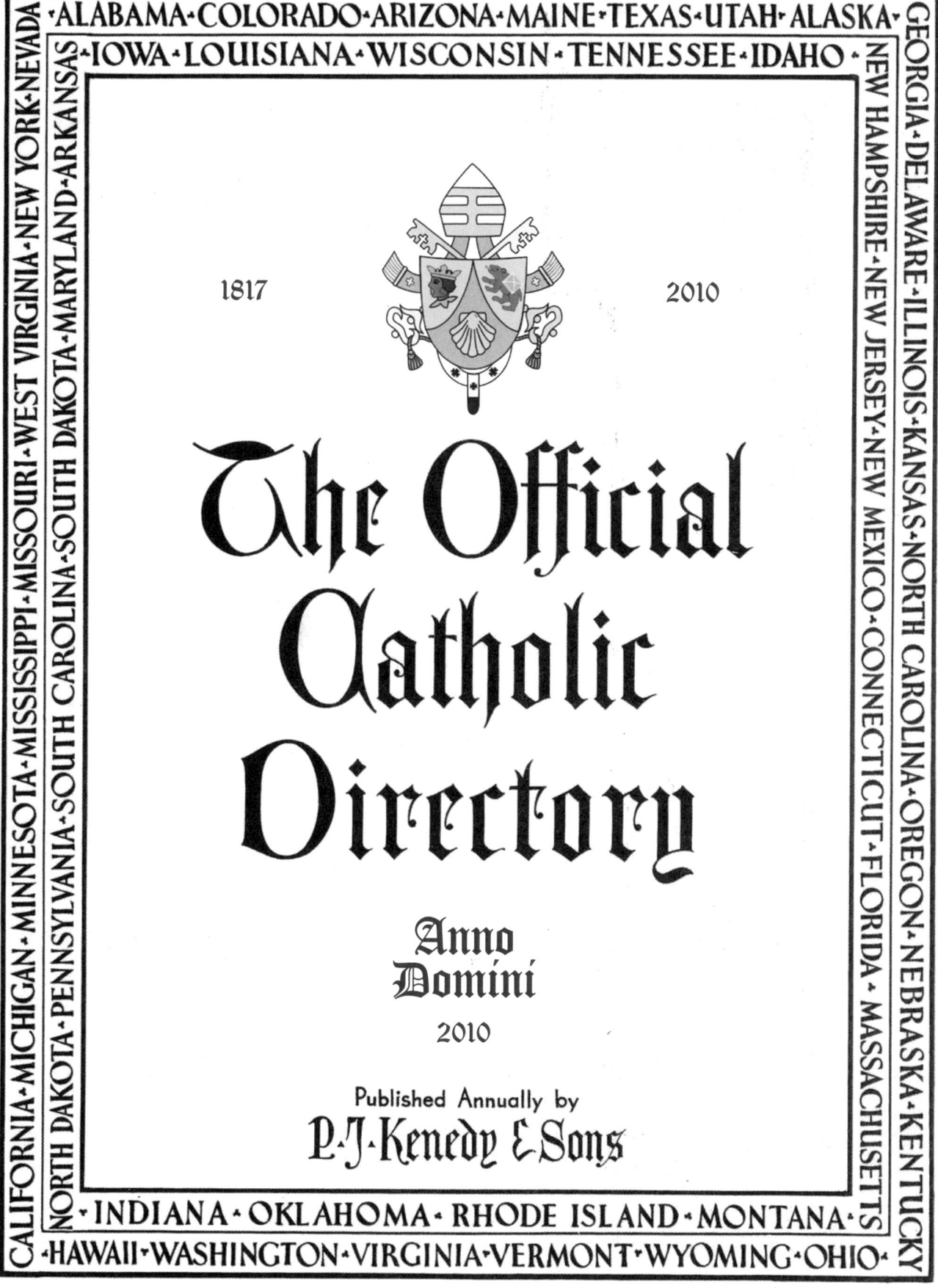

·ALABAMA·COLORADO·ARIZONA·MAINE·TEXAS·UTAH·ALASKA·
·IOWA·LOUISIANA·WISCONSIN·TENNESSEE·IDAHO·

CALIFORNIA·MICHIGAN·MINNESOTA·MISSISSIPPI·MISSOURI·WEST VIRGINIA·NEW YORK·NEVADA
NORTH DAKOTA·PENNSYLVANIA·SOUTH CAROLINA·SOUTH DAKOTA·MARYLAND·ARKANSAS

GEORGIA·DELAWARE·ILLINOIS·KANSAS·NORTH CAROLINA·OREGON·NEBRASKA·KENTUCKY
NEW HAMPSHIRE·NEW JERSEY·NEW MEXICO·CONNECTICUT·FLORIDA·MASSACHUSETTS

1817 2010

The Official Catholic Directory

Anno Domini

2010

Published Annually by

P. J. Kenedy & Sons

·INDIANA·OKLAHOMA·RHODE ISLAND·MONTANA·
·HAWAII·WASHINGTON·VIRGINIA·VERMONT·WYOMING·OHIO·

The Official Catholic Directory

P.J. Kenedy & Sons, Publishers

Jeanne LoGiurato Hanline
Publisher

FOREWORD

It is with great pleasure that we present the 2010 Edition of *The Official Catholic Directory*. This book remains the premier resource for matters relating to the Catholic Church in the United States of America.

In addition to the voluminous facts and statistics regularly furnished in *The Official Catholic Directory*, this volume also includes a special retrospective on the first five years of Benedict XVI's papacy written by noted biographer George Weigel. There is also an overview of the five saints welcomed into the Catholic Church over the past year. Other articles focus on pilgrimage and sacred architecture, the effects of new media in the church, and the growth of the Catholic priesthood towards more effective leadership over the course of the Year for Priests.

With ongoing wars and the ravages of natural disasters, this has been a difficult time for America and the world. In light of current global events, we have included two new sections detailing the work of the Catholic Church as a major force for peace and good. These articles focus on the mission of priests within the U.S. Armed Forces, and the work of Catholic Charities bringing aid to Haiti and Chile in the wake of devastating earthquakes.

Along with Volume One, we have included *The Official Catholic Directory, Part II* in your subscription. Produced in the fall, the supplement contains updates and new listings not present in the main volume, along with the archdioceses and dioceses of the world reprinted with permission from the Vatican.

While we strive to produce a concise and accurate volume, nothing would have been accomplished without the help and cooperation of the many ecclesiastical authorities, diocesan officials, religious and laity who were instrumental in organizing the substantial amount of information needed to publish a successful directory. We would like to thank them all for their tireless work and invaluable assistance.

Sincerely,

Jeanne LoGiurato Hanline
Publisher

890 Mountain Avenue, Suite 300, New Providence, New Jersey 07974 (908) 673-1000 (800) 473-7020

St. Mark Church Interior
Southwest Ranches, FL

St. Mary Church Belltower
Branford, CT

St. Ann Church Interior Renovation Restoration
Hartford, CT

St. Patrick Church Renovation Restoration
Miami Beach, FL

St. Patrick Church Renovation Restoration
Miami Beach, FL

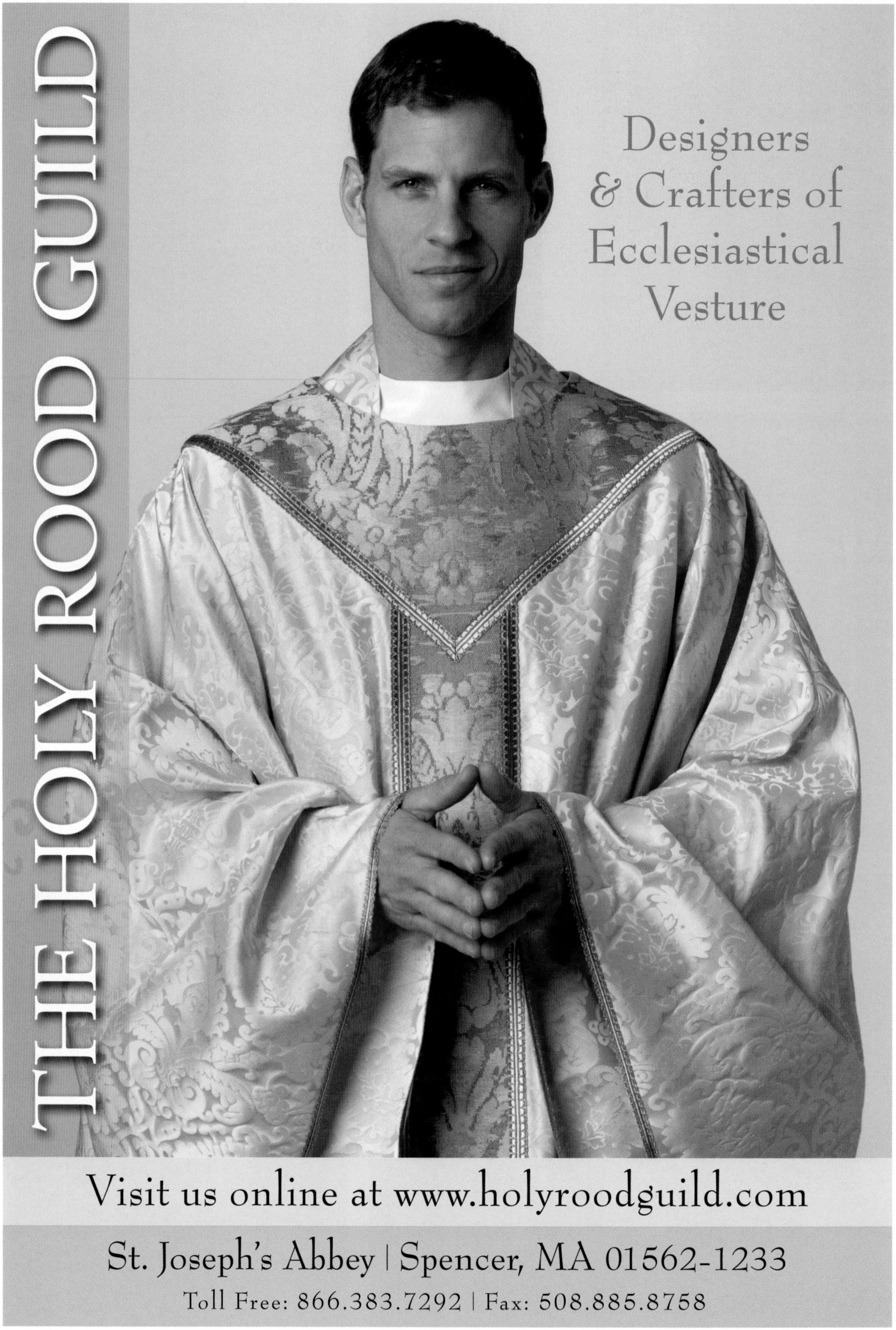
THE HOLY ROOD GUILD
Designers
& Crafters of
Ecclesiastical
Vesture
Visit us online at www.holyroodguild.com
St. Joseph's Abbey | Spencer, MA 01562-1233
Toll Free: 866.383.7292 | Fax: 508.885.8758

KING·OF·KINGS

The Seal of P.J. Kenedy & Sons
The Official Catholic Directory

SIGNIFICANCE:

The shield is the central part of a heraldic device, which is more commonly known as a coat of arms. If that shield is enclosed within a body of text, or other type of surrounding configuration, the device becomes know as a seal, yet it is the shield portion of the design that is the most important, and that which is described technically as the blazon. As the design is examined, it must be remembered that by heraldic tradition the design is described (blazoned) as if being done by the bearer with the shield being worn on the arm. Therefore, the terms dexter and sinister will be reversed as the design is viewed from the front.

The shield of the seal for The Official Catholic Directory has been designed to reflect the character and heritage of this publication of P.J. Kenedy & Sons.

The shield is in two major portions. The right half (sinister impalement) is composed of the blue field on which are seen a silver tree, two candles (in silver or white) in their candleholders (of gold or yellow) and an open book, edged in gold and with a red bookmark. These symbols have been used over the years as the sign of the P.J. Kenedy and Sons publishing organization. These are the traditional symbols of knowledge and learning, so appropriate to a publisher.

The other side of the shield (the dexter impalement) is composed of a silver (white) field on which is seen a red cross, throughout, and a gold eagle. These symbols, combined with the field of the sinister impalement, are represented in the color of the flag of the United States of America and the eagle, the symbol of the United States. The cross represents Christianity and all of this combines to signify that The Official Catholic Directory annually reports on the Catholic Church in the United States.

The shield is surrounded by a laurel wreath of excellence and is enclosed within the legend that states the name of the company, the name of the publication and date (1817) of its founding.

by: Paul J. Sullivan

Historic Photo

Artists' Rendering

Decorative Sample

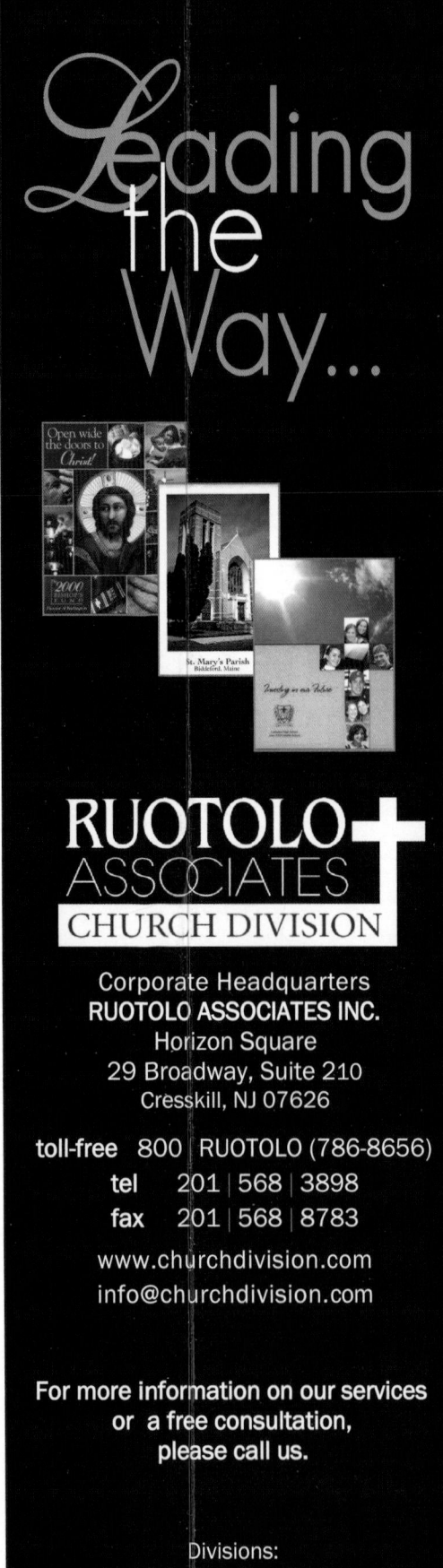

Ciaroscuro: Year in Review: 2009

By Karen A. Walker

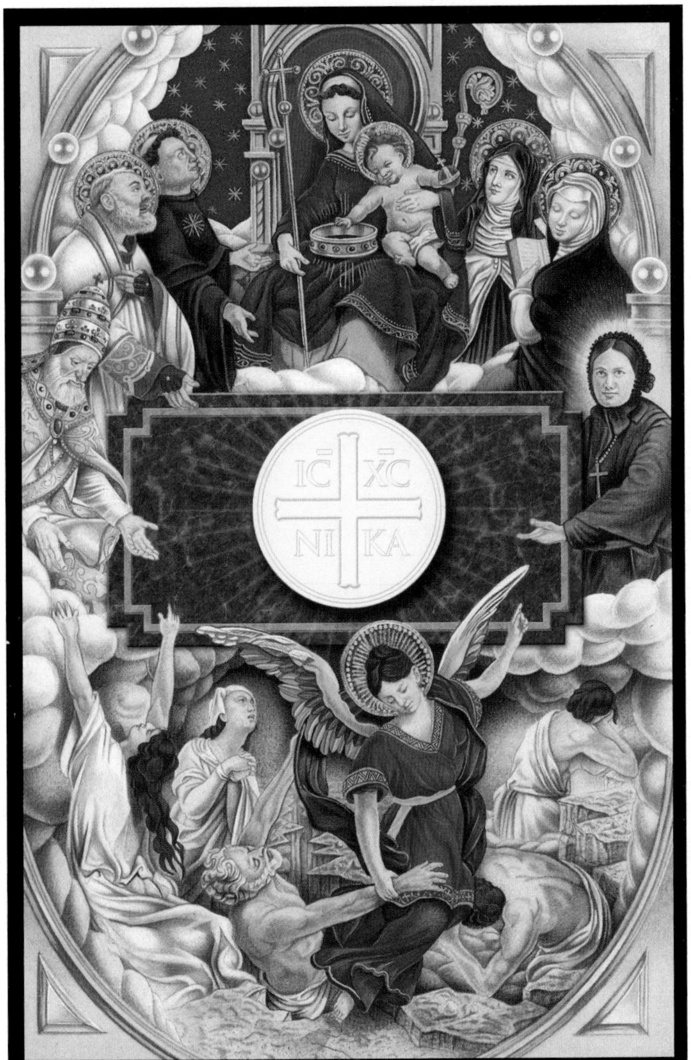

The Communion Of Saints, illumination by Chicago-based artist Jed Gibbons. Commissioned by Our Sunday Visitor, Inc. Image: Artist Jed Gibbons. All rights reserved.

The year 2009 was one of contrasts. As in painting, where light shines brightest against the darkest background (in Italian, *ciaroscuro*), so seemed 2009.

The darkest hues included the continuance of widespread economic instability in the U.S. and globally, leading to increased job losses, home foreclosures and abrupt life changes. U.S. policy direction shifted radically to favor an increased disregard for the inestimable value of each human life, especially for the most vulnerable — the unborn, the frail and infirm, the elderly, the incapacitated, and the suffering. This included the lifting by executive order of long-standing U.S. protections against the unfettered experimentation of embryos. Mandated funding of abortion on demand and removal of conscience clauses became an integral part of unprecedented U.S. healthcare proposals and debate. Aggressive legislative and policy attacks against traditional family values, the most fundamental building block of society, took place in cities and in elementary schools across the U.S. An especially devastating earthquake killed thousands and completely disrupted community life in the capital of Haiti, with an even larger Chilean earthquake a month later. Increased threats of violence in the Middle East and elsewhere threatened civic peace and stability.

Yet amid the *scuro* of 2009, the radiant light of Christ illumined the darkest corners. It took place mostly in hidden ways, and in hidden hearts, which the public will never know. But there were vivid, bold rays of light as well, signs of hope amid suffering.

These bold illuminating rays of 2009 include remarkable feats of heroism such as Captain Sully's landing of a packed airliner in the Hudson River shortly after take-off. Certainly the lives of those passengers and flight crew were unalterably changed! In Rome, Pope Benedict XVI declared A Year for Priests. He released a new and robust social encyclical *Caritas in Veritate*, and opened wide the doors of welcome to Anglican dioceses and communities wishing to enter into full communion with the Church of Rome. Both Pope John Paul II and Pope Pius XII were declared Venerable. Pope Benedict made an historic and memorable Pilgrimage to the Holy Land and also met with artists in the Sistine Chapel, inviting them to embark on a special mission of beauty.

Additionally, a new trend just beginning to surface in the U.S. may be of particular interest to the Church, namely, a new level of lay-driven support for priests and vocations.

Below are snapshots of some of these rays of light from 2009, with special emphasis on one, just-under-the-radar emerging trend in the U.S.

Chiaro Snapshots:

- Pope Benedict XVI's Apostolic Constitution Anglicanorum Coetibus (Groups of Anglicans) welcomes Anglican dioceses and communities who wish to enter into full communion with the Roman Catholic Church by establishing Personal Ordinariates, as needed, and in effect creating an Anglican Rite. An historic moment, nearly 500 years after King Henry III first established The Church of England in 1534.

"When Evening Comes and Work is Done." Illumination: Jed Gibbons. Commissioned by the Pontifical College Josephinum. Image: Jed Gibbons.

- Pope Benedict's new social encyclical Caritas in Veritate builds on the social principles laid out by his predecessors in *Rerum Novarum, Populorum Progressio, Centesimus Annus*, and others. It lays out a litmus test against which one can evaluate organizations, movements, public or economic policy and more. The Pope underscores that man is a creature, made in God's image, whose ultimate fulfillment is found only in God, and therefore any enterprise (political, social, economic) that involves people must give primacy to individual human dignity and value. Any system that does not respect this primacy is, the encyclical states, doomed to cause harm instead of good.

- Pope Benedict's historic pilgrimage to Jerusalem and the Holy Land in May 2009 included an abundant and generous welcome from leaders and citizens, as well as meetings with Israeli and Palestinian Authority top officials, and with the top religious leaders from the Jewish, Muslim and Christian faiths. The visit bolstered the spirits of Christians in the region, especially Catholics, and did much to further respectful dialog and underscore commonly shared beliefs and desires among the three top religious groups co-existing in the region.

- Pope Benedict invited 500 Artists from around the world for a special meeting in the Sistine Chapel – 250 artists attended, including some of international fame. The Holy Father urged them to inject spirituality into their work, saying that beauty can become "a path toward the transcendent, toward the ultimate Mystery, toward God," and contrasting this with: "Too often...the beauty thrust upon us is illusory and deceitful ...it imprisons man within himself and further enslaves him, depriving him of hope and joy."

An emerging trend in the U.S.:

Lay-driven support for priests. The Serra Club, founded in 1934 and named after Spanish missionary Blessed Junipero Serra, "to foster, affirm and promote vocations to ministry in the Catholic Church," remains today one of the most prayerful and practical lay-driven priest and vocation support organizations in the U.S. and in the world. Yet in 2009, several new lay ministries and outreaches, and one intensive leadership training program, point to an emerging trend of lay-led support for priests.

In each of these new ventures, lay founders drew from professional expertise to address festering "occupational challenges" inherent in today's priestly responsibilities.

Good Leaders, Good Shepherds program of the Catholic Leadership Institute (www.CatholicLeaders.org): Clearly at the helm of the new trend toward lay-initiated support for priests, especially in terms of its goals, content, impact and results, this program has been more than five years in development. In 2009, the first 600 graduates emerged from the institute's unique, two-year leadership curriculum for priests. Current enrollment includes an additional 600 priests and 36 bishops, representing a total of 44 dioceses. By the end of 2010, Fr. Bill Dickinson, National Director of Leadership Development for the Catholic Leadership Institute, estimates that more than one-third of the dioceses in the U.S. will have had, or will be enrolled in, the two-year Good Leaders, Good Shepherds program.

"Our mission is to help priests recognize their God-given potential and develop their leadership skills so they can effectively and confidently lead their faith communities in carrying out the mission of Jesus Christ and the Catholic Church," says Fr. Bill Dickinson.

"In the priesthood there are three offices that come with ordination," Fr. Dickinson explains, "to teach, to sanctify and to govern. We made a choice with this program to support the governing office because it's the leadership component and very little is done to support it."

"We have a different program for bishops," says Fr. Dickinson, adding that four bishops have opted instead to go through the priest program with their priests. There is a supporting lay version of the curriculum, accessible only to graduate priests who may choose and recommend key lay associates to attend.

The development of this program, built from the ground-up with priests in mind, underscores the new trend to put lay expertise at the service of the priests.

Dick Lyles, CEO of a global consulting firm, Leadership Legacies, CEO of a Hollywood film-making company, Origin Entertainment, host of The Catholic Business Hour, and author or co-author of more than eight business and leadership books, has literally traveled the world delivering management consulting and training to companies such as Pfizer, Hughes Aircraft, Exxon, Wendy's, the New Zealand Dairy Board, Ericsson, and many others. He is the principal developer of the Good Leaders, Good Shepherd curriculum, and of its accompanying book with the same title.

Using Jesus Christ as the ultimate shepherd and model of leadership, Mr. Lyles explains, the curriculum for clergy was specifically designed to help priests overcome the challenges today of a diminishing number of clergy and more complex circumstances for priestly ministry.

The goal is to minimize the frustration and energy spent on their administrative roles and maximize the joy and time spent on the pastoral duties for which they were uniquely ordained. The impact will be more holy, healthy, and happy shepherds of vibrant parish communities, leading more people to a deeper relationship with Christ.

"The results are truly transformative for priests and parishes," says Mr. Lyles. "We didn't just take a business model and give it a priestly focus. Instead, we developed this program from the ground up to meet the unique demands, challenges and responsibilities of a priest, especially a parish priest. That involved a lot of first-hand research with priests and pastors."

Because the institute's program heralds this new trend, it has been operating enough so that the impact on priests and parishes is more evident than other initiatives. Of all the feedback gathered, perhaps the most significant were the reactions of priests in the first classes.

"In every class I taught, especially at the end of the first module, I'd have a few priests come up to me with tears in their eyes, saying they couldn't believe that someone cared enough about them to put together a program of this caliber and quality. Every class was like that," said Mr. Lyles, who was heavily involved in training during the first years of the program. "One priest told me that he used to walk down the street as a priest and everyone would say 'hi,' welcome him and be positive. But now he walks down the street and people turn away! ...Another priest told me, again with tears in his eyes, that this curriculum has changed his whole attitude about himself, just to know someone cared this much about him.... I heard so many comments from priests like this; 'You can't imagine what it means to me that someone would put something like this together for me, for priests!' 'Thank you for putting something together of this quality to help me be better in what I do.'"

Interviewed priests concur:

Fr. Brian Smith, from the Archdiocese of Boston, is Parochial Vicar at St. Edith Stein Parish. He says, "I would tell any priest, 'You need it more than you think; you'll benefit from Good Leaders, Good Shepherds in ways you cannot imagine...the objectivity it brings is literally invaluable."

"I feel that I am better able to read and relate to people, and that I have a system to better understand where others are coming from," agreed Fr. Michael Phillippino, a pastor from the Diocese of Norwich. "The program gives me a greater advantage in being a more effective priest and evangelizer."

"I found GLGS to be a high level program which takes seriously God's call for priests to act responsibly as leaders. If leading souls to Christ is the call of the priest, then GLGS provides a way to do this with confidence and competence...Leadership skill building founded on a solid understanding of one's own behavior, and that of others, is a great contribution," says Fr. Bill Kelly, Director, Clergy Support Office, for the Archdiocese of Boston.

In the words of one lay person in California who wished to remain anonymous, "Imagine the transformative effect of this leadership training on parishioners and parish communities, in a myriad of parishes nationwide, whose pastors begin to lead their flocks with confidence, clarity of vision and joy in his uniquely priestly ministry." "Hopefully," adds Mr. Lyles, "this is the beginning of an effort by lay people who will rise up to support their priests in tangible ways."

The same year that Catholic Leadership Institute celebrated its first priest graduation class, a handful of other developments echo this trend of lay persons formalizing their professional expertise at the service of priests.

VocationBoom.com
Here I am.

Vocation Boom is a team of passionate advocates dedicated to supporting the priesthood as a life's vocation and mission. www.vocationboom.com

VocationBoom.org is an interactive website with multiple resources for men who are discerning a priestly vocation. Although formally launched in 2009, it is the fruit of more than 20 years of prayer and deliberation. The initiative was founded by Jerry Usher, a pioneer of the recent growth in Catholic Radio over the past decade, and also a young man who spent time discerning his own vocation, especially during a time of priestly formation from 1989 to 1995. VocationBoom.org, with its energy and functionality, clearly reflects full use of this era's new media tools, with easy opportunities for users to connect via blog comments, Twitter, FaceBook and YouTube. The site also is new in its approach. It reflects the vantage point of a person searching, and leads with the kinds of questions and curiosity of today's young man. And it does so in a warm, inviting and simple way; it speaks his language.

Among the website's opportunities to share experiences and questions, a user will find first-hand examples and true stories of others discerning the same vocation. Likewise, there are links to vocation directors, church teachings, the next steps along the discernment process, and much more. In short, a young man seeking to determine his vocation to the priesthood would feel he is not alone in the journey.

"We're building a culture that's open to the priesthood, clearing the path to discovery, and unlocking hearts and minds to God's call," says Mr. Usher, whose site is not limited by locality or priestly options (religious order, diocesan, etc.)

Although spearheaded by Mr. Usher, development of the site and its growing set of tools and resources have been two years in development with the founder's colleagues. As he puts it: "Pope Benedict XVI's recent proclamation of The Year for Priests is a confirmation of our intentions and an indication that now is the time to unveil Vocation Boom!"

EncouragePriests.org. A third initiative, still in its infancy, was just launched in April 2010 by Tom Peterson, founder of Catholics Come Home (www.CatholicsComeHome.org), a nonprofit media apostolate dedicated to producing and airing television ads encouraging Catholics to "come home" to the Church if they have been away. EncouragePriests.org is a communications outreach of Catholics Come Home, Inc. According to the website, its mission is "to encourage priests, and promote priestly vocations through our love and prayers." Television commercials that showcase the humanitarian efforts of priests are slated to begin production and airing in the near future. By June 2010, the organization plans to launch an improved, interactive website enabling Catholics to offer spiritual bouquets, e-cards, printable greeting cards, video messages and blogs with "kind words of gratitude to show appreciation for countless priests around the world."

"Countless priests deserve our true gratitude and love, as so many lead sacrificial and humble lives," says Mr. Peterson, the former CEO of an advertising agency in Phoenix. "These noble men of God need our encouragement and could be uplifted by a simple prayer and a gentle word of appreciation from us."

These lay-driven initiatives indirectly follow on the heels of scattered prayer initiatives for priests and one particularly notable ministry to priests in crisis called Opus Bono Sacerdotii, Work for the Good of the Priesthood, (www.OpusBono.com).

"We've helped about 5,000 priests in crisis in the last eight years," says Opus Bono Sacerdotii founder Joe Maher, a former turnaround CEO who launched his career in the Hollywood entertainment industry and segued to Fortune 500 companies by request. Several years after he relocated his family to the Midwest a local priest was in crisis and needed help. Mr. Maher applied his professional expertise to the situation and his nonprofit apostolate grew from there, ultimately demanding his full commitment.

"We still deal with thousands of priests," Mr. Maher adds. "We work as quietly as we can, since everything we do with a priest is confidential. We now get about a call a day."

Although radically different in its focus from the goals of those groups comprising the emerging trend, Opus Bono Sacerdotii nonetheless exemplifies professional lay expertise brought to the service of priests and the priesthood.

Where this emerging trend will lead is anyone's guess, but the impact is already quietly seeping into parishes nationwide. ◆

KAREN A. WALKER is Editor and Publisher of the *Catholic Business Journal* and Producer of *The Catholic Business Hour* radio show.

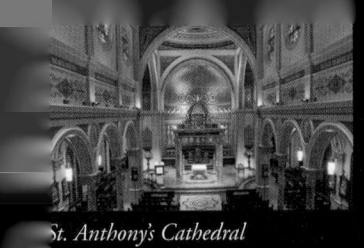

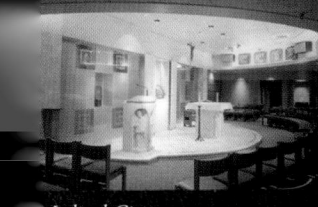

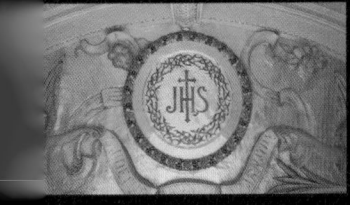

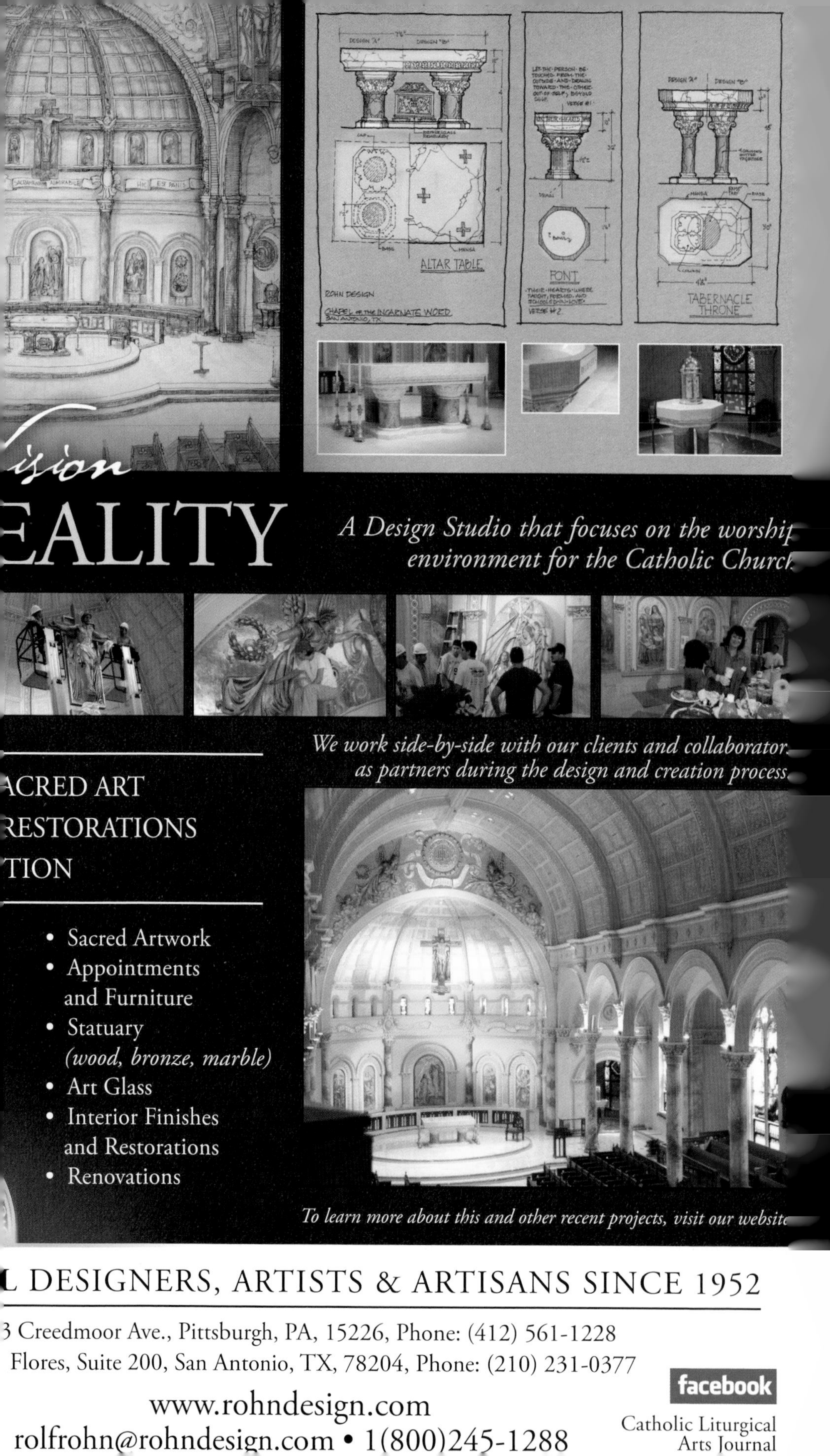
ALTAR TABLE
FONT
TABERNACLE THRONE
ROHN DESIGN
CHAPEL of the INCARNATE WORD
ision
EALITY
A Design Studio that focuses on the worshi
environment for the Catholic Churc
We work side-by-side with our clients and collaborator
as partners during the design and creation process
ACRED ART
RESTORATIONS
TION
• Sacred Artwork
• Appointments and Furniture
• Statuary (wood, bronze, marble)
• Art Glass
• Interior Finishes and Restorations
• Renovations
To learn more about this and other recent projects, visit our websit
L DESIGNERS, ARTISTS & ARTISANS SINCE 1952
3 Creedmoor Ave., Pittsburgh, PA, 15226, Phone: (412) 561-1228
Flores, Suite 200, San Antonio, TX, 78204, Phone: (210) 231-0377
www.rohndesign.com
rolfrohn@rohndesign.com • 1(800)245-1288
facebook
Catholic Liturgical Arts Journal

Pope Benedict XVI:
The First Five Years

By George Weigel

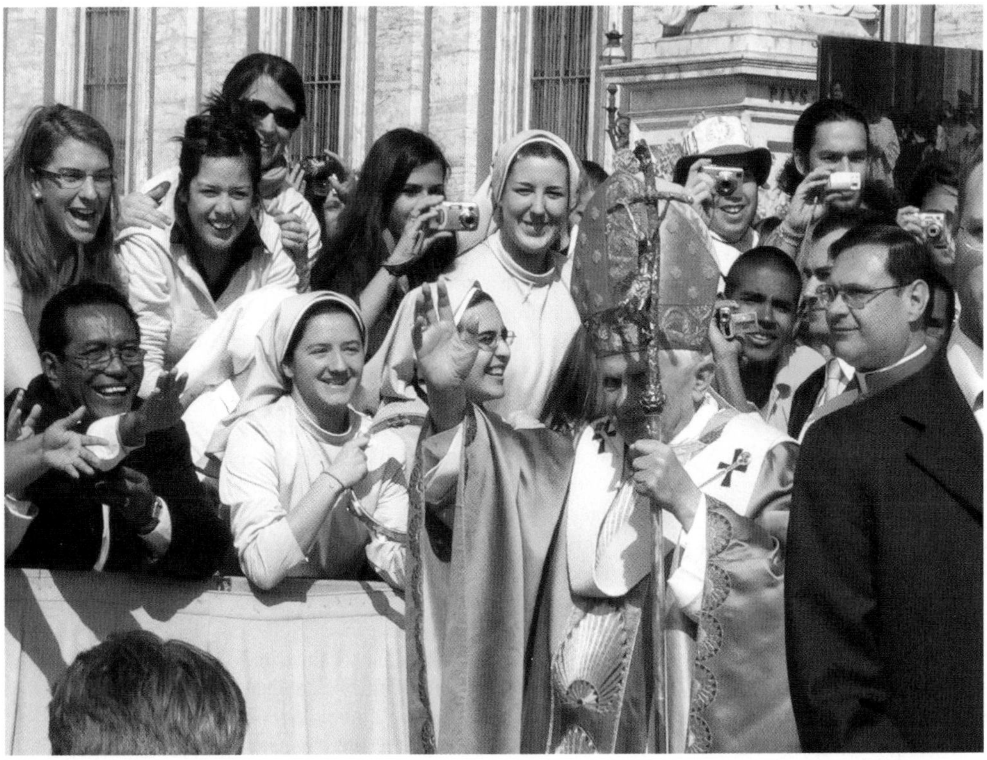

Pope Benedict offers Easter blessings. Photo: Ginger Mortensen, International Theological Institute, Austria

When Cardinal Joseph Ratzinger was elected the 265th Bishop of Rome on April 19, 2005, he brought to the papacy decades of work as one of Christianity's foremost theologians, and more than twenty years experience in the Church's central administration where he had served as prefect of the Congregation for the Doctrine of the Faith [CDF] since his 1981 appointment by John Paul II.

Ratzinger and the man he would succeed as pope formed a unique intellectual partnership for twenty-three years: Ratzinger the theologian and John Paul the philosopher, both men of the Second Vatican Council, had worked in close harness to forge an authoritative interpretation of the Council's work in preparation for the third millennium of Christian history. Ratzinger's election, after one of the shortest conclaves in history, was an expression of the "consensus of esteem" that had quickly formed around him as the "elder brother who stood head and shoulders above the rest," as one cardinal-elector put it. His election also emphasized the cardinals' intention to underscore that John Paul's historic pontificate had not been idiosyncratic, but had set the Church's course for the 21st century and beyond.

Joseph Ratzinger's choice of papal name, "Benedict," reflected the Church's commitment to sanctity – which, Ratzinger and John Paul II believed, was every baptized person's Christian and human destiny. By also evoking the memory of the great founder whose monks saved the civilization of the West, Benedict XVI was also signaling his commitment to the reconversion of Europe, Christianity's historic heartland, which he believed to be suffering from a deep spiritual malaise with grave social consequences.

Elected pope three days after his 78th birthday, Benedict XVI, a shy and retiring personality who had nonetheless displayed an ability to lead millions in prayer during John Paul II's funeral, could not anticipate a pontificate extending over decades. Thus his personal circumstances, his intellectual and pastoral inclinations, and his readings of the signs of the times, especially in Europe, produced a papacy whose first five years called the Church back to the fundamentals of its common life: the universal call to sanctity, the path which the Church discovers in the scriptural word of God, its rich patristic theological heritage, and above all a personal friendship with Jesus Christ, a frequent theme of Benedict's homilies and audience addresses.

Magisterium. While Benedict XVI's papal teaching reflected his remarkably broad and deep learning, it also displayed Joseph Ratzinger's striking ability to explain the densest and most challenging of Christian doctrines in language the theologically untutored could understand. This gift, which Ratzinger had honed in his career as a university professor, was powerfully displayed in his Wednesday general audiences, whose themes reflected his commitment to bringing the world Church into a closer encounter with its roots. In 2005, Benedict picked up the thematic thread of John Paul II's last audiences and continued the late pope's explanation of the psalms and canticles of Vespers, the Church's evening prayer and, in a sense, the primary "hymnbook" of the Catholic Church. Then, in 2006, Benedict turned his attention to the cornerstones on which historic Christianity rests: the apostles, whose personal friendship with Jesus Christ had so transformed their lives that they were compelled to bring the Gospel to the ends of the world they knew. In 2007, Benedict gave a series of audience addresses on figures from the Acts of the Apostles, proceeding directly from there to a multi-year reflection on the eastern and western Fathers of the Church: the men who had turned Christian confession and proclamation into creeds and dogma. The Pope's explication of the thoughts of these early theologians was interrupted in 2008-2009 for a year of reflections on St. Paul, during the Pauline Year the Pope had proclaimed. Benedict returned to the Fathers and then began an explanation of the medieval theological reformers in his late 2009 and early 2010 audiences. These luminously clear catechetical talks often drew large crowds of pilgrims to St. Peter's Square or the Paul VI Audience Hall, and several sets of the addresses were published as books.

Benedict XVI issued three encyclicals in the first five years of his pontificate. *Deus Caritas Est* [God Is Love], was signed on Christmas 2005 and released publicly the following month. In addition to offering a theological exploration of the various meanings of love, the Pope taught that the service of charity is part of the "fundamental structure of the Church," along with the sacraments and the proclamation of God's word. The encyclical also reminded the world that no political system would ever embody justice so fully that there would no longer be a need for love. "There is no ordering of the state so just that it will eliminate the need for love," Benedict wrote; "the state which would provide everything, absorbing everything into itself, would ultimately become a mere bureaucracy incapable of guaranteeing the very thing...every person needs: namely, loving personal concern."

Spe Salvi [Saved in Hope], signed on November 30, 2007, took its title from the letter to the Romans and taught that hope is faith oriented toward the future, thus radically changing the present. *Spe Salvi* urged the post-modern world to consider the possibility – indeed the likelihood – that its great achievements could not endure without a firm grounding in biblical faith and Christian humanism: both of which, Joseph Ratzinger had long been convinced, were crucial building blocks of a genuinely humane civilization.

Caritas in Veritate [Charity in Truth] was signed on June 29, 2009 and evoked the memory of Paul VI's social encyclical, *Populorum Progressio* [The Progress of Peoples], while urging political leaders, economists, and the peoples of the Church to explore what some analysts called an "economy of communion," marked by enlarged philanthropy and new methods of measuring value.

Liturgy. Another significant document of Benedict XVI's magisterium was the 2007 post-synodal apostolic exhortation, *Sacramentum Caritatis* [The Sacrament of Charity], written to complete the work of the 2005 Synod of Bishops, which marked the end of the "Year of the Eucharist" initiated by John Paul II. Throughout his decades as a priest, Joseph Ratzinger, who had been deeply influenced by the mid-century liturgical reform movement in Germany, had emphasized that the liturgy, and especially the Eucharistic liturgy, was the vital center of the Church's life. At his election it was no secret that Ratzinger believed that the implementation of Vatican II's liturgical reforms had not produced the results anticipated, and that a "reform of the reform" was required. *Sacramentum Caritatis* set the theological foundation for such a further reform of the Church's public worship, which the Pope also tried to accelerate by the 2007 apostolic letter *Summorum Pontificum*, which allowed for the universal use of the Roman Missal as reformed by Blessed John XXIII in 1962. Although interpreted by some as an effort to roll back the liturgical reforms of the Council, *Summorum Pontificum* was in fact meant to draw the "reform of the reform" in the direction of a resacralization of the liturgy while providing for the pastoral needs of those who had found it difficult to adjust to the 1970 Missal of Paul VI.

Summorum Pontificum was also a papal gesture toward those Catholics who, because of their devotion to the older liturgy, had separated themselves from full communion with the Church by following the French archbishop Marcel Lefebvre into schism in 1988. In early 2009 the Pope announced a new initiative aimed at reconciling the late French prelate's remaining followers but this effort quickly encountered difficulties when it was revealed that Richard Williamson, one of the bishops Lefebvre had illicitly ordained and whose automatic excommunication Benedict XVI had lifted, was a Holocaust-denier. In the wake of the ensuing international controversy, the Pope moved the Ecclesia Dei Commission, established by John Paul II as a vehicle for reconciling Lefebvrists who wished to return to full communion with Rome, under the authority of the Congregation for the Doctrine of the Faith.

Apostolic Journeys. In the first half-decade of the pontificate, Benedict XVI's pilgrimages to the world Church were focused primarily on Europe. Shortly after his election he returned to his native land to preside over World Youth Day 2005 in Cologne. His May 2006 visit to Poland was an expression of gratitude to the Polish people for having given the Church, John Paul II (whose beatification cause Benedict had started before the normal five-year waiting period was over). The Pope's travels to Spain in July 2006 for the fifth World Meeting of Families, to Austria in September 2007, to France in September 2008, and to the Czech Republic in September 2009 were all intended to call Europe back to its Christian roots as aggressive secularism continued to dominate both European high culture and the institutions of the European Union.

The Pope's second visit to Germany in September 2006 created the first media firestorm of the pontificate when, in a lecture at his old university in Regensburg, Benedict XVI challenged Islam to face its difficulties in accommodating itself to the idea of religious freedom as a universal human right that can be known by reason, and to the separation of religious and political authority in the modern state. Global controversy followed, but the net result of the Regensburg Lecture was that Islamic scholars and religious authorities requested a new dialogue with the Holy See – a dialogue which, in his Christmas

Papal audience January 2010
Photo: Ginger Mortensen, International Theological Institute, Austria

2006 address to the Roman Curia, the Pope insisted must focus on the two crucial issues he had identified at Regensburg.

Benedict XVI visited Ecumenical Patriarch Bartholomew of Constantinople in late 2006, addressed the fifth general conference of Latin American and Caribbean bishops' conferences in Brazil in May 2007, flew around the world to Sydney, Australia for World Youth Day in July 2008, made a week-long visit to Cameroon and Angola in March 2009, and embarked on a pilgrimage to the Holy Land in May 2009. The last must have been an emotional moment for Joseph Ratzinger, who has done more than perhaps any other Catholic theologian to remind the Church of its debt to living Judaism, and who had now, as Bishop of Rome and successor of Peter, come on pilgrimage in the lands where Jesus and his followers had walked.

Benedict XVI addressed the General Assembly of the United Nations in April 2008, proposing that human rights, "the common language and the ethical substratum of international relations," are based on "the natural law inscribed on human hearts and present in different cultures and civilizations." The U.N. address was also the occasion for a pastoral visit to New York and Washington, during which the Pope received a tremendous welcome on the South Lawn of the White House and preached a memorable homily at St. Patrick's in New York, using the cathedral's stained glass and stone as a metaphor for the reality of the Church. In a surprise gesture of apology and reconciliation, Benedict XVI met in Washington with victims of clerical sexual abuse.

After Five Years. At CDF, Joseph Ratzinger dealt firmly with abusive clergy, but sex abuse scandals throughout the

Pope Benedict XVI blesses a family
Photo: Ginger Mortensen, International Theological Institute, Austria

Catholic world plagued the Pope as his first five years in office came to a close. In March 2010, he wrote a stern letter to the Church in Ireland, condemning both the sexual and physical abuse of the young by priests and religious in past decades, and the cravenness of Irish bishops in handling this scandal; the letter seemed to presage major changes in Church leadership there. Early in the pontificate, Benedict had dealt firmly with Father Marcial Maciel, founder of the Legionaries of Christ, convinced that charges of abuse against Maciel which Joseph Ratzinger had ordered investigated had been substantiated. Yet amidst scandals that could not have been anything other than acutely painful to bear, the Pope soldiered on, finishing work in early 2010 on the second volume of his book on Jesus; the first volume, *Jesus of Nazareth*, had been published in 2007 and was an international bestseller.

Five years after his election, it seemed unlikely that Benedict would undertake the thoroughgoing reform of the Roman Curia for which some had hoped in 2005. Curial incompetence had cost the Pope dearly in the Williamson affair; there was little effective Vatican response to attacks on Benedict after his Regensburg lecture; the 2009 presentation of the Pope's decision to create "personal ordinariates" for groups of Anglicans wishing full communion with Rome was poorly handled, with groundless charges of papal "poaching" inevitably following; the president of the Pontifical Academy of Life misstated the Church's teaching on abortion on the front page of *L'Osservatore Romano*. Yet belying the media caricature of him as a stiff disciplinarian, Benedict XVI most often gave those who ill-served him opportunities to do better. Whether such generosity impeded the effective communication of the pontificate's main themes was being actively discussed around the world as the Pope's fifth anniversary approached.

In the first five years of his pontificate, Benedict XVI had shown himself a man of gentleness and courtesy, a compelling preacher and catechist, a priest of deep piety and great personal sanctity, and a man with a unique capacity to put difficult issues on the world agenda. It will be for another pope, it would seem, to repair the broken machinery of curial governance. Meanwhile, Catholics around the world know they have a shepherd who is a master teacher, for whom friendship with Jesus Christ is at the center of Christian discipleship. ◆

GEORGE WEIGEL, Distinguished Senior Fellow of Washington's Ethics and Public Policy Center, is the author of *Witness to Hope: The Biography of Pope John Paul II*, and *God's Choice: Pope Benedict XVI and the Future of the Catholic Church*.

This Special Feature is sponsored in part by
ROHN & ASSOCIATES DESIGN. INC
(www.rohndesign.com)
The sponsor had no input regarding the content.

Catholic Charities - Haiti & Chile

The Face of Love

Catholic response to two devastating quakes that rocked Haiti and Chile

By Karen A. Walker

Close to 50,000 Haitians now call the golf course at the Petionville Club home. CRS is distributing lentils, vegetable oil, and bulgar to those living at the camp. The camp now includes a market, make-shift beauty salons, and a place to make international phone calls. Photo by Lane Hartill/Catholic Relief Services.

"A 7.0 earthquake struck the capital of Haiti today," read news and wire reports circling the globe. A compact, clinical description...until one sees the YouTube videos, listens to first-hand accounts and takes in the ensuing chaos, the cries of anguish, pain, loss and confusion....until one sees the make-shift Petionville camp that quickly swelled to more than 50,000 displaced men, women, and children who chose to sleep and set up temporary quarters on the third hole of a once-swanky golf course in the open air rather than inside a building... until one sees the local and imported doctors and nurses, many local medical professionals still stunned and grieving the loss of medical colleagues, yet all performing triage, amputations and surgery amid the rubble of collapsed and severely damaged hospitals and in makeshift tents.

In 35 to 40 seconds of terror—*only 35 seconds*—lives changed forever in Haiti, and around the world for those in solidarity with their suffering brothers and sisters.

In less than one minute, Haitians in and around the nation's capital of Port-au-Prince had lost their beloved Archbishop Joseph Serge Miot and more than 97 seminarians, as well as popular sports figures and musicians, and at least 85 United Nations personnel, including Mission Chief Hedi Annabi. And in less than one minute more, Catholic Relief Services (CRS) staff, already present in Haiti, began planning their relief efforts.

Entire buildings—including the Cathedral of Port-au-Prince, the National Palace, the Archbishop's residence, the National Major Seminary of Notre Dame of Haiti (the only major seminary in the country), many Catholic schools throughout the region, hospitals and government offices—had collapsed in a plume of dust that rose and then engulfed the city for nearly 20 minutes; leaving hundreds trapped, or worse, in the rubble. Between 92,000 and 230,000 are dead. An accurate death toll may never be known, with mass graves hastily dug to clear unsanitary decay and stench accelerated by the tropical heat. It

What is left of the Eglise Sacre Coeur (Sacred Heart Church), a Catholic Church in downtown Port au Prince, Haiti after a 7.0 magnitude earthquake rattled Haiti on Tuesday, January 12, 2010. Photo by Lane Hartill/Catholic Relief Services

was a race against time. Survivors, the trapped and injured needed immediate attention to survive. The removal of rubble and debris blocking roads, repairs to the region's main airport and control tower, and fixing damaged ports were key to avoid further hampering of aid delivery.

As of mid-March, more than 52 subsequent aftershocks greater than 4.5 had rocked the region.

And then Chile…

A little more than a month after Haiti's monster quake, on February 27, 2010, 3:34 am local time, in the black of early morning, in a country more than 3,500 miles from Haiti, an 8.8 quake lasting only 90 terrifying seconds struck off the coast of the Maule region of Chile. Eighty percent of the country's population felt the quake, as did cities in neighboring Argentina and in southern Peru. A blackout affected 93% of Chile's population, lasting in some places for days. A quake-triggered tsunami devastated several coastal towns in south-central Chile and damaged the port at Talcahuano.

By early March, more than 130 aftershocks had been registered, including 13 above 6.0 on the Richter scale.

Chile's earthquake was 500 times more forceful than Haiti's January quake, yet needs differed radically in the two countries.

Priorities change. Immediately.

CRS workers know the drill. After any disaster, it's impossible to know the extent of damages and human needs, so immediate assessment and planning begin simultaneously. Certain needs are primary—food, sanitation, personal safety and shelter.

"When an earthquake [or any major disaster] strikes," says CRS president Ken Hackett, a 38-year CRS veteran, "we have a set of professionals with various areas of expertise such as logisticians, engineers, shelter, sanitation and water experts, who are accustomed to designing effective disaster response.

"We bring these experts in from around the world to design an immediate and a long-term response to the disaster. They use computers, on-the-ground assessments, and, most importantly, the lessons learned from responding to many other disasters in other parts of the world.... Within hours of the Haitian quake a message had already been sent to these experts, saying: 'Get ready, you're coming to Haiti!'... Some arrived in two or three days, others later. We stagger their arrival and departure so that no one burns out."

But CRS began offering aid even before the special technicians arrived.

"We've had an operational presence in Haiti for 55 years," explains Mr. Hackett, "so we have people, compassion, experience and connections that are long-standing, robust, effective and agile. We were able to get moving quickly. We had supplies in place and people to move those supplies, systems to account for them, and to distribute them effectively."

CRS does not work alone in a major disaster, isolated from other charities or government response teams.

Part of a bigger picture

Catholic Relief Service is the official international outreach of Catholics in the United States to their brothers and sisters—whether Catholic or not—who are in dire need throughout the world. The organization was founded by the bishops of the United States in 1943, during World War II, initially to help Europe and its refugees recover from the ravages of war. As the postwar situation improved, the agency turned its attention to other people and places in need of assistance, opening offices in Africa, Asia and Latin America.

Staff for Catholic Relief Services unload hygiene kits that were packed in the Dominican Republic. The kit includes items such as soap, toothpaste, mosquito nets, toothbrushes, and towels. Nine hundred and sixty eight kits were delivered to the CRS warehouse in Port-au-Prince, in addition to plastic sheeting for shelter, and food kits.

This programming was in response to the 7.0 magnitude earthquake that struck Haiti on Tuesday, January 12, 2010. The earthquake killed and injured thousands of people, primarily the capital, Port-au-Prince. Photo by Lane Hartill/Catholic Relief Services.

"Today we work in 100 countries around the world," says Michael Wiest, a 35-year veteran who began his CRS career at age 24 working in Africa and now serves as the organization's Vice President of Giving and Awareness. "We have about 55 offices overseas in 9 regions... We're part of the Church in the United States, owned by the bishops of the U.S., and mandated to serve the poor of the world on behalf of U.S. Catholics. "

CRS, which serves people in need outside the U.S., and Catholic Charities USA, which serves people in need within the United States, are together considered to be Caritas USA and a member of Caritas International. Caritas International is the umbrella federation consisting of 167 Caritas agencies, which are the bishop-run charitable organizations from each country, i.e. Caritas Brazil, Caritas Canada, Caritas Germany, and Caritas United Kingdom.

"Of all Caritas member organizations," notes Mr. Wiest, "CRS is larger than all the others combined. In terms of operational presence we have about 5,000 staff around the world. So when major disaster strikes, typically CRS can carry the heaviest load in a location. We work together."

"Historical realities of each Caritas agency are different," adds Mr. Wiest. "The size of resources varies, as does cultural background. The tradition of private giving is more developed in the U.S. Interestingly, U.S. Catholics give more than twice per capita than the second most philanthropic nation, the United Kingdom."

In fulfillment of is mission, CRS does more than respond to emergency situations. It helps rebuild societies in need through community-based, sustainable development initiatives. Its programs today include agricultural initiatives, community banks, health education, micro-financing and clean water projects, all of which are developed in a way which ensures that the local population is the central participant in its own development, and that a project can be sustained through the effort and resources of the local community.

In its more than half a century of relief work, CRS has handled a wide range of disasters—from the aftermath of devastating hurricanes or societal instability during intense civil strife, to the psychological and physical destruction left in the wake of the December 26, 2004 Indian Ocean tsunami.

Response and needs different in Chile

The Chilean bishops' Caritas Chile, which CRS developed for the bishops years ago, is now the strongest and most developed Catholic relief organization among Latin American countries. "They were able to walk in quickly and respond to the earthquake disaster with a lot of technical expertise," explains Mr. Hackett. CRS does not have an office in Chile. It is not needed. "Caritas Chile requested two specialty technicians from us, whom we sent down, and they are appreciative of any funds we can send their way.... While no less of an emergency situation, the need is different than in Haiti."

Overall, about $400,000 to $500,000 is anticipated for CRS relief efforts in Chile, whereas more than $170 million is projected for Haiti.

Hope, Courage and Light in the Darkness

Back in Haiti, a country estimated to be 80% Catholic, there's an unexpected note found throughout the makeshift camps. Singing. Heartfelt singing.

"In the camps, the religious spirit of the people was quite noticeable," blogs Cardinal Sean Patrick O'Malley, OFM Cap, Cardinal of the Boston Archdiocese, regarding his early March 2010 trip as part of a U.S. Conference of Catholic Bishops (USCCB) committee to assess the needs of the Church in Haiti.

Volunteers of Caritas Concepci unpack clothing kits that have been prepared to help assist the displaced in the aftermath of an 8.8 magnitude earthquake and ensuing tsunami hit Chile on February 27, 2010. CRS sent technical support to Caritas Chile to help in the relief effort. Photo by Holly Inurreta/Catholic Relief Services

"They would sing religious hymns for hours every night. Everyone talked about how, in the refugee camps, you'd hear people singing hymns all night long."

The Cardinal and his group spent considerable time touring the area with Archbishop Barnardito Auza, apostolic nuncio to Haiti. They brought vestments for priests who had none. By the time of his visit, more than half a million refugees had gone to other provinces of Haiti, with CRS paying for tuition and food for children attending Catholic schools in these provinces.

And there are so many other lights...

"Working side-by-side, CRS and the hospital team pulled mattresses and bed frames from the debris, tunneled out medical supplies, pieced together three operating rooms and sectioned off several outdoor "wards" for patient recovery," reports Sara Fajarado, a CRS communications officer in Haiti.

"Each day the number of surgeries performed at the hospital grows. Wounds are dressed. Antibiotics are dispensed. Charts are dutifully monitored. The St. Francois nursing staff has returned and once again provides 24-hour care. Doctors from Baltimore and CRS work alongside residents, medical students and seasoned Haitian doctors. Signs handwritten in permanent marker direct visitors: the pharmacy, the in-patient clinic, and the pediatric ward. This small touch adds an air of formality to a place ransacked by nature.

"But it's the quiet yet dignified resiliency of the patients that stands out. For a place overrun with the bandaged and amputated, no one complains. They are close enough to one another to hear every sound made by their fellow patients, and yet it's as quiet here as a private room. Patients take comfort in their loved ones and allow the healing to begin."

The most important thing...

Woven into the fabric of CRS relief efforts—the response of the faithful throughout the United States to the needs of most recent overseas disaster victims—a deeper, distinctively Catholic principle is at work than mere humanitarian aid.

"The ministry of charity is as essential to our ministry as Catholics as are the Sacraments," says Mr. Wiest. "The ministry of charity is as much a part of parish life in the United States and elsewhere as are other facets of parish life that might be more immediately visible. It's integral to our life as Catholics. As the Pope says in his first encyclical, Deus Caritas Est, "the ministry of charity is not extra-curricular. It is essential to our lives as Catholics."

"The passion that drives me," echoes Mr. Hackett, "is knowing that you can positively impact millions of peoples' lives. If you do your work correctly, lives can be transformed....it's a good thing to do, to positively improve people's lives in a sustainable way."

"...the exercise of charity is an action of the Church as such, and...like the ministry of Word and Sacrament, it too has been an essential part of her mission from the very beginning," instructs Pope Benedict XVI in *Deus Caritas Est*.

The face of love is the true face of all Catholics, no matter what their circumstances. As Michael Hill, CRS

Chairman of Catholic Relief Services' board, Archbishop of New York Timothy Dolan, right, greets fellow clergy prior to the funeral of Archbishop Joseph Serge Miot and Vicar Charles Benoit, on Saturday, January 23, 2010, in the courtyard of the Notre Dame Cathedral in Port-au-Prince Haiti. The two died as a result of the 7.0 magnitude earthquake that ravaged the Haitian capital. The cathedral collapsed and buried 4 o'clock worshippers in its rubble. In addition to Archbishop Dolan who represented the USCCB and Catholic Relief Services, Bishop Thomas Wenski of Orlando and CRS President, Ken Hackett were also in attendance. Mr. Hackett said of the ceremonies, "It was necessary for all those people there because he (Archbishop Miot) meant a lot to the people there. It was symbolic to have (the ceremony) in the courtyard of the damaged cathedral. This ceremony will help Haitians in their grieving process." Photo by Sara A. Fajardo/Catholic Relief Services.

communications officer for sub-Saharan Africa, based in Baltimore, reports: "During a three-day period of prayer beginning February 12, Haitians across the country took time to observe the one-month marker. Singing could be heard across the city, coming from formal and makeshift churches, from camps and settlements, from people walking to and from prayer services, and even from the CRS offices where a handful of Haitian staff members worked over the weekend."

The work has only begun. Love persists. Writes Mr. Hill: "Now attention is turning to providing shelter as the rainy season looms a month or so away." ◆

KAREN A. WALKER is Editor and Publisher of the *Catholic Business Journal* and Producer of *The Catholic Business Hour* radio show.

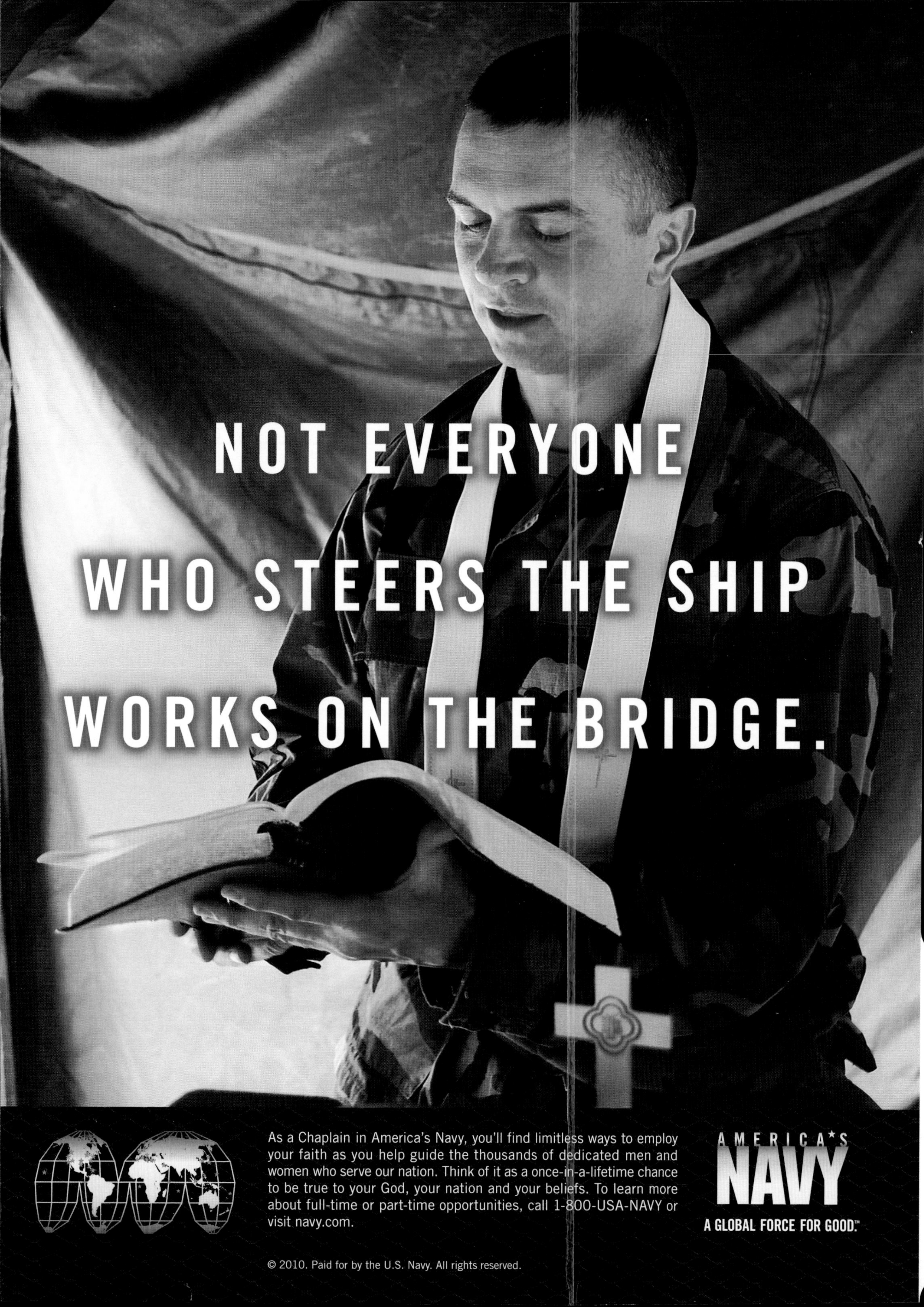
NOT EVERYONE
WHO STEERS THE SHIP
WORKS ON THE BRIDGE.
As a Chaplain in America's Navy, you'll find limitless ways to employ your faith as you help guide the thousands of dedicated men and women who serve our nation. Think of it as a once-in-a-lifetime chance to be true to your God, your nation and your beliefs. To learn more about full-time or part-time opportunities, call 1-800-USA-NAVY or visit navy.com.
AMERICA'S
NAVY
A GLOBAL FORCE FOR GOOD.™
© 2010. Paid for by the U.S. Navy. All rights reserved.

DRILL SERGEANTS STRENGTHEN THEIR MINDS
CHAPLAINS STRENGTHEN THEIR SOULS
There's strong. Then there's Chaplain strong. Do your part to spiritually strengthen our troops and their Families by joining the U.S. Army Chaplaincy. Serve on the frontline of the Soldiers' lives, developing close-knit relationships rarely found in any other ministry. Will you consider the call? For more information, visit www.goarmy.com/info/chaplain/j497.
U.S.ARMY
ARMY STRONG.
©2010. Paid for by the United States Army. All rights reserved.

Called to Serve Catholics in the Military

An interview with Archbishop Timothy Broglio and those who serve with him

By Karen A. Walker

Archbishop Timothy Broglio was installed as the fourth Archbishop of the Military Services, USA, on January 25, 2008. He leads America's only diocese without borders, the Archdiocese for Military Services, USA (AMS). Based out of Washington DC, Archbishop Broglio is charged with the spiritual well-being of U.S. military personnel stationed around the world. In March 2010, *The Official Catholic Directory* interviewed Archbishop Broglio regarding this unique archdiocese, its function and operation, its chaplains, vocations, and the breadth of individuals it serves. In addition to the archbishop's interview, several chaplains and a seminarian studying in Rome offer further insights from their varied perspectives.

Archdiocesan Shield: The coat of arms of the Archdiocese for the Military Services is divided into three sections, one in red, one in silver or white, and one in blue--the traditional colors of the United States. In the uppermost portion, there is an American Bald Eagle holding in each claw the universal symbol of peace, a green olive branch. In the middle portion, there is a silver cross on the outline meridians of the earth. In the lowest, the red portion of these arms, are the gold and silver crossed keys of Saint Peter, the symbol of the Holy See. The composition of the arms conveys the message and mission of the Archdiocese for the Military Services--to be Americans carrying peace; to carry Christ all over the world; and to act as a liaison for the United States and the Holy See.

Credit: the Archdiocese for the Military Services

Q. Archbishop Broglio, what is the unique function of the Archdiocese for the Military Services?

A. The Archdiocese for the Military Services, USA (hereafter AMS) differs from all others in that one is a member not by where he resides, but by the position he or she occupies. Subjects or faithful of the AMS are all Catholic active duty military of the five branches [U.S. Army, U.S. Air Force, U.S. Navy, U.S. Marine Corps, and U.S. Coast Guard] and their immediate family members and dependents or family residing with them, Catholics in the four Military Academies and the Merchant Marine Academy, patients in Veterans' Administration facilities and any personnel of those facilities who reside in them, any Catholic who is employed by the Federal Government (including contractors) and works outside of the boundaries of the United States of America.

The AMS receives no funding from the government and unlike territorial dioceses has no regular source of funding. There is no cathedraticum (a percentage of the Sunday collection given to territorial dioceses). All programs, staff, and travel by the personnel of the AMS must be funded through donations. The geographic area of the AMS is global: anywhere that there are U.S. forces or embassies, the AMS has jurisdiction. With the exception of Holy Trinity at West Point there are no canonically erected parishes in the AMS. All are chapels (some of which are dedicated only for Catholic worship). Any installation that has a Catholic chaplain must also have a Blessed Sacrament Chapel used exclusively for that purpose.

Archbishop Broglio washes soldiers' feet in Camp Victory, Iraq, on Holy Thursday 2009.
Credit for this photograph: Sgt. Neil W. McCabe

Q. What is the unique call of Catholic military chaplains?

A. In the AMS, the term "chaplain" is used exclusively for Catholic priests. They are all ordained for and incardinated in a territorial diocese or a religious order. To serve in the military they must be U.S. citizens. They can choose the branch of the military in which they desire to serve, provided that they meet the requirements of that branch (age, physical condition, etc.).

A chaplain serves the needs of the Catholic community. He becomes their "parish" priest, is the DRE for the religious education program. He must also meet the needs of others who come to him. His is also an ecumenical and interreligious minister. He will also have other military duties to which he must attend.

Q. How would you describe the distinctness of a Catholic military chaplain?

A. Given that all AMS chaplains are priests incardinated in another diocese or religious order, each one has his own vocation story. They are first and foremost called to the Priesthood of Jesus Christ. The specific nature of their calling as a chaplain stems from a variety of factors. Many of our chaplains have served in the military in the past. Remember, 10% of those ordained in the United States for the last several years were prior servicemen. The AMS also has an active co-sponsored seminarian program. There are currently 25 young men studying in seminaries across the U.S. and at the North American College who, in accord with their bishops, will serve three years in a diocesan parish and then serve for a specified number of years in the branch of the military of their choice.

A Catholic military chaplain must be a well-rounded priest who is secure in his role and ministry, able to work in an ecumenical setting, ready and willing to serve in a war zone, creative, a self-starter, and a compassionate man eager to meet the needs of the young entrusted to his care (the average age of Catholics in the military is from 18 to 28). He must be able to move frequently and able to deal with others who move frequently.

A chaplain who works for the VA must be prepared to care for the sick and also the victims of Post Traumatic Stress Disorder. He, too, must work in an ecumenical setting and be ready to deal with a variety of situations and settings that are not always under his control. The independence of each VA center makes very true the adage, "When you have seen one VA hospital, you have seen one VA hospital."

These characteristics allow the priest to serve the faithful in a time of war when there is a severe shortage of priests. Families are particularly victimized by the deployment and the war. The chaplain brings a unique perspective and assists these young families. The VA chaplain must deal with both young and old. He, too, must reach out to the families and console those who mourn.

Q. With no prior military experience, how did you become the archbishop of this diocese?

A. I spent 29 years of ordained ministry either in preparation for, or in service as, a member of the diplomatic corps of the Holy See. When I returned to the United States in 2008, I had not lived in this country since 1979.

I was the Apostolic Nuncio in the Dominican Republic and the Apostolic Delegate in Puerto Rico when the superiors in the Secretariat of State asked if I would accept a nomination as the Archbishop for the Military Services in the U.S.

Q. What are your greatest challenges?

A. My greatest challenges are also my goals. There is a severe shortage of military chaplains (but not of VA chaplains). Religious education must somehow be standardized and improved so that those who frequently change assignments can easily fit into the new setting and program. Finally, given the tenuous financial situation of the AMS, my goal is to assure a constant and regular source of income to allow the AMS to function as it should in the service of its faithful.

Q. What are your greatest joys?

A. The joys of this ministry are the people involved in it. I have been deeply impressed by the men and women I am privileged to serve. Their dedication, willingness to participate, love of country and family are virtues to be cultivated. I am humbled by their appreciation for the little I am able to do. Visiting the military academies has been a great source of hope. The young men and women there are fine, dedicated youth who offer great promise for the future. I am always eager to spend time with them. Their enthusiasm is contagious. Finally, my visits to those who are deployed in the war zone and in other hardship posts have been great lessons in sacrifice, commitment, and duty. The US can be very proud of those who serve our country.

Q. What advice would you give to future chaplains, or to those priests who are considering this service?

A. In terms of advice to future chaplains, the key is ministry which means service. We all respond to a call at ordination and we all have an idea as to how we will live that call, but it is really Almighty God and the Church that ultimately determine the needs and the best use of our talents. Authentic ministry is openness to that call and determination. It is the move from my priesthood to the priesthood of Jesus Christ determined by His Church.

Serving the Flock

The Official Catholic Directory also interviewed three chaplains and a seminarian in Rome.

> After having called the Twelve to follow him, Jesus kept them at his side and lived with them, imparting his teaching of salvation to them through word and example ...
>
> —Pope John Paul II

Q. What is it like to be a chaplain?

A. "A chaplain is a very special vocation. Not everyone is cut out for it," says Fr. Aidan Logan, O.C.S.O., a Cistercian monk who has served nearly 20 years in the U.S. Naval Chaplain Corps. He is now a commander (level O-5, the equivalent of a lieutenant colonel in the Army), and head chaplain of the 2nd U.S. Marine Corps' infantry division on the East Coast, stationed at Camp LeJeune, NC.

"You have to be able to sustain yourself without support of community," explains Fr. Aidan. "Often you're the only priest in a place. You have to be able to stand on your own two feet."

He adds: "You have to be a good priest first. That's why you come in as a chaplain, to be a priest. We don't need more sailors or soldiers. We have plenty. We need priests... You don't want to come into the military because you're uncomfortable with your priesthood. You must be sure and confident in your priesthood....And it helps if you're physically fit – that's important for any priest anyway. You have to be tough to be a priest!"

Certain responsibilities are common to all chaplains—they provide for the sacramental needs of Catholics in their unit as well as for the religious and morale needs of all the troops in their unit, they are not allowed to carry weapons, they live and mingle daily with the troops. Yet each military branch has its own "culture" as well.

"For the Army you have to like the outdoors," says Fr. Paul Anthony Halladay, a chaplain with the rank of captain in the U.S. Army who has been a chaplain for six years, after four prior years as a parish priest in Alabama. "You can't be squeamish about cold and heat, and you can't be afraid to get dirty and wet."

"For the Navy," Fr. Halladay continues, "most everything happens on ships. You don't have to factor in the outdoors as much. The Air Force [chaplain] is more like a parish priest than other branches, and the Marines is most similar to Army chaplains because you're outside a lot."

"Navy chaplains deploy all the time," adds Fr. Aidan. "It's different from the Air Force and Army. The Navy are always on the ships, like cops on the beat, ready to respond to what situations might come up—piracy, threats, keeping sea lanes open. They're kind of the 911 sea response team."

"Commanders call chaplains 'force multipliers,'" says Fr. Halladay. "While we don't bring the heat so to speak, carry weapons, nor are we combatants, we do help keep soldiers focused, prepared and ready to do their job. We help soldiers to be the best soldiers they can be, particularly when that is compromised by what they had to do in defense of this nation."

Different from a parish priest

"As a parish priest, and I was a parish priest for four years before entering the Army, you really live within a Catholic bubble. There's little opportunity to have dialog and interaction with people outside the bubble, you're too busy," Fr. Halladay notes. "But as a military chaplain, you are immediately thrown in the midst of all faiths! As a chaplain, you work every day with chaplains of different faiths, coordinating religious services for the troops and with soldiers of the Catholic faith, another faith, or no faith at all."

"Also, I work right along side these same soldiers—in field exercises, command staff meetings, and in administrative decisions within a battalion. We go out on field exercises together. We'll train for the eventuality of mass casualties and that includes making sure soldiers of all faiths have what they need," continues Fr. Halladay.

Fr. Aidan concurs: "From the first day, we're cheek to jowl with Protestants. We see quickly the strength of our faith and the need for absolute clarity about our Catholic faith because there are other chaplains around to whom the troops can go…You have the opportunity to explain what you believe, and why. Most of the Protestant chaplains have never met a Catholic priest in their lives and now they're living with one! There's a good ecumenical side to it!"

Responsible, Prepared

"A chaplain compiles a religious preference profile for the soldiers in his command, including dietary needs," explains Fr. Halladay. "On Ash Wednesday and Good Friday, a Catholic soldier cannot eat meat, on the feast of Ramadan, a Muslim soldier can only eat before dawn and after sunset —you have to make sure appropriate rations are available. I also must put in for all the things I need for Mass, and I must prepare for a minimum of six months, based on the Catholic population in my battalion—things like the wine and hosts. I have to estimate how many soldiers will attend daily and Sunday Masses, and plan appropriately. When you're on a field exercise, and then later deployed, if you're not prepared, you don't have it!"

On deployment, ensuring soldiers' religious needs are met may often mean bringing in another chaplain from another unit, such as flying in a Navy chaplain to say Mass for Army troops in Afghanistan.

Attentive to the soul, the inner man

Saint Jean Vianney wrote: "The priesthood is the love of the heart of Jesus." Military chaplains live that every day.

A commander relies on his chaplain to know the pulse of the troops under his command. Troops lean on their chaplain for spiritual, religious, personal and morale issues.

"You're right there, right alongside with the troops," explains Fr. Halladay, who clearly loves what he does, just like every chaplain we interviewed. "They might show me a particular weapon, or what they're learning on preventative maintenance of their vehicles, or in grenade training, or at the shooting range."

"I'll ask how they're doing. They'll talk about their personal lives. Just conversation. You're there for them, and they know that what they tell you isn't going anywhere else."

"If a unit is training really hard for deployment and it's starting to show in terms of family problems – for example you start hearing, 'Hey, chaplain, my wife and I aren't getting along. We have different schedules and we're not seeing each other,' etc…"

"You get enough of those comments and you talk to your commander, saying maybe it's time for an Organizational Day—where the commander suspends all operations in the battalion and everyone comes together for recreation, all families included. It might be held in the middle of the week, say on a Wednesday. Troops are on a hard grind for deployment and then they get a day off—it's a huge morale boost. Fr. Halladay continues, "You want soldiers well-prepared for maybe a year deployment. One of biggest things we do as chaplains is to keep up morale in a unit. It's important."

Being there when it counts

Andy Young graduated from the Naval Academy, entered the Marine Corps (USMC), and served two tours, in Afghanistan and Iraq. He was part of the invasion force that went from Kuwait to Iraq after 9-11 and left the military with the rank of Captain, USMC. Now he's a seminarian, studying in Rome for the Diocese of Sioux Falls, SD. He's also a chaplain candidate for the U.S. Navy.

"At Camp Pendleton I'd go to daily Mass and it would be me and the priest, and maybe one or two others," says Mr. Young. "But when we were deployed and in Kuwait, waiting to go into Iraq, we'd have 70 to 80 people at daily Mass, and long lines for confession. When things are tough, people turn to God. When you're in a war zone, when you don't know what the next day will hold for you, you want to be clean of sin, at least I did."

"A chaplain can be a mediator to bring people to know Christ, especially in deployment, away from family and home." Mr. Young adds. "These young soldiers are alone, scared. They're looking for anything—peace, hope, ultimate meaning in life. Christ is the answer to all of it. When things go bad, you turn to the only person who can console you."

Don't forget the veterans!

Fr. James Burnett retired from the Air Force in 1999. For 10 years he's been serving veterans with the Veterans Administration. He is the chief of chaplain services at Hines VA Hospital in Chicago; president, National Conference of Veterans Affairs Chaplains (NCVAC); and a board certified chaplain for NCVAC. The NCVAC has 340 Catholic priests in various salaried positions within the VA system.

Hines is one of the largest hospitals in the VA system, serving 500 patients with needs ranging from spinal cord injuries and blindness rehab, to elder care, hospice and more. He has nine chaplains on his staff. For six of the ten years Fr. Burnett worked in hospice care. He is thrilled that a new hospice wing of the hospital is opening, saying that they serve up to 22 hospice patients at any given time.

"People ask me if it's depressing to be involved in hospice. Not at all!" responds Fr. Burnett. "It's very pleasing to be there in the last days of a veteran, who has served his country well. Now it's our turn to serve him."

Q. Why did you become a military chaplain?

A. "I'd been giving priests retreats for years," says Fr. Aidan. "A number of chaplains came on these retreats. They were the happiest priests I'd ever seen, whereas the others were burned out with low morale. I was impressed with the chaplains. When the Gulf War came on in '91, I got calls to become a chaplain...I asked my superior. He said yes. My spiritual director said yes. So here I am today, back where I first started, in Camp LeJeune."

Fr. Burnett has a different story: "I wanted to see the world. I was priest in southeast Iowa, serving two parishes, and looking for something else. On a visit with friends near Bellville, Ill., we were joined one dinner by someone who was on active duty at nearby Scott Air Force Base. He gave me a tour of the base, showed me the chapel and I met the Catholic chaplain. He wasn't very friendly and I thought, 'I could do better than that.' So I went home, prayed about it, and then asked permission of my bishop to serve in the military. He said OK!"

Upon retirement, Fr. Burnett applied for chief of chaplain services at Hines VA. "I felt a calling from the Lord to get the word out about what's happening with the returning veterans from Afghanistan and Iraq," he says.

Challenges

"One of the greatest challenges is loneliness," says Fr. Paul Halladay, although he's quick to enumerate his abundant joys after explaining what he means. "You're the only chaplain in your battalion. You're the one everyone comes to with personal and religious issues. As a Catholic priest you're typically the only Catholic priest in your brigade so there's not another priest you can talk to close by."

Another challenge is the shortage of priests in the military, especially in the Army. That means a chaplain often pulls double and triple duty.

"My Army rank makes me a battalion chaplain, "says Fr. Halladay. "But because of my religious denomination as a Catholic priest, I often work as the only Catholic priest on a post, which is 25,000 to 35,000 troops...We have more than 1,000 people at Mass each weekend. I run all the Catholic programs, etc."

Fr. Burnett sees another challenge, namely to help to ease the transition of a veteran back home. One lament is that most hometown clergy, who are often too busy, don't understand the unique problems, or what's needed for healing, of a veteran.

"In as little as two weeks, a soldier can go from active duty to a VA hospital," says Fr. Burnett. "It's hard to wrap your head around that; their heads are spinning...It's important for local clergy to understand terms such as traumatic brain injury, post traumatic stress disorder, poly trauma (multiple problems), so they know what they're getting and how to deal with it."

Over the last two years, Fr. Burnett held two well-attended conferences, both funded by his regional VA, to educate non-military priests on how to understand the specific needs of veterans in their community. Topics included the way different cultures express emotions, how female veterans process battle scars differently from men, and the symptoms of traumatic brain injury, which is a hidden wound, a shaking of the brain. A soldier might return not knowing his children, not able to communicate with his spouse, or remember his job even though he's done if for years. "They often end up at the VA as the last ultimatum of his wife," says Fr. Burnett. "There also can be problems in a marriage when the returning veteran feels like a stranger in his own home. He's gone through so much trauma in his deployment while his spouse had to run everything in his absence. It's good for priests to know how to deal with these things."

Joys

"The greatest joys of being a chaplain? There's a lot of those,' says Fr. Halladay without hesitation. "I'd say bringing someone back to their faith—bringing them to a renewed appreciation of faith in their life—that's one of the best feelings in the world."

Fr. Halladay continues: "You run the RCIA program, bring them into church at Easter – beautiful. You prepare for marriage. It's wonderful...just being available for a soldier for what he had to do for our country, psychologically and physically—to know you have that role in someone's life is phenomenal!"

"It's an opportunity to give a masculine face to the Catholic faith," notes Fr. Aiden. "One of the problems of parishes can be that there are not a lot of strong masculine models there, but you're mostly with men in a military environment."

Fr. Aidan adds, "You help soldiers to understand there's an adult way to be a Catholic. Most guys run on fumes. They remember something of their faith from their grandmother and mother but there's not much adult to it – even for those with kids, their faith is centered around their kids. But in the military, you show them it's an adult thing, that there's an adult way to live the faith."

Another of Fr. Aidan's joys happened recently. On an annual pilgrimage with midshipmen from the Naval Academy to Rome, he was surprised to find that a young man he'd known in the medical corps was now in the seminary, inspired by Fr. Aidan.

For Fr. Burnett, his greatest joy is serving the needs of the veterans as a veteran himself, adding "It's a joy to enlighten hometown clergy on returning veterans."

Q. Has it changed you?

A. "Absolutely." says Fr. Aiden. "But that's just life. I think I've become more confirmed in my faith and priesthood;

Father Thomas Falkenthal, CHC, USN celebrates the Eucharist with Marines at the summit of the Sierra Nevada Mountains. Credit: Photograph provided by the Archdiocese for the Military Services, USA

partly because I get to deal with people all the time who don't have the faith and I see what a lack it is. I also see what it means to be a Catholic – to have the faith in extreme situations and to see how it changes people."

Vocations

"The largest single group who enters the seminary has served in military," says Fr. Aidan. "The Naval Academy is 52 percent Catholic. West Point is about 1/3 Catholic."

"You see the need for Catholic chaplains," says Mr. Young. "In an emergency situation, a Catholic priest can run any service, whereas no one else can consecrate the Eucharist or say Mass."

Fr. Burnett is among many chaplains with high praise for their archbishop, crediting him with helping to foster an increased awareness of the chaplaincy and an increase in vocations. "When I applied to the VA 10 years ago," he says, "I was the only Catholic priest applying. Now we have many applications. Three years ago we had 100 VA chaplains. Now we are 340 strong. See what the Lord is doing! Priests who apply to work here want to give back to veterans for serving our country."

But plenty more chaplains are needed.

"There's a huge potential for vocations in the military," Fr. Halladay points out, citing that 18% of all ordinations in the U.S. over the past 10 years have come from those with previous military service or from a military family."

"Any priest who is sent to the military is like an investment. He goes in, and he returns with vocations for you," adds Fr. Halladay. "The backbone of the military is made up of unmarried men between the ages of 18 to 24."

And when Mr. Young describes the marks of a good soldier—love of country and God over self, integrity, obedience, courage—they echo the marks of a good military chaplain, which, for Mr. Young, include dedication to leading his flock and showing his love for Christ. As he puts it, "If you're doing five or six Masses a day, that's tough. We need chaplains who are willing to give 110% every day!...They are living examples of what it means to follow Christ."

"Those who are serving their country need to have Catholic priests serving with them," says Mr. Young. "How else will they receive the sacraments? It's so important and yet it's something we so easily take for granted because most of us can receive sacraments any time we want...at any parish church."

"This is a beautiful way to be a priest," sums up Fr. Halladay. "It's also a very needed ministry." ◆

KAREN A. WALKER is Editor and Publisher of the *Catholic Business Journal* and Producer of *The Catholic Business Hour* radio show.

The Year for Priests: Why St. John Vianney?

June 19, 2009 – June 19, 2010

By Fr. Chris Heath

Christ the Great High Priest Icon © MCzarnecki2010
www.seraphicrestorations.com

Most priests know just enough about the Curé of Ars to consider him only a historical oddity. The patron saint of priests, some would say, was a holy man for his time, but not a model for the modern priesthood, especially here in the United States. But Pope Benedict XVI does not agree. In 2009, he chose a Year for Priests to coincide with the 150th anniversary of St. John Vianney's death. Benedict's choice was no accident. Calling the Church—and especially the clergy—to "interior renewal for the sake of a stronger and more incisive witness to the Gospel in today's world," he invited us during this special year to "learn for ourselves something of the pastoral plan of St. John Vianney." The Year for Priests, which began and ended on the Solemnity of the Sacred Heart of Jesus—also not a coincidence—gave the Church this challenge.

The great Curé first came to the French village of Ars a nobody, relegated to a lost parish in the middle of nowhere. This place—known for its fog, stagnant water and bad roads—had been abandoned for several years following the French Revolution and its ensuing spiritual and material devastation. For the first 10 years of his 40-year pastorate, St. John labored tirelessly for change, at great personal cost.

The church building sat dilapidated, the rectory showed itself a wreck, and for many years the parish was dirt poor. Fr. Vianney's flock numbered just 230 souls living in 60 households.

In his early years as pastor, St. John Vianney performed only a handful of weddings, funerals, baptisms and sick calls. Local townspeople were at best unimpressed with the new pastor. At worst, apathy and active resistance made his task even more daunting. St. John was accused of wrongdoing and even abuse. People whose livelihoods and lifestyles were threatened by his preaching complained to both civil and ecclesiastical authorities to have him removed. Other priests in the diocese thought he was a simpleton or downright dangerous to the Church. The Evil One, too, waged intense spiritual battles to discourage St. John and to frighten his parishioners away.

This situation would have disheartened most priests, but this pastor celebrated Mass prayerfully every day without fail. Slowly his consistency drew the attention of his parishioners, and over time, his small church became filled for daily Mass. St. John knew that his skills as a preacher were limited, but he took his responsibility seriously. He spent hours painstakingly handwriting his Sunday homilies. When preaching, his emotions often overtook him and he would cry as he described the horrors of sin and the dangers his people faced because of their poor choices. He spoke out against dancing, gambling, cursing, missing Sunday Mass and especially against drinking, the cause of much of the village's family discord and poverty. He called people to daily prayer. But the pastor of Ars did even more. He modeled it for them. As people began to see the error of their ways, they sought him out for confession.

Nothing was easy about St. John's pastoral assignment. For example, many village children were forced into manual labor and crime. He opened an orphanage and day school to keep them safe, to teach them the basics of reading and writing, and to teach them the catechism. Often this pastor had little to offer the children for daily meals, but somehow just enough donated food or money would find its way into his hands so that he could provide for their needs one more day. Fr. Vianney named his orphanage "Providence" because he knew it was only by God's hand that he was able to care for so many with so little.

For 10 long years, St. John persevered in his often-thankless pastoral work and prayer. But eventually he converted the desolate and disconsolate place into a hub of Catholic life. By then, most of his parish had returned to the faith, and now people from other towns came to Ars to attend his Masses, and to wait in ever-growing lines for a few moments with him in confession. Even the French railway changed its booking procedures to accommodate the thousands of people who flocked to see Fr.

Priest awaits the presentation of the gifts
Photo: Ginger Mortensen, International Theological Institute, Austria

Vianney year after year. Near the end, St. John was spending 18 hours a day in the confessional. In the last year of his life, some 120,000 people came to Ars to see a man who was ordained initially without the faculties to preach or hear confessions, a man whom the educated and well-placed had written-off as a "half-wit." To disregard his witness to faith, hope, and love—then or now—is to miss the Gospel itself.

Standing in the breach:
An unwitting example and point of reference

In his time, Fr. Vianney was horrified when people gave him honors. What would he think today about a Pope linking him with "a pastoral plan" for the world's priests? Regardless, St. John offers the Church a "point of reference" for dealing with the weakness of her ministers. If only priests and people were aware of the immense gift of this vocation to the Church!

"Were we to fully realize what a priest is on earth, we would die: not of fright, but of love," Fr. Vianney would say, showing us that the ordained and those whom they serve should treat with great care this fragile vocation that helps reveal Christ in the world. Key for priests is the idea of "interior renewal," which begins with an uncompromising approach to the moral and doctrinal truths of the Catholic faith. As a parish priest, St. John stood in the breach against the rationalism and "enlightenment" of the age in which he lived, against the atheists, the intelligentsia, and against the political and economic forces of his time, not with aggression borne of power, but with the power of the Word. Too, his unwavering humility and gentleness in response to accusation, resistance and slander diffused his enemies' attacks. A lack of material resources only increased his faith in Providence. In the face of others' lost faith, he lived his own, modeled it and preached about it in a way that made it credible by example, and thus changed people's lives. Put simply, he brought people to Christ.

For the People of God, this Year for Priests was meant to be a time to pray for priests, to sustain and help them in their ministry, and to rediscover, in the midst of scandal and weakness, the world's absolute need for a purified priesthood to represent the love of God, and the active presence of Jesus Christ in the service of charity and in the Eucharist. Pope Benedict even went so far as to state that the world would be lost without the Real Presence of Christ, and it is the priest who mediates this Real Presence.

When people esteem the priesthood, priests are more conscious of the responsibility they have to model Christ, to strive for spiritual perfection, and to identify themselves more personally with Christ, "to harmonize his life as a minister with the holiness of the ministry he has received." St. John Vianney trembled from a conviction of his personal inadequacy. Three times he ran away from his parish "to weep over his poor life," and each time his parishioners carried him back to the church. His people were ready to support him even when he was overwhelmed by his own weakness. Perhaps it was called "Year 'for' Priests" and not "Year 'of' Priests" precisely to call attention to what the Catholic priesthood needs to thrive in the Church and in the world: a renewed appreciation for the priesthood even as her ministers struggle to live up to its demands and ideals. The Year was "for" priests to benefit them personally, and as they grow the Church will benefit as well.

St. John Vianney said that "the priesthood is the love of the heart of Jesus." Jesus is the perfect and incarnate representation of the Father. His heart, full of love and pierced for all on the Cross, needs to be seen and experienced in the world in every generation. And priests are ordained precisely for this ministry: to show that love personally and sacramentally. Pope Benedict could have pointed to any one of hundreds of priest-saints of the past, or even some who have lived in our lifetime, but he chose the Curé of Ars. He has pointed to his life as a simple parish priest and said our lives should be more like his: personally engaging, completely invested, "enthralled by Christ," not just a functionary but consciously and intentionally striving be a "sign

"Were we to fully realize what a priest is on earth, we would die: not of fright, but of love," Fr. Vianney would say, showing us that the ordained and those whom they serve should treat with great care this fragile vocation that helps reveal Christ in the world.

Newly ordained priest gives his first priestly blessing to his mother. Photo: Ginger Mortensen, International Theological Institute, Austria

and presence of God's infinite mercy," or to use the traditional concept, an alter Christus. The Sacred Heart of Jesus, then, is the perfect symbol for this Year, the most appropriate beginning and ending to the Year for Priests.

Whether priests take their cue from St. John Vianney remains to be seen. Various theological and ecclesiological concepts about the priesthood compete for attention in the Church today. Scandals within the Church force us to look at many facets of priests' lives and psyches and could easily distract our attention away from an element that is foundational to Benedict's main objective: the priest as image of Christ—a sacramental and supernatural reality that St. John, with all his limitations, figured out how to live. Hopefully many will take up the task to study St. John's pastoral activity and unpack it for a new age of the Church. At this tempestuous point in the third millennium, the Curé of Ars could not be more relevant. ◆

FR. CHRIS HEATH is a Priest of the Diocese of Orange in California, and Parochial Vicar of St. Edward the Confessor in Dana Point, California. He has held several parish assignments, most recently as Pastor of La Purisima Church in Orange where he oversaw the building of a new church and parish facilities. He is a law enforcement chaplain, and Chaplain of Catholics at Work OC, the local chapter of a nation-wide business club.

References used in article: Francis Trochu, The Curé d'Ars (Tan Books, 1977); Pope Benedict XVI, Letter Proclaiming a Year for Priests, June 16, 2009; Pope Benedict XVI, Homily on the Solemnity of the Sacred Heart and Opening of the Year for Priests, June 19, 2009; Pope Benedict XVI, General Audience, June 24, 2009; Pope Benedict XVI, General Audience, August 5, 2009.

People's Prayer for Priests

Dear Lord,
we pray that the Blessed Mother
wrap her mantle around your priests
and through her intercession
strengthen them for their ministry.

We pray that Mary will guide your priests
to follow her own words,
"Do whatever He tells you" (Jn 2:5)

May your priests have the heart of St. Joseph,
Mary's most chaste spouse.

May the Blessed Mother's own pierced heart
inspire them to embrace
all who suffer at the foot of the cross.

May your priests be holy,
filled with the fire of your love
seeking nothing but your greater glory
and the salvation of souls.

Amen.

Saint John Vianney, pray for us.

From USCCB for The Year for the Priests

Food for the Journey:

Five Saints and the Bread of Life

By Ricky J. McRoskey

Dr. Drew Peterson is about to sit down to breakfast. It's a humid February morning in Port-au-Prince, and the orthopedic surgeon from San Diego is steeling himself for another day in which he'll operate on people with crushed bones from the massive earthquake that leveled the Caribbean city weeks earlier. He has already finished a set of pushups and a three-mile run before the sun has risen.

Like the many other doctors in Haiti now, Dr. Peterson is here to serve. Over the course of 10 days, he and a group of other surgeons, nurses, and anesthesiologists from San Diego's Scripps Medical Response Team will perform hundreds of operations on wounded Haitians in a packed Catholic hospital. At his disposal are surgical tools, medications, and decades of experience in the operating room. But he needs more. To manage the week's toil—the rigors of surgery, the stench of dead bodies, and the sight of crippled children—he needs to rejuvenate. Constantly. "You need to take care of the body," he says, "especially at a time like this."

It's why, each morning, after he's exercised, showered, and gone to Mass, he and the doctors will convene for a hearty breakfast of eggs and cheese, rice, mangos, cantaloupe, grapes, slices of ham and salami. It's why, to provide for the much-needed energy at the hospital, he will pack himself dried apricots and figs, nuts, PowerBars, powdered Gatorade and bottled water. They came to Haiti on a mission to heal the wounded, and to do it right they need the energy and strength to sustain themselves. In other words, in a land of hunger and death, you need life. You need hope. You need strength.

And, in a land of hunger and death, you need food.

In 2009, Pope Benedict XVI welcomed five new saints to the Catholic Church, saints who had lived in times of hunger and death—ages of physical, emotional, and spiritual longing. Three of them lived through Italy's 19th-century Industrial Revolution, which brought greater efficiency to the nation's businesses, but also longer working hours, sordid factories, and exhausted families. One saint led Portugal in the midst of war. Another lived in medieval Italy during the plague. Throughout their lives, they fought battles, worked in spinning mills, studied law, helped cholera victims, contracted disease, went blind, lost children, and withstood family rejections and heresy accusations.

Yet they succumbed to none of it. Instead of lamenting the circumstances of their lives, we remember them for their endurance. We remember the monastery that St. Bernardo Tolomei founded, or the order of St. Caterina Volpicelli, or St. Nuno's courage on the battlefield and in the convent. We remember St. Arcangelo's advocacy for working women, and St. Geltrude's ministry to poor Italian families. But what is perhaps most fascinating about these five saints is not their different accomplishments, but what unequivocally united them, the singular source of all energy, strength, and nourishment from which they made their societies better: the Eucharist.

In his homily canonizing these five last April, Pope Benedict said, "Nourished with the Eucharistic Bread, the Saints we are venerating today brought their mission of evangelical love to completion."

That's the common thread: they all loved the Eucharist, the true, actual body and blood of Christ. It was the mystery, the spiritual "food," that kept them going. Each of them spent countless hours in front of the Blessed Sacrament and received it frequently at Mass. In doing so, they embraced a strange, remarkable paradox—that we as Catholics derive our strength by remembering and participating in an instance of unimaginable suffering, in which the most powerful person to have ever walked the Earth was punched, spat on, whipped, bloodied, ridiculed, condemned, stripped naked, punctured, and murdered. It's baffling: That's our nourishment? That's supposed to give us strength? That's our hope?

It's hard to believe, until we consider the rest of the story. Because embracing the Eucharist, as these five saints show, means embracing the fact that the story doesn't end at Christ's death. He rises, comes back, and fills his believers with a sense of hope and inspiration that impels them forward. For these five, the Eucharist taught them that every battle for good is worth fighting. You just need to have the strength, the bread—indeed, the spiritual food—to confront it. And, as Catholics, it's something that we have access to, in every church, every day—just as they did.

The Italians of the Industrial Age

Three of the saints came of age in an Italian society that was being wildly transformed. Geltrude Comensoli, Caterina Volpicelli, and Arcangelo Tadini were all born within eight years of one another, in the mid-1800s, just as Italy was joining the Industrial Revolution. Previously rural societies began to morph into technological nations, manufacturing everything from clothing to machinery. But with new opportunity came new dangers. Workplace accidents became prevalent. The poor lived in disease-ridden cities. Children worked long hours, and women had to balance work life with family time. That's when these three made their mark.

Fr. Arcangelo Tadini, a northern Italian priest known for his powerful preaching and zeal, was a workhorse. One gets the sense from his biography that this was a man of incredible grit. While in the seminary, he injured his leg badly—and limped the rest of his life. When he was out of the seminary, he contracted a serious illness—and recovered. He started a soup kitchen, rebuilt a church, and constructed a spinning factory. He never seemed to stop. And how, again, did he have the energy? The Vatican explains: "His parishioners would see him for hours in front of the Blessed Sacrament, despite his disability."

Where others saw work as dismal, he saw it as an opportunity to grow in faith. He founded several Catholic organizations devoted to improving the lives of the working poor. One of them, the Congregation of Worker Sisters of the Holy House of Nazareth, featured sisters who, under his direction, devoted their lives to working alongside other women in Italian factories, encouraging them and offering them hope despite aching joints and acrid air. The organization exists to this day.

If Arcangelo was tireless, **Geltrude Comensoli** was resilient. In 1880, the 33-year-old Italian nun had the chance to directly ask Pope Leo XIII what he thought of her launching an organization devoted to (what else?) Eucharistic adoration. Good, he said, but it wasn't enough in this new society. There were too many women whose spiritual lives were suffering from too much work, he thought; she needed to minister to female factory workers in the process. One can imagine her frustration, like that of an architect who spends years painstakingly sketching a building's design, only to have the master builder say, "It looks good. Now make it twice as big, with more windows."

So she went back to the drawing board, and to the Blessed Sacrament, and spent the next two years forming the Congregation of the Sacramentine Sisters of Bergamo with the bishop's support. It was a resounding—albeit arduous—success. Through the order's example of perpetual adoration and its emphasis on the primacy of family over work, it brought perspective to a nation hypnotized by industry. As for St. Geltrude, her life ended where she spent much of it: in the midst of adoration.

Meanwhile, to the far south in Naples, **Caterina Volpicelli** grew up with wealth, shielded from the indignity of the factory. Early life centered not on the spinning mill, but theaters, ballet, literature, and music. That is, until she decided these things had become too much of a priority. At 15, at the recommendation of a spiritual advisor, she left it all behind, embracing instead the religious life.

It prompts an interesting question: What's more difficult—staying focused on the important things despite work, or despite luxury? Caterina ultimately established—among other things—the Handmaids of the Sacred Heart, an order that emphasized the importance of the family. The Handmaids also focused on care for those suffering from cholera, a debilitating intestinal disease that left its victims weak, nauseous, and dehydrated. It was also extremely contagious, requiring a patience and love that was otherworldly.

Not surprisingly, the Vatican says Caterina was motivated by an "ardent love of the Eucharist," something that prompted her to build a shrine to the Sacred Heart in Naples, for the purpose of Eucharistic adoration.

The Warrior

In 1385, an army of 30,000 Castillians invaded modern-day Portugal, seeking to seize the country. Standing in the Castillians' way was an army less than a quarter its size, led by a 25-year-old

A Brief Look at Forthcoming Saints of 2010

By Ricky J. McRoskey

Mary MacKillop (1842-1909)

Who she was: A 19th-century Australian nun, MacKillop founded the Sisters of Saint Joseph of the Sacred Heart, an order dedicated to education, particularly for the children of the working poor. Today, the congregation has a presence in Australia, New Zealand, Brazil, Peru, Uganda, and Thailand.

Notable: MacKillop, who will be known as St. Mary of the Cross, is slated to become the first Australian saint.

Quotable: "Never see a need without doing something about it."

Andre Bessette (1845-1937)

Who he was: A Canadian Holy Cross brother, Bessette in 1904 founded the St. Joseph's Oratory of Mt. Royal in Montreal, a modern-day 420-foot basilica visited by millions of pilgrims each year. Known for his humility and great devotion to St. Joseph, he became recognized for his healing ministry after thousands of ailing people were cured at his hands in Montreal. But he was always quick to dispel any notion of possessing a personal power: "I do not cure," he would say. "St. Joseph cures."

Notable: Bessette will become the first member of the Holy Cross order to be recognized as a saint.

Quotable: Describing one of his first jobs as a Holy Cross brother, in which he answered the door and welcomed guests at a Montreal college: "At the end of my novitiate, my superiors showed me the door—and I stayed there for 40 years."

Portuguese general named **Nuno de Santa Maria Alvares Pereira**. A devout Christian, Nuno led his troops in an epic battle that drove out the Castillians, secured a long period of peace, and brought the underdog general great notoriety and riches.

It's not hard to imagine the scenes that followed, of doting women and obsequious friends hoping to bask in the glow of his fame. But what's most incredible about Nuno is that the fame and riches didn't go to his head. He realized, as Pope Benedict said, that "in any situation, even of a military and warlike nature, it is possible to act and live out the values and principles of Christian life." He fasted three days a week. He built churches and monasteries. And after his wife and two sons had died, he gave up his wealth and spent the rest of his life in a Carmelite convent, where he prayed, nurtured a deep love for the Eucharist (there it is again!), and distributed bread to the poor.

The Monk

Then there's **Bernardo Tolomei**. A 13th-century knight and law scholar who suffered from partial blindness, he retreated from society at age 41 to work and pray in solitude on his family's farms. He eventually established a Benedictine monastery there in Tuscany, where he would serve as abbot for 27 straight years and live what Pope Benedict called "the Eucharistic life." The monastery, the Abbey of Mt. Oliveto, still stands in the middle of the lush fields today, where its monks work as Bernardo did, cultivating wheat, barley, beans, vineyards and olives for the community.

This begs the question: What sort of person with wealth and an education decides, at age 41, to retreat into the fields and pray, to hunch over the ground and pull weeds, plant seeds, and farm under the Italian sun—while blind? Or, perhaps more importantly, what sort of person, accustomed to this life of prayer and solitude, leaves the monastery at age 76 to help plague-ridden monks at another monastery? And then catches the plague himself and dies?

The answer: a person that is called to it by love. What is most striking about St. Bernardo is that each of the decisions of his life—as strange as they may have appeared to others—came from a humble conviction. Also striking is that this strength of conviction and perseverance, by some remarkable coincidence, has the very same source as that of three other Italians and a Portuguese general who were canonized on the same day.

Perhaps most remarkable about the life of a saint is the incredible energy it requires. Building organizations and treating illnesses requires constant renewal and rejuvenation, as does doing any other good today—operating on an earthquake victim, caring for the elderly, bearing a child.

We live in the same land of hunger and death that these saints did. For them, courage came from the peaceful moments before a tabernacle and the sacrament of the Eucharist.

The question is, today, as we struggle through the aches and pains of work, sickness, and family life, where will we look for the strength to overcome them? That is, in a land of hunger and death, where will we look for the Bread of Life?

RICKY J. MCROSKEY writes for a New York-based financial firm. A 2006 Notre Dame alumnus, he recently graduated from the Columbia Graduate School of Journalism and has written for *Business Week, Silicon Alley Insider* and the *San Diego Daily Transcript*.

Juana Josefa Cipitria Barriola (1845-1912)

Who she was: A Spanish nun known as Mother Candida, she founded the Congregation of the Daughters of Jesus in 1871, an order dedicated to the education of children and the advancement of women in Spain. Today, the Daughters of Jesus teach in 17 countries throughout Latin America, Europe, Asia, and Africa.

Notable: Mother Candida was strongly influenced by the spiritual exercises of St. Ignatius, which seek to deepen faith and understanding through a series of regular meditations, mental exercises, prayers, and visualization techniques.

Quotable: "Where there is no room for the poor, there is no room for me."

Giulia Salzano (1846-1929)

Who she was: A 19th-century nun from southern Italy with a passion for teaching, Salzano founded an order whose mission centered on educating those yet to be baptized or confirmed, called the Congregation of the Catechetical Sisters of the Sacred Heart.

Notable: Giulia was a friend and colleague of Catherine Volpicelli, the Naples-born nun known for her ministry to cholera victims who was canonized in 2009. The two shared a deep devotion to the Sacred Heart.

Quotable: "While I have any life left in me, I will continue to teach the catechism. And then, I assure you, I would be very happy to die teaching the catechism."

Camilla Battista Varano (1458-1524)

Who she was: A 15th-century princess of the central Italian city of Camerino, Camilla eschewed a life of wealth to become a member of the Poor Clares, a Franciscan order of contemplative nuns. She ultimately founded several Poor Clare communities throughout Italy and was known for her extensive writings, which described her ecstatic religious experiences that focused on Christ's Passion.

Notable: Battista died from the plague in 1524, right at the onset of the Protestant Reformation.

Quotable: "You have resurrected me in You, true life who give life to all the living."

Stanislaw Soltys Kazimierczyk (1433-1489)

Who he was: A 15th-century Polish priest, Stanislaw was known as a powerful preacher and confessor who ministered to the poor and sick. He was a member of the Canons Regular of the Lateran, an order of priests who upheld the communal monastic ideals of the early Christians.

Notable: Stanislaw was a scholar of theology and philosophy at the Jagiellonian University in Krakow, one of Europe's oldest universities—and the alma mater of Pope John Paul II.

New Media and the Church

By Karen A. Walker

New media, as defined in Wikipedia (itself the result of new media), "encompasses the emergence of digital, computerized, or networked information and communication technologies in the later part of the 20th century." Important components include two-way (or multi-party) interaction and digital technology. Web 2.0, iPhone, Blackberry, smart phones, Facebook, Twitter, YouTube, Second Life, LinkedIN, Texting, Hulu, hyperlinking, social networking, hypercasting, and iPad—all are part of the new media.

For the Church, the guardian on earth of the timeless teachings of Christ, is this rapidly evolving technology a change to reckon with or merely a passing fad? And, if it is to be reckoned with, how?

Permanence and pace of development

Consider this. Forty-five years ago computers were enormous "main frames," requiring large, air-cooled rooms. Now those technological masterpieces are called dinosaurs.

Only 13 years ago "Google" was a word that didn't make sense! Now it's a verb.

And, in an age of texting and tweets, who remembers pay phones? Yet mobile phones have only become commonplace over the past 10 years or so.

Not only is new technology here to stay, its pace of development over the last few years has been phenomenal. And the number of people affected is enormous. According to Apple, the first two and half years of the iPhone spawned more than 195,000 applications ("apps") created by developers worldwide, and generated more than 4 billion downloads!

Apple's iTunes alone has more than 100 million registered users (and their names, credit card numbers and music choices). More than 8.5 billion songs have been sold, in 23 countries, making iTunes the largest music retailer in the world. Amazon.com is the largest "bookstore" in the world.

Think about it. Anyone over age 35 learned about cell phones as an adult. Students in elementary school today can't imagine life without them!

"My dad is 73; he still takes a newspaper and reads it cover to cover every day," notes Scott Turicchi, CEO of j2Global, an international digital communications firm. "I'm 40, and I rarely read a newspaper these days because I have alternative ways of getting my information. My daughter is 9. She probably won't even know what a newspaper is."

What was unimaginable five years ago is taken for granted today. New media is the "Wild West" of the Third Millennium.

Does it really matter to the Church?

Certainly the Church, its mission and Magisterium has outlived, unphased, more profound social upheavals and cultural revolutions than this technological one. Consider the Roman persecution, the Plague, the Reformation, wars of every sort, even violent godless regimes such as Marxism and Communism. What is texting compared to these?

At first blush, even the juxtaposition of Church and new media seems absurd. Timeless truth, the Holy Trinity, God-made-Man, eternal salvation and each individual's inestimable dignity and value in the eyes of God on the one hand vs. Twitter, texting, Facebook and blogging on the other.

Yet while Church doctrine and mission are linked inexorably to its unchanging, unchangeable founder, Our Lord Jesus Christ, its communication and evangelical outreach can't help but include the technological tools of the era.

Pope John Paul II recognized this, often exhorting the faithful to use every means available to communicate the gospel message. In his Apostolic Letter to those responsible for communications, John Paul II wrote: "...the Church is not only called upon to use the mass media to spread the Gospel but, today more than ever, to integrate the message of salvation into the "new culture" that these powerful means of communication create and amplify. It tells us that the use of the techniques and the technologies of contemporary communications is an integral part of its mission in the third millennium."

Even before Pope John Paul II, other individuals have recognized the power of the "new media" of their era and became early adapters. Archbishop Fulton Sheen, Fr. Patrick Peyton, St. Maximilian Kolbe, even Mother Angelica with her early foray into cable television and satellite broadcasting, were all early adapters for their day and age. But these were individuals who saw and seized the moment, not the Church as a whole.

Reach people where they are

Regardless of whether one "tweets" or uses Facebook, nearly everyone in the U.S. owns at least one computer or smart phone and uses it to search for information. Twenty years ago people used the Yellow Pages and the newspaper. Today they use the Internet.

Newspapers are nearly dead. Why place a classified ad or read the paper, when you can place an ad for free on craigslist? Why page through a newspaper with yesterday's headlines when you can scan the Web for local, regional, state, national and international news. Not only does a reader get news in "real time," the news is delivered in a more engaging, interactive manner (often referred to as "Web 2.0").

Online, a reader can peruse a video, respond immediately with a comment, search for counter opinions and more.... All in a span of 10 minutes.

New media affects even journalism, and journalistic standards. FoxNews, CNN, ABC, NBC, and CBS report a story. But hundreds of thousands of bloggers, so-called "citizen journalists," may tell the same story a different way, reveal another side of the story, show video clips that expose more details and so forth.

In 2009, a dramatic example of the impact of this unfettered access to information took place as the world watched YouTube videos and Twitter posts by Iranians, protesting in massive numbers against presidential election results. The videos and news feeds were posted by citizens on the streets, in the midst of the action, and they revealed a vastly different reality than official Iranian news accounts.

New media users choose what streams and sources of information are important to them, and those sources are available at their fingertips. They are actively engaged in their information gathering and communication process, not passive TV viewers. "Google Wave" is the newest and most robust in a string of new, evolving, free technologies that enable a user to "communicate and collaborate in real time," as Google Wave describes itself.

Put simply: If most people today get their secular news and information online, in an interactive way, then this is how they will search for—and expect to find—news about the Church, especially about their local parish, mass times, Catholic school news and events.

Yet how many parishes and Catholic schools in the U.S. don't have a website, don't have a useful one, or don't keep it current?

What was unimaginable five years ago is taken for granted today. New media is the "Wild West" of the Third Millennium.

Video explosion

Tom Loarie, chairman of Mercador MedSystems, chairman of Silicon BioDevices and a columnist for the Catholic Business Journal, recently attended a trade show featuring the latest in digital advances.

"The use of video and 4G [bandwidth] is increasing dramatically," he reports. "Smart phones are getting smarter, and over the next two to three years video will see exponential growth."

At the time of this article, Apple's iPad was just made public. By next year, it could easily have spawned other digital advances, tools and uses. "The iPad has all kinds of new possibilities," says Mr. Loarie. "People could be going into mass with the readings on their iPad. I don't think we've thought creatively about that yet."

Mr. Turicchi agrees. "We're moving more and more into the video realm, to attract younger crowds... Now there's hypercasting, sending and receiving mini-video messages. Hypercasts can be organized by subject matter, time of year, different ways... What we're seeing is that the next generation is very video-focused. That's how they're used to getting and sending information."

Relevance, Perceived Value and Trust

Mr. Turicchi raises more important concerns: relevance, perceived value and trust.

"The difference between ages past and future ages is that the method of delivery has become as important as the content," says Mr. Turicchi. "So if your message is not visually appealing, it's not going to be heard! People are already getting their information this new way. People are used to getting information – secular information – in this new way.....This generation will give 'packaging' priority."

It is an important point for the Church. Those who can't imagine life without smart phones and video messaging will evaluate and judge the importance and value of all information, including the content and message itself, on the basis of the "package" in which they receive it.

"The Church has content. It has doctrine, teachings, the fullness of truth. That's the advantage," says Mr. Turicchi. "The game going forward, the challenge, is how to present this content in an attractive manner to a visual generation, and, how to make it accessible through varied means of connecting."

Stunted thinking process

The accessibility, speed and immediacy of digital communications does more than deliver content in an interactive way; it affects habits of rumination and critical thinking.

"In this age of new media, there is less critical thinking and more emotional, more reactionary thinking," Mr. Turicchi explains. "In 30 seconds you're told to donate, to buy this or that... It's a tiny window, measured in seconds, to elicit a response from you. It's impulse-driven. You can't do a lot of processing in 35 seconds! You have to make a fast, cursory evaluation and decision."

"You can't fight it," says Mr. Turicchi. "That's a loser. Maybe there are pockets of society that can stem the tide, but it's as much to their detriment as their benefit....so, how can the Church use this tool to disseminate its message? It has to take the core truths, the catechism, and break it down into 35 second messages...You might generate a better understanding of the catechism by pushing out 35-second messages—1,000 of them, delivered once a day, for 3 years—little drops each day!"

twitter

Find us on Facebook

IPhone photo: courtesy of Apple, Inc.
Twitter logo: courtesy of Twitter.
RSS logo: courtesy of RSS.
Facebook logo: Facebook is a registered trademark of Facebook, Inc. ®

Information overload, where's the Church?

"People now expect to get information in real time," says Alan Napleton, CEO of Catholic Marketing Network, a trade association for Catholic retailers and suppliers. During the final days and hours of the national healthcare vote in Congress, Mr. Napleton set his Google Alert to pick up any news related to the issue at hand. In the heat of the final hours of battle, he hoped to get some real time perspective or analysis from a bishop. None came. Even though the final vote took place over a weekend and into late Sunday night—a time when most bishops and priests are especially busy—it was disappointing.

Mr. Napleton's disappointment was not for his own understanding of the issue. Rather, it was a disappointment at not seeing the wisdom of the Church injected into the real time moment of decision, so to speak.

"I wanted the Church to be there, at that moment," he says, even as he acknowledges that the bishops had already been clear and outspoken about their concerns with the proposed legislation. For Mr. Napleton, their statements weren't enough. He says simply: "They needed to have a real time presence."

This points to another serious concern for the Church. Authority.

There are, literally, millions of bloggers and citizen journalists posting opinions, analysis and more. A healthy number of these are commenting on Catholic issues and teachings. But where is the Church, speaking with her wisdom and authority? It creates a vacuum.

"If you have someone of authority blogging on a diocesan site," notes Mr. Turicchi, "then for example, instead of bloggers fueling rumors and speculation about who the next bishop might be, you can have a person of authority quell the rumors with a post that directs them to stop all the nonsense because the new bishop will be appointed and named in due time and it will happen when Rome decides. That's it."

The same holds true for matters of more eternal consequence. Anyone can get people to buy into their views with slick packaging, but many do not have informed consciences that enable them to accurately discern whether something is true or not.

"We're moving out of an age where Imprimatur works, that requires review," says Mr. Turicchi. "We're moving into real time. The Church's challenge is to make very clear what content is officially provided by the church and what is not approved. It's time for the bishops, the Church, to get in the game and be the authority, the leaders and shepherds, within this new media."

The Church has not been entirely out of the loop though. Kevin Perkins, CEO and co-founder of Skweezer, Inc., a company that provides mobile search and advertising solutions to network operators and publishers, points out that the entire Lectionary and Bible are online and that a site called "www.Ebreviary.com" has an online version of the Liturgy of the Hours and common prayers. Even the Vatican has its own iPhone app, giving people access to the Vatican library and resource. "It gives Catholics a way to reacquaint themselves with the gospel while waiting in a long Starbucks line," Mr. Perkins quips. "It's the world we live in—any moments of divine inspiration are positive."

Consequences of denial

On a local level, if potential and existing parishioners, or even out of town visitors, can't find accurate local parish information on the Internet, where will they go to find this information? The Yellow Pages are practically obsolete.

"Where am I getting local diocesan information? Where is it? What about my local parish? I'm still getting printed bulletins!" exclaims Mr. Turicchi. "All this information should be digital. A website is now considered standard operating procedure for business, yet a lot of parishes don't even have a website – that's shocking to me. If I'm traveling around and I want to find parish somewhere, I can't. MassTimes.org is helpful, but it doesn't have all the information I seek, and it's not likely to be as accurate as a local parish would be."

What is the likelihood that someone accustomed to searching for local businesses and citizen referrals (on sites such as Yelp.com) is going to take extra time to call a parish, wait for the receptionist or listen to a recorded message, in order to quickly find mass or confession times? Even more absurd, what is the likelihood that people will drive to every local parish within a 20-mile radius in order to retrieve this information?

Will these seekers miss mass, go elsewhere, or eventually lose interest all together because they consciously or subconsciously come to expect that anything of value – anything worth knowing – is on the Internet. If it's not there, if church leadership isn't posting it there, then maybe it's not that important.

"There's a growing disconnect between what's expected and what is there," notes Mr. Turicchi. "It's ironic that the Vatican has a YouTube channel and Twitter accounts, while the local parish doesn't even have a website...What do most people care about more? The local level."

Citing Holy Week as a good example, Mr. Turicchi points out that if the schedule isn't posted on a parish website, and posted in a manner so that it can be easily viewed without having to download it, then a faithful Catholic has to drive by the local parishes to pick up a bulletin. In the age of real time communication, that puts parishes in the Stone Age.

"The Church at all levels has to find ways to embrace and adopt new communication technologies because it is the standard by which people will judge the relevancy of the local church and its content." says Mr. Turicchi.

The Pope Tweets...

Pope Benedict XVI has been at the forefront to further the banner of his predecessor, emphasizing and encouraging the ready embrace of the new tools of digital mass communications, and using these tools to win souls for Christ.

In March, the Vatican opened six Twitter accounts, one in each of six different languages. Vatican Radio and other Vatican media outlets will "tweet" important news.

Pope Benedict's chosen theme for the 44th World Communications Day, held on May 16, 2010, made the point unmistakably clear: "The Priest and Pastoral Ministry in a Digital World: New Media at the Service of the Word." It was a theme purposefully chosen to coincide with the Church's celebration of the Year for Priest.

In his message, the pope exhorted priests in particular to bring Christ into "cyberspace" likening it to the Lord walking the streets of our cities, knocking on the doors of our homes and hearts, inviting us to open the door and let Him in.

"All priests have as their primary duty the proclamation of Jesus Christ, the incarnate Word of God, and the communication of his saving grace in the sacraments...," the pope exhorts priests. "But how can they call on him in whom they have not believed? And how can they believe in him of whom they have not heard? And how can they hear without someone to preach? And how can people preach unless they are sent?" (Rom 10:11, 13-15).

He continues: "Responding adequately to this challenge amid today's cultural shifts, to which young people are especially sensitive, necessarily involves using new communications technologies...Who better than a priest, as a man of God, can develop and put into practice, by his competence in current digital technology, a pastoral outreach capable of making God concretely present in today's world and presenting the religious wisdom of the past as a treasure which can inspire our efforts to live in the present with dignity while building a better future? ...To priests in particular the new media offer ever new and far-reaching pastoral possibilities..."

The USCCB announced radical communications changes in March, acknowledging: "We are in a paradigm shift in how people receive information, as profound as when the printing press was invented. It is important that the Church not only provide its wisdom regarding the primary dignity of the human person in this information evolution, but also take advantage of the opportunities this new media ecology provides."

"It's a wonderful time for ministry," exudes Mr. Perkins, himself a convert to the faith. "The scale of people to which the gospel can evangelize through new media tools would make Saint Paul marvel. One email, text message, Facebook post can literally be read by millions—all within a few nanoseconds. That's simply amazing!"

Don't do it alone

Perhaps the most important perspective for clergy to keep in mind as they venture into uncharted digital realms, is to lean on digital experts within their own parish and diocese, especially the young.

"I have people daily telling me they want to put their skills to work for the Church," says Mr. Napleton. "Faithful Catholic laity want to help their bishops and pastors get the message out, prudently analyze and respond in real time. There's a goldmine of these individuals in every diocese and parish across the country...They just need to have the door opened to help."

In a phrase immortalized by Nike and used frequently by Mr. Loarie in his work with multi-million dollar venture start-ups in the life sciences field, himself a tireless leader in his parish and diocese, "Just do it!" ◆

KAREN A. WALKER is Editor and Publisher of the *Catholic Business Journal* and Producer of *The Catholic Business Hour* radio show.

O Ancient Beauty Ever New

Thinking About Sacramental Architecture

By Steven Schloeder, Ph.D.

The history of Catholic sacred architecture, at least for the first 1,900 years, concerned the question of how to express something quite beyond words, quite beyond any symbolic structure, quite beyond our imagination. "*Eye has not seen, nor ear heard...*" (1 Cor 2: 9) . [1]

This immediately raises the question as to how immaterial reality – that is to say, *spiritual* things – can be conveyed to us who live our lives in the material world. We know the world outside of ourselves primarily through the senses and through rational thought (the creation of ratios or parallel connections). Yet the very stuff of Catholicism is grounded in immateriality – in God and the heavenly realities. As the Church instructs us, "*Church buildings are to be signs and symbols of heavenly things*." (Sacrosanctum concilium, 122) How then does this occur?

1. The Trinity and All the Saints (Jean Fouquet) 15th cent.

Sacramental distinction

Perhaps the one great insight that distinguishes Catholicism (and the other apostolic Churches) from all other branches of Christianity and all other faiths is the *sacramental principle*. We as human beings – body and soul – come to God precisely through our humanity in a profoundly material world.

It is *through* the material world, and not in spite of the material world, that we connect with the spiritual realities. By God's design all of material creation is, to use the phrase of Dionysius the Areopagite, a *theophany* revealing God to us. It is through the material world that God gives us grace in a loving communion with His beloved: the physical bread and wine that feed and nourish us in the Body and Blood of Christ, the water that washes us physically and spiritually in Baptism, the gift of self in spousal love that is an objective participation in divine love in the sacrament of Matrimony. It is this sacramental insight that mandates our concern for the needy, in the words of Jesus: "*Whatsoever you do to the least of my brothers, you have done to me*." (Matthew 25: 40)

Throughout the scriptures we see that it is through the material world that we participate in the spiritual life. God speaks to humanity through both words and symbols: figures, dreams, language, law, directives, parables, analogies, metaphors, fantastical imagery, visionary language, liturgical arrangement and gestures, and so forth. God communicates to humanity in a manner apprehensible to humanity: through material things knowable to the senses: the dream of Jacob, the three visitors at the oak of Mamre, the burning bush, the pillar of fire and the ark in the desert tabernacle [2], the Glory of the Temple [3], and most perfectly in the Incarnation. Jesus himself then used parables and metaphors to explain the kingdom of God (itself a metaphor), and the writers of the New Testament developed a series of primal and interrelated metaphors to explain the ecclesia.

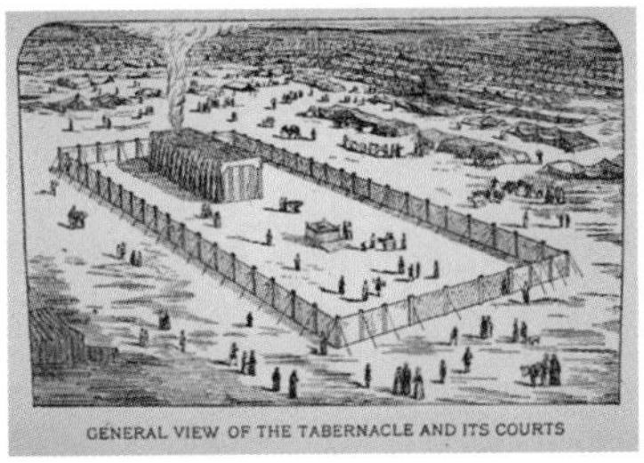

2. The Desert Tabernacle

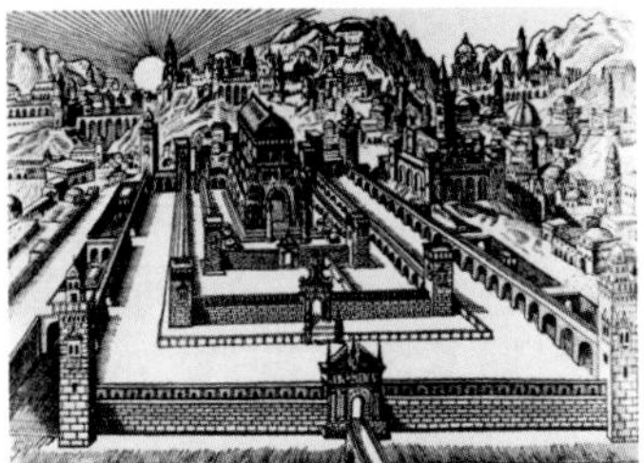

3. The Temple of Solomon

Three core themes

While there are many images used to explain and understand our relationship to God in the Church (the mustard seed, the marital imagery, wine skins, the shepherd and his flock, etc), the three primary metaphors each concern the most fundamental and foundational experiences of the human condition: embodiment, dwelling, and community (Put simply: body, temple, and city).

These three themes are deeply interwoven. The body is a type of house—it is a house for the soul. The house is a shelter, a 'sanctuary' safe from the elements, animals, and marauders.

This human need for shelter precedes and even informs religion. Thus, the temple is a type of house, it is a house for the gods; and the primitive house was an intrinsically religious place dedicated to the family religion of ancestor worship. Archeological investigations show that the earliest temples, the Neolithic earth temples of Malta, symbolically express the woman's body, and Schwaller de Lubicz's works shows an uncanny parallel between the human skeleton and the ancient Egyptian temple. 4 It was with this deep yet now obscure understanding that Jesus could announce that his body was the true temple, and that St. Paul could liken the Body of Christ to the Church. 5 Similarly, the city is a house writ large, primitively as the house of the tribe, the 'body politic.' The king dwelt there, as did the gods. Primitive cities were often both palace-cities and temple-cities, such as Nineveh and Jerusalem. The church in this sense, is a city in which the true God dwells.

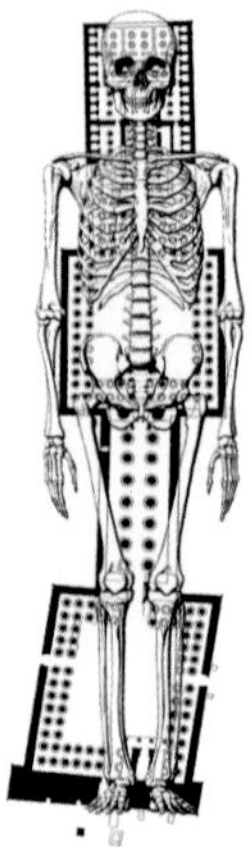

4. The Temple of Luxor (from Schwaller de Lubicz)

5. The Church as the Body of Christ (after Francesco Di Giorgio Martini) 16th cent.

Loss and Recovery

This architectural vocabulary was largely discarded over the course of the 20th century. The loss, or rejection, of this language has coincided with a loss of meaning and vitality in church architecture. Churches of the past century tend to be austere and aniconic, expressive of a functionalistic approach to architecture that was seen in its time as an appropriate response to the Second Vatican Council in speaking to the men and women of that age. Without comment on the myriad of cultural forces that contributed to the loss of this language, it is worth noting that historical architectural styles, and the architectural forms that they engendered, have created the sense of "cultural memory" by which we understand "church" as a built form. Functionalism, which seeks to produce architecture through expressing the material functional relationships in the building, is not concerned with symbolical meaning, historical forms, commonly understood language, or formal typologies through which the "cultural memory" is transmitted and received.

This is why architectural functionalism, or its sister liturgical reductionism can serve neither the Catholic liturgy nor the church building as a sacramental sign. A merely algebraic approach to liturgical symbols guts them of their vitality. Sacramental symbols are perforce complex, multivalent, layered, and even at times ostensibly contradictory. Furthermore, the complexities of the human person and of the communal dynamics of the liturgy call for a richer architecture that engages us in the fullness of our being: body and soul, will and intellect, passions, appetites and emotions, senses, memory and imagination, our capacity for wonderment and delight and awe.

In short, this is a call for a return to, and a recovery of a rich, complex and symbolic architecture. It is not a *stylistic* question, as if building anew Gothic or neo Renaissance temples could adequately respond to the vision of the Second Vatican Council. Rather, it is a *sacramental* question: how to create contemporary churches that help us understand our true place in the Body of Christ, as "living stones" in the Temple of the Holy Spirit, and as dwellers in the Heavenly Jerusalem.

The current challenge

Typically today, parishes want "Catholic churches that look like Catholic churches." Yet simply designing neo Gothic churches, or dressing up centralized modernistic spaces in fancy neo Palladian ball gowns, cannot be the answer. The challenge for today's liturgical architects is how to communicate the meaning behind traditional architectural forms without merely aping those formal elements that constitute the "style."

Each architect will find his or her own expression of what this means; each project will suggest its own solution related to budget, region, architectural vernacular, site context, community expectations, demographics, program, and so forth.

The history of Catholic architecture shows that these central themes of body, temple and city have inflamed the imaginations of architects and builders in every age. Consider the imperial basilica in the patristic age 6, the image of the "city of glass" in the middle ages, the recovery of the Greco-Roman temple in the Renaissance, the image of the body and the expression of the Solomonic temple in the 18th century. Baroque, the fantastical churches of the Rococo age 7, even icons of modern architecture such as Perret's La-Raincy show the perdurance of these themes. 8

6. Saint Paul Outside the Walls (from LeTarouilly)

7. St. Nikolas Mala Strana, Prague. (copyright Steven J Schloeder)

8. Notre-Dame-le-Raincy, Paris (copyright Steven J Schloeder)

However, these themes will always find contemporary expression. Simply put, we are no longer patristics, or medievals, or renaissance thinkers — both our experience of the world and our building materials, methods, and systems are contemporary. It is not that our architecture *must* reflect this reality, but that our architecture *can only* reflect this reality. Furthermore, there is no sense in which either the documents of the Second Vatican Council, or the insights of the mid 20th c. Liturgical Movement, can be responsibly understood as a call to return to the past *per se*, for its own sake. A *retour aux sources* certainly is a call to return to the theological underpinnings of the Liturgy from antiquity onward, but it is not a stylistic return.

The question for today's liturgical architect is how best to express those ineffable relationships that were encoded in traditional architecture, quite apart from the matter of style. Those styles that formed the cultural memory of Catholic architecture are a rich trove of architectural sources from which to work, but it would be a mistake to focus on the matter of style and miss the underpinning theological ideas that the architects and builders of these styles sought to express.

Three Examples

These themes – body, temple, city – all of which seek to express some insight into the heavenly reality find fresh vitality in contemporary projects. At St. Therese in Collinsville OK, the combination of the parish's explicit desire to have "a Catholic church that looks like a Catholic church," the desire for an intimate building with a lateral plan, the budget, and rural location brought forth a design that had strong allusions to late patristic, early Romanesque northern Italian architecture. 9 Themes of the heavenly Jerusalem are expressed in the twelve columns that define the nave and sanctuary and in the twenty-four clearstory windows that allude to the twenty-four elders around the throne in the book of Revelation. Images of the Body are explored in the Greek cross plan and the square –symbols of Christ – overlaid by the octagon which is a symbol of the resurrection. 10 The dedication to the Little Flower is subtly referenced in the 'Mystical Rose" formed at the intersection of the arches in the octagonal ceiling. The building was consecrated on the Feast of the Little Flower in the Jubilee Year, 1 October 2000.

In another, much larger project, the parish of Sts. Anne and Joachim in Fargo desired their new building to recall the local cultural memory of the Northern European Gothic churches that their forebears brought to the Great Plains in the 19th century. 11 Gothic architecture is in essence an expression of "the city of glass" (Revelation 21) and is renowned for the magnificent depictive stained glass, expansive spaces, and durable materiality. 12 The complex arrangement of forms which express clearly the various parts of the church –the great central nave, the monumental bell tower, the daily mass chapel, and the ambulatory with the various side chapels and confessionals – is

9. St. Therese, Collinsville OK. Exterior. (copyright Steven J Schloeder)

11. Sts. Anne and Joachim, Fargo, ND (courtesy of Zerr Berg Architects)

10. St. Therese, Collinsville OK. Interior. (copyright Steven J Schloeder)

12. Sts. Anne and Joachim, Fargo, ND, Interior (copyright Steven J Schloeder)

13. Shrine of Our Lady of Guadalupe, La Crosse WI. Exterior (Duncan G. Stroik Architect, LLC)

14. Shrine of Our Lady of Guadalupe, La Crosse WI. View of Dome (Duncan G. Stroik Architect, LLC)

an organic assemblage of parts that liken the building to the analogy of the body.

For the new Shrine of Our Lady of Guadalupe in La Crosse Wisconsin, Prof. Duncan Stroik employed his signature neo Palladian architecture to evoke the image of the church as the Temple of God. In the tradition of pilgrimage churches, the Shrine is located high upon a hill outside of the city with a campanile and dome which is visible from afar. 13 Since it is a place for prayer and pilgrimage, the Shrine is designed to accommodate flow and movement, with seating in the nave for the liturgy and large open side aisles for circulation and prayer. The dominant baldachin over the high altar 14 – reminiscent of the great patriarchal basilicas in Rome – alludes to the Tent of Dwelling (Exodus 25) which laid the foundation for all subsequent Jewish and Christian liturgical architecture.

These are just three examples of how contemporary church buildings can speak to the ineffable ideal of "heaven wedded to earth." While participating in some of the past architecture that constitute the body of cultural memory in the Catholic tradition, the stylistic allusions are ultimately secondary to the more significant sacramental meaning of the buildings.

The idea of church building as "*signs and symbols of heavenly things*" was largely lost in the middle of the last century. Yet these scriptural themes of the Ecclesia—body, temple and city — have perdured precisely because they are so essential to our comprehension of the human condition. In the history of Catholic architecture these themes have inflamed the imaginations of builders and architects across the ages. Today they can continue both to inspire contemporary architects and to move the hearts and minds of the faithful, responding to the growing desire to once again build churches that move beyond the functional, beyond the stylistic, to a truly sacramental architecture. ◆

STEVEN SCHLOEDER, PhD, a Theologian and Architect, lives in Phoenix, Arizona. He is the author of *Architecture in Communion: Implementing the Second Vatican Council through Liturgy and Architecture* (Ignatius Press 1998).

Pilgrimage, the Human Experience

By Chris Lowney

We humans have been journeying to holy places for over two millennia, and we will likely keep doing so as long as we walk this planet.

Why do we go?

The impulse to pilgrimage spans continents, cultures, and faiths. More than a million Hindus annually descend on Benares to bathe in the sacred Ganges. Some two million Muslims visit Mecca. Eight million pilgrims journey to Lourdes and another five million to Fatima. And millions more will head to shrines great and small, too numerous to count, on every inhabited continent.

At first glance, little seems to link these journeys. Our mind-bogglingly diverse religious traditions spur equally varied motivations for pilgrimage. Buddhists, for example, often visit Bodh Gaya, site of the Buddha's enlightenment, in search of their own illumination. Many Hindus hope that visits to their faith's *Char Dham* (four holy places) might liberate them from the cycle of rebirth. And Catholic visitors to Lourdes often seek healing for themselves or loved ones. What possibly connects the Buddhist serenely meditating under the Bodhi tree, the Catholic petitioning a cancer cure at Bernadette's grotto, and the Hindu seeking deliverance from the wheel of reincarnation?

Well, quite a lot. Underneath the surface concerns that propel pilgrims to holy places is the shared bedrock of human experience. Whatever we believe, wherever we live, and whenever in history we were born, perhaps we humans keep journeying as pilgrims because pilgrimage mirrors the reality of the human condition. Pilgrimage, like life, is a journey. And in pilgrimage, as often in life, we note some need and hope it can be addressed. Put differently, common human themes tie us pilgrims together:

- Desire: Something is missing; we know our world is not perfect; there is a problem to be solved, a need to be addressed.
- Hope: We hope for something better.
- Journey: Pilgrimage is ultimately a metaphor for life itself, a journey that is filled with desires and hopes.

Desire: Something is missing…

A few (*too* few) of us pilgrims set out simply to give thanks for all that we have. More likely, we set out for the opposite reason: we want or need something. We infirm need physical healing; we mentally anguished seek peace; we, the unreconciled want to patch up broken relationships with God, family, or friends. We are restless and feel like there must be more to life than the path we're following; we look for answers to some vexing life dilemma; we yearn for spiritual enlightenment or a deeper connection with our Creator; we are exhausted by modern's life's pace and simply crave a little peace; or we are simply bored and pursue the stimulation of something different. *Our hearts are a little empty; our behavior is a little wanting; or our bodies are suffering.*

Something is missing, however we express that. And so we set out. After all, why would we go anywhere if we lived in perfect bliss? Why would we search for something if we already had everything?

That is not to say—lest the foregoing seem too romantic—that what we search for, on pilgrimage or in life, is necessarily divinely inspired, lofty, noble, or saintly. Pilgrims journey for all sorts of reasons and look for all sorts of things. I once noticed a handsome, twenty-ish male squiring an equally attractive young female along a pilgrim route; a couple of days later I saw them again, she now hobbled by a sore knee; a week later I saw him yet again, miles further along the pilgrimage trail, this time accompanying a different young woman. I imagined the rogue shepherding his first pilgrim-date on a bus back home so that he could once again turn toward his pilgrim goal: finding another woman to accompany. So much for chivalry!

Still, whether our appetites are channeled in lofty or base ways, philosophers of religion find something profoundly spiritual in our insatiable wanting, our unquenchable sense of "something missing." That is, we humans are perennially unsettled because there is ultimately more to us than what we own, eat, earn, or possess; there is more to life than our jobs, homes, entertainments, or bank accounts. No matter what we have, how famous we become, what we earn, who we sleep with, or what we drive, we will always feel at least somewhat incomplete, vaguely dissatisfied, or wanting more.

Our wanting, the forever-restlessness of the human

Detail of Holy Door, Plaza de la Quintana.
Photo: Turismo de Santiago, Rúa do Vilar, 63, 15705
Santiago de Compostela www.santiagoturismo.com

condition, signifies that we are innately geared for more than this earthly lifetime can ever offer, whether or not we ever recognize the fact or forever exhaust ourselves reeling unquenched from one pursuit to another. The fifth century bishop St. Augustine put it this way, "Our hearts are restless, O God, and they will not rest until they rest in Thee." Because we are restless, we are never quite at home here. The New Testament letter to the Hebrews proclaims that, "We are all strangers and exiles on the earth." [Hebrews 11:13] The sentiment is harshly worded. I don't feel an "exile" on this beautiful earth. But I don't feel utterly fulfilled either, and I don't suspect I ever will be. So we restless humans hit the road in search of the healing, enlightenment, answers, or experiences that might complete us, which brings us to the second great human impulse expressed through pilgrimage.

Hope: We indomitably hope for something better….

Every pilgrimage embodies hope. We hope to reach a destination and return home safely. But we also hope that our lives will be bettered through the pilgrim experience. We hope for peace, reconciliation, forgiveness, healing, enlightenment, or a dozen other aspirations. A woman at Lourdes hopes her sick child will be healed, and a Buddhist hopes he too will be enlightened after resting where the Buddha found insight.

I prayed one evening at a small town church during a week-long pilgrimage to Santiago de Compostela. The town was virtually depopulated, a relic of a bygone small-town past struggling to survive a present dominated by large commercial urban centers. Hundred-degree heat had transformed this under populated, dusty place into a ghost town. A handful of us dirty, bedraggled pilgrims straggled into the deserted town; had we been gunslingers on horseback skirting a tumbleweed or two, the scene could have passed for an old western movie.

As dusk fell, church bells tolled to announce the evening mass. Three or four old ladies emerged from shuttered houses and made their way to the same cool church where we pilgrims were resting. After mass, the priest prayed for the pilgrims' continued safety, then closed his prayer book and improvised, "I know you pilgrims are hot and tired, but keep going. If you are looking for answers, you will find answers. If you are looking for peace, you will find peace. If you are looking for God, God will find you." Yes, that's it, isn't it? That's what we humans do. We journey in hope. We hope for peace, answers, and second chances. And we don't give up hoping. We hope indomitably. No diagnosis of terminal illness prevents us from hoping that some miracle or medical breakthrough may yet save our beloved spouse or child. We seize on remarkable stories from our respective traditions, reminding ourselves, for example, of the Jesus who visits a death-struck young girl and says, "*talitha cumi*," "little girl, arise." And she does.

The Biblical patriarch Abraham is considered one of humanity's first great pilgrims, journeying at God's bidding toward a promised land. The letter to the Hebrews reflects on Abraham's long-wandering caravan and observes, "If they had been thinking of that land from which they gone out, they would have had opportunity to return. But, as it is, they desire a better country." [Hebrews 11: 15-16] Yes, we keep going, on our pilgrimage to Lourdes, Mecca, Benares, or Montserrat, or our pilgrimage through life. We hope for something better, and hope pulls us forward on our journey.

Journey: Our life is a journey, and pilgrimage is a metaphor…

Sometimes our hopes are fulfilled and sometimes they are not. Yet we keep going, and frequently we learn from the journey. In this respect, one's pilgrimage to Lourdes or Montserrat is a metaphor for life itself. Most pilgrims learn the truth of the old cliché: it's about the journey, not the destination. That isn't entirely true, of course: no journey will seem worthwhile if it ultimately leads to a meaningless, valueless destination (just ask anyone who late in life suffers regrets after orienting life around some goal that, once finally grasped, turned out to be empty and unfulfilling).

But in pilgrimage as in life, a *lot* of it is about the journey: who we meet along the way, what we see and savor, how we behave, what we learn, and dozens of other things that, in the end, constitute a life well lived or a pilgrimage well walked. No magic will happen simply by reaching a destination like Montserrat, any more than magic happens simply by reaching the company presidency or the comfortable retirement. More often, the magic happens along the way, and pilgrims through life will be wise to keep eyes, hearts, and minds open to what discoveries may await us along the way.

Trekking six or seven hours each day during one pilgrimage, I passed by other trekkers daily (or they bypassed me). Most of us exchanged only a "buen camino" and kept going, each happy

Cathedral and Obradoiro square. Night view.
Photo: Turismo de Santiago, Rúa do Vilar, 63, 15705 Santiago de Compostela www.santiagoturismo.com

in our own solitude. Sometimes we faced the awkward dilemma that we were walking at the same pace; would we remain silent companions for the next three or four hours, each mulling his thoughts accompanied by the soundtrack of the other's footfalls? Faced with the prospect, one might conveniently slow down or speed up a bit, or take an unneeded rest, in order to open up the literal and figurative space we each wanted.

But sometimes pilgrims wanted not space but companionship. After exchanging idle chatter about the weather and our respective home countries, travelers might quickly begin confiding intimate concerns. Some had mulled a quandary for a quiet hour or two and needed to share their insight or anguish with another person. Others were simply taking advantage of the "airline phenomenon" and unburdening themselves anonymously to a walking companion they would never meet again in "normal" life. Walking companions sometimes learn things that bosses, best friends, or lovers didn't know. A savvy young computer engineer walked and wondered if his life and career ought to concern something more than computer engineering. One woman mulled a marriage proposal. Another woman, already married, was resisting her husband's entreaties to start a family. Did her reluctance to have children now say something about her, she wondered? About their relationship? She hoped light would dawn in the five-hundred miles that gaped between her and the famous cathedral in Santiago.

As for me? Nothing like that. I love to walk; I love travel; I'm a religious person; I studied medieval history in college and relished the chance to see Spain's Romanesque and Gothic churches; I enjoy solitude and occasional refuge from the crazed drumbeat of meetings, phone calls, and emails that dominates modern life. Wasn't that reason enough to go on pilgrimage? I had neither a burning conundrum to resolve nor enlightenment to seek. For the first few days of my trek, I good naturedly shrugged aside the oft-repeated mantra that one hears regularly, "Everyone has something to learn on the camino."

But we all do have something to learn, and we more often learn it through the journey than at the destination. One German trekker emailed me after returning home from his trek, undertaken as a long-distance vacation hike, nothing more. He was in terrific shape. We had run into each other various times during the early days of our respective treks. I would arrive in town, sweaty and exhausted at the end of the walking day, to find him relaxing with a beer at some outdoor café; he had arrived two hours ahead of me, showered, washed his clothes and hung them to dry in the late afternoon sun.

After a few days, I didn't see him any more; I was still gutting out thirteen to fifteen miles each day (and grateful to do that much), but he had started pushing himself, ratcheting up his distances from thirteen to fifteen miles, then seventeen and still further. His email reported his safe arrival at Santiago and then back home in Germany, "I felt very good on the camino, my physical condition couldn't be better," he wrote, "Most times I had no problems to walk even long distances. I really enjoyed to see how far I could get, to go to my limits." But to his surprise, his vacation had yielded a challenging insight. Yes, he was exhilarated to push his physical limits and discover his fortitude. But as he walked, the anguishing realization dawned about his life back at home, "I rarely tap my full potential. Or, to say it in the camino way: I walk only 20 km although I could walk 35 km. Now I think it is very helpful to go to your limits from time to time. To feel my energy. For me there is a lot to discover." Everyone has something to learn.

I had my own unexpected thoughts along the way. First came profound solidarity with the millions of my fellow-Christian predecessors who had journeyed the same route over centuries. I particularly imagined the unremembered thousands who died during pilgrim journeys and lied buried in unmarked, makeshift graves along the route. That fact may shock modern minds, but consider that many medieval pilgrims would have been broken-down peasants, released from their feudal obligations for the trip of a lifetime only because they were no longer considered fit for productive labor. If a peasant died three-hundred miles from home in 1000AD, there were neither resources nor inclination to transport the body back home. I began to see myself as metaphorically completing the journey that they couldn't and bearing their hopes to Compostela.

Until that is, I needed someone to bear mine. 250 miles into a five-hundred mile journey, twenty pounds lighter than the day I started, feverish, suffering from chest congestion that required an antibiotic course, a blood-filled blister on one heel and a merely painful one on the other, I was whipped. I gave up. "No mas." I changed plane reservations from a pay phone in a small Spanish town, then took a bus to the nearest city. The bus briefly skirted the pilgrim trail, and I saw two or three trekkers pressing toward the goal I wouldn't reach. I had always understood that I might not complete the pilgrimage; all kinds of things can go wrong during a 500-mile walk; even minor problems like ingrown toenails can turn catastrophic. Yet, in my gut, I was certain I would finish. How could I not? I'm in good shape, had trained, packed the right gear, and prepared for most contingencies. That's who I am, the in-control guy who thinks ahead and gets the job done.

Except that, ultimately, I'm not in control. Everyone has something they have to learn on the camino, so the mantra goes. And, having blithely brushed the slogan aside during the early days of my pilgrimage, I was finally humbled and weakened enough to learn what I was supposed to: it's not my world; it's God's world. I re-learn that truth every couple of years, then slowly push it from consciousness and briefly begin living again as if I can control good health and ill, the vagaries of economies, and how others will choose to behave. But periodic jolts once again remind me that I'm not in control of as much of this world as I would like to believe.

I learned something else during my pilgrimage, at least before those blisters altered my perspective: the sheer joy of being alive. I trekked during early September, counting on an early turn to fall but punished by a late burst of summer. Temperatures climbed to the low hundreds by noon, day after day; so we pilgrims rose earlier and earlier, determined to conquer a chunk of the day's mileage in the pre-dawn cool. I left a pilgrim hostel at 4:30AM one morning, switched on my headlamp, and saw four or five headlamps already strung out ahead of me, bobbing slightly to each walker's particular rhythmic gait.

The file soon strung out as faster walkers out-paced slower ones, and I became a solitary dot of light under an ocean of stars. As we walked west, a dullish gray sky began pursuing us from the east and before long overtook the starry blackness. Then orange rays began warming my back and tinting countless stalks in a harvested grain field. The vague silhouette of a large hill loomed in the distance; over the hours, the hill grew closer (and larger), patches of green appeared, then a road, then trees and bushes. Hours later I stood atop that hill with the fierce sun directly overhead bleaching the colors of all around; I saw my destination for the evening down in the valley. I started down the other side of the hill. Time moves differently when you move slowly.

One Spanish pilgrim put it this way. He had worked in a city along the pilgrim route, and his daily auto commute bypassed one stretch of the camino. He sometimes saw a pilgrim or two as he cruised to work or lurched along in congested traffic. He recounted, "I used to wonder what those people were doing and why they were doing it." Once retired, he decided to walk the camino himself. Some days into his trek, he found himself walking the very same stretch of camino that he had bypassed thousands of times in his commuting lifetime. He stopped walking and beheld Spaniards whizzing by in their cars, a few of them undoubtedly commuting from the same suburb he once had to the same office district where he had once worked, "I looked at them all and I had to laugh to myself, because I found myself wondering what those people were doing and why they were doing it!"

Hit the road. Bring your hopes and questions. You will see some remarkable things as you go. And you will learn something. After all, everyone has something they have to learn on the camino. ◆

CHRIS LOWNEY, formerly a Jesuit seminarian for seven years, was named a Managing Director of J.P. Morgan & Co. while still in his thirties. He held senior positions in New York, Tokyo, Singapore and London until leaving the firm in 2001. He served successively on Morgan's Asia-Pacific, Europe, and Investment Banking Management Committees. Mr. Lowney undertook (but did not complete due to illness) a walking pilgrimage to Santiago de Compostela to raise money for charity. He is author of 3 books: *Heroic Leadership* (#1 best-seller of CBPA, finalist for 2003 Book of the Year Award from ForeWord magazine, translated into 10 languages), *A Vanished World* (nominated for La Coronica award), and *Heroic Living*.

The Official Catholic Directory

for the Year of Our Lord

2010

GIVING STATUS OF THE CATHOLIC CHURCH AS OF JANUARY 1, 2010

Containing Ecclesiastical Statistics of

THE UNITED STATES, PUERTO RICO,
THE VIRGIN ISLANDS, AGANA, CAROLINE AND MARSHALL ISLANDS,
AND FOREIGN MISSIONARY ACTIVITIES.

P.J. KENEDY & SONS
Publishers of the Holy Apostolic See

For inquiries call: 908-673-1000, or write:
890 Mountain Avenue, New Providence, NJ 07974
To place an order call: 1-800-473-7020

The Official Catholic Directory™

Published by P.J. Kenedy & Sons in association with National Register Publishing

Printed and bound in the United States of America
International Standard Book Number: 978-0-87217-001-8
International Standard Serial Number: 0078-3854
Library of Congress Catalog Card Number: 81-30961

CONTENTS

ARCHDIOCESES AND DIOCESES

APOSTOLATE

PRELATURE OF THE HOLY CROSS AND OPUS DEI

EASTERN CHURCHES

TERRITORIAL SEES

MISSION SECTION

RELIGIOUS INSTITUTION SECTION

GENERAL SUMMARY

THE ARCHDIOCESES AND DIOCESES OF THE UNITED STATES—BY STATES

—Indicates Archdiocese. The Archdiocese of Washington includes the District of Columbia and five counties of Maryland. Dioceses traverse state license in the following stances only: Cheyenne includes all of Yellowstone National Park; South Norwich includes Fisher's Island; Wilmington includes the eastern shores of Maryland; and Gallup cludes parts of Arizona and New Mexico.

A USER'S GUIDE TO *THE OFFICIAL CATHOLIC DIRECTORY*

Each year the editors of ***The Official Catholic Directory*** seek added ways of serving their subscribers. Although the book may never answer every question, this is th conscientious goal; its format, arrangement and editorial features are directed toward the convenience and needs of the public. Comments and suggestions are welcome. F the benefit of the subscriber and a more efficient use of ***The Official Catholic Directory*** and its cross references, a summary of the contents and their meaning follow

The Official Catholic Directory **Glossary**
A listing of some of the ecclesiastical terms and organizations found in the *Directory.*

The Governing Bodies in Vatican City
A chronological table of the **Supreme Roman Pontiffs**; the **Pope**, and an alphabetical list of the **College of Cardinals**; the duties of each of the agencies of the **Roman Curia**, and other commissions and institutions associated with the Holy See, along with their officers; a list of the **Seminaries** and **National Colleges** in Rome; the **Apostolic Nunciature** and the **Permanent Observer Mission to the United Nations**, with their staff. As foreign organizations, these entities are not included in the USCCB group tax exemption ruling ("Group Ruling").

The Catholic Church in the United States (Provinces)
The archdioceses and dioceses of the United States arranged under the provinces to which they belong, listed with their active archbishops and bishops.

Ecclesiastical forms of address recognized in the United States. Formal forms of address for correspondence with the clergy in the United States.

U.S. Cardinals, Archbishops, Bishops, Archabbots and Abbots
An alphabetical list of Cardinals, Archbishops, Bishops, Archabbots and Abbots, arranged within their specific title. Also listed is their address and status, followed by a hierarchical/chronological list by year.

United States Conference of Catholic Bishops
The United States Conference of Catholic Bishops is a permanent institute composed of Catholic bishops of the United States of America in and through which the bishops exercise in a communal or collegial manner the pastoral mission entrusted to them by the Lord Jesus of sanctification, teaching, and leadership, especially by devising forms and methods of the apostolate suitably adapted to the circumstances of the times. Such exercise is intended to offer appropriate assistance to each bishop in fulfilling his particular ministry in the local Church, to effect a commonality of ministry addressed to the people of the United States of America, and to foster and express communion with the Church in other nations within the Church universal, under the leadership of its chief pastor, the Pope.

Victims Assistance Coordinators pages.

Alphabetical Places List
The cities, towns, and villages where there is a church with a resident priest, or a Catholic institution, or both, together with the abbreviations of the archdiocese or diocese to which it belongs.

Dioceses and Archdioceses (in alphabetical sequence)
The most detailed information on the Catholic Church in the United States, including the Military Services, Eastern Churches, Personal Prelatures, and Apostolates to the Hungarians and Lithuanians. Listings are in alphabetical order according to the name of the diocese/archdiocese and include the diocesan curia and administrative offices; a parish-by-parish listing of clergy, churches, missions, and parochial schools; information on institutions, and the religious institutes of men and women located in the diocese/archdiocese; and a statistical profile for each diocese/archdiocese.

United States Territorial Sees
This section contains information on U.S. territories similar to that found in the preceding section.

American Foreign Missions
This section highlights the Religious working specifically in foreign countries. Each Province lists their U.S. members and the countries they serve in. For specific address requests, contact the mission office listed.

Missionary Activities
Organizations involved in missionary work in the U.S. and foreign countries.

United States Conference of Secular Institutes
An alphabetical list of secular organizations and their purposes.

U.S. Catholic Mission Association
An alphabetical list of countries served by the U.S. Catholic Mission Association, detailing the number and religious order or laity personnel working there.

Mission Churches
A list, by city, of mission churches in the U.S. and the parishes to which they are attached.

Religious Institutes of Men and Women
An alphabetical list of religious institutes of men and of women, using a P.J. Kenedy identification number. Each listing contains the general headquarters, provinces, provincialates, a summary of legal titles and holdings taken from the individual archdioceses and dioceses within the *Directory*, various forms of ministry and work statistical data of personnel, and representation in the U.S. dioceses and archdiocese Foreign religious institutes are not included in the USCCB Group Ruling.

Special Care Facilities
An alphabetical list of special care facilities by state and diocese.

Religious Order Initials for Men and **Religious Order Initials for Women**
Indexes of abbreviations relevant to the religious institute name and the applicab identification number.

Diocesan and Religious Priests
An alphabetical list of diocesan and religious priests denoting their year of ordinatio the archdiocese or diocese they are assigned to or work in, and the church or instituti with which they are affiliated.

Necrology of U.S. Cardinals, Archbishops, Bishops, Archabbots, Abbots, a Priests
An alphabetical list of the U.S. hierarchy and priests who have died since the last iss of the *Directory*, along with their date of death and last assignment.

The General Summary
A 40+ page general summary of statistics arranged alphabetically by state, listing th archdiocese first within each state, followed by the dioceses. This information, extract from the Statistical Overview of each diocese/archdiocese, pertains to personn parishes, health and welfare, education, and specific sacramental figures, as well Catholic and total population figures for each diocese/archdiocese. U.S. territori and Eastern Church statistics are also included.

Map of Catholic Diocesan and Province Boundaries in the United States
Map defining the diocesan, archdiocesan, provincial, and state boundaries.

Products & Services Guide
Includes a diverse array of products and services offered to the Catholic communi

The Official Catholic Directory
Provides a comprehensive listing of archdioceses and dioceses of the world. Al contains mid-year updates to the U.S. (arch)dioceses. More information on *T OfficialCatholic Directory Part II* can be obtained from the publisher.

SPECIAL NOTATIONS USED IN THE DIRECTORY

An asterisk (*) denotes a tax-exempt organization that has its own IRS exempti status and is not covered by the USCCB Group Ruling. The Group Ruling allows for t exemption from federal income tax of all Catholic institutions listed in *The Offici Catholic Directory* for that year. The exemption was established in 1946 and has be extended every year since then.

[CEM] in a parish listing indicates that a cemetery is connected to the parish.

[JC] indicates a joint cemetery, which is a cemetery being utilized by more than o parish. A number following [CEM] or [JC] indicates the number of cemeteries own by the parish or joint cemeteries shared with other parishes.

A dagger † next to a name in the Necrology denotes a deceased priest. A Maltese cro ✠ denotes a deceased member of the hierarchy.

THE GENERAL SUMMARY

Certain terms used in the General Summary may need additional explanation.

Extern Priests are priests who have not been incardinated into the diocese in whi they are currently working and residing.

Health Care Centers include ancillary care systems, medical centers, sanitorium and hospices.

Specialized Homes refers to institutions which provide aid to abused children adults, halfway homes, AIDS patients, ARC patients, ex-offenders, pregnant wome adjudicated delinquents, or runaway youths.

Special Centers for Social Services are institutions or services that provi assistance, such as hotline centers, food banks, homeless centers, legal aid servic or counseling services.

Residential Care of Children refers to orphanages, as opposed to day care cente

Non-residential Schools for Handicapped are day schools which provide regu and religious education for physically and/or mentally handicapped students.

Received into Full Communion is used to describe people who have been baptiz earlier in life and have now been received into full communion in the Catholic Churc

THE OFFICIAL CATHOLIC DIRECTORY GLOSSARY

bbot

ne superior of an autonomous community of men religious. He has general and cramental jurisdiction over his community. The head of a prominent monastery or congregation consisting of several monasteries is an *archabbot*.

dvocate

n ecclesiastical advocate is someone approved by Church authority to safeguard e rights of a party in a canonical process by arguments regarding the law and the cts of the case. [Cf. c. 1481 and CLSA Comm., p. 967]

postolate

postolate is the mission of Christ and participation in it. Its object is to bring hrist to others, its goal is the greater glory of God, its scope is universal. The work carried out by every human agency by which the life of grace may be given or creased in the soul. A mandate from the Church is essential to the Catholic postolate.

rchbishop

bishop of a main or metropolitan diocese in an ecclesiastical province. The term equivalent to *metropolitan* in the Western Church. It may also be granted to other dinaries and non-residential bishops, and to the ordinary of a diocese outside a rovince.

uditor

n official of a diocesan court, who gathers evidence and testimony and draws up a cord of an ecclesiastical case.

ishop

bishop, by divine institution, carries on the work of the apostles. By reason of piscopal consecration, he shares in the triple apostolic function of teacher of octrine, priest of sacred worship, and minister of church government. Bishops are sponsible for the pastoral care of their dioceses. In addition, bishops have a sponsibility to act in council to guide the Church. The term *eparch* is used in astern-rite churches.

he bishop to whom a particular or local church is entrusted is called a *diocesan shop* or a *residential bishop*. Some other bishops receive *Titular Sees* over which ey exercise no pastoral authority.

hen the pastoral needs of a diocese or archdiocese warrant, an *auxiliary bishop* ay be assigned to aid the residential bishop in governing his diocese. An auxiliary shop is assigned when the residential bishop needs assistance in carrying out his uties because of ill health, advanced age, or amount of work. An auxiliary bishop oes not have the right of succession within his diocese.

special circumstances, such as the advanced age or ill health of a diocesan ishop, a *coadjutator bishop* may be appointed to assist the principal bishop of a iocese. Coadjutator bishops have the *right of succession* in the diocese of their ppointment from the time the See becomes vacant upon the death or retirement f its bishop.

rother

man who is a member of a religious order, but is not ordained or studying for the riesthood.

ana Conference

Catholic family movement, originally designed to aid married couples and families their spiritual and interpersonal relationships. The program is now divided into *re-Cana,* for couples engaged to be married, and *Cana Conferences,* programs for arried people.

atholic Fraternal Organizations

ational Catholic fraternal organizations operating in the United States include e Knights of Columbus and the Knights of Peter Claver. These organizations are ot included in the USCCB group tax exemption ruling.

ensor Librorum

theologian empowered by a bishop to judge a book's soundness in regard to Church eaching before publication.

hancellor

he office of the chancellor (or the *chancery*) evolved from the practice in the early hurch of appointing an official to sign and preserve the letters of the bishop. The first function of the chancellor in the present day is gathering, arranging, and safeguarding the acts of the diocesan curia. Dispensations and other official documents also originate from the chancery. In many dioceses, the chancellor continues to exercise ordinary jurisdiction as delegated by the diocesan bishop. He or she may be assisted by a separate official, the *vice-chancellor.*

Chapter

The *general chapter* of a religious order is an assembly of elected or appointed members and provincials. General chapters are convened for the election of officers, amendments to the constitution, and discussion and legislation of matters of concern to members and the order as a whole.

A *provincial chapter* conducts elections and handles legislation on a provincial level. The assembly is comprised of superiors and representatives of the religious.

A *chapter of canons* is a group of diocesan priests, appointed by the bishop of a diocese, with assigned authority or responsibilities.

College of Cardinals

The College of Cardinals is made up of the cardinals of the Church, who advise the Pope, assist in the central administration of the Church, head the various curial offices and congregations, administer the Holy See during a vacancy, and elect a new Pope. There are three ranks in the College of Cardinals, corresponding to the historical origins of cardinals in the Roman Catholic Church. All cardinals are bishops, but their rank within the College of Cardinals is characterized by one of the hierarchical ranks of bishop, priest, or deacon. Cardinals are given honorary title to churches in the city of Rome. [CF. c. 350; CLSA Comm., pp. 288-289]

1. Cardinal Bishops

There are two types of Cardinal Bishops: 1) those appointed by the Pope as titular bishops to one of the six suburban dioceses of Rome, and 2) Eastern-rite Patriarchs who are heads of Sees with apostolic origins that have been assigned to the College of Cardinals.

2. Cardinal Priests

Heads of Sees outside the city of Rome are assigned a "titular church," one of the churches in Rome. They have no pastoral authority over their titular church.

3. Cardinal Deacons

Cardinals of diaconal rank are bishops without Sees who head the various departments, offices, congregations, committees, and the Secretariat of State of the Roman Curia.

Confraternity of Christian Doctrine [CCD]

A lay organization established for religious education throughout a person's entire life. The term is currently used to describe Catholic parish-based religious education of children from kindergarten through high school. At the diocesan level, the offices are now more commonly known as offices of *religious education* or *Christian formation.* Nationally, the confraternity's religious education component has been taken over by the USCCB's Department of Education. It still exists as a separate entity under the USCCB Administrative Board, with responsibility for licensing religious and spiritual literature.

Consolidated School

The term, as used in the *Directory,* may refer to a school that takes students from more than one parish, or a school that was formed by the consolidation of two or three other schools. In both cases, it is a means of keeping a Catholic school in a given area open by taking students from the surrounding areas, regardless of parish boundaries.

Convent

In common usage, the term refers to a house of women religious. Originally, it referred to a building where members of religious institutes lived, and was not restricted to communities of women.

Cursillo

The *cursillo de cristianidad*, or "little course in Christianity," is a three-day program for achieving spiritual renewal or spiritual awakening. It seeks to convey a new sense of individual and organized apostolic action. The program, conducted by priests and laypeople, consists of a three-day weekend focused on prayer, study, and Christian action, and a follow-up program known as the *post-cursillo.*

Deacons

The diaconate is the first order or grade in ordained ministry. Its origins are in early apostolic times, when deacons preached and baptized under the direction of the presbyters or bishops. Any man who is to be ordained to the priesthood must first be ordained as a *transitional deacon.* Deacons serve in the ministry of liturgy, of the word, and of charity.

In 1967, Pope Paul VI reinstituted the *Permanent Diaconate* for men who do not plan to become ordained priests. Although men ordained as permanent deacons are sometimes referred to as "married deacons," the permanent diaconate is open to both married and unmarried men, with the understanding that after ordination, they may not marry even after the death of a spouse. Under the authority of the diocesan bishop, they perform the same functions as the transitional deacons while, at the same time, retaining their roles in society as family and business men.

Dean/Vicar Forane

The title of a priest appointed by the bishop to aid him in administering the parishes in a certain vicinity, called a "deanery," or "vicariates forane." The function of a dean, or vicar forane, involves promotion, coordination, and supervision of the common pastoral activity within the deanery or vicariate.

Defender of the Bond

A member of a diocesan tribunal, either a cleric or a lay person, holding a graduate degree in canon law, who is appointed by the diocesan bishop for cases concerning the nullity of sacred ordination or the nullity or dissolution of the marriage bond. The defender of the bond is responsible for a review of the evidence, scrutiny of the briefs, examination of witnesses, and maintenance of proper procedures during the trial. The defender also deals with some situations concerning the content of the litigation rather than the legal procedures.

Diocesan Consultors

An advisory council of diocesan priests, as appointed by a diocesan bishop, that assists in the administrative affairs of the diocese.

Diocesan Curia

The personnel and offices assisting the diocesan bishop in directing the pastoral activity, administration, and the exercise of judicial power of his diocese. The curia includes among its officers laity and religious as well as clergy. Principal officers of a diocesan curia are the vicar general of the diocese, the chancellor, officials of the diocesan tribunal, examiners, consultors, auditors, the promoter of justice and the defender of the bond.

Diocese

The standard term for a territorial division of the Church, entrusted to a bishop who rules in his own name as local ordinary, and not as a delegate of another. The chief diocese of a province is an *archdiocese.* It is headed by an archbishop. A diocese is usually limited to a definite territory so that it comprises all the faithful who inhabit that territory. [Cf. cc. 369 and 372, #1] In Eastern-rite churches, the term eparchy is used.

Eastern-rite [Oriental] Church

The term used to describe the Catholic churches which developed in Eastern Europe, Asia, and Africa. The Eastern-rite churches have their own distinctive liturgical and organizational systems. Each is considered equal to the Latin rite within the Church.

Eastern Catholic Association

The eastern catholic association is the association of all Eastern Catholic Bishops in the United States. All Eastern Catholic Bishops, diocesan bishops (and their equivalent in law) and auxiliaries are members. The Association represents the Armenian, Chaldean, Maronite Melikite, Romanian, Ruthenian and Ukrainian Churches. The Syriac, Syro-Malabar and Russian churches are also represented but without a bishop member since they are presently have no established hierarchy in the United States.

Ecumenism/Ecumenical Movement

A movement for spiritual understanding and unity among Christians and their churches. The term is also extended to apply to efforts toward greater understanding and cooperation between Christians and members of other faiths.

Exarch/Exarchy

A church jurisdiction, similar to a diocese, established for Eastern-rite Catholics living outside their native land. The head of an exarchy, usually a bishop, is an *exarch.*

Hierarchy

In general, the term refers to the ordered body of clergy, divided into bisho[p] priests, and deacons. In Catholic practice, the term refers to the bishops of t[h] world or of a particular region.

Holy Name Society

A lay organization which seeks to aid its members in living a genuinely Christi[a] life. The society organizes retreats and other spiritual and devotional exercises.

Holy See

The term refers to the diocese of Rome. Used in reference to the governance of t[h] Church, it refers to the Pontiff, the Roman Curia, and the Sacred College.

Legion of Mary

A lay organization established to assist the clergy in the sanctification of i[ts] members' souls, and the spread of the Christian faith and spiritual service to other[s]. Members participate in almost every form of social service and Catholic actio[n] including evangelization. The organization was founded in 1921.

Metropolitan

The archbishop of an archdiocese in a province. He has limited supervisory powe[r] and influence over the other dioceses and bishops in the province.

Military Ordinariate [Archdiocese for the Military Services, U.S.A.]

A nonterritorial diocese for American Catholics and their dependents who are in t[h] military or affiliated with the armed forces. Personnel employed by or engaged diplomatic missions for the U.S. government in countries where U.S. military forc[es] are stationed also belong to the Military Ordinariate.

Mission

A mission, or *quasi-parish,* is a parish which has not been established because lacks one or more of the following qualifications: a resident pastor; necessa[ry] financial resources; territorial boundaries; or a natural grouping by way of rit[e] nationality, or language. Missions are attached to some parishes under the care their pastors.

Moderator of the Curia

A bishop or priest, appointed by the diocesan bishop, who is concerned primari[ly] with administrative matters and with supervising those working in the curia.

Monastery

An autonomous community house of a religious order, which may or may not be monastic order. The term is used more specifically to refer to a community house men religious or women religious in which they lead a contemplative life separa[te] from the world.

Monsignor

An honorary ecclesiastical title granted by the Pope to some diocesan priests. [In] the United States, the title is given to the vicar general of a diocese. In Europe, t[he] title is also given to bishops.

Newman Apostolate

An apostolate to the Catholic college and university community, now common[ly] known as "campus ministry."

Notary

An elected or appointed ecclesiastical official who acts as a secretary in form[al] church proceedings. The notary records the minutes, testimony, etc., of t[he] proceedings.

Opus Dei

A personal prelature dedicated to spreading through society an awareness of t[he] call to Christian virtue, awareness, and witness in one's life and work. The organizati[on] was founded in 1928 and in 1950, it received Vatican approval as a secular institutio[n]. In 1982, it was designated a personal prelature, the *Prelature of the Holy Cross an[d] Opus Dei.* Members are not members of a religious order, do not take vows, and [do] not live in community.

Ordinary

Diocesan bishops, religious superiors, and certain other diocesan authorities wi[th] jurisdiction over the clergy in a specific geographical area, or the members of religious order.

dination/Ordain

sacramental rite by which a "sacred order" is conferred (diaconate, priesthood, scopacy).

pal Audience

uest for attendance at papal audiences and similar functions may be addressed Bishops' Office for United States Visitors to the Vatican. Postal address: North erican College, Via dell 'Umilta 30, 00187 Rome, Italy. Tel.: 011-39-06-6900-1; Fax: 011-39-06-679-1448. Rev. Msgr. Roger C. Roensch, Dir.

pal Representatives

ere are three types of representatives of the Roman Pontiff:

hose who represent him to particular churches and civil government;

hose who represent him to particular churches;

hose who represent him in international organizations or at various conferences meetings. [Cf. c. 363; CLSA Comm., p. 302]

Apostolic Nuncio

he United States, the papal representative is sent by the Pope to both the local rch and to the government. His title is Apostolic Nuncio.

Legate

individual appointed by the Pope to be his personal representative to a nation, ernational conference, or local church. The legate may be chosen from the local gy of a country.

Permanent Observer to the United Nations

Apostolic See maintains permanent legates below the ambassadorial level several world organizations. Since the papal representative does not enjoy right to vote within the organization, his title at the United Nations is that *Observer*.

rish

pecific community of the Christian faithful within a diocese, which has its own rch building, under the authority of a *pastor* who is responsible for providing m with ministerial service. Most parishes are formed on a geographic basis, but y may be formed along national or ethnic lines.

rish Coordinator

eacon, religious, or lay person who is responsible for the pastoral care of parish. e parish coordinator is in charge of the day-to-day life of the parish in the areas vorship, education, pastoral service and administration.

stor

riest in charge of a parish or congregation. He is responsible for administering sacraments, instructing the congregation in the doctrine of the Church, and er services to the people of the parish.

storal Associate

nember of the laity who is part of a parish ministry team.

storal Council

onsultative body which the pastor or bishop consults concerning the pastoral ivity within the diocese. Its members include laity, religious, and clergy. The storal council's purpose is to study practical situations, difficulties and problems, l make concrete recommendations and proposals to the diocesan bishop. The storal council is always subject to the final authority of the pastor or bishop.

triarch

e Pope is the traditional "Patriarch of the West." All other bishops in the Latin e, even those with the honorary title of "Patriarch," are subject to him. Similarly, riarchs within nations have only an honorary title unless special provisions are de otherwise. Eastern-rite Patriarchs are subject to the Pope while serving as ads of the faithful belonging to their rites throughout the world.

rsonal Prelature

addition to the territorial arrangement of the Church into particular or local rches or dioceses, canon law also provides for non-territorial areas of religious isdiction, incorporating secular clergy and deacons. Membership is also open to lay sons. These *prelatures* are established to meet specific pastoral or missionary needs the regional, national, or international level without infringing on the rights of the al bishops. A prelature is presided over by a *personal prelate,* who is an ordinary with right to establish seminaries and ordain priests as members of the prelature.

non law also allows for laity to be associated in the works of prelatures without ng withdrawn from the jurisdiction of their own diocesan bishop.

Personal prelatures are jurisdictional structures of a secular type which are established by the Holy See as an instrument within the hierarchical pastoral work of the Church to carry out special pastoral or missionary tasks. Personal prelatures are based on the principle of insertion into the local Church. In this they differ essentially from the personal dioceses, such as those constituted for the faithful of a particular rite, which are based on the principle of independence or autonomy in regard to local Churches.

Vatican II provided for setting up personal prelatures (see Decree, Presbyterorum ordinis, no. 10). Additional norms were established in subsequent pontifical legislation (see Motu proprio Ecclesiae Sanctae no. 1, no. 4, August 6, 1966 and the Apostolic Constitution Regimini Ecclesiae Universae, no. 49, no. 1, Aug. 15, 1967). General legislation concerning personal prelatures is contained in canons 294 to 297 of the 1983 Code of Canon Law.

Personal prelatures are to be established by the Holy See after hearing the views of the respective Episcopal Conferences (can. 294). They are governed by a Prelate according to statutes given by the Holy See. The Prelate is their proper Ordinary, who may incardinate priests and must look after their spiritual and temporal welfare (can. 295). Lay people can dedicate themselves by means of a contractual agreement, to the apostolic activities of the prelature; the statutes are to specify the manner of this organic cooperation (can. 296). And the statutes are also to determine the relations of the prelature with the Ordinaries of the places in which the prelature works, with the prior consent of the Ordinaries (can. 297).

Presbyteral Council

Also known as the *priests' council,* the presbyteral council is the principal consultative body mandated by the Code of Canon Law to advise the diocesan bishop in matters of pastoral governance. It consists of bishops and priests serving the diocese.

Propagation of the Faith

An organization, headquartered in Rome, which distributes aid to Catholic missions and organizes the work of missionaries all over the world. The organization has responsibility for fostering missionary vocations, assigning missionaries to field work, defining ecclesiastical boundaries and assigning clergy to them, and encouraging training and installation of native-born clergy.

Promoter of Justice

A cleric or lay person, holding a graduate degree in canon law, who is appointed by the diocesan bishop to serve in the role of a "prosecuting attorney" in trials of crimes against church law and of other judicial litigations in the diocese. A promoter of justice may be appointed for a specific case by the bishop.

Province

A defined geographic area containing an archdiocese, or *Metropolitan See,* and at least one diocese, or *Suffragen See.* The archbishop of the archdiocese has no direct powers over the Suffragen Sees, but does have limited advisory and appellate authority and obligations. The term also refers to a territorial grouping of particular churches or communities, or a territory of a religious order.

Provincial

The superior of the communities of a religious order that constitute a province.

Provincial Council

An assembly of the bishops of an ecclesiastical province, called by the metropolitan archbishop. The term is also used in reference to the provincial superior of a province, along with his or her chief advisors.

Receptions into the Church

Can take two forms: baptism of those not previously validly baptized, or "reception into full communion" with the Church for those who have already been baptized, in which case a profession of faith affects the reception.

Religious Education Department

The ECA has established the ECDD-The Eastern Conference of Diocesan Directors of Religious Education which oversees, through God With Us Publications, all publications of catechtical materials published by it and used in Eastern Catholic Churches, mainly of Byzantine tradition.

Religious Priest/Diocesan Priest

Religious, or regular, priests are those who are professed members of a religious order or institute. Religious clergy live according to the rule of their respective orders. In pastoral ministry, they are under the jurisdiction of their local bishop, as well as the superiors of their order. Diocesan, or secular, priests are under the direction of their local bishop. They commit to serving their congregations and other institutions.

Retreat

A period of time spent in meditation and religious exercise. Retreats may take various forms, from traditional closed forms, to open retreats, which do not disengage the participants from day-to-day life. Both clergy and lay people of all ages participate in retreats. Houses and centers providing facilities for retreats are *retreat houses.*

Rite of Christian Initiation of Adults [RCIA]

The liturgical book containing the norms and rituals of the Catholic Church for people who wish to join the Church. Part of the book is intended for baptized Christians who wish to become Catholics. The term is used in a general sense to refer to the process of entering the Catholic Church.

Roman Curia

The official collective name for the administrative agencies and courts, and their officials, who assist the Pope in governing the Church. Members are appointed and granted authority by the Pope.

St. Vincent DePaul Society

Originally known as the *Conference of Charity,* this is an organization of lay people who serve the poor through spiritual and material works of mercy. The society operates stores, rehabilitation workshops, food centers, shelters, criminal justice and other programs.

Scholastic

A member of a religious order who has completed his novitiate, but has not yet been ordained.

Scholastic Teaching

Usually refers to Scholastic Philosophy, which is the basis for much Catholic Theology. It comes from the canonical "schools" of the 12th-13th centuries, St. Thomas Aquinas, St. Bonaventure, St. Albert the Great, etc., who developed "scholasticism" based mainly on Aristotle. It is the semi-official philosophy of the Church.

Secular Institute

Canonically erected institute of consecrated life for single laity and clerics who strive for the perfection of charity and work for the sanctification of the world while remaining in a lifestyle within the world.

See

The word is taken from the Latin word "sedes" ("seat"), and is used to denote a diocese or ecclesiastical district. The term *Holy See* is reserved to the diocese of Rome whose bishop is the Pope. U.S. Territorial Sees are dioceses located on territory of the United States of America, but are members of episcopal confereences other than the United States Conference of Catholic Bishops.

Seminary

An educational institution for men preparing for *Holy Orders*. The term originates from the time of St. Augustine, when those preparing for the priesthood were educated in the "cathedral school." During the Middle Ages, the clergy were educated in a university setting where faculties of philosophy, theology, and canon law existed. Eventually individual dioceses or provinces came to establish their own schools for educating their clerical students. Traditional seminaries date from the Council of Trent in the 16th century.

A school for the spiritual, academic, and pastoral education and formation of priesthood candidates is known as a *major seminary* in which the focus is on philosophical and theological education. To prepare for entrance into a major seminary, a period of study is set aside for the required courses in the humanities and the sciences in institutions called *minor seminaries*.

Serra Club

Local units of *Serra International,* an organization which promotes vocations to the priesthood and religious life, and offers instruction to lay leaders.

Sister

The term, in the strictest sense, refers to women religious who belong to institutes which have professed simple vows. However, in everyday usage, the term is used for any woman religious.

Sodality

A group of laity established for the promotion of Christian life and worship, or some other religious purpose.

Special Centers for Social Services

This would seem to overlap with Specialized Homes. Some of the categorizatio fairly arbitrary. Catholic Charities might have its own proper distinctions government or private funding purposes.

Specialized Homes

Includes such institutions as homes for handicapped (e.g., Misericordia Hom youth homes (e.g., Maryville, Mercy Boys and Girls, Homes), homes for batte women, drug rehab centers, homes for unwed mothers, etc.

Superior

The head of a religious order or congregation. He or she may be the head province, or an individual house.

Synod

A gathering of designated officials and representatives of a church, that has legisla and policy-making powers.

1. Synod of Bishops

The Synod of Bishops is a consultative body, unless explicitly stated otherwise His Holiness, expressing the communion of the hierarchy. A synod of bishops me in general assembly, either in "Ordinary" or "Extraordinary" session, when matter for treatment concerns the whole Church and in "Special Assembly" w the matter deals directly with a definite region or regions.

2. Synod of Oriental Churches

The synods of the Oriental Churches enjoy various prerogatives including the ri to elect bishops, regulate discipline and exercise pastoral authority in their respec churches.

3. Diocesan Synod

A diocesan synod is an expression of the communion of the particular church diocesan synod enjoys the participation of priests, women and men religious laypersons; the bishop is the sole legislator.

Territorial Sees

Dioceses located on territory of the United States, but are members of episco conferences other than the United States Conference of Catholic Bishops.

Theologate

An institution which provides the last four years of study for candidates for priesthood.

Titular See

A former diocese which no longer physically or geographically exists. Titular Sees given as an honorary title to certain bishop not serving as a chief pastor of a dioc i.e., auxiliary bishops, papal representatives, and bishops of the Roman Curia.

Tribunal

A tribunal (court) is the name given to the person or persons who exercise Church's judicial powers. By its very nature, this procedure involves the determina of a legal controversy. A major concern of tribunals is conducting the process lead to the dissolution or annulment of marriages. In ecclesiastical matters, defi procedural norms for conducting a trial are found in the Code of Canon Law to se disputes. There are various grades of tribunals, including diocesan tribunals, first court of trial for most cases; regional and metropolitan tribunals, located in archdiocese, the appellate court for all cases tried within the province; and tribunals of the Holy See, which act as the Church's central appellate court, cases reserved to the Holy See, deal with questions of procedure and jurisdictio the other courts, and act as the Church's supreme court.

United States Conference of Catholic Bishops

The United States Conference of Catholic Bishops is a permanent instit composed of Catholic bishops of the United States of America in and thro which the bishops exercise in a communal or collegial manner the pasto mission entrusted to them by the Lord Jesus of sanctification, teaching, a leadership, especially by devising forms and methods of the apostolate suita adapted to the circumstances of the times. Such exercise is intended to o appropriate assistance to each bishop in fulfilling his particular ministry in cal Church, to effect a commonality of ministry addressed to the people of the nited States of America, and to foster and express communion with the Church in her nations within the Church universal, under the leadership of its chief pastor, ne Pope.

icar

ne appointment of a priest or a bishop as an *episcopal vicar* is an option given to a diocesan shop when he needs a deputy for governing a specific territory within the diocese, a group persons or a specific rite, or a type of apostolic work within the diocese.

 Church law, the diocesan bishop is the judge of all cases in the diocesan tribunal of st trial. He must appoint a priest with ordinary power to judge cases not reserved to e bishop himself. This priest must have a graduate degree in canon law. He is called e *judicial vicar,* and is sometimes referred to as the chief judge or officialis. He may given another priest as an assistant with the title of *adjutant judicial vicar*.

A bishop or priest appointed to participate in the executive (administrative) governance of the diocese with executive jurisdiction as a deputy of the diocesan bishop is a *vicar general.* The appointment of a vicar general is mandatory for every diocese. This office is designed to facilitate and unify diocesan administration.

Vicar for Religious

A priest appointed by a bishop to act as his representative in dealing with the religious communities in his diocese.

Information for this glossary was taken from the *Catholic News Service's Stylebook on Religion,* the *Modern Catholic Dictionary,* published by Doubleday and Company, Inc., the *Concise Oxford Dictionary of the Christian Church,* published by Oxford University Press, and the *Encyclopedic Dictionary of Religion,* published by the Sisters of St. Joseph of Philadelphia. The publishers of the *Official Catholic Directory* also wish to thank the Vice Chancellors of the Archdiocese of Chicago for their work in the preparation of this glossary.

THE SUPREME ROMAN PONTIFFS

St. Peter of Bethsaida in Galilee, Prince of the Apostles, who received from Jesus Christ the Supreme Pontifical Power to be transmitted to his Successors, resided first at Antioch, then at Rome for twenty-five years where he was martyred in the year 64, or 67 of the common reckoning.

	END OF PONTIFICATE, A.D.
St. Linus	76
St. Anacletus or Cletus	88
St. Clement I	97
St. Evaristus	105
St. Alexander I	115
St. Sixtus I	125
St. Telesphorus	136
St. Hyginus	140
St. Pius I	155
St. Anicetus	166
St. Soterus	175
St. Eleuterius	189
St. Victor I	199
St. Zephyrinus	217
St. Callistus I	222
St. Urban I	230
St. Pontian	235
St. Anterus	236
St. Fabian	250
St. Cornelius	253
St. Lucius I	254
St. Stephen I	257
St. Sixtus II	258
St. Dionysius	268
St. Felix I	274
St. Eutychian	283
St. Caius	296
St. Marcellinus	304
St. Marcellus I	309
St. Eusebius	309
St. Melchiades	314
St. Sylvester I	335
St. Mark	336
St. Julius I	352
Liberius	366
St. Damasus I	384
St. Siricius	399
St. Anastasius I	401
St. Innocent I	417
St. Zozimus	418
St. Boniface I	422
St. Celestine I	432
St. Sixtus III	440
St. Leo I (the Great)	461
St. Hilary	468
St. Simplicius	483
St. Fclix III or II	492
St. Gelasius I	496
Anastasius II	498
St. Symmacus	514
St. Hormisdas	523
St. John I	526
St. Felix IV or III	530
Boniface II	532
John II	535
St. Agapitus	536
St. Silverius	537
Vigilius	555
Pelagius I	561
John III	574
Benedict I	579
Pelagius II	590
St. Gregory I (the Great)	604
Sabinianus	606
Boniface III	607
St. Boniface IV	615

	END OF PONTIFICATE, A.D.
St. Deusdeditus or Adeodatus I	618
Boniface V	625
Honorius I	638
Severinus	640
John IV	642
Theodore I	649
St. Martin I	655
St. Eugene I	657
St. Vitalian	672
Adeodatus II	676
Donus I	678
St. Agathonus	681
St. Leo II	683
St. Benedict II	685
John V	686
Conon	687
St. Sergius I	701
John VI	705
John VII	707
Sisinnius	708
Constantine	715
St. Gregory II	731
St. Gregory III	741
St. Zachary	752
Stephen III	757
St. Paul I	767
Stephen IV	772
Adrian I	795
St. Leo III	816
Stephen V	817
St. Paschal I	824
Eugene II	827
Valentine	827
Gregory IV	844
Sergius II	847
St. Leo IV	855
Benedict III	858
St. Nicholas I (the Great)	867
Adrian II	872
John VIII	882
Marinus I	884
St. Adrian III	885
Stephen VI	891
Formosus	896
Boniface VI	896
Stephen VII	897
Romanus	897
Theodore II	897
John IX	900
Benedict IV	903
Leo V	903
Sergius III	911
Anastasius III	913
Landus	914
John X	928
Leo VI	928
Stephen VIII	931
John XI	935
Leo VII	939
Stephen IX	942
Marinus II	946
Agapitus II	955
John XII	964
Leo VIII	965
Benedict V	966

	END OF PONTIFICATE, A.D.
John XIII	972
Benedict VI	974
Benedict VII	983
John XIV	984
John XV	996
Gregory V	999
Sylvester II	1003
John XVII	1003
John XVIII	1009
Sergius IV	1012
Benedict VIII	1024
John XIX	1032
Benedict IX	1044
Benedict IX	1045
Sylvester III	1045
Gregory VI	1046
Clement II	1047
Benedict IX	1048
Damasus II	1048
St. Leo IX	1054
Victor II	1057
Stephen X	1058
Nicholas II	1061
Alexander II	1073
St. Gregory VII	1085
B. Victor III	1087
B. Urban II	1099
Paschal II	1118
Gelasius II	1119
Callistus II	1124
Honorius II	1130
Innocent II	1143
Celestine II	1144
Lucius II	1145
B. Eugene III	1153
Anastasius IV	1154
Adrian IV	1159
Alexander III	1181
Lucius III	1185
Urban III	1187
Gregory VIII	1187
Clement III	1191
Celestine III	1198
Innocent III	1216
Honorius III	1227
Gregory IX	1241
Celestine IV	1241
Innocent IV	1254
Alexander IV	1261
Urban IV	1264
Clement IV	1268
B. Gregory X	1276
B. Innocent V	1276
Adrian V	1276
John XXI	1277
Nicholas III	1280
Martin IV	1285
Honorius IV	1287
Nicholas IV	1292
St. Celestine V	1296
Boniface VIII	1303
B. Benedict XI	1304
Clement V	1314
John XXII	1334
Benedict XII	1342
Clement VI	1352
Innocent VI	1362

	END OF PONTIFICATE, A.D.
B. Urban V	13
Gregory XI	13
Urban VI	13
Boniface IX	14
Innocent VII	14
Gregory XII	14
Martin V	14
Eugene IV	14
Nicholas V	14
Callistus III	14
Pius II	14
Paul II	14
Sixtus IV	14
Innocent VIII	14
Alexander VI	15
Pius III	15
Julius II	15
Leo X	15
Adrian VI	15
Clement VII	15
Paul III	15
Julius III	15
Marcellus II	15
Paul IV	15
Pius IV	15
St. Pius V	15
Gregory XIII	15
Sixtus V	15
Urban VII	15
Gregory XIV	15
Innocent IX	15
Clement VIII	16
Leo XI	16
Paul V	16
Gregory XV	16
Urban VIII	16
Innocent X	16
Alexander VII	16
Clement IX	16
Clement X	16
B. Innocent XI	16
Alexander VIII	16
Innocent XII	17
Clement XI	17
Innocent XIII	17
Benedict XIII	17
Clement XII	17
Benedict XIV	17
Clement XIII	17
Clement XIV	17
Pius VI	17
Pius VII	18
Leo XII	18
Pius VIII	18
Gregory XVI	18
Pius IX	18
Leo XIII	19
St. Pius X	19
Benedict XV	19
Pius XI	19
Pius XII	19
John XXIII	19
Paul VI	19
John Paul I	19
John Paul II	20
Benedict XVI	now reignin

PART I
Hierarchy of the Catholic Church

The Hierarchy, as the supreme governing body of the Catholic Church, consists of the Roman Pontiff, the successor of Peter, and the Bishops joined together with him and never without him (canons 330,331,336) in one apostolic college to provide for the common good of the Church. The Roman Pontiff in the exercise of his office is assisted by the College of Cardinals, and further by the departments also called "dicasteries" of the Roman Curia. The Bishops, of whom some bear the titles of Patriarch and Archbishop, are united with the Roman Pontiff in the governance of the whole Church; the Bishops, when assigned to particular Sees, are individually responsible for the teaching, sanctification and governance of their particular Church. Apostolic Vicars and Prefects together with certain Abbots and other Prelates are also joined in this work.

HIS HOLINESS THE POPE

Bishop of Rome and Vicar of Jesus Christ,
Successor of St. Peter, Prince of the Apostles,
Supreme Pontiff of the Universal Church.
Primate of Italy.
Archbishop and Metropolitan of the Roman Province,
Sovereign of Vatican City State.
Servant of the Servants of God

Benedict XVI

JOSEPH RATZINGER

The present successor of St. Peter was born in Marktl am Inn, Diocese of Passau, April 16, 1927; ordained Priest, June 29, 1951; appointed Archbishop of Munchen und Freising March 25, 1977 and consecrated May 28, 1977; Proclaimed and created Cardinal June 27, 1977. Elected Pope, April 19, 2005; installed April 24, 2005.

VATICAN CITY

Vatican City is the smallest state in the world, occupying 108.7 acres, of which about one third is covered with buildings and is situated on the right side of the Tiber River. Vatican City has territory, population, and sovereignity. This territory, limited as it is, suffices to guarantee the spiritual and temporal independence needed for the exercise of the Holy See's spiritual mission. In 1870 the Kingdom of Italy seized all Vatican possessions which for several centuries had constituted the papal temporal domain. But even after 1870 the Holy See continued to regard itself as a separate entity in international law, and was recognized as such by numerous states with which it retained normal diplomatic relations. After long discussions the Holy See and the then Kingdom of Italy signed the Lateran Pacts on February 11, 1929, so that the complete and independent authority of the Vatican State was and is recognized by the Italian state.

The Sovereign of this small state is His Holiness, the Pope.

The government presently is administered by a Pontifical Commission of which His Eminence Edmund Casimir Cardinal Szoka is President.

THE COLLEGE OF CARDINALS

The Cardinals constitute a special college and they assist the Roman Pontiff collegially when they are called together to deal with questions of major importance; they do so individually when they assist the Pope especially in the daily care of the universal Church by means of the different offices which they perform (canons 349-350). The Cardinals who are under eighty years of age elect his successor.

The College of Cardinals is divided into three ranks: Cardinal-Bishops, Cardinal-Priests, and Cardinal-Deacons. The College of Cardinals, when complete formerly consisted of 70 members: 6 Cardinal Bishops, 50 Cardinal Priests and 14 Cardinal Deacons, but the late Pontiffs, Pope John XXIII and Pope Paul VI enlarged the College of Cardinals. At the moment the maximum number of Cardinal electors (those under 80 years of age) must not exceed 120.

The Cardinal Bishops (except the Patriarch-Cardinals of the Oriental Rites), have as Titular Sees the Suburban Sees of Rome, which are: Porto Santa Rufina, Albano, Palestrina, Sabina, Frascati, Velletri, Segni. The Cardinal Dean has united to his See the See of Ostia. The Cardinal Priests take their title from the Titular Churches to which they are appointed: the Cardinal Deacons are appointed to other Churches called Deaconries. The first Cardinal Bishop is Dean; the first Cardinal Priest is First Priest; and the first Cardinal Deacon is First Deacon of the Sacred College. The Dean has the right of ordaining the new Pope if he is not already a bishop; the First Deacon has the right of proclaiming him and investing him with the sacred Pallium. On the death of the Pontiff, the Cardinal Camerlengo has the Administration of the affairs of the Holy See.

Sometimes the Roman Pontiff promotes a person to the dignity of Cardinal but does not make public his name and keeps it in pectore. Upon the publication of his name, this Cardinal enjoys his right of precedence from the day on which his name was reserved in pectore by the Pope (cfr. Can. 351¶ 3).

The Cardinals of the Holy Roman Church

(Listed in Alphabetical Order)

Agnelo, Geraldo Majella (Cardinal Priest), Titular of San Gregorio Magno alla Magliana Nuova, Archbishop of Sao Salvador da Bahia; born in Juiz de Fora, October 19, 1933. Created and proclaimed February 21, 2001. Address: Av.

Cardenal da Silva 26, Casa 33-Federação, 40231-250 Salvador, BA, Brazil.

Agré, Bernard (Cardinal Priest), Titular of San Giovanni Crisostomo a Monte Sacro Alto, Archbishop Emeritus of Abidjan; born in Monga, Archdiocese of Abidjan, March 2, 1926. Created and proclaimed February 21, 2001. Address: 01 B.P. 1287, Abidjan 01, Cote D'Ivoire.

Agustoni, Gilberto (Cardinal Priest) Titular of Ss. Urbano e Lorenzo a Primaporta, Prefect Emeritus of the Supreme Tribunal of the Apostolic Signatura; born in Schaffhausen, Switzerland, Diocese of Basel, July 26, 1922. Created and proclaimed November 26, 1994. Address: Piazza della Citta Leonina 9, 00193 Rome, Italy.

Álvarez Martinez, Francisco (Cardinal Priest), Titular of Santa Maria Regina Pacis a Monte Verde, Archbishop Emeritus of Toledo; born in Santa Eulalia de Ferrones Llanera, Archdiocese of Oviedo, July 14, 1925. Created and proclaimed February 21, 2001. Address: Calle Doctor Gómez Ulla 10, 3° drcha., 28028 Madrid, Spain.

Ambrozic, Aloysius Matthew (Cardinal Priest), Titular of Sts. Marcellinus and Peter, Archbishop Emeritus of Toronto, Canada; born in Gabrje, Archdiocese of Ljubljana, January 27, 1930. Created and proclaimed February 21, 1998. Address: Chancery Office, 1155 Yonge St., Toronto, M4T 1W2 Ontario, Canada.

Amigo Vallejo, Carlos, O.F.M. (Cardinal Priest), Titular of Santa Maria di Monserrato degli Spagnoli, Archbishop of Seville; born in Medina de Rioseco, Diocese of Valladolid, August 23, 1934. Created and proclaimed October 21, 2003. Address: Apartado 6, Plaza Virgen de los Reyes s/n, 41004 Sevilla, Spain.

Angelini, Fiorenzo (Cardinal Priest), Titular of S. Spirito in Sassia; President Emeritus of the Pontifical Council for Pastoral Assistance to Health Care Workers; born in Rome, Italy, August 1, 1916. Created and proclaimed June 28, 1991. Address: Via della Conciliazione 15, 00193 Rome, Italy.

Antonelli, Ennio (Cardinal Priest), Titular of Sant'Andrea delle Fratte, President of the Pontifical Council for the Family, Archbishop Emeritus of Florence; born in Todi, Diocese of Orvieto-Todi, November 18, 1936. Created and proclaimed October 21, 2003. Address: Arcivescovado, Piazza S. Calisto 16, 00153 Rome, Italy.

Antonetti, Lorenzo (Cardinal Priest), Titular of Saint Agnes in Agone; President Emeritus of the Administration of the Patrimony of the Apostolic See; born in Romagnano Sesia, diocese of Novara, July 31, 1922. Created and proclaimed February 21, 1998. Address: Casa del Clero, 28010 Miasino (Novara) Italy.

Aponte Martinez, Luis (Cardinal Priest), Titular of S. Maria Madre della Provvidenza a Monte Verde, Archbishop Emeritus of San Juan de Puerto Rico; born in Lajas, diocese of Mayaguez, August 4, 1922. Created and proclaimed March 5, 1973. Address: Urbanizacion San Ignacio, Calle San Alejandro 1763, San Juan, PR 00927-1967.

Araujo, Serafim Fernandes de (Cardinal Priest), Titular of S. Luigi Maria Grignion de Montfort, Archbishop Emeritus of Belo Horizonte, Brazil; born in Minas Novas, Diocese of Aracuai, August 13, 1924. Created and proclaimed February 21, 1998. Address: Av. Brasil 1666, 5 andar, Bairro-dos Funcionários, 30140-003 Belo Horizonte, MG, Brazil.

Arinze, Francis (Cardinal Bishop), Titular of the suburbicarian Church of Velletri-Segni; Prefect Emeritus of the Congregation for Divine Worship and the Discipline of the Sacraments; born in Eziowelle, Archdiocese of Onitsha, November 1, 1932. Created and proclaimed May 25, 1985. Address: Largo del Colonnato 3, 00193 Rome, Italy.

Arns, Paul Evaristo, O.F.M. (Cardinal Priest), Titular of S. Antonio da Padova in Via Tuscolana, Archbishop Emeritus of Sao Paulo; born in Forquilhinha, Diocese of Criciuma, September 14, 1921. Created and proclaimed March 5, 1973. Address: C.P. 916, Rua Antonietta Altenfelder 1000, 02717-170, Sao Paulo, SP, Brazil.

Backis, Audrys Juozas (Cardinal Priest), Titular of Nativita di Nostro Signore Gesu Cristo a Via Gallia, Archbishop of Vilnius; born in Kaunas, February 1, 1937. Created and proclaimed February 21, 2001. Address: Sventaragio 4, 01122 Vilnius, Lithuania.

Bagnasco, Angelo (Cardinal Priest), title of the Gran Madre di Dio, Archbishop of Genoa (Italy), born in Pontevico, Diocese of Brescia, January 14, 1943. Created and proclaimed November 24, 2007. Address: Arcivescovado, Piazza Matteotti 4, 16123 Genova, Italy.

Barbarin, Philippe Xavier Ignace (Cardinal Priest), Titular of Santissima Trinita al Monte Pincio, Archbishop of Lyon; born in Rabat, Morocco, October 17, 1950. Created and proclaimed October 21, 2003. Address: Archeveche, 1 Place de Fourviere, 69321 Lyon, Cedex 05, France.

Baum, William Wakefield (Cardinal Priest), Titular of Santa Croce in Via Flaminia; Major Penitentiary Emeritus; born in Dallas, Texas, November 21, 1926. Created and proclaimed, May 24, 1976. Address: Via Rusticucci 13, 00193 Rome, Italy.

Bergoglio, Jorge Mario, S.J. (Cardinal Priest), Titular of San Roberto Bellarmino, Archbishop of Buenos Aires; born in Buenos Aires, December 17, 1936. Created and proclaimed February 21, 2001. Address: Arzobispado, Av. Rivadavia 415, C1002AAC Buenos Aires, Argentina.

Bertone, Tarcisio, S.D.B. (Cardinal Bishop), Titular of the Suburbicarian Church of Frascati, Secretary of State, Camerlengo of the Holy Roman Church; Archbishop Emeritus of Genova; born in Romano Canavese, Diocese of Ivrea, Italy, December 2, 1934. Created and proclaimed October 21, 2003. Address: 00120 Vatican City State, Europe.

Bevilacqua, Anthony J. (Cardinal Priest), Titular of SS. Redentore e S. Alfonso in Via Merulana, Archbishop Emeritus of Philadelphia; born in Brooklyn, New York, June 17, 1923. Created and proclaimed June 28, 1991. Address: 100 East Wynnewood Road, Wynnewood, PA 19096.

Biffi, Giacomo (Cardinal Priest), Titular of Ss. Giovanni Evangelista e Petronio, Archbishop Emeritus of Bologna; born in Milan, June 13, 1928. Created and proclaimed May 25, 1985. Address: Villa Edera, Via S. Ruffillo 5/A, 40068 S. Lazzaro Di Savena (Bologna), Italy.

Bozanic, Josip (Cardinal Priest), Titular of San Girolamo dei Croati, Archbishop of Zagreb; born in Rijeka, Croatia, March 20, 1949. Created and proclaimed October 21, 2003. Address: Nadbiskupski Duhovni Stol, Kaptol 21, p.p. 553, 10000 Zagreb, Croatia.

Brady, Sean Baptist (Cardinal Priest), Titular of Sts. Quiricus and Julitta, Archbishop of Armagh, Ireland, born in Laragh (Drumcalpin), Diocese of Kilmore, August 16, 1939. Created and proclaimed November 24, 2007. Address: Archbishop's House, Ara Coeli, Cathedral Road, Armagh BT61 7QY, Ireland.

Cacciavillan, Agostino (Cardinal Deacon), Deacon of Holy Guardian Angels at Citta Giardino, President Emeritus of Administration of the Patrimony of the Apostolic See; born in Novale, Diocese of Vincenza, August 14, 1926. Created and proclaimed February 21, 2001. Address: 00120 Vatican City State, Europe.

Caffarra, Carlo (Cardinal Priest), Titular of Saint John the Baptist of the Florentines, Archbishop of Bologna; born in Samboseto di Busseto, Diocese of Fidenza, June 1, 1938. Created and proclaimed March 24, 2006. Address: Via Altabella 6, 40126 Bologna, Italy.

Canestri, Giovanni (Cardinal Priest), Titular of S. Andrea della Valle, Archbishop Emeritus of Genoa; born in Castelspina, Diocese of Alessandria, September 30, 1918. Created and proclaimed June 28, 1988. Address: Via Cernaia 9, 00185 Rome, Italy.

Canizares Llovera, Antonio (Cardinal Priest), Titular of Saint Pancras, Prefect of the Congregation for Divine Worship and the Discipline of the Sacraments, Archbishop Emeritus of Toledo; born in Utiel, Archdiocese of Valencia, October 10, 1945. Created and proclaimed March 24, 2006. Address: Arco de Palacio, 3, 45002 Toledo, Spain.

Carles Gordo, Ricardo Maria (Cardinal Priest), Titular of S. Maria Consolatrice al Tiburtino, Archbishop Emeritus of Barcelona, Spain; born in Valencia, September 24, 1926. Created and proclaimed November 26, 1994, Address: General Vives 29, 08017 Barcelona, Spain.

Cassidy, Edward I. (Cardinal Priest), Titular of S. Maria in Via Lata, President Emeritus of the Pontifical Council for Promoting Christian Unity; born in Sydney, Australia, July 5, 1924. Created and proclaimed June 28, 1991. Address: 16 Coachwood Dr., Warabrook, NSW 2304, Australia.

Castrillón Hoyos, Dario (Cardinal Priest), Titular of the Most Holy Name of Mary at Trajan's Forum, President Emeritus of the Pontifical Commission Ecclesia Dei, Prefect Emeritus of the Congregation for Clergy; born in Medellin July 4, 1929. Created and proclaimed February 21, 1998. Address: Piazza della Citta Leonina 1, 00193 Rome, Italy.

Ce', Marco (Cardinal Priest), Titular of S. Marco, Patriarch Emeritus of Venice; born in Izano, Diocese of Crema, July 8, 1925. Created and proclaimed June 30, 1979. Address: Dorsoduro 2807, 30123 Venezia, Italy.

Cheli, Giovanni (Cardinal Priest), Titular of Ss. Cosmos and Damian at Via Sacra, President Emeritus of the Pontifical Council for the Pastoral Care of Migrants and Itinerant People; born in Torino, October 4, 1918. Created and proclaimed February 21, 1998. Address: Piazza S. Calisto 16, 00153 Rome, Italy.

Cheong Jinsuk, Nicholas (Cardinal Priest), Titular of Mary Immaculate of Lourdes at Boccea, Archbishop of Seoul; born in Seoul, December 7, 1931. Created and proclaimed March 24, 2006. Address: Chung-gu Myong-dong 2-ka, Seoul 100-809, Korea.

Cipriani Thorne, Juan Luis (Cardinal Priest), Titular of San Camillo di Lellis, Archbishop of Lima; born in Lima, December 28, 1943. Created and proclaimed February 21, 2001. Address: Calle Los Nogales 249, San Isidro, Lima 27, Peru.

Clancy, Edward Bede (Cardinal Priest), Titular of S. Maria in Vallicella, Archbishop Emeritus of Sydney; born in Lithgow, Diocese of Bathurst, December 13, 1923. Created and proclaimed June 28, 1988. Address: 54 Cranbrook Rd., Bellevue Hill, NSW 2023, Australia.

Comastri, Angelo (Cardinal Deacon), Deacon of St. Salvatore in Lauro, Vicar General of His Holiness for the Vatican City, Archpriest of the Saint Peter's Basilica and President of the Fabric of Saint Peter's, born in Sorano, Diocese of Pitigliano-Sovano-Orbetello, Italy, September 17, 1943. Created and Proclaimed November 24, 2007. Address: 00120 Vatican City State, Europe.

Connell, Desmond (Cardinal Priest), Titular of San Silvestro in Capite, Archbishop Emeritus of Dublin; born in Dublin, March 24, 1926. Created and proclaimed February 21, 2001. Address: Archbishop's House, 29 Iona Road, Dublin 9, Ireland.

Coppa, Giovanni (Cardinal Deacon), deacon of St. Linus, Apostolic Nuncio Emeritus; born in Alba, Italy, November 9, 1925. Created and proclaimed November 24, 2007.

Cordero Lanza di Montezemolo, Andrea (Cardinal Deacon), Deacon of Saint Mary in Portico, Archpriest Emeritus of the Basilica of St. Paul Outside-the-Walls; born in Turin, August 27, 1925. Created and proclaimed March 24, 2006. Address: Piazza della Citta Leonina, 9, 00193 Rome, Italy.

Cordes, Paul Josef (Cardinal Deacon), Diaconate of St. Lawrence in Piscibus. President of the Pontifical Council "Cor Unum"; born in Kirchhundem, Archdiocese of Paderborn, Germany, September 5, 1934. Created and proclaimed November 24, 2007. Address: 00120 Vatican City State, Europe.

Cottier, Georges Marie Martin, O.P. (Cardinal Deacon), Deacon of Santi Domenico e Sisto, Theologian of the Pontifical Household; born in Geneve, April 25, 1922. Created and proclaimed October 21, 2003. Address: 00120 Vatican City State, Europe.

da Cruz Policarpo, Jose (Cardinal Priest), Titular of St. Anthony in Campo Marzio, Patriarch of Lisbon; born in Alvorninha, Patriarchate of Lisbon, February 26, 1936. Created and proclaimed February 21, 2001. Address: Mosteiro de Sao Vicente De Fora, Campo de Santa Clara 1100-472 Lisbon, Portugal.

Danneels, Godfried (Cardinal Priest), Titular of S. Anastasia, Archbishop of Malines-Brussels; born in Kanegem, Diocese of Brugge, June 4, 1933. Created and proclaimed February 2, 1983. Address: Aartsbisdom, Wollemarkt 15, B-2800 Mechelen, Belgium.

Daoud, Ignace Moussa I (Cardinal Bishop), Patriarch Emeritus of Antioch of the Maronites; born in Meskane, Archeparchy of Homs of the Syrians, September 18, 1930. Created and proclaimed February 21, 2001. Address: 00120 Vatican City State, Europe.

Darmaatmadja, Julius Riyadi, S.J. (Cardinal Priest), Titular of S. Cuore di Maria, Archbishop of Jakarta, Indonesia; born in Muntilan, Archdiocese of Semarang, December 20, 1934. Created and proclaimed November 26, 1994. Address: Keuskupan Agung, Jl. Katedral 7, Jakarta 10710, Indonesia.

De Giorgi, Salvatore (Cardinal Priest), Titular of S. Maria in Ara Coeli, Archbishop Emeritus of Palermo; born in Vernole, Archdiocese of Lecce, September 6, 1930. Created and proclaimed February 21, 1998. Address: Via di Porta Angelica 31, 00193 Roma, Italy.

Delly, Emmanuel III (Cardinal Bishop), Patriarch of Babylon of the Chaldeans, Iraq; born in Telkaif, October 6, 1927; elected Patriarch December 3, 2003. Address: Patriarcat Chaldeen Catholique, P.O. Box 6112, Al-Mansour, Baghdad, Iraq.

Deskur, Andrzej Maria (Cardinal Priest), Titular of S. Cesareo in Palatio, President Emeritus of the Pontifical Council for Social Communications; born in Sancygniow, Diocese of Kielce, February 29, 1924. Created and proclaimed May 25, 1985. Address: 00120 Vatican City State, Europe.

Dias, Ivan (Cardinal Priest), Titular of Spirito Santo alla Ferratella, Archbishop of Bombay; Prefect of the Congregation for the Evangelization of Peoples; born in Mumbai, April 14, 1936. Created and proclaimed February 21, 2001. Address: 00120 Vatican City State, Europe.

DiNardo, Daniel N. (Cardinal Priest), Titular of St. Eusebius, Archbishop of Galveston-Houston, born in Steubenville (Ohio), U.S.A., May 23, 1949. Created and proclaimed November 24, 2007. Address: 1700 San Jacinto St., P.O. Box 907, Houston, TX 77001-0907.

do Nascimento, Alexandre (Cardinal Priest), Titular of San Marco in Agro Laurentino, Archbishop Emeritus of Luanda; born in Malanje, Angola, March 1, 1925. Created and proclaimed February 2, 1983. Address: Rua Américo Júlio de Carvalho 97-99, Luanda, Angola.

Dziwisz, Stanislaw (Cardinal Priest), Titular of Saint Mary del Popolo, Archbishop of Krakow; born in Raba Wyzna, Archdiocese of Krakow, April 27, 1939. Created and proclaimed March 24, 2006. Address: ul. Franciszkanska 3, 31-004 Krakow, Poland.

Egan, Edward M. (Cardinal Priest), Titular of Santi Giovanni e Paolo, Archbishop Emeritus of New York; born in Oak Park, Chicago, February 4, 1932. Created and proclaimed February 21, 2001. Address: 1011 First Ave., New York, NY 10022.

Erdõ, Péter (Cardinal Priest), Titular of Santa Balbina, Archbishop of Esztergom-Budapest; born in Budapest, June 25, 1952. Created and proclaimed October 21, 2003. Address: Primasi es Erseki Hivatal, Uri utca 62, H-1014 Budapest, Hungary.

Errázuriz Ossa, Francisco Javier (Cardinal Priest), Titular of Santa Maria della Pace, Archbishop of Santiago de Chile; born in Santiago de Chile, September 5, 1933. Created and proclaimed February 21, 2001. Address: Simon Bolivar 2845, Santiago, Chile.

Etchegaray, Roger (Cardinal Bishop), Titular of the suburbicarian church of Porto-Santa Rufina, President Emeritus of the Pontifical Council for Justice and Peace; born in Espelette, Diocese of Bayonne, September 25, 1922. Created and proclaimed June 30, 1979. Address: Piazza San Calisto 16, 00153 Rome, Italy.

Falcao, Jose Freire (Cardinal Priest), Titular of S. Luca a Via Prenestina, Archbishop Emeritus of Brasilia; born in Erere, Diocese of Limoeiro do Norte, October 23, 1925. Created and proclaimed June 28, 1988. Address: SHIGS 707, Bl.HL casa 74, Asa Sul, 70351-708 Brazilia, D.F., Brazil.

Farina, Raffaele, S.D.B. (Cardinal Deacon), Deacon of St. John della Pigna, Archivist and Librarian of the Holy Roman Church, born in Buonalbergo, Diocese of Ariano Irpino-Lacedonia, Italy, September 24, 1933. Created and proclaimed November 24, 2007. Address: 00120 Vatican City State, Europe.

Foley, John Patrick (Cardinal Deacon), Deacon of St. Sebastian al Palatino, Grand Master of the Equestrian Order of the Knights of the Holy Sepulchre of Jerusalem; born in Darby, Archdiocese of Philadelphia, November 11, 1935. Created and proclaimed November 24, 2007. Address: 00120 Vatican City State, Europe.

Furno, Carlo (Cardinal Priest), Titular St. Humphrey, Grand Master Emeritus of the Equestrian Order of the Holy Sepulchre of Jerusalem; born in Bairo Canavese, Diocese of Ivrea, December 2, 1921. Created and proclaimed November 26, 1994. Address: Piazza della Citta Leonina 1, 00193 Rome, Italy.

Garcia-Gasco, Vicente Agustin (Cardinal Priest), Titular of St. Marcellus, Archbishop Emeritus of Valencia, Spain, born in Corral de Almaguer, February 12, 1931. Created and proclaimed November 24, 2007. Address: Arzobispado, Palau 2, 46003, Valencia, Spain.

George, Francis E., O.M.I. (Cardinal Priest) Titular of S. Bartolomeo all'Isola, Archbishop of Chicago; born in Chicago, Illinois, U.S.A., January 16, 1937. Created and proclaimed February 21, 1998. Address: 835 N. Rush St., Chicago, IL 60611-2030.

Giordano, Michele (Cardinal Priest), Titular of S. Gioacchino ai Prati di Castello, Archbishop Emeritus of Naples; born in S. Arcangelo, Diocese of Tursi-Lagonegro, September 26, 1930. Created and proclaimed June 28, 1988. Address: Via Capodimonte, 80136 Napoli, Italy.

Glemp, Jozef (Cardinal Priest), Titular of S. Maria in Trastevere, Archbishop Emeritus of Warsaw; born in Inowroclaw, Archdiocese of Gniezno, December 18, 1929. Created and proclaimed February 2, 1983. Address: ul. Miodowa 17-19, 00-246 Warsaw, Poland.

Gracias, Oswald (Cardinal Priest), Titular of St. Paul of the Cross in Corviale. Archbishop of Bombay (India), born in Bombay, December 24, 1944. Created and proclaimed November 24, 2007. Address: Archbishop's House, 21 Nathalal Parekh Marg, Mumbai-400001, India.

Grocholewski, Zenon (Cardinal Deacon), Deacon of St. Nicholas in Prison, Prefect of the Congregation for Catholic Education; born in Brodki, Archdiocese of Poznan, October 11, 1939. Created and proclaimed February 21, 2001. Address: 00120 Vatican City State, Europe.

Gulbinowicz, Henryk Roman (Cardinal Priest), Titular dell'Immacolata Concezione di Maria a Grottarossa, Archbishop Emeritus of Wroclaw; born in Sukiskes, Archdiocese of Vilnius, October 17, 1923. Created and proclaimed May 25, 1985. Address: ul. Katedralna 15, 50-328 Wroclaw, Poland.

Herranz Casado, Julian (Cardinal Deacon), Deacon of Saint Eugenius, President Emeritus of the Pontifical Council for the Interpretation of Legislative Texts; born in Baena, Diocese of Cordoba, March 31, 1930. Created and proclaimed October 21, 2003. Address: 00120 Vatican City State, Europe.

Honoré, Jean (Cardinal Priest), Titular of Santa Maria della Salute a Primavalle, Archbishop Emeritus of Tours; born in Saint-Brice-en-Cogles, Archdiocese of Rennes, August 13, 1920. Created and proclaimed February 21, 2001. Address: 1 Allee de la Rocaille, 37390 La Membrolle-sur-Choisille, France.

Hummes, Claudio, O.F.M. (Cardinal Priest), Titular of Sant' Antonio da Padova in Via Merulana, Prefect of the Congregation for the Clergy; born in Montenegro, Archdiocese of Porto Alegre, August 8, 1934. Created and proclaimed February 21, 2001. Address: 00120 Vatican City State, Europe.

Husar, Lubomyr, M.S.U. (Cardinal Priest), Titular of Santa Sofia a Via Boccea, Major Archbishop of Kyiv-Halye of the Ukrainians; born in Lviv, February 26, 1933. Created and proclaimed February 21, 2001. Address: vol. Riznytcka II -B/28-29, 01011 Kyiv, Ukraine.

Jaworski, Marian (Cardinal Priest), Titular of St. Sisto, Archbishop Emeritus of Lviv of the Latins; born in Lviv August 21, 1926. Created and reserved in pectore February 21, 1998; proclaimed February 21, 2001. Address: Pl. Katedralna 1, 79008 Lviv, Ukraine.

Karlic, Estanislao Esteban (Cardinal Priest), Titular of the Our Lady of Sorrows in Piazza Buenos Aires, Archbishop Emeritus of Paraná. Created and proclaimed November 24, 2007.

Kasper, Walter (Cardinal Deacon), Deacon of All Saints in Via Appia Nuova, President of the Pontifical Council for Promoting Christian Unity; born in Heidenheim/Brenz, Diocese of Rottenburg-Stuttgart, March 5, 1933. Created and proclaimed February 21, 2001. Address: 00120 Vatican City State, Europe.

Keeler, William Henry (Cardinal Priest), Titular of S. Maria degli Angeli, Archbishop Emeritus of Baltimore; born in San Antonio, Texas, March 4, 1931. Created and proclaimed November 26, 1994. Address: 408 N. Charles St., Baltimore, Maryland 21201. U.S.A.

Kitbunchu, Michael Michai (Cardinal Priest), Titular of S. Lorenzo in Panisperna, Archbishop of Bangkok; born in Samphran, Archdiocese of Bangkok, January 25, 1929. Created and proclaimed February 2, 1983. Address: 51 Catholic Mission, Charo en Krung Road 40, Bangrak, Bangkok 10500, Thailand.

Korec, Jan Chryzostom, S.J. (Cardinal Priest), Titular of Ss. Fabiano e Venanzio a Villa Fiorelli, Bishop Emeritus of Nitra; born in Bosany, Diocese of Nitra, January 22, 1924. Created and proclaimed June 28, 1991. Address: Bis Kupstvo Nitra, P.P 46A, 950 50 Nitra, Slovakia.

Lajolo, Giovanni (Cardinal Deacon), Deacon of St. Mary Liberatrice in Monte Testaccio, President of the Pontifical Commission for the Vatican City State and of the Governorate of Vatican City State; born in Novara, Italy, January 3, 1935. Created and proclaimed November 24, 2007. Address: 00120 Vatican City State, Europe.

Law, Bernard Francis (Cardinal Priest), Titular of S. Susanna, Archpriest of the Patriarchal Basilica of Saint Mary Major; born in Torreon, November 4, 1931. Created and proclaimed May 25, 1985. Address: 00120 Vatican City State, Europe.

Lehmann, Karl (Cardinal Priest), Titular of San Leone I, Bishop of Mainz; born in Sigmaringen, Archdiocese of Freiburg im Breisgau, May 16, 1936. Created and proclaimed February 21, 2001. Address: Bischofsplatz 2A, D-55116 Mainz, Germany.

Levada, William Joseph (Cardinal Deacon), Deacon of Saint Mary in Domnica, Prefect of the Congregation for the Doctrine of the Faith; born in Long Beach, Archdiocese of Los Angeles, June 15, 1936. Created and proclaimed March 24, 2006. Address: 00120 Vatican City State, Europe.

Lopez Rodriguez, Nicolas de Jesus (Cardinal Priest), Titular of S. Pio X alla Balduina, Archbishop of Santo Domingo; born in Barranca, Diocese of La Vega, October 31, 1936. Created and proclaimed June 28, 1991. Address: Calle Pellerano Alfau 1, Ciudad Colonial, Santo Domingo, Dominican Republic.

Lourdusamy, D. Simon (Cardinal Priest), Titular of S. Maria delle Grazie alle Fornaci fuori Porta Cavalleggeri, Prefect Emeritus of the Congregation for the Oriental Churches; born in Kalleri, Archdiocese of Pondicherry and Cuddalore, February 5, 1924. Created and proclaimed May 25, 1985. Address: Via dei Corridori 64, 00193 Rome, Italy.

Lozano Barragan, Javier (Cardinal Deacon), Deacon of St. Michael the Archangel, President Emeritus of the Pontifical Council for Pastoral Assistance to Health Care; born in Toluca, Mexico, January 26, 1933. Created and proclaimed October 21, 2003. Address: 00120 Vatican City State, Europe.

Macharski, Franciszek (Cardinal Priest), Titular of S. Giovanni a Porta Latina, Archbishop Emeritus of Krakow; born in Krakow, May 20, 1927. Created and proclaimed June 30, 1979. Address: ul. Franciszkanska 3, 31-004 Krakow, Poland.

Mahony, Roger M. (Cardinal Priest), Titular of Ss. Quattro Coronati, Archbishop of Los Angeles; born in Hollywood, California, Archdiocese of Los Angeles, February 27, 1936. Created and proclaimed June 28, 1991. Address: 555 W. Temple St., Los Angeles, CA 90010-2241, U.S.A.

Maida, Adam Joseph (Cardinal Priest), Titular of Ss. Vitale, Valeria, Gervasio e Protasio, Archbishop Emeritus of Detroit; born in East Vandergrift, Pennsylvania, Diocese of Greensburg, March 18, 1930. Created and proclaimed November 26, 1994. Address: 1234 Washington Blvd., Detroit, Michigan 48226, U.S.A.

Marchisano, Francesco Cardinal (Cardinal Deacon), Deacon of Santa Lucia del Gonfalone, President Emeritus of the Labor Office of the Apostolic See; born in Racconigi, Italy, June 25, 1929. Created and proclaimed October 21, 2003. Address: 00120 Vatican City State, Europe.

Martinez Sistach, Lluis (Cardinal Priest), Titular of St. Sebastian at the Catacombs, Archbishop of Barcelona; Created and proclaimed November 24, 2007.

Martinez Somalo, Eduardo (Cardinal Priest), Titular of SS. Nome di Gesu', Chamberlain Emeritus of the Holy Roman Church; born at Banos de Rio Tobia, Diocese of Calahorra y La Calzada-Logrono, March 31, 1927. Created and proclaimed June 28, 1988. Address: 00120 Vatican City State, Europe.

Martini, Carlo Maria, S.J. (Cardinal Priest), Titular of S. Cecilia, Archbishop Emeritus of Milan; born in Turin, February 15, 1927. Created and proclaimed February 2, 1983. Address: Pontifical Biblical Institute, P.O. Box 497, 91004 Jerusalem, Israel.

Martino, Renato Raffaele (Cardinal Deacon), Deacon of St. Francis of Paola ai Monti, President Emeritus of the Pontifical Council for Justice and Peace, President of the Pontifical Council for the Pastoral Care of Migrants; born in Salerno, Italy, November 23, 1932. Created and proclaimed October 21, 2003. Address: 00120 Vatican City State, Europe.

Mayer, Paul Augustin, O.S.B. (Cardinal Priest), Titular of S. Anselmo all' Aventino, President Emeritus of the Pontifical Commission Ecclesia Dei; born in Altotting, Diocese of Passau, May 23, 1911. Created and proclaimed May 25, 1985. Address: Via Rusticucci 13, 00193 Rome, Italy.

McCarrick, Theodore E. (Cardinal Priest), Titular of Santi Nereo e Achilleo, Archbishop Emeritus of Washington; born in New York, July 7, 1930. Created and proclaimed February 21, 2001. Address: P.O. Box 29260, Washington, DC 20017, U.S.A.

Medina Estévez, Jorge Arturo (Cardinal Priest), Titular of St. Saba, Prefect Emeritus of the Congregation for Divine Worship and the Discipline of the Sacraments; born in Santiago de Chile, December 23, 1926. Created and proclaimed February 21, 1998. Address: Av. Pehuén 7240, depto. 100 Las Condes, Santiago c.p.

6782144 Chile.

Meisner, Joachim (Cardinal Priest), Titular of S. Pudenziana, Archbishop of Cologne; born in Breslau, December 25, 1933. Created and proclaimed February 2, 1983. Address: Kardinal-Frings-Strasse 10, D-50668 Koln 1, Germany.

Mejía, Jorge María (Cardinal Deacon), Deacon of San Girolamo della Carita, Librarian Emeritus and Archivist Emeritus of the Holy Roman Church; born in Buenos Aires, January 31, 1923. Created and proclaimed February 21, 2001. Address: 00120 Vatican City State, Europe.

Murphy-O'Connor, Cormac (Cardinal Priest), Titular of Santa Maria sopra Minerva, Archbishop Emeritus of Westminster; born in Reading, Diocese of Portsmouth, August 24, 1932. Created and proclaimed February 21, 2001. Address: Ambrosden Avenue, Westminster, London SW1P 1QJ, England.

Nagy, Stanislaw, S.C.I. (Cardinal Deacon), Deacon of Santa Maria della Scala; born in Bieru Stary, Archdiocese of Katowice, September 30, 1921. Created and proclaimed October 21, 2003. Address: c/o University of Lublin, UL. Saska 2, 30-715 Krakow, Poland.

Napier, Wilfrid Fox, O.F.M. (Cardinal Priest), Titular of San Francesco d'Assisi ad Acilia, Archbishop of Durban; born in Swartberg, Diocese of Kokstad, March 8, 1941. Created and proclaimed February 21, 2001. Address: 154 Gordon Rd., Durban 4001, Kwazulu-Natal, South Africa.

Navarrete, Urbano, S.J. (Cardinal Deacon), Decon of St. Pontian. Created and proclaimed November 24, 2007.

Nicora, Attilio (Cardinal Deacon), Deacon of St. Filippo Neri in Eurosia, President of the Administration of the Patrimony of the Apostolic See; Pontifical Legate for the Basilicas of St. Francis and St. Mary of the Angels in Assisi; born in Varese, Italy, March 16, 1937. Created and proclaimed October 21, 2003. Address: 00120 Vatican City State, Europe.

Njue, John (Cardinal Priest), Titular of the Most Precious Blood of Our Lord Jesus Christ. Archbishop of Nairobi (Kenya), born in Ngandori, 1944. Created and proclaimed November 24, 2007. Address: Archbishop's House, P.O. Box 14231, Nairobi, Kenya.

Noe', Virgilio (Cardinal Priest), Titular of Regina Apostolorum, Vicar General Emeritus of His Holiness for Vatican City State, Archpriest Emeritus of St. Peter Basilica, President Emeritus of the Fabric of St. Peter; born in Zelata di Bereguardo, Diocese of Pavia, March 30, 1922. Created and proclaimed June 28, 1991. Address: 00120 Vatican City State, Europe.

Obando Bravo, Miguel, S.D.B. (Cardinal Priest), Titular of S. Giovanni Evangelista a Spinaceto, Archbishop Emeritus of Managua; born in La Libertad, Diocese of Juigalpa, February 2, 1926. Created and proclaimed May 25, 1985. Address: Arzobispado, Apartado 2008, Managua, Nicaragua.

O'Brien, Keith Michael Patrick (Cardinal Priest), Titular of Santi Gioacchino e Anna al Tuscolano, Archbishop of Saint Andrews and Edinburgh; born in Ballycastle, County Antrim, Northern Ireland, March 17, 1938. Created and proclaimed October 21, 2003. Address: Archbishop's House, 42 Greenhill Gardens, Edinburgh EH10 4BJ, Scotland, Great Britain.

Okogie, Anthony Olubunmi (Cardinal Priest), Titular of Beata Vergine Maria del Monte Carmelo a Mostacciano, Archbishop of Lagos; born in Lagos, June 16, 1936. Created and proclaimed October 21, 2003. Address: P.O. Box 8, 19 Catholic Mission Street, Lagos, Nigeria.

O'Malley, Sean Patrick, O.F.M.Cap. (Cardinal Priest), Titular of Saint Mary of Victory, Archbishop of Boston; born in Lakewood, Diocese of Cleveland, June 29, 1944. Created and proclaimed March 24, 2006. Address: 66 Brooks Drive, Braintree, MA 02184, U.S.A.

Ortega, Francisco Robles (Cardinal Priest), Titular of St. Mary of the Presentation, Archbishop of Monterrey (Mexico), born in Mascota, Jalisco, Diocese of Tepic, March 2, 1949. Created and proclaimed November 24, 2007. Address: Apardado 7, Zuazua 1100, 64000 Monterrey, N.L., Mexico.

Ortega y Alamino, Jaime Lucas (Cardinal Priest), Titular of Ss. Aquila e Priscilla, Archbishop of San Cristobal de La Habana, Cuba; born in Jaguey Grande, Diocese of Matanzas, October 18, 1936. Created and proclaimed November 26, 1994. Address: Calle Habana 152, Apartado 594, La Habana, 10100 Cuba.

Ouellet, Marc, P.S.S. (Cardinal Priest), Titular of Santa Maria in Traspontina, Archbishop of Quebec; born in Lamotte, Diocese of Amos, June 8, 1944. Created and proclaimed October 21, 2003. Address: 2 rue Port-Douphin, C.P. 459, Quebec, Que. GIC 4R6, Canada.

Panafieu, Bernard Louis Auguste Paul (Cardinal Priest), Titular of San Gregorio Barbarigo alle Tre Fontane, Archbishop Emeritus of Marseille; born in Chatellerault, Archdiocese of Poitiers, January 26, 1931. Created and proclaimed October 21, 2003. Address: 14 Place du Colonel-Edon, 13007 Marseille Cedex 07, France.

Paskai, Laszlo, O.F.M. (Cardinal Priest), Titular of S. Teresa al Corso d'Italia, Archbishop Emeritus of Esztergom-Budapest; born at Szeged, May 8, 1927. Created and proclaimed June 28, 1988. Address: Dobozy Mihaly u. 12, H-2500 Esztergom, Hungary.

Pell, Georges Marie Martin (Cardinal Priest), Titular of Santa Maria Domenica Mazzarello, Archbishop of Sydney; born in Ballarat, Australia, June 8, 1941. Created and proclaimed October 21, 2003. Address: St. Mary's Cathedral, St. Mary's Road, Sydney NSW 2000, Australia.

Pengo, Polycarp (Cardinal Priest), Titular of Nostra Signora de La Salette, Archbishop of Dar-es-Salaam, Tanzania; born in Mwazye, Diocese of Sumbawanga, August 5, 1944. Created and proclaimed February 21, 1998. Address: Archbishop's House, P.O. Box 167, Dar-es-Salaam, Tanzania.

Pham Minh Man, Jean-Baptiste (Cardinal Priest), Titular of San Giustino, Archbishop of Ho Chi Minh; born in Than-Pho, Ca Mau, Diocese of Can Tho, in the year 1934. Created and proclaimed October 21, 2003. Address: Toa Tong Giam Muc, 189 Nguyen Dinh Chieu, Q-3 Thanh-Pho Ho Chi Minh, Vietnam.

Pimenta, Simon Ignatius (Cardinal Priest), Titular of S. Maria Regina Mundi a Torre Spaccata, Archbishop Emeritus of Bombay; born in Marol, Archdiocese of Bombay, March 1, 1920. Created and proclaimed June 28, 1988. Address: Archbishop's House, 21 Nathalal Parekh Marg, Mumbai-400001, India.

Piovanelli, Silvano (Cardinal Priest), Titular of S. Maria delle Grazie a Via Trionfale, Archbishop Emeritus of Florence; born in Ronta di Mugello, Archdiocese of Florence, February 21, 1924. Created and proclaimed May 25, 1985. Address: Via Dante da Castiglione 32, 50010 Trespiano, Italy.

Poggi, Luigi (Cardinal Priest), Titular of S. Lorenzo in Lucina, Librarian Emeritus and Archivist Emeritus of the Holy Roman Church; born in Piacenza, Italy, November 25, 1917. Created and proclaimed November 26, 1994. Address: 00120 Vatican City State, Europe.

Poletto, Severino (Cardinal Priest), Titular of San Giuseppe in Via Trionfale, Archbishop of Turin; born in Salgareda, Diocese of Treviso, March 18, 1933. Created and proclaimed February 21, 2001. Address: Via Arcivescovado 12, 10121 Turin, Italy.

Policarpo, Jose Cardinal da Cruz Patriarchate of Lisbon; born in Alvorninha, February 26, 1936; consecrated June 29, 1978; appointed Coadjutor Archbishop of the Patriarchate of Lisbon March 5, 1997; promoted Patriarch March 24, 1998; elevated to the College of Cardinals February 21, 2001. Address: Mosteiro de Sao Vicente De Fora, Campo de Santa Clara 1100-472 Lisbon, Portugal.

Poupard, Paul (Cardinal Priest), Titular of S. Prassede, President Emeritus of the Pontifical Council of Culture, President Emeritus of the Pontifical Council for Interreligious Dialogue; born in Bouzille, Diocese of Angers, August 30, 1930. Created and proclaimed May 25, 1985. Address: Piazza San Calisto 16, 00153 Rome, Italy.

Pujats, Janis (Cardinal Priest), Titular of Santa Silvia, Archbishop of Riga; born in Nautrani, Diocese of Rezekne-Aglona, November 14, 1930. Created and proclaimed February 21, 2001. Address: Metropolijas Kurija, Maza Pils iela 2/a, 1050 Riga, Latvia.

Puljic, Vinko (Cardinal Priest), Titular of S. Chiara a Vigna Clara, Archbishop of Sarajevo, Bosnia-Herzegovina; born in Prijecani, Diocese of Banja Luka, September 8, 1945. Created and proclaimed November 26, 1994. Address: Nadbiskupski Ordinarijat, Kaptol 7, 71000 Sarajevo, Bosnia Herzegovina.

Quezada Toruño, Rodolfo (Cardinal Priest), Titular of San Saturnino, Archbishop of Guatemala; born in Guatemala City, March 8, 1932. Created and proclaimed October 21, 2003. Address: Arzobispado, Apartado 723, 7a Avenida 6-21, Zona 1, 01001 Ciudad de Guatemala, Guatemala.

Re, Giovanni Battista (Cardinal Bishop), Titular of the suburbicanan Church of Sabina Poggio-Mirteto, Prefect of the Congregation for Bishops; born in Borno, Diocese of Brescia, January 30, 1934. Created and proclaimed February 21, 2001. Address: 00120 Vatican City State, Europe.

Ricard, Jean-Pierre (Cardinal Priest), Titular of Saint Augustine, Archbishop of Bordeaux; born in Marseille, September 26, 1944. Created and proclaimed March 24, 2006. Address: B.P. 79, 183 cours de la Somme, 33034 Bordeaux Cedex, France.

Rigali, Justin Cardinal (Cardinal Priest), Titular of Santa Prisca, Archbishop of Philadelphia; born in Los Angeles, California, April 19, 1935. Created and proclaimed October 21, 2003. Address: 222 North 17th St., Philadelphia, PA 19103-1299.

Rivera Carrera, Norberto (Cardinal Priest), Titular of S. Francesco d' Assisi a Ripa Grande, Archbishop of Mexico City; born in Tepehuanes, Archdiocese of Durango, June 6, 1942. Created and proclaimed February 21, 1998. Address: Camelia 110, Col. Florida, 01030 Mexico D.F., Mexico.

Rode, Franc, C.M. (Cardinal Deacon), Deacon of Saint Francis Xavier at Garbatella, Prefect of the Congregation for the Institutes of Consecrated Life and Societies of Apostolic Life; born in Ljubljana, September 23, 1934. Created and proclaimed March 24, 2006. Address: 00120 Vatican City State, Europe.

Rodríguez Maradiaga, Oscar Andrés, S.D.B. (Cardinal Priest), Titular of Santa Maria della Speranza, Archbishop of Tegucigalpa; born in Tegucigalpa, December 29, 1942. Created and proclaimed February 21, 2001. Address: Apartado 106, 3 y 2 Av. 1113, Tegucigalpa, Honduras.

Rosales, Gaudencio B. (Cardinal Priest), Titular of the Most Holy Name of Mary in Via Latina, Archbishop of Manila; born in Batangas City, Archdiocese of Lipa, August 10, 1932. Created and proclaimed March 24, 2006. Address: 121 Arzobispo St., Intramuros, P.O. Box 132, 1099 Manila, Philippines.

Rouco Varela, Antonio Maria (Cardinal Priest), Titular of S. Lorenzo in Damaso, Archbishop of Madrid, Spain; born in Villalba, Diocese of Mondonedo-Ferrol, August 24, 1936. Created and proclaimed February 21, 1998. Address: Calle San Justo 2, 28005 Madrid, Spain.

Rubiano Sáenz, Pedro (Cardinal Priest), Titular of Trasfigurazione di Nostro Signore Gesu Cristo, Archbishop of Bogotá; born in Cartago, September 13, 1932. Created and proclaimed February 21, 2001. Address: Carrera 7 N. 10-20, Santafe de Bogota, Colombia.

Ruini, Camillo (Cardinal Priest), Titular of S. Agnese Fuori le Mura, Vicar General Emeritus of His Holiness for the Diocese of Rome; born in Sassuolo, Diocese of Reggio Emilia-Guastalla, February 19, 1931. Created and proclaimed June 28, 1991. Address: Piazza San Giovanni in Laterano 4, 00184 Rome, Italy.

Rylko, Stanislaw (Cardinal Deacon), Deacon of the Sacred Heart of Christ the King, President of the Pontifical Council for the Laity; born in Andrychow, Diocese of Bielsko-zywiec, Poland, July 4, 1945. Created and proclaimed November 24, 2007. Address: 00120 Vatican City State, Europe.

Saldarini, Giovanni (Cardinal Priest), Titular of S. Cuore di Gesu' a Castro Pretorio, Archbishop Emeritus of Torino; born in Cantu, Archdiocese of Milan, December 11, 1924. Created and proclaimed June 28, 1991. Address: Via Montenapoleone 22, 20121 Milano, Italy.

Sales, Eugenio de Araujo (Cardinal Priest), Titular of S. Gregorio VII, Archbishop Emeritus of Sao Sebastiao do Rio de Janeiro; born in Acari, Diocese of Caico, November 8, 1920. Created and proclaimed April 28, 1969. Address: Rua Visconde de Piraja 339, 22410-003 Rio de Janeiro, R.J., Brazil.

Sanchez, Jose T. (Cardinal Priest), Titular of St. Pio V, Prefect Emeritus of the Congregation for the Clergy; born in Pandan, Diocese of Virac, March 17, 1920. Created and proclaimed June 28, 1991. Address: 00120 Vatican City State, Europe.

Sandoval Iniguez, Juan (Cardinal Priest), Titular of Nostra Signora di Guadalupe e S. Filippo Martire in Via Aurelia, Archbishop of Guadalajara, Mexico; born in Yahualica, Diocese of San Juan de los Lagos, March 28, 1933. Created and proclaimed November 26, 1994. Address: Morelos 244, 45500 San Pedro Tlaquepaque, Jal., Mexico.

Sandri, Leonardo (Cardinal Deacon), Deacon of Sts. Blaise and Charles ai Catinari, Prefect of the Congregation for the Oriental Churches; born in Buenos Aires, November 18, 1943. Created and proclaimed November 24, 2007. Address: 00120 Vatican City State, Europe.

Santos, Alexandre Jose Maria dos, O.F.M. (Cardinal Priest), Titular of S. Frumenzio ai Prati Fiscali, Archbishop Emeritus of Maputo; born in

Zavala, Diocese of Inhambane, March 18, 1924. Created and proclaimed June 28, 1988. Address: Av. Julius Nyerere 882, Maputo, Mozambique.

Saraiva Martins, José, C.M.F. (Cardinal Bishop), Titular of the Suburbicaria Church of Palestrina, Prefect Emeritus of the Congregation for the Causes of Saints; born in Gagos, Diocese of Guarda, January 6, 1932. Created and proclaimed February 21, 2001. Address: 00102 Vatican City State, Europe.

Sarr, Theodore-Adrien (Cardinal Priest) Titular of St. Lucy a Piazza d'Armi, Archbishop of Dakar (Senegal); born in Fadiouth, Archdiocese of Dakar, November 28, 1936. Created and proclaimed November 24, 2007. Address: Archeveche, B.P. 1908, Avenue Jean XXIII, Dakar, Senegal.

Scheid, Eusebio Oscar, S.C.I. (Cardinal Priest), Titular of Santi Bonifacio e Alessio, Archbishop Emeritus of Sao Sebastiao de Rio de Janeiro; born in Bom Retiro, Diocese of Joacaba, December 8, 1932. Created and proclaimed October 21, 2003. Address: Rua da Glória 446, Glória, 20241-180 Rio de Janeiro, RJ, Brazil.

Scherer, Odilio Pedro (Cardinal Priest) Titular of St. Andrew al Quirinale, Archbishop of Sao Paulo, born in Sao Francisco, Diocese of Santo Angelo, Brazil, September 21, 1949. Created and proclaimed November 24, 2007. Address: Curia Metropolitana, C.P. 1670, 01064-970 Sao Paulo; Av. Higienopolis 890, 01238-000 Sao Paulo, SP, Brazil.

Schönborn, Christoph, O.P. (Cardinal Priest), Titular of Gesu' Divin Lavoratore, Archbishop of Vienna, Austria; born in Skalsko, Diocese of Litomerice, January 22, 1945. Created and proclaimed February 21, 1998. Address: Wollzeile 2, A-1010 Vienna, Austria.

Schwery, Henri (Cardinal Priest), Titular of Ss. Protomartiri a Via Aurelia Antica, Bishop Emeritus of Sion; born in Saint Leonard, Diocese of Sion, June 14, 1932. Created and proclaimed June 28, 1991. Address: C.P. 2334, CH-1950 Sion 2, Switzerland.

Scola, Angelo Cardinal (Cardinal Priest), Titular of Santi XII Apostoli, Patriarch of Venice; born in Malgrate, Archdiocese of Milan, November 7, 1941. Created and proclaimed October 21, 2003. Address: Curia Patriarcale, S. Marco 320/a, 30124 Venice, Italy.

Sebastiani, Sergio (Cardinal Deacon), Deacon of St. Eustach, President Emeritus of the Prefecture for the Economic Affairs of the Holy See; born in Montemonaco, Diocese of San Benedetto del Tronto-Ripatransone-Montalto, April 11, 1931. Created and proclaimed February 21, 2001. Address: 00120 Vatican City State, Europe.

Sepe, Crescenzio (Cardinal Priest), Titular of the Most Merciful Father, Archbishop of Naples; born in Carinaro, Diocese of Aversa, June 2, 1943. Created and proclaimed February 21, 2001.

Sfeir, Nasrallah Pierre (Cardinal Bishop), Patriarch of Antioch of the Maronites, Lebanon; born in Reyfoun, Lebanon, Eparchy of Sarba of the Maronites, May 15, 1920. Created and proclaimed November 26, 1994. Address: Patriarcat Maronite, Bkerke, Lebanon.

Shan Kuo-hsi, Paul, S.J. (Cardinal Priest), Titular of S. Crisogono, Bishop Emeritus of Kaohsiung, Taiwan; born in Puyang, Diocese of Taming, December 3, 1923. Created and proclaimed February 21, 1998. Address: Bishop's House, 125 Szu-wei 3rd Rd., Kaohsiung 80250, Taiwan.

Silvestrini, Achille (Cardinal Priest), Titular of S. Benedetto fuori Porta S. Paolo, Prefect Emeritus of the Congregation for Oriental Churches; born in Brisighella, Diocese of Faenza-Modigliana, October 25, 1923. Created and proclaimed June 28, 1988. Address: Palazzina della Zecca, 00120 Vatican City State, Europe.

Simonis, Adrianus Johannes (Cardinal Priest), Titular of S. Clemente, Archbishop of Utrecht; born in Lisse, Diocese of Rotterdam, November 26, 1931. Created and proclaimed May 25, 1985. Address: Mariapolis Mariënkroon, Abjlaan 8, NL-5253 VP Nienwkuijk nb, Netherlands.

Sodano, Angelo (Cardinal Bishop), Titular of the suburbicarian church of Ostia, Secretary Emeritus of State; Dean of the College of Cardinals; born in Isola d'Asti, Diocese of Asti, November 23, 1927. Created and proclaimed June 28, 1991. Address: 00120 Vatican City State, Europe.

Špidlik, Tomas, S.J. (Cardinal Deacon), Deacon of S. Agata de' Goti; born in Boskovice, Diocese of Brno, December 17, 1919. Created and proclaimed October 21, 2003. Address: Via Paolina, 25 —00184 Roma, Italy.

Stafford, James Francis (Cardinal Priest), Titular of St. Peter in Montorio, Major Apostolic Penitentiary Emeritus. Born in Baltimore, Maryland, U.S.A., July 26, 1932. Created and proclaimed February 21, 1998. Address: 00120 Vatican City State, Europe.

Sterzinsky, Georg M. (Cardinal Priest), Titular of S. Giuseppe all' Aurelio, Archbishop of Berlin; born in Warlack, Archdiocese of Warmia, February 9, 1936. Created and proclaimed June 28, 1991. Address: Postfach 04 0856, 10064 Berlin, Germany.

Swiatek, Kazimierz (Cardinal Priest), Titular of S. Gerardo Maiella, Archbishop Emeritus of Minsk-Mohilev; born in Walga, Ap. Adm. of Estonia, October 21, 1914. Created and proclaimed November 26, 1994. Address: pl. Swobody 9, 220030 Minsk, Belarus.

Szoka, Edmund Casimir (Cardinal Priest), Titular of Ss. Andrea e Gregorio al Monte Celio, President Emeritus of the Pontifical Commission for Vatican City State; President Emeritus of the Governatorate of Vatican City State. Born in Grand Rapids, Michigan, September 14, 1927. Created and proclaimed June 28, 1988. Address: 00120 Vatican City State, Europe.

Tauran, Jean-Louis Pierre (Cardinal Deacon), Deacon of St. Apollonius at the Neronian-Alexandrian Bath; President of the Pontifical Council for Interreligious Dialogue; born in Bordeaux, April 5, 1943. Created and proclaimed October 21, 2003. Address: 00120 Vatican City State, Europe.

Terrazas Sandoval, Julio, C.Ss.R. (Cardinal Priest), Titular of San Giovanni Battista de' Rossi, Archbishop of Santa Cruz de la Sierra; born in Valle Grande, Archdiocese of Santa Cruz de la Sierra, March 7, 1936. Created and proclaimed February 21, 2001. Address: Calle Paquio Esquina Achachairu S/N, Santa Cruz, Bolivia.

Tettamanzi, Dionigi (Cardinal Priest), Titular of Ss. Ambrogio e Carlo, Archbishop of Milan, Italy; born in Renate, Archdiocese of Milan, March 14, 1934. Created and proclaimed February 21, 1998. Address: Palazzo Arcivescovile, Piazza Fontana 2, 20122 Milan, Italy.

Tomko, Jozef (Cardinal Priest), Titular of S. Sabina, Prefect Emeritus of the Congregation for the Evangelization of Peoples; President Emeritus for the Pontifical Committee for International Eucharistic Congresses; born in Udavske, Archdiocese of Kosice, March 11, 1924. Created and proclaimed May 25, 1985. Address: Via della Conciliazione 44, 00193 Rome, Italy.

Tonini, Ersilio (Cardinal Priest), Titular of Ss. Redentore a Val Melaina, Archbishop Emeritus of Ravenna-Cervia, Italy; born in Centovera di San Giorgio Piacentino, Diocese of Piacenza-Bobbio, July 20, 1914. Created and proclaimed November 26, 1994. Address: Via Santa Teresa 8, 48100 Ravenna, Italy.

Toppo, Telesphore Placidus (Cardinal Priest), Titular of Sacro Cuore di Gesu agonizzante a Vitinia, Archbishop of Ranchi; born in Chainpur, India, October 15, 1939. Created and proclaimed October 21, 2003. Address: P.O. Box 5, Purulia Road, Ranchi-834001 Jharkhand, India.

Tucci, Roberto, S.J. (Cardinal Deacon), Deacon of Sant' Ignazio di Loyola a Campo Marzio; born in Naples, Italy, April 19, 1921. Created and proclaimed February 21, 2001. Address: Via Di Porta Pinciana 1, 00187 Rome, Italy.

Tumi, Christian Wiyghan (Cardinal Priest), Titular of Ss. Martiri dell' Uganda a Poggio Ameno, Archbishop of Douala; born in Kikaikelaki, Diocese of Kumbo, October 15, 1930. Created and proclaimed June 28, 1988. Address: Archeveche, B.P. 179, Douala, Cameroon.

Turcotte, Jean-Claude (Cardinal Priest), Titular of Nostra Signora del Ss. Sacramento e Santi Martiri Canadesi, Archbishop of Montreal, Canada; born in Montreal, June 26, 1936. Created and proclaimed November 26, 1994. Address: 1071 rue de la Cathedrale, Montreal, Q.C. H3B 2V4, Canada.

Turkson, Peter Kodwo Appiah (Cardinal Priest), Titular of San Liborio, President of the Pontifical Council for Justice and Peace; born in Wassaw Nsuta, Archdiocese of Cape Coast, October 11, 1948. Created and proclaimed October 21, 2003. Address: 00120 Vatican City State, Europe.

Urosa Savino, Jorge Liberato (Cardinal Priest), Titular of Saint Mary ai Monti, Archbishop of Caracas, Santiago de Venezuela; born in Caracas, August 28, 1942. Created and proclaimed March 24, 2006. Address: Apartado 954, Monajas a Gradillas, Plaza Bolivar, Caracas 1010-A, Venezuela.

Vallini, Agostino (Cardinal Priest), Titular of Saint Peter Damian ai Monti di San Paolo, Vicar General of His Holiness for the Diocese of Rome, Archpriest of the Patriarchal Lateran Basilica; born in Poli, Diocese of Tivoli, April 17, 1940. Created and proclaimed March 24, 2006. Address: 00120 Vatican City State, Europe.

Vanhoye, Albert, S.J. (Cardinal Deacon), Deacon of Saint Mary of Mercy and Saint Adrian at Villa Albani, Former Rector of the Pontifical Biblical Institute and Former Secretary of the Pontifical Biblical Commission; born in Hazebrouck, Diocesi of Lille, July 24, 1923. Created and proclaimed March 24, 2006. Address: Borgo S. Spirito 4, C.P. 6139, 00195 Roma-Prati, Italy.

Vidal, Ricardo J. (Cardinal Priest), Titular of Ss. Pietro e Paolo a Via Stiense, Archbishop of Cebu; born in Mogpoc, Diocese of Boac, February 6, 1931. Created and proclaimed May 25, 1985. Address: 234 D. Jakosalem Str., P.O. Box 52, 6000 Cebu City, Philippines.

Vingt-Trois, Andre (Cardinal Priest) Titular of San Luigi dei Francesi, Archbishop of Paris; born in Paris, November 7, 1942. Created and proclaimed November 24, 2007. Address: 7 Rue Saint-Vincent, 75018 Paris, France.

Vithayathil, Varkey, C.Ss.R. (Cardinal Priest), Titular of San Bernardo alle Terme, Major Archbishop of Ernakulam-Angamaly of the Syro-Malabar; born in Parur, Archeparchy of Ernakulam-Angamaly of the Syro-Malabar, May 29, 1927. Created and proclaimed February 21, 2001. Address: Major Archbishop's House, Mount St. Thomas, P.O. Box 2580, P.O. Kakkanad, Kochi-682031 Kerala, India.

Vlk, Miloslav (Cardinal Priest), Titular of S. Croce in Gerusalemme, Archbishop Emeritus of Prague, Czech Republic; born in Lisnice-Sepekov, Diocese of Ceske Budejovice, May 17, 1932. Created and proclaimed November 26, 1994. Address: Arcibiskupska Kurie, Hradcanske nam. 56/16, 119 02 Praha 1, Czech Republic.

Wamala, Emmanuel (Cardinal Priest), Titular of S. Ugo, Archbishop Emeritus of Kampala, Uganda; born in Kamaggwa, Diocese of Masaka, December 15, 1926. Created and proclaimed November 26, 1994. Address: Archbishop's House, P.O. Box 14125, Mengo- Kampala, Uganda.

Wetter, Friedrich (Cardinal Priest), Titular of S. Stefano al Monte Celio, Archbishop Emeritus of Munich und Freising; born in Landau, Diocese of Speyer, February 20, 1928. Created and proclaimed May 25, 1985. Address: Postfach 100551, Kardinal-Faulhaber Str., 7, D-80079 Munchen, Germany.

Williams, Thomas Stafford (Cardinal Priest), Titular of Gesu' Divin Maestro alla Pineta Sacchetti, Archbishop Emeritus of Wellington; born in Wellington, March 20, 1930. Created and proclaimed February 2, 1983. Address: Archbishop's House, P.O. Box 1937, 21 Eccleston Hill, Wellington 6015, New Zealand.

Zen Ze-kiun, Joseph (Cardinal Priest), Titular of Saint Mary Mother of the Redeemer at Tor Bella Monaca, Archbishop Emeritus of Hong Kong; born in Shanghai, January 13, 1932. Created and proclaimed March 24, 2006. Address: Holy Spirit Seminary, 6 Welfare Rd., Aberdeen, Hong Kong, China.

Zubeir Wako, Gabriel (Cardinal Priest), Titular of Sant' Atanasio a Via Tiburtina, Archbishop of Khartoum; born in Mboro, Diocese of Wau, February 27, 1941. Created and proclaimed October 21, 2003. Address: P.O. Box 49, Khartoum, Sudan.

Patriarchs

Alexandria (Egypt), Coptic Rite— His Beatitude Antonios Naguib, born in Minya, Egypt, March 7, 1935; ordained October 30, 1960; elected Bishop of Minya of the Copts, July 26, 1977; consecrated September 9, 1977; resigned September 29, 2002; elected Patriarch of Alexandria of the Copts, March 30, 2006. Address: Patriarcat Copte Catholique, B.P. 69, 34 Rue Ibn Sandar, Saray El Koubbeh, 11712 Le Caire, Egypte.

Antioch (Syria), Syriac Rite— His Beatitude Ignace Joseph III Younan, born in Hassaké November 15, 1944; elected Patriarch February 15, 2009. Address: Rue Damas, B.P. 116-5087, 1106-2010 Beyrouth, Lebanon.

Maronite Rite— His Beatitude Nasrallah Peter Cardinal Sfeir, born in Reyfoun, May 15, 1920; elected Patriarch April 19, 1986; elevated to the College of Cardinals November 26, 1994. Address: Patriarcat Maronite, Bkerke, Lebanon.

Melkite Greek Catholic— His Beatitude Gregoire III Laham, born December 15, 1933 in Daraya; elected Patriarch November 29, 2000. Address: B.P. 22249, Avenue Az-Zeitoon 12, Bab Charki, Damascus, Syria.

Jerusalem (Israel)— His Beatitude Fouad Twal, born in Madaba, Israel, October 23, 1940; succeeded Patriarch of Jerusalem of the Latins June 21, 2008. Address: Patriarcat Latin, P.O. Box 14152, 91141 Jerusalem (Old City).

Babylon of the Chaldeans— His Beatitude Emmanuel III Delly, born in Telkaif, October 6, 1927;

elected Patriarch December 3, 2003. Address: Patriarcat Chaldeen Catholique, P.O. Box 6112, Al-Mansour, Baghdad, Iraq.

Cilicia of the Armenians— His Beatitude Nerses Bedros XIX Tarmouni, born in LeCaire January 17, 1940; elected Patriarch October 7, 1999. Address: Patriarcat Armenien Catholique, Rue de L'Hopital Orthodoxe, Jeitaoui, 2078 5605 Beyrouth, Lebanon.

East Indies— Most Rev. Filipe Neri António Sebastiaó Do Rosario Ferrao, Archbishop of Goa and Damao; born in Aldona, Archdiocese of Goa, January 20, 1953; promoted Archbishop January 16, 2004. Address: Paco Patriarcal P.O. Box 216, Panaji, Goa-403001, India.

Lisbon, (Portugal)— His Eminence Jose Cardinal da Cruz Policarpo, born in Alvorninha, Patriarchate of Lisbon, February 26, 1936; consecrated June 29, 1978; appointed Coadjutor Archbishop of the Patriarchate of Lisbon March 5, 1997; promoted Patriarch March 24, 1998; elevated to the College of Cardinals February 21, 2001. Address: Mosteiro de Sao Vicente De Fora, Campo de Santa Clara 1100-472 Lisbon, Portugal.

Venice, (Italy)— His Eminence Angelo Cardinal Scola, born in Malgrate, Archdiocese of Milan, November 7, 1941; ordained July 18, 1970; consecrated as Bishop September 21, 1991; elected Patriarch January 5, 2002; elevated to the College of Cardinals October 21, 2003. Address: Curia Patriarcale, S. Marco 320/a, 30124 Venice, Italy.

Synod of Bishops

Synodus Episcoporum President: The Holy Father. Secretary General: Most Rev. Archbishop Nikola Eterovic, General Secretariat: Palazzo del Bramante, Via della Conciliazione, 34, 00193 Rome, Italy. Tel: 69.88.48.21 or 69.88.43.24. Fax: 69.88.33.92.

Office of Labor of the Apostolic See

Officium Laboris Apostolicae Sedia President: His Eminence Francesco Cardinal Marchisano, Vice President: Most Rev. Bishop Franco Croci, Assessor of the Presidency: Prof. Roberto Pessi, Assessor of the Presidency: Prof. Giovanni Giustiniani, Office: Via della Conciliazione, 1, 00193 Rome, Italy. Tel: 69.88.44.49. Fax: 69.88.38.00.

The Roman Curia

he present norms regarding the Roman Curia were publicly announced June 28, 1988, in the Pastor Bonus - Constitutio Apostolica de Romana Curia, and published in A.A.S. LXXX/1988, Commentarium Officiale; pp. 841-934. The Supreme Pontiff usually conducts business of the universal Church by means of the Roman Curia, which fulfills its duty in his name and by his authority for the good and the service of the Churches; it consists of the Secretariat of State or the Papal Secretariat, congregations, tribunals and other institutions, whose structure and competency are defined in special law (can. 360). The Roman curia is the complex of departments and institutes which assist the Roman Pontiff in the exercise of his supreme pastoral function for the good and service of the universal Church and of the particular churches, by which the unity of faith and communion of the people of God is strengthened and the mission is promoted which is proper to the Church in the world.

I. THE SECRETARIAT OF STATE TO HIS HOLINESS

The Secretariat of State

he Secretariat of State is the dicastery of the Roman Curia which works most closely with the Supreme Pontiff in the exercise of his universal mission (*Pastor Bonus*, Art. 39). The Secretariat of State is presided over by a Cardinal who assumes the title of Secretary of State. As the Pope's first Collaborator in the governance of the universal Church, the Cardinal Secretary of State is the one primarily responsible for the diplomatic and political activity of the Holy See, in some circumstances representing the person of the Supreme Pontiff himself.

he Secretariat of State includes two sections, namely: the First Section that is headed by an Archbishop, the *Substitute for General Affairs*, assisted by a Prelate, the *Assessor for General Affairs*; and the Second Section of the Secretariat of State headed by an Archbishop, the *Secretary for Relations with States*, aided by a Prelate, the *Under-Secretary for Relations with States*, and assisted by Cardinals and Bishops.

ecretary of State: His Eminence Tarcisio Cardinal Bertone.

ffice: Apostolic Palace, 00120 Vatican City State, Europe. Tel: 06-69.88.39.13; Fax: 06-69.88.52.55.

First Section: For General Affairs

In conformity with Arts. 41-44 of *Pastor Bonus*, the Section for General Affairs or the First Section is responsible for handling matters regarding the everyday service of the Supreme Pontiff, both in caring for the universal Church and in dealing with the dicasteries of the Roman Curia. It attends to the preparation of whatever documents the Holy Father entrusts to it. It enacts the provisions for appointments within the Roman Curia and keeps custody of the Lead Seal and the Fisherman's Ring. It regulates the duties and activity of the Holy See's Representatives, especially in relation to the local Churches. It attends to all that concerns the Embassies accredited to the Holy See. It supervises the Holy See's official communication agencies and is responsible for publishing the "Acta Apostolicae Sedis" and the "Annuario Pontificio".

Substitute: Most Rev. Archbishop Fernando Filoni.

Assessor: Rev. Msgr. Gabriele Giordano Caccia.

Office: Apostolic Palace, 00120 Vatican City State, Europe. Tel: 06.69.88.34.38 Fax: 06.69.88.50.88.

Second Section: For Relations with States

On the basis of Arts. 45-47 of Pastor Bonus, the Section for Relations with States or Second Section has the specific duty of attending to matters which involve civil governments. It has responsibility for the Holy See's diplomatic relations with States, including the establishing of Concordats or similar agreements; for the Holy See's presence in international organizations and conferences; in special circumstances, by order of the Supreme Pontiff and in consultation with the competent dicasteries of the Curia, provides for appointments to particular Churches, and for their establishment or modification; in close collaboration with the Congregation for Bishops, it attends to the appointment of Bishops in countries which have entered into treaties or agreements with the Holy See in accordance with the norms of international law.

Secretary: Most Rev. Archbishop Dominique Mamberti.

Under-Secretary: Rev. Monsignor Ettore Balestrero.

Office: Apostolic Palace, 00120 Vatican City State, Europe. Tel: 06.69.88.30.14; Fax: 06.69.88.53.64.

II. THE CONGREGATIONS

y the name of department (dicasteria) is understood: the congregations, tribunals, councils and offices, namely the Apostolic Camera, the Administration of the Patrimony of the Apostolic See, and the Prefecture of Economic Affairs of the Holy See. The departments are juridically equal among themselves. Attached to the institutes of the Roman Curia are the Prefecture of the Papal Household and the Office of Liturgical Celebrations of the Supreme Pontiff.

The Congregation for the Doctrine of the Faith

he proper function of the Congregation on the Doctrine of the Faith is to promote and safeguard the doctrine of faith and morals in the whole Catholic world; therefore, those things belong to it which touch this matter in any way. Fulfilling the function of promoting doctrine, it fosters studies in order that the understanding of the faith might grow and that a response can be prepared under the light of faith for new questions arising from developments in science and human culture. It is a help to bishops, whether individually or gathered in assemblies, in the exercise of the function by which they are constituted authentic teachers and doctors of the faith as well as the office by which they are held to safeguard and promote the integrity of that faith. This Sacred Congregation reproves doctrines opposed to the principles of the faith after the interested Bishops of a region have been heard. It studies the books referred to it and, if necessary, reproves them after the author has been heard and has had an opportunity to defend himself and after the Ordinary has been forewarned. It also examines whatever concerns "the privilege of the faith" whether in law and in fact. It is competent to pass judgment on errors about the faith according to the norms of an ordinary process. It safeguards the dignity of the sacrament of Penance. The Congregation proceeds administratively or judicially according to the nature of the question to be treated.

refect: His Eminence William J. Cardinal Levada.

ecretary: Most Rev. Luis Francisco Ladaria Ferrer, S.J.

ffice: Piazza del S. Uffizio 11, 00193 Rome, Italy. Tel: 69.88.33.57; 69.88.34.13; Fax: 69.88.34.09.

The Congregation for the Oriental Churches

his Congregation considers those matters, whether regarding persons or things, which touch on the Eastern Catholic Churches. It treats all questions which pertain either to persons, or to discipline, or to the rites of the Oriental Churches, even if they are mixed in that by the nature of the thing or of persons they involve Latins. Territories in which a major part of the Christians belong to Oriental rites are subject only to this Congregation. Even in Latin territories it carefully supervises the faithful of Oriental rites and provides as much as possible for their spiritual needs even by the establishment of their own hierarchy if the number of faithful and circumstances require this.

Prefect: His Eminence Leonardo Cardinal Sandri.

Secretary: Most Rev. Archbishop Cyril Vasil, S.J.

Office: Via della Conciliazione 34, 00193 Rome, Italy. Tel: 69.88.42.93; Fax: 69.88.43.00.

The Congregation for Divine Worship and the Discipline of the Sacraments

This congregation does those things which pertain to the Apostolic See as to the moderation and promotion of the sacred liturgy, especially the sacraments, with due regard for the competence of the Congregation on Doctrine of the Faith. It fosters and safeguards the discipline of the sacraments, especially what pertains to their valid and licit celebration; moreover, it concedes favors and dispensations for matters which are not contained in the facilities of diocesan bishops in this line. It alone examines the non-consummation of a marriage and the presence of causes for the granting of a dispensation and everything connected with them. It has competence with regard to the obligations connected with major orders and it examines questions about the validity of sacred ordination.

Prefect: His Eminence Antonio Cardinal Canizares Llovera.

Secretary: Most Rev. Archbishop Joseph Augustine J. Di Noia, O.P.

Office: Piazza Pio XII 10, 00193 Rome, Italy. Tel: 69.88.43.16; Fax: 69.88.34.99.

The Congregation for the Causes of Saints

The Congregation for the Causes of Saints is competent in all matters which in any way pertain to the Beatification of Servants of God or to the Canonization of the Blessed or to the Preservation of Relics.

This Congregation is divided into three offices.

Prefect: Most Rev. Archbishop Angelo Amato, S.D.B.

Secretary: Rev. Msgr. Michele Di Ruberto.

Office: Piazza Pio XII 10, 00193 Rome, Italy. Tel: 011 39 06 69.88.42.47; Fax: 011 39 06 6988 1935.

The Congregation for Bishops

This congregation examines what pertains to the constitution and provision of particular churches as well as the exercise of the episcopal function in the Latin Church, except for the competence of the Congregation for the Evangelization of Peoples. It belongs to the Congregation for Bishops to propose to the Roman Pontiff, for approval, the constitution of new dioceses, provinces and regions; to divide, unite and realign them after consulting the interested Episcopal Conferences; it deals also with the erection of the military ordinariates and, after consulting the Episcopal Conference, prelacies for special pastoral ministries for various regions or social groups. This Congregation provides also for the naming of bishops, apostolic administrators, coadjutors and auxiliaries of bishops, military and other vicars and prelates enjoying personal jurisdiction. It is competent for all things that have to do with bishops and publishes norms which, through the Episcopal Conference, provide for the more urgent needs of the faithful.

Prefect: His Eminence Giovanni Battista Cardinal Re

Secretary: Most Rev. Archbishop Manuel Monteiro de Castro.

Office: Piazza Pio XII 10, 00193 Rome, Italy. Tel: 69.88.42.17; Fax: 69.88.53.03.

Pontifical Commission for Latin America

(Directly responsible to Congregation for Bishops)

President: His Eminence Giovanni Battista Cardinal Re.

Vice President: Most Rev. Archbishop José Octavio Ruiz Arenas.

The Congregation for the Evangelization of Peoples or for the Propagation of the Faith

It belongs to this congregation to direct and coordinate throughout the world the work of the evangelization of peoples itself and missionary cooperation, while respecting the competence of the Congregation for Eastern Churches. It is competent for those things which pertain to all the missions established for the spread of the Kingdom of Christ throughout the world and therefore for whatever is connected with the assignment and transferal of the necessary ministers, for describing ecclesiastical boundaries and proposing those who will govern them. It encourages also the development of an indigenous clergy. The congregation sponsors missionary initiatives and promotes missionary vocations and spirituality. In the territories subject to it, the Congregation has charge of all that pertains to the holding of synods and councils, to the establishing of episcopal conferences and to the review of their statutes and decrees. The Congregation has a Supreme Council for the direction of Pontifical Missionary Works, on which depend the general Councils of the Missionary Union of the Clergy, the Society for the Propagation of the Faith, the Society of St. Peter the Apostle, and the Society of the Holy Childhood.

Prefect: His Eminence Ivan Cardinal Dias.

Secretary: Most Rev. Archbishop Robert Sarah.

Office: Palazzo di Propaganda Fide, Piazza di Spagna 48, 00187 Rome, Italy. Tel: 011 39 06 6987 9299; Fax: 011 39 06 6988 01 18.

The Congregation for the Clergy

With due regard for the rights of bishops and their conferences, this congregation examines those things which concern priests and deacons of the secular clergy with regard to their persons, pastoral ministry, matters which are in support of the exercise of these things, and in all this provides opportune assistance to the bishops. The Congregation has many functions: studies, proposes and urges the means and aids by which priests strive for sanctity. This office also has charge of everything which concerns the work and discipline of the diocesan clergy. Particularly it promotes the preaching of the Word of God and the works of the apostolate and organization of catechesis, evaluates and approves pastoral and catechetical directories, fosters national and international Catechetical Congresses and indicates the opportune norms for religious instruction of children, young people and adults. The Congregation looks also to the preservation and administration of the temporal goods of the Church without prejudice to the other Congregations which have temporal goods committed to their vigilance.

Prefect: His Eminence Claudio Cardinal Hummes, O.F.M.

Secretary: Most Rev. Archbishop Mauro Piacenza.

Office: Piazza Pio XII 3, 00193 Rome, Italy. Tel: 69.88.41.51; Fax: 69.88.48.45.

The Congregation for Institutes of Consecrated Life and for Societies of Apostolic Life

The principal function of this congregation is to promote and supervise, in the whole Latin Church, the practices of the evangelical counsels as they are exercised in approved forms of consecrated life and at the same time the activities of societies of apostolic life. The Congregation takes care of Religious Institutes of Consecrated Life and Secular Institutes.

Religious Institutes: the Congregation is entrusted with the affairs of all religious institutes of the Latin Rite and their members. It is also competent in matters which pertain to societies of common life, whose members live like religious, or to Third Orders as such.

Secular Institutes: the Congregation is competent in the same way, all else being equal, for Apostolic Societies which, although not religious, make a true and complete profession of the evangelical counsels in the world.

Prefect: His Eminence Franc Cardinal Rode.

Secretary: Most Rev. Archbishop Gianfranco Gardin, O.F.M.Conv.

Office: Piazza Pio XII 3, 00193 Rome, Italy. Tel: 69.88.41.28; Fax: 69.88.45.26.

The Congregation for Catholic Education (of Seminaries and Institutes of Studies)

This Congregation expresses and exercises the Apostolic See's solicitude for the formation of those who are called to holy orders as well as for the promotion and organization of Catholic education. It is competent for all that pertains to the formation of clerics and the Catholic education both of clerics and of the laity.

The Congregation has many functions and is charged with the direction, discipline and temporal administration of seminaries and whatever touches the education of the diocesan clergy and the scientific form tion of religious and secular institutes.

The Congregation oversees universities, faculti athenaea and any institute of higher learning whi has the name "Catholic" in so far as they depend the authority of the Church, not excluding those rected by religious or the laity.

The Congregation cares for the establishment of pa chial and diocesan schools; watches over all Catho schools below the level of a university and faculty, well as all institutes of instruction or education d pendent on the authority of the Church.

Also within the Congregation is located the Pontific Work for Vocations, which is charged with coordina ing and promoting the work of fostering all ecclesia tical vocations.

Prefect: His Eminence Zenon Cardinal Grocholewski.

Secretary: Most Rev. Archbishop Jean-Louis Brugu O.P.

Office: Piazza Pio XII 3, 00193 Rome, Italy. Tel: 69 41 67; Fax: 69 88 41 72.

III. TRIBUNALS

Apostolic Penitentiary

The competence of this Tribunal is concerned with those matters which pertain to the internal forum, for both the sacramental and non-sacramental internal forum. It is competent in matters pertaining to the granting and use of indulgences.

Major Penitentiary: Most Rev. Archbishop Fortunato Baldelli.

Office: Piazza della Cancelleria 1, 00186 Rome, Italy. Tel: 011 39 06 6988 75 26; Fax: 011 39 06 6988 75 57.

Supreme Tribunal of the Apostolic Signatura

This department, in addition to the function which it exercises as Supreme Tribunal, consults that justice may be correctly administered in the Church.

With the many functions, the Apostolic Signatura judges the matters assigned to it in the Code of Canon Law; it prorogues the competence of tribunals; it extends the forum for strangers in Rome to cases of matrimonial nullity in extraordinary circumstances and for grave reasons; it supervises the proper administration of justice; it provides for the establishment of regional and interregional tribunals; it enjoys the rights assigned to it in concordats between the Holy See and the various nations.

The Tribunal settles questions about the exercise of administrative ecclesiastical power which are referred to it. It also passes on conflicts of competence among the departments of the Holy See; it examines administrative matters referred to it by the Congregations of the Roman Curia as well as questions committed to it by the Holy Father.

Prefect: Most Rev. Archbishop Raymond Leo Burke.

Secretary: Most Rev. Bishop Frans Daneels, O.Praem.

Office: Piazza della Cancelleria 1, 00186 Rome, Italy. Tel: 69.88.75.20; Fax: 69.88.75.53.

Tribunal of the Roman Rota

This tribunal acts as a higher instance at the Aposto See, usually in the grade of appeal, for safeguardi rights in the Church; it fosters the unity of jurispr dence and, through its own sentences, is a help to low tribunals. It is also a court of first instance for cas specified in the law and for others committed to t Rota by the Roman Pontiff. The greater part of i decisions concern the nullity of marriage. In such cas its competence includes marriages between two Cath lics, between a Catholic and non-Catholic, and betwe two non-Catholic parties whether one or both of t baptized parties belongs to a Latin or Oriental Rite

Dean: Most Rev. Bishop Antoni Stankiewicz.

Office: Piazza della Cancelleria 1, 00186 Rome, Ita Tel: 69.88.75.02; Fax: 69.88.75.54.

IV. PONTIFICAL COUNCILS

Pontifical Council for the Laity

This council is competent in those matters which pertain to the Apostolic See in promoting and coordinating the apostolate of the lay persons and, generally, in those things which look to the Christian life of lay persons as such. The norms were published in the apostolic letter, Catholicam Christi Ecclesiam of January 6, 1967 (A.A.S., LIX, pp. 25-28).

President: His Eminence Stanislaw Cardinal Rylko.

Secretary: Most Rev. Bishop Josef Clemens.

Office: Piazza S. Calisto 16, 00153 Rome, Italy. Tel: 69.88.73.22; Fax: 69.88.72.14.

Pontifical Council for Promoting Christian Unity

The function of this Council is to concentrate in an appropriate way on initiatives and ecumenical activities for the restoration of unity among Christians. It has charge of relations with those of other communities; considers the correct interpretation and observance of the principles of ecumenism; promotes Catholic groups and coordinates the efforts at unity, both on the national and international levels; institutes colloquies on ecumenical questions and activities with Churches and ecclesial communities separated from the Holy See; deputes Catholic observers for Christian congresses; invites to Catholic gatherings observers of the separated brethren; orders into practice conciliar decrees on ecumenical matters. Furthermore, it is competent for all questions concerning religious relations with Judaism.

President: His Eminence Walter Cardinal Kasper.

Secretary: Most Rev. Bishop Brian Farrell, L.C.

Office: Via della Conciliazione 5, 00193 Rome, Italy. Tel: 6988 3072; Fax: 6988 53 65.

Commission for Religious Relations with Jews

Secretary: Rev. Norbert Hoffman, S.D.B.

Pontifical Council for the Family

This Council promotes the pastoral care of families and fosters their rights and dignity in the Church and in civil society, in order that they might ever more suitably fulfill their own functions.

President: His Eminence Ennio Cardinal Antonelli.

Secretary: Most Rev. Bishop Jean Laffitte.

Office: Piazza S. Calisto 16, 00153 Rome, Italy. Tel: 69.88.72.43; Fax: 69.88.72.72.

Pontifical Council for Justice and Peace

This Council looks to those things which will promote justice and peace in the world according to the Gospel and the social teaching of the Church.

President: His Eminence Peter Kodwo Appiah Cardinal Turkson.

Secretary: Most Rev. Bishop Mario Toso, S.D.B.

Office: Piazza S. Calisto 16, 00153 Rome, Italy. Tel: 6987.9911; Fax: 69.88.72.05.

Pontifical Council Cor Unum

This Council shows the solicitude of the Catholic Church toward the needy, in order that human fraternity might be fostered and the charity of Christ be made manifest.

President: His Eminence Paul Josef Cardinal Cordes.

Secretary: Rev. Msgr. Karel Kasteel.

Office: Palazzo San Pio X, Via della Conciliazione 5, 3°P, 00193 Rome, Italy. Tel: 69.88.9411; Fax: 69.88.7311.

Pastoral Council for the Pastoral Care of Migrants and Itinerant People

This Council directs the pastoral concern of the Church toward the special needs of those who are forced to leave their own native land or who perhaps lack one; it also sees that there is appropriate study of the questions which touch on this matter.

President: Most Rev. Archbishop Antonio Maria Vegliò.

Secretary: Most Rev. Archbishop Agostino Marchetto.

Office: Piazza S. Calisto 16, 00153 Rome, Italy. Tel: 69.88.71.93; Fax: 69.88.71.11.

Pontifical Council for the Pastoral Assistance to Health Care

This Council shows the solicitude of the Church for the sick by aiding those who carry out a ministry toward the sick and suffering, in order that the apostolate of mercy, which they carry out, may ever more suitably respond to new needs.

President: Most Rev. Archbishop Zygmunt Zimowski.

Secretary: Most Rev. Bishop Jose Luis Redrado Marchite, O.H.

Office: Via della Conciliazione 3, 00193 Rome, Italy. Tel: 69.88.31.38; Fax: 69.88.31.39.

Pontifical Council for the Intepretation of Legislative Texts

The function of this Council consists especially in interpreting the Church's laws.

President: Most Rev. Archbishop Francesco Coccopalmerio.

Secretary: Rev. Msgr. Juan Ignacio Arrieta Ochoa De Chinchetru.

Office: Palazzo delle Congregazioni Piazza Pio XII 10, 00193 Rome, Italy. Tel: 69.88.40.08; Fax: 69.88.47.10.

Pontifical Council for Inter-Religious Dialogue

This Council fosters and moderates relations with members and bodies of religions which do not carry the name of Christian, as well as with those who in any way posses religious spirit. It fosters studies and promotes relatio with non-Christians to bring about an increase in mutu respect and seeks ways to establish a dialogue with the it receives and carefully weighs the wishes of the Ordin ies; it provides for the formation of those who participa in dialogue.

President: His Eminence Jean-Louis Cardinal Tauran.

Secretary: Most Rev. Archbishop Pier Luigi Celata

Office: Via della Conciliazione 5, 00193 Rome, Italy. T 69.88.43.21; Fax: 69.88.44.94.

Commission for Religious Relations with Muslin

Secretary: Rev. Msgr. Khaled Akasheh.

Pontifical Council for Culture

The Council embodies the Church's pastoral concern ov the relationship between faith and cultures. Its tas include: studying unbelief and religious indifference, present in different cultures; supporting the Churc inculturation of the Gospel; promoting initiatives of di logue between faith and culture, as well as dialogue wi those who do not believe in God. Its activities inclu seminars, intercultural exchanges, and coordinating t activities of Pontifical Academies and the Pontifical Co mission for the Cultural Patrimony of the Church. important hope of the Council is to show faith as t inspiration of science, literature and the arts.

President: Most Rev. Archbishop Gianfranco Ravasi.

Secretary: Very Rev. Bernard Ardura, O.Praem.

Office: Piazza S. Calisto 16, 00153 Rome, Italy. T 6989.3811; Fax: 69.88.73.68.

Pontifical Council for Social Communications

This Council is involved in questions touching on the instr ments of social communication so that the proclamati of salvation and human progress might be promot even through them in order to foster civil culture.

President: Most Rev. Archbishop Claudio Maria Celli.

Secretary: Rev. Msgr. Paul Tighe.

Office: Palazzo S. Carlo, 00120 Vatican City State, Euro Tel: 69.88.31.97; Fax: 69.88.53.73.

Apostolic Camera

e Apostolic Camera is presided over by the cardinal chamberlain of the Holy Roman Church, assisted by the vice-chamberlain together with certain prelates chamberlain. It chiefly exercises the function which is given to it in the special law on the vacancy of the Apostolic See.

merlengo: His Eminence Tarcisio Cardinal Bertone, Secretary of State.

Administration of the Patrimony of the Apostolic See

is Office is competent to administer the goods proper to the Holy See, the income from which is destined to support the expenditures necessary for the functions of the Roman Curia.

traordinary Section: Handles the duties committed to it by the Sovereign Pontiff.

sident: His Eminence Attilio Cardinal Nicora.

retary: Most Rev. Archbishop Domenico Calcagno.

fice: 00120 Vatican City State, Europe. Tel: 011 39 06 6989.3403; Fax: 011 39 06 6988 31 41.

V. OFFICES

Prefecture of the Economic Affairs of the Holy See

The Prefecture has the function of supervising and governing the administration of goods which belong to the Holy See or which it is in charge of, no matter what kind of autonomy they may perhaps enjoy. This is directed by a Commission of three Cardinals and coordinates and watches over the administration of the possessions of the Holy See. It receives the reports on the receipts and disbursements of the Church's goods and the various budgets.

President: Most Rev. Archbishop Velasio De Paolis, C.S.

Secretary: Most Rev. Bishop Vincenzo Di Mauro.

Office: Largo del Colonnato 3, 00193 Rome, Italy. Tel: 69.88.42.63; Fax: 69.88.50.11.

Prefecture of the Papal Household

The Prefecture looks after the internal order of the pontifical household and supervises everything which pertains to discipline and service either by clergy or laity who constitute the pontifical chapel and family. It is in charge of the Apostolic Palace and is at the service of the Holy Father, both there and wherever he goes. It arranges audiences with His Holiness and supervises papal ceremonies other than the strictly liturgical.

Prefect: Most Reverend Archbishop James M. Harvey.

Office of the Liturgical Celebrations of the Supreme Pontiff

This Office prepares whatever is necessary for liturgical and other sacred celebrations which are carried out by the Supreme Pontiff or in his name and, in keeping with existing prescription of liturgical law, to supervise them.

Master of Ceremonies: Rev. Msgr. Guido Marini.

Central Office of Statistics of the Church

This Office gathers and organizes the data which seems necessary or useful for a better understanding of the state of the Church and for assistance to its Bishops.

Director: Rev. Msgr. Vittorio Formenti.

VI. COMMISSIONS AND COMMITTEES

ontifical Commission for the Cultural Heritage of the Church

sident: Most Rev. Archbishop Gianfranco Ravasi.

retary: Dr. Francesco Buranelli.

Pontifical Commission for Sacred Archeology

sident: Most Rev. Archbishop Gianfranco Ravasi.

retary: Rev. Msgr. Giovanni Carrù.

Pontifical Biblical Commission

sident: His Eminence William Cardinal Levada

Secretary: Rev. Klemens Stock, S.J.

Pontifical Commission "Ecclesia Dei"

President: His Eminence William Cardinal Levada
Secretary: Rev. Msgr. Guido Pozzo

International Theological Commission

President: His Eminence William Cardinal Levada
Secretary General: Rev. Luis Ladaria, S.J.

Pontifical Commission for the Vatican City State

President: His Eminence Giovanni Cardinal Lojolo

Pontifical Committee for the International Eucharistic Congresses

President: Most Rev. Archbishop Pietro Marini.

Pontifical Committee for Historical Sciences

President: Rev. Msgr. Walter Brandmuller

Secretary: Rev. Cosimo Semeraro, S.D.B.

VII. INSTITUTIONS CONNECTED WITH THE HOLY SEE

Press Office of the Holy See

ector: Rev. Federico Lombardi, S.J.

Vatican Secret Archives

hivist: His Eminence Raffaele Cardinal Farina, S.D.B.
fect: Most Rev. Bishop Sergio B. Pagano.

Vatican Apostolic Library

rarian: His Eminence Raffaele Cardinal Farina, S.D.B.
efect: Rev. Cesare Pasini.

Vatican Polyglot Press

ector General: Rev. Elio Torrigiani, S.D.B.

L'Osservatore Romano

itor-in-Chief: Prof. Giovanni Maria Vian.
retary: Dr. Gaetano Vallini.
glish Language Weekly - Contact Person: Rev. Paul S. Quinter.
Translations of English, French, Spanish, German, Portuguese, and Polish editions available.

Vatican Publishing House

President: Rev. Msgr. Giuseppe Scotti.
Director: Rev. Giuseppe Costa, S.D.B.

Vatican Radio

Director General: Rev. Frederico Lombardi, S.J.

Vatican Television Centre

President of the Administrative Council: Dr. Emilio Rossi.
Director General: Rev. Federico Lombardi, S.J.

St. Peter's Basilica

Archpriest: His Eminence Angelo Cardinal Comastri.

Fabric of St. Peter's

President: His Eminence Angelo Cardinal Comastri.

Office of Papal Charities

Almoner: Most Rev. Archbishop Felix Del Blanco Prieto.

Pontifical Academy of Sciences

President: Prof. Nicola Cabibbo.

Pontifical Academy of Social Sciences

President: Prof. Mary Ann Glendon.

Pontifical Academy for Life

President: Most Rev. Archbishop Salvatore Fisichella.

Pontifical Academy of Theology

President: Rev. Msgr. Marcello Bordoni.

Institute for Works of Religion

Director General: Mr. Paolo Cipriani

VIII. AMERICANS WORKING IN THE ROMAN CURIA

cretariat of State I. Section for General Affairs: Rev. Msgr. Peter Wells; Rev. Msgr. William Millea; Rev. Reginald Foster, O.C.D.; Rev. Daniel Gallagher.

ngregation for the Doctrine of the Faith: His Eminence William J. Cardinal Levada, Prefect; Most Rev. Archbishop Joseph DiNoia, O.P.; Rev. Msgr. Charles Brown; Rev. Msgr. Robert P. Deeley; Rev. Steven Lopes.

ngregation for Divine Worship and the Discipline of the Sacraments: Rev. Msgr. Thomas Fucinaro.

ngregation for Causes of Saints: Rev. Msgr. Robert Sarno.

ngregation for Bishops: Rev. Andrew Baker; Rev. Thomas W. Powers.

ngregation for Evangelization of People: Most Rev. Charles A. Schleck, C.S.C. (Retired).

ngregation for the Clergy: Rev. Msgr. J. Anthony McDaid.

ngregation for The Institutes of Consecrated Life and for Societies of Apostolic Life: Sr. Sharon Holland, I.H.M.

ostolic Penitentiary: His Eminence J. Francis Cardinal Stafford, Major Penitentiary; His Eminence William Cardinal Baum, Major Penitentiary Emeritus.

preme Tribunal of the Apostolic Signatura: Most Rev. Archbishop Raymond L. Burke, Prefect; Rev. Msgr. Joseph Punderson.

Tribunal of the Roman Rota: Rev. Msgr. Kenneth Boccafola; Rev. Msgr. Robert Sable.

Pontifical Council For Promoting Christian Unity: Rev. Msgr. John Radano; Rev. Gregory J. Fairbanks.

Pontifical Council for Justice and Peace: Rev. Msgr. James Reinert; Rev. Msgr. Anthony R. Frontiero.

Pontifical Council for Interreligious Dialogue: Sr. Judith Zoebelein, F.S.E.

Pontifical Council "Cor Unum": Rev. Anthony J. Figueiredo.

Administration for the Patrimony of the Apostolic See: Sr. Judith Zoebelein, F.S.E.

Prefecture of the Papal Household: Most Rev. James M. Harvey, Prefect.

Pontifical Commission Ecclesia Dei: Rev. Msgr. Arthur Calkins.

International Theological Commission: Rev. Peter D. Akpunonu.

Apostolic Vatican Library: Rev. Laurence Spiteri.

Equestrian Order of the Knights of the Holy Sepulchre of Jerusalem: Most Rev. John Foley, Grand Master; Rev. Hans Brouwers.

L'Osservatore Romano: Rev. Paul S. Quinter, Editor. For subscription information for North America please contact: The Cathedral Foundation, Inc., 320 Cathedral St., Baltimore, MD 21201. Tel: 410-547-5380; Fax: 410-385-0113.

Synod of Bishops: Rev. Msgr. John Abruzzese.

Papal Basilica of Saint Mary Major: His Eminence Bernard F. Law, Archpriest; Rev. Msgr. Paul Brendan McInerny.

Residence for American Diocesan Priests working in the Roman Curia: Villa Stritch, Via della Nocetta 63, 00164 Rome, Italy. Tel: 011 39 06 6616 2662; or 6616 2676; Fax: 011 39 06 6616 2700. Rev. Msgr. Robert J. Sarno, Dir.; Rev. Msgr. John Abruzzese, Vice Dir.

INSTITUTES OF GRADUATE STUDIES IN ROME

ntifical Gregorian University (Associated with the Pontifical Biblical Institute and the Pontifical Oriental Institute. Constituted in 1552. *Address*: Piazza della Pilotta 4, 00187 Rome, Italy. His Eminence Zenon Cardinal Grocholewski, Grand Chancellor; Very Rev. Pachó Adolfo Nicolás, S.J. Vice Chancellor; Very Rev. Gianfranco Ghirlanda, S.J., Rector; Very Rev. José Abrego de Lacy, S.J., Rector of the Biblical Institute; Very Rev. Cyril Vasil, S.J., Rector of the Oriental Institute.

ntifical Lateran University Founded in 1824. *Address*: Piazza S. Giovanni in Laterano 4, 00184 Rome, Italy. His Eminence Agostino Cardinal Vallini, Grand Chancellor; Most Rev. Archbishop Salvatore Fisichella, Rector.

Pontifical Urban University Founded in 1627. *Address*: Via Urbano VIII 16, 00165 Rome, Italy. His Eminence Ivan Cardinal Dias, Grand Chancellor; Rev. Cataldo Zuccaro, Rector.

Pontifical University of St. Thomas Aquinas Founded in 1580. *Address*: Largo Angelicum 1, 00184 Rome, Italy. Very Rev. Carlos Alfonso Azpiroz Costa, Master General of the Order of Preachers and Grand Chancellor; Very Rev. Charles Morerod, O.P., Rector.

Pontifical Salesian University Founded in 1940. *Address*: Piazza Ateneo Salesiano 1, 00139 Rome, Italy. Very Rev. Pascual Chávez Villanueva, Grand Chancellor; Very Rev. Carlo Nanni, Rector.

Faculty of Christian and Classical Humanities Very Rev. Pascual Chávez Villanueva, Rector; Very Rev. Mario Maritano, S.D.B., Dean.

Pontifical University of the Holy Cross Founded in 1984. *Address:* Piazza di S. Apollinare, 49, 00186 Rome, Italy. Most Rev. Bishop Javier Echevarría, Prelate of Opus Dei and Grand Chancellor; Rev. Prof. Luis Romero, Rector.

Pontifical Antonianum University Founded in 1933. *Address*: Via Merulana 124, 00185 Rome, Italy. Very Rev. José Rodriguez Carballo, O.F.M., Minister General of the Order of Friars Minor and Grand Chancellor; Very Rev. Johannes Baptist Freyer, O.F.M., Rector.

Pontifical Atheneum of St. Anselm Founded in 1687. *Address*: Piazza Cavalieri di Malta 5, 00153 Rome, Italy. Very Rev. Wolf D. Notker, O.S.B., Abbot Primate of the Benedictine Confederation and Grand Chancellor; Very Rev. Mark Sheridan, O.S.B., Rector.

Pontifical Athenaeum Regina Apostolorum Founded in 1993. *Address*: Via Degli Aldobrandeschi, 190, 00163 Rome, Italy. Very Rev. Alvaro Corcuera, L.C., Grand Chancellor; Very Rev. Pedro Barrajon, L.C., Rector.

Pontifical Institute of Sacred Music Founded in 1911. *Address*: Via di Torre Rossa 21, 00165, Rome, Italy. His Eminence Zenon Cardinal Grocholewski, Grand Chancellor; Rev. Msgr. Valentin Miserachs Grau, President.

Pontifical Institute of Christian Archeology Founded in 1925. *Address*: Via Napoleone III 1, 00185 Rome, Italy. His Eminence Zenon Cardinal Grocholewski, Grand Chancellor; Prof. Nicolai Fiocchi, Rector.

Pontifical Theological Faculty St. Bonaventure Erected in 1935. *Address*: Via del Serafico 1, 00142 Rome, Italy. Very Rev. Marco Tasca, O.F.M.Conv., Grand Chancellor and Minister General of the Order of Friars Minor Conventual; Rev. Zdzislaw Kijas, O.F.M.Conv., President.

Pontifical Theological Faculty Teresianum Founded in 1935. *Address*: Piazza S. Pancrazio 5-A, 00152 Rome, Italy. Very Rev. Luigi Arostegui Gamboa, O.C.D., Grand Chancellor; Very Rev. Aniano Alvarez-Suarez, President.

Pontifical Theological Faculty Marianum Founded in 1666. *Address*: Viale Trenta Aprile 6, 00153 Rome, Italy. Very Rev. Angel M. Ruiz Garnica, Prior General of the Order of Servants of Mary and Grand Chancellor; Very Rev. Silvano M. Maggiani, O.S.M., President.

Pontifical Institute for Arabic and Islamic Studies Founded in 1926. *Address*: Viale di Trastevere 98, 00153 Rome, Italy. His Eminence Zenon Cardinal Grocholewski, Grand Chancellor; Rev. Prof. Gérard Chabanon, Superior General of the Missionarie Africa and Vice Grand-Chancellor; Rev. Prof. Mig Angel Ayuso Gvixot, M.C.C.J., President.

Pontifical Faculty of Educational Scien Auxilium Founded in 1970. *Address:* Via Cremo 141, 00166 Rome, Italy. Very Rev. Pascual Chá Villanueva, Grand Chancellor; Mother Yvor Reungoat, Superior General of the Daughters of M Help of Christians and Vice-Grand Chancellor; Sis Hiang Chu Ausilia Chang, President.

SEMINARIES AND NATIONAL COLLEGES IN ROME

Pontifical Roman Major Seminary Founded in 1565 by Pius IV. Address: Piazza S. Giovanni in Laterano 4, 00184 Rome, Italy. Rev. Msgr. Giovanni Tani, Rector.

Pontifical Roman Minor Seminary Address: Viale Vaticano 42, 00165 Rome, Italy. Rev. Msgr. Paolo Selvadagi, Rector.

North American College (Pontifical) Corporate Title: The American College of the Roman Catholic Church of the United States. A Maryland Corporation. Founded in 1859 by Pope Pius IX. Postal Address: 00120 Vatican City State, Europe. Rev. Msgr. James F. Checchio, Rector. (See AMERICAN COLLEGES ABROAD for further details.)

Armenian College (Pontifical) Founded on March 1, 1883. Address: Salita S. Nicola da Tolentino 17, 00187 Rome, Italy. Rev. Joseph Antoine Kélékian, Rector.

Beda College (Pontifical) Founded in 1852. Address: Viale San Paolo 18, 00146 Rome, Italy. Rev. Charles R. Strange, Rector.

Belgian College (Pontifical) Founded in 1844. Rev. Address: Via G.B. Pagano 35, 00167 Rome, Italy.

Canadian College (Pontifical) Founded in 1888. Address: Via Crescenzio 75, 00193 Rome, Italy. Rev. Charles Langlois, P.S.S., Rector.

Capranica College (Almo) Founded in 1457 by Cardinal Capranica. Address: Piazza Capranica 98, 00186 Rome, Italy. Rev. Msgr. Ermenegildo Manicardi, Rector.

Ethiopian College (Pontifical) Founded on October 1, 1919 and February 12, 1930. Address: 00120 Citta del Vaticano, Europe. Rev. P. Keflemariam Bernhanemeskel, C.M., Rector.

French Seminary (Pontifical) Founded on October 10, 1853. Address: Via di S. Chiara 42, 00186 Rome, Italy. Rev. Yves-Marie Fradet, C.S.Sp., Rector.

German-Hungarian College (Pontifical) Founded on August 31, 1552. Address: Via S. Nicola da Tolentino 13, 00187 Rome, Italy. Rev. P. Franz Meures, S.J., Rector.

American College. Louvain, Belgium. Corporate title: The American College of the Immaculate Conception, Catholic University of Louvain, a corporation of the District of Columbia. Founded in 1857, the American College is the oldest national seminary operated under the auspices of the United States Conference of Catholic Bishops. Most Rev. David L. Ricken, J.C.L., D.D., Chairman. Postal Address: Naamsestraat 100, B-3000 Leuven, Belgium. Tel: 32.16.32.00.11; Fax: 32.16.32.00.12; Website: www.acl.be.

Faculty and Staff: Rev. Msgr. Ross A. Shecterle, S.T.L., Ph.D., Rector-Pres.; Rev. Christopher M. Mahar, Vice Rector; Dr. John A. Steffen, Rector's Asst.; Rev. Rafael Partida, Spiritual Dir.; Rev. Paul Czerwonka, Iconographer.

The American College offers a variety of programs that take advantage of its association with the Faculties of Theology, Philosophy and Canon Law of the Catholic University of Louvain (Leuven). Its primary mission is the formation of seminaries for priestly ministry at either the level of Philosophy/Pre-theology or Theology; The Graduate Studies Programs in Canon Law, Theology and Philosophy; monthly and semester sabbatical Programs and a summer session for ministerial renewal.

Office for Development and Recruitment for the American College of Louvain, Postal Address: The American College, USCCB, 3211 Fourth St., N.E., Washington, DC 20017-1194. Tel: 202-541-3108 (answering service). E-mail: admissions@aci.be or rshecterle@acl.be; alumni@acl.be; guestmaster@acl.be. Quarterly newsletter of the American College, *Sodales*.

Greek College (Pontifical) Founded on January 13, 1577. Address: Via del Babuino 149, 00187 Rome, Italy. Very Rev. Manuel Nin, O.S.B., Rector.

English College (Venerabile) Founded on May 1, 1579. Address: Via Monserrato 45, 00186 Rome, Italy. Rev. Msgr. Nicholas Hudson, Rector.

Irish College (Pontifical) Founded in 1628. Address: Via dei Ss. Quattro 1, 00184 Rome, Italy. Rev. Msgr. Liam Bergin, Rector.

Lithuanian College (Pontifical) Founded on May 1, 1948. Address: Via Casalmonferrato 20, 00182 Rome, Italy. Rev. Msgr. Petras Siurys, Rector.

Maronite College Founded on June 17, 1584. Address: Via Porta Pinciana 18, 00187 Rome, Italy. Rev. Hanna G. Alwan, O.M.M., Rector.

Nepomucene College (Pontifical) Address: Via Concordia 1, 00183 Rome, Italy. Rev. Msgr. Jan Mráz, Rector.

Philippine College (Pontifical) Founded on June 29, 1961. Address: Via Aurelia 490, 00165 Rome, Italy. Rev. Msgr. Ruperto C. Santos, Rector.

Dutch College (Pontifical) Founded on October 26, 1930. Address: Via Ercole Rosa 1, 00153 Rome, Italy.

Brazilian College (Pio Brasiliano) (Pontifical) Founded in 1934 by Pius XI. Address: Via Aurelia 527, 00165 Rome, Italy. Very Rev. Joao Roque Rohr. S.J., Rector.

Latin American College (Pio Latino Americano) (Pontifical) Founded November 21, 1858. Address: Via Aurelia Antica 408, 00165 Rome, Italy. Rev. José A. González Prado, S.J., Rector.

Polish College (Pontifical) Founded in 1582-84. Address: Piazza Remuria 2-A, 00153 Rome, Italy. Rev. Msgr. Tadeusz Karkosz, Rector.

Portuguese College (Pontifical) Founded on October 28, 1900. Address: Via Nicolo V 3, 00165 Rome, Italy. Rev. José Manuel Garcia Cordeiro, Rector.

AMERICAN COLLEGES ABROAD

North American College, Rome, Italy *(Pontifical)* Corporate Title: The American College of the Roman Catholic Church of the United States. A Maryland Corporation. Operates under the auspices of a special committee of the United States Conference of Catholic Bishops. President: His Eminence Cardinal Francis George. Founded in 1859 by Pope Pius IX, to bring American seminarians and student priests into close association with the Holy See. Seminarians live and take their priestly formation at the College, while studying at the theological universities in Rome. Three major departments: Seminary, Graduate and Institute for Continuing Theological Education.

Postal Address: North American College, 00120 Vatican City State, Europe. Tel: (011 39 06) 68 49 31; Administration Fax: (011 39 06) 686 7561; Business office Fax: (011 39 06) 686 4095; Email: pnac@pnac.org; Website: www.pnac.org.

Administration: Rev. Msgr. James F. Checchio, Rector; Lory Mondaini, Secretary, Office of the Rector; Rev. Msgr. Daniel H. Mueggenborg, Vice Rector for Administration and Director of Admissions; Raffaella Granellini, Secretary, Office of the Vice Rector for Administration; Sr. Susan Hooks, O.S.B., Asst. to Vice Rector for Admin. and Comptroller; Ms. Mary DiDonato, Executive Director, Institutional Advancement, Washington, D.C.

Seminary: Rev. Msgr. Robert D. Gruss, Vice Rector for Seminary Life, Director of Human Formation; Elena Panti, Secretary, Office of the Vice Rector and Office of Admissions; Maria Soggiu, Secretary, Office of the Vice Rector; Laura Panarese, Visa Coordinator; F Joseph V. Betschart, Academic Dean; Rev. Jeff Burrill, Director of Apostolic Formation; Rev. Jan Quigley, O.P., Director of Homiletics; Rev. David Songy, O.F.M.Cap., Director of Counseling Servic Rev. Kurt Belsole, O.S.B., Director of Liturgical F mation; Rev. John J. Costello, Director of Pasto Formation; Dr. Gianfranco De Luca, Director of turgical Music, Seminary Choir Director; Rev. seph G. Hanefeldt, Director of Spiritual Formati Spiritual Director; Rev. Brendan G. Lally, S.J., Sp tual Director; Rev. Brendan Hurley, S.J., Spirit Director; Rev. Msgr. William J. Lyons, Spiritual rector; Rev. Michael Hickin, Spiritual Director; F Gregory J. Fairbanks, Adjunct Spiritual Director; F Thomas W. Powers, Adjunct Spiritual Director; F Msgr. Anthony Frontiero, Adjunct Spiritual Direc Rev. Msgr. Anthony Figueiredo, Adjunct Spirit Director; Sr. Rebecca Abel, O.S.B., Librarian.

Institute for Continuing Theological Education, Fal Spring 12-week sabbatical sessions for priests. F Michael Wensing, Director of ICTE, Adjunct For tion Director, romeshabat@pnac.org; Carol Sa Secretary, Institute for Continuing Theological E cation.

Graduate Department: Casa Santa Maria, Residenc North American College for post-gradu priests. Graduate priests 72 from 42 US Dioceses from several other English speaking countries. *Po Address*: Via dell'Umiltà 30, 00187 Rome, Italy. F (011 39 06) 6900 1823. Rev. Msgr. Francis Kelly, perior, fkelly@pnac.org.

Bishops' Office for United States Visitors to the Vatic

Russian College of S. Theresa of the Child Je (Pontifical) Founded on August 15, 1929. Addre Via Carlo Cattaneo 2/A, 00185 Rome, Italy. Rev. Al Cvikl, S.J., Rector.

Ukrainian College of Saint Josephat (Pontific Founded on December 18, 1897. Address: Passeggi del Gianicolo 7, 00165 Rome, Italy. Rev. Gené Viomar, O.S.B.M., Rector.

College of St. Jerome of the Croatians (Pontific Founded on August 1, 1901. Address: Via Tomac 132, 00186 Rome, Italy. Rev. Msgr. Jure Bogdan.

St. Thomas Aquinas Founded in 1948. Address: degli Ibernesi 20, 00184 Rome, Italy. Very Rev. L Douglas Buckles, O.P., Rector.

Scots College (Pontifical) Founded on Decembe 1600. Address: Via Cassia 481, 00189 Rome, It Rev. Paul G. Milarvie, Rector.

Spanish College of St. Joseph (Pontifical) Foun on April 1, 1892. Address: Via Di Torre Rossa 00165 Rome, Italy. Very Rev. Mariano Herrera Fra Rector.

Teutonic College of St. Mary of the Soul (Pont cal Institute) Founded in 1406. Address: Via de Pace 20, 00186 Rome, Italy. Rev. Msgr. Franz Xa Brandmayr, Rector.

Teutonic College (S. Maria in Camposanto), the study of Sacred Archaeology and Ecclesi tical History Founded on November 21, 1876. dress: Via della Sagrestia 17, 00120 Citta del Vatica Europe. Rev. Msgr. Erwin Gatz, Rector.

Polish Ecclesiastical Institute (Pontifical) Foun in 1910. Address: Via Pietro Cavallini, 38, 001 Rome, Italy. Rev. Msgr. Boguslaw Kosmider, Rec

American Church Santa Susanna Address: Via Ve Settembre 15, Postal Address: Via Anto Salandra 6, 00187 Rome, Italy. Tel: 011 3 488.2748; Fax: 011 39 6 474.0236. Very Rev. P G. Robichaud, C.S.P., Rector; Rev. Greg Apparcel, C.S.P., Vice Rector; Rev. Dennis W. Hick C.S.P., Vice Rector.

Postal Address: Via dell'Umiltà 30, 00187 Rome, Italy. Tel: (011 39 06) 6900 1821; Fax: (011 39 06) 679 1448; Email: visitorsoffice@pnac.org; Website: www.pnac.org/general/visiting_vatican.htm. Request for attendance at Papal audiences and similar functions may be addressed to this office. Rev. Msgr. Roger C. Roensch, Dir.

Office for Development of the North American College, *Postal Address*: 3211 Fourth St., N.E., Washington, DC 20017-1194. Tel: 202-541-5403; Fax: 202-722-8804. E-mail: mdodinato@usccb.org. Ms. Mary DiDonato, Executive Director.

The Apostolic Nunciature

Established As Apostolic Delegation January 24, 1893; Nunciature January 10, 1984.
Address: 3339 Massachusetts Ave., N.W., Washington, DC 20008-3610. Tel: 202-333-7121. Fax: 202-337-4036.

APOSTOLIC NUNCIO TO THE UNITED STATES

His Excellency
The Most Reverend

Pietro Sambi, S.T.D., J.C.D.
Titular Archbishop of Belcastro
Apostolic Nuncio

Born in Sogliano al Rubicone, Forli, Italy, June 27, 1938; incardinated in the Diocese of San Marino-Montefeltro and ordained a priest March 14, 1964. He has a Doctorate in Sacred Theology and in Canon Law. Entered the Diplomatic Corps of the Holy See as an Attache, April 1, 1969 in Cameroon; transferred to the Apostolic Delegation in Jerusalem, July 19, 1971 and to the Apostolic Nunciature in Cuba, December 30, 1974, in Algeria, June 16, 1978, in Nicaragua, September 1, 1979, in Belgium, April 27, 1981 and in India, May 14, 1984 with the rank of Counselor. Ordained Archbishop of the Title of Belcastro, on November 9, 1985 in the Cathedral of Rimini, Italy. Nominated Apostolic Pro-Nuncio in Burundi, October 10, 1985 and in Indonesia, November 28, 1991. Nominated Apostolic Nuncio in Israel and Cyprus and Apostolic Delegate in Jerusalem and Palestine, June 6, 1998. Nominated Apostolic Nuncio in the United States and Permanent Observer to the Organization of the American States, December 17, 2005.

Rev. Msgr. Claudio Cricini, J.C.D., *Counselor*; Rev. Msgr. Marco Sprizzi, J.D., S.T.D., J.C.L., *First Secretary*; Rev. Msgr. Mauricio Rueda Beltz, J.C.D., *First Secretary.*

Rev. Msgr. John H. Maksymowicz, S.T.L., *Secretary*; Rev. Msgr. Joseph W. Pokusa, M.A., J.C.D., *Secretary*; Rev. Msgr. Richard E. Marchese, S.T.L., Ph.D., *Secretary*; Rev. Msgr. Gregory W. Gordon, S.T.L., *Secretary*; Rev. Michael McCormack, O.P., S.T.L., *Secretary*.

Former Apostolic Delegates:
His Eminence Francesco Cardinal Satolli 1893-1896
His Eminence Sebastiano Cardinal Martinelli 1896-1902
His Eminence Diomede Cardinal Falconio 1902-1911
His Eminence Giovanni Cardinal Bonzano 1911-1922
His Eminence Pietro Cardinal Fumasoni-Biondi 1922-1933
His Eminence Amleto G. Cardinal Cicognani 1933-1958
His Eminence Egidio Cardinal Vagnozzi 1958-1967
His Eminence Luigi Cardinal Raimondi 1967-1973
His Excellency Most Reverend Jean Jadot 1973-1980
His Eminence Pio Cardinal Laghi 1980-1984

Apostolic Pro-Nuncios:
His Eminence Pio Cardinal Laghi 1984-1990
His Eminence Agostino Cardinal Cacciavillan 1990-1998

Apostolic Nuncios:
His Excellency Most Reverend Gabriel Montalvo 1998-2006
His Excellency Most Reverend Pietro Sambi .... 2006—

The Permanent Observer Mission of the Holy See to the United Nations

Established January 26, 1964

Office Address: 25 E. 39th St., New York, NY 10016. Tel.: 212-370-7885; Fax: 212-370-9622.
E-mail: office@holyseemission.org. Website: www.holyseemission.org.

CONFITEBOR TIBI IN POPULIS

PERMANENT OBSERVER OF THE HOLY SEE TO THE UNITED NATIONS

His Excellency
The Most Reverend

CELESTINO MIGLIORE
Titular Archbishop of Canosa
Apostolic Nuncio

Born in Cuneo, in the Piedmont region of Italy, on July 1, 1952. Ordained a priest on June 25, 1977. Obtained a master's degree in Theology at the Center of Theological Studies in Fossano; finished his Doctorate in Canon Law at the Pontifical Lateran University; joined the Holy See's diplomatic service in 1980. Served in Angola from 1980-1984; then in Washington, D.C., serving also as an Alternate Observer to the Organization of American States. Appointed for a year at the Apostolic Nunciature in Egypt in 1988; served in Warsaw, Poland, a post he held until his appointment on April 14, 1992 as Special Envoy with the role of Permanent Observer of the Holy See to the Council of Europe in Strasbourg, France. From December 1995-October 2002, served as Under-Secretary of the Section for Relations with States of the Vatican Secretariat of State while serving for six years at the Pontifical Lateran University in Rome as Visiting Professor, teaching Ecclesiastical Diplomacy.

Appointed Apostolic Nuncio and Permanent Observer of the Holy See to the United Nations on October 30, 2002. Office Address: 25 E. 39th St., New York, NY 10016. Tel: 212-370-7885; Fax: 212-370-9622.

Rev. Msgr. Kuriakose Bharanikulangara, *Second Counselor;* Rev. Mykhaylo Tkhorovskyy, *First Secretary*; Rev. Christopher Pollard, *Attaché*; Rev. Philip J. Bené, *Attaché*.

Former Permanent Observers:

Rev. Msgr. Alberto Giovannetti	1964-1973
His Eminence Giovanni Cardinal Cheli	1973-1986
His Eminence Renato Cardinal Martino	1986-2002

The United States Embassy to the Holy See

Established United States Embassy to the Holy See January 10, 1984.

Address: Via Delle Terme Deciane, 26 00153 Rome, Italy. Tel: 011-39-06-4674-3428; Fax: 011-39-06-575-8346.
APO Address: U.S. Embassy to the Holy See, PSC 59, Box 66, APO AE 09624.

UNITED STATES AMBASSADOR TO THE HOLY SEE

Your Excellency The Honorable

DR. MIGUEL HUMBERTO DÍAZ

Ambassador Díaz, the first Hispanic to represent the United States at the Vatican earned his bachelor's degree from Saint Thomas University in Miami Gardens, FL and his master's and doctorate from the University of Notre Dame in Indiana. Prior to his appointment, Ambassador Díaz was a professor of theology at the College of Saint Benedict in St. Joseph, MN and St. John's University in Collegeville, MN. He has also taught at Barry University in Miami Shores, FL, Saint Vincent de Paul Regional Seminary in Boyton Beach, FL, the University of Dayton in Ohio and at Notre Dame. Ambassador Díaz is a board member of the Catholic Theological Society of America and former president of the Academy of Catholic Theologians of the United States. He is the author of the book "On Being Human: U.S. Hispanic and Rahnerian Perspectives" which earned him the Hispanic Theological Initiative's 2002 Book of the Year award from Princeton Theological Seminary. He is also co-editor of the book, "From the Heart of Our People" Latino Explorations in Catholic Systematic Theology."

Former Ambassadors to the Holy See:

The Honorable William A. Wilson 1984-1986
The Honorable Frank Shakespeare 1986-1989
The Honorable Thomas Patrick Melady 1989-1993
The Honorable Raymond Flynn 1993-1997
The Honorable Corinne Claiborne Boggs 1997-2001
The Honorable James Nicholson 2001-2005
The Honorable Francis Rooney 2005-2008
The Honorable Mary Ann Glendon 2008-2009

The Catholic Church in the United States

he organizational structure of the Catholic Church in the United States consists of 33 Provinces with as many Archdioceses (Metropolitan Sees); 149 Suffragan Sees (Dioceses); The Military Archdiocese; four Eastern-Rite jurisdictions immediately subject to the Holy See in Rome. The Eparchies of St. Maron (Maronites), Newton (Melkites), St. Thomas the Apostle of Detroit (Chaldeans) and St. George Martyr of Canton, Ohio (Romanians), St. Thomas of Chicago of the Syro-Malabarians. Each of these jurisdictions is under the direction of an Archbishop and Bishop called an Ordinary, who has apostolic responsibility and authority for the pastoral service of the people in his care.

he structure includes the territorial episcopal conference known as the United States Conference of Catholic Bishops. In and through this body, which is strictly ecclesiastical and has defined juridical authority, the Bishops exercise their collegiate pastorate over the Church in the entire country.

elated to the USCCB is the civil corporation and operational secretariat through which the Bishops, in cooperation with other members of the Church, act on a wider-than-ecclesiastical scale for the good of the Church and society in the United States.

The following is a list of the thirteen regions in the United States and provinces within those regions.

Region I: Includes the states of Maine, Vermont, New Hampshire, Massachusetts, Rhode Island, and Connecticut. Provinces of Boston and Hartford; Eparchy of Stamford and Eparchy for Melkites.

Region II: Includes the state of New York. Province of New York and Eparchy of St. Maron.

Region III: Includes the states of New Jersey and Pennsylvania. Provinces of Newark and Philadelphia; Archeparchy of Philadelphia, Ukrainian Archeparchy of Pittsburgh, Byzantine Eparchy of Passaic, and Eparchy of Our Lady of Nareg for Armenian Catholics.

Region IV: Includes the states of Delaware, District of Columbia, Maryland, Virgin Islands, Virginia and West Virginia. Provinces of Baltimore, Washington, and the Military Archdiocese.

Region V: Includes the states of Alabama, Kentucky, Louisiana, Mississippi and Tennessee. Provinces of Louisville, Mobile and New Orleans.

Region VI: Includes the states of Michigan and Ohio. Provinces of Cincinnati, Detroit; Eparchy of Parma, Apostolic Exarchate for Chaldeans, and Apostolic Exarchate for Romanians.

Region VII: Includes the states of Illinois, Indiana and Wisconsin. Provinces of Chicago, Indianapolis, Milwaukee; Eparchy of St. Nicholas in Chicago-Ukrainian.

Region VIII: Includes the states of Minnesota, North Dakota and South Dakota. Provinces of St. Paul and Minneapolis.

Region IX: Includes the states of Kansas, Missouri and Nebraska. Provinces of Dubuque, Kansas City in Kansas, Omaha and St. Louis.

Region X: Includes the states of Arkansas, Oklahoma and Texas (excluding El Paso). Provinces of Galveston-Houston, Oklahoma City and San Antonio.

Region XI: Includes the states of California, Hawaii and Nevada. Provinces of Los Angeles and San Francisco (excluding Salt Lake City); Eparchy of Van Nuys.

Region XII: Includes the states of Alaska, Idaho, Montana, Oregon and Washington. Provinces of Anchorage, Portland and Seattle.

Region XIII: Includes the states of Utah, Arizona, New Mexico, Colorado and Wyoming. Provinces of Denver, Santa Fe, part of San Francisco, Salt Lake City, and El Paso.

Region XIV: Includes the states of Georgia, North and South Carolina and Florida. Provinces of Atlanta and Miami.

lease refer to individual Diocesan and Archdiocesan listing for complete and detailed information. The following list does not include the retired Archbishops or retired Bishops.

PROVINCE OF ANCHORAGE

ncludes the State of Alaska.

rchdiocese of Anchorage, AK—Most. Rev. Roger L. Schwietz, O.M.I., Archbishop of Anchorage.

iocese of Fairbanks, AK—Most Rev. Donald J. Kettler, Bishop of Fairbanks.

iocese of Juneau, AK—Most Rev. Edward J. Burns, Bishop of Juneau.

PROVINCE OF ATLANTA

ncludes the States of Georgia, North Carolina and South Carolina.

rchdiocese of Atlanta, GA—Most Rev. Wilton D. Gregory, Archbishop of Atlanta. Most Rev. Luis R. Zarama, Auxiliary Bishop.

iocese of Charleston, SC—Most Rev. Robert E. Guglielmone, Bishop of Charleston.

iocese of Charlotte, NC—Most Rev. Peter J. Jugis, Bishop of Charlotte.

iocese of Raleigh, NC—Most Rev. Michael F. Burbidge, Bishop of Raleigh.

iocese of Savannah, GA—Most Rev. J. Kevin Boland, Bishop of Savannah.

PROVINCE OF BALTIMORE

ncludes the States of Maryland (except Montgomery, Prince Charles, St. Mary's, Calvert and Charles Counties), Delaware, Virginia and West Virginia.

rchdiocese of Baltimore, MD—Most Rev. Edwin F. O'Brien, Archbishop of Baltimore. Most Rev. Mitchell T. Rozanski, Auxiliary Bishop. Most Rev. Denis J. Madden, Auxiliary Bishop.

iocese of Arlington, VA—Most Rev. Paul S. Loverde, Bishop of Arlington.

iocese of Richmond, VA— Most Rev. Francis X. DiLorenzo, Bishop of Richmond.

iocese of Wheeling-Charleston, WV—Most Rev. Michael J. Bransfield, Bishop of Wheeling-Charleston.

iocese of Wilmington, DE—Most Rev. W. Francis Malooly, Bishop of Wilmington.

PROVINCE OF BOSTON

ncludes the States of Maine, New Hampshire, Vermont and Massachusetts.

rchdiocese of Boston, MA—His Eminence Sean Patrick Cardinal O'Malley, O.F.M.Cap., Archbishop of Boston. Most Rev. Walter J. Edyvean, Auxiliary Bishop. Most Rev. Emilio Allue, S.D.B., Auxiliary Bishop. Most Rev. John A. Dooher, Auxiliary Bishop. Most Rev. Robert F. Hennessey, Auxiliary Bishop.

iocese of Burlington, VT—Most Rev. Salvatore R. Matano, Bishop of Burlington.

Diocese of Fall River, MA—Most Rev. George W. Coleman, Bishop of Fall River.

Diocese of Manchester, NH—Most Rev. John B. McCormack, Bishop of Manchester. Most Rev. Francis J. Christian, Auxiliary Bishop.

Diocese of Portland, ME— Most Rev. Richard J. Malone, Bishop of Portland.

Diocese of Springfield, MA—Most Rev. Timothy A. McDonnell, Bishop of Springfield in Massachusetts.

Diocese of Worcester, MA—Most Rev. Robert J. McManus, Bishop of Worcester.

PROVINCE OF CHICAGO

Includes the State of Illinois.

Archdiocese of Chicago, IL—His Eminence Francis Cardinal George, O.M.I., Archbishop of Chicago. Most Rev. John R. Manz, Auxiliary Bishop. Most Rev. Joseph N. Perry, Auxiliary Bishop. Most Rev. Francis J. Kane, Auxiliary Bishop. Most Rev. Thomas J. Paprocki, Auxiliary Bishop. Most Rev. Gustavo Garcia-Siller, M.Sp.S., Auxiliary Bishop. Most Rev. George J. Rassas, Auxiliary Bishop.

Diocese of Belleville, IL—Most Rev. Edward K. Braxton, Bishop of Belleville.

Diocese of Joliet, IL—Most Rev. James P. Sartain, Bishop of Joliet. Most Rev. Joseph M. Siegel Auxiliary Bishop.

Diocese of Peoria, IL— Most Rev. Daniel R. Jenky, C.S.C., Bishop of Peoria.

Diocese of Rockford, IL—Most Rev. Thomas G. Doran, Bishop of Rockford.

Diocese of Springfield, IL—Vacant See.

PROVINCE OF CINCINNATI

Includes the State of Ohio.

Archdiocese of Cincinnati, OH—Most Rev. Dennis M. Schnurr, Archbishop of Cincinnati.

Diocese of Cleveland, OH—Most Rev. Richard Gerard Lennon, Bishop of Cleveland. Most Rev. Roger W. Gries, O.S.B., Auxiliary Bishop.

Diocese of Columbus, OH—Most Rev. Frederick F. Campbell, Bishop of Columbus.

Diocese of Steubenville, OH—Most Rev. R. Daniel Conlon, Bishop of Steubenville.

Diocese of Toledo, OH—Most Rev. Leonard P. Blair, Bishop of Toledo.

Diocese of Youngstown, OH—Most Rev. George V. Murry, S.J., Bishop of Youngstown.

PROVINCE OF DENVER

Includes the States of Colorado and Wyoming.

Archdiocese of Denver, CO—Most Rev. Charles J. Chaput, O.F.M.Cap., Archbishop of Denver. Most Rev. James D. Conley, Auxiliary Bishop.

Diocese of Cheyenne, WY—Most Rev. Paul D. Etienne, Bishop of Cheyenne.

Diocese of Colorado Springs, CO—Most Rev. Michael J. Sheridan, Bishop of Colorado Springs.

Diocese of Pueblo, CO—Most Rev. Fernando Isern, Bishop of Pueblo.

PROVINCE OF DETROIT

Includes the State of Michigan.

Archdiocese of Detroit, MI—Most Rev. Allen H. Vigneron, Archbishop of Detroit. Most Rev. Francis R. Reiss, Auxiliary Bishop.

Diocese of Gaylord, MI—Most Rev. Bernard A. Hebda, Bishop of Gaylord.

Diocese of Grand Rapids, MI—Most Rev. Walter A. Hurley, Bishop of Grand Rapids.

Diocese of Kalamazoo, MI—Most Rev. Paul J. Bradley, Bishop of Kalamazoo.

Diocese of Lansing, MI—Most Rev. Earl A. Boyea, Bishop of Lansing.

Diocese of Marquette, MI—Most Rev. Alexander K. Sample, Bishop of Marquette.

Diocese of Saginaw, MI—Most Rev. Joseph R. Cistone, Bishop of Saginaw.

PROVINCE OF DUBUQUE

Includes the State of Iowa.

Archdiocese of Dubuque, IA—Most Rev. Jerome Hanus, O.S.B., Archbishop of Dubuque.

Diocese of Davenport, IA—Most Rev. Martin J. Amos, Bishop of Davenport.

Diocese of Des Moines, IA—Most Rev. Richard E. Pates, Bishop of Des Moines.

Diocese of Sioux City, IA—Most Rev. R. Walker Nickless, Bishop of Sioux City.

PROVINCE OF GALVESTON-HOUSTON

Includes the State of Texas except Atascosa, Bandera, Bexar, Comal, Edwards, Frio, Gillespie, Gonzales, Guadalupe, Karnes, Kendall, Kerr, Kinney, McMullen, Medina, Real, Uvalde, Val Verde and Wilson Counties.

Archdiocese of Galveston-Houston, TX—His Eminence Daniel Cardinal DiNardo, Archbishop of Galveston-Houston.

Diocese of Austin, TX— Most Rev. Joe S. Vasquez, Bishop of Austin.

Diocese of Beaumont, TX—Most Rev. Curtis John Guillory, S.V.D., Bishop of Beaumont.

Diocese of Brownsville, TX—Most Rev. Daniel E. Flores, Bishop of Brownsville.

Diocese of Corpus Christi, TX—Most Rev. William M. Mulvey, Bishop of Corpus Christi.

Diocese of Tyler, TX— Most Rev. Alvaro Corrada del Rio, S.J., Bishop of Tyler.

Diocese of Victoria, TX—Most Rev. David E. Fellhauer, Bishop of Victoria in Texas.

PROVINCE OF HARTFORD

Includes the States of Connecticut and Rhode Island.

Archdiocese of Hartford, CT—Most Rev. Henry J. Mansell, Archbishop of Hartford. Most Rev. Peter A. Rosazza, Auxiliary Bishop. Most Rev. Christie A. Macaluso, Auxiliary Bishop.

Diocese of Bridgeport, CT—Most Rev. William E. Lori, Bishop of Bridgeport.
Diocese of Norwich, CT—Most Rev. Michael R. Cote, Bishop of Norwich.
Diocese of Providence, RI—Most Rev. Thomas J. Tobin, Bishop of Providence. Most Rev. Robert C. Evans, Auxiliary Bishop.

PROVINCE OF INDIANAPOLIS

Includes the State of Indiana.
Archdiocese of Indianapolis, IN—Most Rev. Daniel Mark Buechlein, O.S.B., Archbishop of Indianapolis.
Diocese of Evansville, IN—Most Rev. Gerald Andrew Gettelfinger, Bishop of Evansville.
Diocese of Fort Wayne-South Bend, IN—Most Rev. Kevin C. Rhoades, Bishop of Fort Wayne-South Bend.
Diocese of Gary, IN—Most Rev. Dale J. Melczek, Bishop of Gary.
Diocese of Lafayette in Indiana, IN—Most Rev. William L. Higi, Bishop of Lafayette in Indiana.

PROVINCE OF KANSAS CITY, KANSAS

Includes the State of Kansas.
Archdiocese of Kansas City, KS—Most Rev. Joseph F. Naumann, Archbishop of Kansas City.
Diocese of Dodge City, KS—Most Rev. Ronald M. Gilmore, Bishop of Dodge City.
Diocese of Salina, KS—Most Rev. Paul S. Coakley, Bishop of Salina.
Diocese of Wichita, KS—Most Rev. Michael Owen Jackels, Bishop of Wichita.

PROVINCE OF LOS ANGELES

Includes Southern California and Central California.
Archdiocese of Los Angeles, CA—His Eminence Roger Cardinal Mahony, Archbishop of Los Angeles. Most Rev. Jose Horacio Gomez, Coadjutor Archbishop of Los Angeles. Most Rev. Thomas J. Curry, Auxiliary Bishop. Most Rev. Gabino Zavala, Auxiliary Bishop. Most Rev. Gerald E. Wilkerson, Auxiliary Bishop. Most Rev. Edward W. Clark, Auxiliary Bishop. Most Rev. Oscar Azarcon Solis, Auxiliary Bishop. Most Rev. Alexander Salazar, Auxiliary Bishop.
Diocese of Fresno, CA—Most Rev. John T. Steinbock, Bishop of Fresno.
Diocese of Monterey, CA—Most Rev. Richard J. Garcia, Bishop of Monterey.
Diocese of Orange, CA—Most Rev. Tod David Brown, Bishop of Orange in California. Most Rev. Dominic Mai Luong, Auxiliary Bishop. Most Rev. Cirilo Flores, Auxiliary Bishop.
Diocese of San Bernardino, CA—Most Rev. Gerald R. Barnes, Bishop of San Bernardino. Most Rev. Rutilio del Riego, Auxiliary Bishop.
Diocese of San Diego, CA—Most Rev. Robert H. Brom, Bishop of San Diego.

PROVINCE OF LOUISVILLE

Includes the States of Kentucky and Tennessee.
Archdiocese of Louisville, KY—Most Rev. Joseph E. Kurtz, Archbishop of Louisville.
Diocese of Covington, KY—Most Rev. Roger J. Foys, Bishop of Covington.
Diocese of Knoxville, TN—Most Rev. Richard F. Stika, Bishop of Knoxville.
Diocese of Lexington, KY—Most Rev. Ronald W. Gainer, Bishop of Lexington.
Diocese of Memphis, TN—Most Rev. J. Terry Steib, S.V.D., Bishop of Memphis.
Diocese of Nashville, TN—Most Rev. David R. Choby, Bishop of Nashville.
Diocese of Owensboro, KY—William F. Medley, Bishop of Owensboro.

PROVINCE OF MIAMI

Includes the State of Florida.
Archdiocese of Miami, FL—Most Rev. John C. Favalora, Archbishop of Miami. Most Rev. Felipe de Jesus Estevez, Auxiliary Bishop. Most Rev. John G. Noonan, Auxiliary Bishop.
Diocese of Orlando, FL—Most Rev. Thomas G. Wenski, Bishop of Orlando.
Diocese of Palm Beach, FL—Most Rev. Gerald M. Barbarito, Bishop of Palm Beach.
Diocese of Pensacola-Tallahassee, FL—Most Rev. John H. Ricard, S.S.J., Bishop of Pensacola-Tallahassee.
Diocese of St. Augustine, FL—Most Rev. Victor Benito Galeone, Bishop of St. Augustine.
Diocese of St. Petersburg, FL—Most Rev. Robert N. Lynch, Bishop of St. Petersburg.
Diocese of Venice, FL—Most Rev. Frank J. Dewane, Bishop of Venice.

PROVINCE OF MILWAUKEE

Includes the State of Wisconsin.
Archdiocese of Milwaukee, WI—Most Rev. Jerome E. Listecki, Archbishop of Milwaukee. Most Rev. Richard J. Sklba, Auxiliary Bishop. Most Rev. William P. Callahan, Auxiliary Bishop.
Diocese of Green Bay, WI—Most Rev. David L. Ricken, Bishop of Green Bay. Most Rev. Robert F. Morneau, Auxiliary Bishop.
Diocese of La Crosse, WI—Vacant See.
Diocese of Madison, WI—Most Rev. Robert C. Morlino, Bishop of Madison.
Diocese of Superior, WI—Most Rev. Peter F. Christensen, Bishop of Superior.

PROVINCE OF MOBILE

Includes the states of Alabama and Mississippi.
Archdiocese of Mobile, AL—Most Rev. Thomas J. Rodi, Archbishop of Mobile.
Diocese of Biloxi, MS—Most Rev. Roger P. Morin, Bishop of Biloxi.
Diocese of Birmingham, AL—Most Rev. Robert J. Baker, Bishop of Birmingham.
Diocese of Jackson MS—Most Rev. Joseph N. Latino, Bishop of Jackson.

PROVINCE OF NEWARK

Includes the State of New Jersey.
Archdiocese of Newark, NJ—Most Rev. John J. Myers, Archbishop of Newark. Most Rev. Edgar M. da Cunha, S.D.V., Auxiliary Bishop. Most Rev. Thomas A. Donato, Auxiliary Bishop. Most Rev. John W. Flesey, Auxiliary Bishop. Most Rev. Manuel A. Cruz, Auxiliary Bishop.
Diocese of Camden, NJ—Most Rev. Joseph A. Galante, Bishop of Camden.
Diocese of Metuchen, NJ—Most Rev. Paul G. Bootkoski, Bishop of Metuchen.
Diocese of Paterson, NJ—Most Rev. Arthur J. Serratelli, Bishop of Paterson.
Diocese of Trenton, NJ—Most Rev. John M. Smith, Bishop of Trenton.

PROVINCE OF NEW ORLEANS

Includes the State of Louisiana.
Archdiocese of New Orleans, LA—Most Rev. Gregory M. Aymond, Archbishop of New Orleans. Most Rev. Shelton J. Fabre, Auxiliary Bishop.
Diocese of Alexandria, LA—Most Rev. Ronald P. Herzog, Bishop of Alexandria.
Diocese of Baton Rouge, LA—Most Rev. Robert William Muench, Bishop of Baton Rouge.
Diocese of Houma-Thibodaux, LA—Most Rev. Sam G. Jacobs, Bishop of Houma-Thibodaux.
Diocese of Lafayette, LA—Most Rev. Michael C. Jarrell, Bishop of Lafayette.
Diocese of Lake Charles, LA—Most Rev. Glen J. Provost, Bishop of Lake Charles.
Diocese of Shreveport, LA —Most Rev. Michael G. Duca, Bishop of Shreveport.

PROVINCE OF NEW YORK

Includes the State of New York.
Archdiocese of New York, NY—Most Rev. Timothy M. Dolan, Archbishop of New York. Most Rev. Josu Iriondo, Auxiliary Bishop. Most Rev. Dominick J. Lagonegro, Auxiliary Bishop. Most Rev. Dennis J. Sullivan, Auxiliary Bishop. Most Rev. Gerald T. Walsh, Auxiliary Bishop.
Diocese of Albany, NY—Most Rev. Howard J. Hubbard, Bishop of Albany.
Diocese of Brooklyn, NY—Most Rev. Nicholas A. DiMarzio, Bishop of Brooklyn. Most Rev. Ignatius Catanello, Auxiliary Bishop. Most Rev. Guy Sansaricq, Auxiliary Bishop. Most Rev. Frank J. Caggiano, Auxiliary Bishop. Most Rev. Octavio Cisneros, Auxiliary Bishop.
Diocese of Buffalo, NY—Most Rev. Edward U. Kmiec, Bishop of Buffalo. Most Rev. Edward M. Grosz, Auxiliary Bishop.
Diocese of Ogdensburg, NY—Most Rev. Terry R. LaValley, Bishop of Ogdensburg.
Diocese of Rochester, NY—Most Rev. Matthew H. Clar Bishop of Rochester.
Diocese of Rockville Centre, NY—Most Rev. Willia Francis Murphy, Bishop of Rockville Centre. Mo Rev. John C. Dunne, Auxiliary Bishop. Most Rev. Pa H. Walsh, Auxiliary Bishop. Most Rev. Peter Libasci, Auxiliary Bishop.
Diocese of Syracuse, NY—Most Rev. Robert Cunningham, Bishop of Syracuse.

PROVINCE OF OKLAHOMA CITY

Includes States of Arkansas and Oklahoma.
Archdiocese of Oklahoma City, OK—Most Rev. Eusebi J. Beltran, Archbishop of Oklahoma City.
Diocese of Little Rock, AR—Most Rev. Anthony Bas Taylor, Bishop of Little Rock.
Diocese of Tulsa, OK—Most Rev. Edward J. Slatter Bishop of Tulsa.

PROVINCE OF OMAHA

Includes the State of Nebraska.
Archdiocese of Omaha, NE—Most Rev. George J. Luca Archbishop of Omaha.
Diocese of Grand Island, NE—Most Rev. William Dendinger, Bishop of Grand Island.
Diocese of Lincoln, NE—Most Rev. Fabian W. Bruskewit Bishop of Lincoln.

PROVINCE OF PHILADELPHIA

Includes the State of Pennsylvania.
Archdiocese of Philadelphia, PA—His Eminence Justi Cardinal Rigali, Archbishop of Philadelphia. Most Re Robert P. Maginnis, Auxiliary Bishop. Most Rev. J seph P. McFadden, Auxiliary Bishop. Most Rev. Dani E. Thomas, Auxiliary Bishop. Most Rev. Timoth Senior, Auxiliary Bishop.
Diocese of Allentown, PA—Most Rev. John O. Barre Bishop of Allentown.
Diocese of Altoona-Johnstown, PA—Most Rev. Josep V. Adamec, Bishop of Altoona-Johnstown.
Diocese of Erie, PA—Most Rev. Donald W. Trautma Bishop of Erie.
Diocese of Greensburg, PA—Most Rev. Lawrence Brandt, Bishop of Greensburg.
Diocese of Harrisburg, PA—Vacant See.
Diocese of Pittsburgh, PA—Most Rev. David A. Zubi Bishop of Pittsburgh.
Diocese of Scranton, PA—Most Rev. Joseph C. Bamber Bishop of Scranton.

PROVINCE OF PORTLAND IN OREGON

Includes the States of Oregon, Idaho and Montana.
Archdiocese of Portland, OR—Most Rev. John G. Vlazn Archbishop of Portland in Oregon. Most Rev. Ke neth D. Steiner, Auxiliary Bishop.
Diocese of Baker, OR—Most Rev. Robert Francis Vas Bishop of Baker.
Diocese of Boise, ID—Most Rev. Michael P. Drisco Bishop of Boise.
Diocese of Great Falls-Billings, MT—Most Rev. Micha W. Warfel, Bishop of Great Falls-Billings.
Diocese of Helena, MT— Most Rev. George Leo Th mas, Bishop of Helena.

PROVINCE OF ST. LOUIS

Includes the State of Missouri.
Archdiocese of St. Louis, MO—Most Rev. Robert Carlson, Archbishop of St. Louis. Most Rev. Robert Hermann, Auxiliary Bishop.
Diocese of Jefferson City, MO—Most Rev. John Raymor Gaydos, Bishop of Jefferson City.
Diocese of Kansas City-St. Joseph, MO—Most Rev. Ro ert W. Finn, Bishop of Kansas City-St. Joseph.
Diocese of Springfield-Cape Girardeau, MO—Most Re J. Vann Johnston, Jr., Bishop of Springfield-Cap Girardeau.

PROVINCE OF ST. PAUL AND MINNEAPOLIS

Includes the States of Minnesota, South Dakota and Nor Dakota.
Archdiocese of St. Paul and Minneapolis, MN—Mo Rev. John C. Nienstedt, Archbishop of St. Paul ar Minneapolis. Most Rev. Lee A. Piche, Auxiliary Bisho
Diocese of Bismarck, ND—Most Rev. Paul A. Zipfe Bishop of Bismarck.
Diocese of Crookston, MN—Most Rev. Michael Hoeppner, Bishop of Crookston.
Diocese of Duluth, MN—Most Rev. Paul D. Sirba, Bisho of Duluth.

ɔcese of Fargo, ND—Most Rev. Samuel J. Aquila, Bishop of Fargo.
ɔcese of New Ulm, MN—Most Rev. John M. LeVoir, Bishop of New Ulm.
ɔcese of Rapid City, SD—Most Rev. Blase J. Cupich, Bishop of Rapid City.
ɔcese of St. Cloud, MN—Most Rev. John F. Kinney, Bishop of St. Cloud.
ɔcese of Sioux Falls, SD—Most Rev. Paul J. Swain, Bishop of Sioux Falls.
ɔcese of Winona, MN—Most Rev. John M. Quinn, Bishop of Winona.

PROVINCE OF SAN ANTONIO

cludes the State of Texas except Walker, San Jacinto, Galveston, Grimes, Montgomery, Waller, Harris, Fort Bend, Brazoria and Austin Counties.
chdiocese of San Antonio, TX—Vacant See. Most Rev. Oscar Cantu, Auxiliary Bishop.
ɔcese of Amarillo, TX—Most Rev. Patrick J. Zurek, Bishop of Amarillo.
ɔcese of Dallas, TX—Most Rev. Kevin J. Farrell, Bishop of Dallas. Most Rev. John D. Deshotel, Auxiliary Bishop. Most Rev. Mark J. Seitz, Auxiliary Bishop.
ɔcese of El Paso, TX—Most Rev. Armando X. Ochoa, Bishop of El Paso.
ɔcese of Fort Worth, TX—Most Rev. Kevin W. Vann, Bishop of Fort Worth.
ɔcese of Laredo, TX—Most Rev. James A. Tamayo, Bishop of Laredo.
ɔcese of Lubbock, TX—Most Rev. Placido Rodriguez, C.M.F., Bishop of Lubbock.
ɔcese of San Angelo, TX—Most Rev. Michael D. Pfeifer, O.M.I., Bishop of San Angelo.

PROVINCE OF SAN FRANCISCO

cludes Northern California and the States of Nevada, Utah and Hawaii.
chdiocese of San Francisco, CA—Most Rev. George H. Niederauer, Archbishop of San Francisco. Most Rev. William J. Justice, Auxiliary Bishop.
ɔcese of Honolulu, HI—Most Rev. Clarence R. Silva, Bishop of Honolulu.
ɔcese of Las Vegas, NV—Most Rev. Joseph A. Pepe, Bishop of Las Vegas.
ɔcese of Oakland, CA—Most Rev. Salvatore J. Cordileone, Bishop of Oakland.
ɔcese of Reno, NV—Most Rev. Randolph R. Calvo, Bishop of Reno.
ɔcese of Sacramento, CA—Most Rev. Jaime Soto, Bishop of Sacramento.
ɔcese of Salt Lake City, UT—Most Rev. John C. Wester, Bishop of Salt Lake City.
ɔcese of San Jose, CA—Most Rev. Patrick J. McGrath, Bishop of San Jose in California.
ɔcese of Santa Rosa, CA—Most Rev. Daniel F. Walsh, Bishop of Santa Rosa in California.
Diocese of Stockton, CA—Most Rev. Stephen E. Blaire, Bishop of Stockton.

P-ROVINCE OF SANTA FE

Includes the States of New Mexico and Arizona.
Archdiocese of Santa Fe, NM—Most Rev. Michael J. Sheehan, Archbishop of Santa Fe.
Diocese of Gallup, NM—Most Rev. James S. Wall, Bishop of Gallup.
Diocese of Las Cruces, NM—Most Rev. Ricardo Ramirez, C.S.B., Bishop of Las Cruces.
Diocese of Phoenix, AZ—Most Rev. Thomas J. Olmsted, Bishop of Phoenix.
Diocese of Tucson, AZ—Most Rev. Gerald F. Kicanas, Bishop of Tucson.

PROVINCE OF SEATTLE

Includes the State of Washington.
Archdiocese of Seattle, WA—Most Rev. Alexander J. Brunett, Archbishop of Seattle. Most Rev. Eusebio L. Elizondo, M.Sp.S., Auxiliary Bishop. Most Rev. Joseph J. Tyson, Auxiliary Bishop.
Diocese of Spokane, WA—Most Rev. William S. Skylstad, Bishop of Spokane.
Diocese of Yakima, WA—Most Rev. Carlos A. Sevilla, S.J., Bishop of Yakima.

PROVINCE OF WASHINGTON

Includes the District of Columbia, and Montgomery, Prince Georges, Charles, Calvert and St. Mary's Counties in Maryland, also Virgin Islands.
Archdiocese of Washington, DC—Most Rev. Donald W. Wuerl, Archbishop of Washington. Most Rev. Martin D. Holley, Auxiliary Bishop. Most Rev. Francisco Gonzalez, S.F., Auxiliary Bishop. Most Rev. Barry C. Knestout, Auxiliary Bishop.
Diocese of St. Thomas, V.I.—Most Rev. Herbert A. Bevard, Bishop of St. Thomas in the Virgin Islands.
Archdiocese for the Military Services—Most Rev. Timothy P. Broglio, Archbishop for the Military Services. Most Rev. Richard B. Higgins, Auxiliary Bishop. Most Rev. Joseph W. Estabrook, Auxiliary Bishop.

EASTERN CATHOLIC JURISDICTIONS

ANTIOCHENE TRADITION

Maronite Rite—
Eparchy of St. Maron of Brooklyn—Most Rev. Gregory J. Mansour, Bishop of St. Maron.
Eparchy of Our Lady of Lebanon of Los Angeles—Most Rev. Robert J. Shaheen, Bishop of Our Lady of Lebanon of Los Angeles.

Syrian Rite—
Diocese of Our Lady of Deliverance—Most Rev. Yousif Habash, Bishop of Our Lady of Deliverance.

ARMENIAN TRADITION

Armenian Catholic Eparchy of Our Lady of Nareg in the United States of America and Canada—Most Rev. Manuel Batakian, Armenian Catholic Eparch of Our Lady of Nareg.

CHALDEAN TRADITION

Eparchy of St. Thomas the Apostle—Most Rev. Ibrahim N. Ibrahim, Eparch of St. Thomas the Apostle.
Eparchy of St. Peter the Apostle—Most Rev. Sarhad Y. Jammo, Eparch of St. Peter the Apostle.

CONSTANTINOPOLITAN TRADITION

Melkite - Greek Rite—
Eparchy of Newton—Most Rev. Cyrille S. Bustros, S.M.S.P., Eparch of Newton.

Romanian Rite—
Romanian Catholic Diocese of St. George's in Canton—Most Rev. John Michael Botean, Bishop for the Romanian Catholic Diocese of Canton.

Ruthenian Rite—
Metropolitan Archbishop for Pittsburgh Byzantine—Most Rev. Basil M. Schott, O.F.M., Metropolitan Archbishop for Pittsburgh, Byzantine.
Byzantine Eparchy of Parma—Most Rev. John M. Kudrick, Bishop of Parma.
Byzantine Catholic Eparchy of Passaic—Most Rev. William C. Skurla, Bishop of Passaic.
Byzantine Eparchy of Van Nuys—Most Rev. Gerald N. Dino, Bishop of Van Nuys.

Russian Rite—
Two parishes—

Ukrainian Rite—
Metropolitan Archdiocese of Philadelphia Ukrainian—Most Rev. Stefan Soroka, Archbishop of Philadelphia Ukrainian. Most Rev. John Bura, Auxiliary Bishop.
Ukrainian Catholic Diocese of St. Josaphat in Parma—Vacant See. Most Rev. John Bura, Apostolic Administrator of St. Josaphat in Parma.
Diocese of St. Nicholas in Chicago for Ukrainians—Most Rev. Richard S. Seminack, Bishop of St. Nicholas of Chicago.
Ukrainian Catholic Diocese of Stamford—Most Rev. Paul Patrick Chomnycky, O.S.B.M., Bishop of Stamford.

Syro-Malabar—
St. Thomas Syro-Malabar Catholic Diocese of Chicago—Most Rev. Jacob Angadiath, Bishop of St. Thomas Syro-Malabar.

ECCLESIASTICAL FORMS OF ADDRESS RECOGNIZED IN THE UNITED STATES

These are the formal forms of address used in correspondence:

CARDINALS:

Address on envelope: His Eminence (Christian name) Cardinal (Surname)

Salutation: Your Eminence:

Concluding a letter: I have the honor to be, Your Eminence, *etc.*

ARCHBISHOPS:

Address on envelope: Most Reverend N_______ N_______

Salutation: Your Excellency:

Concluding a letter: I have the honor to be, Your Excellency, *etc.*

BISHOPS:

Address on envelope: Most Reverend N_______ N_______

Salutation: Your Excellency:

Concluding a letter: I have the honor to be, Your Excellency, *etc.*

ABBOTS:

Address on envelope: Right Reverend N_______ N_______ *(add religious order initials)*

Salutation: Right Reverend Abbot:

Concluding a letter: I have the honor to be, Right Reverend Abbot, *etc.*

PROTONOTARIES APOSTOLIC:

Address on envelope: Rev. Msgr. N_______ N_______

Salutation: Rev. Msgr.:

Concluding a letter: I am, Rev. Msgr., *etc.*

PRELATE OF HONOR OF HIS HOLINESS:

Address on envelope: Rev. Msgr. N_______ N_______

Salutation: Rev. Msgr.:

Concluding a letter: I am, Rev. Msgr., *etc.*

CHAPLAIN TO HIS HOLINESS:

Address on envelope: Rev. Msgr. N_______ N_______

Salutation: Rev. Msgr.:

Concluding a letter: I am, Rev. Msgr., *etc.*

SECULAR PRIESTS:

Address on envelope: Rev. N_______ N_______

Salutation: Dear Reverend Father:

Concluding a letter: I am, Reverend Father, *etc.*

RELIGIOUS ORDER PRIESTS:

Address on envelope: Rev. N_______ N_______ *(add religious order initials)*

Salutation: Dear Reverend Father:

Concluding a letter: I am, Reverend Father, *etc.*

DEACONS:

Address on envelope: Deacon N_______

Salutation: Dear Deacon N_______

Concluding a letter: I am, Respectfully yours, *etc.*

BROTHERS:

Address on envelope: Brother N_______

Salutation: Dear Brother N_______

Concluding a letter: I am, Respectfully yours, *etc.*

SISTERS:

Address on envelope: Sister N_______

Salutation: Dear Sister N_______

Concluding a letter: I am, Respectfully yours, *etc.*

AN ALPHABETICAL LIST OF THE

Cardinals, Archbishops, Bishops, Archabbots & Abbots of the United States

CARDINALS

His Eminence Luis Aponte Martinez, Archbishop emeritus of San Juan, P.O. Box 9021967, San Juan, PR 00902-1967.
His Eminence William W. Baum, Major Penitentiary emeritus, Via Rusticucci 13, 00193 Rome, Italy.
His Eminence Anthony J. Bevilacqua, Archbishop emeritus of Philadelphia, St. Charles Borromeo Seminary, 100 E. Wynnewood Rd., Wynnewood, PA 19096.
His Eminence Daniel N. DiNardo, Archbishop of Galveston-Houston, 1700 San Jacinto St., Houston, TX 77002.
His Eminence Edward M. Egan, Archbishop emeritus of New York, 1011 First Ave., New York, NY 10022.
His Eminence Francis E. George, o.m.i., Archbishop of Chicago, 835 N. Rush St., Chicago, IL 60611-2030.
His Eminence William H. Keeler, Archbishop emeritus of Baltimore, 320 Cathedral St., Baltimore, MD 21201.
His Eminence Bernard F. Law, Archbishop emeritus of Boston, Archpriest of the Patriarchal Liberian Basilica of St. Mary Major, Patriarcale Basilica Liberiana di Santa Maria Maggiore, 00120 Vatican City.
His Eminence, William J. Levada, Prefect, Congregation for the Doctrine of the Faith, Palazzo del S. Uffizio, 00120 Vatican City State.
His Eminence Roger M. Mahony, Archbishop of Los Angeles, 3424 Wilshire Blvd., Los Angeles, CA 90010-2241.
His Eminence Adam J. Maida, Archbishop emeritus of Detroit, 1234 Washington Blvd., Detroit, MI 48226.
His Eminence Theodore E. McCarrick, Archbishop emeritus of Washington, DC, P.O. Box 29260, Washington, DC 20017.
His Eminence Sean P. O'Malley, o.f.m.cap., Archbishop of Boston, 66 Brooks Dr., Braintree, MA 02184-3839.
His Eminence Justin F. Rigali, Archbishop of Philadelphia, 222 N. 17th St., Philadelphia, PA 19103.
His Eminence J. Francis Stafford, Major Penitentiary, Piazza S. Calisto 16, Vatican City State, Europe 00120.
His Eminence Edmund C. Szoka, President emeritus Pontifical Commission, Vatican City State, Europe. 00120.

ARCHBISHOPS

is Excellency,
The Most Reverend

puron, Anthony Sablan, o.f.m.cap., Archbishop of Agana, 196-B Cuesta San Ramon, Agana, Guam 96910.
ymond, Gregory M., Archbishop of New Orleans, 7887 Walmsley Ave., New Orleans, LA 70125.
eltran, Eusebius J., Archbishop of Oklahoma City, P.O. Box 32180, Oklahoma City, OK 73123.
orders, William D., Archbishop emeritus of Baltimore, 320 Cathedral St., Baltimore, MD 21201.
roglio, Timothy P., Archbishop for the Military Services, 1025 Michigan Ave., N.E., P.O. Box 4469, Washington, DC 20017-0469.
runett, Alexander J., Archbishop of Seattle, 710 9th Ave., Seattle, WA 98104.
uechlein, Daniel M., o.s.b., Archbishop of Indianapolis, 1400 N. Meridian St., P.O. Box 1410, Indianapolis, IN 46206.
ustros, Cyril Salim, s.m.s.p., Archeparch - Eparch of Newton, 3 Veterans of Foreign Wars Pkwy., West Roxbury, MA 02132.
arlson, Robert J., Archbishop of St. Louis, 4445 Lindell Blvd., St. Louis, MO 63108-2497.
haput, Charles J., o.f.m.cap., Archbishop of Denver, 1300 S. Steele St., Denver, CO 80210.
ronin, Daniel A., Archbishop emeritus of Hartford, 469 Bloomfield Ave., Bloomfield, CT 06002.
urtiss, Elden F., Archbishop emeritus of Omaha, 100 N. 62nd St., Omaha, NE 68132-2795.
mino, Joseph T., Archbishop emeritus for the Military Services, P.O. Box 4469, Washington, DC 20017.
olan, Timothy M., Archbishop of New York, 1011 First Ave., New York, NY 10022.
onoghue, John F., Archbishop emeritus of Atlanta, 680 W. Peachtree St., N.W., Atlanta, GA 30308.
avalora, John C., Archbishop of Miami, 9401 Biscayne Blvd., Miami Shores, FL 33138.
orenza, Joseph A., Archbishop emeritus of Galveston-Houston, 1700 San Jacinto, Houston, TX 77002.
ores, Patrick F., Archbishop emeritus of San Antonio, P.O. Box 28410, San Antonio, TX 78228.
ynn, Harry J., Archbishop emeritus of St. Paul and Minneapolis, 226 Summit Ave., St. Paul, MN 55102.
erety, Peter Leo, Archbishop emeritus of Newark, 60 Home Ave., Rutherford, NJ 07070.
omez, Jose H., Coadjutor Archbishop of Los Angeles, 3424 Wilshire Blvd., Los Angeles, CA 90010.
onzalez, Roberto O., o.f.m., Archbishop of San Juan, P.O. Box 9021967, San Juan, PR 00902-1967.
regory, Wilton D., Archbishop of Atlanta, 680 W. Peachtree St., N.W., Atlanta, GA 30308.
annan, Philip M., Archbishop emeritus of New Orleans, 106 Metairie Lawn Dr., Metairie, LA 70001.
anus, Jerome G., o.s.b., Archbishop of Dubuque, 1229 Mt. Loretto Ave., P.O. Box 479, Dubuque, IA 52004-0479.
ughes, Alfred C., Archbishop emeritus of New Orleans, 7887 Walmsley Ave., New Orleans, LA 70125.
unthausen, Raymond G., Archbishop emeritus of Seattle, 710 9th Ave., Seattle, WA 98104.
urley, Francis T., Archbishop emeritus of Anchorage, 225 Cordova St., Anchorage, AK 99501.
eleher, James P., Archbishop emeritus of Kansas City in Kansas, 12615 Parallel Pkwy., Kansas City, KS 66109.
elly, Thomas C., o.p., Archbishop emeritus of Louisville, 212 E. College St., P.O. Box 1073, Louisville, KY 40201.

His Excellency,
The Most Reverend

Kucera, Daniel W., o.s.b., Archbishop emeritus of Dubuque, Villa Raphael, 1155 Mt. Loretta Ave., Dubuque, IA 52003.
Kurtz, Joseph E., Archbishop of Louisville, 212 E. College St., P.O. Box 1073, Louisville, KY 40201.
Lipscomb, Oscar H., Archbishop emeritus of Mobile, 400 Government St., Mobile, AL 36633.
Listecki, Jerome E., Archbishop of Milwaukee, 3501 S. Lake Dr., P.O. Box 070912, Milwaukee, WI 53207-0912.
Lucas, George J., Archbishop of Omaha, 100 N. 62nd St., Omaha, NE 68132-2795.
Mansell, Henry J., Archbishop of Hartford, 134 Farmington Ave., Hartford, CT 06105.
Myers, John Joseph, Archbishop of Newark, 171 Clifton Ave., Newark, NJ 07104-9500.
Naumann, Joseph F., Archbishop of Kansas City in Kansas, 12615 Parallel Pkwy., Kansas City, Kansas 66109.
Niederauer, George H., Archbishop of San Francisco, One Peter Yorke Way, San Francisco, CA 94109-6602.
Nienstedt, John C., Archbishop of St. Paul and Minneapolis, 226 Summit Ave., St. Paul, MN 55102.
O'Brien, Edwin F., Archbishop of Baltimore, 320 Cathedral St., Baltimore, MD 21201.
Pilarczyk, Daniel E., Archbishop emeritus of Cincinnati, 100 E. Eighth St., Cincinnati, OH 45202.
Quinn, John R., Archbishop emeritus of San Francisco, 1100 Woodside Rd., Redwood City, CA 94061.
Rodi, Thomas J., Archbishop of Mobile, 400 Government St., Mobile, AL 36633.
Sanchez, Robert F., Archbishop emeritus of Santa Fe, Catholic Center, St. Joseph's Pl., N.W., Albuquerque, NM 87120.
Schnurr, Dennis M., Archbishop of Cincinnati, 100 E. Eighth St., Cincinnati, OH 45202-2129.
Schott, Basil, o.f.m., Archbishop of Pittsburgh Byzantine, 66 Riverview Ave., Pittsburgh, PA 15214.
Schulte, Francis B., Archbishop emeritus of New Orleans, 320 S. Roberts Rd., Rosemont, PA 19010.
Schwietz, Roger L., o.m.i., Archbishop of Anchorage, 225 Cordova St., Anchorage, AK 99501.
Sheehan, Michael J., Archbishop of Santa Fe, Catholic Center, 4000 St. Joseph's Pl., N.W., Albuquerque, NM 87120.
Soroka, Stefan, Archbishop of the Ukrainian Catholic Archeparchy of Philadelphia, 827 N. Franklin St., Philadelphia, PA 19123.
Sulyk, Stephen, Archbishop emeritus of the Ukrainian Catholic Archeparchy of Philadelphia, 827 N. Franklin St., Philadelphia, PA 19123.
Vigneron, Allen H., Archbishop of Detroit, 1234 Washington Blvd., Detroit, MI 48226.
Vlazny, John G., Archbishop of Portland in Oregon, 2838 E. Burnside St., Portland, OR 97214-1895.
Weakland, Rembert G., o.s.b. Archbishop emeritus of Milwaukee, Wilson Commons, 1400 W. Sonata Dr., #218, Milwaukee, WI 53221.
Wuerl, Donald W., Archbishop of Washington, DC, P.O. Box 29260, Washington, DC 20017.
Zayek, Francis M., Archeparch - Eparch emeritus of St. Maron of Brooklyn, 4010 Galt Ocean Dr., Apt. 1203, Fort Lauderdale, FL 33308.

BISHOPS

Adamec, Joseph V., Bishop of Altoona-Johnstown, 927 S. Logan Blvd., Hollidaysburg, PA 16648.

His Excellency,
The Most Reverend

Ahern, Patrick V., Retired Auxiliary Bishop of New York, John Cardinal O'Connor Clergy Residence, 5665 Arlington Ave., Bronx, NY 10471.
Allue, Emilio, s.d.b., Auxiliary Bishop of Boston, 66 Brooks Dr., Braintree, MA 02184.
Amos, Martin John, Bishop of Davenport, 2706 N. Gaines St., Davenport, IA 52804.
Anderson, Moses B., s.s.e., Retired Auxiliary Bishop of Detroit, 1234 Washington Blvd., Detroit, MI 48226.
Angadiath, Jacob, Bishop of St. Thomas Syro-Malabar Catholic Diocese of Chicago, 372 S. Prairie Ave., Elmhurst, IL 60126-4020.
Angell, Kenneth A., Bishop emeritus of Burlington, 351 North Ave., P.O. Box 489, Burlington, VT 05402-0489.
Aquila, Samuel J., Bishop of Fargo, 5201 Bishops Blvd., Ste. A, Fargo, ND 58104-7605.
Arias, David, o.a.r., Retired Auxiliary Bishop of Newark, St. Joseph of the Palisades Rectory, 6401 Palisade Ave., West New York, NJ 07093.
Baker, Robert J., Bishop of Birmingham, P.O. Box 12047, Birmingham, AL 35202.
Balke, Victor, Retired Bishop of Crookston, 1200 Memorial Dr., Crookston, MN 56716.
Baltakis, Paul A., o.f.m., Bishop emeritus for Lithuanian Catholics Outside Lithuania, St. Anthony's Friary, P.O. Box 980, 28 Beach Ave., Kennebunkport, ME 04046.
Bambera, Joseph C., Bishop of Scranton, 300 Wyoming Ave., Scranton, PA 18503.
Banks, Robert J., Bishop emeritus of Green Bay, P.O. Box 23825, Green Bay, WI 54305-3825.
Barbarito, Gerald, Bishop of Palm Beach, 9995 N. Military Tr., Palm Beach Gardens, FL 33410.
Barnes, Gerald R., Bishop of San Bernardino, 1201 E. Highland Ave., San Bernardino, CA 92404.
Barres, John O., Bishop of Allentown, 4029 W. Tilghman St., Allentown, PA 18104.
Batakian, Manuel, Eparch of Our Lady of Nareg in New York for Armenian Catholics, 167 N. 6th St., Brooklyn NY 11211-3207.
Bevard, Herbert A., Bishop of St. Thomas in the Virgin Islands, P.O. Box 301825, Charlotte Amalie, VI 00803.
Blair, Leonard P., Bishop of Toledo, 1933 Spielbusch Ave., Toledo, OH 43604-5360.
Blaire, Stephen E., Bishop of Stockton, 1105 N. Lincoln St., Stockton, CA 95203.
Boland, J. Kevin, Bishop of Savannah, 601 E. Liberty St., Savannah, GA 31401.
Boland, Raymond J., Bishop emeritus of Kansas City-St. Joseph, 2552 Gillham Rd., Kansas City, MO 64108.
Boles, John P., Retired Auxiliary Bishop of Boston, 841 E. Broadway, Boston, MA 02127.
Bootkoski, Paul G., Bishop of Metuchen, 10 Library Pl., Metuchen, NJ 08840.
Bosco, Anthony G., Bishop emeritus of Greensburg, 723 E. Pittsburgh St., Greensburg, PA 15601.
Botean, John M., Bishop of the Romanian Catholic Eparchy of St. George's in Canton, 1325 Skyway St., N.E., Canton, OH 44721.
Boyea, Earl A., Bishop of Lansing, 300 W. Ottawa, Lansing, MI 48933.
Bradley, Paul J., Bishop of Kalamazoo, 215 N. Westnedge Ave., Kalamazoo, MI 49007-3760.
Brandt, Lawrence E., Bishop of Greensburg, 723 E. Pittsburgh St., Greensburg, PA 15601.

His Excellency,
The Most Reverend

Bransfield, Michael J., Bishop of Wheeling-Charleston, 1300 Byron St., P.O. Box 230, Wheeling, WV 26003.

Braxton, Edward K., Bishop of Belleville, 222 S. Third St., Belleville, IL 62220-1985.

Brom, Robert H., Bishop of San Diego, P.O. Box 85728, San Diego, CA 92186-5728.

Brown, Tod D., Bishop of Orange, Marywood Center, 2811 E. Villa Real Dr., Orange, CA 92867.

Brucato, Robert A., Retired Auxiliary Bishop of New York, John Cardinal O'Connor Clergy Residence, 5655 Arlington Ave., Bronx, NY 10471.

Bruskewitz, Fabian W., Bishop of Lincoln, P.O. Box 80328, Lincoln, NE 68510-0328.

Bullock, William H., Bishop emeritus of Madison, 702 S. High Point Rd., Madison, WI 53744-4983.

Bura, John, Auxiliary Bishop of Philadelphia for Ukrainians & Apostolic Admin. of St. Josaphat in Parma, 5720 State Rd., P.O. Box 347180, Parma, OH 44134-7180.

Burbidge, Michael F., Bishop of Raleigh, 715 Nazareth St., Raleigh, NC 27606.

Burns, Edward J., Bishop of Juneau, 415 Sixth St., #300, Juneau, AK 99801.

Caggiano, Frank J., Auxiliary Bishop of Brooklyn, 310 Prospect Park W., Brooklyn, NY 11215.

Callahan, William P., o.f.m.conv., Auxiliary Bishop of Milwaukee, 3501 S. Lake Dr., P.O. Box 070912, Milwaukee, WI 53207-0912.

Calvo, Randolph R., Bishop of Reno, 290 S. Arlington Ave., Reno, NV 89501-1713.

Camacho, Tomas A., Bishop of Chalan Kanoa, Our Lady of Mt. Carmel, P.O. Box 500745, Saipan, MP 96950.

Campbell, Frederick F., Bishop of Columbus, 198 E. Broad St., Columbus, OH 43215.

Cantu, Oscar, Auxiliary Bishop of San Antonio, 2718 W. Woodlawn Ave., P.O. Box 28410, San Antonio, TX 78228-0410.

Carmody, Edmond, Bishop emeritus of Corpus Christi, 620 Lipan St., P.O. Box 2620, Corpus Christi, TX 78403.

Carmon, Dominic, s.v.d., Retired Auxiliary Bishop of New Orleans, 3270 Continental Dr., Kenner LA 70065-2663.

Casiano-Vargas, Ulises, Bishop of Mayaguez, P.O. Box 2272, Mayaguez, PR 00709.

Catanello, Ignatius, Auxiliary Bishop of Brooklyn, 175-20 74th Ave., Flushing, NY 11366.

Charron, Joseph L., c.pp.s., Retired Bishop of Des Moines, 601 Grand Ave., Des Moines, IA 50309.

Chavez, Gilbert E., Retired Auxiliary Bishop of San Diego, P.O. Box 85728, San Diego, CA 92186.

Chedid, John, Bishop emeritus of Our Lady of Lebanon of Los Angeles, 333 S. San Vicente Blvd., Los Angeles, CA 90048.

Choby, David R., Bishop of Nashville, 2400 - 21st Ave., S., Nashville, TN 37212.

Chomnycky, Paul P., o.s.b.m., Eparch of Stamford Ukrainians, 14 Peveril Rd., Stamford, CT 06902-3019.

Christensen, Peter F., Bishop of Superior, 1201 Hughitt Ave., Box 969, Superior, WI 54880.

Christian, Francis J., Auxiliary Bishop of Manchester, St. Joseph Cathedral, 145 Lowell St., Manchester, NH 03104.

Cisneros, Octavio, Auxiliary Bishop of Brooklyn, Holy Child Jesus, 111-11 86th Ave., Richmond Hill, NY 11418-1613.

Cistone, Joseph R., Bishop of Saginaw, 5800 Weiss St. Saginaw, MI 48603-2762.

Clark, Edward W., Auxiliary Bishop of Los Angeles, Our Lady of the Angels Pastoral Region, 5835 W. Slauson, Culver City, CA, 90230.

Clark, Matthew H., Bishop of Rochester, 1150 Buffalo Rd., Rochester, NY 14624.

Coakley, Paul S., Bishop of Salina, P.O. Box 980, Salina, KS 67402-0980.

Coleman, George W., Bishop of Fall River, 47 Underwood St., Fall River, MA 02720.

Conley, James D., Auxiliary Bishop of Denver, 1300 S. Steele St., Denver, CO 80210.

Conlon, R. Daniel, Bishop of Steubenville, 422 Washington St., Steubenville, OH 43952-5969.

Connolly, Thomas J., Bishop emeritus of Baker, P.O. Box 5999, Bend, OR 97708.

Cooney, Patrick R., Bishop emeritus of Gaylord, 611 W. North St., Gaylord, MI 49735-8349.

Cordileone, Salvatore J., Bishop of Oakland, 2121 Harrison St., Ste. 100, Oakland, CA 94612.

Corrada del Rio, Alvaro, s.j., Bishop of Tyler, 1015 E.S.E. Loop 323, Tyler, TX 75701-9663.

Costello, Thomas J., Retired Auxiliary Bishop of Syracuse, 1515 Midland Ave, P.O. Box 511, Syracuse, NY 13205.

Cote, Michael R., Bishop of Norwich, 201 Broadway, Norwich, CT 06360.

His Excellency,
The Most Reverend

Cruz, Manuel A., Auxiliary Bishop of Newark, 171 Clifton Ave., Newark, NJ 07104.

Cserhati, Ferenc, Bishop to Hungarians, Ung.Kath.Delegatur, Landwehrstr.66, D-80336, Munchen, Germany.

Cullen, Edward P., Bishop emeritus of Allentown, P.O. Box F, 4029 W. Tilghman St., Allentown, PA 18105.

Cummins, John S., Bishop emeritus of Oakland, 617 Prospect Ave., Oakland, CA 94610.

Cunningham, Robert Joseph, Bishop of Syracuse, 240 E. Onondaga St., P.O. Box 511, Syracuse, NY 13201-0511.

Cupich, Blase, Bishop of Rapid City, 606 Cathedral Dr., Rapid City, SD 57701.

Curlin, William G., Bishop emeritus of Charlotte, 3005 Markworth Ave., Charlotte, NC 28210-6432.

Curry, Thomas J., Auxiliary Bishop of Los Angeles, Santa Barbara Pastoral Region, 3240 Calle Pinon, Santa Barbara, CA 93105.

da Cunha, Edgar M., s.d.v., Auxiliary Bishop of Newark, 171 Clifton Ave., Newark, NJ 07104-0500.

Daily, Thomas V., Bishop emeritus of Brooklyn, 7200 Douglaston Pkwy., Douglaston, NY 11362.

Daly, James J., Retired Auxiliary Bishop of Rockville Centre, P.O. Box 9023, Rockville Centre, NY 11571-9023.

D'Arcy, John M., Bishop emeritus of Fort Wayne-South Bend, P.O. Box 390, Fort Wayne, IN 46801.

del Riego, Rutilio J., Auxiliary Bishop of San Bernardino, 1201 E. Highland Ave., San Bernardino, CA 92404.

Dendinger, William J., Bishop of Grand Island, 2708 Old Fair Rd., Grand Island, NE, 68803.

Deshotel, J. Douglas, Auxiliary Bishop of Dallas, 3725 Blackburn, P.O. Box 190507, Dallas, TX 75219.

DeSimone, Louis A., Retired Auxiliary Bishop of Philadelphia, St. Monica Church, St. Justin Martyr Rectory, 1222 Hagysford Rd., Narberth, PA 19072.

Dewane, Frank J., Bishop of Venice, P.O. Box 2006, Venice, FL 34284-2006.

DiLorenzo, Francis X., Bishop of Richmond, 7800 Carousel Lane, Richmond, VA 23294.

DiMarzio, Nicholas A., Bishop of Brooklyn, 310 Prospect Park W., Brooklyn, NY 11215.

Dinh Mai Luong, Dominic, Auxiliary Bishop of Orange, 2811 E. Villa Real Dr., Orange, CA 92613-1595.

Dino, Gerald N., Bishop of Van Nuys Byzantine Eparchy, 8105 N. 16th St., Phoenix, AZ 85020.

Donato, Thomas A., Auxiliary Bishop of Newark, St. Henry's Parish, 82 W. 29th St., Bayonne, NJ 07002.

Donnelly, Robert, Retired Auxiliary Bishop of Toledo, 4227 Bellevue Rd., Toledo, OH 43613.

Donovan, Paul V., Bishop emeritus of Kalamazoo, 1700 Bronson Way, #166, Kalamazoo, MI 49009-3317.

Dooher, John, Auxiliary Bishop of Boston, 236 Pleasant St., Weymouth, MA 02190.

Doran, Thomas G., Bishop of Rockford, P.O. Box 7044, Rockford, IL 61125.

Dorsey, Norbert L., c.p., Bishop emeritus of Orlando, 50 E. Robinson St., Orlando, FL 32801.

Doueihi, Stephen Hector, Bishop emeritus of the Maronite Eparchy of St. Maron of Brooklyn, 113 Remsen St., Brooklyn, NY 11201-4212.

Dougherty, John M., Retired Auxiliary Bishop of Scranton, 300 Wyoming Ave., Scranton, PA 18503.

Driscoll, Michael P., Bishop of Boise, 1501 Federal Way, Boise, ID 83705.

Duca, Michael G., Bishop of Shreveport, 3500 Fairfield Ave., Shreveport, LA 71104.

DuMaine, R. Pierre, Bishop emeritus of San Jose, 20 Willow Rd., Unit 43, Menlo Park, CA 94025.

Dunne, John C., Auxiliary Bishop of Rockville Centre, P.O. Box 39, Farmingdale, NY 11735-0039.

Dupre, Thomas L., Bishop emeritus of Springfield in Massachusetts, P.O. Box 1730, Springfield, MA 01101-1730.

Edyvean, Walter J., Auxiliary Bishop of Boston, St. Patrick, 44 E. Central St., Natick, MA 01760.

Elizondo, Eusebio L., Auxiliary Bishop of Seattle, 710 9th Ave., Seattle, WA 98104.

Elya, John A., b.s.o., Eparch emeritus of Newton, 30 East St., Methuen, MA 01844.

Estabrook, Joseph W., Auxiliary Bishop for the Military Services, P.O. Box 4469, Washington, DC 20017-0469.

Estevez, Felipe J., Auxiliary Bishop of Miami, 9401 Biscayne Blvd., Miami Shores, FL 33138.

Etienne, Paul D., Bishop of Cheyenne, P.O. Box 1468, Cheyenne, WY 82003-1468.

Evans, Robert C., Auxiliary Bishop of Providence, One Cathedral Sq., Providence, RI 02903-3695.

Fabre, Shelton J., Auxiliary Bishop of New Orleans, 7887 Walmsley Ave., New Orleans, LA 70125-3496.

Farrell, Kevin J., Bishop of Dallas, 3725 Blackburn, P.O. Box 190507, Dallas, TX 75219.

Fellhauer, David E., Bishop of Victoria, P.O. Box 4070, Victoria, TX 77903.

His Excellency,
The Most Reverend

Fernandez Torres, Daniel, Auxiliary Bishop of San Ju… P.O. Box 9021967, San Juan, PR 00902-1967.

Fernandez, Gilberto, Retired Auxiliary Bishop of Mia… 5260 N.E. 7th Ave., Miami, FL 33137.

Finn, Robert W., Bishop of Kansas City-St. Joseph, P… Box 419037, Kansas City, MO 64141.

Fitzsimons, George K., Bishop emeritus of Salina, P… Box 980, Salina, KS 67402-0980.

Flanagan, Thomas J., Retired Auxiliary Bishop of S… Antonio, P.O. Box 28410, San Antonio, TX 782… 0410.

Flesey, John W., Auxiliary Bishop of Newark, M… Blessed Sacrament, 787 Franklin Lake Rd., Frank… Lakes, NJ 07417.

Fliss, Raphael M., Bishop emeritus of Superior, 72… Ogden Ave., P.O. Box 3067, Superior, WI 54880.

Flores, Cirilo, Auxiliary Bishop of Orange, 2811 E. Vi… Real Dr., P.O. Box 14195, Orange, CA 92863-159…

Flores, Daniel E., Bishop of Brownsville, 1910 Univ… sity Blvd., P.O. Box 2279, Brownsville, TX 785… 2279.

Foley, David E., Bishop emeritus of Birmingham, 21… Third Ave., N., Birmingham, AL 35203.

Foys, Roger J., Bishop of Covington, P.O. Box 155… Covington, KY 41015-0550.

Franklin, William E., Bishop emeritus of Davenpo… 2706 N. Gaines St., Davenport, IA 52804.

Friend, William B., Bishop emeritus of Shreveport, 35… Broken Woods Dr. #301, Coral Springs, FL 33065…

Gainer, Ronald W., Bishop of Lexington, 1310 W. Ma… St., Lexington, KY 40508-2048.

Galante, Joseph A., Bishop of Camden, 631 Market S… P.O. Box 708, Camden, NJ 08101.

Galeone, Victor B., Bishop of St. Augustine, 11625 O… St. Augustine Rd., Jacksonville, FL 32258.

Garcia, Richard J., Bishop of Monterey, 425 Church S… Monterey, CA 93940.

Garcia-Siller, Gustavo m.sp.s., Auxiliary Bishop of Chi… cago, 2330 W. 118th St., Chicago, IL 60643.

Garland, James H., Bishop emeritus of Marquette, 3… Rock St., Marquette, MI 49855.

Gaydos, John R., Bishop of Jefferson City, P.O. B… 104900, Jefferson City, MO 65110-4900.

Gelineau, Louis E., Bishop emeritus of Providence, … Antoine Residence, 10 Rhodes Ave., North Smithfie… RI 02896.

Gendron, Odore, Bishop emeritus of Manchester, P… Box 310, Manchester, NH 03105-0310.

Gerber, Eugene J., Bishop emeritus of Wichita, 424 … Broadway, Wichita, KS 67202.

Gerry, Joseph J., o.s.b., Bishop emeritus of Portland… Maine, St. Anselm Abbey, 100 St. Anselm Dr., Manch… ter, NH 03102-1310.

Gettelfinger, Gerald A., Bishop of Evansville, 4200 … Kentucky Ave., Evansville, IN 47711.

Gilmore, Ronald M., Bishop of Dodge City, 910 Cent… Ave., Box 137, Dodge City, KS 67801.

Goedert, Raymond E., Retired Auxiliary Bishop of C… cago, P.O. Box 1979, Chicago, IL 60690.

Gonzalez, Francisco, s.f., Auxiliary Bishop of Washi… ton, P.O. Box 29260, Washington, DC 20017.

Gonzalez Medina, Ruben Antonio, c.m.f., Bishop… Caguas, P.O. Box 8698, Caguas, PR 00726.

Gorman, John R., Retired Auxiliary Bishop of Chica… 10731 W. 131st. St., Orland Park, IL 60462.

Gossman, F. Joseph, Bishop emeritus of Raleigh, 24… Crusader Dr., Raleigh, NC 27606.

Gracida, Rene H., Bishop emeritus of Corpus Chris… 620 Lipan St., P.O. Box 2620, Corpus Christi, … 78403.

Grahmann, Charles V., Bishop emeritus of Dallas, 37… Blackburn, P.O. Box 190507, Dallas, TX 75219.

Gries, Roger W., o.s.b., Auxiliary Bishop of Clevela… 1230 Ansel Rd., Cleveland, OH 44109.

Griffin, James A., Bishop emeritus of Columbus, 198… Broad St., Columbus, OH 43215.

Grosz, Edward M., Auxiliary Bishop of Buffalo, … Stanislaus Parish, 123 Townsend St., Buffalo, N… 14212-1299.

Guglielmone, Robert E., Bishop of Charleston, 119 Bro… St., P.O. Box 818, Charleston, SC 29402.

Guillory, Curtis J., Bishop of Beaumont, 703 Archie S… P.O. Box 3948, Beaumont, TX 77704-3948.

Gumbleton, Thomas J., Retired Auxiliary Bishop of D… troit, 1234 Washington Blvd., Detroit, MI 48226.

Habash, Yousif, Bishop of Our Lady of Deliverance, 3… Ave. E. Bayonne, NJ 07002-4678.

Hanifen, Richard C., Bishop emeritus of Colora… Springs, 228 N. Cascade Ave., Colorado Springs, C… 80903.

Harrington, Bernard J., Bishop emeritus of Winona, … W. Sanborn St., P.O. Box 588, Winona, MN 5598…

His Excellency,
The Most Reverend

Hart, Joseph H., Bishop emeritus of Cheyenne, Box 1468, Cheyenne, WY 82003-1468.

Hebda, Bernard A., Bishop of Gaylord, 611 W. North St., Gaylord, MI 49735-8349.

Hennessey, Robert F., Auxiliary Bishop of Boston, 841 E. Broadway, Boston, MA 02127-2302.

Hermann, Robert J., Auxiliary Bishop of St. Louis, 20 Archbishop May Dr., St. Louis, MO 63119.

Hernandez Rivera, Enrique M., Bishop emeritus of Caguas, P.O. Box 8698, Caguas, PR 00726.

Herzog, Ronald P., Bishop of Alexandria, P.O. Box 7417, Alexandria, LA 71306-0417.

Higgins, Richard B., Auxiliary Bishop for the Military Services, P.O. Box 4469, Washington, DC 20017-0469.

Higi, William L., Bishop of Lafayette in Indiana, 610 Lingle Ave., Lafayette, IN 47902.

Hoeppner, Michael J., Bishop of Crookston, 1200 Memorial Dr., Crookston, MN 56716.

Holley, Martin D., Auxiliary Bishop of Washington, P.O. Box 29260, Washington, DC 20017.

Houck, William R., Bishop emeritus of Jackson, P.O. Box 2248, Jackson, MS 39225-2248.

Howze, Joseph L., Bishop emeritus of Biloxi, P.O. Box 6067, Mobile, AL 36660-0067.

Hubbard, Howard J., Bishop of Albany, 125 Eagle St., Albany, NY 12202.

Hughes, Edward T., Bishop emeritus of Metuchen, 914 Milford-Warren Glen Rd., Milford NJ 08848-1619.

Hughes, William A., Bishop emeritus of Covington, Carmel Manor, 100 Carmel Manor Rd., Ft. Thomas, KY 41075-2395.

Hurley, Walter A., Bishop of Grand Rapids, Cathedral Square Center, 360 Division Ave., S., Grand Rapids, MI 49503-4539.

Ibrahim, Ibrahim, Bishop-Eparch to St. Thomas the Apostle (Chaldean), 25603 Berg Rd., Southfield, MI 48033.

Imesch, Joseph L., Bishop emeritus of Joliet, 425 Summit St., Joliet, IL 60435.

Iriondo, Josu, Auxiliary Bishop of New York, St. Anthony Padua Parish, 832 W. 166th St., Bronx, NY 10459.

Irwin, Francis X., Retired Auxiliary Bishop of Boston, Saint Raphael Parish, 30 Boston Ave., Medford, MA 02155.

Isern, Fernando, Bishop of Pueblo, 101 N. Greenwood, Pueblo, CO 81003.

Jackels, Michael O., Bishop of Wichita, 424 N. Broadway, Wichita, KS 67202.

Jacobs, Sam, Bishop of Houma-Thibodaux, P.O. Box 505, Schriever, LA 70395.

Jakubowski, Thad J., Retired Auxiliary Bishop of Chicago, 6002 W. Berteau Ave., Chicago, IL 60634-1630.

Jammo, Sarhad Y., Bishop of St. Peter the Apostle (Chaldean), 1627 Jamacha Way, El Cajon, CA 92019.

Jarrell, Michael, Bishop of Lafayette, 1408 Carmel Dr., Lafayette, LA 70501.

Jenky, Daniel R., c.s.c., Bishop of Peoria, 419 N.E. Madison Ave., Peoria, IL 61603-3720.

Johnston, Jr., James V., Bishop of Springfield-Cape Girardeau, The Catholic Center, 601 S. Jefferson Ave., Springfield, MO 65806.

Jugis, Peter J., Bishop of Charlotte, 1123 S. Church St., Charlotte, NC 28203.

Justice, William J., Auxiliary Bishop of San Francisco, One Peter Yorke Way, San Francisco, CA 94109-6602.

Kane, Francis, Auxiliary Bishop of Chicago, 1641 W. Diversey, Chicago, IL 60614.

Kettler, Donald J., Bishop of Fairbanks, 1316 Peger Rd., Fairbanks, AK 99709.

Kicanas, Gerald F., Bishop of Tucson, P.O. Box 31, Tucson AZ 85702.

Kinney, John F., Bishop of St. Cloud, 214 Third Ave., S., Box 1248, St. Cloud, MN 56302-1248.

Kmiec, Edward U., Bishop of Buffalo, 77 Oakland Pl., Buffalo, NY 14222-1241.

Knestout, Barry C., Auxiliary Bishop of Washington, 5001 Eastern Ave., P.O. Box 29260, Washington, DC 20017.

Kudrick, John M., Bishop of Parma, 1900 Carlton Rd., Parma, OH 44134.

Lagonegro, Dominick J., Auxiliary Bishop of New York, Sacred Heart, 301 Ann St., Newburgh, NY 12550-5467.

Latino, Joseph N., Bishop of Jackson, P.O. 2248, Jackson, MS 39225-2248.

LaValley, Terry R., Bishop of Ogdensburg, P.O. Box 369, Ogdensburg, NY 13669.

Lazaro Martinez, Felix, sch.p., Bishop of Ponce, P.O. Box 32205, Estancion 6, Ponce, PR 00732-2205.

Leibrecht, John J., Bishop emeritus of Springfield-Cape Girardeau, 1152 W. Camino Alto St., Springfield, MO 65810.

His Excellency,
The Most Reverend

Lennon, Richard G., Bishop of Cleveland, 1404 E. Ninth St., Cleveland, OH 44114.

Lessard, Raymond W., Bishop emeritus of Savannah, St. Vincent de Paul Seminary, 10701 S. Military Tr., Boynton Beach, FL 33436-4899.

LeVoir, John M., Bishop of New Ulm, 1400 6th St. N., New Ulm, MN 56073.

Libasci, Peter A., Auxiliary Bishop of Rockville Centre, Eastern Vicariate, P.O. Box 5046, Southampton, NY 11969.

Lohmuller, Martin N., Retired Auxiliary Bishop of Philadelphia, Villa Maria House of Studies, 1410 Almshouse Rd., Jamison, PA 18929.

Lori, William E., Bishop of Bridgeport, 238 Jewett Ave., Bridgeport, CT 06606-2892.

Losten, Basil, Eparch emeritus of Stamford of the Ukrainians, 122 Clovelly Rd., Stamford, CT 06902-3019.

Lotocky, Innocent, o.s.b.m., Bishop emeritus of St. Nicholas in Chicago, 2245 W. Rice St., Chicago, IL 60622.

Loverde, Paul S., Bishop of Arlington, 200 N. Glebe Rd., Arlington, VA 22203.

Lynch, Robert N., Bishop of St. Petersburg, P.O. Box 40200, St. Petersburg, FL 33743-0200.

Lyne, Timothy J., Retired Auxiliary Bishop of Chicago, Holy Name Cathedral, 730 N. Wabash, Chicago, IL 60611.

Macaluso, Christie A., Auxiliary Bishop of Hartford, 134 Farmington Ave., Hartford, CT 06105-3784.

Madden, Denis J., Auxiliary Bishop of Baltimore, 320 Cathedral St., Baltimore, MD 21201.

Madera, Joseph J., m.sp.s., Retired Auxiliary Bishop for the Military Services, P.O. Box 4469, Washington, DC 20017.

Maginnis, Robert P., Auxiliary Bishop of Philadelphia, 222 N. Seventeenth St., Rm. 830, Philadelphia, PA 19103-1299.

Maguire, Joseph F., Bishop emeritus of Springfield, 76 Elliot St., P.O. Box 1730, Springfield, MA 01102-1730.

Mallona Txertudi, Inaki, c.p. Bishop of Arecibo, 206 Dr. Salas St., Box 616, Arecibo, PR 00613-0616.

Malone, Richard J., Bishop of Portland in Maine, 510 Ocean Ave., Portland, ME 04104-7559.

Malooly, W. Francis, Bishop of Wilmington, P.O. Box 2030, Wilmington, DE 19899.

Mansour, Gregory J., Bishop of the Eparchy of St. Maron of Brooklyn, 109 Remsen St., Brooklyn, NY 11201.

Manz, John R., Auxiliary Bishop of Chicago, 1820 S. Leavitt St., Chicago, IL 60608.

Marconi, Dominic A., Retired Auxiliary Bishop of Newark, 71 Washington Ave., Chatham, NJ 07928.

Martino, Joseph F., Bishop emeritus of Scranton, St. Charles Borromeo Seminary, 100 E. Wynnewood Rd., Wynnewood, PA 19096.

Matano, Salvatore R., Bishop of Burlington, 351 North Ave., P.O. Box 489, Burlington, VT 05402-0489.

McCarthy, James F., Retired Auxiliary Bishop of New York, St. Elizabeth Ann Seton, 1377 N. Main St., Shrub Oak, NY 10588.

McCarthy, John E., Bishop emeritus of Austin, 6225 E. Hwy. 290, Austin, TX 78723.

McCormack, John B., Bishop of Manchester, 153 Ash St., P.O. Box 310, Manchester, NH 03105.

McCormack, William J., Retired Auxiliary Bishop of New York, 142 E. 29th St., New York, NY 10016.

McDonald, Andrew J., Bishop emeritus of Little Rock, St. Joseph's Home, 80 W. Northwest Hwy., Palatine, IL 60067.

McDonnell, Charles J., Retired Auxiliary Bishop of Newark, 34 Maple Ave., Hackensack, NJ 07601.

McDonnell, Timothy A., Bishop of Springfield in Massachusetts, P.O. Box 1730, Springfield, MA 01102-1730.

McFadden, Joseph P., Auxiliary Bishop of Philadelphia, 222 N. Seventeenth St., Rm. 530, Philadelphia, PA 19103-1299.

McFarland, Norman F., Bishop emeritus of Orange, Marywood Center, 2811 E. Villa Real Dr., Orange, CA 92867.

McGrath, Patrick J., Bishop of San Jose, 1150 N. First St., Ste. 100, San Jose, CA 95112.

McKinney, Joseph C., Retired Auxiliary Bishop of Grand Rapids, St. Ann's Home, 2161 Leonard, N.W., Grand Rapids, MI 49504.

McLaughlin, Bernard J., Retired Auxiliary Bishop of Buffalo, 204 Knoche Rd., Tonawand, NY 14150.

McManus, Robert J., Bishop of Worcester, 49 Elm St., Worcester, MA 01609.

McRaith, John J., Bishop emeritus of Owensboro, 501 W. Fifth St., Owensboro, KY 42301.

Medley, William F., Bishop of Owensboro, 600 Locust St., Owensboro, KY 42301.

His Excellency,
The Most Reverend

Melczek, Dale J., Bishop of Gary, 9292 Broadway, Merrillville, IN 46410.

Mengeling, Carl F., Retired Bishop of Lansing, 300 W. Ottawa St., Lansing, MI 48933.

Mestice, Anthony F., Retired Auxiliary Bishop of New York, Our Lady of Consolation Residence, 3103 Arlington Ave., Ste. 8, Bronx, NY 10463.

Michaels, James E., s.s.c., Retired Auxiliary Bishop of Wheeling-Charleston, St. Columban's Retirement Home, Silver Creek, NY 14136.

Mikloshazy, Attila, s.j., Retired Bishop for Hungarians, St. Augustine's Seminary, 2661 Kingston Rd., Scarborough, Ontario, Canada, M1M 1M3.

Milone, Anthony M., Bishop emeritus of Great Falls-Billings, 7600 S. 42nd St., Bellevue, NE 68147-1702.

Morin, Roger P., Bishop of Biloxi, 1790 Popps Ferry Rd., Biloxi, MS 39532-2118.

Morlino, Robert C., Bishop of Madison, 702 S. High Point Rd., Madison, WI 53744-4983.

Morneau, Robert F., Auxiliary Bishop of Green Bay, 333 Hilltop Dr., Green Bay, WI 54301-2713.

Moskal, Robert M., Bishop emeritus of St. Josaphat in Parma, 5720 State Rd., Parma, OH 44134.

Moynihan, James M., Bishop emeritus of Syracuse, 240 E. Onondaga St., P.O. Box 511, Syracuse, NY 13201.

Muench, Robert W., Bishop of Baton Rouge, 1800 S. Acadian Thruway, P.O. Box 2028, Baton Rouge, LA 70821-2028.

Mulvee, Robert E., Bishop emeritus of Providence, 30 Fenner St., Providence, RI 02903.

Mulvey, William M., Bishop of Corpus Christi, 620 Lipan St., P.O. Box 2620, Corpus Christi, TX, 78403-2620.

Murphy, William F., Bishop of Rockville Centre, P.O. Box 9023, Rockville Centre, NY 11571-9023.

Murray, James A., Bishop emeritus of Kalamazoo, 215 N. Westnedge Ave., Kalamazoo, MI 49007-3760.

Murry, George V., s.j., Bishop of Youngstown, 144 W. Wood St., Youngstown, OH 44503.

Negron Santana, Hermin, Auxiliary Bishop of San Juan, Urb. Caparra Heights, 1562 C. Encarnacion, San Juan, PR 00920.

Nevins, John J., Bishop emeritus of Venice, P.O. Box 2006, Venice, FL 34284-2006.

Newman, William C., Retired Auxiliary Bishop of Baltimore, 5300 N. Charles St., Baltimore, MD 21201.

Nickless, R. Walker, Bishop of Sioux City, 1821 Jackson St., P.O. Box 3379, Sioux City, IA 51102-3379.

Noonan, John G., Auxiliary Bishop of Miami, 9401 Biscayne Blvd., Miami Shores, FL 33138.

O'Brien, Thomas J., Bishop emeritus of Phoenix, 400 E. Monroe St., Phoenix, AZ 85004-2336.

O'Connell, Anthony J., Bishop emeritus of Palm Beach, 1098 Mepkin Abbey Rd., Moncks Corner, SC 29461-4796.

O'Neill, Arthur J., Bishop emeritus of Rockford, 3330 Maria Linden Dr., Rockford, IL 61114.

Ochoa, Armando, Bishop of El Paso, 499 St. Matthews St., El Paso TX 79907.

Olivier, Leonard J., s.v.d., Retired Auxiliary Bishop of Washington, 619 Tenth St., N.W., Washington, DC 20001-4587.

Olmsted, Thomas J., Bishop of Phoenix, 400 E. Monroe St., Phoenix, AZ 85004-2336.

Ottenweller, Albert H., Bishop emeritus of Steubenville, 2544 Parkwood Ave., Toledo, OH 43610-1317.

Paprocki, Thomas J., Auxiliary Bishop of Chicago, 1400 S. Austin Ave., Chicago, IL 60804.

Pataki, Andrew, Bishop emeritus of Passaic of the Ruthenians, 445 Lackawanna Ave., West Paterson, NJ 07424.

Pates, Richard E., Bishop of Des Moines, 601 Grand Ave., Des Moines, IA 50309.

Pena, Raymundo J., Bishop emeritus of Brownsville, 300 N. Nebraska Ave., San Juan, TX 78589.

Pepe, Joseph A., Bishop of Las Vegas, 336 Cathedral Way, Las Vegas, NV 89109.

Perry, Joseph N., Auxiliary Bishop of Chicago, P.O. Box 733, South Holland, IL 60473-0733.

Pevec, A. Edward, Retired Auxiliary Bishop of Cleveland, 28700 Euclid Ave., Wickliffe, OH 44092.

Pfeifer, Michael D., o.m.i., Bishop of San Angelo, P.O. Box 1829, San Angelo, TX 76902.

Piche, Lee A., Auxiliary Bishop of St. Paul and Minneapolis, 226 Summit Ave., St. Paul, MN 55102.

Pilla, Anthony M., Bishop emeritus of Cleveland, 28700 Euclid Ave., Wickliffe, OH 44092.

Popp, Bernard F., Retired Auxiliary Bishop of San Antonio, Padua Place, 80 Peter Baque Rd., San Antonio, TX 78209.

Provost, Glen J., Bishop of Lake Charles, 414 Iris St., P.O. Box 3223, Lake Charles, LA 70602.

Quinn, A. James, Retired Auxiliary Bishop of Cleveland, 2345 Bassett Rd., Westlake, OH 44145.

His Excellency,
The Most Reverend

Quinn, Francis A., Bishop emeritus of Sacramento, 8840 E. 22nd St., Tucson, AZ 85710.
Quinn, John M., Bishop of Winona, 55 W. Sanborn St., P.O. Box 588, Winona, MN 55987.
Ramirez, Ricardo, c.s.b., Bishop of Las Cruces, 1280 Med Park Dr., Las Cruces, NM 88005.
Ramos Morales, Eusebio, Bishop of Fajardo-Humacao, Apartado 888, Fajardo, PR 00738.
Rassas, George J., Auxiliary Bishop of Chicago, 200 N. Milwaukee Ave., Ste. 200, Libertyville, IL 60048-2250.
Reilly, Daniel P., Bishop emeritus of Worcester, St. Paul Cathedral, 38 High St., Worcester, MA 01609.
Reiss, Francis R., Auxiliary Bishop of Detroit, 36800 Schoolcraft Rd., Livonia, MI 48154.
Reiss, John C., Bishop emeritus of Trenton, Villa Vianney, 2301 Lawrenceville Rd., Trenton, NJ 08648.
Rhoades, Kevin C., Bishop of Fort Wayne-South Bend, P.O. Box 390, Fort Wayne, IN 46801.
Ricard, John H., s.s.j., Bishop of Pensacola-Tallahassee, 11 N. B St., Pensacola, FL 32501.
Ricken, David L., Bishop of Green Bay, 1825 Riverside Dr., Green Bay, WI 54301.
Rivera Perez, Hector M., Retired Auxiliary Bishop of San Juan, P.O. Box 31155, San Juan, PR 00929-2155.
Rizzotto, Vincent M., Retired Auxiliary Bishop of Galveston-Houston, P.O. Box 907, Houston, TX 77001-0907.
Rodimer, Frank J., Bishop emeritus of Paterson, 1082 Greenpond Rd., Newfoundland, NJ 07435.
Rodriguez, Placido, c.m.f., Bishop of Lubbock, P.O. Box 98700, Lubbock, TX 79499-8700.
Roman, Agustin A., Retired Auxiliary Bishop of Miami, 3605 S. Miami Ave., Miami, FL 33133.
Roque, Francis X., Retired Auxiliary Bishop for the Military Services, P.O. Box 4469, Washington, DC 20017.
Rosazza, Peter A., Auxiliary Bishop of Hartford, 1450 Chapel St., New Haven, CT 06511.
Rose, Robert J., Bishop emeritus of Grand Rapids, 1200 104th, Apt. 4, Byron Center, MI 49315.
Rozanski, Mitchell T., Auxiliary Bishop of Baltimore, 320 Cathedral St., Baltimore, MD 21201.
Rueger, George E., Retired Auxiliary Bishop of Worcester, St. Stephen's Rectory, 16 Hamilton St., Worcester, MA 01604.
Ryan, Daniel L., Bishop emeritus of Springfield in Illinois, St. John Vianney Villa, 1464 Green Trail Dr., Naperville, IL 60540-8359.
Ryan, Sylvester D., Bishop emeritus of Monterey, 425 Church St., Monterey, CA 93940.
Salazar, Alexander, Auxiliary Bishop of Los Angeles, 3424 Wilshire Blvd., Los Angeles, CA 90010-2241.
Samo, Amando, Bishop of the Caroline Islands, P.O. Box 939, Chuuk, Caroline Islands, FM 96942.
Sample, Alexander K., Bishop of Marquette, 117 W. Washington St., Ste. 3A, P.O. Box 1000, Marquette, MI 49855.
Samra, Nicholas J., Retired Auxiliary Bishop of Newton, 3 Veterans of Foreign Wars Pkwy., W. Roxbury, MA 02132.
Sansaricq, Guy A., Auxiliary Bishop of Brooklyn, St. Gregory the Great, 224 Brooklyn Ave., Brooklyn, NY 11213-2505.
Sartain, J. Peter, Bishop of Joliet, 425 Summit St., Joliet, IL 60435.
Sartoris, Joseph M., Retired Auxiliary Bishop of Los Angeles, San Pedro Pastoral Region, 1988 Rolling Vista Dr., Unit 12, Lomita, CA 90717-3761.
Schlarman, Stanley G., Bishop emeritus of Dodge City, 2620 Lebanon Ave., Belleville, IL 62221.
Schmitt, Bernard W., Bishop emeritus of Wheeling-Charleston, 1300 Byron St., Box 230, Wheeling, WV 26003.
Schmitt, Mark F., Bishop emeritus of Marquette, 224 Iroquois Ave., Green Bay, WI 54301.
Seitz, Mark J., Auxiliary Bishop of Dallas, 3725 Blackburn, P.O. Box 190507, Dallas, TX 75219.
Seminack, Richard S., Bishop of St. Nicholas in Chicago for Ukrainians, 2245 W. Rice St., Chicago, IL 60622.
Senior, Timothy C., Auxiliary Bishop of Philadelphia, 222 N. 17th St., Rm. 1200, Philadelphia, PA 19103-1299.
Serratelli, Arthur J., Bishop of Paterson, 777 Valley Rd., Clifton, NJ 07013.
Sevilla, Carlos, s.j., Bishop of Yakima, 5301-A Tieton Dr., Yakima, WA 98908.
Shaheen, Robert J., Bishop of Our Lady of Lebanon, 1021 S. 10th St., St. Louis, MO 63104.
Sheldon, Gilbert I., Bishop emeritus of Steubenville, 609 N. Seventh St., Steubenville, OH 43952.
Sheridan, Michael J., Bishop of Colorado Springs, 228 N. Cascade Ave., Colorado Springs, CO 80903.
Sheridan, Patrick J., Retired Auxiliary Bishop of New York, 5655 Arlington Ave., Bronx, NY 10471.

His Excellency,
The Most Reverend

Siegel, Joseph M., Auxiliary Bishop of Joliet, 425 Summit St., Joliet, IL 60435.
Silva, Clarence, Bishop of Honolulu, 1184 Bishop St., Honolulu, HI 96813.
Sirba, Paul D., Bishop of Duluth, 2830 E. Fourth St., Duluth, MN 55812.
Sklba, Richard J., Auxiliary Bishop of Milwaukee, 836 N. Broadway, Milwaukee, WI 53202-3608.
Skurla, William, Bishop of Passaic of the Ruthenians, 445 Lackawanna Ave., Woodland Park, NJ 07424.
Skylstad, William S., Bishop of Spokane, W. 1023 Riverside Ave., Spokane, WA 99201.
Slattery, Edward J., Bishop of Tulsa, P.O. Box 690240, Tulsa, OK 74169.
Smith, John M., Bishop of Trenton, P.O. Box 5147, 701 Lawrenceville Rd., Trenton, NJ 08638-0147.
Snyder, John J., Bishop emeritus of St. Augustine, 5 Casa San Pedro, 1714 State Rd. 13, Ste. 6, Jacksonville, FL 32259.
Soens, Lawrence D., Bishop emeritus of Sioux City, 1703 - W. 25th, Apt. 208, Sioux City, IA 51103-1700.
Solis, Oscar A., Auxiliary Bishop of Los Angeles, 3555 St. Pancratius Pl., Lakewood, CA 90712-1416.
Soto, Jaime, Bishop of Sacramento, 2110 Broadway, Sacramento, CA 95818-2541.
Speyrer, Jude, Bishop Emeritus of Lake Charles, 118 Marcus Dr., Carenco, LA 70502.
Steib, James Terry, s.v.d., Bishop of Memphis, The Catholic Center, P.O. Box 341669, Memphis, TN 38184-1669.
Steinbock, John T., Bishop of Fresno, 1550 N. Fresno St., Fresno, CA 93703-3788.
Steiner, Kenneth D., Auxiliary Bishop of Portland in Oregon, 2838 E. Burnside St., Portland, OR 97214.
Stika, Richard F., Bishop of Knoxville, 805 Northshore Dr., S.W., Knoxville, TN 37919.
Straling, Phillip F., Bishop emeritus of Reno, 290 S. Arlington Ave., Reno, NV 89501-1713.
Sullivan, Dennis J., Auxiliary Bishop of New York, 452 Madison Ave., New York, NY 10022.
Sullivan, Joseph M., Retired Auxiliary Bishop of Brooklyn, 378 Clermont Ave., Brooklyn, NY 11238.
Sullivan, Walter F., Bishop emeritus of Richmond, 3203 Hawthorne Ave., Richmond, VA 23227.
Swain, Paul J., Bishop of Sioux Falls, 523 N. Duluth Ave., Sioux Falls, SD 57104.
Symons, J. Keith, Bishop emeritus of Palm Beach, P.O. Box 7, Alma, MI 48801-0007.
Tafoya, Arthur N., Bishop emeritus of Pueblo, 101 N. Greenwood., Pueblo, CO 81003.
Tamayo, James A., Bishop of Laredo, Chancery, 1901 Corpus Christi St., Laredo, TX 78043.
Taylor, Anthony B., Bishop of Little Rock, 2500 N. Tyler St., P.O. Box 7565, Little Rock, AR 72217.
Thomas, Daniel E., Auxiliary Bishop of Philadelphia, 222 N. 17th St., Rm. 930, Philadelphia, PA 19103.
Thomas, Elliott G., Bishop emeritus of St. Thomas, in the Virgin Islands, Natl. Shrine of Divine Mercy, 2 Prospect Hill Rd., Stockbridge, MA 01262.
Thomas, George, Bishop of Helena, 515 N. Ewing, P.O. Box 1729, Helena, MT 59624-1729.
Thompson, David B., Bishop emeritus of Charleston, 4479 Downing Pl., Mount Pleasant, SC 29466.
Timlin, James C., Bishop emeritus of Scranton, 300 Wyoming Ave., Scranton, PA 18503.
Tobin, Thomas J., Bishop of Providence, One Cathedral Sq., Providence, RI 02903-3695.
Torres Oliver, Fremiot, Bishop emeritus of Ponce, C Marques de Mondejar 24, 3B, Madrid, 28028, Spain.
Trautman, Donald W., Bishop of Erie, 205 W. 9th St., P.O. Box 10397, Erie, PA 16514.
Tyson, Joseph J., Auxiliary Bishop of Seattle, 710 9th Ave., Seattle, WA 98104.
Valero, Rene, Retired Auxiliary Bishop of Brooklyn, 34-43 93rd St., Jackson Heights, NY 11372.
Vann, Kevin W., Bishop of Fort Worth, 800 W. Loop 820 S., Fort Worth, TX 76108.
Vasa, Robert Francis, Bishop of Baker, P.O. Box 5999, Bend, OR 97708.
Vasquez, Joe S., Bishop of Austin, 6225 E. Hwy. 290, Austin, TX 78723.
Wall, James S., Bishop of Gallup, 711 S. Puerco Dr., P.O. Box 1338, Gallup, NM 87305.
Walsh, Daniel F., Bishop of Santa Rosa, 985 Airway Ct., Ste. B, Santa Rosa, CA 95403.
Walsh, Gerald T., Auxiliary Bishop of New York, St. Joseph's Seminary, 201 Seminary Ave., Yonkers, NY 10704.
Walsh, Paul H., Auxiliary Bishop of Rockville Centre, Western Vicariate, Diocese of Rockville Centre, P.O. Box 933, Roosevelt, NY 11575-0933.

His Excellency,
The Most Reverend

Wang, Ignatius, Retired Auxiliary Bishop of San Fra cisco, One Peter Yorke Way, San Francisco, CA 9410
Ward, John J., Retired Auxiliary Bishop of Los Angele 3424 Wilshire Blvd., Los Angeles, CA 90010-2241.
Warfel, Michael, Bishop of Great Falls-Billings, 121 23r St. S., Great Falls, MT 59401-3939.
Wcela, Emil A., Retired Auxiliary Bishop of Rockvil Centre, Church of St. John the Evangelist, 546 S John's Place, Riverhead, NY 11901.
Weigand, William K., Bishop emeritus of Sacrament Pastoral Center, 2110 Broadway, Sacramento C 95818.
Weitzel, John Quinn, m.m., Bishop of Samoa-Pago Pag Fatuoaiga, P.O. Box 596, Pago Pago, American Sa moa 96799.
Wenski, Thomas G., Bishop of Orlando, P.O. Box 180 Orlando, FL 32802.
Wester, John Charles, Bishop of Salt Lake City, 27 C St Salt Lake City, UT 84103-2397.
Wilkerson, Gerald E., Auxiliary Bishop of Los Angele 15101 San Fernando Mission Blvd., Mission Hills, C 91345-1109.
Williams, James K., Bishop emeritus of Lexington, 131 W. Main St., Lexington, KY 40508.
Winter, William J., Retired Auxiliary Bishop of Pitt burgh, St. John Vianney Manor, 2600 Morange Rd Pittsburgh, PA 15205.
Wirz, George O., Retired Auxiliary Bishop of Madiso 702 S. High Point Rd., P.O. Box 44983, Madison W 53714.
Yanta, John W., Bishop emeritus of Amarillo, 1800 N Spring St., P.O. Box 5644, Amarillo, TX 79117-5644
Zarama, Luis R., Auxiliary Bishop of Atlanta, 680 W Peachtree St., N.W., Atlanta, GA 30308.
Zavala, Gabino, Auxiliary Bishop of Los Angeles, Sa Gabriel Pastoral Region, 16009 E. Cypress Ave Irwindale, CA 91706-2122.
Zipfel, Paul A., Bishop of Bismarck, 420 Raymond St Bismarck, ND 58502-1575.
Zubik, David A., Bishop of Pittsburgh, 111 Blvd. of th Allies, Pittsburgh, PA 15222-1618.
Zurek, Patrick J., Bishop of Amarillo, 1800 N. Sprin St., Amarillo, TX 79117.

U.S. HIERARCHY SERVING IN OTHER COUNTRIES

His Excellency,
The Most Reverend

Adams, Edward J., Titular Archbishop of Scala, Arch bishop Apostolic Nuncio in Philippines, 1004 Manil 2140 Taft Ave.; 1099 Manila, P.O. 3604, Philippine
Balvo, Charles D., Titular Archbishop of Castello, Apo tolic Nuncio to New Zealand, Wellington 6041, P.O Box 14-044, 112 Queen's Dr.
Blume, Michael August, s.v.d., Titular Archbishop Alexanum, Apostolic Nuncio in Benin and Togo, B. 20790, Lome, Togo.
Burke, Raymond L., Prefect of the Apostolic Signatur in Rome, Palazzo della Cancelleria, 00186 Roma, P azza della Cancelleria, 1.
Cardone, Christopher, o.p., Bishop of Auki, Solomon Is lands, P. O. Box A 13, Auki, Malaita, Solomon Island
Duffy, Paul F., o.m.i., Bishop of Mongu, Zambia, P. O. Bo 910449, Mongu, Western Province, Zambia.
Echevarria, Javier, Prelate of the Prelature of the Hol Cross and Opus Dei, Viale Bruno Buozzi 73, 0019 Rome, Italy.
Foley, John P. Cardinal, Grand Master of the Equestria Order of the Holy Sepulchre of Jerusalem, 00120 Vatica City State, Europe.
Gilbert, Edward J., c.ss.r., Archbishop of Port of Spai 27 Maraval Rd., St. Clair Port of Spain, Trinidad Tobago.
Gullickson, Thomas E., Titular Archbishop of Bomarz Apostolic Nuncio to Trinidad and Tobago, Port of Spai (Trinidad, W.I.), 11 Mary St., St. Clair, P.O. Box 85
Harvey, James M., Titular Archbishop of Memfi, Prefe of the Papal Household, 00120 Vatican City Stat Europe.
Heim, Capistran F., o.f.m., Bishop Prelate of Itaituba Brazil, C.P. 171, 68181-970 Itaituba, PA, Brazil.
Hermes, Heriberto, o.s.b., Bishop Prelate emeritus Cristalandia, Brazil, C.P. 05, Praca da Catedral s/ 77490-00, Cristalandia, TO, Brazil.
Howaniec, Henry Theophilus, o.f.m., Bishop of Holy Trin ity in Almaty, Kazakhstan, Kabanbai Batyra St., 7 16, 050000 Almaty, Kazakhstan.
Kalisz, Raymond P., s.v.d., Bishop emeritus of Wewak Papua New Guinea, P. O. Box 107, Wewak, E.S.P. 53 Papua New Guinea.

rtz, Robert, c.r., Bishop of Hamilton-in-Bermuda, P.O. Box SN629, Southhampton SNBX Bermuda.
Fay, Michael, o.carm., Bishop Prelate of Sicuani, Peru, Apartado 46, Jiron Hipolio Unanue 236, Plaza de Armas, Sicuani, via Cuzco, Peru.
achyna, Hlib, m.s.u., Titular Bishop of Bareta, Procurator of the Major Archbishop of Kyiv-Halyc of the Ukrainians at Rome, Piazza Madonna dei Monti 3, 00184 Rome, Italy.
anning, Elias James, o.f.m.conv., Bishop of Valenca, Brazil, C.P. 87332, 27600-000 Valenca, RJ, Brazil.
eking, Basil, Bishop emeritus from New Zealand, St. John Fisher House, 190 Brougham St., Sydenham Christchurch 8023 New Zealand.
aldoon, Thomas A., o.f.m., Bishop of Juticalpa, Honduras, Apartado 2, Juticalpa, Olancho 16101, Honduras.
vak, Alfred E., c.ss.r., Bishop emeritus of Paranagua, Brazil, C.P. 531, 83203-970 Paranagua, PR, Brazil.
lletier, Donald L., m.s., Bishop emeritus of Morondava Madagascar, Bishop's House, P.O. Box 132, Morondava 619, Madagascar.
tocnak, Joseph J., s.c.j., Bishop emeritus of De Aar, South Africa, P.O. Box 73, 1 Van Riebeeck Str., De Aar 7000, South Africa.
ichert, Stephen J., o.f.m.cap., Bishop of Mendi, Papua New Guinea, P. O. Box 69, Mendi, Southern Highlands Province 251, Papua New Guinea.
arpone, Gerald, o.f.m., Bishop emeritus of Comayagua, Honduras, Obispado, Calle de la Catedral, Apartado 41, 12101 Comayagua, Honduras.
hleck, Charles A., c.s.c., Titular Archbishop of Africa, former Adjunct Secretary, Congregation for the Evangelization of Peoples, Palazzo di Propaganda Fide, Piazza di Spagna 48, Rome, Italy 00187.
hmitz, Paul Evin, o.f.m.cap., Vicariate Apostolic of Bluefields, Apartado Postal 8, Bluefields, R.A.A.S., Nicaragua, C.A.
eda, Priamo, P., Bishop emeritus of Bani, Dominican Republic, Obispado, Apartado 25, Calle Sanchez s/n, Bani, Republica Dominicana.
rley, Daniel Thomas, o.s.a., Bishop of Chulucanas, Peru, Obispado, Calle Cuzco 381, Chulucanas, Depto. de Piura, Peru.
wiec, David Albin, o.f.m.cap., Auxiliary Bishop, Vicariate Apostolic of Bluefields, Apartado Postal 8, Bluefields, R.A.A.S., Nicaragua, C.A.

OTHER HIERARCHY RESIDING IN THE UNITED STATES

s Excellency,
he Most Reverend

nnett, Gordon D., s.j., Bishop emeritus of Mandeville, P.O. Box 45041, Los Angeles, CA 90045.
land, Ernest B., o.p., Bishop emeritus of Multan, St. Thomas Aquinas Priory, Providence College, Providence, RI 02918-0001.
akovsky, John, s.v.d., Titular Archbishop of Tabalta, Divine Word Residence, 1901 Waukegan Rd., P. O. Box 6000, Techny, IL 60082.
cNabb, John Conway, o.s.a., Bishop emeritus of Chulucanas, Peru, Tolentine Monastery, 20300 Governors Hwy., Olympia Fields, IL 60461.
cNaughton, William J., m.m., Bishop emeritus of Inchon, P.O. Box 304, Maryknoll, NY 10545.
arce, George H., s.m., Archbishop emeritus of Suva, 30 Fenner St., Providence, RI 02903.
abatini, Lawrence, c.s., Bishop emeritus of Kamloops, Canada, Holy Rosary Church, 612 N. Western Ave., Chicago, IL 60612.
wada, Alphonse, o.s.c., Bishop emeritus of Agats, Indonesia, 396 1st Ave., S., St. Cloud, MN 56301.

ARCHABBOTS

e Right Reverend

uVall, Justin, o.s.b., St. Meinrad Archabbey, St. Meinrad, IN 47577.
aebel, Bonaventure, o.s.b., (Resigned), St. Meinrad Archabbey, St. Meinrad, IN 47577.
aher, Paul R., o.s.b., (Resigned) St. Vincent Archabbey, 300 Fraser Purchase Rd., Latrobe, PA 15650-2686.
owicki, Douglas R., o.s.b., St. Vincent Archabbey, 300 Fraser Purchase Rd., Latrobe, PA 15650-2686.
eilly, Lambert, o.s.b., (Resigned) St. Meinrad Archabbey, St. Meinrad, IN 47577.

ABBOTS

e Right Reverend

nderson, Hugh R., o.s.b., St. Procopius Abbey, 5601 College Rd., Lisle, IL 60532.
alsavich, Marion E., o.s.b., Retired. St. Bede Abbey, Peru, IL 61354.
Bamberger, John E., o.c.s.o., Retired. Abbey of Genesee, Piffard, NY 14533.
Barnes, Robert, o.c.s.o., Abbey of Our Lady of the Holy Cross, 901 Cool Spring Ln., Berryville, VA 22611-2700.
Bataille, Vincent, o.s.b., Marmion Abbey, Butterfield Rd., Aurora, IL 60504.
Benedict, Francis, o.s.b., St. Andrew's Abbey, 31001 N. Valyermo Rd., Valyermo, CA 93563.
Benkert, Gerald, o.s.b., Resigned. Marmion Abbey, Butterfield Rd., Aurora, IL 60504.
Berndt, Alan, o.s.b., Retired. Blue Cloud Abbey, P.O. Box 98, Marvin, SD 57252.
Bock, David R., o.c.s.o., Retired. New Melleray Abbey, 6500 Melleray Circle, Peosta, IA 52068.
Boyle, Joseph, o.c.s.o., St. Benedict Monastery, 1012 Monastery Rd., Snowmass, CO 81654.
Burnett, Oscar, o.s.b., Retired. Belmont Abbey, 100 Belmont-Mount Holly Rd., Belmont, NC 28012-1802.
Carr, Christian Aidan, o.c.s.o., Retired. Serving as chaplain in Africa. Our Lady of Mepkin Abbey, HC 69, Box 800, Moncks Corner, SC 29461.
Clark, Victor J., o.s.b., Retired. St. Bernard Abbey, 1600 St. Bernard Dr., Cullman, AL 35055.
Clarke, Brian H., o.s.b., Retired. St. Mary Abbey, Delbarton, Mendham Rd., Morristown, NJ 07960.
Cole, Edwin J., o.s.b., St. Anselm Church, 530 S. Mason Rd., St. Louis, MO 63141.
Confroy, Thomas J., o.s.b., Retired. St. Mary's Abbey, Delbarton, Morristown, NJ 07960.
Connor, James, o.c.s.o., Retired. Assumption Abbey, Rte. 5, P.O. Box 1056, Ava, MO 65608.
Corpus, Roger, o.s.b., Retired. St. Bede Abbey, Peru, IL 61354.
Cyr, David J., o.s.b., Retired. Marmion Abbey, Butterfield Rd., Aurora, IL 60504.
Dagher, George, b.s.o., Retired. American Headquarters, 30 East St., Methuen, MA 01844.
Davis, Thomas X., o.c.s.o., Retired. Our Lady of New Clairvaux Abbey, P.O. Box 80, Vina, CA 96092.
De Wane, Thomas E., o.praem., Retired. St. Norbert Abbey, 1016 N. Broadway, De Pere, WI 54115-2697.
Denburger, John J., o.c.s.o., Abbey of the Genesee, Piffard, NY 14533.
Dimitrijevich, Nicholas, Our Lady of the Valley, P.O. Box 419, Gloverville, SC 29828.
Dosch, Leander, o.c.s.o., Abbey of the Holy Trinity, 1250 S. 9500 E., Huntsville, UT 84317.
Driscoll, William J., o.mar., Monastery of the Most Holy Trinity, 67 Dugway Rd., Petersham, MA 01366-9725.
Dzikowicz, Justin E., o.s.b., Retired. St. Paul Abbey, Newton, NJ 07860.
Eberle, Peter, o.s.b., Mount Angel Abbey, St. Benedict, OR 97373.
Farkasfalvy, Denis, o.cist., Abbey of Our Lady of Dallas, 1 Cistercian Rd., Irving, TX 75039.
Flaherty, Malachy, o.c.s.o., Abbey of Our Lady of the Holy Trinity, 1250 S. 9500 E., Huntsville, UT 84317.
Freeman, Brendan J., o.c.s.o., Abbey of Our Lady of New Melleray, 6500 Melleray Circle, Peosta, IA 52068-9736.
Frerking, Thomas, o.s.b., Abbey of St. Mary and St. Louis, 500 S. Mason Rd., St. Louis, MO 63141.
Garber, Andrew V., o.s.b., Resigned. St. Benedict Abbey, Benet Lake, WI 53102.
Geraets, David, o.s.b., Our Lady of Guadalupe Abbey, Pecos, NM 87552.
Gibbs, Gabriel, o.s.b., St. Benedict Abbey, 252 Still River Rd., P.O. Box 67, Still River, MA 01467-0067.
Hacker, Louis, o.s.b., Corpus Christi Abbey, HCR 2, Box 6300, Sandia, TX 78383.
Harrison, Cyprian, o.c.s.o., Retired. Assumption Abbey, Rte. 5, Box 1056, Ava, MO 65608.
Hayes, Eugene, o.praem., St. Michael Abbey, 19292 El Toro Rd., Silverado, CA 92676-9710.
Hayes, Giles, o.s.b. St. Mary's Abbey, Delbarton, Morristown, NJ 07960.
Heidgen, Warren J., o.s.b., Retired. Holy Cross Abbey, P.O. Box 1510, Canon City, CO 81215-1510.
Hein, Kenneth, o.s.b., Retired Abbot, Holy Cross Abbey, P.O. Box 1510, Canon City, CO 81215-1510.
Hillenbrand, Thomas, o.s.b., Retired. Blue Cloud Abbey, P.O. Box 98, Marvin, SD 57251.
Hinches, Augustine J., o.s.b., Resigned. St. Paul Abbey, Newton, NJ 07860.
Homick, Joseph, Holy Transfiguration Monastery, 17001 Tomki Rd., Redwood Valley, CA 95470.
Keating, Thomas, o.c.s.o., St. Benedict Monastery, 1012 Monastery Rd., Snowmass, CO 81654.
Kelly, Timothy, o.s.b., Newark Abbey, 528 Dr. Martin Luther King Jr. Blvd., Newark, NJ 07102.
Kerndt, James J., o.c.s.o., Retired. New Melleray Abbey, 6500 Melleray Circle, Dubuque, IA 52068.
Kodell, Jerome, o.s.b., New Subiaco Abbey, Subiaco, AR 72865.
Koehler, Ralph, o.s.b., Retired. St. Benedict's, Abbey, Atchison, KS 66002.
Lawrence, Philip, o.s.b., Monastery of Christ in the Desert, Abiquiu, NM 87510.
Leavy, Matthew K., o.s.b., St. Anselm Abbey, Manchester, NH 03102.
Liprie, James, o.s.b., Abbot of Our Lady of Guadalupe Abbey, Pecos, NM 87552.
Logan, John M., o.praem., Daylesford Abbey, 220 S. Valley Rd., Paoli, PA 19301.
Lugo, Martin, o.s.b., Retired. St. Gregory's Abbey, Shawnee, OK 74804.
Macul, Joel P., o.s.b., St. Paul's Abbey, Newton, NJ 07860.
Massoth, Charles, o.s.b., Retired. St. Gregory Abbey, Shawnee, OK 74801.
Matter, Robert, o.c.s.o., Retired. Assumption Abbey, Rte. 5, Box 1056, Ava, MO 65608.
McCaffrey, Edmund F., Former Abbot-Ordinary Belmont Abbey, P.O. Box 70548, Myrtle Beach, SC 29572-0028.
McCarthy, Peter, o.c.s.o., The Cistercian (Trappist) Abbey of Our Lady of Guadalupe, Lafayette, OR 97127.
McCorkell, Edward, o.c.s.o., Retired. Abbey of Our Lady of the Holy Cross, Rte. 2, Box 3870, Berryville, VA 22611-9526.
McDermott, Benedict, o.s.b., Mary Mother of Church Abbey, 12829 River Rd., Richmond, VA 23221.
McGonigle, Kevin, o.s.b., Retired. Conception Abbey, Conception, MO 64433.
Meagher, Cletus D., o.s.b., St. Bernard Abbey, Cullman, AL 35055.
Moore, Patrick, o.s.b., Retired. Assumption Abbey, P.O. Box A, Richardton, ND 58652.
Morcone, Nicholas J., o.s.b., Glastonbury Abbey, 16 Hull St., Hingham, MA 02043.
Neville, Gary, o.praem., Abbot St. Norbert Abbey, DePere, WI 54115-2610.
O'Connor, Philip J., o.c.s.o., Retired. New Melleray Abbey, 6500 Melleray Circle, Peosta, IA 52068.
Odenbrett, Stephen, o.s.b., Our Lady of Guadalupe Abbey, Pecos, NM 87552.
Parcher, Adrian, o.s.b., Retired. St. Martin's Abbey, 5300 Pacific Ave., S.E., Lacey, WA 98503.
Parker, Ladislaus K., o.praem., Retired, St. Michael Abbey, 19292 E. Toro Rd., Silverado, CA 92676.
Polan, Gregory, o.s.b., Abbot of Conception Abbey, Conception, MO 64433.
Purcell, Owen, o.s.b., Retired. St. Benedict's Abbey, Atchison, KS 66002.
Quinkert, Denis, o.s.b., Retired. Blue Cloud Abbey, P.O. Box 98, Marvin, SD 57251.
Rausch, Conrad, o.s.b., Retired. St. Martin's Abbey, 5300 Pacific Ave. S.E., Lacey, WA 98503.
Regan, Patrick, o.s.b., Retired. St. Joseph Abbey, St. Benedict, LA 70457.
Rigby, Luke, o.s.b., Abbey of St. Mary and St. Louis, 500 S. Mason Rd., St. Louis, MO 63141.
Roberts, Augustine, o.c.s.o., St. Joseph Abbey, Spencer, MA 01562.
Rooney, Marcel, o.s.b., Conception Abbey, Conception, MO 64433.
Roth, Neal G., o.s.b., St. Martin's Abbey, 5300 Pacific Ave. S.E., Lacey, WA 98503.
Ryska, Leo M., o.s.b., Retired. St. Benedict's Abbey and Retreat Center, Benet Lake, WI 53102.
Schoofs, Robert, o.s.b., Retired. St. Benedict's Abbey, Benet Lake, WI 53102.
Scott, Mark A., o.c.s.o., Assumption Abbey, Rte. 5, Box 1056, Ava, MO 65608.
Senecal, Barnabas, o.s.b., St. Benedict's Abbey, Atchison, KS 66002.
Serna, Mark, o.s.b., Abbey of St. Gregory, Cory's Ln., Portsmouth, RI 02871.
Shea, Aidan, o.s.b., St. Anselm Abbey, 4501 South Dakota Ave., N.E., Washington, DC 20017-2753.
Solari, Placid D., o.s.b., Belmont Abbey, 100 Belmont-Mount Holly Rd., Belmont, NC 28012-1802.
Spillane, M. Emmanuel, o.c.s.o., Retired. Abbey of Our Lady of the Trinity, 1250 S. 9500 E. Huntsville, UT 84317.
Stark, Matthew, o.s.b., Retired. Abbey of St. Gregory the Great, Cory's Ln., Portsmouth, RI 02871.
Stasyszen, Lawrence, o.s.b., St. Gregory's Abbey, Shawnee, OK 74804.
Thompson, Damien, o.s.c.o., Abbey of Gethsemani, Trappist, KY 40051.
Tremel, Jerome G., o.praem., Admin., Daylesford Abbey Norbertine Canonry, 220 S. Valley Rd., Paoli, PA 19301-1900.
Valvano, Melvin J., o.s.b., Retired. Newark Abbey, 528 Dr. Martin Luther King Jr. Blvd., Newark, NJ 07102.
Veilleux, Armand J., o.s.c.o., Monastery of the Holy Spirit, 2625 Hwy. 212 S.W., Conyers, GA 30094-4044.

Vollmer, Edward J., o.s.b., Retired. Holy Cross Abbey, P.O. Box 1510, Canon City, CO 81215-1510.
Vorderlandwehr, Adrian R., o.s.b., Retired. St. Gregory Abbey, Shawnee, OK 74801.
Wagner, Lawrence, o.s.b., Retired. Assumption Abbey, P.O. Box A, Richardton, ND 58652.
Walsh, Raphael, o.s.b., Mt. Michael Abbey, Elkhorn, NE 68022.
Warles, o.s.b., Prince of Peace Abbey, 650 Benet Hill Rd., Oceanside, CA 92054.
Wechter, David L., o.s.c.o., Retired. New Melleray Abbey, 6500 Melleray Circle, Peosta, IA 52068.
Wiseman, James, o.s.b., Resigned. St. Anselm Abbey Dakota Ave., N.E., Washington, DC 20017-2753.
Wolff, Theodore, o.s.b., Mount Michael Abbey, 22520 M Rd., Elkhorn, NE 68022.
Wood, Joseph, o.s.b., Mt. Angel Abbey, St. Benedict

A LIST OF CARDINALS IN THE UNITED STATES IN THE ORDER OF THEIR SENIORITY

CARDINALS

His Eminence Luis Cardinal Aponte Martinez, San Juan
His Eminence William Cardinal Baum, Vatican City State
His Eminence Bernard Cardinal Law, Vatican City State
His Eminence Edmund Cardinal Szoka, Vatican City State
His Eminence Roger Cardinal Mahony, Los Angeles
His Eminence Anthony Cardinal Bevilacqua, Philadelphia
His Eminence William Cardinal Keeler, Baltimore
His Eminence Adam Cardinal Maida, Detroit
His Eminence Francis Cardinal Stafford, Vatican City State
His Eminence Francis Cardinal George, o.m.i., Chicago
His Eminence Edward Cardinal Egan, New York
His Eminence Theodore Cardinal McCarrick, Washington
His Eminence Justin Cardinal Rigali, Philadelphia
His Eminence William Cardinal Levada, Vatican City State
His Eminence Sean Patrick Cardinal O'Malley, o.f.m.cap., Boston
His Eminence Daniel Cardinal DiNardo, Galveston-Houston

A CHRONOLOGICAL LIST OF CARDINAL, ARCHBISHOP & BISHOP ACTIVITY BY YEAR

1956

ishop

annan, Philip M., Appointed June 16. Ordained Dec. 8, 1939. Auxiliary Bishop of Washington.

1960

ishop

ponte Martinez, Luis, Appointed July 23. Ordained April 10, 1950. Auxiliary of Ponce.

1962

ishops

unthausen, Raymond G., Appointed July 8. Ordained June 1, 1946. Bishop of Helena.

ayek, Francis M., Appointed May 30. Ordained March 17, 1946. Titular Bishop of Callinicum.

1963

ishops

ponte Martinez, Luis, Appointed Nov. 18. Ordained April 16, 1950. Coadjutor Bishop of Ponce to Bishop of Ponce.

'ard, John J., Appointed Oct. 16. Ordained May 4, 1946. Auxiliary Bishop of Los Angeles.

1964

rchbishop

ponte Martinez, Luis, Appointed Nov. 11. Ordained April 10, 1950. Archbishop of San Juan.

ishop

orres, Juan Fremiot, Appointed Nov. 4. Ordained April 10, 1950. Bishop of Ponce.

1965

rchbishop

annan, Philip M., Appointed Sept. 29. Ordained Dec. 8, 1939. Archbishop of New Orleans.

1966

ishops

erety, Peter Leo, Appointed March 4. Ordained June 29, 1939. Coadjutor Bishop of Portland (in Maine).

1967

ishops

roderick, Edwin B., Appointed March 4. Ordained May 30, 1942. Auxiliary Bishop of New York.

Gerety, Peter Leo, Appointed Feb. 18. Ordained June 29, 1939. Apostolic Administrator of Portland (in Maine).

Quinn, John R., Appointed Oct. 21. Ordained July 19, 1953. Auxiliary Bishop of San Diego.

Reiss, John C., Appointed Oct. 21. Ordained May 31, 1947. Auxiliary Bishop of Trenton.

1968

Bishops

Borders, William D., Appointed May 8. Ordained May 18, 1940. Bishop of Orlando.

Cronin, Daniel A., Appointed June 10. Ordained Dec. 20, 1952. Auxiliary Bishop of Boston.

Gossman, F. Joseph, Appointed July 15. Ordained Dec. 17, 1955. Auxiliary Bishop of Baltimore.

Gumbleton, Thomas J., Appointed March 8. Ordained June 2, 1956. Auxiliary Bishop of Detroit.

McKinney, Joseph C., Appointed July 24. Ordained Dec. 20, 1953. Auxiliary Bishop of Grand Rapids.

McLaughlin, Bernard J., Appointed Dec. 28. Ordained Dec. 21, 1935. Retired Auxiliary Bishop of Buffalo.

O'Neill, Arthur J., Appointed Aug. 19. Ordained March 27, 1943. Bishop of Rockford.

1969

Bishops

Broderick, Edwin B., Appointed March 19. Ordained May 30, 1942. Bishop of Albany.

Gerety, Peter Leo, Succeeded to See Sept. 15. Bishop of Portland (in Maine).

1970

Bishops

Ahern, Patrick V., Appointed Feb. 3. Ordained Jan. 27, 1945. Auxiliary Bishop of New York.

Baum, William, Appointed Feb. 18. Ordained May 12, 1951. Bishop of Springfield-Cape Girardeau.

Bosco, Anthony G., Appointed May 14. Ordained June 7, 1952. Auxiliary Bishop of Pittsburgh.

Cronin, Daniel A., Appointed Oct. 30. Ordained Dec. 20, 1952. Bishop of Fall River.

Flores, Patrick F., Appointed March 18. Ordained May 26, 1956. Auxiliary Bishop of San Antonio.

Hurley, Francis T., Appointed Feb. 4. Ordained June 16, 1951. Auxiliary Bishop of Juneau.

Lohmuller, Martin N., Appointed Feb. 11. Ordained June 3, 1944. Auxiliary Bishop of Philadelphia.

McFarland, Norman F., Appointed June 5. Ordained June 15, 1946. Auxiliary Bishop of San Francisco.

Schmitt, Mark F., Appointed May 5. Ordained May 22, 1948. Auxiliary Bishop of Green Bay.

Sullivan, Walter F., Appointed Oct. 20. Ordained May 9, 1953. Auxiliary Bishop of Richmond.

1971

Bishops

Connolly, Thomas J., Appointed May 4. Ordained April 8, 1947. Bishop of Baker.

Donovan, Paul V., Appointed June 15. Ordained May 20, 1950. Bishop of Kalamazoo.

Gelineau, Louis E., Appointed Dec. 6. Ordained June 5, 1954. Bishop of Providence.

Gracida, Rene H., Appointed Dec. 6. Ordained May 23, 1959. Auxiliary Bishop of Miami.

Hurley, Francis T., Appointed July 20. Ordained June 16, 1951. Bishop of Juneau.

Losten, Basil, Appointed March 15. Ordained June 10, 1957. Auxiliary Bishop of Philadelphia Ukrainian.

Maguire, Joseph F., Appointed Dec. 1. Ordained June 29, 1945. Auxiliary Bishop of Boston.

Szoka, Edmund, Appointed June 15. Ordained June 5, 1954. Bishop of Gaylord.

Zayek, Francis M., Appointed Nov. 11. Ordained March 17, 1946. Eparch of St. Maron.

1972

Archbishop

Quinn, John R., Appointed Dec. 13. Ordained July 19, 1953. Archbishop of Oklahoma City.

Bishops

Howze, Joseph L., Appointed Nov. 8. Ordained May 7, 1959. Auxiliary Bishop of Jackson.

McDonald, Andrew J., Appointed July 4. Ordained May 8, 1948. Bishop of Little Rock.

Snyder, John J., Appointed Dec. 19. Ordained June 9, 1951. Auxiliary Bishop of Brooklyn.

1973

Cardinal

Aponte Martinez, Luis Cardinal, Created March 5. Archbishop of San Juan.

Archbishop

Baum, William, Appointed May 9. Ordained May 12, 1951. Archbishop of Washington.

Bishops

Imesch, Joseph L., Appointed Feb. 8. Ordained Dec. 16, 1956. Auxiliary Bishop of Detroit.

Law, Bernard, Appointed Oct. 22. Ordained May 21, 1961. Bishop of Springfield-Cape Girardeau.

Lessard, Raymond W., Appointed March 5. Ordained Dec. 16, 1956. Bishop of Savannah.

Mestice, Anthony F., Appointed March 5. Ordained June 4, 1949. Auxiliary Bishop of New York.

Michaels, James, Appointed March 26. Auxiliary Bishop of Wheeling-Charleston.

Sullivan, Walter F., Appointed April 30. Ordained May 9, 1953. Apostolic Administrator of Richmond.

1974

Archbishops

Borders, William D., Appointed March 25. Ordained May 18, 1940. Archbishop of Baltimore.

Gerety, Peter Leo, Appointed April 2. Ordained June 29, 1939. Archbishop of Newark.

Sanchez, Robert F., Appointed June 1. Ordained Dec. 20, 1959. Archbishop of Santa Fe.

Bishops

Angell, Kenneth A., Appointed Aug. 9. Ordained May 26, 1956. Auxiliary Bishop of Providence.

Chavez, Gilbert E., Appointed April 19. Ordained March 19, 1960. Auxiliary Bishop of San Diego.

Cummins, John S., Appointed Feb. 26. Ordained Jan. 24, 1953. Auxiliary Bishop of Sacramento.

Daily, Thomas V., Appointed Dec. 31. Ordained Jan. 10, 1952. Auxiliary Bishop of Boston.

D'Arcy, John M., Appointed Dec. 31. Ordained Feb. 2, 1957. Auxiliary Bishop of Boston.

Gendron, Odore J., Appointed Dec. 12. Ordained May 31, 1947. Retired Bishop of Manchester.

Hanifen, Richard C., Appointed July 6. Ordained June 6, 1959. Auxiliary Bishop of Denver.

Hughes, William A., Appointed July 23. Ordained April 6, 1946. Auxiliary Bishop of Youngstown.

McFarland, Norman F., Appointed Dec. 6. Ordained June 15, 1946. Apostolic Administrator of Reno-Las Vegas.

Ottenweller, Albert H., Appointed April 17. Ordained June 19, 1943. Auxiliary Bishop of Toledo.

Pilarczyk, Daniel E., Appointed Nov. 12. Ordained Dec. 20, 1959. Auxiliary Bishop of Cincinnati.

Sullivan, Walter F., Succeeded to See June 6. Bishop of Richmond.

1975

Archbishop

Hunthausen, Raymond G., Appointed Feb. 25. Ordained June 1, 1946. Archbishop of Seattle.

Bishops

Fitzsimons, George K., Appointed May 27. Ordained March 18, 1961. Auxiliary Bishop of Kansas City-St. Joseph.

Gossman, F. Joseph, Appointed April 8. Ordained Dec. 17, 1955. Bishop of Raleigh.

Gracida, Rene H., Appointed Oct. 1. Ordained May 23, 1959. Bishop of Pensacola-Tallahassee.

Mahony, Roger M., Appointed Jan. 7. Ordained May 1, 1962. Auxiliary Bishop of Fresno.

Reilly, Daniel P., Appointed June 17. Ordained May 30, 1953. Bishop of Norwich.

1976

Cardinal

Baum, William Cardinal, Created May 24. Prefect of Sacred Congregation for Catholic Education, Vatican.

Archbishop

Hurley, Francis T., Appointed May 4. Ordained June 16, 1951. Archbishop of Anchorage.

Bishops

Balke, Victor, Appointed July 7. Ordained May 24, 1958. Bishop of Crookston.

Broderick, Edwin B., Appointed June 3. Exec. Dir. Catholic Relief Services; resigned Bishop of Albany.

Casiano-Vargas, Ulises, Appointed March 4. Ordained May 30, 1967. Bishop of Mayaguez.

Curtiss, Elden F., Appointed March 4. Ordained May 24, 1958. Bishop of Helena.

Gerber, Eugene J., Appointed Oct. 16. Ordained May 19, 1959. Bishop of Dodge City.

Hart, Joseph H., Appointed July 1. Ordained May 1, 1956. Bishop of Cheyenne.

Hughes, Edward T., Appointed June 14. Ordained May 31, 1947. Auxiliary Bishop of Philadelphia.

Kinney, John F., Appointed Nov. 16. Ordained Feb. 2, 1963. Auxiliary Bishop of St. Paul-Minneapolis.

Losten, Basil H., Appointed June 8. Ordained June 10, 1957. Apostolic Administrator Philadelphia Ukrainian.

Maguire, Joseph F., Appointed April 3. Ordained June 29, 1945. Coadjutor Bishop of Springfield.

Marconi, Dominic A., Appointed May 3. Ordained May 30, 1953. Auxiliary Bishop of Newark.

McFarland, Norman F., Appointed Feb. 10. Ordained June 15, 1946. Bishop of Reno-Las Vegas.

Pena, Raymundo, J., Appointed Oct. 16. Ordained May 25, 1957. Auxiliary Bishop of San Antonio.

Sheldon, Gilbert I., Appointed April 20. Ordained Feb. 28, 1953. Auxiliary Bishop of Cleveland.

Stafford, J. Francis, Appointed Jan. 27. Ordained Dec. 15, 1957. Auxiliary Bishop of Baltimore.

Timlin, James C., Appointed Aug. 3. Ordained July 16, 1951. Auxiliary Bishop of Scranton.

1977

Archbishops

Quinn, John R., Appointed Feb. 22. Ordained July 19, 1953. Archbishop of San Francisco.

Weakland, Rembert, G., o.s.b., Appointed Sept. 20. Ordained June 24, 1951. Archbishop of Milwaukee.

Bishops

Cummins, John S., Appointed May 3. Ordained Jan. 24, 1953. Bishop of Oakland.

Daly, James J., Appointed Feb. 28. Ordained May 22, 1948. Auxiliary Bishop of Rockville Centre.

Howze, Joseph L., Appointed March 1. Ordained May 7, 1959. Bishop of Biloxi from Auxiliary Bishop of Jackson.

Hubbard, Howard J., Appointed Feb. 1. Ordained Dec. 18, 1963. Bishop of Albany.

Kelly, Thomas C., o.p., Appointed July 12. Ordained June 5, 1958. Auxiliary Bishop of Washington.

Kucera, Daniel W., o.s.b., Appointed June 6. Ordained May 26, 1949. Auxiliary Bishop of Joliet.

Losten, Basil H., Appointed Sept. 20. Ordained June 10, 1957. Bishop of Stamford.

Maguire, Joseph F., Succeeded to See Nov. 4. Bishop of Springfield.

McCarrick, Theodore E., Appointed May 24. Ordained May 31, 1958. Auxiliary Bishop of New York.

Mulvee, Robert E., Appointed Feb. 15. Ordained June 30, 1957. Auxiliary Bishop of Manchester.

Ottenweller, Albert H., Appointed Oct. 11. Ordained June 19, 1943. Bishop of Steubenville.

Rodimer, Frank J., Appointed Dec. 13. Ordained May 19, 1951. Bishop of Paterson.

Skylstad, William, Appointed Feb. 22. Ordained May 21, 1960. Bishop of Yakima.

Steiner, Kenneth, Appointed Dec. 6. Ordained May 19, 1962. Auxiliary Bishop of Portland in Oregon.

Wirz, George O., Appointed Dec. 20. Ordained May 31, 1952. Auxiliary Bishop of Madison.

1978

Bishops

Beltran, Eusebius J., Appointed Feb. 28. Ordained May 14, 1960. Bishop of Tulsa.

Costello, Thomas J., Appointed Jan. 10. Ordained June 5, 1954. Auxiliary Bishop of Syracuse.

DuMaine, R. Pierre, Appointed April 28. Ordained June 5, 1957. Auxiliary Bishop of San Francisco.

Flores, Patrick F., Appointed April 4. Ordained May 26, 1956. Bishop of El Paso.

Morneau, Robert F., Appointed Dec. 19. Ordained May 28, 1966. Auxiliary Bishop of Green Bay.

Quinn, Francis A., Appointed April 28. Ordained June 15, 1946. Auxiliary Bishop of San Francisco.

Rosazza, Peter A., Appointed Feb. 28. Ordained June 29, 1961. Auxiliary Bishop of Hartford.

Schmitt, Mark F., Appointed March 21. Ordained May 22, 1948. Bishop of Marquette.

Straling, Phillip F., Appointed July 18. Ordained March 19, 1959. Bishop of San Bernardino.

1979

Archbishop

Flores, Patrick F., Appointed Aug. 28. Ordained May 26, 1956. Archbishop of San Antonio.

Bishops

Clark, Matthew H., Appointed May 2. Ordained Dec. 19, 1962. Bishop of Rochester.

Fiorenza, Joseph A., Appointed Sept. 4. Ordained May 29, 1954. Bishop of San Angelo.

Fliss, Raphael M., Appointed Nov. 6. Ordained May 26, 1956. Coadjutor Bishop of Superior.

Friend, William B., Appointed Aug. 31. Ordained May 7, 1959. Auxiliary Bishop of Alexandria-Shreveport.

Griffin, James A., Appointed June 30. Ordained May 28, 1960. Auxiliary Bishop of Cleveland.

Houck, William R., Appointed March 28. Ordained May 19, 1951. Auxiliary Bishop of Jackson.

Hughes, William A., Appointed April 13. Ordained April 6, 1946. Bishop of Covington.

Imesch, Joseph L., Appointed June 30. Ordained Dec. 16, 1956. Bishop of Joliet.

Keeler, William H., Appointed July 24. Ordained July 17, 1955. Auxiliary Bishop of Harrisburg.

Madera, Joseph J., m.sp.s., Appointed Dec. 18. Ordained June 15, 1957. Coadjutor Bishop of Fresno.

McCarthy, John E., Appointed Jan. 23. Ordained May 26, 1956. Auxiliary Bishop of Galveston-Houston.

Nevins, John J., Appointed Feb. 6. Ordained June 6, 1959. Auxiliary Bishop of Miami.

Pilla, Anthony M., Appointed June 30. Ordained May 23, 1959. Auxiliary Bishop of Cleveland.

Quinn, Francis A., Appointed Dec. 18. Ordained June 15, 1946. Bishop of Sacramento.

Rivera, Hector M., Appointed June 11. Ordained June 12, 1966. Auxiliary Bishop of San Juan.

Rivera, Enrique Hernandez, Appointed June 11. Ordai June 8, 1968. Auxiliary Bishop of San Juan.

Roman, Agustin A., Appointed Feb. 6. Ordained Jul 1959. Auxiliary Bishop of Miami.

Schlarman, Stanley G., Appointed March 13. Ordai July 13, 1958. Auxiliary Bishop of Belleville.

Sklba, Richard J., Appointed Nov. 6. Ordained Dec. 1959. Auxiliary Bishop of Milwaukee.

Snyder, John J., Appointed Oct. 2. Ordained June 1951. Bishop of St. Augustine.

1980

Archbishops

Lipscomb, Oscar H., Appointed July 29. Ordained J 15, 1956. Archbishop of Mobile.

Sulyk, Stephen, Appointed Dec. 29. Archbishop of Phi delphia Ukrainian.

Bishops

Bevilacqua, Anthony, Appointed Oct. 7. Ordained Ju 11, 1949. Auxiliary Bishop of Brooklyn.

Bullock, William H., Appointed June 3. Ordained Ju 7, 1952. Auxiliary Bishop of St. Paul-Minneapolis

Chedid, John, Appointed Oct. 28. Ordained Dec. 1951. Auxiliary Bishop of St. Maron.

Kucera, Daniel W., o.s.b., Appointed March 11. Ordai May 26, 1949. Bishop of Salina.

Madera, Joseph J., m.sp.s., Succeeded to See July Bishop of Fresno.

Mahony, Roger M., Appointed Feb. 26. Ordained May 1962. Bishop of Stockton.

Pena, Raymundo J., Appointed April 29. Ordained M 25, 1957. Bishop of El Paso.

Pilla, Anthony M., Appointed Nov. 18. Ordained May 1959. Bishop of Cleveland.

Reiss, John C., Appointed March 4. Ordained May 1947. Bishop of Trenton.

Speyrer, Jude, Appointed Jan. 29. Ordained July 1953. Bishop of Lake Charles.

Sullivan, Joseph M., Appointed Oct. 7. Ordained Jun 1956. Auxiliary Bishop of Brooklyn.

Tafoya, Arthur N., Appointed July 1. Ordained May 1962. Bishop of Pueblo.

Valero, Rene, Appointed Oct. 7. Ordained June 2, 19 Auxiliary Bishop of Brooklyn.

Weigand, William K., Appointed Sept. 3. Ordained M 25, 1963. Bishop of Salt Lake City.

1981

Archbishops

Kelly, Thomas C., o.p., Appointed Dec. 29. Ordain June 5, 1958. Archbishop of Louisville.

Marcinkus, Paul C., Appointed Sept. 26. Ordained M 3, 1947. Titular Archbishop of Orta, Vatican C State.

Szoka, Edmund C., Appointed March 28. Ordained Ju 5, 1954. Archbishop of Detroit.

Bishops

DeSimone, Louis A., Appointed June 27. Ordained M 10, 1952. Auxiliary Bishop of Philadelphia.

Dumaine, R., Pierre, Appointed Jan. 27. Ordained Ju 5, 1957. Bishop of San Jose.

Grahmann, Charles V., Appointed June 30. Ordain March 17, 1956. Auxiliary Bishop of San Antonio.

Hughes, Alfred C., Appointed July 21. Ordained Dec. 1957. Auxiliary Bishop of Boston.

Lotocky, Innocent, o.s.b.m., Appointed Jan. 29. Ordain Nov. 24, 1940. Bishop of St. Nicholas Chicago.

McCarrick, Theodore E., Appointed Nov. 24. Bishop Metuchen.

Milone, Anthony M., Appointed Nov. 10. Ordained D 15, 1957. Auxiliary Bishop of Omaha.

Moskal, Robert M., Appointed Aug. 3. Ordained Ma 25, 1963. Auxiliary Bishop of the Archeparchy of Phi delphia.

O'Brien, Thomas J., Appointed Nov. 24. Ordained M 7, 1961. Bishop of Phoenix.

Ramirez, Ricardo, c.s.b., Appointed Oct. 27. Ordain Dec. 10, 1966. Auxiliary Bishop of San Antonio.

Rivera, Enrique Hernandez, Appointed Feb. 13. Ordai June 8, 1968. Bishop of Caguas.

Rose, Robert J., Appointed Oct. 13. Ordained Dec. 1955. Bishop of Gaylord.

Ryan, Daniel L., Appointed Aug. 14. Ordained May 1956. Auxiliary Bishop of Joliet.

Santana, Hermin Negron, Appointed June 30. Ordain May 30, 1969. Auxiliary Bishop of San Juan.

Schulte, Francis B., Appointed June 27. Ordained M 10, 1952. Auxiliary Bishop of Philadelphia.

Symons, J. Keith, Appointed Jan. 16. Ordained May 1958. Auxiliary Bishop of St. Petersburg.

Walsh, Daniel F., Appointed June 30. Ordained March 30, 1963. Auxiliary Bishop of San Francisco.

1982

Archbishops

Pilarczyk, Daniel E., Appointed Nov. 2. Ordained Dec. 20, 1959. Archbishop of Cincinnati.

Zayek, Francis M., Appointed Dec. 22. Ordained March 17, 1946. Archbishop of St. Maron, Brooklyn.

Bishops

Anderson, Moses B., s.s.e., Appointed Dec. 3. Ordained May 30, 1958. Auxiliary Bishop of Detroit.

Cooney, Patrick, R., Appointed Dec. 7. Ordained Dec. 20, 1959. Auxiliary Bishop of Detroit.

Friend, William B., Appointed Nov. 23. Bishop of Alexandria-Shreveport.

Gerber, Eugene J., Appointed Nov. 23. Ordained May 19, 1959. Bishop of Wichita.

Grahmann, Charles V., Appointed April 14. Ordained March 17, 1956. Bishop of Victoria.

Kinney, John F., Appointed June 28. Ordained Feb. 2, 1963. Bishop of Bismarck.

Kmiec, Edward V., Appointed Aug. 26. Ordained Dec. 20, 1961. Auxiliary Bishop of Trenton.

McRaith, John J., Appointed Oct. 23. Ordained Feb. 21, 1960. Bishop of Owensboro.

Melczek, Dale J., Appointed Dec. 3. Ordained June 6, 1964. Auxiliary Bishop of Detroit.

Pevec, Edward A., Appointed April 13. Ordained April 29, 1950. Auxiliary Bishop of Cleveland.

Ramirez, Ricardo, c.s.b., Appointed Aug. 31. Ordained Dec. 10, 1966. Bishop of Las Cruces.

Stafford, J. Francis, Appointed Nov. 16. Ordained Dec. 15, 1957. Bishop of Memphis.

1983

Archbishop

Kucera, Daniel, W., Appointed Dec. 20. Archbishop of Dubuque.

Bishops

Apuron, Anthony S., o.f.m.cap., Appointed Dec. 8. Auxiliary Bishop of Agana.

Arias, David, o.a.r., Appointed Jan. 25. Auxiliary Bishop of Newark.

Bevilacqua, Anthony, Appointed Oct. 7. Bishop of Pittsburgh.

Brom, Robert, Appointed March 25. Bishop of Duluth.

Carlson, Robert, J., Appointed Nov. 22. Auxiliary Bishop of St. Paul-Minneapolis.

Dimino, Joseph, Appointed March 29. Auxiliary Bishop of Military Services.

Gracida, Rene, Appointed May 19. Bishop of Corpus Christi.

Gregory, Wilton, Appointed Oct. 31. Auxiliary Bishop of Chicago.

Griffin, James, Appointed Feb. 7. Bishop of Columbus.

Hanifen, Richard, Appointed Nov. 10. Bishop of Colorado Springs.

Keeler, William, Appointed Nov. 10. Bishop of Harrisburg.

Levada, William, J., Appointed March 29. Auxiliary Bishop of Los Angeles.

Lyne, Timothy, Appointed Oct. 31. Auxiliary Bishop of Chicago.

Maida, Adam, Appointed Nov. 8. Bishop of Green Bay.

Moskal, Robert, Appointed Dec. 5. Bishop of St. Josaphat in Parma.

Pataki, Andrew, Appointed May 30. Auxiliary Bishop of Passaic.

Popp, Bernard, Appointed June 7. Auxiliary Bishop of San Antonio.

Quinn, A. James, Appointed Oct. 14. Auxiliary Bishop of Cleveland.

Rodriquez, Placido, Appointed Oct. Auxiliary Bishop of Chicago.

Roque, Francis, Appointed March 29. Auxiliary Bishop of Military Services.

Ryan, Daniel, Appointed Nov. 22. Bishop of Springfield in Illinois.

Schlarmann, Stanley, Appointed March 1. Bishop of Dodge City.

Sheehan, Michael, J., Appointed March 29. Bishop of Lubbock.

Soens, Lawrence, Appointed June 15. Bishop of Sioux City.

Steib, James Terry, s.v.d., Appointed Dec. 6. Auxiliary Bishop of St. Louis.

Symons, J. Keith, Appointed Sept. 29. Bishop of Pensacola-Tallahassee.

Vlazny, John G., Appointed Oct. 31. Auxiliary Bishop of Chicago.

1984

Archbishops

Foley, John, Appointed April 9. Archbishop to the Pontifical Commission for Social Communication.

Law, Bernard, Appointed Jan. 24. Archbishop of Boston.

Bishops

Baltakis, Paul, Appointed June 1. Bishop for the Lithuanian Apostolate.

Camacho, Tomas A., Appointed Nov. 8. Bishop of Chalan Kanoa.

Daily, Thomas, Appointed July 17. Bishop of Palm Beach.

Donnelly, Robert, Appointed March 20. Auxiliary Bishop of Toledo.

Donoghue, John, Appointed Nov. 6. Bishop of Charlotte.

Fiorenza, Joseph, A., Appointed Dec. 18. Bishop of Galveston-Houston.

Fitzsimons, George, Appointed March 22. Bishop of Salina.

Garland, James, H., Appointed June 25. Auxiliary Bishop of Cincinnati.

Higi, William, Appointed April 7. Bishop of Lafayette in Indiana.

Houck, William, Appointed April 24. Bishop of Jackson.

Keleher, James, Appointed Oct. 23. Bishop of Belleville.

Leibrecht, John, Appointed Oct. 23. Bishop of Springfield-Cape Girardeau.

Nevins, John, J., Appointed July 17. Bishop of Venice.

Newman, William, Appointed July 2. Auxiliary Bishop of Baltimore.

O'Malley, Sean, P., o.f.m.cap., Appointed May 30. Coadjutor Bishop of St. Thomas Virgin Islands.

Pataki, Andrew, Appointed June 19. Bishop of Parma.

Ricard, John, s.s.j., Appointed May 29. Auxiliary Bishop of Baltimore.

Steinbock, John T., Appointed May 29. Auxiliary Bishop of Orange.

Timlin, James, Appointed April 24. Bishop of Scranton.

Williams, J. Kendrick, Appointed April 15. Auxiliary Bishop of Covington.

1985

Cardinal

Law, Bernard Cardinal, Created May 25. Archbishop of Boston.

Archbishop

Mahony, Roger, Appointed July 16. Archbishop of Los Angeles.

Bishops

Apuron, Anthony S., o.f.m.cap., Appointed Oct. 27. Apostolic Administrator of Agana.

Banks, Robert J., Appointed June 26. Auxiliary Bishop of Boston.

Corrada del Rio, Alvaro, s.j., Appointed Aug. 4. Auxiliary Bishop of Washington.

D'Arcy, John M., Appointed Feb. 26. Bishop of Fort Wayne-South Bend.

Egan, Edward M., Appointed April 1. Auxiliary Bishop of New York.

Fliss, Raphael M., Succeeded to See June 27. Bishop of Superior.

Ibrahim, Ibrahim, Appointed Sept. 14. Eparch of St. Thomas the Apostle.

McCarthy, John E., Appointed Dec. 24. Bishop of Austin.

Mulvee, Robert E., Appointed Feb. 16. Bishop of Wilmington.

O'Malley, Sean, P., o.f.m.cap., Succeeded to See Oct. 16. Bishop of St. Thomas Virgin Islands.

Pfeifer, Michael, o.m.i., Appointed July 26. Bishop of San Angelo.

Schulte, Francis B., Appointed June 4. Bishop of Wheeling-Charleston.

Trautman, Donald W., Appointed Feb. 27. Auxiliary Bishop of Buffalo.

Wuerl, Donald, Appointed Dec. 3. Auxiliary Bishop of Seattle.

1986

Archbishops

Apuron, Anthony S., o.f.m.cap., Succeeded to See May 11. Archbishop of Agana.

Gerety, Peter, Leo, Retired June. Archbishop of Newark.

Levada, William J., Appointed July 1. Archbishop of Portland in Oregon.

McCarrick, Theodore E., Appointed June 1. Archbishop of Newark.

Stafford, J. Francis, Appointed June 3. Archbishop of Denver.

Bishops

Dorsey, Norbert, c.p., Appointed Jan. 10. Auxiliary Bishop of Miami.

Elya, John A., b.s.o., Appointed April 2. Auxiliary Bishop of Newton.

Favalora, John C., Appointed June 16. Bishop of Alexandria.

Flynn, Harry, Appointed April 19. Coadjutor Bishop of Lafayette.

Foley, David, Appointed May 3. Auxiliary Bishop of Richmond.

Friend, William B., Appointed June 1. Bishop of Shreveport.

Gerry, Joseph J., o.s.b., Appointed April 21. Auxiliary Bishop of Manchester.

Hughes, Edward, Appointed Dec. 11. Bishop of Metuchen.

McCormack, William J., Appointed Dec. 23. Auxiliary Bishop of New York.

McFarland, Norman F., Appointed Dec. 29. Bishop of Orange.

Ochoa, Armando, Appointed Dec. 29. Auxiliary Bishop of Los Angeles.

Weitzel, John Q., m.m., Appointed Oct. 29. Bishop of Samoa-Pago Pago.

1987

Bishops

Adamec, Joseph V., Appointed March 12. Bishop of Altoona-Johnstown.

Bosco, Anthony G., Appointed April 14. Bishop of Greensburg.

Buechlein, Daniel, M., o.s.b., Appointed Jan. 20. Bishop of Memphis.

Bullock, William H., Appointed Feb. 10. Bishop of Des Moines.

Franklin, William, E., Appointed Jan. 29. Auxiliary Bishop of Dubuque.

Guillory, Curtis, Appointed Dec. 29. Auxiliary Bishop of Galveston-Houston.

Hanus, Jerome, G., o.s.b., Appointed July 6. Bishop of St. Cloud.

Milone, Anthony M., Appointed Dec. 14. Bishop of Great Falls-Billings.

Michaels, James, Resigned Sept. Auxiliary Bishop of Wheeling-Charleston.

Myers, John J., Appointed July 14. Coadjutor Bishop of Peoria.

Rueger, George, Appointed Jan. 19. Auxiliary Bishop of Worcester.

Samo, Amando, Appointed May 10. Auxiliary Bishop of The Carolines-Marshalls.

Smith, John M., Appointed Dec. 1. Auxiliary Bishop of Newark.

Steinbock, John T., Appointed March 31. Bishop of Santa Rosa.

Vlazny, John G., Appointed May 19. Bishop of Winona.

Walsh, Daniel F., Appointed June 9. Bishop of Reno- Las Vegas.

1988

Cardinal

Szoka, Edmund Cardinal, Created June 29. Pres. Prefecture for Economic Affairs of the Holy See, Vatican.

Archbishops

Bevilacqua, Anthony J., Appointed Feb. 11. Archbishop of Philadelphia.

Schulte, Francis B., Appointed Dec. 13. Archbishop of New Orleans.

Bishops

Boland, Raymond J., Appointed Feb. 2. Bishop of Birmingham.

Brown, Tod D., Appointed Dec. 27. Bishop of Boise.

Carmody, Edmond, Appointed Nov. 8. Auxiliary Bishop of San Antonio.

Chaput, Charles, o.f.m.cap., Appointed April 11. Bishop of Rapid City.

Curlin, William G., Appointed Dec. 20. Auxiliary Bishop of Washington.

DiLorenzo, Francis, Appointed Jan. 26. Auxiliary Bishop of Scranton.

Dunne, John C., Appointed Oct. 21. Auxiliary Bishop of Rockville Centre.

Egan, Edward, M., Appointed Nov. 8. Bishop of Bridgeport.

Gerry, Joseph, J., o.s.b., Appointed Dec. 27. Bishop of Portland (in Maine).

Gonzalez, Roberto O., o.f.m., Appointed July 19. Auxiliary Bishop of Boston.
Gorman, John R., Appointed Feb. 16. Auxiliary Bishop of Chicago.
Jakubowski, Thaddeus J., Appointed Feb. 16. Auxiliary Bishop of Chicago.
Loverde, Paul S., Appointed Feb. 3. Auxiliary Bishop of Hartford.
McGrath, Patrick, J., Appointed Dec. 6. Auxiliary Bishop of San Francisco.
McLaughlin, Bernard J., Retired Jan. 15. Auxiliary Bishop of Buffalo.
O'Connell, Anthony J., Appointed June 7. Bishop of Knoxville.
Olivier, Leonard J., s.v.d., Appointed Dec. 20. Auxiliary Bishop of Washington.
Schmitt, Bernard W., Appointed May 31. Auxiliary Bishop of Wheeling-Charleston.
Sevilla, Carlos A., s.j., Appointed Dec. 6. Auxiliary Bishop of San Francisco.
Wcela, Emil A., Appointed Oct. 21. Auxiliary Bishop of Rockville Centre.
Williams, J. Kendrick, Appointed March 2. Bishop of Lexington.
Winter, William J., Appointed Dec. 27. Auxiliary Bishop of Pittsburgh.
Wuerl, Donald, Appointed Feb. 11. Bishop of Pittsburgh.

1989

Archbishops

Borders, William D., Retired April. Archbishop of Baltimore.
Hannan, Philip M., Retired Feb. Archbishop of New Orleans.
Keeler, William, Appointed April 6. Archbishop of Baltimore.

Bishops

Brom, Robert, Appointed April 22. Coadjutor Bishop of San Diego.
Charron, Joseph L., c.pp.s., Appointed Nov. 6. Auxiliary Bishop of St. Paul-Minneapolis.
Cooney, Patrick, R., Appointed Nov. 21. Bishop of Gaylord.
Driscoll, Michael P., Appointed Dec. 19. Auxiliary Bishop of Orange.
Favalora, John, C., Appointed March 7. Bishop of St. Petersburg.
Flynn, Harry J., Succeeded to the See May 13. Bishop of Lafayette.
Gettelfinger, Gerald A., Appointed March 11. Bishop of Evansville.
Grahmann, Charles V., Appointed Dec. 18. Coadjutor Bishop of Dallas.
Grosz, Edward, Appointed Nov. 22. Auxiliary Bishop of Buffalo.
Jacobs, Sam, Appointed July 1. Bishop of Alexandria.
Mikloshazy, Attila, s.j., Appointed Aug. 12. Bishop for the Apostolate to the Hungarians.
Rose, Robert J., Appointed July 11. Bishop of Grand Rapids.
Samra, Nicholas J., Appointed June 29. Auxiliary Bishop of Newton.
Schmitt, Bernard W., Appointed March 30. Bishop of Wheeling-Charleston.
Schwietz, Roger L., o.m.i., Appointed Dec. 12. Bishop of Duluth.
Thompson, David B., Appointed May 9. Coadjutor Bishop of Charleston.
Zipfel, Paul A., Appointed May 16. Auxiliary Bishop of St. Louis.

1990

Archbishop

Maida, Adam J., Appointed June 11. Archbishop of Detroit.

Bishops

Banks, Robert J., Appointed Oct. 16. Bishop of Green Bay.
Blaire, Stephen E., Appointed Feb. 17. Auxiliary Bishop of Los Angeles.
Brom, Robert H., Succeeded to the See July 10. Bishop of San Diego.
Daily, Thomas V., Appointed Feb. 20. Bishop of Brooklyn.
Dorsey, Norbert M., c.p., Appointed March 20. Bishop of Orlando.
Dupre, Thomas L., Appointed April 19. Auxiliary Bishop of Springfield in Massachusetts.
Fellhauer, David E., Appointed April 19. Bishop of Victoria.
George, Francis E., o.m.i., Appointed July 10. Bishop of Yakima.
Grahmann, Charles V., Succeeded to See July 14. Bishop of Dallas.
Muench, Robert W., Appointed May 8. Auxiliary Bishop of New Orleans.
Myers, John J., Succeeded to See Jan. 23. Bishop of Peoria.
Ryan, Sylvester D., Appointed Feb. 17. Auxiliary Bishop of Los Angeles.
Sheridan, Patrick J., Appointed Dec. 12. Auxiliary Bishop of New York.
Skylstad, William S., Appointed April 17. Bishop of Spokane.
Symons, J. Keith, Appointed June 2. Bishop of Palm Beach.
Thompson, David B., Succeeded to See Feb. 22. Bishop of Charleston.
Trautman, Donald W., Appointed July 16. Bishop of Erie.

1991

Cardinals

Bevilacqua, Anthony Cardinal, Created June 28. Archbishop of Philadelphia.
Mahony, Roger Cardinal, Created June 28. Archbishop of Los Angeles.

Archbishops

Cronin, Daniel A., Appointed Dec. 9. Archbishop of Hartford.
Dimino, Joseph T., Succeeded to the See June 21. Archbishop of the Military Services.
Hunthausen, Raymond G., Retired Aug. Archbishop of Seattle.

Bishops

Goedert, Raymond E., Appointed July 8. Auxiliary Bishop of Chicago.
Madera, Joseph J., m.sp.s., Appointed May 28. Auxiliary Bishop of the Military Services.
Maguire, Joseph F., Retired Dec. Bishop of Springfield.
Smith, John M., Appointed June 24. Bishop of Pensacola-Tallahassee.
Steinbock, John T., Appointed Oct. 15. Bishop of Fresno.
Txertudi, Inaki Mallona, c.p., Appointed Dec. 14. Bishop of Arecibo.

1992

Archbishops

Beltran, Eusebius J., Appointed Nov. 24. Archbishop of Oklahoma City, from Bishop of Tulsa.
Buechlein, Daniel M., o.s.b., Appointed July 14. Archbishop of Indianapolis, from Bishop of Memphis.

Bishops

Angell, Kenneth A., Appointed Oct. 10. Bishop of Burlington, from Auxiliary Bishop of Providence.
Barnes, Gerald R., Appointed Jan. 28. Auxiliary Bishop of San Bernardino.
Boles, John P., Appointed April 14. Auxiliary Bishop of Boston.
Bruskewitz, Fabian W., Appointed March 24. Bishop of Lincoln.
Carmody, Edmond, Appointed March 24. Bishop of Tyler, from Auxiliary Bishop of San Antonio.
Carmon, Dominic, s.v.d., Appointed Dec. 16. Auxiliary Bishop of New Orleans.
Galante, Joseph A., Appointed Oct. 13. Auxiliary Bishop of San Antonio.
Garland, James H., Appointed Oct. 10. Bishop of Marquette, from Auxiliary Bishop of Cincinnati.
Jarrell, Michael Charles, Appointed Dec. 29. Bishop of Houma-Thibodaux.
Kmiec, Edward Urban, Appointed Oct. 13. Bishop of Nashville, from Auxiliary Bishop of Trenton.
Mansell, Henry J., Appointed Nov. 24. Auxiliary Bishop of New York.
O'Malley, Sean P., o.f.m.cap., Appointed June 16. Bishop of Fall River from Bishop of St. Thomas, Virgin Islands.
Ottenweller, Albert H., Retired April. Bishop of Steubenville.
Ryan, Sylvester D., Appointed Jan. 21. Bishop of Monterey, from Auxiliary Bishop of Los Angeles.
Schmitt, Mark F., Retired Nov. 11. Bishop of Marquette.
Sheldon, Gilbert I., Appointed Jan. 28. Bishop of Steubenville, from Auxiliary Bishop of Cleveland.
Tobin, Thomas J., Appointed Nov. 3. Auxiliary Bishop of Pittsburgh.

1993

Archbishops

Curtiss, Elden F., Appointed May 4. Archbishop of Omah from Bishop of Helena.
Donoghue, John F., Appointed June 22. Archbishop Atlanta, from Bishop of Charlotte.
Keleher, James P., Transferred Sept. 8. Archbishop Kansas City in Kansas, from Bishop of Belleville.
Sanchez, Robert F., Retired April. Archbishop of Santa F
Sheehan, Michael J., Appointed April 6. Archbishop Santa Fe.

Bishops

Boland, Raymond J., Appointed June 22. Bishop of Ka sas City-St. Joseph, from Bishop of Birmingham, Jun
Bullock, William H., Appointed April 13. Bishop of Mad son, from Bishop of Des Moines.
Charron, Joseph L., c.pp.s. Appointed Nov. 12. Bishop Des Moines, from Auxiliary Bishop of St. Paul ar Minneapolis.
Elya, John A., b.s.o. Appointed Dec. 7. Bishop of Nev ton from Auxiliary Bishop of Newton.
Franklin, William E., Appointed Nov. 12. Bishop of Da enport, from Auxiliary Bishop of Dubuque.
Gregory, Wilton, Appointed Dec. 29. Bishop of Bellevil from Auxiliary Bishop of Chicago.
Harrington, Bernard J., Appointed Nov. 23. Auxilia Bishop of Detroit.
Hughes, Alfred C., Appointed Sept. 7. Bishop of Batc Rouge, from Auxiliary Bishop of Boston.
Lotocky, Innocent, Resigned July. Bishop of St. Nichola of Chicago.
Loverde, Paul S., Appointed Nov. 11. Bishop Ogdensburg, from Auxiliary Bishop of Hartford.
Popp, Bernard F., Retired March. Auxiliary Bishop San Antonio.
Quinn, Francis A., Retired Nov. Bishop of Sacrament
Slattery, Edward J., Appointed Nov. 11. Bishop of Tuls
Steib, James Terry, s.v.d. Appointed March 23. Bishc of Memphis, from Auxiliary Bishop of St. Louis.
Tamayo, James A., Appointed Jan. 26. Auxiliary Bisho of Galveston-Houston.
Thomas, Elliot G., Appointed Oct. 10. Bishop of S Thomas, Virgin Islands.
Weigand, William K., Appointed Nov. 3. Bishop of Sa ramento from Bishop of Salt Lake City.
Wiwchar, Michael, c.ss.r. Appointed July 15. Bishop St. Nicholas in Chicago for Ukrainians.

1994

Cardinals

Keeler, William Cardinal, Created Nov. 26. Archbisho of Baltimore.
Maida, Adam Cardinal, Created Nov. 26. Archbishop Detroit.

Archbishops

Favalora, John C., Appointed Nov. 3. Archbishop of Miam
Flynn, Harry J., Appointed Feb. 2. Coadjutor Archbisho of St. Paul-Minneapolis.
Hanus, Jerome, G., o.s.b. Appointed Aug. 23. Coadjutc Archbishop of Dubuque.
Rigali, Justin F., Appointed Jan. 25. Archbishop of S Louis.

Bishops

Ahern, Patrick V., Retired April. Auxiliary Bishop of Ne York.
Barbarito, Gerald, Appointed June 28. Auxiliary Bishop Brooklyn.
Brunett, Alexander J., Appointed April 19. Bishop of He ena.
Burke, Raymond L., Appointed Dec. 10. Bishop of La Cross
Carlson, Robert J., Appointed Jan. 13. Coadjutor Bishop Sioux Falls, from Auxiliary Bishop of St. Paul-Minn apolis.
Catanello, Ignatius, Appointed June 28. Auxiliary Bishc of Brooklyn.
Chedid, John G., Appointed March 1. First Bishop of Ou Lady of Lebanon in Los Angeles, from Auxiliary Bishc of Saint Maron.
Cullen, Edward P., Appointed Feb. 8. Auxiliary Bishop Philadelphia.
Curlin, William G., Appointed Feb. 22. Bishop of Cha lotte, from Auxiliary Bishop of Washington.
Curry, Thomas J., Appointed Feb. 8. Auxiliary Bishop Los Angeles.
DiLorenzo, Francis X., Appointed Oct. 4. Bishop of Hon lulu.
Donovan, Paul V., Retired Nov. Bishop of Kalamazoo.
Doran, Thomas G., Appointed April 19. Bishop of Rock ford.
Foley, David E., Appointed March 22. Bishop of Birming ham, from Auxiliary Bishop of Richmond.

Galante, Joseph A., Appointed April 5. Bishop of Beaumont from Auxiliary Bishop of San Antonio.
Lohmuller, Martin N., Retired Oct. Auxiliary Bishop of Philadelphia.
McDonnell, Charles J., Appointed March 15. Auxiliary Bishop of Newark.
Niederauer, George H., Appointed Nov. 3. Bishop of Salt Lake City.
O'Neill, Arthur J., Retired April. Bishop of Rockford.
Reilly, Daniel P., Appointed Oct. 27. Bishop of Worcester.
Rodriguez, Placido, c.m.f., Appointed April 5. Bishop of Lubbock, from Auxiliary Bishop of Chicago.
Samo, Amando, Appointed Feb. Coadjutor Bishop of the Caroline Islands.
Sartoris, Joseph M., Appointed Feb. 8. Auxiliary Bishop of Los Angeles.
Yanta, John W., Appointed Oct. 27. Auxiliary Bishop of San Antonio.
Zavala, Gabino, Appointed Feb. 8. Auxiliary Bishop of Los Angeles.

1995

Archbishops

Flynn, Harry J., Appointed Sept. 8. From Coadjutor to Archbishop of St. Paul-Minneapolis.
Hanus, Jerome G., o.s.b., Succeeding as Archbishop of Dubuque from status of Coadjutor.
Kucera, Daniel W., Retired Oct. Archbishop of Dubuque.
Quinn, John R., Retired Dec. Archbishop of San Francisco.
Levada, William J., Succeeding as Archbishop of San Francisco Dec.
Schleck, Charles A., c.s.c., Appointed Feb. 10.

Bishops

Barnes, Gerald R., Appointed Dec. 28. Bishop of San Bernardino, from Auxiliary of same Diocese.
Boland, J. Kevin, Appointed Feb. 7. Bishop of Savannah.
Braxton, Edward K., Appointed March 28. Auxiliary Bishop of St. Louis.
Carlson, Robert J., Succeeding as Bishop of Sioux Falls in March, from status of Coadjutor.
Cote, Michael R., Appointed May 9. Auxiliary Bishop of Portland in Maine.
Dougherty, John M., Appointed Feb. 7. Auxiliary Bishop of Scranton.
Dupre, Thomas L., Appointed March 14. Bishop of Springfield, from Auxiliary Bishop of Springfield.
Gonzalez, Roberto O., o.f.m., Appointed May 16. Coadjutor Bishop of Corpus Christi, from Auxiliary Bishop of Boston.
Hughes, William A., Retired July. Bishop of Covington.
Kicanas, Gerald F., Appointed Jan. 24. Auxiliary Bishop of Chicago.
Kinney, John F., Appointed May 8. Bishop of St. Cloud from Bishop of Bismarck.
Lessard, Raymond W., Retired Feb. Bishop of Savannah.
Lori, William E., Appointed Feb. 27. Auxiliary Bishop of Washington.
Lynch, Robert N., Appointed Dec. 4. Bishop of St. Petersburg.
Lyne, Timothy J., Retired Jan. 24. Auxiliary Bishop of Chicago.
Mansell, Henry J., Appointed April 18. Bishop of Buffalo, from Auxiliary Bishop of NewYork.
McCormack, John B., Appointed Nov. Auxiliary Bishop of Boston.
Melczek, Dale J., Appointed Nov. 9. Coadjutor Bishop of Gary.
Mengeling, Carl F., Appointed Nov. Bishop of Lansing.
Moynihan, James M., Appointed April 29. Bishop of Syracuse.
Mulvee, Robert Edward, Appointed Feb. 7. Coadjutor Bishop of Providence from Bishop of Wilmington.
Murphy, William F., Appointed Nov. Auxiliary Bishop of Boston.
Murry, George V., s.j. Appointed Jan. 24. Auxiliary Bishop of Chicago.
Pataki, Andrew, Appointed Bishop of Passaic Nov., from Bishop of Parma.
Pena, Raymundo J., Appointed May 23. Bishop of Brownsville, from Bishop of El Paso.
Samo, Amando, Appointed March. Bishop of the Caroline Islands.
Smith, John M., Named Coadjutor of Trenton from Bishop of Pensacola-Tallahassee.
Straling, Phillip F., Appointed March 21. Bishop of Reno, from Bishop of San Bernadino.
Tobin, Thomas J., Appointed Bishop of Youngstown, from Auxiliary of Pittsburgh.
Walsh, Daniel F., Appointed Bishop of Las Vegas March 21.

1996

Archbishops

George, Francis, E. o.m.i., Appointed Archbishop of Portland in Oregon from Bishop of Yakima, April.
Zayek, Francis M., Retired Archbishop of St. Maron of Brooklyn, Nov.

Bishops

Allue, Emilio, s.d.b., Appointed Auxiliary Bishop of Boston, July 24.
Aymond, Gregory M., Appointed Auxiliary Bishop of New Orleans, Nov. 19.
Botean, John Michael, Appointed Bishop of Romanian Catholic Diocese of St. George in Canton.
Christian, Francis J., Appointed Auxiliary Bishop of Manchester, April 2.
Daly, James J., Retired Auxiliary Bishop of Rockville Centre, July.
DiMarzio, Nicholas A., Appointed Auxiliary Bishop of Newark, Sept.
Doueihi, Hector, Appointed Bishop of St. Maron of Brooklyn.
Irwin, Francis X., Appointed Auxiliary Bishop of Boston, July 24.
Maginnis, Robert P., Appointed Auxiliary Bishop of Philadelphia, Jan. 23.
Manz, John R., Appointed Auxiliary Bishop of Chicago, Jan. 23.
Martino, Joseph F., Appointed Auxiliary Bishop of Philadelphia, Jan. 23.
Melczek, Dale J., Succeeded to Bishop of Gary, June 1.
Muench, Robert W., Appointed Bishop of Covington from Auxiliary Bishop of New Orleans, Jan. 5.
Nienstedt, John C., Appointed Auxiliary Bishop of Detroit, June 11.
O'Brien, Edwin F., Appointed Auxiliary Bishop of New York.
Ochoa, Armando, Appointed Bishop of El Paso from Auxiliary Bishop of Los Angeles, April.
Schott, Basil, o.f.m. , Bishop of Parma (Ruthenians).
Sevilla, Carlos A., s.j. Appointed Bishop of Yakima from Auxiliary Bishop of San Francisco Dec. 31.
Vigneron, Allen H., Appointed Auxiliary Bishop of Detroit June 11.
Ward, John J., Retired Auxiliary Bishop of Los Angeles, July.
Warfel, Michael, Appointed Bishop of Juneau Nov. 19.
Younan, Joseph, Appointed Bishop of Our Lady of Deliverance of Newark.
Zipfel, Paul A., Appointed Bishop of Bismarck from Auxiliary Bishop of St. Louis Dec. 31.

1997

Archbishops

Brunett, Alexander J., Appointed Archbishop of Seattle, Oct.
Chaput, Charles J., o.f.m.cap., Appointed Archbishop of Denver Feb. 18, 1997, from Bishop of Rapid City.
Dimino, Joseph T., Retired Archbishop for the Military Services, Aug.
George, Francis, E. o.m.i., Appointed Archbishop of Chicago from Archbishop of Portland in Oregon from Bishop of Yakima, April.
O'Brien, Edwin F., Appointed Archbishop for the Military Services from Auxiliary Bishop of New York.
Vlazny, John G., Appointed Archbishop of Portland in Oregon, Oct.

Bishops

Bennett, Gordon D., Appointed Auxiliary Bishop of Baltimore, Dec. 23.
Bootkoski, Paul G., Appointed Auxiliary Bishop for the Archdiocese of Newark, July.
Brucato, Robert A., Appointed Auxiliary Bishop for the Archdiocese of New York, July.
Cullen, Edward P., Appointed Bishop of Allentown from Auxiliary Bishop of Philadelphia, Dec 16.
DeSimone, Louis A., Retired Auxiliary Bishop of Philadelphia, April.
DiNardo, Daniel N., Appointed Coadjutor Bishop of Sioux City, Aug. 19.
Fernandez, Gilberto, Appointed Auxiliary Bishop for the Archdiocese of Miami, June 23.
Garcia, Richard J., Appointed Auxiliary Bishop of Sacramento, Nov.
Gaydos, John R., Appointed June 24. Bishop of Jefferson City.
Gelineau, Louis E., Retired Bishop of Providence, June.
Gonzalez, Roberto O., Appointed Bishop of Corpus Christi, March 31.
Gracida, Rene H., Retired Bishop of Corpus Christi, April.
Hughes, Edward T., Retired Bishop of Metuchen, Sept.
Jenky, Daniel R., c.s.c., Appointed Auxiliary Bishop of Fort Wayne-South Bend.
Macaluso, Christie A., Appointed Auxiliary Bishop of Hartford, March 18.
Mulvee, Robert E., Succeeds as Bishop of Providence from Coadjutor Bishop of Providence, June.
Murray, James A., Appointed Bishop of Kalamazoo, Nov. Naumann, Joseph F., Appointed Bishop of St. Louis, July.
Reiss, John C., Retired Bishop of Trenton, July.
Ricard, John H., s.s.j., Appointed Bishop of Pensacola-Tallahassee, Jan.
Sheridan, Michael J., Appointed Auxiliary Bishop of St. Louis, July.
Smith, John M., Succeeds as Bishop of Trenton from Coadjutor Bishop of Trenton, July.
Wenski, Thomas G., Appointed Auxiliary Bishop for the Archdiocese of Miami, June 23.
Wilkerson, Gerald E., Appointed Auxiliary Bishop of Los Angeles, Nov. 5.
Yanta, John W., Appointed Bishop of Amarillo, from Auxiliary of San Antonio in Jan.
Zubik, David A., Appointed Auxiliary Bishop of Pittsburgh Feb. 18.

1998

Cardinals

George, Francis Cardinal, o.m.i., Created Feb. 21. Archbishop of Chicago.
Stafford, Francis Cardinal, Pres.-Pontifical Council for the Laity, Vatican.

Bishops

Brown, Tod D., Appointed Bishop of Orange from Bishop of Boise, June.
Cupich, Blase J., Appointed Bishop of Rapid City, July 6. DiNardo, Daniel N., Appointed Bishop of Sioux City, Dec.
Flanagan, Thomas Joseph, Appointed Auxiliary Bishop of San Antonio, Jan. 5.
Gilmore, Ronald M., Appointed Bishop of Dodge City, May.
Harrington, Bernard J., Appointed Bishop of Winona, from Auxiliary Bishop of Detroit, Nov.
Harvey, James M., Bishop and Prefect of the Papal Household, March.
McCormack, John B., Appointed Bishop of Manchester from Auxiliary Bishop of Boston, July.
McFarland, Norman F., Retired Bishop of Orange, June.
McManus, Robert Joseph, Appointed Auxiliary Bishop of Providence, Dec. 1.
Murry, George V., s.j., Appointed Coadjutor to St. Thomas Virgin Islands, May.
Perry, Joseph N., Appointed Auxiliary Bishop of Chicago, May.
Rivera, Enrique Hernandez, Retired Bishop of Caguas, July.
Schlarman, Stanley G., Retired Bishop of Dodge City, May 12.
Soens, Lawrence D., Retired Bishop of Sioux City, Nov. Symons, Joseph K., Retired Bishop of Palm Beach, June.
Wester, John Charles, Appointed Auxiliary Bishop of San Francisco, June 30.
Zurek, Patrick J., Appointed Auxiliary Bishop of San Antonio, Jan. 5.

1999

Cardinal

Martinez, Luis Cardinal Aponte, Retired Archbishop of San Juan, March.

Bishops

Baker, Robert J. Appointed Bishop of Charleston July 12.
Barbarito, Gerald M., Appointed Bishop of Ogdensburg, from Auxiliary Bishop of Brooklyn.
Blair, Leonard P., Appointed Auxiliary Bishop of Detroit.
Blaire, Stephen E., Appointed Bishop of Stockton, from Auxiliary Bishop of Los Angeles, Sept.
Campbell, Frederick F., Appointed Auxiliary Bishop of St. Paul and Minneapolis, March.
DiMarzio, Nicholas A., Appointed Bishop of Camden.
Dumaine, Pierre, Retired Bishop of San Jose, Nov. Driscoll, Michael P., Appointed Bishop of Boise, from Auxiliary Bishop of Orange, Jan.
Galante, Joseph A., Appointed Coadjutor Bishop of Dallas, from Bishop of Beaumont, Nov. 23.
Kurtz, Joseph E., Appointed Bishop of Knoxville, Dec. Loverde, Paul S., Appointed Bishop of Arlington, from Bishop of Ogdensburg, Jan.

Lucas, George J., Appointed Bishop of Springfield, Illinois, Oct. 19.
McCarthy, James F., Auxiliary Bishop of New York, May.
McGrath Patrick J., Succeeded to Bishop of San Jose, from Coadjutor, Nov. 27.
Morlino, Robert C. Appointed Bishop of Helena July 6.
Murry, George V., s.j., Appointed Bishop to St. Thomas Virgin Islands, June 30.
O'Connell, Anthony J., Resigned Bishop of Palm Beach, from Bishop of Knoxville.
Olmsted, Thomas J., Appointed Coadjutor Bishop of Wichita, Feb.
Ricken, David L., Appointed Coadjutor Bishop of Cheyenne, Dec.
Ryan, Daniel L., Retired Bishop of Springfield in Illinois, Oct.
Sartain, J. Peter, Appointed Bishop of Little Rock, Dec.
Thomas, Elliot G., Retired Bishop of St. Thomas Virgin Islands, June 30.
Thomas, George, Appointed Auxiliary Bishop of Seattle, Nov. 19.
Thompson, David B., Retired Bishop of Charleston, July.
Vasa, Robert F., Appointed Bishop of Baker, Nov. 19.

2000

Archbishops
Egan, Edward M., Appointed Archbishop of New York, from Bishop of Bridgeport, June.
Gonzalez, Roberto O., o.f.m., Archbishop of San Juan.
McCarrick, Theodore E., Appointed Archbishop of Washington from Archbishop of Newark, Dec.
Schwietz, Roger L., o.m.i., Appointed Coadjutor Archbishop of Anchorage from Bishop of Duluth, Jan.
Soroka, Stephen, Appointed Archbishop of the Ukrainian Archeparchy of Philadelphia.
Sulyk, Stephen, Retired Archbishop of Philadelphia Ukrainian, Nov.

Bishops
Aymond, Gregory M., Appointed Coadjutor Bishop of Austin, June.
Batakian, Manuel, Appointed Exarch for Armenian Catholics in U.S.A. and Canada, Nov. 30.
Braxton, Edward K., Appointed Bishop of Lake Charles, Dec. 11.
Carmody, Edmond, Appointed Bishop of Corpus Christi, from Bishop of Tyler, Feb. 2.
Chedid, John G., Retired Bishop of Our Lady of Lebanon, Dec.
Connoly, Thomas J., Retired Bishop of Baker, Jan.
Corrada del Rio, Alvaro, s.j. from Auxiliary Bishop of Washington; Administrator of Caguas to Bishop of Tyler.
Guillory, Curtis J., Appointed Bishop of Beaumont from Auxiliary Bishop of Galveston-Houston, June.
Listecki, Jerome E., Appointed Auxiliary Bishop of Chicago, Nov. 7.
Malone, Richard J., Appointed as Auxiliary Bishop of Boston, Feb.
Malooly, William Frances, Appointed Auxiliary Bishop of Baltimore, Dec. 11.
McDonald, Andrew J., Retired Bishop of Little Rock, Jan.
Serratelli, Arthur J., Appointed Auxiliary Bishop of Newark, July 3.
Shaheen, Robert J., Eparch of Our Lady of Lebanon, Dec. 4.
Snyder, John J., Retired Bishop of St. Augustine, Dec.
Soto, Jaime, Appointed Auxiliary Bishop of Orange, March 23.
Speyrer, Jude, Resigned Bishop of Lake Charles, Dec.
Tamayo, James A., Appointed Bishop of Laredo, July 3.
Torres, Juan Fremiot, Retired Bishop of Ponce, Nov.
Walsh, Daniel F., Appointed Bishop of Santa Rosa, April 4.

2001

Cardinals
Egan, Edward Cardinal, M., Created Feb. 21, Archbishop of New York.
McCarrick, Theodore Cardinal, E., Created Feb., Archbishop of Washington.

Archbishops
Hughes, Alfred C., Coadjutor Archbishop of New Orleans from Bishop of Baton Rouge, Feb.
Hurley, Francis T., Retired Archbishop of Anchorage, March 3.
Myers, John J., Appointed Archbishop of Newark, July.
Schwietz, Roger L., o.m.i., Succeeded March 3, as Archbishop of Anchorage from Coadjutor Archbishop of Anchorage.

Bishops
Amos, Martin John, Appointed Auxiliary Bishop of Cleveland, April 3.
Aquila, Samuel J., Appointed Coadjutor Bishop of Fargo June 12.
Angadiath, Jacob, Appointed Bishop of St. Thomas Syro-Malabar Catholic Diocese of Chicago, March 12.
Aymond, Gregory M., Appointed Bishop of Austin from Coadjutor Bishop of Austin, Jan. 2.
Clark, Edward W., Appointed Auxiliary Bishop of Los Angeles, Jan. 16.
Dolan, Timothy, M., Appointed Auxiliary Bishop of St. Louis, June 19.
Edyvean, Walter, Appointed Auxiliary Bishop of Boston, June 29.
Farrell, Kevin, Appointed Auxiliary Bishop of Washington, D.C., Dec. 28.
Galeone, Victor, Appointed Bishop of St. Augustine, June 26.
Gerber, Eugene J., Retired Bishop of Wichita, Oct.
Gomez, Jose H., Appointed Auxiliary Bishop of Denver, Jan. 22.
Gonzalez, Francisco, Appointed Auxiliary Bishop of Washington, Dec.
Gries, Roger W., o.s.b., Appointed Auxiliary Bishop of Cleveland, April 3.
Hart, Joseph H., Retired Bishop of Cheyenne, Sept. 26.
Howze, Joseph L., Retired Bishop of Biloxi, May 15.
Iriondo, Josu, Appointed Auxiliary Bishop of New York, Oct. 29.
Kicanas, Gerald F., Appointed Coadjutor Bishop of Tucson, from Auxiliary Bishop of Chicago, Oct. 30.
Lagonegro, Dominick J., Appointed Auxiliary Bishop of New York, Oct. 29.
Lennon, Richard, Appointed Auxiliary Bishop of Boston, June 29.
Lori, William E., Bishop of Bridgeport from Auxiliary Bishop of Washington, Jan. 16.
McCarthy, John E., Retired Bishop of Austin, Jan. 2.
McCormack, William J., Retired Auxiliary Bishop of New York, Oct.
McDonnell, Timothy A., Appointed Auxiliary Bishop of New York, Oct. 29.
McKinney, Joseph C., Resigned Auxiliary Bishop of Grand Rapids, Oct.
Medina, Ruben Antonio Gonzalez, c.m.f., Bishop of Caguas.
Mestice, Anthony F., Retired Auxiliary Bishop of New York, Oct.
Muench, Robert W., Appointed Bishop of Baton Rouge, from Bishop of Covington, Dec. 14.
Murphy, William, Appointed Bishop of Rockville Centre from Auxiliary Bishop of Boston June 26.
Myers, John, J., Appointed Archbishop of Newark from Bishop of Peoria, July 24.
Nienstedt, John C., Appointed Bishop of New Ulm, from Auxiliary Bishop of Detroit.
Olmsted, Thomas J., Succeeds as Bishop of Wichita, from Coadjutor Bishop, Oct. 4.
Pates, Richard E., Appointed Auxiliary Bishop of St. Paul and Minneapolis.
Pepe, Joseph A., Appointed Bishop of Las Vegas, April 6.
Pevec, Edward A., Retired Auxiliary Bishop of Cleveland, April.
Ricken, David, Appointed Bishop of Cheyenne, Sept. 26.
Rizzotto, Vincent, Appointed Auxiliary Bishop of Galveston-Houston, June 22.
Rodi, Thomas, Appointed Bishop of Biloxi, May 15.
Schnurr, Dennis M., Appointed Bishop of Duluth, Jan.18.
Sheridan, Michael, Appointed Coadjutor Bishop of Colorado Springs from Auxiliary Bishop of St. Louis Dec. 3.
Sheridan, Patrick, J., Retired Auxiliary Bishop of New York, Jan.
Vasquez, Jose S., Appointed Auxiliary Bishop of Galveston-Houston, Nov. 29.

2002

Cardinal
Law, Bernard, Retired Archbishop of Boston, Dec.

Archbishops
Dolan, Timothy, M., Appointed Archbishop of Milwaukee, June 25.
Hughes, Alfred C., Succeeds as Archbishop of New Orleans from Coadjutor, Jan. 3.
Schott, Basil M., o.f.m., Appointed Archbishop of Pittsburgh Byzantine May 3.
Schulte, Francis B., Retired Archbishop of New Orleans, Jan.
Weakland, Rembert G., o.s.b., Retired Archbishop of Milwaukee, May 24.

Bishops
Aquila, Samuel J., Succeeds as Bishop of Farg March18.
Bootkoski, Paul G., Appointed Bishop of Metuche from Auxiliary Bishop of Newark, Jan. 4.
Boyea Earl A., Appointed Auxiliary Bishop of Detroi July 22.
Burbidge, Michael F., Installed as Auxiliary Bishop Philadelphia, Sept. 5.
Conlon, R. Daniel, Appointed Bishop of Steubenvill June.
Cordileone, Salvatore J., Appointed Auxiliary Bishop San Diego, July.
Curlin, William G., Retired Bishop of Charlotte, Sep 10.
Fernandez, Gilberto, Retired Auxiliary Bishop of M ami, Dec. 10.
Foys, Roger J., Appointed Bishop of Covington, May 3
Gainer, Ronald W., Appointed Bishop of Lexington, De 12.
Hermann, Robert J., Appointed Auxiliary Bishop of S Louis, Oct. 16.
Jammo, Sarhad Y., Appointed Bishop of Eparchy of S Peter the Apostle (Chaldean), May 4.
Jarrell, Michael C., Appointed Bishop of Lafayette Louisiana, Nov. 8.
Jenky, Daniel R., c.s.c., Appointed Bishop of Peori from Auxiliary Bishop of Fort Wayne-South Ben Feb. 11.
Kettler, Donald J., Appointed Bishop of Fairbanks, Ju 6.
Kudrick, John M., Installed as Bishop of Parma, July
Lazaro, Felix, Appointed Coadjutor Bishop of Ponc March.
Marconi, Dominic A., Retired Auxiliary Bishop of Ne ark, July.
McCarthy, James F., Retired Auxiliary Bishop of Ne York, June.
O'Connell, Anthony J., Resigned Bishop of Palm Beac March.
O'Malley, Sean P., o.f.m.cap., Appointed as Bishop Palm Beach, Sept. 3.
Pevec, Edward A., Retired Auxiliary Bishop of Clev land, Sept. 1.
Sartoris, Joseph M., Retired Auxiliary Bishop of L Angeles, Dec. 31.
Sheldon, Gilbert I., Retired as Bishop of Steubenvil Aug. 6.
Skurla, William, Appointed Bishop of the Eparchy Van Nuys, Feb. 19.
Wang, Ignatius, Appointed Auxiliary Bishop of San Fra cisco, Dec. 12.
Williams, J. Kendrick, Retired Bishop of Lexington, Ju 11.

2003

Cardinals
Bevilacqua, Anthony Retired Archbishop of Philadelph July 21.
Rigali, Justin Cardinal, Created Oct. 21, Archbishop Philadelphia.

Archbishops
Burke, Raymond L., Appointed Archbishop of St. Lou Dec. 2.
Cronin, Daniel A., Retired as Archbishop of Hartfo Oct. 20.
Mansell, Henry J., Appointed as Archbishop of Hartfo Oct. 20.
O'Malley, Sean P., o.f.m.cap., Appointed as Archbishop Boston, July 1.
Rigali, Justin F., Appointed as Archbishop of Philad phia, July 21.

Bishops
Anderson, Moses B., s.s.e., Retired Auxiliary Bishop Detroit, Oct. 24.
Baltakis, Paul A., Retired Bishop for the Lithuani Apostolate, July.
Banks, Robert J., Retired Bishop of Green Bay, Oct.
Barbarito, Gerald M., Appointed Bishop of Palm Bea July 1.
Blair, Leonard P., Appointed Bishop of Toledo, Dec. 4
Bullock, William H., Retired Bishop of Madison, May
Coleman, George W., Appointed Bishop of Fall Riv April 30.
Cote, Michael R., Appointed Bishop of Norwich, Ma 10.
Cummins, John S., Retired Bishop of Oakland, Oct. 1
da Cunha, Edgar M., s.d.v., Appointed Auxiliary Bisho Newark, June 27.
Daily, Thomas V., Retired Bishop of Brooklyn, Aug. 1
DiMarzio, Nicholas A., Appointed Bishop of Brook Aug. 1.

nh Mai Luong, Dominic Appointed Auxiliary Bishop of Orange, April 25.
tevez, Felipe J., Appointed Auxiliary Bishop of Miami, Nov. 21.
rcia-Siller, Gustavo, m.sp.s., Appointed Auxiliary Bishop of Chicago, Jan. 23.
edert, Raymond E., Retired Auxiliary Bishop of Chicago, Jan. 23.
rman, John R., Retired Auxiliary Bishop of Chicago, Jan. 23.
nifen, Richard C., Retired Bishop of Colorado Springs, Jan.
uck, William R., Retired Bishop of Jackson, Jan. 3.
rley, Walter A., Appointed Auxiliary Bishop of Detroit, July 7.
cobs, Sam G., Appointed Bishop of Houma-Thibodaux, Aug. 1.
kubowski, Thaddeus J., Retired Auxiliary Bishop of Chicago, Jan. 23.
gis Peter J., Appointed Bishop of Charlotte, Aug. 1.
ne, Francis Appointed Auxiliary Bishop of Chicago, Jan. 23.
canas, Gerald F., Succeeded as Bishop of Tucson, March 7.
tino, Joseph N., Appointed Bishop of Jackson, Jan. 3.
zaro, Felix, Succeeded as Bishop of Ponce, June.
ong, Dominic Mai, Appointed Auxiliary Bishop of Orange in California, April.
rtino, Joseph F., Appointed Bishop of Scranton, July 25.
orin, Roger P., Appointed Auxiliary Bishop of New Orleans, Feb. 11.
orlino, Robert C., Appointed Bishop of Madison, May 22.
wman, William C., Retired Auxiliary Bishop of Baltimore, Aug. 28.
Brien, Thomas J., Resigned Bishop of Phoenix, June 18.
msted, Thomas J., Appointed Bishop of Phoenix, Nov. 25.
procki, Thomas J., Appointed Auxiliary Bishop of Chicago, Jan. 23.
inn, John M., Appointed Auxiliary Bishop of Detroit, July 7.
iss, Francis R., Appointed Auxiliary Bishop of Detroit, July 7.
man, Agustin A., Retired Auxiliary Bishop of Miami, June 6.
se, Robert J., Retired as Bishop of Grand Rapids, Oct. 13.
minack, Richard S. Appointed Bishop of St. Nicholas in Chicago Ukrainian, March 24.
eridan, Michael, J., Succeeded as Bishop of Colorado Springs, Jan. 30.
lis, Oscar A., Appointed Auxiliary Bishop of Los Angeles, Dec. 11.
llivan, Walter F., Retired as Bishop of Richmond, Sept. 16.
mlin, James, C., Retired Bishop of Scranton, July 25.
gneron, Allen H., Appointed Coadjutor Bishop of Oakland Jan. 9; succeeded as Bishop of Oakland, Oct. 1.
alsh, Paul H., Appointed Auxiliary Bishop of Rockville Centre, April 2.
enski, Thomas G., Named Coadjutor Bishop of Orlando, June 30.
bik, David A., Appointed Bishop of Green Bay, Oct. 10.

2004

chbishops

Nardo, Daniel N., Appointed Coadjutor Archbishop of Galveston-Houston from Coadjutor Bishop of Galveston-Houston, Dec. 29.
noghue, John F., Retired Archbishop of Atlanta, Dec. 9.
orenza, Joseph A., Appointed Archbishop of Galveston-Houston, Dec. 29.
ores, Patrick F., Retired Archbishop of San Antonio, Dec. 29.
omez, Jose H., Appointed Archbishop of San Antonio, Dec. 29.
egory, Wilton D., Appointed Archbishop of Atlanta, Dec. 9.
aumann, Joseph F., Named Coadjutor Archbishop of Kansas City in Kansas, Jan. 7.

shops

ias, David, Retired Auxiliary Bishop of Newark, May 21.
sco, Anthony G., Retired Bishop of Greensburg, Jan. 2.
adley, Paul J., Appointed Auxiliary Bishop of Pittsburgh, Dec. 16.
andt, Lawrence E., Appointed Bishop of Greensburg, Jan. 2.
ansfeld, Michael D., Appointed Bishop of Wheeling-Charleston, Dec. 9.
Bustros, Cyrille S., Appointed Eparch of Newton, June 22.
Campbell, Frederick F., Appointed Bishop of Columbus, Oct. 14.
Carlson, Robert J., Appointed Bishop of Saginaw, Dec. 29.
Cistone, Joseph R., Appointed Auxiliary Bishop of Philadelphia, June 8.
Coakley, Paul S., Appointed Bishop of Salina, Oct. 21.
Costello, Thomas J., Retired Auxiliary Bishop of Syracuse, March 23.
Cunningham, Robert Joseph, Appointed Bishop of Ogdensburg, March 9.
Dendinger, William J., Appointed Bishop of Grand Island, Oct. 14.
DiLorenzo, Francis X., Appointed Bishop of Richmond, March 31.
Donato, Thomas A., Appointed Auxiliary Bishop of Newark, May 21.
Dorsey, Norbert L., Retired Bishop of Orlando, Nov. 13.
Doueihi, Hector, Retired Bishop of St. Maron of Brooklyn, Jan. 12.
Dupre, Thomas L., Retired Bishop of Springfield, Feb. 11.
Elya, John A., Retired Eparch of Newton, June 22.
Estabrook, Joseph W., Appointed Auxiliary Bishop for the Military Services, May 7.
Finn, Robert W., Named Coadjutor Bishop of Kansas City-St. Joseph, March.
Fitzsimons, George K., Retired Bishop of Salina, Oct. 21.
Flesey, John W., Appointed Auxiliary Bishop of Newark, May 21.
Galante, Joseph A., Appointed Bishop of Camden from Coadjutor Bishop of Dallas, March 23.
Gerry, Joseph, J., o.s.b., Retired Bishop of Portland, Feb. 10.
Griffin, James A., Retired Bishop of Columbus, Oct. 14.
Herzog, Ronald P., Appointed Bishop of Alexandria, Nov. 4.
Higgins, Richard B., Appointed Auxiliary Bishop for the Military Services, May 7.
Holley, Martin D., Appointed Auxiliary Bishop of Washington, May 18.
Kmiec, Edward U., Appointed Bishop of Buffalo, Aug. 12.
Listecki, Jerome E., Appointed Bishop of La Crosse, Dec. 29.
Madera, Joseph J., Retired Auxiliary Bishop for the Military Services, Sept. 15.
Malone, Richard J., Appointed Bishop of Portland in Maine, Feb.
Mansour, Gregory J., Appointed Bishop of the Eparchy of St. Maron, Brooklyn, Jan.
McDonnell, Charles J., Retired Auxiliary Bishop of Newark, May 21.
McDonnell, Timothy A., Appointed Bishop of Springfield in Massachusetts, March.
McFadden, Joseph P., Appointed Auxiliary Bishop of Philadelphia, June 8.
McManus, Robert J., Appointed Bishop of Worcester, March.
Olivier, Leonard J., Retired Auxiliary Bishop of Washington, May 18.
Reilly, Daniel P., Retired Bishop of Worcester, March.
Rhoades, Kevin C., Appointed Bishop of Harrisburg, Oct. 14.
Rodimer, Frank J., Retired Bishop of Paterson, June 1.
Roque, Francis X., Retired Auxiliary Bishop for the Military Services, Sept. 15.
Rozanski, Mitchell T., Appointed Auxiliary Bishop of Baltimore, July 3.
Salazar, Alexander, Appointed Auxiliary Bishop of Los Angeles, Sept. 7.
Schmitt, Bernard W., Retired Bishop of Wheeling-Charleston, Dec. 9.
Serratelli, Arthur J., Appointed Bishop of Paterson, June 1.
Sullivan, Dennis J., Appointed Auxiliary Bishop of New York June, 28.
Thomas, George, Appointed Bishop of Helena from Auxiliary Bishop of Seattle, March 23.
Walsh, Gerald T., Appointed Auxiliary Bishop of New York, June 28.
Wenski, Thomas G., Succeeded as Bishop of Orlando, Nov. 13.
Wirz, George O., Retired Auxiliary Bishop of Madison, Feb. 10.

2005

Archbishops

Keleher, James P., Retired Archbishop of Kansas City in Kansas, Jan. 15.
Levada, William J., Appointed Prefect of the Congregation for the Doctrine of the Faith, May 13.
Naumann, Joseph F., Succeeded as Archbishop of Kansas City in Kansas, Jan. 15.
Niederauer, George H., Appointed Archbishop of San Francisco, Dec. 15.

Bishops

Angell, Kenneth A., Retired Bishop of Burlington, Nov. 9.
Boland, Raymond, Retired Bishop of Kansas City-St. Joseph, May 24.
Braxton, Edward K., Appointed Bishop of Belleville, March 15.
Calvo, Randolph R., Appointed Bishop of Reno, Dec. 23.
Choby, David R., Appointed Bishop of Nashville, Dec. 20.
del Riego, Rutilio, Appointed Auxiliary Bishop of San Bernardino, July 26.
Elizondo, Eusebio L., Appointed Auxiliary Bishop of Seattle, May 12.
Flanagan, Thomas J., Retired Auxiliary Bishop of San Antonio, Dec. 15.
Finn, Robert W., Succeeded as Bishop of Kansas City-St. Joseph, May 24.
Foley, David E., Retired Bishop of Birmingham, May 10.
Garland, James H., Retired Bishop of Marquette, Dec. 13.
Hurley, Walter A., Appointed Bishop of Grand Rapids, June 21.
Jackels, Michael O., Appointed Bishop of Wichita, Jan. 28.
Madden, Denis J., Appointed Auxiliary Bishop of Baltimore, May 10.
Matano, Salvatore R., Succeeded as Bishop of Burlington from Coadjutor, Nov. 9.
Mulvee, Robert E., Retired Bishop of Providence, March 31.
Nickless, R. Walker, Appointed Bishop of Sioux City, Nov. 10.
Noonan, John, Appointed Auxiliary Bishop of Miami, June 21.
Rueger, George E., Retired Auxiliary Bishop of Worcester, Jan. 25.
Sample, Alexander K., Appointed Bishop of Marquette, Dec. 13.
Samra, Nicholas J., Retired Auxiliary Bishop of Newton, Jan. 11.
Silva, Clarence, Appointed Bishop of Honolulu, May 17.
Straling, Phillip F., Retired Bishop of Reno, June 21.
Sullivan, Joseph, Retired Auxiliary Bishop of Brooklyn, May 12.
Tobin, Thomas J., Appointed Bishop of Providence, March 31.
Tyson, Joseph J., Appointed Auxiliary Bishop of Seattle, May 12.
Valero, Rene A., Retired Auxiliary Bishop of Brooklyn, Oct. 27.
Vann, Kevin W., Succeeded as Bishop of Fort Worth from Coadjutor, July 12.
Winter, William J., Retired Auxiliary Bishop of Pittsburgh, May 20.

2006

Cardinals

Levada, William Cardinal, Created March 24, Prefect of the Congregation for the Doctrine of the Faith.
McCarrick, Theodore Cardinal, Retired Archbishop of Washington DC, May 16.
O'Malley, Sean Patrick Cardinal, Created March 24, Archbishop of Boston.

Archbishops

DiNardo, Daniel N., Succeeded as Archbishop of Galveston-Houston, Feb. 28.
Fiorenza, Joseph A., Retired Archbishop of Galveston-Houston, Feb. 28.
Wuerl, Donald W., Appointed Archbishop of Washington DC, May 16.

Bishops

Amos, Martin, Appointed Bishop of Davenport, Oct. 12.
Boles, John Patrick, Retired Auxiliary Bishop of Boston, Oct. 12.
Brucato, Robert A., Retired Auxiliary Bishop of New York, Oct. 31.
Bura, John, Appointed Auxiliary Bishop of Philadelphia Ukrainian, Jan. 3.
Burbidge, Michael F., Appointed Bishop of Raleigh, June 8.
Caggiano, Frank, Appointed Auxiliary Bishop of Brooklyn, June 6.
Carmon, Dominic, s.v.d., Retired Auxiliary Bishop of New Orleans, Dec. 13.
Chomnycky, Paul, o.s.b.m., Appointed Bishop of Stamford, Jan. 3.

Cisneros, Octavio, Appointed Auxiliary Bishop of Brooklyn, June 6.
Dewane, Frank J., Appointed Coadjutor Bishop of Venice, April 25.
Donnelly, Robert W., Retired Auxiliary Bishop of Toledo, May 30.
Dooher, John, Appointed Auxiliary Bishop of Boston, Oct. 12.
Fabre, Shelton J., Appointed Auxiliary Bishop of New Orleans, Dec. 13.
Flores, Daniel E., Appointed Auxiliary Bishop of Detroit, Oct. 28.
Franklin, William E., Retired Bishop of Davenport, Oct. 12.
Friend, William B., Retired Bishop of Shreveport, Dec. 20.
Garcia, Richard J., Appointed Bishop of Monterey in California, Dec. 19.
Gossman, F. Joseph, Retired Bishop of Raleigh, June 8.
Gumbleton, Thomas J., Retired Auxiliary Bishop of Detroit, Feb. 2.
Hennessey, Robert, Appointed Auxiliary Bishop of Boston, Oct. 12.
Imesch, Joseph J., Retired Bishop of Joliet in Illinois, May 16.
Lennon, Richard G., Appointed Bishop of Cleveland, April 4.
Losten, Basil H., Retired Bishop of Stamford, Jan. 3.
Mikloshazy, Attila, s.j., Retired Bishop of Apostolate to Hungarians, April.
Milone, Anthony M., Retired Bishop of Great Falls, July 12.
Pilla, Anthony M., Retired Bishop of Cleveland, April 4.
Rassas, George J., Appointed Auxiliary Bishop of Chicago, Feb. 2.
Rizzotto, Vincent, Retired Auxiliary Bishop of Galveston-Houston, Nov. 6.
Ryan, Sylvester D., Retired Bishop of Monterey in California, Dec. 19.
Sansaricq, Guy, Appointed Auxiliary Bishop of Brooklyn, June 6.
Sartain, James, Appointed Bishop of Joliet in Illinois, May 16.
Swain, Paul J., Appointed Bishop of Sioux Falls, Aug. 31.
Thomas, Daniel E., Appointed Auxiliary Bishop of Philadelphia, June 8.

2007

Cardinals
DiNardo, Daniel Cardinal, Created Nov. 24, Archbishop of Galveston-Houston.
Keeler, William Cardinal, Retired Archbishop of Baltimore, July 12.

Archbishops
Broglio, Timothy P., Appointed Archbishop for the Military Services Nov. 19.
Kelly, Thomas C., Retired Archbishop of Louisville, June 12.
Kurtz, Joseph E., Appointed Archbishop of Louisville, June 12.
Nienstedt, John C., Appointed Coadjutor Archbishop of St. Paul and Minneapolis, April 24.
O'Brien, Edwin F., Appointed Archbishop of Baltimore, July 12.

Bishops
Baker, Robert J., Appointed Bishop of Birmingham, Aug. 14.
Balke, Victor H. Retired Bishop of Crookston, Sept. 28.
Callahan, William P., Appointed Auxiliary Bishop of Milwaukee, Oct. 30.
Charron, Joseph L., c.pp.s., Retired Bishop of Des Moines, April 10.
Chavez, Gilbert, Retired Auxiliary Bishop of San Diego, June 1.
Christensen, Peter F., Appointed Bishop of Superior, June 28.
Cserhati, Ferenc, Appointed Bishop for the Apostolate to Hungarians, June 15.
Dewane, Frank J., Succeeded as Bishop of Venice, Jan. 19.
Dino, Gerald N., Appointed Bishop of Van Nuys, Dec. 6.
Farrell, Kevin J., Appointed Bishop of Dallas, March 6.
Fernandez Torres, Daniel, Appointed Auxiliary Bishop of San Juan, Feb. 14.
Fliss, Raphael M., Retired Bishop of Superior, June 28.
Grahmann, Charles V., Retired Bishop of Dallas, March 6.
Hoeppner, Michael J., Appointed Bishop of Crookston, Sept. 28.
Libasci, Peter A., Appointed Auxiliary Bishop of Rockville Centre, April 3.
Murry, George V., s.j., Appointed Bishop of Youngstown, Jan. 30.
Nevins, John J., Retired Bishop of Venice, Jan. 19.
Pataki, Andrew, Retired Bishop of Passaic, Dec. 6.
Provost, Glen J., Appointed Bishop of Lake Charles, March 6.
Skurla, William C., Appointed Bishop of Passaic, Dec. 6.
Soto, Jaime, Appointed Coadjutor Bishop of Sacramento, Oct. 11.
Warfel, Michael W., Appointed Bishop of Great Falls-Billings, Nov. 20.
Wcela, Emil A., Retired Auxiliary Bishop of Rockville Centre, April 3.
Wester, John C., Appointed Bishop of Salt Lake City, Jan. 8.
Zubik, David A., Appointed Bishop of Pittsburgh, July 18.

2008

Archbishops
Burke, Raymond L., Resigned Archbishop of St. Louis, June 27.
Flynn, Harry J., Retired Archbishop of St. Paul and Minneapolis, May 2.
Lipscomb, Oscar H., Retired Archbishop of Mobile, April 2.
Nienstedt, John C., Succeeded to Archbishop of St. Paul and Minneapolis, May 2.
Rodi, Thomas J., Appointed Archbishop of Mobile, April 2.
Schnurr, Dennis M., Appointed Coadjutor Archbishop of Cincinnati, Oct. 17.

Bishops
Bevard, Herbert A., Appointed Bishop of St. Thomas in the Virgin Islands, July 7.
Boyea, Earl A., Appointed Bishop of Lansing, Feb. 27.
Cantu, Oscar, Appointed Auxiliary Bishop of San Antonio, April 10.
Conley, James D., Appointed Auxiliary Bishop of Denver, April 10.
Cruz, Manuel A., Appointed Auxiliary Bishop of Newark, June 9.
Duca, Michael G., Appointed Bishop of Shreveport, April 1.
Johnston, Jr., J. Vann, Appointed Bishop of Springfield-Cape Girardeau, Jan. 24.
Justice, William J., Appointed Auxiliary Bishop of San Francisco, April 10.
Knestout, Barry C., Appointed Auxiliary Bishop of Washington, Nov. 18.
Leibrecht, John J., Retired Bishop of Springfield-Cape Girardeau, Jan. 24.
LeVoir, John M., Appointed Bishop of New Ulm, July 14.
Malooly, W. Francis, Appointed Bishop of Wilmington, July 7.
Mengeling, Carl F., Retired Bishop of Lansing, Feb. 27.
Pates, Richard E., Appointed Bishop of Des Moines, April 10.
Quinn, A. James, Retired Auxiliary Bishop of Cleveland, June 14.
Quinn, John M., Appointed Coadjutor Bishop of Winona, Oct. 15.
Ramos Morales, Eusebio, Appointed Bishop of Fajardo-Humacao, March 11.
Ricken, David L., Appointed Bishop of Green Bay, July 9.
Soto, Jaime, Succeeded as Bishop of Sacramento, Nov. 29.
Taylor, Anthony B., Appointed Bishop of Little Rock, April 10.
Weigand, William K., Retired Bishop of Sacramento, Nov. 29.
Yanta, John W., Retired Bishop of Amarillo, Jan. 3.
Zurek, Patrick J., Appointed Bishop of Amarillo, Jan. 3.

2009

Cardinals
Egan, Edward Cardinal, Retired Archbishop of New York, Feb. 23.
Maida, Adam Cardinal, Retired Archbishop of Detroit, Jan. 5.

Archbishops
Aymond, Gregory M., Appointed Archbishop of New Orleans, June 12.
Carlson, Robert J., Appointed Archbishop of St. Louis, April 21.
Curtiss, Elden Francis, Retired Archbishop of Omaha, June 3.
Dolan, Timothy M., Appointed Archbishop of New York, Feb. 23.
Hughes, Alfred C., Retired Archbishop of New Orleans, June 12.
Listecki, Jerome E., Appointed Archbishop of Milwaukee, Nov. 14.
Lucas, George J., Appointed Archbishop of Omaha, June 3.
Pilarczyk, Daniel E., Retired Archbishop of Cincinnati, Dec. 21.
Schnurr, Dennis M., Appointed Archbishop of Cincinn
Dec. 21.
Vigneron, Allen H., Appointed Archbishop of Detr
Jan. 5.

Bishops
Barres, John O., Appointed Bishop of Allentown, M
27.
Bradley, Paul J., Appointed Bishop of Kalamazoo, Apri
Burns, Edward J., Appointed Bishop of Juneau, Jan.
Cistone, Joseph R., Appointed Bishop of Saginaw, M
20.
Cooney, Patrick R., Retired Bishop of Gaylord, Oct.
Cordileone, Salvatore J., Appointed Bishop of Oakla
March 23.
Cullen, Edward P., Retired Bishop of Allentown, M
27.
Cunningham, Robert J., Appointed Bishop of Syracu
April 21.
D'Arcy, John M., Retired Bishop of Fort Wayne-So
Bend, Nov. 14.
Dougherty, John M., Retired Auxiliary Bishop of Scrant
Aug. 31.
Etienne, Paul D., Appointed Bishop of Cheyenne, C
19.
Evans, Robert C., Appointed Auxiliary Bishop of Pro
dence, Oct. 15.
Flores, Cirilo, Appointed Auxiliary Bishop of Oran
Jan. 5.
Flores, Daniel E., Appointed Bishop of Brownsville, D
9.
Guglielmone, Robert E., Appointed Bishop of Char
ton, Jan. 24.
Harrington, Bernard J., Retired Bishop of Winona, M
7.
Hebda, Bernard A., Appointed Bishop of Gaylord, Oct
Irwin, Francis Xavier, Retired Auxiliary Bishop of B
ton, Oct. 12.
Isern, Fernando, Appointed Bishop of Pueblo, Oct. 1
Martino, Joseph F., Retired Bishop of Scranton, A
31.
McRaith, John J., Retired Bishop of Owensboro, Jan
Medley, William F., Appointed Bishop of Owensbo
Dec. 15.
Morin, Roger P., Appointed Bishop of Biloxi, March
Moskal, Robert M., Retired Bishop of St. Josaphat
Parma, July 29.
Moynihan, James M., Retired Bishop of Syracuse, Ap
21.
Murray, James A., Retired Bishop of Kalamazoo, Apri
Pena, Raymundo J., Retired Bishop of Brownsville, Dec
Piche, Lee A., Appointed Auxiliary Bishop of St. P
and Minneapolis, May 27.
Quinn, John M., Appointed Bishop of Winona, May 7
Rhoades, Kevin C., Appointed Bishop of Fort Way
South Bend, Nov. 14.
Rivera, Hector M., Retired Auxiliary Bishop of San Ju
PR, Oct. 31.
Senior, Timothy, Appointed Auxiliary Bishop of Phi
delphia, June 8.
Siegel, Joseph M., Appointed Auxiliary Bishop of Jol
Oct. 28.
Sirba, Paul D., Appointed Bishop of Duluth, Oct. 15
Stika, Richard F., Appointed Bishop of Knoxville, Jan.
Tafoya, Arthur N., Retired Bishop of Pueblo, Oct. 1
Wall, James S., Appointed Bishop of Gallup, Feb. 5.
Wang, Ignatius, Retired Auxiliary Bishop of San Fr
cisco, May 16.
Zarama, Luis R., Appointed Auxiliary Bishop of Atlan
July 27.

2010

Archbishop
Gomez, Jose Horacio, Appointed Coadjutor Archbis
of Los Angeles, April 6.

Bishops
Bambera, Joseph C., Appointed Bishop of Scranton, F
23.
Carmody, Edmond, Retired Bishop of Corpus Chris
Jan. 18.
Camacho, Tomas A., Retired Bishop of Chalan Kan
April 6.
Deshotel, John D., Appointed Auxiliary Bishop of D
las, March 11.
Habash, Yousif, Appointed Bishop of Our Lady of Del
erance, April 12.
LaValley, Terry R., Appointed Bishop of Ogdensbu
Feb. 23.
Mulvey, William M., Appointed Bishop of Corpus Chris
Jan. 18.
Seitz, Mark J., Appointed Auxiliary Bishop of Dall
March 11.
Vasquez, Joe S., Appointed Bishop of Austin, Jan. 2

United States Conference of Catholic Bishops

Address—3211 Fourth St., N.E., Washington, DC 20017-1194. Tel: 202-541-3000; Web Site: www.usccb.org.

The United States Conference of Catholic Bishops is a permanent institute composed of Catholic bishops of the United States of America in and through which the bishops exercise in a communal or collegial manner the pastoral mission entrusted to them by the Lord Jesus of sanctification, teaching, and leadership, especially by devising forms and methods of the apostolate suitably adapted to the circumstances of the times. Such exercise is intended to offer appropriate assistance to each bishop in fulfilling his particular ministry in the local Church, to effect a commonality of ministry addressed to the people of the United States of America, and to foster and express communion with the Church in other nations within the Church universal, under the leadership of its chief pastor, the Pope.

OFFICES

President—Cardinal Francis E. George, O.M.I.
Vice President—Bishop Gerald Frederick Kicanas, D.D.
Treasurer—Archbishop Joseph E. Kurtz
Secretary—Bishop George Vance Murry, S.J.

USCCB GENERAL SECRETARIAT

General Secretary—Rev. Msgr. David J. Malloy
Associate General Secretary—Mr. Bruce E. Egnew
Associate General Secretary—Rev. Msgr. Ronny Jenkins
Associate General Secretary—Ms. Nancy Wisdo
Assistant General Secretary—Rev. J. Brian Bransfield, M.Div., M.A., S.T.L.

STAFF OFFICES

Finance & Accounting—Mrs. Joyce Jones
General Counsel—Mr. Anthony R. Picarello, Esq.
General Services—Mr. Keith Manley
Government Relations—Ms. Nancy Wisdo
Human Resources—Ms. Linda Hunt
Information Technology—Mr. John A. Galotta
Child & Youth Protection—Ms. Teresa M. Kettelkamp

USCCB COMMITTEES

I. EXECUTIVE LEVEL

ADMINISTRATIVE COMMITTEE

Chairman—Cardinal Francis E. George, O.M.I.
Members—Cardinal Sean P. O'Malley, O.F.M.Cap.
Cardinal Justin F. Rigali
Archbishop Roger L. Schwietz, O.M.I., D.D.
Archbishop Timothy M. Dolan
Archbishop Jose H. Gomez, S.T.D.
Archbishop Wilton D. Gregory, S.L.D.
Archbishop George H. Niederauer, D.D., Ph.D.
Archbishop Thomas J. Rodi (Region V)
Archbishop John G. Vlazny
Bishop Earl Boyea (Region VI)
Bishop Michael F. Burbidge, D.D., Ed.D., V.G. (Region XIV)
Bishop Oscar Cantu (Region X)
Bishop Francis J. Christian, Ph.D. (Region I)
Bishop Robert J. Cunningham, D.D., J.C.L. (Region II)
Bishop Blase J. Cupich
Bishop Thomas J. Curry, D.D., Ph.D., V.G.
Bishop Michael J. Hoeppner, D.D. (Region VIII)
Bishop Howard J. Hubbard
Bishop William J. Justice, V.G. (Region XI)
Bishop William E. Lori
Bishop Richard J. Malone
Bishop William F. Murphy, J.C.L., LL.D., S.T.D.
Bishop R. Walker Nickless (Region IX)
Bishop Thomas J. Paprocki, S.T.L., J.D., J.C.D.
Bishop Mitchell T. Rozanski, D.D., V.G. (Region IV)
Bishop J. Peter Sartain (Region VII)
Bishop Carlos Arthur Sevilla, S.J., D.D. (Region XII)
Bishop Michael J. Sheridan, S.T.D. (Region XIII)
Bishop William C. Skurla (Region XV)
Bishop John C. Wester
Bishop David A. Zubik (Region III)
Vice President—Bishop Gerald Frederick Kicanas, D.D.
Treasurer—Archbishop Joseph E. Kurtz
Secretary—Bishop George V. Murry, S.J.

ADMINISTRATIVE COMMITTEE-REGIONAL ALTERNATES

Alternate (Region I)—Bishop Robert Hennessey
Alternate (Region II)—Bishop Ignatius Catanello, D.D., Ph.D., V.E.
Alternate (Region III)—Bishop Edgar M. da Cunha, S.D.V., D.D.
Alternate (Region IV)—Archbishop Timothy Broglio
Alternate (Region V)—Bishop Ronald William Gainer
Alternate (Region VI)—Bishop R. Daniel Conlon
Alternate (Region VII)—Archbishop Jerome E. Listecki
Alternate (Region VIII)—Archbishop John C. Nienstedt
Alternate (Region IX)—Bishop Paul S. Coakley
Alternate (Region X)—Bishop Michael D. Pfeifer, O.M.I.
Alternate (Region XI)—Bishop Rutilio J. del Riego
Alternate (Region XII)—Bishop Joseph J. Tyson
Alternate (Region XIII)—Bishop James S. Wall
Alternate (Region XIV)—Bishop Robert Guglielmone
Alternate (Region XV)—Bishop Jacob Angadiath

EXECUTIVE COMMITTEE

Chairman—Cardinal Francis E. George, O.M.I.
Members—Bishop Arthur J. Serratelli, S.T.D., S.S.L., D.D.
Vice President—Bishop Gerald Frederick Kicanas, D.D.
Treasurer—Archbishop Joseph E. Kurtz
Secretary—Bishop George Vance Murry, S.J.
Staff—Rev. Msgr. David J. Malloy

COMMITTEE ON BUDGET AND FINANCE

Chairman—Archbishop Joseph E. Kurtz
Members—Archbishop Timothy M. Dolan
Coadjutor Archbishop Dennis M. Schnurr
Bishop Joseph R. Cistone, D.D., V.G.
Bishop Felipe de Jesus Estevez
Bishop Kevin Joseph Farrell, D.D.
Bishop Robert N. Lynch
Staff—Mr. Bruce E. Egnew
Mrs. Joyce Jones
Mr. Henry Muhlenberg
Ms. Nancy Wisdo

Audit Subcommittee
Chairman—Bishop William F. Murphy, J.C.L., LL.D., S.T.D.
Members—Bishop Arthur Joseph Serratelli, S.S.L., S.T.D., D.D.
Bishop John C. Wester
Consultants—Ms. Joan Loffredo, CPA
Mr. Kevin Murphy
Mr. Paul Rubacki

COMMITTEE ON PRIORITIES AND PLANS

Chairman—Bishop George Vance Murry, S.J.
Vice Chairman—Archbishop Joseph E. Kurtz
Members—Archbishop Thomas J. Rodi (Region V)
Bishop Earl Boyea (Region VI)
Bishop Michael F. Burbidge, D.D., Ed.D., V.G. (Region XIV)
Bishop Oscar Cantu (Region X)
Bishop Francis J. Christian, Ph.D. (Region I)
Bishop Robert J. Cunningham, D.D., J.C.L. (Region II)
Bishop Michael J. Hoeppner, D.D. (Region VIII)
Bishop William J. Justice, V.G. (Region XI)
Bishop R. Walker Nickless (Region IX)
Bishop Mitchell T. Rozanski, D.D., V.G. (Region IV)
Bishop J. Peter Sartain (Region VII)
Bishop Carlos Arthur Sevilla, S.J., D.D. (Region XII)
Bishop Michael J. Sheridan, S.T.D. (Region X)
Bishop William C. Skurla (Region XV)
Bishop David A. Zubik (Region III)
Consultants—Rev. Msgr. David J. Malloy
Staff Coordinator—Rev. J. Brian Bransfield, M.Div., M.A., S.T.L.
Staff—Mr. Bruce E. Egnew
Rev. Msgr. Ronny Jenkins, S.T.L., J.C.D.
Mr. Paul Henderson, Publishing Dir.
Mrs. Joyce Jones
Ms. Helen Osman
Ms. Nancy Wisdo

II. GENERAL MEMBERSHIP LEVEL STANDING COMMITTEES

COMMITTEE ON CANONICAL AFFAIRS AND CHURCH GOVERNANCE

Chairman—Bishop Thomas J. Paprocki, S.T.L., J.D., J.C.D.
Members—Archbishop John J. Myers, J.C.D., D.D.
Bishop R. Daniel Conlon
Bishop Salvatore J. Cordileone, J.C.D.
Bishop Thomas George Doran, D.D., J.C.D.
Bishop David Eugene Fellhauer
Bishop Peter J. Jugis
Bishop David L. Ricken, D.D., J.C.L.
Bishop Kevin W. Vann
Consultants—Rev. Msgr. Mark L. Bartchak, J.C.D.
Rev. John Coughlin, O.F.M.
Sr. Sharon A. Euart, R.S.M., J.C.D.
Dr. Kurt Martens
Staff—Rev. Msgr. Ronny Jenkins, S.T.L., J.C.D.
Ms. Siobhan M. Verbeek, J.C.L.

COMMITTEE ON CATHOLIC EDUCATION

Chairman—Bishop Thomas J. Curry, D.D., Ph.D., V.G.
Members—Bishop Oscar Cantu
Bishop John C. Dunne
Bishop Walter J. Edyvean, S.T.D.
Bishop Ronald William Gainer
Bishop Francis J. Kane
Bishop Joseph P. McFadden, D.D.
Bishop Richard E. Pates
Bishop John C. Wester, V.G.
Consultants—Bishop Michael J. Sheridan, S.T.D.
Sr. Mary Elizabeth Galt, B.V.M.
Dr. John Convey
Ms. Jennifer Kraska
Dr. Mary McDonald
Rev. Martin Moran
Dr. Karen Ristau
Ms. Mary Ellen Russell
Dr. Richard Yanikoski
Staff—Sr. Suzanne Bellenoit, S.S.J.
Ms. Barbara Humphrey McCrabb
Mrs. Marie A. Powell
Ms. Terry Thames

COMMITTEE ON CLERGY, CONSECRATED LIFE, AND VOCATIONS

Chairman—Cardinal Sean P. O'Malley, O.F.M.Cap., Ph.D.
Chairman-Elect—Archbishop Robert J. Carlson
Members—Archbishop Gregory M. Aymond, D.D.
Archbishop Basil M. Schott, O.F.M.
Bishop Earl Boyea
Bishop Michael F. Burbidge, D.D., Ed.D., V.G.
Bishop William P. Callahan, O.F.M.Conv.
Bishop Octavio Cisneros
Bishop Paul S. Coakley
Bishop J. Terry Steib, S.V.D.
Bishop Daniel E. Thomas
Consultants—Archbishop Edwin F. O'Brien, S.T.D., D.D.
Bishop Robert H. Brom, D.D.
Staff—Rev. W. Shawn McKnight, S.T.D.
Rev. David J. Toups
Sr. Mary Joanna Ruhland, R.S.M.

COMMITTEE ON COMMUNICATIONS

Chairman—Bishop Gabino Zavala, D.D., J.C.L., V.G.
Members—Bishop Michael J. Bransfield
Bishop Randolph Roque Calvo, D.D., J.C.D.
Bishop Thomas J. Costello, D.D., V.G.
Bishop Richard J. Garcia, D.D.
Bishop Martin D. Holley, D.D., V.G.
Bishop Gerald Frederick Kicanas, D.D.
Bishop Richard J. Malone
Bishop John B. McCormack, D.D.
Consultants—Ms. Colleen H. Dolan
Mr. John Bookser Feister
Mr. Clarence Gilyard
Mr. Frank Morock
Mr. Owen Phelps, Ph.D.
Ms. Nancy Wiechec
Ms. Penny Wiegert
Staff—Ms. Helen Osman, Sec. Communications
Mr. Harry Forbes, Dir. Film & Broadcasting
Mr. Anthony J. Spence, Dir./Editor-in-Chief Catholic News Service
Mr. Paul Henderson, Dir. Publishing
Mr. Joseph Larson, Dir. Digital Media

Subcommittee on the Catholic Communications Campaign
Chairman—Bishop Thomas J. Costello, D.D.
Members—Bishop Michael J. Bransfield
Bishop Richard J. Garcia, D.D.
Bishop Martin D. Holley, D.D., V.G.
Bishop Gerald Frederick Kicanas, D.D.
Consultants—Ms. Colleen H. Dolan
Mr. Frank Morock
Mr. Owen Phelps, Ph.D.
Staff—Ms. Helen Osman

COMMITTEE ON CULTURAL DIVERSITY IN THE CHURCH

Chairman—Bishop Jaime Soto
Members—Archbishop Charles J. Chaput, O.F.M.Cap., D.D.
Archbishop John C. Nienstedt
Bishop Edgar M. da Cunha, S.D.V., D.D.
Bishop Felipe de Jesus Estevez
Bishop Richard J. Garcia, D.D.
Bishop Martin D. Holley, D.D., V.G.
Bishop John R. Manz
Bishop Oscar A. Solis, D.D., V.G.
Consultants—Bishop Dominic M. Luong, D.D., V.G.
Bishop J. Terry Steib, S.V.D.
Staff—Rev. Allan F. Deck, S.J., Exec. Dir.

Subcommittee on African American Affairs
Chairman—Bishop Martin D. Holley, D.D., V.G.
Members—Bishop Edward K. Braxton
Bishop Joseph R. Cistone, D.D., V.G.
Bishop Shelton J. Fabre

Bishop Gustavo Garcia-Siller, M.Sp.S.
Bishop Curtis J. Guillory, S.V.D.
Bishop Robert J. Hermann, D.D.
Bishop Dennis J. Madden
Bishop Joseph S. Vasquez
Consultants—Ms. Kathleen Merritt
Mrs. Geralyn Shelvin
Staff—Ms. Beverly A. Carroll

Subcommittee on Asian and Pacific Islanders
Chairman—Bishop Oscar Azarcon Solis
Members—Bishop Jacob Angadiath
Bishop Randolph Roque Calvo, D.D., J.C.D.
Bishop Dominic M. Luong, D.D., V.G.
Bishop Clarence Silva
Bishop Joseph Sullivan
Bishop Ignatius C. Wang
Consultants—Rev. Paul Lee
Sr. Theresa Phan
Staff—Ms. Cecile Motus

Subcommittee on Hispanic Affairs
Chairman—Bishop Richard J. Garcia, D.D.
Members—Archbishop Patrick F. Flores, D.D.
Bishop Octavio Cisneros
Bishop Eusebio Elizondo, M.Sp.S., J.C.D.
Bishop Gustavo Garcia-Siller, M.Sp.S.
Bishop Michael D. Pfeifer, O.M.I.
Bishop Placido Rodriguez, C.M.F.
Consultants—Ms. Enid de Jesus
Ms. Alicia Perez-Nuno
Staff—Mr. Alejandro Aguilera-Titus

Subcommittee on Native American Catholics
Chairman—Archbishop Charles J. Chaput, O.F.M.Cap., D.D.
Members—Archbishop Alexander J. Brunett, D.D., Ph.D.
Bishop Peter F. Christensen, M.A.S.
Bishop Robert J. Cunningham, D.D., J.C.L.
Bishop Ronald P. Herzog, D.D.
Bishop Donald J. Kettler
Bishop Alexander K. Sample
Bishop George L. Thomas
Consultants—Sr. Kateri Mitchell, S.S.A.
Rev. Maurice Henry Sands
Rev. Wayne C. Paysse
Staff—Ms. Beverly A. Carroll

Subcommittee on Pastoral Care of Migrants, Refugees, and Travelers
Chairman—Bishop John R. Manz
Members—Archbishop Jerome E. Listecki
Bishop J. Kevin Boland
Bishop Edgar M. da Cunha, S.D.V., D.D.
Bishop John F. Kinney, D.D., J.C.D.
Bishop Guy Sansaricq
Staff—Sr. Myrna Tordillo, M.S.C.S.

COMMITTEE ON DIVINE WORSHIP

Chairman—Bishop Arthur J. Serratelli, S.T.D., S.S.L., D.D.
Chairman-Elect—Archbishop Gregory M. Aymond, D.D.
Members—Cardinal Justin F. Rigali
Archbishop Daniel M. Buechlein, O.S.B., D.D.
Archbishop Charles J. Chaput, O.F.M.Cap., D.D.
Archbishop Wilton D. Gregory, S.L.D.
Archbishop George H. Niederauer
Bishop Octavio Cisneros
Bishop Kevin Joseph Farrell, D.D.
Bishop Ronald P. Herzog, D.D.
Consultants—Cardinal Roger M. Mahony
Archbishop John G. Vlazny
Sr. Janet Baxendale, S.C., M.A.
Rev. Msgr. John H. Burton
Rev. Msgr. Kevin W. Irwin, S.T.D., M.A.
Rev. Juan J. Sosa
Ms. Lisa A. Tarker
Sr. Julia M. Upton, R.S.M.
Staff—Rev. Richard Hilgartner
Rev. Msgr. Anthony F. Sherman
Sr. Doris M. Turek, S.S.N.D.

Subcommittee on Hispanics and the Liturgy
Chairman—Bishop Octavio Cisneros
Members—Archbishop Jose H. Gomez, S.T.D.
Bishop Ricardo Ramirez, C.S.B.
Bishop Carlos Arthur Sevilla, S.J., D.D.
Bishop James Anthony Tamayo, D.D.
Consultants—Rev. Heliodero Lucatero
Rev. Jorge I. Perales
Mr. Rogelio Zelada
Staff—Mrs. Mar Munoz-Visoso
Sr. Doris M. Turek, S.S.N.D.

COMMITTEE ON DOCTRINE

Chairman—Archbishop Donald W. Wuerl
Members—Archbishop Daniel M. Buechlein, O.S.B., D.D.
Archbishop Jose H. Gomez, S.T.D., D.D.
Archbishop Allen H. Vigneron, D.D.
Bishop Leonard P. Blair
Bishop William E. Lori, S.T.D.
Bishop Robert J. McManus, D.D., S.T.D.
Bishop Kevin C. Rhoades
Bishop Arthur J. Serratelli, S.T.D., S.S.L., D.D.
Consultants—Very Rev. Steven C. Boguslawski, O.P., M.A., M.Div., S.T.M., S.T.L., Ph.D.
Cardinal Francis E. George, O.M.I.
Archbishop John C. Nienstedt
Sr. Sara Butler, M.S.B.T., Ph.D.
Dr. Peter Casarella
Dr. John C. Cavadini, Ph.D.
Rev. John McDermott
Staff—Dr. James Legrys
Ms. Siobhan M. Verbeek, J.C.L.
Rev. Thomas G. Weinandy, O.F.M.Cap.

Subcommittee on the Translation of Scripture Text
Chairman—Bishop Arthur J. Serratelli, S.T.D., S.S.L., D.D.
Members—Cardinal Justin F. Rigali
Bishop Blase J. Cupich
Bishop Richard J. Sklba
Bishop Anthony B. Taylor
Staff—Ms. Siobhan M. Verbeek, J.C.L.
Rev. Thomas G. Weinandy, O.F.M.Cap.

COMMITTEE ON DOMESTIC JUSTICE AND HUMAN DEVELOPMENT

Chairman—Bishop William F. Murphy, J.C.L., LL.D., S.T.D.
Chairman-Elect—Bishop Stephen E. Blaire, D.D.
Members—Archbishop Charles J. Chaput, O.F.M.Cap., D.D.
Bishop Nicholas A. DiMarzio, Ph.D., D.D.
Bishop Curtis J. Guillory, S.V.D.
Bishop Roger P. Morin, D.D.
Bishop George Vance Murry, S.J.
Bishop Ricardo Ramirez, C.S.B.
Bishop David L. Ricken, D.D., J.C.L.
Bishop David A. Zubik
Consultants—Bishop Robert W. Finn
Bishop Howard J. Hubbard
Mr. Ray Boshara
Mr. Pat Clancy
Mr. Arthur McFarland
Rev. Joseph McShane, S.J.
Mr. Tim O'Callaghan
Sr. Marie Sedgwick, D.C.
Mr. John Sweeney
Mr. Anthony Williams
Staff—Ms. Roxanna Barillas
Ms. Cecilia Calvo
Mr. John Carr
Ms. Kathy Saile
Mr. Thomas Shellabarger

Subcommittee on the Catholic Campaign for Human Development
Chairman—Bishop Roger P. Morin, D.D.
Members—Bishop Michael Patrick Driscoll
Bishop Howard J. Hubbard
Bishop Francis J. Kane
Bishop J. Terry Steib, S.V.D.
Bishop David A. Zubik
Consultants—Mr. Robert Gorman, A.C.S.W., B.C.S.W.
Rev. Edward B. Branch
Ms. Christine (Cris) Doby
Mr. Richard Fowler
Rev. Michael Jacques, S.S.E., V.F.
Ms. Martina O'Sullivan, M.S.W.
Ms. Kerry A. Robinson
Dr. Richard Wood
Staff—Mr. Brian Stevens
Ms. Bonita Anderson
Mr. John Carr
Mr. W. Randy Kessler
Ms. Gloria Luna Moorman
Ms. Sandy Mattingly-Paulen
Mr. Ralph McCloud
Ms. Kathy Saile

COMMITTEE ON ECUMENICAL AND INTERRELIGIOUS AFFAIRS

Chairman—Archbishop Wilton D. Gregory, S.L.D.
Members—Archbishop Basil M. Schott, O.F.M.
Bishop Stephen E. Blaire, D.D.
Bishop Daniel E. Flores
Bishop John R. Gaydos
Bishop Denis J. Madden
Bishop William F. Murphy, J.C.L., LL.D., S.T.D.
Bishop Thomas J. Olmsted, J.C.L.
Bishop Kevin C. Rhoades
Consultants—Cardinal William Keeler
Archbishop Oscar H. Lipscomb, D.D., Ph.D.
Archbishop John C. Nienstedt
Archbishop Daniel E. Pilarczyk, S.T.D., Ph.D., D.D.
Bishop Tod D. Brown, D.D.
Bishop Patrick R. Cooney, S.T.B., S.T.L., D.D.
Bishop Ronald P. Herzog, D.D.
Bishop Howard J. Hubbard
Bishop Edward U. Kmiec, D.D., S.T.L.
Bishop John C. Reiss, D.D., J.C.D.
Bishop Placido Rodriguez, C.M.F.
Bishop Carlos Arthur Sevilla, S.J., D.D.
Bishop Richard J. Sklba
Bishop William S. Skylstad, D.D.
Bishop John C. Wester
Staff—Rev. James Massa, Exec. Dir.
Rev. Ronald G. Roberson, C.S.P.
Rev. Francis V. Tiso

COMMITTEE ON EVANGELIZATION AND CATECHESIS

Chairman—Bishop Richard J. Malone
Members—Archbishop Donald W. Wuerl
Bishop Robert Joseph Baker
Bishop Leonard P. Blair
Bishop Paul S. Coakley
Bishop Sam G. Jacobs
Bishop Gregory John Mansour
Bishop Jaime Soto
Bishop Daniel F. Walsh, D.D.
Consultants—Archbishop Alfred C. Hughes, S.T.D.
Mr. Robert McCarty, N.F.C.Y.M.
Rev. John E. Hurley, C.S.P.
Rev. Msgr. John E. Kozar
Ms. Leland Nagel
Ms. Carol Obrokta
Ms. Diana Raiche
Ms. Maruja Sedano
Staff—Rev. J. Brian Bransfield, M.Div., M.A., S.T.L.
Ms. Jeannine Marino
Dr. Michael Steier
Dr. Jem Sullivan

Subcommittee on the Catechism
Chairman—Bishop Leonard P. Blair, D.D., S.T.D.
Members—Cardinal Daniel N. DiNardo
Archbishop George J. Lucas
Archbishop Allen H. Vigneron, D.D.
Bishop Kevin C. Rhoades
Bishop Arthur J. Serratelli, S.T.D., S.S.L., D.D.
Consultants—Archbishop Alfred C. Hughes, S.T.D.
Rev. John Pollard
Staff—Rev. J. Brian Bransfield, M.Div., M.A., S.T.L.
Ms. Jeannine Marino
Dr. Jem Sullivan

COMMITTEE ON INTERNATIONAL JUSTICE AND PEACE

Chairman—Bishop Howard J. Hubbard
Members—Cardinal Theodore E. McCarrick
Archbishop Edwin F. O'Brien, S.T.D., D.D.
Bishop Frank J. Dewane
Bishop Richard E. Pates
Bishop Ricardo Ramírez, C.S.B., D.D.
Bishop John H. Ricard, S.S.J.
Bishop William S. Skylstad, D.D.
Bishop Thomas G. Wenski
Consultants—Cardinal Justin F. Rigali
Archbishop Timothy Broglio
Archbishop Timothy M. Dolan
Bishop William F. Murphy, J.C.L., LL.D., S.T.D.
Bishop Jaime Soto, D.D., M.S.W.
Bishop John C. Wester
Major Gen. William F. Burns, (Ret.)
Ambassador Mary Ann Glendon
Dr. Maryann Cusimano Love
Dr. John Steinbruner
Staff—Mr. John Carr
Dr. Stephen M. Colecchi
Mrs. Virginia L. Farris
Mr. Gerry Flood
Mr. Stephen R. Hilbert
Rev. Juan Jose Molina, O.SS.T.

COMMITTEE ON LAITY, MARRIAGE, FAMILY LIFE, AND YOUTH

Chairman—Archbishop Roger L. Schwietz, O.M.I., D.D.
Chairman-Elect—Bishop Kevin C. Rhoades
Members—Bishop Gregory M. Aymond
Bishop Peter F. Christensen, M.A.S.
Bishop Joseph W. Estabrook
Bishop Sam G. Jacobs
Bishop John Francis Kinney, D.D., J.C.D.
Bishop George J. Rassas
Bishop Jaime Soto, D.D., M.S.W.
Bishop Kevin W. Vann
Consultants—Mr. Robert McCarty, N.F.C.Y.M.
Mr. Carl Anderson
Mr. Paul Jarzembowski
Ms. Kathy Laird
Ms. Charlotte McCorquodale
Staff—Ms. Sheila Garcia
Sr. Eileen McCann, C.S.J.
Dr. H. Richard McCord
Ms. Theresa Notare

Subcommittee on Marriage and Family Life
Chairman—Archbishop Joseph E. Kurtz
Members—Archbishop Charles J. Chaput, O.F.M.Cap., D.D.
Archbishop Joseph F. Naumann
Archbishop Basil M. Schott, O.F.M.
Bishop R. Daniel Conlon
Bishop George J. Rassas
Bishop Gabino Zavala, D.D., J.C.L., V.G.
Consultants—Archbishop Elden F. Curtiss
Bishop J. Kevin Boland
Ms. Helen Alvare, Esq.
Dr. John Grabowski
Mr. Frank Hannigan
Staff—Ms. Sheila Garcia
Dr. H. Richard McCord
Ms. Theresa Notare

COMMITTEE ON MIGRATION

Chairman—Bishop John C. Wester, V.G.
Chairman-Elect—Archbishop Jose H. Gomez, S.T.D.
Members—Cardinal Edward M. Egan
Archbishop Charles J. Chaput, O.F.M.Cap., D.D.
Bishop Michael F. Burbidge, D.D., Ed.D., V.G.
Bishop Felipe de Jesus Estevez
Bishop Richard J. Garcia, D.D.
Bishop John R. Manz
Bishop Jaime Soto, D.D., M.S.W.
Bishop James Anthony Tamayo, D.D.
Consultants—Cardinal Roger M. Mahony
Cardinal Theodore E. McCarrick
Cardinal Sean P. O'Malley, O.F.M.Cap., Ph.D.
Bishop Gerald R. Barnes, D.D.
Bishop J. Kevin Boland
Bishop Edgar M. da Cunha, S.D.V., D.D.
Bishop Nicholas DiMarzio, Ph.D., D.D.
Bishop Kevin Joseph Farrell, D.D.

Bishop Martin D. Holley, D.D., V.G.
Bishop Gerald Frederick Kicanas, D.D.
Bishop John Francis Kinney, D.D., J.C.D.
Bishop Armando X. Ochoa, D.D.
Bishop Thomas Gerard Wenski
Sr. RayMonda DuVall, C.H.S.
Mr. Mark Franken
Mr. Robert Gilligan
Mr. Kenneth Hackett
Staff—Mr. Kevin Appleby
Ms. Anastasia Brown
Sr. Gaye L. Moorhead, R.S.M.
Mr. Johnny Young

COMMITTEE ON NATIONAL COLLECTIONS

Chairman—Bishop Kevin Joseph Farrell, D.D.
Members—Cardinal Theodore E. McCarrick
Cardinal Justin F. Rigali
Bishop Jacob Angadiath
Bishop Thomas J. Costello, D.D., V.G.
Bishop Ronald P. Herzog, D.D.
Bishop Roger P. Morin, D.D.
Bishop John H. Ricard, S.S.J.
Bishop Jaime Soto, D.D., M.S.W.
Bishop Michael W. Warfel
Consultants—Sr. Janice Bader, C.P.P.S.
Mr. Jim Caldarola
Rev. John Cusick
Staff—Ms. Mary Mencarini Campbell
Ms. Gina Laurent
Mr. Patrick Markey
Rev. James M. McCann, S.J.
Rev. Msgr. Carlos Quintana-Puente
Dr. David J. Suley

Subcommittee on Catholic Home Missions
Chairman—Bishop Michael W. Warfel
Members—Archbishop Thomas J. Rodi
Archbishop Basil M. Schott, O.F.M.
Bishop Paul S. Coakley
Bishop George Vance Murry, S.J.
Bishop Robert F. Vasa
Bishop Joseph S. Vasquez
Staff—Mr. Patrick Markey
Mr. Kenneth Ong
Dr. David J. Suley

Subcommittee on the Church in Africa
Chairman—Bishop John H. Ricard, S.S.J.
Members—Cardinal Theodore E. McCarrick
Cardinal Sean P. O'Malley, O.F.M.Cap., Ph.D.
Archbishop Timothy M. Dolan
Archbishop Wilton D. Gregory, S.L.D.
Bishop Martin Holly
Bishop Thomas Wenski
Bishop John C. Wester
Consultants—Rev. Msgr. John E. Kozar
Mr. Paul Miller
Mr. Fritz Zuger
Staff—Mr. Patrick Markey
Rev. James M. McCann, S.J.
Dr. David J. Suley

Subcommittee on the Church in Central and Eastern Europe
Chairman—Cardinal Justin F. Rigali
Members—Cardinal Adam Maida
Cardinal Theodore E. McCarrick
Archbishop John J. Myers, J.C.D., D.D.
Archbishop Francis B. Schulte
Archbishop Stefan Soroka, D.D., Ph.D.
Staff—Mr. Vincent L. Bus
Mr. Patrick Markey
Rev. James M. McCann, S.J.

Subcommittee on the Church in Latin America
Chairman—Bishop Jaime Soto, D.D., M.S.W.
Members—Cardinal Sean P. O'Malley, O.F.M.Cap., Ph.D.
Bishop Roger J. Baker
Bishop Paul G. Bootkowski
Bishop Randolph Roque Calvo, D.D., J.C.D.
Bishop Eusebio Elizondo, M.Sp.S., J.C.D.
Bishop Peter A. Rosazza
Consultant—Bishop John R. Manz
Staff—Mr. Kevin Day
Mr. Patrick Markey
Rev. Msgr. Carlos Quintana-Puente

COMMITTEE ON PRO-LIFE ACTIVITIES

Chairman—Cardinal Daniel N. DiNardo
Members—Cardinal Daniel N. DiNardo
Cardinal Sean P. O'Malley, O.F.M.Cap., Ph.D.
Archbishop Joseph E. Kurtz, D.D.
Archbishop Joseph F. Naumann, V.G., D.D.
Bishop Martin D. Holley, D.D., V.G.
Bishop William E. Lori, S.T.D.
Bishop Gregory John Mansour
Consultants—Cardinal Anthony J. Bevilacqua
Cardinal Edward M. Egan
Cardinal Francis E. George, O.M.I.
Cardinal William Keeler
Cardinal Roger M. Mahony
Cardinal Adam Maida
Cardinal Theodore E. McCarrick
Ms. Helen Alvare, Esq.
Mr. Carl Anderson
Dr. John M. Haas, Ph.D., S.T.L., K.M.
Rev. J. Daniel Mindling, O.F.M.Cap.
Ms. Gail Quinn
Dr. Robert J. Saxer
Mr. Moe Wosepka
Staff—Mr. Richard M. Doerflinger, M.A.
Mr. Thomas Grenchik
Ms. Deirdre McQuade
Ms. Susan Wills

COMMITTEE ON THE PROTECTION OF CHILDREN AND YOUNG PEOPLE

Chairman—Bishop Blase J. Cupich
Members—Bishop Richard J. Malone (Region I)
Bishop Robert J. Cunningham, D.D., J.C.L. (Region II)
Bishop Timothy Senior (Region III)
Bishop Mitchell T. Rozanski, D.D., V.G. (Region IV)
Bishop Ronald William Gainer (Region V)
Archbishop Dennis M. Schnurr, J.C.D., D.D. (Region VI)
Bishop Edward K. Braxton (Region VII)
Bishop John LeVoir (Region VIII)
Bishop Michael O. Jackels, S.T.D. (Region IX)
Bishop Patrick J. Zurek, D.D. (Region X)
Bishop Gerald E. Wilkerson, D.D., V.G. (Region XI)
Bishop Michael W. Warfel (Region XII)
Bishop Michael J. Sheridan (Region XIII)
Bishop John G. Noonan (Region XIV)
Bishop Gerald N. Dino (Region XV)
Consultants—Very Rev. Thomas P. Cassidy, S.C.J.
Rev. Paul Lininger, O.F.M.Conv.
Very Rev. Thomas Picton, C.Ss.R.
Staff—Rev. Msgr. Ronny Jenkins, S.T.L., J.C.D.
Ms. Teresa M. Kettelkamp
Ms. Mary Jane Doerr
Ms. Helen Osman
Mr. Anthony R. Picarello, Esq.
Rev. David J. Toups
Sr. Mary Ann Walsh

AD HOC COMMITTEE FOR THE DEFENSE OF MARRIAGE

Members—Archbishop Joseph E. Kurtz
Bishop William E. Lori, S.T.D.
Bishop Gabino Zavala, D.D., J.C.L., V.G.
Consultant—Mr. Carl Anderson
Staff—Rev. J. Brian Bransfield, M.Div., M.A., S.T.L.
Mr. Andrew Lichtenwalner

TASK FORCE ON CULTURAL DIVERSITY IN THE CHURCH

Chairman—Bishop Ricardo Ramirez, C.S.B.
Members—Archbishop Jose H. Gomez, S.T.D.
Bishop Randolph Roque Calvo, D.D., J.C.D.
Bishop Octavio Cisneros
Bishop Salvatore J. Cordileone, J.C.D.
Bishop Curtis J. Guillory, S.V.D.
Bishop John R. Manz
Bishop Placido Rodriguez, C.M.F.
Bishop Daniel F. Walsh, D.D.
Bishop Thomas G. Wenski
Staff Coordinator—Ms. Cecile Motus

TASK FORCE ON FAITH FORMATION & SACRAMENTAL PRACTICE

Chairman—Bishop J. Peter Sartain
Members—Archbishop Wilton D. Gregory, S.L.D.
Archbishop John G. Vlazny
Archbishop Donald W. Wuerl
Bishop Peter F. Christensen, M.A.S.
Bishop Daniel E. Flores
Bishop Richard J. Garcia, D.D.
Bishop Richard J. Malone
Bishop Joseph P. McFadden, D.D.
Bishop William S. Skylstad, D.D.
Staff Coordinator—Rev. J. Brian Bransfield, M.Div., M.A., S.T.L.
Staff—Ms. Beverly A. Carroll
Mr. Andrew Lichtenwalner
Rev. James M. McCann, S.J.
Sr. Eileen McCann, C.S.J.
Mrs. Marie A. Powell
Rev. Msgr. Anthony F. Sherman
Ms. Mary Elizabeth Sperry
Rev. Thomas G. Weinandy, O.F.M.Cap.

TASK FORCE ON HEALTH CARE

Chairman—Bishop Kevin C. Rhoades
Members—Cardinal Daniel N. DiNardo
Archbishop Charles J. Chaput, O.F.M.Cap., D.D.
Archbishop Henry J. Mansell
Bishop Felipe de Jesus Estevez
Bishop Robert Joseph McManus
Bishop Thomas J. Paprocki, S.T.L., J.D., J.C.D.
Bishop Kevin W. Vann
Bishop Robert F. Vasa
Consultants—Dr. John M. Haas, Ph.D., S.T.L., K.M.
Rev. J. Daniel Mindling, O.F.M.Cap., S.T.D.
Ms. Janice L. Benton
John Brehany, Ph.D., S.T.L.
Sr. Carol Keehan, D.C.
Staff—Mr. John Carr
Mr. Richard M. Doerflinger, M.A.
Mr. Tom Grenchik
Ms. Kathy Saile
Rev. Thomas G. Weinandy, O.F.M.Cap.
Ms. Nancy Wisdo
Mrs. Christina Zvir

TASK FORCE ON PROMOTION OF VOCATIONS TO THE PRIESTHOOD AND CONSECRATED LIFE

Chairman—Archbishop Thomas J. Rodi
Members—Archbishop Robert J. Carlson
Coadjutor Archbishop Dennis M. Schnurr
Archbishop Basil M. Schott, O.F.M.
Bishop Fabian Wendelin Bruskewitz, D.D., S.T.D.
Bishop Michael F. Burbidge, D.D., Ed.D., V.G.
Bishop Blase J. Cupich
Bishop Kevin Joseph Farrell, D.D.
Bishop Dominic M. Luong, D.D., V.G.
Bishop Richard E. Pates
Bishop Jaime Soto
Staff Coordinator—Rev. David Toups, S.T.D.
Staff—Rev. James Steffes
Sr. Suzanne Bellenoit, S.S.J.
Sr. Eileen McCann, C.S.J.
Sr. Myrna Tordillo, M.S.C.S.
Sr. Doris M. Turek, S.S.N.D.
Sr. Mary Ann Walsh

TASK FORCE ON STRENGTHENING MARRIAGE

Chairman—Bishop Gabino Zavala, D.D., J.C.L., V.G.
Members—Archbishop Roger L. Schwietz, O.M.I., D.D.
Archbishop Charles J. Chaput, O.F.M.Cap., D.D.
Archbishop Joseph E. Kurtz
Archbishop George H. Niederauer
Archbishop Allen H. Vigneron, D.D.
Bishop Leonard P. Blair, D.D., S.T.D.
Bishop Nicholas DiMarzio
Bishop John R. Gaydos
Staff—Ms. Sheila Garcia

TASK FORCE ON THE LIFE AND DIGNITY OF THE HUMAN PERSON

Chairman—Bishop Robert W. Finn
Members—Archbishop Gregory M. Aymond, D.D.
Archbishop Joseph F. Naumann
Bishop Michael J. Bransfield
Bishop Felipe de Jesus Estevez
Bishop Martin D. Holley, D.D., V.G.
Bishop Howard J. Hubbard
Bishop William E. Lori, S.T.D.
Bishop Gregory John Mansour
Bishop William F. Murphy, J.C.L., LL.D., S.T.D.
Bishop Michael J. Sheridan
Staff Coordinator—Rev. J. Brian Bransfield, M.Div., M.A., S.T.L.
Staff—Ms. Therese Brown
Mr. John Carr
Dr. Stephen M. Colecchi
Ms. Teresa M. Kettelkamp
Mr. James Kuh
Sr. Joanna Okereke, H.H.C.J.
Mrs. Marie A. Powell
Rev. Thomas G. Weinandy, O.F.M.Cap.

TASK FORCE ON THE SPANISH LANGUAGE BIBLE

Chairman—Archbishop Jose H. Gomez, S.T.D., D.D.
Members—Bishop John R. Manz
Bishop Arthur J. Serratelli, S.T.D., S.S.L., D.D.
Bishop Jaime Soto, D.D., M.S.W.
Bishop Gabino Zavala
Bishop Patrick J. Zurek, D.D., V.G.
Staff—Mr. Alejandro Aguilera-Titus
Sr. Doris M. Turek, S.S.N.D.

BOARD OF BISHOPS FOR THE AMERICAN COLLEGE, LOUVAIN

Chairman—Bishop David L. Ricken, D.D., J.C.L.
Members
Region I—Bishop Francis J. Christian, Ph.D.
Region II—Bishop Octavio Cisneros
Region III—Bishop Arthur Joseph Serratelli, S.S.L., S.T.D., D.D.
Region IV—Bishop Richard B. Higgins, S.T.L., D.D.
Region V—Bishop Shelton J. Fabre
Region VI—Bishop Roger W. Gries, O.S.B., D.D., M.Ed.
Region VII—Bishop David L. Ricken, D.D., J.C.L.
Region VIII—Bishop Lee Piche
Region IX—Bishop Robert Hermann
Region X—Bishop James Anthony Tamayo, D.D.
Region XI—Deacon John Luong
Region XII—Bishop George L. Thomas, D.D., Ph.D., V.G.
Region XIII—Bishop Fernando Isern, D.D.
Region XIV—Bishop John G. Noonan
Region XV—Bishop John Michael Botean, D.D.
Consultant—Rev. Msgr. Ross A. Shecterle, Rector
Staff—Rev. Msgr. Ronny Jenkins, S.T.L., J.C.D.

BOARD OF BISHOPS FOR THE NORTH AMERICAN COLLEGE, ROME

Chairman—Archbishop John J. Myers, J.C.D., D.D.
Vice-Chairman—Archbishop Henry J. Mansell
Treasurer—Bishop Frank J. Dewane
Members
Region I—Archbishop Henry J. Mansell, D.D.
Region II—Bishop William F. Murphy, J.C.L., LL.D., S.T.D.
Region III—Archbishop John J. Myers, J.C.D., D.D.
Region IV—Archbishop Donald W. Wuerl
Region V—Bishop Glen John Provost
Region VI—Bishop Bernard A. Hebda, J.C.L., J.D.
Region VII—Bishop Thomas George Doran, D.D., J.C.D.
Region VIII—Bishop Samuel J. Aquila, D.D.
Region IX—Bishop R. Walker Nickless
Region X—Bishop Patrick J. Zurek, D.D., V.G.
Region XI—Bishop Robert H. Brom, D.D.
Region XII—Bishop Michael W. Warfel
Region XIII—Archbishop Daniel E. Sheehan, D.D.,

J.C.D.
Region XIV—Bishop Frank J. Dewane
Region XV—Bishop John M. Kudrick
Consultant—Mr. James Crowley
Staff—Rev. Msgr. Daniel H. Mueggenborg
Mrs. Mary DiDonato
Rev. Msgr. James Checchio, J.C.D., M.B.A.

CATHOLIC LEGAL IMMIGRATION NETWORK, INC. BOARD OF DIRECTORS

Chairman—Bishop Jaime Soto, D.D., M.S.W.
Members—Archbishop Jose H. Gomez, S.T.D.
Bishop Frank J. Dewane
Bishop Nicholas DiMarzio
Bishop Richard J. Garcia, D.D.
Bishop Joseph A. Pepe, D.D., J.C.D.
Bishop James Anthony Tamayo, D.D.
Bishop Thomas G. Wenski
Bishop John C. Wester
Sr. Anne Curtis, R.S.M.
Sr. Sally Duffy, S.C.
Sr. RayMonda DuVall, C.H.S.
Sr. Maureen Joyce, R.S.M.
Mr. Vincent Pitta
Ms. Nancy Wisdo
Mr. Johnny Young
Secretary—Mr. Mark Franken, Exec. Dir.

CATHOLIC RELIEF SERVICES (CRS) CRS: BOARD OF DIRECTORS

Chairman—Archbishop Timothy M. Dolan
Members—Cardinal Theodore E. McCarrick
Archbishop Timothy Broglio
Archbishop Joseph E. Kurtz
Archbishop Michael Jarboe Sheehan, S.T.L., J.C.D.
Bishop J. Kevin Boland
Bishop Patrick R. Cooney, S.T.B., S.T.L., D.D.
Bishop Daniel E. Flores
Bishop Martin D. Holley, D.D., V.G.
Bishop Denis J. Madden
Bishop George L. Thomas, D.D., Ph.D., V.G.
Bishop John C. Wester
Mr. John H. Griffin, Jr.
Honorable Diana Lewis
Rev. Paul L. Locatelli, S.J.
Rev. Msgr. David J. Malloy
Mr. James N. Perry, Jr.
Mrs. Constance L. Proctor
Mrs. Karen Rauenhorst
Dr. Carolyn Y. Woo
Sr. Carol Keehan, D.C.
Staff—Mr. Kenneth Hackett, Exec. Dir.

CONFRATERNITY OF CHRISTIAN DOCTRINE, INC. BOARD OF TRUSTEES

President—Cardinal Francis E. George, O.M.I.
Members—Archbishop Joseph E. Kurtz
Bishop Gerald Frederick Kicanas, D.D.
Bishop William E. Lori
Bishop George Vance Murry, S.J.
Staff—Ms. Mary Elizabeth Sperry

NATIONAL REVIEW BOARD

Chair—Ms. Diane M. Knight, A.C.S.W., C.I.S.W.
Members—Dr. Emmet M. Kenney, Jr., M.D.
Justice Robert Charles Kohm
Dr. Susan Steibe-Pasalich, Ph.D.
Mr. Stephen A. Zappala, Jr.
Dr. Ana Marie Catanzaro, Ph.D.
Mr. Michael J. Clark
Dr. Antoine M. Garibaldi, Ph.D.
Dr. Charles H. Handel, Ed.D.
Judge Anna Moran, J.D.
Mr. Al Notzon, III
Dr. Thomas Plante, Ph.D.
Judge Geraldine Rivera
Dr. Ruben Gallegos, Ph.D.
Staff—Ms. Mary Jane Doerr
Ms. Teresa M. Kettelkamp

RELATED ORGANIZATIONS

***Catholic Legal Immigration Network, Inc. (CLINIC) Theological College**
National Office, 415 Michigan Ave., N.E. Ste. 200 Washington, DC 20017. Tel: 202-635-2556 Fax: 202-635-2649 Email: national@cliniclegal.org Web: www.cliniclegal.org
Corporate Officers:—Bishop Jaime Soto, Chm. & Pres. ,Bishop James Anthony Tamayo, D.D., Vice Pres.,Sr. Sally Duffy, S.C., Treas.,Mr. Donald Kerwin, Sec.,Mr. Mark Franken, Interim Exec. Dir
Members:—Bishop Jaime Soto, D.D., M.S.W. ,Bishop Thomas J. Flanagan, D.D., V.G.,Bishop Thomas J. Olmsted,Bishop Robert J. Baker, S.T.D.,Bishop Thomas G. Wenski,Bishop John C. Wester, V.G.,Sr. Lourdes Sheehan, R.S.M.,Ms. Margaret Hatton,Ms. Lily Gutierrez,Mr. Mark Franken,Sr. RayMonda DuVail,Mr. Austin T. Fragomen,Jane Belford, Esq.
The Catholic Legal Immigration Network, Inc. (CLINIC), a subsidiary of the United States Catholic Conference of Bishops (USCCB), operates a legal support agency for a rapidly growing national network of Catholic immigration programs. CLINIC advocates for transparent, fair and generous immigration policies, and expresses the Church's commitment to the full membership of migrants in U.S. society.

RELATED ORGANIZATIONS

National Religious Retirement Office
3211 Fourth St. Washington, DC 20017-1194. Tel: 202-541-3215 Sr. Janice Bader, C.P.P.S., Exec. Dir.
The Mission of the National Religious Retirement Office is to coordinate the National Collection for the Retirement Fund for Religious and to distribute these monies to eligible religious institutes for their retirement needs. The office also provides retirement planning and educational assistance to religious institutes. The National Religious Retirement Office is sponsored by the Conference of Major Superiors of Men, the Conference of Major Superiors of Women Religious, the Leadership Conference of Women Religious and the United States Conference of Catholic Bishops.

The USCCB Commission on Certification and Accreditation
3211 South Lake Dr., Ste. 317 St. Francis, WI 53235-3702. Tel: 414-486-0139 Fax: 414-489-0006 Dr. C. Vanessa White, Board Chair, Dr. Kay Sheskaitis, I.H.M., Exec. Dir.
Established in 1982 by the Administrative Board of the United States Conference of Catholic Bishops, the USCCB Commission serves as an accrediting commission of the Catholic Bishops of the United States, establishes accreditation standards, policies, and procedures, and accredits quality ministry formation programs that prepare persons for ministry. The USCCB/CCA also approves certification standards and procedures for the certification of specialized ecclesial ministers by (Arch)Dioceses and organizations.

NATIONAL ORGANIZATIONS

Listing in this category is not related to classification under Canon Law as a public juridic person.

American Catholic Correctional Chaplains Association
c/o Catholic Social Services, 100 E. Eighth St. Cincinnati, OH 45202-2193. Tel: 920-324-6298 Fax: 920-324-6254 Email: info@catholiccorrectionalchaplains.org Web: catholiccorrectionalchaplains.org Auxiliary Bishop Barry C. Knestout, D.D., V.G., Episcopal Advisor,Paul E. Rogers, Pres.,Rev. Michael Koncik, C.Ss.R., Vice Pres.,Mr. Teodoro Rael, Treas.,Christine M. Shimrock, Sec.,Rev. Mark C. Schmieder, Past Pres.,Sr. Peggy Devaney, I.H.M., Certification Chair
The Board of Directors include the Episcopal Advisor and Elected Officers. Address all Communications to the Executive Secretary.
A nonprofit organization for the purposes of unifying and implementing the Church's corrective and restorative efforts for the spiritual welfare of persons committed to the Catholic Chaplains' care, and to foster a Catholic approach to issues of criminal justice in accord with the principles of Sacred Scripture and Catholic social justice teaching. Affiliated with the Social Development and World Peace Department, USCCB, the International Commission of Catholic Prison Pastoral Care, American Correctional Association, American Correctional Chaplains Association, National Council on Crime and Delinquency and The Catholic University of America, it was established with approval of the American Bishops in 1952. Grants USCCB-recognized certification to qualified members.
Publication: tri-annually, ACCCA Newsletter.

American Catholic Historical Association (1919)
The Catholic University of America, Washington, DC 20064. Tel: 202-319-5079 Fax: 202-319-5079 Email: cua-chracha@cua.edu Web: research.cua.edu/acha Rev. Steven M. Avella, Pres.,Rev. Paul G. Robichaud, C.S.P., Gen. Sec.
A membership organization, founded to promote the study of church history understood in the broad sense and to assist American Catholics and other members in all fields of history.

The American College of the Roman Catholic Church of the United States-North American College (1859)
3211 Fourth St., N.E. Washington, DC 20017-1194. Tel: 202-541-5411 Fax: 202-722-8804 Email: nac@usccb.org Archbishop John J. Myers, J.C.D., D.D., Chm.,Rev. Msgr. James Checchio, J.C.D., M.B.A., Rector,Mrs. Mary DiDonato, Exec. Dir., Office of Institutional Advancement
The College is owned and operated by the Bishops of the United States and incorporated under the laws of the State of Maryland.

Apostleship of the Sea of the United States of America (AOSUSA)
1500 Jefferson Dr. Port Arthur, TX 77642-0646. Tel: 409-985-4545 Fax: 409-985-5945 Email: aosusa@sbcglobal.net Bishop Kevin Boland, Bishop Promoter,Rev. Sinclair Oubre, J.C.L., Pres.,Ms. Doreen M. Badeaux, Sec. Gen.
AOSUSA is an association of the faithful of Catholic maritime chaplains, cruise ship Priests, seafarers, deacons, religious lay, ecclesial ministers, and affiliates serving the people of the sea in ports throughout the USA, in collaboration with the Secretariat for Cultural Diversity in the Church of the United States Conference of Catholic Bishops.
Publication: Catholic Maritime News.

Association of Catholic Diocesan Archivists
Archdiocese of Chicago Archives & Record Ctr., 711 W. Monroe Chicago, IL 60661. Tel: 312-831-0711 Bishop Thomas J. Paprocki, Episcopal Moderator,Emile Leumas, Pres.,William Bissenden, Vice Pres. & Pres. Elect,Brian Fahey, Treas.,Janice Cantrell, Sec.
The Association of Catholic diocesan archivists first met in 1979 and formally organized the Association of Catholic Diocesan Archivists in 1982. The organization promotes professionalism in the management of diocesan archives in the United States and Canada, and fosters cooperation between diocesan archivists and others on regional, national and international levels. Membership information is available through the above address and telephone number.

Catholic Academy for Communication Arts Professionals
National Office, 1645 Brook Lynn Dr., Ste. 2 Dayton, OH 45432-1933. Tel: 937-229-2303 Fax: 937-459-0263 Email: admin@catholicacademy.org Web: www.catholicacademy.org Mr. Frank Morock, Pres.,Ms. Sally A. Oberski, 1st. Vice Pres.,Mary Ross Agosta, 2nd Vice Pres.,Jorge Riopedre, Treas.
The Catholic Academy for Communication Arts Professionals is the U.S. affiliate of SIGNIS, the international Vatican-approved organization for communication. The Catholic Academy grew out of the international merger of two other associations founded in the 1920's in Europe: UNDA for radio and television and OCIC the International Catholic Organization for Cinema. These groups joined to form the Catholic Academy in October 2002. The Catholic Academy is a national network of broadcasters, communications directors, public relations personnel, independent producers, syndicators, internet and other media professionals. This national network provides professional support and access to a broad base of experience and resources. Principal activities of the Catholic Academy: annual General Assembly for all members, annual Gabriel Awards for excellence in commercial and religious communications.
Publication: electronic newsletter, White Papers.

Catholic Association of Diocesan Ecumenical and Interreligious Officers (CADEIO)
303 S. Poplar St. Carbondale, IL 62901-2709. Tel: 618-457-4556 Fax: 618-457-7368 Email: rbflan@globaleyes.net Very Rev. Robert B. Flannery, V.F., Pres.,Rev. Msgr. George Appleyard, Vice Pres.,Rev. Msgr. Patrick F. Halfpenny, Treas.,Rev. Donald J. Rooney, Sec.
The purposes of CADEIO are to stimulate an exchange of ideas, experiences and evaluations among the ecumenical officers of the (Arch)Dioceses and Eparchies in union with Rome; to promote programs which further the work of Christian unity and of interreligious cooperation; and to cooperate with the Bishops' Committee for Ecumenical and Interreligious Affairs of the United States Conference of Catholic Bishops, and with other ecumenical and interreligious agencies.
Publication: quarterly Newsletter; annual booklets on various ecumenical and interreligious topics, Handbook for Catholic Ecumenical Officers.

Catholic Association of Teachers of Homiletics (CATH)
St. Meinrad School of Theology, 200 Hill Dr. St. Meinrad, IN 47577.
Officers—Rev. Guerric DeBona, O.S.B., Pres. ,Dr.

Deborah A. Organ, D.Min., Vice Pres.,Rev. Donald J. Heet, O.S.F.S., Sec./Treas.

Catholic Campus Ministry Association

National Office, 1118 Pendleton St., Ste. 300 Cincinnati, OH 45202-8805. Tel: 513-842-0167 Fax: 513-842-0171

Founded in 1969 by campus ministers, the association promotes the mission of the Church in higher education and implements the 1985 Pastoral Letter on Campus Ministry through educational programs and services, leadership, the development of cooperative relationships with other organizations and development activities. Membership is open to individuals interested in campus ministry.

Publications: Crossroads, bimonthly publication; The Catholic Campus Ministry Directory.

Catholic Cemetery Conference

National Office, 1400 S. Wolf Rd., Bldg. 3 Hillside, IL 60162. Tel: 888-850-8131 Web: www.mytriplec.org Dennis Fairbank, Exec. Dir.,Archbishop John G. Vlazny, Episcopal Moderator

The Conference is an organization of Diocesan Directors of Cemeteries and parish cemetery administrators from throughout the United States, Canada, Australia, Italy and Guam. Guided by the principle: "That burial of the dead is one of the Corporal Works of Mercy," the Conference promotes high standards of Catholic cemetery management, development, operation and maintenance consistent with Christian service to the Catholic community; and fosters and promotes the religious, charitable and educational interests of Catholic cemeteries and the people they serve.

Founded in 1949, the Catholic Cemetery Conference (CCC) helps cemetery staff enhance their skills in caring for the deceased and comforting their loved ones through ministry, education, networking and service opportunities.

Publications: monthly magazine, Catholic Cemetery; various booklets on cemetery management & evaluation services; funeral liturgy at the cemetery. Annual Convention; John Carroll University-Summer Seminar on Leadership; smaller cemeteries seminar.

Catholic Relief Services

Catholic Relief Services-USSCB

CRS World Headquarters, 228 W. Lexington St. Baltimore, MD 21201-3413. Tel: 866-608-5978 Web: www.crs.org Mr. Ken Hackett, Pres.

Catholic Relief Services Board of Directors

Chairman—Archbishop Timothy M. Dolan

Members—Bishop J. Kevin Boland ,Bishop Patrick R. Cooney,Bishop Nicholas A. DiMarzio,Mr. John H. Griffin, Jr.,Bishop Curtis J. Guillory, S.V.D.,Sr. Carol Keehan, D.C.,Archbishop Joseph E. Kurtz-,Judge Diana Lewis,Rev. Paul L. Locatelli, S.J.,Bishop Denis J. Madden,Rev. Msgr. David J. Malloy,Cardinal Theodore E. McCarrick,Bishop George Vance Murry, S.J.,Mr. James N. Perry, Jr.,Mrs. Constance L. Proctor,Mrs. Karen Rauenhorst,Archbishop Michael J. Sheehan,Bishop George L. Thomas,Bishop John C. Wester,Dr. Carolyn Y. Woo

Staff—Ms. Annemarie Reilly, Chief of Staff ,Mr. Sean Callahan, Exec. Vice Pres., Overseas Operations,Mr. Mark Palmer, Exec. Vice Pres., Chief Financial Officer,Mr. David Piraino, Exec. Vice Pres., Human Resources,Mr. Michael Wiest, Exec. Vice Pres., Charitable Giving and Awareness,Mr. Ken Hackett, Pres.

Catholic Relief Services is the official international humanitarian agency of the U.S. Catholic community. CRS alleviates suffering and provides assistance to people in need in more than 100 countries, without regard to race, religion or nationality.

CRS was founded in 1943 by the bishops of the United States to assist the poor and disadvantaged outside this country — helping people in need for 65 years.

CRS is efficient and effective directing more than 93 percent of the agency's expenditures directly to programs that benefit the poor overseas. Our agency touches more than 80 million lives, by addressing the root causes and effects of poverty, promoting human dignity, and helping to build more just and peaceful societies.

Our relief and development work is accomplished through programs of emergency response, HIV, health, agriculture, education, microfinance and peacebuilding.

We serve Catholics in the United States by inviting them to live out their faith as part of one human family.

For more information, please visit www.crs.org.

Catholic Charities USA

Sixty-six Canal Center Plaza, Ste. 600 Alexandria, VA 22314. Tel: 703-549-1390 Fax: 703-549-1656 Rev. Larry Snyder, Pres.,Bishop Michael P. Driscoll, D.D., M.S.W., Episcopal Liaison

Catholic Charities USA is a national network of more than 1,700 local Catholic Charities agencies and institutions that provide help and create hope for more than 7.8 million people a year regardless of their religious, social, or economic backgrounds.

For more than 280 years, local Catholic Charities agencies have been providing a wide range of vital services in their communities ranging from day care, adoption, and refugee resettlement to advocacy, counseling, and emergency food and housing. Today, the Catholic Charities network is made up of more than 62,000 staff and 243,000 volunteers. In addition, more than 6,100 individuals serve as volunteer members of local boards.

The National Office-Catholic Charities USA-was founded in 1910 as the National Conference of Catholic Charities by the Most Rev. Thomas J. Shahan and Rt. Rev. Msgr. William J. Kerby in cooperation with lay leaders of the Society of St. Vincent De Paul.

Catholic Charities USA provides its members a national voice, networking opportunities, training and technical assistance, program development, and financial support.

Catholic Charities USA has been commissioned by the U.S. Catholic bishops to represent the Catholic community in times of domestic disaster. Catholic Charities USA also provides disaster preparedness training to dioceses and agencies to mitigate the disruption of business and services consequent to natural disasters.

Catholic Charities USA's president represents North America before Caritas International-the international conference of Catholic Charities-maintaining contact with the Catholic Charities movement throughout the world.

Pope Benedict XVI has named Fr. Larry Synder, President of Catholic Charities USA, to the Dicastery of Cor Unum, which provides disaster-oriented relief in developing countries.

Publications: Charities USA, a quarterly membership magazine; an annual report; an annual survey of Catholic Charities services nationwide; and various publications on issues of concern to Catholic Charities agencies.

The Catholic Communications Foundation (CCF)

c/o 6363 St. Charles Ave. New Orleans, LA 70118. Dr. William H. Hummell, Board Member & Contact Person

The Catholic Communications Foundation was established and is supported by Catholic Fraternal Benefit Societies. Its mission is to assist the communications apostolates of the Catholic Church in the United States, with particular emphasis at the diocesan level. The Foundation awards religious communications training scholarships.

The Catholic Health Association of the United States (1919)

Headquarters, 4455 Woodson Rd. Saint Louis, MO 63134. Tel: 314-427-2500 Fax: 314-427-0029 Web: www.chausa.org Sr. Carol Keehan, D.C., Pres. & CEO,Sr. Patricia A. Talone, R.S.M., Ph.D., Vice Pres. Mission Svcs.,Michael F. Rodgers, Sr. Vice Pres. Public Policy and Advocacy,Rhonda Mueller, Senior Vice Pres. Finance & Opers.,J. Fred Caesar, Sr., Special Asst. to the Pres.,Lisa J. Gilden, Vice Pres. Gen. Counsel,Ed Giganti, Vice Pres. Communications & Mktg.,Elaine Bauer, Vice Pres. Strategic Initiatives

CHA represents the combined strength of its members, more than 2,000 Catholic healthcare sponsors, systems, facilities, and related organizations. Founded in 1915, CHA unites members to advance selected strategic directions. Presents annual awards recognizing contribution to the health ministry by organizations and individuals. Sponsors continuing education for healthcare personnel.

Service Areas: Planning and Policy Development, Public Policy and Advocacy, Communications, Sponsorship, Ethics and Mission Services. Annual Assembly: Annual assembly and membership meeting for Catholic healthcare leaders.

Publications: 6 times-year, Health Progress; bimonthly Catholic Health World; booklets, books & audiovisual on healthcare, Church-related subjects.

Catholic Kolping Society of America (1849)

(Please direct all correspondence to the National Administrator).

1223 Van Houten Clifton, NJ 07013. Patricia Farkas, Natl. Admin.

The Society was founded by Rev. Adolph Kolping in Cologne, Germany, and established in the United States in 1856. The Catholic Kolping Society of America is a part of the world-wide Kolping movement and belongs to the International Kolping Society. There are 12 branches in principal cities of the United States with a combined membership of approximately 2,500. The membership is open to men and women of all ages. The Society's mission statement reads: We, the members of the Catholic Kolping Society of America, extend the vision of our founder, Blessed Adolph Kolping, by promoting the development of the individual and family; we foster a sense of belonging and friendship through our program of spiritual, educational, charitable and social activities.

Catholic Medical Association

National Headquarters, 333 E. Lancaster Ave. #348 Wynnewood, PA 19096. Tel: 215-877-9099 Fax: 215-701-6577 Email: info@cathmed.org Web: www.cathmed.org

Officers (2009-2010)—John Brehany, Ph.D., S.T.L., Exec. Dir. ,Leonard P. Rybak, M.D., Ph.D, Pres.,Mrs. Jan R. Hemstad, M.D., Pres. Elect,Maricela P. Moffitt, M.D., Vice Pres.,John I. Lane, M.D., Treas.,Paul J. Braaton, M.D., Sec.

Upholding the principles of the Catholic faith and morality as related to the science and practice of medicine.

Catholic Network Of Volunteer Service

6930 Carroll Ave., Ste. 820 Takoma Park, MD 20912-4423. Tel: 301-270-0900 Tel: 800-543-5046 Email: cnvsinfo@cnvs.org Web: www.cnvs.org Bishop Oscar Solis, Episcopal Advisor

Catholic Network of Volunteer Service promotes, recruits and refers volunteers to missions in the United States and overseas. We represent nearly 200 faith-based volunteer programs worldwide and work with the U.S. dioceses, religious communities and the private sector to determine their needs for help. Catholic Network of Volunteer Service (CNVS) is committed to the goal that every Catholic man and woman be invited to consider a period of service in the missions, as a vital and important manifestation of the baptismal call of all Catholic people. Currently over 13,000 men and women are serving in CNVS member mission programs offering their gifts and abilities in full-time service to people in need and living their Catholic faith more fully. These volunteers are serving domestically for a summer, six months, a year or more, and they are serving internationally for two or more years at a time. They are single and married, recent college graduates and early retirees, doctors and teachers, parish ministers and social workers, community organizers, computer programmers, legal aides and more. Gatherings: Annual Conference; Formation Workshops, Training Seminars.

Publications: annual, Response: Directory of Volunteer Opportunities; monthly, How Can I Help?; quarterly, FaithWorks.

Awards: The Father George Mader Award, given annually to honor organizations and individuals who promote the value of lay mission service. The Bishop Joseph A. Francis Award to honor organizations and individuals who promote community service.

The Catholic Press Association of the United States and Canada, Inc.

205 W. Monroe St., Ste. 470 Chicago, IL 60606. Tel: 312-380-6789 Fax: 312-361-0256 Web: www.catholicpress.org Bishop Gabino Zavala,Ms. Penny Wiegert, Pres.,Timothy M. Walter, Exec. Dir.,Karen A. Hurley, Deputy Exec. Dir.,Ms. Nancy Wiechec, Vice Pres.,Matthew Schiller, Treas.,Robert DeFrancesco, Sec.,Mr. Robert Zyskowski, Past Pres.

The Catholic Press Association of the United States and Canada, Inc., is the trade and professional association of Catholic newspapers, magazines, and general publishers in the U.S. and Canada and their staff personnel. The CPA was established in 1911. It serves a professional Catholic press market of nearly 2,000 persons working in more than 600 publications with a wide promotion and representation of Catholic press interests in social media, education, and professional development.

The Catholic Theological Society of America

John Carroll University, 20700 N. Park Blvd. University Hts, OH 44118. Tel: 216-397-1631

Fax: 216-397-1804
Board Members—Bryan Massingale, Pres., Milwaukee, WI ,Mary Ann Hinsdale, Pres. Elect., Chestnut Hill, MA,John E. Thiel, Vice Pres., Fairfield, CT,M. Theresa Moser, RSCJ, Sec., San Francisco, CA,Jozef D. Zalot, Treas., Cincinnati, OH,Terrence W. Tilley, Past Pres., Bronx, NY,Nancy Pineda-Madrid, Chestnut Hill, MA,Christine Firer Hinze, Bronx, NY,Kristin E. Heyer, Santa Clara, CA,Vincent Miller, Washington, DC,Dolores L. Christie, Exec. Dir., University Hts., OH

An association of professional theologians. Its purpose is to promote studies and research in theology within the Roman Catholic tradition, to relate theological science to current problems, and to foster a more effective theological education by providing a forum for an exchange of views among theologians and with scholars in other disciplines.

Catholic Youth Foundation USA
415 Michigan Ave., Ste. 40 Washington, DC 20017-4503. Tel: 202-636-3825 Fax: 202-526-7544 Email: info@cyfusa.org Web: cyfusa.org William A. Cubbedge, B.A., J.D., Dir. Devel.

Catholic Youth Foundation USA (CYFUSA) is assuring a faithful future by promoting effective and innovative youth ministry. CYFUSA also provides full financial support to the national youth ministry office of the Catholic Church. CYFUSA makes all of the following possible: scholarships for youth and youth leaders to attend the National Catholic Youth Conference and the National Conference for Catholic Youth Ministry; awards annual grants to local, diocesan, regional, and national youth ministry projects; development of youth ministry programs for culturally diverse communities; outreach to youth in crisis; training of youth ministers; and full support of the work of the National Federation for Catholic Youth Ministry.

Conference for Catholic Facility Management
P.O. Box 016 Kensington, MD 20895-0016. Tel: 301-946-3704 Fax: 301-946-3705 Email: destwolr@adw.org Web: www.ccfm.net Jim Zielinski, Pres.,Richard deStwolinski, Acting Exec. Dir.,William Krammer, Vice Pres.,Janis Balentine, Sec.,Andre Villere, Jr., Treas.

Mindful of their special ministry in the Roman Catholic Church in facility and real estate matters, the members of the CCFM united to be of service to the Church in ministry of facility and real estate concerns. In particular, this organization promotes the spiritual growth of its membership; promotes facility and real estate knowledge and expertise in service to the local and national Church, facilitates the exchange of ideas and information through personal contacts, quarterly newsletters and annual meetings.

The Conference of Major Superiors of Men's Institutes of the United States, Inc.
8808 Cameron St. Silver Spring, MD 20910. Tel: 301-588-4030 Fax: 301-587-4575 Very Rev. Thomas P. Cassidy, S.C.J., Pres.,Very Rev. Thomas H. Smolich, S.J., Vice Pres.,Bro. Francis Carr, F.S.C., Sec. & Treas.,Rev. Paul Lininger, O.F.M-.Conv., Exec. Dir.

A canonical conference of the major superiors of religious communities and institutes of men for the purpose of promoting the spiritual and apostolic welfare of priests and brothers.

The Confraternity of Christian Doctrine, Inc.
3211 Fourth St., N.E. Washington, DC 20017. Tel: 202-541-3098 Fax: 202-541-3089 Mary Elizabeth Sperry, Assoc Dir.
Members—Bishop George V. Murry, S.J.,Cardinal Francis Cardinal George, O.M.I., Ph.D., S.T.D. Bishop William E. Lori,Archbishop Joseph E. Kurtz, D.D.,Bishop Gerald Frederick Kicanas, D.D.

The Confraternity is a distinct entity, separately incorporated and directed by a Board of Trustees from the United States Conference of Catholic Bishops. The purpose of the Corporation is to foster and promote the teachings of Christ as understood and handed down by the Roman Catholic Church. To this end it licenses use of the Lectionary for Mass and the New American Bible, translations made from the original languages.

Council of Major Superiors of Women Religious in the United States of America
1211 Lawrence St., N.E. P.O. Box 4467 Washington, DC 20017-0467. Tel: 202-832-2575 Fax: 202-832-6325 Mother Mary Quentin Sheridan, R.S.M., Chairperson

A canonically erected conference of Major Superiors of women's religious communities established in 1992 to promote mutual support among them and to foster coordination and cooperation with the Bishops' conference and individual Bishops.

Diocesan Fiscal Management Conference
National Office, P.O. Box 60210 San Angelo, TX 76906. Tel: 877-709-3362 Fax: 800-455-9859 Email: lesmaiman@dfmconf.org Bishop Donald W. Trautman, S.T.D., S.S.L., Episcopal Moderator,Leslie Maiman, M.B.A., M.T.S., Exec. Dir.,Daniel Stremel, Pres.,Brian T. Buckingham, Vice Pres.,Deacon Mike Urick, Sec. & Treas.

Mindful of their special ministry in the Roman Catholic Church as the extension of the Diocesan Bishop in fiscal matters, the members of the DFMC unite to be of service to the Church in the ministry of fiscal management.

In particular, this organization promotes the spiritual growth of its members; promotes financial and administrative knowledge and expertise in service to the local and national Church; facilitates the free exchange of ideas and information, and serves as a liaison among the fiscal managers of the Dioceses and Archdioceses of the Church.

Diocesan Information Systems Conference
National Office, 226 Summit Ave. Saint Paul, MN 55102-2197. Tel: 651-291-4439 Fax: 651-290-1627 Email: info@discinfo.org Archbishop Richard E. Pates, D.D., Episcopal Moderator,Mary Jo Jungwirth, Pres.,Lee Jones, Vice Pres.,Dale Jonasson, M.S., Sec. & Treas.

The members of DISC unite to be of service to the Roman Catholic Church in information systems matters. The DISC organization serves as a liaison among technology managers for Archdioceses, Dioceses and related entities.

In particular, this organization promotes the spiritual growth of its members, provides technical expertise in Information Technology, promotes professional technical services to the local and national church communities, encourages the development of professional relationships among its members and facilitates the free exchange of technical information and ideas.

Federation of Diocesan Liturgical Commissions
National Office, 415 Michigan Ave., N.E., Ste. 70 Washington, DC 20017. Tel: 202-635-6990 Fax: 202-529-2452 Web: www.FDLC.org Ms. Lisa A. Tarker, Exec. Dir.,Rev. Msgr. John H. Burton, Chm.,Ms. Dolly Sokol, Vice Chm.,Mrs. Judy Bullock, Treas.,Rev. Robert E. Webster, Delegate-at-Large,Rev. Steven L. Dublinski, V.G., Delegate-at-Large

The FDLC is a voluntary association of all diocesan liturgical commissions/offices from the United States. Two members of each diocesan liturgical commission/office serve as diocesan representatives to the FDLC. From this membership are elected 24 representatives (two from each of the 12 Episcopal regions) to serve as the National Board of Directors. The day-to-day activities of the FDLC are directed by the Executive Director. The FDLC relates closely to the Bishops because its membership consists of their appointees. The Federation serves the Bishops and local commissions in matters of ongoing liturgical renewal. It also serves through education and other coordinated services requested by individual commissions or through consultation and voting at national meetings. The FDLC is organized and operated exclusively for religious and educational purposes.

Instituto Nacional Hispano de Liturgia, Inc.
620 Michigan Ave., N.E. Washington, DC 20064. Tel: 202-319-6450 Fax: 202-319-6449 Rev. Juan J. Sosa, Pres.,Sr. Paulina Hurtado, O.P., Vice Pres.,Mrs. Mary Frances Reza, Sec.

The Instituto is a national organization committed to assist the bishops of the country in promoting the liturgical reforms mandated by the Second Vatican Council, while it studies, reflects and celebrates more authentically the Catholic faith from the various religious traditions of Hispanics who reside in the United States. Instituto members assist the Church at the national, diocesan and parish levels by providing lectures, translations, and other Spanish and bilingual resources that may meet the liturgical needs of Hispanics whenever they surface. Membership to the organization is open to all persons and institutions interested in liturgy. Board members meet twice a year, members meet annually. National Conference every 2 years and/or symposium on liturgical topics.

International Catholic Migration Commission (ICMC) & ICMC, Inc.
c/o USCCB 3211 Fourth St., N.E. Washington, DC 20017-1194. John Klink, Pres.,Johan Ketelers, Sec. Gen.,Jane Bloom, U.S. Liaison Officer

Provides technical assistance and coordination in area of service to migrants and refugees. Non-profit New York Corporation.

Jesuit Conference, Inc.
1016 16th St., N.W., Ste. 400 Washington, DC 20036. Tel: 202-462-0400 Fax: 202-328-9212 Rev. Thomas H. Smolich, S.J., Pres.,Rev. Thomas P. Gaunt, S.J., Exec. Sec.

Ladies of Charity of the United States of America (LCUSA)
National Center, P.O. Box 31697 Saint Louis, MO 63131-0697. Tel: 314-344-1184 ext 102 Fax: 314-344-2989 Web: www.famvin.org/LCUSA MaryAnn Morovitz, Pres. 2007-2008,Bishop Howard James Hubbard, D.D., Episcopal Chm Rev. Richard Gielow, C.M., Spiritual Advisor

Ladies of Charity in the United States of America (LCUSA) is a national organization with local associations of Ladies of Charity as its members. The local Associations are dedicated to the service of the poor in their communities in the spirit of St. Vincent de Paul, St. Louise de Marillac and St. Elizabeth Ann Seton. Nationally about 10,000 members contribute volunteers hours and financial support to services that may include the operation of a thrift shop, food pantry, meal and transportation services. LCUSA participates in social co-responsibility as a member of the International Association of Charities. They are advocates for the disadvantaged and the poor and help to empower the poor to help themselves. National Assembly annually.

Publications; quarterly, Servicette.

Leadership Conference of Women Religious in the United States of America
Office, 8808 Cameron St. Silver Spring, MD 20910. Tel: 301-588-4955 Fax: 301-587-4575 Sr. J. Lora Dambroski, O.S.F., M.S., M.A., Past Pres.,Sr. Marlene Weisenbeck, F.S.P.A., J.C.L., Ph.D., Pres.,Sr. Mary Hughes, O.P., Ed.D., Pres. Elect,Sr. Elizabeth Ney, C.S.J., M.S.W., Treas.,Sr. Ellen Dauwer, S.C., Ph.D, Sec.,Sr. Jane Burke, S.S.N.D., M.S.W., M.Ed, Exec. Dir.

A conference of leaders of U.S. women religious congregations, founded in 1956, canonically approved in 1959 with a name change in 1972 and canonical approval of revised by-laws in 1972 and 1989, to promote a developing understanding and living of religious life, to assist members to carry out more collaboratively their service of leadership, to provide a vehicle for dialogue with the Bishops' Conference and other ecclesiastical authority, and to collaborate with other groups concerned with the needs of society in continuing the mission of Christ in the world today.

Lithuanian Roman Catholic Federation of America
4545 W. 63rd St. Chicago, IL 60629. Tel: 312-585-9500 Bishop Paul Baltakis, O.F.M., Episcopal Advisor,Saulius V. Kuprys, Pres.

A not-for-profit corporation founded in 1906 in Wilkes-Barre, PA, to promote and coordinate religious, educational and charitable activities among Lithuanian American Catholics, their organizations, institutions, religious communities, and parishes (for detailed information regarding religious institutions please refer to the Apostolate for Lithuanians).

Mariological Society of America (1949)
Secretariat: Marian Library, University of Dayton Dayton, OH 45469-1390. Tel: 937-229-4294 Fax: 937-229-4258 Rev. Thomas A. Thompson, S.M., Exec. Sec.

The objects and purposes of this organization are to promote interest and research in the theology of the Virgin Mary. Professional and associate membership. Proceedings of annual meeting published in Marian Studies. Annual convention in late May or early June.

National Apostolate for Inclusion Ministry NAFIM (1968)
Mailing Address, P.O. Box 218 Riverdale, MD 20738-0218. Tel: 800-736-1280 Tel: 301-699-9500 Fax: 240-220-8374 Email: qnafim@aol.com Web: www.nafim.org Bishop Mitchell T. Rozanski, D.D., V.G., Episcopal Moderator, Helaine Arnold, Pres., Barbara J. Lampe, Exec. Dir., Dennis McNulty, E-Journal

Established in 1967 to promote the full participation of persons with intellectual disabilities in the life of the Catholic Church. Formerly known as National Apostolate with Persons with Mental Retardation (NAPMR) 1992-1997, National Apostolate with Mentally Retarded Persons (NAMRP) 1974-1992 and National Apostolate for the Mentally Retarded (NAMR) 1967-1974.

Publications: internet journal; newsletter; pamphlets; training materials.

National Association for Treasurers of Religious Institutes, Inc. (NATRI) (1981)

8824 Cameron St. Silver Spring, MD 20910. Tel: 301-587-7776 Fax: 301-589-2897 Web: www.trcri.org

Serving finance officers and staffs of religious institutes by assisting them in fulfilling their stewardship responsibilities. An annual national conference, seminar for new personnel in financial offices, and a consulting service are key program components. All Roman Catholic religious institutes are eligible for membership in NATRI and currently approximately 585 belong.

Publication: annual membership and service directories and other miscellaneous publications 5 times a year, Accounting and Financial Management.

National Association of African American Catholic Deacons, Inc.

Office of the President, 1418 Glen View Rd. Yellow Springs, OH 45387. Tel: 937-974-1588 Tel: 937-767-5381 Fax: 937-767-7465 Deacon Paul E. Richardson, Pres. Yellow Springs, OH,Deacon Joseph Connor, Vice Pres., Seattle, WA,Deacon Alfred Mitchell, Sec., Atlanta, GA,Deacon Jerry Lett, Treas., Lithonia, GA,Deacon Marvin Threatt, Immediate Past-Pres., Spring Valley, CA

Members At Large:—Deacon Arthur L. Miller, Windsor, CT ,Deacon Jimmie L. Boyd, Sr., Buffalo, NY,Deacon Keith McKnight, Jersey City, NJ,Deacon Ralph Cyrus, Ft. Washington, MD,Deacon Emith Fludd, St. Croix, VI,Deacon Dexter Watson, Chicago, IL,Deacon Oliver Washington, Cincinnati, OH,Deacon Dunn Cumby, Oklahoma City, OK,Deacon A. Stephen Pickett, Lenoir, SC

Wives Representatives:—Magnolia Cumby, Oklahoma City, OK ,Barbara Connor, Seattle, WA

To establish an organization of Permanent deacons of African heritage ordained in the Roman Catholic Church. To promote unity among deacons of African descent by facilitating effective communication network on a national, regional, and diocesan level. To be a pro-active organization in promoting and contributing to the future of the African American family with emphasis on African American men. To promote justice, peace, equality; and end to racism, and the sharing of resources among all peoples in light of the social teachings of the Roman Catholic Church.

National Association of Catholic Chaplains

National Office, 5007 S. Howell Ave., Ste. 120 Milwaukee, WI 53207-6159. Tel: 414-483-4898 Fax: 414-483-6712 Email: info@nacc.org Web: www.nacc.org Bishop Randolph Roque Calvo, D.D., J.C.D.,Sr. Barbara Brumleve, S.S.N.D., Ph.D., Pres. & Chm. Bd.,Mr. David A. Lichter, Exec. Dir.

The National Association of Catholic Chaplains advocates for the profession of spiritual care and educates, certifies, and supports chaplains, clinical pastoral educators, and all members who continue the healing ministry of Jesus in the name of the Church.

Publication: 6 times-year, journal-newsletter, Vision; 26 times-year (every other Monday), email newsletter, NACC Now.

The National Association of Catholic Family Life Ministers

300 College Park Dayton, OH 45469-2512. Tel: 937-431-5443 Fax: 937-431-5443 Email: nacflm@udayton.edu David Abele, CFO,William Urbine, Pres. & Exec. Dir.,Christine Codden, Pres. Elect

The National Association of Church Personnel Administrators (NACPA)

Headquarters, 100 E. Eighth St. Cincinnati, OH 45202. Tel: 513-421-3134 Fax: 513-421-3085 Web: www.nacpa.org Terry Robinson, P.H.R., Bd. Pres.,Mary Jo Moran, Ph.D., S.P.H.R., Exec. Dir.

The National Association of Church Personnel Administrators (NACPA) is a membership association of lay, religious and clergy serving dioceses, parishes, religious congregations and other church-related institutions. The purpose of the Association is to promote justice in the workplace where the Church is the employer through ethical and just standards and to provide programs and resources that assist members in developing competencies in human resource management grounded in gospel values.

National Association of Diaconate Directors (1977)

National Office, 7625 N. High St. Columbus, OH 43215-1498. Tel: 614-985-2276 Email: naddinfo@nadd.org Web: www.nadd.org Deacon Justin Green, Vice Chm.,Deacon J.S. Anzalone, Chm.,Deacon Thomas R. Dubois, Exec. Dir.

Directors, vicars of deacons, and others responsible for the formation of candidates and the ongoing growth and development of deacons in the U.S. Promotes communication and facilitates the exchange of information and resources among members. Seeks to develop professional expertise among members through research, dialogue, formation and self-evaluation procedures. Proposes ways and means for effective implementation of solutions to national and regional issues relating to the diaconate. Maintains library on related issues.

National Association of Diocesan Directors of Campus Ministry

305 Michigan Ave. Detroit, MI 48226. Tel: 313-237-5962 Mrs. Krista Bajoka, Contact Person

National Association of Pastoral Musicians

National Office, 962 Wayne Ave., Ste. 210 Silver Spring, MD 20910-4461. Tel: 240-247-3000 Fax: 240-247-3001 Email: npmsing@npm.org Web: www.npm.org J. Michael McMahon, Pres. & CEO,Ms. Joanne Werner, Chm. Bd. of Dirs.,Cardinal Daniel Cardinal DiNardo, Episcopal Moderator

The National Association of Pastoral Musicians fosters the art of musical liturgy. The members of NPM serve the Catholic Church in the United States as musicians, clergy, liturgists, and other leaders of prayer. Regular parish membership includes both parish musicians and parish clergy. Individual membership is also available.

NPM programs include an annual national convention for musicians, clergy, and other leaders, as well as institutes for cantors, choir directors, organists, guitarists, and ensemble musicians in addition to programs on pastoral liturgy, chant, music with children, and handbells. NPM provides a Job Hotline to assist musicians seeking employment and parishes searching for musicians. The association also sponsors certification programs for organists, cantors, and full-time directors of music ministries.

The Association is directed by a 5-member Board of Directors, advised by a 40-member NPM Council and served by a 9-person staff. There is a division for professional directors of music ministries as well as special interest sections for cantors, choir directors, organists, clergy, ensemble musicians, pianists, composers, diocesan directors of music, music educators, military musicians, campus ministers, youth, pastoral liturgy, chant, and musicians serving African American parishes, Hispanic communities, Asian/Pacific Rim communities, and religious congregations.

Publications include Pastoral Music (quarterly journal); Pastoral Music Notebook (quarterly newsletter), The Liturgical Singer (quarterly), as well as newsletters for clergy, organists, full-time directors, and music educators. Online publications include Pastoral Music E-Notes and Sunday Word for Pastoral Musicians.

National Black Catholic Clergy Caucus

Resurrection Catholic Missions, Office, 2815 Forbes Dr. Montgomery, AL 36110.

Board of Directors:—Rev. Anthony Bozeman, S.S.J., Pres. ,Rev. Kenneth Taylor, V.F., Vice Pres., New Orleans, LA,Rev. Roy Lee, Sec., Atlanta, GA,Deacon Jerry Lett, Treas., Lithonia, GA,Deacon Dunn Cumby, Immediate Past Pres., Oklahoma, OK,Bro. Herman D. Johnson, O.P., Men Religious Representative, New Orleans, LA,Mr. Anthony Onyango, Seminarian Representative,Rev. Jeffrey Ott, New Orleans, LA,Deacon Paul E. Richardson, Pres. NAAACD, Yellow Springs, OH

Members At Large:—Rev. Christopher L. Coleman, Ph.D., Brooklyn, NY ,Rev. Victor H. Cohea, New Orleans, LA

The National Black Catholic Clergy Caucus serves as a fraternity for Black Catholic Clergy and Religious to support the spiritual, theological, educational and ministerial growth of its members. It is a vehicle to bring the contributions of the Black Community to fruition within the Catholic Church.

National Catholic Committee on Scouting Executive Committee (1934)

1325 W. Walnut Hill Ln. P.O. Box 152079 Irving, TX 75015-2079. Fax: 972-580-2535 Bishop Gerald A. Gettelfinger, Bishop of Evansville, IN, Episcopal Liaison,William Davies, Chm. (Minneapolis, MN),Gerard Scanlon, Vice Chm. (New York, NY),Edward Martin, Vice Chm. (Medina, OH),Susan Barriball, Vice Chm. (Chesterton, IN),Dave Moskal, Vice Chm. (New Britain, CT),Bray B. Barnes, Past Chm. (Toms River, NJ),Rev. Stephen B. Salvador, Assoc. Natl. Chap. (Fall River, MA),John Halloran, Vice Chm.,Rev. Roger LaChance, Past Natl. Chap. (Coeur d'Alene, ID),Rev. Raymond L. Fecteau, Natl. Chap. (Darnestown, MD),Mr. Austin Cannon, Vice Chm. (Bellmore, NY)

A voluntary organization of clergy and laymen, members include a chaplain and lay chairman from all of the dioceses in the United States Conferences. It serves as an advisory committee to the Boy Scouts of America. It has the responsibility of promoting and guiding cooperative contracts between the proper authorities of the Catholic Church in the United States and the Boy Scouts of America.

National Catholic Conference for Total Stewardship (NCCTS)

National Office, 300 Liguori Dr. Liguori, MO 63057-9998. Tel: 636-464-3666 Fax: 636-464-4717 Email: fanov@aol.com Archbishop John Francis Donoghue, D.D., Episcopal Moderator,G. William Sefton, Chm.,Rev. Francis A. Novak, C.Ss.R., Pres.,Adelaide Herrell, Sec.

The mission of the National Catholic Conference for Total Stewardship (NCCTS) is to initiate in dioceses and parishes the concept of total stewardship through a pastoral process called Celebrating Life as a Catholic Christian (CLCC). The concept joins the three basic elements of the bible: Evangelization, Discipleship and Service, and through the CLCC process presents them as a single unit not as separate apostolates. The process first updates active church-going Catholics in sound catechetics and eucharistic spirituality. At the same time the process prepares and motivates them to reach out to lapsed, non-regular church-going Catholics making person-to-person contact with them and with RCIA graduates. They join a Small Ecclesial Faith Community (SEFC) connected to the parish. Active parishoners in SEFC's constitute a welcoming environment for those in need of returning to the faith and those in need of retaining it. In them they experience Catholic fellowship, inter-personal sharing, communal and personal prayer and study official church teachings. Through the CLCC process returnees and recent converts are further formed in doctrine and spirituality for full membership in the Church, for encountering Christ in the sacraments, for enjoying "communion" with all Catholics and for Celebrating Life as Catholic Christians both in vocation and mission.

National Catholic Council on Alcoholism and Related Drug Problems, Inc.

Headquarters, 1601 Joslyn Rd. Lake Orion, MI 48360. Tel: 800-626-6910 ext 1200 Fax: 248-391-0210 Email: ncca@guesthouse.org Web: www.ncatoday.org Richard Thibodeau, Exec. Dir.,Rev. Msgr. Thomas M. Haggerty, Pres.,Cardinal Anthony J. Bevilacqua, Episcopal Moderator

NCCA is an agency of the Church, affiliated with the U.S. Conference of Catholic Bishops, and under the auspices of Guest House, Inc., is dedicated to the promotion of adequate treatment for all clergy, men and women religious, and laity who are suffering from alcoholism and other drug dependencies. NCCA also provides educational programs including workshops for dioceses, an Annual Conference, also educational and "Spirituality Support" resources, including free booklet: "Prayers For Addicted Persons and Their Loved Ones", also "Serenity Prayer Bookmarks", "Spirituality and Recovery From Addictions", also: "When They Won't (or Can't) Quit Alcohol or Drugs", also the Blue Book of Conference Proceedings. The NCCA seeks to help those struggling to overcome an addiction and those engaged in pastoral ministry, including outreach to the nation's jail and prison ministries."

National Catholic Development Conference, Inc. (1968)

86 Front St. Hempstead, NY 11550. Tel: 516-481-6000 Web: www.ncdc.org Sr. Georgette Lehmuth, O.S.F., Pres. & CEO,Sr. Cathy Katoski, O.S.F., Chm.,Curtis Yarlott, Vice Chm.,Sharon Untereinner, Sec.,William Hurley, CFRE, Treas.

NCDC leads Catholic organizations toward excellence in their development ministries by providing opportunities for growth in leadership and excellence through conferences and networking. As the United States' largest association of religious philanthropies, NCDC affirms the mission of each of its members by working for and with them as fundraisers. The hallmark of NCDC is the promotion of the integrity of its member organizations to donors, the media and the general public. To this end, all members are required to fully adhere to the NCDC Code of Stewardship and Ethics and support the Donor Bill of Rights. Central to NCDC's existence are the many serivces provided to its membership: advocacy, regional seminars, the annual Conference and Exposition, informative publications, educational resources and other specialized services geared to meet member needs.

Publications: Dimensions (10 times a year); E-Newsletters: Newswire, Essentials, Jobs eBulletin; Stewardship for Mission, Toward a Theology of Fundraising; A Call to Accountability: Where Donors and Mission Meet.

National Catholic Educational Association (1904)

National Headquarters, 1005 N. Glebe Ave., Ste. 225 Arlington, VA 22201. Tel: 800-711-6232 Fax: 703-243-0025 Archbishop Donald W. Wuerl, Board Chair,Karen M. Ristau, Ed.D., Pres.

The National Catholic Educational Association (NCEA) has been providing leadership and service to American Catholic educators since 1904. NCEA's institutional and individual memberships represent Catholic education at all levels and in a variety of settings: preschools, elementary and secondary schools, parish catechetical/religious education programs, diocesan offices, colleges, universities and seminaries. The Association advances the educational and catechetical mission of the Church; provides leadership and service to its members; articulates the contribution of Catholic education to the Church and society; proclaims the uniqueness of Catholic schools; advocates recognition of and support for Catholic education in parish, school, college and university communities; enhances and supports leadership among the members; and fosters local, national and international collaboration.

National Catholic Office for the Deaf (1971)

NCOD Office, 7202 Buchanan St. Landover Hills, MD 20784-2236. Tel: 301-577-1684 Fax: 301-577-1684 Email: info@ncod.org Web: www.ncod.org Teletype: 301-577-4184 Consuelo Wild, Exec. Dir.

The NCOD, established by the Catholic pastoral workers of the deaf in 1971 at Trinity College, Washington, DC is devoted to coordinating the Church's pastoral ministry to deaf and hard-of-hearing persons at the national level; developing special liturgies, catechetical texts and materials; organizing workshops, leadership programs, and national and regional pastoral workers meetings; coordinating a training program for ministers with the deaf; and serving as an information and referral center for all those involved in this special ministry as well as members of the deaf community and their families. Policy is established by a board of directors elected by the members.

Publication: pastoral journal, Vision.

National Catholic Partnership on Disability

415 Michigan Ave., N.E., Ste. 95 Washington, DC 20017-4501. Tel: 202-529-2933 Fax: 202-529-4678 Web: www.ncpd.org Teletype: 202-529-2934 Ms. Janice L. Benton, Exec. Dir.,Stephen Mikochik, Chm.

Established to foster and facilitate the challenges of "Pastoral Statement of U.S. Catholic Bishops on People with Disabilities." Provides resources and enhances visibility of diocesan offices addressing access and inclusion; works with USCCB staff and other national Catholic organizations in advocating for disability involvement and concerns; collaborates with other ministries of the church to enhance meaningful participation; affirms the culture of life through promoting the giftedness of all people with assorted disabilities at all stages of the life cycle. Mission is promoted through appropriate media, consultation, lectures, workshops, and regional gatherings.

National Catholic Rural Life Conference

National Headquarters, 4625 Beaver Ave. Des Moines, IA 50310-2145. Tel: 515-270-2634 Fax: 515-270-9447 Email: ncrlc@aol.com Web: www.ncrlc.com Bishop Frank J. Dewane, Pres. Bd-.,James F. Ennis, Exec. Dir.

The National Catholic Rural Life Conference is a membership organization grounded in a spiritual tradition which brings together the Church, care for creation and care for community. The NCRLC fosters programs of direct service and systemic change. As an educator in the faith, the NCRLC seeks to relate religion to the rural world; develops support services for rural pastoral ministers; serves as a prophetic voice and as a catalyst and convener for social justice.

International Catholic Stewardship Council, Inc. (ICSC)

National Office, 1275 K St., N.W., Ste. 880 Washington, DC 20005. Tel: 800-352-3452 Tel: 202-289-1093 Fax: 202-682-9018 Email: icsc@catholicstewardship.org Web: www.catholicstewardship.org Bishop Paul G. Bootkoski, D.D., Bishop of Metuchen, NJ, Episcopal Moderator,Michael Murphy, Exec. Dir.

Through its annual conference, Stewardship and Development Institutes, publications and audio materials, ICSC allows people committed to Christian stewardship to gather, share ideas, and learn from each other. At one with the universal church, ICSC fosters solidarity of stewardship as a way of life in parishes and dioceses all over the world. Membership in ICSC is extended to several categories of Christian stewards: (Arch)dioceses, parishes, Catholic associations and professional firms from the United States and around the world. Members receive a number of essential benefits to enable them to live stewardship and bring this way of life to others in their communities and organizations.

ICSC encourages the growing professionalism of diocesan stewardship and development procedures and programs, as well as the development of parish-centered stewardship renewal aimed at increasing the time, talent and treasure contributed by parishioners. These principles of stewardship outlined in the 1992 USCCB Pastoral Letter: Stewardship: A Disciple's Response.

For a complete list of services and publications contact the ICSC office or visit the ICSC Website at www.catholicstewardship.org. Membership information is available upon request.

National Catholic Student Coalition (1988)

45 Lovett Ave. Newark, DE 19711. Tel: 302-463-5538 Fax: 302-368-2548 Email: ncsc@catholicstudent.org Web: www.catholicstudent.org Joe Ewing, Natl. Chm.,Jessi Steenbergen, External Affairs Liaison

The National Catholic Student Coalition (NCSC) is a national coalition of Catholic student communities in institutes of higher education. The coalition provides a platform for Catholic students to reflect, speak, and act on issues within the university, the Church and society. The NCSC promotes the development of campus ministry and Catholic lay and religious leaders for the Church and society. The NCSC is a member of the International Movement of Catholic Students. Membership is open to groups or individuals associated with Catholic student groups in higher education. The NCSC holds an annual leadership conference.

Publication: The Catholic Collegian.

The National Center for Urban Ethnic Affairs (1971)

National Office, P.O. Box 20, Cardinal Station Washington, DC 20064. Tel: 202-232-3600 Tel: 202-319-5128 Tel: 202-319-6188 Dr. John A. Kromkowski, Pres.,Rev. Msgr. Salvatore E. Polizzi, Chm.,Rev. George F. McLean, O.M.I., Sec. Treas.

"The great task incumbent on all men of good will is to restore the relations of the human family in truth, in justice, in love, and in freedom." (Pope John XXIII, Peace on Earth.) The independent program of this nonprofit organization has evolved from the efforts initiated by the former Task Force on Urban Problems of the United States Catholic Conference. Its aims and purposes are to continue the expression of the Catholic Church's concern for the problems facing our urban society. NCUEA promotes the celebration of cultural pluralism in America and bridges the gaps between groups of various ethnic and cultural traditions. The Center disseminates information, conducts research, develops and supports programs concerned with ethnic Americans and urban society. The Center in association with various community and church groups develops workshops, conferences, and programs related to the quality of human life, national priorities and the development of an urban mission strategy. The Center is also associated with public and private agencies in developing urban economic, social, and intercultural programs, etc.

The National Conference for Catechetical Leadership (NCCL)

125 Michigan Ave., N.E. Washington, DC 20017. Tel: 202-884-9753 Fax: 202-884-9756 Web: www.nccl.org Dr. Anne D. Roat, Pres.,Mr. Leland Nagel, Exec. Dir.

A voluntary organization composed of diocesan and parish catechetical personnel, academics specializing in religious education, and various associate and affiliated members, including publishers of catechetical materials. The Conference operates on three levels: national, regional and provincial. The purpose of the Conference is to promote and develop professional competence within catechetical leadership and to assist its members in their roles as leaders in the Church's catechetical ministry through networking, resource development, research, training, consultation and advocacy. The Conference is committed to collaboration with other national groups concerned with catechesis/religious education as a means of expanding and coordinating a service to catechetical ministry.

National Conference of Catholic Airport Chaplains (NCCAC)

Chicago O'Hare International Airport, P.O. Box 66353 Chicago, IL 60666-0353. Tel: 773-686-2636 Fax: 773-686-0130 Email: office@nccac.us Web: www.nccac.us Rev. Michael G. Zaniolo, S.T.L., C.A.C., Pres. (Chicago O'Hare International Airport),Rev. John P. Fitzgerald, C.A.C., Vice Pres. (Pittsburgh International Airport-),Deacon Charles Doerpers, C.A.C., Sec. (Cleveland Hopkins International Airport),Deacon Dennis E. Jordan, C.A.C., Treas. (Miami International Airport),Cardinal Francis E. George, O.M.I., Archbishop of Chicago, Episcopal Liaison

This Conference provides support and communication for all Catholics performing pastoral ministry to airport & airline workers, and travelers; in affiliation with the Bishop's Committee on Migration of the National Conference of Catholic Bishops.

National Council of Catholic Women

200 N. Glebe Rd., Ste. 703 Arlington, VA 22203. Tel: 703-224-0990 Fax: 703-224-0991 Email: nccw01@nccw.org Web: www.nccw.org Bobbie Hunt, Pres.,Sheila McCarron, Exec. Dir.

The NCCW consists of Catholic women's organizations in the United States, numbering 5,000+ local, diocesan and national organizations. It programs through its six commissions, Church, Family Concerns, Community Concerns, International Concerns, Legislation and Organization. The program of the Council is furthered through leadership training institutes and national conventions.

Publication: bimonthly, Catholic Woman.

National Federation for Catholic Youth Ministry, Inc. (NFCYM) (1981)

415 Michigan Ave., N.E., Ste. 40 Washington, DC 20017-4502. Tel: 202-636-3825 Bishop Jaime Soto, D.D., M.S.W., Episcopal Liaison,Robert J. McCarty, D.Min., Exec. Dir.,Carole Goodwin, D.Min., Chm.

A membership association of diocesan youth offices and collaborating organizations, founded after a reorganization of the USCC Department of Education and the National CYO Federation. The NFCYM fosters the development of youth ministry in the "United States to, with, by, and for youth." The NFYCM mission is "to serve those who serve the young church". Members of the Federation work through diocesan, regional and national structures to provide national leadership, resources and vision for adults and youth in youth ministry. Key services include the biennial National Conference on Catholic Youth Ministry (for adults working with youth); the biennial National Catholic Youth Conference (for teenagers and their adult chaperones); the development of resources for parish workers; religious recognitions for Catholic Girl Scouts/Camp Fire; position papers on current topics and issues in youth ministry; regional and diocesan consultations and programs for diocesan youth ministry leaders.

National Organization for Continuing Education of Roman Catholic Clergy, Inc. (NOCERCC)
333 N. Michigan Ave., Ste. 1205 Chicago, IL 60601. Tel: 312-781-9450 Fax: 312-442-9709 Email: nocercc@nocercc.org Web: www.nocercc.org Rev. Norbert J. Maduzia, Jr., D.Min., Pres.,Rev. James E. Deiters, Vice Pres.,Rev. Richard Bokinskie, Sec. & Treas.,Dr. Mary Ann Boyarski, Ed.D., Member at Large,Rev. Patrick M. Carrion, Member at Large,Mr. James H. Alphen, Exec. Dir.

The National Organization for Continuing Education of Roman Catholic Clergy (NOCERCC) is a membership association of dioceses and religious communities and other interested organizations and individuals committed to the Church's mission to promote and support ongoing formation for priests and presbyterates. Founded in 1973, NOCERCC's current membership includes approximately 150 Roman Catholic dioceses and religious communities in the United States as well as approximately 40 other organizations and individuals around the world that are part of the ongoing clergy formation community. Professional and formational services offered to members include: an annual national convention; an annual orientation workshop; regional meetings; an expanding menu of formation opportunities that dioceses and religious communities can host for clergy and other pastoral ministers; a membership newsletter; and other practical resources in diverse media. By engaging in dialogue about contemporary pastoral needs and realities, by sponsoring research on issues of presbyteral formation, and by offering educational opportunities, NOCERCC collaborates with others to foster a culture of formation within the Church for all the Church's ministers.

Publications: newsletter, Handbook for Directors of Ongoing Formation of Priests, Sabbatical Opportunities, Priestly Relationships: Freedom through Boundaries.

National Pastoral Center for the Chinese Apostolate, Inc.
Sacred Heart of Jesus, 14277 Preston Rd., Apt. 1027 Dallas, TX 75240. Tel: 972-716-0077 Rev. Paul P. Pang, O.F.M., Dir.

National Pastoral Life Center
Headquarters, 18 Bleecker St. New York, NY 10012-2404. Tel: 212-431-7825 Fax: 212-274-9786 Email: nplc@nplc.org Web: www.nplc.org Rev. John E. Hurley, C.S.P., Exec. Dir.,Hope Villella, Dir. Social Action & Pastoral Planning,Ms. Elizabeth O'Connor, Editor Church Magazine,Mr. Peter Denio, Dir. Catholic Common Ground Initiative and Pastoral Svcs.,Mr. Carl Barnes, Devel. Dir.

The Center is an information, training, and consulting resource for diocesan and parish leaders. The Center conducts and staffs educational and training programs for pastors and others in ministry. It also sponsors pastoral ministry conventions, social justice conferences, the Common Ground Initiative colloquia, conducts pastoral research, and serves as a resource and referral center for parish and diocesan staffs. The Center is home to the roundtable association for Diocesan social action directors and the conference for the pastoral planning and council development The Center publishes Church magazine, books and numerous pastoral pamphlets.

Publications: Church Magazine; Center Papers, books, pastoral pamphlets and other publications.

North American Pastoral Center for Czech Catholics
344 Koch Ave. Placentia, CA 92870-1928. Tel: 714-524-0092 Fax: 714-637-6789 Bishop Peter Esterka, Pres.

The Papal Foundation
Office, 150 Monument Rd., Ste. 609 Bala Cynwyd, PA 19004. Tel: 610-535-6340 Tel: 610-535-6341 Fax: 610-535-6343 Email: jcoffey@thepapalfoundation.com Mr. James V. Coffey, M.A., Vice Pres. Devel.
Trustee Members—Cardinal Anthony J. Bevilacqua, Chm. ,Cardinal Daniel N. DiNardo,Cardinal Edward M. Egan,Cardinal Francis E. George, O.M.I.,Cardinal William Keeler, Vice Chm.,Cardinal Roger M. Mahony,Cardinal Adam Maida,Cardinal Theodore E. McCarrick, Pres.,Cardinal Sean Cardinal O'Malley, O.F.M.Cap.,Cardinal Justin F. Rigali
Trustees—Bishop Michael F. Burbidge ,Archbishop Donald W. Wuerl,Archbishop Timothy M. Dolan-,Archbishop Harry J. Flynn, D.D.,Archbishop John J. Myers, D.D., J.C.D.,Bishop Michael J. Bransfield,Bishop Joseph A. Pepe, D.D., J.C.D-.,Timothy R. Busch,Charles L. Drury, Sr.,Louis B. Eckelkamp, Jr.,Frank J. Hanna, III,E.F. Hansen, Jr., Treas.,Robert C. Hawk,Ken Kenworthy,Judy Rauenhorst Mahoney,Timothy McGuire,Jeremiah O'Connor, Jr.,Gerald A. Rauenhorst, Trustee Emeritus,Antonio Rea,Carol Saeman,John V. Saeman, Jr., Trustee Emeritus,Sir Daniel J. Donohue, Trustee Emeritus

The Parish Evaluation Project
3195 S. Superior St. Milwaukee, WI 53207. Tel: 414-483-7370 Fax: 414-483-7380 Email: pep@pitnet.net Web: www.pepparish.org Rev. Thomas P. Sweetser, S.J., Co-Dir.,Sr. Peg Bishop, O.S.F., Co-Dir.

The Parish Evaluation Project is a nonprofit organization under the laws of Wisconsin, whose purpose is to provide religious and educational services to Catholic parishes in the United States in the areas of surveying, needs assessment, leadership skills, goal setting, evaluation techniques, staff development, pastoral council formation and other resources helpful in parish planning and renewal.

Pax Christi U.S.A., National Catholic Peace Movement
532 W. 8th St. Erie, PA 16502-1343. Tel: 814-453-4955 Fax: 814-452-4784 Etienne de'Jonghe, Intl. Sec.,Bishop Gabino Zavala, Pres.,Pearlette Springer, Chm.,Sr. Kathleen Pritty, R.S.M., Vice Chm.,Sr. Josie Chrosniak, H.M., Treas.

Pax Christi USA is the national Catholic peace movement, reaching more than half a million Catholics in the United States each year. Our membership includes more than 130 U.S. bishops, 800 parishes, 650 religious communities and 275 local groups. Pax Christi USA is a section of Pax Christi International, the international Catholic peace movement with consultative status at the United Nations.

Publications: quarterly newspaper and peace education materials.

Religious Brothers Conference
National Office, 5401 S. Cornell Ave. Chicago, IL 60615. Tel: 773-595-4023 Fax: 773-595-4087 Email: rbc@ctu.edu Web: brothersonline.org Bro. Thomas Osorio, O.H., Pres.,Bro. Herman D. Johnson, O.P., Vice Pres.,Bro. Michael Moran, C.P., Treas.,Bro. John Byrd, F.M.S., Sec.,Bro. Stephen Synan, F.M.S., Exec. Dir.

Publication: Brothers' Voice; Reflections.

Religious Formation Conference
National Office, 8820 Cameron St. Silver Spring, MD 20910-4152. Tel: 301-588-4938 Fax: 301-585-7649 Sr. Violet Grennan, M.F.I.C., Exec. Dir.,Sr. Jeanine Tisot, R.S.M., Chm.

A national organization which assists Women and Men Religious who are engaged in the ministry of initial and on-going formation in their congregations.

The Resource Center for Religious Institutes
8824 Cameron St. Silver Spring, MD 20910. Tel: 301-589-8143 Fax: 301-589-2897 Email: trcri@trcri.org Web: www.trcri.org Rev. Daniel Ward, O.S.B., Exec. Dir.

The Slovak Catholic Federation (1911)
301 S. State St. Clarks Summit, PA 18411-1544. Tel: 570-587-5191 Fax: 570-585-7382 Email: frfrosty@epix.net Web: www.slovakcatholicfederation.org Rev. Philip A. Altavilla, M.Th., V.E., Pres.,Bishop Joseph Victor Adamec, D.D., S.T.L., Episcopal Advisor,Rev. Msgr. Thomas A. Derzack, M.Div., Spiritual Dir.,Dolores M. Evanko, Sec. & Treas.

Founded by Father Joseph Murgas at Wilkes-Barre, Pennsylvania as a nonprofit corporation to promote and coordinate religious and social activities among Slovak Catholic fraternal benefit societies, religious communities, Slovak parishes and individuals in order to address the pastoral needs of Slovak Catholics at home and abroad.

United States Catholic Mission Association
Hecker Center, 3025 Fourth St., N.E., Ste. 100 Washington, DC 20017. Tel: 202-832-3112 Fax: 202-832-3688 Email: uscma@uscatholicmission.org Web: www.uscatholicmission.org Teresita Gonzalez de la Maza, Pres.,Rev. Michael Montoya, M.J., Exec Dir.

The USCMA was juridically established September 1, 1981. Its members include U.S. missioners, mission organizations, diocesan mission offices, and others concerned about the mission of the Church and global solidarity. The Association seeks to help missioners to stay up-to-date on mission and world trends, to promote greater global awareness, sensibility, and solidarity in the U.S., and periodically to be a voice for U.S. missioners speaking out in defense of the poor and oppressed throughout the world. USCMA activities include a national conference that highlights specific mission themes and issues, liaison and cooperation with missionary bodies of other Christian churches. The USCMA is responsible for gathering statistical data on the U.S. missionary personnel, which is published biannually.

Publications: quarterly newsletter, Mission Update; reports, U.S. Catholic Missionary Statistics, and education programs on mission and global awareness.

NATIONAL ORGANIZATIONS WITH INDIVIDUAL I.R.S. RULINGS

Beginning Experience
International Ministry Center, 1657 Commerce Dr. South Bend, IN 46628. Tel: 574-283-0279 Tel: 866-610-8877 Fax: 574-283-0287 Email: imc@beginningexperience.org Web: www.beginningexperience.org Bishop Patrick J. Zurek, D.D., Episcopal Moderator,Kathleen Murphy, Exec. Dir.,Steven Oldham, Pres.,Beverly Howell, Vice Pres.,Susan Ackerman, Sec.,Carolyn Rhode, Treas.

Beginning Experience is a copyrighted weekend program to help divorced, separated and widowed persons, as well as their families, work through the trauma of the loss of their spouse and make a new beginning in life. The program was designed by and for Catholics and has its roots in sound Catholic tradition and the sacramental life of the Church. True to the ecumenical spirit in the Church since Vatican II, it has been open to persons of all faiths from the beginning. The Beginning Experience weekend was originated in 1974 by Sr. Josephine Stewart in Fort Worth, TX. It has spread throughout the United States as well as other countries. Trained teams make the Beginning Experience weekend available on a regular basis. It also serves as an informational and materials resource for the establishment of support groups to minister to the needs of the divorced, separated and widowed and their families at various points in their growth process.

Canon Law Society of America
The Hecker Center, 3025 4th St., N.E., Ste. 111 Washington, DC 20017-1102. Tel: 202-832-2350 Fax: 202-832-2331 Email: coordinator@clsa.org Sr. Sharon A. Euart, R.S.M., J.C.D., Exec. Coord.,Rev. Lawrence Jurcak, J.C.L., Pres.,Rev. Michael Joyce, J.C.D., Vice Pres.,Ms. Siobhan M. Verbeek, J.C.L., Sec.,Rev. Thomas Anslow, C.M., J.C.L., Treas.

A membership association of Bishops, Clergy, Religious and Laity for the purpose of promoting research and professional collaboration in the area of Canon Law.

Catholic Engaged Encounter, Inc.
4239 Shirley Rd. Richmond, VA 23225. Tel: 800-339-9790 Jim Dyk,Sandy Dyk,Rev. Jay Biber

Catholic Library Association
100 North St., Ste. 224 Pittsfield, MA 01201-5178. Tel: 413-443-2252 Fax: 413-442-2252 Email: cla@cathla.org Web: www.cathla.org Sr. Jean R. Bostley, S.S.J., Exec. Dir.

The Catholic Mutual Relief Society of America
10843 Old Mill Rd. Omaha, NE 68154-2600. Tel: 402-551-8765 Mr. Joseph Beveridge, Pres. & CEO,Mr. Michael Intrieri, Exec. Vice Pres. & Chief Operating Officer

The Catholic Relief Insurance Company of America
76 St. Paul St., Ste. 500 Burlington, VT 05401. Tel: 402-551-8765 Mr. Joseph Beveridge, Pres.,Mr. Michael Intrieri, Treas.

Conference for Pastoral Planning and Council Development
P.O. Box 45625 Philadelphia, PA 19149. Tel: 215-333-0993 Email: cppcd@cppcd.org Web: www.cppcd.org Mr. Robert Choiniere, Chair,Fran Stratton, Acting Admin. Dir.

National Association for Lay Ministry (NALM)
National Office, 6896 Laurel St., N.W. Washington,

DC 20012. Tel: 202-291-4100 Fax: 202-291-8550 Email: nalm@nalm.org Web: www.nalm.org Christopher Anderson, Exec. Dir.

The National Association for Lay Ministry is a professional organization which supports, educates and advocates for lay ministers and promotes the development of lay ministry in the Catholic Church. Rejoicing in our baptismal call to be disciples of Jesus Christ and claiming our vocation to minister in the Roman Catholic Church, we value: 1) the universal call to holiness; 2) sharing in the mission and ministry of Jesus; 3) faith that works for justice; 4) the dignity of each person and the richness that results from diversity; 5) the ongoing conversion of persons and structures; 6) collaboration in ministry and participative Church leadership, and; 7) the life experiences lay ministers bring to ministry from their unique relationships and responsibilities as family members, workers, and citizens.

Publications: quarterly, Lay Ministry; National Certification Standards for Lay Ecclesial Ministers; Moving Ministry Forward; Study Guide: CoWorkers in the Vineyard of the Lord; National Certification Standards for Pastoral Ministers; A Call to Collaborative Ministry, Video and Workbook.

National Catholic Conference for Interracial Justice (NCCIJ) (1959)

Office, 1200 Varnum St., N.E. Washington, DC 20017-2796. Tel: 202-529-6480 Fax: 202-526-1262 Archbishop Charles J. Chaput, O.F.M-.Cap., D.D., Co. Chm.,Hon. Lindy Boggs, Co. Chm.,Deacon Joseph M. Conrad, Exec. Dir.

Established to implement the teaching of the Catholic Church on cultural and racial justice and to promote the church's vision of multicultural, multiracial understanding, mutual respect and collaboration.

The National Catholic Risk Retention Group, Inc.

National Office, 801 Warrenville Rd., Ste. 175 Lisle, IL 60532-4334. Tel: 630-725-0986 Tel: 877-486-2774 Fax: 630-725-1374 Michael J. Bemi, Pres. & CEO,Rev. Jay C. Haskin, M.Ch.A., Chm. Bd.,Bro. William Walz, F.S.C., Vice Chm.,Mr. John M. Scholl, C.P.C.U., A.I.M., Vice Pres.,Mr. John J. Maxwell, CPA, Treas.

The Company is wholly owned by 65 Catholic (Arch)Dioceses and one Catholic Risk Pooling Trust. It underwrites excess liability insurance for Dioceses and other Church organizations listed in the Official Catholic Directory. Coverage is always subject to a minimum self-insured retention or underlying coverage of $250,000. Maximum limits of coverage available are $14,750,000. The company has the capability to underwrite insurance in all states, Territories and Possessions of the U.S.

National Catholic Young Adult Ministry Association

c/o Diocese of Joliet Young Adult Ministry, Chicago Office, 402 S. Independence Blvd. Romeoville, IL 60446. Tel: 815-334-4047 Fax: 773-508-2844 Email: info@ncyama.org Web: www.ncyama.org Rakhi Roy McCormick, Pres.,Paul Jarzembowski, Exec. Dir.,Lauren Gaffey, Treas.

Founded in 1982, NCYAMA is an organization supporting those who minister to and with single and married people in their late teens, twenties or thirties. We develop and promote programs and resources while providing opportunities for networking and communication. We advocate for the full integration of young adults in the life of the Catholic faith community in order to connect them with Jesus, the Church, the mission of the Church and their peers.

Publication: electronic newsletter.

National Conference of Diocesan Vocation Directors (1962)

National Office, 440 W. Neck Rd. Huntington, NY 11743. Tel: 631-645-8210 Fax: 631-812-0249 Email: office@ncdvd.org Rev. Leonard Plazewski, Pres.,Mrs. Rosemary C. Sullivan, Exec. Dir.

NCDVD is a professional organization that supports, educates and provides resources for diocesan vocation directors as they promote all Church vocations, but particularly diocesan priesthood. This organization serves all dioceses associated with the United States Conference of Catholic Bishops.

Publications: four times a year, Newsletter; documents of interest & training institutes; Meetings annually for Regional Conferences and a National Convention.

The National Federation of Priests' Councils (1968)

National Office, 333 N. Michigan Ave., Ste. 1205 Chicago, IL 60601-4002. Tel: 312-442-9700 Tel: 888-271-6372 Fax: 312-442-9709 Email: nfpc@nfpc.org Web: www.nfpc.org Rev. Richard Vega, Pres.,Mr. Victor J. Doucette, Dir. Programs & Publications,Mr. Terry Oldes, Business Mgr.,Mr. David Philippart, Dir. Devel.,Mr. Alan Szafsaniec, Research Asst.

The NFPC promotes priestly fraternity by facilitating communication among priests' councils, provides a forum for priests to discuss pastoral matters, enables priests' councils to speak with a common voice, promotes and collaborates on programs of pastoral research, furthers the spiritual renewal of priestly life, collaborates with national lay and religious groups in ways that promote renewal in the Church, collaborates with the USCCB in addressing the needs of the Church in the U.S.A., encourages priests' councils to promote justice in light of the social teachings of the Church, and participates in developing a national and universal perspective of church and ministry.

The NFPC represents over 116 priests' councils, priests' associations and affiliates. Elected delegates of member councils meet annually to set policy, and a national executive board meets regularly to carry out the work of the NFPC, assisted by standing committees. Member councils represent approximately 26,000 priests.

Publications: quarterly newsletter, Touchstone; weekly; NFPC This Week; books, Income Tax for Priests Only, The Laborer Is Worthy of His Hire, International Priests in America, The First Five Years of Priesthood, Evolving Visions of the Priesthood, Stewards of God's Mysteries.

National Institute for the Word of God

Headquarters, 487 Michigan Ave., N.E. Washington, DC 20017. Tel: 203-562-6193 ext 147 Email: wjburke@dhs.edu Web: www.wordofgodinstitute.org

Episcopal Advisory Board—Archbishop John R. Quinn ,Bishop David E. Foley, D.D.,Bishop Patrick R. Cooney, S.T.B., S.T.L., D.D.,Bishop William G. Curlin, D.D.

Staff—Rev. John W. Burke, O.P., Exec. Dir. ,William H. Graham, Assoc. Dir.,Mary Graham, Sec.,Very Rev. Joseph P. Allen, O.P., B.A., Admin. & Treas.

Board of Advisors—Rev. Msgr. Raymond East ,Rev. James Patrick Moroney,Rev. Rutilio J. del Riego,Rev. James Walsh,Martha Fernandez,Carol Graham Lehan,Mary Ann McGuire,Michael M. McGuire

The Institute is an unaffiliated nonprofit organization incorporated under the laws of the District of Columbia, whose purpose is to promote, support, conduct and assist in any way whatsoever educational, liturgical, and remedial programs and activities, public and private, through the use of any and all media, to further effective communication of the revealed word of God, as the primary pastoral work of the Church. Ongoing efforts include the dissemination of scriptural, theological and pastoral aids such as books, films and tape albums, and the conducting of parish missions, conferences and retreats for clergy and laity.

National Service Committee of the Catholic Charismatic Renewal of the United States, Inc.

P.O. Box 628 Locust Grove, VA 22508-0628. Rev. Richard J. Loch, V.E., Chm.,Walter Matthews, Exec. Dir.

Our focus is to foster baptism in the Holy Spirit in the life of the Church in the United States and throughout the world, to broaden and deepen the understanding that baptism in the Holy Spirit is the Christian inheritance of all, and to strengthen the Catholic Charismatic Renewal. The National Service Committee has established and supported numerous programs to help further our mission. Some of the activities and programs include the establishment of Chariscenter USA, which serves as the national headquarters for our committee and a national office for the Catholic Charismatic Renewal.

Publications: Magazine, "Pentecost Today"; Leaders' training materials as well as an annual national conference, outreach to youth ministers, and evangelization training. The NSC has supported the International Catholic Charismatic Renewal Office in Rome.

The North American Forum on the Catechumenate

125 Michigan Ave., N.E. Washington, DC 20017-1102. Tel: 202-884-9758 Fax: 202-884-9747 James Schellman, Exec. Dir.

The North American Forum on the Catechumenate is an international network committed to the implementation of the Rite of Christian Initiation of Adults. The work of FORUM is overseen by a Board of Directors of seven elected representatives. A variety of institutes are offered in co-sponsorship with a hosting diocese to serve the local Church. FORUM networks with other U.S., Canadian and international groups, promotes research into issues raised by Christian Initiation (including outreach to the inactive through a process of Re-Membering Church), and provides a newsletter which focuses on the impact of Christian Initiation on the Church as well as key issues related to its implementation.

Worldwide Marriage Encounter

National Office, 2210 E. Highland Ave., Ste. 106 San Bernardino, CA 92404. Tel: 909-863-9963 Fax: 909-863-9986

Secretariat Team—Rev. Emile Frische, M.H.M. ,Anthony Witczak,Catherine Witczak

Organized to foster a program of Christian information to instruct married couples in the means to find God's plan and matrimony in their lives, for their own spiritual development and the betterment of all humankind; and to develop, foster and disseminate an adult catechesis supporting, furthering and building upon such instruction. Worldwide Marriage Encounter offers the marriage encounter weekend experience in 150 dioceses in the United States as well as in 88 foreign countries. In the United States over 1,500,000 couples and over 5,000 priests and bishops have experienced the Worldwide weekend.

Publication: EMatrimony online at ematrimony.org.

MISCELLANEOUS

Catholic Committee for Refugees & Children

3211 Fourth St., N.E. Washington, DC 20017-1194. Fax: 202-722-8755 Mr. Mark Franken, Pres.

In operation since January 4, 1937, and incorporated since 1954, the Catholic Committee for Refugees and Children was founded to counsel and cooperate with European refugees during and after World War II. Since that time its mission has been expanded to include service to refugees worldwide. It has a special mandate from the bishops concerning its work with children through international child welfare, child care or placement, and international adoption. The USCCB Committee on Migration serves as the Board of Directors for CCRC.

National Association of State Catholic Conference Directors

An Association of the Directors of the State Catholic Conferences, organized in 1968 to facilitate and encourage the exchange of information among its members pertaining to the activities, programs and organization of the Conferences. A State Catholic Conference is a Church agency composed of the dioceses within a state to provide for the coordination of the public policy concerns of the Church. Thus a Conference of the Church communicates with state government, other Church Agencies, non-Catholic churches and secular agencies. Bishops, priests, religious and lay persons are involved in the work of the State Conferences. National Association: USCCB, 3211 4th St., N.E., Washington, DC 20017-1194.

ALASKA

Alaska Conference of Catholic Bishops, 225 Cordova St., Anchorage, AK 99501. Tel: 907-297-7700; Fax: 907-279-3885
Executive Director: Ms. Mary Gore

ARIZONA

Arizona Catholic Conference, 400 E. Monroe St., Phoenix, AZ 85004-2336. Tel: 602-354-2391; Fax: 602-354-2466
Chairman: Bishop Thomas J. Olmsted, J.C.D.
Executive Director: Ron Johnson

CALIFORNIA

California Catholic Conference, 1119 K St., 2nd Fl., Sacramento, CA 95814. Tel: 916-313-4000; Fax: 916-313-4066; Email: conference@cacatholic.org; Web: www.cacatholic.org
President: Bishop Stephen E. Blaire, D.D.
Vice President: Bishop Daniel F. Walsh, D.D.
Secretary-Treasurer: Bishop Gerald E. Wilkerson, D.D., V.G.
Executive Director: Mr. Edward Dolejsi

COLORADO

Colorado Catholic Conference, 1535 Logan St., Denver, CO 80203. Tel: 303-894-8808; Fax: 303-894-7939; Email: ccc@cocatholicconference.org; Web: www.cocatholicconference.org
Executive Director: Jennifer Kraska

CONNECTICUT

Connecticut Catholic Conference, 134 Farmington Ave., Hartford, CT 06105. Tel: 860-524-7882; Fax: 860-525-0750; Email: ccc@ctcatholic.org
President and Chairman of the Board: Archbishop Henry J. Mansell
Secretary: Bishop Michael Richard Cote, D.D.
Executive Director: Marie T. Hilliard, J.C.L., Ph.D., R.N.

FLORIDA

Florida Catholic Conference, 201 W. Park Ave., Tallahassee, FL 32301-7760. Tel: 850-222-3803; Fax: 850-681-9548
President: Archbishop John Clement Favalora
Executive Director: Dr. D. Michael McCarron, Ph.D.

GEORGIA

Georgia Catholic Conference, Office Building, 3200 Deans Bridge Rd., Augusta, GA 30906. Tel: 706-798-1719; Fax: 706-798-6037
President: Cheatham E. Hodges
Executive Director: Francis J. Mulcahy, Esq.

HAWAII

Hawaii Catholic Conference, 6301 Pali Hwy., Kaneohe, HI 96744. Tel: 808-203-6704; Fax: 808-261-7022; Email: hcc@rcchawaii.org
Director: Vacant

ILLINOIS

Catholic Conference of Illinois, 65 E. Wacker Pl., Ste. 1620, Chicago, IL 60601. Tel: 312-368-1066 108 E. Cook St., Springfield, IL 62701. Tel: 217-528-9200
Chairman: His Eminence Francis Cardinal George, O.M.I., Ph.D., S.T.D.
Executive Director: Robert F. Gilligan
Associate Director: Zachary Wichmann
Associate Director: Marilou Gervacio

INDIANA

Indiana Catholic Conference, 1400 N. Meridian St., P.O. Box 1410, Indianapolis, IN 46206. Tel: 317-236-1455; Fax: 317-236-1456; Email: icc@archindy.org
General Chairman: Archbishop Daniel M. Buechlein, O.S.B., D.D.
Executive Director: Glenn Tebbe

IOWA

Iowa Catholic Conference, 530-42nd St., Des Moines, IA 50312-2707. Tel: 515-243-6256; Fax: 515-243-6257; Email: info@iowacatholicconference.org; Web: www.iowacatholicconference.org
President: Archbishop Jerome Hanus, O.S.B.
Directors: Bishop Martin J. Amos, D.D.
Bishop Richard E. Pates
Secretary-Treasurer-Director: Bishop Ralph Walker Nickless
Executive Director: Thomas Chapman

KANSAS

Kansas Catholic Conference, 6301 Antioch, Merriam, KS 66202. Tel: 913-722-6633; Web: www.kscathconf.org
Chairman: Archbishop Joseph F. Naumann, V.G., D.D.
Executive Director: Michael M. Schuttloffel
Associate Director: Ms. Beatrice E. Swoopes

KENTUCKY

Catholic Conference of Kentucky, 1042 Burlington Ln., Frankfort, KY 40601. Tel: 502-875-4345; Fax: 502-875-2841
Chairman: Archbishop Joseph E. Kurtz, D.D.
Executive Director: Mr. Robert J. Castagna

LOUISIANA

Louisiana Conference of Catholic Bishops, 3423 Hundred Oaks Ave., Baton Rouge, LA 70808. Tel: 225-344-7120; Fax: 225-383-9591
Chairman: Archbishop Gregory M. Aymond, D.D.
Executive Director: Mr. Daniel J. Loar
Associate Director: Mr. Robert M. Tasman
Business Manager: Mrs. Barbara Bovard

MARYLAND

Maryland Catholic Conference, 10 Francis St., Annapolis, MD 21401-1714. Tel: 410-269-1155; Fax: 410-269-1790
Chairman: Archbishop Edwin F. O'Brien, S.T.D., D.D.
Executive Director: Mary Ellen Russell

MASSACHUSETTS

Massachusetts Catholic Conference, 150 Staniford St. W. End Pl., Ste. 5, Boston, MA 02114. Tel: 617-367-6060
Executive Director: Edward F. Saunders

MICHIGAN

Michigan Catholic Conference, 510 S. Capitol Ave., Lansing, MI 48933. Tel: 517-372-9310; Fax: 517-372-3940
Chairman: Archbishop Allen Vigneron
Vice Chairman: Bishop Walter Allison Hurley
President & CEO: Sr. Monica Kostielney, R.S.M.
Secretary-Treasurer: Mr. Robert Asmussen

MINNESOTA

Minnesota Catholic Conference, 475 University Ave. W., Ste. B, Saint Paul, MN 55103-1959. Tel: 651-227-8777; Fax: 651-227-2675
President: Archbishop John C. Nienstedt
Secretary-Treasurer: Bishop John LeVoir
Executive Director: Christopher Leifeld
Education Department Director: Dr. Peter Noll
Social Concerns Director: Alexandra Fitzsimmons

MISSOURI

Missouri Catholic Conference, 600 Clark Ave., P.O. Box 1022, Jefferson City, MO 65102. Tel: 573-635-7239; Fax: 573-635-7431
General Chairman: Archbishop Robert J. Carlson
Executive Chairman: Bishop John R. Gaydos
General Counsel Executive Director: Vacant
Interim Director: J. Michael Hoey
Staff Associate: Rita Linhardt
Communications Director: Kayla Muck

MONTANA

Montana Catholic Conference, P.O. Box 1708, Helena, MT 59624. Tel: 406-442-5761; Fax: 406-442-9047; Email: mccadmin@bresnan.net; Web: www.montanacc.org
President: Mr. James Ziegler
Vice President: Mr. Craig Eddy
Secretary/Treasurer: Mr. Richard Martin
Executive Director: Mr. Moe Wosepka

NEBRASKA

Nebraska Catholic Conference, 215 Centennial Mall South, Ste. 310, Lincoln, NE 68508-1890. Tel: 402-477-7517
President: Archbishop George J. Lucas
Directors: Bishop Fabian Wendelin Bruskewitz, D.D., S.T.D.
Bishop William J. Dendinger, D.D., M.A.
Executive Director: James R. Cunningham

NEVADA

Nevada Catholic Conference, 290 S. Arlington Ave., Ste. 200, Reno, NV 89501-1713. Tel: 775-684-9028; Fax: 775-348-8619
Executive Director: John Cracchiolo

NEW JERSEY

New Jersey Catholic Conference, 149 N. Warren St., Trenton, NJ 08608. Tel: 609-989-1120; Fax: 609-989-1152; Email: info@njcathconf.com; Web: www.njcathconf.com
President: Archbishop John J. Myers, D.D., J.C.D.
Executive Director: Patrick R. Brannigan

NEW YORK

New York State Catholic Conference, 465 State St., Albany, NY 12203. Tel: 518-434-6195
President: Archbishop Timothy M. Dolan
Vice President: Bishop Nicholas A. DiMarzio, D.D., Ph.D.
Secretary-Treasurer: Bishop William Francis Murphy, S.T.D., L.H.D.
Chairman-Public Policy Committee: Bishop Howard James Hubbard, D.D.
Executive Director: Richard E. Barnes

NORTH DAKOTA

North Dakota Catholic Conference, 103 S. 3rd St., Ste. 10, Bismarck, ND 58501. Tel: 701-223-2519; Fax: 701-223-6075
President: Bishop Paul Albert Zipfel
Vice President: Bishop Samuel J. Aquila, D.D.
Executive Director: Christopher Dodson

OHIO

Catholic Conference of Ohio, 9 E. Long St., Ste. 201, Columbus, OH 43215. Tel: 614-224-7147; Email: cco@cdeducation.org
President: Archbishop Daniel E. Pilarczyk, S.T.D., Ph.D., D.D.
Vice President: Bishop Richard G. Lennon
Secretary-Treasurer: Bishop Frederick F. Campbell, Ph.D., D.D.
Executive Director: Carolyn M. Jurkowitz

OREGON

Oregon Catholic Conference, 2838 E. Burnside St., Portland, OR 97214. Tel: 503-234-5334; Fax: 503-234-2545
President: Archbishop John G. Vlazny
Vice President: Bishop Robert F. Vasa
Secretary-Treasurer: Rev. Msgr. Dennis O'Donovan

PENNSYLVANIA

Pennsylvania Catholic Conference, 223 North St., P.O. Box 2835, Harrisburg, PA 17105. Tel: 717-238-9613; Fax: 717-238-1473
Chairman: His Eminence Justin Cardinal Rigali
President: Bishop Kevin C. Rhoades, Pres.
Vice President: Rev. Msgr. Lawrence T. Persico, J.C.L., V.G.
Secretary: Rev. Msgr. Peter Waslo, J.C.L.
Executive Director: Dr. Robert J. O'Hara
Treasurer: Rev. Msgr. Michael E. Servinsky, S.T.L., J.C.L., D.Min., V.G.

TEXAS

Texas Catholic Conference, 1625 Rutherford Ln., Bldg. D, Austin, TX 78754-5105. Tel: 512-339-9882
Co-Chairmen: Archbishop Jose H. Gomez, S.T.D., D.D.
His Eminence Daniel Cardinal DiNardo
Executive Director: Mr. Andrew Rivas
Associate Director: Jennifer Carr
Director of Education: Margaret McGettrick
Director, Catholic Archives of Texas: Susan Eason
Director of Accreditation: Marsha Solana

WASHINGTON

Washington State Catholic Conference, 710 Ninth Ave., Seattle, WA 98104. Tel: 206-301-0556; Fax: 206-301-0558; Web: www.thewscc.org
President: Archbishop Alex J. Brunett, Ph.D.
Executive Director: Sr. Sharon Park, O.P.
Office Manager: Theresa Ferguson

WEST VIRGINIA

Catholic Conference of West Virginia, 1114 Virginia St. E., Charleston, WV 25301. Tel: 304-342-8175; Fax: 304-344-3907
Director: Rev. Msgr. P. Edward Sadie, S.T.L., V.F.
Executive Secretary: Rev. Brian P. O'Donnell, S.J., Ph.D.

WISCONSIN

Wisconsin Catholic Conference, 131 W. Wilson St., Rm. 1105, Madison, WI 53703. Tel: 608-257-0004; Fax: 608-257-0376
Chairman: Archbishop Jerome E. Listecki
Vice Chairman: Bishop Robert C. Morlino
Executive Director: John Huebscher
Associate Director Respect Life & Social Concerns: Barbara A. Sella
Associate Director Education & Health Care: Kim Wadas

Alphabetical List of Places in the United States

This comprehensive list includes all cities and towns in the United States in which a Catholic Institution is located.

The abbreviations identify each city or town to the corresponding Diocese or Archdiocese.

Abbeville, LA	LAF
SC	CHR
Abbotsford, WI	LC
Abbott, TX	FWT
Abbottstown, PA	HBG
Aberdeen, ID	B
MD	BAL
MS	JKS
SD	SFS
WA	SEA
Abernathy, TX	LUB
Abilene, KS	SAL
TX	SAN
Abingdon, IL	PEO
MD	BAL
VA	RIC
Abington, MA	BO
PA	PH
Abiquiu, NM	SFE
Abita Springs, LA	NO
Absecon, NJ	CAM
Ackerman, MS	JKS
Acme, MI	GAY
Acton, MA	BO
ME	PRT
Acushnet, MA	FR
Ada, MI	GR
MN	CR
OH	COL
OK	OKL
Adams, MA	SPR
MN	WIN
NY	OG
WI	LC
Adamstown, MD	BAL
Adamsville, AL	BIR
Addison, IL	JOL
NY	ROC
Adel, GA	SAV
IA	DM
Adelanto, CA	SB
Adelphi, MD	WDC
Adena, OH	STU
Adrian, MI	LAN
MN	WIN
Advance, MO	SPC
Affton, MO	STL
Agawam, MA	SPR
Agua Dulce, TX	CC
Aguilar, CO	PBL
Ahoskie, NC	R
Aiea, HI	HON
Aiken, SC	CHR
Ainsworth, NE	GI
Aitkin, MN	DUL
Ajo, AZ	TUC
Akron, CO	DEN
IA	SC
NY	BUF
OH	CLV
OH	NTN
OH	SJP
OH	PRM
Alakanuk, AK	FBK
Alameda, CA	OAK
Alamo, TX	BWN
Alamogordo, NM	LSC
Alamosa, CO	PBL
Albany, CA	OAK
GA	SAV
IL	RCK
KY	L
LA	BR
MN	SCL
NY	ALB
OR	P
TX	FWT
WI	MAD
Albemarle, NC	CHL
Albers, IL	BEL
Albert Lea, MN	WIN
Albertville, MN	STP
Albia, IA	DAV

Albion, IN	FTW
MI	KAL
NE	OM
NY	BUF
PA	E
RI	PRO
Albuquerque, NM	SFE
NM	VNN
Alburgh, VT	BUR
Alcoa, TN	KNX
Alden, NY	BUF
Aledo, IL	PEO
TX	FWT
Alexander City, AL	BIR
Alexandria, IN	LFT
KY	COV
LA	ALX
MN	SCL
SD	SFS
VA	ARL
VA	WDC
Alexandria Bay, NY	OG
Alexis, IL	PEO
Alfred, ME	PRT
NY	BUF
Algoma, WI	GB
Algona, IA	SC
Algonquin, IL	RCK
Alhambra, CA	LA
Alice, TX	CC
Alief, TX	GAL
Aliquippa, PA	PBR
PA	PIT
PA	SJP
Aliso Viejo, CA	ORG
Allegan, MI	KAL
Allegany, NY	BUF
Allen, TX	DAL
Allen Park, MI	DET
MI	PRM
Allendale, MI	GR
NJ	NEW
Allenspark, CO	DEN
Allenton, MI	DET
WI	MIL
Allentown, NJ	TR
PA	ALN
PA	PSC
Alleyton, TX	VIC
Alliance, NE	GI
OH	Y
Allison Park, PA	PIT
Allston, MA	BO
Alma, MI	SAG
Alma Center, WI	LC
Almond, NY	BUF
WI	LC
Aloha, OR	P
Alpena, MI	GAY
Alpha, NJ	MET
Alpharetta, GA	ATL
Alpine, AZ	GLP
CA	SD
MI	GR
TX	ELP
Alsip, IL	CHI
Alta Loma, CA	SB
Altadena, CA	LA
Altamont, IL	SFD
NY	ALB
Altamonte Springs, FL	ORL
Alton, IA	SC
IL	SFD
TX	BWN
Altona, NY	OG
Altoona, IA	DM
PA	ALT
PA	SJP
WI	LC
Alturas, CA	SAC
Altus, AR	LR
OK	OKL
Alva, OK	OKL

Alvin, TX	GAL
Alviso, CA	SJ
Ama, LA	NO
Amargosa Valley, NV	LAV
Amarillo, TX	AMA
Ambia, IN	LFT
Ambler, PA	PH
PA	SYM
Amboy, IL	RCK
Ambridge, PA	PBR
PA	PIT
PA	SJP
Amelia, LA	HT
OH	CIN
VA	RIC
Amenia, NY	NY
American Canyon, CA	SR
American Fork, UT	SLC
Americus, GA	SAV
Amery, WI	SUP
Ames, IA	DUB
Amesbury, MA	BO
Amherst, MA	SPR
NY	BUF
OH	CLV
VA	RIC
WI	LC
Amite, LA	BR
Amity, OR	P
Amityville, NY	RVC
Amory, MS	JKS
Amsterdam, NY	ALB
NY	STF
OH	STU
Anaconda, MT	HEL
Anacortes, WA	SEA
Anacostia, Washington, DC	WDC
Anadarko, OK	OKL
Anaheim, CA	ORG
CA	VNN
Anaheim Hills, CA	LA
Anahuac, TX	BEA
Anamoose, ND	FAR
Anamosa, IA	DUB
Anchorage, AK	ANC
AK	VNN
Andale, KS	WCH
Andalusia, AL	MOB
IL	PEO
Anderson, CA	SAC
IN	LFT
SC	CHR
TX	GAL
Andice, TX	AUS
Andover, KS	WCH
MA	BO
NJ	PAT
OH	Y
Andrews, NC	CHL
TX	SAN
Angels Camp, CA	STO
Angleton, TX	GAL
Angola, IN	FTW
NY	BUF
Angus, MN	CR
Aniak, AK	FBK
Anita, IA	DM
Ankeny, IA	DM
Ann Arbor, MI	LAN
MI	OLL
Anna, IL	BEL
OH	CIN
Annandale, MN	STP
VA	ARL
VA	PSC
Annapolis, MD	BAL
Annawan, IL	PEO
Anniston, AL	BIR
Annville, PA	HBG
Anoka, MN	STP
Anson, TX	LUB
Ansonia, CT	HRT
CT	STF

Anthem, AZ	PHX
Anthon, IA	SC
Anthony, NM	LSC
Antigo, WI	GB
Antioch, CA	OAK
IL	CHI
TN	NSH
Anton Chico, NM	SFE
Antonito, CO	PBL
Anza, CA	SB
Apache Junction, AZ	TUC
Apalachicola, FL	PT
Apex, NC	R
Apollo, PA	GBG
Apopka, FL	ORL
FL	SJP
Apple Creek, MO	STL
Apple Valley, CA	SB
Applegate, CA	SAC
Appleton, MN	NU
WI	GB
Appomattox, VA	RIC
Aptos, CA	MRY
Arabi, LA	NO
Aransas Pass, TX	CC
Arbor Vitae, WI	SUP
Arcade, NY	BUF
Arcadia, CA	LA
FL	VEN
IA	SC
WI	LC
Arcata, CA	SR
Archbald, PA	SCR
Archbold, OH	TOL
Arcola, IL	SFD
Arden, NC	CHL
Ardmore, OK	OKL
PA	PH
Ardsley, NY	NY
PA	PH
Arena, WI	MAD
Argo, IL	CHI
Argyle, MI	SAG
MN	CR
MO	JC
WI	MAD
Arkadelphia, AR	LR
Arkansas City, KS	WCH
Arkansaw, WI	LC
Arlington, IL	PEO
MA	BO
MN	NU
TX	FWT
VA	ARL
VT	BUR
WA	SEA
Arlington Heights, IL	CHI
Arma, KS	WCH
Armada, MI	DET
Armonk, NY	NY
Armour, SD	SFS
Armstrong, IA	SC
Armstrong Creek, WI	GB
Arnaudville, LA	LAF
Arnold, MO	STL
PA	SJP
Arroyo Grande, CA	MRY
Arroyo Seco, NM	SFE
Artesia, CA	LA
NM	LSC
Arvada, CO	DEN
Arvin, CA	FRS
Asbury Park, NJ	TR
Ash Fork, AZ	PHX
Ashaway, RI	PRO
Ashburn, VA	ARL
Ashburnham, MA	WOR
Ashdown, AR	LR
Asheboro, NC	CHL
Asherton, TX	LAR
Asheville, NC	CHL
Ashford, CT	NOR
Ashfork, AZ	PHX

Ashkum, IL	JOL
Ashland, IL	SFD
KS	DOD
KY	LEX
MA	BO
MT	GF
NE	LIN
OH	CLV
OR	P
PA	ALN
VA	RIC
WI	SUP
Ashland City, TN	NSH
Ashley, PA	SCR
Ashtabula, OH	Y
Ashton, IA	SC
Aspen, CO	DEN
Aspinwall, PA	PIT
Assonet, MA	FR
Assumption, IL	SFD
Aston, PA	PH
Astoria, NY	BRK
OR	P
Atascadero, CA	MRY
Atchison, KS	KCK
Atco, NJ	CAM
Athens, AL	BIR
GA	ATL
NY	ALB
OH	STU
TN	KNX
TX	TYL
WI	LC
WV	WH
Atherton, CA	SFR
Athol, MA	WOR
Athol Springs, NY	BUF
Atkins, AR	LR
Atkinson, IL	PEO
NE	OM
Atlanta, GA	ATL
GA	SAM
GA	NTN
TX	TYL
Atlantic, IA	DM
Atlantic Beach, FL	STA
Atlantic City, NJ	CAM
Atlantic Highlands, NJ	TR
Atmore, AL	MOB
Attica, IN	LFT
NY	BUF
OH	TOL
Attleboro, MA	FR
Attleboro Falls, MA	FR
Atwater, CA	FRS
Atwood, KS	SAL
Au Sable Forks, NY	OG
AuGres, MI	SAG
Auburn, AL	MOB
CA	SAC
IA	SC
IL	SFD
IN	FTW
KY	OWN
MA	WOR
ME	PRT
MI	SAG
NE	LIN
NH	MAN
NY	ROC
NY	STF
WA	SEA
Auburn Hills, MI	DET
Auburndale, WI	LC
Audubon, IA	DM
NJ	CAM
PA	PH
Augusta, GA	NTN
GA	SAV
KS	WCH
KY	COV
ME	PRT
MI	KAL
MO	STL
Ault, CO	DEN
Aumsville, OR	P
Auriesville, NY	ALB
Aurora, CO	DEN
IL	JOL
IL	RCK
IL	ROM
IN	IND
KS	SAL
MN	DUL
MO	SPC
NE	LIN
NY	ROC
OH	Y
Austin, MN	WIN
TX	AUS
TX	OLL
Austintown, OH	Y
OH	SJP
Ava, IL	BEL
MO	SPC
Avalon, CA	LA
NJ	CAM
Ave Maria, FL	VEN
Avella, PA	PBR
PA	PIT
Avenal, CA	FRS
Avenel, NJ	MET
Aventura, FL	MIA
Avenue, MD	WDC
Averill Park, NY	ALB
Avilla, IN	FTW
Aviston, IL	BEL
Avoca, IA	DM
PA	SCR
Avon, CT	HRT
MA	BO
MN	SCL
NY	ROC
OH	CLV
Avon By The Sea, NJ	TR
Avon Lake, OH	CLV
Avon Park, FL	VEN
Avondale, AZ	PHX
CO	PBL
LA	NO
PA	PH
Avonmore, PA	GBG
Axtell, KS	KCK
Ayer, MA	BO
Aztec, NM	GLP
Azusa, CA	LA
Babbitt, MN	DUL
Babylon, NY	RVC
Bad Axe, MI	SAG
Baden, PA	PIT
Badger, MN	CR
Bagdad, AZ	PHX
Bagley, MN	CR
Bailey, CO	COS
Baileyville, KS	KCK
ME	PRT
Bainbridge, GA	SAV
NY	SY
Bainbridge Island, WA	SEA
Bairdford, PA	PIT
Baker, MT	GF
OR	BAK
Baker City, OR	BAK
Bakersfield, CA	FRS
Bala Cynwyd, PA	PH
Baldwin, KS	KCK
LA	LAF
MI	GR
NY	RVC
Baldwin Park, CA	LA
Baldwinsville, NY	SY
Baldwinville, MA	WOR
Ballinger, TX	SAN
Ballston Lake, NY	ALB
Ballston Spa, NY	ALB
Ballwin, MO	STL
Bally, PA	ALN
Balmorhea, TX	ELP
Balsam Lake, WI	SUP
Baltic, CT	NOR
Baltimore, MD	BAL
MD	PHU
MD	PSC
Bancroft, IA	SC
Bandera, TX	SAT
Bandon, OR	P
Bangall, NY	NY
Bangor, ME	PRT
MI	KAL
PA	ALN
WI	LC
Banks, OR	P
Bannister, MI	SAG
Banquete, TX	CC
Bantam, CT	HRT
Baptistown, NJ	MET
Bar Harbor, ME	PRT
Baraboo, WI	MAD
Baraga, MI	MAR
Barberton, OH	CLV
OH	PRM
Barbourville, KY	LEX
Bardonia, NY	NY
Bardstown, KY	L
Bardwell, KY	OWN
Barefoot Bay, FL	ORL
Barhamsville, VA	RIC
Bark River, MI	MAR
Barker, NY	BUF
Barling, AR	LR
Barnegat, NJ	TR
Barnesville, MD	WDC
MN	CR
OH	STU
PA	ALN
Barneveld, WI	MAD
Barnwell, SC	CHR
Barre, MA	WOR
VT	BUR
Barrett Station, TX	GAL
Barrington, IL	CHI
NJ	CAM
RI	PRO
Barron, WI	SUP
Barrow, AK	FBK
Barryville, NY	NY
Barstow, CA	SB
Bartelso, IL	BEL
Bartlesville, OK	TLS
Bartlett, IL	CHI
TN	MEM
Barton, VT	BUR
Bartonville, IL	PEO
Bartow, FL	ORL
Bascom, OH	TOL
Basehor, KS	KCK
Basile, LA	LAF
Basking Ridge, NJ	MET
Bassfield, MS	BLX
Bastrop, LA	SHP
TX	AUS
Batavia, IL	RCK
NY	BUF
OH	CIN
Batesburg–Leesville, SC	CHR
Batesville, AR	LR
IN	IND
MS	JKS
Bath, ME	PRT
NY	ROC
PA	ALN
Bathgate, ND	FAR
Baton Rouge, LA	BR
Battle Creek, MI	KAL
NE	OM
Battle Ground, WA	SEA
Battle Lake, MN	SCL
Battle Mountain, NV	RNO
Baudette, MN	CR
Baxley, GA	SAV
Bay City, MI	PRM
MI	SAG
TX	VIC
Bay Head, NJ	TR
Bay Minette, AL	MOB
Bay Point, CA	OAK
Bay Shore, NY	RVC
Bay St. Louis, MS	BLX
Bay Village, OH	CLV
Bayard, NM	LSC
Bayfield, WI	SUP
Bayonne, NJ	NEW
NJ	PSC
Bayou LaBatre, AL	MOB
Bayport, MN	STP
Bayside, NY	BRK
Baytown, TX	GAL
Bayville, NJ	TR
NY	RVC
Beach, ND	BIS
Beacon, NY	NY
Beacon Falls, CT	HRT
Bear, DE	WIL
Bear Creek, PA	SCR
WI	GB
Beardsley, MN	NU
Beardstown, IL	SFD
Beatrice, NE	LIN
Beattie, KS	KCK
Beattyville, KY	LEX
Beaufort, SC	CHR
Beaumont, CA	SB
TX	BEA
Beaver, PA	PBR
PA	PIT
Beaver Crossing, NE	LIN
Beaver Dam, KY	OWN
WI	MIL
Beaver Falls, PA	PIT
Beaver Island, MI	GAY
Beaver Meadows, PA	PSC
Beavercreek, OH	CIN
Beaverdale, PA	PBR
Beaverton, OR	P
Beaverville, IL	JOL
Beckemeyer, IL	BEL
Becker, MN	SCL
Beckley, WV	WH
Bedford, IN	IND
MA	BO
NH	MAN
NY	NY
OH	CLV
OH	PRM
PA	ALT
TX	FWT
VA	RIC
Beebe, AR	LR
Beech Grove, IN	IND
Beemer, NE	OM
Beeville, TX	CC
Bel Air, MD	BAL
Belchertown, MA	SPR
Belcourt, ND	FAR
Belding, MI	GR
Belen, NM	SFE
Belfield, ND	BIS
ND	STN
Belgium, WI	MIL
Belgrade, MN	SCL
Bell City, LA	LKC
Bell Gardens, CA	LA
Bella Vista, AR	LR
Bellaire, MI	GAY
OH	STU
Belle, MO	JC
WV	WH
Belle Chasse, LA	NO
Belle Fontaine, AL	MOB
Belle Fourche, SD	RC
Belle Glade, FL	PMB
Belle Harbor, NY	BRK
Belle Plaine, IA	DUB
MN	STP
Belle Rose, LA	BR
Belle Vernon, PA	GBG
Belleair, FL	SP
Bellechester, MN	STP
Bellefontaine, OH	CIN
Bellefonte, PA	ALT
Bellerose, NY	BRK
Belleview, FL	ORL
Belleville, IL	BEL
KS	SAL
MI	DET
NJ	NEW
WI	MAD
Bellevue, IA	DUB
KY	COV
MI	LAN
NE	OM
OH	TOL
PA	PIT
WA	SEA
Bellflower, CA	LA
Bellingham, MA	BO
WA	SEA
Bellmawr, NJ	CAM
Bellmore, NY	RVC
Bellows Falls, VT	BUR
Bellport, NY	RVC
Bellville, TX	GAL
Bellwood, IL	CHI
IL	SYM
NE	LIN
PA	ALT
Belmar, NJ	TR
Belmond, IA	DUB
Belmont, CA	SFR
MA	BO
MA	OLN
MI	GR
NC	CHL
NH	MAN
NY	BUF
WI	MAD
Beloit, KS	SAL
WI	MAD
WI	MIL
Belpre, KS	DOD
Belt, MT	GF
Belton, MO	KC
TX	AUS
Beltsville, MD	PSC
MD	WDC
Belvidere, IL	RCK
NJ	MET
Belzoni, MS	JKS
Bemidji, MN	CR
Bemus Point, NY	BUF
Ben Bolt, TX	CC
Benavides, TX	CC
Bend, OR	BAK
Bendena, KS	KCK
Benedict, MD	WDC
Benedicta, ME	PRT
Benet Lake, WI	MIL
Benicia, CA	SAC
Benkelman, NE	LIN
Bennington, VT	BUR
Bensalem, PA	PH
Bensenville, IL	JOL
Benson, AZ	TUC
MN	NU

VT	BUR
Bentleyville, PA	PIT
Benton, AR	LR
IL	BEL
MO	SPC
WI	MAD
Benton City, WA	YAK
Benton Harbor, MI	KAL
Bentonville, AR	LR
Benwood, WV	WH
Berea, KY	LEX
OH	CLV
Beresford, SD	SFS
Bergen, NY	BUF
Bergenfield, NJ	NEW
Berkeley, CA	OAK
Berkeley Heights, NJ	NEW
Berkeley Springs, WV	WH
Berkley, MI	DET
Berlin, MA	WOR
MD	WIL
NH	MAN
NJ	CAM
WI	MAD
Bernalillo, NM	SFE
Bernard, IA	DUB
Bernardsville, NJ	MET
Berryville, AR	LR
VA	ARL
Bertha, MN	SCL
Bertram, TX	AUS
Berwick, LA	LAF
ME	PRT
PA	HBG
PA	PHU
Berwyn, IL	CHI
PA	PH
Bessemer, AL	BIR
MI	MAR
Bethalto, IL	SFD
Bethany, MO	KC
OK	OKL
WV	WH
Bethany Beach, DE	WIL
Bethel, AK	FBK
CT	BGP
OH	CIN
VT	BUR
Bethel Park, PA	PIT
Bethesda, MD	WDC
Bethlehem, CT	HRT
PA	ALN
PA	PHU
PA	PSC
Bethpage, NY	RVC
Bettendorf, IA	DAV
Beulah, ND	BIS
Beverly, MA	BO
OH	STU
Beverly Hills, CA	LA
FL	SP
MI	DET
Beverly Shores, IN	GRY
Bicknell, IN	EVN
Biddeford, ME	PRT
Big Bear Lake, CA	SB
Big Bend, WI	MIL
Big Lake, AK	ANC
LA	LKC
MN	SCL
TX	SAN
Big Pine Key, FL	MIA
Big Rapids, MI	GR
Big Spring, TX	SAN
Big Stone City, SD	SFS
Big Stone Gap, VA	RIC
Big Sur, CA	MRY
Big Timber, MT	GF
Bigelow, AR	LR
Bigfork, MN	DUL
MT	HEL
Billerica, MA	BO
Billings, MO	SPC
MT	GF
Biloxi, MS	BLX
Binghamton, NY	SY
NY	PSC
Birch Run, MI	SAG
Bird Island, MN	NU
Birmingham, AL	BIR
AL	NTN
AL	OLL
MI	DET
Birmingham (Hoover), AL	BIR
Birnamwood, WI	GB
Bisbee, AZ	TUC
ND	FAR
Biscoe, NC	CHL
Bishop, CA	FRS
TX	CC
Bismarck, ND	BIS

Biwabik, MN	DUL
Bixby, OK	TLS
Black Canyon City, AZ	PHX
Black Creek, WI	GB
Black Diamond, WA	SEA
Black Eagle, MT	GF
Black River, NY	OG
Black River Falls, WI	LC
Blackfoot, ID	B
Blacksburg, VA	RIC
Blackstone, MA	WOR
VA	RIC
Blackwell, OK	OKL
Blackwood, NJ	CAM
Bladensburg, MD	WDC
Blaine, MN	STP
Blair, NE	OM
Blairstown, NJ	MET
Blairsville, GA	ATL
PA	GBG
Blakely, GA	SAV
Blanchardville, WI	MAD
Blanco, TX	AUS
Blasdell, NY	BUF
Blauvelt, NY	NY
NY	CAM
Blessing, TX	VIC
Blissfield, MI	LAN
Block Island, RI	PRO
Bloomer, WI	LC
Bloomfield, CT	HRT
IN	EVN
NJ	NEW
NJ	PAT
NM	GLP
Bloomfield Hills, MI	DET
Blooming Prairie, MN	WIN
Bloomingdale, IL	JOL
NY	OG
OH	STU
Bloomington, CA	SB
IL	PEO
IN	IND
MN	STP
TX	VIC
WI	MAD
Bloomsburg, PA	HBG
Bloomsbury, NJ	MET
Bloomsdale, MO	STL
Blountstown, FL	PT
Blue Anchor, NJ	CAM
Blue Bell, PA	PH
Blue Earth, MN	WIN
Blue Grass, IA	DAV
Blue Island, IL	CHI
Blue Point, NY	RVC
Blue Ridge, GA	ATL
Blue Springs, MO	KC
Bluefield, WV	WH
Bluffton, IN	FTW
MN	SCL
OH	TOL
SC	CHR
Blythe, CA	SB
Blytheville, AR	LR
Blythewood, SC	CHR
Boardman, OH	Y
OH	PBR
OH	ROM
OR	BAK
Bobtown, PA	PIT
Boca Grande, FL	VEN
Boca Raton, FL	PMB
Boerne, TX	SAT
Bogalusa, LA	NO
Bogota, NJ	NEW
Bohemia, NY	RVC
Boise, ID	B
Bokeelia, FL	VEN
Bolingbrook, IL	JOL
Bolivar, MO	SPC
NY	BUF
OH	COL
PA	GBG
TN	MEM
Bolton, CT	NOR
Bolton Landing, NY	ALB
Bonduel, WI	GB
Bonesteel, SD	RC
Bonfield, IL	JOL
Bonham, TX	DAL
Bonifay, FL	PT
Bonita, CA	LA
CA	SD
Bonita Springs, FL	VEN
Bonne Terre, MO	STL
Bonner, MT	HEL
Bonners Ferry, ID	B
Bonnots Mill, MO	JC
Boone, IA	SC
NC	CHL

Booneville, AR	LR
MS	JKS
Boonton, NJ	PAT
Boonville, IN	EVN
MO	JC
NC	CHL
NY	SY
Boothwyn, PA	PH
Bordelonville, LA	ALX
Bordentown, NJ	TR
Borger, TX	AMA
Borrego Springs, CA	SD
Boscobel, WI	MAD
Bossier City, LA	SHP
Boston, MA	BO
NY	BUF
Boswell, PA	ALT
Bothell, WA	SEA
Botkins, OH	CIN
Bottineau, ND	FAR
Boulder, CO	DEN
MT	HEL
Boulder City, NV	LAV
Boulder Creek, CA	MRY
Boulder Junction, WI	SUP
Boulevard, CA	SD
Bound Brook, NJ	MET
Bountiful, UT	SLC
Bourbonnais, IL	JOL
Bourg, LA	HT
Bovina, TX	AMA
Bowdle, SD	SFS
Bowie, MD	WDC
Bowling Green, KY	OWN
MO	JC
OH	TOL
Bowlus, MN	SCL
Bowman, ND	BIS
Bowmansville, NY	BUF
Box Elder, MT	GF
Boyce, LA	ALX
Boyceville, WI	LC
Boyd, WI	LC
Boyers, PA	PIT
Boyertown, PA	ALN
Boylston, MA	WOR
Boyne City, MI	GAY
Boynton Beach, FL	PMB
Boys Town, NE	OM
Bozeman, MT	HEL
Brackettville, TX	SAT
Braddock, PA	PBR
PA	PIT
Bradenton, FL	VEN
Bradenton Beach, FL	VEN
Bradenville, PA	PBR
Bradford, IN	IND
NY	ROC
OH	CIN
PA	E
RI	PRO
VT	BUR
Bradley, IL	JOL
Bradley Beach, NJ	TR
Bradshaw, MD	BAL
Brady, TX	SAN
Brady's Bend, PA	GBG
Braham, MN	SCL
Braidwood, IL	JOL
Brainard, NE	LIN
Brainerd, MN	DUL
Braintree, MA	BO
Braithwaite, LA	NO
Branchville, NJ	PAT
Brandenburg, KY	L
Brandon, FL	SP
MN	SCL
SD	SFS
VT	BUR
Brandywine, MD	WDC
Branford, CT	HRT
FL	STA
Branson, MO	SPC
Brant Beach, NJ	TR
Brasher Falls, NY	OG
Brattleboro, VT	BUR
Brawley, CA	SD
Brazil, IN	IND
Brazoria, TX	GAL
Brea, CA	ORG
Breaux Bridge, LA	LAF
Breckenridge, MN	SCL
TX	FWT
Brecksville, OH	CLV
OH	PRM
Breda, IA	SC
Breese, IL	BEL
Bremen, IN	FTW
OH	COL
Bremerton, WA	SEA
Bremond, TX	AUS

Brenham, TX	AUS
Brentwood, CA	OAK
MO	STL
NY	RVC
TN	NSH
Brevard, NC	CHL
Brewerton, NY	SY
Brewster, MA	FR
NY	NY
OH	Y
WA	SPK
Brewton, AL	MOB
Briarcliff Manor, NY	NY
Briarwood, NY	BRK
Brick, NJ	TR
Brick Town, NJ	TR
Bridal Veil, OR	P
Bridge City, TX	BEA
Bridgehampton, NY	RVC
Bridgeport, CT	BGP
CT	STF
MI	SAG
NE	GI
NY	SY
OH	STU
PA	PH
PA	PHU
TX	FWT
WV	WH
Bridger, MT	GF
Bridgeton, MO	STL
NJ	CAM
Bridgeview, IL	CHI
Bridgeville, PA	PIT
Bridgewater, MA	BO
NJ	MET
SD	SFS
Bridgman, MI	KAL
Bridgton, ME	PRT
Brigantine, NJ	CAM
Briggsville, WI	MAD
Brigham City, UT	SLC
Brighton, CO	DEN
IL	SFD
MA	BO
MI	DET
MI	LAN
Brillion, WI	GB
Brimfield, IL	PEO
MA	SPR
Brimley, MI	MAR
Brinkley, AR	LR
Bristol, CT	HRT
IN	FTW
PA	PH
PA	PHU
RI	PRO
SD	SFS
VA	RIC
VT	BUR
WI	MIL
Bristow, IN	IND
VA	ARL
Britt, IA	DUB
Britton, SD	SFS
Broad Brook, CT	HRT
Broadalbin, NY	ALB
Broadus, MT	GF
Broadview, IL	CHI
Broadview Heights, OH	CLV
Brockport, NY	ROC
Brockton, MA	BO
MA	SAM
Brockway, PA	E
Brodhead, WI	MAD
Brodheadsville, PA	SCR
Broken Arrow, OK	TLS
Broken Bow, NE	GI
Bronson, MI	KAL
Bronx, NY	NY
NY	BRK
NY	SYM
NY	STF
Bronxville, NY	NY
Brook Park, OH	CLV
Brookeville, MD	WDC
Brookfield, CT	BGP
IL	CHI
MO	JC
WI	MIL
Brookhaven, MS	JKS
PA	PH
Brookings, OR	P
SD	SFS
Brooklandville, MD	BAL
Brooklawn, NJ	CAM
Brookline, MA	BO
MA	ROM
Brooklyn, CT	NOR
IA	DAV
MI	LAN

NY	BRK
NY	OLN
NY	STF
NY	SAM
NY	NTN
OH	CLV
OH	NTN
OH	SJP
Brooklyn Center, MN	STP
Brooklyn Park, MN	STP
Brooksville, FL	SP
FL	SJP
KY	COV
MS	JKS
Brookville, IN	IND
NY	RVC
PA	E
Broomall, PA	PH
Broomfield, CO	DEN
Brooten, MN	SCL
Broussard, LA	LAF
Browerville, MN	SCL
Brown Deer, WI	MIL
Brown's Valley, MN	SCL
Brownfield, TX	LUB
Browning, MT	HEL
Browns Mills, NJ	TR
Browns Valley, MN	SCL
Brownsburg, IN	IND
Brownsville, PA	GBG
PA	PBR
TN	MEM
TX	BWN
Brownville, NY	OG
Brownwood, TX	SAN
Bruce, MS	JKS
Bruno, NE	LIN
Brunswick, GA	SAV
MD	BAL
ME	PRT
MO	JC
OH	CLV
OH	PRM
Brush, CO	DEN
Brushton, NY	OG
Brusly, LA	BR
Brussels, IL	SFD
WI	GB
Bryan, OH	TOL
TX	AUS
Bryant, IN	LFT
Bryantown, MD	WDC
Bryn Mawr, PA	PH
Bryson City, NC	CHL
Buchanan, MI	KAL
NY	NY
Buckeye, AZ	PHX
Buckeye Lake, OH	COL
Buckeystown, MD	BAL
Buckhannon, WV	WH
Buckingham, PA	PH
Buckley, WA	SEA
Buckner, MO	KC
Bucksport, ME	PRT
Bucyrus, KS	KCK
OH	TOL
Buda, TX	AUS
Budd Lake, NJ	PAT
Buena Park, CA	ORG
Buena Vista, CO	COS
Buffalo, IA	DAV
MN	STP
MO	SPC
NY	BUF
NY	STF
SD	RC
TX	TYL
WY	CHY
Buffalo Grove, IL	CHI
Buford, GA	ATL
Buhl, ID	B
MN	DUL
Bulger, PA	PIT
Bullhead City, AZ	PHX
Bumpass, VA	RIC
Buna, TX	BEA
Bunkie, LA	ALX
Bunnell, FL	STA
Burbank, CA	LA
IL	CHI
Burgaw, NC	R
Burgettstown, PA	PIT
Burien, WA	SEA
Burkburnett, TX	FWT
Burke, SD	RC
VA	ARL
Burleson, TX	FWT
Burley, ID	B
Burlingame, CA	SFR
Burlington, CO	COS
IA	DAV

KS	KCK
KY	COV
MA	BO
NC	R
NJ	TR
TX	AUS
VT	BUR
WA	SEA
WI	MIL
Burnet, TX	AUS
Burney, CA	SAC
Burnham, IL	CHI
Burns, OR	BAK
Burnsville, MN	STP
Burr Ridge, IL	JOL
Burton, MI	LAN
OH	PRM
Burtonsville, MD	WDC
Bushnell, FL	ORL
IL	PEO
Bushton, KS	WCH
Bushwood, MD	WDC
Butler, AL	MOB
MO	KC
NJ	PAT
PA	PBR
PA	PIT
WI	MIL
Butner, NC	R
Butte, MT	HEL
NE	OM
Butternut, WI	SUP
Buttonwillow, CA	FRS
Buxton, NC	R
Buzzards Bay, MA	FR
Byers, CO	DEN
Byron, CA	OAK
IL	RCK
MN	WIN
Byron Center, MI	GR
MI	KAL
Cabery, IL	JOL
Cable, WI	SUP
Cabot, PA	PIT
Cadet, MO	STL
Cadillac, MI	GAY
Cadiz, KY	OWN
OH	STU
Cadogan, PA	GBG
Cadott, WI	LC
Cadyville, NY	OG
Cahokia, IL	BEL
Cairo, IL	BEL
NY	ALB
Calais, ME	PRT
Caldwell, ID	B
KS	WCH
NJ	NEW
OH	STU
TX	AUS
Caledonia, MI	GR
MN	WIN
NY	ROC
WI	MIL
Calexico, CA	SD
Calhan, CO	COS
Calhoun, GA	ATL
KY	OWN
Caliente, NV	LAV
Califon, NJ	MET
California, KY	COV
MO	JC
PA	PIT
California City, CA	FRS
Calimesa, CA	SB
CA	VNN
Calipatria, CA	SD
Calistoga, CA	SR
Callahan, FL	STA
Callaway, MN	CR
Callicoon, NY	NY
Calmar, IA	DUB
Calumet, MI	MAR
Calumet City, IL	CHI
Calumet Park, IL	CHI
Calvert City, KY	OWN
Camanche, IA	DAV
Camarillo, CA	LA
Camas, WA	SEA
Cambria, CA	MRY
Cambria Heights, NY	BRK
Cambridge, MA	BO
MD	WIL
MN	SCL
NE	LIN
NY	ALB
OH	STU
VT	BUR
WI	MAD
Cambridge City, IN	IND
Cambridge Springs, PA	E

Camden, AL	MOB
AR	LR
ME	PRT
MS	JKS
NJ	CAM
NY	SY
SC	CHR
TN	MEM
WV	WH
Camdenton, MO	JC
Cameron, LA	LKC
MO	KC
TX	AUS
Camillus, NY	SY
Camp Douglas, WI	LC
Camp Hill, PA	HBG
Camp Springs, KY	COV
MD	WDC
Camp Verde, AZ	PHX
Campbell, CA	SJ
CA	SPA
MO	SPC
NE	LIN
OH	Y
OH	PBR
Campbell Hall, NY	STF
Campbellsport, WI	MIL
Campbellsville, KY	L
Campo, CA	SD
Campti, LA	ALX
Campus, IL	PEO
Canaan, CT	HRT
Canadaigua, NY	ROC
Canadensis, PA	SCR
Canadian, TX	AMA
Canal Fulton, OH	Y
Canal Winchester, OH	COL
Canandaigua, NY	ROC
Canaseraga, NY	BUF
Canastota, NY	SY
Canby, MN	NU
OR	P
Candia, NH	MAN
Candler, FL	ORL
NC	CHL
Cando, ND	FAR
Candor, NC	CHL
Caney, KS	WCH
Canfield, OH	Y
Cankton, LA	LAF
Cannon Falls, MN	STP
Canoga Park, CA	LA
Canon City, CO	PBL
Canonsburg, PA	PBR
PA	PIT
Canterbury, CT	NOR
Canton, GA	ATL
IL	PEO
MA	BO
MI	DET
MO	JC
MS	JKS
NY	OG
OH	Y
OH	ROM
PA	SCR
SD	SFS
TX	TYL
Cantonment, FL	PT
Canutillo, TX	ELP
Canyon, TX	AMA
Canyon Lake, TX	SAT
Capac, MI	DET
Cape Charles, VA	RIC
Cape Coral, FL	VEN
Cape Elizabeth, ME	PRT
Cape Girardeau, MO	SPC
Cape May, NJ	CAM
Cape May Court House, NJ	CAM
Cape May Point, NJ	CAM
Cape Vincent, NY	OG
Capitola, CA	MRY
Captain Cook, HI	HON
Capulin, CO	PBL
Carbondale, CO	DEN
IL	BEL
PA	SCR
Cardington, OH	COL
Carefree, AZ	PHX
Carencro, LA	LAF
Carey, OH	TOL
Caribou, ME	PRT
Carle Place, NY	RVC
Carleton, MI	DET
Carlin, NV	RNO
Carlinville, IL	SFD
Carlisle, AR	LR
IA	DM
KY	LEX
MA	BO
PA	HBG

Carlos, MN	SCL
Carlsbad, CA	SD
NM	LSC
TX	SAN
Carlton, MN	DUL
Carlyle, IL	BEL
Carmel, CA	MRY
IN	LFT
NY	NY
Carmel Valley, CA	MRY
Carmi, IL	BEL
Carmichael, CA	SAC
PA	PIT
Carmichaels, PA	PIT
Carnegie, PA	PIT
PA	SAM
PA	SJP
Carney's Point, NJ	CAM
Carneys Point, NJ	CAM
Caro, MI	SAG
Carol Stream, IL	JOL
Carolina, RI	PRO
Carpentersville, IL	RCK
Carpinteria, CA	LA
Carrington, ND	FAR
Carrizo Springs, TX	LAR
Carrizozo, NM	LSC
Carroll, IA	SC
Carrollton, GA	ATL
IL	SFD
KY	COV
MO	KC
OH	STU
TX	DAL
TX	SYM
TX	FWT
Carrolltown, PA	ALT
Carson, CA	LA
ND	BIS
Carson City, MI	GR
NV	RNO
Carter Lake, IA	DM
Carteret, NJ	MET
NJ	PHU
NJ	PSC
Cartersville, GA	ATL
Carterville, IL	BEL
Carthage, MO	SPC
MS	JKS
NY	OG
TX	TYL
Carthagena, OH	CIN
Caruthersville, MO	SPC
Carver, MA	BO
MN	STP
Cary, IL	RCK
NC	R
NC	PSC
NC	SAM
Casa Grande, AZ	TUC
Cascade, CO	COS
IA	DUB
Casco, ME	PRT
WI	GB
Caseville, MI	SAG
Casey, IL	SFD
Caseyville, IL	BEL
Cashion, AZ	PHX
Cashmere, WA	YAK
Cashton, WI	LC
Casper, WY	CHY
Caspian, MI	MAR
Cass City, MI	SAG
Cass Lake, MN	DUL
Cassandra, PA	ALT
Casselberry, FL	ORL
Casselton, ND	FAR
Cassopolis, MI	KAL
Cassville, MO	SPC
WI	MAD
Castine, ME	PRT
Castle Hayne, NC	R
Castle Rock, CO	COS
WA	SEA
Castleton, NY	ALB
VT	BUR
Castleton On Hudson, NY	ALB
Castro Valley, CA	OAK
Castroville, CA	MRY
TX	SAT
Catasauqua, PA	ALN
Catawissa, MO	STL
PA	HBG
Catharine, KS	SAL
Cathedral City, CA	SB
Cato, WI	GB
Catonsville, MD	BAL
Catskill, NY	ALB
Cattaraugus, NY	BUF
Cavalier, ND	FAR
Cave Creek, AZ	PHX

Cayucos, CA	MRY
Cazenovia, NY	SY
WI	LC
Cecil, PA	PIT
WI	GB
Cecilia, LA	LAF
Cedar, MI	GAY
Cedar City, UT	SLC
Cedar Falls, IA	DUB
Cedar Grove, NJ	NEW
WI	MIL
Cedar Knolls, NJ	PAT
Cedar Lake, IN	GRY
Cedar Park, TX	AUS
Cedar Rapids, IA	DUB
NE	OM
Cedarburg, WI	MIL
Cedarhurst, NY	RVC
Cedartown, GA	ATL
Cedarville, NJ	CAM
Celebration, FL	ORL
Celestine, IN	EVN
Celina, OH	CIN
Centennial, CO	DEN
Center, CO	PBL
ND	BIS
TX	TYL
Center Harbor, NH	MAN
Center Line, MI	DET
Center Moriches, NY	RVC
Center Ossipee, NH	MAN
Center Ridge, AR	LR
Center Valley, PA	ALN
Centereach, NY	RVC
Centerline, MI	DET
Centerport, NY	RVC
Centerville, IA	DAV
LA	LAF
MA	FR
MN	STP
OH	CIN
SD	SFS
TN	NSH
Central City, IA	DUB
KY	OWN
NE	OM
PA	ALT
Central Falls, RI	PRO
Central Islip, NY	RVC
Central Point, OR	P
Central Square, NY	SY
Central Valley, UT	SLC
Centralia, IL	BEL
MO	JC
WA	SEA
Centreville, MD	WIL
Ceres, CA	SPA
CA	STO
Cerrillos, NM	SFE
Chadds Ford, PA	PH
Chadron, NE	GI
Chaffee, MO	SPC
Chagrin Falls, OH	CLV
Chalfont, PA	PH
Chalmette, LA	NO
Chama, NM	SFE
Chamberino, NM	LSC
Chamberlain, SD	SFS
Chambersburg, PA	HBG
Chamblee, GA	ATL
Chamois, MO	JC
Champaign, IL	PEO
Champion, MI	MAR
Champlain, NY	OG
Chandler, AZ	PHX
OK	OKL
Chanhassen, MN	STP
Channahon, IL	JOL
Channelview, TX	GAL
Channing, MI	MAR
Chantilly, VA	ARL
Chanute, KS	WCH
Chaparral, NM	LSC
Chapel Hill, NC	R
Chapin, SC	CHR
Chapman, KS	SAL
Chappaqua, NY	NY
Chappell, NE	GI
Chappell Hill, TX	AUS
Chaptico, MD	WDC
Chardon, OH	CLV
Charenton, LA	LAF
Chariton, IA	DM
Charleroi, PA	PBR
PA	PIT
Charles City, IA	DUB
Charles Town, WV	WH
Charleston, AR	LR
IL	SFD
MO	SPC
MS	JKS
SC	CHR
WV	WH
Charlestown, IN	IND
MA	BO
NH	MAN
Charlevoix, MI	GAY
Charlotte, IA	DAV
MI	LAN
NC	CHL
TX	SAT
VT	BUR
Charlotte Hall, MD	WDC
Charlottesville, VA	RIC
Charlton, MA	WOR
Charlton City, MA	WOR
Chaska, MN	STP
Chassell, MI	MAR
Chataignier, LA	LAF
Chatawa, MS	JKS
Chateaugay, NY	OG
Chatfield, MN	WIN
Chatham, IL	SFD
MA	FR
NJ	PAT
NY	ALB
Chatsworth, CA	LA
IL	PEO
Chattahoochee, FL	PT
Chattanooga, TN	KNX
Chauvin, LA	HT
Chazy, NY	OG
Chebanse, IL	JOL
Cheboygan, MI	GAY
Cheektowaga, NY	BUF
Chefornak, AK	FBK
Chehalis, WA	SEA
Chelan, WA	YAK
Chelmsford, MA	BO
Chelsea, MA	BO
MI	LAN
Cheltenham, PA	PH
Cheney, WA	SPK
Cheneyville, LA	ALX
Chenoa, IL	PEO
Chepachet, RI	PRO
Cheraw, SC	CHR
Cherokee, IA	SC
Cherokee Village, AR	LR
Cherry, IL	PEO
Cherry Hill, NJ	CAM
NJ	PHU
Cherry Valley, NY	ALB
Cherryvale, KS	WCH
Chesaning, MI	SAG
Chesapeake, OH	STU
VA	RIC
Cheshire, CT	HRT
MA	SPR
Chest Springs, PA	ALT
Chester, CT	NOR
IL	BEL
MD	WIL
MT	GF
NJ	PAT
NY	NY
PA	PH
SC	CHR
VT	BUR
WV	WH
Chesterfield, MO	JC
MO	STL
NJ	TR
VA	RIC
Chesterland, OH	CLV
OH	ROM
Chesterton, IN	GRY
Chestertown, MD	WIL
NY	ALB
Chestnut Hill, MA	BO
Chetek, WI	SUP
Chevak, AK	FBK
Cheverly, MD	WDC
Chewelah, WA	SPK
Cheyenne, WY	CHY
Cheyenne Wells, CO	COS
Chicago, IL	CHI
IL	EST
IL	STN
IL	SYM
IL	LIT
IL	DET
Chicago Heights, IL	CHI
Chicago Ridge, IL	CHI
Chickasaw, AL	MOB
Chickasha, OK	OKL
Chico, CA	SAC
Chicopee, MA	SPR
Chicora, PA	PIT
Chiefland, FL	STA
Childress, TX	AMA
Childs, MD	WIL
Chillicothe, IL	PEO
MO	KC
OH	COL
Chillum, MD	WDC
Chiloquin, OR	BAK
Chilton, WI	GB
Chimayo, NM	SFE
China, TX	BEA
China Spring, TX	AUS
Chincoteague Island, VA	RIC
Chinle, AZ	GLP
Chino, CA	SB
Chino Hills, CA	SB
Chino Valley, AZ	PHX
Chinook, MT	GF
Chipley, FL	PT
Chippewa Falls, WI	LC
Chippewa Lake, OH	CLV
Chisholm, MN	DUL
Chittenango, NY	SY
Chokio, MN	SCL
Choteau, MT	HEL
Chowchilla, CA	FRS
Chrisney, IN	EVN
Christiansburg, VA	RIC
Christopher, IL	BEL
Christoval, TX	SAN
Chula Vista, CA	SD
Church Point, LA	LAF
Churchville, NY	ROC
Churdan, IA	SC
Churubusco, IN	FTW
NY	OG
Cibecue, AZ	GLP
Cicero, IL	CHI
IN	LFT
NY	SY
Cimarron, NM	SFE
Cincinnati, OH	CIN
OH	OLL
Cinnaminson, NJ	TR
Circle, MT	GF
Circleville, OH	COL
Citronelle, AL	MOB
Citrus Heights, CA	SAC
Citrus Springs, FL	SP
Claflin, KS	DOD
Clairton, PA	PBR
PA	PIT
Clanton, AL	BIR
Clara City, MN	NU
Clare, MI	SAG
Claremont, CA	LA
NH	MAN
Claremore, OK	TLS
Clarence, NY	BUF
PA	ALT
Clarendon, TX	AMA
Clarendon Hills, IL	JOL
Clarinda, IA	DM
Clarion, IA	DUB
PA	E
Clarissa, MN	SCL
Clark, NJ	NEW
SD	SFS
Clarkesville, GA	ATL
Clarklake, MI	LAN
Clarks Green, PA	SCR
Clarks Summit, PA	SCR
Clarksburg, CA	SAC
WV	WH
Clarksdale, MS	JKS
Clarkson, KY	OWN
NE	OM
Clarkston, MI	DET
WA	SPK
Clarksville, AR	LR
IN	IND
MD	BAL
PA	PIT
TN	NSH
TX	TYL
VA	RIC
Clawson, MI	DET
Claxton, GA	SAV
Clay Center, KS	SAL
Claymont, DE	WIL
Clayton, MO	STL
NC	R
NJ	CAM
NM	SFE
NY	OG
Clayville, NY	SY
Cle Elum, WA	YAK
Clear Lake, IA	DUB
MN	SCL
SD	SFS
WI	SUP
Clearfield, PA	E
Clearlake, CA	SR
Clearville, PA	ALT
Clearwater, FL	SP
MN	STP
Clearwater Beach, FL	SP
Cleburne, TX	FWT
Clemmons, NC	CHL
Clemson, SC	CHR
Clermont, FL	ORL
IA	DUB
Cleveland, GA	ATL
MN	STP
MS	JKS
NY	SY
OH	CLV
OH	OLL
OH	SJP
OH	ROM
OH	PRM
TN	KNX
TX	BEA
Cleveland Heights, OH	CLV
Clewiston, FL	VEN
Clifford, PA	SCR
Cliffside Park, NJ	NEW
NJ	NTN
Clifton, AZ	TUC
IL	JOL
NJ	PAT
TX	FWT
VA	ARL
Clifton Forge, VA	RIC
Clifton Heights, PA	PH
PA	PHU
Clifton Park, NY	ALB
Clifton Springs, NY	ROC
Clint, TX	ELP
Clinton, AR	LR
CT	NOR
IA	DAV
IL	PEO
IN	IND
KY	OWN
MA	WOR
MD	WDC
MI	LAN
MO	KC
MS	JKS
NC	R
NJ	MET
NY	SY
OK	OKL
TN	KNX
WI	MAD
Clinton Corners, NY	NY
Clinton Township, MI	DET
MI	PRM
Clinton Twp., MI	DET
Clintwood, VA	RIC
Clio, MI	LAN
Cloquet, MN	DUL
Closter, NJ	NEW
Cloudcroft, NM	LSC
Cloutierville, LA	ALX
Cloverdale, CA	SR
OH	TOL
Cloverport, KY	OWN
Clovis, CA	FRS
NM	SFE
Clute, TX	GAL
Clyde, KS	SAL
MO	KC
NY	ROC
OH	TOL
Clymer, NY	BUF
PA	GBG
Coachella, CA	SB
Coal City, IL	JOL
Coal Township, PA	HBG
Coal Valley, IL	PEO
Coalinga, CA	FRS
Coalport, PA	E
Coalton, WV	WH
Coatesville, PA	PH
PA	PSC
Cobden, IL	BEL
Cobleskill, NY	ALB
Cockeysville, MD	BAL
Cocoa, FL	ORL
Cocoa Beach, FL	ORL
Coconut Creek, FL	PSC
Coconut Grove, FL	MIA
Coden, AL	MOB
Cody, WY	CHY
Coeur d'Alene, ID	B
Coffeyville, KS	WCH
Coggon, IA	DUB
Cohasset, MA	BO
Cohoes, NY	ALB
NY	STF
Colbert, WA	SPK
Colby, KS	SAL

WI	LC
Colchester, CT	NOR
CT	STF
VT	BUR
Cold Spring, KY	COV
MN	SCL
NY	NY
Coldwater, MI	KAL
OH	CIN
Colebrook, NH	MAN
Coleman, MI	SAG
TX	SAN
WI	GB
Colerain, OH	STU
Coleraine, MN	DUL
Colfax, CA	SAC
IA	DAV
IL	PEO
LA	ALX
WA	SPK
College Park, MD	WDC
College Point, NY	BRK
College Station, TX	AUS
Collegeville, MN	SCL
PA	PH
Colleyville, TX	FWT
Collierville, TN	MEM
Collingdale, PA	PH
Collings Lakes, NJ	CAM
Collingswood, NJ	CAM
Collinsville, CT	HRT
IL	SFD
OK	TLS
Collyer, KS	SAL
Colma, CA	SFR
Colo, IA	DUB
Cologne, MN	STP
Colon, NE	LIN
Colona, IL	PEO
Colonia, NJ	MET
Colonial Beach, VA	ARL
Colonial Heights, VA	RIC
Colonie, NY	ALB
Colorado City, TX	SAN
Colorado Springs, CO	COS
Colstrip, MT	GF
Colton, CA	SB
NY	OG
WA	SPK
Colts Neck, NJ	TR
Columbia, CT	NOR
IL	BEL
MD	BAL
MO	JC
MS	BLX
PA	HBG
SC	CHR
TN	NSH
VA	RIC
Columbia City, IN	FTW
Columbia Falls, MT	HEL
Columbia Heights, MN	STP
Columbia Station, OH	CLV
Columbiana, OH	Y
Columbus, GA	SAV
IN	IND
KS	WCH
MS	JKS
MT	GF
NE	OM
OH	COL
OH	PRM
OH	SYM
TX	VIC
WI	MAD
Columbus Grove, OH	TOL
Columbus Junction, IA	DAV
Colusa, CA	SAC
Colver, PA	ALT
Colville, WA	SPK
Colwich, KS	WCH
Combined Locks, WI	GB
Comfort, TX	SAT
Comfrey, MN	NU
Commack, NY	RVC
Commerce, CA	LA
TX	DAL
Commerce City, CO	DEN
Compton, CA	LA
Conception, MO	KC
Conception Junction, MO	KC
Concord, CA	SJ
CA	OAK
MA	BO
MI	LAN
NC	CHL
NH	MAN
Concord Twp., OH	CLV
Concordia, KS	SAL
Conde, SD	SFS
Condon, OR	BAK

Conejos, CO	PBL
Conemaugh, PA	ALT
PA	PBR
Congers, NY	NY
Conifer, CO	DEN
Conklin, MI	GR
Conneaut, OH	Y
Conneaut Lake, PA	E
Conneautville, PA	E
Connell, WA	SPK
Connellsville, PA	GBG
Connersville, IN	IND
Conrad, MT	HEL
Conroe, TX	GAL
Conshohocken, PA	PH
Constable, NY	OG
Constableville, NY	OG
Convent, LA	BR
Convent Station, NJ	PAT
Converse, TX	SAT
Conway, AR	LR
MI	GAY
MO	SPC
PA	PIT
SC	CHR
Conway Springs, KS	WCH
Conyers, GA	ATL
GA	SJP
Conyngham, PA	SCR
Cook, MN	DUL
Cookeville, TN	NSH
Cooksville, MD	BAL
Coolidge, AZ	TUC
Coon Rapids, IA	SC
MN	STP
Coon Valley, WI	LC
Cooper City, FL	MIA
Coopersburg, PA	ALN
Cooperstown, ND	FAR
NY	ALB
Coopersville, MI	GR
Coos Bay, OR	P
Copake Falls, NY	ALB
Copemish, MI	GAY
Copenhagen, NY	OG
Copiague, NY	RVC
Coplay, PA	ALN
Copley, OH	CLV
Coppell, TX	DAL
Copperas Cove, TX	AUS
Copperhill, TN	KNX
Copperopolis, CA	STO
Copperton, UT	SLC
Coquille, OR	P
Coral, PA	GBG
Coral Gables, FL	MIA
Coral Springs, FL	MIA
FL	SYM
Coralville, IA	DAV
Coram, NY	RVC
Coraopolis, PA	PIT
Corbin, KY	LEX
Corcoran, CA	FRS
Cordele, GA	SAV
Cordova, AK	ANC
TN	MEM
Corfu, NY	BUF
Corinth, MS	JKS
NY	ALB
Cornelius, OR	P
Cornell, WI	LC
Corning, AR	LR
CA	SAC
IA	DM
KS	KCK
NY	ROC
OH	COL
Cornville, AZ	PHX
Cornwall, NY	NY
PA	HBG
Cornwall–on–Hudson, NY	NY
Corona, CA	SB
NY	BRK
Coronado, CA	SD
Corpus Christi, TX	CC
Corrales, NM	SFE
Corralitos, CA	MRY
Corry, PA	E
Corsicana, TX	DAL
Cortaro, AZ	TUC
Cortez, CO	PBL
Cortland, NE	LIN
NY	SY
OH	Y
Cortlandt Manor, NY	NY
NY	SYM
Corvallis, OR	P
Corydon, IN	IND
Coshocton, OH	COL
Costa Mesa, CA	ORG
Cotati, CA	SR

Cottage City, MD	WDC
Cottage Grove, MN	STP
OR	P
WI	MAD
Cottonport, LA	ALX
Cottonwood, AZ	PHX
ID	B
MN	NU
Cotulla, TX	LAR
Coudersport, PA	E
Coulee City, WA	YAK
Council Bluffs, IA	DM
Council Grove, KS	WCH
Country Club Hills, IL	CHI
Countryside, IL	CHI
Coupon, PA	ALT
Coushatta, LA	SHP
Coventry, CT	NOR
RI	PRO
Covina, CA	LA
Covington, GA	ATL
IN	LFT
KY	COV
LA	NO
OH	CIN
TN	MEM
VA	RIC
WA	SEA
Coweta, OK	TLS
Cowiche, WA	YAK
Cox's Creek, KY	L
Coxsackie, NY	ALB
Cozad, NE	GI
Crabtree, PA	GBG
Craig, AK	JUN
CO	DEN
Cranberry Township, PA	PIT
Crandon, WI	GB
WI	SUP
Crane, TX	SAN
Cranford, NJ	NEW
Cranston, RI	PRO
Crawford, NE	GI
Crawfordsville, IN	LFT
Crawfordville, FL	PT
Creighton, NE	OM
PA	PIT
Cresaptown, MD	BAL
Crescent, PA	PIT
Crescent City, CA	SR
FL	STA
Crescent Springs, KY	COV
Cresco, IA	DUB
PA	PSC
PA	SCR
Cresskill, NJ	NEW
Cresson, PA	ALT
Crest Hill, IL	JOL
Crestline, CA	SB
OH	TOL
Creston, IA	DM
Crestone, CO	PBL
Crestview, FL	PT
Crestview Hills, KY	COV
Crestwood, KY	L
MO	STL
NY	NY
Crete, NE	LIN
Creve Coeur, IL	PEO
MO	STL
Crivitz, WI	GB
Crockett, CA	OAK
TX	TYL
Crofton, MD	BAL
NE	OM
Croghan, NY	OG
Cromwell, CT	NOR
Crookston, MN	CR
Crooksville, OH	COL
Cropwell, AL	BIR
Crosby, MN	DUL
ND	BIS
TX	GAL
Cross Plains, WI	MAD
Cross Village, MI	GAY
Crossett, AR	LR
Crosslake, MN	DUL
Crossville, TN	KNX
Croswell, MI	SAG
Croton Falls, NY	NY
Croton–on–Hudson, NY	NY
Crow Agency, MT	GF
Crowley, LA	LAF
TX	FWT
Crown, PA	E
Crown Point, IN	GRY
Crownpoint, NM	GLP
Crownsville, MD	BAL
Croydon, PA	PH
Crozet, VA	RIC
Crystal, MN	STP

Crystal City, MO	STL
TX	LAR
Crystal Falls, MI	MAR
Crystal Lake, IL	RCK
Crystal River, FL	SP
Crystal Springs, MS	JKS
Cuba, MO	JC
NM	GLP
NY	BUF
Cuba City, WI	MAD
Cudahy, CA	LA
WI	MIL
Cuero, TX	VIC
Cullman, AL	BIR
Cullom, IL	PEO
Culpeper, VA	ARL
Culver, IN	FTW
Culver City, CA	LA
Cumberland, IA	DM
KY	LEX
MD	BAL
RI	PRO
WI	SUP
Cumming, GA	ATL
Cunningham, KS	WCH
Cupertino, CA	SJ
Curdsville, KY	OWN
Curtis, NE	LIN
Curtis Bay, MD	BAL
Curwensville, PA	E
Cushing, OK	TLS
Custar, OH	TOL
Custer, MI	GR
SD	RC
WI	LC
Cut Bank, MT	HEL
Cut–Off, LA	HT
Cutchogue, NY	RVC
Cutler, CA	FRS
Cutler Bay, FL	MIA
Cuyahoga Falls, OH	CLV
Cynthiana, KY	COV
Cypress, CA	ORG
D'Hanis, TX	SAT
D'Iberville, MS	BLX
Dade City, FL	SP
Dahlgren, IL	BEL
Dahlonega, GA	ATL
Daingerfield, TX	TYL
Dakota Dunes, SD	SFS
Dale, IN	EVN
Dale City, VA	ARL
Dalhart, TX	AMA
Dallas, GA	ATL
OR	P
PA	SCR
TX	DAL
Dallastown, PA	HBG
Dalton, GA	ATL
MA	SPR
PA	SCR
Daly City, CA	SFR
Dalzell, IL	PEO
Damar, KS	SAL
Damascus, MD	WDC
Damiansville, IL	BEL
Damon, TX	GAL
Dana Point, CA	ORG
Danbury, CT	BGP
CT	NTN
CT	SAM
CT	PSC
IA	SC
TX	GAL
Dane, WI	MAD
Dania Beach, FL	MIA
Danielson, CT	NOR
Dannemora, NY	OG
Dante, SD	SFS
Danvers, MA	BO
Danville, CA	OAK
IL	PEO
IN	IND
KY	LEX
OH	COL
PA	HBG
VA	RIC
Daphne, AL	MOB
Darby, PA	PH
Dardanelle, AR	LR
Dardenne Prairie, MO	STL
Darien, CT	BGP
IL	JOL
Darien Center, NY	BUF
Darlington, PA	PIT
WI	MAD
Darnestown, MD	SYM
MD	WDC
Darwin, MN	NU
Dauphin, PA	HBG
Dauphin Island, AL	MOB

Davenport, CA	MRY
IA	DAV
WA	SPK
Davey, NE	LIN
David City, NE	LIN
Davidson, NC	CHL
Davidsonville, MD	BAL
Davidsville, PA	ALT
Davie, FL	MIA
Davis, CA	SAC
Davisburg, MI	DET
Davison, MI	LAN
Dawson, MN	NU
NE	LIN
Dawson Springs, KY	OWN
Dawsonville, GA	ATL
Dayton, KY	COV
MN	STP
NV	RNO
OH	CIN
OH	PRM
OH	OLL
TN	KNX
TX	BEA
WA	SPK
WY	CHY
Daytona Beach, FL	ORL
Dayville, CT	NOR
De Forest, WI	MAD
De Funiak Springs, FL	PT
De Motte, IN	LFT
De Pere, WI	GB
De Queen, AR	LR
De Ridder, LA	LKC
De Smet, SD	SFS
De Soto, MO	STL
De Witt, MI	LAN
DeBary, FL	ORL
DeKalb, IL	RCK
DeLand, FL	ORL
DePue, IL	PEO
DeQuincy, LA	LKC
DeSmet, ID	B
DeTour, MI	MAR
DeWitt, IA	DAV
NY	SY
Deal, NJ	TR
Dearborn, MI	DET
MI	ROM
MI	STN
Dearborn Heights, MI	DET
MI	STN
Deatsville, AL	MOB
Decatur, AL	BIR
GA	ATL
IL	SFD
IN	FTW
MI	KAL
TX	FWT
Decherd, TN	NSH
Decorah, IA	DUB
Dedham, IA	SC
MA	BO
Deep River, CT	NOR
Deephaven, MN	STP
Deer Lodge, MT	HEL
Deer Park, NY	RVC
TX	GAL
WA	SPK
Deer River, MN	DUL
Deerbrook, WI	GB
Deerfield, IL	CHI
KS	DOD
MI	LAN
Deerfield Beach, FL	MIA
Defiance, IA	DM
MO	STL
OH	TOL
Deford, MI	SAG
Del City, OK	OKL
Del Norte, CO	PBL
Del Rio, TX	SAT
Deland, FL	ORL
Delano, CA	FRS
MN	STP
Delanson, NY	ALB
Delavan, IL	PEO
WI	MIL
Delaware, OH	COL
Delaware City, DE	WIL
Delcambre, LA	LAF
Delhi, IA	DUB
NY	ALB
Dell Rapids, SD	SFS
Delmar, IA	DAV
NY	ALB
Delmont, PA	GBG
Delphi, IN	LFT
Delphos, OH	TOL
Delran, NJ	TR
Delray Beach, FL	NTN
FL	PMB
Delta, CO	PBL
Delta Junction, AK	FBK
Delton, MI	KAL
Deltona, FL	ORL
Demarest, NJ	NEW
Deming, NM	LSC
Demopolis, AL	BIR
Demotte, IN	LFT
Denham Springs, LA	BR
Denison, IA	SC
TX	DAL
Denmark, WI	GB
Dennison, OH	COL
Dent, MN	SCL
Denton, NE	LIN
TX	FWT
Denver, CO	DEN
CO	STN
CO	VNN
NC	CHL
Denver City, TX	LUB
Denville, NJ	PAT
Depauw, IN	IND
Depew, NY	BUF
Deposit, NY	SY
Deptford, NJ	CAM
Dequincy, LA	LKC
Derby, CT	HRT
KS	WCH
NY	BUF
Derby Line, VT	BUR
Derry, NH	MAN
PA	GBG
Derwood, MD	WDC
Des Allemands, LA	NO
Des Moines, IA	DM
WA	SEA
Des Plaines, IL	CHI
Descanso, CA	SD
Desert Hot Springs, CA	SB
Deshler, OH	TOL
Destin, FL	PT
Destrehan, LA	NO
Detroit, MI	DET
MI	ROM
MI	STN
MI	OLL
MI	EST
Detroit Lakes, MN	CR
Deville, LA	ALX
Devils Lake, ND	FAR
Devine, TX	SAT
Devon, PA	PH
Dewey, OK	TLS
Dexter, ME	PRT
MI	LAN
MO	SPC
NM	LSC
Diamond Bar, CA	LA
Diamondhead, MS	BLX
Diberville, MS	BLX
Diboll, TX	TYL
Dickeyville, WI	MAD
Dickinson, ND	BIS
TX	GAL
Dickson, TN	NSH
Dickson City, PA	SCR
Dieterich, IL	SFD
Dighton, KS	DOD
MA	FR
Dilley, TX	SAT
Dillingham, AK	ANC
Dillon, MT	HEL
SC	CHR
Dilworth, MN	CR
Dime Box, TX	AUS
Dimmitt, TX	AMA
Dimock, SD	SFS
Dinuba, CA	FRS
Dittmer, MO	STL
Dix Hills, NY	RVC
Dixon, CA	SAC
IL	RCK
MO	JC
NM	SFE
Dobbs Ferry, NY	NY
Dodge, NE	OM
WI	LC
Dodge Center, MN	WIN
Dodge City, KS	DOD
Dodgeville, WI	MAD
Doland, SD	SFS
Dolgeville, NY	ALB
Dona Ana, NM	LSC
Donaldson, IN	FTW
Donaldsonville, LA	BR
Donegal, PA	GBG
Doniphan, MO	SPC
NE	LIN
Donna, TX	BWN
Donora, PA	PBR
PA	PIT
Doral, FL	ARL
FL	MIA
Doraville, GA	ATL
Dorchester, MA	BO
Dorr, MI	KAL
Dos Palos, CA	FRS
Dothan, AL	MOB
Douglas, AZ	TUC
GA	SAV
MA	WOR
MI	KAL
WY	CHY
Douglassville, PA	ALN
Douglaston, NY	BRK
Douglasville, GA	ATL
Dousman, WI	MIL
Dover, DE	WIL
MA	BO
NH	MAN
NH	SAM
NJ	PAT
OH	COL
TN	NSH
Dover Plains, NY	NY
Dow City, IA	SC
Dowagiac, MI	KAL
Downers Grove, IL	JOL
Downey, CA	LA
Downieville, CA	SAC
Downingtown, PA	PH
Downs, IL	PEO
Doylesburg, PA	HBG
Doylestown, OH	CLV
PA	PH
WI	MAD
Dracut, MA	BO
Drake, ND	FAR
Draper, UT	SLC
Drayton, ND	FAR
Dresden, OH	COL
Drexel Hill, PA	PH
Dripping Springs, TX	AUS
Drummond, MT	HEL
Drums, PA	SCR
Dryden, MI	DET
Du Bois, PA	E
PA	PBR
Du Quoin, IL	BEL
Duarte, CA	LA
Dublin, CA	OAK
GA	SAV
OH	COL
Dubois, IL	BEL
IN	EVN
Dubuque, IA	DUB
Dudley, MA	WOR
PA	ALT
Dufur, OR	BAK
Dulac, LA	HT
Dulce, NM	GLP
Duluth, GA	ATL
MN	DUL
MN	SUP
Dumas, AR	LR
TX	AMA
Dumfries, VA	ARL
Dumont, NJ	NEW
Dunbar, PA	GBG
Duncan, OK	OKL
Duncansville, PA	ALT
Duncanville, TX	DAL
Dundee, IL	RCK
MI	DET
Dunedin, FL	SP
Dunellen, NJ	MET
NJ	PSC
Dunkerton, IA	DUB
Dunkirk, IN	LFT
NY	BUF
Dunlap, IA	DM
TN	KNX
Dunmore, PA	PSC
PA	SCR
Dunn, NC	R
Dunnellon, FL	ORL
Dunseith, ND	FAR
Dunsmuir, CA	SAC
Dunwoody, GA	ATL
Dupo, IL	BEL
Dupont, LA	ALX
PA	SCR
Duquesne, PA	PBR
PA	PIT
Durand, IL	RCK
MI	LAN
WI	LC
Durango, CO	PBL
Durant, OK	TLS
Durham, CT	NOR
NC	R
NH	MAN
Durhamville, NY	SY
Duryea, PA	SCR
Dushore, PA	SCR
Duson, LA	LAF
Dutton, MT	HEL
Duvall, WA	SEA
Duxbury, MA	BO
Dwight, IL	PEO
NE	LIN
Dyer, IN	GRY
Dyersburg, TN	MEM
Dyersville, IA	DUB
Dysart, PA	ALT
Eagan, MN	STP
Eagle, ID	B
WI	MIL
Eagle Butte, SD	RC
Eagle Grove, IA	DUB
Eagle Harbor, MI	STN
Eagle Lake, TX	VIC
Eagle Pass, TX	LAR
Eagle River, AK	ANC
WI	SUP
Earlimart, CA	FRS
Earling, IA	DM
Earlington, KY	OWN
Earlville, IA	DUB
IL	PEO
Early, IA	SC
Earth City, MO	STL
East Aurora, NY	BUF
East Berlin, CT	HRT
East Bernard, TX	VIC
East Bethany, NY	BUF
East Bloomfield, NY	ROC
East Boston, MA	BO
East Brady, PA	E
PA	GBG
East Bridgewater, MA	BO
East Brookfield, MA	WOR
East Brunswick, NJ	MET
NJ	PSC
East Carbon, UT	SLC
East Chicago, IN	GRY
IN	ROM
East China, MI	DET
East Dubuque, IL	RCK
East Elmhurst, NY	BRK
East Falmouth, MA	FR
East Freetown, MA	FR
East Glendale, NY	BRK
East Grand Forks, MN	CR
East Grand Rapids, MI	GR
East Greenbush, NY	ALB
East Greenwich, RI	PRO
East Hampton, CT	NOR
NY	RVC
East Hanover, NJ	PAT
East Hartford, CT	HRT
East Haven, CT	HRT
East Helena, MT	HEL
East Islip, NY	RVC
East Jordan, MI	GAY
East Lansdowne, PA	PH
East Lansing, MI	LAN
East Liverpool, OH	Y
East Longmeadow, MA	SPR
East Lyme, CT	NOR
East McKeesport, PA	PIT
East Meadow, NY	RVC
East Millinocket, ME	PRT
East Moline, IL	PEO
East Newark, NJ	NEW
East Norriton, PA	PH
East Northport, NY	RVC
East Orange, NJ	NEW
East Palestine, OH	Y
East Palo Alto, CA	LA
CA	SFR
East Patchogue, NY	RVC
East Peoria, IL	PEO
IL	RCK
East Pittsburgh, PA	PBR
PA	PIT
East Providence, RI	PRO
East Rochester, NY	ROC
East Rockaway, NY	RVC
East Rutherford, NJ	NEW
East Saint Louis, IL	BEL
East Sandwich, MA	FR
East St. Louis, IL	BEL
East Stroudsburg, PA	SCR
East Syracuse, NY	SY
East Taunton, MA	FR
East Tawas, MI	GAY
East Templeton, MA	WOR
East Troy, WI	MIL
East Vandergrift, PA	GBG
East Wenatchee, WA	YAK

East Windsor, CT	HRT
Easthampton, MA	SPR
Eastlake, OH	CLV
Eastman, GA	SAV
WI	LC
Easton, CA	FRS
CT	BGP
KS	KCK
MD	WIL
MO	KC
PA	ALN
PA	SAM
Eastpointe, MI	DET
Eaton, OH	CIN
Eaton Rapids, MI	LAN
Eatontown, NJ	TR
NJ	CAM
Eau Claire, WI	LC
Eau Galle, WI	LC
Ebensburg, PA	ALT
Ebony, VA	RIC
Echo, LA	ALX
Ecorse, MI	DET
Edcouch, TX	BWN
Eddystone, PA	PH
Eddyville, KY	OWN
Eden, NC	CHL
NY	BUF
SD	SFS
TX	SAN
WI	MIL
Eden Prairie, MN	STP
Eden Valley, MN	SCL
Edenton, NC	R
Edgar, WI	LC
Edgard, LA	NO
Edgefield, SC	CHR
Edgeley, ND	FAR
Edgerton, KS	KCK
OH	TOL
WI	MAD
Edgewater, MD	BAL
NJ	NEW
Edgewood, IA	DUB
KY	COV
MD	BAL
Edina, MN	STP
MO	JC
Edinboro, PA	E
Edinburg, TX	BWN
Edinburgh, IN	IND
Edison, NJ	MET
Edisto Island, SC	CHR
Edmond, OK	OKL
Edmonds, WA	SEA
Edmonton, KY	L
Edmore, MI	GR
Edna, TX	VIC
Edroy, TX	CC
Edwards, CO	DEN
Edwardsburg, MI	KAL
Edwardsville, IL	SFD
PA	PHU
Effingham, IL	SFD
KS	KCK
Egg Harbor, WI	GB
Egg Harbor City, NJ	CAM
Egg Harbor Township, NJ	CAM
Eggertsville, NY	BUF
Egypt, OH	CIN
El Cajon, CA	SD
CA	SPA
CA	OLL
El Campo, TX	VIC
El Centro, CA	SD
El Cerrito, CA	OAK
El Dorado, AR	LR
KS	WCH
El Dorado Hills, CA	SAC
CA	SPA
El Dorado Springs, MO	SPC
El Mirage, AZ	PHX
El Monte, CA	LA
El Paso, IL	PEO
TX	ELP
TX	OLL
El Reno, OK	OKL
El Rito, NM	SFE
El Segundo, CA	LA
CA	NTN
El Sobrante, CA	OAK
Elberon, NJ	TR
Elberta, AL	MOB
Elbow Lake, MN	SCL
Elburn, IL	RCK
Elcho, WI	GB
Eldersburg, MD	BAL
Eldon, MO	JC
Eldora, IA	DUB
Eldorado, IL	BEL
TX	SAN

WI	MIL
Eldred, PA	E
Eldridge, IA	DAV
Elgin, IL	RCK
NE	OM
OK	OKL
OR	BAK
TX	AUS
Elizabeth, CO	COS
IL	RCK
MN	SCL
NJ	NEW
NJ	PHU
NJ	PSC
PA	PIT
Elizabeth City, NC	R
Elizabethton, TN	KNX
Elizabethtown, IL	BEL
KY	L
NY	OG
PA	HBG
Elk City, OK	OKL
Elk Grove, CA	SAC
Elk Grove Village, IL	CHI
Elk Mound, WI	LC
Elk Point, SD	SFS
Elk Rapids, MI	GAY
Elk River, MN	SCL
Elkader, IA	DUB
Elkhart, IA	DM
IL	PEO
IN	FTW
KS	DOD
Elkhart Lake, WI	MIL
Elkhorn, NE	OM
WI	MIL
Elkins, WV	WH
Elkins Park, PA	PH
Elkland, PA	SCR
Elko, NV	RNO
Elkridge, MD	BAL
Elkton, FL	STA
KY	OWN
MD	WIL
VA	RIC
Elkview, WV	WH
Ellenburg, NY	OG
Ellenburg Center, NY	OG
Ellendale, ND	FAR
Ellensburg, WA	YAK
Ellenville, NY	NY
Ellicott City, MD	BAL
Ellicottville, NY	BUF
Ellijay, GA	ATL
Ellington, CT	NOR
Ellinwood, KS	DOD
Ellis, KS	SAL
Ellis Grove, IL	BEL
Ellisville, MO	STL
Ellsworth, KS	SAL
ME	PRT
WI	LC
Ellwood City, PA	PIT
Elm Creek, NE	GI
Elm Grove, WI	MIL
Elma, IA	DUB
NY	BUF
WA	SEA
Elmendorf, TX	SAT
Elmer, NJ	CAM
Elmhurst, IL	JOL
IL	SYM
NY	BRK
PA	SCR
Elmira, MI	GAY
NY	ROC
Elmira Heights, NY	STF
Elmont, NY	RVC
Elmore, AL	MOB
OH	DET
Elmsford, NY	NY
Elmwood, IL	PEO
WI	LC
Elmwood Park, IL	CHI
NJ	NEW
Elon, NC	R
Eloy, AZ	TUC
Elrama, PA	PIT
Elrosa, MN	SCL
Elsa, TX	BWN
Elsberry, MO	STL
Elsmere, KY	COV
Elton, LA	LKC
Eltopia, WA	SPK
Elverson, PA	PH
Elwood, IN	LFT
Ely, MN	DUL
NV	LAV
Elyria, OH	CLV
Elyria Township, OH	CLV
Elysburg, PA	HBG

Elysian, MN	STP
Emerson, NE	OM
NJ	NEW
Emery, SD	SFS
Emeryville, CA	OAK
Emily, MN	DUL
Emlenton, PA	E
Emmaus, PA	ALN
Emmetsburg, IA	SC
Emmett, ID	B
MI	DET
Emmitsburg, MD	BAL
Emmonak, AK	FBK
Empire, MI	GAY
Emporia, KS	KCK
Emporium, PA	E
Encinal, TX	LAR
Encinitas, CA	SD
Encino, CA	LA
Enderlin, ND	FAR
Endicott, NY	SY
Endwell, NY	SY
Enfield, CT	HRT
NH	MAN
England, AR	LR
Englewood, CO	DEN
FL	VEN
NJ	NEW
OH	CIN
Englewood Cliffs, NJ	NEW
Enid, OK	OKL
Ennis, TX	DAL
Enola, PA	HBG
Enosburg Falls, VT	BUR
Enterprise, AL	MOB
OR	BAK
Enumclaw, WA	SEA
Ephraim, UT	SLC
Ephrata, PA	HBG
WA	YAK
Epping, NH	MAN
Epworth, IA	DUB
Equality, IL	BEL
Erath, LA	LAF
Erdenheim, PA	PH
Erie, KS	WCH
MI	DET
PA	E
PA	PBR
Erlanger, KY	COV
Ernest, PA	PBR
Escanaba, MI	MAR
Escondido, CA	SD
Esmond, ND	FAR
Esopus, NY	NY
Espanola, NM	SFE
Essex, CT	NOR
MA	BO
Essex Junction, VT	BUR
Essexville, MI	SAG
Essington, PA	PH
Estacada, OR	P
Estes Park, CO	DEN
Estherville, IA	SC
Ettrick, WI	LC
Euclid, MN	CR
OH	CLV
OH	PRM
Eudora, KS	KCK
Eufaula, AL	MOB
Eugene, MO	JC
OR	P
Eunice, LA	LAF
Eupora, MS	JKS
Eureka, CA	SR
IL	PEO
KS	WCH
MO	STL
MT	HEL
NV	RNO
SD	SFS
Eureka Springs, AR	LR
Eustis, FL	ORL
Eutaw, AL	BIR
Evangeline, LA	LAF
Evans City, PA	PIT
Evans Mills, NY	OG
Evanston, IL	CHI
WY	CHY
Evansville, IL	BEL
IN	EVN
WI	MAD
Evart, MI	GR
Eveleth, MN	DUL
Everett, MA	BO
PA	ALT
WA	SEA
Evergreen, CO	DEN
LA	ALX
Evergreen Park, IL	CHI
Everson, PA	GBG

Ewa, HI	HON
Ewa Beach, HI	HON
Ewen, MI	MAR
Ewing, MO	JC
NE	OM
Excelsior, MN	STP
Excelsior Springs, MO	KC
Exeter, CA	FRS
NE	LIN
NH	MAN
PA	SCR
RI	PRO
Export, PA	GBG
Exton, PA	PH
Eynon, PA	SCR
Fabens, TX	ELP
Fair Haven, NJ	TR
VT	BUR
Fair Lawn, NJ	NEW
Fair Oaks, CA	SAC
Fairbank, IA	DUB
Fairbanks, AK	FBK
Fairborn, OH	CIN
Fairbury, IL	PEO
NE	LIN
Fairchance, PA	GBG
Fairchild, WI	LC
Fairdale, KY	L
Fairfax, CA	SFR
IA	DUB
MN	NU
OK	TLS
SD	RC
VA	ARL
VT	BUR
Fairfield, CA	SAC
CT	BGP
IA	DAV
IL	BEL
KY	L
MT	HEL
NJ	NEW
OH	CIN
PA	HBG
TX	TYL
VT	BUR
Fairfield Bay, AR	LR
Fairfield Glade, TN	KNX
Fairhaven, MA	FR
Fairhope, AL	MOB
Fairlawn, OH	CLV
OH	OLL
Fairless Hills, PA	PH
Fairmont, MN	SFS
MN	WIN
WV	WH
Fairmont City, IL	BEL
Fairmount, ND	FAR
NY	SY
Fairport, NY	ROC
Fairport Harbor, OH	CLV
Fairview, NJ	NEW
PA	E
Fairview Heights, IL	BEL
Fairview Park, OH	CLV
OH	PRM
Faith, SD	RC
Falcon, CO	COS
Falconer, NY	BUF
Falfurrias, TX	CC
Fall Creek, WI	LC
Fall River, MA	FR
MA	STF
MA	SAM
Fallbrook, CA	SD
Fallentimber, PA	ALT
Fallon, NV	RNO
Falls Church, VA	ARL
Falls City, NE	LIN
TX	SAT
Falls Creek, PA	E
Fallsington, PA	PH
Fallston, MD	BAL
Falmouth, KY	COV
KY	SYM
MA	FR
ME	PRT
Fancy Farm, KY	OWN
Far Hills, NJ	MET
Far Rockaway, NY	BRK
Fargo, ND	FAR
Faribault, MN	STP
Farley, IA	DUB
Farmer City, IL	PEO
Farmers Branch, TX	DAL
Farmersville, IL	SFD
Farmingdale, NJ	TR
NY	RVC
Farmington, CT	HRT
IA	DAV
IL	PEO

ME	PRT
MI	DET
MI	SYM
MI	OLN
MN	STP
MO	STL
NH	MAN
NM	GLP
PA	GBG
Farmington Hills, MI	DET
Farmingville, NY	RVC
Farmville, NC	R
VA	RIC
Farnham, NY	BUF
Farrell, PA	E
Faulkner, MD	WDC
Faulkton, SD	SFS
Fayette, IA	DUB
MO	JC
MS	JKS
OH	TOL
Fayetteville, AR	LR
GA	ATL
IL	BEL
NC	R
NC	SAM
NY	SY
OH	CIN
TN	NSH
TX	AUS
Feasterville, PA	PH
Federal Way, WA	SEA
Feeding Hills, MA	SPR
Fellsmere, FL	PMB
Felton, CA	MRY
Fenelton, PA	PIT
Fennimore, WI	MAD
Fennville, MI	KAL
Fenton, LA	LKC
MI	LAN
MO	STL
Ferdinand, IN	EVN
Fergus Falls, MN	SCL
Ferguson, MO	STL
Fernandina Beach, FL	STA
Ferndale, CA	SR
MI	DET
WA	SEA
Fernley, NV	RNO
Ferriday, LA	ALX
Ferris, TX	DAL
Fertile, MN	CR
Fessenden, ND	FAR
Festus, MO	STL
Fife, WA	SEA
Fillmore, CA	LA
NY	BUF
Fincastle, VA	RIC
Findlay, OH	TOL
Finleyville, PA	PIT
Firebaugh, CA	FRS
Fisher, MN	CR
Fishers, IN	LFT
Fishers Island, NY	NOR
Fishkill, NY	NY
Fiskdale, MA	WOR
Fitchburg, MA	WOR
Flagler Beach, FL	STA
Flagstaff, AZ	PHX
Flanders, NJ	PAT
NJ	PSC
Flandreau, SD	SFS
Flasher, ND	BIS
Flat Rock, MI	DET
Flatonia, TX	VIC
Fleming Island, FL	STA
Flemingsburg, KY	COV
Flemington, NJ	MET
Flint, MI	LAN
MI	OLL
TX	TYL
Flint Hill, MO	STL
Floodwood, MN	DUL
Flora, IL	BEL
Floral City, FL	SP
Floral Park, NY	BRK
NY	RVC
Florence, AL	BIR
AZ	TUC
CO	PBL
KY	COV
MA	SPR
OR	P
SC	CHR
SD	SFS
TX	AUS
WI	GB
Floresville, TX	SAT
Florham Park, NJ	PAT
Florida, NY	NY
Florissant, MO	STL

Flossmoor, IL	CHI
Flourtown, PA	PH
Flowery Branch, GA	ATL
Flowood, MS	JKS
Floydada, TX	LUB
Floyds Knobs, IN	IND
Flushing, MI	LAN
MI	PRM
NY	BRK
OH	STU
Foley, AL	MOB
MN	SCL
Follansbee, WV	WH
Folly Beach, SC	CHR
Folsom, CA	SAC
LA	NO
Fond Du Lac, WI	MIL
Fond du Lac, WI	MIL
Fonda, IA	SC
NY	ALB
Fontana, CA	SB
CA	VNN
WI	MIL
Footville, WI	MAD
Force, PA	E
Ford City, PA	GBG
PA	SJP
Fordsville, KY	OWN
Fordyce, AR	LR
NE	OM
Foreman, AR	LR
Forest, MS	JKS
Forest City, IA	DUB
NC	CHL
PA	SCR
Forest Grove, OR	P
Forest Hill, MD	BAL
Forest Hills, NY	BRK
Forest Lake, MN	STP
Forest Park, IL	CHI
Forestburgh, NY	NY
Foreston, MN	SCL
Forestport, NY	SY
Forestville, CT	HRT
MD	WDC
Forked River, NJ	TR
Forks, WA	SEA
Forman, ND	FAR
Forney, TX	DAL
Forrest City, AR	LR
Forsyth, MO	SPC
MT	GF
Fort Ann, NY	ALB
Fort Ashby, WV	WH
Fort Atkinson, WI	MAD
Fort Benton, MT	GF
Fort Bragg, CA	SR
Fort Branch, IN	EVN
Fort Calhoun, NE	OM
Fort Collins, CO	DEN
Fort Covington, NY	OG
Fort Davis, TX	ELP
Fort Defiance, AZ	GLP
Fort Dodge, IA	SC
Fort Edward, NY	ALB
Fort Gratiot, MI	DET
Fort Hancock, TX	ELP
Fort Jennings, OH	TOL
Fort Jones, CA	SAC
Fort Kent, ME	PRT
Fort Lauderdale, FL	MIA
Fort Leavenworth, KS	KCK
Fort Lee, NJ	NEW
Fort Loramie, OH	CIN
Fort Lupton, CO	DEN
Fort Madison, IA	DAV
Fort McClellan, AL	BIR
Fort Mill, SC	CHR
Fort Mitchell, AL	MOB
KY	COV
Fort Monroe, VA	RIC
Fort Morgan, CO	DEN
Fort Myers, FL	VEN
Fort Myers Beach, FL	VEN
Fort Oglethorpe, GA	ATL
Fort Payne, AL	BIR
Fort Pierce, FL	PMB
FL	PSC
Fort Pierre, SD	RC
Fort Plain, NY	ALB
Fort Recovery, OH	CIN
Fort Scott, KS	WCH
Fort Shaw, MT	GF
Fort Smith, AR	LR
Fort Stockton, TX	SAN
Fort Sumner, NM	SFE
Fort Thomas, KY	COV
Fort Thompson, SD	SFS
Fort Totten, ND	FAR
Fort Walton Beach, FL	PT
Fort Washington, MD	WDC

Fort Wayne, IN	FTW
Fort Worth, TX	FWT
Fort Wright, KY	COV
Fort Yates, ND	BIS
Fortuna, CA	SR
Fortville, IN	IND
Fosston, MN	CR
Foster, RI	PRO
Foster City, CA	SFR
Fostoria, OH	TOL
Fountain City, WI	LC
Fountain Hill, PA	ALN
Fountain Hills, AZ	PHX
Fountain Valley, CA	ORG
Fowler, CA	FRS
IN	LFT
KS	DOD
MI	LAN
Fowlerville, MI	LAN
Fox Chase Manor, PA	PH
PA	PHU
Fox Lake, WI	MIL
Fox Point, WI	MIL
Foxborough, MA	BO
Foxfield, CO	DEN
Foxholm, ND	BIS
Frackville, PA	ALN
PA	PHU
Framingham, MA	BO
MA	SYM
Francis Creek, WI	GB
Frankenmuth, MI	SAG
Frankfort, IL	JOL
IN	LFT
KS	KCK
KY	LEX
MI	GAY
NY	ALB
Franklin, IN	IND
KY	OWN
LA	LAF
MA	BO
MN	NU
NC	CHL
NH	MAN
NJ	PAT
OH	CIN
PA	E
TN	NSH
TX	AUS
VA	RIC
WI	MIL
WV	WH
Franklin Furnace, OH	STU
Franklin Lakes, NJ	NEW
Franklin Park, IL	CHI
Franklin Square, NY	RVC
Franklinton, LA	NO
Franklinville, NJ	CAM
NY	BUF
Fraser, MI	DET
Frazee, MN	CR
Frazier Park, CA	FRS
Frederic, WI	SUP
Frederick, CO	DEN
MD	BAL
Fredericksburg, TX	SAT
VA	ARL
Fredericktown, MO	SPC
PA	PIT
Fredonia, KS	WCH
NY	BUF
WI	MIL
Free Soil, MI	GR
Freeburg, IL	BEL
MO	JC
Freedom, PA	PIT
WI	GB
Freehold, NJ	TR
Freeland, MI	SAG
PA	PSC
PA	SCR
Freeport, IL	RCK
MN	SCL
NY	RVC
PA	GBG
TX	GAL
Freer, TX	CC
Freeville, NY	ROC
Fremont, CA	SJ
CA	SYM
CA	OAK
MI	GR
NE	OM
OH	TOL
French Lick, IN	IND
French Settlement, LA	BR
Frenchburg, KY	LEX
Frenchtown, MT	HEL
Frenchville, ME	PRT
PA	E

Fresh Meadows, NY	BRK
NY	STF
Fresno, CA	FRS
Friday Harbor, WA	SEA
Fridley, MN	STP
Friend, NE	LIN
Friendsville, PA	SCR
Friendswood, TX	GAL
Friona, TX	AMA
Frisco, CO	DEN
TX	DAL
Front Royal, VA	ARL
Frontenac, KS	WCH
MN	STP
MO	STL
Frostburg, MD	BAL
Fruita, CO	PBL
Fruitland, ID	B
Fryburg, PA	E
Fulda, MN	WIN
Fullerton, CA	OLL
CA	ORG
NE	OM
Fulton, IL	RCK
KY	OWN
MD	BAL
MO	JC
NY	SY
TX	CC
Fultonville, NY	ALB
Fuquay–Varina, NC	R
Gadsden, AL	BIR
Gaffney, SC	CHR
Gagetown, MI	SAG
Gahanna, OH	COL
Gaines, MI	LAN
Gainesville, FL	STA
GA	ATL
TX	FWT
VA	ARL
Gaithersburg, MD	WDC
Galena, AK	FBK
IL	RCK
MD	WIL
Galena Park, TX	GAL
Gales Ferry, CT	NOR
Galesburg, IL	PEO
Galeton, PA	E
Galion, OH	TOL
Gallatin, TN	NSH
Galliano, LA	HT
Gallipolis, OH	STU
Gallitzin, PA	ALT
Galloway, NJ	CAM
Gallup, NM	GLP
Galt, CA	SAC
Galva, IL	PEO
Galveston, TX	GAL
Gambrills, MD	BAL
Ganado, AZ	GLP
TX	VIC
Garberville, CA	SR
Garciasville, TX	BWN
Garden, MI	MAR
Garden City, KS	DOD
MI	DET
NY	RVC
SC	CHR
TX	SAN
Garden Grove, CA	ORG
Garden Plain, KS	WCH
Gardena, CA	LA
Gardendale, AL	BIR
Gardiner, NY	NY
Gardner, KS	KCK
MA	WOR
Gardnerville, NV	RNO
Garfield, NJ	NEW
NJ	SYM
NM	LSC
Garfield Heights, OH	CLV
Garland, TX	DAL
TX	SYM
Garner, IA	DUB
NC	R
NC	SJP
Garnerville, NY	NY
Garnett, KS	KCK
Garretson, SD	SFS
Garrett, IN	FTW
Garrett Park, MD	WDC
Garrettsville, OH	Y
Garrison, MN	DUL
ND	BIS
NY	NY
Garwood, NJ	NEW
Gary, IN	GRY
WV	WH
Garyville, LA	NO
Gas City, IN	LFT
Gassaway, WV	WH

Gastonia, NC	CHL
Gate City, VA	RIC
Gates Mills, OH	CLV
Gatesville, TX	AUS
Gatlinburg, TN	KNX
Gautier, MS	BLX
Gaylord, MI	GAY
MN	NU
Gays Mills, WI	LC
Geddes, SD	SFS
Genesee, ID	B
Genesee Depot, WI	MIL
Geneseo, IL	PEO
ND	FAR
NY	ROC
Geneva, IL	RCK
IN	FTW
NE	LIN
NY	ROC
OH	Y
Genoa, IL	RCK
NE	OM
OH	TOL
WI	LC
George West, TX	CC
Georgetown, CA	SAC
CT	BGP
DE	WIL
IL	PEO
IN	IND
KY	LEX
MA	BO
MN	CR
OH	CIN
SC	CHR
TX	AUS
Georgiaville, RI	PRO
Gering, NE	GI
Germantown, IL	BEL
MD	WDC
NY	ALB
OH	CIN
TN	MEM
WI	MIL
Gervais, OR	P
Gettysburg, PA	HBG
SD	SFS
Getzville, NY	BUF
Ghent, MN	NU
Gibbon, MN	NU
Gibbsboro, NJ	CAM
Gibbstown, NJ	CAM
Gibraltar, MI	DET
Gibson, LA	HT
Gibson City, IL	JOL
Gibsonburg, OH	TOL
Gibsonia, PA	PBR
PA	PIT
Giddings, TX	AUS
Gig Harbor, WA	SEA
Gilbert, AZ	PHX
AZ	VNN
IA	DUB
MN	DUL
Gilberts, IL	RCK
Gilbertville, IA	DUB
MA	WOR
Gilford, NH	MAN
Gillespie, IL	SFD
Gillett, WI	GB
Gillette, WY	CHY
Gilman, IL	JOL
MN	SCL
WI	SUP
Gilmer, TX	TYL
Gilroy, CA	SJ
Girard, KS	WCH
OH	Y
PA	E
PA	PBR
Girardville, PA	ALN
Gladewater, TX	TYL
Gladstone, MI	MAR
MO	KC
NJ	PAT
Gladwin, MI	SAG
Gladwyne, PA	PH
Glandorf, OH	TOL
Glasco, NY	NY
Glasgow, KY	L
MO	JC
MT	GF
Glassboro, NJ	CAM
Glassport, PA	PIT
Glastonbury, CT	HRT
CT	STF
Glen Allen, VA	RIC
VA	SAM
Glen Burnie, MD	BAL
Glen Carbon, IL	SFD
Glen Cove, NY	RVC
NY	STF
Glen Dale, WV	WH
Glen Echo, MD	WDC
Glen Ellyn, IL	JOL
Glen Head, NY	RVC
Glen Lyon, PA	SCR
Glen Mills, PA	PH
Glen Rock, NJ	NEW
Glen Rose, TX	FWT
Glen Ullin, ND	BIS
Glenburn, ND	BIS
Glencoe, MN	NU
Glendale, AZ	PHX
AZ	SPA
CA	LA
CA	OLN
NY	BRK
WI	MIL
Glendale Heights, IL	JOL
Glendive, MT	GF
Glendora, CA	LA
MS	JKS
Glenmora, LA	ALX
Glennallen, AK	ANC
Glenns Ferry, ID	B
Glenolden, PA	PH
Glenrock, WY	CHY
Glens Falls, NY	ALB
Glenshaw, PA	PIT
Glenside, PA	PH
Glenview, IL	CHI
Glenville, NY	ALB
WV	WH
Glenwood, IA	DM
IL	CHI
MN	SCL
Glenwood Springs, CO	DEN
Globe, AZ	TUC
Gloucester, MA	BO
NJ	CAM
VA	RIC
Gloversville, NY	ALB
Gloverville, SC	CHR
Gluckstadt, MS	JKS
Glyndon, MD	BAL
Gobles, MI	KAL
Goddard, KS	WCH
Godfrey, IL	SFD
Goetzville, MI	MAR
Goffstown, NH	MAN
Gold Hill, OR	P
Golden, CO	DEN
Golden Meadow, LA	HT
Golden Valley, MN	STP
Goldendale, WA	YAK
Goldsboro, NC	R
Goldthwaite, TX	AUS
Goleta, CA	LA
Goliad, TX	VIC
Gonic, NH	MAN
Gonzales, CA	MRY
LA	BR
TX	SAT
Goodhue, MN	STP
Gooding, ID	B
Goodland, KS	SAL
Goodman, WI	GB
Goodrich, MI	LAN
Goodyear, AZ	PHX
AZ	TUC
Goose Creek, SC	CHR
Gordon, NE	GI
PA	ALN
Gorham, KS	SAL
ME	PRT
NH	MAN
Goshen, CT	HRT
IN	FTW
NY	NY
Gouldsboro, PA	SCR
Gouverneur, NY	OG
Gowanda, NY	BUF
Graceville, MN	NU
Graettinger, IA	SC
Graford, TX	FWT
Grafton, IL	SFD
MA	WOR
ND	FAR
NY	ALB
OH	CLV
WI	MIL
WV	WH
Graham, TX	FWT
Grambling, LA	SHP
Grampian, PA	E
Granada Hills, CA	LA
Granbury, TX	FWT
Granby, CO	DEN
CT	HRT
MA	SPR
Grand Bay, AL	MOB
Grand Blanc, MI	LAN
Grand Canyon, AZ	PHX
Grand Chenier, LA	LKC
Grand Coteau, LA	LAF
Grand Coulee, WA	YAK
Grand Forks, ND	FAR
Grand Haven, MI	GR
Grand Island, NE	GI
NY	BUF
Grand Isle, LA	HT
Grand Junction, CO	PBL
IA	SC
Grand Ledge, MI	LAN
Grand Marais, MI	MAR
MN	DUL
Grand Meadow, MN	WIN
Grand Mound, IA	DAV
Grand Prairie, TX	DAL
Grand Rapids, MI	GR
MI	STN
MN	DUL
OH	TOL
Grand Rivers, KY	OWN
Grand Ronde, OR	P
Grand Terrace, CA	SB
Grandview, MO	KC
WA	YAK
Grandville, MI	GR
Granger, IA	DM
IN	FTW
TX	AUS
WA	YAK
Grangeville, ID	B
Granite City, IL	SFD
Granite Falls, MN	NU
Graniteville, VT	BUR
Grant, NE	LIN
Grants, NM	GLP
Grants Pass, OR	P
Grantsville, MD	BAL
Granville, IA	SC
IL	PEO
NY	ALB
OH	COL
Grapevine, TX	FWT
Grass Lake, MI	LAN
Grass Valley, CA	SAC
Gratiot, WI	MAD
Gray, LA	NO
LA	PBR
ME	PRT
Grayling, MI	GAY
Grayslake, IL	CHI
Grayson, KY	LEX
Great Barrington, MA	SPR
Great Bend, KS	DOD
PA	SCR
Great Falls, MT	GF
VA	ARL
Great Meadows, NJ	MET
Great Mills, MD	WDC
Great Neck, NY	RVC
Greeley, CO	DEN
KS	KCK
Green Bay, WI	GB
Green Harbor, MA	BO
Green Isle, MN	NU
Green Lake, WI	MAD
Green Pond, NJ	PAT
Green River, WY	CHY
Green Valley, AZ	TUC
Greenacres, FL	PMB
FL	SAM
Greenbelt, MD	WDC
Greenbush, MN	CR
Greencastle, IN	IND
PA	HBG
Greendale, WI	MIL
Greene, IA	DUB
NY	SY
Greeneville, TN	KNX
Greenfield, CA	MRY
IA	DM
IL	SFD
IN	IND
MA	SPR
OH	CIN
WI	MIL
Greenfield Center, NY	ALB
Greenlawn, NY	RVC
Greenleaf, WI	GB
Greenport, NY	RVC
Greensboro, GA	ATL
NC	CHL
Greensburg, IN	IND
KS	DOD
PA	GBG
PA	PBR
PA	PIT
Greenup, IL	SFD
Greenville, AL	MOB
IL	SFD
ME	PRT
MI	GR
MS	JKS
NC	R
NH	MAN
NY	ALB
OH	CIN
PA	E
RI	PRO
SC	CHR
SC	SAM
TX	DAL
WI	GB
Greenwald, MN	SCL
Greenwell Springs, LA	BR
Greenwich, CT	BGP
NY	ALB
Greenwood, IN	IND
MS	JKS
SC	CHR
WI	LC
Greenwood Lake, NY	NY
Greer, SC	CHR
Gregory, SD	RC
TX	CC
Grenada, MS	JKS
Grenora, ND	BIS
Grenville, SD	SFS
Gresham, OR	P
WI	GB
Gretna, LA	NO
NE	OM
Grey Eagle, MN	SCL
Greybull, WY	CHY
Gridley, CA	SAC
Griffin, GA	ATL
Griffith, IN	GRY
Grinnell, IA	DAV
KS	SAL
Griswold, CT	NOR
IA	DM
Groom, TX	AMA
Grosse Ile, MI	DET
Grosse Pointe, MI	DET
Grosse Pointe Farms, MI	DET
Grosse Pointe Park, MI	DET
Grosse Tete, LA	BR
Groton, CT	NOR
NY	ROC
SD	SFS
Grove, OK	TLS
Grove City, MN	NU
OH	COL
PA	E
Grove Hill, AL	MOB
Groveport, OH	COL
Groves, TX	BEA
Groveton, NH	MAN
Grovetown, GA	SAV
Grulla, TX	BWN
Gruver, TX	AMA
Guadalupe, AZ	PHX
CA	LA
Guasti, CA	SB
Guerneville, CA	SR
Guernsey, WY	CHY
Gueydan, LA	LAF
Guilderland, NY	ALB
Guilderland Center, NY	ALB
Guilford, CT	HRT
IN	IND
Gulf Breeze, FL	PT
Gulf Shores, AL	MOB
Gulfport, FL	SP
MS	BLX
Gun Barrel City, TX	TYL
Gunnison, CO	PBL
Guntersville, AL	BIR
Gurnee, IL	CHI
Gustine, CA	FRS
Guthrie, KY	OWN
OK	OKL
Guthrie Center, IA	DM
Guttenberg, IA	DUB
Guymon, OK	OKL
Guys Mills, PA	E
Gwinn, MI	MAR
Gwynedd Valley, PA	PH
Hacienda Heights, CA	LA
Hackberry, LA	LKC
Hackensack, MN	DUL
NJ	NEW
Hackettstown, NJ	MET
Haddon Heights, NJ	CAM
Haddonfield, NJ	CAM
Hadley, MA	SPR
Hagaman, NY	ALB
Hagerstown, MD	BAL
MD	SYM
Hague, ND	BIS

Hahnville, LA	NO
Haiku, HI	HON
Hailey, ID	B
Haines, AK	JUN
Haines City, FL	ORL
Haines Falls, NY	ALB
Hainesport, NJ	TR
NJ	CAM
Halbur, IA	SC
Hale, MI	GAY
Hale Center, TX	LUB
Haledon, NJ	PAT
Hales Corners, WI	MIL
Halethorpe, MD	BAL
Half Moon Bay, CA	SFR
Hallandale Beach, FL	MIA
Hallettsville, TX	VIC
Hallock, MN	CR
Hallowell, ME	PRT
Halstead, KS	WCH
Haltom City, TX	FWT
Ham Lake, MN	STP
Hamburg, IA	DM
NJ	PAT
NY	BUF
PA	ALN
Hamden, CT	HRT
Hamel, MN	STP
Hamilton, AL	BIR
GA	SAV
MA	BO
MO	KC
MT	HEL
NJ	TR
NY	SY
OH	CIN
TX	AUS
VA	ARL
Hamilton Square, NJ	TR
Hamlet, IN	GRY
NC	CHL
Hamlin, NY	ROC
Hammond, IN	GRY
IN	NTN
LA	BR
WI	SUP
Hammondsport, NY	ROC
Hammonton, NJ	CAM
Hampden, MA	SPR
Hampshire, IL	RCK
Hampstead, NC	R
NH	MAN
Hampton, IA	DUB
MN	STP
NH	MAN
NJ	MET
VA	RIC
Hampton Bays, NY	RVC
Hamptonville, NC	CHL
Hamtramck, MI	DET
MI	STN
Hana, HI	HON
Hanahan, SC	CHR
SC	NTN
Hanceville, AL	BIR
Hancock, MD	BAL
MI	MAR
NY	ALB
Hanford, CA	FRS
Hankinson, ND	FAR
Hannibal, MO	JC
NY	SY
Hanover, IL	RCK
KS	SAL
MA	BO
MD	BAL
NH	MAN
PA	HBG
Hanover Park, IL	CHI
Hanover Township, PA	SCR
Hanoverton, OH	Y
Hanson, MA	BO
Hapeville, GA	ATL
Happy, TX	AMA
Harahan, LA	NO
Harbor Beach, MI	SAG
Harbor Springs, MI	GAY
Harborcreek, PA	E
Hardin, IL	SFD
KY	OWN
MT	GF
Hardinsburg, KY	OWN
Hardwick, VT	BUR
Harker Heights, TX	AUS
Harlan, IA	DM
KY	LEX
Harleigh, PA	SCR
Harlingen, TX	BWN
Harlowton, MT	HEL
Harmony, MN	WIN
Harper, KS	WCH
TX	SAT
Harper Woods, MI	DET
Harriman, NY	NY
TN	KNX
Harrington, WA	SPK
Harrington Park, NJ	NEW
Harrisburg, IL	BEL
PA	HBG
PA	PSC
Harrison, AR	LR
MI	SAG
NJ	NEW
NY	NY
OH	CIN
Harrison City, PA	GBG
Harrison Township, MI	DET
Harrisonburg, VA	RIC
Harrisonville, MO	KC
Harrisville, MI	DET
MI	GAY
NY	OG
RI	PRO
WV	WH
Harrodsburg, KY	LEX
Hart, MI	GR
Hartford, CT	HRT
CT	SYM
CT	STF
MI	KAL
SD	SFS
WI	MIL
Hartford City, IN	LFT
Hartington, NE	OM
Hartland, WI	MIL
Hartman, AR	LR
Hartsdale, NY	NY
Hartshorne, OK	TLS
Hartsville, SC	CHR
Hartwell, GA	ATL
Harvard, IL	RCK
MA	WOR
NE	LIN
Harvey, IL	CHI
LA	NO
ND	FAR
Harvey Cedars, NJ	TR
Harveys Lake, PA	SCR
Harwichport, MA	FR
Harwick, PA	PIT
Harwinton, CT	HRT
Harwood, ND	FAR
Harwood Heights–Norridge, IL	CHI
Hasbrouck Heights, NJ	NEW
Haskell, NJ	PAT
Hastings, MI	KAL
MN	STP
NE	LIN
PA	ALT
Hastings–On–Husdon, NY	NY
Hastings–on–Hudson, NY	NY
Hatboro, PA	PH
Hatch, NM	LSC
Hatfield, MA	SPR
PA	PH
Hatley, WI	LC
Hattiesburg, MS	BLX
Hattieville, AR	LR
Haubstadt, IN	EVN
Hauppauge, NY	RVC
Havana, IL	PEO
Havelock, NC	R
Haverford, PA	PH
Haverhill, MA	BO
Haverstraw, NY	NY
Havertown, PA	PH
Havre, MT	GF
Havre de Grace, MD	BAL
Hawaiian Gardens, CA	LA
Hawarden, IA	SC
Hawesville, KY	OWN
Hawi, HI	HON
Hawk Point, MO	STL
Hawk Run, PA	PBR
Hawley, MN	CR
PA	SCR
Haworth, NJ	NEW
Hawthorne, CA	LA
NJ	PAT
NV	RNO
NY	NY
Hayden, AZ	TUC
Haydenville, MA	SPR
Hayfield, MN	WIN
Hays, KS	SAL
MT	GF
Haysville, KS	WCH
Hayward, CA	OAK
WI	SUP
Hazard, KY	LEX
Hazel Crest, IL	CHI
Hazel Green, WI	MAD
Hazel Park, MI	DET
Hazelton, ND	BIS
Hazelwood, MO	STL
Hazen, ND	BIS
Hazleton, PA	PSC
PA	SCR
Healdsburg, CA	SR
Healy, AK	FBK
Hearne, TX	AUS
Heart Butte, MT	HEL
Heath, OH	COL
Hebbronville, TX	CC
TX	LAR
Heber Springs, AR	LR
Hebron, CT	NOR
IN	GRY
ND	BIS
NE	LIN
Hecker, IL	BEL
Hector, MN	NU
Hedgesville, WV	WH
Helena, AR	LR
MT	HEL
OH	TOL
Helenwood, TN	KNX
Hellertown, PA	ALN
Helmetta, NJ	MET
Helmville, MT	HEL
Helotes, TX	SAT
Helper, UT	SLC
Hemet, CA	SB
Hemlock, MI	SAG
Hemphill, TX	TYL
Hempstead, NY	RVC
NY	STF
TX	GAL
Henderson, KY	OWN
MN	NU
NC	R
NV	LAV
NV	SYM
TX	TYL
Hendersonville, NC	CHL
TN	NSH
Hennessey, OK	OKL
Henniker, NH	MAN
Henning, MN	SCL
Henrietta, NY	ROC
TX	FWT
Henry, IL	PEO
SD	SFS
Henryetta, OK	TLS
Heppner, OR	BAK
Herculaneum, MO	STL
Hercules, CA	OAK
Hereford, AZ	TUC
TX	AMA
Herington, KS	SAL
Herkimer, NY	ALB
Hermann, MO	JC
Herminie, PA	GBG
PA	PBR
Hermiston, OR	BAK
Hermitage, MO	JC
PA	E
PA	PBR
Hermosa Beach, CA	LA
Hernando, MS	JKS
Herndon, VA	ARL
Herreid, SD	SFS
Herrin, IL	BEL
Herron, MI	GAY
Herscher, IL	JOL
Hershey, PA	HBG
Hesperia, CA	SB
Hessmer, LA	ALX
Hettinger, ND	BIS
Heuvelton, NY	OG
Hewitt, NJ	PAT
WI	LC
Hewlett, NY	RVC
Hialeah, FL	MIA
Hiawatha, IA	DUB
KS	KCK
Hibbing, MN	DUL
Hickman, KY	OWN
Hickory, NC	CHL
Hickory Hills, IL	CHI
Hicksville, NY	RVC
OH	TOL
Hidalgo, TX	BWN
Higganum, CT	NOR
Higgins Lake, MI	GAY
Higginsville, MO	KC
High Bridge, NJ	MET
High Point, NC	CHL
High Ridge, MO	STL
High Springs, FL	STA
Highland, CA	SB
IL	SFD
IN	GRY
MI	DET
NY	NY
WI	MAD
Highland Beach, FL	PMB
Highland Falls, NY	NY
Highland Heights, KY	COV
OH	CLV
Highland Lakes, NJ	PAT
Highland Mills, NY	NY
Highland Park, IL	CHI
MI	DET
NJ	MET
Highland Springs, VA	RIC
Highlands, NJ	TR
TX	GAL
Highlands Ranch, CO	COS
Highmore, SD	SFS
Hightstown, NJ	TR
Highwood, IL	CHI
Higley, AZ	PHX
Hilbert, WI	GB
Hill City, KS	SAL
MN	DUL
Hillcrest Heights, MD	WDC
Hilliard, OH	COL
Hillman, MI	GAY
MN	SCL
Hills, IA	DAV
Hillsboro, IL	SFD
MO	STL
ND	FAR
OH	CIN
OR	P
TX	FWT
WI	LC
Hillsborough, NC	R
NH	MAN
NJ	MET
NJ	PHU
Hillsborough Township, NJ	PSC
Hillsdale, MI	LAN
NJ	NEW
Hillside, IL	CHI
NJ	NEW
NJ	PHU
Hillsville, PA	PIT
Hilltown, PA	PH
Hilmar, CA	FRS
Hilo, HI	HON
Hilton, NY	ROC
Hilton Head Island, SC	CHR
Hinckley, MN	DUL
NY	SY
OH	CLV
Hinesburg, VT	BUR
Hinesville, GA	SAV
Hingham, MA	BO
Hinsdale, IL	JOL
Hinton, WV	WH
Hitchcock, TX	GAL
Hobart, IN	GRY
Hobbs, NM	LSC
Hobe Sound, FL	PMB
Hoboken, NJ	NEW
Hobson, TX	SAT
Hockessin, DE	WIL
Hodge, LA	SHP
Hodgenville, KY	L
Hoffman Estates, IL	CHI
Hogansburg, NY	OG
Hohenwald, TN	NSH
Hohokus, NJ	NEW
Hoisington, KS	DOD
Holbrook, AZ	GLP
MA	BO
NY	RVC
Holden, MO	KC
Holdingford, MN	SCL
Holdrege, NE	LIN
Holgate, OH	TOL
Holiday, FL	SP
Holland, MI	GR
NY	BUF
PA	PH
Holland Patent, NY	SY
Hollandale, WI	MAD
Holley, NY	BUF
Hollidaysburg, PA	ALT
Hollis, NY	BRK
Hollis Hills, NY	BRK
Hollister, CA	MRY
Holliston, MA	BO
Holly, CO	PBL
MI	DET
Holly Springs, MS	JKS
Hollywood, CA	STN
FL	MIA
MD	WDC
Holmdel, NJ	TR
Holmen, WI	LC
Holstein, IA	SC

Holton, KS	KCK
Holts Summit, MO	JC
Holtville, CA	SD
Holy Cross, AK	FBK
IA	DUB
Holyoke, CO	DEN
MA	SPR
Homer, AK	ANC
NY	SY
Homer City, PA	PBR
Homer Glen, IL	JOL
IL	PRM
Homestead, FL	MIA
PA	PIT
Hometown, IL	CHI
Homewood, IL	CHI
IL	JOL
Homosassa, FL	SP
Hondo, TX	SAT
Honeoye, NY	ROC
Honeoye Falls, NY	ROC
Honesdale, PA	SCR
Honey Brook, PA	PH
Honokaa, HI	HON
Honolulu, HI	HON
HI	STN
Hood River, OR	BAK
Hooksett, NH	MAN
Hoopa, CA	SR
Hooper, NE	OM
Hooper Bay, AK	FBK
Hoopeston, IL	PEO
Hoosick Falls, NY	ALB
Hooversville, PA	ALT
Hopatcong, NJ	PAT
Hope, AR	LR
Hope Mills, NC	R
Hope Valley, RI	PRO
Hopedale, MA	WOR
OH	STU
Hopelawn, NJ	MET
Hopewell, NJ	TR
VA	RIC
Hopewell Junction, NY	NY
Hopkins, MN	STP
Hopkins Park, IL	JOL
Hopkinsville, KY	OWN
Hopkinton, IA	DUB
MA	BO
Hoquiam, WA	SEA
Horace, ND	FAR
Horicon, WI	MIL
Horizon City, TX	ELP
Hornell, NY	ROC
Horse Branch, KY	OWN
Horseheads, NY	ROC
Horseshoe Bay, TX	AUS
Horseshoe Bend, AR	LR
Horsham, PA	PH
Horton, KS	KCK
Hortonville, WI	GB
Hoschton, GA	ATL
Hospers, IA	SC
Hot Springs, SD	RC
VA	RIC
Hot Springs National Park, AR	LR
Hot Springs Village, AR	LR
Houck, AZ	GLP
Houghton, IA	DAV
MI	MAR
Houlton, ME	PRT
Houma, LA	HT
Housatonic, MA	SPR
House Springs, MO	STL
Houston, MN	WIN
MO	SPC
TX	GAL
TX	SYM
TX	STN
TX	OLL
TX	PBR
Houtzdale, PA	E
Hoven, SD	SFS
Howard, SD	SFS
Howard Beach, NY	BRK
Howard City, MI	GR
Howardstown, KY	L
Howell, MI	LAN
NJ	TR
Howells, NE	OM
Howes, SD	RC
Howland, ME	PRT
Hoxie, KS	SAL
Hoyt Lakes, MN	DUL
Hubbard, OH	Y
Hubertus, WI	MIL
Hudson, FL	SP
MA	BO
MI	LAN
NH	MAN
NY	ALB

NY	STF
OH	CLV
WI	SUP
Hudson Falls, NY	ALB
Huffman, TX	GAL
Hughestown, PA	SCR
Hughson, CA	STO
Hugo, MN	STP
OK	TLS
Hugoton, KS	DOD
Hulbert, OK	TLS
Hull, MA	BO
Humble, TX	GAL
Humboldt, IA	SC
KS	WCH
SD	SFS
TN	MEM
Humphrey, NE	OM
Hungerford, TX	GAL
TX	VIC
Hunlock Creek, PA	SCR
Hunt Valley, MD	BAL
Hunter, NY	STF
Huntersville, NC	CHL
Huntingburg, IN	EVN
Huntingdon, PA	ALT
Huntingdon Valley, PA	PH
Huntington, IN	FTW
MA	SPR
NY	RVC
WV	WH
Huntington Beach, CA	ORG
Huntington Park, CA	LA
Huntington Station, NY	RVC
Huntingtown, MD	WDC
Huntley, IL	RCK
Huntsville, AL	BIR
AR	LR
OH	CIN
TX	GAL
UT	SLC
Hurley, NM	LSC
NY	NY
WI	SUP
Huron, CA	FRS
OH	TOL
SD	SFS
Hurricane, WV	WH
Hurst, TX	FWT
Hurt, VA	RIC
Hurtsboro, AL	MOB
Huslia, AK	FBK
Hutchinson, KS	WCH
MN	NU
Hutto, TX	AUS
Huttonsville, WV	WH
Hyannis, MA	FR
Hyattsville, MD	WDC
Hyde Park, MA	BO
NY	NY
UT	SLC
Hydes, MD	BAL
Iberia, MO	JC
Ida, MI	DET
Ida Grove, IA	SC
Idabel, OK	TLS
Idaho Falls, ID	B
Idaho Springs, CO	DEN
Idalou, TX	LUB
Idyllwild, CA	SB
Ignacio, CO	PBL
Ijamsville, MD	BAL
Ilion, NY	ALB
Illiopolis, IL	SFD
Imlay City, MI	DET
Immaculata, PA	PH
Immokalee, FL	VEN
Imogene, IA	DM
Imperial, CA	SD
MO	STL
NE	LIN
PA	PIT
Inchelium, WA	SPK
Incline Village, NV	RNO
Independence, IA	DUB
KS	WCH
KY	COV
LA	BR
MO	KC
OH	CLV
OR	P
WI	LC
Indialantic, FL	ORL
Indian Creek, IL	CHI
Indian Head, MD	WDC
Indian Lake, NY	OG
Indian River, MI	GAY
Indian Rocks Beach, FL	SP
Indiana, PA	GBG
Indianapolis, IN	IND
IN	PRM

Indianola, IA	DM
MS	JKS
NE	LIN
Indiantown, FL	PMB
Indio, CA	SB
Inez, TX	VIC
Ingalls, KS	DOD
Ingleside, IL	CHI
TX	CC
Inglewood, CA	LA
Ingram, TX	SAT
Inkster, MI	DET
Interlachen, FL	STA
Interlaken, NY	ROC
International Falls, MN	DUL
Intervale, NH	MAN
Inver Grove Heights, MN	STP
Inverness, FL	SP
IL	CHI
Inwood, NY	RVC
WV	WH
Iola, KS	WCH
Ione, CA	SAC
WA	SPK
Ionia, MI	GR
Iota, LA	LAF
Iowa, LA	LKC
Iowa City, IA	DAV
Iowa Falls, IA	DUB
Iowa Park, TX	FWT
Ipswich, MA	BO
SD	SFS
Ira Township, MI	DET
Ireland, IN	EVN
Irene, SD	SFS
Iron Mountain, MI	MAR
Iron River, MI	MAR
WI	SUP
Irons, MI	GR
Ironton, MO	SPC
OH	STU
Ironwood, MI	MAR
Irvine, CA	ORG
KY	LEX
Irving, TX	DAL
TX	PBR
Irvington, KY	OWN
NJ	NEW
Irvington–on–the–Hudson, NY	NY
Irwin, PA	GBG
Irwindale, CA	LA
Isanti, MN	SCL
Iselin, NJ	MET
Ishpeming, MI	MAR
Island Park, NY	RVC
Island Pond, VT	BUR
Isle La Motte, VT	BUR
Isleta, NM	SFE
Isleton, CA	SAC
Islip, NY	RVC
Islip Terrace, NY	RVC
Issaquah, WA	SEA
Italy, TX	DAL
Itasca, IL	JOL
Ithaca, MI	SAG
NY	ROC
Ivanhoe, MN	NU
Ivesdale, IL	PEO
Jabor, Jaluit, MI	MI
Jackman, ME	PRT
Jackson, CA	SAC
GA	ATL
KY	LEX
MI	LAN
MN	WIN
MO	SPC
MS	JKS
NE	OM
NJ	TR
OH	COL
PA	SCR
TN	MEM
WY	CHY
Jackson Heights, NY	BRK
Jacksonville, AL	BIR
AR	LR
FL	OLD
FL	SAM
FL	STA
IL	SFD
NC	R
TX	TYL
Jacksonville Beach, FL	STA
Jaffrey, NH	MAN
Jal, NM	LSC
Jamaica, NY	NY
NY	BRK
Jamaica Estates, NY	NY
NY	BRK
Jamaica Plain, MA	BO
MA	SAM

MA	STF
Jamesburg, NJ	MET
Jamestown, KY	L
ND	FAR
NY	BUF
OH	CIN
RI	PRO
Jamison, PA	PH
Jamul, CA	SD
Janesville, MN	WIN
WI	MAD
Jarrell, TX	AUS
Jasper, AL	BIR
GA	ATL
IN	EVN
TX	BEA
Jay, ME	PRT
Jeanerette, LA	LAF
Jeannette, PA	GBG
PA	SJP
Jefferson, IA	SC
LA	NO
MA	WOR
NC	CHL
OH	Y
SD	SFS
TX	TYL
WI	MAD
Jefferson City, MO	JC
TN	KNX
Jefferson Hills, PA	PIT
Jeffersonville, IN	IND
NY	NY
Jemez Pueblo, NM	SFE
Jemez Springs, NM	SFE
Jena, LA	ALX
Jenison, MI	GR
Jenkins, KY	LEX
Jenkintown, PA	PH
PA	PHU
Jennings, LA	LKC
Jensen Beach, FL	PMB
Jermyn, PA	SCR
Jerome, ID	B
Jersey City, NJ	NEW
NJ	PSC
NJ	PHU
Jersey Shore, PA	SCR
Jerseyville, IL	SFD
Jessup, PA	PSC
PA	SCR
Jesup, GA	SAV
IA	DUB
Jetmore, KS	DOD
Jewett City, CT	NOR
Jim Falls, WI	LC
Jim Thorpe, PA	ALN
Joanna, SC	CHR
Jobstown, NJ	TR
Joelton, TN	NSH
Johannesburg, MI	GAY
John Day, OR	BAK
Johns Creek, GA	ATL
Johns Island, SC	CHR
Johnsburg, IL	RCK
Johnson City, NY	SY
NY	STF
TN	KNX
Johnson Creek, WI	MAD
Johnsonburg, PA	E
Johnston, IA	DM
RI	PRO
Johnston City, IL	BEL
Johnstown, CO	DEN
NY	ALB
OH	COL
PA	ALT
PA	SJP
PA	PBR
Joliet, IL	JOL
Jolon, CA	MRY
Jonesboro, AR	LR
GA	ATL
Jonesburg, MO	JC
Jonestown, MS	JKS
Jonesville, VA	RIC
Joplin, MO	SPC
Joppa, MD	BAL
Jordan, MN	STP
NY	SY
Jordan Valley, OR	BAK
Joshua Tree, CA	SB
Jourdanton, TX	SAT
Julesburg, CO	DEN
Julian, CA	SD
Junction, TX	SAN
Junction City, KS	SAL
OH	COL
OR	P
WI	LC
Juneau, AK	JUN

Jupiter, FL	PMB
Justice, IL	CHI
Kahoka, MO	JC
Kahuku, HI	HON
Kahului, HI	HON
Kailua, HI	HON
Kailua–Kona, HI	HON
Kalaheo, HI	HON
Kalamazoo, MI	KAL
Kalaupapa, HI	HON
Kalida, OH	TOL
Kalispell, MT	HEL
Kalkaska, MI	GAY
Kalona, IA	DAV
Kalskag, AK	FBK
Kaltag, AK	FBK
Kamiah, ID	B
Kamuela, HI	HON
Kanab, UT	SLC
Kandiyohi, MN	NU
Kane, PA	E
Kaneohe, HI	HON
Kankakee, IL	JOL
Kannapolis, NC	CHL
Kansas City, KS	KCK
MO	KC
Kansasville, WI	MIL
Kapaa, HI	HON
Kaplan, LA	LAF
Kapolei, HI	HON
Karnes City, TX	SAT
Kathleen, GA	SAV
Katonah, NY	NY
Katy, TX	GAL
Kaufman, TX	DAL
Kaukauna, WI	GB
Kaunakakai, HI	HON
Kawkawlin, MI	SAG
Kayenta, AZ	GLP
Keams Canyon, AZ	GLP
Keansburg, NJ	TR
Kearney, MO	KC
NE	GI
Kearneysville, WV	WH
Kearns, UT	SLC
Kearny, AZ	TUC
NJ	NEW
Keene, NH	MAN
NY	OG
Keeseville, NY	OG
Keizer, OR	P
Kekaha, HI	HON
Keller, TX	FWT
WA	SPK
Kelley's Island, OH	TOL
Kelliher, MN	CR
Kellnersville, WI	GB
Kellogg, ID	B
Kelly, KS	KCK
Kelso, MO	SPC
WA	SEA
Kemmerer, WY	CHY
Kenai, AK	ANC
Kenansville, NC	R
Kendall, WI	LC
Kendall Park, NJ	MET
Kendallville, IN	FTW
Kenedy, TX	SAT
Kenilworth, NJ	NEW
Kenmare, ND	BIS
Kenmore, NY	BUF
NY	STF
Kennebunkport, ME	PRT
Kenner, LA	NO
Kennesaw, GA	ATL
Kennett, MO	SPC
Kennett Square, PA	PH
Kennewick, WA	YAK
Kenosha, WI	MIL
Kensington, CA	OAK
CT	HRT
MD	WDC
Kent, CT	HRT
MN	SCL
OH	Y
PA	GBG
WA	SEA
Kentfield, CA	SFR
Kentland, IN	LFT
Kenton, KY	COV
OH	COL
Kenyon, MN	STP
Keokuk, IA	DAV
Keota, IA	DAV
Kerhonkson, NY	STF
Kerman, CA	FRS
Kermit, TX	ELP
WV	WH
Kernersville, NC	CHL
Kerrville, TX	SAT
Kersey, PA	E

Keshena, WI	GB
Ketchikan, AK	JUN
Kettering, OH	CIN
Kewanee, IL	PEO
Kewaskum, WI	MIL
Kewaunee, WI	GB
Key Biscayne, FL	MIA
Key Largo, FL	MIA
Key West, FL	MIA
Keyport, NJ	TR
Keyser, WV	WH
Keystone Heights, FL	STA
Kickapoo (Edwards), IL	PEO
Kiel, WI	GB
Kieler, WI	MAD
Kihei, HI	HON
Kilgore, TX	TYL
Kilkenny, MN	STP
Killdeer, ND	BIS
Killeen, TX	AUS
Killingworth, CT	NOR
Kilmarnock, VA	ARL
Kiln, MS	BLX
Kimball, MN	SCL
NE	GI
SD	SFS
Kimberling City, MO	SPC
Kimberly, WI	GB
Kimberton, PA	PH
Kincaid, IL	SFD
Kinde, MI	SAG
Kinder, LA	LKC
Kindred, ND	FAR
King City, CA	MRY
King of Prussia, PA	PH
Kingfisher, OK	OKL
Kingman, AZ	PHX
KS	WCH
Kings Park, NY	RVC
Kingsburg, CA	FRS
Kingsford, MI	MAR
Kingsland, TX	AUS
Kingsley, MI	GAY
Kingsport, TN	KNX
Kingston, MA	BO
NY	NY
PA	PSC
PA	SCR
RI	PRO
Kingstree, SC	CHR
Kingsville, OH	Y
TX	CC
Kingwood, TX	GAL
WV	WH
Kinnelon, NJ	PAT
Kinsley, KS	DOD
Kinston, NC	R
Kiowa, KS	DOD
Kirkland, WA	SEA
Kirksville, MO	JC
Kirkwood, MO	STL
NY	SY
Kirtland, OH	CLV
Kissimmee, FL	ORL
Kittanning, PA	GBG
Kittery, ME	PRT
Kitty Hawk, NC	R
Klamath Falls, OR	BAK
Klawock, AK	JUN
Knights Landing, CA	SAC
Knightstown, IN	IND
Knottsville, KY	OWN
Knox, IN	GRY
Knox City, TX	FWT
Knoxville, IA	DAV
TN	KNX
TN	PBR
Kodiak, AK	ANC
Kohler, WI	MIL
Kokomo, IN	LFT
Koloa, HI	HON
Konawa, OK	OKL
Koppel, PA	PIT
Kosciusko, MS	JKS
Kotlik, AK	FBK
Kotzebue, AK	FBK
Kountze, TX	BEA
Kouts, IN	GRY
Koyukuk, AK	FBK
Krakow, WI	GB
Kranzburg, SD	SFS
Krebs, OK	TLS
Kremmling, CO	DEN
Krotz Springs, LA	LAF
Kula, HI	HON
Kulpmont, PA	HBG
Kutztown, PA	ALN
Kyle, TX	AUS
L'Anse, MI	MAR
La Canada Flintridge, CA	LA
La Conner, WA	SEA

La Crescent, MN	WIN
La Crescenta, CA	LA
La Crosse, WI	LC
La Feria, TX	BWN
La Follette, TN	KNX
La Grande, OR	BAK
La Grange, IL	CHI
TX	AUS
TX	VIC
La Grange Park, IL	CHI
La Habra, CA	ORG
La Jolla, CA	SD
La Joya, NM	SFE
TX	BWN
La Junta, CO	PBL
La Marque, TX	GAL
La Mesa, CA	SD
CA	OLD
CA	STN
NM	LSC
La Mirada, CA	LA
La Moure, ND	FAR
La Pine, OR	BAK
La Place, LA	NO
La Plata, MD	WDC
La Porte, IN	GRY
TX	GAL
La Porte City, IA	DUB
La Pryor, TX	LAR
La Puente, CA	LA
La Quinta, CA	SB
La Salle, IL	PEO
La Valle, WI	MAD
La Verne, CA	LA
La Vernia, TX	SAT
La Villa, TX	BWN
LaBelle, FL	VEN
LaCenter, KY	OWN
LaCoste, TX	SAT
LaCrosse, KS	DOD
LaFollette, TN	KNX
LaGrange, GA	ATL
IN	FTW
KY	L
TX	AUS
LaGrangeville, NY	NY
Labadieville, LA	BR
Lac du Flambeau, WI	SUP
Lacey, WA	SEA
Laceyville, PA	SCR
Lackawanna, NY	BUF
NY	STF
Lacombe, LA	NO
Lacon, IL	PEO
Lacona, IA	DM
Laconia, NH	MAN
Ladd, IL	PEO
Ladera Ranch, CA	ORG
Ladue, MO	STL
Lady Lake, FL	ORL
Ladysmith, VA	RIC
WI	SUP
Lafayette, CA	OAK
CO	DEN
IN	LFT
LA	LAF
MN	NU
NY	SY
OR	P
TN	NSH
Lafayette Hill, PA	PH
Lafferty, OH	STU
Lafitte, LA	NO
Laflin, PA	SCR
Lagarto, TX	CC
Lago Vista, TX	AUS
Laguna, NM	GLP
Laguna Beach, CA	ORG
Laguna Heights, TX	BWN
Laguna Niguel, CA	ORG
Laguna Woods, CA	ORG
Lagunitas, CA	SFR
Lahaina, HI	HON
Laingsburg, MI	LAN
Lake Andes, SD	SFS
Lake Ariel, PA	SCR
Lake Arrowhead, CA	SB
Lake Arthur, LA	LKC
Lake Benton, MN	SFS
Lake Charles, LA	LKC
Lake City, FL	STA
IA	SC
MI	GAY
MN	WIN
SC	CHR
Lake Clear, NY	OG
Lake Dallas, TX	FWT
Lake Elmo, MN	STP
Lake Forest, CA	ORG
IL	CHI
Lake Geneva, WI	MIL

Lake George, NY	ALB
Lake Harmony, PA	ALN
Lake Havasu City, AZ	PHX
Lake Hopatcong, NJ	PAT
Lake Jackson, TX	GAL
Lake Katrine, NY	NY
Lake Leelanau, MI	GAY
Lake Linden, MI	MAR
Lake Mills, WI	MAD
Lake Milton, OH	Y
Lake Nebagamon, WI	SUP
Lake Odessa, MI	GR
Lake Orion, MI	DET
Lake Oswego, OR	P
Lake Ozark, MO	JC
Lake Park, MN	CR
Lake Placid, FL	VEN
NY	OG
Lake Providence, LA	SHP
Lake Ridge, VA	ARL
Lake Ronkonkoma, NY	RVC
Lake Saint Louis, MO	STL
Lake St. Croix Beach, MN	STP
Lake Station, IN	GRY
Lake Stevens, WA	SEA
Lake View, NY	BUF
Lake Villa, IL	CHI
Lake Village, AR	LR
IN	LFT
Lake Wales, FL	ORL
Lake Worth, FL	PMB
Lake Zurich, IL	CHI
Lakehurst, NJ	TR
Lakeland, FL	ORL
LA	BR
Lakemont, Altoona, PA	ALT
Lakeport, CA	SR
MI	DET
NH	MAN
Lakeshore, MS	BLX
Lakeside, AZ	GLP
CA	SD
Lakeview, OR	BAK
Lakeville, CT	HRT
MA	BO
MN	STP
Lakeway, TX	AUS
Lakewood, CA	LA
CO	DEN
CO	OLL
NJ	TR
NY	BUF
OH	CLV
OH	PRM
WA	SEA
WI	GB
Lakewood Ranch, FL	VEN
Lakin, KS	DOD
Lakota, ND	FAR
Lamar, CO	PBL
MO	SPC
Lamberton, MN	NU
Lambertville, NJ	MET
Lame Deer, MT	GF
Lamesa, TX	LUB
Lamont, CA	FRS
Lamoure, ND	FAR
Lampasas, TX	AUS
Lanai City, HI	HON
Lanark Village, FL	PT
Lancaster, CA	LA
KY	LEX
MA	WOR
NH	MAN
NY	BUF
NY	STF
OH	COL
PA	HBG
SC	CHR
TX	DAL
WI	MAD
Lancing, TN	KNX
Land O'Lakes, FL	SP
WI	SUP
Lander, WY	CHY
Landisville, NJ	CAM
Landover Hills, MD	WDC
Lanesville, IN	IND
Lanett, AL	BIR
Langdon, ND	FAR
Langhorne, PA	PH
Langley, OK	TLS
WA	SEA
Lanham, MD	WDC
Lansdale, PA	PH
Lansdowne, MD	BAL
PA	PH
Lansford, ND	FAR
PA	ALN
PA	PSC
Lansing, IA	DUB

IL	CHI
KS	KCK
MI	LAN
MI	NTN
NY	ROC
Lantana, FL	PMB
Laona, WI	GB
Lapeer, MI	DET
Laramie, WY	CHY
Larchmont, NY	NY
Larchwood, IA	SC
Laredo, TX	LAR
Largo, FL	SP
MD	WDC
Larimore, ND	FAR
Larkspur, CA	SFR
Larned, KS	DOD
Larose, LA	HT
Las Animas, CO	PBL
Las Cruces, NM	LSC
Las Vegas, NM	SFE
NV	LAV
NV	SPA
NV	VNN
NV	OLL
Lastrup, MN	SCL
Latham, NY	ALB
Lathrop, CA	STO
Laton, CA	FRS
Latrobe, PA	GBG
PA	SJP
PA	PBR
Lauderdale Lakes, FL	MIA
Lauderdale–by–the–Sea, FL	MIA
Laughlin, NV	LAV
Laupahoehoe, HI	HON
Laurel, MD	BAL
MD	WDC
MS	BLX
MT	GF
NE	OM
Laurence Harbor, NJ	MET
Laurie, MO	JC
Laurinburg, NC	R
Lavallette, NJ	TR
Laveen, AZ	PHX
Laverock, PA	PH
Lawler, IA	DUB
Lawrence, KS	KCK
MA	BO
MA	SAM
MA	NTN
NE	LIN
Lawrenceburg, IN	IND
KY	LEX
TN	NSH
Lawrenceville, GA	ATL
IL	BEL
NJ	TR
Lawtell, LA	LAF
Lawton, OK	OKL
Layton, UT	SLC
Le Center, MN	STP
Le Mars, IA	SC
Le Roy, NY	BUF
Le Sueur, MN	STP
LeClaire, IA	DAV
LeRoy, NY	BUF
Lead, SD	RC
Leadville, CO	COS
League City, TX	GAL
Leavenworth, KS	KCK
WA	YAK
Leawood, KS	KCK
Lebanon, CT	NOR
IL	BEL
IN	LFT
KY	L
MO	SPC
NH	MAN
OH	CIN
OR	P
PA	HBG
TN	NSH
VA	RIC
Lebanon Junction, KY	L
Lebeau, LA	LAF
Lecanto, FL	SP
Leckrone, PA	GBG
Lecompte, LA	ALX
Ledyard, IA	SC
Lee, IL	RCK
MA	SPR
Lee Center, NY	SY
Lee's Summit, MO	KC
Leechburg, PA	GBG
Leeds, AL	BIR
Lees Summit, MO	KC
Leesburg, FL	ORL
VA	ARL
Leesville, LA	ALX
Leetonia, OH	Y
Lefor, ND	BIS
Lehigh Acres, FL	VEN
Lehighton, PA	ALN
Leicester, MA	WOR
Leigh, NE	OM
Leipsic, OH	TOL
Leisenring, PA	PBR
Leisure City, FL	MIA
Leitchfield, KY	OWN
Leland, MS	JKS
Lemay, MO	STL
Lemhi, ID	B
Lemmon, SD	RC
Lemon Grove, CA	SD
Lemont, IL	CHI
Lemoore, CA	FRS
Lena, IL	RCK
Lenexa, KS	KCK
Lenni, PA	PH
Lennox, SD	SFS
Lenoir, NC	CHL
Lenoir City, TN	KNX
Lenox, IA	DM
MA	SPR
Lenox Dale, MA	SPR
Leominster, MA	WOR
Leon, IA	DM
Leonardtown, MD	WDC
Leonia, NJ	NEW
Leonville, LA	LAF
Leopold, IN	IND
MO	SPC
Leoti, KS	DOD
Leslie, MI	LAN
Levelland, TX	LUB
Levittown, NY	RVC
PA	PH
PA	PSC
Lewes, DE	WIL
Lewis Run, PA	E
Lewisburg, PA	HBG
TN	NSH
Lewisport, KY	OWN
Lewiston, ID	B
ME	PRT
MI	GAY
MN	WIN
NY	BUF
Lewistown, IL	PEO
MT	GF
PA	HBG
Lewisville, TX	FWT
TX	OLL
Lexington, KY	LEX
MA	BO
MA	OLN
MI	SAG
MO	KC
MS	JKS
NC	CHL
NE	GI
OH	TOL
SC	CHR
TN	MEM
VA	RIC
Lexington Park, MD	WDC
Libby, MT	HEL
Liberal, KS	DOD
Liberty, IL	SFD
IN	IND
KY	L
MO	KC
NY	NY
TN	NSH
TX	BEA
Liberty Township, OH	CIN
Libertytown, MD	BAL
Libertyville, IL	CHI
Lidderdale, IA	SC
Lidgerwood, ND	FAR
Liebenthal, KS	DOD
Lighthouse Point, FL	MIA
Ligonier, IN	FTW
PA	GBG
Liguori, MO	STL
Lihue, HI	HON
Lilburn, GA	ATL
Lillian, AL	MOB
Lilly, PA	ALT
Lima, NY	ROC
OH	TOL
Lime Ridge, WI	MAD
Limerick, ME	PRT
PA	PH
Limestone, NY	BUF
Limon, CO	COS
Lincoln, CA	SAC
IL	PEO
KS	SAL
ME	PRT
NE	LIN
NH	MAN
RI	NTN
RI	PRO
RI	SAM
Lincoln City, OR	P
Lincoln Park, MI	DET
NJ	PAT
Lincolnton, NC	CHL
Lincroft, NJ	TR
Lindale, TX	TYL
Linden, CA	STO
NJ	NEW
NJ	PSC
VA	ARL
Lindenhurst, NY	RVC
NY	STF
Lindenwold, NJ	CAM
Lindsay, CA	FRS
NE	OM
TX	FWT
Lindsborg, KS	WCH
Lindstrom, MN	STP
Linesville, PA	E
Linn, MO	JC
Lino Lakes, MN	STP
Linthicum Heights, MD	BAL
Linton, IN	EVN
ND	BIS
Linwood, MA	WOR
MI	SAG
NJ	CAM
PA	PH
Lisbon, ND	FAR
NY	OG
OH	Y
Lisbon Falls, ME	PRT
Lisle, IL	JOL
Lismore, MN	WIN
Litchfield, CT	HRT
IL	SFD
MN	NU
NH	MAN
OH	CLV
Lithia Springs, GA	ATL
Lithonia, GA	ATL
Lititz, PA	HBG
Little Canada, MN	STP
Little Chute, WI	GB
Little Compton, RI	PRO
Little Falls, MN	SCL
NJ	OLN
NJ	PAT
NY	ALB
Little Ferry, NJ	NEW
Little Hocking, OH	STU
Little Meadows, PA	NTN
Little Neck, NY	BRK
Little Rock, AR	LR
Littlefield, TX	LUB
Littlestown, PA	HBG
Littleton, CO	COS
CO	DEN
MA	BO
NH	MAN
Live Oak, FL	STA
Livermore, CA	OAK
Liverpool, NY	SY
Livingston, AL	BIR
CA	FRS
IL	SFD
MT	GF
NJ	NEW
TX	BEA
Livingston Manor, NY	NY
Livonia, LA	BR
MI	DET
MI	PRM
MI	OLL
NY	ROC
Llano, TX	AUS
Lock Haven, PA	ALT
Lockeford, CA	STO
Lockhart, TX	AUS
Lockport, IL	JOL
LA	HT
NY	BUF
Locust Valley, NY	STF
Lodge Grass, MT	GF
Lodi, CA	STO
NJ	NEW
OH	CLV
WI	MAD
Logan, IA	DM
KS	SAL
OH	COL
WV	WH
Logansport, IN	LFT
Loganville, GA	SYM
Loma Linda, CA	SB
Lombard, IL	JOL
IL	OLL
Lomira, WI	MIL
Lomita, CA	LA
Lompoc, CA	LA
Lonaconing, MD	BAL
London, KY	LEX
OH	COL
Londonderry, NH	MAN
Lone Pine, CA	FRS
Lone Tree, IA	DAV
Lonedell, MO	STL
Long Beach, CA	LA
MS	BLX
NY	RVC
Long Branch, NJ	TR
Long Grove, IA	DAV
Long Island City, NY	BRK
NY	ROM
NY	STF
Long Lake, MN	STP
Long Prairie, MN	SCL
Long Valley, NJ	PAT
Longboat Key, FL	VEN
Longmeadow, MA	SPR
Longmont, CO	DEN
Longport, NJ	CAM
Longview, TX	TYL
WA	SEA
Longville, MN	DUL
Longwood, FL	ORL
Lonsdale, MN	STP
Loogootee, IN	EVN
Lookout Mountain, GA	ATL
Loomis, CA	SAC
Loose Creek, MO	JC
Lorain, OH	CLV
OH	SJP
OH	PRM
Lords Valley, PA	SCR
Lordsburg, NM	LSC
Loreauville, LA	LAF
Loretto, KY	L
MN	STP
PA	ALT
TN	NSH
TN	SYM
Los Alamitos, CA	ORG
Los Alamos, NM	SFE
Los Altos, CA	SJ
Los Altos Hills, CA	SJ
Los Angeles, CA	LA
CA	OLN
CA	OLL
Los Banos, CA	FRS
Los Fresnos, TX	BWN
Los Gatos, CA	SJ
CA	MRY
CA	VNN
Los Lunas, NM	SFE
Los Nietos, CA	LA
Los Ojos, NM	SFE
Los Osos, CA	MRY
Lost Nation, IA	DAV
IA	DUB
Lott, TX	AUS
Loudonville, NY	ALB
OH	CLV
Louisa, KY	LEX
Louisburg, KS	KCK
NC	R
Louisiana, MO	JC
Louisville, CO	DEN
KY	L
KY	SYM
MS	JKS
OH	Y
Loup City, NE	GI
Loveland, CO	DEN
OH	CIN
Lovell, WY	CHY
Lovelock, NV	RNO
Loves Park, IL	RCK
Lovilia, IA	DAV
Loving, NM	LSC
Lovingston, VA	RIC
Lovington, NM	LSC
Lowell, IN	GRY
MA	BO
MI	GR
OH	STU
VT	BUR
Lowellville, OH	Y
Lower Brule, SD	RC
SD	SFS
Lower Burrell, PA	GBG
Lowry, MN	SCL
Lowville, NY	OG
Loyal, WI	LC
Lubbock, TX	LUB
Lucan, MN	NU
Lucerne Valley, CA	SB

Lucinda, PA	E
Ludington, MI	GR
Ludlow, KY	COV
MA	SPR
MA	STF
VT	BUR
Lufkin, TX	TYL
Lukachukai, AZ	GLP
Luling, LA	NO
TX	AUS
Lumberton, MS	BLX
NC	R
NM	GLP
TX	BEA
Lunenburg, MA	WOR
Luray, VA	ARL
Lusk, WY	CHY
Lutherville, MD	BAL
Lutz, FL	SP
Luverne, MN	WIN
Luxemburg, IA	DUB
WI	GB
Luzerne, PA	SCR
Lydia, LA	LAF
Lyford, TX	BWN
Lykens, PA	HBG
Lyman, ME	PRT
Lynbrook, NY	RVC
Lynch, NE	OM
Lynchburg, VA	RIC
Lynden, WA	SEA
Lyndhurst, NJ	NEW
OH	CLV
Lyndon Station, WI	LC
Lyndora, PA	PBR
PA	SJP
Lynn, MA	BO
Lynnfield, MA	BO
Lynnwood, WA	SEA
Lynwood, CA	LA
CA	SJ
Lyon Mountain, NY	OG
Lyons, IL	CHI
KS	WCH
NE	OM
NY	ROC
WI	MIL
Lytle, TX	SAT
Mableton, GA	ATL
Mabton, WA	YAK
Macclenny, FL	STA
Macdona, TX	SAT
Macedon, NY	ROC
Macedonia, OH	CLV
Machias, ME	PRT
Mackinac Island, MI	MAR
Mackinaw City, MI	GAY
Macomb, IL	PEO
MI	DET
Macon, GA	SAV
MO	JC
Madawaska, ME	PRT
Madeira Beach, FL	SP
Madelia, MN	WIN
Madera, CA	FRS
Madill, OK	OKL
Madison, AL	BIR
CT	HRT
FL	PT
IL	SFD
IL	STN
IN	IND
MN	NU
MS	JKS
NE	OM
NJ	PAT
OH	CLV
SD	SFS
TN	NSH
VA	ARL
WI	MAD
WV	WH
Madison Heights, MI	DET
Madison Lake, MN	STP
MN	WIN
Madisonville, KY	OWN
LA	NO
TN	KNX
TX	TYL
Madras, OR	BAK
Madrid, IA	SC
NY	OG
Magee, MS	JKS
Maggie Valley, NC	CHL
Magna, UT	SLC
Magnolia, AR	LR
DE	WIL
NJ	CAM
TX	GAL
Magnolia Springs, AL	MOB
Mahanoy City, PA	ALN
PA	PSC
Mahnomen, MN	CR
Mahomet, IL	PEO
Mahopac, NY	NY
Mahtomedi, MN	STP
Mahwah, NJ	NEW
Maine, NY	SY
Makawao, HI	HON
Makoti, ND	BIS
Malaga, NJ	CAM
Malakoff, TX	TYL
Malden, MA	BO
Malibu, CA	LA
Mallard, IA	SC
Malone, NY	OG
Malta, MT	GF
Malvern, AR	LR
PA	PH
Malverne, NY	RVC
Mamaroneck, NY	NY
Mammoth, AZ	TUC
Mammoth Lakes, CA	STO
Mamou, LA	LAF
Man, WV	WH
Manahawkin, NJ	TR
Manalapan, NJ	TR
Manasquan, NJ	TR
Manassas, VA	ARL
Manawa, WI	GB
Mancelona, MI	GAY
Manchaug, MA	WOR
Manchester, CT	HRT
IA	DUB
MD	BAL
MI	LAN
MO	STL
NH	MAN
NH	NTN
NH	PRT
NH	STF
TN	NSH
Manchester Center, VT	BUR
Manchester Township, NJ	TR
Manchester by the Sea, MA	BO
Mandan, ND	BIS
Mandaree, ND	BIS
Manderson, SD	RC
Mandeville, LA	NO
Mangum, OK	OKL
Manhasset, NY	RVC
Manhattan, IL	JOL
KS	SAL
Manhattan Beach, CA	LA
Manheim, PA	HBG
Manilla, IA	SC
Manistee, MI	GAY
Manistique, MI	MAR
Manitou Beach, MI	LAN
Manitowish Waters, WI	SUP
Manitowoc, WI	GB
WI	MIL
Mankato, KS	SAL
MN	WIN
Manley, NE	LIN
Manlius, NY	SY
Manly, IA	DUB
Manning, IA	SC
Mannington, WV	WH
Manomet, MA	BO
Manor, TX	AUS
Manorville, NY	RVC
Mansfield, LA	SHP
MA	FR
OH	TOL
PA	SCR
TX	FWT
Manson, IA	SC
Mansura, LA	ALX
Mantador, ND	FAR
Manteca, CA	STO
Manteno, IL	JOL
Mantua, NJ	CAM
OH	Y
Manvel, ND	FAR
TX	GAL
Manville, NJ	MET
RI	PRO
Many, LA	SHP
Maple City, MI	GAY
Maple Glen, PA	PH
Maple Grove, MN	STP
Maple Heights, OH	CLV
Maple Hill, KS	KCK
Maple Lake, MN	STP
Maple Mount, KY	OWN
Maple Park, IL	RCK
Maple Shade, NJ	TR
Mapleton, IA	SC
MN	WIN
Mapleville, RI	PRO
Maplewood, MN	STP
MO	STL
NJ	NEW
WI	GB
Maquoketa, IA	DUB
Marana, AZ	TUC
Marathon, FL	MIA
NY	SY
WI	LC
Marathon City, WI	LC
Marble, MN	DUL
Marble Falls, TX	AUS
Marblehead, MA	BO
OH	PRM
OH	TOL
Marbury, AL	MOB
Marceline, MO	JC
Marcellus, NY	SY
Marco Island, FL	VEN
Marcus, IA	SC
Marcus Hook, PA	PH
Marengo, IA	DAV
IL	RCK
Marfa, TX	ELP
Margaretville, NY	ALB
Margate, FL	MIA
FL	SYM
NJ	CAM
Maria Stein, OH	CIN
Mariah Hill, IN	EVN
Marianna, AR	LR
FL	PT
Maricopa, AZ	TUC
Marienthal, KS	DOD
Marietta, GA	ATL
NY	SY
OH	STU
Marina, CA	MRY
Marine, IL	SFD
Marine City, MI	DET
Marine on St. Croix, MN	STP
Marinette, WI	GB
Marion, IA	DUB
IL	BEL
IN	LFT
KS	WCH
KY	OWN
MA	FR
OH	COL
SD	SFS
VA	RIC
Marionville, MO	SPC
Mariposa, CA	FRS
Marked Tree, AR	LR
Markesan, WI	MAD
Markham, IL	CHI
Marksville, LA	ALX
Marlboro, NJ	TR
NY	NY
NY	SYM
Marlborough, CT	HRT
MA	BO
Marlette, MI	SAG
Marlin, TX	AUS
Marlinton, WV	WH
Marlton, NJ	TR
Marmora, NJ	CAM
Marne, MI	GR
Marquette, MI	MAR
Marrero, LA	NO
Marriottsville, MD	BAL
Mars Hill, NC	CHL
Marseilles, IL	PEO
Marshall, AK	FBK
IL	SFD
MI	KAL
MN	NU
MO	JC
TX	TYL
WI	MAD
Marshalltown, IA	DUB
Marshfield, MA	BO
MO	SPC
WI	LC
Marthasville, MO	STL
Martin, KY	LEX
OH	TOL
SD	RC
TN	MEM
Martindale, TX	AUS
Martinez, CA	OAK
Martins Creek, PA	ALN
Martins Ferry, OH	STU
Martinsburg, MO	JC
WV	WH
Martinsville, IN	IND
NJ	MET
VA	RIC
Marty, SD	SFS
Marvin, SD	SFS
Mary Esther, FL	PT
Marydel, MD	WIL
Maryknoll, NY	NY
Maryland Heights, MO	STL
Marylhurst, OR	P
Marysville, CA	SAC
KS	KCK
MI	DET
OH	COL
PA	HBG
WA	SEA
Maryville, IL	SFD
MO	KC
Masaryktown, FL	SP
Mascoutah, IL	BEL
Mashpee, MA	FR
Mason, MI	LAN
OH	CIN
Mason City, IA	DUB
Masontown, PA	GBG
Maspeth, NY	BRK
Massapequa, NY	RVC
Massapequa Park, NY	RVC
Massena, IA	DM
NY	OG
Massillon, OH	Y
OH	PBR
Mastic Beach, NY	RVC
Masury, OH	Y
Matamoras, PA	SCR
Matawan, NJ	TR
NJ	MET
NJ	PSC
Mathews, VA	RIC
Mathis, TX	CC
Mattapan, MA	BO
Mattapoisett, MA	FR
Mattawa, WA	YAK
Mattawan, MI	KAL
Matteson, IL	CHI
Matthews, NC	CHL
Mattoon, IL	SFD
Mauldin, SC	CHR
Maumee, OH	TOL
Maurepas, LA	BR
Maurice, LA	LAF
Mauriceville, TX	BEA
Mauston, WI	LC
Maximo, OH	Y
May's Lick, KY	COV
Maybee, MI	DET
Maybrook, NY	NY
Mayer, AZ	PHX
Mayetta, KS	KCK
Mayfield, KY	OWN
PA	SCR
Maynard, MA	BO
OH	STU
Mays Landing, NJ	CAM
Maysel, WV	WH
Maysville, KY	COV
Mayville, MI	SAG
ND	FAR
WI	MIL
Maywood, CA	LA
IL	CHI
IL	SYM
NJ	NEW
Mazomanie, WI	MAD
Mc Connellsburg, PA	ALT
Mc Kean, PA	E
Mc Keesport, PA	PBR
PA	PIT
Mc Lean, VA	WDC
Mc Leansboro, IL	BEL
Mc Pherson, KS	WCH
Mc Sherrystown, PA	HBG
McAdoo, PA	ALN
PA	PSC
PA	PHU
McAfee, NJ	PAT
McAlester, OK	TLS
McAllen, TX	BWN
McCall, ID	B
McCamey, TX	SAN
McCloud, CA	SAC
McComb, MS	JKS
McConnellsburg, PA	ALT
McConnelsville, OH	STU
McCook, NE	LIN
McDonald, OH	Y
PA	PIT
McDonough, GA	ATL
McEwen, TN	NSH
McFarland, CA	FRS
WI	MAD
McGehee, AR	LR
McGrath, AK	FBK
McGregor, MN	DUL
TX	AUS
McHenry, IL	RCK
McKees Rocks, PA	PBR
PA	PIT

PA	SJP
McKeesport, PA	PBR
PA	PIT
PA	ROM
PA	SJP
McKenzie Bridge, OR	P
McKinleyville, CA	SR
McKinney, TX	DAL
McLaughlin, SD	RC
McLean, VA	ARL
VA	WDC
VA	NTN
McLeansboro, IL	BEL
McLoud, OK	OKL
McMechen, WV	WH
McMinnville, OR	P
TN	NSH
McMurray, PA	PIT
McNary, AZ	GLP
McPherson, KS	WCH
McRae, GA	SAV
McSherrystown, PA	HBG
Mcallen, TX	BWN
Mead, NE	LIN
Meade, KS	DOD
Meadow Lands, PA	PIT
Meadowbrook, PA	PH
Meadville, PA	E
Mecca, CA	SB
Mechanicsburg, OH	CIN
PA	HBG
Mechanicsville, IA	DAV
MD	WDC
VA	RIC
Mechanicville, NY	ALB
Medfield, MA	BO
Medford, MA	BO
MN	WIN
NJ	TR
NY	RVC
OK	OKL
OR	P
WI	SUP
Media, PA	PH
Medical Lake, WA	SPK
Medicine Lodge, KS	DOD
Medina, NY	BUF
OH	CLV
Medway, MA	BO
Meeker, CO	DEN
Megargel, TX	FWT
Melbourne, FL	ORL
KY	COV
Melbourne Beach, FL	ORL
Melcher, IA	DAV
Mellen, WI	SUP
Mellette, SD	SFS
Melrose, IA	DAV
MA	BO
MN	SCL
WI	LC
Melrose Park, IL	CHI
PA	PHU
Melville, LA	LAF
NY	RVC
Melvindale, MI	DET
Memphis, MI	DET
MO	JC
TN	MEM
TX	AMA
Mena, AR	LR
Menahga, MN	SCL
Menands, NY	ALB
Menard, TX	SAN
Menasha, WI	GB
Mendham, NJ	PAT
Mendocino, CA	SR
Mendon, MA	WOR
MI	KAL
NY	ROC
Mendota, CA	FRS
IL	PEO
MN	STP
Mendota Heights, MN	STP
Menlo Park, CA	SFR
Menoken, ND	BIS
Menominee, MI	MAR
Menomonee Falls, WI	MIL
Menomonie, WI	LC
Mentor, MN	CR
OH	CLV
Mentor–on–the–Lake, OH	PRM
Mequon, WI	MIL
Meraux, LA	NO
Merced, CA	FRS
Mercedes, TX	BWN
Mercer, PA	E
WI	SUP
Mercer Island, WA	SEA
Merchantville, NJ	CAM
Meredith, NH	MAN

Meriden, CT	HRT
KS	KCK
Meridian, ID	B
MS	JKS
Merion Station, PA	PH
Mermentau, LA	LAF
Merrick, NY	RVC
Merrill, IA	SC
MI	SAG
OR	BAK
WI	SUP
Merrillville, IN	GRY
IN	PRM
Merrimac, MA	BO
WI	MAD
Merrimack, NH	MAN
Merritt Island, FL	ORL
Mesa, AZ	PHX
ID	B
Mescalero, NM	LSC
Mesilla, NM	LSC
Mesilla Park, NM	LSC
Mesquite, NV	LAV
TX	DAL
TX	SYM
Metairie, LA	NO
Metaline Falls, WA	SPK
Metamora, IL	PEO
Methuen, MA	BO
MA	NTN
Metropolis, IL	BEL
Metuchen, NJ	MET
Mexia, TX	AUS
Mexico, MO	JC
NY	SY
Meyersdale, PA	ALT
Meyersville, TX	VIC
Miami, AZ	TUC
FL	ARL
FL	PSC
FL	SJP
FL	SAM
FL	NTN
FL	MIA
OK	TLS
Miami Beach, FL	MIA
Miami Gardens, FL	MIA
Miami Lakes, FL	MIA
Miami Shores, FL	MIA
Miami Springs, FL	MIA
Miamisburg, OH	CIN
Michigan Center, MI	LAN
Michigan City, IN	GRY
Middle Village, NY	BRK
Middleborough, MA	BO
Middlebourne, WV	WH
Middleburg, FL	STA
VA	ARL
Middleburg Heights, OH	CLV
Middleburgh, NY	ALB
Middlebury, CT	HRT
VT	BUR
Middlefield, CT	NOR
OH	CLV
Middlesboro, KY	LEX
Middlesex, NJ	MET
Middleton, MA	BO
WI	MAD
Middletown, CA	SR
CT	NOR
DE	WIL
MD	BAL
NJ	TR
NY	NY
NY	STF
OH	CIN
PA	HBG
RI	PRO
Middletown Springs, VT	BUR
Midland, MD	BAL
MI	SAG
PA	PIT
TX	SAN
TX	SAT
Midland Park, NJ	NEW
Midlothian, IL	CHI
VA	RIC
Midvale, UT	SLC
Midway City, CA	ORG
Midwest City, OK	OKL
Miesville, MN	STP
Mifflintown, PA	HBG
Milaca, MN	SCL
Milan, IL	PEO
MI	LAN
MO	JC
NM	GLP
OH	TOL
Milbank, SD	SFS
Miles, TX	SAN
Miles City, MT	GF

Milford, CT	HRT
DE	WIL
IA	SC
MA	WOR
MI	DET
NH	MAN
NJ	MET
OH	CIN
PA	SCR
UT	SLC
Mililani, HI	HON
Mililani Town, HI	HON
Mill Creek, WA	SEA
Mill Valley, CA	SFR
Milladore, WI	LC
Millbrae, CA	OLL
CA	SFR
Millbrook, NY	NY
Millbury, MA	WOR
Milledgeville, GA	ATL
Millen, GA	SAV
Miller, SD	SFS
Miller City, OH	TOL
Millersburg, OH	COL
PA	HBG
Millersville, MD	BAL
Millington, TN	MEM
Millis, MA	BO
Millstadt, IL	BEL
Millstone Township, NJ	TR
Milltown, NJ	MET
Millville, MA	WOR
NJ	CAM
NJ	PHU
Milmont Park, PA	PH
Milnor, ND	FAR
Milpitas, CA	SJ
Milroy, MN	NU
Milton, FL	PT
LA	LAF
MA	BO
NY	NY
PA	HBG
VT	BUR
WI	MAD
Milton Freewater, OR	BAK
Milwaukee, WI	MIL
WI	NTN
WI	STN
Milwaukie, OR	P
Mims, FL	ORL
Minden, LA	SHP
NE	LIN
Mineola, NY	RVC
TX	TYL
Mineral, VA	RIC
Mineral Point, WI	MAD
Mineral Ridge, OH	Y
Mineral Wells, TX	FWT
Minersville, PA	ALN
PA	PHU
PA	PSC
Minerva, OH	STU
Minetto, NY	SY
Mingo Junction, OH	PBR
OH	STU
Minneapolis, KS	SAL
MN	OLL
MN	STN
MN	PRM
MN	STP
Minneota, MN	NU
Minnetonka, MN	STP
Minong, WI	SUP
Minonk, IL	PEO
Minooka, IL	JOL
Minot, ND	BIS
Minster, OH	CIN
Minto, ND	FAR
Minturn, CO	DEN
Mio, MI	GAY
Miramar, FL	MIA
Miramar Beach, FL	PT
Mishawaka, IN	FTW
IN	STN
Mishicot, WI	GB
Misquamicut, RI	PRO
Mission, KS	KCK
SD	RC
TX	BWN
Mission Hill, SD	SFS
Mission Hills, CA	LA
Mission Viejo, CA	ORG
Missoula, MT	HEL
Missouri City, TX	GAL
TX	SYM
Missouri Valley, IA	DM
Mitchell, IN	IND
NE	GI
SD	SFS
Mitchellville, MD	WDC

Moab, UT	SLC
Moberly, MO	JC
Mobile, AL	MOB
Mobridge, SD	SFS
Mocanaqua, PA	SCR
Mocksville, NC	CHL
Modesto, CA	STO
Modoc, IL	BEL
Mogadore, OH	Y
Mohall, ND	BIS
Mohawk, NY	ALB
Mohnton, PA	ALN
Mokane, MO	JC
Mokena, IL	JOL
Molalla, OR	P
Moline, IL	PEO
KS	WCH
Momence, IL	JOL
Monaca, PA	PIT
Monahans, TX	ELP
Moncks Corner, SC	CHR
Mondovi, WI	LC
Monee, IL	JOL
Monessen, PA	GBG
PA	PBR
Moneta, VA	RIC
Monett, MO	SPC
Monkton, MD	BAL
Monmouth, IL	PEO
OR	P
Monmouth Beach, NJ	TR
Monmouth Junction, NJ	MET
Monona, IA	DUB
Monongah, WV	WH
Monongahela, PA	PIT
Monponsett, MA	BO
Monroe, CT	BGP
GA	ATL
LA	SHP
MI	DET
NC	CHL
NY	NY
OH	CIN
WA	SEA
WI	MAD
Monroe City, MO	JC
Monroe Township, NJ	MET
Monroeville, AL	MOB
IN	FTW
OH	TOL
PA	PBR
PA	PIT
Monrovia, CA	LA
Monsey, NY	NY
Monson, MA	SPR
Mont Belvieu, TX	BEA
Mont Clare, PA	PSC
Montague, MI	GR
NJ	PAT
Montauk, NY	RVC
Montclair, CA	SB
NJ	NEW
Monte Vista, CO	PBL
Montebello, CA	LA
Montegut, LA	HT
Montello, WI	MAD
Monterey, CA	MRY
IN	LFT
Monterey Park, CA	LA
Montevallo, AL	BIR
Montevideo, MN	NU
Montezuma, OH	CIN
Montfort, WI	MAD
Montgomery, AL	MOB
IN	EVN
MN	STP
NY	NY
WV	WH
Montgomery City, MO	JC
Monticello, AR	LR
IA	DUB
IL	PEO
IN	LFT
KY	LEX
MN	STP
NY	NY
UT	SLC
Montoursville, PA	SCR
Montpelier, IN	LFT
OH	TOL
VA	RIC
VT	BUR
Montrose, CA	LA
CA	OLN
CO	PBL
IA	DAV
IL	SFD
MI	LAN
MO	KC
NY	NY
PA	SCR

SD	SFS
Montvale, NJ	NEW
Montville, NJ	PAT
Monument, CO	COS
Moodus, CT	NOR
Mooers, NY	OG
Mooers Forks, NY	OG
Moon Township, PA	PIT
Moore, OK	OKL
Moore Haven, FL	VEN
Moorefield, WV	WH
Moorestown, NJ	TR
Mooresville, IN	IND
NC	CHL
Mooreton, ND	FAR
Moorhead, MN	CR
Moorpark, CA	LA
Moose Lake, MN	DUL
Moosup, CT	NOR
Mora, MN	SCL
NM	SFE
Moraga, CA	OAK
Moreauville, LA	ALX
Morehead, KY	LEX
Morehead City, NC	R
Morenci, AZ	TUC
Moreno Valley, CA	SB
Morgan, MN	NU
Morgan City, LA	HT
LA	LAF
Morgan Hill, CA	SJ
Morganfield, KY	OWN
Morganton, NC	CHL
Morgantown, KY	OWN
WV	WH
WV	PBR
Morganza, LA	BR
MD	WDC
Moriarty, NM	SFE
Morrice, MI	LAN
Morrilton, AR	LR
Morris, IL	JOL
IN	IND
MN	SCL
NY	ALB
Morris Plains, NJ	PAT
Morrisdale, PA	E
Morrison, IL	RCK
Morrisonville, IL	SFD
NY	OG
Morristown, NJ	PAT
NY	OG
TN	KNX
Morrisville, NC	SYM
NY	SY
PA	PH
VT	BUR
Morro Bay, CA	MRY
Morrow, LA	LAF
OH	CIN
Morse, LA	LAF
Morse Bluff, NE	LIN
Morton, IL	PEO
MN	NU
PA	PH
TX	LUB
WA	SEA
Morton Grove, IL	CHI
Moscow, ID	B
PA	SCR
TN	MEM
Moses Lake, WA	YAK
Mosinee, WI	LC
Moss Beach, CA	SFR
Moss Bluff, LA	LKC
Moss Point, MS	BLX
Mott, ND	BIS
Moulton, AL	BIR
TX	VIC
Moultrie, GA	SAV
Mound, MN	STP
Mound Bayou, MS	JKS
Mound City, IL	BEL
Moundsville, WV	WH
Mount Airy, MD	BAL
Mount Angel, OR	P
Mount Arlington, NJ	PAT
Mount Calvary, WI	MIL
Mount Carmel, IL	BEL
PA	HBG
PA	PHU
Mount Carroll, IL	RCK
Mount Clemens, MI	DET
Mount Dora, FL	ORL
Mount Ephraim, NJ	CAM
Mount Holly, NJ	TR
Mount Hope, KS	WCH
Mount Horeb, WI	MAD
Mount Ida, AR	LR
Mount Jewett, PA	E
Mount Joy, PA	HBG

Mount Laurel, NJ	TR
Mount Morris, MI	LAN
Mount Olive, IL	SFD
NC	R
Mount Pleasant, IA	DAV
MI	SAG
PA	GBG
SC	CHR
TX	TYL
Mount Pocono, PA	SCR
Mount Rainier, MD	WDC
Mount Savage, MD	BAL
Mount Shasta, CA	SAC
Mount St. Francis, IN	IND
Mount St. Joseph, OH	CIN
Mount Sterling, IL	SFD
KY	LEX
Mount Union, PA	ALT
Mount Vernon, AL	MOB
IA	DUB
IL	BEL
IN	EVN
KY	LEX
MO	SPC
NY	NY
TX	TYL
WA	SEA
Mount Victoria, MD	WDC
Mount Washington, KY	L
Mount Zion, IL	SFD
Mountain City, TN	KNX
Mountain Grove, MO	SPC
Mountain Home, AR	LR
ID	B
TX	SAT
Mountain Home A F B, ID	B
Mountain Home Air Force Base, ID	B
Mountain Lakes, NJ	PAT
Mountain Top, PA	SCR
Mountain View, AR	LR
CA	SJ
HI	HON
MO	SPC
Mountain Village, AK	FBK
Mountainair, NM	SFE
Mountainside, NJ	NEW
Mountaintop, PA	SCR
Mountlake Terrace, WA	SEA
Moville, IA	SC
Moweaqua, IL	SFD
Moxee, WA	YAK
Mt Zion, IL	SFD
Mt. Airy, NC	CHL
Mt. Angel, OR	P
Mt. Hope, KS	WCH
Mt. Kisco, NY	NY
Mt. Lebanon, PA	PIT
Mt. Pleasant, SC	CHR
Mt. Prospect, IL	CHI
Mt. Shasta, CA	SAC
Mt. Sterling, KY	LEX
Mt. Vernon, IN	EVN
NY	NY
OH	COL
Muenster, TX	FWT
Mukwonago, WI	MIL
Muleshoe, TX	LUB
Mullen, NE	GI
Mullens, WV	WH
Mullica Hill, NJ	CAM
Mulvane, KS	WCH
Muncie, IN	LFT
Muncy, PA	SCR
Munday, TX	FWT
Mundelein, IL	CHI
Munger, MI	SAG
Munhall, PA	PBR
PA	PIT
Munich, ND	FAR
Munising, MI	MAR
Munjor, KS	SAL
Munnsville, NY	SY
Munster, IN	GRY
IN	PRM
IN	STN
Murdock, MN	NU
Murfreesboro, TN	NSH
Murphy, NC	CHL
Murphysboro, IL	BEL
Murray, KY	OWN
UT	OLL
UT	SLC
Murrieta, CA	SB
Murrysville, PA	GBG
Muscatine, IA	DAV
Muscoda, WI	MAD
Muse, PA	PIT
Muskego, WI	MIL
Muskegon, MI	GR
Muskegon Heights, MI	GR
Muskogee, OK	TLS

Mustang, OK	OKL
Myerstown, PA	HBG
Myrtle Beach, SC	CHR
Myrtle Creek, OR	P
Mystic, CT	NOR
Naches, WA	YAK
Nachitoches, LA	ALX
Nacogdoches, TX	TYL
Nada, TX	VIC
Nadeau, MI	MAR
Nahant, MA	BO
Nampa, ID	B
Nanakuli, HI	HON
Nanticoke, PA	PHU
PA	SCR
Nantucket, MA	FR
Nanty-Glo, PA	ALT
PA	PBR
Nanuet, NY	NY
Napa, CA	SR
Naperville, IL	JOL
Naples, FL	VEN
Napoleon, IN	IND
ND	FAR
OH	TOL
Napoleonville, LA	BR
Naranja, FL	MIA
Narberth, PA	PH
Narragansett, RI	PRO
Narrowsburg, NY	NY
Nashotah, WI	MIL
Nashua, IA	DUB
NH	MAN
Nashville, AR	LR
IL	BEL
IN	IND
KS	WCH
TN	NSH
Nashwauk, MN	DUL
Nassau, NY	ALB
Nassau Bay, TX	GAL
Natchez, LA	ALX
MS	JKS
Natchitoches, LA	ALX
Natick, MA	BO
National City, CA	SD
National Park, NJ	CAM
Natrona Heights, PA	PIT
Naugatuck, CT	HRT
Nauvoo, IL	PEO
Navajo, NM	GLP
Navarre, FL	PT
OH	Y
Navasota, TX	GAL
Nazareth, KY	L
MI	KAL
PA	ALN
TX	AMA
Nebraska City, NE	LIN
Necedah, WI	LC
Nederland, TX	BEA
Needham, MA	BO
Needles, CA	SB
Needville, TX	GAL
Neenah, WI	GB
Neffs, OH	STU
Negaunee, MI	MAR
Neillsville, WI	LC
Nekoosa, WI	LC
Neligh, NE	OM
Nelsonville, OH	STU
Nenana, AK	FBK
Neodesha, KS	WCH
Neola, IA	DM
Neopit, WI	GB
Neosho, MO	SPC
WI	MIL
Neptune, NJ	TR
Nerinx, KY	L
Nesbit, MS	JKS
Nesconset, NY	RVC
Nespelem, WA	SPK
Nesquehoning, PA	ALN
PA	PSC
Ness City, KS	DOD
Netcong, NJ	PAT
Nevada, MO	KC
Nevada City, CA	SAC
Nevis, MN	CR
New Albany, IN	IND
MS	JKS
OH	COL
New Alexandria, PA	GBG
New Almelo, KS	SAL
New Athens, IL	BEL
New Baden, IL	BEL
New Baltimore, MI	DET
PA	ALT
New Bavaria, OH	TOL
New Bedford, MA	FR
MA	SAM

PA	PIT
New Berlin, IL	SFD
NY	SY
WI	MIL
New Bern, NC	R
New Bethlehem, PA	E
New Blaine, AR	LR
New Bloomfield, PA	HBG
New Boston, MI	DET
OH	COL
TX	TYL
New Braintree, MA	WOR
New Braunfels, TX	SAT
New Bremen, OH	CIN
New Brighton, MN	STP
PA	PIT
New Britain, CT	HRT
CT	PSC
CT	STF
New Brunswick, NJ	MET
NJ	PHU
NJ	PSC
New Buffalo, MI	KAL
New Cambria, MO	JC
New Canaan, CT	BGP
New Caney, TX	GAL
New Carlisle, IN	FTW
OH	CIN
New Castle, DE	WIL
IN	IND
PA	PIT
PA	SAM
VA	RIC
New City, NY	NY
New Cumberland, PA	HBG
WV	WH
New Cuyama, CA	LA
New Derry, PA	GBG
New Egypt, NJ	TR
New England, ND	BIS
New Fairfield, CT	BGP
New Franken, WI	GB
New Freedom, PA	HBG
New Hampton, IA	DUB
New Harmony, IN	EVN
New Hartford, CT	HRT
NY	SY
New Haven, CT	HRT
CT	STF
IN	FTW
KY	L
MO	STL
New Hill, NC	R
New Holland, PA	HBG
New Holstein, WI	GB
WI	MIL
New Hope, KY	L
MN	STP
PA	PH
New Hyde Park, NY	RVC
New Iberia, LA	LAF
New Ipswich, NH	MAN
New Kensington, PA	GBG
New Lebanon, NY	ALB
New Lenox, IL	JOL
New Lexington, OH	COL
New Lisbon, WI	LC
New London, CT	NOR
NH	MAN
OH	TOL
WI	GB
New Lothrop, MI	SAG
New Madrid, MO	SPC
New Market, MN	STP
New Martinsville, WV	WH
New Melle, MO	STL
New Middletown, OH	Y
New Milford, CT	HRT
NJ	NEW
New Monmouth, NJ	TR
New Munich, MN	SCL
New Munster, WI	MIL
New Orleans, LA	NO
LA	PBR
New Oxford, PA	HBG
New Paltz, NY	NY
New Philadelphia, OH	COL
PA	ALN
New Port Richey, FL	SP
FL	PSC
New Prague, MN	STP
New Providence, NJ	NEW
New Richland, MN	WIN
New Richmond, OH	CIN
WI	SUP
New Riegel, OH	TOL
New Ringgold, PA	ALN
New Roads, LA	BR
New Rochelle, NY	NY
New Rockford, ND	FAR
New Salem, ND	BIS

PA	GBG
PA	PBR
New Smyrna Beach, FL	ORL
New Town, ND	BIS
New Ulm, MN	NU
TX	VIC
New Vernon, NJ	PAT
New Vienna, IA	DUB
New Washington, OH	TOL
New Waverly, TX	GAL
New Windsor, NY	NY
New York, NY	NY
NY	PSC
NY	STF
New York Mills, NY	SY
Newark, CA	OAK
DE	WIL
NJ	NEW
NJ	PSC
NJ	PHU
NY	ROC
OH	COL
Newaygo, MI	GR
Newberg, OR	P
Newberry, MI	MAR
SC	CHR
Newburg, MD	WDC
WI	MIL
Newburgh, IN	EVN
NY	NY
Newbury, OH	CLV
Newbury Park, CA	LA
Newburyport, MA	BO
Newcastle, WY	CHY
Newcomb, NY	OG
Newcomerstown, OH	COL
Newfane, NY	BUF
Newfield, NJ	CAM
Newington, CT	HRT
Newkirk, OK	OKL
Newman, CA	STO
Newmarket, NH	MAN
Newnan, GA	ATL
Newport, KY	COV
MI	DET
NH	MAN
NY	ALB
OR	P
RI	PRO
TN	KNX
VT	BUR
WA	SPK
Newport Beach, CA	ORG
Newport News, VA	RIC
Newry, PA	ALT
Newtok, AK	FBK
Newton, IA	DAV
IL	BEL
IL	SFD
KS	WCH
MA	BO
NC	CHL
NJ	PAT
WI	GB
Newton Falls, OH	Y
OH	PBR
Newton Grove, NC	R
Newtown, CT	BGP
PA	PH
Newtown Square, PA	PH
PA	SAM
Nez Perce, ID	B
Niagara, WI	GB
Niagara Falls, NY	BUF
NY	STF
Niagara University, NY	BUF
Niantic, CT	NOR
Niceville, FL	PT
Nicholasville, KY	LEX
Nichols, IA	DAV
Nicholson, PA	SCR
Nicktown, PA	ALT
Nicollet, MN	NU
Nicoma Park, OK	OKL
Nightmute, AK	FBK
Niles, IL	CHI
MI	KAL
OH	Y
Nine Mile Falls, WA	SPK
Nipomo, CA	MRY
Nisswa, MN	DUL
Nitro, WV	WH
Nixa, MO	SPC
Nixon, TX	SAT
Noblesville, IN	LFT
Nogales, AZ	TUC
Nokomis, FL	VEN
IL	SFD
Nome, AK	FBK
Norco, CA	SB
LA	NO
Norcross, GA	ATL
GA	SYM
Norfolk, MA	BO
NE	OM
NY	OG
VA	RIC
Norge, VA	RIC
Normal, IL	PEO
Norman, OK	OKL
Normandy, MO	STL
Norridge, IL	CHI
Norris, TN	KNX
Norristown, PA	PH
North Adams, MA	SPR
North Andover, MA	BO
North Arlington, NJ	NEW
North Attleboro, MA	FR
North Augusta, SC	CHR
North Aurora, IL	RCK
North Baltimore, OH	TOL
North Bangor, NY	OG
North Bay, NY	SY
North Beach, MD	WDC
North Bend, NE	OM
OH	CIN
OR	P
North Bennington, VT	BUR
North Bergen, NJ	NEW
North Bethesda, MD	WDC
North Branch, MI	DET
MN	STP
North Branford, CT	HRT
North Brookfield, MA	WOR
North Brunswick, NJ	MET
North Caldwell, NJ	NEW
North Canton, OH	Y
North Cape May, NJ	CAM
North Charleston, SC	CHR
North Chili, NY	ROC
North Collins, NY	BUF
North Conway, NH	MAN
North Creek, NY	ALB
North Dartmouth, MA	FR
North Dighton, MA	FR
North East, PA	E
North Easton, MA	FR
North English, IA	DAV
North Evans, NY	BUF
North Falmouth, MA	FR
North Fond du Lac, WI	MIL
North Grafton, MA	WOR
North Grosvenordale, CT	NOR
North Guilford, CT	HRT
North Haledon, NJ	PAT
North Haven, CT	HRT
North Highlands, CA	SAC
North Hills, CA	LA
North Hollywood, CA	LA
CA	NTN
CA	OLD
CA	SPA
North Huntingdon, PA	GBG
PA	PBR
North Jackson, OH	Y
OH	OLL
North Judson, IN	GRY
North Kingstown, RI	PRO
North Lake, WI	MIL
North Las Vegas, NV	LAV
North Lauderdale, FL	MIA
North Lima, OH	Y
North Little Rock, AR	LR
North Manchester, IN	FTW
North Mankato, MN	NU
North Merrick, NY	RVC
North Miami, FL	MIA
North Miami Beach, FL	MIA
North Muskegon, MI	GR
North Myrtle Beach, SC	CHR
North Olmsted, OH	CLV
North Oxford, MA	WOR
North Palm Beach, FL	PMB
North Plainfield, NJ	MET
North Plains, OR	P
North Platte, NE	GI
NE	LIN
North Pole, AK	FBK
North Port, FL	SJP
FL	VEN
North Providence, RI	PRO
North Reading, MA	BO
North Ridgeville, OH	CLV
North Riverside, IL	CHI
North Royalton, OH	CLV
OH	PRM
North Saint Paul, MN	STP
North Scituate, RI	PRO
North Smithfield, RI	PRO
North Stonington, CT	NOR
North Syracuse, NY	SY
North Tonawanda, NY	BUF
North Topsail Beach, NC	R
North Vernon, IN	IND
North Wales, PA	PH
North Wildwood, NJ	CAM
North Wilkesboro, NC	CHL
Northampton, MA	SPR
PA	ALN
PA	PHU
Northboro, MA	WOR
Northbridge, MA	WOR
Northbrook, IL	CHI
Northern Cambria, PA	ALT
PA	PBR
PA	SJP
Northfield, IL	CHI
MA	SPR
MN	STP
NJ	CAM
OH	CLV
VT	BUR
Northford, CT	HRT
Northglenn, CO	DEN
Northlake, IL	CHI
IL	NTN
Northport, NY	RVC
WA	SPK
Northridge, CA	LA
Northvale, NJ	NEW
Northville, MI	DET
NY	ALB
Northwood, OH	PRM
Norton, KS	SAL
MA	FR
OH	CLV
VA	RIC
Nortonville, KS	KCK
Norwalk, CA	LA
CT	BGP
IA	DM
OH	TOL
Norway, ME	PRT
MI	MAR
Norwell, MA	BO
Norwich, CT	NOR
NY	SY
Norwichtown, CT	NOR
Norwood, MA	BO
MN	STP
NJ	NEW
NY	OG
PA	PH
Notre Dame, IN	FTW
Novato, CA	SFR
Novi, MI	DET
Nulato, AK	FBK
Nutley, NJ	NEW
Nyack, NY	NY
Nyssa, OR	BAK
O Fallon, IL	BEL
O'Donnell, TX	LUB
O'Fallon, IL	BEL
MO	STL
O'Neill, NE	OM
Oak Brook, IL	JOL
Oak Creek, WI	MIL
Oak Forest, IL	CHI
Oak Grove, KY	OWN
LA	SHP
MN	STP
Oak Harbor, OH	TOL
WA	SEA
Oak Hill, WV	WH
Oak Lawn, IL	CHI
Oak Park, IL	CHI
MI	DET
MI	EST
Oak Ridge, NJ	PAT
TN	KNX
Oak Ridge–Milton, NJ	PAT
Oakbrook Terrace, IL	JOL
IL	OLL
Oakdale, CA	STO
CT	NOR
IL	BEL
LA	LKC
MN	STP
NE	OM
NY	RVC
PA	PIT
Oakes, ND	FAR
Oakfield, NY	BUF
Oakhurst, CA	FRS
Oakland, CA	OAK
MD	BAL
NJ	NEW
Oakland City, IN	EVN
Oakland Gardens, NY	BRK
Oakland Park, FL	MIA
Oakley, CA	OAK
KS	SAL
MI	SAG
Oaklyn, NJ	CAM
Oakmont, PA	PIT
Oakridge, OR	P
Oakville, CA	SR
CT	HRT
MO	STL
Oberlin, KS	SAL
LA	LKC
OH	CLV
Obernburg, NY	NY
Ocala, FL	ORL
Occidental, CA	SR
Ocean Beach, NY	RVC
Ocean City, MD	WIL
NJ	CAM
Ocean Grove, NJ	TR
Ocean Springs, MS	BLX
Oceanside, CA	SD
NY	RVC
Oconee, IL	SFD
Oconomowoc, WI	MIL
Oconto, WI	GB
Oconto Falls, WI	GB
Odebolt, IA	SC
Odell, IL	PEO
Odem, TX	CC
Odenton, MD	BAL
Odessa, MO	KC
TX	SAN
Oelwein, IA	DUB
Ogallala, NE	GI
Ogden, IA	SC
UT	SLC
Ogdensburg, NJ	PAT
NY	OG
Ogema, MN	CR
Oglala, SD	RC
Oglesby, IL	PEO
Ohio, IL	PEO
Ohkay Owingeh, NM	SFE
Oil City, PA	E
Ojai, CA	LA
Okanogan, WA	SPK
Okarche, OK	OKL
Okawville, IL	BEL
Okeechobee, FL	PMB
Okeene, OK	OKL
Okemos, MI	LAN
Oklahoma City, OK	OKL
OK	SYM
Oklee, MN	CR
Okmulgee, OK	TLS
Olathe, KS	KCK
Old Bridge, NJ	MET
Old Fields, WV	WH
Old Forge, NY	OG
PA	PSC
PA	SCR
Old Hickory, TN	NSH
Old Lyme, CT	NOR
Old Monroe, MO	STL
Old Orchard Beach, ME	PRT
Old Saybrook, CT	NOR
Old Tappan, NJ	NEW
Old Town, ME	PRT
Old Westbury, NY	RVC
Oldenburg, IN	IND
Oldsmar, FL	SP
Olean, NY	BUF
NY	SAM
NY	PSC
Olema, CA	SFR
Olive Branch, MS	JKS
Olive Hill, KY	LEX
Olivia, MN	NU
Olmito, TX	BWN
Olmitz, KS	DOD
Olmsted Falls, OH	CLV
Olney, IL	BEL
MD	WDC
Olpe, KS	KCK
Olympia, WA	ROM
WA	SEA
WA	VNN
Olympia Fields, IL	CHI
Olyphant, PA	PHU
PA	SCR
Omaha, NE	OM
NE	STN
Omak, WA	SPK
Omer, MI	PRM
Omro, WI	GB
Ona, WV	WH
Onaga, KS	KCK
Onalaska, WI	LC
Onamia, MN	SCL
Onawa, IA	SC
Onaway, MI	GAY
Oneida, NY	SY
WI	GB
Onekama, MI	GAY

Oneonta, AL	BIR
NY	ALB
Onida, SD	SFS
Onley, VA	RIC
Onset, MA	FR
Onsted, MI	DET
Ontario, CA	SB
NY	ROC
OR	BAK
Ontonagon, MI	MAR
Opelika, AL	MOB
Opelousas, LA	LAF
Oquossoc, ME	PRT
Oracle, AZ	TUC
Oradell, NJ	NEW
Oran, MO	SPC
Orange, CA	ORG
CT	HRT
MA	SPR
NJ	NEW
TX	BEA
VA	ARL
Orange Beach, AL	MOB
Orange Cove, CA	FRS
Orange Grove, TX	CC
TX	SYM
Orange Park, FL	STA
Orangeburg, NY	NY
SC	CHR
Orangevale, CA	SAC
Orbisonia, PA	ALT
Orchard Lake, MI	DET
Orchard Park, NY	BUF
Ord, NE	GI
Orefield, PA	ALN
Oregon, IL	RCK
OH	TOL
WI	MAD
Oregon City, OR	P
Oreland, PA	PH
Orem, UT	SLC
Orient, SD	SFS
Oriental, NC	R
Orinda, CA	OAK
Orion, IL	PEO
Oriska, ND	FAR
Oriskany Falls, NY	SY
Orland, CA	SAC
Orland Hills, IL	CHI
Orland Park, IL	CHI
Orlando, FL	ORL
FL	PSC
FL	SAM
Orleans, MA	FR
NE	LIN
Ormond Beach, FL	ORL
Oro Valley, AZ	TUC
Orofino, ID	B
Orono, ME	PRT
Oroville, CA	SAC
WA	SPK
Orr, MN	DUL
Orrtanna, PA	HBG
Orrville, AL	MOB
OH	CLV
Ortonville, MI	DET
MN	NU
Orwell, OH	Y
VT	BUR
Orwigsburg, PA	ALN
Osage, IA	DUB
Osage City, KS	KCK
Osakis, MN	SCL
Osawatomie, KS	KCK
Osborne, KS	SAL
Osceola, AR	LR
IA	DM
NE	LIN
WI	SUP
Oscoda, MI	GAY
Osgood, IN	IND
OH	CIN
Oshkosh, WI	GB
Oskaloosa, IA	DAV
Oslo, MN	CR
Osmond, NE	OM
Osprey, FL	VEN
Osseo, MN	STP
Ossian, IA	DUB
Ossineke, MI	GAY
Ossining, NY	NY
Osterville, MA	FR
Oswego, IL	JOL
KS	WCH
NY	SY
Othello, WA	SPK
Otis Orchards, WA	SPK
Otisville, MI	LAN
NY	NY
Otsego, MI	KAL
Ottawa, IL	PEO
KS	KCK
OH	TOL
Ottawa (Naplate), IL	PEO
Otter River, MA	WOR
Ottoville, OH	TOL
Ottsville, PA	PH
Ottumwa, IA	DAV
Ouray, CO	PBL
Overgaard, AZ	GLP
Overland, MO	STL
Overland Park, KS	KCK
Overton, NV	LAV
Ovid, MI	LAN
NY	ROC
Oviedo, FL	ORL
Owasso, OK	TLS
Owatonna, MN	WIN
Owego, NY	ROC
Owen, WI	LC
Owensboro, KY	OWN
Owensville, MO	JC
OH	CIN
Owings, MD	WDC
Owings Mills, MD	BAL
Owingsville, KY	LEX
Owosso, MI	LAN
Oxford, CT	HRT
IA	DAV
IN	LFT
MA	WOR
MI	DET
MS	JKS
NJ	MET
OH	CIN
PA	PH
WI	LC
Oxnard, CA	LA
Oxon Hill, MD	WDC
Oyster Bay, NY	RVC
Ozark, AL	MOB
AR	LR
MO	SPC
Ozona, TX	SAN
Ozone Park, NY	BRK
NY	STF
Pacific, MO	STL
Pacific Grove, CA	MRY
Pacific Palisades, CA	LA
Pacifica, CA	SFR
Pacoima, CA	LA
Paden City, WV	WH
Paducah, KY	OWN
Page, AZ	GLP
Pagosa Springs, CO	PBL
Pahala, HI	HON
Pahoa, HI	HON
Pahokee, FL	PMB
Pahrump, NV	LAV
Paia, HI	HON
Paincourtville, LA	BR
Painesville, OH	CLV
Paintsville, KY	LEX
Pala, CA	SD
Palacios, TX	VIC
Palatine, IL	CHI
IL	STN
Palatka, FL	STA
Palestine, TX	TYL
Palisades Park, NJ	NEW
Palm Bay, FL	ORL
Palm Beach, FL	PMB
Palm Beach Gardens, FL	PMB
Palm City, FL	PMB
Palm Coast, FL	STA
Palm Desert, CA	SB
Palm Harbor, FL	SP
Palm Springs, CA	SB
FL	PMB
Palmdale, CA	LA
Palmer, AK	ANC
MA	SPR
Palmerton, PA	ALN
PA	PHU
Palmetto, FL	VEN
Palms, MI	SAG
Palmview, TX	BWN
Palmyra, MO	JC
NE	LIN
NY	ROC
PA	HBG
VA	RIC
WI	MAD
Palo Alto, CA	SJ
Palos Heights, IL	CHI
Palos Hills, IL	CHI
Palos Park, IL	CHI
IL	STN
Pampa, TX	AMA
Pana, IL	SFD
Panama, IA	DM
Panama City, FL	PT
Panama City Beach, FL	PT
Panhandle, TX	AMA
Panna Maria, TX	SAT
Panora, IA	DM
Panorama City, CA	LA
Paola, KS	KCK
Paoli, IN	IND
PA	PH
Paonia, CO	PBL
Papaikou, HI	HON
Papillion, NE	OM
Paradis, LA	NO
Paradise, CA	SAC
MI	MAR
Paradox, NY	ALB
Paragould, AR	LR
Paramount, CA	LA
Paramus, NJ	NEW
Parchment, MI	KAL
Pardeeville, WI	MAD
Paris, AR	LR
IL	SFD
KY	LEX
TN	MEM
TX	TYL
Park, KS	SAL
Park City, UT	SLC
Park Falls, WI	SUP
Park Forest, IL	CHI
IL	JOL
Park Hills, KY	COV
MO	STL
Park Rapids, MN	CR
Park Ridge, IL	CHI
NJ	NEW
Park River, ND	FAR
Parker, AZ	TUC
CO	COS
SD	SFS
Parkers Prairie, MN	SCL
Parkersburg, WV	WH
Parkesburg, PA	PH
Parkland, FL	MIA
Parkman, OH	CLV
Parks, LA	LAF
Parkston, SD	SFS
Parkville, MD	BAL
Parlier, CA	FRS
Parlin, NJ	MET
Parma, OH	CLV
OH	PRM
OH	SJP
Parma Heights, OH	CLV
Parnell, MO	KC
Parrish, FL	VEN
Parshall, ND	BIS
Parsippany, NJ	PAT
Parsons, KS	WCH
Pasadena, CA	LA
MD	BAL
TX	GAL
Pascagoula, MS	BLX
Pasco, WA	SPK
Pascoag, RI	PRO
Paso Robles, CA	MRY
Pass Christian, MS	BLX
Passaic, NJ	PAT
NJ	PHU
NJ	PSC
Patagonia, AZ	TUC
Patchogue, NY	RVC
Paterson, NJ	PAT
Patterson, CA	STO
LA	LAF
NY	NY
Pattison, TX	GAL
Patton, PA	ALT
PA	PBR
Paulding, OH	TOL
Paulina, LA	BR
Pauls Valley, OK	OKL
Paulsboro, NJ	CAM
Pavilion, NY	BUF
Paw Paw, MI	KAL
Pawcatuck, CT	NOR
Pawhuska, OK	TLS
Pawleys Island, SC	CHR
Pawling, NY	NY
Pawnee Rock, KS	DOD
Pawtucket, RI	PRO
Paxico, KS	KCK
Paxton, IL	JOL
MA	WOR
Paynesville, MN	SCL
Payneville, KY	L
Payson, AZ	PHX
AZ	TUC
UT	SLC
Pe Ell, WA	SEA
Peabody, MA	BO
Peachtree City, GA	ATL
Pearblossom, CA	ROM
Pearce, AZ	TUC
Pearisburg, VA	RIC
Pearl, MS	JKS
Pearl City, HI	HON
Pearl River, LA	NO
NY	NY
Pearland, TX	GAL
Pearsall, TX	SAT
Pecatonica, IL	RCK
Peckville, PA	SCR
Pecos, NM	SFE
TX	ELP
Peebles, OH	CIN
Peekskill, NY	NY
NY	PSC
Peetz, CO	DEN
Pekin, IL	PEO
Pelham, AL	BIR
NH	MAN
NY	NY
Pelham Manor, NY	NY
Pelican Rapids, MN	SCL
Pell City, AL	BIR
Pella, IA	DAV
Pellston, MI	GAY
Pembina, ND	FAR
Pembine, WI	GB
Pembroke, MA	BO
Pembroke Pines, FL	MIA
FL	SYM
Pen Argyl, PA	ALN
Pena Blanca, NM	SFE
Penacook, NH	MAN
Penasco, NM	SFE
Pence Springs, WV	WH
Pender, NE	OM
Pendleton, OR	BAK
Penelope, TX	FWT
Penfield, IL	PEO
NY	ROC
Peninsula, OH	CLV
Penitas, TX	BWN
Penn Hills, PA	PIT
Penn Yan, NY	ROC
Penndel, PA	PH
Penngrove, CA	SR
Pennington, NJ	TR
Pennsauken, NJ	CAM
Pennsburg, PA	PH
Pennsville, NJ	CAM
Pensacola, FL	PT
Peoria, AZ	PHX
IL	OLL
IL	PEO
Peoria Heights, IL	PEO
Peosta, IA	DUB
Peotone, IL	JOL
Pepper Pike, OH	CLV
Pepperell, MA	BO
Pequannock, NJ	PAT
Pequot Lakes, MN	DUL
Peralta, NM	SFE
Perham, MN	SCL
Perkins, MI	MAR
Perris, CA	SB
CA	SPA
Perry, FL	PT
IA	DM
KS	KCK
ME	PRT
MO	JC
NY	BUF
OH	CLV
OK	OKL
Perryopolis, PA	GBG
PA	PBR
Perrysburg, OH	TOL
Perryton, TX	AMA
Perryville, MD	WIL
MO	STL
Perth Amboy, NJ	MET
NJ	PHU
NJ	PSC
Peru, IL	PEO
IN	LFT
NY	OG
Peshtigo, WI	GB
Pesotum, IL	PEO
Petal, MS	BLX
Petaluma, CA	SR
Peterborough, NH	MAN
Petersburg, AK	JUN
IL	SFD
IN	EVN
NE	OM
TX	LUB
VA	RIC
WV	WH
Petersham, MA	SAM
MA	WOR

Petoskey, MI	GAY
Pettus, TX	CC
Pevely, MO	STL
Pewamo, MI	GR
Pewaukee, WI	MIL
Pewee Valley, KY	L
Pflugerville, TX	AUS
Pharr, TX	BWN
TX	SYM
Phelan, CA	SB
Phenix City, AL	MOB
Philadelphia, MS	JKS
PA	PH
PA	SYM
PA	PHU
PA	SAM
PA	PSC
Philip, SD	RC
Philippi, WV	WH
WV	OLL
Philipsburg, PA	ALT
Phillips, WI	SUP
Phillipsburg, KS	SAL
NJ	MET
NJ	PSC
Philo, IL	PEO
Philpot, KY	OWN
Phlox, WI	GB
Phoenicia, NY	NY
Phoenix, AZ	NTN
AZ	OLL
AZ	PHX
AZ	STN
AZ	VNN
AZ	SYM
NY	SY
Phoenixville, PA	PH
Picayune, MS	BLX
Pickens, SC	CHR
Pickerel, WI	GB
Pickerington, OH	COL
Pico Rivera, CA	LA
Piedmont, CA	OAK
MO	SPC
OK	OKL
SD	RC
Pierce, NE	OM
Pierce City, MO	SPC
Pierceton, IN	FTW
Piermont, NY	NY
Pierre, SD	SFS
Pierre Part, LA	BR
Pierron, IL	SFD
Pierz, MN	SCL
Piffard, NY	ROC
Pigeon, MI	SAG
Pigeon Forge, TN	KNX
Pikeville, KY	LEX
Pilot Grove, MO	JC
Pilot Knob, MO	SPC
Pilot Point, TX	FWT
Pilot Rock, OR	BAK
Pilot Station, AK	FBK
Pinckney, MI	LAN
Pinckneyville, IL	BEL
Pinconning, MI	SAG
Pine Apple, AL	MOB
Pine Bluff, AR	LR
Pine Bluffs, WY	CHY
Pine Bush, NY	NY
Pine City, MN	DUL
NY	ROC
Pine Grove, PA	SCR
Pine Island, MN	STP
NY	NY
Pine Mountain, GA	SAV
Pine Plains, NY	NY
Pine Prairie, LA	LAF
Pine Ridge, SD	RC
Pine River, MN	DUL
Pinecrest, FL	MIA
Pinedale, WY	CHY
Pinehurst, NC	R
Pinellas Park, FL	SP
Pinetop, AZ	GLP
Pineville, LA	ALX
WV	WH
Pinole, CA	OAK
Pinon, AZ	GLP
Piper City, IL	JOL
Pipestone, MN	WIN
Piqua, OH	CIN
Pirtleville, AZ	TUC
Piscataway, NJ	MET
Pisek, ND	FAR
Pismo Beach, CA	MRY
Pitcairn, PA	PIT
Pitman, NJ	CAM
Pittsboro, NC	R
Pittsburg, CA	OAK
KS	WCH
TX	TYL
Pittsburgh, PA	PBR
PA	SJP
PA	PIT
Pittsfield, IL	SFD
MA	SPR
MA	STF
NH	MAN
Pittsford, NY	ROC
VT	BUR
Pittston, PA	PSC
PA	SCR
Pittstown, NJ	MET
Pittsville, WI	LC
Placentia, CA	NTN
CA	ORG
Placerville, CA	SAC
Plain, WI	MAD
Plain City, OH	COL
Plainfield, CT	NOR
IL	JOL
IN	IND
NJ	NEW
WI	GB
Plains, KS	DOD
MT	HEL
PA	SCR
Plainsboro, NJ	MET
Plainview, MN	WIN
NE	OM
NY	RVC
TX	LUB
Plainville, CT	HRT
KS	SAL
MA	BO
Plaistow, NH	MAN
Planada, CA	FRS
Plankinton, SD	SFS
Plano, IL	JOL
TX	DAL
Plant City, FL	SP
Plantation, FL	MIA
Plantation Key, FL	MIA
Plantersville, TX	GAL
Plantsville, CT	HRT
Plaquemine, LA	BR
Platte, SD	SFS
Platte Center, NE	OM
Platte City, MO	KC
Plattekill, NY	NY
Platteville, CO	DEN
WI	MAD
Plattsburg, MO	KC
Plattsburgh, NY	VG
Plattsmouth, NE	LIN
Plaucheville, LA	ALX
Playa del Rey, CA	LA
Plaza, ND	BIS
Pleasant City, OH	PBR
Pleasant Grove, AL	BIR
Pleasant Hill, CA	OAK
MO	KC
Pleasant Mount, PA	SCR
Pleasant Prairie, WI	MIL
Pleasant Valley, NY	NY
Pleasanton, CA	OAK
TX	SAT
Pleasantville, NJ	CAM
NY	NY
Plentywood, MT	GF
Plover, WI	LC
WI	SUP
Plum, PA	PIT
Plum City, WI	LC
Plymouth, IN	FTW
MA	BO
MI	DET
MI	LAN
MI	NTN
MN	STP
NC	R
NH	MAN
OH	TOL
PA	PHU
PA	SCR
WI	MIL
Plymouth Meeting, PA	PH
Pocahontas, AR	LR
IA	SC
Pocasset, MA	FR
Pocatello, ID	B
Pocomoke City, MD	WIL
Pocono Pines, PA	SCR
Pocono Summit, PA	PSC
Point Arena, CA	SR
Point Lookout, NY	RVC
Point Pleasant, NJ	TR
WV	WH
Point Pleasant Beach, NJ	TR
Point Richmond, CA	OAK
Pointe A La Hache, LA	NO
Poland, OH	Y
Polo, IL	RCK
Polonia, WI	LC
Polson, MT	HEL
Pomeroy, OH	STU
WA	SPK
Pomfret, CT	NOR
MD	WDC
Pomona, CA	LA
NJ	CAM
Pompano Beach, FL	MIA
Pompey, NY	SY
Pompton Lakes, NJ	NY
NJ	PAT
Pompton Plains, NJ	PAT
Ponca, NE	OM
Ponca City, OK	OKL
Ponchatoula, LA	BR
LA	NO
Ponte Vedra Beach, FL	STA
Pontiac, IL	PEO
MI	DET
Pontotoc, MS	JKS
Poolesville, MD	WDC
Poplar, MT	GF
Poplar Bluff, MO	SPC
Poquonock, CT	HRT
Porcupine, SD	RC
Port Allegany, PA	E
Port Allen, LA	BR
Port Angeles, WA	SEA
Port Aransas, TX	CC
Port Arthur, TX	BEA
Port Austin, MI	SAG
Port Barre, LA	LAF
Port Carbon, PA	ALN
Port Charlotte, FL	VEN
Port Chester, NY	NY
Port Clinton, OH	TOL
Port Crane, NY	SY
Port Edwards, WI	LC
Port Ewen, NY	NY
Port Gibson, MS	JKS
Port Henry, NY	OG
Port Huron, MI	DET
Port Isabel, TX	BWN
Port Jefferson, NY	RVC
Port Jefferson Station, NY	RVC
Port Jervis, NY	NY
Port Lavaca, TX	VIC
Port Leyden, NY	OG
Port Murray, NJ	MET
Port Neches, TX	BEA
Port Orange, FL	ORL
Port Orchard, WA	SEA
Port Reading, NJ	MET
Port Richey, FL	SP
Port Sanilac, MI	SAG
Port St. Joe, FL	PT
Port St. Lucie, FL	PMB
Port Sulphur, LA	NO
Port Tobacco, MD	WDC
Port Townsend, WA	SEA
Port Vue, PA	PIT
Port Washington, NY	RVC
WI	MIL
Port Wentworth, GA	SAV
Portage, IN	GRY
MI	KAL
PA	ALT
PA	PBR
WI	MAD
Portage Des Sioux, MO	STL
Portageville, MO	SPC
Portales, NM	SFE
Porterfield, WI	GB
Porterville, CA	FRS
Portland, CT	NOR
IN	LFT
ME	PRT
MI	GR
OR	P
OR	OLL
TX	CC
Portola, CA	SAC
Portola Valley, CA	SFR
Portsmouth, IA	DM
NH	MAN
OH	COL
RI	PRO
VA	RIC
Posen, IL	CHI
MI	GAY
Poseyville, IN	EVN
Post, TX	LUB
Post Falls, ID	B
Poteau, OK	TLS
Poteet, TX	SAT
Poth, TX	SAT
Potomac, MD	WDC
Potomac Falls, VA	ARL
Potosi, MO	STL
WI	MAD
Potsdam, NY	OG
Pottstown, PA	PH
PA	PSC
PA	PHU
Pottsville, PA	ALN
Poughkeepsie, NY	NY
Poulsbo, WA	SEA
Poultney, VT	BUR
Poway, CA	SD
Powell, OH	COL
WY	CHY
Powhatan, LA	ALX
VA	RIC
WV	WH
Poynette, WI	MAD
Prague, NE	LIN
OK	OKL
Prairie Du Rocher, IL	BEL
Prairie View, TX	GAL
Prairie Village, KS	KCK
Prairie du Chien, WI	LC
Prairie du Rocher, IL	BEL
Prairie du Sac, WI	MAD
Prairieburg, IA	DUB
Prairieville, LA	BR
Pratt, KS	DOD
Prattville, AL	MOB
Prayer Town, TX	AMA
Premont, TX	CC
Prescott, AZ	PHX
MI	GAY
WI	LC
Prescott Valley, AZ	PHX
Presho, SD	RC
Presidio, TX	ELP
Presque Isle, ME	PRT
Preston, CT	NOR
IA	DUB
Prestonsburg, KY	LEX
Price, UT	SLC
Prichard, AL	MOB
Priest River, ID	B
Primos, PA	PH
Prince Frederick, MD	WDC
Princess Anne, MD	WIL
Princeton, FL	MIA
IL	PEO
IN	EVN
KY	OWN
MA	WOR
NJ	TR
NJ	MET
WI	MAD
WV	WH
Princeton Jct., NJ	TR
Princeville, IL	PEO
Prineville, OR	BAK
Prior Lake, MN	STP
Proctor, MN	DUL
VT	BUR
WV	WH
Progreso, TX	BWN
Prophetstown, IL	RCK
Prospect, CT	HRT
KY	L
PA	PIT
Prospect Heights, IL	CHI
Prospect Park, NJ	PAT
Prosser, WA	YAK
Protivin, IA	DUB
Providence, RI	OLD
RI	PRO
Provincetown, MA	FR
Prudenville, MI	GAY
Pryor, MT	GF
OK	TLS
Pueblo, CO	PBL
Pueblo of Acoma, NM	GLP
Pulaski, NY	SY
TN	NSH
WI	GB
Pullman, WA	SPK
Punta Gorda, FL	VEN
Punxsutawney, PA	E
PA	PBR
Purcell, OK	OKL
Purcellville, VA	ARL
Put–In–Bay, OH	TOL
Putnam, CT	BUR
CT	NOR
Putney, VT	BUR
Puyallup, WA	SEA
Pylesville, MD	BAL
Quaker Hill, CT	NOR
Quakertown, PA	PH
Quarryville, PA	HBG
Queen Creek, AZ	PHX
Queens, NY	BRK
Queens Village, NY	BRK

Queensbury, NY	ALB
Quemado, NM	GLP
Questa, NM	SFE
Quincy, CA	SAC
FL	PT
IL	SFD
MA	BO
WA	YAK
Quinebaug, CT	NOR
Quinlan, TX	DAL
Quinque, VA	RIC
Quinton, VA	RIC
Raceland, LA	HT
Racine, WI	MIL
Radcliff, KY	L
Radnor, PA	PH
PA	OLN
Radom, IL	BEL
Raeford, NC	R
Rahway, NJ	NEW
NJ	PSC
Rainelle, WV	WH
Rainier, OR	P
Raleigh, NC	R
NC	SJP
Ralls, TX	LUB
Ralston, NE	OM
Ramah, NM	GLP
Ramey, PA	E
PA	SJP
Ramona, CA	SD
Ramsey, IL	SFD
MN	STP
NJ	NEW
Rancho Cordova, CA	SAC
Rancho Cucamonga, CA	SB
Rancho Dominguez, CA	LA
Rancho Palos Verdes, CA	LA
Rancho Santa Fe, CA	SD
Rancho Santa Margarita, CA	ORG
Ranchos De Taos, NM	SFE
Rancocas, NJ	TR
Randall, MN	SCL
Randallstown, MD	BAL
Randolph, MA	BO
NE	OM
NJ	PAT
VT	BUR
Random Lake, WI	MIL
Rangely, CO	DEN
Ranger, TX	FWT
Ransom, IL	PEO
Ransomville, NY	BUF
Rantoul, IL	PEO
Rapid City, SD	RC
Rapid River, MI	MAR
Rapids City, IL	PEO
Rapson, MI	SAG
Raritan, IL	PEO
NJ	MET
Ratcliff, AR	LR
Raton, NM	SFE
Ravena, NY	ALB
Ravenna, KY	LEX
MI	GR
NE	GI
OH	Y
Ravenswood, WV	WH
Rawlins, WY	CHY
Ray Township, MI	DET
Raymond, IL	SFD
MS	JKS
WA	SEA
Raymondville, TX	BWN
Rayne, LA	LAF
Raynham Center, MA	FR
Raytown, MO	KC
Rayville, LA	SHP
Raywick, KY	L
Raywood, TX	BEA
Reading, MA	BO
OH	CIN
PA	ALN
PA	PHU
Readsboro, VT	BUR
Readville, MA	BO
Red Bank, NJ	TR
Red Bluff, CA	SAC
Red Bud, IL	BEL
Red Cloud, NE	LIN
Red Hook, NY	NY
Red Lake, MN	CR
Red Lake Falls, MN	CR
Red Lodge, MT	GF
Red Oak, IA	DM
Red Springs, NC	R
Red Wing, MN	STP
Redding, CA	SAC
Redding Ridge, CT	BGP
Redfield, SD	SFS
Redford, MI	DET
NY	OG
Redford Township, MI	DET
Redgranite, WI	GB
Redlands, CA	SB
Redmond, OR	BAK
WA	SEA
Redondo Beach, CA	LA
Redwood City, CA	SJ
CA	SFR
Redwood Falls, MN	NU
Redwood Valley, CA	STN
Reed, KY	OWN
Reed City, MI	GR
Reedley, CA	FRS
Reedsburg, WI	MAD
Reedsport, OR	P
Reese, MI	SAG
Reeseville, WI	MIL
Refugio, TX	CC
Regent, ND	BIS
Rego Park, NY	BRK
Rehoboth Beach, DE	WIL
Reidsville, NC	CHL
Reinbeck, IA	DUB
Remington, IN	LFT
Remsen, IA	SC
Remus, MI	GR
Renault, IL	BEL
Reno, NV	RNO
Renovo, PA	ALT
Rensselaer, IN	LFT
NY	ALB
Renton, WA	SEA
Renville, MN	NU
Republic, MI	MAR
MO	SPC
PA	GBG
WA	SPK
Reseda, CA	LA
Reserve, LA	NO
NM	GLP
Reston, VA	ARL
Revere, MA	BO
Revillo, SD	SFS
Reynolds, IN	LFT
ND	FAR
Reynoldsburg, OH	COL
Reynoldsville, PA	E
Rhinebeck, NY	NY
Rhineland, MO	JC
Rhinelander, WI	SUP
Rhodell, WV	WH
Rialto, CA	SB
Rib Lake, WI	SUP
Ribera, NM	SFE
Rice, MN	SCL
Rice Lake, WI	SUP
Riceville, IA	DUB
Rich Fountain, MO	JC
Richardson, TX	DAL
Richardton, ND	BIS
Richboro, PA	PH
Richeyville, PA	PIT
Richfield, MN	STP
OH	CLV
Richfield Springs, NY	ALB
Richford, VT	BUR
Richland, IA	DAV
NJ	CAM
NY	SY
WA	YAK
Richland Center, WI	LC
Richmond, CA	OAK
IL	RCK
IN	IND
KY	LEX
MI	DET
MN	SCL
MO	KC
OH	STU
TX	GAL
VA	RIC
VT	BUR
Richmond Heights, MO	STL
Richmond Hill, GA	SAV
NY	BRK
Richwood, TX	GAL
WV	WH
Richwoods, MO	STL
Ridge, MD	WDC
Ridge Manor, FL	SP
Ridgecrest, CA	FRS
Ridgefield, CT	BGP
NJ	NEW
Ridgefield Park, NJ	NEW
Ridgeland, SC	CHR
Ridgeley, WV	WH
Ridgely, MD	WIL
Ridgeway, WI	MAD
Ridgewood, NJ	NEW
NY	BRK
Ridgway, IL	BEL
PA	E
Ridley Park, PA	PH
Riegelsville, PA	PH
Rifle, CO	DEN
Ringtown, PA	ALN
Ringwood, NJ	PAT
Rio Bravo, TX	LAR
Rio Grande, OH	STU
Rio Grande City, TX	BWN
Rio Hondo, TX	BWN
Rio Rancho, NM	SFE
Rio Rico, AZ	TUC
Rio Vista, CA	SAC
Ripley, MS	JKS
OH	CIN
Ripon, CA	STO
WI	MIL
Rittman, OH	CLV
Ritzville, WA	SPK
River Edge, NJ	NEW
River Falls, WI	LC
WI	SUP
River Forest, IL	CHI
River Grove, IL	CHI
River Ridge, LA	NO
River Rouge, MI	DET
Riverbank, CA	STO
Riverdale, CA	FRS
GA	ATL
IL	CHI
MD	WDC
NY	NY
Riverdale Park, MD	WDC
Riverhead, NY	RVC
NY	STF
Riverside, CA	SB
CT	BGP
IA	DAV
IL	CHI
NJ	TR
RI	PRO
Riverton, IL	SFD
NJ	TR
UT	SLC
WY	CHY
Riverview, FL	SP
MI	DET
Riviera, TX	CC
Riviera Beach, FL	PMB
Roanoke, IL	PEO
IN	FTW
TX	FWT
VA	RIC
VA	SAM
Roanoke Rapids, NC	R
Roaring Spring, PA	ALT
Robbinsdale, MN	STP
Robertsdale, AL	MOB
Robesonia, PA	ALN
Robinson, IL	SFD
Robinsonville, MS	JKS
Robstown, TX	CC
Rochelle, IL	RCK
Rochelle Park, NJ	NEW
Rochester, IL	SFD
IN	LFT
MI	DET
MN	WIN
NH	MAN
NY	NTN
NY	ROC
NY	STF
PA	PIT
Rochester Hills, MI	DET
Rock Creek, OH	Y
Rock Falls, IL	RCK
Rock Hill, SC	CHR
Rock Island, IL	PEO
Rock Rapids, IA	SC
Rock Springs, WY	CHY
Rock Valley, IA	SC
Rockaway, NJ	PAT
OR	P
Rockaway Beach, NY	BRK
Rockaway Park, NY	BRK
Rockaway Point, NY	BRK
Rockdale, IL	JOL
TX	AUS
Rockford, IA	DUB
IL	RCK
MI	GR
OH	CIN
Rockland, MA	BO
WI	LC
Rockledge, FL	ORL
Rocklin, CA	SAC
Rockport, IN	EVN
TX	CC
Rocksprings, TX	SAT
Rockville, CT	NOR
IN	IND
MD	WDC
MN	SCL
VA	RIC
Rockville Centre, NY	RVC
Rockwall, TX	DAL
Rockwell, IA	DUB
Rockwell City, IA	SC
Rockwood, MI	DET
Rocky Ford, CO	PBL
Rocky Hill, CT	HRT
Rocky Mount, MO	STL
NC	R
VA	RIC
Rocky Point, NY	RVC
Rocky River, OH	CLV
Rodeo, CA	OAK
Roebling, NJ	TR
NJ	PSC
NJ	ROM
Roeland Park, KS	KCK
Rogers, AR	LR
MN	STP
TX	AUS
Rogers City, MI	GAY
Rogersville, TN	KNX
Roggen, CO	DEN
Rohnert Park, CA	SR
Rolette, ND	FAR
Rolla, MO	JC
ND	FAR
Rolling Meadows, IL	CHI
Rolling Prairie, IN	GRY
Rollingstone, MN	WIN
Roma, TX	BWN
Rome, GA	ATL
NY	SY
Rome City, IN	FTW
Romeo, MI	DET
Romeoville, IL	JOL
Romney, WV	WH
Romulus, MI	DET
Ronan, MT	HEL
Ronceverte, WV	WH
Ronkonkoma, NY	RVC
Roosevelt, NY	RVC
UT	SLC
Roosevelt Island, NY	NY
Rootstown, OH	Y
Rosalia, WA	SPK
Rosamond, CA	FRS
Roscoe, PA	PIT
SD	SFS
Roscommon, MI	GAY
Roseau, MN	CR
Rosebud, SD	RC
Roseburg, OR	P
Rosebush, MI	SAG
Rosedale, MS	JKS
NY	BRK
Roseland, NE	LIN
NJ	NEW
Roselle, IL	JOL
NJ	NEW
Roselle Park, NJ	NEW
Rosemead, CA	LA
Rosemont, IL	CHI
PA	PH
Rosemount, MN	STP
Rosenberg, TX	GAL
Rosendale, NY	NY
Rosenhayn, NJ	CAM
Roseto, PA	ALN
Roseville, CA	SAC
MI	DET
MN	STP
Rosholt, SD	SFS
WI	LC
Roslindale, MA	BO
Roslyn, NY	RVC
PA	PH
Rosman, NC	CHL
Ross, CA	SFR
Rossford, OH	SJP
OH	TOL
Rossville, KS	KCK
Roswell, GA	ATL
GA	PSC
NM	LSC
Rotan, TX	LUB
Rothschild, WI	LC
Rotterdam Junction, NY	ALB
Round Lake, IL	CHI
NY	ALB
Round Rock, TX	AUS
Roundup, MT	GF
Rouses Point, NY	OG
Rowena, TX	SAN
Rowland Heights, CA	LA
Rowlett, TX	DAL
Roxboro, NC	R

Roxbury, MA	BO
Roy, NM	SFE
Royal, IA	SC
Royal City, WA	YAK
Royal Oak, MI	DET
Royal Palm Beach, FL	PMB
Royalton, IL	BEL
MN	SCL
Royersford, PA	PH
Rubicon, WI	MIL
Ruby, AK	FBK
Rudolph, WI	LC
Rudyard, MI	MAR
Rugby, ND	FAR
Ruidoso, NM	LSC
Rulo, NE	LIN
Rumford, ME	PRT
RI	PRO
Rumson, NJ	TR
Runge, TX	SAT
Runnemede, NJ	CAM
Running Springs, CA	SB
Rupert, ID	B
Rush, NY	ROC
Rush City, MN	STP
Rushford, MN	WIN
NY	BUF
Rushville, IL	PEO
IN	IND
Ruskin, FL	SP
Russell, KS	SAL
MA	SPR
Russells Point, OH	CIN
Russellton, PA	PIT
Russellville, AL	BIR
AR	LR
KY	OWN
MO	JC
Russia, OH	CIN
Ruston, LA	SHP
Ruth, MI	SAG
Rutherford, NJ	NEW
Ruthven, IA	SC
Rutland, MA	WOR
VT	BUR
Ryan, IA	DUB
Rydal, PA	PH
Rye, NY	NY
Rye Beach, NH	MAN
Sabattus, ME	PRT
Sabetha, KS	KCK
Sabinal, TX	SAT
Sabula, IA	DUB
Sac City, IA	SC
Sacaton, AZ	PHX
Sackets Harbor, NY	OG
Saco, ME	PRT
Sacramento, CA	NTN
CA	SAC
CA	VNN
CA	STN
Saddle Brook, NJ	NEW
Saddle River Borough, NJ	NEW
Safety Harbor, FL	SP
Safford, AZ	TUC
Sag Harbor, NY	RVC
Saginaw, MI	SAG
Sahuarita, AZ	TUC
St. Agatha, ME	PRT
St. Albans, ME	PRT
NY	BRK
VT	BUR
WV	WH
St. Amant, LA	BR
St. Ann, MO	STL
St. Anne, IL	JOL
St. Anthony, ID	B
IN	EVN
MN	STP
ND	FAR
St. Augustine, FL	STA
St. Benedict, KS	KCK
LA	NO
Saint Benedict, LA	NO
St. Benedict, OR	P
Saint Benedict, OR	P
Saint Bernard, LA	NO
St. Bonaventure, NY	BUF
Saint Bonaventure, NY	BUF
St. Bonifacius, MN	STP
St. Catharine, KY	L
St. Charles, IL	RCK
Saint Charles, IL	RCK
St. Charles, MI	SAG
MN	WIN
MO	STL
St. Clair, MI	DET
MO	STL
PA	ALN
PA	PHU
Saint Clair, PA	ALN
St. Clair Shores, MI	DET
St. Clairsville, OH	STU
St. Cloud, FL	ORL
Saint Cloud, FL	ORL
St. Cloud, MN	SCL
Saint Cloud, MN	SCL
St. Cloud, MN	SYM
WI	MIL
St. Columbans, NE	OM
St. Croix, IN	IND
St. David, AZ	TUC
St. Edward, NE	OM
St. Elizabeth, MO	JC
St. Francis, KS	SAL
KY	L
MN	SCL
SD	RC
WI	MIL
St. Francisville, LA	BR
St. Gabriel, LA	BR
St. George, UT	SLC
St. Hedwig, TX	SAT
Saint Helen, MI	GAY
St. Helena, CA	SR
Saint Helena, CA	SR
St. Helena Island, SC	CHR
St. Helens, OR	P
St. Henry, OH	CIN
Saint Henry, OH	CIN
St. Ignace, MI	MAR
St. Ignatius, MT	HEL
St. Inigoes, MD	WDC
St. James, LA	BR
MN	WIN
MO	JC
Saint James, MO	JC
St. James, NY	RVC
Saint James, NY	RVC
St. John, FL	STA
IN	GRY
KS	DOD
ND	FAR
WA	SPK
Saint John, WA	SPK
St. Johns, AZ	GLP
FL	STA
MI	LAN
St. Johnsbury, VT	BUR
Saint Johnsbury, VT	BUR
St. Joseph, LA	ALX
MI	KAL
MN	SCL
Saint Joseph, MN	SCL
St. Joseph, MO	KC
MO	STN
St. Leo, FL	SP
Saint Leo, FL	SP
St. Leo, MN	NU
St. Libory, IL	BEL
NE	GI
St. Louis, MI	SAG
MO	OLL
MO	PRM
Saint Louis, MO	STL
MO	OLL
St. Louis, MO	STN
MO	STL
St. Louis County, MO	STL
St. Louis Park, MN	STP
St. Lucas, IA	DUB
St. Maries, ID	B
St. Martin, MN	SCL
OH	CIN
St. Martinville, LA	LAF
St. Mary, MO	STL
St. Mary Of The Woods, IN	IND
Saint Mary Of The Woods, IN	IND
St. Mary's, IA	DM
MO	BEL
St. Mary's City, MD	WDC
St. Mary–of–the–Woods, IN	IND
St. Marys, AK	FBK
GA	SAV
IA	DM
KS	KCK
OH	CIN
PA	E
WV	WH
St. Meinrad, IN	IND
Saint Meinrad, IN	IND
St. Michael, AK	FBK
MN	STP
ND	FAR
PA	ALT
Saint Michael, PA	ALT
St. Michaels, AZ	GLP
St. Nazianz, WI	GB
St. Paul, KS	WCH
MN	OLL
MN	STP
Saint Paul, MN	STP
St. Paul, MO	STL
NE	GI
OR	P
VA	RIC
St. Paul Park, MN	STP
St. Pete Beach, FL	SP
St. Peter, MN	NU
Saint Peter, MN	NU
St. Peters, MO	STL
St. Petersburg, FL	SP
Saint Petersburg, FL	PSC
FL	SP
St. Petersburg, FL	SJP
St. Regis Falls, NY	OG
St. Robert, MO	JC
St. Rose, IL	BEL
St. Simons Island, GA	SAV
St. Stephen, MN	SCL
Saint Stephens, WY	CHY
St. Theresa, WI	MIL
St. Thomas, MO	JC
St. Xavier, MT	GF
Salado, TX	AUS
Salamanca, NY	BUF
Salem, IL	BEL
IN	IND
MA	BO
MA	STF
MO	SPC
NH	MAN
NJ	CAM
NY	ALB
OH	Y
OR	P
SD	SFS
VA	RIC
WV	WH
Salida, CO	COS
Salina, KS	SAL
Salinas, CA	MRY
Saline, MI	LAN
Salisbury, MA	BO
MD	WIL
MO	JC
NC	CHL
Salix, IA	SC
Sallisaw, OK	TLS
Salmon, ID	B
Salt Lake City, UT	SLC
Salt Point, NY	NY
Saltaire, NY	RVC
Salyersville, KY	LEX
Sammamish, WA	SEA
San Andreas, CA	STO
San Angelo, TX	SAN
San Anselmo, CA	SFR
San Antonio, FL	SP
TX	OAK
TX	SYM
TX	SAT
TX	OLL
San Benito, TX	BWN
San Bernardino, CA	SB
CA	NTN
San Bruno, CA	SFR
San Carlos, AZ	TUC
CA	SFR
San Clemente, CA	ORG
San Diego, CA	SD
CA	NTN
CA	SPA
CA	VNN
TX	CC
San Dimas, CA	LA
San Elizario, TX	ELP
San Fernando, CA	LA
CA	SYM
San Fidel, NM	GLP
San Francisco, CA	SFR
CA	STN
San Gabriel, CA	LA
San Isidro, TX	BWN
San Jacinto, CA	SB
San Jose, CA	SJ
CA	NTN
CA	SYM
San Juan, TX	BWN
San Juan Bautista, CA	MRY
San Juan Capistrano, CA	ORG
San Leandro, CA	OAK
San Lorenzo, CA	OAK
San Luis, AZ	TUC
CO	PBL
San Luis Obispo, CA	MRY
CA	VNN
San Manuel, AZ	TUC
San Marcos, CA	SD
TX	AUS
San Marino, CA	LA
San Mateo, CA	SFR
San Miguel, CA	MRY
NM	LSC
San Pablo, CA	OAK
San Patricio, NM	LSC
San Pedro, CA	LA
TX	BWN
San Pierre, IN	GRY
San Rafael, CA	SFR
San Ramon, CA	OAK
San Saba, TX	AUS
San Ysidro, CA	SD
Sanborn, IA	SC
MN	NU
Sanbornville, NH	MAN
Sand Lake, MI	GR
Sand Springs, OK	TLS
Sanderson, TX	SAN
Sandia, TX	CC
Sandoval, IL	BEL
Sandpoint, ID	B
Sandstone, MN	DUL
Sandusky, MI	SAG
OH	TOL
Sandwich, IL	RCK
Sandy, OR	P
UT	SLC
Sandy Hook, KY	LEX
Sandyston, NJ	PAT
Sanford, FL	ORL
ME	PRT
MI	SAG
NC	R
Sanger, CA	FRS
Sanibel, FL	VEN
Santa Ana, CA	ORG
CA	SYM
CA	SPA
Santa Barbara, CA	LA
Santa Clara, CA	SJ
CA	STN
NM	LSC
Santa Clarita, CA	LA
Santa Claus, IN	EVN
Santa Cruz, CA	MRY
NM	SFE
Santa Fe, NM	SFE
Santa Fe Springs, CA	LA
Santa Margarita, CA	MRY
Santa Maria, CA	LA
Santa Monica, CA	LA
Santa Paula, CA	LA
Santa Rosa, CA	SR
NM	SFE
TX	BWN
Santa Rosa Beach, FL	PT
Santa Susana Knolls, CA	LA
Santa Ynez, CA	LA
Santa Ysabel, CA	SD
Santee, CA	SD
SC	CHR
Sapulpa, OK	TLS
Saranac, MI	GR
Saranac Lake, NY	OG
Sarasota, FL	VEN
Saratoga, CA	SJ
NY	ALB
WY	CHY
Saratoga Springs, NY	ALB
Sardinia, NY	BUF
Sarita, TX	CC
Sartell, MN	SCL
Satanta, KS	DOD
Saugerties, NY	NY
Saugus, MA	BO
Sauk Centre, MN	SCL
Sauk City, WI	MAD
Sauk Rapids, MN	SCL
Sauk Village, IL	CHI
Saukville, WI	MIL
Sault Sainte Marie, MI	MAR
Sausalito, CA	SFR
Savage, MN	STP
Savanna, IL	RCK
Savannah, GA	SAV
MO	KC
TN	MEM
Saxon, WI	SUP
Sayre, PA	PHU
PA	SCR
Sayreville, NJ	MET
Sayville, NY	RVC
Scales Mound, IL	RCK
Scammon Bay, AK	FBK
Scandia, MN	STP
Scappoose, OR	P
OR	VNN
Scarborough, ME	PRT
Scarsdale, NY	NY
Schaghticoke, NY	ALB
Schaller, IA	SC
Schaumburg, IL	CHI
Scheller, IL	BEL

Schenectady, NY	ALB
Schererville, IN	GRY
Schertz, TX	SAT
Schiller Park, IL	CHI
Schnellville, IN	EVN
Schofield, WI	LC
Schriever, LA	HT
Schroon Lake, NY	OG
Schulenburg, TX	VIC
Schuyler, NE	OM
Schuylerville, NY	ALB
Schuylkill Haven, PA	ALN
Schwenksville, PA	PH
Scio, OR	P
Scituate, MA	BO
Scobey, MT	GF
Scotch Plains, NJ	NEW
Scotia, CA	SR
NY	ALB
Scotland, SD	SFS
Scott, LA	LAF
Scott AFB, IL	BEL
Scott City, KS	DOD
MO	SPC
Scott Twp., PA	SCR
Scottdale, PA	GBG
PA	PBR
Scotts Valley, CA	MRY
Scottsbluff, NE	GI
Scottsboro, AL	BIR
Scottsburg, IN	IND
Scottsdale, AZ	PHX
AZ	SPA
Scottsville, KY	OWN
NY	ROC
VA	RIC
Scottville, MI	GR
Scranton, AR	LR
IA	SC
PA	NTN
PA	PSC
PA	PHU
PA	SAM
PA	SCR
Sea Cliff, NY	RVC
Sea Girt, NJ	TR
Sea Isle City, NJ	CAM
Seaford, DE	WIL
NY	RVC
Seahurst, WA	SEA
Seal Beach, CA	ORG
Sealy, TX	GAL
Searcy, AR	LR
Seaside, CA	MRY
OR	P
Seaside Heights, NJ	TR
Seaside Park, NJ	TR
Seat Pleasant, MD	WDC
Seattle, WA	NTN
WA	VNN
WA	STN
WA	SEA
Seaview, WA	SEA
Sebastian, FL	PMB
Sebastopol, CA	SR
Sebewaing, MI	SAG
Seboyeta, NM	GLP
Sebree, KY	OWN
Sebring, FL	VEN
OH	Y
Secane, PA	PH
Secaucus, NJ	NEW
Secretary, MD	WIL
Security, CO	COS
Sedalia, CO	COS
MO	JC
Sedro Woolley, WA	SEA
Seekonk, MA	FR
Seelyville, IN	IND
Seffner, FL	SP
Seguin, TX	SAT
Selah, WA	YAK
Selby, SD	SFS
Selden, KS	SAL
NY	RVC
Seligman, AZ	PHX
Selinsgrove, PA	HBG
Sellersburg, IN	IND
Sellersville, PA	PH
Selma, AL	MOB
CA	FRS
TX	SAT
Selmer, TN	MEM
Selz, ND	FAR
Seminole, FL	SP
OK	OKL
TX	LUB
Semmes, AL	MOB
Senatobia, MS	JKS
Seneca, IL	PEO
KS	KCK
MO	SPC
WI	LC
Sentinel Butte, ND	BIS
Sequim, WA	SEA
Sesser, IL	BEL
Setauket, NY	RVC
Severn, MD	BAL
Severna Park, MD	BAL
Seward, AK	ANC
KS	DOD
NE	LIN
PA	GBG
Sewell, NJ	CAM
Sewickley, PA	PIT
Seymour, CT	HRT
IL	PEO
IN	IND
TN	KNX
TX	FWT
WI	GB
Shady Cove, OR	P
Shadyside, OH	STU
Shafter, CA	FRS
Shaker Heights, OH	CLV
Shakopee, MN	STP
Shallotte, NC	R
Shallowater, TX	LUB
Shamokin, PA	HBG
PA	PHU
Shandon, OH	CIN
Shannon, IL	RCK
Sharon, CT	HRT
KS	DOD
MA	BO
PA	E
WI	MIL
Sharon Hill, PA	PH
Sharpsburg, PA	PIT
Sharpsville, PA	E
Shavertown, PA	SCR
Shaw, MS	JKS
Shaw Island, WA	SEA
Shawano, WI	GB
Shawnee, KS	KCK
OK	OKL
Shawnee Mission, KS	KCK
Shawneetown, IL	BEL
Sheboygan, WI	MIL
Sheboygan Falls, WI	MIL
Sheffield, MA	SPR
OH	CLV
PA	E
PA	PBR
Sheffield Lake, OH	CLV
Shelbina, MO	JC
Shelburne, VT	BUR
VT	SAM
Shelburne Falls, MA	SPR
Shelby, MI	GR
MS	JKS
MT	HEL
NC	CHL
NE	LIN
OH	TOL
Shelby Twp., MI	DET
MI	EST
Shelbyville, IL	SFD
IN	IND
KY	L
TN	NSH
Sheldon, IA	SC
Sheldon Springs, VT	BUR
Shell Knob, MO	SPC
Shell Lake, WI	SUP
Shelter Island Heights, NY	RVC
Shelton, CT	BGP
WA	SEA
Shenandoah, IA	DM
PA	ALN
PA	PHU
Shepherd, MI	SAG
Shepherdstown, WV	WH
Shepherdsville, KY	L
Sheppton, PA	ALN
Sherborn, MA	BO
Sherburne, NY	SY
Sheridan, AR	LR
MT	HEL
WY	CHY
Sherman, CT	BGP
IL	SFD
TX	DAL
Sherman Oaks, CA	LA
CA	VNN
CA	ROM
Sherrill, NY	SY
Sherwood, AR	LR
OR	P
WI	GB
Shieldsville, MN	STP
Shillington, PA	ALN
Shiloh, IL	BEL
Shiner, TX	VIC
Shinglehouse, PA	E
Shinnston, WV	WH
Shippensburg, PA	HBG
Shiprock, NM	GLP
Shirley, MA	BO
Shohola, PA	SCR
Shoreham, NY	RVC
Shoreline, WA	SEA
Shoreview, MN	STP
Shorewood, IL	JOL
WI	MIL
Short Hills, NJ	NEW
Shoshone, ID	B
Show Low, AZ	GLP
Shreveport, LA	SHP
Shrewsbury, MA	WOR
MO	STL
Shrub Oak, NY	NY
Shullsburg, WI	MAD
Shumway, IL	SFD
Sibley, IA	SC
Sicklerville, NJ	CAM
Sidney, MT	GF
NE	GI
NY	ALB
OH	CIN
Sierra Madre, CA	LA
Sierra Vista, AZ	TUC
Sigel, IL	SFD
Signal Mountain, TN	KNX
Sigourney, IA	DAV
Sikeston, MO	SPC
Siler City, NC	R
Silex, MO	STL
Siloam Springs, AR	LR
Silsbee, TX	BEA
Silver Bay, MN	DUL
Silver City, NM	LSC
Silver Creek, NE	OM
NY	BUF
Silver Lake, MN	NU
Silver Spring, MD	PHU
MD	WDC
Silverado, CA	ORG
Silverton, OR	P
Silvis, IL	PEO
Simi Valley, CA	LA
Simmesport, LA	ALX
Simpson, PA	PHU
PA	SCR
Simpsonville, SC	CHR
Simsbury, CT	HRT
Sinking Spring, PA	ALN
Sinsinawa, WI	MAD
Sinton, TX	CC
Sioux City, IA	SC
Sioux Falls, SD	SFS
Sioux Rapids, IA	SC
Siren, WI	SUP
Sisseton, SD	SFS
Sisters, OR	BAK
Sistersville, WV	WH
Sitka, AK	JUN
Skaneateles, NY	SY
Skiatook, OK	TLS
Skidmore, TX	CC
Skillman, NJ	MET
Skokie, IL	CHI
Skowhegan, ME	PRT
Slater, MO	JC
Slatersville, RI	PRO
Slatington, PA	ALN
Slaton, TX	LUB
Slayton, MN	WIN
Sleepy Eye, MN	NU
Sleepy Hollow, NY	NY
Slickville, PA	GBG
Slidell, LA	NO
Slinger, WI	MIL
Slingerlands, NY	ALB
Slippery Rock, PA	PIT
Sloan, NY	BUF
Sloatsburg, NY	NY
NY	STF
Smethport, PA	E
Smiley, TX	SAT
Smith Center, KS	SAL
Smithfield, NC	R
RI	PRO
VA	RIC
Smithton, IL	BEL
Smithtown, NY	RVC
Smithville, MO	KC
TN	NSH
TX	AUS
Smock, PA	GBG
Smyrna, DE	WIL
GA	ATL
TN	NSH
Sneedville, TN	KNX
Snellville, GA	ATL
Snohomish, WA	SEA
Snoqualmie, WA	SEA
Snowflake, AZ	GLP
Snowmass, CO	DEN
Snyder, NE	OM
NY	BUF
TX	LUB
Sobieski, WI	GB
Socorro, NM	SFE
Soda Springs, ID	B
Soddy Daisy, TN	KNX
Solana Beach, CA	SD
Soldotna, AK	ANC
Soledad, CA	MRY
Solomon, AZ	TUC
KS	SAL
Solomons, MD	WDC
Solon, IA	DAV
OH	CLV
OH	SJP
OH	PRM
Solon Springs, WI	SUP
Solvang, CA	LA
Solvay, NY	SY
Somers, NY	NY
Somers Point, NJ	CAM
Somerset, KY	LEX
MA	FR
NJ	MET
NJ	PSC
NJ	SYM
NJ	SAM
OH	COL
PA	ALT
TX	SAT
WI	SUP
Somersville, CT	NOR
Somersworth, NH	MAN
Somerton, AZ	TUC
Somerville, MA	BO
NJ	MET
TN	MEM
TX	AUS
Somonauk, IL	RCK
Sonoita, AZ	TUC
Sonoma, CA	SR
Sonora, CA	STO
TX	SAN
Soquel, CA	MRY
Sorrento, LA	BR
Sound Beach, NY	RVC
Sour Lake, TX	BEA
South Abington Township, PA	SCR
South Amboy, NJ	MET
South Amherst, OH	CLV
South Attleboro, MA	FR
South Barre, MA	WOR
South Beloit, IL	RCK
South Bend, IN	FTW
IN	NTN
South Boston, MA	BO
VA	RIC
South Bound Brook, NJ	MET
South Burlington, VT	BUR
South Charleston, OH	CIN
WV	WH
South Dartmouth, MA	FR
South Deerfield, MA	SPR
MA	STF
South Easton, MA	FR
South El Monte, CA	LA
South Euclid, OH	CLV
South Fork, PA	ALT
South Gate, CA	LA
CA	SYM
South Glastonbury, CT	HRT
South Glens Falls, NY	ALB
South Grafton, MA	WOR
South Hadley, MA	SPR
South Haven, MI	KAL
South Heart, ND	BIS
South Hero, VT	BUR
South Hill, VA	RIC
South Holland, IL	CHI
South Houston, TX	GAL
South Huntington, NY	RVC
South Hutchinson, KS	WCH
South Kingstown, RI	PRO
South Lake Tahoe, CA	SAC
South Lyon, MI	DET
MI	SYM
South Mantoloking, NJ	TR
South Milwaukee, WI	MIL
South Orange, NJ	NEW
South Ozone Park, NY	BRK
South Park, PA	PIT
South Pasadena, CA	LA
South Pittsburg, TN	KNX
South Plainfield, NJ	MET

South Portland, ME	PRT
South Richmond Hill, NY	BRK
South River, NJ	MET
South San Francisco, CA	SFR
South Sioux City, NE	OM
South St. Paul, MN	STP
South Tucson, AZ	TUC
South Wilmington, IL	JOL
South Windsor, CT	HRT
South Yarmouth, MA	FR
Southampton, NY	RVC
PA	PH
Southaven, MS	JKS
Southborough, MA	WOR
Southbridge, MA	WOR
Southbury, CT	HRT
Southern Pines, NC	R
Southfield, MI	DET
MI	OLD
MI	EST
MI	SYM
Southgate, KY	COV
MI	DET
Southington, CT	HRT
Southold, NY	RVC
Southport, NC	R
Southwest Ranches, FL	MIA
Southwick, MA	SPR
Spalding, MI	MAR
NE	GI
Sparkill, NY	NY
Sparks, MD	BAL
NV	RNO
Sparta, IL	BEL
MI	GR
NJ	PAT
TN	NSH
WI	LC
Spartanburg, SC	CHR
Spearfish, SD	RC
Spearman, TX	AMA
Spearville, KS	DOD
Speculator, NY	OG
Spencer, IA	SC
IN	IND
MA	WOR
WV	WH
Spencerport, NY	ROC
Spencerville, OH	TOL
Spicer, MN	NU
Spillville, IA	DUB
Spirit Lake, IA	SC
Splendora, TX	GAL
Spokane, WA	SPK
Spokane Valley, WA	SPK
WA	VNN
Spooner, WI	SUP
Spotswood, NJ	MET
Spotsylvania, VA	ARL
Spreckels, CA	MRY
Spring, TX	GAL
Spring Branch, TX	SAT
Spring City, PA	PH
Spring Green, WI	MAD
Spring Grove, IL	RCK
PA	HBG
Spring Hill, FL	SP
TN	NSH
Spring House, PA	PH
Spring Lake, MI	GR
NJ	TR
Spring Mills, PA	ALT
Spring Valley, CA	SD
IL	PEO
MN	WIN
NY	NY
NY	STF
WI	LC
Springbrook, IA	DUB
NY	BUF
Springdale, AR	LR
PA	PIT
Springer, NM	SFE
Springerville, AZ	GLP
Springfield, CO	PBL
GA	SAV
IL	SFD
KY	L
MA	SAM
MA	SPR
MN	NU
MO	SPC
NE	OM
NJ	NEW
OH	CIN
OR	P
OR	STN
PA	PH
SD	SFS
TN	NSH
VA	ARL

VT	BUR
Springfield Gardens, NY	BRK
Springville, IA	DUB
NY	BUF
Spruce Pine, NC	CHL
Spur, TX	LUB
Stafford, TX	GAL
TX	SYM
VA	ARL
Stafford Springs, CT	NOR
Stamford, CT	BGP
CT	STF
NY	ALB
TX	LUB
Stanberry, MO	KC
Standish, ME	PRT
MI	SAG
Stanford, CA	SJ
MT	GF
Stanley, ND	BIS
NY	ROC
WI	LC
Stanton, CA	ORG
KY	LEX
NE	OM
TN	MEM
TX	SAN
Stanwood, WA	SEA
Staples, MN	SCL
Stapleton, NE	GI
Star City, AR	LR
IN	LFT
WV	WH
Star Lake, NY	OG
Starke, FL	STA
Starkville, MS	JKS
State College, PA	ALT
PA	PBR
Staten Island, NY	NY
NY	STF
Statesboro, GA	SAV
Statesville, NC	CHL
Staunton, IL	SFD
VA	RIC
Stayton, OR	P
Ste. Genevieve, MO	STL
Ste. Marie, IL	SFD
Steamboat Springs, CO	DEN
Stebbins, AK	FBK
Steele, ND	FAR
Steelton, PA	HBG
Steger, IL	JOL
Steinauer, NE	LIN
Stella Niagara, NY	BUF
Stephen, MN	CR
Stephenson, MI	MAR
Stephenville, TX	FWT
Sterling, CO	DEN
IL	RCK
MA	WOR
VA	ARL
Sterling Heights, MI	DET
MI	PRM
Stetsonville, WI	SUP
Steubenville, OH	STU
Stevens Point, WI	LC
Stevenson, MD	BAL
Stevensville, MT	HEL
Stewart, MN	NU
Stewartsville, NJ	MET
Stewartville, MN	WIN
Stickney, IL	CHI
Still River, MA	WOR
Stillwater, MN	STP
NY	ALB
OK	TLS
PA	SCR
Stirling, NJ	PAT
Stockbridge, MA	SPR
WI	GB
Stockdale, TX	SAT
Stockholm, NJ	PAT
Stockton, CA	STO
IL	RCK
Stone Harbor, NJ	CAM
Stone Lake, WI	SUP
Stone Mountain, GA	ATL
Stoneboro, PA	E
Stoneham, MA	BO
Stoneville, NC	CHL
Stonewall, TX	SAT
Stonewood, WV	WH
Stonington, CT	NOR
IL	SFD
Stony Point, NY	NY
Storm Lake, IA	SC
Storrs, CT	NOR
Stoughton, MA	BO
WI	MAD
Stow, MA	BO
OH	CLV

Stowe, PA	PH
VT	BUR
Strafford, PA	PH
Strandquist, MN	CR
Strasburg, ND	BIS
VA	ARL
Stratford, CT	BGP
TX	AMA
WI	LC
Stratton, CO	COS
Strawberry Point, IA	DUB
Streamwood, IL	CHI
Streator, IL	PEO
Streetsboro, OH	Y
Strongsville, OH	CLV
Stroudsburg, PA	SCR
Struthers, OH	Y
Strykersville, NY	BUF
Stuart, FL	PMB
IA	DM
NE	OM
Studio City, CA	LA
Sturgeon Bay, WI	GB
Sturgis, KY	OWN
MI	KAL
SD	RC
Sturtevant, WI	MIL
Stuttgart, AR	LR
Stuyvesant, NY	ALB
Suamico, WI	GB
Subiaco, AR	LR
Sublette, IL	RCK
Sublimity, OR	P
Succasunna, NJ	PAT
Sudbury, MA	BO
Suffern, NY	NY
Suffield, CT	HRT
Suffolk, VA	RIC
Sugar Creek, MO	KC
MO	PRM
Sugar Grove, IL	RCK
OH	COL
Sugar Land, TX	GAL
Sugar Notch, PA	SCR
Sugarloaf, PA	PSC
Suitland, MD	WDC
Sulligent, AL	BIR
Sullivan, IL	SFD
IN	EVN
MO	STL
WI	MAD
Sullivan's Island, SC	CHR
Sulphur, LA	LKC
Sulphur Springs, TX	TYL
Summerfield, FL	ORL
KS	KCK
Summerhill, PA	ALT
Summersville, WV	WH
Summerton, SC	CHR
Summerville, SC	CHR
Summit, IL	CHI
NJ	NEW
Summit Hill, PA	ALN
Sumner, IA	DUB
WA	SEA
Sumter, SC	CHR
Sun City, AZ	PHX
CA	SB
Sun City Center, FL	SP
Sun City West, AZ	PHX
Sun Lakes, AZ	PHX
Sun Prairie, WI	MAD
Sun Valley, CA	LA
ID	B
NV	RNO
Sunapee, NH	MAN
Sunbury, OH	COL
PA	HBG
Suncook, NH	MAN
Sunfish, KY	OWN
Sunland Park, NM	LSC
Sunman, IN	IND
Sunny Hills, FL	PT
Sunny Isles Beach, FL	MIA
Sunnyside, WA	YAK
Sunnyvale, CA	SJ
Sunrise, FL	MIA
Sunriver, OR	BAK
Sunset Hills, MO	STL
Superior, AZ	TUC
NE	LIN
WI	SUP
Suring, WI	GB
Surprise, AZ	PHX
Susanville, CA	SAC
Susquehanna, PA	SCR
Sussex, NJ	PAT
Sutherlin, OR	P
Sutter Creek, CA	SAC
Sutton, MA	WOR
NE	LIN

Suttons Bay, MI	GAY
Swainsboro, GA	SAV
Swampscott, MA	BO
Swan Lake, MT	HEL
Swannanoa, NC	CHL
Swansboro, NC	R
Swansea, MA	FR
Swanton, OH	TOL
VT	BUR
Swarthmore, PA	PH
Swartswood, NJ	PAT
Swartz Creek, MI	LAN
Swedesboro, NJ	CAM
Swedesburg, PA	PH
Sweeny, TX	GAL
Sweet Home, OR	P
TX	VIC
Sweetwater, TX	SAN
Swinomish, WA	SEA
Switzerland, FL	STA
Swormville, NY	BUF
Swoyersville, PA	SCR
Sybertsville, PA	PSC
Sycamore, IL	RCK
OH	TOL
Sykeston, ND	FAR
Sykesville, PA	E
PA	PBR
Sylacauga, AL	BIR
Sylmar, CA	LA
Sylva, NC	CHL
Sylvania, GA	SAV
OH	TOL
Syosset, NY	RVC
Syracuse, IN	FTW
KS	DOD
NE	LIN
NY	SY
NY	STF
Tabb, VA	RIC
Taberg, NY	SY
Tabernacle, NJ	TR
Tabor, SD	SFS
Tacoma, WA	SEA
Taft, CA	FRS
TX	CC
Taftville, CT	NOR
Tahlequah, OK	TLS
Tahoe City, CA	SAC
Takoma Park, MD	WDC
Talkeetna, AK	ANC
Talladega, AL	BIR
Tallahassee, FL	PT
Tallassee, AL	MOB
Tallmadge, OH	CLV
Tallulah, LA	ALX
Tama, IA	DUB
Tamaqua, PA	ALN
Tamarac, FL	MIA
Tamaroa, IL	BEL
Tampa, FL	SP
FL	SAM
FL	SYM
Tampico, IL	RCK
Tanana, AK	FBK
Taneytown, MD	BAL
Tannersville, PA	SCR
Taos, NM	SFE
Tappahannock, VA	RIC
Tappan, NY	NY
Tarboro, NC	R
Tarentum, PA	PBR
PA	PIT
Tariffville, CT	HRT
Tarkio, MO	KC
Tarpon Springs, FL	SP
Tarrytown, NY	NY
Taunton, MA	FR
Tavernier, FL	MIA
Tawas City, MI	GAY
Taylor, MI	DET
TX	AUS
Taylor Mill, KY	COV
Taylors, SC	CHR
Taylors Falls, MN	STP
Taylorsville, NC	CHL
UT	SLC
Taylorville, IL	SFD
Tazewell, VA	RIC
Tea, SD	SFS
Teaneck, NJ	NEW
Techny, IL	CHI
IL	OLD
Tecumseh, MI	LAN
NE	LIN
Tehachapi, CA	FRS
Tekamah, NE	OM
Tekoa, WA	SPK
Tell City, IN	IND
Teller, AK	FBK
Telluride, CO	PBL

Temecula, CA	SB
Tempe, AZ	PHX
AZ	STN
Temperance, MI	DET
Temple, TX	AUS
Temple City, CA	LA
Temple Terrace, FL	SP
Tenafly, NJ	NEW
Tennessee Ridge, TN	NSH
Tequesta, FL	PMB
Terre Haute, IN	IND
Terrell, TX	DAL
Terrytown, LA	NO
Terryville, CT	HRT
CT	STF
Teutopolis, IL	SFD
Tewksbury, MA	BO
Texarkana, AR	LR
TX	TYL
Texas City, TX	GAL
The Colony, TX	FWT
TX	STN
The Dalles, OR	BAK
The Rock, GA	ATL
The Woodlands, TX	GAL
Theriot, LA	HT
Thermopolis, WY	CHY
Thibodaux, LA	HT
Thief River Falls, MN	CR
Thomas, WV	WH
Thomasboro, IL	PEO
Thomaston, CT	HRT
Thomasville, GA	SAV
NC	CHL
Thompson, CT	NOR
ND	FAR
OH	CLV
Thompson Falls, MT	HEL
Thomson, GA	ATL
Thoreau, NM	GLP
Thornton, CO	DEN
Thornwood, NY	NY
Thorp, WI	LC
Thousand Oaks, CA	LA
CA	OLL
Three Bridges, NJ	MET
Three Forks, MT	HEL
Three Lakes, WI	SUP
Three Oaks, MI	KAL
Three Rivers, CA	FRS
MA	SPR
MI	KAL
TX	CC
Throop, PA	SCR
Tiburon, CA	SFR
Tickfaw, LA	BR
Ticonderoga, NY	OG
Tidioute, PA	E
Tierra Amarilla, NM	SFE
Tiffin, OH	TOL
Tifton, GA	SAV
Tigard, OR	P
Tigerton, WI	GB
Tijeras, NM	SFE
Tilden, NE	OM
Tillamook, OR	P
Tilton, NH	MAN
Tiltonsville, OH	STU
Timber Lake, SD	RC
Timonium, MD	BAL
Tinley Park, IL	CHI
Tintah, MN	SCL
Tioga, LA	ALX
ND	BIS
Tipp City, OH	CIN
Tipton, CA	FRS
IA	DAV
IN	LFT
KS	SAL
MO	JC
Titusville, FL	ORL
NJ	TR
PA	E
Tiverton, RI	PRO
Tivoli, NY	NY
TX	CC
Tobyhanna, PA	SCR
Toccoa, GA	ATL
Tohatchi, NM	GLP
Tok, AK	FBK
Toksook Bay, AK	FBK
Toledo, OH	TOL
WA	SEA
Tolland, CT	NOR
Tolleson, AZ	PHX
Tolono, IL	PEO
Toluca, IL	PEO
Tomah, WI	LC
Tomahawk, WI	SUP
Tomales, CA	SFR
Tomball, TX	GAL

Tombstone, AZ	TUC
Tome, NM	SFE
Toms River, NJ	TR
NJ	PHU
NJ	PSC
Tonawanda, NY	BUF
Tonganoxie, KS	KCK
Tonica, IL	PEO
Tonkawa, OK	OKL
Tonopah, NV	LAV
Tontitown, AR	LR
Tooele, UT	SLC
Topawa, AZ	TUC
Topeka, KS	KCK
Toppenish, WA	YAK
Topping, VA	RIC
Topsfield, MA	BO
Toronto, OH	PBR
OH	STU
Torrance, CA	LA
Torrington, CT	HRT
CT	SAM
WY	CHY
Totowa, NJ	PAT
Towanda, KS	WCH
PA	SCR
Tower, MN	DUL
Town and Country, MO	STL
Towner, ND	FAR
Townsend, MA	BO
MT	HEL
TN	KNX
Towson, MD	BAL
Tracy, CA	STO
MN	NU
Tracyton, WA	SEA
Traer, IA	DUB
Trafford, PA	GBG
Tranquillity, CA	FRS
Trappist, KY	L
Travelers Rest, SC	CHR
Traverse City, MI	GAY
Tremont, PA	ALN
Trempealeau, WI	LC
Trenary, MI	MAR
Trenton, IL	BEL
MI	DET
MO	KC
NE	LIN
NJ	TR
NJ	PHU
NJ	ROM
NJ	PSC
OH	CIN
Tres Pinos, CA	MRY
Trevorton, PA	HBG
Triangle, VA	ARL
Tribes Hill, NY	ALB
Tribune, KS	DOD
Trinidad, CO	PBL
Trinity, FL	SP
TX	TYL
Tripp, SD	SFS
Troy, AL	MOB
IL	SFD
KS	KCK
MI	DET
MI	EST
MO	STL
NY	ALB
NY	STF
NY	SAM
OH	CIN
VT	BUR
Truckee, CA	SAC
Trumansburg, NY	ROC
Trumbull, CT	BGP
CT	PSC
Trussville, AL	BIR
Truth or Consequences, NM	LSC
Truxton, NY	SY
Tryon, NC	CHL
Tualatin, OR	P
Tuba City, AZ	GLP
Tubac, AZ	TUC
Tuckahoe, NY	NY
Tuckerton, NJ	TR
Tucson, AZ	STN
AZ	TUC
AZ	VNN
Tucumcari, NM	SFE
Tujunga, CA	LA
CA	OLN
Tukwila, WA	SEA
Tulare, CA	FRS
Tularosa, NM	LSC
Tulelake, CA	SAC
Tulia, TX	AMA
Tullahoma, TN	NSH
Tully, NY	SY
Tulsa, OK	OLL

OK	TLS
Tum Tum, WA	SPK
Tumwater, WA	SEA
Tunkhannock, PA	SCR
Tununak, AK	FBK
Tupelo, MS	JKS
Tupper Lake, NY	OG
Turlock, CA	SPA
CA	STO
Turners Falls, MA	SPR
Turnersville, NJ	CAM
Turtle Creek, PA	PIT
Turton, SD	SFS
Tuscaloosa, AL	BIR
Tuscola, IL	SFD
Tuscon, AZ	TUC
Tuscumbia, AL	BIR
Tuskegee Institute, AL	MOB
Tustin, CA	ORG
Tutwiler, MS	JKS
Tuxedo, NY	NY
Twain Harte, CA	STO
Twentynine Palms, CA	SB
Twin Falls, ID	B
Twin Lake, MI	GR
Twin Lakes, WI	MIL
Twin Rocks, PA	ALT
Twinsburg, OH	CLV
Twisp, WA	SPK
Two Harbors, MN	DUL
Two Rivers, WI	GB
Tybee Island, GA	SAV
Tyler, MN	NU
TX	TYL
Tyndall, SD	SFS
Tyngsborough, MA	BO
Tyringham, MA	SPR
Tyrone, GA	ATL
PA	ALT
Ubly, MI	SAG
Uhland, TX	AUS
Ukiah, CA	SR
CA	STN
Ulysses, KS	DOD
NE	LIN
Umbarger, TX	AMA
Unadilla, NY	ALB
Unalakleet, AK	FBK
Unalaska, AK	ANC
Uncasville, CT	NOR
Underhill Center, VT	BUR
Underwood, MN	SCL
ND	BIS
Union, KY	COV
MO	STL
NJ	NEW
OR	BAK
SC	CHR
Union City, CA	OAK
CT	HRT
IN	LFT
NJ	NEW
NJ	OLD
OK	OKL
PA	E
TN	MEM
Union Gap, WA	YAK
Union Grove, WI	MIL
Uniondale, NY	RVC
Uniontown, KY	OWN
OH	Y
OH	CLV
PA	GBG
PA	SAM
PA	PBR
Unionville, CT	HRT
United, PA	GBG
Universal, IN	IND
University City, MO	STL
University Heights, OH	CLV
University Park, PA	ALT
Upland, CA	SB
Upper Darby, PA	PH
Upper Marlboro, MD	WDC
Upper Montclair, NJ	NEW
Upper Saddle River, NJ	NEW
Upper Sandusky, OH	TOL
Upper St. Clair, PA	PBR
Upton, MA	WOR
Urbana, IL	PEO
OH	CIN
Urbandale, IA	DM
Utica, IL	PEO
KY	OWN
MI	DET
NY	SY
NY	NTN
NY	STF
NY	SAM
OH	COL
Uvalde, TX	SAT

Uwchlan, PA	PH
Uxbridge, MA	WOR
Vacaville, CA	SAC
Vacherie, LA	BR
Vail, AZ	TUC
IA	SC
Valatie, NY	ALB
Valdez, AK	ANC
Valdosta, GA	SAV
Vale, NC	CHL
OR	BAK
Valentine, NE	GI
Valhalla, NY	NY
Valier, MT	HEL
Valinda, CA	LA
Vallejo, CA	SAC
Valley, NE	OM
WA	SPK
Valley Center, CA	SD
KS	WCH
Valley City, ND	FAR
OH	CLV
Valley Lee, MD	WDC
Valley Park, MO	STL
Valley Stream, NY	RVC
Valley View, TX	FWT
Valmeyer, IL	BEL
Valparaiso, IN	GRY
NE	LIN
Valrico, FL	SP
FL	SYM
Valyermo, CA	LA
CA	ROM
Van Alstyne, TX	DAL
Van Buren, AR	LR
ME	PRT
Van Horn, TX	ELP
Van Horne, IA	DUB
Van Nuys, CA	LA
Van Wert, OH	TOL
Vanceburg, KY	COV
Vancleave, MS	BLX
Vancouver, WA	SEA
Vandalia, IL	SFD
MO	JC
OH	CIN
Vanderbilt, TX	VIC
Vandergrift, PA	GBG
Vanderwagen, NM	GLP
Vashon, WA	SEA
Vassar, MI	SAG
Vaughn, NM	SFE
Vega, TX	AMA
Velva, ND	FAR
Veneta, OR	P
Venice, CA	LA
FL	VEN
Ventnor, NJ	CAM
PA	PH
Ventura, CA	LA
CA	ROM
Verdigre, NE	OM
Vergennes, VT	BUR
Vermilion, OH	TOL
Vermillion, MN	STP
SD	SFS
Vernal, UT	SLC
Verndale, MN	SCL
Vernon, CA	LA
CT	NOR
NY	SY
TX	FWT
Vernon Hills, IL	CHI
Vernonia, OR	P
Vero Beach, FL	PMB
Verona, NJ	NEW
NY	SY
PA	PIT
WI	MAD
Verplanck, NY	NY
Versailles, KY	LEX
OH	CIN
Veseli, MN	STP
Vesper, WI	LC
Vestaburg, MI	GR
Vestal, NY	SY
Vicksburg, MI	KAL
MS	JKS
Victor, IA	DAV
NY	ROC
Victoria, KS	SAL
MN	STP
TX	VIC
Victorville, CA	SB
Vidalia, GA	SAV
LA	ALX
Vidor, TX	BEA
Vienna, IL	BEL
MO	JC
OH	Y
VA	ARL

WV	WH
Viera, FL	ORL
Villa Grove, IL	SFD
Villa Hills, KY	COV
Villa Maria, PA	PIT
Villa Park, IL	JOL
Villa Ridge, MO	STL
Villanova, PA	PH
Villanueva, NM	SFE
Villas, NJ	CAM
Ville Platte, LA	LAF
Vina, CA	SAC
Vincennes, IN	EVN
Vine Grove, KY	L
Vineland, NJ	CAM
Vineyard Haven, MA	FR
Vinita, OK	TLS
Vinton, IA	DUB
LA	LKC
Viola, KS	WCH
Virden, IL	SFD
Virgil, IL	RCK
Virginia, IL	SFD
MN	DUL
Virginia Beach, VA	RIC
Virginia City, NV	RNO
Virginia Dale, CO	DEN
Viroqua, WI	LC
Visalia, CA	FRS
Vista, CA	SD
Vivian, LA	SHP
Volga, IA	DUB
Volo, IL	CHI
Voluntown, CT	NOR
Von Ormy, TX	SAT
Voorheesville, NY	ALB
Vulcan, MI	MAR
WaKeeney, KS	SAL
Wabash, IN	FTW
Wabasha, MN	WIN
Wabasso, MN	NU
Wabeno, WI	GB
Waco, TX	AUS
Waconia, MN	STP
Waddington, NY	OG
Wadena, MN	SCL
Wading River, NY	RVC
Wadsworth, IL	CHI
OH	CLV
Waggaman, LA	NO
Wagner, SD	SFS
Wagon Mound, NM	SFE
Wagoner, OK	TLS
Wahiawa, HI	HON
Wahkon, MN	SCL
Wahoo, NE	LIN
Wahpeton, ND	FAR
Waialua, HI	HON
Waianae, HI	HON
Waihee, HI	HON
Wailuku, HI	HON
Waimanalo, HI	HON
Waipahu, HI	HON
Waite Park, MN	SCL
Wake Forest, NC	R
Wakefield, MA	BO
MI	MAR
RI	PRO
Wakeman, OH	TOL
Walbridge, OH	TOL
Walden, NY	NY
Waldorf, MD	WDC
Waldport, OR	P
Waldron, AR	LR
Walhalla, ND	FAR
Walker, IA	DUB
MN	DUL
Walkersville, MD	BAL
Walkerton, IN	FTW
IN	GRY
Wall, PA	PBR
SD	RC
TX	SAN
Wall Lake, IA	SC
Walla Walla, WA	SPK
Wallace, ID	B
NE	LIN
Walled Lake, MI	DET
Wallingford, CT	HRT
PA	PH
VT	BUR
Wallington, NJ	NEW
Wallis, TX	GAL
Walls, MS	JKS
Walnut, CA	LA
IL	PEO
Walnut Creek, CA	OAK
Walnut Grove, CA	SAC
MN	NU
Walnut Ridge, AR	LR
Walnutport, PA	ALN

Walpole, MA	BO
Walsenburg, CO	PBL
Walsh, IL	BEL
Walterboro, SC	CHR
Waltham, MA	BO
Walton, KY	COV
NY	ALB
Wamego, KS	KCK
Wanatah, IN	GRY
Wantagh, NY	RVC
Wapakoneta, OH	CIN
Wapato, WA	YAK
Wapella, IL	PEO
Wappingers Falls, NY	NY
Wapwallopen, PA	SCR
War, WV	WH
Warba, MN	DUL
Ward, SC	CHR
Ware, MA	SPR
Wareham, MA	FR
Warminster, PA	PH
Warner, NH	MAN
Warner Robins, GA	SAV
Warren, AR	LR
IL	RCK
MA	WOR
MI	DET
MI	OLL
MI	STN
MI	NTN
MN	CR
NJ	MET
OH	Y
OH	PBR
PA	E
RI	PRO
Warren Center, PA	NTN
Warrens, WI	LC
Warrensburg, MO	KC
NY	ALB
Warrenton, MO	STL
NC	R
VA	ARL
Warrenville, IL	JOL
Warrington, PA	PH
PA	PHU
Warroad, MN	CR
Warsaw, IL	PEO
IN	FTW
KY	COV
MO	JC
NY	BUF
Warson Woods, MO	STL
Warwick, NY	NY
RI	PRO
Wasco, CA	FRS
OR	BAK
Waseca, MN	WIN
Washburn, WI	SUP
Washington, DC	PHU
DC	SAM
DC	WDC
GA	ATL
IA	DAV
IL	PEO
IN	EVN
KS	SAL
LA	LAF
MI	DET
MO	STL
NC	R
NJ	MET
PA	PIT
TX	AUS
VA	ARL
Washington Court House, OH	COL
Washington Depot, CT	HRT
Washington Township, NJ	NEW
Washingtonville, NY	NY
Wasilla, AK	ANC
Watchung, NJ	MET
Waterbury, CT	HRT
CT	SAM
VT	BUR
Waterflow, NM	GLP
Waterford, CT	NOR
CT	NTN
MI	DET
NJ	CAM
NY	ALB
PA	E
WI	MIL
Waterloo, IA	DUB
IL	BEL
IN	FTW
NY	ROC
WI	MAD
Watersmeet, MI	MAR
Watertown, CT	HRT
MA	BO
MN	STP

NY	OG
SD	SFS
WI	MAD
Waterville, ME	PRT
ME	SAM
MN	STP
NY	SY
WA	YAK
Watervliet, MI	KAL
NY	ALB
NY	STF
Watford City, ND	BIS
Wathena, KS	KCK
Watkins, MN	NU
MN	SCL
Watkins Glen, NY	ROC
Watseka, IL	JOL
Watsonville, CA	MRY
Waubun, MN	CR
Wauchula, FL	VEN
Waucoma, IA	DUB
Wauconda, IL	CHI
Waukee, IA	DM
Waukegan, IL	CHI
Waukesha, WI	MIL
Waukon, IA	DUB
Waumandee, WI	LC
Waunakee, WI	MAD
Waupaca, WI	GB
Waupun, WI	MIL
Wauregan, CT	NOR
Wausau, WI	LC
Wausaukee, WI	GB
Wauseon, OH	TOL
Wautoma, WI	GB
Wauwatosa, WI	MIL
Wauzeka, WI	LC
Waveland, MS	BLX
Waverly, IA	DUB
KY	OWN
MN	STP
NE	LIN
OH	COL
Waxahachie, TX	CHL
TX	DAL
Waycross, GA	SAV
Wayland, MA	BO
MI	KAL
NY	ROC
Waymart, PA	SCR
Wayne, IL	JOL
MI	DET
NE	OM
NJ	PAT
PA	PH
WV	WH
Waynesboro, GA	SAV
MS	BLX
PA	HBG
VA	RIC
Waynesburg, OH	Y
OH	STU
PA	PIT
Waynesville, NC	CHL
OH	CIN
Wayside, NJ	TR
Wayzata, MN	STP
Weatherford, OK	OKL
TX	FWT
Weatherly, PA	ALN
Weaverville, CA	SAC
Webb City, MO	SPC
Webster, MA	WOR
MN	STP
NY	ROC
SD	SFS
WI	SUP
Webster City, IA	DUB
Webster Groves, MO	STL
Webster Springs, WV	WH
Wedron, IL	PEO
Weed, CA	SAC
Weedsport, NY	ROC
Weehawken, NJ	NEW
Weimar, TX	VIC
Weiner, AR	LR
Weirton, WV	WH
WV	PBR
Weiser, ID	B
Welch, WV	WH
Wellesley, MA	BO
Wellesley Hills, MA	BO
Wellfleet, MA	FR
Wellington, FL	PMB
KS	WCH
OH	CLV
TX	AMA
Wellpinit, WA	SPK
Wells, ME	PRT
MN	WIN
NV	RNO

Wellsboro, PA	SCR
Wellsburg, WV	WH
Wellston, OH	COL
Wellsville, NY	BUF
OH	Y
Wellton, AZ	TUC
Welsh, LA	LKC
Wenatchee, WA	YAK
Wendell, NC	R
Wendover, UT	SLC
Wenona, IL	PEO
Wentzville, MO	STL
Wernersville, PA	ALN
Weslaco, TX	BWN
Wesley, IA	SC
Wesley Hills, NY	NY
Wessington Springs, SD	SFS
West, TX	AUS
West Allis, WI	MIL
West Babylon, NY	RVC
West Bend, IA	SC
WI	MIL
West Bethesda, MD	WDC
West Bloomfield, MI	DET
MI	EST
West Boylston, MA	WOR
West Branch, IA	DAV
MI	GAY
West Brandywine, PA	PH
West Bridgewater, MA	BO
West Brookfield, MA	WOR
West Brooklyn, IL	RCK
West Burlington, IA	DAV
West Chazy, NY	OG
West Chester, OH	CIN
PA	PH
West Chicago, IL	JOL
West Clarksville, NY	BUF
West Collingswood, NJ	CAM
West Conshohocken, PA	PH
West Covina, CA	LA
CA	OLL
West Des Moines, IA	DM
West Easton, PA	PHU
West End, NJ	TR
West Falls, NY	BUF
West Fargo, ND	FAR
West Frankfort, IL	BEL
West Greenwich, RI	PRO
West Grove, PA	PH
West Harrison, IN	IND
NY	NY
West Hartford, CT	HRT
West Harwich, MA	FR
West Haven, CT	HRT
UT	SLC
West Hazleton, PA	SCR
West Hempstead, NY	RVC
NY	SYM
West Hollywood, CA	LA
FL	MIA
West Hyattsville, MD	WDC
West Islip, NY	RVC
West Jefferson, OH	COL
West Jordan, UT	SLC
West Lafayette, IN	LFT
West Lawn, PA	ALN
West Leyden, NY	OG
West Liberty, IA	DAV
KY	LEX
WV	WH
West Long Branch, NJ	TR
West Memphis, AR	LR
West Middlesex, PA	E
West Mifflin, PA	PIT
West Milford, NJ	PAT
West Milton, OH	CIN
West Monroe, LA	SHP
West New York, NJ	NEW
West Newton, PA	GBG
West Nyack, NY	NY
West Orange, NJ	NEW
West Palm Beach, FL	PMB
West Park, FL	MIA
NY	NY
West Paterson, NJ	NTN
NJ	PAT
West Peoria, IL	PEO
West Pittston, PA	SCR
West Plains, MO	SPC
West Point, IA	DAV
MS	JKS
NE	OM
NY	NY
VA	RIC
West Portsmouth, OH	COL
West Redding, CT	BGP
West River, MD	BAL
West Roxbury, MA	BO
MA	NTN
West Rutland, VT	BUR

West Sacramento, CA	SAC
West Salem, OH	CLV
WI	LC
West Salisbury, PA	ALT
West Sedona, AZ	PHX
West Seneca, NY	BUF
West Simsbury, CT	HRT
West Springfield, MA	SPR
West St. Paul, MN	STP
West Stockbridge, MA	SPR
West Terre Haute, IN	IND
West Trenton, NJ	TR
West Union, IA	DUB
OH	CIN
West Valley, NY	BUF
West Valley City, UT	SLC
West Warren, MA	WOR
West Warwick, RI	PRO
West Yellowstone, MT	HEL
Westampton, NJ	TR
Westborough, MA	WOR
Westbrook, CT	NOR
ME	PRT
Westbury, NY	PSC
NY	RVC
Westchester, IL	CHI
Westcliffe, CO	PBL
Westerly, RI	PRO
Western Springs, IL	CHI
Westernport, MD	BAL
Westerville, OH	COL
OH	NTN
Westfield, IN	LFT
MA	SPR
NJ	NEW
NY	BUF
VT	BUR
Westford, MA	BO
Westhampton Beach, NY	RVC
Westhope, ND	FAR
Westlake, LA	LKC
OH	CLV
Westlake Village, CA	LA
Westland, MI	DET
Westminster, CA	ORG
CO	DEN
MA	WOR
MD	BAL
Westmont, IL	JOL
NJ	CAM
Westmorland, CA	SD
Weston, CT	BGP
FL	MIA
MA	BO
MO	KC
NE	LIN
PA	SCR
VT	BUR
WI	LC
WV	WH
Westphalia, IA	DM
MI	LAN
MO	JC
Westport, CT	BGP
MA	FR
SD	SFS
Westville, IL	PEO
NJ	CAM
Westville Grove, NJ	CAM
Westwego, LA	NO
Westwood, CA	SAC
MA	BO
NJ	NEW
Wethersfield, CT	HRT
Wever, IA	DAV
Wexford, PA	PIT
Weyauwega, WI	GB
Weyerhaeuser, WI	SUP
Weymouth, MA	BO
Wharton, NJ	PAT
TX	VIC
Wheat Ridge, CO	DEN
Wheatfield, IN	LFT
Wheatland, IA	DAV
WY	CHY
Wheaton, IL	GB
IL	JOL
MN	SCL
Wheelersburg, OH	COL
Wheeling, IL	CHI
WV	WH
WV	OLL
WV	SJP
Whippany, NJ	PAT
NJ	PHU
Whistler, AL	MOB
White Bear Lake, MN	STP
White Castle, LA	BR
White Cloud, MI	GR
White Deer, TX	AMA
White Haven, PA	SCR

White Lake, MI	DET
SD	SFS
WI	GB
White Mills, KY	L
White Oak, PA	PIT
White Pigeon, MI	KAL
White Pine, MI	MAR
White Plains, NY	NY
NY	PSC
White River, SD	RC
White River Junction, VT	BUR
White Salmon, WA	YAK
White Sulphur Springs, MT	HEL
WV	WH
White Swan, WA	YAK
Whitefield, ME	PRT
Whitefish, MT	HEL
Whitefish Bay, WI	MIL
Whitehall, MT	HEL
NY	ALB
PA	ALN
WI	LC
Whitehouse, OH	TOL
TX	TYL
Whitehouse Station, NJ	MET
Whitelaw, WI	GB
Whiteriver, AZ	GLP
Whitesboro, NY	SY
Whitestone, NY	BRK
Whitesville, KY	OWN
Whitethorn, CA	SR
Whiteville, NC	R
Whitewater, CO	PBL
WI	MIL
Whiting, IN	GRY
IN	PRM
NJ	TR
Whitinsville, MA	WOR
Whitley City, KY	LEX
Whitman, MA	BO
Whitney, PA	GBG
Whitney Point, NY	SY
Whittemore, IA	SC
MI	GAY
Whittier, CA	LA
Wichita, KS	STN
KS	WCH
Wichita Falls, TX	FWT
Wickatunk, NJ	TR
Wickenburg, AZ	PHX
Wickford, RI	PRO
Wickliffe, OH	CLV
Wiggins, MS	BLX
Wilber, NE	LIN
Wilbraham, MA	SPR
Wilbur, WA	SPK
Wilburton, OK	TLS
Wilder, KY	COV
Wildomar, CA	SB
CA	NTN
Wildwood, FL	ORL
MO	STL
NJ	CAM
PA	PIT
Wilkes Barre, PA	PSC
PA	SCR
Wilkes Barre Township, PA	SCR
Wilkes–Barre, PA	PHU
PA	SCR
PA	PSC
PA	SAM
Willard, OH	TOL
WI	LC
Willcox, AZ	TUC
Williams, AZ	PHX
CA	SAC
IA	DUB
Williamsburg, IA	DAV
KY	LEX
PA	ALT
VA	PSC
VA	RIC
Williamson, WV	WH
Williamsport, IN	LFT
MD	BAL
PA	SCR
Williamston, MI	LAN
NC	R
Williamstown, KY	COV
MA	SPR
NJ	CAM
PA	HBG
Williamsville, NY	BUF
NY	SAM
Willimantic, CT	NOR
CT	STF
Willingboro, NJ	TR
Willington, CT	NOR
Williston, FL	STA
ND	BIS
VT	BUR

Williston Park, NY	RVC
Willits, CA	SR
Willmar, MN	NU
Willoughby, OH	CLV
Willoughby Hills, OH	CLV
Willow City, ND	FAR
Willow Grove, PA	PH
Willow River, MN	DUL
Willow Springs, IL	CHI
MO	SPC
Willowick, OH	CLV
Willows, CA	SAC
Willsboro, NY	OG
Wilmerding, PA	PIT
Wilmette, IL	CHI
Wilmington, CA	LA
DE	PHU
DE	WIL
IL	JOL
MA	BO
NC	R
OH	CIN
VT	BUR
Wilmore, PA	ALT
Wilmot, SD	SFS
Wilson, KS	SAL
NC	R
Wilsonville, OR	P
Wilton, CT	BGP
IA	DAV
ND	BIS
ND	STN
Wilton Manors, FL	MIA
Wimberley, TX	AUS
Wimbledon, ND	FAR
Winamac, IN	LFT
Winchendon, MA	WOR
Winchester, CA	SB
IL	SFD
KY	LEX
MA	BO
VA	ARL
Winchester Center, CT	HRT
Wind Lake, WI	MIL
Windber, PA	ALT
PA	PBR
Winder, GA	ATL
Windham, CT	NOR
ME	PRT
NH	MAN
NY	ALB
OH	Y
Windom, MN	WIN
Windsor, CA	SR
CO	DEN
CT	HRT
ME	PRT
NC	R
NY	SY
VT	BUR
Windsor Locks, CT	HRT
Windsor Mill, MD	BAL
Windthorst, TX	FWT
Winfield, AL	BIR
IL	JOL
KS	WCH
Winlock, WA	SEA
Winnebago, NE	OM
Winneconne, WI	GB
Winnemucca, NV	RNO
Winner, SD	RC
Winnetka, CA	LA
IL	CHI
Winnfield, LA	ALX
Winnie, TX	BEA
Winnsboro, LA	ALX
Winona, MN	WIN
Winooski, VT	BUR
Winslow, AR	LR
AZ	GLP
ME	PRT
Winsted, CT	HRT
MN	NU
Winston–Salem, NC	CHL
Winter, WI	SUP
Winter Garden, FL	ORL
Winter Haven, FL	ORL
Winter Park, FL	ORL
Winter Springs, FL	ORL
Winterhaven, CA	SD
Winters, CA	SAC
TX	SAN
Winterset, IA	DM
Wintersville, OH	STU
Winthrop, MA	BO
MN	NU
Wisconsin Dells, WI	MAD
Wisconsin Rapids, WI	LC
WI	SUP
Wishek, ND	FAR
Wisner, NE	OM

Wittenberg, WI	LC
Woburn, MA	BO
Wofford Heights, CA	FRS
Wolcott, CT	HRT
NY	ROC
Wolf Point, MT	GF
Wolfeboro, NH	MAN
Wolfforth, TX	LUB
Wonder Lake, IL	RCK
Wonewoc, WI	LC
Wood Dale, IL	JOL
Wood Ridge, NJ	NEW
Wood River, IL	SFD
NE	GI
Woodbine, NJ	CAM
Woodbourne, NY	NY
Woodbridge, CT	HRT
NJ	MET
VA	ARL
Woodburn, OR	P
Woodbury, CT	HRT
MN	STP
NJ	CAM
NY	RVC
Woodbury Heights, NJ	CAM
Woodcliff Lake, NJ	NEW
Woodhaven, MI	DET
NY	BRK
Woodhull, IL	PEO
Woodinville, WA	SEA
Woodlake, CA	FRS
Woodland, CA	SAC
WA	SEA
Woodland Hills, CA	LA
Woodland Park, CO	COS
NJ	PSC
Woodlawn, VA	RIC
Woodlynne, NJ	CAM
Woodridge, IL	JOL
Woodruff, WI	SUP
Woods Hole, MA	FR
Woodsboro, TX	CC
Woodsfield, OH	STU
Woodside, NY	BRK
Woodstock, GA	ATL
IL	RCK
MD	BAL
NY	NY
VA	ARL
VT	BUR
Woodstown, NJ	CAM
Woodsville, NH	MAN
Woodville, FL	PT
MS	JKS
TX	BEA
Woodward, OK	OKL
Woodworth, LA	ALX
Woonsocket, RI	NTN
RI	STF
RI	PRO
SD	SFS
Wooster, OH	CLV
Worcester, MA	NTN
MA	SAM
MA	WOR
NY	ALB
Worland, WY	CHY
Worthington, IA	DUB
MN	WIN
OH	COL
Wrangell, AK	JUN
Wray, CO	DEN
Wrentham, MA	BO
Wright, KS	DOD
Wrightsville Beach, NC	R
Wurtsboro, NY	NY
Wyalusing, PA	SCR
Wyandanch, NY	RVC
Wyandotte, MI	DET
Wyckoff, NJ	NEW
Wylie, TX	DAL
Wymore, NE	LIN
Wynantskill, NY	ALB
Wyncote, PA	PH
Wyndmere, ND	FAR
Wyndmoor, PA	PH
Wynne, AR	LR
Wynnewood, PA	PH
PA	OLN
Wynot, NE	OM
Wyoming, IL	PEO
MI	GR
OH	CIN
PA	SCR
Wytheville, VA	RIC
Xenia, OH	CIN
Yakima, WA	YAK
Yakutat, AK	JUN
Yale, MI	DET
Yalesville, CT	HRT
Yamhill, OR	P

Yankton, SD	SFS
Yardley, PA	PH
Yardville, NJ	TR
Yarmouth, ME	PRT
Yatesboro, PA	GBG
Yazoo City, MS	JKS
Yeadon, PA	PH
Yellow Springs, OH	CIN
Yellville, AR	LR
Yelm, WA	SEA
Yerington, NV	RNO
Yoakum, TX	VIC
Yoder, IN	FTW
Yonges Island, SC	CHR
Yonkers, NY	NY
NY	NTN
NY	STF
Yorba Linda, CA	ORG
York, ME	PRT
NE	LIN
PA	HBG
SC	CHR
York Haven, PA	HBG
Yorktown, TX	VIC
VA	RIC
Yorktown Heights, NY	NY
Yorkville, IL	JOL
Yosemite National Park, CA	FRS
Youngstown, NY	BUF
OH	Y
OH	SJP
OH	PBR
OH	OLL
Youngsville, LA	LAF
PA	E
Youngtown, AZ	PHX
Youngwood, PA	GBG
Yountville, CA	SR
Ypsilanti, MI	LAN
Yreka, CA	SAC
Yuba City, CA	SAC
Yucaipa, CA	SB
Yucca Valley, CA	SB
Yukon, OK	OKL
PA	GBG
Yulan, NY	NY
Yuma, AZ	TUC
CO	DEN
Zachary, LA	BR
Zaleski, OH	COL
Zanesville, OH	COL
OH	NTN
Zapata, TX	LAR
Zelienople, PA	PIT
Zenda, KS	WCH
Zephyr Cove, NV	RNO
Zephyrhills, FL	SP
Zillah, WA	YAK
Zimmerman, MN	SCL
Zion–Beach Park, IL	CHI
Zionsville, IN	LFT
Zumbrota, MN	STP
Zuni, NM	GLP
Zwolle, LA	SHP

Diocesan Abbreviations

ARCHDIOCESES AND DIOCESES

(ALB) Albany (New York)
(ALN) Allentown (Pennsylvania)
(ALT) Altoona-Johnstown (Pennsylvania)
(ALX) Alexandria (Louisiana)
(AGN) Agana (Guam)
(AMA) Amarillo (Texas)
(ANC) Anchorage (Alaska)
(ARE) Arecibo (Puerto Rico)
(ARL) Arlington (Virginia)
(ATH) Apostolate To Hungarians (Washington, DC)
(ATL) Atlanta (Georgia)
(AUS) Austin (Texas)
(B) Boise (Idaho)
(BAK) Baker (Oregon)
(BAL) Baltimore (Maryland)
(BEA) Beaumont (Texas)
(BEL) Belleville (Illinois)
(BGP) Bridgeport (Connecticut)
(BIR) Birmingham (Alabama)
(BIS) Bismarck (North Dakota)
(BLX) Biloxi (Mississippi)
(BO) Boston (Massachusetts)
(BR) Baton Rouge (Louisiana)
(BRK) Brooklyn (New York)
(BUF) Buffalo (New York)
(BUR) Burlington (Vermont)
(BWN) Brownsville (Texas)
(CAM) Camden (New Jersey)
(CC) Corpus Christi (Texas)
(CGS) Caguas (Puerto Rico)
(CHI) Chicago (Illinois)
(CHK) Chalan Kanoa
(CHL) Charlotte (North Carolina)
(CHR) Charleston (South Carolina)
(CHY) Cheyenne (Wyoming)
(CI) Caroline Islands
(CIN) Cincinnati (Ohio)
(CLV) Cleveland (Ohio)
(COL) Columbus (Ohio)
(COS) Colorado Springs (Colorado)
(COV) Covington (Kentucky)
(CR) Crookston (Minnesota)
(DAL) Dallas (Texas)
(DAV) Davenport (Iowa)
(DEN) Denver (Colorado)
(DET) Detroit (Michigan)
(DM) Des Moines (Iowa)
(DOD) Dodge City (Kansas)
(DUB) Dubuque (Iowa)
(DUL) Duluth (Minnesota)
(E) Erie (Pennsylvania)
(ELP) El Paso (Texas)
(EST) Eparchy of Saint Thomas the Apostle
(EVN) Evansville (Indiana)
(FAJ) Fajardo-Humacao (Puerto Rico)
(FAR) Fargo (North Dakota)
(FBK) Fairbanks (Alaska)
(FgM) Foreign Mission Section
(FR) Fall River (Massachusetts)
(FRS) Fresno (California)
(FTW) Fort Wayne-South Bend (Indiana)
(FWT) Fort Worth (Texas)
(GAL) Galveston-Houston (Texas)
(GAY) Gaylord (Michigan)
(GB) Green Bay (Wisconsin)
(GBG) Greensburg (Pennsylvania)
(GF) Great Falls-Billings (Montana)
(GI) Grand Island (Nebraska)
(GLP) Gallup (New Mexico)
(GR) Grand Rapids (Michigan)
(GRY) Gary (Indiana)
(HBG) Harrisburg (Pennsylvania)
(HEL) Helena (Montana)
(HON) Honolulu (Hawaii)
(HRT) Hartford (Connecticut)
(HT) Houma-Thibodaux (Louisiana)
(IND) Indianapolis (Indiana)
(JC) Jefferson City (Missouri)
(JKS) Jackson (Mississippi)
(JOL) Joliet in Illinois
(JUN) Juneau (Alaska)
(KAL) Kalamazoo (Michigan)
(KC) Kansas City-St. Joseph (Missouri)
(KCK) Kansas City in Kansas
(KNX) Knoxville (Tennessee)
(L) Louisville (Kentucky)
(LA) Los Angeles (California)
(LAF) Lafayette (Louisiana)
(LAN) Lansing (Michigan)
(LAR) Laredo (Texas)
(LC) La Crosse (Wisconsin)
(LEX) Lexington (Kentucky)
(LFT) Lafayette in Indiana
(LIN) Lincoln (Nebraska)
(LIT) Lithuanian Apostolate for Lithuanian Catholics
(LKC) Lake Charles (Louisiana)
(LR) Little Rock (Arkansas)
(LSC) Las Cruces (New Mexico)
(LUB) Lubbock (Texas)
(LAV) Las Vegas (Nevada)
(MAD) Madison (Wisconsin)
(MAN) Manchester (New Hampshire)
(MAR) Marquette (Michigan)
(MEM) Memphis (Tennessee)
(MET) Metuchen (New Jersey)
(MGZ) Mayaguez (Puerto Rico)
(MI) Marshall Islands
(MIA) Miami (Florida)
(MIL) Milwaukee (Wisconsin)
(MO) Military Services (Maryland)
(MOB) Mobile (Alabama)
(MRY) Monterey in California
(NEW) Newark (New Jersey)
(NO) New Orleans (Louisiana)
(NOR) Norwich (Connecticut)
(NSH) Nashville (Tennessee)
(NTN) Newton (Melkite, United States)
(NU) New Ulm (Minnesota)
(NY) New York (New York)
(OAK) Oakland (California)
(OG) Ogdensburg (New York)
(OKL) Oklahoma City (Oklahoma)
(OLD) Our Lady of Deliverance Syriac (Union City, New Jersey)
(OLL) Our Lady of Lebanon of Los Angeles (California)
(OLN) Our Lady of Nareg for Armenian Catholics (New York)
(OM) Omaha (Nebraska)
(ORG) Orange in California
(ORL) Orlando (Florida)
(OWN) Owensboro (Kentucky)
(P) Portland in Oregon
(PAT) Paterson (New Jersey)
(PBL) Pueblo (Colorado)
(PBR) Pittsburgh Byzantine (Pennsylvania)
(PCE) Ponce (Puerto Rico)
(PEO) Peoria (Illinois)
(PH) Philadelphia (Pennsylvania)
(PHU) Philadelphia Ukrainian (Pennsylvania)
(PHX) Phoenix (Arizona)
(PIT) Pittsburgh (Pennsylvania)
(PMB) Palm Beach (Florida)
(POD) Prelature of the Holy Cross and Opus Dei
(PRM) Parma Byzantine (Ohio)
(PRO) Providence (Rhode Island)
(PRT) Portland (Maine)
(PSC) Passaic Byzantine (New Jersey)
(PT) Pensacola-Tallahassee (Florida)
(R) Raleigh (North Carolina)
(RC) Rapid City (South Dakota)
(RCK) Rockford (Illinois)
(RIC) Richmond (Virginia)
(RNO) Reno (Nevada)
(ROC) Rochester (New York)
(ROM) Romanian (Byzantine) (Ohio)
(RVC) Rockville Centre (New York)
(SAC) Sacramento (California)
(SAG) Saginaw (Michigan)
(SAL) Salina (Kansas)
(SAM) St. Maron of Brooklyn (U.S.A.)
(SAN) San Angelo (Texas)
(SAT) San Antonio (Texas)
(SAV) Savannah (Georgia)
(SB) San Bernadino (California)
(SC) Sioux City (Iowa)
(SCL) St. Cloud (Minnesota)
(SCR) Scranton (Pennsylvania)
(SD) San Diego (California)
(SEA) Seattle (Washington)
(SFD) Springfield in Illinois
(SFE) Santa Fe (New Mexico)
(SFR) San Francisco (California)
(SFS) Sioux Falls (South Dakota)
(SHP) Shreveport (Louisiana)
(SJ) San Jose in California
(SJN) San Juan (Puerto Rico)
(SJP) St. Josaphat in Parma (Ohio)
(SLC) Salt Lake City (Utah)
(SP) St. Petersburg (Florida)
(SPA) Eparchy of St. Peter the Apostle (Chaldean)
(SPC) Springfield-Cape Girardeau (Missouri)
(SPK) Spokane (Washington)
(SPP) Samoa-Pago Pago
(SPR) Springfield in Massachusetts
(SR) Santa Rosa in California
(STA) St. Augustine (Florida)
(STF) Stamford Ukrainian (Connecticut)
(STL) St. Louis (Missouri)
(STN) St. Nicholas in Chicago Ukrainian
(STO) Stockton (California)
(STP) St. Paul and Minneapolis (Minnesota)
(STU) Steubenville (Ohio)
(STV) St. Thomas, Virgin Islands
(SUP) Superior (Wisconsin)
(SY) Syracuse (New York)
(SYM) St. Thomas Syro-Malabar (Illinois)
(TLS) Tulsa (Oklahoma)
(TOL) Toledo (Ohio)
(TR) Trenton (New Jersey)
(TUC) Tucson (Arizona)
(TYL) Tyler (Texas)
(VEN) Venice (Florida)
(VIC) Victoria in Texas
(VNN) Van Nuys Byzantine (California)
(WCH) Wichita (Kansas)
(WDC) Washington (District of Columbia)
(WH) Wheeling-Charleston (West Virginia)
(WIL) Wilmington (Delaware)
(WIN) Winona (Minnesota)
(WOR) Worcester (Massachusetts)
(Y) Youngstown (Ohio)
(YAK) Yakima (Washington)

Diocese of Albany

(Dioecesis Albanensis)

Most Reverend

HOWARD J. HUBBARD, D.D.

Bishop of Albany; ordained December 18, 1963; appointed February 1, 1977; ordained and installed March 27, 1977. *Res.: 125 Eagle St., Albany, NY 12202.* Tel: 518-462-3804.

REJOICE WE ARE HIS PEOPLE

Chancery Office: Pastoral Center, 40 N. Main Ave., Albany, NY 12203. Tel: 518-453-6600; Fax: 518-453-6795.

Web: www.rcda.org

Email: chancery@rcda.org

ESTABLISHED APRIL 23, 1847.

Square Miles 10,419.

(Incorporated by a special act of the Legislature of the State of New York, April 12, 1941, with the title "The Roman Catholic Diocese of Albany, New York").

Comprises the entire Counties of Albany, Columbia, Delaware, Fulton, Green, Montgomery, Otsego, Rensselaer, Saratoga, Schenectady, Schoharie, Warren and Washington and that part of Herkimer and Hamilton Counties, south of the northern line of the townships of Ohio and Russia, as existing in 1872 in the State of New York.

For legal titles of parishes and diocesan institutions, consult the Chancery Office.

STATISTICAL OVERVIEW

Personnel	
Bishop	1
Priests: Diocesan Active in Diocese	113
Priests: Diocesan Active Outside Diocese	4
Priests: Retired, Sick or Absent	96
Number of Diocesan Priests	213
Religious Priests in Diocese	79
Total Priests in Diocese	292
Extern Priests in Diocese	4
Ordinations:	
Diocesan Priests	1
Transitional Deacons	4
Permanent Deacons in Diocese	111
Total Brothers	76
Total Sisters	702
Parishes	
Parishes	136
With Resident Pastor:	
Resident Diocesan Priests	98
Resident Religious Priests	9
Without Resident Pastor:	
Administered by Priests	6
Administered by Deacons	4
Administered by Religious Women	9
Administered by Lay People	10
Missions	16
Pastoral Centers	5
New Parishes Created	14
Closed Parishes	42
Professional Ministry Personnel:	
Brothers	3
Sisters	32
Lay Ministers	196
Welfare	
Catholic Hospitals	3
Total Assisted	1,250,000
Health Care Centers	17
Total Assisted	72,000
Homes for the Aged	7
Total Assisted	1,200
Residential Care of Children	4
Total Assisted	135
Day Care Centers	3
Total Assisted	269
Specialized Homes	37
Total Assisted	326
Special Centers for Social Services	75
Total Assisted	110,972
Residential Care of Disabled	15
Total Assisted	101
Other Institutions	16
Total Assisted	848
Educational	
Diocesan Students in Other Seminaries	11
Total Seminarians	11
Colleges and Universities	3
Total Students	6,670
High Schools, Diocesan and Parish	4
Total Students	1,249
High Schools, Private	3
Total Students	975
Elementary Schools, Diocesan and Parish	23
Total Students	5,146
Elementary Schools, Private	2
Total Students	321
Catechesis/Religious Education:	
High School Students	8,393
Elementary Students	20,749
Total Students under Catholic Instruction	43,514
Teachers in the Diocese:	
Priests	3
Sisters	13
Lay Teachers	545
Vital Statistics	
Receptions into the Church:	
Infant Baptism Totals	3,315
Minor Baptism Totals	108
Adult Baptism Totals	74
Received into Full Communion	156
First Communions	3,982
Confirmations	3,067
Marriages:	
Catholic	704
Interfaith	304
Total Marriages	1,008
Deaths	3,686
Total Catholic Population	331,908
Total Population	1,312,642

Former Bishops—His Eminence JOHN CARDINAL MCCLOSKEY, D.D., ord. Jan. 12, 1834; appt. Bishop of Axiere and Coadjutor to the Bishop of New York, Nov. 21, 1843; cons. March 10, 1844; transferred to Albany, May 21, 1847; promoted to New York, May 6, 1864; created Cardinal Priest of the Holy Roman Church, March 15, 1875, under the title Sanctae Mariae supra Minervam; died Oct. 10, 1885; Rt. Rev. JOHN J. CONROY, ord. May 21, 1842; appt. Bishop July 7, 1865; cons. Oct. 15, 1865; resigned Oct. 16, 1877; transferred to the See of Curium, March 22, 1878; died Nov. 20, 1895; Rt. Rev. Msgrs. FRANCIS MCNEIRNY, D.D., ord. Aug. 17, 1854; appt. Bishop of Rhesina and Coadjutor to the Bishop of Albany, Dec. 22, 1871; cons. April 21, 1872; appt. Administrator of the Diocese of Albany, Jan. 18, 1874; Bishop of Albany, by right of succession, Oct. 16, 1877; died Jan. 2, 1894; THOMAS M. A. BURKE, D.D., ord. June 30, 1864; preconized May 18, 1894; cons. July 1, 1894; died Jan 20, 1915; THOMAS F. CUSACK, D.D., ord. May 30, 1885; cons. Titular Bishop of Themiscyra and Auxiliary to the Archbishop of New York, April 25, 1904; transferred to Albany, July 5, 1915; died July 12, 1918; Most Revs. EDMUND F. GIBBONS, D.D., ord. May 27, 1893; appt. Bishop, Feb. 1, 1919; cons. March 25, 1919; resigned Nov. 10, 1954; transferred to See of Verbe; died June 19, 1964; WILLIAM A. SCULLY, D.D., ord. Sept. 20, 1919; appt. Coadjutor Bishop "cum jure successionis," Aug. 21, 1945; cons. Oct. 24, 1945; succeeded to See, Nov. 10, 1954; died Jan. 5, 1969; EDWIN B. BRODERICK, D.D., ord. May 30, 1942; appt. Titular Bishop of Tizica and Auxiliary of New York, March 8, 1967; cons. April 21, 1967; transferred to Albany, March 19, 1969; resigned June 2, 1976; appt. Exec. Dir. Catholic Relief Services, June 3, 1976; retired Sept. 1985; died July 2, 2006.

Pastoral Center—Pastoral Center, 40 N. Main Ave., Albany, 12203. Tel: 518-453-6600; Fax: 518-453-6793. Office Hours: Mon.-Fri. 8:30-4:30.

Vicar General and Moderator of the Curia—Rev. MICHAEL A. FARANO, Pastoral Center, 40 N. Main Ave., Albany, 12203-1422. Tel: 518-453-6612.

Chancellors—Pastoral Center, 40 N. Main Ave., Albany, 12203. Tel: 518-453-6612. Rev. KENNETH DOYLE, Chancellor Pub. Information; ELIZABETH SIMCOE, Chancellor Pastoral Svcs.

Chief Financial Officer—Mr RICHARD FARRELL, 40 N. Main Ave., Albany, 12203. Tel: 518-453-6640.

Insurance Office—Catholic Mutual Group, 33 Elk St., Albany, 12207. Tel: 518-445-6250. SAL CARPONE, Property Inspector, 40 N. Main Ave., Albany, 12203. Tel: 518-453-6790.

Office of Human Resources—JOYCE C. TARANTINO, Esq., Dir. Email: joyce.tarantino@rcda.org; PAMELA BENNETT, Administrative Asst., 40 N. Main Ave., Albany, 12203. Tel: 518-453-6635. Email: pamela.bennett@rcda.org.

Pastoral Planning—Deacon FRANK C. BERNING, Office of Pastoral Planning: Tel: 518-453-6661. Email: frank.berning@rcda.org.

Archivist—Sr. NOLA BRUNNER, C.S.J., 40 N. Main Ave., Albany, 12203. Tel: 518-453-6669. Email: nola.brunner@rcda.org.

Office of Canonical Services—40 N. Main Ave., Albany, 12203. Tel: 518-453-6620; Fax: 518-453-6778. Office Hours: 8:30-4:30 (By appointment only)

Vicar Judicial—Rev. JAMES I. DONLON, J.C.D.

Adjutant Vicar Judicial—Rev. PETER J. SULLIVAN III, J.C.L.

Judges—Revs. DAVID V. BERBERIAN, J.C.L.; ANTHONY M. BARRATT; JAMES I. DONLON, J.C.D.; PETER J. SULLIVAN III, J.C.L.

Defender of the Marriage Bond in First Instance—Sr. MARY ANN HAYES, C.S.J., J.C.L.

Promoter of Justice—Sr. MARY ANN HAYES, C.S.J., J.C.L.

Advocates—Revs. THOMAS KRUPA; JAMES LEFEBVRE; JOSEPH O'BRIEN; JOHN L. MOYNA; ARTHUR BECKER; MEG BERGH; MARY MORIARITY; Deacon CHARLES TAYLOR.

Bishop's Delegate for Marriage Dispensations—Revs. JAMES I. DONLON, J.C.D.; PETER J. SULLIVAN III, J.C.L.

Notaries—MARTHA MCEWAN; MARY FIORILLO.

Interdiocesan Tribunal for the Province of NY Archdiocese— (Second Instance Appeal Court), Rev. Msgr. GEORGE P. GRAHAM, Vicar Judicial;

Rev. MICHAEL T. MARTINE, Admin. & Chief Exec. Sec., 201 Seminary Ave., Yonkers, 10704-1852. Tel: 914-968-4301; 800-293-6598; Fax: 914-968-4466.

Presbyteral Council—Most Rev. HOWARD JAMES HUBBARD, D.D., Pres.; Revs. PAUL BUTLER, Chm.; JAMES KANE; JOSEPH BENINTENDE; ANTHONY KALL, O.F.M.Conv.; THOMAS BERARDI; ANTHONY LIGATO; JAMES FITZMAURICE; PETER PAGONES; JOSEPH FALLETTA; THOMAS MORETTE; DOMINIC INGEMIE; JOSEPH O'BRIEN; KENNETH DOYLE, Chancellor; JAMES I. DONLON, J.C.D.; Mr RICHARD FARRELL, CFO; Rev. MICHAEL A. FARANO, Vicar Gen. & Moderator of the Curia.

Diocesan Board of Consultors—Revs. JAMES KANE; JOSEPH FALLETTA; PAUL BUTLER; DOMINIC INGEMIE; ANTHONY KALL, O.F.M.Conv.; THOMAS BERARDI; ANTHONY LIGATO; JOSEPH BENINTENDE; THOMAS MORRETTE; JAMES FITZMAURICE; PETER PAGONES; JOSEPH O'BRIEN; JAMES I. DONLON, J.C.D., Canonical Consultant to the Bd.

Deans—Revs. JOHN BRADLEY, Albany County-City; GEOFFREY D. BURKE, Albany County Suburban Deanery; JOHN MOLYN, Colombia County; JOHN BURNS, Delaware County and Otsego County; DONALD CZELUSNIAK, Fulton County and Montgomery County; JOHN L. MOYNA, Greene County; ANTHONY M. BARRATT, Herkimer County; RANDALL P. PATTERSON, Northern Albany County and Northern Rensselaer County; THOMAS KRUPA, Southern Rensselaer County; Very Rev. THOMAS J. HAYES, Saratoga; Revs. PETER PAGONES, Schenectady County; THOMAS HOLMES, Schoharie County; THOMAS ZELKER, Warren County & Washington County.

Diocesan Offices and Directors

Unless otherwise indicated all Diocesan Offices and Directors are located at: *The Pastoral Center, 40 N. Main Ave., Albany, 12203*. Tel: 518-453-6600; Fax: 518-453-6793.

Office of Real Property—NOEL A. OLSEN, Dir. Tel: 518-453-6623.

Administrative Review Board (Due Process)—Rev. DAVID V. BERBERIAN, J.C.L., Chm. Tel: 518-439-4951, Ext. 121. Email: dvberberian@msn.com.

Apostleship of Prayer—Rev. ROBERT MCGUIRE, S.J., Fultonville, 12072. Tel: 518-853-3033, Ext. 233.

Bishop's Appeal—THOMAS PRINDLE, Exec. Dir. Tel: 518-453-6680.

Black Apostolate—Rev. KOFI NTSIFUL-AMISSAH, Admin., St. Joan of Arc Church, 76 Menand Rd., Albany, 12204. Tel: 518-462-9604.

Korean Apostolate of the Roman Catholic Diocese of Albany, New York—Rev. SIMON (KWANGGUN) YOU, 80 Slingerland St., Albany, 12202. Tel: 518-275-0350.

Vietnamese Apostolate—Rev. LOUIS VAN THANH, c/o St. Patrick's Rectory, 55 Grand St., Newburgh, 12550. Tel: 845-561-0888.

Campus Ministry—Rev. EDWARD KACERGUIS, Diocesan Dir., Christ Sun of Justice, 10 Tom Phelan Place, Troy, 12180.

Catholic Deaf Ministry—Rev. JAMES E. CLARK, Chap., 40 N. Main Ave., Albany, 12203-1422. Tel: 518-686-5064 (Office); 518-423-1883. Email: deaf@rcda.org. Web: www.deafalbany.catholicweb.com.

Cemeteries—Mr RICHARD TOUCHETTE, Dir., Albany Diocesan Cemeteries, 48 Cemetery Ave., Menands, Albany, 12204. Tel: 518-432-4953. Web: www.rcdacemeteries.org. Email: rick.touchette@rcda.org.

Censor Librorum—Rev. JOHN R. ROOS, J.C.D.

Architecture and Building Commission—Rev. RANDALL P. PATTERSON, Chm.; LORI CHERA, Coord. Tel: 518-453-6622; Fax: 518-453-6792.

Public Information—Rev. KENNETH DOYLE, Chancellor. Tel: 518-453-6612; KENNETH GOLDFARB, Dir. Communications. Tel: 518-453-6618.

Cursillo in Christian Living—Sr. BETSY VAN DEUSEN, C.S.J., Spiritual Dir., St. Helen's Church, 1803 Union St., Niskayuna, 12309. Tel: 518-377-3119; JOE THOUIN, Lay Dir., 446 Baker Ave., Cohoes, 12047. Tel: 518-233-7119. Web: www.cursillo.org/albany.

Diocesan Service Committee for Charismatic Renewal—Liaisons: Deacon JERRY GRIGAITIS; MARIE GRIGAITIS, 25 Par Del Rio, Clifton Park, 12065. Tel: 518-371-7911. Email: dcnjmgrigaitis@aol.com.

Diocesan Stewardship Office—THOMAS PRINDLE, Exec. Dir. Tel: 518-453-6680.

Office of Information Technology—GERALYN A. FOX, Dir. Tel: 518-453-6685; Fax: 518-453-6779.

Catholic Charities of Diocese of Albany, Inc.; St. Vincent's Child Care Society, Inc.—Sr. MAUREEN JOYCE, R.S.M., CEO & Sec. to the Bishop for Health & Social Svcs. & Sec. St. Vincent's Child Care Society, Inc. Tel: 518-453-6650; Fax: 518-453-6792; MICHELE KELLY, CFO.

Catholic Charities Agencies and Commissions—TOM GILLESPIE, Dir., Catholic Charities of Columbia & Greene Counties, 431 E. Allen St., Hudson, 12534. Tel: 518-828-8660; JOHN NASSO, Dir., Catholic Charities of Fulton & Montgomery Counties, 4 Nicholas St., Johnstown, 12095. Tel: 518-762-8313; TERRY LEONARD, Dir., Catholic Charities of Herkimer County, 61 West St., Ilion, 13357. Tel: 315-894-9917; KATHIE GREENBLATT, Dir., Catholic Charities of Delaware & Otsego Counties, 176 Main St., Oneonta, 13820. Tel: 607-432-0061; Sisters CHARLA COMMINS, C.S.J., Dir., Catholic Charities of Saratoga, Warren & Washington Counties, 142 Regent St., Saratoga, 12866. Tel: 518-587-5000; MAUREEN JOYCE, R.S.M., Dir., Catholic Charities of Schenectady County. Tel: 518-453-6650; MAUREEN JOYCE, R.S.M., Dir. Roarke Center - Troy, NY. Tel: 518-453-6650; TIMOTHY MULLIGAN, Dir., Catholic Charities of Schoharie County, 489 W. Main St., Cobleskill, 12043. Tel: 518-234-3581; JOSEPH POFIT, Dir., Commission on Aging. Tel: 518-453-6650; Rev. GEORGE BRENNAN, Dir. Commission on Restorative Justice. Tel: 518-453-6650; BARBARA DITOMMASO, Dir., Commission on Peace & Justice. Tel: 518-453-6650; MARTHA POFIT, Dir. Public Policy for the Diocese of Albany. Tel: 518-453-6650; RENEE BENSON, Dir., Catholic Charities Caregivers Support Svcs., 100 Slingerland St., Albany, 12202. Tel: 518-449-2001; Sr. MARY ANN LOGIUDICE, R.S.M., Dir., Community Maternity Svcs., 27 N. Main Ave., Albany, 12203. Tel: 518-482-8836; GARY SIEGEL, Dir., Catholic Charities Disabilities Svcs., 1 Park Place, Ste. 200, Albany, 12205. Tel: 518-783-1111; DEBORAH DAMM O'BRIEN, Dir., Diocesan Housing, Svcs. & Property, 41 N. Main Ave., Albany, 12203. Tel: 518-459-0183; Sr. MAUREEN JOYCE, R.S.M., Dir., Catholic Charities of Rensselaer County. Tel: 518-453-6650; ELAINE ESCOBALES, Dir., Hispanic Outreach Svcs., 40 N. Main Ave., Albany, 12203. Tel: 518-453-6655; ANGELA KELLER, Dir., Catholic Charities AIDS Svcs., 100 Slingerland St., Albany, 12202. Tel: 518-449-3581; JOSEPH POFIT, Dir. Diocesan Community Health Alliance, 40 N. Main Ave., Albany, 12203. Tel: 518-453-6650; MARY PAT HICKEY, Dir. Diocesan Jail Ministry, 40 N. Main Ave., Albany, 12203. Tel: 518-453-6650.

United Tenants of Albany—Co Directors: ROGER MARKOVICS; MARIA MARKOVICS, 33 Clinton Ave., Albany, 12207. Tel: 518-436-8997.

Catholic Campaign for Human Development—MARY OLSEN, Dir., Catholic Campaign for Human Devel., 40 N. Main Ave., Albany, 12203. Tel: 518-453-6650.

Catholic Relief Services—MARY OLSEN, Dir., Catholic Relief Svcs.; DAVID MEYERS, Dir., Immigration Svcs., Catholic Charities of the Diocese of Albany, 40 N. Main Ave., Albany, 12203. Tel: 518-453-6650.

Health and Hospitals Office—Sr. MAUREEN JOYCE, R.S.M., Bishop's Rep. Tel: 518-453-6650.

Catholic Women's Service League—CHRISTINE VANDE LOO, Pres.; Bro. JAMES MARTINO, F.S.C., Moderator; Rev. ROBERT J. HOHENSTEIN, Spiritual Advisor, c/o LaSalle School, 391 Western Ave., Albany, 12203. Tel: 518-242-4731.

Ladies of Charity—LUANN WILSON, Pres., 46 Meadowbrook Dr., Slingerlands, 12159. Tel: 518-438-9104. Email: msluann1022@aol.com.

Spiritual Director—Rev. PATRICK J. BUTLER, St. Edward the Confessor, 569 Clifton Park Rd., Clifton Park, 12065. Tel: 518-371-7372.

Society of St. Vincent de Paul—EDWARD NARE, Diocesan Central Council Pres., 202 S. Ballston Ave., Scotia, 12302. Tel: 518-374-2548; EMMET J. LYNCH, Pres. Emeritus.

St. Luke's Guild of Catholic Physicians—c/o Chancery, 40 N. Main Ave., Albany, 12203. Tel: 518-453-6612. Email: stlukes.guild@rcda.org. Deacon FRANK THOMAS, M.D., Contact.

Consultation Center of the Diocese of Albany— A nonprofit Mental Health Center which provides quality professional psychological counseling services and educational programs in the area of mental health to individuals and groups.

Office—Rev. ANTHONY J. CHIARAMONTE, Ph.D., Dir.; Sr. MARY FRANCES BECK, S.N.J.M., Admin. Dir.; Revs. JOHN J. MALECKI, Ph.D., Psychologist (Retired); THOMAS E. KONOPKA, L.M.S.W., Counselor; KATHLEEN STIFFEN, Sec., 790 Lancaster St., Albany, 12203. Tel: 518-489-4431; Fax: 518-489-5189. Email: consultation.center@rcda.org. Web: consultationcenteralbany.org.

Psychological Counseling— Provides individual therapy, marriage and couples counseling, psychological testing and consultative services to individuals and groups in matters calling for psychological expertise.

Group Therapy— Provides a variety of different kinds of therapy groups.

Educational Programs— Offers lectures and workshops in the area of mental health and personal growth. The Center also offers specialized workshops and training programs to meet the needs of various groups.

Spiritual Direction— Provides a program of individual spiritual direction for any person interested in developing a deeper relationship with God.

Counseling for Laity—Sr. ANNE BRYAN SMOLLIN, C.S.J., Ph.D., Exec. Dir. Tel: 518-453-6625; Fax: 518-453-6793. Email: anne.smollin@rcda.org. Provides individual, family, marital and group psychological counseling-therapy by certified trained therapists. The staff provides services for the Young Married program and assessments for second marriages. Consultation and training programs are offered upon request. Workshops and lectures offered on select topics.

Diocesan Coordinator of Pastoral Care—Ms. HARLEY MCDEVITT, Pastoral Center: 40 N. Main Ave., Albany, 12203-1422. Tel: 518-641-6823. Email: harley.mcdevitt@rcda.org.

Diocesan Pastoral Council—Mr. DAVID AMICO, Admin., Pastoral Center, 40 N. Main Ave., Albany, 12203-1422. Tel: 518-453-6670. Email: david.amico@rcda.org.

Prevention Services - Catholic Schools Office—CATHY GOLAS, Prog. Dir. Tel: 518-453-6771; Fax: 518-453-6667 Services students, faculty and parents of Catholic schools in the diocese.

Ecumenical and Interreligious Affairs of the Roman Catholic Diocese of Albany, Commission for—Mrs. AUDREY HUGHES; Deacons WILLIAM GAFFNEY; RAYMOND SULLIVAN, Assoc. Dir.; JOAN HOLMAN; JOAN LIPSCOMB; KATHLEEN DUFF; Mr. FRANK M. PELL; Deacon MAURICE DROWN, Protestant Min.; Revs. JAMES KANE, Dir.; DAVID MICKIEWICZ; GEORGE BRENNAN; Bro. ROBERT GILROY, C.S.C.; Mr. EDWARD FALTERMAN; Ms. ANNE SNYDER; MARYANN POSTAVA-DAVIGNON, Sec.

"The Evangelist"— Diocesan Newspaper, Albany Catholic Press Assoc., Inc. CHRISTOPHER D. RINGWALD, Editor. Tel: 518-453-6688; Fax: 518-453-8448.

Holy Name Societies—VACANT, Dir.

Initial & Ongoing Formation Cluster—Tel: 518-453-6670. DAVID G. AMICO, Dir. Office of Ministry Formation. Tel: 518-453-6670.

Formation for Priesthood/Vocation Awareness—Sr. ROSEMARY ANN CUNEO, C.R.; Rev. JAMES WALSH. Tel: 518-453-6670.

Legion of Mary, North Hudson Valley Curia—FRANK DALY, Pres. Tel: 518-793-3473.

Office of Evangelization, Catechesis and Family Life—JEANNE SCHREMPF, Diocesan Dir.; STEPHEN MAWN, Assoc. Dir., Catechist Formation & Respect Life; CAROL ROMANINI, Coord. Video & Resource Center/Pre-Cana Registrar; DAVID STAGLIANO, Assoc. Dir., Youth & Young Adult Ministry; JOYCE SOLIMINI, Assoc. Dir., Adult, Family and Intergenerational Catechesis; Rev. ROBERT LONGOBUCCO, Clergy Assoc.; MARY FAY, Assoc. Dir. Marriage Preparation & Enrichment; MARGARET LEATHEM, Consultant: Catechesis of Persons with Developmental Disabilities/Special Needs.

Permanent Deacons Office—Deacons MICHAEL MCDONALD, Administrative Advocate for Deacons & Dir. Office of Diaconate. Tel: 518-453-6678; FRANK C. BERNING, Dir. Diaconate Formation. Tel: 518-453-6670; RAYMOND SULLIVAN, Dir. Ongoing Formation & Continuing Education of Deacons. Tel: 518-453-6678.

Catholic Foundation—Most Rev. HOWARD JAMES HUBBARD, D.D., Pres.; NICOLE PEZZULO, Exec. Dir.

Office of Prayer & Worship—ELIZABETH SIMCOE, Dir. & Chancellor for Pastoral Svcs.; MARYANN POSTAVA-DAVIGNON, Sec., 40 N. Main Ave., Albany, 12203. Tel: 518-453-6645; Fax: 518-453-6793. Email: prayer&worship@rcda.org.

Administrative Advocate for Priests—Rev. RONALD MENTY. Tel: 518-453-6643.

Priests Placement Committee—Revs. RONALD MENTY, Chm. Tel: 518-453-6643; L. EDWARD DEIMEKE; ROBERT J. HOHENSTEIN; DAVID V. BERBERIAN, J.C.L.; JAMES J. WALSH.

Priestly Life and Ministry Council—Tel: 518-453-6643. Revs. DAVID MICKIEWICZ, Chm.; JOSEPH MANEROWSKI; RONALD MENTY, Admin. Advocate; ANTHONY F. LIGATO; STEVEN P. MOORE; CHRISTOPHER DEGIOVINE; G. ANTHONY CHILDS; THOMAS KRUPA.

Ministers to Active Priests and Priests in Special Circumstances—Revs. ARTHUR BECKER; THOMAS BERARDI.

Ministers to Retired Priests—Revs. PAUL COX (Retired); GEORGE G. ST. JOHN (Retired); JOHN D. KIRWIN; RICHARD J. LESKOVAR (Retired).

Ongoing Formation and Continuing Education for Priests—Members: Revs. STEVEN P. MOORE; PAUL BUTLER; MARK CUNNINGHAM, Chm.; Very Rev. THOMAS J. HAYES; Revs. DENNIS MURPHY; RONALD MENTY, Administrative Advocate for Priests - Advisory; JAMES SCHIFFER; ANTHONY J. CHIARAMONTE, Ph.D.

Priests Retirement Board/Priests Retirement Plan Board—Revs. JOHN T. PROVOST, Chm. Tel: 518-674-3818; JOSEPH ANSELMENT (Retired); JOSEPH A. BARKER (Retired); WINSTON L. BATH; J. THOMAS CONNERY (Retired); JOSEPH DWORAK; JAMES LEFEBVRE; RICHARD J. LESKOVAR (Retired); RONALD MENTY, Administrative Advocate for Priests & Ex Officio; ERWIN H. SCHWEIGARDT; Mr RICHARD FARRELL, CFO & Ex Officio.

Administrative Advocate for Deacons—Deacon MICHAEL MCDONALD, Administrative Advocate for Deacons & the Office of Diaconate. Tel: 518-453-6678.

Propagation of the Faith-Pontifical Society—Tel: 518-453-6675. Rev. MICHAEL A. FARANO, Dir.

Schools: Diocesan School Board—

Chair—KATE BURGESS, Esq. Tel: 518-439-4493.

Diocesan School Office—Sr. MARY JANE HERB, I.H.M., Ph.D., Supt. Schools. Tel: 518-453-6602; Mr. JOHN SOJA, Asst. Supt., Admin. Svcs. Tel: 518-453-6666; Ms. TERRI MCGRAW, Asst. Supt. for Instructional Svcs. Tel: 518-453-6666; CATHY GOLAS, Prevention Svcs. Prog. Tel: 518-453-6771; CURTIS A. MCEWAN, Business Mgr. Tel: 518-453-6604; SAL CARBONE, Safety Coord. Tel: 518-853-4001; Sr. DEBORAH TIMMIS, C.S.J., Dir. Educational Technology. Tel: 518-453-6666.

Scouting—Deacon WILLIAM H. GAUL JR., Diocesan Chap., 12 Woodlake Dr., Gansevoort, 12831-1817. Tel: 518-587-4631.

St. Bernard's School of Theology and Ministry—Sr. KATHERINE HANLEY, C.S.J., Dir. & Assoc. Dean. Tel: 518-453-6760; Fax: 518-453-6793. Email: stbernards@rcda.org.

Vicar for Religious—Sr. NOLA BRUNNER, C.S.J. Tel: 518-453-6669.

Women's Commission—c/o Chancery, 40 N. Main Ave., Albany, 12203. Tel: 518-453-6612. Email: lrose@nycap.rr.com. LINDA ROSE, Contact.

Assistance Coordinator—THERESA F. RODRIGUES. Tel: 518-453-6646. Email: assistance.coordinator@rcda.org.

Vocations and Vocation Awareness Program—Sr. ROSEMARY ANN CUNEO, C.R. Tel: 518-674-3818. Email: rosemary.cuneo@rcda.org. Web: www.albanyvocations.org; Rev. JAMES WALSH. Tel: 518-453-6670.

CLERGY, PARISHES, MISSIONS AND PAROCHIAL SCHOOLS

CITY OF ALBANY

(ALBANY COUNTY)

1—CATHEDRAL OF THE IMMACULATE CONCEPTION (1848) Rev. William H. Pape, Rector; Deacon Raymond J. Sullivan. In Res., Most Rev. Howard James Hubbard.
Rectory Office—125 Eagle St., 12202. Tel: 518-463-4447; Fax: 518-436-5177. Email: ecathedr@nycap.com. Web: www.cathedralic.com.
Religious Education Office—Tel: 518-436-7918.
Cathedral Social Services—Tel: 518-463-2279.
Catechesis/Religious Program—(Combined with St. James & St. John/St. Ann) Sr. Maria Mercurio, D.R.E. Students 65.
Convent—93 Park Ave., 12202. Tel: 518-436-7697. Sisters 10.

2—ALL SAINTS CATHOLIC CHURCH Rev. Paul Butler; Deacon Gary O'Connor, D.R.E.
Parish Office: 1168 Western Ave., 12203. Tel: 518-482-4497; Fax: 518-482-4719. Email: stmargm2@csdsl.net.
School—All Saints Catholic Academy, (Grades PreK-8), 10 Rosement St., 12203. Tel: 518-438-0066; Fax: 518-438-0066. Sr. Mary Ellen Owens, Prin. Sisters 1; Lay Teachers 16; Students 291.
Catechesis/Religious Program—(Combined with Holy Cross) Students 189.

3—BLESSED SACRAMENT Revs. John J. Bradley; Thomas Lawless; Pat Pasternak, Pastoral Assoc.; Deacon William Fitzgerald. In Res., Revs. George G. St. John (Retired); Anthony Gully.
Res.: 607 Central Ave., 12206. Tel: 518-482-3375; Fax: 518-482-3376.
School—(Grades PreK-8), 605 Central Ave., 12206. Tel: 518-438-5854; Fax: 518-438-1532. Sr. Patricia Lynch, R.S.M., Prin. Sisters of Mercy 2; Lay Teachers 16; Students 250.
Catechesis/Religious Program—Tel: 516-446-0997. Rosemarie Reed, D.R.E.; Cathy Fredette, D.R.E. Clustered with St. Mary. Students 202.

4—ST. CASIMIR, Consolidated with Our Lady of Angels, Albany & St. Patrick, Albany to form Holy Family Parish, Albany. For inquiries for parish records, please contact Holy Family Parish.

5—ST. CATHERINE OF SIENA, Merged with St. Theresa of Avila, Albany to form Parish of Mater Christi, Albany. Worship Site.

6—CHURCH OF THE HOLY CROSS, Merged with St. Margaret Mary, Albany to form All Saints Catholic Church, Albany.

7—ST. GEORGE, Closed. For inquiries for Sacramental records, please contact St. Joan of Arc/The Black Apostolate, Menands.

8—HOLY FAMILY PARISH (2005) [JC], Clustered with Our Lady of Angels Parish Cemetery, Albany Revs. Anthony Kall, O.F.M.Conv., Admin.; Joseph Angelini, O.F.M.Conv., Sacramental Min.; Alvin Somerville, O.F.M.Conv., Chap., Resurrection Nursing Home, Castleton; Bro. Greg Spuhler, O.F.M.Conv., Parish Social Min.; Deacon Miguel Fabian.
283 Central Ave., 12206. Tel: 518-465-3685; Fax: 518-462-5487.
Catechesis/Religious Program—Janice Galazzo, D.R.E. Students 50.

9—ST. JAMES Revs. Cabell B. Marbury, Sacramental Min. (Retired); Paul Smith, Sacramental Min. (Retired); Leo P. O'Brien, Sacramental Min. (Retired); Deacon Andy Cohen; Dorothy A. Sokol, Parish Life Dir.; Sr. Patricia Houlihan, C.S.J., Pastoral Assoc. Prayer & Worship; Jo-Ann Garrison, Pastoral Assoc. for Admin.
Res.: 391 Delaware Ave., 12209. Tel: 518-434-4028; Fax: 518-434-1097.
Catechesis/Religious Program—Tel: 518-465-2876. Sr. Phyllis Mauger, C.S.J., Dir. Faith Formation. Students 57.

10—ST. JOHN-ST. ANN Sr. Natalie Runfola, R.S.C.J., Parish Life Coord.
Office: 88 Fourth Ave., 12202. Tel: 518-472-9091; Fax: 518-427-5983.
Catechesis/Religious Program—Tel: 518-472-9091, Ext. 18. Ann Marie Carswell, D.R.E. Students 50.

11—ST. JOSEPH, Records are kept at Sacred Heart of Jesus, Albany.
Parish Office—33 Walter St., 12204. Tel: 518-463-3286; Fax: 518-462-0506.

12—ST. MARGARET MARY, Merged with Church of the Holy Cross, Albany to form All Saints Catholic Church, Albany. Worship Site.

13—ST. MARY Rev. James Lefebvre; Deacon George Witko; Rev. Lloyd Rebeyro.
Res.: 10 Lodge St., 12207. Tel: 518-462-4254; Fax: 518-462-4255.
Catechesis/Religious Program— Clustered with Blessed Sacrament.
Chapel— 111 Washington Ave., 12203.

14—OUR LADY HELP OF CHRISTIANS, (German), Closed. For inquiries for parish records please see Cathedral of the Immaculate Conception.

15—OUR LADY OF ANGELS, [CEM], Consolidated with St. Casimir, Albany & St. Patrick, now called Holy Family Parish, Albany. For inquiries for parish records please contact Holy Family Parish Tel: 518-465-3685.

16—PARISH OF MATER CHRISTI Rev. Kenneth Doyle; Deacon Gerald Ladouceur; Sr. Margery Halpin, R.S.M., Pastoral Assoc. In Res., Rev. John Tallman.
40 Hopewell Ave., 12208. Email: sstcathe@nycap.rr.com.
Res.: 40 Collins Pl., 12208. Tel: 518-489-3204; Fax: 518-482-3721.
School—*St. Catherine of Siena School*, (Grades PreK-8), 35 Hurst Ave., 12208. Tel: 518-489-3111; Fax: 518-489-5863. Theresa L. Ewell, Prin. Lay Teachers 20; Students 229.
Catechesis/Religious Program—Bernadette McSparron, D.R.E. Students 406.

17—ST. PATRICK, Consolidated with St Casimir, Albany & Our Lady of Angels now called Holy Family Parish, Albany. For inquiries for parish records please contact Holy Family Parish.

18—SACRED HEART OF JESUS Rev. Kofi Ntsiful Amissah.
31 Walter St., 12204. Tel: 518-434-0680.

19—ST. TERESA OF AVILA, Merged with St. Catherine of Siena, Albany to form Parish of Mater Christi, Albany.

20—ST. VINCENT DE PAUL C. Elizabeth Rowe-Manning, Parish Life Dir.; Deacons Edward R. Solomon; Martin Beckman.
Parish Office: 900 Madison Ave., 12208. Tel: 518-489-5408; Fax: 518-489-5474.
Catechesis/Religious Program—Susan Sweeney, D.R.E. Students 170.

OUTSIDE THE CITY OF ALBANY

ALTAMONT, ALBANY CO., ST. LUCY Sr. Mary Lou Liptak, R.S.M., Parish Life Dir.; Rev. Paul Smith, Sacramental Min. (Retired).
Parish House—P.O. Box 678, 12009. Tel: 518-861-8770; Fax: 518-861-8770. 1757 Helderberg Tr., Berne, 12023. Tel: 518-872-1131. Email: slucys@nycap.rr.com.
Catechesis/Religious Program—Tel: 518-861-5810. Leah Kedik, D.R.E. Students 112.
Mission—St. Bernadette 1763 Helderberg Tr., Berne, Albany Co. 12023. Tel: 518-872-1131.

AMSTERDAM, MONTGOMERY CO.

1—ST. CASIMIR, (Lithuanian), [CEM] Closed. For inquiries for parish records, contact St. Mary's, Amsterdam.

2—ST. JOHN THE BAPTIST, (Polish), [CEM] Closed. For inquiries for parish records, contact St. Stanislaus, Amsterdam

3—ST. JOSEPH, See separate listing. Canonically merged in 1980 into St. Joseph-St. Michael-Our Lady of Mount Carmel. All inquiries should be directed to the listed address, 39 St. John St. & 58 Grove St., Amsterdam, NY 12010.

4—ST. JOSEPH-ST. MICHAEL-OUR LADY OF MOUNT CARMEL, [CEM 3], Canonically merged parishes in 1980. Rev. Lawrence J. Decker.
Mailing Address: 39 John St., P.O. Box 699, 12010.
Office: 39 St. John St. & 58 Grove St., 12010. Tel: 518-843-3250; Fax: 518-843-4070. Email: mt.carmel699@verizon.net.
Res.: 39 St. John St., 12010.
Catechesis/Religious Program— Mary A. Califano, D.R.E.; Cynthia Kuzia, D.R.E. Students 83.

5—ST. MARY, [CEM] Rev. John M. Medwid.
Res.: 156 E. Main St., 12010. Tel: 518-842-4500; Fax: 518-843-1068.
School—*St. Mary Institute*, (Grades PreK-8), Upper Church St., 12010. Tel: 518-842-4100; Fax: 518-842-0217. Giovanni Virgilio, Prin. Sisters 2; Lay Teachers 32; Students 200.
Catechesis/Religious Program—Sr. Agnes Clare, S.A., D.R.E. Students 736.

6—ST. MICHAEL THE ARCHANGEL, See separate listing. Canonically merged in 1980 into St. Joseph-St. Michael-Our Lady of Mount Carmel. All inquiries should be directed to the listed address, 39 St. John St. & 58 Grove St., Amsterdam, NY 12010.

7—OUR LADY OF MT. CARMEL, (Italian), See separate listing. Canonically merged in 1980 into St. Joseph-St. Michael-Our Lady of Mount Carmel. All inquiries should be directed to the listed address, 39 St. John St. & 58 Grove St., Amsterdam, NY 12010.

8—ST. STANISLAUS, (Polish), [CEM] Rev. David Mickiewicz.
Res.: 73 Reid St., 12010. Tel: 518-842-2771; Fax: 518-842-2771.
Convent—46 Cornell St., 12010. Tel: 518-842-2621.

ATHENS, GREENE CO, ST. PATRICK Rev. Richard D. Shaw, Sacramental Min.; Sr. Mary L. Mazza, C.N.D., Parish Life Dir.
Res.: 19 N. Franklin St., 12015. Tel: 518-945-1656; Fax: 518-947-6362. Email: patrickofathens@aol.com. Web: www.stpatrickofathens.org.
Catechesis/Religious Program—Email: stpatsff@yahoo.com. Mrs. Theresa E. St. Germain, D.R.E. Tel: 518-947-9444. Students 113.

AVERILL PARK, RENSSELAER CO., ST. HENRY (1868) [CEM 2] Rev. John T. Provost; Deacons Frank S. Lukovits; John W. Novak; Robert Pasquarelli.
Res.: Crystal Lake Rd., P.O. Box 550, 12018. Tel: 518-674-3818; Fax: 518-674-1043.
Catechesis/Religious Program—Mary Lee Kopache, Coord. Faith Formation (High School); Marie Frost, Coord. Faith Formation (Elem. School). Students 448.

BALLSTON LAKE, SARATOGA CO., OUR LADY OF GRACE (1922) Deacon Neil Hook, Parish Life Dir. In Res., Rev. John N. Varno, Sacramental Min.
Res.: 73 Midline Rd., 12019. Tel: 518-399-5713; Fax: 518-399-5761. Web: www.ourladyofgracechurchny.com.
Catechesis/Religious Program—Tel: 518-384-0109. Mary Salm, D.R.E. Students 646.

BALLSTON SPA, SARATOGA CO., ST. MARY, [CEM] Revs. Thomas J. Kelly; James A. Ebert; Deacon Ronald Hogan.
Res.: 167 Milton Ave., 12020. Tel: 518-885-7411; Fax: 518-885-6863.
School—(Grades PreK-5), 40 Thompson St., 12020. Tel: 518-885-7300; Fax: 518-855-7378. Michelle Lezon, Prin. Sisters 2; Lay Teachers 23; Students 237.
Catechesis/Religious Program—Jake Stomieroski, D.R.E. Students 806.

BERLIN, RENSSELAER CO., SACRED HEART, Merged with St. John Francis Regis, Grafton to form Parish of Our Lady of the Snow, Grafton.

BOLTON LANDING, WARREN CO., BLESSED SACRAMENT, [CEM] Kathleen L. Sousa, Parish Life Dir.; Rev. Thomas F. Berardi, Sacramental Min.
Res.: 12 Goodman Ave., P.O. Box 266, 12814.
Church: Goodman Ave., P.O. Box 266, 12814. Tel: 518-644-3861.

BROADALBIN, FULTON CO., ST. JOSEPH Rev. Thomas Morrette, Admin.
Res.: 7 North St., P.O. Box 538, 12025. Tel: 518-883-3774; Fax: 518-883-6381. Email: stjosephschurch@yahoo.com.
Catechesis/Religious Program—Patricia Cardone, D.R.E. Students 131.

CAIRO, GREENE CO., SACRED HEART Rev. Jeremiah Nunan.
Mailing Address: P.O. Box 778, 12413.
Res.: 35 Church St., 12413. Tel: 518-622-3319; Fax: 518-622-0131.
Catechesis/Religious Program—Mrs. Camille Thiesen, D.R.E. Students 153.
Shrine—Our Lady of Knock Shrine P.O. Box 223, East Durham, Greene Co. 12423. Tel: 518-634-7448. Email: sacredheartofficecairony@verizon.net.
Mission—St. Mary 2052 Rte. 145, East Durham, Greene Co. 12423.

CAMBRIDGE, WASHINGTON CO., ST. PATRICK, [CEM] Rev. Liam Condon, Sacramental Min.; Michele Ruland, Parish Life Assoc.
Res.: 17 S. Park St., 12816-1248. Tel: 518-677-2757; Fax: 518-677-2810. Email: stpatrick18@verizon.net.
Catechesis/Religious Program—Students 85.

CANAJOHARIE, MONTGOMERY CO., ST. PETER'S AND PAUL'S, [CEM] Merged with St. James, Fort Plain & St. Patrick, St. Johnsville to form Parish of Our Lady of Hope, Fort Plain. Worship Site.

CASTLETON ON HUDSON, RENSSELAER CO., SACRED HEART, [CEM 2] Rev. Thomas Krupa.
Res.: 3 Catholic Way, 12033-1543. Tel: 518-732-2155; Fax: 518-732-4906.
Catechesis/Religious Program—Tel: 518-732-1106; Fax: 518-732-4960. Jane Forget, D.R.E. Students 387.

CATSKILL, GREENE CO., ST. PATRICK Sr. Mary L. Mazza, C.N.D., Parish Life Dir.; Rev. Richard D. Shaw, Sacramental Min.; Mrs. Theresa E. St. Germain, Pastoral Assoc. for Faith Formation.
Res.: 157 Bridge St., 12414. Tel: 518-943-3150; Fax: 518-943-5257. Email: patrickcatskill@gmail.com. Web: home.catholicweb.com/stpatrickchurch.
School—(Grades PreK-8), 80 Woodland Ave., 12414. (School closed June 6, 2007.)
Catechesis/Religious Program—Students 94.

CHATHAM, COLUMBIA CO., ST. JAMES Rev. Gary Paul Gelfenbien; Deacon Peter Trawinski.
Res.: 129 Hudson Ave., 12037. Tel: 518-392-4991; Fax: 518-392-9205.
Catechesis/Religious Program—C. Cain, D.R.E. Students 244.

CHERRY VALLEY, OTSEGO CO., ST. THOMAS THE APOSTLE Mrs. Karen J. Walker, Parish Life Assoc.; Rev. John Roos, Sacramental Min. (Retired).
Mailing Address: P.O. Box 246, 13320.
Res.: 24 Maple Ave., 13320. Tel: 607-264-3779. Email: stthomas@pronetisp.net. Web: turnpikecatholics.com.
Catechesis/Religious Program—Mrs. Karen J. Walker, Faith Formation Coord. Students 43.

CHESTERTOWN, WARREN CO.
1—ST. JOHN THE BAPTIST, Merged with Blessed Sacrament, Hague to form Parish of St. Isaac Jogues, Chestertown. Worship Site.
2—PARISH OF ST. ISAAC JOGUES Rev. John O'Kane; Sr. Francesca Husselbeck, R.S.M., Parish Life Dir.
Res.: 86 Riverside Dr., P.O. Box 471, 12817. Tel: 518-494-5229. Email: northernpointscluster@frontiernet.net. Web: northernpointscluster.org.
Catechesis/Religious Program—Barbara Carlozzi, D.R.E. Students 64.

CLAVERACK, COLUMBIA CO., ST. JOHN VIANNEY, Merged with St. Bridget, Copake Falls to form Parish of Our Lady of Hope, Copake Falls. Worship Site.

CLIFTON PARK, SARATOGA CO., ST. EDWARD THE CONFESSOR Rev. Patrick J. Butler; Deacons Jerry Grigaitis; Walter MacKinnon; Charles Taylor; Eugene Kelenski.
Office: Tel: 518-371-7372; Fax: 518-371-1206. Email: stedwards@stedwardsny.org. Web: stedwardsny.org.
Church: 569 Clifton Park Center Rd., 12065-4838.
Catechesis/Religious Program— Richard Amico, D.R.E. Students 1,530.

CLINTON HEIGHTS, RENSSELAER CO., ST. MARY Rev. David R. LeFort.
Res.: 163 Columbia Tpke., East Greenbush, 12144-3521. Tel: 518-449-2232; Fax: 518-449-2234.
School— Closed. For further information, contact St. Mary's Parish.
Catechesis/Religious Program—Austin J. Byrnes, D.R.E. Students 227.

COBLESKILL, SCHOHARIE CO., ST. VINCENT DE PAUL, [CEM] Rev. Thomas Holmes, Sacramental Min.; Deacon Gary Surman; Sisters Connie James, S.N.D., Parish Life Dir.; Helen Farrell, S.N.D., Pastoral Assoc.
Res.: 138 Washington Ave., 12043. Tel: 518-234-2892; Fax: 518-234-3699. Email: vincentdepaul@verizon.net.
Catechesis/Religious Program—Students 143.

COHOES, ALBANY CO.
1—ST. AGNES-ST. PATRICK, Merged with St. Marie, Cohoes to form Holy Trinity, Cohoes.
2—ST. BERNARD, Closed. For inquiries for parish records, contact St. Michael, Cohoes.
3—HOLY TRINITY, [CEM] Rev. Arthur Becker; Deacons Albert Schrempf; Gerard Matthews; Denise Miller, Youth Min.
Res.: 122 Vliet Blvd., 12047-1842. Tel: 518-237-2373; Fax: 518-238-9427. Email: holytrinity@nycap.rr.com. Web: www.holytrinity.cohoesonline.com.
See Cohoes Catholic School, Cohoes under Consolidated Elementary Schools located in the Institution section.
Catechesis/Religious Program—Email: htpfaithformation@nycap.rr.com. Karen T. Beattie, C.R.E. Students 203.
4—ST. JOSEPH, (French), [CEM] Closed. For inquiries for parish records, contact St. Michael, Cohoes.
5—ST. MARIE, Merged with St. Agnes-St. Patrick, Cohoes to form Holy Trinity, Cohoes.
6—ST. MICHAEL, [CEM] Rev. Peter Tkocz.
Res.: 36 Page Ave., 12047. Tel: 518-237-5151.
Office: 20 Page Ave., 12047. Fax: 518-237-5151 (Call First). Email: parishinfo@stmichaelsofcohoes.org; stmichaelscohoes@hotmail.com. Web: www.stmichaelsofcohoes.org.
Catechesis/Religious Program—Karen T. Beattie, D.R.E. Students 54.
7—ST. RITA-SACRED HEART, Closed. For inquiries for parish records, contact Holy Trinity, Cohoes.

COLONIE, ALBANY CO.
1—ST. CLARE Rev. Thomas E. Konopka, Sacramental Min.; Nancy A. Volks, Parish Life Dir.; Deacons George Nahm; Gary Riggi. In Res., Very Rev. Ronald A. Menty.
Res.: 1947 Central Ave., 12205-4299. Tel: 518-456-3112; Fax: 518-456-1072. Email: rstclare@nycaprr.com. Web: www.stclares.nycap.rr.com.
Catechesis/Religious Program—Tel: 518-456-3113. Email: stclarefaithformsec@nycap.rr.com. Patti Voerg, Coord. Faith Formation & Youth Ministry. Students 440.
2—OUR LADY OF MERCY, Merged with St. Francis de Sales, Loudonville to form Christ Our Light Roman Catholic Church, Loudonville.

COOPERSTOWN, OTSEGO CO., ST. MARY, [CEM 2] Rev. John P. Rosson.
Res.: 31 Elm St., 13326. Tel: 607-547-2213; Fax: 607-547-5742.

COPAKE FALLS, COLUMBIA CO.
1—ST. BRIDGET, [CEM] Merged with St. John Vianney, Claverack to form Parish of Our Lady of Hope, Copake Falls. Worship Site.
2—PARISH OF OUR LADY OF HOPE Rev. Joseph Falletta; Mary Burntitius, Pastoral Assoc. for Faith Formation; Steven M. Gubler, Pastoral Assoc. for Admin & Liturgy.
Res.: 8074 State Rte. 22, 12517. Tel: 518-329-4711; Fax: 518-329-4240. Email: stbridgets@yahoo.com. Web: www.stbridgets.net.
Catechesis/Religious Program—Students 55.

CORINTH, COLUMBIA CO.
1—HOLY MOTHER AND CHILD PARISH Rev. Charles A. Gaffigan.
Office: 45 Palmer Ave., 12822. Tel: 518-654-2113; 518-654-9119; Fax: 518-654-9119. Email: angel409@frontiernet.net.
Res.: 323 Lake Ave., P.O. Box 470, Lake Luzerne, 12846. Tel: 518-696-2625; Fax: 518-696-2625. Email: hiicl@localnet.com.
Catechesis/Religious Program—Margaret Watkins, D.R.E.; Pat Melillo, D.R.E. Students 160.
2—IMMACULATE CONCEPTION, [CEM] Merged with Holy Infancy, Lake Luzerne to form Holy Mother and Child Parish, Corinth. Worship Site.

COXSACKIE, GREENE CO., ST. MARY, [CEM] Rev. John L. Moyna; Deacon Michael McDonald.
Res.: 80 Mansion St., 12051. Tel: 518-731-8800; Fax: 518-731-8505.
Catechesis/Religious Program— Mr. Robert DesRosiers, D.R.E. Students 215.

CRESCENT, SARATOGA CO., ST. MARY'S CHURCH Very Rev. Thomas J. Hayes.
Parish Center—86 Church Hill Rd., Waterford, 12188. Tel: 518-371-9632; Fax: 518-371-7235. Email: gutiguy@nycap.rr.com. Web: rcda.org/churches/StMarysCrescent.
Catechesis/Religious Program—Tel: 518-371-9521. Email: smcff@nycap.rr.com. Mary Anne Cureau, C.R.E. Students 402.

DELANSON, SCHENECTADY CO., OUR LADY OF FATIMA Lynn O'Rourke, Parish Life Dir.; Rev. Paul Engel, Sacramental Min. (Retired); Angela Caraher, Pastoral Assoc.
Res.: 1735 Alexander Rd., P.O. Box 219, 12053-0219. Tel: 518-895-2788; Fax: 518-895-2788. Email: 13flamingos@nycap.rr.com. Web: rcda.org/churches/ourladyoffatima.
Catechesis/Religious Program—Students 75.

DELHI, DELAWARE CO., ST. PETER Rev. Matthew H. Frisoni.
Res.: 8 Franklin St., 13753. Tel: 607-746-2503.
Catechesis/Religious Program—Sharon Gruver, Faith Formation Moderator. Students 49.

DELMAR, ALBANY CO., ST. THOMAS THE APOSTLE Revs. David V. Berberian; James D. Daley, Pastor Emeritus (Retired); Richard J. Leskovar (Retired) (Weekend Assistant); Deacon Alfred Manzella.
Res.: 35 Adams Pl., 12054. Tel: 518-439-4951; Fax: 518-439-0108. Email: office@stthomaschurch-delmar.org. Web: www.stthomaschurch-delmar.org.
School—(Grades PreK-8), 42 Adams Pl., 12054. Tel: 518-439-5573; Fax: 518-478-9773. Web: www.stthomas-school.org. Mr. Thomas Kane, Prin. Lay Teachers 25; Students 206.
Catechesis/Religious Program—Tel: 518-439-3945. Students 1,075.

DOLGEVILLE, HERKIMER CO., ST. JOSEPH, [CEM 2] Rev. William A. Gorman; Deacon Peter Manno, Pastoral Asst.
Res.: 31 N. Helmer Ave., 13329. Tel: 315-429-8338. Email: stjoe@capital.net.
Catechesis/Religious Program—Students 36.

EAST GREENBUSH, RENSSELAER CO., HOLY SPIRIT Rev. Joseph O'Brien; Deacon William Dringus.
Res.: 667 Columbia Tpke., 12061. Tel: 518-477-7925; Fax: 518-477-7926. Email: holyspiriteg@nycap.rr.com. Web: www.rcda.org/churches/holyspiritchurch.
School—(Grades PreK-8), 54 Highland Dr., 12061. Tel: 518-477-5739; Fax: 518-477-5743. Email: albhss@rcdaschools.org. Web: rcdaschools.org/holyspirit/. Roger Rooney, Prin. Lay Teachers 23; Students 242.
Catechesis/Religious Program—Tel: 518-477-8108. Tracy Penk-Masucci, Coord. Youth Ministry; Maria Collins, Coord. Faith Formation. Students 242.

EDMESTON , OSWEGO CO., NATVITY OF B.V.M., Closed. For inquiries for parish records, contact Holy Cross, Morris.

FONDA, MONTGOMERY CO., ST. CECILIA, [CEM] Rev. Patrick Gallagher, O.F.M.Conv.
Mailing Address: P.O. Box 837, 12068.
Res.: 26 Broadway, 12068. Tel: 518-853-4195.
Catechesis/Religious Program—Lenora Fiorenza, D.R.E. Students 82.

FORT ANN, WASHINGTON CO., ST. ANN Rev. Michael Flannery.
Res.: 85 George St., P.O. Box 226, 12827. Tel: 518-639-5218; Fax: 518-639-4073. Email: frpastor@nycap.rr.com.
Catechesis/Religious Program—(Combined with Our Lady of Hope, Whitehall) Students 67.

FORT EDWARD, WASHINGTON CO., ST. JOSEPH, [CEM] Revs. Thomas Babiuch; Harold Wessell, Assoc. for Faith Formation.
Res.: 166 Broadway, 12828. Tel: 518-747-5117; Fax: 518-747-3444.
Catechesis/Religious Program—Tel: 518-747-5117, Ext. 816. Students 119.

FORT PLAIN, MONTGOMERY CO.
1—ST. JAMES, Merged with St. Peter's and Paul's, Canajoharie & St. Patrick, St. Johnsville to form Parish of Our Lady of Hope, Fort Plain. Worship Site.
2—PARISH OF OUR LADY OF HOPE Rev. James E. Clark; Deacon Joseph Cechnicki.
Office: 115 Reid St., P.O. Box 287, 13339-0287. Tel: 518-993-3822. Email: ourladyofhope@frontier.com.
Catechesis/Religious Program—Debra DiVisconti, D.R.E. Students 99.

FRANKFORT, HERKIMER CO.
1—ST. MARY, Merged with SS. Peter & Paul, Frankfort, to form Our Lady Queen of Apostles, Frankfort, Jan. 8, 1995.
2—OUR LADY QUEEN OF APOSTLES (1995) [CEM] Rev. Anthony M. Barratt.
Res.: 414 Frankfort St., 13340. Tel: 315-894-2025; 315-894-2360; Fax: 315-894-2025.
Catechesis/Religious Program—Phyllis Luczka, D.R.E. Students 262.
3—SS. PETER & PAUL, Merged with St. Mary, Frankfort, to form Our Lady Queen of Apostles, Frankfort, Jan. 8, 1995.

GERMANTOWN, COLUMBIA CO., RESURRECTION, [CEM] Merged with Church of St. Mary, Hudson to form Parish of the Holy Trinity, Hudson. Worship Site.

GLENS FALLS, WARREN CO.
1—ST. ALPHONSUS, [CEM] Rev. Thomas Babiuch,

Admin.; Deacon William F. Bazinet.
Res.: 4 Crandall St., 12801. Tel: 518-792-1574. Email: ustalphonsusch@nycap.rr.com.
Merged with St. Mary's Academy to form St. Mary's/St. Alphonsus Regional School under St. Mary's, Glens Falls.
2—ST. MARY Rev. Joseph Manerowski; Deacons F. David Powers. Tel: 518-792-0989, Ext. 35; Joseph Tyrrell. Tel: 518-792-0989, Ext. 35.
Res.: 62 Warren St., 12801-4530. Tel: 518-792-0989; Fax: 518-792-0251. Email: dwoodward@nycap.rr.com; rmattes@nycap.rr.com. Web: www.stmaryglensfalls.parishesonline.com.
School—St. Mary's / St. Alphonsus Regional School, (Grades PreK-8), 10-12 Church St., 12801. Tel: 518-792-3178; Fax: 518-792-6056. Mrs. Kathryn Mahoney Fowler, Prin.
Catechesis / Religious Program—Tel: 518-792-0989, Ext. 15. Jo Kaczmarek, Pastoral Assoc. for Faith Formation. Tel: 518-792-0798; Fax: 518-792-0798; Maria Polidore, Pastoral Assoc. Youth Min. Email: molidire@nycap.rr.com. Students 350.

GLENVILLE, SCHENECTADY CO., IMMACULATE CONCEPTION Rev. Jerome R. Gingras; Deacon Michael Melanson. In Res., Rev. Thomas Connery.
Res.: 400 Saratoga Rd., 12302. Tel: 518-399-9168; Fax: 518-384-3278. Email: icchurch@nycap.rr.com. Web: www.ic-glenville.com.
Catechesis / Religious Program—Tel: 518-399-9210. Email: ic400saratoga@yahoo.com. Christine Goss, Pastoral Assoc. for Youth Ministries; Madeline Fretto, Pastoral Assoc. Faith Formation. Students 780.

GLOVERSVILLE, FULTON CO.
1—CHURCH OF THE HOLY SPIRIT Rev. Donald Czelusniak.
Res.: 149 S. Main St., 12078. Tel: 518-725-3143; Fax: 518-725-7245. Email: smmcrectory@nycap.rr.com.
Catechesis / Religious Program—Tel: 518-725-1213. Karen Hoose, D.R.E. Students 140.
2—ST. MARY, See separate listing. Canonically merged with Our Lady of Mount Carmel in 1990. See St. Mary of Mount Carmel.
3—ST. MARY OF MT. CARMEL, [CEM], Consolidated from Our Lady of Mount Carmel and St. Mary in 1990.; Merged with Sacred Heart, Gloversville to form Church of the Holy Spirit, Gloversville.; Worship Site.
4—SACRED HEART, Merged with St. Mary of Mt. Carmel, Gloversville to form Church of the Holy Spirit, Gloversville.

GRAFTON, RENSSELAER CO.
1—ST. JOHN FRANCIS REGIS, Merged with Sacred Heart, Berlin to form Parish of Our Lady of the Snow, Grafton. Worship Site.
2—PARISH OF OUR LADY OF THE SNOW Jeffrey C. Peck, Parish Life Dir. Fax: 518-279-3055; Rev. Kenneth Gregory, Sacramental Min.; Vici Armsby, Pastoral Assoc. Faith Formation.
13 Owen Rd., P.O. Box 234, 12082. Tel: 518-279-4943. Email: ourladyofthesnow@verizon.com.
Catechesis / Religious Program—Students 40.

GRAND GORGE, DELAWARE CO., ST. PHILIP NERI, Merged with Sacred Heart, Stamford to form Sacred Heart/St. Philip Neri, Stockton

GRANVILLE, WASHINGTON CO.
1—ST. MARY, Closed. For inquiries for parish records contact the chancery.
2—ST. MARY'S ROMAN CATHOLIC CHURCH ROMAN CATHOLIC COMMUNITY OF GRANVILLE, Consolidated St. Mary's, All Saints, and Our Lady of Mount Carmel. Rev. Thomas Zelker.
Res.: 23 Bulkley Ave., 12832. Tel: 518-642-1262.
Parish Center—All Saints House, Morrison Ave., 12832.
Catechesis / Religious Program—Mary King, D.R.E. Students 207.

GREEN ISLAND, ALBANY CO., ST. JOSEPH, Merged with St. Brigid's, Immaculate Conception, Our Lady of Mt. Carmel, St. Patrick's & Sacred Heart of Mary, Watervliet to form Immaculate Heart of Mary, Watervliet. Church not closed.

GREENFIELD CENTER, SARATOGA CO., ST. JOSEPH Deacon Gary Pilcher, Parish Life Dir.
Res.: 3159 Rte. 9N, 12833-0568. Tel: 518-893-7680; Fax: 518-893-0472.
Mission—St. Paul 771 Rte. 29, P.O. Box 136, Rock City Falls, Saratoga Co. 12863. Tel: 518-885-4877.

GREENVILLE, GREENE CO., ST. JOHN THE BAPTIST Rev. James Schiffer, C.P.; Deacon Peter Sedlmeir; Connie Parente, Pastoral Assoc.
Office: 4987 Rte. 81, P.O. Box 340, 12083. Tel: 518-966-8317; Fax: 518-966-4652.
Catechesis / Religious Program—Students 173.

GREENWICH, WASHINGTON CO., ST. JOSEPH Rev. Martin J. Fisher; Deacon Herbert Howley.
Res.: 36 Bleecker St., 12834. Tel: 518-692-2159; Fax: 518-692-8706.

GUILDERLAND, ALBANY CO.
1—CHRIST THE KING Revs. James Fitzmaurice, Admin.; Paul G. Catena; Deacon Joseph Markham.
Res.: 20 Sumpter Ave., 12203. Tel: 518-456-1644; Fax: 518-456-4070. Email: CTKathy@nycap.rr.com. Web: CTKparishny.org.
School—(Grades PreK-8) Tel: 518-456-5400; Fax: 518-456-5506. Web: www.christthekingschoolalb.org. Judith Smith, Prin. Lay Teachers 18; Students 156.
Catechesis / Religious Program—Nancy Paino, D.R.E. Students 439.
2—ST. MADELEINE SOPHIE Revs. James Belogi; Robert Powhida; Deacons Earle Flatt; Mark Leonard.
Res.: 3500 Carman Rd., Schenectady, 12303. Tel: 518-355-0421; Fax: 518-355-0412. Email: pstmadel@nycap.rr.com. Web: www.smsparish.org.
School—(Grades PreK-5), 3510 Carman Rd., Schenectady, 12303. Tel: 518-355-3080; Fax: 518-355-3106. Email: stmadeleinesophie@yahoo.com. Miss Teresa Kovarovic, Prin. Lay Teachers 17; Students 155.
Catechesis / Religious Program—Sisters Marilyn Hickey, R.S.M., D.R.E.; Sheila Christensen, R.S.M., D.R.E. Students 1,100.
Convent—3514 Carman Rd., Schenectady, 12303. Tel: 518-355-8052.

HAGAMAN, MONTGOMERY CO., ST. STEPHEN, [CEM] Rev. Martin DeRose.
Res.: 46 Pawling St., P.O. Box 81, 12086. Tel: 518-843-2951.
Mission—St. Mary's Galway, Saratoga Co.
Catechesis / Religious Program—Therese DeBiere Craig, D.R.E.; Patti Canterbury, D.R.E. Students 204.

HAGUE, WARREN CO., BLESSED SACRAMENT, Merged with St. John the Baptist, Chestertown to form Parish of St. Isaac Jogues, Chestertown. Worship Site-Summer only.

HAINES FALLS, GREENE CO.
1—IMMACULATE CONCEPTION, [CEM] Merged with Sacred Heart, Palenville to form Immaculate Conception, Haines Falls. Worship Site.
2—SACRED HEART-IMMACULATE CONCEPTION CHURCH Rev. Anthony Motta.
67 N. Lake Rd., P.O. Box 379, 12436. Tel: 518-589-5577.
Res.: Mountain House Rd., 12436.
Mission—St. Mary's Church Rte. 23A, Hunter, 12442.
Shrine—Wayside Shrine, Greene Co.

HANCOCK, DELAWARE CO., ST. PAUL THE APOSTLE, [CEM 2] Rev. Christopher J. Welch.
Res.: 330 W. Main St., 13783. Tel: 607-637-2571; Fax: 607-637-3203. Email: stpauls@hancock.net. Web: www.stpaulshancock.org.
Catechesis / Religious Program—Patricia Brown, D.R.E. Students 58.

HERKIMER, HERKIMER CO.
1—ST. ANTHONY-ST. JOSEPH, Unassigned.
Res.: 228 S. Main St., 13350. Tel: 315-866-2892; 315-866-6373 (Parish Office); Fax: 315-867-6186.
Catechesis / Religious Program—Carole Powers, D.R.E., (Grades K-6). Tel: 315-866-6821.
2—ST. FRANCIS DE SALES, [CEM] Rev. Mark Cunningham; Deacon William Henkel.
Parish Center—219 N. Bellinger St., 13350. Tel: 315-866-4282; Fax: 315-866-9043.
Res.: 25 Park Pl. S., 13350. Tel: 315-866-7103.
School—(Grades PreK-6), 220 Henry St., 13350. Tel: 315-866-4831. Sr. Rosalie Kelly, C.S.J., Prin. Sisters of St. Joseph of Carondolet 3; Lay Teachers 8; Students 150.
Catechesis / Religious Program—Students 265.
Convent—One Park Pl., 13350. Tel: 315-866-4492.

HOOSICK FALLS, RENSSELAER CO., IMMACULATE CONCEPTION, [CEM] Rev. Vincent Ciotoli.
Res.: 67 Main St., Box 269, 12090. Tel: 518-686-5064; Fax: 518-686-1625. Email: immconcept@roadrunner.com. Web: hoosick-falls-catholicchurch.org.
School—St. Mary Academy, (Grades PreK-8), 4 Parsons Ave., 12090. Tel: 518-686-4314; Fax: 518-686-5957. Email: rebeccamartin15@gmail.com. Web: stmaryshf.com. Mrs. Rebecca Martin, Prin. Lay Teachers 13; Students 157.

HUDSON FALLS, WASHINGTON CO.
1—CHURCH OF ST. MARY'S/ST. PAUL'S (Sandy Hill) [CEM 2], The Roman Catholic Community of Hudson Falls/Kingsbury. Rev. Joseph Dworak; Mrs. Doroth Michon, Pastoral Assoc. for Admin.
Res.: 11 Wall St., 12839. Tel: 518-747-4823; Fax: 518-747-2265.
Catechesis / Religious Program—Peter Durway, D.R.E. Students 270.
2—IMMACULATE HEART OF MARY (Sandy Hill), (French), See separate listing. Canonically merged with St. Paul, Hudson Falls. Now called Church of St. Mary's/St. Paul's, Roman Catholic Community of Hudson Falls/Kingsbury.
3—ST. PAUL (Sandy Hill), (French), See separate listing. Canonically merged with Immaculate Heart of Mary parish, Hudson Falls. Now called Church of St. Mary's/St. Paul's, Roman Catholic Community of Hudson Falls/Kingsbury.

HUDSON, COLUMBIA CO.
1—CHURCH OF ST. MARY, Canonically merged with Our Lady of Mount Carmel and Our Lady of Perpetual Help-Sacred Heart in 1991. ; Merged with Resurrection, Germantown to form Parish of the Holy Trinity, Hudson.; Worship Site.
2—OUR LADY OF MT. CARMEL, See separate listing. Canonically merged with Church of St. Mary in 1991. All inquiries should be directed to P.O. Box 323, Hudson, NY 12534. Tel: 518-828-1334.
3—OUR LADY OF PERPETUAL HELP-SACRED HEART, (Polish), See separate listing. Canonically merged with Church of St. Mary in 1991. All inquiries should be directed to P.O. Box 323, Hudson, NY 12534. Tel: 518-828-1334.
4—PARISH OF THE HOLY TRINITY Rev. Winston L. Bath; Deacon Charles O'Neill. In Res., Rev. Edward F. Cantwell (Retired).
Res.: 429 E. Allen St., 12534. Tel: 518-828-1334. Email: stmaryhudson@mhcable.com.
Catechesis / Religious Program—Students 141.
Mission—Nativity Linlithgo, Columbia Co.

ILION, HERKIMER CO., ANNUNCIATION, [CEM] Rev. Anthony M. Barratt; Deacon James Bower.
Res.: 109 West St., 13357. Tel: 315-894-3766; Fax: 315-894-1550. Web: www.annunciationilion.org.
Catechesis / Religious Program—Students 201.

JOHNSONVILLE, RENSSELAER CO., ST. MONICA'S CHURCH, Merged with St. John the Baptist, Schaghticoke to form Church of the Holy Trinity, Schaghticoke.

JOHNSTOWN, FULTON CO.
1—ST. ANTHONY, (Slovak), [CEM] Consolidated with Immaculate Conception, Johnstown and St. Patrick, Johnstown to form Holy Trinity, Johnstown.
2—HOLY TRINITY PARISH Rev. Kenneth J. Swain. Email: kswain001@nycap.rr.com.
Mailing Address: P.O. Box 930, 12095. Tel: 518-762-2636; 518-762-2011; Fax: 518-762-6920. Email: rcchurch@holytrinityjohnstown.com. Web: www.holytrinityjohnstown.com.
Catechesis / Religious Program—Cynthia Kollar, D.R.E. Students 247.
3—IMMACULATE CONCEPTION, (Italian), [CEM 3] Consolidated with St. Anthony, Johnstown and St. Patrick, Johnstown to form Holy Trinity, Johnstown.
4—ST. PATRICK, [CEM] Consolidated with Immaculate Conception, Johnstown and St Anthony, Johnstown to form Holy Trinity Parish, Johnstown.

LAKE GEORGE, WARREN CO., SACRED HEART Rev. Thomas F. Berardi, Temporary Admin.
Res.: 50 Mohican St., 12845. Tel: 518-668-2046; Fax: 518-668-4377. Web: www.sacredheartcatholiccommunity.com.
Catechesis / Religious Program—Irene Filippelli, D.R.E.; Torie Wattendorf, D.R.E. Students 270.
Mission—Our Lady of the Assumption Ridge Rd., Queensbury, Warren Co. 12804. Tel: 518-668-2046.

LAKE LUZERNE, WARREN CO., HOLY INFANCY, [JC] Merged with Immaculate Conception, Corinth to form Holy Mother and Child Parish, Corinth. Worship Site.

LATHAM, ALBANY CO.
1—ST. AMBROSE Rev. Francis J. DuBois; Deacon Helmut Neurohr.
Res.: 347 Old Loudon Rd., 12110. Tel: 518-785-1351; Fax: 518-785-1951. Email: office@churchofstambrose.org. Web: www.churchofstambrose.org.
School—(Grades PreK-8) Tel: 518-785-6453; Fax: 518-785-8370. James Leveskas, Prin. Email: albstamb@rcdaschools.org. Sisters 2; Lay Teachers 21; Students 172.
Catechesis / Religious Program—Mary Kay Frederick, D.R.E.; Mark Trudeau, Life Teen Youth Min. Students 679.
2—OUR LADY OF THE ASSUMPTION Rev. Geoffrey D. Burke.
Res.: 498 Watervliet-Shaker Rd., 12110. Tel: 518-785-0234; Fax: 518-785-0420. Web: www.rcda.org/churches/ourladyoftheassumption.
Catechesis / Religious Program—Tel: 518-785-1605. Linda Berkery, D.R.E.; Rosemary Gavin, Youth Min. Students 588.

LITTLE FALLS, HERKIMER CO.
1—HOLY FAMILY, [CEM] Rev. Anthony F. Ligato; Sr. Marilyn Hayes, C.S.J., Pastoral Assoc.; Deacons Michael Carbone; Joseph DeLorenzo; Mary Puznowski, Music Dir. (1992 Merger of St. Mary's, St. Joseph's & Sacred Heart)
Office: 763 E. Main St., 13365. Tel: 315-823-3410; Fax: 315-823-2701. Email: hfplf@ntcnet.com. Web: www.rcda.org/churches/holy_family_parish_sts_anthony_joseph.
Catechesis / Religious Program—Lisa LaCoppola, D.R.E. & Youth Min. Students 168.
2—ST. JOSEPH, Consolidated with St. Mary and Sacred Heart to form Holy Family Parish, Little Falls.
3—ST. MARY, Consolidated with St. Joseph and

Sacred Heart to form Holy Family Parish, Little Falls.

4—SACRED HEART, (Polish), Consolidated with St. Joseph and St. Mary to form Holy Family Parish, Little Falls.

LOUDONVILLE, ALBANY CO.

1—CHRIST OUR LIGHT ROMAN CATHOLIC CHURCH Rev. David E. Noone.
Church & Offices: 1 Maria Dr., 12211. Tel: 518-489-8386; Fax: 518-489-6910.
Res.: 15 Exchange St., 12205. Tel: 518-489-8386.
Old Church—15 Exchange St., 12205.

2—ST. FRANCIS DE SALES (1972) Merged with Our Lady of Mercy, Colonie to form St. Francis de Sales, Loudonville. Worship Site.

3—ST. PIUS X Revs. Michael A. Farano; Stephen P. Moore.
Mailing Address: 23 Crumitie Rd., 12211. In Res., Rev. James J. Walsh.
School—(Grades PreK-8), 79 Upper Loudon Rd., 12211. Tel: 518-465-4539; Fax: 518-465-4895. Dennis Mullahy, Prin. Students 630.
Catechesis/Religious Program—Judy Rinalli, D.R.E.; Brian Evers, D.R.E. Students 725.
Convent—Tel: 518-449-9024.

MARGARETVILLE, DELAWARE CO., SACRED HEART Rev. Paul G. Catena.
Res.: Academy St., 12455. Tel: 845-586-2665.
Catechesis/Religious Program—Students 122.
Mission—St. Ann Andes, Delaware Co.
Mission—Our Lady of Good Counsel Roxbury, Delaware Co.

MECHANICVILLE, SARATOGA CO., ASSUMPTION-ST. PAUL Rev. James J. Kane, Sacramental Admin.; Deacon Gregory Mansfield.
Rectory—52 William St., P.O. Box 308, 12118. Tel: 518-664-6196; Fax: 518-664-6782. Email: assumptionst@nycap.rr.com.
Catechesis/Religious Program—Victoria Giulianelli, Dir. Youth Ministry; Bro. Ron Davis, Dir. Faith Formation. Students 366.
Convent—Sisters of St. Joseph, 8 Farrell St., 12118. Tel: 518-664-4053.

MENANDS, ALBANY CO., ST. JOAN OF ARC Rev. Kofi Ntsiful Amissah.
Parish Office & Res.: 76 Menand Rd., 12204. Tel: 518-463-0378; Fax: 518-463-0489. Email: sjoa@nycap.rr.com.
Catechesis/Religious Program—Students 76.

MIDDLEBURGH, SCHOHARIE CO.

1—ST. CATHERINE, Merged with St. Joseph, Schoharie to form Parish of Our Lady of the Valley, Middleburgh. Worship Site.

2—PARISH OF OUR LADY OF THE VALLEY Rev. Thomas Holmes.
Res.: 111 Wells Ave., 12122. Tel: 518-827-5132. Email: stcath56@midtel.net.
Catechesis/Religious Program—Tel: 518-239-6587. Martha Conroy, D.R.E. Students 72.

MOHAWK, HERKIMER CO., BLESSED SACRAMENT Sr. Mary Jo Tallman, C.S.J., Parish Life Dir.; Rev. Mark Cunningham, Sacramental Min.
Res.: 54 E. Main St., 13407. Tel: 315-866-1752.
Catechesis/Religious Program—Students 241.

MORRIS, OTSEGO CO., HOLY CROSS Rev. John Burns.
Res.: 96 Main St., P.O. Box 118, 13808-0118. Tel: 607-263-5143. Email: hcchurch@frontiernet.net.
Catechesis/Religious Program—Maureen E. Joy, A.R.E. Students 31.

NASSAU, RENSSELAER CO., ST. MARY, [CEM] Revs. John T. Provost; Antone Kandra, O.F.M.Conv., Pastor Emeritus; Deacon John Skelly.
Res.: 26 Church St., P.O. Box 435, 12123. Tel: 518-766-2701; Fax: 518-766-7535.
Catechesis/Religious Program—Linda Ridzi, D.R.E. Students 124.

NEW LEBANON, COLUMBIA CO., IMMACULATE CONCEPTION, [CEM] Rev. John Close; Deacon Peter Quinn.
Church and Shrine of Our Lady of Lourdes: 732 U.S. Rte. 20, 12125. Tel: 518-794-7651; 518-766-5651; Fax: 518-766-5651.
Mission—St. Joseph's Stephentown, Rensselaer Co.

NEWPORT, HERKIMER CO., ST. JOHN THE BAPTIST Rev. William A. Gorman.
Res.: Main St., Box 475, 13416. Tel: 315-845-8017.
Mission—St. Mary of the Assumption [CEM] Middleville, Herkimer Co.

NORTH CREEK, WARREN CO., ST. JAMES, [CEM] Rev. John O'Kane; Sr. M. Francesca Husselbeck, R.S.M., Parish Life Dir.
Parish Center: 223 Main St., P.O. Box 23, 12853. Tel: 518-251-2518; Fax: 518-251-2518.
Catechesis/Religious Program— Karen Smith, D.R.E.; Joyce Parker, D.R.E. Students 45.

NORTHVILLE, FULTON CO., ST. FRANCIS OF ASSISI Rev. Thomas Morrette, Admin.
Mailing Address: P.O. Box 126, 12134.
Res.: 501 Bridge St., 12134. Tel: 518-863-4736; Fax: 518-863-4128.

ONEONTA, OTSEGO CO., ST. MARY, [CEM] Rev. Joseph Benintende; Lawrence Curran, Campus Ministry, Neuman House, 77 Spruce St., 13820. Tel: 607-432-4400; Fax: 607-432-6437.
Res.: 39 Walnut St., 13820. Tel: 607-432-3920; Fax: 607-432-6437. Web: stmarysoneonta.org/church.
School—(Grades N-6), 5588 State Hwy. 7, 13820. Tel: 607-432-1450; Fax: 607-433-1656. Web: stmarysoneonta.org/school. Patricia Bliss, Prin.; Nancy Jankura, Librarian. Religious 1; Lay Teachers 16; Students 122.
Catechesis/Religious Program—Tel: 607-431-9320. Carmel Ann Sperti DeArmas, D.R.E. Students 275.

PALENVILLE, GREENE CO., SACRED HEART, Merged with Immaculate Conception, Haines Falls to form Sacred Heart-Immaculate Conception, Haines Falls. Worship Site.

PHILMONT, COLUMBIA CO., SACRED HEART, [CEM] Merged with Holy Cross, West Taghkanic to form St. John Vianney, Philmont.

PITTSTOWN, RENSSELAER CO., ST. GEORGE, Closed. For inquiries for parish records, contact Immaculate Conception, Hoosick Falls.

QUEENSBURY, WARREN CO., OUR LADY OF THE ANNUNCIATION Rev. Joseph Busch.
Res.: 448 Aviation Rd., 12804. Tel: 518-793-9677; Fax: 518-793-9678.
Catechesis/Religious Program— Catherine Vesterby, C.R.E.; Tammy Casey, Youth Min. Students 604.

RAVENA, ALBANY CO., ST. PATRICK, [CEM] Rev. Stuart Gullan-Steele.
Res.: 21 Main St., 12143. Tel: 518-756-3145; Fax: 518-756-8411. Web: www.tcosp.com.
Catechesis/Religious Program—Frank Julian, Faith Formation Min. Students 183.

RENSSELAER, RENSSELAER CO.

1—ST. JOHN THE EVANGELIST, [CEM] Consolidated with St. Joseph, Rensselaer to form Parish of St. John the Evangelist and St. Joseph's, Rensselaer.

2—ST. JOSEPH (1915) Consolidated with St. John the Evangelist, Rensselaer to form Parish of St. John the Evangelist and St. Joseph's, Rensselaer.

3—PARISH OF ST. JOHN THE EVANGELIST AND ST. JOSEPH'S Rev. R. Adam Forno.
Res.: 50 Herrick St., 12144. Tel: 518-465-2209.
Parish Office—P.O. Box 256, 12144. Tel: 518-465-0482; 518-463-4401; Fax: 518-449-7088. Email: sjesjparish@aol.com. Web: www.churchofstjohn.org.
School—St. Joseph-St. John, 1641 Third St., 12144. Closed.
Catechesis/Religious Program—Combined program with St. Joseph. Linda Remington, D.R.E. Students 153.
Convent—20 Lawrence St., 12144. Tel: 518-465-1514. Sisters 9.

RICHFIELD SPRINGS, OTSEGO CO.

1—ST. JOSEPH, [CEM] Merged with St. Joseph, West Winfield to form St. Joseph the Worker, Richfield Springs. Worship Site.

2—ST. JOSEPH THE WORKER Rev. Terence P. Healy, Sacramental Min.; Nancy Brown, Pastoral Assoc. 35 Canadarago St., 13439.
Res.: 305 W. Main St., West Winfield, 13491. Tel: 315-858-1682; Fax: 315-858-1682. Email: stjosephsrichfield@verizon.net.
Catechesis/Religious Program—Students 40.

ROTTERDAM, SCHENECTADY CO., ST. GABRIEL THE ARCHANGEL Ms. Annette Brooks, Parish Life Dir.; Revs. James Belogi, Sacramental Min.; Robert Powhida, Sacramental Min. In Res., Rev. Kenneth Tunney (Retired).
Res.: 3040 Hamburg St., Schenectady, 12303. Tel: 518-355-6600; Fax: 518-355-6604. Email: stgaberectory@aol.com. Web: www.stgabrielschurch.com.
Catechesis/Religious Program—Tel: 518-355-4193. Email: chs3040@msn.com. Clementina Carlin, A.R.E. Students 395.

ROTTERDAM JUNCTION, SCHENECTADY CO., ST. MARGARET OF CORTONA Rev. Michael Hogan.
2 Putnam St., 12150.
Res.: 248 Elm St., 12202. Tel: 518-887-5288; Fax: 518-369-4580.
Catechesis/Religious Program—Tel: 518-399-1888. Katherine Skelly, D.R.E. Students 17.

ST. JOHNSVILLE, MONTGOMERY CO., ST. PATRICK, Merged with St. James, Fort Plain & St. Peter's & Paul's, Canajoharie to form Parish of Our Lady of Hope, Fort Plain. Worship Site.

SALEM, WASHINGTON CO., HOLY CROSS, [CEM] Rev. Liam Condon.
Res.: 247 Main St., P.O. Box 357, 12865. Tel: 518-854-7626.

SARATOGA SPRINGS, SARATOGA CO.

1—ST. CLEMENT Revs. Paul Borowski, C.Ss.R.; Francis E. Sullivan, C.Ss.R.; Arthur Tuttle, C.Ss.R.; Deacons Larry Willette, Pastoral Assoc.; Arthur Turcotte, Pastoral Assoc.; Lee Hanson, Pastoral Assoc.; William H. Gaul Jr.
Res.: 231 Lake Ave., 12866. Tel: 518-584-6122; Fax: 518-584-2644. Web: stclementschurch.com.
School—(Grades PreK-5), 231 Lake Ave., 12866. Tel: 518-584-7350; Fax: 518-587-2623. Mrs. Jane E. Kromm, Prin. Lay Teachers 21; Students 258.
Catechesis/Religious Program—Tel: 518-587-3611. Rev. Cornelius Draves-Arpaia (PHX), Dir. Whole Community Catechesis; Bonnie Thornton, Co-Dir. Youth Ministry; Kurt Lawrence, Co-Dir. Youth Ministry; Denise Salage, C.R.E.; Kathleen M. Donnellan, C.R.E. Students 1,124.
Chapel—Gansevoort, St. Therese, Tel: 518-587-3180. Deacon Danny Boyd.

2—ST. PETER, [CEM] Revs. Dominic Ingemie; Robert J. LeFevre, Pastor Emeritus (Retired); Michael Cambi.
Rectory—241 Broadway, 12866. Tel: 518-584-2375; Fax: 518-584-5471. Email: stpetersar@nycap.rr.com. Web: www.stpeteronline.org.
Priest Res.: 88 Regent St., 12866. Tel: 518-584-8127.
Catechesis/Religious Program— Rita Usher. Tel: 518-587-4487. Students 534.

SCHAGHTICOKE, RENSSELAER CO.

1—CHURCH OF THE HOLY TRINITY, [CEM], 2001 merger of St. John the Baptist & Our Lady of Good Counsel, Valley Falls, NY & St. Monica's, Johnsonville. Rev. George Fleming; Deacon Walter Rehder, (Retired).
Mailing Address: P.O. Box 300, 12154. Tel: 518-753-4554; Fax: 518-753-0456.
Res.: 50 Hillview Dr., Troy, 12182. Tel: 518-235-0337.
Catechesis/Religious Program—Tel: 518-753-6228; Fax: 518-753-6228. Cheri Foster, D.R.E. Students 210.

2—ST. JOHN THE BAPTIST, Merged with St. Monica, Johnsonville to form Church of the Holy Trinity, Schaghticoke.

SCHENECTADY, SCHENECTADY CO.

1—ST. ANTHONY, (Italian), Revs. Richard A. Carlino; Anthony De Franco, Pastor Emeritus (Retired); Sr. Maria Rose Querini, M.P.V., Pastoral Assoc.
Parish Office—331 Seward Pl., 12305. Tel: 518-374-4591; Fax: 518-377-5245. Web: stanthonyschurch.net.
School—Early Childhood Education Center, 1840 Van Vranken Ave., 12308. Tel: 518-372-5961; Fax: 518-372-7337. Web: stanthonysdaycare.com.
Catechesis/Religious Program—Tel: 518-393-0748; 518-847-3044. Sr. Dolores Puglis, M.P.V., D.R.E. Students 202.
Convent—1834 Van Vranken Ave., 12308. Tel: 518-346-2060.

2—CHURCH OF ST. ADALBERT, (Polish), [CEM] Rev. Carl A. Urban; Sr. Bernadette Filter, C.R., Pastoral Assoc. for Elderly.
Res.: 550 Lansing St., 12303-1195. Tel: 518-346-4204; Fax: 518-346-0348.
Catechesis/Religious Program—Tel: 518-372-8372. Jacqueline Burgoyne, D.R.E. Students 78.

3—SS. CYRIL AND METHODIUS, Closed. For inquiries for parish records contact Our Lady of Mount Carmel, Schenectady.

4—ST. HELEN Rev. Robert Longobucco.
Res.: 1803 Union St., 12309. Tel: 518-346-6137; Fax: 518-346-5390. Email: helen1803@aol.com.
School—(Grades PreK-5), 1801 Union St., 12309. Tel: 518-382-8225; Fax: 518-382-2226. Jennifer Chatain, Prin. Lay Teachers 18; Students 180.
Catechesis/Religious Program—Tel: 518-377-3119. Students 585.

5—HOLY CROSS, Closed. For inquiries for parish records, contact St. John the Evangelist, Schenectady.

6—IMMACULATE CONCEPTION Rev. O. Robert De Martinis.
Res. & Office: 523 Thompson St., 12306. Tel: 518-382-0451; Fax: 518-382-3243. Email: icchurch1@juno.com.
Catechesis/Religious Program—Deborah Ploetz, D.R.E. Students 114.

7—ST. JOHN THE BAPTIST, [CEM] Closed. For inquiries for parish records, contact St. John the Evangelist, Schenectady.

8—ST. JOHN THE EVANGELIST Revs. Richard A. Carlino; Anthony Curran; Deacon Frank Schickel. In Res., Revs. Anthony De Franco (Retired); Leopold Kamundo; Richard W. Dybas (Retired).
Res.: 802 Union St., 12308. Fax: 518-372-0992.
Office: 816 Union St., 12308. Tel: 518-372-3381; Fax: 518-372-0992.
School—(Grades PreK-6), 806 Union St., 12308. Tel: 518-393-5331; Fax: 518-374-4663. Marie Keenan, Prin. Lay Teachers 171; Students 231.
Catechesis/Religious Program—Tel: 518-372-3381, Ext. 110; Fax: 518-372-0962. Jeanne Marie Hawkey, D.R.E. Combined with St. Mary and Holy Cross Students 650.

9—ST. JOSEPH, (German), [CEM 2] Rev. Michael Hogan. In Res., Rev. Brian Cronin (Retired).
Res.: 225 Lafayette St., 12305. Tel: 518-374-4466; Fax: 518-374-4466.
Church: 600 State St., 12305.
Catechesis/Religious Program—Donna Simone, D.R.E. Students 13.

10—ST. LUKE Rev. Dominic Isopo.
Res.: 1241 State St., 12304. Tel: 518-346-3405; Fax: 518-346-3406. Email: slrcc7@aol.com. Web: stlukesofschenectady.org.
Catechesis/Religious Program—Doreen Wright, D.R.E. Students 184.

11—ST. MARY, (Polish), [CEM] Closed. For inquiries for parish records, contact St. John the Evangelist, Schenectady.

12—OUR LADY OF FATIMA Deacon Richard J. Thiesen, Parish Life Dir.
Res.: 2216 Rosa Rd., 12309. Tel: 518-370-3136; Fax: 518-370-3137. Email: admin@olfatima.cc. Web: www.olfatima.cc.
Catechesis/Religious Program—Tel: 518-370-0027. Patricia Policastro, C.R.E. Students 205.

13—OUR LADY OF MT. CARMEL, (Italian), Revs. Robert J. Hohenstein; Anastacio Segura, Diocesan Ministry to Spanish Apostolate.
Res.: 1255 Pleasant St., 12303. Tel: 518-393-4109; Fax: 518-393-4100. Email: olmc1255@aol.com. Web: olmc-schenectady.com.
Our Lady of Mt. Carmel Center—1274 Pleasant St., 12303. Tel: 518-372-0336.
Catechesis/Religious Program—Tel: 518-372-8372. Jacquline Burgoyne, D.R.E. Students 82.

14—OUR LADY OF THE ASSUMPTION Rev. Joseph Cebula; Deacon Joseph Brennan.
Res.: 3034 Ford Ave., 12306. Tel: 518-346-4926; Fax: 518-374-5670. Web: olarotterdam.org.
Catechesis/Religious Program—Debbie Ploetz, D.R.E. Students 420.

15—ST. PAUL THE APOSTLE Rev. Peter Pagones; Deacon Owen South. In Res., Revs. Anthony Curran; Dennis Murphy.
Res.: 2777 Albany St., 12304. Tel: 518-377-8886; Fax: 518-377-4371.
School—Closed., 16 Van Zandt St., 12304. Tel: 518-377-0506.
Catechesis/Religious Program—Marilyn Friguletto, D.R.E. (K-6); Arlene Parisi, D.R.E. (7-8); David Oakes, D.R.E. (9-12). Students 230.

16—SACRED HEART-ST. COLUMBA, Merged with St. Joseph, Schenectady. For inquiries for parish records contact St. Joseph.

17—ST. THOMAS THE APOSTLE, Closed. For inquiries for parish records please see Our Lady of Mt. Carmel, Schenectady.

SCHOHARIE, SCHOHARIE CO., ST. JOSEPH, Merged with St. Catherine, Middleburgh to form Parish of Our Lady of the Valley, Middleburgh.

SCHUYLERVILLE, SARATOGA CO.

1—NOTRE DAME-VISITATION, [CEM 2] Rev. Martin J. Fisher.
Parish House—18 Pearl St., 12871. Tel: 518-695-3391; Fax: 518-695-4651.
Catechesis/Religious Program—Tel: 518-695-3318; Fax: 518-695-4854. Sr. Rene Drolet, D.R.E. Students 130.
Convent—P.O. Box 55, 12871. Tel: 518-695-3318.

2—VISITATION OF THE BLESSED VIRGIN MARY, Closed. For inquiries for parish records contact Notre Dame de Lourdes Parish, Schuylerville.

SCOTIA, SCHENECTADY CO., ST. JOSEPH Rev. Peter Russo; Deacons John P. Crane; Frank C. Berning.
Res.: 231 Second St., 12302.
Parish Center—45 MacArthur Dr., 12302. Tel: 518-346-2316; Fax: 518-374-3383. Email: stjosephs1@verizon.net. Web: mysite.verizon.net/stjosephs1.
Catechesis/Religious Program—Tel: 518-374-3382. Donna Simone, D.R.E.; Ruth Moon, Youth Min. Students 309.

SIDNEY, DELAWARE CO., SACRED HEART Rev. Gordon Polenz; Deacons Thomas E. Luby; Michael R. Donnell.
Res.: 15 Liberty St., 13838. Tel: 607-563-1591; Fax: 607-563-7066. Email: revgordon@mkl.com.
Catechesis/Religious Program—Fax: 607-563-7066. Email: revgordon@frontiernet.net. Paula Ciborowski, D.R.E.; Kimberly Ayres, Youth Min. Students 150.
Mission—St. Ambrose Unadilla, Otsego Co. (Closed)
Mission—St. Paul Franklin, Delaware Co. (Closed)

SOUTH GLENS FALLS, SARATOGA CO., ST. MICHAEL THE ARCHANGEL Rev. Guy A. Childs, Admin.
Res.: 80 Saratoga Ave., 12803. Tel: 518-792-5859; Fax: 518-792-5850. Email: smichael@nycap.rr.com. Web: stmichaelssgf.com.
Catechesis/Religious Program—James M. Gorman, D.R.E. Students 305.

SOUTH KORTRIGHT, DELAWARE CO., CHURCH OF THE MOST PRECIOUS BLOOD OF JESUS, Merged with Sacred Heart, Stamford.

SPEIGLETOWN, RENSSELAER CO., ST. BONAVENTURE Rev. George Fleming.
Res.: 50 Hillview Dr., Troy, 12182. Tel: 518-235-0337; Fax: 518-235-8726.
Catechesis/Religious Program—Tel: 518-235-0337, Ext. 4. Barbara Colangione, D.R.E. Students 146.

STAMFORD, DELAWARE CO.

1—SACRED HEART, Merged with St. Philip Neri, Grand Gorge to form Sacred Heart/St. Philip Neri, Stamford

2—SACRED HEART/ST. PHILIP NERI, [CEM] Rev. Joseph Arockiassamy; Marlies Kneis, Pastoral Assoc. for Faith Formation.
Res.: 27 Harper St., P.O. Box 38, 12167. Tel: 607-652-7170; Fax: 607-652-9250. Email: sheartchurch@stny.rr.com; pastorshc2@stny.rr.com.
Catechesis/Religious Program—Combined with St. Philip Neri Mission. Louise Evans, D.R.E. Students 100.

STILLWATER, SARATOGA CO., ST. PETER THE APOSTLE, [CEM] Rev. James Kane.
Res.: 271 N. Hudson Ave., P.O. Box 519, 12170. Tel: 518-664-3354; Fax: 518-664-3891.
Catechesis/Religious Program—Tel: 518-664-3891. Carol Ford, D.R.E. Students 312.
Mission—St. Isaac Jogues Saratoga Lake, Saratoga Co. (Summer)

STOTTVILLE, COLUMBIA CO., HOLY FAMILY, Merged with St. Mary/Nativity, Stuyvesant Falls to form Church of St. Joseph, Stuyvesant. Worship Site.

STUYVESANT, COLUMBIA CO.

1—CHURCH OF ST. JOSEPH Rev. Frank O'Connor.
Res.: 2824 Atlantic Ave., Stottville, 12172. Tel: 518-828-1889; Fax: 518-822-9238. Email: holyfamily@localnet.com. Web: www.rcda.org/churches/holyfamilychurch.
Church: 1820 Rte. 9, 12173. Tel: 518-799-5411; Fax: 518-799-3144.
Catechesis/Religious Program—Students 39.

2—NATIVITY/ST. MARY'S, Merged with Holy Family, Stottville to form Church of St. Joseph, Stuyvesant. Worship Site.

STUYVESANT FALLS, COLUMBIA CO., ST. MARY/NATIVITY, [CEM] Merged with Holy Family, Stottville to form Church of St. Joseph, Stuyvesant.

SUMMIT, SCHOHARIE CO., ST. ANNA, Closed. For inquiries for parish records, contact St. Vincent de Paul, Cobleskill.

TRIBES HILL, MONTGOMERY CO., SACRED HEART Rev. Patrick Gallagher, O.F.M.Conv.
Res.: 111 Third Ave., P.O. Box 264, 12177. Tel: 518-829-7301. Email: usacredh@nycap.rr.com.
Catechesis/Religious Program—Tel: 518-762-7732. Wendy Hall, D.R.E. Students 53.

TROY, RENSSELAER CO.

1—ST. ANTHONY OF PADUA (SHRINE CHURCH), (Italian), Rev. Mario F. Julian, O.F.M.; Bro. Philip Hira, O.F.M., Parish Asst.; Deacon Moises Gutierrez.
Friary: 28 State St., 12180-3916. Tel: 518-273-8622; Fax: 518-273-2731.
Catechesis/Religious Program—(Combined with St. Joseph, Troy), Tel: 518-283-5760. Students 6.

2—ST. AUGUSTINE Revs. James Spenard, O.S.A.; Alfred J. Ellis, O.S.A.; Joseph Getz, O.S.A.
Res.: 25 115th St., 12182. Tel: 518-235-3861; Fax: 518-233-0284. Email: jass@nycap.rr.com.
School—(Grades N-6), 525 Fourth Ave., 12182. Tel: 518-235-7287; Fax: 518-237-7943. Email: staug@nycap.rr.com. James R. Clement, Prin. Lay Teachers 12; Students 195.
Catechesis/Religious Program—Cindy Brisson, D.R.E. Students 198.

3—ST. FRANCIS DE SALES, Closed. For inquiries for parish records, contact Our Lady of Victory, Troy.

4—HOLY TRINITY, (Polish), Rev. Romaeus Cooney, O.Carm., Admin.
Mailing Address: *St. Joseph's Priory*, 416 Third St., 12180. Tel: 518-274-6720; Fax: 518-272-6503.

5—ST. JOSEPH, [CEM] Revs. Timothy Ennis, O.Carm.; Albert Pavlik, O.Carm.; Deacon Charles Wojton. In Res., Rev. Romaeus Cooney, O.Carm.
Res.: 416 Third St., 12180. Tel: 518-274-6720; Fax: 518-272-6503.
Catechesis/Religious Program—Mary Lou Kane, D.R.E. Students 56.

6—ST. LAWRENCE, Closed. For inquiries for parish records contact St. Joseph Parish, Troy.

7—ST. MARY Revs. James O'Neill (Retired); Peter Nabozny, Sacramental Min. (Retired); Sam Marro, Pastoral Assoc.
Res.: 196 Third St., 12180. Tel: 518-272-5820; Fax: 518-271-7880. Email: pstmaryschurch@nycap.rr.com.
Catechesis/Religious Program—Sam Marro, D.R.E. Students 55.

8—ST. MICHAEL THE ARCHANGEL Sr. Katherine Arseneau, C.S.J., Parish Life Dir.; Revs. Arthur A. Toole, Sacramental Min. (Retired); James Mackey, Sacramental Min. (Retired); Barbara Berger, Pastoral Assoc. Tel: 518-283-6110, Ext. 13.
Church: 175 Williams Rd., 12180. Tel: 518-283-6110; Fax: 518-283-3938.
Catechesis/Religious Program—Students 330.
Mission—Van Rensselaer Manor, County Nursing Home North Greenbush, Rensselaer Co.
Mission—The Springs Nursing Home, Rensselaer Co.

9—OUR LADY OF VICTORY Rev. Randall P. Patterson; Deacons Gerald Christiano; Brian Lewis. In Res., Rev. Joseph A. Barker (Retired).
Res.: 55 N. Lake Ave., 12180. Tel: 518-273-7609; 518-273-7602 (Office); Fax: 518-273-0310. Email: olvparish01@aol.com. Web: olv-troy.4lpi.com.
School—Our Lady of Victory Education Center, (Grades PreK-6), 451 Marshland Ct., 12180. Tel: 518-274-6202; Fax: 518-271-8680. Email: tourlady@nycap.rr.com. Web: olvtroy.com. Ms. Karen Snyder, Prin. Lay Teachers 11; Students 121.
Catechesis/Religious Program—Email: mtuiteolv@nycap.rr.com. Maryanne Tuite, D.R.E. Students 376.

10—ST. PATRICK Revs. David J. Jones, M.M., Admin.; Cyril F. Pereira (Retired); Anna E. Denney, D.R.E.
Res.: 3027 Sixth Ave., 12180. Tel: 518-272-4666; Fax: 518-272-4666. Email: stpatroy@nycap.rr.com. Web: www.stpatrickstroy.org.

11—ST. PAUL THE APOSTLE, Closed. For inquiries for parish records, contact Our Lady of Victory, Troy.

12—ST. PETER, [CEM] Closed. For inquiries for parish records, contact St. Anthony of Padua, Troy.

13—SACRED HEART Revs. John Yanas; James Vaughan, Pastor Emeritus (Retired); Augustine Tufail; Sr. Rita Duggan, C.S.J., Admin. Email: ritacsj@yahoo.com.
Res.: 310 Spring Ave., 12180. Tel: 518-274-1363; Fax: 518-274-8720.
School—(Grades PreK-6), 308 Spring Ave., 12180. Tel: 518-274-3655; Fax: 518-274-8270. Susan Holland, Prin. Lay Teachers 17; Students 172.
Catechesis/Religious Program—Margaret Leathem, D.R.E. Students 236.

14—ST. WILLIAMS, Closed. For inquiries for parish records, contact Sacred Heart, Troy.

USHERS, SARATOGA CO., CORPUS CHRISTI Rev. Edward Golding; Deacon John Tierney.
Mailing Address: P.O. Box 628, Round Lake, 12151-0628. Email: ccorpus@nycap.rr.com.
Res.: 23 Pepperbush Pl., Ballston Spa, 12020. Tel: 518-877-8506 (Office); Fax: 518-877-5620 (Office).
Catechesis/Religious Program—Tel: 518-877-8506, Ext. 302. Sr. Sue Wieczynski, R.S.M., Dir. Whole Community Catechesis. (Generations of Faith Program) 900.

VALATIE, COLUMBIA CO., ST. JOHN THE BAPTIST, [CEM] Rev. John Molyn.
Res.: 1025 Kinderhook St., 12184. Tel: 518-758-9401; Fax: 518-758-9409. Email: stjohnthebapistch@nycap.rr.com. Web: home.nycap.rr.com/stjohn.
Catechesis/Religious Program—Tel: 518-758-1828. Email: faithformation@fairpoint.net. Connie Smith, D.R.E. Students 436.

VOORHEESVILLE, ALBANY CO., ST. MATTHEW Rev. Thomas H. Chevalier; Deacon Paul M. Davignon; Ms. Ellie Dorn, Youth Min.
Res.: 25 Mountain View St., P.O. Box 346, 12186-9551. Tel: 518-765-2805; Fax: 518-765-3701. Email: stmatthewschurch@net2dish.net. Web: www.stmatthewsvoorheesville.org.
Catechesis/Religious Program—Ms. Suzanne Schultz, D.R.E. Students 325.

WALTON, DELAWARE CO., ST. JOHN THE BAPTIST Rev. Matthew H. Frisoni, Admin.
Mailing Address: 25 Benton Ave., 13856-0315.
Res.: 15 Benton Ave., 13856-0315. Tel: 607-865-4720.
Catechesis/Religious Program—Ann Burkin, Faith Formation Moderator. Students 78.
Mission—Holy Family 14918 State Hwy. 30, Downsville, Delaware Co. 13755.

WARRENSBURG, WARREN CO., ST. CECILIA, [CEM] Rev. Paul Cox, Sacramental Min. (Retired); Sr. Linda Hogan, C.S.J., Parish Life Dir.
Res.: 3802 Main St., 12885-1629. Tel: 518-623-3021. Web: www.stceciliaschurch.com.
Catechesis/Religious Program—Tel: 518-361-3765. Students 70.

WATERFORD, SARATOGA CO.

1—ST. ANNE, Closed. For inquiries for parish records, contact St. Mary of the Assumption, Waterford.

2—ST. MARY OF THE ASSUMPTION, [CEM] Rev. David Kelley, O.S.A. In Res., Rev. Michael Stanley, O.S.A.
Res.: 119 Broad St., 12188-2397. Tel: 518-237-3131; Fax: 518-237-9625.
School—St. Mary's Catholic School, 12 Sixth St., 12188. Tel: 518-237-0652; Fax: 518-233-0898. Mary Rushkoski, Prin. Lay Teachers 20; Students 245.
Catechesis/Religious Program—Wally Decker, D.R.E. Faith Formation Program is located at St. Mary of the Assumption. Students 152.

WATERVLIET, ALBANY CO.

1—ST. BRIGID, Merged with Immaculate Conception, Our Lady of Mt. Carmel, St. Patrick's and Sacred Heart of Mary, Watervliet & St. Joseph, Green Island, to form Immaculate Heart of Mary, Watervliet. Church not closed.

2—IMMACULATE CONCEPTION, (Polish), [CEM] Merged with St. Brigid's, Our Lady of Mt. Carmel, St. Patrick's, Sacred Heart of Mary, Watervliet & St.

Joseph's, Green Island to form Immaculate Heart of Mary, Watervliet. Church not closed.

3—IMMACULATE HEART OF MARY Leadership Team:, Rev. L. Edward Deimeke; Deacon Thomas Nash. In Res., Revs. Donald J. Ophals (Retired); George Brennan.

Parish Office: 2416 7th Ave., 12189. Tel: 518-273-6020; Fax: 518-273-3978. Email: ihm@rcpw.org. Web: www.rcpw.org.

Rectory—695 Fifth Ave., 12189. Tel: 518-687-2107.

School—St. Brigid's Regional School, (Grades PreK-8), 700 Fifth Ave., 12189. Tel: 518-273-3321; Fax: 518-273-9355. Web: www.rcdaschools.org/stbrigid/. Ralph Provenza, Prin. (Regional) Sisters 3; Lay Teachers 17; Students 174.

Catechesis/Religious Program—Sharon C. Kowalski, D.R.E. Students 216.

4—OUR LADY OF MT. CARMEL, (Italian), Merged with St. Brigid's, Immaculate Conception, St. Patrick's, Sacred Heart of Mary, Watervliet & St. Joseph, Green Island to form Immaculate Heart of Mary, Watervliet. Church not closed.

5—ST. PATRICK, Merged with St. Brigid's, Immaculate Conception, Our Lady of Mt. Carmel, Sacred Heart of Mary, Watervliet & St. Joseph's Green Island, to form Immaculate Heart of Mary, Watervliet. Church not closed.

6—SACRED HEART OF MARY, Closed. Consolidated with St. Brigid's, Immaculate Conception, Our Lady of Mt. Carmel, St. Patrick's, Watervliet & St. Joseph's, Green Island to form Immaculate Heart of Mary, Watervliet.

WEST TAGHKANIC, COLUMBIA CO., HOLY CROSS, Merged with Sacred Heart, Philmont, to form St. John Vianney, Claverack, NY 12153-0477. Tel: 518-851-1333.

WEST WINFIELD, HERKIMER CO., ST. JOSEPH, [CEM] Merged with St. Joseph, Richfield Springs to form St. Joseph the Worker, Richfield Springs. Worship Site.

WHITEHALL, WASHINGTON CO.

1—NOTRE DAME DES VICTOIRES, Merged with Our Lady of Angels, Whitehall to form Our Lady of Hope, Whitehall.

2—OUR LADY OF ANGELS, Merged with Notre Dame des Victoires, Whitehall to form Our Lady of Hope, Whitehall.

3—OUR LADY OF HOPE Rev. Michael Flannery.

Res.: 9 Wheeler Ave., 12887. Tel: 518-499-1656; Fax: 518-499-2489.

Catechesis/Religious Program—Combined with Chapel of the Assumption. Patti Abbott, A.R.E. & Youth Min. Students 53.

Chapel—Assumption, Huletts Landing

WINDHAM, GREENE CO., ST. THERESA OF CHILD JESUS Rev. James Schiffer, C.P.

Res.: Main St., 12496. Tel: 518-734-3352.

Catechesis/Religious Program—Tel: 518-734-9685; Fax: 518-734-3352. Margaret Reinold Gulino, D.R.E. Students 128.

Mission—St. Joseph's Chapel Ashland, Greene Co.

WORCESTER, OTSEGO CO., ST. JOSEPH Rev. Edward Golding.

Res.: 181 Main St., P.O. Box 156, 12197. Tel: 607-397-9373; Fax: 607-397-7732.

Mission—St. Mary [CEM] Schenevus, Otsego Co.

WYNANTSKILL, RENSSELAER CO., ST. JUDE THE APOSTLE Rev. Anthony Ligato, Admin.

Res.: 43 Brookside Ave., P.O. Box 347, 12198-0347. Tel: 518-283-1162; Fax: 518-286-2808. Email: stjude@nycap.rr.com. Web: stjude-church.com.

Parish Office: 42 Dana Ave., 12198-0347.

School—(Grades PreK-6), 35 Dana Ave., 12198. Tel: 518-283-0333; Fax: 518-283-0475. Email: albsjs@rcdaschools.org. Web: www.rcdaschools.org/stjude/. Cathleen Carney, Admin. Lay Teachers 18; Students 203.

Chaplains of Public Institutions

ALBANY. *Albany County Jail*. (Assigned to Deanery Priests).

Albany County Nursing Home. Rev. Anthony Curran, Rev. Anthony C. Nicklas, (Orthodox).

Albany Medical Center Hospital. Revs. Charles R. Celeste, Kenneth Gregory, Robert E. DeLeon, C.S.C.

Capital District Psychiatric Center. Deacon Charles Hall.

Columbia County Jail. Rev. Theodore J. Gerken (Retired).

Memorial Hospital. Rev. John T. Kelly.

New York State Department of Corrections. Deacon Donald Thomas Sharrow, Ministerial Prog. Coord. Tel: 518-457-8106.

St. Peter's Hospital. Rev. John Tallman, Chap., Deacon Martin Beckman, Chap., David Dietsche, Chap., Mr. Younas Azad, Chap., Ms. Sally Conklin, Chap., Rev. Terrence O'Neil, Chap., Mr. J. Erik Swift, Chap.

University Heights Nursing Home. Sr. Jane Carr, R.S.M., Chap.

Veterans' Administration Hospital. Deacon Gerald Ladouceur.

COMSTOCK. *Great Meadows Correctional Institution*. Ann Narcisso, Chap., Bro. Dennis E. Tamburello, O.F.M., Sacramental Min.

COXSACKIE. *Coxsackie Correctional Facility*. Rev. Richard D. Shaw, Sacramental Min., Deacon Lawrence Groesbeck, Chap.

Greene Correctional Facility. Deacon Angel Garcia-Lopez, Chap., Rev. Richard D. Shaw, Sacramental Min.

Regional Medical Unit. Rev. John L. Moyna.

GLENS FALLS. *Glens Falls Hospital*. Sr. Donna Irvine, S.S.N.D., Chap.

Hudson Correctional Facility. Gerald Van Alstine, Chap.

SCHENECTADY. *Ellis Hospital*. Deacon Gary Riggi.

Hallmark Nursing Home. Deacon Earle Flatt, Chap.

Schenectady County Nursing Home. Sharyn R. Sabatini, Chap.

TROY. *Samaritan Hospital*. Deacons Frank S. Lukovits, Moses Guitterrez.

Seton Health. Deacon Albert Schrempf.

Van Rensselaer Manor. Vacant.

WILTON. *Mount McGregor Correctional Facility*. Revs. Matthew T. Conlin, O.F.M., Sacramental Min., Jamie Lippincot-Pino, Chap.

Special Assignment:

Most Rev.—

Hubbard, Howard James, D.D., Bishop, Roman Catholic Diocese of Albany

Revs.—

Brennan, George, Sacramental Min. & Catholic Charities, 695 Fifth Ave., Watervliet, 12189.

Broderick, Richard, Pueblo to Pueblo Program, 330 Brownell Rd., Cambridge, 12816.

Butler, Paul, 28 Tudor Rd., 12203.

Chepaitis, Peter, O.F.M., 26C Mill Ln., P.O. Box 42, Middleburgh, 12122.

Chiaramonte, Anthony J., Ph.D., 790 Lancaster St., 12203. Consultation Center

Cullinane, Briant, O.F.M.Conv., P.O. Box 629, Rensselaer, 12144.

Curran, Anthony, St. Paul the Apostle Rectory, 277 Albany St., Schenectady, 12304.

DeGiovine, Christopher, 432 Western Ave., 12203. College of St. Rose

DeLeon, Robert E., C.S.C., 495 Maple Ln., Valatie, 12184.

Donlon, James I., J.C.D., 40 N. Main Ave., 12203. Judicial Vicar, Tribunal, Pastoral Center

Farano, Michael A., Vicar Gen. & Dir. Society of the Propagation of Faith, 2 Fairview Rd., Loudonville, 12211.

Finn, Firmin, O.F.M.Conv., 1 Jeanne Jugan Ln., Latham, 12110.

Fragomeni, Richard, 5401 S. Cornell Ave., Chicago, IL 60615.

Gregory, Kenneth, Chap., Albany Medical Center, 12208.

Kelly, John T., Chap., Memorial Hospital, 600 N. Blvd., 12010.

Konopka, Thomas E., L.M.S.W., Consultation Center, Advanced Studies, Sacramental Min., 465 State St., 12203.

L'Arche, Jeffrey, M.S., B.S., S.T.B., Our Lady of LaSalette Shrine, Lessome Ln., Altamont, 12009.

Menty, Ronald, Administrative Advocate, 40 N. Main Ave., 12203.

Murray, Peter J., S.J., 136 Shrine Rd., Fultonville, 12072.

Shaw, Richard D., Chap., Coxsackie Correctional Facility, P.O. Box 232, New Baltimore, 12124. Sacramental Min., Greene County Correctional Facility

Sheldon, William W., C.M.

Sullivan, Peter J., III, J.C.L., 40 N. Main Ave., 12203. Adjutant Vicar Judicial Tribunal, Pastoral Center

Tallman, John, Chap., St. Peter's Hospital, Mater Christi, 40 Collins Pl., 12208.

Tufail, Augustine, 310 Spring Ave., Troy, 12180.

Van Thanh, Louis, Vietnamese Apostolate, 55 Grand St., Newburgh, 12550.

Vosko, Richard, Liturgical Design Consultant, 4611 Foxwood Dr., P.O. Box 2217, Clifton Park, 12605.

Weider, Gregory, Chap., St. Mary's Hospital, Amsterdam, NY

You, Simon (Kwanggun), Korean Apostolate, 80 Slingerlands St., 12202.

On Duty Outside the Diocese:

Revs.—

Fragomeni, Richard, Chicago Theological Institute, 5401 S. Cornell Ave., Chicago, IL 60615-5698.

Hurst, Thomas R., S.S., Theological College, 401 Michigan Ave., N.E., Washington, DC 20017.

Military Chaplains:

Rev.—

Rutherford, Donald I., CH (COL.), Headquarters US Army Europe, CMR 420-Box 208, APO AF 09063-0208.

Leave of Absence:

Revs.—

Celeste, Charles R.

Cournoyer, Michael R.

Raiche, Brian

Rossi, Desmond

Tressic, David L.

Retired:

Revs.—

Ahern, Bernard, 4418 Poppy Tree Ln., Jacksonville, FL 32258.

Allie, Stanley J., 1201 Bogard Rd., Wasilla, AK 99643.

Amato, Joseph, 1056 Nantucke Rd., Venice, FL 34293.

Anselment, Joseph, 23 Tiffany Dr., Glens Falls, 12801.

Antos, Paul J., 1149 Highland Park Rd., Niskayuna, 12309.

Baniak, Walter, 520 Second St., Troy, 12180.

Brucker, George W., 25 St. Anthony Ln., Rensselaer, 12144.

Cairns, John L., 23 Oak Brook Commons, Clifton Park, 12065.

Campagnone, Nicholas, Wesley Health Care Center, 131 Lawrence St., Hathorn Residence, Rm. 117, Saratoga Springs, 12866.

Cantwell, Edward F., 429 E. Allen St., Hudson, 12534.

Clemente, Michael, 100 E. Palmer Ave., Schenectady, 12303.

Cox, Paul, P.O. Box 134, Kattskill Bay, 12844.

Cronin, Brian, 1807 Mariner Pl., Deerfield Beach, FL 33442.

Cyvas, Matthew, 555 68th Ave., St. Petersburg Beach, FL 33706.

D'Agostino, Joseph, 6 Bircher Ave., Poughkeepsie, 12601.

Daley, James D., 69 Murray Ave., Delmar, 12054.

De Franco, Anthony, Teresian House, 200 Washington Ave. Ext., 12203.

De Pascale, Daniel, CDR, 2750 Biarritz Ct., Ponte Vedra Beach, FL 32802.

Donnelly, Robert, Apt. #109, East Greenbush, 12061.

Douglas, Louis, 1880 Superfine Ln., #8, Wilmington, DE 19802.

Doyle, Donald, 178 E. Sanford St., Glens Falls, 12801.

Dunbar, Francis, 20 1/2 Williams St., Whitehall, 12887.

Dybas, Richard W., 1786 Union St., Rm. 336, Schenectady, 12309.

Engel, Paul, 3 Raymond Dr., Altamont, 12009.

Esmond, William, Ledgewood Village, Rte. 149, 17 Ledgewood Dr., Lake George, 12845.

Facci, John, S.A.C., 802 Union St., Schenectady, 12308.

French, John F., 15 Priorslee Ln., Williamsburg, VA 23185.

Gaffigan, William J., 111 Stewart St., Amsterdam, 12010.

Gerken, Theodore J., 207 S. Main St., P.O. Box 335, Germantown, 12526.

Girzone, Joseph, 107 Joshua Ln., Altamont, 12209.

Gulley, Anthony D., Blessed Sacrament, 607 Central Ave., 12206.

Gulley, James, Teresian House, 200 Washington Ave. Ext., 12203.

Halloran, Joseph, 2256 Burdett Ave., Apt. 1022, Troy, 12180.

Ianotti, Pascal, 15 Steadwell Ave., Amsterdam, 12010.

Jupin, Alan D., Rosegarden Apts., Bldg. 7, Apt. 6, Latham, 12110.

Kelly, Donald F., 38 Paine St., Green Island, 12183.

Kirwin, John, 94 Lincoln Ave., Saratoga Springs, 12866.

Lamanna, Alfred, The Prospect Inn, 20 N. Prospect St., Apt. J, Herkimer, 13350.

LeFevre, Robert J., 2 Jaipur Ln., Saratoga Springs, 12866.

Leskovar, Richard J., 4 Woodlake Rd., Apt. 7, 12203.

Lonergan, J. Barry, 187 E. Sanford St., Glens Falls, 12801.

Lynch, Patrick J., c/o Mary Ellen Tracy, 116 Denise Dr., Latham, 12110.

Mackey, James, 38 Oak Brook Commons, Clifton Park, 12065.

Maher, Daniel J., 2305 Florence Dr., Latham, 12110.

Malecki, John J., Ph.D., Teresian House, 200 Washington Ave. Ext., 12203.
Marbury, Cabell B., 99 Slingerland St., 12202.
Markert, Leo, 133 Saratoga Rd., Bldg. S, Apt. #5, Glenville, 12302.
Matulewicz, Ronald, St. Joseph Rectory, 7 North St., P.O. Box 538, Broadalbin, 12025.
McCloskey, Francis G., 1094 Mountain Ave., #4, Purling, 12470.
McTavey, Lawrence, V.F., 89B Church Hill Rd., Waterford, 12188.
Murphy, John, 40 Brunswick Ave., Troy, 12180.
Nabozny, Peter, 27 St. Anthony Ln., Rensselaer, 12144.
Nusbaum, Daniel C., Ph.D., 2701 Chicago Blvd., Detroit, MI 48206.
O'Brien, Leo P., Avila, 100 White Pine Dr., 12203.
O'Grady, John F., S.S.D., S.T.D., 1000 Quayside Ter., #2104, Miami, FL 33138.
O'Keefe, Joseph, P.O. Box 793, Enfield, NH 03748.
O'Neill, James, 38 Middletown Rd., P.O. Box 421, Waterford, 12188.
Ophals, Donald J., 695 5th Ave., Watervliet, 12189.
Pereira, Cyril F., 3027 Sixth Ave., Troy, 12180.
Piechocki, Raymond S., 6 Tremont Ave., Amsterdam, 12010.
Potvin, Leo F., 73 1st St., Ilion, 13357.
Powers, Thomas M., 1255 Pleasant St., Schenectady, 12303.
Purcell, Robert, P.O. Box 169, Margaretville, 12455.
Redmond, Paul V., P.O. Box 458, Emmitsburg, MD 21727.
Riley, John F., 2256 Burdett Ave., Apt. 1009, Troy, 12180.
Roman, Paul, 1066 Palmer Rd., Broadalbin, 12025. Tel: 518-882-9649
Rooney, John J., St. Joseph Apts., #4115, 2 Jeanne Jugan Ln., Latham, 12110.
Roos, John, 203 Elm St., Apt. 7, Cobleskill, 12043.
Ryan, Edward J., 204 Washington St., Troy, 12180.
Schmitt, Michael T., 133 Saratoga Rd. Bldg. H, Apt. 12, Glenville, 12302.
Schweigardt, Erwin, 1570 Kingston Ave., Schenectady, 12303.
Shanley, Owen F., P.O. Box 914, Broadalbin, 12025.
Sipperly, Edward, P.O. Box 317, Clifton Park, 12065.
Smith, Paul, 37 Parkwood St. E., 12203.
St. John, George G., 607 Central Ave., 12206.
Swierzowski, Stanislaus J., 48 Van Derveer St., Amsterdam, 12010.
Tartaglia, Paul, 465 State St., 12203. (June-Nov.)
Testa, Richard, St. Joseph Apts., 2 Jeanne Jugan Ln., Latham, 12110.
Titta, Santino, 19 Juniper Pl., Grant City, 10306.
Toole, Arthur A., 38 Oak Brook Commons, Clifton Park, 12065.
Touchette, Marc L., 140 Washington Ave., Apt. 29B, 12203.
Tremblay, Nellis, P.O. Box 134, Kattskill Bay, 12844.
Tunny, Kenneth J., St. Gabriel's Rectory, 3040 Hamburg St., Schenectady, 12303.
Turnbull, William, 89A Church Hill Rd., Waterford, 12188.
Vail, Thomas, 76 Moreland St., Little Falls, 13365.
Varno, John J., 73 Midline Rd., Ballston Lake, 12019.
Vaughan, James, 310 Spring Ave., Troy, 12180.
Watroba, Boleslaus M., 2416 Seventh Ave., Watervliet, 12189.

Permanent Deacons:
Ackerson, Dana J.
Baechel, Kenneth, Saint Augustine, FL 32080.
Bandel, Arthur, Blessed Sacrament, Bolton Landing
Bazinet, William, St. Alphonsus, Glens Falls
Beckman, Martin L., St. Vincent de Paul, Albany
Berning, Frank C., St. Joseph's, Scotia; Dir. Initial Formation for the Diaconate
Bower, James W., Annunciation, Ilion
Boyd, Danny S., St. Therese Mission, Gansevoort
Brady, Robert, (Retired), 316 Lark St., Scotia, 12302.
Brennan, Joseph, Our Lady of the Assumption
Brett, William, Chap. Our Lady of Mercy Life Center, Guilderland; Legion of Mary
Brown, Richard Dr., St. Joseph the Worker, West Winfield
Carbone, Michael S., Holy Family, Little Falls
Cechnicki, Joseph, St. James, Fort Plain; St. Peter's & Paul's, Canajoharie; St. Patrick's; St. Johnsville
Christiano, Gerald, (Retired), 14 Woods Path, Troy, 12182-1636.
Cohen, Andrew
Colton, Thomas, St. Mary's, Crescent
Crane, John, St. Joseph's, Scotia
Davignon, Paul M., St. Matthews, Voorheesville
DeLorenzo, Joseph, Holy Family, Little Falls
DeMauro, Gerald, Our Lady of Assumption, Rotterdam
Devine, Patrick, (On Duty Outside Diocese)
Donnell, Michael, Sacred Heart, Sidney
Dorsch, Warren, St. John Vianney; Parish of Our Lady of Hope, Copake Falls
Dringus, William, Holy Spirit Church, East Greenbush
Fabian, Miguel, Holy Family Parish, Hispanic Community, Albany
Fitzgerald, William, Blessed Sacrament, Albany
Flatt, Earle, St. Madeleine Sophie, Guiderland
Gaffney, William, (Retired)
Garcia-Lopez, Angel, Holy Family Parish, Hispanic Community, Albany; Coxsackie & Greene Correctional
Gaul, William H., Jr., St. John Newman Residence, Saratoga Springs; Diocesan Scouting
Glennon, Dr. John E., (Retired), Advocate for HIV/AIDS
Gorman, William, D.Min., Ph.D., (On Duty Outside Diocese)
Grigaitis, Jerry, Co-liaison for Catholic Charismatic Renewal; St. Edward the Confessor, Clifton Park
Groesbeck, Lawrence, Sacred Heart & Our Lady of Mt. Carmel, Gloversville; Hale Creek Correctional Facility
Gutierrez, Moises, St. Anthony of Padua, Troy; Samaritan Hospital, Troy
Hall, Charles H., III, Capitol District Psychiatric Center, Albany
Hanson, Lee, St. Clement, Saratoga Springs
Henkel, William, St. Francis de Sales, Herkimer; Office of Evangelization, Catechesis, & Family Life
Herlihy, Frank, Sacred Heart, Lake George
Hewitt, William, (Retired)
Hook, J. Neil, Our Lady of Grace, Ballston Lake, Parish Life Dir.
Jones, Dennis, St. Anthony and St. Joseph, Herkimer
Kelenski, Eugene, St. Edward's, Clifton Park
Ladouceur, Gerald J., Mater Christi, Albany; Stratton VA Hospital, Albany
Leonard, Mark J., St. Madeleine Sophie, Schenectady
Levine, Brian, St. Peter's, Saratoga Springs
Lewis, Brian, Our Lady of Victory, Troy
Luby, Thomas T., Rural Ministry, Sacred Heart, Sidney
Lukovits, Frank S., St. Henry, Averill Park; Samaritan Hospital, Troy
MacKinnon, Walter, St. Edward, Clifton Park
Manno, Peter, St. Joseph's, Dolgeville
Mansfield, E. Gregory, Assumption-St. Paul's, Mechanicville
Manzella, Alfred R., St. Thomas, Delmar
Markham, Joseph, Christ the King, Albany; Pre-Cana Coord.
Matthews, Gerard, Holy Trinity, Cohoes
McAuliffe, Timothy J.
McDonald, Michael, Administrative Advocate for Deacons; St. Mary's, Coxsackie
Melanson, Michael, Immaculate Conception, Glenville
Nahm, George H., (Retired)
Nash, Thomas, Immaculate Heart of Mary, Watervliet; Green Island
Neurohr, Helmut N., St. Ambrose, Latham
Novak, John W., (Retired)
O'Connell, Thomas, (Retired)
O'Connor, Gary, All Saints Catholic Church, Albany
O'Connor, Gerard, (Retired)
O'Neill, Charles, Parish of the Holy Trinity, Hudson
Pagano, Joseph, St. Francis of Assisi, Northville; St. Joseph, Broadalbin
Pasquarelli, Robert, St. Henry's, Averill Park
Picher, Gary, St. Joseph, Greenfield Center, Parish Life Director
Powers, David F., St. Mary's, Glen Falls
Quinn, Peter, Immaculate Conception, New Lebanon
Rehder, Walter, (Retired)
Riggi, Gary, Ellis Hospital, Schenectady
Roemer, Paul W., St. Patrick's, Catskill
Rucinski, Robert T., (Retired)
Ryba, Michael, St. Stanislaus, Amsterdam; Montgomery County Convalescent Home, Fulton
Safford, Warren A., St. Jude the Apostle, Wynantskill
Sakowicz, Albert, Parish of Our Lady of Hope, Fort Plain
Salamone, Sam, (Retired)
Schickel, Frank, St. Mary & St. John the Evangelist, Schenectady
Schrempf, Albert G., Holy Trinity, Cohoes; Seton Health, Troy
Sedlmeir, Peter, St. John the Baptist, Greenville
Sharrow, Thomas, New York State Dept. of Corrections; St. Helen's, Schenectady
Sheppeck, Michael, (Retired)
Skelly, John, St. Mary's, Nassau
Solar, Richard, (Retired)
Solomon, Edward R., St. Vincent de Paul, Albany
South, Owen D., St. Paul the Apostle, Schenectady
Stosiek, Martin, (Retired)
Sullivan, Raymond, Cathedral of the Immaculate Conception, Albany; Commission for Ecumenical Affairs; Ongoing Formation of Ordained Deacons
Surman, Dr. Gary, St. Vincent, Cobleskill; Office of Evangelization, Catechesis, & Family Life
Tapia, Raymon
Taylor, Charles A., St. Edward the Confessor, Clifton Park; Diocesan Office of Canonical Services
Thiesen, Richard J., Our Lady of Fatima, Schenectady, Parish Life Director
Thomas, Frank, M.D., Our Lady of Grace, Ballston Spa; St. Luke's Guild
Tierney, John, Corpus Christi, Round Lake (Ushers)
Trawinski, Peter, St. James, Chatham
Turcotte, Arthur W., (Retired)
Tyrell, Joseph, St. Mary's, Glens Falls
Valenti, Charles
Velez, Randy, St. Mary's, Cooperstown
Washburn, Richard, Church of St. Joseph, Stuyvesant; Brookwood Secure Center, Claverack
Willette, Lawrence, St. Clement, Saratoga Springs
Wilson, Gerald, Our Lady of Annunciation, Queensbury
Witko, George, St. Mary, Albany
Wojton, Charles, St. Joseph, Troy
Wubbenhorst, Robert H., Blessed Sacrament, Hague; St. John the Baptist, Chestertown; Parish of St. Isaac Jogues, Chestertown
Yankowski, Frank, St. Michael the Archangel, Troy
Zoltowski, Gregory, St. John the Evangelist, Schenectady

INSTITUTIONS LOCATED IN THE DIOCESE

[A] SEMINARIES, RELIGIOUS OR SCHOLASTICATES

CATSKILL. *St. Anthony Friary*, 24 Harrison St., P.O. Box 487, 12414-0487. Tel: 518-943-3451; Fax: 518-943-1573. Revs. Michael Dominic W. Ledoux, O.F.M.; Regis Gallo, O.F.M.; Frederick Fusco, O.F.M.; Valerian Faugno, O.F.M.; Albin Fusco, O.F.M.; James Tuxbury, O.F.M.; Thomas Nicastro, O.F.M.; Albert McMahon, O.F.M.; Marcellinus Borg, O.F.M.; Bros. Lawrence Stumpo, O.F.M.; Vincent de Paul Ciaravino, O.F.M., Guardian, Dir. of Health Care. Order of Friars Minor.

RENSSELAER. *Conventual Franciscan Friars Immaculate Conception Province, Provincialate Office of the Treasurer*, P.O. Box 629, 12144. Tel: 518-472-1000; 518-472-1016; Fax: 518-472-1013. Email: brorayl@juno.com. Web: www.franciscanseast.org. 77 St. Francis Pl., 12144. Very Rev. Justin Biase, O.F.M.Conv., Min. Prov.; Friar Raymond Sobocinski, O.F.M. Conv., Province Treas. Order Friars Minor Conventual. Priests 1; Brothers 1.

[B] COLLEGES AND UNIVERSITIES

ALBANY. *St. Bernard's School of Theology and Ministry at Albany*, 40 N. Main Ave., 12203. Tel: 518-453-6760; Fax: 518-453-6793. Email: stbernards@rcda.org. Web: stbernards.edu. Sr. Katherine Hanley, C.S.J., Assoc. Dean. Extension Program of St. Bernard's School of Theology and Ministry, Rochester, NY. Graduate School of Theology & Ministry Studies.

The College of Saint Rose (Corporate Name), 432 Western Ave., 12203. Tel: 518-454-5111; 800-657-8556; Fax: 518-458-5447. Web: www.strose.edu. Dr. Mark Sullivan, Pres.; Dr. David Szczerbacki, Provost & Vice Pres. Academic Affairs; Marcus Buckley, Vice Pres. Fin. & Admin.; Karin Carr, Vice Pres. Inst. Advancement; Judith A. Kelly, Registrar; Dennis McDonald, Vice Pres. Student Affairs; Mary Grondahl, Vice Pres. Enrollment Planning & Undergraduate Admissions; Rev. Christopher DeGiovine, Chap. & Dean Spiritual Life; Peter Koonz, Librarian. Founded by the Sisters of St. Joseph of Carondelet in 1920. Priests 1; Sisters 2; Lay Teachers 209; Students 4,675.

Maria College, 700 New Scotland Ave., 12208. Tel: 518-438-3111; Fax: 518-438-7170. Web: MariaCollege.edu. Sr. Laureen Fitzgerald, Pres.; Dr. Margie Byrd, Dean for Academic Affairs; Ms. Laurie Gilmore, Dir. Admissions; Ms. Deborah Corrigan, Dean Students; Mrs. Frances Bernard, Dir. Business Affairs; Sr. Rose Hobbs, R.S.M., Librarian. Two-Year College. Sisters of Mercy 9; Sisters of St. Joseph 1; Lay Teachers 32; Students 800.

LOUDONVILLE. *Siena College* 12211. Tel: 518-783-2300; Fax: 518-783-4293. Web: www.siena.edu. Revs. Kevin Mullen, O.F.M., Ph.D., Pres.; Kenneth Paulli, O.F.M., Chief of Staff, President's Cabinet; Linda Richardson, Ph.D., Vice Pres. Academic Affairs; Paul Stec, Vice Pres. Fin. & Admin.; David Smith, Vice Pres. Develop. & External Affairs; Ned Jones, Vice Pres. Enrollment Mgmt.; Dr. Maryellen Gilroy, Vice Pres. Student Affairs; Rev. Greg Jakubowicz, O.F.M., Chap.; Mary Lawyer, Asst. Vice Pres., Financial Aid; Mark Frost, Asst. Vice Pres. Facilities; James A. Serbalik, Registrar; Gary B. Thompson, Dir. of Library; Debra Del Belso, Dir. of Career Center.

Siena College, Founded in 1937 by the Franciscan Friars, Order of Friars Minor, Province of the Most Holy Name of Jesus. Students 3,355.

The Friary: Revs. Greg Jakubowicz, O.F.M., Chap.; Richard Biasiotto, O.F.M.; Matthew T. Conlin, O.F.M., Chap.; Julian A. Davies, O.F.M.; Ambrose Donehue, O.F.M.; Mattias Doyle, O.F.M.; Daniel P. Dwyer, O.F.M.; Peter A. Fiore, O.F.M.; Capistran Hanlon, O.F.M., Vicar, Siena College Friary; Linh Hoang, O.F.M.; Gregory P. Jakubowicz, O.F.M.; Gerard Lee, O.F.M., Dir., St. Francis Chapel; Kevin Mullen, O.F.M., Ph.D.; Gerald R. Mudd, O.F.M.; Daniel C. Nelson, O.F.M.; Kenneth Paulli, O.F.M.; Reginald J. Reddy, O.F.M.; Blaise R. Reinhart, O.F.M.; Dennis Tamburello, O.F.M.; John E. Van Hook, O.F.M.; Bros. Brian Belanger, O.F.M., Siena Friary Guardian; Romuald Chinetsky, O.F.M.; Walter Liss, O.F.M.

[C] HIGH SCHOOLS, DIOCESAN

ALBANY. *Bishop Maginn High School*, 99 Slingerland St., 12202. Tel: 518-463-2247; Fax: 518-463-9880. Email: principal@bishopmaginn.org. Web: www.bishopmaginn.org. Mr. Joseph Grasso, Prin.; Annemarie Barkman, Head of School. Priests 1; Sisters 1; Lay Teachers 20; Students 230.

AMSTERDAM. *Bishop Scully High School*, Upper Church St., 12010. Tel: 518-842-4100. Closed.

SARATOGA SPRINGS. *Saratoga Central Catholic High School*, (Grades 7-12), 247 Broadway, 12866. Tel: 518-587-7070; Fax: 518-587-0678. Email: scc@saratogacentralcatholic.org. Web: www.saratogacentralcatholic.org. Mr. Christopher A. Signor, Prin.; Rev. Christopher J. Welch. Lay Teachers 22; Students 200.

SCHENECTADY. *Notre Dame-Bishop Gibbons School*, (Grades 6-12), (Coed), 2600 Albany St., 12304. Tel: 518-393-3131; Fax: 518-370-3817. Email: info@ndbg.org. Michael Piatek Jr., Prin. Brothers 2; Lay Teachers 37; Students 350.

TROY. *Catholic Central High School*, (Grades 7-12), 625 Seventh Ave., 12182. Tel: 518-235-7100; Fax: 518-237-1796. Email: cchsprincipal@yahoo.com. Web: www.cchstroy.org. Mr. Christopher Bott, Prin.; Charlene Markham, Librarian. Sisters 3; Lay Teachers 38; Students 535.

[D] HIGH SCHOOLS, PRIVATE

ALBANY. *Academy of the Holy Names Upper, Middle and Lower Schools*, (Grades PreK-12), 1073 New Scotland Rd., 12208. Tel: 518-438-7895; Fax: 518-438-7368. Web: www.ahns.org. Dr. Eva C. Joseph, Pres. (PreK-12); Ms. Mary Anne Vigliante, Prin. (Grades 9-12); Mrs. Maureen Ferris, Prin. (Grades PreK-8). Sisters 6; Lay Teachers 71; Students 294.

The Christian Brothers' Academy of Albany, (Grades 6-12), 12 Airline Dr., 12205. Tel: 518-452-9809; Fax: 518-452-9804. Web: www.cbaalbany.org. Mr. James Schlegel, Prin.; Ms. Diane Babbie, Librarian. Brothers of the Christian Schools., JROTC College Prep. Program. Brothers 6; Lay Teachers 36; Students 402.

Mercy High, Private School for Girls Closed., c/o 40 N. Main Ave., 12203.

TROY. *LaSalle Institute*, (Grades 6-12), 174 Williams Rd., 12180. Tel: 518-283-2500; Fax: 518-283-6265. Email: info@lasalleinstitute.org. Web: www.lasalleinstitute.org. Bro. Carl Malacalza, F.S.C., Prin.; Mrs. Frances Lengua, Librarian. Brothers of the Christian Schools. Brothers 8; Sisters 1; Lay Teachers 42; Students 401.

[E] ELEMENTARY SCHOOLS, PRIVATE

LOUDONVILLE. *Saint Gregory's School*, (Grades N-8), 121 Old Niskayuna Rd., 12211-1399. Tel: 518-785-6621; Fax: 518-782-1364. Email: marrao@saintgregoryschool.org. Web: www.saintgregorysschool.org. Jeffry P. Loomis, Head of School; Theresa C. Braaten, Librarian. An independent Catholic day school for boys staffed by laity (Nursery-8). Girls admitted in Nursery through Kindergarten classes. Lay Teachers 30; Students 135.

[F] CONSOLIDATED ELEMENTARY SCHOOLS

ALBANY. *Cathedral Academy*, 75 Park Ave., 12202. Tel: 518-449-5232. Closed.

COHOES. *Cohoes Catholic School* Closed., One St. Marie's Ln., 12047. Tel: 518-235-5202; Fax: 518-453-6666.

GLEN FALLS. *St. Mary's/St. Alphonsus Regional Catholic School*, (Grades PreK-8), 10-12 Church St., Glens Falls, 12801. Tel: 518-792-3178; Fax: 518-792-6056. Web: www.smsaschool.org. Mrs. Kathryn Mahoney-Fowler, Prin.

WATERFORD. *St. Mary's School*, (Grades PreK-8), 12 Sixth St., 12188. Tel: 518-237-0652; Fax: 518-233-0898. Email: stmarys1@nycap.rr.com. Web: www.smswaterford.org. Mary Rushkoski, Prin. Lay Teachers 22; Students 249.

[G] RESIDENTIAL INSTITUTIONS FOR CHILDREN & ADOLESCENTS

ALBANY. *Saint Anne Institute*, 160 N. Main Ave., 12206. Tel: 518-437-6500; Fax: 518-437-6555. Email: rriccio@s-a-i.org. Web: www.stanneinstitute.org. Richard C. Riccio, Exec. Dir. Email: rriccio@s-a-i.org. Residential and Community-based Preventive Service Center. Regents accredited and certified junior and senior H.S. for the emotionally handicapped and Preschool program for 3-4 year olds who are speech-impaired and emotionally disturbed. Residential care, critical care, and Day Treatment for young women ages 12-18. Family Services, Vocational Training, Sex Abuse Prevention and Juvenile Sex Offender Programs for male and female adolescents in crisis and their families. Residential 129; Day Treatment 40; Juvenile Sex Offender & Sex Abuse Prevention Families 90.

Saint Catherine's Center for Children, 40 N. Main Ave., 12203. Tel: 518-453-6700; Fax: 518-453-8443. Web: www.st-cath.org. Ms. Helen Hayes, Exec. Dir. Residential and day treatment, group homes and foster family programs for children with special needs. Community based prevention programs; Parent aides; Parent Training; Transitional Program for Homeless Families. Total Assisted Annually 1,250.

LaSalle School, Inc., 391 Western Ave., 12203. Tel: 518-242-4731; Fax: 518-242-4747. Email: information@lasalle-school.org. Web: www.lasalle-school.org. Mr. William Wolff, Exec. Dir. Residential and day programs, independent living program, sexual victim/offender program, licensed substance abuse treatment program, and preventative services for boys (ages 12-18) and their families in New York State. Registered New York State Junior and Senior High School and certified School of Special Education. Brothers of the Christian Schools 8; Prevention Families 64; Resident Students 83; Day Students 44; Community Connections 21.

The La Salle School Foundation of Albany Tel: 518-242-4731; Fax: 518-242-4744.

WATERVLIET. *St. Colman's Home* 12189. Tel: 518-273-4911; Fax: 518-273-3312. Sr. Mary Regina, Dir.; Rev. Kenneth Gregory, Chap. Sisters of the Presentation of the B.V.M. Children 45.

[H] GENERAL HOSPITALS

ALBANY. *St. Clare's Holding Company, Inc.*, 40 N. Main Ave., 12203-1422. Tel: 518-453-6650. Web: www.stclares.org.

St. Clare's Hospital, 40 N. Main Ave., 12203-1422. Tel: 518-453-6650.

St. Peter's Health Care Services, 315 S. Manning Blvd., 12208. Tel: 518-525-1550; Fax: 518-525-1520. Email: sboyle@stpetershealthcare.org. Web: www.stpetershealthcare.org. Mr. Steven P. Boyle, Pres. & CEO.

St. Peter's Addiction Recovery Center, 8 Mercycare Ln., Guilderland, 12084. Tel: 518-452-6700.

St. Peter's Hospital of the City of Albany, 315 S. Manning Blvd., 12208. Tel: 518-525-1550; 518-525-1388 (Education Sites for Natural Family Planning); Fax: 518-525-1520. Email: sboyle@sphcs.org. Web: www.sphcs.org. Mr. Steven P. Boyle, Pres. & CEO; Rev. John Tallman, Chap. Bed Capacity 442; Patients Assisted Annually 500,000.

AMSTERDAM. *St. Mary's Hospital*, 427 Guy Park Ave., 12010. Tel: 518-842-1900; Fax: 518-842-0107. Web: smha.org. Mr. Victor Giulianelli, FACHE, Pres. & CEO; Rev. Gregory Weider. Sisters of St. Joseph of Carondelet 14; Sisters of the Resurrection 1; Bed Capacity 143; Patients Assisted Annually 191,673.

RENSSELAER. *The Community Hospice*, 295 Valley View Blvd., 12144. Tel: 518-285-8150; Fax: 518-285-8151. Web: www.communityhospice.org. Ronald F. Watson, Pres. & CEO.

TROY. *Seton Health System, Inc.*, 1300 Massachusetts Ave., 12180. Tel: 518-268-5000; Fax: 518-268-5257. Email: info@setonhealth.org. Web: www.setonhealth.org. Mr. Gino J. Pazzaglini, FACHE - Pres. & CEO; Shafi Thomas, Dir. Spiritual Care; Sr. Clarisse Correia, Chm. Bd. of Directors.

Seton Health System, Inc. Daughters of Charity of St. Vincent de Paul. Sisters 8; Bed Capacity 196; Patients Assisted Annually 315,000.

Seton Health at Schuyler Ridge aka Leonard Nursing Home One Abele Dr., Clifton Park, 12065. Tel: 518-371-1400. Email: ssmith@setonhealth.org. Web: schuylerridge.org. Sandy Smith, Exec. Dir.

[I] SERVICES FOR ELDERLY

ALBANY. *St. Peter's Licensed Home Care Agency*, 159 Wolf Rd., 12205. Tel: 518-525-6099; Fax: 518-525-6002. Email: bsmith@stpetershealthcareservices.org. Sr. Jean McGinty, R.S.M.

GERMANTOWN. *The Carmelite System, Inc.*, 646 Woods Rd., 12526-5617. Tel: 518-537-7500; Fax: 518-537-7501. Email: xsusansan@carmelitesystem.org. Web: Carmelitesystem.org. Sr. M. Mark Louis Anne Randall, O.Carm., Chair.

[J] NURSING AND AGED HOMES

ALBANY. *McAuley Living Services*, 310 S. Manning Blvd., 12208. Tel: 518-437-8400; Fax: 518-437-8418. Email: mhulihan@stpetershealthcare.org. Sisters Amy Kennedy, Exec. Dir.; Stella Dillon, R.S.M., Diocesan Contact Person for Pastoral Care. Tel: 518-437-8400. Sisters of Mercy of the Americas - Northeast Community.

Teresian House (1974) 200 Washington Ave. Ext., 12203. Tel: 518-456-2000; Fax: 518-456-1142. Email: info@teresianhouse.com. Web: www.teresianhouse.com. Sisters Pauline Brecanier, O.Carm., Admin.; Joan Lewis, O.Carm., Coord. Pastoral Care; Rev. Jeffrey L'Arche, M.S., B.S., S.T.B., Chap. Carmelite Sisters for the Aged and Infirm., Corporate Title: Teresian House Nursing Home Co., Inc. Bed Capacity 300; Respite Beds 2.

Teresian House Foundation

Villa Mary Immaculate dba St. Peter's Nursing & Rehabilitation Center 301 Hackett Blvd., 12208. Tel: 518-525-7600; Fax: 518-525-7673. Email: gcooper@stpetershealthcare.org. Web: www.stpetershealthcare.org. Glen Cooper, Exec. Dir.

AMSTERDAM. *Mt. Loretto Nursing Home*, 302 Swart Hill Rd., 12010. Tel: 518-842-6790; Fax: 518-843-5993. Email: mtloretto@superior.net. Web: www.MountLoretto.com. Mr. Brian Chamberlin, Admin.; Sr. Joan Thomas, C.S.J., Dir. Pastoral Care. Health Care Facility, 24 Hour Skilled Nursing Care, Hospice, IV Therapy & Rehab.; Conducted by the Sisters of the Holy Family of Nazareth and the Sisters of the Resurrection. Capacity 120.

CASTLETON. *Resurrection Nursing Home* 12033. Tel: 518-732-7617; Fax: 518-732-4211. Email: rnh@resnursinghome.org. Web: www.resnursinghome.org. Conducted by the Sisters of the Holy Family of Nazareth and the Sisters of Resurrection., Nursing Home (Established 1962); Corporate Name: Resurrection Nursing Home, Inc. Bed Capacity 80.

CATSKILL. *St. Joseph's Villa Senior Living Services*, 38 Prospect Ave., 12414. Tel: 518-453-6650; Fax: 518-453-6650.

CLIFTON PARK. *Seton Health at Schuyler Ridge aka Leonard Nursing Home* One Abele Dr., 12065. Tel: 518-371-1400; Fax: 518-371-1240. Email: ssmith@setonhealth.org. Web: schuylerridge.org. Sandy Smith, Exec. Dir.

GERMANTOWN. *Avila Institute of Gerontology, Inc.*, 600 Woods Rd., 12526. Tel: 518-537-5000; Fax: 518-537-4725. Email: srpeter@avilainstitute.org. Web: www.avilainstitute.org. Sisters Michelle Anne Reho, O.Carm., Pres.; Peter Lillian, O.Carm., Dir. Carmelite Sisters for the Aged and Infirm., (Educational Institute)

GUILDERLAND. *Our Lady of Mercy Life Center*, 2 Mercycare Ln., 12084. Tel: 518-464-8100; Fax: 518-464-8111. Web: www.stpetershealthcare.org. Wesley I. Hale, Exec. Dir.

LATHAM. *Our Lady of Hope Residence*, Little Sisters of the Poor, 1 Jeanne Jugan Ln., 12110. Tel: 518-785-4551; Fax: 518-213-4499. Email: lmmothersuperior@littlesistersofthepoor.org.

Sr. Celine Therese Vadukkoot, Pres.; Rev. Firmin Finn, O.F.M.Conv. Nursing Facility 36; Apartments for the Elderly 48.

[K] APARTMENTS FOR ELDERLY

ALBANY. *Bishop Broderick Apartments Housing Development Fund Co., Inc. dba Bishop Broderick Apts.* 50 Prescott St., 12205. Tel: 518-869-7441; Fax: 518-869-0443. Email: communitymanagerbba@nycap.rr.com. Web: www.depaulhousing.com. Pamela Rost, Community Mgr. Affordable housing for seniors and people with physical disabilities.

C.S.C. Housing Development Fund Co., Inc. dba Sanderson Court Senior Apts. 6 Carondelet Dr., Watervliet, 12189. Tel: 518-782-1123; Fax: 518-782-1125. Email: scfm6@yahoo.com. Web: www.depaulhousing.com. Caitlin Fraser, Community Mgr. Affordable housing for seniors.

Cusack Community Service Corporation, 40 N. Main Ave., 12203. Tel: 518-459-0183; Fax: 518-459-0202. Email: Deborah.DammOBrien@rcda.org.

DePaul Housing Management Corp., 41 N. Main Ave., 12203. Tel: 518-459-0183; Fax: 518-459-0202. Email: diocesan.housing@rcda.org. Web: www.depaulhousing.com. Deborah Damm O'Brien, Exec. Dir.; Jill McLellan Phelps, Dir. Affordable Housing Admin.; Rhonda Finehout, Dir. Housing Mgmt. Managing diocesan sponsored housing for persons who are elderly or mobility impaired.

Teresian House Housing Corporation dba Avila Retirement Community 100 White Pine Dr., 12203. Tel: 518-452-4250; Fax: 518-452-4251. Email: cpolacko@avilaretirement.com. Web: www.avilaretirement.com. Christy Polacko Durant, Dir. Senior Retirement Community. Apartments and cottages.

St. Vincent Apartments Housing Development Fund Co., Inc. dba St. Vincent's Apts. 475 Yates St., 12208. Tel: 518-482-8915; Fax: 518-489-1220. Email: mrmsva@nycap.rr.com. Web: www.depaulhousing.com. Lorraine Caroccia, Community Mgr. Affordable housing for seniors and people with physical disabilities. Total Apartments 59.

CLIFTON PARK. *Halfmoon Housing Development Fund Co., Inc. dba Bishop Hubbard Senior Apartments* 54 Katherine Dr., 12065. Tel: 518-383-2705; Fax: 518-383-6350. Email: diocesan.housing@rcda.org. Web: www.depaulhousing.com. Affordable housing for seniors and people with physical disabilities. Total Apartments 49.

DELHI. *Delhi Housing Development Fund Co., Inc. I and II dba Delhi Senior Community* 7 Main St., 13753. Tel: 607-746-8142; Fax: 607-746-6546. Email: dsc7@delhitel.net. Web: www.depaulhousing.com. Rick Ackerly, Community Mgr. Total Apartments 45.

LATHAM. *LSOP Housing, Inc.*, 2 Jeanne Jugan Ln., 12110. Tel: 518-785-4551; Fax: 518-213-4499. Email: lmmothersuperior@littlesistersofthepoor.org. Sr. Celine Therese Vadukkoot, Pres.

NORTH GREENBUSH. *S.J. Housing Development Fund Company, Inc. dba St. Jude's Apartments* 50 Dana Ave., Wynantskill, 12198. Tel: 518-283-5690; Fax: 518-283-5893. Email: bwsjabmsa@yahoo.com. Web: www.depaulhousing.com. Barbara Weatherwax, Community Mgr. Affordable housing for seniors and people with physical disabilities. Apartments 49.

RENSSELAER. *East Greenbush Housing Development Fund Co., Inc. dba Branson Manor Senior Apartments* 3 Grandview Dr., 12144. Tel: 518-283-8280; Fax: 518-283-8292. Email: bwsjabmsa@yahoo.com. Web: www.depaulhousing.com. Barbara Weatherwax, Community Mgr. Affordable housing for seniors and people with physical disabilities. Total Apartments 49.

Franciscan Heights Community Service Corp. dba Franciscan Heights Senior Community 1 St. Anthony Ln., 12144. Tel: 518-432-3555; Fax: 518-432-3553. Web: www.depaulhousing.com. Cheryl Walton, Community Mgr. Apartments and Cottages 85.

ROTTERDAM. *Rotterdam Housing Development Fund Co., Inc. dba Father Leo O'Brien Senior Community* 3151 Marra Ln., Schenectady, 12303. Tel: 518-357-4424; Fax: 518-357-9377. Email: flobtlc@nycap.rr.com. Web: www.depaulhousing.com. Carrin Swanson, Community Mgr. Affordable housing for seniors. Total Apartments 49.

SCHENECTADY. *LCS Housing Development Fund Company, Inc. dba The Lawrence Commons* 2660 Albany St., 12304. Tel: 518-393-2412; Fax: 518-346-2686. Email: flobtlc@nycap.rr.com. Web: www.depaulhousing.com. Carrin Swanson, Community Mgr. Affordable housing for people with physical disabilities. Apartments 12.

SLINGERLANDS. *Marie-Rose Manor HDFCI dba Marie Rose Manor* 100 Marquis Dr., 12159. Tel: 518-459-0204; Fax: 518-459-0527. Email: mrmsva@nycap.rr.com. Web: www.depaulhousing.com. Lorraine Caroccia, Community Mgr. Affordable housing for seniors. Total Apartments 49.

WATERVLIET. *Delatour Housing Development Fund Company, Inc. dba Carondelet Commons Senior Apartments* 2 Carondelet Dr., 12189. Tel: 518-783-0444; Fax: 518-783-0456. Email: cccakrom@yahoo.com. Web: www.depaulhousing.com. Brenda Krom, Community Mgr. Affordable housing for seniors and people with physical disabilities. Total Apartments 49.

Fontbonne Manor Housing Development Fund Company, Inc. dba Fontbonne Manor Senior Apts. 10 Carondelet Dr., 12189. Tel: 518-782-2780; Fax: 518-782-2778. Email: scfm6@yahoo.com. Web: www.depaulhousing.com. Caitlin Fraser, Community Mgr. Affordable housing for seniors. Total Apartments 49.

Italian-American Housing Development Fund Co., Inc. dba Cabrini Acers Senior Apts. 4 Carondelet Dr., 12189. Tel: 518-785-0050; Fax: 518-785-0110. Email: cccakrom@yahoo.com. Web: www.depaulhousing.com. Brenda Krom, Community Mgr. Affordable housing for seniors and people with physical disabilities. Total Apartments 49.

[L] MONASTERIES AND RESIDENCES OF PRIESTS AND BROTHERS

ALBANY. *Vincentian Fathers Residence*, 96 Menands Rd., 12204-1499. Tel: 518-433-1003. Email: svinz@nycap.rr.com. Priests 1.

LAKE GEORGE. *St. Mary of the Lake*, P.O. Box 31, 12845. Tel: 518-668-5594. c/o 40 N. Main Ave., 12203. Rev. Ken McGuire, C.S.P., Dir. Summer retreat of the Paulist Fathers.

RENSSELAER. *Franciscan Mission House*, 517 Washington Ave., 12144. Tel: 518-465-0062; Fax: 518-472-1013. Web: www.thefma.org. Rev. Antone Kandra, O.F.M.Conv.; Bro. Leo Merriman, O.F.M.Conv. Promotion Center for Order's Missions.

Provincialate, Immaculate Conception Friary - Order of Friars Minor Conventual (1872) (Immaculate Conception Province), P.O. Box 629, 12144. Tel: 518-472-1000; Fax: 518-472-1013. Email: Biasej@aol.com. Web: www.franciscanseast.org. Very Rev. Justin Biase, O.F.M.Conv., Min. Prov.; Bro. Raymond Sobocinski, O.F.M.Conv., Province Treas.; Revs. Briant Cullinane, O.F.M.Conv., Guardian; Henry Madigan, O.F.M.Conv.; Rufino Maloney, O.F.M.Conv.; Friars Dominic McGee, O.F.M.Conv.; Leo Merriman, O.F.M.Conv.; Revs. Firmin Finn, O.F.M.Conv., Chap.; Antone Kandrac, O.F.M.Conv.; Friars Placid Kazczorek, O.F.M.Conv.; Duane Mastangelo, O.F.M.Conv., Archivist; Rev. Giles Van Wormer, O.F.M.Conv.; Bro. Andre Picotte, O.F.M.Conv. (Corporate Name: Order Minor Conventuals, Inc.)

SARATOGA SPRINGS. *St. John Neumann Residence*, 233 Lake Ave., 12866-2729. Tel: 518-584-7500; Fax: 518-581-8421. Revs. George H. Bridge, C.Ss.R.; Robert Gaugler, C.Ss.R.; Thomas F. O'Toole, C.Ss.R.; Richard Knappik, C.Ss.R.; Vincent J. Kelly, C.Ss.R.; Andrew Skeabeck, C.Ss.R.; Edward Dunne, C.Ss.R; Joseph Oppitz, C.Ss.R.; John Salamon, C.Ss.R.; James Ferris, C.Ss.R.; Edward Tardiff, C.Ss.R.; Donald Bolton, C.Ss.R.; Francis Freel, C.Ss.R.; George Deimel, C.Ss.R.; John O'Toole, C.Ss.R.; William Biffar, C.Ss.R.; Charles Gildea, C.Ss.R.; Joseph Buono, C.Ss.R.; George Drew, C.Ss.R.; John Graham, C.Ss.R.; John Drum, C.Ss.R.; Bros. Barnabas Hipkins, C.Ss.R.; Francis Alfone, C.Ss.R.; John Bosco Hammond, C.Ss.R.; David Skarda, C.Ss.R.; Gilbert Hunter, C.Ss.R.; Thomas Kuhn, C.Ss.R. Redemptorist Priests and Brothers of the Baltimore Province.

VALATIE. *St. Joseph Center* Residence for retired Holy Cross Brothers and Priests., 495 Maple Ln., 12184. Tel: 518-784-9481; Fax: 518-784-9494. Email: BEBCSC@hotmail.com. Rev. Robert E. DeLeon, C.S.C., Pastoral Care Albany Medical Center & Chap. In Res. Rev. James P. Madden, C.S.C.; Bro. Edward Boyer, C.S.C., B.A., M.M.Ed., Dir.

[M] CONVENTS AND RESIDENCES FOR SISTERS

ALBANY. *De Paul Provincial House* (Corporate Name: Daughters of Charity of St. Vincent de Paul, N.E. Prov., Inc.), 96 Menand Rd., 12204-1499. Tel: 518-462-5593; Fax: 518-462-5025. Email: dcinfo@dc-northeast.org. Web: www.dc-northeast.org. Rev. William W. Sheldon, C.M.; Sr. Louise Gallahue, D.C., Prov. Supr.; Rev. Gerard H. Luttenberger, C.M., S.T.D., Prov. Dir.

Religious of the Sacred Heart, 128 W. Lawrence St., 12203. Tel: 518-489-8280; Fax: 518-489-8280. Sr. Marie Buonato, R.S.C.J., Area Dir.

Sisters of Mercy of the Americas - Northeast Community, 310 S. Manning Blvd., 12208. Tel: 518-437-3000; Fax: 518-437-3030. Sr. Jane Somerville, R.S.M., Life & Ministry Admin. Sisters 110.

Sisters of the Holy Names of Jesus and Mary, U.S. - Ontario Province, Regional Center, 258 Partridge St., 12208. Tel: 503-675-7125; Fax: 503-675-7138. Email: meholohan@snjmuson.org. Web: www.snjmusontario.org. (Corporate Name: Sisters of the Holy Names of Jesus and Mary of the New York Province, Inc.)

CASTLETON ON HUDSON. *Provincial House, Juniorate and Novitiate of the Sisters of Resurrection*, 35 Boltwood Ave., 12033-1097. Tel: 518-732-2226; Fax: 518-732-2898. Email: crsister@resurrectionsisters.org. Web: www.resurrectionsisters.org. Sisters Cecilia Mary Berdar, C.R., Prov. Supr.; Christine Bykowski, C.R., Local Supr.; Dolores Palermo, C.R., Dir. Novices. Sisters 24. *Chaplain's Residence*, 34 Boltwood Ave., 12033.

Retreat and Vacation Home, 325 Madonna Lake Rd., Cropseyville, 12052-1819. Tel: 518-279-1673.

DEL MAR. *Franciscan House, Mill Hill Sisters* Regional House, 703 Derzee Ct., Delmar, 12054. Tel: 518-512-4362; Fax: 518-512-4362. Sr. Judith Dever, F.M.S.J., Admin. Sisters 2.

GERMANTOWN. *St. Teresa's Motherhouse*, Avila on the Hudson, 600 Woods Rd., 12526-5639. Tel: 518-537-5000; Fax: 518-537-5226. Email: smrc@stteresasmotherhouse.org. Web: www.carmelitesisters.com. Sr. M. Mark Louis Anne Randall, O.Carm., Supr. Gen.; Rev. Joseph E. Finch, Chap. Carmelite Sisters for the Aged and Infirm., Motherhouse and Novitiate. Sisters 31.

Postulation Office Tel: 518-537-5000; Fax: 518-537-5226. Sr. M. Angeline Teresa, O.Carm., Servant of God; Rev. Mario Esposito, O.Carm., Vice Postulator; Andrea Ambrosi, Postulator.

LATHAM. *Provincial House of the Sisters of St. Joseph of Carondelet (Albany Province)* 12110-4799. Tel: 518-783-3500; Fax: 518-783-3672. Email: sszczerbacki@csjalbany.org. Web: www.csjalbany.org. Rev. Geoffrey D. Burke, Chap.; Sisters Mary Anne Rodgers, C.S.J., Province Leadership Team; Nancy Gregg, C.S.J., Province Leadership Team; Ann Christi Brink, C.S.J., Province Leadership Team; Charla Commins, C.S.J., Province Leadership Team; Mary Jo Tallman, C.S.J., Province Leadership Team; Eileen McCann, C.S.J., Province Leadership Team. Sisters 402.

WATERVLIET. *St. Colman's Convent* 12189. Tel: 518-273-4911; Fax: 518-273-3312. Sr. M. Carmel, P.B.V.M., Supr. Motherhouse and Novitiate of Sisters of the Presentation of the B.V.M.

[N] HOUSES OF PRAYER AND RETREAT HOUSES

AURIESVILLE. *Jesuit Retreat House (Auriesville) - Inactive, Shrine of Our Lady of Martyrs*, 136 Shrine Rd., Fultonville, 12072. Tel: 518-853-3033; Fax: 518-853-3051. Web: www.martyrshrine.org.

Shrine of Our Lady of Martyrs, Fultonville, 12072. Tel: 518-853-3033; Fax: 518-853-3051. Email: office@martyrshrine.org. Web: www.martyrshrine.org. Revs. Peter J. Murray, S.J., Supr. & Dir.; Robert McGuire, S.J., Vice Postulator Cause of Kateri Tekakwitha; Bro. Ted Bender, S.J. National Shrine of the Jesuit Martyrs of North America. Priests 2; Brothers 1.

CHESTERTOWN. *The Priory of St. Benedict, Inc.*, 135 Priory Rd., P.O. Box 336, 12817-0336. Tel: 518-494-3733; Fax: 518-494-3733. Email: prioryretreat@yahoo.com. Web: www.prioryretreathouse.org. Sr. Constance M. Messitt, C.S.J., Dir.

MIDDLEBURGH. *Bethany Ministries*, 176 Mill Ln., P.O. Box 432, 12212. Tel: 518-827-4699. Email: bethmin@midtel.net. Web: www.midtel.net/~bethmin. Rev. Peter Chepaitis, O.F.M., Dir.

PARADOX. *Pyramid Life Center* Corporation Name: Albany Catholic Youth Association, Inc., 12858. Tel: 518-585-7545; Fax: 518-585-7545. Email: monicaplc@aol.com. Web: www.pyramidlife.org. Sr. Monica Murphy, C.S.J., Dir. Summer, fall and winter retreat house, located at Pyramid Lake.

QUEENSBURY. *Wellsprings*, 230 Robert Gardens N., #5, 12804. Tel: 518-745-1617. Email: info@wsprings.org. Web: www.wsprings.org. Michael Laratonda, F.M.S., Dir. Programs in Spirituality (Holistic Retreats & Workshops)

SCHENECTADY. *Dominican Retreat and Conference Center*, 1945 Union St., 12309. Tel: 518-393-4169; Fax: 518-393-4525. Email: dslcny@nycap.rr.com. Web: www.dslcny.org. Sr. Susan M. Zemgulis, O.P., Admin. Residence Facilities for 50; Non-resident

Facilities for 90 to 100.

STILLWATER. *Still Point Interfaith Retreat House*, 20 Still Point Rd., Mechanicville, 12118. Tel: 518-587-4967; Fax: 518-587-4967. Email: stillpt423@aol.com. Web: www.stillpointretreatcenter.com. Sisters Rowena Fay, Dir.; Anne Leger, Dir.; Nicole St. John, Dir.

UNADILLA. *Gilead, Inc.*, 1011 State Hwy. 7, 13849. Tel: 607-369-2845. Email: tngilead@aol.com. Eucharistic Community

VALATIE. *St. Joseph Center*, 495 Maple Ln., 12184. Tel: 518-784-9481; Fax: 518-784-9494. Email: bebcsc@hotmail.com. Bros. Edward Boyer, C.S.C., B.A., M.M.Ed., Dir.; Renatus Foldenauer, C.S.C., B.A., M.A., Dir. Retreats.

[O] YOUTH TREATMENT FACILITIES

ALBANY. *Hospitality House Therapeutic Community Inc.*, 271 Central Ave., 12206. Tel: 518-434-6468; Fax: 518-434-6302. Email: lbecker@hospitalityhouse.info. A private, not-for-profit, intensive residential treatment program for males, 18 years or older, with a history of drug and/or substance abuse.

ALTAMONT. *Bernard and Caroline Cobb Memorial School*, 100-300 Mt. Presentation Way, P.O. Box 503, 12009. Tel: 518-861-6446; Fax: 518-861-5228. Email: cobbmemorialschool@verizon.net. Web: www.cobbmemorialschool.org. Sr. Mary Thomas, P.B.V.M., Prin. 12-month special education program for students 5-21 years.

[P] SHRINES

ALTAMONT. *La Salette Shrine* 1109 Berne-Altamont Rd., 12009-3440. Tel: 518-861-8159; Fax: 518-861-7052. Email: fr.jeff@verizon.net. Rev. Jeffrey L'Arche, M.S., B.S., S.T.B., Dir.; Bros. Anthony Casso, M.S., B.A., Assoc.; Donald Wininski, M.S., B.A., Assoc. Corporate Titles: Missionaries of Our Lady of La Salette Inc., Altamont, NY; La Salette Seminary, Altamont, NY.

FONDA. *The National Shrine of Blessed Kateri Tekakwitha and Friary* P.O. Box 627, 12068. Tel: 518-853-3646; Fax: 518-853-3371. Email: katerishrine@nycap.rr.com. Web: www.katerishrine.com. Friar Kevin Kenny, O.F.M.Conv., Shrine Dir. & Guardian; Bro. James Amrhein, O.F.M.Conv., Assoc. Dir.; Friar Patrick Gallagher, O.F.M.Conv., Local Pastor.

[Q] CAMPUS MINISTRY

ALBANY. *New York State University at Albany* , (Albany Collegiate Interfaith Center, Inc.) with offices at Albany-Chapel House., 1400 Washington Ave., 12222. Tel: 518-489-8573; Fax: 518-489-8573. Email: pbutler@uamail.albany.edu. Rev. Paul Butler, Chap.

COBLESKILL. *State University of New York College of Agricultural & Technology at Cobleskill* Main St., P.O. Box 124, 12175. Tel: 518-234-2892. Rev. Thomas F. Berardi.

DELHI. *State University of New York College of Agricultural & Technology at Delhi* St. Peter Rectory, 8 Franklin St., 13753. Tel: 607-746-2503. Rev. Matthew H. Frisoni.

GLENS FALLS. *Adirondack Community College* c/o 40 N. Main Ave., 12203. Tel: 518-793-9677.

HUDSON. *Columbia-Greene Community College* P.O. Box 1000, 12534. Tel: 518-828-4181.

LOUDONVILLE. *Siena College* 12211. Tel: 518-783-2332; Fax: 518-783-2549. Email: ministry@siena.edu. Web: www.siena.edu. Rev. Greg Jakubowicz, O.F.M., Chap.; Diana King, Sec.; Michele Stefanik, Assoc. Campus Min.

ONEONTA. *New York State University at Oneonta and Hartwick College* Newman House, 77 Spruce St., 13820. Tel: 607-432-4400. Email: newmanhouse@stny.rr.com. Web: www.dmcom.net/newmanhouse/. Susan Nesbitt, Campus Min. Tel: 607-432-4400; Maureen DeBonis, Pres. of Foundation & Bd. of Dir.; Michelle Gardner, Office Admin. Corporate Title: Oneonta Newman Foundation.

SARATOGA. *Skidmore College* 815 N. Broadway, 12866. Tel: 518-580-5682; Fax: 518-580-5555. Email: cminnery@skidmore.edu. Catherine W. Minnery, Coord. Catholic Student Life.

SCHENECTADY. *Catholic Chaplain, Union College Silliman Hall*, 807 Union St., 12308-3152. Tel: 518-388-6087. Email: bolandt@union.edu. Web: www.union.edu/studentlife/religious_programs/catholic. Dr. Thomas J. Gutch, Chap.

TROY. *Hudson Valley Community College* 80 Vandenburgh Ave., 12180. Tel: 518-629-7168. Email: langhnan@hvcc.edu. Web: www.hvcc.edu. Sr. Nancy Langhart, O.S.F., Campus Min.

The Rensselaer Newman Foundation RPI Chaplains Office-RU # 3514, 110 Eighth St., 12180. Tel: 518-276-6518; Fax: 518-274-5945. Email: fred@rpi.edu. Web: www.rpi.edu/web/c+cc. Richard M. Hartt, Pres.; Rev. Edward Kacerguis, Chap.

University Parish of Christ Sun of Justice 12180. Tel: 518-274-7793; Fax: 518-274-5945. Rev. Edward Kacerguis.

Chapel + Cultural Center 10 Tom Phelan Pl., 12180. Tel: 518-274-7793; Fax: 518-274-5945. 10 Phelan Pl., 12180.

Russell Sage College Campus Ministry Office, Rm. #304 Student Center, 12180. Tel: 518-244-4507. Email: cuneor@sage.edu. Sr. Rosemary Ann Cuneo, C.R.

[R] MISCELLANEOUS LISTINGS

ALBANY. *Birthright of Albany*, 586 Central Ave., 12206. Tel: 518-438-2978; Fax: 518-438-2978.

Burke Community Service Corp., Inc., 40 N. Main Ave., 12203. Tel: 518-453-6623; Fax: 518-453-6792. Email: noel.olsen@rcda.org.

The Cathedral Restoration Corp., 40 N. Main Ave., 12203. Tel: 518-463-4447; Fax: 518-436-5177. Email: ecathedra@nycap.rr.com. Rev. William H. Pape, Sec. & Treas.

Diocesan AIDS Services, 100 Slingerlands St., 12202. Tel: 518-449-3581; Fax: 518-426-3662.

Diocesan Investment and Loan Trust, 40 N. Main Ave., 12203-1422.

Emmaus House, 45 Trinity Pl., 12202. Tel: 518-482-4966. Albany Catholic Worker Community.

Family Rosary Albany Office, 16 Cornell Ave., 12203. Tel: 518-452-3082; Fax: 518-452-3956. Email: lrhatigan@hcfm.org. Web: www.hcfm.org. Laetitia Rhatigan, Albany Mission Dir. Sponsored by Congregation of Holy Cross (Eastern Prov.)

Crusade for Family Prayer, Inc., North Easton, MA. Tel: 508-238-4095; Fax: 508-238-3953. Rev. John P. Phalen, C.S.C., Pres. Sponsored by Congregation of Holy Cross (Eastern Prov.)

The Foundation of the Roman Catholic Diocese of Albany, New York, Inc., 40 N. Main Ave., 12203. Tel: 518-453-6680; Fax: 518-453-8440.

St. Francis Chapel Wolf Road Shoppers Park, 145A Wolf Rd., 12205. Tel: 518-459-2854; Fax: 518-783-4195. Web: www.TimesUnion/communities/StFrancischapel. Revs. Gerard Lee, O.F.M., Dir. Email: catglee@aol.com; Richard Biasiotto, O.F.M.; Ambrose Donehue, O.F.M.; Reginald J. Reddy, O.F.M.; Gerald R. Mudd, O.F.M. Order of Friars Minor Province of the Most Holy Name of Jesus.

Kenwood Braille Association, Inc., Kenwood Convent of the Sacred Heart, 799 S. Pearl St., 12202. Tel: 518-465-3341; Fax: 518-465-3663. Sr. Priscilla Meier, R.S.C.J., Dir.

Korean Apostolate of the Roman Catholic Diocese of Albany, New York, 80 Slingerland St., 12202. Tel: 518-275-0350.

LaSalle Albany, Inc., Christian Brothers Academy, 12 Airline Rd., 12205. Tel: 518-452-9809; Fax: 518-452-9804. Email: schlegel@cbaalbany.org. Web: www.cbaalbany.org. Mr. James Schlegel, Prin.

The Marillac-N.E. Charitable Trust, 96 Menand Rd., 12204-1499. Tel: 518-462-6096; Fax: 518-462-5192. Email: patbouza@gmail.com.

McCloskey Community Service Corporation, 41 N. Main Ave., 12203. Tel: 518-459-0183; Fax: 518-459-0202. Email: Diocesan.Housing@rcda.org. Deborah Damm O'Brien, Exec. Dir.

Mercy Cares for Kids, 310 S. Manning Blvd., 12208. Tel: 518-525-5437; Fax: 518-525-6514. Web: www.stpetershealthcare.org. Mr. Steven P. Boyle, Pres. & CEO.

Mill Hill Sisters Charitable Trust, 703 Derzee Ct., Delmar, 12054. Tel: 518-512-4362. Email: jdever001@nycap.rr.com.

New York State Catholic Conference, 465 State St., 12203. Tel: 518-434-6195; Fax: 518-434-9796. Email: info@nyscatholic.org. Web: www.nyscatholic.org. Richard E. Barnes, Exec. Dir.

Noonan Community Service Corporation, 40 N. Main Ave., 12203-1422. Tel: 518-453-6641; Fax: 518-453-8454. Rev. Joseph Benintende, Contact Person.

St. Peter's Auxiliary, 315 S. Manning Blvd., 12208. Tel: 518-525-1550; Fax: 518-525-1003. Mr. Steven P. Boyle, Pres. & CEO.

St. Peter's Licensed Home Care Agency, 159 Wolf Rd., 12205. Tel: 518-525-6000; Fax: 518-525-6002. Web: www.stpetershealthcare.org. Mr. Steven P. Boyle, Pres. & CEO.

Sisters of the Holy Names of Jesus & Mary of the New York Province, Inc., 1061 New Scotland Ave., 12208-1198. Tel: 503-675-7125; Fax: 503-675-7138. Email: meholohan@snjmuson.org. Continuing Support Charitable Trust to provide for the needs of the Tutwiler Clinic, Tutwiler, Mississippi.

St. Peter's Hospital Foundation, Inc., 319 S. Manning Blvd., Ste. 309, 12208. Tel: 518-482-4433; Fax: 518-482-4593. Web: www.stpetershealthcare.org. Peter D. Semenza, Exec. Dir.

Support Fund Trust of the Province of St. Thomas of Villanova, c/o 40 N. Main Ave., 12203.

Warde Services Corporation, Inc., 159 Wolf Rd., 12205. Tel: 518-525-1550; Fax: 518-525-1520. Mr. Steven P. Boyle, Pres. & CEO.

CASTLETON ON HUDSON. *Cooperative Christian Ministries of Schodack, Inc. aka CCMS The Anchor* 92 S. Main St., 12033-0092. Tel: 518-732-4120. Formal Name: C.C.M. of Schodack

COHOES. *Apostolate for the Suffering, c/o St. Rita Rectory*, 50 St. Rita Ln., 12047. Tel: 518-237-4444. Rev. John Facci, S.A.C. (Retired).

GERMANTOWN. *Oneness in Peace Center, Inc.*, 49 Main St., 12526. Tel: 518-537-5678; Fax: 518-537-5678. Email: info@onenessinpeace.org. Web: www.onenessinpeace.org. Sr. Vergilia Jim, O.S.F., Co-Dir, Prog. Presenter & Peace Educator; Claire Langie, Co-Dir, Prog. Presenter & Peace Educator.

GUILDERLAND CENTER. *Christ Child Society of Albany*, P.O. Box 423, 12085. Tel: 518-355-0739. Annette Guido, Pres.

LATHAM. *The Sister M. Athanasia Gurry Trust Fund of the Sisters of St. Joseph*, 385 Watervliet-Shaker Rd., 12110-4799. Tel: 518-783-3538; Fax: 518-783-1123.

MECHANICVILLE. *Albany, New York Chapter of Magnificat, Inc.*, 178 George Thompson Rd., 12118.

NISKAYUNA. *Villa Fusco Child Day Care*, 955 Balltown Rd., 12309. Tel: 518-377-1613; Fax: 518-377-1613. Email: fcppschaloux@yahoo.com. Sr. Maria Goretti Chaloux, Supr. Daughters of Charity of the Most Precious Blood. Capacity 14.

NORTH CREEK. *North Country Ministry, Inc., Leaven House*, 32 Circle Ave., P.O. Box 111, 12853. Tel: 518-251-4460; Fax: 518-251-5483. Email: ncm32@frontiernet.net. Bro. James Posluszny, C.S.C., Dir.

RENSSELAER. *Assisi in Albany, Inc.*, 77 St. Francis Pl., 12144. Tel: 518-265-0747; Fax: 518-472-1013. Rev. Anthony Kall, O.F.M.Conv.

Circles of Mercy, Inc., 11 Washington St., Ste. A, 12144. Tel: 518-462-0899; Fax: 518-462-2892. Email: circlesofmercy@nycap.rr.com. Web: www.circlesofmercy.org. Richard S. Zazycki, Dir.

Franciscans in Collaborative Ministry, Inc., 77 St. Francis Pl., 12144. Tel: 518-472-1000; Fax: 518-472-1013. Very Rev. Justin Biase, O.F.M.Conv., Minister Prov.

Franciscorps, Inc., 77 St. Francis Pl., 12144. Tel: 518-472-1000; Fax: 518-472-1013. Email: francorps@gmail.com. Web: www.Franciscanseast.org.

Order of Friars Minor Conventual Immaculate Conception Province Charitable Trust (Established 1990), P.O. Box 629, 12144. Tel: 518-472-1000; Fax: 518-472-1013. Email: brorayl@juno.com. Web: www.Franciscanseast.org. Bro. Raymond Sobosinski, Trustee & Treas.

The Community Hospice Foundation, Inc., 295 Valley View Blvd., 12144. Tel: 518-285-8150; Fax: 518-285-8192. Web: www.communityhospice.org. Ronald F. Watson, Pres. & CEO.

SCHENECTADY. *Secular Order of Discalced Carmelites*, P.O. Box 408, 12301. Tel: 518-393-5027. Email: carmel1352@localnet.com. Pamela Taranto, Pres.

TROY. *Catholic School Administrators' Association of New York State*, 406 Fulton St., Ste. 512, 12180. Tel: 518-273-1205; Fax: 518-273-1206. Email: nysadm@csdsl.net; csaanys@csdsl.net. Web: www.csaanys.org. Carol Geddis, Exec. Dir.

Seton Auxiliary, Inc., 1300 Massachusetts Ave., 12180. Tel: 518-268-5505. Email: amarsolais@setonhealth.org. Web: setonhealth.org. Anne Marsolais, Dir.

Seton Health Foundation, Inc., 1300 Massachusetts Ave., P.O. Box 985, 12180. Tel: 518-268-5503; Fax: 518-268-5799. Email: msteiner@setonhealth.org. Web: setonhealth.org. Marica M. Steiner, Exec. Dir.

Seton Licensed Home Care, Inc., 70-102nd St., 12180. Tel: 518-233-1802. Email: kmelkun@setonhealth.org. Web: setonhealth.org. Kathy Melkun, Exec. Dir.

[S] SUMMER CAMPS

ALBANY. *Camp Scully*, 40 N. Main Ave., 12203. Tel: 518-453-6613; 518-283-1617 (Synders Lake); Fax: 518-453-6792 (Synders Lake). Web: campscully.squarespace.com. *Summer Address*, 24 Camp Scully Way, Wynantskill, 12198. Tel: 518-283-1617. A program of Catholic Charities of Albany County; Summer Residential Camp for children 7-17. Under direction of Catholic Charities of the Diocese of Albany. Financed by local Youth Bureaus, the Albany Catholic Diocese, USDA Summer Program and by contributions. Capacity 110.

TROY. *Troy CYO Day Camp*, 237 Fourth St., Box 867, 12180. Tel: 518-274-2630; Fax: 518-274-2734.

Raymond R. Piscitelli, Exec. Dir. Sponsored by Troy Youth Organization, Inc. for Boys and Girls, ages 5-12 yrs.

RELIGIOUS INSTITUTES OF MEN REPRESENTED IN THE DIOCESE

For further details refer to the corresponding bracketed number in the Religious Institutes of Men or Women section.

[0140]—*The Augustinians*—O.S.A.
[0330]—*Brothers of the Christian Schools* (New York Prov.)—F.S.C.
[0600]—*Brothers of the Congregation of Holy Cross* (Eastern Prov.)—C.S.C.
[0310]—*Congregation of Christian Brothers* (Eastern US)—C.F.C.
[1330]—*Congregation of the Mission* (Eastern Prov.)—C.M.
[]—*Franciscan Friars* (Immaculate Conception Prov.)—O.F.M.
[0480]—*Friars Minor Conventual* (Prov. of Immaculate Conception)—O.F.M.Conv.
[0690]—*Jesuit Fathers and Brothers* (New York Prov.)—S.J.
[0720]—*The Missionaries of Our Lady of La Salette* (Prov. of Our Lady of Seven Dolors)—M.S.
[0520]—*Order of Friars Minor* (Most Holy Name Prov.)—O.F.M.
[1070]—*Redemptorist Fathers* (Baltimore Prov.)—C.SS.R.

RELIGIOUS INSTITUTES OF WOMEN REPRESENTED IN THE DIOCESE

[0330]—*Carmelite Sisters for the Aged and Infirm*—O.Carm.
[2980]—*Congregation of Notre Dame*—C.N.D.
[0760]—*Daughters of Charity of St. Vincent de Paul*—D.C.
[0740]—*Daughters of Charity of the Most Precious Blood*—D.C.P.B.
[1070-17]—*Dominican Sisters - Congregation of St. Catherine de Ricci*—O.P.
[1105]—*Dominican Sisters of Hope*—O.P.
[1170]—*Felician Sisters*—C.S.S.F.
[1180]—*Franciscan Sisters of Allegany, New York*—O.S.F.
[1190]—*Franciscan Sisters of the Atonement*—S.A.
[2340]—*Little Sisters of the Poor*—L.S.P.
[2070]—*Religious of the Holy Union of the Sacred Hearts*—S.U.S.C.
[4180]—*Religious Venerini Sisters*—M.P.V.
[2970]—*School Sisters of Notre Dame*—S.S.N.D.
[2150]—*Sister Servants of the Immaculate Heart of Mary* (Michigan)—I.H.M.
[2160]—*Sister Servants of the Immaculate Heart of Mary* (Pennsylvania)—I.H.M.
[2575]—*Sisters of Mercy of the Americas* (Albany)—R.S.M.
[2990]—*Sisters of Notre Dame de Namur*—S.N.D.
[3830-14]—*Sisters of St. Joseph of Rochester*
[1660]—*Sisters of St. Francis of the Providence of God*—O.S.F.
[3840]—*Sisters of St. Joseph of Carondelet*—C.S.J.
[1830]—*Sisters of the Good Shepherd of Mary*—R.G.S.
[1990]—*Sisters of the Holy Names of Jesus and Mary*—S.N.J.M.
[3320]—*Sisters of the Presentation of the B.V.M.*—P.B.V.M.
[3480]—*Sisters of the Resurrection*—C.R.
[4070]—*Society of the Sacred Heart*—R.S.C.J.

DIOCESAN CEMETERIES

COHOES. *St. Agnes Cemetery*, St. Agnes Hwy., 12047. Tel: 518-463-0134.

COLONIE. *St. Patrick Cemetery*, Troy Rd., 12205. Tel: 518-463-0134.

GLENMONT. *Our Lady Help of Christians Cemetery*, Mailing Address: 48 Cemetery Ave., Menands, 12204. Jolley Rd., 12077. Tel: 518-463-0134.

GLENVILLE. *St. Anthony Cemetery*, Glenridge Rd., Schenectady, 12302. Tel: 518-374-5319.

MENANDS. *St. Agnes Cemetery*, 48 Cemetery Ave., 12204. Tel: 518-463-0134; Fax: 518-427-8035. Web: rcdacemeteries.org.

ROTTERDAM. *Holy Cross Cemetery*, Mailing Address: 2501 Troy-Schenectady Rd., Schenectady, 12309. Dunnsville Rd., 12306. Tel: 518-374-5319.

SCHENECTADY. *St. Cyril & St. Methodius Cemetery*, Mailing Address: 2501 Troy-Schenectady Rd., 12309. Duanesburg Rd., Rotterdam, 12306. Tel: 518-374-5319.

St. Mary's Cemetery, Mailing Address: 2501 Troy-Schenectady Rd., 12309. McClellan St., 12304. Tel: 518-374-3519.

Most Holy Redeemer Cemetery, 2501 Troy Rd., 12309. Tel: 518-374-5319. Email: putortit@rcda.org. Web: rcdacemeteries.org.

TROY. *St. Jean Baptiste Cemetery*, Mailing Address: 48 Cemetery Ave., Menands, 12204. Spring Ave. Rd., 12180. Tel: 518-463-0134. Web: rcdacemeteries.org.

St. John Cemetery, Gurley Ave., 12180. Tel: 518-272-0931.

St. Mary's Cemetery of Troy, Inc., 79 Brunswick Rd., 12180. Tel: 518-463-0134. Web: rcdacemeteries.org.

NECROLOGY

† Jones, Rev. Msgr. John L., (Retired)—Died July 10, 2009
† Bondi, Paul, (Retired)—Died Feb. 27, 2009
† Ciani, Francis P., (Retired)—Died March 7, 2009
† Czechowicz, Walter, (Retired)—Died May 11, 2009
† Delos, Bernard M., (Retired)—Died Aug. 20, 2009
† Jillisky, William F., (Retired)—Died Aug. 27, 2009
† Lemoyne, William, (Retired)—Died Aug. 15, 2009
† Nugent, Robert, (Retired)—Died April 14, 2009
† Polewczak, Michael J., (On Duty Outside the Diocese)—Died June 23, 2009
† Zakens, Michael W., Albany, NY St. Mary—Died April 29, 2009

An asterisk (*) denotes an organization that has established tax-exempt status directly with the IRS and is not covered by the USCCB Group Ruling.

Diocese of Alexandria

(Dioecesis Alexandrina in Louisiana)

Most Reverend

RONALD P. HERZOG

Bishop of Alexandria; ordained June 1, 1968; appointed Bishop of Alexandria October 27, 2004; ordained and installed January 5, 2005. *Mailing Address: P.O. Box 7417, Alexandria, LA 71306-0417.* Tel: 318-445-6424, Ext. 201; Fax: 318-767-1230. Email: rherzog@diocesealex.org.

Chancery Office: 4400 Coliseum Blvd., P.O. Box 7417, Alexandria, LA 71306. Tel: 318-445-2401 (Receptionist); 318-445-6424 (Auto Attendant); Fax: 318-448-6121.

Web: www.diocesealex.org

ERECTED AS DIOCESE OF NATCHITOCHES JULY 29, 1853.

Square Miles 11,108.

Transferred to Alexandria August 6, 1910 and became Diocese of Alexandria.

Redesignated Diocese of Alexandria-Shreveport on January 12, 1977; split, forming two Dioceses, the Diocese of Alexandria and the Diocese of Shreveport as of June 16, 1986.

Comprises the Counties (parishes) of Rapides, Avoyelles, Concordia, Catahoula, LaSalle, Grant, Natchitoches, Vernon, Tensas, Caldwell, Winn, Franklin and Madison.

For legal titles of parishes and diocesan institutions, consult the Chancery Office.

STATISTICAL OVERVIEW

Personnel	
Bishop	1
Priests: Diocesan Active in Diocese	32
Priests: Diocesan Active Outside Diocese	5
Priests: Retired, Sick or Absent	18
Number of Diocesan Priests	55
Religious Priests in Diocese	14
Total Priests in Diocese	69
Extern Priests in Diocese	18
Ordinations:	
Transitional Deacons	2
Permanent Deacons in Diocese	6
Total Brothers	4
Total Sisters	32
Parishes	
Parishes	49
With Resident Pastor:	
Resident Diocesan Priests	27
Resident Religious Priests	5
Without Resident Pastor:	
Administered by Priests	17
Missions	23
Professional Ministry Personnel:	
Lay Ministers	15
Welfare	
Catholic Hospitals	1
Total Assisted	210,657
Health Care Centers	1
Total Assisted	350
Special Centers for Social Services	8
Total Assisted	840
Residential Care of Disabled	2
Total Assisted	308
Other Institutions	1
Total Assisted	57,990
Educational	
Diocesan Students in Other Seminaries	12
Total Seminarians	12
High Schools, Diocesan and Parish	3
Total Students	684
Elementary Schools, Diocesan and Parish	7
Total Students	1,925
Catechesis/Religious Education:	
High School Students	1,028
Elementary Students	2,144
Total Students under Catholic Instruction	5,793
Teachers in the Diocese:	
Brothers	3
Sisters	8
Lay Teachers	185
Vital Statistics	
Receptions into the Church:	
Infant Baptism Totals	660
Minor Baptism Totals	103
Adult Baptism Totals	48
Received into Full Communion	152
First Communions	600
Confirmations	465
Marriages:	
Catholic	130
Interfaith	64
Total Marriages	194
Deaths	520
Total Catholic Population	44,003
Total Population	387,579

Former Bishops—Rt. Revs. AUGUSTUS M. MARTIN, ord. May 31, 1828; cons. Nov. 30, 1853; died Sept. 29, 1875; FRANCIS XAVIER LERAY, ord. March 19, 1852; cons. Bishop of Natchitoches, April 22, 1877; named Bishop of Janopolis, Coadjutor of New Orleans, and Administrator of Natchitoches, Oct. 23, 1879; promoted to the See of New Orleans, Dec. 1883; died Sept. 23, 1887; ANTHONY DURIER, D.D., ord. 1856; cons. March 19, 1885; died Feb. 28, 1904; Most Revs. CORNELIUS VAN DE VEN, ord. May 31, 1890; cons. Nov. 30, 1904; made assistant at the Pontifical Throne, Nov. 12, 1929; died May 8, 1932; DANIEL FRANCIS DESMOND, D.D., ord. June 9, 1911; cons. Bishop of Alexandria Jan. 5, 1933; died Sept. 11, 1945; CHARLES P. GRECO, D.D., ord. July 25, 1918; cons. Feb. 25, 1946; retired May 22, 1973; died Jan. 20, 1987; LAWRENCE P. GRAVES, D.D., J.C.L., ord. June 11, 1942; cons. April 25, 1969; installed Bishop of Alexandria, Sept. 18, 1973; retired July 14, 1982; died Jan. 15, 1994; WILLIAM B. FRIEND, ord. Oct. 30, 1979; installed Bishop of Alexandria-Shreveport Jan. 11, 1983; then after Diocese of Alexandria-Shreveport was divided into two dioceses June 16, 1986; installed Bishop of Shreveport July 30, 1986; JOHN C. FAVALORA, ord. Dec. 20, 1961; appt. Bishop of Alexandria June 16, 1986; ord. and installed July 29, 1986; installed Bishop of St. Petersburg May 16, 1989; installed Archbishop of Miami Dec. 20, 1994; SAM G. JACOBS, ord. June 6, 1964; appt. Bishop of Alexandria July 1, 1989; ord. and installed Aug. 24, 1989; appt. Bishop of Houma-Thibodaux Aug. 1, 2003; installed Oct. 10, 2003.

St. Joseph Catholic Center—Diocese of Alexandria, 4400 Coliseum Blvd., Alexandria, 71303-3597. Mailing Address: P.O. Box 7417, Alexandria, 71306-0417. Tel: 318-445-2401 Receptionist; 318-445-6424 Auto-Attendant; Fax: 318-448-6121. Web: www.diocesealex.org. Office Hours: Mon.-Thurs. 8-5, Fri. 8-12:30.

All offices as above unless listed otherwise. Send requests for matrimonial dispensations to the Diocesan Tribunal

Coordinating Staff

Vicar General—Rev. STEPHEN SCOTT CHEMINO, V.G., J.C.L. Tel: 318-445-6424, Ext. 202. Email: frschemino@diocesealex.org.

Moderator of the Curia—Rev. BRUCE MILLER, J.C.L., M.C., J.V. Tel: 318-445-6424, Ext. 261; Fax: 318-767-0872. Email: frbmiller@diocesealex.org.

Director of Catholic Charities and Special Ministries—(family life and worship) Rev. RICKEY J. GREMILLION, Chief Technology Officer. Tel: 318-445-6424, Ext. 226. Email: frgrem@diocesealex.org.

Superintendent of Catholic Schools—Sr. ANN LACOUR, M.S.C. Tel: 318-445-6424, Ext. 227. Email: annlacour@diocesealex.org.

Director of Development and Public Affairs—ANN MASDEN. Tel: 318-445-6424, Ext. 209. Email: amasden@diocesealex.org.

Chief Financial Officer—DAVID BROOK. Tel: 318-445-6424, Ext. 215. Email: dbrook@diocesealex.org.

Director of Pastoral Planning and Lay Ecclesial Ministry—Rev. STEPHEN SCOTT CHEMINO, V.G., J.C.L. Tel: 318-445-6424, Ext. 202. Email: frschemino@diocesealex.org.

Director of Personnel—PATRICK MCCUSKER. Tel: 318-445-6424, Ext. 206. Email: pmccusker@diocesealex.org.

Director of Religious Formation and Training—(includes youth ministry and Steubenville Conference) CHRISTINA THERIOT. Tel: 318-445-6424, Ext. 221. Email: ctheriot@diocesealex.org.

Secretary to the Bishop—DEBORAH DEOROSAN. Tel: 318-445-6424, Ext. 201. Email: ddeorosan@diocesealex.org.

Other Diocesan Services

Archivist and Chancellor—Rev. Msgr. JOSEPH M. SUSI (Retired). Tel: 318-445-6424, Ext. 208. Email: msgrjsusi@diocesealex.org.

Vicar for Clergy—Rev. CRAIG SCOTT, Mailing Address: P.O. Box 7056, Alexandria, 71306-0056. Tel: 318-445-7141, Ext. 12. Email: frcscott@strita.org.

Communications—ANN MASDEN, Communications Dir. Tel: 318-445-6424, Ext. 210. Email: amasden@diocesealex.org; JEANNIE PETRUS, Editor of The Church Today & Coord. Evangelization. Tel: 318-445-6424, Ext. 255. Email: jpetrus@diocesealex.org.

Continuing Education of the Clergy—Rev. ADAM FREDERICK TRAVIS, Mailing Address: P.O. Box 7056, Alexandria, 71306-0056. Email: fathertravis@gmail.com.

Diaconate Program—Rev. DANIEL O'CONNOR, V.F., Dir., 401 21st St., Alexandria, 71301-6500. Tel: 318-445-9748, Ext. 16. Email: frdan@bellsouth.net.

Diocesan Tribunal— (canonical services) PATRICIA THOMAS, Moderator of the Tribunal Chancery. Tel: 318-445-6424, Ext. 263; Fax: 318-767-0872. Email: pthomas@diocesealex.org.

Judges—Revs. BRUCE MILLER, J.C.L., M.C., J.V. Tel: 318-445-6424, Ext. 263. Email: frbmiller@diocesealex.org; ALBI G. MULLOTH, J.C.L., A.J.V. Tel: 318-445-6424, Ext. 229. Email: fralbi@diocesealex.org; STEPHEN SCOTT CHEMINO, V.G., J.C.L. Tel: 318-445-6424, Ext. 223. Email: frschemino@diocesealex.org.

Defender of the Bond and Promoter of Justice—Rev. JAMES A. FERGUSON, J.C.L. Tel: 318-445-6424, Ext.

265. Email: frjferguson@diocesealex.org.
Notary—MARY ANN MANUEL. Tel: 318-445-6424, Ext. 262. Email: mmanuel@diocesealex.org.
Hispanic Ministry—Mr. JOSE COLLS, Mailing Address: P.O. Box 7417, Alexandria, 71306-0417. Tel: 318-445-6424, Ext. 258. Email: jcolls@diocesealex.org; Rev. MARTIN L. LAIRD.
Liturgy Commission—Rev. JOSE A. ROBLES-SANCHEZ, Chm., 2211 E. Texas Ave., Alexandria, 71301-4207. Tel: 318-445-4588. Email: frjose@cabrinichurch.com.
Maryhill Renewal Center—Mr. PAUL ANDRIES, Property Mgr., 600 Maryhill Rd., Pineville, 71360-4196. Tel: 318-640-1378; 318-792-1570. Email: cnorris@diocesealex.org.
Protection of Children—
Program Director—PATRICK MCCUSKER. Tel: 318-445-6424, Ext. 206. Email: pmccusker@diocesealex.org.
Victim Assistance Minister—MARY GIRARD, L.M.F.T., L.P.C., 5501 C John Eskew Blvd., Alexandria, 71303-3725. Tel: 318-449-8571, Ext. 13.
Administrator and Assessor, Code of Pastoral Conduct—Rev. STEPHEN SCOTT CHEMINO, V.G., J.C.L. Tel: 318-445-6424, Ext. 223. Email: frschemino@diocesealex.org.
Coordinator for Religious—VACANT.
Vocations and Seminarians—Revs. KENNETH J. MICHIELS, Dir.; BLAKE PAUL DESHAUTELLE, Assoc. Dir., Mailing Address: 105 South St., Leesville, 71446. Tel: 337-239-2656. Email: stmichaelschurch@bellsouth.net.
College of Consultors—Revs. ANTONY AELAVANTHARA, V.F.; FERREOLUS D'CRUZ, V.F.; JAMES A. FERGUSON, J.C.L.; Rev. Msgr. RONALD C. HOPPE (Retired); Revs. KENNETH J. MICHIELS; BRUCE MILLER, J.C.L., M.C., J.V.; DANIEL P. O'CONNOR, V.F.; Rev. Msgrs. JOSEPH M. SUSI, Chancellor (Retired); STEVE J. TESTA, V.F.
Presbyteral Council—Elected Members: Revs. JAMES A. FERGUSON, J.C.L.; RYAN P. HUMPHRIES; KEITH E. ISHMAEL; DWIGHT DE JESUS; HAROLD IMAMSHAH; CHAD A. PARTAIN; DANIEL P. O'CONNOR, V.F. Appointed Members: Revs. ANTONY AELAVANTHARA, V.F.; FERREOLUS D'CRUZ, V.F.; KENNETH J. MICHIELS, Vice Chm.; LOUIS E. SKLAR; CRAIG SCOTT, Vicar for Clergy; Rev. Msgrs. STEVE J. TESTA, V.F.; JOSEPH M. SUSI, Chancellor (Retired). Ex Officio: Rev. STEPHEN SCOTT CHEMINO, V.G., J.C.L., Ex Officio.
Deans—Revs. ANTONY AELAVANTHARA, V.F., Natchitoches Deanery; FERREOLUS D'CRUZ, V.F., Eastern Deanery; DANIEL P. O'CONNOR, V.F., Central Deanery; Rev. Msgr. STEVE J. TESTA, V.F., Avoyelles Deanery.

Diocesan Representatives

Boy Scouts of America—
Region 5 Chaplain—Rev. CHARLES J. MORGAN, Mailing Address: P.O. Box 9, Plaucheville, 71362-0009. Tel: 318-922-3131.
Diocesan, Region 5 & Louisiana Purchase Council Chaplain—Rev. STEPHEN J. BRANDOW, Mailing Address: P.O. Box 39, Tioga, 71477-0039. Tel: 318-473-0010, Ext. 2539.
Catholic Relief Services—Rev. RICKEY J. GREMILLION. Tel: 318-445-6424, Ext. 226. Email: frgrem@diocesealex.org.
Louisiana Interchurch Council—Rev. STEPHEN SCOTT CHEMINO, V.G., J.C.L., Ecumenical Liaison. Tel: 318-445-6424, Ext. 202. Email: frschemino@diocesealex.org.
Holy Childhood Association—Rev. Msgr. STEVE J. TESTA, V.F., Dir. Tel: 318-445-6424, Ext. 225.
Propagation of the Faith and Foreign Mission Education—Rev. Msgr. STEVE J. TESTA, V.F., Dir. Tel: 318-445-6424, Ext. 225.

CLERGY, PARISHES, MISSIONS AND PAROCHIAL SCHOOLS

CITY OF ALEXANDRIA

(RAPIDES PARISH)
1—ST. FRANCIS XAVIER CATHEDRAL (1834) Revs. James A. Ferguson, Rector; Peter A. Faulk.
Res.: 626 Fourth St., 71301-8424. Tel: 318-445-1451; Fax: 318-445-1433. Email: info@sfxcathedral.org. Web: www.sfxcathedral.org.
Catechesis/Religious Program—Students 18.
2—ST. FRANCES XAVIER CABRINI (1947) Revs. Jose A. Robles-Sanchez (Puerto Rico); Thomas Elmus Paul.
Office: 2211 E. Texas Ave., 71301-4207. Tel: 318-445-4588; Fax: 318-443-7156.
Res.: 2012 Wedgewood Ave., 71301. Tel: 318-445-4588; Fax: 318-443-7156. Web: www.cabrinichurch.com.
School—(Grades PreK-8), 2215 E. Texas Ave., 71301. Tel: 318-448-3333; Fax: 318-448-3343. Web: www.cabrinischool.com. Joseph Wiederholt, Prin. Lay Teachers 14; Students 140.
Catechesis/Religious Program—Students 94.
3—ST. JAMES MEMORIAL (1911) Rev. Remigius Owuamanam, S.M.M.M. (Nigeria).
Res.: 900 Daspit St., 71302.
Church: 714 Winn St., 71301. Tel: 318-487-9512; Fax: 318-445-9826.
Catechesis/Religious Program—Students 24.
4—ST. JULIANA (1959) Rev. Remigius Owuamanam, S.M.M.M. (Nigeria).
Res.: 900 Daspit St., 71302-5343. Tel: 318-445-6700; Fax: 318-445-9826.
Catechesis/Religious Program—Students 38.
5—OUR LADY OF PROMPT SUCCOR (1947) Revs. Daniel P. O'Connor; Martin L. Laird. In Res., Rev. Christudas Nayak (India).
Res.: 401 21st St., 71301-7022. Tel: 318-445-3693; Fax: 318-445-8471. Email: olpsc@bellsouth.net. Web: www.olpschurch.org.
School—(Grades PreK-6), 420 21st St., 71301. Tel: 318-487-1862; Fax: 318-473-9321. Email: olpsoffice@promptsuccor.org. Jo Tassin, Prin.; Jackie Whitcher, Librarian. Lay Teachers 33; Students 519.
Catechesis/Religious Program—Paul Hood, D.R.E. Students 192.
6—ST. RITA (1940) Revs. Michael Craig Scott, V.C.; Adam Frederick Travis.
Mailing Address: P.O. Box 7056, 71306.
Office: 3822 Bayou Rapides Rd., 71303. Tel: 318-445-7120; Fax: 318-448-0704. Email: strita@strita.org. Web: www.strita.org.
Res.: 214 N. 17th St., 71301. Tel: 318-445-7120.
Church: 4401 Bayou Rapides Rd., 71303. Tel: 318-448-9599.
Child Development Center—1005 Seip Dr., 71303. Tel: 318-448-9999; Fax: 318-445-3003. Email: cdc@strita.org.
Catechesis/Religious Program—Tel: 318-445-7141, Ext. 15. Sr. Nell Murray, M.S.C., D.R.E. Students 148.

OUTSIDE THE CITY OF ALEXANDRIA

BELLEDEAU, AVOYELLES PARISH, ST. MARTIN OF TOURS (1950) [CEM] Rev. Edwin Rodriguez-Hernandez (Puerto Rico). In Res., Rev. Daniel Corkery (Ireland) (Retired).
Res.: P.O. Box 98, Hessmer, 71341-4234.
Catechesis/Religious Program—Tel: 318-563-8772. Roxanna Moreau, D.R.E. Students 28.
BORDELONVILLE, AVOYELLES PARISH, ST. PETER (1903) [CEM] Rev. Msgr. Steve J. Testa.
Mailing Address: P.O. Box 31, 71320-0031.
Res.: 4702 Hwy. 451, 71320-0031. Tel: 318-997-2151; Fax: 318-997-2159. Email: stpeter@cebridge.net.
Catechesis/Religious Program—Tel: 318-997-2502. Rachel Rachal, D.R.E. Students 38.
BOYCE, RAPIDES PARISH, ST. MARGARET (1936) Rev. Kurian Zachariah (India).
Res.: 402 Ryan St., 71409. Tel: 318-793-8811; Fax: 318-793-8815.
Mission—St. Cyril Flatwoods, Rapides Parish.
Mission—St. Margaret Mary Gorum, Natchitoches Parish.
BROUILLETTE, AVOYELLES PARISH, ST. GENEVIEVE (1953) [CEM] Rev. Jose Pallipurath, O.S.B.Silv. (India).
Res.: 4052 Hwy. 452, Marksville, 71351-3530. Tel: 318-253-9237; Fax: 318-253-0703.
Catechesis/Religious Program—Cindy Dupuy, D.R.E. Students 35.
BUNKIE, AVOYELLES PARISH, ST. ANTHONY OF PADUA (1904) [CEM] Rev. Jack H. Michalchuk (Canada).
Res.: 409 St. John St., P.O. Box 719, 71322-0719. Tel: 318-346-7274; Fax: 318-346-7475. Email: stanthonyscatho@bellsouth.net. Web: stanthony_bunkie.org.
School—(Grades PreK-8), 116 S. Knoll St., 71322. Tel: 318-346-2739; Fax: 318-346-9191. Martha Coulon, Prin. Sisters 2; Lay Teachers 13; Students 243.
Catechesis/Religious Program—Karen McCoy, D.R.E. Students 49.
CAMPTI, NATCHITOCHES PARISH, NATIVITY OF THE BLESSED VIRGIN MARY (1831) [CEM 3] Rev. Robert Garrione.
Res.: 119 Tally St., 71411. Tel: 318-476-2116; Fax: 318-476-2815.
Mission—St. Joseph Trichel, Natchitoches Parish.
Mission—Our Lady of the Holy Rosary Black Lake, Natchitoches Parish.
Catechesis/Religious Program—Students 21.
CHENEYVILLE, RAPIDES PARISH, ST. JOSEPH (1966) [CEM] Rev. S. Scott Chemino.
Res.: P.O. Box 446, 71325-0446. Tel: 318-279-2394; Fax: 318-279-2394.
CLOUTIERVILLE, NATCHITOCHES PARISH, ST. JOHN THE BAPTIST (1816) [CEM] Revs. Harold Imamshah (Trinidad and Tobago); Kenneth Obrikwe (Nigeria), Pastoral Admin.
Mailing Address: P.O. Box 40, 71416-0040.
Res.: 423 Hwy. 495, 71416-0040. Tel: 318-379-2231; Fax: 318-379-2236.
Catechesis/Religious Program—Students 40.
Mission—Holy Rosary Emmanuel, Natchitoches Parish.
Mission—Holy Family Monet Ferry, Natchitoches Parish.
COLFAX, GRANT PARISH, ST. JOSEPH (1897) Rev. Matthew Thayil, M.S.F.S. (India).
Res.: 139 Second St., P.O. Box 243, 71417-0243. Tel: 318-627-5442; Fax: 318-627-3011.
Mission—St. Patrick P.O. Box 243, Montgomery, Grant Parish 71417. Tel: 318-542-2332.
Catechesis/Religious Program—Students 25.
COTTONPORT, AVOYELLES PARISH, ST. MARY ASSUMPTION (1889) [CEM 4] Rev. Anthony Dharmaraj, M.S.F.S. (India).
Mailing Address: P.O. Box 1123, 71327-1123. In Res., Rev. Blake Paul Deshautelle.
Res.: 820 Front St., 71327-1123. Tel: 318-876-3681; Fax: 318-876-3686. Email: stmarychurch@kricket.net.
School—(Grades PreK-8) Tel: 318-876-3651; Fax: 318-876-2955. Email: smsangels@kricket.net. Gale Jeansonne, Prin. Lay Teachers 12; Students 243.
Catechesis/Religious Program—Students 108.
DEVILLE, RAPIDES PARISH, ST. JOHN THE BAPTIST (1942) [CEM 2] Revs. John O'Brien (Canada); Joy Antony Retnazihamoni (India); Peter Kuligowski (Poland).
Res.: 1024 Hwy. 1207, P.O. Box 7, 71328-0007. Tel: 318-466-5587; Fax: 318-466-5265.
Catechesis/Religious Program—Students 188.
Mission—Sts. Francis and Anne Kolin, Rapides Parish.
Mission—St. Winifred Effie, Avoyelles Parish.
DUPONT, AVOYELLES PARISH, IMMACULATE CONCEPTION (1945) [CEM] Rev. Charles J. Morgan.
Res.: P.O. Box 385, 71329-0385. Tel: 318-922-3243.
Catechesis/Religious Program—Tel: 318-922-3707. Angie Dixon, D.R.E. Students 25.
ECHO, RAPIDES PARISH, ST. FRANCIS DE SALES (1894) [CEM] Rev. S. Scott Chemino.
Res.: P.O. Box 37, 71330-0037. Tel: 318-563-4530; Fax: 318-563-4530.
Catechesis/Religious Program—Tel: 318-564-4340. Students 82.
EVERGREEN, AVOYELLES PARISH, LITTLE FLOWER (1928) [CEM 2] Rev. Bartholomew Ibe (Nigeria).
Mailing Address: P.O. Box 20, 71333-0020.
Res.: 2912 Main St., 71333-0020. Tel: 318-346-2840; Fax: 318-346-4989. Email: litflowr@bellsouth.net.
Catechesis/Religious Program—Students 8.
Mission—St. Charles Goudeau, Avoyelles Parish.
FERRIDAY, CONCORDIA PARISH, ST. PATRICK (1952) [JC] Rev. Louis E. Sklar.
Res.: P.O. Box 369, 71334. Tel: 318-757-3834.
Mission—St. Gerard P.O. Box 863, Jonesville, Catahoula Parish 71343. Tel: 318-339-6143.
GLENMORA, RAPIDES PARISH, ST. LOUIS (1941) Rev. Binochan Pallipparambil, O.S.B.Silv. (India).
Res.: 826 8th St., P.O. Box 636, 71433-0636. Tel: 318-748-8324.
Catechesis/Religious Program—Students 37.
Mission—St. Peter [CEM] Elmer, Rapides Parish.
Mission—St. Jude Sieper, Rapides Parish.
HESSMER, AVOYELLES PARISH, ST. ALPHONSUS (1898) [CEM] Rev. Edwin Rodriguez-Hernandez (Puerto Rico).
Mailing Address: P.O. Box 66, 71341-0066.
Res.: 3659 Main St., 71341-0066. Tel: 318-563-4550; Fax: 318-563-8395.
Catechesis/Religious Program—Tel: 318-563-8529. Tina Laborde, D.R.E. Students 144.
ISLE BREVELLE, NATCHITOCHES PARISH, ST. AUGUSTINE'S (1856) [CEM] Rev. Jacob Thomas (India).
Res.: 2262 Hwy. 484, Natchez, 71456-3622. Tel: 318-379-2521; Fax: 318-379-6085.
Catechesis/Religious Program—Tommy Roque, D.R.E. Students 50.
Mission—St. Charles Bermuda, Natchitoches Parish.
Mission—St. Anne Old River, Natchitoches Parish.
JENA, LASALLE PARISH, ST. MARY (1949) Rev. Keith E. Ishmael.
Mailing Address: P.O. Box 2240, 71342. Tel: 318-992-1019; Fax: 318-765-2530.
Catechesis/Religious Program—Students 43.
Mission—St. Edward Fishville, Grant Parish 71467. P.O. Box 669, Pollock, 71467. Tel: 318-765-3798.
LECOMPTE, RAPIDES PARISH, ST. MARTIN (1860) Rev. Pedro J. Sierra-Posada (Colombia).
Res.: 1904 Union St., P.O. Box 459, 71346-0459. Tel: 318-776-5980; Fax: 318-776-9921. Email: stmartinscatholi@bellsouth.net. Web: www.diocesealex.org/stmartin.
Catechesis/Religious Program—Tel: 318-748-7389;

Fax: 318-748-7389. Kim Litton, D.R.E. Students 42.
Mission—Our Lady of Guadalupe 10 Butter Cemetery Rd., P.O. Box 370, Forest Hill, Rapides Parish 71430. Tel: 318-308-9021.
Catechesis/Religious Program—Tel: 318-448-1068. Students 75.

LEESVILLE, VERNON PARISH, ST. MICHAEL (1946) Rev. Kenneth J. Michiels.
Res.: 202 W. Harriet, 71446. Tel: 337-239-2670; Fax: 337-239-2657.
Catechesis/Religious Program—Tel: 337-238-4941. Tammy Cecil, D.R.E. Students 160.

MANSURA, AVOYELLES PARISH

1—OUR LADY OF PROMPT SUCCOR (1937) Rev. Jose Palathara, C.M.I. (India).
Res.: 1910 Escude St., P.O. Box 67, 71350-0067. Tel: 318-964-2654; Fax: 318-964-5469.
Catechesis/Religious Program—Students 8.

2—ST. PAUL THE APOSTLE (1796) [CEM] Rev. Chad A. Partain.
Mailing Address: P.O. Box 130, 71350-0130.
Res.: 1879 Leglise St., 71350-0130. Tel: 318-964-2921; Fax: 318-964-2921.
Catechesis/Religious Program—Students 72.

MARKSVILLE, AVOYELLES PARISH

1—HOLY GHOST (1919) [CEM 2] Rev. Ignatius A. Ibe, S.M.M.M. (Nigeria).
Res.: 121 S. Preston St., 71351-3034. Tel: 318-253-7131; Fax: 318-253-7136. Email: holyghostchur783@bellsouth.net.
Catechesis/Religious Program—Students 81.
Mission—St. Richard, Avoyelles Parish 71351.

2—ST. JOSEPH'S (1869) [CEM 2] Revs. Rusty P. Rabalais; Jose Pallipurath, O.S.B.Silv. (India).
Res.: 141 S. Washington, 71351-3025. Tel: 318-253-7561 (Office); Fax: 318-253-8871. Email: stjosephofc@kricket.net.
Catechesis/Religious Program—Students 204.

3—OUR LADY OF LOURDES (1948) [CEM 4] Rev. Paul Kunnumpuram, M.S.F.S. (India).
Res.: 1315 Eggbend Rd., 71351-4223. Tel: 318-253-9936; Fax: 318-253-6300. Email: lourdeschurch@bellsouth.net.
Mission—St. John the Baptist Moncla, Avoyelles Parish.
Catechesis/Religious Program—Students 111.

MOREAUVILLE, AVOYELLES PARISH

1—OUR LADY OF SORROWS (1944) [CEM] Rev. Marc A. Noel (Canada).
Mailing Address: P.O. Box 247, 71355-0247.
Res.: 524 Main St., 71355-0247. Tel: 318-985-2968. Email: ladyofsorrow@cebridge.net.
Catechesis/Religious Program—Students 9.

2—SACRED HEART (1860) [CEM] Rev. Marc A. Noel (Canada).
Res.: 9986 Bayou Des Glaises St., 71355-9702. Tel: 318-985-2774; Fax: 318-985-2397. Email: shc_moreauville@yahoo.com. Web: www.shcmoreauville.org.
School—(Grades PreK-8), 9968 Bayou Des Glaises, P.O. Box 179, 71355. Tel: 318-985-2772; Fax: 318-985-2164. Email: shs@kricket.net. Sr. Anthony Castellani, O.L.S., Prin.; Deborah Veade, Librarian. Sisters of Our Lady of Sorrows 3; Lay Teachers 22; Students 316.
Catechesis/Religious Program—Students 114.

NATCHITOCHES, NATCHITOCHES PARISH

1—ST. ANTHONY OF PADUA (1935) [JC] Rev. Jamie Medina-Cruz (Puerto Rico).
Res.: 911 Fifth St., P.O. Box 432, Nachitoches, 71458-0432. Tel: 318-352-2559; Fax: 318-352-2528. Email: spadua@bellsouth.net.
Catechesis/Religious Program—Students 114.

2—HOLY CROSS (1968) Rev. Jason E. Gootee.
Res.: 129 Second St., P.O. Box 211, Nachitoches, 71458-0211. Tel: 318-352-2615; Fax: 318-352-8989.
Catechesis/Religious Program—Students 29.

3—IMMACULATE CONCEPTION (1728) [CEM] Revs. James A. Foster; Ryan P. Humphries.
Res.: 145 Church St., P.O. Box 13, Nachitoches, 71458-0013. Tel: 318-352-3422; Fax: 318-352-3822.
School—St. Mary, (Grades PreK-8), 1101 E. Fifth St., P.O. Box 2070, 71458-2070. Tel: 318-352-8394; Fax: 318-352-5798. Alan Powers, Prin. & High School Prin. Lay Teachers 24; Students 284.
High School—Lay Teachers 18; Students 136.
Catechesis/Religious Program—Students 119.

PINEVILLE, RAPIDES PARISH, SACRED HEART (1933) Revs. Bruce Miller; Luke A. Melcher.
Res.: 600 Lakeview, P.O. Drawer 3009, 71361-3009. Tel: 318-445-2496; Fax: 318-443-0808.
Catechesis/Religious Program—Students 262.

PLAUCHEVILLE, AVOYELLES PARISH, MATER DOLOROSA (1879) [CEM] Rev. Charles J. Morgan.
Res.: P.O. Box 9, 71362-0009. Tel: 318-922-3131; Fax: 318-922-3664.
School—(Grades PreK-8) Tel: 318-922-3401; Fax: 318-922-3776. Bro. Anthony Dugas, F.S.E., Prin. Brothers of the Holy Eucharist 2; Marianites of Holy Cross 1; Lay Teachers 10; Students 180.
High School—Bro. Anthony Dugas, F.S.E., Prin. Brothers of the Holy Eucharist 3; Sisters 2; Lay Teachers 5; Students 71.
Catechesis/Religious Program—Bro. Paul Casey, F.S.E., D.R.E. Students 75.

POWHATAN, NATCHITOCHES PARISH, ST. FRANCIS OF ASSISI (1952) Rev. Anthony Aelavanthara (India).
Res.: P.O. Box 82, 71066-0082. Tel: 318-352-8819; Fax: 318-352-8008.
Catechesis/Religious Program—Students 20.
Mission—St. Anne [CEM] Spanish Lake, Natchitoches Parish.

REXMERE, AVOYELLES PARISH, ST. MICHAEL (1964) [CEM] Rev. Msgr. Steve J. Testa.
Res.: 4702 Hwy. 451, P.O. Box 31, Bordelonville, 71320-0031. Tel: 318-997-2151; Fax: 318-997-2159. Email: stpeter@cebridge.net.
Catechesis/Religious Program—

ST. JOSEPH, TENSAS PARISH, ST. JOSEPH (1940) [JC] Rev. Jose Nediyakala, C.M.I. (India).
Mailing Address: P.O. Box 198, 71366-0198. Email: frmiclepoovath@catholic.org.
Res.: 919 Plank Rd., 71366-0198. Tel: 318-766-3565; Fax: 318-766-3560. Email: nediyakalajose@yahoo.com.
Catechesis/Religious Program—Students 12.
Mission—St. Francis of Assisi Waterproof, Tensas Parish.

SIMMESPORT, AVOYELLES PARISH, CHRIST THE KING (1935) [CEM] Rev. James Nellikunnell, C.M.I. (India).
Res.: 657 Main St., P.O. Box 186, 71369-0186. Tel: 318-941-2381; Fax: 318-941-2381. Email: cthe@centurytel.net.
Catechesis/Religious Program—Tel: 318-941-5159. Liz Jeansonne, D.R.E. Students 92.

TALLULAH, MADISON PARISH, ST. EDWARD (1936) Rev. Ferreolus D'Cruz (India).
Res.: 204 Hwy. 80 E., P.O. Box 1308, 71282-1308. Tel: 318-574-1677; Fax: 318-574-1677. Email: stedward@bellsouth.net.
Catechesis/Religious Program—Tel: 318-574-2916; Fax: 318-574-2916. Ann Keene, D.R.E. Students 47.

TIOGA, RAPIDES PARISH, IMMACULATE HEART OF MARY (1971) Rev. George Krosfield (India).
P.O. Box 687, 71477-0687. Tel: 318-640-5314 (Res.); 318-640-9446 (Office); Fax: 318-640-3864. Email: ihmarychurch@suddenlink.net.
Res.: 1220 Tioga Rd., Ball, 71405.
Catechesis/Religious Program—Helen Craig, D.R.E. Students 114.

VIDALIA, CONCORDIA PARISH, OUR LADY OF LOURDES (1887) [JC] Rev. George Pookkattu, C.M.I. (India).
Res.: 503 Texas St., P.O. Box 460, 71373. Tel: 318-336-5450; Fax: 318-336-9770. Email: ollourdes@bellsouth.net.
Catechesis/Religious Program—Tel: 601-446-5757. Brigid Martin, D.R.E. Students 35.

WINNFIELD, WINN PARISH, OUR LADY OF LOURDES (1988) Rev. Christian Iheanyichukwu Ogbonna (Nigeria).
Res.: 772 Country Club Rd., P.O. Box 1412, 71483-1412. Tel: 318-628-2561; Fax: 318-628-4653.
Mission—St. William 4580 Main St., P.O. Box 1232, Olla, La Salle Parish 71465. Tel: 318-495-5356; Fax: 318-495-3579.
Catechesis/Religious Program—Students 24.

WINNSBORO, FRANKLIN PARISH, ST. MARY (1945) Rev. Dwight De Jesus (Philippines).
Res.: 1712 West St., 71295-3240. Tel: 318-435-8580; Fax: 318-435-2002. Email: stmaryscc@bellsouth.net.
Catechesis/Religious Program—Cindy Futch, D.R.E. Students 32.
Mission—St. John 7900 Hwy. 165, Columbia, Caldwell Parish 71295.

WOODWORTH, RAPIDES PARISH, CONGREGATION OF MARY, MOTHER OF JESUS ROMAN CATHOLIC CHURCH, WOODWORTH, LOUISIANA Rev. John Pardue.
9323 Hwy. 165 S., P.O. Box 408, 71485. Tel: 318-487-9894. Email: mmjwoodworth@att.net.
Catechesis/Religious Program—Donna Smith, D.R.E. Students 13.

Chaplains of Public Institutions

ALEXANDRIA. *Christus St. Frances Cabrini Hospital*, 3330 Masonic Dr., 71301. Tel: 318-487-1122. Rev. Christudas Nayak (India).
Rapides Regional Medical Center, 211 4th St., 71301. Tel: 318-769-3000. Rev. Peter A. Faulk.

PINEVILLE. *Central Louisiana State Hospital*, W. Shamrock Ave., P.O. Box 5031, 71361. Tel: 318-484-6357; 318-484-6352. Rev. Stephen J. Brandow.
Veterans Administration Medical Center, Shreveport Hwy., 71360. Tel: 318-473-0010. Rev. Stephen J. Brandow, Staff Chap.

On Duty Outside the Diocese:
Revs.—
Braquet, David J., Archdiocese of New Orleans
DeCoste, Wade (Canada)
Mathews, Ronald J., Disciples of the Lord Jesus Christ, Channing, TX
Vead, Victor P., Federal Correctional Complex, Beaumont, TX

Military Chaplains:
Rev.—
Brocato, John K.

Absent on Leave:
Rev.—
Deevy, Edward

Retired:
Rev. Msgrs.—
Bordelon, Roland
Hoppe, Ronald C.
Lyons, Frederick J.
Susi, Joseph M.
Timmermans, John (The Netherlands)
Revs.—
Allen, Terry
Corkery, Daniel (Ireland)
Cunningham, John H.
Fey, Thomas J.
Hasieber, Joseph S.
Lemoine, Russell J.
Messina, Angelo
Montalbano, Joseph E.
Roy, James
Ryan, John (Ireland)
Thompson, August L.
Viviano, Nino
Zagst, Bernard L.

Permanent Deacons:
Daigrepont, William, Avoyelles Prison Ministry
Foster, John, (Retired)
Giaco, Vincent, Chap., Christus St. Frances Cabrini Hospital
Gremillion, Norman, Immaculate Conception, Dupont
Peltier, Joseph, (Retired), St. Augustine, Isle Brevelle
Plaisance, Paul J., (Retired)

INSTITUTIONS LOCATED IN THE DIOCESE

[A] HIGH SCHOOLS, DIOCESAN

ALEXANDRIA. *Holy Savior Menard Central*, (Grades 7-12), 4603 Coliseum Blvd., 71303. Tel: 318-445-8233; Fax: 318-448-8170. Email: hsmenard@centuryinter.net. Mr. Joel Desselle, Prin.; Revs. Michael Craig Scott, V.C., Pres.; James A. Ferguson, J.C.L., Coord. Chap. Junior & High School. Lay Teachers 34; Students 486.

[B] GENERAL HOSPITALS

ALEXANDRIA. *Christus Health Central Louisiana dba Christus St. Frances Cabrini Hospital* 3330 Masonic Dr., 71301. Tel: 318-487-1122; Fax: 318-448-6754. Web: www.cabrini.org. Mr. Stephen Wright, Regl. Pres. & CEO; Rev. Christudas Nayak (India), Dir. Pastoral Care. Sisters of Charity of the Incarnate Word 2; Bed Capacity 280; Total Staff 1,749; Patients Assisted Annually 210,657.

Christus St. Frances Cabrini Hospital Foundation of Alexandria, Inc., 3330 Masonic Dr., 71301. Tel: 318-448-6580; Fax: 318-443-3072. Email: michael.davis@christushealth.org. Web: www.christuscabrinifoundation.org.

Dubuis Hospital of Alexandria, 3330 Masonic Dr., 71301. Tel: 318-448-4938; Fax: 318-483-4033. Web: www.dubuis.org. Mr. Gary Kemps, Admin. Bed Capacity 33; Total Staff 100; Patients Assisted Annually 350.

[C] PROTECTIVE INSTITUTIONS

ALEXANDRIA. *St. Mary's Residential Training School, Inc.*, P.O. Drawer 7768, 71306. Tel: 318-445-6443; Fax: 318-449-8520. Email: sistercarla@stmarys-rts.org. Web: www.stmarys-rts.org. Sr. Carla Bertani, O.L.S., Admin. Congregation of the Sisters of Our Lady of Sorrows of the U.S.A., Inc. Sisters 2; Lay Staff 308; Bed Capacity 202; Students 202.
Our Lady of Sorrows Community Homes, 347 Browns Bend Rd., 71303. Tel: 318-487-8897; Fax: 318-487-9987. Email: carlabols@aol.com. Congregation of the Sisters of Our Lady of Sorrows of the U.S.A., Inc. Sisters 3; Lay Staff 23; Bed Capacity 20; Residents 20.

[D] HOMES FOR AGED

ALEXANDRIA. *Our Lady's Manor, Inc.*, 402 Monroe St., 71301. Tel: 318-473-2560; Fax: 318-443-2449. Ms. Christina Brumley, Admin. Apartments 104.

[E] RESIDENCES OF PRIESTS AND BROTHERS

PLAUCHEVILLE. *Brothers of the Holy Eucharist*, P.O. Box 25, 71362. Tel: 318-922-3630. Bro. Andre M. Lucia, F.S.E., Supr. Brothers 4.

[F] CONVENTS AND RESIDENCES FOR SISTERS

ALEXANDRIA. *Congregation of the Marianites of Holy Cross, St. Rita Convent*, 1717 Ashley Ave., 71301. Tel: 318-448-8001. Sisters 3.

Congregation of the Sisters of Charity of the Incarnate Word, Nazareth Community, 340 Park Pl., 71301-3942. Tel: 318-473-9329; Fax: 318-473-9377. Sisters 3.

Sisters of Our Lady of Sorrows, St. Joseph Convent, 440 Browns Bend Rd., 71303. Tel: 318-443-1553; Fax: 318-443-0994. Email: stjoe97@aol.com. Sisters 4.

Sisters of the Holy Family, 4609 Coliseum Blvd., 71303. Tel: 318-443-4495. Sr. Patricia Ann Williams, S.S.F., Local Leader. Sisters 5.

MOREAUVILLE. *Sisters of Our Lady of Sorrows, Sacred Heart Convent*, P.O. Box 179, 71355. Tel: 318-985-2994. Sisters 2.

[G] RETREAT HOUSES

PINEVILLE. *Maryhill Renewal Center*, 600 Maryhill Rd., 71360. Tel: 318-640-1378; 318-792-1570; Fax: 318-640-8604. Email: cnorris@diocesealex.org. Web: www.diocesealex.org.

[H] CATHOLIC CHARITIES AND SPECIAL MINISTRIES

ALEXANDRIA. *Catholic Charities and Special Ministries*, 4400 Coliseum Blvd., P.O. Box 7417, 71306. Tel: 318-445-2401; Fax: 318-448-6121. Email: frgrem@diocesealex.org. Web: www.diocesealex.org. Rev. Rickey J. Gremillion, Dir.

[I] NEWMAN CENTERS

ALEXANDRIA. *Louisiana State University at Alexandria Catholic Student Center*, 8100 Hwy. 71-S, 71302-9633. Tel: 318-473-6494. Mrs. Lynn Ray, Dir.

NATCHITOCHES. *Northwestern State University Holy Cross Catholic Student Center*, 129 Second St., P.O. Box 211, 71458. Tel: 318-352-2615; Fax: 318-352-8989. Email: holycross@cp.tel.net. Rev. Jason E. Gootee, Chap.

[J] MISCELLANEOUS

ALEXANDRIA. *Catholic Charitable Endowment of Alexandria*, 4400 Coliseum Blvd., 71303. Tel: 318-445-2401; Fax: 318-448-6121.

The Catholic Foundation of North-Central Louisiana, Inc., P.O. Box 8021, 71306. Tel: 318-487-9222. Joseph L. Hebert, Pres.; Mrs. Betty Chop, Sec.

Manna House, 2655 Lee St., P.O. Box 6011, 71307. Tel: 318-445-9053. Mr. Chuck Westerchil, Pres. Board of Directors.

HESSMER. *Magnificat - Central Louisiana Chapter of the Diocese of Alexandria*, P.O. Box 37, 71341. Tel: 318-563-8213; Fax: 318-563-8213. Email: msgd_@bellsouth.net. M. Sue Dauzat, Coord.

RELIGIOUS INSTITUTES OF MEN REPRESENTED IN THE DIOCESE

For further details refer to the corresponding bracketed number in the Religious Institutes of Men or Women section.

[]—*Apostles of Jesus (Uganda)*—A.J.
[]—*Benedictine Monks* (India)—O.S.B.Silv.
[0620]—*Brothers of the Holy Eucharist*—F.S.E.
[0275]—*Carmelites of Mary Immaculate*—C.M.I.
[0520]—*Franciscan Friars*—O.F.M.
[]—*Missionaries of St. Francis de Sales* (France)—M.S.F.S.
[]—*Sons of Mary Mother of Mercy (Nigeria)*—S.M.M.M.

RELIGIOUS INSTITUTES OF WOMEN REPRESENTED IN THE DIOCESE

[2410]—*Congregation of the Marianites of Holy Cross*—M.S.C.
[0470]—*Congregation of the Sisters of Charity of the Incarnate Word*—C.C.V.I.
[1950]—*Congregation of the Sisters of the Holy Family*—S.S.F.
[1010]—*Sisters of Divine Providence of San Antonio, Texas*—C.D.P.
[3120]—*Sisters of Our Lady of Sorrows*—O.L.S.
[]—*Sisters of the Living Word*—S.L.W.

DIOCESAN CEMETERIES

LECOMPTE. *Lecompte Cemetery*
PINEVILLE. *Maryhill Cemetery for Clergy*

NECROLOGY

† Murphy, Rev. Msgr. Patrick J., (Retired)—Died 2009

† Roy, Kenneth Jude, Alexandria, LA Pres., Holy Savior Menard Central High School—Died June 16, 2009

An asterisk (*) denotes an organization that has established tax-exempt status directly with the IRS and is not covered by the USCCB Group Ruling.

Diocese of Allentown

(Dioecesis Alanopolitana)

Most Reverend

JOHN O. BARRES

Bishop of Allentown; ordained October 21, 1989; appointed Bishop of Allentown May 27, 2009; installed July 30, 2009. *Office: 4029 W. Tilghman St., Allentown, PA 18104.*

Most Reverend

EDWARD P. CULLEN, D.D.

Retired Bishop of Allentown; appointed Auxiliary Bishop of Philadelphia and Titular Bishop of Paria in Preconsilare February 8, 1994; consecrated April 14, 1994; appointed Bishop of Allentown December 16, 1997; installed Third Bishop of Allentown February 9, 1998; retired May 27, 2009. *Office: 4029 W. Tilghman St., Allentown, PA 18104. Mailing Address: Bishop's Office, P.O. Box F, Allentown, PA 18105.*

Chancery Office: 4029 W. Tilghman St., Allentown, PA 18104. Mailing Address: P.O. Box F, Allentown, PA 18105-1538. Tel: 610-437-0755; Fax: 610-433-7822.

ESTABLISHED JANUARY 28, 1961.

Square Miles 2,773.

Comprises the Counties of Berks, Carbon, Lehigh, Northampton and Schuylkill in the State of Pennsylvania.

STATISTICAL OVERVIEW

Personnel	
Bishop	1
Retired Bishops	1
Priests: Diocesan Active in Diocese	150
Priests: Diocesan Active Outside Diocese	8
Priests: Retired, Sick or Absent	50
Number of Diocesan Priests	208
Religious Priests in Diocese	63
Total Priests in Diocese	271
Extern Priests in Diocese	3
Ordinations:	
Diocesan Priests	3
Religious Priests	1
Transitional Deacons	1
Permanent Deacons in Diocese	108
Total Brothers	12
Total Sisters	350
Parishes	
Parishes	104
With Resident Pastor:	
Resident Diocesan Priests	97
Resident Religious Priests	4
Without Resident Pastor:	
Administered by Priests	3
Missions	2
Pastoral Centers	26
New Parishes Created	13
Closed Parishes	60
Professional Ministry Personnel:	
Brothers	12
Sisters	350
Welfare	
Catholic Hospitals	2
Total Assisted	488,955
Health Care Centers	2
Total Assisted	4,356
Homes for the Aged	10
Total Assisted	735
Day Care Centers	1
Total Assisted	39
Specialized Homes	2
Total Assisted	39
Special Centers for Social Services	7
Total Assisted	24,983
Residential Care of Disabled	2
Total Assisted	807
Educational	
Diocesan Students in Other Seminaries	14
Total Seminarians	14
Colleges and Universities	2
Total Students	6,117
High Schools, Diocesan and Parish	8
Total Students	3,641
Elementary Schools, Diocesan and Parish	45
Total Students	9,485
Non-residential Schools for the Disabled	3
Total Students	116
Catechesis/Religious Education:	
High School Students	206
Elementary Students	16,252
Total Students under Catholic Instruction	35,831
Teachers in the Diocese:	
Priests	10
Sisters	54
Lay Teachers	916
Vital Statistics	
Receptions into the Church:	
Infant Baptism Totals	3,043
Adult Baptism Totals	117
First Communions	3,363
Confirmations	3,824
Marriages:	
Catholic	618
Interfaith	317
Total Marriages	935
Deaths	3,101
Total Catholic Population	272,300
Total Population	1,161,932

Former Bishops—Most Revs. JOSEPH MCSHEA, D.D., appt. Titular Bishop of Mina and Auxiliary Bishop of Philadelphia Feb. 8, 1952; cons. March 19, 1952; appt. Bishop of Allentown Feb. 15, 1961; installed April 11, 1961; retired Feb. 8, 1983; died Nov. 28, 1991; THOMAS J. WELSH, D.D., J.C.D., appt. Titular Bishop of Scattery Island and Auxiliary Bishop of Philadelphia, Feb. 18, 1970; cons. April 2, 1970; appt. First Bishop of Arlington, June 4, 1974; installed Aug. 13, 1974; appt. Bishop of Allentown, Feb. 8, 1983; installed Second Bishop of Allentown, March 21, 1983; retired Dec. 16, 1997; died Feb. 19, 2009; EDWARD PETER CULLEN, D.D., ord. May 19, 1962; appt. Auxiliary Bishop of Philadelphia and Titular Bishop of Paria in Preconsilare Feb. 8, 1994; cons. April 14, 1994; appt. Bishop of Allentown Dec. 16, 1997; installed Third Bishop of Allentown Feb. 9, 1998; retired May 27, 2009.

Vicar General—Rev. Msgr. ALFRED A. SCHLERT, J.C.L., V.G., 4029 W. Tilghman St., Allentown, 18105-1538. Mailing Address: P.O. Box F, Allentown, 18105-1538. Tel: 610-437-0755; Fax: 610-433-7822.

Chancellor—Rev. Msgr. GERALD E. GOBITAS, Th.M., 4029 W. Tilghman St., Allentown, 18105-1538. Mailing Address: P.O. Box F, Allentown, 18105-1538. Tel: 610-437-0755; Fax: 610-433-7822.

Secretary to the Bishop—Rev. Msgr. GERALD E. GOBITAS, Th.M., 4029 W. Tilghman St., Allentown, 18105. Mailing Address: P.O. Box F, Allentown, 18105-1538. Tel: 610-437-0755; Fax: 610-433-7822.

Victim Assistance Coordinator—Mrs. HELEN P. KELLEHER, L.S.W. Tel: 800-791-9209; Fax: 610-791-1878. Email: hkelleher@allentowndiocese.org.

Censor of Books—Rev. Msgr. JAMES J. MULLIGAN, S.T.L.

Diocesan Tribunal—Very Rev. JOHN J. PAUL, M.S.C., V.J., S.T.L., J.C.D., Judicial Vicar, 202 N. 17th St., Allentown, 18104. Tel: 610-434-3200; Fax: 610-433-3104.

Judges—Rev. Msgrs. DAVID J. MORRISON (Retired); THOMAS P. KOONS, V.R., J.C.L., M.A., M.Div.; VICTOR F. FINELLI, J.C.L., Th.M., M.Div.

Promoter of Justice—Rev. Msgr. DAVID L. JAMES, V.E., J.C.L.

Defenders of the Bond—Rev. Msgr. DAVID L. JAMES, V.E., J.C.L.; Rev. DAVID J. KOZAK, J.C.L.; Rev. Msgr. ALFRED A. SCHLERT, J.C.L., V.G.

Secretary—Deacon EUGENE J. WYRWA.

Advocates—Rev. Msgr. DAVID L. JAMES, V.E., J.C.L.; Deacon EUGENE J. WYRWA.

Notaries—Mrs. JUDITH CHUSS; Mrs. PATRICIA ECHTERNACH; Mrs. DIANE SELDOMRIDGE; Mrs. COLETTE SNYDER.

Vicar for Religious—Rev. Msgr. THOMAS P. KOONS, V.R., J.C.L., M.A., M.Div., Diocesan Tribunal, 202 N. 17th St., Allentown, 18104-5605. Tel: 610-434-3200; Fax: 610-433-3104. Email: tkoons@allentowndiocese.org.

Vicars Forane—Rev. Msgrs. JOHN G. CHIZMAR, V.F., M.Div., Carbon Deanery; DANIEL J. YENUSHOSKY, V.F., Th.M., Lehigh Deanery; DENNIS T. HARTGEN, V.F., Berks Deanery; STEPHEN J. RADOCHA, V.F., M.Div., Northampton Deanery; EDWARD J. O'CONNOR, M.Th., M.S.W., V.F., Schuylkill Deanery.

Secretariat for Clergy—Rev. Msgr. GERALD E. GOBITAS, Th.M., Sec., Mailing Address: P.O. Box F, Allentown, 18105-1538. Tel: 610-437-0755; Fax: 610-433-7822. Email: ggobitas@allentowndiocese.org.

Priest Personnel Office—Rev. Msgr. GERALD E. GOBITAS, Th.M., Dir., Mailing Address: P.O. Box F, Allentown, 18105-1538. Tel: 610-437-0755; Fax: 610-433-7822.

Holy Family Villa for Priests—VACANT, 1325 Prospect Ave., Bethlehem, 18018-4916. Tel: 610-694-0395; Fax: 610-694-9990.

Permanent Diaconate Office—Rev. Msgr. MICHAEL J. CHABACK, S.T.D., Dir., 2145 Madison Ave., Bethlehem, 18018-4642. Tel: 610-866-0581; Fax: 610-867-8702. Email: diaconate@allentowndiocese.org.

Vocations Office—Rev. ANDREW N. GEHRINGER, M.Div., M.A., S.T.B., Dir., 4029 W. Tilghman St., Allentown, 18105-1538. Tel: 610-437-0755; Fax:

610-433-7822. Email: agehringer@ allentowndiocese.org. Web: beapriest.com.

Priestly Life and Ministry Office—Rev. Msgr. JAMES J. MULLIGAN, S.T.L., Dir., Queenship of Mary Rectory, 1324 Newport Ave., Northampton, 18067-1442. Tel: 610-262-1885; Fax: 610-262-4192.

Secretariat for Catholic Life and Evangelization—Very Rev. E. MICHAEL CAMILLI, M.S.C., S.T.L., M.S.L.S., H.E.L., Sec., 900 S. Woodward St., Allentown, 18103-4179. Tel: 610-289-8900; Fax: 610-289-7917. Email: mcamilli@allentowndiocese.org; Rev. SCOTT R. ARDINGER, M.Div., M.A., S.T.B., Deputy Sec. Tel: 610-289-8900, Ext. 227; Fax: 610-289-7917. Email: sardinger@allentowndiocese.org.

Office of Ecumenical and Interreligious Dialogue—Rev. Msgr. JOHN S. MRAZ, M.A., M.Ed., M.Div., Dir., 2174 Lincoln Ave., Northampton, 18067-1257. Tel: 610-965-2426; Fax: 610-967-1099. Email: churchofstann@rcn.com.

Office of Worship—Rev. SCOTT R. ARDINGER, M.Div., M.A., S.T.B., Dir., 900 S. Woodward St., Allentown, 18103-4179. Tel: 610-289-8900; Fax: 610-289-7917. Email: sardinger@ allentowndiocese.org.

Office of Hispanic Affairs—VACANT, 900 S. Woodward St., Allentown, 18103-4179. Tel: 610-289-8900, Ext. 233; Fax: 610-289-7917.

Liaison to Hispanic Community—Sr. MARY MARTHA ZAMMATORE, O.S.F. Tel: 610-289-8900; Fax: 610-289-7917. Email: mzammator@allentowndiocese.org.

Office of Communications—Mr. MATTHEW T. KERR, Dir., Mailing Address: P.O. Box F, Allentown, 18105-1538. Tel: 610-871-5200, Ext. 265; Fax: 610-439-7694. Email: mkerr@ allentowndiocese.org.

Office of Family Life Ministries—Dr. WILLIAM F. URBINE, Dir. Tel: 610-289-8900, Ext. 224; Fax: 610-289-7917. Email: wurbine@ allentowndiocese.org. Family Life Coordinators: Mrs. CARLA NEUPAUER. Tel: 610-289-8900, Ext. 238. Email: cneupauer@allentowndiocese.org; Mrs. SANDY MAAS, 900 S. Woodward St., Allentown, 18103-4179. Tel: 610-289-8900, Ext. 239. Email: smaas@allentowndiocese.org.

Office for Ministry with Persons with Disabilities—Sr. JANICE MARIE JOHNSON, R.S.M., 900 S. Woodward St., Allentown, 18103-4179. Tel: 610-289-8900, Ext. 245; Fax: 610-289-7917. Email: jjohnson@allentowndiocese.org.

The A.D. Times—Mrs. JILL M. CARAVAN, Editor, P.O. Box F, Allentown, 18105-1538. Tel: 610-871-5200, Ext. 264; Fax: 610-439-7694. Email: adtimes@ allentowndiocese.org.

Campus Ministry Office—Rev. WAYNE E. KILLIAN, M.A., M.S., Dir., The Newman Center at Lehigh University, Bldg. 41, 661 Taylor St., Bethlehem, 18015-3127. Tel: 610-758-4148; Fax: 610-758-6392.

Office of Youth and Young Adult Ministry—Mrs. MARY ELLEN JOHNS, B.A., Dir. Email: mjohns@ allentowndiocese.org; Mrs. MARY MATUNIS, Asst. Dir., 47 Wiggins St., New Philadelphia, 17959-1119. Tel: 570-277-0123; Fax: 570-277-0183. Email: mmatunis@allentowndiocese.org.

Pontifical Mission Societies in the United States—Rev. Msgr. JOHN P. MURPHY, Diocesan Dir., St. Thomas More, 1040 Flexer Ave., Allentown, 18103-5520. Tel: 610-433-7413; Fax: 610-433-2308.

Office for Social Action—Mrs. MARYANN HARTZELL, Dir., 900 S. Woodward St., Allentown, 18103-4179. Tel: 610-289-8900, Ext. 231; Fax: 610-289-7917. Email: mhartzell@ allentowndiocese.org.

Office of Pro-Life Activities—Mrs. MARYANN W. DUNN, Dir., 900 S. Woodward St., Allentown, 18103-4179. Tel: 610-289-8900, Ext. 229; Fax: 610-289-7917. Email: mdunn@ allentowndiocese.org.

Office of Adult Formation—MARY FRAN HARTIGAN, M.A., Dir., 900 S. Woodward St., Allentown, 18103-4179. Tel: 610-289-8900, Ext. 226; Fax: 610-289-7917. Email: mhartigan@ allentowndiocese.org.

Secretariat for Temporal Affairs—Mr. MARK E. SMITH, CPA, CFO & Sec., P.O. Box F, Allentown, 18105-1538. Tel: 610-871-5200, Ext. 205; Fax: 610-871-5211. Email: msmith@allentowndiocese.org.

Banking and Investments—Mr. MARK D. HULLINGER, Dir., P.O. Box F, Allentown, 18105-1538. Tel: 610-871-5200, Ext. 288; Fax: 610-871-5211. Email: mhullinger@ allentowndiocese.org.

Strengthening Our Future in Faith (SOFF)—Rev. Msgr. JOHN G. CHIZMAR, V.F., M.Div., Campaign Chm., 1101 W. Hamilton St., P.O. Box F, Allentown, 18105-1538. Tel: 800-831-4443 (toll free).

Accounting Services—JEFFREY K. BUCK, Controller. Tel: 610-871-5200, Ext. 102; Fax: 610-871-5211. Email: jbuck@allentowndiocese.org; Mr. ALEXANDER J. NAGURNEY, Mgr. Tel: 610-871-5200, Ext. 229; Fax: 610-871-5211. Email: anagurney@allentowndiocese.org; Mr. THOMAS O. KERN, C.E.B.S., Benefits & Payroll Mgr. Tel: 610-871-5200, Ext. 109; Fax: 610-871-5211. Email: tkern@allentowndiocese.org.

Parish and School Support Services—Mr. CHRISTOPHER E. DOMYAN, Dir. Tel: 610-871-5200, Ext. 238; Fax: 610-871-5211. Email: cdomyan@ allentowndiocese.org.

Information Systems—Mrs. NANCY A. TORO, Dir. Tel: 610-871-5200, Ext. 239; Fax: 610-871-5211. Email: ntoro@allentowndiocese.org.

Cemeteries—Rev. Msgr. WILLIAM F. BAVER, M.Div., Th.M., C.C.C.E., K.C.H.S., Dir., P.O. Box F, Allentown, 18105-1538. Tel: 610-871-5200, Ext. 234; Fax: 610-871-5211. Email: wbaver@ allentowndiocese.org.

Human Resources—Mr. RONALD J. JACOBS, SPHR, Dir., P.O. Box F, Allentown, 18105-1538. Tel: 610-871-5200, Ext. 204; Fax: 610-871-5211. Email: rjacobs@allentowndiocese.org.

Diocesan Benefit Programs—Mr. THOMAS O. KERN, C.E.B.S., CEBS Benefits Mgr. Tel: 610-871-5200, Ext. 109. Email: tkern@allentowndiocese.org.

Insurance and Real Estate—Ms. KELLY C. BRUCE, A.R.M., Dir. Tel: 610-871-5200, Ext. 203. Email: kbruce@allentowndiocese.org.

Office of Stewardship and Development—Mr. JAMES S. FRIEND JR., P.O. Box F, Allentown, 18105-1538. Tel: 610-871-5200, Ext. 210; Fax: 610-871-5211. Email: jfriend@ allentowndiocese.org.

Government Affairs—Mr. MATTHEW T. KERR, Dir., P.O. Box F, Allentown, 18105-1538. Tel: 610-871-5200, Ext. 265; Fax: 610-871-5211. Email: mkerr@allentowndiocese.org.

Secretariat for Catholic Education—Mr. PHILIP J. FROMUTH, M.Ed., Sec., 2145 Madison Ave., Bethlehem, 18017-4642. Tel: 610-866-0581; Fax: 610-867-8702. Email: pfromuth@ allentowndiocese.org.

Elementary School Religious Education—Ms. BARBARA AMABILE, Asst. Supt. Email: bamabile@ allentowndiocese.org.

Religious Education—Ms. BARBARA AMABILE, Asst. Supt. Email: bamabile@allentowndiocese.org.

Curriculum, Supervision and Professional Development (Elementary/Secondary Schools)—Sr. ANITA PATRICK GALLAGHER, I.H.M., Asst. Supt. Email: agallagher@ allentowndiocese.org.

Personnel (Elementary and Secondary)—Sr. ROBERTA PETERS, I.H.M., Asst. Supt. Email: rpeters@allentowndiocese.org.

Early Childhood Education—Sr. ANITA PATRICK GALLAGHER, I.H.M., Asst. Supt. Email: agallagher@allentowndiocese.org.

Secondary Schools—VACANT, Asst. Supt.

Special Education Programs—Mr. LOUIS RUSNOCK, Dir. Tel: 610-866-0581, Ext. 25; Fax: 610-867-8702. Email: lrusnock@allentowndiocese.org.

Government Programs—Sr. ANN MONICA BUBSER, I.H.M., Asst. Supt. Email: abubser@ allentowndiocese.org.

Board of Education—Deacon WILLIAM R. KASE, Pres. Tel: 610-372-4010.

Secretariat for Catholic Human Services—Mrs. HELEN P. KELLEHER, L.S.W., Sec., 2141 Downyflake Ln., Allentown, 18103-4774. Tel: 610-791-3888; Fax: 610-791-1878. Email: hkelleher@ allentowndiocese.org.

Catholic Charities—Mrs. HELEN P. KELLEHER, L.S.W., Exec. Dir., 2141 Downyflake Ln., Allentown, 18103-4774. Tel: 610-791-3888; Fax: 610-791-1878. Web: catholiccharityad.org.

Catholic Senior Housing and Health Care Services, Inc.—

Holy Family Manor—Mrs. HEATHER KESSLER, N.H.A., Admin., 1200 Spring St., Bethlehem, 18018. Tel: 610-865-5595; Fax: 610-997-5442. Web: www.hfmanor.org.

Holy Family Residential Services—Mrs. KAREN ABRUZZESE, Coord., 1200 Spring St., Bethlehem, 18018. Tel: 610-865-5595; Fax: 610-997-8454. Web: www.hfmanor.org.

Collaborative Residential and Home Care Services—SANDRA LEE LEVENGOOD, M.B.A., R.N., Dir., 2615 Perkiomen Ave., Reading, 19606. Tel: 610-779-6432; 800-300-3007; Fax: 610-779-5002. Email: slevengood@covenanthc.org. Web: www.covenanthc.org.

Diocesan Medical Ethicist—Rev. Msgr. JAMES J. MULLIGAN, S.T.L., Dir., Queenship of Mary Rectory, 1324 Newport Ave., Northampton, 18067-1442. Tel: 610-262-1885; Fax: 610-262-4192.

Saint Vincent De Paul Society—Rev. FRANCIS P. STRAKA, Spiritual Advisor; Ms. ELIZABETH HARRISON, Pres. Diocesan Council, 969 Port Carbon St., Pottsville, 17901. Tel: 570-622-6289.

Council of Priests/Diocesan Consultors—4029 W. Tilghman St., P.O. Box F, Allentown, 18105. Tel: 610-437-0755; Fax: 610-433-7822.

College of Consultors—Rev. Msgrs. ALFRED A. SCHLERT, J.C.L., V.G.; THOMAS D. BADDICK, Th.M.; THOMAS A. DERZACK, M.Div.; Rev. ROBERT T. FINLAN, M.A., M.Div.; Rev. Msgrs. JOHN P. MURPHY; GERALD E. GOBITAS, Th.M.; DAVID L. JAMES, V.E., J.C.L.; STEPHEN J. RADOCHA, V.F., M.Div.; JAMES J. REICHERT.

Ex Officio Members—Rev. Msgrs. ALFRED A. SCHLERT, J.C.L., V.G.; GERALD E. GOBITAS, Th.M.; Very Rev. E. MICHAEL CAMILLI, M.S.C., S.T.L., M.S.L.S., H.E.L.

Elected Members—Rev. Msgr. JOHN P. MURPHY; Revs. KENNETH A. MEDVE; RICHARD H. CLEMENT, M.Div.; Rev. Msgr. EDWARD R. SACKS, M.Ed.; Revs. MICHAEL J. STONE; THOMAS P. BORTZ, M.Div., S.T.B.; RONALD P. BOWMAN, M.Div., M.A.; ANDREW N. GEHRINGER, M.Div., M.A., S.T.B.; ROBERT T. FINLAN, M.A., M.Div.; Rev. Msgr. VICTOR F. FINELLI, J.C.L., Th.M., M.Div.; Revs. JOSEPH F. TOBIAS, M.S.C.; MICHAEL J. BRIGGMAN (Retired).

Appointed Members—Revs. SCOTT R. ARDINGER, M.Div., M.A., S.T.B.; ERIC R. ARNOUT, M.Div.; ADAM C. SEDAR, M.Div., M.A.; Rev. Msgr. JOSEPH A. DESANTIS, M.Div.; Rev. WILLIAM T. BAKER, S.T.L.; Rev. Msgr. DAVID L. JAMES, V.E., J.C.L.; Rev. JEROME A. TAUBER, M.Div., S.T.B.

Finance Council—Most Rev. JOHN O. BARRES, S.T.D., J.C.L., D.D.; Rev. Msgr. ALFRED A. SCHLERT, J.C.L., V.G., 4029 W. Tilghman St., P.O. Box F, Allentown, 18105-1538. Tel: 610-437-0755; Fax: 610-433-7822; Mr. DENNIS DOMCHEK; Mr. P. MICHAEL EHLERMAN; Mr. JOHN F. HORRIGAN JR.; Mr. HERMAN L. RIJ; Mr. ROBERT J. SNYDER; Mr. JAMES A. TIEFENBRUNN; THOMAS F. TRAUD, Esq.

Affiliated Organizations

American Catholic Overseas Aid Fund—Mailing Address: P.O. Box F, Allentown, 18105-1538. Tel: 610-437-0755; Fax: 610-433-7822.

Blue Army of Our Lady of Fatima—2483 Community Dr., Bath, 18014. Tel: 610-614-1218. Email: thesixfamily@enter.net. Mr. MICHAEL A. SIX, Pres.; Rev. DOMINIC THAO PHAM, M.Div., Spiritual Dir.

Catholic Daughters of the Americas—Rev. FLOYD CAESAR JR., Diocese Committee Chap.

Ashland - Court St. Joan of Arc #225—Rev. JOHN W. BAMBRICK, Chap.

Easton - Court Easton #358—Rev. Msgr. EDWARD S. ZEMANIK, M.Div., Chap.

Frackville - Court St. James #1029—Rev. J. MICHAEL BEERS, Ph.D., S.S.L., Chap.

Girardville - Court St. Cecilia #1529—Rev. EDWARD B. CONNOLLY, M.Div., M.Ed., Chap.

Jim Thorpe - Court Ryan #911—Rev. JAMES J. WARD, M.Div., Chap.

Pottsville - Court Santa Maria #26—Rev. Msgr. EDWARD J. O'CONNOR, M.Th., M.S.W., V.F., Chap.

Shenandoah - Court Annunciation #175—Rev. Msgr. BERNARD A. FLANAGAN, M.Div., Chap.

Charismatic Renewal—Rev. LARRY J. HESS, M.A., Bishop's Liaison. Assistants: Rev. CLIFTON E. BISHOP; Deacon ANTHONY T. CAMPANELL, Our Lady of Good Counsel Rectory, 436 S. 2nd St., Bangor, 18013-2514. Tel: 610-588-5445; Fax: 610-599-6997. Email: olgc2002@epix.net.

Courage—Mailing Address: P.O. Box F, Allentown, 18105-1538. Tel: 610-217-5557.

Cursillo Movement—Rev. MARTIN F. KERN, Spiritual Dir., St. Columbkill Rectory, 200 Indian Spring Rd., Boyertown, 19512-2008. Tel: 610-367-2371; Fax: 610-369-0242.

Father Walter Ciszek Prayer League, Inc. (The)—Rev. Msgr. RONALD C. BOCIAN, M.Ed., Bd. Pres., The Ciszek Center, 231 N. Jardin St., Shenandoah, 17976-1642. Tel: 570-462-2270; Fax: 570-462-2274. Email: fwccenter@verizon.net. Web: www.ciszek.org.

Holy Name Societies—Rev. EDWARD B. CONNOLLY, M.Div., M.Ed., Spiritual Moderator, St. Joseph Rectory, 211 W. Main St., Girardville, 17935. Tel: 570-276-6239. Email: stjospar@verizon.net.

Knights of Columbus—

St. Peter the Fisherman Council #10772, Lake Harmony—DAVID MICHAEL, District Deputy #41, Mailing Address: P.O. Box 612, Albrightsville, 18210-0612. Tel: 570-722-1234. Email: dprm@ ptd.net.

St. Joseph the Worker Council #10921, Orefield—Rev. RONALD J. MINNER, M.Div., Chap.; JEFFREY JOYCE, Grand Knight, 3516 Woodlea Rd., Orefield, 18069-2312. Tel: 610-391-1362. Email: jrj_rmj@hotmail.com.

St. Paul Council #10922, Allentown—JOHN M. LEVCHAK, Grand Knight, 2437 S. 5th St.,

Allentown, 18103. Tel: 610-791-4876.

Calvary Council #528, Allentown—Deacon EUGENE M. FLANLEY JR., Grand Knight, 2008 Wehr Ave., Allentown, 18104-1130. Tel: 610-434-9620; Fax: 610-434-6154.

Sarto Council #1322, Ashland—THOMAS P. COLIHAN, Grand Knight, 75 S. Hoffman Blvd., Ashland, 17921-1951. Tel: 570-875-2091.

Father DeNisco Council #3862, Bangor—JOHN PAGER, Grand Knight, 402 N. Harding Ave., Pen Argyl, 18072. Tel: 610-863-4390.

Trinity Council #313, Bethlehem—PHILIP B. COMITO, Grand Knight, 4110 Donegal Dr., Bethlehem, 18020-7639. Tel: 610-866-4883. Email: philkath51@verizon.net. Web: www.kofc313.org; Rev. ANTHONY P. MONGIELLO, Chap.

Union Council #345, Easton—FRANK S. GUALANO, Grand Knight, 328 Ellwood St., Easton, 18045-3719. Tel: 610-253-6933. Email: sagfsg@aol.com.

St. Ann Council #12886, Emmaus—CRAIG R. SCHARADIN, Grand Knight, 415 S. 6th St., Emmaus, 18049-2908. Tel: 610-965-2426.

Rev. James A. Hogan Council #2580, Frackville—SAMUEL A. BENDER, Grand Knight, 156 N. Center St., Frackville, 17931-1226. Tel: 570-874-1438; Rev. Archpriest JOHN M. FIELDS, B.A., M.A., J.D., Chap.

Father Sheridan Council #748, Girardville—WADE O. RICHARDS, Grand Knight, 223 W. Main St., Girardville, 17935-1705. Tel: 570-278-1014; Fax: 570-276-1444.

Damien Council #598, Jim Thorpe— (Serving Jim Thorpe, Lehighton, Nesquehoning and the surrounding areas). CHRISTOPHER A. HEERY, Grand Knight, 383 S. Third St., Lehighton, 18235. Tel: 610-379-0406. Email: heeryc@nwlehighsd.org.

District #32— (Serving most of Carbon County). MICHAEL A. HEERY, District Deputy #32, 68 White Pine Ln., Lehighton, 18235-9612. Tel: 570-386-2297. Email: jttraindon@yahoo.com.

Archbishop Ryan Council #1552, Lansford—FRANK SERINA, Grand Knight, 107 W. Bertsch St., Lansford, 18232-1908. Tel: 570-645-5221.

Mahanoy City Council #549, Mahanoy City—WILLIAM A. KUBILUS, Grand Knight, 321 W. Center St., Mahanoy City, 17948. Tel: 570-773-1365.

Our Lady of the Sacred Heart Council #4282, Nazareth—WILLIAM J. TANZOSH, Grand Knight, 615 Hill Ave., Nazareth, 18064-9507. Tel: 610-759-3161; Fax: 610-746-7069. Email: billtanzosh@aol.com.

Queenship of Mary Council #4050, Northampton—BRUCE WERMANN, Grand Knight, Mailing Address: P.O. Box 121, Northampton, 18067. Cell: 610-905-7817. Email: spundt2@ptd.net.

Lafayette Council #2522, Palmerton—ALBERT KOHLER, Grand Knight, 456 Lafayette Ave., Palmerton, 18071-1619. Tel: 610-826-6072; Rev. JAMES J. WARD, M.Div., Chap.

Schuylkill Council #431, Pottsville—GEORGE F. HALCOVAGE JR., Grand Knight, Mailing Address: 106 N. 6th St., Pottsville, 17901. Tel: 570-628-3333. Email: schuylkillkofc@verizon.net; Rev. Msgr. EDWARD J. O'CONNOR, M.Th., M.S.W., V.F., Chap.

Reading Council #793, Reading—WILLIAM PETTIT, Grand Knight, 950 Weiser St., Reading, 19601-2031. Tel: 610-376-5734. Email: quantum3@msn.com.

Holy Eucharist Council #4198, Reading—EDWARD W. KOSAK, Grand Knight, 210 Fairway Dr., Reading, 19606-3667. Tel: 610-370-0739.

Francis Cardinal Brennan Council #618, Shenandoah—FRANK WASKO JR., Grand Knight, 415 W. Columbus St., Shenandoah, 17976-2150. Tel: 570-462-9996. Email: mwasko@localnet.com.

Holy Name Council #7179, Shillington—MICHAEL V. SHARER, Grand Knight, 488 Walnuttown Rd., Fleetwood, 19522. Tel: 610-944-6626. Email: msharer@ecycle.com.

Light of Christ Council #8726, Sinking Spring—KEN LYTZ, Grand Knight, 1213 Fox Rd., Leesport, 19533. Tel: 610-823-6751.

Father Henry Baker Council #2711, Tamaqua—WILLIAM SOMMERS, Grand Knight, RR 1, Box 329, Tamaqua, 18252-9474.

Father Henry Baker Council #12105, Weatherly—JOSEPH D'ANDREA, Grand Knight, 411 6th St., Weatherly, 18255-1214. Tel: 570-427-4137. Email: joetd@verizon.net; Rev. FLOYD CAESAR JR., Chap.

Legatus—25 Pinewood Rd., Wyomissing, 19610-1972. Tel: 610-478-1148; Fax: 610-288-5801. Mr. LEN MARRELLA; Mrs. DEE MARRELLA; Rev. JOHN A. KRIVAK, M.Div., Th.M., M.Ed., Ed.D., Chap.

Legion of Mary—Mr. JOE AKKARA, Pres., 29 Mulligan Dr., Reading, 19606. Tel: 610-301-5139.

National Shut-In Visitation Society—Rev. Msgr. FELIX A. LOSITO, Natl. Dir., Holy Rosary, 237 Franklin St., Reading, 19602-1034. Tel: 610-373-5579.

Operation Rice Bowl—Rev. Msgr. JOHN P. MURPHY, Dir., St. Thomas More, 1040 Flexer Ave., Allentown, 18103-5520. Tel: 610-433-7413; Fax: 610-433-2308.

Our Lady's Missionaries of the Eucharist—VACANT A Public Association of Christ's Faithful. Magnificat House, 640 E. Main St., Birdsboro, 19508. Tel: 610-582-3333; Fax: 610-582-2456. Email: olme@olme.org. Web: www.olme.org.

Secular Franciscan Order - St. Francis Fraternity—St. Francis Retreat House, 3918 Chipman Rd., Easton, 18045-3014. Tel: 610-258-3053; Fax: 610-258-2412. Mr. DONALD FOOTE, S.F.O., Mailing Address: R.R. 5, P.O. Box 5080A, Stroudsburg, 18360. Tel: 570-420-0670.

Serra Clubs—

Serra Club of Allentown—Rev. Msgr. DANIEL J. YENUSHOSKY, V.F., Th.M., Chap.; Mr. JOHN MCHALE, Pres., 301 Windsor Place, Macungie, 18062. Tel: 610-965-0184. Email: jmchale81@yahoo.com.

Forks of the Delaware Serra—Rev. PATRICK H. LAMB, Chap.; Mr. VINCENT PRESTO, Pres., 59 Central Dr., Easton, 18045. Tel: 610-253-0223.

Serra Club of Bethlehem—Rev. ANTHONY P. MONGIELLO, Chap.; JOHN M. TOBIN, Pres., 872 Media St., Bethlehem, 18017. Tel: 610-868-0250. Email: jmt872@msn.com.

Serra Club of Reading—Rev. RONALD P. BOWMAN, M.Div., M.A., Chap.; Mr. AL F. FRANCHOWIAK, 4001 Grant St., Reiffton, Reading, 19606. Tel: 610-779-6068. Email: aalfiel@verizon.net.

Carbon/Schuylkill Serra Club—Rev. JAMES C. BECHTEL, M.Div., Chap.; DIANE SURAVICZ, Vice Pres. Programs, 1877 Quakake Rd., Weatherly, 18255. Tel: 570-427-8724.

Third Order Dominican Expectation of Blessed Virgin Mother Chapter—Dr. FELICIDAD QUILO, Moderator, Notre Dame of Bethlehem Church, 1861 Catasauqua Rd., Bethlehem, 18018-1298. Tel: 610-691-6761.

Third Order Secular Carmelites—Holy Rosary Parish, 237 Franklin St., Reading, 19602-1034. Tel: 610-373-5579. Rev. Msgr. FELIX A. LOSITO, Dir.

Miscellaneous Affiliated Organizations

Catholic Men of Good News (CMOGN)—Rev. LARRY J. HESS, M.A., Our Lady of Good Counsel, 436 S. 2nd St., Bangor, 18013-2514. Tel: 610-588-5445; Fax: 610-599-6997.

Dayspring Homes, Inc.—Mr. DWAYNE ALBRIGHT, CEO; CATHY BEWLEY, Dir. Mission; Sr. FRANCIS BISLAND, C.P.S., Mailing Address: P.O. Box 158, Reading, 19607-0172. Tel: 610-374-9036; Fax: 610-374-9086. Email: dayspringhomes@dayspringhomes.org.

Mary's Shelter—BRENDA GEHRING, M.S.W., Prog. Dir.; DANIELLE MONAHAN, M.S.W., Asst. Exec. Dir., 325 S. 12th St., Reading, 19602-2021. Tel: 610-376-1973; Fax: 610-376-5391. Email: maryshelterrdg@verizon.net. Web: www.marysshelter.org.

Mary's Home—CHRISTINE FOLK, Exec. Dir., 736 Upland Ave., Reading, 19607. Tel: 610-603-8010; Fax: 610-603-8012. Email: chris@marysshelter.org; marysshelterrdg@verizon.net. Web: www.marysshelter.org.

Stephen's Place, Inc.—Sr. VIRGINIA LONGCOPE, M.S.C., M.S.W., Dir., 729 Ridge Ave., Bethlehem, 18015-3621. Tel: 610-861-7677; Fax: 610-861-7677. Email: vlongcope@msn.com. Web: www.stephens-place.com.

CLERGY, PARISHES, MISSIONS AND PAROCHIAL SCHOOLS

CITY OF ALLENTOWN

(LEHIGH COUNTY)

1—CATHEDRAL OF ST. CATHARINE OF SIENA (1919), (Indian), Rev. Msgr. Andrew R. Baker; Revs. Eric R. Arnout; Thomas P. Bortz; Allen J. Hoffa; Deacon William Hassler. Students 350. In Res., Rev. Msgr. Alfred R. Ott, Pastor Emeritus (Retired).
Res.: 1825 W. Turner St., 18104. Tel: 610-433-6461; Fax: 610-433-5452. Email: cathsec@ptd.net.
School—(Grades PreK-8), 210 N. 18th St., 18104. Tel: 610-435-8981; Fax: 610-437-7951. Mrs. Robin Fredericks, Prin. Lay Teachers 21; Students 237.
Catechesis/Religious Program—Tel: 610-432-7655. Sr. Laura Berryman, S.C.C., D.R.E. Students 150.

2—ST. FRANCIS OF ASSISI (1928) Rev. Msgr. David L. James; Deacon Robert P. Young. In Res., Rev. Msgr. Thomas P. Koons.
Res.: 801 N. 11th St., 18102-1304. Tel: 610-433-6102; Fax: 610-434-6972.
Business Office—1046 W. Cedar St., 18102-1304. Tel: 610-433-6102; Fax: 610-434-6972. Email: stephe@ptd.net.
School—(Grades PreK-8), 1035 W. Washington St., 18102-1305. Tel: 610-435-0364; Fax: 610-435-2666. Email: altlsf@ptd.net. Lay Teachers 11; Students 110.
Parish Center—1046 W. Cedar St., 18102-1304.
Catechesis/Religious Program—Tel: 610-433-6102, Ext. 35. Email: sfadre@aol.com. Marianne Schubert, D.R.E. Students 156.

3—IMMACULATE CONCEPTION (1857) [CEM], (Declared National Shrine of Our Lady of Guadalupe, Mother of the Americas 1974). Rev. Msgr. Albert J. Byrne; Deacons Brian J. Monahan; Richard L. Benkovic. In Res., Rev. Edwin V. Schwartz (Retired).
Res.: 501 Ridge Ave., 18102. Tel: 610-433-4404; Fax: 610-433-8401.
Schools-See Holy Spirit School, Allentown under Regional Catholic Elementary Schools, Diocesan located in the Institution section.
Catechesis/Religious Program—Students 89.

4—ST. JOHN THE BAPTIST, (Slovak), [CEM] Rev. Msgr. Robert F. Kozel.
Res.: 924 N. Front St., 18102-1912. Tel: 610-432-0034; Fax: 610-432-2776. Email: stjohn924@aol.com. Web: www.saintjohnthebaptist.net.
See Holy Spirit School, Allentown under Regional Catholic Elementary Schools, Diocesan located in the Institution section.
Convent—920 N. Front St., 18102-1998. Tel: 610-434-1471.

5—OUR LADY HELP OF CHRISTIANS (1927) Rev. John S. Pendzick; Deacon Julian Corchado. In Res., Rev. Clifton E. Bishop; Rev. Msgr. Robert M. Forst (Retired).
Res.: 444 N. Jasper St., 18109-2666. Tel: 610-432-9384; Fax: 610-782-9297.
School—934 Hanover Ave., 18109-2011. Tel: 610-433-1592; Fax: 610-434-7123. Ms. Mary K. Vanya, Prin.
Catechesis/Religious Program—Students 156.
Convent—922 Hanover Ave., 18109-2011. Tel: 610-433-4915.

6—OUR LADY OF MT. CARMEL (1911), (Italian), [CEM] Consolidated at Sacred Heart of Jesus, Allentown.

7—ST. PAUL (1928) Rev. Msgr. Joseph R. Sobiesiak; Rev. Stephen L. Maco; Deacons Gary Granato; Cu T. Than. In Res., Rev. Gregory R. Karpyn, Pastoral Ministry, Allentown Hospitals & Nursing Homes.
Res.: 920 S. Second St., 18103. Tel: 610-797-9733; Fax: 610-797-9537. Email: sprcc1@rcn.com.
Church: Second St. & Susquehanna St., 18103.
School—(Grades K-8), 219 W. Susquehanna St., 18103-3496. Tel: 610-797-5321; Fax: 610-791-5356. Email: altlsp@ptd.net. Janet Brogan, Prin. Students 131.
Catechesis/Religious Program—Students 100.

8—SS. PETER AND PAUL (1912), (Polish), Rev. Raymond P. Slezak.
Res.: 1065 Fullerton Ave., 18102. Tel: 610-432-2252; Fax: 610-432-0247.
See Holy Spirit School, Allentown under Regional Catholic Elementary Schools, Diocesan located in the Institution section.
Catechesis/Religious Program—Students 4.

9—SACRED HEART OF JESUS (1869) [CEM] Rev. Msgr. John J. Grabish; Rev. Angel L. Garcia Almodovar; Deacons Saul Hernandez; Roberto Reyes; Julian Corchado.
Res.: 336 N. Fourth St., 18102-3008. Tel: 610-434-5171; Fax: 610-434-2441.
School—(Grades PreK-8), 325 N. Fourth St., 18102-3007. Tel: 610-437-3031; Fax: 610-437-2724. Email: altlsh@ptd.net. James Krupka, Prin. Lay Teachers 10; Students 233.
Catechesis/Religious Program—317 N. 4th St., 18102. Tel: 610-434-5171, Ext. 21; Fax: 610-434-2441. Mrs. Nilsa Martinez-Fernandez, D.R.E. Students 320.

10—ST. STEPHEN OF HUNGARY (1915), (Hungarian), Rev. William N. Seifert.
Res.: 510 W. Union St., 18101-2307. Tel: 610-439-0111; Fax: 610-439-6048. Email: ststephenofhun@aol.com.
See Sacred Heart School, Allentown under Regional Catholic Elementary Schools, Diocesan located in the Institution section.

11—ST. THOMAS MORE (1966) Rev. Msgr. John P. Murphy; Revs. Christopher S. Butera; Keith A. Mathur; Deacons James R. Duncan; James Toolan; Ralph J. Jaccodine; Fredic W. Lash Jr.; Thomas F. Schubella.
Res.: 1040 Flexer Ave., 18103-5520. Tel: 610-433-7413; Fax: 610-433-2308. Email: rectory@stmchurchallentown.org. Web: www.stmchurchallentown.org.
School—Tel: 610-432-0396; Fax: 610-432-1395. Email: altlstm@ptd.com. Web: www.stmschoolpa.com. Dr. Carl P. Weber, Prin. Bernardine Sisters 2; Lay Teachers 47; Students 640.

Catechesis/Religious Program—Tel: 610-437-3491; Fax: 610-437-4935. Kevin Damitz, D.R.E. Students 601.
Convent—992 Flexer Ave., 18103-3664. Tel: 610-437-9520; Fax: 610-432-9359.

OUTSIDE CITY OF ALLENTOWN

ASHLAND, SCHUYLKILL CO.
1—ST. JOSEPH (1856) [CEM] Rev. John W. Bambrick. 1115 Walnut St., 17921-1845.
Res.: 802 Pine St., 17921-1845. Tel: 570-875-1521; Fax: 570-875-2635.
See Trinity Academy at the Father Walter J. Ciszek Education Center, Shenandoah under Regional Catholic Elementary Schools, Diocesan located in the Institution section.
Catechesis/Religious Program—Students 55.
2—ST. MAURITIUS (1856), (German), [CEM] Rev. John W. Bambrick.
Office: 1115 Walnut St., 17921. Tel: 570-875-1521; Fax: 570-875-2635.
Res.: 802 Pine St., 17921. Fax: 570-875-2635.
See Trinity Academy at the Father Walter J. Ciszek Education Center, Shenandoah under Regional Catholic Elementary Schools, Diocesan located in the Institution section.
Catechesis/Religious Program—Tel: 570-875-1521. Students 30.

BALLY, BERKS CO., MOST BLESSED SACRAMENT (1741) [CEM] Rev. Msgr. Edward J. Coyle; Revs. Michael J. Briggman, Pastor Emeritus (Retired); Robert Freed (Retired); Deacons Thomas J. Murphy; Michael J. Boyle.
Res.: 610 Pine St., Box C, 19503-1003. Tel: 610-845-2460; Fax: 610-845-2660.
See St. Francis Academy, Bally under Regional Catholic Elementary Schools, Diocesan located in the Institution section.
Catechesis/Religious Program—Students 220.

BANGOR, NORTHAMPTON CO., OUR LADY OF GOOD COUNSEL (1915) [CEM] Rev. Msgr. Thomas A. Derzack.
Res.: 436 S. Second St., 18013-2514. Tel: 610-588-5445; Fax: 610-599-6997. Email: olgc2002@epix.net.
See Our Lady of Mt. Carmel School, Roseto under Regional Catholic Elementary Schools, Diocesan located in the Institution section.
Catechesis/Religious Program—Tel: 570-897-6941; 610-588-2602. Elizabeth Thompson, D.R.E.; Pricilla Pecca, D.R.E. Students 136.
Mission—St. Vincent de Paul 720 Delaware Ave., Portland, Northampton Co. 18351.

BARNESVILLE, SCHUYLKILL CO., ST. RICHARD (1950) Rev. Joseph T. Whalen.
Res.: 799 Barnesville Dr., 18214-9747. Tel: 570-467-2315; Fax: 570-467-2462.
Catechesis/Religious Program—

BATH, NORTHAMPTON CO., SACRED HEART OF JESUS (1920) [CEM] Rev. Msgr. Francis A. Nave; Deacon Lewis T. Ferris.
Res.: 210 E. Northampton St., 18014-1625. Tel: 610-837-7874; Fax: 610-837-4570. Email: office@sacredheartchurch.com. Web: www.sacredheartchurch.com.
School—(Grades PreK-8), 115 Washington St., 18014-1524. Tel: 610-837-6391; Fax: 610-837-2469. Email: office@shschool.us. Web: www.sacred-heart-school.com. Mrs. Donna M. Blaszka, Prin. Students 150.
Catechesis/Religious Program—Mrs. Rose Prentice, D.R.E. Tel: 610-837-7874, Ext. 26. Students 189.

BEAVER MEADOWS, CARBON CO., ST. MARY (1841) [CEM] Merged with St. Nicholas, Weatherly to form Our Lady of Lourdes Parish, Weatherly.

BETHLEHEM, LEHIGH CO.
1—ASSUMPTION B.V.M. (1927) Rev. Msgrs. John J. Martin; Robert J. Coll, Pastor Emeritus (Retired); Deacons Richard Thoden; Donald W. Elliott; William F. Urbine; Mrs. Carole Chuk, Dir. Christian Ministries.
Res.: 4101 Old Bethlehem Pike, 18015-9097. Tel: 610-867-7424; Fax: 610-867-8301. Email: abvmrect@ptd.net. Web: www.assumptionbethlehem.com.
See St. Michael the Archangel School, Bethlehem under Regional Catholic Elementary Schools, Diocesan located in the Institution section.
Catechesis/Religious Program—Tel: 610-814-0712. Christina Bigatel Durback, D.R.E. Students 595.
2—NOTRE DAME OF BETHLEHEM (1954) Rev. Msgr. Thomas D. Baddick; Rev. Joel E. Kiefer; Deacon Michael W. Doncsecz. In Res., Revs. Achilles Ayaton; Bernard J. Ezaki.
Res.: 1861 Catasauqua Rd., 18018-1298. Tel: 610-866-4371; Fax: 610-866-9065. Web: www.churchofndbeth.org.
School—(Grades K-8), 1835 Catasauqua Rd., 18018-1211. Tel: 610-866-2231; Fax: 610-866-4374. Email: altlndb@ptd.net. Web: www.ndbeth.org. Mrs. Kathy Maziarz, Prin.; Mrs. Rosalie Weitman, Librarian. Lay Teachers 28; Students 376.
Catechesis/Religious Program—Tel: 610-866-1418. Mrs. Stephanie Kalavoda, D.R.E. Students 404.
3—SS. SIMON AND JUDE (1917) Rev. Msgr. William F. Baver; Deacons Reuben H. Hartzell Jr.; Jeffrey R. Trexler.
Res.: 730 W. Broad St., 18018. Tel: 610-866-5582; Fax: 610-866-2992.
See Seton Academy, Bethlehem under Regional Catholic Elementary Schools.
Catechesis/Religious Program—Tel: 610-866-5582, Ext. 7. Students 65.
Convent—714 W. Broad St., 18018. Tel: 610-867-9546.

BETHLEHEM, NORTHAMPTON CO.
1—ST. ANNE (1929) Revs. Anthony P. Mongiello; Thomas P. Bortz; Deacons Francis J. Cosgrove; Richard L. Gergar.
Res.: 450 E. Washington Ave., 18017-5944. Tel: 610-867-5039; Fax: 610-882-4094. Email: st.annes.rectory@verizon.net. Web: www.stannebethlehem.catholicweb.com.
School—(Grades PreK-8), 375 Hickory St., 18017-5944. Tel: 610-868-4182; 610-868-7513 (preschool); Fax: 610-868-8709. Email: altnsa@ptd.net. Web: www.stannebethlehem.org. Mrs. Annette M. Filler, Prin. Students 447.
Catechesis/Religious Program—
2—SS. CYRIL AND METHODIUS (1891), (Slovak), [CEM] Merged with Our Lady of Pompeii, St. John Capistrano, St. Joseph & St. Stanislaus, Bethlehem to form Incarnation of Our Lord Parish, Bethlehem.
3—HOLY GHOST (1871), (German), [CEM] Rev. Wayne E. Killian; Rev. Msgr. Richard J. Loeper, Pastor Emeritus (Retired); Deacon Franklin J. Chiles.
See Seton Academy, Bethlehem under Regional Catholic Elementary Schools, Diocesan located in the Institution section.
Holy Ghost Pre-School—Tel: 610-867-5939. Mrs. Jane Zakovitch, Dir.
Catechesis/Religious Program—Tel: 610-867-9382. Mrs. Mary C. Elliott, D.R.E.
4—HOLY INFANCY (1861) [CEM] Rev. Msgr. Robert J. Biszek; Rev. Robson Luis Weber; Deacons Nicasio Rodriguez; Manuel Ramirez; Rodoberto Matos.
Res.: 312 E. Fourth St., 18015-1706. Tel: 610-866-1121; Fax: 610-866-7094. Email: holyinfancy@aol.com.
School—(Grades PreK-8), 127 E. 4th St., 18015-1707. Tel: 610-868-2621; Fax: 610-868-5402. Email: altnhi@ptd.net. Sr. Joyce Valese, S.S.J., Prin. Students 170.
Catechesis/Religious Program— Sr. Moira Frawley, O.S.F., D.R.E. Tel: 610-866-1121, Ext. 12. Students 353.
Convent—Sisters of St. Joseph, 202 E. 4th St., 18015-1704. Tel: 610-867-7384. Email: sjoyce@onecommail.com.
Convent—Poor Sisters of St. Joseph, Casa Belen, 305 E. Fourth St., 18015. Tel: 610-867-4030. Email: hnasbelen@att.net. Sr. Rosa B. But, P.S.S.J., Supr.
5—INCARNATION OF OUR LORD PARISH (2008) [CEM], Formed by the merger of Our Lady of Pompeii, St. John Capistrano, St. Joseph, St. Stanislaus and SS. Cyril and Methodius, Bethlehem. Rev. William T. Baker.
Thomas and Buchanan Sts., 18015.
Rectory—617 Pierce St., 18015-3498. Tel: 610-866-3391; Fax: 610-866-6490.
See Seton Academy, Bethlehem under Regional Catholic Elementary Schools, Diocesan located in the Institution section.
Convent—520 Buchanan St., 18015-3499. Tel: 610-866-0275.
6—ST. JOHN CAPISTRANO (1903), (Hungarian), Merged with SS. Cyril and Methodius, Our Lady of Pompeii, St. Joseph & St. Stanislaus, Bethlehem to form Incarnation of Our Lord, Bethlehem.
7—ST. JOSEPH (1913), (Slovenian—Croatian), Merged with SS. Cyril and Methodius, Our Lady of Pompeii, St. John Capistrano & St. Stanislaus, Bethlehem to form Incarnation of Our Lord Parish, Bethlehem.
8—OUR LADY OF PERPETUAL HELP (1963) Rev. Msgr. Edward R. Sacks; Rev. Richard C. Brensinger; Deacons Joseph G. Buragino; George C. Kelly Jr. In Res., Rev. Msgr. David J. Morrison (Retired).
Res.: 3219 Santee Rd., 18020. Tel: 610-867-8409; Fax: 610-867-4870.
School—3221 Santee Rd., 18020. Tel: 610-868-6570; Fax: 610-868-7941. Lay Teachers 14; Students 295.
Catechesis/Religious Program—Students 502.
9—OUR LADY OF POMPEII (1902), (Italian), Merged with SS. Cyril and Methodius, St. John Capistrano, St. Joseph & St. Stanislaus, Bethlehem to form Incarnation of Our Lord Parish, Bethlehem.
10—SACRED HEART OF JESUS (1936) Rev. Robert J. George; Deacons Hugh E. McShane; Hugh Carlin. In Res., Rev. Robert T. Finlan.
Res.: 1817 First St., 18020. Tel: 610-865-5042; Fax: 610-865-1912. Email: shchbeth@etd.net.
School—(Grades K-8), 1814 Second St., 18020. Tel: 610-867-0221; Fax: 610-867-8351. John Schulte, Prin. Lay Teachers 11; Students 167.
Catechesis/Religious Program—Tel: 610-867-0221. Students 100.
11—ST. STANISLAUS (1906), (Polish), Merged with SS. Cyril and Methodius, Our Lady of Pompeii, St. John Capistrano & St. Joseph, Bethlehem to form Incarnation of Our Lord Parish, Bethlehem.

BOYERTOWN, BERKS CO., ST. COLUMBKILL (1921) Revs. Martin F. Kern; Robert J. McConaghy; Deacons Michael Woodall; Joseph L. Paschall Jr.
Res.: 200 Indian Spring Rd., 19512-2008. Tel: 610-367-2371; Fax: 610-369-0242. Email: pastor@stcolumbkill.com. Web: stcolumbkill.com.
See St. Francis Academy, Bally under Regional Catholic Elementary Schools, Diocesan located in the Institution section.
Catechesis/Religious Program—Tel: 610-367-5975. Sr. Nancy Kramer, S.S.J., D.R.E.; Constance Boyer, D.R.E. Students 664.

BRANCHDALE, SCHUYLKILL CO., ST. MARY STAR OF THE SEA (1886) [CEM] Merged with St. Stanislaus Kosta, St. Barbara & St. Francis of Assisi, Minersville to form St. Matthew the Evangelist, Minersville.

BROCKTON, SCHUYLKILL CO., ST. BARTHOLOMEW (1846) [CEM] Consolidated at St. Jerome, Tamaqua.

CATASAUQUA, LEHIGH CO., ANNUNCIATION B.V.M.-ST. MARY'S (1857), (German), [CEM] Rev. Msgr. Victor F. Finelli, Admin.; Deacon Joseph H. Bogusky.
Res.: 122 Union St., 18032-1923. Tel: 610-264-0332; Fax: 610-264-5271.
Catechesis/Religious Program—Tel: 610-264-9383. Christina Moriarty, D.R.E. Students 103.

CATASAUQUA, NORTHAMPTON CO.
1—ST. ANDREW (1902), (Slovak), [CEM] Rev. Eric J. Gruber, Admin.
Mailing Address: 1001 2nd St., 18032-2764. Tel: 610-264-1972; Fax: 610-264-2105.
Church: 1229 3rd St., North Catasauqua, 18032.
Schools-See Our Lady of Hungary Regional School, Northampton under Regional Catholic Elementary Schools, Diocesan located in the Institution section.
Catechesis/Religious Program—Tel: 610-264-1972. Regina Marhefka, D.R.E. Located at St Lawrence, Catasauqua Students 14.
2—ST. LAWRENCE THE MARTYR (Lehigh Co.) (1858) [CEM 2] Rev. Eric J. Gruber, Admin.; Deacon Thomas B. Reimer.
Res.: 1001 Second St., 18032. Tel: 610-264-1972; Fax: 610-264-2105.
School— Please see separate listing under Regional Catholic Elementary Schools, Diocesan in the Institutions section.
Catechesis/Religious Program—Students 70.

COALDALE, SCHUYLKILL CO.
1—SS. CYRIL AND METHODIUS (1920), (Slovak), [CEM] Merged with St. John the Baptist & St. Mary, Coaldale; St. Michael, St. Ann & SS. Peter and Paul, Lansford to form St. Katharine Drexel Parish, Lansford.
2—ST. JOHN THE BAPTIST (1914), (Lithuanian), [JC] Merged with SS. Cyril and Methodius & St. Mary, Coaldale; St. Michael, St. Ann & SS. Peter and Paul, Lansford to form St. Katharine Drexel Parish, Lansford.
3—ST. MARY OF THE ASSUMPTION (1892) Merged with SS. Cyril and Methodius & St. John the Baptist, Coaldale; St. Michael, St. Ann & SS. Peter and Paul, Lansford to form St. Katharine Drexel Parish, Lansford.

COPLAY, LEHIGH CO., ST. PETER (1927), (Austrian—Hungarian), [CEM] Rev. Msgrs. William E. Handges; John A. Auchter.
Res.: 4 S. Fifth St., 18037. Tel: 610-262-2417; Fax: 610-262-2652.
See Christ the King School, Whitehall under Regional Catholic Elementary Schools, Diocesan located in the Institution section.
Catechesis/Religious Program—Students 90.

CUMBOLA, SCHUYLKILL CO., ST. ANTHONY OF PADUA (1907), (Polish), [CEM] Merged with Holy Family & Sacred Heart, New Philadelphia to form Holy Cross Parish, New Philadelphia.

DOUGLASSVILLE, BERKS CO., IMMACULATE CONCEPTION (1916) [CEM 2] Rev. Msgrs. John B. McCann; Voltaire Rono; Deacon Paul J. Hiryak Jr. In Res., Rev. Msgrs. Richard J. Loeper (Retired); Thomas J. Birch (Retired).
Res.: 905 Chestnut St., 19518-9006. Tel: 610-582-2411; Fax: 610-404-2609. Email: secretary@icbvm.com. Web: www.icbvm.org.
School—Immaculate Conception Academy, (Grades K-8), 903 Chestnut St., 19518. Tel: 610-404-8645; Fax: 610-404-4890. Mrs. Christine Foley, Prin. Students 209.
Catechesis/Religious Program—Tel: 610-582-3880; Fax: 610-404-2609. Patricia Tarquinio, D.R.E. Students 470.

EASTON, NORTHAMPTON CO.
1—ST. ANTHONY OF PADUA (1909), (Italian), [CEM] Rev. Msgr. Edward S. Zemanik; Deacon Charles A. DeBellis.
Res.: 900 Washington St., 18042-4342. Tel: 610-253-7188; Fax: 610-253-6184.
See Easton Catholic School, Easton under Regional Catholic Elementary Schools, Diocesan, located in the Institution section.
Catechesis/Religious Program—Mrs. Karen Donato, D.R.E. Students 191.
Convent—910 Washington St., 18042. Tel: 610-258-7792; Fax: 610-258-7792.
2—ST. BERNARD (1829) [CEM] [JC] Merged with St. Joseph & St. Michael, Easton to form Our Lady of Mercy Parish, Easton.
3—ST. JANE FRANCES DE CHANTAL (1920) [JC] Rev. Msgr. Stephen J. Radocha; Revs. Keith R. Laskowski; Robert R. Fagan (Retired); Eric N. Tolentino; Deacons Robert W. Rodgers; Ranulfo Raymundo; John A. Hanni; Noreen McDonough, Business Mgr.
4049 Hartley Ave., 18045.
Res.: 123 S. Nulton Ave., 18045-3791. Tel: 610-253-3553; Fax: 610-253-5711. Web: www.stjanesofeastonpa.com.
School—(Grades PreK-8), 1900 Washington Blvd., 18042-4619. Tel: 610-253-8442; Fax: 610-253-2427. Email: altnsjf@ptd.net. Mrs. Isabel Conlin, Prin.; Jeane Corradino, Librarian. Lay Teachers 23; Students 457.
Catechesis/Religious Program—Tel: 610-253-7794, Ext. 13. Kevin Kimmel, D.R.E. Students 613.
4—ST. JOSEPH (1852) [CEM 2] Merged with St. Bernard & St. Michael, Easton to form Our Lady of Mercy Parish, Easton.
5—ST. MICHAEL (1916), (Lithuanian), [CEM] Merged with St. Bernard & St. Joseph, Easton to form Our Lady of Mercy Parish, Easton.
6—OUR LADY OF MERCY PARISH (2008), Formed by the merger of St. Bernard, St. Joseph and St. Michael, Easton. Public oratory for weekday masses: St. Bernard, 134 S. 5th St. Revs. Deogratias Rwegasira, A.J. (Tanzania); Constantine Oduori, A.J.; Deacons Jose F. DeCastro; Henry J. Fleck Jr. St. Joseph and Davis Sts., 18042. In Res., Rev. Avitus Siriwa, A.J., Catholic Ministry to the Sick.
Office: 132 S. Fifth St., 18042-4418. Tel: 610-252-7381; Fax: 610-252-6757. Email: info@olomercy.com. Web: www.olomercy.com.
Rectory—129 Davis St., 18042-6295.
Catechesis/Religious Program—Mrs. Kelly DeRaymond, D.R.E.
ELLENGOWAN, SCHUYLKILL CO., ST. AIDAN, Closed. Parish from November 1919 to July 9, 1948. Records at the Annunciation B.V.M. Church, Shenandoah (Phone: 570-462-1916).
EMMAUS, LEHIGH CO., ST. ANN (1931) [CEM] Rev. Msgr. John S. Mraz; Rev. Dominic Thao Pham; Deacon Dominic F. Amedeo Jr.
Res.: 415 S. Sixth St., 18049-3703. Tel: 610-965-2426; Fax: 610-967-1099.
School—(Grades PreK-8), 435 S. 6th St., 18049. Tel: 610-965-9220; Fax: 610-967-4521. Diana Kile, Prin. Sisters 1; Lay Teachers 23; Students 282.
Catechesis/Religious Program—Tel: 610-965-6888. Cris Kimock, D.R.E. Students 385.
Convent—526 Fairview St., 18049. Tel: 610-965-6818.
FOUNTAIN HILL, LEHIGH CO., ST. URSULA (Bethlehem P.O.) (1919) Rev. Robert J. Potts; Deacon David K. Rohner. In Res., Rev. Stephen V. Mallya, A.J.
Res.: 1300 Broadway, 18015-4099. Tel: 610-867-5122; Fax: 610-867-6569.
See Bethlehem under Regional Catholic Elementary Schools, Diocesan located in the Institution section.
Catechesis/Religious Program—Tel: 610-861-2897. Students 31.
FRACKVILLE, SCHUYLKILL CO.
1—ST. ANN (1924), (Polish), Rev. Edward J. Essig.
Res.: 7 S. Broad Mountain Ave., 17931-1800. Tel: 570-874-0842; Fax: 570-874-2265.
Schools-See Trinity Academy at the Father Walter J. Ciszek Education Center, Shenandoah under Regional Catholic Elementary Schools, Diocesan located in the Institution section.
Catechesis/Religious Program—William Blickly, D.R.E. Students 30.
2—ANNUNCIATION B.V.M. (1917), (Lithuanian), [CEM] Rev. Edward J. Essig.
Res.: 7 S. Broad Mountain Ave., 17931-1800. Tel: 570-874-0842; Fax: 570-874-2265.
Schools-See Trinity Academy at the Father Walter J. Ciszek Education Center, Shenandoah under Regional Catholic Elementary Schools, Diocesan located in the Institution section.
Catechesis/Religious Program—William Blickly, D.R.E. Students 30.
3—ST. JOSEPH (1909) [CEM] Rev. J. Michael Beers.
Res.: 14 N. Nice St., 17931-1310. Tel: 570-874-0610; Fax: 570-874-0969. Email: stjoes@chilitech.net.
See Trinity Academy at the Father Walter J. Ciszek Education Center, Shenandoah under Regional Catholic Elementary Schools, Diocesan located in the Institution section.
GIRARDVILLE, SCHUYLKILL CO.
1—ST. JOSEPH (1870) [CEM] Rev. Edward B. Connolly.
Mailing Address & Parish Center: 260 N. 2nd, 17935-1338. Tel: 570-276-6033; Fax: 570-276-6032. Email: stjospar@verizon.net.
See Trinity Academy at the Father Walter J. Ciszek Education Center, Shenandoah under Regional Catholic Elementary Schools, Diocesan located in the Institution section.
2—ST. VINCENT DE PAUL (1907), (Lithuanian), [CEM] Revs. Edward B. Connolly; David M. Liebner, Pastor Emeritus (Retired).
Res.: 260 N. Second St., 17935. Tel: 570-276-6033; 570-276-6239; Fax: 570-276-6032. Email: stvdppar@verizon.net.
See Immaculate Heart Elementary School, Girardville under Regional Catholic Elementary Schools, Diocesan located in the Institution section.
Catechesis/Religious Program—Students 10.
GORDON, SCHUYLKILL CO., OUR LADY OF GOOD COUNSEL (1922) Revs. John W. Bambrick, 1115 Walnut St., Ashland, 17921; Thomas A. Horan, Pastor Emeritus (Retired), 802 Pine St., Ashland, 17921.
Res.: 220 W. Biddle St., P.O. Box 9, 17936-9999. Tel: 570-875-1521; Fax: 570-875-2635.
See Trinity Academy at the Father Walter J. Ciszek Education Center, Shenandoah under Regional Catholic Elementary Schools, Diocesan located in the Institution section.
Catechesis/Religious Program—Sr. Elizabeth Kealy, I.H.M., D.R.E. Students 11.
HAMBURG, BERKS CO., ST. MARY (1854) [CEM] Revs. Donald W. Cieniewicz; James M. Torpey; Deacon Henry G. Gordon.
Res.: 94 Walnut Rd., P.O. Box 189, 19526. Tel: 610-562-7657; Fax: 610-562-0379. Email: stmary@stmaryhamburg.org. Web: www.rc.net/allentown/stmaryhamb.
Catechesis/Religious Program—Email: stmaryprep@stmaryhamburg.org. Mrs. Brenda Cordier, D.R.E. Students 185.
Station—Hamburg State School and Hospital, Tel: 610-562-6063.
HECKSCHERVILLE, SCHUYLKILL CO., ST. KIERAN (1857) [CEM] Merged with Our Lady of Mount Carmel & St. Vincent de Paul, Minersville to form St. Michael the Archangel Parish, Minersville.
HELLERTOWN, NORTHAMPTON CO., ST. THERESA OF THE CHILD JESUS (1925) Rev. Msgr. Alfred A. Schlert; Rev. Jerome A. Tauber.
Res.: 1408 Easton Rd., 18055-1127. Tel: 610-838-7045; Fax: 610-838-0932. Email: sttheresacj@enter.net.
School—(Grades PreK-8), 300 Leonard St., 18055-1199. Tel: 610-838-8161; Fax: 610-838-1915. Email: altnst@ptd.net. Mrs. Louise Glass, Prin.; Kenneth Westgate, Librarian. Lay Teachers 15; Students 120.
Catechesis/Religious Program—Tel: 610-838-7645. Students 112.
Convent—255 Wilson Ave., 18055-1454.
JIM THORPE, CARBON CO.
1—IMMACULATE CONCEPTION (1848) [CEM] Rev. James J. Ward.
Res.: 180 W. Broadway, 18229. Tel: 570-325-2791; Fax: 570-325-2427.
See St. Joseph Regional Academy, Jim Thorpe under Regional Catholic Elementary Schools, Diocesan located in the Institution section.
Catechesis/Religious Program—Mrs. Kathleen D. Merkel, C.R.E. Students 65.
2—ST. JOSEPH (1871) [CEM] Rev. Francis J. Baransky.
Res.: 526 North St., 18229. Tel: 570-325-3731; Fax: 570-325-2523.
Schools-See St. Joseph Regional Academy, Jim Thorpe under Regional Catholic Elementary Schools, Diocesan located in the Institution section.
Catechesis/Religious Program—Mrs. Kathleen D. Merkel, D.R.E. Students 54.
KELAYRES, SCHUYLKILL CO., IMMACULATE CONCEPTION (1899), (Italian), [CEM] Merged with St. Kunegunda, St. Mary & St. Patrick, McAdoo; St. Michael & St. Bartholomew, Tresckow to form All Saints Parish, McAdoo.
KUTZTOWN, BERKS CO., ST. MARY (1919) Rev. Msgr. Walter T. Scheaffer.
Res.: 14833 Kutztown Rd., 19530. Tel: 610-683-7443; 610-683-7466 (Church); Fax: 610-683-7625. Email: stmarysktown@verizon.net. Web: www.stmaryskutztown.com.
Catechesis/Religious Program—Tel: 610-683-6454. Students 385.
LAKE HARMONY, CARBON CO., ST. PETER THE FISHERMAN (1982) Rev. Msgrs. John G. Chizmar; John A. Auchter, Pastor Emeritus; Deacon John F. Thompson.
Res.: Lake Dr., P.O. Box 237, 18624-0237. Tel: 570-722-2034; Fax: 570-722-1348. Email: stpeter@ptd.net.
Catechesis/Religious Program—Students 118.
LANSFORD, CARBON CO.
1—ST. ANN, Merged with SS. Cyril and Methodius, St. John the Baptist & St. Mary, Coaldale; St. Michael & SS. Peter and Paul, Lansford to form St. Katharine Drexel Parish, Lansford.
2—ST. KATHARINE DREXEL PARISH (2008) [CEM 3], Formed by the merger of St. John the Baptist, St. Mary & SS. Cyril and Methodius Parishes, Coaldale and St. Ann, St. Michael & SS. Peter and Paul Parishes, Lansford. Rev. Kenneth A. Medve; Deacon James P. Henninger.
Mailing Address: 124 E. Abbott St., 18232-0177. Tel: 570-645-2282; Fax: 570-645-2754.
Rectory—41 E. Ruddle St., Coaldale, 18218-1206.
See Our Lady of the Angels Academy, Lansford under Regional Catholic Elementary Schools, Diocesan located in the Institution section.
3—ST. MICHAEL (1891), (Slovak), [CEM] Merged with SS. Cyril and Methodius, St. John the Baptist & St. Mary, Coaldale; St. Ann & SS. Peter and Paul, Lansford to form St. Katharine Drexel Parish, Lansford.
4—SS. PETER AND PAUL (1907), (Polish), [CEM] Merged with SS. Cyril and Methodius, St. John the Baptist & St. Mary, Coaldale; St. Michael & St. Ann, Lansford to form St. Katharine Drexel Parish, Lansford.
LEHIGHTON, CARBON CO., SS. PETER AND PAUL (1885), (German), [CEM] Rev. Michael E. Ahrensfield.
Res.: 260 N. Third St., 18235-1595. Tel: 610-377-3690; Fax: 610-377-0721. Email: sspp@ptd.net. Web: www.ssppchurch.com.
School—307 Coal St., 18235-1458. Tel: 610-377-4466; Fax: 610-377-8881. Email: altcspp@ptd.net. Web: www.sppschool.org. Mrs. Sherry Ambrose, Prin. Students (Early childhood to 8) 100.
Catechesis/Religious Program—Students 105.
LIMEPORT, LEHIGH CO., ST. JOSEPH (1926) [CEM] Rev. Thomas R. Buckley; Deacon Dennis P. Meyer.
Res.: 5050 St. Joseph's Rd., Coopersburg, 18036-8920. Tel: 610-965-2877; Fax: 610-965-8317. Email: stjoes@ptd.net. Web: www.st-mikes.com.
See St. Michael the Archangel School, Limeport & Colesville under Regional Catholic Elementary Schools, Diocesan located in the Institution section.
Catechesis/Religious Program—Tel: 610-965-0590. Students 278.
LOST CREEK, SCHUYLKILL CO., ST. MARY MAGDALEN (1879) [JC] Rev. Msgr. Bernard A. Flanagan.
Res. & Parish Office: 218 W. Cherry St., Shenandoah, 17976-2226. Tel: 570-462-1916; Fax: 570-462-1980. Email: rccos@shenhgts.net. Web: saintmarymagdalen.catholicweb.com.
See Trinity Academy at the Father Walter J. Ciszek Education Center, Shenandoah under Regional Catholic Elementary Schools, Diocesan located in the Institution section.
Catechesis/Religious Program—Students 4.
MAHANOY CITY, SCHUYLKILL CO.
1—ASSUMPTION B.V.M. (1892), (Slovak), [CEM] Merged with St. Canicus, St. Casimir, St. Fidelis, St. Joseph & Sacred Heart, Mahanoy City; Our Lady of Siluva, Maizeville to form Blessed Teresa of Calcutta Parish, Mahanoy City.
2—BLESSED TERESA OF CALCUTTA PARISH, Formed by the merger of Assumption B.V.M., St. Canicus, St. Casimir, St. Fidelis, St. Joseph & Sacred Heart, Mahanoy City; Our Lady of Siluva, Maizeville. Rev. Kevin P. Gallagher; Deacon Joseph J. Costa.
600 W. Mahanoy Ave., 17948.
Office: 614 W. Mahanoy Ave., 17948-2416. Tel: 570-773-2771; Fax: 570-773-1937. Email: btoc@ptd.net.
See Academy of the Blessed Virgin Mary, Mahanoy City under Regional Catholic Elementary Schools, Diocesan located in the Institution section.
3—ST. CANICUS (1862), (Irish), [CEM] Merged with Assumption B.V.M., St. Casimir, St. Fidelis, St. Joseph & Sacred Heart, Mahanoy City; Our Lady of Siluva, Maizeville to form Blessed Teresa of Calcutta Parish, Mahanoy City.
4—ST. CASIMIR (1893), (Polish), [CEM] Merged with Assumption B.V.M., St. Canicus, St. Fidelis, St. Joseph & Sacred Heart, Mahanoy City; Our Lady of Siluva, Maizeville to form Blessed Teresa of Calcutta Parish, Mahanoy City.
5—ST. FIDELIS (1863), (German), [CEM] Merged with Assumption B.V.M., St. Canicus, St. Casimir, St. Joseph & Sacred Heart, Mahanoy City; Our Lady of Siluva, Maizeville to form Blessed Teresa of Calcutta Parish, Mahanoy City.
6—ST. JOSEPH (1888), (Lithuanian), [CEM] Merged with Assumption B.V.M., St. Canicus, St. Casimir, St. Fidelis & Sacred Heart, Mahanoy City; Our Lady of Siluva, Maizeville to form Blessed Teresa of Calcutta Parish, Mahanoy City.
7—SACRED HEART (1907), (Italian), [CEM] Merged

with Assumption B.V.M., St. Canicus, St. Casimir, St. Fidelis & St. Joseph, Mahanoy City; Our Lady of Siluva, Maizeville to form Blessed Teresa of Calcutta Parish, Mahanoy City.

MAHANOY PLANE, SCHUYLKILL CO., HOLY ROSARY (1988) Closed. Parish records at St. Joseph's, Girardville.

MAIZEVILLE, SCHUYLKILL CO., OUR LADY OF SILUVA (1907), (Lithuanian), [CEM] Merged with Assumption B.V.M., St. Canicus, St. Casimir, St. Fidelis, St. Joseph & Sacred Heart, Mahanoy City to form Blessed Teresa of Calcutta Parish, Mahanoy City.

MARTINS CREEK, NORTHAMPTON CO., ST. ROCCO (1929) Rev. Msgr. James J. Reichert.
Res.: 6658 School St., Box 421, 18063-0010. Tel: 610-258-9059; Fax: 610-258-4780. Email: strocco@enter.net. Web: strocco.org.
See Immaculate Conception School, Pen Argyl under Regional Catholic Elementary Schools, Diocesan located in the Institution section.
Catechesis/Religious Program—Students 106.

MCADOO, SCHUYLKILL CO.
1—ALL SAINTS PARISH (2008), Formed by the merger of Immaculate Conception, Kelayres; St. Kunegunda, St. Mary & St. Patrick, McAdoo; St. Michael & St. Bartholomew, Tresckow. Rev. Ronald J. Minner.
Mailing Address: 36 E. Washington Ave., 18237-1842. Tel: 570-929-1073; Fax: 570-929-1073. Email: churchofallsaints@earthlink.net. In Res., Rev. George R. Winne, Dir. Spiritual Activities.
Church: 21 N. Cleveland St., 18237.
High School—Marian High School, Tamaqua.
2—ST. KUNEGUNDA (1893), (Polish), [CEM] Merged with Immaculate Conception, Kelayres; St. Mary & St. Patrick, McAdoo; St. Michael & St. Bartholomew, Tresckow to form All Saints Parish, McAdoo.
3—ST. MARY (1893), (Slovak), [CEM] Merged with Immaculate Conception, Kelayres; St. Kunegunda & St. Patrick, McAdoo; St. Michael & St. Bartholomew, Tresckow to form All Saints Parish, McAdoo.
4—ST. PATRICK (1869), (Irish), [CEM] Merged with Immaculate Conception, Kelayres; St. Kunegunda & St. Mary, McAdoo; St. Michael & St. Bartholomew, Tresckow to form All Saints Parish, McAdoo.
5—ST. STEPHEN, (Hungarian), Closed. Formerly a mission of St. Kunegonda, McAdoo. For inquiries for parish records contact Mother church (phone/fax: 570-929-1073).

MINERSVILLE, SCHUYLKILL CO.
1—ST. BARBARA (1913), (Italian), [CEM] Merged with St. Stanislaus Kostka & St. Francis of Assisi, Minersville; St. Mary, Star of the Sea, Branchdale to form St. Matthew the Evangelist, Minersville.
2—ST. FRANCIS OF ASSISI (1895), (Lithuanian), [CEM] Merged with St. Stanislaus Kostka & St. Barbara, Minersville; St. Mary, Star of the Sea, Branchdale to form St. Matthew the Evangelist, Minersville.
3—ST. MATTHEW THE EVANGELIST (2008), Formed by the merger of St. Stanislaus Kostka, St. Francis of Assisi & St. Barbara, Minersville; St. Mary, Star of the Sea, Branchdale. Rev. Leo J. Maletz.
135 Spruce St., 17954.
Parish Center: 120 Oak St. Tel: 570-544-5485.
Rectory—139 Spruce St., 17954-1642. Tel: 570-544-2211; Fax: 570-544-2317. Email: ssk1905@verizon.net. Web: www.stmatthewtheevangelistparish.org.
See All Saints Regional School, Pottsville, under Regional Catholic Elementary Schools, Diocesan located in the Institution section.
Catechesis/Religious Program—Tel: 570-544-3766. Ms. Rosalie Novack, D.R.E. Students 90.
4—ST. MICHAEL THE ARCHANGEL PARISH (2008), Formed by the merger of Our Lady of Mount Carmel & St. Vincent de Paul, Minersville; St. Kieran, Heckscherville. Rev. Adam C. Sedar.
541 Sunbury St., 17954.
Rectory—538 Sunbury St., 17954-1015. Tel: 570-544-4741; 540-544-4360 (Parish Center); Fax: 570-544-4742. Email: st.michaelthearchangelminers@hotmail.com.
See All Saints Regional School, Pottsville, under Regional Catholic Elementary Schools, Diocesan located in the Institution section.
Catechesis/Religious Program—Sr. Catherine T. Brennan, S.S.J., D.R.E.
Convent—Tel: 570-544-2016. Email: ssjmin@comcast.net.
5—OUR LADY OF MOUNT CARMEL (1855), (German), [CEM] Merged with St. Vincent de Paul, Minersville & St. Kieran, Heckscherville to form St. Michael the Archangel Parish, Minersville.
6—ST. STANISLAUS KOSTKA (1905), (Polish), [CEM 2] Merged with St. Barbara & St. Francis of Assisi, Minersville; St. Mary, Star of the Sea, Branchdale to form St. Matthew the Evangelist, Minersville.
7—ST. VINCENT DE PAUL (1842) [CEM 2] Merged with Our Lady of Mount Carmel, Minersville & St. Kieran, Heckscherville to form St. Michael the Archangel Parish, Minersville.

MOHNTON, BERKS CO., ST. BENEDICT'S (1955) Rev. Philip F. Rodgers. In Res., Rev. Robert C. Quinn (Retired).
Res.: 2020 Chesnut Hill Rd., 19540-8243. Tel: 610-856-1006; Fax: 610-856-1035. Email: stbenedict2020@dejazzd.com.
See La Salle Academy and Early Childhood Center, Shillington under Regional Catholic Elementary Schools, Diocesan located in the Institution section.
Catechesis/Religious Program—Tel: 610-370-0199; 610-856-5146. Ms. Valerie Christo-Pinheiro, D.R.E. Students 274.

MOUNT CARBON, SCHUYLKILL CO., ST. FRANCIS DE SALES (Pottsville P.O.) (1922) Consolidated at St. Patrick, Pottsville.

NAZARETH, NORTHAMPTON CO., HOLY FAMILY (1908) [CEM 2] Revs. Joseph F. Tobias, M.S.C.; Simione Vola Vola, M.S.C. (Fiji); Antony Lazar, M.S.C. (India); Deacons Donald J. Dupont, Gracedave Ministry; Frank J. Danyi Jr., Parish Ministry.
Res.: 23 Forest Dr., 18064-1300. Tel: 610-759-0870; Fax: 610-746-2026. Email: hfp23@rcn.com. Web: holyfamilyonline.org.
School—(Grades PreK-8), 17 Convent Ave., 18064-1324. Tel: 610-759-5642; Fax: 610-759-0386. Web: holyfamilynazareth.org. Mrs. Colette Fisher, Prin. Lay Teachers 22; Students 299.
Catechesis/Religious Program—Tel: 610-759-2623 (Grades K-8). Email: elyd@holyfamily-edu.org. Donna Ely, D.R.E. Students 665.

NESQUEHONING, CARBON CO.
1—ST. FRANCIS OF ASSISI PARISH (2008), Formed by the merger of Immaculate Conception, Sacred Heart and Our Lady of Mount Carmel Parishes, Nesquehoning. Rev. Anthony M. Drounchеck.
Mill and Radcliff Sts., 18240.
Rectory—15 E. Garibaldi Ave., 18240-1109. Tel: 570-669-6321; Fax: 570-669-9440. Email: iccnesq@ptd.net.
See Our Lady of the Angels Academy, Lansford under Regional Catholic Elementary Schools, Diocesan located in the Institution section.
2—IMMACULATE CONCEPTION OF B.V.M. (1914), (Slovak), Merged with Our Lady of Mt. Carmel & Sacred Heart, Nesquehoning to form St. Francis of Assisi Parish, Nesquehoning.
3—OUR LADY OF MOUNT CARMEL (1913), (Italian), [CEM] Merged with Immaculate Conception of B.V.M. & Sacred Heart, Nesquehoning to form St. Francis of Assisi Parish, Nesquehoning.
4—SACRED HEART (1839) [CEM 2] Merged with Immaculate Conception of B.V.M. & Our Lady of Mount Carmel, Nesquehoning to form St. Francis of Assisi Parish, Nesquehoning.

NEW PHILADELPHIA, SCHUYLKILL CO.
1—HOLY CROSS PARISH (2008) [CEM 3], Formed by the merger of Holy Family & Sacred Heart, New Philadelphia; St. Anthony of Padua, Cumbola. Rev. Joseph J. Kweder.
101 Valley St., 17959.
Office & Rectory: 99 Valley St., 17959-1103. Tel: 570-277-6800; Fax: 570-277-0528. Email: hfchurch@f-tech.net.
See St. Stephen Regional Elementary School, Port Carbon under Regional Catholic Elementary Schools, Diocesan located in the Institution section.
Catechesis/Religious Program—Students 22.
2—HOLY FAMILY (1866) Merged with Sacred Heart, New Philadelphia & St. Anthony of Padua, Cumbola to form Holy Cross Parish, New Philadelphia.
3—SACRED HEART (1895), (Lithuanian), [CEM] Merged with Holy Family, New Philadelphia & St. Anthony of Padua, Cumbola to form Holy Cross Parish, New Philadelphia.

NEWTOWN, SCHUYLKILL CO., SACRED HEART (1896) [CEM] Merged with Immaculate Conception, Tremont & SS. Peter and Paul, Tower City to form Most Blessed Trinity Parish, Tremont.

NORTHAMPTON, NORTHAMPTON CO.
1—ASSUMPTION OF THE BLESSED VIRGIN MARY (1922), (Slovak), [CEM] Rev. Francis P. Straka; Deacon Anthony L. Brasten.
Res.: 2174 Lincoln Ave., 18067-1257. Tel: 610-262-2559; Fax: 610-262-1613. Email: bvm1922@rcn.com. See Our Lady of Hungary Regional School, Northampton under Regional Catholic Elementary Schools, Diocesan located in the Institution section.
Catechesis/Religious Program—Tel: 610-262-7343. Mrs. Linda Santucci, C.R.E. Students 200.
2—ST. MICHAEL (1914), (Polish), [JC] Merged with Our Lady of Hungary, Northampton to form Queenship of Mary Parish, Northampton.
3—OUR LADY OF HUNGARY (1907) [CEM] Merged with St. Michael, Northampton to form Queenship of Mary Parish, Northampton.
4—QUEENSHIP OF MARY PARISH (2008), Formed by the merger of Our Lady of Hungary & St. Michael, Northampton. Rev. Msgr. John S. Campbell; Deacon Joseph F. Godiska.
1308 Newport Ave., 18067. In Res., Rev. Msgrs. Michael J. Chaback, Dir. Office of Permanent Diaconate; James J. Mulligan, Dir. Office of Priestly Life and Ministry.
Rectory—1324 Newport Ave., 18067-1442. Tel: 610-262-2227; Fax: 610-262-4192. Email: queenshipofmary@rcn.com.
See Our Lady of Hungary Regional School, Northampton under Regional Catholic Elementary Schools, Diocesan located in the Institution section.

OREFIELD, LEHIGH CO., ST. JOSEPH THE WORKER (1948) Rev. Msgr. Robert J. Wargo; Revs. Kevin M. Gualano; Michael E. Mullins; Deacons Anthony T. Campanell; Bruno Schettini; Charles A. Coyle. In Res., Rev. Scott R. Ardinger; Rev. Msgr. Joseph P.T. Smith.
Res.: 1879 Applewood Dr., 18069-9507. Tel: 610-395-2876; Fax: 610-395-2616. Email: stjc@ptd.net. Web: stjoseph-theworker.org.
School—(Grades K-8), 1858 Applewood Dr., 18069-9535. Tel: 610-395-7221; Fax: 610-395-7904. Email: altlsj@ptd.net. Mrs. Jody Myers, Prin. Students 400.
Catechesis/Religious Program—Tel: 610-395-4920. Students 938.

PALMERTON, CARBON CO., SACRED HEART (1908) [CEM] Rev. William T. Campion; Deacon William P. Pitts.
Res.: 243 Lafayette Ave., 18071-1511. Tel: 610-826-2335; Fax: 610-826-5360. Email: shpmtn@ptd.net. Web: www.shcpalmerton.org.
See St. John Neumann Regional School, Palmerton-Slatington under Regional Catholic Elementary Schools, Diocesan located in the Institution section.
Catechesis/Religious Program—Tel: 610-826-2849. Mrs. Kathleen D. Merkel, D.R.E.

PEN ARGYL, NORTHAMPTON CO., ST. ELIZABETH OF HUNGARY (1929) [CEM] Rev. Msgr. Vincent P. York. In Res., Rev. Patrick H. Lamb.
Res.: 300 W. Babbitt Ave., 18072-0126. Tel: 610-863-4777; Fax: 610-863-7449.
See Immaculate Conception School, Pen Argyl under Regional Catholic Elementary Schools, Diocesan located in the Institution section.
Catechesis/Religious Program—Tel: 610-863-8509. Suzanne Engler, C.R.E.; Susan Sampson, C.R.E. Students 155.
Convent—111-115 Lobb Ave., 18072. Tel: 610-863-9214. Email: ddimpa@epix.net.

PORT CARBON, SCHUYLKILL CO., ST. STEPHEN (1847) [CEM] Rev. David W. Karns.
Res.: 218 Valley St., 17965-1636. Tel: 570-622-6600; Fax: 570-622-3689. Email: st.stephen@fast.net. Cemetery office 570-622-9817
See St. Stephen Regional School, Port Carbon under Regional Catholic Elementary Schools, Diocesan located in the Institution section.
Catechesis/Religious Program—

POTTSVILLE, SCHUYLKILL CO.
1—ST. JOHN THE BAPTIST (1841), (German), [CEM 3] Rev. David J. Loeper; Deacon Luis R. Visot.
Res.: 913 Mahantongo St., 17901-3024. Tel: 570-622-5470; Fax: 570-622-4589. Email: stjohnthebaptist@verizon.net.
See All Saints Elementary School, Pottsville under Regional Catholic Elementary Schools, Diocesan located in the Institution section.
Catechesis/Religious Program—Students 126.
2—ST. JOSEPH (1906), (Italian), [CEM] Consolidated at St. Patrick, Pottsville.
3—MARY QUEEN OF PEACE (1920) Consolidated at St. Patrick, Pottsville.
4—ST. PATRICK (1827) [CEM 3] Rev. Msgr. Edward J. O'Connor; Deacon John E. Quirk. In Res., Rev. Christopher L. Wakefield.
Res.: 319 Mahantongo St., 17901-3012. Tel: 570-622-1802; Fax: 570-622-2593.
See All Saints Elementary School, Pottsville under Regional Catholic Elementary Schools, Diocesan located in the Institution section.
Catechesis/Religious Program—Mrs. Peterine Wojcik, D.R.E. Students 179.

READING, BERKS CO.
1—ST. ANTHONY (1913) Closed. Records kept at Church of St. Peter the Apostle, Reading, Tel: 610-372-9652.
2—ST. ANTHONY OF PADUA (1914), (Polish), Rev. Larry J. Hess.
Res.: 501 Summit Ave., 19611-1964. Tel: 610-685-5505; Fax: 610-685-1101. Email: stanthony2009@stanthonyreading.org. Web: www.stanthonyreading.org.
LaSalle Academy & Early Childhood Center, Shillington— See separate listing.
Catechesis/Religious Program—
Convent—234 Grace St., 19611-1946. Tel: 610-372-8578; Fax: 610-372-0263.
3—ST. CATHARINE OF SIENA (1925) Rev. Msgr. Edward R. Domin; Revs. Ronald P. Bowman; Eugene P. Ritz, Parochial Vicar; Deacons Richard A. Horst; Craig A. Fry.

Res.: 2427 Perkiomen Ave., 19606. Tel: 610-779-4005; Fax: 610-779-0859.
Church: 4975 Boyertown Pike, 19606. Tel: 610-779-4090.
School—(1925) 2330 Perkiomen Ave., 19606-2048. Tel: 610-779-5810; Fax: 610-779-6888. Email: altbscs@ptd.net. Sr. M. Teresa Ballisty, I.H.M., Prin. Sisters 3; Lay Teachers 20; Students 261.
Catechesis/Religious Program—Tel: 610-779-8535. Constance Fry, D.R.E., (K-5); Lorraine Gajewski, D.R.E., (6-8). Students 500.
Convent—2328 Perkiomen Ave., 19606. Tel: 610-779-5583.

4—SS. CYRIL AND METHODIUS (1895), (Slovak), Rev. Charles S. Sperlak; Deacon John J. Allison.
Res.: 449 S. Sixth St., 19602-2410. Tel: 610-373-0627; Fax: 610-371-9532.
Catechesis/Religious Program—Kathleen Shaulis, D.R.E. Students 34.
Convent—502 S. Sixth St., 19602-2706. Tel: 610-375-8001.

5—HOLY GUARDIAN ANGELS (1929) Rev. Msgrs. Dennis T. Hartgen; Francis X. Barrett, Pastor Emeritus (Retired); Rev. Christopher M. Zelonis; Deacon John B. Gallagher.
Res.: 3121 Kutztown Rd., 19605-2659. Tel: 610-921-2729; Fax: 610-921-8886. Web: www.hgaparish.com.
Schools-see Holy Guardian Angels Regional School, Reading under Regional Catholic Elementary Schools, Diocesan located in the Institution section.
Catechesis/Religious Program—3125 Kutztown Rd., 19605. Tel: 610-929-1416; Fax: 610-929-1623. Mrs. Rose Quaglia, D.R.E. Students 228.

6—HOLY ROSARY (1904), (Italian), Rev. Msgr. Felix A. Losito.
Res.: 237 Franklin St., 19602-1034. Tel: 610-373-5579; Fax: 610-372-0130. Email: holyrosarychurch01@comcast.net. Web: www.holyrosaryreading.com.
School—Cabrini Academy, (Grades PreK-8), 240 Franklin St., 19602-1099. Tel: 610-374-8483; Fax: 610-374-0369. Email: altbcab@ptd.net. Students 182.
Catechesis/Religious Program—Sr. Marita Olango, F.D.Z., D.R.E. Students 22.
Convent—234 Franklin St., 19602-1035. Tel: 610-375-9072; Fax: 610-375-4895. Email: srdivinezeal@hotmail.com. Sr. Angelie Marie Inoferio, F.D.Z., Supr.
Mission—Holy Rosary Chapel Schuylkill Ave., Berks Co. 19601. Tel: 610-376-4383.

7—ST. JOSEPH (1891) Deacons Peter M. LaFata; Francisco De La Garcia Colon.
Res.: 1018 N. Eighth St., 19604-2210. Tel: 610-376-2976; Fax: 610-376-2825. Email: stjosephchurchreading@yahoo.com.
See Holy Guardian Angels Regional School, Reading under Regional Catholic Elementary Schools, Diocesan located in the Institution section.
Catechesis/Religious Program—Located at Holy Guardian Angels, Reading & St. Joseph Church. Students 95.

8—ST. MARGARET (1920) Rev. John M. Gibbons; Deacons John P. Konopelski; Ramon L. Rolon; Gregory G. Schneider.
Res.: 925 Centre Ave., 19601-2105. Tel: 610-376-2919; Fax: 610-376-2462. Email: stmrgrt@att.net.
School—Tel: 610-375-1882; Fax: 610-376-2291. Email: stmargaretoffice@comcast.net. Web: www.sm-sreading.com. Sr. Marian Michele Smith, I.H.M., Prin. Students 186.
Catechesis/Religious Program—Tel: 610-376-2919. Sr. Honoria Smith, D.R.E.
Convent—233 Spring St., 19601-2121. Tel: 610-372-1302. Email: stmgrtconvent@holmail.com.

9—ST. MARY (1888), (Polish), [CEM] Rev. Leo S. Stajkowski.
250 S. 12th St., 19602-2046. Tel: 610-376-6321; Fax: 610-376-1378. In Res., Rev. Robert Tobolski, M.S.C.
Catechesis/Religious Program—Students 9.

10—ST. PAUL (1860), (German), [CEM] Revs. Andrew A. Ulincy; Amiro Jimenez; Quyet A. Pham.
Res.: 151 N. 9th St., 19601. Tel: 610-372-1531; Fax: 610-372-7478. Email: stpaulsrcchurch@comcast.net.
Catechesis/Religious Program—Students 412.

11—ST. PETER THE APOSTLE (1752) [CEM] Rev. Msgr. Thomas J. Orsulak; Rev. David J. Kozak; Deacons Jesus Centeno; Mariano Torres; Julio Colon; Fernando L. Torres; Leopoldo Alvarado.
Res.: 322 S. Fifth St., 19602-2311. Tel: 610-372-9652; Fax: 610-374-3351. Email: stpeterchurch@comcast.net.
School—225 S. Fifth St., 19602-1816. Tel: 610-374-2447; Fax: 610-374-3415. Email: altbsp@ptd.com. Sr. Anna Musi, I.H.M., Prin. Students 210.
Catechesis/Religious Program—Sr. Margaret Pavluchuk, I.H.M., D.R.E. Students 275.
Convent—218 S. Fifth St., 19602-1841. Tel: 610-373-6185. Email: speter7@aol.com. Sr. Mary Heffron, I.H.M., Supr.

RINGTOWN, SCHUYLKILL CO., ST. MARY (1923) [CEM] Rev. Richard A. Schware.
Mailing Address: P.O. Box F, 17967-9731.
Res.: 84 N. Center, P.O. Box F, 17967-9731. Tel: 570-889-3850; Fax: 570-889-5005.
See Trinity Academy at the Father Walter J. Ciszek Education Center, Shenandoah under Regional Catholic Elementary Schools, Diocesan located in the Institution section.
Catechesis/Religious Program—

ROBESONIA, BERKS CO., ST. FRANCIS DE SALES (1982) Rev. Joseph P. Jocco, O.S.F.S.; Sr. Mary Heffron, I.H.M., Pastoral Assoc.
Res.: 320 N. Church St., 19551. Tel: 610-693-5851; Fax: 610-693-5852. Email: stfrancisrob82@verizon.net. Web: www.stfrancisroby.org.
Catechesis/Religious Program—Email: marijoccd@verizon.net. Students 157.

ROSETO, NORTHAMPTON CO., OUR LADY OF MT. CARMEL (1897), (Italian), [CEM 2] Revs. James G. Prior, C.M.; Thomas W. Prior, C.M.
P.O. Box 422, 18013.
Rectory—560 N. Sixth St., P.O. Box 422, Bangor, 18013. Tel: 610-588-2183; Fax: 610-588-6973.
See Our Lady of Mt. Carmel School, Roseto under Regional Catholic Elementary Schools, Diocesan located in the Institution section.
Catechesis/Religious Program—Students 90.

SAINT CLAIR, SCHUYLKILL CO.

1—ST. BONIFACE (1854), (German), [CEM] Merged with St. Mary, Immaculate Conception, St. Casimir & SS. Peter and Paul, St. Clair to form St. Clare of Assisi Parish, St. Clair.

2—ST. CASIMIR (1912), (Lithuanian), [CEM] Merged with St. Boniface, St. Mary, Immaculate Conception & SS. Peter and Paul, St. Clair to form St. Clare of Assisi Parish, St. Clair.

3—ST. CLARE OF ASSISI PARISH (2008), Formed by the merger of St. Mary, Immaculate Conception, St. Casimir, SS. Peter and Paul & St. Boniface. Rev. Msgr. William F. Glosser; Deacons John F. Pogash; John A. Setlock.
Mill and Hancock Sts., 17970.
Rectory—250 E. Hancock St., St. Clair, 17970-1049. Tel: 570-429-0701; 570-429-0370 (Office); Fax: 570-429-0630. Email: scassisi@ptd.net.
See St. Stephen Regional School, Port Carbon under Regional Catholic Elementary Schools, Diocesan located in the Institution section.
Catechesis/Religious Program—Mrs. Kazimiera Hornberger, D.R.E. Students 75.

4—IMMACULATE CONCEPTION (1905), (Slovak), [CEM] Merged with St. Mary, St. Casimir, St. Boniface & SS. Peter and Paul, St. Clair to form St. Clare of Assisi Parish, St. Clair.

5—ST. MARY (1864) [CEM 2] Merged with Immaculate Conception, St. Casimir, St. Boniface & SS. Peter and Paul, St. Clair to form St. Clare of Assisi Parish, St. Clair.

6—SS. PETER AND PAUL (1918), (Polish), [CEM] Merged with St. Mary, Immaculate Conception, St. Casimir, & St. Boniface, St. Clair to form St. Clare of Assisi Parish, St. Clair.

SCHUYLKILL HAVEN, SCHUYLKILL CO., ST. AMBROSE (1851) [CEM] Revs. Michael J. Stone; Abraham Ha; Deacons Richard K. Braun; Edward E. Freed.
Res.: 201 Randel St., 17972-1495. Tel: 570-385-1031; Fax: 570-385-1035. Email: sambrosel@comcast.net.
School—(Grades PreK-8), 302 Randel St., 17972-1421. Tel: 570-385-2377; Fax: 570-385-2387. Email: altssa@ptd.net. Web: www.pottsville.com/stambrose. Anne B. Curry, Prin. Students 158.
Catechesis/Religious Program—Tel: 570-385-2472. Sr. Dolorita Nachajska, C.S.F.N., D.R.E.

SHENANDOAH, SCHUYLKILL CO.

1—ANNUNCIATION (1870) [CEM] Rev. Msgr. Bernard A. Flanagan. In Res., Rev. Charles J. Dene.
Res. & Office Center: 129 S. Jardin St., 17976-2209. Tel: 570-462-1916; Fax: 570-462-1980.
See Trinity Academy at the Father Walter J. Ciszek Education Center, Shenandoah under Regional Catholic Elementary Schools, Diocesan located in the Institution section.
Convent—229 W. Cherry St., 17976. Tel: 570-462-1024.
Catechesis/Religious Program—Students 43.

2—ST. CASIMIR (1872), (Polish), [CEM] Rev. Msgr. Ronald C. Bocian; Teofil Galezniak, Music Min.; Stanley Pietkiewicz, Business Mgr.
Res.: 108 W. Cherry St., 17976-2207. Tel: 570-462-1968; Fax: 570-462-1388.
See Trinity Academy at the Father Walter J. Ciszek Education Center, Shenandoah under Regional Catholic Elementary Schools, Diocesan located in the Institution section.
Catechesis/Religious Program—Tel: 570-773-1142. Kay Hornberger, D.R.E. Students 25.
Convent—233 N. Jardin St., 17976. Tel: 570-462-0877; Fax: 570-462-9318.

3—ST. GEORGE (1891), (Lithuanian), [CEM 5] Rev. Msgr. Bernard A. Flanagan.
Res.: 129 S. Jardin St., 17976. Tel: 570-462-1989; Fax: 570-462-1980.
See Trinity Academy at the Father Walter J. Ciszek Education Center, Shenandoah under Regional Catholic Elementary Schools, Diocesan located in the Institution section.
Catechesis/Religious Program—Kay Hornberger, D.R.E. Students 23.

4—HOLY FAMILY (1870-1934) Closed. Records kept at Annunciation, Shenandoah Tel: 570-462-1916.

5—OUR LADY OF MT. CARMEL (1914), (Italian), [CEM] Rev. Msgr. Bernard A. Flanagan.
Res.: 129 S. Jardin St., 17976. Tel: 570-462-1989; Fax: 570-462-1980.
See Trinity Academy at the Father Walter J. Ciszek Education Center, Shenandoah under Regional Catholic Elementary Schools, Diocesan located in the Institution section.
Catechesis/Religious Program—Students 16.

6—ST. STANISLAUS (1898), (Polish), [CEM] Rev. Msgr. Ronald C. Bocian; Maria Rittle, Music Min.; Stanley Pietkiewicz, Business Mgr.
Res.: 108 W. Cherry St., 17976. Tel: 570-462-1968; Fax: 570-462-1388.
See Trinity Academy at the Father Walter J. Ciszek Education Center, Shenandoah under Regional Catholic Elementary Schools, Diocesan located in the Institution section.
Catechesis/Religious Program—Tel: 570-773-1142. Kay Hornberger, D.R.E. Students 11.

7—ST. STEPHEN (1899), (Slovak), [CEM] Rev. Msgr. Ronald C. Bocian.
Church: 14-16 E. Oak St., 17976.
Res.: 108 W. Cherry St., 17976-2207. Tel: 570-462-1968; Fax: 570-462-1388.
See Trinity Academy at the Father Walter J. Ciszek Education Center, Shenandoah under Regional Catholic Elementary Schools, Diocesan located in the Institution section.
Catechesis/Religious Program—Students 9.

SHEPPTON, SCHUYLKILL CO., ST. JOSEPH (1894) [CEM] [JC] Rev. Richard A. Schware.
Res.: 14 E. Oak St., P.O. Box 118, 18248-0118. Tel: 570-384-0517. Email: smrc@epix.net.
Catechesis/Religious Program—Students 11.
Mission—St. John the Baptist P.O. Box 118, Oneida, Schuykill Co. 18248.

SHILLINGTON, BERKS CO., ST. JOHN BAPTIST DE LA SALLE (1948) Rev. Richard H. Clement; Rev. Msgr. Thomas J. Birch, Pastor Emeritus (Retired); Deacon Sylvester F. Simchick.
Mailing Address: 420 Holland St., 19607. Tel: 610-777-1697; Fax: 610-777-4468. Email: stjohnbaptist.delasalle@verizon.net. Web: www.catholic-church.org/baptist-delasalle. In Res., Rev. John A. Frink.
Res.: 400 Holland St., 19607. Tel: 610-777-1365.
See La Salle Academy and Early Childhood Center, Shillington under Regional Catholic Elementary Schools, Diocesan located in the Institution section.
Catechesis/Religious Program—Bernadette H. Yohn, D.R.E. Students 255.

SINKING SPRING, BERKS CO., ST. IGNATIUS LOYOLA (1965) Rev. Msgr. James A. Treston; Revs. Cletus S. Onyegbule; Paul L. Rothermel; Deacon William L. Autrey.
Res.: 2810 St. Alban's Dr., 19608-1028. Tel: 610-678-3767; Fax: 610-678-4483. Email: ignatiusrect@aol.com. Web: www.stignatiusreading.org.
School—(Grades PreK-8), 2700 St. Albans Dr., Reading, 19609. Tel: 610-678-0111; Fax: 610-670-5795. Mr. Robert Birmingham, Prin.; Mrs. Ann Rutkoski, Librarian. Sisters of the Third Order of St. Francis 1; Lay Teachers 37; Students 518.
Catechesis/Religious Program—2710 St. Alban's Dr., Reading, 19609. Tel: 610-678-0676; Fax: 610-678-4274. Students 658.
Convent—2601 St. Alban's Dr., West Lawn, 19609. Tel: 610-678-2769.

SLATINGTON, LEHIGH CO., ASSUMPTION B.V.M. (1883) [CEM] Rev. Joseph L. Grembocki; Deacon Fredic Bloom.
Res.: 633 W. Washington St., 18080-1618. Tel: 610-767-2214; Fax: 610-767-2702.
See St. John Neumann Regional School, Palmerton-Slatington under Regional Catholic Elementary Schools, Diocesan located in the Institution section.
Catechesis/Religious Program—Students 149.

SUMMIT HILL, CARBON CO.

1—ST. JOSEPH (1850) [CEM 3] Rev. James J. Burdess.
Mailing Address & Res.: 118 N. Market St., 18250-1108. Tel: 570-645-2664; Fax: 570-645-3037. Email: stjs@ptd.net. Web: www.stjscatholicchurch.org.
Church: 468 W. Ludlow St., 18250-1108.
See Our Lady of the Angels Academy, Lansford

under Regional Catholic Elementary Schools, Diocesan located in the Institution section.
Catechesis/Religious Program— Twinned with Coaldale/Lansford. Students 40.
2—ST. STANISLAUS (1924), (Polish), [CEM] Consolidated at St. Joseph, Summit Hill.
TAMAQUA, SCHUYLKILL CO.
1—ST. JEROME (1833) Rev. James C. Bechtel.
Res.: 266 W. Broad St., 18252-1819. Tel: 570-668-2301; Fax: 570-668-4406. Email: stjeromes@verizon.net.
School—250 W. Broad St., 18252-1819. Tel: 570-668-2757; Fax: 570-668-6101. Email: altssj@ptd.net. Mary Ann Mansell, Prin.; Mrs. Michelle Bates, Pre-School Dir. Tel: 570-668-2651. Lay Teachers 9; Students 163.
Catechesis/Religious Program—Tel: 570-668-4416. Jane Habel, D.R.E. Students 173.
2—SS. PETER AND PAUL (1911), (Lithuanian), [CEM] [JC] Rev. William J. Linkchorst.
Res.: 307 Pine St., 18252. Tel: 570-668-1150; Fax: 570-668-6933.
Catechesis/Religious Program—Tel: 570-668-4416. Students 64.
TOWER CITY, SCHUYLKILL CO., SS. PETER AND PAUL (1896) [CEM] Merged with Immaculate Conception, Tremont & Sacred Heart, Newtown to form Most Blessed Trinity Parish, Tremont.
TREMONT, SCHUYLKILL CO.
1—IMMACULATE CONCEPTION (1853) [CEM] Merged with Sacred Heart, Newtown & SS. Peter and Paul, Tower City to form Most Blessed Trinity Parish, Tremont.
2—MOST BLESSED TRINITY PARISH (2008), Formed by the merger of Immaculate Conception, Tremont, Sacred Heart, Newtown & SS. Peter and Paul, Tower City. Rev. Dominic P. Kalata.
Mailing Address: P.O. Box 35, 17981-0035. Tel: 570-695-3648; Fax: 570-695-2275. Email: mostbt@wtvaccess.com.
Rectory—113 Cherry St., 17981.
See Good Shepherd Regional School, Minersville, under Regional Catholic Elementary Schools, Diocesan located in the Institution section.
TRESCKOW, CARBON CO.
1—ST. BARTHOLOMEW (1917), (Italian), Merged with Immaculate Conception, Kelayres; St. Kunegunda, St. Mary & St. Patrick, McAdoo; St. Michael, Tresckow to form All Saints Parish, McAdoo.
2—ST. MICHAEL (1908) [CEM] Merged with Immaculate Conception, Kelayres; St. Kunegunda, St. Mary & St. Patrick, McAdoo; St. Bartholomew, Tresckow to form All Saints Parish, McAdoo.
TUSCARORA, SCHUYLKILL CO., ST. BERTHA (1922) [CEM] Consolidated at St. Jerome, Tamaqua.
WALNUTPORT, NORTHAMPTON CO., ST. NICHOLAS (1974) [CEM] Rev. Francis P. Schoenauer; Deacon Michael W. Kudla.
4412 Mountain View Dr., 18088-9728.
Res.: 1152 Oak Rd., 18088-9728. Tel: 610-767-3107; Fax: 610-760-6241. Email: stnickll@ptd.net. Web: stnicholaswalnutport.parishesonline.com.
See St. John Neumann Regional School, Palmerton-Slatington under Regional Catholic Elementary Schools, Diocesan located in the Institution section.
Catechesis/Religious Program—Students 152.
WEATHERLY, CARBON CO.
1—ST. NICHOLAS (1874) [CEM 2] [JC] Merged with St. Mary, Beaver Meadows to form Our Lady of Lourdes Parish, Weatherly.
2—OUR LADY OF LOURDES PARISH (2008), Formed by the merger of St. Nicholas, Weatherly and St. Mary, Beaver Meadows. Rev. Floyd Caesar Jr.
Rectory—318 Plane St., 18255-1012. Tel: 570-427-4123; Fax: 570-427-4615. Email: 011318@verizon.net.
See McAdoo Catholic Elementary School, McAdoo under Regional Catholic Elementary Schools, Diocesan located in the Institution section.
Catechesis/Religious Program—Barbara Brown, D.R.E. Students 91.
WEST BANGOR, NORTHAMPTON CO., ST. ROCH (1937) [CEM] Consolidated at St. Elizabeth of Hungary, Pen Argyl.
WEST READING, BERKS CO., SACRED HEART (1917), (German), Rev. Msgr. Joseph A. DeSantis; Deacon William R. Kase.
Lakeview Dr. at Cherry St., P.O. Box 6217, Reading, 19610-0217. Tel: 610-372-4010; Fax: 610-372-4926. Email: shc6217@aol.com. Web: www.rc.net/allentown/sacredheartwr/.
Res.: 740 Cherry St., 19611.
School—701 Franklin St., 19611-1029. Tel: 610-373-3316; Fax: 610-375-7299. Email: altbsh@ptd.net. Mrs. Katherine Napolitano, Prin. Lay Teachers 12; Students 164.
Catechesis/Religious Program—Tel: 610-374-5430. Ms. Valerie Christo-Pinheiro, D.R.E. Students 123.
WHITEHALL, LEHIGH CO.
1—ST. ELIZABETH (1941) Rev. Msgr. Anthony D. Muntone, S.T.L.; Rev. Stanley M. Moczydlowski; Deacon Alexander L. Maggitti Sr.
Res.: 618 Fullerton Ave., 18052-6726. Tel: 610-266-0695; Fax: 610-266-1548. Email: adm1936@sercc.org. Web: www.sercc.org.
See St. Elizabeth Regional School, Whitehall under Regional Catholic Elementary Schools, Diocesan located in the Institution section.
2—HOLY TRINITY (1928) Rev. Msgr. Daniel J. Yenushosky; Deacons Eugene J. Wyrwa; Michael J. Laroche. In Res., Rev. Andrew N. Gehringer.
Res.: 4102 S. Church St., 18052-2415. Tel: 610-262-9315; Fax: 610-261-3576.
See Christ the King School, Whitehall under Regional Catholic Elementary Schools, Diocesan located in the Institution section.
Catechesis/Religious Program—Mrs. Barbara Majkowski, C.R.E. Students 352.
3—ST. JOHN THE BAPTIST (1927) [CEM] Rev. Joseph J. Campion.
Res.: 3024 S. Ruch St., 18052. Tel: 610-262-2260; Fax: 610-262-1935. Email: stjohnsstiles@verizon.net.
See Christ the King School, Whitehall under Regional Catholic Elementary Schools, Diocesan located in the Institution section.
Catechesis/Religious Program—Ms. Irene M. Quigley, D.R.E. Students 55.

Chaplains of Public Institutions

ALLENTOWN. *Country Meadows*. (St. Catharine of Siena)
Devon House Personal Care Home (1930). (St. Thomas More)
Good Shepherd Home and Rehabilitation Hospital. Rev. Gregory R. Karpyn, B.A., M.A., M.Div., Deacon Cu T. Than. (St. Paul)
Lehigh County Prison. (Sacred Heart)
Lehigh Valley Hospital, Allentown Campus, 17th and Chew Sts., 18103. (St. Catharine of Siena)
Lehigh Valley Hospital at Cedar Crest, Tel: 610-402-8465 Pastoral Care. Rev. Joseph P. Becker, O.S.F.S., M.A., Deacon Anthony L. Brasten. (St. Thomas More)
Liberty Nursing Center. (St. Catharine of Siena)
St. Luke's Hospital, Allentown Campus. (St. Catharine of Siena)
Luthercrest. (St. Joseph, Orefield)
Manor Care Nursing Home, 1265 S. Cedar Crest Blvd., 18103. Rev. Gregory R. Karpyn, B.A., M.A., M.Div., (St. Paul).
New Seasons Personal Care Home. (St. Thomas More)
Phoebe Devitt Home. (St. Catharine of Siena)
Westminster Village. (Our Lady Help of Christians)
ASHLAND. *Ashland Regional Medical Center*. Administered by St. Mauritius, Ashland; St. Joseph, Ashland; St. Joseph, Girardville; St. Vincent de Paul, Girardville; Our Lady of Good Counsel, Gordon.
BETHLEHEM. *Atria*. (Notre Dame of Bethlehem)
Lehigh Valley Muhlenberg Medical Center. (Notre Dame of Bethlehem)
Lehigh Valley Muhlenberg Rehab Center. (Notre Dame of Bethlehem)
Lutheran Manor of the Lehigh Valley, Inc. (Notre Dame of Bethlehem)
Manor Care Nursing and Rehabilitation Centers I and II. (Notre Dame of Bethlehem)
COALDALE. *Edgemont Lodge Assisted Living Personal Care Home*. St. Katharine Drexel, Lansford
St. Luke's Miners Memorial Medical Center. St. Katharine Drexel, Lansford
EASTON. *Easton Home*. (Our Lady of Mercy)
Easton Hospital. (Priests of Easton Area)
Easton Nursing Center. (Our Lady of Mercy)
Northampton County Prison. (Our Lady of Mercy)
Praxis. (Our Lady of Mercy)
FOUNTAIN HILL. *Cedarbrook*. (Lehigh County Home) St. Ursula.
St. Luke's Hospital. (St. Ursula)
FRACKVILLE. *SCI-Mahoney*. Vacant. (State Correctional Institution)
HAMBURG. *Hamburg Center*. (St. Mary)
Laurel Nursing Center. (St. Mary)
LEHIGHTON. *Gnaden Huetten Memorial Hospital*. (SS. Peter and Paul)
Gnaden Huetten Nursing Home. (SS. Peter & Paul)
Mahoning Valley Nursing Home. (SS. Peter & Paul)
MACUNGIE. *Lehigh Center Nursing Home*, 1718 Spring Creek Rd., 18062. Rev. Gregory R. Karpyn, B.A., M.A., M.Div. St. Paul, Allentown
Lehigh Commons Personal Care Home, 1680 Spring Creek Rd., 18062. Rev. Gregory R. Karpyn, B.A., M.A., M.Div. St. Paul, Allentown
MINERSVILLE. *Federal Correctional Institution Schuylkill*, P.O. Box 700, 17954-0700. Tel: 570-544-7191; Fax: 570-544-7196. Sr. Patricia Weldman, Chap. Email: pweldman@bop.gov.
NAZARETH. *Gracedale*. Deacon Donald J. Dupont. (Northampton County Home) Holy Family.
NEW TRIPOLI. *Jenny's Country Manor*. (St. Joseph the Worker, Orefield)
ORWIGSBURG. *Orwigsburg Center*. (St. Ambrose, Schuylkill Haven)
Pinebrook Personal Care Center. (St. Ambrose, Schuylkill Haven)
PALMERTON. *Palmerton Hospital*. Rev. William T. Campion, M.Div., Th. M, Chap. (Sacred Heart)
POTTSVILLE. *Luther Ridge*. (St. Patrick)
Manor Care. (St. Patrick)
Pottsville Hospital and Warne Clinic, Tel: 570-621-5449; Fax: 570-622-8221. Email: ssj825@infi.net. Sr. Marjorie Sweeney, S.S.J., Chap.
Providence Place. (St. Patrick)
Schuylkill County Prison. St. Patrick, Pottsville
Schuylkill Manor. (St. Patrick)
York Terrace Nursing Home. (St. John)
READING. *Berks County Prison*. (St. Ignatius Loyola, Sinking Spring; St. Peter, Reading - Spanish Speaking Inmates)
Berks-Heim. (Berks County Home; St. Ignatius Loyola, Sinking Spring)
Villa St. Elizabeth, 1201 Museum Rd., 19611. (Sacred Heart, West Reading)
Wyomissing Nursing and Rehabilitation Center, 1000 E. Wyomissing Blvd., 19611. (Sacred Heart)
SCHUYLKILL HAVEN. *Rest Haven County Home*. (St. Ambrose)
SINKING SPRING. *Columbia Cottage*. (St. Ignatius Loyola)
TREXLERTOWN. *Mosser Nursing Home*. (St. Joseph the Worker, Orefield)
WEATHERWOOD. *Carbon County District Home*. (Our Lady of Lourdes, Weatherly)
Heritage Hill (Personal Care). Our Lady of Lourdes, Weatherly
WERNERSVILLE. *Phobe Berks Village*. (St. Ignatius Loyola)
State Hospital. Deacon Richard A. Horst.
WESCOSVILLE. *Lehigh County Home*. (Cedarbrook) St. Catharine of Siena, Allentown.
WEST READING. *Manorcare Health Services*, 425 Buttonwood St., 19611. (Sacred Heart)
Reading Hospital and Medical Center. Rev. Sunnychan Vadakkedath Skaria, O.C.D., Chap. (Sacred Heart)
Spruce Manor Nursing and Rehabilitation Center, 220 S. Fourth Ave., 19611. (Sacred Heart)
WYOMISSING. *County Meadows*. (St. Ignatius Loyola, Sinking Spring)
Highlands at Wyomissing, 2000 Cambridge Ave., 19610. (Sacred Heart, West Reading)

On Duty Outside the Diocese:
Rev. Msgrs.—
Bartkus, Algimantas A. (BRK), St. Stanislaus Rectory, 57-15 61st St., Maspeth, NY 11378.
Callaghan, Aloysius R., Rector & Vice Pres., The Saint Paul Seminary School of Divinity, 2260 Summit Ave., St. Paul, MN 55105-5050. Tel: 651-962-5050
Klinger, Nevin J., M.A., J.C.L., CNWEA, 1011 First Ave., New York, NY 10022-4195. Residence: 339 E. 62nd St., New York, NY 10065. Tel: 212-826-1480, Ext. 214
Revs.—
Czartoryński, David F., 437 Arch Ridge Loop, Seffner, FL 33584-3703.
Gillis, David C., St. Ann Church, P.O. Box 530218, Debary, FL 32753-0218. Tel: 386-668-8270
Thomas, James J., 905 N. Allerton Rd., Belleville, IL 62221.

Military Chaplains:
Revs.—
Connolly, James M.T., Lt., CHC, St. Peter Rectory, 70 Lady's Island Dr., Beaufort, SC 29907.
Dermott, William R., Chap., 100 East Ocean View, Ave., Apt. 511, Norfolk, VA 23503-1632. Tel: 757-227-3490

Unassigned:
Revs.—
Brennan, Edmund J.
Czaus, Joseph C.
DaDamio, Paul A.
Donahue, Edward J.
Gaffney, James F.
Kuzmann, Robert J., 14325 Sandhurst St., Brooksville, FL 34613.
Margarito, Luis A. Bonilla, M.Div.
Nachajski, Richard E.
Onushco, William J.

Retired:
Rev. Msgrs.—
Barrett, Francis X., Saw Creek Estates, #89, Bushkill, 18324-9403.
Benestad, Thomas J., M.Div., 1299 Ocean Blvd. K-2, Boca Raton, FL 33432-7729.

Birch, Thomas J., 113 Pinoak Dr., Jim Thorpe, 18229-9404.
Coll, Robert J., P.O. Box 1363, Marco Island, FL 34145.
Dooley, Joseph P., Carver House, 337 Carver Dr., Bethlehem, 18017.
Forst, Robert M., Our Lady Help of Christians Rectory, 444 N. Jasper St., 18109-2699.
Hoban, Thomas E., St. John the Baptist, 3024 Ruch Ave., Whitehall, 18052.
Loeper, Richard J., M.A., Immaculate Conception Rectory, 905 Chestnut St., Douglassville, 19518-9006.
Merman, Raymond F., Holy Family Villa, 1325 Prospect Ave., Bethlehem, 18018.
Morrison, David J., Our Lady of Perpetual Help Parish Center, 3219 Santee Rd., Bethlehem, 18020-2833.
Ott, Alfred R., V.F., M.Div., Holy Family Villa, 1325 Prospect Ave., Bethlehem, 18018.
Rigney, Dennis A., 580 Yellow Pine Dr., Auburn, 17922.
Smith, James, St. Joseph the Worker, 1879 Applewood Dr., Orefield, 18069-9536.
Wassel, Anthony F., 36 Clay St., New Philadelphia, 17959.

Revs.—
Bolez, Edward C., 1340 W. Linden St., 18102.
Brady, James J., Holy Family Villa, 1325 Prospect Ave., Bethlehem, 18018-4916.
Braudis, Joseph M., Holy Family Villa, 1325 Prospect Ave., Bethlehem, 18018-4916.
Briggman, Michael J., Holy Family Villa, 1325 Prospect Ave., Bethlehem, 18018-4916.
Conte, John P., Holy Family Villa, 1325 Prospect Ave., Bethlehem, 18018-4916.
Dagle, Harold F., M.A., St. Mary, 2N. 8th St., Lebanon, 17046.
della Picca, Paul B., Via Piave 1, 33036 Pantianicco, Udine, Italy.
Fromholzer, Francis J., P.O. Box F, 18105.
Gillespie, Francis T., Holy Family Villa, 1325 Prospect Ave., Bethlehem, 18018-4916.
Grundowski, Francis M., P.O. Box 13553, Reading, 19612-3553.
Halabura, Stephen J., 403 E. Broad St., 2nd Fl., Tamaqua, 18252.
Hulko, Joseph D., Holy Family Villa, 1325 Prospect Ave., Bethlehem, 18018-4916.
Jones, William P., Holy Family Manor Nursing Home, 1200 Spring St., Bethlehem, 18018-4915.
Kerestus, Thomas J., P.O. Box F, 18105.
Lawrence, Michael S., P.O. Box F, 18105-1538.
Lofton, James J., 1759 Tanglewood Rd., Orwigsburg, 17961.
Martinkovic, Joseph (Slovakia), Frantiskanska 7, Trnava 91701 Slovakia.
McElduff, Edward W., Holy Family Villa, 1325 Prospect Ave., Bethlehem, 18018-4916.
McKenna, F. Charles, Holy Family Villa, 1325 Prospect Ave., Bethlehem, 18018-4916.
Mihalak, James J., P.O. Box F, 18105-1538.
O'Donnell, William J., Holy Family Villa, 1325 Prospect Ave., Bethlehem, 18018-4916.
Paskowicz, Marian, 469 Ridge Line Ct., Dayton, OH 45458.
Pavlosky, John J., 531 Morris St., Frackville, 17931-1622.
Puza, Paul G., P.O. Box F, 18105-1538.
Quinn, Robert C., St. Benedict Rectory, 2020 Chestnut Hill Rd., Mohnton, 19540.
Sattler, Frederick F., Holy Family Villa, 1325 Prospect Ave., Bethlehem, 18018.
Schwartz, Edwin V., Immaculate Conception, 501 Ridge Ave., 18102.

Permanent Deacons:
Allison, John J., SS. Cyril and Methodius, Reading
Alvarado, Leopoldo, St. Peter, Reading
Amedeo, Dominick F., Jr., St. Ann, Emmaus
Autrey, William L., St. Ignatius Loyola, Sinking Spring
Benkovic, Richard L., Immaculate Conception, Allentown
Bloom, Fredic, Assumption B.V.M., Slatington
Bogusky, Joseph H., Annunciation B.V.M., Catasauqua
Boyle, Michael J., Most Blessed Sacrament, Bally
Brasten, Anthony L., Assumption B.V.M., Northampton; Lehigh Valley Hospital Center, Allentown
Braun, Richard K., St. Ambrose, Schuylkill Haven
Buragino, Joseph G., Our Lady of Perpetual Help, Bethlehem
Campanell, Anthony T., St. Joseph the Worker, Orefield
Carlin, Hugh, Sacred Heart, Bethlehem (Miller Heights)
Centeno, Jesus, St. Peter, Reading
Chiles, Franklin J., (Retired)
Close, Richard B., (Serving outside diocese)
Colon, Francisco De La Garcia, St. Joseph, Reading
Colon, Julio, St. Peter, Reading
Corchado, Julian, Sacred Heart of Jesus, Allentown
Cosgrove, Francis J., St. Anne, Bethlehem
Costa, Joseph J., Blessed Teresa of Calcutta, Mahanoy City
Coyle, Charles A., St. Joseph the Worker, Orefield
Cummings, John D., (On Duty Outside the Diocese)
Danyi, Frank J., Jr., Holy Family, Nazareth
De Bellis, Charles A., St. Anthony of Padua, Easton
De Jesus, Roberto
DeCastro, Jose F., Our Lady of Mercy, Easton
Doncsecz, Michael W., Notre Dame of Bethlehem, Bethlehem
Duncan, James R., St. Thomas More, Allentown
Dupont, Donald J., Holy Family, Nazareth; Northampton County Home, Gracedale
Elliott, Donald W., Assumption B.V.M., Bethlehem
Ferris, Lewis T., Sacred Heart, Bath
Flanley, Eugene M., Jr.
Fleck, Henry J., Jr., Our Lady of Mercy, Easton
Freed, Edward E., St. Ambrose, Schuylkill Haven
Fry, Craig A., St. Catharine of Siena, Reading
Gallagher, John B., Holy Guardian Angels, Reading
Gergar, Richard L., St. Anne, Bethlehem
Godiska, Joseph F., Queenship of Mary, Northampton
Gonzalez, Jose
Gordon, Henry G., St. Mary, Hamburg
Granato, Gary J., St. Paul, Allentown
Hanni, John A., St. Jane Frances de Chantal, Easton
Hartzell, Reuben H., Jr., SS. Simon and Jude, Bethlehem
Hassler, William R., Cathedral of St. Catharine of Siena, Allentown
Henninger, James P., St. Katharine Drexel, Lansford
Hernandez, Saul, Sacred Heart of Jesus, Allentown
Hiryak, Paul J., Jr., Immaculate Conception Blessed Virgin Mary, Douglassville
Horst, Richard A., Wernersville State Hospital, Wernersville; St. Catharine of Siena, Reading
Hunkele, Thomas H.
Jaccodine, Ralph J., St. Thomas More, Allentown
Kase, William R., Sacred Heart, West Reading
Kelly, George C., Jr., Our Lady of Perpetual Help, Bethlehem
Konopelski, John P., St. Margaret, Reading
Koval, Edward P.
Kudla, Michael W., St. Nicholas, Walnutport
Lafata, Peter M., St. Joseph, Reading
LaPolice, George D., St. Joseph, Summit Hill
Laroche, Michael J., Holy Trinity, Whitehall
Lash, Fredic W., Jr., St. Thomas More, Allentown
Maggitti, Alexander L., Sr., St. Elizabeth, Whitehall
Matos, Rodoberto, Holy Infancy, Bethlehem
McShane, Hugh E., Sacred Heart, Miller Heights, Bethlehem
Meyer, Dennis P., St. Joseph, Coopersburg
Miller, Thomas H., St. Mary, Kutztown
Monahan, Brian J., Immaculate Conception, Allentown
Morales, Edison
Murphy, John W., Jr., St. Ignatius Loyola, Sinking Spring
Murphy, Thomas J., St. Francis Academy and Most Blessed Sacrament, Bally
Najera-Ramirez, Francisco, St. Paul, Reading
Paschall, Joseph L., Jr., St. Columbkill, Boyertown
Pitts, William P., Sacred Heart, Palmerton
Pogash, John F., St. Clare of Assisi, St. Clair
Pufko, Joseph H., St. Jane Frances de Chantel, Easton
Quirk, John E., St. Patrick, Pottsville
Ramirez, Manuel L., Holy Infancy, Bethlehem
Raymundo, Ranulfo, St. Jane Frances de Chantal, Easton
Reimer, Thomas B., St. Lawrence the Martyr, Catasauqua
Reyes, Roberto, Sacred Heart of Jesus, Allentown
Rodgers, Robert W., St. Jane Frances de Chantal, Easton
Rodriguez, Nicasio, Holy Infancy, Bethlehem
Rohner, David K., St. Ursula, Fountain Hill
Rolon, Ramon L., St. Margaret, Reading
Schettini, Bruno, St. Joseph the Worker, Orefield
Schmidt, Gerald R., St. Theresa of the Child Jesus, Hellertown
Schneider, Gregory G., St. Margaret, Reading
Setlock, John A., St. Clare of Assisi, St. Clair
Shubella, Thomas F., St. Thomas More, Allentown
Simchick, Sylvester F., St. John Baptist de la Salle, Shillington
Solis, Alfonso D.
Than, Cu T., Good Shepherd Home and Rehabilitation Hospital; St. Paul, Allentown
Thoden, Richard M., Jr., Assumption B.V.M., Bethlehem
Thompson, John F., St. Peter the Fisherman, Lake Harmony
Toolan, James, St. Thomas More, Allentown
Torres, Fernando L., St. Peter, Reading
Torres, Mariano, St. Peter, Reading
Trejo, Jose N. Rodriguez
Trexler, Jeffrey R., Ph.D., SS. Simon & Jude, Bethlehem
Tyson, Robert J.
Visot, Luis R., St. John the Baptist, Pottsville
Wagner, William J., (Retired)
Wilkinson, Raymond, (Retired)
Wisser, Bernard M.
Woodall, Michael V., St. Columbkill, Boyertown
Wyrwa, Eugene J., Holy Trinity, Whitehall
Young, Robert P., St. Francis of Assisi, Allentown
Urbine, William F., Assumption B.V.M, Bethlehem

INSTITUTIONS LOCATED IN THE DIOCESE

[A] SEMINARIES, RELIGIOUS OR SCHOLASTICATES

CENTER VALLEY. *Sacred Heart Villa, Missionaries of the Sacred Heart*, 3300 Station Ave., 18034-9563. Tel: 610-282-1415, Ext. 21; Fax: 610-282-0610. Email: mscvilla@aol.com. Web: www.misacor-usa.org. Very Revs. E. Michael Camilli, M.S.C., S.T.L., M.S.L.S., H.E.L., Supr./Rector; John J. Paul, M.S.C., V.J., S.T.L., J.C.D.; Revs. Thomas Carney, M.S.C.; Raymond Costello, M.S.C.; Walter Downs, M.S.C.; Ronald Leinen, M.S.C., Ph.D.; Joseph T. Muller, M.S.C.; Leo Petit, M.S.C., M.A.; Jacob Welle, M.S.C., M.A.L.S.; Bros. John Peralta, M.S.C.; Robert Murphy, M.S.C.; Alois Schirmers, M.S.C.; Michael Tomcics, M.S.C.; Anton Freitas, M.S.C.; George Farkas, M.S.C.; John Rose, M.S.C. Priests 9; Brothers 6; Total Staff 7.

WERNERSVILLE. *Jesuit Center-Jesuit Community* (1930) P.O. Box 223, 19565-0223. 501 N. Church Rd., 19565-0223. Tel: 610-678-8085; Fax: 610-678-8747. Email: jescntsec@jesuitcenter.org. Web: www.jesuitcenter.org. Rev. Lucien F. Longtin, S.J., Rector. Priests 23; Brothers 3; Sisters 2; Lay Staff 21; Total Staff 28. In Res. Revs. John P. Barron, S.J.; Henry G. Coster, S.J.; James J. Ditillo, S.J.; Robert J. Dullahan, S.J.; Stephen M. Garrity, S.J.; John J. Keenan, S.J.; Joseph A. Kemme, S.J.; James J. Keogh, S.J.; William D. Lynn, S.J.; John J. Martinez, S.J.; John T. McCaslin, S.J.; Joseph A. Newell, S.J.; Richard W. Norman, S.J.; Edwin J. Sanders, S.J.; Joseph P. Sanders; William J. Sneck, S.J.; D. Gilbert Sweeney, S.J.; Justin Whittington, S.J.; Bros. Robert A. Larouere, S.J.; Thomas R. Williams, S.J.

[B] COLLEGES AND UNIVERSITIES

CENTER VALLEY. *DeSales University*, 2755 Station Ave., 18034-9568. Tel: 610-282-1100; Fax: 610-282-2254. Email: admiss@desales.edu. Web: www.DeSales.edu. Very Rev. Bernard F. O'Connor, O.S.F.S., Ph.D., Pres.; Rev. Alexander T. Pocetto, O.S.F.S., Ph.D., Senior Vice Pres.; Mrs. Linda Zerbe, Dean Students; Mrs. Mary Birkhead, Dean Enrollment Mgmt.; Mr. Thomas Mantoni, Registrar; Mr. Robert J. Snyder, Vice Pres. Admin., Fin. & Environment; Mr. Thomas Campbell, Vice Pres. Devel.; Dr. Karen Doyle Walton, Vice Pres. Academic Affairs & Provost; Rev. John A. Hanley, O.S.F.S., M.Div., M.R.E., Dir. Campus Min.; Mr. Michael Sweetana, Dir. Fin. & Treas.; Dr. Gerard Joyce, Vice Pres. for Student Life; Dr. Galen Godbey, Dir. Gov. Rels.; Revs. Joseph P. Becker, O.S.F.S., M.A.; Douglas C. Burns, O.S.F.S., M.Div.; Thomas F. Dailey, O.S.F.S., S.T.D., Dir. Salesian Ctr. for Faith & Culture; Marc Gherardi, O.S.F.S., J.D., Asst. Prof.; Daniel G. Gambet, O.S.F.S., Ph.D., Pres. Emeritus; John F. Harvey, O.S.F.S., S.T.D.; Christopher J. Hudgin, O.S.F.S., M.A.; Peter J. Leonard, O.S.F.S., Ph.D., Dean of Graduate Educ.; Deacon George Kelly, M.A., Dir. Inst. Research; Rev. Gerard J. Schubert, O.S.F.S., Ph.D.; Very Rev. Mark Plaushin, O.S.F.S., M.A., M.Div., Dir. Emergency Management & Rel. Supr.; Mrs. Debbie Malone, Dir., Library. Coeducational liberal arts college conducted by the Oblates of St. Francis de Sales (1965); Accredited. Priests 8; Lay Teachers 187; Students 3,150.

READING. *Alvernia University* (1958) 19607. Tel: 610-796-8200; Fax: 610-796-8324. Email: tom.flynn@alvernia.edu. Web: www.alvernia.edu. Thomas F. Flynn, Ph.D., Pres.; Ms. Sharon Neal, Dir. Library & Educ. Svcs.; Dr. Shirley Williams, Provost; Dr. Joseph Cicula, Vice Pres. Univ. Life & Student Learning Experience; Sr. Rosemary Stets, O.S.F., M.A., Vice Pres., Mission; Mr. Douglas Smith, Vice

Pres., Fin. & Admin.; Mr. Michael Pressimone, Vice Pres., Inst. Advancement; Mr. John McCloskey Jr., Vice Pres., Enrollment Mgmt; Ms. Beki Stein, Registrar; Dr. Evelina Panayotova, Dir., Inst. Research; Ms. Ginny Hand, Exec. Dir., Center for Community Engagement; Dr. Gerald Vigna, Exec. Dir., Center for Ethics & Leadership. Bernardine Sisters of the Third Order of St. Francis., Catholic Franciscan University, coeducational, accredited, offering undergraduate & graduate education in Liberal Arts & Professional Programs & Doctoral Program in Leadership. Sisters 2; Lay Teachers 87; Students 4,214.

[C] HIGH SCHOOLS, DIOCESAN

ALLENTOWN. *Allentown Central Catholic High School*, 301 N. Fourth St., 18102-3098. Tel: 610-437-4601; Fax: 610-437-6760. Email: altlcchs@ptd.net. Web: www.acchs.info. Mrs. Yvonne G. McCarthy, Prin.; Mr. William F. Tielman Jr., Vice Prin.; Miss Kathleen Closkey, Dir. Campus Ministry. Priests 3; Lay Teachers 58; Students 870.

BANGOR. *Pius X High School*, 580 Third Ave., 18013-1399. Tel: 610-588-3291; Fax: 610-599-3048. Email: altnpxhs@ptd.net. Web: www.piusxhs.com. Mr. James Angeline, Prin.; Rev. Patrick H. Lamb, Pres. Sisters 3; Lay Teachers 20; Students 252.

BETHLEHEM. *Bethlehem Catholic High School*, 2133 Madison Ave., 18017-4699. Tel: 610-866-0791; Fax: 610-866-9892. Email: altnbchs@ptd.net. Web: www.BethlehemCatholichs.org. Rev. Robert T. Finlan, M.A., M.Div., Pres.; Mrs. Diane Young, Vice Prin.; Mr. Michael Grasso, Dean of Student Life; Mr. Richard F. Mazza, Dir. Admissions; Rev. Bernard J. Ezaki, Dir. Spiritual Activities; Very Rev. Peter J. Hosak, M.S., Guidance Counselor; Ms. Christine M. Chew, Dir. Institutional Advancement; Mrs. Mary Ann Harmanos, Librarian. Founded as two-year commercial high school, 1897.; Founded as four-year comprehensive high school, 1925. Sisters of St. Joseph 1; Priests 2; Lay Teachers 39; Students 777.

EASTON. *Notre Dame High School*, 3417 Church Rd., 18045-2999. Tel: 610-868-1431; Fax: 610-868-6710. Email: altnndhs@ptd.net. Web: www.notredamehseastonpa.org. Mr. Joseph R. Kramer Jr., Prin.; Mr. James E. Steiner, Vice Prin.; Rev. Robert J. George, M.Div., Chap.; Michelle Bonner, Librarian. Priests 1; Lay Teachers 39; Students 580.

POTTSVILLE. *Nativity B.V.M. High School*, One Lawtons Hill, 17901-2795. Tel: 570-622-8110; Fax: 570-622-0454. Email: nativitybvm@nativitybvm.net. Web: www.nativitybvm.net. Rev. Christopher L. Wakefield, Pres.; Mr. Bruce Hess, Prin.; Mrs. Shirley Stiles, Admin. for Curriculum; Mrs. Jennifer Daubert, Dir. Devel. Lay Teachers 20; Students 200.

READING. *Central Catholic High School*, 1400 Hill Rd., 19602-1499. Tel: 610-373-4178; Fax: 610-375-4898. Email: admins@cchscardinals.org. Web: www.cchscardinals.org. Mrs. Joanne Heintz, M.Ed., Prin.; Sr. Jonathan Moyles, S.C.C., Asst. Prin.; Amy Zeigler, Librarian. Priests 2; Sisters 3; Lay Teachers 31; Administrators 3; Students 325.

The Aquinas Program (Secondary Level), 1400 Hill Rd., 19602-1499. Tel: 610-373-4178; Fax: 610-375-4898. Mr. Louis Rusnock, Supvr.; Mrs. Joanne Heintz, M.Ed., Prin.; Amy Zeigler, Librarian.

Holy Name High School, 955 E. Wyomissing Blvd., 19611-1799. Tel: 610-374-8361; Fax: 610-374-4309. Email: altbhnhs@ptd.net. Web: www.gohnhs.org. Keith Laser, Prin.; William Hess, Dir. Student Life; Rev. John A. Frink, M.Div., Pres.; Mrs. Alice Einolf, Dir. Studies. Priests 1; Lay Teachers 26; Students 453.

TAMAQUA. *Marian Catholic High School*, 166 Marian Ave., 18252. Tel: 570-467-3335; Fax: 570-467-0186. Email: altsmhs@ptd.net. Web: www.mariancatholicshs.org. Sr. Bernard Agnes, I.H.M., Prin.; Mr. Paul Coombe, Vice Prin.; Rev. George R. Winne. Priests 1; Sisters (Servants of the Immaculate Heart of Mary) 2; Lay Teachers 27; Students 328.

[D] REGIONAL CATHOLIC ELEMENTARY SCHOOLS, DIOCESAN

ALLENTOWN. *Holy Spirit School*, (Grades K-8), 510 Ridge Ave., 18102. Tel: 610-434-4044; Fax: 610-434-5458. Email: altlhs@ptd.net. Web: holyspiritschoolallentown.com. Sr. Catherine Bones, S.S.J., Prin. Serving St. John the Baptist, Immaculate Conception, SS. Peter & Paul, Allentown.

Primary School (Grades K-2), 920 N. Front St., 18102. Tel: 610-820-0220. Sr. Catherine Bones, S.S.J., Prin.

Middle School (Grades 3-8), 510 Ridge Ave., 18102. Tel: 610-434-4044; Fax: 610-434-5458. Sr. Catherine Bones, S.S.J., Prin. Sisters 1; Lay Teachers 9; Teacher Aides 1; (K to 8) 95.

Sacred Heart School, (Grades PreK-8), 325 N. Fourth St., 18102-3007. Tel: 610-437-3031; Fax: 610-437-2724. Email: altlsh@ptd.net. James Krupka, Prin. Serving Sacred Heart & St. Stephen, Allentown. Lay Teachers 10; Students 275.

BALLY. *St. Francis Academy*, 668 Pine St., 19503. Tel: 610-845-7364; Fax: 610-845-2223. Email: sfacademy@aol.com. Web: www.sfabally.org. Deacon Thomas J. Murphy, Prin. Serving Most Blessed Sacrament, Bally, St. Columbkill, Boyertown, and St. Mary, Kutztown. Lay Teachers 10; Students 210.

BETHLEHEM. *St. Michael the Archangel School* Serving Assumption B.V.M., Colesville; St. Joseph, Limeport.

Primary Bldg. (Grades K-4), 5040 St. Joseph's Rd., Coopersburg, 18036. Tel: 610-965-4441; Fax: 610-965-1030; Tel: 610-965-9383 (PreSchool).

Middle School (Grades 5-8), Main Office., 4121 Old Bethlehem Pike, 18015. Tel: 610-867-8422; 610-867-7892 (Pre-school); Fax: 610-865-2098. Stephen W. Mickulik, M. Ed., Prin.; Mary Ellen Kitchen, Librarian. Priests 2; Lay Teachers 24; Students (K-8) 314.

Seton Academy, 623 6th Ave., 18018-5224. Tel: 610-867-9530; Fax: 610-868-6784. Email: altlset@ptd.net. Web: www.setonacademypa.org. Lori L. Rutkiewicz, Prin. Serving SS. Simon and Jude, Holy Ghost, St. Ursula & Incarnation of Our Lord. Sisters 1; Lay Teachers 11; Students 140.

The Aquinas Program (Elementary Level), 623 6th Ave., 18018-5224. Tel: 610-867-5930; Fax: 610-868-6784. Mr. Louis Rusnock, Supvr.; Lori L. Rutkiewicz, Prin.

COPLAY. *Christ the King School* (1983) 22 S. Fifth St., 18037. Tel: 610-262-5822; Fax: 610-262-5632. Email: altlck@ptd.net. Web: www.ctk-wc.org. Ms. Irene M. Quigley, M.Ed., Prin.; Christine Siebler, Librarian. Serving St. Peter, Coplay; St. John the Baptist, Whitehall; Holy Trinity, Egypt. Lay Teachers 11; Students 142.

JIM THORPE. *St. Joseph Regional Academy*, (Grades K-8), 25 W. 6th St., 18229-2120. Tel: 570-325-3186; Fax: 570-325-9451. Email: altcsjra@ptd.net. Jo-Ann Novatnack, Prin. Serving St. Joseph, Immaculate Conception, Jim Thorpe, St. Peter the Fisherman, and Lake Harmony. Lay Teachers 8; Students 128.

LANSFORD. *Our Lady of the Angels Academy* (1999) (Grades PreK-8), 123 E. Water St., 18232-2001. Tel: 570-645-7170; Fax: 570-645-5278. Email: altcola@ptd.net. Web: www.oloa.net. Sr. Regina Elinich, I.H.M., Prin. Serving St. Katharine Drexel, Lansford; St. Francis of Assisi, Nesquehoning & St. Joseph, Summit Hill. Sisters 2; Lay Teachers 8; Students 111.

MCADOO. *McAdoo Catholic Elementary School*, (Grades PreK-8), 35 N. Cleveland St., 18237-1915. Tel: 570-929-1442; Fax: 570-929-3016. Email: altsmacc@ptd.net. Sr. Amy Summers, I.H.M., Prin.; Mrs. Rita Prekopa, Librarian. Serving St. Patrick, St. Kunegunda, St. Mary, McAdoo; St. Bartholomew, St. Michael, Tresckow; Immaculate Conception, Kelayres; St. Nicholas, Weatherly; St. Mary, Beaver Meadows; Church of All Saints, McAdoo; Our Lady of Lourdes, Weatherly. Sisters 2; Lay Teachers 10; Students 123.

NORTHAMPTON. *Our Lady of Hungary Regional School*, 1300 Newport Ave., 18067. Tel: 610-262-9171; Fax: 610-262-2202. Email: altnolh@ptd.net. Web: www.olhrs.com. Sr. Deborah Reho, M.S.C., Prin. Serving Our Lady of Hungary, Assumption B.V.M., Northampton; St. Lawrence and St. Andrew, Catasauqua. Sisters 1; Lay Teachers 13; Students 203.

PALMERTON-SLATINGTON. *St. John Neumann Regional School* Serving St. Nicholas, Berlinsville; Sacred Heart, Palmerton; Assumption B.V.M., Slatington.

(Grades K-3), 641-645 W. Washington St., Slatington, 18080. Tel: 610-767-2935; Fax: 610-767-2948. Email: altcsjn@ptd.net.

(Grades 4-8), 259 Lafayette Ave., 18071. Tel: 610-826-2354; Fax: 610-826-6444. Sr. Virginia Stephanie, S.S.J., M.S., Prin. Sisters 1; Lay Teachers 8; Students 80.

PEN ARGYL. *Immaculate Conception School*, (Grades K-6), Babbitt Ave. & Heller Ave., 18072. Tel: 610-863-4816; Fax: 610-863-8158. Email: altnics@ptd.net. Web: www.immaculateconceptionschool.net. Sr. Maria Luz, O.P., Prin. Serving St. Elizabeth, Pen Argyl; St. Rocco, Martins Creek; St. Roch, West Bangor. Sisters 6; Lay Teachers 2; Students 144.

PORT CARBON. *St. Stephen Regional School* (1886) (Grades PreK-8), 214 Valley St., 17965. Tel: 570-622-3063; Fax: 570-622-3689. Email: altsss@ptd.net. Web: www.ststephenregionalschool.com. Mrs. Mildred T. Scarbinsky, Prin. Serving the following parishes: St. Stephen, Port Carbon; St. Clare of Assisi, St. Clair; Holy Cross, New Philadelphia. Sisters 1; Lay Teachers 10; Students 121.

POTTSVILLE. *All Saints Elementary School*, (Grades K-8), 112 S. Seventh St., 17901-3079. Tel: 570-622-0106; 570-622-1765; Fax: 570-622-4737. Email: altsase@ptd.net. Web: www.all-saintscatholicschool.net. Miss Kimberly A. Fetter, Prin. Serving St. Patrick, St. John the Baptist, Pottsville, St. Matthew the Evangelist, St. Michael the Archangel, Minersville & Most Blessed Trinity, Tremont. Lay Teachers 12; Students 144.

READING. *Holy Guardian Angels Regional School, Reading*, (Grades PreK-8), 3125 Kutztown Rd., 19605-2659. Tel: 610-929-4124; Fax: 610-929-1623. Email: altbhga@ptd.net. Web: www.hgaparish.com. Mrs. Maureen Wallin, Prin.; Carolyn Santoro, Librarian. Serving Holy Guardian Angels and St. Joseph, Reading. Lay Teachers 24; Students 419.

ROSETO. *Our Lady of Mt. Carmel School* (1953) 80 Ridge St., 18013-1398. Tel: 610-588-2629; Fax: 610-588-3423. Email: altnolmc@ptd.net. Web: www.olmc-roseto.org. Mr. Joseph Yannuzzi, Prin. Serving Our Lady of Mt. Carmel, Roseto and Our Lady of Good Counsel, Bangor. Lay Teachers 12; Students 148.

SHENANDOAH. *Trinity Academy at the Father Walter J. Ciszek Education Center*, (Grades PreK-8), 233 W. Cherry St., 17976. Tel: 570-462-3927; Fax: 570-462-4603. Email: altsta@ptd.net. Sr. Mary Ann Spaetti, I.H.M., Prin.; Barbara Eiche, Librarian. Serving Annunciation, St. Casimir, St. George, Our Lady of Mt. Carmel, St. Stanislaus, St. Stephen, Shenandoah; St. Mary Magdalen, Lost Creek; St. Mary, Ringtown; St. Joseph, Annunciation, St. Ann, Frackville; Our Lady of Good Counsel, Gordon; St. Joseph, St. Vincent de Paul, Girardville; St. Joseph, St. Mauritius, Ashland; Blessed Theresa of Calcutta, Mahanoy City. Religious 4; Lay Teachers 10; Students 176.

SHILLINGTON. *La Salle Academy and Early Childhood Center*, (Grades PreK-8), 440 Holland St., 19607-3260. Tel: 610-777-7392; Fax: 610-777-1280. Email: altblsa@ptd.net. Web: www.lsabear.org. Dr. Patti Fisher, Psy.D., M.Ed., Prin.; Diana McNamara, Librarian. Serving St. John Baptist de La Salle, Shillington; St. Benedict, Mohnton; St. Anthony, Millmont. Lay Teachers 18; Students 242.

TAMAQUA. *St. Jerome Regional School* (1919) 250 W. Broad St., 18252-1819. Tel: 570-668-2757; Fax: 570-668-6101. Email: altssj@ptd.net. Web: www.saintjeromeregionalschool.com. Mary Ann Mansell, Prin. Serving St. Jerome, SS. Peter and Paul, Tamaqua. Lay Teachers 9; Students 153.

WEST LAWN. *St. Ignatius Loyola School*, (Grades PreK-8), 2700 St. Alban's Dr., 19609. Tel: 610-678-0111; Fax: 610-670-5795. Email: altbsil@ptd.net. Web: www.stignatiusvikings.org. Mr. Robert Birmingham, Prin.; Mrs. Ann Rutkoski, Librarian. Serving St. Ignatius Loyola, Sinking Spring; St. Francis de Sales, Robesonia. Sisters 1; Lay Teachers 32; Students 486.

WHITEHALL. *St. Elizabeth Regional School* (1953) 433 Pershing Blvd., 18052. Tel: 610-264-0143; Fax: 610-264-1563. Email: altlse@ptd.net. Web: www.sercc.org/school. Sr. Bonita Smith, R.S.M., Prin.; Mrs. Lisa Capece, Librarian. Serving St. Elizabeth, Whitehall; Annunciation, Catasauqua. Religious 1; Lay Teachers 9; Students 121.

[E] SPECIAL SCHOOLS

ALLENTOWN. *Mercy Special Learning Center* (1954) 830 S. Woodward St., 18103-3440. Tel: 610-797-8242; Fax: 610-797-9092. Email: altlmslc@pdt.net. Web: www.mercyspeciallearning.org. Bridget L. Muehlemkamp, Prin.; Mr. Louis Rusnock, Supvr. Ages: 18 months to post 21. Lay Teachers 8; Students 99.

EASTON. *The Aquinas Program - Secondary Level Notre Dame High School*, 3417 Church St., 18045-2999. Tel: 610-868-1431; Fax: 610-868-8710. Email: altnndhs@ptd.net. Mr. Joseph R. Kramer Jr., Prin.; Mr. Louis Rusnock, Supvr. Students 62.

POTTSVILLE. *St. Joseph Center for Special Learning*, 2075 W. Norwegian St., 17901-1907. Tel: 570-622-4638; Fax: 570-622-3420. Email: altssjc@ptd.net. Web: www.pottsville.com/stjosephctr. Julia Leibensperger, Prin. Lay Teachers 3; Students 30.

READING. *The Aquinas Program St. Margaret School*, 233 Spring St., 19601-2121. Tel: 610-375-1882; Fax: 610-376-2291. Email: altbsmg@ptd.net. Sr. Marian Michele Smith, I.H.M., Prin.; Mr. Louis Rusnock, Supvr. Tel: 610-866-0581, Ext. 25; Fax: 610-867-8702. Students 18.

SHILLINGTON. *John Paul II Center for Special Learning* (1982) 1092 Welsh Rd., 19607-0097. Tel: 610-777-0605; Fax: 610-777-0682. Email: jp2center@comcast.net. Web: www.johnpaulIIcenter.org. Mrs. Mary A. Adams, Prin.; Mrs. Camille Stock, Dir. Devel. Lay Teachers 4; Students 42.

WEST READING. *Alvernia Montessori School at Sacred Heart School* (1969) (Grades N-K), 211 Grace St., 19611. Tel: 610-396-0882. Sr. Ann Marie Coll, Prin. Bernardine Sisters, O.S.F. 4; Lay Teachers 1; Students 65.

[F] CATHOLIC CHARITIES AND SOCIAL AGENCIES

ALLENTOWN. *Catholic Charities*, 2141 Downyflake Ln., 18103-4774. Tel: 610-791-3888; Fax: 610-791-1878. Web: www.catholiccharityad.org. Mrs. Helen P. Kelleher, L.S.W., Exec. Dir. of Catholic Charities. Parish-based Counseling Centers: St. Columbkill, Boyertown; St. Joseph, Jim Thorpe; St. Mary's, Kutztown; St. Jerome, Tamaqua, Sacred Heart, Bath; St. Katharine Drexel, Lansford.

Branch Offices: (For Lehigh and Northampton Cos.); (For Schuylkill and Carbon Cos.); (For Berks Co.)

Branch Office, 530 Union Blvd., 18109-3230. Tel: 610-435-1541; Fax: 610-435-4367.

13 Westwood Rd., Pottsville, 17901-1800. Tel: 570-628-0466; Fax: 570-628-3343.

Berks County Branch Office, The Madison Building, 400 Washington St., Ste. 100, Reading, 19601-3966. Tel: 610-376-7144; Fax: 610-376-7145.

[G] GENERAL HOSPITALS

ALLENTOWN. *Sacred Heart Hospital* (1912) 421 Chew St., 18102-3490. Tel: 610-776-4500; Fax: 610-776-4559. Web: shh.org. Mr. John Nespoli, Pres. & CEO; Rev. John G. Hilferty, Chap. & Dir. Pastoral Care. Priests 1; Deacons 1; Sisters 1; Bed Capacity 196; Skilled Nursing Beds 22; Patients Assisted Annually 169,612; Total Staff 1,309.

READING. *Bornemann Health Corporation* (1990) *c/o Saint Regional Health Network*, 2500 Bernville Rd., P.O. Box 316, 19603-0316. Tel: 610-378-2300; Fax: 610-378-2798. Web: www.sjmcberks.org. Mr. John Morahan, Pres. & CEO. Total Assisted (Physician Visits) 12,118; Total Staff 22.

Saint Joseph Medical Center, 2500 Bernville Rd., P.O. Box 316, 19603-0316. Tel: 610-378-2000; Fax: 610-378-2798. John R. Morahan, Pres. & CEO; Sr. Janet Henry, Vice Pres., Mission & Ministry. Opened Aug. 26, 1873. Sisters 5; Total Staff 1,323; Bed Capacity 212; Bassinets 22; Patients Assisted Annually 319,793.

[H] SKILLED NURSING FACILITIES

BETHLEHEM. *Holy Family Manor of Catholic Senior Housing and Health Care Services, Inc.* (1963) Holy Family Manor: a division of Catholic Senior Housing and Health Care Services, Inc., 1200 Spring St., 18018. Tel: 610-865-5595; Fax: 610-997-8454. Email: hkessler@hfmanor.org. Web: www.hfmanor.org. Judee Bavaria, Pres.; Mrs. Heather Kessler, N.H.A., Admin.; Mr. Robert Rakow, Interim Exec. Dir.; Rev. Clifton E. Bishop, Chap. Skilled and intermediate nursing care facility for the aged, chronically ill, or invalid. Capacity 208; Total Assisted 421; Total Staff 323.

POTTSVILLE. *Covenant Home Care*, 1510 Hwy. 61 S., 17901-8409. Tel: 570-385-5522; 800-726-8761; Fax: 570-385-5287. Email: slevengood@covenanthc.org. Web: www.covenanthc.org. Sandra Lee Levengood, M.B.A., R.N., Exec. Dir.

[I] HOMES AND SERVICES FOR THE ELDERLY AND CONVALESCENT

BETHLEHEM. *Grace Mansion Assisted Living Residence of Catholic Senior Housing and Health Care Services, Inc.*, 1200 Spring St., 18018. Tel: 610-865-6748; Fax: 610-997-8444. Email: kabruzzese@HFManor.org. Web: www.hfmanor.org. Mrs. Karen Abruzzese, Admin. Personal care/assisted living facility for 25 elderly. Total in Residence 23; Total Staff 13; Total Assisted 33.

Holy Family Apartments of Catholic Housing Corporation of Bethlehem, 330-338 13th Ave., 18018. Tel: 610-866-4603; Fax: 610-866-1622. Email: hfabeth@epix.net. Josephine Vecchio, Admin. Catholic housing for the elderly. Total Staff 2; Apartments 50; Residents 50.

Trexler Pavilion, Assisted Living Residence of Catholic Senior Housing and Health Care Services, Inc., 1220 Prospect Ave., 18018. Tel: 610-868-7776; Fax: 610-865-7775. Email: kabruzzese@HFManor.org. Web: www.hfmpc.org. Mary Jo Kuebler, Admin. Personal care/assisted living facility for 23 elderly. Total in Residence 23; Total Staff 10; Total Assisted 27.

EASTON. *Antonian Towers*, 2405 Hillside Ave., 18042. Tel: 610-258-2033; Fax: 610-258-6541. Email: antoniantowers@verizon.net. Gordon Griffiths, Dir.; Mrs. Judith Kern, Mgr. Catholic housing for the elderly. Apartments 50; Total in Residence 50; Total Staff 2.

NEW PHILADELPHIA. *Holy Family Apartments of Catholic Housing Corporation of New Philadelphia, c/o Neumann Apartments*, 25 N. Nichols St., St. Clair, 17970. Tel: 570-429-0699; Fax: 570-429-2368. Email: neumann@ptd.com. Apartments 11; Total Staff 2.

ORWIGSBURG. *Holy Family Adult Day Care at St. Francis Center of Catholic Charities of the Diocese of Allentown, Inc.*, 900 W. Market St., 17961. Tel: 570-366-2924; Fax: 570-366-2301. Email: lherb@allentowndiocese.org. Mrs. Linda Herb, Dir. Day care for the elderly. Total Staff 7; Clients 34.

Holy Family Assisted Living Residence of Catholic Senior Housing and Health Care Services, Inc., 900 W. Market St., 17961. Tel: 570-366-2912; Fax: 570-366-7781. Web: www.hfmanor.org. Debra Bayliff, Admin.; Mr. James Polaski, Dir. Residential Svcs.; Mrs. Karen Abruzzese, Coord. Personal care/assisted living facility for 59 elderly of Holy Family Manor. Total in Residence 55; Total Staff 21; Total Assisted 73.

POTTSVILLE. *Queen of Peace Apartments of Catholic Housing Corporation of Schuylkill County*, 777 Water St., 17901. Tel: 570-628-4504; Fax: 570-628-4712. Email: qpeace@comcast.net. Gordon Griffiths, Dir.; Mrs. Diana Hess, Mgr. Catholic housing for the elderly. Apartments 48; Total in Residence 48; Total Staff 2.

READING. *Queen of Angels Apartments of Catholic Housing Corporation of Northern Berks County*, 22 Rothermel St., Hyde Park, 19605. Tel: 610-921-3115; Fax: 610-921-8576. Email: qangels@comcast.net. Hazel C. Black, Mgr. Catholic housing for the elderly. Apartments 45; Total in Residence 47; Total Staff 3.

Sacred Heart Villa - Assisted Living Community of the Missionary Sisters of the Most Sacred Heart of Jesus (2003) 51 Seminary Ave., 19605. Tel: 610-929-5751; Fax: 610-929-0762. Email: sacredheart-villa@comcast.com. Web: sacredheartvilla-readingpa.org. Sr. Mary Anne Bigos, M.S.C., Admin. Bed Capacity 100; Total Assisted 78; Total Staff 56.

SAINT CLAIR. *Neumann Apartments of Catholic Housing Corporation of St. Clair*, 25 N. Nichols St., St. Clair, 17970. Tel: 570-429-0699; Fax: 570-429-2368. Email: neumann@ptd.com. Rev. Ronald V. Jankaitis, Pres.; Mrs. Shannon Marlow, Mgr. Catholic housing for the elderly. Apartments 24; Total in Residence 24; Total Staff 2; Total in Residence 24; Total Staff 2.

[J] HOMES FOR PRIESTS

BETHLEHEM. *Holy Family Villa*, 1325 Prospect Ave., 18018-4916. Tel: 610-694-0395; Fax: 610-694-9990. In Res. Rev. Msgrs. Raymond F. Merman (Retired); Alfred R. Ott, V.F., M.Div. (Retired); Revs. James J. Brady (Retired); Joseph M. Braudis (Retired); Michael J. Briggman (Retired); Francis T. Gillespie (Retired); Thomas Horan (Retired); Joseph D. Hulko (Retired); Paul E. Masiar; Edward W. McElduff (Retired); F. Charles McKenna (Retired); William J. O'Donnell (Retired); Luigi Palmieri (Retired); John J. Duminiak (Retired); John P. Conte (Retired); Joseph A. Sheehan (Retired); Frederick F. Sattler (Retired); Robert J. Reed (Retired).

ORWIGSBURG. *St. Francis Villa for Priests*, 900 W. Market St., 17961-1008. Rev. Thomas Shanfelt, Rector.

[K] MONASTERIES AND RESIDENCES OF PRIESTS AND BROTHERS

BETHLEHEM. *The Barnabite Fathers Barnabite Spiritual Center*, 4301 Hecktown Rd., 18020-9704. Tel: 610-691-8648; Fax: 610-691-8649. Email: BarnabiteSpiritualCenter@gmail.com. Web: www.catholic-church.org/barnabites. Revs. Anthony M. Bianco, C.R.S.P., M.A., Vicar, House Sec.; Robert B. Kosek, C.R.S.P., Ph.D., Supr., Mod. of Spiritual Center; Paul M. Marconi, C.R.S.P.

CENTER VALLEY. *Oblates of St. Francis de Sales*, Wills Hall, 2755 Station Ave., 18034-9568. Tel: 610-282-3300; Fax: 610-282-3962. Email: mark.plaushin@desales.edu. Web: www.desales.edu. Total in Residence 14. In Res. Revs. Joseph P. Becker, O.S.F.S., M.A.; Douglas C. Burns, O.S.F.S., M.Div.; Thomas F. Dailey, O.S.F.S., S.T.D.; Daniel G. Gambet, O.S.F.S., Ph.D.; Marc Gherardi, O.S.F.S., J.D.; John A. Hanley, O.S.F.S., M.Div., M.R.E.; John F. Harvey, O.S.F.S., S.T.D.; Christopher J. Hudgin, O.S.F.S., M.A.; Peter J. Leonard, O.S.F.S., Ph.D.; Very Revs. Bernard F. O'Connor, O.S.F.S., Ph.D., Pres.; Mark Plaushin, O.S.F.S., M.A., M.Div., Supr.; Revs. Alexander T. Pocetto, O.S.F.S., Ph.D.; Gerard J. Schubert, O.S.F.S., Ph.D.

EASTON. *St. Francis Friary*, 3908 Chipman Rd., 18045-3014. Tel: 610-515-0867; Fax: 610-515-0902. Web: www.catholic-church.org/stfran-retreat. Revs. William Reisteter, O.F.M.; Miles Pfalzer, O.F.M., Guardian; Daniel Havron, O.F.M.; Bros. Mark Ligett, O.F.M., Vicar; Edward Skutka, O.F.M.; Edward Demyanovich, O.F.M. Franciscan Province of St. John the Baptist. Brothers 3; Total in Residence 6.

NEW RINGGOLD. *Cistercian Monastery, St. Mary's Priory*, 70 Schuylkill Rd., 17960-9703. Tel: 570-943-2645; Fax: 570-943-3035. Very Rev. Luke Anderson, S.O.Cist., Th.M., Ph.D., Prior; Rev. Hugh Montague, S.O.Cist., M.A., Th.M. Fathers 3.

[L] CONVENTS AND RESIDENCES OF SISTERS

BETHLEHEM. *Casa Belen* (1880) 305 E. Fourth St., 18015-1705. Tel: 610-867-4030. Email: hnasbelen@verizon.net. Sr. Rosa B. But, P.S.S.J., Supr. Residence of the Poor Sisters of St. Joseph who minister to the Spanish speaking people of the area. Sisters 4.

St. Joseph Convent, 2133 Madison Ave., 18017-4642. Tel: 610-865-4691; Fax: 610-866-9892. Email: ssj2133@aol.com. Sisters 12.

Monocacy Manor (1947) 395 Bridle Path Rd., 18017. Tel: 610-866-2597; Fax: 610-861-7478. Web: www.catholic-church.org/stfrancis-cfn. Sr. Elaine Hromulak, O.S.F., Prov. Min. School Sisters of the Third Order Regular United States Prov. Professed Sisters 17; Retreat Center Total Staff 4.

COOPERSBURG. *Carmelite Monastery* (1931) St. Therese of the Child Jesus and St. Mary Magdalen de Pazzi, St. Therese's Valley., 3551 Lanark Rd., 18036-9324. Tel: 610-797-3721. Sr. Mary Therese, O.Carm., Mother Prioress; Rev. Msgr. Thomas P. Koons, V.R., J.C.L., M.A., M.Div., Chap. Carmelite Nuns of the Ancient Observance (Calced) O.Carm. Professed Nuns 8.

EMMAUS. *Transfiguration Monastery* (1998) 526 Fairview St., 18049-3837. Tel: 610-965-6818. Email: monasteryosb@enter.net. Sr. Martina Revak, O.S.B., Supr. Corporate Title: Benedictine Sisters of Emmaus, Ministries in the fields of education, pastoral ministry, hospitality and spirituality. Charter Members 3.

MAHANOY CITY. *St. Joseph Convent*, 536 W. South St., 17948-2422. Tel: 570-773-1420. Sr. M. Taissa, M.C., Supr. Missionaries of Charity. Sisters 4.

NESQUEHONING. *Our Lady of Perpetual Help House of Prayer*, 140 W. Mill St., 18240-1225. Tel: 570-669-9858. Email: hopnesq@ptd.net. Sr. Anne Elise Darreff, I.H.M., Supr. Sister Servants of the Immaculate Heart of Mary. Sisters 4.

PEN ARGYL. *Dominican Daughters of the Immaculate Mother*, 115 Lobb Ave., 18072. Tel: 610-863-9214; Fax: 610-863-9214. Email: ddimpa@epix.net. Sr. Maria Angelita, O.P., Supr. Sisters 6.

READING. *The Bernardine Sisters of the Third Order of Saint Francis*, 450 St. Bernardine St., 19607-1737. Tel: 484-334-6976; Fax: 484-334-6977. Email: RobertaAnn@bfranciscan.org. Web: www.bfranciscan.org. Sr. Madonna Marie Harvath, O.S.F., Congregational Min.

The Bernardine Sisters of the Third Order of Saint Francis, Generalate, (aka Bernardine Franciscan Sisters).

Bethany Convent, 1214 N. 14th St., 19604. Tel: 610-372-1753. Web: www.mscreading.org. Sisters Theresa Molchanow, M.S.C., Dir. Lay MSC; Barbara Daniels, M.S.C., Prov. Leadership Team & Treas. Sisters 3.

Chevalier House, 43 Seminary Ave., 19605. Tel: 610-929-8348; Fax: 610-929-0762. Email: mabigos1@aol.com. Web: www.mscreading.org. Sr. Virginia Marie Chnapko, M.S.C., Coord. Sisters 3.

St. Clare Convent, 465 St. Bernardine St., 19607-1736. Tel: 610-777-4590; Fax: 610-777-3973. Web: www.bfranciscan.org. Sr. Paula Nowak, O.S.F., Contact Person. Bernardine Franciscan Sisters. Sisters 2.

Hannibal House - Spiritual Center (1887) *Daughters of Divine Zeal, F.D.Z.*, 1526 Hill Rd., 19602-1410. Tel: 610-375-1738; 610-375-9072; Fax: 610-375-2188. Email: srdivinezeal@aol.com. Sisters 3.

House of Nazareth (Casa Nazaret), 532 Spruce St., 19602. Tel: 610-378-1947; Fax: 610-374-3351. Email: nazarethouse@comcast.net. Sr. Delfina Gomez, Supr. Residence of the Poor Sisters of St. Joseph who work in Spanish Apostolate of Berks County. Sisters 3.

Saint Ignatius Convent, 2601 St. Alban Dr., 19609-1132. Tel: 610-678-2769. Sr. M. Patricia Brennan, O.S.F., Local Min. Sisters 2.

St. Joseph Villa (1967) 464 Bernardine St., 19607. Tel: 610-777-5556; Fax: 610-777-5545. Email: jeananthony@saintjosephvilla.com. Web:

www.bfranciscan.org. Sisters Jean Anthony Rodgers, O.S.F., Admin.; La Verne Grippe, O.S.F., Sisters Care Coord.; Rev. Msgr. Edward W. Sarzynski, Chap. Home of the Retired Bernardine Sisters of the Third Order of St. Francis. Sisters 91.

MSC Province Center, 2811 Moyers Ln., 19605. Tel: 610-929-5944; Fax: 610-929-3634. Email: mscsisters@aol.com. Web: www.mscreading.org. Sr. Lorraine Molchanow, M.S.C., Province Leader. Provincial offices of Missionary Sisters of the Sacred Heart of Jesus. Sisters 3. *Our Lady of the Sacred Heart Convent*, 2811 Moyers Ln., 19605. Tel: 601-929-5944; Fax: 610-929-3634. Email: mscsisters@aol.com. Sisters 3.

Our Lady of the Assumption Convent, 1500 Eckert Ave., 19602. Tel: 610-373-8203. Faculty House of Sisters of Christian Charity, teaching in Central Catholic High School. Sisters 3.

Precious Blood Convent (1885) 1094 Welsh Rd., P.O. Box 97, 19607-0097. Tel: 610-777-1624; Fax: 610-777-3359. Email: cps.shillington@comcast.net. Web: cpsmissionarysisters.com. Sisters Mary William Verhoeven, C.P.S, Prov. Supr.; Margaret Teufer, C.P.S., Local Supr. Residence for Missionary Sisters of the Precious Blood and Novitiate. Sisters 23.

Sacred Heart Convent, 460 St. Bernardine St., 19607-1737. Tel: 484-334-7000; Fax: 484-334-6808. Email: skateri@bfranciscan.org. Web: www.bfranciscan.org. Sr. Kateri Peake, O.S.F., Admin. Tel: 610-777-7221; Rev. Msgr. Edward W. Sarzynski, Chap. Motherhouse; Residence for Bernardine Sisters of Third Order of St. Francis. Professed Sisters 47; Total Staff 4.

Sacred Heart Villa, 51 Seminary Ave, 19605-2621. Tel: 610-929-5751; Fax: 610-929-0762. Email: mscsisters_shv@comcast.net. Sisters Marie Raymond Gazo, M.S.C., Local Supr.; Lorraine Molchanow, M.S.C., Prov. Supr. Motherhouse, Retirement Home of Missionary Sisters of the Most Sacred Heart of Jesus., Attended by Chaplain. Professed Sisters 35.

WEATHERLY. *Sisters of Peace Pentecost*, 484 Pump House Rd., 18255. Tel: 570-427-2467; Fax: 570-427-2545. Email: pentecosty@hanmail.net.

[M] RETREAT HOUSES

BETHLEHEM. *St. Francis Center for Renewal (Monocacy Manor)* (1948) 395 Bridle Path Rd., 18017. Tel: 610-867-8890; Fax: 610-861-7478. Email: stfranciscenter@gmail.com. Web: www.catholic-church.org/stfrancis-cfn. Sr. M. Marguerite Stewart, O.S.F., Dir. Weekend retreats (68) and days of recollection (70); retreats for men and women, marriage encounter; engaged encounters; parish retreats; workshops; youth groups; weekends; privately directed retreats; private retreats, spiritual direction. Professed Sisters 6; Lay Staff 2; Total Staff 8.

EASTON. *St. Francis Retreat House*, 3918 Chipman Rd., 18045-3014. Tel: 610-258-3053; Fax: 610-258-2412. Email: stfranrh@localnet.com. Web: www.stfrancisretreathouse.org. Rev. Daniel Havron, O.F.M., Dir. of Retreat & Prog.; Mr. Michael Markle, Exec. Dir. Retreatants 129.

ORWIGSBURG. *St. Francis Center*, 900 W. Market St., 17961-1006. Tel: 570-366-1016; Fax: 570-366-1017. Diocesan Agencies with Facilities in the St. Francis Center:

Holy Family Adult Day Care Tel: 570-366-2924; Fax: 570-366-2301. Email: lherb@allentowndiocese.org. Mrs. Linda Herb, Dir.

Holy Family Assisted Living Tel: 570-366-2912; Fax: 570-366-7781. Email: dbayliff@hfmanor.com. Deborah Bayliff, L.P.N., Admin.

READING. *Mariawald Renewal Center*, 1094 Welsh Rd., P.O. Box 97, 19607-0097. Tel: 610-777-0135; Fax: 610-777-3359. Email: mariawald@aol.com. Web: www.mariawaldrenewal.com. Diane Ross, Admin. Single, double, and triple occupancy. Units 16.

[N] CENTERS FOR SPIRITUAL GROWTH

READING. *Bernardine Franciscan Sisters Spirituality and Conference Center*, 460 St. Bernardine St., 19607-1737. Tel: 484-334-6807; Fax: 484-334-6808. Email: bfcc@bfranciscan.org. Sr. Christen Shukwit, O.S.F., Dir. The Center shares space at the Bernardine Franciscan Motherhouse. Able to provide space for days of reflection and workshops for groups up to 125 persons. Spiritual direction and directed/private retreats available. Total Staff 2.

WERNERSVILLE. *Jesuit Center* (1971) 19565. Tel: 610-670-3640; Fax: 610-670-3650. Email: jescntsec@jesuitcenter.org. Web: www.jesuitcenter.org. Rev. Thomas F. Gleeson, S.J., Rector; Susan Bowers, Dir. of Spiritual Growth Programs; Revs. John P. Barron, S.J.; William J. Sneck, S.J.; Lucien F. Longtin, S.J.; Kathryn M. Fitzgerald, D.Min.; Sisters Maria McCoy, S.S.J.; Sarah Lamb, I.H.M. Directed retreats, programs in prayer, discernment, psychology and spirituality. Priests 3; Total Assisted (9710 overnight & 822 day only) 10,532; Total Staff 7.

[O] NEWMAN CENTERS

ALLENTOWN. *The Newman Center* 2339 Liberty St., 18104. Tel: 484-664-3122; Fax: 484-664-3123. Rev. John A. Krivak, M.Div., Th.M., M.Ed., Ed.D., Diocesan Dir., Campus Ministry.

Albright College (Reading) Christopher House, 15207 Kutztown Rd., Kutztown, 19530-9281. Tel: 610-223-6206; Fax: 610-683-8467. Email: christopherhouse@kutztown.edu. Web: www.kutztown.edu/activities/clubs/newmancenter/home.htm/. Rev. Frans J. Berkhout, M.Div., M.Ed., Campus Ministry.

DeSales University (Center Valley) 2755 Station Ave., Center Valley, 18034-9568. Tel: 610-282-1100, Ext. 1898; Fax: 610-282-1772. Email: johnhanley@desales.edu. Rev. John A. Hanley, O.S.F.S., M.Div., M.R.E.

Alvernia College Office of Campus Ministry, 400 St. Bernardine St., Reading, 19607. Tel: 610-796-8300; Fax: 610-796-8324.

Cedar Crest College (Allentown) Rev. John A. Krivak, M.Div., Th.M., M.Ed., Ed.D. See Muhlenberg College

Kutztown University (Kutztown) Christopher House, 15207 Kutztown Rd., Kutztown, 19530-9218. Tel: 610-683-8380; Fax: 610-683-8467. Email: christopherhouse@kutztown.edu. Web: www.kutztown.edu/activities/clubs/newmancenter/home.htm/. Rev. Frans J. Berkhout, M.Div., M.Ed.

Lafayette College (Easton) Newman House, 119 McCartney St., Easton, 18042-7647. Tel: 610-253-5044; Fax: 610-253-1391. Email: normanc@lafayette.edu. Rev. Charles Norman, O.S.F.S.

Lehigh University (Bethlehem) Newman Center at Lehigh University, 661 Taylor St., Bldg. 41, Bethlehem, 18015-3127. Tel: 610-758-4148; Fax: 610-758-6392. Email: wek4@lehigh.edu. Rev. Wayne E. Killian, M.A., M.S.

Moravian College (Bethlehem) Newman Center at Moravian College, 1309 Main St., Bethlehem, 18018-6650. Tel: 610-625-7922; Fax: 610-625-7885. Email: killian@moravian.edu. Rev. Wayne E. Killian, M.A., M.S.

Muhlenberg College (Allentown) Newman Center, 2339 Liberty St., 18104-5586. Tel: 484-664-3122; Fax: 464-664-3123. Rev. John A. Krivak, M.Div., Th.M., M.Ed., Ed.D.

Penn State University Campus Ministry Coordinator Office: Penn State Schuylkill Campus. Tel: 570-385-6262.

[P] MISCELLANEOUS

ALLENTOWN. *Eastern Pennsylvania Scholarship Foundation*, P.O. Box F, 18105-1538. Tel: 610-871-5200, Ext. 244; Fax: 610-871-5211. Email: bshotwell@allentowndiocese.org. Web: www.allentowndiocese.org/giving. Mr. James S. Friend Jr., Dir. Devel.; Mrs. Barbara Ann Shotwell, Asst. Dir. Devel.

BATH. *Blue Army of Our Lady of Fatima*, 2483 Community Dr., 18014. Tel: 610-614-1218. Email: thesixfamily@gmail.com. Rev. Dominic Thao Pham, M.Div., Spiritual Dir.

BETHLEHEM. *Stephen's Place*, 729 Ridge Ave., 18015-3621. Tel: 610-861-7677. Email: vlongcope@msn.com. Sr. Virginia Longcope, M.S.C., Dir. A nonprofit residential community designed to meet the needs of the adult non-violent offender with a history of substance abuse.

Third Order Dominican Expectation of the Blessed Mother Chapter, Notre Dame of Bethlehem Church, 1861 Catasqusqua Rd., 18018-1298. Tel: 610-691-6761. Dr. Felicidad Quilo, Mod.

CENTER VALLEY. *Mission Vehicle Association, Inc.*, 3300 Station Ave., 18034-9563.

EASTON. *Secular Franciscan Fraternity, Secular Franciscan Order, St. Francis Retreat House*, 3918 Chipman Rd., 18045-3014. Tel: 610-258-3053; Fax: 610-258-2412.

NORTHAMPTON. *Apostles of Jesus* (1968) 829 Main St., 18067-1838. Tel: 610-502-1732; Fax: 610-502-1733. Email: worldaj@email.com. Web: www.apostlesofjesus.org. Rev. Paul O. Gaggawala, A.J., Supr.

ORWIGSBURG. *Seton Manor, Inc.*, 1000 Seton Dr., 17961. Tel: 570-366-0400; Fax: 570-366-1970. Email: apostupak@setonmanor.org. Web: www.setonmanor.org. Lynn Bressi Esq., Chairperson, Bd. Dirs.; Mrs. Arlene Postupak, Admin./ CEO. Total Staff 180; Bed Capacity 120. Board of Directors: Mr. Joseph P. Tray Esq., Vice Chairperson; Mary Paspalas Lazare, Treas.; Ms. Darnell Furer; Mr. Gary D. Hennis; Robert Cash Jr., Sec.; Sr. Margaret Walker, D.C.

READING. *Bernardine Franciscan Sisters Congregational Leadership Offices*, 450 St. Bernardine St., 19607-1737. Tel: 484-334-6976; Fax: 484-334-6977.

Bernardine Franciscan Sisters Mission and Ministries Charitable Trust, 450 St. Bernardine St., 19607-1737. Tel: 484-334-6976; Fax: 484-334-6927. Email: RobertaAnn@bfranciscan.org. Web: www.bfranciscan.org. Sr. Madonna Marie Harvath, O.S.F., Congregational Min.

Bernardine Franciscans, Delaware County, 450 St. Bernardine St., 19607-1737. Tel: 484-334-6976; Fax: 484-334-6977. Email: RobertaAnn@bfranciscan.org. Web: www.bfranciscan.org. Sr. Madonna Marie Harvath, O.S.F., Congregational Min.

Mary's Home (2001) 736 Upland Ave., 19607. Tel: 610-603-8010; Fax: 610-603-8012. Email: dani@marysshelter.org. Web: www.marysshelter.org. Christine Folk, Exec. Dir. Transitional home for mothers and babies. Bed Capacity 10; Total Assisted Annually 35; Total Staff 10.

Mary's Shelter, 325 S. 12th St., 19602-2021. Tel: 610-376-1973; Fax: 610-376-5391. Email: brenda@maryshelter.org. Web: www.marysshelter.org. Christine Folk, Exec. Dir.; Danielle Monahan, M.S.W., Asst. Exec. Dir. A residence for pregnant, homeless young women and teens.

SHENANDOAH. *Apostles of Jesus*, P.O. Box 215, 17976-0215. Tel: 570-462-1236; Fax: 570-462-1235. Email: worldaj@email.com. Web: www.apostlesofjesus.org. Revs. Paul O. Gaggawala, A.J., Regl. Supr. & Dir.; Peter C. Mainza, A.J., Sec.

RELIGIOUS INSTITUTES OF MEN REPRESENTED IN THE DIOCESE

For further details refer to the corresponding bracketed number in the Religious Institutes of Men or Women section.

[]—*Apostles of Jesus*—A.J.

[]—*Cistercian Monks of the Strict Observance*—O.Cist.

[0160]—*Clerics Regular of St. Paul* (Bernabite Fathers)—C.R.S.P.

[1330]—*Congregation of the Mission (Vincentian Fathers)* (Eastern Prov.)—C.M.

[0520]—*Franciscan Fathers* (St. John the Baptist Province)—O.F.M.

[0690]—*Jesuit Fathers* (Maryland Prov.)—S.J.

[1110]—*Missionaries of the Sacred Heart* (American Prov.)—M.S.C.

[0920]—*Oblates of St. Francis de Sales*—O.S.F.S.

RELIGIOUS INSTITUTES OF WOMEN REPRESENTED IN THE DIOCESE

[0120]—*Angelic Sisters of St. Paul*—A.S.S.P.

[1810]—*Bernardine Sisters of the Third Order of St. Francis (Bernardine Franciscan Sisters)*—O.S.F.

[0320]—*Carmelite Nuns of the Ancient Observance*—O.Carm.

[]—*Congregation of Sisters of Holy Family of Nazareth*—C.S.F.N.

[0795]—*Daughters of Divine Zeal*—F.D.Z.

[1065]—*Dominican Daughters of the Immaculate Mother*—O.P.

[2710]—*Missionaries of Charity*—M.C.

[]—*Missionary Sisters of the Most Sacred Heart of Jesus*—M.S.C.

[2850]—*Missionary Sisters of the Precious Blood*—C.P.S.

[3250]—*Poor Sisters of St. Joseph*—P.S.S.J.

[1700]—*School Sisters of the Third Order of St. Francis* (United States Prov.)—O.S.F.

[0660]—*Sisters of Christian Charity*—S.C.C.

[]—*Sisters of Mercy* (Mid-Atlantic Community)—R.S.M.

[3700]—*Sisters of St. Benedict*—O.S.B.

[]—*Sisters of St. Francis of Philadelphia* (Glen Riddle)—O.S.F.

[3830]—*Sisters of St. Joseph*—S.S.J.

[2170]—*Sisters, Servants of the Immaculate Heart of Mary*—I.H.M.

[]—*Sisters, Servants of the Immaculate Heart of Mary* (Scranton Province)—I.H.M.

DIOCESAN CEMETERIES

ALLENTOWN. *Resurrection*, 547 N. Krocks Rd., 18106-9732. Tel: 610-395-3819; Fax: 610-366-3713. Email: pkosloff@allentowndiocese.org. Mr. Peter J. Kosloff, Supt.

BETHLEHEM. *Holy Saviour*, 2575 Linden St., 18017-3842. Tel: 610-866-2372; Fax: 610-866-9277. Mr. Peter J. Kosloff, Supt.; Mr. Larry Hillanbrand, Asst. Supt.; Mr. James D. Reich, Sales Mgr.

NECROLOGY

† Barnes, Joseph A., Douglassville, PA Immaculate Conception—Died Feb. 2, 2009

† Flynn, Stephen F.X., Bath, PA Sacred Heart of Jesus—Died Feb. 1, 2009

† King, Thomas J., Bethlehem, PA Holy Family Villa—Died April 4, 2009

† Strassner, Henry E., (Retired)—Died Nov. 20, 2009

An asterisk (*) denotes an organization that has established tax-exempt status directly with the IRS and is not covered by the USCCB Group Ruling.

Diocese of Altoona-Johnstown

(Dioecesis Altunensis-Johnstoniensis)

Most Reverend

JOSEPH V. ADAMEC, D.D., S.T.L.

Bishop of Altoona-Johnstown; ordained July 3, 1960; appointed Bishop of Altoona-Johnstown March 17, 1987; ordained and installed May 20, 1987. *Mailing Address: Chancery Office, 927 S. Logan Blvd., Hollidaysburg, PA 16648.*

The Chancery: 927 S. Logan Blvd., Hollidaysburg, PA 16648. Tel: 814-695-5579; Fax: 814-695-8894.

Web: www.ajdiocese.org

Email: tdegol@dioceseaj.org

ESTABLISHED DIOCESE OF ALTOONA, MAY 27, 1901.

Square Miles 6,674.

Redesignated Diocese of Altoona-Johnstown, October 9, 1957.

Comprises the Counties of Bedford, Blair, Cambria, Centre, Clinton, Huntingdon and Somerset in the State of Pennsylvania.

For legal titles of parishes and diocesan institutions, consult the Chancery Office.

STATISTICAL OVERVIEW

Personnel	
Bishop	1
Priests: Diocesan Active in Diocese	78
Priests: Diocesan Active Outside Diocese	4
Priests: Retired, Sick or Absent	41
Number of Diocesan Priests	123
Religious Priests in Diocese	61
Total Priests in Diocese	184
Ordinations:	
Diocesan Priests	3
Religious Priests	1
Transitional Deacons	2
Permanent Deacons	4
Permanent Deacons in Diocese	32
Total Brothers	9
Total Sisters	71
Parishes	
Parishes	91
With Resident Pastor:	
Resident Diocesan Priests	72
Resident Religious Priests	15
Without Resident Pastor:	
Administered by Deacons	3
Administered by Religious Women	1
Missions	5
New Parishes Created	1
Closed Parishes	5
Welfare	
Catholic Hospitals	1
Total Assisted	407,279
Health Care Centers	1
Total Assisted	253
Homes for the Aged	3
Total Assisted	390
Special Centers for Social Services	2
Total Assisted	25,712
Educational	
Diocesan Students in Other Seminaries	4
Total Seminarians	4
Colleges and Universities	2
Total Students	4,322
High Schools, Diocesan and Parish	3
Total Students	953
Elementary Schools, Diocesan and Parish	20
Total Students	3,608
Catechesis/Religious Education:	
High School Students	3,094
Elementary Students	6,708
Total Students under Catholic Instruction	18,689
Teachers in the Diocese:	
Priests	2
Brothers	1
Sisters	8
Lay Teachers	322
Vital Statistics	
Receptions into the Church:	
Infant Baptism Totals	974
Minor Baptism Totals	33
Adult Baptism Totals	62
Received into Full Communion	136
First Communions	1,251
Confirmations	1,928
Marriages:	
Catholic	299
Interfaith	192
Total Marriages	491
Deaths	1,523
Total Catholic Population	94,284
Total Population	638,969

Former Bishops—Rt. Rev. EUGENE A. GARVEY, D.D., ord. Sept. 22, 1869; cons. Sept. 8, 1901; died Oct. 22, 1920; Most Revs. JOHN JOSEPH MCCORT, D.D., ord. Oct. 14, 1883; cons. Titular Bishop of Azotus and Auxiliary to the Archbishop of Philadelphia, Sept. 17, 1912; appt. Coadjutor cum jure successionis to the Bishop of Altoona, Jan. 27, 1920; appt. Bishop of Altoona, Oct. 22, 1920; appt. Assistant at the Pontifical Throne, Oct. 5, 1933; died April 21, 1936; RICHARD T. GUILFOYLE, D.D., ord. June 2, 1917; appt. Aug. 8, 1936; cons. Nov. 30, 1936; died June 10, 1957; HOWARD J. CARROLL, D.D., ord. April 2, 1927; appt. Dec. 5, 1957; cons. Jan. 2, 1958; died March 21, 1960; J. CARROLL MCCORMICK, D.D., ord. July 10, 1932; cons. April 20, 1947; appt. June 25, 1960; transferred to See of Scranton March 4, 1966; retired Feb. 15, 1983; died Nov. 2, 1996; JAMES J. HOGAN, D.D., ord. Dec. 8, 1937; appt. Titular Bishop of Philomelium and Auxiliary of Trenton, Nov. 27, 1959; cons. Feb. 25, 1960; appt. to the See of Altoona-Johnstown May 23, 1966; retired Oct. 17, 1986; died June 14, 2005.

Diocesan Officials

Bishop—Most Rev. JOSEPH VICTOR ADAMEC, D.D., S.T.L., 927 S. Logan Blvd., Hollidaysburg, 16648. Tel: 814-695-5579; Fax: 814-695-8894.

Secretary to the Bishop—Deacon ROBERT D. BAILEY, Episcopal Master of Ceremonies, 927 S. Logan Blvd., Hollidaysburg, 16648. Tel: 814-695-5579; Fax: 814-695-8894. Email: rbailey@dioceseaj.org.

Secretary for Communications—Mr. TONY DEGOL, 927 S. Logan Blvd., Hollidaysburg, 16648. Tel: 814-695-5579; Fax: 814-695-8894. Email: tdegol@dioceseaj.org.

Vicar General—Rev. Msgr. MICHAEL E. SERVINSKY, S.T.L., J.C.L., D.Min., V.G. Tel: 814-944-6676 (Res.). 927 S. Logan Blvd., Hollidaysburg, 16648. Tel: 814-695-5579; Fax: 814-695-8894.

Judicial Vicar—Very Rev. JOHN D. BYRNES, J.V., J.C.L., 927 S. Logan Blvd., Hollidaysburg, 16648. Tel: 814-693-9485; 814-886-2235 (Res.); Fax: 814-695-8894.

Bishop's Vicar for Religious—Very Rev. ANTHONY FRANCIS SPILKA, O.F.M.Conv., St. Francis of Assisi, 120 Barron Ave., Johnstown, 15906. Tel: 814-539-1632; Fax: 814-536-7024.

Chancellor—Mrs. TERESA M. STAYER, 927 S. Logan Blvd., Hollidaysburg, 16648. Tel: 814-695-5579; Fax: 814-695-8894. Email: teresaaj@dioceseaj.org.

Episcopal Master of Ceremonies—Deacon ROBERT D. BAILEY, 927 S. Logan Blvd., Hollidaysburg, 16648. Tel: 814-695-5579; Fax: 814-695-8894. Email: rbailey@dioceseaj.org.

Vicars Forane

Allegheny Deanery—Very Rev. RONALD V. OSINSKI, V.F., Our Lady of the Sacred Heart Rectory, 601 Mountain Ave., Portage, 15946. Tel: 814-736-4239; Fax: 814-736-9285. Email: ronvo812@hotmail.com.

Altoona Deanery—Very Rev. MARK S. BEGLY, V.F., St. John the Evangelist Rectory, 311 Lotz Ave., Lakemont, Altoona, 16602. Tel: 814-942-5503; Fax: 814-943-8832.

Cambria Deanery—Very Rev. LEONARD E. VOYTEK, V.F., St. Elizabeth Ann Seton Rectory, 605 Graham Ave., Windber, 15963. Tel: 814-467-7191.

Northern Deanery—Very Rev. NEIL R. DADEY, V.F., St. John the Evangelist Rectory, 134 E. Bishop St., Bellefonte, 16823. Tel: 814-355-3134.

Juniata Deanery—Very Rev. CLEMENT G. GARDNER, V.F., St. Michael Rectory, 301 Spruce St., Hollidaysburg, 16648. Tel: 814-695-0912.

Johnstown Deanery—Very Rev. PAUL E. TURNBULL, V.F., Our Mother of Sorrows Rectory, 407 Tioga St., Johnstown, 15905. Tel: 814-535-7646.

Prince Gallitzin Deanery—Rev. Msgr. TIMOTHY J. SWOPE, V.F., Basilica of St. Michael the Archangel Rectory, 321 St. Mary's St., P.O. Box 10, Loretto, 15940-0010. Tel: 814-472-8551 Minor Basilica.

Southern Deanery—Very Rev. JAMES M. DUGAN, V.F., SS. Philip & James Rectory, 247 High St., Meyersdale, 15552. Tel: 814-634-8150.

Diocesan Offices

Building Commission—Mr. GERALD MCMULLEN, Chm., 728 Ben Franklin Hwy., Ebensburg, 15931. Tel: 814-472-0603. Email: jmcmulln@dioceseaj.org.

Campus Ministry—Rev. Msgr. MICHAEL A. BECKER, Coord., Mailing Address: St. Michael Rectory, 751 Locust St., Box 103, St. Michael, 15951-0103. Tel: 814-495-9640; Fax: 814-495-9424.

Catholic Charities—Mrs. JEAN JOHNSTONE, Exec. Dir., 1300 12th Ave., P.O. Box 1349, Altoona, 16603. Tel: 814-944-9388; Fax: 814-941-2677. Email: cssaltpa@dioceseaj.org.

Altoona Offices—1300 12th Ave., P.O. Box 1349, Altoona, 16603. Tel: 814-944-9388; Fax: 814-941-2677.

Johnstown Offices—741 Railroad St., Johnstown, 15901. Tel: 814-535-6538; Fax: 814-535-2235. Email: cssjtown@dioceseaj.org.

Bellefonte Offices—213 E. Bishop St., Bellefonte, 16823. Tel: 814-353-0502; Fax: 814-353-0515. Email: cyoung@dioceseaj.org.

"The Catholic Register"—Rev. Msgr. TIMOTHY P. STEIN, Editor, Mailing Address: P.O. Box 413,

Hollidaysburg, 16648. Tel: 814-695-7563; Fax: 814-695-7517. Email: tstein@dioceseaj.org.

Catholic Relief Services & Foreign Mission Outreach—Rev. ROBERT J. KELLY, Ph.D., Dir. Email: bkelly@dioceseaj.org; Sr. PATTI ROSSI, C.S.J., Assoc. Dir.. Email: srpatti@dioceseaj.org; 933 S. Logan Blvd., Hollidaysburg, 16648. Tel: 814-695-5579; Fax: 814-696-6725.

Cemetery Commission—Rev. DAVID H. ROESCH, St. Joseph Rectory, 623 E. Third St., Bellwood, 16617. Tel: 814-742-7075; Fax: 814-695-7517. Email: sanjoe3@nb.net.

Chancery—Mrs. TERESA M. STAYER, Chancellor, 927 S. Logan Blvd., Hollidaysburg, 16648. Tel: 814-695-5579; Fax: 814-695-8894. Email: teresaaj@dioceseaj.org.

Children and Youth Protection/Safe Environment Office—Sr. DONNA MARIE LEIDEN, S.C., Dir., 933 S. Logan Blvd., Hollidaysburg, 16648. Tel: 814-693-9333; Fax: 814-696-6725. Email: dleiden@dioceseaj.org.

Communications—Mr. TONY DEGOL, 927 S. Logan Blvd., Hollidaysburg, 16648. Tel: 814-695-5579; Fax: 814-695-8894. Email: tdegol@dioceseaj.org.

Commission for Life and Justice—Co Chairs: Dr. CAROLYN NICKERSON; Mr. ROBERT NICKERSON; Mrs. SUSAN STITH, Diocesan Liaison, 5379 Portage St., Lilly, 15938. Tel: 814-886-5551. Email: sstith@dioceseaj.org.

Development—Mr. CHRISTOPHER F. RINGKAMP, Dir., 925 S. Logan Blvd., P.O. Box 409, Hollidaysburg, 16648. Tel: 814-695-5577; Fax: 814-696-9516. Email: ringkamp@dioceseaj.org.

Diaconal Formation—Deacon GENE P. NERAL, 925 S. Logan Blvd., Hollidaysburg, 16648. Tel: 814-693-9870; Fax: 814-695-8894. Email: gneral@dioceseaj.org.

Diocesan Liturgy Committee—Mrs. DEBORAH HETRICK, Chm., 925 S. Logan Blvd., Hollidaysburg, 16648. Tel: 814-944-2044; 814-693-9870. Email: dhetrick@dioceseaj.org; jnoonan@dioceseaj.org.

Dmitri Manor - Priests' Residence - St. Mary's Lane—Rev. Msgr. ROBERT J. SALY, 927 S. Logan Blvd., Hollidaysburg, 16648. Tel: 814-696-4698; 814-696-4126 (Res.).

Ecumenical Minister—Rev. DANIEL SINISI, T.O.R., St. Francis University, P.O. Box 600, Loretto, 15940-0600. Tel: 814-472-3001; Fax: 814-472-3003.

Education—Sr. DONNA MARIE LEIDEN, S.C., Dir.. Email: dleiden@dioceseaj.org; VACANT, Administrative Asst.. Email: fwope@dioceseaj.org; 933 S. Logan Blvd., Hollidaysburg, 16648. Tel: 814-693-1401; Fax: 814-696-6725.

Elementary Education—Sr. MARK PLESCHER, C.S.A., Asst. Dir., 933 S. Logan Blvd., Hollidaysburg, 16648. Tel: 814-693-1401; Fax: 814-696-6725. Email: srmark@dioceseaj.org.

Facilities Manager—Mr. GERALD MCMULLEN, 728 Ben Franklin Hwy., Ebensburg, 15931. Tel: 814-472-7500, Ext. 109; Fax: 814-472-8020. Email: jmcmulln@dioceseaj.org.

Family Life Office—Mrs. SUSAN STITH, Dir.. Email: sstith@dioceseaj.org; 5379 Portage St., Lilly, 15938-1091. Tel: 814-886-5551; Fax: 814-886-7697. Email: familylife@dioceseaj.org.

Finance—Mr. LARRY R. SUTTON, CFO. Email: sutton@dioceseaj.org; Mr. MATTHEW REILLY, CPA, Comptroller. Email: mreilly@dioceseaj.org; Mrs. JEANNE BRYAN, Accounting Asst.. Email: jbryan@dioceseaj.org; 927 S. Logan Blvd., Hollidaysburg, 16648. Tel: 814-695-5579; Fax: 814-695-8894.

Fulton County Catholic Mission—Sr. MARGIE MONAHAN, C.C.W.. Email: sistermargie@comcast.net; 110 S. Third St., Mc Connellsburg, 17233. Tel: 717-485-5917; 717-485-0661; Fax: 717-485-3855.

Holy Childhood—Rev. ROBERT J. KELLY, Ph.D., Dir.. Email: bkelly@dioceseaj.org; Sr. PATTI ROSSI, C.S.J., Assoc. Dir.. Email: srpatti@dioceseaj.org; 933 S. Logan Blvd., Hollidaysburg, 16648. Tel: 814-695-5579; Fax: 814-696-6725.

Information Technology—Mr. DON LAYO, Dir., 927 S. Logan Blvd., Hollidaysburg, 16648. Tel: 814-695-5579; Fax: 814-695-8894. Email: dlayo@dioceseaj.org.

Network Support Specialist—Mr. DAVID EGER, 927 S. Logan Blvd., Hollidaysburg, 16648. Tel: 814-695-5579; Fax: 814-695-8894. Email: deger@dioceseaj.org.

Network Support Technicians—Mr. GREGORY CLAPPER. Email: gclapper@dioceseaj.org; Mr. JAMES ECKENRODE, 927 S. Logan Blvd., Hollidaysburg, 16648. Tel: 814-695-5579; Fax: 814-695-8894. Email: jeckenrode@dioceseaj.org.

Technology/Implementation Coordinator—Mrs. ALISON LINK. Email: alink@dioceseaj.org.

Inter-Faith Minister—Very Rev. MARK S. BEGLY, V.F., St. John the Evangelist Rectory, 309 Lotz Ave., Lakemont, Altoona, 16602. Tel: 814-942-5503. Email: stjohnpastor@atlanticbb.net.

Liturgy—Rev. Msgr. ROBERT C. MAZUR, 925 S. Logan Blvd., Hollidaysburg, 16648. Tel: 814-693-9871; Fax: 814-695-8894.

Ongoing Formation of the Clergy—Rev. Msgr. TIMOTHY J. SWOPE, V.F., Mailing Address: P.O. Box 99, Loretto, 15940-0099. Tel: 814-472-5441; Fax: 814-472-5446.

Parish Life Office—Rev. Msgr. ROBERT C. MAZUR, Dir.; Mrs. JEAN SCHNEIDERBAUER, Administrative Asst.. Email: jschneider@dioceseaj.org; 925 S. Logan Blvd., Hollidaysburg, 16648. Tel: 814-693-9605; Fax: 814-696-9516.

Adult Enrichment—Mrs. JEAN SCHNEIDERBAUER, Ministerial Coord. Tel: 814-693-9605; Fax: 814-696-9516. Email: jschneider@dioceseaj.org.

Christian Initiation of Adults—Mrs. JEANNE THOMPSON, Ministerial Coord. Tel: 814-693-9605; Fax: 814-696-9516. Email: jtchrin@dioceseaj.org.

Lay Ecclesial Ministry—Mrs. JEAN SCHNEIDERBAUER, Ministerial Coord. Tel: 814-693-9605; Fax: 814-696-9516. Email: jschneider@dioceseaj.org.

Diocesan Contact for Parish Pastoral Councils—Rev. Msgr. ROBERT C. MAZUR, Ministerial Coord. Tel: 814-693-9605; Fax: 814-696-9516.

Sacramental Preparation/Confirmation Process/Religious Education—Mrs. FRANCINE M. SWOPE, Ministerial Coord., 933 S. Logan Blvd., Hollidaysburg, 16648. Tel: 814-693-1401; Fax: 814-696-6725. Email: fswope@dioceseaj.org.

Stewardship—Rev. Msgr. ROBERT C. MAZUR, Ministerial Coord. Tel: 814-693-9605; Fax: 814-696-9516.

Ministerial Coordinator of Evangelization/Catholics Returning—Sr. LINDA LAMAGNA, C.C.W., Ministerial Coord., Sacred Heart Formation Center, 511 20th St., Altoona, 16602. Tel: 814-944-3922. Email: LindaLccw@verizon.net.

Youth Ministry—Mrs. FRANCINE M. SWOPE, Ministerial Coord., 933 S. Logan Blvd., Hollidaysburg, 16648. Tel: 814-693-1401; Fax: 814-696-6725. Email: fswope@dioceseaj.org.

Permanent Deacons Formation Ministry and Life—Deacon GENE P. NERAL, 925 S. Logan Blvd., Hollidaysburg, 16648. Tel: 814-693-9870; 814-695-8894; Fax: 814-695-8894. Email: gneral@dioceseaj.org.

Presbyteral Council—Rev. ANGELO J. PATTI, Chm., St. Andrew Rectory, 1621 Ferndale Ave., Johnstown, 15905. Tel: 814-288-4324; Fax: 814-288-6750. Email: frpatti@quixnet.net.

Priests' Personnel Board—Rev. Msgr. MICHAEL E. SERVINSKY, S.T.L., J.C.L., D.Min., V.G., 927 S. Logan Blvd., Hollidaysburg, 16648. Tel: 814-695-5579; Fax: 814-695-8894.

Priests' Retirement Plan—Rev. WALTER J. MOLL JR., 927 S. Logan Blvd., Hollidaysburg, 16648. Tel: 814-695-5579; Fax: 814-696-8894.

Propagation of the Faith—Rev. ROBERT J. KELLY, Ph.D., Dir.. Email: bkelly@dioceseaj.org; Sr. PATTI ROSSI, C.S.J., Assoc. Dir.. Email: srpatti@dioceseaj.org; 933 S. Logan Blvd., Hollidaysburg, 16648. Tel: 814-695-5579; Fax: 814-696-6725.

Retreat & Conference Center—Mailing Address: St. John the Baptist Retreat Center, P.O. Box 10, New Baltimore, 15553. Tel: 814-733-2210; Fax: 814-733-2966.

St. Vincent de Paul Society—Mr. ANTHONY CONSIGLIO, Exec. Dir., 927 Franklin St., Johnstown, 15905. Tel: 814-539-4627; Fax: 814-536-1272. Email: avcdepaul@verizon.net. Web: www.svdpcares.org.

Scouting—Rev. JOSEPH T. ORR, St. Matthew Rectory, 1105 Cameron Ave., Tyrone, 16686. Tel: 814-684-1480. Email: saintmat@nb.net.

Self Insurance Program—Mr. DAVE ROSS, Gallagher Bassett Insurance Service, 540 Pellis Rd., Ste. 3000, Greensburg, 15601. Tel: 800-831-3247; Fax: 724-836-8684.

Temporalities—Mr. LARRY R. SUTTON, CFO, 927 S. Logan Blvd., Hollidaysburg, 16648. Tel: 814-695-5579; Fax: 814-695-8894. Email: sutton@dioceseaj.org.

Tribunal—Very Rev. JOHN D. BYRNES, J.V., J.C.L.. Email: jbyrnes@dioceseaj.org; Rev. DAVID R. RIZZO, 927 S. Logan Blvd., Hollidaysburg, 16648. Tel: 814-693-9485; 814-886-2235 (Res.); Fax: 814-695-8894.

Victims' Advocate—Sr. MARILYN WELCH, C.C.W., 927 S. Logan Blvd., Hollidaysburg, 16648. Tel: 814-695-5579; Fax: 814-695-8894.

Vocation—Rev. BRIAN R. SAYLOR, Dir., Prince Gallitzin Chapel House, 357 St. Mary's St., P.O. Box 99, Loretto, 15940-0099. Tel: 814-472-5441; Fax: 814-472-5446. Email: bsaylor@dioceseaj.org.

CLERGY, PARISHES, MISSIONS AND PAROCHIAL SCHOOLS

CITY OF ALTOONA

(BLAIR COUNTY)

1—CATHEDRAL OF THE BLESSED SACRAMENT (1851) Rev. Msgrs. Robert C. Mazur, Rector; Roy F. Kline (Retired); Revs. Aron M. Maghsoudi; Chinemere R.U. Onyeocha; Deacons James F. Leap, (Retired); John R. Rys.
Church: One Cathedral Square, Altoona, 16601-3315. Tel: 814-944-4603; Fax: 814-942-4337. Email: altcathedral@dioceseaj.org. Web: www.altoonacathedral.org.
Catechesis/Religious Program—Nicholas J. Will, Music Min. Students 157.

2—HOLY ROSARY (1901) Rev. Msgr. Michael E. Servinsky.
Res.: 900 N. Fourth St., Altoona, 16601. Tel: 814-944-6676; Fax: 814-946-9207.
Catechesis/Religious Program—Tel: 814-944-4611. Mrs. Margaret M. McCulloch, D.R.E. Students 83.

3—IMMACULATE CONCEPTION (1860) [CEM], (St. Mary's) Rev. Msgr. Timothy P. Stein.
Res.: 1405 Fifth Ave., Altoona, 16602. Tel: 814-942-2416.
See Altoona Central Catholic School, Altoona under Elementary Diocesan Schools located in the Institution section.
Catechesis/Religious Program—Mr. James Mock, D.R.E. Students 100.

4—ST. JOHN THE EVANGELIST (1921) Very Rev. Mark S. Begly; Deacon Gene P. Neral.
Res.: 309 Lotz Ave., Lakemont, Altoona, 16602. Tel: 814-942-5503. Email: stjohnchurch@atlanticbb.net.
School—311 Lotz Ave., Altoona, 16602. Tel: 814-943-4966; Fax: 814-943-8832. Cheryl Zuiker, Prin. Lay Teachers 9; Students 100.
Catechesis/Religious Program—Tel: 814-943-4966. Mrs. Jane Adams, D.R.E. Students 145.

5—ST. LEO THE GREAT (1911) Merged with SS. Peter & Paul to form Our Lady of Fatima, Altoona.

6—ST. MARK'S (1889) Rev. James B. Coveney.
Catechesis/Religious Program—Tel: 814-942-2488. Students 75.
Chapel—Valley View Home for the Aged, Tel: 814-944-0845.
Chapel—Bellemeade Manor, Tel: 814-942-2423.

7—OUR LADY OF FATIMA (1995) [CEM] Rev. James D. Zatalava.
Res.: 2010 12th Ave., Altoona, 16601. Tel: 814-942-0371; Fax: 814-942-0372. Email: olfoffio@hotmail.com. Web: www.ourladyoffatimaaltoona.org.
See Altoona Central Catholic School, Altoona under Elementary Diocesan Schools located in the Institution section.
Catechesis/Religious Program—1304 13th Ave., Altoona, 16603. Tel: 814-943-7423. Students 20.

8—OUR LADY OF LOURDES (1923) Rev. David R. Rizzo.
Res.: 2716 Broad Ave., Altoona, 16601. Tel: 814-943-6185; Fax: 814-943-1968.
Catechesis/Religious Program—Tel: 814-943-1685. Colleen Sheehan, D.R.E. Students 68.

9—OUR LADY OF MT. CARMEL (1905), (Italian), Revs. Frank Scornaienchi, T.O.R.; Robert Juroszek, T.O.R. In Res., Revs. Edward J. Sabo, T.O.R., Chap. Altoona Hospital; William Santre, T.O.R. (Retired).
Res.: 806 11th St., Altoona, 16602. Tel: 814-942-8501; Fax: 814-944-2208. Email: olmc806@aol.com. Web: www.mountcarmelaltoona.com.
See Altoona Central Catholic School, Altoona under Elementary Diocesan Schools located in the Institution section.
Catechesis/Religious Program—Tel: 814-931-3995. Mrs. Dona Baughman, C.R.E. Students 141.
Convent—
Mission—Our Lady of the Assumption (1925) 15 1/2 Hileman St., Altoona, Blair Co. 16602.

10—SS. PETER AND PAUL (1911), (Polish), Merged with St. Leo the Great to form Our Lady of Fatima, Altoona.

11—ST. ROSE OF LIMA (1924) Rev. Brian R. Saylor. In Res., Rev. Carl A. Spishak (Retired).
Res.: 5514 Roselawn Ave., Altoona, 16602. Tel: 814-944-8509; Fax: 814-942-8345. Web: www.stroselima.com.
School—5519 Sixth Ave., Altoona, 16602. Tel: 814-942-7835; Fax: 814-942-1095. Patricia Ronan, Prin. Lay Teachers 15; Students 226.
Catechesis/Religious Program—Students 128.

12—SACRED HEART (1890) Rev. Msgr. Stanley B. Carson.
Res.: 511 20th St., Altoona, 16602. Tel: 814-943-8553; Fax: 814-943-1556. Email: sacredheart511@verizon.net.

Web: www.sacredheartaltoona.org.
Formation Center—2009 Sixth Ave., Altoona, 16602. Tel: 814-944-3922.
Catechesis/Religious Program—Students 166.

13—ST. THERESE OF THE CHILD JESUS (1927) Rev. D. Timothy Grimme.
Res.: 2301 5th St., Altoona, 16601-3863. Tel: 814-942-4479; Fax: 814-942-1873. Email: sttheresealtoona@catholicweb.com. Web: http://homes.catholicweb.com/sttheresealtoona.
See Altoona Central Catholic School, Altoona under Elementary Diocesan Schools located in the Institution section.
Catechesis/Religious Program—Mary Beth Schmidhamer, D.R.E. Students 146.

CITY OF JOHNSTOWN

(CAMBRIA COUNTY)

1—ST. JOHN GUALBERT CATHEDRAL (1835) [CEM 2] Revs. James F. Crookston, Rector; John F. Brezovec; Clarence S. Bridges; Deacons John J. Concannon, (Retired); Thomas M. Buige.
Res.: 117 Clinton St., P.O. Box 807, Johnstown, 15907. Tel: 814-536-0117; Fax: 814-535-6771. Email: cathedral@floodcity.net. Web: www.stjohngualbertcathedral.org.
Catechesis/Religious Program—124 Maple Ave., Johnstown, 15901. Tel: 814-535-4228. Students 65.

2—ST. ANDREW (1956) Rev. Angelo J. Patti.
Res.: 1621 Ferndale Ave., Johnstown, 15905. Tel: 814-288-4324; Fax: 814-288-6750. Email: pastor@standrewschurch.com. Web: www.standrewschurch.com.
School—(Grades PreK-8), 1621 Ferndale Ave., Johnstown, 15905. Tel: 814-288-2811; Fax: 814-288-6750. Email: gguaetta@standrewschurch.com. Lay Teachers 11; Students 192.
Catechesis/Religious Program—Email: mclark@standrewschurch.com. Students 81.

3—ST. ANTHONY'S (1905), (Italian), Merged with SS. Peter & Paul, Johnstown to form St. Clare of Assisi, Johnstown.

4—ST. BARNABAS (1954), (Slovenian), Merged with St. Gregory, Johnstown to form SS. Gregory & Barnabas, Johnstown.

5—ST. BENEDICT'S (1930) Revs. David S. Peles; Derek Fairman; Michael Wolfe.
Res.: 2310 Bedford St., Johnstown, 15904. Tel: 814-266-9718, Ext. 101; Fax: 814-269-4220. Email: SBpastor@atlanticbb.net. Web: www.stbenedictchurch.org.
School—2306 Bedford St., Johnstown, 15904. Tel: 814-266-3837; Fax: 814-266-7718. Web: www.sbpanthers.org. Sr. Carol Ann Ziecina, C.S.J., Prin. Lay Teachers 25; Students 301.
Catechesis/Religious Program—Sr. Cindy Burns, D.R.E. (High School). Tel: 814-266-9718, Ext. 301; Mrs. Michelle Robatin, D.R.E. (Elem). Tel: 814-266-9718, Ext. 302. Students 361.

6—SS. CASIMIR & EMERICH (1997), (Polish—Hungarian), [CEM 2] Closed. For inquiries for parish records contact the chancery.

7—ST. CLARE OF ASSISI (2000), (Italian—Slovak), [CEM 2] Rev. Leo Arnone; Deacon Samuel M. Cammarata.
Office: 110 Maple Ave., Johnstown, 15901. Tel: 814-535-1133; Fax: 814-535-1664. Email: stclareofassisi@atlanticbb.net.
Res.: 124 Maple Ave., Johnstown, 15901.
See Central Catholic Academy, Johnstown under Elementary Diocesan Schools located in the Institution section.
Catechesis/Religious Program—Tel: 814-535-2360. Students 60.

8—ST. CLEMENT'S (1956) Rev. William E. Rosenbaum; Very Rev. Robert Radasky.
Res. & Church: 114 Lindberg Ave., Johnstown, 15905. Tel: 814-255-4422; Fax: 814-255-2623. Email: stclementchurch@atlanticbb.net. Web: www.stclementaj.org.
See Cathedral Catholic Academy under Education Consolidated Elementary Schools located in the Institution section.
Catechesis/Religious Program—Sr. Dolores Partsch, C.S.J., D.R.E. Students 133.

9—ST. COLUMBA'S (1888) [CEM] Closed. For inquiries for parish records contact the chancery.

10—ST. EMERICH'S (1905), (Hungarian), Merged with St. Casimir's, Johnstown to form SS. Casimir & Emerich, Johnstown.

11—ST. FRANCIS OF ASSISI (1922), (Slovak), [CEM] Very Rev. Anthony Francis Spilka, O.F.M.Conv.
Res.: 120 Barron Ave., Johnstown, 15906. Tel: 814-539-1632; Fax: 814-539-5888. Email: sfassisich@atlanticbbn.net.
Catechesis/Religious Program—Students 63.

12—SS. GREGORY & BARNABAS (2001) Rev. Robert L. Ruston; Deacon Thomas M. Papinchak.
Res.: 120 Boltz St., Johnstown, 15902. Tel: 814-536-6818; Fax: 814-534-0651. Email: sgsb925@hotmail.com. Web: www.gregbar.org.
Catechesis/Religious Program—Students 133.

13—ST. GREGORY'S (1919) Merged with St. Barnabas, Johnstown to form SS. Gregory & Barnabas, Johnstown.

14—IMMACULATE CONCEPTION (1859), (German), [CEM] Closed. For inquiries for parish records contact the chancery.

15—ST. JOSEPH'S (1852), (German), Merged with Our Lady of Mercy to form St. John Gualbert Cathedral, Johnstown.
See Central Catholic Elementary School, Johnstown under Elementary Diocesan Schools located in the Institution section.

16—ST. MICHAEL'S (1910), (German), Very Rev. Anthony Francis Spilka, O.F.M.Conv.
Mailing Address: 180 Gilbert St., Johnstown, 15906.
Res.: 120 Barron Ave., Johnstown, 15906. Tel: 814-539-1632; Fax: 814-539-5888.
Catechesis/Religious Program— (Clustered with St. Francis of Assisi) Students 63.

17—OUR LADY OF MERCY (1921) Merged with St. Joseph to form St. John Gualbert Cathedral, Johnstown.

18—OUR MOTHER OF SORROWS (1920) Very Rev. Paul E. Turnbull.
Res.: 407 Tioga St., Johnstown, 15905. Tel: 814-535-7646; Fax: 814-536-7850. Email: parishsecretary@omosjohnstownpa.org. Web: www.omosjohnstownpa.org.
School—430 Tioga St., Johnstown, 15905. Tel: 814-539-5315; Fax: 814-539-5315. Mrs. Pamela Seidel, Prin. Lay Teachers 20; Students 275.
Catechesis/Religious Program—Tel: 814-255-1264. Mrs. Karen Fink, D.R.E. Students 180.

19—ST. PATRICK'S (1904) Rev. Matthew A. Reese, Admin.
Res.: 609 Park Ave., Johnstown, 15902. Tel: 814-539-2186; Fax: 814-539-2410.
Catechesis/Religious Program—Students 41.

20—SS. PETER AND PAUL'S (1918) Merged with St. Anthony, Johnstown to form St. Clare of Assisi, Johnstown.

21—RESURRECTION ROMAN CATHOLIC CHURCH (2009) [CEM] Rev. Alan E. Thomas.
Parish Office: 408 Eighth Ave., Johnstown, 15906. Tel: 814-539-5788; Fax: 814-539-8845.
Worship Site: 324 Chestnut St., Johnstown, 15906.
Catechesis/Religious Program—Tel: 814-535-5409. Students 123.

22—ST. ROCHUS (1900), (Croatian), [CEM] Closed. For inquiries for parish records contact the chancery.

23—ST. STEPHEN, FIRST KING OF HUNGARY (1891), (Slovak), [CEM] Closed. For inquiries for parish records contact the chancery.

24—ST. THERESE OF THE CHILD JESUS (1929), (Slovenian), [CEM] Rev. Bernard Karmanocky, O.F.M.
Res.: 536 Decker Ave., Johnstown, 15906. Tel: 814-539-7633; Fax: 814-539-7633.
See West End Catholic School, Johnstown under Elementary Diocesan Schools located in the Institution section.
Convent—702 Saybrook Pl., Johnstown, 15906.
Mission—St. Anne's (1935) 533 Woodland Ave., Moxham, Cambria Co. 15902. Tel: 814-539-7633.
Catechesis/Religious Program—Tel: 814-536-2287. Students 45.

25—VISITATION OF THE B.V.M. (1927) Rev. Barry J. Baroni; Deacon John E. Sroka.
Res.: 1127 McKinley Ave., Johnstown, 15905. Tel: 814-536-6110; Fax: 814-536-3709. Email: visitation@floodcity.net. Web: www.visitationchurch.net.
Catechesis/Religious Program—Tel: 814-535-2341. Students 42.

OUTSIDE THE CITIES OF ALTOONA AND JOHNSTOWN

ACOSTA, SOMERSET CO., ST. JOHN THE BAPTIST'S (1912) Merged with St. Joseph, Boswell, and St. Stanislaus, Boswell, to form All Saints Church, Boswell.

ASHVILLE, CAMBRIA CO., ST. THOMAS AQUINAS (1889) [CEM] Rev. Sean K. Code.
Mailing Address: 692 Glendale Valley Blvd., Fallentimber, 16639. Tel: 814-943-5437. Email: ssjoanandthomasonpa53@dishmail.net.
Catechesis/Religious Program—Tel: 814-736-3774. Mrs. Jean Vasilko, D.R.E. Students 58.

BAKERTON, CAMBRIA CO., SACRED HEART (1904) Merged with St. Patrick, Spangler, to form St. Jude, Elmora.

BARNESBORO, CAMBRIA CO.

1—CHRIST THE KING (1993) Merged with St. Stanislaus Kostka, Barnesboro; St. John the Baptist, Northern Cambria; Our Lady of Mt. Carmel, Northern Cambria; Holy Cross, Northern Cambria to form Prince of Peace, Northern Cambria.

2—ST. STANISLAUS KOSTKA (1906), (Polish), Merged with Christ the King, Barnesboro; St. John the Baptist, Northern Cambria; Our Lady of Mt. Carmel, Northern Cambria; Holy Cross, Northern Cambria to form Prince of Peace, Northern Cambria.

BEANS COVE, BEDFORD CO., SEVEN DOLORS B.V.M. (1878) [CEM] Rev. Norman P. Imgrund, Canonical Pastor.
Mailing Address: 2174 Beans Cove Rd., Clearville, 15535-7901. Tel: 814-767-9522; Fax: 814-767-8158.
Res.: 161 E. First Ave., Everett, 15537. Tel: 814-652-5854.
Catechesis/Religious Program—Students 7.

BEAVERDALE, CAMBRIA CO.

1—ST. AGNES (1909) Merged with St. Joseph, Beaverdale, and Corpus Christi, Dunlo, to form Holy Spirit Church, Beaverdale.

2—HOLY SPIRIT (1995) [CEM 2] Closed. For inquiries for parish records contact the chancery.

3—ST. JOSEPH'S (1904), (Slovak), Merged with St. Agnes, Beaverdale, and Corpus Christi, Dunlo, to form Holy Spirit Church, Beaverdale.

BEDFORD, BEDFORD CO., ST. THOMAS (1816) [CEM 2] Rev. Donald W. Dusza.
Res.: 215 E. Penn St., 15522. Tel: 814-623-5526; Fax: 814-623-1741. Web: www.stthomasbedford.com.
School—129 W. Penn St., 15522. Tel: 814-623-8873; Fax: 814-623-1208. Joyce Wityk, Prin. Lay Teachers 7; Students 56.
Catechesis/Religious Program—Tel: 814-623-6023. Mrs. Amelie Regester, D.R.E. Students 133.

BELLEFONTE, CENTRE CO., ST. JOHN THE EVANGELIST'S (1828) [CEM 2] Very Rev. Neil R. Dadey; Rev. Valentine J. Bradley; Deacon Thomas E. Boldin.
Res.: 134 E. Bishop St., 16823. Tel: 814-355-3134; Fax: 814-355-4820. Email: stjcatholic@comcast.net. Web: www.catholicchurchbellefonte.catholicweb.com.
School—(Grades PreK-5), 116 E. Bishop St., 16823. Tel: 814-355-7859; Fax: 814-355-2939. Email: twendt@saintjohnsch.com. Web: www.stjohnsch.com. Mrs. Pamela Vaiana, Prin.; Mrs. Karen Moore, Librarian. Lay Teachers 8; Students 118.
Catechesis/Religious Program—Tel: 814-355-3134. Students 315.

BELLWOOD, BLAIR CO., ST. JOSEPH'S (1890) Rev. David H. Roesch.
Res.: 623 E. Third St., 16617. Tel: 814-742-7075. Email: sanjoe3@aol.com. Web: stjosephbellwood.org.
Catechesis/Religious Program—Tel: 814-742-7894. Students 105.

BOSWELL, SOMERSET CO.

1—ALL SAINTS (1995) [CEM 3] Rev. Justin A. Ratajczak, O.F.M.Conv.
Res.: 325 Quemahoning St., 15531. Tel: 814-629-5551; Fax: 814-629-5677. Email: allsaints.parish@verizon.net.
Catechesis/Religious Program—Students 48.

2—ST. STANISLAUS (1901), (Polish), Merged with St. John the Baptist, Acosta to form All Saints Church, Boswell.

CARROLLTOWN, CAMBRIA CO., ST. BENEDICT'S (1846) [CEM 3] Rev. Jude W. Brady, O.S.B.; Bro. Jeremy Heppler, O.S.B.
Res.: 100 Main St., P.O. Box 447, 15722. Tel: 814-344-6548; Fax: 814-344-8656. Email: sbcjwb@comcast.net. Web: saintbenedictchurch.com.
School—119 S. Church St., 15722. Tel: 814-344-6512; Fax: 814-344-8530. Email: sbsct@dioceseaj.org. Sisters 1; Brothers 1; Lay Teachers 11; Students 155.
Catechesis/Religious Program—Suzanne Bills, D.R.E. Students 190.

CASSANDRA, CAMBRIA CO., ST. AGNES (1909) Rev. Charles F. Bodziak.
Res.: P.O. Box 56, 15925. Tel: 814-736-8314.
Catechesis/Religious Program—Tel: 814-495-5360.

CENTRAL CITY, SOMERSET CO.

1—ST. JOHN THE BAPTIST (1917), (Slovak), Merged with Sacred Heart of Jesus, Central City to form Our Lady Queen of Angels, Central City.

2—OUR LADY QUEEN OF ANGELS (1999) [CEM 2] Rev. Joseph D. Maurizio Jr.
Res.: 738 Sunshine Ave., 15926-1233. Tel: 814-754-5224; Fax: 814-754-4447 (24 hrs a day). Email: queenofangels@wpia.net. Web: www.ladyqueenofangels.org.
Catechesis/Religious Program—Students 50.

3—SACRED HEART OF JESUS (1914), (Polish), Merged with St. John the Baptist, Central City to form Our Lady Queen of Angels, Central City.

CHEST SPRINGS, CAMBRIA CO., ST. MONICA'S (1859) [CEM] Rev. Joseph W. Fleming.
Res.: 803 St. Augustine Rd., Dysart, 16636. Tel: 814-674-8550.
Church: 3037 Colonel Drake Hwy., 16624. Tel: 814-674-3712.
Catechesis/Religious Program—Students 47.

CLARENCE, CENTRE CO.

1—ST. MICHAEL'S (1900), (Slovak), [CEM] Merged with St. Mary's, Snow Shoe to form Queen of Archangels, Clarence.

2—QUEEN OF ARCHANGELS (2005) [CEM 2] Rev. Lubomir J. Strecok.
102 Church St., 16829. Tel: 814-387-6762.

Email: queenofarchangelspa@verizon.net.
Catechesis/Religious Program—Tel: 814-387-6762. Students 97.
Mission— 204 S. 4th St., Snow Shoe, Centre Co. 16874.

COLVER, CAMBRIA CO., HOLY FAMILY (1912), (Polish), [CEM] Rev. Bernard F. Grega.
Res.: 562 Fifth St., P.O. Box 543, 15927. Tel: 814-748-7054; Fax: 814-748-7254.
Catechesis/Religious Program—Sr. Anna Marie, S.A., D.R.E. Students 52.

CONEMAUGH, CAMBRIA CO.
1—ASSUMPTION OF B.V.M. (1910) [CEM] Merged with Sacred Heart, Conemaugh to form Church of the Transfiguration, Conemaugh.
2—CHURCH OF THE TRANSFIGURATION (2008) [CEM 2] Rev. Robert C. Hall.
Res.: 340 Second St., 15909. Tel: 814-535-2250; Fax: 814-536-9770. Email: shasec@comcast.net.
Catechesis/Religious Program—Mrs. Louise Brezovic, D.R.E. Students 61.
3—SACRED HEART (1902) [CEM] Merged with Assumption of B.V.M., Conemaugh to form Church of the Transfiguration, Conemaugh.

COUPON, CAMBRIA CO., ST. JOSEPH'S (1855) [CEM 2] Rev. Brian R. Saylor; Deacon Steve A. Luke.
Res.: 3224 Coupon-Gallitzin Rd., 16629. Tel: 814-943-8464.
Catechesis/Religious Program—Students 35.

CRESSON, CAMBRIA CO.
1—ST. ALOYSIUS (1838) [CEM] Very Rev. John D. Byrnes.
Res.: 7911 Admiral Peary Hwy., 16630. Tel: 814-886-2235. Email: stals16630@yahoo.com. Web: www.saintaloysiuscresson.org.
See All Saints Catholic School under Elementary Diocesan Schools located in the Institution section.
Catechesis/Religious Program—Tel: 814-886-2669. Marcia E. Hammond, D.R.E. Students 107.
2—ST. FRANCIS XAVIER (1908) [CEM] Rev. George M. Gulash.
Res.: 211 Powell Ave., 16630. Tel: 814-886-2374; Fax: 814-886-2498.
See All Saints Catholic School under Elementary Diocesan Schools located in the Institution section.
Catechesis/Religious Program—Tel: 814-886-2374. Mrs. Tracey Ingold, Dir. Faith Formation. Students 114.

DAVIDSVILLE, SOMERSET CO., ST. ANNE (1911) [CEM 2] Rev. Michael Lewandowski, O.F.M.Conv.
Mailing Address: 205 Woodstown Hwy., P.O. Box 500, 15928. Tel: 814-479-2664; Fax: 814-479-7702. Email: sannep@atlanticbb.net. In Res., Revs. Karl Kolodziejski, O.F.M.Conv.; Justin A. Ratajczak, O.F.M.Conv.
Catechesis/Religious Program—Students 46.

DUDLEY, HUNTINGDON CO., IMMACULATE CONCEPTION (1856) [CEM] Rev. Bernard L. White.
Res.: 1416 Dudley Rd., P.O. Box 188, 16634. Tel: 814-635-2919.
Catechesis/Religious Program—Students 45.

DUNCANSVILLE, BLAIR CO., ST. CATHERINE OF SIENA (1963) Rev. Msgr. Robert J. Saly.
Mailing Address: Old Rte. 22, P.O. Box 88, 16635. Tel: 814-696-4126; Fax: 814-693-7518. Email: sienaelm@verizon.net.
Res.: 417 Elm Ln., 16635.
Catechesis/Religious Program—P.O. Box 88, 16635. Debra Terchanik, D.R.E. Students 80.

DUNLO, CAMBRIA CO., CORPUS CHRISTI (1903) Merged with St. Agnes and St. Joseph, Beaverdale to form Holy Spirit Church, Beaverdale.

EBENSBURG, CAMBRIA CO., HOLY NAME (1816) [CEM] Rev. Msgr. Arnold L. Gaus; Rev. Mark Robert Reid.
Res.: 500 N. Julian St., 15931. Tel: 814-472-7244; Fax: 814-472-7249. Email: holynameebg@verizon.net. Web: www.holynameebg.org.
School—Tel: 814-472-8817; Fax: 814-471-0500. Email: holynameelementary@comcast.net. Ms. Joan Meintel, Prin. Lay Teachers 16; Students 220.
Catechesis/Religious Program—Students 389.

EHRENFELD, CAMBRIA CO., OUR LADY OF MT. CARMEL (1892) Merged with St. James and St. Anthony's, South Fork to form Most Holy Trinity, South Fork.

ELMORA, CAMBRIA CO., ST. JUDE (1995) Closed. For inquiries for parish records contact the chancery.

EMEIGH, CAMBRIA CO., MOST PRECIOUS BLOOD, See separate listing. See Christ the King, Barnesboro.

EVERETT, BEDFORD CO., ST. JOHN THE EVANGELIST (1971) Rev. Norman P. Imgrund.
Res.: 161 E. First Ave., 15537. Tel: 814-652-5854. Church: 163 E. First Ave., 15537.
Catechesis/Religious Program—Students 16.

FALLENTIMBER, CAMBRIA CO.
1—ST. JOAN OF ARC (1995) Rev. Sean K. Code.
Res.: 692 Glendale Valley Blvd., 16639. Tel: 814-943-5437. Email: ssjoanandthomasonpa53@dishmail.net.
Catechesis/Religious Program—Tel: 814-672-5123. Mrs. Nancy Francisco, D.R.E. Students 25.
2—ST. MARY MAGDALEN'S (1889) Closed. Merged with St. Richard's Mission, Blandburg to form St. Joan of Arc Church, Fallentimber.

GALLITZIN, CAMBRIA CO.
1—ST. DEMETRIUS (2000) [CEM 2] Rev. Albert H. Ledoux.
Res.: 811 Church St., 16641. Tel: 814-886-7941; Fax: 814-886-5673.
Catechesis/Religious Program—Students 97.
Mission— 616 Church St., Cambria Co. 16641. Tel: 814-886-4203.
2—OUR LADY OF CZESTOCHOWA (1903), (Polish), Merged with St. Patrick, Gallitzin to form St. Demetrius, Gallitzin.
3—ST. PATRICK'S (1850) Merged with Our Lady of Czestochowa, Gallitzin to form St. Demetrius, Gallitzin.

HASTINGS, CAMBRIA CO., ST. BERNARD (1890) [CEM 2] Rev. Thaddeus E. Rettger, O.S.B.
Res.: 148-Apt. 2 Seventh Ave., P.O. Box 497, 16646. Tel: 814-247-6558; Fax: 814-247-8522.
Catechesis/Religious Program—Tel: 814-674-5841. Mrs. Aileen Ropp, D.R.E. Students 132.
Mission—St. Boniface Chapel 1278 Main St., St. Boniface, Cambria Co. 16675.

HOLLIDAYSBURG, BLAIR CO.
1—ST. MARY'S (1841) [CEM 2] Rev. Anthony J. Legarski; Deacon John A. Tiernan, (Retired).
Res.: 312 Clark St., 16648. Tel: 814-695-0622; Fax: 814-696-9609. Email: smcforyou@hotmail.com. Web: www.webparish.com/aj/saintmarys.
See Hollidaysburg Consolidated Catholic Elementary, Hollidaysburg under Elementary Diocesan Schools located in the Institution section.
Catechesis/Religious Program—Tel: 814-695-5678. Mrs. Connie Curfman, D.R.E. Students 199.
2—ST. MICHAEL'S (1862), (German), [CEM] Very Rev. Clement G. Gardner.
Res.: 301 Spruce St., 16648. Tel: 814-695-0912; Fax: 814-693-9820. Web: www.stmichael-hldg-pa.org.
See Hollidaysburg Consolidated Catholic Elementary, Hollidaysburg under Elementary Diocesan Schools located in the Institution section.
Catechesis/Religious Program—Tel: 814-695-9735. Email: susu194@aol.com. Susan M. Teske, D.R.E. Students 320.

HOOVERSVILLE, SOMERSET CO., HOLY FAMILY (1911) [CEM] Rev. Karl Kolodziejski, O.F.M.Conv.
Res.: 321 Sugar St., P.O. Box 187, 15936. Tel: 814-798-2933; Fax: 814-798-8601.
Catechesis/Religious Program—Students 32.

HUNTINGDON, HUNTINGDON CO., MOST HOLY TRINITY (1826) [CEM] Rev. David J. Arseneault.
Res.: 524 Mifflin St., 16652. Tel: 814-643-0160; Fax: 814-643-0160. Email: mhtcc@comcast.net. Web: www.mhtcc.org.
Catechesis/Religious Program—Students 183.

LILLY, CAMBRIA CO.
1—ST. BRIGID'S (1883) Merged with Our Lady of Mount Carmel, Lilly to form Our Lady of the Alleghenies, Lilly.
2—OUR LADY OF MT. CARMEL (1910), (Polish), Merged with St. Brigid, Lilly to form Our Lady of the Alleghenies, Lilly.
3—OUR LADY OF THE ALLEGHENIES (1995) [CEM 2] Rev. Msgr. John R. Sasway.
Res.: 608 Main St., 15938. Tel: 814-886-2504; Fax: 814-884-4952. Email: olallegh@comcast.net.
Catechesis/Religious Program—Tel: 814-886-2161. Sr. Theresa M. Kukla, S.S.C.J., D.R.E. Students 109.

LOCK HAVEN, CLINTON CO.
1—ST. AGNES (1873) [CEM] Rev. Jozef Kovacik; Deacon Philip Gibson.
Res.: 3 E. Walnut St., 17745. Tel: 570-748-4594; Fax: 570-893-8229. Email: stagnespa@comcast.net. Web: www.stagneslh.org.
See Lock Haven Catholic School under Immaculate Conception, Lock Haven.
Catechesis/Religious Program—Tel: 570-748-4828. Email: stagnespa.pat@comcast.net. Students 96.
2—IMMACULATE CONCEPTION (1852) [CEM] Rev. Richard B. Tomkosky; Deacon Calvin J. Young.
Res.: 310 W. Water St., 17745. Tel: 570-748-4535; Fax: 570-748-1674. Email: ic1852@comcast.net.
School—Lock Haven Catholic School, Tel: 570-748-7252. Michele Alexander, Interim Prin. Lay Teachers 17; Students 146.
Catechesis/Religious Program—Tel: 570-748-4828; Fax: 570-893-8229. Students 170.

LORETTO, CAMBRIA CO., BASILICA OF ST. MICHAEL THE ARCHANGEL (1799) [CEM] Rev. Msgr. Timothy J. Swope; Deacon Michael Condor Jr. Tel: 814-886-4948. In Res., Rev. Dennis M. Kurdziel.
Res.: 321 St. Mary, P.O. Box 10, 15940. Tel: 814-472-8551; Fax: 814-471-4959. Web: www.basilica-loretto.com.
School—301 St. Elizabeth St., 15940. Tel: 814-472-9117; Fax: 814-472-9117. Judy M. Noel, Prin. Lay Teachers 9; Students 180.
Catechesis/Religious Program—Tel: 814-471-4890. Robert Sutton, D.R.E. (Elementary & High School). Students 133.

MCCONNELLSBURG, FULTON CO., ST. STEPHEN'S (1962) Rev. Joseph C. Nale.
Res.: 303 Lincoln Way E., 17233. Tel: 717-485-3723; Fax: 717-485-3855.
Catechesis/Religious Program—Tel: 717-485-0661. Students 30.

MEYERSDALE, SOMERSET CO., SS. PHILIP AND JAMES (1850) [CEM 2] Very Rev. James M. Dugan.
Res.: 247 High St., 15552. Tel: 814-634-8150; Fax: 814-634-0983.
Catechesis/Religious Program—Students 68.
Mission—St. Gregory (1907) Church St., Berlin, Somerset Co. 15530.

MOUNT UNION, HUNTINGDON CO., ST. CATHERINE OF SIENA (1912) [CEM] Rev. George D. Koharchik.
Res.: 205 W. Market St., 17066. Tel: 814-542-4582. Email: stcatherine@comcast.net.
Catechesis/Religious Program—Students 42.

MUNDYS CORNER, CAMBRIA CO., ST. JOHN VIANNEY'S (1950) Rev. Andrew C. Stanko.
Res.: 3513 William Penn Ave., Johnstown, 15909. Tel: 814-322-4789; Fax: 814-322-3799. Email: stjohnvianney@atlanticbb.net. Web: www.sjvcc.com.
Catechesis/Religious Program—Tel: 814-322-1149. Yvonne Allbaugh. Students 115.

NANTY-GLO, CAMBRIA CO., ST. MARY'S (1902) [CEM] Rev. Martin A. Cingle; Deacon James J. Janosik.
Res.: 1020 Caroline St., 15943. Tel: 814-749-9103; Fax: 814-749-5463. Email: mirrorsmcl@aol.com.
Catechesis/Religious Program—Mrs. Patricia LaMantia, D.R.E. Students 84.

NEW BALTIMORE, ST. JOHN THE BAPTIST (1829) [CEM] Rev. Allen P. Zeth.
Res.: 101 Findley St., P.O. Box 10, 15553. Tel: 814-733-2210; Fax: 814-733-2966.
Catechesis/Religious Program— Linda Little, D.R.E.; Julie Hoover, D.R.E. Students 80.

NEWRY, BLAIR CO., ST. PATRICK'S (1816) [CEM 2] Rev. Msgr. Anthony B. Little.
P.O. Box 398, 16665.
Res.: 704 Patrick Ln., 16665. Tel: 814-695-3413; Fax: 814-695-1733. Email: pastor@saintpatricknewry.org. Web: www.saintpatricknewry.org.
School—Tel: 814-695-3819; Fax: 814-695-5274. Sisters 1; Lay Teachers 10; Students 91.
Catechesis/Religious Program—Mrs. Linda Guiffre, D.R.E. Students 90.

NICKTOWN, CAMBRIA CO., ST. NICHOLAS (1861) [CEM] Rev. Job Foote, O.S.B.
Res.: 1169 Alverda Rd., P.O. Box 37, 15762. Tel: 814-948-9614; Fax: 814-948-5232. Email: info@saintnicholasparish.org. Web: www.saintnicholasparish.org.
See Northern Cambria Catholic School, Nicktown under Elementary Schools Diocesan located in the Institution section.
Catechesis/Religious Program—Students 147.

NORTHERN CAMBRIA, CAMBRIA CO.
1—HOLY CROSS (1893) Merged with St. Stanislaus Kostka, Barnesboro; Christ the King, Barnesboro; St. John the Baptist, Northern Cambria; Our Lady of Mt. Carmel, Northern Cambria to form Prince of Peace, Northern Cambria.
2—ST. JOHN THE BAPTIST (1896), (Slovak), Merged with St. Stanislaus Kostka, Barnesboro; Christ the King, Barnesboro; Holy Cross, Northern Cambria; Our Lady of Mt. Carmel, Northern Cambria to form Prince of Peace, Northern Cambria.
3—OUR LADY OF MT. CARMEL (1908), (Italian), Merged with St. Stanislaus Kostka, Barnesboro; Christ the King, Barnesboro; Holy Cross, Northern Cambria; St. John the Baptist, Northern Cambria to form Prince of Peace, Northern Cambria.
4—PRINCE OF PEACE (2000) [CEM 5] Rev. Lawrence L. Lacovic.
Res.: 811 Chestnut Ave., 15714. Tel: 814-948-6842; Fax: 814-948-6585.
School—Tel: 814-948-8900. See Elementary Diocesan Schools under Institutions Located in the Diocese.
Catechesis/Religious Program—Deacon Bernard J. Zernick, D.R.E. Students 213.

ORBISONIA, HUNTINGDON CO., ST. MARY'S (1840) [CEM 2] Rev. Joseph C. Nale.
Mailing Address: 20896 Croghan Pike, 17243-9000. Tel: 814-447-3172; Fax: 814-447-9030. Email: valumbra@embarqmail.com.
Res.: 303 Lincoln Way E., Mc Connellsburg, 17233. Tel: 717-485-3723.
Catechesis/Religious Program—Students 27.

PATTON, CAMBRIA CO.
1—ST. GEORGE (1907), (Slovak), Merged with Our Lady of Perpetual Help, Patton and St. Lawrence to form Queen of Peace, Patton.
2—OUR LADY OF PERPETUAL HELP (1892) Merged with St. George, Patton, and St. Lawrence to form Queen of Peace, Patton.

3—QUEEN OF PEACE (1995) [CEM 2] Rev. Ananias Buccicone, O.S.B. In Res., Rev. Robert Roche, O.S.B. Tel: 814-674-8986.
Res.: 907 Sixth Ave., 16668. Tel: 814-674-8983; Fax: 814-674-8805. Email: quopchurch@nb.net.
Catechesis/Religious Program—Tel: 814-674-3645. Marlene Price, D.R.E. Students 166.

PENNS VALLEY, CENTRE CO., BLESSED KATERI TEKAKWITHA (1986) [JC] Very Rev. Neil R. Dadey; Rev. Valentine J. Bradley.
Res.: 3503 Penns Valley Rd., Spring Mills, 16875. Tel: 814-422-8983.
Catechesis/Religious Program—Students 78.

PHILIPSBURG, CENTRE CO., SS. PETER AND PAUL (1868) [CEM] [JC] Rev. Robert J. Kelly.
Res.: 400 S. Fourth St., 16866. Tel: 814-342-1700; Fax: 814-342-5480. Email: rjkll@psu.edu.
Catechesis/Religious Program—William J. Slother Jr., D.R.E. Students 110.

PORTAGE, CAMBRIA CO.
1—ASSUMPTION B.V.M. (1907), (Slovak), Merged with Sacred Heart of Jesus to form Our Lady of the Sacred Heart, Portage
2—ST. JOHN THE BAPTIST (1923), (Hungarian), [CEM] Merged with Our Lady of the Sacred Heart, Portage.
3—ST. JOSEPH'S (1898) Rev. Walter J. Moll Jr.
Res.: 509 Caldwell Ave., 15946. Tel: 814-736-4279; Fax: 814-736-4764.
Catechesis/Religious Program—Tel: 814-736-9214. Mary E. Heinrich, D.R.E. Students 148.
4—OUR LADY OF THE SACRED HEART (1999), (Polish—Slovak), [CEM 3] Very Rev. Ronald V. Osinski.
601 Mountain Ave., 15946. Tel: 814-736-4239; Fax: 814-736-9285. Email: OLSHparish@hotmail.com. Web: www.sdmnet.com.
Res.: 806 Hammers St., 15946. Tel: 814-736-9770.
Catechesis/Religious Program—Students 94.
5—SACRED HEART OF JESUS (1909), (Polish), Merged with Assumption of the Blessed Virgin Mary, Portage to form Our Lady of the Sacred Heart, Portage.

RENOVO, CLINTON CO., ST. JOSEPH'S (1869) [CEM 3] Sr. Nancy E. Spence, C.C.W., Parochial Admin.
Res.: 925 Huron Ave., 17764. Tel: 570-923-0172; Fax: 570-923-0317.
Catechesis/Religious Program—Judy M. Kurutz, D.R.E. Students 35.

REVLOC, CAMBRIA CO., MOST HOLY REDEEMER (1920) Closed. For inquiries for parish records contact the chancery.

ROARING SPRING, BLAIR CO., ST. THOMAS MORE (1969) Rev. Msgr. William E. Shultz.
Res.: 825 Williams St., 16673. Tel: 814-224-4522; Fax: 814-224-4522.
Catechesis/Religious Program—Students 80.

ST. AUGUSTINE, CAMBRIA CO., ST. AUGUSTINE (1847) [CEM] Rev. Joseph W. Fleming.
Res.: 803 St. Augustine Rd., Dysart, 16636. Tel: 814-674-8550.
Catechesis/Religious Program—Students 90.

ST. BONIFACE, CAMBRIA CO., ST. BONIFACE CHAPEL (1859) Merged to form St. Bernard, Hastings.

ST. LAWRENCE, CAMBRIA CO., ST. LAWRENCE'S (1853) Merged with Our Lady of Perpetual Help and St. George, Patton to form Queen of Peace, Patton.

ST. MICHAEL, CAMBRIA CO., ST. MICHAEL'S (1913) [CEM] Rev. Msgr. Michael A. Becker.
Res.: 751 Locust St., Box 103, 15951. Tel: 814-495-9640; Fax: 814-495-9424. Email: saintmichaelsecretaries@yahoo.com. Web: www.saintmichaelchurch.us.
Catechesis/Religious Program—Students 178.

SNOW SHOE, CENTRE CO., ST. MARY'S (1865), (Irish), [CEM] Merged with St. Michael, Clarence to form Queen of Archangels, Clarence.

SOMERSET, SOMERSET CO.
1—ST. PETER IN CHAINS (1995) Mailing Address: *S.C.I.-Somerset*, 1590 Walters Mill Rd., 15501-0001. Tel: 814-443-8100.
2—ST. PETER'S (1920) [CEM] Rev. Daniel J. O'Neill.
Res.: 433 W. Church St., 15501. Tel: 814-443-6574; Fax: 814-445-7766.
School—Tel: 814-445-6662. Mrs. Jill Harris, Prin. Lay Teachers 7; Students 99.
Catechesis/Religious Program—Students 215.

SOUTH FORK, CAMBRIA CO.
1—ST. ANTHONY'S (1905), (Polish), Merged with St. James, South Fork and Our Lady of Mt. Carmel, Ehrenfeld to form Most Holy Trinity, South Fork.
2—ST. JAMES (1906) Merged with St. Anthony, South Fork and Our Lady of Mt. Carmel, Ehrenfeld to form Most Holy Trinity, South Fork.
3—MOST HOLY TRINITY (1995) [CEM 2] Rev. Robert P. Reese.
Res.: 550 Main St., 15956. Tel: 814-495-4419; Fax: 814-495-9104. Email: rectory@mostholytrinitychurch.com. Web: www.mostholytrinitychurch.com.
Catechesis/Religious Program—Tel: 814-495-4028. Mrs. Betty Rosmus, D.R.E. Students 53.

SPANGLER, CAMBRIA CO., ST. PATRICK'S (1902) Merged with Sacred Heart, Bakerton to form St. Jude, Elmora.

STATE COLLEGE, CENTRE CO.
1—GOOD SHEPHERD (1989) Rev. Philip M. Bender; Deacons Michael A. Ondik Jr. Tel: 814-237-1857; Jack E. Orlandi. Tel: 814-692-7472.
Res.: 867 Gray's Woods Blvd., P.O. Box 8186, 16805. Email: gsoffice@goodshepherd-sc.org. Web: www.goodshepherd-sc.org.
Church: Tel: 814-238-2110; Fax: 814-238-3484.
Catechesis/Religious Program—Tel: 814-238-0649. Email: dirred@goodshepherd-sc.org. Barbara E. Ballenger, Dir. Faith Formation. Students 471.
2—OUR LADY OF VICTORY (1908) Rev. Msgr. David A. Lockard; Revs. Matthew Baum; Charles Chidindu Ugo; Deacon David C. Lapinski.
Res.: 820 Westerly Pkwy., 16801. Tel: 814-237-7832; Fax: 814-237-6709. Email: churchoffice@ourladyofvictory.com. Web: ourladyofvictory.com.
Preschool—Tel: 814-238-6616. Lay Teachers 11; Students 72.
School—800 Westerly Pkwy., 16801. Tel: 814-238-1592; Fax: 814-238-4553. Web: olvcatholicschool.org. Kathleen Bechdel, Prin. Lay Teachers 23; Students 280.
Catechesis/Religious Program—Tel: 814-237-7832, Ext. 213. Email: hmanfred@ourladyofvictory.com. Students 468.

SUMMERHILL, CAMBRIA CO., ST. JOHN (1903) [CEM] Rev. Alfred Patterson, O.S.B.
Res.: 538 Main St., P.O. Box 248, 15958. Tel: 814-495-5241; Fax: 814-495-9522. Email: stjic@verizon.net.
Mission—Immaculate Conception (1855) 1640 New Germany Rd., P.O. Box 248, New Germany, Cambria Co. 15958.
Catechesis/Religious Program—Melissa Long, C.R.E. Students 174.

TWIN ROCKS, CAMBRIA CO.
1—ST. CHARLES (1917) Merged with Immaculate Conception Mission, Vintondale to form SS. Timothy & Mark Church, Twin Rocks & SS. Timothy & Mark Chapel, Vintondale.
2—SS. TIMOTHY & MARK (1995) [CEM], 116 Church St., P.O. Box 275, 15960. Tel: 814-749-9331; Fax: 814-749-8000. Email: timothymchurch@comcast.net.
Catechesis/Religious Program—Students 26.
Mission—SS. Timothy & Mark Chapel 116 Church St., Cambria Co. 15960.

TYRONE, BLAIR CO., ST. MATTHEW'S (1853) [CEM 2] Rev. Joseph T. Orr.
Res.: 1205 Cameron Ave., 16686. Tel: 814-684-1480; Fax: 814-684-7969. Email: stmatthewtyrone@verizon.net. Cemeteries: Oak Grove & St Luke's.
School—1105 Cameron Ave., 16686. Tel: 814-684-3510; Fax: 814-684-7833. Melissa McMullen, Prin. Lay Teachers 6; Students 63.
Catechesis/Religious Program—Students 100.

WEST SALISBURY, SOMERSET CO., ST. MICHAEL'S (1887) [CEM 2] Deacon William R. Underhill, Parochial Admin.; Rev. Nathan Munsch, O.S.B., Sacramental Min.
Res.: 1316 St. Paul Rd., 15565-0036. Tel: 814-662-2958.
Mission—St. Mary's (1906) 215 Warrens Mill Rd., Pocahontas, Somerset Co. 15565. Tel: 814-662-2958. P.O. Box 36, Salisbury, 15558-0036.
Catechesis/Religious Program—Tel: 301-689-9189. Students 45.

WILLIAMSBURG, BLAIR CO., ST. JOSEPH (1861) [CEM 2] Rev. Leo A. Lynch.
Res.: 628 W. First St., 16693. Tel: 814-832-2137; Fax: 814-832-1025. Email: frleo52@comcast.net.
Catechesis/Religious Program—Students 30.

WILMORE, CAMBRIA CO., ST. BARTHOLOMEW'S (1840) [CEM] Rev. Charles F. Bodziak.
185 Church Hill Rd., P.O. Box 95, 15962.
Res.: P.O. Box 56, Cassandra, 15925. Tel: 814-736-8314.
Catechesis/Religious Program—Students 45.

WINDBER, SOMERSET CO.
1—ST. ANTHONY OF PADUA (1908), (Italian), [CEM] Most Rev. Bonaventure N. Midili, T.O.R.; Revs. Roderick N. Soha, T.O.R.; Adrian Tirpak, T.O.R.; Mark Reifel, T.O.R.
Res.: 2201 Graham Ave., 15963. Tel: 814-467-7292; Fax: 814-467-9182.
School—St. Benedict School, Tel: 814-266-3837; Fax: 814-266-7718. Students 3.
School—St. Andrew School, Tel: 814-288-2811; Fax: 814-288-6750.
School—St. Clement School, Tel: 814-255-1964; Fax: 814-255-2623.
Catechesis/Religious Program—Tel: 814-467-9670. Violet Bunk, D.R.E.; Roxann Newcomer, D.R.E. Students 106.
2—SS. CYRIL AND METHODIUS (1906), (Slovak), [CEM 2] Rev. Matthew Misurda.
Res.: 604 Graham Ave., 15963. Tel: 814-467-7042; Fax: 814-467-0183. Email: mmisurda@verizon.net.
Catechesis/Religious Program—600 Graham Ave., 15963. Tel: 814-467-9670. Students 28.
3—ST. ELIZABETH ANN SETON (2000) [CEM 2] Very Rev. Leonard E. Voytek; Deacon Thaddeus J. Janisko.
Res.: 605 Graham Ave., 15963. Tel: 814-467-7191; Fax: 814-467-1621.
Catechesis/Religious Program—P.O. Box 36, 15963. Tel: 814-467-9670; Fax: 814-467-9670. Violet Bunk, D.R.E. Students 145.
4—HOLY CHILD JESUS (1921), (Irish), Closed. For inquiries for sacramental records, please contact SS. Cyril & Methodius.
5—ST. JOHN CANTIUS (1898), (Polish), Merged with St. Mary's, Windber to form St. Elizabeth Ann Seton, Windber.
6—ST. MARY'S (1914), (Hungarian), Merged with St. John Cantius, Windber to form St. Elizabeth Ann Seton, Windber.

Chaplains of Public Institutions

ALTOONA. *Altoona Regional Health System, Altoona Hospital Campus*, Howard Ave. & Seventh St., 16601. Tel: 814-946-2011.
Altoona Hospital Campus, 620 Howard Ave., 16601. Tel: 841-946-2011. Rev. Edward J. Sabo, T.O.R., Chap.
Bon Secours-Holy Family Campus, 2500 Seventh Ave., 16602. Tel: 814-944-1681; Fax: 814-889-7690. Rev. Bradley Baldwin, T.O.R., Dir.
Catholic Chaplaincy Ministry. Revs. Bradley Baldwin, T.O.R., Chap., Edward J. Sabo, T.O.R., Chap.
Hospitality House, Bon Secours-Holy Family Campus, 16602-2099. Tel: 814-949-9718. Sr. Mary Aquinas, C.S.F.N. Tel: 814-944-1681.
Veterans Medical Center, 2907 Pleasant Valley Blvd., 16602. Tel: 814-943-8164. Revs. David H. Roesch, Chap., Anthony J. Legarski, Assoc. Chap.

JOHNSTOWN. *Conemaugh Health System*.
Memorial Medical Center, 1086 Franklin St., 15905. Tel: 814-534-9000. Rev. John F. Brezovec, Chap. Tel: 814-534-9250; Fax: 814-534-3507.
Good Samaritan Medical Center, 1020 Franklin St., 15905. Tel: 814-534-9000. Rev. James Smyka, O.F.M.Conv., Chap.
Memorial Medical Center Lee Campus, 320 Main St., 15901. Tel: 814-534-6000. Rev. James Smyka, O.F.M.Conv., Chap.
Pastoral Care Department Memorial & Good Samaritan, 1086 Franklin St., 15905. Tel: 814-534-1646. Email: dkline@conemaugh.org. Sr. Dorothy Kline, R.S.M., Staff Chap.
Good Samaritan Nursing Care Center, 1020 Franklin St., 15905. Tel: 814-534-1934.

BELLEFONTE. *State Correctional Institution - Rockview Our Lady of the Mount*, Box A, 16823. Tel: 814-355-4874, Ext. 232. Deacon Thomas E. Boldin, Catholic Chap. & Admin., 2139 Zion Rd., 16823. Tel: 814-355-4234, Rev. Valentine J. Bradley, Sacramental Min. Tel: 814-355-3134 (Res.).

CRESSON. *State Correctional Institution*, P.O. Box A, 16630. Tel: 814-886-8181. Rev. Aron M. Maghsoudi, Chap. Tel: 814-944-4603 (Res.).

EBENSBURG. *Laurel Crest Rehabilitation & Special Care Center*, 429 Manor Dr., 15931. Tel: 814-472-8100, Ext. 3119. Vacant.

HUNTINGDON. *State Correctional Institution*, St. Dismas, 1100 Pike St., 16652. Tel: 814-643-6520, Ext. 213. Deacon Bruce L. Becker, Chap. & Admin.

LORETTO. *Federal Correctional Institution*, P.O. Box 1000, 15940. Tel: 814-472-4140, Ext. 155. Sr. Maryann Palko, C.C.W., Chap.

SMITHFIELD. *State Correctional Institution*, 1120 Pike St., Huntingdon, 16652. Tel: 814-643-6520; 814-832-2137 (Res.). Rev. David J. Arseneault, Sacramental Min. Tel: 814-643-0160 (Res.), Deacon Bruce L. Becker, Chap.

SOMERSET. *State Correctional Institution*, St. Peter in Chains, 1590 Walters Mill Rd., 15510. Tel: 814-443-8100. Very Rev. James M. Dugan, V.F., Chap. & Pastor.
State Correctional Institution, Laurel Highlands, 5706 Glades Pike Rd., P.O. Box 631, 15501. Tel: 814-445-6501. Sr. Kathleen Marie Todora, Chap.

On Duty Outside the Diocese:
Rev.—
Slovikovski, John J., Theological College, 401 Michigan Ave., N.E., Washington, DC 20017.

Military Chaplains:
Rev.—
Halka, Frantisek A., CMR 464, Box 2943, Apo, AE 09226. U.S. Army

On Sabbatical:
Rev.—
Amershek, Charles M., Jr., V.F.

Absent on Leave:
Revs.—
Kuligowski, Peter J.
Leahey, Patrick R.
Norcavage, Albert R.
Petracca, Anthony

Retired:
Rev. Msgrs.—
Biller, Bernard N., 201 W. High St., Apt. 202, Ebensburg, 15931.
Fleming, Patrick V., Delray Beach, FL 33445. Tel: 561-498-7646
Kline, Roy, Blessed Sacrament Cathedral, One Cathedral Sq., P.O. Box 33, Altoona, 16601. Tel: 814-944-1909
Lenz, Paul A., Bureau of Catholic Indian Missions, 2021 H. St., N.W., Washington, DC 20006-4207.
Mabon, Thomas K., 703 Lincoln-Lee Manor, 231 Walnut St., Johnstown, 15904. Tel: 814-535-2991
Panza, Paul D., P.A., 150 Saint Marys Ln., Apt./Ste. 1, 16648.
Przybocki, Bernard A., 7923 Admiral Peary Hwy., Cresson, 16630.
Saylor, Philip, Mid Town Square, 310 S. Allen St., State College, 16801.
Tomaselli, Samuel J., 855 W. Sanner St., 15501.
Valko, George J.
Wadas, Ignatius C., 221 Luray Ave., Johnstown, 15904. Tel: 814-266-8415
Revs.—
Anselmi, Albert J., 404 E. Honeoye St., Shinglehouse, 16748.
Balestino, Francis P., P.O. Box 817, Johnstown, 15907.
Becker, David R., 505 McIntosh Ln., 16648. Tel: 814-935-3588
Bendzella, Sylvester J., 150 Saint Marys Ln., Apt./Ste. 3, 16648.
Boslett, Donald E., 3037 Colonel Drake Hwy., Box 132, Chest Springs, 16624. Tel: 814-674-8327
Crosser, Raymond G., 100 Beckman Dr., 6F, Altoona, 16602.
Dykas, Benjamin, Town House Towers, 420 Vine St., Apt. 2402, Johnstown, 15906. Tel: 814-539-4776
Ellias, John J., 118 Mechanic St., Everett, 15537.
George, J. Clark, 150 Saint Marys Ln., Apt./Ste. 2, 16648.
Gergel, Stephen J., Lt. USN, 116 Lake Manor Dr., Kingsland, GA 31548.
Joly, Henry L., 228 Piedmont Dr., Duncansville, 16635.
Knapik, Andrew G., P.O. Box 111, Bellefonte, 16823.
Mulvehill, Louis J., John Paul II Manor, 856 Cambria St., Cresson, 16630.
Myers, Regis F., 150 Saint Marys Ln., Apt./Ste. 10, 16648.
Pollack, Anthony, 513 - 27th Ave., Altoona, 16601.
Robine, Paul M., 21 Country Club Rd., Cresson, 16630. Tel: 814-866-2573
Spishak, Carl A., St. Rose of Lima, 5514 Roselawn Ave., Altoona, 16602. Tel: 814-944-8509

Permanent Deacons:
Bailey, Robert D., Secretary to the Bishop and Episcopal Master of Ceremonies
Beavers, Thomas T., St. John the Baptist, New Baltimore
Becker, Bruce L., St. Benedict, Johnstown; Catholic Chap. State Correctional Institution, Smithfield; Catholic Chap. & Admin. St. Dismas, State Correctional Institution, Huntingdon
Boldin, Thomas E., Chap., St. John the Evangelist, Bellefonte, Catholic Chap. & Admin.; Our Lady of the Mount-SCI, Rockview
Buige, Thomas M., St. John Gualbert Cathedral, Johnstown
Cammarata, Samuel M., St. Clare of Assisi, Johnstown
Concannon, John J., Senior Deacon, Johnstown
Condor, Michael, Jr., Basilica of St. Michael, Loretto
Dalla Valle, Joseph R., St. Patrick, Johnstown
Gibson, Philip, St. Agnes, Lock Haven
Ivanits, Laszlo P., Penn State Catholic Campus Ministry
Janisko, Thaddeus J., St. Elizabeth Ann Seton, Windber
Janosik, James J., St. Mary, Nanty Glo
Kolonich, Ronald A., St. Peter, Somerset
Lapinski, David C., Our Lady of Victory, State College
Leap, James F., Senior Deacon
Little, Scott Q., Our Mother of Sorrows and Saint Michael, Johnstown
Luke, Steve A., St. Joseph, Coupon
Neral, Gene P., St. John the Evangelist, Lakemont
O'Dowd, Daniel J., (On Duty Outside Diocese)
Ondik, Michael A., Jr., Senior Deacon
Orlandi, Jack E., Good Shepherd, State College
Papinchak, Thomas M., SS. Gregory & Barnabas, Johnstown
Pyle, Jay A., All Saints, Boswell
Rys, John R., Cathedral of the Blessed Sacrament, Altoona
Sroka, John E., Senior Deacon, Johnstown
Tiernan, John A., Senior Deacon
Underhill, William R., SS. Philip & James, Meyersdale; St. Gregory, MacDonaldton; Admin. St. Michael, West Salisbury; St. Mary, Pocahontas
Visinsky, Joseph W., Holy Family, Hooversville
Young, Calvin J., Immaculate Conception, Lock Haven; Sacramental Min. Lock Haven Univ., Lock Haven; St. Joseph, Renovo
Zernick, Bernard J., Prince of Peace, Northern Cambria

INSTITUTIONS LOCATED IN THE DIOCESE

[A] COLLEGES AND UNIVERSITIES
(NON-DIOCESAN)

CRESSON
Mount Aloysius College (1853) 7373 Admiral Peary Hwy., 16630. Tel: 814-886-4131; Fax: 814-886-2978. Email: cmiller@mtaloy.edu. Web: www.mtaloy.edu. Sr. Mary Ann Dillon, R.S.M., Pres.; Mr. Frank Crouse, Vice Pres. Enrollment Management; Dr. Ron Cromwell, Senior Vice Pres. Academic Affairs; Dr. Jane Grassadonia, Vice Pres. Student Affairs. Sisters of Mercy. Priests 1; Sisters 8; Lay Teachers 61; Total Staff 197; Students 2,000.

LORETTO
St. Francis University, P.O. Box 600, 15940-0600. Tel: 814-472-3001; Fax: 814-472-3003. Email: vsoyka@francis.edu. Web: www.francis.edu. Rev. Gabriel Zeis, T.O.R., Pres.; Ms. Patricia Serotkin, Vice Pres. Strategic Initiatives; Dr. Wayne Powel, Vice Pres. Academic Affairs; Erin McCloskey, Vice Pres. Enrollment Mgmt.; Robert Datsko, Vice Pres. Finance; Mr. Raymond Ponchione, Vice Pres. Advancement; Mr. Randy Frye, Dean Business; Ms. Glenda Griffith, Dir. Residence Life; Ms. Sandra Balough, Dean Library Svcs.; Ms. Julie Barris, Dir. Career Devel.; Mr. George Pyo, Dir. Computer Svcs.; Mr. Dominick Peruso, Assoc. Dir. Student Activities; Ms. Denise Kovach, Dir. Academic Center for Enrichment; Robert Krimmel, Dir. Athletics; Mr. David Wilson, Dir. Counseling; Rev. Daniel Sinisi, T.O.R., Vice Pres. Mission Effectiveness & Ministry; Bro. Gabriel Mary Amato, T.O.R., Dir. Dorothy Day Center; Revs. Nathan Malavolti, T.O.R., Asst. Professor Chemistry; Malachi VanTassell, T.O.R., Adjunct Asst. Professor Accounting; Joseph Chancler, T.O.R., Adjunct Instructor Math; Christopher Dobson, T.O.R., Dir. Campus Ministry; Bros. Richard Gates, T.O.R., Dir. OASIS; Shamus McGrenra, T.O.R., Dir. Intl. Admissions; Rev. Shawn Roberson, T.O.R., Campus Min. Priests 10; Lay Professors 109; Students 2,322.

[B] HIGH SCHOOLS, DIOCESAN

ALTOONA. **Bishop Guilfoyle Catholic High School*, 2400 Pleasant Valley Blvd., 16602. Tel: 814-944-4014; Fax: 814-944-8695. Email: kubitza.bernard@daj.k12.pa.us. Web: www.bishopguilfoyle.org. Bernard G. Kubitza, Pres. & Prin.; Sr. Beverly Hmel, I.H.M., Asst. Prin.; Joan Donnelly, Vice Prin.; Linda Alianiello, Librarian. Sisters 1; Lay Teachers 24; Total Staff 48; Students 323.

JOHNSTOWN. **Bishop McCort Catholic High School*, 25 Osborne St., 15905. Tel: 814-536-8991; Fax: 814-535-4118. Email: salem.kenneth@daj.k12.pa.us. Web: www.mccort.org. Mr. Kenneth S. Salem, Prin. & Contact Person; Mrs. Janet Skelly, Librarian; Sr. Donna Marie Leiden, S.C., Dir. Educ. Priests 2; Deacons 1; Sisters 1; Lay Teachers 34; Students 408.

EBENSBURG. **Bishop Carroll Catholic High School*, 728 Ben Franklin Hwy., 15931. Tel: 814-472-7500; Fax: 814-472-8020. Email: wolfe.kristie@daj.k12.pa.us. Web: bishopcarroll.com. Mrs. Kristie L. Wolfe, Prin.; Rasha Shawarby, Librarian. Priests 2; Lay Teachers 18; Students 221.

[C] ELEMENTARY DIOCESAN SCHOOLS

ALTOONA. *Altoona Central Catholic School*, (Grades PreK-8), 1400 4th Ave., 16602. Tel: 814-944-1250; Fax: 814-944-1452. Email: altoonaccs1@aol.com. Web: altoonacentralcatholic.com. Jeffery F. Maucieri, Prin. Lay Teachers 25; Students 330.

424 Wopsononock Ave., 16601. Tel: 814-381-7011; Fax: 814-381-7015.

1400 4th Ave., 16602. Tel: 814-944-1250; Fax: 814-944-1452. Email: altoonaccs@aol.com.

CRESSON. *All Saints Catholic School*, (Grades PreK-8), 220 Powell Ave., 16630. Tel: 814-886-7942; Fax: 814-886-7942. Email: allsaints@daj.k12.pa.us. Mrs. Susan Glass, Prin. Consolidation of the following parishes: St. Francis Xavier; St. Aloysius; St. Agnes; Our Lady of the Alleghenies; St. Thomas Aquinas; Our Lady of the Sacred Heart; St. Demetrius. Sisters 2; Lay Teachers 10; Preschool 44; Students 111.

HOLLIDAYSBURG. *Hollidaysburg Consolidated Catholic Elementary School*, (Grades PreK-8), Spruce & Wayne Sts., P.O. Box 599, 16648. Tel: 814-695-6112; Fax: 814-696-8960. Email: spencer.elaine@daj.k12.pa.us. Web: www.daj.k12.pa.us/hcs/. Mrs. Elaine Spencer, Prin. Consolidation of the following parishes: St. Michael's; St. Mary's. Lay Teachers 10; Students 154.

NICKTOWN. *Northern Cambria Catholic School*, 3278 Blue Goose Rd., P.O. Box 252, 15762. Tel: 814-948-8900; Fax: 814-948-8720. Email: nccs@daj.k12.pa.us. Sr. Mary Lee Przybylski, C.S.S.F., Prin.; Ellen Hoover, Librarian. Consolidation of the following parishes: St. Nicholas & Prince of Peace. Sisters 1; Lay Teachers 13; Students 119.

[D] EDUCATION CONSOLIDATED ELEMENTARY SCHOOLS

JOHNSTOWN. *Cathedral Catholic Academy*, (Grades PreK-8), Consolidated schools of St. John Gualbert Cathedral, St. Clement & St. Clare of Assisi., 110 Lindberg Ave., 15905. Tel: 814-255-1964; Fax: 814-255-1964. Email: batzel.rosemary@daj.k12.pa.us. Mrs. Rosemary Batzel, Prin. Lay Teachers 12.

[E] GENERAL HOSPITALS
(NON-DIOCESAN)

ALTOONA
Altoona Regional Health System - Bon Secours Hospital Campus (1910) 2500 Seventh Ave., 16601. Tel: 814-889-2011; Fax: 814-889-7808. Email: bstrawser@altoonaregional.org. Web: www.altoonaregional.org. Jerry Murray, Acting Pres./CEO; Revs. Christopher Panagoplos, T.O.R., Chap.; Edward J. Sabo, T.O.R., Chap. Patients Assisted Annually 407,026; Total Assisted 407,026; Total Staff 2,340; Bed Capacity 497.

JOHNSTOWN
Good Samaritan Medical Center, 1020 Franklin St., 15905. Tel: 814-534-9000; Fax: 814-539-0264. Email: stucker@conemaugh.org. Sr. Dorothy Kline, R.S.M., Staff Chap.; Mr. Steven E. Tucker, Pres. Skilled Nursing Care Center Beds 74; Patients Assisted Annually 253; Total Staff 58.

[F] HOMES FOR AGED
(NON-DIOCESAN)

HOLLIDAYSBURG
Garvey Manor (1965) 128 Logan Blvd., 16648. Tel: 814-695-5571; Fax: 814-695-8516. Web: www.garveymanor.org. Sr. M. Joachim Anne Ferenchak, O.Carm., Admin. Senior Care Complex: Nursing, Personal Care, Independent Living. Carmelite Sisters for the Aged and Infirm 7; Aged Residents 180; Patients Assisted Annually 300; Total Staff 310; Bed Capacity 180.

St. Leonard's Home, Inc., 601 N. Montgomery St., 16648. Tel: 814-695-9581; Fax: 814-695-2606. Email: srcindy@juno.com. Sr. Cynthia Meyer, C.S.F.N., Exec. Dir.

St. Leonard's Home, Inc. Sisters of the Holy Family of Nazareth 1; Bed Capacity 23; Total Staff 15; Total Assisted Annually 35.

(DIOCESAN)

HOLLIDAYSBURG
Dmitri Manor Priests' Residence, St. Mary's Ln., 16648. Tel: 814-696-4698. Rev. Msgr. Robert J. Saly. Aged Residents 5; Staff 1; Bed Capacity 12.

[G] MONASTERIES AND RESIDENCES OF PRIESTS AND BROTHERS
(NON-DIOCESAN)

HOLLIDAYSBURG
St. Joseph Friary, 501-503 Walnut St., 16648. Tel: 814-695-5802. Bro. Stephen P. Baker, T.O.R.; Very Rev. Adalbert Wolski, T.O.R. (Retired); Rev. Bradley Baldwin, T.O.R., Priest Chap. Altoona Regional Health System.

LORETTO
St. Bonaventure Friary, P.O. Box 155, 15940-0155. Tel: 814-693-2824; Fax: 814-693-2831. Revs. Bernard Tickerhoof, T.O.R., Dir. Novices;

Shawn Roberson, T.O.R., Dir. Postulants. Priests 2; Novices 3; Postulants 6.

St. Francis Friary at Mount Assisi, 141 St. Francis Dr., P.O. Box 40, 15940. Tel: 814-693-2819; Fax: 814-471-1766. Web: www.franciscanstor.org. Revs. Patrick George, T.O.R. Tel: 814-472-5324, Ext. 302; Augustine Belinda, T.O.R.; Alex Bombera, T.O.R.; David Bonarrigo, T.O.R., Faculty Bishop Carroll H.S.; Gervase Cain, T.O.R.; Marion Deck, T.O.R.; Simon Mary Engler, T.O.R.; Jack Grinnen, T.O.R.; Bede Hines, T.O.R.; Colman J. McGarril, T.O.R.; Francis Moyher, T.O.R.; Daniel J. Mulkern, T.O.R.; Aidan Mullaney; Christian R. Oravec, T.O.R., Prov. Tel: 814-472-3001; Arnold Petrosky, T.O.R.; Emil Resconich, T.O.R.; Shawn Roberson, T.O.R., Postulants Dir., Dir. Retreats; Bernard Tickerhoof, T.O.R., Novices Dir.; Kevin Queally, T.O.R.; Andre Strittmatter, T.O.R.; Benjamin Medeiros, T.O.R., Archivist; Malachi VanTassell, T.O.R., Faculty-St. Francis Univ./Prov. Econome/Vicar; Jude Ventiquattro, Dir. Healthcare; Robert Yetsko, Local Min., Dir Liturgy; Matthew Russick, Faculty-Bishop Carrol H.S.; Ronan Deegan, T.O.R.; Sean Sullivan, T.O.R.; Bros. Gabriel Mary Amato, T.O.R., Dir., Dorothy Day Center; Callistus Gerardi, T.O.R.; Damien Koehler, T.O.R.; Stephen Liebal; Bernard Nicolosi; Francis M. Haworth, T.O.R., Assoc. Dir. Liturgy; Norman MeNelis; Stephen Prenatt. Priests 26; Brothers 8; Novices 3; Postulants 6.

NEWRY

St. Bernardine Monastery (1925) P.O. Box 208, 16665. Tel: 814-695-3992; 814-693-0166; Fax: 814-695-1611. Email: xtofertor@aol.com. Web: www.franciscanfriarstor.com. Revs. Christopher Panagoplos, T.O.R., Local Min.; Camillus Angle, T.O.R. (Retired); Kenneth La Pan, T.O.R. (Retired); Leonard Blostic, T.O.R. (Retired); Fabian Sheganoski, T.O.R. (Retired); Very Rev. Eugene Kubina, T.O.R. (Retired); Rev. Gerard M. Connolly, T.O.R. Priests 7. *Franciscan Mass Association Office*, P.O. Box 139, 16648. Tel: 814-695-3802; Fax: 814-695-1611. Email: toroffice@aol.com. Tim Beresnyek, Dir. Devel. & Mass Association. *Province Econome's Office* (1925) P.O. Box 117, 16648. Tel: 814-696-3321; Fax: 814-695-1611. Email: wlinhares@gmail.com. Web: www.franciscanfriarstor.com. Revs. William P. Linhares, T.O.R., Provincial Econome; Gerard M. Connolly, T.O.R.

[H] CONVENTS AND RESIDENCES FOR SISTERS
(NON-DIOCESAN)

ALTOONA

Our Lady of Perpetual Help Convent, 445 Baynton Ave., #A, 16602. Tel: 814-942-3819. Sisters, Servants of the Immaculate Heart of Mary. Total in Residence 1; Total Staff 1.

St. John of the Cross Convent, 35 Seneca Ave., 16602. Tel: 814-942-5747; Fax: 814-942-8052. Email: lindalccw@verizon.net; altoonallw@verizon.net. Carmelite Community of the Word. Total in Residence 2.

CRESSON

Sister Servants of the Most Sacred Heart of Jesus (1894) Provincial House, 866 Cambria St., 16630-1713. Tel: 814-886-4223; Fax: 814-886-4735. Email: sscjusa@pngusa.net. Sr. Ryszarda Wittbrodt, S.S.C.J., Prov. Supr. Personnel 26. *John Paul II Manor Personal Care Home* Tel: 814-886-7961; Fax: 814-886-7987. Email: johnpaul2manor@juno.com. Total in Residence 45; Total Staff 18.

EBENSBURG

Carmelite Community of the Word (1971) St. Therese Convent, 218 W. Lloyd St., 15931. Tel: 814-472-9457; Fax: 814-472-5105. Email: ebensburgccw@aol.com. Total in Residence 3.

Sisters of St. Ann Mother House, 1120 N. Center St., P.O. Box 328, 15931. Tel: 814-472-9354; Fax: 814-472-9354. Email: sistersann@verizon.net. Sr. Melany Pereira, S.S.A., Supr. Sisters of St. Ann. Total in Residence 4.

GALLITZIN

Carmelite Community of the Word-Incarnation Center, 394 Bem Rd., 16641. Tel: 814-886-4098; Fax: 814-886-7115. Web: ccwsisters.org. Sr. Marilyn Welch, C.C.W., Admin. Gen. Total in Residence 3.

Little Sisters of Jesus, 347 Tunnel Hill St., 16641. Tel: 814-886-4679. Sr. Laura Lee Seubert, Supr. Total in Residence 3.

LORETTO

Carmel of St. Therese of Lisieux (1927) P.O. Box 57, 15940. Tel: 814-472-8620. Sr. John of the Cross, O.C.D., Prioress. Discalced Carmelite Nuns. Nuns with Solemn Vows 10.

MCCONNELLSBURG

Carmelite Community of the Word, Fulton County Mission, 110 S. Third St., 17223. Tel: 717-485-5917; 717-485-0661; Fax: 717-485-3855. Email: sistermargie@comcast.net. Total in Residence 2.

PORTAGE

Sister Servants of the Most Sacred Heart of Jesus, Sacred Heart Novitiate, 1872 Munster Rd., 15946. Tel: 814-886-4459. Sr. Jacinta Miryam Hanley, S.S.C.J., Novice Mistress. Sisters 4.

[I] CAMPUS MINISTRY

HOLLIDAYSBURG. *Office of Youth and Campus Ministry Saint Michael Rectory*, 751 Locust St., Saint Michael, 15951. Tel: 814-495-9640; Fax: 814-495-9424. Rev. Msgr. Michael A. Becker, Coord.

Juniata College 1905 More St., Huntington, 16652. Tel: 814-641-3362 (Office); Fax: 814-641-3317. Ms. Lisa Baer, Campus Min.; Rev. David J. Arseneault, Chap.

Lock Haven University (Lock Haven) Newman Center, 445 W. Main St., Lock Haven, 17745. Tel: 570-748-8592; Fax: 570-748-8592 (Call ahead). Ms. Carol Schaffer, Campus Min.; Mr. Jeff Schaffer, Campus Min.; Rev. Richard B. Tomkosky.

Mount Aloysius College (Cresson) 7373 Admiral Peary Hwy., Cresson, 16630. Tel: 814-886-6476; Fax: 814-886-2978. Sr. Nancy Donovan, R.S.M., Dir. Campus Ministry; Ann Schwartz, Campus Min.

Penn State University, Altoona Edith Davis Eve Chapel Room 113, 3000 Ivyside Park, Altoona, 16601. Tel: 814-949-5137. Mary Claire Curtis, Campus Min.

Penn State University, University Park 205C Pasquerilla Spiritual Center, University Park, 16802. Tel: 814-865-4281; Fax: 814-865-2972. Revs. Matthew T. Laffey, O.S.B., Dir. Campus Ministry; David R. Griffin, O.S.B., Campus Min.; Deacon Laszlo P. Ivanits, Campus Min.; Mr. Phillip Torbert, Dir. Music & Liturgy; Andres Diaz, Hispanic Min.

St. Francis University (Loretto) P.O. Box 600, Loretto, 15940. Tel: 814-472-3329; Fax: 814-472-2776. Rev. Christopher Dobson, T.O.R., Dir. Campus Ministry. Tel: 814-472-3391; Mr. Paul Girardi, Campus Min. Tel: 814-472-3367; Rev. Shawn Roberson, T.O.R., Campus Min.; Ms. Susan Maurer, Campus Min.; Rev. Zygmunt Mazanowksi, T.O.R., Campus Min.

University of Pittsburgh at Johnstown 450 Schoolhouse Rd., Johnstown, 15904. Tel: 814-269-2007; Fax: 814-269-7128. Sr. Corinne Kirsch, C.S.J., Campus Min.; Rev. Msgr. Michael A. Becker, Chap.

[J] NEWMAN CENTERS
(NON-DIOCESAN)

UNIVERSITY PARK

Penn State Catholic Community 205 Pasquerilla Spiritual Center, 16802. Tel: 814-865-4281; Fax: 814-865-2972. Email: catholic@psu.edu. Web: www.psu.edu/catholic. Revs. Matthew T. Laffey, O.S.B., Dir.; David R. Griffin, O.S.B., Campus Min.; Deacon Laszlo P. Ivanits, Campus Min. Catholic Students attending Penn State University 9,500; Total in Residence 2; Total Staff 6.

[K] MISCELLANEOUS LISTINGS
(NON-DIOCESAN)

BEDFORD

St. Mary's House of Greater Solitude, Passionist Community, 2970 Imlertown Rd., 15522-8101. Tel: 814-623-1796; Fax: 814-623-2457. Rev. Silvan Rouse, C.P., Supr.

HOLLIDAYSBURG

Conference of Slovak Clergy (1985) 927 S. Logan Blvd., 16648. Tel: 814-695-5579; Fax: 814-695-8894. Email: queenofarchangelspa@verizon.net. Most Rev. Joseph Victor Adamec, D.D., S.T.L., Chm.; Rev. Msgr. Michael J. Chaback, S.T.D., Vice Chm.; Rev. Lubomir J. Strecok, Sec. The Conference was founded April 22, 1985, and incorporated on June 14, 2000. It associates bishops, priests and deacons of Slovak ancestry in the United States for the purposes of mutual pastoral support and financial assistance to those preparing themselves for ordained ministry of the churches in union with Rome, particularly those of Slovak ancestry.

Second Century Scholarship Fund (2001) *Diocese of Altoona-Johnstown*, 925 S. Logan Blvd., 16648. Tel: 814-695-5577; Fax: 814-696-9516. Email: ringkamp@dioceseaj.org. Web: www.secondcentury-fund.org. Mr. Christopher F. Ringkamp, Devel. Dir.; Mr. Larry R. Sutton, Corporate Sec. Student Scholarships 1,082.

LORETTO

American Parish Youth Center, Inc., P.O. Box 40, 15940. Tel: 814-693-2885; Fax: 814-693-2881. Email: framarco@aol.com.

Prince Gallitzin Chapel House (Diocesan), P.O. Box 99, 15940. Tel: 814-472-5441; Fax: 814-472-5446. Email: bsaylor@dioceseaj.org.

Office of Vocations, Prince Gallitzin Chapel House, 357 St. Mary's St., P.O. Box 99, 15940-0099. Tel: 814-472-5444; Fax: 814-472-5446. Email: bsaylor@dioceseaj.org. Rev. Brian R. Saylor, Dir.

Office of Ongoing Formation of Clergy, P.O. Box 99, 15940-0099. Tel: 814-472-5441; Fax: 814-472-5446. Rev. Msgr. Timothy J. Swope, V.F.

NEW BALTIMORE

St. John The Baptist Retreat Center, P.O. Box 10, 15553. Tel: 814-733-2210; Fax: 814-733-2966. Total in Residence 1; Total Staff 6.

RELIGIOUS INSTITUTES OF MEN REPRESENTED IN THE DIOCESE

For further details refer to the corresponding bracketed number in the Religious Institutes of Men or Women section.

[0200]—*Benedictine Monks*—O.S.B.
[0470]—*The Capuchin Friars*—O.F.M.Cap.
[1000]—*Congregation of the Passion*—C.P.
[0480]—*Conventual Franciscans* (St. Anthony of Padua Prov.)—O.F.M.Conv.
[0520]—*Franciscan Friars*—O.F.M.
[0560]—*Third Order Regular of Saint Francis* (Provs. of Sacred Heart, Immaculate Conception)—T.O.R.

RELIGIOUS INSTITUTES OF WOMEN REPRESENTED IN THE DIOCESE

[0100]—*Adorers of the Blood of Christ*—A.S.C.
[0315]—*Carmelite Community of the Word*—C.C.W.
[0330]—*Carmelite Sisters for the Aged and Infirm*—O.Carm.
[3710]—*Congregation of the Sisters of Saint Agnes*—C.S.A.
[0420]—*Discalced Carmelite Nuns*—O.C.D.
[1070-03]—*Dominican Sisters*—O.P.
[1170]—*Felician Sisters*—C.S.S.F.
[2330]—*Little Sisters of Jesus*—L.S.J.
[3630]—*Servants of the Most Sacred Heart of Jesus*—S.S.C.J.
[0570]—*Sisters of Charity of Seton Hill, Greensburg, Pennsylvania*—S.C.
[2575]—*Sisters of Mercy of the Americas* (Dallas Regional Community)—R.S.M.
[1620]—*Sisters of Saint Francis of Millvale, Pennsylvania*—O.S.F.
[3780]—*Sisters of Ss. Cyril and Methodius*—SS.C.M.
[3718]—*Sisters of St. Ann* (Italy)—S.S.A.
[3830]—*Sisters of St. Joseph*—C.S.J.
[1970]—*Sisters of the Holy Family of Nazareth*—C.S.F.N.
[3260]—*Sisters of the Precious Blood (Ohio)*—C.PP.S.
[2160]—*Sisters, Servants of the Immaculate Heart of Mary* (Scranton, PA)—I.H.M.
[4160]—*Vincentian Sisters of Charity*—V.S.C.

NECROLOGY

† Flinn, Rev. Msgr. George B., Johnstown, PA St. John Gualbert Cathedral—Died Sept. 6, 2009
† Walsh, Rev. Msgr. Richard J., (Retired)—Died Aug. 15, 2009
† Crouse, William S., (Retired)—Died July 11, 2009
† Stange, A. Henry, (Retired)—Died July 21, 2009

An asterisk (*) denotes an organization that has established tax-exempt status directly with the IRS and is not covered by the USCCB Group Ruling.

Diocese of Amarillo

(Dioecesis Amarillensis)

Most Reverend

PATRICK J. ZUREK, D.D.

Bishop of Amarillo; ordained June 29, 1975; appointed Auxiliary Bishop of San Antonio and Titular Bishop of Tamugadi January 5, 1998; consecrated February 16, 1998; appointed Bishop of Amarillo January 3, 2008; installed Feb. 22, 2008.

Most Reverend

JOHN W. YANTA, D.D.

Retired Bishop of Amarillo; ordained March 17, 1956; appointed Titular Bishop of Naratcata and Auxiliary Bishop of San Antonio October 27, 1994; consecrated December 30, 1994; appointed Bishop of Amarillo January 21, 1997; installed March 17, 1997; retired January 3, 2008.

Diocesan Pastoral Center: 1800 N. Spring St., P.O. Box 5644, Amarillo, TX 79117-5644. Tel: 806-383-2243; Fax: 806-383-8452.

Web: www.amarillodiocese.org

ERECTED A DIOCESE BY POPE PIUS XI, AUGUST 25, 1926.

Square Miles 25,800.

Comprises that part of the State of Texas known as the Panhandle, and extending thence southward; bounded on the east by Oklahoma, and by the eastern county line of Childress and by the southern lines Childress, Hall, Briscoe, Swisher, Castro and Parmer Counties; the western boundary is the New Mexico state line from the southern line of Parmer County, Texas, northward to the northwestern corner of the Panhandle of Texas. There are 26 counties.

For legal titles of parishes and diocesan institutions, consult the Chancery Office.

STATISTICAL OVERVIEW

Personnel	
Bishop	1
Retired Bishops	1
Priests: Diocesan Active in Diocese	22
Priests: Diocesan Active Outside Diocese	4
Priests: Retired, Sick or Absent	15
Number of Diocesan Priests	41
Religious Priests in Diocese	5
Total Priests in Diocese	46
Extern Priests in Diocese	14
Ordinations:	
Diocesan Priests	1
Religious Priests	1
Transitional Deacons	1
Permanent Deacons in Diocese	52
Total Brothers	1
Total Sisters	97
Parishes	
Parishes	38
With Resident Pastor:	
Resident Diocesan Priests	18
Resident Religious Priests	2
Without Resident Pastor:	
Administered by Priests	18
Administered by Deacons	1
Missions	11
Professional Ministry Personnel:	
Brothers	1
Sisters	2
Lay Ministers	20
Welfare	
Homes for the Aged	1
Total Assisted	72
Day Care Centers	1
Total Assisted	89
Specialized Homes	3
Total Assisted	360
Special Centers for Social Services	1
Total Assisted	4,500
Other Institutions	1
Total Assisted	4
Educational	
Diocesan Students in Other Seminaries	11
Total Seminarians	11
High Schools, Diocesan and Parish	1
Total Students	139
Elementary Schools, Diocesan and Parish	5
Total Students	723
Catechesis/Religious Education:	
High School Students	1,723
Elementary Students	4,081
Total Students under Catholic Instruction	6,677
Teachers in the Diocese:	
Priests	1
Sisters	5
Lay Teachers	80
Vital Statistics	
Receptions into the Church:	
Infant Baptism Totals	1,211
Minor Baptism Totals	82
Adult Baptism Totals	53
Received into Full Communion	181
First Communions	921
Confirmations	498
Marriages:	
Catholic	175
Interfaith	39
Total Marriages	214
Deaths	345
Total Catholic Population	40,310
Total Population	422,500

Former Bishops—Most Revs. RUDOLPH ALOYSIUS GERKEN, D.D., ord. June 10, 1917; cons. April 26, 1927; installed Bishop of Amarillo, April 28, 1927; elevated to the Metropolitan See of Santa Fe, NM, June 2, 1933; died March 2, 1943; ROBERT E. LUCEY, ord. May 14, 1916; cons. May 1, 1934; installed May 16, 1934; elevated to the Metropolitan See of San Antonio, Jan. 22, 1941; LAURENCE J. FITZSIMON, D.D., ord. May 17, 1921; cons. Oct. 22, 1941; installed Nov. 5, 1941; died July 2, 1958; JOHN L. MORKOVSKY, appt. Auxiliary of Amarillo, Dec. 22, 1955; named Bishop of Amarillo, Aug. 18, 1958; transferred to as Coadjutor Bishop of Galveston-Houston "cum jure successionis," April 16, 1963; LAWRENCE M. DEFALCO, D.D., ord. June 11, 1942; appt. April 16, 1963; cons. May 30, 1963; installed June 13, 1963; retired Aug. 28, 1979; died Sept. 22, 1979; LEROY T. MATTHIESEN, D.D., M.A., LITT.D, ord. March 10, 1946; appt. March 25, 1980; ord. Bishop, May 30, 1980; retired Jan. 21, 1997; died March 22, 2010.; JOHN W. YANTA, D.D., ord. March 17, 1956; appt. Titular Bishop of Naratcata and Auxiliary Bishop of San Antonio Oct. 27, 1994; cons. Dec. 30, 1994; appt. Bishop of Amarillo Jan. 21, 1997; installed March 17, 1997; retired Jan. 3, 2008.

Diocesan Officials

Diocesan Pastoral Center—1800 N. Spring St., Amarillo, 79107. Tel: 806-383-2243; Fax: 806-383-8452. Web: www.amarillodiocese.org. *Mailing Address: P.O. Box 5644, Amarillo, 79117-5644.*

Vicar General—Very Rev. PHU PHAN, J.C.L.

Moderator of the Curia—Rev. Msgr. HAROLD L. WALDOW.

Vicar of Clergy—Rev. Msgr. HAROLD L. WALDOW.

Vicars Forane—Revs. JOHN VALDEZ, South Deanery; HECTOR MADRIGAL, Central Deanery; FRANCISCO PENEZ, East Deanery; SCOTT RAEF, North Deanery.

Diocesan Tribunal—

Judicial Vicar—Very Rev. PHU T. PHAN, J.C.L.

Defenders of the Bond—Rev. Msgr. JAMES C. GURZYNSKI (Retired); Rev. MIECZYSLAW "MITCHELL" PRZEPIORA.

Advocates—Rev. Msgr. JOSEPH T. TASH; Revs. JOSE GOMEZ; DAVID CONTRERAS; HECTOR MADRIGAL; FRANCISCO PEREZ.

Notaries—Ms. CAROL SANFORD; Ms. SUSAN GARNER; Deacon FLOYD ASHLEY.

Chancellor—Rev. FRANCISCO PEREZ.

Archivist—Ms. SUSAN GARNER.

Executive Assistant to the Bishop—Deacon FLOYD ASHLEY.

Administrative Assistant to the Bishop—Deacon BLAINE WESTLAKE.

Diocesan Advisory Councils

Presbyteral Council—Rev. Msgrs. JOSEPH T. TASH, Chm.; JOSEPH BIXENMAN; Rev. LUPE MAYORGA. Bishop's Appointee: Rev. GABRIEL CARDIEL, O.F.M., Rel. Representative. Ex Officio: Very Rev. PHU PHAN, J.C.L., Vicar Gen.; Rev. Msgr. HAROLD L. WALDOW, Vicar of Clergy; Revs. JOHN VALDEZ, Dean; HECTOR MADRIGAL, Dean; FRANCISCO PEREZ, Dean; SCOTT RAEF, Dean.

College of Consultors—Rev. Msgrs. HAROLD L. WALDOW; REX NICHOLL; Rev. JOHN VALDEZ; Rev. Msgrs. MICHAEL P. COLWELL; JOSEPH T. TASH; Very Rev. PHU PHAN, J.C.L., Vicar Gen.; Rev. Msgr. JOSEPH BIXENMAN; Rev. FRANCISCO PEREZ.

Diocesan Pastoral Council—Rev. Msgr. HAROLD L. WALDOW, Liaison.

Priests' Pension Plan Retirement Committee—Rev. Msgrs. JOSEPH T. TASH; RAYMOND CROSIER; Revs. FRANCISCO PEREZ; DAVID CONTRERAS.

Vocation Development Team—Very Rev. PHU PHAN, J.C.L., Dir.; Revs. JOHN VALDEZ; FRANCISCO PEREZ; TONY NEUSCH; SCOTT RAEF.

Deacon Director—Deacon BLAINE WESTLAKE.

Diocesan Departments

Director of Youth—OSCAR GUZMAN.

Office for the Catholic Schools—Ms. BERNICE NOGGLER, Supt.

Christian Formation Commission—Sr. JANET ABBACHI, S.S.N.D.

Department of Communications—CHRIST ALBRACHT, Editor "The West Texas Catholic".
Department of Finances and Ecclesiastical Properties—
Fiscal Manager—PHIL WHITSON, CFO.
Director of Administrative Services—PATSY GRAHAM.
Office of Development and Stewardship—KIM RICHARD, Dir.
United Catholic Appeal—KIM RICHARD, Dir.
Webmaster/IT Manager—JOE GARCIA.

General Auxiliary Pastoral Services

Diocesan Attorney—FREDERICK J. GRIFFIN, 504 S. Polk, Amarillo, 79101.
Promoter of Justice—Rev. Msgr. MICHAEL P. COLWELL. Email: mcolwell@amarillodiocese.org.
Victim Assistance Coordinator—BELINDA TAYLOR GONZALEZ, Mailing Address: P.O. Box 5644, Amarillo, 79117-5644. Tel: 806-372-7960.
Charter Review Board—LOUISE ROSS, Chm.; BELINDA TAYLOR GONZALEZ; FRANK JONES; DOROTHY GUGGEMOS; MICHAEL ROZARIO; ZEKE CASTRO; CHARLES MESTAS.
Ex Officio—Very Rev. PHU PHAN, J.C.L.; Rev. Msgr. HAROLD L. WALDOW; FREDERICK J. GRIFFIN.
Coalition for Catholic Social Services - CCSS—VACANT.
Catholic Historical Society—VACANT, Pres.; ANN WELD, Museum Cur.
Rural Life Director—DALE ARTHO.
Holy Childhood Association—Ms. BERNICE NOGGLER.
Propagation of the Faith—Rev. MIECZYSLAW "MITCHELL" PRZEPIORA.
Rite of Christian Initiation of Adults Commission—Sr. JANET ABBACHI, S.S.N.D.; Rev. Msgr. HAROLD L. WALDOW.

Auxiliary Pastoral Services for Laity

Diocesan Council of Catholic Women—Rev. Msgr. REX NICHOLL, Diocesan Moderator; TERESA SARZYNSKI, Pres., 1200 S. Washington, Amarillo, 79102.
Director of Prison Ministry—Deacons BLAINE WESTLAKE; MARK SEIDLITZ, Coord.
Marriage Encounter—Rev. Msgr. MICHAEL P. COLWELL.
Engaged Encounter—Directors: Deacon BLAINE WESTLAKE; LOUISE WESTLAKE. Contact Couple: JERRY BALLARD; AGNES BALLARD. Tel: 806-353-0907.
Catholic Student Center at West Texas A & M University—Rev. DANIEL A. DREHER, Dir. & Chap.; BETTY ARAGON, Asst. Dir., 2614 Fourth Ave., Canyon, 79015. Tel: 806-655-4345.
Scouting—Deacon ROBERT SMITH.
Serra Club—TOM RINEY, Pres.
Natural Family Planning—Dr. FAYE USALA, Coord. Tel: 806-379-9224.
Cursillo Movement—Rev. Msgr. REX NICHOLL, Spiritual Dir. Lay Directors: LUPE GOMEZ, Amarillo; MARISOL CASTANON, Amarillo.
A.C.T.S. Movement—Rev. Msgr. HAROLD L. WALDOW, Spiritual Dir. Retrouvallie: ROB GRIFFITH; MARY GRIFFITH. Tel: 806-477-6262.
Family Life Commission—STEPHANIE FRAUSTO.
Vicar for Religious—Sr. MARY ANA STEELE, S.S.S.F., Mailing Address: Sancta Maria Convent, P.O. Box 906, Pampa, 79068-0906. Tel: 806-537-3182.
Office for the Permanent Diaconate—Deacon BLAINE WESTLAKE, Coord.
Continuing Education of Clergy—Rev. Msgr. HAROLD L. WALDOW.
Priests' Retirement—PATSY GRAHAM.

CLERGY, PARISHES, MISSIONS AND PAROCHIAL SCHOOLS

CITY OF AMARILLO

(POTTER COUNTY)

1—SACRED HEART CATHEDRAL, Closed. This parish ceased to exist 1/19/75. For inquiries contact the Diocese of Amarillo: P.O. Box 5644, Amarillo, TX 79117-5644. Tel: 806-383-2243.

2—BLESSED SACRAMENT Rev. Msgr. Arturo Meza; Deacon Mark Seidlitz.
Res.: 4112 S.E. 25th St., 79103. Tel: 806-374-1132; Fax: 806-372-3631.
Catechesis/Religious Program—Students 182.

3—ST. FRANCIS Rev. Barnabas Radke, Parochial Admin.
Res.: 5005 Klinke Rd., 79108-9628. Tel: 806-335-1872.
Catechesis/Religious Program—Verlyn Walunas, C.R.E. Students 29.

4—ST. HYACINTH'S Rev. Msgr. Raymond Crosier.
Res.: 4500 W. Hills Tr., 79106. Tel: 806-358-1351; Fax: 806-467-1708.
Catechesis/Religious Program—Lori Greer, C.R.E. Students 38.

5—ST. JOSEPH'S Rev. Hector Madrigal; Deacons Leo Ramos; Willy Montao. In Res., Rev. John Ohlig (LUB).
Res.: 4122 Bonham St., 79110. Tel: 806-355-5621; Fax: 806-355-5622.
See St. Joseph's School, Amarillo under Elementary Schools, City-Wide located in the Institution section.
St. Joseph Day Care Center—4108 Bonham, 79110. Tel: 806-353-7043; Fax: 806-353-3340. Gail Sands, Dir. Students 89.
Catechesis/Religious Program—Students 54.

6—ST. LAURENCE CATHEDRAL Revs. Gabriel Cardiel, O.F.M.; Juan Rubio, O.F.M.; Adam Vallejo; Bro. Alberto Alvarado, O.F.M.; Deacons Pete Valdez; Alfredo Alarcon; David Duenes.
Res.: 2300 N. Spring St., 79107. Tel: 806-383-2261; Fax: 806-383-2266.
Catechesis/Religious Program—Sr. Benicia Ramirez, D.R.E. Students 480.

7—ST. MARTIN DE PORRES MISSION Rev. Msgr. Rex Nicholl.
Res.: 1507 N. Adams St., 79107. Tel: 806-376-8871.

8—ST. MARY'S Rev. Msgr. Harold L. Waldow; Deacons Floyd Ashley; Robert Smith; John Peters; Bill Allein. In Res., Rev. Nicholas J. Gerber.
Res.: 1200 Washington St., 79102. Tel: 806-376-7204; Fax: 806-376-7972.
See St. Mary's School and St. Mary's Montessori Preschool, Amarillo under Elementary Schools, City-Wide located in the Institution section.
Catechesis/Religious Program—Ms. Bernice Noggler, D.R.E. Students 299.

9—OUR LADY OF GUADALUPE Rev. Jose Gomez; Deacons Hector Gallegos; Armando Esparza.
Res.: 1210 E. 11th Ave., 79102. Tel: 806-372-1128; Fax: 806-372-2225.
See Our Lady of Guadalupe School, Amarillo under Elementary Schools, City-Wide located in the Institution section.
Catechesis/Religious Program—Elizabeth Martinez, D.R.E. Students 191.

10—OUR LADY OF VIETNAM Rev. Francis Xavir M. Vinh Van Vu, C.M.C.
Res.: 2001 N. Grand, 79107. Tel: 806-383-0467; Fax: 806-383-0467.
Catechesis/Religious Program—Students 89.

11—ST. THOMAS THE APOSTLE Rev. Msgr. Joseph T. Tash; Deacons Terry Pevehouse; Blaine Westlake.
Res.: 4100 Coulter Dr., 79109. Tel: 806-358-2461; Fax: 806-358-2529.
Catechesis/Religious Program—Eileen Dolan, D.R.E. Students 469.

OUTSIDE THE CITY OF AMARILLO

BORGER, HUTCHINSON CO., ST. JOHN THE EVANGELIST Rev. Msgr. Michael P. Colwell; Deacons Zeferino Jimenez; Isaac Driedger.
Res.: 201 St. John's Rd., 79007. Tel: 806-274-7064.
Catechesis/Religious Program—Jennifer Crittenden, D.R.E. Students 216.
Mission—*St. Ann's* Stinnett, Hutchinson Co.

BOVINA, PARMER CO., ST. ANN'S Rev. George William Yeddanapalli, Parochial Admin.
Res.: Box 660, 79009. Tel: 806-251-1511.
Catechesis/Religious Program—Nancy Trimble, D.R.E. Students 172.

CANADIAN, HEMPHILL CO., SACRED HEART Rev. Salibindla Balashowreddy; Deacon Jose Jesus Gutierrez.
Rectory—721 Main St., 79014. Tel: 806-323-6608; Fax: 806-323-9643.
Church: 804 Kingman Ave., P.O. Box 938, 79014.
Catechesis/Religious Program—Students 29.

CANYON, RANDALL CO., ST. ANN'S Very Rev. Phu T. Phan; Deacon Gabriel Rivas.
Mailing Address: P.O. Box 59, 79015. In Res., Rev. Daniel A. Dreher.
Res.: 605 38th St., 79015. Tel: 806-655-3302; Fax: 806-655-3384.
Catechesis/Religious Program—Ms. Carol Sanford, D.R.E. Students 248.

CHILDRESS, CHILDRESS CO., HOLY ANGELS Rev. James Schitmeyer.
Res.: 308 Ave. B, S.W., P.O. Box 608, 79201. Tel: 940-937-3946; Fax: 940-937-0668.
Catechesis/Religious Program—Students 45.

CLARENDON, DONLEY CO., ST. MARY'S Rev. Arokia Raj Samala; Deacon Pedro Juarez.
Res.: 815 McClelland St., P.O. Drawer C, 79226. Tel: 806-874-3910.
Catechesis/Religious Program—Debra Kuhl, C.R.E. Students 11.

DALHART, HARTLEY CO., ST. ANTHONY OF PADUA Rev. Scott Raef; Deacon Ronald Hein.
Res.: 411 Texas Blvd., Box 1029, 79022. Tel: 806-244-4128; Fax: 806-244-7128.
School—(Grades K-6), 1302 Oak St., 79022. Tel: 806-244-4811; Fax: 806-244-0462. Nicole Barber, Prin. School Sisters of the Third Order of St. Francis 3; Lay Teachers 6; Students 105.
Catechesis/Religious Program—Javita Anzaldua, C.R.E.; Suzanne Foley, C.R.E. Students 225.
Convent—1301 Oak Ave., 79022. Tel: 806-244-2390. Email: stanthon@xit.net. School Sisters of St. Francis 2.
Mission—*St. Mary's* Texline, Dallum Co.

DIMMITT, CASTRO CO., IMMACULATE CONCEPTION Revs. Guadalupe Mayorga; Ken Keller, Sacramental Min.; Deacons Paul Garcia; Jose Garcia.
Res.: 710 W. Halsell St., 79027. Tel: 806-647-4219 (Church); 806-647-0105 (Office).
Catechesis/Religious Program—Mary Helen Flores, D.R.E. Students 140.
Mission—*St. John's* Hart, Castro Co.

DUMAS, MOORE CO., SS. PETER AND PAUL Revs. Juan Carlos Barragan; Marco Antonio Salazar; Deacons Joseph A. Schwertner; Jim Clements.
Res.: 815 S. Maddox, Box 503, 79029. Tel: 806-935-5002; Fax: 806-934-3382.
Catechesis/Religious Program—Maria Guttierrez, D.R.E. Students 210.
Mission—*Christ the King* P.O. Box 681, Sunray, Moore Co. 79086. Rev. Joseph Papaiah; Deacon Wayne Norrell.

FRIONA, PARMER CO., ST. TERESA OF JESUS Rev. George William Yeddanapalli.
Res.: 401 W. 17th, 79035-9601. Tel: 806-250-2871; Fax: 806-250-3549.
Catechesis/Religious Program—Olga De Lao, C.R.E. Students 164.

GROOM, CARSON CO., IMMACULATE HEART OF MARY, [CEM] Rev. Arokia Raj Samala.
Res.: 411 Ware Ave., P.O. Box 130, 79039. Tel: 806-248-7584.
Catechesis/Religious Program—Students 33.

GRUVER, HANSFORD CO., CRISTO REDENTOR Rev. Gregory Bunyan.
Res. & Mailing Address: P.O. Box 238, 79040. Tel: 806-733-5236.
Catechesis/Religious Program—Olivia Salgado, C.R.E. Students 47.

HAPPY, SWISHER CO., HOLY NAME OF JESUS, [CEM] Rev. George Kalampatt; Rev. Msgr. Mario Stortz (Retired).
Res.: 317 W. Main, P.O. Box 128, 79042. Tel: 806-558-2871.
Catechesis/Religious Program—Students 24.

HEREFORD, DEAF SMITH CO.

1—ST. ANTHONY'S Rev. John Valdez; Deacon Jerry Duenes.
Business Office—114 Sunset Dr., 79045. Tel: 806-364-6150; Fax: 806-364-0969.
Res.: 115 N. 25 Mile Ave., 79045. Tel: 806-364-2793; Fax: 806-364-0969.
School—(Grades PreK-5), 120 W. Park Ave., 79045. Tel: 806-364-1952. Ann Lueb, Prin.; Susan Hicks, Librarian. Lay Teachers 11; Students 115.
Catechesis/Religious Program—Students 275.

2—SAN JOSE Rev. David Contreras; Deacons Emilio Fuentes; Vicente H. Garcia.
Res.: 735 Brevard, 79045. Tel: 806-364-5053; Fax: 806-364-2880.
Catechesis/Religious Program—Tel: 806-364-5053. Students 425.

MEMPHIS, HALL CO., SACRED HEART Rev. Gregory Bunyan; Deacon John Nino, Parish Life Coord.
Mailing Address: 213 N. Third St., P.O. Box 239, 79245. Tel: 806-259-2178.
Catechesis/Religious Program—Mrs. Juanita Garza, D.R.E. Students 45.

NAZARETH, CASTRO CO., HOLY FAMILY Rev. Ken Keller; Deacon Jerome Brockman.
Res.: 210 St. Joseph, P.O. Box 100, 79063. Tel: 806-945-2616; Fax: 806-945-2564.
Catechesis/Religious Program—Gladys Fortenberry, D.R.E. Students 144.

PAMPA, GRAY CO., ST. VINCENT DE PAUL Revs. Francisco Perez; Joseph Ravi.
Res.: 810 W. 23rd St., 79065. Tel: 806-665-8933; Fax: 806-665-2840.
School—Temporarily closed., 2300 N. Hobart, 79065. Tel: 806-665-5665. Amy Unruh, Prin.
Catechesis/Religious Program—Students 244.

PANHANDLE, CARSON CO., ST. THERESA Rev. Mieczyslaw "Mitchell" Przepiora.
Res.: P.O. Box 366, 79068. Tel: 806-537-3677.
Catechesis/Religious Program—Judy Neusch, D.R.E. Students 43.

PERRYTON, OCHILTREE CO., IMMACULATE CONCEPTION Rev. Msgr. Joseph Bixenman; Deacons Jose Cano; Serigo Estrada.
Res.: 1000 S.W. 15th Ave., 79070. Tel: 806-435-3802; Fax: 806-648-1490.
Catechesis/Religious Program—Maria Gallardo, C.R.E. (Elementry); Manuel Moreno, C.R.E.; Lupe Moreno, C.R.E. Students 396.

Mission—St. Peter Booker, Lipscomb Co. Deacon Felix Tudon.

SPEARMAN, HANSFORD CO., SACRED HEART Rev. Gregory Bunyan.
Res.: 901 S. Roland, P.O. Box 127, 79081. Tel: 806-659-2166; Fax: 806-659-2166.
Catechesis/Religious Program—Oliva Salgado, D.R.E. Students 148.
Mission—Cristo Redentor P.O. Box 238, Gruver, Hansford Co. 79040.

STRATFORD, SHERMAN CO., ST. JOSEPH'S Rev. Joseph Papaiah; Deacon Willie F. Artho.
Mailing Address: Box 28, 79084. Tel: 806-366-5687.
Catechesis/Religious Program—Johnny Garza, D.R.E.
Mission—Our Lady of Guadalupe Box 28, Cactus, Sherman Co. 79084. Tel: 806-396-5687. Deacon Vacilio Anaya.

TULIA, SWISHER CO., CHURCH OF THE HOLY SPIRIT Rev. Fernando Ruge.
Res.: 513 S. Austin, P.O. Box 25, 79088. Tel: 806-995-3191; Fax: 806-995-3286.
Catechesis/Religious Program—Mike Huseman, D.R.E.
Mission—St. Paul the Apostle P.O. Box 231, Kress, Swisher Co. 79052. Tel: 806-823-2548.

UMBARGER, RANDALL CO., ST. MARY'S, [CEM] Rev. George Kalampatt; Deacon Bill Dorsey.
22830 Pondaseta St., 79091.
Res.: P.O. Box 105, 79091. Tel: 806-499-3531.
Catechesis/Religious Program—Students 40.

VEGA, OLDHAM CO., IMMACULATE CONCEPTION Rev. Antony Punnackal, C.M.I., Parochail Admin.; Deacon Raymond Artho.
Res.: P.O. Box 250, 79092. Tel: 806-267-0154.
Catechesis/Religious Program—Michelle Baca, D.R.E. Students 44.

WELLINGTON, COLLINGSWORTH CO., OUR MOTHER OF MERCY Rev. Tony Neusch; Deacon Jose Velasco.
Church: 1108 Floydada, P.O. Box 686, 79095. Tel: 806-256-5358; Fax: 806-256-2829.
Catechesis/Religious Program—Students 14.
Mission—St. Patrick Shamrock, Wheeler Co.

WHITE DEER, CARSON CO., SACRED HEART Rev. Mieczyslaw "Mitchell" Przepiora, Admin.
Box 427, 79097. Tel: 806-883-4781.
Catechesis/Religious Program—Karen Storey, D.R.E. Students 17.

On Duty Outside the Diocese:
Revs.—
Afunugo, Emmanuel, D.D.
Busch, Robert
Pavone, Frank
Rosolen, Emil

Unassigned:
Rev.—
Lindley, Philip

Retired:
Rev. Msgrs.—
Corcoran, Clifton J., P.O. Box 1179, Panhandle, 79068.
Greka, David, Allpena, MI
Gurzynski, James C., 2229 Loucust, 79109.
Hickey, John, Corpus Christi, TX
Kuehler, Norbert, Chaplain Franciscan Sisters
Malnar, Matthew, Independence, WI
Stalter, Cal, 3811 Hancock, 79118.
Stortz, Mario, Rt. 1, Box 174, Tulia, 79088.
Revs.—
Chen, Raphael, 9170 Graham, Cypress, CA 90630.
Choong, Norbert, 5906 Aspen Ave., N.E., Albuquerque, NM 87110.
McGhee, Jim, Keller, TX
Sherry, Brendan, Ireland
Sweeney, Edward, 2400 E. Willow Creek, 79108.
Wood, Michael, Baltic, CT

Permanent Deacons:
Alarcon, Alfredo, St. Laurence Cathedral, Amarillo
Allein, Bill, St. Mary's, Amarillo
Ambs, James R., (Retired)
Artho, Raymond, Immaculate Conception, Vega
Artho, Willie F., (Retired), St. Joseph's Church, Stratford
Ashley, Floyd, St. Mary's Church, Amarillo; Admin. Asst. to Bishop Zurek
Blunt, Orvel Ray, (Retired)
Brock, Kennith, (Leave of Absence)
Brockman, Jerome, Holy Family, Nazareth
Brown, Jim, (Retired)
Campos, Tony, (On Leave of Absence)
Cano, Jose, Immaculate Conception, Perryton
Castillo, Esteban, (On Leave of Absence)
Clements, Jim, Sts. Peter & Paul, Dumas
Cloud, Jonny E., (Retired)
Correa, Jose, St. Teresa's Church, Friona
Dollins, Belvin G., (Retired)
Dorsey, Bill, St. Mary's, Umbarger
Driedger, Isaac, St. John's, Borger
Duenes, David, St. Laurence Cathedral, Amarillo
Duenes, Jerry, St. Anthony's, Hereford
Esparza, Armando, Our Lady of Guadalupe, Amarillo
Estrada, Sergio, Immaculate Conception, Perryton
Frausto, Joseph, (Unassigned)
Fuentes, Emilio, Sr., (Retired), San Jose Church, Hereford
Gallegos, Hector, Our Lady of Guadalupe Church, Amarillo; (Sick Leave)
Garcia, Paul, Immaculate Conception, Dimmitt
Garcia, Vicente H., San Jose Church, Hereford
Gonzales, Roberto, (Retired), St. John's, Hart
Grossman, Jerry, (On Leave of Absence)
Guerrero, Jesse, (Prison Ministry) St. Ann's, Bovina
Gutierrez, Jose Jesus, Sacred Heart Church, Canadian
Gutierrez, Robert, (Retired)
Hein, Ronald, St. Anthony's Church, Dalhart
Hernandez, Mauro, (Retired)
Hesse, August, III, (Retired)
Jimenez, Zeferino, St. John's Church, Borger
Juarez, Pedro, St. Mary's, Clarendon
Keller, Robert C., (On Duty Outside the Diocese)
Mason, Wilbur, (Retired)
Montano, Willie, St. Joseph's, Amarillo
Nino, John, Sacred Heart, Memphis
Norrell, Wayne, Christ the King Church, Sunray
Peters, John, St. Mary's, Amarillo
Pevehouse, Terry, St. Thomas the Apostle Church, Amarillo
Ramos, Leo, St. Joseph, Amarillo
Reid, Timothy, (On Duty Outside the Diocese)
Rivas, Gabriel, St. Ann's Church, Canyon
Ruiz, Jesse P., (On Duty Outside the Diocese)
Schwertner, Joseph A., SS. Peter & Paul Church, Dumas
Seidlitz, Mark, Blessed Sacrament Church, Amarillo and Prison Ministry
Smith, Robert, St. Mary's Church, Amarillo
Tudon, Felix, Sts. Peter and Paul, Booker
Valdez, Pete, St. Laurence Cathedral, Amarillo
Velasco, Jose, Our Lady of Mercy, Wellington
Velo, Jose, (On Leave)
Westlake, Blaine, St. Thomas Church, Amarillo; Coord. Deacons/Safe Environment

INSTITUTIONS LOCATED IN THE DIOCESE

[A] HIGH SCHOOLS, CITY-WIDE

AMARILLO. *Holy Cross Catholic Academy*, (Grades 6-12), (Coed), 4114 S. Bonham, 79110-1113. Tel: 806-355-9637; Fax: 806-353-9520. Email: hcca124@swbell.net. Web: www.holycrosscatholicacademy.org. Deacon Jim Clements, Prin.; Laveta Peters, Librarian. Lay Teachers 18; Students 136.

[B] ELEMENTARY SCHOOLS, CITY-WIDE

AMARILLO. *St. Joseph's School*, (Grades K-5), 4118 Bonham St., 79110. Tel: 806-359-1604; Fax: 806-355-5622. Email: stjosephelem@catholicexchange.com. Web: www.rc.net/amarillo/stjosephschool. Angie Seidenbenger, Prin.; Evelyn Mula, Librarian. Priests 1; Sisters 3; Lay Teachers 4; Students 109.

St. Mary School and St. Mary's Montessori Preschool, 1200 S. Washington, 79102. Tel: 806-376-9112; Fax: 806-376-9112. Email: lreynolds@stmarysamarillo.com. Kathi Lewis, Prin.; Amanda McDonald, Librarian. Sisters 1; Lay Teachers 13; Students 219.

Our Lady of Guadalupe School, (Grades K-5), 1108 S. Houston, 79102. Tel: 806-372-2629; Fax: 806-372-2225. Marissa Cochran, Prin.; Patsy Preciado, Librarian. Sisters 2; Lay Teachers 5; Students 97.

[C] HOMES FOR THE AGED

PANHANDLE. *St. Ann's Nursing Home*, P.O. Box 1179, 79068. Tel: 806-537-3194; Fax: 806-537-3003. Email: stannsnh@amaonline.com. Jimmie Sue Chisum, Admin. In Res. Rev. Msgr. Clifton J. Corcoran (Retired).

St. Joseph's Home for Retired Priests, P.O. Box 1179, 79068. Rev. James Hutzler (Retired).

[D] COALITION OF CATHOLIC SOCIAL SERVICES

AMARILLO. **Catholic Family Service, Inc.*, 200 S. Tyler, 79101. Tel: 806-376-4571; Fax: 806-345-7911. Email: gbcree@catholicfamily.net. Web: www.catholicfamilyservice.org. Box 15127, 79105-5127. Bernard Johnson, Exec. Dir.

Downtown Women's Center, Inc., 409 S. Monroe, 79101. Tel: 806-372-3625; Fax: 806-372-9026. Email: diann@dwcenter.org. Diann Gilmore, Exec. Dir.

[E] CATHOLIC CHILDREN'S DEVELOPMENT CENTERS

AMARILLO. *Amarillo Catholic Children's Development Centers*

St. Joseph Campus, 4108 Bonham St., P.O. Box 19726, 79114. Tel: 806-353-7043. Gail Sands, Dir. Teachers 5; Caregivers 11; Students 98.

[F] RETREAT HOUSE

AMARILLO. *Bishop DeFalco Retreat Center*, 2100 N. Spring St., 79107. Tel: 806-383-1811; Fax: 806-383-6919. Email: bdrc@1s.net. Web: www.bdrc.org. Deacon Robert Smith, Admin.

Bishop DeFalco Retreat Center Foundation

CANYON. *St. Benedict Monastery Retreat/Spirituality Center*, 17825 S. Western St., 79015. Tel: 806-655-9317; Fax: 806-655-9736. Email: nuns@osbcanyontx.org. Web: www.osbcanyontx.org. Sr. Hildegard Varga, O.S.B., Dir.

CHANNING. *Prayer Town Emmanuel Retreat House*, 404 Holy Way, P.O. Box 64, Prayer Town, 79010. Tel: 806-534-2312; Fax: 806-534-2223. Email: sisters@dljc.org. Web: www.dljc.org. Sr. Magdalena Casas-Nava, Coord. The Disciples of the Lord Jesus Christ.

[G] CONVENTS AND RESIDENCES FOR SISTERS

AMARILLO. *St. Francis Convent, Novitiate and U.S. Provincial House*, 4301 N.E. 18th, 79107. Tel: 806-383-5769; Fax: 806-383-6545. Email: francpro@worldnet.att.net. Web: www.members.cox.net/franciscansistersofmaryimmaculate. Sr. Sol Diaz, Prov. Supr. Franciscan Sisters of Mary Immaculate of the Third Order of St. Francis. Sisters 14.

St. Francis Mission Community, O.S.F., LaVerna Convent, 203 S. Avondale, 79106. Tel: 806-352-2981. Email: franciscan@erfwireless.net. Sr. Charlotte Lyjan, O.S.F., Prov., Lubbock House. Sisters 4.

Madres Clarisas Capuchinas, Capuchin Nuns of St. Clare, 4201 N.E. 18th Ave., 79107. Tel: 806-383-9877. Sr. Theresa Cortes, O.S.C., Abbess. Convent of the Blessed Sacrament and Our Lady of Guadalupe. Professed Nuns 14; Apostulants 3.

CANYON. *St. Benedict's Monastery*, 17825 S. Western, 79015. Tel: 806-655-9317; Fax: 806-655-9736. Email: nuns@osbcanyontx.org. Web: www.osbcanyontx.org. Sr. Mary Hawkins, O.S.B., Prioress. Sisters 3.

CHANNING. *Disciples of the Lord Jesus Christ*, P.O. Box 64, Prayer Town, 79010. Tel: 806-534-2312; Fax: 806-534-2223. Email: sisters@dljc.org. Web: www.dljc.org. Sr. Lucy Lukasiewicz, Supr. Gen.

PANHANDLE. *Sancta Maria Convent (North American Region and Novitiate)*, 119 Franciscan Way, P.O. Box 906, 79068-0906. Tel: 806-537-3182; Fax: 806-537-5498. Email: schsrs@gmail.com. Web: www.panhandlefranciscans.org. Sr. Mary Ana Steele, Regl. Supr. School Sisters of the Third Order of St. Francis. Sisters 25.

[H] CAMPUS MINISTRY

CANYON. *Catholic Student Center at West Texas A & M University* 2610 Fourth Ave., 79015. Tel: 806-655-4345; Fax: 806-655-0534. Email: cscwtamu@arn.net. Web: www.wtcsc.org. Rev. Daniel A. Dreher, Chap.; Betty Aragon, Asst. Dir.

[I] MISCELLANEOUS LISTINGS

AMARILLO. *Amarillo Catholic School System*, 1800 N. Spring St., 79109. Tel: 806-383-2243, Ext. 110; Fax: 806-383-8452. Email: bnoggler@amarillodiocese.org.

Amarillo Scholarship Endowment and Assistance Fund, 1800 N. Spring St., 79107. Tel: 806-383-2243; Fax: 806-383-8452.

**Catholic Radio of the Texas High Plains*, 701 S. Pierce, Ste. 101, 79101. Tel: 806-350-1360; Fax: 806-350-1361.

Engaged Encounter, 3600 Torre, 79109. Tel: 806-352-2607. Deacon Blaine Westlake, Dir.; Louise Westlake, Dir.; Jerry Ballard, Contact. Tel: 806-353-0907.

Holy Family Parish of Nazareth, Texas Endowment Foundation, Diocese of Amarillo, 1800 N. Spring St., 79107. Tel: 806-383-2243; Fax: 806-383-8452. Email: pwhitson@amarillodiocese.org. Phil Whitson, CFO; Most Rev. Patrick J. Zurek, D.D., Bd.; Rev. Ken Keller.

Marriage Encounter, 1800 N. Spring, 79107. Tel: 806-376-6498. Email: pvkrat@msn.com. Rev. Msgr. Michael P. Colwell; Patrick Kratochvil, Ecclesiastical Team; Virginia Kratochvil, Ecclesiastical Team.

Monsignor B.A. Erpen Trust Fund (1985) Diocese of Amarillo, 1800 N. Spring, 79107. Tel: 806-383-2243; Fax: 806-383-8452. Email: joelo2046@dellnet.com. Phil Whitson, CFO; Most Rev. Patrick J. Zurek, D.D., Trustee; Rev. Msgr. Harold L. Waldow, Trustee.

Pope John Paul II House of Discernment (2005) 1501 N. Adams, 79107. Tel: 806-373-5400. Email: mcolwell@amarillodiocese.org. Rev. Msgr. Michael P. Colwell, Vocation Dir.

Project Solidarity (1999) Diocese of Amarillo, 1800 N. Spring, 79107. Tel: 806-383-2243; Fax: 806-383-8452. Email: mcolwell@amarillodiocese.org. Rev. Msgr. Michael P. Colwell, Chancellor & Vicar Gen.

Roman Catholic Diocese of Amarillo Deposit and Loan Fund, P.O. Box 5644, 79117. Tel: 806-383-2243; Fax: 806-383-8452. Email: pwhitson@amarillodiocese.org. Phil Whitson, CFO; Most Rev. Patrick J. Zurek, D.D.; Very Rev. Joseph E. Bixenman.

Texas Panhandle Catholic Endowment Foundation (1985) 1800 N. Spring, 79107. Tel: 806-383-2243; Fax: 806-383-8452. Email: pwhitson@amarillodiocese.org. Most Rev. Patrick J. Zurek, D.D., Trustee; Robert Neslage, Trustee; Ed Wieck, Trustee; Frank Walsh, Trustee; Daniel Martinez, Trustee; Dr. Anh My Do, Trustee.

RELIGIOUS INSTITUTES OF MEN REPRESENTED IN THE DIOCESE

For further details refer to the corresponding bracketed number in the Religious Institutes of Men or Women section.

[0275]—*Carmelite of Mary Immaculate*—C.M.I.

[]—*Congregation of Mother Coredemptrix*—C.M.C.

[]—*Provincia de los SS. Francisco and Santiago* (Mexico)—A.R.

RELIGIOUS INSTITUTES OF WOMEN REPRESENTED IN THE DIOCESE

[0230]—*Benedictine Sisters of Pontifical Jurisdiction* (Little Rock, AR)—O.S.B.

[]—*Congregation of the School Sisters of Notre Dame*—S.S.N.D.

[0460]—*Congregation of the Sisters of Charity of the Incarnate Word*—C.C.V.I.

[0965]—*Disciples of the Lord Jesus Christ*—D.L.J.C.

[1500]—*Franciscan Sisters of Mary Immaculate of the Third Order of St. Francis of Assisi*—F.M.I.

[]—*Missionary Catechist Sisters of St. Joseph* (Mexico)—O.F.M.

[1695]—*School Sisters of the Third Order of St. Francis, (Panhandle, Texas)*—O.S.F.

[1705]—*Sisters of the Third Order of St. Francis of Assisi*—O.S.F.

[]—*St. Clare Capuchin Sisters*—C.P.C.

NECROLOGY

✠ Matthiesen, Most Rev. Leroy T., Retired Bishop of Amarillo—Died March 22, 2010

† Hand, Rev. Msgr. Kevin, (Retired)—Died Aug. 9, 2009

An asterisk (*) denotes an organization that has established tax-exempt status directly with the IRS and is not covered by the USCCB Group Ruling.

Archdiocese of Anchorage

(Archidioecesis Ancoragiensis)

Most Reverend

ROGER L. SCHWIETZ, O.M.I., D.D.

Archbishop of Anchorage; ordained December 20, 1967; appointed Bishop of Duluth December 12, 1989; consecrated and installed Bishop of Duluth February 2, 1990; appointed Coadjutor Archbishop of Anchorage January 18, 2000; succeeded to the See March 3, 2001.

Most Reverend

FRANCIS T. HURLEY

Archbishop Emeritus of Anchorage; ordained June 16, 1951; appointed Titular Bishop of Daimlaig and Auxiliary of Juneau February 4, 1970; consecrated March 19, 1970; appointed Bishop of Juneau July 20, 1971; installed September 8, 1971; appointed Archbishop of Anchorage May 4, 1976; installed July 8, 1976; retired March 3, 2001.

ESTABLISHED FEBRUARY 9, 1966.

Square Miles 138,985.

Comprises the Third Judicial Division of Alaska.

For legal titles of parishes and archdiocesan institutions, consult the Chancery Office.

Chancery Office: 225 Cordova St., Anchorage, AK 99501. Tel: 907-297-7700; Fax: 907-279-3885.

Web: www.archdioceseofanchorage.org

Email: mail@caa-ak.org

STATISTICAL OVERVIEW

Personnel	
Archbishops	1
Retired Archbishops	1
Priests: Diocesan Active in Diocese	9
Priests: Diocesan Active Outside Diocese	1
Priests: Diocesan in Foreign Missions	1
Priests: Retired, Sick or Absent	5
Number of Diocesan Priests	16
Religious Priests in Diocese	11
Total Priests in Diocese	27
Extern Priests in Diocese	11
Ordinations:	
Permanent Deacons	6
Permanent Deacons in Diocese	19
Total Brothers	2
Total Sisters	25
Parishes	
Parishes	23
With Resident Pastor:	
Resident Diocesan Priests	16
Resident Religious Priests	5
Without Resident Pastor:	
Administered by Religious Women	1
Administered by Lay People	1
Missions	6
Professional Ministry Personnel:	
Brothers	2
Sisters	25
Lay Ministers	25
Welfare	
Catholic Hospitals	1
Total Assisted	82,396
Health Care Centers	5
Total Assisted	18,273
Homes for the Aged	1
Total Assisted	641
Residential Care of Children	2
Total Assisted	19
Special Centers for Social Services	3
Total Assisted	33,751
Educational	
Diocesan Students in Other Seminaries	2
Total Seminarians	2
High Schools, Diocesan and Parish	1
Total Students	80
Elementary Schools, Diocesan and Parish	3
Total Students	306
Catechesis/Religious Education:	
High School Students	743
Elementary Students	1,797
Total Students under Catholic Instruction	2,928
Teachers in the Diocese:	
Priests	1
Brothers	2
Sisters	2
Lay Teachers	67
Vital Statistics	
Receptions into the Church:	
Infant Baptism Totals	474
Minor Baptism Totals	94
Adult Baptism Totals	26
Received into Full Communion	79
First Communions	451
Confirmations	272
Marriages:	
Catholic	50
Interfaith	46
Total Marriages	96
Deaths	120
Total Catholic Population	37,089
Total Population	401,610

Former Archbishops—Most Revs. JOSEPH T. RYAN, D.D., Archbishop of Anchorage; ord. June 3, 1939; cons. March 25, 1966; installed April 14, 1966; transferred to as Coadjutor Military Vicar of U.S. Armed Forces Dec. 13, 1975; appt. First Archbishop of the Archdiocese for the Military Services, U.S.A., March 16, 1985; died Oct. 9, 2000; FRANCIS T. HURLEY, D.D. (Retired), Archbishop of Anchorage; ord. June 16, 1951; appt. Titular Bishop of Daimlaig and Auxiliary of Juneau, Feb. 4, 1970; cons. March 19, 1970; appt. Bishop of Juneau, July 20, 1971; installed Sept. 8, 1971; appt. Archbishop of Anchorage, May 4, 1976; installed July 8, 1976; retired March 3, 2001.

Vicars General—Most Rev. FRANCIS T. HURLEY, D.D. (Retired); Very Rev. STEVEN C. MOORE, S.T.D.

Pastoral Center—

Moderator of the Curia—Revs. THOMAS T. BRUNDAGE, J.C.L.; WILLIAM J. FOURNIER, Chancellor; Mrs. EILEEN T. KRAMER, Vice Chancellor, 225 Cordova St., Anchorage, 99501. Tel: 907-297-7712; Fax: 907-279-3885.

Secretary to Archbishop Emeritus—Ms. JOANN WHITE.

Secretary to Archbishop Roger L. Schwietz, O.M.I.—KIMBERLY BAKIC.

Office of Stewardship/Development—Mr. JAMES CALDAROLA.

Tribunal—225 Cordova St., Anchorage, 99501-2409. Tel: 907-297-7724.

Judicial Vicar—Rev. THOMAS T. BRUNDAGE, J.C.L.

Judge—Deacon WILLIAM FINNEGAN, J.C.L.

Defenders of the Bond—Rev. SCOTT GARRETT, J.C.L.; Mrs. MIRIAM DONOHUE.

Case Manager and Data Entry—Sr. JOAN OBERLE, C.PP.S.; JENNIFER MICHAELSON, Auditor.

Notaries—Sr. JOAN OBERLE, C.PP.S.; Mrs. EILEEN T. KRAMER; KIMBERLY BAKIC; Revs. VINCENT BLANCO; WILLIAM HANRAHAN.

Diocesan Consultors—Revs. FRANCIS LE, O.P.; RICHARD D. TERO; THOMAS C. LILLY; Very Rev. STEVEN C. MOORE, S.T.D.; Revs. FRED BUGARIN; WILLIAM HANRAHAN; THOMAS T. BRUNDAGE, J.C.L.

Archdiocesan Offices and Directors

Apostleship of the Sea— Port Chaplain: SALLY BOSTWICK, Anchorage.

Archdiocesan Newspaper— "Catholic Anchor" JOEL DAVIDSON, Editor, Pastoral Center, 225 Cordova St., Anchorage, 99501. Tel: 907-297-7730.

Magadan Mission—Rev. MICHAEL SHIELDS.

Campaign for Human Development—Deacon THEODORE GREENE.

Catholic Relief Services—Ms. BONNIE CLER.

Catholic Social Services—SUSAN BOMALASKI, Exec. Dir.; ELLEN KRSNAK, Dir. Community Rels.; MARY BETH BRAGIEL, Deputy Dir., 3710 E. 24th St., Anchorage, 99508. Tel: 907-276-5590; Fax: 907-258-1091.

Board Members—BILLIE R. BOWEN; ROGER CHAN; ROSE CARROLL SUWANNEE; Rabbi MICHAEL OBLATH, Ex Officio; Rev. SCOTT MEDLOCK, Ex Officio; MIKE STOPHLET; MAURICE COYLE, M.D.; Ms. MONICA ANDERSON; HARRIETT FENERTY; PATRICK GILMORE; PATRICIA PETRIVELLI; Ms. ERNESTINE FLEECE; CAROL COMEAU; MICHELLE EGAN; WILLIAM GRANGER; LOTTIE MICHAEL; MARIA TAGLIAVENTO.

Hispanic Ministry—Rev. DOMINIC DEMAIO, O.P.; Sr. LORRAINE REAUME, O.P.

Korean Ministry—Rev. AN KWANG-SUNG, 7206 Lake Otis Pkwy., Anchorage, 99507. Tel: 907-333-5307; Fax: 907-333-2888; Sisters MARTHA HWANG; CECILIA PARK.

Native Ministry—Sr. DONNA KRAMER, D.C., Dir.

Office of Finance—Sr. CHARLOTTE DAVENPORT, C.S.J.P., CFO.

Office of Evangelization and Worship Service—VACANT. Tel: 907-297-7778.

Permanent Diaconate—Deacon JAMES "MICK" FORNELLI.

Propagation of the Faith—Mr. JAMES CALDAROLA, Dir.

Retreats—ALAN MUISE, Dir., Holy Spirit Center, 10980 Hillside Dr., Anchorage, 99507. Tel: 907-346-2343, Ext. 205.

Superintendent of Schools—Sr. ANN FALLON, O.P., 225 Cordova St., Anchorage, 99501. Tel: 907-297-7790. Email: afallon@caa-ak.org.

Victim Assistance Coordinator—ROSEMARY INSLEY. Tel: 907-297-7786. Email: rinsley@aol.com.

Vocations—Revs. THOMAS C. LILLY, Dir.; BENJAMIN TORRETO, Assoc. Dir.

CLERGY, PARISHES, MISSIONS AND PAROCHIAL SCHOOLS

CITY OF ANCHORAGE

1—HOLY FAMILY CATHEDRAL (1915) [JC] Revs. Francis Le, O.P.; Dominic DeMaio, O.P.; Vincent M. Kelber, O.P.; Deacon Gerald Grewe, Pastoral Assoc.; Bro. Dominic Maichrowicz, O.P.
Mailing Address: 811 W. 6th Ave., 99501-2093. Tel: 907-276-3455; Fax: 907-258-9785. Email: holyfamilycathedral@alaska.com.
Catechesis/Religious Program—Mrs. Theresa Lutes, D.R.E. Students 219.

2—ST. ANTHONY Rev. Fred Bugarin; H. William Goehring, Business Mgr.
Res.: 825 S. Klevin St., 99508-2698. Tel: 907-333-5544; Fax: 907-338-3864.
Catechesis/Religious Program—Students 75.

3—ST. BENEDICT Very Rev. Steven C. Moore; Deacons Ted Greene; Desiderio L. Martinez.
Res.: 8110 Jewel Lake Rd., 99502. Tel: 907-243-2195; Fax: 907-243-0088. Email: info@stbenedictsak.com. Web: www.stbenedictsak.com.
Catechesis/Religious Program—Students 213.

4—CORP. OF ST. CHRISTOPHER BY THE SEA CHURCH Very Rev. Steven C. Moore, Canonical Pastor.
P.O. Box 405, Unalaska, 99685. Tel: 907-581-4022; Fax: 907-581-2979.

5—CORP. OF OUR LADY OF THE LAKE CHURCH (2007) Revs. William J. Fournier, Canonical Pastor; Luzvimindo Flores, Parochial Vicar; Katherine Bishop, Parish Dir.
P.O. Box 520769, Big Lake, 99652. Tel: 907-892-6492; Fax: 907-892-6497.
Catechesis/Religious Program—Students 28.
Mission—St. Christopher P.O. Box 412, Willow, 99688.

6—CORP. OF ST. ANDREW KIM PARISH OF THE KOREAN COMMUNITY Rev. An Kwang-Sung.
7206 Lake Otis Pkwy., 99507. Tel: 907-333-5307; Fax: 907-333-2888.
Catechesis/Religious Program—Sisters Martha Hwang, D.R.E.; Cecilia Park, D.R.E.; Phillip W. Lee, D.R.E. Students 50.

7—ST. ELIZABETH ANN SETON (1975) Revs. Thomas C. Lilly; Jaime Mencias; Deacon Kenneth Donohue.
2901 E. Huffman Rd., 99516. Tel: 907-345-4466; Fax: 907-345-6361.
Catechesis/Religious Program—Students 466.
Mission—Our Lady of the Snows Girdwood, 99587. Tel: 907-783-1171. Email: reservations@chapelourladyofthesnows.org. Web: www.chapelourladyofthesnows.org.

8—HOLY CROSS (1984) Rev. Daniel J. Hebert; Sr. Loretta Luecke, C.PP.S., Parish Admin.
Res.: 2627 Lore Rd., 99507. Tel: 907-349-8388; Fax: 907-344-3388. Email: parish@holycrossalaska.net. Web: www.holycrossalaska.net.
Catechesis/Religious Program—Mrs. Janine Redding, D.R.E.; Theresa Austin, Youth Min. Students 154.

9—OUR LADY OF GUADALUPE (1970) Rev. Vincent Blanco.
Res.: 3900 Wisconsin St., 99517. Tel: 907-248-2000; Fax: 907-245-1600. Email: olg@olgalaska.org.
Catechesis/Religious Program—Leandra Childs, D.R.E. Students 141.

10—ST. PATRICK (1971) Revs. Scott Medlock; Richard Tero, Canonical Pastor; Deacons Felix Maguire; James Fornelli; Jon Hermon.
Res.: 2111 Muldoon Rd., 99504-3699. Tel: 907-337-1538; Fax: 907-337-5460. Email: stpatricks@st.patsak.org. Web: www.st.patsak.org.
Catechesis/Religious Program—Julia Thomas, D.R.E. Students 264.

11—ST. PAUL MIKI, Closed. For inquiries for parish records contact St. Elizabeth Ann Seton Parish, Anchorage.

OUTSIDE THE CITY OF ANCHORAGE

CORDOVA, VALDEZ-CORDOVA CO., ST. JOSEPH Rev. Thomas Killeen, O.M.I.
Res.: 220 Adams Ave., P.O. Box 79, 99574. Tel: 907-424-3637. Email: stjoecor@gci.net.
Catechesis/Religious Program—Students 30.

DILLINGHAM, DILLINGHAM CO., HOLY ROSARY Rev. Scott Garrett.
Res.: P.O. Box 810, 99576. Tel: 907-842-5581. Email: holyrosaryalaska@hotmail.com. Web: www.holyrosaryalaska.org.
Catechesis/Religious Program—Students 6.
Mission—St. Theresa P.O. Box 269, Naknek, Bristol Bay Borough 99633. Tel: 907-246-6652.

EAGLE RIVER, ANCHORAGE BOROUGH, ST. ANDREW (1968) Revs. Benjamin Torreto (Philippines); Eric Wiseman; Sr. Camilla Menting, S.S.S.F., Pastoral Assoc.; Deacons James Hostman; Jim Lee.
Res.: 16300 Domain Ln., 99577. Tel: 907-694-2170; Fax: 907-694-1385. Email: fr.ben@aksaintandrews.org. Web: www.aksaintandrews.org.
Catechesis/Religious Program—Email: deb@aksaintandrews.org. Mrs. Debbie Marino, Dir. Faith Formation. Students 263.

GLENNALLEN, VALDEZ-CORDOVA CO., HOLY FAMILY (1955) Rev. Thomas T. Brundage.
Mailing Address: P.O. Box 126, 99588. Tel: 907-745-3229; Fax: 907-822-4208. Email: tbrundage@caa-ak.org.
Catechesis/Religious Program—Students 15.

HOMER, KENAI PENINSULA BOROUGH, ST. JOHN THE BAPTIST, 255 Ohlson Ln., 99603. Tel: 907-235-8436; Fax: 907-235-5251. Email: stjohn@gci.net. Pastoral Team:, Revs. Roger Bergkamp, O.M.I.; Andrew Sensenig, O.M.I., Priest Mod.; Joseph Dowling, O.M.I.; Bro. Craig Bonham, O.M.I., Pastoral Assoc.
Res.: 222 W. Redoubt Ave., Soldotna, 99669.
Mission—St. Peter the Apostle Box 39290, Ninilchik, 99639. Tel: 907-567-3490.
Catechesis/Religious Program—Students 52.

KENAI, KENAI PENINSULA BOROUGH, OUR LADY OF THE ANGELS Pastoral Team:, Revs. Roger Bergkamp, O.M.I.; Andrew Sensenig, O.M.I., Priest Mod.; Joseph Dowling, O.M.I.; Bro. Craig Bonham, O.M.I., Pastoral Assoc.
Res.: 225 S. Spruce Rd., 99611. Tel: 907-283-4555.
Catechesis/Religious Program—Ms. Margaret Menting, D.R.E. Students 120.

KODIAK, KODIAK ISLAND BOROUGH, ST. MARY'S Rev. Ron Licayan (Philippines).
Res.: 2934 Mill Bay Rd., 99615. Tel: 907-486-5411; Fax: 907-486-3117.
School—(Grades K-8) Tel: 907-486-3513. Joshua Lewis, Prin. Lay Teachers 10; Students 96.
Catechesis/Religious Program—Students 31.

PALMER, MATANUSKA-SUSITNA BOROUGH, ST. MICHAEL (1935) Rev. Thomas T. Brundage.
Res.: 432 E. Fireweed Ave., 99645. Tel: 907-745-3229; Fax: 907-746-7040. Email: tbrundage@st-mikesparish.org. Web: www.st-mikesparish.org.
Catechesis/Religious Program—Mrs. Joanne Rousculp, D.R.E.; Matthew Beck, Pastoral Assoc. Students 108.

SEWARD, KENAI PENINSULA BOROUGH, SACRED HEART Rev. Richard Tero; Deacon Walter Corrigan.
Res.: 409 Fifth Ave., P.O. Box 207, 99664. Tel: 907-224-5414; Fax: 907-224-5093. Email: walcor@arctic.net.
Catechesis/Religious Program—Mrs. Kim Reierson, D.R.E. Teachers 4; Students 24.
Mission—St. John Neumann Church P.O. Box 737, Cooper Landing, 99572. Tel: 907-595-1300.

SOLDOTNA, KENAI PENINSULA BOROUGH, OUR LADY OF PERPETUAL HELP (1961) Pastoral Team:, Revs. Roger Bergkamp, O.M.I.; Andrew Sensenig, O.M.I., Priest Mod.; Joseph Dowling, O.M.I.; Bro. Craig Bonham, O.M.I., Pastoral Assoc.; Marlys Verba, Parish Dir.
Res.: 222 Redoubt Ave., 99669. Tel: 907-262-4749; Fax: 907-262-5542 (Call 907-262-4725 before sending fax).
Catechesis/Religious Program—Students 95.

TALKEETNA, MATANUSKA-SUSITNA BOROUGH, ST. BERNARD (1970) Renamary Rauchenstein, Dir.; Rev. William J. Fournier, Canonical Pastor.
Res.: P.O. Box 510, 99676. Tel: 907-733-2424; Fax: 907-733-2425. Email: rstein@matnet.com.
Mission—St. Philip Benizi P.O. Box 13475, Trapper Creek, 99683.

VALDEZ, VALDEZ-CORDOVA CO., ST. FRANCIS XAVIER (1908) Sr. Marie Ann Brent, S.H.F., Dir.; Rev. Thomas C. Lilly, Canonical Pastor; Deacon Daniel Stowe.
Res.: 341 Pioneer Dr., P.O. Box 908, 99686. Tel: 907-835-4556; Fax: 907-835-3583. Email: stfrnxav@cvalaska.net.
Catechesis/Religious Program—Tiana Schnider, D.R.E.; Jamie Schnider, D.R.E. Students 45.

WASILLA, MATANUSKA-SUSITNA BOROUGH, SACRED HEART, [CEM] Rev. William J. Fournier.
Res.: 1201 Bogard Rd., 99654-6523. Tel: 907-376-5087; Fax: 907-373-1156. Email: shparish@mtaonline.net. Web: www.sacredheartwasilla.org.
Catechesis/Religious Program—Students 142.

On Duty Outside Archdiocese:
Revs.—
Shields, Michael, Magadan, Russia
Walsh, Leo, S.T.D.

Retired:
Rev. Msgr.—
Murphy, Francis A., P.O. Box 1625, Cuba, NM 87013.
Revs.—
Abele, Alan Carl, 340 N. Worthy, Marblehead, OH 43440.
Desso, Leo C., 1925 Gaylord St., Butte, MT 59701.
Hornick, J. Michael, 225 Cordova St., 99501.
Houck, Peter, 4140 Folker St., 99508.

Permanent Deacons:
Allor, Raymond W., (Retired), Albany, OR
Cable, Jay, Wasilla
Corrigan, Walter, Seward
Donohue, Kenneth, Anchorage
Ernst, Richard, Kenai
Foreman, Dennis, (Retired), Anchorage
Fornelli, James, Anchorage
Frost, William, Wasilla
Greene, Theodore, Anchorage
Grewe, Gerald, Anchorage
Hermon, Jon, Anchorage
Hoffman, Louis, (Retired)
Hostman, James, Eagle River
Larroque, Robert, (Retired), Portland, OR
Lee, Jim, St. Andrew, Eagle River
Luenberger, Curt, Palmer
Maguire, Felix M., Anchorage
Martinez, Dez, Anchorage
Moore, Harry, Palmer
Pearson, Bill, Loxley, AL
Schutt, David E., Wasilla
Stowe, Daniel, Valdez

INSTITUTIONS LOCATED IN THE ARCHDIOCESE

[A] GRADE SCHOOLS, HIGH SCHOOLS PAROCHIAL

ANCHORAGE. *St. Elizabeth Ann Seton School*, (Grades K-6), 2901 E. Huffman Rd., 99516. Tel: 907-345-3712; Fax: 907-345-2910. Email: jimbailey@akseas.com. Web: www.akseas.com. James Bailey, Prin.; Beth Lottridge, Librarian. Lay Teachers 12; Students 164.

Lumen Christi High School, (Grades 7-12), 8110 Jewel Lake Rd., Bldg. D., 99502. Tel: 907-245-9231; Fax: 907-245-9232. Email: lchsprincipal@alaska.net. Web: www.lumenchristiak.com. Mrs. Colleen Larson, Prin.; Marty Osredker, Librarian. Students 80; Total Staff 11.

KODIAK. *St. Mary's*, (Grades PreK-8), 2932 Mill Bay Rd., 99615. Tel: 907-486-3513; Fax: 907-486-3117. Joshua Lewis, Prin.; Frances Le, Librarian. Lay Teachers 10; Students 96.

WASILLA. *Corp. of Our Lady of the Valley Catholic School, Inc.*, (Grades K-8), 260 Nelson Ave., 99654. Tel: 907-376-0883; Fax: 907-376-0853. Suzanne Hammons, Prin. Staff 7; Students 48.

[B] PRIVATE SCHOOLS

ANCHORAGE. *Holy Rosary Academy*, (Grades K-12), 1010 W. Fireweed Ln., 99503. Tel: 907-276-5822; Fax: 907-258-1055. Email: ewassell@gci.net. Web: www.holyrosaryacademy.net. Mr. Edward Wassell, Exec. Dir.; Mrs. Barbara Dorner, Prin. Lay Teachers 17; Students 146.

[C] GENERAL HOSPITALS

ANCHORAGE. *Providence Alaska Medical Center*, 3200 Providence Dr., P.O. Box 196604, 99519. Tel: 907-212-2211; Fax: 907-212-3041. Mr. E. Al Parrish, CEO; Ms. Monica Anderson, Chief Integration Officer. Properties, entities, and divisions owned or operated: Providence Health System--Washington; Providence Alaska Medical Center, Anchorage, AK, Providence Extended Care Center, Anchorage, AK, Providence Health System Housing* dba- Providence Horizon House, Anchorage, AK, Mary Conrad Center, Anchorage, AK. Bed Capacity 364; Patients Assisted

Annually 82,396; Staff 2,480.

KODIAK. *Providence Kodiak Island Medical Center*, 1915 E. Rezanof Dr., 99615. Tel: 907-486-3281; Fax: 907-486-2336. Bed Capacity 25; Skilled Nursing 19; Total Assisted Annually 3,924; Total Staff 179.

SEWARD. *Providence Seward Medical Center*, 417 First Ave., 99664. Tel: 907-224-5205; Fax: 907-224-7248. Bed Capacity 6; Total Assisted Annually 3,504; Total Staff 104.

VALDEZ. *Providence Valdez Medical Center*, 911 Meals Ave., P.O. Box 550, 99686-0550. Tel: 907-835-2249; Fax: 907-835-1980. Bed Capacity 10; Skilled Nursing 11; Total Assisted 14,250; Total Staff 76.

[D] NURSING HOMES

ANCHORAGE. *Providence Extended Care Center*, 4900 Eagle St., 99503. Tel: 907-562-2281; Fax: 907-762-0280. Jody Howorth, Admin.
Sisters of Providence in Washington. Bed Capacity 224; Patients Assisted Annually 641; Staff 336.

[E] CATHOLIC SOCIAL SERVICES

ANCHORAGE. *Brother Francis Shelter*, 1021 E. Third Ave., 99501. Tel: 907-277-1731. Mr. Dewayne Harris, Dir. Overnight shelter for homeless men and women.
Catholic Social Services Center, 3710 E. 20th St., 99508. Tel: 907-276-5590; Fax: 907-258-1091. Email: sbomalaski@cssalaska.org. Web: www.cssalaska.org.
Catholic Social Services Center, 3710 E. 20th Ave., 99508. Tel: 907-276-5590; Fax: 907-258-1091. Email: sbomalaski@cssalaska.org. Karen Ferguson, Dir., Immigration & Refugee Svcs.; Karen Hollar, Pregnancy Support & Adoption Dir.; Ms. Jennifer Nieves, Prog. Mgr., St. Francis House.
Charlie Elder House, 1513 Wintergreen, 99508. Tel: 907-277-8622; Fax: 907-277-2326. Mary Beth Bragiel, Deputy Dir.
Clare House, 420 W. 54th Ave., 99518. Tel: 907-563-4545. Barbara Neeson, Deputy Dir. Temporary shelter for homeless women and women with children.
McAuley Manor, 3015 Yale Dr., 99508. Tel: 907-279-5772; Fax: 907-279-5774. Mary Beth Bragiel, Deputy Dir. Residence for homeless teenage girls.

KODIAK. *Marian Center, Inc.*, P.O. Box 8756, 99615. Tel: 907-486-3820; Fax: 907-486-2605. Email: mariancenter@alaska.com.

[F] MONASTERIES AND RESIDENCES OF PRIESTS AND BROTHERS

ANCHORAGE. *Anchorage Jesuit Community*, 1500 Birchwood, 99508. Tel: 907-279-4389. Rev. Vincent Beuzer, S.J. Oregon Province of Society of Jesus.

[G] CONVENTS AND RESIDENCES FOR SISTERS

ANCHORAGE. *Daughters of Charity*, 3424 E. 15th Ave., 99508. Tel: 907-258-3424. Email: docanchorage@aol.com. Sisters 3.
Sisters of Perpetual Adoration, 2645 E. 72nd Ave., 99507. Tel: 907-344-3330; Fax: 907-522-2945. Sisters 3.
Sisters of St. Paul de Chartres, 7206 Lake Otis Pkwy., 99507. Tel: 907-258-3273; Fax: 907-333-2888. Sisters 2.

[H] RETREAT HOUSES

ANCHORAGE. *Holy Spirit Center*, 10980 Hillside Dr., 99507. Tel: 907-346-2343; Fax: 907-346-2140. Email: hsc@holyspiritcenterak.org. Web: www.holyspiritcenterak.org.

[I] MISCELLANEOUS

ANCHORAGE. *Archdiocese of Anchorage Priests Pension Trust*, 225 Cordova St., 99501. Tel: 907-297-7700; Fax: 907-279-3885.
Catholic Foundation of Alaska, 225 Cordova St., 99501. Tel: 907-297-7700; Fax: 907-279-3885. James P. Caldarola, Dir.
Catholic Retreat House Ministries, Inc., 225 Cordova St., 99501. Tel: 907-297-7700; Fax: 907-279-3885.
Covenant House Alaska, 609 F St., 99501. Tel: 907-272-1255; Fax: 907-272-1466. Ms. Deirdre Cronin, Exec. Dir. Program for homeless and runaway youth.
Providence Alaska Foundation, Anchorage, Alaska, 3200 Providence Dr., P.O. Box 196604, 99519-6604. Tel: 907-261-3600; Fax: 907-212-3048. Email: jsix@provak.org. Web: www.providence.org/alaska. Janice Six, Devel. Officer; Susan Ruddy, Pres.
Providence Health System Housing dba Providence Horizon House 4140 Folker Ave., 99508. Tel: 907-261-4140; Fax: 907-562-4160. Email: ssamet@provak.org. Jamie Benard, Prog. Dir. Staff 53; Patients Assisted Annually 85; Guests 80.
Providence Home Health Care, Anchorage, Alaska, 3546 Latouche St., Ste. 101, 99508. Tel: 907-563-0130; Fax: 907-563-0135. Email: klum@provak.org. Deborah Seidl, Prog. Dir.

PALMER. *Bishop's Attic II, Inc.*, 840 S. Bailey St., 99645. Tel: 907-745-1316; Fax: 907-745-4209. Email: batwo@mtaonline.net.

RELIGIOUS INSTITUTES OF MEN REPRESENTED IN THE ARCHDIOCESE

For further details refer to the corresponding bracketed number in the Religious Institutes of Men or Women section.

[0690]—*Jesuit Fathers and Brothers* (Oregon Prov.)—S.J.
[0854]—*Missionary Society of St. Paul of Nigeria*—M.S.P.
[0910]—*Oblates of Mary Immaculate*—O.M.I.
[0430]—*Order of Preachers-Dominicans* (Oakland Prov.)—O.P.

RELIGIOUS INSTITUTES OF WOMEN REPRESENTED IN THE ARCHDIOCESE

[1070]—*Adrian Dominican Sisters, Congregation of the Most Holy Rosary*—O.P.
[0760]—*Daughters of Charity of St. Vincent DePaul*—D.C.
[2330]—*Little Sisters of Jesus*—L.S.J.
[3190]—*Nuns of Perpetual Adoration of the Blessed Sacrament* (Mexico)—A.P.
[1680]—*School Sisters of St. Francis*—S.S.S.F.
[2575]—*Sisters of Mercy of the Americas* (Merion, PA)—R.S.M.
[3890]—*Sisters of St. Joseph of Peace* (Bellevue)—C.S.J.P.
[3980]—*Sisters of St. Paul de Chartres*—S.P.C.
[1960]—*Sisters of the Holy Family*—S.H.F.
[2183]—*Sisters of the Immaculate Heart of Mary, Mother of Christ*
[3270]—*Sisters of the Most Precious Blood* (O'Fallon, MO)—C.PP.S.
[4110]—*Ursuline Nuns*—O.S.U.

NECROLOGY

(No Deaths)

An asterisk (*) denotes an organization that has established tax-exempt status directly with the IRS and is not covered by the USCCB Group Ruling.

Diocese of Arlington

(Dioecesis Arlingtonensis)

Most Reverend

PAUL S. LOVERDE, D.D., S.T.L., J.C.L.

Bishop of Arlington; ordained December 18, 1965; appointed Titular Bishop of Ottabia and Auxiliary Bishop of Hartford February 3, 1988; consecrated April 12, 1988; appointed Bishop of Ogdensburg November 11, 1993; installed as Eleventh Bishop of Ogdensburg January 17, 1994; appointed Bishop of Arlington January 25, 1999; installed as Third Bishop of Arlington March 25, 1999.

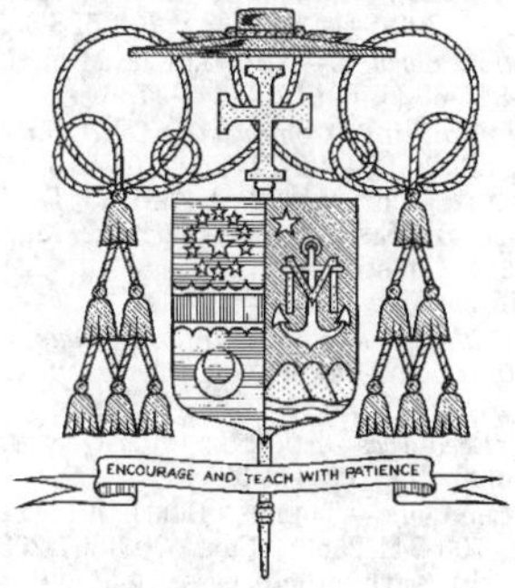

The Chancery: 200 N. Glebe Rd., Ste. 914, Arlington, VA 22203. Tel: 703-841-2500; Fax: 703-524-5028.

ESTABLISHED AUGUST 13, 1974.

Square Miles 6,541.

Comprises the following 21 Counties in Northern Virginia: Arlington, Clarke, Culpeper, Fairfax, Fauquier, Frederick, King George, Lancaster, Loudoun, Madison, Northumberland, Orange, Page, Prince William, Rappahannock, Richmond, Shenandoah, Spotsylvania, Stafford, Warren and Westmoreland and the 7 independent cities of Alexandria, Fairfax City, Falls Church, Fredericksburg, Manassas, Manassas Park and Winchester.

For legal titles of parishes and diocesan institutions, consult the Chancery Office.

STATISTICAL OVERVIEW

Personnel	
Bishop	1
Retired Bishops	1
Abbots	1
Retired Abbots	2
Priests: Diocesan Active in Diocese	129
Priests: Diocesan Active Outside Diocese	8
Priests: Diocesan in Foreign Missions	2
Priests: Retired, Sick or Absent	21
Number of Diocesan Priests	160
Religious Priests in Diocese	62
Total Priests in Diocese	222
Extern Priests in Diocese	28
Ordinations:	
Diocesan Priests	3
Transitional Deacons	3
Permanent Deacons in Diocese	63
Total Brothers	15
Total Sisters	140
Parishes	
Parishes	68
With Resident Pastor:	
Resident Diocesan Priests	57
Resident Religious Priests	11
Missions	6
Professional Ministry Personnel:	
Lay Ministers	141
Welfare	
Specialized Homes	2
Special Centers for Social Services	10
Total Assisted	29,162
Other Institutions	1
Educational	
Diocesan Students in Other Seminaries	37
Total Seminarians	37
Colleges and Universities	4
Total Students	6,122
High Schools, Diocesan and Parish	4
Total Students	3,456
High Schools, Private	2
Total Students	724
Elementary Schools, Diocesan and Parish	38
Total Students	13,025
Elementary Schools, Private	1
Total Students	200
Catechesis/Religious Education:	
High School Students	2,794
Elementary Students	34,659
Total Students under Catholic Instruction	61,017
Teachers in the Diocese:	
Sisters	19
Lay Teachers	803
Vital Statistics	
Receptions into the Church:	
Infant Baptism Totals	6,692
Minor Baptism Totals	910
Adult Baptism Totals	553
Received into Full Communion	1,211
First Communions	8,291
Confirmations	6,373
Marriages:	
Catholic	972
Interfaith	472
Total Marriages	1,444
Deaths	1,630
Total Catholic Population	431,386
Total Population	2,826,999

Former Bishops—Most Revs. THOMAS J. WELSH, D.D., J.C.D., appt. Titular Bishop of Scattery Island and Auxiliary Bishop of Philadelphia on Feb. 18, 1970; cons. April 2, 1970; appt. as 1st Bishop of Arlington on June 4, 1974; installed on Aug. 13, 1974; transferred to the See of Allentown, Feb. 8, 1983; resigned Dec. 16, 1997; appt. Diocesan Administrator; retired Feb. 9, 1998; JOHN R. KEATING, D.D., J.C.D., ord. Dec. 20, 1958; appt. Second Bishop of Arlington on June 7, 1983; cons. and installed on Aug. 4, 1983; died March 22, 1998.

The Chancery

The Chancery—200 N. Glebe Rd., Ste. 914, Arlington, 22203. Tel: 703-841-2500; Fax: 703-524-5028. Office Hours: Mon.-Fri. 8:30-4:30; Address all official business to this office.

Bishop—Most Rev. PAUL S. LOVERDE, D.D., S.T.L., J.C.L., 200 N. Glebe Rd., Ste. 914, Arlington, 22203. Tel: 703-841-2511.

Secretary to the Bishop—Bro. DAVID S. EDDY, C.F.X., 200 N. Glebe Rd., Ste. 914, Arlington, 22203. Tel: 703-841-2511; Fax: 703-524-5028.

Vicar General for Administration and Moderator of the Curia—Rev. MARK S. MEALEY, O.S.F.S., J.C.D., Ph.D., V.G., J.V., 200 N. Glebe Rd., Ste. 914, Arlington, 22203. Tel: 703-841-2563; Fax: 703-524-5028.

Vicar General for Pastoral Services—Rev. FRANK J. READY, V.G., 200 N. Glebe Rd., Ste. 901, Arlington, 22203. Tel: 703-841-3857; Fax: 703-841-8472.

Chancellor and General Counsel—MARK E. HERRMANN, Esq., 200 N. Glebe Rd., Ste. 914, Arlington, 22203. Tel: 703-841-2524; Fax: 703-524-5028.

Episcopal Vicar for Faith Formation and Director of the Diaconate Formation Program—Rev. THOMAS P. FERGUSON, J.C.L., 200 N. Glebe Rd., Ste. 914, Arlington, 22203. Tel: 703-841-2563; Fax: 703-524-5028.

Bishop's Delegate for Clergy—Rev. JOHN C. CREGAN, V.F., 200 N. Glebe Rd., Ste. 901, Arlington, 22203. Tel: 703-841-3809; Fax: 703-841-8472.

Diocesan Finance Officer—TIMOTHY R. COTNOIR, CPA, 200 N. Glebe Rd., Ste. 914, Arlington, 22203. Tel: 703-841-2543; Fax: 703-524-5028.

Finance & Accounting Office—ANN DEPUE, CPA, Controller. Tel: 703-841-3813; Fax: 703-524-5028; JOEL GORZA, Asst. Controller, 200 N. Glebe Rd., Ste. 914, Arlington, 22203. Tel: 703-841-3842; Fax: 703-524-5028.

Director of Diocesan Charities—STEPHEN LUTERAN, M.S.W., L.C.S.W., 200 N. Glebe Rd., Ste. 506, Arlington, 22203. Tel: 703-841-3835; Fax: 703-841-3840.

Deans—Revs. ROBERT J. RIPPY, J.C.L., V.F.; JOHN C. CREGAN, V.F.; WILLIAM P. SAUNDERS, Ed.D., V.F.; LEO J. ZONNEVELD, C.I.C.M., V.F., Ph.D.; ROBERT C. CILINSKI, V.F.; JOHN D. KELLY, V.F.

Vicar for Religious—Rev. FRANK J. READY, V.G. Tel: 703-841-3857; Fax: 703-841-8472.

The Tribunal

The Tribunal—200 N. Glebe Rd., Ste. 524, Arlington, 22203. Tel: 703-841-2555; Fax: 703-841-0693.

Judicial Vicar—Rev. MARK S. MEALEY, O.S.F.S., J.C.D., Ph.D., V.G., J.V. Tel: 703-841-2563; Fax: 703-841-0693.

Adjutant Judicial Vicar—Rev. LEE R. ROOS, J.C.L. Tel: 703-841-2563; Fax: 703-841-0693.

Diocesan Judges—Revs. PAUL F. DELADURANTAYE, S.T.D.; THOMAS P. FERGUSON, J.C.L.; Mrs. TARA A. MCINTOSH, J.C.L.; Revs. MARK S. MEALEY, O.S.F.S., J.C.D., Ph.D., V.G., J.V.; LEE R. ROOS, J.C.L.; WILLIAM J. RUHL, O.S.F.S., S.T.D.; DAVID A. WHITESTONE, J.C.L.

Defenders of the Bond—Revs. ROBERT E. AVELLA; PAUL A. BERGHOUT; Deacons CHARLES A. COUTU; WILLIAM J. DONOVAN, J.C.L.; Revs. THOMAS J. LEHNING, S.T.L., Ph.D.; JAMES G. MERCER; JOHN P. MOSIMANN; RICHARD A. MULLINS; DONALD J. PLANTY, J.C.D.; GREGORY S. THOMPSON; MATTHEW H. ZUBERBUELER.

Promoter of Justice—VACANT.

Auditor—Mrs. JOYCE M. KIDD MACDONALD, J.C.L.

Advocates—Revs. BRIAN G. BASHISTA; RONALD J. GRIPSHOVER JR.; DANIEL F. HANLEY; JAMES M. POUMADE; JAMIE R. WORKMAN.

Advocate & Procurator—Rev. SYMPHORIEN LOPOKE-OHAMAMBOYA, J.C.L.

Notaries—Revs. RAMON A. BAEZ; PHILLIP M. COZZI; KEVIN J. FIMIAN; PAUL M. GRANKAUSKAS; ANDREW J. HEINTZ; EDWARD R. HORKAN; ANTHONY J. KILLIAN; WILSON I. KORPI; BJORN C. LUNDBERG; MARK MULLANEY; CHARLES C. SMITH; DIEM JOSEPH QUANG VU; AUGUSTINE MINH HAI TRAN; CHRISTOPHER T. VACCARO.

Diocesan Offices

Diocesan Offices— Unless otherwise noted, all offices are located at: *200 N. Glebe Rd., Arlington, 22203.*

Accounting Office—MONICA GRIFFIN, Accounting Dir., Ste. 600. Tel: 703-841-2756.

Archives—MARK E. HERRMANN, Esq., Ste. 914. Tel: 703-841-2524.

Arlington Catholic Herald, Inc.—MICHAEL F. FLACH, Editor & Gen. Mgr.; ANN AUGHERTON, Mng. Editor, Ste. 600. Tel: 703-841-2590; Fax: 703-524-2782. Web: www.catholicherald.com.

Bishop's Lenten Appeal—ROBERT P. MUELLER, Prog. Dir., Ste. 811. Tel: 703-841-2545; Fax: 703-528-3057; JUANITA PADGETT, Pledge Coord., Ste. 811. Tel: 703-841-2570; Fax: 703-528-3057.

Campus Ministry—Rev. PETER W. NASSETTA, Y.A., Bishop's Liaison, 4515 Roberts Rd., Fairfax, 22032. Tel: 703-425-0022.

*Catholic Charities of the Diocese of Arlington—Ste. 506*Web: www.ccda.net. STEPHEN LUTERAN, M.S.W., L.C.S.W., Exec. Dir. Tel: 703-841-3835; Fax: 703-841-3840; J. MICHAEL LANIGAN, Assoc. Dir. Finance & Admin. Tel: 703-841-2542.

Catholic Charities Fredericksburg Office—305 Hanson Ave., Ste. 180, Fredericksburg, 22401. Tel: 540-371-1124.

Western Regional Office—100 Dry Mill Rd., Unit 102, Leesburg, 20175. Tel: 703-443-2481.

Parish Based Catholic Charities Loudoun Office—At Christ the Redeemer Parish, 46833 Harry Byrd Hwy., Sterling, 20164. Tel: 703-421-2317.

Parish Based Catholic Charities Prince William Office—All Saints Church, 9300 Stonewall Rd., Manassas, 20110. Tel: 703-368-4500.

Children's Services—TERESA MCDONOUGH, M.S.W., L.C.S.W., Prog. Dir., 5294 Lyngate Ct., Burke, 22015. Tel: 703-425-0100.

Christ House Emergency Shelter—131 S. West St., Alexandria, 22314. Tel: 703-549-8644.

Catholic Charities Communications—JEANNE SPAETH, Coord. Tel: 703-841-3833.

Elderly Services—CAROL AUGUSTINE, M.A., Prog. Dir., St. Martin de Porres Senior Center, 4650 Taney Ave., Alexandria, 22304. Tel: 703-751-2766.

Emergency Assistance—131 S. West St., Alexandria, 22314. Tel: 703-548-4227.

Family Services—DAVID CAVANAUGH, M.S.W., L.C.S.W., Prog. Dir., 3838 Cathedral Ln., Arlington, 22203. Tel: 703-841-2531.

Hogar Hispano-Legal Assistance to Immigrants—JOHN ODENWELDER, M.B.A., Prog. Dir., 6201 Leesburg Pike, Ste. 307, Falls Church, 22044. Tel: 703-534-9805.

Parish Social Ministry—SALLY O'DWYER, Prog. Dir. Tel: 703-841-3831.

Prison Ministry—Sr. CONSTANCIA V. PARCASIO, S.N.D.S., Prog. Dir. Tel: 703-841-3832.

Saint Margaret of Cortona Transitional Residences—CHRISTINE NEIJSTROM, Prog. Dir., 1423 G St., Apt. K, Woodbridge, 22191. Tel: 703-910-4845.

Services for Disabled Persons/Car Ministry—HARRY BURKE, Prog. Dir., 3838 Cathedral Ln., Arlington, 22203. Tel: 703-841-2531.

Volunteer Coordinator—SALLY O'DWYER, Assoc. Dir. Community Svc. Tel: 703-841-3838.

Catholic Education, Office of Catechetics—Rev. PAUL F. DELADURANTAYE, S.T.D., Sec. Relg. Educ. & The Liturgy, Ste. 503. Tel: 703-841-2554; Fax: 703-524-8670; Mrs. PROVIE RYDSTROM, Coord. Pastoral Ministry for the Hearing Impaired. Tel: 703-978-7997 (V-TTD); Mrs. NADINE HALLUMS, Dir., Spec. Rel. Educ. (SPRED). Tel: 703-569-2428.

Office of Catholic Schools—Sisters BERNADETTE MCMANIGAL, B.V.M., Supt. of Schools, Ste. 503. Tel: 703-841-2519; Fax: 703-524-8670; KARL ANN HOMBERG, S.S.J., Asst. Supt. for Elementary Educ.; ELIZABETH ROACH, Asst. Supt. for Instruction and Personnel; DANIEL FERRIS, Asst. Supt. for Educational Progs.; DIANE ELLIOTT, M.Ed., Special Svcs. Coord.; ROBERT QUARTUCCIO, CPA, School Finance Officer.

Child Protection and Safety—Rev. TERRY W. SPECHT, Dir., Ste. 914. Tel: 703-841-3847.

Communications Office—JOELLE SANTOLLA, Dir., Ste. 914. Tel: 703-841-2517; Fax: 703-524-5028. Email: communications@arlingtondiocese.org.

Development Office—ROBERT P. MUELLER, Dir., Ste. 811. Tel: 703-841-2545; Fax: 703-528-3057.

Information Services—KIMBERLY T. MURPHY, Dir. Tel: 703-841-3825; Fax: 703-841-4786.

Office of Planning, Construction and Facilities—Ste. 704. Tel: 703-841-2572; Fax: 703-276-9486. J. REID HERLIHY, Dir.; MARK ANTHONY, Dir. Planning; PETER B. FISHER, Construction Mgr.; FRANCIS PAREK, Construction Mgr.; JOHN AMARANTIDES, Facilities Mgr.

Ecumenical and Interreligious Affairs Commission—Rev. DONALD J. ROONEY, Chm. Tel: 540-373-6491.

Human Resources—EUGENE F. RITZENTHALER, Dir., Ste. 600. Tel: 703-841-3854.

Family Life Office—THERESE BERMPOHL, Dir., Ste. 523. Tel: 703-841-2550; Fax: 703-807-2032. Email: familylife@arlingtondiocese.org.

Gabriel Project-Pregnancy Assistance Program—SARAH LAPIERRE, Prog. Dir., Ste. 814. Tel: 703-841-3812; ANA DELEON, Prog. Coord. Tel: 703-841-3810.

Marriage Preparation & Enrichment— Conferences for the Engaged TOM O'NEILL. Tel: 703-841-3807.

Natural Family Planning—Tel: 703-841-2550.

Project Rachel Post-Abortion Outreach—SARAH LAPIERRE, Prog. Dir. Tel: 703-841-2504; 888-456-4673 (24 hrs.). Email: projectrachel@arlingtondiocese.org; JO BALSAMO, Prog. Coord. Tel: 703-841-2504.

Respect Life/Pro-Life Activities—Sr. CLARE HUNTER, F.S.E., Prog. Dir. Tel: 703-841-2550. Email: respectlife@arlingtondiocese.org.

Young Adult Ministry—KATERI SCHMIDT, Prog. Dir. Tel: 703-841-2549. Email: yam@arlingtondiocese.org.

Liturgy, Office of Sacred—Rev. PAUL F. DELADURANTAYE, S.T.D., Sec. for the Liturgy, Ste. 503. Tel: 703-841-2554; RICHARD GIBALA, Diocesan Music Coord. Tel: 703-524-2815.

Permanent Diaconate—Rev. JOHN C. CREGAN, V.F., Ste. 901. Tel: 703-841-3809; Fax: 703-841-8472.

Diaconal Formation Program—Revs. THOMAS P. FERGUSON, J.C.L., Dir. Tel: 703-841-2563; FRANK J. READY, V.G., Coord. Spiritual Formation. Tel: 703-841-3857.

Propagation of the Faith—Rev. PATRICK L. POSEY, Dir. Tel: 703-532-8815.

Spanish Apostolate—Rev. JOSE EUGENIO HOYOS, Dir.; IVONNE GRANADOS, Prog. Coord., Ste. 820. Tel: 703-841-3882.

Office of Migration and Refugee Services—SEYOUM BERHE, Dir., 80 N. Glebe Rd., Arlington, 22203. Tel: 703-524-2154; Fax: 703-524-2741.

Risk Management, Office of—GRETCHEN KRIEBEL, Dir., Ste. 600. Tel: 703-841-2503; Fax: 703-841-4786.

Victim Assistance Coordinators—PATRICIA MUDD, M.S.W., A.C.S.W. Tel: 703-841-2530; KATHRYN KRAMER, M.A., M.S.W., L.C.S.W., 200 N. Glebe Rd., Ste. 914, Arlington, 22203. Tel: 703-841-2759.

Vocations, Office of—Revs. BRIAN G. BASHISTA, Dir. & Promoter of Vocations; ANDREW J. FISHER, Coord. Hispanic Men Vocations; Sr. ELOINA ALVAREZ, P.S.S.J., Coord. Hispanic Women Vocations, Ste. 901. Tel: 703-841-2514; Fax: 703-841-8472.

Youth Ministry, Office of—KEVIN BOHLI, Dir., Ste. 519. Tel: 703-841-2559; Fax: 703-807-2032.

Catholic Scouting Information—Rev. EDWARD R. HORKAN, Chap., Ste. 519. Tel: 703-841-2559; Fax: 703-807-2032.

Scouting & Camp Fire, Diocesan Committee on—PATRICK BERNEY, Chm., 1701 Gelding Lane, Vienna, 22182. Tel: 730-255-2445. Email: pmberney@hotmail.com.

Consultative Bodies

Clergy Personnel Board—Rev. JOHN C. CREGAN, V.F., 200 N. Glebe Rd., Ste. 901, Arlington, 22203. Tel: 703-841-3809; Fax: 703-841-8472.

Diaconal Council—Deacons THOMAS M. BELLO, Chm. Tel: 703-448-9677; NICHOLAS LADUCA, Vice Chm. Tel: 703-323-4608.

Diocesan Consultors—Revs. ROBERT C. CILINSKI, V.F.; MARK S. MEALEY, O.S.F.S., J.C.D., Ph.D., V.G., J.V.; FRANK J. READY, V.G.; ROBERT J. RIPPY, J.C.L., V.F.; WILLIAM P. SAUNDERS, Ed.D., V.F.; DAVID P. MENG; JOHN P. MOSIMANN; TERRY W. SPECHT; DAVID A. WHITESTONE, J.C.L.

Diocesan Finance Council—Most Rev. PAUL S. LOVERDE, D.D., S.T.L., J.C.L., Chm. Tel: 703-841-2511; TIMOTHY R. COTNOIR, CPA, Diocesan Finance Officer. Tel: 703-841-2543.

Diocesan School Board—MAUREEN BLAKE, Chm. Tel: 703-494-3879.

Presbyteral Council—Most Rev. PAUL S. LOVERDE, D.D., S.T.L., J.C.L., Pres.; Rev. PHILLIP M. COZZI, Recording Sec.

Sisters' Council—Sr. CECILIA DWYER, O.S.B., Pres. Tel: 703-361-0106.

CLERGY, PARISHES, MISSIONS AND PAROCHIAL SCHOOLS

COUNTY OF ARLINGTON

1—CATHEDRAL OF ST. THOMAS MORE (1938) Revs. Robert J. Rippy; Jamie R. Workman; Deacons Jason Weber; Samuel M. Taub, (Retired); Claudio F. Benedi, (Retired). In Res., Revs. Paul F. deLadurantaye; Paul A. Berghout.
Res.: 3901 Cathedral Ln., 22203. Tel: 703-525-1300; 703-525-0450; Fax: 703-528-5760. Web: www.cathedralstm.org.
School—(Grades PreK-8), 105 N. Thomas St., 22203. Tel: 703-528-6781; Fax: 703-528-5048. Email: stmoffice@stmschool.org. Web: www.stmschool.org. Ms. Eleanor S. McCormack, Prin. Lay Teachers 25; Students 331.
Catechesis/Religious Program—Tel: 703-528-7104. Luke Swantek, D.R.E. Students 94.

2—ST. AGNES (1936) Revs. Lee R. Roos; Carroll L. Oubre. In Res., Revs. Frank J. Ready; Cedric M. Wilson, O.S.A.
Res. & Office: 1910 N. Randolph St., 22207. Tel: 703-525-1166; Fax: 703-243-2840. Email: parishoffice.stagnes@verizon.net. Web: www.saintagnes.org.
School—(Grades PreK-8), 2024 N. Randolph St., 22207. Tel: 703-527-5423; Fax: 703-527-6325. Kristine Carr, Prin. Lay Teachers 28; Students 360.
Catechesis/Religious Program—Tel: 703-527-1129. Email: re.stagnes@verizon.net. Bernadette Michael, D.R.E. Students 292.

3—ST. ANN (1947) Revs. Donald C. Greenhalgh; Paul M. Grankauskas; Deacon William J. Donovan.
Res.: 5300 10th St. N., 22205. Tel: 703-528-6276; Fax: 703-522-4758.
School—(Grades PreK-8), 980 N. Frederick St., 22205. Tel: 703-525-7599; Fax: 703-525-2687. Ms. Mary E. Therrell, Prin.; Mary Herrington, Librarian. Lay Teachers 16; Students 186.
Catechesis/Religious Program—Tel: 703-528-6199. Students 389.

4—ST. CHARLES BORROMEO (1909) Revs. Gerard Creedon; John T. O'Hara. In Res., Rev. Clement Aapengnuo.
Res.: 3304 N. Washington Blvd., 22201. Tel: 703-527-5500; Fax: 703-527-5505. Email: parishoffice@stcharleschurch.org. Web: www.stcharleschurch.org.
School—(Grades PreK-8), 3299 N. Fairfax Dr., 22201. Tel: 703-527-0608; Fax: 703-526-0262. Email: office@stcharles.k12.va.us. Web: www.stcharles.k12.va.us. Mrs. Linda Lacot, Prin. Sisters of St. Benedict 1; Lay Teachers 14; Students 200.
Catechesis/Religious Program—Tel: 703-527-5500, Ext. 19. Mrs. Anne Marie Kaufman, D.R.E. Students 575.
Convent—Benedictine Sisters of Virginia, 3299 N. Fairfax Dr., 22201. Tel: 703-527-1026; Fax: 703-526-0262.

5—HOLY MARTYRS OF VIETNAM (1979), (Vietnamese), Revs. John Baptist Vuong Duc Nguyen, O.P.; Thich Ngo, O.P.; Luan Pho, O.P.; Deacon Michael Kien Minh Pham, D.R.E.
Res.: 915 S. Wakefield St., 22204. Tel: 703-553-0370; Fax: 703-553-0371. Email: cttdarlington@yahoo.com. Web: www.cttdva.net.
Catechesis/Religious Program—Tel: 703-471-0137. Students 483.

6—OUR LADY OF LOURDES (1946) Revs. Robert E. Avella; Richard J. Ley. In Res., Revs. Brian G. Bashista; Joseph J. Loftus (Retired).
Res.: 830 S. 23rd St., 22202. Tel: 703-684-9261; 703-684-9211; Fax: 703-684-6342. Email: olol@comcast.net. Web: www.ololcc.net.
Catechesis/Religious Program—Marian Hartzell, D.R.E. Students 68.

7—OUR LADY, QUEEN OF PEACE (1945) Revs. Timothy J. Hickey, C.S.Sp.; Thomas P. Tunney, C.S.Sp., Parochial Vicar; Deacon Eugene D. Betit. In Res., Rev. Robert J. Richter.
Res.: 2700 S. 19th St., 22204. Tel: 703-979-5580; Fax: 703-979-5590. Email: office@ourladyqueenofpeace.org. Web: ourladyqueenofpeace.org.
Catechesis/Religious Program—Email: kremedios@ourladyqueenofpeace.org. Kathleen Remedios, D.R.E. Students 223.

OUTSIDE THE COUNTY OF ARLINGTON

ALEXANDRIA, ALEXANDRIA CO.

1—BLESSED SACRAMENT (1946) Revs. John C. Cregan; Anthony J. Killian; Terry A. Cramer.
1427 W. Braddock Rd., 22302. In Res., Rev. Msgr. Frank E. Mahler (Retired).
Res.: 1407 W. Braddock Rd., 22302. Tel: 703-998-6100. Web: www.blessedsacramentcc.org.
School—(Grades PreK-8), 1417 W. Braddock Rd., 22302. Tel: 703-998-4170; Fax: 703-998-5033. Mrs. Valerie Garcia, Prin.; Sue Knight, Librarian. Lay Teachers 40; Students 326.
Catechesis/Religious Program— Susan Doyle, D.R.E. Students 399.

2—ST. JOSEPH'S (1915) Rev. Francis M. Hull, S.S.J.
Res.: 711 N. Columbus St., 22314. Tel: 703-836-3725; Fax: 703-837-9066.
Catechesis/Religious Program—Tel: 703-924-5448. Mrs. Beverly Anderson, D.R.E. Students 36.

3—ST. MARY'S (1795) [CEM] Revs. Dennis W. Kleinmann; John C. De Celles; Robert L. Ruskamp; Brian W. Belli. In Res., Rev. Jean-Claude Atusameso.
Res.: 310 Duke St., 22314. Tel: 703-836-4100; Fax: 703-549-3605. Web: www.saintmaryparish.net.
School—(Grades PreK-8), 400 Green St., 22314. Tel: 703-549-1646; Fax: 703-519-0840. Web: www.stmarys-alexva.org. Mrs. Janet Cantwell, Prin.; Karen Kelly, Librarian. Lay Teachers 48; Students 713.
Catechesis/Religious Program—Tel: 703-836-5450. Luis Brown, D.R.E. Students 262.

4—ST. RITA (1914) Revs. Denis M. Donahue; Edward R. Horkan. In Res., Rev. Edwin E. Perez.
Res.: 3815 Russell Rd., 22305. Tel: 703-836-1640; Fax: 703-836-7825. Email: saintritarectory@speakeasy.net. Web: www.strita-parish.org.
School—(Grades K-8), 3801 Russell Rd., 22305. Tel: 703-548-1888. Email: saintritaalexandria@worldnet.att.net. Web: www.saintrita-school.org. Mrs. Mary Pat Schlickenmaier, Prin. Sisters of St. Joseph 2; Lay Teachers 13; Students 168.

Catechesis/Religious Program—Tel: 703-836-1356. Betsy Nunn, D.R.E. Students 180.
Convent—Sisters of St. Joseph, 231 W. Glebe Rd., 22305. Tel: 703-683-1929.

ALEXANDRIA, FAIRFAX CO.

1—GOOD SHEPHERD (1965) Rev. Charles C. McCoart; Deacon Thomas G. White, Jr. In Res., Most Rev. Joseph W. Estabrook; Revs. Juan Alvarez; Ricardo Martin Pinillos.
Church & Mailing Address: 8710 Mount Vernon Hwy., 22309. Tel: 703-780-4055; Fax: 703-360-5385. Email: office@gs-cc.org. Web: www.gs-cc.org.
Res.: 3510 Surry Dr., 22309.
Catechesis/Religious Program—Joan Sheppard, D.R.E. Students 1,300.

2—ST. LAWRENCE (Franconia) (1967) Rev. Christopher J. Mould. In Res., Revs. Tomasz Medrek; James G. Mercer.
Res.: 6222 Franconia Rd., 22310. Tel: 703-971-4378; Fax: 703-971-0331. Email: st.lawrence@cox.net. Web: saintlawrenceparish.com.
Catechesis/Religious Program—Tel: 703-971-8541. Miss Mary Ann McGrath, D.R.E. Students 230.

3—ST. LOUIS (1949) Revs. Richard A. Mullins; Mark F. Carrier. In Res., Rev. Idomor Da Mota.
Res.: 2907 Popkins Ln., 22306. Tel: 703-765-4421; Fax: 703-765-1750.
School—(Grades K-8), 2901 Popkins Ln., 22306. Tel: 703-768-7732; Fax: 703-768-3836. Daniel Baillargeon, Prin. Lay Teachers 24; Students 408.
Catechesis/Religious Program— Mrs. Carol Anne Jones, D.R.E. Students 376.

4—QUEEN OF APOSTLES (1963) Revs. Thomas P. Vander Woude; Andrew J. Heintz. In Res., Deacon Richard C. Caporiccio.
Res.: 4329 Sano St., 22312. Tel: 703-354-8711; Fax: 703-354-0766. Web: www.queenofapostles.org.
School—(Grades K-8), 4409 Sano St., 22312. Tel: 703-354-0714; Fax: 703-354-1820. Joanne Yates, Prin. Lay Teachers 16; Students 252.
Catechesis/Religious Program—Marielisa Puigbo, D.R.E. Students 291.

ANNANDALE, FAIRFAX CO.

1—ST. AMBROSE (1966) Revs. Andrew J. Fisher; John Edwin Thayer Tewes. In Res., Rev. Charles W. Merkle III.
Church & Office Mailing Address: 3901 Woodburn Rd., 22003. Tel: 703-280-4400; Fax: 703-280-1123. Email: information@stambroseva.org. Web: www.stambroseannandale.org.
Res.: 3825 Woodburn Rd., 22003. Tel: 703-280-4400; Fax: 703-280-1123.
School—(Grades K-8), 3827 Woodburn Rd., 22003. Tel: 703-698-7171; Fax: 703-698-7170. Web: stambroseschool.org. Barbara Dalmut, Prin. Lay Teachers 15; Students 210.
Catechesis/Religious Program—Tel: 703-280-1122; Fax: 703-280-1123. Email: dre@stambroseannandale.org. Sr. Cecilia Thuy Nguyen, C.C.S.S., D.R.E. & Dir. Youth Activities. Students 262.

2—HOLY SPIRIT (1964) Revs. Terry W. Specht; Joseph R. Kenna, Parochial Vicar; Christopher T. Vaccaro, Parochial Vicar.
Mailing Address: 5121 Woodland Way, 22003. Email: holyspiritparish@cox.net. Web: www.holyspiritchurch.us.
School—(Grades PreK-8), 8800 Braddock Rd., 22003. Tel: 703-978-7117; Fax: 703-978-7438. Mrs. Sarah L. Schmitt, Prin. (Extended Day Care available) Lay Teachers 27; Students 366.
Catechesis/Religious Program—Tel: 703-978-8925. Email: religious.ed@holyspiritchurch.us. Ms. Ana Lisa Pinon, D.R.E.; Gerard-Marie Anthony, Asst. D.R.E.; Ryan Stohlman, Asst. D.R.E. Students 603.

3—ST. MICHAEL (1953) Revs. Jerry Pokorsky; John T.B. Trong; Kevin J. Beres; Deacons David S. McCaffrey; Roger T. Ostrom. In Res., Rev. Joseph J. Clark.
Res.: 7401 St. Michael's Ln., 22003. Tel: 703-256-7822; Fax: 703-256-7122. Web: www.stmikes22003.org.
School—(Grades K-8) Tel: 703-256-1222; Fax: 703-941-9474. Web: www.stmikes22003.org. Sr. Therese Elizabeth Bauer, Prin. Sisters (Servants of the Immaculate Heart of Mary) 5; Lay Teachers 15; Students 228.
Catechesis/Religious Program—Tel: 703-941-9403. Email: dre@stmikes22003.org. Deacon David S. McCaffrey, D.R.E. Students 150.
Convent—Sisters, Servants of the Immaculate Heart of Mary, 7421 St. Michael's Ln., 22003. Tel: 703-256-2130.

ASHBURN, LOUDOUN CO., ST. THERESA (1991) Revs. Richard M. Guest; Daniel S. Spychala.
Mailing Address: P.O. Box 526, 20146-0526. Tel: 703-729-2287; Fax: 703-729-9036. Email: office@sttheresa-ashburn.com. Web: www.sttheresa-ashburn.com.
Rectory—43367 Icepond Dr., 20147.
Church: 21371 St. Theresa Ln., 20147.
School—(Grades K-8) Tel: 703-729-3577; Fax: 703-729-8068. Web: sttheresa-ashburn.com. Carol Krichbaum, Prin.; Mrs. Kit McKeon, Librarian. Lay Teachers 28; Students 463.
Catechesis/Religious Program—Tel: 703-729-3714; Fax: 703-729-9036. Email: reoffice@sttheresa-ashburn.org. Students 1,800.

BURKE, FAIRFAX CO., CHURCH OF THE NATIVITY (W. Springfield) (1973) Revs. Richard B. Martin; J. Kevin O'Keefe.
Mailing Address: 6400 Nativity Ln., 22015. Tel: 703-455-2400; Fax: 703-455-6832.
Res.: 9523 Lyra Ct., 22015. Tel: 703-913-2306. Web: www.nativityburke.org.
School—(Grades PreK-8), 6398 Nativity Ln., 22015. Tel: 703-455-2300; Fax: 703-569-8109. Web: www.nativityschool.org. Miss Maria E. Kelly, Prin. Lay Teachers 18; Students 312.
Catechesis/Religious Program—Tel: 703-455-0372. Sisters Donatella Merulla, A.R., D.R.E.; Mary Attilia Todaro, A.R., D.R.E. Students 1,260.
Convent—Handmaids of Reparation of the Sacred Heart of Jesus, 6300 Capella Ave., 22015. Tel: 703-455-4180.

CHANTILLY, FAIRFAX CO.

1—ST. TIMOTHY (1969) Revs. Gerald Weymes; William M. Aitcheson; Stephen J. Schultz, Parochial Vicar; Deacon David E. Conroy. In Res., Rev. Anthony J. Pinizzotto, O.S.F.S.
Res.: 13807 Poplar Tree Rd., 20151. Tel: 703-378-7461; 703-378-7646; Fax: 703-378-7552. Web: www.sttimothyparish.org.
School—(Grades K-8), 13809 Poplar Tree Rd., 20151. Tel: 703-378-6932; Fax: 703-378-1273. Patricia Kobyra, Prin. Sisters 1; Lay Teachers 32; Students 565.
Catechesis/Religious Program—Tel: 703-378-9143; Fax: 703-378-7552. Maria Ho, D.R.E. Students 1,009.

2—ST. VERONICA (1999) Revs. Edward C. Hathaway; Stephen Holmes.
3460 Centreville Rd., 20151. Tel: 703-773-2000; Fax: 703-773-2001. Email: info@stveronica.net. Web: www.stveronica.net.
School—(Grades K-8), 3460B Centreville Rd., 20151. Tel: 703-773-2020; Fax: 703-773-2021. Web: www.stveronicaschool.org. Mary Baldwin, Prin. Students 348; Lay Staff 45.
Catechesis/Religious Program—Michael Sirotniak, D.R.E. Students 520.

CLIFTON, FAIRFAX CO.

1—ST. ANDREW THE APOSTLE (1989) Revs. John D. Kelly; Mark Mullaney, Parochial Vicar.
Res.: 6720 Union Mill Rd., 20124. Tel: 703-817-1770; Fax: 703-817-0928.
School—(Grades PreK-8) Tel: 703-817-1774; Fax: 703-817-1721. Glenda Sigg, Prin. Lay Teachers 15; Students 245.
Catechesis/Religious Program—Tel: 703-817-1773. Mrs. Delores Nelson, D.R.E. Students 875.

2—ST. CLARE OF ASSISI (1981) Rev. Thomas J. Lehning.
Church & Rectory: 12409 Henderson Rd., 20124. Tel: 703-266-1310; 703-266-7293; Fax: 703-266-7011. Email: stclareva@cox.net. Web: www.stclareclifton.org.
Catechesis/Religious Program—Peggy Mattei, D.R.E. Students 68.

COLONIAL BEACH, WESTMORELAND CO., ST. ELIZABETH OF HUNGARY (1906) [JC] Revs. John A. Ziegler; Francis M. de Rosa.
Res.: 21 Irving Ave., 22443. Tel: 804-224-7221; Fax: 804-224-3137.
Catechesis/Religious Program—Sally Cullin, D.R.E. Students 114.
Mission—St. Anthony's [CEM] 11 Irving Ave., Westmoreland Co. 22443.

CULPEPER, CULPEPER CO., PRECIOUS BLOOD (1880) [CEM] Rev. Leo J. Zonneveld, C.I.C.M.; Deacon Ramon Tirado.
Res.: 114 E. Edmondson St., 22701. Tel: 540-825-8945; Fax: 540-825-8987.
Catechesis/Religious Program—Tel: 540-825-1339. Ms. Patricia Reed, D.R.E. Students 387.

DALE CITY, PRINCE WILLIAM CO., HOLY FAMILY (1970) Revs. Donald J. Planty; Stephen F. McGraw; Deacons Vincent Einsmann; Richard L. Demers. In Res., Rev. Matthew H. Zuberbueler.
Res.: 14160 Ferndale Rd., 22193. Tel: 703-670-8161; Fax: 703-670-8323. Email: parishoffice@holyfamilydalecity.org. Web: www.holyfamilycatholicchurchdalecity.org.
School—(Grades PreK-8) Tel: 703-670-3138. Web: www.holyfamilyinfolink.com. Joseph M. McLaughlin, Prin. Email: principal@hfccdc.com; Judi Peacott, Dir. (PreK); Jacqueline Manaspal, Librarian. Lay Teachers 22; Students 245.
Catechesis/Religious Program—Tel: 703-670-8161, Ext. 230. Reyes Ruiz, D.R.E. Students 832.

FAIRFAX, FAIRFAX CO.

1—ST. MARY OF SORROWS (1858) [CEM] Revs. James S. Barkett; Stefan P. Starzynski. In Res., Rev. Cyprien Ephrem Houndje, O.P.
Mailing & Parish Center Address: 5222 Sideburn Rd., 22032-2640. Tel: 703-978-4141; Fax: 703-978-2568. Web: stmaryofsorrows.org. Email: kathyc@stmaryofsorrows.org.
Historic Church—5612 Ox Rd., Fairfax Station, 22039.
Res.: 11112 Fairfax Station Rd., Fairfax Station, 22039.
Catechesis/Religious Program— Margaret Telesca, D.R.E., (PreK-8); Brian Kissinger, Youth Min. Students 848.

2—ST. PAUL CHUNG (1986), (Korean), Revs. Peter Hoin Kwak; Dominic Hyi Jeong Yang; Deacon Paul Lee.
Res.: 4708 Rippling Pond Dr., 22033-5077. Tel: 703-818-9707; Fax: 703-968-3013. Email: sthasang@earthlink.net. Web: www.stpaulchung.org.
Church & Mailing Address: 4712 Rippling Pond Dr., 22033-5077. Tel: 703-968-3010.
Catechesis/Religious Program—Students 520.

FAIRFAX CITY, FAIRFAX CO., ST. LEO'S (1957) Revs. David A. Whitestone; Ramon A. Baez; Deacons Nicholas LaDuca; Noel Vivaldi. In Res., Rev. J.D. Jaffe.
Res.: 3700 Old Lee Hwy., 22030. Tel: 703-273-5369; Fax: 703-273-2371.
School—(Grades PreK-8), 3704 Old Lee Hwy., 22030. Tel: 703-273-1211; Fax: 703-273-6913. Mr. David DiPippa, Prin.; Cynthia Washington, Asst. Prin. Lay Teachers 30; Students 521.
Catechesis/Religious Program—Tel: 703-273-4868; Fax: 703-273-0994. Lee Cena, D.R.E.; Erik Teter, Asst. Youth Min. Tel: 703-591-6089; Nina Deboeck, Youth Min. Students 742.
Station—Fairfax Nursing Home, Tel: 703-273-7705.
Station—Commonwealth Care Center 22030. Tel: 703-934-5060.
Station—The Gardens at Fair Oaks 22030. Tel: 703-278-1001.
Station—Sunrise Assisted Living at George Mason 22030. Tel: 703-934-5069.

FALLS CHURCH, FAIRFAX CO.

1—ST. ANTHONY'S (1952) Rev. Horace H. Grinnell; Deacon Mario Mendoza. In Res., Revs. Jean Vanes Nicolas; Jorge Acho; Augustine Owusu-Sekyere.
Res.: 3305 Glen Carlyn Rd., 22041. Tel: 703-820-7111; Fax: 703-379-9195.
Catechesis/Religious Program—Tel: 703-820-2158. Lia Salinas, D.R.E. Students 776.

2—ST. JAMES (1892) [CEM] Revs. Patrick L. Posey; Daniel F. Hanley; Philip S. Majka; Deacons James A. Fishenden; Thomas M. Bello. In Res., Revs. James C. Hudgins; Symphorien Lopoke; Joseph Elamparayil, O.C.D.
Res.: 905 Park Ave., 22046. Tel: 703-532-8815; Fax: 703-533-7644. Email: rectory@stjamescatholic.org; sjcc@stjamescatholic.org. Web: www.stjamescatholic.org.
School—(Grades K-8), 830 W. Broad St., 22046. Tel: 703-533-1182, Ext. 100; Fax: 703-532-8316. Email: mainoffice@saintjamesschool.org. Sr. Nancy J. Kindelan, I.H.M., Prin. Sisters (Servants of the Immaculate Heart of Mary) 5; Lay Teachers 40; Students 598.
Catechesis/Religious Program—Sr. Joyce Carolyn Bell, I.H.M., D.R.E. Students 364.
Convent—Sisters, Servants of the Immaculate Heart of Mary, 101 N. Spring St., 22046. Tel: 703-532-2388.

3—ST. PHILIP (1963) Revs. Kevin B. Walsh; Joseph Q. Vu. In Res., Revs. Jose Eugenio Hoyos; Alex Diaz Amaya.
Res.: 7500 St. Philip's Ct., 22042. Tel: 703-573-3808; Fax: 703-560-2832. Email: stphilipparish@gmail.com. Web: www.stphilipsparish.com.
Convent—7504 St. Philip's Ct., 22042. Tel: 703-204-0837. Sisters 5.
Catechesis/Religious Program—Tel: 703-573-1899. Students 345.

FREDERICKSBURG, FREDERICKSBURG CO.

1—ST. JUDE (2003) Rev. David L. Martin. Email: pastoratstjude@verizon.net; Deacon Robert F. Borchert.
Mailing and Office Address: 5610 Southpoint Center Blvd., Ste. 105, 22407.
Church: 10800B Courthouse Rd., 22408. Tel: 540-891-7350; Fax: 540-891-1810. Email: stjudeinpotsy@verizon.net. Web: www.stjudespotsy.org.
Res.: 10101 Chatham Ct., 22408. Tel: 540-710-1060.
Catechesis/Religious Program—Tel: 540-891-1262. Joyce Franklin, D.R.E. Students 248.

2—ST. MARY OF THE IMMACULATE CONCEPTION (1858) Revs. Donald J. Rooney; Bjorn C. Lundberg, Parochial Vicar; Wilson I. Korpi, Parochial Vicar; Deacon Robert A. Lyons.

In Res., Rev. Frederick H. Edlefsen.
Res.: 1009 Stafford Ave., 22401-5418. Tel: 540-373-6491; Fax: 540-371-0251. Email: stmary@stmaryfred.org. Web: www.stmaryfred.org.
Catechesis/Religious Program—Tel: 540-373-7770. Diane K. McFall, D.R.E. Students 933.
Convent—Oblate Sisters of St. Francis de Sales, St. Mary Convent, 1316 Royston St., 22401. Tel: 540-371-1652; Fax: 540-371-1652.

3—ST. PATRICK (1983) Revs. Michael G. Taylor; Ronald J. Gripshover Jr.; Deacons David Conroy; William D. Pivarnik.
Church & Res.: 9149 Elys Ford Rd., 22407. Tel: 540-785-5299; Fax: 540-785-5692. Email: stpatschurch@comcast.net. Web: www.saintpatrickparish.org.
School—(Grades PreK-8), 9151 Ely's Ford Rd., 22407. Tel: 540-786-2277; Fax: 540-785-2213. Email: saintpatrick123@yahoo.com. Web: saintpatrick-school.com. Mr. George Elliott, Prin. Lay Teachers 16; Students 281.
Catechesis/Religious Program—Tel: 540-785-7857; Fax: 540-785-5758. Email: stpatsreligioused@adelphia.net. Philip Camill, D.R.E. Students 439.

FRONT ROYAL, WARREN CO., ST. JOHN THE BAPTIST (1884) Revs. Jerome W. Fasano; Richard T. Carr.
Res.: 123 W. Main St., 22630. Tel: 540-635-3780; Fax: 540-635-2683. Email: stjohns@shentel.net. Web: www.sjtb.org.
Catechesis/Religious Program—Dr. Onalee McGraw, D.R.E. Students 360.

GAINESVILLE, PRINCE WILLIAM CO., HOLY TRINITY (2001) Revs. Francis J. Peffley; Jerry A. Wooton; Deacon Lawrence B. Henry.
Church: 8213 Linton Hall Rd., 20155. Web: www.holytrinityparish.net.
Res.: 13260 McCartney Ct., Bristow, 20136. Tel: 703-753-6700; Fax: 703-753-6286. Web: www.holytrinityparish.net.
Catechesis/Religious Program—Email: ReligiousEd@holytrinityparish.net. Michele Leary, D.R.E. Students 1,470.

GORDONSVILLE, ORANGE CO., ST. MARK'S (1972) Merged with St. John's, Orange to form St. Isidore the Farmer, Orange.

GREAT FALLS, FAIRFAX CO., ST. CATHERINE OF SIENA (1979) Rev. Alexander R. Drummond.
Mailing Address: 1020 Springvale Rd., 22066. Tel: 703-759-4350; Fax: 703-759-3753.
School—Siena Academy, Tel: 703-759-4129. Email: SienaAcademy@cox.net. Laura Bell, Head of School. Students 125.
Catechesis/Religious Program—Tel: 703-759-3530; Fax: 703-759-7941. Anson Groves, D.R.E. Students 155.

HERNDON, FAIRFAX CO., ST. JOSEPH (1950) Revs. James Angert, T.O.R.; Patrick Donahoe, T.O.R., Parochial Vicar; Timothy Harris, T.O.R., Parochial Vicar.
Res.: 750 Peachtree St., 20170. Tel: 703-880-4300; Fax: 703-880-4320. Web: www.sjcherndon.org.
School—(Grades K-8) Tel: 703-880-4350. Mrs. Joan Cargill, Prin.; Mrs. Patty Andres, Librarian. Lay Teachers 29; Students 579.
Catechesis/Religious Program—Students 593.

KILMARNOCK, LANCASTER CO., ST. FRANCIS DE SALES (1966) [CEM 2] Revs. James C. Bruse; John M. O'Donohue.
Res.: 154 E. Church St., P.O. Box 759, 22482-0759. Tel: 804-435-1511; Fax: 804-436-9614. Email: stfrancis@vametrocast.net.
Catechesis/Religious Program—Fax: 804-436-9614. Nancy Weber, D.R.E. Students 67.
Mission—St. Paul P.O. Box 65, Hague, Westmoreland Co. 22469. Tel: 804-472-3090; Fax: 804-423-3092. Email: saintpaul@hughes.net.

LAKE RIDGE, PRINCE WILLIAM CO., ST. ELIZABETH ANN SETON (1976) Revs. David P. Meng; James R. Searby, Parochial Vicar; Deacon Emil P. Myskowski.
Mailing Address: 12805 Valleywood Dr., 22192. Tel: 703-494-4008; Fax: 703-494-1995.
Catechesis/Religious Program—Tel: 703-494-3966; Fax: 703-494-8005. Jackie Ezersky, D.R.E. (Grades K-5); Kathy Lord, D.R.E. (Middle School); Kevin Heider, Youth Min. Students 534.

LEESBURG, LOUDOUN CO., ST. JOHN THE APOSTLE (1926) [CEM] Revs. John P. Mosimann; Augustine Minh Hai Tran.
Mailing Address: 101 Oakcrest Manor Dr., N.E., 20176-2221. Tel: 703-777-1317; Fax: 703-771-9016. Email: church@stjohnleesburg.com. Web: stjohnleesburg.com.
Res.: 302 N. King St., N.E., 20176. Tel: 703-777-6477.
Catechesis/Religious Program—Tel: 703-777-3891. Email: dre@stjohnleesburg.com. Edward V. Spinelli, D.R.E. Students 1,237.

LURAY, PAGE CO., OUR LADY OF THE VALLEY (1954) Rev. Christopher Lemme, T.O.R.
Mailing Address: 200 Collins Ave., 22835. Tel: 540-743-4919; Fax: 540-743-2490.
Catechesis/Religious Program—Mrs. Elizabeth Hutchins, D.R.E. Students 52.

MADISON, MADISON CO., OUR LADY OF THE BLUE RIDGE (1977) Rev. Michael T. Orlowsky.
Res.: 692 Lonnie Burke Rd., 22727. Tel: 540-948-4144; Fax: 540-948-3325.
Catechesis/Religious Program—Students 56.

MANASSAS, PRINCE WILLIAM CO.

1—ALL SAINTS (1929) Revs. Robert C. Cilinski; Matthew J. DeForest, Parochial Vicar; Francisco Mendez de Dios, Parochial Vicar; Gregory S. Thompson, Parochial Vicar; Deacons John W. Eberlein; Richard O'Connell; Edward J. Bresnahan.
Res.: 9300 Stonewall Rd., 20110. Tel: 703-368-4500; Fax: 703-257-9299. Web: www.allsaintsvachurch.org.
School—(Grades PreK-8), 9294 Stonewall Rd., 20110. Tel: 703-368-4400; Fax: 703-393-2157. Web: www.allsaintsschool.org. Mr. David E. Conroy Jr., Prin.; Mrs. Elba Campagna, Asst. Prin. Lay Teachers 27; Students 530.
Catechesis/Religious Program—Tel: 703-393-2142. Samantha Welsh, D.R.E., (Elementary-English); Clarissa Maciel, D.R.E. (Elementary-Spanish); Rob Tessier, Youth Min. (Junior-Senior High School & College). Students 1,290.

2—SACRED HEART (1984) [CEM] Rev. Michael J. Bazan; Deacons Thomas W. Wolter; Gerald J. Moore.
Mailing Address: 12975 Purcell Rd., 20112-3217. Tel: 703-590-0030; Fax: 703-590-0141. In Res., Rev. Jude Onogbosele.
Res.: 6258 Terrapin Dr., 20112. Tel: 703-791-5131.
Catechesis/Religious Program—Tel: 703-590-0256. Kathleen Burr, D.R.E. Students 369.

MCLEAN, FAIRFAX CO.

1—ST. JOHN THE BELOVED (1913) Revs. Paul D. Scalia; James M. Poumade; Deacon Joseph G. Benin. In Res., Revs. Franklyn M. McAfee; Michael T. McClane; James E. Kruse.
Res.: 6420 Linway Ter., 22101. Tel: 703-356-7916; Fax: 703-356-4517.
School—(Grades PreK-8), 6422 Linway Ter., 22101. Tel: 703-356-7554; Fax: 703-448-3811. Web: www-.stjohnacademy.org. Peter Schultz, Headmaster; Barbara Gray, Librarian. Lay Teachers 26; Students 273.
Catechesis/Religious Program—Tel: 703-356-5275. Ms. Laura Pennefather, D.R.E. Students 296.

2—ST. LUKE (1961) Rev. Martin McGuill. In Res., Rev. Thomas P. Ferguson.
Res.: 7001 Georgetown Pike, 22101. Tel: 703-356-1255; Fax: 703-442-0848. Email: parishoffice@saintlukemclean.org. Web: www.saintlukemclean.org.
School—(Grades K-8), 7005 Georgetown Pike, 22101. Tel: 703-356-1508; Fax: 703-356-1141. Web: www.saintlukeschool.com. Renee Quiros White, Prin. Lay Teachers 18; Students 218.
Catechesis/Religious Program—Tel: 703-356-8419; Fax: 703-356-5988. Nancy Griswold, D.R.E. Students 750.

MIDDLEBURG, LOUDOUN CO., ST. STEPHEN THE MARTYR (1975) Rev. William B. Schardt; Deacon Jack M. Ligon.
Mailing Address: 23331 Sam Fred Rd., 20117-3221. Tel: 540-687-6433; Fax: 540-687-5170. Web: www.saint-stephen.org.
Res.: 23309 Sam Fred Rd., 20117.
Church: Intersection of Rtes. 50 & Sam Fred Rd., 20117.
Catechesis/Religious Program—Students 827.
Mission—St. Katharine Drexel Mission 14535 John Marshall Hwy., Ste. 210, Gainesville, Prince William Co. 20155. Tel: 703-754-8444; Fax: 703-754-7443.
Mission—Corpus Christi Mission 15100 Enterprise St., Ste. 300, Chantilly, 20151. Tel: 703-378-1037; Fax: 703-378-4442. Rev. Sean K. Rousseau, Admin.

ORANGE, ORANGE CO.

1—ST. ISIDORE THE FARMER (2002) Rev. Terrence R. Staples.
Res.: 14405 St. Isidore Way, 22960. Tel: 540-672-4933; Fax: 540-661-4204. Email: stisidore@nexet.net.
Church: 14414 St. Isidore Way, 22960-2573.
Catechesis/Religious Program—Tel: 540-854-7526. Mollie McMahon, D.R.E. Students 57.

2—ST. JOHN'S (1946) Merged with St. Mark's, Gordonsville to form St. Isidore the Farmer, Orange.

POTOMAC FALLS, LOUDOUN CO., OUR LADY OF HOPE (2000) Revs. William P. Saunders; Kevin J. Fimian; Deacon William P. Emley.
Res.: 20648 Belwood Ct., 20165. Email: info@ourladyofhope.net. Web: www.ourladyofhope.net.
School—46633 Algonkian Pkwy., 20165. Tel: 703-433-6760; Fax: 703-433-6761. Email: school@ourladyofhope.net. Web: www.school.ourladyofhope.net. Mary Beth Pittman, Prin. Lay Teachers 15; Students 202.
Catechesis/Religious Program—Cathy Plummer, D.R.E. Students 715.

PURCELLVILLE, LOUDOUN CO., ST. FRANCIS DE SALES (1967) Rev. Ronald S. Escalante; Deacon Lawrence V. Hammel. In Res., Revs. Cesar A. Serrano Prada; Gerard Ramotso.
Res.: 37730 St. Francis Ct., 20132. Tel: 540-338-6381; Fax: 540-338-6431. Email: secretary@saintfrancisparish.org. Web: stfrancisdesalescatholicchurch.org.
Catechesis/Religious Program—Tel: 540-338-4497. Melissa Gobs, D.R.E.; Janice Rees, C.R.E. Students 895.

RESTON, FAIRFAX CO.

1—ST. JOHN NEUMANN (1979) Revs. Thomas E. Murphy, O.S.F.S.; William N. Dougherty, O.S.F.S.; Robert Mancini, O.S.F.S. In Res., Rev. William M. Rutledge, O.S.F.S.
Res.: 11900 Lawyers Rd., 20191-4299. Tel: 703-860-8510; Fax: 703-860-2136. Web: www.saintjn.org.
Catechesis/Religious Program—Tel: 703-860-2815. Mrs. Mary Lyons, D.R.E. Students 1,103.

2—ST. THOMAS A BECKET (1970) Rev. Mark E. Moretti.
Res.: 1421 Wiehle Ave., 20190. Tel: 703-437-7113; Fax: 703-689-3814. Web: www.stthomasabecketparish.org.
Catechesis/Religious Program—Tel: 703-689-3816. Betsy Coffey, Coord. of Middle & High School Faith Formation (6-12); Susan Reilly, Coord. of Pre-K-Grade 5 Faith Formation. Students 640.

SPOTSYLVANIA, SPOTSYLVANIA CO., ST. MATTHEW (1999) Revs. John J. Riley; Michael R. Duesterhaus, Parochial Vicar; Deacons Edward F. Whelan Jr.; John A. Hubbarth.
Mailing Address: 8200 Robert E. Lee Dr., 22553. Tel: 540-582-5575; Fax: 540-582-8639.
Catechesis/Religious Program—Tel: 540-582-8469. Joanne Warren, D.R.E. Students 393.

SPRINGFIELD, FAIRFAX CO.

1—ST. BERNADETTE (1959) Revs. Kevin J. Larsen; Marcus A. Pollard; M. Paul Richardson. In Res., Rev. Luis Fernando Franco Henao.
Res.: 7600 Old Keene Mill Rd., 22152-2022. Tel: 703-451-8576; Fax: 703-269-1121. Email: office@stbernpar.org. Web: www.stbernpar.org.
School—(Grades K-8), 7602 Old Keene Mill Rd., 22152-2099. Tel: 703-451-8696. Email: school@stbernschool.org. Web: www.stbernpar.org. Mrs. Patricia Beeks, Prin. Lay Teachers 30; Students 461.
Catechesis/Religious Program—Tel: 703-451-8576, Ext. 36. Email: religioused@stbernpar.org. David Wallace, D.R.E. Students 462.

2—ST. RAYMOND OF PENAFORT (1997) Revs. James R. Gould; Mark A. Pilon; Deacon Charles C. Allen. In Res., Rev. Peter Odhiambo Okola, A.J.
Parish Office & Res.: 8750 Pohick Rd., 22153. Tel: 703-440-0535; Fax: 703-440-0538.
Catechesis/Religious Program—Email: strayccd@aol.com. Maria Ammirati, D.R.E.; Matthew Wheeler, Youth Min.; Jill Wheeler, Youth Min. Students 757.

STAFFORD, STAFFORD CO., ST. WILLIAM OF YORK (1971) Revs. Robert J. DeMartino; Geronimo A. Magat, Parochial Vicar; Deacon Richard P. Smith.
Res. & Mailing Address: 3130 Jefferson Davis Hwy., 22554. Tel: 540-659-1102; Fax: 540-659-5637. Web: www.swoycc.org.
School—(Grades PreK-8) Tel: 540-659-5207; Fax: 540-659-9863. Web: www.stwillschool.org. Sr. Lisa Lorenz, F.M.I.J., Prin. Franciscan Missionary Sisters of the Infant Jesus 3; Lay Teachers 17; Students 227.
Catechesis/Religious Program—Tel: 540-659-5705. Mr. Jim Benisek, D.R.E. Students 706.
Convent—Franciscan Missionary Sisters of the Infant Jesus, 13 Emerson Ct., 22554. Tel: 540-288-0201.

STERLING, LOUDOUN CO., CHRIST THE REDEEMER (1972) Revs. C. Donald Howard, S.A.; William F. Schmidt, S.A.; Arthur M. Johnson, S.A. In Res., Rev. Lino Rico-Rostro (Mexico).
Res.: 12494 Cliff Edge Dr., Herndon, 20170. Tel: 703-430-1686.
Church: 46833 Harry Byrd Hwy., 20164. Tel: 703-430-0811; Fax: 703-430-1590.
Catechesis/Religious Program—Tel: 703-430-0813; Fax: 703-430-1590. Ms. Haresta Greene Williams, D.R.E.; Mr. Jay Cuasay, D.R.E.; Mrs. M. Amelia Silva, D.R.E. Hispanic. Students 965.

TRIANGLE, PRINCE WILLIAM CO., ST. FRANCIS OF ASSISI (1957) Revs. Charles J. Miller, O.F.M.; Robert Menard, O.F.M.; John J. Heffernan, O.F.M.
Res.: 18414 Cabin Rd., 22172. Tel: 703-221-4575. Web: www.stfrncis.org.
Church: 18825 Fuller Heights Rd., 22172. Tel: 703-221-4044; Fax: 703-221-3246.
School—(Grades PreK-8) Tel: 703-221-3868; Fax: 703-221-0700. Dr. Tricia Barber, Prin.; Geri Weindelmayer, Librarian. Lay Teachers 16; Students 337.
Catechesis/Religious Program—Tel: 703-221-4978.

Mrs. Margaret Bruni, D.R.E. Students 988.
VIENNA, FAIRFAX CO.
1—ST. MARK (1965) [CEM] Rev. Patrick Holroyd. In Res., Rev. Msgr. Thomas J. Cassidy (Retired).
Res.: 9970 Vale Rd., 22181. Tel: 703-281-9100; Fax: 703-281-0675. Web: www.stmark.org.
School—(Grades PreK-8), 9972 Vale Rd., 22181. Tel: 703-281-9103. Roberta Etzel, Prin.; Elizabeth Posey, Librarian. Lay Teachers 28; Students 400.
Catechesis / Religious Program—Tel: 703-938-1948. Mickey Edwards, D.R.E.; Clem Gross, D.R.E. Students 680.
2—OUR LADY OF GOOD COUNSEL (1956) Revs. William J. Metzger, O.S.F.S.; Thomas J. McGee, O.S.F.S.; Lewis S. Fiorelli, O.S.F.S., Parochial Vicar; William J. Ruhl, O.S.F.S. In Res., Rev. Mark S. Mealey, O.S.F.S.
Office & Mailing Address: P.O. Box 97, 22183-0097. Tel: 703-938-2828; Fax: 703-938-2829. Email: administration_receptionist@olgcva.org. Web: www.olgcva.org.
Res.: 8601 Wolftrap Rd., 22182.
School—(Grades K-8) Tel: 703-938-3600; Fax: 703-938-2933. Web: olgcschool.org. Mr. Austin Poole, Prin.; Susan McFaden, Librarian. Lay Teachers 34; Students 443.
Catechesis / Religious Program—Tel: 703-896-7414. Loyes Spayd, D.R.E. Students 621.
WARRENTON, FAUQUIER CO., ST. JOHN THE EVANGELIST (1874) Revs. John H. Melmer; Phillip M. Cozzi, Parochial Vicar; Deacon W. Bernard Ragan.
Res.: 271 Winchester St., 20186. Tel: 540-347-2922; Fax: 540-347-1274. Email: info@stjohntheevangelist.org. Web: www.stjohntheevangelist.org.
School—(Grades PreK-8), 111 King St., 20186. Tel: 540-347-2458; Fax: 540-349-8007. Edward Hoffman, Prin. Lay Teachers 21; Students 250.
Catechesis / Religious Program—Linda Durney, D.R.E. Email: ldurney@stjohntheevangelist.org. Students 550.
WASHINGTON, RAPPAHANNOCK CO., ST. PETER (2005) Rev. Paul L. Dudzinski; Deacon Charles A. Coutu. P.O. Box 27, 22747. Tel: 540-675-3432; Fax: 540-675-1053.
Catechesis / Religious Program—Mrs. Carole Pechie, D.R.E. Students 53.
WINCHESTER, FREDERICK CO., SACRED HEART OF JESUS (1870) [CEM] Revs. Stanley J. Krempa; Michael J. Dobbins, Parochial Vicar; Deacons Edward L. Christianson; Paul E. Ruffo.
Res.: 130 Keating Dr., 22601-2806. Tel: 540-662-5858; Fax: 540-667-6156.
School—(Grades PreK-8), 110 Keating Dr., 22601-2806. Tel: 540-662-7177. Mrs. Rebecca McTavish, Prin.; Mrs. Dolores Sirbaugh, Librarian. Lay Teachers 15; Students 190.
Catechesis / Religious Program—Tel: 540-662-2651. Douglas Koenker, D.R.E. Students 805.
Mission—St. Bridget of Ireland Berryville, Clarke Co.
WOODBRIDGE, PRINCE WILLIAM CO., OUR LADY OF ANGELS (1959) Rev. Paul M. Eversole; Deacons Danny E. Johnson; Jose I. Pardo. In Res., Rev. Milton Acevedo.
Res.: 13752 Mary's Way, 22191. Tel: 703-494-2444; 703-494-5015; Fax: 703-494-0005. Web: www.olacc.org.
Catechesis / Religious Program—Tel: 703-494-3696; Fax: 703-494-3117. Email: religioused@olacc.org. Students 571.
WOODSTOCK, SHENANDOAH CO., ST. JOHN BOSCO (1888) Rev. Wilhelm J. Ettner. In Res., Rev. Zacharis Martinez.
Res.: 315 N. Main St., 22664. Tel: 540-459-4448; Fax: 540-459-4406. Email: donbosco@shentel.net.
Catechesis / Religious Program—Tel: 540-436-9342. Linda Spiker, D.R.E. Students 174.
Mission—Our Lady of the Shenandoah 240 Fretzel Way, P.O. Box 654, Basye, Shenandoah Co. 22810. Tel: 540-856-2411; Fax: 540-856-3043. Rev. Tarsicio Buitrago, Parochial Vicar.

DIOCESAN MISSION PARISH

DOMINICAN REPUBLIC
1—SAN FRANCISCO DE ASIS, BANICA Revs. Keith M. O'Hare; Christopher D. Murphy.
Mailing Address: BM #7038, 3508 NW114 Ave., Doral, FL 33178.
2—SAN JOSE, PEDRO SANTANA Revs. Keith M. O'Hare; Christopher D. Murphy.
Mailing Address: BM #7038, 3508 NW 114 Ave., Doral, FL 33178.

On Duty Outside the Diocese:
Revs.—
Albertson, Eric J., Chap. Lt.Col., Fort Belvoir, VA
Duesterhaus, Michael R., Chap., LCDR, Camp LeJeune, NC
Gross, Lee W., S.T.L., Mount St. Mary Seminary, Emmitsburg, MD
Heisler, John F., Pontifical College Josephinum, Columbus, OH
Mode, Daniel L., Chap., LCDR, Groton, CT
Murphy, Christopher D., St. Joseph, Pedro Santana & Banica, Domincan Republic
O'Hare, Keith M., St. Francis of Assisi, Bonica & Pedro Santana, Dominican Republic
Pollard, Christopher J., Permanent Observer, Mission of the Holy See to the United Nations, New York, NY
Terrien, Lawrence B., S.S., Dir. Spiritual Life Progs., Systematic Theology, St. Mary's Seminary & University, 5400 Roland Ave., Baltimore, MD 21210-1994
Wagner, Robert J., Pontifical North American College 00120 Vatican City State.
Weston, Michael D., Basilica of the National Shrine of the Immaculate Conception, Washington D.C.

Military Chaplains:
Revs.—
Albertson, Eric J., Chap., Lt.Col., Fort Belvoir, VA
Duesterhaus, Michael R., Chap., LCDR, Camp LeJeune, NC
Mode, Daniel L., Chap., CRMD, Virgina Beach, VA

On Leave of Absence:
Revs.—
Bork, Vincent P.
Buckner, Christopher M.
Erbacher, William J.
Hamilton, Daniel E.
Tran, Nhi Dinh
Tucker, James A.

Retired:
Rev. Msgrs.—
Cassidy, Thomas J., St. Mark, Vienna
Cosby, R. Roy, M.A., V.G., Rockville, VA
Hendrick, Frank J., Pinehurst, NC
Mahler, Frank E., Blessed Sacrament, Alexandria
Revs.—
Biniek, Joseph P., New Orleans, LA
Brooks, Robert C., Arlington, VA
Dair, Richard J., Fairfax
Daly, Jerome R., Fort Belvoir, VA
Irace, Dominic P., Lakeworth, FL
Lange, Robert A., Fort Valley
Loftus, Joseph J., Our Lady of Lourdes, Arlington
O'Brien, Cornelius, County Cork, Ireland
Trinkle, Clarence M., Fort Valley
Watkins, Clarence N., Falls Church

Permanent Deacons:
Allen, Charles C., St. Raymond of Penafort, Fairfax Station
Arquette, Lester K., (Retired)
Bayne, James L., (Leave of Absence)
Bello, Thomas M., St. James, Falls Church
Benedi, Claudio F., (Retired)
Benin, Joseph G., St. John the Beloved, McLean
Betit, Eugene D., (Leave of Absence)
Borchert, Robert F., St. Jude, Fredericksburg
Braun, Richard L., (Leave of Absence)
Burrell, Richard L., (Leave of Absence)
Canonica, Donald A., St. Mary, Opelika, AL
Caporiccio, Richard C., Queen of Apostles, Alexandria
Christianson, Edward L., Sacred Heart of Jesus, Winchester
Conroy, David E., St. Timothy, Chantilly; St. Patrick, Fredericksburg
Coutu, Charles A., St. Peter, Washington
deLadurantaye, Robert E., (Retired)
Demers, Richard L., Holy Family, Dale City
Donovan, William J., J.C.L., St. Ann, Arlington
Doyle, James B., St. Anthony, Falls Church
Eberlein, John W., All Saints, Manassas
Einsmann, W. Vincent, Holy Family, Dale City
Emley, William P., Our Lady of Hope, Potomac Falls
Fishenden, James A., St. James, Falls Church
Galvez, Rene A., Annunciation, West Hollywood, FL
Garcia, Meliton H., Queen of Apostles, Alexandria
George, Paul J., (Leave of Absence)
Hammel, Lawrence V., St. Francis de Sales, Purcellville
Henry, Lawrence B., Holy Trinity, Gainesville
Hubbarth, John A., St. Matthew, Spotsylvania
Johnson, Danny E., Our Lady of Angels, Woodbridge
Kenski, Frank G., (Retired)
LaDuca, Nicholas J., St. Leo the Great, Fairfax
Lee, Paul, St. Paul Chung, Fairfax
Ligon, Jack M., St. Stephen the Martyr, Middleburg
Lyons, Robert A., St. Mary of the Immaculate Conception, Fredericksburg
Malinowski, Leonard P., (Retired)
Mallon, John B., (Leave of Absence)
McCaffrey, David S., St. Michael, Annandale
Mendoza, Mario L., St. Anthony, Falls Church
Moore, Gerald J., Sacred Heart, Manassas
Myskowski, Emil P., St. Elizabeth Ann Seton, Lake Ridge
Nickle, Dennis E., (Leave of Absence)
O'Connell, Richard T., All Saints, Manassas
Ostrom, Roger T., St. Michael, Annandale
Pardo, Jose I., Our Lady of Angels, Woodbridge
Pham, Kien Minh, Holy Martyrs of Vietnam, Arlington
Pivarnik, William D., St. Patrick, Fredericksburg
Prien, Richard K., (Leave of Absence)
Pyrek, William J., St. Jude the Apostle, Lewes, DE
Ragan, W. Bernard, St. John the Evangelist, Warrenton
Ramirez, Eduardo A., (Leave of Absence)
Resendes, Daniel F., (Retired)
Ruffo, Paul E., Sacred Heart of Jesus, Winchester
Singer, Joseph R., (Retired)
Smith, Richard P., St. William of York, Stafford
Soutuyo, Francisco R., (Leave of Absence)
Taub, Samuel M., (Retired)
Tirado, Ramon, Precious Blood, Culpeper
Tynan, Thomas, Blessed Sacrament, Alexandria
Vivaldi, Noel, St. Leo the Great, Fairfax
Whelan, Edward F., Jr., St. Matthew, Spotsylvania
White, Jr., Thomas G., Good Shepherd, Alexandria
Wolter, Thomas W., Sacred Heart, Manassas

INSTITUTIONS LOCATED IN THE DIOCESE

[A] COLLEGES AND UNIVERSITIES

ARLINGTON. *Marymount University*, 2807 N. Glebe Rd., 22207. Tel: 703-522-5600; Fax: 703-284-1595. Email: admissions@marymount.edu. Web: www.marymount.edu. Dr. James E. Bundschuh, Pres.; Rev. David M. Sharland, Y.A., Campus Min.; Zary Mostashari, Librarian. Religious of the Sacred Heart of Mary., Resident and Non-resident coed students. Sisters 6; Lay Faculty & Staff 593; Students 3,600.

FRONT ROYAL. *Christendom College*, 134 Christendom Dr., 22630. Tel: 540-636-2900; Fax: 540-636-1655. Web: www.christendom.edu. Timothy T. O'Donnell, S.T.D., K.C.H.S., Pres.; Andrew Armstrong, Library Dir. Resident and Non-resident students. Priests 5; Sisters 1; Lay Teachers 45; Students 450. In Res. Rev. Daniel N. Gee, Chap.

[B] GRADUATE SCHOOLS

ARLINGTON. **The Institute for the Psychological Sciences, Inc.*, 2001 Jefferson Davis Hwy., Ste. 511, 22202. Tel: 703-416-1441; Fax: 703-416-8588. Email: info@ipsciences.edu. Web: www.ipsciences.edu. Gladys Sweeney, Ph.D., Dean; Rev. Charles Sikorsky, L.C. Dedicated to the development and promotion of approaches to psychology founded in the Catholic vision of the human person. Master of Science (M.S.) and Doctor of Psychology (Psy.D.) degrees in Clinical Psychology. Priests 2; Lay Facility 12; Lay Adjunct Faculty 5; Total Staff 11; Total Enrollment 72.

ALEXANDRIA. *Notre Dame Graduate School of Christendom College*, 4407 Sano St., 22312. Tel: 703-658-4304; Fax: 703-658-2318. Email: ndgs@christendom.edu. Web: www.christendom.edu. Kristin P. Burns, Ph.D., Dean; Heidi Kalian, Registrar & Business Officer; Joseph Arias, Librarian. Priests 9; Sisters 1; Lay Teachers 12; Total Staff 4; Total Enrollment 200.

[C] DISTANCE UNIVERSITY

HAMILTON. *The Catholic Distance University*, 120 E. Colonial Hwy., 20158-9012. Tel: 888-254-4238; Fax: 540-338-4788. Email: cdu@cdu.edu. Web: www.cdu.edu. Most Rev. Paul S. Loverde, D.D., S.T.L., J.C.L., Bd. Chm.; Marianne Evans Mount, Pres.; Dr. Robert Royal, Ph.D., Dean Graduate Progs.; Sr. Mary Margaret Ann Schlather, S.N.D., Dean Catechetical Progs.; Dr. Carol Ann Cirbee, Ph.D., Dean of Students; Rev. Bevil Bramwell, O.M.I., Ph.D., Dean Undergraduate Progs. Accredited University and Catechetical Institute offering M.A. in theology, B.A. degree completion in theology, catechetical diploma, advanced catechist certificate, continuing education, online seminars. All programs through distance and online education. No residency required. Adjunct Faculty 32; Staff 18; Total Staff 50; Students 1,800.

[D] HIGH SCHOOLS, DIOCESAN

ARLINGTON. *Bishop Denis J. O'Connell High School*, 6600 Little Falls Rd., 22213. Tel: 703-237-1400; Fax: 703-237-1465. Email: mrohrbach@bishopoconnell.org. Web: www.bishopoconnell.org. Barry Edward Breen, Pres.; Dr. Joseph E. Vorbach III, Ph.D., Prin.; Mr. John J. Gutter, Asst. Prin.; Sr. Regina Joseph Ryan, I.H.M., Asst. Prin.; Rev. James C. Hudgins, Chap. & Asst. Prin.; Mrs. Sue Baxter, Librarian. Priests 1; Sisters 6; Teachers 114; Total Staff 46; Students 1,364.

ALEXANDRIA. *Bishop Ireton High School*, 201 Cambridge Rd., 22314. Tel: 703-751-7606; Fax: 703-212-8173. Email: info@bishopireton.org. Web: www.bishopireton.org. Mr. Tim Hamer, Prin.; Rev. Edwin E. Perez, Chap.; Lindagale Dube, Librarian. Priests 1; Brothers 1; Sisters 2; Lay Teachers 63; Students 828.

DUMFRIES. *Pope John Paul the Great Catholic High School*, (Grades 9-11), 17700 Dominican Drive, 22026. Tel: 703-445-0300; Fax: 703-445-0301. Web: www.jpthegreat.org. Sr. Mary Jordan Hoover, O.P., Prin.; Shawn McNulty, Asst. Prin. Student Life; Carl Patton, Asst. Prin. Academics; Rev. Matthew H. Zuberbueler, Chap.; Mrs. Cynthia Trax, Librarian; Donald Turner, Dir. Facilities; Dr. Patricia Smith, Dir. Guidance; Jennifer Cole, Dir. Admissions; Lori Strickland, Registrar; Dianna Tillgtson, Dir. Devel.; Joseph Redding, Business Mgr. Priests 1; Sisters 3; Lay Staff 26; Students 330.

FAIRFAX. *Paul VI Catholic High School*, 10675 Fairfax Blvd., 22030. Tel: 703-352-0925; Fax: 703-273-9845. Email: website@paulvi.net. Web: www.paulvi.net. Mrs. Virginia Colwell, Prin.; Thomas G. Opfer, Asst. Prin. & Dean of Academics; Eileen Hanley, Dir. of Admissions & Asst. Prin.; Rev. Joel D. Jaffe, Chap. & Asst. Prin.; Brenda Lande, Librarian. Priests 1; Deacons 1; Lay Teachers 90; Students 1,018.

[E] ELEMENTARY SCHOOLS, PRIVATE

BRISTOW. *Linton Hall*, (Grades PreK-8), 9535 Linton Hall Rd., 20136. Tel: 703-368-3157; Fax: 703-368-3036. Email: lintonhall@aol.com. Web: www.lintonhall.edu. Mrs. Elizabeth Poole, Prin. Benedictine Sisters of Virginia 4; Lay Teachers 22; Students 194.

[F] INTERPAROCHIAL SCHOOLS

CULPEPER. *Epiphany School*, (Grades PreK-8), Precious Blood, 114 E. Edmondson St., 22701. Tel: 540-825-9017; Fax: 540-825-8987. Email: office@epiphanycatholicschool.org. Web: www.epiphanycatholicschool.org. Mrs. Barbara Terry, Prin. Sponsoring parishes: Precious Blood, Culpeper; Our Lady of the Blue Ridge, Madison; St. Isidore, Orange and St. Peter Mission, Washington, VA. Lay Teachers 16; Students 142.

FALLS CHURCH. *Corpus Christi School*, (Grades PreK-8), And Early Childhood Center, 3301 Glen Carlyn Rd., 22041. Tel: 703-820-7450; Fax: 703-820-9635. Email: info@corpuschristischool.org. Web: www.corpuschristischool.org. Laura Zybrick, Prin.; Ann Stich, Dir. Early Childhood Center. Sponsoring parishes: St. Anthony and St. Philip. Lay Teachers 25; Students 450.

FREDERICKSBURG. *Holy Cross Academy*, (Grades PreK-8), 250 Stafford Lakes Pkwy., 22406. Tel: 540-286-1600; Fax: 540-286-1625. Email: holycrossacademy@verizon.net. Web: www.holycrossweb.com. Sr. Susan Louise Eder, O.S.F.S., Prin.; Jennifer Buer, Librarian. Sponsoring parish: St. Mary, Fredericksburg. Oblate Sisters of St. Francis de Sales 3; Lay Teachers 28; Total Staff 42; Students 533.

WOODBRIDGE. *St. Thomas Aquinas Regional School*, (Grades PreK-8), 13750 Mary's Way, 22191. Tel: 703-491-4447; Fax: 703-492-8828. Email: office@aquinastars.org. Web: www.aquinastars.org. Sr. Maria Goretti Baker, O.P., Prin.; Mrs. Judy Beda, Librarian. Sponsoring parishes: Our Lady of Angels, Woodbridge; St. Elizabeth Ann Seton, Lake Ridge; and Sacred Heart, Manassas. Dominican Sisters, Congregation of St. Cecilia 4; Lay Teachers 34; Total Staff 64; Students 520.

[G] DAY CARE AND CHILD LEARNING CENTERS

ARLINGTON. *Holy Martyrs of Vietnam Child Enrichment Day Care Center* (Children 2 1/2-5 years), 915 S. Wakefield St., 22204. Tel: 703-920-1049; Fax: 703-553-0371. Email: tamila915@cs.com. Dr. Tamila Mostamandy, Dir. Lay Teachers 2; Students 50.

ALEXANDRIA. *Blessed Sacrament Grade School and Early Childhood Center*, (Grades PreK-8), 1417 W. Braddock Rd., 22302. Tel: 703-998-4170; Fax: 703-998-5033. Email: schoolinfo@blessedsacramentcc.org. Web: www.BlessedSacramentcc.org. Mrs. Valerie Garcia, Prin. Lay Teachers 40; Students 329.

St. Gabriel's (Children 2-5 years), 4319 Sano St., 22312. Tel: 703-354-0395; Fax: 703-354-0395. Sr. Maria D. Gonzalez, P.S.S.J., Local Supr. Poor Sisters of St. Joseph (Buenos Aires). Sisters 5; Lay Teachers 6; Students 90.

FALLS CHURCH. *Corpus Christi Early Childhood Center* (Children 3-5 years), 7506 St. Philip's Ct., 22042. Tel: 703-573-4570; Fax: 703-573-6832. Laura Zybrick, Prin.; Amy Fry, Dir.; Ann Stich, Dir. Sponsoring Parishes: St. Anthony and St. Philip. Lay Teachers 7; Students 174.

St. Joseph's Preschool (Children 2-12 years), 203 N. Spring St., 22046. Tel: 703-533-8441; Fax: 703-462-8621. Rodney Torp, Dir. Lay Teachers 22; Students 100.

[H] MONASTERIES AND RESIDENCES OF PRIESTS AND BROTHERS

ARLINGTON. *Missionhurst, C.I.C.M.-Central House and Provincialate*, 4651 N. 25th St., 22207. Tel: 703-528-3800; Fax: 703-528-5355. Email: provincial@missionhurst.org. Web: www.missionhurst.org. Revs. Anselme Malonda Nkuanga, C.I.C.M., Prov. Supr.; Joseph Giordano, C.I.C.M., Provincial Treas. & Dir. Promotion; Michael Hann, C.I.C.M., Rector; William Wyndaele, C.I.C.M.; John B. Peters, C.I.C.M.; Roger Van Cauwenbergh, C.I.C.M.; Joseph Dewaele, C.I.C.M.; Charles Denys, C.I.C.M.; Randy Gonzales, C.I.C.M., Asst. Dir. Promotion; John Morel, C.I.C.M.

American I.H.M. Province, Inc.

Immaculate Heart Missions, Inc.

Missionhurst, Inc., Congregation of the Immaculate Heart of Mary foreign and home missions.

BERRYVILLE. *Cistercian Abbey of Our Lady of the Holy Cross*, 901 Cool Spring Ln., 22611-2700. Tel: 540-955-1425; Fax: 540-955-1356. Email: holycross@hcava.org. Web: www.hcava.org. Rt. Revs. Robert T. Barnes, O.C.S.O., Abbot; Edward McCorkell, O.C.S.O. (Retired); Mark Delery, O.C.S.O., Retreat House (Retired); Revs. Edmund Flynn, O.C.S.O., Prior & Treas.; Paschal Balkan, O.C.S.O.; Andrew Gries, O.C.S.O.; Vincent Collins, O.C.S.O.; Maurice Flood, O.C.S.O.; Joseph Wittstock, O.C.S.O.; James Orthmann, O.C.S.O., Novice Master & Vocation Dir.; Malachy Marrion, O.C.S.O.; Bros. Stephen Maguire, O.C.S.O.; Michael Desilets, O.C.S.O., Cellarer; Barnabas Brownsey, O.C.S.O.; Christopher Harmon, O.C.S.O.; Edward McLean, O.C.S.O.; Luke Scheuerell, O.C.S.O.; Benedict Simmonds, O.C.S.O.; James Sommers, O.C.S.O.; Martin Statz, O.C.S.O.; Joseph Vantu, O.C.S.O.; Efrain Sosa, O.F.M.Cap. Order of Cistercians of the Strict Observance (Trappist). Community 22; Residents 17; Priests 11; Solemnly Professed Non-priest Monks 11.

[I] CONVENTS AND RESIDENCES FOR SISTERS

ARLINGTON. *Religious of the Sacred Heart of Mary*, 2807 N. Glebe Rd., 22207-4299. Tel: 703-284-1495; Fax: 703-284-5992. Email: sister.bennett@marymount.edu. Web: www.rshm.org. Sisters Irene Cody; Francisca Grace; Catherine Bennett; Jacqueline Murphy. Sisters 4.

Sisters Servants of the Immaculate Heart of Mary, 6600 Little Falls Rd., 22213. Tel: 703-237-1424; Fax: 703-237-1465. Email: ihmdjo@yahoo.com. Web: www.ihmimmaculata.org. Sr. Rose Marie DeCarlo, I.H.M., Supr. Sisters 8.

ALEXANDRIA. *Congregation of the Sisters of the Holy Cross*, 5582 First Statesman Ln., 22312. Tel: 703-658-9519.

Sisters of the Holy Cross, Inc. Sisters 2.

St. Gabriel Convent, 4319 Sano St., 22312. Tel: 703-354-0395; Fax: 703-354-0395. Email: mgonzalezruiz@verizon.net. Sr. Maria D. Gonzalez, P.S.S.J., Local Supr. Poor Sisters of St. Joseph's Buenos Aires Regional House and Novitiate 3.

Poor Clare Monastery of Mary, Mother of the Church, 2505 Stonehedge Dr., 22306. Tel: 703-768-4918; Fax: 703-765-2985. Observing the Primitive Rule of St. Clare. Solemnly Professed 13; Postulants 1; Novices 1.

BRISTOW. *St. Benedict Monastery*, Benedictine Sisters of Virginia, 9535 Linton Hall Rd., 20136-1217. Tel: 703-361-0106; Fax: 703-361-0254. Email: cdwyerosb@comcast.net. Web: www.osbva.org. Sr. Cecilia Dwyer, O.S.B., Prioress. Tel: 703-368-4848. B.E.A.C.O.N.: Benedictine Educational Assistance Community Outreach to Neighbors, Benedictine Pastoral Center, Linton Hall School, Benedictine Counseling Center. Professed Sisters 31; Sisters Resident at Motherhouse 26.

FAIRFAX. *Adorers of the Holy Cross*, 10917 Marilta Ct., 22030. Tel: 703-591-0862; Fax: 703-591-0862. Email: tuvienmtgva@hotmail.com. Sr. Elizabeth Lien Nguyen, M.T.G., Supr. Sisters 8.

Sisters of Our Lady of La Salette (Grenoble, France), 10600 Cedar Ave., 22030. Tel: 703-691-4294; Fax: 703-691-1767. Email: marijosnds@verizon.net; lasalettesisters@yahoo.com. Web: www.geocities.com/lasalettesisters. Sr. Maria Josephine S. Valenton, S.N.D.S., U.S.A. Regl. Supr.

FRONT ROYAL. *Pax Christi Institute*, 118 Jamestown Rd., 22630. Tel: 540-635-7690; Fax: 540-635-9139. Email: paxchristisisters@yahoo.com. Sr. Mercedes Martinez, P.C.I., Supr. Sisters 3.

LINDEN. *Saint Dominic's Monastery, Dominican Nuns (Contemplative)*, 2636 Monastery Rd., 22642-5371. Tel: 540-635-3259; Fax: 540-635-5086. Email: lindenopnuns@aol.com. Sr. Mary Fidelis Stoll, O.P., Prioress. Solemnly Professed 6; Novices 2; Postulants 2.

STRASBURG. *Sisters of Mercy of the Americas*, 112 N. Funk St., 22657-2402. Tel: 540-465-9368. Email: mwharton@su.edu. Web: www.sistersofmercy.org. Sr. Margaret Mary Wharton, R.S.M., Contact Person.

Sisters of Notre Dame de Namur, 112 N. Funk St., 22657-2402. Tel: 540-465-9368; Fax: 540-465-9368. Email: carolsnd@aol.com. Web: www.sndden.org. Sr. Carol A. Symons, S.N.D.deN., Contact Person.

WOODBRIDGE. *Dominican Sisters Convent* (Congregation of St. Cecilia), 5009 Bobcat Ct., 22193. Tel: 703-878-7823; Fax: 703-878-7824. Email: smj.hoover@jpthegreat.org. Sr. Mary Jordan Hoover, O.P., Supr. Dominican Sisters. Sisters 6.

[J] RETREAT HOUSES

BERRYVILLE. *Retreat House, Holy Cross Abbey*, 901 Cool Spring Ln., 22611-2700. Tel: 540-955-4383; Fax: 540-955-1356. Email: information@hcava.org. Web: www.hcava.org. Rt. Rev. Mark Delery, O.C.S.O., Retreat House Counselor (Retired).

MCLEAN. *Dominican Retreat House*, 7103 Old Dominion Dr., 22101-2799. Tel: 703-356-4243; Fax: 703-893-4502. Email: dominicanretreat@cox.net. Web: www.dominicanretreat.org. Dominican Sisters of St. Catherine De Ricci., Accommodations for 41 persons. Sisters 6.

[K] CAMPUS MINISTRY

ARLINGTON. *Marymount University* 2807 N. Glebe Rd., 22207. Tel: 703-284-1607; Fax: 703-284-3850. Email: father.david@marymount.edu. Web: www.marymount.edu. Revs. John P. Peterson, Y.A., Asst. Chap.; David M. Sharland, Y.A., Chap. & Dir. Campus Ministry

FAIRFAX. *George Mason University, Catholic Campus Ministry* 4515 Roberts Rd., 22032. Tel: 703-425-0022; Fax: 703-425-0753. Email: pnassett@gmu.edu. Web: gmuccm.org. Rev. Peter W. Nassetta, Y.A., Chap. & Dir. Campus Ministry; John More, Asst. Campus Min.

St. Robert Bellarmine Chapel George Mason University, 4515 Roberts Rd., 22032. Tel: 703-425-0022; Fax: 703-425-0753. Rev. Peter W. Nassetta, Y.A.; Catherine Horan, Asst. Campus Min. Catholic Campus Ministry.

FREDERICKSBURG. *University of Mary Washington* Catholic Campus Ministry, 1614 College Ave., 22401. Tel: 540-373-6746; Fax: 540-518-9086. Email: father@umwccm.org. Web: umwccm.org. Rev. Frederick H. Edlefsen, Chap.; Rita Richardson, Asst. to the Chap.; Veronica Knickerbocker, Admin. Asst.

[L] MISCELLANEOUS

ARLINGTON. *Rooted in Faith-Forward in Hope, Inc.*, 200 N. Glebe Rd., Ste. 914, 22203. Tel: 703-841-2500; Fax: 703-524-5028. Rev. Mark S. Mealey, O.S.F.S., J.C.D., Ph.D., V.G., J.V., Pres.

The Women's Apostolate to Youth, 5600 N. 16th St., 22205. Tel: 703-534-5821. Email: robinmass@verizon.net. Web: www.rc.net/arlington/way. Dr. Robin Maas, Dir.

Youth Apostles Institute, An Association of Christian Faithful, 1600 Carlin Ln., McLean, 22101-4100. Tel: 703-556-0914; Fax: 703-556-9455. Email: administrator@youthapostles.org. Web: www.youthapostles.org. Revs. John P. Peterson, Y.A., Dir.; Ramon Dominguez, Y.A.; Michael F. Kuhn, Y.A.; Peter W. Nassetta, Y.A.; David M. Sharland, Y.A.; Mr. Thomas Duesterhaus; Mr. Thomas Yehl.

ALEXANDRIA. *Pauline Book and Media (Daughters of St. Paul)*, 1025 King St., 22314. Tel: 703-549-3806; 703-549-1323 (Convent); Fax: 703-683-2568. Email: alexandria@pauline.org. Web: www.pauline.org. Sr. Christine Virginia, F.S.P. An international congregation of women religious who serve the church with the communications media.

FAIRFAX. *Alpha Omega Clinic and Consultation Services*, 3607A Chain Bridge Rd., Ste. 105, 22030. Tel: 301-767-1733; Fax: 301-767-1743. Email: alphaomegaclinic@verizon.net. Web: www.aoccs.org. Art Bennett, Dir.

Divine Mercy Care, 11135B Lee Hwy., 22030. Tel: 703-934-5552, Ext. 304; Fax: 703-766-5500. Email: info@divinemercycare.org. Web: www.divinemercycare.org. John Bruchalski, M.D., Board Chm.

FRONT ROYAL. **Human Life International*, 4 Family Life Ln., 22630. Tel: 540-635-7884; Fax: 540-622-6247. Email: hli@hli.org. Web: www.hli.org. Rev. Thomas J. Euteneuer, Pres.

**Seton Home Study School*, 1350 Progress Dr., 22630. Tel: 540-636-9990; Fax: 540-636-1602. Email: info@setonhome.org. Web: www.setonhome.org. Dr. Mary K. Clark, Dir.

MCLEAN. *Crusaders of St. Mary*, 2001 Great Falls St., 22101. Tel: 703-536-3546. Email: aperezalca@cox.net. Antonio Perez-Alcala, Dir.

SPOTSYLVANIA. *St. Francis Catholic Worker West*, 9631 Peppertree Rd., 22553. Tel: 540-972-3218. Web: www.catholicworker.org. Mr. John Mahoney, Vice Pres. Total in Residence 2.

STAFFORD. **American Life League, Inc.*, P.O. Box 1350, 22555. Tel: 540-659-4171; Fax: 540-659-2586. Email: jbrown@all.org. Web: www.all.org. Mrs. Judie Brown, Pres.

VIENNA. *Mount Tabor Society, Inc.*, 2363 Hunter Mill Rd., 22181. Tel: 703-938-2564. Rev. Paul G. Wynants, C.I.C.M., Dir. A House of Prayer and Christian Community.

RELIGIOUS INSTITUTES OF MEN REPRESENTED IN THE DIOCESE

For further details refer to the corresponding bracketed number in the Religious Institutes of Men or Women section.

[]—*Apostles of Jesus*—A.J.
[1350]—*Brothers of St. Francis Xavier*—C.F.X.
[0350]—*Cistercians Order of the Strict Observance* (Trappists)—O.C.S.O.
[0650]—*Congregation of the Holy Spirit*—C.S.Sp.
[0260]—*Discalced Carmelite Friars*—O.C.D.
[]—*Disciples of the Hearts of Jesus and Mary*—D.C.J.M.
[0520]—*Franciscan Friars* (Holy Name Prov.)—O.F.M.
[0530]—*Franciscan Friars of the Atonement*—S.A.
[0860]—*Missionhurst Congregation of the Immaculate Heart of Mary*—C.I.C.M.
[0920]—*Oblates of St. Francis de Sales* (Wilmington-Philadelphia Prov.)—O.S.F.S.
[]—*Order of St. Augustine (Augustinians)*—O.S.A.
[]—*Order of the Canons Regular of Premontre (Norbertines)*—O.Praem
[0975]—*Society of Our Lady of the Most Holy Trinity*—S.O.L.T.
[0700]—*St. Joseph's Society of the Sacred Heart* (Baltimore, MD)—S.S.J.
[0560]—*Third Order Regular of Saint Francis* (Sacred Heart Prov.)—T.O.R.
[]—*Vietnamese Dominican Fathers* (Calgary, Alberta, Canada)—O.P.
[]—*Youth Apostles*—Y.A.

RELIGIOUS INSTITUTES OF WOMEN REPRESENTED IN THE DIOCESE

[4155]—*Adorers of the Holy Cross*—M.T.G.
[0230]—*Benedictine Sisters of Virginia*—O.S.B.
[1920]—*Congregation of the Sisters of the Holy Cross*—C.S.C.
[0960]—*Daughters of Wisdom*—D.W.
[1070-17]—*Dominican Sisters Congregation of St. Catherine deRicci*—O.P.
[1070-07]—*Dominican Sisters Congregation of St. Cecilia*—O.P.
[1365]—*Franciscan Missionary Sisters of the Infant Jesus*—F.M.I.J.
[1250]—*Franciscan Sisters of the Eucharist*—F.S.E.
[1880]—*Handmaidens of Reparation of the Sacred Heart of Jesus*—A.R.
[3060]—*Oblate Sisters of St. Francis de Sales*—O.S.F.S.
[3760]—*Order of St. Clare (Cloistered)*—P.C.C.
[]—*Pax Christi Institute* (Corpus Christi, TX)—P.C.I.
[0950]—*Pious Society of Daughters of St. Paul*—F.S.P.
[3250]—*Poor Sisters of St. Joseph*—P.S.S.J.
[3465]—*Religious of the Sacred Heart of Mary* (Eastern North Amer. Prov.)—R.S.H.M.
[2575]—*Sisters of Mercy of the Americas*—R.S.M.
[2990]—*Sisters of Notre Dame*—S.N.D.
[3000]—*Sisters of Notre Dame de Namur*—S.N.D.deN.
[]—*Sisters of Our Lady of La Salette* (Grenoble, France)—S.N.D.S.
[1650]—*Sisters of St. Francis of Philadelphia*—O.S.F.
[3893]—*Sisters of St. Joseph of Chestnut Hill* (Philadelphia)—S.S.J.
[]—*Sisters of St. Paul of Chartres*—S.P.C.
[]—*Sisters of the Humility of Mary*—H.M.
[2170]—*Sisters, Servants of the Immaculate Heart of Mary*—I.H.M.

NECROLOGY

† Cilinski, Rev. Msgr. John T., (Retired)—Died Aug. 14, 2009
† Griffin, George J., Orange, VA St. Isidore the Farmer—Died Dec. 25, 2008
† Hughes, John J., (Retired)—Died Feb. 13, 2009
† Kelly, Michael C., Purcellville, VA St. Francis de Sales—Died Dec. 31, 2008

An asterisk (*) denotes an organization that has established tax-exempt status directly with the IRS and is not covered by the USCCB Group Ruling.

Archdiocese of Atlanta

(Archidioecesis Atlantensis)

Most Reverend

WILTON D. GREGORY, S.L.D.

Archbishop of Atlanta; ordained May 9, 1973; appointed Auxiliary Bishop of Chicago and Titular Bishop of Oliva October 31, 1983; consecrated December 13, 1983; appointed Bishop of Belleville December 29, 1993; installed February 10, 1994; appointed Archbishop of Atlanta December 9, 2004; installed January 17, 2005.

Most Reverend

JOHN FRANCIS DONOGHUE, D.D.

Retired Archbishop of Atlanta; ordained June 4, 1955; appointed Bishop of Charlotte November 6, 1984; appointed Archbishop of Atlanta June 22, 1993; installed August 18, 1993; retired December 9, 2004.

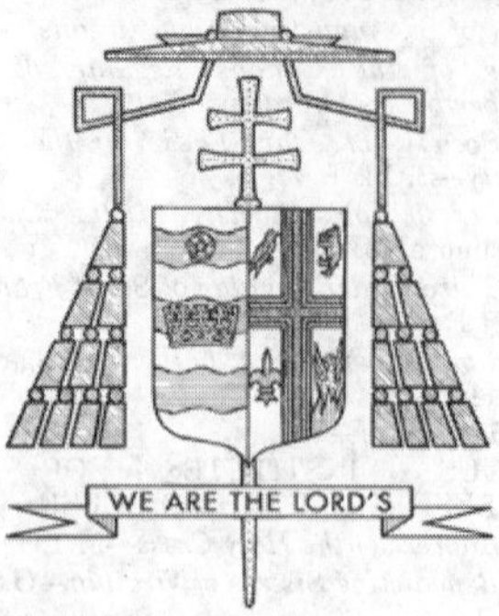

Catholic Center Archdiocese of Atlanta: 680 W. Peachtree St., N.W., Atlanta, GA 30308. Tel: 404-888-7800; 404-885-7214 (after office hours only) In Emergency; Fax: 404-885-7230.

Web: www.archatl.com

Most Reverend

LUIS R. ZARAMA

Auxiliary Bishop of Atlanta; ordained November 27, 1993; appointed Auxiliary Bishop of Atlanta and Titular Bishop of Bararus July 27, 2009; consecrated September 29, 2009.

ESTABLISHED JULY 2, 1956.

Square Miles 21,445.

Canonically Erected November 8, 1956; created an Archdiocese February 21, 1962.

Comprises the 69 Counties in the northern part of the State of Georgia, north of and including the following counties: Lincoln, McDuffie, Warren, Hancock, Baldwin, Putnam, Jasper, Monroe, Upson, Meriwether and Troup

Patrons of the Archdiocese: I. Our Blessed Lady under the title of the Immaculate Heart of Mary; II. Saint Pius X.

For legal titles of parishes and archdiocesan institutions, consult the Archbishop's office.

STATISTICAL OVERVIEW

Personnel	
Archbishops	1
Retired Archbishops	1
Auxiliary Bishops	1
Abbots	1
Priests: Diocesan Active in Diocese	150
Priests: Diocesan Active Outside Diocese	6
Priests: Retired, Sick or Absent	29
Number of Diocesan Priests	185
Religious Priests in Diocese	67
Total Priests in Diocese	252
Extern Priests in Diocese	16
Ordinations:	
Diocesan Priests	8
Transitional Deacons	7
Permanent Deacons	12
Permanent Deacons in Diocese	232
Total Brothers	9
Total Sisters	81
Parishes	
Parishes	87
With Resident Pastor:	
Resident Diocesan Priests	77
Resident Religious Priests	10
Missions	12
Professional Ministry Personnel:	
Brothers	1
Sisters	18
Lay Ministers	192
Welfare	
Catholic Hospitals	5
Total Assisted	348,724
Homes for the Aged	3
Total Assisted	99
Special Centers for Social Services	5
Total Assisted	7,350
Educational	
Diocesan Students in Other Seminaries	42
Seminaries, Religious	8
Total Seminarians	42
Colleges and Universities	1
Total Students	240
High Schools, Diocesan and Parish	3
Total Students	2,217
High Schools, Private	4
Total Students	1,857
Elementary Schools, Diocesan and Parish	15
Total Students	6,266
Elementary Schools, Private	4
Total Students	1,473
Catechesis/Religious Education:	
High School Students	11,383
Elementary Students	34,088
Total Students under Catholic Instruction	57,566
Teachers in the Diocese:	
Priests	14
Brothers	2
Sisters	7
Lay Teachers	957
Vital Statistics	
Receptions into the Church:	
Infant Baptism Totals	11,070
Minor Baptism Totals	478
Adult Baptism Totals	496
Received into Full Communion	1,260
First Communions	9,599
Confirmations	4,853
Marriages:	
Catholic	1,133
Interfaith	442
Total Marriages	1,575
Deaths	1,331
Total Catholic Population	850,000
Total Population	6,887,670

Former Bishops—Most Revs. FRANCIS E. HYLAND, D.D., J.C.D., appt. Titular Bishop of Gomphi and Auxiliary Bishop of Savannah-Atlanta, Oct. 15, 1949; cons. Dec. 21, 1949; First Bishop of Atlanta, July 17, 1956; installed on Nov. 8, 1956; resigned and appointed Titular Bishop of Bisica, Oct. 11, 1961; died Jan. 31, 1968; PAUL J. HALLINAN, D.D., appt. Bishop of Charleston, Sept. 9, 1958; cons. Oct. 28, 1958; elevated to the Archiepiscopal dignity, Feb. 21, 1962; installed First Archbishop of Atlanta, March 29, 1962; died March 27, 1968; JOSEPH L. BERNARDIN, D.D., appt. Auxiliary of Atlanta, March 9, 1966; cons. April 26, 1966; appt. Gen. Sec. U.S.C.C., April 5, 1968; died Nov. 14, 1996.; THOMAS A. DONNELLAN, appt. Bishop of Ogdensburg, March 4, 1964; cons. April 9, 1964; appt. to Atlanta, May 29, 1968; installed July 16, 1968; died Oct. 15, 1987; EUGENE A. MARINO, S.S.J., D.D., appt. Auxiliary of Washington, July 15, 1974; appt. Archbishop of Atlanta, March 14, 1988; installed May 5, 1988; resigned July 10, 1990; died Nov. 12, 2000; JAMES P. LYKE, O.F.M., Ph.D., appt. Auxiliary Bishop of Cleveland and Titular Bishop of Fornos Maggiore, June 30, 1979; cons. Aug. 1, 1979; appt. Apostolic Administrator Archdiocese of Atlanta, July 10, 1990; appt. Archbishop of Archdiocese of Atlanta, April 30, 1991; installed June 24, 1991; Palium conferred June 29, 1991; died Dec. 27, 1992; JOHN FRANCIS DONOGHUE, D.D., ord. June 4, 1955; appt. Bishop of Charlotte Nov. 6, 1984; installed second Bishop Dec. 18, 1984; appt. Archbishop of Atlanta June 22, 1993; installed Aug. 18, 1993; retired Dec. 9, 2004.

Vicars General—Most Rev. LUIS R. ZARAMA, J.C.L., V.G., J.V. Tel: 404-885-7490; Fax: 404-885-7230. Email: lzarama@archatl.com; Rev. Msgr. W. JOSEPH CORBETT, V.G., Moderator of the Curia. Tel: 404-888-7805; Fax: 404-885-7230. Email: jcorbett@archatl.com. Senior Executive Assistants: KIRIAL DEROZAS-MILES. Tel: 404-885-7490; Fax: 404-885-7230. Email: kderozas-miles@archatl.com; CECELIA THOMPSON. Tel: 404-885-7284; Fax: 404-885-7230. Email: cthompson@archatl.com.

Chancellor—Deacon DENNIS J. DORNER. Tel: 404-885-7407; Fax: 404-885-7462. Email: ddorner@archatl.com; PHILLIS CURRY, Exec. Asst. Tel: 404-885-7296; Fax: 404-885-7462. Email: pcurry@archatl.com; MARDESSA SMITH, Administrative Asst. Tel: 404-885-7445; Fax: 404-885-7462. Email: mwsmith@archatl.com.

Judicial Vicar—Most Rev. LUIS R. ZARAMA, J.C.L., V.G., J.V., 680 W. Peachtree St., N.W., Atlanta, 30308. Tel: 404-885-7805; Fax: 404-885-7230. Email: lzamara@archatl.com.

Secretary for Finance—BRADLEY WILSON, CFO, 680 W. Peachtree St., N.W., Atlanta, 30308. Tel: 404-888-7808; Fax: 404-885-7223. Email: bwilson@archatl.com.

Secretary for Catholic Charities—JOSEPH J. KRYGIEL, 680 W. Peachtree St., N.W., Atlanta, 30308. Tel: 404-881-6571; Fax: 404-888-7816. Email: jkrygiel@archatl.com.

Secretary for Communications—PATRICIA CHIVERS, 680 W. Peachtree St., N.W., Atlanta, 30308. Tel: 404-885-7420; Fax: 404-978-2770. Email: pchivers@archatl.com.

Secretary for Schools—DIANE STARKOVICH, 680 W. Peachtree St., N.W., Atlanta, 30308. Tel: 404-888-7883; Fax: 404-885-7430. Email: dstarkovich@archatl.com.

Secretary for Office of Formation and Discipleship—DENNIS LEE JOHNSON JR., 680 W. Peachtree St.,

N.W., Atlanta, 30308. Tel: 404-885-7413; Fax: 404-885-7473. Email: djohnsonjr@archatl.com.

Secretary for Human Resources—CHARLES THIBAUDEAU, 680 W. Peachtree St., N.W., Atlanta, 30308. Tel: 404-885-7227; Fax: 404-885-7497. Email: cthibaudeau@archatl.com.

Archbishop's Office—Most Rev. WILTON D. GREGORY, S.L.D., Office of the Archbishop, 680 W. Peachtree St., N.W., Atlanta, 30308-1984. Tel: 404-888-7812; Fax: 404-885-7282. Email: archbishop@archatl.com. Web: www.archatl.com; KENYA GRAHAM, Senior Exec. Asst. Tel: 404-888-7812; Fax: 404-885-7282. Email: kgraham@archatl.com; LAURA DOROSKI, Administrative Asst. Tel: 404-885-7241; Fax: 404-885-7282. Email: ldoroski@archatl.com.

College of Consultors—Most Rev. LUIS R. ZARAMA, J.C.L., V.G., J.V.; Rev. Msgr. W. JOSEPH CORBETT, V.G.; Revs. FRANCIS G. MCNAMEE; JOSE DUVAN GONZALEZ-FLORES; Rev. Msgrs. STEPHEN T. CHURCHWELL, J.C.D., V.F.; JAMES J. FENNESSY; Revs. RICARDO BAILEY; PAUL W. BERNY; PAUL D. WILLIAMS JR.; Very Rev. ALBERT W. JOWDY, V.F., M.Div.; Rev. GREGORY J. HARTMAYER, O.F.M.Conv.; Very Rev. JOHN WALSH, V.F.

Deans—Very Rev. PETER J. RAU, V.F., North Metro Deanery; Rev. Msgr. TERRY W. YOUNG, V.F., Southeast Deanery; Very Revs. ALBERT W. JOWDY, V.F., M.Div., Northeast Metro Deanery; RICHARD P. WISE, V.F., Northeast Deanery; MICHAEL KINGERY, V.F., South Deanery; DAVID MCGUINNESS, V.F., East Deanery; CARL ZDANCEWICZ, O.F.M.Conv., V.F., Southwest Deanery; RANDALL MATTOX, V.F., Northwest Deanery; JAMES A. SCHILLINGER, S.T.L., V.F., Central Deanery; JOHN WALSH, V.F., Northwest Metro Deanery.

Priest Personnel—680 W. Peachtree St., N.W., Atlanta, 30308-1984. Rev. FRANCIS G. MCNAMEE, Dir. Email: frfrank@ctking.com; SUSIE BRISKI, Exec. Asst. Tel: 404-885-7255; Fax: 404-885-7230. Email: sbriski@archatl.com.

Vicars for Clergy—Rev. Msgr. FRANCIS PHUONG; Rev. FRANCIS G. MCNAMEE; Very Revs. VICTOR A. GALIER, M.Div.; RICHARD B. MORROW (Retired); Rev. PEDRO POLOCHE, J.C.L.; Rev. Msgr. HENRY C. GRACZ.

Vicar for Consecrated Life—Sr. JOAN MCCANN, O.P., 3230 Oakbrook Lane, Clarkston, 30021. Tel: 404-294-8685; Fax: 404-294-8685. Email: jmccannop@bellsouth.net.

Archdiocesan Offices

Archives and Records—680 W. Peachtree St., N.W., Atlanta, 30308-1984. Tel: 404-885-7253; Fax: 404-885-7462. Deacon DENNIS J. DORNER, Chancellor. Email: ddorner@archatl.com; CAROLYN DENTON, Dir. Archives & Records. Tel: 404-885-7253; Fax: 404-885-7462. Email: cdenton@archatl.com; BRIDGET T. LERETTE, C.A., Asst. Archivist. Tel: 404-978-2772; Fax: 404-885-7462. Email: blerette@archatl.com.

Black Catholic Ministry—680 W. Peachtree St., N.W., Atlanta, 30308-1984. Tel: 404-888-7848; Fax: 404-885-7481. Web: www.obcm.org. CHARLES PREJEAN, Dir. Tel: 404-888-7848; Fax: 404-885-7481. Email: cprejean@archatl.com; GRACIELA MULERO, Administrative Asst. Tel: 404-978-2776; Fax: 404-885-7481. Email: gmulero@archatl.com; ASHLEY MORRIS, Consultant. Tel: 404-885-7283; Fax: 404-885-7481. Email: amorris@archatl.com.

Campus Ministry—680 W. Peachtree St., N.W., Atlanta, 30308-1984. Tel: 404-885-7413; Fax: 404-885-7473. Web: www.archatl.com. DENNIS LEE JOHNSON JR., Dir., Office of Formation & Discipleship and Member of the Secretariat, 680 W. Peachtree St., Atlanta, 30308. Tel: 404-885-7413; Fax: 404-885-7473. Email: djohnsonjr@archatl.com.

Catholic Charities of the Archdiocese of Atlanta, Inc.—680 W. Peachtree St., N.W., Atlanta, 30308-1984. Tel: 404-881-6571; Fax: 404-888-7816; 404-885-7477 (Confidential Fax). Web: www.catholiccharitiesatlanta.org. JOSEPH J. KRYGIEL, Sec. Catholic Charities, CEO & Member of the Secretariat. Tel: 404-885-7476; Fax: 404-885-7477. Email: jkrygiel@archatl.com. Village of St. Joseph Counseling Services, Pregnancy, Parenting & Adoption Program, Immigration Legal Services Program, Refugee Resettlement Services, Disaster Preparedness & Response, Family Enrichment Program, Parish Social Justice Ministries; JOHN NEE, Catholic Charities Bd. Chm. Tel: 678-419-1576. Email: john.d.nee@us.pwc.com; JOSEPH GALVIN, COO. Tel: 404-885-7258; Fax: 404-885-7477. Email: jgalvin@archatl.com; Rev. THOMAS J. MEEHAN, Chap. & Pastor, Sacred Heart Catholic Church, 353 Peachtree St., N.E., Atlanta, 30308. Tel: 404-552-6800; Fax: 404-524-5440. Email: tjmeehan@sacredheartatlanta.org.

Catholic Housing Initiatives, Inc.—JOSEPH J. KRYGIEL, 680 W. Peachtree St., N.W., Atlanta, 30308. Tel: 404-888-7826; Fax: 404-885-7477.

Good Shepherd Place—198 N. Corners Pkwy., Cumming, 30040. Tel: 404-766-7121; Fax: 404-766-4344. MARILYN CONSALAZIO, Mgr.

Saint Joseph Place—2973 Butner Rd., S.W., Atlanta, 30331. Tel: 404-346-0745; Fax: 404-346-0747. LARGINE JOHNSON, Mgr.

Catholic Construction Services, Inc.—2969-C Butner Rd., S.W., Atlanta, 30331-7860. Tel: 404-888-7838; Fax: 404-885-7299. GEORGE BARRIE, Pres., CEO & Member of the Secretariat. Tel: 404-885-7294; Fax: 404-885-7299. Email: gbarrie@archatl.com; DONNA L. WORLEY, Office Mgr. & Land Acquisitions. Tel: 404-885-7295; Fax: 404-885-7299. Email: dworley@archatl.com; RACHEL WHITE, Administrative Asst. Tel: 404-885-7291; Fax: 404-885-7299. Email: rwhite@archatl.com.

Field Representatives/Quality Control—RANDY HOOD. Tel: 404-494-4202; Fax: 404-885-7299. Email: rhood@archatl.com; DICK JANSEN. Tel: 404-885-7229; Fax: 404-885-7299. Email: djansen@archatl.com.

Project Managers—DENNIS W. KELLY. Tel: 404-885-7228; Fax: 404-885-7299. Email: dkelly@archatl.com; STEVE LARKIN. Tel: 404-885-7297; Fax: 404-885-7299. Email: slarkin@archatl.com; CARL TREVATHAN. Tel: 404-494-4203; Fax: 404-885-7299. Email: ctrevathan@archatl.com.

Catholic Foundation of North Georgia—780 Johnson Ferry Rd., Ste. 750, Atlanta, 30342. Tel: 404-497-9440; Fax: 404-497-9442. Web: www.cfnga.org. NANCY DINKA COVENY, Exec. Dir. Email: ncoveny@cfnga.org; DIANE DUQUETTE, Dir. Gift Planning. Email: dduquette@cfnga.org; MARY ELLEN CENZALLI, Exec. Asst. Email: mcenzalli@cfnga.org.

Catholic Schools—680 W. Peachtree St., N.W., Atlanta, 30308-1984. Tel: 404-888-7883; Fax: 404-885-7430. Web: www.archatl.com. DIANE STARKOVICH, Supt. & Member of the Secretariat. Tel: 404-885-7428; Fax: 404-885-7430. Email: dstarkovich@archatl.com; THOMAS R. CAMPBELL, Assoc. Supt. Tel: 404-885-7429; Fax: 404-885-7430. Email: tcampbell@archatl.com; LISA JONES, Asst. to Supt. Tel: 404-885-7431; Fax: 404-885-7430. Email: ljones@archatl.com; NANCY DILLY, School Psychologist. Tel: 404-885-7233; Fax: 404-885-7430. Email: ndilly@archatl.com; TERRY GRAHAM, Dir. Parish Pre-Schools. Tel: 404-885-7492; Fax: 404-885-7430. Email: tgraham@archatl.com; CECI MCAULIFFE, Dir. Special Svcs. Tel: 404-885-7491; Fax: 404-885-7430. Email: cmcauliffe@archatl.com; DONNA TOMLINSON, Administrative Asst. to School Psychologist. Tel: 404-885-7225; Fax: 404-885-7430. Email: dtomlinson@archatl.com; JACK KNIGHT, Receptionist & Administrative Asst. Tel: 404-885-7424; Fax: 404-885-7430. Email: jknight@archatl.com.

Child and Youth Protection—680 W. Peachtree St., N.W., Atlanta, 30308-1984. Tel: 404-885-7234; Fax: 404-978-2778. Web: www.archatl.com. MARY SUSAN STUBBS, Dir. & Victim Asst. Coord. Tel: 404-885-7459; Cell: 404-456-4043; Tel: 888-437-0764 24 Hour Reporting Hotline; Fax: 404-978-2778. Email: sstubbs@archatl.com; JENNIFER BROEL, Dir. Safe Environment. Tel: 404-978-2765; 888-437-0764 (24 Hour Reporting Hotline); Fax: 404-978-2778; MARIANNE "MAC" FRONEK, Sec. Tel: 404-885-7234; Fax: 404-978-2778. Email: mfronek@archatl.com.

Communications—680 W. Peachtree St., N.W., Atlanta, 30308-1984. Tel: 404-885-7420; Fax: 404-978-2770. Web: www.archatl.com. PATRICIA CHIVERS, Dir. & Member of the Secretariat. Tel: 404-885-7420; Fax: 404-978-2770. Email: pchivers@archatl.com; MEAGHAN SCHROEDER, Asst. Dir. Communications. Tel: 404-978-2766; Fax: 404-978-2770. Email: mschroeder@archatl.com; JONATHON HANTEN, Web Devel. Tel: 404-877-5508; Fax: 404-978-2770. Email: jhanten@archatl.com; DAVID PACE, Creative Dir. Tel: 404-885-7469; Fax: 404-978-2770. Email: dpace@archatl.com; JOY PLACE, Administrative Asst. Tel: 404-885-7201; Fax: 404-978-2770. Email: jplace@archatl.com.

Court of Appeals - Province of Atlanta—680 W. Peachtree St., N.W., Atlanta, 30308-1984. Tel: 404-888-7813; Fax: 404-888-7845.

Judicial Vicar—Very Rev. PAUL J. HACHEY, S.M., J.C.L., M.C.L., M.Div. Email: phachey@archatl.com; MARGUERITE V. FORTINO, B.M., Sec. Email: mfortino@archatl.com.

Defenders of the Bond—Rev. Msgr. PETER A. DORA, M.Div.; Rev. DANIEL J. MCCORMICK, B.A.; Ms. ROBERTA I. SIEGWALD; Most Rev. JOHN F. DONOGHUE, J.C.L. (Retired).

Judges—Revs. JOHN C. DRUDING, M.Div. (Retired); GREGORY D. GOOLSBY, M.Div., J.D.; Very Rev. ALBERT W. JOWDY, V.F., M.Div.; Rev. Msgr. R. DONALD KIERNAN, P.A., D.P.A., Ph.D., LL.D.; Very Rev. RICHARD B. MORROW (Retired); Rev. Msgr. PAUL H. REYNOLDS; Very Rev. JAMES A. SCHILLINGER, S.T.L., V.F.

Advocates—Rev. Msgr. HENRY C. GRACZ; Rev. JAMES D. DUFFY, S.M., M.Div.; Mrs. MARY CANDEE ELROD, M.R.E.; Rev. VICTOR J. REYES, M.Div.; Very Rev. VICTOR A. GALIER, M.Div.; Deacon MICHAEL J. O'BRIEN.

Notaries—MARGUERITE V. FORTINO, B.M.; MARIANNE "MAC" FRONEK.

Promoter of Justice—Rev. DANIEL J. MCCORMICK, B.A.

Office of Evangelization—Rev. TIMOTHY M. HEPBURN, Dir., Catholic Center at Georgia Tech, 172 Fourth St., N.W., Atlanta, 30313. Tel: 404-892-6759; Fax: 404-892-6759. Email: frhepburn@gmail.com.

Office of Formation and Discipleship—680 Peachtree St., N.W., Atlanta, 30308-1984. Tel: 404-885-7413; Fax: 404-885-7473. Web: www.archatl.com.

Family Ministry/Pastoral Care Ministry—LYNN CRUTCHFIELD, Assoc. Dir. Tel: 404-885-7450; Fax: 404-885-7473. Email: lcrutchfield@archatl.com; IVONNE S. VREELAND, Office Mgr. Tel: 404-885-7484; Fax: 404-885-7473. Email: ivreeland@archatl.com.

Family Ministry—

Retrouvaille—REED POLOMSKY. Tel: 770-495-8592; SUSAN POLOMSKY, 680 W. Peachtree St., N.W., Atlanta, 30308-1984. Tel: 404-888-7818. Web: www.retrouvailleofatlanta.org.

Engaged Encounter—Coordinators: JEFF CROWELL; AMY CROWELL, 680 W. Peachtree St., N.W., Atlanta, 30308. Tel: 770-973-1147. Web: www.retrouvailleofatlanta.org.

LLASU-Hispanic Marriage Preparation Program—MIGUEL ZUMARAN; VANGIE ZUMARAN, 680 W. Peachtree St., N.W., Atlanta, 30308-1984. Tel: 770-216-0371. Web: www.archatl.com.

Finance Office—680 W. Peachtree St., N.W., Atlanta, 30308-1984. Tel: 404-888-7808; Fax: 404-885-7223. BRADLEY WILSON, CFO & Member of the Secretariat. Tel: 404-885-7408; Fax: 404-885-7223. Email: bwilson@archatl.com; MICHAEL WARREN, Controller. Tel: 404-885-7261; Fax: 404-885-7223. Email: mwarren@archatl.com; ELSA RULLAN, Planning Mgr. Tel: 404-885-7427; Fax: 404-885-7223. Email: erullan@archatl.com; PATRICK WARNER, Parish Systems Mgr. Tel: 404-885-7246; Fax: 404-885-7223. Email: pwarner@archatl.com; ANN PITRA, Office Mgr. Tel: 404-885-7417; Fax: 404-885-7223. Email: apitra@archatl.com; DIANE RAY, Accounting Asst. Tel: 404-885-7203; Fax: 404-885-7223. Email: dray@archatl.com; MELISSA CHAPMAN, Accounting Mgr. Tel: 404-885-7411; Fax: 404-885-7223. Email: mchapman@archatl.com; MARY ANN BROWN, Accounting Asst. Tel: 404-885-7262; Fax: 404-885-7223. Email: mabrown@archatl.com; MARIA TERESA VELEZ, Deposit & Loan Mgr. Tel: 404-885-7416; Fax: 404-885-7223. Email: mvelez@archatl.com.

"Georgia Bulletin, The"—680 W. Peachtree St., N.W., Atlanta, 30308-1984. Tel: 404-877-5500; Fax: 404-877-5505. Web: www.georgiabulletin.org. Most Rev. WILTON D. GREGORY, S.L.D., Publisher. Tel: 404-888-7812; Fax: 404-885-7282. Email: archbishop@archatl.com; MARY ANNE CASTRANIO, Exec. Editor. Tel: 404-877-5506; Fax: 404-877-5505. Email: mcastranio@archatl.com; GRETCHEN KEISER, Editor. Tel: 404-877-5518; Fax: 404-877-5505. Email: gkeiser@archatl.com.

Hispanic Ministry—680 W. Peachtree St., N.W., Atlanta, 30308-1984. Tel: 404-885-7289; Fax: 404-885-7479. Web: www.archatl.com. JAIRO MARTINEZ, Dir. Tel: 404-885-7202. Email: jemartinez@archatl.com; ROCIO ZAMARRON, Office Mgr. Tel: 404-885-7289; Fax: 404-885-7479. Email: rzamarron@archatl.com.

Human Resources—688 W. Peachtree St., N.W., Atlanta, 30308-1984. Tel: 404-978-2775; Fax: 404-885-7497. Web: www.archatl.com. CHARLES THIBAUDEAU, Dir. & Member of the Secretariat. Tel: 404-885-7227; Fax: 404-885-7497. Email: cthibaudeau@archatl.com; MARQUITA RICHBURG, Human Resources Mgr. Tel: 404-885-7254; Fax: 404-885-7497. Email: mrichburg@archatl.com; LILY GALLAGHER, Benefits Mgr. Tel: 404-885-7409; Fax: 404-885-7497. Email: lgallagher@archatl.com; ROSA MONTANO-PARKER, Senior Benefits Specialist. Tel: 404-885-7406; Fax: 404-885-7497. Email: rmontano-parker@archatl.com; STEPHANIE LANDRUM, Volunteer Coord. Tel: 404-885-7220; Fax: 404-885-7497; CHAUNDRA LOUARD, Human Resources Specialist. Tel: 404-885-7437; Fax: 404-885-7497. Email: clouard@archatl.com; ANGELA GRAHAM, Receptionist. Tel: 404-885-7403. Email: agraham@archatl.com. Human Resources Assistants: BRENDA POLLOCK. Tel: 404-885-7204; Fax: 404-885-7497. Email: bpollock@archatl.com; DALIA KINSEY. Tel: 404-978-2775; Fax: 404-885-7497. Email: dkinsey@archatl.com.

Information Technology—680 W. Peachtree St., N.W., Atlanta, 30308-1984. TOM POPE, Dir. Tel: 404-885-7432; Fax: 404-885-7223.

Email: tpope@archatl.com; TOMASZ KASPRZYK, Information Technology Mgr. Tel: 404-978-2774; Fax: 404-885-7223. Email: tkasprzyk@archatl.com; CHAD SIGLER, Sr. Systems Analyst. Tel: 404-751-2383; Fax: 404-885-7223. Email: csiglar@archatl.com; BEN VIGIL, Sr. Systems Analyst. Tel: 404-751-2383; Fax: 404-885-7223. Email: bvigil@archatl.com; SANDRA LONG, Sr. Software Analyst. Tel: 404-626-6009; Fax: 404-885-7223. Email: slong@archatl.com; ANGEL ROSA, Support Specialist I. Tel: 404-885-7241; Fax: 404-885-7223. Email: arosa@archatl.com; CHANDLER RICHBURG, Assoc. Support Specialist & iPortal Trainer. Tel: 404-885-7241; Fax: 404-885-7223. Email: crichburg@archatl.com.

Metropolitan Tribunal—680 W. Peachtree St., N.W., Atlanta, 30308-1984. Tel: 404-888-7815; Fax: 404-885-7242. Web: www.archatl.com/offices/tribunal. Email: tribunal@archatl.com.

Judicial Vicar—Most Rev. LUIS R. ZARAMA, J.C.L., V.G., J.V., 680 W. Peachtree St., N.W., Atlanta, 30308. Tel: 404-885-7805; Fax: 404-885-7230. Email: lzarama@archatl.com.

Executive Secretary to the Judicial Vicar—DIANE GILSDORF. Tel: 404-885-7446; Fax: 404-885-7242. Email: dgilsdorf@archatl.com.

Adjutant Judicial Vicars—Rev. Msgr. STEPHEN T. CHURCHWELL, J.C.D., V.F.; Rev. MICHAEL U. ONYEKURU, J.C.D.

Court Administrator—Dr. DAVID CASTRONOVO, J.D., Court Admin. Email: dcastronovo@archatl.com.

Archdiocesan Judges—Rev. Msgr. EDWARD J. DILLON, J.C.D.; Rev. MICHAEL U. ONYEKURU, J.C.D.; Dr. DAVID CASTRONOVO, J.D., Court Admin.

Court Expert—Dr. ED YAROSZ, Ed.D.

Defenders of the Bond—Deacon ALFRED T. SAMORANSKI; Mrs. ELYN MACEK, J.D.

Auditors—Bro. NICHOLAS WOLFLA, O.F.M.Conv., J.C.L., Chief Auditor; CATHERINE MCCARTY; ROBERT BROOKS, J.D.

Advocates—Rev. PEDRO POLOCHE, J.C.L., Chief Advocate; JEAN GUETTLER; DOROTHY WESSELMAN; JOSEPH TOVAR.

Notaries—WENDY A. ABRAHAM, Case Mgr. & Chief Notary; MICHELE CHAMORRO; KARREN DEBOW; PAM ROQUE; MARCO GALLARDO.

Case Sponsor Coordinator—Deacon WHITNEY ROBICHAUX.

Permanent Diaconate—680 W. Peachtree St., N.W., Atlanta, 30308-1984. Tel: 404-885-7407; Fax: 404-885-7462. Deacon DENNIS J. DORNER, Dir. Office of Permanent Diaconate. Tel: 404-885-7407; Fax: 404-885-7462. Email: ddorner@archatl.com; Rev. TIMOTHY M. HEPBURN, Office of Permanent Diaconate & Spiritual Dir., Catholic Center at Georgia Tech, 172 Fourth St., NW, Atlanta, 30313. Tel: 404-892-6759; Fax: 404-892-6759. Email: frhepburn@gmail.com; Deacon STEVE SWOPE, Assoc. Dir. Formation, Office of Permanent Diaconate. Tel: 404-885-7265; Fax: 404-885-7462. Email: sswope@archatl.com; PHILLIS CURRY, Exec. Asst. Tel: 404-885-7296; Fax: 404-885-7462. Email: pcurry@archatl.com; Most Rev. LUIS R. ZARAMA, J.C.L., V.G., J.V., Episcopal Delegate. Tel: 404-888-7805; Fax: 404-885-7230. Email: lzarama@archatl.com; KIRIAL DEROZAS-MILES. Tel: 404-885-7490; Fax: 404-885-7230. Email: kderozas-miles@archatl.com.

Stewardship—680 W. Peachtree St., N.W., Atlanta, 30308-1984. Tel: 404-885-7423; Fax: 404-885-7494. Web: www.archatl.com. STEVE SILER, Exec. Dir. Stewardship. Tel: 404-885-7226; Fax: 404-885-7494. Email: ssiler@archatl.com; CHRISTINE HEUSINGER, Stewardship Coord. Tel: 404-885-7277; Fax: 404-885-7494. Email: cheusinger@archatl.com; GEORGIA BABIC, Administrative Asst. Tel: 404-751-2382; Fax: 404-885-7494. Email: gbabic@archatl.com; TRACY ZELCZAK, Administrative Asst. Tel: 404-885-7423; Fax: 404-885-7494. Email: tzelczak@archatl.com; BILL WIDER, Devel. Assoc. Tel: 404-885-7264; Fax: 404-888-7816. Email: bwider@archatl.com.

The Disabilities Ministry—680 W. Peachtree St., N.W., Atlanta, 30308-1984. Tel: 404-888-7809; Fax: 404-885-7439. Web: www.archatl.com. Mr. ED MCCOY, Dir. Tel: 404-888-7809; Fax: 404-885-7439. Email: emccoy@archatl.com; Mrs. DEB GARNER, Coord. Deaf Svcs. Tel: 404-888-7846; Fax: 404-885-7439. Email: dgarner@archatl.com.

Respect Life—680 W. Peachtree St., N.W., Atlanta, 30308-1984. Tel: 404-888-7821; Fax: 404-885-7286. Web: www.archatl.com. MARY BOYERT, Dir. Tel: 404-885-7442; Fax: 404-885-7286. Email: mboyert@archatl.com.

Office of Formation and Discipleship—680 W. Peachtree St., N.W., Atlanta, 30308. Tel: 404-885-7413; Fax: 404-885-7473. Web: www.archatl.com. DENNIS LEE JOHNSON JR., Dir., Admin. & Member of the Secretariat. Tel: 404-885-7413; Fax: 404-885-7473. Email: djohnsonjr@archatl.com; IVONNE S. VREELAND, Office Mgr. Tel: 404-885-7484; Fax: 404-885-7473. Email: ivreeland@archatl.com; AIXA MCLEAN, Administrative Asst. Tel: 404-885-7413; Fax: 404-885-7473. Email: amclean@archatl.com.

Catechetical Ministry—SORANGEL GOVIN, Assoc. Dir. Tel: 404-885-7235; Fax: 404-885-7473. Email: sgovin@archatl.com.

Office for Youth Ministry—MARILYN SANTOS, Assoc. Dir. Tel: 404-885-7231; Fax: 404-885-7473. Email: msantos@archatl.com; ANA NAGEL, Administrative Asst., 680 W. Peachtree St., N.W., Atlanta, 30308. Tel: 404-885-7458; Fax: 404-885-7473. Email: anagel@archatl.com.

Inculturation Ministry—MARILYN SANTOS, Assoc. Dir. Tel: 404-885-7231; Fax: 404-885-7473.

Office for Young Adult Ministry—DOROTHY POLCHINSKI, Assoc. Dir. Tel: 404-885-7248; Fax: 404-885-7473. Email: dpolchinski@archatl.com; JULIANA BARROSO, Prog. Coord., 680 W. Peachtree St., N.W., Atlanta, 30308. Tel: 404-885-7222; Fax: 404-885-7473. Email: jbarroso@archatl.com.

Office for Adult Ministry—DOROTHY POLCHINSKI, Assoc. Dir. Tel: 404-885-7248; Fax: 404-885-7473. Email: dpolchinski@archatl.com.

Vocations—680 W. Peachtree St., N.W., Atlanta, 30308-1984. Tel: 404-888-7844; Fax: 404-888-7849. Web: www.calledbychrist.com. Very Rev. LUKE R. BALLMAN, S.T.L., Dir. Tel: 404-888-7844; Fax: 404-888-7849. Email: lballman@archatl.com. Secretaries: SALLY SCARDASIS. Tel: 404-978-2779; Fax: 404-888-7849. Email: sscardasis@archatl.com; LIVIA DOMINGUES. Tel: 404-885-7298; Fax: 404-888-7849. Email: ldomingues@archatl.com.

Other Archdiocesan Offices

AACCW—SHIRLEY TOWLE, Pres., 58 Kentucky Ave., Sharpsburg, 30277. Tel: 770-683-0060. Email: stowle@numail.org; Rev. TIMOTHY GADZIALA, J.C.L., Spiritual Moderator, Saint Anthony of Padua Catholic Church, 928 Ralph David Abernathy Blvd., S.W., Atlanta, 30310. Tel: 404-758-8861; Fax: 404-755-6755. Email: stanthny@hotmail.com.

Cursillo—Sr. MARGARET MCANOY, I.H.M., Dir., 3731 Embry Cir., Atlanta, 30341. Tel: 770-455-1500.

Georgia Catholic Conference—FRANK MULCAHY, c/o Tinsley, Bacon & Tinsley, L.L.C., 3600 Mansell Rd., Ste. 300, Alpharetta, 30022. Tel: 770-521-8799. Email: fmulcahy@tbtlaw.com.

Boy Scouts—Rev. Msgr. WILLIAM G. HOFFMAN, Chap. (Retired), St. George Village, Apt. 2124, 11350 Woodstock Rd., Roswell, 30075. Tel: 770-645-2340. Email: msgrbill@yahoo.com; Rev. ROBERT A. FREDERICK, Asst. Chap., St. Luke the Evangelist Catholic Church, 91 N. Park St., Dahlonega, 30533. Tel: 706-864-4779; Fax: 706-864-2536. Email: frbobfred@gmail.com.

Archdiocesan Councils, Boards, Commissions, and Committees

Atlanta Conference of Sisters—Sr. JOAN MCCANN, O.P., 3230 Oakbrook Lane, Clarkston, 30021. Tel: 404-294-8685; Fax: 404-294-8685. Email: jmccannop@bellsouth.net.

Audit Committee—KIERAN QUINN, Chm.

Benefits Committee—PAT MANNELLY, Chm.

Budget and Operations Committee—PAT MANNELLY, Chm.

Catholic Charities of the Archdiocese of Atlanta, Inc.—JOHN NEE, Chm.

Council of Priests—Rev. EDWARD B. BRANCH, Chm., Atlanta University - Lyke House. Tel: 404-755-2646. Email: ebranch@intergate.com.

Eucharistic Congress Committee—Deacon DENNIS J. DORNER, Chancellor & Dir. Office of Permanent Diaconate. Tel: 404-885-7407; Fax: 404-885-7462. Email: ddorner@archatl.com; MARDESSA SMITH, Administrative Asst. Tel: 404-885-7445; Fax: 404-885-7462. Email: mwsmith@archatl.com.

Finance Council—GEORGE AULBACH, Chm.

Investment Committee—MATT MCDANIEL, Chm.

Advisory Board on Sexual Abuse of Minors—Rev. Msgr. EDWARD J. DILLON, J.C.D., Promoter of Justice.

Liturgical Commission—Rev. THEODORE BOOK, S.L.D., 680 W. Peachtree St., N.W., Atlanta, 30308-1984. Tel: 404-888-7801; Fax: 404-885-7230. Email: tbook@archatl.com.

Project Review Committee—GEORGE AULBACH, Chm.

St. George Village—Catholic Community Retirement Center, 11350 Woodstock Rd., Roswell, 30075. Mr. MARK A. LOWELL, Exec. Dir. Tel: 678-987-0404; ZANDRA ANDERSON, Concierge Supvr.

Board of Directors—Most Revs. WILTON D. GREGORY, S.L.D.; LUIS R. ZARAMA, J.C.L., V.G., J.V.; GEORGE AULBACH; Rev. Msgr. W. JOSEPH CORBETT, V.G., Moderator of the Curia; BRADLEY WILSON, CFO, Archdiocese of Atlanta; HAL BARRY; MATT MCDANIEL; MICHAEL REILLY; STEPHEN BACHMAN.

Council of Deacons—Deacon MICHAEL T. BYRNE, Chm.

Diaconate Advisory Board—Deacon DENNIS J. DORNER, Facilitator.

Archdiocese of Atlanta Pastoral Council—Most Rev. WILTON D. GREGORY, S.L.D., Chm.

Archdiocesan School Advisory Council—CHRIS REYNOLDS, Chm.

CLERGY, PARISHES, MISSIONS AND PAROCHIAL SCHOOLS

CITY OF ATLANTA

(FULTON COUNTY)

1—CATHEDRAL OF CHRIST THE KING (1936) [CEM] Most Rev. Wilton D. Gregory, Archbishop of Atlanta; Rev. Francis G. McNamee; Very Rev. Richard B. Morrow (Retired); Revs. Neil Dhabliwala, Parochial Vicar; Jorge Arevalo, Parochial Vicar; Deacons Whitney Robichaux; Scott J.N. McNabb; John J. McManus.
Church: 2699 Peachtree Rd., N.E., 30305. Tel: 404-233-2145; Fax: 404-233-9711. Web: www.cathedralofchristtheking.org.
See Cathedral of Christ the King Catholic School, Atlanta under Archdiocesan Schools, located in the Institution section.
Catechesis/Religious Program—Tel: 404-267-3694; Fax: 404-233-4984. Web: www.religioused.com. Students 1,212.

2—ST. ANTHONY OF PADUA (1903) Rev. Timothy Gadziala; Deacons Joseph Barker; Leviticus Jelks; William H. Simmons III.
Church: 928 Ralph David Abernathy Blvd., S.W., 30310. Tel: 404-758-8861; Fax: 404-755-6755. Web: parishesonline.com/scripts/hostedsites/org.asp?ID=12639.
Catechesis/Religious Program—Fax: 404-755-6755. Students 44.

3—HOLY CROSS (1964) Revs. Richard Tibbetts; Gregory Anatuanya, Parochial Vicar; F. Javier Munoz, Parochial Vicar; Deacons Cece Reimer; Tom Silvestri; James Weiss; Whitney Robichaux. In Res., Rev. Edward A.J. Danneker (Retired).
Res.: 3175 Hathaway Ct., 30341.
Church: 3773 Chamblee-Tucker Rd., 30341. Tel: 770-939-3501; Fax: 770-723-7013. Email: office@holycrossatlanta.org. Web: www.holycrossatlanta.org.
Catechesis/Religious Program—Tel: 770-939-3501, Ext. 233 (English); 770-939-3501, Ext. 235 (Spanish). Sr. Pilar Dalmau, C.R.E.; Aida Buseta, C.R.E. Students 1,328.
Mission—Holy Vietnamese Martyr's Mission (2003) Revs. Tuan Quoc Tran, Admin.; Tran Duy Hung, Parochial Vicar.

4—HOLY SPIRIT (1964) Rev. Msgr. Edward J. Dillon; Revs. Paul A. Burke, Parochial Vicar; James Flanagan, Parochial Vicar; Deacons Thomas B. Shuler; William F. McCarthy; Joseph Ruberte; Allen Underwood; Stephen G. Demko. In Res., Rev. John C.K. Fallon.
Church: 4465 Northside Dr., N.W., 30327. Tel: 404-252-4513; Fax: 404-252-1162. Web: hsccatl.com.
See Holy Spirit Preparatory School, Atlanta, under Independent Schools located in the Institution Section
Catechesis/Religious Program—Students 521.
Mission—Centro Catolico del Espiritu Santo 120 Northwood Dr., Ste. B5-8, Fulton Co. 30342. Tel: 404-303-9927; Fax: 404-303-0620. Rev. Fausto Marquez.

5—IMMACULATE HEART OF MARY (1958) Very Rev. James A. Schillinger; Rev. Juan Anzora, Parochial Vicar.
Church: 2855 Briarcliff Rd., N.E., 30329. Tel: 404-636-1418; Fax: 404-636-4394. Web: www.ihmatlanta.org.
See Immaculate Heart of Mary Catholic School, Atlanta under Archdiocesan Schools, located in the Institution section.
Catechesis/Religious Program—Tel: 404-636-4458. Students 750.

6—ST. JUDE (1960) [CEM] Rev. Msgr. James J. Fennessy; Revs. Rosenilton Do Carmo Araujo, Parochial Vicar; Fausto Marquez, Parochial Vicar; Daniel Ketter, Parochial Vicar; Deacons Robert Riddett; James A. Tramonte.
Church: 7171 Glenridge Dr. N.E., 30328. Tel: 770-394-3896; Fax: 770-399-7866. Web: www.stjudeatlanta.net.
See St. Jude the Apostle Catholic School, Atlanta

under Archdiocesan Schools, located in the Institution section.
Catechesis/Religious Program—Students 378.

7—MOST BLESSED SACRAMENT (1960) Rev. Bruce W. Wilkinson; Deacon Fred Tocca.
Church: 2971 Butner Rd., S.W., 30331. Tel: 404-349-0176; Fax: 404-349-0178. Web: www.mbschurch.com.
Rectory—1926 Austin Rd., 30331. Tel: 404-349-1406.
Catechesis/Religious Program—Tel: 404-629-1287. Students 75.

8—OUR LADY OF LOURDES (1912) Rev. John S. Adamski; Deacon Chester H. Griffin.
Church: 25 Boulevard, N.E., 30312. Tel: 404-522-6776; Fax: 404-222-0202. Web: www.lourdesatlanta.org.
Catechesis/Religious Program—Students 182.

9—OUR LADY OF THE ASSUMPTION (1951) Revs. James D. Duffy, S.M.; John J. Sullivan, S.M., Parochial Vicar; Eugene E. Hughes, S.M. (Retired); Bro. Ernest Morasci, S.M.; Deacons Bill Bevacqua; Michael J. O'Brien; William Garrett; Chris Thompson; Terry Biglow; Bob Gregerson; Antonius Anugerah; Edward Patterson.
Church: 1350 Hearst Dr., N.E., 30319. Tel: 404-261-7181; Fax: 404-364-1913. Web: www.olachurch.org.
See Our Lady of the Assumption Catholic School, Atlanta under Archdiocesan Schools, located in the Institution section.
Catechesis/Religious Program—Students 267.
Chapel—Marist School 3790 Ashford Dunwoody Rd., 30319. Tel: 770-457-7201; Fax: 770-457-8402. Web: www.marist.com.
Chapel—St. Joseph's Hospital 5665 Peachtree Dunwoody Rd., NE, 30319. Tel: 404-851-7001; Fax: 404-851-5901. Web: www.stjosephsatlanta.org.
Chapel—Sisters of Mercy Convent at St. Joseph's Hospital, Tel: 404-255-6427.

10—ST. PAUL OF THE CROSS (1954) Rev. Jerome McKenna, C.P.; Deacons George Smith; Hilliard M. Lee Jr.; Joseph Goolsby.
Church: 551 Harwell Rd., N.W., 30318. Tel: 404-696-6704; Fax: 404-696-4735. Email: info@spcatl.catholicweb.com. Web: www.spcatl.catholicweb.com.
Catechesis/Religious Program—Students 108.

11—SACRED HEART OF JESUS (1880) Rev. T. J. Meehan; Deacons Wayne D. Smith; Michael K. Balfour; Marino Gonzalez. In Res., Rev. Pedro Poloche Rodriguez.
Church: 353 Peachtree St., N.E., 30308. Tel: 404-522-6800; Fax: 404-524-5440. Web: www.sacredheartatlanta.org.
Catechesis/Religious Program—Students 770.
Mission—San Felipe de Jesus 925 Conley Rd., Forest Park, Clayton Co. 30297. Tel: 404-675-0540. Rev. Jacques E. Fabre, C.S., Admin.

12—SHRINE OF THE IMMACULATE CONCEPTION (1848) Rev. Msgr. Henry C. Gracz; Deacons William Payne; Bart DeSandre.
Church: 48 Martin Luther King, Jr. Dr., S.W., 30303-3599. Tel: 404-521-1866; Fax: 404-524-2297. Email: theshrine@mindspring.com. Web: www.catholicshrineatlanta.org.
Catechesis/Religious Program—Students 30.

OUTSIDE CITY OF ATLANTA

ALPHARETTA, FULTON CO., ST. THOMAS AQUINAS (1972) [CEM] Revs. Gregory D. Goolsby; Mansueto P. Palang, Parochial Vicar; Very Rev. Jose Duvan Gonzalez-Florez, Parochial Vicar; Deacons William W. Keeling; Edmund LaHouse; John Strachan; Kevin F. Tracy; Arthur Lerma; Jose I. Pupo.
Church: 535 Rucker Rd., 30004. Tel: 770-475-4501; Fax: 770-772-0355. Web: www.sta.org.
Catechesis/Religious Program—Tel: 770-475-4508. Students 1,459.

ATHENS, CLARKE CO., ST. JOSEPH (1873) Very Rev. David McGuinness; Rev. Juan Carlos Betancourt; Deacon Jim Gaudin.
Church: 134 Prince Ave., 30601. Tel: 706-548-6332; Fax: 706-354-1783.
See St. Joseph's Catholic School, Athens under Archdiocesan Schools, located in the Institution section.
Catechesis/Religious Program—Tel: 706-548-5487; Fax: 706-548-5487. Students 416.
Chapel—St. Mary's Hospital, Tel: 706-389-3000; Fax: 706-389-3931. Email: ploome@stmarysathens.org. Web: www.stmarysathens.org. Nurses 342; Total Staff 1,421.
Chapel—Catholic Student Center at The University of Georgia 1344 S. Lumpkin St., 30605-1345. Tel: 706-543-2293; Fax: 706-543-2541. Web: www.uga.edu/cc. Revs. Thomas F. Vigliotta, O.F.M., Dir. Campus Ministry; David L. Hyman, O.F.M., Assoc. Campus Min.

BLAIRSVILLE, UNION CO., ST. FRANCIS OF ASSISI (1966) [CEM] [JC] Very Rev. Richard P. Wise; Rev. Arturo Haro-Palos, Parochial Vicar; Deacons Lawrence Casey; Paul Dietz.
Church: 3717 Hwy. 515 E., 30512-3288. Tel: 706-745-6400; Fax: 706-745-1468. Email: saintfrancis@windstream.net.
Catechesis/Religious Program—Tel: 706-781-4291. Students 125.

BLUE RIDGE, FANNIN CO., ST. ANTHONY (1976) [CEM] Rev. John T. Conway; Deacons Loris Sinanian; John Mason.
E. Main St., P.O. Box 1448, 30513. Tel: 706-632-5970; Fax: 706-632-2120. Email: stanthony@tds.net. Web: www.stanthonyblueridge.parishesonline.com.
Catechesis/Religious Program—Students 23.

CALHOUN, GORDON CO., ST. CLEMENT (1958) Rev. Joseph Shaute; Deacon Bradford Krupa.
Mailing Address: 875 Hwy. 53, S.W., 30701. Tel: 706-629-2345; Fax: 706-625-5219. Email: stclementcalhoun@yahoo.com. Web: www.stclementsga.org.
Catechesis/Religious Program—Students 363.

CANTON, CHEROKEE CO., OUR LADY OF LASALETTE (1984) Rev. Victor J. Reyes; Deacon Charles E. Carignan.
2941 Sam Nelson Rd., 30114. Tel: 770-479-8923 (Office); Fax: 770-479-6025 (Office).
Catechesis/Religious Program—Students 176.

CARROLLTON, CARROLL CO., CHURCH OF OUR LADY OF PERPETUAL HELP (1962) [CEM] Rev. Rafael Carballo; Deacon Jon Gary Atkinson.
Church: 210 Old Center Point Rd., 30117. Tel: 770-832-8977; Fax: 770-832-1666.
Newman Center West Georgia College—
Catechesis/Religious Program—Students 315.

CARTERSVILLE, BARTOW CO., ST. FRANCIS OF ASSISI (1969) [JC] Very Rev. Daniel Stack; Deacon James H. Williams.
Church: 850 Douthit Ferry Rd., 30120. Tel: 770-382-4549; Fax: 770-382-4506. Web: www.st-francis-cartersville.org.
Catechesis/Religious Program—Noel Parro, C.R.E. (English); Cecilia Betancourt, C.R.E. (Spanish); Cynthia Winn, Youth Min. Students 254.

CEDARTOWN, POLK CO., ST. BERNADETTE'S (1941) [JC] Rev. Rafael Castano Fernandez.
Church: 101 S. College St., 30125. Tel: 770-748-1517.
Catechesis/Religious Program—Fax: 770-748-1517. Students 137.

CLARKESVILLE, HABERSHAM CO., ST. MARK (1964), (Hispanic), Rev. Abel Guerrero Orta; Deacons Richard Marinchak; John J. Barone.
Mailing Address: 5410 Hwy. 197 S., 30523. Tel: 706-754-4518; Fax: 706-754-9751.
Res.: 128 Rolling Hills Dr., 30523. Tel: 706-754-6504.
Catechesis/Religious Program—Students 134.
Mission—St. Helena P.O. Box 534, Clayton, Rabun Co. 30525. Tel: 706-782-5152; Fax: 706-782-5152. Email: sthelenachurchclayton@windstream.net. Deacon David Hanson.

CLEVELAND, WHITE CO., ST. PAUL THE APOSTLE (1964) Revs. Vincent Sullivan; Arturo Haro-Palos, Parochial Vicar.
1243 Hulsey Rd., 30528. Tel: 706-865-4474; Fax: 706-219-3009. Web: stpaulclevelandga.parishesonline.com.
Catechesis/Religious Program—Laurie Vitek, D.R.E. Students 135.

CONYERS, ROCKDALE CO., ST. PIUS X (1974) Revs. John C. Kieran; Timothy Gallagher, Parochial Vicar; Deacons Brian Kilkelly; Fred Johns; Joseph Rhodes; Stuart A. Mead.
Church: 2621 Hwy. 20, S.E., 30013-2424. Tel: 770-483-3660; Fax: 770-483-7006.
Catechesis/Religious Program—Tel: 770-929-1017. Students 546.

COVINGTON, NEWTON CO., ST. AUGUSTINE OF HIPPO (1977) Rev. Roberto Orellana; Deacons Thomas J. Metzger; Richard A. Mickle.
Church: 11524 Hwy. 278 E., 30014. Tel: 770-787-1064; Fax: 770-787-0871. Email: office@staugcc.org. Web: home.catholicweb.com/StAugustineCovington/.
Catechesis/Religious Program—Tel: 770-787-9052. Students 161.
Mission—St. James 562 Vine St., Madison, Morgan Co. 30650. Tel: 706-342-9661; Fax: 706-342-2860. Deacon Herbert C. Berding, Admin.

CUMMING, FORSYTH CO.

1—ST. BRENDAN THE NAVIGATOR (2000) Revs. John T. Howren; Fabio A. Alvarez, Parochial Vicar; Deacons Roger A. Fraser; William J. Monahan; Paul Lee Doppel; Eduardo J. Rubio.
4633 Shiloh Rd., 30040. Tel: 770-205-7969; Fax: 770-205-5040. Web: www.stbrendansatl.com.
Catechesis/Religious Program—Students 1,221.

2—GOOD SHEPHERD (1975) Revs. Francis X. Richardson; Alvaro Avendano, Parochial Vicar; Deacons Donald N. Nadeau; Ralph LaMachia.
Church: 3740 Holtzclaw Rd., 30041. Tel: 770-887-9861; Fax: 770-887-2241. Web: www.goodshepherdcumming.com.
Catechesis/Religious Program—Tel: 770-887-9861, Ext. 16; Fax: 770-887-9861. Students 667.

DAHLONEGA, LUMPKIN CO., ST. LUKE (1960) Revs. Robert A. Frederick; Alvaro Avendano, Parochial Vicar; Deacon Dennis J. Dorner.
Church: 91 N. Park St., 30533. Tel: 706-864-4779; Fax: 706-864-2568. Email: pastor@stlukercc.org. Web: www.stlukercc.org.
Catechesis/Religious Program—Michael Ferrin, Youth Min. & Campus Min.; Kelly Peffer, D.R.E. Students 173.
Station—North Georgia College (Newman Club) 91 N. Park St., 30597. Email: college@stlukercc.org. Web: www.ngcsucatholic.org.

DALLAS, PAULDING CO., ST. VINCENT DE PAUL (2003) Rev. Adrian C.H. Pleus; Deacons Jose Perez; James McDermott; Stephen J. Bek.
680 W. Memorial Dr., 30132. Tel: 770-443-0566 (Office); Fax: 770-443-1612 (Office). Email: svdpchurch@bellsouth.net. Web: saintvincentdepaulchurch.org.
Catechesis/Religious Program—Tel: 770-443-0566; Fax: 770-443-1612. Students 300.

DALTON, WHITFIELD CO., ST. JOSEPH'S (1941) [JC] Revs. Paul D. Williams Jr.; Juan de Dios Oliveros, Parochial Vicar.
Res.: 969 Haigmill Lake Rd., 30720.
Church: 968 Haigmill Lake Rd., 30720. Tel: 706-278-3107; Fax: 706-278-6902. Web: www.sjccdalton.com.
Catechesis/Religious Program—Cathy Blevins, D.R.E. Students 1,200.

DAWSONVILLE, DAWSON CO., CHRIST REDEEMER CATHOLIC CHURCH (1982) Rev. Msgr. Stephen T. Churchwell; Deacons Kenneth Williams; Ray Richardson.
Church: 991 Kilough Church Rd., 30534. Tel: 706-265-1361; Fax: 706-265-1363.
Catechesis/Religious Program—Students 71.

DECATUR, DEKALB CO.

1—STS. PETER AND PAUL (1959) [JC] Rev. Eric J. Hill; Deacons Jerry Lett; Alfred Mitchell.
Res: 2372 Collier Dr., 30032. Tel: 404-241-5862 (Office); Fax: 404-241-5839 (Office). Web: www.stspandp.com.
Church: 2560 Tilson Rd., 30032.
See St. Peter Claver Regional Catholic School, Decatur under Archdiocesan Schools, located in the Institution section.
Catechesis/Religious Program—Gloria George-Patrick, D.R.E. Students 102.

2—ST. THOMAS MORE (1949) Rev. Msgr. Paul Fogarty; Rev. Brian Lorei, Parochial Vicar.
Church: 636 W. Ponce de Leon Ave., 30030. Tel: 404-378-4588; Fax: 404-378-0506. Web: www.stmgaparish.org.
See St. Thomas More Catholic School, Decatur under Archdiocesan Schools, located in the Institution section.
Catechesis/Religious Program—Students 250.

DORAVILLE, DEKALB CO., KOREAN MARTYRS CATHOLIC CHURCH (1977) Revs. Isidore Jeong-Ho An, S.J.; Hyong-Nyol Ryu, S.J., Parochial Vicar.
6003 Buford Hwy., N.E., 30340. Tel: 770-455-1380; Fax: 770-455-4262. Web: www.kmccga.org.
Catechesis/Religious Program—Students 250.

DOUGLASVILLE, DOUGLAS CO., ST. THERESA (1985) Revs. Fernando Molina-Restrepo; William T. Hao, Parochial Vicar; Deacons Ronald A. St. Michel; Terry M. Holmer; Charles Patrick; Israel D. Melara.
Church: 4401 Prestley Mill Rd., 30135. Tel: 770-489-7115; Fax: 770-489-4873. Web: www.sainttheresacatholicchurch.org.
Catechesis/Religious Program—Tel: 770-942-9765. Students 645.

DULUTH, GWINNETT CO., ST. MONICA (1994) Revs. John F. Durkin Jr.; Pavol Brenkus, Parochial Vicar; Deacons Bob Tipton; John Koppenaal; Edward Rademacher; Joseph R. Carter.
1700 Buford Hwy., 30097. Tel: 678-584-9947; Fax: 678-584-9760. Web: www.saintmonicas.com.
Rectory—3393 Forrestwood Dr., Suwanee, 30024.
Catechesis/Religious Program—Tel: 678-584-9947. Students 1,280.

DUNWOODY, DEKALB CO., ALL SAINTS (1977) Rev. Msgr. R. Donald Kiernan; Revs. Daniel J. McCormick, Parochial Vicar; Brian J. Higgins, Parochial Vicar; Deacon William Garrett. In Res., Most Rev. John F. Donoghue, Archbishop Emeritus (Retired).
Church: 2443 Mount Vernon Rd., 30338-3099. Tel: 770-393-3255; Fax: 770-913-0140. Web: www.allsaints.us.
Catechesis/Religious Program—Students 670.

ELLIJAY, GILMER CO., GOOD SAMARITAN CATHOLIC CHURCH (1986) Very Rev. Randall Mattox.
55 Church St., 30540. Tel: 706-636-2772; Fax: 706-636-2776.
Catechesis/Religious Program—Students 90.

FAYETTEVILLE, FAYETTE CO., ST. GABRIEL (1993) Rev. Michael L. McWhorter; Deacons I. Carl McBride; Donald S. Parker.
Church: 152 Antioch Rd., 30215-5702. Tel: 770-461-0492; Fax: 770-461-0374. Email: stgabrielchurch@comcast.net. Web: www.stgabrielaga.com.
Catechesis/Religious Program—Tel: 770-461-0493. Students 414.

FLOWERY BRANCH, HALL CO., PRINCE OF PEACE (1978) Revs. Paul W. Berny; Ignacio Morales, Parochial Vicar; Deacons Michael R. Jones; William Speed; Al Samoranski; Michael Woods; Nicholas Johnson.
Church: 6439 Spout Springs Rd., 30542. Tel: 770-945-2244; Fax: 770-945-4599. Email: princeofpeace@popcatholicchurch.org. Web: www.popcatholicchurch.org.
Catechesis / Religious Program—Students 1,447.

FORT OGLETHORPE, CATOOSA CO., ST. GERARD MAJELLA (1952) Rev. Liam Coyne.
3049 LaFayette Rd., 30742. Tel: 706-861-9410; Fax: 706-866-0574. Email: stgeradmin@bellsouth.net.
Catechesis / Religious Program—Tel: 706-861-0563. Students 53.

GAINESVILLE, HALL CO., ST. MICHAEL (1933) Revs. Fabio A. Sotelo-Pena; William Canales, Parochial Vicar; Kizito Okeke, Parochial Vicar; Thad B. Rudd, Parochial Vicar (Retired); Deacons Michael Kennedy; Gary Roche; Gilberto Perez; Luis Londono; Richard Thibodeau.
Church: 1440 Pearce Cir., N.E., 30501-2457. Tel: 770-534-3338; Fax: 770-535-2440. Web: www.saintmichael.cc.
Catechesis / Religious Program—Students 1,335.

GREENSBORO, GREENE CO., CHRIST OUR KING AND SAVIOR (1992), Consolidation of Christ Our Savior, Eatonton, and Christ Our King, Greensboro. Rev. G. Philip Ryan.
Church: 6341 Lake Oconee Pkwy., 30642. Tel: 706-453-7292; Fax: 706-453-7095. Email: admin@cokas.org. Web: www.cokas.org.
Catechesis / Religious Program—Students 84.

GRIFFIN, SPALDING CO., SACRED HEART (1941) Rev. Dennis R. Juan; Deacons Felix Marrero; Kenneth P. Bishop.
Church: 1323 MacArthur Dr., 30224. Tel: 770-227-2378; Fax: 770-227-6440. Email: shpriest@comcast.net.
Catechesis / Religious Program—Tel: 770-227-2898. Students 117.

HAPEVILLE, DEKALB CO., ST. JOHN THE EVANGELIST (1954) Revs. Edward Thein; Hernan Queuedo Rodriguez, Parochial Vicar; Deacons Henry Akers; Tom Stonecipher.
Res.: 3370 Sunset Ave., 30354.
Church: 230 Arnold St., 30354-1530. Tel: 404-768-5647; Fax: 404-767-6416.
See St. John the Evangelist School, Hapeville under Archdiocesan Schools, located in the Institution section.
Catechesis / Religious Program—Fax: 404-767-6416. Mrs. Daphny Keel, C.R.E. Students 246.

HARTWELL, HART CO., SACRED HEART OF JESUS (1977) [CEM] [JC] Rev. Terence Kane; Deacon Jerry Korte.
Church: 1009 Benson St., 30643. Tel: 706-376-4112; 706-522-5723 (Rectory); Fax: 706-376-6207. Email: shj.parish@gmail.com. Web: www.sacredheartofhartwell.com.
Catechesis / Religious Program—Tel: 864-958-0601. Email: stgus8@bellsouth.net. Students 151.

JACKSON, BUTTS CO., SAINT MARY, MOTHER OF GOD CATHOLIC CHURCH (1960) Rev. Msgr. Terry W. Young.
359 Old Griffin Rd., P.O. Box 901, 30233. Tel: 770-775-4162; Fax: 770-775-4174. Email: stmarysinjackson@bellsouth.net.
Catechesis / Religious Program—Students 70.

JASPER, PICKENS CO., OUR LADY OF THE MOUNTAINS (2004) Rev. Charles A. Byrd Jr.
Church: 1908 Waleska Hwy. 108, 30143. Tel: 706-253-3078; 706-268-1902 (Res.); Fax: 706-253-3077. Email: ladyofthemts@ellijay.com.
Catechesis / Religious Program—Students 178.

JOHNS CREEK, FULTON CO.

1—ST. BENEDICT (1987) Revs. Paul Flood; Carlos-Mario Bustamante-Agudelo, Parochial Vicar; Joseph Mullakkara, M.S.F.S., Parochial Vicar; Deacons Gerard G. Kazin; John D. Puetz; Ronald Carr.
Res.: 11085 Parson's Rd., Duluth, 30097.
Church: 11045 Parson's Rd., 30097. Tel: 770-442-5903; Fax: 770-442-0744. Web: www.stbenedict.net.
Catechesis / Religious Program—Tel: 678-992-2511; Fax: 770-442-0744. Students 1,732.
Mission—Mision del Divino Nino Jesus 11045 Parsons Rd., Duluth, Gwinnett Co. 30097.

2—ST. BRIGID (1998) [CEM] Rev. Msgr. Paul H. Reynolds; Revs. Gilbert Exume, Parochial Vicar; Diosmar Natad, Parochial Vicar; Deacons Dennis J. Dorner; James A. LaFreniere; Leo Gahafer; Tom Huff.
3400 Old Alabama Rd., 30022. Tel: 678-393-0060; Fax: 678-393-0071. Email: office@saintbrigid.org. Web: www.saintbrigid.org.
See Holy Redeemer Catholic School, Alpharetta under Archdiocesan Schools located in the Institution section
Catechesis / Religious Program—Students 1,180.

JONESBORO, CLAYTON CO., ST. PHILIP BENIZI (1965) Revs. Gregory J. Hartmayer, O.F.M.Conv.; Abelardo Huanca Martinez, O.F.M.Conv., Parochial Vicar; John Koziol, O.F.M.Conv., Parochial Vicar; Deacons Joseph C. Anzalone; Peter B. Swan Sr.; Richard P. Tolcher; Etienne Francisco Rodriguez; Gregory L. Pecore; Matias A. Casal.
Church: 591 Flint River Rd., 30238-3452. Tel: 770-478-0178; 770-478-4201 (Res.); Fax: 770-471-2079. Web: www.stphilipbenizi.org.
Catechesis / Religious Program—Mary M. Mauldin, D.R.E. Students 537.

KENNESAW, COBB CO., ST. CATHERINE OF SIENA (1981) Revs. John M. Matejek, Admin.; Manuel de Jesus Rivas, Parochial Vicar; Deacons Pat O'Connor; Richard Conti; Burgess "David" Grubbs; Stanley B. Ford; Stephen Ponichtera; Thomas J. Ryan; Miguel A. Echevarria.
Res.: 1644 Ben King Rd., 30144. Tel: 770-419-9112. Web: saintcatherineofsiena.org.
Church: 1618 Ben King Rd., N.W., 30144. Tel: 770-428-7139; Fax: 770-428-0131.
See St. Catherine of Siena Catholic School, Kennesaw under Archdiocesan Schools, located in the Institution section.
Catechesis / Religious Program— Joan Hennes, C.R.E. Students 1,302.

LAGRANGE, TROUP CO., ST. PETER (1936) Rev. Kevin J. Hargaden.
Church: 200 LaFayette Pkwy., 30241. Fax: 706-884-1624. Web: www.stpeterslagrange.org.
Catechesis / Religious Program—Lyss Feria, D.R.E. Students 146.
Mission—St. Elizabeth Seton P.O. Box 638, Warm Springs, Meriwether Co. 31830. Tel: 706-846-5223.

LAWRENCEVILLE, GWINNETT CO.

1—ST. LAWRENCE (1974) Very Rev. Albert W. Jowdy; Rev. Roberto Herrera-Castaneda, Parochial Vicar; Deacons A.B. King III; Patrick Fagan; Terry D. Millinger; John R. Peterson; Richard Downey.
Church: 319 Grayson Hwy., 30046. Tel: 770-963-8992; Fax: 770-963-1710. Web: www.saintlaw.org.
Catechesis / Religious Program—Tel: 770-962-2765. Students 609.

2—ST. MARGUERITE D'YOUVILLE (1994) Revs. James Harrison; Joseph Mendes, M.S.F.S.; Marek Ciesla, S.Chr., Parochial Vicar; Deacon George D. Angelich.
Church: 85 Gloster Rd., 30044. Tel: 770-381-7337; 770-931-0099 (Res.); Fax: 770-381-6568.
Catechesis / Religious Program—Students 246.

LILBURN, GWINNETT CO.

1—ST. JOHN NEUMANN (1977) Rev. Msgr. David P. Talley; Rev. Armando Herrejon-Lopez, Parochial Vicar; Deacons Gary Womack; Michael T. Byrne; Greg Ollick; William H. Marten.
Church: 801 Tom Smith Rd., 30047-2299. Tel: 770-923-6633; Fax: 770-381-7856. Web: www.sjnlilburn.com.
See St. John Neumann Catholic School, Lilburn under Archdiocesan Schools located in the Institution section.
Catechesis / Religious Program—Laura Todd, D.R.E. Students 726.

2—ST. STEPHEN THE MARTYR (1999) Revs. Patrick H.M. Donaghey; John Paul Ezeonyido, Parochial Vicar; Deacons Evelio Garcia-Carreras; Michael K. Mobley Sr.; Lawrence French.
Church & Res.: 5373 Wydella Rd., 30047. Tel: 770-381-7488; Fax: 770-923-8061. Web: www.ststephenthemartyr.info.
Catechesis / Religious Program—Students 131.

LITHIA SPRINGS, DOUGLAS CO., ST. JOHN VIANNEY (1958) Very Rev. Carl Zdancewicz, O.F.M.Conv.; Revs. Paulino Matus Castillo, O.F.M.Conv., Parochial Vicar; Martin Breski, O.F.M. Conv., Parochial Vicar.
Church: 1920 Skyview Dr., 30122. Tel: 770-941-2807; 770-745-5445 (Res.); Fax: 770-941-5821. Web: www.sjvpar.com.
Catechesis / Religious Program—Students 396.

LITHONIA, DEKALB CO., CHRIST OUR HOPE (1984) Rev. Guyma Noel; Deacon Gerald A. Collins.
1786 Wellborn Rd., 30058. Tel: 770-482-5017; Fax: 770-482-9476. Web: www.christourhopeatl.org.
Catechesis / Religious Program—Students 88.

LOOKOUT MOUNTAIN, WALKER CO., OUR LADY OF THE MOUNT (1947) [JC] Rev. Msgr. Leo P. Herbert.
Church: 1227 Scenic Hwy., 30750. Tel: 706-820-0680; 706-820-2691 (Res.); Fax: 706-820-2797. Web: www.olmga.org. (Memorial Garden For Ashes)
Catechesis / Religious Program—Students 94.
Mission—St. Katherine Drexel 109 New England Rd., P.O. Box 1032, Trenton, Dade Co. 30753-1032.

MABLETON, COBB CO., ST. FRANCIS DE SALES (1999) Revs. Mark F. Fischer, F.S.S.P.; Thomas M. Fritschen, F.S.S.P., Parochial Vicar; Deacon Douglas J. Anderson.
Church: 587 Landers Dr., 30126. Tel: 770-948-6888; 770-745-3464 (Res.); Fax: 770-948-6888. Web: www.francisdesales.com.
Catechesis / Religious Program—Randall Mandock, D.R.E. Students 52.

MARIETTA, COBB CO.

1—ST. ANN (1978) Revs. Thomas A. Reilly, M.S.; Raymond G. Cadran, M.S., Parochial Vicar; Joseph G. Aquino, M.S., Parochial Vicar; John Gabriel, M.S., Parochial Vicar; Deacons Edmund M. Grabowy; J. Nicholas Morning; Bobby Allen Jennings.
Church: 4905 Roswell Rd., N.E., 30062. Tel: 770-552-6400; 770-552-6400 (Res.); Fax: 770-552-6420. Web: www.st-ann.org.
Catechesis / Religious Program—Tel: 770-552-6400, Ext. 6044; Fax: 770-552-6421. Students 2,000.

2—CHURCH OF THE TRANSFIGURATION (1977) Rev. Msgr. Patrick A. Bishop; Revs. Arcangel Cardenas-Martinez, S.S.P., Parochial Vicar; Dominic Tran, Parochial Vicar; Deacons Tom Coffey; Jim Easterwood; Jose G. Espinosa; Paul A. Gorski.
Church: 1815 Blackwell Rd., N.E., 30066-2911. Tel: 770-977-1442; 770-977-2756 (Res.); Fax: 770-578-1415. Email: staff@transfiguration.com. Web: www.transfiguration.com.
Catechesis / Religious Program—Joyce Guris, D.R.E. Students 1,695.

3—HOLY FAMILY (1973) Revs. Darragh Griffith; Casmir Maduakor, Parochial Vicar; Manuel de Jesus Rivas, Parochial Vicar; Adam Z. Ozimek, Parochial Vicar; Deacons Ronald A. Comeau; Al Gallagher; John P. Duffield.
Church: 3401 Lower Roswell Rd., 30068-3974. Tel: 770-973-0038; Fax: 770-578-0475. Web: www.holyfamilycc.org.
Catechesis / Religious Program—Students 282.

4—ST. JOSEPH (1952) Revs. John P. Walsh; Michael S. Sherliza, Parochial Vicar; Omar Loggiodice, Parochial Vicar; Deacons Thomas Shaver; Joseph C. Eustace; Bruce Reed.
Church: 87 Lacy St., N.W., 30060. Tel: 770-422-5633; Fax: 770-422-1148. Web: www.saintjosephcc.org.
See St. Joseph Catholic School, Marietta under Archdiocesan Schools, located in the Institution section.
Catechesis / Religious Program—Tel: 770-422-5633, Ext. 51; Fax: 770-422-1472. Students 1,205.

MCDONOUGH, HENRY CO., ST. JAMES THE APOSTLE (1979) Revs. John Murphy; Jose Kochuparampil, C.M.F., Parochial Vicar; Deacon Patrick (Pat) J. Gillespie.
1000 Decatur Rd., Hwy. 155, 30252. Web: www.stjamesmcdonough.com.
Church: 1000 Decatur Rd., 30252. Tel: 770-957-5441; Fax: 770-957-0383. Email: stjammcd@bellsouth.net.
Catechesis / Religious Program—Email: stjfaithformation@bellsouth.net. Students 568.

MILLEDGEVILLE, BALDWIN CO., SACRED HEART OF JESUS (1874) Rev. Dung Nguyen; Deacon Cesar Basilio.
Church: 110 N. Jefferson St., P.O. Box 754, 31061. Tel: 478-452-2421 (Res.); Fax: 478-454-1110.
Catechesis / Religious Program—Students 99.

MONROE, WALTON CO., ST. ANNA (1951) [JC] Rev. Daniel R. Toof.
Church: 836 E. Spring St., 30655. Tel: 770-267-7637 (Res.); Fax: 770-267-0465. Web: www.st-annas.com.
Catechesis / Religious Program—Tel: 770-267-0420. Students 205.

NEWNAN, COWETA CO.

1—ST. GEORGE (1952) [JC] Rev. Austin Forgarty; Deacons James R. Bishop; Steve Beers; David C. Corbett; Paul S. Swope Jr.
Church: 771 Roscoe Rd., 30263. Tel: 770-251-5353; Fax: 770-251-2053. Email: lbrunelle@numail.org. Web: www.stgeorgecatholicchurch.org.
Catechesis / Religious Program—Tel: 770-254-9933. Students 226.

2—ST. MARY MAGDALENE (1999) Rev. Daniel J. Fleming; Deacon David C. Sandlin.
3 Village Rd., 30265-6162. Tel: 770-253-1888; Fax: 770-253-1290. Email: smmcc@smmcatholic.org. Web: www.smmcatholic.org.
Catechesis / Religious Program—Tel: 770-253-1888. Students 440.

NORCROSS, GWINNETT CO.

1—MARY OUR QUEEN CATHOLIC CHURCH (1994) Revs. David M. Dye, Admin.; Stephen J. Lyness, Parochial Vicar; Deacons James E. Stone; William McKenzie.
Church: 6260 The Corners Pkwy., 30092. Tel: 770-416-0002; Fax: 770-416-1846. Email: office@maryourqueen.com. Web: www.maryourqueen.com.
Catechesis / Religious Program—Tel: 770-416-9799. Email: reled@maryourqueen.com. Students 193.

2—SAINT PATRICK (1968) Revs. Thomas J. Hennessy; Cyril Soo-Gil Chae, Parochial Vicar; Dairo Rico, Parochial Vicar; Deacon Jose Narvaez. In Res., Rev. Joseph Peek.
Church & Res.: 2140 Beaver Ruin Rd., 30071. Tel: 770-448-2028; 770-446-2041 (Res.); Fax: 770-448-7046. Web: www.stpatricks-norcross.org.

Catechesis/Religious Program—Tel: 770-448-6386. Students 1,946.

Mission—Our Lady of the Americas 4603 Lawrenceville Hwy., Lilburn, Gwinnet Co. 30047. Tel: 770-717-1517; Fax: 770-717-1312. Revs. Luis Guillermo-Cordoba, Admin.; Roberto L. Jaramillo, Parochial Vicar; Fabian Cabarcas-Rua, Parochial Vicar.

PEACHTREE CITY, FAYETTE CO., HOLY TRINITY (1973), (Hispanic), Very Rev. Michael G. Kingery; Rev. Salomon Garcia, Parochial Vicar; Deacons Anthony F. Cuomo; Nemour Michel Landaiche; Terry S. Blind; Hector M. Vargas; Robert J. Kepshire.

Church: 101 Walt Banks Rd., 30269. Tel: 770-487-7672; Fax: 770-486-9152. Web: www.holytrinitypt-c.org.

See Our Lady of Mercy Catholic High School, Fairburn under Archdiocesan Schools located in the Institution section.

See St. Pius X Catholic High School, Atlanta under Archdiocesan Schools located in the Institution section

Catechesis/Religious Program—Tel: 770-487-0175. Students 1,268.

RIVERDALE, CLAYTON CO., OUR LADY OF VIETNAM (1989), (Vietnamese), [JC] Rev. Msgr. Francis Pham Van Phuong; Rev. Peter Duc Vu, Parochial Vicar; Deacons Peter Hung Viet Huynh; Joseph Phu Nguyen.

Church: 91 Valley Hill Rd., 30274. Tel: 770-472-9963; 770-471-8453 (Res.); Fax: 770-473-5211.

Catechesis/Religious Program—Students 460.

THE ROCK, UPSON CO., ST. PETER THE ROCK (2005) Rev. Neil Herlihy; Deacon Tilton (T.C.) Meuninck.

3594 Barnesville Hwy., P.O. Box 280, 30285. Tel: 706-648-2599; Fax: 706-648-4040. Web: www.stpetertherock.com.

Catechesis/Religious Program—Sherre Rohling, C.R.E. Students 58.

ROME, FLOYD CO., ST. MARY'S (1930) Rev. Patrick J. Kingery; Deacons Stuart L. Neslin; Jose M. Orellana.

Res.: 911 N. Broad St., 30161. Tel: 706-290-9100; Fax: 706-295-1717. Web: www.smcrome.org.

See St. Mary Catholic School, Rome under Archdiocesan Schools, located in the Institution section.

Catechesis/Religious Program—Ballard Betz, Youth Dir. Students 180.

ROSWELL, FULTON CO.

1—ST. ANDREW (1981) Rev. Msgr. Hugh M. Marren; Rev. Juan Areiza, Parochial Vicar; Deacons William Keen; Thomas E. Gotschall; Jose G. Campos.

Res.: 115 River Lake Ct., 30075. Tel: 770-552-0485.

Church: 675 Riverside Rd., 30075. Tel: 770-641-9720; Fax: 770-641-8584. Email: admin@standrewcatholic.com. Web: www.standrewcatholic.com.

Catechesis/Religious Program—Tel: 770-641-9720, Ext. 228; Fax: 770-641-8584. Email: religioused@standrewcatholic.com. Students 298.

2—ST. PETER CHANEL (1998) Very Rev. Peter J. Rau; Rev. Henry Atem, Parochial Vicar; Deacons Keith M. Kolodziej; Martin J. Lampe; Jesus Nerio; Michael Bickerstaff; Scott A. Sparks; Tom Blond, Business Mgr.; Jane Jackson, Music Min.; Megan Busch, Youth Min.

11330 Woodstock Rd., 30075. Tel: 678-277-9424; 678-461-9717 (Res.); Fax: 678-277-9423. Web: www.stpeterchanel.org. In Res., Rev. Augustine Hoa T. Tran.

See Queen of Angels Catholic School, Roswell under Archdiocesan Schools located in the Institution section

See Blessed Trinity Catholic High School, Roswell under Archdiocesan Schools located in the Institution section

Catechesis/Religious Program—Tel: 678-832-1230. Cathy Marbury, D.R.E. Students 1,233.

SMYRNA, COBB CO., ST. THOMAS THE APOSTLE (1966) Revs. James H. Kuczynski, M.S.; Eugene Barrette, M.S., Parochial Vicar; Jaime Molina-Juarez, M.N.M., Parochial Vicar; Jose Manjaly, M.S., Parochial Vicar; Deacons Albert G. Weber; Harold Michael Garrett; Earl D. Jackson.

Church: 4300 King Springs Rd., 30082. Tel: 770-432-8579; Fax: 770-432-8570. Email: stthomasga@stthomastheapostle.org. Web: stthomastheapostle.org.

Catechesis/Religious Program—Tel: 770-432-5296. Email: ssenecal@stthomastheapostle.org. Students 1,200.

SNELLVILLE, GWINNETT CO., ST. OLIVER PLUNKETT (1978) Revs. James A. Henault, M.S.; Neil G. Jones, M.S., Parochial Vicar; Juan de la Cruz, Parochial Vicar; Martin Kopchik, M.S.F.S., Parochial Vicar; Deacons William Jindrich; Rafael Cintron; Albert L. Feliu.

Church & Res.: 3200 Brooks Dr., 30078. Tel: 770-979-2500; 770-979-3827 (Res.); Fax: 770-985-6590. Email: oplunkett@stolivers.com. Web: www.stolivers.com.

Catechesis/Religious Program—Tel: 770-978-6751. Students 875.

STONE MOUNTAIN, DEKALB CO., CORPUS CHRISTI (1971) [JC] Revs. Len Brown, C.M.F.; John Molyneux, C.M.F., Parochial Vicar; Daniel Onyeayana, C.M.F., Parochial Vicar; Deacons John J. McManus; Ken W. Melvin. In Res., Rev. Gregory D. Kenny, C.M.F.

Church: 600 Mountain View Dr., 30083. Tel: 770-469-0395; Fax: 770-469-0568. Web: www.corpuschristicc.org.

Catechesis/Religious Program—Tel: 770-469-0597; Fax: 770-469-0568. Richard Dick, D.R.E. Students 562.

THOMSON, MCDUFFIE CO., QUEEN OF ANGELS (1955) Rev. William M. Williams.

Church: 1326 Washington Rd., 30824. Tel: 706-595-2913; Fax: 706-595-9636.

Catechesis/Religious Program—Email: ourladyqofa@comcast.net. Students 50.

TOCCOA, STEPHENS CO., ST. MARY (1956) [JC] Rev. Terence Crone; Deacon John Burke.

Res.: 231 Rothell Rd. Ext., 30577. Tel: 706-886-2819; Fax: 706-886-8770. Email: stmary@windstream.net. Web: www.stmarystoccoaga.com.

Catechesis/Religious Program—Students 97.

Mission—St. Catherine Laboure 180 Elrod Rd., P.O. Box 653, Jefferson, Jackson Co. 30549. Tel: 706-367-7220.

TYRONE, FULTON CO., ST. MATTHEW (1979) Very Rev. Victor A. Galier; Deacons William Hampton; Jim G. Weeks; Gayle P. Peters; King E. Cooper.

Church: 215 Kirkley Rd., 30290-9549. Tel: 770-964-5804; Fax: 770-964-1228. Web: www.saintmatthew.us.

See Our Lady of Victory Catholic School, Tyrone under Archdiocesan Schools located in the Institution section

Catechesis/Religious Program—Students 325.

WASHINGTON, WILKES CO., ST. JOSEPH (1840) [CEM] [JC 2] Rev. Christopher Williamson.

Church: 1015 N. By Pass Hwy. 78 W., P.O. Box 632, 30673. Tel: 706-678-2110; Fax: 706-678-3353. Email: stjosephs@nu-z.net.

Catechesis/Religious Program—Students 24.

Mission—St. Mary's P.O. Box 632, Elbert Co. 30678.

Mission—Purification Hwy. 47, Sharon, Talifero Co. 30631.

WINDER, BARROW CO., ST. MATTHEW (1999) Rev. Jaime Barona; Deacon Tim Kirksey.

25 Wilkins Rd., S.W., 30680-1009. Tel: 770-867-4876; Fax: 770-867-6034. Email: busmgr@saintmatthewcc.org. Web: www.saintmatthewcc.org.

Rectory—450 Winston Manor Dr., 30680. Tel: 770-307-9612.

Catechesis/Religious Program—Students 312.

WOODSTOCK, CHEROKEE CO., ST. MICHAEL THE ARCHANGEL (1995) Revs. Larry Niese; Jaime Rivera, Parochial Vicar; Deacons William H. Heinsch; Bernard J. Casey; Victor L. Taylor.

Church & Res.: 490 Arnold Mill Rd., 30188. Tel: 770-516-0009. Web: www.stmichaelthearchangelwoodstock.catholicweb.com.

Catechesis/Religious Program—Tel: 770-516-9699; Fax: 770-516-4664. Students 1,331.

Chaplains of Public Institutions

ATLANTA. *Atlanta Veterans Administration Hospital*, 2442 Mt. Vernon Rd., Dunwoody, 30338. Tel: 770-395-6302. Rev. Daniel J. McCormick, B.A.

Cobb County Jail, 1825 County Services Pkwy., Marietta, 30060. Tel: 770-499-4200. Rev. Yuen Caballejo.

Dobbins Air Force Base. Vacant.

94 AW/HC, 1311 Patrol Rd., Dobbins Air Force Base, 30069-5003. Tel: 404-919-4955; 404-919-4956.

Fort McPherson.

Office of the Garrison Chaplain, Bldg. 51, Fort McPherson, 30330-5000. Tel: 404-752-2616. Rev. Fred W. Wendel, Chap.

Office of the FORSCOM Chap., 1777 Hardee Ave., S.W., Fort McPherson, 30330. Tel: 404-464-6030. Vacant.

Hartsfield Jackson International Airport, Interfaith Airport Chaplaincy, P.O. Box 20801, 30320. Tel: 404-762-1051. Web: www.airportchapel.org. Deacons Donald A. Kelsey, Nemour Michel Landaiche.

Prison Apostolate. Rev. John C. Fallon, Chap.

U.S. Penitentiary, 601 McDonough Blvd., 30315. Tel: 404-635-5100. Vacant.

JACKSON. *Georgia Diagnostic & Classification Center, Diagnostic & Classification*, 2978 Hwy. 36 W., 30233. Tel: 770-504-2000. Deacon Thomas O. Silvestri, Chap.

Special or Other Archdiocesan Assignment:

Rev. Msgrs.—

Corbett, W. Joseph, V.G., Vicar Gen. & Moderator of the Curia

Giusta, Frank J., Chap. (Retired), Emory Crawford Long Hospital, Emory University Hospital, The Emory Clinic, Winship Cancer Institute & Wesley Woods Center Complex, Emory University Orthopaedics and Spine Hospital

Lopez, Richard J., Chap., Our Lady of Perpetual Help Cancer Home & Faculty, St. Pius X High School

Very Revs.—

Ballman, Luke R., S.T.L., Dir. Vocations & Rector, St. Charles Borromeo House of Formation

Hachey, Paul J., S.M., J.C.L., M.C.L., M.Div., Judicial Vicar, Court of Appeals

Williams, Paul, V.F.

Revs.—

Adams, James P., Chap., Our Lady of Mercy High School

Bailey, Ricardo, Chap., Blessed Trinity High School

Branch, Edward B., Chap., Atlanta University

Brown, Leonard, C.M.F., Chap., DeKalb Community College

Caballejo, Yuen, Chap., Prison Ministry Catholic Charities of the Archdiocese of Atlanta

Frederick, Robert A., Chap., North Georgia College

Hargaden, Kevin J., Chap., LaGrange College

Hepburn, Timothy M., Chap., Georgia Institute of Technology

Hernandez-Ayala, Jose Luis, Faculty & Chap. St. Pius X High School, Atlanta

Hyman, David L., O.F.M., Chap., University of Georgia

Kopchik, Martin, M.S.F.S., Chap., North Metro Sierra Club

Lyness, Stephen J., Chap., Georgia State University

McWhorter, Michael L., Chap., Georgia College & State University

Morris, Joseph E., Chap., Kennesaw State University

Mullakkara, Joseph, M.S.F.S., Chap. Our Lady of Perpetual Help Cancer Home, Atlanta

Natad, Diosmar, Master of Ceremonies for the Most Reverend Wilton D. Gregory

Small, Bryan, Chap., Emory University & Agnes State College

Vigliotta, Thomas F., O.F.M., Chap., University of Georgia

Wilber, Stewart, Counselor, Catholic Charities of the Archdiocese of Atlanta

---

Without Archdiocesan Assignment or Faculties:

Revs.—

Anderson, John

Calle-Perez, Sergio

Doyle, N. Brendan

Duggan, Karl

Fuchs, Ronald G.

Lacey, Mark W., (Leave of Absence)

Zivic, Richard A.

On Duty Outside the Archdiocese:

Revs.—

Kinast, Robert L., Center for Theological Reflection, 102 Gulf Blvd. #301, Indian Rocks Beach, FL 33785.

McBrearity, Gerald D., S.S., 5408 Roland Ave., Baltimore, MD 21210-1984.

Patterson, David L., 911 Ocean Blvd., St. Simons Island, 31522. Diocese of Savannah, GA

Graduate Studies:

Revs.—

Azar, Nicholas G., Pontifical North American College 00120 Vatican City State.

Selvaraj, Balapa, Casa Santa Maria, Pontifical North American College, 00120 Vatican City State, Italy.

Military Chaplains:

Revs.—

David, Craig, VA Health Care System, 5901 E. 7th St., Long Beach, CA 90822.

Ha, Hieu Minh, United States Regular Army

McCormick, Patrick J., 850 Ticonderoga St., Ste. 100, Pearl Harbor, HI 96860.

Niemeier, Dennis, Fort McPherson, 1236 Haney Plaza, S.W., 30330-1050.

Peek, Kevin T., B.A., M.Div., United States Regular Army, 1397 Diamond Head Cir., Decatur, 30033.

Wendel, Fred W., United States Regular Army, 1236 Haney Plaza, S.W., Fort Mcpherson, 30330.

On Leave of Absence:

Revs.—

Doyle, N. Brendan

Duggan, Karl

Heninger, Michael B.
Jean, Thony R.
Kieran, Richard A.
Mateus, Norberto
Schoenfield, Andrew
Shramko, John
St. Fleur, Maxis

Retired:
Most Rev.—
Donoghue, John F., J.C.L., All Saints Catholic Church, 2443 Mt. Vernon Rd., 30338.
Rev. Msgrs.—
Donovan, Walter J., St. George Village, 11350 Woodstock Rd., Apt. 2122, Roswell, 30075. Sacred Heart Church, 353 Peachtree St., 30308.
Giusta, Frank J., P.O. Box 160019, 30316.
Hoffman, William G., St. George Village, 11350 Woodstock Rd., Apt. 2124, Roswell, 30075. Tel: 770-645-2340. Email: msgrbill@yahoo.com
Hogan, Michael, 1439 Summit Chase Dr., Snellville, 30076.
O'Connor, Daniel, 7090 Glenridge Dr., 30328.
Very Rev.—
Morrow, Richard B., 2699 Peachtree Rd., 30305. Cathedral of Christ the King
Revs.—
Curran, Anthony T., 915 N. Rock St., Shamokin, PA 17872.
Danneker, Edward A.J., Holy Cross Catholic Church, 3175 Hathaway Ct., NE, 30341.
Dillman, Alan M., 3957 Woodridge Way, Tucker, 30084.
Druding, John C., M.Div., St. George Village, 11350 Woodstock Rd., Apt. 2120, Roswell, 30075.
Dullea, Denis, 11350 Woodstock Rd., Roswell, 30075.
Foley, Walter W., 561 Raindrop Circle, Hartwell, 30643.
Horan, Ray, 318 Memory Ln., Martin, 30557.
Medlin, Douglas S., P.O. Box 224, Sautee Nacoochee, 30571.
Redden, Michael J., 1413 Oak Knoll Dr., Conyers, 30012.
Rudd, Thad B., 540 Ascension Trail, Cleveland, 30528.
Sanches, Joseph A., 227 Cana Cir., Nashville, TN 37205.
Scherer, James F., 28 Brookway Dr., Greensboro, NC 27410.
Sexstone, James H., Saint George Village, 11350 Woodstock Rd., Apt. 2116, Roswell, 30075.

Permanent Deacons:
Akers, Henry, St. John the Evangelist, Hapeville
Anderson, Douglas J., St. Francis De Sales, Mableton
Angelich, George D., St. Marguerite D'Youville, Lawrenceville
Anugerah, Antonius, Our Lady of the Assumption, Atlanta
Anzalone, Joseph C., St. Philip Benizi, Jonesboro
Anzalone, Joseph S., (On Duty Outside the Archdiocese)
Atkinson, Jon G., Our Lady of Perpetual Help, Bremen
Balfour, Michael K., Sacred Heart, Atlanta
Barker, Joseph J., St. Anthony, Atlanta
Barone, John J., St. Mark, Clarkesville
Basilio, Cesar, Sacred Heart, Milledgeville
Bathea, Val, (On Duty Outside the Archdiocese)
Beckman, Richard F., (Retired)
Bedard, Walter T., Sr., (Retired)
Beers, Steven (Steve), St. George's, Newnan
Bek, Stephen J., St. Vincent de Paul, Dallas
Berding, Herbert C., (Retired), St. James, Madison
Bevacqua, Bill J., Our Lady of the Assumption, Atlanta
Bickerstaff, Michael, St. Peter Chanel, Roswell
Biglow, Ernest, Our Lady of the Assumption, Atlanta
Bishop, James R., St. George's, Newnan
Bishop, Kenneth P., Sacred Heart, Griffin
Blind, Terry S., Holy Trinity, Peachtree City
Bobb, William, St. George Village, Roswell
Borsavage, Charles T., (Inactive)
Brown, Raymond E., (On Duty Outside the Archdiocese)
Burke, John, St. Mary's, Toccoa
Byrne, Michael T., St. John Neumann, Lilburn
Campos, Jose G., St. Andrew, Roswell
Carignan, Charles E., Our Lady of LaSalette, Canton
Carr, Ronald, St. Benedict, Johns Creek
Carter, Joseph R., St. Monica, Duluth
Casal, Matias A., St. Philip Benizi, Jonesboro
Casey, Bernard J., St. Michael the Archangel, Woodstock
Casey, Lawrence B., St. Francis of Assisi, Blairsville
Cintron, Rafael, St. Oliver, Plunkett, Snellville
Coffey, Thomas, Church of the Transfiguration, Marietta
Collins, Gerald A., Christ Our Hope, Lithonia
Comeau, Ronald A., Holy Family, Marietta
Connell, Jerry F., (Retired)
Conti, Richard J., St. Catherine of Siena, Kennesaw
Cooper, King E., St. Matthew, Tyrone
Corbett, David C., St. George, Newnan
Coughlin, Frank F., (Retired)
Cuomo, Anthony F., Holy Trinity, Peachtree City
Demko, Stephen G., Holy Spirit, Atlanta
DeSandre, Bart R., Shrine of the Immaculate Conception, Atlanta
Dietz, Paul E., St. Francis of Assisi, Blairsville
Doppel, Paul Lee, St. Brendan the Navigator, Cumming
Dorner, Dennis J., Chancellor, Dir. Permanent Diaconate, St. Brigid, Alpharetta; St. Luke the Evangelist, Dahlonega
Duffield, John P., Holy Family, Marietta
Easterwood, James M., (Retired)
Echevarria, Miguel A., St. Catherine of Siena, Kennesaw
Egan, Raymond F., Chancery, Atlanta
Espinosa, Jose G., Transfiguration, Marietta
Eustace, Joseph C., St. Joseph, Marietta
Fagan, Patrick, St. Lawrence, Lawrenceville
Feliu, Albert L., St. Oliver Plunkett, Snellville
Figueredo, Alberto, (Inactive)
Ford, Stanley B., Catherine of Siena, Kennesaw
Fraser, Roger A., St. Brendan, Cumming
French, Lawrence, St. Stephen the Martyr, Lilburn
Gahafer, Leo, St. Brigid, Alpharetta
Gallagher, Alexander S., Holy Family, Marietta
Galvis, Enrique L., (Retired)
Garcia-Carreras, Evelio, St. Stephen the Martyr, Lilburn
Garrett, Harold Michael, St. Thomas the Apostle, Smyrna
Garrett, William, All Saints, Dunwoody
Gaudin, James M., Jr., St. Joseph's, Athens
Gillespie, Patrick (Pat) J., St. James the Apostle, McDonough
Gonzalez, Marino, Sacred Heart, Atlanta
Goolsby, Joseph B., (Retired)
Gorski, Paul A., Transfiguration, Marietta
Gotschall, Thomas E., St. Andrew, Roswell
Grabowy, Edmund M., St. Ann's, Marietta
Gregerson, Robert J., Our Lady of the Assumption, Atlanta
Griffin, Chester H., Our Lady of Lourdes, Atlanta
Gross, Benedict, (Retired)
Grubbs, Burgess "David", St. Catherine of Siena, Kennesaw
Hampton, William (Bill) L., St. Matthew's, Tyrone
Hanson, David, St. Helena Catholic Mission, Clayton
Heinsch, William H., St. Michael the Archangel, Woodstock
Henrich, Robert A., (On Duty Outside the Archdiocese)
Hettel, Louis A., (Retired)
Holmer, Terry M., St. Theresa, Douglasville
Huff, Tom, St. Brigid, Alpharetta
Hunkele, Thomas H., (Retired)
Huynh, Hung Viet (Vic), Our Lady of Vietnam, Riverdale
Jackson, Earl D., St. Thomas the Apostle, Smyrna
Jelks, Leviticus St. Anthony's, Atlanta
Jennings, Bobby Allen, St. Ann, Marietta
Jimenez, Arturo P., (On Leave of Absence)
Jindrich, William L., St. Oliver Plunkett, Snellville
Johns, Fred, St. Pius X, Conyers
Johnson, Nicholas, Prince of Peace, Flowery Branch
Jones, Frederick T., (Retired)
Jones, Michael R., Prince of Peace, Flowery Branch
Kazin, Gerard G., St. Benedict, Duluth
Keeling, William W., St. Thomas Aquinas, Alpharetta
Keen, William, St. Andrew's, Roswell
Kelsey, Donald A., (Retired)
Kennedy, Michael L., St. Michael's, Gainesville
Kepshire, Robert J., Holy Trinity, Peachtree City
Kilkelly, Brian, St. Pius X, Conyers
King, A.B., III, St. Lawrence, Lawrenceville
Kirksey, Timothy K., St. Matthew's Church, Winder
Kolodziej, Keith M., St. Peter Chanel Church, Roswell
Korte, Jerry R., Sacred Heart of Jesus, Hartwell
Krupa, Bradford, St. Clement, Calhoun
LaFreniere, James A., St. Brigid, Alpharetta
LaHouse, Edmund J., St. Thomas Aquinas, Alpharetta
LaMachia, Ralph, Good Shepherd, Cumming
Lampe, Martin J., St. Peter Chanel Church, Roswell
Landaiche, Nemour Michel Holy Trinity, Peachtree City
Lange, William G., (Retired)
Lee, Hilliard M., Jr., St. Paul of the Cross, Atlanta
Lerma, Arthur, St. Thomas Aquinas, Alpharetta
Lett, Jerry M., Sts. Peter & Paul, Decatur
Londono, Luis St. Michael, Gainesville
Mac Donald, Will, (Retired)
Makin, Thomas F., (Retired)
Marchildon, Donald W., (Retired)
Marinchak, Richard J., St. Mark's, Clarkesville
Marrero, Felix, Sacred Heart, Griffin
Marten, William H., St. John Neumann, Lilburn
Martorell, Gerardo G., (Retired)
Mason, John, St. Anthony's, Blue Ridge
Mc Carthy, Kevin J., (On Duty Outside the Archdiocese)
McBride, Carl I., St. Gabriel's, Fayetteville
McCarthy, William F., Holy Spirit, Atlanta
McDermott, James, St. Vincent de Paul, Dallas
McGrane, Thomas J., (On Duty Outside the Archdiocese)
McHugh, Al C., (Retired)
McKenzie, William, Mary Our Queen, Norcross
McManus, John J., J.D., J.C.L. , Cathedral of Christ the King, Atlanta; Corpus Christi, Stone Mountain
McNabb, Scott J.N., Cathedral of Christ the King, Atlanta
Mead, Stuart A., St. Pius X, Conyers
Melara, Israel D., St. Theresa, Douglasville
Melvin, Ken W., Corpus Christi, Stone Mountain
Metzger, Thomas J., St. Augustine, Covington
Meuninck, Tilton (T.C.), St. Peter the Rock, The Rock, GA
Mickle, Richard (Rich) A., St. Augustine, Covington
Millinger, Terry D., St. Lawrence, Lawrenceville
Mitchell, Alfred, Sts. Peter & Paul, Decatur
Mobley, Michael K., Sr., St. Stephen the Martyr, Lilburn
Monahan, William J., St. Brendan Church, Cumming
Moncrief, Wayland, (On Duty Outside the Archdiocese)
Moore, Dennis, (Retired)
Morning, J. Nicholas, St. Ann, Marietta
Mure, Samuel M., (Retired)
Nadeau, Donald N., Good Shepard, Cumming
Narvaez, Jose A., St. Patrick's, Norcross
Nerio, Jesus, St. Peter Chanel Church, Roswell
Neslin, Stuart L., St. Mary, Rome
Nguyen, Joseph Phu, Our Lady of Vietnam, Riverdale
O'Brien, Michael J., Our Lady of the Assumption, Atlanta
O'Connor, D. Patrick, St. Catherine of Siena, Kennesaw
O'Neill, Robert A., (Retired)
Ollick, Gregory, St. John Neumann, Lilburn
Orellana, Jose M., St. Mary, Rome
Parker, Donald S., St. Gabriel, Fayetteville
Patrick, Charles, St. Theresa, Douglasville
Patterson, Edward, Our Lady of the Assumption, Atlanta
Payne, William E., Jr., Shrine of the Immaculate Conception, Atlanta
Pecore, Gregory L., St. Philip Benizi, Jonesboro
Perez, Gilberto, Saint Michael, Gainesville
Perez, Jose, St. Vincent de Paul, Dallas
Peters, Gayle P., St. Matthew, Tyrone
Peterson, John R., St. Lawrence, Lawrenceville
Ponichtera, Stephen, St. Catherine of Siena, Kennesaw
Publicover, Bruce C., (Retired)
Puetz, John D., St. Benedict, Duluth
Pupo, Jose I., St. Thomas Aquinas, Alpharetta
Rademacher, Edward, St. Monica, Duluth
Readdy, Robert G., (Retired)
Reed, William Bruce, Jr., St. Joseph, Marietta
Reimer, Cecil R., Holy Cross, Atlanta
Rhodes, Joseph, St. Pius X, Conyers
Rich, Robert M., (Unassigned)
Richardson, Raymond L., Christ the Redeemer Mission, Dawsonville
Riddett, Robert, St. Jude the Apostle, Atlanta
Rivera, Prudencio I., (Retired)
Robichaux, Whitney F., Jr., Cathedral of Christ the King, Atlanta; Holy Cross, Atlanta
Roche, Gary J., St. Michael's, Gainesville
Rodriguez, Etienne Francisco, St. Philip Benizi, Jonesboro
Ruberte, Joseph, Holy Spirit, Atlanta
Rubio, Eduardo J., St. Brendan the Navigator, Cumming
Russell, Philippe, (Leave of Absence)
Ryan, Thomas J., St. Catherine of Siena, Kennesaw
Sambrone, Fred J., Jr., (Retired)
Samoranski, Alfred T., Prince of Peace, Buford
Sandlin, David C., St. Mary Magdalene, Newnan
Shaver, Thomas R., St. Joseph's, Marietta
Shoemaker, John W., (Retired)
Shuler, Thomas B., Holy Spirit, Atlanta
Silvestri, Thomas D., Holy Cross, Atlanta; Chap., Georgia Diagnostic and Correctional Center, Jackson

Simmons, William H., III, St. Anthony of Padua, Atlanta
Sinanian, Loris R., St. Anthony's, Blue Ridge
Smith, George, St. Paul of the Cross, Atlanta
Smith, Robert B., (Retired)
Smith, Wayne D., Sacred Heart, Atlanta
Sparks, Scott A., St. Peter Chanel, Roswell
Speed, William (Bill) E., Prince of Peace, Flowery Branch
St. Michel, Ronald A., St. Theresa, Douglasville
Stagg, James A., (On Duty Outside the Archdiocese)
Stewart, James M., (Retired)
Stone, James E., Mary Our Queen, Norcross
Stonecipher, Thomas L., St. John the Evangelist, Hapeville
Strachan, John S., St. Thomas Aquinas, Alpharetta
Suever, Richard M., (Retired)
Sutter, Edward L., (Leave of Absence)
Swan, Peter B., Sr., St. Philip Benizi, Jonesboro
Swope, Paul S., Jr., Assoc. Dir. Formation, St. George, Newnan
Thibodeau, Richard, St. Michael, Gainesville
Thompson, Chris, Our Lady of Assumption, Atlanta
Tipton, Robert F., St. Monica, Duluth
Tocca, Fred, Most Blessed Sacrament, Atlanta
Tolcher, Richard P., St. Philip Benizi, Jonesboro
Tracy, Kevin F., St. Thomas Aquinas, Alpharetta
Tramonte, James A., St. Jude the Apostle, Sandy Springs
Underwood, Froilan (Allen) V., Holy Spirit, Atlanta
Vargas, Hector M., Holy Trinity, Peachtree City
Weber, Albert G., St. Thomas the Apostle, Smyrna
Weeks, Jim G., St. Matthew's, Tyrone
Weiss, Dr. James (Jim), Holy Cross, Atlanta
Whitmeyer, Eugene, (Retired)
Williams, James H., St. Francis of Assisi, Cartersville
Williams, Kenneth, Christ Redeemer Mission, Dawsonville
Womack, Gary D., St. John Neumann, Lilburn
Woods, Michael, Prince of Peace, Flowery Branch
Zaworski, Thomas E., (Retired)

INSTITUTIONS LOCATED IN THE ARCHDIOCESE

[A] SEMINARIES, RELIGIOUS OR SCHOLASTICATES

ATLANTA. *Aquinas Center of Theology at Emory University*, 1256 Briarcliff Rd, Bldg. A, Rm. 221, 30306. Tel: 404-727-8860; Fax: 404-727-8862. Email: colane@emory.edu. Web: www.aquinas.emory.edu. Joseph Soltz Esq., Chair; Dr. Phillip Thompson, Dir. Total Staff 2.

[B] COLLEGES AND UNIVERSITIES

DAWSONVILLE. *Southern Catholic College*, 330 Southern Catholic Dr., 30534. Tel: 706-344-4005; Fax: 706-344-4003. Email: dwalters@southerncatholic.org. Web: www.southerncatholic.org. Revs. Shawn Aaron, L.C., Pres.; Theodore Book, S.L.D., Adjunct Prof.; Paul A. Burke, J.C.L., Adjunct Prof.; Sheryl L. Exley, M.L.I.S., Library Dir. Priests 2; Lay Teachers 22.

[C] ARCHDIOCESAN SCHOOLS, PARISH

ATLANTA. *Cathedral of Christ the King Catholic School* (1937) (Grades K-8), (Co-ed), 46 Peachtree Way N.E., 30305. Tel: 404-233-0383; Fax: 404-266-0704. Email: pmwarner@christking.org. Web: www.christking.org. Mrs. Peggy Warner, Prin.; Tricia Ward, Asst. Prin.; Melanie Brent, Librarian. Lay Teachers 44; Students 567.

Immaculate Heart of Mary Catholic School (1958) (Grades K-8), 2855 Briarcliff Rd., N.E., 30329. Tel: 404-636-4488; Fax: 404-636-1853. Web: www.ihmschool.org. Tricia DeWitt, Prin.; Bob Baldonado, Asst. Prin.; Sandy Wilson, Librarian. Lay Teachers 37; Students 499.

St. Jude the Apostle Catholic School (1962) (Grades K-8), 7171 Glenridge Dr., N.E., 30328. Tel: 770-394-2880; Fax: 770-804-9248. Web: saintjude.net. Patty Childs, Prin.; Eleneora Straub, Librarian. Lay Teachers 31; Students 504.

Our Lady of the Assumption Catholic School (1952) (Grades PreK-8), 1320 Hearst Dr., N.E., 30319. Tel: 404-364-1902; Fax: 404-364-1914. Email: office@olaschool.org. Web: olaschool.org. Anita Nagel, Prin.; Diane Miller-Deasy, Librarian. Lay Teachers 40; Students 474.

St. Pius X Catholic High School (1958) (Coed), 2674 Johnson Rd., N.E., 30345. Tel: 404-636-3023; Fax: 404-633-8387. Email: spellman@spx.org. Web: spx.org. Mr. Stephen Spellman, Prin.; Ruth McCullough, Dean Academics; Rachel Braham, Dean Students; Edye Simpson, Dean Students; Mark Kelly, Athletic Dir.; Chuck Byrd, Admissions; Rev. Msgr. Richard J. Lopez; Revs. Dan Rogaczewski; Jose Luis Hernandez-Ayala, Faculty & Chap.; Robin Tanis, Librarian. Priests 3; Teachers 87; Students 1,071; Total Staff 38.

ATHENS. *St. Joseph Catholic School* (1949) (Grades PreK-8), 134 Prince Ave., 30601. Tel: 706-543-1621; Fax: 706-543-0149. Email: kpetti@sjsathens.org. Web: sjsathens.org. Donovan Yarnall, Prin.; Karen Roberts, Librarian. Lay Teachers 20; Students 300.

DECATUR. *St. Peter Claver Regional Catholic School* (2001) (Grades PreK-8), 2560 Tilson Rd., 30032. Tel: 404-241-3063; Fax: 404-241-4382. Email: pclaver@spc-school.org. Web: www.spc-school.org. Catherine Spencer, M.Ed., Prin.; Jocelyn Lyons, Admission & Devel. Dir.; Eileen Rice, Librarian. Lay Teachers 15; Students 130.

St. Thomas More Catholic School (1950) (Grades K-8), 630 W. Ponce De Leon Ave., 30030. Tel: 404-373-8456; Fax: 404-377-8554. Email: stm@stmga.org. Web: www.stmga.org. Mrs. Terry Collis, Prin.; Eileen Maron, Admissions; Ansley Murphey, Devel.; Laura Ayala, Librarian. Lay Teachers 31; Students 477.

FAYETTEVILLE. *Our Lady of Mercy Catholic High School*, 861 Evander Holyfield Hwy., 30214. Tel: 770-461-2202; Fax: 770-461-9353. Email: ddorsel@olmbobcats.org. Web: www.olmbobcats.org. Daniel Dorsel, Prin.; Sandra Livsey-Martin, Admissions; William Schmitz, Athletic Dir.; Timothy Wojcik, Librarian; Rev. James P. Adams, Chap. Priests 1; Lay Teachers 32; Total Staff 48; Total Enrollment 275.

HAPEVILLE. *St. John the Evangelist Catholic School* (1954) (Grades PreK-8), 240 Arnold St., 30354. Tel: 404-767-4312; Fax: 404-767-0359. Web: sjccs.org. Karen Vogtner, B.S., M.Ed., Prin.; Kathy Van Meter, Librarian. Lay Teachers 22; Students 287.

JOHN'S CREEK. *Holy Redeemer Catholic School* (1999) (Grades K-8), 3380 Old Alabama Rd., Johns Creek, 30022. Tel: 770-410-4056; Fax: 770-410-1454. Email: ewestley@hrcatholicschool.org. Web: www.hrcatholicschool.org. Eric Westley, Ed.D., Prin.; Sue Kalinauskas, Asst. Prin.; Derin Thompson, Librarian. Lay Teachers 33; Students 500.

KENNESAW. *St. Catherine of Siena Catholic School* (2002) (Grades K-8), 1618 Ben King Rd., 30144. Tel: 770-419-8601; Fax: 678-626-0000. Web: www.scsiena.org. Sr. Mary Jacinta, O.P., Prin.; Vinita John, Librarian. Sisters 4; Lay Teachers 33; Total Enrollment 372.

LILBURN. *St. John Neumann Regional* (1986) (Grades K-8), (Regional), 791 Tom Smith Rd., S.W., 30047. Tel: 770-381-0557; Fax: 770-381-0276. Email: crusader@sjnrcs.org. Web: www.sjnrcs.org. James Anderson, Prin.; Janet Kent. Lay Teachers 40; Students 547.

MARIETTA. *St. Joseph Catholic School* (1953) (Grades K-8), 81 Lacy St., 30060. Tel: 770-428-3328; Fax: 770-424-2960. Email: mdunn@stjosephschool.org. Web: stjosephschool.org. Patricia Allen, Ed.S., Prin.; Jill Ramsey, Vice Prin. Lay Teachers 28; Students 489.

ROME. *St. Mary's Catholic School* (1945) (Grades PreK-8), 401 E. Seventh St., 30161. Tel: 706-234-4953; Fax: 706-234-3030. Web: www.smsrome.org. Alex Porto, Prin.; Theresa Cox, Librarian. Lay Teachers 31; Students 341.

ROSWELL. *Blessed Trinity Catholic High School* (2000) 11320 Woodstock Rd., 30075. Tel: 678-277-9083; Fax: 678-277-9756. Email: fmoore@btcatholic.org. Web: www.btcatholic.org. Frank Moore, Prin.; Mr. Richard Martin, Asst. Prin.; Brian Marks, Asst. Prin.; Susan Dorner, Asst. Prin.; Alan Keel, Librarian; Revs. Ricardo Bailey, Chap.; Augustine Tran, J.C.L. . Priests 2; Lay Teachers 77; Total Staff 102; Total Enrollment 871.

Queen of Angels Catholic School (1999) (Grades K-8), 11340 Woodstock Rd., 30075. Tel: 770-518-1804; Fax: 770-518-0945. Email: kwood@qaschool.org. Web: www.qaschool.org. Dr. Kathy Wood, Ph.D., Prin.; Mrs. Molly Carlin, Asst. Prin.; Mrs. Sue VanRooyen, Librarian. Lay Teachers 35; Students 504; Total Staff 60.

TYRONE. *Our Lady of Victory Catholic School* (1999) (Grades PreK-8), 211 Kirkley Rd., 30290. Tel: 770-306-9026; Fax: 770-306-0323. Web: www.olvpatriots.org. Linda Grace, Prin. Lay Teachers 21; Total Staff 39; Total Enrollment 275; Admin/Facilities Staff 18.

[D] INDEPENDENT SCHOOLS

ATLANTA. *Holy Spirit Preparatory School*, 4449 Northside Dr., 30327. Tel: 678-904-2811 (Office); Fax: 678-904-2811. Web: www.holyspiritprep.org. Gareth N. Genner, Pres.; Bob Pelletier, High School Prin.; Rev. Paul Moreau, L.C., B.A., Head Chap.; Kelly Corsetti, Librarian. Priests 1; Lay Teachers 114.

(Grades 7-12), Upper School Campus: 4449 Northside Dr., 30327. Tel: 678-904-2811. Bob Pelletier, High School Prin.

(Grades K-6), Lower School Campus: 4820 Long Island Dr., 30342. Tel: 404-255-0900. Linda Anthony, Prin.; Linda Ehlers, Librarian.

(Grades PreK), Preschool: 4465 Northside Dr., 30327. Tel: 404-252-8008. Dara Liberatore, Early Childhood Prin.; Linda Ehlers, Librarian.

Marist School, (Grades 7-12), 3790 Ashford-Dunwoody, N.E., 30319-1899. Tel: 770-457-7201; 770-451-1316 (Res.); Fax: 770-457-8402. Email: marist@marist.com. Web: www.marist.com. Revs. Joel M. Konzen, S.M., Prin.; Francis J. Kissel, S.M.; Ralph F. Olek, S.M., Supr.; David D. Musso, S.M., Chap.; John H. Harhager, S.M., Pres.; John Walls, S.M., Dir. Campus Ministry. A Private Catholic School.; College Preparatory Day School conducted by The Marist Fathers and Brothers. Corporate Title: Marist School, Inc. Priests 6; Lay Faculty 112; Total Staff 194; Students 1,077. In Res. Revs. Lawrence R. Schmuhl, S.M. (Retired); Charles A. Girard, S.M., Prov. Archivist; Very Rev. Paul J. Hachey, S.M., J.C.L., M.C.L., M.Div., Court of Appeals.

**The Solidarity School, Inc.*, 120 Northwood Dr., Ste. 106, 30342. Tel: 404-236-0868; Fax: 404-843-2739. Email: jarthur@solidarityschool.org. Web: www.solidarityschool.org. Jamie Arthur, Head of School; Martha Manrique, Asst. Dir. Lay Teachers 2; Total Staff 6; Students 33.

ATHENS. **Monsignor Donovan Catholic High School* (2003) 590 Lavender Rd., 30606. Tel: 706-433-0223; Fax: 706-433-0229. Email: jnasworthy@mdchs.org. Web: www.mdchs.org. Barbara Bankston, Prin.; Virginia Stutsman, Asst. Prin.; Liz Edwards, Librarian. Teachers 17; Total Staff 9; Students 121.

CUMMING. **Pinecrest Academy, Inc.* (1993) (Grades PreK-12), 955 Peachtree Pkwy., 30041. Tel: 770-888-4477; Fax: 770-888-0404. Email: pinecrestacademy@pinecrestacademy.org. Web: www.pinecrestacademy.org. Rick Swygman, Exec. Dir.; John Tarpley, Prin. High School; Magdalena Faine, Formation Dir. Girls & Lower School; Robert Bruckner, Admissions; Rev. Eamonn Shelly, L.C., Chap.; Bro. Gabriel Lewis, L.C.; Rev. Todd Belardi, L.C.; Emily Smolynsky, Librarian. Priests 2; Brothers 2; Female Consecrated 3; Lay Teachers 90; Students 915.

DULUTH. *Notre Dame Academy* (2005) (Grades PreK-8), 4635 River Green Pkwy., 30096. Tel: 678-387-9385 (Office); Fax: 678-990-9353. Email: dorr@ndacademy.org. Web: www.ndacademy.org. Debra Orr, Pres.; John Findley, Prin. Middle School; Julia Derucki, Prin. Elem. School; Anne Mancini, Advancement Dir.; Gary Hegarty, Dir. Finance. Independent, Marist Sponsored School, Preschool program for children ages 3 & 4

Early Years School, Notre Dame Academy, 3345 Peachtree Industrial Blvd., 30096. Tel: 678-387-9385 (Office); Fax: 678-990-9353. Email: mhole@ndacademy.org. Web: www.ndacademy.org. Molly Hole, Prin. Early Years. Independent, Marist Sponsored School Lay Teachers 50.

[E] GENERAL HOSPITALS

ATLANTA. *Saint Joseph's Hospital of Atlanta, Inc.* (1890) 5665 Peachtree Dunwoody Rd., N.E., 30342. Tel: 678-843-7120; Fax: 404-851-7339. Email: sjgerety@sjha.org. Web: www.stjosephsatlanta.org. Kirk Wilson, CEO; Rev. Steven L. Yander, Resident Chap.; Sr. Jane Gerety, R.S.M., Exec. Board Officer. Sisters of Mercy of Americas, South Central Community, Inc. Sisters 6; Bed Capacity 410; Inpatients 21,647; Patients Assisted Annually 196,339; Total Staff 2,568.

ATHENS. *St. Mary's Health Care System*, 1230 Baxter St., 30606-3791. Tel: 706-389-3930; Fax: 706-389-3931. Email: dmckenna@stmarysathens.org. Web: www.stmarysathens.org. Mr. Don McKenna, Pres. & CEO. Sisters of Mercy, South Central Region. Other Sister Personnel 4; Nurses 497; Bed Capacity 196; Patients Assisted Annually 130,000; Total Staff 1,413.

[F] SPECIAL HOSPITALS

ATLANTA. *Saint Joseph's Mercy Care Services* (1985) 424 Decatur St., 30312-1848. Tel: 678-843-8500; Fax: 678-843-8501. Email: aebberwein@sjha.org. Division of Saint Joseph's Health System. Operates Saint Joseph's Mercy Care Services

(Atlanta, Georgia). Operates Mercy Senior Care (Rome, Georgia). Total Staff 140; Sisters 1; Total Assisted 22,000.

Our Lady of Perpetual Help Home, 760 Pollard Blvd., S.W., 30315. Tel: 404-688-9515; Fax: 404-588-9568. Web: olphhome.org. Sr. Miriam Smith, O.P., Supr.; Rev. Joseph Mullakkara, M.S.F.S., Chap.

Servants of Relief for Incurable Cancer Dominican Sisters of Hawthorne, Nursing Home for Free Care of Cancer Patients. Priests 1; Sisters 11; Total Staff 32; Patients Assisted Annually 150; Bed Capacity 35.

ROME. *Mercy Senior Care, Inc.*, P.O. Box 866, 30162-0866. Tel: 706-291-8496; Fax: 706-295-5953. Email: rlawler@sjha.org. Sr. Angela Marie Ebberwein, R.S.M., Vice Pres.; Rita Lawler, Dir. Total Staff 20; Total Assisted 350.

[G] MONASTERIES AND RESIDENCES OF PRIESTS

ATLANTA. *Marist Provincial Office, Society of Mary - Atlanta Province*, P.O. Box 81144, 30366-1144. Tel: 770-458-1435; Fax: 770-458-1044. Email: provincialoffice@marist.com; tgkeating@msn.com. Web: maristsociety.org. Res.: 1485 Ashford Pl., 30319. Very Rev. Timothy G. Keating, S.M., Prov.

CONYERS. *The Monastery of the Holy Spirit*, 2625 Hwy. 212 S.W., 30094-4044. Tel: 770-483-8705; Fax: 770-760-0989. Email: monastery@trappist.net. Web: www.trappist.net. Rev. Anthony Delisi, O.C.S.O.; Bro. Elias Marechal, O.C.S.O., Master of Novices; Revs. Francis Michael Stiteler, O.C.S.O., Abbot; Richard Donarski, O.C.S.O.; Methodius Telnack, O.C.S.O., Prior; Malachy Corley, O.C.S.O.; Gerard Gross, O.C.S.O., Office Sub Prior; Jerome J. Hickey, O.C.S.O. (Retired); Luke C. Kot, O.C.S.O. (Retired); Ed Morley, O.C.S.O.; John M. O'Brien, O.C.S.O.; Eduardo Rodriguez, O.C.S.O.; Isaac Gonzalez, O.C.S.O., Novice; Thomas F. Smith, O.C.S.O.; Matt G. Torpey, O.C.S.O., Master of Juniors. Priests 15; Professed Brothers 20; Postulants 2; Novices 2.

Located Elsewhere: Rev. James Stephen Behrens, O.C.S.O.

NORCROSS. *Legionaries of Christ, Incorporated*, 4040 Gunnin Rd., 30092. Tel: 770-671-8778; Fax: 678-916-7543. Email: vtran@legionaries.org. Web: www.legionariesofchrist.org. Revs. Scott Reilly, L.C., Territorial Dir.; Emilio Diaz-Torre, L.C., Supr. Asst. to Territorial Dir.; Bros. Viet Tran, L.C., Spiritual Formation; E.N. Barnett, L.C.; Rev. Peter Devereux, L.C. Total in Residence 5.

Norcross Pastoral Center, Inc., 55 Club Ct., Alpharetta, 30005. Tel: 770-394-2158; Fax: 770-393-0934. Email: atlanta@legionaries.org. Web: www.legionariesofchrist.org. Revs. Paul Moreau, L.C., B.A., Vice Rector & Retreat Work; Chap. Holy Spirit Preparatory School; Dominic Pham, L.C., Chap. Holy Spirit; Kevin Baldwin, Retreats & Promotion; Timothy Moran, Retreats & Promotion Work; Todd Belardi, L.C., Formation Dir. Pinecrest Academy; Eamonn Shelly, L.C., Chap. Pinecrest Academy; David Daly, L.C., Supr. & Retreat Work. Email: ddaly@legionaries.org; Juan Gabriel Guerra, L.C., Retreat Work; Bros. Nicholas Carlson; Juan Jose Hernandez, L.C.; David Joyce, L.C., Asst. to Formation Dir. at Pinecrest. Total in Residence 11.

SNELLVILLE. *The Missionaries of St. Francis De Sales* (1838) 3474 Pate Dr., 30039. Tel: 770-972-0202; Fax: 770-963-3774. Web: www.basilluyethop.org. Revs. Joseph Mullakkara, M.S.F.S., Local Supr.; John C. DeVore, M.S.F.S.; Martin Kopchik, M.S.F.S., Dir. Vocations & Spirituality Center; Jose Maliekal, M.S.F.S.; Joseph Mendes, M.S.F.S.; Abraham Puthiaparampil, M.S.F.S.

[H] CONVENTS AND RESIDENCES OF SISTERS

ATLANTA. *Missionaries of Charity* (1993) 995 St. Charles Ave., N.E., 30306-4211. Tel: 404-892-5111. Sisters 4; Total Assisted 300.

Sisters of Good Shepherd, 3244 Wanda Woods Dr., 30340-4510. Tel: 770-491-6292; Fax: 770-908-8777. Email: srmak77@bellsouth.net. Sr. M. Anita Kristofco, Contact Person. Sisters 4.

BUFORD. *Missionary Sisters of the Sacred Heart "Ad Gentes"* (1949) 6401 New Bethany Rd., 30518. Tel: 678-482-1530; Fax: 678-482-1530. Email: xeniagonzalez@bellsouth.net. Sisters Inés G. Ramos Tapia, M.A.G., B.A., M.A., Gen. Coord. of M.A.G. Sisters in U.S.A.; Beatriz Taneco Bieira, M.A.G., B.A., L.P., Pastoral Assoc.; Xenia Gonzalez, M.A.G., B.A., M.A., Treas. & Pastoral Assoc.; Veronica F. Ramos, M.A.G., B.A., M.A., Pastoral Assoc.; Esther Ordonez, M.A.G., B.A., Pastoral Assoc.; Maria L. Ramos, M.A.G., Pastoral Assoc.; Pilar Hinojosa, M.A.G., B.A., Pastoral Assoc. To serve the Hispanic Community. Sisters 7.

SNELLVILLE. *Monastery of the Visitation* (Maryfield), 2055 Ridgedale Dr., 30078. Tel: 770-972-1060. Sr. Mary Jane Frances Williams, V.H.M., Supr. Strictly cloistered contemplative Office of First Federation. Private retreats for women interested in a religious vocation. U.S. Professed Sisters 10; Novices 1.

[I] RETREAT HOUSES

ATLANTA. *Ignatius House*, 6700 Riverside Dr., N.W., 30328-2710. Tel: 404-255-0503; Fax: 404-256-0776. Email: ihsecretary@bellsouth.net. Web: www.ignatiushouse.org. Revs. Albert C. Louapre, S.J., Retreat Dir.; Niel Jarreau, S.J., Retreat Dir.; Edward P. Buvens, S.J., Retreat Dir.; Maria Greta Cressler, Lay Exec. Dir.; Rev. Edward Salazar, Retreat Dir. Total in Residence 4; Total Staff 9.

CONYERS. *Monastery of the Holy Spirit*, 2625 Hwy. 212, S.W., 30094. Tel: 770-760-0959; Fax: 770-760-0989. Email: rhouse@trappist.net. Web: www.trappist.net. Private retreats for men and women.

HOSCHTON. *Sisters of the Cenacle*, 5913 Jackson Trail Rd., 30548. Tel: 706-654-3460; Fax: 706-654-1459. Sisters Susan Arcaro, R.C.; Barbara Young, R.C. Congregation of Our Lady of the Retreat in the Cenacle., Retreat Ministry, Spiritual Development Programs, Spiritual Direction, and Other Forms of Spiritual Ministry. Sisters 2.

[J] CAMPUS MINISTRY CENTERS

ATLANTA. *Campus Ministry Archdiocese of Atlanta*, 680 W. Peachtree St., N.W., 30308-1984. Tel: 404-885-7413; Fax: 404-885-7473. Email: djohnson@archatl.com. Dennis Lee Johnson Jr., Dir., Office of Formation & Discipleship, Member of the Secretariat.

Atlanta University Complex-The Catholic Center 809 Beckwith St., S.W., 30314-3720. Tel: 404-755-9394; Fax: 404-755-3460. Rev. Edward B. Branch, Campus Min.

Kennesaw State University 3487 Campus Loop Rd., Kennesaw, 30144. Tel: 770-423-9909; Fax: 770-423-9605. Web: www.kennesaw.edu. Rev. Joseph E. Morris, Chap.

Emory University, Agnes Scott College 1753 N. Decatur Rd., N.E., 30307. Tel: 404-636-7237; Fax: 404-636-6099. Web: www.emory.edu. Rev. Bryan Small, Chap.

Georgia Institute of Technology 172 4th St., N.W., 30313. Tel: 404-892-6759; Fax: 404-829-6759. Web: www.gatech.edu. Rev. Timothy M. Hepburn, Chap.

Oglethorpe University 4484 Peachtree Rd., N.E., 30319. Tel: 404-261-1441. Web: www.oglethorpe.edu.

University of Georgia - Catholic Student Center 1344 S. Lumpkin St., Athens, 30605. Tel: 706-543-2293; Fax: 706-543-2541. Web: www.uga.edu/cc. Revs. Thomas F. Vigliotta, O.F.M., Dir. Campus Ministry; David L. Hyman, O.F.M., Assoc. Campus Min. (Athens)

North Georgia College , (Dahlonega), *St. Luke the Evangelist Church*, 301 Hawkins St., Dahlonega, 30533. Tel: 706-864-2568; Fax: 706-864-4294. Web: www.ngcsu.edu. Rev. Robert A. Frederick.

Dalton Junior College , (Dalton), *Church of St. Joseph*, 1775 Old Haigmill Rd., Dalton, 30720. Tel: 706-278-3107; Fax: 706-278-6902. Web: www.daltonstate.edu.

Brenau College St. Michael's Catholic Church - 1440 Pearce Cir., N.E., Gainesville, 30501-2457. Tel: 706-534-3338; Fax: 706-535-2440. Web: www.onlinebrenau.edu. (Gainesville)

LaGrange Jr. College 200 LaFayette Pkwy., LaGrange, 30240. Tel: 706-884-4224; Fax: 706-884-1624. Web: www.lagrange.edu. Rev. Kevin J. Hargaden, Chap. (LaGrange)

Georgia College & State University , (Milledgeville), *Sacred Heart Church*, 1730 Columbine Rd., Milledgeville, 31061. Tel: 478-453-7758. Email: cesar.basilio@thielekanolin.com.

Shorter College , (Rome), *St. Mary's Church*, 911 N. Broad St., Rome, 30161. Tel: 706-295-7014; Fax: 706-295-1717. Web: www.shorter.edu.

Dekalb Community College , (Stone Mountain), *Corpus Christi Church*, 600 Mountain View Dr., Stone Mountain, 30083. Tel: 770-469-0395; Fax: 770-469-6822. Web: www.dekalbtech.org. Rev. Leonard Brown, C.M.F.

Catholic Center Georgia State University Student Center, Ste. 330, P.O. Box 3965, 30302. Rev. Stephen J. Lyness, Chap.

[K] CATHOLIC CONTINUING CARE RETIREMENT CENTER

ROSWELL. *St. George Village-Catholic Community Retirement Center*, 11350 Woodstock Rd., 30075. Tel: 770-645-2340. Web: www.stgeorgevillage.com. Mr. Mark A. Lowell, Exec. Dir.

[L] MISCELLANEOUS LISTINGS

ATLANTA. *Allegre Point Senior Residences, Inc.*, 621 North Ave., Ste. A150, 30308. Tel: 404-549-5349; Fax: 877-693-2333. Web: www.mercyhousing.org.

AOA Properties Holding, Inc., 680 W. Peachtree St., N.W., 30308. Tel: 404-885-7408; Fax: 404-885-7223. Bradley Wilson, CFO & Sec.

The Catholic Charismatic Renewal for the Archdiocese of Atlanta, 1786 Wellborn Rd., Lithonia, 30058. Tel: 770-482-5017; Fax: 770-482-9476. Email: contact@atlccr.org. Web: www.atlccr.org.

Catholic Education of North Georgia, Inc., 680 W. Peachtree St., N.W., 30308. Tel: 404-885-7408; Fax: 404-885-7223.

Good Shepherd Services of Atlanta, Inc. (1993) (Incorporated as Good Shepherd Corporation)

Main Office, 2426 Shallowford Terr., 30341. Tel: 770-455-9379; Fax: 770-451-0156. Email: shepherdatlanta@bellsouth.net. Sr. Christine Truong, M.S.W., M.A., Exec. Dir. Tel: 770-455-9379; 770-986-8279.

Good Shepherd Outreach Center, 2426 Shallowford Ter., 30341. Tel: 770-455-9379; Fax: 770-451-0156. Sr. M. Catherine Massei, Pres. Sisters 2.

G.R.A.C.E. Scholars, Inc., 680 W. Peachtree St., N.W., 30308. Tel: 404-888-7800; Fax: 404-978-2770. Web: www.archatl.com. Diane Starkovich, Supt. Schools.

Greater Northwest Atlanta Serra Club #1070, Dist. #169, 680 W. Peachtree St., N.W., 30308. Web: serraatlanta.org. Edward Schaeffer, Pres. Tel: 678-230-9803.

St. Joseph Research Institute, Inc. (2003) 5673 Peachtree - Dunwoody Rd., N.E., Ste. 675, 30342. Tel: 678-843-6067; Fax: 678-843-6051. Email: asimon@sjha.org. Web: www.stjosephatlanta.org. Nichlas Chronos, M.D., Vice Pres. Clinical Research Operations; Paul G. Justice Esq., Vice Pres. & General Counsel.

St. Joseph's 125th Anniversary Capital Campaign, Inc., 5673 Peachtree Dunwoody Rd., N.E., 30342.

Saint Joseph's at East Georgia, Inc., 5665 Peachtree Dunwoody Rd., N.E., 30342. Tel: 706-453-5031; Fax: 706-453-2812. Paul G. Justice Esq., Asst. Sec.

Saint Joseph's Health System, Inc. (1985) 5665 Peachtree Dunwoody Rd., N.E., 30342. Tel: 678-843-7120; Fax: 678-843-7339. Email: sjgerety@sjha.org. Web: www.stjosephsatlanta.org. Kirk Wilson, CEO; Sr. Jane Gerety, R.S.M., Senior Vice Pres. for Sponsorship. Sponsorship. Holding Company Sponsored by Sisters of Mercy of Americas, South Central Community Inc., which operates: Saint Joseph's Hospital of Atlanta, Inc.; Saint Joseph's Mercy Foundation, Inc.; Saint Joseph's Mercy Care Services, Inc.; Saint Joseph's Research Institute Inc. and Saint Joseph's East Georgia.

Saint Joseph's Mercy Foundation (1981) 5673 Peachtree Dunwoody Rd., Ste. 650, 30342-1746. Tel: 404-851-5710; Fax: 404-851-4986. Email: bgarrett@sjha.org. Web: www.stjosephsatlanta.org. William Garrett, Pres. Priests 1; Total Staff 11; Total Assisted 5,000.

Mercy Housing Pembroke, Inc., 621 North Ave., N.E. Ste. A-150, 30308. Tel: 404-873-3887; Fax: 877-693-2333. Email: pwalker@mercyhousing.org. Pete Walker, Pres.

National Christ Child Society of Atlanta, Georgia Inc., P.O. Box 88646, 30356. Tel: 770-352-9636. Email: christchildatl@bellsouth.net.

National Consultants for Education, Inc., 5 Concourse Pkwy., Ste. 750, 30328. Tel: 770-828-4950; Fax: 770-828-4955. Email: businessoffice@nceducation.org; egrandio@nceducation.org. Web: www.nceducation.org. Eduardo Grandio, Dir.

Patrons of the Arts in the Vatican Museums, Inc., 4449 Northside Dr., 30328. Tel: 678-904-2811, Ext. 235; Fax: 404-221-1006. Gareth N. Genner, Dir. & Sec.

Renovacion Carismatica Catolica Hispana De Atlanta, 490 Arnold Mill Rd., Woodstock, 30188. Tel: 678-213-0685; Fax: 770-516-4664. Email: rcchatlanta@yahoo.com.

Serra Club #120, Dist. 169 Metro Atlanta, 680 W. Peachtree St., N.W., 30308. Web: serraatlanta.org. Frank Murphy, Pres. Tel: 770-432-4333.

Serra Club #684, Dist. 169 North Metro Atlanta, 680 W. Peachtree St., N.W., 30308. Web: serraatlanta.org. Tom Jankowski, Pres.

The Solidarity Association, 4449 Northside Dr., 30327. Frank J. Hanna III, Moderator & Trustee; Most Rev. John F. Donoghue, J.C.L., Trustee (Retired); Gareth N. Genner, Trustee, Sec. & Pres.; Rev. Msgr. Edward J. Dillon, J.C.D., Spiritual Advisor; Elizabeth Hanna, Trustee; David Hanna, Trustee; Sally Hanna, Trustee.

ALPHARETTA. **Mission Network USA, Inc.*, 6445 Shiloh Rd., Ste. B, 30005. Tel: 628-679-2480; Fax: 678-679-2481. Web: www.cywn.net.

College Compass, Inc., 6445 Shiloh Rd., Ste. B, 30005. Tel: 914-773-1368. Email: jfortega@legionaries.org. Rev. Jose F. Ortega, L.C., Sec. & Treas.

Youth for the Third Millennium, Inc., 6445 Shiloh Rd., Ste. B, 30005. Tel: 914-773-1368. Email: jfortega@legionaries.org. Rev. Jose F. Ortega, L.C., Sec. & Treas.

BLAIRSVILLE. *Faith Enrichment Institute, Inc.* (1989) 5939 Dills Rd., 30512. Tel: 404-402-4022; Fax: 706-781-3673. Email: peglor@alltel.net. Deacon Loris Sinanian.

CONYERS. *Magnificat - Joyful Visitation Chapter, Inc.* (1922) 3295 Creekside Dr., 30094. Tel: 770-929-0405. Email: gowa@bellsouth.net. Susie Goodrow, Coord.

**Rosary Army Corp.*, 1805 Overlake Dr. Ste. C, 30013. Tel: 770-918-1101. Email: greg@rosaryarmy.com. Web: rosaryarmy.com. P.O. Box 82721, 30013. Greg Willits, Pres.; Jennifer Willits, Sec. & Treas.

COVINGTON. *Society of Our Lady of the Most Holy Trinity, SOLT Lay Community*, 326-B Dry Pond Rd., 30016-5637. Tel: 706-819-9215. Email: frpauldamian@netzero.net. Revs. John S. Zachary, Lay Formation Dir.; Paul Johnston, Chap.

CUMMING. *Vocation Action Circle, Inc.*, 2820 Bordeaux Blvd., 30041. Tel: 678-528-7514. Email: jgonzales@vocation.com.

NORCROSS. *Home and Family, Inc.* (1996) 3240 Pointe Pkwy., Ste. 200, 30092. Tel: 770-396-2363; Fax: 678-578-5297. Email: office@missionnetworkatlanta.org. Revs. Dominic Pham, L.C., Supr.; Todd Belardi, L.C.; Eamonn Shelly, L.C.; Peter Devereux, L.C.; Paul Moreau, L.C., B.A., Dir.

ROSWELL. **Catholics Come Home*, 560 W. Crossville Rd., Ste. 101, 30075.

**Virtue Media, Inc.*, 560 W. Crossville Rd., Ste. 101, 30075.

SANDY SPRINGS. *LCNA Atlanta, Incorporated*, 55 Club Ct., Alpharetta, 30005. Tel: 914-773-1368. Email: jfortega@legionaries.org. Rev. Jose F. Ortega, L.C., Asst. Sec.

Legion of Christ, Atlanta, Inc., 55 Club Ct., Alpharetta, 30005. Tel: 770-671-8778. Bro. Viet Tran, L.C., Vice Pres.

RELIGIOUS INSTITUTES OF MEN REPRESENTED IN THE ARCHDIOCESE

For further details refer to the corresponding bracketed number in the Religious Institutes of Men or Women section.

[0350]—*Cistercians Order of the Strict Observance-Trappists*—O.C.S.O.

[0360]—*Claretian Missionaries* (Eastern Province)—C.M.F.

[1000]—*Congregation of the Passion* (Prov. of St. Paul of the Cross)—C.P.

[0480]—*Conventual Franciscans* (Prov. of St. Anthony of Padua, Baltimore)—O.F.M.Conv

[0520]—*Franciscan Friars* (Prov. of the Most Holy Name of Jesus)—O.F.M.

[0690]—*Jesuit Fathers and Brothers* (New Orleans Prov.)—S.J.

[0730]—*Legionaries of Christ*—L.C.

[0780]—*Marist Fathers* (San Francisco-Washington Prov.)—S.M.

[0720]—*The Missionaries of Our Lady of La Salette*—M.S.

[]—*Missionaries of St. Francis de Sales* (Annecy, France)—M.S.F.S.

[]—*Missionaries of the Nativity of Mary*—M.N.M.

[1065]—*The Priestly Fraternity of St. Peter*—F.S.S.P.

[]—*Society of Christ*—S.Chr.

[]—*Society of Our Lady of the Most Holy Trinity*—SOLT

[]—*Society of St. Paul*—S.S.P.

RELIGIOUS INSTITUTES OF WOMEN REPRESENTED IN THE ARCHDIOCESE

[3110]—*Congregation of Our Lady of the Retreat in the Cenacle*—R.C.

[1070-13]—*Dominican Sisters (Adrian, MI)*—O.P.

[]—*Dominican Sisters of St. Cecilia* (Nashville, TN)

[1070-23]—*Dominican Sisters of St. Rose of Lima (Hawthorne, NY)*—O.P.

[]—*Dominican Sisters of Vietnam*

[1070-03]—*Dominican Sisters (Sinsinawa, WI)*—O.P.

[]—*Franciscan Sisters of Our Lady of Refuge* (Mexico)—R.F.R.

[1840]—*Grey Nuns of the Sacred Heart (Yardley, PA)*—G.N.S.H.

[1870]—*Handmaids of the Sacred Heart of Jesus (Philadelphia, PA)*—A.C.J.

[]—*Holy Family Sisters of the Needy* (Nigeria)—H.F.S.N.

[2575]—*Institute of the Sisters of Mercy of the Americas* (Merion, PA; Rochester, NY; Baltimore, MD)—R.S.M.

[2710]—*Missionaries of Charity*—M.C.

[]—*Missionary Sisters of the Most Sacred Heart* (Reading, PA)

[2800]—*Missionary Sisters of the Most Sacred Heart of Jesus of Hiltrup* (Reading, PA)—M.S.C.

[]—*Missionary Sisters of the Sacred Heart "Ad Gentes"* (Mexico)—M.A.G.

[]—*Sisters of Jesus of Kkottongnae* (Korea)

[3840]—*Sisters of St. Joseph of Carondelet (St. Louis, MO)*—C.S.J.

[3830-15]—*Sisters of St. Joseph of Concordia (Concordia, KS)*—C.S.J.

[]—*Sisters of the Blessed Sacrament* (Nigeria)

[1830]—*The Sisters of the Good Shepherd (Silver Spring, MD)*—R.G.S.

[4190]—*Sisters of the Visitation*—V.H.M.

[]—*Sisters of the Visitation of Holy Mary*

[2150]—*Sisters, Servants of the Immaculate Heart of Mary (Monroe, MI)*—I.H.M.

ARCHDIOCESAN CEMETERIES

CARROLLTON. *Our Lady of Perpetual Help, Our Lady of Help Church*, 210 Old Center Point Rd., 30117. Tel: 770-832-8977; Fax: 770-832-1666. Email: olphcc@gmail.com.

SHARON. *Locust Grove, Archdiocese of Atlanta*, 680 W. Peachtree St., N.W., 30308-1984. Tel: 404-885-7805.

Purification, St. Joseph's Catholic Church, U.S. Hwy. 78, P.O. Box 632, Washington, 30673.

SPARTA. *Sparta, Archdiocese of Atlanta*, 680 W. Peachtree St., N.W., 30308-1984. Tel: 404-888-7805.

WASHINGTON. *Saint Patrick's, St. Joseph's*, US Hwy. 78, P.O. Box 632, 30673. Email: frtom4nfp@stpatricks-norcross.org.

NECROLOGY

† Miceli, James A., (Retired)—Died Dec. 8, 2009

An asterisk (*) denotes an organization that has established tax-exempt status directly with the IRS and is not covered by the USCCB Group Ruling.

Diocese of Austin

(Dioecesis Austiniensis)

Most Reverend

JOE S. VASQUEZ

Bishop of Austin; ordained June 30, 1984; appointed Titular Bishop of Cova and Auxiliary Bishop of Galveston-Houston November 30, 2001; ordained January 23, 2002; appointed Bishop of Austin January 26, 2010; installed March 8, 2010. *Office: P.O. Box 15405, Austin, TX 78761.*

Most Reverend

JOHN E. McCARTHY, D.D.

Retired Bishop of Austin; ordained May 26, 1956; appointed Titular Bishop of Pasadena and Auxiliary Bishop of Galveston-Houston January 15, 1979; appointed Bishop of Austin December 19, 1985; retired January 2, 2001.

Pastoral Center: 6225 E. Hwy. 290, Austin, TX 78723. Tel: 512-949-2400; Fax: 512-949-2520.

Web: www.austindiocese.org

Email: info@austindiocese.org

ERECTED 1947.

Square Miles 19,511.

Comprises the Counties of Mills, Hamilton, San Saba, Lampasas, Coryell, McLennan, Limestone, Bell, Falls, Robertson, Mason, Llano, Burnet, Williamson, Milam, Brazos, Blanco, Travis, Bastrop, Lee, Burleson, Washington, Hays, Caldwell and the part of Fayette County north of the Colorado River in the State of Texas.

For legal titles of parishes and diocesan institutions, consult the Chancery Office.

STATISTICAL OVERVIEW

Personnel	
Bishop	1
Retired Bishops	1
Priests: Diocesan Active in Diocese	92
Priests: Diocesan Active Outside Diocese	11
Priests: Retired, Sick or Absent	28
Number of Diocesan Priests	131
Religious Priests in Diocese	50
Total Priests in Diocese	181
Extern Priests in Diocese	43
Ordinations:	
Diocesan Priests	5
Transitional Deacons	5
Permanent Deacons in Diocese	197
Total Brothers	46
Total Sisters	107
Parishes	
Parishes	101
With Resident Pastor:	
Resident Diocesan Priests	74
Resident Religious Priests	26
Without Resident Pastor:	
Administered by Priests	1
Missions	22
Pastoral Centers	1
Professional Ministry Personnel:	
Sisters	25
Lay Ministers	165
Welfare	
Catholic Hospitals	4
Total Assisted	1,508,356
Homes for the Aged	3
Total Assisted	334,253
Day Care Centers	2
Total Assisted	300
Specialized Homes	2
Total Assisted	160
Special Centers for Social Services	7
Total Assisted	24,524
Residential Care of Disabled	1
Total Assisted	1,900
Educational	
Diocesan Students in Other Seminaries	46
Total Seminarians	46
Colleges and Universities	1
Total Students	5,285
High Schools, Diocesan and Parish	4
Total Students	615
High Schools, Private	2
Total Students	550
Elementary Schools, Diocesan and Parish	16
Total Students	3,626
Elementary Schools, Private	1
Total Students	367
Catechesis/Religious Education:	
High School Students	8,108
Elementary Students	29,416
Total Students under Catholic Instruction	48,013
Teachers in the Diocese:	
Priests	6
Brothers	3
Sisters	13
Lay Teachers	629
Vital Statistics	
Receptions into the Church:	
Infant Baptism Totals	8,182
Minor Baptism Totals	642
Adult Baptism Totals	467
Received into Full Communion	1,107
First Communions	7,453
Confirmations	4,308
Marriages:	
Catholic	1,186
Interfaith	414
Total Marriages	1,600
Deaths	1,676
Total Catholic Population	321,197
Total Population	2,699,324

Former Bishops—Most Revs. LOUIS J. REICHER, D.D., ord. Dec. 6, 1918; appt. first Bishop of Austin Nov. 29, 1947; cons. April 14, 1948; died Feb. 23, 1984; VINCENT M. HARRIS, D.D., ord. March 19, 1938; appt. Bishop of Beaumont July 4, 1966; cons. Sept. 28, 1966; transferred to Austin April 21, 1971; succeeded to the See Nov. 16, 1971; retired Feb. 25, 1986; died March 31, 1988; JOHN E. McCARTHY, D.D. (Retired), Bishop of Austin; ord. May 26, 1956; appt. Titular Bishop of Pasadena and Auxiliary Bishop of Galveston-Houston, Jan. 23, 1979; cons. March 14, 1979; appt. Bishop of Austin, Dec. 24, 1985; installed Feb. 25, 1986; retired Jan. 2, 2001; GREGORY M. AYMOND, ord. May 10, 1975; appt. Titular Bishop of Acolla and Auxiliary Bishop of New Orleans Nov. 19, 1996; ord. Jan. 10, 1997; appt. Coadjutor Bishop of Austin June 1, 2000; installed Aug. 3, 2000; succeeded to the See of Austin Jan. 2, 2001; appt. Archbishop of New Orleans, June 12, 2009; installed Aug. 20, 2009.

Vicar General—VACANT.

Moderator of the Curia—Deacons RON WALKER, Chancellor; BILL HOBBY, Vice Chancellor.

Pastoral Center—Mailing Address: 6225 Hwy. 290 E., Austin, 78723. Tel: 512-949-2400, Ext. 2452; Fax: 512-949-2524. Office Hours: Mon.-Fri. 8:30-5.

Notary—Deacon RON WALKER.

Deans—VACANT.

Presbyteral Council—VACANT.

Consultors—Rev. Msgr. FRED BOMAR; Very Rev. DANIEL E. GARCIA; Rev. Msgr. ELMER HOLTMAN (Retired); Revs. DAVID LEIBHAM; GLYNN (BUD) ROLAND JR.; Rev. Msgrs. MICHAEL J. SIS; LONNIE A. URBAN.

Canonical and Tribunal Services—6225 E. Hwy. 290, Austin, 78723-1025. Tel: 512-949-2400; Fax: 512-949-2522. Direct all inquiries concerning marriage nullity, dispensation and permissions to this address.

Judicial Vicar—Very Rev. CHRISTOPHER FERRER, M.F., J.C.L.

Adjutant Judicial Vicar—Rev. JOZEF MUSIOL, S.D.S., J.C.D.

Diocesan Tribunal Judges—Rev. ROBERT L. KINCL, J.C.L.; Very Rev. CHRISTOPHER FERRER, M.F., J.C.L.; Revs. ANTHONY NWUDAH, J.C.L.; DAVID WILLIAMS, J.C.L., J.D.

Defenders of the Bond—Revs. KIRBY GARNER; JOZEF MUSIOL, S.D.S., J.C.D.

Notaries—Deacons RAYMOND SANDERS JR., M.S., M.A., Ed.D.; RALPH AREVALO JR.; DON GESSLER, M.D., M.B.A.; KEVIN NISSEN; LARRY TERRELL; HARVEY BOLLICH, Ph.D.; Mrs. JOANNE SANDERS, M.R.E.; Mrs. DEBORAH R. PATIN, Senior Administrative Asst. Administrative Assistants: Mrs. JANIE CUELLAR; ROBERT PINE, M.Sc.

Advocates— Priests, Deacons, Religious, and Parish Associates exercising ministry in the Diocese of Austin. Advocates for the Respondent in English: Deacons DON GESSLER, M.D., M.B.A.; KEVIN NISSEN; RALPH AREVALO JR., Advocate for the Respondent in Spanish.

Auditors—Deacon LARRY TERRELL; HARVEY BOLLICH, Ph.D.; Mrs. JOANNE SANDERS, M.R.E.; ROBERT PINE, M.Sc.

Assessors—Deacons JOHN PICKWELL; RAYMOND SANDERS JR., M.S., M.A., Ed.D.; ROBERT PINE, M.Sc.

Finance Office—MARY BETH KOENIG, CFO, Mailing Address: 6225 Hwy. 290 E., Austin, 78723. Tel: 512-949-2400; Fax: 512-949-2528.

Finance Council—DON E. COX; Deacon SWITZER DEASON; CAMPBELL MCGINNIS; KARL KUYKENDALL; JIM SMOLIK; MARY BETH KOENIG; JOSE MONTEMAYOR; PATRICIA OHLENDORF; JOHN MCGOVERN.

Diocesan Archives and Records—Deacon RON WALKER, Chancellor, Mailing Address: 6225 Hwy. 290 E., Austin, 78723. Tel: 512-949-2400.

Office of Black Catholics—Mr. JOHNNIE DORSEY, Dir., Mailing Address: 6225 Hwy. 290 E., Austin, 78723. Tel: 512-949-2449. Email: johnnie-dorsey@austindiocese.org.

Facility Planning—Deacon TOM JOHNSON, Dir., Mailing Address: 6225 Hwy. 290 E., Austin, 78723. Tel: 512-949-2418; Fax: 512-949-2525.

Catholic Campaign for Human Development—BARBARA BUDDE, M.A., Mailing Address: 6225 Hwy. 290 E., Austin, 78723. Tel: 512-949-2471.

Catholic Charities of Central Texas—CYNTHIA COLBERT, Exec. Dir., 1817 E. 6th St., Austin, 78702. Tel: 512-651-6102.

Immigration Legal Services—CARMEN CORTES-HARMS, Dir., Catholic Charities of Central Texas, 1817 E. 6th St., Austin, 78702. Tel: 512-651-6110.

Catholic Schools Office—NED F. VANDERS, Ph.D., Supt., Mailing Address: 6225 Hwy. 290 E., Austin, 78723. Tel: 512-949-2498; Fax: 512-949-2520.

Stewardship and Development—SCOTT WHITAKER, Dir., Mailing Address: 6225 Hwy. 290 E., Austin, 78723. Tel: 512-949-2441; Fax: 512-949-2520.

"Catholic Spirit" Newspaper—SHELLEY METCALF, Editor, Mailing Address: 6225 Hwy. 290 E., Austin, 78723. Tel: 512-949-2443; Fax: 512-949-2523. Email: catholic.spirit@austindiocese.org.

Office of Youth, Young Adult and Campus Ministry—CHRIS BARTLETT, Dir., Mailing Address: 6225 Hwy. 290 E., Austin, 78723. Tel: 512-949-2465; Fax: 512-949-2520; Rev. JESUS FERRAS, I.S.P., Assoc. Dir. Hispanic Young Adult Ministry. Tel: 512-949-2466; ALISON KOEDERITZ, Prog. Coord. Young Adult Ministry. Tel: 512-949-2467.

Cemeteries—Deacon TOM JOHNSON, Mailing Address: 6225 Hwy. 290 E., Austin, 78723. Tel: 512-949-2418.

Charismatic Renewal—Deacon JESSE MARTINEZ, Dir., 1104 Turtle Creek, Austin, 78745. Tel: 512-447-8977.

Communications—CHRISTIAN GONZALEZ, Dir., Mailing Address: 6225 Hwy. 290 E., Austin, 78723. Tel: 512-949-2456.

Human Resources—TADIM LEASURE, Dir., Mailing Address: 6225 Hwy. 290 E., Austin, 78723. Tel: 512-949-2451; Fax: 512-949-2524.

Priestly Life and Formation Committee—Rev. HARRY DEAN, Chm.

Council of Catholic Women—MARCY YOUNGMAN, Pres., 1448 Seminole Trail, Dale, 78616. Tel: 512-601-1677. Web: www.adccw.com.

Cursillo—Our Lady of Guadalupe Cursillo Center, Jarrell, 76537. Tel: 512-746-2041. LOUIS RUIZ, Center Dir., 3201 Shady Hill, Temple, 76502. Tel: 254-773-5905. Spanish: JUAN M. LOPEZ, 2825 S. University Dr., Waco, 76706. Tel: 254-753-5697. English: ADOLFO ALVAREZ, Pres., Mailing Address: P.O. Box 142486, Austin, 78714-2486. Tel: 512-784-7964. Email: wu_doc1@hotmail.com.

Deaf Ministry—Deacon PATRICK MURRAY, Dir., St. Ignatius Church, 2309 Euclid St., Austin, 78704. Email: mpatrick@austin.rr.com.

Diaconate—Deacon RON WALKER, Dir., Mailing Address: 6225 Hwy. 290 E., Austin, 78723. Tel: 512-949-2452.

Diaconate Formation—Deacon TOM JOHNSON, Assoc. Dir.

Ecumenism—Rev. CHARLES L. COVINGTON, Dir., St. Louis Church, 7601 Burnet Rd., Austin, 78757. Tel: 512-454-0384.

Catholic Family Counseling and Family Life Office—JOSEPH WHITE, Ph.D., Dir., Mailing Address: 6225 Hwy. 290 E., Austin, 78723. Tel: 512-949-2493; Fax: 512-949-2527.

Holy Childhood—CHARLENE O'CONNELL, M.A., 6225 Hwy. 290 E., Austin, 78723. Tel: 512-949-2470.

Criminal Justice Ministry—Deacon E. GENERES (DOOTS) DUFOUR, Dir., 1817 E. 6th St., Austin, 78702. Tel: 512-651-6108.

Mission Council—BARBARA BUDDE, M.A., Contact, Mailing Address: 6225 Hwy. 290 E., Austin, 78723. Tel: 512-949-2471.

Office of Hispanic Ministry—Sr. CELIA ANN CAVAZOS, M.C.D.P., Dir.; PEDRO MORENO, Assoc. Dir., Hispanic Catechesis, Mailing Address: 6225 Hwy. 290 E., Austin, 78723. Tel: 512-949-2468; Fax: 512-949-2520.

Social Concerns and Parish Social Ministries—BARBARA BUDDE, M.A., Dir., Mailing Address: 6225 Hwy. 290 E., Austin, 78723. Tel: 512-949-2471.

Propagation of the Faith—Deacon BILL HOBBY, Dir. Tel: 512-949-2427.

Department of Religious Education & Formation—GERI TELEPAK, D.Min., Dir. Tel: 512-949-2469; Fax: 512-949-2520; CHARLENE O'CONNELL, M.A., Assoc. Dir. Catholic School Relg. Educ. Tel: 512-949-2470; Sr. CELIA ANN CAVAZOS, M.C.D.P., Assoc. Dir. Hispanic Relg. Educ., Mailing Address: 6225 Hwy. 290 E., Austin, 78723. Tel: 512-949-2468; Fax: 512-949-2520.

Office of Pro-Life Activities & Chaste Living—MARIE SEALE, Dir., Mailing Address: 6225 Hwy. 290 E., Austin, 78723. Tel: 512-949-2487; Fax: 512-949-2520.

Rural Life—Rev. Msgr. EMILIAN FOLTYN, Dir., 8626 FM 1105, Jarrell, 76537-1522. Tel: 512-863-3020.

Serra Club - Austin—Rev. JAMES EKEOCHA, Chap.-Austin; JEFFREY BRUNS, Pres., 11101 Sierra Blanca, Austin, 78726. Tel: 512-918-0519. Email: jbruns@austinaerotech.com.

Serra Club - Central Texas—C. DAVID BROECKER, Pres., 1417 Elizabeth Circle, Salado, 76571. Tel: 254-247-1776. Email: cbroecker@vum.com.

Special Collections—SCOTT WHITAKER, Dir., Mailing Address: 6225 Hwy. 290 E., Austin, 78723. Tel: 512-949-2400; Fax: 512-949-2520.

Vicar for Clergy—Rev. HARRY DEAN, Mailing Address: 6225 Hwy. 290 E., Austin, 78723. Tel: 512-949-2431; Fax: 512-949-2524. Email: fr-harry-dean@austindiocese.org.

Office for Religious—Executive Co Directors: Sisters KATHLEEN SKOG, O.S.F.; HELEN BREWER, D.C., Mailing Address: 6225 Hwy. 290 E., Austin, 78723. Tel: 512-949-2401.

Ethics and Integrity in Ministry—EMILY HURLIMANN, Dir., Mailing Address: 6225 Hwy. 290 E., Austin, 78723. Tel: 512-949-2447.

Victim Assistance Coordinator—PATRICIA STANKUS. Tel: 512-949-2400. Email: pat-stankus@austindiocese.org.

Vocations—Rev. BRIAN MCMASTER, Dir., Mailing Address: 6225 Hwy. 290 E., Austin, 78723. Tel: 512-949-2405. Email: fr-brian-mcmaster@austindiocese.org. Associate Directors: Rev. DAVID KONDERLA, St. Mary's Catholic Center, 603 Church Ave., College Station, 77840. Tel: 979-846-5717; Very Rev. DANIEL E. GARCIA, St. Vincent de Paul, 9500 Neenah Dr., Austin, 78717. Tel: 512-255-1389; Revs. ALBERTO J. BORRUEL, St. William Church, 620 Round Rock West Dr., Round Rock, 78681. Tel: 512-255-3825; KEITH KOEHL, St. Patrick's Church, 2500 Limmer Loop, Hutto, 78634. Tel: 512-759-3712; JAMES EKEOCHA, St. Thomas More, 10205 RR 620 N., Austin, 78726. Tel: 512-258-1161; RAFAEL PADILLA, Santa Teresa, 1212 Lucky, Bryan, 77803. Tel: 979-822-2932; LE-MINH PHAM, St. Margaret Mary, 1101 W. New Hope Dr., Cedar Park, 78613. Tel: 512-259-3126; CELINA GALVAN, Admin. Asst. Tel: 512-949-2430.

Diocesan Institute for Ecclesial Ministry—6225 Hwy. 290 E., Austin, 78723. Tel: 512-949-2400. Rev. BRIAN MCMASTER, Dir. Tel: 512-949-2405.

Legal Services—6225 Hwy. 290 E., Austin, 78723. Tel: 512-949-2400. Deacon RON WALKER, Gen. Counsel. Tel: 512-949-2452.

Worship Office—Mailing Address: 6225 Hwy. 290 E., Austin, 78723. Tel: 512-949-2400. CHERYL MAXWELL, Dir. Tel: 512-949-2453.

Foundations, Endowments and Trusts

Charitable Trusts—

Father Bernard C. Goertz Scholarship Trust Fund—Sacred Heart Church, 4045 FM 535, Bastrop, 78602.

John J. Kearns Memorial Charitable Trust Fund—Mailing Address: P.O. Box 5040, Waco, 78708.

Clerical Endowment Fund—Very Rev. EDWARD KARASEK, Mailing Address: P.O. Box 276, West, 76691. Tel: 254-826-3705.

Sts. Cyril & Methodius School Endowment—Very Rev. JOSEPH NISARI, Mailing Address: Sts. Cyril & Methodius, P.O. Box 201, Granger, 76530.

Clergy Medical and Retirement Trust of the Diocese of Austin— The Diocese of Austin Pension Plan Committee VACANT, Chm.

St. Joseph's Foundation of Bryan—THOMAS J. POOL, Exec., 2801 Franciscan Dr., Bryan, 77802. Tel: 979-774-4087.

St. Jude Foundation, Inc.—1306 N. Park, Brenham, 77833.

St. Joseph's School Memorial Endowment Fund—Rev. Msgr. JOHN A. MCCAFFREY, St. Joseph, 600 E. 26th St., Bryan, 77803. Tel: 979-822-2721; Fax: 979-779-3120.

CLERGY, PARISHES, MISSIONS AND PAROCHIAL SCHOOLS

CITY OF AUSTIN

(TRAVIS COUNTY)

1—ST. MARY CATHEDRAL (1852) Revs. Albert Laforet Jr., Rector; Daniel Liu, Parochial Vicar; Germanus Rayen, O.F.M.Cap., Parochial Vicar; Deacons Willie Cortez; Ron Walker; Vincent A. Boyle.
Res.: 203 E. 10th St., 78701. Tel: 512-476-6182; Fax: 512-476-8799. Email: office@smcaustin.org. Web: www.smcaustin.org.
School—Cathedral School of St. Mary, (Grades PreK-8), 910 San Jacinto, 78701. Tel: 512-476-1480; Fax: 512-476-9922. David O'Connell, Prin. Lay Teachers 17; Students 205.
Catechesis/Religious Program—Tel: 512-476-4801; Fax: 512-476-8799. Students 300.

2—ST. ALBERT THE GREAT (1987) [CEM] Rev. Isidore Ndagizimana (Uganda); Deacon Al Cuevas; Storm Knien, Music Min.
Res.: 12041 Bittern Hollow, 78758. Tel: 512-837-7825; Fax: 512-834-2377.
Catechesis/Religious Program— Annemarie Weis, D.R.E. Students 805.

3—ST. ANDREW KIM TAEGON KOREAN CATHOLIC CHURCH (1984), (Korean), Rev. Francis Chung.
Church: 6523 Emerald Forest, 78745. Tel: 512-326-3225.
Catechesis/Religious Program—Students 55.

4—ST. AUSTIN (1908) Revs. John E. Hurley, C.S.P., Temp. Admin.; Steven Bell, C.S.P. In Res., Revs. Edward C. Nowak, C.S.P.; Robert P. Michele, C.S.P.; Robert T. Scott, C.S.P.
Res.: 2026 Guadalupe St., 78705. Tel: 512-477-9471; Fax: 512-477-9430.
School—(Grades PreK-8), 1911 San Antonio St., 78705. Tel: 512-477-3751; Fax: 512-477-3079. Web: www.staustinschool.org. Barbara Kennedy, Prin.; Kathy Hymal, Librarian. Lay Teachers 19; Students 208.
Catechesis/Religious Program—Tel: 512-477-9471, Ext. 302. Students 253.

5—ST. CATHERINE OF SIENA (1979) Revs. Patrick Coakley, M.S.C.; Masilamani Rajamanickam; Deacons Larry Terrell; Christopher Schroeder.
Church: 4800 Convict Hill Rd., 78749. Tel: 512-892-2420; Fax: 512-892-0488.
Catechesis/Religious Program—Tel: 512-892-2426; Fax: 512-892-0488. Pamela Neuman, D.R.E. Students 1,200.

6—CHURCH OF THE RESURRECTION, EMMAUS (1963) [CEM] [JC] Very Rev. Samuel Hose; Deacons Boyce Foreman; John Hill; Jesse Martinez.
Mailing Address & Res.: 1718 Lohman's Crossing, Lakeway, 78734. Tel: 512-261-8500; Fax: 512-261-8200.
Catechesis/Religious Program—Students 700.
Chapel—Queen of Angels 20600 Siesta Shores Rd., Spicewood, Travis Co. 78669. Tel: 512-264-3355. P.O. Box 448, Spicewood, 78669-0448.

7—CRISTO REY (1950), (Hispanic), Rev. Jayme Mathias, O.F.M.Conv.; Deacon Agapito Lopez.
2208 E. 2nd St., 78702. Fax: 512-480-9604 (Office).
Res.: 2107 E. 2nd St., 78702. Tel: 512-474-6376.
Catechesis/Religious Program—2215 E. 2nd St., 78702. Tel: 512-477-1099. Sisters Maria Becerrill, F.M.A.; Maria Rodriguez, F.M.A., Dir. Faith & Educ.; M. Guadalupe Medina, F.M.A., Dir. Evangelization; Elizabeth Villanueua, F.M.A., Mother Supr.; Mary Gloria Mar, F.M.A., Dir. Vides. Students 875.

8—HOLY CROSS (1936), (African American), Rev. Michael Ajewole, M.S.P.
1610 E. 11th St., 78702. Tel: 512-472-3741; Fax: 512-472-3783. Email: holycrossaustin@grandecom.net. Web: www.holycrossaustin.org.
Res.: 1607 E. 11th St., 78702. Tel: 512-322-0603.
Catechesis/Religious Program—Tel: 512-276-7924. Joann Meadows, D.R.E. Students 61.

9—HOLY VIETNAMESE MARTYRS CATHOLIC CHURCH - AUSTIN, TEXAS (1990), (Vietnamese), Rev. Msgr. Joe Van Anh Nguyen.
Res.: 1107 E. Yager Ln., 78753. Tel: 512-834-8483; Fax: 512-821-1155.
Catechesis/Religious Program—Hoa Mai, D.R.E. Students 530.

10—ST. IGNATIUS MARTYR (1937) Revs. William A. Wack, C.S.C.; Michael Couhig, C.S.C.; Deacons Patrick Murray; Rudy Rios; Tony Ross, Parish Admin.
Res.: 2308 Euclid Ave., 78704. Tel: 512-442-3602; Fax: 512-916-4440.
School—(Grades PreK-8), 120 W. Oltorf St., 78704. Tel: 512-442-8547; Fax: 512-442-8685. Todd Blahnik, Prin.; Deborah Stavely, Librarian. Aides 3; Lay Teachers 20; Students 273.
Catechesis/Religious Program—Tel: 512-442-8656. Sirene Brunell, D.R.E. Students 424.

11—ST. JOHN NEUMANN (1984) Revs. Glynn (Bud) Roland Jr.; James L. Evans; Deacon Mike Gesch.
Res.: 5455 Bee Cave Rd., 78746. Tel: 512-328-3220;

Fax: 512-328-3226.
Rectory—Tel: 512-494-6335.
Catechesis/Religious Program—Students 629.

12—St. Julia (1957), (Hispanic), Revs. Chris Ferrer; Eliecer Patino; Deacons Ralph Arevalo Jr.; Kevin Nissen.
Mailing Address: 3010 Lyons Rd., 78702. Tel: 512-926-4186; Fax: 512-926-7414.
Res.: 900 Tillery Rd., 78702.
Catechesis/Religious Program—Students 250.

13—St. Louis (1952) Revs. Larry Covington; Abraham Puentes-Mejia; Oliver Weerakkody; Deacons Rob Embry; Donald Turner; Richard Bigelow; Tony Pynes; William Vidal Vela.
Res.: 7601 Burnet Rd., 78757. Tel: 512-454-0384; Fax: 512-454-2010.
School—(Grades PreK-8) Tel: 512-454-0384, Ext. 242; Fax: 512-454-7252. Carol Bruns, Prin.; Brian Kemp, Librarian. Lay Teachers 31; Students 328.
Catechesis/Religious Program—Tel: 512-454-0384, Ext. 225. Tommy Sustaita, D.R.E. Youth Ministries; Amy Allert, D.R.E., Adult Ministries; Dr. Tina Juarez Bailey, D.R.E., Childhood Ministries. Students 784.

14—St. Margaret of Scotland (1984) Closed. For inquiries for parish records contact the chancery.

15—Nuestra Senora De Dolores (1952), (Hispanic), Rev. Albert Capello Ruiz; Deacon Hector Rosales.
Res.: 1111 Montopolis Dr., 78741. Tel: 512-385-4333; Fax: 512-385-6116.
Catechesis/Religious Program—Tel: 512-385-4333. Sr. Rose Moreno, F.H.M., D.R.E. Students 645.
Convent—Hijas De La Misericordia, Tel: 512-385-5090; Fax: 512-389-0692. Sisters 2.

16—Our Lady of Guadalupe (1907), (Hispanic), Rev. Francisco Munoz Villegas; Deacon Mario Renteria.
1206 E. 9th St., 78702.
Rectory—912 Lydia, 78702. Tel: 512-478-7955; 512-478-4132; Fax: 512-478-8377.
Catechesis/Religious Program—Students 292.

17—St. Paul (1989) Revs. Barry E. Cabell, C.S.C.; James Martin, C.S.C.; Deacons John Pickwell; Solomon Villegas.
Res.: 10000 David Moore Dr., 78748. Tel: 512-280-7230.
Catechesis/Religious Program—Tel: 512-280-4460, Ext. 122; Fax: 512-280-7219. Ana Jackoskie, D.R.E. Students 352.

18—St. Peter the Apostle (1962) Rev. Msgr. Fred Bomar.
Res.: 4600 E. Ben White Blvd., P.O. Box 17575, 78760. Tel: 512-442-0655.
Catechesis/Religious Program—Tel: 512-444-7477. Students 119.

19—Sacred Heart (1958) Revs. Matthew C. Iwuji; Manuel Montenegro; Deacons Jesse M. Garza; Robert Martinez; Nelson Fahlund. In Res., Rev. Anthony Nwudah.
Res.: 5909 Reicher Dr., 78723. Tel: 512-926-2552; Fax: 512-926-5138.
Catechesis/Religious Program—Tel: 512-926-2116; Fax: 512-926-2983. Angelica Mishoe, D.R.E. Students 665.

20—San Francisco (1941), (Hispanic), Rev. Cesar Jaime Guzman Diaz.
Res.: 9110 Hwy. 183 S., 78747. Tel: 512-243-1404; Fax: 512-243-2995.
Catechesis/Religious Program—Fax: 512-243-2995. Students 507.
Mission—San Juan Diego 216 Stony Point Dr., Del Valle, Travis Co. 78617. Tel: 512-247-2476. Web: www.sanjuandiego.org.

21—San Jose (1939), (Hispanic), Rev. Msgr. Tom Frank; Rev. Kevin Rai; Deacons Joe Gutierrez; John Rivera; Romeo Sanchez; Alfred Benavides; Richard Botello.
Res.: 2435 Oak Crest Ave., 78704. Tel: 512-444-7587; Fax: 512-443-1212.
Catechesis/Religious Program—Tel: 512-444-4664. Students 1,300.

22—Santa Barbara Catholic Church -Austin, Texas (1991), (Hispanic), Rev. Melesio Peter Espinosa; Deacons Joe Arellano; Cruz Banda Jr.
Mailing Address: 13713 FM 969, 78724. Tel: 512-276-7718.
Catechesis/Religious Program—Students 145.

23—St. Theresa (1968) Rev. Msgr. William C. Brooks; Rev. Justin Udomah; Deacons Ray James; Don Gessler; George Zacek.
Res.: 4311 Small Dr., 78731. Tel: 512-451-5121; Fax: 512-453-6824.
Rectory—4405 Enclove Cove, 78731.
School—(Grades PreK-8) Tel: 512-451-7105; Fax: 512-451-8808. Gracie Burback, Prin.; Jayne Uglum, Librarian. Lay Teachers 40; Students 433.
Catechesis/Religious Program—Tel: 512-451-2940; Fax: 512-453-6824. Sandy Nevills, D.R.E. Students 701.

24—St. Thomas More (1978) Rev. Msgr. Michael J. Sis; Rev. James Ekeocha; Deacons Peter Schwab; Thomas Mallinger; Thomas Johnson; Daniel Wright; Ronald Clapp.
Office: 10205 Ranch Rd., 620 N., 78726. Tel: 512-258-1161; Fax: 512-258-8812.
Catechesis/Religious Program—Tel: 512-258-1944; Fax: 512-331-9248. Cynthia Klaer-Jordan, D.R.E. Students 1,704.

25—St. Thomas More Chapel (1958) Closed. For inquiries for sacramental records please see St Mary's Cathedral, (512-476-6182). Res: 1600 N. Congress, Austin, TX 78701.

26—St. Vincent de Paul (1995) Very Rev. Daniel E. Garcia; Rev. Evaristus Uche Obikwelu; Deacon David Boren.
Mailing Address: 9500 Neenah Ave., 78717. Tel: 512-255-1389; Fax: 512-246-2373.
Rectory—13007 Partridge Bend, 78729. Tel: 512-249-1549.
Catechesis/Religious Program—Fax: 512-246-2373. Judy Falgout, D.R.E.; Jeremy Miller, Youth Min. Students 601.

OUTSIDE CITY OF AUSTIN

Andice, Williamson Co., Santa Rosa (1937) [CEM] Rev. Eliseus Ibeh, M.S.P.; Deacon Marc Washburne.
Mailing Address: 6571 FM 970, Florence, 76527. Tel: 254-793-2047; Fax: 254-793-3247. 6571 FM 970, 78628.
Catechesis/Religious Program—Tel: 254-793-2056; 254-793-2047 (Church); Fax: 254-793-3247. Debra Cahill, D.R.E. Students 182.

Bastrop, Bastrop Co., Ascension Catholic Church (1864) Revs. Ricardo Aguilar; Rito Davila; Deacon Bill Hobby.
905 Water St., 78602. Tel: 512-321-3552; Fax: 512-303-6539.
Res.: 905 Pecan St., 78602.
Catechesis/Religious Program—Sr. Cal Leopold, O.S.F., D.R.E. Students 408.

Belton, Bell Co., Christ the King (1969) Rev. Richard Hudson; Deacons Armando Aguirre; Steve Pina; William Shoemake.
Res.: 310 E. 24th Ave., 76513. Tel: 254-939-0806; 254-939-6109 (Rectory); Fax: 425-962-6914.
Catechesis/Religious Program—Krissie Lastovica, D.R.E. Students 341.

Bertram, Burnet Co., Holy Cross (1941) Attended by Our Mother of Sorrows, Burnet. Rev. Anthony Alphonse.
Mailing Address: P.O. Box 94, 78605. Tel: 512-355-2972.
Catechesis/Religious Program—Tel: 512-699-0376. Liz Barta, D.R.E. Students 70.

Blanco, Blanco Co., St. Ferdinand (1940) [CEM] Rev. Nichodemus Ejimabo.
Res.: 25 Main St., 78606. Tel: 830-833-4447; Fax: 830-833-9978.
Catechesis/Religious Program—Tel: 830-833-0444. Students 67.
Mission—Good Shepherd P.O. Box 1608, Johnson City, Blanco Co. 78636. Tel: 830-868-0370.
Mission—St. Mary's Help of Christians CR 473, Twin Sisters, Blanco Co. 78606.

Bremond, Robertson Co., St. Mary (1879) [CEM] Rev. Celso A. Yu, M.F. (Philippines).
Res.: 715 N. Main St., 76629. Tel: 254-746-7789; Fax: 254-746-7789.
Catechesis/Religious Program—Tel: 254-746-7789. Students 100.

Brenham, Washington Co., St. Mary of the Immaculate Conception (1870) [CEM] Revs. David J. Ivey (LA); Bradford Hernandez; Deacon Bill Januszewski.
Office: 701 Church St., 77833.
Rectory—Res.: 608 S. Baylor, 77833. Tel: 979-836-4441; Fax: 979-836-9383.
Catechesis/Religious Program—Tel: 979-830-8331. Sisters Kathleen Skog, O.S.F., D.R.E.; Mary Kay Bailey, Dir. Faith Formation. Students 576.
Mission—Sacred Heart Latium, 77833.

Bryan, Brazos Co.

1—St. Anthony (1896), (Italian), [JC] Rev. Patrick Ebner; Deacons Ellis Abraham; Glen Milton; Andy Perrone; Bill Scarmardo.
Res.: 401 S. Parker, 77803. Tel: 979-823-8145; Fax: 979-823-6001.
Catechesis/Religious Program—Tel: 979-822-3700. Students 370.
Mission—San Salvador, Brazos Co. 77803.

2—St. Joseph (1873) [CEM 2] Rev. Msgr. John A. McCaffrey; Rev. Thanh Vincent Nguyen, C.Ss.R.; Deacons Gary Nelson; Patrick Gallagher.
Res.: 600 E. 26th St., 77803. Tel: 979-822-2721; Fax: 979-779-3120.
School—(Grades PreK-12), 600 S. Coulter Dr., 77803. Tel: 979-822-6641; Fax: 979-779-2810. Mrs. Beatrice Janssen, Pres. & Prin.; Melissa Slater, Librarian. Lay Teachers 46; Students 452.
Catechesis/Religious Program—Tel: 979-823-5568; Fax: 979-779-3120. John Valentino, Youth Min.; Lisa Storemski, D.R.E. Students 513.

3—San Salvador, Attended by St. Ann, Rosebud Rev. Patrick Ebner.
Mailing Address: 401 S. Parker, 77803. Tel: 979-823-8145.

4—Santa Teresa (1940), (Hispanic), Revs. Raymundo Chavez Vazquez; Rafael Padilla; Deacon Fred Molina.
Res.: 1212 Lucky, 77803. Tel: 979-822-2932; Fax: 979-822-6957. Email: st.teresa@verizon.net.
Catechesis/Religious Program—Tel: 979-822-5557. Laura Cisneros, English & Spanish D.R.E. Students 630.

Buda, Hays Co., Santa Cruz (1941) Revs. Kirby Garner; Filadelfo Secundo Angulo Viloria; Deacons Rodolfo Gonzalez; Rey Garza; John Riojas; Benjamin Garcia; Robert Johnson, Business Mgr.; Juanita Rodriguez, Parish Sec.
Res.: 1100 Main St., 78610. Tel: 512-312-2520; Fax: 512-295-2034.
School—(Grades PreK-3), 1100 Main St., P.O. Box 160, 78610. Tel: 512-312-2137; Fax: 512-312-2143. Martha Owen, Prin. Students 950.
Catechesis/Religious Program—Tel: 512-312-2520, Ext. 138; 512-312-2520, Ext. 129. Joanna Rubio, D.R.E.; Lupita Bodony, High D.R.E./Youth Ministry. Students 63.

Burlington, Milam Co., St. Michael, Attended by St. Ann, Rosebud. Rev. Joseph Suneet, I.M.S.
P.O. Box 85, 76519. Tel: 254-869-2525.

Burnet, Burnet Co., Our Mother of Sorrows (1941) Rev. Anthony Alphonse; Deacons Eugene Montag; Edward Holicky.
Res.: 507 Buchanan Dr., 78611-2304. Tel: 512-756-4410; Fax: 512-756-1573.
Catechesis/Religious Program—Tel: 512-756-2323. Liz Barta, D.R.E. Students 211.
Mission—Holy Cross P.O. Box 94, Bertram, Burnet Co. 78605. Tel: 512-355-2972.

Caldwell, Burleson Co., St. Mary (1895), (Hispanic), [CEM] Rev. Dimitrij Colankin; Deacons John Young; Samuel Reyes.
Res.: 509 N. Thomas, 77836. Tel: 979-567-3667; Fax: 979-567-0749.
Catechesis/Religious Program—Students 420.
Mission—Holy Rosary [CEM] 8610 FM 2774, Burleson Co. 77836. Tel: 979-535-7704.

Calvert, Robertson Co., St. Mary (1876), (Hispanic), [CEM] Closed. See St. Mary's Church, Hearne.

Cameron, Milam Co., St. Monica (1883) [CEM] Rev. Juan Carlos Lopez; Deacon Earl Colley.
Mailing Address: P.O. Box 673, 76520. Tel: 254-697-2107; Fax: 254-697-3334.
Church: 306 S. Nolan, 76520.
Catechesis/Religious Program—Tel: 254-697-4544. Betty Brenek, D.R.E. Students 250.

Cedar Park, Williamson Co., St. Margaret Mary (1942) Revs. Le-Minh Pham; Javier Toscano; Deacons Phillip Roberge; Paul Rodriguez; Toby Romero.
Res.: 1101 W. New Hope Dr., 78613. Tel: 512-259-3126.
Catechesis/Religious Program—Tel: 512-260-0162; Fax: 512-259-9658. Robin Hambright, D.R.E. Students 1,169.

Chappell Hill, Washington Co., St. Stanislaus (1889), (Polish), [CEM] [JC 2] Rev. Vincent Chacko, I.M.S. (India).
Res.: 9175 FM 1371, 77426. Tel: 979-836-3030; Fax: 979-836-7170.
Catechesis/Religious Program—Students 30.

China Spring, McLennan Co., St. Philip Catholic Church - China Spring, Texas (1996) Attended by Mission of St. Eugene, McGregor. Rev. Hilario Guajardo, Pastoral Admin.
Mailing Address: P.O. Box 430, 76633. Tel: 254-836-4425; Fax: 254-751-8428.
Catechesis/Religious Program—Tel: 254-836-1969; Fax: 254-836-0600. Students 89.

College Station, Brazos Co.

1—St. Mary (1926) Revs. David Konderla; Christopher J. Downey; Deacons Bill Scott Jr.; David Reed; Switzer Deason.
Res.: 603 Church Ave., 77840. Tel: 979-846-5717; Fax: 979-846-4493.
Catechesis/Religious Program—Students 54.

2—St. Thomas Aquinas (1982) Very Rev. Michael J. O'Connor; Rev. Nock W. Russell; Deacons Theodore Baker; Frank Ashley; Dave Mayes.
Res.: 2541 Earl Rudder Fwy. S., 77845. Tel: 979-680-1412; 979-693-6994 (Office); Fax: 979-260-4502.
Catechesis/Religious Program—Nancy Blanco, D.R.E. Students 824.

Copperas Cove, Coryell Co., Holy Family (1963) Rev. James E. Robertson; Deacon Tim Dorsey.
Res.: 1001 Georgetown Rd., 76522. Tel: 254-547-3735; Fax: 254-547-3735.
Catechesis/Religious Program—Tel: 254-547-0090. Natalie Czajka, D.R.E. Students 290.

Cyclone, Bell Co., St. Joseph (1902), (Czech—German), [CEM] Rev. Walter J. Matus.
Mailing Address: 20120 FM 485, Burlington, 76519.
Catechesis/Religious Program—1201 S. St. Joseph

Rd. #400, Burlington, 76519. Tel: 817-985-2257. Students 70.
Mission—Ss. Cyril & Methodius Burlington. FM 485, Marak, Milam Co. 76519. Tel: 254-985-2280. Res.: 6633 FM 2269, Buckholts, 76518.

DIME BOX, LEE CO., ST. JOSEPH (1909) [CEM] Rev. Ramon Frayna.
Mailing Address: 8282 FM 141, 77853.
Church: Farm-Market Rd. 141, 77853.
Catechesis/Religious Program—Students 17.
Mission—Holy Family (1990) P.O. Box 541, Lexington, Lee Co. 78947. Tel: 949-773-2500.

DRIPPING SPRINGS, HAYS CO., ST. MARTIN DE PORRES (1974) Rev. Edward Koharchik, C.S.P.; Deacon Edward Rositas; Sr. Yvonne Feeney, O.P.
Mailing Address: P.O. Box 1062, 78620. Tel: 512-858-5667; Fax: 512-858-1467. Email: stmartindp@austin.rr.com. Web: stmartindp.org.
Church: 26160 Ranch Rd. 12, P.O. Box 1062, 78620.
Catechesis/Religious Program— Mary Armatta, D.R.E. Students 325.

ELGIN, BASTROP CO., SACRED HEART (1908), (Hispanic), [JC] Very Rev. George Joseph; Deacons Larry Dunne; Juan Lopez; Channing Fell.
Res.: 206 W. 12th St., 78621. Tel: 512-281-4478; Fax: 512-281-2527.
Catechesis/Religious Program—Tel: 512-281-3536, Ext. 205. Students 800.

ELK, MCLENNON CO., ST. JOSEPH (1925) [CEM] Attended by St. Martin, Tours. Rev. Msgr. Isidore Rozycki.
Mailing Address: 301 St. Martins Church Rd., West, 76691. Tel: 254-822-1145; Fax: 254-822-0171.
Res.: 9656 Elk Rd., West, 76691.
Catechesis/Religious Program—Tel: 254-863-5919. Tami Kadlacek, D.R.E. Students 78.

FAYETTEVILLE, FAYETTE CO., ST. JOHN THE BAPTIST (1872), (Czech), [CEM] Rev. Steven Nesrsta.
Mailing Address: P.O. Box 57, 78940. Tel: 979-378-2277; Fax: 979-378-4407.
Res.: 205 E. Bell St., 78940. Tel: 979-378-2003.
Catechesis/Religious Program—Tel: 979-378-2244. Janice Kasmiersky, D.R.E. Students 87.
Mission—St. Mary Ellinger/Hostyn Hill, Fayette Co. 78940.
Mission—St. Martin Warrenton, Fayette Co. 78940.

FRANKLIN, ROBERTSON CO., ST. FRANCIS OF ASSISI (1997) Rev. Melvin Dornak; Deacon Luis Doriocourt.
Mailing Address: P.O. Box 543, 77856. Tel: 979-828-9025 (Rectory); 979-828-1269 (Office).
Res.: 1371 W. FM 1644, 77856.
Catechesis/Religious Program—Students 60.

FRENSTAT, BURLESON CO., HOLY ROSARY (1888), (Czech), [CEM 2] Attended by St. Mary's, Caldwell Rev. Dimitrij Colankin.
Mailing Address: 6978 SH 36 S., Caldwell, 77836-5462. Tel: 979-567-4994.
Church: 8610 FM 2774, Caldwell, 77836. Fax: 979-535-7704.
Rectory—509 N. Thomas, Caldwell, 77836. Tel: 979-535-7704.
Catechesis/Religious Program—Tel: 979-596-2606. Students 20.

GATESVILLE, CORYELL CO., OUR LADY OF LOURDES CATHOLIC CHURCH - GATESVILLE, TEXAS (1946) Rev. Anthony Mbanefo, M.S.P.
Res.: 1108 W. Main St., 76528-1123. Tel: 254-865-6710.
Catechesis/Religious Program— Deborah Grmela, D.R.E. Students 100.

GEORGETOWN, WILLIAMSON CO., ST. HELEN (1932) Rev. Msgr. Louis Pavlicek; Rev. William R. Straten; Deacons Frank Monroe; Joe Ruiz; Vern Dawson.
Res.: 2700 E. University Ave., 78626-7300. Tel: 512-868-0086; Fax: 512-863-8558.
School—(Grades PreK-8) Tel: 512-868-0744; Fax: 512-869-3244. Sr. Mary Jean Olsovsky, Prin.; Laura Zarate, Librarian.
Catechesis/Religious Program—Tel: 512-863-0799. Sr. Felice Mojica, M.C.D.P., D.R.E. Students 705.

GIDDINGS, LEE CO., ST. MARGARET (1944), (German—Hispanic), [JC] Very Rev. James Robert Olnhausen; Rev. Luis Albert Caceres.
Res.: 526 S. Grimes St., 78942. Tel: 979-542-0217; Fax: 979-542-4186.
Catechesis/Religious Program— Suzanne Peschke, D.R.E. (Upper Grades); Roxanna Madero, D.R.E. (Lower Grades). Students 228.
Mission—St. Mary's in Pin Oak Smithville. 732 FM 2104, Pin Oak, Bastrop Co. 78957.

GOLDTHWAITE, MILLS CO., ST. PETER (1885) [JC] Attended by St. Mary, San Saba. Rev. Gilber Ibarguen-Gomez; Deacon Richard Menchaca, Pastoral Admin.
Res.: 1212 Reynolds St., P.O. Box 352, 76844. Tel: 325-648-3732; Fax: 325-648-3732.
Catechesis/Religious Program—Tel: 325-648-2903. Tani Menchaca, D.R.E. Students 68.

GRANGER, WILLIAMSON CO., SS. CYRIL AND METHODIUS (1891), (Czech), [CEM 2] [JC] Very Rev. Joseph Nisari (Pakistan).
Mailing Address: P.O. Box 608, 76530.
Res.: 300 W. Davilla, 76530. Tel: 512-859-2223; Fax: 512-859-2030.
School—(Grades PreK-6), P.O. Box 248, 76530. Tel: 512-859-2927; Fax: 512-859-2649. Mrs. Crystal Blahnik, Prin.; Monica Schwertner, Librarian. Lay Teachers 14; Students 64.
Catechesis/Religious Program—104 N. Brazas, P.O. Box 956, 76530. Tel: 512-859-2634. Cara Finn, D.R.E. Students 124.

HAMILTON, HAMILTON CO., ST. THOMAS CATHOLIC CHURCH - HAMILTON, TEXAS (1965) [JC] Attended by Our Lady of Lourdes, Gatesville Rev. Anthony Mbanefo, M.S.P.; Deacon Victor Beltran, Pastoral Admin.
Res.: 843 Nicholson Ave., 76531. Tel: 254-386-5513.
Catechesis/Religious Program—Students 27.

HARKER HEIGHTS, BELL CO., ST. PAUL CHONG HASANG (1986) Very Rev. Richard O'Rourke, M.S.C.; Rev. Peter Dong Ho Shin, C.P.; Deacons Peter Kim; Klaus Adam; Ms. Margaret Hunt, Pastoral Assoc.
Mailing Address: P.O. Box 2414, 76548.
Res.: 1000 E. FM 2410, 76548. Tel: 254-698-4110; 254-698-4338; Fax: 254-698-4608.
Catechesis/Religious Program—Mrs. Victoria Biehle, D.R.E. Students 477.

HEARNE, ROBERTSON CO., ST. MARY (1872), (Italian—Mexican-American), [CEM] Rev. Robert Herald.
Res.: 402 W. First St., 77859. Tel: 979-279-2233; Fax: 979-279-9606.
Catechesis/Religious Program— Madeline Zeig, D.R.E. Students 215.
Mission—St. Mary, Calvert 505 Logan St., Calvert, Robertson Co. 77837.

HORSESHOE BAY, BURNET CO., ST. PAUL THE APOSTLE (1982) Rev. Ruben M. Patino, C.S.P.
Mailing Address: P.O. Box 8019, 78657. Tel: 830-598-8342; Fax: 830-598-1274.
Res.: 201 Dalton Cir., 78657.
Catechesis/Religious Program—Students 27.

HOSTYN HILL, FAYETTE CO., ST. MARY (1855), (Czech), [CEM] Attended by St. John, Fayetteville. Rev. Steven Nesrsta.
Mailing Address: P.O. Box 57, Fayetteville, 78940. Tel: 979-378-2277; Fax: 979-378-4407.
Catechesis/Religious Program—209 E. Bell St., Fayetteville, 78940. Tel: 979-378-2244; Fax: 979-378-2244. Students 25.

HUTTO, WILLIAMSON CO., ST. PATRICK (2000) Rev. Keith Koehl; Deacons Allen Desorcie; Gumisindo Gonzales.
Mailing Address: 2500 Limmer Loop, 78634. Tel: 512-759-3712; Fax: 512-759-3728.
Res.: 536 Will Smith Cir., 78634. Tel: 512-846-2118.
Catechesis/Religious Program—Students 210.

JARRELL, WILLIAMSON CO., HOLY TRINITY CATHOLIC CHURCH - CORN HILL, TEXAS (1889), (Czech—German), [CEM] Rev. Msgr. Emilian Foltyn; Deacon Gene (Roy) Davis.
Res.: 8626 FM 1105, 76537. Tel: 512-863-0401; Fax: 512-868-9505. Email: trinity@thegateway.net.
Catechesis/Religious Program—Tel: 512-863-3020. Debie Klaus, D.R.E. Students 73.

KILLEEN, BELL CO., ST. JOSEPH (1954) Revs. Adam Martinez; Karel Fink; Deacons Michael Aaronson; Rafael Ozuna.
Res.: 2903 E. Rancier Ave., 76543. Tel: 254-634-7878; Fax: 254-634-1508.
School—(Grades PreK-5), 2901 E. Rancier Ave., 76543. Tel: 254-634-7272; Fax: 254-634-1224. Becky Kirkland, Prin. Lay Teachers 13; Students 119.
Catechesis/Religious Program—Tel: 254-634-7878, Ext. 107; Fax: 254-634-1508. Students 431.

KINGSLAND, LLANO CO., ST. CHARLES BORROMEO CATHOLIC CHURCH - KINGSLAND, TEXAS (1965) Rev. Bernard Nguyen Hung; Deacons Larry Crochet; Ronald Woods.
Mailing Address: P.O. Box 1748, 78639. 205 Trinity Dr., 78639.
Church: 1927 Hwy. 1431, 78639.
Rectory—1927 Hwy. 1431, 78639. Tel: 325-388-3742.
Catechesis/Religious Program—Tel: 830-598-7327. Students 45.
Mission—Our Lady of the Lake (Sunrise Beach) 304 Hillview Dr., Horseshoe Bay, Burnet Co. 78657-6043.

KOVAR, BASTROP CO., STS. PETER AND PAUL (1909), (Czech), Now a mission of St. Paul, Smithville. Mailing Address: 204 Mills St., Smithville, TX 78957. Tel: 512-237-2179.

KYLE, HAYS CO., ST. ANTHONY MARIE DE CLARET (1909), (Hispanic), Very Rev. Howard Goertz; Rev. Francisco Morales; Deacons John Peca; Joe Flores; Richard Duecker; Aurelio Medina.
Res.: 801 N. Burleson St., P.O. Box 268, 78640. Tel: 512-268-5311 (Church); Fax: 512-268-0144.
Rectory—279 Greene, 78640. Tel: 512-268-5312.
Catechesis/Religious Program—Maryrae Stein, D.R.E. Students 850.

LA GRANGE, FAYETTE CO., SACRED HEART OF JESUS (1886) [JC] Rev. Joseph Varickamackal (India); Deacon Mike Meismer.
Mailing Address: Box 548, 78945. Tel: 979-968-3430; Fax: 979-968-5740.
Res.: 539 E. Pearl, 78945. Tel: 979-968-6030.
School—(Grades PreK-6) Tel: 979-968-3223; Fax: 979-968-6382. Elmer Faykus, Prin. Lay Teachers 23; Students 210.
Catechesis/Religious Program—Tel: 979-968-3430, Ext. 6. Susan Graves, D.R.E. Students 147.

LAGO VISTA, TRAVIS CO., OUR LADY OF THE LAKE CATHOLIC CHURCH - LAGO VISTA, TEXAS (1970) [CEM] Rev. Msgr. Joseph J. Schmitt; Deacon Terry Martin.
Mailing Address: 6100 Lohman Ford Rd., 78645. Tel: 512-267-2644; Fax: 512-267-2649.
Rectory—6502 Avenida Ann, 78645. Tel: 512-267-1336.
Catechesis/Religious Program—Students 78.

LAMPASAS, TRAVIS CO., ST. MARY OF THE IMMACULATE CONCEPTION (1885) Rev. Pedro Castillo; Deacons Carlos Jasso; Frank J. (Jay) Vocelka.
Mailing Address: 701 N. Key Ave., 76550-0866. Tel: 512-556-5544; Fax: 512-556-6967.
Church: 701 N. Key Ave., Lampassas, 76550.
Catechesis/Religious Program—Students 134.
Mission—Good Shepherd Catholic Church (1927) 411 W. Main St., Lometa, Lampasas Co. 76853.

LATIUM, WASHINGTON CO., SACRED HEART CATHOLIC CHURCH - LATIUM, TEXAS (1872) [CEM] Attended by St. Mary, Brenham., 701 Church St., Brenham, 77833. Tel: 979-836-4441.
Res.: Off FM Rd. 389, corner of County Rd. 18 & 16, 77833.

LEXINGTON, LEE CO., HOLY FAMILY CATHOLIC CHURCH - LEXINGTON, TEXAS (1990) [JC], Mission of St. Joseph, Dime Box. Rev. Ramon Frayna.
Mailing Address: 8282 FM 141, Dime Box, 77853. Tel: 979-884-3100.
Res.: 1027 FM 696 East of Hwy. 77, 78947. Tel: 979-773-2500.
Catechesis/Religious Program—Students 46.

LLANO, LLANO CO., HOLY TRINITY CATHOLIC CHURCH - LLANO, TEXAS (1890) Rev. Gabriel Uzondu, S.O.L.T.; Deacon George Lillard.
Mailing Address: P.O. Box 698, 78643. Tel: 325-247-4481; Fax: 325-248-0691. 708 Bessemer, 78643.
Catechesis/Religious Program—Students 45.
Mission—St. Joseph 216 Ave. B, Mason, Mason Co. 76856. Tel: 325-347-6932.

LOCKHART, CALDWELL CO., ST. MARY (1887) [CEM 2] Rev. Robert Becker; Deacons Guadalupe Aguilar; William Long; William Haywood; Patrick Venglar.
Res.: 205 W. Pecan, 78644. Tel: 512-398-4649; 512-376-3634; Fax: 512-398-2285.
Catechesis/Religious Program—Tel: 512-398-3506. Eva Mendez, D.R.E. Students 532.

LOMETA, LAMPASAS CO., GOOD SHEPHERD (1927) Attended by St. Mary, Lampasas. Rev. Pedro Castillo; Deacon Carlos Jasso.
Mailing Address: 701 N. Key Ave., Lampasas, 76550-0866. Tel: 512-556-5544; Fax: 512-556-6967.
Church: 500 W. Main St., 76853.
Catechesis/Religious Program—Students 6.

LOTT, FALLS CO., SACRED HEART (1905), (Italian—German), [CEM] Attended by St. Joseph, Marlin. Rev. John Kelley.
Mailing Address: P.O. Box 371, Marlin, 76661. Tel: 254-803-8888; Fax: 254-803-8888.
Res.: 213 N. 6th St., 76656.
Catechesis/Religious Program— Clustered with St. Joseph, Marlin

LULING, CALDWELL CO., ST. JOHN THE EVANGELIST (1879) [CEM] Rev. Jose Luis Azcona; Deacon Wilfred Dub Hargraves.
Res.: 400 S. Pecan Ave., 78648. Tel: 830-875-9484; Fax: 830-875-3533.
Catechesis/Religious Program—Students 273.

MANOR, TRAVIS CO., ST. JOSEPH (1876), (Hispanic), [JC] Rev. Ernesto Elizondo; Deacon Jose Chavez.
Mailing Address: P.O. Box 389, 78653. Tel: 512-272-4004 (Rectory); Fax: 512-272-8939.
Catechesis/Religious Program—Students 375.

MARAK, MILAM CO., SS. CYRIL AND METHODIUS CATHOLIC CHURCH - MARAK, TEXAS (1903), (Czech), [CEM] [JC 2], Attended from St. Joseph's, Cyclone. Rev. Walter J. Matus.
Mailing Address: 20120 FM 485, Burlington, 76519. Tel: 254-985-2280.
Res.: 6633 FM 2266, Buckholts, 76518.
Catechesis/Religious Program—Tel: 254-697-4861. Students 50.

MARBLE FALLS, BURNET CO., ST. JOHN THE EVANGELIST (1961) Very Rev. Jairo Lopez; Deacons Eraclio Solarzno; Paul Lavallee.
Church: 105 Hwy. 1431 E., 78654. Tel: 830-693-5134; Fax: 830-798-9574.
Catechesis/Religious Program—Tel: 830-693-3279. Students 280.

MARLIN, FALLS CO., ST. JOSEPH (1872), (Italian—Polish), Rev. John Kelley, Admin.; Deacon Sidney Prewitt.
Mailing Address: Box 371, 76661. Tel: 254-803-8888; Fax: 254-803-8888.
Church: 311 Oakes St., 76661.
Catechesis/Religious Program— Mr. Eddie Roberts, D.R.E. Students 132.
Mission—Sacred Heart [CEM] 6th & Hackberry, Lott, Falls Co. 76656.

MARTINDALE, CALDWELL CO., IMMACULATE HEART OF MARY (1908), (Hispanic), Rev. Victor Mayorga (Colombia); Deacon Johnny Ojeda; Anna M. Ramirez, Admin.
Mailing Address: P.O. Box 117, 78655. Tel: 512-357-6573; Fax: 512-357-2667.
Church: 312 Lockhart St., 78655.
Catechesis/Religious Program—Tel: 512-357-9076. Georgina Cruz, D.R.E. Students 180.

MASON, MASON CO., ST. JOSEPH (1873) Attended by Holy Trinity, Llano. Rev. Gabriel Uzondu, S.O.L.T.; Deacon George Keller. Tel: 325-347-5678.
Mailing Address: P.O. Box 698, Llano, 78643. Fax: 325-248-0691.
Church: 216 Ave. B, 76856. Tel: 325-347-6932.
Catechesis/Religious Program—Tel: 325-347-5327. Gladys Garner, D.R.E. Students 38.

MCGREGOR, MCLENNAN CO., ST. EUGENE CATHOLIC CHURCH - MCGREGOR, TEXAS (1958), (Hispanic), [JC] Rev. Hilario Guajardo.
Res.: 207 N. Johnson Dr., 76657. Tel: 254-840-3174; Fax: 254-840-0174.
Catechesis/Religious Program—Students 230.
Mission—Our Lady of San Juan 207 N. Johnson Dr., Moody, McLennan Co. 76657. Tel: 254-853-9011.
Mission—St. Philip 13095 Old China Spring Rd., P.O. Box 430, China Spring, McLennan Co. 76633. Tel: 254-836-4425.

MEXIA, LIMESTONE CO., ST. MARY (1886) [JC] Rev. Carlo Benjamin Magnaye, M.F.; Deacons Daniel Ramirez; Dwight Mahoney.
Mailing Address: 506 E. Sumpter, 76667.
Res.: 606 N. Bonham, 76667. Tel: 254-562-3619; Fax: 254-562-6377.
Catechesis/Religious Program—Dot Mushinski, D.R.E.; Ines Flores, D.R.E. Students 282.

MOODY, MCLENNAN CO., OUR LADY OF SAN JUAN CATHOLIC MISSION CHURCH - MOODY, TEXAS (1991), (Hispanic), Mission of St. Eugene, McGregor. Rev. Hilario Guajardo.
Church: 207 N. Johnson Dr., Mc Gregor, 76657. Tel: 254-840-3174; Fax: 254-840-0174.
Catechesis/Religious Program—Tel: 254-853-9011. Students 55.

OLD WASHINGTON-ON-THE-BRAZOS, WASHINGTON CO., BLESSED VIRGIN MARY (1849), (African American), Attended by St. Ann, Somerville. Rev. Joseph F. Geleney Jr.; Deacon Limas Sweed Sr.
Mailing Address: P.O. Box 485, Washington, 77880.
Catechesis/Religious Program—Students 12.

PFLUGERVILLE, TRAVIS CO., ST. ELIZABETH (1932) Revs. Pedro Garcia-Ramirez; James Misko; Deacons Alejandro Lara; Barry Ryan.
Mailing Address: 1520 N. Railroad Ave., 78660. Tel: 512-251-9838; Fax: 512-251-9868.
Res.: 1104 Lincoln Sparrow Cove, 78660. Tel: 512-670-3526.
Catechesis/Religious Program—Tel: 512-251-9842; Fax: 572-251-9868. Students 1,330.

PIN OAK, BASTROP CO., ST. MARY (1866), (German), [CEM] Attended by St. Margaret, Giddings. Very Rev. James Robert Olnhausen.
Mailing Address: *c/o St. Margaret Catholic Church*, 526 S. Grimes St., Giddings, 78942. Tel: 979-542-0217; Fax: 979-542-4186.
Church: 732 FM 2104, Smithville, 78957.
Catechesis/Religious Program—Roxanna Madero, D.R.E.; Suzanne Peschke, D.R.E. Students 7.

ROCKDALE, MILAM CO., ST. JOSEPH (1880) Rev. Gregory Hanks, Admin.; Deacons Gus Coelho; Donald Sims.
Mailing Address: P.O. Box 548, 76567. Tel: 512-446-2049; Fax: 512-446-0411.
Rectory—521 E. Davilla St., 76567. Tel: 512-446-2196.
Church: 234 San Gabriel St., 76567.
Catechesis/Religious Program—Theresa Alvarez, D.R.E. Students 169.

ROCKNE, BASTROP CO., SACRED HEART (1876), (German), [CEM] Rev. Dariusz Ziebowicz, S.D.S.; Deacon Roger Muehr.
Mailing Address: 4045 FM 535, Bastrop, 78602. Tel: 512-321-7991; Fax: 512-303-2723.
Church: Farm-Market Rd., 78602.
Catechesis/Religious Program—Tel: 512-303-3311. Dr. Alvin Frerich, D.R.E. Students 170.
Mission—Assumption of the Blessed Virgin Mary [CEM] String Prairie, Bastrop Co. Tel: 830-839-4580.

ROGERS, BELL CO., ST. MATTHEW (1991) Revs. Tom Chamberlain; Ramiro Tarazona.
Mailing Address: 707 S. 6th St., Temple, 76504.
Church: 10451 E. Hwy. 1290, 76569. Tel: 254-773-6779.
Catechesis/Religious Program—Students 58.

ROSEBUD, FALLS CO., ST. ANN (1915) [CEM] Rev. Joseph Suneet, I.M.S.
Mailing Address: 85 Church Ave., Burlington, 76519. Tel: 254-869-2525.
Church: 511 S. Stalworth St., 76570.
Catechesis/Religious Program—Tel: 254-583-0309. Students 103.
Mission—St. Michael (1879) Burlington.

ROUND ROCK, WILLIAMSON CO.

1—ST. JOHN VIANNEY (1997) Rev. Edwin Kagoo; Deacons Gene Saienga; Frank McCormick.
Catechesis/Religious Program—Fax: 512-218-8272. Students 385.

2—ST. WILLIAM (1956) Revs. Dean E. Wilhelm; Alberto J. Borruel; Jonathan D. Raia; Deacons Concho Castillo; Richard Kotrola; Dennis Egan.
Mailing Address & Office: 620 Round Rock W. Dr., 78681. Tel: 512-255-4473; Fax: 512-255-8126. Email: office@saintwilliams.org. Web: www.saintwilliams.org.
Rectory—1105 Deer Run, 78681. Tel: 512-358-6063.
Catechesis/Religious Program—Tel: 512-600-8172. Students 1,702.

SALADO, BELL CO., ST. STEPHEN (1989) Rev. Gregory McLaughlin; Deacon Jose Jimenez.
Mailing Address: P.O. Box 662, 76571. Tel: 254-947-8037; Fax: 254-947-8091.
Rectory—601 FM 2268, 76751. Tel: 254-947-5582.
Church: 601 FM 2268 (Holland Rd.), P.O. Box 662, 76751. Tel: 254-947-8037; Fax: 254-947-8091.
Catechesis/Religious Program—Tel: 254-947-8091. Laura Snyder, D.R.E. Students 130.

SAN MARCOS, HAYS CO., ST. JOHN THE EVANGELIST (1883) Revs. Larry Stehling; Segundo Enrique Diaz; Deacons Domingo Vargas; Jesse Mojica; Jorge Guerrero; Luis F. Silguero.
Res.: 624 E. Hopkins, 78666. Tel: 512-353-8969; Fax: 512-396-7522.
Catechesis/Religious Program—Tel: 512-353-5065. Students 584.
Mission—Guadalupe Chapel 218 Roosevelt, Hays Co. 78666.

SAN SABA, SAN SABA CO., ST. MARY (1967), (Hispanic), Rev. Gilber Ibarguen-Gomez.
Mailing Address: P.O. Box 415, 76877. Tel: 325-372-3679; Fax: 325-372-6569. Email: stmarys@centex.net.
Church: 504 W. Wallace, 76877.
Catechesis/Religious Program—Tani Menchaca, D.R.E., (Goldthwaite); Michael Bohensky, D.R.E (San Saba). Students 87.

SATIN, SATIN FALLS CO., SANTA RITA SHRINE (1917), (Hispanic), Attended by St. Francis, Waco., Mailing Address: 301 Jefferson Ave., Waco, 76701. Tel: 254-752-8434; Fax: 254-752-2415.

SMITHVILLE, BASTROP CO., ST. PAUL THE APOSTLE (1896) Rev. Jozef Musiol, S.D.S.; Deacon Bernard Meuth.
Res.: 204 Mills St., 78957.
Catechesis/Religious Program—Tel: 512-237-3299. Students 175.
Mission—Sts. Peter and Paul Kovar, Bastrop Co.

SOMERVILLE, BURLESON CO., ST. ANN (1913) Rev. Joseph F. Geleney Jr.
Mailing Address: P.O. Box 99, 77879. Tel: 979-596-1966; Fax: 979-596-2857.
Church: 333 Thornberry Rd., 77879.
Catechesis/Religious Program—Sr. Mary John Della Morte, D.R.E. Students 20.
Mission—Blessed Virgin Mary Chapel (1849) [JC] Washington. 17370 Sweed Rd., Old Washington, Washington Co. 77880. Tel: 936-878-2659.

STONY POINT, TRAVIS CO., SAN JUAN DIEGO MISSION OF DOLORES - STONEY POINT (1987), (Mexican), Attended by San Francisco Javier, Austin. Rev. Cesar Jaime Guzman Diaz.
Mailing Address: 9110 U.S. Hwy. 183 S., 78747.
Church: 216 Stoney Point Dr., Del Valle, 78617. Tel: 512-247-2476; Fax: 512-243-2995.
Catechesis/Religious Program—Students 107.

STRING PRAIRIE, BASTROP CO., ST. MARY OF THE ASSUMPTION (1876), (German), [CEM] Attended by Sacred Heart, Rockne. Rev. Dariusz Ziebowicz, S.D.S.
Mailing Address: 4045 FM 535, Bastrop, 78602. Tel: 830-839-4580; Fax: 512-303-2723.
Catechesis/Religious Program—Tel: 830-540-4089. Mrs. Deanna Seidel, D.R.E. Students 38.

SUNRISE BEACH, FALLS CO., OUR LADY OF THE LAKE, Attended by St. Charles Borromeo, Kingsland Rev. Bernard Nguyen Hung.
304 Hillview Dr., Horseshoe Bay, 78657. Tel: 830-598-7327.

TAYLOR, WILLIAMSON CO.

1—ST. MARY OF THE ASSUMPTION (1877) [CEM] Rev. Msgr. Lonnie A. Urban; Deacon Dan Ozuna.
Res.: 408 Washburn St., 76574. Tel: 512-352-2175; 512-365-2175; Fax: 512-365-5313.
School—(Grades PreK-8) Tel: 512-352-2313. Dr. Barbara Gibson, Prin.; Dolores Hernandez, Librarian. Sisters 2; Lay Teachers 18; Students 184.
Catechesis/Religious Program—Tel: 512-352-2133. Frances Albert, D.R.E. Students 261.
Convent—317 E. 4th St., 76574. Tel: 512-352-2144.

2—OUR LADY OF GUADALUPE (1914), (Hispanic), [CEM] Rev. Efrain Villanueva; Deacon Alfredo Torres.
Res.: 113 Dickey St., 76574. Tel: 512-365-2380; Fax: 512-365-1733.
Catechesis/Religious Program—Students 260.

TEMPLE, BELL CO.

1—ST. LUKE (1969) [CEM] [JC] Revs. Don Loftin; Justin M. Nguyen; Deacons Jerome J. Klement; James Madsen; Robert George.
Res.: 2807 Oakdale, 76502. Tel: 254-773-1561; Fax: 254-773-4623.
Catechesis/Religious Program—Tel: 254-773-2330. Students 425.

2—ST. MARY (1883) [JC] Revs. Sales T. (Ranjan) Cletus; James Deaconson; Deacons Bonfacio (Barney) Rodriguez; Robert J. Snigger.
Res.: 1018 S. 7th St., 76504. Tel: 254-773-4541; Fax: 254-774-7044.
Rectory—1004 S. 7th St., 76504. Tel: 254-773-3238.
School—(Grades PreK-8), 1019 S. 7th St., 76504. Tel: 254-778-8141; Fax: 254-778-1396. James Melone, Prin.; Bernadette Hickman, Librarian. Lay Teachers 23; Students 230.
Catechesis/Religious Program—Tel: 254-773-1980. Loris Edwards, D.R.E. Students 190.

3—OUR LADY OF GUADALUPE CATHOLIC CHURCH - TEMPLE, TEXAS (1952), (Hispanic), Revs. Tom Chamberlain; Ramiro Tarazona; Deacons J. Margarito Alvarado; Jose Cruz Perez; Joe Vela.
Res.: 707 S. 6th St., 76504. Tel: 254-778-1304; Fax: 254-773-5469.
Catechesis/Religious Program—Students 450.

TOURS, MCLENNAN CO., ST. MARTIN (1870), (German—Czech), [CEM] Rev. Msgr. Isidore Rozycki.
Res.: 301 St. Martin's Church Rd., West, 76691-2135. Tel: 254-822-1145; Fax: 254-822-0171.
Catechesis/Religious Program—Tel: 254-822-1026. Jennifer Varga, D.R.E.; Kayla Sinkule, D.R.E. Students 139.
Mission—St. Joseph Elk, McLennon Co. 76691.

UHLAND, HAYS CO., ST. MICHAEL (1924), (Hispanic), [CEM] [JC] Rev. Victor Mayorga (Colombia); Deacon W. J. Ham.
Church and Mailing: 80 S. Old Spanish Tr., 78640. Tel: 512-398-7475; Fax: 512-398-7156.
Catechesis/Religious Program—Tel: 512-398-5720. Carolyn Martinez, D.R.E. Students 60.

WACO, MCLENNAN CO.

1—ST. FRANCIS ON THE BRAZOS (1924), (Hispanic), [JC] Very Rev. Roman Burgos, T.O.R.; Deacon Jessie C. Garza.
Mailing Address: 315 Jefferson Ave., 76701.
Res.: 301 Jefferson Ave., 76701. Tel: 254-752-8434; Fax: 254-752-2415.
Nursery & Kindergarten—612 N. 3rd St., 76701. Tel: 254-753-5565; Fax: 254-757-0537. Sr. Maria Izquierdo, F.H.M., Prin. Sisters 4; Lay Teachers 6; Students 131.
Catechesis/Religious Program—Tel: 254-752-1159. Students 530.
Convent—612 N. 3rd St., 76701. Tel: 254-753-5565.
Mission—Santa Rita Satin, Satin Falls Co.

2—ST. JEROME (1982) Revs. Rakshaganathan Selvaraj; Brion Zarsky; Deacons Joseph Potter; Rae Carter; Greg George; Raymond Jones.
Res.: 9820 Chapel Rd., 76712. Tel: 254-666-7722; Fax: 254-666-4848.
Catechesis/Religious Program—Tel: 254-666-6222. Lisa Sanders, D.R.E. Students 348.

3—ST. JOHN THE BAPTIST (1953), (African American), Attended by St. Mary's, Waco. Rev. Cyril Ngbede Ejaidu, Admin.; Sylvia Glenn, Business Admin.
Mailing Address: P.O. Box 585, 76704-0585.
Res.: 1312 Dallas St., 76704-0585. Tel: 254-753-6742.
Catechesis/Religious Program—Students 4.

4—ST. JOSEPH (1950) Rev. Timothy V. Vaverek.
Res.: 1011 Boston St., 76705.
Catechesis/Religious Program—Tel: 254-799-6646. Rosemary Berrios, D.R.E. Students 120.

5—ST. LOUIS (1964) Revs. David Leibham; Pius T. Mathew.
Res.: 2001 N. 25th St., P.O. Box 5040, 76708. Tel: 254-754-1221; Fax: 254-754-4019.
School—(Grades PreK-8) Tel: 254-754-2041; Fax: 254-754-2091. Louis Gonzales, Prin.; Linda Adkins, Librarian. Lay Teachers 37; Students 360.
Catechesis/Religious Program—Antonia Duran, D.R.E. Students 73.

6—ST. MARY OF THE ASSUMPTION (1870) Rev. Irudayaraj Nelapatti-Thomas; Deacons James Fitzpatrick; James Poole.

Church & Mailing Address: 1401 Washington Ave., 76701. Tel: 254-753-0146; Fax: 254-753-5100.
Catechesis/Religious Program—Tel: 254-754-1622. Terri Bukowski, D.R.E. Students 90.

7—SACRED HEART CATHOLIC CHURCH - WACO, TEXAS (1957), (Spanish), Rev. Lawrence Soler, T.O.R.; Deacons Tony Arocha; Lorenzo Garcia; George Shields; Robert Wehrer.
Res.: 2621 Bagby Ave., 76711. Tel: 254-756-0449; Fax: 254-756-6302.
Catechesis/Religious Program—Tel: 254-756-2390. Students 448.

8—SANTA RITA CATHOLIC CHURCH - SATIN, TEXAS (1917) Attended by St. Francis on the Brazos, Waco., 315 Jefferson Ave., 76701.

WARRENTON, FAYETTE CO., ST. MARTIN CATHOLIC CHURCH - WARRENTON, TEXAS, Historic chapel, mission of St John, Fayetteville., Mailing Address: P.O. Box 57, Fayetteville, 78940.

WEST, MCLENNAN CO., ST. MARY, CHURCH OF THE ASSUMPTION (1892), (Czech), [CEM] Very Rev. Edward Karasek; Rev. Anthony Odiong (Nigeria).
Mailing Address: P.O. Box 276, 76691. Tel: 254-826-3705; Fax: 254-826-5497.
Church: 303 S. Harrison, 76691. Tel: 254-826-3705; Fax: 254-826-5497.
School—(Grades PreK-8) Tel: 254-826-5991; Fax: 254-826-7047. Ericka Sammons, Prin. Lay Teachers 11; Students 150.
Catechesis/Religious Program—Mrs. Charlotte Klaus, D.R.E.; Kim Foitek, D.R.E. Students 240.

WESTPHALIA, FALLS CO., CHURCH OF THE VISITATION (1883), (German), [CEM] Rev. Walter Dhanwar, I.M.S.; Deacons Bill Smetana; Charlie Wright.
Res.: 144 County Rd. 3000, Lott, 76656-3827. Tel: 254-584-4983; Fax: 254-584-7063.
Catechesis/Religious Program—Tel: 254-584-4407. Marilyn Rudloff, D.R.E. Students 131.

WIMBERLEY, HAYS CO., ST. MARY (1956) [CEM] Revs. Fulgencio Vincent Mayorga; Everett Trebtoske, Pastor Emeritus (Retired).
Res.: 14711 Ranch Rd. 12, 78676. Tel: 512-847-9181 (Church); Fax: 512-847-5573.
Catechesis/Religious Program—Tel: 512-847-1662. Minerva Martinez, D.R.E. Students 249.

Chaplains of Public Institutions

AUSTIN. *St. David's Hospital*. Attended by St. Austin Catholic Church., 2010 Guadalupe, 78705. Tel: 512-477-9471. Vacant.
School for the Blind. Attended by St. Louis Church., 7601 Burnet Rd., 78757. Tel: 512-454-0384. Vacant.
School for the Deaf, 2309 Euclid St., 78704. Tel: 512-442-3602. Attended by St. Ignatius Catholic Church.
Seton/Brackenridge Hospital, Tel: 512-324-7480; 512-324-7106. Revs. Paulinus Iwuji, S.M.M.M., Chap., Seton Healthcare Facilities, Richard Tijerina, Chap., Frank Zlotkowski, C.S.C., Chap., Brackenridge Hospital.
State Hospital, 4110 Guadalupe, 78751. Tel: 512-836-1213. Attended by St. Austin Church, Tel: 512-477-9471.

GATESVILLE. *Texas Department of Criminal Justice*, P.O. Box 665, 76528. Vacant.

GIDDINGS. *State School*, Tel: 979-542-0217. Very Rev. James Robert Olnhausen. Attended by St. Margaret, Giddings. Tel: 409-542-3380.

MEXIA. *State School*, 606 N. Bonham, 76667. Tel: 254-562-3619. Rev. Carlo Benjamin Magnaye, M.F., M.F.

TEMPLE. *V.A. Hospital*, 1901 S. First St., 76501. Tel: 254-778-4811, Ext. 4879. Rev. Richard Beyer.

WACO. *V.A. Hospital*, 4800 Memorial Dr., 76711. Tel: 254-752-6581. Rev. Richard Beyer.

Chaplains of the Military:
Revs.—
George, George C., Chap., 15519 Luna Ridge, Helotes, 78023.
Johnson, Charles W., (LT), C.H.C., U.S.N., CRMD USS Theodore Roosevelt, CVN 71, Apo, AE 09599-2871.
Lee, Sang Yil, Fort Hood, TX
Moss, Donald G. (SP), C.H.C, U.S.N.R, Nuss Theodore Roosevelt Cvn 71, Apo, AE 09599-2871.
Nielson, Kenneth (Karl), U.S. Army

On Duty Outside the Diocese:
Rev. Msgrs.—
Elmer, Charles, St. Mary Seminary, 9845 Memorial Dr., Houston, 77024.
Jenkins, Ron, USCCB, 3211 4th St. N.E., Washington, DC 20017. Tel: 202-541-3100, Ext. 11
Revs.—
Heimsoth, Larry
Kim, Sae-Eul
Manion, Kevin
McNeil, Joel
Strieder, Leon, St. Mary Seminary, University of St. Thomas, Houston, Texas, 9845 Memorial Dr., Houston, 77024.

Retired:
Rev. Msgrs.—
Brennan, Ralph, 921 St. Edward's Dr., 78704. Tel: 512-493-0130
Deane, Joseph
Deering, Mark, 4700 Westchester, 76710. Tel: 254-772-5263
Goertz, Victor, 2610 E. University Ave., #202, Georgetown, 78626.
Holtman, Elmer
Johnson, Oliver F., John Paul II Residence for Priests, 2620 E. University Ave., Georgetown, 78626.
Malinowski, John C., P.O. Box 3931, Bryan, 77805.
Mazurkiewicz, Ben, 2836 Ehlinger-Becker Rd., Fayetteville, 78940.
Mazurkiewicz, Harry, 2848 Ehlinger-Becker, Fayetteville, 78940.
Miller, Frank, 434 FM 1242, Abbott, 76621.
Reyes, Lonnie C.
Tydlacka, George
Wozniak, Louis, 2212 Rifle Bend Dr., Georgetown, 78626. Tel: 512-864-1907
Zientek, Benedict, P.O. Box 2447, Brenham, 77834.
Revs.—
Benish, William, 450 Discovery Blvd., Room 210, Cedar Park, 78613. Tel: 254-741-1412
Carr, Walter, 1006 Salem Ln., 78753.
Chalupa, Fred, J.C.L., John Paul II Residence for Priests, 2610 E. University Ave., Georgetown, 78626.
Clancy, "Ray", 13836 W. Sola Dr., Sun City West, AZ 85375.
Frazer, Joseph, P.O. Box 1083, Penney Farms, FL 32079.
Goertz, Bernard C., 585 Shiloh Rd., Bastrop, 78602.
Hanus, Thomas J.
Leddy, Leonard, Western Hill Village, 3000 W. Adams Ave., #301, Temple, 76504.
Mahoney, Bernard, 1722 Chippendale, Houston, 77018.
McCabe, Peter
McCallum, Paul F., John Paul II Residence for Priests, 2610 E. University Ave., Georgetown, 78626.
Mikkelson, Scott, John Paul II Residence for Priests, 2610 E. University, Georgetown, 78626.
Romanski, Gregory A.
Shepard, Eugene
Smith, Gerald, 4800 Convict Hill, 78749.
Trebtoske, Everett, 14711 Ranch Rd. 12, Wimberley, 78676.
Tzanakas, George M., John Paul II Residence for Priests, 2610 E. University Ave., #102, Georgetown, 78626.

Permanent Deacons:
Aaronson, Michael, St. Joseph, Killeen
Abraham, Ellis, St. Anthony, Bryan
Adam, Klaus, St. Paul Chong Hasang, Harker Heights
Aguilar, Guadalupe, St. Mary, Lockhart
Aguirre, Armando, Christ the King, Belton
Alvarado, J. Margarito, Our Lady of Guadalupe, Temple
Arellano, Joe, Santa Barbara, Austin
Arevalo, Ralph, St. Julia, Austin
Arocha, Antonio, Sacred Heart, Waco
Ashley, Frank, St. Thomas Aquinas, College Station
Baker, Ted, St. Thomas Aquinas, College Station
Banda, Cruz, Jr., Santa Barbara, Austin
Barkley, Roy, St. Joseph, Manor
Beltran, Victor, St. Thomas, Hamilton
Benavides, Alfred, San Jose, Austin
Bigelow, Richard, St. Louis, Austin
Boren, David, St. Vincent de Paul, Austin
Botello, Richard, San Jose, Austin
Boyle, Vincent A., St. Mary Cathedral, Austin
Caceras, Luis Alberto, St. Mary's Seminary, Houston
Cardona, David, Serving in Diocese of St. Petersburg, FL
Carter, Rae, St. Jerome, Waco
Castillo, Concepcion, St. William, Round Rock
Chavez, Jose, St. Joseph, Manor
Clapp, Ron, St. Thomas More, Austin
Coelho, Gus, St. Joseph, Rockdale
Colley, Earl, St. Monica, Cameron
Collins, Roger, (Retired)
Colon, Willie, (Retired)
Consentino, John, Holy Family, Copperas Cove
Cortez, Willie, St. Mary Cathedral
Crochet, Larry, St. Charles Borromeo, Kingsland
Cuevas, Alfonso, St. Albert the Great, Austin
Davis, Gene (Roy), Holy Trinity, Corn Hill
Dawson, Vern, St. Helen, Georgetown
De La Garza, John, University Catholic Center, Austin
Deason, Switzer, St. Mary, College Station
Desorcie, Allen, St. Patrick, Hutto
Diaz, Johnny R., St. Elizabeth Ann Seton, Killeen
Doriocourt, Luis, St. Francis of Assisi, Franklin
Dorsey, Timothy, Holy Family, Copperas Cove
Duecker, Richard, St. Anthony, Kyle
Dufour, Generes "Doots", Diocesan Criminal Justice Ministry
Dunne, Larry, Sacred Heart, Elgin
Duran, Everardo "Lalo", (Retired)
Egan, Dennis, St. William, Round Rock
Embry, Rob, St. Louis, Austin
Endris, Lou, (Retired)
Fahlund, Nelson, Sacred Heart, Austin
Fell, Channing, Scared Heart, Elgin
Fitzpatrick, Jim, St. Mary, Church of the Assumption, Waco
Flores, Joe, St. Anthony, Kyle
Foreman, Boyce A., (Retired), Emmaus, Lakeway
Franklin, John, (Retired)
Fuller, James, Serving in Diocese of Fort Worth, TX
Gallagher, Pat, St. Joseph, Bryan
Garcia, Ben, Santa Cruz, Buda
Garcia, Lorenzo, Sacred Heart, Waco
Garza, Jesse M., Sacred Heart, Austin
Garza, Jessie C., St. Francis, Waco
Garza, Juan, (Retired)
Garza, Rey, Santa Cruz, Buda
George, Gregory, St. Jerome, Waco
George, Robert, St. Luke, Temple
Gesch, Michael, St. John Neumann, Austin
Gessler, Don, M.D., M.B.A., St. Theresa, Austin
Gonzales, Gumisindo, St. Patrick, Hutto
Gonzalez, Rodolfo, Santa Cruz, Buda
Guerrero, Jorge, St. John, San Marcos
Gutierrez, Joe, San Jose, Austin
Ham, W. J., St. Michael, Uhland
Hamlet, Mark
Hansen, Clarence, (Inactive)
Hargraves, Wilfred (Dub), St. John, Luling
Haywood, Daryl, St. Mary, Lockhart
Hill, John, Jr., Emmaus, Lakeway
Hipskind, Gregory, (Inactive)
Hobby, Bill, Ascension, Bastrop; Diocesan Vice Chancellor
Holicky, Edward, Jr., Our Mother of Sorrows, Burnet; Holy Cross, Bertram
James, Ray, (Retired)
Januszewski, Bill, (Retired)
Jasek, Frank, St. Peter Catholic Student Center, Waco
Jasso, Carlos, St. Mary, Lampasas
Jimenez, Jose, St. Stephen, Salado
Johnson, Tom, St. Thomas More, Austin; Diocesan Dir., Facilities/Maintenance
Jones, Fred, Catholic Community, Fort Hood
Jones, Ray, St. Jerome, Waco
Keller, George, St. Joseph, Mason
Kennedy, Pat, (Retired)
Kim, Peter, St. Paul Chong Hasang, Harker Heights
Klement, Jerry, St. Luke, Temple
Kotrola, Richard, St. William, Round Rock
Krotzer, Philip, (Inactive)
Lara, Alejandro, St. Elizabeth, Pflugerville
Lastovica, Ronnie, Our Lady's Maronite, Austin
Lavallee, Paul, St. John the Evangelist, Marble Falls
Lawrence, John, (Retired)
Ledesma, Robert, (Inactive)
Lilliard, George, Holy Trinity, Llano
Long, Bill, St. Mary, Lockhart
Lopez, Agapito, Cristo Rey, Austin
Lopez, Juan, Sacred Heart, Elgin
Luna, Conception, St. Mary, Hearne
Luna, Willie, St. Matthew, Rogers
Madsen, James, St. Luke, Temple
Mahoney, Dwight, St. Mary, Mexia
Mallinger, Thomas, St. Thomas More, Austin
Martin, Terry, St. Mary, Lago Vista
Martinez, Jesse, Emmaus, Lakeway
Martinez, Roberto, Sacred Heart, Austin
Mayes, Dave, St. Thomas Aquinas, College Station
McCormick, Frank, St. John Vianney, Round Rock
Medina, Aurelio, St. Anthony, Kyle
Meismer, Mike, (Inactive)
Menchaca, Richard, St. Peter, Goldthwaite
Meuth, Bernard, St. Paul, Smithville
Milton, Glen, St. Anthony, Bryan
Mojica, Jessie, St. John, San Marcos
Molina, Fred, Santa Teresa, Bryan
Monroe, Frank, J.D., St. Helen, Georgetown
Montag, Eugene J., Our Mother of Sorrows, Burnet; Holy Cross, Bertram
Moore, Ray, Santa Rosa, Andice
Morales, David, (Retired)
Moran, Elias, (Inactive)
Morse, Eugene, St. Joseph, Killeen
Muehr, Roger, Sacred Heart, Rockne

Murray, Patrick, St. Ignatius, Austin
Nelson, Gary, St. Joseph, Bryan
Nissen, Kevin, St. Julia, Austin
O'Neill, John, (Retired)
Ojeda, Johnny, Immaculate Heart of Mary, Martindale
Orton, Dick, (Retired)
Ozuna, Dan, St. Mary, Taylor
Ozuna, Rafael, St. Joseph, Killeen
Peca, John M., St. Anthony, Kyle
Perez, Jose Cruz, Our Lady of Guadalupe, Temple
Perrone, Andy, St. Anthony, Bryan
Pfuntner, Jordan, (Retired)
Pickwell, John, St. Paul, Austin; Canonical & Tribunal Services
Pina, Steve, Christ the King, Belton
Poole, James, St. Mary, Church of the Assumption, Waco
Potter, Joseph, St. Jerome, Waco
Prewitt, Sidney, Sacred Heart, Lott; St. Joseph, Marlin
Pynes, Tony, St. Louis, Austin
Ramirez, Daniel, St. Mary, Mexia
Reed, David, St. Mary, College Station
Renteria, Mario, Our Lady of Guadalupe, Austin
Reyes, Samuel, St. Mary, Caldwell
Riojas, John, Santa Cruz, Buda
Rios, Rudy, St. Ignatius, Martyr, Austin
Rivera, John, San Jose, Austin
Roberge, Philip R., St. Margaret Mary, Cedar Park
Rodriguez, Bonifacio, St. Mary, Temple
Rodriguez, Guadalupe, St. William, Round Rock
Rodriguez, J. Paul, St. Margaret Mary, Cedar Park
Romero, Toby, St. Margaret Mary, Cedar Park
Rosales, Hector, Dolores, Austin
Rositas, Edward, St. Martin de Porres, Dripping Springs
Ruiz, Joe, St. Helen, Georgetown
Ryan, Barry, St. Elizabeth, Pflugerville
Saienga, Gene, St. John Vianney, Round Rock
Sanchez, Romeo, San Jose, Austin
Sanders, Raymond, Jr., M.S., M.A., Ed.D., (Retired)
Scarmardo, Bill, St. Anthony, Bryan
Schroeder, Christopher, St. Catherine, Austin
Schwab, Peter, Ph.D., St. Thomas More, Austin
Scott, Bill, (Retired)
Shieldes, George, Sacred Heart, Waco
Shoemake, William, Christ the King, Belton
Silguero, Luis F., St. John, San Marcos
Sims, Donald, St. Joseph, Rockdale
Sis, Ray, (Retired)
Smetana, Bill, Visitation, Westphalia
Snigger, Robert J., St. Mary, Temple
Solarzno, Eraclio, St. John the Evangelist, Marble Falls
Sweed, Limas, Blessed Virgin Mary, Washington
Terrell, John Larry, St. Catherine of Sienna, Austin
Thornton, Johnnie, Sts. Cyril & Methodius, Granger
Torres, Alfredo, Our Lady of Guadalupe, Taylor
Turner, Donald, St. Louis, Austin
Tyboroski, Julian, (Retired)
Vargas, Domingo, St. John, San Marcos
Vela, Joe, Our Lady of Guadalupe, Temple
Vela, William, St. Louis, Austin
Venglar, Patrick, St. Mary, Lockhart; H.L. Grant Student Center, Texas State, San Marcos
Villegas, Solomon, St. Paul, Austin
Vocelka, Frank J. (Jay), St. Mary, Lampasas
Vogler, Fred, (Inactive)
Walker, Ron, St. Mary Cathedral, Austin; Dir. of Diaconal Ministry; Chancellor
Washburne, Marc, Santa Rosa, Andice
Wearden, Glen, (Retired)
Wehrer, Robert, Sacred Heart, Waco
Weilert, Otto, (Inactive)
Weynand, Joe, (Retired)
Woods, Ronald, St. Charles Borromeo, Kingsland
Wright, Charlie, Visitation, Westphalia
Wright, Dan, St. Thomas More, Austin
Young, John, St. Mary, Caldwell
Zacek, George, St. Theresa, Austin

INSTITUTIONS LOCATED IN THE DIOCESE

[A] COLLEGES AND UNIVERSITIES

AUSTIN. *St. Edward's University*, 3001 S. Congress Ave., 78704-6489. Tel: 512-448-8400; Fax: 512-448-8492. Email: seu.admit@stedwards.edu. Web: www.stedwards.edu. Dr. George E. Martin, Pres. Established in 1878 by the Congregation of Holy Cross and chartered by the state in 1885. Priests 2; Holy Cross Brothers 14; Sisters 4; Lay Professors 522; Total Staff 960; Students 5,285.
Officers: Revs. Louis Brusatti, C.M., Dean School of Humanities; Rick Wilkinson, C.S.C., Dir. Campus Ministry; Sr. Donna M. Jurick, S.N.D., Exec. Vice Pres.; Bros. Thomas Chady, C.S.C.; Richard Daly, C.S.C., B.A., M.A.; James DeTemple, C.S.C.; Joseph Harris, C.S.C.; George Klawitter, C.S.C.; Gerald Muller, C.S.C.; John Perron, C.S.C.; Edwin Reggio, C.S.C.; Paige Booth, Vice Pres. Mktg. & Enrollment; David Waldron, Vice Pres. Information Technology; Rhonda Cartwright, Vice Pres. Financial Affairs; Walter Pearson, Dean of New College; Dr. Lance Hayes, Registrar; Dr. Marianne F. Hopper, Dean Univ. Programs; Michael Larkin, Vice Pres. for Univ. Advancement; Marsha C. Kelliher, Dean School of Mgmt. & Business; Dr. George E. Martin, Pres.; Molly Minus, Assoc. Vice Pres. Acadmic Affairs; Dr. Sandra L. Pacheco, Vice Pres. Student Affairs; Bro. Stephen Walsh, C.S.C., B.A., MED, Ph.D., Dir., Holy Cross Institute; Cynthia Naples, Interim Dean, School Natural Sciences; Dr. Thomas Evans, Assoc. Vice Pres.; J. Frank Smith, Dean, School Educ.; Dr. Brenda Vallance, Dean, School Behavioral & Social Sciences; Cristina Bordin, Pres. Asst.; Josie Barrett, Pres. Asst.; Bhuban Pandey, Assoc. Vice Pres., Inst. Effectiveness & Research.

[B] HIGH SCHOOL, DIOCESAN

AUSTIN. *St. Dominic Savio Catholic High School*, (Grades 9-10), 9400 Neenah Ave., 78717. Mr. Kevin J. Calkins, Prin. Priests 1; Sisters 1; Lay Teachers 6.
San Juan Diego Catholic High School (2002) 800 Herndon Ln., 78704. Tel: 512-804-1935; Fax: 512-804-1937. Email: info@sjdchs.org. Web: sjdchs.org. Pamela S. Jupe, Prin.; Ann Walters, Asst. Prin.; Lori Jasper, Librarian. Priests 1; Brothers 1; Sisters 1; Lay Teachers 19; Total Staff 20; Total Enrollment 172.

BRYAN. *St. Joseph High School*, 600 S. Coulter, 77803. Tel: 979-822-6641; Fax: 979-779-2810. Mrs. Beatrice Janssen, Prin.; Melissa Slater, Librarian. Lay Teachers 46.

WACO. *Reicher Catholic High School* (1954) 2102 N. 23rd St., 76708. Tel: 254-752-8349; Fax: 254-752-8408. Email: ajones@reicher.org. Web: www.reicher.org. Mrs. Arlene Anderson Jones, Prin.; Michele Lacina, Librarian. Deacons 1; Sisters 2; Lay Teachers 22; Students 229.

[C] HIGH SCHOOL, PRIVATE

AUSTIN. *St. Michael's Catholic Academy* (1984) 3000 Barton Creek Blvd., 78735. Tel: 512-328-2323; Fax: 512-328-2327. Email: sscarmardo@smca.com. Web: www.smca.com. Sharon S. Scarmardo, Prin.; Ayne Ray, Librarian. Priests 1; Lay Teachers 47; Students 463.

TEMPLE. *Holy Trinity Catholic High School* (1997) 418 N. 11th, 76501. Tel: 254-771-0787; Fax: 254-771-2285. Email: info@holytrinitychs.org; holytrinity@hot.rr.com. Web: www. holytrinitychs.org. Christopher Mosmeyer, Prin.; Mary Ann Clark, Librarian. Priests 2; Lay Teachers 16; Total Enrollment 87; Total Staff 14.

[D] ELEMENTARY SCHOOL, PRIVATE

AUSTIN. *St. Gabriel's Catholic School*, (Grades PreK-8), (Legal name: Southwest Austin Catholic School Inc.), 2500 Wimberly Ln., 78735. Tel: 512-327-7755; Fax: 512-327-4334. Web: sgs-austin.org. Steve Balak, Head School; Misty Poe, Head Middle School; Janet Ickert, Head Lower School; Jennifer Coleman, Librarian. Lay Teachers 37; Total Enrollment 367.
Holy Family Catholic School (2000) (Grades PreK-8), 9400 Neenah Ave., 78717. Tel: 512-246-4455; Fax: 512-246-4454. Email: hfcs@holyfamilycs.org. Web: www.holyfamilycs.org. Ms. Joan Wagner, Ph.D., Prin.; Donald Kenner, Librarian. Lay Teachers 26; Total Staff 42; Students 471.

[E] GENERAL HOSPITALS

AUSTIN. **Seton Healthcare*, 1345 Philomena St., 78723. Tel: 512-324-1923. Web: www.seton.net. Charles J. Barnett, Pres. & CEO. d/b/a's: Dell Children's Medical Center, Austin; Seton Bertram Healthcare Center, Bertram; Seton Burnet Healthcare Center, Burnet; Seton Edgar B. Davis Hospital, Luling; Seton Highland Lakes Hospital, Burnet; Seton Kozmetsky Community Health Center, Austin; Seton Lampasas Healthcare Center, Lampasas; Seton Lockhart Family Health Center, Lockhart; Seton Marble Falls Healthcare Center, Marble Falls; Seton McCarthy Community Health Center, Austin; Seton Medical Center Austin, Austin; Seton Medical Center Williamson, Round Rock; Seton Northwest Hospital, Austin; Seton Pflugerville Healthcare Center, Pflugerville; Seton Shoal Creek Hospital, Austin; Seton Southwest Hospital, Austin; Seton Topfer Community Health Center, Austin. Bed Capacity 1,649; Total Assisted Annually 929,240; Staff 10,596.

BRYAN. *Burleson St. Joseph Health Center of Caldwell, Texas*, 2801 Franciscan Dr., 77802. Tel: 979-776-2599; Fax: 409-774-4590. Email: info@mail.st-joseph.org. Web: www.st-joseph.org. Anthony D. Pfitzer, Pres. & CEO; Reed Edmundson, Vice Pres., Rural Hospitals. Patients Assisted Annually 31,996; Total Staff 86; Bed Capacity 25.
St. Joseph Regional Health Center, 2801 Franciscan Dr., 77802. Tel: 979-776-3777; Fax: 979-774-4590. Email: tpfitzer@st-joseph.org. Web: www.st-joseph.org. Anthony D. Pfitzer, CEO; Rev. Msgr. John C. Malinowski, Chap. (Retired); Mrs. Caroline McDonald, Bd. Chm. Sisters of St. Francis of Sylvania, OH 6; Bed Capacity 304; Patients Assisted Annually 247,000; Total Staff 1,535.
St. Joseph Services Corp., 2801 Franciscan Dr., 77802. Tel: 979-776-3777; Fax: 979-774-4590. Email: info@mail.st-joseph.org. Web: www.st-joseph.org. Anthony D. Pfitzer, CEO; George Nelson, Bd. Chm. Sisters of St. Francis of Sylvania, OH 5; Bed Capacity 354; LTC Beds 233; Patients Assisted Annually 332,116; LTC Staff 191; Total Staff 2,465.

WACO. *Providence Healthcare Network* (1904) 6901 Medical Pkwy., P.O. Box 2589, 76702-2589. Tel: 254-751-4000; Fax: 254-751-4769. Email: kkeahey@phn-waco.org. Web: www.providence.net. Kent A. Keahey, M.B.A., B.B.A., Pres. & CEO; Sr. Cecile Matushek, D.C., Vice Pres. Mission. Medical/Surgical/OB/Pediatrics acute care; DePaul Center - Psychiatric care; Providence Park - Independent living, Assisted living & Long Term care facilities & Home Health. Daughters of Charity of St. Vincent de Paul 11; Bed Capacity 603; Patients Assisted Annually 302,141; Total Staff 2,482.

[F] SPECIAL HOSPITAL

WACO. *DePaul Center*, 301 Londonderry Dr., 76712. Tel: 254-776-5970; 800-777-5043. Psychiatric Hospital Daughters of Charity 1; Bed Capacity 45; Patients Assisted Annually 1,900.

[G] MONASTERIES AND RESIDENCES OF PRIESTS AND BROTHERS

AUSTIN. *Brother Andre Residence* (1985) 2111 Brackenridge St., 78704. Tel: 512-351-9780. Web: www.southerncsc.org. Rev. Charles Van Winkle, C.S.C.
Brothers of the Holy Cross of Texas Inc. (1837) Tel: 512-442-7856; Fax: 512-444-3133. Web: www.holycross-sw.org. *Brother John Baptist Province Center* (1956) 1101 St. Edward's Dr., 78704-6512. Tel: 512-442-7856; Fax: 512-444-3133. Web: www.holycross-sw.org. Bros. Donald Blauvelth, C.S.C, B.A., M.A., M.A. Ed. Admin., Prov. Supr.; Johnny Juno, C.S.C., B.A., Province Accounting Office; Richard Daly, C.S.C., Councilor; Joel Giallanza, C.S.C., B.A., M.A., Councilor; Richard Kelly, C.S.C, Administrative Asst. Total in Province 8. *Brother Vincent Pieau Residence* (1997) 921 St. Edward Dr., 78704. Tel: 512-493-0121; Fax: 512-493-0158. Bro. Harold Ehlinger, C.S.C., B.S., M.Ed., Dir.
Dominican Friars of Austin (1960) 2502 Comburg Castle Way, 78748-5258. Tel: 512-282-3908; Fax: 512-280-9011. Email: chiefop@att.net. Revs. James A. McDonough, O.P., Supr.; Gerardo Guerra-Mayaudon, O.P. Tel: 512-292-3381; Gerald Mendoza, O.P.; Ralph Rogawski, O.P., 6008 Club Terrace, 78741. Tel: 512-385-1719; Bro. Angel Mendez, O.P.
Missionary of St. Paul, MSP, 1610 E. 11th St., 78702. Tel: 512-472-3741; Fax: 512-472-3783. Rev. Michael Ajewole, M.S.P.
Moreau House, St. Edward University, #1069, 3001 S. Congress, 78704. Tel: 512-448-8595; Fax: 512-448-8638. Email: larrya@stedwards.edu. Web: holycrossbrothers.org. Bros. Larry Atkinson, C.S.C., M.Ed.; John Perron, C.S.C.
Schoenstatt Fathers, 7839 Wheel Rim Cir., 78749. Tel: 512-301-8762; Fax: 512-301-8564. Revs. Christian Christensen, I.S.P.; Jesus Ferras, I.S.P.
St. Joseph's Hall, 3001 S. Congress Ave., 78704. Tel: 512-448-8628; Fax: 512-448-8638. Email: nosopher@aol.com. Web: www.stedwards.edu/holycross/. Bro. Patrick Sopher, C.S.C., B.A., Dir. Brothers 18.

BREMOND. *Clerical Congregation Missionaries of Faith* (1972) 715 N. Main St., 76629-5173. Tel: 254-746-7789; Fax: 254-746-7789. Email: jyucmf@hotmail.com. Web: www.mftexas.catholicweb.com. Rev. Celso A. Yu, M.F., M.F. (Philippines), Supr.

GEORGETOWN. *Pope John Paul II, Residence for Priests*, 2610 E. University Ace., #1001, 78626. Tel: 512-949-2431; Fax: 512-949-2520.

[H] CONVENTS AND RESIDENCES FOR SISTERS

AUSTIN. *Congregation of Marianites of Holy Cross, M.S.C.*, 2809 Onslow Dr., 78748. Tel: 512-904-9070; Fax: 512-804-1937. Sr. Stephanie Brignac, M.S.C., Contact Person.

Congregation of the Sisters of the Holy Cross, La Casa Convent, 2213 Euclid Ave., 78704. Tel: 512-441-6693.

Congregation of the Sisters of the Holy Cross (1975) Loretto Convent, 2301 E. Side Dr., 78704-5214. Tel: 512-441-3850; Fax: 512-441-3850. Email: alicecondon@aol.com. Sisters 4.

Daughters of Charity of St. Vincent De Paul, 1018 W. 31st St., 78705-2002. Tel: 512-453-9655; Fax: 512-459-5629. Email: dc31st@yahoo.com. Web: www.daughters-of-charity.org.index.php. Sisters 8.

Other Addresses: *Daughters of Charity of St. Vincent De Paul*, 5803 Fairlane Dr., 78757-4414. Tel: 512-452-8980. Email: docfairlane@sbcglobal.net. Sisters 4. *Daughters of Charity of St. Vincent De Paul*, 8013 Greenslope Dr., 78759. Tel: 512-340-0081; Fax: 512-324-0794. Email: austindc1633@sbcglobal.net. Sisters 3.

Daughters of Mary Help of Christians (Salesian Sisters of St. John Bosco), St. Mary Mazzarello Convent, 2109 E. Second St., 78702. Tel: 512-474-2312; Fax: 512-474-2314. Email: evillanueva@craustin.com. Sisters 5.

Franciscan Sisters Daughters of Mercy (Hermanas Franciscanas Hijas de la Misericordia) (1856) *House of Formation*, 1207 Montopolis Dr., 78741. Tel: 512-389-3411; 512-385-5090; Fax: 512-389-0692. Sr. Rose Moreno, F.H.M., M.A., Regl. Supr. Sisters 2.

St. Francis Convent, 612 N. 3rd St., Waco, 76701. Tel: 254-753-6816; Fax: 254-757-0537. Sisters 4.

Missionary Catechists of Divine Providence (1946) 921 St. Edward's Dr., 78704. Tel: 512-793-0123; 512-949-2468; Fax: 512-949-2520. Email: sr_celia_ann_cavazos@austindiocese.org.

Missionary Sisters of the Immaculate Conception of the Mother of God, 4211-B Shoalwood, 78756. Tel: 512-451-2890. Email: jreisch@prodigy.net.

Sinsinawa Dominican Sisters (1848) 6008 Club Terr., 78741. Tel: 512-385-1719. Sisters 2.

Sisters of Charity of the Incarnate Word, 8233 Summer Side Dr., 78759. Tel: 512-451-0272; Fax: 512-451-0284.

Sisters of Divine Providence, 4604 Molera Dr., 78749. Tel: 512-324-1000.

Sisters of Mercy of New Jersey, R.S.M. (Watchung, NJ), 4604 Molera Dr., 78749. Tel: 512-280-7343. Email: slchebro@earthlink.net. Sr. Linda Chebro, Contact Person.

Sisters of the Holy Cross, Our Lady of Victory Convent, 2215 Euclid Ave., 78704-5214. Tel: 512-441-2927. Sisters 3.

Sisters, Servants of the Immaculate Heart of Mary, 2606 Eastside Dr., 78704. Sisters 2.

BRENHAM. *Monastery of St. Clare* (1985) 9300 Hwy. 105, 77833. Tel: 979-836-2444. Email: srangela@franciscanpoorclares.org. Web: www.franciscanpoorclares.org. Sr. Angela Chandler, O.S.C., Abbess. Sisters 3.

Sisters of St. Francis of Our Lady of Lourdes (O.S.F.) (1916) 605A Church St., 77833. Tel: 979-836-9481; Fax: 979-830-2277. Sisters 3.

BRYAN. *Sisters of St. Francis of Our Lady of Lourdes*, 2514 Clare Ct. Apt. C, 77802. Tel: 979-777-0578; Fax: 409-774-4590. Email: info@mail.st-joseph.org. Web: www.st-joseph.org. Sisters 5.

BURNET. *Sisters of the Holy Cross, Inc.*, 1910 Sunset Cliff, 78611. Sr. Judith Hallock, C.S.C., Contact Person.

SOMERVILLE. *Missionary Ecumenical*, P.O. Box 367, 77879. Tel: 979-595-1494; Fax: 979-596-1494. Sisters 2.

TAYLOR. *Sisters of St. John Bosco* (1938) St. John's Convent, 1101 Symes, 76574. Tel: 512-352-2802.

WACO. *Daughters of Charity of St. Vincent De Paul*, 2416 Colcord, 76707. Tel: 254-753-3817. Email: dcswaco@email.com. Sisters 4. 6901 Old McGregor Rd., 76712. Tel: 254-399-7575. Email: hewittdc@aol.com. Sisters 5.

Franciscan Sisters Daughters of Mercy (Franciscanas Hijas de la Misericordia), 612 N. Third St., 76701. Tel: 254-753-5565. Sisters 4. 1207 Montopolis Dr., 78741. Sisters 2.

[I] HOMES FOR THE AGED & HANDICAPPED

BRENHAM. *Trinity Care Center* (1999) 400 E. Sayles, 77833. Tel: 979-836-9770; Fax: 979-836-6100. Web: www.trinitymed.org. Del Waggoner, Exec. Dir.; Sr. Patricia Zielinski, O.S.F., Dir. of Pastoral Care & Mission Integration. Bed Capacity 128; Total Assisted 190; Total Staff 110.

BRYAN. *St. Joseph Manor* (1999) 2333 Manor Dr., 77802. Tel: 979-821-7330; Fax: 979-821-7301. Email: hcottrell@st-joseph.org. Carol Seibert, Office Mgr.; Harold O. Cottrell, BBA, Exec. Dir. Bed Capacity 121; Total Staff 95; Total Assisted Annually 116.

CALDWELL. *Burleson St. Joseph Manor*, 1022 Presidential Corridor, Hwy. 21E, 77836. Tel: 979-567-0920; Fax: 979-567-4811. Email: pbeathard@st-joseph.org. Paul Beathard, Exec. Dir. Bed Capacity 112; Staff 96.

[J] MISSION CENTERS

SOMERVILLE. *St. Ann Mission Center*, P.O. Box 367, 77879. Tel: 979-596-1696; Fax: 979-596-1496. Sr. M. John DellaMorte, M.E., Supr. Missionary Ecumenical. Day Care Students 20; Total Staff 2.

WACO. *St. Francis Mission Center*, 612 N. Third St., 76701. Tel: 254-753-5565; Fax: 254-757-0537. Email: barbarajhtexas@hotmail.com. Sisters Jacinta Amengual, F.H.M., Supr.; Maria Izquierdo, F.H.M., Catechetical, Kindergarten & Nursery; Catherine Vallespir, F.H.M., Catechetical, Kindergarten & Nursery. Franciscan Sisters Daughters of Mercy. Sisters 4; Total Staff 12.

[K] RENEWAL CENTERS

BELTON. *Cedarbrake Renewal Center* (1979) 5602 S. Hwy. 317 N., P.O. Box 58, 76513-0058. Tel: 254-780-2436; Fax: 254-780-2684. Email: cedarbrake@austindiocese.org. Total in Residence 1; Total Staff 11.

[L] NEWMAN APOSTOLATE

AUSTIN. *University Catholic Center* 2010 University Ave., 78705. Tel: 512-476-7351; Fax: 512-476-7377. Email: catholic@utcatholic.org. Web: www.utcatholic.org. Revs. Edward C. Nowak, C.S.P., B.S., M.Div.; Jamie Baca, C.S.P., M.Div., Assoc. Dir.; Deacon John De La Garza. Serving the Catholic community at the University of Texas. Total Staff 15.

BRENHAM. *Blinn College Catholic Student Union* Blinn College, 902 College Ave., 77833. Tel: 979-830-4417. For Catholic students attending Blinn Jr. College. Staff 2.

COLLEGE STATION. *St. Mary's Catholic Center* 603 Church Ave., 77840. Tel: 979-846-5717; Fax: 979-846-4493. Email: info@aggiecatholic.org. Web: www.aggiecatholic.org. Revs. David Konderla; Christopher J. Downey; Deacons Bill Scott Jr.; David Reed; Switzer Deason. Campus ministry at Texas A & M University and Blinn College. Total in Residence 2; Total Staff 35.

SAN MARCOS. *Texas State University, H.L. Grant Catholic Student Center* 100 Concho St., 78666. Tel: 512-392-5925; Fax: 512-392-5922. Email: office@txstatecatholic.org. Web: www.txstatecatholic.org. Rev. Brian Joseph Eilers, Dir.; Melinda Habingreither, Assoc. Dir. Catholic Students attending Texas State University.

WACO. *St. Peter Catholic Student Center at Baylor University* 1415 S. 9th St., P.O. Box 6060, 76706-0060. Tel: 254-757-0636; Fax: 254-714-0639. Email: stpeter-waco@austindiocese.org. Web: www.baylorcatholic.org. Rev. Anthony Odiong (Nigeria), Dir.; Deacon Frank Jasek, Spiritual Dir.; Jerry Opperman, Admin. For Catholic students attending Baylor University, Texas State Technical College, and McLennan Community College.

[M] FOUNDATIONS, ENDOWMENTS & TRUSTS

AUSTIN. *Blue Ladies Minerals, Inc.*, 1201 W. 38th St., Ste. 4200, 78705-1056. Tel: 512-324-1990; Fax: 512-324-1989. Gene Attal, Pres.

Catholic Foundation - Diocese of Austin, Mailing Address: P.O. Box 13327, 78711-3327. Tel: 512-949-2400; Fax: 512-949-2520.

Holy Family Catholic School Foundation (2000) 9400 Neenah Ave., 78717. Tel: 512-246-4455; Fax: 512-246-4454. Email: hfcs@holyfamilycs.org. Web: www.holyfamilycs.org. Ms. Joan Wagner, Ph.D., Contact Person.

Seton Hays Foundation, 6001 Kyle Pkwy., Kyle, 78764. Tel: 512-504-5061; Fax: 512-268-8710. Gerald Hill, Exec. Dir.

Vincare Services of Austin Foundation (2000) 2026 Guadalupe St., 78705. Tel: 512-302-0027; Fax: 512-326-2290. Email: vincare@vincare.org. Web: vincare.org. Sharon Bieser, Exec. Dir.

BRYAN. *St. Joseph Memorial Endowment Fund*, St. Joseph's, 600 E. 26th, 77803. Tel: 979-822-2721; Fax: 979-779-3120. Email: frjohn@stjosephbcs.org. Web: www.stjosephbcs.org. Rev. Msgr. John A. McCaffrey.

[N] MISCELLANEOUS

AUSTIN. *Catholic Archives of Texas*, P.O. Box 13124, 78711-3124. Tel: 512-476-6296; Fax: 512-476-3715. Email: archives@txcatholic.org. Web: www.catholicarchivesoftx.org. Susan Eason, Archive Dir.; Eric J. Hartmann, Asst. Archivist. Historical collection of the Church in the Southwest and Texas from 1519.

Catholic Family Fraternal of Texas. KJZT, P.O. Box 18896, 78760-8896. Tel: 512-444-9586; Fax: 512-444-6887. Lucille Ulcak, Pres.

Catholic Southwest, 1600 Congress Ave., Ste. B, 78701. Tel: 817-251-5451; Fax: 512-339-8670. Email: roy.barkley@sbcglobal.net. P.O. Box 13285, 78711. Dr. Roy Barkley, Editor.

Juan Diego Missionary Society, 4606 E. St. Elmo, 78744. Tel: 512-731-8434; Fax: 512-441-0928. Email: jdms2003@yahoo.com. Elias and Christina Limon, Dir.

Juan Diego Work/Study Program, Inc., 800 Herndon Ln., 78704. Tel: 512-804-1935; Fax: 512-804-1937. Web: www.sjdchs.org. Pamela S. Jupe, Prin.

Ladies of Charity of Austin, TX (1890) P.O. Box 9566, 78766. Tel: 512-507-0068; Fax: 512-267-5578. Email: mmoya@aol.com. Web: www.main.org/locaustin/index.html. Monique Urtado, Pres.

Ladies of Charity of Lake Travis, P.O. Box 340026, 78734. Tel: 512-266-1606; Fax: 512-261-8200. Email: emmaus@emmauslakeway.com. Web: www.emmauslakeway.com. Cindy Balfour, Pres.; Alicia Gray, Vice Pres.

North Central Catholic School Corporation (1996) 9400 Neenah Ave., 78717. Tel: 512-246-4455; Fax: 512-246-4454. Email: hfcs@holyfamilycs.org. Web: www.holyfamilycs.org.

Society of St. Katharine Drexel, 503 Vale St., 78746. Tel: 512-329-5052. Merlie Morales, Pres.

**Society of St. Vincent de Paul, Diocesan Council of Austin*, P.O. Box 9070, 78766.

Texas Catholic Conference, P.O. Box 13285, 78711. 1600 N. Congress Ave., Suite B, 78701. Tel: 512-339-9882; Fax: 512-339-8670. Web: www.txcatholic.org. Mr. Andrew Rivas, Exec. Dir.

Texas Catholic Historical Society, c/o Texas Catholic Conference, P.O. Box 13285, 78711. 1600 N. Congress Ave., Ste. B, 78701. Tel: 512-339-9882; Fax: 512-339-8670. Dr. Roy Barkley, Pres.

VIDES Volunteers International Development Education and Solidarity, 2109 E. 2nd St., 78702. Tel: 512-477-1099. Email: director@vides.us. Web: www.vides.us. Sr. Mary Gloria Mar, F.M.A., Prog. Dir. VIDES USA (Central Office) and VIDES East USA (Satellite Office)

BASTROP. *Ladies of Charity of Bastrop, TX*, P.O. Box 1060, 78602. Tel: 512-321-9819; Fax: 512-321-1647. Email: locb@ev1.net. Putzie Martin, Pres.

BRENHAM. *Trinity Medical Center Auxiliary*, 700 Medical Pkwy., 77833. Tel: 979-830-2207. Email: aahrens@trinitymed.org. Arlene Ahrens, Contact Person.

BUDA. *St. Mary's Academy Alumnae Association*, 16005 Scenic Oak Tr., 78610. Tel: 512-312-0836. Email: cattal@austin.rr.com. Catherine Attal, Contact Person.

LAGRANGE. *Catholic Union of Texas, The K.J.T.* (1889) P.O. Box 297, 78945-0297. Tel: 979-968-5877; Fax: 979-968-5823. Email: president@kjt.net.org. Web: www.kjtnet.org. Christopher L. Urban, Pres. KJT NEWS (official publication).

ROUND ROCK. *Christ the Child Society of Texas, Capital Area, Inc.* (2004) P.O. Box 5953, 78683. Tel: 512-388-1528. Email: lschuckman@fox7.com; lallen09@austin.rr.com. Lorraine Schuckman, Co-Pres.; Linda Allen, Co-Pres.

WACO. *Ladies of Charity of Waco, TX* (1895) 622 N. 36th St., 76710. Tel: 254-752-2009; Fax: 254-753-5059. Email: Lbb622@aol.com. Lorraine Brooks, Financial Sec.

RELIGIOUS INSTITUTES OF MEN REPRESENTED IN THE DIOCESE

For further details refer to the corresponding bracketed number in the Religious Institutes of Men or Women section.

[0600]—*Brothers of the Congregation of Holy Cross* (South-West Province)—C.S.C.

[0480]—*Conventual Franciscans* (Mt. Francis, IN)—O.F.M.Conv.

[]—*Indian Missionary Society* (Varanasi, UP, India)—I.M.S.

[0690]—*Jesuit Fathers and Brothers* (New Orleans Province, LA)—S.J.

[]—*Missionaries of Faith* (U.S. Region, Bremond, TX)—M.F.

[]—*Missionaries of St. Paul* (Houston, TX)—M.S.P.

[1110]—*Missionaries of the Sacred Heart* (San Antonio, TX)—M.S.C.

[0430]—*Order of Preachers-Dominicans* (New Orleans, LA)—O.P.

[1030]—*Paulist Fathers* (Jamaica Estates, NY)—C.S.P.

[0610]—*Priests of the Congregation of Holy Cross* (Indiana Prov., Notre Dame, IN)—C.S.C.

[]—*Redemptorist Fathers*—C.Ss.R.

[]—*Schoenstatt Fathers*—I.S.P.

[0975]—*Society of Our Lady of the Most Holy Trinity* (Robstown TX)—S.O.L.T.

[1200]—*Society of the Divine Savior* (Polish Province, US, Porth, TX)—S.D.S.

[0470]—*The Capuchin Friars*—O.F.M.Cap.

[0560]—*Third Order Regular of Saint Francis of Waco, TX* (Vice-Province of Santa Maria de Guadalupe, Mexico)—T.O.R.

RELIGIOUS INSTITUTES OF WOMEN REPRESENTED IN THE DIOCESE

[]—*Apostles of the Interior Life*—A.V.I.

[2410]—*Congregation of Marianites of the Holy Cross* (New Orleans, LA)—M.S.C.

[1855]—*Congregation of the Handmaids of the Holy Child Jesus*—H.H.C.J.

[0470]—*Congregation of the Sisters of Charity of the Incarnate Word* (Houston, Texas)—C.C.V.I.

[1920]—*Congregation of the Sisters of the Holy Cross* (Notre Dame, IN)—C.S.C.

[0760]—*Daughters of Charity of St. Vincent de Paul* (St. Louis, MO)—D.C.

[0850]—*Daughters of Mary Help of Christian* (San Antonio, TX)—F.M.A.

[]—*Daughters of Mary, Mother of Mercy* (Nigeria)—D.M.M.M.

[]—*Daughters of St. Theresa of the Child Jesus* (Uganda)—D.S.T.

[1070-19]—*Dominican Sisters* (Houston, TX)—O.P.

[1070-03]—*Dominican Sisters* (Sinsinawa, WI)—O.P.

[]—*Dominican Sisters - Congregation of Sacred Heart*—O.P.

[]—*Dominican Sisters of Mary, Mother of the Eucharist*—O.P.

[]—*Eudist Servants of the Eleventh Hour* (Tijuana, Mexico)—E.S.E.H.

[1235]—*Franciscan Sisters Daughters of Mercy (Franciscanas Hijas de la Misericordia)* (U.S. delegation: Waco, TX)—F.H.M.

[1430]—*Franciscan Sisters of Our Lady of Perpetual Help* (St. Louis, MO)—O.S.F.

[2690]—*Missionary Catechists of Divine Providence* (San Antonio, TX)—M.C.D.P.

[]—*Missionary Ecumenical* (Rome, Italy)—M.E.

[2760]—*Missionary Sisters of the Immaculate Conception of the Mother of God* (Paterson, NJ)—S.M.I.C.

[3760]—*Order of St. Clare* (Brenham, TX)—O.S.C.

[2970]—*School Sisters of Notre Dame* (St. Louis, MO; Dallas, TX)—S.S.N.D.

[]—*Sisters for Christian Community*—S.F.C.C.

[]—*Sisters of Christian Community*—S.F.C.C.

[1010]—*Sisters of Divine Providence* (San Antonio, TX)—C.D.P.

[]—*Sisters of Jesus the Savior*—S.J.S.

[3000]—*Sisters of Notre Dame de Namur* (Cincinnati, OH)—S.N.D.deN.

[]—*Sisters of Sacred Sciences* (India)—S.S.S.

[]—*Sisters of St. Francis of Assisi*—O.S.F.

[1530]—*Sisters of St. Francis of the Congregation of Our Lady of Lourdes* (Sylvania, OH)—O.S.F.

[]—*Sisters of St. John Bosco* (Taylor, TX)—S.J.B.

[2150]—*Sisters, Servants of the Immaculate Heart of Mary* (Monroe, MI)—I.H.M.

NECROLOGY

† Dokupil, Rev. Msgr. Edward J., Bastrop, TX Ascension—Died Jan. 18, 2009

† Frizelle, Rev. Msgr. John D., (Retired)—Died Feb. 19, 2009

† Matocha, Rev. Msgr. Edward C., (Retired)—Died Nov. 11, 2009

† McCabe, Rev. Msgr. Richard, (Retired)—Died Sept. 12, 2009

† Davis, Charles A., (Retired)—Died Dec. 18, 2009

† Euresti, Jesse E., Austin, TX Christo Rey—Died April 5, 2009

† Mahoney, Robert, (Retired)—Died Sept. 12, 2009

An asterisk (*) denotes an organization that has established tax-exempt status directly with the IRS and is not covered by the USCCB Group Ruling.

Diocese of Baker

(Dioecesis Bakeriensis)

Most Reverend

ROBERT FRANCIS VASA

Bishop of Baker; ordained May 22, 1976; appointed November 19, 1999; consecrated and installed January 26, 2000.

Most Reverend

THOMAS J. CONNOLLY, D.D., J.C.D.

Retired Bishop of Baker; ordained April 8, 1947; appointed May 4, 1971; consecrated June 30, 1971; retired January 2000. *Res.: P.O. Box 5999, Bend, OR 97708.*

Diocesan Pastoral Office: P.O. Box 5999, Bend, OR 97708. Tel: 541-388-4004; Fax: 541-388-2566.

Email: chancellor@dioceseofbaker.org

ESTABLISHED JUNE 19, 1903.

Square Miles 66,826.

Comprises the Counties of Baker, Crook, Deschutes, Gilliam, Grant, Harney, Hood River, Jefferson, Klamath, Lake, Malheur, Morrow, Sherman, Umatilla, Union, Wallowa, Wasco and Wheeler in the State of Oregon.

For legal titles of parishes and diocesan institutions, consult the Chancery Office.

STATISTICAL OVERVIEW

Personnel	
Bishop	1
Retired Bishops	1
Priests: Diocesan Active in Diocese	17
Priests: Diocesan Active Outside Diocese	2
Priests: Diocesan in Foreign Missions	1
Priests: Retired, Sick or Absent	16
Number of Diocesan Priests	36
Religious Priests in Diocese	15
Total Priests in Diocese	51
Extern Priests in Diocese	10
Ordinations:	
Diocesan Priests	1
Transitional Deacons	1
Permanent Deacons in Diocese	12
Total Sisters	11
Parishes	
Parishes	36
With Resident Pastor:	
Resident Diocesan Priests	21
Resident Religious Priests	9
Without Resident Pastor:	
Administered by Priests	6
Missions	23
Professional Ministry Personnel:	
Lay Ministers	49
Welfare	
Catholic Hospitals	5
Total Assisted	481,068
Homes for the Aged	4
Total Assisted	220
Day Care Centers	3
Total Assisted	80
Special Centers for Social Services	7
Total Assisted	72,469
Educational	
Diocesan Students in Other Seminaries	2
Total Seminarians	2
Elementary Schools, Diocesan and Parish	5
Total Students	592
Catechesis/Religious Education:	
High School Students	687
Elementary Students	1,829
Total Students under Catholic Instruction	3,110
Teachers in the Diocese:	
Lay Teachers	50
Vital Statistics	
Receptions into the Church:	
Infant Baptism Totals	977
Minor Baptism Totals	115
Adult Baptism Totals	37
Received into Full Communion	208
First Communions	1,166
Confirmations	844
Marriages:	
Catholic	144
Interfaith	34
Total Marriages	178
Deaths	237
Total Catholic Population	32,799
Total Population	493,996

Former Bishops—Most Revs. CHARLES J. O'REILLY, D.D., ord. June 29, 1890; appt. June 24, 1903; cons. Bishop of Baker City, Aug. 25, 1903; transferred to the See of Lincoln March 20, 1918; died Feb. 4, 1923; LEO F. FAHEY, D.D., ord. May 29, 1926; appt. Titular Bishop of Ipsus and Coadjutor "cum jure successionis" March 13, 1948; cons. May 26, 1948; died March 31, 1950; JOSEPH F. MCGRATH, D.D., appt. assistant at the Pontifical Throne, Bishop of Baker City; ord. Dec. 21, 1895; appt. Dec. 21, 1918; cons. March 25, 1919; died April 12, 1950; FRANCIS P. LEIPZIG, D.D., ord. April 14, 1920; appt. Bishop of Baker July 18, 1950; cons. Sept. 12, 1950; retired May 4, 1971; died Jan. 17, 1981; THOMAS J. CONNOLLY, D.D., J.C.D. (Retired), ord. April 8, 1947; appt. May 4, 1971; cons. June 30, 1971; retired Nov. 19, 1999.

Vicar General—Very Rev. JAMES P. LOGAN.

Judicial Vicar—Very Rev. JAMES P. LOGAN.

Chancellor—Very Rev. JAMES P. LOGAN.

Diocesan Pastoral Office—Mailing Address: P.O. Box 5999, Bend, 97708. Tel: 541-388-4004; Fax: 541-388-2566. *911 S.E. Armour, Bend, 97702.*

Receptionists and Secretaries—PATTI RAUSCH; VIRGINIA MOHR.

Diocesan Tribunal—Tel: 541-388-4010.

Judicial Vicar and Chief Judge—Very Rev. JAMES P. LOGAN.

Judge—VACANT.

Defenders of the Bond and Promoters of Justice—Revs. LEO F. WECKERLE (Retired); CHRISTOPHER AGOHA, S.M.M.M.

Coordinator and Notary—VIRGINIA MOHR.

Council of Priests and Diocesan Consultors—Most Rev. ROBERT F. VASA, Pres. Ex Officio; Very Rev. ROBERT C. IRWIN; Revs. JAMES A. RADLOFF; CHARLES CHIKA NNABUIFE; Very Rev. JAMES P. LOGAN; Revs. BAILEY CLEMENS; CHRISTOPHER AGOHA, S.M.M.M.; STANISLAUS STRZYZ (Retired); FRANCIS EKWUGH; FRANCIS AKANO.

Deans—Central: Very Rev. JOSEPH REINIG. Eastern: Very Rev. ROBERT C. IRWIN. Northern: Very Rev. GERALD W. CONDON. Southern: Very Rev. RICHARD O. FISCHER. Western: Very Rev. RONALD E. MAAG.

Diocesan Offices and Directors

Board of Education—Most Rev. ROBERT F. VASA; ROGER RICHMOND, Supt.; Very Revs. TODD UNGER; JOSEPH REINIG; Rev. CHRISTOPHER AGOHA, S.M.M.M.; Very Rev. ROBERT C. IRWIN, Principals of Schools and Representatives from each Parish School Board.

Building Committee—Most Rev. ROBERT F. VASA; HOPE BURKE; JOHN G. SCHIEMER; Very Rev. JAMES P. LOGAN.

Campus Ministry Apostolate—Very Rev. ROBERT C. IRWIN, 829 S.W. Second Ave., Ontario, 97914. Tel: 541-889-8469.

Catholic Services—JEAN WHITMORE, 67016 End Rd., Summerville, 97876.

Church Property, Administration of—Most Rev. ROBERT F. VASA, Pres.; JOSEPH LA CASSE, Realtor.

Diocesan Attorney—Mr. GREGORY LYNCH.

Diocesan Development Office—JOHN G. SCHIEMER, Mailing Address: P.O. Box 5999, Bend, 97708. Tel: 541-388-4004.

Diocesan Finance Minister—HOPE BURKE.

Diocesan Financial Board—Most Rev. ROBERT F. VASA; HOPE BURKE; JOHN G. SCHIEMER; RICHARD GRALL; JOSEPH LA CASSE; CRAIG MINNIS.

Diocesan Superintendent of Schools—ROGER RICHMOND, Mailing Address: P.O. Box 5999, Bend, 97708. Tel: 541-388-4004; Fax: 541-388-2566.

Director of Campaign for Human Development—Very Rev. RONALD E. MAAG, Mailing Address: St. Mary Church, P.O. Box 693, Hood River, 97031. Tel: 541-386-3373.

Director of Catholic Hospitals—Very Rev. JAMES P. LOGAN, Mailing Address: P.O. Box 5999, Bend, 97708.

Friends of the Catholic University of America—Very Rev. JAMES P. LOGAN, Mailing Address: P.O. Box 5999, Bend, 97708. Tel: 541-388-4004.

Health and Retirement Board—Most Rev. ROBERT F. VASA, Ex Officio Pres.; Very Rev. RONALD E. MAAG; Rev. ROBERT GREINER, Vice Chm.; Very Rev. TODD UNGER, Sec. & Treas.; Revs. STANISLAUS STRZYZ, Chm. (Retired); JULIAN CASSAR.

Office of Worship and Spirituality—VACANT.

Natural Family Planning—PATTY MARX, Pro-Life Dir., Mailing Address: P.O. Box 5999, Bend, 97708. Tel: 541-388-4004.

Director of Youth Ministry—Rev. JAMES A. RADLOFF, Mailing Address: P.O. Box 5999, Bend, 97708. Tel: 541-388-4004.

Director of Religious Education—Rev. JAMES A. RADLOFF.

Director of Hispanic Ministry and Adult Faith Development—Deacon GUSTAVO RUIZ, Mailing Address: P.O. Box 5999, Bend, 97708. Tel: 541-388-4004.

Priests' Continuing Education Committee—Most Rev. ROBERT F. VASA; Very Rev. RONALD E. MAAG.

R.C.I.A. Office—VACANT.

Diocesan Scout Director—TED YAROSH, 5160 S. Etna St., Klamath Falls, 97603. Tel: 541-882-4611.

Victim Assistance Coordinator—ANGELINA MONTOYA. Tel: 541-388-9271.

Vocations—

Director of Seminarians—VACANT.

Vocation Promoter—Rev. JAMES A. RADLOFF, Mailing Address: P.O. Box 5999, Bend, 97708. Tel: 541-388-4004.

CLERGY, PARISHES, MISSIONS AND PAROCHIAL SCHOOLS

BAKER CITY

(COUNTY OF BAKER), CATHEDRAL OF ST. FRANCIS DE SALES (1871) [CEM] Rev. Julian Cassar (Malta), Rector.
Res.: 2235 First St., Baker, 97814. Tel: 541-523-4521; Fax: 541-523-8362. Email: julianmlt@uci.net. Web: www.saintfranciscathedral.com.
Catechesis/Religious Program—Tamara Skidmore, D.R.E. Students 150.
Mission—St. Therese Halfway, Baker Co.

OUTSIDE BAKER CITY

ARLINGTON, GILLIAM CO., ST. FRANCIS (1931) Rev. Peter Obinna Umekwe (Nigeria), Admin.
Mailing Address: P.O. Box 485, Condon, 97823. Tel: 541-384-5271; Fax: 541-384-5271.

BEND, DESCHUTES CO., ST. FRANCIS OF ASSISI (1904) Very Rev. Joseph Reinig; Rev. Daniel J. Maxwell; Deacons Bob Walling; Joseph Levine.
Office: 2450 N.E. 27th St., 97701. Tel: 541-382-3631; Fax: 541-385-8879. Web: www.stfrancisbend.org.
School—(Grades PreK-8) Tel: 541-382-4701; Fax: 541-312-9111. Web: www.saintfrancisschool.net. Julie Roberts, Head Teacher; Jennifer Brewer, Librarian. Lay Teachers 22; Students 254.
Day Care—Tel: 541-389-3906. Students 15.
Catechesis/Religious Program—Duke Johnson, D.R.E. Students 245.
Diocese of Baker - Latino Community Association—Tel: 541-312-2084.

BOARDMAN, MORROW CO., OUR LADY OF GUADALUPE Rev. Saul Alba Infante.
Mailing Address: P.O. Box 1277, 97818. Tel: 541-481-2024.

BURNS, HARNEY CO., HOLY FAMILY (1899) Rev. Francis Xavier Ekwugha (Nigeria).
Res.: 685 N. Fairview Ave., 97720. Tel: 541-573-2613.
Catechesis/Religious Program—620 N. Egan St., 97720. Andrea Nichols, D.R.E. Students 80.
Mission—Our Lady of Loretto Drewsey, Harney Co.
Mission—St. Thomas Crane, Harney Co.
Mission—St. Charles Juntura, Malheur Co.

CHILOQUIN, KLAMATH CO., OUR LADY OF MT. CARMEL (1927) Rev. Innocent Onwukwe Diala (Nigeria).
Res.: 503 W. Chocktoot, P.O. Box 396, 97624. Tel: 541-783-2411.
Catechesis/Religious Program—Students 7.
Mission—St. James the Apostle Bly, Klamath Co.

CONDON, GILLIAM CO., ST. JOHN (1925) Rev. Peter Obinna Umekwe (Nigeria), Admin.
Res.: P.O. Box 485, 97823. Tel: 541-384-5271; Fax: 541-384-5271.
Catechesis/Religious Program—Students 4.
Mission—St. Catherine Fossil, Wheeler Co.

DUFUR, WASCO CO., ST. ALPHONSUS (1911) Rev. Fabian Nwokorie (Nigeria).
Res.: P.O. Box 395, 97021. Tel: 541-467-2580.
Catechesis/Religious Program—
Mission—St. Mary Maupin, Wasco Co. 97037.

ELGIN, UNION CO., ST. MARY (1966) Attended by Our Lady of the Valley, La Grande. Deacon Joseph Garlitz.
Res.: P.O. Box 97, 97827. Tel: 541-437-8101.
Catechesis/Religious Program—Nancy Wheeling, D.R.E. Students 26.

ENTERPRISE, WALLOWA CO., ST. KATHERINE'S (1923) Rev. Peter Fernando (Sri Lanka), Admin.
Res.: 301 E. Garfield St., P.O. Box 370, 97828. Tel: 541-426-3043.
Parish Office—Tel: 541-426-4008.
Catechesis/Religious Program—Students 36.
Mission—St. Pius X S. Pine St., Wallowa, Wallowa Co. 97885.

HEPPNER, MORROW CO., ST. PATRICK'S (1887) Very Rev. Gerald W. Condon.
Res.: 525 Gale St., P.O. Box 633, 97836. Tel: 541-676-9462.
Catechesis/Religious Program—Mary Ann Elguezabal, D.R.E. Students 65.

HERMISTON, UMATILLA CO., OUR LADY OF ANGELS (1910) Revs. Paul Mbatia, A.J.; Elias M. Dissi, A.J.; Deacon Jesus Esparaza; Kay Edwards, Administrative Asst.
Res.: 565 Hermiston Ave., 97838. Tel: 541-567-5812; Fax: 541-564-0933.
Catechesis/Religious Program—Tel: 541-567-3825. Michelle Edwards, D.R.E. Students 365.

HOOD RIVER, HOOD RIVER CO., IMMACULATE CONCEPTION (1906) [CEM] Very Rev. Ronald E. Maag; Deacons Lou DeSitter, Pastoral Assoc.; David Raj, Pastoral Assoc.
Res.: 1501 Belmont Ave., P.O. Box 693, 97031. Tel: 541-386-3373; Fax: 541-386-1451.
Catechesis/Religious Program—Tel: 541-387-6797. Maria Ramirez, D.R.E., (Spanish); Sharon Foss, D.R.E., (English); Patricia Romero, Youth Min. Students 304.

IONE, MORROW CO., ST. WILLIAM Very Rev. Gerald W. Condon.
Mailing Address: P.O. Box 633, Heppner, 97836. Tel: 541-676-9462.
Church: 110 Main St., 97843.
Catechesis/Religious Program—Jeri Mc Elligott, D.R.E. Students 38.

JOHN DAY, GRANT CO., ST. ELIZABETH (1939) Rev. Bartholomew Ifionu, S.M.M.M. (Nigeria).
Res.: 111 S.W. 2nd St., P.O. Box 189, 97845. Tel: 541-575-1459; Fax: 541-575-1459.
Catechesis/Religious Program—Tel: 541-575-0415.
Mission—St. Anne Monument, Grant Co.
Mission—St. Charles Seneca, Grant Co.
Mission—St. Katherine Long Creek, Grant Co.

JORDAN VALLEY, MALHEUR CO., ST. BERNARD (1915) Rev. Jude Nwachukwu, S.M.M.M. (Nigeria).
Res.: P.O. Box 186, 97910. Tel: 541-586-2266; Fax: 541-586-2448.
Catechesis/Religious Program—Lily Garrard, D.R.E. Students 12.
Mission—Holy Family Arock Rd., Arock, Malheur Co. 97902.

KLAMATH FALLS, KLAMATH CO.

1—ST. PIUS X (1957) [CEM] Very Rev. Richard O. Fischer. In Res., Rev. Ildefonce Mapara, O.S.B. (Tanzania).
Res.: 4880 Bristol Ave., 97603. Tel: 541-884-4242; Fax: 541-885-8724.
Catechesis/Religious Program—Tel: 541-882-7593; Fax: 541-882-7593. Corina Moore, D.R.E. Students 156.

2—SACRED HEART (1904) Revs. Rogatian Urassa; Theodore Nnabaugo (Nigeria).
Res.: 815 High St., 97601. Tel: 541-884-4566; Fax: 541-882-0472.
Catechesis/Religious Program—Tel: 541-882-4864. Michele Laughlin, D.R.E. Students 137.

LA GRANDE, UNION CO., OUR LADY OF THE VALLEY (1914), (Under the title of the Immaculate Conception) Rev. Christopher Agoha, S.M.M.M. (Nigeria). In Res., Revs. Louis Henry Albrecht (Retired); Francis Obijokwu, S.M.M.M. (Nigeria).
Parish Office: 1002 L Ave., 97850. Tel: 541-963-7341; Fax: 541-963-7341.
Res.: 1101 4th St., 97850. Tel: 541-963-0006.
School—Marian Academy, (Grades PreSchool-K) Lay Teachers 2; Students 10.
Catechesis/Religious Program—Tel: 541-963-0861. Charlene Storoe, D.R.E. Students 60.
Mission—St. Anthony North Powder, Union Co.

LA PINE, DESCHUTES CO., HOLY REDEEMER (1983) Rev. Jose Thomas Mudakodiyil (India).
Res.: 16137 Burgess Rd., P.O. Box 299, 97739. Tel: 541-536-3571; 541-536-1177 (Rectory); Fax: 541-536-5647.
Catechesis/Religious Program—Tel: 541-536-1992. Debbie Garrett, D.R.E. Students 43.
Mission—Our Lady of the Snows Gilchrist, Klamath Co.
Mission—Holy Family Christmas Valley, Lake Co.
Mission—Holy Trinity 18143 Cottonwood Rd., Sunriver, Deschutes Co. 97707.

LAKEVIEW, LAKE CO., ST. PATRICK (1912) Rev. Anthony Mbaegbu (Nigeria).
Res.: 12 G St. N., P.O. Drawer 29, 97630. Tel: 541-947-2741; Fax: 541-947-2756. Email: saintpatrick@tnet.biz.
Catechesis/Religious Program—185 S. G St., 97630. Tel: 541-947-3875. Students 62.
Mission—St. Richard Adel, Lake Co.
Mission—St. Thomas Plush, Lake Co.
Mission—St. John the Apostle Paisley, Lake Co.

MADRAS, JEFFERSON CO., ST. PATRICK (1955) Rev. Luis M. Flores-Alva.
Res.: 341 S.W. J St., P.O. Box 786, 97741. Tel: 541-475-2936; Fax: 541-475-0539. Email: stpat@crestviewcable.com.
Catechesis/Religious Program—Tel: 541-475-2444. Elouise Kirsch, D.R.E. Students 125.
Mission—Blessed Kateri Tekakwitha P.O. Box 764, Warm Springs, Jefferson Co. 97761. Tel: 541-553-1235. (Indian Reservation)

MERRILL, KLAMATH CO., ST. AUGUSTINE (1939) Rev. Francis Akano (Nigeria).
Res.: 905 E. Front St., P.O. Box 340, 97633. Tel: 541-798-5823.
Catechesis/Religious Program—Tel: 541-891-6907. Debbie Wallace, D.R.E. Students 22.
Mission—St. Frances Cabrini Bonanza, Klamath Co. Tel: 541-545-6002.
Catechesis/Religious Program—Students 17.

MILTON FREEWATER, UMATILLA CO., ST. FRANCIS OF ASSISI (1940) Rev. Gabriel U. Ezeh, S.M.M.M. (Africa).
Res.: 925 Vining, 97862. Tel: 541-938-5436; Fax: 541-938-3536.
Catechesis/Religious Program—
Mission—Sacred Heart 5th St. & College St., Athena, Umatilla Co. 97813.

NYSSA, MALHEUR CO., ST. BRIDGET OF KILDARE (1951) Rev. Andrew Szymakowski, F.S.S.P.
Res.: 504 Locust, 97913-3235. Tel: 541-372-3133; Fax: 541-372-5620.
Catechesis/Religious Program—Students 120.

ONTARIO, MALHEUR CO., BLESSED SACRAMENT (1911) Very Rev. Robert C. Irwin; Rev. Jude Nwachukwu, S.M.M.M. (Nigeria); Mrs. Frances A. Schaffer, Pastoral Assoc.
Office: 829 S.W. Second Ave., 97914-2695. Tel: 541-889-8469; Fax: 541-889-8483.
School—Saint Peter, (Grades K-5), 98 S.W. Ninth St., 97914. Tel: 541-889-7363; Fax: 541-889-2852. Lay Teachers 6; Students 66.
Catechesis/Religious Program—Tel: 541-889-8404. Angelica Corona, D.R.E.; Tim Cables, Youth Min. Students 177.

PENDLETON, UMATILLA CO.

1—ST. ANDREW'S INDIAN MISSION (1847) [CEM] Revs. Michael J. Fitzpatrick, S.J.; John Apel, S.J.
Res.: 48022 St. Andrews Rd., 97801. Tel: 541-276-6155; Fax: 541-276-0767.
Catechesis/Religious Program—Tel: 541-276-0767. Fern Oliver, D.R.E. Students 40.

2—ST. MARY (1902) [CEM] Rev. Bailey Clemens; Deacons Martin Omar Tores; Daniel Martinez. In Res., Rev. Desmond Chilagorom.
Res.: 800 S.E. Court Ave., 97801. Tel: 541-276-3615; Fax: 541-276-7484.
Catechesis/Religious Program—Tel: 541-276-6163. Shirley Baker, C.R.E. Students 95.

PILOT ROCK, UMATILLA CO., ST. HELEN (1930) Attended by St. Mary's, Pendleton. Rev. Albert Lakra.
Res.: 740 S.W. Birch, P.O. Box V, 97868. Tel: 541-443-3151.
Catechesis/Religious Program—Students 4.

PRINEVILLE, CROOK CO., ST. JOSEPH (1943) Rev. Robert Greiner.
Res.: 150 E. First, P.O. Box 1315, 97754. Tel: 541-447-6475; Fax: 541-416-9141.
Catechesis/Religious Program—200 E. First St., P.O. Box 721, 97754. Tel: 541-447-1227; Fax: 541-389-0888. Dolores Wettstein, D.R.E. Students 90.

REDMOND, DESCHUTES CO., ST. THOMAS (1941) Very Rev. Todd Unger. In Res., Rev. Stanislaus Strzyz (Retired).
Res.: 1720 N.W. 19th, 97756. Tel: 541-923-3390; Fax: 541-548-6630.
School—St. Thomas Academy, (Grades PreSchool-4), 1740 N.W. 9th St., 97756. Tina Hinchcliff, Prin. Lay Teachers 6; Students 64.
Catechesis/Religious Program—535 S. 11th St., 97756. Tel: 541-923-0597. Mary Lehnertz, D.R.E. Students 100.

SISTERS, DESCHUTES CO., ST. EDWARD (1984) Very Rev. James P. Logan. In Res., Rev. James A. Radloff.
Res.: 123 Trinity Way, P.O. Box 489, 97759-0489. Tel: 541-549-0751 (Rectory); 541-549-9391 (Office); Fax: 541-549-1057.
Catechesis/Religious Program—Marcia Rietmann, C.R.E. Students 40.

THE DALLES, WASCO CO., ST. PETER (1848) [CEM] Rev. Charles Chika Nnabuife. In Res., Rev. Fabian Nwokorie (Nigeria).
Res.: 1222 W. 10th St., P.O. Box 41, 97058. Tel: 541-296-2026; Fax: 541-296-5835.
School—St. Mary, (Grades PreK-8), 1112 Cherry Heights Rd., 97058. Tel: 541-296-6004; Fax: 541-296-7858. Kim Koch, Admin. Lay Teachers 13; Students 198.
Catechesis/Religious Program—1111 W. 10th, P.O. Box 41, 97058. Students 41.

UNION, UNION CO., SACRED HEART (1905) Attended by Our Lady of the Valley, La Grande.
Church: 340 S. 10th St., P.O. Box 473, 97883. Tel: 541-562-5486.

Catechesis/Religious Program—Tel: 541-562-5486. Kathy Goodman, D.R.E.; Sherry Mendoza, D.R.E. Students 16.

VALE, MALHEUR CO., ST. PATRICK (1946) Rev. Camillus Fernando (Sri Lanka).
Res.: 690 A St. W., P.O. Box J, 97918. Tel: 541-473-3906; Fax: 541-473-3906.
Catechesis/Religious Program—Tel: 541-473-3848. Susan Seals, D.R.E. Students 55.
Mission—St. Joseph Unity, Baker Co.

WASCO, MALHEUR CO., ST. MARY (1954) Rev. Augustine Okwuzu, S.M.M.M. (Nigeria).
Res.: 807 Barnett St., P.O. Box 14, 97065. Tel: 541-442-8560; Fax: 541-442-8569. Email: okwuzuan@yahoo.com.
Catechesis/Religious Program—Bob O'Dell, D.R.E.; Cindy Brown, Youth Min. Students 24.
Mission—St. John the Baptist Grass Valley, Sherman Co.

Military Services:
Rev.—
Colvin, Andrew, CHC, USN, 5527 N.W. Lause Way, Silverdale, WA 98383.

On Duty Outside the Diocese:
Revs.—
Hickie, J. Noel, Sacred Heart General Hospital, 1305 Willagillespie Rd., Eugene, 97401.
Kiely, Cornelius, Iglesia La Immaculada Concepcion, Puerto Lopez, Manabi, Ecuador.

Retired:
Revs.—
Albrecht, Louis Henry, 1002 Lave, La Grande, 97850. Tel: 541-963-7341
Bower, Lawrence C., 215 Woodward Blvd., Summerville, SC 29483. Tel: 843-815-1285
Cribbin, Austin J., 220 Newcastle Rd., Klamath Falls, 97601.
Dreisbach, Charles V., 2308 Newcastle, Klamath Falls, 97601. Tel: 541-882-6016
Fisher, A. J., 1200 W. Dimond #14105, Anchorage, AK 99515.
Homes, Dennis, Rainbow Retirement Home, 20-3rd St. N., Great Falls, MT 59401. Tel: 406-452-1994
Hopp, Raymond, 1800 N. 4th St. #28, Lakeview, 97630.
Jarboe, Raymond, P.O. Box 562, Adrian, MI 49221.
Jasper, John, 4300 Albany Dr., Apt. L132, San Jose, CA 95129.
Reeves, Joseph, 15612 N.W. Clubhouse Dr., Portland, 97729. Tel: 503-690-3643
Scanlan, Thomas R., 11055 S.W. Summerfield Dr., #7, Tigard, 97224.
Strzyz, Stanislaus
Van Sickler, Robert, 3911 S.E. Milwaukie, Portland, 97202. Tel: 541-206-6514
Weckerle, Leo F., 10979 S.W. Shad Rd., Terrebonne, 97760. Tel: 541-923-6828

INSTITUTIONS LOCATED IN THE DIOCESE

[A] GENERAL HOSPITALS

BAKER CITY. *St. Elizabeth Health Services, Inc.*, 3325 Pocahontas Rd., 97814. Tel: 541-523-6461 (Hospital); 541-523-4452 (Nursing Care); Fax: 541-523-8151. Email: leanneirsik@chiwest.com. Leanne Irsik, CEO. Bed Capacity 25; Nursing Home Beds 90; Patients Assisted Annually 9,848; Nursing Home 159; Staff 223.

BEND. *St. Charles Medical Center*, 2500 N.E. Neff Rd., 97701. Tel: 541-382-4321; Fax: 541-388-7723. Web: www.cascadehealthcare.org. Mr. James A. Diegel, Pres. & CEO; Alan Burke, Team Leader. Bed Capacity 261; Total Staff 2,395; Patients Assisted Annually 183,011.

HOOD RIVER. *Providence Hood River Memorial Hospital*, 811 13th St., 97031. Tel: 541-386-3911; Fax: 541-387-6462. Email: mark.thomas@providence.org. Web: www.providence.org. Ty W. Erickson, CEO. Total Staff 457; Bed Capacity 25; Patients Assisted Annually 160,000.

ONTARIO. *Holy Rosary Medical Center*, 351 S.W. Ninth St., 97914. Tel: 541-881-7000; Fax: 541-881-7184. Web: holyrosary-ontario.org. Mr. Mark Dalley, Pres. & CEO; Mr. Kenneth Hart, Bd. Chm.; Mr. Mark Bekkadahl, Vice Pres. Mission Integration. Bed Capacity 49; Total Staff 463; Patients Assisted Annually 73,189.

PENDLETON. *St. Anthony Hospital*, 1601 S.E. Court Ave., 97801. Tel: 541-276-5121; Fax: 541-278-3227. Email: vonnismonton@chiwest.com. Web: www.sahpendleton.org. Randall L. Mee, Pres. & CEO. Sisters of St. Francis of Philadelphia 3; Bed Capacity 49; Patients Assisted Annually 55,020; Staff 319.

[B] MONASTERIES AND RESIDENCES FOR PRIESTS AND BROTHERS

GILCHRIST. *Monastery of Annunciation Hermitage*, 146640 Hwy. 97, La Pine, 97739-9127. Tel: 541-433-2903; Fax: 207-433-2900. Email: w146640@hotmail.com. Rev. Arsenius.

[C] ST. VINCENT DE PAUL SOCIETY

BEND. *St. Vincent de Paul Society - Bend, St. Francis Conference*, P.O. Box 1011, 97709. Tel: 541-389-6643; Fax: 541-389-5093. Stan Brock, Pres. Bd. of Directors.
Bend Social Services Conference, 950 S.E. 3rd St., 97702. Tel: 541-389-6643; Fax: 541-389-5093. Email: stvincentbend@qwest.net.
St. Vincent de Paul - Klamath Falls, St. Pius X Conference

HERMISTON. *St. Vincent de Paul Society - Hermiston, Our Lady of Angels Conference*, 565 W. Hermiston Ave., 97838. Tel: 541-567-5812; Fax: 541-564-0933.

LA PINE. *St. Vincent de Paul Society - La Pine, Holy Redeemer Conference*, P.O. Box 1008, 97739. Tel: 541-536-1956; Fax: 541-536-6135. Email: arlene@qwestoffice.net. Corinne Martinez, Pres.

PRINEVILLE. *St. Vincent de Paul Society - Prineville, St. Joseph Conference*, P.O. Box 545, 97754. Tel: 541-447-7662; Fax: 541-447-9163. Marcella Edmonds, Pres.
De Paul's, 298 E. 1st St., 97754. Tel: 541-447-7570.
Re-Store, 940 N.E. Court St., 97754.

REDMOND. *St. Vincent de Paul Society - Redmond, St. Thomas Conference*, 1612 S.W. Veterans Way, 97756. 1616 S.W. Veterans Way, 97756. Tel: 541-923-5264; Fax: 541-923-5264. Stephanie Swee, Pres.

THE DALLES. *St. Vincent de Paul Society - The Dalles, St. Peter Conference*, 505 W. 9th St., 97058. Tel: 541-298-7837; Fax: 541-298-7940. Email: svdptd@gorge.net. Mike Kilkenny, Chm. Bd.

[D] MISCELLANEOUS

BEND. *Baker Diocese Investment and Loan Corporation*, P.O. Box 5999, 97708.
Bend Volunteer Corps, P.O. Box 682, 97709. Tel: 541-318-4636. Email: charlotte@bendvolunteercorps.org. Web: www.bendvolunteercorps.org. Charlotte Roe, Dir. Recruiting; Richard Coon, Exec. Dir.
Church Resource Institute, Inc, P.O. Box 5999, 97708. Tel: 541-388-4004; Fax: 541-388-2566.
The Health and Retirement Association of the Diocese of Baker, Oregon, 911 S.E. Armour St., P.O. Box 5999, 97708. Tel: 541-296-7979; Fax: 541-296-5835. Email: tunger@netcnct.net. Very Rev. Todd Unger, Plan Admin.
The Legacy of Faith Catholic Community Foundation of Oregon, P.O. Box 5999, 97708. Tel: 541-388-4004; Fax: 541-388-2566. John G. Schiemer, Exec. Dir.
Serra Club of the Diocese of Baker, P.O. Box 5999, 97708.

HOOD RIVER. *Dethman Manor*, 1205 Montello St., 97031. Tel: 541-386-5111; Fax: 541-387-6356.
Providence Brookside Manor, 1550 Brookside Dr., 97031. Tel: 541-387-6370; Fax: 541-387-8272.
Providence Down Manor, 1950 Sterling Pl., 97031. Tel: 541-386-5115; Fax: 541-386-2456.
Providence Hood River Memorial Hospital Foundation, 811 13th St., P.O. Box 149, 97031. Tel: 541-387-6474; Fax: 541-387-6462.

SUNRIVER. *Holy Trinity Community Outreach Care and Share*, 18160 Cottonwood Rd., PMB 763, 97707. Tel: 541-593-5990; Fax: 541-593-5991.

RELIGIOUS INSTITUTES OF MEN REPRESENTED IN THE DIOCESE

For further details refer to the corresponding bracketed number in the Religious Institutes of Men or Women section.

[0470]—*Apostles of Jesus*—A.J.
[0690]—*Jesuit Fathers and Brothers* (Oregon Prov.)—S.J.
[]—*Salesians of Don Bosco*—S.D.B.
[]—*Sons of Mary Mother of Mercy*—S.M.M.M.

RELIGIOUS INSTITUTES OF WOMEN REPRESENTED IN THE DIOCESE

[2470]—*Maryknoll Sisters of St. Dominic*—M.M.
[]—*Sisters of Providence, Mother Joseph Providence*
[1650]—*Sisters of St. Francis of Philadelphia*—O.S.F.
[1990]—*Sisters of the Holy Names of Jesus and Mary*—S.N.J.M.

NECROLOGY

† Crotty, Rev. Msgr. Matthew M., (Special Assignment)—Died Sept. 24, 2009

An asterisk (*) denotes an organization that has established tax-exempt status directly with the IRS and is not covered by the USCCB Group Ruling.

Archdiocese of Baltimore

(Archidioecesis Baltimorensis)

His Eminence

WILLIAM CARDINAL KEELER, D.D., J.C.D.

Retired Archbishop of Baltimore; ordained July 17, 1955; appointed Titular Bishop of Ulcinium and Auxiliary Bishop of Harrisburg July 24, 1979; ordained Bishop September 21, 1979; appointed Bishop of Harrisburg November 10, 1983; installed January 4, 1984; appointed Archbishop of Baltimore April 6, 1989; installed as Fourteenth Archbishop of Baltimore May 23, 1989; created Cardinal Priest November 26, 1994; retired July 12, 2007. *Office: 320 Cathedral St., Baltimore, MD 21201.* Tel: 410-547-5437.

Most Reverend

WILLIAM DONALD BORDERS, D.D.

Retired Archbishop of Baltimore; ordained May 18, 1940; appointed Bishop of Orlando May 2, 1968; consecrated June 14, 1968; appointed Archbishop of Baltimore March 25, 1974; installed June 26, 1974; retired April 6, 1989. *Office: 320 Cathedral St., Baltimore, MD 21201.* Tel: 410-547-5439.

Most Reverend

WILLIAM C. NEWMAN, D.D., V.G.

Retired Auxiliary Bishop of Baltimore; ordained May 29, 1954; appointed Auxiliary Bishop of Baltimore and Titular Bishop of Numluli May 25, 1984; installed Bishop July 2, 1984; retired August 28, 2003. *Office: 320 Cathedral St., Baltimore, MD 21201.* Tel: 410-547-5438. *Res.: 5300 N. Charles St., Baltimore, MD 21201.*

Most Reverend

EDWIN F. O'BRIEN, S.T.D., D.D.

Archbishop of Baltimore; ordained May 29, 1965; appointed Titular Bishop of Tizica and Auxiliary Bishop of New York February 6, 1996; consecrated March 25, 1996; appointed Coadjutor April 8, 1997; succeeded as Ordinary to the Military Services August 12, 1997; appointed Archbishop of Baltimore July 12, 2007; installed as 15th Archbishop of Baltimore October 1, 2007. *Office: 320 Cathedral St., Baltimore, MD 21201.* Tel: 410-547-5437.

Chancery Office: 320 Cathedral St., Baltimore, MD 21201. Tel: 410-547-5446; Fax: 410-727-8234.

Web: www.archbalt.org

Email: chancery@archbalt.org

Most Reverend

MITCHELL T. ROZANSKI

Auxiliary Bishop of Baltimore; ordained November 24, 1984; appointed Auxiliary Bishop of Baltimore and Titular Bishop of Walla Walla July 3, 2004; installed August 24, 2004. *Office: 320 Cathedral St., Baltimore, MD 21201.* Tel: 410-547-5438.

Most Reverend

DENIS J. MADDEN

Auxiliary Bishop of Baltimore; ordained April 1, 1967; appointed Auxiliary Bishop of Baltimore and Titular Bishop of Baia May 10, 2005; ordained August 24, 2005. *Office: 320 Cathedral St., Baltimore, MD 21201.* Tel: 410-547-5452.

Square Miles 4,801.

Established a Diocese November 6, 1789; Established an Archdiocese April 8, 1808.

Comprises the City of Baltimore and Allegany, Anne Arundel, Baltimore, Carroll, Frederick, Garrett, Harford, Howard and Washington Counties.

By a Decree of the Sacred Congregation of the Propaganda, July 19, 1858, approved by His Holiness, Pius IX, July 25, 1858, "Prerogative of Place" was conferred on the Archdiocese of Baltimore. By the explicit words of said decree of the Holy See, the Archbishop of Baltimore takes precedence over all Archbishops of the United States (not Cardinals) in Councils, gatherings and meetings of whatever kind of the Hierarchy (in concillis, coetibus et comitiis quibuscumque) regardless of the seniority of other Archbishops in promotion or ordination. Decree signed by Cardinal Barnabo, August 15, 1858.

For legal titles of parishes and archdiocesan institutions, consult the Chancery Office.

STATISTICAL OVERVIEW

Personnel	
Retired Cardinals	1
Archbishops	1
Retired Archbishops	1
Auxiliary Bishops	2
Retired Bishops	1
Priests: Diocesan Active in Diocese	197
Priests: Diocesan Active Outside Diocese	11
Priests: Retired, Sick or Absent	46
Number of Diocesan Priests	254
Religious Priests in Diocese	246
Total Priests in Diocese	500
Extern Priests in Diocese	52
Ordinations:	
Diocesan Priests	4
Transitional Deacons	2
Permanent Deacons	12
Permanent Deacons in Diocese	158
Total Brothers	69
Total Sisters	934
Parishes	
Parishes	153
With Resident Pastor:	
Resident Diocesan Priests	90
Resident Religious Priests	27
Without Resident Pastor:	
Administered by Priests	20
Administered by Deacons	5
Administered by Lay People	4
Completely Vacant	11
Missions	6
Professional Ministry Personnel:	
Brothers	1
Sisters	31
Lay Ministers	176
Welfare	
Catholic Hospitals	5
Total Assisted	1,665,874
Health Care Centers	4
Total Assisted	2,690
Homes for the Aged	26
Total Assisted	3,950
Residential Care of Children	9
Total Assisted	1,050
Day Care Centers	7
Total Assisted	2,220
Specialized Homes	5
Total Assisted	396
Special Centers for Social Services	56
Total Assisted	659,558
Residential Care of Disabled	1
Total Assisted	261
Other Institutions	1
Total Assisted	12,000
Educational	
Seminaries, Diocesan	2
Students from This Diocese	23
Students from Other Diocese	193
Diocesan Students in Other Seminaries	7
Total Seminarians	30
Colleges and Universities	4
Total Students	11,673
High Schools, Diocesan and Parish	8
Total Students	3,753
High Schools, Private	13
Total Students	7,641
Elementary Schools, Diocesan and Parish	53
Total Students	18,544
Elementary Schools, Private	7
Total Students	1,338
Non-residential Schools for the Disabled	1
Total Students	121
Catechesis/Religious Education:	
High School Students	3,199
Elementary Students	24,955
Total Students under Catholic Instruction	71,254
Teachers in the Diocese:	
Priests	34
Brothers	18
Sisters	79
Lay Teachers	3,487
Vital Statistics	
Receptions into the Church:	
Infant Baptism Totals	6,229
Adult Baptism Totals	483
Received into Full Communion	910
First Communions	6,099
Confirmations	5,529
Marriages:	
Catholic	958
Interfaith	554
Total Marriages	1,512
Deaths	4,510
Total Catholic Population	499,529
Total Population	3,093,068

Former Archbishops—Most Revs. JOHN CARROLL, D.D., cons. Aug. 15, 1790; Archbishop, April 8, 1808; died Dec. 3, 1815; LEONARD NEALE, D.D., cons. Coadjutor, Dec. 7, 1800; acceded to the Dec. 3, 1815; died June 18, 1817; AMBROSE MARECHAL, S.S., D.D., cons. Dec. 14, 1817; died Jan. 29, 1828; JAMES WHITFIELD, D.D., cons. May 25, 1828; died Oct. 19, 1834; SAMUEL ECCLESTON, S.S., D.D., cons. Sept. 14, 1834; died April 22, 1851; FRANCIS PATRICK KENRICK, D.D., cons. June 6, 1830; Coadjutor Bishop of Philadelphia; promoted to Aug. 19, 1851; died July 8, 1863; MARTIN JOHN SPALDING, D.D., cons. Sept. 10, 1848; Coadjutor Bishop of Louisville; promoted to May 6, 1864; died Feb. 7, 1872; JAMES ROOSEVELT BAYLEY, D.D., cons. Oct. 30, 1853; Bishop of Newark; promoted to July 30, 1872; died Oct. 3, 1877; His Eminence JAMES CARDINAL GIBBONS, D.D., cons. Vicar Apostolic of North Carolina, Aug. 16, 1868; transferred to See of Richmond, July 30, 1872; promoted to See of Baltimore, Oct. 3, 1877; created Cardinal Priest of S. Maria in Trastevere, June 7, 1886; died March 24, 1921; Most Revs. MICHAEL J. CURLEY, D.D., cons. Bishop of St. Augustine, June 30, 1914; promoted to Aug. 10, 1921; died May 16, 1947; FRANCIS P. KEOUGH, D.D., cons. Bishop of Providence, May 22, 1934; promoted to Nov. 29, 1947; died Dec. 8, 1961; LAWRENCE CARDINAL SHEHAN, cons. Auxiliary Bishop of Baltimore, Dec. 12, 1945; transferred to Diocese of Bridgeport, Aug. 25, 1953; appt. Coadjutor Archbishop of Baltimore, July 10, 1961; acceded to the Dec. 8, 1961; created Cardinal Priest of S. Clemente, Feb. 22, 1965; retired March 25, 1974; died Aug. 26, 1984; WILLIAM DONALD BORDERS, D.D. (Retired), appt. Bishop of Orlando, May 2, 1968; cons. June 14, 1968; promoted to March 25, 1974; installed June 26, 1974; retired April 6, 1989; His Eminence WILLIAM CARDINAL KEELER, ord. July 17, 1955; appt. Titular Bishop of Ulcinium and Auxiliary Bishop of Harrisburg July 24, 1979; ord. Bishop

Sept. 21, 1979; appt. Bishop of Harrisburg Nov. 10, 1983; installed Jan. 4, 1984; appt. Archbishop of Baltimore April 6, 1989; installed as Fourteenth Archbishop of Baltimore May 23, 1989; created Cardinal Priest Nov. 26, 1994; retired July 12, 2007.

Vicars General—Most Revs. WILLIAM C. NEWMAN, D.D., V.G. (Retired); MITCHELL T. ROZANSKI, D.D., V.G.; DENIS J. MADDEN, D.D., V.G.; Rev. Msgr. RICHARD WOY, V.G., Moderator of the Curia.

Office of the Cardinal Archbishop Emeritus—In Res.: 320 Cathedral St., Baltimore, 21201. Tel: 410-547-5440.

Office of the Former Archbishop—Most Rev. WILLIAM DONALD BORDERS (Retired), 320 Cathedral St., Baltimore, 21201. Tel: 410-547-5439.

Chancery Office—320 Cathedral St., Baltimore, 21201. Tel: 410-547-5446; Fax: 410-727-8234. Office Hours: Mon.-Fri. 9-5; Closed holidays.

Chancellor—Dr. DIANE L. BARR, J.C., J.C.D. Tel: 410-547-5446.

Canonical Adviser, Office of—Canonical & Theological Consultants to the Archbishop: Rev. Msgr. RONNY JENKINS, J.C.D.; Rev. JAMES J. CONN, S.J. Tel: 410-547-5435.

Consultors—Most Revs. MITCHELL T. ROZANSKI, D.D., V.G.; DENIS J. MADDEN, D.D., V.G.; Rev. Msgrs. PAUL G. COOK; ROBERT A. ARMSTRONG; JAMES O. MCGOVERN, V.F. (Retired); G. MICHAEL SCHLEUPNER, V.F.; ARTHUR F. VALENZANO; RICHARD W. WOY; RICHARD E. CRAMBLITT, V.F.; JAMES W. HANNON; Rev. DONALD GRZYMSKI, O.F.M.Conv.

Neumann Vicar, Office of the—Most Rev. MITCHELL T. ROZANSKI, D.D., V.G., Eastern Vicar. Tel: 410-547-5438. Email: mrozanski@archbalt.org; Deacons PAUL MANN, Coord. Planning & Council Svcs., 320 Cathedral St., Baltimore, 21201. Tel: 410-547-5438; Fax: 410-727-5432. Email: pmann@archbalt.org; CHARLES H. HIEBLER JR., Coord. Planning & Council Svcs. Tel: 410-547-5456. Email: chiebler@archbalt.org.

Interdiocesan Tribunal of Appeals of the Province of Baltimore—320 Cathedral St., Baltimore, 21201. Tel: 410-547-5512; Fax: 410-576-6932. Email: interdiocesan.tribunal@archbalt.org.

Judicial Vicar—Rev. WILLIAM GRAHAM, O.F.M.Cap., J.C.L.; Rev. Msgr. THOMAS SHREVE, Adjutant Judicial Vicar & Judge.

Metropolitan Tribunal—320 Cathedral St., Baltimore, 21201. Tel: 410-547-5533; Fax: 410-576-6932.

Judicial Vicar—Rev. GILBERT J. SEITZ, J.C.L.

Adjutant Judicial Vicar—Rev. JOHN B. WARD, J.C.L., J.D. Email: wcollins@archbalt.org.

Judge—Rev. MICHAEL J. CARRION.

Defenders of the Bond—Rev. Msgr. ROBERT A. ARMSTRONG; Rev. ALBAN HARMON, C.P., J.C.L.

Promoter of Justice—VACANT.

Advocates—Mr. STEPHEN R. BEARD; Sisters KATHERINE BELL, R.S.M.; JUDITH CIANFROGNA, S.S.J.; Rev. JOSEPH E. COTE; Sisters ANGELA DEFONTES, O.S.F.; SUSAN ENGEL, M.H.S.H.; Deacon NICHOLAS FEURER; Ms. MARGARET GAUGHAN; Rev. Msgrs. JAMES W. HANNON; ROBERT HARTNETT; Deacon JOHN L. MANLEY; Mrs. TERESA MARTH; Deacon LAWRENCE G. MATHENY; Rev. Msgr. EDWARD M. MILLER; Deacon HUGH H. MILLS JR.; Mr. JOE MULICK; Deacon WILLIAM NAIRN; Rev. G. EUGENE NICKOL; Ms. CAROLYN NOLAN; Mr. GERARD NOVAK; Rev. DONALD J. PARSON; Ms. CAMILLA RAWE; Deacon EDWARD SULLIVAN.

Notaries—Deacon NEIL A. CRISPO; Mrs. M. TERESA EWEN; Mrs. PATRICIA WALLS.

Neumann Vicar, Office of the—Most Rev. DENIS J. MADDEN, D.D., V.G.; Mr. ALBERT SCHARBACH, Pastoral Assoc. to the Neumann Vicar. Tel: 410-547-5488; Fax: 410-727-5432; KATHERINE SWANSON, Coord. Planning & Council Svcs., 320 Cathedral St., Baltimore, 21201. Tel: 410-547-5452; Fax: 410-727-5432.

Archdiocesan Offices and Directors

African American Ministries, Archdiocesan Office of—THERESE WILSON FAVORS, Dir., 320 Cathedral St., Baltimore, 21201. Tel: 410-625-8472; Fax: 410-727-5432. Email: tfavors@archbalt.org.

Archdiocesan Directory—VACANT, Mailing Address: P.O. Box 777, Baltimore, 21203. Tel: 443-524-3150 Official directory of the Archdiocese of Baltimore. Published annually by The Catholic Review. $45 per copy.

Archdiocesan Pastoral Council— (See Pastoral Council Archdiocesan)

Archives-Archivist—TRICIA PYNE, Ph.D., 5400 Roland Ave., Baltimore, 21210. Tel: 410-864-3691 (By appointment); Fax: 410-864-3690. Email: tpyne@stmarys.edu. Web: stmarys.edu/archives.

Boy Scouts— (See Catholic Youth Activities)

Building Commission—NOLAN MCCOY, Contact Person. Tel: 410-547-5335.

Catholic Campaign For Human Development, Archdiocese of Baltimore, Inc.—Rev. Msgr. WILLIAM F. BURKE, Dir., 320 Cathedral St., Baltimore, 21201. Tel: 410-235-5136; 410-547-5446.

The Cathedral Foundation, Inc.—Most Rev. EDWIN F. O'BRIEN, S.T.D., D.D., Pres. & Publisher; Mr. CHRISTOPHER GUNTY, Assoc. Publisher & Editor, Mailing Address: P.O. Box 777, Baltimore, 21203. Tel: 443-524-3150; Fax: 443-524-3155 Publishers of The Catholic Review, Official Archdiocesan Directory, Catholic International and Cathedral Foundation Press.

Catholic Charities, Inc.—Mr. WILLIAM J. MCCARTHY JR., Exec. Dir., 320 Cathedral St., Baltimore, 21201. Tel: 410-547-5490. Web: www.cc-md.org.

Catholic Education Ministries, Department of—VACANT, 320 Cathedral St., Baltimore, 21201. Tel: 410-547-5393; Fax: 410-547-5566.

"The Catholic Review"—Most Rev. EDWIN F. O'BRIEN, S.T.D., D.D., Publisher; Mr. CHRISTOPHER GUNTY, Assoc. Publisher & Editor; PAUL MCMULLEN, Mng. Editor, Mailing Address: P.O. Box 777, Baltimore, 21203. Tel: 443-263-0259. Web: www.catholicreview.org. Newspaper of the Archdiocese of Baltimore. Established 1913. Published every Thursday by the Cathedral Foundation, Inc.

Catholic Schools, Division of—VACANT, Supt., Catholic Center, 320 Cathedral St., Baltimore, 21201. Tel: 410-547-5391; Fax: 410-547-5566. Email: schools@archbalt.org.

Clergy Personnel, Division of—Rev. Msgr. JAY F. O'CONNOR, Div. Dir. Tel: 410-547-5558. Email: joconnor@archbalt.org. Administrative Assistants: Mrs. CINDY ORR. Tel: 410-547-5550. Email: corr@archbalt.org; Mrs. CAROL PURWIN. Tel: 410-547-5427. Email: cpurwin@archbalt.org; 320 Cathedral St., Rm. 620, Baltimore, 21201.

Commission for Ecumenical and Interreligious Affairs—Rev. Msgr. RICHARD H. TILLMAN, 10431 Twin Rivers Rd., Columbia, 21044. Tel: 410-964-1425; Fax: 410-730-9253.

Communications Office—SEAN CAIN, Dir. Communications, 320 Cathedral St., Baltimore, 21201. Tel: 410-547-5379; Fax: 410-625-8480. Email: scain@archbalt.org.

Deacon Personnel Board—Deacons RON THOMPSON, Asst. Dir.; DEAN LOPATA; JAMES A. RYAN; LAWRENCE "TEX" TEIXEIRA; FRED MAUSER; MARTIN WOLF; RAY H. BRITT; PAUL MANN; Mrs. DARLENE ZEILER; Mrs. JANICE SMITH. Email: deacons@archbalt.org.

Development, Department of—PATRICK MADDEN, Exec. Dir.; GEORGE LEITNER, Dir. Devel.; BRENT DAILEY, Dir. Devel.; JAMES EDWARDS, Dir. Catholic Family Foundation; CESSY TORSELLA, Exec. Asst.; JENNIFER SMITH, Dir. Advancement Svcs.; MELANIE TORSELLA, Research Mgr.; JENNIFER HAMMOND, Grants Admin.; MATTHEW ANTHONY, Devel. Assoc. Partners In Excellence; CHARLENE MC CONNELL, Devel. Assoc.; BETH BOWIE, Devel. Assoc.; LYNNETTE GUSLEY, Devel. Assoc.

Employee Benefits, Division of—PETRA PHELPS, Dir., 320 Cathedral St., Baltimore, 21201. Tel: 410-547-5563; Fax: 410-783-5993. Email: pphelps@archbalt.org.

Evangelization and Catechesis, Division of—Ms. CAROL A. AUGUSTINE, Dir., 320 Cathedral St., Baltimore, 21201. Tel: 410-547-5403; Fax: 410-347-7896. Email: caugustine@archbalt.org.

Financial Administration, Board of—Most Rev. EDWIN F. O'BRIEN, S.T.D., D.D., Chm.; JOSEPH A. SPADARO, CPA, Exec. Dir. Mgmt. Svcs. & CFO, 320 Cathedral St., Baltimore, 21201. Tel: 410-547-5587.

Fiscal Services, Division of—JOHN M. MATERA, CPA, Controller, 320 Cathedral St., Baltimore, 21201. Tel: 410-547-5313; Fax: 410-332-8233. Email: fiscal@archbalt.org.

Gay and Lesbian Ministries, Office of—Deacon PAUL WEBER, Dir., 320 Cathedral St., Baltimore, 21201. Tel: 410-547-5486.

Hispanic Ministries, Office of—MARIA T.P. JOHNSON, Dir., 320 Cathedral St., Baltimore, 21201. Tel: 410-547-5363; Fax: 410-625-8485. Email: mtpjohnson@archbalt.org.

Holy Childhood Association—Deacon RODRIGUE MORTEL, M.D., 320 Cathedral St., Baltimore, 21201. Tel: 410-625-8450. Email: rmortel@archbalt.org.

Human Resource Services, Division of—MICHELLY B. MERRICK, SPHR, Dir., 320 Cathedral St., Baltimore, 21201. Tel: 410-547-5448; Fax: 410-234-2953. Email: mmerrick@archbalt.org.

Human Resources Committee—LEONARD STROM, Exec. Dir. Tel: 410-547-5556.

Information Technology, Division of—WILLIAM A. GLOVER, Dir., 320 Cathedral St., Baltimore, 21201. Tel: 410-547-5539; Fax: 410-332-8233. Email: it@archbalt.org.

Insurance Committee—WILLIAM FRANEY, Chm.; PETRA PHELPS, Sec., 320 Cathedral St., Baltimore, 21201. Tel: 410-547-5317; Fax: 410-783-5993. Email: pphelps@archbalt.org.

Lay Employees Retirement Board—JAYNE MCGEEHAN, Chm.; PETRA PHELPS, Sec., 320 Cathedral St., Baltimore, 21201. Tel: 410-547-5317; Fax: 410-783-5993. Email: pphelps@archbalt.org.

League of the Little Flower—Ms. CAROL A. AUGUSTINE, Dir., 320 Cathedral St., Baltimore, 21201. Tel: 410-547-5361. Email: llf@archbalt.org.

Management Services, Department of—JOSEPH A. SPADARO, CPA, Exec. Dir. & CFO, 320 Cathedral St., Baltimore, 21201. Tel: 410-547-5587; Fax: 410-332-8233. Email: mgmtserv@archbalt.org.

Maryland Catholic Conference—Mrs. MARY ELLEN RUSSELL, Exec. Dir., 10 Francis St., Annapolis, 21401. Tel: 410-269-1155 (Bal.); 301-261-1979 (Wash.); Fax: 410-269-1790. Email: info@mdcathcon.org. Web: www.mdcathcon.org.

Ministry Formation and Development, Division of—RUTH A. PULS, Dir. Email: rpuls@archbalt.org; ARMANDO GARCIA, Coord. Hispanic Formation Programs; Mrs. JULIE KLINE-RYBEZNSKI, Coord. Church Leadership Institute, 320 Cathedral St., Baltimore, 21201. Tel: 410-547-5470; Fax: 410-234-2953.

Missions Office—Most Rev. EDWIN F. O'BRIEN, S.T.D., D.D., Gen. Dir.; Deacon RODRIGUE MORTEL, M.D., Dir., 320 Cathedral St., Baltimore, 21201. Tel: 410-547-5498; Fax: 410-625-8486. Email: rmortel@archbalt.org.

Moderator of the Curia—Rev. Msgr. RICHARD WOY, V.G., 320 Cathedral St., Baltimore, 21201. Tel: 410-547-5591. Email: rwoy@archbalt.org.

New Cathedral Cemetery—4300 Old Frederick Rd., Baltimore, 21229. Tel: 410-566-7770; Fax: 410-566-0709.

Office of Diaconate—Rev. Msgr. JAY F. O'CONNOR, Dir. Tel: 410-547-5558. Administrative Assistants: Mrs. CINDY ORR; Mrs. CAROL PURWIN, 320 Cathedral St., Rm. 620, Baltimore, 21201. Tel: 410-547-5427. Email: deacons@archbalt.org.

Office of Pastoral Service for Senior and Retired Clergy—Rev. SALVATORE LIVISNI, Dir., 320 Cathedral St., Baltimore, 21201. Tel: 410-547-5382.

Pastoral Council, Archdiocesan—320 Cathedral St., Baltimore, 21201. Tel: 410-547-5435.

Permanent Deacon Formation Program—Rev. Msgr. JAY F. O'CONNOR, Dir.

Presbyteral Council—Rev. Msgrs. JAMES BARKER, Vice Chm.; DAMIEN G. NALEPA, V.F.; THOMAS L. PHILLIPS; Revs. M. SHAWN MAHON; JOSEPH F. BARR; Rev. Msgr. EDWARD M. MILLER; Rev. PETER A. LYONS, T.O.R.; Rev. Msgr. ROBERT L. HARTNETT; Revs. JAMES P. KIESEL; CHRISTOPHER WHATLEY; Rev. Msgr. MARTIN EUGENE FEILD; Revs. KEVIN FARMER; SYLVESTER PETERKA, C.M.; DONALD J. PARSON; RICHARD HILGARTNER; GILBERT J. SEITZ, J.C.L.; Rev. Msgr. F. DENNIS TINDER; Revs. JAMES A. CASCIOTTI, S.J.; KEVIN MILTON, C.Ss.R.; DONALD GRZYMSKI, O.F.M.Conv.; Rev. Msgrs. KEVIN T. SCHENNING; J. BRUCE JARBOE; Rev. ERIK A. ARNOLD.

Ex Officio—Most Revs. MITCHELL T. ROZANSKI, D.D., V.G.; DENIS J. MADDEN, D.D., V.G Consultors: Rev. Msgrs. ROBERT A. ARMSTRONG; RICHARD W. WOY; PAUL G. COOK; JAMES O. MCGOVERN, V.F (Retired); G. MICHAEL SCHLEUPNER, V.F.; ARTHUR F. VALENZANO; RICHARD E. CRAMBLITT, V.F.; Rev. JOHN DIETZENBACH; Rev. Msgr. JAMES W. HANNON; Rev. DONALD GRZYMSKI, O.F.M.Conv.

Priest Personnel Board—Rev. Msgrs. LLOYD AIKEN; A. THOMAS BAUMGARTNER (Retired); RICHARD H. TILLMAN; Revs. ANDREW AARON; RICHARD T. LAWRENCE, Vice Chm.; EDWARD KENNY; JOHN A. WILLIAMSON; Rev. Msgrs. KEVIN T. SCHENNING; EDWARD M. MILLER; Revs. MICHAEL DEASCANIS; JEFFREY DUASES; CHRISTOPHER P. MOORE.

Prison Ministry for the Archdiocese of Baltimore—Sr. DOLORES CHEPIGA, S.S.J., Coord. Prison Outreach, St. Vincent de Paul. Tel: 443-263-1931.

Real Estate and Facilities Management, Division of—NOLAN MCCOY, Dir. Facilities & Real Estate; HUGH ANDES, Project Mgr.; MATTHEW REGAN, Capital Project Mgr.; DOUG JOHNSON, Capital Project Mgr.; MYRTLE BUCHANAN, Office Mgr.; GEORGE KEITZ, Bldg. Mgr.; DAVE OWENS, Capital Projects Mgr.; ROBERT CLANCY, Project Mgr., 320 Cathedral St., Baltimore, 21201. Tel: 410-547-5366; Fax: 410-837-2932.

St. Vincent de Paul Society— Baltimore Council: Most Rev. EDWIN F. O'BRIEN, S.T.D., D.D., Honorary Pres.; Rev. JOHN J. LOMBARDI, Spiritual Advisor; KEVIN G. MEYD, Pres.; JOHN J. SCHIAVONE, Exec. Dir., 2305 N. Charles St., Baltimore, 21218. Tel: 410-547-5377; Fax: 410-625-8483. Web: www.vincentbaltimore.org.

Senior Priests' Retirement Board—Rev. Msgr. JAMES O. MCGOVERN, V.F., Chm. (Retired); PETRA PHELPS, Sec.

Technology Advisory Committee—JOHN MCFADDEN, Chm.

Vicar for African-American Affairs—Rev. Msgr. DAMIEN G. NALEPA, V.F.

Vicar for Hispanic Affairs—Most Rev. MITCHELL T. ROZANSKI, D.D., V.G.

Vicar for Religious—VACANT.

Office of Child and Youth Protection—ALISON J. D'ALESSANDRO, Dir. Tel: 410-547-5348. Email: adalessandro@archbalt.org.

Vocation Office—Rev. GERARD C. FRANCIK, Dir. Tel: 410-547-5426; Fax: 410-234-2953. Email: vocations@archbalt.org.

Youth and Young Adult Ministry, Division of—VACANT, Dir., 320 Cathedral St., Baltimore, 21201. Tel: 410-547-5372; Fax: 410-625-8481. Email: mpacione@archbalt.org.

Associated Catholic Charities, Inc.

Catholic Charities— Associated Catholic Charities, Inc. (Catholic Charities) is Maryland's leading private provider of human services. The agency welcomes and serves people in need, regardless of faith, race or other circumstances. Through more than 80 programs, Catholic Charities improves the lives of children and families, seniors, the disadvantaged, and people with developmental disabilities. Headquartered in Baltimore, the agency operates in the city and nine Maryland counties under the auspices of the Roman Catholic Archdiocese of Baltimore. *Catholic Charities, 320 Cathedral St., Baltimore, 21201.* Tel: 410-547-5490. Email: info@catholiccharities-md.org. Web: www.catholiccharities-md.org. For detailed information on specific Catholic Charities and its programs, please refer to the Institution Section.

Executive Director—Mr. WILLIAM J. MCCARTHY JR., Catholic Charities, 320 Cathedral St., 3rd Fl., Baltimore, 21201-4493. Tel: 410-547-5495; Fax: 410-752-2873.

CLERGY, PARISHES, MISSIONS AND PAROCHIAL SCHOOLS

METROPOLITAN BALTIMORE

(BALTIMORE CITY AND BALTIMORE COUNTY)

1—CATHEDRAL OF MARY OUR QUEEN (1954) [CEM] Rev. Msgrs. J. Bruce Jarboe, Rector; Robert A. Armstrong, Rector Emeritus; Rev. Silvester T. Kim; Deacons Charles Hiebler; Ray Moreau. In Res., Most Rev. Mitchell T. Rozanski; Revs. Joseph F. Breighner; Gerard C. Francik; Rev. Msgr. Robert Jaskot.
Res.: 5200 N. Charles St., 21210-2098. Tel: 410-464-4000; Fax: 410-464-4060. Web: www.cathedralofmary.org.
School—(Grades K-8), 111 Amberly Way, 21210-2098. Tel: 410-464-4100; Fax: 410-464-4137. Sr. Josephann Wagoner, S.S.N.D., Prin. Lay Teachers 30; Students 423.
Catechesis/Religious Program—5200 N. Charles St., 21210. Tel: 410-464-4004. Dr. Jack Buchner, D.R.E. Students 210.
Youth & Family Life—Tel: 410-464-4012. Ms. Meghan Cosgrove, Dir.
Office of Music Ministry—Tel: 410-464-4020. Daniel Sansone.

2—ST. AGNES (Catonsville) (1852) [CEM] Rev. Timothy J. Fell, Temporary Admin.; Deacon John Ames.
Res.: 5422 Old Frederick Rd., 21229. Tel: 410-744-2900; Fax: 410-744-8304. Email: stagnes@archbalt.org. Web: www.stagnescatholicchurch.org.
School—(Grades PreK-8), 603 St. Agnes Ln., 21229. Tel: 410-747-4070; Fax: 410-747-0138. Ms. Susan Banks, Prin. Lay Teachers 21; Religious 1; Students 339.
Catechesis/Religious Program—Amanda Barrick, D.R.E. Students 185.

3—ST. ALPHONSUS, SHRINE OF (1845), (Lithuanian), Rev. Msgr. Arthur Bastress. In Res., Rev. William F. Spacek, Univ. of Maryland Hospital Chap.; Deacon Hugh H. Mills Jr., Business Mgr.
Res.: 114 W. Saratoga St., 21201. Tel: 410-685-6090; Fax: 410-244-1670. Email: alphonsus@verizon.net. Web: www.stalphonsusbalt.org.

4—ST. AMBROSE (1907), (African American), Rev. Paul Zaborowski, O.F.M.Cap.; Deacons Seigfried Presberry; Steven Rubio. In Res., Revs. Roman Kozacheson, O.F.M.Cap; Mark Carter, O.F.M.Cap.; Bill Graham, O.F.M.Cap.; Roger White, O.F.M.Cap.; Bro. Mark Pattock, O.F.M.Cap.
Res.: 4502 Park Heights Ave., 21215. Tel: 410-367-9918; Fax: 410-542-6056. Email: pastor@stambrose.org. Web: www.stambrose.org.
School—(Grades K-8), 4506 Park Heights Ave., 21215. Tel: 410-664-2373; Fax: 410-664-0857. Email: principal@stambrose.org. Pamela Sanders, Prin. Lay Teachers 24; Students 187.
Catechesis/Religious Program—Mrs. Annett Bruce, D.R.E. Students 50.
Outreach Center—, (St. Vincent de Paul Society), 3445 Park Heights Ave., 21215. Tel: 410-225-0870. Ms. Laura Spada, Dir.

5—ST. ANDREW, Closed. 1974. Parish records available at the Chancery. Tel: 410-547-5446.

6—ST. ANN (1873), (African American), Twinned with St. Wenceslaus, Baltimore. Rev. Peter A. Lyons, T.O.R.; Deacon J. Edward Bee; Sr. Jeanne Barasha, S.S.N.D., Pastoral Admin.
Res.: 528 E. 22nd St., 21218. Tel: 410-235-8169; Fax: 410-235-8253.
Catechesis/Religious Program—Students 35.

7—ANNUNCIATION (1968) Rev. Thomas E. Walsh, O.F.M.Conv.; Sr. Susan Engel, M.H.S.H., Pastoral Assoc.
Res.: 5212 McCormick Ave., 21206. Tel: 410-866-4020; Fax: 410-866-2754. Email: cota.parish@verizon.net.
Catechesis/Religious Program—Tel: 410-866-4706. Mrs. Kathy Brotzman, C.R.E. Students 63.

8—ST. ANTHONY OF PADUA (1884), Twinned with Most Precious Blood. Rev. Anthony Abiamiri. Email: akabiamiri@comcast.net; Deacons Joseph C. Krysiak, Temporary Admin.; Joseph Schultz.
Res.: 4414 Frankford Ave., 21206. Tel: 410-488-0400; Fax: 410-488-0032. Email: sapmpb@comcast.net. Web: www.stampb.org.
Catechesis/Religious Program—Tel: 410-488-0400; Fax: 410-488-0032. Students 22.

9—ASCENSION (Halethorpe) (1913) Rev. John A. Williamson; Mary Beth Barnes, Pastoral Assoc.; Deacon Thomas J. Yannuzzi.
Res.: 4603 Poplar Ave., 21227. Tel: 410-242-2292; Fax: 410-242-6807. Email: ascebalt@archbalt.org. Web: www.ascensionbaltimore.org.
School—(Grades PreK-8), 4601 Maple Ave., 21227. Tel: 410-242-2020; Fax: 410-242-2384. Web: www.ascension-school.org. Mrs. Virginia Bahr, Prin. Lay Teachers 15; Students 180.
Catechesis/Religious Program—Mrs. Marie Murphy, D.R.E. Students 105.

10—ST. ATHANASIUS (1891) Rev. Robert A. DiMattei Jr.; Deacon Michael Dodge.
Res.: 4708 Prudence St., Curtis Bay, 21226. Tel: 410-355-5740; Fax: 410-355-8122. Web: www.athanasius.org.
Catechesis/Religious Program—Tel: 410-355-2540. Mary Beth Barnes, D.R.E. Students 70.

11—ST. AUGUSTINE (Elkridge) (1844) [CEM] Rev. Gerard J. Bowen.
Res.: 5976 Old Washington Rd., Elkridge, 21075. Tel: 410-796-1520; Fax: 410-796-8172. Web: www.staugustinechurch.org.
School—(Grades PreK-8), 5990 Old Washington Rd., Elkridge, 21075. Tel: 410-796-3040; Fax: 410-579-1165. Web: www.staug-md.org. Mrs. Patricia Schratz, Prin. School Sisters of Notre Dame 2; Lay Teachers 9; Students 262.
Catechesis/Religious Program—Tel: 410-796-8150. Cathy Carlin, C.R.E.; Mary Jane Thomas, Dir. Adult Faith Formation; Marty Link, Coord. Youth Min. Students 455.

12—ST. BARNABAS, Closed. 1931. Parish records available at St. Pius V Church. Tel: 410-523-1930.

13—BASILICA OF THE NATIONAL SHRINE OF THE ASSUMPTION OF THE BLESSED VIRGIN MARY (1806), (Co-Cathedral). Corporate Title: The Trustees of the Catholic Cathedral Church of Baltimore (The Basilica); Basilica of the Assumption Historic Trust, Inc. Established for the Preservation of the Basilica as a National Landmark of American Architecture. Rev. Jeffrey S. Dauses, Rector. In Res., Rev. Adam Parker.
The Archbishop's Residence—408 N. Charles St., 21201. Tel: 410-727-3564; Fax: 410-539-0407. Web: www.baltimorebasilica.org. Most Rev. Edwin F. O'Brien.
Parish Office—Tel: 410-727-3565; Fax: 410-539-0407.

14—ST. BENEDICT (1893) Rt. Rev. Paschal A. Morlino, O.S.B.; Deacon Edward Whitesell; Sr. Catherine Fitzgerald, D.C., Pastoral Assoc.; Mrs. Maggie Barrick, Pastoral Coord. In Res., Rev. David Ho, O.S.B.
Res.: 2612 Wilkens Ave., 21223. Tel: 410-947-4988; Fax: 410-947-6009. Email: pamorlino@aol.com. Web: www.stbenedict.org.
Catechesis/Religious Program—Theresa Lingenfelter, D.R.E.; Mr. Kenneth Podowski, Youth Min. Students 38.

15—ST. BERNARD, (Korean), Closed. For parish records prior to 1989 contact the chancery office. For parish records past 1989 contact Holy Korean Martyrs, Baltimore.

16—ST. BERNARDINE (1928), (African American), Rev. Msgr. Edward M. Miller; Deacons Wardell Barksdale; Philip W. Harcum, (Retired); Natalie Austin, Parish Community Outreach.
Res.: 3812 Edmondson Ave., 21229. Tel: 410-362-8664; Fax: 410-945-0459. Email: stbernardine@archbalt.org. Web: www.stbernardinechurch.org.
School—(Grades K-8), 3601 Old Frederick Rd., 21229. Tel: 410-624-5088; Fax: 410-947-5439. Email: admin@stbernardineschool.org. Web: stbernardineschool.org. Dr. Antoinette Lyles, Prin. Aides 4; Lay Teachers 16; Students 215.
Catechesis/Religious Program—618 Mt. Holly St., 21229. Tel: 410-362-8978. Email: bwhite@stbernardineschool.org. Beverly White, D.R.E. Students 122.

17—BLESSED SACRAMENT CHURCH (1911) Rev. P. Edward Kenny Jr.; Deacon Paul D. Shelton; Sr. Marie Mack, S.S.N.D., Pastoral Admin.
Res.: 4103 Old York Rd., 21218-1237. Tel: 410-323-0424; Fax: 410-323-4478. Email: blesssac@aol.com.
Catechesis/Religious Program—Sr. Marie Mack, S.S.N.D., D.R.E. Students 7.

18—ST. BRIGID (1854) Rev. Joseph G. Bochenek; Deacon Paul T. Mann; Bette Brocato, Pastoral Assoc.
Res.: 900 S. East Ave., 21224. Tel: 410-563-1717; Fax: 410-563-1776. Email: sbrigid@archbalt.org. Web: www.saintbrigid-canton.com.
Catechesis/Religious Program—Tel: 410-558-3125. Jo Ellen Shorb, C.R.E., Youth Min. Students 50.

19—ST. CASIMIR (1902) Rev. Ross Syracuse, O.F.M.Conv.; Bernadette Vece, Pastoral Assoc. In Res., Revs. Timothy Kulbicki, O.F.M.Conv.; Romuald Meogrossi, O.F.M.Conv.
Res.: 2736 O'Donnell St., 21224. Tel: 410-276-1981; Fax: 410-732-7436. Email: st.casimir@verizon.net. Web: www.stcasimir.org.
School—*St. Casimir Catholic School*, (Grades PreK-8), 1035 S. Kenwood Ave., 21224. Tel: 410-342-2681; Fax: 410-342-5715. Email: school@stcasimirschool.us. Web: www.stcasimirschool.us. Melanie Conley, Prin. See separate listing.
Catholic Community at Relay— (1972) 5025 Cedar Ave., 21227. Tel: 410-247-4033; Fax: 410-247-2557. Email: catholic.relay@verizon.net. Peg Mooney, Admin.; Gary Ribar, Coord. Total Staff 2.

20—ST. CECILIA (1902), Twinned with Immaculate Conception, Baltimore. Rev. Sylvester Peterka, C.M.; Bro. William Stover, C.M., Pastoral Assoc. In Res., Rev. Abel Agbulu.
Res.: 3300 Clifton Ave., 21216. Tel: 410-624-3600; Fax: 410-945-0157. Email: ourchurches@verizon.net.
Catechesis/Religious Program—Joseph Parham Sr., D.R.E. Students 39.

21—ST. CHARLES BORROMEO (Pikesville) (1849) [CEM] Rev. Raymond Chase; Christopher Welsh, Pastoral Assoc.
Res.: 101 Church Ln., 21208. Tel: 410-486-5400; Fax: 410-486-5421. Email: charlesst@comcast.net. Web: www.ourstcharles.org.
Catechesis/Religious Program—Elizabeth Schmedes, Youth Min. Students 92.

22—CHRIST THE KING (Dundalk) (1957) Closed. For inquiries for parish records please see St. Rita, Baltimore.

23—CHURCH OF THE IMMACULATE CONCEPTION (Towson) (1883) [CEM] Rev. Msgrs. F. Dennis Tinder; Edward J. Lynch, Pastor Emeritus (Retired); Revs. Michael Foppiano; Bert Akers, S.J. In Res., Rev. T. Austin Murphy Jr.
Res.: 200 Ware Ave., Towson, 21204. Tel: 410-427-4700; Fax: 410-427-4795. Email: info@theimmaculate.org. Web: www.immaculateconception.net.
School—(Grades PreK-8), 112 Ware Ave., Towson, 21204. Tel: 410-427-4800; Fax: 410-427-4895. Mrs. Madeline Meaney, Prin.
Catechesis/Religious Program—*School of Religion* Glenda Sorteberg, Dir. Students 140.

24—ST. CLARE (Essex) (1956) Rev. C. Lou Martin.
Res.: 714 Myrth Ave., 21221-4898. Tel: 410-687-6011; Fax: 410-687-3054. Web: www.saintclare.org.
School—(Grades PreK-8), 716 Myrth Ave., 21221-4898. Tel: 410-687-7787; Fax: 410-687-2715. Mrs. Dorothy Williams, Prin. Sisters 1; Lay Teachers 20; Students 275.
Catechesis/Religious Program—Tel: 410-686-7693; Fax: 410-687-2518. Mrs. Susan Bangert, Adult Religious Education. Students 140.

25—ST. CLEMENT (Lansdowne) (1891) Deacon Paul A. Gifford, Pastoral Life Dir.; Revs. Thomas R. Malia; Jesus Aguirre. Serving the Spanish and English speaking communities of Lansdowne, Baltimore Highlands, Riverview, Lakeland, Westport, and

Morrel Park.
Res.: 2700 Washington Ave., 21227. Tel: 410-242-1025; Fax: 410-536-0636.
Catechesis/Religious Program—Tel: 410-242-1025. Students 80.

26—ST. CLEMENT MARY HOFBAUER (Rosedale) (1925) Revs. Donald Grzymski, O.F.M.Conv.; Thomas E. Walsh, O.F.M.Conv.; Deacons Nicholas Feurer; Francis Zeiler. In Res., Rev. Bernard Dudek, O.F.M. Conv.
Res. & Parish Office: 1212 Chesaco Ave., 21237. Tel: 410-686-6188; Fax: 410-686-6198. Email: parishoffice@stclementmh.org. Web: www.stclementmh.org.
School—(Grades PreK-8), 1216 Chesaco Ave., 21237. Tel: 410-686-3316. Email: inquiry@stclemmh.org. Web: www.stclemmh.org. Mr. Gary M. Rand, Prin. Lay Teachers 20; Students 308.
Catechesis/Religious Program—Tel: 410-391-5028. Mrs. Patricia Wagner, C.R.E. Email: pwagner@archbalt.org. Students 90.

27—CORPUS CHRISTI (1881) Rev. Msgr. Richard J. Bozzelli; Deacons Frank Hodges; Fritz Bauerschmidt; Ms. Betty W. Lafferty, Pastoral Assoc.
Res.: 110 W. Lafayette Ave., 21217. Tel: 410-523-4161; Fax: 410-523-5745. Email: cchristi@archbalt.org. Web: www.corpuschristibaltimore.org.
Catechesis/Religious Program—Stephanie Roberts, D.R.E. Students 70.

28—ST. DOMINIC (1906) Rev. James P. Kiesel; Sr. Catherine Manning, S.S.N.D., Pastoral Assoc.; Deacon James L. Mann. In Res., Most Rev. Denis J. Madden.
Res.: 5310 Harford Rd., 21214. Tel: 410-426-0360; Fax: 410-444-6963. Email: stdominic@archbalt.org.
Catechesis/Religious Program—Tel: 410-426-0360. Susan Donnelly, D.R.E. Students 30.

29—ST. EDWARD (1880) Rev. Evod E. Shao, C.S.Sp.; Sr. Anita B. Smith, O.S.F., Pastoral Assoc.; Deacon Carl A. Anderson.
Res.: 901 Poplar Grove St., 21216-4350. Tel: 410-362-2000; Fax: 410-945-7113. Email: stedwardsparish@verizon.net. Web: www.stedwardschurchmd.org.
Catechesis/Religious Program—Dr. Cre Saundra Sills, D.R.E. Students 70.

30—ST. ELIZABETH OF HUNGARY (1895) Rev. Robert Sisk, T.O.R. In Res., Bros. Finbar Gallagher, T.O.R.; Edward Bennett, T.O.R.
Mailing & Office Address: 2638 E. Baltimore St., 21224. Tel: 410-675-8260; Fax: 410-675-2530. Email: stliz1@comcast.net. Web: www.stelizabethofhungarychurchmd.org.
Res.: 2638 E. Baltimore St., 21224.
Catechesis/Religious Program—Students 20.

31—FOURTEEN HOLY MARTYRS, Closed. 1964. Parish records available at St. Martin Church. Tel: 410-947-1242.

32—ST. FRANCIS OF ASSISI (1927) Rev. Msgr. William F. Burke; Sr. Katherine Bell, R.S.M., Pastoral Assoc.
Res.: 3615 Harford Rd., 21218. Tel: 410-235-5136; Fax: 410-467-9503. Email: sfabalt@archbalt.org.
School—(Grades PreK-8), 3617 Harford Rd., 21218. Tel: 410-467-1683; Fax: 410-467-9449. J. Kevin Frye, Prin. Lay Teachers 19; Students 233.
Catechesis/Religious Program—Sr. Katherine M. Bell, D.R.E.; Frederick Buettner, Dir. Youth Min. Students 50.

33—ST. FRANCIS XAVIER (1793) Revs. James E. McLinden, S.S.J.; Nixon Ambe Mulah.
Res.: 1501 E. Oliver St., 21213. Tel: 410-727-3103; 410-727-3104; Fax: 410-625-9587. Email: j1mclinden@aol.com. Web: www.josephite.com/parish/md/sfx.
Catechesis/Religious Program—Tel: 410-837-0556. Sr. Magdala Marie Gillbert, O.S.P., D.R.E. Students 117.

34—ST. GABRIEL (1997), Formerly St. Lawrence and Our Lady of Perpetual Help, Woodlawn. Rev. Msgr. Thomas L. Phillips; Rev. Wilson Saldana, Spanish Vicar; Deacon Clifford L. Britton.
Parish Office: 6950 Dogwood Rd., 21244-2697. Tel: 410-298-8888; Fax: 410-944-7409. Email: stgabriel@archbalt.org. Web: www.stgabrielch.org.
See John Paul Regional Catholic School, Inc., Baltimore under Elementary/Middle Schools, Private located in the Institution section.
Catechesis/Religious Program—Sr. Sonia Marie Fernandez, M.H.S.H., Dir. Christian Formation.

35—ST. GREGORY THE GREAT (1884), (African American), Rev. Msgr. Damien G. Nalepa; Sisters Anthonia Ugwu, O.S.P., Pastoral Assoc.; Mary Charlotte Marshall, O.S.P., Dir. Evangelization.
Res. & Church: 1542 N. Gilmor St., 21217-2304. Tel: 410-523-0061; 410-523-0063; Fax: 410-669-1385. Email: sggreat@archbalt.org.
Catechesis/Religious Program—Louise G. Tildon, D.R.E. Students 52.

36—HOLY CROSS (1858), (German), [CEM] Rev. Patrick Carrion; Deacon Rick Clemens; Sisters Catherine Cress, S.N.D.deN., Pastoral Assoc.; Vicki Staub, S.S.J., Dir. Ministry & Volunteers.
Res.: 110 E. West St., 21230. Tel: 410-752-8498; Fax: 410-752-2703. Web: www.southbaltcatholic.org.
Catechesis/Religious Program— Dorris van Gaal, Dir. Faith Formation. Students 35.

37—HOLY KOREAN MARTYRS (1989), (Korean), [CEM] Rev. Joseph Y. Kim.
Res.: 5801 Security Blvd., 21207. Tel: 410-265-8885; Fax: 410-265-1655. Email: kmartyrs@archbalt.org.
Catechesis/Religious Program—Students 165.

38—HOLY ROSARY (1887), (Polish), [CEM] Rev. Jan Michalski, S.Ch.
Res.: 408 S. Chester St., 21231. Tel: 410-732-3960; Fax: 410-675-4917. Web: www.holyrosarypl.org.
Catechesis/Religious Program—Students 35.

39—ST. IGNATIUS CHURCH (1856) Revs. William J. Watters, S.J.; Edward M. Ifkovits, S.J.; Deacon Paul Webber.
Church: 740 N. Calvert St., 21202. Tel: 410-727-3848; Fax: 410-837-8883. Email: parish@st-ignatius.net. Web: www.st-ignatius.net.
Jesuit Community of St. Ignatius Parish: 102 E. Madison St., 21202. Tel: 410-727-8729.
School—St. Ignatius Loyola Academy, (Grades 6-8) Tel: 410-539-8268; Fax: 410-539-4821. John Ciccone, Pres.; Mr. Jeffrey Sindler, Prin.
Catechesis/Religious Program—Students 30.

40—IMMACULATE CONCEPTION (1850), (African American), Twinned with St. Cecilia, Baltimore. Rev. Sylvester Peterka, C.M.; Bro. William Stover, C.M., Pastoral Assoc. In Res., Rev. Abel Agbulu.
Res.: 3300 Clifton Ave., 21216. Tel: 410-624-3600; Fax: 410-945-0157.
Catechesis/Religious Program—Debra Curry, D.R.E. Students 26.

41—IMMACULATE HEART OF MARY (Baynesville) (1948) Rev. Michael W. Carrion; Deacons John R. Martin; Kenneth Pivec. In Res., Rev. James Risacher.
Res.: 8501 Loch Raven Blvd., 21286. Tel: 410-668-7935; Fax: 410-661-6560. Web: www.immaculateheartofmary.com.
School—(Grades PreK-8) Tel: 410-668-8466; Fax: 410-668-6171. Amy Belz, Prin. Lay Teachers 33; Students 505.
Catechesis/Religious Program—Tel: 410-661-3820; Fax: 410-661-3838. Amie Post, Dir. Faith Formation. Students 138.

42—ST. ISAAC JOGUES (1968) Rev. H. Martin Hammond; Sr. Patricia Tryon, S.N.D.deN., Pastoral Assoc.; Deacons Al Rose, (Retired); James Westwater; Frank O'Keefe.
Church Office: 9215 Old Harford Rd., 21234. Tel: 410-661-4888; Fax: 410-882-1484. Email: sij@archbalt.org. Web: www.sij.org.
Res.: 9400 Old Harford Rd., 21234.
Catechesis/Religious Program—Tel: 410-665-2561; 410-668-3686 Youth Ministry Office. Sr. John Francis Kearney, S.S.N.D., Dir. Faith Formation; Barbara Ward, Dir. Evangelization; Kenneth Goedeke, Coord. Youth Ministry. Students 452.

43—ST. JAMES AND ST. JOHN, Closed. 1986. Parish records available at the Chancery. Tel: 410-547-5446.
See Queen of Peace Elementary Cluster, St. James and St. John School, Baltimore under Elementary Schools, Regional and Community located in the Institution section.

44—ST. JEROME (1887) Merged with St. Martin and St. Peter the Apostle, Baltimore to form Transfiguration Roman Catholic Church, Baltimore.

45—ST. JOHN GERMAN CATHOLIC CHURCH, Closed. in 1841. Original records, stored at The Catholic Center, are available to researchers on microfilm at the Maryland State Archives in Annapolis.

46—ST. JOHN THE EVANGELIST, Closed. in 1966. Parish records available at the Chancery. Tel: 410-547-5446.

47—ST. JOSEPH, Closed. in 1962. Parish records available at Holy Cross Rectory. Tel: 410-752-8498.

48—ST. JOSEPH (Fullerton) (1850), (German), [CEM] Rev. Msgr. Kevin T. Schenning; Rev. Roque G. Lim; Deacons William J. DeAngelis; Charles A. Baynes; William S. Albaugh. In Res., Rev. Msgr. A. Thomas Baumgartner.
Res.: 8420 Belair Rd., 21236. Tel: 410-256-1630; Fax: 410-529-2990. Web: www.stjoefullerton.org.
School—(Grades PreK-8), 8416 Belair Rd., 21236. Tel: 410-256-8026; Fax: 410-529-7234. Email: office@stjoefullerton.org. Web: www.stjoeschool.org. Mrs. Phyllis Karko, Prin. Lay Teachers 25; Students 490.
Catechesis/Religious Program—Tel: 410-256-8235. Vacant, D.R.E. Students 421.

49—ST. JOSEPH PASSIONIST MONASTERY PARISH (1868) Rev. William Murphy, C.P.; Frank J. McGloin, Pastoral Assoc. In Res., Revs. Robert Carbonneau, C.P.; Alban Harmon, C.P.; Thomas McCain, C.P.
Res.: 251 S. Morley St., 21229. Tel: 410-566-0877; Fax: 410-233-4974. Email: info@sjmp.org. Web: www.sjmp.org.
Catechesis/Religious Program—Students 80.

50—ST. JUDE SHRINE (1917), (Italian), Revs. Louis F. Micca, S.A.C.; Joseph Kuchar, S.A.C. In Res., Rev. John G. Biermann, S.A.C.
Res.: 308 N. Paca St., P.O. Box 1455, 21203. Tel: 410-685-6026; Fax: 410-244-5728.
St. Jude Shrine Corp.—Tel: 410-685-6026. Web: www.stjudeshrine.org.

51—ST. KATHARINE OF SIENNA, Closed. in 1986. Parish records available at St. Wenceslaus Church. Tel: 410-675-7304.

52—ST. LAWRENCE (1962) Merged with The Shrine of Our Lady of Perpetual Help, Baltimore, to form St. Gabriel Parish, Baltimore. Records available at St. Gabriel Parish.

53—ST. LEO (1881), (Italian), Rev. Salvatore C. Furnari, S.A.C.
Res.: 227 S. Exeter St., 21202-4451. Tel: 410-675-7275; Fax: 410-675-8292.
School—St. Casimir Catholic School, (Grades PreK-8), See separate listing., Tel: 410-685-8505. Melanie Conley, Prin.
Catechesis/Religious Program—Mary Ann Blattermann, D.R.E.

54—LITTLE FLOWER, SHRINE OF (1926) Rev. Michael J. Orchik; Deacon Henry L. Siarkowski; Tony Magliano, Pastoral Assoc. In Res., Rev. James Miles.
Res.: 2854 Brendan Ave., 21213. Tel: 410-483-1700; Fax: 410-488-6482. Email: slflower@netzero.net. Web: www.shrineofthelittleflower.org.
Catechesis/Religious Program—Barbara G. Talley, C.R.E. Students 17.

55—ST. LUKE (Edgemere) (1888) Rev. Msgr. Joseph S. Lizor Jr.
Res.: 7517 North Point Rd., 21219-1499. Tel: 410-477-5200; Fax: 410-477-5996. Email: stlukromcathchur@yahoo.com. Web: www.stlukeedgemere.org.
School—Our Lady of Hope/St. Luke's School, (Grades PreK-8) Tel: 410-288-2793. Sr. Irene Mary Pryle, S.S.N.D., Prin.
Catechesis/Religious Program—Tel: 410-477-5201; Fax: 410-477-2022. Doris Lundin, C.R.E. Students 91.

56—ST. MARK (Catonsville) (1888) Rev. Christopher Whatley; Deacon Seigfried Presberry. In Res., Rev. Peter Tianzhi Chen.
Res.: 30 Melvin Ave., Catonsville, 21228. Tel: 410-744-6560; Fax: 410-747-3182. Email: smcatons@archbalt.org. Web: www.stmarkchurch-catonsville.org.
School—(Grades PreK-8), 26 Melvin Ave., 21228. Tel: 410-744-6560, Ext. 250; Fax: 410-747-3188. Email: mwarthen@stmark-school.org. Web: www.stmark-school.org. Mary Jo Warthen, Prin.
Catechesis/Religious Program—Anne Kidwell, D.R.E. Students 869.

57—ST. MARTIN (1865), (African American), Merged with St. Jerome and St. Peter the Apostle, Baltimore to form Transfiguration Roman Catholic Church, Baltimore.

58—ST. MARY OF THE ASSUMPTION (1849) [CEM] Deacons Miguel Sainz; Paul D. Shelton; Dianne McHale, Parish Admin. In Res., Rev. Rochus Vu Dinh Hoat (Retired).
Res.: 5502 York Rd., 21212. Tel: 410-435-5900; Fax: 410-435-1287.
Catechesis/Religious Program—Miss Lisa O'Reily, D.R.E., Coord. Youth Min. Students 13.

59—ST. MARY, STAR OF THE SEA (1868) Rev. Patrick Carrion; Deacon Rick Clemens; Sr. Catherine Cress, S.N.D.deN., Pastoral Assoc.
Res.: 110 E. West St., 21230. Tel: 410-685-2255; Fax: 410-752-2703. Email: smstar@archbalt.org. Web: www.southbaltcatholic.org.
See Catholic Community School of South Baltimore, Baltimore under Elementary Schools, Regional and Community located in the Institution section.
Catechesis/Religious Program—1528 E. Fort Ave., 21230. Tel: 410-752-8498. Dorris van Gaal, Dir. Faith Formation. Twinned with Holy Cross & Good Counsel Students 35.
Convent—Sisters of St. Joseph, 1410 Riverside Ave., 21230. Tel: 410-752-4344; Fax: 410-685-0692.

60—ST. MATTHEW (1949) Rev. Joseph L. Muth.
Res.: 5401 Loch Raven Blvd., 21239. Tel: 410-433-2300; Fax: 410-433-5263. Email: stmattrc@verizon.net. Web: www.stmattrc.org.
See Cardinal Shehan School, Baltimore under Elementary Schools, Regional and Community located in the Institution section.
Catechesis/Religious Program—Tel: 410-444-4563; Fax: 410-444-6502. Email: skeating@archbalt.org. Students 90.
Convent—Comboni Missionary Sisters, 5405 Loch

Raven Blvd., 21239. Tel: 410-323-1469; Fax: 410-323-9632. Email: sisters@combonisrs.com. Web: www.combonisrs.com.

61—ST. MICHAEL (Broadway) (1852), (Hispanic), Merged with St. Patrick 1995. Revs. Robert Wojtek, C.Ss.R.; Andrew Carr, C.Ss.R.; Charles McDonald, C.Ss.R.; Deacons Richard Novak; Edison Morales; Michael Flamini.
Res.: 7 S. Wolfe St., 21231-1913. Tel: 410-276-1646; Fax: 410-522-0789. Email: smikepat@juno.com.
Catechesis/Religious Program—Tel: 410-563-0064; Fax: 410-563-0310. Olga E. Diaz, D.R.E., RCIA Coord. Students 145.

62—ST. MICHAEL (Overlea) (1913) Rev. James L. Sorra; Deacon Henry C. Davis, Pastoral Assoc. In Res., Rev. Msgr. Jay F. O'Connor; Rev. Salvatore Livigni (Retired).
Res.: 2 Willow Ave., 21206. Tel: 410-665-1054; Fax: 410-665-4024. Email: parish@smoverlea.org.
School—(Grades K-8), 10 Willow Ave., 21206. Tel: 410-668-8797; Fax: 410-663-9277. Mrs. Patricia Rohde Kelly, Prin. Lay Teachers 16; Students 395.
Catechesis/Religious Program—Nikki Lux, D.R.E.; Mr. Michael Boyer, Coord. Youth Ministry. Students 125.

63—ST. MILDRED CHURCH, Closed. in 1967. Parish records available at Our Lady of Hope Rectory. Tel: 410-284-6600.

64—ST. MONICA, Closed. 1959. Parish records available at the Chancery. Tel: 410-547-5446.

65—MOST PRECIOUS BLOOD (1948), Twinned with St. Anthony of Padua, Baltimore. Deacons Joseph C. Krysiak, Temporary Admin.; Joseph Schultz.
Office: 4414 Frankford Ave., 21206. Tel: 410-488-0400; Fax: 410-488-0032. Email: sapmpb@comcast.net. Web: www.stampb.org.
Church: 5010 Bowleys Ln., 21206.
Catechesis/Religious Program— Twinned with St. Anthony of Padua, Baltimore.

66—THE NEW ALL SAINTS (1912), (African American), Rev. Donald A. Sterling.
Res.: 4408 Liberty Heights Ave., 21207. Tel: 410-542-0445; Fax: 410-542-8852. Email: office@newallsaintschurch.org. Web: www.newallsaintschurch.org.
Catechesis/Religious Program—Laura Thomas, D.R.E.; Kirk Johnson, Dir. Youth Ministry. Students 35.

67—OUR LADY OF FATIMA (1951) Revs. Kevin Milton, C.Ss.R.; Richard K. Poetzel, C.Ss.R.; Bro. DeSales Zimpfer, C.Ss.R.; Sr. Julianne Hau, M.H.S.H., Pastoral Assoc.; Deacon Alphonse Bankard III. In Res., Rev. Edwin Foley, C.Ss.R.
Res.: 6420 E. Pratt St., 21224. Tel: 410-633-9393; Fax: 410-631-7239.
School—(Grades PreK-8), 6400 E. Pratt St., 21224. Tel: 410-633-5882; Fax: 410-633-5268. Mr. Paul Llufrio, Prin. Sisters 3; Lay Teachers 16; Students 149.
Catechesis/Religious Program—Tel: 410-633-6526. Sr. Rita Dorn, S.S.N.D., D.R.E. Students 47.

68—OUR LADY OF GOOD COUNSEL (1859) Rev. Patrick Carrion; Sr. Catherine Cress, S.N.D.deN., Pastoral Assoc.; Deacon Rick Clemens; Mary Beth Barnes, Pastoral Assoc.
Office: 1532 E. Fort Ave., 21230. Tel: 410-752-0205; Fax: 410-576-0929. Web: www.southbaltcatholic.org.
See Catholic Community School of South Baltimore, Baltimore under Elementary Schools, Regional and Community located in the Institution section.
Catechesis/Religious Program—Fax: 410-752-2703. Dorris van Gaal, Dir. Faith Formation. Students 35.

69—OUR LADY OF HOPE (1967) Rev. John B. Ward; Deacon Herman S. Wilkins.
Res.: 1727 Lynch Rd., 21222. Tel: 410-284-6600; Fax: 410-282-9361. Email: lhope@archbalt.org.
School—(Grades PreK-8), 8003 N. Boundary Rd., 21222. Tel: 410-288-2793; Fax: 410-288-2850. Email: olhsls@aol.com. Web: www.olhsls.com. Sr. Irene Mary Pryle, S.S.N.D., Prin. School Sisters of Notre Dame 2; Lay Teachers 24; Students 311.
Catechesis/Religious Program—8003 N. Boundary Rd. Tel: 410-282-3120; Fax: 410-282-9361. Mrs. Bonnie Nagel, Youth Min. Students 155.
Convent—8001 N. Boundary Rd., 21222. Tel: 410-282-3800; Fax: 410-288-2850.

70—OUR LADY OF LA VANG (2000) Rev. Francis Nhi Nguyen.
335 Sollers Point Rd., 21222. Tel: 410-282-1497. Email: lavangchurch335@verizon.net.
Catechesis/Religious Program—Nhung Le, D.R.E.

71—OUR LADY OF LOURDES, Closed. 1995. Parish records available at The New All Saints Church. Tel: 410-542-0445.

72—OUR LADY OF MOUNT CARMEL (Middle River) (1887) Rev. Msgr. Robert L. Hartnett; Rev. John Rapisarda; Deacon Charles A. Baynes, Pastoral Assoc.
Res.: 1704 Old Eastern Ave., 21221. Tel: 410-686-4972; Fax: 410-574-8785. Web: www.olmcmd.org.
School—(Grades PreK-8), 1702 Old Eastern Ave., 21221. Tel: 410-686-0859; Fax: 410-686-4916. Ms. Lisa Shipley, Prin. Sisters of St. Francis of Philadelphia 2; Lay Teachers 28; Students 417.
High School—1706 Old Eastern Ave., 21221. Tel: 410-686-1023; Fax: 410-686-2361. Mrs. Kathleen Sipes, Prin. Lay Teachers 22; Students 231.
Catechesis/Religious Program—Tel: 410-238-1167; Fax: 410-574-8785. Caroline Hemling, D.R.E.; Missy Lawrence, Youth Min. Students 187.

73—OUR LADY OF PERPETUAL HELP (1936) Merged with St. Lawrence, Baltimore, to form St. Gabriel Parish, Baltimore. Records available at St. Gabriel.

74—OUR LADY OF POMPEI (1924) Revs. Luigi Esposito; Luis Cremis.
Res.: 3600 Claremont St., 21224. Tel: 410-675-7790; Fax: 410-563-9067. Email: lpompei@archbalt.org. Web: www.olpmd.org.
School—Archbishop Borders School, (Grades PreK-8), 201 S. Conkling St., 21224. Tel: 410-276-6534; Fax: 410-276-6915. Ms. Mary Catherine Marshal, Prin. Lay Teachers 10; Students 160.
Catechesis/Religious Program—Mrs. Dorothy Locco, D.R.E.; Jorge Santisteban, D.R.E.

75—OUR LADY OF SORROWS, Closed. 1935. Parish records available at Holy Cross Rectory. Tel: 410-752-8498.

76—OUR LADY OF THE ANGELS CATHOLIC COMMUNITY (Catonsville) (1993), Service senior citizens w/in community. Rev. Leo J. Larrivee, S.S.; Sisters Victoria Kessler, S.S.N.D., Pastoral Assoc.; Patricia Huesman, S.S.N.D., Pastoral Assoc.; Deacon Jack Coster.
Mailing Address: 711 Maiden Choice Ln., Catonsville, 21228. Tel: 410-247-4779; Fax: 410-737-8826. Email: llarrive@archbalt.org.

77—OUR LADY OF VICTORY (Arbutus) (1952) Rev. Timothy Klunk; Sr. Mary McFadden, S.N.D.deN., Pastoral Assoc.; Deacon William Jauquet.
Res.: 4414 Wilkens Ave., 21229. Tel: 410-242-0131; 410-242-0180; Fax: 410-242-6963. Email: ol.victory@verizon.net. Web: www.olvictory.org.
School—(Grades PreK-8), 4416 Wilkens Ave., 21229. Tel: 410-242-3688; Fax: 410-242-8867. Thomas E. Riddle, Prin. Lay Teachers 24; Students 475.
Catechesis/Religious Program—Tel: 410-242-9533. Email: smithgl@mail.olvschool.com. Gloria Smith, Dir. Students 57.

78—OUR LADY, QUEEN OF PEACE (1953), (Middle River) Deacons George Jenkins, (Retired); Robert Keenan, (Retired). In Res., Rev. Paul C. Sparklin.
Res.: 10003 Bird River Rd., 21220. Tel: 410-686-3085; Fax: 410-687-1916. Email: qpeace@archbalt.org. Web: www.olqpmd.org.
Catechesis/Religious Program—Tel: 410-686-3085, Ext. 120; Fax: 410-687-1916. Kathy Shadrach, C.R.E.; Debbie Boblitz, C.R.E. Students 98.

79—ST. PATRICK (Broadway) (1792), (Hispanic), Revs. Robert Wojtek, C.Ss.R.; Charles McDonald, C.Ss.R.; Andrew Carr, C.Ss.R.; Bro. Raphael Rock, C.Ss.R.; Deacons Richard Novak; Edison Morales; Michael Flamini. Twinned with St. Michael (Wolfe St.) 1995.
Res.: 7 S. Wolfe St., 21231. Tel: 410-276-1646; Fax: 410-522-0789. Email: smikepat@juno.com.
Catechesis/Religious Program—Tel: 410-276-1998; Fax: 410-563-0310. Olga E. Diaz, D.R.E. Students 145.

80—ST. PAUL'S (1888) Closed. Parish records available at St. Francis Xavier. Tel: 410-727-3103.

81—ST. PETER CLAVER (1888), (African American), Revs. Ray P. Bomberger, S.S.J.; Henry Harper, S.S.J.
Res.: 1546 N. Fremont Ave., 21217. Tel: 410-669-0512; Fax: 410-383-8227. Email: spclaver@verizon.net.
School—Father Charles A. Hall School, (Grades PreK-5), 1526 N. Fremont Ave., 21217. Tel: 410-225-7555; Fax: 410-225-7721. M. Kathleen Filippelli, Prin. Lay Teachers 11; Students 198.
Catechesis/Religious Program—Students 54.

82—ST. PETER THE APOSTLE (1842) Merged with St. Jerome and St. Martin, Baltimore to form Transfiguration Roman Catholic Church, Baltimore.

83—SS. PHILIP AND JAMES (1897) Rev. William A. Au; Linda Boswell, Parish Mgr.
Res.: 2801 N. Charles St., 21218. Tel: 410-235-2294; Fax: 410-243-5262. Email: stspandj@aol.com.
Catechesis/Religious Program—Sr. Jean Marie Hobbs, R.S.M., D.R.E.

84—ST. PIUS V (1878), (African American), [JC] Rev. Ray P. Bomberger, S.S.J.
Res.: 907 Edmondson Ave., P.O. Box 16550, 21217-0550. Tel: 410-523-1930; Fax: 410-523-8164. Email: stpiusv@archbalt.org.
Catechesis/Religious Program—Mrs. Jean Brent, D.R.E. Students 11.

85—ST. PIUS X (1957) Carol J. Pacione, Pastoral Life Dir.; Rev. Samuel Lupico (Retired). In Res., Rev. Bogdan Palka, S.D.S.
Parish Office—6428 York Rd., 21212. Tel: 410-427-7500; Fax: 410-377-2651.
School—(Grades PreK-8), 6432 York Rd., 21212. Tel: 410-427-7400; Fax: 410-377-9738. Email: spschool10@aol.com. Mrs. Geri Morrison, Prin. Lay Teachers 26; Students 402; School Sisters of Notre Dame 3.
Catechesis/Religious Program—Tel: 410-427-7500. Mrs. Pinky Howard, Dir. Adult & Family Min.; Mrs. Kristin Rupprechy, Dir. Children's Ministry; Ed Rogers, Dir. Youth Ministry. Students 240.

86—ST. RITA (1922) Deacons John Langmead, Pastoral Life Dir.; George T. Evans; Herman Wilkens. In Res., Revs. Richard Gray, M.S.A.; Greg Ferri.
Res.: 2907 Dunleer Rd., 21222. Tel: 410-284-0388; Fax: 410-284-3998.
Catechesis/Religious Program—Tel: 410-284-7355. Sr. Michael Marie Hartman, I.H.M., Adult Faith Formation. Students 85.

87—ST. ROSE OF LIMA (1914) Rev. Joseph O'Meara (Retired).
Res.: 3803 4th St., 21225. Tel: 410-355-8515; Fax: 410-354-3392. Web: www.stroseparish.org.
School—(Grades PreK-8), 410 Jeffrey St., 21225. Tel: 410-355-1050; Fax: 410-355-2408. Email: srlschool@archbalt.org. Web: www.stroseschool.org. Madeleine Hobik, Prin. Lay Teachers 15; Students 179.
Catechesis/Religious Program—Madeleine Hobik, C.R.E. & Youth Ministry. Students 43.

88—SACRED HEART OF JESUS (1873) Revs. Gerard J. Knapp, C.Ss.R.; John Bauer, C.Ss.R.; Deacon James S. Clack. In Res., Bro. Raphael Rock, C.Ss.R.
Res.: 600 S. Conkling St., 21224-4294. Tel: 410-342-4336; Fax: 410-522-2022. Email: shjesus@archbalt.org.
Catechesis/Religious Program—Joan Turowski, Admin. Rel. Educ. Students 45.

89—SACRED HEART OF MARY (1925) [CEM] Rev. George J. Gannon, Admin.; Rev. Msgr. Richard E. Parks, Pastor Emeritus (Retired); Rev. William Ciganek, C.F.X.
Res.: 6736 Youngstown Ave., 21222-1097. Tel: 410-633-2828; Fax: 410-633-0349. Email: stmary@archbalt.org. Web: www.shmparish.org.
School—(Grades PreK-8), 6726 Youngstown Ave., 21222-1098. Tel: 410-633-7040; Fax: 410-633-7491. Mrs. Pamela Walters, Prin. Lay Teachers 12; Students 229.
Catechesis/Religious Program—Michael Demski, D.R.E.; Noel Fell, Youth Coord. Students 123.

90—SHRINE OF THE SACRED HEART (Mt. Washington) (1867) Rev. Msgr. Richard E. Cramblitt; Sr. Carol Czyzewski, F.S.S.J., Pastoral Assoc.; Deacon Mark Soloski.
Res.: 1701 Regent Rd., 21209. Tel: 410-466-6884; Fax: 410-664-0523. Email: shshrine@archbalt.org. Web: www.theshrine.org.
School—(Grades PreK-8), 5800 Smith Ave., 21209. Tel: 410-542-7406; Fax: 410-664-1463. Email: shrineschool@aol.com. Martha Pierorazio, Prin. Lay Teachers 12; Students 166.
Catechesis/Religious Program—Tel: 410-466-6884, Ext. 14. Bernetta Palasik, C.R.E. Students 168.

91—ST. STANISLAUS KOSTKA (1880), (Polish), Closed. For inquiries for parish records please contact St. Casimir, Baltimore. Tel: 410-276-1981; 732-7436 (fax).

92—ST. THOMAS AQUINAS (1867) Rev. M. Shawn Mahon; Deacon Richard W. Montalto; Donna Dougherty, Pastoral Assoc.
Res.: 1008 W. 37th St., 21211. Tel: 410-366-4488; Fax: 410-366-8352. Email: staquinas@archbalt.org. Web: www.stthomasaquinasbaltimore.parishesonline.com.
School—(Grades PreK-8), 3710 Roland Ave., 21211. Tel: 410-889-4618; Fax: 410-889-1956. Email: stasch@archbalt.org. Web: www.stthomasaquinasschool.us. Sr. Marie Rose Gustatus, S.S.N.D., Prin. School Sisters of Notre Dame 3; Lay Teachers 24; Students 185.
Catechesis/Religious Program— Susan Sousa, C.R.E.; Annemarie Vallonga, Youth Min. Students 40.

93—ST. THOMAS MORE (1961) Rev. Brian A. Zielinski, O.Praem.; Deacon Michael McCoy; Sr. Kathleen Haughey, S.N.D., Pastoral Assoc.
Parish Center & Mailing Address: 6806 McClean Blvd., 21234. Tel: 410-444-6500; Fax: 410-444-6502.
See Cardinal Shehan School, Baltimore under Elementary Schools, Regional and Community located in the Institution section.
Catechesis/Religious Program—Tel: 410-444-4563. Susan Keating, D.R.E. & Youth Ministry. Students 39.

94—TRANSFIGURATION CATHOLIC COMMUNITY (2004) Rev. Roger White, O.F.M.Cap.; Deacon Tony Roberts; Sr. Suzanne Baumgartner, D.C., Pastoral Assoc.
Office: 848 Hollins St., 21201. Tel: 410-685-5044 (Office); Fax: 410-625-2406. Email: spabalt@archbalt.org.
Res.: *St. Ambrose Friary*, 4502 Park Heights Ave., 21215. Tel: 410-685-5044.
Catechesis/Religious Program—Students 84.

95—ST. URSULA (Parkville) (1937) Rev. Msgrs. James Farmer; A. Thomas Baumgartner, Pastor Emeritus; Sr. Kathleen White, O.S.B., Pastoral Ministry; Deacons Richard F. Morris; Frank Rongione Sr.; Robert G. Keenan; Michael Baker. In Res., Rev. Gerald Hynes, C.P. (Retired).
Res.: 8801 Harford Rd., 21234. Tel: 410-665-2111; Fax: 410-665-0758. Email: stursula@comcast.net. Web: www.stursulaparish.com.
School—(Grades K-8), 8900 Harford Rd., 21234. Tel: 410-665-3533; Fax: 410-661-1620. Sr. Joan Kelly, S.N.D.deN., Prin.
Catechesis/Religious Program—Tel: 410-655-4106. Laura Wetherington, D.R.E.; Elizabeth Schmedes, Dir. Youth Ministry. Students 716.

96—ST. VERONICA (1945), (African American), Rev. Augustine Etemma Inwang, M.S.P. (Nigeria); Deacons Jhan Harris; Williard Pinkney Jr., (Retired).
Res.: 806 Cherry Hill Rd., 21225. Tel: 410-355-7466; Fax: 410-355-7741.
Catechesis/Religious Program—Cathy McClain, Youth Min. Students 108.

97—ST. VINCENT DE PAUL (1841) [CEM] Rev. Richard T. Lawrence; Colleen McCahill, Pres. Parish Council.
Res.: 120 N. Front St., 21202-4804. Tel: 410-962-5078; Fax: 410-962-8427. Web: stvchurch.org.
St. Vincent de Paul Church Historic Trust, Inc.—Tel: 410-962-5078.
Jonestown Planning Council, Inc.—Tel: 410-962-5078.
Jonestown Day Care Center, Inc.—
Catechesis/Religious Program—Students 55.

98—ST. WENCESLAUS (1872) Rev. Peter A. Lyons, T.O.R. In Res., Rev. Jordan Hite, T.O.R.
Res.: 2111 Ashland Ave., 21205. Tel: 410-675-7304; Fax: 410-675-5746. Web: www.stwen.org.
See Queen of Peace Elementary Cluster, St. James and St. John School, Baltimore under Elementary Schools, Regional and Community located in the Institution section.
Catechesis/Religious Program—Students 43.

99—ST. WILLIAM OF YORK (1914) Rev. Martin H. Demek.
Res.: 600 Cooks Ln., 21229. Tel: 410-566-2140; Fax: 410-362-5475. Web: www.stwilliamofyorkchurch.org.
School—(Grades PreK-8) Tel: 410-945-1442; Fax: 410-945-4036. Noreen Heffner, Prin. Lay Teachers 11; Students 190.
Catechesis/Religious Program—Tel: 410-566-6152. Peggy Mrozek, D.R.E. (Children); Rochelle Hubbard, D.R.E. (Adult); Wayne Hipley, Youth Min. Students 45.

OUTSIDE METROPOLITAN BALTIMORE

ABERDEEN, HARFORD CO., ST. JOAN OF ARC (1920) Rev. Samuel V. Young; Deacons Daniel Kopczyk; Paul R. Ciesla, (Retired).
Office: 222 S. Law St., 21001. Tel: 410-272-4535; 410-575-6909; Fax: 410-272-9025. Email: parish@stjoanarc.org. Web: www.stjoanarc.org.
Res.: 223 S. Law St., 21001.
School—(Grades K-8), 230 S. Law St., 21001. Tel: 410-272-1387; Fax: 410-272-1959. Email: school@stjoanarc.org. Dr. Jane Towery, Prin. Lay Teachers 16; Students 199.
Catechesis/Religious Program—Tel: 410-272-6944. Richard Berndt, C.R.E. Students 152.

ABINGDON, HARFORD CO., ST. FRANCIS DE SALES (1866) [CEM] Rev. Charles M. Wible; Deacons Richard Stine; James Sullivan; Alex Rodriguez; Beth Marchiano, Parish Mgr.
Res.: 1450 Abingdon Rd., 21009. Tel: 410-676-5119; 410-679-4555; Fax: 410-676-7520. Email: sfabing@archbalt.org. Web: www.stfrancisabingdon.org.
Catechesis/Religious Program—Tel: 410-676-3354. Doris McKibbon, Dir. Preschool; Elizabeth Taneyhill, Dir. Evangelization & Adult Catechesis; Betty Burlin, Coord. High School Catechesis & Sacramental Prep (9-12); Patrick Perkins, Coord. Middle School Catechesis; Diane Lewis, C.R.E. Elementary Catechesis & Youth Minister. Students 700.

ANNAPOLIS, ANNE ARUNDEL CO.

1—ST. ANDREW BY THE BAY (Annapolis) (1981) Rev. Martin J. Burnham; Deacons James C. Monaghan Jr., Pastoral Assoc.; David Tengwell; Mrs. Stephany Crane, Family Min.; Mr. Zachary Stachowski, Music Min. & Liturgy.
Parish Center—701 College Pkwy., 21409. Tel: 410-974-4366; Fax: 410-974-4339. Email: sabbanna@archbalt.org. Web: www.standrewbythebay.org.
Catechesis/Religious Program—Sr. Mary Teresa Day, S.N.D.deN., D.R.E.; Debra Alwan-Humkey, Coord. Youth Ministry. Students 609.

2—ST. MARY (1853) [CEM] Revs. John Kingbury, C.Ss.R.; Patrick Flynn, C.Ss.R.; Eric Hoog, C.Ss.R.; John Harrison, C.Ss.R.; George Blasick, C.Ss.R.; Andrew Costello, C.Ss.R.; Fabio Mavin, C.Ss.R.; Deacons Leroy S. Moore; Anthony F. Norcio. In Res., Rev. Alphonsus Olive, C.Ss.R.
Res.: 109 Duke of Gloucester St., 21401. Tel: 410-263-2396; 410-269-6092; Fax: 410-263-3027.
School—(Grades K-8), 111 Duke of Gloucester St., 21401. Tel: 410-263-2869; Fax: 410-269-6513. Mrs. Margaret Dammeyer, Prin. Sisters 1; Lay Teachers 43; Students 869.
High School—113 Duke of Gloucester St., 21401. Tel: 410-263-3294; Fax: 410-269-7843. Richard Bayhan, Prin. School Sisters of Notre Dame 1; Lay Teachers 37; Students 515.
Catechesis/Religious Program—Tel: 410-990-4779; Fax: 410-263-7381. Stephen Beard, D.R.E. Students 1,498.
Convent—4 Shipwright St., 21401. Tel: 410-269-0568. School Sisters of Notre Dame 2.
Mission—St. John Neuman 620 N. Bestgate Rd., Anne Arundel Co. 21401. Tel: 410-266-2498; Fax: 410-266-2497.

BEL AIR, HARFORD CO., ST. MARGARET (1905) Rev. Msgr. G. Michael Schleupner; Revs. Francis X. Callahan, Pastor Emeritus (Retired); Jesse Bolger; John Cunningham; Mrs. Mary Ellen Bates, Business Mgr.; Michael Britt, Music Mgr.; Jane O'Hara, Outreach Coord.; Deacons Patrick J. Goles; Victor Petrosino; Martin Wolf; John Chott; James DeCapite. In Res., Rev. Msgr. Martin Stempeck.
Res.: 141 Hickory Ave., 21014. Tel: 410-838-6969; Fax: 410-879-2518. Web: www.stmargaret.org.
School—(Grades PreK-8), 205 Hickory Ave., 21014. Tel: 410-879-1113. Email: smsch@archbalt.org. Mrs. Jane Dean, Prin. Lay Teachers 30; Students 863.
Catechesis/Religious Program—Tel: 410-838-4224. Mrs. Marge Troilo, C.R.E. Preschool; Mrs. Karen Clemens, D.R.E. Youth & Young Adult Ministry; Mrs. Kim O'Brien, Youth & Young Adult Ministry Coord.; Mr. Dick Gatto, Dir. Faith Formation. Students 1,600.
Mission—St. Mary Magdalen 1716 Churchville Rd., Harford Co. 21015.

BRADSHAW, BALTIMORE CO., ST. STEPHEN (1863) [CEM] Revs. Lawrence F. Kolson; Paul Breczinski; Deacons Gilbert J. Hartlieb; Frank R. Laws; Timothy D. Maloney.
Res.: 8030 Bradshaw Rd., 21087. Tel: 410-592-7071; Fax: 410-592-6803. Email: ssbradsh@archbalt.org. Web: www.ststephenbradshaw.org.
School—(Grades PreK-8), 8028 Bradshaw Rd., 21087. Tel: 410-592-7617; Fax: 410-592-7330. Email: sssch@archbalt.org. Mrs. Mary M. Patrick, Prin. Lay Teachers 25.
Catechesis/Religious Program—Tel: 410-592-8666. Sr. Angela DeFontes, O.S.F., D.R.E. Students 402.

BRUNSWICK, FREDERICK CO., ST. FRANCIS OF ASSISI (1893) [CEM] Deacons Lawrence "Tex" Teixeira, Pastoral Life Dir.; Chuck McCandless; Faye Williams, Business Mgr.
Res.: 113 First Ave., 21716. Tel: 301-834-9185; Fax: 301-834-4162. Email: stsmparishoffice@verizon.net. Web: www.stfrancis-stmary.org.
Catechesis/Religious Program—Patricia Martz, Faith Formation Coord.; Deirdre Shurland, Faith Formation Coord. Students 90.
Mission—St. Mary's Petersville, Frederick Co. 21758.

BUCKEYSTOWN, FREDERICK CO., ST. JOSEPH-ON-CARROLLTON MANOR (1811) [CEM] Rev. Lawrence K. Frazier.
Mailing Address: P.O. Box 33, 21717. Tel: 301-663-0907; Fax: 301-874-0247. Email: office@stjoesbuckeystown.org. Web: www.stjoesbuckeystown.org.
Res.: 5843 Manor Woods Rd., Frederick, 21703.
Catechesis/Religious Program—Tel: 301-663-0907, Ext. 12; Fax: 301-874-0247. Therese Ivanisin, D.R.E.; Justin Orlando, Coord. Youth Ministry. Students 354.

CLARKSVILLE, HOWARD CO., ST. LOUIS (1855) [CEM] Rev. Msgr. Joseph L. Luca; Revs. Dominique Pridons; James L. Sorra; Deacons Fred Mauser; Matthew A. Podwiesinski; Marianne M. Faulstich, Pastoral Assoc.; Mary S. Helfrich, Dir. Devel.
Res.: 12500 Clarksville Pike, 21029. Tel: 410-531-6040; Fax: 410-531-6191. Email: parishoffice@stlouisparish.org. Web: www.stlouisparish.org.
School—(Grades PreK-8) Tel: 410-531-6664; Fax: 410-531-6690. Web: www.stlouisparish.org/school. Mrs. Mary Theresa Weiss, Prin. Sisters 1; Lay Teachers 27; Students 475.
Catechesis/Religious Program—Tel: 410-531-6688; Fax: 410-531-6689. Web: www.stlouisparish.org/reled. Victoria Yozwiak, D.R.E.; Patrick Sprankle, Dir. Youth Ministry. Students 1,330.

COCKEYSVILLE, BALTIMORE CO., ST. JOSEPH (1852) [CEM] Rev. Msgr. Paul G. Cook; Rev. Gonzalo Cadavid-Rivera; Sr. Rose Lindner, S.S.N.D., Pastoral Assoc.; Deacon Edward Sulivan; Ann Marie Labin, Pastoral Assoc. & Parish Nurse.
Res.: 101 Church Ln., 21030. Tel: 410-683-0600; Fax: 410-628-2956.
School—(Grades K-8), 105 Church Ln., 21030. Fax: 410-628-6814. Sr. Anne O'Donnell, R.S.M., Prin. Sisters 2; Lay Teachers 25; Students 406.
Catechesis/Religious Program—Fax: 410-628-6814. Marie Lybolt, D.R.E.; Kathleen Harrigan-Paul, Youth & Young Adult Ministry. Students 442.

COLUMBIA, HOWARD CO., ST. JOHN THE EVANGELIST (1967) Revs. Richard H. Tilman; Ferdinand Ezenwachi; Antonio Velez, T.C., Hispanic Ministry; Deacon James J. Benjamin.
5885 Robert Oliver Pl., 21045. Tel: 410-964-1434; Fax: 410-740-9323.
Interfaith Centers—10431 Twin Rivers Rd., 21044. Tel: 410-964-1425; Fax: 410-730-9253. Web: www.sjerc.org. (Wilde Lake)
Catechesis/Religious Program—Tel: 410-964-1440. Wyman A. Scott IV, D.R.E., Youth & Young Adults; Kathleen Armstrong, D.R.E.; Mr. Peter Barbernitz, Evangelization. Students 490.

CRESAPTOWN, ALLEGANY CO., ST. AMBROSE (1886) [CEM] Revs. James Kurtz, O.F.M.Cap.; Bernard Finerty, O.F.M.Cap.; Ms. Margaret Gaughan, Pastoral Assoc.
Res.: P.O. Box 5130, 21505-5130. Tel: 301-729-2790; Fax: 301-729-2436. Email: sacresap@archbalt.org.
Catechesis/Religious Program—Monica Beck, C.R.E. Students 136.

CROFTON, ANNE ARUNDEL CO., ST. ELIZABETH ANN SETON (1976) Rev. Edward C. Connelly; Sr. Katherine O'Donnell, R.S.M., Pastoral Assoc.; Deacon Frederick Seibold; Mr. Jack O'Malley, Administrative Assoc.
Office: 1800 Seton Dr., 21114. Tel: 410-721-5770; Fax: 410-721-5508. Email: setonparish@seaton.org. Web: www.seaseton.org.
See School of the Incarnation, Inc., Gambrills under Elementary Schools, Regional and Community located in the Institution section.
Catechesis/Religious Program—Tel: 410-721-5774. Michael MacDonald, Coord. Youth Ministry; Nancy Connell, Admin. Faith Formation. Students 280.

CUMBERLAND, ALLEGANY CO.

1—ST. MARY (1900), (Italian), [CEM] Rev. Ty S. Hullinger; Deacon David A. Conley; Joan Ruppenkamp, Parish Mgr.
Res.: 300 E. Oldtown Rd., 21502. Tel: 301-777-2990; Fax: 301-777-1108. Email: smcumber@archbalt.org.
School—Bishop Walsh School, (Grades PreK-12) Sr. Phyllis McNally, S.S.N.D., Prin.
Catechesis/Religious Program—Tel: 301-722-3445. Students 80.

2—ST. PATRICK (1790), (Irish), [CEM] Deacons Paul H. Dignan; Loren Mooney; Francis L. Werner Jr.; Teresa Files, Admin. Asst.; J. J. Klapka, Dir. Music.
Res.: 201 N. Centre St., 21502. Tel: 301-777-1750; Fax: 301-777-2669. Email: spcumber@archbalt.org.
Catechesis/Religious Program—Tel: 301-724-0288. Deacon Loren L. Mooney, D.R.E. Students 74.

3—SS. PETER AND PAUL (1848), (German), [CEM] Revs. James Kurtz, O.F.M.Cap.; Bernard Finerty, O.F.M.Cap. In Res., Revs. Jerome Dunn, O.F.M.Cap.; Michael Masich, O.F.M.Cap.
Res.: 109 N. Smallwood St., 21502-2992. Tel: 301-777-3131; Fax: 301-759-3568. Email: ppaul@archbalt.org. Web: www.ss-peterandpaul.net.
Catechesis/Religious Program—Mary Ann Peer, C.R.E. Students 124.

DAVIDSONVILLE, ANNE ARUNDEL CO., HOLY FAMILY (1929) Rev. Joseph F. Barr; Deacon Thomas W. Beales.
Res.: 826 W. Central Ave., P.O. Box 130, 21035-0130. Tel: 410-269-0586; 301-261-7399; Fax: 410-798-5315. Email: office@hfccmail.org. Web: www.holy-familychurch.com.
See School of the Incarnation under Elementary Schools, Regional and Community located in the Institution section.
Catechesis/Religious Program—Tel: 410-798-5680. Sharon Graham, Admin. Rel. Educ.; Meg O'Neill, Adult Enrichment Coord.; Ben Lorenz, Youth Min. Students 576.

EDGEWATER, ANNE ARUNDEL CO., OUR LADY OF PERPETUAL HELP (1976) Rev. Joseph J. Cosgrove; Deacon Stephen H. Cooley.
Res.: 515 Loch Haven Rd., 21037. Tel: 443-203-1002; Fax: 410-798-0076. Web: www.olph.net.
See School of the Incarnation, Gambrills under Elementary Schools, Regional and Community in the Institution Section.
Catechesis/Religious Program—Patricia Dixon, C.R.E. Students 125.

EDGEWOOD, HARFORD CO., PRINCE OF PEACE (1977)
Office Address—2600 Willoughby Beach Rd., 21040.

Tel: 410-679-5912; Fax: 410-676-0326. Email: ppedgewd@archbalt.org.
Catechesis/Religious Program—Sr. Susanne Bunn, M.H.S.H., Dir. Faith Formation. Students 84.

ELLICOTT CITY, HOWARD CO.

1—OUR LADY OF PERPETUAL HELP (1893) [CEM] Revs. Erik J. Arnold; McLean Cummings; Sr. Lorraine McGraw, O.S.F., Pastoral Assoc.
Res.: 4795 Ilchester Rd., 21043. Tel: 410-747-4334; Fax: 410-747-4399. Email: olphparish@archbalt.org. Web: www.olphparish.org.
School—4801 Ilchester Rd., Elliott City, 21043. Tel: 410-744-4251; Fax: 410-788-5210. Nancy Malloy, Prin. Lay Teachers 22; Students 230.
Catechesis/Religious Program—Tel: 410-747-0131; Fax: 410-788-8905. Mrs. Judy Gruel, D.R.E.; Mrs. Kristen Fisher, Youth Min. (Middle School); Erin Cooney, Dir. Youth Ministry (High School). Students 561.

2—ST. PAUL (1838) [CEM] Revs. Matthew T. Buening, Pastoral Admin.; Thomas J. Donaghy (Retired).
Res.: 3755 St. Paul St., 21043. Tel: 410-465-1670; Fax: 410-313-8551. Email: stpaulsrc@aol.com.
Catechesis/Religious Program—Tel: 410-465-0622. Sr. Dorothy Franz, O.S.F.; Becky Clark, Youth Min. Students 237.

3—RESURRECTION (1974) Rev. Msgr. John A. Dietzenbach; Rev. Michael Triplett; Deacons Ray H. Britt, (Retired); John Comegna. In Res., Rev. Edward S. Szymanski, Chap. Howard Co. General Hospital.
Office: 3175 Paulskirk Dr., 21042. Tel: 410-461-9111; Fax: 410-203-9419. Web: www.res-ec.org.
School—Resurrection/St. Paul, (Grades K-8), 315 Paulskirk Dr., 21042-2698. Fax: 410-461-8621. Web: www.resstpaul.org. Karen Murphy, Prin. Lay Teachers 32; Students 452.
Catechesis/Religious Program—Tel: 410-461-9111, Ext. 221. Kate Kleintank, D.R.E.; Ginny Ryan, C.R.E.; Martha Bode, Dir. Adult Education. Students 820.

EMMITSBURG, FREDERICK CO.

1—ST. ANTHONY SHRINE (1805) [CEM] Ms. Barbara Anderson, Parish Life Dir.; Deacon John A. Hawkins.
Res. & Office Address: 16150 St. Anthony Rd., 21727. Tel: 301-447-2367; Fax: 301-447-3618. Email: sasolmc@archbalt.org. Web: www.emmitsburg.net/sasolmc.
Catechesis/Religious Program—Tel: 301-271-4099; Fax: 301-271-7127. Sr. M. Valent Rusin, F.S.S.J., D.R.E. & Pastoral Min. Students 36.

2—ST. JOSEPH (1793) [CEM 2] Revs. Vincent J. O'Malley, C.M.; Stephen P. Trzecieski, C.M.; Paul M. Murphy, C.M.; Deacon Robert L. Baker. In Res., Revs. Michael J. Kennedy, C.M., Chap. St. Elizabeth Seton Shrine; Walter T. Menig, C.M., Chap. St. Michael Villa.
Res.: 47 DePaul St., P.O. Box 376, 21727. Tel: 301-447-2326; Fax: 301-447-3579. Email: stjosephemmitsburg@comcast.net. Web: www.emmitsburg.net/st.josephparish.
Catechesis/Religious Program—Rina Roca, Dir. Faith Formation; Roberta Alvarez, Coord. Youth Ministry. Students 110.

FALLSTON, HARFORD CO., ST. MARK (1887) Rev. Edward B. Hemler; Deacons Charles W. Hicks; Marty Perry; Mrs. Charlotte Henderson, Pastoral Assoc.
Res.: 812 Reckord Rd., 21047. Tel: 410-879-9110; Fax: 410-877-0576.
Catechesis/Religious Program—Tel: 410-879-1706; Fax: 410-877-3502. Mrs. Bridget Goedekl, D.R.E. Students 554.

FREDERICK, FREDERICK CO.

1—ST. JOHN THE EVANGELIST (1763) [CEM] Rev. Msgr. Richard J. Murphy; Revs. Richard Gray, M.S.A.; Daniel Goulet; Deacons John L. Manley; Daniel C. Roff.
Res.: 112 E. Second St., 21701. Tel: 301-662-8288; Fax: 301-698-1832. Web: www.stjohn-frederick.org.
See St. John Regional Catholic School, Frederick under Elementary Schools, Regional and Community located in the Institution section.
Catechesis/Religious Program—Tel: 301-662-6722; Fax: 301-695-7024. Julie St. Croix, D.R.E., Elementary and Family Catechesis; Mr. Joseph Mele, Dir. Youth Min.; Ms. Amy Spessard, Dir. Evangelization. Students 387.

2—ST. KATHARINE DREXEL ROMAN CATHOLIC CONGREGATION, INC. (2000) Rev. Keith W. Boisvert; Deacons Jeff Sutterman; Doug Nathan; Leah Huber, Pastoral Assoc.; Brian McCrohan, Pastoral Assoc.; Laura Webber, Pastoral Assoc.
8428 Opossumtown Pike, 21702. Tel: 301-360-9581; Fax: 301-360-9582. Email: stkatharinedrexel@saintdrexel.org. Web: www.saintdrexel.org.
Catechesis/Religious Program—Laura Weber, D.R.E. Students 175.

FROSTBURG, ALLEGANY CO., ST. MICHAEL (1852) [CEM] Rev. Msgr. James W. Hannon; Deacon W. Frederick Passquer, Pastoral Assoc.
Res.: 44 E. Main St., 21532. Tel: 301-689-6767; Fax: 301-689-6411. Email: smfrostb@archbalt.org.
Catechesis/Religious Program—Tel: 301-689-2898. Camilla Rawe, D.R.E.; Kathleen Broadwater, Coord. Youth Ministry. Students 95.

FULTON, HOWARD CO., ST. FRANCIS OF ASSISI (1988) Rev. Dennis P. Diehl; Deacon Joseph McKenna; Berta Sabrio, Dir. Liturgy & Music; Tracey Eberhardt, Dir. Health Ministry.
Office: 8300 Old Columbia Rd., 20759. Tel: 410-792-0470; Fax: 410-792-0472. Email: office@instrumentofpeace.org. Web: www.instrumentofpeace.org.
Res.: 10681 Glen Hannah Dr., Laurel, 20723. Tel: 410-880-3068.
Catechesis/Religious Program—Becki Kaman, Youth Min. Students 491.

GAMBRILLS, ANNE ARUNDEL CO., CHURCH OF THE HOLY APOSTLES (2004) Rev. Kevin A. Mueller; Sr. Angela Case, S.S.J., Asst. for Community Life & Adult Prog.; Deacon Keith D. Chase.
Res.: 1755 Urby Dr., Crofton, 21114. Tel: 410-451-8285. Web: www.holyapostlesmd.org.
See School of the Incarnation, Inc., Gambrills under Elementary Schools, Regional and Community located in the Institution section.
Church of the Holy Apostles Roman Catholic Congregation, Inc.—Tel: 410-519-2291; Fax: 410-519-2299.
Catechesis/Religious Program—Michele Dougherty, Faith Formation, Sacramental Prep & Youth Ministry; Nancy Lerch, C.R.E. Students 200.

GLEN BURNIE, ANNE ARUNDEL CO.

1—CHURCH OF THE GOOD SHEPHERD (1972) Rev. Msgr. J. Bruce Jarboe; Revs. John L. Kelly, Pastor Emeritus (Retired); Michael DeAscanis.
Res.: 1451 Furnace Ave., 21060. Tel: 410-761-4607; Fax: 410-761-6019.
See Arthur Slade Regional Catholic School, Glen Burnie under Elementary Schools, Regional and Community located in the Institution section.
Catechesis/Religious Program—Students 48.

2—CRUCIFIXION, CHURCH OF THE (1972) Rev. Msgr. J. Bruce Jarboe; Rev. Michael DeAscanis.
Rectory—100 Scott Ave., 21060. Tel: 410-768-4880; Fax: 410-768-5025.
Catechesis/Religious Program—Sandy Klohr, C.R.E. Students 68.

3—HOLY TRINITY (1919) Rev. Msgr. J. Bruce Jarboe; Deacons John J. Boscoe; Leroy Beimel; Kevin T. Brown; Kristin Walsh, Business Mgr. In Res., Revs. Jesus Aguirre Guzman, (Diocese of Oruro); Michael DeAscanis.
Res.: 126 Dorsey Rd., 21061. Tel: 410-766-1214. Email: office@holytrinitycc.org. Web: www.holytrinitycc.org.
Parish Center—126 Dorsey Rd., 21061. Tel: 410-766-5070; Fax: 410-760-6738.
See Monsignor Slade Catholic School, Glen Burnie under Elementary Schools, Regional and Community located in the Institution section.
Catechesis/Religious Program—Tel: 410-768-3890; Fax: 410-760-6738. Pat Stanley, D.R.E. (PreK-5); Karen Ng, D.R.E. (6-12). Students 500.

GLYNDON, BALTIMORE CO., SACRED HEART (1873) Rev. Msgr. Lloyd E. Aiken; Rev. Marc L. Lanoue; Sr. Judith Cianfrogna, S.S.J., Pastoral Assoc.; Deacon James A. Ryan; Sr. Helen Wiegman, S.S.J., Health Care Ministry.
65 Sacred Heart Ln., P.O. Box 3672, 21071-3672. Tel: 410-833-1696; Fax: 410-833-2676. Email: parish@shgparish.org. Web: www.shgparish.org.
School—(Grades PreK-8), 63 Sacred Heart Ln., P.O. Box 3672, 21071-3672. Tel: 410-833-0857; Fax: 410-833-0914. Email: school@shgschool.org. Web: www.shgsc.org. Mrs. Sherri Wright, Prin.; Jeanne Cossentino, Asst. Prin.; Ms. Mary Renehan, Asst. Prin. Sisters 1; Lay Teachers 39; Students 775.
Catechesis/Religious Program—Tel: 410-833-8515. Ms. Mae Richardson, Coord. Youth Ministry. Students 574.
Convent—Sacred Heart, 81 Sacred Heart Ln., P.O. Box 3672, 21071-3677. Tel: 410-526-1327.

GRANTSVILLE, NORTHERN GARRETT CO., ST. ANN (1976) Rev. Msgr. James W. Hannon; Rev. Patrick Besel; Deacon W. Frederick Passauer, Pastoral Assoc.
Res.: 12814 New Germany Rd., 21536. Tel: 301-689-6767; Fax: 301-689-6411. Email: sagrants@archbalt.org.
Catechesis/Religious Program—Camilla Rawe, C.R.E.; Kathleen Broadwater, Youth Min. Students 37.

HAGERSTOWN, WASHINGTON CO.

1—ST. ANN (1966) Rev. C. Douglas Kenney; Deacons William Nairn; Richard Kunkel, (Retired); Gary Fulmer.
Res.: 12817 Cathedral Ave., 21742. Tel: 301-791-2727. Email: church@stannchurch.com. Web: www.stannhagerstown.parishesonline.com.
Church: 1525 Oak Hill Ave., 21742. Tel: 301-733-0410; Fax: 301-733-6218.
Catechesis/Religious Program—Tel: 301-733-0410, Ext. 20. Linda Snyder, D.R.E., Youth Min.; Karen Gullace, Confirmation & Life Teen Dir.; Rita Mahoney, Adult Faith Formation Coord. Students 284.

2—ST. JOSEPH (1951) Rev. Christopher P. Moore.
Res.: 17630 Virginia Ave., 21740. Tel: 301-797-9445; Fax: 301-797-2490. Email: stjoe319@verizon.net. Web: www.parishesonline.com/stjosephhagerstown.
Catechesis/Religious Program—Tel: 301-790-1610. Denise Kuhna, D.R.E.; Neil Becker, Youth Min. Students 160.

3—ST. MARY (1790) Revs. J. Collin Poston, Admin.; James Nirappel.
Res.: 224 W. Washington St., 21740. Tel: 301-739-0390; Fax: 301-739-7082.
School—(Grades K-8), 218 Washington St., Hagerstown, 21740. Tel: 301-733-1184; Fax: 301-745-4997. Web: www.stmarycatholicschool.org. Mrs. Patricia McDermott, Prin. School Sisters of Notre Dame 2; Lay Teachers 24; Students 260.
Catechesis/Religious Program—Tel: 301-790-2444. Jan McCarter, Exec. Sec. Rel. Educ. Students 166.
Mission—St. Michael 31 S. Martin St., Clear Spring, Washington Co. 21722.

HANCOCK, WASHINGTON CO., ST. PETER'S (1834) [CEM] Rev. John F. Lesnick.
Res. & Mailing Address: 16 E. High St., 21750. Tel: 301-678-6339; Fax: 301-678-6608. Email: officestpeter@verizon.net.
Mission—St. Patrick's (1860) [CEM] 12517 St. Patrick Rd., S.E., Little Orleans, Allegany Co. 21766.
Catechesis/Religious Program—Miss Susan Taylor, D.R.E. Students 85.

HAVRE DE GRACE, HARFORD CO., ST. PATRICK'S (1847) [CEM] Rev. William J. O'Brien III; Sr. Frances Schiminsky, O.S.F., Pastoral Assoc.; Mary Wancowicz, Admin.; Richard Allen, Dir. Music.
Res.: 615 Congress Ave., 21078. Tel: 410-939-2525; 410-575-6741; Fax: 410-575-6490. Email: sphgrace@archbalt.org.
Catechesis/Religious Program—Tel: 410-939-2544. Nancy Elder, C.R.E. Students 145.

HICKORY, HARFORD CO., ST. IGNATIUS (1792) [CEM] Rev. Msgr. James Barker; Revs. Charles L. Lafferty, Pastor Emeritus (Retired); Stephen Sutton; Mark Bialek; Deacons Robert Lehr, Dir. Operations; Ralph Trautwein, Pastoral Assoc.; Peter J. Calabrese; Lee A. Benson; Deborah Czawlytko, Pastoral Assoc. & Parish Nurse. In Res., Rev. Kennard Muller (Retired).
Res.: 533 E. Jarrettsville Rd., Forest Hill, 21050. Tel: 410-879-1926; Fax: 410-879-1352.
Catechesis/Religious Program—Tel: 410-879-9390. Mary Lou Hare, Dir. Faith Formation; Doris Wheeler, Coord. Faith Formation; Cetta York, Coord. Family Ministry; Susan Strickroth, Dir. Youth Ministry. Students 1,280.

HUNT VALLEY, BALTIMORE CO., CATHOLIC COMMUNITY OF ST. FRANCIS XAVIER (1988) Rev. Frank J. Brauer; Deacon Donald Murray.
13717 Cuba Rd., P.O. Box 407, 21030. Tel: 410-785-0356; Fax: 410-785-1628. Email: info@ccsfx.net. Web: www.ccsfx.org.
Catechesis/Religious Program—Patricia Allshouse, C.R.E.; Ms. Joanie Carlson, Coord. Middle School; Mr. John Mojzisek, Youth Min. Students 445.

HYDES, BALTIMORE CO., ST. JOHN THE EVANGELIST (1822) [CEM] Rev. William F. Franken; Rev. Msgrs. John C. Collopy (Retired); Charles F. Meisel (Retired); Deacon Frederick X. Schoennagel. In Res., Most Rev. William C. Newman (Retired).
Res.: 13305 Long Green Pike, 21082. Tel: 410-592-6206; Fax: 410-817-4432. Email: sjehydes@sjehydes.org. Web: www.stjohnhydes.org.
School—(Grades PreK-8), 13311 Long Green Pike, 21082. Tel: 410-592-9585, Ext. 120; Fax: 410-817-4548. Email: school@stjohnhydes.org. Web: www.stjohnhydes.org. Mrs. Genevieve Delcher, Prin. Lay Teachers 30; Students 323.
Catechesis/Religious Program—M. Theresa Konitzer, D.R.E.; Mrs. M. Colleen Sisolak, Youth & Young Adult Ministry. Students 427.

IJAMSVILLE, FREDERICK CO., ST. IGNATIUS OF LOYOLA (1983) Rev. Michael J. Jendrek; Deacon Larry Matheny.
Office: 4103 Prices Distillery Rd., 21754. Tel: 301-695-8845; Fax: 301-695-0259. Email: pastor@e-stignatius.org. Web: www.e-stignatius.org.
Res.: 4914 Bush Creek Dr., Monrovia, 21770. Tel: 301-865-5783.
See St. John Regional Catholic School, Frederick under Elementary Schools, Regional and Community located in the Institution section.
Catechesis/Religious Program—Carol Smith, Coord. Faith Formation & Youth Ministry. Students 764.

JESSUP, ANNE ARUNDEL CO., ST. LAWRENCE MARTYR (1866) [CEM] Revs. Juan Vazquez-Rubio, O.SS.T.; John Dorn, O.SS.T.; Deacon John Sedlevicius.

In Res., Rev. Aaron M. Dowdell, O.SS.T.
Res.: 7669 Clark Rd., Hanover, 21076. Tel: 410-799-1970; Fax: 410-799-1143. Email: office@stlawrencemartyr.org. Web: www.saintlawrencemartyr.org.
See Arthur Slade Regional Catholic School, Glen Burnie under Elementary Schools, Regional and Community located in the Institution section.
Catechesis / Religious Program—St. Lawrence School of Religion, P.O. Box 1188, 2821 Jessup Rd., 20794. Tel: 410-799-7790; Fax: 410-799-7291. Mrs. Valerie Magnuson, D.R.E. Students 76.

JOPPA, HARFORD CO., CHURCH OF THE HOLY SPIRIT (1963) Rev. Joseph C. Simmons.
Res.: 540 Joppa Farm Rd., 21085. Tel: 410-679-2191; Fax: 410-679-2874. Email: hspiritchurch@aol.com. Web: www.hspiritchurch.org. Office: Tel: 410-679-0378; Fax: 410-679-2874.
Catechesis / Religious Program—Sr. Susanne Bunn, M.H.S.H., Dir. Faith Formation. Students 99.

LAUREL, ANNE ARUNDEL CO., RESURRECTION OF OUR LORD (1968) Rev. John T. Wielebski; Michael Ruzicki, Pastoral Assoc. Liturgy & Music.
Res.: 407 Forest Bridge Ct., 20724. Tel: 301-498-7107; Fax: 410-792-8337. Email: rollaure@archbalt.org. Web: www.resurrectionofourlord.com.
Office Address: 8402 Brock Bridge Rd., 20724. Email: office@resurrectionofourlord.com.
Catechesis / Religious Program—Tel: 301-498-9803. Danica Tarantino, Dir. Faith Formation; Mr. Fernando Cartagena, Youth & Young Adult Ministry. Students 174.

LIBERTYTOWN, FREDERICK CO., ST. PETER (1821) [CEM] Rev. Jason Worley; Deacon Michael Misulia.
P.O. Box 278, 21762.
Res.: 9201 Green Valley Rd., 21762. Tel: 301-898-5111 (Office); 301-898-9069 (Rectory); Fax: 301-898-0465. Web: www.stpeters-libertytown.org.
Catechesis / Religious Program—Anne Mason, C.R.E. (Children); Ms. Caroline Nolan, C.R.E. (Adults); Harry Ford, C.R.E. (Youth). Students 713.

LINTHICUM HEIGHTS, ANNE ARUNDEL CO., ST. PHILIP NERI (1964) Rev. Dale Picarella; Deacons Robert Keeley; David Tengwall. In Res., Rev. John L. Lippold (Retired).
Parish Center—6405 S. Orchard Rd., 21090-2628. Tel: 410-859-0571; Fax: 410-859-5047.
School—(Grades K-8), 6401 Orchard Rd., 21090. Tel: 410-859-1212; Fax: 410-859-5840. Email: spnschool@archbalt.org. Mrs. Shirley T. Wise, Prin. Lay Teachers 24; Students 389.
Catechesis / Religious Program—Tel: 410-859-4950, Ext. 224. Anne Nelson, D.R.E.; Hilary Bateman, Dir. Youth Ministry. Students 310.

LONACONING, ALLEGANY CO., ST. MARY OF THE ANNUNCIATION (1865) [CEM] Rev. Msgr. James W. Hannon; Deacon W. Frederick Passauer, Pastoral Assoc.
Res.: 16102 St. Mary Church Ter., 21539. Tel: 301-463-6770; Fax: 301-463-6729. Email: smlonaco@archbalt.org.
Catechesis / Religious Program—Kathleen Broadwater, C.R.E. Students 3.

MANCHESTER, CARROLL CO., ST. BARTHOLOMEW (1864) Rev. Michael J. Roach.
Mailing Address & Parish Center: 3071 Park Ave., 21102. Tel: 410-239-8881.
Res.: 2940 Park Ave., P.O. Box 448, 21102-0448. Tel: 410-239-8207; Fax: 410-239-3216.
Catechesis / Religious Program—Tom Abbott, C.R.E. (Adult); Lynn Szymanski, C.R.E.; Linda Sterner, C.R.E. (Youth Coord.). Students 466.

MIDDLETOWN, FREDERICK CO., HOLY FAMILY CATHOLIC COMMUNITY (1986) Revs. J. Kevin Farmer; John C. Moore, Pastor Emeritus (Retired); Deacon George Sisson.
Mailing Address: 321 Burkittsville Rd., 21769. Tel: 301-473-4800; Fax: 301-371-6810. Email: info@hfccmd.org. Web: www.hfccmd.org.
Res.: 3240 Old National Pike, 21769. Tel: 301-371-3239.
Church: 7321 Burkittsville Rd., 21769. Tel: 301-473-4800; Fax: 301-371-6810.
Catechesis / Religious Program—Mr. Ricardo Valdez, Dir. Faith Formation; Carolyn Kilonsky, Coord. Youth Ministry. Students 522.

MIDLAND, ALLEGANY CO., ST. JOSEPH (1891), (Irish), [CEM] Rev. Msgr. James W. Hannon; Deacon W. Frederick Passauer.
Mailing Address: 19925 Church St., P.O. Box 1, 21542. Tel: 301-463-6770; Fax: 301-463-6729. Email: stjoemid@archbalt.org.
Catechesis / Religious Program—Kathleen Broadwater, C.R.E. & Youth Ministry. Students 23.

MILLERSVILLE, ANNE ARUNDEL CO., OUR LADY OF THE FIELDS (1902) [CEM] Rev. G. Eugene Nickol; Deacons Anthony Grillo; Edward Stoops. In Res., Rev. Jose Opalda.
Res.: 1070 Cecil Ave. S., 21108. Tel: 410-987-1551; Fax: 410-987-9723. Email: lfields@archbalt.org. Web: www.ourladyofthefields.org.
See School of the Incarnation, Inc., Gambrills under Elementary Schools, Regional and Community located in the Institution section.
Catechesis / Religious Program—Tel: 410-923-2195. Donna Fischer, D.R.E. (Children); Scott Link, Youth Min.; Sue Dobryzkowski, C.R.E. (Adult). Students 1,052.

MOUNT SAVAGE, ALLEGANY CO., ST. PATRICK (1863) [CEM] Rev. Ty S. Hullinger, Admin.
Mailing Address: 15706 St. Patrick Church Rd., N.W., 21545. Tel: 301-264-3521; Fax: 301-264-3603. Email: spmtsav@archbalt.org.
Catechesis / Religious Program—Denise Lowery, C.R.E. Students 37.

OAKLAND, GARRETT CO., ST. PETER THE APOSTLE (1852) [CEM] Rev. Donald J. Parson.
Res.: 208 S. Fourth St., 21550. Tel: 301-334-2202; Fax: 301-334-9006. Email: spsecretary@archbalt.org. Web: www.catholicchurchofsoutherngarrettcounty.org.
Catechesis / Religious Program—Betty Eaton, D.R.E. Students 67.
Mission—St. Peter at the Lake Deep Creek Lake, Garrett Co. Dolores Gloeckl, Lake Center Coord.

ODENTON, ANNE ARUNDEL CO., ST. JOSEPH (1924) Rev. William L. Viola; Deacons Richard C. Swann; David A. Page; Mr. Robert Sutliff, Pastoral Assoc.
Mailing Address & Church: 1283 Odenton Rd., 21113. Tel: 410-551-9238; Fax: 410-674-4761. Email: parish@sjodenton.org. Web: www.stjosephodenton.org.
See School of the Incarnation, Inc., Gambrills under Elementary Schools, Regional and Community located in the Institution section.
Catechesis / Religious Program—Patricia Dieterich, D.R.E.; Michele Fulk, Coord. Youth Activities. Students 236.

PARKTON, BALTIMORE CO., OUR LADY OF GRACE (1974) Rev. Msgr. Nicholas P. Amato; Sr. Mary Therese White, O.S.F., Pastoral Assoc.
Res.: 425 Everett Rd., Monkton, 21111. Fax: 410-329-6830. Web: www.olgrace.com.
School—(Grades PreK-8) Tel: 410-329-6956; Fax: 410-357-5793. Web: www.olgs.org. Mrs. Byrdie Ricketts, Prin.
Parish Center—18310 Middletown Rd., 21120. Tel: 410-329-6826; Fax: 410-329-6830. Email: ehagner@earthlink.net.
Catechesis / Religious Program—Dr. Jack Buchner, D.R.E.; Deborah Webber, Coord. Youth Ministries. Students 472.

PASADENA, ANNE ARUNDEL CO.
1—ST. JANE FRANCES DE CHANTAL (Riviera Beach) (1946) Rev. Msgr. Carl F. Cummings; Rev. John J. Jicha; Deacon Robert Vlcej.
Res.: 8499 Virginia Ave., 21122. Tel: 410-255-4646; Fax: 410-437-5191. Web: www.stjane.org.
School—(Grades PreK-8), 8513 Saint Jane Dr., 21122. Tel: 410-255-4750; Fax: 410-360-6720. Mrs. Michelle Jones, Prin.; Renee Hammond, Vice Prin. Lay Teachers 28; Students 574.
Catechesis / Religious Program—Tel: 410-437-4727. Timothy Burkhart, D.R.E.; Melissa Serafin, Youth Ministry. Students 361.

2—OUR LADY OF THE CHESAPEAKE (1980) Revs. Brian M. Rafferty; Walter J. Paulits, Pastor Emeritus (Retired).
Church: 8325 Ventnor Rd., 21122. Tel: 410-255-3677; Fax: 410-437-7527. Email: info@olchesapeake.org. Web: www.olchesapeake-.org.
See Arthur Slade Regional Catholic School, Glen Burnie under Elementary Schools, Regional and Community in the Institution Section.
Catechesis / Religious Program—Fax: 410-437-7527. Carole Dowell, C.R.E.; Mr. Brian Harrison, C.R.E.; Tim Janiszewski, Youth Ministry. Students 456.

POPLAR SPRINGS, HOWARD CO., ST. MICHAEL (1879) [CEM] Rev. Michael J. Ruane; Deacon Harbey Santiago.
Res.: 1200 St. Michaels Rd., Mount Airy, 21771-3202. Tel: 410-489-4211; 410-442-2845. Email: smpoplar@archbolt.org. Web: www.stmichaelpoplarsprings.org.
Parish Center—Tel: 410-489-7667; 410-442-1717; Fax: 410-442-1486. Email: smpoplar@archbalt.org. Web: www.stmichaelspoplarsprings.org.
Catechesis / Religious Program—Tel: 410-489-7667; Fax: 410-442-1486. Stacey Ford, D.R.E.; Theodore P. Burkhardt, Youth & Young Adult Ministry. Students 820.

PYLESVILLE, HARFORD CO., ST. MARY (1855) [CEM] Rev. A. Henry Kunkel III; Deacons Simon M. Driesen; Gary Dumer; Phillip Seneschal.
Res.: 1021 St. Mary's Rd., 21132. Tel: 410-838-7471; 410-879-4015; Fax: 410-452-8493. Web: www.stmaryspylesville.org.
Catechesis / Religious Program— Janet Young, Coord. Christian Formation; Rachel Bittner, Youth Min. Students 353.

RANDALLSTOWN, BALTIMORE CO., HOLY FAMILY (1876) [CEM] Revs. Andrew S. Mohl; Walter J. McGovern, Senior Priest (Retired); Dennis W. Kast, Business Mgr. In Res., Rev. Msgr. William A. Collins.
Res., Church & Office: 9531 Liberty Rd., 21133. Tel: 410-922-3800; Fax: 410-922-3804.
School—(Grades K-8), 9535 Liberty Rd., 21133. Tel: 410-922-3677; Fax: 410-521-9764. Web: www.holyfamilyschool.org. Mr. Christopher M. Ashby, Prin. Lay Teachers 10; Students 141.
Catechesis / Religious Program—9531 Liberty Rd., 21133. Tel: 410-922-2805. Students 107.

SEVERN, ANNE ARUNDEL CO., ST. BERNADETTE (1972) Ann McDonald, Pastoral Life Dir. Tel: 410-969-2785.
Res.: 801 Stevenson Rd., 21144. Tel: 410-969-2783; Fax: 410-969-2789. Web: www.stbernadette.org.
See Arthur Slade Regional Catholic School, Glen Burnie under Elementary Schools, Regional and Community located in the Institution section.
Catechesis / Religious Program—Tel: 410-969-2786. Theresa Platania, D.R.E.; Marge Sholl, Coord. Youth Ministry; Andrea Montrose, Coord. Youth Educ. Students 225.

SEVERNA PARK, ANNE ARUNDEL CO., ST. JOHN THE EVANGELIST (1927) Revs. James Proffitt; Stewart Bullock; Deacons Ronald Thompson; Dean Lopata. In Res., Rev. Msgr. John J. Auer (Retired).
Res.: 689 Ritchie Hwy., S.E., 21146. Tel: 410-647-4884; Fax: 410-544-3047. Web: www.stjohnsp.org.
School—(Grades K-8), 669 Ritchie Hwy., 21146. Tel: 410-647-2283; Fax: 410-431-5438. Sr. Linda Larsen, S.S.J., Prin. Sisters of St. Joseph, Chestnut Hill 5; Lay Teachers 30; Students 460.
Catechesis / Religious Program—Tel: 410-647-4892; Fax: 410-431-8912. John Poland, D.R.E.; Jen Mayer, Adult Faith Formation; Cassandra Anderson, Youth Min. Students 770.
Convent—679 Ritchie Hwy., 21146. Tel: 410-647-2041. Sisters of St. Joseph 6.

SYKESVILLE, CARROLL CO., ST. JOSEPH (1868) [CEM] Revs. Terence Weik, S.M.; Paul A. Reich, S.M.; David McGuigan, S.M.; Deacons Todd Smith; Karl Bayhi.
Office: 915 Liberty Rd., 21784. Tel: 443-920-9191; Fax: 410-795-7516. Email: parishoffice@saintsjoseph.cc. Web: www.stjosepheldersburg.org.
Res.: 6049 Kennard Ct., Eldersburg, 21784. Tel: 410-795-2722.
Catechesis / Religious Program—Tel: 410-552-5402; Fax: 410-795-7516. Nora Rozelle, D.R.E.; Thomas Hild, Youth Min.; Jackie Antkowiak, Adult Formation. Students 1,295.

TANEYTOWN, CARROLL CO., ST. JOSEPH (1797) [CEM] Rev. Msgr. Martin Eugene Feild; Deacons Darrell W. Smith; Stanley Wise, (Retired).
Res.: 44 Frederick St., 21787. Tel: 410-756-2500; Fax: 410-756-1260. Email: sjtaney@archbalt.org.
Catechesis / Religious Program—Tel: 410-876-8108. Terry Smith, C.R.E. Students 182.

THURMONT, FREDERICK CO., OUR LADY OF MOUNT CARMEL (1856) [CEM] Ms. Barbara Anderson, Parish Life Dir.; Sr. M. Valenta Rusin, F.S.S.J., Pastoral Min. & Dir. Rel. Educ.
Office: 16150 St. Anthony Rd., Emmitsburg, 21727. Email: saolmc@archbalt.org. Web: www.emmitsburg.net/sasolmc.
Church: 103 N. Church St., 21788.
Catechesis / Religious Program—18 N., Altamont Ave., 21788. Tel: 301-271-4099; Fax: 301-271-7127. Sr. M. Valent Rusin, F.S.S.J., Pastoral Min./DRE. Tel: 301-271-4099. Students 94.

TIMONIUM, BALTIMORE CO., CHURCH OF THE NATIVITY (1968) Rev. Michael J. White; Tom Corcoran, Pastoral Assoc.
20 E. Ridgely Rd., 21093. Tel: 410-252-6080; Fax: 410-252-2657. Web: www.churchnativity.org.
Catechesis / Religious Program—Students 562.

WALKERSVILLE, FREDERICK CO., ST. TIMOTHY (1980) Rev. Andrew Aaron.
Res.: 200 Glade Blvd., 21793. Tel: 301-845-8043; Fax: 301-845-4902.
Church: 8651 Biggs Rd., 21793. Tel: 301-845-8025.
Catechesis / Religious Program—Tel: 301-845-8025. Yvette Leith, D.R.E.; Marissa Alspaugh, Dir. Youth Faith Formation. Students 275.

WEST RIVER, ANNE ARUNDEL CO., OUR LADY OF SORROWS (1866) [CEM] Rev. Mark Logue.
Res.: 101 Owensville Rd., 20778. Tel: 410-867-2059; 410-269-6803; Fax: 410-867-8276. Email: frmark@olos.us. Web: www.olos.us.
Catechesis / Religious Program—Tel: 410-867-1941. Mary Catherine Haines, D.R.E. Students 309.

WESTERNPORT, ALLEGANY CO., ST. PETER (1857) [CEM] Rev. Msgr. James W. Hannon; Deacon W. Frederick Passauer, Pastoral Assoc.
Res.: 127 Church St., 21562. Tel: 301-359-3055; Fax: 301-359-0657. Email: stpeter127@verizon.net.
Catechesis / Religious Program—Tel: 301-359-9832. Kathleen Broadwater, C.R.E. & Youth Ministry.

Students 71.
Mission—St. Gabriel Barton, 21521.

WESTMINSTER, CARROLL CO., ST. JOHN (1853) [CEM] Rev. Msgr. Arthur F. Valenzano; Revs. Hector Mateus-Ariza; D. Martin; Deacons Donald W. Miller; Joseph M. Cinquino; Mark Ripper.
Res.: 43 Monroe St., 21157. Tel: 410-848-4744; 410-876-2248; Fax: 410-857-1519. Email: sjwestmi@archbalt.org. Web: www.sjwest.org.
School—(Grades K-8), 45 Monroe St., 21157. Tel: 410-848-7455; Fax: 410-848-2822. Web: sjwest.org. Mrs. Harriann Walker, Prin. Lay Teachers 30; Students 520.
*Catechesis/Religious Program—*Tel: 410-848-8443. Paul D. Gallagher, D.R.E.; Ruth Hartman, C.R.E. (PreK-4); Jordan Tippett, C.R.E. (5-8). Students 968.

WILLIAMSPORT, WASHINGTON CO., ST. AUGUSTINE (1854) Revs. Stephen Hook; John T. Carter, Pastor Emeritus (Retired); Rev. Msgr. Alfred E. Smith, Pastor Emeritus (Retired); April Dietrich, Pastoral Assoc.
Res.: 32 E. Potomac St., 21795. Tel: 301-223-7959; Fax: 301-223-9506. Web: www.staugustinemd.org.
*Catechesis/Religious Program—*Sherry Brodnan, C.R.E.; David Gentile, Youth Ministry High School. Students 35.

WOODSTOCK, BALTIMORE CO., ST. ALPHONSUS RODRIGUEZ (1869) [CEM] Rev. Joseph P. Lacey, S.J.; Dee Papania, Pastoral Assoc.
Res.: 10800 Old Court Rd., 21163. Tel: 410-461-5267; Fax: 410-750-7286. Email: stalphonsus@comcast.net.
*Catechesis/Religious Program—*De Papania, D.R.E.; Valerie Herrington, Youth Min. Students 246.

SHRINES, NATIONAL SHRINE OF ST. ELIZABETH ANN SETON Mrs. Karen Harding, Dir.
333 S. Seton Ave., Emmitsburg, 21727. Tel: 301-447-6606; Fax: 301-447-6061. Email: office@setonshrine.org. Web: www.setonshrine.org.

Chaplains of Public Institutions

BALTIMORE. *Baltimore City Detention Center - Men*, 401 Eager St., 21202. Tel: 410-523-0061. Rev. Msgr. Damien G. Nalepa, V.F., Chap.
Baltimore City Jail Detention Center - Women, 401 Eager St., 21202. Tel: 410-209-4216. Sr. Patricia Ash, S.S.J., Chap.
Carroll County Detention Center. Debbie Loveland, Volunteer Coord. Tel: 410-857-1201.
Franklin Square Hospital Center. Covered on rotating basis by Our Lady of Mt. Carmel; St. Clare; St. Elizabeth; St. Rita; Church of the Annunciation, St. Clement Mary Hofbauer; Sacred Heart of Mary, St. Anthony; Most Precious Blood.
Greater Baltimore Medical Center, Tel: 410-427-4700. Immaculate Conception, Towson
Harbor Hospital (1959)Tel: 410-685-2255. St. Mary Star of the Sea
James Lawrence Kernan Hospital, Tel: 410-298-8888. St. Gabriel, Woodlawn
Johns Hopkins Bayview Medical Center, Tel: 410-633-9393. Our Lady of Fatima
Johns Hopkins Hospital. Rev. Paul C. Sparklin.
Maryland Correctional Adjustment Center, 401 E. Madison St., 21201. Tel: 410-539-5445. Rev. Charles J. Canterna.
Maryland General Hospital. St. Ignatius; Church of the Immaculate Conception
Maryland Penitentiary Complex, 954 Forest St., 21202. Rev. Chuck Canterna, Chap. Tel: 410-539-5445.
Mt. Washington Pediatric Hospital, Tel: 410-466-6884. Shrine of the Sacred Heart
Northwest Hospital Center, Tel: 410-922-3800. Holy Family, Randallstown
Sheppard Pratt Hospital, Tel: 410-427-4700. Immaculate Conception, Towson
Sinai Hospital of Baltimore. Covered on rotating basis by St. Ambrose; Shrine of the Sacred Heart
Union Memorial Hospital. SS. Philip & James, Blessed Sacrament & St. Thomas Aquinas
University of Maryland Medical System. St. Leo; St. Mary, Star of the Sea
University of Maryland- R. Adams Crowley Shock Trauma. Rev. Lawrence Schulmeister, O.F.M.

ANNAPOLIS. *Anne Arundel Medical Center*, Tel: 410-263-2397. St. Andrew by the Bay (Cape St. Clare)

COLUMBIA. *Howard County General Hospital*, Tel: 410-964-1425. St. John the Evangelist, Columbia

CUMBERLAND. *Federal & State Correctional Facilities* 21505. Rev. Ty S. Hullinger, S.T.B. Tel: 301-777-2990. St. Mary's, Cumberland
Memorial Hospital & Medical Center, Tel: 301-777-2990. St. Mary, Cumberland

ELLICOTT CITY. *Taylor Manor Hospital*, Tel: 410-465-1670. St. Paul, Ellicott City

FALLSTON. *Fallston General Hospital*, Tel: 410-879-9110. St. Mark, Fallston; Our Lady of LaVang

FREDERICK. *Frederick Memorial Hospital*. Tel: 301-662-8288. St. John the Evangelist, Frederick

HAGERSTOWN. *Brook Lane Psychiatric Hospital*, Tel: 301-733-0410. St. Ann, Hagerstown
Maryland Correction Training Center 21740. Tel: 240-420-1601. Mr. Bob Lashinsky, Volunteer Coord. Tel: 240-420-1601.
Maryland Correctional Institution- Hagerstown 21740. Tel: 240-420-1601. Mr. Bob Lashinsky, Volunteer Coord. Tel: 240-420-1601.
Roxbury Correctional Institution 21740. Tel: 240-420-1601. Mr. Bob Lashinsky, Volunteer Coord. Tel: 240-420-1601.

HAVRE DE GRACE. *Harford Memorial Hospital*, Tel: 410-939-2525. St. Patrick, Havre de Grace

GLEN BURNIE. *Baltimore Washington Medical Center*. Covered on rotating basis by Holy Trinity; Good Shepherd; St. Bernadette (Severn), Our Lady of the Chesapeake; St. Joseph (Odenton); St. Jane Francis de Chantal

JESSUP. *Brockbridge Correction Facility*, 7931 Brockbridge Rd., 20794. Tel: 410-792-0470. Tracey Eberhardt, Volunteer Coord.
Clifton T. Perkins Hospital 20794. Tel: 410-547-5475. Rev. Msgr. John J. Auer (Retired).
Jessup Pre-Release Unit 20794. Tel: 410-566-0877. Terrie McGill, Volunteer Coord.
Maryland Correctional Institution for Women 20794. Tel: 410-547-5475. Kathy Reid, Volunteer Coord. Tel: 410-795-7838, Ext. 113.
Maryland Correctional Institution-Jessup 20794. Tel: 410-964-1438. Jim Sanders, Chap. Tel: 410-799-0100, Ext. 2836.
Patuxent Institution 20794. Tel: 410-518-9977. Bill Cornolius, Volunteer Coord.
Toulson Correctional Boot Camp 20794. Tel: 410-547-5475. John Reinhard, Volunteer Coord. Tel: 410-730-6289.

OAKLAND. *Garrett County Memorial Hospital*, Tel: 301-334-2204. St. Peter the Apostle, Oakland

WESTMINSTER. *Carroll County General Hospital*, Tel: 410-848-4744. St. John, Westminster

---

Special Assignment:
Rev. Msgrs.—
FitzGerald, John L., Apostleship of the Sea Chaplaincy for Port of Baltimore
Jaskot, Robert, S.T.B., S.T.L., J.C.L., Office of Worship
O'Connor, Jay F., Dir., Div. of Clergy Personnel
Woy, Richard W., Dir. Office Worship, St. Mary's Seminary
Revs.—
Besel, Patrick, Assoc. Vocation Dir., Dir. Keeler House of Discernment
Breighner, Joseph F., Retreats & Missions
Canterna, Charles J., Chap., Prison Ministry
Chase, Raymond, Chap., St. Charles Borromeo & Catholic Charities
Cote, Joseph J., Chap., SSND Motherhouse
Ferri, Gregory J., Hospital Chap., John Hopkins Hospital Bayview Center
Francik, Gerard C., Vocation Dir., 320 Cathedral St., 21201.
Gosnell, Stephen D., Chap., 320 Cathedral St., 21201. Mercy Medical Center
Hendricks, Edward S., Campus Min. & Dir. Higher Education, Frostburg State
Henry, Paul J., Jr., Retreats & Missions
Jakopac, George I., St. John Catholic Prep
Johnson, Lawrence M., Chap., Stella Maris
Malia, Thomas R., Chap., Mercy Medical Center, St. Clements
Martin, Raymond D., Pastoral Care, Carroll Hospital Center
Murphy, Michael A., Chap. & Teacher, Mt. St. Joseph High School
Murphy, T. Austin, Jr., Chap., Newman Center, Towson University
Nocchi, Martin S., Dir., Msgr. O'Dwyer Retreat House, Sparks, 21152. O'Dwyer Retreat House
Nolan, Brian P., Dir. Campus Min., Mount St. Mary's University
Parker, Adam, Sec. to the Archbishop, Secretary to Archbishop
Patalinghug, Leo E., S.T.L., Dir. Pastoral Formation, Mount St. Mary's Seminary
Reusing, James M., Chap., Good Samaritan Hospital
Rock, Larry G., Faculty, Maria Goretti High School, Hagerstown
Ryan, Thomas, Chap., John Hopkins Univ., Newman Apostolate. Neuman Center - John Hopkins Hospital
Seitz, Gilbert J., J.C.L., Interim Judicial Vicar of the Metropolitan Tribual, 320 Cathedral St., 21201.
Spacek, William F., Chap., Univ. of MD Hospital
Sparklin, Paul C., Chap., Johns Hopkins Hospital
Szymanski, Edward S., Hospital Chap., Chaplain Healthcare Facilities, Howard County

---

On Duty Outside the Archdiocese:
Revs.—
Hilgartner, Richard B., USCCB, 4001 14th St., N.E., Washington, DC 20017.
Lesnick, John F., Belmont Abbey
Lobert, Richard C., Chap. & Head Theology Dept., 9841 Hamburg Rd, Brighton, MI 48116. Father Gabriel Richard High School
Maillet, Paul A., S.S., B.Mus., M.M., M.Div., S.T.L., Society of St. Sulpice, 401 Michigan Ave., N.E., Washington, DC 20017.
Morey, Robert E., Holy Family, 24 Pope Ave., Hilton Head Island, SC 29928. Extern in diocese of Charlston
Peach, D. Patrick, Carmelite Hermitage
Warman, William C., VA Hospital, P.O. Box 31, Lyons, NJ 07939. VA Hospital

---

Graduate Studies:
Revs.—
Byrne, Glenn F., Theology, Somerville, MA
Cibelli, Ernest W., Pontifical North American College
Harris, Raymond L., St. Paul College, 3015 4th St., NE, Washington, DC 20017-1102. CUA - Cannon Law Studies
Maillet, Paul A., S.S., B.Mus., M.M., M.Div., S.T.L., St. Mary's Seminary

---

Military Chaplains:
Revs.—
Gills, Thomas, 75 ABW/HC, 5711 East Ave., Hill Air Force Base, UT 84056. U.S.A.F.
Kruse, David B., 1st Lt., PSC2, P.O. Box 13365, Apo, AE 09012-0087. U.S.A.F.
Ochalek, Arkdiusz, Chaplain Basic Officer Leader Course US Army
Spencer, F. Richard, CH LTC, HHC, 2-ID, Unit 15041, Apo, AP 96258. U.S. Army
Wood, Tyson J., 5321 Tarkington Pl., Columbia, 21044. US Army

---

Priests Sick or Absent:
Rev. Msgr.—
Kinsella, John
Revs.—
Bianco, Louis A.
Bonderenko, Thomas
Eckard, John
Golueke, Thomas J.
Kenny, P. Edward, Jr.
Kightlinger, Jon T.
Kucharczyk, John J.
McFadden, Frank
Messina, John
Metzger, Thomas
O'Brien, John E.
Pietropaoli, David
Rice, Charles
Richardson, Stephen S.
Rouse, Charles Owen
Schenk, Raymond C.
Thornsberry, Michael J.
Waudby, Lawrence
Zeller, Leonard H.

Retired:
His Eminence—
Keeler, William Cardinal, 14th Archbishop of Baltimore, 408 N. Charles St., 21201.
Most Revs.—
Borders, William Donald, 13th Archbishop of Baltimore, Mercy Ridge S201, 2525 Pot Spring Rd., Timonium, 21093.
Newman, William C., D.D., V.G., Auxiliary Bishop of Baltimore, 6536 Cherry Hill Rd., Baldwin, 21013.
Rev. Msgrs.—
Armstrong, Robert
Auer, John J., St. John the Evangelist, 689 Ritchie Hwy., Severna Park, 21146.
Baumgartner, A. Thomas, St. Dominic, 5302 Harford Rd., 21214.
Bozel, Robert A., Mercy Ridge S635, 2525 Pot Spring Rd., Timonium, 21093-2764.
Byrnes, Paul A., 210 Hazelhurst Ln., Swanton, 21561.
Collopy, John C., Mercy Ridge S733, 2525 Pot Spring Rd., Timonium, 21093.
Donellen, Thomas J., Hampton House, 204 E. Joppa Rd., #515, 21204.
Hobbs, James V., 206 E. Main St., Thurmont, 21788.
Kenney, Jeremiah F.
Lynch, Edward J., Mercy Ridge S735, 2525 Pot Spring Rd., Timonium, 21093.
McGovern, James O., V.F.
Meisel, Charles F., Mercy Ridge S614, 2525 Pot Spring Rd., Timonium, 21093.

Mieczkowski, Chester J., 3215 Fleet St., 21224.
Moeller, George B.
Parks, Richard E., 205 Robwood Rd., 21222.
Smith, Alfred E., 224 Sunbrook Ln., Hagerstown, 21742.
Strempeck, Martin R., St. Margaret, 141 Hickory Ave., Bel Air, 21014.
Tewes, Thomas J., 3905 Darleigh Rd., #E3, Nottingham, 21236.
Tinder, Frederick D.

Revs.—
Abrahams, John J., 46 Abraham Rd., Port Deposit, 21904.
Albright, Robert E., 7415 Chesapeake Rd., 21220.
Bayer, Edward J., Sacred Heart Seminary, Kokopom, East New Britain, Papua, New Guinea Oceania.
Buettner, George J., Mercy Ridge SSG313, 2525 Pot Spring Rd., Timonium, 21093.
Buttner, Michael T., 600 Squire Ln., #2G, Bel Air, 21014.
Callahan, Francis X., 8820 Blairwoods Ct., Apt. 103, 21236.
Carey, David M., 6 Econway Ct., Apt. 3D, Towson, 21286.
Carney, John J.
Carr, Brendan
Carter, John T., Mercy Ridge - S618, 2525 Pot Spring Rd., Timonium, 21093.
Collins, William A.
Donaghy, Thomas J., Ph.D., 233 Mohawk Ave., Norwood, PA 19074-1208.
Fullen, John N., 4820 Piney Branch Rd., Fairfax, VA 22030.
Gallagher, John J.
Gesy, Lawrence J., 7121 Queen St., Kearneysville, WV 25430.
Hill, Edward T., 4614 Eugene Ave., 21206.
Hipsley, Milton A., Mercy Ridge, S728, 2525 Pot Spring Rd., Timonium, 21093.
Hoat, Rochus Vu Dinh
Holthaus, Paul G.
Huesman, Edward G.
Hughes, Joseph B., 2034 Park Ave., 21217.
Karoor, Isaac M.
Kelly, John L., St. Mark Rectory, 30 Melvin Rd., Catonsville, 21228.
Klein, Charles R., Harbor Hospital Center, 3001 S. Hanover St., 21225.
Lafferty, Charles L., Mercy Ridge S717, 2525 Pot Spring Rd., Timonium, 21093.
Lardner, Gerald V., S.S., S.T.B., M.A., Ph.D.
Limmer, George A., 716 Naples Dr., Hagerstown, 21740.
Lippold, John L., St. Philip Neri, 6405 S. Orchard Rd., Linthicum Heights, 21090.
Livigni, Salvatore, Annunciation, 5212 McCormick Ave., 21206.
Lupico, Samuel, St. Edward Parish, 901 Poplar Grove St., 21216.
Mattingly, John F., S.S., M.A., M.S.L.S., S.S.L.
McGovern, Walter J., Holy Family Rectory, 9533 Liberty Rd., Randallstown, 21133.
Messer, Joseph V., Mercy Ridge S628, 2525 Pot Spring Rd., Timonium, 21093.
Moody, William J., 86 Mt. Pleasant St., Frostburg, 21532.
Moore, John C., Ruxton Towers, Apt. 715, 8415 Bellone Ln., Towson, 21204.
Muller, Kennard, 7 Joppawood Ct. A-1, 21236.
Muller, Myles, Mercy Ridge S727, 2525 Pot Spring Rd., Timonium, 21093.
O'Meara, Joseph
Paulits, Walter J., Ph.D., 513 Sylview Dr., Pasadena, 21222.
Peterson, Casimir M., S.T.L., J.C.D., 7920 Beverly Ave., 21234.
Polk, Thomas T., Cooper Ridge, C009, 710 O'Brecht Rd., Sykesville, 21784.
Purvey, John J., Mercy Ridge, S635, 2525 Pot Spring Rd., Timonium, 21093.
Reitz, Louis M., S.S., S.T.L., M.S.L.S., M.Ed.
Roman, Manuel R., 4 Wimsap Ct., Apt. H, 21228.
Rose, Alphonse G., 5510 Woodlawn Rd., 21210.
Shaum, David W., Ph.D., Mount St. Mary's College, 16300 Old Emmitsburg Rd., Emmitsburg, 21727.
Snouffer, Philip T., 8820 Walther Blvd., Apt. 1401, 21234.
Thomas, Paul K., 637 Dover St., 21230.
Tittler, Leo R., St. John the Evangelist, 116 E. Second St., Frederick, 21701.
Wenderoth, Joseph R., 16745 Wesley Chapel Rd., Monkton, 21111.
West, Gerald F., 3725 Ellerslie Ave., 21218.
Wilson, Stuart T., 5269 North Spring Pointe Pl., Tucson, AZ 85749.
Witthauer, Paul G., Briarwood Estates, 719 Gregwood Ct., 21222.
Wojciechowski, Richard P., Stella Maris P612, 2525 Pot Spring Rd., Timonium, 21093.
Zoubek, Ronald, 1 Greenwood Ave., 21206.

Permanent Deacons:
Albaugh, William S., St. Joseph, Fullerton
Ames, John, St. Agnes
Anderson, Carl A., St. Edward, Baltimore
Antczak, George, Holy Rosary (part-time)
Bagley, Kevin, (Unassigned)
Baker, Robert L., St. Joseph Parish, Emmitsburg
Bankard, Alphonse C., III, Our Lady of Fatima, Baltimore
Barbernitz, Peter, Dir. Evangelization, St. John, Columbia
Barksdale, Wardell, St. Bernardine
Barth, James F., St. Timothy Parish, Walkersville
Bauerschmidt, Frederick C., Corpus Christi
Baxter, Michael R., St. Ursula
Bayhi, Karl, St. Joseph's, Sykesville
Baynes, Charles A., Our Lady of Mount Carmel
Beales, Thomas W., Holy Family, Davidsonville
Bee, J. Edward, St. Ann, Baltimore
Beimel, Leroy W., Holy Trinity, Glen Burnie
Benjamin, James, St. John the Evangelist, Columbia
Benson, Lee A., St. Ignatius, Hickory
Boscoe, John J., Holy Trinity, Glen Burnie
Britt, Ray H., Resurrection, Ellicott City
Britton, Clifford L., St. Gabriel Parish
Brown, Kevin T., Holy Trinity, Glen Burnie
Calabrese, Peter J., St. Ignatius, Hickory
Chase, Keith D., Church of the Holy Apostles
Chesnavage, Albert W., (Retired)
Chott, John, St. Margaret, Bel Air
Ciesla, Paul R., (Retired)
Cinquino, Joseph M., St. John, Westminster
Clack, James S., Sacred Heart of Jesus
Clemens, Richard W., Holy Cross; St. Mary, Star of the Sea; Our Lady of Good Counsel
Comegna, John, Resurrection, Ellicott City
Conley, David A., St. Mary, Cumberland
Connor, Jack, (Retired)
Cook, Charles E., (Retired)
Cook, Thomas P., Our Lady of Sorrows, Owensville
Cooley, Stephen H., Our Lady of Perpetual Help, Edgewater
Coster, John E., Charlestown
Crispo, Neil A., St. Joseph Parish in Dallastown, PA & Tribunal Office
Davis, Henry C., St. Michael the Archangel, Overlea
DeAngelis, William J., St. Joseph, Fullerton
DeCapite, James, St. Margaret, Bel Air
Dignan, Paul H., (Retired)
Dodge, Michael, St. Athanasius
Driesen, Simon M., St. Mary's, Pylesville
Dumer, Gary, St. Mary's, Pylesville
Evans, George T., St. Rita
Fallon, William L., St. Alphonsus Rodriguez, Woodstock
Feurer, Nicholas E., St. Clement Mary Hofbauer
Flamini, Michael, St. Michael/St. Patrick, Fells Point
Fulmer, Gary Lee, St. Ann, Hagerstown
Gifford, Paul A., PLD at St. Clement I, Lansdowne
Goles, Patrick J., St. Margaret, Bel Air
Gramling, John C., Immaculate Conception, Towson
Grillo, Anthony, Our Lady of the Fields
Gross, Theodore C., (Retired)
Hacker, Robert, (Retired)
Harcum, Philip W., (Retired)
Harris, Jhan M., St. Veronica, Baltimore
Hartlieb, Gilbert J., St. Stephen, Bradshaw
Hawkins, John A., (Unassigned)
Herzog, Robert, Holy Trinity, Good Shepherd & Crucifixion
Hicks, Charles W., St. Mark, Fallston
Hiebler, Charles H., Jr., Cathedral of Mary Our Queen
Hodges, Frank P., Corpus Christi
Ingold, Gary, Minitary Diaconate, United States Navel Academy
Jauquet, William, Our Lady of Victory
Keeley, Robert L., St. Philip Neri
Keenan, Robert G., St. Ursula
Kendzierski, Douglas P., Sacred Heart of Mary Parish
Knepper, Joseph E., St. Paul, Ellicott City
Kopczyk, Daniel R., St. Joan of Arc
Kosla, Albert F., (Retired)
Krysiak, Joseph C., Temp. Admin., St. Anthony/ Most Precious Blood
Kunkel, Richard, St. Ann, Hagerstown
Langmead, John T., St. Rita Parish (PLD)
Latrick, Donald P., Our Lady of the Chesapeake
Laws, Francis R., St. Stephen, Bradshaw
Lehr, Robert I., St. Ignatius, Hickory
Lopata, Dean M., St. John, Severna Park
Lynne, Robert O., (Retired)
MacKnew, J. Donald, (Retired)
Malinowski, Bob A., (Retired)
Maloney, Timothy D., St. Stephen Parish
Manley, John L., St. John, Frederick
Mann, James L., St. Dominic
Mann, Paul T., St. Brigid
Martin, John, Immaculate Heart of Mary; Good Samaritan Hospital
Martin, John R., St. Peter Parish, Libertytown
Matheny, Lawrence G., St. Ignatius of Loyola, Ijamsville
Matthews, Russell, St. Francis Xavier, Baltimore
Mauser, Fred, St. Louis, Clarksville
McCandless, Charles, Petersville
McCoy, Michael, St. Thomas More
McKenna, John I., St. Clement, Lansdown
McKenna, Joseph, St. Francis of Assisi, Fulton
Miller, Donald W., St. John, Westminster
Miller, Eugene J., (Unassigned)
Mills, Hugh H., Jr., St. Alphonsus, Baltimore
Misulia, Michael, (Retired), St. Peter the Apostle, Libertown
Monaghan, James C., St. Andrew by the Bay
Montalto, Richard W., St. Thomas Aquinas
Mooney, Loren, St. Patrick, Cumberland
Moore, LeRoy S., St. Mary, Annapolis
Moreau, Ray, Cathedral of Mary Our Queen
Morris, Richard F., St. Ursula
Mortel, Rodrigue, M.D., Missions Office
Murray, J. Donald, St. Francis Xavier, Hunt Valley
Nairn, William P., St. Ann, Hagerstown
Nathan, Douglas J., St. Katherine Drexel
Norcio, Anthony F., Deacon Formation
Novak, Richard D., Catholic Community of St. Michael and St. Patrick
O'Keefe, Francis, St. Issac Jogues
O'Neill, Harry, Oak Crest
Page, David A., St. Joseph, Odenton
Passauer, W. Fred, St. Joseph, Midland; St. Michael, Frostburg; St. Mary of the Annunciation, Lonaconing; St. Patrick, Mt. Savage; St. Ann, Grantsville; St. Peter, Westernport and St. Gabriel, Barton
Pearson, William J., St. Vincent dePaul Parish
Perry, Martin, St. Mark, Fallston
Petrosino, Victor R., St. Margaret, Bel Air
Piet, Stanley G., (Retired)
Pinkney, Willard A., Jr., (Retired)
Pitocco, Nickolas, Archdiocese of Washington, D.C.
Pivec, J. Kenneth, Immaculate Heart of Mary and Loch Raven Nursing Home
Podniesinski, Matthew, St. Louis, Clarksville
Presberry, Seigfried, St. Mark, Catonsville
Prosser, James J., Our Lady of Grace Parish, Parkton
Rafter, John J., Jr., St. Jane Frances de Chantal
Rapisarda, Gregory A., St. Margaret, Bel Air
Rausch, P. Gregory, St. Joseph-on-Carrollton Manor
Reid, Kevin, Immaculate Conception, Towson
Ripper, Mark, St. John, Westminster
Roberts, Gerald A., Our Lady Queen of Peace
Rodriguez, Alex, St. Francis de Sales
Roff, Daniel, St. John, Frederick
Rongione, Frank, St. Ursula
Rose, Alan, St. Isaac Jogues
Rubio, Steven, St. Matthew
Ryan, James A., Sacred Heart, Glyndon
Sainz, Miguel E., St. Mary of the Assumption, Govans/Hispanic
Santiago, Harbey, St. Michael, Poplar Springs
Schoennagel, Frederick, St. John the Evangelist, Hydes
Schultz, Joseph L., St. Anthony of Padua/Most Precious Blood
Sedlevicius, John, St. Lawrence the Martyr, Jessup
Seibold, Frederick, St. Elizabeth Ann Seton, Crofton
Seneschal, Phillip, St. Mary, Pylesville
Shelton, Paul D., St. Mary's; Blessed Sacrament
Shepard, Robert M.
Siarkowski, Henry L., (Retired), Shrine of the Little Flower
Sisson, George, Holy Family CC, Middletown
Smith, Darrell, St. Joseph, Taneytown
Smith, H. Todd, St. Joseph, Sykesville
Soloski, Mark, Shrine of the Sacred Heart, Mt. Washington
Stine, Richard J., St. Francis de Sales, Abingdon
Stoops, Edward, Our Lady of the Fields
Sullivan, Edward C., St. Joseph, Cockeysville
Sullivan, James, St. Francis de Sales, Abingdon
Sutterman, Jeffrey, St. Katharine Drexel
Swann, C. Richard, (Retired)
Teixeira, Lawrence "Tex", St. Francis of Assisi, Brunswick
Tengwall, David, St. Andrew by the Bay
Thompson, Ronald, St. John, Severna Park and Liaison to the Deacon Personnel Board
Trautwein, Ralph, St. Ignatius, Hickory
Vlcej, Robert, St. Jane Frances de Chantel
Wachter, George C., Springfield Hospital Center
Weber, Paul, St. Ignatius, Baltimore
Werner, Francis L., Jr., St. Patrick, Cumberland
Westwater, James, St. Isaac Jogues and Asst. Dir. Clergy Personnel for Deacon Formation

Whitesell, Edward, St. Benedict
Wiedel, Verdan, (Retired)
Wilkins, Herman S., Our Lady of Hope
Wilson, J. Larry, St. Andrew by the Bay
Wise, Stanley, St. Joseph, Taneytown
Witherspoon, Willard, Jr., St. Peter Claver & St. Pius V
Wolf, Martin, Maryland Correctional Institutions; St. Margaret's, Bel Air
Yannuzzi, Thomas J., Ascension Parish
Zeiler, Francis, St. Clement Mary Hofbauer & Clergy Liaison at Project Rachel

INSTITUTIONS LOCATED IN THE ARCHDIOCESE

[A] SEMINARIES, ARCHDIOCESAN

BALTIMORE. *St. Mary's Seminary and University*, 5400 Roland Ave., 21210-1994. Tel: 410-864-4000; Fax: 410-864-4278. Web: www.stmarys.edu. Most Rev. Edwin F. O'Brien, S.T.D., D.D., Archbishop of Baltimore, Chancellor, Chm. Board of Trustees.

St. Mary's Seminary and University Priests 14; Diocesan Seminarians 70; Diocesan Seminarians on Pastoral Leave 5; Lay Teachers 3.

Officers of the Administration: Revs. Thomas R. Hurst, S.S., S.T.L., Ph.D., Pres. Rector; Timothy Kulbicki, O.F.M.Conv., B.A., S.T.B., H.E.D., Assoc. Prof. Church History & Academic Dean & Vice Rector, School of Theology; Richard G. Childs, M.B.A., Vice Pres. for Admin. & Finance; Michael J. Gorman, Dean, Ecumenical Institute of Theology; Mrs. Patricia Grega, M.A., Univ. Registrar and Dir. of Information Svcs.; Mrs. Elizabeth L. Visconage, B.S., Vice Pres. Inst. Advancement; Thomas Raszewski, Dir. Library Svcs.

Academic Faculty: Revs. Michael L. Barre, S.S., S.T.L., Ph.D., Prof., Sacred Scripture; Luis R. Corneli Esq., S.S., J.D., J.C.L., Asst. Prof. Canon Law; Daniel J. Doherty, S.S., B.A., M.A., M.Div., S.T.L., Asst. Prof. Pastoral Theology; John J. Donahue, S.J., S.T.L., Ph.D.; Patricia Fosarelli, M.D., D.Min., Lecturer Pastoral Theology; Rev. Msgr. David I. Fulton, J.C.L., S.T.D., Asst. Prof. Canon Law; Michael J. Gorman, Dean, Ecumenical Institute of Theology & Prof. Sacred Scripture; Revs. Thomas R. Hurst, S.S., S.T.L., Ph.D., Assoc. Prof. Sacred Scripture; Robert F. Leavitt, S.S., S.T.D., Prof. Systematic Theology; Renato Lopez, S.S., S.S.L., Asst. Prof. Sacred Scripture & Dir. Liturgy; Stephen Miles, Ph.D., Asst. Prof. Moral Theology; Revs. William Miller, S.J., M.Div., Ph.D., Assoc. Prof. Sacred Scripture; Hy K. Nguyen, S.S., M.Div., M.A., S.T.D., Asst. Prof. Systematic Theology; Peter Paul Seaton, Ph.L., Ph.D., Asst. Prof. Philosophy; Rev. Lawrence B. Terrien, S.S., Ph.D., S.T.D.

Adjunct Academic Faculty: Myrelle D'Abreu, ESL Coord.; Rev. Edward Griswold, M.Div., Ph.D., Instructor Homiletics; Rev. Msgr. Robert Jaskot, S.T.B., S.T.L., J.C.L., Instructor Sacramental Theology; Bill Scalia, Lecturer English; Leo White, Instructor Philosophy; Rev. Jonathan Woodhall, M.A., Ph.D., Lecturer Pastoral Theology.

Ecumenical Institute of Theology, 5400 Roland Ave., 21210. Tel: 410-864-4200; Fax: 410-864-4205. Michael J. Gorman, M.Div., Ph.D., Dean. Students 258.

EMMITSBURG. *Mount St. Mary's Seminary* (1808) 21727-7797. Tel: 301-447-5295; Fax: 301-447-5895. Email: seminaryinfo@msmary.edu. Web: www.msmary.edu/seminary.

An integral part of the corporation known as Mount St. Mary's University and Seminary. Priests 19; Lay Teachers 9; Lay Administrators 3; Support Staff 4; Diocesan Seminarians 142; Religious Seminarians 4; Total Enrollment 146.

Administration: Most Rev. Edwin F. O'Brien, S.T.D., D.D., Chancellor & Chm. of Seminary Committee; Dr. Thomas H. Powell, Pres.; Rev. Msgr. Steven P. Rohlfs, S.T.L., S.T.D., Vice Pres. & Rector; Revs. Brett A. Brannen, M.Div., Vice Rector & Dir. of Formation Advising Prog.; Lee W. Gross, S.T.L., Dean of Students; J. Daniel Mindling, O.F.M.Cap., S.T.D., Academic Dean; John J. Dietrich, M.A., M.Div., Dir. Spiritual Formation; Leo Patalinghug, Dir. Pastoral Field Educ.; Rev. Msgr. Stuart W. Swetland, S.T.D.; Dr. D. Stephen Rockwood, Ph.D., M.L.S., Dir. Library; Mrs. Amelia Y. Rodriguez, Seminary Registrar; Mrs. Rosemary S. Mick, Seminary Records & Canonicals.

Full Time Faculty: Revs. Frederick L. Miller; Thomas J. Lane, S.S.L., S.T.D.; Peter F. Ryan, S.J., S.T.L., S.T.D.; Brett A. Brannen, M.Div.; John J. Dietrich, M.A., M.Div.; Lawrence J. Donohoo, O.P., Assoc. Prof. Systematic Theology, Formation Advising, Spiritual Direction; Lee W. Gross, S.T.L.; Kenneth D. Brighenti, Asst. Prof. Homiletics & Pastoral Theology, Asst. Dir. Pastoral Field Education Formation Advising, Spiritual Direction; McLean Cummings, Spiritual Direction & Formation Advising; Dr. Christopher J. Anadale; William A. Bales, Ph.D.; Dr. Cynthia Fraga-Canadas; Dr. Paige E. Hochschild, Adjunct Faculty; Dr. John D. Love; Mr. Phil McGlade, Dir. Seminary Devel. & Alumni Rels.; Dr. Owen M. Phelan; Dr. Steven C. Smith; Deborah Wentling, M.A., ESL Coord.; Mr. Frederick J. Ziegler, Organist/Dir. Liturgical Music.

Part Time Faculty: Revs. Ronald S. Gillis, S.T.L., J.C.D.; Michael J. Roach; Lawrence J. McNeil, D.Min., M.Div.; Dr. Carol L. Houghton, S.T.D., J.C.D.; Dr. Patrick J. DiVietri, Ph.D.; Mrs. Caroline Purcell, M.A., ESL Instructor.

[B] COLLEGES AND UNIVERSITIES

BALTIMORE. *College of Notre Dame of Maryland*, 4701 N. Charles St., 21210. Tel: 410-435-0100; Fax: 410-532-5791. Web: www.ndm.edu. Hon. Kathleen O'Ferrall Friedman, Chm. Bd. of Trustees; Dr. Mary Pat Seurkamp, Ph.D., Pres.; Dr. Sally A. White, Vice Pres. Academic Affairs; Ms. Heidi Fletcher, Vice Pres. Enrollment Mgmt.; Richard Staisloff, Vice Pres. Fin. & Admin.; Sharon Bogdan, Registrar; Dr. Irene Ferguson, Vice Pres. Student Devel.; Andrea Trisciuzzi, Vice Pres. Institutional Advancement; Sr. Eileen O'Dea, Vice Pres. Mission. School Sisters of Notre Dame. Sisters 23; Lay Professors 83; Students 3,402; Residents 288; Total Staff 207.

**Loyola University in Maryland*, 4501 N. Charles St., 21210. Tel: 410-617-2000; Fax: 410-617-2176. Web: www.loyola.edu. Rev. Brian F. Linnane, S.J., Pres. Priests 15; Lay Teachers 549; Total Staff 1,338; Total Enrollment 6,067.

Loyola Graduate Center-Columbia Campus, 8890 McGaw Rd., Columbia, 21045-5245. Tel: 410-617-7600; Fax: 410-617-7643.

Loyola Graduate Center-Timonium Campus, 2034 Greenspring Dr., Timonium, 21093. Tel: 410-617-1500; Fax: 410-617-1518. Rev. Brian F. Linnane, S.J., Pres.; Dr. Timothy Law Snyder, Vice Pres. Academic Affairs; Dr. James Buckley, Dean College of Arts and Sciences; Dr. Karyl Leggio, Dean Sellinger School of Business & Mgmt.; Dr. Susan Donovan, Vice Pres. Student Devel. & Dean Students; John Palmucci, Vice Pres. Finance & Treas.; Terrence Sawyer, Vice Pres. Admin.; Marc Camille, Vice Pres. Enrollment Mgmt. & Communications; David Sears, Vice Pres. Advancement; Ilona McGuiness, Ph.D., Dean of First Year Students & Academic Svcs.; Revs. Charles Borges, S.J.; C. Kevin Gillespie, S.J.; Hank Hilton, S.J.; Joseph S. Rossi, S.J.; James F. Salmon, S.J.

Jesuit Community of Loyola University, Inc. Tel: 410-617-2318; Fax: 410-617-2125. Revs. Ronald J. Amiot, S.J.; Charles Borges, S.J.; Timothy B. Brown, S.J.; John Conley, S.J.; John M. Dennis, S.J., M.Ed.; Frank R. Haig, S.J.; Francis G. Hilton, S.J.; James Kelly, S.J.; Brian F. Linnane, S.J.; Brian O. McDermott, S.J.; Francis J. Nash, S.J.; Joseph S. Rossi, S.J.; James F. Salmon, S.J.; Mr. Samuel J. Sawyer, S.J.; Rev. Luis A. Tampe, S.J.

Mount St. Agnes College Tel: 410-617-2271; Fax: 410-617-5413. Sisters of Mercy of the Americas., (Merged with Loyola College.)

EMMITSBURG. *Mount Saint Mary's University* (1808) 21727. Tel: 301-447-6122; Fax: 301-447-5634. Email: communications@msmary.edu. Web: www.msmary.edu. Dr. Thomas Powell, Pres.; Dr. Stephen Rockwood, Librarian; Mr. David C. Reeder, Dir. Fin. Aid; Dr. David Rehm, Vice Pres. for Academic Affairs; Mr. John Butler, Vice Pres. Inst. Advancement; Ms. Leona Sevick, Assoc. Vice Pres. Academic Affairs; Mr. Michael Post, Interim Dean of Admissions & Enrollment; Ms. Margot Rhoades, Registrar; Mr. Dan Soller, Exec. Vice Pres.; Michael Malewicki, Vice Pres., Business & Finance; Rev. Msgr. Steven P. Rohlfs, S.T.L., S.T.D., Vice Pres. & Rector; Revs. Brian P. Nolan, Chap.; Paul V. Redmond (Retired); David W. Shaum, Ph.D. (Retired); James Donohue, C.R. Priests 1; Sisters 2; Lay Teachers 171; Total Enrollment 1,944.

[C] HIGH SCHOOLS, ARCHDIOCESAN

BALTIMORE. *Archbishop Curley High School* (1961) 3701 Sinclair Ln., 21213. Tel: 410-485-5000; Fax: 410-483-2545. Email: mmartin@archbishopcurley.org. Web: www.archbishopcurley.org. Revs. Michael Martin, O.F.M.Conv., Pres. & Guardian; Vincent Gluc, O.F.M.Conv., Vocation Dir.; Matthew Foley, O.F.M.Conv., Teacher; Bros. Daniel Lutolf, O.F.M.Conv., Teacher; Douglas McMillan, O.F.M.Conv., Teacher; Mr. Barry Brownlee, Prin.; Ms. Ann Kennedy, Librarian. Administered by Order of Friars Minor Conventual, St. Anthony of Padua Province (USA). Priests 2; Brothers 2; Lay Teachers 43; Students 570; Total Staff 66.

The Seton Keough High School (1988) 1201 Caton Ave., 21227-1092. Tel: 410-646-4444; Fax: 443-573-0107. Email: info@setonkeough.com. Web: setonkeough.com. Patricia Anne Bossle, D.C., Pres.; Mr. Dennis J. Meehan, Prin.; Clare Pitz, Vice Prin.; Ms. Laurie Manuel, Librarian. Priests 1; Sisters 5; Lay Teachers 38; Students 475.

SEVERN. *Archbishop Spalding High School* (1966) 8080 New Cut Rd., 21144. Tel: 410-969-9105; Fax: 410-969-1026. Email: info@archbishopspalding.org. Web: www.archbishopspalding.org. Dr. Michael Murphy, Pres.; Kathleen K. Mahar, Prin. Lay Teachers 92; Students 1,100.

[D] HIGH SCHOOLS, PRIVATE

BALTIMORE. *Calvert Hall* (1845) 8102 La Salle Rd., 21286. Tel: 410-825-4266; Fax: 410-825-6826. Email: chc@calverthall.com. Web: www.calverthall.com. Bro. Thomas Zoppo, F.S.C., Pres.; Mr. Joseph Baker, Asst. Prin. Academic Affairs; Mr. Charles Stembler, Asst. Prin. Student Affairs; Mr. Louis Heidrick, Prin.; Carole Russell, Contact Person; Ms. Elsie Paliath, Librarian. Conducted by the Brothers of the Christian Schools (F.S.C.). Brothers 11; Lay Teachers 90; Students 1,212.

The Catholic High School of Baltimore (1939) 2800 Edison Hwy., 21213. Tel: 410-732-6200; Fax: 410-732-7639. Email: chsb@thecatholichighschool.org. Web: www.thecatholichighschool.org. Dr. Barbara Nazelrod, Pres.; Keith Harmeyer, Prin.; Jan Bandzwolck, Vice Prin. Sisters of St. Francis of Philadelphia. Sisters 7; Lay Teachers 30; Students 330; Total Staff 60.

Cristo Rey Jesuit High School, 420 Chester St., 21231. Tel: 410-727-3255; Fax: 443-573-9898. Rev. John W. Swope, S.J., Pres.; Thomas A. Malone, Prin.; Katherine Sorci, Librarian. Priests 1; Scholastics 2; Lay Teachers 21; Staff 51; Students 273.

St. Frances Academy (1828) (Coed), 501 E. Chase St., 21202. Tel: 410-539-5794; Fax: 410-685-2650. Email: sfa@sfacademy.org. Web: www.sfacademy.org. Sr. John Francis Schilling, O.S.P., Pres.; Deacon Curtis Turner, Prin.; Ms. Mary Missouri, Asst. Prin.; Mr. Doral Palley, Asst. Prin.; Ms. Linda Wilson, Guidance. Oblate Sisters of Providence. Brothers 1; Sisters 3; Lay Teachers 27; Students 300.

Institute of Notre Dame (1847) 901 Aisquith St., 21202. Tel: 410-522-7800; Fax: 410-522-7810. Email: indofmd@indofmd.org. Web: indofmd.org. Ms. Charisse Wernecke, Pres.; Ann Seeley, Prin.; Mrs. Diana Franz, Asst. Prin.; Anders Alicea, Dean, Students.

Institute of Notre Dame, Inc. Sisters 1; Lay Teachers 27; Lay Employees 17; Counselors 2; Students 318.

Loyola Blakefield (1952) (Grades 6-12), P.O. Box 6819, 21285-6819. Tel: 410-823-0601; Fax: 410-823-5277. Email: admin@blakefield.loyola.edu. Web: www.loyolablakefield.org. Revs. Thomas A. Pesci, S.J., Pres.; F. Joseph Michini, S.J., Chap.; Lloyd George, S.J.; Mrs. Gail P. Kujawa, Prin. (Middle School); Mr. Anthony I. Day, Prin. (Upper School); Mrs. Theresa K. Darr, Librarian. Priests 3; Lay Teachers 85; Students 1,002.

Mercy High School (1960) 1300 E. Northern Pkwy., 21239-1998. Tel: 410-433-8880; Fax: 410-323-8816. Email: mercy@mercyhighschool.com. Web: www.mercyhighschool.com. Sr. Carol E. Wheeler, R.S.M., Pres.; Jo Ann Lazzeri, Vice Pres. Academic Affairs; Pegeen D'Agostino, Dir. Library Svcs. Sisters of Mercy of the Americas. Sisters 6; Lay Teachers 54; Students 450; Total Staff 94.

Mount de Sales Academy (1952) 700 Academy Rd., 21228. Tel: 410-744-8498; Fax: 410-747-5105. Email: mdsa@mountdesales.org. Web: www.mountdesales.org. Sr. Anne Catherine, Prin.; Judi Lanciotti, Vice Prin.; Kathleen Sinkinson, Ph.D., Vice Prin.; Mrs. Alice Carpenter, Librarian. Sisters 5; Lay Teachers 57; Students 500.

Mt. St. Joseph College High School (1876) 4403 Frederick Ave., 21229. Tel: 410-644-3300; Fax: 410-646-6220. Email: barry@admin.msjnet.edu. Web: www.msjnet.edu. Bro. James M. Kelly, C.F.X., Pres.; Mr. Barry J. Fitzpatrick, Prin. Xaverian Brothers. Priests 1; Brothers 3; Lay Teachers 93; Students 1,025; Total Staff 148.

BEL AIR. *The John Carroll School* (1964) 703 Churchville Rd., 21014. Tel: 410-879-2480; Fax: 410-836-8514. Email: jcs@johncarroll.org. Web: www.johncarroll.org. Mr. Paul G. Barker, Prin.; Mrs. Patti Murphy Dohn, Campus Min.; Ann Barker, Librarian. Priests 1; Sisters 1; Lay Teachers 60; Students 828; Total Staff 110.

CUMBERLAND. *Bishop Walsh School* (1966) (Grades PreK-12), 700 Bishop Walsh Rd., 21502. Tel: 301-724-5360; Fax: 301-722-0555.

Email: pmcnally@bishopwalsh.org. Web: www.bishopwalsh.org. Sisters Phyllis McNally, S.S.N.D., M.Ed., Pres. & Acting Prin.; Kathleen Jancuk, S.S.N.D., M.Ed., Reading Specialist; Shelby Webb, Asst. Prin.; Wendy Walker, Librarian. Brothers of the Christian Schools, School Sisters of Notre Dame. Brothers 1; Sisters 3; Lay Teachers 39; Students 465.

FREDERICK. *Saint John's Catholic Prep* (1829) (Coed), 889 Butterfly Ln., 21703. Tel: 301-662-4210; Fax: 301-662-5166. Email: mschultz@saintjohnsprep.org. Web: www.saintjohnsprep.org. Dr. John Campbell, Pres.; Mr. Christopher Cosentino, Prin.; Mrs. Traci Brossart, Librarian. Priests 1; Lay Teachers 29; Total Staff 60; Students 264.

HAGERSTOWN. *St. Maria Goretti High School* (1955) (Coed), 1535 Oak Hill Ave., 21742. Tel: 301-739-4266; Fax: 301-739-4261. Email: goretti@goretti.org. Web: www.goretti.org. Monica Des Jarles, Pres.; Mr. Richard E. Fairley, Prin.; Rev. Larry G. Rock, Chap.; Debra Ruffner, Librarian. Priests 1; Lay Teachers 25; Students 230; Total Staff 38.

[E] MIDDLE/HIGH SCHOOLS, ARCHDIOCESAN

BALTIMORE. *Cardinal Gibbons School for Boys* (1962) 3225 Wilkens Ave., 21229-4286. Tel: 410-644-1770; Fax: 410-525-3747; 410-525-3757. Email: cgschool@archbalt.org. Web: www.cardinal-gibbons.org. David F. Brown, Prin.; Mr. Steven A. Cole, Vice Pres. Academics; Bro. Kevin P. Strong, F.S.C., M.A., Pres. Emeritus. Priests 1; Brothers 1; Lay Teachers 28; Students 297.

[F] MIDDLE/HIGH SCHOOLS, PRIVATE

BROOKLANDVILLE. *Maryvale Preparatory School* (1945) (Grades 6-12), (Girls), 11300 Falls Rd., 21022-1490. Tel: 410-252-3366; Fax: 410-308-1497. Email: grahamm@maryvale.com. Web: www.maryvale.com. Sr. Shawn Marie Maguire, S.N.D.deN., Headmistress; Donna Bridickas, Prin.; Kelly McDowell, Librarian. Sisters of Notre Dame de Namur 1; Lay Teachers 49; Students 386; Total Staff 25.

TOWSON. *Notre Dame Preparatory School* (1873) (Grades 6-12), 815 Hampton Ln., 21286. Tel: 410-825-6202; Fax: 410-832-2625. Web: www.notredameprep.com. Sr. Patricia McCarron, S.S.N.D., Headmistress; Ms. Laurie Jones, Prin.; Mrs. Ellen Cullen, Librarian.

Notre Dame Preparatory School, Inc. Sisters 5; Lay Teachers 89; Students 758; Total Staff 137.

[G] ELEMENTARY/MIDDLE SCHOOLS, PRIVATE

COOKSVILLE. *Woodmont Academy* (1995) (Grades PreK-8), 2000 Woodmont Dr., 21723. Tel: 443-574-8100; Fax: 410-465-9162. Email: admissions@woodmontacademy.org. Web: www.woodmontacademy.org. Mr. John Farrell, Prin. Priests 1; Lay Teachers 16; Students 257.

[H] ELEMENTARY/MIDDLE SCHOOLS, REGIONAL AND COMMUNITY

BALTIMORE. *John Paul Regional Catholic School, Inc.*, (Grades PreK-8), 6946 Dogwood Rd., 21244. Tel: 410-944-0367; Fax: 410-265-5316. Email: office@jprcs.org. Web: www.jprcs.org. Mrs. Theresa Brooks, Prin.; Mrs. Patricia Little, Librarian. Early Childhood Program. Lay Teachers 16; Students 205.

[I] ELEMENTARY SCHOOLS, PRIVATE

BALTIMORE. *Mother Seton Academy*, (Grades 6-8), 2215 Greenmount Ave., 21218-5421. Tel: 410-563-2833; Fax: 410-563-7353. Web: www.mothersetonacademy.org. Laura Peterson-Minakowski, Prin.; Sisters Charmaine Krohe, S.S.N.D., Pres.; Karen Pourby, O.S.F., Librarian. Innovative Middle School for Inner City Youth. Brothers 2; Sisters 8; Lay Teachers 5; Lay Volunteers 3; Students 66.

Sisters Academy of Baltimore, Inc. (2004) (Grades 5-8), 139 First Ave., 21227. Tel: 410-242-1212; Fax: 410-242-5104. Web: www.sistersacademy.org. Sisters Delia Dowling, S.S.N.D., Pres.; Debra Liesen, S.S.N.D., Prin.; Dorothy Daiger, S.S.N.D., Librarian; Kathleen Donnelly, Admin. Asst.; Sr. Virginia Maria Brune, S.S.N.D., Teacher. Religious 1; Lay Teachers 8.

ELLICOTT CITY. *Trinity School* (1941) (Grades PreK-8), 4985 Ilchester Rd., 21043. Tel: 410-744-1524; Fax: 410-744-3617. Email: admintrin@trinityschoolmd.org. Web: trinityschoolmd.org. Sr. Catherine Phelps, S.N.D.deN., Prin.; Anne Howard, Librarian. Sisters of Notre Dame de Namur 2; Lay Teachers 30; Students 360.

EMMITSBURG. *Mother Seton School*, (Grades PreK-8), 100 Creamery Rd., 21727. Tel: 301-447-3161; Fax: 301-447-3914. Email: office@mothersetonschool.org. Web: www.mothersetonschool.org. Sr. JoAnne Goecke, D.C., Prin.; Ms. Teri Monacelli, Librarian. Daughters of Charity of St. Vincent de Paul 1; Lay Teachers 21; Students 360.

FREDERICK. *The Visitation Academy* (1846) (Grades PreK-8), 200 E. 2nd St., 21701. Tel: 301-662-2814; Fax: 301-695-8549. Email: schase@thevisitationacademy.org. Web: www.thevisitationacademy.org. Ms. Susan Chase, Prin.; Lynne Kirby, Asst. Prin.; Ms. Danielle Adams, Librarian. Lay Teachers 21; Students 126.

[J] ELEMENTARY SCHOOLS, REGIONAL AND COMMUNITY

BALTIMORE. *Archbishop Borders School*, (Grades PreK-8), 201 S. Conkling St., 21224. Tel: 410-276-6534; Fax: 410-276-6915. Email: principal@abbschool.com. Mary C. Marshall, Prin. Students 160; Lay Staff 15.

Cardinal Shehan School, (Grades PreK-8), 5407 Loch Raven Blvd., 21239-2996. Tel: 410-433-2775; Fax: 410-323-6131. Web: cardinalshehanschool.org. Paula Redman, Prin.; Maggie Dates, Asst. Prin. Serving St. Matthew and St. Thomas More Parishes. Lay Teachers 22; Students 290.

St. Ignatius Loyola Academy (1993) (Grades 6-8), 740 N. Calvert St., 21202. Tel: 410-539-8268; Fax: 410-539-4821. Email: chriswilson@saintignatius.org. John Ciccone, Pres.; Mr. Christopher Wilson, Prin. Middle School for boys from low income families. Lay Teachers 12; Students 75.

Mother Mary Lange Catholic School, (Grades PreK-8), 4410 Frankford Ave., 21206. Tel: 410-488-4848; Fax: 410-323-4003. Email: mmlange@archbalt.org. Rev. C. Lou Martin; Sr. Rita Michele Proctor, O.S.P., Prin.; Ms. Mary Lu Farnsworth, Librarian. Sisters 4; Lay Teachers 16.

Queen of Peace Elementary Cluster, St. James and St. John School (1847) (Grades PreK-5), 1012 Somerset St., 21202. Tel: 410-342-3222; Fax: 410-675-8262. Mrs. LaUanah King-Cassell, Prin. Sisters 2; Lay Teachers 14; Students 232.

St. Katherine of Sienna School (Grades PreK-8), 1201 N. Rose St., 21213. Tel: 410-327-4738; Fax: 410-327-1835. Ms. Angela Calamari, Prin. Lay Teachers 11; Students 253.

BRADSHAW. *St. Stephen School* (1863) (Grades PreK-8), 8028 Bradshaw Rd., 21087-1807. Tel: 410-592-7617; Fax: 410-592-7330. Email: sssch@archbalt.org. Web: www.ststephenbradshaw.org. Mrs. Mary M. Patrick, Prin.; Mrs. Linda Boschert, Librarian. Lay Teachers 20; Instructional Aides 4.

FREDERICK. *St. John Regional Catholic School*, (Grades PreK-8), 8414 Opossumtown Pike, 21702. Tel: 301-662-6722; Fax: 301-695-7024. Email: ksmith@SJRCS.org. Web: www.sjrcs.org. Mrs. Karen Smith, Prin.; Mr. Paul Fer, Asst. Prin.; Mrs. Rosanna Rensberger, Librarian. Lay Teachers 35; Students 575.

GAMBRILLS, ANNE ARUNDEL. *School of the Incarnation, Inc.* (1999) (Grades K-8), 2601 Symphony Ln., 21054. Tel: 410-519-2285; Fax: 410-519-2286. Email: bedmondson@schooloftheincarnation.org. Web: www.schooloftheincarnation.org. Dr. Barbara Edmondson, Prin.; Anne Umerlik, Librarian. An interparish school of the Archdiocese of Baltimore established 1999. Parishes: Church of the Holy Apostles, Gambrills; Our Lady of the Fields, Millersville; St. Joseph, Odenton; Our Lady of Perpetual Help, Edgewater; Holy Family, Davidsonville and St. Elizabeth Ann Seton, Crofton. Lay Staff 31; Lay Teachers 42; Students 785.

GLEN BURNIE. *Monsignor Slade Catholic School* (1954) (Grades K-8), 120 Dorsey Rd., 21061. Tel: 410-766-7130; Fax: 410-787-0594. Email: mscs@msladeschool.com. Web: www.mslade.com. Gregory E. Jones, Prin.; Laura Lodowski, Librarian. Serving Glen Burnie, Pasadena, Hanover and Severn Parishes. Lay Teachers 41; Students 851.

[K] SPECIAL EDUCATION

BALTIMORE. *St. Elizabeth School, Inc.*, 801 Argonne Dr., 21218-1998. Tel: 410-889-5054; Fax: 410-889-2356. Email: info@stelizabeth-school.org. Web: www.stelizabeth-school.org. Christine Manlove, Ed.D., Exec. Dir.; Mr. Andy Parsley, Prin.; Ed McAnnulla, Librarian. Sisters of St. Francis of Assisi 3; Lay Teachers 23; Other Lay Staff 56; Aides 60; Children 116.

TIMONIUM. *Villa Maria School* (Timonium Campus), 2300 Dulaney Valley Rd., 21093. Tel: 410-252-6343; Fax: 410-560-1347. Jack Pumphrey, Admin. & Dir. Education. Non-public (Level V and VI) special education for children with emotional/multiple disabilities, ages 11-15. Lay Teachers 22; Teacher Aides 20; Children 120.

Villa Maria School at St. Vincent's Center, 2600 Pot Spring Rd., 21093. Tel: 410-252-3725; Fax: 410-561-8109. Non-public level V & VI special education for children with emotional/multiple disabilities ages 4-11. Lay Teachers 7; Teacher Aides 9; Children 60.

Villa Maria School, 1501 Ashburton St., 21216. Tel: 410-624-0534; Fax: 410-624-0596. Non-public level V special education for children with emotional/multiple disabilities ages 6-14. Lay Teachers 7; Teacher Aides 5; Children 45.

Villa Maria School of Harford County, 1370 Brass Mill Rd., Belcamp, 21017. Tel: 410-297-4100; Fax: 410-273-9555. Non-public level 5 special education for children with emotional/multiple disabilities ages 5-15. Lay Teachers 9; Teacher Aides 6; Children 45.

[L] CHILD CARE CENTERS

BALTIMORE. *Bon Secours Family Support Center*, 26 N. Fulton Ave., 21223. Tel: 410-362-3629; Fax: 410-362-3649. Web: www.bonsecours.org/bshsi. Brenda K. Jones, Svc. Coord.; Lori H. Fagan, Exec. Dir.

Bon Secour of Maryland Foundation, Inc. Total Staff 14; Total Assisted 200.

St. Frances Outreach Center, 1026 Brentwood Ave., 21202-4203. Tel: 410-685-1975; Fax: 410-332-1299. Sr. Brenda Motte, O.S.P., Dir. Total Assisted 20; Total Staff 1.

Good Shepherd Center, 4100 Maple Ave., 21227. Tel: 410-247-2770; Fax: 410-247-3242. Email: info@goodshepherdcenter.org. Web: www.goodshepherdcenter.org. Derrick Boone, Psy.D., Pres. & CEO; Sr. Mary Carol McClenon, Mission Integration Coord.

House of the Good Shepherd of the City of Baltimore, Residential psychiatric treatment for adolescent girls with emotional and behavioral problems. Sisters 9; Capacity 105; Students 99; Total Assisted 189; Total Staff 306.

Mount Providence Child Development Center, 701 Gun Rd., 21227. Tel: 410-247-0449; Fax: 410-247-1150. Web: www.oblatesisters.com. Sr. Brenda Cherry, O.S.P., Dir. Oblate Sisters of Providence. Sisters 3; Lay Teachers 10; Students 80; Total Staff 14.

TIMONIUM. *Francis X. Gallagher Services*, 2520 Pot Spring Rd., 21093. Tel: 410-252-4005; Fax: 410-560-3495. Email: jhillman@cc-md.org. Web: www.catholiccharities-md.org/programs/gallagher. Mark J. Schulz, Admin. Residential, day habilitation and medical day programs for the people with developmental disabilities. Residential Capacity 262; Day Capacity 240; Total Assisted 360; Total Staff 410.

Villa Maria Continuum, 2300 Dulaney Valley Rd., 21093. Tel: 410-252-4700; Fax: 410-252-3040. Email: jhackbar@catholiccharities-md.org. Web: www.catholiccharities-md.org. Mark Greenberg, Div. Dir.; Rev. Raymond Chase, Chap.; Chandra Smith, Spiritual Devel. Coord. We operate a full continuum of different mental health and special education programs for children and their families. Clients 2,900; Total Staff 550.

St. Vincent's Center, 2600 Pot Spring Rd., 21093. For additional information please see the Associated Catholic Charities section.

[M] GENERAL HOSPITALS

BALTIMORE. *St. Agnes HealthCare, Inc.*, 900 Caton Ave., 21229-5299. Tel: 410-368-6000; Fax: 410-368-2109. Email: info@stagnes.org. Web: www.stagnes.org. Dr. Ann Hazelwood, Dir. Pastoral Care; Bonnie Phipps, Pres. & CEO; Revs. Christy Arockiaraj, Chap.; Simonraj Savarimathu. Ascension Health. Priests 2; Sisters 11; Bed Capacity 318; Patients Assisted Annually 478,365; Total Staff 2,824.

St. Agnes Foundation, Inc. Tel: 410-368-3155; Fax: 410-368-3533. (Subsidiary of St. Agnes Health-Care, Inc.)

Bon Secours Baltimore Health Corporation, Inc. (1919) 2000 W. Baltimore St., 21223. Tel: 410-362-3000; Fax: 410-362-3126. Email: inforequest@bshsi.org. Web: www.bonsecoursbaltimore.org. Samuel L. Ross, M.D., M.S., CEO; Sr. Anne Lutz, C.B.S., Bd. Pres.; Glendora Hughes, Bd. Chair; Sr. Mary Skopal, S.S.J., Dir. of Pastoral Care. Bon Secours Ministry. Sisters of Bon Secours 4; Bed Capacity 126; Patients Assisted Annually 182,151; Total Staff 931.

The following are tax exempt subsidiaries of the Bon Secours Baltimore Health Corporation, Inc.

Bon Secours Hospital Baltimore, Inc. (1920)

Bon Secours Community Health Services, Inc. (1994)

Bon Secours of Maryland Foundation, Inc. (1991)

Good Samaritan Hospital, 5601 Loch Raven Blvd.,

21239. Tel: 443-444-8000; Fax: 443-444-4599. Web: www.goodsam-md.org. Lawrence M. Beck, Pres.; Shirley Roth, Vice Pres. Nursing; Rev. James M. Reusing, Dir. Pastoral Care; Deborah Bena, R.N., Health Min. Coord.; Anthony Read, Board Chm. Adult acute care teaching hospital with a strong tradition of community care and home to more than 200 hospital based physicians. Bed Capacity 303.

Mercy Health Services Inc., 301 St. Paul Pl., 21202. Tel: 410-332-9000; Fax: 410-962-1303. Email: rrice@mdmercy.com. Web: www.mdmercy.com. Thomas Mullen, Pres. & CEO; Revs. Theodore E.A. Brady, S.J.; Thomas R. Malia, Chap.; Sr. Mary Harper, R.S.M., Chap.; Rev. Augustine Inwang, M.S.P.; Mary C. Webb, Dir. Pastoral Care. Institute of the Sisters of Mercy of the Americas., Subsidiaries: Mercy Medical Center Inc.; St. Paul Place Specialists, Inc.; Healthcare for the Homeless; Maryland Family Care; Mercy Transitional Care; Stella Maris, Inc.; Cardinal Shehan Center, Inc.; Mercy Health Foundation, Inc.; Mercy Ridge. Sisters 14; Employees 3,312; Patients Assisted Annually 634,000; Bed Capacity 244; Total Staff 3,432.

TOWSON. *St. Joseph Medical Center, Inc.* (1864) 7601 Osler Dr., 21204. Tel: 410-337-1000; Fax: 410-337-1024. Email: susannedecrane@catholichealth.net. Web: www.sjmcmd.org. Robert Lovell, Interim CEO; Susanne De Crane, Ph.D., Dir. Spiritual Care. Sisters of St. Francis of Philadelphia. Sisters 6; Nurses 740; Beds 354; Patients Assisted Annually 234,646; Total Staff 2,426.
Chaplains: Affiliate of Catholic Health Initiatives. Revs. Bogdan Palka, S.D.S.; William J. Moorman, O.SS.T., Ph.D.; Robert Phillips, S.J.; Sr. Anna M. Keenaghan, O.S.F., Chap.; Jane Mayrer; Maureen O'Brien, Ph.D.; Janette Silva; Kathy Edelmann.

[N] NURSING HOMES (SKILLED) AND REHABILITATION CENTERS

BALTIMORE. *Belvedere Green at Good Samaritan*, 1651 E. Belvedere Ave., 21239. Tel: 410-433-7255. Lawrence M. Beck, Pres.; Shirley Roth, Vice Pres. Nursing; Rev. James M. Reusing, Dir. of Pastoral Care; Deborah Bena, R.N., Health Min. Coord.; Anthony Read, Board Chm.

Dismas House West, 105 S. Mount St., 21223-0435. Tel: 410-566-9400; Fax: 410-233-1622. P.O. Box 4435, 21223-0435. Joseph J. Kruse Jr., Exec Dir.; Barbara Fleming, Admin. Svcs. Facilitator. Non-Sectarian-Use Diocesan Property Rehabilitation center under contract to the Maryland Division of Corrections to provide inmate services. Total Staff 26; Total Assisted Annually 200.

St. Elizabeth Rehabilitation and Nursing Center, 3320 Benson Ave., 21227-1035. Tel: 410-644-7100; Fax: 410-646-6589. Email: info@catholiccharities-md.org. Web: www.catholiccharities-md.org. Ms. Christine Mour, N.H.A., Admin.; Rev. Godswill Agbagwa, Chap.
St. Elizabeth Rehabilitation and Nursing Center., Sponsored by Associated Catholic Charities. Sisters 1; Bed Capacity 162; Total Assisted 285; Total Staff 220.

Good Samaritan Nursing Center, 1651 E. Belvedere Ave., 21239. Tel: 410-532-5600. Lawrence M. Beck, Pres.; Nancy Lawrence, Long Term Care; Rev. James M. Reusing, Dir. Pastoral Care; Deborah Bena, R.N., Health Min. Coord.

EMMITSBURG. *Villa St. Catherine, Inc.*, 331 S. Seton Ave., 21727. Tel: 301-447-7000; Fax: 301-447-7015. Email: info@stcatherinesnursingcenter.com. Web: stcatherinesnursingcenter.com. Louis Vogel III, Admin. & CEO. Sponsored by Ascension Health. Bed Capacity 69; Total Assisted 68; Total Staff 92.

[O] HOMES FOR AGED

BALTIMORE. *St. Charles Villa*, 603 Maiden Choice Ln., 21228-3697. Tel: 410-747-1211; Fax: 410-747-2460. Revs. John L. Bitterman, S.S., S.T.B., M.A., Dir.; Joseph J. Bonadio, S.S., M. Rel.Ed., D.Min., S.T.L. (Retired); John W. Bowen, S.S., M.A., S.T.L. (Retired); Albert C. Giaquinto, S.S., M.A., S.T.L. (Retired); Claude H. Dukehart, S.S., M.A., S.T.D. (Retired); Edward J. Frazer, S.S., M.A., S.T.L. (Retired); John F. Mattingly, S.S., M.A., M.S.L.S., S.S.L. (Retired); John E. McMurry, S.S., S.T.L., Ph.D. (Retired); Vincent deP. McMurry, S.S., M.A., S.T.L. (Retired); John H. Olivier, S.S., M.A., S.T.B. (Retired). Priests 10; Total in Residence 10; Total Staff 5.

St. Joseph's Nursing Home (1934) 1222 Tugwell Dr., 21228. Tel: 410-747-0026; Fax: 410-747-0386. Email: st.josephs@stjosephs.net. Rev. Joseph Dorniak, O.F.M.Conv.; Sr. Krystyna Mroczek, Admin.
Sisters Servants of Mary Immaculate, Inc. Sisters 11; Residents 44; Total Assisted 80; Total Staff 63.

St. Martin's Home for Aged, Little Sisters of the Poor, 601 Maiden Choice Ln., 21228. Tel: 410-744-9367; Fax: 410-747-6380. Email: msbaltlsp@mindspring.com. Web: www.littlesistersofthepoor.org. Sisters 17; Intermediate Care Beds 42; Assisted Living 22; Apartments 16; Aged Residents 80; Total Staff 122; Total Assisted 94.

TIMONIUM. *Stella Maris* (1953) 2300 Dulaney Valley Rd., 21093. Tel: 410-666-0698 (office); Fax: 410-560-9675. Email: ljohnson@stellamorisinc.com. Web: www.stellamarisinc.com. Sr. Karen McNally, R.S.M., Chief Admin. Officer; Rev. Lawrence M. Johnson, Dir. of Pastoral Care. The management corporation for all programs of Stella Maris. Long-term care; subacute care; home health; rehabilitative services; hospice services; hospice inpatient; home/hospice care; outreach ministries program; independent living; group home; and counseling/bereavement services for adults and children. All applications for the facilities of the Center are processed directly through the Admissions Office at Stella Maris. Lay Personnel 716; Sisters 7; Staff 723; Residents 384; Bed Capacity 412; Total Assisted 141,000.
Cardinal Shehan Center, Inc.

[P] SOCIAL SERVICES

BALTIMORE. *Franciscan Center* (1968) 101 W. 23rd St., 21218. Tel: 410-467-5340; Fax: 410-467-4569. Email: kheyward-west@franciscancenterbaltimore.org. Web: www.franciscancenterbaltimore.org. Karen Heyward-West, B.S., M.A., Pres. & CEO. Sisters of St. Francis of Assisi. Total Assisted 180,000; Total Staff 21.

Mount Providence Reading Center, 701 Gun Rd., 21227. Tel: 410-247-0448; Fax: 410-242-4963. Email: sisterconstance@oblatesisters.com. Web: www.oblatesisters.com. Sr. M. Constance Fenwick, O.S.P., Dir. Oblate Sisters of Providence. Students 56; Total Assisted 56; Total Staff 7.

Trinitarian Counseling Services, Inc., 8400 Park Heights Ave., P.O. Box 5719, 21282. Tel: 410-486-5764; Fax: 410-486-0614. Email: treasurer@trinitarians.org. Rev. William J. Moorman, O.SS.T., Ph.D., Dir. Total Assisted 12; Total Staff 1.

EMMITSBURG. *Seton Center, Inc.*, 16840 S. Seton Ave., 21727. Tel: 301-447-6102; Fax: 301-447-1748. Email: setoncenterinc@doc.org. Web: www.setoncenterinc.org. Sr. Carol Durkin, D.C., Admin. Daughters of Charity., Social Service; Outreach; Thrift Shop. Total Assisted 8,000; Total Staff 4.

PASADENA. *Mary's Center, Inc.* (1990) P.O. Box 1804, 21123-1804. Tel: 410-761-8082; 301-739-1234 (Hagerstown); Fax: 410-761-0330. 7567 Ritchie Hwy., Glen Burnie, 21061. Pregnancy Support Svcs. Free pregnancy tests; material assistance to women & babies in need. Additional offices in Hagerstown, MD (1200 Dual Hwy.) & Baltimore, MD (805 N. Calvert St.) Total Assisted 801; Total Staff 28.

[Q] ASSOCIATED CATHOLIC CHARITIES

BALTIMORE. *Associated Catholic Charities, Inc. (Catholic Charities)*
For more information on Catholic Charities and its programs please contact:
Catholic Charities, 320 Cathedral St., 3rd Floor, 21201-4421. Tel: 410-547-5469. Email: info@catholiccharities-md.org. Web: www.catholiccharities-md.org.
Management Team:

Associated Catholic Charities Inc., 320 Cathedral St., 3rd Floor, 21201-4421. Tel: 410-547-5495; Fax: 410-752-2873. Mr. William J. McCarthy Jr., Exec. Dir.

Associated Catholic Charities Inc., 28 W. Lexington St., 21201-3432. Tel: 410-261-6775; Fax: 410-889-0203. Mary Anne O'Donnell, Dir. Community Svcs. Div.

Associated Catholic Charities Inc., 320 Cathedral St., 3rd Floor, 21201-4421. Tel: 410-547-5459; Fax: 410-752-2873. James Gabriel, Assoc. Dir. & CFO.

Associated Catholic Charities Inc., 320 Cathedral St., 21201-4421. Tel: 410-547-5481; Fax: 410-576-2179. Angelo Boer, Dir., Devel. and Communications Div.

Associated Catholic Charities Inc., 2520 Pot Spring Rd., Timonium, 21093-2795. Tel: 410-252-4005, Ext. 104; Fax: 410-560-3495. Mark J. Schulz, Dir., Lifetime Svcs. Division.

Associated Catholic Charities Inc., 1966 Greenspring Dr., Ste. 200, Timonium, 21093. Tel: 443-798-3416; Fax: 410-561-3056. Dale R. McArdle, Dir., Housing Svcs. Div.

Associated Catholic Charities Inc., 1966 Greenspring Dr., Ste. 200, Timonium, 21093. Tel: 443-798-3390; Fax: 410-561-7728. Kathleen H. Mills, Dir., Human Resources Div.

Associated Catholic Charities Inc., 2300 Dulaney Valley Rd., Timonium, 21093-2739. Tel: 410-252-4700, Ext. 101; Fax: 410-252-3040. Mark Greenberg, Dir., Children & Family Svcs. Division Management Team: Mr. William J. McCarthy Jr.; Jim Gabriel; Angelo Boer; Mark Greenburg; Dale R. McArdle; Kathy Mills; Mary Anne O'Donnell; Mark J. Schulz; Scott Becker.

Associated Catholic Charities Inc., 2300 Dulaney Valley Rd., Timonium, 21093. Tel: 410-252-4700, Ext. 103; Fax: 410-252-3040. Mary Rode, Admin. Villa Maria Continuum.

Associated Catholic Charities Inc., 1966 Greenspring Dr., Ste. 200, Timonium, 21093. Tel: 443-798-3443; Fax: 410-561-7741. Scott Becker, Sr. Dir. Finance.
Services For Children and Families:

Catholic Charities Early Head Start, Harford County, 34 N. Philadelphia Blvd., Aberdeen, 21001. Tel: 410-273-5650; Fax: 410-272-6082. 1980 Brookside Dr., Edgewood, 21040. Tel: 410-612-1760; Fax: 410-612-1763.

Catholic Charities Head Start, Carroll County, 255 Clifton Blvd., Ste. 101, Westminster, 21157. Tel: 410-871-2450; 410-876-8503; Fax: 410-876-8630.

Center for Family Services - Domestic and International Adoptions, 11 E. Mount Royal Ave., 3rd Fl., 21202. Tel: 410-659-4050; Fax: 410-659-4060.

Center for Family Services - Family to Family Respite, 11 E. Mount Royal Ave., 21202-2714. Tel: 410-685-2363; Fax: 410-685-2364.

Center for Family Services - Hope, 11 E. Mount Royal Ave., 21202. Tel: 410-685-2363; Fax: 410-685-2364.

Center for Family Services - Pregnancy, Parenting and Adoption Svcs., 11 E. Mount Royal Ave., 3rd Fl., 21202. Tel: 410-659-4050; Fax: 410-659-4060.

Center for Family Services - Therapeutic Alternative Shelter Care (TASC), 1301 Continental Dr., Ste. 101, Abingdon, 21009. Tel: 410-538-3388; Fax: 410-538-3376.

Center for Family Services - Resource Services, 11 E. Mount Royal Ave., 21202-2714. Tel: 410-685-2363; Fax: 410-685-2364.

Center for Family Services - Treatment Foster Care, 11 E. Mount Royal Ave., 21202. Tel: 410-685-2363; Fax: 410-685-2364.
1301 Continental Dr., Suite 101, Abingdon, 21009. Tel: 410-538-3388; Fax: 410-538-3376.

St. Jerome's Head Start, 915 Sterrett St., 21230-2502. Tel: 410-685-1700; Fax: 410-685-2546.

St. Vincent's Center, 2600 Pot Spring Rd., Timonium, 21093-2732. Tel: 410-252-4000; Fax: 410-561-8109.

St. Vincent's Child Abuse Prevention Programs, 2600 Pot Spring Rd., Timonium, 21093. Tel: 410-666-7113; Fax: 410-561-8109.

(HOPE) Program for Medically Fragile Infants and Children, 11 E. Mt. Royal Ave., 21202. Tel: 410-685-2363; Fax: 410-685-2364.

Villa Maria Continuum, 2300 Dulaney Valley Rd., Timonium, 21093. Tel: 410-252-4700; Fax: 410-252-3040.

Villa Maria Baltimore Child and Adolescent Response System (B-CARS), 1118 S. Light St., 21230. Tel: 410-727-4800; Fax: 410-727-5853.

Villa Maria Behavioral Health Clinics, 2300 Dulaney Valley Rd., Timonium, 21093. Tel: 410-252-7664; Fax: 410-561-9073.
Villa Maria - Behavioral Health Clinics: (10 locations)

Villa Maria Anne Arundel County, 1438 Defense Hwy., Ste. 202, Gambrills, 21054. Tel: 410-451-0682; Fax: 410-451-0701.

Villa Maria At St. Clements Church, 2700 Washington Ave., 21227. Tel: 410-242-1025; Fax: 410-536-0636.

Villa Maria Harford County, 1301 Continental Dr., Suite 103, Abingdon, 21009. Tel: 410-676-4002; Fax: 410-676-7365.

Villa Maria Carroll County, 255 Clifton Blvd., Ste. 302, Westminster, 21157. Tel: 410-848-2037; Fax: 410-848-5273.

Villa Maria of Frederick County, 116 E. 2nd St., Frederick, 21701. Tel: 301-694-6654; 301-898-7900 (Voicemail); Fax: 301-694-8221.

Villa Maria of Washington County, 229 N. Potomac St., Hagerstown, 21740-3812. Tel: 301-733-5858; Fax: 301-733-5626.

Villa Maria of Mountain Maryland, 921 Seton Dr., Ste. G, P.O. Box 916, Cumberland, 21502. Tel: 301-777-8685; Fax: 301-777-8687.

Villa Maria Behavioral Health Clinic-Outreach Program at Fallstaff, 6999 Reisterstown Rd., 21215. Tel: 410-585-0598; Fax: 410-585-0589.

Falstaff Clinic Counseling Services, 6999 Reisterstown Rd., 21215. Tel: 410-585-0598; Fax: 410-585-0589.

Villa Maria - Bridges to Success, 1301 Continental Dr., Ste. 103, Abingdon, 21009-2338. Tel: 410-676-4002; Fax: 410-676-7365.

Villa Maria - Home-Based Respite Program, 118 S.

Light St., 21230. Tel: 410-230-0540; Fax: 410-727-3520.
Villa Maria - In-Home Intervention Program, 1118 S. Light St., Ste. 200, 21230. Tel: 410-230-0540; Fax: 410-727-5520.
Villa Maria - Residential Treatment Center (Villa Maria, Inc.), 2300 Dulaney Valley Rd., Timonium, 21093-2739. Tel: 410-252-4700; Fax: 410-252-3040.
Villa Maria - Safe Start, 1301 Continental Dr., Ste. 103, Abingdon, 21009-2338. Tel: 410-676-4002; Fax: 410-676-7365; Tel: 410-272-2844.
Villa Maria School at the Main Campus, 2300 Dulaney Valley Rd., Timonium, 21093-2739. Tel: 410-252-6343; Fax: 410-560-1347.
Villa Maria School at Hartford County, 1370 Brass Mill Rd., Belcamp, 21017. Tel: 410-297-4101; Fax: 410-273-9555. Rick Frank, Prin.
Villa Maria School at St. Vincent's Center, 2600 Pot Spring Rd., Timonium, 21093-2732. Tel: 410-252-3725; Fax: 410-453-9712.
Villa Maria School at Dr. Lillie M. Jackson, 1501 N. Ashburton St., 21216. Tel: 410-624-0593; Fax: 410-624-0592.
Villa Maria School-Based Mental Health Programs Baltimore County, Hartford County, Baltimore City, 2300 Dulaney Valley Rd., Timonium, 21093. Tel: 410-252-4700; Fax: 410-252-3040. Carl Fornoff, Contact Person (Balt. Co.); Diane Shannon, Contact Person (Balt. City); Crystal Taylor, Contact Person (Hartford Co.).
Villa Maria School Consultation Program, 1118 Light St., 21230. Tel: 410-252-4700; Fax: 410-252-3040.
Villa Maria Therapeutic Group Home, 1422 Gibsonwood Rd., Catonsville, 21228-2523. Tel: 410-788-9440; Fax: 410-788-4668.
Villa Maria Lansdowne After School Program at St. Clement Church, 2700 Washington Ave., 21227. Tel: 410-368-3984; Fax: 410-536-1290.
Villa Maria Therapeutic After School Program in Timonium, 2300 Dulaney Valley Rd., Timonium, 21093-2739. Tel: 410-252-4700; Fax: 410-252-3040.
Villa Maria Respite Program, 2300 Dulaney Valley Rd., Timonium, 21093. Tel: 410-252-4700; Fax: 410-252-3040.
Community Services:
Anna's House, P.O. Box 88, Bel Air, 21014-0088. Tel: 410-803-2130; Fax: 410-638-1753.
Esperanza Center/Immigration Legal Services, 430 S. Broadway, 21231-2410. Tel: 410-522-2668; 410-534-8015; Fax: 410-675-1451.
**Cherry Hill Town Center (Cherry Hill Town Center, Inc.)* Program now part of Lifetime Services Division.
Christopher Place Employment Academy, 725 Fallsway, 21202. Tel: 443-983-9046; Fax: 410-962-8933.
Families That Work, 17 W. Franklin St., 21201. Tel: 410-659-3750; Fax: 410-244-6069.
Holden Hall, 761 W. Hamburg St., 21230. Tel: 410-347-9830; Fax: 410-347-9831.
Legislative Education Group Advocacy Networks (LEG), 228 W. Lexington St., Ste. 220, 21201-3432. Tel: 410-261-6783; Fax: 410-889-0203.
My Sister's Place Women's Center, 17 W. Franklin St., 21201. Tel: 410-727-3523; Fax: 410-727-1611.
My Sister's Place Lodge, 111 W. Mulberry St., 21201-3619. Tel: 410-528-9002; Fax: 410-528-9004.
Our Daily Bread, 725 Fallsway, 21202. Tel: 443-986-9027; Fax: 410-962-8932.
Parish Social Ministry, 228 W. Lexington St., Ste. 220, 21201-3432. Tel: 410-261-6782; Fax: 410-889-0203.
Project FRESH Start (Family Relocation, Empowerment, and Self-Help), 228 W. Lexington St., Ste. 220, 21201-3432. Tel: 410-261-6777; Fax: 410-889-0203.
Project SERVE (Service and Education through Residential Volunteer Experience), 725 Fallsway, 21202. Tel: 413-986-9029; Fax: 410-962-8931.
Alternative Spring Break, 725 Fallsway, 21202. Tel: 443-986-9029; Fax: 410-962-8931.
Employment Services, 725 Fallsway, 21202. Tel: 443-986-9040; Fax: 410-962-8930.
Samaritan Center, 17 W. Franklin St., 21201. Tel: 410-659-4020; Fax: 410-659-0642.
Sarah's House, 2015 20th St., Fort Meade, 20755-1301. Tel: 410-551-7722; Fax: 410-551-7279.
Social Concerns, 228 W. Lexington St., Ste. 220, 21201-3432. Tel: 410-261-6783; Fax: 410-889-0203.
Senior Community Service Employment Program (SCSEP), 228 W. Lexington St., Ste. 220, 21201-3432. Tel: 410-261-6765; Fax: 410-235-5781.
Services for Seniors:
Abingdon Senior Housing, 30014 St. Clair Dr., Abingdon, 21009. Tel: 410-569-3630. Debbie Seigle, Contact Person.
Answers for the Aging, 3320 Benson Ave., 21227-1035. Tel: 410-646-0100; 888-502-7587; Fax: 410-646-0500.
Caritas House Assisted Living, 3308 Benson Ave., 21227. Tel: 410-646-6600; Fax: 410-646-6565.
**Catholic Charities Senior Housing at Arundel Woods (Glen Burnie Senior Housing, Inc.)*, 403 W. Ordnance Rd., Glen Burnie, 21061. Tel: 410-424-3535; Fax: 410-424-4484.
Catholic Charities Senior Housing at Basilica Place (The Catholic Charities Housing, Inc.), 124 W. Franklin Street, 21201-4576. Tel: 410-539-0418; Fax: 410-752-6207.
**Catholic Charities Senior Housing at Coursey Station (Coursey Station Apartments, Inc.)*, 200 First Ave., Lansdowne, 21227. Tel: 410-242-6167; Fax: 410-242-3459.
Catholic Charities Senior Housing at DePaul House (DePaul House, Inc.), 3300 Benson Ave., 21227-1030. Tel: 410-644-8484; Fax: 410-644-1334.
**Catholic Charities Senior Housing at Friendship Station (Odenton Senior Housing, Inc.)*, 1212 Odenton Rd., Odenton, 21113-1629. Tel: 410-519-6085; Fax: 410-519-6092.
**Catholic Charities Senior Housing at Owings Mills New Town (Owings Mills Senior Housing, Inc.)*, 9733 Groffs Mill Dr., Owings Mills, 21117. Tel: 410-902-8222; Fax: 410-902-0250.
**Catholic Charities Senior Housing at Reister's Clearing (Reisterstown Gardens Senior Housing, Inc.)*, 304 Cantata Ct., Reisterstown, 21136-6471. Tel: 410-517-4994; Fax: 410-517-0095.
**Catholic Charities Senior Housing at Reister's View (Reisterstown Village Senior Housing, Inc.)*, 306 Cantata Ct., Reisterstown, 21136-6472. Tel: 410-517-4994; Fax: 410-517-4995.
Catholic Charities Senior Housing at St. Charles House (St. Charles House, Inc.), 11 Church Ln., Pikesville, 21208-6607. Tel: 410-484-6125; Fax: 410-484-8713.
**Catholic Charities Senior Housing at Aberdeen Senior Housing, Inc.*, 901 Barnett La., Aberdeen, 21001. Tel: 410-273-0435; Fax: 410-273-0439.
**Catholic Charities Senior Housing at St. Joachim House (St. Joachim House, Inc.)*, 3310 Benson Ave., 21227-1075. Tel: 410-644-8269; Fax: 410-525-9227.
**Catholic Charities Senior Housing at St. Luke's Place (St. Luke's Apartments, Inc.)*, 2825 Lodge Farm Rd., Sparrows Point, 21219-1347. Tel: 410-477-3661; Fax: 410-477-0199.
**Catholic Charities Senior Housing at Starner Hill Apartments (Backbone Housing, Inc.)*, 25 N. Pennsylvania Ave., Grantsville, 21536-0489. Tel: 301-895-5842; Fax: 301-895-3762.
**Catholic Charities Senior Housing at Trinity House Apartments (Trinity House Apartments, Inc.)*, 409 Virginia Ave., Towson, 21286-5372. Tel: 410-825-5288; Fax: 410-825-5592.
**Catholic Charities Senior Housing at Holy Korean Martyrs (Woodlawn Senior Housing, Inc.)*, 5500 Lexington Rd., Woodlawn, 21207. Tel: 410-944-5959; Fax: 410-944-0555.
Cherry Hill SeniorLife Center, 606 Cherry Hill Rd., Ste. 201, 21225-1229. Tel: 410-354-5101; Fax: 410-354-5103.
Congregate Housing Services Program, 1966 Greenspring Dr., Timonium, 21093. Tel: 443-798-3417; Fax: 410-561-3056.
Everall Gardens, 6100 Everall Ave., Overlea, 21206. Tel: 410-444-5850; Fax: 410-444-0190.
Friendship Village, 1208 Odenton Rd., Odenton, 21113. Tel: 410-305-0480; Fax: 410-305-0481.
Kessler Park, 4230 Hollins Ferry Rd., Lansdowne, 21227. Tel: 410-247-9244; Fax: 410-247-4251.
Pastoral Care at the Jenkins Senior Living Community, 3320 Benson Ave., 21227. Tel: 410-646-6513; Fax: 410-646-0500.
Our Lady of Fatima I, 6400 E. Pratt St., 21224. Tel: 443-798-3423; Fax: 410-561-3056.
St. Ann Adult Day Services, 3320 Benson Ave., 21227-1001. Tel: 410-646-6533; Fax: 410-644-0840.
St. Elizabeth Rehabilitation and Nursing Center (Jenkins Memorial Nursing Home, Inc.), 3320 Benson Ave., 21227-1035. Tel: 410-644-7100; Fax: 410-646-6589.
St. Mark's, 19 Winters Ln., Catonsville, 21228. Tel: 410-788-0972.
Services for People with Developmental Disabilities:
Francis X. Gallagher Services, 2520 Pot Spring Rd., Timonium, 21093-2795. Tel: 410-252-4005; Fax: 410-560-3495. Programs include vocational, adult medical day & residential services.
The Bethany Community, Inc. Tel: 410-252-4005; Fax: 410-560-3495.
Group homes constructed and operated under the U.S. Dept. of Housing and Urban Development's Section 202-8 Program:
3731 Ellerslie Ave., 21218.
2421 Pot Spring Rd., Timonium, 21093.
2292 Dulaney Valley Rd., Timonium, 21093.
18314 Middletown Rd., Parkton, 21120.
3400 Benson Ave., 21227.
8240 Jumpers Hole Rd., Millersville, 21108.
4607 Mountain Rd., Pasadena, 21122.
2560 Pot Spring Rd., Timonium, 21093.
625 Belfast Rd., Sparks, 21152.
4605 Mountain Rd., Pasadena, 21122.
751 Argonne Dr., 21218.
47 Church Rd., Arnold, 21012.
1925 Rockhaven Ave., 21228.
Other Associated Catholic Charities, Inc. Corporations:
661 Corporation, 320 Cathedral St., 21201. Tel: 410-547-5469.
The Children's Fund, Inc., 320 Cathedral St., 21201. Tel: 410-547-5469; Fax: 410-752-2873.
OLF Senior Housing, Inc., 320 Cathedral St., 21201. Tel: 443-798-3416; Fax: 410-561-3056. Web: www.cc-md.org. Dale R. McArdle, Vice Pres.
OLF Senior Housing II, Inc., 320 Cathedral St., 21201. Tel: 443-798-3416; Fax: 410-561-3056. Web: www.cc-md.org. Dale R. McArdle, Vice Pres. & Contact Person.

[R] RETREAT HOUSES FOR MEN, WOMEN AND YOUTH

BALTIMORE. *St. Mary's Spiritual Center* (1988) (Historic Site), 600 N. Paca St., 21201-1920. Tel: 410-728-6464; Fax: 410-669-8140. Email: SMSCBalto@verizon.net. Web: www.stmaryspiritualcenter.org. Rev. John C. Kemper, S.S., M.Div., M.A., D.Min., Dir. The Mother Seton House and the Historic Seminary Chapel are under the direction of St. Mary's Spiritual Center and Historic Site. Tours and pilgrims are welcome to the site. The site is owned and managed by the Society of St. Sulpice (Sulpicians) USA. Adjunct Staff 14; Auxiliary Staff 4.

SPARKS. *Msgr. Clare J. O'Dwyer Retreat House*, 15523 York Rd., P.O. Box 310, 21152. Tel: 410-666-2400; Fax: 410-472-3281. Email: odwyer@archbalt.org. Web: www.msgrodwyer.org. Rev. Martin S. Nocchi, Dir. Total Staff 11.

[S] MONASTERIES AND RESIDENCES OF PRIESTS AND BROTHERS

BALTIMORE. *St. Ambrose Friary*, 4502 Park Heights Ave., 21215. Tel: 410-367-0334; Fax: 410-542-6056. Revs. William Graham, O.F.M.Cap., J.C.L., Tribunal Office, Archdiocese of Baltimore; Paul Zaborowski, O.F.M.Cap., Pastor St. Ambrose Parish; Roger White, O.F.M.Cap., Pastor of Transfiguration Parish; Bro. Mark Pattock, O.F.M.Cap.; Rev. Roman Kozacheson, O.F.M.Cap, Pastoral Min. Good Shepherd Hospital.
Congregation of the Holy Spirit, 2846 W. Lafayette Ave., 21216. Revs. Christopher Promis, C.S.Sp. Tel: 410-951-7372; Gerald Kasule, C.S.Sp.
Ferdinand Wheeler Jesuit Community, 3048 Guilford Ave., 21218. Tel: 410-338-1296. Email: kgillespie@loyola.edu. Bro. Paul Cawthorne, S.J.; Revs. Michael Simone, S.J.; Brian Pereira, S.J.; Desmond Bughagar, S.J.; Theodore E.A. Brady, S.J.; Kevin Gillespie, S.J.; William Walsh, S.J.; Irsan Maurus, S.J.; Christopher Dumadag. Priests 8; Brothers 1.
Holy Trinity Monastery, 8400 Park Heights Ave., P.O. Box 5719, 21282-0719. Tel: 410-486-5171; Fax: 410-486-0614. Web: trinitarians.org. Priests 59. Leadership Very Revs. Victor Scocco, O.SS.T., Min. Provincial; Thomas Cerulo, O.SS.T., Vicar Provincial & Dir. Holy Trinity Spiritual Center; Revs. Kurt J. Klismet, O.SS.T., Prov. Treas, Dir. Devel. & Prov. Sec.; Carl M. Frisch, O.SS.T., Dir. Vocations Baltimore, MD Rev. Thomas J. Burke, O.SS.T., S.T.M., S.T.D.; Very Rev. Thomas Cerulo, O.SS.T.; Revs. David Colella, O.SS.T; John Dorn, O.SS.T.; Aaron M. Dowdell, O.SS.T., M.A., S.T.B.; Carl M. Frisch, O.SS.T.; Joseph J. Gross, O.SS.T; Kurt J. Klismet, O.SS.T.; William J. Moorman, O.SS.T., Ph.D.; Juan Antonio Perez-Ojeda, O.SS.T.; Very Rev. Victor Scocco, O.SS.T.; Rev. Juan Vasquez-Rubio, O.SS.T.
Assigned But Serving Elsewhere: The Trinitarians in Italy (Rome) Very Rev. Albeet M. Anuszewski, O.SS.T., Gen. Councilor & Economer Gen.; Most Rev. Jose T. Narlaly, O.SS.T., Minister Gen., Via Massimi, 114/C, Rome 00136 Italy. Tel: 011-39-063-542-0529; Fax: 011-39-063-534-1673 The Trinitarians in Egypt (Cairo) Bro. Richard J. Micka, O.SS.T., Trinity House, 1511 E. Commercial St., Victoria, TX 77901-7021; Rev. Alfonso Serna, O.SS.T., 440 S. Chester St., 21231. Tel: 410-732-5425; Fax: 410-732-5427 The Trinitarians in India (Bangalore & Trichur) Revs. Binoy Akkalayil, O.SS.T., Holy Trinity Ashram, S.O.S. Post, Bannerghatta Rd., Bangalore 560076 India. Tel: 011-91-80-6585596; Janil Joseph Chakkiath, O.SS.T.; Poulose Chalackal, O.SS.T., Holy Trinity Ashram, S.O.S. Post, Bannerghatta Rd., Bangalore 560076 India. Tel: 011-91-80-6585596; Simine G. Fernandez, O.SS.T., Holy Trinity Ashram, P.O. Aranttukara, Kerala State, Trichur 680618 India. Tel: 011-91-80-487-360379; Fax: 011-91-80-487-361596; Sajeev Joseph, O.SS.T.;

Xavier Kachappilly, O.SS.T.; Roy Kurian Kalachalil, O.SS.T.; Santhosh George Kozhippandan, O.SS.T.; Francis Kulathingal, O.SS.T., Holy Trinity Ashram, S.O.S. Post, Bannerghatta Rd., Bangalore 560076 India. Tel: 011-91-80-6585596; Mathew Maniamkerry, O.SS.T., Holy Trinity Ashram, P.O. Aranttukara, Kerala State, Trichur 680618 India. Tel: 011-91-80-487-360379; Fax: 011-91-80-487-361596; Joseph Muthuplackal, O.SS.T., Holy Trinity Ashram, P.O. Aranttukara, Kerala State, Trichur 680618 India. Tel: 011-91-80-487-360379; Fax: 011-91-80-487-361596; Baiju Parakkal, O.SS.T., Holy Trinity Ashram, S.O.S. Post, Bannerghatta Rd., Bangalore 560076 India. Tel: 011-91-80-6585596; Anthony Pullukattu, O.SS.T., Holy Trinity Ashram, P.O. Aranttukara, Kerala State, Trichur 680618 India. Tel: 011-91-80-487-360379; Fax: 011-91-80-487-361596; Binoj Mathew Puthenpurackal, O.SS.T.; Bitaju Puthenpurakal, O.SS.T.; Pradeep Puthenveettil, O.SS.T., Holy Trinity Ashram, S.O.S. Post, Bannerghatta Rd., Bangalore 560076 India. Tel: 011-91-80-6585596; Jolly Pappachan Thekkinen, O.SS.T.; Augustine Varghese Vadakathalakal, O.SS.T. *The Trinitarians in Texas (Victoria & vicinity)* Revs. Raphael Baidoo, O.SS.T., Immaculate Conception Church, 238 N. Commercial St., P.O. Box 49, Goliad, TX 77963-0049; Stanley W. DeBoe, O.SS.T., 2410 Jefferson Point Dr., Apt. 537, Arlington, TX 76006. Tel: 817-676-3086; Adelson S. Moreira, O.SS.T., St. Clare of Assisi Parish, 321 Calumet Ave., Dallas, TX 75211. Tel: 214-623-0800; Fax: 214-333-9148; Bro. Patrick G. Wildgen, O.SS.T., 440 S. Chester St., 21231. Tel: 410-732-5425; Fax: 410-732-5427. *Novitiate House (Victoria, Texas)* Rev. Juan Antonio Perez-Ojeda, O.SS.T., Dir., Novices, Trinity House, 1511 E. Commercial St., Victoria, TX 77901-7021 (Dallas, Texas) Revs. Michael Conway, O.SS.T.; Alberto Rodriquez, O.SS.T., Our Lady of Sorrows Catholic Church, 208 W. River St., Victoria, TX 77901-2548. Tel: 361-575-2293; Fax: 361-582-0405 The Trinitarians in Bristol, Pennsylvania Rev. Vincent Bechamps, O.SS.T.; Very Rev. James R. Day, O.SS.T., Prov. Councilor; Rev. Thomas A. Morris, O.SS.T., 357 Dorrance St., P.O. Box 1175, Bristol, PA 19007-1175. Tel: 215-788-2128; Fax: 215-781-9782 The Trinitarian Community in Adelphi, Maryland Very Rev. Damian Anuzewski, O.SS.T., Prov. Councilor; Revs. Lawrence C. Hernandez, O.SS.T., 8612 Laverne Dr., Adelphi, 20783. Tel: 301-422-0155; Fax: 301-422-0070; Joseph K. Mitko, O.SS.T.; Juan Molina, O.SS.T., St. Clare of Assisi Parish, 321 Calumet Ave., Dallas, TX 75211. Tel: 214-623-0800; Fax: 214-333-9148 The Trinitarians in New Jersey Revs. Ken Borgesen, O.SS.T., St. James Church, 29 E. Paul Ave., P.O. Box 5877, Trenton, NJ 08638-0877. Tel: 609-393-4403; Fax: 609-303-6078; Philip Cordisco, O.SS.T., St. James Church, 29 E. Paul Ave., P.O. Box 5877, Trenton, NJ 08638-0877. Tel: 609-393-4403; Fax: 609-393-6078; Ireneusz Ekiert, O.SS.T.; Charles J. Flood, O.SS.T., Our Lady of Mt. Carmel Church, 805 Pine St., Asbury Park, NJ 07712-5747. Tel: 732-775-1056; Fax: 732-775-8767; Daniel Houde, O.SS.T., Our Lady of Mt. Carmel Church, 805 Pine St., Asbury Park, NJ 07712-5747. Tel: 732-775-1056; Fax: 732-775-8767; Boby Kurian Kumbakeel, O.SS.T., St. James Church, 29 E. Paul Ave., P.O. Box 5877, Trenton, NJ 08638-0877. Tel: 609-393-4403; Fax: 609-393-6078; Gerard Lynch, O.SS.T., Our Lady of Mt. Carmel Church, 805 Pine St., Asbury Park, NJ 07712-5747. Tel: 732-775-1056; Fax: 732-775-8767 The Trinitarians in California Revs. William J. Axe, O.SS.T., Ave Maria Retreat Center, 8089 Barataria Blvd., Crown Point, LA 70072. Tel: 504-689-3837; Frank Whatley, O.SS.T., Ave Maria Retreat Center, 8089 Barataria Blvd., Crown Point, LA 70072. Tel: 504-689-3837 Individuals in Other Locations: Bro. Eric Beardsley, O.SS.T., Meredith Memorial Home, 16 S. Illinois St., #604, Belleville, IL 62220-2107. Tel: 618-277-2139; Rev. Tom Dymowski, O.SS.T.; Very Rev. J. Edward Owens, O.SS.T., Prov. Councilor; Rev. Damon Geiger, O.SS.T., 440 S. Chester St., 21231. Tel: 410-732-5425; Fax: 410-732-5427; Bro. Alfonso Serna Ornelas, O.SS.T; Revs. William Sullivan, O.SS.T., 8612 Laverne Dr., Adelphi, 20783. Tel: 301-422-0155; Fax: 301-422-0070; Edward Wagner, O.SS.T., 900 E. Desert Inn Rd., #417, Las Vegas, NV 89109. Tel: 702-735-5989.

Immaculate Heart of Mary Friary, 4220 Erdman Ave., 21213. Tel: 410-485-5511; Fax: 410-483-2545. Email: mmartin@archbishopcurley.org. Revs. Michael Martin, O.F.M.Conv., Pres. & Guardian; Vincent Gluc, O.F.M.Conv.; Joseph Benicewicz, O.F.M.Conv.; Matthew Foley, O.F.M.Conv.; Bros. Douglas McMillan, O.F.M.Conv., Vicar; Daniel Lutolf, O.F.M.Conv. Residence of Franciscan Friars, O.F.M.Conv., conducting Archbishop Curley High School. Priests 4; Brothers 2; Total Staff 6.

Jesuit Community of Loyola University, Inc., Loyola University, 4603 Millbrook Rd., 21212-4721. Tel: 410-617-2318; Fax: 410-617-2125. Email: bomcdermott@loyola.edu. Revs. David G. Allen, S.J.; Ronald J. Amiot, S.J.; Ronald J. Anton, S.J. (Retired); Charles Borges, S.J.; Timothy B. Brown, S.J.; John Conley, S.J.; James L. Connor, S.J.; Edwin H. Convey, S.J.; John M. Dennis, S.J., M.Ed.; John R. Donahue, S.J.; Frank R. Haig, S.J.; Francis G. Hilton, S.J.; James Kelly, S.J.; Brian F. Linnane, S.J., Pres. Loyola College; Dominic W. Maruca, S.J.; Bienvenu Matanzonga, S.J.; Brian O. McDermott, S.J., Rector; William K. McGroarty, S.J.; William T. Miller, S.J.; Francis J. Nash, S.J.; Konrad Noronha, S.J.; Rolland Rabenarivo, S.J.; Joseph S. Rossi, S.J.; Peter F. Ryan, S.J., S.T.L., S.T.D.; James F. Salmon, S.J.; Mr. Samuel J. Sawyer, S.J.; Revs. James M. Shea, S.J.; Luis A. Tampe, S.J. Total in Residence 25.

Jesuit Mission Bureau, Maryland Province Inc., 8600 LaSalle Rd., Ste. 620, Towson, 21286-2014. Tel: 443-921-1332; Fax: 443-921-1313. Email: missionbureau@mdsj.org. Web: www.mdsj.org. Mr. Edward F. Plocha, Dir. Advancement & Contact Person.

Jesuit Seminary Guild, Maryland Province, Inc., 8600 La Salle Rd., Ste. 620, Towson, 21286-2014. Tel: 443-921-1332; Fax: 443-921-1313. Email: seminaryguild@mdsj.org. Web: www.mdsj.org. Mr. Edward F. Plocha, Dir. Advancement & Contact Person.

St. Joseph Society of the Sacred Heart House of Central Administration, 1130 N. Calvert St., 21202. Tel: 410-727-3386; Fax: 410-727-1006. Email: superiorgeneral@josephite.com. Web: www.josephite.com. Very Revs. Edward J. Chiffriller, S.S.J., Supr. Gen.; Roger J. Caesar, S.S.J., Vicar Gen.; John G. Harfmann, S.S.J., Consultor Gen.; Nelson A. Moreira, S.S.J., Treas. & Rector; Mrs. Bernice Jones, Asst. Archivist; Revs. Peter C. Weiss, S.S.J., Vocations Dir.; John F. Byrne, S.S.J. (Retired); N. Wilfrid DesRosiers, S.S.J. (Retired); James A. Hayes, S.S.J. (Retired); Joseph J. Rimshaw, S.S.J. (Retired); Louis R. Saporito, S.S.J. (Retired). Priests 12.

St. Joseph's Manor, 911 W. Lake Ave., 21210-1022. Tel: 410-323-3829; Fax: 410-435-1853. Very Revs. Stephen F. Brett, S.S.J., Rector; Matthew J. O'Rourke, S.S.J., Vice Rector; Revs. Paul Banet, S.S.J.; Joseph M. Calamari, S.S.J.; Michael J. Farrell, S.S.J.; Vincent P. Keenan, S.S.J.; Peter J. Kenney, S.S.J.; Joseph Kennedy, S.J.; Edward J. Lawlor, S.S.J. (Retired); Eugene J. Moynihan, S.S.J. (Retired); Edward J. Mullowney, S.S.J.; Joseph V. Tyson, S.S.J.; Bros. Charles Douglas, S.S.J.; Ricardo Gourrier, S.S.J. Home for retired priest & brothers of St. Joseph's Society of the Sacred Heart. Priests 15; Brothers 2.

St. Joseph's Passionist Community, 251 S. Morley St., 21229. Tel: 410-566-0877; Fax: 410-233-4974. Email: info@sjmp.org. Web: www.sjmp.org. Revs. Robert Carbonneau, C.P.; Alban Harmon, C.P., J.C.L.; Thomas McCann, C.P.; William Murphy, C.P. Congregation of the Most Holy Cross and Passion of Our Lord Jesus Christ. Priests 4.

Pallottine Center for Apostolic Causes, 512 W. Saratoga St., 21201. Tel: 410-685-3063; Fax: 410-234-1459. Rev. Peter T. Sticco, S.A.C., Dir.

St. Jude Shrine-Pallottine Missions; Pallottine Center for Apostolic Causes, Inc., Promotional Center for St. Jude Shrine.

Society of Mary (Marianists), Marianist Community, 317 S. Broadway, 21231-2408. Tel: 410-522-1568; Fax: 410-522-1569. Rev. Richard Kuhn, S.M.; Bros. Frank O'Donnell, S.M.; Gerard Sullivan, S.M. Priests 1; Brothers 2.

Society of St. Sulpice, Province of the United States (Associated Sulpicians of the United States), 5408 Roland Ave., 21210-1988. Tel: 410-323-5070; Fax: 410-433-6524. Email: provincial@sulpicians.org. Web: sulpicians.org. Very Revs. Ronald D. Witherup, S.S., S.T.L., S.T.M., Ph.D., Supr. General, 6 rue du Regard, Paris 75006 France; Thomas R. Ulshafer, S.S., S.T.L., Ph.D., Prov. Supr., Dubourg House, 4210 N. Charles St., Apt. 6, 21218-1041; Rev. Gerald D. McBrearity, S.S., M.A., S.T.B., D.Min., Dir. Formation & Personnel, Coord. Human & Spiritual Formation, Dir. Basselins Advisor & Spiritual Dir. Theological College of The Catholic University of America, 401 Michigan Ave., NE, Washington, DC 20017-1578. Represented in the Archdioceses and Dioceses of: Baltimore, Bridgeport, Dallas, Lansing, Los Angeles, Monterey, Oakland, Scranton, San Antonio, San Francisco, San Jose, Springfield-Cape Girardeau, and Washington, DC. Also in France, Mexico & Italy.; Missions: Kabwe & Lusaka in Zambia, Central Africa Priests in Society of St. Sulpice 62; Priests at Provincial House 2; Priest Candidates 7.

Members and Candidates on Individual Assignments: Revs. Francis M. Musonda, S.S., B.D., S.T.L., Dean, Students, Liturgy & African Studies, St. Augustine's Major Seminary, P.O. Box 81011, Kabwe, Zambia; Robert L. Russell, S.S., S.T.L. (Retired), Casa de Nuestra Senora Dolorosa, Calle 31 no. 78, Apdo. #712, Chuburna de Hildalgo, Merida, Yucatan 97200 Mexico. Tel: 011-52-99-81-07-48; Cornelius Hankomoone, S.S., S.T.L., S.T.D., Rector & Faculty, Emmaus Spirituality Center, Emmaus Spirituality Center, P.O. Box 320084-Woodlands, Lusaka, Zambia; Timothy C. Chikweto, B.D., Graduate Studies, Pontifical Gregorian Univ., College Pontifical Canadien, 75 Via Crescenzio, Rome 00193 Italy; Lewis B. Chilufya, S.T.L., Graduate Studies in Accademia Alfonsiana, College Pontifical Canadien, 75 Via Crescenzio, Rome 00193 Italy; Smart H. Chinyanwa, S.S., B.D., Graduate Studies, Catholic Univ. America, Theological College at The Catholic University of America, 401 Michigan Ave., NE, Washington, DC 20017-1578; Thomas R. Hurst, S.S., S.T.L., Ph.D., Pres.-Rector, Vice Chancellor, St. Mary's Seminary & University, 5400 Roland Ave., 21210-1994; Melvin C. Blanchette, S.S., M.A., Ph.D., Rector, Theological College of The Catholic University of America, 401 Michigan Ave, N.E., Washington, DC 20017-1578. Tel: 202-756-4915; Fax: 202-756-4909; Daniel J. Doherty, S.S., B.A., M.A., M.Div., S.T.L., Pastoral Theology & Asst. Dir. Pastoral Formation, St. Mary's Seminary & University, 5400 Roland Ave., 21210-1994; Paul A. Maillet, S.S., B.Mus., M.M., M.Div., S.T.L., Grad. Studies, St. Mary's Seminary & University, 5400 Roland Ave., 21210-1994. Tel: 202-756-5400; Fax: 202-756-4909; Daniel F. Moore, S.S., M.A., S.T.L., S.T.D., Dir. Discernment & Admissions, Vice Rector, Advisor & Spiritual Dir., Theological College of The Catholic University of America, 401 Michigan Ave., NE, Washington, DC 20017-1578. Tel: 202-756-4914; Fax: 202-756-4909; Anthony J. Pogorelc, S.S., M.Div., M.S., Ph.D., Dir. Pastoral Formation Prog., Advisor & Spiritual Dir., Theological College of The Catholic University of America, 401 Michigan Ave, N.E., Washington, DC 20017-1578. Tel: 202-756-4912; Fax: 202-756-4909; David D. Thayer, S.S., S.T.L., Ph.D., Advisor/Spirit. Dir. & Dir. of Intellectual Formation, Catholic University of America, c/o Theological College, 401 Michigan Ave, N.E., Washington, DC 20017-1578. Tel: 202-756-4911; Fax: 202-756-4909; Victor S. Shikaputo, S.S., S.T.L., S.T.D., St. Dominic Seminary Academic Dean, Moral Theology & Regl. Coord. Discernment, St. Dominic's Major Seminary, P.O. Box 320191, Woodlands, Lusaka, Zambia; Joseph T. Ky, S.S., M.A. (Retired), The Congregation of the Mother Co-Redemptrix, 1900 Grand Ave., Carthage, MO 64836-3500. Tel: 417-358-7137; William E. Hartgen Jr., S.S., M.A. (Retired), 634 E St., N.E., Washington, DC 20002-5230. Tel: 202-236-7745; John S. Kselman, S.S., S.T.L., Ph.D., Sacred Scripture, St. Patrick's Seminary & University, 320 Middlefield Rd., Menlo Park, CA 94025-3596; Addison G. Wright, S.S., M.A., S.S.L., S.T.D. (Retired), 24 Killian Ave., Trumbull, CT 06611-4118. Tel: 203-268-3610; James W. Lothamer, S.S., S.T.B., M.A., Ph.D., St. Agnes Parish, 855 E. Grand River Ave., Fowlerville, MI 48836-9529. Tel: 517-223-8684; Fax: 517-223-0813; James P. Oberle, S.S., S.T.B., S.T.L., Ph.D., Dir. Spiritual & Liturgical Formation, Holy Trinity Seminary, 3131 Vince Hagen Dr., Irving, TX 75062; James S. Tucker, S.S., M.A., M.S., Ph.D., Spiritual Advisor, Assumption Seminary, 2600 W. Woodlawn Ave., San Antonio, TX 78228-5196. Tel: 210-734-5137, Ext. 36; Cale J. Crowley, S.S., M.Div., Ph.D., Rector, Philosophy, Regl. Supr. of Sulpicians in Zambia, St. Augustine's Major Seminary, P.O. Box 81011, Kabwe 157101 Zambia. Tel: 011-2605-226023; Fax: 001-2605-226023; Patrick Simutowe, S.S., S.T.L., Graduate Studies, Accademia Alfonsiana, College Pontifical Canadien, 75 Crescenzio, Rome 00193 Italy. Tel: 011-260-95-915273; Fax: 001-260-1-263-404; Gerald V. Lardner, S.S., S.T.B., M.A., Ph.D. (Retired), 3601 Greenway, Apt. 102, 21218-2450. Tel: 443-983-5992; Fax: 410-747-2460; Joseph J. Bonadio, S.S., M. Rel.Ed., D.Min., S.T.L., Chap. Oak Crest Retirement Center (Retired), St. Charles Villa, 603 Maiden Choice Ln., 21228-3697. Tel: 410-747-2055; Fax: 410-747-2460; John W. Bowen, S.S., M.A., S.T.L., St. Mary Seminary & Univ. Alumni News Ed. (Retired), St. Charles Villa, 603 Maiden Choice Ln., 21228-3697. Tel: 410-719-2842; Fax: 410-747-2460; C. Henry Dukehart, S.S., M.A., S.T.D. (Retired), St. Charles Villa, 603 Maiden Choice Ln., 21228-3697. Tel: 410-455-5382; Fax: 410-747-2460; Edward J. Frazer, S.S., M.A., S.T.L. (Retired), St. Charles Villa, 603 Maiden Choice Ln., 21228-3697. Tel: 410-719-7191; Fax: 410-747-2460; Albert C. Giaquinto, S.S., M.A., S.T.L. (Retired), St. Charles Villa, 603 Maiden Choice Ln., 21228-3697. Tel: 410-744-2049; Fax: 410-747-2460; John F. Mattingly, S.S., M.A., M.S.L.S., S.S.L. (Retired), St. Charles Villa, 603 Maiden Choice Ln., 21228-3697. Fax:

410-747-2460; Vincent deP. McMurry, S.S., M.A., S.T.L. (Retired), St. Charles Villa, 603 Maiden Choice Ln., 21228-3697. Fax: 410-747-2460; John H. Olivier, S.S., M.A., S.T.B. (Retired), St. Charles Villa, 603 Maiden Choice Ln., 21228-3697. Tel: 410-747-3587; Fax: 410-747-2460; Hy K. Nguyen, S.S., M.Div., M.A., S.T.D., Systematic Theology, St. Mary's Seminary and University, 5400 Roland Ave., 21210-1994. Tel: 410-864-4258; Fax: 410-864-4278; William J. Flynn, S.S., S.T.L., M.S., D.Min. (Retired), Villa St. Joseph, 1600 Green Ridge St., Dunmore, PA 18509. Tel: 570-254-6233; Fax: 570-254-6233; Peter F. Chirico, S.S., S.T.D., B.B.A. (Retired), St. Martin's Home for the Aged, 601 Maiden Choice Ln., 21228-3698. Tel: 410-744-1528; William J. Lee, S.S., M.A., Ph.D. (Retired), St. Martin's Home for the Aged, 601 Maiden Choice Ln., 21228-3698. Tel: 410-788-0455; Peter W. Gray, S.S., M.A., Ph.D., Special Assignment, 113 Maple Ridge Rd., Reisterstown, 21136-6518; John E. McMurry, S.S., S.T.L., Ph.D. (Retired), St. Charles Villa, 603 Maiden Choice Ln., 21201-3697; John C. Kemper, S.S., M.Div., M.A., D.Min., Vice Pres. Advancement & Dir. St. Mary's Spiritual Center & Historic Site, St. Mary's Spiritual Center & Historic Site, 600 N. Paca St., 21201-1920; Leo J. Larrivee, S.S., M.A. (Theol.), M.A. (Hist.), Dubourg House, 4210 N. Charles St., Apt. 3, 21218-1041. Fax: 410-737-8826; John L. Bitterman, S.S., S.T.B., M.A., Dir./Supr Sulpician Retirement Community, St. Charles Villa, 603 Maiden Choice Ln., 21228-3697. Tel: 410-323-5070; Fax: 410-433-6524; Gerald L. Brown, S.S., M.Div., Ph.D., Sabbatical, St. Patrick's Seminary & University, 320 Middlefield Rd., Menlo Park, CA 94025-3596. Tel: 650-289-3357; Fax: 650-322-0997; Phillip J. Brown, J.D., S.T.B., J.C.D., Faculty, Catholic University of America School of Canon Law, Theological College of The Catholic University of America, 401 Michigan Ave., N.E., Washington, DC 20017-1578. Tel: 202-756-4910; Fax: 202-756-4909; Vincent D. Bui, S.S., M.A., S.T.B., J.C.L., Dean, Students, St. Patrick's Seminary & University, 320 Middlefield Rd., Menlo Park, CA 94025; Frederick J. Cwiekowski, S.S., M.A., S.T.D., Systematic Theology (Retired), St. Patrick's Seminary & University, 320 Middlefield Rd., Menlo Park, CA 94025-3596. Tel: 650-328-2544; Fax: 650-322-0997; Philip S. Keane, S.S., S.T.D., Prov. Sec. & Province Dir. Communications Ethical Consultant, St. Mary's Seminary & University, 5400 Roland Ave., 21210-1994; Nam J. Kim, S.S., M.A., S.T.L., S.T.D., Systematic Theology, Moderator, Pontifical Degree Prog. & Dir. Pastoral Year Prog., St. Patrick's Seminary & University, 320 Middlefield Rd., Menlo Park, CA 94025-3563. Tel: 408-533-5073; Fax: 650-322-0997; Eugene J. Konkel, S.S., M.A., S.T.L., Spiritual Direction (Retired), St. Patrick's Seminary & University, 320 Middlefield Rd., Menlo Park, CA 94025-3596. Tel: 650-326-3825; Fax: 650-322-0997; Gerald D. Coleman, S.S., M.A., S.T.L., Ph.D., Vice Pres. Corp. Ethics Daughters of Charity Health System, St. Pius Rectory, 1100 Woodside Rd., Redwood City, CA 94061-3627. Tel: 650-298-9953; 650-298-9953; Louis M. Reitz, S.S., S.T.L., M.S.L.S., M.Ed. (Retired), St. Pius X Rectory, 6428 York Rd., 21212-2111. Tel: 410-377-5417; Lawrence B. Terrien, S.S., Ph.D., S.T.D., Dir. Spiritual Life Programs, Systematic Theology, St. Mary's Seminary & University, 5400 Roland Ave., 21210-1994; James E. Myers, S.S., M.Div., Dir. of Vatican II Institute, Vatican II Institute, St. Patrick's Seminary & University, 320 Middlefield Rd., Menlo Park, CA 94025-3596. Tel: 650-328-1731; Fax: 650-325-6765; James L. McKearney, S.S., M.Div., S.T.L., S.T.D., Pres., Rector & Vice Chancellor, St. Patrick's Seminary and University, 320 Middlefield Rd., Menlo Park, CA 94025-3563. Tel: 650-839-1290; Fax: 650-322-0997; J. Michael Strange, S.S., M.A., M.T.S., St. Vincent de Paul Parish, 2320 Green St., San Francisco, CA 94123-4625. Tel: 415-922-7203; Howard P. Bleichner, S.S., M.A., Dr. Theol., Prof. Systematic Theol. (Retired), 2-1151 E. Cliff Dr., Santa Cruz, CA 95062-4835. Tel: 831-475-5724; Richard M. Gula, S.S., S.T.L., S.T.M., Ph.D., Moral Theology, Franciscan School of Theology, 1514 Oxford St., Apt. 303, Berkeley, CA 94709-1502. Tel: 510-649-8259; Fax: 510-549-9466; Richard B. MacDonough, S.S., S.T.L., Ph.D., Adjunct Spiritual Direction, St. John's Seminary (Retired), 647 Bluewater Way, Port Hueneme, CA 93041-3559. Tel: 805-482-3470. *St. Mary's Seminary & University*, 5400 Roland Ave., 21210-1994. Tel: 410-864-4000; Fax: 410-864-4278. Revs. Michael L. Barre, S.S., S.T.L., Ph.D., Sacred Scripture, St. Mary's Seminary & University, 5400 Roland Ave., 21210-1994. Tel: 410-435-1973; Robert F. Leavitt, S.S., S.T.D., Systematic Theology, St. Mary's Seminary & University, 16131 Old York Rd., Monkton, 21111. Tel: 410-864-3611; Luis R. Corneli Esq., S.S., J.D., J.C.L., Adjunct Prof. Canon Law, Pastoral Theology, St. Mary's Seminary & University, 5400 Roland Ave., 21210-1994; Gladstone H. Stevens, S.S., M.A., S.T.L., Ph.D., Vice Rector, Academic Dean, Systematic Theology, St. Patrick's Seminary & University, 320 Middlefield Rd., Menlo Park, CA 94025-3563; Shoba Nyambe, B.D., Vice Rector, Liturgy, Emmaus Spirituality Centre, P.O. Box 320084, Woodlands, Lusaka, Zambia; Renato Lopez, S.S., S.S.L., New Testament, Introduction to Theology, Dir. Liturgy, St. Mary's Seminary & University, 5400 Roland Ave., 21210-1994; Jeffrey A. Hubbard, B.A., S.T.B., M.Div., Faculty, Pre-Theology Christian Doctrine, St. Patrick's Seminary & University, 320 Middlefield Rd., Menlo Park, CA 94025-3563; Noel R. de Lira, A.B., S.T.B., S.T.L., Catholic Doctrine, Spiritual Dir. & Advisor, St. Patrick's Seminary & University, 320 Middlefield Rd., Menlo Park, CA 94025-3563; Victor Mwanamwambwa, B.D., Scripture, Emmaus Spirituality Centre, P.O. Box 320084, Woodlands, Lusaka, Zambia; John J. Slovikovski, M.Div., M.A., Ph.D. (Cand.), Advisor & Spiritual Dir., Theological College of The Catholic University of America, 401 Michigan Ave., NE, Washington, DC 20017-1578.

Xaverian Brothers Generalate, 4409 Frederick Ave., 21229. Tel: 410-644-0034; Fax: 410-644-2762. Email: brother@xaverianbrothers.org. Web: xaverianbrothers.org. Bros. Lawrence Harvey, C.F.X., Gen. Supr.; Daniel Skala, C.F.X., Vicar Gen.; Ms. Alice Hession, Dir. Xaverian Sponsored Schools; Bros. Paul J. Murray, C.F.X., Gen. Councillor U.S. Personnel; Thomas Klar, C.F.X., Properties Mgr.; John Hamilton, C.F.X., Gen. Councillor Formation; Cornelius Hubbuch, C.F.X., Pastoral Care; Mr. Shawn Lynch, Business Mgr.; Bros. Jeremiah O'Leary, C.F.X., Peace & Justice; James Connolly, C.F.X., Dir. Memberships: Vocations/Volunteers; Peter Campbell, C.F.X., J.D., Treas. & Finance Officer. Legal Titles and Schools Sponsored: Xaverian Brothers USA, Inc. (f/k/a The American Central Province of the Xaverian Brothers Inc., The American Northeast Province of the Xaverian Brother, Inc., and the Working Boys Home, Inc.); St. Mary's-Ryken High School, Inc.; Our Lady of Good Counsel High School, Inc.; St. Xavier High School, Inc.; Xaverian High School, Inc.; Mt. St. Joseph High School, Inc.; Xaverian Brothers Auxiliary; St. Michael's High School Alumni Association; Nazareth Regional High School, Inc.; St. John's Preparatory School, Inc.; St. John's High School, Inc.; Xaverian Brothers High School, Inc.; Malden Catholic High School, Inc.; Xavier High School, Inc.; Isidore Charitable Trust. Brothers 235.

ADAMSTOWN. *Christian Brothers of Frederick*, P.O. Box 29, 21710. Tel: 301-874-5188; Fax: 301-874-5674. Web: fscbaltimore.org. Bros. Dennis Malloy, F.S.C., Prov.; Timothy J. Froehlich, F.S.C., Dir. Finance; Charles Mrozinski, F.S.C., District Sec.; Ernest Miller, F.S.C., Dir. Educ. & Lasallian Mission Formation.

Christian Brothers of Frederick, Inc. Brothers of the Christians Schools, District of Eastern North America. Brothers 4; Total 171; Total Staff 5.

CUMBERLAND. *SS. Peter and Paul Friary*, 109 N. Smallwood St., 21502. Tel: 301-777-3131; 301-777-7946; Fax: 301-759-3568. Email: ppaul@archbalt.org. Revs. James Kurtz, O.F.M.Cap., Vicar and Pastor, Ss. Peter and Paul (Cumberland); Pastor, St. Ambrose (Cresaptown); Bernard Finerty, O.F.M.Cap., Guardian & Assoc. Pastor; Michael Masich, O.F.M.Cap., Chap. Western MD Health System; Jerome Dunn, O.F.M.Cap., Pastoral Assoc.

Province of St. Augustine of the Capuchin Order Priests 4.

ELLICOTT CITY. *Friary of St. Joseph Cupertino*, 12290 Folly Quarter Rd., 21042-1425. Tel: 410-531-2800; Fax: 410-531-2801. Revs. Bart Karwacki, O.F.M.Conv.; Jude Winkler, O.F.M.Conv., Dir. Evangelization; Joseph Dorniak, O.F.M.Conv.; Timothy Lyons; Bros. Gerry Seipp, O.F.M.Conv., Dir. Hospitality; Vincent Vivan, O.F.M.Conv., Guardian & Exec. Dir. Shrine. Conventual Franciscan Friars., Corporate Title: Franciscan Friars Minor Conventuals of MD, Inc. *Friars Minor Conventual Shrine of St. Anthony* Tel: 410-531-2800; Fax: 410-531-2801. *Companions of St. Anthony*, 12290 Folly Quarter Rd., 21042. Tel: 410-531-2800; Fax: 410-531-2801. *Companions Evangelization & Mail Order Office* Tel: 410-988-9833; Fax: 410-988-9705.

Order of Friars Minor Conventual, 12300 Folly Quarter Rd., 21042-1419. Tel: 410-531-1400; Fax: 410-531-4881. Email: vicar@saprov.org. Web: www.stanthonyprovince.org. Rev. Joachin Giermek, O.F.M.Conv.; Very Rev. Michael Kolodziej, O.F.M.Conv., Min. Prov.; Rev. Robert Twele Esq., O.F.M.Conv., Counselor; Bro. Brian Newbigging, O.F.M.Conv.; Rev. Thomas Lavin, O.F.M.Conv., Province Sec.

Order of Friars Minor Conventual, St. Anthony of Padua Province, U.S.A., Inc.; Franciscan Minor Conventuals of Maryland, Inc. of Ellicott City, MD.; The Franciscan Fathers, Minor Conventuals, of St. Stanislaus Church of Baltimore City, Inc.; Franciscan Friars, St. Anthony of Padua Province, Education Fund, Inc.; Franciscan Friars, St. Anthony of Padua Province, Fund for the Aged and Infirm Friars, Inc.; St. Francis of Assisi Community, Inc., Companions of St. Anthony. St. Stanislaus Cemetery Inc; AnthonyCorps, Inc. Fr. Justin Ministry Fund, Inc. Total in Residence 147.

On Assignment Outside the U.S.A.: Revs. Matteo Luo, O.F.M.Conv., Curia Generale dei Frati Minori Conventualli, Piazza Ss. Apostoli 51, Rome 00187 Italy. Tel: 011-39-06-699-571; Fax: 011-39-06-699-57321; Donald Kos, O.F.M.Conv., Convento S. Antonio, 56, Viale Guido Baccelli, 56, Rome 00153 Italy. Tel: 011-39-06-572-993-11; Fax: 011-39-06-572-993-42; David Blowey, O.F.M.Conv., Mag-9sawang 11at, 4120, P.O. Box 080, Tagaytay, Cavite, Philippines. Tel: 046-431-12-74-; Fax: 011-254-2-88420; Vincent Lachendro, O.F.M.Conv., Asato Catholic Church, 3-7-2 Asato, Naha, Okinawa 902-0067 Japan. Tel: 011-81-98-863-2020; Fax: 011-81-98-863-8474 Metro Manila; James McCurry, O.F.M.Conv.; Thomas Reist, O.F.M.Conv.; Giles Zakowicz, O.F.M.Conv., St. Francis of Assisi Friary, P.O. Box 238, Saltpond, Ghana. Tel: 011-233-42-34555; Fax: 011-233-27-5403-76; Michael Heine, O.F.M.Conv.; John Voytek, O.F.M.Conv.; Bro. Michael Duffy, O.F.M.Conv.

Individual Assignment Within the U.S.A.: Revs. Callistus Juras, O.F.M.Conv. (Retired), Stella Maris, 2300 Dulaney Valley Rd., Timonium, 21093; Gregory Kwapisz, O.F.M.Conv. *Sisters of Providence Infirmary*, 1233 Main St., Holyoke, MA 01040-5399.

EMMITSBURG. *Vincentian House*, P.O. Box 376, 21727. Tel: 301-447-2326; Fax: 301-447-3579. Email: stjosephemmitsburg@comcast.net. Web: www.emmitsburg.net/stjosephparish. Revs. Vincent J. O'Malley, C.M., Pastor, Supr.; Michael J. Kennedy, C.M., Chap.; Stephen P. Trzecieski, C.M., Chap.; Paul M. Murphy, C.M., Asst. Supr.; Devasia Pudussery, Parochial Vicar. Priests 5.

TOWSON. *Jesuit Jamshedpur Mission Society, Inc.*, 8600 La Salle Rd., Ste. 620, 21286-2014. Tel: 443-921-1332; Fax: 443-921-1313. Email: jamshedpur@mdsj.org. Web: www.mdsj.org. Mr. Edward F. Plocha, Dir. Advancement & Contact Person.

Maryland Province of the Society of Jesus, 8600 LaSalle Rd., Ste. 620, 21286-2014. Tel: 443-921-1310; Fax: 443-921-1313. Web: www.mdsj.org. Revs. James M. Shea, S.J., Provincial; James A. Casciotti, S.J., Socius; William P. Ryan, S.J., Treas.; William C. Rickle, S.J., Asst. Latino Ministries; Liborio J. LaMartina, S.J., Resident Archivist; David A. Sauter, S.J., Asst. Education; Ronald J. Amiot, S.J., Asst. Healthcare Planning.

Corporation of the Roman Catholic Clergymen, Maryland Colombiere Jesuit Community St. Claude La Colombiere Jesuit Community., 5704 Roland Ave., 21210-1399. Tel: 410-532-1400; Fax: 410-532-1419. Revs. William C. Rickle, S.J., Supr., Asst. for Latino Ministries & Dir., Institute on Migration, Culture & Ministry. Tel: 443-451-1659; 443-921-1335 (Office); Bert Akers, S.J.; Michael L. Barber, S.J.; C. Jefferies Burton, S.J. Tel: 410-532-1422; James A. Casciotti, S.J., Socius, Admonitor to Prov. & Prov. Consultor. Tel: 410-532-1423; 443-921-1317; William A. Dawson, S.J.; James M. English, S.J.; Edward Glynn, S.J., Min. Tel: 410-532-1431; Joseph M. Hamernick, S.J.; Robert K. Judge, S.J.; Joseph Kennedy, S.J.; Liborio J. LaMartina, S.J., Resident Archivist & Sacristan. Tel: 410-532-1420; Thomas P. Martin, S.J., Subminister, Asst. Community Treas. & House Confessor; Neil P. McLaughlin, S.J. Tel: 410-321-1405; Francis X. Metzbower, S.J.; Francis X. Moan, S.J., House Consultor; Bro. Claude L. Ory, S.J.; Revs. Joseph A. Panuska, S.J.; Thomas E. Peacock, S.J. Tel: 410-532-1438; Joseph M. Ritzman, S.J.; William P. Ryan, S.J., Prov. Treas. & Revisor for Houses & Apostolic Works. Tel: 410-532-1433; 443-921-1321 (Office).

Military Chaplains: Rev. Paul J. Shaughnessy, S.J., Naval War College, 686 Cushing Rd., Newport, RI 02841-1207. Tel: 760-763-3510.

Priests of the Province Serving Abroad: Rev. Eugene J. Barber, S.J., Resid. S. Pedro Claver, Casilla 452, Africa, Chile. Tel: 011-56-58-22-9402; Fax: 011-56-58-22-9402; Mr. Cesare Campagna, S.J.; Revs. James J. Conn, S.J., Pont. Univ. Greg., Piazza della Pilotta 4, Rome 00187 Italy. Tel: 011-36-06-6701-5467; Fax: 011-39-06-6701-5440; Vincent J. Capuano, S.J., Parroq. San Jose Obrero, Juan Larrea 1161, Barrio San Jose 4400 Salta Argentina. Tel: 011-54-387-42-5519; Jeffrey G.L. Chang, S.J., Fu Jen University Theologate, P.O. B 1-107, Hsinchuang, Tai Pei Hsien, Taiwan 242. Tel:

X 342; 011-886-2-29017270; Fax: 011-886-2-29080835; Edgar J. Debany, S.J., P.O. Box 223, Surulere, Lagos State, Nigeria. Tel: 011-234-1-7733535; James M. Desjardins, S.J., UL. Levitana 38, P.O. Box "Inigo", 630051 Novosibirsk, Russia. Tel: 011-7-3832-77-2013; Fax: 011-7-3832-77-1413; Mr. Mark P. Fusco, S.J.; Revs. Eugene M. Geinzer, S.J.; Robert E. Hamm, S.J., P.O. Box 854, Benin City, Edo State, Nigeria. Tel: 011-234-52-258610; John F. Henry, S.J., Resid. S. Pedro Claver, Casilla 452, Arica, Chile. Tel: 011-56-58-22-9402; Fax: 011-56-58-22-9402; Brendan Hurley, S.J.; Michael J. Kuchera, S.J., Pont. Ist Orientale, Piazza S. Maria Maggiore 7, Rome 00187 Italy. Tel: 011-39-06-44741-7154; Fax: 011-39-06-446-5576; Brendan G. Lally, S.J., Pontifical North American College, 00120 Vatican City State, Vatican City. Tel: 011-39-06-684-931; Michael J. Lynch, S.J.; Mr. William A. Noe, S.J.; Rev. Eugene M. Rooney, S.J., San Ignacio, Casilla 597, Santiago, Chile. Tel: 011-56-2-582-7569; Fax: 011-56-2-582-7549; Mr. Paul K. Rourke, S.J., Collegium Internationale del gesu, Piazza del Gesu 45, Rome 00186 Italy; Revs. Joseph C. Sands, S.J.; Dominic J. Totaro, S.J., P.O. Box 854, Benin City, Edo State, Nigeria. Tel: 011-234-52-258610; Eric A. Zimmer, S.J.

Priests of the Province Serving Elsewhere: Revs. David E. Barry, S.J.; G. Richard Dimler, S.J.; Bernard G. Filmyer, S.J., 9784 Guisante Ter., San Diego, CA 92124-1621. Tel: 858-278-1027; Leigh A. Fuller, S.J., St. Mary's Hospital, 2900 First Ave., Huntington, WV 25702-1271. Tel: 304-526-1342; Raymond T. Gawronski, S.J., St. John Vianney Theological Seminary, 1300 S. Steele St., Denver, CO 80210-2599. Tel: 303-282-3404; 303-282-3449 (Office); James N. Gelson, S.J., 3510 S. Ocean Blvd., Highland Beach, FL 33487-3326. Tel: 561-272-4409; Fax: 561-278-8509; Robert J. McTeigue, S.J.; John J. Rock, S.J., 801 Dominican Dr., Nashville, TN 37228. Tel: 615-255-5863; A. Richard Sotelo, S.J., P.O. Box 972141, El Paso, TX 79997-2141. Tel: 915-845-3899; Fax: 915-298-5325; David F. Stokes.

[T] CONVENTS AND RESIDENCES FOR SISTERS

BALTIMORE. *Carmelite Communities Assoc.*, 1318 Dulaney Valley Rd., 21286-1399. Tel: 410-823-7415. Email: info@baltimorecarmel.org. Web: www.ccacarmels.org.

Carmelite Sisters of Baltimore (1790) 1318 Dulaney Valley Rd., 21286-1399. Tel: 410-823-7415; Fax: 410-823-7418. Email: info@baltimorecarmel.org. Web: www.baltimorecarmel.org. Sr. Colette Ackerman, O.C.D., Prioress. Discalced Carmelite Nuns. Professed Sisters 16.

Chesapeake Province of the Sisters of Notre Dame de Namur, Provincial Offices, 305 Cable St., 21210-2511. Tel: 410-243-1993; Fax: 410-243-2279. Email: ches.prov@sndden.org. Web: www.sndden.org.

Chesapeake Province of the Sisters of Notre Dame de Namur, Inc. Sisters in Province 61; Sisters in Baltimore Diocese 43.

Administrative Team: Sisters Mary Donohue, S.N.D-.deN.; Edithann Kane, S.N.D.deN., Pres.

Comboni Missionary Sisters, 5405 Loch Raven Blvd., 21239-2902. Tel: 410-323-1469; Fax: 410-323-9632. Email: sisters@combonisrs.com. Web: www.combonisrs.com. Sr. Andre T. Rothschild, C.M.S., Supr. Sisters 7.

Contemplative Sisters of the Good Shepherd (CGS), 4140 Maple Ave., Halethorpe, 21227-4099. Tel: 410-247-1485; Fax: 410-247-1513. Web: goodshepherdsisters.org. Sr. Frances Marie, Local Supr. Sisters 4.

Daughters of Charity, 900 S. Caton Ave., 21229. Tel: 410-368-2885; Fax: 410-368-3509. Email: stagneshouse@stagnes.org. Sr. Suzanne Baumgartner, D.C., Local Supr. Total in Residence 11.

Little Sisters of Jesus-Regional Residence, 400 N. Streeper St., 21224-1230. Tel: 410-327-7863. Web: www.rc.net/org/littlesisters. Sr. Lynn Flear, Regl. Supr. Sisters 5.

Little Sisters of the Poor-Provincial Residence (1869) 601 Maiden Choice Ln., 21228-3698. Tel: 410-744-9367; Fax: 410-747-0601. Email: mpbaltimore@littlesistersofthepoor.org. Web: www.littlesistersofthepoor.org. Sisters Alice Marie Jones, L.S.P., Supr.; Loraine Maguire, L.S.P., Provincial. Sisters 18; Total Assisted 80; Total Staff 122.

Maria Health Care Center, Inc., 6401 N. Charles St., 21212. Tel: 410-377-3011; Fax: 410-377-6042. Email: gsciamanna@ssndba.org. Sr. Grace Sciamanna, S.S.N.D., Admin. Health Center for School Sisters of Notre Dame and other Religious Congregations.

Mission Helper Center, 1001 W. Joppa Rd., 21204-3787. Tel: 410-823-8585; Fax: 410-825-6355. Email: csbassist@missionhelpers.org. Web: www.missionhelpers.org. Sisters Loretta Cornell, M.H.S.H., Pres.; Dolores Glick, Vice Pres.; Susan Engel, M.H.S.H., Treas.; Claire Cartier, Office Mgr. Sisters 20; Sisters in Diocese 49; Total Staff 7.

Missionaries of Charity (1950) Gift of Hope Convent, 818 N. Collington Ave., 21205. Tel: 410-732-6056. Sr. Vineeth, M.C., Supr. Sisters 6; Total Assisted Annually 800; Total in Residence 10.

Our Lady of Mt. Providence Convent-Motherhouse, 701 Gun Rd., 21227. Tel: 410-242-8500; Fax: 410-242-4963. Email: srcrescentia@oblatesisters.com. Sisters Mary Crescentia, Proctor, Sec.; Sharon Young, Treas. Oblate Sisters of Providence., Attended by Sulpician Fathers and Josephite Fathers. Sisters in the Motherhouse 57; Oblate Sisters 76; Sisters in the Diocese 63; Total Staff 30.

The School Sisters of Notre Dame Atlantic-Midwest Province (1876) 6401 N. Charles St., 21212. Tel: 410-377-7774; Fax: 410-377-5363. Email: kcornell@amssnd.org. Web: www.atlanticmidwest.org. Sr. Kathleen Cornell, S.S.N.D., Prov. Leader; Rev. E. Joseph Cote, Chap. Sisters in Province 587; Sisters in Diocese 232.

Atlantic-Midwest Province of the School Sisters of Notre Dame, Inc.

SSND Service Corporation

SSND Care, Inc.

SSND Real Estate Holding Corporation

SSND Real Estate Trust

SSND Continuing Care Trust

SSND Charitable Annuity Trust

Atlantic-Midwest Province Endowment Trust

Sisters of the Good Shepherd (1864) 4100 Maple Ave., 21227-4099. Tel: 410-247-2770; Fax: 410-242-5890. Email: mregina@goodshepherdcenter.org. Sr. M. Regina Long, Supr. Sisters 11; Total Staff 3.

Sisters of the Good Shepherd-St. Joseph Residence (1864) 4130 Maple Ave., 21227-4007. Tel: 410-247-3898; Fax: 410-242-5890. Email: sr.morrisroe@goodshepherdcenter.org. Sr. Mary Frances Altavilla, Coord. Infirmary for the Mid-North America Province. Sisters 16; Total Staff 36.

Sisters Servants of Mary Immaculate, Inc., 1220 Tugwell Dr., 21228. Tel: 410-747-1353; Fax: 410-747-0386. Sr. Krystyna Mroczek, Prov. Supr. Convent and Novitiate. Sisters 19.

St. Anthony, 4500 Frankford Ave., 21206. Tel: 410-488-0054. Sisters 6.

St. Clare of Assisi, Inc. (2003) 3725 Ellerslie Ave., 21218. Tel: 410-235-9277; Fax: 410-243-2569. Email: etcarr@msn.com. Web: www.lakeosfs.org. Sisters Ellen Carr, O.S.F., Admin. Dir.; Jodene Wydeven, O.S.F., Local Coord.; Rev. Gerald F. West, Chap. (Retired). Clare of Assisi, Inc. operates Clare Court Convent, a retirement residence for members of The Sisters of St. Francis of Assisi, Inc. These sisters were Franciscan Sisters of Baltimore prior to the merger of the two congregations in 2001. Priests 1; Sisters 9; Staff 10.

The Villa (1971) 6806 Bellona Ave., 21212-1299. Tel: 410-377-2450; Fax: 410-377-2501. Mrs. Carol Zaicko, Admin.

The Villa-Joint Retirement Convent, Inc., Convent for Retired Sisters of Mercy, Mission Helpers of the Sacred Heart, and other religious. Sisters 70; Total Staff 70.

EMMITSBURG. *Daughters of Charity of St. Vincent de Paul, Emmitsburg Province* 21727. Tel: 301-447-3121; Fax: 301-447-6038. Web: www.thedaughtersofcharity.org. Sr. Claire Debes, D.C., Prov.

Sisters of Charity of St. Joseph's, Emmitsburg, MD, (St. Joseph's Provincial House) Sisters at Provincial House 23; Sisters in Diocese 105; Sisters in Province 155.

Villa St. Michael, 333 S. Seton Ave., 21727-9299. Tel: 301-447-3121; Fax: 301-447-7082. Web: www.thedaughtersorcharity.org. Retirement Home of Daughters of Charity of St. Vincent de Paul. Daughters of Charity 56; Sisters of Notre Dame 35; Visitation Sisters 2.

LUTHERVILLE. *Emmanuel Monastery* (1971) 2229 W. Joppa Rd., 21093-4601. Tel: 410-821-5792; Fax: 410-296-9560. Email: bensrs@emmanuelosb.org. Web: www.emmanuelosb.org. Benedictine Sisters of Baltimore., Ministering in Education, Pastoral Ministry and Counseling, Retreats and Spiritual Direction, Social Services, Justice Ministry, Hospital Ministry, and Business Admin. Sisters 14.

MARRIOTTSVILLE. *Sisters of Bon Secours, C.B.S., Provincial House* (1824) 21104. Tel: 410-442-1333; Fax: 410-442-1394. Web: www.bonsecours.org. Sr. Rose Marie Jasinski, C.B.S., Pres. Retired Sisters 16; Total in Residence (Baltimore) 20; Total in Residence (In Province) 35; Total Staff 49.

STEVENSON. *Maryland Province Center* (1934) 1531 Greenspring Valley Rd., 21153. Tel: 410-486-5599; Fax: 410-486-5466. Email: sndmd@aol.com. Web: www.sndden.org. Sisters Marian Schaechtel, S.N.D.deN., Prov. Moderator; Rosemary Donohue, S.N.D.deN., Prov. Leadership; Florence Maier, S.N.D.deN., Prov. Leadership; Bernadette Glodek, S.N.D.deN., Prov. Leadership.

Baltimore Province of the Sisters of Notre Dame de Namur, Inc.

Sisters of Notre Dame de Namur, Maryland Province, Charitable Trust

Cemetery Perpetual Trust, Additional Projects Sponsored: Maryland Province Center, Stevenson, MD; Villa Julie Residence, Stevenson, MD; Notre Dame Academy, Villanova, PA; Trinity School, Ellicott City, MD; Maryvale Preparatory School, Brooklandville, MD.; Additional Projects Co-Sponsored: The Development Office, a joint project of the Maryland, Chesapeake & Notre Dame Base Communities Provinces; Director: Ms. Marion Connolly; Sisters Academy of Baltimore, co-sponsored by the School Sisters of Notre Dame, The Sisters of Bon Secours, The Sisters of Notre Dame de Namur and The Sisters of Mercy. Sisters in Province 96; Sisters in Diocese 67; Total Staff 16.

Villa Julie Residence, 1531 Greenspring Valley Rd., 21153. Tel: 410-486-6946; Fax: 410-484-6930. Email: sndvilla@aol.com. Web: www.sndden.org. Residence for retired Sisters of Notre Dame de Namur Sisters 22.

St. Vincent Care Center, 333 S. Seton Ave., Emmitsburg, 21727-9200. Tel: 301-447-3121. Sisters of Notre Dame de Namur 17.

St. Julie Hall, 333 S. Seton Ave., Emmitsburg, 21727-9200. Tel: 301-447-5935. Sisters of Notre Dame de Namur 12.

Maria Health Care, 6401 N. Charles St., 21212-1016. Tel: 410-377-7774.

The Villa, 6806 Bellona Ave., 21212. Tel: 410-377-2450. Sisters of Notre Dame de Namur 2.

[U] NEWMAN CENTERS

BALTIMORE. *Archdiocesan Office-Newman Center* (1966) 7909 York Rd., 21204. Tel: 410-828-0622; Fax: 410-828-4825. Email: newmanctr@verizon.net. Rev. T. Austin Murphy, Campus Min. Total in Residence 2; Total Staff 4.

Johns Hopkins University Newman House, 2941 N. Charles St., 21218. Tel: 410-243-7066; Fax: 410-243-5489. Rev. Thomas Ryan, Campus Min.

Morgan State University St. Matthew Church, 5401 Loch Raven Blvd., 21239. Tel: 410-433-2300.

Towson University Newman Center, 7909 York Rd., 21204. Tel: 410-828-0622; Fax: 410-828-4825. Rev. T. Austin Murphy, Campus Min.

University of Maryland-Baltimore County St. Rita Church, 2907 Dunleer Rd., 21222. Tel: 410-960-6549; Fax: 410-284-3998.

Frostburg State University Osborne Center, 130 S. Broadway, Frostburg, 21532. Tel: 301-689-5041; Fax: 301-689-8910. Rev. Edward S. Hendricks, Campus Min.

McDaniel College Westminster, 21157. Tel: 410-857-2223; Fax: 410-857-2411. Contact St. John Church, Westminster, 21157. Tel: 410-848-4744.

[V] FOUNDATIONS, FUNDS AND TRUSTS

BALTIMORE. *Archbishop Curley High School Endowment Trust*, 3701 Sinclair Ln., 21213. Tel: 410-485-5000; Fax: 410-483-2545. Rev. Michael Martin, O.F.M.Conv.

Bon Secours of Maryland Foundation, Inc. (1919) 26 N. Fulton Ave., 21223. Tel: 410-362-3199; Fax: 410-362-3443. Email: george_kleb@bshsi.com. Total Staff 27; Total Assisted 3,235.

The following are tax exempt subsidiaries of the Bon Secours of Maryland Foundation, Inc.

Bon Secours Housing, Inc. aka Hollins Terrace (1983)

Bon Secours Housing II, Inc. aka Benet House (1987)

Unity Properties, Inc. (1993)

Bon Secours Baltimore Development, Inc. (2005)

The Catholic Family Foundation of the Archdiocese of Baltimore, Inc., 320 Cathedral St., 21201. Tel: 410-625-8497; Fax: 410-625-8485. Email: jedwards@archbalt.org. Web: www.archbalt.org/cff. Jim Edwards, Dir.

Chancery Office, 320 Cathedral St., 21201. Tel: 410-547-5444; Fax: 410-727-8234. Email: chancery@archbalt.org. Web: www.archbalt.org. Dr. Diane L. Barr, J.C., J.C.D., Chancellor. Tel: 410-547-5446.

Archbishop of Baltimore Annual Appeal Trust/ Cardinal's Lenten Appeal Tel: 410-547-5439; Fax: 410-727-8234.

Archdiocesan Health Plan Trust Fund Agreement Tel: 410-547-5317; Fax: 410-783-5993.

Archdiocesan General Insurance Program Trust Tel: 410-547-5317; Fax: 410-783-5993.

Archdiocesan Priests Post-Retirement Benefits Plan Trust Fund, 320 Cathedral St., 21201. Tel: 410-547-5317; Fax: 410-783-5993. Email: pphelps@archbalt.org. Petra R. Phelps, Contact Person.

Cemetery Continuing Care Trust St. Patrick's Havre de Grace, Cemetery Continuing Care Trust; Holy Cross Cemetery Continuing Care Trust; St. Joseph, Fullerton, Cemetery-Continuing Care Trust Agreement; St. Mary of the Assumption, Govans, Cemetery Continuing Care Trust; St. Mary's, Pylesville Cemetery, Continuing Care Trust

Christian Brothers Community Support Charitable Trust Tel: 301-874-5188.

Corpus Christi Jenkins Memorial Trust, Inc. Tel: 410-523-4161; Fax: 410-523-5745.

Dart, Inc.

The Dr. Charles J. Foley Sr. and Mildred H. Foley Memorial Endowment Trust Tel: 410-547-5322; Fax: 410-332-8233. Provides annual support for over 300 programs and agencies of the Archdiocese.

Franciscan Sisters of Baltimore, Inc., Trust Tel: 410-235-2496; Fax: 410-243-2569.

The Gallagher Family Fund, 320 Cathedral St., 21201. Tel: 410-547-5322; Fax: 410-332-8233.

**G S Housing, Inc.*

John Paul II Regional School, Inc. (Grades PreK-8) Tel: 410-944-0367; Fax: 410-265-5316.

The Marion Burk Knott Scholarship Fund, Educational Trust Tel: 301-603-9501.

Marianist Charitable Trust Tel: 410-366-1300; Fax: 410-889-5743.

Maryvale Educational Fund, Inc. Tel: 410-252-3366; Fax: 410-561-1826.

Mercy Primary Care Group, Inc. Tel: 410-332-9000; Fax: 410-962-1303.

The National Black Catholic Congress, Inc. Tel: 410-547-8496; Fax: 410-752-3958. Email: nbcc@nbccongress.org. Web: www.nbccongress.org.

Neumann Early Childhood Center, Inc. Tel: 410-547-5495.

Our Lady of Good Counsel Historic Trust, Inc. Tel: 410-752-0205; Fax: 410-576-0929.

Plan of Self-Insurance Trust Tel: 410-547-5317; Fax: 410-783-5993.

The Priests Continuing Education and Formation Endowment Trust Tel: 410-547-5317; Fax: 410-783-5993.

St. Gregory the Great Housing Committee, Inc. Tel: 410-523-0061; Fax: 410-669-1385.

St. Jane Frances Educational Endowment Trust Tel: 410-255-4750; Fax: 410-350-6720.

St. John Neumann Regional School, Inc. Tel: 301-724-4055; Fax: 301-724-4827.

St. John the Evangelist School Endowment Trust, 689 Ritchie Hwy., Severna Park, 21146. Tel: 410-647-2283.

St. Jude Shrine Corporation Tel: 410-685-6026; Fax: 410-244-5728.

St. Mark's Parish School Endowment Trust Tel: 410-747-6613; Fax: 410-747-3188.

St. Peter's Cemetery Restoration Fund, Inc. Tel: 410-547-5300; Fax: 410-332-8233.

St. Pius V Housing Committee, Inc. Tel: 410-523-1930; Fax: 410-523-8164.

St. Vincent De Paul Historic Trust, Inc. Tel: 410-547-5377; Fax: 410-625-8483.

Sacred Heart Community Health Services, Inc. Tel: 301-723-5222.

Sacred Heart Foundation, Inc. Tel: 301-723-5222.

Sacred Heart Hospital of the Sisters of Charity, Inc. Tel: 410-723-5222.

School Sisters of Notre Dame in the City of Baltimore Charitable Trust, Inc. Tel: 410-377-7774; Fax: 410-377-5363.

Sisters of Notre Dame de Namur Charitable Trusts Tel: 410-255-1577.

Sisters of Notre Dame de Namur, Maryland Province, Charitable Trust Tel: 410-486-5382; Fax: 410-486-5466.

Women's Auxiliary Board Tel: 410-547-5356. Funds provide partial tuition for thousands of low income students in designated Baltimore City Catholic Schools.

**St. Elizabeth School Foundation, Inc.*, 801 Argonne Dr., 21218-1998. Tel: 410-889-5054; Fax: 410-889-2356. Email: info@stelizabeth-school.org. Web: www.stelizabeth-school.org. Diane Darrah, Pres.

The Immaculate Heart of Mary School Endowment Trust, 8501 Loch Raven Blvd., 21286. Tel: 410-668-7935; Fax: 410-668-6171. Rev. Michael W. Carrion.

St. Joseph Manor Foundation, Inc., 1130 N. Calvert St., 21202. Tel: 410-727-3386; Fax: 410-727-1006. Email: superiorgeneral@josephite.com. Web: www.josephite.com. Very Rev. Edward J. Chiffriller, S.S.J., Contact Person.

The Josephite Retirement and Disability Benefits Trusts (2003) 1130 N. Calvert St., 21202. Tel: 410-727-3386; Fax: 410-727-1006. Email: superiorgeneral@josephite.com. Web: www.josephite.com. Very Rev. Edward J. Chiffriller, S.S.J., Supr. Gen.

The Josephite Seminarian Education Trust (2003) 1130 N. Calvert St., 21202. Tel: 410-727-3386; Fax: 410-727-1006. Email: superiorgeneral@josephite.com. Web: www.josephite.com. Very Rev. Edward J. Chiffriller, S.S.J., Supr. Gen.

St. Luke Parish Education Endowment Trust, 7517 N. Point Rd., 21219. Tel: 410-477-5200; Fax: 410-477-5996. Email: stlukecathchur@yahoo.com. Purpose: to support the youth of the parish who attend catholic schools. Total Assisted 43; Total Staff 1.

St. Matthew's Parish Endowment Trust, 5401 Loch Raven Blvd., 21239. Tel: 410-433-2300. Email: stmattrc@verizon.net. Rev. Joseph L. Muth, Contact Person.

Mercy Health Foundation, Inc., 301 St. Paul Pl., 21202. Tel: 410-332-9874; Fax: 410-685-7464. Email: nkoas@mdmercy.com. Web: mdmercy.com. Thomas R. Mullen, Pres.

Partners in Excellence - Inner City Scholarship, 320 Cathedral St., 21201. Tel: 410-547-5356. Fund provides partial tuition for thousands of low income students in designated Baltimore City Catholic Schools.

The Paul Van Gerwin Religious & Charitable Trust, 4409 Frederick Ave., 21229. Tel: 941-484-9641. Email: pecampbellcfx@comcast.net. Bro. Peter Campbell, C.F.X., J.D., Contact Person.

The Sacred Heart of Mary Cemetery Continuing Care Trust, 6736 Youngstown Ave., 21222. Tel: 410-633-2828; Fax: 410-633-0349. Rev. George J. Gannon.

The Seton Keough High School Endowment Trust, 1201 Caton Ave., 21227. Tel: 410-646-4444; Fax: 443-573-0107. Email: info@setonkeough.com. Web: setonkeough.com.

St. Thomas Aquinas School Foundation Trust, 3710 Roland Ave., 21211. Tel: 410-889-4618; Fax: 410-889-1956. Email: starch@archbalt.org. Larry Glose, Contact Person.

BEL AIR. *John Carroll Foundation of the Roman Catholic Archdiocese of Baltimore, The John Carroll School*, 703 E. Churchville Rd., 21014. Tel: 410-879-2480; Fax: 410-836-8514.

ANNAPOLIS. *St. Andrew by the Bay Endowment Trust*, 701 College Pkwy., 21409. Tel: 410-974-4366; Fax: 410-974-4339. Email: sabbanna@archbalt.org. Web: standrewbythebay.org. Rev. Martin J. Burnham.

COCKEYSVILLE. *St. Joseph, Texas Endowment Trust*, 101 Church Ln., 21030. Tel: 410-683-0600; Fax: 410-628-2956. Email: pcook@sjpmd.org. Rev. Msgr. Paul G. Cook, Contact Person; Rev. Gonzalo Cadavid-Rivera.

CUMBERLAND. *The SS. Peter & Paul Parish Endowment Trust*, 109 N. Smallwood St., 21502-2992. Tel: 301-777-3131, Ext. 5; Fax: 301-759-3568. Email: ppaul@archbalt.org.

ELKRIDGE. *St. Augustine School Education Endowment Trust*, 5990 Old Washington Rd., 21075. Tel: 410-796-3040; Fax: 410-579-1165. Web: www.staug-md.org. Mrs. Patricia Schratz, Prin.

ELLICOTT CITY. *The St. Paul's Parish Endowment Trust*, 3755 St. Paul St., 21043. Tel: 410-465-1670; Fax: 410-313-8551. Email: stpaulsrc@aol.com. Rev. Matthew T. Buening.

FROSTBURG. *St. Michael School Endowment Trust*, 44 E. Main St., 21532. Tel: 301-689-6767; Fax: 301-689-6411. Email: smfrostb@archbalt.org. Rev. Msgr. James W. Hannon.

GLEN BURNIE. *The Church of the Good Shepherd Parish Endowment Trust*, 1451 Furnace Ave., 21060. Tel: 410-761-4607; Fax: 410-761-6019. Rev. Msgr. J. Bruce Jarboe; Revs. Michael DeAscanis; Charles R. Klein (Retired).

KINGSVILLE. *St. Stephen School Endowment Trust*, 8028 Bradshaw Rd., 21087-1807. Tel: 410-592-7617; Fax: 410-592-7330.

MARRIOTTSVILLE. *Bon Secours Health System, Inc.*, 1505 Marriottsville Rd., 21104. Tel: 410-442-3505; Fax: 410-442-3256. Web: www.bshsi.org. Sr. Patricia A. Eck, C.B.S., Chair & Bd. of Directors; Richard J. Statuto, CEO & Pres.

Bon Secours, Inc., 1505 Marriottsville Rd., 21104. Tel: 410-442-3505; Fax: 410-442-3256. Web: www.bshsi.org.

MIDLAND. *St. Joseph Midland Parish Endowment Trust*, 19925 Church St., P.O. Box 1, 21542. Tel: 301-463-6770; Fax: 301-463-6729. Deacon W. Fred Passauer.

St. Joseph, Midland Cemetery Continuing Care Trust, 19925 Church St., P.O. Box 1, 21542. Tel: 301-463-6770; Fax: 301-463-6729. Deacon W. Fred Passauer.

PASADENA. *St. Jane Frances Educational Endowment Trust*, 8499 Virginia Ave., 21122. Tel: 410-255-4646; Fax: 410-437-5191. Email: postmaster@stjane.org. Web: stjane.org.

SYKESVILLE. *St. Joseph Catholic Community Endowment Trust*, 915 Liberty Rd., 21784. Tel: 443-920-9191; Fax: 443-920-9192. Email: parishoffice@saintjoseph.cc. Web: www.stjosepheldersburg.org. Revs. Terence Weik, S.M.; David McGuigan, S.M.; Deacons Karl Bayhi; Todd Smith.

TOWSON. *The Immaculate Conception Elementary School Endowment Trust*, 200 Ware Ave., 21204. Tel: 410-427-4700; Fax: 410-427-4795. Email: info@theimmaculate.org. Web: immaculateconception.net. Rev. Msgr. F. Dennis Tinder, Contact Person.

Towson Catholic High School Endowment Trust, 200 Ware Ave., 21204. Tel: 410-427-4700; Fax: 410-427-4795. Email: info@theimmaculate.org. Web: immaculateconception.net. Rev. Msgr. F. Dennis Tinder, Contact Person.

[W] MISCELLANEOUS

BALTIMORE. *Saint Agnes Hospital Foundation, Inc.*, 900 S. Caton Ave., SAHC Box 123, 21229. Tel: 410-368-3155; Fax: 410-368-3533. Web: www.stagnes.org/foundation-main.htm. Sherry Welch, Pres.

Alhambra, International Order of (1904) Supreme Headquarters, 4200 Leeds Ave., 21229. Tel: 410-242-0660; Fax: 410-536-5729. Email: salaamone@covad.net. Web: www.OrderAlhambra.org. Roger J. Reid, Exec. Dir. Nonprofit organization dedicated to assisting the developmentally disabled.

The Baltimore Catholic League, Inc., 2850 N. Ridge Rd., #207, Ellicott City, 21043. Tel: 410-461-4612; Fax: 410-480-3764.

Basilica of the Assumption Historic Trust, Inc., 408 N. Charles St., 21201. Tel: 410-727-3565; Fax: 410-539-0407. Web: www.baltimorebasilica.org. Mark Potter, Exec. Dir.

Bon Secours Baltimore Development, Inc., 26 N. Fulton Ave., 21223. Tel: 410-362-3199; Fax: 410-362-3443. Email: george_kleb@bshsi.com.

**Cardijn Associates, Inc.* (1994) 4513 Bayonne Ave., 21206. Tel: 410-488-7936. Ms. Nancy Lee Conrad, Sec.

Caroline Center (1996) 900 Somerset St., 21202. Tel: 410-563-1303; Fax: 410-563-1302. Email: carolinecenter@caroline-center.org. Web: Caroline-Center.org. Sr. Patricia McLaughlin, S.S.N.D., Exec. Dir.

The Caroline Freiss Center, Inc., Employment training education for low income women. Total Assisted Annually 180; Total Staff 20.

Cathedral Library, 5200 N. Charles St., 21210. Tel: 410-464-4041. Laura M. Perry, Dir. Staffed by the Catholic Evidence League.; Maintain a lending library open to anyone in the archdiocese on Sunday & Monday, from 10:00 AM-2:00 PM. Total Staff 11.

Catholic Alumni Club of Baltimore (1961) P.O. Box 22305, 21203-2305. Tel: 410-580-1250; Fax: 410-771-7191. Email: info@cacbaltimore.org. Web: www.cacbaltimore.org.

Catholic Evidence League, c/o Cathedral of Mary Our Queen, 5200 N. Charles St., 21210. Tel: 410-308-3113; Fax: 410-464-4060. Email: lindacorbett@comcast.net.

Catholic Fraternity Incorporated 1910., 951 Rosedale Ave., 21237. Tel: 410-687-8787; Fax: 410-780-0319. Email: jfesons@comcast.net.

Catholic Relief Services Foundation, Inc., 228 W. Lexington St., 21201. Tel: 410-951-7546; Fax: 410-951-7546. Rev. Robert Twele Esq., O.F.M.Conv., Sec.

Catholic Relief Services, U.S.C.C.B. World Headquarters, 228 W. Lexington St., 21201. Tel: 410-625-2220; Fax: 410-234-2986. Web: www.crs.org. Mr. Kenneth Hackett, Pres. For a more detailed explanation of this organization, please consult the A-pages located in the front of the Directory.

Catholic Single Again Council of Baltimore, The Villa, 6806 Belona Ave., 21212-1219. Tel: 410-485-8313. Email: singleagaincouncil@yahoo.com. Web: www.singleagain.itgo.com. Mary Ann Leard, Pres.

Christian Life Community Regional Information Center (1967) 615 Rest Ave., Catonsville, 21228. Tel: 410-465-1312; Fax: 410-646-0500. Email: cazieba@yahoo.com. Web: www.clc-usa.org. Carol A. Zieba, Regional Chm.; Carol Montagnese, Treas. CLC is a lay organization that forms and sustains men and women, adults and youth, who commit themselves to the church and its mission in the world and feel the urgent need to unite their human life in all its dimensions with the fullness of their Christian faith and to work for social justice. Members come together in community to share their experience of Ignatian spirituality and mission.

Cristo Rey Corporate Internship Program, Inc., 420 S. Chester St., 21231. Tel: 410-727-3255; Fax: 443-573-9898. Janet Shock, Dir.

Disciples Now Ministries Inc. (1999) c/o *Youth & Young Adult Ministries*, 320 Cathedral St., 21201. Tel: 503-922-0317; Fax: 503-210-8077. Email: support@disciplesnow.com. Web: www.disciplesnow.com. Sherry Raspa, Managing Editor.

Food for Thought, Inc., 1625 E. Baltimore, 21231. Tel: 410-563-0081; Fax: 410-327-1345. Email: srmaryannh@aol.com. Sr. Mary Ann Hartnett, S.S.N.D., Dir. Tutorial program for children & adult literacy.

**Franciscan Youth Center, Inc.* (1985) Stone House, Clare Court, 3725 Ellersile Ave., 21218. Tel: 410-235-3577; Fax: 410-243-8191. Email: asmith.fyc@verizon.net. Web: www.fycbaltimore.org. Antwaine R. Smith, Exec. Dir.; Derryck Fletcher, Dir. of Programs; Ruth Maria Allen, Office Mgr.; Cathy Haggerty, Dir. Devel. Staff 26; Total Assisted 110.

**G S Properties, Inc.*, 5601 Loch Raven Blvd., 21239. Tel: 410-772-6719. Web: www.medstarhealth.org.

Holy Name Society (Union) (1911) P.O. Box 919, Millersville, 21108. Tel: 410-987-2009; Fax: 410-987-6392. Rev. Michael W. Carrion, Archdiocesan Dir.; Michael F. Armetta, Treas. Purpose: Support Right to Life, Anti-Pornography, High School Scholarship Grants, Canonization of Blessed John of Vercelli, Support the Archbishop's discernment supper fund and works of charity.

Ignatian Volunteer Corps, 801 St. Paul St., 21202. Tel: 410-752-4686; Fax: 410-752-8480. Email: info@ivcusa.org. Web: www.ivcusa.org. Ms. Suzanne Geaney, Exec. Dir.; Rev. James R. Conroy, S.J., Founder; Meg Mannix, Dir. Programs & Operations.

Johns Hopkins Hospital, Dept. of Pastoral Care, 600 N. Wolfe St., Halsted 144, 21287-4170. Tel: 410-955-5842; Fax: 410-502-6765. Email: caoffice@jhmi.edu. Rev. Paul C. Sparklin. Total Staff 20.

Legion of Mary, 502 Old Stone Pl., Bel Air, 21015-1812. Tel: 410-893-3607. Elissa Passalacqua, Pres. Baltimore Comitium, governing body for the Legion of Mary in the Baltimore Archdiocese.

Marian House, Inc., 949 Gorsuch Ave., 21218. Tel: 410-467-4121; Fax: 410-467-6709. Web: www.marianhouse.org. Katie Allston, LCSW-C, Exec. Dir.

Maryland Family Care, Inc., 301 St. Paul Pl., 21202. Tel: 410-332-1902; Fax: 410-332-9134. Email: hleek@mercymed.com. Helen Leek, Vice Pres.

Mission Helper Productions, Inc., 1001 W. Joppa Rd., 21204-3787. Tel: 410-823-8585, Ext. 241; Fax: 410-296-4050. Email: missionhelperproductions@missionhelpers.org. Web: missionhelperproductions.org. Sisters Anne Guinan, M.H.S.H., Dir.; Caritas Kennedy, R.S.M., Assoc. Dir. A nonprofit video production house which provides full service professional relatively low-cost video production for independent producers and nonprofit socially concerned groups or individuals.

Mother Seton House on Paca Street, Inc., 600 N. Paca St., 21201. Tel: 410-523-3443; Fax: 410-669-8140. Web: www.mothersetonhouse.org. Rev. John C. Kemper, S.S., M.Div., M.A., D.Min., Dir. The Mother Seton House on Paca Street is part of the St. Mary's Spiritual Center and Historic Site. The federal style house served as home (1808) and school for St. Elizabeth Ann Seton, America's first native-born canonized saint. Also on the site is the Historic Seminary Chapel that served the needs of our nation's first Roman Catholic Seminary (1791). The Historic Site is owned and operated by the Society of St. Sulpice, Province of the US. The site is open Monday-Friday from 12 noon to 3:30 pm and Saturday-Sunday from 1-3 pm. Entrance to the site is free.

The Mount Saint Agnes Theological Center for Women, Inc., 909 Poplar Hill Rd., 21210. Tel: 410-435-7500; Fax: 410-435-9522. Email: wisdom@mountsaintagnes.org. Web: www.mountsaintagnes.org. Dr. Dianne Caplin, Ph.D., Dir.; Sr. Mary Aquin O'Neill, R.S.M., Theologian. Total Staff 4.

**Murphy Initiative for Justice and Peace*, 1001 W. Joppa Rd., 21204. Tel: 410-823-8585, Ext. 244. Sr. Diane Bardol, G.N.S.H., Exec. Dir.

My Sister's Place Women's Center Fund, Inc., 320 Cathedral St., 21201. Tel: 410-547-5469. Email: jgabriel@catholiccharities.org. Mr. William J. McCarthy Jr., Contact Person.

Nigeria-Igbo Catholic Community, P.O. Box 66027, 21239. Tel: 443-850-6673. Email: office@niccchurch.org. Web: www.niccchurch.org. Frank Okechukwu, Chm. Tel: 443-850-6673; Clement Anyadike, Vice Chm. Tel: 443-910-3647; Felix Opara, Sec. Tel: 202-250-0889. Purpose: to provide an environment for all Igbos in the Baltimore Metropolitan area to worship in their native language.

Our Daily Bread Employment Center Fund, Inc., 320 Cathedral St., 21201. Tel: 410-547-5469. Email: jgabriel@catholiccharities.org. Mr. William J. McCarthy Jr., Contact Person.

Pallottine Charitable, Educational and Apostolic Ministry Trust, 512 W. Saratoga St., 21201. Tel: 410-685-3064.

Radio Mass of Baltimore, Inc., St. Ignatius Church, 740 N. Calvert St., 21202. Tel: 410-539-7812; Fax: 410-727-1573. Rev. James A. Casciotti, S.J., Dir.; Mrs. Carolyn Dunne, Admin. Mass is broadcast every Sunday morning from St. Ignatius Church at 9:30 A.M., WBAL, 1090 AM Radio Dial.

Redemptorist Office for Mission Advancement, 7401 German Hill Rd., 21222. Tel: 410-288-8755; Fax: 410-288-8757. Web: redemptorists.net. Rev. Daniel Francis, C.Ss.R., Dir.

Reparation Society of the Immaculate Heart of Mary, Inc. (1946) Fatima House, 7920 Beverly Ave., 21234. Tel: 410-665-1199. Rev. Casimir M. Peterson, S.T.L., J.C.D., Pres. & Spiritual Dir. (Retired). Purpose: To promote prayer and penance in reparation to the Immaculate Heart of Mary in accordance with the message of Fatima. Volunteers 4; Total in Residence 1.

Sarah's House Fund, Inc., 320 Cathedral St., 21201. Tel: 410-547-5469. Email: jgabriel@catholiccharities.org. Mr. William J. McCarthy Jr., Contact Person.

Serra Club, 320 Cathedral St., 21201. Tel: 410-547-5426; Fax: 410-234-2953. Email: gfrancik@archbalt.org. Web: www.becomeapriest.org. Rev. Gerard C. Francik, Chap.; Mr. Joseph M. Reynolds, Chairperson.

Stella Maris Maritime Center, 320 Cathedral St., 21201. Tel: 443-845-7227; Fax: 410-288-5504. Email: aosbalt@gmail.com. Web: www.aosbalt.org. Rev. Msgr. John L. FitzGerald, Dir. Member of Apostleship of the Sea (USA).; Christian hospitality services in the Catholic tradition with spiritual, temporal, and emotional support for seafarers and their families. Also, transportation to and from ships for their crew members to the local Stella Maris Maritime Center and the city.

**The Thomas O'Neill Catholic Health Care Fund, Inc.*, 5601 Lock Raven Blvd., 21239.

Union of Catholic Apostolate USA, Inc., 512 W. Saratoga St., 21201. Tel: 410-685-6026, Ext. 1355; Fax: 410-244-5728. Email: usncc@sacapostles.org. Rev. Frank S. Donio, S.A.C., Pres.

BEL AIR. *St. Thomas More Society of Maryland Inc.*, 31 E. Lee St., 21014-8876. Tel: 410-838-8338. Stuart Schadt, Pres. The local branch of the St. Thomas More Society.

ANNAPOLIS. *Christ Child Society of Annapolis*, P.O. Box 561, Severna Park, 21146. Tel: 410-991-3845. Mary Morris, Pres.

Mid-Atlantic Catholic Schools Consortium, 10 Francis St., 21401. Tel: 301-908-7812; Fax: 410-269-1790. Email: mehrutka@gmail.com. Mary Ellen Hrutka, Contact Person.

CROWNSVILLE. **Springhill Center for Family Development*, 1134 Bacon Ridge Rd., 21032. Tel: 410-923-8900. Rev. John Hopkins, L.C., Exec. Dir.; Mrs. Diane Nicholson, Contact Person. A Catholic organization enriching and strengthening family life in the community; addresses the needs of the modern family through quality programs and counseling services.

CUMBERLAND. *Catholic Education Ministries of Western Maryland*, 300 E. Oldtown Rd., 21502. Tel: 301-777-9082; Fax: 301-722-6114. Email: catholicwmd@archbalt.org. Margaret Meyers, Dir.

DUNKIRK. *Family of the Americas Foundation, Inc.* (1977) P.O. Box 1170, 20754-1170. Tel: 301-627-3346; 800-443-3395; Fax: 301-627-0847. Email: familyplanning@yahoo.com. Web: familyplanning.net.

ELLICOTT CITY. *AnthonyCorps, Inc.* (2003) 12300 Folly Quarter Rd., 21042. Tel: 410-531-1400; Fax: 410-531-4881. Email: treasurer1@saprov.org. Rev. Joseph Benicewicz, O.F.M.Conv., Treas.

The Baltimore Evidence League, 9051 Baltimore National Pike, 21042. Tel: 410-461-4612. John E. Degele Jr.

Christlife, Inc. (1995) 12280 Folly Quarter Rd., 21042. Tel: 410-531-7701; Fax: 410-531-7702. Email: info@christlife.org. Web: www.christlife.org. Mr. Dave Nodar, Dir.

**Faith Journeys Foundation, Inc.*, P.O. Box 1222, 21041. Tel: 410-744-0305; Fax: 410-744-4910. Email: fjourneys@aol.com. Web: www.faithjourneys.org. Ms. Lynn A. Cassella-Kapusinski, B.A., M.F.A., Pres. & Founder.

Fr. Justin Ministry Fund, Inc., 12300 Folly Quarter Rd., 21042. Tel: 410-531-1400; Fax: 410-531-4881. Email: treasurer1@saprov.org. Revs. Joseph Benicewicz, O.F.M.Conv.; Thomas Lavin, O.F.M.Conv.

LINTHICUM. *Catholic Daughters of the Americas*, 3601 Cliffmar Rd., Windsor Mill, 21244. Tel: 410-922-9423. Debra Williams, State Regent. Religious, charitable and educational to serve the needs of the Church and community through apostolate, renewal, community and youth. Catholic women 18 years or older in good standing with the Church are eligible for membership.

OWINGS MILLS. *Knights of Columbus, Maryland State Council*, 10815 Stang Rd., 21117-4607. Tel: 410-521-6200; Fax: 410-521-0203. Email: kc-md@comcast.net. Rev. Donald Grzymski, O.F.M.Conv., State Chap.; Richard V. Siejack, State Deputy; Romeo Gauthier, Exec. Sec.

TIMONIUM. *Odenton Senior Housing II, Inc.*, 1966 Greenspring Dr., Ste. 200, 21093. Tel: 443-798-3416; Fax: 410-561-3056. Web: www.cc-md.org. Dale R. McArdle, Contact Person.

TOWSON. *Jesuit Educational Association of Maryland, Inc.*, 8600 LaSalle Rd., Ste. 620, 21286-2014. Tel: 443-921-1310; Fax: 443-921-1313. Email: dsauter@mdsj.org. Web: www.mdsj.org. Rev. David A. Sauter, S.J. Tel: 301-214-1265.

WESTERNPORT. *St. Peter's, Westernport, School Endowment Trust*, 127 Church St., 21562. Tel: 301-359-3055; Fax: 301-359-0657.

WOODSTOCK. *Catholic War Veterans, Inc.*, CWV Post 736, P.O. Box 252, 21163. Tel: 410-933-0766. James Barlow, Post Commander; Rev. Msgr. Carl F. Cummings, Post Chap.

RELIGIOUS INSTITUTES OF MEN REPRESENTED IN THE ARCHDIOCESE

For further details refer to the corresponding bracketed number in the Religious Institutes of Men or Women section.

[0200]—*Benedictine Monks (Latrobe, PA)*—O.S.B.
[1350]—*Brothers of St. Francis Xavier*—C.F.X.
[0330]—*Brothers of the Christian Schools* (Baltimore Prov.)—F.S.C.
[0470]—*The Capuchin Friars* (Prov. of St. Augustine)—O.F.M.Cap.
[1330]—*Congregation of the Mission/Vincentians* (Eastern Prov.)—C.M.
[1000]—*Congregation of the Passion* (Prov. of St. Paul of the Cross)—C.P.
[0480]—*Conventual Franciscans* (Ellicott City, MD)—O.F.M.Conv
[0400]—*Crosier Fathers*—O.S.C.
[0520]—*Franciscan Friars (Most Holy Name)*—O.F.M.
[0690]—*Jesuit Fathers and Brothers* (Maryland Prov.)—S.J.
[0730]—*Legionaries of Christ*—L.C.
[0854]—*Missionary Society of St. Paul of Nigeria*—M.S.P.
[]—*Norbertine Fathers* (Immaculate Conception Priory, DE)—O.Praem.
[1310]—*Order of the Most Holy Trinity, Immaculate Heart of Mary Province*—O.SS.T.
[1070]—*Redemptorist Fathers* (Baltimore Prov.)—C.SS.R.
[1260]—*Society of Christ*—S.Ch.
[0760]—*Society of Mary*—S.M.
[0990]—*Society of the Catholic Apostolate* (Immaculate Conception Prov.)—S.A.C.
[1200]—*Society of the Divine Saviour*—S.D.S.
[]—*Society of the Missionaries of the Sacred Heart*
[1290]—*Society of the Priests of St. Sulpice*—S.S.
[0700]—*St. Joseph's Society of the Sacred Heart*—S.S.J.
[]—*Sulpicians*—S.S.
[0560]—*Third Order Regular of St. Francis*—T.O.R.

RELIGIOUS INSTITUTES OF WOMEN REPRESENTED IN THE ARCHDIOCESE

[0230]—*Benedictine Sisters of Pontifical Jurisdiction* (Baltimore)—O.S.B.
[0690]—*Comboni Missionary Sisters*—C.M.S.
[0270]—*Congregation of Bon Secours*—C.B.S.
[2030]—*Congregation of the Holy Spirit (Spiritans)*—C.S.Sp.
[]—*Congregation of the Sisters of Merciful Jesus*—C.S.M.J.
[0760]—*Daughters of Charity of St. Vincent de Paul*—D.C.
[0420]—*Discalced Carmelite Nuns*—O.C.D.
[1070-03]—*Dominican Sisters*—O.P.
[1070-13]—*Dominican Sisters*—O.P.
[1070-07]—*Dominican Sisters*—O.P.
[1115]—*Dominican Sisters of Peace*—O.P.
[1470]—*Franciscan Sisters of St. Joseph*—F.S.S.J.
[1840]—*Grey Nuns of the Sacred Heart* (Pennsylvania)—G.N.S.H.
[2575]—*Institute of the Sisters of the Mercy of the Americas* (Baltimore, Merion)—R.S.M.
[2330]—*Little Sisters of Jesus*—L.S.J.

[2340]—*Little Sisters of the Poor*—L.S.P.
[2470]—*Maryknoll Sisters* (New York)—M.M.
[2490]—*Medical Missionary Sisters* (Pennsylvania)—M.M.S.
[2720]—*Mission Helpers of the Sacred Heart*—M.H.S.H.
[2710]—*Missionaries of Charity* (New York)—M.C.
[3040]—*Oblate Sisters of Providence*—O.S.P.
[]—*Oblates of St. Martha*
[2070]—*Religious of the Holy Union of the Sacred Hearts*—S.U.S.C.
[3465]—*Religious of the Sacred Heart of Mary* (New York)—R.S.H.M.
[2970]—*School Sisters of Notre Dame*—S.S.N.D.
[]—*Sisters for Christian Community*—C.F.C.C.
[0640]—*Sisters of Charity* (Halifax)—S.C.
[3000]—*Sisters of Notre Dame de Namur*—S.N.D.deN.
[4080]—*Sisters of Social Service*
[1705]—*Sisters of St. Francis of Assisi*—O.S.F.
[1650]—*Sisters of St. Francis of Philadelphia*—O.S.F.
[]—*Sisters of St. Francis of Rochester* (Minnesota)—O.S.F.
[3893]—*Sisters of St. Joseph*—S.S.J.
[3890]—*Sisters of St. Joseph of Peace*—C.S.J.P.
[1030]—*Sisters of the Divine Savior*—S.D.S.
[1830]—*Sisters of the Good Shepherd* (Mid North -American Prov.)—R.G.S.
[1920]—*Sisters of the Holy Cross*—C.S.C.
[1990]—*Sisters of the Holy Names of Jesus and Mary*—S.N.J.M.
[]—*Sisters of the Humility of Mary* (Villa Maria, PA)—H.M.
[3610]—*Sisters Servants of Mary Immaculate*—S.S.M.I.
[2160]—*Sisters, Servants of the Immaculate Heart of Mary*—I.H.M.
[4120]—*Ursuline Nuns, of the Congregation of Kentucky*—O.S.U.

ARCHDIOCESAN CEMETERIES

BALTIMORE. *New Cathedral Cemetery*, 4300 Old Frederick Rd., 21229. Tel: 410-566-7770; Fax: 410-566-0709.

NECROLOGY

† McGowan, Rev. Msgr. Myles, Baltimore, MD St. Ursula—Died Aug. 29, 2009
† Kitko, Joseph F., Laurel, MD Resurrection of Our Lord—Died July 22, 2009
† Riepe, Charles K., (Retired)—Died Feb. 7, 2009

An asterisk (*) denotes an organization that has established tax-exempt status directly with the IRS and is not covered by the USCCB Group Ruling.

Diocese of Baton Rouge

(Dioecesis Rubribaculensis)

Most Reverend

ROBERT WILLIAM MUENCH, D.D.

Bishop of Baton Rouge; ordained May 18, 1968; appointed Titular Bishop of Mactaris and Auxiliary Bishop of New Orleans May 8, 1990; consecrated June 29, 1990; appointed Bishop of Covington January 5, 1996; installed March 19, 1996; appointed Fifth Bishop of Baton Rouge December 15, 2001; installed March 14, 2002. *Office: Bishop's Office, P.O. Box 2028, Baton Rouge, LA 70821-2028.* Tel: 225-242-0247; Fax: 225-336-8768. Email: Bishop@diobr.org.

Chancery Office: Catholic Life Center, 1800 S. Acadian Thruway, P.O. Box 2028, Baton Rouge, LA 70821-2028. Tel: 225-387-0561; Fax: 225-336-8789.

Web: www.diobr.org

Email: chancery@diobr.org

ESTABLISHED JULY 20, 1961.

Square Miles 5,513.

Comprises the civil parishes (counties) of Ascension, Assumption, East Baton Rouge, West Baton Rouge, Iberville, Pointe Coupee, East Feliciana, West Feliciana, St. Helena, Tangipahoa, Livingston and St. James in the State of Louisiana.

For legal titles of parishes and diocesan institutions, consult the Chancery Office.

STATISTICAL OVERVIEW

Personnel	
Bishop	1
Priests: Diocesan Active in Diocese	52
Priests: Diocesan Active Outside Diocese	1
Priests: Retired, Sick or Absent	19
Number of Diocesan Priests	72
Religious Priests in Diocese	32
Total Priests in Diocese	104
Extern Priests in Diocese	4
Ordinations:	
Diocesan Priests	2
Permanent Deacons in Diocese	59
Total Brothers	18
Total Sisters	95
Parishes	
Parishes	68
With Resident Pastor:	
Resident Diocesan Priests	42
Resident Religious Priests	12
Without Resident Pastor:	
Administered by Priests	13
Administered by Lay People	1
Professional Ministry Personnel:	
Brothers	1
Sisters	10
Lay Ministers	117
Welfare	
Catholic Hospitals	3
Total Assisted	637,597
Homes for the Aged	7
Total Assisted	714
Specialized Homes	5
Total Assisted	302
Special Centers for Social Services	8
Total Assisted	225,335
Educational	
Diocesan Students in Other Seminaries	18
Total Seminarians	18
Colleges and Universities	1
Total Students	2,016
High Schools, Diocesan and Parish	6
Total Students	2,286
High Schools, Private	2
Total Students	1,962
Elementary Schools, Diocesan and Parish	24
Total Students	11,481
Catechesis/Religious Education:	
High School Students	3,496
Elementary Students	7,456
Total Students under Catholic Instruction	28,715
Teachers in the Diocese:	
Priests	1
Brothers	4
Sisters	12
Lay Teachers	1,051
Vital Statistics	
Receptions into the Church:	
Infant Baptism Totals	2,257
Minor Baptism Totals	138
Adult Baptism Totals	105
Received into Full Communion	264
First Communions	2,455
Confirmations	2,155
Marriages:	
Catholic	515
Interfaith	185
Total Marriages	700
Deaths	1,648
Total Catholic Population	211,149
Total Population	935,440

Former Bishops—Most Revs. ROBERT E. TRACY, D.D., LL.D., appt. Titular Bishop of Sergentza and Auxiliary of Lafayette March 18, 1959; cons. May 19, 1959; appt. First Bishop of Baton Rouge Aug. 10, 1961; retired March 21, 1974; died April 4, 1980; JOSEPH V. SULLIVAN, S.T.D., appt. Titular Bishop of Tagamuta and Auxiliary of Kansas City-St. Joseph March 3, 1967; cons. April 3, 1967; appt. Second Bishop of Baton Rouge Aug. 5, 1974; died Sept. 4, 1982; STANLEY JOSEPH OTT, S.T.D., appt. Titular Bishop of Nicives and Auxiliary of New Orleans May 24, 1976; cons. June 29, 1976; appt. Third Bishop of Baton Rouge Jan. 18, 1983; died Nov. 28, 1992; ALFRED C. HUGHES, S.T.D., ord. Dec. 15, 1957; appt. Auxiliary of Boston and Titular Bishop of Massimiana in Bizacena, July 21, 1981; cons. Sept. 14, 1981; appt. to Baton Rouge Sept. 7, 1993; installed Fourth Bishop of Baton Rouge, Nov. 4, 1993; appt. Coadjutor Archbishop of New Orleans, Feb. 16, 2001; installed May 2, 2001.

Vicar General/Moderator of the Curia—Very Rev. THAN N. VU, S.T.L., V.G.

Chancery Office—Catholic Life Center, 1800 S. Acadian Thruway, P.O. Box 2028, Baton Rouge, 70821-2028. Tel: 225-387-0561; Fax: 225-336-8789. Email: chancery@diobr.org. Office Hours: Mon.-Fri. 8:30-4:30.

Chancellor—Very Rev. THOMAS C. RANZINO.

Diocesan Tribunal—Catholic Life Center, 1800 S. Acadian Thruway, P.O. Box 1087, Baton Rouge, 70821-1087. Tel: 225-336-8755; Fax: 225-242-0229. Email: tribunal@diobr.org.

Judicial Vicar—Very Rev. PAUL D. COUNCE, J.C.L., M.C.L.

Promoter of Justice—Very Rev. VINCENT J. DUFRESNE, S.T.L., J.C.L., V.F.

Judges—Rev. Msgrs. WILLIAM L. GREENE (Retired); GERALD M. LEFEBVRE (Retired); Revs. FRANK M. UTER; MICHAEL J. MORONEY; Mrs. JACLYN O'BRIEN MCEACHERN, J.C.L.

Defenders of the Bond—Very Rev. VINCENT J. DUFRESNE, S.T.L., J.C.L., V.F.; Rev. GARLAND T. BELSOME; Very Rev. THAN N. VU, S.T.L., V.G.; Revs. MATTHEW P. LORRAIN; GERARD R. MARTIN; PAUL A. MCDUFFIE.

Notaries—Mrs. V. EILEEN BOURGEOIS; Mrs. PATRICIA F. SONIAT; Mrs. ANN T. BOLTIN.

College of Consultors—Very Revs. PAUL D. COUNCE, J.C.L., M.C.L.; THAN N. VU, S.T.L., V.G.; Revs. THOMAS P. DUHE, M.Ed.; MICHAEL J. SCHATZLE; MATTHEW C. DUPRE.

Diocesan Pro-Vicar—

Pro-Vicar for Religious Men and Women—Sr. LUCY SILVIO, C.S.J.

Diocesan Corporation (The Roman Catholic Church of the Diocese of Baton Rouge)—Most Rev. ROBERT WILLIAM MUENCH, D.D., Pres.; Very Revs. THAN N. VU, S.T.L., V.G., Vice Pres.; THOMAS C. RANZINO, Sec.; Mr. JOSEPH E. INGRAHAM, Treas.

Diocesan Offices and Directors

Apostolate to the Deaf—Mr. WILLIAM G. DUGAS, Dir., 2585 Brightside Lane, Baton Rouge, 70820-3504. Tel: 225-766-9320; 225-769-0223; Fax: 225-766-9320. Email: hearingimpaired@diobr.org.

Archives and Records Management—Mrs. ANN T. BOLTIN, Mailing Address: P.O. Box 2028, Baton Rouge, 70821-2028. Tel: 225-242-0224; Fax: 225-242-0299. Email: archives@diobr.org.

Black Catholics—Deacon ALFRED P. ADAMS SR., Mailing Address: P.O. Box 30, Convent, 70723-0030. Tel: 225-562-3255. Email: bcatholics@diobr.org.

Campus Ministry—Very Rev. THAN N. VU, S.T.L., V.G., Mailing Address: P.O. Box 25131, Baton Rouge, 70894-5131. Tel: 225-383-1574; Fax: 225-344-1920. Email: tvu@ctk-lsu.org.

Catholic Charismatic Renewal—Rev. HENRY W. GAUTREAU, Ph.D. (Retired), 421 D Longwood Ct., Baton Rouge, 70806-4048. Tel: 225-346-8873. Email: hgautreau@diobr.org.

Catholic Charities of the Diocese of Baton Rouge, Inc.—Mr. DAVID C. AGUILLARD, M.P.A., M.H.A., Exec. Dir., Office, 1900 S. Acadian Thruway, P.O. Box 1668, Baton Rouge, 70821-1668. Tel: 225-336-8770; Fax: 225-336-8745. Email: ccsgen@ccdiobr.org. Web: www.ccdiobr.org.

Catholic Social Services— Maternity & Adoption Dept. Mrs. JANICE ALLEN, 1900 S. Acadian Thruway, P.O. Box 1668, Baton Rouge, 70821-1668. Tel: 225-336-8770; Fax: 225-336-8745. Email: adopt@ccdiobr.org. Web: www.adoptbatonrouge.com.

Social Responsibility Department—Ms. LYNN GAUDET. Email: lgaudet@ccdiobr.org.

Cemeteries—Rev. FRANK M. UTER, P.O. Box 1609, Denham Springs, 70727-1609. Tel: 225-665-5359; Fax: 225-665-4422. Email: futer@diobr.org.

Child and Youth Protection Office—Mrs. AMY J. CORDON, Dir., Mailing Address: P.O. Box 2028, Baton Rouge, 70821-2028. Tel: 225-242-0202; Fax: 225-242-0233. Email: childprotection@diobr.org.

Clergy Personnel—Rev. ROBERT F. STINE, Dir., St. Mary of False River, 348 W. Main St., New Roads, 70760-3587. Tel: 225-638-9665; Fax: 225-638-6346. Email: rstine@diobr.org.

Board Members—Rev. GERALD R. MARTIN; Very Rev. CLEO J. MILANO, S.T.L., V.F.; Revs. MATTHEW P. LORRAIN; GARLAND T. BELSOME.

Ecumenical Affairs—Rev. MICHAEL J. MORONEY, 14040 Greenwell Springs Rd., Greenwell Springs, 70739-3302. Tel: 225-261-4650; Fax: 225-261-5650. Email: ecumenism@diobr.org.

Evangelization Office—Ms. GREER G. GORDON, Ph.D. (cand.), Dir., Mailing Address: P.O. Box 2028, Baton Rouge, 70821-2028. Tel: 225-242-0137; Fax: 225-242-0245. Email: evangelization@diobr.org.

Communications—Mr. WILLIAM MICHELET, Media Liaison. Tel: 225-242-0256. Email: bmichelet@diobr.org; Mr. STEVE LEE, Mailing Address: Catholic Life Channel 15, P.O. Box 2028, Baton Rouge, 70821-2028. Tel: 225-242-0215; Fax: 225-242-0134. Email: television@diobr.org.

Continuing Formation for the Clergy—Rev. THOMAS P. DUHE, M.Ed., Dir., Mailing Address: 11441 Goodwood Blvd., Baton Rouge, 70815-6222. Tel: 225-275-3940; Fax: 225-275-1407. Email: clergyformation@diobr.org.

Stewardship Office—Mr. MARK J. BLANCHARD, Dir., Mailing Address: P.O. Box 2028, Baton Rouge, 70821-2028. Tel: 225-336-8790; Fax: 225-336-8710. Email: stewardship@diobr.org.

Finance—Mr. JOSEPH E. INGRAHAM, Fiscal Officer, Mailing Address: P.O. Box 2028, Baton Rouge, 70821-2028. Tel: 225-387-0561; Fax: 225-336-8789. Email: jingraham@diobr.org.

Christian Formation—Mr. CHARLES JUMONVILLE, M.R.E.; Mrs. RHONDA PARENTON, Asst. D.R.E., Mailing Address: P.O. Box 2028, Baton Rouge, 70821-2028. Tel: 225-336-8760; Fax: 225-336-8765. Email: formation@diobr.org.

Hispanic Apostolate—Rev. RAPHAEL JUANTORENA, S.T.L., Ph.D., Dir., 7520 Florida Blvd., Baton Rouge, 70806-4702. Tel: 225-927-8700; Fax: 225-927-8787. Email: hapostol@bellsouth.net.

Newspaper "The Catholic Commentator"—Mrs. LAURA G. DEAVERS, Exec. Editor & Gen. Mgr., Office, 1800 S. Acadian Thruway, Baton Rouge, 70821-1668. Email: tcc@diobr.org; Mailing Address: P.O. Drawer 14746, Baton Rouge, 70898-4746. Tel: 225-387-0983; Fax: 225-336-8710.

Marriage and Family Life Department—Deacon MICHAEL T. CHIAPPETTA, Dir., Office: 1800 S. Acadian Thruway, P.O. Box 2028, Baton Rouge, 70821-2028. Tel: 225-336-8770; Fax: 225-336-8745. Email: mflgen@diobr.org.

Permanent Diaconate Office—Deacon JAMES J. MORRISSEY, Dir., Mailing Address: 42021 Hwy. 621, Gonzales, 70737-9354. Tel: 225-647-8461. Email: diaconate@diobr.org.

Presbyteral Council—Revs. GARLAND T. BELSOME; THOMAS P. DUHE, M.Ed.; Very Rev. PAUL D. COUNCE, J.C.L., M.C.L.; Revs. MATTHEW C. DUPRE; CHARLES R. LANDRY; CHRISTOPHER J. DECKER; N. JOHN NUTTER III; AYO E. EFODIGBUE, M.S.P.; MICHAEL J. MORONEY; EDWARD E. EVERITT, O.P.; Very Revs. MILES D. WALSH, S.T.D., V.F.; THAN N. VU, S.T.L., V.G.; Rev. MICHAEL J. SCHATZLE.

Propagation of the Faith and Association of Holy Childhood—Rev. N. JOHN NUTTER III, Dir., P.O. Box 2028, Baton Rouge, 70821-2028. Tel: 225-242-0115; Fax: 225-242-0343. Email: missions@diobr.org.

Catholic Schools—Dr. MELANIE B. VERGES, Ed.D., Supt.; Mr. JOSEPH M. SCIMECA, Asst. Supt., Mailing Address: P.O. Box 2028, Baton Rouge, 70821-2028. Tel: 225-336-8735; Fax: 225-336-8711. Email: secretary@csobr.org.

Separated and Divorced—Rev. FRED A. YOUNGS, Dir., 5657 Thomas Rd., Baton Rouge, 70811-7356. Tel: 225-775-8850; Fax: 225-775-7072. Email: fyoungs@diobr.org.

Serra Clubs—Rev. MATTHEW P. LORRAIN, Spiritual Advisor, Mailing Address: P.O. Box 2028, Baton Rouge, 70821-2028. Tel: 225-336-8778; Fax: 225-336-8710. Email: vocations@diobr.org.

Society of St. Vincent De Paul—Mr. MICHAEL J. ACALDO, CEO. Email: macaldo@svdpbr.com; Deacon ESNARD F. GREMILLION, Spiritual Advisor, Mailing Address: P.O. Box 127, Baton Rouge, 70821-0127. Tel: 225-383-7837.

Victim Assistance Coordinator—Mrs. AMY J. CORDON, Mailing Address: P.O. Box 2028, Baton Rouge, 70821-2028. Tel: 225-242-0202; Fax: 225-242-0233. Email: childprotection@diobr.org.

Vietnamese Apostolate—Rev. FRANCIS MINH HAI NGUYEN, I.C.M., Dir., 2580 Tecumseh St., Baton Rouge, 70805-7999. Tel: 225-357-4787; Fax: 225-355-9794.

Vocations—Rev. MATTHEW P. LORRAIN, Dir.; Sr. LUCY SILVIO, C.S.J., Assoc. Dir., Mailing Address: P.O. Box 2028, Baton Rouge, 70821-2028. Tel: 225-336-8778; Fax: 225-336-8710. Email: vocations@diobr.org.

Worship, Office of—Very Rev. THOMAS C. RANZINO, Dir., Mailing Address: P.O. Box 2028, Baton Rouge, 70821-2028. Tel: 225-387-0561; Fax: 225-336-8789. Email: worship@diobr.org.

Youth Ministry—Mrs. BRIGITTE BURKE, Dir., Mailing Address: P.O. Box 2028, Baton Rouge, 70821-2028. Tel: 225-336-8751; Fax: 225-336-8765. Email: youth@diobr.org.

CLERGY, PARISHES, MISSIONS AND PAROCHIAL SCHOOLS

CITY OF BATON ROUGE

(EAST BATON ROUGE PARISH)

1—ST. JOSEPH CATHEDRAL (1792) Very Rev. Paul D. Counce. In Res., Deacon Jodi A. Moscona.
Res.: 412 North St., 70802-5496. Tel: 225-387-5928; Fax: 225-387-5929. Email: office@cathedralofstjoseph.org. Web: www.cathedralofstjoseph.org.
Catechesis/Religious Program—Students 20.

2—ST. AGNES (1917) Rev. Msgr. Robert H. Berggreen; Deacon Thomas Traylor. In Res., Revs. Clifton Hill, C.S.Sp.; Michael Jung, O.S.B.
Res.: 749 East Blvd., 70802-6398. Tel: 225-383-4127; Fax: 225-383-4154. Email: saintagnes@bellsouth.net.
Catechesis/Religious Program—Tel: 225-338-1511. Ms. Margaret Granger, C.R.E. Students 147.

3—ST. ALOYSIUS (1955) Rev. Gerald H. Burns; Deacon John A. Jung Jr.
Mailing Address: 2025 Stuart Ave., 70808-3998. Tel: 225-343-6657; Fax: 225-344-6847. Email: saghb@cox.net. Web: www.aloysius.org.
School—(Grades PreK-8) Tel: 225-383-3871; Fax: 225-383-4500. Mr. John L. Bennett, Prin.; Anne Blanchard, Librarian. Lay Teachers 75; Students 1,158.
Catechesis/Religious Program—Mrs. Patricia Greely, D.R.E.; Mr. Steven Brooksher, D.R.E. Students 169.

4—STS. ANTHONY OF PADUA AND LE VAN PHUNG (1920) Rev. Minh Hai Nguyen, I.C.M.
Res.: 2305 Choctaw Dr., 70805-7910. Tel: 225-357-4800; Fax: 225-354-0611. Email: revminhnguyen@cox.net. Web: www.gxvnbatonrouge.org.
Catechesis/Religious Program—Students 369.

5—ST. CHARLES BORROMEO (1964) Closed. For inquiries for parish records contact St. Gerard Majella, Baton Rouge.

6—CHRIST THE KING (1980) Very Rev. Than N. Vu; Rev. Andrew J. Merrick; Deacon John A. Ellis.
Mailing Address: P.O. Box 25131, 70894-5131. In Res., Rev. Matthew P. Lorrain.
Office: 11 Fraternity Ln., 70803. Tel: 225-344-8595; Fax: 225-344-1920. Email: tvu@ctk-lsu.org. Web: www.ctk-lsu.org.
Catechesis/Religious Program—Mrs. Rebecca East, D.R.E. Students 34.

7—ST. FRANCIS DE SALES PARISH (1979), (Center for Hearing Impaired) Mr. William G. Dugas, Exec. Dir.
Res.: 2585 Brightside Dr., 70820-3504. Tel: 225-766-9320; 225-769-0223 (Voice/TDD); Fax: 225-766-6615. Email: hearingimpaired@diobr.org.
Catechesis/Religious Program—Fax: 225-766-6615. Mr. William G. Dugas, D.R.E. Students 10.

8—ST. FRANCIS XAVIER (1918) Rev. Michael L. Thompson, S.S.J.
Res.: 1143 S. 11th St., 70802-4997. Tel: 225-246-2727; Fax: 225-343-4259. Email: stfrancisxavier@bellsouth.net. Web: www.stfrancisxavierchurch.net.
School—(Grades K-8) Tel: 225-387-6639; Fax: 225-383-1215. Sr. Joseph Charles, S.S.F., Prin. Lay Teachers 15; Students 128.
Catechesis/Religious Program—Students 84.

9—ST. GEORGE (1908) [CEM] Revs. Michael J. Schatzle; Frank B. Bass; Deacon Albert R. Ellis.
Office: 7808 St. George Dr., 70809-4699. Tel: 225-293-2212; Fax: 225-291-8063. Web: www.st-george.org.
School—(Grades PreK-8), 7880 St. George Dr., 70809-4699. Tel: 225-293-1298. Mrs. Lizette Leader, Prin. Lay Teachers 85; Students 1,076.
Catechesis/Religious Program—Mrs. Cherry Riggs, D.R.E.; Mrs. Karen Fawley, D.R.E. Students 98.

10—ST. GERARD MAJELLA (1944) Rev. Samuel C. Maranto, C.Ss.R.
Res.: 3808 Gerard St., 70805-2834. Tel: 225-355-2553; Fax: 225-356-7472. Email: stgmc@earthlink.net.
School—(Grades PreK-6), 3655 St. Gerard Ave., 70805-2898. Tel: 225-355-1437; Fax: 225-355-1879. Ms. Joanie Hudson, Prin. Lay Teachers 17; Students 206.
Catechesis/Religious Program—Students 8.

11—IMMACULATE CONCEPTION (1953) Very Rev. Thomas F. Clark, S.J. In Res., Rev. George F. Lundy, S.J.
Res.: 1565 Curtis St., 70807-4906. Tel: 225-775-7067; Fax: 225-775-0775. Email: clarktf@hotmail.com.
Catechesis/Religious Program—Students 84.

12—ST. JEAN VIANNEY (1975) Very Rev. Thomas C. Ranzino; Deacons Brent Duplessis; Tommy J. St. Pierre.
Res.: 16166 S. Harrell's Ferry Rd., 70816-3199. Tel: 225-753-7950; Fax: 225-753-7965. Email: churchinfo@stjeanvianney.org. Web: www.stjeanvianney.org.
School—(Grades K-8), 16266 S. Harrell's Ferry Rd., 70816-3103. Tel: 225-751-1831; Fax: 225-752-8774. Mrs. Wendy Gilmore, Prin.; Kerry Ferrara, Librarian. Lay Teachers 49; Students 493.
Preschool—Tel: 225-752-5356. Mrs. Amie Williams, Dir. Lay Teachers 15; Students 91.
Catechesis/Religious Program—Students 98.

13—ST. JUDE THE APOSTLE (1966) Rev. Caye A. Nelson III; Deacons Frank E. Bains; Curt P. Reeson.
Res.: 9150 Highland Rd., 70810-4096. Tel: 225-766-2431; Fax: 225-766-0722. Email: stjude@stjudecatholic.org. Web: stjudecatholic.org.
School—(Grades PreK-8) Tel: 225-769-2344; Fax: 225-769-0671. Web: stjudebr.org. Mrs. Karen Jackubak, Prin.; Mrs. Terri Legendre, Librarian. Lay Teachers 33; Students 594.
Catechesis/Religious Program—Students 127.

14—ST. LOUIS, KING OF FRANCE (1966) Rev. Nicholas John Nutter III. In Res., Rev. Msgr. Leo Guillot (Retired).
Res.: 2121 N. Sherwood Forest Dr., 70815-1962. Tel: 225-275-7280; Fax: 225-275-5845. Email: slkfadm@bellsouth.net. Web: www.slkfbr.org.
School—(Grades PreK-8), 2311 N. Sherwood Forest Dr., 70815-1997. Tel: 225-273-3932; Fax: 225-273-3978. Mrs. Mary Clare Polito, Prin.; Carol Speyrer, Librarian. Lay Teachers 17; Students 238.
Early Learning Center—Tel: 225-272-6438; Fax: 225-275-5845. Mrs. Jo Ellen Frederick, Dir. Lay Teachers 11; Students 34.
Catechesis/Religious Program—Students 45.

15—MOST BLESSED SACRAMENT (1979) Rev. Michael J. Collins; Deacon Donald J. Musso.
Res.: 15165 Old Jefferson Hwy., 70817-6311. Tel: 225-752-6230; Fax: 225-756-5014. Web: www.mbsparish.org.
School—(Grades K-8), 8033 Barringer Rd., 70817-6000. Tel: 225-751-0273; Fax: 225-753-7259. Mrs. Maria I. Cloessner, Prin.; Ellen Manint, Librarian. Lay Teachers 28; Students 553.
Catechesis/Religious Program—Tel: 225-751-5867; Fax: 225-751-6738. Mr. David P. Planche, D.R.E. Students 318.

16—OUR LADY OF MERCY (1947) Very Rev. Miles D. Walsh; Rev. Ju Hyung Paul Yi; Deacon Richard H. Grant.
Office: 445 Marquette Ave., 70806-4497. Tel: 225-926-1883; Fax: 225-923-0448.
Res.: 450 Marquette Ave., 70806-4497. Tel: 225-927-7106. Email: admin@olomchurch.com.
School—(Grades PreK-8), 400 Marquette Ave., 70806-4498. Tel: 225-924-1054; Fax: 225-923-2201. Email: eguidry@olomschool.org. Web: www.olomschool.org. Mrs. Tina Villa, Prin.; Kirsten Steintrager, Librarian. Lay Teachers 48; Students 814.
Catechesis/Religious Program—Students 131.

17—ST. PATRICK (1974) Rev. Gerard R. Martin; Deacon J. Peter Walsh.
Res.: 12424 Brogdon Ln., 70816-4801. Tel: 225-753-5750; Fax: 225-756-9636. Email: stpatrickbr@aol.com. Web: www.stpatrickbr.org.
Catechesis/Religious Program—Ms. Lisa Trahan, D.R.E. Students 174.

18—ST. PAUL THE APOSTLE (1960) Rev. Vincent Alexius, S.V.D.; Deacon Benjamin J. Dunbar.
Res.: 3912 Gus Young Ave., 70802-1727. Tel: 225-383-2537; Fax: 225-383-3702. Email: stpaulbr@aol.com. Web: www.stpaulbr.org.
Catechesis/Religious Program—Mrs. Vera Dunbar, D.R.E. Students 98.

19—ST. PIUS X (1963) Rev. Alexander J. Sheldon; Deacon Esnard F. Gremillion.
Res.: 6380 Hooper Rd., 70811-2499. Tel: 225-357-5935; Fax: 225-357-6005. Email: stpius@stpius.brcoxmail.com.
Catechesis/Religious Program—Students 47.

20—SACRED HEART OF JESUS (1928) Rev. Paul A. McDuffie.

Res.: 2250 Main St., 70802-3198. Tel: 225-387-6671; Fax: 225-387-6674. Email: info@sacredheartbtr.com. Web: www.sacredheartbtr.com.
School—(Grades PreK-8) Tel: 225-383-7481; Fax: 225-383-1810. Bro. Augustine B. Kozdroj, F.S.E., Prin.; Catherine Fontenot, Librarian. Sisters of St. Joseph 2; Lay Teachers 30; Students 497.
Catechesis/Religious Program—Ms. Vicki Nacol, D.R.E. Students 49.

21—ST. THOMAS MORE (1959) Revs. Thomas P. Duhe; Christopher J. Decker; Deacon Clayton Hollier.
Office: 11441 Goodwood Blvd., 70815-6299. Tel: 225-275-3940; Fax: 225-275-1407. Email: info@stmchurch.org. Web: stmchurch.org.
School—(Grades PreK-8), 11400 Sherbrook Dr., 70815. Tel: 225-275-2820; Fax: 225-275-0376. Dr. Judy Armstrong, Prin.; Mrs. Felice Bourg, Librarian. Lay Teachers 8; Students 917.
Preschool—11500 Sherbrook Dr., 70815. Tel: 225-272-3477; Fax: 225-272-0468. Ms. Angie Ducote, Dir. Lay Teachers 12; Students 120.
Catechesis/Religious Program—Students 54.

OUTSIDE THE CITY OF BATON ROUGE

ALBANY, LIVINGSTON PARISH, ST. MARGARET QUEEN OF SCOTLAND (1910) [CEM] Rev. Joseph Arogyasami, I.M.S. (India); Deacon Warren Fortenberry.
Res.: P.O. Box 100, 70711-0100. Tel: 225-567-3573; Fax: 225-567-2031.
Catechesis/Religious Program—Mrs. Tamara Grace, D.R.E. Tel: 225-294-9471. Students 120.
Chapel—Springfield, St. Thomas

AMITE, TANGIPAHOA PARISH, ST. HELENA (1868) Rev. Joseph M. Camilleri; Deacon Michael A. Agnello.
Res.: 121 S. First St., 70422-2701. Tel: 985-748-9057; Fax: 985-748-9094. Email: sthelenacatholic@bellsouth.net.
Catechesis/Religious Program—Students 156.
Chapel—Greensburg, St. Jude; Kentwood, St. Elizabeth

BAKER, EAST BATON ROUGE PARISH, ST. ISIDORE THE FARMER (1958) Rev. Fred A. Youngs; Deacons Bruno Rizzo; Willie Berthelot; Micheal J. Joseph.
Res.: 5657 Thomas Rd., 70811-7356. Tel: 225-775-8850 (Office); Fax: 225-775-7072. Email: parishoffice@stisidorecommunity.org. Web: www.stisidorecommunity.org.
School—(Grades PreK-6) Tel: 225-775-3336; Fax: 225-775-3351. Ms. Linda March, Prin. Lay Teachers 11; Students 139.
Catechesis/Religious Program—Ms. Marlene Ortego, D.R.E. Students 40.

BAYOU PIGEON, IBERVILLE PARISH, ST. JOAN OF ARC (1965) Rev. Joey F. Angeles.
Res.: 39315 Hwy. 75, Plaquemine, 70764-9629. Tel: 225-545-8213; Fax: 225-545-8213.
Catechesis/Religious Program—Students 28.
Chapel—Bayou Sorrell, St. Catherine Laboure

BELLE ROSE, ASSUMPTION PARISH, ST. JULES (1912) [CEM 2] Rev. Jason M. Labbe.
Res.: P.O. Box 38, 70341-0038. Tel: 225-473-8569; Fax: 225-473-2950. Email: stjuleschurch@charterinternet.com.
Catechesis/Religious Program—Students 13.
Chapel—Brusly/St. Martin, St. Martin

BRUSLY, WEST BATON ROUGE PARISH, ST. JOHN THE BAPTIST (1835) Rev. Matthew C. Dupre; Deacon Samuel C. Collura.
Res.: P.O. Box 248, 70719-0248. Tel: 225-749-2189; 225-749-3387; Fax: 225-749-1921. Email: sjbcc@sjbcc.brcoxmail.com.
Catechesis/Religious Program—Mrs. Peggy LeBlanc, D.R.E. Students 407.

CONVENT, ST. JAMES PARISH, ST. MICHAEL THE ARCHANGEL (1812) [CEM 2] Very Rev. Vincent J. Dufresne; Rev. Mark B. Beard; Deacon Alfred P. Adams Sr.
Mailing Address: P.O. Box 129, Paulina, 70763. Tel: 225-869-5751; Fax: 225-869-4166. Email: riverroadcatholic@att.net. Web: www.riverroadcatholic.com.
Church: 6490 LA Highway 44, 70763.
Catechesis/Religious Program—Students 77.

DARROW, ASCENSION PARISH, ST. ANTHONY OF PADUA (1962) Rev. Michael A. Galea.
Mailing Address: P.O. Box 9, Sorrento, 70778. Tel: 225-675-8126; Fax: 225-675-6150.
Church: 37311 LA Highway 22, 70725.
Catechesis/Religious Program—Tel: 225-675-6528. Combined with St. Anne, Sorrento

DENHAM SPRINGS, LIVINGSTON PARISH, IMMACULATE CONCEPTION (1960) Revs. Frank M. Uter; Paul A. Gros; Deacons Peter Schlette; Michael T. Chiappetta; Rudolph W. Stahl.
Mailing Address: P.O. Box 1609, 70727-1609.
Res.: 865 Hatchell Ln., 70726. Tel: 225-665-5359; Fax: 225-665-4422. Web: www.icc-msh.org.
Catechesis/Religious Program—Tel: 225-665-5926. Mrs. Dianne Fontenot, D.R.E. Students 1,139.
Chapel—Livingston, Sacred Heart of Jesus, Tel: 225-686-7322.

DONALDSONVILLE, ASCENSION PARISH

1—ASCENSION OF OUR LORD JESUS CHRIST (1772) [CEM] Rev. Philip F. Spano.
Res.: P.O. Box 508, 70346-0508. Tel: 225-473-3176; Fax: 225-473-3256.
Catechesis/Religious Program—Students 7.

2—ST. CATHERINE OF SIENA (1924) Rev. Ayo E. Efodigbue, M.S.P.
Res.: P.O. Box 428, 70346-0428. Tel: 225-473-8350; Fax: 225-473-9978.
Catechesis/Religious Program—Mrs. Ivory Joseph, D.R.E. Students 98.

3—ST. FRANCIS OF ASSISI (1884) [CEM] Rev. Philip F. Spano.
Res.: 818 W. Tenth St., 70346-9501. Tel: 225-473-8302; Fax: 225-474-0348.
Catechesis/Religious Program—

FRENCH SETTLEMENT, LIVINGSTON PARISH, ST. JOSEPH (1849) [CEM] Rev. Jason P. Palermo; Deacon James A. Little.
Res.: 15710 Louisiana Hwy. 16, 70733-9802. Tel: 225-698-3110; Fax: 225-698-1512. Email: stjosephfs@eatel.net.
Catechesis/Religious Program—Tel: 225-698-6318. Mrs. Barbara Bethelot, D.R.E. Students 184.

GONZALES, ASCENSION PARISH

1—ST. MARK (1973) Rev. Rubin R. Reynolds; Deacon James J. Morrissey.
Res.: 42021 Hwy. 621, 70737-9354. Tel: 225-647-8461; Fax: 225-647-5125. Email: mail@stmarkgonzales.org. Web: www.stmarkgonzales.org.
Catechesis/Religious Program—Peggy Villavaso, D.R.E. Students 682.

2—ST. THERESA OF AVILA (1918) [CEM] Rev. Gary T. Belsome; Deacons Thomas E. Labat Sr.; William Blair.
Res.: 1022 N. Burnside Ave., 70737-2551. Tel: 225-647-6588; Fax: 225-647-2223. Email: sttheresa@eatel.net. Web: www.sttheresaofavila.org.
School—212 E. New River St., 70737-2499. Tel: 225-647-2803; Fax: 225-647-7814. Ms. Chris Musso, Prin. Sisters 1; Lay Teachers 36; Students 428.
Catechesis/Religious Program—Mrs. Alice Blair, D.R.E. Students 31.

GRAMERCY, ST. JAMES PARISH, MOST SACRED HEART OF JESUS (1961) Very Rev. Vincent J. Dufresne; Rev. Mark B. Beard.
Mailing Address: P.O. Box 129, Paulina, 70763-0129. Tel: 225-869-5751; Fax: 225-869-4166. Email: sacredheart3@cox.net. Web: www.riverroadcatholic.com.
Church: 616 E. Main St., 70052.
Catechesis/Religious Program—Mrs. Diana Cantillo, D.R.E. (Elementary); Mrs. Melissa Laurent, D.R.E. (High School). Students 173.

GREENWELL SPRINGS, EAST BATON ROUGE PARISH, ST. ALPHONSUS LIGUORI (1962) Rev. Michael J. Moroney; Deacons J. Phillip BeJeaux; Robert J. Kusch.
Res.: 14040 Greenwell Springs Rd., 70739-3302. Tel: 225-261-4650; Fax: 225-261-5650. Web: www.st-alphonsus.net.
School—(Grades PreK-8), 13940 Greenwell Springs Rd., 70739. Tel: 225-261-5299; Fax: 225-261-2795. Web: www.stalphonsusbr.org. Mrs. Cynthia Ryals, Prin.; Melissa Bordelon, Librarian. Lay Teachers 26; Students 459.
Catechesis/Religious Program—Olga Johnson, D.R.E. Students 343.

GROSSE TETE, IBERVILLE PARISH, ST. JOSEPH (1904) [CEM] Revs. Arun John, I.M.S.; John Joseph Kunnaseril, I.M.S.
Res.: P.O. Box 8, 70740-0008. Tel: 225-625-2438; Fax: 225-625-3513. Email: ajohn@diobr.org.
Catechesis/Religious Program—Tel: 225-625-2485; Fax: 225-625-3513. Students 66.

HAMMOND, TANGIPAHOA PARISH, HOLY GHOST (1902) Revs. Edward E. Everitt, O.P.; Henry B. Groover, O.P.; Cayet N. Mangiaracina, O.P.; Deacon Wallace L. Gainey Jr.
Res.: 601 N. Oak St., 70401-2529. Tel: 985-345-3360; Fax: 985-542-4191. Email: holyghostchurch@I-55.com. Web: www.i-55.com/holyghost.
School—(Grades PreK-8), 507 Oak St., 70401-2598. Tel: 985-345-0977; Fax: 985-542-6545. Ms. Tangee Daugereaux, Prin. Lay Teachers 44; Students 775.
Catechesis/Religious Program—Tel: 985-345-3360, Ext. 28; Fax: 985-542-4191. Mrs. Trisha Labbe, D.R.E. Students 113.

INDEPENDENCE, TANGIPAHOA PARISH, MATER DOLOROSA (1908) Rev. Howard R. Adkins; Deacons Alfred P. Zeringue; Roger A. Navarra; Natale J. Garofalo.
620 3rd St., 70443.
Res.: P.O. Box 349, 70443-0349. Tel: 985-878-9639; Fax: 985-878-6260.
School—(Grades PreK-8), P.O. Box 380, 70443-0380. Tel: 985-878-4295; Fax: 985-878-4888. Mr. Alfred Donaldson, Prin. Lay Teachers 12; Students 173.
Catechesis/Religious Program—Tel: 985-878-2852. Ms. Carol A. Young, D.R.E. Students 148.
Chapel—Husser, St. Dominic

LABADIEVILLE, ASSUMPTION PARISH, ST. PHILOMENA (1847) [CEM] Rev. Michael J. Alello.
Res.: P.O. Box 99, 70372-0099. Tel: 985-526-4247; Fax: 985-526-4128. Email: stphilomena@charterinternet.com. Web: www.stphilomenachurch.org.
Catechesis/Religious Program—Students 233.

LAKELAND, POINTE COUPEE PARISH, IMMACULATE CONCEPTION (1859) [CEM 2] Rev. Gregory J. Daigle.
Res.: P.O. Box 158, 70752-0158. Tel: 225-627-5124; Fax: 225-627-5125.
Catechesis/Religious Program—Students 265.

LIVONIA, POINTE COUPEE PARISH, ST. FRANCES XAVIER CABRINI (1955) [CEM] Revs. Arun John, I.M.S.; John Joseph Kunnaseril, I.M.S.
Res.: 3523 Hwy. 78, P.O. Box 128, 70755-0128. Tel: 225-637-2396; Fax: 225-637-2390. Email: stfrances@spillwaycable.com.
Catechesis/Religious Program—Students 252.
Chapel—Fordoche, St. Catherine of Siena

MARINGOUIN, IBERVILLE PARISH, IMMACULATE HEART OF MARY (1964) [CEM] Revs. Arun John, I.M.S.; John Joseph Kunnaseril, I.M.S.
Mailing Address: P.O. Box 8, Grosse Tete, 70740-0008.
Res.: 11140 Hwy. 77, 70757-9703. Tel: 225-625-2438; Fax: 225-625-3513.
Catechesis/Religious Program—Students 48.

MAUREPAS, LIVINGSTON PARISH, ST. STEPHEN THE MARTYR (1964) Rev. Jason P. Palermo.
Res.: 22494 Hwy. 22, 70449-3404. Tel: 225-695-6310; Fax: 225-695-6039. Email: saintstephen@eatel.net.
Catechesis/Religious Program—Tel: 225-695-6310; Fax: 225-695-6039. Students 67.

MORGANZA, POINTE COUPEE PARISH, ST. ANN (1872) [CEM 3] Rev. Keun-Soo Lee.
Res.: 182 Church St., P.O. Box 128, 70759-0128. Tel: 225-694-3781; Fax: 225-694-3711. Email: stanns@bellsouth.net.
Catechesis/Religious Program—Tel: 225-694-2132. Mrs. Sharon LeCoq, D.R.E. Students 45.
Chapel—Innis, St. Vincent De Paul

NAPOLEONVILLE, ASSUMPTION PARISH

1—ST. ANNE (1874) [CEM 2] Rev. J. Joel LaBauve.
Res.: P.O. Box 99, 70390-0090. Tel: 985-369-6656; Fax: 985-369-9718. Email: stanne@charterinternet.com. Web: www.renewthebcc.com.
Catechesis/Religious Program—Tel: 985-369-2130. Kathy Landry, D.R.E. Students 192.

2—ST. BENEDICT THE MOOR (1911) [CEM 2] Rev. John Osom, M.S.P.
Res.: 5479 Hwy. 1, 70390-2410. Tel: 985-369-7225; Fax: 985-369-2772. Email: stbenedictchurch@charter.net.
Catechesis/Religious Program—twinned with St. Augustine. Mr. Jerry Carter, D.R.E.; Mrs. Catherine Moore, D.R.E. Tel: 225-473-4322. Students 59.
Chapel—Klotzville, St. Augustine, Tel: 225-473-9670.

NEW ROADS, POINTE COUPEE PARISH

1—ST. AUGUSTINE (1923) Rev. John J. McBrearty, S.S.J.; Deacon Thomas Robinson.
Res.: 809 New Roads St., P.O. Box 548, 70760-0548. Tel: 225-638-7553; Fax: 225-638-2947. Email: staug812@bellsouth.net.
Catechesis/Religious Program—Students 159.

2—ST. MARY OF FALSE RIVER (1865) [CEM 2] Rev. Robert F. Stine; Deacon Thomas M. Robinson.
Res.: 348 W. Main St., 70760-3587. Tel: 225-638-9665; Fax: 225-638-6346. Email: rstine@diobr.org. Web: www.stmarysfr.org.
Catechesis/Religious Program—Tel: 225-638-6508. Mrs. Emily Froeba, D.R.E. Students 77.
Chapel—Pointe Coupee, St. Francis

PAINCOURTVILLE, ASSUMPTION PARISH, ST. ELIZABETH (1840) [CEM] Rev. Jason M. Labbe.
Mailing Address: P.O. Box 1, 70391-0001.
Res.: 6057 St. Elizabeth St., 70391. Tel: 985-369-7398; Fax: 985-369-9892. Email: stelizabeth@charter.net.
Catechesis/Religious Program—Students 44.

PAULINA, ST. JAMES PARISH, ST. JOSEPH (1900) [CEM] Very Rev. Vincent J. Dufresne; Rev. Mark B. Beard.
Mailing Address: P.O. Box 129, 70763-0129.
Church: 2130 Rectory St., 70763-0129. Tel: 225-869-5751; Fax: 225-869-4166. Email: riverroadcatholic@att.net. Web: www.riverroadcatholic.com.
Catechesis/Religious Program—Mrs. Melissa Laurent, D.R.E. (High School); Mrs. Donna Waguespack, D.R.E. (Elementary). Students 471.
Chapel—Lutcher, Our Lady of Prompt Succor

PIERRE PART, ASSUMPTION PARISH, ST. JOSEPH THE WORKER (1858) [CEM 2] Rev. Clarence J. Waguespack.
Res.: 1022 Bayou Dr., P.O. Box 190, 70339-0190. Tel: 985-252-6008; Fax: 985-252-8011. Email: office@sjworker.org.
Catechesis/Religious Program—Tel: 985-252-6633.

Mrs. Georgiana C. Cox, D.R.E. Students 409.

PLAQUEMINE, IBERVILLE PARISH

1—ST. CLEMENT OF ROME (1964) Closed. For inquiries for parish records contact St. John the Evangelist, Plaquemine.

2—ST. JOHN THE EVANGELIST (1850) [CEM] Very Rev. Cleo J. Milano.
Office:—57805 Main St., 70764-2531.
Res.: 57810 Plaquemine St., 70764-2538. Tel: 225-687-2402; Fax: 225-687-1587.
Catechesis/Religious Program—Students 122.

PLATTENVILLE, ASSUMPTION PARISH, ASSUMPTION OF THE BLESSED VIRGIN MARY (1793) [CEM] Rev. J. Joel LaBauve.
Mailing Address: P.O. Box 99, Napoleonville, 70390-0099. Tel: 985-369-6656; Fax: 985-369-9718. Email: stanne@charter.net.
Church: Hwy. 308, 70393.

PONCHATOULA, TANGIPAHOA PARISH, ST. JOSEPH (1875) [CEM] Revs. John D. Sims, O.P.; Ramon J. Gonzales, O.P.; Deacon Larry Melancon.
Res.: 330 W. Pine St., P.O. Box 368, 70454-0368. Tel: 985-386-3749; Fax: 985-386-4188. Email: Kauchak@i-55.com.
School—(Grades PreK-8), 175 N. Eighth St., 70454-3306. Tel: 985-386-6421; Fax: 985-386-0560. Dr. Gerard Toups, Prin. Lay Teachers 24; Students 356.
Catechesis/Religious Program—Ms. Daphne Griffin, D.R.E. Students 160.

PORT ALLEN, WEST BATON ROUGE PARISH, HOLY FAMILY (1920) Rev. David E. Allen.
Res.: P.O. Box 290, 70767-0290. Tel: 225-383-1838; Fax: 225-383-1839. Email: pastorholyfamily@brcoxmail.com.
School—(Grades K-8), 335 N. Jefferson Ave., 70767-2798. Tel: 225-344-4100; Fax: 225-344-1928. Mrs. Brenda Fremin, Prin. Lay Teachers 30; Students 427.
Preschool—415 N. Jefferson Ave., 70767-2727. Tel: 225-343-6541; Fax: 225-344-4100. Mrs. Diane Harkins, Dir. Lay Teachers 3; Students 43.
Catechesis/Religious Program—Tel: 225-336-4463. Students 57.

PRAIRIEVILLE, ASCENSION PARISH, ST. JOHN THE EVANGELIST (1919) Revs. Eric V. Gyan; William Egedegbe, M.S.P.; Deacons Randy Clement; Claude H. Bourgeois Jr.
Res.: 15208 Hwy. 73, 70769-3507. Tel: 225-673-8307; Fax: 225-673-8680. Email: stjohnchurch@eatel.net.
School—St. John Primary School, (Grades PreK-K), 37407 Duplessis Rd., 70769-4321. Tel: 225-677-8238 (Office). Mrs. Tina Schexnaydre, Prin. Lay Teachers 9; Students 186.
Catechesis/Religious Program—Tel: 225-673-8680. Mr. Horace Shows, D.R.E. Students 1,321.

ST. AMANT, ASCENSION PARISH, HOLY ROSARY (1905) [CEM 2] Revs. Jon C. Koehler; Boby Alex (India); Deacon Eliazar Salinas Jr.
Res.: 44450 Hwy. 429, 70774-4597. Tel: 225-647-5321; Fax: 225-647-5322. Email: holyrosary@eatel.net. Web: www.holyrcc.org.
Catechesis/Religious Program—Students 710.
Chapel—Lake, Sacred Heart

ST. FRANCISVILLE, WEST FELICIANA PARISH, OUR LADY OF MOUNT CARMEL (1874) Rev. J. Cary Bani.
Res.: P.O. Box 1249, 70775-1249. Tel: 225-635-3630; Fax: 225-635-2344. Email: olmcchurch@bellsouth.net.
Catechesis/Religious Program—Students 125.
Chapel—Jackson, Our Lady of Perpetual Help, Tel: 225-634-5331.
Chapel—Angola, St. Augustine, Louisiana State Penitentiary [CEM]Tel: 225-655-4411, Ext. 2028; Fax: 225-634-5331.

ST. GABRIEL, IBERVILLE PARISH, ST. GABRIEL THE ARCHANGEL (1769) [CEM] Rev. Charles R. Landry.
Res.: 3625 Hwy. 75, 70776-9411. Tel: 225-642-8441; Fax: 225-642-8491. Email: stgabrielcatholi@bellsouth.net.
Catechesis/Religious Program—Students 42.

ST. JAMES, ST. JAMES PARISH, ST. JAMES (1767) [CEM] Rev. Louis T. Oubre; Deacon Henry Zeringue.
Res.: 6613 Hwy. 18, 70086-9054. Tel: 225-265-4210; Fax: 225-265-4225.
Catechesis/Religious Program—Tel: 225-265-9549. Mrs. Janel W. Gordon, D.R.E. Students 132.

SORRENTO, ASCENSION PARISH, ST. ANNE (1963) Rev. Michael A. Galea; Deacon Jerry Braud.
Res.: P.O. Box 9, 70778-0009. Tel: 225-675-8126; Fax: 225-675-6150.
Catechesis/Religious Program—Tel: 225-675-6528. Mrs. Lisa Westerfield, C.R.E. Attended by St. Anthony of Padua, Darrow Students 140.

TICKFAW, TANGIPAHOA PARISH, OUR LADY OF POMPEII (1973) Revs. Edward E. Everitt, O.P.; Cayet N. Mangiaracina, O.P.; Henry B. Groover, O.P.
14450 Hwy. 442, 70466.
Res.: P.O. Box 276, 70466-0276. Tel: 985-345-8957; Fax: 985-542-8490.
Catechesis/Religious Program—Students 55.

VACHERIE, ST. JAMES PARISH

1—OUR LADY OF PEACE (1864) [CEM] Very Rev. Michael A. Miceli.
Res.: 13281 Hwy. 644, 70090-3102. Tel: 225-265-3953; Fax: 225-265-2507. Email: olopeace@bellsouth.net.
Catechesis/Religious Program—Students 333.

2—ST. PHILIP (1873) [CEM] Rev. Louis T. Oubre; Deacon Francis Waguespack.
Res.: 1175 Hwy. 18, 70090-9527. Tel: 225-265-4085; Fax: 225-265-9348. Email: stphilip@bellsouth.net.
Catechesis/Religious Program—Mrs. Janel W. Gordon, D.R.E. Students 75.

WHITE CASTLE, IBERVILLE PARISH, OUR LADY OF PROMPT SUCCOR (1899) [CEM 2] Rev. Joey F. Angeles.
Mailing Address: P.O. Box 249, 70788-0249. Tel: 225-545-3635; Fax: 225-545-8615. Email: olpschurch@cox.net. 32615 Bowie St., 70788.
Catechesis/Religious Program—Students 91.

ZACHARY, EAST BATON ROUGE PARISH, ST. JOHN THE BAPTIST (1964) Rev. M. Jeffery Bayhi; Deacons Ronald D. LeGrange; Christopher Surek.
Res.: 4727 McHugh Dr., 70791-3935. Tel: 225-654-5778; Fax: 225-654-5796.
Catechesis/Religious Program—Tel: 225-654-5885; Fax: 225-654-5294. Mrs. Dorothy Kuhlman, D.R.E. Students 36.
Chapel—Clinton, Our Lady of the Assumption

Chaplains of Public Institutions

BATON ROUGE. *Baton Rouge General Medical Center*, P.O. Box 3611, 70821-3611. Tel: 225-387-7000. Rev. Michael Jung, O.S.B., Chap.

ANGOLA. *Louisiana State Penitentiary*, P.O. Box 428, 70712-0428. Tel: 225-655-4411, Ext. 2028; 225-655-3243. Rev. J. Cary Bani, Deacon Angelo S. Nola. St. Augustine Chapel.

ST. GABRIEL. *Hunt Correctional Institute*. Jules Tolivar, Chap.
Mailing Address: P.O. Box 174, 70776-0174. Tel: 225-642-3306. Deacon Claude H. Bourgeois Jr.
LA Correctional Institute For Women, Mailing Address: P.O. Box 26, 70726-0026. Tel: 225-642-5529, Ext. 240. Sr. Linda Songy, S.C.S.C., Chap.

Special Assignment:
Revs.—
Ferrier, Francis V., S.J., 4101 Plaza Tower Dr. #233, 70816-4381. Tel: 225-291-2444 Nursing homes not under Catholic auspices.
Jamin, David S., St. Stephen Martyr Church, 2436 Pennsylvania Ave., N.W., Washington, DC 20037-1717. Tel: 202-785-0983, Ext. 21. Email: djavid@diobr.org

---

Retired:
Rev. Msgrs.—
Frey, Andrew F., 274 Marquette Ave., 70806-4417. Tel: 225-929-8917
Greene, William L., 3111 Kleinert Ave., 70806-6833. Tel: 225-336-0903
Guillot, Leo, St. Louis King of France, 2121 N. Sherwood Forest Dr., 70815-1962. Tel: 225-275-7280
Lefebvre, Gerald M., P.O. Box 84126, 70884-4126. Tel: 225-925-8241
Revs.—
Blanchard, Donald V., St. Aloysius Parish, 9124 Old Hammond Hwy., #46, 70809-1380. Tel: 225-361-0818
Brunet, Jules A., 604 Country Club Blvd., Thibodaux, 70301. Tel: 985-209-5701
Carville, John, S.T.D., 3553 Hyacinth St., 70808-2849. Tel: 225-383-8320
Dugas, Jerome A., 24520 Ferdinand St., Plaquemine, 70764. Tel: 225-687-1291
Gautreau, Henry W., Ph.D., 421-D Longwood Ct., 70806. Tel: 225-346-8873
Hall, Howard B., P.O. Box 457, 70821-0457. Tel: 225-245-1862
Laird, Kenneth W., 3331 Myrtle Grove, 70810-1232. Tel: 225-262-1517
Marcell, Robert G., P.O. Box 80783, 70898-0783. Tel: 225-346-8258
Mascarella, Patrick J., 144 Highland Park Dr., 70808-5631. Tel: 225-252-2806
McDonald, A. John, 333 Lee Dr., #323, 70808-4974. Tel: 225-767-8237
Messina, Victor G., 438 Alello Dr., 70806-4531. Tel: 225-927-7633
Palang, Mansueto P., 2699 Peachtree Rd., N.E., Atlanta, GA 30305-3666. Tel: 404-233-2145
Russo, Anthony J., P.O. Box 83573, 70884-3573. Tel: 225-226-8569
Vavasseur, Henry C., St. Mary of False River Parish, 348 Main St., New Roads, 70760-3587. Tel: 225-939-1924
Young, Gerard F., c/o 412 North St., 70802. Tel: 225-278-2466

Permanent Deacons:
Adams, Alfred P., Sr., St. Michael the Archangel, Convent
Agnello, Michael A., St. Helena, Amite
Bains, Frank E., St. Jude the Apostle, Baton Rouge
BeJeaux, J. Phillip, St. Alphonsus Liguori, Greenwell Springs
Berthelot, Willie M., St. Isidore the Farmer, Baker
Blair, William B., St. Theresa of Avila, Gonzales
Bourgeois, Claude H., Jr., St. John the Evangelist, Prairieville
Brady, Eugene F., Nursing Homes Coord., Baton Rouge
Braud, Jerry W., St. Anne Church, Sorrento
Campeaux, Barry G., (Retired), (Diocese of New Orleans)
Chiappetta, Michael T., Dir. Marriage & Family Life, Immaculate Conception, Denham Springs
Christophe, Norman, (Retired), Oklahoma City
Clement, Randall A., St. John the Evangelist, Prairieville
Collura, Samuel C., St. John the Baptist, Brusly
Decker, Guy E., (Retired)
Dunbar, Benjamin J., St. Paul the Apostle, Baton Rouge
Duplessis, W. Brent, St. Jean Vianney, Baton Rouge
Ellis, Albert R., St. George, Baton Rouge
Ellis, John A., Christ the King Catholic Center & Parish, Baton Rouge
Ferguson, H. John, III, (On Leave)
Fortenberry, Warren D., St. Margaret, Albany
Furlow, Robert E., Jr., (Leave of Absence)
Gainey, Wallace L., Jr., Holy Ghost, Hammond
Garofalo, Natale J., Mater Dolorosa, Tangipahoa Prison
Grant, Richard H., Our Lady of Mercy, Baton Rouge
Gremillion, Esnard F., St. Pius X, Baton Rouge
Hollier, Clayton A., St. Thomas More Church, Baton Rouge
Holtman, Williams H., Most Blessed Sacrament, Baton Rouge
Joseph, Micheal J., St. Isidore the Farmer, Baker
Jung, John A., Jr., St. Aloysius & Nursing Home Ministry, Baton Rouge
Kusch, Robert J., St. Alphonsus Liguori, Greenwell Springs
Labat, Thomas E., Sr., St. Theresa of Avila, Gonzales
LeGrange, Ronald D., St. John the Baptist, Zachary
Little, James A., St. Joseph Church, French Settlement
Malinoski, Thomas J., (Retired)
Melancon, Larry, St. Joseph, Ponchatoula
Morrissey, James J., St. Mark, Gonzales
Moscona, Jodi A., St. Joseph Cathedral, Baton Rouge
Musso, Donald J., Most Blessed Sacrament, Baton Rouge
Navarra, Roger A., Mater Dolorosa, Independence
Nola, Angelo S., Holy Family, Port Allen; LA State Penitentiary, Angola
Reeson, Curles P., St. Jude The Apostle, Baton Rouge
Rhodes, Frank W., (Retired), Denham Springs
Ricard, Alfred J., II, St. John & St. Clement, Plaquemine
Rizzo, Bruno, St. Isidore the Farmer Church, Baker
Robinson, Thomas H., St. Mary & St. Augustine, New Roads
Salinas, Eliazar, Jr., Holy Rosary, St. Amant
Schanzbach, Dr. Milton, (Retired)
Schlette, Peter, Immaculate Conception, Denham Springs
St. Pierre, Tommy J., St. Jean Vianney, Baton Rouge
Stahl, Rudolph W., Immaculate Conception, Denham Springs; Jetson Correctional Institute
Surek, Christopher, St. John, Zachary
Traylor, John T., St. Agnes, Baton Rouge
Waguespack, Francis, Jr., St. Philip Church, Vacherie
Walsh, J. Peter, St. Patrick, Baton Rouge
Wax, James E., (Retired)
Zeringue, Alfred P., Mater Dolorosa, Independence
Zeringue, Henry J., St. James, St. James

INSTITUTIONS LOCATED IN THE DIOCESE

[A] COLLEGES AND UNIVERSITIES

BATON ROUGE. *Our Lady of the Lake College*, 7434 Perkins Rd., 70808-4380. Tel: 225-768-1710; Fax: 225-768-1726. Email: sandra.harper@ ololcollege.edu. Web: www.ololcollege.edu. Dr. Sandra Harper, Pres. Lay Teachers 120; Students 2,046.

[B] DIOCESAN HIGH SCHOOLS, INTERPAROCHIAL

BATON ROUGE. *Redemptorist Diocesan Regional High School*, (Grades 7-12), 4000 St. Gerard Ave., 70805-2999. Tel: 225-357-0936; Fax: 225-357-4555. Email: redemptortist@rhsbr.org. Web: www.rhsbr.com. John W. Sanders, Prin.; Kathy Mendoza, Librarian. Serving parishes in Baton Rouge, Baker, Brusly, Denham Springs, Greenwell Springs, Lakeland, New Roads, Gonzales, Port Allen, St. Gabriel, Zachary, Plaquemine, Maringouin, Prairieville and Clinton. Lay Teachers 42; Students 470.

St. Michael the Archangel Diocesan Regional High School, 17521 Monitor Ave., 70817-2640. Tel: 225-753-9782; Fax: 225-753-0605. Email: stmichaelhigh@csobr.org. Web: www.smhsbr.org. P.O. Box 86110, 70879-6110. Mrs. Myra T. Patureau, Prin.; Ms. Amy Donaldson, Librarian. Sisters 1; Lay Teachers 61; Students 689.

DONALDSONVILLE. *Ascension Catholic Diocesan Regional School*, 311 St. Vincent St., 70346-2697. Tel: 225-473-9227; Fax: 225-473-9235. Email: dawn@ascensioncatholic.org. Mr. Gerald Mahoney, Prin. Serving parishes in Donaldsonville, St. James, Belle Rose, Vacherie, White Castle, Darrow, Gonzales, Convent, Paincourtville and Plattenville. Lay Teachers 15; Students 190.

HAMMOND. *St. Thomas Aquinas Regional Catholic High School*, 14520 Voss Dr., 70401-9801. Tel: 985-542-7662; Fax: 985-542-4010. Email: stthomasaquinas@csobr.org. Web: www.stafalcons.org. Mr. Jose Becerra, Prin.; Ms. Virginia Bravata, Librarian. Dominican Sisters, Springfield, IL. Lay Teachers 32; Students 388.

NEW ROADS. *Catholic High School of Pointe Coupée*, (Grades 7-12), 504 Fourth St., 70760-3499. Tel: 225-638-9313; Fax: 225-638-6471. Email: catholichighpc@csobr.org. Web: www.catholicpc.com. Mrs. Colleen Caillet, Prin. Serving parishes in Lakeland, Livonia, Morganza, New Roads and Maringouin. Lay Teachers 21; Students 320.

PLAQUEMINE. *St. John Interparochial High School*, 24250 Regina St., 70764-3598. Tel: 225-687-3056; Fax: 225-687-3530. Email: info@stjohnschool.org. Web: www.stjohnschool.org. Mr. David W. Dean, Admin.; Mrs. Cherie Schlatre, Prin.; Mrs. Tonya Orcino, Librarian. Serving parishes in Plaquemine, Brusly, Port Allen, Grosse Tete, St. Gabriel and White Castle. Lay Teachers 16; Students 166.

[C] HIGH SCHOOLS, PRIVATE

BATON ROUGE. *Catholic High School*, (Grades 8-12), 855 Hearthstone Dr., 70806-5599. Tel: 225-383-0397; Fax: 225-383-0381. Email: info@ catholichigh.org. Web: www.catholichigh.org. Mr. Gerald E. Tullier, Pres.; Bro. Barry Landry, S.C., Prin.; Mrs. Amanda Graves, Librarian. Brothers of the Sacred Heart 4; Lay Teachers 82; Boys 1,044.

St. Joseph's Academy, 3015 Broussard St., 70808-1198. Tel: 225-383-7207; Fax: 225-344-5714. Email: harvisol@sjabr.org. Web: www.sjabr.org. Sr. Adele Lambert, C.S.J., Pres.; Mrs. Linda Harvison, Prin.; Mrs. Rebecca V. Stagg, Librarian. Sisters of St. Joseph 4; Lay Teachers 74; Girls 918.

[D] DIOCESAN ELEMENTARY SCHOOLS, INTERPAROCHIAL

DONALDSONVILLE. *Ascension Catholic Interparochial School*, (Grades K-8), 311 St. Vincent St., 70346-3499. Tel: 225-473-8559; Fax: 225-473-8559. Email: dawn@ascensioncatholic.org; ascensionelem@csobr.org. Mr. Mark Shambuger, Admin.; Mrs. Janice M. Burns, Prin. Serving parishes in Donaldsonville, St. James, Belle Rose, Vacherie, White Castle, Darrow, Gonzales, Convent, Paulina, Paincourtville, and Plattenville. Lay Teachers 22; Students 402.

NEW ROADS. *Catholic Elementary School of Pointe Coupee*, (Grades PreK-6), 304 Napoleon St., 70760-3527. Tel: 225-638-9313; Fax: 225-638-9953. Email: catholicelemofpc@csobr.org. Web: www.catholicpc.com. Mrs. Melissa Cline, Prin.; Ms. Kathy Holloway, Librarian. Serving parishes in Lakeland, Livonia, Morganza, New Roads and Maringouin. Lay Teachers 21; Students 393.

PAINCOURTVILLE. *St. Elizabeth Interparochial*, (Grades PreK-8), P.O. Drawer M, 70391-0420. Tel: 985-369-7402; Fax: 985-369-1527. Email: St.Elizabeth@csobr.org. Ms. Paula Simoneaux, Prin.; Ms. Celeste Comeaux, Librarian. Serving parishes in Belle Rose, Bertrandville, Napoleonville, Paincourtville, Pierre Part, Plattenville and Labadieville. Lay Teachers 22; Students 225.

PAULINA. *St. Peter Chanel Interparochial School*, (Grades PreK-8), 2590 LA Hwy 44, 70763. Tel: 225-869-5778; Fax: 225-869-8131. Email: chanel.school@stpchanel.org. Web: www.stpchanel.org. Mrs. Joanna Foltz, Prin.; Mrs. Sharon Poche, Librarian. Serving parishes in Paulina, Gramercy, Convent, Vacherie, St. James and Grand Point. Lay Teachers 16; Students 250.

PLAQUEMINE. *St. John Interparochial Elementary/ Middle School*, (Grades PreK-3), 58645 St. Clement Ave., 70764-3599. Tel: 225-687-6616; Fax: 225-687-6280. Email: info@stjohnschool.org. Web: www.stjohnschool.org. Mrs. Bernardine Legendre, Prin.; Ms. Amy John, Librarian. Serving parishes in Plaquemine, Brusly, Grosse Tete, White Castle, Baton Rouge, St. Gabriel, Maringouin, Bayou Pigeon, and Donaldsonville. Lay Teachers 27; Students 526.

[E] SCHOOL, EXCEPTIONAL CHILDREN

BATON ROUGE. *Department of Special Education*, 4000 St. Gerard Ave, 70805. Tel: 225-356-4239; Fax: 225-356-4239. Email: jhollowell@rhsbr.org. Web: www.csobr.org. Mrs. Janie Hollowell, Dir. Special Educ. Guardian Angels Center (6-13 yrs.) and Career Ed. Center (14-21 yrs.); Housed on St. Gerard Elementary Campus and at Redemptorist High School. Teachers 5; Speech Therapist 1; Students 61.

[F] GENERAL HOSPITALS

BATON ROUGE. *Our Lady of the Lake Regional Medical Center*, 5000 Hennessy Blvd., 70808-4398. Tel: 225-765-6565; Fax: 225-766-5645. Web: www.ololrmc.com. Sr. Barbara Arceneaux, O.S.F., Supr.; Mr. K. Scott Wester, CEO; Revs. Thomas Danso (Ghana); Donatus O. Ajoko (Nigeria). Franciscan Missionaries of Our Lady (North American Province). Bed Capacity 736; Sisters 19; Patients Assisted Annually 332,597.

Tau Center, 8080 Margaret Ann Dr., 70809-3444. Tel: 225-767-1320; Fax: 225-767-1327.

GONZALES. *St. Elizabeth Hospital*, 1125 W. Hwy. 30, 70737-5000. Tel: 225-647-5071; Fax: 225-647-6066. Web: www.steh.com. Mrs. Dolores LeJeune, R.N., Pres. & CEO. Bed Capacity 87; Total Staff 740; Patients Assisted Annually 255,000.

NAPOLEONVILLE. *Our Lady of the Lake Assumption Community Hospital, Inc.*, 135 Highway 402, 70390-2217. Tel: 985-369-3600; Fax: 985-369-4271. Mr. Wayne M. Arboneaux, CEO. Bed Capacity 60; Total Staff 72.

[G] HOMES AND SPECIAL CARE FACILITIES

BATON ROUGE. *Elderly Housing of Our Lady of the Lake Medical Center*, 5000 Hennessy Blvd., 70808-4398. Tel: 225-765-6565. Ms. Patricia Hima, Dir.

Chateau Louise, 7565 Bishop Ott Dr., 70806. Tel: 225-926-5918. Ms. Patricia Hima, Exec. Dir. Housing for elderly and handicapped persons.

Assisi Village, Inc., of Our Lady of the Lake Medical Center, 7585 Bishop Ott Dr., 70806-8922. Tel: 225-926-5918; Fax: 225-927-1742. Housing facilities for elderly persons.

Calais House, Inc., of Our Lady of the Lake Medical Center, 7545 Bishop Ott Dr., 70806-8900. Tel: 225-927-1889; Fax: 225-927-1742. Housing facilities for elderly persons.

Villa St. Francis, Inc., of Our Lady of the Lake Medical Center, 7575 Bishop Ott Dr., 70806-8906. Tel: 225-927-0070; Fax: 225-927-1742. Housing facilities for elderly and handicapped persons.

Ollie Steele Burden Manor, 4250 Essen Ln., 70809-2196. Tel: 225-926-0091; Fax: 225-926-4937. Ms. Susan Folse, M.S., N.F.A., Admin. Our Lady of the Lake Regional Medical Center, Our Lady of the Lake Pastoral Care. Total Staff 172; Bed Capacity 164.

[H] MONASTERIES AND RESIDENCES OF PRIESTS OR BROTHERS

BATON ROUGE. *Brothers of the Sacred Heart*, 4345 Woodside Dr., 70808. Tel: 225-223-6920. Bro. Xavier Werneth, S.C., Supr. Brothers 5; Ordained 1.

St. Gerard Residence, P.O. Box 53900, 70892-3900. Tel: 225-355-3377; Fax: 225-355-6200. Web: www.novp.org. Priests 6; Brothers 2. In Res. Rev. Samuel C. Maranto, C.Ss.R.; Bro. Clement J. Furno, C.Ss.R.

Incarnatio Consecratio Missio (Vietnamese Institute), 2580 Choctaw Dr., 70805-7999. Tel: 225-357-1204; Fax: 225-354-0611. Email: nvhung@ bellsouth.net. Very Rev. Hung Viet Nguyen, I.C.M. (Vietnam), Supr. General; Revs. Minh Hai Nguyen, I.C.M., Dir.; Martin Thanh Nguyen, I.C.M.; Thomas Tranh Dinh, I.C.M.; Peter Neuman, I.C.M.

[I] CONVENTS AND RESIDENCES FOR SISTERS

BATON ROUGE. *Congregation of St. Joseph*, 3134 Hundred Oaks Ave., 70808. Tel: 225-332-2999; Fax: 225-379-7930. Email: lamberta@sjabr.org. Web: sistersofstjoseph.org. Sr. Patricia Sullivan, C.S.J., Admin. Sisters of St. Joseph 7.

St. Joseph Spirituality Center, 2980 Kleinert Ave., 70806-6800. Tel: 225-383-3349; Fax: 225-336-4874.

Maryville Novitiate and Provincial House, 4200 Essen Ln., 70809-2196. Email: barcenea@ ololrmc.com. Web: www.fmolsisters.com. *North American Province*, 4200 Essen Ln., 70809-2196. Tel: 225-927-7481; 225-926-1627; Fax: 225-925-5268. Sr. Barbara Arceneaux, O.S.F., Prov. Supr. Final Vows 23.

[J] RETREAT HOUSES

BATON ROUGE. *Bishop Robert E. Tracy Center*, P.O. Box 2028, 70821-2028. Tel: 225-336-8750; Fax: 225-336-8725. Email: tracycenter@diobr.org. 1800 S. Acadian Thruway, P.O. Box 2028, 70821-2028. Mr. Samuel N. Scimeca, Admin.

CONVENT. *Manresa House of Retreats*, Office: P.O. Box 89, 70723-0089. Tel: 225-562-3596; 800-782-9431; Fax: 225-562-3147. Email: manresahr@ bellsouth.net. Mr. Tim Murphy, Dir.; Revs. Peter J. Callery, S.J., Assoc. Dir.; John J. Callahan, S.J., Assoc. Dir.; Clyde Le Blanc, S.J., Assoc. Dir.

PONCHATOULA. *Rosaryville/Spirit Life Center*, 39003 Rosaryville Rd., 70454-7001. Tel: 225-294-5039; 800-627-9183; Fax: 225-294-3510. Email: dsslc@I-55.com. Web: www.rosaryvillela.com. Ms. Mary Herbert, Acting Dir.

[K] CAMPUS MINISTRY

BATON ROUGE. *Christ the King Parish and Catholic Center Louisiana State University*, P.O. Box 25131, 70894-5131. Tel: 225-344-8595; Fax: 225-344-1920. Email: tvu@ctk-lsu.org. Web: www.ctk-lsu.org. Very Rev. Than N. Vu, S.T.L., V.G.; Revs. Andrew J. Merrick; Matthew P. Lorrain; Deacon John A. Ellis.

11 Fraternity Ln., 70803. Total Catholic Students 10,413.

Martin Luther King, Jr. Catholic Student Center St. Joseph Chapel, Southern University, 586 Harding Blvd., 70807-5301. Tel: 225-775-8691; Fax: 225-775-2702. Email: glundysj@aol.com. Rev. George F. Lundy, S.J., Chap. & Dir. Total Catholic Students 3,000.

HAMMOND. *St. Albert the Great Catholic Student Center* 409 W. Dakota St., 70401-2517. Tel: 985-345-7206; Fax: 985-345-7223. Email: saintal@ bellsouth.net. Very Rev. Randy M. Cuevas, S.T.L., V.F., Dir. Serving Southeastern Louisiana University. Catholic Students 4,500.

[L] MISCELLANEOUS

BATON ROUGE. *Bishop Stanley J. Ott Shelter Program*, P.O. Box 127, 70821-0127. Tel: 225-383-7343; Fax: 225-383-6623. Email: macaldo@svdpbr.com. Mr. Michael J. Acaldo, CEO.

Catholic Charities of the Diocese of Baton Rouge, Inc., 1900 S. Acadian Thruway, 70808-1688. Tel: 225-336-8770; Fax: 225-336-8745. Email: daguillard@ccdiobr.org. Web: www.ccdiobr.org. Mailing Address: P.O. Box 1668, 70821-1668. Mr. David C. Aguillard, M.P.A., M.H.A., Exec. Dir.

Joseph Homes, Inc.

Child Nutrition Program, P.O. Box 66578, 70896-6578. Lynda Carville, Supvr.

FMOL Health Systems, Inc., 4200 Essen Ln., 70809-2196. Tel: 225-923-2701; Fax: 225-926-4846. Email: jfinan@fmolhs.com. Web: www.fmolhs.org. Mr. John J. Finan Jr., Pres. & CEO.

Franciscan Ministry Fund, Inc., 4200 Essen Ln., 70809. Sr. Brendan Mary Ronayne, O.S.F., Contact Person.

Haiti Mission, Inc., 4200 Essen Ln., 70809-2196. Tel: 225-926-1627; Fax: 225-925-5268. Email: barcenea@ololrmc.com. Sr. Barbara Arceneaux, O.S.F., Pres. Organized and under the supervision of the Franciscan Missionaries of Our Lady, North American Province.

MAGNIFICAT-Baton Rouge Chapter, 16047 Hickory Knoll, 70810-9515. Tel: 225-752-5678. Mrs. Mary Kestler, Coord. A Ministry to Catholic Women.

Maternity & Adoption, 1900 S. Acadian Thruway, 70808. Tel: 225-336-8708; Fax: 225-336-8703. Email: adopt@ccdiobr.org. Web: www.adoptbatonrouge.com. Mailing Address: P.O. Box 4785, 70821-4785. Mrs. Janice Allen, Dir.

St. Michael's Home (Vietnamese), 2305 Choctaw Dr., 70805-7999. Tel: 225-357-1204; Fax: 225-354-0611. Email: nvhung@bellsouth.net. 2580 Tecumseh St., 70805-7999. Very Rev. Hung Viet Nguyen, I.C.M. (Vietnam), Supr. Gen. Tel: 225-355-9794.

Missionaries of Charity Queen of Peace Home and Soup Kitchen, 737 East Blvd., 70802-6399. Tel: 225-383-8367. Missionaries of Charity.

PACE, Inc., Franciscan Missionaries of Our Lady, 4200 Essen Ln., 70809. Tel: 225-923-2701; Fax: 225-926-4846. Sr. Brendan Mary Ronayne, O.S.F., Contact Person.

Redemptorist Fathers of Baton Rouge, Inc., Redemptorist Residence, P.O. Box 53900, 70892. 5354 Plank Rd., 70805. Tel: 225-355-3377; Fax: 225-355-6200. Rev. Samuel C. Maranto, C.Ss.R.; Bro. Clement J. Furno, C.Ss.R.

**Sisters of St. Joseph - St. Paul Center*, 3920 Gus Young Ave., 70802-1727. Tel: 225-344-8590; Fax: 225-387-5169. Email: spalc@juno.com. Mr. David Jones, Dir.; Sr. Kathleen Bahlinger, C.S.J., Asst. Dir.

**St. Vincent DePaul Community Pharmacy, Inc.*, Mailing Address: P.O. Box 127, 70821-0127. Tel: 225-383-7450; Fax: 225-383-4774. Email: macaldo@svdpbr.com. Mr. Michael J. Acaldo, CEO.

St. Vincent DePaul Dining Room, Mailing Address: P.O. Box 127, 70821-0127. Tel: 225-383-7837; 225-383-7439; Fax: 225-383-6623. Email: macaldo@svdpbr.com. Mr. Michael J. Acaldo, CEO.

St. Vincent DePaul Stores, Mailing Address: P.O. Box 127, 70821-0127. Tel: 225-267-5447; Fax: 225-267-5157. Email: macaldo@svdpbr.com. Mr. Michael J. Acaldo, CEO. Tel: 225-383-7837.

[M] FOUNDATIONS, FUNDS AND TRUSTS

BATON ROUGE. *Baton Rouge Chancery Office*, Mailing Address: P.O. Box 2028, 70821-2028. 1800 S. Acadian Thruway, 70808-1698. Tel: 225-387-0561; Fax: 225-336-8789. Email: chancery@diobr.org.

Ascension Catholic Interparochial School Endowment Fund, Donaldsonville. Tel: 225-473-9227; Fax: 225-473-9235.

Bishop Stanley J. Ott Works of Mercy Trust Tel: 225-387-0561; Fax: 225-336-8789.

Diocese of Baton Rouge Clergy Retirement Plan Tel: 225-387-0561; Fax: 225-336-8789.

Diocese of Baton Rouge Lay Retirement Plan Tel: 225-387-0561; Fax: 225-336-8715.

Catholic Foundation of the Diocese of Baton Rouge Tel: 225-387-0561; Fax: 225-336-8715.

Nim Pecquet Holy Family School Foundation, Port Allen. Tel: 225-344-4100; Fax: 225-344-1928.

Our Lady of Perpetual Help Trust Tel: 225-635-3630; Fax: 225-635-2344.

Pamphile and Mabyn Donaldson Trust for St. Louis King of France Church Tel: 225-275-7280; Fax: 225-275-5845.

Pointe Coupee Catholic Interparochial School Endowment Fund, New Roads. Tel: 225-638-9313; Fax: 225-638-6471.

The Roman Catholic Church of The Diocese of Baton Rouge, Deposit and Loan Fund, Inc., 1800 S. Acadian Thruway, 70808-1698. Tel: 225-387-0561; Fax: 225-336-8789. Mr. Joseph E. Ingraham, CFO.

Sacred Heart School Endowment Fund Tel: 225-383-7481; Fax: 225-383-1810.

St. Aloysius School Endowment Fund Tel: 225-383-3871; Fax: 225-383-4500.

St. Joseph Cathedral Cemetery Fund Tel: 225-387-5928; Fax: 225-387-5929.

St. Joseph Cathedral Trust Tel: 225-387-5928; Fax: 225-387-5929.

St. Theresa of Avila Catholic School Educational Foundation, Gonzales. Tel: 225-647-2803; Fax: 225-647-7814.

St. Thomas More School Endowment Trust Tel: 225-275-2820; Fax: 225-275-0376.

Veritas Foundation, Hammond. Tel: 985-542-7662; Fax: 985-542-4010.

CHS Foundation, 4345 Woodside Dr., 70808. Tel: 225-223-6920; Fax: 225-389-0983. Mr. Gerald E. Tullier, Pres.

Our Lady of the Lake Foundation, 5000 Hennessy Blvd., 70808-9907. Tel: 225-765-5000; Fax: 225-765-6480.

CONVENT. *Hynes Fund*, Tel: 800-782-9431; Fax: 225-562-3147. Mailing Address: P.O. Box 89, 70723-0089. Mr. Tim Murphy, Dir. Email: timmurphy@bellsouth.net.

The Administrators of the Rev. John W. Hynes, S.J., Manresa Memorial Endowment Fund, Inc.

RELIGIOUS INSTITUTES OF MEN REPRESENTED IN THE DIOCESE

For further details refer to the corresponding bracketed number in the Religious Institutes of Men or Women section.

[0200]—*Benedictine Monks* (St. Joseph Abbey, St. Benedict, LA)—O.S.B.

[0620]—*Brothers of the Holy Eucharist*—F.S.E.

[1100]—*Brothers of the Sacred Heart* (New Orleans Prov.)—S.C.

[1070]—*Congregation of the Most Holy Redeemer-Redemptorists*—C.Ss.R.

[]—*Incarnatio Consecratio Missio*—I.C.M.

[]—*Indian Missionary Society*—I.M.S.

[0854]—*Missionaries of St. Paul*—M.S.P.

[0430]—*Order of Preachers-Dominicans* (Prov. of St. Martin de Porres)—O.P.

[0690]—*Society of Jesus* (New Orleans Prov.)—S.J.

[0420]—*Society of the Divine Word* (Southern Prov.)—S.V.D.

[0700]—*St. Joseph's Society of the Sacred Heart-Josephites*—S.S.J.

RELIGIOUS INSTITUTES OF WOMEN REPRESENTED IN THE DIOCESE

[]—*Congregation of the Mother of Carmel*—C.M.C.

[3832]—*Congregation of the Sisters of St. Joseph*—C.S.J.

[]—*Congregation of the Sisters of the Holy Family*—S.S.F.

[]—*Dominican Sisters of St. Mary*—O.P.

[1115]—*Dominican Sisters of Peace*—O.P.

[1380]—*Franciscan Missionaries of Our Lady*—O.S.F.

[2187]—*Incarnatio Consecratio Missio*—I.C.M.

[2410]—*Marianites of Holy Cross*—M.S.C.

[2590]—*Mercedarian Sisters of the Blessed Sacrament*—H.M.S.S.

[2710]—*Missionaries of Charity*—M.C.

[2970]—*School Sisters of Notre Dame*—S.S.N.D.

[2630]—*Sisters of Mercy of the Holy Cross*—S.C.S.C.

[]—*Sisters of Notre Dame de Namur*—S.N.D.deN.

[3830-16]—*Sisters of St. Joseph of Springfield, Mont Marie*—S.S.J.

[2940]—*Sisters of the Most Holy Sacrament*—M.H.S.

[4070]—*Society of the Sacred Heart*—R.S.C.J.

[4110]—*Ursuline Nuns (Roman Union)* (Northeastern Prov.)—O.S.U.

NECROLOGY

† Faschan, Matthew John, (Retired)—Died Jan. 3, 2009

An asterisk (*) denotes an organization that has established tax-exempt status directly with the IRS and is not covered by the USCCB Group Ruling.

Diocese of Beaumont

(Dioecesis Bellomontensis)

Most Reverend

CURTIS JOHN GUILLORY, S.V.D., D.D.

Bishop of Beaumont; ordained December 16, 1972; appointed Titular Bishop of Stagno and Auxiliary Bishop of Galveston-Houston December 29, 1987; consecrated February 19, 1988; appointed Bishop of Beaumont June 2, 2000; installed July 28, 2000. *Mailing Address: P.O. Box 3948, Beaumont, TX 77704-3948. Office: 703 Archie St., Beaumont, TX 77701-2899.* Tel: 409-924-4310; Fax: 409-838-4511.

Catholic Pastoral Center: 703 Archie St., Beaumont, TX 77701. Mailing Address: P.O. Box 3948, Beaumont, TX 77704-3948. Tel: 409-924-4300; Fax: 409-838-4511.

Web: www.dioceseofbmt.org

Email: chancery@dioceseofbmt.org

ESTABLISHED SEPTEMBER 29, 1966.

Square Miles 7,878.

Comprises the counties of Chambers, Hardin, Jasper, Jefferson, Liberty, Newton, Orange, Polk and Tyler.

For legal titles of parishes and diocesan institutions, consult the Catholic Pastoral Center.

STATISTICAL OVERVIEW

Personnel	
Bishop	1
Priests: Diocesan Active in Diocese	32
Priests: Diocesan Active Outside Diocese	2
Priests: Retired, Sick or Absent	15
Number of Diocesan Priests	49
Religious Priests in Diocese	22
Total Priests in Diocese	71
Extern Priests in Diocese	7
Permanent Deacons in Diocese	40
Total Brothers	1
Total Sisters	23
Parishes	
Parishes	44
With Resident Pastor:	
Resident Diocesan Priests	26
Resident Religious Priests	16
Without Resident Pastor:	
Administered by Priests	2
Missions	7
Pastoral Centers	2
Closed Parishes	1
Professional Ministry Personnel:	
Brothers	1
Sisters	8
Lay Ministers	27
Welfare	
Catholic Hospitals	2
Total Assisted	406,633
Special Centers for Social Services	3
Total Assisted	32,140
Educational	
High Schools, Diocesan and Parish	1
Total Students	437
Elementary Schools, Diocesan and Parish	5
Total Students	1,260
Catechesis/Religious Education:	
High School Students	1,439
Elementary Students	6,632
Total Students under Catholic Instruction	9,768
Teachers in the Diocese:	
Sisters	2
Lay Teachers	139
Vital Statistics	
Receptions into the Church:	
Infant Baptism Totals	1,272
Adult Baptism Totals	139
First Communions	1,407
Confirmations	670
Marriages:	
Catholic	212
Interfaith	89
Total Marriages	301
Deaths	776
Total Catholic Population	73,327
Total Population	597,684

Former Bishops—Most Revs. VINCENT M. HARRIS, D.D., ord. March 19, 1938; appt. Bishop of Beaumont, July 4, 1966; cons. Sept. 28, 1966; installed as First Bishop of Beaumont, Sept. 29, 1966; appt. Titular Bishop of Rotaria and Coadjutor with right of succession to the Bishop of Austin, TX, April 21, 1971; succeeded to See as Second Bishop of Austin, Nov. 16, 1971; died March 31, 1988; WARREN L. BOUDREAUX, J.C.D., D.D., ord. May 30, 1942; appt. Titular Bishop of Calynda and Auxiliary Bishop of Lafayette, LA, May 19, 1962; cons. July 25, 1962; appt. second Bishop of Beaumont, June 4, 1971; installed Aug. 25, 1971; appt. first Bishop of Houma-Thibodaux, March 2, 1977; installed as first Bishop of Houma-Thibodaux, June 5, 1977; died Oct. 6, 1997; BERNARD J. GANTER, D.D., ord. May 22, 1952; appt. first Bishop of Tulsa, Dec. 19, 1972; cons. and installed, Feb. 7, 1973; appt. third Bishop of Beaumont, Oct. 3, 1977; installed Dec. 13, 1977; died Oct. 9, 1993; JOSEPH A. GALANTE, D.D., J.C.D., ord. May 16, 1964; appt. Titular Bishop of Equilum & Auxiliary Bishop of San Antonio Oct. 13, 1992; cons. Dec. 11, 1992; appt. Bishop of Beaumont, April 5, 1994; installed May 9, 1994; appt. Coadjutor Bishop of Dallas, Nov. 23, 1999; installed Jan. 14, 2000; appt. Bishop of Camden, March 23, 2004; installed April 30, 2004.

Catholic Pastoral Center—703 Archie St., Beaumont, 77701-2899. Tel: 409-924-4300; Fax: 409-838-4511 Office Hours: 8-5. *Mailing Address: P.O. Box 3948, Beaumont, 77704-3948.*

Vicar General and Moderator of the Curia—Rev. Msgr. MICHAEL A. JAMAIL, J.C.D., Ed.D., Mailing Address: P.O. Box 3948, Beaumont, 77704-3948. Tel: 409-924-4300, Ext. 4303; Fax: 409-838-4511.

Episcopal Vicars—Central Vicariate: Rev. Msgr. WILLIAM MANGER, M.Ed., E.V., Mailing Address: St. Anne, P.O. Box 3429, Beaumont, 77704-3429. Eastern Vicariate: Very Rev. JOSEPH P. DALEO, Mailing Address: St. Mary Church, 912 W. Cherry Ave., Orange, 77630-5017. Northern Vicariate: Very Rev. RONALD B. FOSHAGE, M.S., St. Michael, P.O. Box 239, Jasper, 75951. Southern Vicariate: Rev. Msgr. DONALD GOLASINSKI, E.V., Mailing Address: Immaculate Conception Church, P.O. Box 967, Groves, 77619. Western Vicariate: Very Rev. JOSEPH KHANH HO, S.T.L., J.C.L., St. Louis Church, 315 W. Bucaneer, Winnie, 77665-9711.

Diocesan College of Consultors—Very Rev. JOSEPH KHANH HO, S.T.L., J.C.L.; Rev. Msgr. MICHAEL A. JAMAIL, J.C.D., Ed.D.; Rev. CLIFTON LABBE, S.V.D.; Rev. Msgr. KENNETH R. GREIG; Rev. JOHN CLANCY COON, MA.P.S.; Rev. Msgr. BENNIE J. PATILLO, M.Ed.; Revs. THOMAS E. PHELAN, M.S.W.; STEPHEN MCCRATE, S.T.L.; CHARLES ATUAH, M.S.P.; DAVID A. EDWARDS, M.Div.; Very Rev. LUONG QUANG TRAN, J.C.L.

Presbyteral Council—Very Rev. JOSEPH KHANH HO, S.T.L., J.C.L.; Rev. Msgr. MICHAEL A. JAMAIL, J.C.D., Ed.D.; Rev. CLIFTON LABBE, S.V.D.; Rev. Msgr. KENNETH R. GREIG; Rev. ANDREW MOORE, M.Div.; Rev. Msgr. BENNIE J. PATILLO, M.Ed.; Revs. THOMAS E. PHELAN, M.S.W.; M. SHANE BAXTER, S.T.L.; CHARLES ATUAH, M.S.P.; DAVID A. EDWARDS, M.Div.; Very Rev. LUONG QUANG TRAN, J.C.L.

Clergy Personnel Board—Rev. Msgr. BENNIE J. PATILLO, M.Ed., Chm., Mailing Address: P.O. Box 3948, Beaumont, 77704-3948.

Chancellor—Sr. ESTHER DUNEGAN, I.W.B.S., J.C.L., Mailing Address: Catholic Pastoral Center, P.O. Box 3948, Beaumont, 77704-3948. Tel: 409-924-4304; Fax: 409-838-4511.

Chief Financial Officer—LAURA J. WILLIAMS, CPA, Mailing Address: Catholic Pastoral Center, P.O. Box 3948, Beaumont, 77704-3948. Tel: 409-924-4313; Fax: 409-838-4511.

Diocesan Finance Council—LAURA J. WILLIAMS, CPA, Mailing Address: P.O. Box 3948, Beaumont, 77704-3948.

Human Resources Director—BEVERLY ESCAMILLA, P.H.R., Mailing Address: Catholic Pastoral Center, P.O. Box 3948, Beaumont, 77704-3948. Tel: 409-924-4314; Fax: 409-924-4396; 409-838-4511.

Diocese of Beaumont Retirement Committee—JOE BROUSSARD IV, J.D., Chm., Mailing Address: P.O. Box 3948, Beaumont, 77704-3948. Tel: 409-924-4314.

Tribunal—703 Archie St., P.O. Box 3948, Beaumont, 77704-3948. Tel: 409-924-4300, Ext. 4319; Fax: 409-838-4511.

Judicial Vicar—Very Rev. LUONG QUANG TRAN, J.C.L.

Diocesan Judges—Very Rev. LUONG QUANG TRAN, J.C.L., Judicial Vicar; Rev. Msgr. KENNETH R. GREIG; Very Rev. JOSEPH KHANH HO, S.T.L., J.C.L.; Revs. MARTIN LESTER NELSON, J.C.L.; SINCLAIR OUBRE, J.C.L.; Rev. Msgr. BENNIE J. PATILLO, M.Ed.; Sr. ESTHER DUNEGAN, I.W.B.S., J.C.L.

Promoter of Justice—Rev. Msgr. MICHAEL A. JAMAIL, J.C.D., Ed.D.

Defender of Bond—Rev. Msgr. MICHAEL A. JAMAIL, J.C.D., Ed.D.

Psychologists for the Tribunal—RAY COXE, Ph.D.; Rev. Msgr. MICHAEL A. JAMAIL, J.C.D., Ed.D.

Secretary-Notary—MARILYN PRICE; Sr. BARBARA ANNE OSTERHAUS, C.V.I., Sec.

Victim Assistance Coordinator—Mrs. BECKY RICHARD, M.S., L.P.C., Mailing Address: 2780 Eastex Freeway, Beaumont, 77703. Tel: 409-924-4400, Ext. 4433; Fax: 409-832-0145. Email: brichard@catholiccharitiesbmt.org.

Diocesan Departments

Apostleship of the Sea—Rev. SINCLAIR OUBRE, J.C.L., Diocesan Dir., 1500 Jefferson Dr., Port Arthur,

77642. Tel: 409-982-5111; Fax: 409-985-5945. Email: aos-beaumont@dioceseofbmt.org.

Lifelong Catholic Formation/Education—LORRAINE S. DELUCA, Ed.D., Dir., Mailing Address: P.O. Box 3948, Beaumont, 77704-3948. Tel: 409-924-4323; Fax: 409-838-4511.

Catholic Schools—NANCY SIMS COLLINS, M.Ed., Supt., Mailing Address: P.O. Box 3948, Beaumont, 77704-3948. Tel: 409-924-4322; Fax: 409-838-4511.

Office of Stewardship & Communications—LETTY LANZA, Dir., Mailing Address: P.O. Box 3948, Beaumont, 77704-3948. Tel: 409-924-4300, Ext. 4302; Fax: 409-838-4511.

East Texas Catholic Newspaper—703 Archie St., Beaumont, 77701-2899. Tel: 409-924-4300, Ext. 4350; Fax: 409-838-4511. Ms. KAREN GILMAN, Editor.

Diaconate, Permanent Diaconate—Rev. Msgr. JEREMIAH J. MCGRATH, D.Min., Vicar, Mailing Address: St. Anthony Cathedral Basilica, P.O. Box 3309, Beaumont, 77704-3309. Tel: 409-833-6433; Fax: 409-833-6688; Deacon KEITH FONTENOT, Dir., 2240 Oak S., Nederland, 77627-4740. Tel: 409-727-3768; Fax: 409-838-4511.

Diaconate Formation—Rev. Msgr. MICHAEL A. JAMAIL, J.C.D., Ed.D., Dir. Tel: 409-924-4300, Ext. 4303; Fax: 409-838-4511; Sr. ESTHER DUNEGAN, I.W.B.S., J.C.L., Assoc. Dir., Diocese of Beaumont, P.O. Box 3948, Beaumont, 77704-3948. Tel: 409-924-4304; Fax: 409-838-4511.

Holy Childhood—LETTY LANZA, Mailing Address: P.O. Box 3948, Beaumont, 77704-3948. Tel: 409-924-4300, Ext. 4316; Fax: 409-838-4511.

Propagation of the Faith: Mission Coop—LETTY LANZA, Mailing Address: P.O. Box 3948, Beaumont, 77704-3948. Tel: 409-924-4300, Ext. 4316; Fax: 409-838-4511.

Hispanic Ministry, Diocesan—Mr. JESUS ABREGO, Dir., Mailing Address: P.O. Box 3948, Beaumont, 77704-3948. Tel: 409-924-4331; Fax: 409-838-4511.

African American Ministry—LINDA DUHON-LACOUR, Dir., Mailing Address: P.O. Box 3948, Beaumont, 77704-3948. Tel: 409-924-4300, Ext. 4325; Fax: 409-838-4511.

Worship; Liturgical Commission; Diocesan Choir—Mrs. ROSALIND SANCHEZ, M.A., Dir., Mailing Address: P.O. Box 3948, Beaumont, 77704-3948. Tel: 409-924-4321; Fax: 409-838-4511.

Principal Master of Episcopal Ceremonies—Deacon DAVID LUTHER, Mailing Address: Rte. 7, Box 46-1, Jasper, 75951-9294. Tel: 409-384-1521.

Family Life Ministry & Respect Life Liaison—LINDA DUHON-LACOUR, Dir., Mailing Address: P.O. Box 3948, Beaumont, 77704-3948. Tel: 409-924-4300, Ext. 4306; Fax: 409-838-4511.

Criminal Justice Ministry—Deacon HARRY DAVIS, Dir., Mailing Address: P.O. Box 3948, Beaumont, 77704-3948. Tel: 409-924-4300, Ext. 4329; Fax: 409-838-4511.

Director of Seminarians—Rev. ANDREW MOORE, M.Div., Mailing Address: Infant Jesus Church, P.O. Box 8180, Lumberton, 77657. Tel: 409-755-1734; Fax: 409-755-2833.

Vocations—Rev. M. SHANE BAXTER, S.T.L., Mailing Address: P.O. Box 10095, Beaumont, 77710. Tel: 409-924-4300, Ext. 4361; Fax: 409-832-4129.

Office of Youth Ministry—Mr. TOMMY CHATLOSH, Dir., Mailing Address: P.O. Box 10095, Beaumont, 77710. Tel: 409-924-4300, Ext. 4362; Fax: 409-832-4129.

Ecumenical Interreligious Affairs Officer—Rev. Msgr. JEREMIAH J. MCGRATH, D.Min., Mailing Address: St. Anthony Cathedral Basilica, P.O. Box 3309, Beaumont, 77704-3309. Tel: 409-833-6433; Fax: 409-833-6688.

Committees, Boards, Commissions

Diocesan Review Board—Mailing Address: P.O. Box 3948, Beaumont, 77704-3948.

Diocesan African American Commission—Mr. WILLIAM JAMES CARTER, Chm., Mailing Address: P.O. Box 3948, Beaumont, 77704-3948. Tel: 409-924-4325; Fax: 409-838-4511.

Diocesan Building Commission—Rev. Msgr. RICHARD A. DESTEFANO, Chm. (Retired), Mailing Address: P.O. Box 3948, Beaumont, 77704. Tel: 409-924-4313.

Catholic Committee on Scouting—Mrs. CHRISTINE MCGINNIS, Chm., 2815 Westmont, Beaumont, 77706. Tel: 409-892-6733.

Catholic Daughters of America—OLIVIA GONZALES, District Deputy, Mailing Address: P.O. Box 7851, Beaumont, 77726. Tel: 409-832-0101.

Catholic Women, Council of—Rev. Msgr. DONALD GOLASINSKI, E.V., Moderator, Mailing Address: Immaculate Conception Church, P.O. Box 967, Groves, 77619-0967.

Charismatic Prayer Renewal—Rev. Msgr. WILLIAM MANGER, M.Ed., E.V., Group Liaison, Mailing Address: St. Anne Church, P.O. Box 3429, Beaumont, 77704-3429.

Southeast Texas ACTS Mission Chapter—Rev. Msgr. WILLIAM MANGER, M.Ed., E.V., Liaison, Mailing Address: St. Anne Church, P.O. Box 3429, Beaumont, 77704-3429. Tel: 409-832-9963; Fax: 409-832-9964.

Commission for Continuing Education of Clergy & Religious—Rev. PETER C. FUNK, Chm., Holy Family Retreat Center, 9920 N. Major Dr., Beaumont, 77713-7618. Tel: 409-899-5617; Fax: 409-899-3161.

R.C.I.A. Commission—LORRAINE S. DELUCA, Ed.D., Chm., Mailing Address: P.O. Box 3948, Beaumont, 77704-3948.

Diocesan School Board—Mr. GREG THOMPSON, Pres., 2615 Calder, Ste. 300, Beaumont, 77702. Tel: 409-838-2343 (Office); 409-284-2767 (Home); BILL DARLING, Vice Pres., 5730 Fleetwood Ln., Beaumont, 77706. Tel: 409-880-1215.

Vocation Board—Rev. M. SHANE BAXTER, S.T.L., Vocations Dir.

CLERGY, PARISHES, MISSIONS AND PAROCHIAL SCHOOLS

CITY OF BEAUMONT

(JEFFERSON COUNTY)

1—ST. ANTHONY CATHEDRAL BASILICA (1879) Rev. Msgr. Jeremiah J. McGrath; Deacons Laurence David; Keith Fontenot. In Res., Revs. George Kalappura, C.M.I.; Klaudiusz Rokicki, M.I.C.
Res.: 700 Jefferson St., P.O. Box 3309, 77704-3309. Tel: 409-833-6433; Fax: 409-833-8996. Email: support@stanthonycathedral.org. Web: stanthonycathedral.org.
School—(Grades PreK-8), 850 Forsythe, 77701-2890. Tel: 409-832-3486; Fax: 409-838-9051. Email: kvaldez@stanthonycathedralschool.org. Phyllis Walters, Prin.; Sherridan Shakour, Librarian. Lay Teachers 19; Students 225.
Catechesis/Religious Program—Students 140.

2—ST. ANNE (1937) Rev. Msgr. William Manger; Rev. Rodel Faller; Deacon Jude Arceneaux. In Res., Rev. Msgr. Michael A. Jamail.
Res.: Calder Ave. & 11th, P.O. Box 3429, 77704-3429. Tel: 409-832-9963; Fax: 409-832-9964. Email: stannechurch@gtbizclass.com. Web: www.stannebmt.org.
School—(Grades PreK-8), 375 N. 11th St., 77702-1834. Web: www.stannecatholic.org. Todd Higginbotham, Prin.; Ana Wallace, Librarian. (Formerly St. Anne Tri-Parish School) Lay Teachers 45; Students 588.
Catechesis/Religious Program—Tel: 409-832-8107; Fax: 409-832-5099. Web: www.stannecatholic.org. Email: ccdstanne@gt.bizclass.org. Students 124.

3—BLESSED SACRAMENT (1915), (African American), [CEM] Revs. Henry Davis, S.S.J.; Godwin Imoru; Robert Zawacki, S.S.J.
Res.: 780 Porter St., 77701-7198. Tel: 409-833-6089; Fax: 409-833-6091. Email: bsc@catholic.org.
Catechesis/Religious Program—Tel: 409-833-1909. Students 32.

4—CRISTO REY (1951), (Hispanic), Rev. Luis Urriza, O.S.A.
Res.: 767 Ave. A, 77701. Tel: 409-835-7788; Fax: 409-835-7788.
Catechesis/Religious Program—Tel: 409-835-7240. Students 677.

5—ST. JOSEPH (1905), (Italian—Vietnamese), Rev. Khue Si Bui.
Res.: 1115 Orange St., 77701-4392. Tel: 409-835-5662; Fax: 409-832-7717. Email: josephcbmt@aol.com.
Catechesis/Religious Program—Students 193.

6—ST. JUDE THADDEUS (1978) Revs. John Hughes; Constantino Barrera; Deacon Gordon Cabra.
Res.: 6825 Gladys, 77706-3239. Tel: 409-866-5088; Fax: 409-866-1866. Email: stjude@stjudebmt.org. Web: www.stjudebmt.org.
Catechesis/Religious Program—Tel: 409-866-9595. Students 387.

7—OUR LADY OF THE ASSUMPTION (1951) Rev. Eathan Oakes; Deacon Harry Davis. In Res., Rev. M. Shane Baxter.
Res.: 4445 Ave. A, 77705-4998. Tel: 409-835-5343; Fax: 409-835-5344. Email: oloa4445@gt.rr.com.
Catechesis/Religious Program—Students 45.

8—OUR MOTHER OF MERCY (1937), (African American), Revs. Henry Davis, S.S.J.; Godwin Imoru; Robert Zawacki, S.S.J.
Res.: 3390 Sarah St., 77705-3098. Tel: 409-842-5533; Fax: 409-842-4710. Email: omomchurch@catholic.org. Web: josephitecom/parish/tx/omom.
School—(Grades PreK-6) Dorothy Wheaton, Prin. Lay Teachers 8; Students 59.
Catechesis/Religious Program—Tel: 409-842-0112. Students 114.

9—ST. PIUS X (1954) Rev. Joseph Dang, S.V.D.
Res.: 5075 Bigner Rd. at East Lucas, 77708-5299. Tel: 409-892-3316; Fax: 409-892-8916. Email: stpiusx50@stpiusxbmt.com. Web: catholic.web.com/stpiusxbmt.
Catechesis/Religious Program—Tel: 409-892-6052. Students 40.

OUTSIDE THE CITY OF BEAUMONT

AMES, LIBERTY CO., OUR MOTHER OF MERCY (1903), (African American), [CEM] Rev. Ikeokwu Nduh, M.S.P.
Res.: P.O. Box 264, Liberty, 77575-0264. Tel: 936-336-3004; Fax: 936-336-5955. Email: ommc@sbcglobal.net.
Catechesis/Religious Program—Students 23.

ANAHUAC, CHAMBERS CO., OUR LADY OF LIGHT (1938) Rev. Neil A. Arce, Parochial Admin.
Res.: Rte. 2, Box 1-F, 77514-9001. Tel: 409-267-3158; Fax: 409-267-4047. Email: neilofjesus@hotmail.com.
Catechesis/Religious Program—Students 130.

BRIDGE CITY, ORANGE CO., ST. HENRY (1948) Rev. Steven L. Leger; Deacons Hazen Kenney; Steven Obernuefemann; Chris Penning.
Mailing Address: P.O. Box 427, 77611-0427.
Res.: 475 W. Round Bunch Rd., 77611-2448. Tel: 409-735-2422; Fax: 409-738-2158. Email: office@sthenrybctx.org. Web: www.sthenrybctx.org.
Catechesis/Religious Program—Tel: 409-735-8642; Fax: 409-697-1013. Students 275.

BUNA, JASPER CO., ST. FRANCIS OF ASSISI MISSION (1968) Rev. Delphyn J. Meeks.
Mailing Address: P.O. Box 1688, 77612-1688. Tel: 409-994-3456. Email: stfrancism@att.net.
Catechesis/Religious Program—Tel: 409-994-3456. Students 18.

CHEEK, JEFFERSON CO., ST. MARTIN DE PORRES MISSION (1972), (African American), Rev. Joseph Kattakkara, C.M.I., Parochial Admin.
Mailing Address: 9894 Gilbert, 77705. Tel: 409-794-2548; Fax: 409-794-3411. Email: stmarycc@hotmail.com.
Catechesis/Religious Program—Tel: 409-794-1725. With St. Mary, Fannett. Students 17.

CHINA, JEFFERSON CO., OUR LADY OF SORROWS (1918) Very Rev. Luong Quang Tran.
Res.: P.O. Box 38, 77613-0038. Tel: 409-752-3571; Fax: 409-752-5134. Email: olos1@sbcglobal.net.
Catechesis/Religious Program—Students 49.

CLEVELAND, LIBERTY CO., ST. MARY (1950) Rev. Eric Groner, S.V.D.; Deacons David Mueller; Larry Terrell.
Res.: P.O. Box 816, 77328-0816. Tel: 281-592-2985; Fax: 281-592-7247. Email: stmarycleveland01@sbcglobal.net. Web: www.stmarycleveland-tx.org.
Catechesis/Religious Program—Students 394.

CORRIGAN, POLK CO., ST. MARTIN DE PORRES MISSION (1971), (Hispanic), Rev. Clifton Labbe, S.V.D.; Deacon Jose A. Vitela.
Mailing Address: P.O. Box 930, Livingston, 77351-0930. Tel: 936-967-8385; Fax: 936-967-4657.
104 Gossett Rd., 75939. Tel: 936-398-2807. Email: stjoe@eastex.net. Web: stjoseph-livingston-tx.org.
Catechesis/Religious Program—Students 48.

DAYTON, LIBERTY CO., ST. JOSEPH THE WORKER (1945) [CEM] Rev. James McClintock, Parochial Admin.; Deacon Eugene R. LeBlanc.
Res.: P.O. Box 640, 77535-0640. Tel: 936-258-5735; Fax: 936-258-7220. Email: stjosephdayton@yahoo.com.
Catechesis/Religious Program—Students 123.

EASTGATE, LIBERTY CO., ST. ANNE MISSION (1918) Rev. James McClintock, Parochial Admin.; Deacon Eugene R. LeBlanc.
Mailing Address: P.O. Box 640, Dayton, 77535-0640. Tel: 936-258-5735; Fax: 936-258-7220. Email: stjosephdayton@yahoo.com.

FANNETT, JEFFERSON CO., ST. MARY (1964), Formerly St. Mary, Hamshire (1899). Rev. Joseph Kattakkara, C.M.I., Parochial Admin.; Deacon Allan Santos.
Res.: 9894 Gilbert Rd., 77705-8878. Tel: 409-794-2548; Fax: 409-794-3411. Email: stmarycc@hotmail.com.
Catechesis/Religious Program—Tel: 409-794-1725; Fax: 409-794-3411. Students 247.

GROVES, JEFFERSON CO.

1—IMMACULATE CONCEPTION (1928) Rev. Msgr. Donald Golasinski.
Res.: 6250 Washington, P.O. Box 967, 77619-0967. Tel: 409-962-0255; Fax: 409-963-3464. Email: icc-groves@gtbizclass.com.
Catechesis/Religious Program—Students 125.

2—ST. PETER THE APOSTLE (1972) Rev. Msgr. Kenneth R. Greig; Deacon Thomas Ewing Jr.
Res.: 2049 Taft Ave., 77619-4953. Tel: 409-962-8365; Fax: 409-962-8366.

Email: stpeters4072@sbcglobal.net.
Catechesis/Religious Program—Tel: 409-962-3661. Students 266.

JASPER, JASPER CO., ST. MICHAEL (1952) Very Rev. Ronald B. Foshage, M.S.; Rev. Anil Thomas, S.V.D.; Deacons David Luther; William (Bill) Lawrence.
Res.: P.O. Box 239, 75951-0239. Tel: 409-384-2447; Fax: 409-384-2447. Email: stm@jas.net.
Catechesis/Religious Program—Students 112.
Station—Toledo Village

KIRBYVILLE, JASPER CO., OUR LADY OF LA SALETTE MISSION (1948) Very Rev. Ronald B. Foshage, M.S.; Rev. Anil Thomas, S.V.D.; Deacons David Luther; William (Bill) Lawrence.
Mailing Address: P.O. Box 239, Jasper, 75951-0239. Tel: 409-384-2447; Fax: 409-384-2447. Email: stm@jas.net.
Catechesis/Religious Program—Students 41.

KOUNTZE, HARDIN CO., HOLY SPIRIT MISSION (1986) Rev. Andrew Moore.
470 Monroe, 77625-5414. Tel: 409-246-4457 (Office); Fax: 409-246-4623. Email: spiritchurch@sbcglobal.net.
Catechesis/Religious Program—Students 37.

LIBERTY, LIBERTY CO., IMMACULATE CONCEPTION (1756) [CEM] Revs. Joseph Jessing, S.V.D.; Anil Thomas, S.V.D., Parochial Vicar; Deacon Luther Wells.
Res.: 411 Milam, 77575-4730. Tel: 936-336-7267; Fax: 936-336-9740. Email: iccliberty@comcast.net.
Catechesis/Religious Program—Students 292.

LIVINGSTON, POLK CO., ST. JOSEPH (1970) Rev. Clifton Labbe, S.V.D.; Deacons Rudy Cockburn; John G. Stanley; Mike Marion.
Res.: P.O. Box 930, 77351-0930. Tel: 936-967-8385; Fax: 936-967-4657. Email: stjoe@eastex.net. Web: www.stjoseph-livingston-tx.org.
Catechesis/Religious Program—Tel: 936-646-4685. Students 179.

LUMBERTON, HARDIN CO., INFANT JESUS (1948) Rev. Andrew Moore.
Res.: P.O. Box 8180, 77657-0180. Tel: 409-755-1734; Fax: 409-755-2833. Email: infantjesus@gtbizclass.com.
Catechesis/Religious Program—Students 208.

MAURICEVILLE, ORANGE CO., ST. MAURICE (1966) Rev. Delphyn J. Meeks.
Res.: P.O. Box 940, 77626-0940. Tel: 409-745-4060; Fax: 409-745-4272. Email: stmaurice2@aol.com.
Catechesis/Religious Program—Students 60.

MONT BELVIEU, CHAMBERS CO., HOLY TRINITY (2003) Rev. David A. Edwards; Deacon Eugene R. LeBlanc.
Mailing Address: P.O. Box 290, 77580-0290.
Church: 3515 Trinity, 77580. Email: office@htcc-mb.org. Web: www.holytrinitymb.org.
Catechesis/Religious Program—Students 225.

NEDERLAND, JEFFERSON CO., ST. CHARLES BORROMEO (1923) Revs. Dan Malain; David D. Placette, Parochial Vicar; Deacon Dallas Broussard.
Res.: 130 Hardy Ave., 77627-7326. Tel: 409-722-3413; Fax: 409-722-2020. Email: stcharles@gt.bizclass.com. Web: stcharlesnederland.com.
Catechesis/Religious Program—Tel: 409-722-0421; Fax: 409-722-5848. Students 756.

ORANGE, ORANGE CO.

1—ST. FRANCIS OF ASSISI (1978) Rev. Thomas E. Phelan; Deacons Harvey Dubois; Hector Maldonado.
Church: 4300 Meeks Dr., 77632-4508. Tel: 409-883-9153; Fax: 409-883-9154. Email: tsullivan@gtbizclass.com. Web: www.stfrancisorange.org.
Catechesis/Religious Program—Tel: 409-883-8232. Email: jbroussard@gtbizclass.com. Students 169.

2—ST. MARY (1880) [CEM] Very Rev. Joseph P. Daleo; Deacon Melvin Payne.
Res.: 912 W. Cherry St., 77630-5017. Tel: 409-883-2883; Fax: 409-883-3547. Email: stmary@gtbizclass.com.
School—(Grades PreK-8), 2600 Bob Hall Rd., 77630-2418. Tel: 409-883-8913; Fax: 409-883-0827. Dr. Frances Droddy, Prin. Lay Teachers 26; Students 208.
Catechesis/Religious Program—Tel: 409-886-0841; Fax: 409-886-0841. Students 95.

3—ST. THERESE (1924), (African American), Rev. Anselm Eke, M.S.P.; Deacon Julian Richard.
Res.: 1409 N. Sixth St., 77630-3927. Tel: 409-883-3783; Fax: 409-883-4918. Email: sttherese@gt.rr.com.
Catechesis/Religious Program—Students 20.

ORANGEFIELD, ORANGE CO., ST. HELEN (1938) Rev. George Kindangen, C.M.I., Parochial Admin.; Deacon Timothy Istre.
Res.: 8105 FM 1442, 77630-8197. Tel: 409-735-2200 (Office); Fax: 409-735-7786. Email: sthelen@pnx.com.
Catechesis/Religious Program—Tel: 409-735-7028. Students 95.

PORT ARTHUR, JEFFERSON CO.

1—ST. CATHERINE OF SIENA (1954) Rev. Duc Duong; Deacon Jim Gard.
Res.: 3706 Woodrow Dr., 77642-2320. Tel: 409-962-5715; Fax: 409-962-4775.
School—(Grades PreK-8) Michael Collins, Prin. Lay Teachers 18; Students 178.
Catechesis/Religious Program—Students 80.

2—ST. JAMES (1929) Rev. John Clancy Coon; Deacon James DeLee.
Res.: 3617 Gulfway Dr., 77642-3675. Tel: 409-985-8865; Fax: 409-985-3847. Email: jefferyhlewis@sbcglobal.net. Web: www.patx.us/stjames.
Catechesis/Religious Program—Students 24.

3—ST. JOHN (1951), (African American), Rev. Sinclair Oubre; Deacon Willie Posey.
Res.: P.O. Box 123, 77641-0123. Tel: 409-985-8010; Fax: 409-982-8691. Email: aos-beaumont@dioceseofbmt.org.
Catechesis/Religious Program—Tel: 409-985-8010; Fax: 409-982-8691. Students 50.

4—ST. JOSEPH (1951) Rev. D. Stephen McCrate, S.T.L.; Deacon Luis Javier Magana.
Res.: 4600 Procter St., 77642-1365. Tel: 409-982-6409; Fax: 409-983-5383. Email: stjochurch@sbcglobal.net. Web: www.patx.us/stjoseph.
Catechesis/Religious Program—Tel: 409-982-0667. Students 401.

5—ST. MARY (1903), (African American), Merged with Sacred Heart, Port Arthur to form Sacred Heart-St. Mary Parish, Port Arthur.

6—OUR LADY OF GUADALUPE (1927), (Hispanic), Rev. Telesforo R. Blanco, O.S.A.
Res.: 3648 S. Sgt. Lucian Adams Dr., 77642-6100. Tel: 409-962-6777; Fax: 409-963-0669. Email: trb@gtbizclass.com. Web: www.patx.us/olgchurch.
Catechesis/Religious Program—Tel: 409-962-2247. Students 456.

7—QUEEN OF VIETNAM (1977), (Vietnamese), Revs. John Tinh Tran, C.M.C.; Martin Vanban Tran, C.M.C., Parochial Vicar.
Res.: 801 Ninth Ave., 77642-3329. Tel: 409-983-7676; Fax: 409-982-1212. Email: queenofvnchurch@hotmail.com.
Catechesis/Religious Program—Students 200.
Convent—1148 Ninth Ave., 77642. Tel: 409-985-5102; Fax: 409-985-5102. Dominican Sisters 4.

8—SACRED HEART (1915), (African American), Merged with St. Mary, Port Arthur to form Sacred Heart-St. Mary Parish, Port Arthur.

9—SACRED HEART-ST. MARY PARISH (2006) Rev. Charles Atuah, M.S.P.
920 Booker T. Washington Ave., 77640-4923. Tel: 409-985-5104; Fax: 409-982-0106. Email: sacredheart@gt.rr.com.
Catechesis/Religious Program—Students 56.

10—ST. THERESE THE LITTLE FLOWER OF JESUS (1928) Rev. Rejimon George, C.M.I., Parochial Admin.; Deacon Jimmy Bourgeois.
Res.: 6412 Garnet Ave., 77640-1308. Tel: 409-736-1536; Fax: 409-736-2113. Email: officelittleflower@gtbizclass.com. Web: www.patx.us/sttherese.
Catechesis/Religious Program—Students 65.

PORT NECHES, JEFFERSON CO., ST. ELIZABETH (1922) Rev. Msgr. Bennie J. Patillo.
Res.: 2006 Nall St., 77651-3714. Tel: 409-727-8874; Fax: 409-727-8875. Email: stebeth@stelizabethchurch.net. Web: stelizabethchurch.net.
Catechesis/Religious Program—Tel: 409-722-5941. Students 392.

RAYWOOD, LIBERTY CO., SACRED HEART (1952), (African American), [CEM] Rev. George Okeahialam, M.S.P.
Res.: P.O. Box 429, 77582. Tel: 936-587-4631; Fax: 936-587-1012. Email: sacredheartchurchraywood@yahoo.com.
Catechesis/Religious Program—Students 20.

SABINE PASS, JEFFERSON CO., ST. PAUL MISSION (1955) Closed. For inquiries for parish records contact St. John, Port Arthur.

SAM RAYBURN, JASPER CO., ST. RAYMOND MISSION (1970) Very Rev. Ronald B. Foshage, M.S.
Mailing Address: P.O. Box 239, Jasper, 75951-0239. Tel: 409-384-2447.

SILSBEE, HARDIN CO., ST. MARK THE EVANGELIST (1940) Rev. Msgr. James Vanderholt (Retired); Deacon Glen Hebert.
Res.: 905 N. Ninth St., 77656. Tel: 409-287-3287; Fax: 409-385-0806. Email: mevangelist@sbcglobal.net.
Catechesis/Religious Program—Students 75.

SOUR LAKE, HARDIN CO., OUR LADY OF VICTORY (1906) 225 Barkley, P.O. Box 1359, 77659. In Res., Rev. Martin Lester Nelson.
Res.: 210 W. Barkley, P.O. Box 1359, 77659. Tel: 409-287-3287; Fax: 409-287-3271.
Catechesis/Religious Program—Students 120.

VIDOR, ORANGE CO., OUR LADY OF LOURDES (1938) Rev. Paul Sumler.
Res.: 1600 N. Main, 77662-3014. Tel: 409-769-2865; Fax: 409-769-2865. Email: ourladyoflourdes@sbcglobal.net. Web: ololvidor.c-paluch.com.
Catechesis/Religious Program—Tel: 409-769-6758. Students 168.

WINNIE, CHAMBERS CO., ST. LOUIS (1947) Very Rev. Joseph Khanh Ho.
Res.: 315 W. Buccaneer Dr., 77665-9711. Tel: 409-296-4200; Fax: 409-296-9715. Email: josepheaux@yahoo.com. Web: www.slcc-winnie.org.
Catechesis/Religious Program—Tel: 409-296-4925. Students 240.

WOODVILLE, TYLER CO., OUR LADY OF THE PINES (1950) Rev. Michael A. Strother.
Res.: P.O. Box 2029, 75979-2029. Tel: 409-283-5367; Fax: 409-283-2219. Email: olopcc@sbcglobal.net.
Catechesis/Religious Program—Students 36.

Chaplains of Public Institutions

BEAUMONT. *Memorial Hermann Baptist Hospital*. Rev. Charles Atuah, M.S.P.

PORT ARTHUR. *Convalescent Home Ministry*. Rev. George Kalappura, C.M.I.

Prisons

LIVINGSTON. *Beaumont - Federal Correctional Complex*. Rev. Victor P. Vead (ALX), Chap.
Livingston: Polunsky Unit - Death Row. Deacon Jose A. Vitela, Chap.

On Duty Outside the Diocese:
Rev.—
DeFrancisco, Joseph, S.T.D., St. Ambrose University, Davenport, IA 52803.

On Leave:
Revs.—
Badeaux, Kevin, J.C.L., J.C.L.
Baluyot, Michael

Military Chaplains:
Rev.—
Beck, R. Patrick, PSC37 - Box 4636, Apo, AE 09459.

Retired:
Rev. Msgrs.—
Culotta, Salvador J.
Dempsey, James
DeStefano, Richard A.
DiStefano, John
Montondon, Walter, Chap. Col.
Revs.—
Delarue, Louis
Iglesias, Clement
Mudd, Earl
Pucar, August, M.Div.
Romero, Joseph J.
Stratman, Joseph, M.Th.
Sumler, Kevin

Permanent Deacons:
Arceneaux, Jude, St. Anne, Beaumont
Blankenstein, Eddie, (Retired)
Bourgeois, Jimmy, St. Therese the Little Flower of Jesus, Port Arthur
Broussard, Dallas, St. Charles Borromeo, Nederland
Cabra, Gordon, St. Jude Thaddeus, Beaumont
Cockburn, Rudy, St. Joseph, Livingston
David, Laurence, St. Anthony Cathedral Basilica, Beaumont
Davis, Harry, Dir., Office of Criminal Justice Ministry, Our Lady of the Assumption, Beaumont
DeLee, James, St. James, Port Arthur
Dubois, Harvey, St. Francis, Orange
Ewing, Thomas, Jr., St. Peter the Apostle, Groves
Fontenot, Keith, Dir., Permanent Diaconate, St. Anthony Cathedral Basilica, Beaumont
Gard, Jim, St. Catherine of Siena, Port Arthur
Gros, Robert, (Retired)
Hebert, Glen, St. Mark, the Evangelist Church, Silsbee
Istre, Timothy, St. Helen, Orangefield
Kenny, Hazen, St. Henry, Bridge City
Landry, Nolen, (Retired)
Lawrence, William (Bill), St. Michael, Jasper; Our Lady of LaSalette, Kirbyville and St. Raymond, Rayburn
LeBlanc, E. R., Holy Trinity, Mont Belvieu; St. Joseph, Dayton
Luther, David, Principal Master of Episcopal Ceremonies, St. Michael, Jasper; Our Lady of LaSalette, Kirbyville; St. Raymond, Rayburn
Magana, Luis Javier, St. Joseph, Port Arthur
Maldonado, Hector, St. Francis of Assisi, Orange
Marion, Mike, St. Joseph, Livingston
McBride, Stronnie, (Retired)
Mueller, David, St. Mary, Cleveland
Obernuefemann, Steven, St. Henry, Bridge City

Payne, Melvin, St. Mary, Orange
Penning, Chris, St. Henry, Bridge City
Posey, Willie, St. John, Port Arthur; Apostleship of the Sea
Richard, Julian, St. Therese, Orange
Rudolph, William, (Retired)
Santos, Allan, St. Mary, Fannett
Scheurich, Joseph, (Retired)
Smith, Morris, (Retired)
Stanley, John G., St. Joseph, Livingston; State Jail, Travis City
Terrell, Larry, St. Mary, Cleveland
Vitela, Joe, St. Joseph, Livingston; St. Martin de Porres, Corrigan; Criminal Justice Ministry
Wells, Luther, (Retired)
Wycliff, Wilbert, (Retired)

INSTITUTIONS LOCATED IN THE DIOCESE

[A] HIGH SCHOOLS, DIOCESAN

BEAUMONT. *Monsignor Kelly Catholic High School*, 5950 Kelly Dr., 77707. Tel: 409-866-2351; Fax: 409-866-0917. Email: rbemis@kelly.beaumont.tx.us. Web: www.kelly.beaumont.tx.us. Mr. Roger Bemis, Prin.; Rev. Constantino Barrera. Sisters 1; Lay Teachers 44; Students 451.

[B] GENERAL HOSPITALS

BEAUMONT. *CHRISTUS Health Southeast Texas - CHRISTUS Hospital - St. Elizabeth* (1962) 2830 Calder Ave., P.O. Box 5405, 77726-5405. Tel: 409-892-7171; Fax: 409-899-8191. Web: www.christusste.org. Ms. Ellen Jones, CEO & Pres.; Revs. Jerome Robinson (MOB), Vice Pres., Mission Integration; Emmanuel Chikezie (Nigeria), Chap.; Leonard Ogbonna (Nigeria), Chap. Operated by CHRISTUS Health Southeast Texas Bed Capacity 434; Patients Assisted Annually 241,336.

JASPER. *CHRISTUS Health Southeast Texas dba Jasper Memorial Hospital* 1275 Marvin Hancock Dr., 75951. Tel: 409-384-5461; Fax: 409-383-0622. Email: deborah.wiegand@christushealth.org. Deborah Wiegand, R.N., CEO Admin. Operated by CHRISTUS Health Southeast Texas. Bed Capacity 59; Patients Assisted Annually 42,613.

PORT ARTHUR. *CHRISTUS Health Southeast Texas - CHRISTUS Hospital - St. Mary* (1930) 3600 Gates Blvd., P.O. Box 3696, 77643. Tel: 409-985-7431; Fax: 409-989-1033. Web: www.christushospital.org. Ms. Ellen Jones, CEO & Pres.; Mr. Wayne Moore, Admin.; Revs. Jerome Robinson (MOB), Vice Pres. Mission Integration; Donald E. Donahugh (RCK), Chap. Operated by CHRISTUS Health Southeast Texas. Sisters 2; Bed Capacity 227; Patients Assisted Annually 122,684.

[C] MONASTERIES AND RESIDENCES OF PRIESTS AND BROTHERS

BEAUMONT. *Holy Cross Monastery*, 9920 N. Major Dr., 77713-7618. Tel: 409-899-3554; Fax: 409-899-3558. Email: porter@holycrossmonks.org. Web: www.holycrossmonks.org. Benedictine Monks

[D] NEWMAN CENTERS

BEAUMONT. *Lamar University-Catholic Student Center* 1010 E. Virginia, P.O. Box 10095, 77710. Tel: 409-924-4360; Fax: 409-832-4129. Email: vocationsandcampus@dioceseofbmt.org. Rev. M. Shane Baxter, S.T.L., Dir.

[E] RETREAT CENTERS

BEAUMONT. *Holy Family Retreat Center*, 9920 N. Major Dr., 77713-7618. Tel: 409-899-5617; Fax: 409-899-3161. Email: retreatcenter@dioceseofbmt.org. Web: www.dioceseofbmt.org/holyfamily/index.html. Rev. Peter C. Funk, Dir.; Bro. Michael Gallagher, Asst. Dir.

[F] SOCIAL AGENCIES - Catholic Charities of Southeast Texas

BEAUMONT. *Catholic Charities of Southeast Texas*, P.O. Box 829, 77704-0829.

Physical Address, 2780 Eastex Freeway, 77703-4617. Tel: 409-924-4400; Fax: 409-832-0145. Email: catholiccharities@catholiccharitiesbmt.org. Web: www.catholiccharitiesbmt.org. Carol R. Fernandez, Pres. & CEO.

Child Care Contractor Services, 304 Pearl St., 77701. Tel: 409-835-1411; Fax: 409-833-9706. P.O. Box 829, 77704-0829. Raymond J. Broussard, Dir.

Counseling Services, P.O. Box 829, 77704-0829. Tel: 409-924-4418; Fax: 409-832-0145. 2780 Eastex Fwy., 77703-4617. Ms. Christie Byrne, M.S., L.P.C., Dir.

Elijah's Place (2003) P.O. Box 829, 77704. Tel: 409-924-4419; Fax: 409-832-0145. JoAnna Schrock, Coord.

Hospitality Center, 3959 Gulfway Dr., Port Arthur, 77642. Tel: 409-982-4842; Fax: 409-983-7145. P.O. Box 829, 77704-0829. Christina Green, Dir.

Immigration Services, P.O. Box 829, 77704-0829. Tel: 409-924-4413; Fax: 409-832-0145. 2780 Eastex Fwy., 77703-4617. Alma Garza-Cruz, Dir.

Parish Social Ministry, P.O. Box 829, 77704-0829. Tel: 409-924-4415; Fax: 409-832-0145. 2780 Eastex Fwy., 77703-4617. Ginny Smith, L.M.S.W., Coord.

Disaster Trauma & Loss, P.O. Box 829, 77704-0829. 2780 Eastex Freeway, 77703-4617. Randi Fertitta, M.S., L.P.C., L.P.A., Dir. Tel: 409-924-4426; Fax: 409-832-0145.

[G] FOUNDATIONS, ENDOWMENTS AND TRUSTS

BEAUMONT. *St. Anthony School Foundation, Inc.*, 850 Forsythe, 77701. Tel: 409-832-3486; Fax: 409-838-9051. Web: stanthonycathedralschool.org. Tom Flanagan, Pres.

Catholic Clerical Student Fund, P.O. Box 3948, 77704-3948. Ms. Renella Primeaux, Diocesan Representative.

The Catholic Foundation of the Diocese of Beaumont, Inc., P.O. Box 3948, 77704-3948. Tel: 409-924-4313; Fax: 409-838-4511. Rev. Msgr. Richard A. DeStefano, Pres. (Retired); Laura J. Williams, CPA, Sec. Treas.

CHRISTUS Health Foundation of Southeast Texas, 2830 Calder Ave., 77702. Tel: 409-899-7555; Fax: 409-899-7346. Web: www.christushealthfoundationofsetx.org.

Monsignor Kelly Catholic High School Foundation, Inc., 5950 Kelly Dr., 77707. Tel: 409-866-2351; Fax: 409-866-0917. Hubert Oxford III, Pres.

NEDERLAND. *Rev. Herman Vincent Scholarship Fund* Nederland, 130 Hardy St., 77627. Tel: 409-722-3413; Fax: 409-722-2020. Rev. Dan Malain, D.Min., Admin.

ORANGE. *St. Mary School Foundation, Inc.*, 912 Cherry St., 77630. Tel: 409-883-2883; Fax: 409-883-3547. Email: stmary@gtbizclass.com.

[H] MISCELLANEOUS

BEAUMONT. *Abiding Place Catholic Charismatic Renewal Center*, 4440 Chaison, 77705. Email: ncl890@aol.com. Ms. Nita Chavis, Dir.

St. Thomas More Society of Southeast Texas, 470 Orleans, Ste. 950, 77701-3018. Tel: 409-832-8811; Fax: 409-832-8812. Email: pat@pcmcginnis.com. Mr. Patrick Connell McGinnis, J.D., Pres.; Very Rev. Luong Quang Tran, J.C.L., Chap.

PORT ARTHUR. *Apostleship of the Sea of the United States of America (AOSUSA)* (1976) 1500 Jefferson Dr., 77642-0646. Tel: 409-985-4545; Fax: 409-985-5945. Email: aosusa@sbcglobal.net. Web: www.aos-usa.org. Rev. Sinclair Oubre, J.C.L., Pres. Email: aos-beaumont@dioceseofbmt.org; Sr. Myrna Tordillo, AOS National Dir.; Ms. Doreen M. Badeaux, Sec. General.

RELIGIOUS INSTITUTES OF MEN REPRESENTED IN THE DIOCESE

For further details refer to the corresponding bracketed number in the Religious Institutes of Men or Women section.

[0140]—*The Augustinians* (Prov. of Castile, Spain)—O.S.A.
[0600]—*Brothers of the Congregation of Holy Cross* (Southwest Prov.)—C.S.C.
[0275]—*Carmelites of Mary Immaculate* (Chanda, India)—C.M.I.
[]—*Congregation of Marian Fathers of the Immaculate Conception of the B.V.M.* (Mother of Mercy Province)—M.I.C.
[]—*Congregation of the Mother Coredemptrix* (Missouri)—C.M.C.
[0720]—*The Missionaries of Our Lady of La Salette* (Prov. of Mary Queen)—M.S.
[]—*Missionary Society of St. Paul*—M.S.P.
[0420]—*Society of the Divine Word* (Southern Province of St. Augustine)—S.V.D.
[0700]—*St. Joseph's Society of the Sacred Heart* (Baltimore)—S.S.J.

RELIGIOUS INSTITUTES OF WOMEN REPRESENTED IN THE DIOCESE

[2190]—*Congregation of the Incarnate Word and Blessed Sacrament* (Houston, TX)—C.V.I.
[0470]—*Congregation of the Sisters of Charity of the Incarnate Word* (Houston, TX)—C.C.V.I.
[1070-19]—*Dominican Sisters*—O.P.
[1115]—*Dominican Sisters of Peace*—O.P.
[]—*Missionary Carmelites of St. Teresa* (Houston)—C.M.S.T.
[]—*Sisters of the Destitute* (India)—S.D.
[2205]—*Sisters of the Incarnate Word and Blessed Sacrament* (Corpus Christi)—I.W.B.S.
[]—*Vietnamese Dominican Sisters* (Houston)—O.P.

DIOCESAN CEMETERIES

BEAUMONT. *Blessed Sacrament Cemetery*, c/o Blessed Sacrament Church, 780 Porter St., 77701. Tel: 409-833-6089; Fax: 409-833-6091.

Hebert Catholic Cemetery-Stivers Lane, c/o Diocese of Beaumont, P.O. Box 3948, 77704-3948. Tel: 409-924-4313. Laura J. Williams, CPA, CFO.

AMES. *Our Mother of Mercy Cemetery*, c/o Our Mother of Mercy Church, P.O. Box 264, Liberty, 77575-0264. Tel: 936-336-3004; Fax: 936-336-5955.

EASTGATE. *St. Anne Cemetery*, c/o St. Joseph, the Worker Church, P.O. Box 640, Dayton, 77535-0640. Tel: 936-258-5735; Fax: 936-258-7220.

LIBERTY. *Immaculate Conception Cemetery*, c/o Immaculate Conception Church, 411 Milam, 77575-4730. Tel: 936-336-7267; Fax: 936-336-9740.

ORANGE. *St. Mary Cemetery, c/o St. Mary Church*, 912 W. Cherry St., 77630-5017. Tel: 409-883-7390; Fax: 409-883-7390.

PORT ARTHUR. *Calvary Cemetery, Diocese of Beaumont*, P.O. Box 3948, 77704-3948. Tel: 409-924-4313; Fax: 409-722-8312; 409-838-4511.

NECROLOGY

(No Deaths)

An asterisk (*) denotes an organization that has established tax-exempt status directly with the IRS and is not covered by the USCCB Group Ruling.

Diocese of Belleville

(Dioecesis Bellevillensis)

Most Reverend

EDWARD K. BRAXTON, PH.D., S.T.D.

Bishop of Belleville; ordained May 13, 1970; appointed Auxiliary Bishop of St. Louis and Titular Bishop of Macomades Rusticiana March 28, 1995; ordained May 17, 1995; appointed Bishop of Lake Charles December 12, 2000; installed February 22, 2001; appointed Bishop of Belleville March 15, 2005; installed June 22, 2005. *Mailing Address: The Chancery, 222 S. Third St., Belleville, IL 62220.* Tel: 618-277-8181.

The Chancery: 222 S. Third St., Belleville, IL 62220-1985. Tel: 618-277-8181; Fax: 618-277-0387.

Web: www.diobelle.org

Email: info@diobelle.org

ERECTED JANUARY 7, 1887.

Square Miles 11,678.

Comprises Illinois south of the northern limits of the Counties of St. Clair, Clinton, Marion, Clay, Richland and Lawrence.

For legal titles of parishes and diocesan institutions, consult the Chancery Office.

STATISTICAL OVERVIEW

Personnel	
Bishop	1
Retired Bishops	1
Priests: Diocesan Active in Diocese	72
Priests: Diocesan Active Outside Diocese	3
Priests: Retired, Sick or Absent	47
Number of Diocesan Priests	122
Religious Priests in Diocese	36
Total Priests in Diocese	158
Extern Priests in Diocese	1
Ordinations:	
Transitional Deacons	3
Permanent Deacons	1
Permanent Deacons in Diocese	28
Total Brothers	6
Total Sisters	90
Parishes	
Parishes	119
With Resident Pastor:	
Resident Diocesan Priests	67
Resident Religious Priests	5
Without Resident Pastor:	
Administered by Priests	36
Administered by Deacons	3
Administered by Religious Women	4
Administered by Lay People	4
Professional Ministry Personnel:	
Sisters	12
Lay Ministers	27
Welfare	
Catholic Hospitals	5
Total Assisted	434,372
Homes for the Aged	3
Total Assisted	186
Day Care Centers	3
Total Assisted	212
Specialized Homes	1
Total Assisted	14
Special Centers for Social Services	3
Total Assisted	250,000
Educational	
Diocesan Students in Other Seminaries	2
Total Seminarians	2
High Schools, Diocesan and Parish	3
Total Students	1,227
Elementary Schools, Diocesan and Parish	30
Total Students	4,488
Catechesis/Religious Education:	
High School Students	340
Elementary Students	5,020
Total Students under Catholic Instruction	11,077
Teachers in the Diocese:	
Priests	3
Sisters	5
Lay Teachers	549
Vital Statistics	
Receptions into the Church:	
Infant Baptism Totals	1,073
Minor Baptism Totals	210
Adult Baptism Totals	127
Received into Full Communion	186
First Communions	1,256
Confirmations	1,375
Marriages:	
Catholic	266
Interfaith	226
Total Marriages	492
Deaths	1,150
Total Catholic Population	91,550
Total Population	850,200

Former Bishops—Most Revs. JOHN JANSSEN, D.D., ord. Nov. 19, 1858; cons. April 25, 1888; died July 2, 1913; HENRY J. ALTHOFF, D.D., ord. July 26, 1902; appt. Dec. 4, 1913; cons. Feb. 24, 1914; died July 3, 1947; ALBERT R. ZUROWESTE, D.D., ord. June 8, 1924; appt. Nov. 29, 1947; cons. Jan. 29, 1948; retired Sept. 3, 1976; died March 28, 1987; WILLIAM M. COSGROVE, D.D., ord. Dec. 18, 1943; Auxiliary Bishop of Cleveland June 19, 1968; cons. Sept. 3, 1968; appt. Bishop of Belleville Sept. 3, 1976; installed Oct. 28, 1976; retired May 19, 1981; died Dec. 11, 1992; JOHN N. WURM, S.T.D., Ph.D., ord. April 3, 1954; Auxiliary Bishop of St. Louis June 25, 1976; cons. Aug. 17, 1976; appt. Bishop of Belleville Sept. 19, 1981; installed Nov. 4, 1981; died April 27, 1984; JAMES P. KELEHER, S.T.D., M.Ed., ord. April 12, 1958; appt. Bishop of Belleville Oct. 23, 1984; cons. Dec. 11, 1984; transferred to Kansas City, KS Sept. 8, 1993; WILTON D. GREGORY, S.L.D., ord. May 9, 1973; appt. Auxiliary Bishop of Chicago and Titular Bishop of Oliva Oct. 31, 1983; cons. Dec. 13, 1983; appt. Bishop of Belleville Dec. 29, 1993; installed Feb. 10, 1994; appt. Archbishop of Atlanta Dec. 9, 2004; installed Jan. 17, 2005.

Diocese of Belleville Chancery Office—222 S. Third St., Belleville, 62220-1985. Tel: 618-277-8181; Fax: 618-277-0387.

Diocesan Pastoral Center—2620 Lebanon Ave., Belleville, 62221. Tel: 618-235-9601; Fax: 618-235-7416.

Vicar General—Very Rev. JOHN W. MCEVILLY, V.G.

Moderator of the Curia—Very Rev. JOHN W. MCEVILLY, V.G.

Chancellor for Canonical Affairs—Rev. KENNETH J. YORK, J.C.L.

Chancellor of Administration & Pastoral Services—Mr. DAVID R. SPOTANSKI.

Vicar for Priests—Most Rev. STANLEY G. SCHLARMAN, D.D. (Retired).

Administrative Assistant to the Bishop—Ms. CAROL COSTELLO, Interim Administrative Asst.

Administrative Assistant to the Vicar General & Chancellor—Mrs. LINDA KREHER.

Archivist—Sr. MARY KENAN WOLFF, S.S.N.D., Diocesan Pastoral Center, 2620 Lebanon Ave., Bldg. 6, Belleville, 62221-3299. Tel: 618-235-9601, Ext. 156; Fax: 618-235-7115.

Diocesan Tribunal—Diocesan Pastoral Center, 2620 Lebanon Ave., Belleville, 62221. Tel: 618-212-0050; Fax: 618-212-0055. Address all rogatory commissions to the Chancellor at the Chancery.

Judicial Vicar—Very Rev. JAMES M. NALL, J.C.L.

Judges—Very Rev. JAMES M. NALL, J.C.L.; Rev. Msgr. JAMES E. MARGASON, M.Div., J.C.L.

Promoter Justitiae—Rev. PAUL R. WIENHOFF, J.C.L.

Defensores Vinculi—Rev. Msgrs. DONALD W. EICHENSEER; THOMAS D. FLACH, V.F.; Rev. PAUL R. WIENHOFF, J.C.L.

Advocate—Very Rev. JOHN T. MYLER, S.T.D., V.F.

Notaries—Mrs. RENEE QUIRIN; Mrs. JACQUELINE MATT.

Diocesan Consultors—Very Rev. JOHN W. MCEVILLY, V.G.; Rev. Msgrs. HARRY J. JEROME; WILLIAM P. MCGHEE; JEROME D. HARTLEIN; Revs. KENNETH J. YORK, J.C.L., Chancellor; JAMES E. DEITERS; Very Rev. DANIEL J. JUREK, V.F.; Rev. PAUL R. WIENHOFF, J.C.L.; Most Rev. STANLEY G. SCHLARMAN, D.D. (Retired); Very Rev. JOHN T. MYLER, S.T.D., V.F.; Revs. TREVOR K. MURRY; DAVID M. WILKE.

Diocesan Deans—Very Revs. JOHN T. MYLER, S.T.D., V.F., Belleville Deanery; RAYMOND C. SCHULTZ, V.F., East St. Louis Deanery; Rev. Msgrs. JOSEPH A. LAWLER, V.F., East Deanery; JAMES A. BUERSTER, V.F., North Central Deanery; Very Revs. DANIEL J. JUREK, V.F., West Deanery; ROBERT B. FLANNERY, V.F., South Deanery.

Diocesan Finance Office—Mr. WILLIAM J. KNAPP, CFO; Mr. DAVID WAELTZ, Comptroller, Chancery Office. Tel: 618-277-8181; Fax: 618-277-0819.

Diocesan Finance Council—Most Rev. EDWARD K. BRAXTON, Bishop of Belleville; Mrs. DEBI EDWARDS; Very Rev. JOHN W. MCEVILLY, V.G.; Mr. WILLIAM J. KNAPP, CFO; Deacon LINUS KLOSTERMANN; Mr. DAVID FIELDS; Sr. THERESA MARKUS, S.S.N.D.; Rev. Msgr. DONALD W. EICHENSEER; Mr. JAMES L. BURKE; Mr. MARK KABAT; Mr. JAMES FREDERICH; Rev. KENNETH J. YORK, J.C.L.; Mr. DAVID R. SPOTANSKI; Mr. JOHN SMITH, Chm.; Rev. DENNIS F. VOSS.

Diocesan Pastoral Council—Most Rev. EDWARD K. BRAXTON, Bishop of Belleville; Mr. JERRY DESOTO; Mr. DARREN EULTGEN, M.Div.; Mr. DAVID R. SPOTANSKI, Chancellor of Admin. & Pastoral Svcs.; Mr. DENNIS LAAKE; Ms. PHYLLIS MENSING; Mr. FRANCIS MYER; Mr. BRIAN NIERMAN; Deacon DONALD DEITZ; Sr. DIANE M. TURNER, S.S.N.D.; Rev. VON C. DEEKE; Ms. KATHY MULVIN. Tel: 618-277-8181; Fax: 618-277-0387.

Building Commission, Chancery Office—Rev. Msgr. JEROME D. HARTLEIN, Chm.; Deacon DONALD DEITZ; Mr. HERB FOPPE; Mr. MAURICE BEUCKMAN.

Catholic Campaign for Human Development—2620 Lebanon Ave., Belleville, 62221. Tel: 618-235-9601.

Catholic Charities of Southern Illinois— Formerly Catholic Charities *8601 W. Main St., Belleville, 62223.* Tel: 618-394-5900.

Catholic Social Service of Southern Illinois—Mr. GARY HUELSMANN, Dir. Email: ghuelsmann@cssil.org.

Main Office—

Belleville—8601 W. Main St., Ste. 201, Belleville, 62223. Tel: 618-394-5900. Mr. BRAD BECK, Regl. Dir. Tel: 618-688-1161.

Carbondale—214 S. University, Carbondale, 62901. Tel: 618-351-0743. Ms. MARY LOU LOOS, Regl. Dir.

Mount Vernon—219 Withers Dr., Mount Vernon, 62864. Tel: 618-244-0344; Fax: 618-244-1445. Ms. PAM FLOTA, Regl. Dir.

Mount Carmel—120 W. Fifth St., P.O. Box 23, Mount Carmel, 62863. Tel: 618-263-3863; Fax: 618-263-4559. Mr. DON GOFF, Regl. Dir.

Belleville—Don Bosco Children's Center, 900 Royal Heights Rd., Ste. 200, Belleville, 62226. Tel: 618-688-1150; Fax: 618-277-7084. Mr. GEORGE FERGUSON, M.S.W., Dir.

Olney—Fox River Assisted Living, 1016 Parker St., Olney, 62450. Tel: 618-392-6168; Fax: 618-392-6170. Ms. JESSICA SLATER, Dir.

Catholic Urban Programs—Coordinators: Mr. JOSEPH P. HUBBARD; Mr. GERARD F. HASENSTAB; VACANT, Case Mgr., #7 Vieuxcarre Dr., East Saint Louis, 62203. Tel: 618-398-5616. Mailing Address: P.O. Box 3310, East Saint Louis, 62203.

Holy Angels Shelter—Ms. PATRICIA LEWIS, Dir., 1410 N. 37th St., East St. Louis, 62204. Tel: 618-874-4079.

Griffin Center—Sr. JULIA HUISKAMP, D.C., Dir., 2630 Lincoln Ave., East St. Louis, 62204. Tel: 618-874-2500. De Shields-Robinson Center, 1235 McCasland, East St. Louis, 62201. Tel: 618-874-0637. Roosevelt Center, 1328 N. 44th St., East St. Louis, 62204. Tel: 618-271-9859. Weather-Owens Center, 1400 Missouri Ave., East St. Louis, 62201. Tel: 618-271-1250.

Family Center—Sisters CAROL LEHMKUHL, O.P., Site Dir.; MARY ANN BUHR, O.P., Asst. Site Dir.; MARY KAY MCKENZIE, I.W.B.S., Dir. East Side Heart & Home; ANN GREGORY BISCHOFF, O.P., Prog. Dir., 705 Summit, East St. Louis, 62201. Tel: 618-875-7295.

Neighborhood Law Office—7 Vieux Carre, East Saint Louis, 62203. Mailing Address: P.O. Box 3310, East Saint Louis, 62203. Tel: 618-398-1100; Fax: 618-398-1101. Ms. KATHLEEN O'KEEFE, Advocate.

Catholic Diocese of Belleville Cemetery Association, Chancery Office—

Child Protection Office and Victim Assistance Coordinator—Mrs. LYNN MUSCARELLO, Dir., Diocesan Pastoral Center, 2620 Lebanon Ave., Bldg. 5, Belleville, 62221. Tel: 618-212-0050; Fax: 618-212-0055.

Clergymen's Aid Society—Rev. DENNIS F. VOSS, St. Liborius Parish, 911 Sparta, P.O. Box 331, Saint Libory, 62282. Tel: 618-768-4921.

Communications—Mr. DAVID R. SPOTANSKI, Dir. Tel: 618-277-8181.

Diocesan Development Office—Mr. DAVID R. SPOTANSKI, Chancellor of Admin. & Pastoral Svcs.; Mr. RANDY FLACHSBART, Dir. Planned Giving; Ms. JUDY PHILLIPS, Dir. Foundations & Corporations, Chancery Office. Tel: 618-277-8181; Fax: 618-277-0387.

Diocesan Liturgical Commission—Rev. DAVID M. DARIN, Chm. Tel: 618-235-9601.

Diocesan Outreach Apostolate— Serving Alexander and Pulaski Counties. Daystar Community Program, *909 Washington Ave., Cairo, 62914.* Tel: 618-734-0178. Mrs. SHERRY MILLER, Dir. Email: sherrym47@yahoo.com.

Diaconate, Office of Permanent—Rev. Msgr. MARVIN C. VOLK, Vicar for Deacons. Tel: 618-476-3513; Deacons ROBERT LANTER, Coord. of Deacon, Diocesan Pastoral Center, 2620 Lebanon Ave., Belleville, 62221. Tel: 618-235-9601, Ext. 148; DONALD DEITZ, Pres. Deaconate Community; Rev. EUGENE H. WOJCIK, Dir. Deacon Formation.

Office of Vocation and Deacon Formation—Mrs. PATTI WARNER, Administrative Asst., Diocesan Pastoral Center. Tel: 618-235-9601, Ext. 145.

Diocesan Council of Catholic Women—Rev. DENNIS F. VOSS, Diocesan Moderator; Mrs. MARIE MILLER, Pres., Diocesan Pastoral Center.

Ecumenical and Interreligious Affairs—Very Rev. ROBERT B. FLANNERY, V.F., 303 S. Poplar St., Carbondale, 62901. Tel: 618-457-4556.

Formation of Priests—Very Rev. JOHN T. MYLER, S.T.D., V.F., Chm., Cathedral of St. Peter, 200 W. Harrison St., Belleville, 62220. Tel: 618-234-1166; Rev. JAMES R. DEITERS, 1411 Cross, Shiloh, 62269. Tel: 618-632-3562.

Office of Education—Mr. THOMAS H. POSNANSKI, Dir., Diocesan Pastoral Center.

Religious Education and Catechesis—Mr. RUSSELL PETERSON, Assoc. Dir.

Diocesan Board of Education—Mr. BEN FUEHNE, Pres.

Hispanic Ministry—Sr. CECILIA MARIE HELLMANN, A.S.C., Dir., 2620 Lebanon Ave., Belleville, 62221. Tel: 618-235-9601, Ext. 129.

Holy Childhood Association—Very Rev. JOHN T. MYLER, S.T.D., V.F., Cathedral of St. Peter, 200 W. Harrison St., Belleville, 62220. Tel: 618-234-1166.

Hospitals—Rev. EUGENE J. NEFF, Delegate, Ministry to Sick and Aged, 2620 Lebanon Ave., Belleville, 62221. Tel: 618-235-9991.

Insurance Commission—Mr. WILLIAM J. KNAPP, Dir., Chancery Office.

Catholic Mutual Group—Mr. WILLIAM P. JOHNSON, Claims & Risk Mgr., Diocesan Pastoral Center. Tel: 618-233-1090.

Office of Worship—Mrs. SUE HUETT, Dir. Worship, Diocesan Pastoral Center.

Newman Catholic Student Center—Mr. TIM TAYLOR, Dir., 715 S. Washington St., Carbondale, 62901. Tel: 618-529-3311; Rev. PATTINIKUTTIGE KINGSLEY NONIS, Campus Min.

Newman Auxiliary—Ms. MARGE MANGAN, Pres., 9741 Stilley's Mill Dr., Marion, 62959. Tel: 618-982-2218.

Newspaper, "The Messenger"—Ms. LIZ QUIRIN, Editor, Diocesan Pastoral Center.

Ondessonk, Camp— Diocese of Belleville, Department of Outdoor Education: Mr. DAN KING, Exec. Dir., 3760 Ondessonk Rd., Ozark, 62972. Tel: 618-695-2489; Fax: 618-695-3593.

Respect Life/Project Rachel Pastoral Center—Pastoral Center. Mrs. LAURIE EDWARDS, Diocesan Pastoral Center, 2620 Lebanon Ave., Belleville, 62221. Tel: 618-235-9601, Ext. 133.

Propagation of the Faith—Very Rev. JOHN T. MYLER, S.T.D., V.F., Cathedral of St. Peter, 200 W. Harrison St., Belleville, 62220. Tel: 618-234-1166.

Office of Review Board—Ms. JOANN PISEL, Chancery - Diocese of Belleville: 222 S. Third St., Belleville, 62220. Tel: 800-640-3044 (Hotline).

Office of Youth Ministry—Ms. COLETTE KENNETT, Dir.; Rev. BERNARD C. GOEDDE JR., Spiritual Moderator.

Rural Life Conference—Deacon DOUG SPARLING, Dir., 1945 Etherton Rd., Murphysboro, 62966. Tel: 618-687-9618. Email: dsparling@siu.edu.

St. Vincent DePaul Society—Mr. MICHAEL JOHNSON, Store Mgr.; Ms. BONNIE DAVIS, Pres.; Ms. PATRICIA HOGREBE, Dir. Devel., 13 Vieux Carre Dr., Ste. 2, East St. Louis, 62205. Tel: 618-271-6230. Mailing Address: P.O. Box 3310, East Saint Louis, 62205.

Sick and Aged (Ministry)—Rev. EUGENE J. NEFF, Dir., Diocesan Pastoral Center. Tel: 618-235-9991.

Vocation Office—Pastoral Center, 2620 Lebanon Ave., Belleville, 62221. Tel: 618-235-9601. Co Directors: Rev. Msgr. WILLIAM P. MCGHEE, Diocesan Pastoral Center; Revs. TREVOR K. MURRY; DAVID M. WILKE.

CLERGY, PARISHES, MISSIONS AND PAROCHIAL SCHOOLS

CITY OF BELLEVILLE

(ST. CLAIR COUNTY)

1—CATHEDRAL OF ST. PETER (1842) [CEM] Very Rev. John T. Myler, Rector; Rev. Steven L. Beatty; Deacons Robert Becker; Joseph Stock; Donald Deitz.
Res.: 200 W. Harrison St., 62220-2090. Tel: 618-234-1166; Fax: 618-234-2957. Web: www.stpeterscathedral.info.
School—Cathedral School, 200 S. Second St., 62220. Tel: 618-233-6414; Fax: 618-233-3587. Email: cgsoffice@stclair.k12.il.us. Dr. Kay Bennett, Prin. School Sisters of Notre Dame 1; Lay Teachers 14; Students 200.
Catechesis/Religious Program—Sr. Theresa Markus, S.S.N.D., D.R.E.; Miss Jane Stock, D.R.E.; Mr. Charles York, Business Mgr. Students 107.
Convent—300 S. Second St., 62220. Tel: 618-233-3580.

2—ST. AUGUSTINE OF CANTERBURY (1955) Rev. Patrick Okwumuo (Nigeria).
Res.: 1910 W. Belle St., 62226. Tel: 618-233-3813; Fax: 618-233-3946.
School—St. Mary - St. Augustine School, 1900 W. Belle, 62226. Tel: 618-234-4958; Fax: 618-234-3360. Ms. Linda Putz, Prin.; Ms. Mary Sachtleben, Librarian. Merged school with St. Mary. Lay Teachers 22; Students 137.
Catechesis/Religious Program—(Combined with St. Mary, Belleville) Students 25.

3—BLESSED SACRAMENT (1927) Very Rev. John W. McEvilly; Rev. Matthew Elie.
Res.: 8707 W. Main St., 62223. Tel: 618-397-2287; Fax: 618-397-2269.
School—8801 W. Main St., 62223. Tel: 618-397-1111; Fax: 618-397-8431. Ms. Claire Hatch, Prin. Lay Teachers 18; Students 197.
Catechesis/Religious Program—Students 21.
Convent—

4—CHAPEL OF ST. JOHN CHILDREN'S HOME, [CEM] Very Rev. John W. McEvilly.
Mailing Address: *Chancery Office*, 222 S. Third St., 62220. Tel: 618-277-8181; Fax: 618-277-0387.

5—ST. HENRY (1925) Rev. Kenneth J. York.
Res.: 5315 W. Main St., 62226. Tel: 618-233-2423; Fax: 618-233-9879.
Catechesis/Religious Program—Students 85.

6—ST. LUKE (1883) Revs. David M. Darin, Canonical Pastor; Nicholas G. Junker, Sacramental Min.; Deacon Robert Lanter; Sr. Grace Marie Mueller, S.S.N.D., Parish Life Coord.
Res.: 301 N. Church St., 62220. Tel: 618-236-1124; Fax: 618-236-1125. Email: stluke301@aol.com. Web: www.stlukebelleville.org.
Catechesis/Religious Program—Tel: 618-236-1839. Students 43.

7—ST. MARY (1893) Rev. Msgr. William P. McGhee.
Res.: 1706 W. Main St., 62226. Tel: 618-233-2391; Fax: 618-233-9201. Email: stmarychurch1893@sbcglobal.net. Web: www.st-marybelleville.org.
See St. Mary - St. Augustine School under St. Augustine of Canterbury, Belleville for details.
Catechesis/Religious Program— Ms. Ann Bach, D.R.E. Tel: 618-277-1652. Twinned with St. Augustine, Belleville. Students 88.

8—OUR LADY QUEEN OF PEACE (1955) Very Rev. John W. McEvilly; Rev. Matthew Elie; Ms. Karen Ferrara, Business Mgr.
Res.: 5923 N. Belt W., 62223. Tel: 618-234-6196; Fax: 618-234-6217. Email: qpparish@qpfp.com.
School—5915 N. Belt W., 62223. Tel: 618-234-1206; Fax: 618-234-6123. Email: qpschool@qofp.com. Web: www.qofp.com. Ms. Sharon Needham, Prin. Lay Teachers 17; Students 222.
Catechesis/Religious Program—Students 28.

9—ST. TERESA OF THE CHILD JESUS (1926), (Little Flower) Revs. David M. Darin; Nicholas G. Junker, Parochial Vicar.
Res.: 1201 Lebanon Ave., 62221. Tel: 618-233-3500; Fax: 618-233-9703. Email: stteresa@charter.net. Web: www.stteresa.pvt.k.12.il.us.
School—1108 Lebanon Ave., 62221. Tel: 618-235-4066; Fax: 618-235-7930. Mr. Dennis Grimmer, Prin. Lay Teachers 18; Students 281.
Catechesis/Religious Program—Students 80.

OUTSIDE THE CITY OF BELLEVILLE

ALBERS, CLINTON CO., ST. BERNARD (1908) [CEM] Rev. Msgr. Donald W. Eichenseer.
Res.: 202 N. Broadway, P.O. Box 10, 62215. Tel: 618-248-5112; Fax: 618-248-5595. Email: stbernard@plantnet.com.
Catechesis/Religious Program—Tel: 618-248-5134; Fax: 618-248-5134 (Call First). Sr. Joan Stoverink, A.S.C., D.R.E. Students 102.

ANNA, UNION CO., ST. MARY (1857) Rev. Federico Higuera; Sr. Joan Backes, S.S.N.D., Pastoral Assoc. & D.R.E.
Res.: 402 Freeman, 62906. Tel: 618-833-5835; Fax: 618-833-8220. Email: stmaryanna@live.com.
Catechesis/Religious Program—Tel: 618-833-3131. Students 88.

AVA, JACKSON CO., ST. ELIZABETH (1890) Rev. Leo J. Hayes.
Res.: 606 W. George St., 62907. Tel: 618-426-3321; Fax: 608-426-3321.
Catechesis/Religious Program—Tel: 618-497-8724. Students 14.

AVISTON, CLINTON CO., ST. FRANCIS OF ASSISI (1865), (German), [CEM] Rev. Daniel L. Friedman; Deacon Charles Litteken, Ministry Dir.
Res.: 251 S. Clinton, Box 93, 62216-0093. Tel: 618-228-7219; Fax: 618-228-7320. Email: parish@stfrancisav.org. Web: www.stfrancisav.org.
Catechesis/Religious Program—Students 358.

BARTELSO, CLINTON CO., ST. CECILIA (1885), (German), Rev. Henry J. Fischer.
Res.: 304 S. Washington St., P.O. Box 176, 62218. Tel: 618-765-2162; Fax: 618-765-2264. Email: cechbart@frontier.com.
Catechesis/Religious Program— Ms. Betty Budde, D.R.E.; Ms. Ellen Huegen, D.R.E. Students 22.

BEAVER PRAIRIE, CLINTON CO., ST. FELICITAS (1883) [CEM] Revs. Edward F. Schaefer; Larry Nickels, O.F.M., Sacramental Min.; Benjamin Stern; Sr. Diane M. Turner, S.S.N.D., Pastoral Life Coord.
Mailing Address: 13322 Church Rd., Carlyle, 62231. Tel: 618-594-3040; Fax: 618-594-3040.
Catechesis/Religious Program—Students 22.

BECKEMEYER, CLINTON CO., ST. ANTHONY (1905) [CEM] Rev. Charles W. Tuttle; Deacon Robert Lippert, Parish Life Coord.
Res.: 451 W. 3rd St., P.O. Box 305, 62219. Tel: 618-227-8236; Fax: 618-227-8630. Email: stanthony@papadocs.com.
Catechesis/Religious Program— Combined with All Saints, Breese. Students 53.

BENTON, FRANKLIN CO., ST. JOSEPH (1872) [CEM] Rev. Joseph L. Trapp.
Res.: 506 W. Main, 62812. Tel: 618-438-9941; Fax: 618-438-9941. Email: stjoecc@verizon.net. Web: www.stjoecc.org.
Catechesis/Religious Program—Students 46.

BREESE, CLINTON CO.
1—ST. AUGUSTINE (1912) [CEM] Rev. Charles W. Tuttle; Deacon Robert Lippert, Parish Life Coord.
Res.: 525 S. Third St., 62230. Tel: 618-526-4362; Fax: 618-526-4362. Email: augustine306@att.net.
Catechesis/Religious Program—Students 120.
2—ST. DOMINIC (1858) [JC] Revs. Patrick N. Peter; Benjamin Stern.
Res.: 493 N. Second St., 62230. Tel: 618-526-7746; Fax: 618-526-7755. Email: saintdominic@papadocs.com.
Catechesis/Religious Program— Ms. Phyllis Mensing, D.R.E. Students 91.

BRIDGEPORT, LAWRENCE CO., IMMACULATE CONCEPTION (1856) [CEM] Rev. Bernardine Nganzi (Uganda).
Mailing Address: 1006 Collins, Lawrenceville, 62439. Tel: 618-943-5255. Email: slfxic@shawneelink.net.
Catechesis/Religious Program—Students 18.

CAHOKIA, ST. CLAIR CO.
1—ST. CATHERINE LABOURE (1959) Closed. For inquiries for parish records contact the chancery.
2—HOLY FAMILY (1699) [CEM 3] Rev. Paul R. Wienhoff.
Res.: 116 Church St., 62206. Tel: 618-337-4548; Fax: 618-332-1699.
School—116 E. First St., 62206. Tel: 618-337-2880; Fax: 618-337-7898. Ms. Lindy Graves, Prin.; Ms. Janet Sickinger, Bookkeeper. Lay Teachers 5; Students 73.
Catechesis/Religious Program—Joint with Sacred Heart, Dupo Students 3.

CAIRO, ALEXANDER CO., ST. PATRICK (1838) [CEM] Rev. John Agbasiere, S.M.M.M. (Nigeria).
Res.: 517 Walnut, Mound City, 62963. Tel: 618-734-2061; Fax: 618-734-9823.
Church: 312 Ninth St., 62914.
Catechesis/Religious Program—Ms. Mary Helen Wissinger, D.R.E.

CARBONDALE, JACKSON CO., ST. FRANCIS XAVIER (1900) Very Rev. Robert B. Flannery.
Res.: 303 S. Poplar St., 62901-2709. Tel: 618-457-4556; Fax: 618-457-7368. Email: sfrancis@globaleyes.net. Web: wwwstfx.org.
Catechesis/Religious Program—Ms. Toni Intravaia, D.R.E. Students 102.

CARLYLE, CLINTON CO., ST. MARY (1853) [CEM], (Immaculate Conception) Rev. George A. Mauck.
Res.: 1171 Jefferson St., Box 179, 62231. Tel: 618-594-2225; Fax: 618-594-4638. Email: stmary@sbcglobal.net. Web: www.carlylecatholicchurch.com.
Catechesis/Religious Program—Tel: 618-594-2284. Ms. Ellen Knolhoff, D.R.E. Students 257.

CARMI, WHITE CO., ST. POLYCARP (GERMAN) (1847) [CEM] Rev. Stephen A. Rudolphi.
Res.: 209 Fourth St., 62821. Tel: 618-382-7732. Email: wccath@verizon.net.
Catechesis/Religious Program—Students 22.

CARTERVILLE, WILLIAMSON CO., CHURCH OF THE HOLY SPIRIT (1974) Very Rev. Robert B. Flannery, Canonical Pastor; Rev. Pattinikuttige Kingsley Nonis, Sacramental Min.; Sr. Carol Karnitsky, SSCM, Parish Life Coord.
Office: 300 N. Pine St., 62918. Tel: 618-985-2900; 618-925-5099. Email: holyspirit300@verizon.net.
Catechesis/Religious Program—Tel: 618-985-6929. Students 75.

CASEYVILLE, ST. CLAIR CO., ST. STEPHEN (1893) Rev. Joseph C. Rascher.
Res.: 901 S. Main St., P.O. Box 458, 62232. Tel: 618-397-0666; Fax: 618-397-4430. Email: ststephenoffice@charterinternet.com. Web: www.ststephencaseyville.org.
Catechesis/Religious Program—Email: ststephencarolyn@charterinternet.com. Students 43.

CENTRALIA, MARION CO., ST. MARY (1857) [CEM] Rev. Justin Olisaemeka (Nigeria), Admin.
Rectory—645 S. Lincoln Blvd., 62801. Tel: 618-532-5041; Fax: 618-532-4758. Email: parish@stmarycentralia.org.
Church Office: 424 E. Broadway, 62801. Tel: 618-532-6291.
School—Tel: 618-532-3473; Fax: 618-532-5180. Mrs. Helen Donsbach, Prin. Lay Teachers 6; Students 93.
Catechesis/Religious Program—Sr. Annette Kaba, O.S.F., D.R.E. Students 29.

CENTREVILLE, ST. CLAIR CO., IMMACULATE CONCEPTION (1858) [CEM] Closed. For inquiries for parish records contact the chancery.

CHESTER, RANDOLPH CO., ST. MARY HELP OF CHRISTIANS (1842) [CEM] Rev. Eugene H. Wojcik.
Res.: 911 Swanwick St., 62233. Tel: 618-826-2444; Fax: 618-826-2444.
School—Tel: 618-826-3120; Fax: 618-826-3486. Mrs. Janelle Robinson, Prin. Email: stmarychester@hotmail.com. Web: www.stmaryschester.com. Lay Teachers 10; Preschool 26; Students (K-8) 79.
Catechesis/Religious Program—Tel: 618-826-2526. Ms. Cheryl Gross, D.R.E. Students 23.

CHRISTOPHER, FRANKLIN CO., ST. ANDREW (1905) [CEM] Rev. Steven F. Poole.
Res.: 412 E. Washington St., 62822. Tel: 618-724-4114; Fax: 618-724-4114. Email: standrew@11.net. Web: www.standrewandmary.org.
Catechesis/Religious Program—Ms. Tammy Valette, D.R.E. Students 42.

COBDEN, UNION CO., ST. JOSEPH (1883) [CEM] Rev. Uriel Salamanca Cipagauta; Deacon Patrick Patterson.
Res.: 101 Centennial St., P.O. Box 237, 62920. Tel: 618-893-2276. Email: stjoseph2005@verizon.net.
Catechesis/Religious Program—Tel: 618-893-2368. Students 102.

COLUMBIA, MONROE CO., IMMACULATE CONCEPTION OF THE B.V.M. (1846) [CEM] Rev. Msgr. Carl E. Scherrer; Rev. Steve Gira, C.R.
Res.: 117 E. Madison, 62236. Tel: 618-281-5105; Fax: 618-281-6848. Web: www.ics-columbia-il.us.
School—321 S. Metter, 62236. Tel: 618-281-5353; Fax: 618-281-6044. Email: mkish@htc.net. Web: www.ics.k12.il.us. Mr. Michael Kish, Prin. Lay Teachers 21; Students 297.
Catechesis/Religious Program—Students 189.

COULTERVILLE, RANDOLPH CO., ST. ANTHONY, Closed. For inquiries for parish records contact the chancery.

DAHLGREN, HAMILTON CO., ST. JOHN NEPOMUCENE (1893), (German), [CEM] Rev. Msgr. Joseph A. Lawlor; Rev. Slawomir Ptak (Poland).
Church: 7th & Main Sts., P.O. Box 220, 62828. Tel: 618-736-2878; 618-643-3552. Email: catholic@hamiltoncom.net. Web: www.hamiltoncom.net/~catholic.
Res.: Rte. 3, Box 170, McLeansboro, 62859. Tel: 618-648-2490.
Catechesis/Religious Program—Ms. Amy Wade, D.R.E. Students 35.

DAMIANSVILLE, CLINTON CO., ST. DAMIAN (1861), (German—Hispanic), [CEM] Rev. Msgr. Donald W. Eichenseer.
One W. Main St., 62215. Tel: 618-248-5134; Fax: 618-248-5134. Email: stdamian@plantnet.com.
Res.: 202 N. Broadway, Albers, 62215. Tel: 618-248-5112; Fax: 618-248-5112.
Catechesis/Religious Program—Students 84.

DU QUOIN, PERRY CO., SACRED HEART OF JESUS (1863) [CEM] Unassigned.
Res.: 17 N. Walnut St., 62832. Tel: 618-542-3423; Fax: 618-542-5061. Email: lsherman@egyptian.net.
Catechesis/Religious Program—Students 21.

DUBOIS, WASHINGTON CO., ST. CHARLES BORROMEO (1877) [CEM] Rev. Oliver Nwachukwu, Admin.
Res.: 223 S. 3rd. St., P.O. Box 6, 62831. Tel: 618-787-2781; Fax: 618-787-2171. Email: nwaodike@yahoo.com.
Catechesis/Religious Program—Students 8.

DUPO, ST. CLAIR CO., SACRED HEART OF JESUS (1914) Rev. Paul R. Wienhoff.
100 S. 3rd St., P.O. Box 35, 62239. Tel: 618-286-3224.
Catechesis/Religious Program—Tel: 618-337-4548.

EAST ST. LOUIS, ST. CLAIR CO.
1—ST. AUGUSTINE OF HIPPO (2006) Rev. Carroll Mizicko, O.F.M.
408 Columbia Pl., East Saint Louis, 62205. Email: staugustineofhippo@sbcglobal.net.
Catechesis/Religious Program—Ms. Diane Sonnemann, D.R.E. Students 49.
Chapel—Sister Thea Bowman Chapel 8313 Church Ln., East Saint Louis, 62203.
2—IMMACULATE CONCEPTION (1895), (Lithuanian), Rev. Kenneth J. York, Admin.
1509 Baugh Ave., 62205. Tel: 618-874-0162.

ELDORADO, SALINE CO., ST. MARY (1900) [CEM] Rev. Ignatius Okonkwo.
Parish Center/Office: 1158 N. 2nd St., 62930. Tel: 618-273-6947; Fax: 618-273-3134. Email: stmarys1@clearwave.com.
Catechesis/Religious Program—Students 65.

ELIZABETHTOWN, HARDIN CO., ST. JOSEPH (1897) [CEM] Rev. Ignatius Okonkwo.
Res.: IL 146-185 E Rd., Box 140, 62931-9711. Tel: 618-285-3332.
Catechesis/Religious Program—Tel: 618-287-4824. Students 16.

ELLIS GROVE, RANDOLPH CO., DIVINE MATERNITY OF THE B.V.M. (1933) Deacon Omer E. DuBois.
Res.: 7362 Shawneetown Tr., 62241. Tel: 618-859-3541.
Catechesis/Religious Program—Students 68.

ENFIELD, WHITE CO., ST. PATRICK (1830), (Irish), [CEM] Rev. Stephen A. Rudolphi.
St. Polycarp Church & Office: 209 Fourth St., Carmi, 62821. Tel: 618-382-7732. Email: wccath@verizon.net.
Catechesis/Religious Program—Tel: 618-963-2431. Students 13.

EQUALITY, GALLATIN CO., ST. JOSEPH (1873) [CEM] Rev. Mark D. Stec.
Mailing Address: P.O. Box 99, 62934. Tel: 618-276-4252. Email: stjoe@shawneelink.com. Web: www.gallatincountycatholics.org.
Res.: P.O. Box 190, Ridgway, 62979. Tel: 618-272-7059; Fax: 618-272-5400.
Catechesis/Religious Program—Students 9.

EVANSVILLE, RANDOLPH CO., ST. BONIFACE (1860) [CEM] Rev. Rafi Kuttukaran.
Res.: 1007 Olive St., 62242. Tel: 618-853-4453; Fax: 618-853-4453. Email: sbonifce@htc.net.
Catechesis/Religious Program—Students 45.

FAIRFIELD, WAYNE CO., ST. EDWARD (1881) Rev. Michael Mbonu, Admin.
Res.: 300 N.W. 5th St., 62837. Tel: 618-847-7931; Fax: 618-842-7393. Email: stedseb@fairfieldwireless.net.
Catechesis/Religious Program—Ms. Peggy Garrison, C.R.E. Students 32.

FAIRMONT CITY, ST. CLAIR CO., HOLY ROSARY (1922) Rev. David M. Wilke, Pastor.
Res.: 2716 N. 42nd St., 62201. Tel: 618-274-3486; Fax: 618-274-1814.
Catechesis/Religious Program—Students 150.

FAIRVIEW HEIGHTS, ST. CLAIR CO., HOLY TRINITY CATHOLIC CHURCH (1951) Very Rev. Raymond C. Schultz.
505 Fountains Pkwy., 62208.
Rectory—9879 Old Lincoln Tr., 62208. Tel: 618-628-8825; Fax: 618-628-8866. Web: www.holytrinityil.org.
School—504 Fountains Pkwy., 62208. Tel: 618-628-7395; Fax: 618-628-1570. Mr. Michael Oslance, Prin. Students 192.
Catechesis/Religious Program—Email: htdre@sbcglobal.net. Students 92.

FAYETTEVILLE, ST. CLAIR CO., ST. PANCRATIUS (1837) [CEM] Revs. Kenneth J. York; Edward Hauf, O.M.I.
Res.: 2213 N. 2nd St., 62258. Tel: 618-677-2717.
Catechesis/Religious Program—Students 7.

FLORA, CLAY CO., ST. STEPHEN (1854) [CEM] Rev. Martin E. Ohajunwa (Nigeria), Pastoral Admin.
Res.: 812 N. Main St., 62839. Tel: 618-662-6261; Fax: 618-662-8121. Email: ststephen_flora@yahoo.com. Web: www.floracatholic.com.
Catechesis/Religious Program—Tel: 618-662-8121. Students 34.

FREEBURG, ST. CLAIR CO., ST. JOSEPH (1857) [CEM] Rev. Mark D. Reyling.
Res.: 9 N. Alton St., 62243. Tel: 618-539-3209; Fax: 618-539-4772. Web: www.stjoefreeburg.org.
School—(Grades K-8), 2 N. Alton St., 62243. Tel: 618-539-3930. Email: office@stjosephfreeburg.org. Web: www.stjosephfreeburg.org. Ms. Kimberly Ruef, Prin.; Ms. Julie Neuner, Librarian. Students 95.
Catechesis/Religious Program—Students 138.

GERMANTOWN, CLINTON CO., ST. BONIFACE (1837) [CEM] Rev. Msgr. James A. Buerster; Deacon Richard Bagby.
Res.: 402 Munster St., Box 280, 62245. Tel: 618-523-4271; Fax: 618-523-4263. Email: stboniface@charter.net.
Catechesis/Religious Program—Email: stbonifaceff@charter.net. Students 365.

GRAND CHAIN, PULASKI CO., ST. CATHERINE (1891) [CEM] Rev. John Agbasiere, S.M.M.M. (Nigeria).
517 N. Walnut St., Box 67, Mound City, 62963. Tel: 618-748-9113; Fax: 618-748-9260.
Catechesis/Religious Program—

HARRISBURG, SALINE CO., ST. MARY (1907) [CEM] Rev. Ignatius Okonkwo.
2000 W. Poplar St., 62946.
Res.: 1158 N. 2nd St, Eldorado, 62930.
Office: 2000 W. Poplar St., 62946. Tel: 618-253-7408; Fax: 618-252-7874. Email: stmaryhb@shawneelink.net.
Catechesis/Religious Program—Tel: 618-252-7874. Students 62.

HECKER, MONROE CO., ST. AUGUSTINE OF CANTERBURY (1824) [CEM] Rev. Robert D. Gore.
Res.: 310 N. Main St., P.O. Box 126, 62248. Tel: 618-473-2217; Fax: 618-473-9141. Email: staug@htc.net.

HERRIN, WILLIAMSON CO., OUR LADY OF MOUNT CARMEL (1900) [CEM] Rev. Msgr. Kenneth J. Schaefer.
Res.: 316 W. Monroe St., 62948. Tel: 618-942-3114;

Fax: 618-988-1375. Email: belpolmc@shawneelink.net.
School—Tel: 618-942-4484; Fax: 618-942-2864. Ms. Cheryl Patterson-Dreyer, Prin. Lay Teachers 16; Students 266.
Catechesis/Religious Program—Students 68.

JOHNSTON CITY, WILLIAMSON CO., ST. PAUL (1904) Rev. Msgr. Kenneth Schaefer; Sr. Catherine Wellinghoff, A.S.C., Parish Life Coord.
1103 Washington Ave., 62951. Tel: 618-983-5073. Email: stpaulcc@gmail.com.
Catechesis/Religious Program—Students 25.

KASKASKIA, RANDOLPH CO., IMMACULATE CONCEPTION (1675), (French—Native American), [CEM], (Independent Mission), Mailing Address: 6450 Klein Ln., St. Mary's, MO 63673. Tel: 618-366-2633; Fax: 618-826-2667. Email: elyons@pdwrup.net.

KINMUNDY, MARION CO., ST. ELIZABETH ANN SETON (1878) Mr. Darren Eultgen, Parish Life Coord.; Rev. James P. Thomas, Sacramental Min.
Mailing Address: 812 W. Main St., Salem, 62881. Tel: 618-548-0899; Fax: 618-548-0269. Email: st.theresa@gosalem.com. Web: www.holywomen.org.
Catechesis/Religious Program—N. Madison St., 62854. Tel: 618-245-6221. Ms. Mary Kay Sigrist, D.R.E. Students 8.

LAWRENCEVILLE, LAWRENCE CO., ST. LAWRENCE (1909) [JC] Rev. Bernardine Nganzi (Uganda).
Res.: 1006 Collins, 62439. Tel: 618-943-5255.
Catechesis/Religious Program—Students 50.

LEBANON, ST. CLAIR CO., ST. JOSEPH (1862) [CEM] Rev. Msgr. James E. Margason, Canonical Pastor; Rev. Eugene J. Neff, Sacramental Min.; Deacon Peter Cerneka III; Mrs. Brenda Pehle, Parish Life Coord.
901 N. Alton St., 62254. Tel: 618-537-2221; 618-537-2575; Fax: 618-537-0147. Email: lebstjbp@sbcglobal.net.
Catechesis/Religious Program—Students 26.

LIVELY GROVE, WASHINGTON CO., ST. ANTHONY (1868) [CEM] Rev. Dennis F. Voss.
Church: 6101 St. Anthony Church Rd., Oakdale, 62268. Tel: 618-824-6271; Fax: 618-768-4921.
Catechesis/Religious Program—Students 30.

MADONNAVILLE, MONROE CO., IMMACULATE CONCEPTION (1833) Rev. Jose K. Jacob, S.M.M.
Mailing Address: 5676 LL Rd., Waterloo, 62298. Tel: 618-935-2247.
Catechesis/Religious Program—Students 7.

MARION, WILLIAMSON CO., ST. JOSEPH (1940) Rev. Msgr. Thomas D. Flach.
Res.: 600 N. Russell St., 62959. Tel: 618-993-3194; Fax: 618-997-9391. Email: rgm13@midamer.net. Web: www.stjosephmarion.org.
Catechesis/Religious Program—Tel: 618-997-7373. Mr. William T. Harper III, D.R.E. Students 186.

MARYDALE, CLINTON CO., ST. TERESA OF AVILA (1919) Revs. George A. Mauck, Canonical Pastor; Lawrence M. Nickels, O.F.M., Sacramental Min.; Deacons Charles Litteken, Admin.; John Hempen.
18021 Marydale Rd., Carlyle, 62231. Tel: 618-594-3266. Email: stteresa@papadocs.com.
Catechesis/Religious Program—Students 44.

MASCOUTAH, ST. CLAIR CO., HOLY CHILDHOOD OF JESUS (1857) [CEM] Rev. Msgr. Jerome D. Hartlein.
Res.: 104 N. Independence St., P.O. Box 160, 62258. Tel: 618-566-2958; Fax: 618-566-4447. Email: holychildhoodchurch@cbnstl.com. Web: www.holychildhoodchurch.com.
School—215 N. John St., 62258. Tel: 618-566-2922; Fax: 618-566-2720. Email: hcs@holychildhoodschool.com. Web: www.holychildhoodschool.com. Mr. Ronald Karcher, Prin. Lay Teachers 12; Students 151.
Catechesis/Religious Program—Students 109.

MCLEANSBORO, HAMILTON CO., ST. CLEMENT (1881), (German), [CEM] Rev. Msgr. Joseph A. Lawler; Rev. Slawomir Ptak (Poland).
Res.: 103 N. Hancock, 62859. Tel: 618-643-3552; 618-648-2490; Fax: 618-643-3112. Email: catholic@hamiltoncom.net. Web: www.hamiltoncom.net/~catholic.
Catechesis/Religious Program—Tel: 618-643-4400. Students 70.

METROPOLIS, MASSAC CO., ST. ROSE OF LIMA (1872) Rev. Christopher Michael Mujule (Uganda).
Res.: 315 E. Third St., 62960-2229. Tel: 618-524-9006; Fax: 618-524-9006. Email: strosechurch@comcast.net. Web: www.strosemetropolis.com.
Catechesis/Religious Program—405 E. Third St., 62960. Tel: 618-524-8202. Students 23.

MILLSTADT, ST. CLAIR CO., ST. JAMES (1851) [CEM] Rev. Msgr. Marvin C. Volk; Deacon Ronald Karcher.
Res.: 405 W. Madison St., 62260. Tel: 618-476-3513; Fax: 618-476-1281. Email: stjrectory@htc.net.
School—Tel: 618-476-3510. Email: principalstj@htc.net. Web: www.stjames.pvt.k12.il.us. Mrs. Rebecca Chell, Prin. Sisters 1; Lay Teachers 10; Students 116.
Catechesis/Religious Program—Tel: 618-476-1923. Students 132.

MODOC, RANDOLPH CO., ST. LEO (1893) [CEM] Very Rev. Daniel J. Jurek.
5895 St. Leo Rd., 62261. Tel: 618-284-3314; Fax: 618-284-3314. Mailing Address: 802 Middle St., P.O. Box 365, Prairie Du Rocher, 62277-0365.

MOUND CITY, PULASKI CO., CHURCH OF THE IMMACULATE CONCEPTION-ST. MARY (1863) [CEM] Rev. John Agbasiere, S.M.M.M. (Nigeria).
Res.: 517 N. Walnut St., P.O. Box 67, 62963. Tel: 618-748-9113; Fax: 618-748-9260. Email: rcchurch-pastorstmpc@yahoo.com.
Catechesis/Religious Program—Students 6.

MOUNT CARMEL, WABASH CO., ST. MARY (1836) [CEM] Rev. William J. Rowe; Deacon Charles Speaks.
Res.: 125 W. Fifth St., 62863. Tel: 618-262-5337; Fax: 618-262-5333. Email: smsparish@hotmail.com.
School—417 Chestnut St., 62863. Tel: 618-263-3183; Fax: 618-263-3596. Mrs. Alice Wirth, Prin. Lay Teachers 13; Students 132.
Catechesis/Religious Program—Students 40.

MOUNT VERNON, JEFFERSON CO., ST. MARY (1871) [CEM] Rev. John C. Iffert, Admin.
Res.: 115 N. 14th St., 62864. Tel: 618-244-1559; Fax: 618-244-1793. Email: saintmary@mvn.net. Web: www.saintmary.mvn.net.
School—1416 Main St., 62864. Tel: 618-242-5353; Fax: 618-242-5365. Mr. Brett Heinzman, Prin. Lay Teachers 10; Students 140.
Catechesis/Religious Program—Students 238.

MURPHYSBORO, JACKSON CO., ST. ANDREW (1868) [CEM] Rev. Gary P. Gummersheimer; Deacon Don Sparling, Pastoral Assoc.
Res.: 724 Mulberry St., 62966. Tel: 618-687-2012; Fax: 618-684-3431.
School—723 Mulberry St., 62966. Tel: 618-687-2013; Fax: 618-684-4969. Email: nborgsmiller@neondsl.com. Web: saintandrewschool.org. Ms. Nancy Borgmiller, Prin. Lay Teachers 14; Students 138.
Catechesis/Religious Program—Email: cre@stamboro.org. Paulette Sparling, C.R.E. Students 40.

NASHVILLE, WASHINGTON CO., ST. ANN (1874) [CEM] Rev. Andrew J. Knopik.
Res.: 631 S. Mill St., 62263. Tel: 618-327-3232; Fax: 618-327-4904.
Parish Office: 695 S. Mill St., 62263.
School—Tel: 618-327-8741. Mrs. Bonnie Paszkiewicz, Prin. Lay Teachers 9; Students 97.
Catechesis/Religious Program—Students 45.

NEW ATHENS, ST. CLAIR CO., ST. AGATHA (1870) [CEM] Very Rev. James M. Nall.
Res.: 205 S. Market St., 62264. Tel: 618-475-2331; Fax: 618-475-3177.
School—207 S. Market St., 62264. Tel: 618-475-2170; Fax: 618-475-3177. Email: cnewbold@stagathaschool.org. Mrs. Charlotte Newbold, Prin. Lay Teachers 6; Students 54.
Catechesis/Religious Program—Tel: 618-295-2686. Students 27.

NEW BADEN, CLINTON CO., ST. GEORGE (1894) [CEM] Rev. Eugene J. Neff.
Res.: 200 N. 3rd St., 62265. Tel: 618-588-4323; Fax: 618-588-2413. Email: saintg@cbnst1.com. Web: www.stgeorgefamily.org.
Catechesis/Religious Program—Students 130.

O'FALLON, ST. CLAIR CO.
1—ST. CLARE (1867) [CEM] Revs. James E. Deiters; Von C. Deeke, Parochial Vicar; Deacon Dennis W. Vander Ven.
Office: 1411 Cross St., 62269.
Res.: 205 W. Third, 62269. Tel: 618-632-3562; Fax: 618-632-9036. Web: www.stclarechurch.org.
School—214 W. 3rd St., 62269. Tel: 618-632-6327; Fax: 618-632-5587. Mr. Ken Pajares, Prin. Lay Teachers 24; Students 412.
Catechesis/Religious Program—Students 182.
2—ST. NICHOLAS (1982) Rev. Msgr. William J. Hitpas; Deacon Richard H. Olson; Ann Daniels, Admin.
Res., Church & Office: 625 St. Nicholas Dr., 62269. Tel: 618-632-1997; 618-632-1797; Fax: 618-632-7703. Email: busadmin@stnicholasofallon.org. Web: www.stnicholasofallon.org.
Catechesis/Religious Program—Tel: 618-632-1137. Email: liturgy@stnicholasofallon.org. Sr. Judith McKenna, Liturgy Director. Tel: 618-632-1007; Ms. Barbara Furdek, D.R.E. Students 310.

OKAWVILLE, WASHINGTON CO., ST. BARBARA (1867) [CEM] Rev. John J. Joyce.
Res.: 305 N. Front St., P.O. Box 106, 62271. Tel: 618-243-6236; Fax: 618-243-5270.
Catechesis/Religious Program—Students 55.

OLNEY, RICHLAND CO., ST. JOSEPH (1857) [CEM] Rev. Jerry E. Wirth.
220 S. Elliott St., 62450.
Res.: 220 S. Elliott St., 62450. Tel: 618-392-6711; 618-392-8181; Fax: 618-395-8500. Email: stjosephchurch_olney@yahoo.com. Web: www.omegabbs.com/stjosephchurch_olney.
School—Tel: 618-395-3081. Ms. Carol Potter, Prin. Lay Teachers 15; Students 103.
Catechesis/Religious Program—Students 50.

PADERBORN, ST. CLAIR CO., ST. MICHAEL (1843), (German), [CEM] Rev. James A. Voelker, Admin.
Church: 4576 Buss Branch Rd., Waterloo, 62298. Tel: 618-473-2798; Fax: 618-473-9180. Email: stmichaels4@aol.com.
Catechesis/Religious Program—Tel: 618-473-2915. Ms. Jackie Billings, C.R.E. Students 46.

PINCKNEYVILLE, PERRY CO., ST. BRUNO (1872) [CEM] Rev. Brian Barker.
Res.: 204 N. Gordon St., 62274. Tel: 618-357-5510; Fax: 618-357-6050. Web: www.stbrunoparish.org.
School—210 N. Gordon St., 62274. Tel: 618-357-8276; Fax: 618-357-6425. Ms. Sandra Kabat, Prin. Lay Teachers 7; Students 121.
Catechesis/Religious Program—Tel: 618-758-2055. Ms. Kathy Sprehe, D.R.E. Students 65.

PIOPOLIS, HAMILTON CO., ST. JOHN THE BAPTIST (1841) [CEM] Rev. Msgr. Joseph A. Lawler; Rev. Slawomir Ptak (Poland).
Res.: Route 3, Box 170, McLeansboro, 62859. Tel: 618-648-2490. Email: catholic@hamiltoncom.net. Web: www.hamiltoncom.net/~catholic.
Catechesis/Religious Program—Tel: 618-648-2586. Students 82.

POND SETTLEMENT, GALLATIN CO., ST. PATRICK (1842) Rev. Mark D. Stec.
Mailing Address: P.O. Box 579, Shawneetown, 62984. Tel: 618-269-3318; Fax: 618-272-5400.
Catechesis/Religious Program—Tel: 618-272-7059; Fax: 618-277-7059. Students 6.

POSEN, WASHINGTON CO., OUR LADY OF PERPETUAL HELP (1901) [CEM] Rev. Bernard C. Goedde Jr.
Res.: 19824 Posen Rd., Nashville, 62263-6122. Tel: 618-327-3556; Fax: 618-327-3556.
Catechesis/Religious Program—Students 6.

PRAIRIE DU ROCHER, RANDOLPH CO., ST. JOSEPH (1721) [CEM] Very Rev. Daniel J. Jurek.
Res.: 802 Middle St., 62277. Tel: 618-284-3314.
Catechesis/Religious Program—Students 81.

RADDLE, JACKSON CO., ST. ANN (1875) Rev. Leo J. Hayes.
101 Raddle Ln., P.O. Box 157, Ava, 62907. Tel: 618-426-3321; Fax: 618-426-3321.
Catechesis/Religious Program—Tel: 618-965-3621. Students 4.

RADOM, WASHINGTON CO., ST. MICHAEL (1874), (Polish), [CEM] Rev. Robert J. Zwilling, Admin.
Church: 52 S. Third St., P.O. Box 128, 62876. Fax: 618-485-2272. Email: stmichaelradom@hughes.net.
Res.: 52 S. Third St., P.O. Box 15, 62876. Tel: 618-485-2265. Email: Godislove333@hotmail.com.
School—Tel: 618-485-6461. Mrs. Sherri Beckham, Prin. Lay Teachers 5; Students 57.

RED BUD, RANDOLPH CO., ST. JOHN THE BAPTIST (1862) [CEM] Rev. Msgr. Dennis R. Schaefer.
Res.: 515 Locust St., 62278. Tel: 618-282-3222; Fax: 618-282-6867.
School—519 Hazel St., 62278. Tel: 618-282-3215; Fax: 618-282-6790. Web: www.sjbredbud.com. Ms. Kristine Hill, Prin. Lay Teachers 10; Students 111.
Catechesis/Religious Program—Students 98.

RENAULT, MONROE CO., OUR LADY OF GOOD COUNSEL (1879) [CEM] Rev. Roger R. Karban, Admin.
Office: 2038 Washington St., P.O. Box 98, 62279. Tel: 618-458-7710; Fax: 618-458-7710.
Catechesis/Religious Program—Students 16.

RIDGWAY, GALLATIN CO., ST. JOSEPH (1870) [CEM] Rev. Mark D. Stec.
Res.: 205 W. South St., P.O. Box 190, 62979. Tel: 618-272-7059; Fax: 618-272-5400. Email: stjoe@shawneelink.com. Web: www.gallatincountycatholics.org.
Catechesis/Religious Program—Students 45.

ROYALTON-ZEIGLER, FRANKLIN CO., ST. ALOYSIUS/SACRED HEART (1919) [JC] Rev. Trevor Murray; Sr. Laura Reynolds, O.S.F., Pastoral Assoc.
Res.: 212 Pecan St., P.O. Box 100, 62983. Tel: 618-984-2146; Fax: 618-984-2146. Email: srlaura@neonds1.com.
Catechesis/Religious Program—Students 51.

RUMA, RANDOLPH CO., ST. PATRICK (1818) [CEM] Rev. Msgr. Dennis R. Schaefer; Rev. J. Clyde Grogan.
Res.: #1 Pioneer Ln.-Ruma, Red Bud, 62278. Tel: 618-282-3176; Fax: 618-282-3176.

ST. FRANCISVILLE, LAWRENCE CO., ST. FRANCIS XAVIER (1836), (French), [CEM] Rev. Bernardine Nganzi (Uganda).
Mailing Address: 1006 Collins St., Lawrenceville, 62439. Tel: 618-943-5255. Email: slfxic@shawneelink.net.
Catechesis/Religious Program—Students 11.

ST. LIBORY, ST. CLAIR CO., ST. LIBORIUS (1838) [CEM] Rev. Dennis F. Voss; Deacon Andrew Lintker.
Res.: 911 Sparta St., P.O. Box 331, 62282. Tel: 618-768-4921; Fax: 618-768-4207.
Catechesis/Religious Program—Ms. Mona Mense, D.R.E. Students 98.

ST. ROSE, CLINTON CO., ST. ROSE (1868) [CEM] Rev. Edward F. Schaefer.

Res.: 18010 St. Rose Rd., 62230-2506. Tel: 618-526-4118; Fax: 618-526-0004. Email: belpsros@papadocs.com.
Catechesis / Religious Program—Tel: 618-526-4886. Sr. Justina Schaefer, A.S.C., D.R.E. Students 205.

ST. SEBASTIAN, WABASH CO., ST. SEBASTIAN (1871) [CEM] Rev. Michael Mbonu, Admin.
Church: 4921 N. 1400 Blvd., Mount Carmel, 62863. Tel: 618-298-2589.
Res.: 300 N.W. Fifth St., Fairfield, 62837. Tel: 618-847-7931; Fax: 618-842-7393.
Catechesis / Religious Program—Students 62.

SALEM, MARION CO., ST. THERESA OF AVILA (1868) [CEM] Revs. John C. Iffert, Admin.; James P. Thomas, Sacramental Min.; Mr. Darren Eultgen, Parish Life Coord.
Res.: 719 Markland St., 62881. Tel: 618-548-5098; Fax: 618-548-0269. Email: sttheresa@gosalem.com. Web: www.holywomen.org.
School—190 Ohio St., 62881. Tel: 618-548-3492; Fax: 618-548-9673. Email: rascals@ussonet.net. Web: www.sttheresagradeschool.com. Sr. Margaret Schmidt, S.S.N.D., Prin. Lay Teachers 5; Students 50.
Catechesis / Religious Program—Ms. Denise McGormack, D.R.E. Students 15.

SANDOVAL, MARION CO., ST. LAWRENCE (1871) [CEM] Rev. Msgr. James A. Buerster, Canonical Pastor; Rev. Justin Olisaemeka (Nigeria), Sacramental Min.; Cindy M. Eultgen, Parish Life Coord.
Mailing Address: P.O. Box 278, 62882.
Office: 412 N. Vine St., P.O. Box 278, 62882.
Church: 311 W. Missouri St., 62882. Tel: 618-247-3300; Fax: 618-247-3300. Email: stlawrence@frontiernet.net. Web: www.saintlawrencesandoval.org.
Catechesis / Religious Program—Students 17.

SCHELLER, JEFFERSON CO., ST. BARBARA (1898) Rev. Robert J. Zwilling, Parochial Admin.
4281 N. Scheller Ln., 62883. Tel: 618-279-7207; Fax: 618-279-7207. Email: godislove333@otmail.com.
Catechesis / Religious Program—Students 40.

SESSER, FRANKLIN CO., ST. MARY (1909) Rev. Steven F. Poole, Admin.
Church: 100 N. Poplar St., P.O. Box 568, 62884. Tel: 618-625-5053.
Res.: 412 E. Washington St., Christopher, 62822. Tel: 618-724-4114.
Catechesis / Religious Program—Students 21.

SHAWNEETOWN, GALLATIN CO., ST. MARY (1842) [CEM] Rev. Mark D. Stec.
Mailing Address: 655 W. Marshall St., P.O. Box 579, 62984. Tel: 618-269-3318; Fax: 618-272-5400. Email: stjoe@shawneelink.com. Web: www.gallatincountycatholics.org.
Catechesis / Religious Program—Tel: 618-272-7059. Students 19.

SHILOH, ST. CLAIR CO., CORPUS CHRISTI (1913) Rev. Msgr. James E. Margason.
Res.: 206 Rasp St., 62269. Tel: 618-632-7614; Fax: 618-632-7614.
Catechesis / Religious Program—Tel: 618-632-7614. Students 75.

SMITHTON, ST. CLAIR CO., ST. JOHN THE BAPTIST (1867) [CEM] Rev. Gerald R. Hechenberger; Deacon Donald R. Deitz.
Res.: 10 S. Lincoln St., 62285-1614. Tel: 618-234-2068; Fax: 618-234-0179.
School—Tel: 618-233-0581. Web: www.stjohnschool.us. Ms. Jennifer Miller, Prin. Lay Teachers 10; Students 70.
Catechesis / Religious Program—Students 130.

SPARTA, RANDOLPH CO., OUR LADY OF LOURDES (1897) Rev. Lawrence Mariasossai, O.M.I., Parochial Admin.
Res.: 611 W. Broadway, 62286. Tel: 618-443-2811. Web: www.ollandspv.com.
Catechesis / Religious Program—Tel: 618-443-2878. Ms. Lila Lehnherr, D.R.E. Students 33.

STONEFORT, WILLIAMSON CO., ST. FRANCIS DE SALES (1879) Rev. Thomas M. Barrett.
Mailing Address: 2020 State Rte. 146 E., P.O. Box 1325, Vienna, 62995. Tel: 618-658-4501. Email: spccil@verizon. et. Students attend Vie.

STRINGTOWN, RICHLAND CO., ST. JOSEPH (1841) [CEM], Mailing Address: 6004 N. Shell Rd., Olney, 62450. Tel: 618-752-5671 (Res.); 618-754-3676; Fax: 618-754-3356. Email: stjoestringtown@hotmail.com. Web: www.stringtown.org.
Church: 6342 N. Stringtown Rd., Olney, 62450.
Catechesis / Religious Program—Tel: 618-754-3049. Ms. Donna Zwilling, C.R.E. Students 40.

TAMAROA, PERRY CO., IMMACULATE CONCEPTION (1904) Rev. Oliver Nwachukwu, Admin.
Res.: 533 W. 2nd North St., 62888. Tel: 618-496-5867. Email: immaculateconception@frontiernet.net.
Catechesis / Religious Program—Tel: 618-496-3100. Students 8.

TIPTON, MONROE CO., ST. PATRICK (1850) [CEM] Rev. Jose K. Jacob, S.M.M.
Res.: 5675 LL Rd., Waterloo, 62298. Tel: 618-458-6875; Fax: 618-458-6875.
Catechesis / Religious Program—Students 7.

TODDS MILL, PERRY CO., ST. MARY MAGDALEN (1868) [CEM] Rev. Bernard C. Goedde Jr.
5047 Todds Mill Rd., Pinckneyville, 62274-2235.
Res. & Business Office: 19824 Posen Rd., Nashville, 62263-6122. Tel: 618-327-3556; Fax: 618-327-3556. Email: olph-smm@hughes.net.
Catechesis / Religious Program—Students 3.

TRENTON, CLINTON CO., ST. MARY (1858), (German), [CEM] Rev. Eugene A. Kreher; Sr. Angela J. Schrage, A.S.C., Pastoral Assoc. & D.R.E.; Deacon John P. Dilley.
Res.: 215 W. Kentucky St., 62293. Tel: 618-224-9335; Fax: 618-224-9346. Web: www.stmarytrenton.com.
Office: 218 W. Kentucky St., 62293. Email: stmary@stmarytrenton.com. Web: www.stmarytrenton.com.
Catechesis / Religious Program—Students 145.

ULLIN, PULASKI CO., OUR LADY OF FATIMA (1949) [CEM] Closed. For inquiries for parish records contact the chancery.

VALMEYER, MONROE CO., SEVEN DOLORS OF THE B.V.M. (1921) Rev. Urban Osuji, C.M.
Res.: 101 S. Meyer Ave., 62295. Tel: 618-935-2247; Fax: 618-935-2410. Email: urbanosuji@yahoo.co.uk; smoffice@htc.net (Office).
Catechesis / Religious Program—Ms. Karen Limestall, D.R.E. Students 79.

VIENNA, JOHNSON CO., ST. PAUL (1895) [JC] Rev. Thomas M. Barrett.
Res.: 2020 State Rte. 146 E., P.O. Box 1325, 62995. Tel: 618-658-4501.
Catechesis / Religious Program—Tel: 618-658-4701. Ms. Madonna Slife, C.R.E. Students 14.

WALSH, RANDOLPH CO., ST. PIUS V (1905) Rev. Lawrence Mariasoosai, O.M.I.
7681 Walsh Rd., 62297. Tel: 618-853-4404. Email: stpius@accessus.net.
Catechesis / Religious Program—Students 14.

WASHINGTON PARK, ST. CLAIR CO., ST. MARTIN OF TOURS, Closed. For inquiries for parish records contact the chancery.

WATERLOO, MONROE CO., SS. PETER AND PAUL (1843) [CEM] Revs. Osang Idagbo, C.M. (Nigeria), Admin.; Stan J. Konieczny; Deacon Douglas L. Boyer, Admin.; Ms. Karen Seaborn, Pastoral Assoc.
Res.: 204 W. Mill St., 62298. Tel: 618-939-6426; Fax: 618-939-2011.
School—Tel: 618-939-7217; Fax: 618-939-5994. Ms. Lisa Buchheit, Prin. Lay Teachers 24; Students 380.
Catechesis / Religious Program—Ms. Anita Toth, D.R.E. Students 300.

WENDELIN, CLAY CO., HOLY CROSS (1870) [CEM]
Res.: 5782 Ingraham Ln., Newton, 62448. Tel: 618-752-5671; Fax: 618-752-6006.
Catechesis / Religious Program—Ms. Melissa Weber, C.R.E.; Ms. Joyce Reis, C.R.E. Students 122.

WEST FRANKFORT, FRANKLIN CO., ST. JOHN THE BAPTIST (1916) [CEM] Rev. Trevor K. Murry.
Res.: 703 E. Main St., 62896. Tel: 618-932-2828; Fax: 618-932-2828. Email: stjohnthebaptist@mchsi.com.
School—Tel: 618-937-2017; Fax: 618-937-2287. Mr. Kevin Spiller, Prin. Franciscan Sisters of Our Lady of Perpetual Help 2; Lay Teachers 8; Students 93.
Catechesis / Religious Program—Sr. Laura Reynolds, O.S.F., D.R.E. Students 10.

WILLISVILLE, PERRY CO., ST. JOSEPH (1903) [CEM] Rev. Leo J. Hayes.
Mailing Address: 606 W. George St., Ava, 62907. Tel: 618-426-3321.
Catechesis / Religious Program—Tel: 618-965-3621; Fax: 618-426-3321. Students 23.

ZEIGLER, FRANKLIN CO., SACRED HEART, Merged with St. Aloysius, Royalton to form St. Aloysius/Sacred Heart, Royalton-Zeigler.

SACRAMENTAL RECORDS LOCATED IN CHANCERY ARCHIVES:
ST. ADALBERT CHURCH, EAST ST. LOUIS—
St. Anthony, Coulterville—
St. Augustine Church, East St. Louis—
SS. Cyril and Methodius Church, East St. Louis—
St. Elizabeth Church, East St. Louis—
St. Henry Church, East St. Louis—
Holy Angels Church, East St. Louis—
Immaculate Conception, Centreville—
Immaculate Conception, East St. Louis—
Immaculate Conception, Kaskaskia—
St. John Francis Regis, East St. Louis—
St. John's Orphanage, Belleville—
St. Joseph Church, Wetaug—
St. Joseph, East St. Louis—
St. Martin of Tours, Washington Park—
St. Mary Church, East St. Louis—
Our Lady of Fatima, Ullin—
St. Patrick, East St. Louis—
St. Philip, East St. Louis—
Sacred Heart Church, East St. Louis—
St. Catherine Labourne, Cahokia—
St. Thomas Church, Millstadt—

Chaplains of Correctional Institutions and State Hospitals

ANNA. *Anna State Hospital*. Vacant. Attended from St. Mary Church, Anna.

CENTRALIA. *Centralia Correctional Center*, P.O. Box 1266, 62801. Rev. George A. Mauck.

CHESTER. *Chester Mental Health Center*, P.O. Box 31, 62233. Tel: 618-826-4571.

HARRISBURG. *Illinois Youth Center*, P.O. Box 300, 62946. Vacant.

INA. *Big Muddy River Correctional Center*. Very Rev. Daniel J. Jurek, V.F.

MARION. *Federal Maximum Security Prison*, P.O. Box 2000, 62959. Deacon Pat Patterson, Chap. Tel: 618-964-1441.
Veterans Hospital. Attended from St. Joseph, Marion.

MENARD. *Menard Correctional Center*, P.O. Box 711, 62259. Vacant. Tel: 618-826-5071.

VIENNA. *Dixon Springs Work Camp* 62995. Vacant.
Shawnee Correctional Center, Box 400, 62995. Rev. Christian Reuter, O.F.M.
Vienna Correctional Center. Rev. Christian Reuter, O.F.M.

Military Chaplains:
Revs.—
Gegotek, Tadeusz, U.S.N.R.
Voelker, David A., U.S.A.F.

Special Assignment:
Rev.—
Geller, Charles H., Fort Stockton, TX

Leave of Absence:
Revs.—
Harbaugh, Paul E.
Higgins, John
Lemay, Larry
O'Guinn, Jon
Ruppert, Alan E.
Sebescak, Gary
Unverferth, Steven R.
Witte, Steven D.

Retired:
Most Rev.—
Schlarman, Stanley G., D.D., Fiat House, 113 N. Ottawa, Joliet, 60432. Tel: 618-277-6814
Rev. Msgrs.—
Blazine, James A.
Dobkowski, Paulin J., Hincke Residence for Priests, 2620 Lebanon Ave., 62221.
Haselhorst, Vincent, Hincke Residence, 2620 Lebanon Ave., 62221.
Schwaegel, Joseph R., 222 S. Third St., 62220. (On Leave)
Revs.—
Balestrieri, Edward, (On Leave)
Blaes, Donald A., 205 N. 3rd St., New Baden, 62265.
Chlopecki, Robert J., (On Leave)
Crook, David G., (On Leave)
Daly, Richard L., Hincke Residence for Priests, 2620 Lebanon Ave., 62221.
Dougherty, James R.
Engelhart, Henry R.
Frerker, Jack W., 7315 Henderson, S.E., Olympia, WA 98501.
Hibner, Jerome H., Rosewood Care Center, 100 Rosewood Village Dr., Swansea, 62226.
Hsu, Peter, 123 S. Pine, Ziegler, 62999.
Humphrey, Steven, 2613 S. 16th St., Saint Louis, MO 63118.
Iffert, Wilbert J., 147 Juniper Dr., Oak Grove Terrace, Mount Vernon, 62864.
Kastner, Edwin H., 222 S. Third St., 62220. (On Leave)
Koehr, Louis, 203 N. Franklin, P.O. Box 56, Albers, 62215-0056.
Kownacki, Raymond F.
Kribs, Charles R., Hincke Residence, 2620 Lebanon Ave., 62221.
Lenzini, Donald J., Hincke Residence for Priests, 2620 Lebanon Ave., 62221.
Linnemann, Eugene C., (On Leave)
Long, James T.
Lopardo, Vito R., Hincke Residence for Priests, 2620 Lebanon Ave., 62221.
MacPherson, Walter E., 222 S. Third St., 62220. (On Leave)
Miriani, Gerald C., 7158 E. Charro Cir., Tuscan, AZ 85715.
Peterson, Louis P., (On Leave)
Ratermann, Jerome B., 303 Hillcrest Dr., 62286-1203. (On Leave)
Reinhardt, Leo S., Hincke Residence for Priests, 2620 Lebanon Ave., 62221.

Rensing, William F., (On Leave)
Stauder, Paul W., Hincke Residence for Priests, 2620 Lebanon Ave., 62221.
Thoonkuzhy, Joseph (TLS), 6526-E South Memorial Dr., Tulsa, OK 74133.

Permanent Deacons:
Bach, Gerald, Sr.
Bagby, Richard
Becker, Robert H.
Boyer, Douglas
Cerneka, Peter
Coates, John
Dietz, Donald
Dilley, John P.
DuBois, Omer E.
Hampton, Arthur
Hempen, John
Karcher, Ronald
Klostermann, Linus
Lanter, Robert
Lintker, Andrew
Lippert, Robert
Litteken, Charles
Mills, George, Jr.
Munie, George J.
Netemeyer, Glennon J.
Olson, Richard H.
Patterson, Pat
Pautler, Stephen
Rickert, Dennis
Sparling, Don
Speaks, Charles
Stock, Joseph E.
Vander Ven, Dennis W.
Welch, Thomas

INSTITUTIONS LOCATED IN THE DIOCESE

[A] HIGH SCHOOLS, DIOCESAN

BELLEVILLE. *Althoff Catholic High School*, 5401 W. Main St., 62226-4796. Tel: 618-235-1100; Fax: 618-235-9535. Email: althoff@norcom2000.com. Web: www.althoff.net. Mr. David L. Harris, Prin.; Ms. Luann Toennies, Librarian. Lay Teachers 38; Students 472.

BREESE. *Mater Dei High School*, 900 N. Mater Dei Dr., 62230. Tel: 618-526-7216; Fax: 618-526-8310. Email: mda@lcls.org. Web: www.materdei.breese.il.us. Mr. Dennis Litteken, Prin.; Mrs. Maria Zurliene, Asst. Prin.; Rev. Charles W. Tuttle, Dir. Institution Advancement; Ms. Carol Bandre, Librarian. Central Catholic High School for Clinton Co. Priests 1; Lay Teachers 42; Students 518.

WATERLOO. *Gibault Catholic High School*, 501 Columbia Ave., 62298. Tel: 618-939-3883; Fax: 618-939-7215. Email: russhart@htc.net. Web: www.gibaultonline.com. Mr. Russell Hart, Prin.; Ms. Michelle Posey, Librarian. Sisters 2; Teachers 27; Students 236.

[B] ELEMENTARY SCHOOLS

BREESE. *All Saints Academy*, (Grades PreK-8), 295 N. Clinton St., 62230. Tel: 618-526-4323; Fax: 618-526-2547. Email: RobinBooth@asasaints.com. Web: www.asasaints.com. Ms. Robin Booth, Prin.; Ms. Jane Klostermann, Librarian; Ms. Marietta Kuhl, Librarian. Consolidated schools of Saint Augustine, Saint Dominic parishes, Breese, IL, and St. Anthony Parish, Beckemeyer, IL. Lay Teachers 24; Students 342.

EAST ST. LOUIS. *Sister Thea Bowman Catholic School*, (Grades K-8), 8213 Church Ln., 62203. Tel: 618-397-0316; Fax: 618-397-0337. Email: thea_bowman@yahoo.com. Sr. Janet McCann, A.S.C., M.A., Prin. Sisters 3; Lay Teachers 10; Students 105.

FAIRVIEW HEIGHTS. *Holy Trinity Catholic School*, (Grades PreSchool-8), Consolidated schools of St. Stephen Parish, Caseyville, IL; Our Lady of the Assumption Parish, Fairview Heights, IL; St. Albert the Great and Elizabeth Seton School., 504 Fountains Pkwy., 62208. Tel: 618-628-7395; Fax: 618-628-1570. Email: htschool504@sbcglobal.net. Web: www.holytrinitycatholicchurch.com. Mr. Michael Oslance, Prin. Priests 1; Lay Teachers 14; Students 222.

[C] DAY CARE CENTERS

BELLEVILLE. *St. Henry Creative Learning Center* (1980) 5303 W. Main St., 62226. Tel: 618-234-6061; Fax: 618-234-6801. Email: sthdaycare@peaknet.net. Ms. Judy Shovlin, Dir.; Ms. Mary Haas, Co-Dir. Lay Teachers 10; Children 56.

St. John Children's Home, 2620 Lebanon Ave., 62221.

Chancery Office, 222 S. Third St., 62220. Tel: 618-277-8181. Very Rev. John W. McEvilly, V.G.

St. John Day Care Center, 2620 Lebanon Ave., 62221. Tel: 618-235-6717; Fax: 618-235-8485. Email: director79@aol.com. Ms. April Jones, Dir. Lay Women 11; Children 75.

EAST ST. LOUIS. *Catholic Day Care Center* (1973) 617 Summit Ave., 62201. Tel: 618-874-7178; Fax: 618-261-2005. Email: catholicdcc@sbcglobal.net. Nursery and Kindergarten.; Conducted by the Cordi-Marian Sisters.
2417 Ridge Ave., 62205. Tel: 618-875-1447. Email: irenejua@htctech.net. Sr. Gema Juarez, M.C.M., Dir. Brothers 1; Sisters 2; Lay Teachers 4; Children 40.

Cathedral Grade School Early Learning Center, 200 S. 2nd St., 62220. Tel: 618-233-6414. Ms. Patty Birkner, Dir.

[D] GENERAL HOSPITALS

BELLEVILLE. *St. Elizabeth Hospital* (1875) 211 S. Third St., 62220-1998. Tel: 618-234-2120; Fax: 618-222-4650. Web: www.steliz.org. Mr. Kevin Shrake, CEO. Hospital Sisters of the Third Order of St. Francis, Clinically Affiliated with St. Louis University School of Medicine. Sisters 5; Staff 1,673; Bed Capacity 506; Patients Assisted Annually 187,113.

BREESE. *St. Joseph Hospital* (1897) 9515 Holy Cross Ln., 62230. Tel: 618-526-4511; Fax: 618-526-8022. Email: sniemann@sjb.hshs.org; ljones@sjb.hshs.org. Web: www.stjoebreese.com. Mr. Lowell Jones, CEO; Sr. Dorothy Niemann, S.C.S.C., Pastoral Care. Hospital Sisters of the Third Order of St. Francis. Sisters 2; Staff 418; Bed Capacity 85; Patients Assisted Annually 90,020.

CENTRALIA. **St. Mary's Hospital*, 400 N. Pleasant Ave., 62801. Tel: 618-436-8000; Fax: 618-436-8038. Web: www.smgsi.com. Mr. Bruce A. Merrell, Pres. Felician Sisters 4; Staff 850; Bed Capacity 180; Patients Assisted Annually 139,968.

MOUNT VERNON. **Good Samaritan Regional Health Center*, 605 N. 12th St., 62864. Tel: 618-242-4600; Fax: 618-242-3196. Web: www.smgsi.com. Mr. Mike Warren, Pres.; Mr. Jeffrey Stewart, Dir. Pastoral Care. Member of SSM Health Care. Bed Capacity 161; Staff 1,042; Patients Assisted Annually 106,786.

MURPHYSBORO. *St. Joseph Memorial Hospital*, 2 S. Hospital Dr., 62966. Tel: 618-684-3156; Fax: 618-529-0529. Web: www.sih.net. Mr. Scott Seaborn, Admin.; Sr. Clara Ternes, A.S.C., Corp. Dir. of Missions, Values & Ethics. Adorers of the Blood of Christ., A service of Southern Illinois Healthcare. Sisters 2; Total Staff 250; Bed Capacity 25; Patients Assisted Annually 16,229.

[E] HOMES FOR SENIOR CITIZENS

BELLEVILLE. *Charles and Bertha Hincke Residence for Priests and Sense Residence*, 2620 Lebanon Ave., 62221. Tel: 618-234-5722; Fax: 618-234-5792. Email: hinckehome@aol.com. Ms. Joline Beck, Mgr. Owned by Diocese of Belleville. Guests 16; Staff 8; Bed Capacity 21.

Meredith Memorial Home, 16 S. Illinois St., 62220. Tel: 618-233-8780; Fax: 618-233-9602. Email: sueneuharth@aol.com. Web: www.ccsil.org. Ms. Sue Neuharth, Admin. Owned by the Diocese of Belleville. Total Staff 23; Total Apartments 69; Total Assisted 40.

Our Lady of the Snows Apartment Community Retirement Home, 726 Community Dr., 62223. Tel: 618-394-6400; Fax: 618-394-9051. Email: bob.mccardle@apartmentcommunity.org. Web: apartmentcommunity.org. Mr. D. Robert McCardle, Exec. Vice Pres.; Rev. George Capen, O.M.I. Independent Apartments 125; Skilled Care 57; Assisted Living 38.

[F] MONASTERIES AND RESIDENCES OF PRIESTS AND BROTHERS

BELLEVILLE. *Missionary Oblates of Mary Immaculate - St. Henry's Oblate Residence*, 200 N. 60th St., 62223. Tel: 618-233-2991. Email: sthenryomi@charter.net. Revs. George Capen, O.M.I.; Andrew G. Chalkey, O.M.I.; William Clark, O.M.I.; Rene DuFour, O.M.I.; Urban Figge, O.M.I.; Thomas J. Hayes, O.M.I.; Justin H. Huelsing, O.M.I.; Michael Hussey, O.M.I.; George Kuryvial, O.M.I.; Elmar Mauer, O.M.I; Thomas Meyer, O.M.I.; Thomas J. Singer, O.M.I.; James E. Taylor, O.M.I., Supr. Oblate Community; James Wynne, O.M.I.; Clarence Zachman, O.M.I. Priests 17.

Shrine of Our Lady of the Snows, 442 S. DeMazenod Dr., 62223-1023. Tel: 618-397-6700; Fax: 618-397-1210. Email: info@snows.org. Web: www.snows.org. Revs. Allen Maes, O.M.I., Area Councillor; Gregory Gallagher, O.M.I., Dir.; J. C. Cain, O.M.I.; William Hagen, O.M.I.; Edward Hauf, O.M.I.; John Leddy, O.M.I.; John Louis, O.M.I. (Retired); John R. Madigan, O.M.I.; Leo Miller, O.M.I. (Retired); Joseph Pitts, O.M.I.; Charles Prass, O.M.I. (Retired); Frank A. Ryan, O.M.I. (Retired); Boniface Wittenbrink, O.M.I. (Retired); Bros. William Johnson, O.M.I., Councillor-at-large; Thomas Ruhmann, O.M.I. Missionary Oblates of Mary Immaculate.

EAST ST. LOUIS. *St. Benedict the Black Friary* (2002) 404 N. 14th St., 62205. Tel: 618-482-5570; Fax: 618-482-5574. Revs. Fernand Cheri, O.F.M., Dir. Gospel Choir; Christian Reuter, O.F.M., Diocesan Coord. of Prison Ministry; Carroll Mizicko, O.F.M., Pastor St. Augustine of Hippo.

Marianist House of Intercession Marianist Community, 641 N. 7th St., 62201. Tel: 618-271-0204; Fax: 618-261-2005. Email: mrnstes1@att.net. Bro. John Laudenbach, S.M, Contact Person.

[G] CONVENTS AND RESIDENCES FOR SISTERS

BELLEVILLE. *Hospital Sisters of St. Francis* (1844) 1031 Golfview Ct., 62223-3261. Tel: 618-538-6033; Fax: 618-538-6033. Web: www.springfieldfranciscans.org. Sisters 4.

Hospital Sisters of The Third Order of St. Francis (1844) 1000 Royal Heights Rd., Apt. 58, 62226. Tel: 618-233-1687; Fax: 618-233-1687. Email: sistertk1948@yahoo.com. Web: www.springfieldfranciscans.org.

Poor Clare Monastery of Our Lady of Mercy (1986) 300 N. 60th St., 62223. Tel: 618-235-4407; Fax: 618-235-4426. Web: www.poorclares-belleville.info. Sr. Mary Giovanna, P.C.C., Abbess. Sisters 9.

CAIRO. *Mary Katherine Convent, Poor Handmaids of Jesus Christ*, 725 22nd St., 62914. Tel: 618-734-0778; Fax: 618-734-0778. Email: mkccairo@onemain.com. Sisters 2.

EAST ST. LOUIS. *Daughters of Charity*, 3500 Market St., 62207-1637. Tel: 618-274-2513; Fax: 618-274-2513. Email: regisdc@juno.com. Sr. Julia Huiskamp, D.C., Supr.

RUMA. *Adorers of the Blood of Christ Ruma Center*, 2 Pioneer Ln. - Ruma, Red Bud, 62278. Tel: 618-282-3848; Fax: 618-282-3266. Email: grossm@adorers.org. Web: www.adorers.org. Sr. Mildred Gross, A.S.C., Dir., Community Life & Mission. Sisters 65; Total Membership of the Province 295.

[H] RETREAT HOUSES

BELLEVILLE. *King's House Retreat and Renewal Center* (1951) 700 N. 66th St., 62223-3949. Tel: 618-397-0584; Fax: 618-397-5123. Email: info@kingsretreatcenter.org. Web: www.kingsretreatcenter.org. Revs. James Brobst, O.M.I., Dir.; David E. Kraus, O.M.I.; Bros. Victor Capek, O.M.I.; Edward Driggins, O.M.I.; William Johnson, O.M.I., Dir.

[I] NEWMAN CENTERS

CARBONDALE. *The Newman Catholic Student Center* Southern Illinois University, 715 S. Washington, 62901. Tel: 618-529-3311; Fax: 618-549-9401. Web: www.siucnewman.org. Mr. Tim Taylor, Dir.

[J] MISCELLANEOUS LISTINGS

BELLEVILLE. *Althoff Catholic High School Educational Endowment Trust*, 222 S. 3rd St., 62220. Tel: 618-277-8181. Mr. William Knapp, C.P.A., Contact Person.

Ancient Order of Hibernians, 1520 Weil Rd., Lebanon, 62254. Tel: 618-632-4538. Mr. Gish A. Johnson Jr., Contact Person.

Ancient Order of Hibernians (LAOH), P.O. Box 23193, 62223. Tel: 618-277-9620. 16 Catherine Dr., Fairview Heights, 62208. Ms. Marcia Gilhausen, Pres.

Catholic Committee on Scouting of the Diocese of Belleville, 2243 Havenford Dr., Shiloh, 62221. Email: tderousse@charter.net. Mr. Tim DeRousse, Contact Person.

Catholic Community Foundation for the Diocese of Belleville, 222 S. 3rd St., 62220-1985. Tel: 618-277-8181.

The Catholic Diocese of Belleville Custodial Fund, 222 S. Third St., 62220. Tel: 618-277-8181; Fax: 618-277-0819. Email: dwaeltz@diobelle.org. Web: diobelle.org. Most Rev. Edward Kenneth Braxton, Ph.D., S.T.D., Pres.; Very Rev. John W. McEvilly, V.G., Sec.; Mr. William Knapp, C.P.A., CFO.

The Catholic Diocese of Belleville Deposit and Loan Fund, 222 S. Third St., 62220. Tel: 618-277-8181; Fax: 618-277-0819. Email: dwaeltz@diobelle.org. Web: diobelle.org. Most Rev. Edward Kenneth Braxton, Ph.D., S.T.D., Pres.; Very Rev. John W. McEvilly, V.G., Sec.; Mr. William Knapp, C.P.A., CFO.

The Catholic Diocese of Belleville Group Health Insurance Fund, 222 S. Third St., 62220. Tel: 618-277-8181; Fax: 618-277-0819. Email: dwaeltz@diobelle.org. Web: diobelle.org. Most Rev. Edward Kenneth Braxton, Ph.D., S.T.D., Pres.; Very Rev. John W. McEvilly, V.G., Sec.; Mr. William Knapp, C.P.A., CFO.

The Catholic Diocese of Belleville Ministry Formation Fund, 222 S. Third St., 62220. Tel: 618-277-8181; Fax: 618-277-0819. Email: dwaeltz@diobelle.org. Web: diobelle.org. Most Rev. Edward K. Braxton, Pres.; Very Rev. John W. McEvilly, V.G., Sec.; Mr. William Knapp, C.P.A., CFO.

The Catholic Diocese of Belleville Property Insurance Fund, 222 S. Third St., 62220. Tel: 618-277-8181; Fax: 618-277-0819. Email: dwaeltz@diobelle.org. Web: diobelle.org. Most Rev. Edward Kenneth Braxton, Ph.D., S.T.D., Pres.; Very Rev. John W. McEvilly, V.G., Sec.; Mr. William Knapp, C.P.A., CFO.

Catholic Holy Family Society, Mary Barbara Kurtz, P.O. Box 327, 62222. Tel: 618-233-0286; Fax: 618-277-8259. Email: mbkurtz@chfsociety.org. Web: www.chfsociety.org.

Catholic Social Services of Southern Illinois, 8601 W. Main St., Ste. 201, 62223. Tel: 618-394-5900; Fax: 619-394-5909. Email: admin@cssil.org. Web: www.cssil.org. Mr. Gary Huelsmann, Exec. Dir.

Catholic War Veterans, Mailing Address: P.O. Box 325, 62222. 3535 State Rte. 159, Freeburg, 62243. Tel: 618-234-3074.

Cursillos in Christianity, Belleville Diocese, 6735 Stoneridge Est., Columbia, 62236. Tel: 618-476-7302; Fax: 618-327-9795. Web: www.bellevillecursillo.blogspot.com. Email: julie@wisperhome.com. Ms. Julie Bostick, Lay Dir.

Engaged Encounter, 2620 Lebanon Ave., 62221. Tel: 618-397-0386. Web: www.eeofs-il.org. Mr. Bob Libby, Coord.; Ms. Lori Libby, Coord.

St. Francis Thrift Shop, 800 E. Main St., 62220. Tel: 618-233-6998. Mr. Leroy Forness, Mgr. Tel: 618-233-1669.

Minds Eye Information Service, 9541 Church Circle Dr., 62223. Tel: 618-394-6221; Fax: 618-394-6438. Email: mindseye@oblatesusa.org. Ms. Marjorie Williams, Exec. Dir. Closed Circuit Radio for the blind and print handicapped.

Missionary Association of Mary Immaculate-Missionary Oblates of Mary Immaculate, 9480 N. De Mazenod Dr., 62223-1160. Tel: 618-398-4848; Fax: 618-398-0588. Email: mami@oblatesusa.org. Web: www.oblatesusa.org. Rev. John R. Madigan, O.M.I., Oblate Dir.; Mrs. Rosalee Cavataio, Charitable Gift Advisor. Serving the missions of the Missionary Oblates, the National Shrine of Our Lady of the Snows, and the Tekakwitha Indian Missions.

Secular Franciscan Order, 200 W. Harrison, 62220. Email: Fransfo@aol.com. Ms. Mary Ellen Herman, S.F.O. Tel: 618-234-4945. St. Peter Fraternity.

Serra Club of St. Clair County, 39 Signal Hill Blvd., 62223. Tel: 618-398-1778. Mr. James Gomric, Pres.
1333 Goldfinch Dr., 62223. Tel: 618-632-7541.

TEC (Teens Encounter Christ), 2620 Lebanon Ave., 62221. Email: chairperson@bellevilletec.com. Web: www.bellevilletec.com. Ms. Carissa Cushman, Chairperson.

Victorious Missionaries, 442 S. DeMazenod Dr., 62223-1097. Tel: 618-394-6281 (Voice/TDD); Fax: 618-397-1210. Email: truhmann@oblatesusa.org. Web: www.vmusa.org. Bro. Thomas Ruhmann, O.M.I., National Dir. Spiritual Support Network for people with disabilities, chronic illness, and those who want to share the journey.

World Apostolate of Fatima, The Blue Army, U.S.A., c/o 222 S. 3rd St., 62220-1985. Very Rev. John T. Myler, S.T.D., V.F., Spiritual Advisor. Tel: 618-233-2391. Priests 3; Total Staff 45; Total Assisted 150.

AVISTON. *Daughters of Isabella, Precious Blood Circle #718*, 248 W. Elm, P.O. Box 375, 62216. Tel: 618-228-7372. Ms. Amelia Wesselmann, Diocesan Chairperson.

CARLYLE. *Carlyle Priest Center*, 222 S. Third St., 62220. 17440 Highline Rd., 62231. Contact the Chancery, Tel: 618-277-8181.

CENTRALIA. **St. Mary's - Good Samaritan, Inc.*, 400 N. Pleasant Ave., 62801. Tel: 618-436-8000. Web: www.smgsi.com. Mr. Philip Gustafson, Pres., CEO. Co-Sponsored by the Franciscan Sisters of Mary and the Felician Sisters.

CHRISTOPHER. *Catholic Daughters of the Americas*, 805 S. Jesse, 62822. Tel: 618-724-4364. Mrs. Frances Furlin, Diocesan Chm.

SCOTT AFB. *Scott Air Force Base*, Scott AFB Chapel, 375 AW/HC, 320 Ward Dr., Bldg. 1620, 62225-5256. Tel: 618-256-3303; Fax: 618-256-8010.

WATERLOO. *Worldwide Marriage Encounter*, 721 Ridge Rd., 62298. Tel: 618-939-3846. Email: hermes@htc.net. Web: www.aweekendofdiscovery.org. Mr. John Hermes, Exec. Couple; Mrs. Karen Hermes, Exec. Couple.

INCORPORATED CEMETERIES

BELLEVILLE. *Green Mount Catholic Cemetery of the Cathedral Congregation of Belleville*

BREESE. *St. Dominic Roman Catholic Cemetery of Breese*

FAIRVIEW HEIGHTS. *St. Adalbert Association (An Illinois Religious Corporation)*

O'FALLON. *Mount Calvary Cemetery of St. Clare Roman Catholic Congregation*

VILLA RIDGE. *Calvary Cemetery of St. Patrick Roman Catholic Church of Cairo*

NECROLOGY

† Driscoll, Rev. Msgr. Maurice F., (Retired)—Died Sept. 9, 2009
† Jansen, Rev. Msgr. James H., (Retired)—Died Feb. 11, 2009
† Voss, Rev. Msgr. Bernard L., Belleville, IL St. Henry—Died May 12, 2009
† Braun, David L., Wendelin, IL Holy Cross; Stringtown, IL St. Joseph.—Died Dec. 30, 2009
† Dollar, Robert J., (Retired)—Died Dec. 1, 2009
† Meskenas, Vincent A., (Retired)—Died Feb. 27, 2010
† Misho, Lloyd P., (Retired)—Died July 31, 2009
† O'Shea, Robert J., (Retired)—Died Oct. 20, 2009
† Perjak, Edmond J., (Retired)—Died Sept. 3, 2009
† Stout, Thomas, Red Bud, IL St. John the Baptist—Died Sept. 18, 2009

An asterisk (*) denotes an organization that has established tax-exempt status directly with the IRS and is not covered by the USCCB Group Ruling.

Diocese of Biloxi

(Dioecesis Biloxiensis)

Most Reverend

ROGER P. MORIN

Bishop of Biloxi; ordained April 15, 1971; appointed Auxiliary Bishop of New Orleans and Titular Bishop of Aulon February 11, 2003; ordained April 22, 2003; appointed Bishop of Biloxi March 2, 2009; installed April 27, 2009. *Office: 1790 Popps Ferry Rd., Biloxi, MS 39532-2118.*

Most Reverend

JOSEPH LAWSON HOWZE, D.D.

Bishop Emeritus of Biloxi; ordained May 7, 1959; appointed Titular Bishop of Maxita and Auxiliary of Natchez-Jackson, November 8, 1972; ordained Bishop January 28, 1973; appointed Bishop of Biloxi March 1, 1977; installed June 6, 1977; retired May 15, 2001. *Mailing Address: P.O. Box 6067, Mobile, AL 36660-0067.*

WALK HUMBLY AND ACT JUSTLY

Chancery Office: 1790 Popps Ferry Rd., Biloxi, MS 39532-2118. Tel: 228-702-2100; Fax: 228-702-2125.

ESTABLISHED MARCH 1, 1977.

Square Miles 9,653.

Comprises 17 counties in southern Mississippi: Jackson, Harrison, Hancock, George, Stone, Pearl River, Greene, Perry, Forrest, Lamar, Marion, Walthall, Wayne, Jones, Covington, Jefferson Davis and Lawrence.

Legal Title: "Catholic Diocese of Biloxi". For legal titles of parishes and diocesan institutions, consult the Chancery Office.

STATISTICAL OVERVIEW

Personnel	
Bishop	1
Retired Bishops	1
Priests: Diocesan Active in Diocese	39
Priests: Retired, Sick or Absent	12
Number of Diocesan Priests	51
Religious Priests in Diocese	24
Total Priests in Diocese	75
Extern Priests in Diocese	10
Ordinations:	
Diocesan Priests	1
Transitional Deacons	1
Permanent Deacons	8
Permanent Deacons in Diocese	35
Total Brothers	9
Total Sisters	39
Parishes	
Parishes	42
With Resident Pastor:	
Resident Diocesan Priests	32
Resident Religious Priests	7
Without Resident Pastor:	
Administered by Priests	3
Missions	11
Professional Ministry Personnel:	
Sisters	9
Lay Ministers	37
Welfare	
Homes for the Aged	7
Total Assisted	469
Special Centers for Social Services	9
Total Assisted	362,661
Other Institutions	1
Total Assisted	5,450
Educational	
Diocesan Students in Other Seminaries	8
Total Seminarians	8
High Schools, Diocesan and Parish	4
Total Students	1,117
High Schools, Private	1
Total Students	375
Elementary Schools, Diocesan and Parish	11
Total Students	2,717
Catechesis/Religious Education:	
High School Students	1,287
Elementary Students	3,168
Total Students under Catholic Instruction	8,672
Teachers in the Diocese:	
Brothers	5
Sisters	3
Lay Teachers	339
Vital Statistics	
Receptions into the Church:	
Infant Baptism Totals	996
Minor Baptism Totals	93
Adult Baptism Totals	140
Received into Full Communion	181
First Communions	1,014
Confirmations	847
Marriages:	
Catholic	163
Interfaith	123
Total Marriages	286
Deaths	657
Total Catholic Population	62,494
Total Population	775,538

Former Bishop—Most Revs. JOSEPH LAWSON HOWZE, D.D. (Retired), ord. May 7, 1959; appt. Titular Bishop of Maxita and Auxiliary of Natchez-Jackson Nov. 8, 1972; ord. Bishop Jan. 28, 1973; appt. Bishop of Biloxi March 1, 1977; installed June 6, 1977; retired May 15, 2001; THOMAS J. RODI, ord. May 20, 1978; appt. Bishop of Biloxi May 15, 2001; ord. and installed July 2, 2001; appt. Archbishop of Mobile April 2, 2008; installed June 6, 2008.

Office of the Bishop—1790 Popps Ferry Rd., Biloxi, 39532-2118. Tel: 228-702-2111.

Vicar General—Very Rev. T. DOMINICK FULLAM, J.C.L., V.G., 1790 Popps Ferry Rd., Biloxi, 39532-2118. Tel: 228-702-2112.

Moderator of Curia—Very Rev. T. DOMINICK FULLAM, J.C.L., V.G., 1790 Popps Ferry Rd., Biloxi, 39532-2118. Tel: 228-702-2112.

Chancery Office—1790 Popps Ferry Rd., Biloxi, 39532-2118. Tel: 228-702-2100; Fax: 228-702-2125. Office Hours: Mon.-Fri. 8:30-5; All offices are at this address unless otherwise noted.

Pastoral Services—Deacon GAYDEN R. HARPER. Tel: 228-702-2107.

Special Delegate for Matrimonial Dispensations—Very Rev. JOHN R. MCGRATH, J.C.L., J.V., V.F. Tel: 228-702-2117.

Chancellor—Sr. REBECCA A. RUTKOWSKI, O.S.F., A.C.S.W. Tel: 228-702-2136.

Office for Planning and Development—Deacon ROBERTO JIMENEZ, Dir. Tel: 228-702-2100.

Marriage Tribunal—

Judicial Vicar—Very Rev. JOHN R. MCGRATH, J.C.L., J.V., V.F. Tel: 228-702-2117.

Promoter of Justice—Rev. Msgr. MICHAEL J. THORNTON, J.C.L.

Tribunal Judge—Very Rev. JOHN R. MCGRATH, J.C.L., J.V., V.F.

Defenders of the Bond—Very Revs. T. DOMINICK FULLAM, J.C.L., V.G.; THOMAS S. CONWAY, V.F.; Rev. Msgr. MICHAEL J. THORNTON, J.C.L.

Pro-Synodal Judge—Rev. Msgr. JAMES P. MCGOUGH, J.C.D. (Retired).

Advocates—Rev. PATRICK J. MOCKLER; Deacons JOHN R. HENDERSON; JOHN E. JENNINGS; ROBERTO JIMENEZ.

Secretaries and Ecclesiastical Notaries (Court of First Instance)—Mrs. CLAIRE D. JONES; Ms. BRENDA C. SMITH.

Auditors—Sr. REBECCA A. RUTKOWSKI, O.S.F., A.C.S.W.; Rev. CHARLES W. NUTTER.

Deans—Very Revs. DENNIS J. CARVER, V.F., West Coast Deanery; PETER F. MOCKLER, V.F., Central Coast Deanery; JOHN R. MCGRATH, J.C.L., J.V., V.F., East Central Coast Deanery; MICHAEL P. AUSTIN, V.F., East Coast Deanery; THOMAS S. CONWAY, V.F., Northern Deanery.

College of Consultors—Very Revs. DENNIS J. CARVER, V.F.; T. DOMINICK FULLAM, J.C.L., V.G.; Rev. LOUIS LOHAN; Very Rev. JOHN R. MCGRATH, J.C.L., J.V., V.F.; Rev. CHARLES E. MCMAHON, S.S.J.; Very Rev. PETER F. MOCKLER, V.F.; Revs. CUTHBERT R. O'CONNELL; I. ANTHONY ARGUELLES, V.F.; MICHAEL P. O'CONNOR; Rev. Msgr. MICHAEL J. THORNTON, J.C.L.

Diocesan Attorney—KEVIN J. NECAISE, Mailing Address: P.O. Box 636, Gulfport, 39502. Tel: 228-586-0933.

Department of Administration and Finance Comptroller—TAMMY W. DILORENZO, CPA, Dir. Tel: 228-702-2118.

Office of Information Technology—RICHARD A. YOUNG, Dir. Tel: 228-702-2171.

Diocesan Risk Management for Property and Medical—Mr. A. J. SCARDINO, Contact Person. Tel: 228-702-2100.

Office of Human Resources—Deacon GAYDEN R. HARPER. Tel: 228-702-2107.

Catholic Foundation of the Diocese of Biloxi, Inc.—Deacon ROBERTO JIMENEZ, Exec. Dir. Tel: 228-702-2100.

Mission Office—Very Rev. MICHAEL P. AUSTIN, V.F. Tel: 228-475-0777.

Office of Communication—SHIRLEY HENDERSON, Dir., 1790 Popps Ferry Rd., Biloxi, 39532-2118. Tel: 228-702-2126; Fax: 228-702-2128. Email: smhenderson@biloxidiocese.org.

"Gulf Pine Catholic Newspaper"—SHIRLEY HENDERSON, Editor. Tel: 228-702-2126; 228-702-2127; Fax: 228-702-2128. Email: gulfpinecatholic@biloxidiocese.org.

Radio Ministry—SHIRLEY HENDERSON. Tel: 228-702-2126; Fax: 228-702-2128.

Department of Education—
Office of Superintendent of Catholic Schools—Dr. MIKE LADNER, Supt. Tel: 228-702-2130; 228-702-2129; Dr. RHONDA P. CLARK, Asst. Supt. Tel: 228-702-2130; 228-702-2151.
Office of Resource Center—Mr. LEO TRAHAN; JOY LANDRY.
Office of Special Education—Dr. MIKE LADNER; Dr. RHONDA P. CLARK.
Office of Religious Education—Mr. LEO TRAHAN, Dir. Tel: 228-702-2131.
CDB Religious Education, Inc.—Mr. LEO TRAHAN, Contact Person, 1790 Popps Ferry Rd., Biloxi, 39532-2118. Tel: 228-702-2131.
Office of Youth Ministry—BRAGG MOORE, Dir. Tel: 228-702-2142.
Catholic Boy Scouts—JUDITH BRADFORD. Tel: 228-467-7452.
Campus Ministry—Very Rev. THOMAS S. CONWAY, V.F., Dir., 3117 W. Fourth St., Hattiesburg, 39401. Tel: 601-264-5192.
Priests' Continuing Education and Retreat Programs—Rev. CUTHBERT R. O'CONNELL, 236 S. Beach Blvd., Waveland, 39576.
Ecumenical & Interreligious Affairs—Mr. LEO TRAHAN, Contact Person. Tel: 228-702-2131.
Liturgy, Office of—Very Rev. MICHAEL P. AUSTIN, V.F., Dir., Mailing Address: St. Joseph the Worker Parish, P.O. Box 8549, Moss Point, 39562-0008. Tel: 228-475-0777.
Diocesan Liturgical Commission—Very Rev. MICHAEL P. AUSTIN, V.F., Chm.; Mr. PHIL BEINING, Music Liaison; Mr. KEVIN BENEFIELD; Rev. ROBERT FISHER, S.V.D.; Ms. PAULA SPEARS; Sr. MARIE FRANCIS TRAN, F.M.S.R.; Deacons WILLIAM VRAZEL; BEN WIMBERLY JR.
Catholic Charities— Legal Title: Catholic Social and Community Services, Inc. All offices are at this address unless otherwise noted. *1790 Popps Ferry Rd., Biloxi, 39532-2118.* Tel: 228-702-2137. JENNIFER WILLIAMS, L.S.W., Diocesan Dir. Tel: 228-702-2167.
Hattiesburg Regional Office—2707 McInnis Loop, Hattiesburg, 39402. Tel: 601-261-5308; 601-261-5320. POLLY SUMRALL, Office Mgr.; JANNIE GREENE, A.I.D.S. Ministry.
Pascagoula Regional Office—1810 Old Mobile Hwy., Pascagoula, 39567. Tel: 228-567-0001; 228-567-0002. JENNIFER STACKHOUSE, Case Mgr.
Adoption Services—NANCY LOFTUS, 1790 Popps Ferry Rd., Biloxi, 39532-2118. Tel: 228-702-2137.
Emergency Assistance—MARGOT SWETMAN, 1450 North St., Gulfport, 39501. Tel: 228-297-4982.
Office of Long Term Recovery—VACANT, 1450 North St., Gulfport, 39507. Tel: 228-701-0555.
St. Gerard Community Outreach—ANNE HALE, Office Mgr., 200 Hwy. 90, Ste. C, Waveland, 39520. Tel: 228-467-2600.
Morning Star Pregnancy Care Center— (Unplanned pregnancy services) ANN RIVERA, Office Mgr., 2204 24th Ave., Gulfport, 39503. Tel: 228-864-4221.
12 Baskets Food Bank—JENNIFER KNUE, Dir., 1520 29th Ave., Gulfport, 39501. Tel: 228-822-0836.
Refugee Resettlement—MAGDA LELEAUX, Dir., 800 Division St., Biloxi, 39531. Tel: 228-374-6554.
Family Life Office—Tel: 228-702-2137.
Catholic Charities Housing Association of Biloxi, Inc.—
Santa Maria Retirement Apartments; Villa Maria Retirement Apartments—Most Rev. ROGER P. MORIN, D.D., Pres.; GREG CRAPO, Contact Person. Tel: 228-702-2100.
Samaritan Housing, Inc.—Most Rev. ROGER P. MORIN, D.D., Pres.; GREG CRAPO, Contact Person. Tel: 228-702-2100.
Notre Dame de la Mer, Inc.—Most Rev. ROGER P. MORIN, D.D., Pres.; GREG CRAPO, Contact Person. Tel: 228-702-2100.
Gabriel Manor, Inc.—Most Rev. ROGER P. MORIN, D.D., Pres.; GREG CRAPO, Contact Person. Tel: 228-702-2100.
Caritas Manor, Inc.—Most Rev. ROGER P. MORIN, D.D., Pres.; GREG CRAPO, Contact Person. Tel: 228-702-2100.
Carlow Manor—Most Rev. ROGER P. MORIN, D.D., Pres.; GREG CRAPO, Contact Person. Tel: 228-702-2100.
Gabriel Manor II, Inc.—Most Rev. ROGER P. MORIN, D.D., Pres.; GREG CRAPO, Contact Person. Tel: 228-702-2100.
Apostleship of the Sea—Port of Gulfport: Deacon JOHN R. HENDERSON.
Vietnamese Apostolate—VACANT.
Prison Apostolate—Jackson County Jails: Deacon AL STOCKERT. Tel: 228-702-2107. Harrison County Jails: Deacon AL STOCKERT. Tel: 228-702-2107. Hancock County Jails: Deacon AL STOCKERT. Tel: 228-702-2107. South Mississippi Correctional Facility: Rev. Msgr. MICHAEL J. THORNTON, J.C.L.
Diocesan Boards and Committees—
Association of Priests (Diocese of Biloxi and Jackson)—Most Revs. ROGER P. MORIN, D.D., Bishop of Biloxi & Co-Chm.; JOSEPH N. LATINO, Bishop of Jackson & Co-Chm.; Rev. PATRICK FARRELL, Pres.; Rev. Msgr. MICHAEL J. THORNTON, J.C.L., Sec., Treas. & Pres.-Elect. Trustees: Rev. PATRICK J. MOCKLER; Very Rev. THOMAS S. CONWAY, V.F.; Revs. CHARLES BUCCIANTINI; THOMAS MCGING.
Building and Real Estate Committee—Very Rev. MICHAEL P. AUSTIN, V.F., Chm.; CHUCK COLLINS; GEORGE DENMARK; KELEAL HASSIN JR.; GERALD HOPKINS; BOB MANDAL; HOPPY ALLRED; ROBERT STARKS; STEPHEN STOJCICH; WESLEY TOCHE III.
Catholic Foundation-Diocese of Biloxi—Most Rev. ROGER P. MORIN, D.D., Pres.; Very Rev. T. DOMINICK FULLAM, J.C.L., V.G., Vice Pres.; Deacon ROBERTO JIMENEZ, Exec. Dir.; MARIAN C. HARRISON; JOSEPH HUDSON; JERRY L. LEVENS; TED LONGO; DAVID LORD; VONRETTA J. SINGLETON; ROBERT TUCEI; TAMMY W. DILORENZO, CPA, Advisor.
Catholic Housing Board—Most Rev. ROGER P. MORIN, D.D., Pres.; GREG CRAPO, Sec.; Very Rev. T. DOMINICK FULLAM, J.C.L., V.G.; Rev. BERNARD P. FARRELL; TAMMY W. DILORENZO, CPA; SALVADOR DOMINO; GARY YOUNG; Very Rev. JOHN R. MCGRATH, J.C.L., J.V., V.F.
Finance Council—Most Rev. ROGER P. MORIN, D.D.; Very Rev. T. DOMINICK FULLAM, J.C.L., V.G.; RICHARD ECKERT; JOSEPH P. HUDSON; THEODORE LONGO; DAVID L. LORD, Chm.; Very Rev. PETER F. MOCKLER, V.F.; STEVE MONTAGNET; JOHN P. MYERS; Deacon ROBERTO JIMENEZ.
Insurance Committee—Most Rev. ROGER P. MORIN, D.D.; BOBBY TROSCLAIR; Very Rev. T. DOMINICK FULLAM, J.C.L., V.G.; Dr. MIKE LADNER; Sr. MARY JO MIKE, O.S.F.; GREG CRAPO. Advisors: TAMMY W. DILORENZO, CPA; Mr. A. J. SCARDINO.
Mission Board—Most Rev. ROGER P. MORIN, D.D.; Very Rev. MICHAEL P. AUSTIN, V.F.
Personnel Board—Rev. Msgr. MICHAEL J. THORNTON, J.C.L.; Very Rev. DENNIS J. CARVER, V.F.; Rev. BERNARD P. FARRELL; Very Rev. T. DOMINICK FULLAM, J.C.L., V.G.; Rev. ROBERT P. HIGGINBOTHAM.
Presbyteral Council—Most Rev. ROGER P. MORIN, D.D., Pres.; Very Revs. JOHN R. MCGRATH, J.C.L., J.V., V.F.; MICHAEL P. AUSTIN, V.F.; DENNIS J. CARVER, V.F.; THOMAS S. CONWAY, V.F.; PETER F. MOCKLER, V.F.; T. DOMINICK FULLAM, J.C.L., V.G.; Revs. SERGIO A. BALDERAS; LOUIS LOHAN; PATRICK J. MOCKLER; MICHAEL P. O'CONNOR; JOSEPH TRUONG Q. TRINH; JOSEPH M. UKO; STEVEN WILSON, C.Ss.R.
Miscellaneous Apostolates—
Campaign for Human Development—GREG CRAPO, 1790 Popps Ferry Rd., Biloxi, 39532-2118. Tel: 228-702-3001.
Catholic Relief Services—GREG CRAPO, 1790 Popps Ferry Rd., Biloxi, 39532-2118. Tel: 228-702-3001.
Catholic University, Friends of—Very Rev. T. DOMINICK FULLAM, J.C.L., V.G., 1790 Popps Ferry Rd., Biloxi, 39532-2118.
Charismatic Renewal—Rev. GEORGE R. KITCHIN, Dir., St. James Parish, 366 Cowan-Lorraine Rd., Gulfport, 39507.
Council of the St. Vincent de Paul Society—MARY FRANCIS FORD, Pres. Tel: 228-388-1837.
Cursillo and Retreats—Rev. MICHAEL P. O'CONNOR, Spiritual Dir., 14595 Vidalia Rd., Pass Christian, 39571. Tel: 228-255-7560.
Deaf and Disabled, Office of the—Mr. GREGORY K. CRAPO, B.S., M.B.A, Dir., de l'Epee Deaf Center, Inc., 1450 North St., Gulfport, 39507. Tel: 228-897-2280 (Voice-TTY); 228-896-2280 (Video Phone); Fax: 228-897-2462.
Latin American Apostolate— Mission-Saltillo, Mexico, co-sponsored with Diocese of Jackson Rev. BENJAMIN PIOVAN, Parroquia San Miguel Arcangel, Av. Central 4649, Col. Vista Hermosa, Saltillo, Coah CP 25010 Mexico.
Legion of Mary—Contact: Office of Pastoral Svcs. Tel: 228-702-2107.
Permanent Diaconate Program—1790 Popps Ferry Rd., Biloxi, 39532. Tel: 228-702-2107. Deacons GAYDEN R. HARPER, Dir.; RICHARD A. HOLLINGSWORTH, Assoc. Dir. Formation; RALPH TORRELLI, Continuing Educ.
Pontifical Association of the Holy Childhood—Very Rev. MICHAEL P. AUSTIN, V.F., Dir., Mailing Address: P.O. Box 8549, Moss Point, 39563-0549. Tel: 228-475-0777.
Propagation of the Faith—Very Rev. MICHAEL P. AUSTIN, V.F., Dir., Mailing Address: P.O. Box 8549, Moss Point, 39563-0549. Tel: 228-475-0777.
Vocations—Very Rev. DENNIS J. CARVER, V.F., Dir., 22342 Evangeline Rd., Pass Christian, 39571. Tel: 228-452-4686; Rev. SERGIO A. BALDERAS, Asst. Vocations Dir. to Hispanic Seminarians, 2090 Pass Rd., Biloxi, 39531-3130. Tel: 228-388-3887.
CDB Seminarian Education, Inc.—Very Rev. DENNIS J. CARVER, V.F., Contact Person, 1790 Popps Ferry Rd., Biloxi, 39532-2118. Tel: 228-452-4686.
Victim Assistance Coordinator—Sr. MARY JO MIKE, O.S.F., 1046 Beach Blvd., Biloxi, 39530. Tel: 228-806-5677. Email: smaryjm@aol.com.
Construction Manager for the Diocese of Biloxi—STEVE LABARRE. Tel: 228-702-2148; Cell: 228-216-5222. Email: slabarre@biloxidiocese.org; JACK ROUSSO. Tel: 228-702-2149; Cell: 251-689-8483. Email: jrousso@biloxidiocese.org.

CLERGY, PARISHES, MISSIONS AND PAROCHIAL SCHOOLS

CITY OF BILOXI

(HARRISON COUNTY)

1—CATHEDRAL OF THE NATIVITY OF THE BLESSED VIRGIN MARY (1843) Very Rev. John R. McGrath, Rector; Rev. George Manchapilly, C.M.I.; Deacon Ben Wimberly Jr. In Res., Rev. Gregory Barras.
Res.: 870 Howard Ave., P.O. Box 367, 39533. Tel: 228-374-1717; Fax: 228-374-1773. Email: office@nativitybvmcathedral.org.
School—(Grades PreK-6) Tel: 228-432-2269; Fax: 228-432-9421. Web: www.nativitybvm.org. Sr. Mary Jo Mike, O.S.F., Prin.; Barbara Ziz, Librarian. Sisters 1; Lay Teachers 20; Students 179.
Catechesis/Religious Program— Twinned with Nativity BVM Parish. Students 55.

2—BLESSED FRANCIS XAVIER SEELOS (2005) Rev. Steven Wilson, C.Ss.R.
Mailing Address: P.O. Box 347, 39533-0347. Tel: 228-374-0117; Fax: 228-374-0118.
Res.: 724 Bradford St., 39530. Tel: 228-374-0117; Fax: 228-374-0118.
Catechesis/Religious Program—P.O. Box 347, 39533. Tel: 228-374-0117. Students 26.

3—CHURCH OF THE VIETNAMESE MARTYRS (2000), (Vietnamese), [JC] Rev. James Chau Pham, C.Ss.R.
Res.: 172 Oak St., 39530. Tel: 228-374-1116; Fax: 228-374-9344.
Catechesis/Religious Program—Tel: 228-432-7724. Students 184.

4—ST. LOUIS (1957) Closed. For inquiries for sacramental records, please see Blessed Francis Xavier Seelos, Biloxi.

5—ST. MARY (1967) Very Rev. T. Dominick Fullam.
Res.: 8343 Woolmarket Rd., 39532. Tel: 228-392-7500; Fax: 228-392-4552.
Catechesis/Religious Program—Tel: 228-392-1999; Fax: 228-392-4552. Students 163.

6—ST. MICHAEL (1917) Rev. Gregory Barras.
Res.: 177 First St., P.O. Box 523, 39533. Tel: 228-435-5578; Fax: 228-435-5579. Email: stmichaelschurch@megagate.com. Web: www.stmichaelchurchbiloxi.com.
Catechesis/Religious Program—Students 15.

7—OUR LADY OF FATIMA (1957) Revs. Patrick J. Mockler; Sergio A. Balderas; Satish Baburao Adhav (India). In Res., Rev. Msgr. Francis Farrell (Retired).
Res.: 2090 Pass Rd., 39531. Tel: 228-388-3887; Fax: 228-388-7069. Email: fatima@cableone.net. Web: www.fatima-biloxi.com.
School—(Grades PreK-6), 320 Jim Money Rd., 39531. Tel: 228-388-3602; Fax: 228-385-1140. Web: www.fatimafalcons.org. Susie Bass, Prin. Lay Teachers 14; Students 295.
Catechesis/Religious Program—Tel: 228-388-5737. Students 173.

8—OUR MOTHER OF SORROWS (1914), (African American), Rev. Steven Wilson, C.Ss.R.
Mailing Address: P.O. Box 347, 39533-0347.
Res.: 803 Division St., 39530. Tel: 228-435-0007; Fax: 228-435-7555.
Catechesis/Religious Program—Students 23.

9—SACRED HEART (1921) Revs. Robert P. Higginbotham; Thomas J. Pazheparambil.
Res.: 10446 Le Moyne Blvd., P.O. Box 6819, D'Iberville, 39540. Tel: 228-392-4526.
School—(Grades PreK-6), 10482 Le Moyne Blvd., D'Iberville, 39540. Tel: 228-392-4180; Fax: 228-392-4859. Jane Sema, Prin.; Gerri Weldon, Librarian. Lay Teachers 9; Students 73.
Catechesis/Religious Program—Tel: 228-392-4180; 228-392-5509. Sr. Julia Marie Burke, R.S.M., D.R.E. Students 180.

OUTSIDE THE CITY OF BILOXI

BASSFIELD, JEFFERSON DAVIS CO., ST. PETER (1904), (Irish), [CEM 2] [JC 2] Rev. Eappen Joseph; Deacon Robert Everard.

Res.: 4135 Hwy. 42, P.O. Box 10, 39421. Tel: 601-943-5104; 601-943-6688 (Office); Fax: 601-943-8055.
Catechesis/Religious Program—Tel: 601-943-6259. Russ Palmeri, D.R.E. Students 60.
Mission—St. Mary's Prentiss, Jefferson Davis Co.
Mission—St. Lawrence P.O. Box 16, Monticello, Lawrence Co. 39654. Tel: 601-587-8017.

BAY ST. LOUIS, HANCOCK CO.

1—OUR LADY OF THE GULF (1847) [CEM] Rev. Michael Tracey; Deacons Eddie Renz; Mike Harris; Kathleen LeBlanc, Pastoral Assoc.
Res.: 228 S. Beach Blvd., 39520. Tel: 228-467-6509; Fax: 228-467-2960. Email: olgchurc@bellsouth.net. Web: www.olgchurch.net.
School—Holy Trinity Catholic Elementary, (Grades PreK-6), 301 Second St., 39520. Tel: 228-467-5158; Fax: 228-467-9742. Web: www.holytrinitycatholic.net. Janet Buras, Prin.; Mrs. Barbara Hancock, Librarian. Lay Teachers 23; Students 394.
Catechesis/Religious Program—Tel: 228-467-6509. Students 73.

2—ST. ROSE DE LIMA (1924), (African American), Rev. Sebastian Myladiyil, S.V.D.
Res.: 301 S. Necaise Ave., 39520. Tel: 228-467-7357; Fax: 228-467-7740.
Catechesis/Religious Program—Tel: 228-363-1017. Mrs. Joan Thomas, D.R.E. Students 62.

CLERMONT HARBOR, HANCOCK CO., ST. ANN (1915) [CEM] Rev. Christopher Louis Munsch.
Mailing Address: P.O. Box 1037, Lakeshore, 39558.
Res.: 5858 Lower Bay Rd., Bay Saint Louis, 39520. Tel: 228-467-5128; Fax: 228-467-5638. Email: stannscathparish@att.net.
Catechesis/Religious Program—Students 46.
Chapel—St. Joseph 5383 Hwy. 604, Pearlington, 39572.

COLUMBIA, MARION CO., MOST HOLY TRINITY (1959) Rev. Martin Joseph Gillespie.
Res.: 1429 N. Park Ave., 39429. Tel: 601-736-3136; Fax: 601-736-1920. Email: holytrinity5230@yahoo.com. Web: www.holytrinityonline.com.
Catechesis/Religious Program—Audrey Rink, D.R.E. (St. Paul the Apostle). Students 10.
Mission—St. Paul the Apostle 702 Union St., P.O. Box 646, Tylertown, Walthall Co. 39667. Tel: 601-876-6422; Fax: 601-876-6422.

DELISLE, HARRISON CO., ST. STEPHEN (1874) Revs. David A. Hamm, S.T.; Joseph Keenan, S.T., Parochial Vicar.
Res.: 25220 St. Stephen Rd., Pass Christian, 39571. Tel: 228-255-1294; Fax: 228-255-7479.
Catechesis/Religious Program—Melanie Walrod, D.R.E. Students 133.
Mission—St. Ann 9520 Vidalia Rd., Dubuisson, Harrison Co. 39571.
Mission—St. William 9600 Edwin Ladner Rd., Rotten Bayou, Harrison Co. 39571.

GAUTIER, JACKSON CO., ST. MARY (1968) Rev. Charles W. Nutter.
Res.: 809 De La Pointe Rd., 39553. Tel: 228-497-2364; Fax: 228-497-5887. Email: stmarygautier@yahoo.com.
Catechesis/Religious Program— Donna Harper, D.R.E. Students 109.

GULFPORT, HARRISON CO.

1—ST. ANN (1939) Very Rev. Peter F. Mockler.
Res.: 23529 Hwy. 53, 39503. Tel: 228-832-2560; Fax: 228-832-2560. Web: www.stannparishlizana.org.
Catechesis/Religious Program—Tel: 228-831-9452. Robert Earl Lizana, D.R.E. Students 82.
Mission—Our Lady of Chartres Big Creek Rd., Delmas Dedeaux, Harrison Co. 39503. Tel: 228-832-2560; Fax: 228-832-2560.

2—ST. JAMES (1898) [CEM] Revs. George R. Kitchin; Khoa Phi Vo, Parochial Vicar; Deacons John R. Henderson, Pastoral Assoc.; Rick Conason.
Res.: 366 Cowan Rd., 39507. Tel: 228-896-6059; Fax: 228-896-5498.
School—(Grades PreK-6), 603 West Ave., 39507. Tel: 228-896-6631; Fax: 228-896-6638. Mrs. Jennifer Broadus, Prin.; Connie Favret, Librarian. Sisters of Mercy (Ennis, Ireland) 2; Lay Teachers 18; Students 322.
Catechesis/Religious Program— Rob Russo, D.R.E. Students 107.

3—ST. JOHN THE EVANGELIST (1900) Revs. Joseph Uko; Gerard M. Cleary.
Res.: 2414 17th St., P.O. Box 970, 39501. Tel: 228-864-2272; Fax: 228-864-2273. Email: stjohnthee@cableone.net.
School—(Grades PreK-6) Tel: 228-863-1606; Fax: 228-863-9677. Email: webmaster@stjohnelementary.com. Web: www.stjohncatholicschool.net. Cynthia Hahn, Prin.; Shelly Motyka, Librarian. Lay Teachers 12; Students 105.
High School—St. Patrick High School, 18300 Hwy. 67, 39532-8655. Tel: 228-702-0500; Fax: 228-702-0511. Email: btrosclair@biloxidiocese.org. Web: www.stpatrickhighschool.net. Bobby Trosclair, Prin. Brothers 1; Lay Teachers 37; Students 510.
Catechesis/Religious Program—Sr. Mary Kealy, P.B.V.M., D.R.E. Students 48.

4—ST. JOSEPH CATHOLIC CHURCH (Northwood Hills) (1966) Rev. George E. Murphy.
Res.: 12290 DePew Rd., 39503. Tel: 228-832-3244; 228-832-1166; Fax: 228-832-1166. Email: stjosephgulfport@bellsouth.net. Web: www.stjosephcc.com.
Catechesis/Religious Program— Mrs. Michele Stoner, D.R.E. & Youth Min. Students 119.

5—ST. THERESE (1932), (African American), Rev. Raymond P. Carignan, S.S.J.
Res.: 3521 19th St., 39501. Tel: 228-863-0624; Fax: 228-863-2531.
Catechesis/Religious Program—Sr. Carmelita Mulry, S.H.Sp., D.R.E. Students 67.

HATTIESBURG, FORREST CO.

1—HOLY ROSARY (1949), (African American), Rev. William J. Vollor.
Res.: 900 Dabbs St., 39401. Tel: 601-584-6528; Fax: 601-584-9533.

2—SACRED HEART (1900) [CEM] Rev. Kenneth G. Ramon-Landry; Deacons Warren Goff; Tom LeBlanc.
Res.: 313 Walnut St., P.O. Box 1027, 39401. Tel: 601-583-9404; Fax: 601-583-9486. Email: sacheartchurch@aol.com. Web: www.sacredhearthattiesburg.org.
School—(Grades PreK-12), 608 Southern Ave., 39401. Tel: 601-583-8683; Fax: 601-583-8684. Email: bmccrory@biloxidiocese.org. Web: www.shshattiesburg.com. Brian McCrory, Prin.; Karen Walsh, Librarian. Lay Teachers 52; Students 580.
Catechesis/Religious Program—Tel: 601-583-9404; Fax: 601-583-9486. Email: jbeck02@hotmail.com. Jean Beckett, D.R.E. Students 89.

3—ST. THOMAS AQUINAS (1968), (University of Southern Mississippi-Student Parish) Very Rev. Thomas Conway; Nora Dagg, Youth Min.
Res.: 3117 W. Fourth St., 39401. Tel: 601-264-5192; Fax: 601-264-0834.
Catechesis/Religious Program—Tel: 601-325-3462. Karen Jones, D.R.E. Students 353.

KILN, HANCOCK CO., ANNUNCIATION (1869) [CEM] Very Rev. John T. Noone.
Res.: 5370 Kiln-DeLisle Rd., 39556. Tel: 228-255-1800; Fax: 228-255-1894. Email: annunciationkiln@hughes.net.
Catechesis/Religious Program—Candice Plouffe, D.R.E. Students 85.

LAUREL, JONES CO., IMMACULATE CONCEPTION (1887) Rev. Msgr. Michael J. Thornton; Revs. Anthony Doan Tran; Jose Vasquez; Deacons Richard Hollingsworth; David Hughes Sr.; Larry Pressly; Mrs. Suzie Middleton, Youth Min.
Res.: 833 W. Sixth St., 39440. Tel: 601-426-3473; Fax: 601-426-3890.
Catechesis/Religious Program—Tel: 601-426-3473. Students 87.

LONG BEACH, HARRISON CO., ST. THOMAS THE APOSTLE (1903) Rev. Louis Lohan; Sr. Teresa Baugh, P.B.V.M., Pastoral Assoc.
Mailing Address: P.O. Box 1529, 39560.
Res.: 725 N. Nicholson, P.O. Box 1529, 39560. Tel: 228-863-1610; Fax: 228-868-6068. Email: stthomaschurch@cableone.net. Web: www.stthomaschurchlb.org.
School—St. Vincent de Paul Elementary, (Grades PreK-6), 4321 Espy Ave., 39560. Tel: 228-863-6876; Fax: 228-863-9537. Email: emfortenberry@biloxidiocese.org. Web: www.svdpcatholicschool.org. Mrs. Elizabeth Fortenberry, Prin.; Susan Hughes, Librarian. Lay Teachers 38; Students 388.
Catechesis/Religious Program—Tel: 228-868-3774. Students 290.

LUMBERTON, LAMAR CO., OUR LADY OF PERPETUAL HELP (1922) [CEM] Rev. Truong Quang Trinh; Deacon Harold Gaule.
Res.: 379 W. Seneca Rd., 39455-7728. Tel: 601-796-3051 (Office); 601-796-3053 (Rectory); Fax: 601-796-3023. Email: olphst@megagate.com.
Catechesis/Religious Program—Students 27.
Mission—St. Joseph P.O. Box 202, Poplarville, Pearl River Co. 39470. Tel: 601-795-9164. Email: stjoseph@megagate.com.

MOSS POINT, JACKSON CO., ST. JOSEPH (1950) Very Rev. Michael P. Austin; Deacon Emery E. Elder.
Res.: 4114 First St., P.O. Box 8549, 39562-8549. Tel: 228-475-0777; Fax: 228-475-3672. Email: stjosephmoss@aol.com.
Catechesis/Religious Program— Mrs. Diane Stewart, D.R.E. (St. Ann). Tel: 228-641-3937. Students 65.
Mission—St. Ann P.O. Box 8549, Hurley, Jackson Co. 39562-8549. Tel: 228-588-0599; Fax: 228-588-0599.

OCEAN SPRINGS, JACKSON CO.

1—ST. ALPHONSUS (1860) Revs. Henry McInerney; Thomas White; Deacon Gregory Miller.
Res.: 502 Jackson Ave., 39564. Tel: 228-875-5419; Fax: 228-875-5410. Email: stals@cableone.net.
School—(Grades PreK-6), 504 Jackson Ave., 39564. Tel: 228-875-5329; Fax: 228-875-3584. Dr. Pamela Rogers, Prin.; Rebecca Young, Librarian. Lay Teachers 17; Students 218.
Catechesis/Religious Program—Tel: 228-872-2652. Pat Cronin, D.R.E. Students 256.

2—ST. ELIZABETH ANN SETON (1975) Rev. Bernard P. Farrell; Deacon Martin Finnegan.
Res.: 4900 Riley Rd., 39564. Tel: 228-875-0654; Fax: 228-875-6852. Email: stelizabethseton@bellsouth.net.
Catechesis/Religious Program—Linda Holtorf, D.R.E. Students 330.

PASCAGOULA, JACKSON CO.

1—OUR LADY OF VICTORIES (1855) Rev. I. Anthony Arguelles.
Res.: 503 Convent St., P.O. Box 368, 39568. Tel: 228-762-1653; Fax: 228-762-2546. Email: ourladyofvictori@bellsouth.net.
Catechesis/Religious Program—Tel: 228-497-6893. Michele Hill, D.R.E. Students 17.

2—ST. PETER THE APOSTLE (1907), (African American), [CEM] Rev. Charles E. McMahon, S.S.J.
Mailing Address: P.O. Box 876, 39568.
Res.: 1715 Telephone Rd., 39567. Tel: 228-762-1759; Fax: 228-762-1709.
Catechesis/Religious Program—Lena Sanders, D.R.E.; Sr. Mary Kay Schreier, D.C., D.R.E. Students 39.

3—SACRED HEART (1963) Rev. Michael Kelleher.
Mailing Address: P.O. Box 2190, 39569. Tel: 228-762-1837; Fax: 228-762-1958.
Res.: 3702 Quinn Dr., 39581. Tel: 228-762-1837.
School—Resurrection School-Elementary, (Grades PreK-6), 3704 Quinn Dr., 39581-2356. Tel: 228-762-7207; Fax: 228-762-0611. Elizabeth K. Benefield, Prin.; Linda Wiggins, Librarian; Cathy Groff, Librarian. Lay Teachers 25; Students 332.
Catechesis/Religious Program—Students 14.

PASS CHRISTIAN, HARRISON CO.

1—HOLY FAMILY PARISH (2005, Pineville) Very Rev. Dennis J. Carver; Rev. Peter Varghese, C.M.I.; Deacon William Vrazel; Sr. Jackie Tarrant, R.S.M., Pastoral Assoc.
Res.: 22342 Evangeline Dr., 39571. Tel: 228-452-4686; Fax: 228-452-5488. Web: www.holyfamilyparish.cc.
School—St. Vincent de Paul Elementary, (Grades PreK-6) Tel: 228-863-6876; Fax: 228-863-9537. Mrs. Elizabeth Fortenberry, Prin.; Susan Hewes, Librarian. Lay Teachers 48; Students 385.
Catechesis/Religious Program— Linden Williams, D.R.E.; Craig Spence, Youth Dir. Students 90.

2—OUR MOTHER OF MERCY (1911), (African American), [JC] Rev. Batholomew Enslow, S.S.J.
Res.: 216 Saucier Ave., 39571. Tel: 228-452-4514; 228-452-6309; Fax: 228-452-4514.
Catechesis/Religious Program—Tel: 228-452-4002. Students 189.

3—ST. PAUL, Closed. For inquiries for parish records contact Holy Family, Pass Christian.

4—SACRED HEART (Dedeaux) (1967) Rev. Michael P. O'Connor; Deacon Roberto Jimenez.
Res. & Office: 14595 Vidalia Rd., 39571. Tel: 228-255-3381; 228-255-7560 (Office); Fax: 228-255-7888 (Office).
Catechesis/Religious Program—Students 159.
Station—Cursillo Center, (Dedeaux), Tel: 228-255-0430. Students 121.

PEARLINGTON, HANCOCK CO., ST. JOSEPH (1939) [JC] Closed. For inquiries for sacramental records, please see St. Ann, Clermont Harbor.

PICAYUNE, PEARL RIVER CO., ST. CHARLES BORROMEO (1950) Rev. Michael E. Snyder.
Res.: 1020 Fifth St., 39466. Tel: 601-798-4779. Email: stcborromeo@att.net. Web: www.scborromeo.org.
School—St. Charles Borromeo Catholic Elementary School, (Grades PreK-4), 1006 Goodyear Blvd., 39466. Tel: 601-799-0860; Fax: 601-798-4749. Email: stcb@att.net. Web: scborromeo.org/school. Ellen Loper, Prin. Lay Teachers 8; Students 77.
Catechesis/Religious Program—Tel: 601-798-7574 (Youth Min.); 601-799-0860 (Children's Min.); Fax: 601-798-4749. Ellen Loper, D.R.E. & Prin. Students 340.

PINEVILLE, HARRISON CO., OUR LADY OF LOURDES (Pass Christian) (1973) Closed. Please see Holy Family, Pass Christian.

VANCLEAVE, JACKSON CO., HOLY SPIRIT CATHOLIC CHURCH (1980) Rev. Thang John Pham; Deacon John E. Jennings.
Res.: 6705 Jim Ramsey Rd., 39565. Tel: 228-826-4008; Fax: 228-826-1650.
Catechesis/Religious Program—Students 166.
Mission—Christ the King 10601 Daisy Vestry, Latimer, Jackson Co. 39565. Tel: 228-392-0340.

WAVELAND, HANCOCK CO., ST. CLARE (1919) Rev. Cuthbert R. O'Connell.

Res.: 236 S. Beach Blvd., P.O. Box 500, 39576. Tel: 228-467-9275; Fax: 228-466-5653. Email: stclarecatholic@yahoo.com.
Catechesis/Religious Program—Tel: 228-424-8771. Noel Phillips, D.R.E. Students 96.

WAYNESBORO, WAYNE CO., ST. BERNADETTE (1977) [JC 2] Rev. Msgr. Michael J. Thornton; Rev. Anthony Doan Tran.
Res.: 401 Mississippi Dr., 39367. Tel: 601-735-9420.
Catechesis/Religious Program—Students 11.
Mission—Holy Trinity 911 Jackson Ave., P.O. Box 896, Leakesville, Perry Co. 39451. Tel: 601-394-6761.

WHITE CYPRESS, HANCOCK CO., ST. MATTHEW THE APOSTLE (1982) Rev. Noel Fannon.
Mailing Address: P.O. Box 919, Kiln, 39556.
Res.: 27074 St. Matthew Church Rd., Perkinston, 39573. Tel: 228-255-7720; Fax: 228-255-7786.
Catechesis/Religious Program—Students 144.

WIGGINS, STONE CO., ST. FRANCIS XAVIER (1961) [JC] Rev. Fintan J. Kilmurray.
Res.: 1026 E. Central Ave., 39577. Tel: 601-928-2182; Fax: 601-928-2182.
Church: Tel: 601-928-2182.
Catechesis/Religious Program—Tel: 601-528-9778. Leona O'Neil, D.R.E. Students 70.
Mission—St. Lucy CB6308, Lucedale, George Co. 39452. Tel: 601-947-9968. Deacon Caruba L. Merrill.
Station—Perkinston Junior College Perkinston.

Chaplains of Public Institutions

BILOXI. *Keesler Airforce Base*. Revs. Richard B. Dunn, Colonel, Frank E. Lowe, Lieutenant, Ruben Covos, Lieutenant.
V.A. Center. Rev. Maryon Jordan, O.S.B.

COLUMBIA. *Industrial and Training School*. Rev. Martin Joseph Gillespie.

GULFPORT. *Naval Const. Bn. Center*. Vacant.

HATTIESBURG. *University of Southern Mississippi*. Very Rev. Thomas Conway, V.F.

LEAKESVILLE. *South Mississippi Correctional Institution*. Rev. Msgr. Michael J. Thornton, J.C.L.

Retired:
Most Rev.—
Howze, Joseph Lawson, D.D.
Rev. Msgrs.—
Farrell, Francis
McGough, James P., J.C.D.
Mercier, Joseph
Revs.—
Harlow, Denis
Izral, John
Kelly, John J.
Kozak, Remigius A.
Lynch, Antone, V.F.
O'Shaughnessy, Patrick
Phan, Dominic

Permanent Deacons:
Baglioni, Victor, (Retired)
Bradford, L. Paul, Sr., Our Lady of Fatima, Biloxi
Conason, Rick, St. James, Gulfport
Elder, Emery, St. Joseph, Moss Point
Everard, Robert, St. Peter, Bassfield
Finnegan, Martin, St. Elizabeth Seton, Ocean Springs
Gaule, Harold, Our Lady of Perpetual Help, Lumberton
Gilly, Michael, Our Lady of Victories, Pascagoula
Goff, Warren P., Sr., Sacred Heart, Hattiesburg
Hamm, David, Our Lady of Perpetual Help, Lumberton
Harper, Gayden R., St. Mary, Gautier
Harris, Michael M., Our Lady of the Gulf, Bay St. Louis
Henderson, John R., St. James, Gulfport
Hollingsworth, Richard A., Immaculate Conception, Laurel
Hughes, David O., St. Bernadette, Waynesboro
Hunter, Jack, (Retired)
Jennings, John E., Holy Spirit, Vancleave
Jimenez, Roberto, Sacred Heart, Pass Christian
Jones, Bob, St. Mary, Woolmarket
Landry, Melvin J., Blessed Francis Xavier Seelos, Biloxi
LeBlanc, Tom, Sacred Heart, Hattiesburg
Martin, Frank W., St. Ann Mission, Hurley
McNair, Douglas R., St. Charles Borromeo, Picayune
Merrill, Caruba L., St. Lucy, Lucedale
Miller, Gregory, St. Alphonsus, Ocean Springs
Miller, Tom, (Retired)
Moragas, Lucien F., Jr., Keesler Air Force Base
Pressly, Larry L., Immaculate Conception, Laurel
Renz, Edward, Our Lady of the Gulf, Bay St. Louis
Stockert, Al, St. Mary, Biloxi
Torrelli, Ralph, St. Thomas, Hattiesburg
Vancourt, Ernest, St. Thomas the Apostle, Long Beach
Vrazel, William, Holy Family, Pass Christian
Walker, Charles, (Retired)
Wimberly, Ben, Jr., Nativity B.V.M. Cathedral, Biloxi

INSTITUTIONS LOCATED IN THE DIOCESE

[A] HIGH SCHOOLS, INTERPAROCHIAL

BILOXI. *St. Patrick Catholic High School*, (Grades 7-12), (Coed), 18300 St. Patrick Rd., 39532. Tel: 228-702-0500; Fax: 228-702-0511. Email: btrosclair@biloxidiocese.org. Web: www.stpatrickhighschool.net. Bobby Trosclair, Prin.; Margaret Evans, Librarian. Brothers 1; Lay Teachers 41; Students 506.

BAY ST. LOUIS. *Our Lady Academy*, (Grades 7-12), (Girls), 222 S. Beach Blvd., 39520-4320. Tel: 228-467-7048; Fax: 228-467-1666. Email: sue.goggins@ourladyacademy.com. Web: www.ourladyacademy.com. Susan Goggins, Prin.; Virginia Gex, Librarian. Sisters of Mercy 2; Lay Teachers 20; Students 235.

PASCAGOULA. *Resurrection Middle/Sr. School*, (Grades 7-12), (Coed), 520 Watts Ave., 39567. Tel: 228-762-3353; Fax: 228-769-1226. Email: dcuevas@rcseagles.com. Web: www.rcseagles.com. Darnell Cuevas, Prin.; Laura Thompson, Librarian; Linda Wiggins, Librarian. Lay Teachers 25; Students 197.
Resurrection Elementary School (Grades PreK-6), 3704 Quinn, 39581. Tel: 228-762-7207. Elizabeth K. Benefield, Prin.; Linda Wiggins, Librarian. Lay Teachers 30; Students 307.

[B] HIGH SCHOOLS AND ELEMENTARY SCHOOLS, PRIVATE

BAY ST. LOUIS. *St. Stanislaus College* (1854) 304 S. Beach Blvd., 39520-4301. Tel: 228-467-9057; Fax: 228-466-2972. Email: admissions@ststan.com. Web: www.ststan.com. Bro. Ronald Hingle, S.C., Pres.; Mr. Paul Verlander, Prin.; Dolores Richmond, Dir. Admissions; Virginia Gex, Librarian. Brothers of the Sacred Heart., Boys boarding and day school, secondary and elementary. Brothers 6; Lay Teachers 38; Students 375.
Camp Stanislaus Tel: 228-467-9057; Fax: 228-466-2972. Boys' summer program for ages 9-15.

[C] HOUSING FOR THE ELDERLY

BILOXI. *Gabriel Manor*, 2321 Atkinson Rd., 39531. Tel: 228-388-1013; Fax: 228-388-1176. Email: gabrielmanor@bellsouth.net. Ms. Brenda Mulvaney, Mgr. Total Staff 3; Total in Residence 51.
Gabriel Manor II, Inc.
Santa Maria Retirement Apartments, 1790 Popps Ferry Rd., 39532. Tel: 228-702-2137. Mr. Gregory K. Crapo, B.S., M.B.A, Sec. Bed Capacity 209; Total Assisted Annually 250; Total Staff 3.

BAY ST. LOUIS. *Notre Dame de la Mer Retirement Apartments*, 292 Hwy. 90, 39520. Tel: 228-467-2885; Fax: 228-466-6300. Email: mftine@bellsouth.net. Ms. Michele Tine, Mgr. Total Staff 2; Total in Residence 66.

GULFPORT. *Carlow Manor*, 15195 Barbara Dr., 39503. Tel: 228-539-0707; Fax: 228-539-0704. Email: carlow@bellsouth.net. Donna G. Holliman, Mgr. Bed Capacity 40; Total Assisted Annually 39; Total Staff 3.

OCEAN SPRINGS. *Samaritan House* (1987) 642 Jackson Ave., 39564. Tel: 228-875-1087; Fax: 228-872-9500. Email: samaritanhousere@bellsouth.net. Ms. Sharon Ballow, Mgr. Total Staff 2; Total in Residence 52.
Villa Maria Retirement Apartments, 921 Porter Ave., 39564. Tel: 228-875-8811; Fax: 228-875-8889. Email: villacindy@aol.com. Mrs. Cindy A. Ladnier, Mgr. Total Staff 15; Total in Residence 209.

PETAL. *Caritas Manor*, 145 W. 10th Ave., 39465. Tel: 601-545-7744; Fax: 601-545-7740. Email: caritaspetal@att.net. Total Staff 2; Total in Residence 32.

[D] MONASTERIES AND RESIDENCES OF PRIESTS AND BROTHERS

BAY ST. LOUIS. *St. Augustine's Residence* (1920) 199 Seminary Dr., 39520. Tel: 228-467-6414; Fax: 228-466-4393. Very Rev. Augustine Wall, S.V.D., Rector; Revs. Thaddeus Boucree, S.V.D.; Walter Bracken, S.V.D., Chap. Retreat Center; Robert Fisher, S.V.D.; George Gormley, S.V.D., House Fin. Admin.; Very Rev. James Pawlicki, S.V.D., Provincial Supr.; Revs. Stanley Plutz, S.V.D.; Thomas Potts, S.V.D.; Benignus Wego, S.V.D.; Bros. Samuel Adjei, S.V.D., (Leave of Absence); Richard Chambers, S.V.D.; James Heeb, S.V.D Priests 9; Brothers 2; Permanent Staff Priests 9; Permanent Staff Brothers 2. *St. Augustine's Retreat Center* Tel: 228-467-1097; Fax: 228-466-4393. Very Rev. Augustine Wall, S.V.D., Retreat Center Supvr.
Brothers of the Sacred Heart, 114 Bookter St., 39520. Tel: 228-466-4974; Fax: 228-466-2972. Email: bgcouvillion@gmail.com. Bros. Ronald Hingle, S.C.; Edwardo Baldisceda, S.C., Sub-Dir.; Raymond Sylve, S.C.; Bernard Couvillion, S.C., Dir.; Malcolm Melcher, S.C.; Dwight Kenney, S.C. Total in Residence 6. *Media Production Center* Tel: 228-467-1097; Fax: 228-466-5618. Email: pawlicki@inaword.com. Very Rev. James Pawlicki, S.V.D., Dir. Media Production Center.
Media Production Center "In A Word", 199 Seminary Dr., 39520. Tel: 228-467-1097; Fax: 228-466-5618. Email: editor@inaword.com. Web: www.inaword.com. Very Rev. James Pawlicki, S.V.D., Dir. & Editor.
Southern Province of St. Augustine - Provincial Offices, 199 Seminary Dr., 39520. Tel: 228-467-4322; Fax: 228-466-5618. Email: provincial@inaword.com. Very Rev. James Pawlicki, S.V.D., Prov.; Revs. Paul Kahan, S.V.D., Vice Prov.; George Gormley, S.V.D., Treas. Society of the Divine Word. Priests 61; Brothers 4; Parishes 29; Mission Stations 4; Elementary Schools 5. *Province Development Office* Tel: 228-467-3815; Fax: 228-466-5618. Rev. Thomas Potts, S.V.D., Dir.

[E] CONVENTS AND RESIDENCES FOR SISTERS

BILOXI. *Sisters of Mercy Convent*, 11454 Spring Ln., 39532. Sr. Kim Marie Lajoie, R.S.M., Contact Person. Religious Sisters of Mercy of the Americas 4.

LONG BEACH. *Congregation of the Holy Rosary* (Vietnamese), 5122 N. Gates Ave., 39560. Tel: 228-863-3045. Sisters 3.
Presentation Sisters, 18091 Commission Rd., 39560. Tel: 228-864-8418; Fax: 228-864-1627. Email: pres18091@cableone.net. Web: www.tbvmunion.org. Union of the Sisters of the Presentation of the Blessed Virgin Mary.

[F] NEWMAN CENTERS

HATTIESBURG. *University of Southern Mississippi* St. Thomas Aquinas Catholic Church, 3117 W. Fourth St., 39401. Tel: 601-264-5192; Fax: 601-264-0834. Email: church@stthomas-usm.org. Web: www.stthomas-usm.org. Rev. Tommy Conway, Chap.; Carrie Bell, Campus Min. Priests 1; Staff 8.

[G] MISCELLANEOUS

BILOXI. *Magnificat - Mississippi Gulf Coast Chapter*, 1501 Popps Ferry Rd., 39532. Tel: 228-392-0697. Mrs. Yvette D. Livaccari, Contact Person.

DIAMONDHEAD. *Magnificat of Diamondhead*, 883 Manini Way, 39525. Tel: 228-255-8490. Cindy Burnett, Coord.

RELIGIOUS INSTITUTES OF MEN REPRESENTED IN THE DIOCESE

For further details refer to the corresponding bracketed number in the Religious Institutes of Men or Women section.

[1100]—*Brothers of the Sacred Heart*—S.C.
[]—*Carmelites of Mary Immaculate*—C.M.I.
[]—*Heralds of Good News*—H.G.N.
[0840]—*Missionary Servants of the Most Holy Trinity*—S.T.
[]—*Order of St. Benedict*—O.S.B.
[1070]—*Redemptorist Fathers*—C.Ss.R.
[0420]—*Society of the Divine Word*—S.V.D.
[0700]—*St. Joseph's Society of the Sacred Heart*—S.S.J.

RELIGIOUS INSTITUTES OF WOMEN REPRESENTED IN THE DIOCESE

[0760]—*Daughters of Charity of St. Vincent De Paul*—D.C.
[]—*Daughters of Our Lady of the Holy Rosary*—F.M.S.R.
[]—*Dominican Sisters*—O.P.
[2575]—*Institute of the Sisters of Mercy of the Americas*—R.S.M.
[]—*Missionaries of the Infant Jesus of Good Health*
[3530]—*Missionary Sisters Servants of the Holy Spirit*—S.H.Sp.
[3280]—*Presentation of the Blessed Virgin Mary Sisters*—P.B.V.M.

[]—*Sisters for Christian Community*—S.F.C.C.

[1510]—*Sisters of St. Francis*—O.S.F.

[]—*Sisters of the Blessed Sacrament*—S.B.S.

NECROLOGY

† Murray, Rev. Msgr. Andrew L., Gulfport, MS St. John the Evangelist—Died Oct. 20, 2009

† O'Brien, John T., (Retired)—Died May 18, 2009

An asterisk (*) denotes an organization that has established tax-exempt status directly with the IRS and is not covered by the USCCB Group Ruling.

Diocese of Birmingham

(Dioecesis Birminghamiensis)

Most Reverend

ROBERT J. BAKER, S.T.D.

Bishop of Birmingham; ordained March 21, 1970; appointed Bishop of Charleston July 12, 1999; ordained and installed September 29, 1999; appointed Bishop of Birmingham August 14, 2007; installed October 2, 2007.

Most Reverend

DAVID E. FOLEY, D.D.

Bishop Emeritus of Birmingham; ordained May 26, 1956; appointed Auxiliary Bishop of Richmond, Virginia May 3, 1986; ordained Bishop June 27, 1986; appointed Bishop of Birmingham March 22, 1994; installed May 13, 1994; retired May 10, 2005.

ESTABLISHED JUNE 28, 1969.

Square Miles 28,091.

Comprises the Counties of North Alabama in an irregular line between the Counties (west to east) of Sumter and Choctaw and following the base of the following Counties: Marengo, Perry, Chilton, Coosa, Tallapoosa and Chambers or comprising the Counties of: Bibb, Blount, Calhoun, Chambers, Cherokee, Chilton, Clay, Cleburne, Colbert, Coosa, Cullman, DeKalb, Etowah, Fayette, Franklin, Greene, Hale, Jackson, Jefferson, Lamar, Lauderdale, Lawrence, Limestone, Madison, Marengo, Marion, Marshall, Morgan, Perry, Pickens, Randolph, St. Clair, Shelby, Sumter, Talladega, Tallapoosa, Tuscaloosa, Walker and Winston.

Legal Title: The Catholic Bishop of Birmingham in Alabama, a Corporation Sole.
For legal titles of institutions, consult the Chancery Office

Chancery Office: Catholic Diocese of Birmingham, P.O. Box 12047, Birmingham, AL 35202-2047. Tel: 205-838-8322; Fax: 205-836-1910.

Web: www.bhmdiocese.org

STATISTICAL OVERVIEW

Personnel	
Bishop	1
Retired Bishops	1
Abbots	1
Retired Abbots	1
Priests: Diocesan Active in Diocese	58
Priests: Diocesan Active Outside Diocese	3
Priests: Retired, Sick or Absent	23
Number of Diocesan Priests	84
Religious Priests in Diocese	27
Total Priests in Diocese	111
Ordinations:	
Transitional Deacons	2
Permanent Deacons in Diocese	56
Total Brothers	22
Total Sisters	155
Parishes	
Parishes	54
With Resident Pastor:	
Resident Diocesan Priests	36
Resident Religious Priests	13
Without Resident Pastor:	
Administered by Priests	2
Administered by Lay People	3
Missions	19
Professional Ministry Personnel:	
Brothers	1
Sisters	10
Lay Ministers	57
Welfare	
Catholic Hospitals	4
Total Assisted	689,500
Health Care Centers	1
Total Assisted	42,000
Special Centers for Social Services	19
Total Assisted	87,323
Educational	
Diocesan Students in Other Seminaries	8
Total Seminarians	8
High Schools, Diocesan and Parish	5
Total Students	203
High Schools, Private	1
Total Students	160
Elementary Schools, Diocesan and Parish	18
Total Students	3,809
Elementary Schools, Private	1
Total Students	247
Non-residential Schools for the Disabled	1
Total Students	120
Catechesis/Religious Education:	
High School Students	1,775
Elementary Students	6,902
Total Students under Catholic Instruction	13,224
Teachers in the Diocese:	
Priests	4
Brothers	1
Sisters	14
Lay Teachers	263
Vital Statistics	
Receptions into the Church:	
Infant Baptism Totals	2,436
Minor Baptism Totals	175
Adult Baptism Totals	206
Received into Full Communion	576
First Communions	1,948
Confirmations	1,369
Marriages:	
Catholic	273
Interfaith	138
Total Marriages	411
Deaths	628
Total Catholic Population	89,489
Total Population	2,944,890

Former Bishops—Most Revs. JOSEPH G. VATH, ord. June 7, 1941; appt. Auxiliary Bishop of Mobile-Birmingham March 25, 1966; cons. May 26, 1966; transferred to the Diocese of Birmingham Dec. 9, 1969; died July 14, 1987; RAYMOND J. BOLAND, D.D., ord. June 16, 1957; appt. Bishop of Birmingham Feb. 2, 1988; cons. March 25, 1988; transferred to Kansas City-St. Joseph Sept. 9, 1993; DAVID E. FOLEY, D.D., ord. May 26, 1956; appt. Titular Bishop of Ottaba and Auxiliary Bishop of Richmond May 3, 1986; cons. June 27, 1986; appt. Bishop of Birmingham March 22, 1994; installed May 13, 1994; retired May 10, 2005.

Chancery Office—Catholic Diocese of Birmingham, 2121 Third Ave. N., Birmingham, 35203. Tel: 205-838-8322; Fax: 205-836-1910. *Mailing Address: P.O. Box 12047, Birmingham, 35202-2047*Web: www.bhmdiocese.org. Address all Diocesan Correspondence to the above Post Office Box unless otherwise indicated. Telephones listed below.

Office of the Bishop—ALLISON SCHUMACHER, Sec. Tel: 205-838-8318; GERRY NABORS, Exec. Asst. Tel: 205-833-0175.

Chancellor—Very Rev. KEVIN M. BAZZEL, J.C.L.

Priests'/Presbyteral Council—Most Rev. ROBERT JOSEPH BAKER, Pres.; Very Revs. JOSEPH G. CULOTTA, Chair; RAYMOND J. REMKE, Vice-Chair; J. THOMAS ACKERMAN, Sec.; KEVIN M. BAZZEL, J.C.L.; PATRICK P. CULLEN; JEREMIAH DEASY; MICHAEL J. DEERING, V.G.; Revs. JOHN H. HARTSFIELD; JOSEPH DELANO LODY JR.; Very Revs. WILLIAM P. LUCAS; MICHAEL MAC MAHON; Rev. Msgrs. MARTIN M. MULLER; PAUL L. ROHLING, V.G.; MICHAEL F. SEXTON; Very Rev. GREGORY T. BITTNER, J.C.L., J.D., Observer.

Diocesan College of Consultors—Very Revs. J. THOMAS ACKERMAN; KEVIN M. BAZZEL, J.C.L.; PATRICK P. CULLEN; JOSEPH G. CULOTTA; JEREMIAH DEASY; MICHAEL J. DEERING, V.G.; WILLIAM P. LUCAS; MICHAEL MAC MAHON; Rev. Msgr. MARTIN M. MULLER; Very Rev. RAYMOND J. REMKE; Rev. Msgrs. PAUL L. ROHLING, V.G.; MICHAEL F. SEXTON.

Diocesan College of Vicars—Rev. Msgr. PAUL L. ROHLING, V.G.; Very Revs. MICHAEL J. DEERING, V.G.; GREGORY T. BITTNER, J.C.L., J.D., Judicial Vicar; KEVIN M. BAZZEL, J.C.L., Adjutant Judicial Vicar; Rev. Msgr. MICHAEL F. SEXTON, Vicar for Clergy, Southeast Deanery; Very Revs. JOSEPH G. CULOTTA, Vicar for Ecumenical & Interfaith Dialogue; BRYAN K. LOWE, Vicar for Vocations; VERNON HUGULEY, Vicar for Black Catholic Ministry; JOHN G. MCDONALD, Vicar for Hispanic Ministry; RICHARD E. DONOHOE, Vicar for Catholic Charities; PATRICK P. CULLEN, West Birmingham Deanery; JEREMIAH DEASY, Southwest Deanery; WILLIAM P. LUCAS, East Birmingham Deanery; MICHAEL MAC MAHON, Northeast Deanery; Rev. Msgr. MARTIN M. MULLER, Central Birmingham Deanery; Very Rev. RAYMOND J. REMKE, Northwest Deanery.

Diocesan Pastoral Council—Most Rev. ROBERT JOSEPH BAKER, Pres., Members include lay representatives of the Diocesan Deaneries, four Vicars for Deaneries, four religious and a staff representative.

Diocesan Finance Council—Most Rev. ROBERT JOSEPH BAKER, Pres.; Very Rev. RICHARD E. DONOHOE; ROGER MCLAUGHLIN, Chm. Members: Very Rev. GREGORY T. BITTNER, J.C.L., J.D.; RAY G. DYER JR., CPA; PAUL J. SHARBEL; J. STANLEY MACKIN JR.; BILLY RICHARDSON; JIM FRANKLIN; FRANK COMENSKY. Staff Members: ROBERT M. SELLERS JR., CFO; GERRY NABORS, Exec. Asst., Plus members of Diocesan Committees: Audit, Investment, Property, Personnel.

Tribunal—Very Revs. GREGORY T. BITTNER, J.C.L., J.D., Judicial Vicar. Tel: 205-838-8307; KEVIN M. BAZZEL, J.C.L., Adjutant Judicial Vicar; CYWILLA FABIJANIC, Moderator of Tribunal Chancery &

Notary; JACKIE HELLINGER, Sec. & Notary.
Judges—Sr. LYNN MCKENZIE, O.S.B., J.C.L., Ad Causum, Defender of the Bond; Rev. LOUIS GIARDINO; Rev. Msgr. PAUL ROHLING, V.G.
Defender of the Bond—Deacon DANIEL J. LAURITA, Please address all Rogatory to the Office of the Tribunal, Catholic Diocese of Birmingham.
Catholic Social Services—ALBERT MANZELLA, Exec. Dir. Tel: 205-838-8316.
Catholic Family Services—TOM COOK, D.S.W., Rgnl. Dir., 1515 12th Ave. S., Birmingham, 35205. Tel: 205-324-6561.
Catholic Family Services Offices—LAURA DINWIDDIE, M.S.W., Rgnl. Dir., 1010 Church St., Huntsville, 35804. Tel: 256-536-0073; Sr. CAROL ANN GRAY, M.H.S.H., Dir., Catholic Family Service Center, 608 37th St., Tuscaloosa, 35405. Tel: 205-759-9384; ELLEN BEADLE, M.S.W., Social Worker, 1111 E. College St., Florence, 35630. Tel: 256-768-1550.
Catholic Centers of Concern— Birmingham; Anniston; Gadsden; Hamilton; Huntsville; Eutaw; Winfield; Sulligent; Tuscaloosa.
Apostolate to the Aged—Deacon AL GERMANN, Dir., 369 Midwood Ave., Birmingham, 35228. Tel: 205-923-7108.
Engaged Encounter—DAN CATT; TERRY CATT, 2116 Bailey Brook Dr., Birmingham, 35244. Tel: 205-988-3962.
Natural Family Planning—HAROLD GRAY; CATHY GRAY, 2771 Cox Cove Rd., Hayden, 35079. Tel: 205-590-1792.
Department of Education—FRANK X. SAVAGE, Dir., Catholic Educ. & Lifelong Formation.
Catholic Schools—FRAN LAWLOR, Supt. Tel: 205-838-8303.
Religious Education—MICKY ZIELINSKI, Dir. Tel: 205-838-8312.
Apostolate with Mentally Retarded Persons—Very Rev. PATRICK P. CULLEN, Dir.; Sr. MARY VERNON GENTLE, R.S.M., Assoc. Dir., The Nazareth House, 751 Academy Dr., Bessemer, 35020. Tel: 205-424-2984; Fax: 205-426-5753. Email: mvgentle@aol.com.
Catholic Youth Ministry—DONALD SCHWARZHOFF, Dir. Tel: 205-838-8301.
Campus Ministry—JOHN MARTIGNONI, Dir. Tel: 205-776-7186. Email: jmartignoni@bhmdiocese.org.
Catholic Scouting—DONALD SCHWARZHOFF, Dir. Tel: 205-838-8301.
Toy Bowl Association—FRANK X. SAVAGE, Diocesan Contact, Mailing Address: P.O. Box 12047, Birmingham, 35202-2047. Tel: 205-838-8308.
Board of Education—MARK RICHARDS, Chm. Tel: 256-721-9572, Ext. 149 (Office); 256-985-9117 (Res.).
Finance Office and Administration—
Diocesan Finance Officer—ROBERT M. SELLERS JR. Tel: 205-833-0173.
Annual Catholic Charities Appeal— Catholic Relief Services, and National and Special Collections Very Rev. RICHARD E. DONOHOE, Dir. Tel: 205-838-8309.
Human Resources—JAMES H. WARREN II, Dir. Tel: 205-838-8321.
Family Life Ministry—JOHN MARTIGNONI, Dir. Tel: 205-776-7186. Email: jmartignoni@bhmdiocese.org.
Office of Pastoral Services—
Beginning Experience—TOM GARNER. Tel: 205-969-8509.
Children's Beginning Experience—JEANNETTE CAMPISI, 936 5th Ave., N.W., Alabaster, 35007. Tel: 205-664-0401.
Cursillo Program—KEVIN KISBY-GREEN, Lay Dir., 1735 Woodland St., N.W., Cullman, 35055. Tel: 256-736-2091. Email: kisbygreen@aol.com.
Hispanic Ministries—Sr. ROSA HERNANDEZ, M.G.Sp.S., Dir. Tel: 205-838-8308.
Services to Hispanics—VACANT. Tel: 205-987-4771.
Catholic Social Services Center - Hoover—VACANT. Tel: 205-987-4771.
Lay Ministries Program—Sr. MARIE LEONARD, O.S.B., Dir. Tel: 205-838-8300.
Marriage Encounter—KARL BRADY; MARY BRADY. Email: kbrady0816@aol.com.
Black Catholic Ministry—JAMES WATTS, Dir.
Pro-Life Activities—JOHN MARTIGNONI, Dir. Tel: 205-776-7186.
Propagation of the Faith and Holy Childhood—Very Rev. RAYMOND J. REMKE, Dir.; THERESA PETRUZELLA, Asst. Dir. Tel: 205-776-7181.
Serra Club of Birmingham—TIM HESS, Pres. Tel: 205-991-5301.
Vocations—JOHN MARTIGNONI, Coord. Tel: 205-838-2184.
"One Voice"— Diocesan weekly MARY ALICE CROCKETT, Mng. Editor. Tel: 205-838-8305; ANN LANZI, Circulation, The Birmingham Catholic Press, Inc., P.O. Box 10822, Birmingham, 35202. Tel: 205-838-8305; Fax: 205-838-8319.
Retrouvaille of Alabama, Inc.—Coordinators: LEE HINES; FRAN HINES. Tel: 205-967-3458.
Diocesan Council of Catholic Women—RUTH MAYS, Pres., 84 Muirfield Circle, Oneonta, 35121. Tel: 205-274-4101.
Priests' Retirement Fund—Mr. HENRY SMITH, c/o Priests' Retirement Fund, P.O. Box 10247, Birmingham, 35202-2047. Tel: 205-833-0173.
Victim Assistance Coordinator—Deacon FRANK R. SLAPIKAS. Email: fslapikas@bhmdiocese.org.
Office of the New Evangelization and Stewardship—JOHN MARTIGNONI, Dir. Tel: 205-776-7186. Email: jmartignoni@bhmdiocese.org.

CLERGY, PARISHES, MISSIONS AND PAROCHIAL SCHOOLS

CITY OF BIRMINGHAM

(JEFFERSON COUNTY)

1—ST. PAUL'S CATHEDRAL (1871) Very Rev. Kevin M. Bazzel, Rector & Adjutant Judicial Vicar; Rev. Show Reddy Kasu; Deacon Neal Kay.
Mailing Address: P.O. Box 10044, 35202-0044. Tel: 205-251-1279; Fax: 205-251-1284. In Res., Rev. Desmond Regan (Retired).
Res.: 2120 Third Ave. N., 35203. Tel: 205-328-7209.
Catechesis/Religious Program—Students 135.
Mission—St. Stephen the Martyr and Campus Center 1515 12th Ave. S., Jefferson Co. 35205. Tel: 205-933-2508. Sr. Karen Ann Lortscher, O.S.B., Campus Min.

2—ST. ANTHONY'S (1900) Closed. For inquiries for parish records contact St. Paul Cathedral, Birmingham.

3—ST. BARNABAS (1908) Rev. Msgr. Eugene O'Connor. Mailing Address: P.O. Box 610304, 35261. In Res., Rev. Michael Wrigley.
Res.: 7921 First Ave. N., 35206. Tel: 205-833-0334; 205-833-5695; Fax: 205-833-0272.
School—(Grades K-8), 7901 First Ave. N., 35206. Tel: 205-836-5385; Fax: 205-833-0272. Marilyn Coman, Prin. Lay Teachers 10; Students 112.
Mailing Address: P.O. Box 610347, 35261.
Catechesis/Religious Program—Tel: 205-836-4567. Rosemary Gagliano, D.R.E. Students 18.

4—ST. BERNARD'S (Inglenook) (1928) Closed. For inquiries for parish records contact St. Paul Cathedral, Birmingham.

5—BLESSED SACRAMENT (1910) [CEM] Rev. Jose Manjaly.
Res.: 1460 Pearson Ave., S.W., P.O. Box 110006, 35211. Tel: 205-785-9840.
Catechesis/Religious Program—Ann Noblitt, D.R.E. Students 3.

6—ST. FRANCIS XAVIER (1953) Rev. Robert J. Sullivan; Very Rev. John G. McDonald; Deacon George Mickwee; Sr. Jane Bishop, O.S.B., Pastoral Assoc. In Res., Very Rev. Gregory T. Bittner, Diocesan Judicial Vicar.
Res.: P.O. Box 130669, 35213. Tel: 205-871-1153; Fax: 205-871-9831.
School—(Grades K-8) Tel: 205-871-1687; Fax: 205-871-1674. Nathan Wright, Prin. Sisters 1; Lay Teachers 17; Students 176.
Catechesis/Religious Program—Julie McLean, D.R.E. Students 262.

7—HOLY FAMILY (1938), (African American), Rev. Robert Crossmyer, C.P.; Deacon Benjamin Jett. In Res., Rev. Alex Steinmiller, C.P.
Res.: 1910 19th St., 35218. Tel: 205-780-3440; Fax: 205-780-5272.
School—(Grades K-8), 1916 19th St., Ensley, 35218. Tel: 205-785-5858; Fax: 205-785-2666. William Kindall, Pres.; Chandra Farrier, Prin. Lay Teachers 12; Students 155.
Catechesis/Religious Program—Fax: 205-780-3440. Rose Sturdivant, D.R.E. Students 45.
Mission—St. Mary's (1943) 6101 Dr. Martin Luther King Dr., Fairfield, Jefferson Co. 35064. Tel: 205-923-0202 (Office); 205-780-9683 (Res.); Fax: 205-923-2276. Rev. Philip Paxton, C.P.; Deacon Walter Henderson.
Catechesis/Religious Program—Wade White, D.R.E. Students 345.
School—St. Mary's Early Childhood Center, (Grades PreK-2), 6124 Myron Massey Blvd., Fairfield, 35064. Tel: 205-923-5161; Fax: 205-923-5166. Shilisha Logan, Prin. Lay Teachers 5; Students 45.

8—HOLY ROSARY (Gate City) (1889) Revs. Anthony D'Angelo, S.D.B.; Kenneth Germaine, S.D.B. 7414 Georgia Rd., 35212. Tel: 205-595-0652.

9—ST. JOHN BOSCO (1973) Closed. For inquiries for parish records, please contact Holy Rosary, Birmingham.

10—ST. JOSEPH'S (1921), (Italian), Rev. Guillermo Castillo DelGadillo, Admin.
Res.: 3020 Avenue K, 35218. Tel: 205-788-5721; Fax: 205-788-7146.
Catechesis/Religious Program—Antonia Casas, D.R.E. Students 50.

11—KOREAN CATHOLIC COMMUNITY, ST. LUKE HWANG (1995), (Korean), Rev. Jeong Sang-Ki.
Res.: 759 Valley St., 35226. Tel: 205-823-2301.

12—ST. MARGARET'S (1986) Closed. For inquiries for parish records contact Blessed Sacrament Parish, Birmingham.

13—ST. MARK THE EVANGELIST (1999) Very Rev. Joseph G. Culotta.
Mailing Address: P.O. Box 380396, 35238-0396. Tel: 205-980-1810; Fax: 205-980-9208.
Catechesis/Religious Program—Susan Webb, C.R.E. Students 436.

14—ST. MARK'S (1904) Closed. For inquiries for parish records contact St. Paul's Cathedral, Birmingham.

15—OUR LADY OF FATIMA (1905), (African American), Rev. Paul Oberg, S.S.J.; Deacon Douglass C. Moorer.
Res.: 708 First St. S., 35205. Tel: 205-322-1205; Fax: 205-714-5056.
School—(Grades K-8), 630 First St. S., 35205. Tel: 205-251-8395; Fax: 205-251-8393. Velda Gilyot, Prin. Sisters of The Blessed Sacrament, PA 5; Lay Teachers 14; Students 212.
Catechesis/Religious Program—Mrs. Theresa Nalls, D.R.E. Students 100.

16—OUR LADY OF LOURDES (1959) Rev. Andrew Kennedy; Deacon William F. Brandt.
Res.: 980 Huffman Rd., 35215.
Office: Tel: 205-836-2274; Fax: 205-836-5436.
Catechesis/Religious Program—Students 176.

17—OUR LADY OF SORROWS (1887) Rev. Msgr. Martin M. Muller; Revs. Jim W. Booth; Jaya Prathap Duggimpudi; Sr. Pat Sullivan, M.S.B.T., Pastoral Assoc.
1730 Oxmoor Rd., 35209. Tel: 205-871-8121; Fax: 205-871-8180. In Res., Rev. Msgr. Brian Egan (Retired).
Res.: 1728 Oxmoor Rd., 35209. (Homewood)
School—(Grades K-8) Tel: 205-879-3237; Fax: 205-879-9332. Mary Jane Dorn, Prin. Lay Teachers 30; Students 484.
Catechesis/Religious Program—Tel: 205-871-1431; Fax: 205-871-1487. Elizabeth Sutton, D.R.E.; Sarah Pflaum, D.R.E. Students 464.

18—OUR LADY OF THE VALLEY (1974) Rev. Msgr. Paul L. Rohling; Rev. Richard A. Chenault Jr.; Sr. Madeline Contorno, O.S.B., Pastoral Min.; Deacon Bob Martin; Rev. Michael J. White, Pastor Emeritus (Retired).
Res.: 5514 Double Oak Ln., 35242. Tel: 205-991-5488; Fax: 205-991-5181.
Church: Tel: 205-991-5488; Fax: 205-991-5181.
School—(Grades K-8) Tel: 205-991-5963; Fax: 205-991-1251. Sandra Roden, Prin. Lay Teachers 33; Students 483.
Catechesis/Religious Program—Tel: 205-991-5489; Fax: 205-991-5181. Deacon Dan Whitaker, D.R.E. Students 522.

19—OUR LADY QUEEN OF THE UNIVERSE (1955), (African American), Rev. Jose Brahmakulam Chacko.
Res.: 961 Center St. N., 35204. Tel: 205-328-7729; Fax: 205-328-7703.
Catechesis/Religious Program—Carol Washington, D.R.E. Students 52.
Mission—Sacred Heart 3401 27th Ct. N., Collegeville, Jefferson Co. 35207. Tel: 205-252-8909.

20—ST. PETER THE APOSTLE (1962) Rev. Thomas M. Kelly; Very Rev. John G. McDonald; Rev. John Michael Adams; Deacon Sam Anzalone. In Res., Rev. John Robinson.
Res.: 2061 Patton Chapel Rd., 35216. Tel: 205-822-4480; Fax: 205-822-4534.
Catechesis/Religious Program—Tel: 205-823-4480, Ext. 24. Marcella Stobert, D.R.E. Students 388.

21—PRINCE OF PEACE (1984) Rev. John Fallon; Deacons Andres Eduardo Rodriguez Tejeda; Jose Vasquez. In Res., Rev. Henry McDaid (Retired).
Church & Mailing Address: 4600 Preserve Pkwy., Birmingham (Hoover), 35226. Tel: 205-822-9125; Fax: 205-822-9127.
Res.: 10-A Shades Crest Rd., 35226. Tel: 205-682-0460.
School—(Grades PreK-8) Tel: 205-824-7886; Fax: 205-827-2093. Connie Angstadt, Prin. Lay Teachers 35; Students 360.
Catechesis/Religious Program—Tel: 205-822-9125; Fax: 205-822-9127. Kathleen Dunne, D.R.E. Students 775.

22—SACRED HEART (1955) See separate listing. See Our Lady Queen of the Universe, Birmingham for details.

23—ST. STANISLAUS (1914) Very Rev. Vernon Huguley.
Mailing Address: 904 Indiana St., 35224. Tel: 205-785-9625.
Catechesis/Religious Program—Students 9.

24—ST. STEPHEN THE MARTYR (1991) See separate listing. Now a mission of Cathedral of St. Paul, Birmingham.
25—ST. THERESA'S, Closed. For inquiries for parish records contact St. Paul's Cathedral, Birmingham.
26—VIETNAMESE CATHOLIC COMMUNITY OUR LADY OF LAVANG PARISH AT ST. JOHN BOSCO CHURCH (2005) Rev. Andrew M. Nguyen.
142 52nd Pl. N., 35212.

OUTSIDE THE CITY OF BIRMINGHAM

ADAMSVILLE, JEFFERSON CO., ST. PATRICK'S (1983) [CEM] Very Rev. Vernon Huguley.
301 Shamrock Tr., 35005.
Res.: 404 Brian Dr., 35005. Tel: 205-674-7090.
Church: Tel: 205-798-5326; Fax: 205-798-5330.
Catechesis/Religious Program—Students 64.
Family Life Center—Tel: 205-798-0372.

ALEXANDER CITY, TALLAPOOSA CO., ST. JOHN THE APOSTLE (1948) Rev. Joseph Delano Lody Jr.
Res.: 454 N. Central Ave., 35010. Tel: 256-234-3631; Fax: 256-234-3789.
Catechesis/Religious Program—Tel: 256-329-8204; Fax: 256-234-3789. Susie Kelley, D.R.E. Students 40.
Mission—St. Mark (1994) 460 Country Club Rd., P.O. Box 98, Ashland, Clay Co. 36251. Tel: 256-354-3598; Fax: 256-354-3599. P.O. Box 98, Ashland, 36251.

ANNISTON, CALHOUN CO.
1—ALL SAINTS (1939) B. Dianne Green, Parish Dir.
Mailing Address: P.O. Box 4862, 36204. 1112 W. 15th St., 36201. Tel: 256-237-9230; Fax: 256-237-9230.
Catechesis/Religious Program—Rose Munford, D.R.E.
2—SACRED HEART OF JESUS (1886) Very Rev. Bryan K. Lowe.
Res.: P.O. Box 5010, 36205. Tel: 256-237-3011; Fax: 256-241-2048.
School—(Grades K-12), 16 Morton Rd., Fort McClellan, 36205. Tel: 256-237-4231; Fax: 256-241-2353. Charles Maniscalco, Prin. Lay Teachers 24; Students 200.
Catechesis/Religious Program—Carla Keith, D.R.E. Students 132.

ASHLAND, CLAY CO., ST. MARK'S, See separate listing. See St. John the Apostle, Alexander City for details.

ATHENS, LIMESTONE CO., ST. PAUL'S (1959) Rev. Charles Alookaran.
Mailing Address: P.O. Box 998, 35612.
Res.: 1900 Hwy. 72 W., 35611. Tel: 256-232-4191; Fax: 256-232-4191 (call first).
Catechesis/Religious Program—Elizabeth Niedzwiecki, D.R.E. Students 195.

BESSEMER, JEFFERSON CO.
1—ST. ALOYSIUS CHURCH (1886) Very Rev. Patrick P. Cullen; Stephanie Gerson, Pastoral Assoc.
Mailing Address: 751 Academy Dr., 35022. Tel: 205-424-2984; Fax: 205-426-5753.
Res.: Tel: 205-424-1839.
School—(Grades K-8) Tel: 205-425-0045; Fax: 205-425-0046. Dr. Bette Kirsting Bell, Prin.; Marcia Reid, Librarian. Lay Teachers 21; Students 175.
Catechesis/Religious Program—Students 68.
2—ST. FRANCIS OF ASSISI (1940), (African American), Rev. Paul Asih, M.S.P. In Res., Revs. Raphael Obatama; Emmanuel Isi.
Res.: 2400 Seventh Ave. N., 35020.
Catechesis/Religious Program—2410 7th Ave. N., 35020. Tel: 205-428-4758; Fax: 205-428-4751. Students 18.

CLANTON, CHILTON CO., CHURCH OF THE RESURRECTION Rev. Bruce Bumbarger, M.SS.CC.
P.O. Box 735, 35046. Tel: 205-755-5498; Fax: 205-755-5498.
Catechesis/Religious Program—Regina Phillips, D.R.E.

CULLMAN, CULLMAN CO., SACRED HEART (1877), (German), [CEM] Revs. Patrick Egan, O.S.B.; John O'Donnell, O.S.B.; Deacons William Roberson; Mike Branch.
Res.: 217 Second St., S.E., P.O. Box 1085, 35056. Tel: 256-734-3730; Fax: 256-734-3476.
School—(Grades K-6), 112 2nd Ave. S.E., 35055. Tel: 256-734-4563; Fax: 256-734-5882. Earnest Hauk, Prin. Lay Teachers 13; Students 128.
Catechesis/Religious Program—Fharis Richter, D.R.E. Students 155.
Mission—St. Boniface [CEM] P.O. Box 1085, Cullman Co. 35056.

DECATUR, MORGAN CO.
1—ST. ANN'S (1870) [JC], For more information please see Annunciation of the Lord, Decatur.
2—ANNUNCIATION OF THE LORD (2003) Very Rev. Raymond J. Remke; Sr. Teresa Walsh, C.S.J., Pastoral Assoc.; Deacons Javier Ramirez; Ramon D. Rodriguez.
Res.: 3910 Spring Ave., S.W., 35603. Tel: 256-353-2667; Fax: 256-353-8994.
School—(Grades PreK-8) Tel: 256-353-6543. Christine Wright, Prin. Lay Teachers 15; Students 180.
Catechesis/Religious Program—Jan Gile, D.R.E. Students 162.

DEMOPOLIS, MARENGO CO., ST. LEO (1936) Rev. Lawrence E. Shinnick.
Res.: 306 S. Walnut Ave., P.O. Box 937, 36732. Tel: 334-289-2767; Fax: 334-289-6085.
Catechesis/Religious Program—Diane Busby, D.R.E. Students 34.
Mission—Our Lady of Lourdes 8 Erwin Woods Dr., Greensboro, Hale Co. 37644.
Mission—St. Mary (1948) 274 Wilson Ave., Eutaw, Greene Co. 35462. (African American)

EUTAW, GREENE CO., ST. MARY (1948), (African American), See separate listing. See St. Leo, Demopolis for details.

FAIRFIELD, JEFFERSON CO., ST. MARY (1943) See separate listing. See Holy Family, Birmingham for details.

FLORENCE, LAUDERDALE CO.
1—ST. JOSEPH'S (1898) Rev. Andrew A. Sullivan; Kathie Franck, Pastoral Min.
Res.: 1111 E. College St., 35630. Tel: 256-764-3303; 256-767-9069 (Rectory); Fax: 256-718-0208.
School—(Grades K-8) Tel: 256-766-1923; 256-766-1955; Fax: 256-766-1713. Kelley Dewberry, Prin. Lay Teachers 21; Students 204.
Catechesis/Religious Program—Students 77.
2—ST. MICHAEL (1873) [CEM] Rev. Edward P. Markley, O.S.B.
Res.: 2751 County Rd. 30, 35634. Tel: 256-764-1885; Fax: 256-764-8933.
Catechesis/Religious Program—Karen Holden, D.R.E., (High School). Students 83.

FORT PAYNE, DE KALB CO., OUR LADY OF THE VALLEY (1959) Revs. Mark T. Spruill, English & Spanish Masses; E. Gray Bean, Spanish Mass; Deacon Hector Garcia, Admin.
Church & Mailing Address: 2910 Gault Ave., N., 35967. Tel: 256-845-4774; Fax: 256-845-4708.
Catechesis/Religious Program—Students 522.

GADSDEN, ETOWAH CO.
1—ST. JAMES (1912) Rev. E. Gray Bean.
Mailing Address: P.O. Box 38, 35902.
Res.: 225 Carleen St., 35901. Tel: 256-546-5339.
Church: 622 Chestnut St., 35901. Tel: 256-546-2975; Fax: 256-546-2930.
School—(Grades K-8) Tel: 256-546-0132; Fax: 256-546-0134. John Parker, Prin. Lay Teachers 14; Students 181.
Catechesis/Religious Program—Sandra Ashley, C.R.E. Students 215.
2—ST. MARTIN DE PORRES, Closed. For inquiries for parish records contact St. James, Gadsden.

GARDENDALE, JEFFERSON CO., ST. ELIZABETH ANN SETON (1976) Very Rev. Michael J. Deering; Margaret Wiley, Pastoral Assoc.
Mailing Address: 334 Main St., P.O. Box 1027, 35071. Tel: 205-631-9398 (Office); Fax: 205-631-5781.
Res.: 205 Powell Dr., P.O. Box 1027, 35071. Tel: 205-631-8582.
Catechesis/Religious Program—Fax: 205-631-5781. Jeanne Busby, D.R.E.; Jim Jernigan, D.R.E. Students 119.
Mission—St. Henry [CEM] 211 5th St., Warrior, Jefferson Co. 35180.

GUNTERSVILLE, MARSHALL CO., ST. WILLIAM (1952) Very Rev. J. Thomas Ackerman; Rev. Manuel Ruiz; Deacon Edwin M. Santos.
929 Gunter Ave., 35976. Tel: 256-582-4245 (Office); 256-572-3796 (Hispanic Min); Fax: 256-582-7954.
Res.: 1002 Blount Ave., 35976.
Catechesis/Religious Program—Ms. Cecilia Hall, D.R.E. Students 414.
Mission—Chapel of the Holy Cross 1534 Whitesville Rd., Albertville, Marshall Co. 35950. Tel: 256-891-0550.

HUNTSVILLE, MADISON CO.
1—GOOD SHEPHERD (1981) Rev. Louis Giardino; Deacons Ron Puent; Helmut Sassenfeld.
Res.: 13550 Chaney Thompson Rd. S.E., 35803-2326. Tel: 256-882-1844; Fax: 256-882-1841.
Catechesis/Religious Program— Katherine Maxwell, D.R.E. Students 427.
2—HOLY SPIRIT (1965) Very Rev. Michael Mac Mahon; Rev. Bryan W. Jerabek; Bro. Benedict Stoegbauer, S.D.S.; Deacons Samuel Dias; Lawrence E. Sisterman; Michael P. Sudnik.
Res.: 625 Airport Rd. S.W., 35802. Tel: 256-881-4781; Fax: 256-881-5510.
School—(Grades K-8) Tel: 256-881-4852. James Bell, Prin.; Karen McDaniel, Librarian. Lay Teachers 27; Students 437.
Catechesis/Religious Program—Tel: 256-881-0345. Mrs. Tracy Finke, D.R.E. Students 306.
3—ST. JOSEPH'S (1952) [CEM] Revs. Gary New, S.D.S.; Patrick Nelson, S.D.S. In Res., Rev. Robert Wagner, S.D.S. (Retired).
Res.: 2300 Beasley Ave., N.W., 35816. Tel: 256-534-8459; Fax: 256-534-8450.
School—Holy Family School, (Grades K-8) Tel: 256-539-5221; Fax: 256-533-0747. Mary Tomaine, Prin. Sisters of the Divine Savior 1; Lay Teachers 17; Students 189.
Catechesis/Religious Program—Tel: 256-534-1310. Carmen Amato, D.R.E. Students 61.
4—ST. MARY OF THE VISITATION (1861) Rev. Glen W. Sayers, S.D.S.; Deacon James G. Bodine.
Res.: 222 N. Jefferson St., 35801. Tel: 256-536-6349; Fax: 256-536-6349.
Catechesis/Religious Program—Tel: 256-536-6760. Mark C. Canney, D.R.E. Students 40.
5—OUR LADY QUEEN OF THE UNIVERSE (1965) Rev. Joy Chalissery; Deacon Daniel Melchoir.
Mailing Address: P.O. Box 3268, 35810.
Res.: 3701 Grizzard, 35810. Tel: 256-852-0788.
Church: 2421 Shady Lane Dr., N.W., 35810. Fax: 256-852-0199.
Catechesis/Religious Program—Susan Turner, D.R.E. Students 110.

JACKSONVILLE, CALHOUN CO., ST. CHARLES (1964) Rev. James R. Macey.
Church: 308 Seventh St., N.E., 36265. Tel: 256-435-3238; Fax: 256-435-4942.
Res.: 400 Seventh St., N.E., 36265. Tel: 256-435-1307.
Catechesis/Religious Program—Peggy Sugar, D.R.E. Students 39.
Mission—St. Joachim c/o 308 7th St., N.E., Piedmont, Calhoun Co. 36265. Deacon Donald Ash.

JASPER, WALKER CO., ST. CECILIA (1964) Rev. David Buchanan.
Mailing Address: 2159 Hwy. 195, 35503.
Res.: Tel: 205-384-4800 (Office); Fax: 205-384-1009.
Catechesis/Religious Program—Dan Gardener, D.R.E. Students 50.

LANETT, CHAMBERS CO., HOLY FAMILY (1915) [CEM] Rev. Antoo Alappat, Temp. Admin.
Res.: 705 N. Third Ave., 36863-0325. Tel: 334-644-4405; Fax: 706-645-6783.
Catechesis/Religious Program—Students 49.
Mission—Immaculate Conception 1256 Main St., Roanoke, Randolph Co. 36274. Tel: 334-853-4418.

LEEDS, JEFFERSON CO., ST. THERESA'S (1951) Rev. James J. Naughton, S.D.B.; Deacon Silverio Rubio Roman.
Res.: 1390 Ashville Ct., P.O. Box 525, 35094. Tel: 205-699-8534; Fax: 205-702-4010.
Catechesis/Religious Program—Sr. Rita Vogelsang, D.R.E. Students 70.

LIVINGSTON, SUMTER CO., ST. FRANCIS OF ASSISI (1972), Administered by The Catholic Church in West Central Alabama. Rev. Lawrence E. Shinnick.
Mailing Address: P.O. Box 1035, 35470. Tel: 334-289-2767; Fax: 334-289-0544.
Church: Hwy. 28 E., 35470.
Catechesis/Religious Program—Grace Neel, D.R.E. Students 1.

MADISON, MADISON CO., ST. JOHN THE BAPTIST (1973) Revs. Philip N. O'Kennedy; Mark T. Spruill; Deacons Dan Laurita; Darrell Diem; Carmelo Graffagnini; Lawrence Howell.
Res.: 1059 Hughes Rd., 35758. Tel: 256-722-0130; Fax: 256-722-0303.
School—(Grades K-8), 1057 Hughes Rd., 35758. Tel: 256-722-0772; Fax: 256-722-0151. Sherry Lewis, Prin.; Rosemary Terry, Librarian. Lay Teachers 29; Students 455.
Catechesis/Religious Program—Tel: 256-722-8590. Tandra Lavallee, D.R.E. Students 725.

MONTEVALLO, SHELBY CO., ST. THOMAS THE APOSTLE (1951) Rev. Raymond A. Dunmyer; Deacon William P. Alexiou.
Res. & Mailing Address: 80 St. Thomas Way, 35115. Tel: 205-663-3936; Fax: 205-663-3929.
Catechesis/Religious Program—Claire Murrell, D.R.E.; Mike Haughton, D.R.E. Students 270.

MOULTON, LAWRENCE CO., RESURRECTION CATHOLIC CHAPEL (1993) Unassigned.
Res.: 7363 Alabama Hwy. 33, 35650. Tel: 256-905-0330; Fax: 256-905-0330 (Call First).
Catechesis/Religious Program—Students 8.

ONEONTA, BLOUNT CO., CORPUS CHRISTI (1983) Rev. John H. Hartsfield; Deacon Paul I. Mullen.
Res.: 115 Androse Dr., 35121. Tel: 205-274-0343.
Church: 32015 State Hwy. 75, 35121. Tel: 205-625-6078; Fax: 205-625-6078.
Catechesis/Religious Program—Charlene Makofsky, C.R.E.; Yolanda Torres, D.R.E. (Spanish). Students 118.

PELL CITY, ST. CLAIR CO., OUR LADY OF THE LAKE (1969) Rev. Msgr. Michael R. Sexton; Deacon Terrence L. Rumore.
Mailing Address: Hwy. 231 S., P.O. Box 388, 35125.
Res.: 117 Ingram Lane, Cropwell, 35054. Tel: 205-525-5161 (Church); Fax: 205-525-5162.
Catechesis/Religious Program—Parma Boyle, D.R.E. Students 141.

RUSSELLVILLE, FRANKLIN CO., GOOD SHEPHERD CHURCH (1973) Rev. James A. Hedderman.
Res.: 1700 N. Jackson Ave., P.O. Box 878, 35653. Tel: 256-332-4861.

Catechesis/Religious Program—Students 152.

SCOTTSBORO, JACKSON CO., ST. JUDE (1971) Rev. Alan C. Mackey; Deacon Jerome P. Raispis.
Res.: 17205 Hwy. 35, 35768. Tel: 205-574-6156.
Catechesis/Religious Program—Carol Miller, C.R.E. Students 30.

SYLACAUGA, TALLADEGA CO., ST. JUDE (1947) Rev. Thomas F. Woods; Sr. Therese Francis Walker, M.S.B.T., Parish Dir.
Res.: 310 W. Bay St., P.O. Box 111, 35150. Tel: 256-245-7741.
Catechesis/Religious Program—Students 45.
Mission—Holy Name of Jesus 4th St., S.W. at 5th Ave., Childersburg, Talladega Co. 35044.

TALLADEGA, TALLADEGA CO., ST. FRANCIS OF ASSISI (1951) [CEM] Rev. Thomas F. Woods.
Res.: 722 East St. S., P.O. Box 1142, 35161. Tel: 256-362-5372; Fax: 256-362-5312.
Catechesis/Religious Program—Wendy Struzik, D.R.E. Students 10.

TRUSSVILLE, JEFFERSON CO., HOLY INFANT OF PRAGUE (1941) Very Rev. William P. Lucas; Deacons Ed Pruet; E. Lee Robinson Sr.
Res.: 8090 Gadsden Hwy., P.O. Box 43, 35173. Tel: 205-655-2541; Fax: 205-661-9231.
Catechesis/Religious Program—Terry Pruet, D.R.E. Students 282.

TUSCALOOSA, TUSCALOOSA CO.

1—ST. FRANCIS OF ASSISI UNIVERSITY PARISH (1929) Rev. Gerald Holloway; Deacons J. Adrian Straley; William J. Remmert; Susan Nelms, Campus Min.
Res.: 811 Fifth Ave., 35401. Tel: 205-758-5672; Fax: 205-758-5673.
Catechesis/Religious Program—Nancy Woodbury, D.R.E. Students 145.
Mission—St. Robert 407 2nd St., S.W., Reform, Pickens Co. 35481. Tel: 205-375-2638.

2—HOLY SPIRIT (1961) Very Rev. Jeremiah Deasy; Deacons Francis N. Viselli Jr.; Frank R. Slapikas.
Res.: 733 37th St. E., 35405. Tel: 205-553-9733; Fax: 205-553-7014.
School—(Grades K-6), 711 37th St., 35405. Tel: 205-553-9630; Fax: 205-553-8880. Sr. Elaine Sebera, R.S.M., Pres. & Prin. (Grades K-6). Tel: 205-553-5606; Judith H. Halli, Prin. (Grades 7-12). Tel: 205-553-5606. Lay Teachers 47; Students 672.
Catechesis/Religious Program—Mary Jane Wagner, D.R.E. Students 72.
Mission—St. John c/o Rev. Jeremiah Deasy at Holy Spirit, 8th & Lurleen Wallace Blvd., Tuscaloosa Co. 35401.

TUSCUMBIA, COLBERT CO., OUR LADY OF THE SHOALS (1869) [CEM] Rev. Patrick Don Bosco Forsythe.
Church & Res.: 200 E. Commons St. N., 35674. Tel: 256-383-7207 (Church); 256-381-2699 (Res.); Fax: 256-383-7883.
Catechesis/Religious Program—Elizabeth Gargis, D.R.E. Students 82.

WINFIELD, MARION CO., HOLY SPIRIT (1965) Rev. Timothy Pfander; Deacon John D. DeBlieux.
2710 U.S. Hwy. 43 N., 35594. Tel: 205-487-3616; Fax: 205-487-3616.
Catechesis/Religious Program—Tracy Rao, D.R.E. Students 40.
Mission—Holy Family 423 19th St., N.W., Fayette, Fayette Co. 35555. Tel: 205-932-6242.
Mission—Our Lady of Guadalupe 485 Layne Hill Dr., Haleyville, Winston Co. 35565. Tel: 205-487-3616.

On Special or Other Diocesan Assignment:
Most Rev.—
Marino, Joseph, Apostolic Nuncio to Bangladesh, U.N. Rd. 2, Baridhana, P.O. Box 6003, Dhaka 1212 Bangladesh.
Rev.—
O'Donnell, John, O.S.B., 112 Second Ave., S.E., Cullman, 35055.

On Duty Outside the Diocese:
Revs.—
Fisher, Albert, Chap., St. Joseph's Hospital, 9 Brackenston Sq., Savannah, GA 31406.
Reynolds, Jeffrie S. (Retired), 2159 S. McKenzie, #290, Foley, 36535. Tel: 352-228-3138

Absent on Leave:
Revs.—
Klauck, Michael
Summitt, James A.

Retired:
Rev. Msgr.—
Egan, Brian, 1728 Oxmoor Rd., 35209. Tel: 205-879-2257
Very Rev.—
Tierney, Patrick J., V.F., 340 Woodland Meadows, Albertville, 35951.
Revs.—
Blazak, Camillus, 533 Alexian Way #111, Signal Mountain, TN 37377.
Brennan, Matthew. Tel: 205-525-4711
Keiser, Raymond W., 3011 Massey Rd., Apt. E, Vestavia, 35216.
McDaid, Henry, 10-B Shades Crest Rd., 35226. Tel: 205-989-4060
Mulvaney, James J., 400 University Park Dr., Somerby, Apt. 203, 35209.
Murrin, Raymond J., 18 Merrion Ct., Ailesbury Rd., Dublin 4, Ireland.
Muscolino, Frank J., 2600 Arlington Ave., Apt. 52, 35205. Tel: 205-933-5252
O'Donoghue, Patrick, Haleyville, St. Anne's Rd., Killarney, County Kerry, Ireland.
Regan, Desmond, 2120 3rd Ave., N., 35205.
Reynolds, Jeffrie S., 2159 S. McKenzie, #290, Foley, 36535. Tel: 352-228-3138
Sheehan, J. Peter, 653 S.E. Lakeview Dr., Sebring, FL 33870. Tel: 863-471-0378
Thorsen, Henry, 700 Connell Dr., Pensacola, FL 32507. Tel: 850-469-0919
Underwood, Joseph, 6520 Court K, 35228. Tel: 205-925-8329
White, Michael J., Pastor Emeritus, Our Lady of the Valley, 837 Greystone Highlands Dr., 35242-2651. Tel: 205-408-1034

Permanent Deacons:
Alexiou, William P., St. Thomas the Apostle, Montevallo
Anzalone, J.S., St. Peter the Apostle, Birmingham
Ash, Donald J., St. Joachim, Piedmont
Bodine, James G., St. Mary's, Huntsville
Branch, Michael E., Sacred Heart of Jesus, Cullman
Brandt, William F., Our Lady of Lourdes, Birmingham
Cholewinski, Stan, St. George the Great, Birmingham
Cova, Michael A., (Unassigned)
DeBlieux, John D., Holy Spirit, Winfield; Holy Family, Fayette
Dias, Sam A., Holy Spirit, Huntsville
Diem, Darrell, St. John the Baptist, Madison
Garcia, Hector, Our Lady of the Valley, Ft. Payne
Germann, Aloysius A., (Retired)
Graffagnini, Carmelo, St. John the Baptist, Madison
Henderson, Walter J., St. Mary, Fairfield
Howell, Lawrence, (Retired)
Hunkele, Thomas H., Holy Family, Lanett
Iovino, Frank, Prince of Peace, Birmingham
Jett, Benjamin, Holy Family, Birmingham
Joly, Walter Jerome, (On Leave)
Kay, G. Neal, Cathedral of St. Paul, Birmingham
Laremore, Robert, (Retired)
Larsen, Alf B., St. Joseph, Huntsville
Laurita, Dan, St. John the Baptist, Madison
Machus, Paul, (Retired)
Martin, Robert A., Jr., Our Lady of the Valley, Birmingham
Mickwee, George, St. Francis Xavier, Birmingham
Moorer, Douglass C., Our Lady of Fatima, Birmingham
Motherway, Gerald, Holy Family, Birmingham
Mullen, Paul I., Corpus Christi, Oneonta
Pruet, Ed, Holy Infant of Prague, Trussville
Puent, Ron, Good Shepherd, Huntsville
Raispis, Jerome P., (Retired)
Ramirez, Javier, Annunciation of the Lord, Decatur
Remmert, William J., St. Francis University Parish, Tuscaloosa
Ritchey, Seraphim (NTN), St. George the Great Martyr, Birmingham
Roberson, William, Sacred Heart, Cullman
Robinson, E. Lee, Sr., Holy Infant of Prague, Trussville
Rodriguez, Ramon D., Annunciation of the Lord, Decatur
Roman, Silverio Rubio, St. Theresa, Leeds
Rosko, Christopher J., St. Peter the Apostle, Birmingham
Rumore, Terrence L., Our Lady of the Lake, Pell City
Santos, Edwin M., St. William, Guntersville
Sassenfeld, Helmut, Good Shepherd, Huntsville
Sisterman, Lawrence E., Holy Spirit, Huntsville
Slapikas, Frank R., Holy Spirit, Tuscaloosa
Stagg, James A., Archdiocese of Atlanta
Steltemeier, R. William, Shrine of the Most Blessed Sacrament, Hanceville
Stephens, Joseph R., Jr., St. Elias (Marionite Rite), Birmingham
Straley, J. Adrian, Holy Spirit, Tuscaloosa
Sudnik, Michael P., Holy Spirit, Huntsville
Sullivan, Paul Mark, Our Lady of the Valley, Birmingham
Tejeda, Andres Eduardo Rodriguez, Prince of Peace, Birmingham
Vazquez, Jose R., Prince of Peace, Birmingham
Viselli, Francis N., Jr., Holy Spirit, Tuscaloosa
Wehby, Samuel J.
Whitaker, Dan, Our Lady of the Valley, Birmingham
Zieverink, Edward Walter, Jr., (Unassigned)

INSTITUTIONS LOCATED IN THE DIOCESE

[A] HIGH SCHOOLS, DIOCESAN

BIRMINGHAM. *John Carroll Catholic High School*, 300 Lakeshore Pkwy., P.O. Box 19907, 35209. Tel: 205-940-2400; Fax: 205-945-7429. Web: www.jcchs.org. Very Rev. John G. McDonald, Prin.; Rev. Richard A. Chenault Jr. Priests 2; Sisters 3; Lay Teachers 50; Students 615.

FORT MCCLELLAN. *Sacred Heart Catholic High School*, 16 Morton Rd., 36205. Tel: 256-237-4231; Fax: 256-237-4231. Email: principal@sacredheartcardinals.org. Charles Maniscalco, Prin. Lay Teachers 18; Students 235.

HUNTSVILLE. *Pope John Paul II Catholic High School*, 4810 Bradford Dr., 35805. Tel: 256-430-1760; Fax: 256-430-1766. Email: vaquila@chsfalcons.org. Web: www.chsfalcons.org. Vince Aquila, Prin.; Revs. Mark T. Spruill; Bryan W. Jerabek, Chap.; Kathy Smith, Librarian. Priests 2; Lay Teachers 33; Students 333.

TUSCALOOSA. *Holy Spirit High School*, (Grades 7-12), 601 37th St. E., 35405. Tel: 205-553-5606; Fax: 205-556-7103. Email: jhalli@holyspirit-al.com. Web: www.holyspirit-al.com. Judi Halli, Prin. Lay Teachers 27; Students 250.

[B] HIGH SCHOOLS, PRIVATE

BIRMINGHAM. *Holy Family Cristo Rey Catholic High School*, 2001 19th St. Ensley, 35218. Tel: 205-787-9937; Fax: 205-787-8530. Web: www.hfcristorey.org. Rev. Alex Steinmiller, C.P., Pres.; Elbert M. Morrow, Prin.; Mary Harris, Librarian. Passionist Community of Chicago, IL. Priests 1; Lay Teachers 11; Students 160.

CULLMAN. *St. Bernard Preparatory School*, (Grades 7-12), 1600 St. Bernard Dr., SE, 35055. Tel: 256-739-6682; Fax: 256-734-2925. Email: sbprep@hiwaay.net. Web: www.stbernardprep.com. Revs. Marcus J. Voss, O.S.B., Pres.; Joel W. Martin, O.S.B., Headmaster. Priests 3; Brothers 3; Lay Teachers 21; Students 153.

[C] ELEMENTARY SCHOOLS, PRIVATE

BIRMINGHAM. *St. Rose of Lima Academy*, (Grades K-8), 1401 22nd St. S., 35205. Tel: 205-933-0549; Fax: 205-933-0591. Email: smseton@saintroseacademy.com. Web: www.saintroseacademy.com. Sr. Mary Seton, Prin. Dominican Sisters of Nashville, TN. Sisters 4; Staff 11; Lay Teachers 16; Students 215.

[D] GENERAL HOSPITALS

BIRMINGHAM. *St. Vincent's Health System*, 810 St. Vincent's Dr., 35205. Tel: 205-939-7184; Fax: 205-930-2284. Email: Rhonda.Buzbee@stvhs.com. Web: www.stvhs.com. John O'Neil, Pres. & COO. Ascension Health Sisters 3.

St. Vincent's Birmingham, P.O. Box 12407, 35202-2407. Tel: 205-939-7000; Fax: 205-930-2157. Email: christine.lacek@stvhs.com. Web: www.stvhs.com. 810 St. Vincent's Dr., 35205. Neeysa D. Biddle, COO. Ascension Health Total Staff 1,940; Nurses 723; Patients Assisted Annually 457,000; Bed Capacity 372.

St. Vincent's East, 50 Medical Park E. Dr., 35235. Tel: 205-838-3000; Fax: 205-838-3326. Email: Nancy.Lawrence@stvhs.com. Web: www.stvhs.com. Todd Kennedy, Pres. & COO. Ascension Health Total Staff 1,381; Nurses 194; Total Assisted Annually 190,000; Bed Capacity 282.

St. Vincent's Blount, 150 Gilbreath Dr., Oneonta, 35121. Tel: 205-274-3000; Fax: 205-274-3002. Email: Michelle.Brown@stvhs.com. Web: www.stvhs.com. Sean Tinney, Pres. & COO. Ascension Health Total Staff 195; Nurses 40; Total Assisted Annually 41,000; Bed Capacity 40.

St. Vincent's St. Clair, 2850 Dr. John Haynes Dr., Pell City, 35125. Tel: 205-338-3301; Fax: 205-814-2145. Email: Joanna.Murphree@stvhs.com. Web: www.stvhs.com. Terrell Vick, Pres. & COO. Ascension Health Total Staff 159; Nurses 56; Total Assisted Annually 1,500; Bed Capacity 82.

[E] MONASTERIES AND RESIDENCES OF PRIESTS AND BROTHERS

BIRMINGHAM. *Franciscan Missionaries of the Eternal Word, A Public Association of the Christian Faithful*, 5821 Old Leeds Rd., 35210. Tel: 205-271-2937; Fax: 205-271-2949.

Web: www.franciscanmissionaries.com. Revs. Anthony Mary Stelten, M.F.V.A., Community Servant; Joseph M. Wolfe, M.F.V.A.; Mark Mary Cristina, M.V.F.A.; Miguel Marie Soeherman, M.F.V.A.; Dominic Mary Garner, M.F.V.A., Community Vicar. Professed 15; Total in Residence 19.

St. John Vianney Residence for Priests, 2724 Hanover Cir., 35205.

CULLMAN. *St. Bernard Abbey* (Corporate Title: Benedictine Society of Alabama, Inc.), 1600 St. Bernard Dr., S.E., 35055. Tel: 256-734-8291; Fax: 256-734-3885. Email: abcletus@stbernardprep.com. Web: www.stbernardabbey.com. Rt. Revs. Cletus D. Meagher, O.S.B., Abbot; Victor J. Clark, O.S.B., Retired Abbot (Retired); Revs. Roger R.S. Lott, O.S.B. (Retired); Francis M. Reque, O.S.B.; Marcus J. Voss, O.S.B.; Very Rev. Kevin D. McGrath, O.S.B.; Revs. Joel W. Martin, O.S.B.; Howard R. Moussier, O.S.B. Total Priests of Abbey 12; Brothers 17.

[F] CONVENTS AND RESIDENCES OF SISTERS

BIRMINGHAM. *Sister Servants of the Eternal Word*, Casa Maria Retreat House, 3721 Belmont Rd., 35210. Tel: 205-956-6760; Fax: 205-951-0386. Sr. Mary Gabriel, Supr.

CULLMAN. *Sacred Heart Monastery*, 916 Convent Rd., 35055. Tel: 256-734-4622; 256-734-2199; Fax: 256-734-7592. Email: sjmf@shmon.org. Sr. Janet Marie Flemming, O.S.B., Prioress. Benedictine Sisters. Professed Sisters 46.

HANCEVILLE. *Our Lady of the Angels Monastery, Inc. and Shrine of the Most Blessed Sacrament*, 3222 County Rd. 548, 35077. Tel: 205-271-2917; Fax: 205-795-5702. Web: www.olamshrine.com. Sr. M. Angelica, P.C.P.A., Abbess & Pres.; Deacon R. William Steltemeier. Poor Clare Nuns of Perpetual Adoration. Sisters 34; Novices 4; Postulants 7.

[G] DIOCESAN SOCIAL SERVICE

BIRMINGHAM. *Catholic Center of Concern* (Div. of Catholic Charities), 712 Fourth Ct. W., 35204. Tel: 205-786-4388; Fax: 205-786-6321. P.O. Box 12701, 35202. Email: czamboni@cssbhm.org. Sr. Cecilia Zamboni, M.C. Consolata Missionary Sisters. Total Staff 6; Total Assisted 29,840.

Catholic Family Services, 1515 12th Ave., S., 35205. Tel: 205-324-6561; Fax: 205-323-0475. Email: tcook@cfsbhm.org. Web: www.cfsbhm.org. Thomas Cook, D.S.W., Dir. Total Staff 6; Total Assisted 1,095.

ANNISTON. *All Saints Interfaith Center of Concern*, 1029 W. 15th St., 36201. Tel: 256-236-7793; Fax: 256-236-7793. Email: sister.roy@worldnet.att.net. Sr. Mary Roy, D.H.S., Dir. Tel: 256-238-1365. Total Staff 3; Total Assisted 14,000.

EUTAW. *Consolata Apostolate*, 331 Boligee St., P.O. Box 538, 35462. Tel: 205-372-3497; Fax: 205-372-3497. Total Staff 2; Total Assisted 8,450.

FLORENCE. *Catholic Family Services*, 1111 E. College St., P.O. Box 3633, 35630. Tel: 256-768-1550; Fax: 256-768-1551. Ellen Beadle, M.S.W., Social Worker. Total Assisted 342.

GADSDEN. *Catholic Center of Concern*, 612 Chestnut St., 35901. Tel: 866-546-4883; Fax: 256-547-1730. Total Assisted 15,601.

HAMILTON. *Christian Center of Concern*, P.O. Box 973, 35570. Tel: 205-921-3470. Catherine Brown, Co-Dir.; Sonja Leonelli, Co-Dir. Total Assisted 1,694.

HUNTSVILLE. *Catholic Center of Concern*, 1010 Church St., N.W., P.O. Box 745, 35804. Tel: 256-536-0041; Fax: 256-534-3141. Email: shgcctr@knology.net. Sr. Helen Gaffney, M.S.B.T., Dir. Total Assisted 4,306.

Catholic Family Services, 1010 Church St., N.W., P.O. Box 745, 35804. Tel: 256-536-0073; Fax: 256-534-3141. Email: cfshsv@knology.net. Web: www.cfsbhm.org. Laura Dinwiddie, M.S.W., Regl. Dir. Total Staff 3; Total Families Served 885.

SULLIGENT. *Christian Center of Concern*, P.O. Box 1154, 35586. Tel: 205-698-7197. Martha Richards, Dir. Total Staff 11; Total Assisted 1,029.

WINFIELD. *Christian Center of Concern*, 197 State Hwy. 253, 35594. Tel: 205-487-6230. Judy Sobrak, Bookkeeper. Total Assisted 3,641.

[H] CAMPUS MINISTRY

BIRMINGHAM. *The Chapel of St. Stephen the Martyr Campus Center* 1515 12th Ave. S., 35205. Tel: 205-933-2500; Fax: 205-939-1500. Email: saintst@bellsouth.com. Very Rev. Kevin M. Bazzel, J.C.L.; Rev. Show Reddy Kasu; Sr. Karen Ann Lortscher, O.S.B., Campus Min. Parish Serves: University of Alabama at Birmingham, Samford University, Birmingham-Southern College. Total Staff 2; Students 100.

FLORENCE. *University of North Alabama* St. Joseph's Church, 1111 E. College St., 35630. Tel: 256-764-3303; Fax: 256-718-0208. Email: stjoseph@catholichill.com. Rev. Andrew A. Sullivan.

HUNTSVILLE. *Campus Ministry - University of Alabama in Huntsville c/o St. Joseph*, 2300 Beasley Ave., 35805. Tel: 256-534-8459; Fax: 256-534-8450. Email: stjoseph52@aol.com. Rev. Gary New, S.D.S., Contact Person.

JACKSONVILLE. *Jacksonville State University* St. Charles Church, 308 Seventh St., N.E., 36265. Tel: 256-435-3238; Fax: 256-435-4942. Email: stcharleschurch@aol.com. Rev. James R. Macey. Total Staff 2; Total in Program 15.

MONTEVALLO. *University of Montevallo* St. Thomas the Apostle Catholic Campus Ministry, 80 St. Thomas Way, 35115. Tel: 205-663-3936; Fax: 205-663-3929. Rev. Raymond A. Dunmyer.

TALLADEGA. *Talladega College Catholic Campus Ministry St. Francis of Assisi*, P.O. Box 1142, 35160. Tel: 256-362-5372; Fax: 256-362-5312. Email: stfrassisi@bellsouth.net. Rev. Thomas F. Woods.

TUSCALOOSA. *Diocesan Campus Ministry Office* St. Francis University Parish, 811 Fifth Ave., 35401. Tel: 205-758-5672; Fax: 205-758-5673. Email: frgerald@stfrancisuofa.com. Web: stfrancisuofa.com. Rev. Gerald Holloway. Total Staff 1; Total in Residence 1.

University of Alabama in Tuscaloosa St. Francis University Parish, 811 Fifth Ave., 35401. Tel: 205-758-5672; Fax: 205-758-5673. Email: office@stfrancisuofa.com. Web: stfrancisuofa.com. Rev. Gerald Holloway, Campus Min. Total Staff 2; Total in Residence 1.

[I] MISCELLANEOUS LISTINGS

BIRMINGHAM. *St. Barnabas Regional School Educational Foundation*, 7921 First Ave. N., 35206. Tel: 205-833-0334; Fax: 205-833-0270.

Bruno Family's Catholic Diocesan Trust, P.O. Box 12047, 35202-2047. Tel: 205-838-8322; Fax: 205-836-1910. Email: gnabors@bhmdiocese.org. Web: www.bhmdiocese.org.

Casa Maria Retreat House, 3721 Belmont Rd., 35210. Tel: 205-956-6760; Fax: 205-951-0386. Sr. Mary Gabriel, Dir.

Catholic Housing of Birmingham, Inc., P.O. Box 12047, 35202. Tel: 205-838-8311; Fax: 205-836-1910. 2121 3rd Ave. N., 35203. William M. Moran, Pres.; Rev. Msgr. Paul L. Rohling, V.G.

Congregation of the Passion: Holy Family Community, Inc. (House of Religious Men), 1910 19th St., Ensley, 35218. Tel: 205-780-3440; Fax: 205-780-5272. Email: rcrossmyer@aol.com. Revs. Robert Crossmyer, C.P., Local Supr.; Alex Steinmiller, C.P.; Guillermo Casadillo. Corporation for Holy Family Church, and Holy Family Elementary, Birmingham, and St. Mary's Church, Fairfield, St. Mary Elementary, Fairfield.

Contemplative Outreach Birmingham, 106 Red Stick Rd., Pelham, 35124. Tel: 205-991-6964. Email: tschached@bellsouth.net. Web: www.bham.net/cobweb. Diana Tschache, Coord.; Aloysius Golden, Area Contact Person. Tel: 205-592-3930.

The Fatima Educational Foundation, 708 First St. S., 35205. Tel: 205-322-1205. Web: olf.schoolinsites.com. Rev. Paul Oberg, S.S.J., Contact Person.

St. Francis Xavier Catholic School Education Foundation, 2 Xavier Cir., 35213. Tel: 205-871-1687; Fax: 205-871-1674. Email: jnwrightiii@hotmail.com. Web: www.saintfrancisxavierschool.com. Nathan Wright, Prin. & Contact Person.

Holy Family Educational Foundation, 1910 19th St., 35218. Tel: 205-780-3440; Fax: 205-782-5272. Email: lmlang@bellsouth.net. Web: www.passionist.org. Melva Langford, Bd. Chair.

Holy Name of Jesus Hospital Trust (Senior Citizen Housing), c/o Regions Bank, P.O. Box 11426, 35202. Tel: 205-326-7219; Fax: 205-581-7433. Email: sidney.roebuck@regions.com. Sidney O. Roebuck Jr., Trustee, Vice Pres. & Senior Trust Officer, Regions Bank. Total Assisted 350.

John Carroll Catholic High School Educational Foundation, Inc., 300 Lakeshore Pkwy., 35209. Tel: 205-940-2400; Fax: 205-945-7429. Web: www.jcchs.org.

Ladies of Charity of Central Alabama aka Servants of Charity 810 St. Vincent's Dr., 35205.

Magnificat: Mary, Woman of Faith Chapter, 1341 Forest Ridge Ct., 35226. Tel: 205-941-0144; Fax: 205-941-0144. Email: carolynwright@gmail.com. Web: www.magnificat-birminghamal.org. Carolyn Mathis Wright, Coord.

Our Lady of Sorrows Educational School Foundation, 1728 Oxmoor Rd., 35209. Tel: 205-871-8121; Fax: 205-871-8180.

Our Lady of the Valley Educational Foundation, 5514 Double Oak Ln., 35242. Tel: 205-991-5488; Fax: 205-991-5181. Email: olvchurch@olvsch.com.

St. Peter's Endowment Foundation, 2061 Patton Chapel Rd., 35216. Email: stpeterapostle@bellsouth.net. Rev. Thomas M. Kelly. Total Assisted 149; Total Staff 35.

St. Thomas More Society of Metro Birmingham, 2001 Park Pl. N., Ste. 400, 35203. Tel: 205-639-5300. Email: jwhitaker@wmslawfirm.com. G. Rick DiGiorgio, Chm.; John Whitaker, Pres.

Tuxedo Junction Catholic Community, Inc., 1910 19th St., Ensley, 35218. Tel: 205-780-3440; Fax: 205-780-5272.

Villa Maria, 500 82nd St. S., 35206. Tel: 205-836-7839; Fax: 205-836-0664. Judy Murphree, Mgr. Total Staff 7; Total in Residence 63.

St. Vincent's Foundation, 2800 University Blvd., Ste. 304, 35205. Tel: 205-939-7825; Fax: 205-930-2525. Web: www. stvfoundation.org. William M. Moran, Exec. Dir.; Susann Montgomery Clark, Dir. Planned Giving; Jeffrey Scott Powell, Dir. Devel.; Jacqueline Godby Gardner, Dir. Capital Campaign.

BESSEMER. *St. Aloysius Educational Foundation*, 751 Academy Dr., 35022. Tel: 205-424-2984; Fax: 205-426-5753. Email: staloysius@bellsouth.net. Very Rev. Patrick P. Cullen.

CULLMAN. *Benedictine Manor Retirement Home, Inc.*, 200 Janeway Dr., 35055. Tel: 256-739-2853; Fax: 256-739-2860 (Call First). Email: bmanor1@hiwaay.net. Web: www.shmon.org. Sr. Cecilia MacDermott, Dir. Resident Capacity 35.

Benedictine Sisters Retreat Center, 916 Convent Rd., 35055-2019. Tel: 256-734-8302; Fax: 256-734-8302 (Call First). Email: thereseosb@shmon.org. Web: www.shmon.org. Sr. Therese Haydel, O.S.B., Dir. Bed Capacity 72; Total Staff 7.

St. Bernard Abbey Foundation, 1600 St. Bernard Dr., S.E., 35055. Tel: 256-734-8291; Fax: 256-734-3885. Web: www.stbernardabbey.com. Rt. Rev. Cletus Meagher, O.S.B., Chm.

St. Bernard Preparatory School Educational Foundation, 1600 St. Bernard Dr., S.E., 35055. Tel: 256-739-6682; Fax: 256-734-2925. Email: frmarcus@stbernardprep.com. Web: www.stbernardprep.com. Rt. Rev. Cletus Meagher, O.S.B., Chm.

Sacred Heart Monastery of Cullman, Alabama Foundation, 916 Convent Rd., 35055-2019. Tel: 256-734-4622; 256-734-3835; Fax: 256-734-7592. Web: www.shmon.org. Sr. Janet Marie Flemming, O.S.B., Prioress.

DECATUR. *St. Ann's Educational Foundation*, 3910 A Spring Ave., 35603. Tel: 256-353-6543; Fax: 256-353-0705. Email: cwright@saintanncatholicschool.com. Web: st-ann-school.com. Christine Wright.

FLORENCE. *St. Joseph School Foundation, Florence*, 115 Plum St., 35630. Tel: 256-766-1923. Email: ceckleck@aol.com.

Society of St. Vincent de Paul, St. Joseph Conference, 659 S. Poplar St., 35630-6818. Tel: 256-718-0901; Fax: 256-718-0901. Email: hrlong@bellsouth.net. Roy E. Long, Spiritual Advisor; Roberta Bergner, Treas. Email: eberg20653@aol.com.

GADSDEN. *St. James Educational Foundation*, 700 Albert Rains Blvd., 35901. Tel: 256-546-0132; Fax: 256-546-0134. Email: jparker@st.jamesgadsden.org. Total Staff 22.

HANCEVILLE. *Knights of the Holy Eucharist*, 3222 County Rd. 548, 35077. Tel: 205-795-5720; Fax: 205-795-5705. Email: knightsinfo@gmail.com. Web: www.knightsoftheholyeucharist.com. Total in Residence 11.

HUNTSVILLE. *Holy Spirit Regional School Foundation*, 625 Airport Rd., 35802. Tel: 256-881-4852, Ext. 137; Fax: 256-881-4904. Email: foundation89@comcast.net. Web: www.hstigers.org. Lee Dumbacher, Admin.

Society of St. Vincent dePaul, District Council of Huntsville, 625 Airport Rd., 35802. Tel: 256-883-0157. Email: hsvsvdp@knology.net. John Wolfsberger, Pres., District Council of Huntsville; Deacon Sam A. Dias, Spiritual Advisor; Patricia Schuessler, Treas.

St. Vincent De Paul Thrift Store, 2140 Jonathan Dr., 35810-3453. Tel: 256-851-8881. Patricia Schuessler, Mgr.

MADISON. *St. John's Educational Foundation*, 1055 Hughes Rd., 35758. Tel: 256-722-0130; Fax: 256-722-0303. Rev. Philip N. O'Kennedy.

PLEASANT GROVE. *Queen of Heaven Radio, Inc.*, P.O. Box 483, 35127. Tel: 205-744-4456; Fax: 205-744-4457.

TUSCALOOSA. *The Harrison Family Endowment Trust for the Benefit of Holy Spirit School*, 711 37th St. E., 35405. Tel: 205-553-9630; Fax: 205-553-8880. Web: holyspirit-al.com. Very Rev. Jeremiah Deasy.

RELIGIOUS INSTITUTES OF MEN REPRESENTED IN THE DIOCESE

For further details refer to the corresponding bracketed number in the Religious Institutes of Men or Women section.

[0200]—*Benedictine Monks*—O.S.B.

[0820]—*Congregation of the Fathers of Mercy*—C.P.M.

[1000]—*Congregation of the Passion*—C.P.

[]—*Franciscan Missionaries of the Eternal Word*—M.F.V.A.

[1120]—*Missionaries of the Sacred Hearts of Jesus and Mary*—M.SS.CC.

[1190]—*Salesians of Don Bosco*—S.D.B.

[1200]—*Society of the Divine Savior*—S.D.S.

[0700]—*St. Joseph's Society of the Sacred Heart* (Baltimore, MD)—S.S.J.

RELIGIOUS INSTITUTES OF WOMEN REPRESENTED IN THE DIOCESE

[0230]—*Benedictine Sisters of Pontifical Jurisdiction*—O.S.B.

[0260]—*Blessed Sacrament Sisters*—S.B.S.

[0720]—*Consolata Missionary Sisters*—M.C.

[0760]—*Daughters of Charity of St. Vincent de Paul*—D.C.

[0820]—*Daughters of the Holy Spirit*—D.H.S.

[1070-03]—*Dominican Sisters* (Adrian, MI)—O.P.

[1070-07]—*Dominican Sisters* (Nashville, TN)—O.P.

[1845]—*Guadalupan Missionaries of the Holy Spirit*—M.G.Sp.S.

[2720]—*Mission Helpers of the Sacred Heart*—M.H.S.H.

[2790]—*Missionary Servants of the Most Blessed Trinity*—M.S.B.T.

[3210]—*Poor Clares of Perpetual Adoration*—P.C.P.A.

[]—*Sister Servants of the Eternal Word*—S.S.E.W.

[2575]—*Sisters of Mercy of the Americas*—R.S.M.

[1650]—*Sisters of St. Francis of Philadelphia*—O.S.F.

[3840]—*Sisters of St. Joseph of Carondelet*—C.S.J.

[1030]—*Sisters of the Divine Savior*—S.D.S.

[3320]—*Sisters of the Presentation of the B.V.M.*—P.B.V.M

[4048]—*Society of Sisters Faithful Companions of Jesus*—F.C.J.

NECROLOGY

† Hill, Timothy, (Retired)—Died April 18, 2009

An asterisk (*) denotes an organization that has established tax-exempt status directly with the IRS and is not covered by the USCCB Group Ruling.

Diocese of Bismarck

(Dioecesis Bismarckiensis)

Most Reverend

PAUL A. ZIPFEL, D.D.

Bishop of Bismarck; ordained March 18, 1961; appointed Titular Bishop of Walla Walla and Auxiliary Bishop of St. Louis May 16, 1989; consecrated June 29, 1989; appointed Bishop of Bismarck December 31, 1996; installed February 20, 1997.

ESTABLISHED DECEMBER 31, 1909.

Square Miles 34,268.

Comprises the Counties of Adams, Billings, Bowman, Burke, Burleigh, Divide, Dunn, Emmons, Golden Valley, Grant, Hettinger, McKenzie, McLean, Mercer, Morton, Mountrail, Oliver, Renville, Sioux, Slope, Stark, Ward and Williams in the State of North Dakota.

For legal titles of parishes and diocesan institutions consult the Chancery Office.

Chancery Office: 420 Raymond St., P.O. Box 1575, Bismarck, ND 58502-1575. Tel: 701-223-1347; Fax: 701-223-3693.

STATISTICAL OVERVIEW

Personnel	
Bishop	1
Abbots	1
Retired Abbots	1
Priests: Diocesan Active in Diocese	39
Priests: Diocesan Active Outside Diocese	4
Priests: Retired, Sick or Absent	24
Number of Diocesan Priests	67
Religious Priests in Diocese	29
Total Priests in Diocese	96
Extern Priests in Diocese	12
Ordinations:	
Diocesan Priests	3
Transitional Deacons	1
Permanent Deacons in Diocese	79
Total Brothers	20
Total Sisters	95
Parishes	
Parishes	99
With Resident Pastor:	
Resident Diocesan Priests	32
Resident Religious Priests	13
Without Resident Pastor:	
Administered by Priests	53
Administered by Deacons	1
Professional Ministry Personnel:	
Sisters	3
Lay Ministers	26
Welfare	
Catholic Hospitals	4
Total Assisted	329,137
Homes for the Aged	4
Total Assisted	570
Educational	
Diocesan Students in Other Seminaries	23
Total Seminarians	23
Colleges and Universities	1
Total Students	2,830
High Schools, Diocesan and Parish	3
Total Students	627
Elementary Schools, Diocesan and Parish	11
Total Students	1,537
Catechesis/Religious Education:	
High School Students	1,713
Elementary Students	5,02
Total Students under Catholic Instruction	11,75
Teachers in the Diocese:	
Priests	[illegible]
Sisters	[illegible]
Lay Teachers	18
Vital Statistics	
Receptions into the Church:	
Infant Baptism Totals	89
Minor Baptism Totals	10
Adult Baptism Totals	3
Received into Full Communion	8
First Communions	91
Confirmations	1,05
Marriages:	
Catholic	22
Interfaith	11
Total Marriages	33
Deaths	73
Total Catholic Population	61,27
Total Population	264,08

Former Bishops—Most Revs. VINCENT DE PAUL WEHRLE, O.S.B., D.D., appt. Bishop of Bismarck, April 9, 1910; cons. May 19, 1910; retired Dec. 11, 1939; named Titular Bishop of Teos by Pope Pius XII; died Nov. 2, 1941; VINCENT J. RYAN, D.D., L.L.D., appt. March 19, 1940; cons. May 28, 1940; died Nov. 10, 1951; LAMBERT A. HOCH, D.D., L.L.D., appt. Jan. 23, 1952; cons. March 25, 1952; transferred to Diocese of Sioux Falls, Dec. 5, 1956; died June 27, 1990; HILARY B. HACKER, D.D., appt. Bishop, Dec. 29, 1956; retired June 28, 1982; died Nov. 6, 1990; JOHN F. KINNEY, D.D., J.C.D., appt. June 28, 1982; Episcopal Ord. Jan. 25, 1977; installed Aug. 23, 1982; transferred to Diocese of St. Cloud, July 6, 1995.

Vicar General—Rev. JOHN G. GUTHRIE.

Chancery Office—420 Raymond St., P.O. Box 1575, Bismarck, 58502-1575. Tel: 701-223-1347; Fax: 701-223-3693.

Chancellor—Deacon JOEL MELARVIE.

Center for Pastoral Ministry Office—520 N. Washington St., P.O. Box 1137, Bismarck, 58502-1137. Tel: 701-222-3035.

Office of Canonical Affairs (Marriage Tribunal)—520 N. Washington St., P.O. Box 1137, Bismarck, 58502-1137. Tel: 701-222-3035. Marriage papers are sent to this office.

Judicial Vicar—Rev. CHRISTOPHER J. KADRMAS, J.C.L., Dir.

Defensor Vinculi—Revs. GENE E. LINDEMANN, J.C.L.; DAVID L. ZIMMER, J.C.L.

Promoter of Justice—Rev. DAVID L. ZIMMER, J.C.L.

Pro-Synodal Judges—Revs. MARVIN J. KLEMMER; BRUCE D. KREBS; KEITH N. STREIFEL; DAVID RICHTER; SHANNON G. LUCHT; CHAD GION.

Auditors—RUTH MOERICKE; HELEN SCHERR-BOURGOIS.

Notary—SANDRA BREINER.

Presbyteral Council—Revs. PATRICK A. SCHUMACHER, S.T.L.; GENE E. LINDEMANN, J.C.L., Chm.; BRUCE D. KREBS, Sec.; DENNIS R. SCHAFER; JOHN G. GUTHRIE, Ex Officio; SHANNON G. LUCHT, Treas.; Rt. Rev. BRIAN WANGLER, O.S.B., M.A.; Revs. THOMAS E. KRAMER, Vice Chm. (Retired); CHRISTOPHER J. KADRMAS, J.C.L.

Diocesan Corporate Board—Most Rev. PAUL A. ZIPFEL, Pres.; Revs. JOHN G. GUTHRIE, Vice Pres.; DANIEL J. BERG; JAMES B. BRAATEN; Deacon JOEL MELARVIE, Sec.

Diocesan Finance Council—Most Rev. PAUL A. ZIPFEL, Pres.; Revs. JOHN G. GUTHRIE, Chm.; JAMES B. BRAATEN; DANIEL J. BERG; MIKE SCHWINDT; MARVIN HEINERT, Consultant; THOMAS BAIR, Consultant; TIM CONLIN; KEVIN DVORAK; JIM LONG; BRIAN RUMMEL; GREG VETTER. Ex Officio: LAURA J. HUBER; Deacon JOEL MELARVIE; RON SCHATZ.

Diocesan Offices and Directors

Archives—Deacon JOEL MELARVIE, Mailing Address: P.O. Box 1137, Bismarck, 58502-1137. Tel: 701-222-3035.

Boy Scouts—

National Catholic Committee on Scouting—Deacon DOYLE SCHULZ, 513 Munich Dr., Bismarck, 58504-7038.

Catholic Campaign For Human Development—Mr. RONALD SCHATZ, Dir., Mailing Address: P.O. Box 1137, Bismarck, 58502-1137. Tel: 701-222-3035.

Catholic Charities North Dakota—LARRY BERNHARDT, Exec. Dir., 5201 Bishops Blvd., Ste. B, Fargo, 58104-7605. Tel: 701-235-4457. Other Locations: 919 7th St. S., Ste. 607, Bismarck, 58504-5881. Tel: 701-255-1793. 216 S. Broadway, Ste. 103, Minot, 58701-3852. Tel: 701-852-2854.

Catholic Relief—Mr. RONALD SCHATZ, Dir., Mailing Address: P.O. Box 1137, Bismarck, 58502-1137. Tel: 701-222-3035.

Office of Vocations—Rev. THOMAS J. RICHTER, Dir., Mailing Address: P.O. Box 1137, Bismarck, 58502-1137. Tel: 701-222-3035.

Vicar for Presbyters—Rev. MARVIN J. KLEMMER, Mailing Address: 1905 S. 3rd St., Bismarck, 58504-7118. Tel: 701-223-3606.

Office of Worship—Rev. GENE E. LINDEMANN, J.C.L. Interim Dir., Mailing Address: P.O. Box 1575, Bismarck, 58502-1575. Tel: 701-223-1347.

Continuing Education for Clergy—Rev. AUSTIN VETTER, 105 1st St., S.E., Minot, 58701-3901. Tel: 701-838-1026.

Newspaper— "Dakota Catholic Action" Deacon JOEL MELARVIE, Editor, Mailing Address: P.O. Box 1575, Bismarck, 58502-1575. Tel: 701-223-1347.

North Dakota Catholic Conference—CHRISTOPHER DODSON, 103 S. 3rd St., Ste. 10, Bismarck, 58501-3800. Tel: 701-223-2519; Fax: 701-223-6075.

Permanent Diaconate Office—

Vicar for Deacons—Rev. THOMAS J. RICHTER, Mailing Address: P.O. Box 1137, Bismarck, 58502-1137. Tel: 701-222-3035.

Director of Deacons—DAVID FLECK, Mailing Address: P.O. Box 1137, Bismarck, 58502-1137. Tel: 701-222-3035.

Priests' Benefit Association—Most Rev. PAUL A. ZIPFEL, Pres.; Revs. KENNETH G. PHILLIPS, Vice Chm.; DANIEL J. BERG; CHARLES A. HEIDT, Treas. (Retired); DAVID G. MORMAN; CASIMIR S. PALUCK, Chm. (Retired); JOHN PAUL GARDNER, Sec.; LAURA J. HUBER, Agent of Record.

Priests' Personnel Board—Revs. FRED R. HARVEY, Chm.; KENNETH G. PHILLIPS, Sec.; DAVID L. ZIMMER, J.C.L., Vice Chm.; TODD KREITINGER; THOMAS J. RICHTER, Ex Officio; MARVIN J. KLEMMER, Ex Officio; Most Rev. PAUL A. ZIPFEL, Ex Officio.

Propagation of the Faith—Mr. RONALD M. SCHATZ, Mailing Address: P.O. Box 1137, Bismarck, 58502-1137. Tel: 701-222-3035.

Communications Office—Deacon JOEL MELARVIE, Dir. Mailing Address: P.O. Box 1575, Bismarck, 58502-1575. Tel: 701-223-1347.

Office of Catechesis (Faith Formation)—BETTY E. GREFF, Dir., Mailing Address: P.O. Box 1137, Bismarck, 58502-1137. Tel: 701-222-3035. Email: bgreff@bismarckdiocese.com.

Provision for the Future—LAURA J. HUBER, Contact Person, 520 N. Washington St., P.O. Box 1137, Bismarck, 58502-1137. Tel: 701-222-3035. Email: lhuber@bismarckdiocese.com.

Stewardship and Resource Development Office—Mr. RONALD SCHATZ, Dir., Mailing Address: P.O. Box 1137, Bismarck, 58502-1137. Tel: 701-222-3035. Email: rschatz@bismarckdiocese.com.

Youth Ministry—KENNETH H. ROSHAU, Dir., 11010 41st St., S.W., Dickinson, 58601-9512. Tel: 701-290-4137. Email: kroshau@bismarckdiocese.com.

Search Program—KENNETH H. ROSHAU, 11010 41st St., S.W., Dickinson, 58601-9512. Tel: 701-290-4137. Email: kroshau@bismarckdiocese.com.

Victim Assistance Coordinator—Deacon JOEL MELARVIE, Mailing Address: P.O. Box 1575, Bismarck, 58502-1575. Tel: 701-223-1347. Email: jmelarvie@bismarckdiocese.com.

Finance Officer—LAURA J. HUBER, Mailing Address: P.O. Box 1137, Bismarck, 58502-1137. Tel: 701-222-3035. Email: lhuber@bismarckdiocese.com.

Family Ministry—JOYCE MCDOWALL, Dir., Mailing Address: P.O. Box 1137, Bismarck, 58502-1137. Tel: 701-222-3035. Email: jmcdowall@bismarckdiocese.com.

Parish Planning—Deacon LYNN CLANCY, Mailing Address: P.O. Box 1137, Bismarck, 58502-1137. Tel: 701-222-3035. Email: lclancy@bismarckdiocese.com.

Risk Management—ROMAN WEILER, Dir., Mailing Address: P.O. Box 1137, Bismarck, 58502-1137. Tel: 701-222-3035. Email: rweiler@bismarckdiocese.com.

Ecumenism—Rev. MARVIN J. KLEMMER, Mailing Address: 1905 S. 3rd St., Bismarck, 58504-7118. Tel: 701-223-3606.

Respect Life—AMANDA ELLERKAMP, 733 1st Ave., S.W., Dickinson, 58601-5911. Tel: 701-590-2837.

Native American Ministry—Mr. RONALD SCHATZ, Mailing Address: P.O. Box 1137, Bismarck, 58502-1137. Tel: 701-222-3035.

CLERGY, PARISHES, MISSIONS AND PAROCHIAL SCHOOLS

CITY OF BISMARCK

(BURLEIGH COUNTY)

1—CATHEDRAL OF THE HOLY SPIRIT (1947) [JC] Revs. John G. Guthrie; Russell P. Kovash; Deacons Richard Fettig; Gary Mizeur; Ralph von Ruden; Wilfred Wolf, (Retired).
Mailing Address: 519 Raymond St., 58501. Tel: 701-223-1033; Fax: 701-223-1438. Email: cathchrch@bismarckdiocese.com. Web: www.cathedralparish.com.
School—Tel: 701-223-5484; Fax: 701-223-5485. Leann Binde, Prin. Lay Teachers 18; Students 234.
Catechesis/Religious Program—Tel: 701-222-2259. Marie Gabel, D.R.E. Students 350.

2—ST. ANNE (1957) [JC] Rev. Edwin P. Wehner; Deacons Wayne Jundt; Joe Krupinsky; Mary Ann Meyer, Business & Operations Mgr. In Res., Rev. Thomas J. Richter, Dir. Office of Vocations.
Res.: 1321 Braman Ave., 58501. Tel: 701-223-1549; Fax: 701-250-9214. Web: www.stannebismarck.org.
School—(Grades PreK-8) Tel: 701-223-3373. Web: www.st-anneschool.org. Cori Hilzendeger, Prin.; Sheila Krogstad, Librarian. Lay Teachers 13; Students 202.
Catechesis/Religious Program—Tel: 701-224-0847. Marilyn Geiger, C.R.E. Students 411.

3—ASCENSION (1974) [JC] Rev. Marvin J. Klemmer; Deacons Ray Grabar, (Retired); Tony J. Finneman; Doyle F. Schulz.
Res.: 1905 S. Third St., 58504-7118. Tel: 701-223-3606; Fax: 701-223-5783. Email: ascension@midconetwork.com. Web: ascensionbismarck.org.
Catechesis/Religious Program—Tel: 701-223-5783. Cheryle Gagner, D.R.E. Students 231.

4—CORPUS CHRISTI (1964) [JC] Rev. Paul D. Becker; Sr. Ivo Schoch, Pastoral Assoc.; Deacons Harry M. Deichert, (Retired); Michael Fix; Joseph J. Mathern, (Retired); Rex McDowell; John Tharaldsen.
Res.: 1919 N. Second St., 58501. Tel: 701-255-4600 (Church); Fax: 701-255-4616.
Catechesis/Religious Program—Tel: 701-255-3104. Tara Brooke, D.R.E.; Tracy Kraft, D.R.E.; Patrick Hall, D.R.E. Students 496.

5—ST. MARY (1877) [JC] Rev. Gene E. Lindemann; Deacons Tony Dworshak, (Retired); Terry Glatt, Outreach Min.; Harvey Hanel; Kenneth Klein; Michael Marback; Steve Braus, Admin.; Sheila Gilbertson, Pastoral Min.; Diane Huck, Pastoral Min.
Res.: 816 E. Broadway, 58501. Tel: 701-223-5562; Fax: 701-530-0864. Email: smpf@stmarysparishfamily.net. Web: stmarysbismarck.org.
School—Tel: 701-223-0225; Fax: 701-250-9918. Email: tom.hesford@sendit.nodak.edu. Web: st-marys.k12.nd.us. Tom Hesford, Prin. Lay Teachers 14; Students 212.
Catechesis/Religious Program—Email: sheila@stmarysparishfamily.net. Students 198.

OUTSIDE THE CITY OF BISMARCK

ALEXANDER, MCKENZIE CO., OUR LADY OF CONSOLATION (1907), Served from Watford City. Rev. John M. Pfeifer.
c/o Epiphany, P.O. Box 670, Watford City, 58854-0670. Tel: 701-842-3791.

ALMONT, MORTON CO., ST. MARY, QUEEN OF PEACE (1907), Served from New Salem. Rev. Amalraj Roche, M.S.F.X. (India).
c/o St. Pius V, P.O. Box C, New Salem, 58563-0429. Tel: 701-843-7061.
Catechesis/Religious Program—Students 11.

ALPHA, GOLDEN VALLEY CO., MOST HOLY REDEEMER (1919) Closed. For inquiries for parish records contact the chancery.

AMIDON, SLOPE CO., SS. PETER & PAUL (1918) Closed. For inquiries for parish records contact the chancery.

BEACH, GOLDEN VALLEY CO., ST. JOHN THE BAPTIST (1909) [CEM] Rev. David A. Richter; Bro. Samuel Larson, S.D.S.; Deacons Donald Nistler; James Wosepka.
Res.: 162 2nd Ave., S.E., Box 337, 58621-0337. Tel: 701-872-4153; Fax: 701-872-4153.
Catechesis/Religious Program—Kathy Hollar, D.R.E. Students 88.

BELFIELD, STARK CO., ST. BERNARD (1910) [CEM] Rev. Shannon G. Lucht.
Res.: P.O. Box 38, 58622. Tel: 701-575-4295; Fax: 701-575-8457. Email: stbernardbelfield@ndsupernet.com.
Catechesis/Religious Program—Tel: 701-575-4099. Diane Procive, D.R.E. (High School). Students 66.

BENTLEY, HETTINGER CO., SACRED HEART (1920) Closed. For inquiries for parish records contact the chancery.

BERTHOLD, WARD CO., ST. ANN (1903), Served from Stanley. Rev. Mike Millard.
c/o Queen of the Most Holy Rosary, P.O. Box 159, Stanley, 58784-0159. Tel: 701-628-3405.
Catechesis/Religious Program—Rhonda Hanson, D.R.E. Students 21.

BEULAH, MERCER CO.

1—ST. BENEDICT (1911) Closed. For inquiries for parish records contact the chancery.

2—ST. JOSEPH (1915), (German—Russian), [CEM] Rev. Johnson Kuriappilly; Deacon Daniel Wallach. 115 3rd St., N.E., 58523. Email: sjcc@westriv.com. Web: sanjoscommunity.org. Mailing Address: P.O. Box 146, 58523.
Res.: 508 1st Ave., N.E., 58523. Tel: 701-873-5397; Fax: 701-873-5614. Email: sjcc@westriv.com. Web: sanjoscommunity.org.
Catechesis/Religious Program—Tel: 701-873-5006; Fax: 701-873-5614. Email: sjccd@westriv.com; sjyouth@westriv.com. Students 143.

BLAISDELL, MOUNTRAIL CO., ST. MARGARET (1912) Closed. For inquiries for parish records contact the chancery.

BOWBELLS, BURKE CO., ST. JOSEPH (BOWBELLS) (1905), (German—Scandinavian), Rev. Selvaraj Periannan, M.S.F.X. (India).
Res.: 409 E. Division, P.O. Box 488, Kenmare, 58746. Tel: 701-385-4311; Fax: 701-385-4321.
Church: 102 3rd St., N.W., 58721. Tel: 701-377-2611 (Parish Center).
Catechesis/Religious Program—Students 1.

BOWMAN, BOWMAN CO., ST. CHARLES (1910) Rev. David G. Morman.
Res.: 202 First Ave. S.W., 58623. Tel: 701-523-5292; Fax: 701-523-5415.
Catechesis/Religious Program—Tel: 701-523-5415. Tobiann Andrews, D.R.E. (Grades 1-6); Shannon Schmit, D.R.E. (Grades 7-12). Students 98.

BRADDOCK, EMMONS CO., ST. KATHERINE (1908), Served from Linton. Rev. Gary Benz.
c/o St. Anthony, 613 N. Broadway, Linton, 58552-7311. Tel: 701-254-4588.

BRISBANE, GRANT CO., HOLY INFANT JESUS (1911) Closed. For inquiries for parish records contact the chancery.

BURLINGTON, WARD CO., ST. FRANCIS OF ASSISI (1889) Closed. For inquiries for parish records contact the chancery.

BUTTE, MCLEAN CO., HOLY GHOST (1939) Closed. For inquiries for parish records contact the chancery.

CANNON BALL, SIOUX CO., ST. ELIZABETH (1897), Served from Fort Yates. Rev. Basil Atwell, O.S.B.
c/o St. Peter, P.O. Box 394, Fort Yates, 58538-0394. Tel: 701-854-3473.

CARSON, GRANT CO., ST. THERESA THE CHILD JESUS (1920) [JC] Rev. Daniel J. Berg.
204 2nd Ave., N.E., 58529.
Res.: 421 Court St., Flasher, 58535-7216. Tel: 701-597-3570; 701-597-3228; Fax: 701-597-3228.
Catechesis/Religious Program—Tel: 701-597-3228. Students 33.

CARTWRIGHT, MCKENZIE CO., ST. JOSEPH (1913) Closed. For inquiries for parish records contact the chancery.

CENTER, OLIVER CO., ST. MARTIN (1914) [CEM 3] [JC] Rev. Amalraj Roche, M.S.F.X. (India).
Res.: 322 2nd St. E., P.O. Box 2766, 58530. Tel: 701-794-3329; Fax: 701-794-3601.
Catechesis/Religious Program—Tel: 701-794-3191. Judith McNulty, D.R.E.; Alice Henderscheid, D.R.E. Students 46.

COLUMBUS, BURKE CO., ST. MICHAEL (1905) Closed. For inquiries for parish records contact the chancery.

CROSBY, DIVIDE CO., ST. PATRICK (1912) [CEM 4] [JC 2] Rev. Biju Chitteth (India).
Res.: 205 1st. St. N.W., P.O. Box 89, 58730. Tel: 701-965-6537; Fax: 701-965-6537.
Catechesis/Religious Program—Tel: 701-965-6674. Students 17.

CROWN BUTTE, MORTON CO., ST. VINCENT (1896) [CEM] Deacon Steve M. Brannan; Nancy J. Brannan, Pastoral Assoc.
Res.: 2119 S. 3rd St., 58504.
Catechesis/Religious Program—Students 12.

DE LACS, WARD CO., ST. VINCENT DE PAUL (1912) Closed. For inquiries for parish records contact the chancery.

DICKINSON, STARK CO.

1—ST. JOSEPH (1902), (German—Russian), [CEM] Rev. Keith N. Streifel; Deacons Terry B. Quintus; Al Schwindt.
Res.: 240 E. Broadway, 58601. Tel: 701-483-2223; Fax: 701-483-0648. Email: stjoseph@ndsupernet.com.
Catechesis/Religious Program—Kris Quintus, D.R.E. Students 123.

2—ST. PATRICK (1885) Rev. Todd Kreitinger; Deacons Anton Wanner; Ron Keller.
Res.: 229 Third Ave. W., 58601. Tel: 701-483-6700; Fax: 701-483-6702. Email: stpatrick@goesp.com.
Catechesis/Religious Program—Tel: 701-225-8831; Fax: 701-225-8831. Jessica Emter, D.R.E. Students 98.

3—QUEEN OF PEACE CHURCH (1973) [JC] Revs. Jeffrey Zwack; Joshua J. Ehli, Parochial Vicar.
Office: 725 12th St. W., 58601-3516. Tel: 701-483-2134; 701-483-2991 (Res.); Fax: 701-483-1379. Web: www.queenofpeacedickinson.org.
Catechesis/Religious Program—Sr. Phoebe Schwartze, O.S.B., D.R.E. Students 158.

4—ST. WENCESLAUS (1912), (Bohemian), [CEM] [JC] Rev. James B. Braaten; Deacons Eugene F. Morman, (Retired); Raymond Jilek, (Retired); Robert Stockert; Robert Zent.
Res.: 525 Third St. E., 58601. Tel: 701-225-3972; Fax: 701-225-4146.
School—515 3rd St. E., 58601. Tel: 701-225-9463; 701-483-6083; Fax: 701-225-0474. Sr. Dorothy Zeller, S.S.N.D., Supt.; Mr. Rocky Cofer, Prin. High Sch. & Jr. High; Peggy Mayer, Elem. Prin. Lay Teachers 11; Students 121.
See Dickinson Catholic School, Dickinson under High Schools Interparochial and Parish located in the Institution section.
Catechesis/Religious Program—Gini Zent, D.R.E. Students 112.

DODGE, DUNN CO.

1—ST. MARTIN (1908) Closed. For inquiries for parish records contact the chancery.

2—PRECIOUS BLOOD (1920) Closed. For inquiries for parish records contact the chancery.

DONNYBROOK, WARD CO., ST. ANTHONY (1902), Served from Kenmare. Rev. Selvaraj Periannan, M.S.F.X. (India).
c/o St. Agnes, P.O. Box 488, Kenmare, 58746-0488. Tel: 701-385-4311.
Catechesis/Religious Program—Deb Zettinger, D.R.E.; Andrea Hager, D.R.E. Students 8.

DOUGLAS, WARD CO., HOLY CROSS (1908) Closed. For inquiries for parish records contact the chancery.

DRISCOLL, BURLEIGH CO., ST. ANTHONY (1906) Closed. For inquiries for parish records contact the chancery.

EMMONS, EMMONS CO.

1—ST. BERNARD (1884) Closed. For inquiries for parish records contact the chancery.

2—ST. JOSEPH (1918) Closed. For inquiries for parish records contact the chancery.

ENDRES, MCLEAN CO., ST. ADOLPH (1906) Closed. For inquiries for parish records contact the chancery.

EPPING, WILLIAMS CO., ST. MARY (1915) Closed. For inquiries for parish records contact the chancery.

FALLON, MORTON CO., SS. PETER & PAUL (1907) Closed. For inquiries for parish records contact the chancery.

FAYETTE, DUNN CO., ST. EDWARD (1914) Closed. For inquiries for parish records contact the chancery.

FLASHER, MORTON CO., ST. LAWRENCE (1912) [CEM] Rev. Daniel J. Berg.
Res.: 421 Court St., 58535-7216. Tel: 701-597-3570. Email: stlwrnce@westriv.com.
Catechesis/Religious Program—Tel: 701-597-3228. Students 44.

FORT RICE, MORTON CO. , IMMACULATE CONCEPTION (1908) Closed. For inquiries for parish records contact the chancery.

FORT YATES, SIOUX CO., ST. PETER - CATHOLIC INDIAN MISSION (1878), (Native American), [CEM], (Standing Rock Indian Reservation) Rev. Basil Atwell, O.S.B.; Bro. George Maufort, S.D.S.
Res.: P.O. Box 394, 58538. Tel: 701-854-3473; Fax: 701-854-3474.
School—St. Bernard Mission School, Tel: 701-854-7413. Sr. Richarde Wolf, S.S.N.D., Prin. Sisters 2; Lay Teachers 4; Students 60.
Catechesis/Religious Program—Tel: 701-854-3447.

FORTUNA, DIVIDE CO., ST. BERNARD (1918) Closed. For inquiries for parish records contact the chancery.

FOXHOLM, WARD CO., ST. MARY (1887) [CEM] [JC] Rev. Victor Paulraj Pichiamuthu, M.S.F.X. (India).
Res.: 17901 128th Ave. N.W., 58718-9643. Tel: 701-468-5925.
Catechesis/Religious Program—Tel: 701-468-5648. Students 95.

GARRISON, MCLEAN CO., ST. NICHOLAS (1905) [JC 8] Rev. Joseph John Kandathiparambil (India).
Res.: 235 Second St. N.E., P.O. Box 870, 58540. Tel: 701-463-2327; Fax: 701-463-2323.
Catechesis/Religious Program—Students 72.

GAYLORD, STARK CO., OUR LADY OF LOURDES (1910) Closed. For inquiries for parish records contact the chancery.

GLADSTONE, STARK CO., ST. THOMAS (1903), Served from Richardton. Rev. Boniface Muggli, O.S.B.
c/o St. Mary, 332 2nd St. N., Richardton, 58652-7141. Tel: 701-974-3569.
Catechesis/Religious Program—Dennise Miller, D.R.E. Twinned with St. Mary's, Richardton. Students 8.

GLEN ULLIN, MORTON CO.

1—ST. JOSEPH (1918), Served from Glen Ullin. Rev. Arul Joseph Irudamoney (India).
c/o Sacred Heart, P.O. Box 609, 58631-0609. Tel: 701-348-3527. 5210 62nd Ave., 58631.
Catechesis/Religious Program— Twinned with Sacred Heart, Glen Ullin. Students 9.

2—SACRED HEART OF JESUS (1883), (German—Russian), [CEM 2] Rev. Arul Joseph Irudamoney (India).
Res.: 204 E. Ash Ave., Box 609, 58631-0609. Tel: 701-348-3518. Email: aruljoe@gmail.com.
Catechesis/Religious Program—Tel: 701-348-3527. Mrs. Peggy Krebs, D.R.E. Students 95.

GLENBURN, RENVILLE CO., ST. PHILOMENA (1948), (German—Scandinavian), [CEM] Rev. Victor Paulraj Pichiamuthu, M.S.F.X. (India).
Res.: 310 3rd Ave., P.O. Box 68, 58740. Tel: 701-362-7571; Fax: 701-362-7571.
Catechesis/Religious Program—Kelly Zelinski, D.R.E. Students 12.

GOLVA, GOLDEN VALLEY CO., ST. MARY'S GOLVA (1906), Served from Beach. Rev. David Richter.
c/o St. John the Baptist, P.O. Box 337, Beach, 58621-0337. Tel: 701-872-4153.
Catechesis/Religious Program—Kathy Hollar, D.R.E.; Pam Knopp, Asst. D.R.E. High School twinned with St. John, Beach. Students 9.

GRASSNA, EMMONS CO., HOLY TRINITY (1900) Closed. For inquiries for parish records contact the chancery.

GRASSY BUTTE, MCKENZIE CO., ST. PETER CANSIUS (1927) Closed. For inquiries for parish records contact the chancery.

GRENORA, WILLIAMS CO., ST. BONIFACE (1912) [CEM 2] [JC] Rev. Raymond A. Aydt.
Church: P.O. Box 37, 58845. Tel: 701-694-3743.
Res.: 118 Fifth St. W., Williston, 58801. Tel: 701-572-6732.
Catechesis/Religious Program—Tel: 701-694-4285. Kari Pittenger, D.R.E. Students 12.

HAGUE, EMMONS CO.

1—ST. ALOYSIUS (1899) Closed. For inquiries for parish records contact the chancery.

2—ST. MARY (1890), (German—Russian), [CEM 2] Rev. Paul Eberle.
Church: P.O. Box 156, 58542.
Res.: Box 322, Strasburg, 58573. Tel: 701-336-7172.
Catechesis/Religious Program—Tel: 701-336-7102. Kathleen Kramer Nagel, D.R.E. Students 27.

HALEY, BOWMAN CO., ST. STANISLAUS (1908) Closed. For inquiries for parish records contact the chancery.

HALLIDAY, DUNN CO., ST. PAUL (1952) [CEM] [JC], (Quasi-Parish) Rev. Darnis Selvanayakam, M.S.F.X. (India).
Res.: 152 3rd Ave. N.W., P.O. Box 299, Killdeer, 58640. Tel: 701-764-5357; Fax: 701-764-6246. Email: stjoseph@ndsupernet.com.
Catechesis/Religious Program—Tel: 701-938-4504. Margaret Senger, D.R.E. Students 5.

HANKS, WILLIAMS CO., OUR LADY OF GOOD COUNSEL (1918) Closed. For inquiries for parish records contact the chancery.

HAYMARSH, MORTON CO., ST. CLEMENT (1887), Served from Hebron. Rev. Arul Joseph Irudamoney (India).
c/o St. Ann, P.O. Box 12, Hebron, 58638-0012. Tel: 701-878-4658.
Catechesis/Religious Program— Twinned with St. Ann's. Students 2.

HAYNES, ADAMS CO., ST. PETER (1908) Closed. For inquiries for parish records contact the chancery.

HAZELTON, EMMONS CO., ST. PAUL (1905) Rev. Gary Benz; Deacon Kenneth Wolbaum.
Church: 372 Harold St., 58544. Tel: 701-254-4588.
Res.: 613 N. Broadway St., Linton, 58552.
Catechesis/Religious Program—Tel: 701-782-6281. Charlotte Beastrom, D.R.E. Students 42.

HAZEN, MERCER CO., ST. MARTIN (1914), (German—Russian), [CEM] Rev. Johnson Kuriappilly.
Mailing Address: 103 3rd Ave., S.W., P.O. Box 387, 58545. Tel: 701-748-2121. Email: stmhazen@westriv.com.
Res.: 508 1st. Ave. N.E., P.O. Box 146, Beulah, 58523. Tel: 701-214-5575; Fax: 701-873-5614.
Catechesis/Religious Program— LuAnn Woeste, D.R.E. Students 110.

HEBRON, MORTON CO., ST. ANN (1906), (German), [CEM 3] Rev. Irudamoney Arul Joseph, M.S.F.X.
Res.: P.O. Box 12, 58638. Tel: 701-878-4658; Fax: 701-878-4658.
Catechesis/Religious Program—Tel: 701-878-4686. Irene Wehri, D.R.E. Students 56.

HETTINGER, ADAMS CO., HOLY TRINITY (1916), (German), [CEM] [JC] Rev. Joseph Chipson (India).
Res.: 405 3rd St. N., 58639. Tel: 701-567-2772; Fax: 701-567-2772.
Catechesis/Religious Program—Tamara Schneider, D.R.E. Tel: 701-567-2524. (includes missions) 71.

HIRSCHVILLE, STARK CO., ST. PHILIP (1908) Closed. For inquiries for parish records contact the chancery.

HUFF, MORTON CO., ST. MARTIN (1911), Served from Mandan. Rev. Chad Gion.
c/o Spirit of Life, Box 247, Mandan, 58554. Tel: 701-663-8842.
Catechesis/Religious Program—Students 12.

KENMARE, WARD CO., ST. AGNES (1901), (Scandinavian—German), [CEM] Rev. Selvaraj Periannan, M.S.F.X. (India).
Res.: 409 E. Division, P.O. Box 488, 58746. Tel: 701-385-4311; Fax: 701-385-4321.
Catechesis/Religious Program—Tel: 701-386-2403. Deb Zeltinger, D.R.E.; Andrea Hager, D.R.E. Students 43.

KENNEDY, BOWMAN CO., ST. HELENA (1912) Closed. For inquiries for parish records contact the chancery.

KILLDEER, DUNN CO., ST. JOSEPH (1917) [CEM] [JC 2] Rev. Darnis Selvanayakam, M.S.F.X. (India).
Res.: 152 3rd Ave., N.W., P.O. Box 299, 58640. Tel: 701-764-5357; Fax: 701-764-6246. Email: stjoseph@ndsupernet.com.
Catechesis/Religious Program—Tel: 701-548-8068. Sarah McFadden, D.R.E. Students 87.

LANSFORD, BOTTINEAU CO., ST. JOHNS (1949), Served from Mohall. Rev. Chris B. Walter (Retired).
c/o St. Jerome, P.O. Box 457, Mohall, 58761-0457. Tel: 701-756-6601.
Catechesis/Religious Program—Eileen Savelkoul, D.R.E. Students 13.

LEFOR, STARK CO., ST. ELIZABETH (1898) [CEM] Rt. Rev. Patrick Moore, O.S.B.
Rectory—10 - 5th & Mckenzie, New England, 58647. Email: stmarysne@ndsupernet.com.
Parish Office: 437 Main St., P.O. Box 369, New England, 58647-0369.
Catechesis/Religious Program—Anne Wolf, D.R.E. Students 5.

LIGNITE, BURKE CO., ST. MARY (1920) Closed. For inquiries for parish records contact the chancery.

LINTON, EMMONS CO.

1—ST. ANTHONY (1909) [CEM] Rev. Gary Benz; Deacon Kenneth Wolbaum.
Res.: 613 N. Broadway, 58552-7311. Tel: 701-254-4588; Fax: 701-254-4588.
Catechesis/Religious Program—Susan Schumacher, D.R.E.; Denice Kautz, D.R.E. Students 154.

2—ST. MICHAEL (1916), Served from Strasburg. Rev. Paul Eberle.
c/o SS. Peter & Paul, P.O. Box 322, Strasburg, 58573-0322. Tel: 701-336-7172.
Catechesis/Religious Program—Marie Vetter, D.R.E. Students 31.

MAKOTI, WARD CO., ST. ELIZABETH (1948), Served from Parshall. Rev. Roger A. Synek.
4th & Edwards St., 58756. *c/o St. Bridget*, P.O. Box 519, Parshall, 58770-0519. Tel: 701-862-3484.
Catechesis/Religious Program—Students 9.

MANDAN, MORTON CO.

1—CHRIST THE KING (1957) [CEM] Rev. Kenneth G. Phillips; Deacon Dennis Rohr.
Res.: 505-10th Ave., N.W., 58554-2552. Tel: 701-663-8842; Fax: 701-667-1730. Web: christthekingmandan.org.
School—Tel: 701-663-6200; Fax: 701-667-1730. Lay Teachers 13; Students 108.
Catechesis/Religious Program—Andrea Helbing, D.R.E.; Sandra Breiner, Sacramental Prep. Students 139.

2—ST. JOSEPH (1879) [CEM] Rev. Patrick A. Schumacher; Deacons Peter Hoffman, (Retired); Larry Dorrheim; Randall Frohlich.
Res.: 108 Third St. N.E., 58554. Tel: 701-663-9562; Fax: 701-663-6522. Email: stjosephmandan@goesp.com. Web: www.stjosephmandan.com.
School—(Grades K-6), 110 Collins Ave., 58554. Tel: 701-663-9563; Fax: 701-663-0183. Josephine Greff, Librarian. Lay Teachers 14; Students 141.
Catechesis/Religious Program—Michele Himmelspach, D.R.E. Students 145.

3—SPIRIT OF LIFE (1978) Rev. Chad Gion; Deacons David Vaughn; Joel Melarvie.
Mailing Address: Box 247, 58554. Web: myspiritoflife.com.
Res.: 809 First St. S.E., 58554. Tel: 701-663-1660; Fax: 701-667-2021.
Catechesis/Religious Program—Students 372.

MANDAREE, DUNN CO., ST. ANTHONY, (Native American), [CEM] Rev. Stephen Kranz, O.S.B.
Res.: Fr. Berthold Reservation, 9385 BIA Rte. 12, 58757-9269. Tel: 701-759-3412; Fax: 701-759-3412 (Call first). Email: skranz@restel.net.
Catechesis/Religious Program—Students 63.

MARMARTH, SLOPE CO., ST. MARY (1915), Served from Bowman. Rev. David G. Morman.
c/o St. Charles, 202 1st Ave., S.W., Bowman, 58623-4216. Tel: 701-523-5292.
Catechesis/Religious Program—Students 9.

MAX, MCLEAN CO., IMMACULATE CONCEPTION (1908), Served from Garrison. Rev. Joseph John Kandathiparambil (India).
c/o St. Nicholas, P.O. Box 870, Garrison, 58540-0870. Tel: 701-463-2327.
Catechesis/Religious Program—Peggy Bingham, D.R.E. Students 26.

MEDORA, BILLINGS CO., ST. MARY (MEDORA) (1886) [JC], Served from Beach. Rev. David Richter.
c/o St. John the Baptist, P.O. Box 337, Beach, 58621-0337. Tel: 701-872-4153.
Catechesis/Religious Program—Kathy Hollar, D.R.E. Twinned with St. John the Baptist, Beach. Students 1.

MENOKEN, BURLEIGH CO., ST. HILDEGARD (1947) [JC] Rev. Christopher J. Kadrmas.
Res.: 17200 Hwy. 10, 58558-9604. Tel: 701-673-3177; Fax: 701-673-3177. Email: sthildegard@bektel.com.
Catechesis/Religious Program—Tel: 701-673-3452. Janice Aberle, D.R.E. Students 61.

MINER, GRANT CO., MARY IMMACULATE (1912) Closed. For inquiries for parish records contact the chancery.

MINOT, WARD CO.

1—ST. JOHN THE APOSTLE (1961) Rev. David L. Zimmer; Deacons Stephen B. Mays, (Retired); Charles Kramer; Hans G. Gayzur.
Mailing Address: 2600 Central Ave. W., 58701.
Res.: 109-25th St. N.W., 58703-2862. Tel: 701-839-7076; Fax: 701-839-2553. Email: stjohnchurch@srt.com. Web: www.stjohnminot.com.
Catechesis/Religious Program—Monica Perry, D.R.E. Teachers 17; Students 194.

2—ST. LEO (1886), (German), [CEM] Revs. Austin Vetter; Justin P. Waltz, Parochial Vicar; Victor Paulraj Pichiamuthu, M.S.F.X. (India); Deacon Robert A. Dangel.
Res.: 305 1st. St., S.E., 58701. Tel: 701-838-1026; Fax: 701-852-4683.
Catechesis/Religious Program— Cynthia Clark, D.R.E. Students 229.

3—MINOT AIR FORCE BASE CHAPEL (1954) Rev. John Schuetze.
5BW/HC—230 Missile Ave., 58505-5003. Tel: 701-723-2456; Fax: 701-723-3052.
Catechesis/Religious Program—Tel: 701-723-6442. Email: colleen.moore@minot.af.mil. Students 100.

4—OUR LADY OF GRACE (1959) Rev. Bruce D. Krebs; Deacon Steven F. Streitz.
Res.: 707 16th Ave., S.W., 58701. Tel: 701-839-6834; 701-852-3002; Fax: 701-837-1080.

Catechesis/Religious Program—Darlene Demars, D.R.E., (Grades K-5); Brian Krebs, D.R.E., (Grades 6-12). Students 339.

5—ST. THERESE THE LITTLE FLOWER (1954) [JC] Rev. Frederick R. Harvey; Julie Eisenbraun, Business Mgr.
Res.: 800 University Ave. W., 58703. Tel: 701-838-1520; Fax: 701-838-1520. Email: lfp@brhs.com. Web: littleflowerminot.com.
See Little Flower School, Minot under Miscellaneous located in the Institution section.
Catechesis/Religious Program—Tel: 701-839-8567. Deb Carroll, D.R.E. Students 82.

MOHALL, RENVILLE CO., ST. JEROME (1906) [CEM] [JC] Rev. Chris B. Walter, Admin. (Retired).
Res.: 303 E. Main St., P.O. Box 457, 58761-0457. Tel: 701-756-6601; Fax: 701-756-6901.
Catechesis/Religious Program—Students 34.

MORTON, MORTON CO., SS. PETER & PAUL (1904) Closed. For inquiries for parish records contact the chancery.

MOTT, HETTINGER CO., ST. VINCENT DE PAUL (1907) [CEM] Rev. Charles A. Zins; Deacons Ervin Schneider; David M. Crane.
Res.: 408 Iowa Ave., 58646. Tel: 701-824-2651; Fax: 701-824-2651.
Catechesis/Religious Program—Students 95.

NEW ENGLAND, HETTINGER CO., ST. MARY (1910) [CEM] Rt. Rev. Patrick Moore, O.S.B.; Deacon Victor F. Dvorak.
Rectory—10 - 5th & McKenzie, 58647. Tel: 701-579-4312; Fax: 701-579-4874. Email: stmarysne@ndsupernet.com.
Parish Office: 437 Main St., P.O. Box 369, 58647.
Catechesis/Religious Program—Anne Wolf, D.R.E. Students 81.

NEW HRADEC, DUNN CO., SS. PETER AND PAUL (1898), Served from Belfield. Rev. Shannon G. Lucht.
c/o St. Bernard, P.O. Box 38, Belfield, 58622-0038. Tel: 701-575-4295.

NEW LEIPZIG, GRANT CO., ST. JOHN THE BAPTIST (1911), Served from Mott. Rev. Charles A. Zins.
c/o St. Vincent de Paul, 408 Iowa Ave., Mott, 58646-7260. Tel: 701-824-2651.
Catechesis/Religious Program—Students 4.

NEW SALEM, MORTON CO., ST. PIUS V (1912) [CEM] Rev. Amalraj Roche, M.S.F.X. (India).
Res.: 202 N. 3rd St., P.O. Box C, 58563-0429. Tel: 701-843-7144. Email: stpiusv@westriv.com.
Catechesis/Religious Program—Tel: 701-843-7061. Students 101.

NEW TOWN, MOUNTRAIL CO., ST. ANTHONY (1954), (Native American), [CEM 4] [JC] Revs. Stephen Kranz, O.S.B.; Denis Fournier, O.S.B.; Deacon Daniel Barone.
Res.: 206 Eagle Dr., P.O. Box 715, 58763. Tel: 701-627-4423.
Catechesis/Religious Program—Students 71.

NOONAN, DIVIDE CO. , ST. LUKE (1914), Served from Crosby. Rev. Biju Chitteth (India).
c/o St. Patrick, P.O. Box 89, Crosby, 58730-0089. Tel: 701-965-6537.

ODENSE, MORTON CO., ST. JOHN (1905) Closed. For inquiries for parish records contact the chancery.

PARSHALL, MOUNTRAIL CO., ST. BRIDGET (1917), (German—Norwegian), [CEM 4] [JC 3] Rev. Roger A. Synek.
Res.: 12 First Ave., N.E., Box 519, 58770-0519. Tel: 701-862-3484. Email: stbridget@restel.com.
Catechesis/Religious Program—Tel: 701-862-3484. Students 24.

PLAZA, MOUNTRAIL CO., SACRED HEART (1910), Served from Parshall. Rev. Roger A. Synek.
58771. *c/o St. Bridget*, P.O. Box 519, Parshall, 58770-0519. Tel: 701-862-3484.
Catechesis/Religious Program—Students 6.

PORCUPINE, SIOUX CO., ST. JAMES (1897), Served from Fort Yates. Rev. Basil Atwell, O.S.B.
c/o St. Peter, P.O. Box 394, Fort Yates, 58538-0394. Tel: 701-854-3473.

PORTAL, BURKE CO., ST. JOHN THE BAPTIST (1900), Served from Crosby. Rev. Biju Chitteth (India).
c/o St. Patrick, P.O. Box 89, Crosby, 58730-0089. Tel: 701-965-6537.
Catechesis/Religious Program—Students 9.

POWERS LAKE, BURKE CO., ST. JAMES (1910), Served from Tioga. Rev. Benny D. Putharayil (India).
c/o St. Thomas the Apostle, P.O. Box 667, Tioga, 58852-0667. Tel: 701-664-2445.
Catechesis/Religious Program—Jane Streifel, D.R.E. Students 16.

RALEIGH, GRANT CO., ST. GERTRUDE (1913) [CEM] Rev. Daniel J. Berg.
Mailing Address: 421 Court St., Flasher, 58535-7216. Tel: 701-597-3570.
Church: 7785 St. Gertrude Ave., 58564. Tel: 701-597-3570.
Catechesis/Religious Program—Tel: 701-597-3228. Students 3.

RAY, WILLIAMS CO., ST. MICHAEL (1903), Served from Tioga. Rev. Benny D. Putharayil (India).
c/o St. Thomas the Apostle, P.O. Box 667, Tioga, 58852-0667. Tel: 701-664-2445.
Catechesis/Religious Program—Rebecca Jungemann, D.R.E. Students 14.

REEDER, ADAMS CO., SACRED HEART (1908), Served from Hettinger. Rev. Joseph Chipson (India).
c/o Holy Trinity, 405 3rd St. N., Hettinger, 58639-7125. Tel: 701-567-2772.

REGENT, HETTINGER CO., ST. HENRY (1913) [JC] Rev. Charles A. Zins; Deacon Don J. Gion.
Res.: 150 W. Fifth, P.O. Box 155, 58650-0155. Tel: 701-563-4595.
Catechesis/Religious Program— Twinned with St. Vincent's, Mott. Students 27.

RHAME, BOWMAN CO., ST. MEL (1914), Served from Bowman. Rev. David G. Morman.
c/o St. Charles, 202 1st Ave., S.W., Bowman, 58623-4216. Tel: 701-523-5292.
Catechesis/Religious Program—Theresa Fischy, D.R.E. Students 23.

RICHARDTON, STARK CO., ST. MARY (1895) [CEM] Rev. Boniface Muggli, O.S.B.
332 2nd St. N., 58652-7141. Web: www.marychurch.org.
Res.: 418 N. 3rd Ave. W., 58652. Tel: 701-974-3569. Web: www.marychurch.org.
Catechesis/Religious Program—Dennise Miller, D.R.E. (Grades K-12). Students 88.

RIVERDALE, MCLEAN CO., ST. JOHN (1947) Closed. For inquiries for parish records contact the chancery.

ROSENTHAL, EMMONS CO., SACRED HEART (1907) Closed. For inquiries for parish records contact the chancery.

ROSS, MOUNTRAIL CO., ST. FRANCIS (1911) Closed. For inquiries for parish records contact the chancery.

RYDER, WARD CO., ST. CHARLES (1907) Closed. For inquiries for parish records contact the chancery.

ST. ANTHONY, MORTON CO., ST. ANTHONY (1894), Served from Mandan. Rev. Chad Gion.
c/o Spirit of Life, Box 247, Mandan, 58554. Tel: 701-663-1660.
Catechesis/Religious Program—Jonathan Marohl, D.R.E. Students 23.

SCRANTON, BOWMAN CO., SACRED HEART (1928), Served from Hettinger. Rev. Joseph Chipson (India).
c/o Holy Trinity, 405 3rd St. N., Hettinger, 58639-7125. Tel: 701-567-2772.
Catechesis/Religious Program—Diaune Pierce, D.R.E. Students 43.

SELFRIDGE, SIOUX CO., ST. PHILOMENA (1919), (German—Russian), [CEM] Rev. Basil Atwell, O.S.B.
Res.: P.O. Box 394, Fort Yates, 58538-0394. Tel: 701-854-3473; Fax: 701-854-3474.
Catechesis/Religious Program—Sr. Frances Marie Voigt, D.R.E.

SENTINEL BUTTE, GOLDEN VALLEY CO., ST. MICHAEL (1891) Closed. For inquiries for parish records contact the chancery.

SHEFFIELD, STARK CO., ST. PIUS (1912) Closed. For inquiries for parish records contact the chancery.

SHERWOOD, RENVILLE CO., ST. JAMES (1911), Served from Mohall. Rev. Chris B. Walter (Retired).
c/o St. Jerome, 303 E. Main St., P.O. Box 457, Mohall, 58761-0457. Tel: 701-756-6601.
Catechesis/Religious Program—Lori Feland, D.R.E. Students 30.

SHIELDS, MORTON CO., ST. GABRIEL (1912) Closed. For inquiries for parish records contact the chancery.

SOLEN, SIOUX CO., SACRED HEART (1913), Served from Ft. Yates Rev. Basil Atwell, O.S.B.
c/o St. Peter, P.O. Box 394, Fort Yates, 58538-0394. Tel: 701-854-3473.

SOUTH HEART, STARK CO., ST. MARY (1923) [CEM] Rev. Shannon G. Lucht.
Res.: P.O. Box 189, 58655. Tel: 701-677-5886; Fax: 701-677-5886.
Catechesis/Religious Program—Tel: 701-575-4838. Students 83.

STANLEY, MOUNTRAIL CO., QUEEN OF THE MOST HOLY ROSARY (1908) [JC] Rev. Glen Michael Millard.
Res.: 425 1st St. S.E., P.O. Box 159, 58784. Tel: 701-628-2323; Fax: 701-628-3406. Email: mikemillardeagl@hotmail.com.
Catechesis/Religious Program—Tel: 701-628-3405. Students 70.

STARK, STARK CO., ST. STEPHEN (1900), Served from Ricardton. Rev. Boniface Muggli, O.S.B.
c/o St. Mary, 332 2nd St. N., Richardton, 58652-7141. Tel: 701-974-3569.
Catechesis/Religious Program—Dennise Miller, D.R.E. Twinned with St. Mary's, Richardton. Students 8.

STRASBURG, EMMONS CO., STS. PETER AND PAUL (1889), (German—Russian), [CEM] Rev. Paul Eberle.
Res.: P.O. Box 322, 58573-0322. Tel: 701-336-7172.
Catechesis/Religious Program—Tel: 701-336-4607. Kathleen Kramer Nagel, D.R.E. Students 78.

TAYLOR, STARK CO., ST. PETER (1883) Closed. For inquiries for parish records contact the chancery.

TIOGA, WILLIAMS CO., ST. THOMAS (1914) [JC] Rev. Benny D. Putharayil (India).
Res.: 213 N. Gilbertson St., P.O. Box 667, 58852. Tel: 701-664-2445; Fax: 701-664-3531.
Catechesis/Religious Program—Students 18.

TOLLEY, WARD CO., SS. PETER & PAUL (1906) Closed. For inquiries for parish records contact the chancery.

TRENTON, WILLIAMS CO., ST. JOHN THE BAPTIST (1890), Served from Williston. Rev. Dennis R. Schafer.
c/o St. Joseph, P.O. Box K, Williston, 58802-1115. Tel: 701-572-6731.
Catechesis/Religious Program—Students 50.

TURTLE LAKE, MCLEAN CO., ST. CATHERINE (1913), Served from Underwood. Rev. Frank Schuster.
c/o St. Bonaventure, P.O. Box 240, Underwood, 58576-0240. Tel: 701-442-5229.
Catechesis/Religious Program—Diane Cullum, D.R.E. Students 24.

TWIN BUTTES, DUNN CO., ST. JOSEPH (1951), Served from Mandaree. Rev. Stephen Kranz, O.S.B.
c/o St. Anthony, 9385 BIA Rte. 12, Mandaree, 58757-9269. Tel: 701-759-3412.
Catechesis/Religious Program—Students 24.

UNDERWOOD, MCLEAN CO., ST. BONAVENTURE (1913) [CEM] Rev. Frank J. Schuster.
Res.: 505 Grant Ave., P.O. Box 240, 58576. Tel: 701-442-5229; Fax: 701-442-5259. Email: stbonaventurechurch@westriv.com.
Catechesis/Religious Program—Students 34.

WASHBURN, MCLEAN CO., ST. EDWIN'S CHURCH (1903), Served from Underwood. Rev. Frank Schuster.
c/o St. Bonaventure, P.O. Box 240, Underwood, 58576-0240. Tel: 701-442-5229.
Catechesis/Religious Program—Jill Grumbo, D.R.E. Students 77.

WATFORD CITY, MCKENZIE CO., EPIPHANY (1915) Rev. John M. Pfeifer.
Res.: 112 6th Ave., N.E., P.O. Box 670, 58854. Tel: 701-842-3505.
Catechesis/Religious Program—Tel: 701-842-3791; 701-444-5150. Leah Voll, D.R.E. Students 75.

WHITE EARTH, MOUNTRAIL CO., ST. FRANCIS OF ASSISI (1894) Closed. For inquiries for parish records contact the chancery.

WHITE SHIELD, MCLEAN CO., SACRED HEART (1953), Served from Garrison. Rev. Joseph John Kandathiparambil (India).
c/o St. Nicholas, P.O. Box 870, Garrison, 58540-0870. Tel: 701-463-2327.
Catechesis/Religious Program—Students 6.

WILDROSE, DIVIDE CO., SACRED HEART OF JESUS (1916) Closed. For inquiries for parish records contact the chancery.

WILLA, STARK CO., ST. PLACIDUS (1903) Closed. For inquiries for parish records contact the chancery.

WILLISTON, WILLIAMS CO., ST. JOSEPH (1901) [JC] Rev. Dennis R. Schafer.
124 Sixth St. W., P.O. Box K, 58802.
Res.: 524 First Ave. W., P.O. Box K, 58802. Tel: 701-572-6731; Fax: 701-572-4203. Email: stjoech@nemont.net.
School—Tel: 701-572-6384; Fax: 701-774-0998. Peter Lingen, Prin. Lay Teachers 13; Students 172.
Catechesis/Religious Program—Tel: 701-572-0201. Email: charley.epperson@sendit.nodak.edu. Charley Epperson, D.R.E. Students 185.

WILTON, MCLEAN CO., SACRED HEART (1906) [CEM] [JC] Deacon James Nistler.
Res.: 421 Bismarck Ave., P.O. Box 128, 58579-0128. Tel: 701-734-6384. Email: jhnistler@bismarckdiocese.com.
Catechesis/Religious Program—Tel: 701-734-8136; 701-734-6377. Jeanette Fox, D.R.E. Students 30.

WING, BURLEIGH CO., ST. IGNATIUS (1914) Closed. For inquiries for parish records contact the chancery.

Chaplains of Public Institutions

BISMARCK. *North Dakota State Penitentiary* 58504. Tel: 701-328-6357. Deacon David Vaughn.

MANDAN. *North Dakota Youth Correctional Center*, 701-16th Ave. S.W., 58554-5800. Tel: 701-667-1400. Deacon John Tharaldsen.

On Duty Outside the Diocese:
Revs.—
Brown, Phillip, Theological College, 401 Michigan Ave., N.E., Washington, DC 20017-1518.
Deichert, Joseph, HQ USAFA/HCX, 2348 Sijan Dr. Ste. 100, U S A F Academy, CO 80840-8280.
Kuss, Allen R., Office of the Chaplain, PSC 561, Box 1236, Fpo, AP 96310-0013.

Graduate Studies:
Rev.—
Schneider, Nick L., Pontifical North American College 00120 Vatican City State.

Retired:

Rev. Msgr.—

Walsh, Gerald J., 3037 W. Avenida Destino, Tucson, AZ 85746-8268.

Revs.—

Bova, Eugene R., 360 Pinon Rd., Bailey, CO 80421-1837.

Cervinski, Paul, P.O. Box 1425, New Town, 58763-1425.

Cosgrove, William P., P.O. Box 263, New Leipzig, 58562.

Dignan, Thomas L., 211 W. Sutton Sq., Stafford, TX 77477-4715.

Dukart, George, Emmaus Place, 1020 N. 26th St., Apt. 3, 58501-3186.

Dukart, Norman J., 140 4th Ave., S.E., Dickinson, 58601.

Eckroth, Leonard A., P.O. Box 116, Bowbells, 58721.

Heidt, Charles A., 4199 13th St., N.W., Lot #28, Garrison, 58540-9423.

Kautzman, Jerome G., Emmaus Place, 1020 N. 26th St., Apt. 5, 58501-3186.

Kramer, Thomas E., Emmaus Place, 1020 N. 26th St., Apt. 7, 58501-3187.

Krank, Michael T.

Leary, Albert R., P.O. Box 329, Strasburg, 58573-0329.

O'Leary, John P., Emmaus Place, 1020 N. 26th St., Apt. 1, 58501-3186.

Owens, John J., 9670 210th St. Crt N, Forest Lake, MN 55025-9106.

Paluck, Casimir S., P.O. Box 283, South Heart, 58655-0283.

Rushford, William A., Emmaus Place, 1020 N. 26th St., Apt. 2, 58501-3186.

Schneider, Henry W., 1900 28th St. S.W., Minot, 58701-8135.

Schumacher, Jacob J., Emmaus Place, 1020 N. 26th St., Apt. 6, 58501-3186.

Wald, Kenneth J., 267 N. Rice Lake Rd., Douglas, 58735-9512.

Walter, Chris B., P.O. Box 457, Mohall, 58761-0457.

Zastoupil, Stephen R., Little Knife Cottage Site, Box 14, New Town, 58763.

Permanent Deacons:

Barone, Daniel, St. Anthony, New Town

Brannan, Steve M., St. Vincent de Paul, Crown Butte

Clancy, Lynn, (Retired)

Crane, David M., St. Vincent de Paul, Mott

Cunningham, Patrick M., (Unassigned)

Dangel, Robert A., St. Leo, Minot

Dean, Dennis L., St. John, Lansford

Deichert, Harry M., (Retired)

Dorrheim, Larry L., St. Joseph, Mandan

Dukart, Herman, (Retired)

Dvorak, Victor F., St. Mary, New England

Dworshak, Anton T., (Retired)

Fettig, Richard H., Cathedral of the Holy Spirit, Bismarck

Finneman, Tony, Ascension, Bismarck

Fischer, Leonard, St. Charles, Bowman

Fix, Michael, Corpus Christi, Bismarck

Frohlich, Randall, St. Joseph, Mandan

Gayzur, Hans, St. John the Apostle, Minot

Gion, Donald J., St. Henry, Regent

Glatt, Terry, St. Mary, Bismarck

Grabar, Ray A., (Retired)

Haga, James A., St. Joseph, Williston

Hanel, Harvey, St. Mary, Bismarck

Helbing, Douglas, Christ the King, Mandan

Hibl, Albert W., (Retired)

Hoffman, Peter, (Retired)

Hogan, Ronald, (Unassigned)

Jilek, Raymond, (Retired)

Johnson, Ed J., Sr., Rolla, ND

Johnson, Ward A., (Retired)

Jundt, Wayne M., St. Anne, Bismarck

Keller, Ronald, St Patrick, Dickinson

Klein, Kenneth M., St. Mary, Bismarck

Knopik, Martin, (Retired)

Kordonowy, Leonard J., Ukrainian Church of St. Demetrius, Fairfield

Kramer, Charles L., St. John the Apostle, Minot

Krupinsky, Joseph M., St. Anne, Bismarck

Marback, Michael, St. Mary, Bismarck

Martin, Morris E., (Retired)

Mathern, Joseph J., (Retired)

Mattson, Joseph M., Holy Trinity, Hettinger

Mays, Stephen B., (Retired)

McDowall, Rexford R., Corpus Christi, Bismarck

Melarvie, Joel D., Spirit of Life, Mandan

Mizeur, Gary, Cathedral of the Holy Spirit, Bismarck

Morgel, Edmund D., (Retired)

Morman, Eugene F., (Retired)

Nistler, Donald R., (Retired)

Nistler, James A., Co-Dir. African Mission, Sacred Heart, Wilton

Olson, Robert C., (Retired)

Quintus, Gary, St. Mary, Richardton

Quintus, Terry B., St. Joseph, Dickinson

Ressler, James V., (Retired)

Riehl, Emil J., (Retired)

Ringwall, Kris, Queen of Peace, Dickinson

Rohr, Dennis, Christ the King, Mandan

Rustand, Gerald T., (Unassigned)

Schmit, Kenneth, St. Charles, Bowman

Schneider, Ervin H., St. Vincent de Paul, Mott

Schulz, Doyle, Ascension, Bismarck

Schwindt, Alvin W., St. Joseph, Dickinson

Stockert, Ralph F., (Retired)

Stockert, Robert, St. Wenceslaus, Dickinson

Streitz, Steven F., Our Lady of Grace, Minot

Tharaldsen, John, Corpus Christi, Bismarck; Youth Correctional Center, Mandan

Vaughn, David L., Spirit of Life, Mandan; North Dakota State Penitentiary, Bismarck

Volk, Jerome, Queen of Peace, Dickinson

Von Ruden, Ralph, Cathedral of the Holy Spirit, Bismarck

Wallach, Daniel, St. Joseph, Beulah

Wanner, Anton, Jr., St. Patrick, Dickinson

Wesolowski, Edwin A., St. Mary, Bismarck

Wolbaum, Kenneth J., St. Katherine, Braddock

Wolberg, Ronald R., Queen of Peace, Dickinson

Wolf, Wilfred P., (Retired)

Wosepka, James, St. John the Baptist, Beach

Zent, Robert, St. Wenceslaus, Dickinson

Ziman, Edward J., (Retired)

INSTITUTIONS LOCATED IN THE DIOCESE

[A] SEMINARIES, RELIGIOUS OR SCHOLASTICATES

RICHARDTON. *Assumption Abbey* (1893) P.O. Box A, 58652. Tel: 701-974-3315; Fax: 701-974-3317. Email: monks@assumptionabbey.com. Web: www.assumptionabbey.com. Rt. Revs. Brian Wangler, O.S.B., M.A., Abbot; Lawrence Wagner, O.S.B., Abbot (Retired); Rev. Valerian Odermann, O.S.B., Ph.D., Teacher & Chap.; Bro. Basil Kirsch, O.S.B., Prior; Revs. Claude Seeberger, O.S.B., M.A., Chap.; Gerald Ruelle, O.S.B. (Retired); Raymond Dietlein, O.S.B. (Retired); John Odermann, O.S.B. (Retired); Stephen Kranz, O.S.B.; Damian Dietlein, O.S.B., S.T.L., Seminary Prof.; Sebastian Schmidt, O.S.B., Subprior; Denis Fournier, O.S.B., Ph.D.; Francis Wehri, O.S.B., M.A., (Overseas); Terrence Kardong, O.S.B., M.A.; Victor Feser, O.S.B., Ph.D., Teacher; Odo Muggli, O.S.B., Business Mgr.; Daniel Maloney, O.S.B., M.A., Chap. & Teacher; Philip Vanderlin, O.S.B., Prior, (Overseas); Francis dos Remedios, O.S.B. (Retired); Julian Nix, O.S.B., Hospital Chap.; Hugo L. Blotsky, O.S.B.; Efraim Villegas, O.S.B., Business Mgr., (Overseas); Boniface Muggli, O.S.B.; Gonzalo Blanco, O.S.B., (Overseas); Thomas Wordekemper, O.S.B., Chap.; Nicolas Cano, O.S.B., (Overseas); James Kilzer, O.S.B., Asst. Business Mgr.; Basil Atwell, O.S.B.; Manuel Cely, (Overseas); Warren Heidgen, O.S.B., Chap.; Benedict Fischer, O.S.B., Teacher; Carlos Suarez, O.S.B., (Overseas); Bro. Aaron Jensen, O.S.B., Librarian; Rt. Rev. Patrick Moore, O.S.B., Resigned Abbot. Priests 33; Brothers 20; Monks 57.

[B] COLLEGES AND UNIVERSITIES

BISMARCK. *University of Mary* (1959) 7500 University Dr., 58504-9652. Tel: 701-255-7500; Fax: 701-255-7687. Email: marauder@umary.edu. Web: www.umary.edu. Rev. James P. Shea, Pres.; Dr. Diane Fladeland, Vice Pres. Academic Affairs; Revs. Victor Feser, O.S.B., Ph.D.; Benedict Fischer, O.S.B.; Daniel Maloney, O.S.B., M.A.; Valerian Odermann, O.S.B., Ph.D., Chap.; Cheryl Bailey, Librarian. Priests 5; Sisters 11; Lay Teachers 83; Students 2,830.

[C] HIGH SCHOOLS, INTERPAROCHIAL AND PARISH

BISMARCK. *St. Mary's Central High School*, 1025 N. Second St., 58501. Tel: 701-223-4113; Fax: 701-223-8629. Email: smchs@smchs.org. Web: www.smchs.org. John Jankowski, Supt.; Tom Eberle, Prin.; Rev. Joshua K. Waltz, Chap. & Instructor; Connie Tschider, Librarian. Priests 1; Lay Teachers 27; Students 315.

DICKINSON. *Dickinson Catholic Schools*, (Grades PreK-12), P.O. Box 1177, 58601. Tel: 701-483-6081; Fax: 701-483-1450. Email: dorothy.a.zeller@sendit.nodak.edu. Sr. Dorothy Zeller, S.S.N.D., Supt.; Mr. Rocky Cofer, Prin. (Trinity High Sch.); Rachel Ebach, Librarian (Trinity High Sch.); Peggy Mayer, Prin. (Trinity Elem. Sch. East & West); Andrea Krebs, Librarian (Trinity Elem. Sch. East & West). Priests 1; Sisters 2; Lay Teachers 40; K-12 Students 465; Pre-K Students 58.

Trinity High School (1961) (Grades 7-12), 810 Empire Rd., P.O. Box 1177, 58602-1177. Tel: 701-483-6081; Fax: 701-483-1450. Web: www.trinityhighschool.com. Email: rocklyn.g.cofer@sendit.nodak.edu. Rocklyn Cofer, Prin.; Rev. Joshua J. Ehli; Rachel Ebach, Librarian. Lay Teachers 18; Students 231; Total Staff 21; Sisters 1; Priests 1.

MINOT. *Bishop Ryan High School* (1958) 316 11th Ave. N.W., 58703-2260. Tel: 701-852-4004; Fax: 701-839-4651. Email: rlimke@brhs.com. Web: www.brhs.com. Richard Limke, Supt.; Terry Voiles, Prin.; Cindy Lientz, Librarian. Priests 1; Teachers 23; Students 258.

[D] GENERAL HOSPITALS

BISMARCK. *St. Alexius Medical Center* (1885) P.O. Box 5510, 58506-5510. Tel: 701-530-7000; Fax: 701-530-7284. Web: www.st.alexius.org. Andrew L. Wilson, Admin. & CEO; Sr. Renee Zastoupil, Dir. Pastoral Care. Sisters of St. Benedict. Priests 3; Sisters 4; Bed Capacity 306; Total Staff 2,108; Patients Assisted Annually 216,330.

DICKINSON. *St. Joseph's Hospital and Health Center*, 30 W. Seventh St., 58601. Tel: 701-456-4271; Fax: 701-456-4800. Web: stjoeshospital.org. Reed E. Reyman, Pres. & CEO. Nurses 152; Total Staff 414; Bed Capacity 106; Patients Assisted Annually 40,307.

GARRISON. *Garrison Memorial Hospital*, P.O. Box 39, 58540. Tel: 701-463-2275; Fax: 701-463-2886; 701-463-6569. Email: dmattern@primecare.org. Web: garrisonmh.com. Dean Mattern, Admin. Sisters of St. Benedict (Bismarck) 3; Nurses 48; Bed Capacity 50; Total Staff 135; Patients Assisted Annually 12,500.

WILLISTON. *Mercy Medical Center - Affiliate of Catholic Health Initiatives*, 1301 15th Ave. W., 58801. Tel: 701-774-7400; Fax: 701-774-7479. Web: www.mercy-williston.org. Dennis Goebel, Pres. & CEO. Bed Capacity 35; Patients Assisted Annually 60,000; Total Staff 454.

Mercy Medical Foundation, 1301 15th Ave. W., 58801. Tel: 701-774-7404; Fax: 701-774-7479. Email: warrensundet@catholichealth.net. Web: www.mercy-williston.org. Bed Capacity 35; Patients Assisted Annually 60,000; Total Staff 454.

[E] SPECIAL CARE FACILITIES

DICKINSON. *Benedictine Living Communities, Inc. dba St. Benedicts Health Center* 851 Fourth Ave. E., 58601. Tel: 701-456-7242; Fax: 701-456-7250. Email: Jon.frantsvog@bhshealth.org. Web: www.saint-benedicts.org. Jon Frantsvog, Admin. Operated by Benedictine Living Communities, Inc. Bed Capacity 164; Total Staff 250; Total Assisted Annually 164.

Benedictine Living Communities, Inc. dba Benedict Court (2003) 830 2nd Ave. E., 58601. Tel: 701-456-7242; Fax: 701-456-7250. Email: Jon.frantsvog@bhshealth.org. Web: www.benedict-court.org. Jon Frantsvog, Admin. & Contact Person. Bed Capacity 26; Total Assisted Annually 26; Total Staff 10.

GARRISON. *Benedictine Living Communities, Inc. dba Benedictine Living Center of Garrison* (1969) 609 4th Ave., N.E., P.O. Box 219, 58540. Tel: 701-463-2226; Fax: 701-463-2650. Email: scott.foss@bhshealth.org. Scott Foss, Admin. Operated by Benedictine Health System Long Term Care, Inc. Bed Capacity 63; Total Staff 75; Total Assisted Annually 125.

[F] PROTECTIVE INSTITUTIONS

SENTINEL BUTTE. *Home On The Range* (1950) 16351 I-94, 58654-9500. Tel: 701-872-3745; Fax: 701-872-3748. Email: jorluck@gohotr.org. Web: www.gohotr.org. Mr. Jay Johnson, M.S.W., L.I.C.S.W., Exec. Dir.; Rev. David Richter, Chap. Total Staff 75; Total Assisted 120; Bed Capacity 62.

[G] HOMES FOR AGED

BISMARCK. *Emmaus Place*, 1020 N. 26th St., 58501. Tel: 701-258-2618. Revs. George Dukart (Retired); Jerome G. Kautzman (Retired); Thomas E. Kramer (Retired); John P. O'Leary (Retired); William A. Rushford (Retired); Jacob J. Schumacher (Retired). Priests retirement home. Total Staff 5; Total Assisted Annually 8; Total in Residence 6.

Marillac Manor (1977) 1016 N. 28th St., 58501. Tel: 701-258-8702; Fax: 701-250-4898. Email: awilz@mohs.org. Web: marillacmanor.com. Angie Wilz, Office Mgr. Retirement Apartments 77; Total Staff 5; Total in Residence 85.

**Medcenter One St. Vincent's Care Center* (1943) 1021 N. 26 St., 58501-3199. Tel: 701-323-1999; Fax: 701-323-1989. Email: kgreff@mohs.org. Kirk Greff, Admin. Sisters of St. Benedict 1; Total Staff 180; Resident Patients 101; Total Assisted Annually 170; Bed Capacity 101.

[H] CONVENTS AND RESIDENCES FOR SISTERS

BISMARCK. *Annunciation Monastery* (1947) 7520 University Dr., 58504-9653. Tel: 701-255-1520; Fax: 701-255-1440. Web: www.annunciationmonastery.org. Sr. Nancy Miller, O.S.B., Prioress; Rev. Daniel Maloney, O.S.B., M.A., Resident Chap. Motherhouse and Novitiate of the Benedictine Sisters of the Annunciation, B.M.V. Professed Sisters 60.

RICHARDTON. *Sacred Heart Monastery*, 8969 Hwy. 10 W., P.O. Box 364, 58652. Tel: 701-974-2121; Fax: 701-974-2124. Email: busoffice@sacredheartmonastery.com. Web: www.sacredheartmonastery.com. Sr. Ruth Fox, O.S.B., Prioress & Pres. Motherhouse and Novitiate of the Sisters of the Order of St. Benedict. Professed Sisters 27.

[I] MISCELLANEOUS

BISMARCK. *Benedictine Living Communities - Bismarck, Inc.*, 1839 E. Capitol Ave., 58501.

The St. Mary's Central High School Endowment for Operations and Tuition Aid for Students at SMCHS, 1025 N. 2nd St., 58501.

World Apostolate of Fatima, 2114 N. 3rd St., 58501. Tel: 701-222-0185; 701-391-1172. Email: wafbismarck@gmail.com. Web: www.wafbismarck.org. Shirlein Vetter, Pres.

DICKINSON. *Subiaco Manor* (1990) 2441 10th Ave. W. #10, 58601. Tel: 701-483-2350. Email: reneeosb@ndsupernet.com. Sr. Renee Branigan, O.S.B., Resident Mgr. Sponsored by the Benedictine Sisters of Sacred Heart Monastery in Richardton. Total Staff 2; Total in Residence 13.

MINOT. *Minot Catholic Schools Corporation* (1994) 316 11th Ave., N.W., 58703-2299. Tel: 701-852-4004; Fax: 701-837-8914. Email: rlimke@brhs.com. Web: www.brhs.com. Richard Limke, Supt. Total Staff 35.

Bishop Ryan High School, 316 11th Ave., N.W., 58703-2260. Tel: 701-838-3355; Fax: 701-839-4651. Email: rlimke@brhs.com. Web: www.brhs.com. Richard Limke, Supt.; Gary Volk, Prin.; Rev. Justin P. Waltz, Chap. & Instructor. Priests 1; Lay Teachers 23; Students 258.

Little Flower School, 800 University Ave. W., 58703. Tel: 701-839-5882; Fax: 701-839-8567. Gary Volk, Prin. Lay Teachers 11; Students 136.

St. Leo's School, 305 First St., S.E., 58701. Tel: 701-838-2597; Fax: 701-838-2597. Email: gary.volk@sendit.nodak.edu. Gary Volk, Prin. Lay Teachers 9; Students 107.

RICHARDTON. *Benedictine Sponsorship Board*, 8969 Hwy. 10 W., P.O. Box 364, 58652-0364. Tel: 701-974-2121; Fax: 701-974-2124. Email: ruthfox36@sacredheartmonastery.com. Web: www.sacredheartmonastery.com. Sr. Ruth Fox, O.S.B., Pres. & Contact Person.

PIA Tegler Benedictine Foundation, 8969 Hwy. 10 W., P.O. Box 364, 58652-0364. Tel: 701-974-2121; Fax: 701-974-2124. Email: busoffice@sacredheartmonastery.com. Web: www.sacredheartmonastery.com. Sisters Michael Emond, O.S.B., Pres.; Brigid McLean, O.S.B., Vice Pres.; Phoebe Schwartze, O.S.B., Sec. & Treas.

Sacred Heart Benedictine Foundation, 8969 Hwy. 10 W., P.O. Box 364, 58652-0364. Tel: 701-974-2121; Fax: 701-974-2124. Email: busoffice@sacredheartmonastery.com. Web: www.sacredheartmonastery.com. Sr. Ruth Fox, O.S.B., Pres.

Sacred Heart Mission, 418 3rd Ave. W., 58652-7100. Tel: 701-974-3315; Fax: 701-974-3317. Email: odo@assumptionabbey.com. Rev. Odo Muggli, O.S.B., Sec. & Treas.

SENTINEL BUTTE. *Home On The Range Foundation* (1999) 16351 I-94, 58654. Tel: 701-872-3745; Fax: 701-872-3748. Email: jjohnson@gohotr.org. Web: www.gohotr.org. Rev. David G. Morman, Pres.

RELIGIOUS INSTITUTES OF MEN REPRESENTED IN THE DIOCESE

For further details refer to the corresponding bracketed number in the Religious Institutes of Men or Women section.

[0200]—*Benedictine Monks* (Richardton, ND)—O.S.B.

[]—*Missionary Society of St. Francis Xavier* (Chennai, India)—M.S.F.X.

[1200]—*Society of the Divine Savior* (Milwaukee, WI)—S.D.S.

RELIGIOUS INSTITUTES OF WOMEN REPRESENTED IN THE DIOCESE

[0230]—*Benedictine Sisters of Pontifical Jurisdiction* (Bismarck; Richardton, ND; Duluth, MN)—O.S.B.

[2970]—*School Sisters of Notre Dame* (Mankato Prov.; St. Louis, MO)—S.S.N.D.

[0990]—*Sisters of Divine Providence* (Alison Park, PA)—C.D.P.

[]—*Sisters of Mary of the Presentation* (Valley City, ND)—S.M.P.

NECROLOGY

(No Deaths)

An asterisk (*) denotes an organization that has established tax-exempt status directly with the IRS and is not covered by the USCCB Group Ruling.

Diocese of Boise

(Dioecesis Xylopolitana)

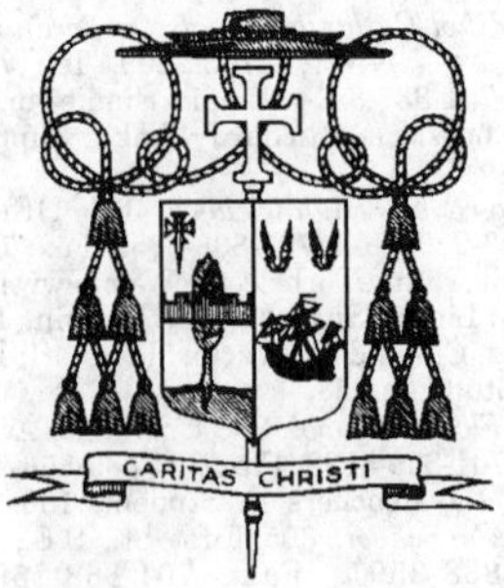

Most Reverend

MICHAEL P. DRISCOLL, M.S.W., D.D.

Bishop of Boise; ordained May 1, 1965; appointed Titular Bishop of Massita and Auxiliary Bishop of Orange December 19, 1989; consecrated March 6, 1990; appointed Bishop of Boise January 19, 1999; installed March 18, 1999. *Res.: 1501 Federal Way, Boise, ID 83705.*

Chancery Office: 1501 Federal Way, Boise, ID 83705. Tel: 208-342-1311; Fax: 208-342-0224.

Email: mwilske@rcdb.org

ESTABLISHED AS A VICARIATE-APOSTOLIC MARCH 3, 1868.

Square Miles 83,557.

Erected a Diocese by His Holiness Pope Leo XIII, August 26, 1893

Comprises the State of Idaho, with a Total Population of 1,532,200.

Legal Title: "Roman Catholic Diocese of Boise". For legal titles of parishes and diocesan institutions, consult the Chancery Office.

STATISTICAL OVERVIEW

Personnel	
Bishop	1
Priests: Diocesan Active in Diocese	49
Priests: Diocesan Active Outside Diocese	7
Priests: Retired, Sick or Absent	27
Number of Diocesan Priests	83
Religious Priests in Diocese	15
Total Priests in Diocese	98
Ordinations:	
Diocesan Priests	2
Transitional Deacons	5
Permanent Deacons in Diocese	65
Total Brothers	5
Total Sisters	86
Parishes	
Parishes	51
With Resident Pastor:	
Resident Diocesan Priests	39
Resident Religious Priests	2
Without Resident Pastor:	
Administered by Priests	7
Administered by Deacons	2
Administered by Lay People	1
Missions	29
Pastoral Centers	28
Professional Ministry Personnel:	
Sisters	3
Lay Ministers	80
Welfare	
Catholic Hospitals	5
Total Assisted	648,274
Day Care Centers	4
Total Assisted	168
Special Centers for Social Services	19
Total Assisted	380,000
Educational	
Diocesan Students in Other Seminaries	11
Total Seminarians	11
High Schools, Diocesan and Parish	1
Total Students	629
Elementary Schools, Diocesan and Parish	13
Total Students	2,227
Catechesis/Religious Education:	
High School Students	2,350
Elementary Students	5,778
Total Students under Catholic Instruction	10,995
Teachers in the Diocese:	
Sisters	1
Lay Teachers	210
Vital Statistics	
Receptions into the Church:	
Infant Baptism Totals	2,596
Minor Baptism Totals	224
Adult Baptism Totals	168
Received into Full Communion	203
First Communions	2,401
Confirmations	1,191
Marriages:	
Catholic	324
Interfaith	140
Total Marriages	464
Deaths	732
Total Catholic Population	167,620
Total Population	1,523,816

Former Bishops—Rt. Revs. LOUIS LOOTENS, D.D., ord. June 14, 1851; appt. first Vicar-Apostolic of Idaho, March 3, 1868; cons. Bishop of Castabala, Aug. 9, 1868; resigned July 16, 1876; died Jan. 13, 1898; ALPHONSE JOSEPH GLORIEUX, D.D., ord. Aug. 17, 1867; appt. second Vicar-Apostolic of Idaho, Feb. 27, 1885; cons. Titular Bishop of Apolonia, April 19, 1885; appt. first Bishop of the Diocese of Boise, Aug. 26, 1893; died Aug. 25, 1917; DANIEL MARY GORMAN, D.D., LL.D., ord. June 24, 1892; cons. May 1, 1918; died June 9, 1927; Most Revs. EDWARD JOSEPH KELLY, D.D., ord. June 2, 1917; cons. March 6, 1928; died April 21, 1956; JAMES J. BYRNE, D.D., S.T.D., ord. June 3, 1933; appt. Titular Bishop of Etenna and Auxiliary of St. Paul, July 2, 1947; cons. July 2, 1947; transferred to Boise June 16, 1956; appt. Archbishop of Dubuque, March 19, 1962; retired Aug. 23, 1983; died Aug. 2, 1996; SYLVESTER WILLIAM TREINEN, D.D., ord. June 11, 1946; appt. May 19, 1962; cons. July 25, 1962; retired Aug. 17, 1988; died Sept. 30, 1996; TOD D. BROWN, D.D., ord. May 1, 1963; appt. Dec. 27, 1988; ord. and installed April 3, 1989; appt. Bishop of Orange, June 30, 1998.

Executive Secretary to Bishop/Administration—BARBARA BIRD.

Vicars General—Rev. Msgrs. JOSEPH DA SILVA, V.G.; DENNIS WASSMUTH, V.G.

Administrative Assistant to Vicar General—CYNTHIA TALBOY.

Chancery Office—1501 Federal Way, Boise, 83705. Tel: 208-342-1311; Fax: 208-342-0224.

Chancellor—Ms. MARCELLA M. WILSKE, M.A.

Assistant to the Chancellor—CAROLINE CARTHY-WICKHAM.

Office of Cultural Ministries—Ms. CHRISTINE KING, Dir., 1501 Federal Way, Boise, 83705. Tel: 208-342-1311.

Coordinator of Multicultural Ministries—SANTIAGO ROBLES.

Notaries—DOVE MIZELL; Ms. MARCELLA M. WILSKE, M.A.; CYNTHIA TALBOY.

Diocesan Tribunal—1501 Federal Way, Boise, 83705. Tel: 208-344-1344; Fax: 208-342-0224. (Direct all correspondence here.)

Director—MARK L. RAPER, J.C.L., M.C.L.

Staff Canonist—VACANT.

Judicial Vicar—Very Rev. HENRY CARMONA, J.C.L., J.V.

Adjutant Judicial Vicars—Rev. WILLIAM CROWLEY; Very Rev. GERALD FUNKE, J.C.L., V.F.

Promoters of Justice—Rev. JOSEPH F. MCDONALD III, J.C.L.; MARK L. RAPER, J.C.L., M.C.L.

Notaries—Rev. Msgr. DENNIS WASSMUTH, V.G.; MARK L. RAPER, J.C.L., M.C.L.; COLLEEN CUNNINGHAM; Deacon MIKE SERVATIUS; CAROLINE CARTHY-WICKHAM.

Judges—Very Rev. HENRY CARMONA, J.C.L., J.V.; Revs. WILLIAM CROWLEY; SEAN CAULFIELD (Retired); W. THOMAS FAUCHER, J.C.L., V.U.; Very Rev. GERALD FUNKE, J.C.L., V.F.; Rev. Msgr. GEORGE L. KING (Retired); Rev. JAIRO RESTREPO, J.C.L.; MARK L. RAPER, J.C.L., M.C.L.; Rev. JOHN MORGAN.

Defenders of the Bond—Rev. Msgr. ANDREW SCHUMACHER (Retired); Rev. JAIRO RESTREPO, J.C.L.; MARK L. RAPER, J.C.L., M.C.L.

College of Consultors—Very Revs. BRADLEY NEELY, V.F., Chm.; DENNIS C. DAY, V.F.; GERALD FUNKE, J.C.L., V.F.; Rev. TIMOTHY M. RITCHEY; Very Revs. HENRY CARMONA, J.C.L., J.V.; BENJAMIN UHLENKOTT, V.F.; MICHAEL ST. MARIE, V.F.; Rev. ROB COOK; Rev. Msgr. ANDREW SCHUMACHER (Retired); Very Rev. ENRIQUE TERRIQUEZ, V.F.

Ex Officio—Rev. Msgrs. DENNIS WASSMUTH, V.G.; JOSEPH DA SILVA, V.G.

Deans—Very Revs. DENNIS C. DAY, V.F., Northern Deanery; ENRIQUE TERRIQUEZ, V.F., Eastern Deanery; GERALD FUNKE, J.C.L., V.F., Western Deanery; BENJAMIN UHLENKOTT, V.F., West Central Deanery; MICHAEL ST. MARIE, V.F., Southern Deanery; BRADLEY NEELY, V.F., North Central Deanery.

Presbyteral Council— See College of Consultors.

Priest Personnel Commission—Rev. TIMOTHY M. RITCHEY; Very Revs. BRADLEY NEELY, V.F.; BENJAMIN UHLENKOTT, V.F.; Revs. FRANCISCO FLORES; RAUL R. COVARRUBIAS, V.U.; CALEB VOGEL; PAUL WANDER; JUSTIN BRADY; Rev. Msgrs. DENNIS WASSMUTH, V.G., Ex Officio; JOSEPH DA SILVA, V.G., Ex Officio.

Finance Council—Rev. Msgrs. DENNIS WASSMUTH, V.G., Chm.; JOSEPH DA SILVA, V.G., Ex Officio; JAMES BRUCE; LARRY HELLHAKE; STANLEY WELSH; CHARLES HUMMEL; SUSAN COPPLE; GLENN SCHUMACHER; Ms. MARCELLA M. WILSKE, M.A.; PATRICK CRISLER, CPA, Finance Office Consultant; Most Rev. MICHAEL P. DRISCOLL, D.D., M.S.W., Ex Officio.

Building Commission—Rev. Msgr. DENNIS WASSMUTH, V.G., Chm.; Deacon JACK PELOWITZ; DAVID DAVIES; TIMOTHY HAENER; MICHAEL JONES; JAMES MESPLAY; PETER ROCKWELL; PATRICIA NORBERG; PATRICK CRISLER, CPA; TOM MANNSCHRECK.

Priest Retirement Committee—Rev. Msgr. DENNIS WASSMUTH, V.G., Chm.; Revs. JOSEPH MUHA (Retired); TIMOTHY M. RITCHEY; JOHN WORSTER; RAUL R. COVARRUBIAS, V.U.; FRANCISCO FLORES, 1501 Federal Way, Boise, 83705. Tel: 208-342-1311.

Ex Officio—Rev. Msgr. JOSEPH DA SILVA, V.G.

Diocesan Offices and Directors

Apostleship of Prayer—VACANT.

Bureau of Information— "Idaho Catholic Register" *1501 Federal Way, Boise, 83705.*

Catholic Campaign for Human Development—Ms. MARCELLA M. WILSKE, M.A., 1501 Federal Way, Boise, 83705-5925.

Catholic Charities of Idaho, Inc.—ROSIO GONZALEZ, Exec. Dir.; Most Rev. MICHAEL P. DRISCOLL, D.D., M.S.W., Pres.; LYNNE TIDDENS, Admin. Mgr., 1501 Federal Way, Boise, 83705. Tel: 208-345-6031; Fax: 208-345-5674.

Catholic Communications Center—MICHAEL BROWN, 1501 Federal Way, Boise, 53705.

Catholic Relief Services—Ms. MARCELLA M. WILSKE, M.A., 1501 Federal Way, Boise, 83705.

Catholic Scouts—DAVID L. DAVIS, Chm., 142 N. 9th St., Pocatello, 83201. Tel: 208-232-2098; Rev. ROGER LACHANCE, V.F., Chap., St. Pius X, 625 E. Haycraft, Coeur d'Alene, 83815. Tel: 208-765-5108.

Catholic Daughters of the Americas—VALERIE "SUNNY" STORCH, State Regent, 1569 Rovian St., Boise, 83701. Tel: 208-424-7971.

Catholic Schools—DAN MAKLEY, Supt., 1501 Federal Way, Boise, 83705.

Catholic Hospitals—VACANT, 1501 Federal Way, Boise, 83705. Tel: 208-342-1311.

Catholic Liturgical Commission—LETITIA THORNTON. Email: tthornton@rcdb.org; Deacons RICK BONNEY, Chm.; GERALD PERA; ELWOOD KLEAVER; LARRY HARRISON; Rev. Msgr. DENNIS WASSMUTH, V.G.

Censor Librorum—Rev. Msgr. ANDREW SCHUMACHER (Retired), 3213 Fifth St., Unit I, Lewiston, 83501. Tel: 208-746-3362.

Charismatic Renewal—VACANT.

Children, Youth and Adult Protection Coordinator—Dr. ROBERT FONTAINE. Tel: 208-342-1311.

Priest Retirement Plan— Direct Inquiries to the Chancery, *1501 Federal Way, Boise, 83705*.

Cursillo Movement—Deacon BILL BOOTH, Spiritual Dir. - English, 13249 W. Blue Bonnet Ct., Boise, 83713. Tel: 208-939-7568; Rev. MAURICIO MEDINA, Spiritual Dir. - Spanish (Retired), 931 Eastland Dr. N., Twin Falls, 83301. Tel: 208-734-2432.

Development/Stewardship Office—JIM HUGHES, Dir., 1501 Federal Way, Boise, 83705. Tel: 208-342-1311; Fax: 208-342-0224; Cell: 208-861-2202.

Diocesan Pastoral Council—BETTY WUNDERLE, Pres.

Ecumenical Commission—Rev. Msgr. JOSEPH DA SILVA, V.G., 11511 Lake Hazel Rd., Boise, 83709.

Parish Life and Faith Formation—Mr. MICHAEL BENTON, Dir.; PATRICIA THOMAS, Events Coord.; VERONICA CHILDERS, Admin. Asst./Resource Ctr., 1501 Federal Way, Boise, 83705. Tel: 208-342-1311.

Parish Life & Faith Formation West, West Central Deanery's—MICHAEL BEATON.

Parish Life & Faith Formation North, North Central Deanery's—Sr. MEG SASS, O.S.B.

Parish Life & Faith Formation Southern & Eastern Deanery's—JAIME GIL.

Finance Officer—PATRICK CRISLER, CPA.

Human Resources—Dr. ROBERT FONTAINE.

Idaho Council of Catholic Women—LOUANNA CHAVEZ MAHERAS, Pres.

Idaho Catholic Foundation—Most Rev. MICHAEL P. DRISCOLL, D.D., M.S.W., Pres.

Knights of Columbus—BRIAN SIMER, State Deputy; Rev. JUSTIN BRADY, State Chap.

Campus Ministry—Deacon CHARLES L. SKORRO, Dir., 1915 University Dr., Boise, 83706.

Newspaper— "Idaho Catholic Register" Most Rev. MICHAEL P. DRISCOLL, D.D., M.S.W., Publisher; MICHAEL BROWN, Exec. Editor; ANN BIXBY, Advertising/Business/Circulation; LORETTA GOSSI, Sec., Library, 1501 Federal Way, Boise, 83705. Tel: 208-342-1311.

Deacon Life and Ministry—Deacons GARY MCSWAIN, Dir., 625 E. Haycraft, Coeur d'Alene, 83815. Tel: 208-667-9233; JAMES KELLY, 1323 Johnson St., Boise, 83705. Tel: 208-343-9619.

Deacon Formation Director—Deacon RICHARD KULLECK, 1501 Federal Way, Boise, 83705. Tel: 208-342-1311.

Prison Ministry—Rev. JESUS CAMACHO, 322 S. Manville St., Boise, 83705. Tel: 208-429-9196.

Propagation of the Faith—Ms. MARCELLA M. WILSKE, M.A., 1501 Federal Way, Boise, 83705.

Diocesan Respect Life Coordinator—Deacon PIERCE MURPHY.

St. Vincent de Paul Society—Very Rev. GERALD FUNKE, J.C.L., V.F., Diocesan Spiritual Dir., 1515 8th St., S., Nampa, 83651. Tel: 208-466-7031.

State Trustee—IDA FISK, 314 Jackson, Boise, 83705. Tel: 208-344-6947.

Vocations—Rev. ROB COOK, Dir., 804 N. 9th St., Boise, 83702. Tel: 208-342-1328.

CLERGY, PARISHES, MISSIONS AND PAROCHIAL SCHOOLS

CITY OF BOISE

(ADA COUNTY)

1—CATHEDRAL OF ST. JOHN THE EVANGELIST (1906) Very Rev. Henry Carmona, Rector; Rev. Mariusz Majewski, Parochial Vicar; Deacons Ken Hiner; Tom Dominick; Jack Pelowitz; Sr. Maria Elena, O.S.B., Pastoral Assoc.; Ms. Bobbi Dominick, Pastoral Assoc.
Res.: 775 N. 8th St., 83702. Tel: 208-342-3511; 208-342-3512; Fax: 208-342-1564.
School—St. Joseph's School, (Grades K-8), 825 W. Fort St., 83702. Tel: 208-342-4909; Fax: 208-342-0997. Ms. Antonia Bicandi, Prin. Lay Teachers 19; Students 351.
Catechesis/Religious Program—Jackie Hopper, D.R.E. Students 331.

2—ST. MARK'S (1970) Revs. Steven Rukavina; Bruno Mgaya; Deacons Ralph Pierce; James Bowen; Joseph Rodriguez; Mike Lowe; Diana Tetreault, Pastoral Assoc.; Phyllis Sawyer, Pastoral Assoc.
Res.: 3021 Ash Park, 83704.
7960 Northview, 83704.
School—(Grades K-8), 7503 Northview, 83704. Tel: 208-375-6654; Fax: 208-375-9471. Dan Maloney, Prin. Lay Teachers 16; Students 327.
Catechesis/Religious Program—Students 294.

3—ST. MARY'S Revs. W. Thomas Faucher; Jesus Camacho; Arnie Miller; Deacons William Petzak; Francis Hess; Jorge Gonzalez.
Res.: 2612 W. State St., 83702. Tel: 208-344-2597; Fax: 208-344-9337. Email: mbaca@gmail.com. Web: www.stmarysboise.org.
School—(Grades K-8), 2620 W. State St., 83702. Tel: 208-342-7476; Fax: 208-345-5154. Marianne White, Prin.; Tammy Morrison, Librarian. Lay Teachers 12; Students 158.
Catechesis/Religious Program—Students 150.

4—OUR LADY OF THE ROSARY (1947) Rev. Msgr. Dennis Wassmuth; Deacons Michael Dessert; Pierce Murphy; Chuck Skoro; Mike Servatius.
Res.: 1500 E. Wright, 83706. Tel: 208-343-9041; Fax: 208-343-2644.
Catechesis/Religious Program—Rosie Skoro, D.R.E. Students 284.
Chapel—Idaho City, St. Joseph's
Chapel—Boise, St. Paul's Student Center

5—ST. PAUL'S, Closed. See Our Lady of the Rosary, Boise for details.

6—RISEN CHRIST CATHOLIC COMMUNITY (1992) [CEM] Rev. Msgr. Joseph da Silva; Very Rev. Benjamin Uhlenkott; Deacons Richard Kulleck; C. J. Harris.
Res.: 11511 W. Lake Hazel Rd., 83709. Tel: 208-362-6584; Fax: 208-362-9545.
Catechesis/Religious Program—Mark Henry, D.R.E. Students 207.

7—SACRED HEART Deacon Michael Eisenbeiss, Parish Life Dir.; Rev. Msgr. Dennis Wassmuth, Priest Moderator; Rev. Evarist Shiyo, Parochial Vicar; Deacon James R. Kelly.
Mailing Address: 811 S. Latah St., 83705-0127. Tel: 208-344-8311; Fax: 208-343-1876.
School—(Grades PreK-8), 3901 Cassia St., 83705. Tel: 208-344-9738; Fax: 208-343-1939. Brock Carpenter, Prin.; Jane Collins, Librarian. Sisters 1; Lay Teachers 12; Students 150.
Catechesis/Religious Program—Deborah Fischer, D.R.E. Students 215.

OUTSIDE THE CITY OF BOISE

ABERDEEN, BINGHAM CO., BLESSED SACRAMENT, Merged with St. Mary, American Falls to form Presentation of the Lord, Aberdeen.

AMERICAN FALLS, POWER CO.

1—ST. MARY, Merged with Blessed Sacrament, Aberdeen to form Presentation of the Lord, Aberdeen.

2—PRESENTATION OF THE LORD Rev. Carlos Camargo, Admin.
Res.: 635 S. 4th W., Aberdeen, 83210. Tel: 208-220-0868; Fax: 208-226-1125.
Catechesis/Religious Program—Zulma Ceana, D.R.E. Students 156.
Chapel—Pingree, St. John
Chapel—St. Mary 376 Roosevelt, 83211. Tel: 208-226-5217.
Chapel—Aberdeen, Blessed Sacrament 667 S. 4th W., Aberdeen, 83210.

ARCO, BUTTE CO., ST. ANN'S, See separate listing. See St. Charles, Salmon for details.

BLACKFOOT, BINGHAM CO., ST. BERNARD'S Revs. John Worster; Reginald Nwauzor, Parochial Vicar.
Res.: 584 W. Sexton St., 83221. Tel: 208-785-1935; Fax: 208-785-7382.
Catechesis/Religious Program—Students 153.
Chapel—Blessed Kateri Tekakwitha Sheepskin Rd., Fort Hall, 83203.

BONNERS FERRY, BOUNDARY CO., ST. ANN'S (1800) Rev. Carlos Perez, Admin.; Deacon Joseph Nicholas.
Res.: 6712 El Paso, 83805. Tel: 208-267-2852; Fax: 208-267-8222. Email: st-anns@peoplepc.com.
Catechesis/Religious Program—Students 55.

BUHL, TWIN FALLS CO., IMMACULATE CONCEPTION Very Rev. Michael St. Marie, Admin.; Rev. Camilo Garcia, Parochial Vicar.
Res.: 1701 Poplar, Box 626, 83316. Tel: 208-543-5136; Fax: 208-543-5714.
Catechesis/Religious Program—Jacqueline Machado, D.R.E. Students 132.
Station—Hagerman, St. Catherine's Hagerman.

BURLEY, CASSIA CO., ST. THERESA Revs. Justin Brady; Marcos Sanchez, Parochial Vicar.
Res.: 1550 Oakley, 83318. Tel: 208-678-5453; Fax: 208-678-5479.
Catechesis/Religious Program—Eugene Kramer, D.R.E.; Melissa Santana, D.R.E. Students 92.

CALDWELL, CANYON CO.

1—ST. MARY'S, Merged to form Our Lady of the Valley, Caldwell.

2—OUR LADY OF THE VALLEY Revs. Francisco Flores; Eladio Vieyra, Parochial Vicar; Deacon Humberto Almeida.
Office: 1122 W. Linden St., 83605. Tel: 208-459-3653; Fax: 208-454-8789.
Catechesis/Religious Program—Students 670.
Chapel—Marsing, Good Shepherd
Chapel—Homedale, St. Hubert's

CHUBBUCK, BANNOCK CO., ST. PAUL'S, Merged with St. Anthony's, Pocatello and St. Joseph, Pocatello to form Holy Spirit Catholic Community, Pocatello.

COEUR D'ALENE, KOOTENAI CO.

1—ST. PIUS X Rev. Roger LaChance; Deacons Gary McSwain; Leonard Trueworthy.
Res.: 625 E. Haycraft, 83815. Tel: 208-765-5108; Fax: 208-664-5325.
Catechesis/Religious Program—Deacon Gary McSwain, D.R.E. Students 200.

2—ST. THOMAS (1890) Rev. William Crowley; Deacon Gary Jacobs.
Res.: 919 E. Indiana Ave., 83814. Tel: 208-664-9259; Fax: 208-667-8321.
Catechesis/Religious Program—John Kastelic, D.R.E. Students 53.

COTTONWOOD, IDAHO CO., ST. MARY'S (1890) [CEM] Rev. Richard S. Haldane.
Mailing Address: 503 Garrett St., P.O. Box 425, 83522-0425. Tel: 208-962-3214; Fax: 208-962-5477.
Church: 508 Church St., 83522-0425.
Catechesis/Religious Program—Students 71.
Chapel—Keuterville, Holy Cross

COUNCIL, ADAMS CO., ST. JUDE STATION, See separate listing. See St. Agnes, Weiser for details.

DESMET, BENEWAH CO., SACRED HEART (1842) Rev. Thomas Connolly, S.J.; Sr. Dolores Ellwart, S.P., Pastoral Assoc.; Deacon Nick Vietri.
Res.: Box 306, 83824. Tel: 208-274-5871; Fax: 208-274-3015.
Catechesis/Religious Program—Students 74.
Station—Plummer, Our Lady of Perpetual Help Plummer.
Station—Worley, St. Michael's Worley.

EAGLE, ADA CO., ST. MATTHEW, Merged with Holy Spirit, Meridian to form Holy Apostles, Meridian.

EMMETT, GEM CO., SACRED HEART Rev. Oscar Jaramillo; Deacon Alan Shaber.
Res.: 211 E. First Street, 83617. Tel: 208-365-4320; Fax: 208-365-0754.
Catechesis/Religious Program—Students 116.
Station—Garden Valley, St. Jude Garden Valley.

FERDINAND, IDAHO CO., ASSUMPTION (1900) Rev. Richard S. Haldane.
Mailing Address: P.O. Box 425, Cottonwood, 83522-0425.
Catechesis/Religious Program—Students 31.

FRUITLAND, PAYETTE CO., CORPUS CHRISTI CATHOLIC CHURCH (1999) Rev. Calvin Blankinship; Deacons Harley Salazar; Juan Tamayo.
Mailing Address: 900 N.W. 7th St., 83619.
Res.: 1104 Partridge St., 83619. Tel: 208-452-5778; Fax: 208-452-6778.
Catechesis/Religious Program—Students 178.

GARDEN VALLEY, BOISE CO., ST. JUDE'S, See separate listing. See Sacred Heart, Emmett for details.

GENESEE, LATAH CO., ST. MARY STATION, See St. Mary's, Moscow for details. In Res., Rev. Robert Finucane (Retired).
Res.: 138 N. Jackson, P.O. Box 36, 83832. Tel: 208-285-1218; Fax: 208-285-1139.
Catechesis/Religious Program—Connie Myers, D.R.E. Students 28.

GLENNS FERRY, ELMORE CO., OUR LADY OF LIMERICK STATION (1892), See Our Lady of Good Counsel, Mountain Home for details. In Res., Rev. Eugene Esch, O.S.B.
Res.: 21 W. Arthur St., Box 216, 83623. Tel: 208-366-7721.
Catechesis/Religious Program—Students 70.

GOODING, GOODING CO., ST. ELIZABETH'S Very Rev. Michael St. Marie, Priest Mod.; Rev. John Koelsch, Sacramental Min. (Retired); Deacons Javier Leiga; John McKinley, Parish Life Dir.
Res.: 1515 California St., Box 147, 83330-0147. Tel: 208-934-5634; Fax: 208-934-4910. Email: stelizabethgooding@yahoo.com.
Catechesis/Religious Program—Bridget Arkoosh, D.R.E.; Maria Garcia, D.R.E. (Gooding). Students 82.
Station—Wendell, St. Anthony's P.O. Box 811, Wendell, 83355.

GRANDVIEW, OWYHEE CO., ST. HENRY CHAPEL, See Our Lady of Good Counsel, Mountain Home for details.

GRANGEVILLE, IDAHO CO., SS. PETER AND PAUL (1892) Very Rev. Bradley Neely; Deacon Don Sokolowski.
Office: 625 Lake St., 83530.
Res.: 622 S. W. 1st St., 83530. Tel: 208-983-0403; Fax: 208-983-0115.
School—330 S. B St., 83530. Tel: 208-983-2182. Teresa Groom, Prin. Lay Teachers 6; Students 82.
Catechesis/Religious Program—Students 30.
Station—Nez Perce, Holy Trinity P.O Box 65, Nez Perce, 83543. Tel: 208-937-2300.
Chapel—White Bird, Sacred Heart, See Sts. Peter & Paul, Grangeville for details.

GREENCREEK, IDAHO CO., ST. ANTHONY'S (1900) [CEM] Rev. Richard S. Haldane.
Res.: P.O. Box 425, Cottonwood, 83522.
Catechesis/Religious Program—Patricia Schmidt, D.R.E. Students 29.

HAGERMAN, GOODING CO., ST. CATHERINE'S, See separate listing. See Immaculate Conception, Buhl for details.

HAILEY, BLAINE CO., ST. CHARLES BORROMEO (1881) Rev. Jorge E. Garcia.
Res.: 313 1st. Ave. S., Box 789, 83333. Tel: 208-788-3024; Fax: 208-788-0726. Email: stcharles@qwestoffice.net.
Catechesis/Religious Program—Students 197.
Chapel—Fairfield, Immaculate Conception

HOMEDALE, OWYHEE CO., ST. HUBERT, Merged with St. Mary's, Caldwell and Sacred Hearts of Jesus and Mary, Parma to form Our Lady of the Valley, Caldwell.

HORSESHOE BEND, BOISE CO., OUR LADY QUEEN OF ANGELS CHAPEL, See separate listing. See Holy Apostle, Meridian for details.

IDAHO CITY, BOISE CO., ST. JOSEPH'S CHAPEL, See separate listing. See Our Lady of the Rosary, Boise for details.

IDAHO FALLS, BONNEVILLE CO.

1—CHRIST THE KING Revs. Raul R. Covarrubias; Jairo Restrepo, Parochial Vicar; Joseph F. McDonald III, Moderator; Deacons Richard Bonney, Pastoral Assoc.; Alvaro Ponce; Wence Rodriquez; Eric Shaber; Chris Reilly.
Res.: 145 E. 9th St., 83404. Tel: 208-523-3827; Fax: 208-523-3827.
Catechesis/Religious Program—(Combined with Holy Rosary, Idaho Falls) Mary Haley, D.R.E.; Marie Tracy, D.R.E.; Mary Lou Hart, D.R.E.; Raquel Delgadillo, D.R.E. (Hisp. Youth). Students 783.
Chapel—Shelley, Our Lady of Guadalupe

2—HOLY ROSARY Revs. Raul R. Covarrubias; Joseph F. McDonald III, Moderator; Jairo Restrepo; Deacons Richard Bonney, Pastoral Assoc.; Wence Rodriquez; Alvaro Ponce; Eric Shaber; Chris Reilly.
Res.: 145 E. Ninth St., 83404-6392. Tel: 208-522-4366; Fax: 208-523-3827.
School—(Grades K-8), 161 Ninth St., 83404. Tel: 208-522-7781; Fax: 208-522-7782. Marilyn Reilly, Prin. Lay Teachers 12; Students 165.
Catechesis/Religious Program—Combined with Christ the King, Idaho Falls. Mary Haley, D.R.E.; Marie Tracy, D.R.E.; Raquel Delgadillo, Hispanic Youth Min.; Marilou Hart, D.R.E. Students 805.
Station—Roberts, St. Anthony's Roberts.
Station—Mud Lake, St. Ann's Mud Lake.

JEROME, JEROME CO., ST. JEROME'S Rev. Ronald Wekerle; Deacons William Last, (Retired); John Baumbach; Marino Perea, Pastoral Assoc.
Res.: 216 2nd Ave. E., Box 169, 83338. Tel: 208-324-8794; Fax: 208-324-4141.
Catechesis/Religious Program—Generations of Faith Students 262.

KAMIAH, LEWIS CO., ST. CATHERINE'S OF SIENA (1964) Rev. Msgr. George L. King (Retired).
Res.: 407 7th St., Box 685, 83536-0685. Tel: 208-935-2130; 208-935-2984; Fax: 208-476-5632.
Catechesis/Religious Program—Students 33.

KELLOGG, SHOSHONE CO., ST. RITA'S Rev. Thomas Loucks.
Res.: 27 Kellogg Ave., 83837-2626. Tel: 208-784-7361; Fax: 208-784-7361.
Catechesis/Religious Program—Students 7.

KEUTERVILLE, IDAHO CO., HOLY CROSS, Merged with St. Mary's, Cottonwood.

LEWISTON, NEZ PERCE CO.

1—ST. JAMES (1970) Revs. Leslie P. Kish; Dat Vu, Parochial Vicar.
Office: 1519 Ripon Ave., 83501. Tel: 208-743-8231; Fax: 208-798-8407. Email: stjameschurch@cableone.net. Web: www.allsaintslewiston.org.
Catechesis/Religious Program—Students 113.
Station—Lapwai, Sacred Heart 203 Birch Ave., Lapwai, 83840. Tel: 208-843-2562; Fax: 208-843-2562.

2—OUR LADY OF LOURDES Revs. Leslie P. Kish; Dat Vu, Parochial Vicar; Deacon Fred Schmidt.
Church & Res.: 2015 13th Ave., 83501. Tel: 208-743-6101 (Church); Fax: 208-743-5301. Email: ourladyoflourdes@cableone.net. Web: www.lewistoncatholics.org.
Catechesis/Religious Program—Students 115.

3—ST. STANISLAUS Revs. Leslie P. Kish; Dat Vu, Parochial Vicar; Ralph Smith Jr., Pastoral Assoc.
Res.: 633 5th Ave., 83501. Tel: 208-743-7331; Fax: 208-746-7134.
School—Tri-Parish School, (Grades PreSchool-6) Denise Hammrich, Prin. Lay Teachers 18; Students 128.
Catechesis/Religious Program—Heidi Munoz, D.R.E. Students 115.

MCCALL, VALLEY CO., OUR LADY OF THE LAKE (1916) Rev. Donald D. Fraser.
Res.: 501 Cross Rd., Box 821, 83638. Tel: 208-634-5474; Fax: 208-634-5475.
Catechesis/Religious Program—Students 11.
Station—St. Katharine Drexel, Cascade
Chapel—Riggins, St. Jerome's

MERIDIAN, ADA CO.

1—HOLY APOSTLES (1998) [CEM] Revs. Len MacMillan; Paul Materu, A.L.C.P., Parochial Vicar; Deacons Ralph Flager; Gerald Pera; Charles Rasmussen; Malherbe Desert; Carolyn Bailey, Pastoral Assoc.
Res.: Box 708, 83680. Tel: 208-888-1182; Fax: 208-884-1800. Web: www.holyapostlesmeridian.net.
Holy Apostles Columbarium— (2008), [CEM]
Catechesis/Religious Program—Mary Ossenkop, D.R.E.; Brandie Navarro, Youth Min.; Rusty Bang, Youth Min. Students 834.
Chapel—Horseshoe Bend, Our Lady Queen of Angels

2—HOLY SPIRIT, Merged Sacramental records are at Holy Apostles, Meridian.

MOSCOW, LATAH CO.

1—ST. AUGUSTINE'S, (Catholic Center) Rev. Caleb Vogel; Katie Goodson, Campus Min.
Res.: 628 Deakin Ave., P.O. Box 3457, 83843. Tel: 208-882-4613.
Station—Potlatch, St. Mary's P.O. Box 143, Potlatch, 83855.

2—ST. MARY'S (1882) Rev. Joseph F. Schmidt; Deacons George Canney; Verne Geidl.
Res.: 618 E. First St., Box 9106, 83843. Tel: 208-882-4813; Fax: 208-883-0608.
School—(Grades PreSchool-6), 412 N. Monroe, 83843. Tel: 208-882-2121. Sr. Margaret Johnson, O.S.U., Prin. Lay Teachers 8; Students 97.
Kindergarten & Preschool—St. Rose, 412 N. Howard, 83843. Tel: 208-882-4014; Fax: 208-882-0970. Owned by the Ursuline Nuns, affiliated with St. Mary's School.
Catechesis/Religious Program—Students 110.
Station—Genessee, St. Mary's Genessee.

MOUNTAIN HOME AIR FORCE BASE, ELMORE CO., ST. MARY'S Rev. Hoang Nguyen.
Res.: 366 FW/HC, 420 Gunfighter Ave., 83648. Tel: 208-828-6417; Fax: 208-828-4570.
Catechesis/Religious Program—Students 150.

MOUNTAIN HOME, ELMORE CO., OUR LADY OF GOOD COUNSEL Very Rev. Henry Carmona, Admin.; Rev. Julio Vicente, Parochial Vicar.
Res.: 115 N. 4th St. E., Box 310, 83647. Tel: 208-587-3046; Fax: 208-587-5114.
Catechesis/Religious Program—Tina Barrie, C.R.E.; Karen Bermensolo, Youth Min. Students 179.
Station—Bruneau, St. Bridget Bruneau.
Station—Glenns Ferry, Our Lady of Limerick Glenn's Ferry.
Chapel—Grand View, St. Henry's

NAMPA, CANYON CO.

1—OUR LADY OF GUADALUPE CHAPEL, Closed. See St. Paul's, Nampa for details.

2—ST. PAUL'S, [CEM] Very Rev. Gerald Funke; Rev. Saul Reyes, Parochial Vicar; Deacons Michael Collins; Jose Luis Grandos; Sisters Maria Velia Huchin, H.M.R.F., Pastoral Assoc. & Hispanic Ministry; Pilar Casillas, H.M.R.F., Pastoral Assoc. & Hispanic Ministry.
Res.: 1515 8th St. S., 83651. Tel: 208-466-7031; Fax: 208-467-7203.
School—(Grades PreSchool-8) Tel: 208-467-3601; Fax: 208-467-6485. Bill Graham, Prin. Lay Teachers 14; Students 194.
Catechesis/Religious Program—Students 566.
Station—Melba, St. Joseph
Chapel—Silver City, Our Lady of Tears
Chapel—Oreana, Queen of Heaven

NEW PLYMOUTH, PAYETTE CO., ST. ALOYSIUS, Merged to form Corpus Christi Catholic Community, Fruitland.

NEZPERCE, LEWIS CO., HOLY TRINITY, See SS. Peter and Paul, Grangeville for details.
Res.: 506 Willow St., Box 65, Nez Perce, 83543. Tel: 208-937-2300.
Catechesis/Religious Program—Students 34.

OREANA, OWYHEE CO., QUEEN OF HEAVEN CHAPEL, See separate listing. See St. Paul's, Nampa for details.

OROFINO, CLEARWATER CO., ST. THERESA'S (1926) Rev. Msgr. George L. King (Retired).
Res.: 446 Brown Ave., Box 1169, 83544. Tel: 208-476-5121.
Catechesis/Religious Program—Students 20.
Chapel—Pierce, Our Lady of Woodland

PARMA, CANYON CO., SACRED HEARTS OF JESUS AND MARY, Merged with St. Mary's, Caldwell and St. Hubert's, Homedale to form Our Lady of the Valley, Caldwell.

PAYETTE, PAYETTE CO., HOLY FAMILY, Merged with St. Aloysius, New Plymouth to form Corpus Christi, Fruitland.

POCATELLO, BANNOCK CO.

1—ST. ANTHONY'S, Merged with St. Joseph, Pocatello and St. Paul, Chubbuck to form Holy Spirit Catholic Community, Pocatello.

2—HOLY SPIRIT CATHOLIC COMMUNITY (2003) Very Rev. Enrique Terriquez; Rev. Adrian Vasquez, Parochial Vicar; Kathy Barkdull, Pastoral Assoc. In Res., Rev. Anthony DeLoreto (Retired).
Res.: 524 N. 7th Ave., 83201. Tel: 208-232-1196; Fax: 208-234-1624. Web: www.holyspirit.org.
School—(Grades PreK-6), 540 N. 7th Ave., 83205. Tel: 208-232-5763; Fax: 208-232-7142. Nancy Corgiat, Prin. Lay Teachers 16; Students 168.
Catechesis/Religious Program—Students 145.
St. John's Catholic Student Center—920 E. Lovejoy St., I.S.U., Box 8129, 83209-0001. Tel: 208-233-0880; Fax: 208-233-5745.
Chapel—Pocatello, St. Anthony of Padua Chapel 504 N. 7th Ave., 83201.
Chapel—Pocatello, St. Joseph Chapel 439 N. Hayes St., 83204.
Chapel—Chubbuck, St. Paul Chapel 820 W. Chubbuck Rd., 83202.

3—ST. JOSEPH'S, Merged with St. Anthony, Pocatello and St. Paul, Chubbuck to form Holy Spirit Catholic Community, Pocatello.

POST FALLS, KOOTENAI CO., ST. GEORGE'S (1917) Revs. William R. Gould; Colman J. Nolan, S.T.
Res.: Box 10, 83854-0010. Tel: 208-773-4715; Fax: 208-777-1549.
Catechesis/Religious Program—Rosemary McDougall, D.R.E. Students 126.
Chapel—St. Joan of Arc, Coeur D'Alene Rev. Chad Ripperger, F.S.S.P.
Chapel—Rathdrum, St. Stanislaus
Chapel—Spirit Lake, St. Joseph

POTLATCH, LATAH CO., ST. MARY'S STATION, See separate listing. See St. Augustine's, Moscow for details.

PRIEST RIVER, BONNER CO., ST. CATHERINE'S Rev. Lawrence L. Gooley, S.J., Admin.
Res.: P.O. Box 445, 83856. Tel: 208-290-4635.
Catechesis/Religious Program—Students 18.
Station—St. Blanche Priest Lake.

RATHDRUM, KOOTENAI CO., ST. STANISLAUS CHAPEL, See separate listing. See St. George, Post Falls for details.

RUPERT, MINIDOKA CO., ST. NICHOLAS Revs. Justin Brady; Marcos Sanchez, Parochial Vicar; Deacons Paul Henscheid; Orville Rathe.
Res.: 802 F St., Box 115, 83350-0115. Tel: 208-436-3781; Fax: 208-436-0628.
School—(Grades K-6), P.O. Box 26, 83350. Tel: 208-436-6320. Diane Brumley, Prin. Lay Teachers 9; Students 101.
Catechesis/Religious Program—Students 148.

ST. ANTHONY, FREMONT CO., MARY IMMACULATE Rev. Jose de Jesus Gonzales, Parochial Vicar.
Res.: 328 W. First N., P.O. Box 527, 83445. Tel: 208-624-7459; Fax: 208-624-7479.
Catechesis/Religious Program—Paula Hanlon, D.R.E.; Maria Castillo, D.R.E.; Marla Franco, D.R.E. Students 95.
Station—Rexburg, St. Patrick's Rexburg.
Station—Driggs, Good Shepherd Driggs.
Chapel—Island Park, Chapel of the Pines Island Park.

SAINT MARIES, BENEWAH CO., ST. MARY IMMACULATE (1912) Rev. Timothy M. Ritchey; Deacon Floyd Turner.
Res.: 921 W. Jefferson Ave., P.O. Box 335, St. Maries, 83861. Tel: 208-245-2977; Fax: 208-245-3143. Web: stmstm.com.
Catechesis/Religious Program—Students 35.

Station—Harrison, Our Lady of Perpetual Help Pine St., Harrison, 83833.

SALMON, LEMHI CO., ST. CHARLES (1908) Revs. Paul Wander; Gordon A. Taylor (Retired).
Res.: 508 Hope Ave., P.O. Box 550, 83467. Tel: 208-756-2432; Fax: 208-756-1190.
Catechesis/Religious Program—Kate Curet, D.R.E.; Kathy Tracy, D.R.E. Students 32.
Station—Arco, St. Ann Box 61, Arco, 83213. Tel: 208-521-3035.
Station—Challis, St. Louise Challis, 83229.
Station—Mackay, St. Barbara Box 452, Mackay, 83251. Tel: 208-527-3035.
Chapel—Leadore, St. Joseph Leadore, 83464.

SANDPOINT, BONNER CO., ST. JOSEPH'S (1907) Very Rev. Dennis C. Day.
Res.: 601 S. Lincoln, P.O. Box 279, 83864-0279. Tel: 208-263-3720; Fax: 208-265-4974. Web: www.st-joseph-church.net.
Catechesis/Religious Program—Irene Sundquist, D.R.E. Students 160.
Chapel—Clark Fork, Sacred Heart

SHOSHONE, LINCOLN CO., ST. PETER'S Very Rev. Michael St. Marie, Priest Mod.; Rev. John Koelsch, Sacramental Min. (Retired); Deacons Javier Leiga; John McKinley, Parish Life Dir.
Res.: 215 W. B St., Box 336, 83352. Tel: 208-886-2002; 208-934-5634.
Catechesis/Religious Program—Students 16.

SODA SPRINGS, CARIBOU CO., GOOD SHEPHERD CATHOLIC COMMUNITY (1910) Rev. Gabriel F. Vargas, Admin.
Res.: 99 W. Center, 83276. Tel: 208-547-3200; Fax: 208-547-3200.
Catechesis/Religious Program—Students 70.
Chapel—Montpelier, Blessed Sacrament Montpelier.
Chapel—Soda Springs, St. Mary's
Chapel—Preston, St. Peter's Preston.
Chapel—Lava Hot Springs, Our Lady of Lourdes Lava Hot Springs.

SUN VALLEY, BLAINE CO., OUR LADY OF THE SNOWS (1970) Revs. Ronald Wekerle, Priest Mod.; Jorge E. Garcia, Sacramental Min.; Teresa Gregory, Parish Life Dir.
Res.: Sun Valley Rd., Box 1650, 83353. Tel: 208-622-3432; Fax: 208-622-4348. Email: parishoffice@ourladyofthesnowssunvalley.net. Web: www.ourladyofthesnowssunvalley.net.
Catechesis/Religious Program—Students 75.

TWIN FALLS, TWIN FALLS CO.
1—ST. EDWARD THE CONFESSOR (1920) Very Rev. Michael St. Marie; Rev. Camilo Garcia, Parochial Vicar; Deacons Lloyd LeClair, (Retired); James Herrett; John Hurley.
Res.: 212 7th Ave. E., 83301-6321. Tel: 208-733-3907; Fax: 208-733-3935.
School—(Grades K-6), 139 Sixth Ave. E., 83301-6316. Tel: 208-734-3872; Fax: 208-734-1214. Kevin Bushman, Prin. Lay Teachers 14; Students 143.
Catechesis/Religious Program—Students 210.
2—ST. EDWARD'S, Merged with Our Lady of Guadalupe, Twin Falls to form St. Edward The Confessor, Twin Falls.
3—OUR LADY OF GUADALUPE, Merged with St. Edward's, Twin Falls to form St. Edward The Confessor, Twin Falls.

WALLACE, SHOSHONE CO., ST. ALPHONSUS Rev. Thomas Loucks.
Res.: 214 Pine St., 83873. Tel: 208-752-3551.
Catechesis/Religious Program—Students 24.
Chapel—Mullan, St. Michael's

WEISER, WASHINGTON CO., ST. AGNES (1878) Revs. Victor Manuel, Admin.; Thomas Keller; Deacons Francis Wander, (Retired); Ignacio Cornejo.
Res.: 214 E. Liberty, P.O. Box 87, 83672. Tel: 208-549-0088; Fax: 208-549-1080.
Email: saintagnes@qwest.net.
Catechesis/Religious Program—Students 160.
Station—Cambridge, Holy Rosary P.O. Box 335, Cambridge, 83610-0335. Tel: 208-257-3559.
Station—Council, St. Jude the Apostle 2054 Hwy. 95 N., Council, 83612. Tel: 208-253-6470.

WENDELL, GOODING CO., ST. ANTHONY'S, See separate listing. See St. Elizabeth's, Gooding for details.

Chaplains of Public Institutions

BOISE. *Elks Rehabilitation*, 204 Fort Pl., 83702. Vacant. Attended by St. John's Cathedral, 775 N. 8th St., Boise, ID 83702. Tel: 208-342-3511.
St. Luke's Medical Center, 190 E. Bannock, 83712. Vacant. Attended by St. John Cathedral, 775 N. 8th St., Boise, ID, 83702. Tel: 208-342-3511.
VA Hospital, 5th St. & Fort St., 83401. Vacant. Attended by St. John Cathedral, 775 N. 8th St., Boise, ID, 83702. Tel: 208-342-3511.

COTTONWOOD. *Monastery of St. Gertrude*, HC 3 Box 121, 83522-9408. Tel: 208-962-3224. Rev. Eamonn McNerney.

On Duty Outside the Diocese:
Revs.—
Dolan, Raymond, M.H. Station, Box 217, Staten Island, NY 10303.
Legerski, John, Bishop Manogue High School, 110 Bishop Manogue Dr., Reno, NV 89511.
Ramirez, Jorge, St. Patrick's Church, Dio of Kansas - St. Joseph.
Segatta, Bruno
Stravinskas, Peter M.J., Newman House, 5401 S. 33rd St., Omaha, NE 68107.
Zuletta, Nondier, Columbia, Diocese of California.

On Sabbatical:
Rev.—
Worster, John

Retired:
Rev. Msgrs.—
Hallissey, James T., 855 Galena Ct., Box 370, Mountain Home, 83647.
McGoldrick, John T., 106 N. 12th St., #4C, Payette, 83661.
Morgan, John W.
O'Donovan, Timothy John, 1802 W. Ontario St., Sand Point, 83864-6380.
Schumacher, Andrew, 3213 S. M St., Unit 1, Lewiston, 83501.
Revs.—
Caulfield, Sean, 505 7th Ave., Lewiston, 83501.
Daws, Dominic, 541 E. 100 S., Jerome, 83338.
Dennis, Patrick
DiLoreto, Anthony, 524 N. 7th Ave., Pocatello, 83201.
Dohman, William, J.C.L., 5972 Via Casitas Ave., Carmichael, CA 95608-6541.
Fernandez, Marcellus
Finucane, Robert, P.O. Box 36, Genesee, 83832.
Koelsch, John
Medina, Mauricio, 931 Eastland Dr. N., Twin Falls, 83301.
Muha, Joseph, 2711 N. 29th St., 83703.
O'Sullivan, John, 700 E. Fairview, #116, Meridian, 83642-3315.
Pu, Matthew, P.O. Box 9012, 83707.
Riffle, David
Riffle, Donald J.
Riffle, Douglas H., 13601 W. McMillan Rd., Ste. 102, PMB 303, 83713.
Scarcello, Michael S., 3427 W. Scarcello Rd., Rathdrum, 83858-3427.
Sprute, Mel, (Medical Retirement)
Steinhoff, Henry, P.O. Box 626, Eureka, MT 59917.
Taylor, Gordon A., P.O. Box 161, Arco, 83213.
Taylor, William

Permanent Deacons:
Almeida, Humberto, Our Lady of the Valley, Caldwell
Arndt, Ralph, (Retired)
Aslett, Devon H., St. Peter, Shoshone
Baumbach, John, St. Jerome's, Jerome
Bonney, Richard, Christ the King, Idaho Falls; Holy Rosary, Idaho Falls
Booth, William, (Retired), St. Mark's, Boise
Bowen, James E., St. Mark's, Boise
Canney, George, St. Mary's, Moscow
Collins, Michael, St. Paul's, Nampa
Cornejo, Ignacio, St. Agnes, Weiser
Desert, Malherbe, Holy Apostles, Meridian
Dessert, Michael, Our Lady of the Rosary, Boise
Dominick, Thomas, St. John's Cathedral, Boise
Duggan, Bill
Eisenbeiss, Michael, Sacred Heart, Boise
Finan, Charles, St. Pius X, Coeur d'Alene
Flager, Ralph, Holy Apostles, Meridian
Geidl, Verne, St. Mary's, Moscow
Gonzalez, Jorge, St. Mary's, Boise
Granados, Jose Luis, St. Paul's, Nampa
Hamm, Richard, (Retired), St. Catherine of Siena, Priest River
Harris, C. J., Risen Christ Catholic Community, Boise
Henscheid, Paul, St. Nicholas, Rupert
Herrett, James, St. Edward's, Twin Falls
Hess, Francis, St. Mary's, Boise
Hiner, Kenneth, (Retired), St. John Cathedral, Boise
Hurley, John, Immaculate Conception, Buhl
Jacobs, Gary, St. Thomas, Coeur D'Alene
Kelly, James, Sacred Heart, Boise
Kelso, Richard
Kreilcamp, Ben, (Retired)
Last, William, (Retired)
Le Clair, Lloyd, (Retired)
Leija, Javier, St. Elizabeth's, Gooding
Lowe, Michael, St. Mark's, Boise
McKinley, John D., Jr., St. Elizabeth's, Gooding
McSwain, Gary, St. Pius X, Coeur d'Alene
Murphy, Pierce, Risen Christ, Boise
Nicholas, Joseph, St. Ann's, Bonners Ferry
Pelowitz, Jack, St. John's Cathedral, Boise
Pera, Gerald D., Holy Apostles, Meridian
Perea, Marino, St. Jerome, Jerome
Petzak, William, St. Mary, Boise
Pierce, Ralph, St. Mark, Boise
Ponce, Alvaro, Holy Rosary, Idaho Falls
Rasmussen, Charles, Holy Apostles, Meridian
Rathe, Orville, St. Nicholas, Rupert
Reilly, Christopher, Holy Rosary, Idaho Falls
Rodriguez, Wence, Idaho Falls
Rodriquez, Joseph, St. Marks's, Boise
Rueda, Reynaldo, St. Bernard's, Blackfoot
Salazar, Harley, Corpus Christi, Fruitland
Schmidt, Fred, Our Lady of Lourdes, Lewiston
Servatius, Michael, Our Lady of the Rosary, Boise
Shaber, Alan, Sacred Heart, Emmett
Shaber, Eric, Holy Rosary, Idaho Falls
Skoro, Chuck, Our Lady of The Rosary, Boise
Sokolowski, Don, Sts. Peter & Paul, Grangeville
Solbrig, Charles W., (Retired)
Souza, Edward, (On Duty Outside the Diocese)
Tamayo, Juan, Corpus Christi Community, Fruitland
Trueworthy, Leonard, (Retired), St. Pius X, Coeur d' Alene
Turner, Floyd, St. Mary Immaculate, St. Maries
Vietri, Nick, Sacred Heart Indian Mission, DeSmet
Wander, Francis, (Retired), St. Agnes, Weiser

INSTITUTIONS LOCATED IN THE DIOCESE

[A] HIGH SCHOOLS, INTER-PAROCHIAL

BOISE. *Bishop Kelly High School*, 7009 Franklin Rd., 83709-0922. Tel: 208-375-6010; Fax: 208-375-3626. Robert Wehde, Prin. Lay Teachers 43; Students 645.

COEUR D'ALENE. *Holy Family Catholic School of Coeur d'Alene*, (Grades PreK-8), 3005 Kathleen Ave., 83815. Tel: 208-765-4327; Fax: 208-664-2903. Karen Durgin, Prin. Lay Teachers 14; Students 198.

[B] GENERAL HOSPITALS

BOISE. *St. Alphonsus Regional Medical Center, Inc.* (1894) 1055 N. Curtis Rd., 83706-1370. Tel: 208-367-2121. Sally Jeffcoat, Pres. & CEO.
St. Alphonsus Regional Medical Center.
St. Alphonsus Building Co., Inc.
St. Alphonsus Diversified Care. Sisters of the Holy Cross 4; Bed Capacity 387; Patients Assisted Annually 298,851.

COTTONWOOD. *St. Mary's Hospital*, 701 N. Lewiston St., P.O. Box 137, 83522. Tel: 208-962-3251; Fax: 208-962-3722. Ms. Casey Meza, Admin.; Rev. Eamonn McNerney, Chap.; Sr. Corinne Forsman, Dir., Mission Svc. Sponsored by Sisters of St. Benedict, Duluth, MN. Sisters 1; Bed Capacity 25; Patients Assisted Annually 10,000.

JEROME. *St. Benedicts Family Medical Center*, 709 N. Lincoln, 83338-1851. Tel: 208-324-4301; Fax: 208-324-3878. Email: davisc@stbenshospital.org. Alan Stevenson, Admin. Critical access hospital with adjoining long-term care facility & medical clinics. Sisters 1; Bed Capacity 50; Patients Assisted Annually 64,000.
Divine Medical Services, 240 E. Main St., 83338. Tel: 208-324-7775; Fax: 208-324-3878. Email: davisc@stbenshospital.org. Alan Stevenson, Contact Person. Ambulance service in connection with medical center.

LEWISTON. *St. Joseph Regional Medical Center*, 415 6th St., P.O. Box 816, 83501-0816. Tel: 208-743-2511; Fax: 208-799-5528. Howard A. Hayes, Pres. & CEO. Nursing Education is in affiliation with Lewis-Clark State College and with Walla-Walla Community College, Clarkston Branch. Bed Capacity 161; Patients Assisted Annually 106,403.

NAMPA. *Mercy Medical Center*, 1512 12th Avenue Rd., 83686. Tel: 208-463-5000. Joseph A. Messmer, Pres. & CEO; Rev. Mark Bekkedahl, Vice Pres. Mission Integration; Sr. Alice Marie Schmid, O.P.; Jim Hoff, Dir. Spiritual Care Resources & Chap. Sisters 1; Bed Capacity 152; Patients Assisted Annually 169,020.

[C] MONASTERIES AND RESIDENCES OF PRIESTS AND BROTHERS

JEROME. *Monastery of the Ascension*, 541 E. 100 S., 83338. Tel: 208-324-2377; Fax: 208-324-2377. Revs. Boniface Lautz, O.S.B., Prior; Norbert Novak, O.S.B.; Meinrad Schallberger, O.S.B.; Andrew Baumgartner, O.S.B., Subprior; Hugh Feiss, O.S.B.; Eugene Esch, O.S.B.;

Rt. Rev. Kenneth C. Hein, O.S.B. (Retired); Bros. Sylvester Sonnen, O.S.B.; Selby Coffman, O.S.B.; Tobiah Urrutia, O.S.B.; Jose Echanove, O.S.B.

The Benedictine Monks of Idaho, Inc. The Benedictine Monks of Idaho, Inc.

LEMHI. *Hermitage of St. Joseph*, Box 37, 83465. Bro. Maurice Mansfield, H.M.C. Hermits of Mt. Carmel.

[D] CONVENTS AND RESIDENCES OF SISTERS

COTTONWOOD. *Monastery of St. Gertrude, Motherhouse and Novitiate*, 465 Keuterville Rd., 83522-5183. Tel: 208-962-3224; Fax: 208-962-7212. Rev. Eamonn McNerney, Chap.; Sisters Clarissa Goeckner, O.S.B., Prioress; Mary Marge Goeckner, O.S.B., Asst. Prioress. Sisters of St. Benedict 60.

MESA. *Marymount Hermitage, Inc., Hermit Sisters of Mary*, 2150 Hermitage Ln., 83643-5005. Tel: 208-256-4354 (msg. only). Web: www.marymount-hermitage.org. Sr. Mary Beverly Greger, H.S.M., Supr. Sisters 2.

[E] RETREAT HOUSES

BOISE. *Nazareth*, 4450 N. Five Mile Rd., 83713-2709. Tel: 208-375-2932; Fax: 208-376-5787. Web: www.nazarethretreatcenter.org. Marjorie DiLorenzo, Dir.; Fred DiLorenzo, Dir.

COTTONWOOD. *Spirit Center*, 465 Keuterville Rd., 83522-5183. Tel: 208-962-2000; Fax: 208-962-2003. Mary Schmidt, Admin.

[F] CAMPUS MINISTRY

BOISE. *Boise State University, St. Paul's Catholic Center* 1915 University Dr., 83706. Tel: 208-343-2128; Fax: 208-343-2128. Email: chuck@stpaulsboise.org. Deacon Charles L. Skorro, Coord. Campus Ministry.

CALDWELL. *The College of Idaho c/o Our Lady of The Valley*, 1122 W. Linden St., 83605. Tel: 208-459-3653; Fax: 208-454-8789. Rev. Francisco Flores.

COEUR D'ALENE. *North Idaho College* St Pius X, 625 E. Haycraft, 83815. Tel: 208-765-5108; Fax: 208-664-5325. Email: frlachance@roadrunner.com. Rev. Roger LaChance.

LEWISTON. *Lewis Clark State College* St. Stanislaus, 633 5th Ave., 83501. Tel: 208-743-7331; Fax: 208-746-7134. Rev. Leslie P. Kish, Pastor.

MOSCOW. *St. Augustine Catholic Center* 628 Deakin Ave., Box 3457, 83843-1911. Tel: 208-882-4613; Fax: 208-882-0810. Email: auggiesecretary@moscow.com. Rev. Caleb Vogel. (Serving University of Idaho)

POCATELLO. *Idaho State University, St. John's Catholic Student Center* 920 E. Lovejoy, I.S.U., Box 8129, 83209. Tel: 208-233-0880; Fax: 208-233-5745. Email: stjohns@isu.edu. Web: www.bannockcatholic.net. Jennifer Seaich, Dir.

TWIN FALLS. *College of Southern Idaho* 212 7th Ave. E., 83301-6321. Tel: 208-733-3907; Fax: 208-734-4145. Very Rev. Michael St. Marie, V.F. Attended by St. Edward the Confessor, Twin Falls.

[G] MISCELLANEOUS

BOISE. *Catholic Charities of Idaho, Inc.*, 1501 S. Federal Way, Ste. 450, 83705. Tel: 208-345-6031; Fax: 208-350-7499. Rosio Gonzalez, Exec. Dir.; Most Rev. Michael P. Driscoll, D.D., M.S.W., Pres. Bd. of Dirs.; Lynne Johnson, Admin. Mgr.

The Catholic Migrant Farmworker Network, Inc., P.O. Box 50026, 83705. Web: www.cmfn.org. Hector R. Rodriquez, Exec. Dir.

Society of St. Vincent de Paul - Southwest Idaho District Council, 3217 W. Overland Rd., 83705. Tel: 208-331-4809. Ida Fisk, Pres.

St. Vincent de Paul Society, St. Mark's Conference, 7960 Northview, 83704. Tel: 208-853-2593. Kevin Ankrom, Pres.

St. Vincent de Paul Society, Our Lady of the Rosary Conference, 1500 E. Wright St., 83706-5358. Tel: 208-343-9041. John Gilderman, Pres.

St. Vincent de Paul Society Thrift Stores, 6464 W. State St., 83703. Tel: 208-853-4921; Fax: 208-853-4935. Email: stateSVDP@aol.com. Vicky Rowell, Store Dir.

St. Vincent de Paul Society St. John's Conference., 775 N. 8th St., 83702. Tel: 208-331-2208. Tom Aden, Pres.

St. Vincent de Paul Society Sacred Heart Conference., 1241 E. Ringneck Cir., Meridian, 83642. Tel: 208-888-7574. Pete Murray, Pres.

St. Vincent de Paul Society Risen Christ Conference., 5059 Silverspur, 83709. Tel: 208-362-3778. Karen Kotts, Pres.

CALDWELL. *Society of St. Vincent de Paul* Society of St. Vincent de Paul, 17281 Ustick Rd., 83607. Tel: 208-459-7658. Jerry Phillips, Store Mgr.

COEUR D'ALENE. *St. Vincent de Paul Salvage Bureau* St. Thomas Conference., 108 E. Walnut, 83814. Tel: 208-664-3095; Fax: 208-664-1772. John Bruning, Pres.; Jeff Conroy, Exec. Dir.

EAGLE. *Mercy Housing Idaho, Inc.*, 540 N. Eagle Rd., #117, 83616. Tel: 208-939-6838; Fax: 208-939-9480.

Mercy Properties II, Inc., 83616.
Mercy Idaho Properties, Inc., 83616.
Mercy Twin Falls, Inc., 83616.
Mercy Moscow, Inc., 83616.
Mercy Southeast Idaho, Inc., 83616.
Eagle Senior Village, Inc., 83616.
Mercy Independence Hill, Inc.

IDAHO FALLS. *St. Vincent de Paul Society of Idaho Falls*, P.O. Box 50951, 83405-0951. Tel: 208-522-6280; Fax: 208-522-6280. Bryan Forsmann, Pres.

KELLOGG. *Society of St. Vincent de Paul* St. Rita Conference., 104 E. Riverside, 83837. Tel: 208-783-5551. Gary Strope, Pres.; Cindy Patton, Store Mgr.

LEWISTON. *Lewis and Clark District Council of St. Vincent de Paul*, 906 Grelle Ave., 83501. Tel: 208-746-1542. Mel Lewis, Board Pres.

MERIDIAN. *Holy Apostles Conference*, P.O. Box 708, 83680-0708. Tel: 208-888-1182. Jack Crane, Pres.

NAMPA. *Our Lady of Guadalupe Conference*, 2227 Andy Pl., 83651. Tel: 208-442-3089. Jim Daniels, Pres. Tel: 208-466-3400 Message.

POCATELLO. *PortNeuf Valley Conference (St. Vincent de Paul)*, 855 S. 2nd St., 83201. Tel: 208-233-2555. Barbara Nusbaum, Pres.; Brice Boland, Social Svcs. Dir.

TWIN FALLS. *St. Michael Conference (St. Vincent de Paul)* 83301. Tel: 208-734-9143. Email: svdptf@yahoo.com. Mary Lou Howard, Pres.; Rick Mesaros, Store Mgr.

RELIGIOUS INSTITUTES OF MEN REPRESENTED IN THE DIOCESE

For further details refer to the corresponding bracketed number in the Religious Institutes of Men or Women section.

[]—*Apostolic Life Community of Priests*—A.L.C.P.
[0200]—*Benedictine Monks*—O.S.B.
[]—*Hermits of Mt. Carmel*—H.M.C.
[0690]—*Jesuit Fathers* (Oregon Prov.)—S.J.
[0840]—*Missionary Servants of the Most Holy Trinity*—S.T.
[1065]—*Priestly Fraternity of St. Peter*—F.S.S.P.
[1070]—*Redemptorist Fathers* (Oakland Prov.)—C.SS.R.

RELIGIOUS INSTITUTES OF WOMEN REPRESENTED IN THE DIOCESE

[0230]—*Benedictine Sisters of Pontifical Jurisdiction*—O.S.B.
[1920]—*Congregation of the Sisters of the Holy Cross*—C.S.C.
[1070-21]—*Dominican Sisters*—O.P.
[]—*Hermit Sisters of Mary*—H.S.M.
[1250]—*Institute of the Franciscan Sisters of the Eucharist*—F.S.E.
[2575]—*Institute of the Sisters of Mercy of the Americas*—R.S.M.
[]—*Missionary Sisters of the Sacred Heart of the Rosary of Fatima*—H.M.R.F.
[3340]—*Sisters of Providence*—S.P.
[3830]—*Sisters of St. Joseph*—C.S.J.
[1990]—*Sisters of the Holy Names of Jesus and Mary*—S.N.J.M.
[]—*Society of Sisters of the Church*—S.S.C.
[4110]—*Ursuline Nuns* (Western Prov.)—O.S.U.

NECROLOGY

† Donoghue, Rev. Msgr. John F., (Retired)—Died Jan. 5, 2009
† Dodds, Perry W., (Retired)—Died May 17, 2009

An asterisk (*) denotes an organization that has established tax-exempt status directly with the IRS and is not covered by the USCCB Group Ruling.

Archdiocese of Boston

(Archidioecesis Bostoniensis)

His Eminence

SEÁN PATRICK CARDINAL O'MALLEY, O.F.M.CAP.

Archbishop of Boston; ordained priest August 29, 1970; ordained Coadjutor Bishop of St. Thomas in the Virgin Islands August 2, 1984; succeeded to the See, October 16, 1985; Named sixth Bishop of Fall River, MA June 16, 1992; installed August 10, 1992; Named fourth Bishop of Palm Beach, FL September 3, 2002; installed October 19, 2002; Named ninth Bishop and sixth Metropolitan Archbishop of Boston July 1, 2003; installed July 30, 2003; Named Cardinal Priest with the title of Santa Maria della Vittoria, in the consistory of March 24, 2006; installed October 1, 2006. *Office: 66 Brooks Dr., Braintree, MA 02184-3839.* Tel: 617-782-2544; Fax: 617-779-3820. *Residence: Cathedral of the Holy Cross, 75 Union Park St., Boston, MA 02118.* Tel: 617-542-5682; Fax: 617-542-5926.

Chancery Office: 66 Brooks Dr., Braintree, MA 02184-3839. Tel: 617-254-0100; Fax: 617-779-4571.

Web: www.bostoncatholic.org

Most Reverend

EMILIO SIMEON ALLUE, S.D.B.

Titular Bishop of Croe, Auxiliary Bishop of Boston, Vicar General and Vicar for Hispanic Affairs; ordained priest December 22, 1966; ordained Bishop September 17, 1996. *Office: 66 Brooks Dr., Braintree, MA 02184-3839.* Tel: 617-746-5916; Fax: 617-746-5614. *Res.: Saint Theresa of Avila Rectory, 10 Saint Theresa Ave., Boston, MA 02132.* Tel: 617-325-1300; Fax: 617-325-0380.

Most Reverend

WALTER JAMES EDYVEAN

Titular Bishop of Aeliae, Auxiliary Bishop of Boston, Vicar General and Regional Bishop-West; ordained priest December 16, 1964; ordained Bishop September 14, 2001. *Office: 5 Wilson St., Natick, MA 01760.* Tel: 508-647-0296; Fax: 508-647-1542. *Res. & Mailing Address: Saint Patrick Rectory, 44 E. Central St., Natick, MA 01760.* Tel: 508-647-1860.

Most Reverend

JOHN ANTHONY DOOHER

Titular Bishop of Theveste, Auxiliary Bishop of Boston, Vicar General and Regional Bishop-South; ordained priest May 21, 1969; ordained Bishop December 12, 2006. *Office: 236 Pleasant St., Weymouth, MA 02190-2599.* Tel: 781-337-4413; Fax: 781-337-3625. *Res.: Saint Jerome Rectory, 632 Bridge St., Weymouth, MA 02191.* Tel: 781-335-2038; Fax: 781-340-7165.

Most Reverend

ROBERT FRANCIS HENNESSEY

Titular Bishop of Tigias, Auxiliary Bishop of Boston, Vicar General and Regional Bishop-Central; ordained priest May 20, 1978; ordained Bishop December 12, 2006. *Office: 841 E. Broadway, Boston, MA 02127-2302.* Tel: 617-269-4001; Fax: 617-269-4006. *Res.: Saint James the Greater Parish, 135 Harrison Ave., Boston, MA 02111.* Tel: 617-542-8498; Fax: 617-542-2708.

Most Reverend

JOHN PATRICK BOLES

Titular Bishop of Nova Sparsa and Vicar General; ordained priest February 2, 1955; ordained Bishop May 21, 1992; retired October 12, 2006. *Office: 841 E. Broadway, Boston, MA 02127-2302.* Tel: 617-269-4001; Fax: 617-269-4006. *Res.: Regina Cleri Residence.* Tel: 617-523-1861; Fax: 617-720-0585.

Most Reverend

FRANCIS XAVIER IRWIN

Titular Bishop of Ubaza and Vicar General; ordained priest February 2, 1960; ordained Bishop September 17, 1996; retired October 12, 2009. *Office & Res.: Saint Raphael Parish, 30 Boston Ave., Medford, MA 02155.* Tel: 781-488-5444; Fax: 781-483-3375.

Square Miles 2,465.

Created a Diocese April 8, 1808; Made Metropolitan Archdiocese February 12, 1875.

Comprises the Counties of Essex, Middlesex, Norfolk, Suffolk and Plymouth (the towns of Marion, Mattapoisett and Wareham excepted) in the Commonwealth of Massachusetts.

For legal titles of parishes and archdiocesan agencies and institutions, consult the Chancery Office.

STATISTICAL OVERVIEW

Personnel	
Cardinals	1
Auxiliary Bishops	4
Retired Bishops	2
Retired Abbots	1
Priests: Diocesan Active in Diocese	406
Priests: Diocesan Active Outside Diocese	27
Priests: Diocesan in Foreign Missions	5
Priests: Retired, Sick or Absent	306
Number of Diocesan Priests	744
Religious Priests in Diocese	491
Total Priests in Diocese	1,235
Extern Priests in Diocese	75
Ordinations:	
Diocesan Priests	6
Permanent Deacons in Diocese	258
Total Brothers	144
Total Sisters	1,945
Parishes	
Parishes	291
With Resident Pastor:	
Resident Diocesan Priests	275
Resident Religious Priests	16
Pastoral Centers	1
Closed Parishes	2
Professional Ministry Personnel:	
Sisters	36
Lay Ministers	241
Welfare	
Catholic Hospitals	8
Total Assisted	708,219
Health Care Centers	3
Total Assisted	7,511
Homes for the Aged	15
Total Assisted	2,832
Residential Care of Children	1
Total Assisted	921
Day Care Centers	11
Total Assisted	1,110
Specialized Homes	21
Total Assisted	1,722
Special Centers for Social Services	43
Total Assisted	206,000
Other Institutions	3
Total Assisted	35,410
Educational	
Seminaries, Diocesan	3
Students from This Diocese	44
Students from Other Diocese	95
Diocesan Students in Other Seminaries	2
Seminaries, Religious	1
Students Religious	37
Total Seminarians	83
Colleges and Universities	6
Total Students	24,900
High Schools, Diocesan and Parish	3
Total Students	1,150
High Schools, Private	29
Total Students	15,155
Elementary Schools, Diocesan and Parish	79
Total Students	24,067
Elementary Schools, Private	9
Total Students	2,264
Non-residential Schools for the Disabled	2
Total Students	139
Catechesis/Religious Education:	
High School Students	26,624
Elementary Students	97,419
Total Students under Catholic Instruction	191,801
Teachers in the Diocese:	
Priests	7
Brothers	31
Sisters	91
Lay Teachers	3,177
Vital Statistics	
Receptions into the Church:	
Infant Baptism Totals	15,718
Minor Baptism Totals	3,196
Adult Baptism Totals	347
Received into Full Communion	387
First Communions	18,643
Confirmations	14,842
Marriages:	
Catholic	2,972
Interfaith	744
Total Marriages	3,716
Deaths	15,642
Total Catholic Population	1,681,533
Total Population	3,682,588

Former Bishops—His Eminence JOHN LEFEVRE CARDINAL DE CHEVERUS, ord. Dec. 18, 1790; appt. first Bishop of Boston, April 8, 1808; ord. Bishop Nov. 1, 1810; Apostolic Administrator of New York, NY (1810-1815); transferred to Montauban, May 3, 1823; appt. Archbishop of Bordeaux Oct. 2, 1826; named Cardinal, Feb. 1, 1836 (died before receiving red hat and titular church); died July 19, 1836; Most Revs. BENEDICT J. FENWICK, S.J., ord. June 11, 1808; appt. second Bishop of Boston, May 10, 1825; ord. Bishop Nov. 1, 1825; died Aug. 11, 1846; JOHN BERNARD FITZPATRICK, ord. June 13, 1840; appt. Titular Bishop of Callipolis and Coadjutor of Boston, Nov. 21, 1843; ord. Bishop March 24, 1844; Succeeded as third Bishop of Boston, Aug. 11, 1846; died Feb. 13, 1866; JOHN JOSEPH WILLIAMS, D.D., ord. May 17, 1845; appt. Titular Bishop of Tripolis and Coadjutor of Boston, Jan. 8, 1866; ord. fourth Bishop of Boston, March 11, 1866; named first Archbishop of Boston, Feb. 12, 1875; died Aug. 30, 1907; His Eminence WILLIAM HENRY CARDINAL O'CONNELL, ord. June 7, 1884; appt. third Bishop of Portland, Maine, Feb. 8, 1901; ord. Bishop May 19, 1901; appt. Titular Archbishop of Constantia and Coadjutor with right of succession to the Archbishop of Boston, Feb. 8, 1906; appt. fifth Bishop and second Archbishop of Boston, April 30, 1907; named Cardinal, Nov. 27, 1911, Titular Church, San Clemente; died April 22, 1944; RICHARD JAMES CARDINAL CUSHING, ord. May 26, 1921; appt. Titular Bishop of Mela and Auxiliary of Boston, June 10, 1939; ord. Bishop June 29, 1939; appt. sixth Bishop and third Archbishop of Boston, Sept. 25, 1944; named Cardinal December 15, 1958, Titular Church, Santa Susanna; died Nov. 2, 1970; HUMBERTO SOUSA CARDINAL MEDEIROS, ord. June 15, 1946; appt. second Bishop of Brownsville, Texas April 14, 1966;

ord. Bishop June 9, 1966; named seventh Bishop and fourth Archbishop of Boston, Sept. 8, 1970; installed Oct. 7, 1970; named Cardinal March 5, 1973, Titular Church, Santa Susanna; died Sept. 17, 1983; BERNARD FRANCIS CARDINAL LAW, ord. priest May 21, 1961; appt. fourth Bishop of Springfield-Cape Girardeau Oct. 22, 1973; ord. Bishop of Springfield-Cape Girardeau Dec. 5, 1973; appt. eighth Bishop and fifth Archbishop of Boston Jan. 11, 1984; installed March 23, 1984; named Cardinal Priest May 25, 1985; Titular Church, Santa Susanna; resigned Dec. 13, 2002; named Archpriest of the Patriarchal Basilica of St. Mary Major, Rome, Italy, May 27, 2004.

Vicars General—Most Revs. EMILIO S. ALLUE, S.D.B.; JOHN P. BOLES; JOHN A. DOOHER; WALTER J. EDYVEAN, S.T.D.; ROBERT F. HENNESSEY; FRANCIS X. IRWIN; Very Rev. RICHARD M. ERIKSON, V.G.

Regional Bishops and Vicars—

Central Region—Most Rev. ROBERT F. HENNESSEY. Tel: 617-269-4001; Fax: 617-269-4006. Vicariate I: Rev. Msgr. FRANCIS H. KELLEY, V.F., Sacred Heart, Roslindale. Tel: 617-325-3322; Fax: 617-325-2145. Vicariate II: Very Rev. ROBERT E. CASEY, V.F., Gate of Heaven and St. Brigid, South Boston. Tel: 617-268-2122; Fax: 617-268-2666. Vicariate III: Very Rev. KEVIN J. O'LEARY, V.F., Cathedral of the Holy Cross, Boston. Tel: 617-542-5682; Fax: 617-542-5926. Vicariate IV: Very Rev. WALTER A. CARREIRO, V.F., St. Anthony of Padua, Cambridge. Tel: 617-547-5593; Fax: 617-547-1505.

North Region—Most Rev. FRANCIS X. IRWIN. Tel: 978-531-1013; Fax: 978-531-5312. Vicariate I: Very Rev. JOHN E. FARRELL, V.F., Our Lady of the Assumption, Lynnfield. Tel: 781-598-4313; Fax: 781-598-0055. Vicariate II: Rev. Msgr. PAUL V. GARRITY, V.F., St. Mary, Lynn. Tel: 781-598-4907; Fax: 781-599-2088. Vicariate III: Very Rev. THOMAS F. NESTOR, V.F., St. Eulalia, Winchester. Tel: 781-729-8220; Fax: 781-729-0919. Vicariate IV: Very Rev. JAMES J. BARRY, V.F., Our Lady of Grace, Chelsea. Tel: 617-884-0030; Fax: 617-884-0957.

Merrimack Region—Very Rev. ARTHUR M. COYLE. Tel: 978-399-0000; Fax: 978-399-0123. Vicariate I: Very Rev. PAUL E. RITT, V.F., St. John the Evangelist, Chelmsford. Tel: 978-251-8571; Fax: 978-251-7873. Vicariate II: Very Rev. DANIEL D. MAGNI, V.F., St. Rita, Lowell. Tel: 978-452-4812; Fax: 978-459-8969. Vicariate III: Very Rev. JOHN W. DELANEY, V.F., St. Michael, North Andover. Tel: 978-686-4050; Fax: 978-686-5408. Vicariate IV: Very Rev. JAMES M. CARROLL, V.F., St. Mary, Georgetown. Tel: 978-352-2024; Fax: 978-352-5513.

North Region—Most Rev. FRANCIS X. IRWIN. Tel: 978-531-1013; Fax: 978-531-5312. Vicariate I: Very Rev. JOHN E. FARRELL, V.F., Our Lady of the Assumption, Lynnfield. Tel: 781-598-4313; Fax: 781-598-0055 Sacred Heart; Middleton - Saint Agnes; Saugus - Blessed Sacrament, Saint Margaret. Vicariate II: Rev. Msgr. PAUL V. GARRITY, V.F., Saint Mary, Lynn. Tel: 781-598-4907; Fax: 781-599-2088. Vicariate III: Very Rev. THOMAS F. NESTOR, V.F., Saint Eulalia, Winchester. Tel: 781-729-8220; Fax: 781-729-0919. Vicariate IV: Very Rev. JAMES J. BARRY, V.F., Our Lady of Grace, Chelsea. Tel: 617-884-0030; Fax: 617-884-0957.

West Region—Most Rev. WALTER J. EDYVEAN, S.T.D. Tel: 508-647-0296; Fax: 508-647-1542. Vicariate I: Very Rev. JAMES J. LAUGHLIN, J.C.L., V.F., St. Ann and St. Zepherin, Wayland. Tel: 508-358-2985; Fax: 508-358-3415. Vicariate II: Very Rev. RICHARD W. FITZGERALD, V.F., St. Paul, Wellesley. Tel: 781-235-1060; Fax: 781-235-4620. Vicariate III: Very Rev. JOHN J. GRIMES, V.F., Most Precious Blood, Dover. Tel: 508-785-0305; Fax: 508-785-0432. Vicariate IV: Rev. Msgr. TIMOTHY J. MORAN, V.F., St. Joseph, Medway. Tel: 508-533-6500; Fax: 508-533-1236.

Vicar General and Moderator of the Curia—Very Rev. RICHARD M. ERIKSON, V.G., 66 Brooks Dr., Braintree, 02184-3839. Tel: 617-254-0100; Fax: 617-746-5920. Email: vicar_general@rcab.org.

Assistant to the Moderator of the Curia for Canonical Affairs—Bro. JAMES M. PETERSON, O.F.M.Cap., J.D., J.C.L., 66 Brooks Dr., Braintree, 02184-3839. Tel: 617-746-5635; Fax: 617-746-5920. Email: peters_j@rcab.org.

Archives—Mr. ROBERT JOHNSON-LALLY, Archivist, 66 Brooks Dr., Braintree, 02184-3839. Tel: 617-746-5797; Fax: 617-746-4561.

Pontifical Association of the Holy Childhood—

Pontifical Society for the Propagation of the Faith—

Pontifical Society of Saint Peter the Apostle—Rev. THOMAS A. KOPP, Dir., 66 Brooks Dr., Braintree, 02184-3839. Tel: 617-779-3865. Email: officestaff@propfaithatboston.org.

Metropolitan Tribunal

Ecclesiastical Court of the Archdiocese of Boston—66 Brooks Dr., Braintree, 02184-3839. Tel: 617-746-5900; Fax: 617-779-4566.

Judicial Vicar of the Archdiocese—Very Rev. MARK O'CONNELL, J.C.D.

Archdiocesan Judges—Tribunal Court: Rev. Msgr. MICHAEL S. FOSTER, J.C.D.; Very Rev. MARK O'CONNELL, J.C.D.; Rev. JOSEPH F. MOZER JR., J.C.L.; Sr. MARGARET L. SULLIVAN, C.S.J., J.C.L.; Ms. MARIA GALINDEZ-BIANCO, J.C.L., J.D. Associates: Revs. JOSEPH M. HENNESSEY, J.C.L.; ROBERT OLIVER, B.H., S.T.D., J.C.D.

Court Advocate/Petitioner—Rev. WLODZIMIERZ SOBOLEWSKI, C.R.; Ms. AMY JILL STRICKLAND, J.C.L.

Court Advocate/Respondent—Rev. PETER G. GORI, O.S.A., J.C.D.

Defenders of the Bond—Revs. JAMES G. BURKE, J.C.L.; RODNEY J. COPP, J.C.L.; AIDAN J. WALSH, J.C.L.

Promoter of Justice—Rev. RODNEY J. COPP, J.C.L.

Notary—Ms. MARSHA A. STATEN.

Staff—Ms. ROSE GRENIER; Ms. ELLEN OBSHATKIN; Ms. JULIANNE SHANKLIN; Ms. MARSHA A. STATEN.

Canonical Affairs Committee—Very Rev. MARK O'CONNELL, J.C.D., Chm.; Most Rev. WALTER J. EDYVEAN, S.T.D.; Revs. JAMES G. BURKE, J.C.L.; RODNEY J. COPP, J.C.L.; PETER G. GORI, O.S.A., J.C.D.; Very Rev. JAMES J. LAUGHLIN, J.C.L., V.F.; Revs. JOSEPH F. MOZER JR., J.C.L.; JAMES A. O'DONOHUE, J.C.D.; WALTER J. WOODS, S.T.D.; Bro. JAMES M. PETERSON, O.F.M.Cap., J.D., J.C.L.; Sr. MARGARET L. SULLIVAN, C.S.J., J.C.L.; Ms. AMY JILL STRICKLAND, J.C.L.

Presbyteral Council—His Eminence SEAN CARDINAL O'MALLEY, O.F.M.Cap.; Most Revs. EMILIO S. ALLUE, S.D.B.; JOHN P. BOLES; JOHN A. DOOHER; WALTER J. EDYVEAN, S.T.D.; ROBERT F. HENNESSEY; FRANCIS X. IRWIN; Rev. Msgrs. FRANCIS H. KELLEY, V.F.; FRANCIS J. MCGANN (Retired); DENNIS F. SHEEHAN; Very Revs. EDWIN D. CONDON (Retired); ARTHUR M. COYLE; RICHARD M. ERIKSON, V.G.; THOMAS S. FOLEY, V.F.; PAUL E. RITT, V.F.; PETER J. UGLIETTO, M.Div., S.T.L., S.T.D.; Revs. IGNACIO D. BERRIO; ROBERT M. BLANEY, V.F.; MARK J. COIRO; ARNOLD F. COLETTI; ROBERT L. CONNORS; DONALD R. DELAY; STEPHEN S. DONOHOE, M.Div.; MATHIAS DOYLE, O.F.M.; GEORGE F. EMERSON (Retired); GEORGE P. EVANS, M.Div., S.T.D.; DANIEL J. FINN; PETER G. GORI, O.S.A., J.C.D.; THOMAS GRIFFITHS, S.V.D.; JOHN W. HANLEY, O.M.I., V.F.; MICHAEL A. HOBSON; HERBERT J. JONES, O.Carm.; THOMAS A. KOPP; J. MICHAEL LAWLOR; MICHAEL D. LINDEN, S.J.; PATRICK J. MCLAUGHLIN; VINCENT P. MELLONE; ANTHONY G. NGUYEN; GERARD PETRINGA; MARC A. PICHE; LAWRENCE E. PRATT (Retired); PETER F. QUINN; JOHN J. RONAGHAN; NICHOLAS A. SANELLA; MICHAEL L. STEELE; WILLIAM G. WILLIAMS.

College of Consultors—His Eminence SEAN CARDINAL O'MALLEY, O.F.M.Cap.; Most Revs. EMILIO S. ALLUE, S.D.B.; JOHN P. BOLES; JOHN A. DOOHER; WALTER J. EDYVEAN, S.T.D.; ROBERT F. HENNESSEY; FRANCIS X. IRWIN; Very Revs. ARTHUR M. COYLE; RICHARD M. ERIKSON, V.G.; PETER J. UGLIETTO, M.Div., S.T.L., S.T.D.; Revs. GEORGE F. EMERSON (Retired); J. MICHAEL LAWLOR.

Finance Council—President: His Eminence SEAN CARDINAL O'MALLEY, O.F.M.Cap. Members: Very Rev. RICHARD M. ERIKSON, V.G.; Sr. JOAN DUFFY, C.S.J.; Mr. JOHN J. CONNORS JR.; Mr. JOHN A. KANEB; Mr. PETER S. LYNCH; Mr. WILLIAM F. MCCALL; Mr. JOHN MCCARTHY; Mr. JAMES P. MCDONOUGH; Mr. SEAN P. MCGRATH; Mr. JOHN A. MCNIECE; Mr. JAMES MOONEY; Mr. ROBERT J. MORRISSEY; Mr. GILES MOSHER; Mr. PAUL W. SANDMAN; Ms. MARY RYAN.

Archdiocesan Pastoral Council—President: His Eminence SEAN CARDINAL O'MALLEY, O.F.M.Cap. Ex Officio: Very Revs. RICHARD M. ERIKSON, V.G.; ARTHUR M. COYLE. Appointed: Revs. LEONARD F. O'MALLEY; FRANK J. SILVA; Deacon PHILIP H. LAFOND; Bro. JOHN F. KERR, C.F.X.; Sisters SUZANNE FONDINI, M.F.I.C.; MARK LOUIS RANDALL, O.Carm.; Mr. PETER A. BAILEY; Mr. KEVIN M. CASEY; Mr. VINCENT J. DEBAGGIS; Mr. KEVIN DELEHANTY; Mr. ARMAND J. DI LANDO; Mr. ROBERT GADBOIS; Mr. MARK GARVEY; Mr. MICHAEL F. GILROY; Dr. EDWARD GOTGART; Mr. JOHNNY IP; Mr. TIMOTHY J. KELLEY; Mr. JOSEPH KOSCIUSZEK; Mr. HERB LYNCH, Attorney; Mr. JOHN F. MORAN; Mr. PHILLIP MORAN; Mr. JOHN T. MULCAHY; Mr. THOMAS J. NUTTALL; Mr. THONG PHAMDUY; Mr. PETER POUND; Mr. JIM SULLIVAN; Mr. PHILIP J. WALSH; Ms. ANDREA S. ALBERTI; Ms. SANDRA BISHOP; Ms. NANCY D. CIRONE; Ms. ELLEN H. CONNELL; Ms. JANE DEVLIN; Ms. PATRICIA M. DINNEEN; Ms. ANTONIA GARCIA-VEGA; Ms. NANCY HARRINGTON; Ms. PATRICIA MEUSE; Ms. SHARON M. MOORE; Ms. LINDA RILEY; Ms. SUZANNE ROBOTHAM; Ms. BETTY SNIEGOSKI; Ms. BUFFY WALSH.

Administration and Financial Services—Mr. JAMES P. MCDONOUGH, Sec. & Chancellor, 66 Brooks Dr., Braintree, 02184-3839. Tel: 617-746-5670; Fax: 617-779-4571. Email: jpm@rcab.org.

Cemeteries—Mr. ROBERT VISCONTI, Dir., 175 Broadway, Malden, 02148-6097. Tel: 781-322-6300; Fax: 781-322-3801. Email: rvisconti@rcab.org. Web: ccemetery.org.

Finance and Technology—Mr. GLEN MATTERA, Dir., 66 Brooks Dr., Braintree, 02184-3839. Tel: 617-746-5878; Fax: 617-779-4564.

Human Resources—CAROL GUSTAVSON, Dir., 66 Brooks Dr., Braintree, 02184-3839. Tel: 617-746-5829; Fax: 617-779-4571. Email: carol_gustavson@rcab.org.

Parish Services and Risk Management—Mr. JOSEPH F. MCENNESS, Dir., 66 Brooks Dr., Braintree, 02184-3839. Tel: 617-746-5740; Fax: 617-779-4510. Email: jmcenness@rcab.org.

Planning and Projects—Mr. KEVIN KILEY, Dir., 66 Brooks Dr., Braintree, 02184-3839. Tel: 617-746-5671; Fax: 617-746-5456. Email: peter_silva@rcab.org.

Planning Office for Urban Affairs—Ms. LISA ALBERGHINI, Dir., 84 State St., Boston, 02109. Tel: 617-350-8885; Fax: 617-350-8889. Email: lba@poua.org.

Health Benefit Trust, Insurance and Pension Trusts, Caritas Christi Retirement Plan—His Eminence SEAN P. CARDINAL O'MALLEY, O.F.M.Cap.; Very Rev. RICHARD M. ERIKSON, V.G.; Bro. JAMES M. PETERSON, O.F.M.Cap., J.D., J.C.L., Alternate for Cardinal O'Malley; Very Rev. JOSEPH K. RAEKE, V.F.; Mr. ROBERT GUYON; Mr. JAMES P. MCDONOUGH; Mr. WILSON D. ROGERS, Esq.; Mr. DAVID WOONTON; Ms. HELEN DRINAN; Ms. ANNA-MARIE FERRARO. Plan Administrator: Mr. JAMES M. WALSH. Plan Manager: Ms. MARY REGAN. Caritas Christi Delegate: PAMELA DONOVAN. Attorney for the Trust: LINDA SHERMAN, Consultants: JP Morgan Compensation and Benefit Strategies for the pension plans and Mercer for the health plan.

Insurance Advisory Committee—Chair: Mr. JAMES P. MCDONOUGH. Members: Mr. JOHN P. RIORDON; Mr. JAMES M. WALSH; Mr. EDWARD WAYSTACK. Counsel: Mr. WILSON D. ROGERS, Esq. Consultant: Mr. JOSEPH F. MCENNESS.

Massachusetts Catholic Self Insurance Group—President: Mr. JAMES P. MCDONOUGH. Treasurer: Mr. JAMES M. WALSH. Directors: Mr. ROBERT CANTWELL; Mr. STEVEN FISCHER; Mr. JOSEPH P. WELCH. Counsel: TIMOTHY MCCRYSTAL, Esq. Clerk: Rev. CHARLES J. HIGGINS. Administrator: Mr. JOSEPH F. MCENNESS.

Investment Advisory Committee—Chair: Deacon CHARLES I. CLOUGH; Very Rev. RICHARD M. ERIKSON, V.G.; Mr. GERALD CURTIS; Mr. JAMES J. MAHONEY; Mr. JAMES P. MCDONOUGH; Mr. THOMAS M. O'NEIL; Mr. THOMAS STAKEM; Ms. MAUREEN E. CULLINANE; Ms. KATHLEEN HEGENBART.

Audit Committee—Chair: Mr. JOHN MCCARTHY. Members: Mr. JOSEPH FINN; Mr. JAMES F. O'CONNOR.

Archdiocesan Building Commission—Chair: Mr. JAMES P. MCDONOUGH. Members: Revs. JOSEPH A. ANTONELLIS; WILLIAM D. COUGHLIN; BRIAN F. MANNING; ROBERT MCMILLAN, S.J. Consultants: Mr. RAFIK AYOUB; Mr. ROBERT A. CASSIDY; Mr. DANIEL J. DIESO; Mr. PETER J. FORTE; Mr. PETER G. SILVA.

Delegate for Religious—Sr. MARIAN BATHO, C.S.J., Sec., 66 Brooks Dr., Braintree, 02184-3839. Tel: 617-746-5637; Fax: 617-746-5754. Email: sr_marian_batho@rcab.org.

Airport Chaplaincy—Rev. RICHARD A. UFTRING, Chap., Logan International Airport, Boston, 02128. Tel: 617-567-2800. Email: fatherrichard@massport.com.

Office of Black Catholics—Ms. LORNA DESROSES, 66 Brooks Dr., Braintree, 02184-3839. Tel: 617-746-5810; Fax: 617-746-5614. Email: ldesroses@rcab.org; Ms. LINDA RUSSO. Tel: 617-746-5794. Email: lrusso@rcab.org.

Black Catholic Choir—Ms. RUTH VILLARD. Tel: 617-288-2252.

African-American—Ms. LORNA DESROSES. Tel: 617-746-5810.

Cape Verdean—Rev. EGIDIO ALVES DOS SANTOS. Tel: 617-445-7615.

Congolese—Ms. JACQUELINE KALONJI. Tel: 781-599-6662.

Eritrean—Rev. ABAYNEH GEBREMICHAEL. Tel: 508-583-1121.

Ethiopian—Rev. ABAYNEH GEBREMICHAEL. Tel: 508-583-1121.

Ghanaian—Mr. PATRICK SOSSOU. Tel: 617-323-6458.

Haitian—Rev. GABRIEL MICHEL. Tel: 617-298-0080.
Kenyan—Rev. MICHAEL KUMO. Tel: 978-459-0713.
Nigerian—Rev. ANSELM NWAGBARA. Tel: 617-445-8915.
Ugandan—Mr. HENRY NDAWULA. Tel: 781-935-0610.
Boston Catholic Directory—Rev. ROBERT M. O'GRADY, Mng. Editor, 66 Brooks Dr., Braintree, 02184-3839. Tel: 617-746-5873; Fax: 617-779-4560. Email: rmogrady@thebostonpilot.com.
Campus Ministry—Rev. RICHARD F. CLANCY, Dir., 66 Brooks Dr., Braintree, 02184-3839. Tel: 617-746-5856; Fax: 617-782-0213. Email: father_richard_clancy@rcab.org.
Boston—
Boston University—Rev. PAUL D. HELFRICH, B.H., Campus Min., 211 Bay State Rd., Boston, 02215. Tel: 617-353-3632; Fax: 617-358-2049. Email: frpaul@bu.edu. Web: bu.edu.
Emerson College—Ms. KRISTELLE ANGELLI, Campus Min., 120 Boylston St., Boston, 02116. Tel: 617-783-3924. Email: volservice@aol.com.
Emmanuel College—Rev. STEPHEN M. BOYLE, Campus Min., 400 The Fenway, Boston, 02115. Tel: 617-735-9780; Fax: 617-735-9877. Email: boyles@emmanuel.edu. Web: emmanuel.edu.
Northeastern University—Bro. JOSEPH DONOVAN, B.H., Campus Min., 68 Saint Stephen St., Boston, 02115. Tel: 617-373-8964. Email: jj.donovan@neu.edu. Web: northeastern.edu.
Babson Park—
Babson College—VACANT, Campus Min., Galvin Family Chapel, Babson Park, 02457-0310. Tel: 781-239-5623. Web: babson.edu.
Bridgewater—
Bridgewater State College—Ms. JENNIFER SPARROW, Campus Min., 122 Park Ave., Bridgewater, 02324. Tel: 508-531-1346. Email: gatorfan@gmail.com. Web: bridgew.edu.
Cambridge—
Harvard University—Rev. MICHAEL E. DREA, Campus Min., 20 Arrow St., Cambridge, 02138. Tel: 617-868-6585. Email: mdrea@stpaulparish.org. Web: harvard.edu.
Massachusetts Institute of Technology—Rev. RICHARD F. CLANCY, Campus Min., 40 Massachusetts Ave., Cambridge, 02139-4312. Tel: 617-253-2981; Fax: 617-253-3260. Email: frclancy@mit.edu.
Chestnut Hill—
Boston College—Rev. TONY PENNA, Dir., McElroy 233, Chestnut Hill, 02467-3805. Tel: 617-552-3475; Fax: 617-552-3473. Email: ministry@bc.edu. Web: bc.edu.
Dorchester—
Laboure College—Rev. JOHN J. STAGNARO, Campus Min., 2120 Dorchester Ave., Dorchester, 02124-5698. Tel: 617-296-8300; Fax: 617-296-7947. Email: jstagnaro@labourecollege.org. Web: labourecollege.org.
University of Massachusetts-Boston—Ms. JENNIFER SPARROW, Campus Min., Harbor Campus, Dorchester, 02125-3393. Tel: 617-287-5839; Fax: 617-287-5815. Email: gatorfan@gmail.com. Web: umb.edu.
Framingham—
Framingham State College—Ms. HAI OK HWANG, M.Div., Campus Min., 100 State St., Framingham, 01701-9101. Tel: 508-626-4610; Fax: 508-626-4939. Email: hhwang@frc.mass.edu. Web: frc.mass.edu.
Lowell—
University of Massachusetts-Lowell—Ms. BERNADINE KENSINGER, Campus Min., Mailing Address: Box 360, Lowell, 01853-0360. Tel: 978-934-5032. Email: bernadine_kensinger@uml.edu. Web: uml.edu.
Medford—
Tufts University—Ms. LYNN COOPER, Campus Min., Three The Green, Medford, 02155-5300. Tel: 781-391-7272; Fax: 617-571-5269. Email: lynn.cooper@tufts.edu. Web: tufts.edu.
Milton—
Curry College—VACANT, Spiritual Life Coord., Curry College, Milton, 02186. Tel: 617-333-2289; Fax: 617-333-2014. Web: curry.edu.
North Andover—
Merrimack College—Sr. MARY ELLEN DOW, S.N.D., Campus Min., Grace J. Palmisano Center, North Andover, 01845. Tel: 978-837-5450; Fax: 978-837-5004. Email: maryellendow@merrimack.edu. Web: merrimack.edu.
Salem—
Salem State College—Rev. GERARD R. MCKEON, S.J., Campus Min., Interfaith Office, 352 Lafayette St., Salem, 01970. Tel: 978-542-6074.
Waltham—
Bentley College—Rev. CLAUDE GRENACHE, A.A., B.A., S.T.B., S.T.L., Campus Min., 175 Forest St., Waltham, 02452-4705. Tel: 781-891-2754; Fax: 781-891-2839. Email: cgrenache@bentley.edu. Web: bentley.edu.
Brandeis University—Rev. WALTER H. CUENIN, Campus Min., Mail Stop 205, Waltham, 02454-9110. Tel: 781-736-3574; Fax: 781-736-3577. Email: whcuenin@hotmail.com.
Wellesley—
Wellesley College—Sr. NANCY CORCORAN, C.S.J., Campus Min., Chaplaincy Center, Wellesley, 02481. Tel: 781-283-2688. Email: ncorcora@wellesley.edu. Web: wellesley.edu.
Weston—
Regis College—Sr. ROSEMARY MULVIHILL, R.S.M., Campus Min., 235 Wellesley St., Weston, 02493-1571. Tel: 781-768-7063; Fax: 781-768-8339. Email: rosemary.mulvihill@regiscollege.edu. Web: regiscollege.edu.
Catholic Charitable Bureau of the Archdiocese of Boston, Inc.—His Eminence SEAN PATRICK CARDINAL O'MALLEY, O.F.M.Cap., Archbishop of Boston; Rev. J. BRYAN HEHIR, Pres., 51 Sleeper St., Boston, 02110. Tel: 617-482-5440; Fax: 617-451-0337. Email: info@ccab.org. Web: www.rcab.org.
Community Service Centers and Divisions— El Centro del Cardenal; Greater Boston Catholic Charities; Haitian Multi-Service Center; Laboure Center; Merrimack Valley Catholic Charities; Catholic Charities North; Catholic Charities South; Catholic Charities West; Behavioral Health Division; Child Care Division; Refugee and Immigration Services Division
Catholic Charities Senior Management—JENNIFER MENDELSOHN, CFO; Rev. PHILLIP B. EARLEY ESQ., Sec. & Gen. Counsel; DEBORAH KINCADE RAMBO, L.I.C.S.W., Vice Pres. Programs; JOSEPH BURNIEIKA, Vice Pres. External Affairs; DAVID I. WALSH, Chief Information Officer; CAROL REILLY, Dir. Human Resources; KENNETH P. BINDER, Vice Pres. Devel.; JUDITH WHITMARSH, Dir. Public Policy; BRIDGET RYAN SNELL, Dir. Mktg. & Public Rels.; BARRY VERONESI, Controller; DANIEL DORMER, Dir. Real Estate.
Greater Boston Catholic Charities—VIVIAN SOPER, L.I.C.S.W., Dir.; BETH CHAMBERS, Dir. Community Svcs. Services: Basic Needs Emergency Services, Sunset Point Camp, Youth Empowerment, Family Stabilization, Foster Grandparents, Friendly Visitor and Elderly Outreach, Healthy Families, Housing and Transitional Living, Adoption Search. 185 Columbia Rd., Dorchester, 02121. Tel: 617-506-6600; Fax: 617-474-1009.
Greater Boston Catholic Charities at Somerville—270 Washington St., Somerville, 02143. Tel: 617-625-1920; Fax: 617-629-2246.
Teen Center at St. Peter's—278 Bowdoin St., Dorchester, 02122. Tel: 617-506-6600; Fax: 617-282-3483.
Sunset Point Camp—2 10th St., Hull, 02045. Tel: 781-925-0710; Fax: 781-925-3840.
Saint Ambrose Family Shelter—Tel: 617-288-7675; Fax: 617-288-7037.
Brigid's Crossing—Tel: 978-454-0081; Fax: 978-454-0210.
Robert McBride House—Tel: 617-236-8319; Fax: 617-236-8219.
Seton Manor—Tel: 617-277-7133; Fax: 617-227-7288.
Genesis II—Tel: 617-332-9905; Fax: 617-964-4354.
Nazareth Residence for Mothers and Children—Tel: 617-541-0100; Fax: 617-541-8781.
St. Patrick's Shelter for Homeless Women—Tel: 617-628-3015; Fax: 617-629-2246.
Caritas Saint Mary Women and Children's Center—Ms. JUDITH BECKLER, Exec. Dir., 90 Cushing Ave., Boston, 02125. Tel: 617-436-8600; Fax: 617-288-8961. Email: jbeckler@smwic.org. Web: smwic.org. Region: Central.
Laboure Center—Sr. MARYADELE ROBINSON, D.C., M.S.W., Dir., 275 W. Broadway, South Boston, 02127. Tel: 617-268-9670; Fax: 617-268-3088 Services: Basic Needs Emergency Services, Pregnancy Counseling, T.E.A.M., Youth Tutoring Youth, Family Intervention, Visiting Nurse Services.
Metro Boston—
El Centro del Cardenal—DEBORAH KINCADE RAMBO, L.I.C.S.W., Interim Dir.; ROBERT HIBBARD, Dir. Adult Educ.; EDWARD CASTRO, Dir. Youth Educ.; BETH CHAMBERS, Dir. Community Svcs. Services: Basic Needs Emergency Services, Adult Basic Education, English for Employment, English for Speakers of Other Languages, Career Pathways, Alternative High School (Diploma), Pa'lante (English and Spanish GED), Parenting Support. 76 Union Park St., Boston, 02118. Tel: 617-542-9292; Fax: 617-542-6912.
Haitian Multi-Service Center—VIVIAN SOPER, L.I.C.S.W., Interim Dir. Services: Basic Needs Emergency Services, Outpatient Counseling, Sante Manman se Sante Petite, Elder Services, Adult Education ESOL Classes, Health and Human Services Management Certificate Program. 185 Columbia Rd., Dorchester, 02121. Tel: 617-506-6600; Fax: 617-474-1009.
Merrimack Valley Catholic Charities—VIRGINIA DOOCEY, Dir. Services: Basic Needs Emergency Services, Outpatient Counseling, Latino Outreach, Young Parents Program, Grandparents as Parents, Parent Aide Program, Adoption Search. 354 Merrimack St., Bldg. 1, Rm. 305, Lawrence, 01843. Tel: 978-685-5930; Fax: 978-685-0329.
Merrimack Valley Catholic Charities at Lowell—70 Lawrence St., Lowell, 01852. Tel: 978-452-1421; Fax: 978-454-9968.
Open Hand Food Pantry—16 Ashland St., Haverhill, 01830. Tel: 978-372-2828.
Food Pantry of Merrimack Valley—174 Central St., Lowell, 01852. Tel: 978-454-9946.
Merrimack Valley Young Parents Program—45 Merrimack St., Ste. 225, Lowell, 01852. Tel: 978-459-2387; Fax: 978-459-2801.
Catholic Charities North—VIRGINIA DOOCY, M.A., Dir. Services: Basic Needs Emergency Services, Education and Parenting Skills Center, Teenstart, Youthworks, The Asian Center, Office Works, Companions to the Aging, Fathers Support, Young Parents, Pregnancy Counseling, Parent Aide, Family Preservation, Healthy Families, Adoption Search.
Catholic Charities North at Lynn—55 Lynn Shore Dr., Lynn, 01902. Tel: 781-593-2312; Fax: 781-581-3270.
Catholic Charities North at Salem—280 Washington St., Salem, 01970. Tel: 978-740-6923; Fax: 978-745-1863.
Catholic Charities North at Gloucester—74 Pleasant St., Gloucester, 01930. Tel: 978-283-3055.
Healthy Families North Shore—117 Franklin St., Lynn, 01902. Tel: 781-593-4515; Fax: 781-593-4615.
Asian Center—12 Orchard St., Lynn, 01905. Tel: 781-593-2312; Fax: 781-581-3270.
Haverhill Area Healthy Families—191 Merrimack St., Haverhill, 01830. Tel: 978-521-6265.
Catholic Charities South—DAVID PHILLIPS, Dir. Services - Basic Needs Emergency Services, Nursing Assistant Training, ESOL, Youth Tracking and Mentoring, SOAR, Pregnancy Counseling, Parent Support Program, Adoption Search. 686 N. Main St., Brockton, 02301. Tel: 508-587-0815; Fax: 508-580-0837.
Nursing Assistant Home Health Aide Training Program—250 Thatcher St., Mater Dei Bldg., Brockton, 02302. Tel: 508-587-0815; Fax: 508-580-0837.
Thrifty Pilgrim Thrift Shop—36 Cordage Park Cir., Plymouth, 02360. Tel: 508-746-6133.
Catholic Charities West—BETH CHAMBERS, Dir. Community Svcs. Services: Basic Needs Emergency Services. 126 Main St., Rm. 6, Milford, 01757. Tel: 508-478-9632.
Behavioral Health - Family Counseling & Guidance Center—DEBORAH KINCADE RAMBO, Interim Dir.
Brockton Clinic—686 N. Main St., Brockton, MA 01923. Tel: 508-587-0815; Fax: 508-586-9446.
Driver Alcohol Education—686 N. Main St., Brockton, 01923. Tel: 508-587-0815.
Danvers Clinic—152 Sylvan St., Danvers, 01923. Tel: 978-774-6820; Fax: 978-777-4242.
Refugee and Immigration Services—MARJEAN PERHOT, Dir., 275 W. Broadway, South Boston, 02210. Tel: 617-451-7979; Fax: 617-629-5768.
Refugee Resettlement—275 W. Broadway, South Boston, 02210. Tel: 617-451-7979.
Refugee Employment Services—275 W. Broadway, South Boston, 02210. Tel: 617-451-7979.
Community Interpreter Services—275 W. Broadway, South Boston, 02210. Tel: 617-451-7979; Fax: 617-629-5768. Email: cis_request@ccab.org.
Immigration Legal Services—275 W. Broadway, South Boston, 02210. Tel: 617-451-7979.
Child Care—MARY ANN ANTHONY, M.S., Dir., Child Care Division Office: c/o Nazareth, 19 Saint Joseph St., Jamaica Plain, 02130. Tel: 617-524-9595; Fax: 617-832-7448.
Child Care Sites—Lynn Child Care, JANET MACDOUGALL, Dir. Child Care Svcs.; BEVERLY PRIFTI, (Peabody) - Family Child Care Dir., 37 N. Federal St., Lynn, 01905. Tel: 781-598-2759; Fax: 781-581-9740. *Peabody Child Care*, CHUCK JOHNSON, Dir. Child Care Svcs.; BEVERLY PRIFTI, (Peabody) - Family Child Care Dir.; NADINE LADA, Preschool Prog. Dir.; RALPH LAMONDA, School-Age Prog. Dir., 13 Pulaski St., Peabody, 01960. Tel: 978-532-6860; Fax: 978-531-7429. *Cambridge/Somerville/Malden*, RICHARD MURPHY, Dir. Child Care Svcs.; SHARON RICHARDSON-O'CONNELL, Family Child Care Dir., 187 Central St., Somerville, 02145. Tel: 617-623-8555; Fax: 617-623-5014. *Cambridge Children's Center*, CINDY GREEN, Dir. Child Care Svcs., 21C Walden Square Rd., Cambridge, 02140.

Tel: 617-876-0503; Fax: 617-497-6464. *Malden High Teen Parent Child Care*, DIANA MAKHLOUF, Dir. Child Care Svcs., 77 Salem St., Malden, 02148. Tel: 781-397-1556; Fax: 781-322-4309. *Malden Early Education & Learning Program*, DIANA MAKHLOUF, Prog. Dir., 77 Salem St., Malden, 02148. Tel: 781-397-1556; Fax: 781-322-4309. *Laboure Child Care Center*, PEGGY KELLY, Dir. Child Care Svcs., 275 W. Broadway, Boston, 02127. Tel: 617-464-8533; Fax: 617-269-1386. *Yawkey Konbit-Kreyol Center for Early Education & Care*, Sr. ESTHER GARCIA, S.A., Dir. Child Care Svcs., 185 Columbia Rd., Dorchester, 02121. Tel: 617-506-6600. *Nazareth Child Care Center*, PAMELA J. PENTON, Dir. Child Care Svcs., 19 Saint Joseph St., Jamaica Plain, 02130. Tel: 617-522-4040; Fax: 617-983-0460. *Caritas Saint Mary Women and Children's Center*, Ms. JUDITH BECKLER, Exec. Dir., 90 Cushing Ave., Boston, 02125. Tel: 617-436-8600; Fax: 617-288-8961. Email: jbeckler@smwic.org. Web: smwic.org.

Education—Dr. MARY GRASSA O'NEILL, Sec., Catholic School Office, 66 Brooks Dr., Braintree, 02184-3839. Tel: 617-779-3604; Fax: 617-746-5702.

Catholic School Office—66 Brooks Dr., Braintree, 02184-3839. Tel: 617-779-3601; Fax: 617-746-5702. Web: catholicschoolsboston.org.

Superintendent of Schools—Dr. MARY GRASSA O'NEILL.

Associate Superintendent for Administration/Finance—Mr. JAMES M. WALSH. Email: walsh_j@rcab.org.

Associate Superintendent for Academic Excellence—Mr. WILLIAM MCKERSIE. Email: william_mckersie@rcab.org.

Deputy Director for Academic Excellence—Mr. CHRIS FLIEGER. Email: cflieger@rcab.org.

Associate Superintendent for Government Funded Programs—Mr. JOHN SHEEHAN. Email: sheehan_j@rcab.org.

Special Assistant to the Superintendent (Interim)—Dr. IRENE MCCARTHY. Email: mccart_i@rcab.org.

Network Administrator—Ms. NANCY MORRISON. Email: nmorrison@rcab.org.

Administrative Assistants—Ms. BARBARA DEVINE. Email: devine_b@rcab.org; Ms. NINA MAYO. Email: mayo_n@rcab.org.

Executive Assistant—Mrs. ROBIN MOBLEY. Email: robin-marie_mobley@rcab.org.

Catholic Television—Rev. ROBERT P. REED, Dir., Mailing Address: 34 Chestnut St., Box 9196, Watertown, 02471-9196. Tel: 617-923-0220. Email: reed@catholictv.org. Web: catholictv.com.

Archdiocesan Cemeteries—

The Catholic Cemetery Association of the Archdiocese of Boston, Inc.—Mr. ROBERT VISCONTI, Exec. Dir., 175 Broadway, Malden, 02148-6097. Tel: 888-919-7926; 781-322-6300; Fax: 781-322-3801. Web: ccemetery.org.

Boston—Saint Francis de Sales, 313 Bunker Hill St., Boston, 02129-1826. Pastoral Region Central

Andover—Sacred Heart, Corbett Rd., Andover, 01810. Pastoral Region Merrimack

Arlington—Saint Paul, 30 Broadway, Arlington, 02179-5523. Pastoral Region North

Beverly—Saint Mary, 106 Brimbal Ave., Beverly, 01915-1936. Pastoral Region North

Cambridge—North Cambridge Catholic, 244 Rindge Ave., Cambridge, 02140-2526. Pastoral Region Central

Framingham—Saint George, 177 Cherry St., Framingham, 01706. Pastoral Region West

Gloucester—Calvary, 151 Eastern Ave., Gloucester, 01930. Pastoral Region North. Oak Hill, 55 Poplar St., Gloucester, 01930. Pastoral Region North

Haverhill—Saint James, 360 Primrose St., Haverhill, 01830-3198. Pastoral Region Merrimack. Saint Joseph, 892 Hilldale Ave., Haverhill, 01830. Pastoral Region Merrimack. St. Patrick, 395 N. Broadway, Haverhill, 01830. Pastoral Region Merrimack

Lynn—Saint Jean, 134 Broadway, Lynn, 01904-1868. Pastoral Region North. Saint Joseph, 134 Broadway, Lynn, 01904-1868. Pastoral Region North. Saint Mary, 190 Lynnfield St., Lynn, 01904. Pastoral Region North

Malden—Holy Cross, 175 Broadway, Malden, 02148-6097. Pastoral Region North. Saint Mary, 304 Fellsway E., Malden, 02148. Pastoral Region North

Marblehead—Star of the Sea, 140 Lafayette St., Marblehead, 01947. Pastoral Region North

Marlborough—Immaculate Conception, Beach St., Marlborough, 01752. Pastoral Region West. Saint Mary, Beach St., Marlborough, 01752. Pastoral Region West

Salem—Saint Mary, 226 North St., Salem, 01970-1645. Pastoral Region North

Stoneham—Saint Patrick, 120 Elm St., Stoneham, 02180. Pastoral Region North

Waltham—Calvary, 250 High St., Waltham, 02154-5914. Pastoral Region West

Watertown—Catholic Mount Auburn, 64 Cottage St., Watertown, 02472-1516. Pastoral Region West. Saint Patrick, Belmont St., Watertown, 02472. Pastoral Region West

Winchester—Calvary, 686 Washington St., Winchester, 01890. Pastoral Region North

Boston—Saint Augustine, 225 Dorchester Ave., Boston, 02127. Tel: 617-268-1230. Parish: Saint Monica and Saint Augustine Parish. Region: Central

Abington—Saint Patrick, 455 Plymouth St., Abington, 02351. Tel: 781-982-8974. Parish: Saint Bridget Parish. Region: South

Amesbury—Saint Joseph, 6 Allen's Court, Amesbury, 01913. Tel: 978-388-0330. Parish: Holy Family Parish. Region: Merrimack

Avon—Saint Michael, 87 N. Main St., Avon, 02322. Tel: 508-586-7210. Parish: Saint Michael Parish. Region: South

Ayer—Saint Mary, 31 Shirley St., Ayer, 01432. Tel: 978-772-2414. Parish: Saint Mary Parish. Region: Merrimack

Bridgewater—Saint Thomas Aquinas, 103 Center St., Bridgewater, 02324. Tel: 508-697-9528. Parish: Saint Thomas Aquinas Parish. Region: South

Brockton—Calvary, 331 Main St., Brockton, 02301. Tel: 508-586-4840 Parish: Saint Patrick Parish. Region: South. *Saint Patrick, 331 Main St., Brockton, 02301*. Tel: 508-586-4840. Parish: Saint Patrick Parish. Region: South

Canton—Saint Mary, 700 Washington St., Canton, 02021. Tel: 781-828-0090. Parish: Saint John the Evangelist Parish. Region: South

Concord—Saint Bernard, 70 Monument Square, Concord, 01742. Tel: 978-369-7442. Parish: Holy Family Parish. Region: West

Danvers—Annunciation, 24 Conant St., Danvers, 01935. Tel: 978-774-0340 Parish: Saint Mary of the Annunciation Parish. Region: West. *Saint Mary, 24 Conant St., Danvers, 01935*. Tel: 978-774-0340. Parish: Saint Mary of the Annunciation Parish. Region: West

Dedham—Saint Mary, 420 High St., Dedham, 02026. Tel: 781-326-0550. Parish: Saint Mary Parish. Region: West

Foxborough—Saint Mary, 58 Carpenter St., Foxboro, 02035. Tel: 508-543-7726. Parish: Saint Mary Parish. Region: West

Framingham—Saint Stephen, 221 Concord St., Framingham, 01702. Tel: 508-875-4788 Parish: Saint Stephen Parish. Region: West. *Saint Tarcisius, Winthrop St., Framingham, 01702*. Tel: 508-875-8623 Parish: Saint Tarcisius Parish. Region: West.

Franklin—Saint Mary, Beaver St., Franklin, 02038. Tel: 508-528-6826. Parish: Saint Mary Parish. Region: West

Hingham—Saint Paul, 147 North St., Hingham, 02043. Tel: 781-749-0587. Parish: Saint Paul Parish. Region: South

Holliston—Saint Mary, Washington St., Holliston, 01746. Tel: 508-429-4427. Parish: Saint Mary Parish. Region: West

Hopkinton—Saint John the Evangelist, 20 Church St., Hopkinton, 01748. Tel: 508-435-3313. Parish: Saint John the Evangelist Parish. Region: West

Kingston—Saint Joseph, Elm St., Kingston, 02364. Tel: 781-585-6679. Parish: Saint Joseph Parish. Region: South

Lawrence—Saint Mary, 29 Barker St., Lawrence, 01841. Tel: 978-682-8181. Parish: Our Lady of Good Counsel Parish. Region: Merrimack

Lowell—Holy Trinity, 140 Boston Rd., Lowell, 01852. Tel: 978-452-2564 Parish: Holy Trinity Parish. Region: Merrimack. *Saint Mary, 384 Stevens St., Lowell, 01851*. Tel: 978-458-8464 Parish: Saint Margaret Parish. Region: Merrimack. *Saint Patrick, 384 Stevens St., Lowell, 01851*. Tel: 978-458-8464 Parish: Saint Margaret Parish. Region: Merrimack.

Maynard—Saint Bridget, One Percival St., Maynard, 01754. Tel: 978-897-2171. Parish: Saint Bridget Parish. Region: West

Middleborough—Saint Mary, Wood St., Middleboro, 02346. Tel: 508-947-0444. Parish: Sacred Heart Parish. Region: South

Needham—Saint Mary, 270 Elliot St., Newton, 02462. Tel: 781-235-1841. Parish: Mary Immaculate of Lourdes Parish. Region: West

Newburyport—Saint Mary, Green St., Newburyport, 01950. Tel: 978-462-2724. Parish: Immaculate Conception Parish. Region: Merrimack

North Andover—Holy Sepulchre, 114 S. Broadway, Lawrence, 01843. Tel: 978-683-9416. Parish: Saint Patrick Parish. Region: Merrimack

Pepperell—Saint Joseph, Jersey St., Pepperell, 01463. Tel: 978-433-9725. Parish: Saint Joseph Parish. Region: Merrimack

Plymouth—Saint Joseph, 86 Court St., Plymouth, 02360. Tel: 508-746-0663. Parish: Saint Peter Parish. Region: South

Quincy—Saint Mary, 95 Crescent St., Quincy, 02169. Tel: 617-773-0120. Parish: Saint Mary Parish. Region: South

Randolph—Saint Mary, 211 N. Main St., Randolph, 02368. Tel: 781-961-9323. Parish: Saint Mary Parish. Region: South

Rockland—Holy Family, 403 Union St., Rockland, 02370. Tel: 781-878-2306. Parish: Holy Family Parish. Region: South

Shirley—Saint Anthony of Padua, 12 Phoenix St., Shirley, 01464. Tel: 978-425-4588. Parish: Saint Anthony of Padua Parish. Region: Merrimack

Stoughton—Holy Sepulchre, Central St., Stoughton, 02072. Tel: 781-344-2073. Parish: Immaculate Conception Parish. Region: South

Walpole—Saint Francis, Diamond St., Walpole, 02081. Tel: 508-668-4700. Parish: Blessed Sacrament Parish. Region: West

Wayland—Saint Zepherin, 99 Main St., Wayland, 01778. Tel: 508-653-8013. Parish: Saint Zepherin Parish. Region: West

Westford—Saint Catherine of Alexandria, 107 N. Main St., Westford, 01886. Tel: 978-692-6353. Parish: Saint Catherine of Alexandria Parish. Region: Merrimack

Weymouth—Saint Francis Xavier, 234 Pleasant St., Weymouth, 02190. Tel: 781-337-3144. Parish: Saint Francis Xavier Parish. Region: South

Whitman—Saint James, School St., Whitman, 02382. Tel: 781-447-4421. Parish: Holy Ghost Parish. Region: South

Private Cemeteries—

Boston—Mount Benedict Cemetery, 409 Corey St., West Roxbury, 02132. Tel: 617-323-8389 Owner: Boston Catholic Cemetery Association. Region: Central. *Mount Calvary Cemetery, 366 Cummins Hwy., Roslindale, 02131*. Tel: 617-325-0883 Owner: Boston Catholic Cemetery Association. Region: Central. *New Calvary Cemetery, 800 Harvard St., Mattapan, 02126*. Tel: 617-296-2339 Owner: Boston Catholic Cemetery Association. Region: Central. *Saint Joseph Cemetery, 990 Lagrange St., West Roxbury, 02132*. Tel: 617-327-1010 Owner: Holyhood Cemetery Association. Region: Central. *Saint Mary Cemetery, Bernard St., Dorchester, 02124*. Tel: 617-325-6830 Owner: Boston Catholic Cemetery Association. Region: Central. *Saint Michael Cemetery, 500 Canterbury St., Forest Hills, 02131*. Tel: 617-524-1036. Owner: Saint Michael Cemetery Association. Region: Central

Brookline—Holyhood Cemetery, Heath St., Brookline, 02467. Tel: 617-327-1010. Owner: Holyhood Cemetery Association. Region: Central.

Chelmsford—Saint Joseph Cemetery, 96 Riverneck Rd., Chelmsford, 01824-2941. Tel: 978-458-4851. Owner: Saint Joseph Cemetery, Inc. Region: Merrimack.

Charismatic Renewal—Mr. VINCENT CERASUOLO, Dir. & Liaison, 30 Pond St., Waltham, 02451-4514. Tel: 781-891-3592; Fax: 781-874-9467. Email: staff@crsboston.org.

Chrism—Ms. CELIA SIROIS, Coord., 236 Pleasant St., Weymouth, 02190-2507. Tel: 781-331-5194; Fax: 781-337-3225.

Clergy Services Group—66 Brooks Dr., Braintree, 02184-3839.

Clergy Personnel—Rev. ROBERT J. DEEHAN, Dir. Tel: 617-779-3685; Fax: 617-746-5614. Email: reverend_robert_deehan@rcab.org; Deacon PATRICK E. GUERRINI, Asst. Dir. Tel: 617-746-5658; Fax: 617-746-5498. Email: deacon_patrick_guerrini@rcab.org.

Pastoral Care of Clergy—Very Rev. EDWIN D. CONDON, Vicar (Retired). Tel: 617-746-5601; Fax: 617-779-4570. Email: edwinduxb@aol.com.

Pastoral Care of Priests and Clergy Fund—Rev. JAMES A. FLAVIN, Dir. Tel: 617-746-5928; Fax: 617-779-4576. Email: reverendjames_flavin@rcab.org.

Priests' Recovery Program—Rev. BRIAN M. CLARY, Dir., 5 Linden Pl., Brookline, 02445-7311. Tel: 617-473-0444; Fax: 617-734-3001. Email: frbrian2002@yahoo.com.

Senior Priests—Rev. JAMES L. MCCUNE, Chap. (Retired), 60 William Cardinal O'Connell Way, Boston, 02114-2729. Tel: 617-723-3976; Fax: 617-523-0092.

Support and Ongoing Formation—Rev. WILLIAM T. KELLY, Dir. Tel: 617-746-5601; Fax: 617-779-4570. Email: reverendwilliam_kelly@rcab.org; Deacon PATRICK E. GUERRINI, Asst. Dir. Tel: 617-746-5658; Fax: 617-746-5614. Email: deacon_patrick_guerrini@rcab.org.

Clergy Personnel Board—Ex Officio: Very Revs. RICHARD M. ERIKSON, V.G.; THOMAS S. FOLEY, V.F.; Rev. ROBERT J. DEEHAN. Designated: Rev. Msgr. DENNIS F. SHEEHAN; Rev. JOHN E. MACINNIS. Elected: Rev. Msgrs. PETER V. CONLEY, V.F., Block I; GEORGE F. CARLSON, Block II; Revs. JOHN P. TACKNEY, Block III; WILLIAM B. PALARDY, Ph.D., Block IV; Very Rev. KEVIN M. SEPE, V.F., Block V; Rev. GEORGE C. HINES, Block VI.

Communications and Public Affairs—Mr. TERRENCE C. DONILON, Sec., 66 Brooks Dr., Braintree, 02184-3839. Tel: 617-746-5775; Fax: 617-779-4572. Email: tdonilon@rcab.org.

Cor Unum Meal Center—Ms. DIANE JARVIS, Dir., 191 Salem St., Lawrence, 01843-1427. Tel: 978-688-8900; Fax: 978-681-5808. Email: corunummealcenter@comcast.net. Web: www.corunummealcenter.org.

Courage—Rev. JOHN M. SULLIVAN, Spiritual Dir., 46 Myrtle St., Melrose, 02176-3827. Tel: 781-665-0152; Fax: 781-665-2750. Email: info@bostoncourage.org.

Cursillo—Rev. JOHN E. SASSANI, Spiritual Dir., 66 Brooks Dr., Braintree, 02184-3839. Tel: 617-779-3640; Fax: 617-779-4570. Email: jsassani@ourladys.com; Ms. MARYANN MCLAUGHLIN, Lay Dir. Tel: 617-779-3640; Fax: 617-779-4570. Email: maryann_mclaughlin@rcab.org.

Office of the Deaf Apostolate—66 Brooks Dr., Braintree, 02184-3839. Tel: 617-997-8025; Fax: 617-746-5614. Web: www.deafcatholic.org.

Director—Rev. JEREMY P. ST. MARTIN. Tel: 617-746-5645 (Work); 617-997-8025 (Text); 774-217-3000 (Video Phone). Email: frjeremy@deafcatholic.org.

Assistant Director of the Office of the Deaf Apostolate—Rev. SHAWN P. CAREY. Email: frshawn@deafcatholic.org; frshawn@sprint.blackberry.net (Emergency)Tel: 866-572-8386 (Video Phone); 781-267-7109 (Video Phone).

Interpreters / Coordinators—Mrs. JENNY CORBIN. Tel: 617-746-5815. Email: jenny.corbin@deafcatholic.org; Miss CELIA MOJICA. Tel: 617-746-5815 (Work). Email: mojica.celia@deafcatholic.org.

Assistant Coordinator of the Deaf Senior Wellness Program—Mrs. MARY BROOKS. Tel: 617-746-5815 (Work). Email: mary.k.brooks@deafcatholic.org. Mass in American Sign Language and Deaf Senior Wellness Program take place at Sacred Heart Parish, 1317 Centre St., Newton, MA 02459. Tel: 617-969-2248.

American Sign—

Bellingham—Saint Blaise. Tel: 508-966-1258.

Boston—Cathedral of the Holy Cross. Tel: 617-542-5682.

Danvers—New England Home for the Deaf. Tel: 978-774-0445.

Hopkington—Saint John the Evangelist. Tel: 508-435-3313.

Middleborough—Sacred Heart. Tel: 508-947-0444.

Newton—Sacred Heart. Tel: 617-969-2248.

Stoneham—Saint Patrick. Tel: 781-438-0960.

Whitman—Holy Ghost. Tel: 781-447-4421.

Disabilities—Ms. KAREN MURRAY, 66 Brooks Dr., Braintree, 02184-3839. Tel: 617-746-5679; Fax: 617-779-4570. Email: kmurray@rcab.org.

Divine Worship and Spiritual Life—66 Brooks Dr., Braintree, 02184-3839. Tel: 617-779-3640; Fax: 617-779-4570. Rev. JONATHAN M. GASPAR, Dir. Divine Worship. Tel: 617-746-5880. Email: jgaspar@rcab.org.

Ecumenical and Interreligious Affairs—Rev. EDWARD F. O'FLAHERTY, S.J., Dir., 66 Brooks Dr., Braintree, 02184-3839. Tel: 617-435-0019; Fax: 617-783-5642.

EnCourage—Rev. ALBERT A. SYLVIA, Spiritual Dir., 558 South Ave., Weston, 02493. Tel: 781-899-5500; Fax: 781-899-9057.

Ethnic Ministries—Sr. MARY CORRIPIO, S.N.D., Dir., 66 Brooks Dr., Braintree, 02184-3839. Tel: 617-746-5818; Fax: 617-746-5614. Email: mcorripio@rcab.org; Ms. LINDA RUSSO. Tel: 617-746-5794. Email: lrusso@rcab.org.

Brazilian—Rev. EDUARDO MARQUES. Tel: 617-783-2121.

Cambodian—Deacon AN ROS. Tel: 978-459-0561.

Chinese—Ms. LAURA CHAN. Tel: 781-438-4772.

Filipino—Rev. CELESTINO V. PASCUAL. Tel: 617-726-1947.

French—Office of Cultural Diversity. Tel: 617-746-5818.

German—Rev. HARRY J. KAUFMAN. Tel: 617-268-2122.

Hmong—Dr. PAULE VERDET. Tel: 617-965-2499.

Indian—Ms. DEEPA PRABHU. Tel: 781-724-5179.

Irish—Sr. MARGUERITE KELLY, M.F.I.C. Tel: 617-479-7404.

Italian—Rev. ANTONIO NARDOIANNI, O.F.M. Tel: 617-523-2110.

Japanese—Office of Cultural Diversity. Tel: 617-746-5794.

Korean—Rev. DOMINIC JUNG, C.PP.S. Tel: 617-244-9685.

Lithuanian—Rev. STEPHAN ZUKAS. Tel: 617-268-0353.

Polish—Rev. ANDRZEJ URBANIAK, O.F.M.Conv. Tel: 617-268-4355.

Portuguese—Very Rev. WALTER A. CARREIRO, V.F. Tel: 617-547-5593.

Vietnamese—Rev. HOANG V. LE. Tel: 617-265-5302.

Health Care—

Caritas Christi Health Care Corporation—Dr. RALPH DE LA TORRE, M.D., Pres., 736 Cambridge St., Boston, 02135-2997. Tel: 617-789-5050; Fax: 617-789-2124. Email: patricia.prichette@caritaschristi.org. Web: caritaschristi.org.

Hispanic Apostolate—Most Rev. EMILIO S. ALLUE, S.D.B., Vicar Gen., 66 Brooks Dr., Braintree, 02184-3839. Tel: 617-746-5916; Fax: 617-746-5614. Email: bishop_emilio@rcab.org; Mr. FERNANDO FERNANDEZ-ARELLANO, Coord. Programs, 66 Brooks Dr., Braintree, 02184-3839. Tel: 617-746-5816; Fax: 617-746-5614. Email: fernando_fernandez@rcab.org.

Boston—Cathedral of the Holy Cross. Tel: 617-542-5682. *Saint Anthony Shrine*. Tel: 617-542-6440. *Saint Francis Chapel*. Tel: 617-437-7117.

Hispanic Ministry Sites—

Brighton—Saint Columbkille. Tel: 617-782-5774.

Charlestown—Saint Mary-Saint Catherine of Siena. Tel: 617-242-4664.

Dorchester—Holy Family. Tel: 617-445-9553. *Saint Ambrose*. Tel: 617-265-5302. *Saint Christopher*. Tel: 617-436-7273.

East Boston—Madonna Queen Shrine. Tel: 617-569-2100. *Most Holy Redeemer*. Tel: 617-567-3227. *Our Lady of the Assumption*. Tel: 617-567-1223.

Jamaica Plain—Our Lady of Lourdes. Tel: 617-524-0434. *Saint Thomas Aquinas*. Tel: 617-524-0240.

Roslindale—Sacred Heart. Tel: 617-325-3322.

Roxbury—Our Lady of Perpetual Help-Mission Church. Tel: 617-445-2600. *Saint Mary of the Angels*. Tel: 617-445-1524. *Saint Patrick*. Tel: 617-445-7645.

South Boston—Saint Monica and Saint Augustine. Tel: 617-268-1230.

Brockton—Saint Patrick. Tel: 508-586-4840.

Cambridge—Saint Mary of the Annunciation. Tel: 617-547-0120.

Chelsea—Saint Rose of Lima. Tel: 617-889-2774.

Everett—Saint Anthony of Padua. Tel: 617-387-0310. *Immaculate Conception*. Tel: 617-389-5660.

Framingham—Saint Stephen. Tel: 508-875-4788.

Haverhill—Saint James. Tel: 978-372-8537.

Lawrence—Corpus Christi. Tel: 978-685-1711. *Saint Mary of the Assumption*. Tel: 978-685-1111. *Saint Patrick*. Tel: 978-683-9416.

Lowell—Saint Patrick. Tel: 978-459-0561.

Lynn—Saint Joseph. Tel: 781-599-7040.

Marlborough—Immaculate Conception. Tel: 508-485-0016.

Newton—Saint Ignatius Loyola Church. Tel: 617-552-6100.

Peabody—Saint John the Baptist. Tel: 978-531-0002.

Revere—Immaculate Conception. Tel: 781-289-0735.

Salem—Immaculate Conception. Tel: 978-745-6303.

Somerville—Saint Ann. Tel: 617-625-1904. *Saint Benedict*. Tel: 617-625-0029.

Waltham—Saint Mary. Tel: 781-891-1730.

Woburn—Saint Charles Borromeo. Tel: 781-933-0300.

Holy Name Societies—Mr. ROBERT QUAGAN, 35 Cass St., Boston, 02132-4411. Tel: 617-325-5905. Email: rquagan@comcast.net.

Hospital Chaplain Ministry—Deacon JAMES F. GREER, Dir., 66 Brooks Dr., Braintree, 02184-3839. Tel: 617-746-5843; Fax: 617-746-5754.

Boston—

Arbour Hospital—49 Robinwood Ave., Boston, 02130. Tel: 617-522-4400. Pastoral Care: Our Lady of Lourdes, Jamaica Plain

Beth Israel Deaconess Medical Center—330 Brookline Ave., Boston, 02215. Tel: 617-667-4205. Pastoral Care: Rev. BRUCE TEAGUE.

Boston Medical Center - Harrison Avenue Campus—818 Harrison Ave., Boston, 02118. Tel: 617-414-7560. Pastoral Care: Sr. MARYANNE RUZZO, S.C.

Boston Medical Center - Newton Street Campus—One Medical Center Pl., Boston, 02118-2393. Tel: 617-638-6851. Pastoral Care: Rev. ROGER BOURGEA, S.M.

Brigham and Women's Hospital—75 Francis St., Boston, 02115-6195. Tel: 617-732-7480; Fax: 617-232-2746. Pastoral Care: Sr. KATHLEEN GALLIVAN, S.N.D.

Caritas Carney Hospital—2100 Dorchester St., Boston, 02124-5666. Tel: 617-296-4000; Fax: 617-296-9513. Pastoral Care: Sr. PAULA TINLIN, S.N.D.

Caritas Saint Elizabeth Medical Center—736 Cambridge St., Boston, 02135-2997. Tel: 617-789-3228; Fax: 617-789-2281. Pastoral Care: Ms. CHERYL AMRICH.

Children's Hospital—300 Longwood Ave., Boston, 02115. Tel: 617-355-4775. Pastoral Care: Ms. MARIA CATALDO-CUNNIFF.

Dana Farber Cancer Institute—44 Binney St., Boston, 02115. Tel: 617-632-3000.

Faulkner Hospital—1153 Centre St., Boston, 02130. Tel: 617-983-7000, Ext. 1556. Pastoral Care: Ms. REGINA CLARE GAVIN.

Franciscan Children's Hospital—30 Warren St., Boston, 02135. Tel: 617-779-1645. Pastoral Care: Sr. JEAN MULLOY, C.S.J.

Hebrew Rehabilitation Center—1200 Centre St., Boston, 02131. Tel: 617-361-5249. Pastoral Care: Sacred Heart, Roslindale and Holy Name, West Roxbury

Jewish Memorial Hospital—59 Townsend St., Boston, 02119. Tel: 617-989-8315. Pastoral Care: Saint Patrick and Saint Mary of the Angels, Roxbury

Kindred Hospital Boston—1515 Commonwealth Ave., Brighton, 02135. Tel: 617-254-1100. Pastoral Care: Saint Columbkille, Brighton

Lemuel Shattuck Hospital—170 Morton St., Boston, 02130. Tel: 617-522-8110. Pastoral Care: Our Lady of Lourdes, Jamaica Plain

Massachusetts General Hospital—55 Fruit St., Boston, 02114. Tel: 617-724-3226; Fax: 617-726-2220. Pastoral Care: Mr. MICHAEL MCELHINNY.

New England Baptist Hospital—91 Parker Hill Ave., Boston, 02120. Tel: 617-754-5160. Pastoral Care: Rev. ANDREW ALBERT, S.M.

New England Medical Center—750 Washington St., Boston, 02111. Tel: 617-636-5896. Pastoral Care: Rev. JAMES SHAUGHNESSEY, S.J.

Shriners Burns Institute—51 Blossom St., Boston, 02114. Tel: 617-722-3000. Pastoral Care: Saint Joseph and Saint Leonard of Port Maurice, Boston

Spaulding Rehabilitation Hospital—125 Nashua St., Boston, 02114-1198. Tel: 617-572-2780; Fax: 617-573-2419. Pastoral Care: Ms. JOAN HORGAN.

Veterans Administration Health Care System - West Roxbury—1400 VRW Pkwy., Boston, 02132. Tel: 617-323-7700. Pastoral Care: Rev. CLAUDIUS NOWINSKI, M.S.

Veterans Administration Health Care System - Jamaica Plain—150 S. Huntington Ave., Boston, 02130. Tel: 857-364-5065. Pastoral Care: Rev. PHILIP SALOIS, M.S.

Ayer—

Nashoba Valley Medical Center—200 Groton St., Ayer, 01432. Tel: 978-772-2414. Pastoral Care: Saint Constance Gagnon, S.U.S.C.

Bedford—

Veterans Administration Health Care System - Bedford—200 Spring Rd., Bedford, 01730. Tel: 781-687-2384. Pastoral Care: Rev. SEBASTIAN A. UGOCHUKWU.

Belmont—

McLean Hospital—115 Mill St., Belmont, 02178. Tel: 617-855-2000. Pastoral Care: Saint Luke, Belmont and local parishes

Beverly—

Beverly Hospital—75 Herrick St., Beverly, 01915. Tel: 978-922-3000, Ext. 2790. Pastoral Care: Mr. JOHN KWIATEK.

Braintree—

Health South Braintree Hospital—250 Pond St., Braintree, 02184. Tel: 781-348-2500. Pastoral Care: Saint Francis of Assisi

Northeast Specialty Hospital—2001 Washington St., Braintree, 02185. Tel: 781-952-2254. Pastoral Care: Saint Clare, Braintree

Brockton—

Brockton Hospital—680 Centre St., Brockton, 02302. Tel: 508-941-7000, Ext. 2550. Pastoral Care: Sr. BARBARA HARRINGTON, O.P.

Caritas Good Samaritan Medical Center—235 N. Pearl St., Brockton, 02301. Tel: 508-427-2376. Pastoral Care: Rev. RICHARD W. VISBISKY.

McLean Hospital Brockton—940 Belmont St., Brockton, 02402. Tel: 508-894-8420. Pastoral Care: Our Lady of Lourdes, Brockton

Veterans Administration Health Care System - Brockton—930 Belmont St., Brockton, 02402. Tel: 508-583-4500. Pastoral Care: Rev. HENRY P. NICHOLS.

Brookline—

Bournewood Health System—300 South St., Brookline, 02146. Tel: 617-469-0300. Pastoral Care: Saint Mary of the Assumption, Brookline

Burlington—

Lahey Clinic—41 Mall Rd., Burlington, 01805. Tel: 781-744-8800. Pastoral Care: Mr. WILLIAM W. HOUGHTON.

Cambridge—
Cambridge Hospital—1493 Cambridge St., Cambridge, 02139. Tel: 617-665-1000. Pastoral Care: Local Cambridge Parishes
Mount Auburn Hospital—330 Mt. Auburn St., Cambridge, 02238. Tel: 617-499-5206. Pastoral Care: Ms. MARY HARRISON.
Youville Lifecare—1575 Cambridge St., Cambridge, 02138-4398. Tel: 617-758-5495. Pastoral Care: Mr. ROBERT SHORT.
Canton—
Massachusetts Hospital School—Randloph St., Canton, 02121. Tel: 781-828-2440. Pastoral Care: Saint Gerard Mejella, Canton
Chelsea—
Quigley Memorial Hospital—91 Crest St., Chelsea, 02150. Tel: 617-889-7146. Pastoral Care: Rev. PATRICK F. HEALY, O.M.I.
Concord—
Emerson Hospital—Rte. 2 ORNAC, Box 9120, Concord, 01742-9120. Tel: 978-287-3015. Pastoral Care: Ms. GEORGIA GOJMERAC-LEINER.
Everett—
Whidden Memorial Hospital—103 Garland St., Everett, 02149. Tel: 617-381-7202. Pastoral Care: Sr. THERESA CARLOW, S.N.D.
Framingham—
Metro West Medical Center - Framingham Campus—115 Lincoln St., Framingham, 01701-9167. Tel: 508-383-1007. Pastoral Care: Sr. URSULA TISDALL, O.S.F.
Gloucester—
Addison Gilbert Hospital—298 Washington St., Gloucester, 01930. Tel: 978-283-4000. Pastoral Care: Holy Family and Our Lady of Good Voyage, Gloucester
Haverhill—
Merrimack Valley Hospital—140 Lincoln Ave., Haverhill, 01830. Tel: 978-374-2000. Pastoral Care: Saint John the Baptist, Haverhill and local parishes
Whittier Rehabilitation Hospital—76 Summer St., Haverhill, 01830. Tel: 978-372-8000. Pastoral Care: Saint James, Haverhill
Lawrence—
Lawrence General Hospital—One General St., Lawrence, 01842. Tel: 978-683-4000. Pastoral Care: Ms. ARLENE LARSEN.
Lowell—
Lowell General Hospital—295 Varnum Ave., Lowell, 01854. Tel: 978-937-6418. Pastoral Care: Mrs. CAROL GAGNE.
Saints Memorial Medical Center—One Hospital Dr., Lowell, 01852. Tel: 978-458-1411; Fax: 978-934-8526. Pastoral Care: Ms. CATHERINE SEELEY.
Lynn—
Northshore Medical Center - Lynn—500 Lynnfield St., Lynn, 01904. Tel: 781-477-3955. Pastoral Care: Rev. ROBERT G. LABRIE.
Marlborough—
Marlborough Hospital—155 Union St., Marlborough, 01752. Tel: 508-958-3536. Pastoral Care: Immaculate Conception, Marlborough and local parishes
Medford—
Lawrence Memorial Hospital—170 Governor's Ave., Medford, 02155. Tel: 781-306-6665. Pastoral Care: Ms. ROSEMARY BURKE.
Melrose—
Melrose Wakefield Hospital—585 Lebanon St., Melrose, 02176. Tel: 781-979-3011. Pastoral Care: Rev. WILLIAM F. LUCEY (Retired).
Methuen—
Caritas Holy Family Medical Center—70 East St., Methuen, 01844. Tel: 978-687-0156. Pastoral Care: Mr. WILLIAM SWEENEY JR.
Milton—
Milton Hospital—92 Highland St., Milton, 02186. Tel: 617-696-4600, Ext. 1801. Pastoral Care: Ms. VIRGINIA ALLEN.
Natick—
Metro West Medical Center - Natick Campus—67 Union St., Natick, 01760. Tel: 508-650-7331. Pastoral Care: Saint Patrick, Natick and local parishes
Needham—
Beth Israel Deaconess Hospital - Needham—148 Chestnut St., Needham, 02192. Tel: 781-453-3000. Pastoral Care: Needham Parishes
Newburyport—
Anna Jacques Hospital—25 Highland Ave., Newburyport, 01950. Tel: 978-463-1000. Pastoral Care: Immaculate Conception, Newburyport and local parishes
Newton—
Newton Wellesley Hospital—2014 Washington St., Newton, 02462. Tel: 617-243-6634. Pastoral Care: Ms. ANN LOMUTO.
Norwood—
Caritas Norwood Hospital—800 Washington St., Norwood, 02062. Tel: 781-278-6045. Pastoral Care: Bro. GERALD PACIELLO, O.F.M.
Peabody—
Kindred Hospital Northshore—15 King St., Peabody, 01960. Tel: 978-531-2900. Pastoral Care: Saint John the Baptist, Peabody
Plymouth—
Jordan Hospital—275 Sandwich St., Plymouth, 02360. Tel: 508-830-2626. Pastoral Care: Ms. KAREN FARRELL.
Quincy—
Quincy Hospital—114 Whitwell St., Quincy, 02169. Tel: 617-376-5501. Pastoral Care: Ms. KATHLEEN HALLEE.
Salem—
Northshore Medical Center Salem—57 Highland Ave., Salem, 01970. Tel: 978-741-1215, Ext. 7698. Pastoral Care: Ms. JANE KORINS.
Somerville—
Somerville Hospital—230 Highland Ave., Somerville, 02143. Tel: 617-666-4400. Pastoral Care: Saint Catherine of Genoa, Somerville and local parishes
Stoughton—
New England Sinai Hospital—150 York St., Stoughton, 02072. Tel: 617-344-0600; Fax: 617-297-1302. Pastoral Care: Sr. ELLEN REILLY, S.N.D.
Tewksbury—
Tewksbury Hospital—365 East St., Tewksbury, 01876. Tel: 978-851-7321, Ext. 2889. Pastoral Care: Ms. PATRICIA HARDY.
Waltham—
Fernald Development Center—200 Trapelo Rd., Waltham, 02452-6302. Tel: 781-894-3600. Pastoral Care: Rev. WILLIAM T. LEONARD.
Westwood—
Westwood Lodge Hospital—45 Clapboardtree St., Westwood, 02090. Tel: 781-762-7764. Pastoral Care: Saint Margaret Mary, Westwood
Weymouth—
South Shore Hospital—55 Fogg Rd., Weymouth, 02190. Tel: 781-340-8589. Pastoral Care: Deacon CHARLES P. WEBB.
Winchester—
Winchester Hospital—41 Highland Ave., Winchester, 01890. Tel: 781-756-2295. Pastoral Care: Ms. MARY BETH MORAN.
Woburn—
Health South - New England Rehabilitation Hospital—Two Rehabilitation Way, Woburn, 01801. Tel: 781-935-5050. Pastoral Care: Saint Barbara, Woburn
Wrentham—
Wrentham Development Center—131 Emerald St., Wrentham, 02093. Tel: 508-384-3114. Pastoral Care: Saint Mary, Wrentham

Institutional Advancement—Mr. SCOT LANDRY, Sec. Advancement & Chief Devel. Officer, 66 Brooks Dr., Braintree, 02184-3839. Tel: 617-779-3700; Fax: 617-779-3731. Email: slandry@rcab.org; Mr. DOM BETTINELLI, Mgr. Gift Processing & Donor Rels. Tel: 617-779-3708; Fax: 617-779-3721. Email: dbettinelli@rcab.org; Ms. JUDY CHOHARIS, Senior Gifts Processor. Tel: 617-779-3707; Fax: 617-779-3721. Email: jchoharis@rcab.org; Mr. DAMIEN DEVASTO, Chief Leadership Giving Officer. Tel: 617-779-3703; Fax: 617-779-3721. Email: ddevasto@rcab.org; Mr. RICHARD ELY, Dir. Gift Planning & Stewardship. Tel: 617-779-3702; Fax: 617-779-3721. Email: rely@rcab.org; Mr. PATRICK GIPSON, Catholic Appeal Mgr. Tel: 617-779-3711; Fax: 617-779-3721. Email: pgipson@rcab.org; Mr. JOHN IRWIN, Leadership Giving Officer. Tel: 617-779-3712; Fax: 617-779-3721. Email: jirwin@rcab.org; Ms. ANNA JOHNSON, Gift Processing Assoc. Tel: 617-779-3705; Fax: 617-779-3721. Email: ajohnson@rcab.org; Ms. MARY JO KRIZ, Sr. Oper. Assoc. & Parish Stewardship Coord. Tel: 617-779-3706; Fax: 617-779-3731. Email: mkriz@rcab.org; Mr. GEORGE MARTELL, Dir. Digital Communications & New Media. Tel: 617-779-3705; Fax: 617-779-3721. Email: gmartell@rcab.org; Mr. TIMOTHY REGELE, Oper. Assoc. Tel: 617-779-3709; Fax: 617-779-3731. Email: tregele@rcab.org.

The Catholic Foundation Board of Trustees—Mr. CRAIG B. GIBSON, Pres.; Ms. JANE MANCINI PULIAFICO, Vice Pres. Trustees: His Eminence SEAN CARDINAL O'MALLEY, O.F.M.Cap.; Very Rev. RICHARD M. ERIKSON, V.G.; Rev. Msgrs. PAUL V. GARRITY, V.F.; WILLIAM M. HELMICK; CORNELIUS M. MCRAE; FRANCIS V. STRAHAN, V.F.; Revs. RODNEY J. COPP, J.C.L.; PAUL B. O'BRIEN; BRYAN K. PARRISH, V.F.; GEORGE SZAL, S.M.; WALTER J. WALDRON; Deacon DANIEL C. NELSON; R. STEPHEN BARRETT; MARY CORCORAN; JACK DUNN; JANICE JUDGE FOX; Mr. CRAIG B. GIBSON; KEVIN GILL; JOHN J. GRIFFIN; MICHAEL HALLORAN; CHRISTOPHER HAUGHEY; PHILIP HAUGHEY; RICHARD HORAN; JEFFREY J. KANEB; Mr. SCOT LANDRY; JANE MANCINI PULIAFICO; JAMES P. MCDONOUGH; JOANN MCGRATH; JOHN A. MCNEICE; JAMES F. MOONEY; MANUEL PIRES; JOHN M. RILEY; JACK J. SHAUGHNESSY; MARSHALL SLOANE.

Jewish Relations—Rev. DAVID C. MICHAEL, Dir., 4750 Washington St., Boston, 02132. Tel: 617-323-4410; Fax: 617-323-0423.

Labor Guild—Rev. PATRICK SULLIVAN, C.S.C., Dir., 85 Commercial St., Weymouth, 02188. Tel: 781-340-7887; Fax: 781-340-5885. Email: laborguild@aol.com. Web: www.laborguild.com.

L'Arche Irenicon, Inc.—SWANNA CHAMPLIN, Exec. Dir., Mailing Address: Box 1177, Haverhill, 01831. Tel: 978-374-6928; Fax: 978-373-9097. Email: office@larcheirenicon.org.

League of Catholic Women—Ms. MARY SULLIVAN, Pres., 39 Washington Park Rd., Braintree, 02184. Tel: 781-843-6616.

Legatus Boston—Mr. SCOT LANDRY, Pres., 66 Brooks Dr., Braintree, 02184-3839. Web: legatus.org.

Legion of Mary—Mr. JAMES KJELLANDER, Pres., 75 Union Park St., Boston, 02118-2141. Tel: 617-542-5682; Fax: 617-542-5926.

Life Resources— Residential and Community Services to Adolescents. Ms. LYNNE MARIE BIELECKI, Pres., 100 River St., Braintree, 02184-2021. Tel: 781-849-7751; Fax: 781-849-7754. Email: lbielecki@liferesourcesinc.org. Web: www.liferesourcesinc.org.

The Listening Place—Rev. ALPHONSE FERREIRA, O.F.M., Dir., 36 Michigan Ave., Lynn, 01902-1934. Tel: 781-592-7396; Fax: 781-595-6724.
American Sign—
Boston—Cathedral of the Holy Cross. Tel: 617-542-5682.
Bellingham—Saint Blaise. Tel: 508-966-1258.
Danvers—New England Home for the Deaf. Tel: 978-774-0445.
Hopkington—Saint John the Evangelist. Tel: 508-435-3313.
Middleborough—Sacred Heart. Tel: 508-947-0444.
Newton—Sacred Heart. Tel: 617-969-2248.
Stoneham—Saint Patrick. Tel: 781-438-0960.
Whitman—Holy Ghost. Tel: 781-447-4421.
Amharic—
Boston—Cathedral of the Holy Cross. Tel: 617-542-5682.
Chinese—
Boston—Saint James the Greater. Tel: 617-542-8498.
Congolese French—
Lynn—Saint Mary. Tel: 781-598-4907.
Haitian Creole—
Brockton—Christ the King. Tel: 508-586-1575.
Cambridge—Saint John the Evangelist. Tel: 617-547-4880.
Chelsea—Our Lady of Grace. Tel: 617-884-0030.
Dorchester—Saint Matthew. Tel: 617-436-3590.
Everett—Immaculate Conception. Tel: 617-389-5660.
Lynn—Saint Mary. Tel: 781-598-4907.
Mattapan—Saint Angela Merici. Tel: 617-298-0080.
Somerville—Saint Ann. Tel: 617-625-1904.
Igbo (Nigerian)—
Roxbury—Saint Katherine Drexel. Tel: 617-445-8915.
Italian—
Boston—Saint Leonard of Port Maurice. Tel: 617-523-2110.
Cambridge—Saint Francis of Assisi. Tel: 617-876-6754.
East Boston—Sacred Heart. Tel: 617-567-5776.
Everett—Saint Anthony of Padua. Tel: 617-387-0310.
Lawrence—Corpus Christi. Tel: 978-685-1711.
Khmer (Cambodian)—
Lowell—Saint Patrick. Tel: 978-459-0561.
Kiswahili (Kenyan)—
Lowell—Saint Michael. Tel: 617-846-7400.
Quincy—Sacred Heart. Tel: 978-459-0713.
Winthrop—Saint John the Evangelist. Tel: 617-328-8666.
Korean—
Newton—Saint Philip Neri. Tel: 617-244-9685.
Lithuanian—
Lawrence—Corpus Christi. Tel: 978-685-1711.
South Boston—Saint Peter. Tel: 617-268-0353.
Polish—
Chelsea—Saint Stanislaus. Tel: 617-889-0261.
Hyde Park—Saint Adalbert. Tel: 617-361-0565.
Lawrence—Corpus Christi. Tel: 978-685-1711.
Lowell—Holy Trinity. Tel: 978-452-2564.
Salem—Saint John the Baptist. Tel: 978-744-1278.
South Boston—Our Lady of Czestochowa. Tel: 617-268-4355.
Portuguese (Brazilian)—
Allston—Saint Anthony of Padua. Tel: 617-782-0775.
Cambridge—Saint Anthony of Padua. Tel: 617-547-5593.

East Boston—Madonna Queen Shrine. Tel: 617-569-2100.
Everett—Saint Anthony of Padua. Tel: 617-387-0310.
Framingham—Saint Tarcisius. Tel: 508-875-8623.
Gloucester—Holy Family. Tel: 978-281-4820.
Hudson—Saint Michael. Tel: 978-562-2552.
Lowell—Holy Family. Tel: 978-453-2134.
Marlborough—Immaculate Conception. Tel: 508-485-0016.
Maynard—Saint Bridget. Tel: 978-897-2171.
Peabody—Our Lady of Fatima. Tel: 978-532-0272.
Plymouth—Saint Mary. Tel: 508-746-0426.
Rockland—Holy Family. Tel: 781-878-0160.
Somerville—Saint Anthony of Padua. Tel: 617-625-4530.
Stoughton—Immaculate Conception. Tel: 781-344-2073.
Woburn—Saint Charles Borromeo. Tel: 781-933-0300.

Portuguese (Cape Verdean)—
Brockton—Saint Edith Stein. Tel: 508-586-6491.
Dorchester—Saint Peter. Tel: 617-265-1132.
Roxbury—Saint Patrick. Tel: 617-445-7645.
Scituate—Saint Mary of the Nativity. Tel: 781-545-3335.

Portuguese (European)—
Cambridge—Saint Anthony of Padua. Tel: 617-547-5593.
Framingham—Saint Tarcisius. Tel: 508-875-8623.
Gloucester—Our Lady of Good Voyage. Tel: 978-283-1490.
Hudson—Saint Michael. Tel: 978-562-2552.
Lawrence—Corpus Christi. Tel: 978-685-1711.
Lowell—Saint Anthony of Padua. Tel: 978-452-1506.
Peabody—Our Lady of Fatima. Tel: 978-532-0272.
Stoughton—Immaculate Conception. Tel: 781-344-2073.

Spanish—
Boston—Cathedral of the Holy Cross. Tel: 617-542-5682. *Saint Anthony Shrine*. Tel: 617-542-6440. *Saint Francis Chapel*. Tel: 617-437-7117.
Brighton—Saint Columbkille. Tel: 617-782-5774.
Brockton—Saint Patrick. Tel: 508-586-4840.
Cambridge—Saint Mary of the Annunciation. Tel: 617-547-0120.
Charlestown—Saint Mary-Saint Catherine of Siena. Tel: 617-242-1750.
Chelsea—Saint Rose of Lima. Tel: 617-889-2774.
Dorchester—Holy Family. Tel: 617-445-9553. *Saint Ambrose*. Tel: 617-265-5302. *Saint Christopher*. Tel: 617-436-7273.
East Boston—Madonna Queen Shrine. Tel: 617-569-2100. *Most Holy Redeemer*. Tel: 617-567-3227. *Oud Lady of the Assumption*. Tel: 617-567-1223.
Everett—Saint Anthony of Padua. Tel: 617-387-0310.
Framingham—Saint Stephen. Tel: 508-875-4788.
Haverhill—Saint James. Tel: 978-372-8537.
Jamaica Plain—Our Lady of Lourdes. Tel: 617-524-0434.
Lawrence—Corpus Christi. Tel: 978-685-1711. *Saint Mary of the Assumption*. Tel: 978-685-1111. *Saint Patrick*. Tel: 978-683-9416.
Lowell—Saint Patrick. Tel: 978-459-0561.
Lynn—Saint Joseph. Tel: 781-599-7040.
Marlborough—Immaculate Conception. Tel: 508-485-0016.
Newton—Saint Ignatius Loyola. Tel: 617-552-6100.
Peabody—Saint John the Baptist. Tel: 978-531-0002.
Revere—Immaculate Conception. Tel: 781-289-0735.
Roslindale—Sacred Heart. Tel: 617-325-3519.
Roxbury—Our Lady of Perpetual Help. Tel: 617-445-1524. *Saint Mary of the Angels*. Tel: 617-445-1524. *Saint Patrick*. Tel: 617-445-7645.
Salem—Immaculate Conception. Tel: 978-745-6303.
Somerville—Saint Ann. Tel: 617-625-1904. *Saint Benedict*. Tel: 617-625-0029.
South Boston—Saint Monica and Saint Augustine. Tel: 617-269-6760.
Waltham—Saint Mary. Tel: 781-891-1730.
Woburn—Saint Charles Borromeo. Tel: 781-933-0300.

Tagalog—
Malden—Saint Joseph. Tel: 781-324-0402.
Quincy—Saint John the Baptist. Tel: 617-773-1021.
West Roxbury—Holy Name. Tel: 617-325-4865.

Tigrinya—
Boston—Cathedral of the Holy Cross. Tel: 617-542-5682.
Vietnamese—Chelsea, Saint Rose of Lima. Tel: 617-889-2774. *Dorchester, Saint Ambrose*. Tel: 617-265-5302. *East Boston, Sacred Heart*. Tel: 617-567-5776. *Haverhill, Saint James*. Tel: 978-372-8537. *Lawrence, Saint Patrick*. Tel: 978-683-9416. *Lowell, Saint Patrick*. Tel: 978-459-0561. *Malden, Sacred Heart*. Tel: 781-324-0728. *Randolph, Saint Bernadette*. Tel: 781-963-1327.

Maria Droste Services—Sr. LORRAINE BERNIER, R.G.S., Admin., 1354 Hancock St., Quincy, 02169. Tel: 617-471-5686; Fax: 617-471-6622. Email: mariadroste@verizon.net.
Marian Devotions—Rev. WILLIAM R. CARROLL, Spiritual Dir., 46 Myrtle St., Melrose, 02176-3827. Tel: 781-665-0152; Fax: 781-665-2750.
Marriage Ministry—Ms. KARI COLELLA, Coord. Tel: 617-746-5801; Fax: 617-783-5642. Email: kari_colella@rcab.org.
Massachusetts Catholic Conference—Mr. EDWARD F. SAUNDERS ESQ., Exec. Dir., 150 Staniford St., Boston, 02114-2511. Tel: 617-367-6060; Fax: 617-367-2767.
Natural Family Planning—Ms. MARY FINNIGAN, Coord. Tel: 617-746-5803; Fax: 617-746-5782. Email: mary_finnigan@rcab.org.
New Ecclesial Movements—
Focolare—Ms. MARIA C. FERREIRA, Dir., 29 Jackson Terr., Newton, 02458-1430. Tel: 617-965-4879; Fax: 617-965-4879. Email: focolareboston@rcn.com. Web: focolare.org.
New Evangelization of Youth and Young Adults—Rev. MATTHEW M. WILLIAMS, Dir., 66 Brooks Dr., Braintree, 02184-3839. Tel: 617-746-5752; Fax: 617-779-4572. Email: fr.matt@rcab.org.
Notre Dame Education Center—50 W. Broadway, Boston, 02127-1093. Tel: 617-268-1912; Fax: 617-464-7924. Email: ndecboston@aol.com.
Notre Dame Mission Center—Sr. RUTH DUFFY, S.N.D., Dir., 30 Jeffreys Neck Rd., Ipswich, 01938. Tel: 978-682-6441; Fax: 978-356-3552. Email: ndcimps@aol.com. Web: sndden.org.
Notre Dame Education Center—Sr. MARY MURPHY, S.N.D., Ph.D., Dir., 301 Haverhill St., Lawrence, 01842-9998. Tel: 978-682-6441; Fax: 978-974-8940. Email: sndmemurphy@aol.com.
Outreach and Cultural Diversity—Sr. MARY CORRIPIO, S.N.D., Dir., 66 Brooks Dr., Braintree, 02184-3839. Tel: 617-746-5818; Fax: 617-746-5614. Email: mcorripio@rcab.org.
Parish Life and Leadership—Very Rev. THOMAS S. FOLEY, V.F., Sec. & Episcopal Vicar, 66 Brooks Dr., Braintree, 02184-3839. Tel: 617-746-5834; Fax: 617-779-4576. Email: reverendthomas_foley@rcab.org.
Pastoral Centers—
Brazilian Pastoral Centers—
Saint Anthony of Padua Social Action—43 Holton St., Allston, 02134. Tel: 617-783-2121.
Centro Bom Samaritano—Good Samaritan Center, 116 Concord St., Ste. 3, Framingham, 01702. Tel: 508-628-3721; Fax: 508-875-6358. Email: centrobomsamaritano@hotmail.com.
Centro Comunitario Scalabrini—Sr. ELISETE SIGNOR, M.S.C.S., 63 Oakes St., Everett, 02149. Tel: 617-387-0822.
Chinese Pastoral Center—Sr. MADELINE GALLAGHER, M.H.S.H., 78 Tyler St., Boston, 02111-1831. Tel: 617-482-2949; Fax: 617-482-2949.
Irish Pastoral Center—Sr. MARGUERITE KELLY, M.F.I.C., 953 Hancock St., Quincy, 02170-2322. Tel: 617-479-7404; Fax: 617-479-0541. Email: ipcboston@yahoo.com.
Other Pastoral Centers—
Our Lady's Guild House—ANDREA BEALL, 20 Charlesgate W., Boston, 02215-2703. Tel: 617-536-3000; Fax: 617-536-8508.
Salesian Boys and Girls Club—Rev. JOHN NAZZARO, S.D.B., 150 Byron St., Boston, 02128. Tel: 617-667-6626; Fax: 617-567-0418.
Don Guanella Center—Sr. RHONDA BROWN, D.S.M.P., 37 Nichols St., Chelsea, 02150-1225. Tel: 617-889-0179.
Pastoral Planning—Rev. DAVID COUTERIER, O.F.M.Cap., Dir., 66 Brooks Dr., Boston, 02135-3193. Tel: 617-746-5865; Fax: 617-746-5614. Email: reverenddavid_couturier@rcab.org.
Pauline Books and Media—Sr. DONNA GIAIMO, F.S.P., Dir., 885 Providence Hwy., Dedham, 02026. Tel: 781-326-5385; Fax: 781-461-1013. Email: dedham@paulinemedia.com. Web: pauline.org.
Pauline Center for Media Studies—Sr. MARY SOPHIE STEWART, F.S.P., Dir., 50 Saint Paul's Ave., Boston, 02130-3491. Tel: 617-522-8911; Fax: 617-522-4081. Web: pauline.org.
Pilgrimages—Rev. MICHAEL E. DREA, Coord., 29 Mount Auburn St., Cambridge, 02138. Tel: 617-491-8400; Fax: 617-354-7092.
The Pilot—Mr. ANTONIO ENRIQUE, Editor, 66 Brooks Dr., Braintree, 02184-3839. Tel: 617-746-5890; Fax: 617-779-4563. Email: aenrique@thebostonpilot.com. Web: thebostonpilot.com.
Pregnancy Help— Supporting women in crisis pregnancies. MARY B. GIRARD, R.N., Dir. 77 Warren St., Ste. 251, Brighton Marine Mental Health Center; Caritas Saint Elizabeth Medical Center, Boston, MA 02135Tel: 888-771-3914 (Toll Free In State); 617-782-5151; Fax: 617-782-1662.
Metro-West—5 Wilson St., Natick, 01760. Tel: 508-651-0753; Fax: 508-651-0754. Email: help@pregnancyhelpboston.org. Web: pregnancyhelpboston.org.
Prison Ministry—Deacon JAMES F. GREER, Interim Dir., 66 Brooks Dr., Braintree, 02184-3839. Tel: 978-746-5842; Fax: 617-742-5754. Email: jgreer@rcab.org.
State Facilities—
Bay State Correctional Facility—Rev. THOMAS F. STANTON, Chap., 28 Clark St., Norfolk, 02056. Tel: 508-668-1687.
Bridgewater State Hospital—Ms. PEG NEWMAN, Coord., 20 Administration Rd., Bridgewater, 02324. Tel: 508-279-4500.
Longwood Treatment Center—Ms. PEG NEWMAN, Coord., Two Administration Rd., Bridgewater, 02324. Tel: 508-279-3500.
Massachusetts Correctional Institution - Cedar Junction—Rev. THOMAS F. STANTON, Chap., Rte. 1A, Norfolk, 02056. Tel: 508-660-8000.
Massachusetts Correctional Institution - Concord—Rev. GEORGE WILLIAMS, S.J., Chap., 965 Elm St., Concord, 01742. Tel: 978-405-6100.
Massachusetts Correctional Institution - Framingham—Sr. MAUREEN CLARK, C.S.J., Coord., Mailing Address: Box 9007, Framingham, 01701-9007. Tel: 508-532-5100.
Massachusetts Correctional Institution - Norfolk—Ms. MARY BETH ROBINSON, Coord., 2 Clark St., Norfolk, 02056. Tel: 508-660-5900.
Massachusetts Correctional Institution - Plymouth—Deacon THOMAS HANLON, Mailing Address: Box 207, Carver, 02355-0207. Tel: 508-295-2647.
Massachusetts Correctional Institution - Shirley—Deacon ARTHUR F. ROGERS JR., Coord., Mailing Address: Box 1218, Shirley, 01464-1218. Tel: 978-425-4341.
Massachusetts Treatment Center—Deacon THOMAS HANLON, Coord., 30 Administration Rd., Bridgewater, 02324. Tel: 508-279-8100.
Northeast Correctional Center—Rev. GEORGE WILLIAMS, S.J., Chap., Barretts Mill Rd., Concord, 01742. Tel: 978-369-4120.
Old Colony Correction Center—VACANT, One Administration Rd., Bridgewater, 02324. Tel: 508-879-6000.
Pondville Correctional Center—Ms. MARY BETH ROBINSON, Coord., Mailing Address: Box 146, Norfolk, 02056-0146. Tel: 508-660-3924.
Shattuck Hospital Correctional Unit—180 Morton St., Boston, 02130. Tel: 617-522-7585.
South Middlesex Correctional Center—Sr. MAUREEN CLARK, C.S.J., Coord., 135 Western Ave., Framingham, 01701-0850. Tel: 508-879-1241.
County Facilities—
Essex County Correctional Facility—Deacon CARROLL H. TAYLOR, Coord., 20 Manning Ave., Middleton, 01949. Tel: 978-750-1900.
Middlesex County - House of Correction—Deacon WILLIAM R. EMERSON, Coord., 269 Treble Cove Rd., Billerica, 01821. Tel: 978-667-1711.
Middlesex County Jail—Deacon WILLIAM R. EMERSON, 40 Thorndike St., Cambridge, 02146. Tel: 617-494-4410.
Suffolk County Jail—200 Nashua St., Boston, 02118. Tel: 617-635-1100.
Norfolk County Correctional Facility—Rev. ROBERT M. JONES, S.V.D., Chap., 200 West St., Dedham, 02026. Tel: 781-329-3705.
Plymouth County Correctional Center—VACANT, 20 Long Pond Rd., Plymouth, 02360. Tel: 508-830-6200.
Suffolk County - House of Correction—VACANT, 20 Brandston St., Boston, 02118. Tel: 617-635-1000.
Youth Facilities—
Metro Youth Service Center—Rev. JOSEPH J. BAGGETTA, Chap., 425 Harvard St., Boston, 02124-2737. Tel: 617-727-6603.
Private Associations of Christ's Faithful—
Foyer of Charity—Rev. MATTHEW BRADLEY, Dir., 74 Hollett St., Scituate, 02066. Tel: 781-545-1080; Fax: 240-332-5826. Email: fb@foyerofcharity.org. Web: foyerofcharity.org.
Little Brothers of Saint Francis—785 Parker St., Boston, 02120-3021. Tel: 617-442-2556. Web: littlebrothersofstfrancis.org.
Marian Community—Sr. MARGARET CATHERINE SIMS, C.S.J., Dir., 154 Summer St., Medway, 02053-0639. Tel: 508-533-5377; Fax: 508-533-2877. Web: mariancommunity.org.
Professional Standards and Oversight—Rev. JOHN J. CONNOLLY, 66 Brooks Dr., Braintree, 02184-3839. Tel: 617-782-2544; Fax: 617-779-3820.
Background Screening—Mrs. ANN LALLY, 66 Brooks Dr., Braintree, 02184-3839. Tel: 617-746-5840; Fax: 617-779-4565.

Child Advocacy, Implementation and Oversight—Deacon ANTHONY RIZZUTO, 66 Brooks Dr., Boston, 02315-3193. Tel: 617-746-5994; Fax: 617-746-5702. Web: www.rcab.org/childadvocacy/homepage.html.

Delegate for Investigations—Mr. JAY CROWLEY, Delegate, 66 Brooks Dr., Braintree, 02184-3839. Tel: 617-746-5639; Fax: 617-746-5696.

Pastoral Support and Outreach—Ms. BARBARA THORP, Dir., 25 Braintree Hill Office Park, Ste. 300, Braintree, 02184. Tel: 866-244-9603 (Toll Free); 781-794-2581 (Local); Fax: 781-794-2584. Email: barbara_thorp@pastoralsupportandoutreach.org. Web: www.rcab.org/oha/homepage.htm.

Project Hope— Little Sisters of the Assumption Family Health Services, Inc. Sr. MARGARET LEONARD, L.S.A., Exec. Dir., 550 Dudley St., Roxbury, 02119. Tel: 617-442-1880; Fax: 617-238-0473. Email: mleonard@prohope.org.

Project Rachel— Post-Abortion Reconciliation and Healing. Mrs. MARIANNE P. LUTHIN, Dir., 5 Wilson St., Natick, 01760. Tel: 508-651-3100; Fax: 508-651-0754. Email: help@projectrachelboston.com. Web: projectrachelboston.com. Est. 1986.

Pro-Life Office—Mrs. MARIANNE P. LUTHIN, Dir., 5 Wilson St., Natick, 01760. Tel: 508-651-1900; Fax: 508-651-0754. Email: prolifeoffice@rcab.org. Web: bostoncatholic.org/prolifeoffice.aspx.

Public Association of Christ's Faithful—

Association of Saint Francis De Sales—Ms. CATHERINE CULLEN, Area Dir., 10 Wright Ln., Duxbury, 02332. Tel: 781-934-7228. Email: kateycullen@msn.com. Web: desalesassociation.org.

Brotherhood of Hope—194 Summer St., Somerville, 02143-2525. Tel: 617-623-9592; Fax: 617-625-1837. Email: info@brotherhoodofhope.org. Web: brotherhoodofhope.org.

Franciscans of the Primitive Observance—Bro. JOHN M. SWEENEY, F.P.O., 30 Trinity St., Lawrence, 01841.

Radio—Rev. ROBERT P. REED, Dir., Mailing Address: 34 Chestnut St., Box 9196, Watertown, 02471-9196. Tel: 617-923-0220.

Regina Cleri—Mr. STEPHEN J. GUST, Interim Dir., 60 William Cardinal O'Connell Way, Boston, 02114-2729. Tel: 617-523-1861; Fax: 617-720-0585. Email: sgust@reginacleri.org.

Religious Education—Ms. SUSAN LANG ABBOTT, Dir., 66 Brooks Dr., Braintree, 02184-3839. Tel: 617-779-3625; Fax: 617-746-5702; Ms. SUSAN J. KAY, Asst. Dir. Catechetical Leadership, 66 Brooks Dr., Braintree, 02184-3839. Tel: 617-779-3625; Fax: 617-746-5702; Ms. M. PILAR LATORRE, Assoc. Dir. Hispanic Catechesis, 66 Brooks Dr., Braintree, 02184-3839. Tel: 617-779-3625; Fax: 617-746-5702; Ms. BARBARA RICHARDS, Administrative Asst., 66 Brooks Dr., Braintree, 02184-3839. Tel: 617-779-3625; Fax: 617-746-5702.

Respect Life Education Office—KATHLEEN DARDIS, Asst. Dir., 66 Brooks Dr., Braintree, 02184-3839. Tel: 617-746-5684; Fax: 617-747-5702. Email: respectlifeed@rcab.org. Web: respectlifeeducation.com.

Saint Ann's Home, Inc.—Mr. DENIS GRANDBOIS, Pres. & CEO, 100-A Haverhill St., Methuen, 01844. Tel: 978-685-5276; Fax: 978-688-4932. Email: dgrandbois@st.annshome.org. Web: st.annshome.org.

Society of Saint James the Apostle—Rev. Msgr. TIMOTHY F. O'LEARY, Dir., 24 Clark St., Boston, 02109-1127. Tel: 617-742-4715; Fax: 617-723-7389.

Society of Saint Vincent de Paul—Mr. EDWARD RESNICK, Controller, 18 Canton St., Stoughton, 02072. Tel: 781-344-3100; Fax: 617-341-4560. Email: execdir@svdpboston.com. Web: svdpboston.com.

Seaport Chaplaincy—Rev. RICHARD A. UFTRING, Chap., Logan International Airport, Boston, 02128. Tel: 617-567-2800. Email: fatherrichard@massport.com.

Secular Institutes—

Oblate Missionaries of Mary Immaculate—Ms. PAULINE LABBE, Dir., 9 Bayberry Dr., Atkinson, NH 03811. Tel: 603-362-9960. Email: pjlabbe1@juno.com.

Caritas Christi—Ms. ANNE M. RYAN, Sec., 537 Winter St., Framingham, 01702-5632. Tel: 508-875-7990. Email: aryan1211@aol.com. Web: ccinfo.org.

Institute of the Heart of Jesus—Rev. FREDERICK W. O'BRIEN, Coord. (Retired), 60 William Cardinal O'Connell Way, Boston, 02114. Tel: 617-720-4655. Email: federico22@verizon.net.

Secular Orders—

Secular Augustinians—Rev. JORGE A. REYES, O.S.A., Dir., 205 Hampshire St., Lawrence, 01841. Tel: 978-685-1111; Fax: 978-686-5555.

Secular Carmelites—Ms. LORETTA L. GALLAGHER, O.D.C.S., 36 Virginia Ln., Newburyport, 01950. Tel: 978-462-1057. Email: lorluceri@yahoo.com.

Lay Dominicans—Mr. RAYMOND A. DIBONA, O.P., Dir., 45 Trafford St., Quincy, 02169. Tel: 617-472-4446. Email: kmcaldwell@verizon.net.

Secular Franciscans—Ms. JACQUELYN D. WALSH, Regl. Min., 102 Everett Cir., Stoughton, 02072-5101. Tel: 781-344-7719. Email: jackiesfo@juno.com.

Social Services—

Catholic Relief Services—Rev. J. BRYAN HEHIR, 66 Brooks Dr., Braintree, 02184-3839. Tel: 617-746-5733; Fax: 617-779-4571. Email: bryan-hehir@harvard.edu.

Labor Guild—Rev. PATRICK SULLIVAN, C.S.C., Dir., 85 Commercial St., Weymouth, 02188. Tel: 781-340-7887; Fax: 781-340-5885. Email: laborguild@aol.com. Web: www.laborguild.com.

Life Resources— Residential and Community Services to Adolescents Ms. LYNNE MARIE BIELECKI, Pres., 100 River St., Braintree, 02184-2021. Tel: 781-849-7751; Fax: 781-849-7754. Email: lbielecki@liferesourcesinc.org. Web: www.liferesourcesinc.org.

L'Arche Irenicon, Inc.—SWANNA CHAMPLIN, Exec. Dir., Mailing Address: Box 1177, Haverhill, 01831. Tel: 978-374-6928; Fax: 978-373-9097. Email: office@larcheirenicon.org.

Pregnancy Help— Supporting women in crisis pregnancies. MARY B. GIRARD, R.N., Dir. 77 Warren St., Ste. 251, Brighton Marine Mental Health Center; Caritas Saint Elizabeth Medical Center, Boston, MA 02135Tel: 888-771-3914 (Toll Free In State); 617-782-5151; Fax: 617-782-1662.

Metro-West—5 Wilson St., Natick, 01760. Tel: 508-651-0753; Fax: 508-651-0754. Email: help@pregnancyhelpboston.org. Web: pregnancyhelpboston.org.

Project Rachel— Post-Abortion Reconciliation and Healing. Mrs. MARIANNE P. LUTHIN, Dir., 5 Wilson St., Natick, 01760. Tel: 508-651-3100; Fax: 508-651-0754. Email: help@projectrachelboston.com. Web: projectrachelboston.com. Est. 1986.

Pro-Life Office—Mrs. MARIANNE P. LUTHIN, Dir., 5 Wilson St., Natick, 01760. Tel: 508-651-1900; Fax: 508-651-0754. Email: prolifeoffice@rcab.org. Web: bostoncatholic.org/prolifeoffice.aspx.

Respect Life Education Office—KATHLEEN DARDIS, Asst. Dir., 66 Brooks Dr., Braintree, 02184-3839. Tel: 617-746-5684; Fax: 617-747-5702. Email: respectlifeed@rcab.org. Web: respectlifeeducation.com.

Saint Ann's Home, Inc.—Mr. DENIS GRANDBOIS, Pres. & CEO, 100-A Haverhill St., Methuen, 01844. Tel: 978-685-5276; Fax: 978-688-4932. Email: dgrandbois@st.annshome.org. Web: st.annshome.org.

Related Services—

Cor Unum Meal Center—Ms. DIANE JARVIS, Dir., 191 Salem St., Lawrence, 01843-1427. Tel: 978-688-8900; Fax: 978-681-5808. Email: corunummealcenter@comcast.net. Web: www.corunummealcenter.org.

The Listening Place— Counseling and Spiritual Services. Rev. ALPHONSE FERREIRA, O.F.M., Dir., 36 Michigan Ave., Lynn, 01902-1934. Tel: 781-592-7396; Fax: 781-595-6724.

Maria Droste Services— Counseling Service. Sr. LORRAINE BERNIER, R.G.S., Admin. & Interim Dir., 1354 Hancock St., Rm. 203, Quincy, 02169. Tel: 617-471-5686; Fax: 617-471-6622. Email: mariadroste@verizon.net.

Project Hope— Little Sisters of the Assumption Family Health Services, Inc. Sr. MARGARET LEONARD, L.S.A., Exec. Dir., 550 Dudley St., Roxbury, 02119. Tel: 617-442-1880; Fax: 617-238-0473. Email: mleonard@prohope.org.

Society of Saint Vincent De Paul—PAUL MCNEIL, Exec. Dir.; Mr. EDWARD RESNICK, 18 Canton St., Stoughton, 02072. Tel: 781-344-3100; Fax: 781-341-4560. Email: exdir@svdpboston.com. Web: www.svdpboston.com.

Specialized Catholic Organizations—

Ancient Order of Hibernians - Ladies Auxiliary—Rev. THOMAS B. MORGAN, Chap., 18 Beach Rd., Salisbury, 01953-1436. Tel: 978-465-3334; Fax: 978-465-5524. Email: starsea@seacoast.com. Web: laoh.massboard.org.

Ancient Order of Hibernians—Mr. RICHARD J. THOMPSON, Pres., 7 Derby Rd., Watertown, 02472. Tel: 617-924-9765. Email: rthomp521@comcast.net. Web: massaoh.org.

Archdiocesan Union of Holy Name Societies—Mr. ROBERT QUAGAN, 35 Cass St., Boston, 02132-4411. Tel: 617-325-5905. Email: rquagan@comcast.net.

Boston Catholic Men's Conference and Fellowship—Mr. ROBERT ALLARD, Coord., 350 Massachusetts Ave., Arlington, 02474. Tel: 617-851-5800. Email: info@bostoncatholicmen.org. Web: bostoncatholicmen.org.

Casa Monte Cassino—11 Tileston St., Boston, 02113. Tel: 617-227-1613; Fax: 617-227-1613. Email: casamontecassino@earthlink.net. Web: casamontecassino.org.

Catholic Alumni Club—Mr. THOMAS LITRENTA, Pres., 40 Nowell Rd., Melrose, 02176-1242. Tel: 617-261-9600. Email: cachubbub@yahoo.com. Web: caci.org.

Catholic Association of Foresters—Mr. JOHN F. ANDERSON, Treas., 132 Forbes Rd., Braintree, 02184-2693. Tel: 781-848-8221; Fax: 781-848-0311. Email: john@catholicforesters.org. Web: catholicforesters.org.

Catholic Daughters of the Americas—Ms. JOYCE A. FLEMING, Regent, 62 Cushing St., Medford, 02155. Tel: 781-391-1069. Email: jatfleming@comcast.net.

Catholic Lawyers Guild—HON. JOSEPH R. NOLAN, Pres., 100 Cambridge St., Boston, 02114. Tel: 617-723-1100.

Cor Unum Meal Center—Ms. DIANE JARVIS, Dir., 191 Salem St., Lawrence, 01843-1427. Tel: 978-688-8900; Fax: 978-681-5808. Email: corunummealcenter@comcast.net. Web: corunummealcenter.org.

Daughters of Isabella—Ms. THERESA LEWIS, Regent, 72 Seabreeze Dr., South Dartmouth, 02748. Tel: 508-993-5085.

Equestrian Order of the Holy Sepulchre of Jerusalem—Mr. JOHN W. SPILLAINE, Lieutenant, 23 Institute Rd., Worcester, 01609. Tel: 508-749-2920; Fax: 508-572-2234. Email: eohsjne@aol.com.

Guild of the Infant Savior—Ms. SHARON DEEHAN, Pres., 162 Pineridge Rd., North Andover, 01845. Tel: 978-683-9846. Email: sdeehan@comcaset.net.

Healing and Restoration Ministry—Rev. EDWARD J. MCDONOUGH, C.SS.R., Dir., 1545 Tremont St., Boston, 02120. Tel: 617-442-2008; Fax: 617-442-2845.

International Order of the Alhambra—Mr. CORNELIUS M. MURPHY, Sec., 15 Carolina St., Medford, 02155-4806. Tel: 781-396-1979.

Knights of Columbus—470 Washington St., Norwood, 02062-0194. Tel: 781-551-0628; Fax: 781-551-0490. Email: mastatekofc@verizon.net. Web: massachusettsstatekofc.org.

Knights of Peter Claver—Mr. MEYER CHAMBERS, Grand Knight, 32 Courtney Rd., Boston, 02132-1044. Tel: 617-552-1298; Fax: 617-552-3044. Email: meyer.chambers.1@bc.edu. Web: kofpc.org.

League of Catholic Women—Ms. MARY SULLIVAN, Pres., 39 Washington Park Rd., Braintree, 02184. Tel: 781-843-6616.

Legatus Boston—Mr. SCOT LANDRY, Pres., 66 Brooks Dr., Braintree, 02184-3839. Web: legatus.org.

Legion of Mary—Mr. JAMES KJELLANDER, Pres., 75 Union Park St., Boston, 02118-2141. Tel: 617-542-5682; Fax: 617-542-5926.

Magnificat Joy of Boston—Ms. LOUISE SCIPIONE, Coord., 42 Packard Rd., Stoughton, 02072. Tel: 781-344-6616.

Maria Droste Services—Sr. LORRAINE BERNIER, R.G.S., Admin., 1354 Hancock St., Quincy, 02169. Tel: 617-471-5686; Fax: 617-471-6622. Email: mariadroste@verizon.net.

Nocturnal Adoration Society—Mr. GEORGE J. HALLETT, Pres., 45 Courtland Cir., Milton, 02186-4303. Tel: 617-698-6321. Email: geojoshal@aol.com.

Pax Christi USA—Rev. WILLIAM T. KREMMELL, Advisor, 27 Bainbridge Rd., Reading, 01867-1810. Tel: 781-944-0330; Fax: 781-944-1266. Email: pax_2_you@yahoo.com.

Pieta—Ms. BARBARA WATERS, Coord., 66 Enoch Pond Rd., Wrentham, 02093-1391. Tel: 508-384-6663. Email: hanknann@verizon.net.

Pro Maria Committee—Ms. IRENE TREMBLAY, Dir., 112 Norris Rd., Tyngsborough, 01879. Tel: 978-649-1813. Email: irene_tremblay@hotmail.com.

Pro Parvulis—Ms. BEVERLY C. BAKER, Treas., 286 Turtle Pond Pkwy., Boston, 02136-1224.

Project Hope—Sr. MARGARET LEONARD, L.S.A., Exec. Dir., 550 Dudly St., Boston, 02119. Tel: 617-442-1880; Fax: 617-238-0473. Email: mleonard@prohope.org. Web: prohope.org.

Serra Boston—Leaders: BRIAN GALLAGHER; LORETTA GALLAGHER, 36 Virginia Ln., Newburyport, 01950. Tel: 978-462-1057. Email: information@serraboston.org. Web: serraboston.org.

Seton Club—Ms. JOSEPH WELLER, Pres., 14 Summer St., Saugus, 01906-2139. Tel: 781-233-2497; Fax: 781-231-5569.

Simon of Cyrene Society—Sr. MARGARET YOUNGCLAUS, S.N.D., Dir., Mailing Address: Box 54, Boston, 02127-0054. Tel: 617-268-8393. Email: sndbol@aol.com. Web: simonofcyrene.com.

Society of Saint Vincent de Paul—Mr. EDWARD RESNICK, Controller, 18 Canton St., Stoughton, 02072. Tel: 781-344-3100; Fax: 617-341-4560. Email: execdir@svdpboston.com. Web: svdpboston.com.
The Gathering Place—Sr. PATRICIA BRENNAN, R.G.S., Dir., 3 Common St., Waltham, 02451-4401. Tel: 781-647-0012; Fax: 781-647-0055. Email: gather1997@aol.com. Web: thegatheringplace@homestead.com.
The Listening Place—Rev. ALPHONSE FERREIRA, O.F.M., Dir., 36 Michigan Ave., Lynn, 01902-1934. Tel: 781-592-7396; Fax: 781-595-6724.
Women Affirming Life—Ms. FRANCES X. HOGAN, Pres., Mailing Address: Box 35532, Boston, 02135-0532. Tel: 617-254-2277; Fax: 617-254-2299.
World Apostolate of Fatima—Ms. LYNN KENN, Pres., Mailing Address: Box 308, East Bridgewater, 02333-0308. Tel: 508-378-7431. Email: elk314@comcast.net.
Special Needs—
Braintree— Cardinal Cushing Centers, Inc. Mr. RON SHEPHERD, Prin., 85 Washington St., Braintree, 02184. Tel: 781-848-6250; Fax: 781-848-0640. Web: www.coletta.org/cardinal/braintree/braintree.htm. Email: rshepherd@coletta.org.
Hanover— Cardinal Cushing Centers, Inc. Mrs. ROBERTA PULASKI, Dir. Educ., 405 Washington St., Hanover, 02339. Tel: 781-826-6371; Fax: 781-826-1559. Web: www.coletta.org/cardinal/hanoverprogs/hanover.htm. Email: rpulaski@coletta.org.
Spiritual Life—66 Brooks Dr., Braintree, 02184-3839. Tel: 617-779-3640; Fax: 617-779-4570. Ms. MARYANN MCLAUGHLIN, Dir. Spiritual Life. Tel: 617-779-3641. Email: mmclaugh@rcab.org; Sr. ANNE D'ARCY, C.S.J., Assoc. Dir. Spiritual Life. Tel: 617-779-3648; Fax: 617-779-4570. Email: sdarcy@rcab.org; Revs. DANIEL O'CONNELL, Assoc. Dir. Spiritual Life. Tel: 617-779-3643; Fax: 617-779-4570. Email: roconnell@rcab.org; JOHN E. SASSANI, Assoc. Dir. Spiritual Life. Tel: 617-527-7560, Ext. 215; Fax: 617-779-4570. Email: jsassani@ourladys.com; Ms. PATRICIA DEBAISE, Administrative Asst. Tel: 617-779-3645; Fax: 617-779-4570. Email: patricia_debaise@rcab.org.
ARISE: Together in Christ—Ms. MARYANN MCLAUGHLIN, Archdiocesan Coord. Tel: 617-779-3640; Fax: 617-779-4570. Email: mmclaugh@rcab.org; Ms. ANN M. CUSSEN, Oper. Asst. Tel: 617-779-3640; Fax: 617-779-4570. Email: ann_cussen@rcab.org.
Vocations—Revs. DANIEL F. HENNESSEY, Dir., 127 Lake St., Boston, 02135. Tel: 617-746-5949; Fax: 617-779-5470. Email: reverend_daniel_hennessey@rcab.org; MICHAEL C. HARRINGTON, Assoc. Dir. Tel: 617-746-5939; Fax: 617-779-5470. Email: michael_harrington@rcab.org; ALONSO E. MACIAS, Assoc. Dir. Tel: 617-746-5987; Fax: 617-779-5470. Email: reverend_alonso_macias@rcab.org.

CLERGY, PARISHES, MISSIONS AND PAROCHIAL SCHOOLS

BOSTON

(SUFFOLK COUNTY)

1—CATHEDRAL OF THE HOLY CROSS (1788) Very Rev. Kevin J. O'Leary, Admin.; Rev. Carlos A. Lopez (Puerto Rico), Parochial Vicar; Sr. Tania Santander-Atauchi, C.D.P., Pastoral Assoc.; Mr. Robert V. Travers, Pastoral Assoc.; Deacon Ricardo M. Mesa.
Res.: 75 Union Park St., Boston, 02118. Tel: 617-542-5682; Fax: 617-542-5926. Email: cathedral2@rcab.org. Web: www.holycrossboston.com.
School—Cathedral Grammar School, 595 Harrison Ave., Boston, 02118. Tel: 617-422-0042. Sr. Dorothy Burns, C.S.J., Prin. Sisters 2; Lay Teachers 13; Students 201.
See Cathedral High School under High Schools, Archdiocesan in the Institution section.
Catechesis/Religious Program—
Convent—Mission Helpers of Sacred Heart, 286 Shuwmut Ave., Boston, Suffolk Co. 02118. Tel: 617-542-1143.

2—ST. ADALBERT (1913), (Polish), Rev. Msgr. Stanislaus T. Sypek.
Res.: 1450 River St., Hyde Park, 02136-2150. Tel: 617-361-0565; Fax: 617-361-7788. Email: stadalberts@homeofpeace.org.
Catechesis/Religious Program—Kathleen A. Lynch, D.R.E.

3—ALL SAINTS (1894), All Saints, Roxbury was suppressed. This parish's records are located at St. Patrick, Boston.

4—ST. AMBROSE (1914) Revs. Thomas F. Bouton, Admin.; Hoang V. Le, Parochial Vicar; Joseph Chinh Nguyen (Vietnam), Parochial Vicar; Sr. Mary Damien Powers, O.S.M., Pastoral Assoc.; Deacon Marcio O. Fonseca. In Res., Rt. Rev. John J. Ahern; Revs. Richard C. Conway; Huy H. Nguyen.
Res.: 240 Adams St., Dorchester, 02122-1380. Tel: 617-265-5302; Fax: 617-265-0886. Email: stambroseparish@comcast.net.

5—ST. ANDREW (1918), St. Andrew the Apostle, Forest Hills was suppressed. This parish's records are located at Sacred Heart, Boston.

6—ST. ANGELA MERICI (1907) Revs. William P. Joy; Gabriel Michel (Haiti), Parochial Vicar.
Res.: 1544 Blue Hill Ave., Mattapan, 02126. Tel: 617-298-0080; Fax: 617-298-2388.
School—120 Babson St., Mattapan, 02126. Tel: 617-296-1161. Sr. Gail Donahue, C.S.J., Prin. Lay Teachers 11; Students 201.
Catechesis/Religious Program—Josette Rameau, D.R.E.
Convent—47 Fremont St., Mattapan, 02126. Tel: 617-298-5585.

7—ST. ANN (1889) Rev. Sean M. Connor. In Res., Revs. Michael C. Harrington; John J. Connelly.
Res.: 243 Neponset Ave., Dorchester, 02122-3239. Tel: 617-825-6180. Email: saintanneponset@gmail.com. Web: www.saintanneponset.com.
School—239 Neponset Ave., Dorchester, 02122. Tel: 617-825-6262. Cynthia Duggan, Prin. Religious 5; Lay Teachers 13; Students 275.
Catechesis/Religious Program—Marie Mannion, D.R.E.
Convent—241 Neponset Ave., Dorchester, 02122. Tel: 617-288-1202.

8—ST. ANN (1945), St. Ann, Back Bay was suppressed. This parish's records are located at St. Cecilia, Boston.

9—ST. ANNE (1919) Rev. William F. Joyce. In Res., Rev. William F. Sweeney, S.S.C.
Res.: 79 W. Milton St., Readville, 02136-1929. Tel: 617-361-3443; Fax: 617-361-6690.
School—20 Como Rd., Readville, 02136. Tel: 617-361-3563. Grace Alexander, Prin. Religious 1; Lay Teachers 11; Students 225.
Catechesis/Religious Program—Joanna Imbaro, D.R.E.
Convent—85 W. Milton St., Readville, 02136. Tel: 617-361-8224.

10—ST. ANTHONY OF PADUA (1896) Revs. Francis M. Glynn; Jose E. Marques (Brazil), Parochial Vicar. In Res., Revs. Walter H. Cuenin; Paul E. Kilroy.
Res.: 43 Holton St., Allston, 02134-1397. Tel: 617-782-0775; Fax: 617-782-2008. Email: glynnfrank@hotmail.com.

11—ST. AUGUSTINE (1868), St. Augustine, South Boston was suppressed. This parish's records are located at St. Monica and St. Augustine, Boston.

12—BLESSED MOTHER TERESA OF CALCUTTA (2004) Rt. Rev. John J. Ahern; Revs. Richard C. Conway, Parochial Vicar; Huy H. Nguyen, Parochial Vicar.
Mailing Address & Res.: 240 Adams St., Dorchester, 02122. Tel: 617-436-2190; Fax: 617-282-5428. Web: www.motherteresadorchester.org.
School—100 Savin Hill Ave., Dorchester, 02125. Tel: 617-265-7110. Claire Sheridan, Prin.

13—BLESSED SACRAMENT (1891), Blessed Sacrament, Jamaica Plain was suppressed. This parish's records are located at Our Lady of Lourdes, Boston.

14—ST. BRENDAN (1929) Rev. John J. Connolly. In Res., Revs. John M. McCarthy (Ireland); Brian F. McMahon.
Res.: 15 Rita Rd., Dorchester, 02124-5321. Tel: 617-436-0310; Fax: 617-436-1386. Email: stbrndn@gis.net.
School—29 Rita Rd., Dorchester, 02124-5321. Tel: 617-282-3388. Ellen Leary, Prin. Lay Teachers 12; Students 209.
Catechesis/Religious Program—Tel: 617-825-8622. Jean Curley, D.R.E.

15—ST. BRIGID (1908) Very Rev. Robert E. Casey; Revs. Edward F. Doughty, Parochial Vicar; William C. Palladino, Parochial Vicar; Mr. Stephen Fahrig, Pastoral Assoc. In Res., Rev. Daniel J. Sheehan (Retired).
Res.: 841 E. Broadway, South Boston, 02127-2302. Tel: 617-268-2122; Fax: 617-268-2666. Email: stbrigidparish@aol.com. Web: www.stbrigidparish.com.
School—866 E. Broadway, South Boston, 02127-2302. Tel: 617-268-2326. Joseph F. Cirigliano, Prin. Sisters 2; Lay Teachers 7; Students 275.
Catechesis/Religious Program—James Fowkes, D.R.E.
Convent—100 N St., South Boston, 02127.

16—ST. CATHERINE OF SIENA (1887), St. Catherine of Siena, Charlestown was suppressed. This parish's records are located at St. Mary - St. Catherine of Siena, Boston.

17—ST. CECILIA (1888) Rev. John J. Unni; Mr. Mark Donohoe, Pastoral Assoc.; Ms. Kathleen McCabe, Pastoral Assoc. In Res., Rev. Thomas A. Mahoney.
Res.: 30 St. Cecilia St., Boston, 02115-3132. Tel: 617-536-4548; Fax: 617-536-1781. Email: info@stceciliaboston.org. Web: www.stceciliaboston.org.
Catechesis/Religious Program—Scott MacDonald, D.R.E.

18—ST. CHRISTOPHER (1956) Rev. George A. Carrigg, Admin.; Ms. Louise Tardif, Pastoral Assoc.
Res.: 263 Mt. Vernon St., Dorchester, 02125. Tel: 617-436-7273; Fax: 617-265-2704. Web: www.stchristopherchurch.org.
Catechesis/Religious Program—

19—ST. COLUMBKILLE (1871) Rev. Msgr. William P. Fay; Rev. F. Augustin Anda Gomez, Parochial Vicar. In Res., Revs. Carney E. Gavin; Joseph F. Keville; James J. O'Rourke (Retired).
Res.: 321 Market St., Brighton, 02135-2126. Tel: 617-782-5774; Fax: 617-782-7283. Web: www.brightoncatholic.org.
School—25 Arlington St., Brighton, 02135-2199. Tel: 617-254-3110. Michael A. McCarthy, Prin. Sisters 4; Lay Teachers 10; Students 200.
Catechesis/Religious Program—Christopher Carmody, D.R.E.

20—CONGREGATION OF SAINT ATHANASIUS Rev. Richard S. Bradford, Admin.
Res.: 767 W. Roxbury Pkwy., Boston, 02132-2121. Tel: 617-325-5232; Fax: 617-325-5232. Web: www.locator.net.

21—ST. FRANCIS DE SALES (1859) Rev. Daniel J. Mahoney. In Res., Rev. Martin Okwir (Uganda).
Res.: 303 Bunker Hill St., Charlestown, 02129-1826. Tel: 617-242-0147; Fax: 617-242-3026. Email: stfran303@aol.com. Web: www.stfrancisdesales-charlestown.com.

22—ST. FRANCIS DE SALES-ST. PHILIP (1867), St. Francis de Sales, Roxbury was suppressed. This parish's records are located at St. Katherine Drexel, Boston.

23—ST. GABRIEL (1934), St. Gabriel, Brighton was suppressed. This parish's records are located at St. Columbkille, Boston.

24—GATE OF HEAVEN (1862) Very Rev. Robert E. Casey; Revs. Edward F. Doughty, Parochial Vicar; William C. Palladino, Parochial Vicar; Stephen Fahrig, Pastoral Assoc.
Res.: 841 E. Broadway, South Boston, 02127-2302. Tel: 617-268-3344; Fax: 617-268-2666. Email: gateofheavensb@aol.com. Web: www.gateofheavenparish.com.
School—609 E. 4th, South Boston, 02127. Tel: 617-268-8431. Sr. Patricia McCarthy, C.S.J., Prin. Sisters 3; Lay Teachers 17; Students 483.
Catechesis/Religious Program—James Fowkes, D.R.E.

25—ST. GREGORY (1863) Revs. Vincent E. Daily (Retired); Laurence J. Borges, Parochial Vicar. In Res., Rev. Richard F. Clancy.
Res.: 2223 Dorchester Ave., Dorchester, 02124-5607. Tel: 617-298-2460; Fax: 617-298-9232. Email: stgregoryparish@gmail.com. Web: www.stgregoryparish.com.
School—2214 Dorchester Ave., Dorchester, 02124. Tel: 617-296-1210. Margaret Donovan, Prin. Lay Teachers 18; Students 225.
Catechesis/Religious Program—Elizabeth Labbe, D.R.E.

26—HOLY FAMILY (1995) Rt. Rev. John J. Ahern; Revs. Richard C. Conway, Parochial Vicar; Huy H. Nguyen, Parochial Vicar; Senior Deacon Francisco Guerrios.
Mailing Address: 240 Adams St., Dorchester, 02122. Tel: 617-445-9553; Fax: 617-265-0463. Email: holyfamdor@aol.com.
School—St. Kevin, 516 Columbia Rd., Dorchester, 02125. Tel: 617-825-3883. Sr. Paula Kelley, S.C.H., Prin.
Catechesis/Religious Program—336 Saratoga St., East Boston, 02128. Tel: 617-567-6509; Fax: 617-567-2561.

27—HOLY NAME (1927) Rev. Msgr. George F. Carlson; Revs. Martin G. Dzengelski, Parochial Vicar; Oscar J. Pratt, Parochial Vicar; Fran M. Hauck, Pastoral Assoc. In Res., Very Rev. Richard M. Erikson.
Res.: 1689 Centre St., West Roxbury, 02132-1292. Tel: 617-325-4865; Fax: 617-325-5571. Email: holyname.parish@verizon.net. Web: www.holynameparish.com.
School—525 W. Roxbury Pkwy., West Roxbury, 02132-1292. Tel: 617-325-9338. Linda Workman, Prin. Sisters 2; Lay Teachers 40; Students 572.
Convent—525 W. Roxbury Pkwy., West Roxbury, 02132. Tel: 617-325-5089.

28—HOLY TRINITY (1844), (German), Rev. John J. Connolly, Admin.
Res.: 140 Shawmut Ave., Boston, 02118-2227. Tel: 617-426-6142; Fax: 617-426-5409. Email: htparish@aol.com. Web: www.holytrinitygerman.org.
Catechesis/Religious Program—Patti Strom, D.R.E.

29—ST. JAMES THE GREATER (1854) Very Rev. Kevin J. O'Leary, Admin. In Res., Most Rev. Robert F. Hennessey; Rev. Joseph J. Baggetta.
Res. & Parish: 135 Harrison Ave., Boston, 02111. Tel: 617-542-8498; Fax: 617-542-2708. Email: stjameschinatown@hotmail.com.
Catechesis/Religious Program—Susan Ho, D.R.E.; Teresa Yuen, D.R.E.

30—ST. JOHN CHRYSOSTOM (1952) Rev. David C. Michael; Sr. Maureen Taaffe, S.C.N., Pastoral Assoc.
Res.: 4740 Washington St., West Roxbury, 02132. Tel: 617-323-4410; Fax: 617-323-0423. Email: stjohnoffice1@msn.com. Web: rc.net/boston/stjohnchrysostom.
Catechesis/Religious Program—

31—ST. JOHN THE BAPTIST (1921), St. John the Baptist, East Boston was suppressed. This parish's records are located at Sacred Heart, Boston.

32—ST. JOHN-ST. HUGH (1901), St. John-St. Hugh was suppressed. This parish's records are located at St. Katherine Drexel, Boston.

33—ST. JOSEPH (1845), St. Joseph, Roxbury was suppressed. This parish's records are located at St. Patrick, Boston.

34—ST. JOSEPH (1862), St. Joseph, East Boston was suppressed. This parish's records are located at St. Joseph-St. Lazarus, Boston.

35—ST. JOSEPH (1938), St. Joseph, Hyde Park was suppressed. This parish's records are located at St. Angela Merici, Boston.

36—ST. JOSEPH (1862) Rev. Daniel C. O'Connell.
68 William Cardinal O'Connell Way, Boston, 02114. Tel: 617-523-4342; Fax: 617-523-8459. Email: st.josephs01@verizon.net. Web: www.stjosephboston-.com. In Res., Revs. Robert P. Reed; Celestino V. Pascual (Philippines).
Catechesis/Religious Program—Denise Tompkins, D.R.E.

37—ST. JOSEPH-ST. LAZARUS (1892) Revs. John Kilmartin, F.D.P.; Miroslaw Kowalczyk, F.D.P., Parochial Vicar.
Res.: 59 Ashley St., East Boston, 02128. Tel: 617-569-0406; Fax: 617-569-8212. Email: stjstl50@aol.com.
School—St. Mary Star of the Sea, 58 Moore St., East Boston, 02128. Tel: 617-567-6609. Joan Lawrence, Prin.
Catechesis/Religious Program—Maria Zolla, D.R.E.

38—ST. KATHARINE DREXEL (2005) Revs. Gerald J. Osterman, Admin.; Anselm Nwagbara (Nigeria), Parochial Vicar; Deacon John W. McHugh; Sisters Mary Hart, R.G.S., Pastoral Assoc.; Christine Smith, S.B.S., Pastoral Assoc.; Mr. Tipp Harris, Pastoral Assoc.
Mailing Address: 175 Ruggles St., Boston, 02120.
Rectory—26 Lawrence Ave., Roxbury, 02120. Tel: 617-445-8915; Fax: 617-445-1652.

39—ST. KEVIN (1945), St. Kevin, Dorchester was suppressed. This parish's records are located at Holy Family, Boston.

40—ST. LAZARUS (1892), St. Lazarus, East Boston was suppressed. This parish's records are located at St. Joseph-St. Lazarus, Boston.

41—ST. LEO (1902), St. Leo, Dorchester was suppressed. This parish's records are located at St. Angela Merici, Boston.

42—ST. LEONARD OF PORT MAURICE (1873), (Italian), Revs. Antonio Nardoianni, O.F.M./I.C.; Claude Scrima, O.F.M./I.C., Parochial Vicar.
Res.: 14 N. Bennett St., Boston, 02113-1913. Tel: 617-523-2110; Fax: 617-367-0456. Email: stleonard@catholic-church.org. Web: www.catholic-church.org/stleonard.
School—St. John, 9 Moon St., Boston, 02113-1913. Tel: 617-227-3143. Sr. Eileen Harvey, C.S.J., Prin.
Chapel—St. Mary 150 Endicott St., Boston, 02113.

43—ST. MARGARET (1893), St. Margaret, Dorchester was suppressed. This parish's records are located at Blessed Mother Teresa of Calcutta, Boston.

44—ST. MARK (1905) Rev. Daniel J. Finn; Sr. Helen Roberts, O.S.F., Pastoral Assoc.; Deacon Hon H. Nguyen. In Res., Rev. Leonard Kayondo (Rwanda).
Res.: 20 Roseland St., Dorchester, 02124. Tel: 617-825-2852; Fax: 617-825-0514. Email: judy.stmarks@comcast.net. Web: www.stmarkparish.com.
School—197 Centre Ave., Dorchester, 02124. Tel: 617-282-2577. Edward Butler, Prin. Sisters 7; Lay Teachers 15; Students 512.
Catechesis/Religious Program—Kathy Wall, D.R.E.; Mary Swanton, D.R.E.

45—ST. MARY, St. Mary, North End was suppressed. This parish's records are located at St. Leonard of Port Maurice, Boston.

46—ST. MARY (1828), St. Mary, Charlestown was suppressed. This parish's records are located at St. Mary - St. Catherine of Siena, Boston.

47—ST. MARY - ST. CATHERINE OF SIENA (2006) Rev. James J. Ronan; Sr. Nancy Citro, S.N.D., Pastoral Assoc.
Mailing Address: 46 Winthrop. St., Boston, 02129. In Res., Rev. James A. Flavin.
Res.: Vine St., Boston, 02129. Tel: 617-242-4664; Fax: 617-242-0016. Web: www.charlestown.cc.
Catechesis/Religious Program—Sr. Kathleen Carven, S.C., D.R.E.

48—ST. MARY OF THE ANGELS (1904) Rev. Robert F. VerEecke, S.J., Admin.; Ms. Jen Roy, Pastoral Assoc.
Res.: 377 Walnut Ave., Roxbury, 02119. Tel: 617-445-1524; Fax: 617-442-6455. Email: stmaryoftheangels@msn.com. Web: www.stmaryoftheangelsroxbury.org.
Catechesis/Religious Program—Tel: 617-524-0913.

49—ST. MARY, STAR OF THE SEA (1864), St. Mary Star of the Sea, East Boston was suppressed. This parish's records are located at St. Joseph-St. Lazarus, Boston.

50—ST. MATTHEW (1900) Revs. William P. Joy; Jean Gabriel Charles (Haiti), Parochial Vicar.
Res.: 33 Stanton St., Dorchester, 02124-3716. Tel: 617-436-3590; Fax: 617-287-2741.
School—29 Stanton St., Dorchester, 02124. Tel: 617-825-7955. Mary Lanata, Prin. Sisters 2; Lay Teachers 10; Students 247.
Catechesis/Religious Program—Josette Rameau, D.R.E.

51—ST. MONICA (1907), St. Monica, South Boston was suppressed. This parish's records are located at St. Monica and St. Augustine, Boston.

52—ST. MONICA-ST. AUGUSTINE (1907) [CEM] Rev. Robert R. Kennedy.
Res.: 70 Devine Way, South Boston, 02127. Tel: 617-268-1230; Fax: 617-269-3831. Email: stmonicastaugustine@hotmail.com.

53—MOST HOLY REDEEMER (1844) Rev. Thomas S. Domurat; Deacons Antonio M. Perea; Pedro LaTorre. Member Central Catholic School of East Boston. In Res., Rev. Alexander J. Keenan.
Res.: 65 London St., East Boston, 02128-1924. Tel: 617-567-3227; Fax: 617-569-6950.
See East Boston Central Catholic School under Sacred Heart, 69 London St., East Boston.
Catechesis/Religious Program—Angelina Monge, D.R.E.

54—MOST PRECIOUS BLOOD (1880) Rev. Peter P. Nolan, C.S.Sp.
Res.: 43 Maple St., Hyde Park, 02136-2755. Tel: 617-364-9500; Fax: 617-364-2590. Email: ppnmpb@aol.com. Web: www.mostpreciousbloodhydepark.com.
Catechesis/Religious Program—Joseph Shaughnessy, D.R.E.

55—OUR LADY OF CZESTOCHOWA (1893), (Polish), Revs. Andrzej Urbaniak, O.F.M.Conv.; Wieslaw Ciemiega, O.F.M.Conv. (Poland), Parochial Vicar. In Res., Rev. Janusz Chmielecki, O.F.M.Conv.
Res.: 655 Dorchester Ave., South Boston, 02127. Tel: 617-268-4355; Fax: 617-268-4599. Email: parish@ourladyofczestochowa.com. Web: www.ourladyofsczestochowa.com.
School—52 Boston St., South Boston, 02127. Tel: 617-268-3766. Mrs. Linda Klotzbeecher, Prin. Lay Teachers 12; Students 190.
Convent—666 Dorchester Ave., Boston, 02127.

56—OUR LADY OF KAZAN, Our Lady of Kazan, South Boston was suppressed. This parish's records are located at St. Vincent de Paul, Boston.

57—OUR LADY OF LOURDES (1908) Rev. Brendan P. Buckley, O.F.M.Cap.; Deacons Jesus M. Ortiz; Luciano Herrera.
Res.: 45 Brookside Ave., Jamaica Plain, 02130-2370. Tel: 617-524-0434; Fax: 617-524-1888. Email: ololjp@comcast.net. Web: www.ourladyoflourdesjpma.org.
School—54 Brookside Ave., Jamaica Plain, 02130. Tel: 617-524-6136. Janice C. Wilson, Prin. Sisters 2; Lay Teachers 10; Students 220.
Catechesis/Religious Program—Lourdes Ortiz, D.R.E.

58—OUR LADY OF MT. CARMEL (1905), (Italian), Our Lady of Mt. Carmel, East Boston was suppressed. This parish's records are located at Sacred Heart, Boston.

59—OUR LADY OF OSTROBRAMA, Our Lady of Ostrobrama, West End was suppressed. This parish's records are located at Archives, Boston.

60—OUR LADY OF PERPETUAL HELP (1868) Revs. Raymond Collins, C.Ss.R.; John Furey, C.Ss.R., Parochial Vicar; Philip Dabney, C.Ss.R., Parochial Vicar. In Res., Revs. John C. Devin, C.Ss.R.; John J. Hennessey, C.Ss.R.; Philip A. Cabasino, C.Ss.R.; Sean McGillicuddy, C.Ss.R.
Res.: 1545 Tremont St., Boston, 02120-2909. Tel: 617-445-2600; Fax: 617-445-1857. Web: www.themissionchurch.com.
School—(Grades 1-6), 94 St. Alphonsus St., Boston, 02120. Tel: 617-442-2660. Maura Bradley, Prin. Sisters 4; Lay Teachers 3; Students 152.
Catechesis/Religious Program—Alyson Perry, D.R.E.

61—OUR LADY OF POMPEII, Our Lady of Pompeii, South End was suppressed. This parish's records are located at Archives, Boston.

62—OUR LADY OF THE ASSUMPTION (1869) Rev. Oscar Martin (NEW). Member East Boston Central Catholic School Consortium.
Res.: 404 Sumner St., East Boston, 02128. Tel: 617-567-1223. Email: ola_boston@familink.com.
See East Boston Central Catholic School under Sacred Heart, 69 London St., East Boston.

63—OUR LADY OF THE PRESENTATION (1909), Our Lady of the Presentation, Brighton was suppressed. This parish's records are located at St. Columbkille, Boston.

64—OUR LADY OF THE ROSARY, Our Lady of the Rosary, South Boston was suppressed. This parish's records are located at St. Vincent de Paul, Boston.

65—OUR LADY OF VICTORIES (1880), (French), Revs. Gerard A. Demers, S.M.; John Granato, S.M., Parochial Vicar.
Res.: 27 Isabella St., Boston, 02116-5216. Tel: 617-426-4448; Fax: 617-426-1884. Email: olvbboston@yahoo.com. Web: www.geocities.com/olvboston.tripod.com.

66—ST. PATRICK (1836) Revs. Walter J. Waldron; Christopher Gomes, O.F.M.Conv., Parochial Vicar; Carlos A. Lopez (Puerto Rico), Parochial Vicar; Sisters Gerard Ndagano, I.H.M.R., Pastoral Assoc.; Christine Smith, S.B.S., Pastoral Assoc.; Mary Thomasine Twomey, M.S.B.T., Pastoral Assoc.; Luisa Vasconcelos, F.I.C., Pastoral Assoc.; Maria Macedo, F.I.C., Pastoral Assoc.; Antonia Soares, F.I.C., Pastoral Assoc.; Laura Lopes, F.I.C., Pastoral Assoc. In Res., Revs. Russell W. Best; Jonas Christal (Brazil).
Res.: 10 Magazine St., Roxbury, 02119-2706. Tel: 617-445-7645; Fax: 617-445-6166. Email: stpatrickrox@comcast.net.
School—131 Mt. Pleasant Ave., Roxbury, 02119. Tel: 617-427-3881. Mary Lanata, Prin. Religious Brother 1; Sisters 4; Lay Teachers 17; Students 251.

67—ST. PAUL (1907), St. Paul, Dorchester was suppressed. This parish's records are located at Holy Family, Boston.

68—ST. PETER (1872) Rt. Rev. John J. Ahern; Revs. Richard C. Conway, Parochial Vicar; Huy H. Nguyen, Parochial Vicar.
Res.: 240 Adams St., Dorchester, 02122-1834. Tel: 617-265-1132; Fax: 617-265-0463. Email: stpeter.dor@verizon.net.

69—ST. PETER (1904), (Lithuanian), Rev. Stephen P. Zukas.
Res.: 50 Orton Marotta Way, South Boston, 02127-2006. Tel: 617-268-0353; Fax: 617-268-2585. Email: klebonas@verizon.net. Web: www.stpeterlithparish.catholicweb.com.
Catechesis/Religious Program—Mrs. Aldona Lingertat, D.R.E.; Mrs. Glorija Adonkaitis, D.R.E.

70—SS. PETER AND PAUL (1844), SS. Peter and Paul, South Boston was suppressed. This parish's records are located at St. Vincent de Paul, Boston.

71—ST. PHILIP, St. Philip, Roxbury was suppressed. This parish's records are located at St. Katherine Drexel, Boston.

72—ST. RICHARD, St. Richard, Roxbury was suppressed. This parish's records are located at St. Patrick, Boston.

73—SACRED HEART (1873) Very Rev. Wayne L. Belschner; Deacon Anthony J. Constantino.
Res.: 303 Paris St., East Boston, 02128-3063. Tel: 617-567-5776; Fax: 617-567-3042. Email: mtalluto@yahoo.com. Web: www.rc.net/boston/sacredhearteast.
School—East Boston Central Catholic School Consortium, 69 London St., East Boston, 02128. Tel: 617-567-7456. Mary Ann Manfredonia, Prin. Sisters 1; Lay Teachers 12; Students 229.
Catechesis/Religious Program—See Holy Family, Boston, Tel: 617-567-6509. Sharon A. Rozzi, D.R.E.

74—SACRED HEART (1888), (Italian), Sacred Heart, North End was suppressed. This parish's records are located at St. Leonard of Port Maurice, Boston.

75—SACRED HEART (1893) Rev. Msgr. Francis H. Kelley; Rev. John M. Mendicoa, Parochial Vicar; Senior Deacon Jesus M. Quiles; Mr. John Scanlon, Pastoral Assoc.; Ms. Kathy Sherrod, Pastoral Assoc.
Res.: 169 Cummins Hwy., Roslindale, 02131-3739. Tel: 617-325-3322; Fax: 617-325-2145. Email: sacredheartparish@verizon.net. Web: www.sh-roslindale.org.
School—1035 Canterbury St., Roslindale, 02131. Tel: 617-323-2500. Sr. Gail Ripley, C.S.J., Prin. Sisters 2; Lay Teachers 15; Students 464.

Catechesis/Religious Program—Caroline Quiles, D.R.E.

76—St. Stephen Rev. Msgr. Timothy F. O'Leary (Wales), Admin.
24 Clark St., Boston, 02109-9923. Tel: 617-523-1230; Fax: 617-723-7389. Email: info@socstjames.com. In Res., Rev. Patrick J. Universal (GLP) (Retired).

77—St. Stephen, St. Stephen, North End was suppressed. This parish's records are located at St. Leonard of Port Maurice, Boston.

78—St. Theresa of Avila (1895) Rev. Msgr. William M. Helmick; Revs. Andreas R. Davison, Parochial Vicar; Robert J. Blaney, Parochial Vicar. In Res., Most Rev. Emilio S. Allue, S.D.B.; Rev. Raymond G. Helmick, S.J.
Res.: 10 St. Theresa Ave., West Roxbury, 02132. Tel: 617-325-1300; Fax: 617-325-0380. Email: sttheresarectory@msn.com. Web: www.rc.net/boston/st_theresa.
School—40 St. Theresa Ave., West Roxbury, 02132. Tel: 617-323-1050. Jane Gibbons, Prin. Sisters 2; Lay Teachers 20; Students 589.
Catechesis/Religious Program—Ann Barden, D.R.E.; Diane Flynn, D.R.E.; Jennifer McKiernan, D.R.E.
Convent—20 Pine Lodge Rd., West Roxbury, 02132. Tel: 617-325-9171.

79—St. Thomas Aquinas (1869) Rev. Michael J. Harkins.
Res.: 97 South St., Jamaica Plain, 02130. Tel: 617-524-0240; Fax: 866-339-5148. Email: stthosq@comcast.net.
Catechesis/Religious Program—Ms. Nancy Thompson, D.R.E.

80—St. Vincent de Paul (1872) Rev. Joseph M. White; Ms. Nicole Feeley, Pastoral Assoc.
Res.: 363 E St., South Boston, 02127. Tel: 617-268-8100; Fax: 617-268-1277. Email: stvincentdepaul@comcast.net. Web: www.stvincent-depaulparish.org.

81—St. William (1909), St. William, Dorchester was suppressed. This parish's records are located at Blessed Mother Teresa of Calcutta, Boston.

OUTSIDE THE CITY OF BOSTON

Abington, Plymouth Co.

1—St. Bridget (1863) [JC] Revs. James M. Mahoney; Joseph G. Arsenault, Parochial Vicar; Deacon James V. McLaughlin; Ms. Terri Raymond, Pastoral Assoc. Tel: 781-857-3224.
Res.: 455 Plymouth St., 02351-1889. Tel: 781-878-0900; Fax: 781-878-6566. Web: www.rc.net/boston/saintbridget/.
School—Joseph F. Cirigliano, Prin. Lay Teachers 11; Students 249.
Catechesis/Religious Program—Tel: 781-878-5950. Anne Fennell, D.R.E.

2—St. Nicholas (1964), St. Nicholas, Abington was suppressed. This parish's records are located at St. Edith Stein, Brockton.

Acton, Middlesex Co., St. Elizabeth of Hungary (1945) Rev. Walter J. Woods; Mr. Stephen J. Ryan, Pastoral Assoc.
Res.: 89 Arlington St., 01720-2503. Tel: 978-263-4305; Fax: 978-263-9014. Email: office@seoh.org. Web: www.seoh.org.
Catechesis/Religious Program—Barbara M. Dane, D.R.E.; Cindy K. Harrington, D.R.E.; Mr. James Flanagan, D.R.E.

Amesbury, Essex Co.

1—Holy Family (1998) [CEM] Rev. Conrad Salach, O.F.M.Conv., Admin.; Deacon Raymond E. Doucette.
Office & Rectory: 9 Sparhawk St., 01913. Tel: 978-388-0330; Fax: 978-388-1451. Email: parishoffice@hfamesbury.com. Web: www.hfamesbury.com.
Catechesis/Religious Program—Tel: 978-388-3477. Doreen Keller, D.R.E.

2—St. Joseph, St. Joseph, Amesbury was suppressed. This parish's records are located at Holy Family, Amesbury.

3—Sacred Heart, Sacred Heart, Amesbury was suppressed. This parish's records are located at Holy Family, Amesbury.

Andover, Essex Co.

1—St. Augustine (1866) [CEM] Revs. Peter G. Gori, O.S.A.; Joseph L. Narog, O.S.A., Parochial Vicar.
Res.: 43 Essex St., 01810-3748. Tel: 978-475-0050; Fax: 978-475-3078. Email: info@staugustineparish.org. Web: www.staugustineparish.org.
School—26 Central St., 01810. Tel: 978-475-2414. Ann Kendall, Prin. Sisters 1; Lay Teachers 28; Students 493.
Catechesis/Religious Program—Tel: 978-475-7612; Fax: 978-475-9825. Bridget Rao, D.R.E.
Mission—St. Joseph's (1881) Ballardville.
Convent—Sisters of Notre Dame, 47 Essex St., Essex Co. 01810. Tel: 978-475-0087.

2—St. Robert Bellarmine (1961) Rev. Richard T. Conway.
Res.: 198 Haggetts Pond Rd., 01810-4218. Tel: 978-683-8922; Fax: 978-689-8878. Web: www.saintroberts.net.
Catechesis/Religious Program—Amanda Roberts, D.R.E.

Arlington, Middlesex Co.

1—Saint Agnes (1872) Revs. Brian M. Flatley; John J. Graham, Parochial Vicar; Joseph J. D'Onofrio, Parochial Vicar.
Res.: 51 Medford St., 02474-3197. Tel: 781-648-0220; Fax: 781-643-7883. Email: parish@saintagnes.net. Web: www.saintagnes.net.
School—39 Medford St., 02474. Tel: 781-643-9031. Sr. Patricia Randall, R.S.M., Prin. Religious 3; Lay Teachers 20; Students 400.
High School—Arlington Catholic High School, 16 Medford St., 02474. Tel: 781-646-7770. Stephen J. Biagioni, Prin. Religious 10; Lay Teachers 40; Students 800.
Catechesis/Religious Program—Tel: 781-646-5579. Ms. Joyce Patriacca, D.R.E.

2—St. Camillus (1950) Rev. James E. O'Leary. In Res., Rev. Robert M. O'Grady.
Res.: 1175 Concord Tpke., 02476-7262. Tel: 781-643-3132; Fax: 781-643-8228. Email: stcamillus@aol.com.
Catechesis/Religious Program—Catherine Robinson, D.R.E.; John Flahery, D.R.E.

3—St. James the Apostle (1914), St. James the Apostle, Arlington was suppressed. This parish's records are located at St. Camillus, Arlington.

4—St. Jerome (1934), St. Jerome, Arlington was suppressed. This parish's records are located at St. Agnes, Arlington.

Ashland, Middlesex Co., St. Cecilia (1885) Rev. Richard P. Cornell.
Res.: 54 Esty St., 01721-2126. Tel: 508-881-1107; Fax: 508-881-8606. Email: business.stcecilia@comcast.net. Web: www.saintcecilia.org.
Catechesis/Religious Program—Tel: 508-881-6107. Janet Wilkinson, D.R.E.; Jason Giombetti, D.R.E.

Avon, Norfolk Co., St. Michael (1908) [CEM] Rev. Louis R. Palmieri.
Res.: 87 N. Main St., 02322-1286. Tel: 508-586-7210; Fax: 508-586-7211.
Catechesis/Religious Program—Carol Prance, D.R.E.

Ayer, Middlesex Co., St. Mary (1858) [CEM] Rev. Edmond M. Derosier; Sr. Joan Guertin, S.U.S.C., Pastoral Assoc.
31 Shirley St., 01432-1219. Tel: 978-772-2414; Fax: 978-772-0727. Email: stmary-ayer@verizon.net. Web: www.stmarysayer.org.
Catechesis/Religious Program—

Bedford, Middlesex Co., St. Michael (1931) Rev. Mark S. Sheehan; Deacon Guy C. Saint Sauveur. In Res., Rev. Isaac Ebo Mensah (Ghana).
Res.: 90 Concord Rd., 01730. Tel: 781-275-6318; Fax: 781-271-9879. Email: office@saintmichaelparishbedford.org. Web: www.saintmichaelparishbedford.org.
Catechesis/Religious Program—Tel: 781-275-6324; Fax: 781-271-0133. Patricia Marks, D.R.E.

Bellingham, Norfolk Co.

1—Assumption (1927), Assumption, Bellingham was suppressed. This parish's records are located at St. Blaise, Bellingham.

2—St. Blaise (1962) Rev. Michael J. Kearney. In Res., Rev. Albert J. Sallese (Retired).
Res. & Office: 1158 Main St., 02019-1597. Tel: 508-966-1258; Fax: 508-966-0310. Email: fathermike@saintblaise.org. Web: www.stblaise.org.
Catechesis/Religious Program—Cheryl Langevin, D.R.E.

3—St. Brendan (1945) Rev. David J. Mullen; Senior Deacon Robert T. Hackett.
Res.: 384 Hartford Ave., 02019-1217. Tel: 508-966-0260; Fax: 508-966-4404. Email: fr.mullen.saintsbrendan@comcast.net. Web: www.saintbrendansparish.org.
Catechesis/Religious Program—Gladys Griffin, D.R.E.

Belmont, Middlesex Co.

1—St. Joseph (1900) Rev. Albert M. Faretra. In Res., Rev. David M. O'Leary.
Res.: 345 Waverley St., 02478-2418. Tel: 617-484-0279; Fax: 617-489-5445. Email: frfaretra@stjoseph.belmont.ma.us. Web: www.stjoseph.belmont.ma.us.
Catechesis/Religious Program—Tel: 617-484-1770. Ann Marie Mahoney, C.R.E.

2—St. Luke (1919) Rev. Gerard Petringa; Sr. Kathleen Moran, C.S.J., Pastoral Assoc.
Res.: 132 Lexington St., 02478. Tel: 617-484-1996; Fax: 617-484-7831. Email: stlukebelmont@verizon.net. Web: www.stlukesbelmont.org.
Catechesis/Religious Program—Tel: 617-484-9357. Robert Flaherty, D.R.E.

3—Our Lady of Mercy (1926), Our Lady of Mercy, Belmont was suppressed. This parish's records are located at St. Luke, Belmont.

Beverly, Essex Co.

1—St. Alphonsus (1917), St. Alphonsus, Beverly was suppressed. This parish's records are located at St. Mary Star of the Sea, Beverly.

2—St. John the Evangelist (1955) Rev. William H. McLaughlin.
Res.: 552 Cabot St., 01915. Tel: 978-922-5542; Fax: 978-921-4563.
School—111 New Balch St., 01915. Tel: 978-922-0048. Karen P. McCarthy, Prin.
Catechesis/Religious Program—Jean Sword, D.R.E. (Elem. School); Jude Odimone Milan, D.R.E. (High School).

3—St. Margaret (1905) Rev. Edward M. Keohan, Admin. (Retired).
Res.: 672 Hale St., 01915-2119. Tel: 978-927-0069; Fax: 978-927-9359. Email: stmargaretbeverlyfarms@comcast.net.
Catechesis/Religious Program—Miss Mary Murray, D.R.E.

4—St. Mary Star of the Sea (1870) Rev. David J. Barnes.
Res.: 253 Cabot St., 01915-4597. Tel: 978-922-0113; Fax: 978-922-8501. Web: www.stmarystar.org.
School—13 Chapman St., 01915. Tel: 978-927-3259. Patricia Diglio, Prin.
Catechesis/Religious Program—Christine O'Brien, D.R.E.
Convent—St. Mary, 15 Chapman St., 01915-4597.

Billerica, Middlesex Co.

1—St. Andrew (1868) Rev. Michael Parise; Ms. Adrienne Cullen, Pastoral Assoc.
Res.: 45 Talbot Ave., 01862-1414. Tel: 978-663-3624; Fax: 978-670-1433. Email: pastormichael1@juno.com. Web: www.saintandrewbillerica.com.
Catechesis/Religious Program—Tel: 978-667-9024. Ann Marie Huff, D.R.E.

2—St. Mary (1937) Rev. Francis E. Sullivan; Deacon Allan R. Shanahan.
Res.: 796 Boston Rd., 01821. Tel: 978-663-2215; Fax: 978-663-0127. Email: parish@stmarybillerica.com. Web: www.stmarybillerica.com.
Catechesis/Religious Program—Roberta Breen, D.R.E.; James J. Spinale, D.R.E.

3—St. Theresa of Lisieux (1945) Revs. Eugene D. Tully; Tinh Van Nguyen, Parochial Vicar; Deacon Phillip T. DiBello. In Res., Rev. John J. McCormick (Retired).
Res.: One Grace Ave., 01821-2504. Tel: 978-663-8816; Fax: 978-663-0577. Email: rectory_parish@sttheresaparishbillerica.com. Web: www.sttheresaparishbillerica.com.
Catechesis/Religious Program—Stephanie Tuzzolo, D.R.E.; Lorraine Ronan, D.R.E.; Theresa Grejdus, D.R.E.; Carol Roncari, D.R.E.

Braintree, Norfolk Co.

1—St. Clare (1959) Rev. Paul S. Sughrue; Deacon Michael J. Cavanaugh.
Res.: 1244 Liberty St., 02184-8299. Tel: 781-848-7480; Fax: 781-356-8380. Email: stclare1@verizon.net.
Catechesis/Religious Program—Tel: 781-848-7481. Gilbert Capone, D.R.E.

2—St. Francis of Assisi (1903) Very Rev. Kevin M. Sepe; Rev. Darin V. Colarusso, Parochial Vicar; Linda M. Muldoon, Pastoral Assoc. In Res., Very Rev. Mark O'Connell.
Res.: 856 Washington St., 02184-6464. Tel: 781-843-1332; Fax: 781-848-0976. Email: parish@sfab.org. Web: www.sfab.org.
School—850 Washington St., 02184. Tel: 781-848-0842. Victoria DeBenedictis, Prin.
Catechesis/Religious Program—Tel: 781-848-3238. Margaret L. Donaher, D.R.E.

3—St. Thomas More (1938) Rev. James J. McCarthy; Deacon Charles P. Webb; Ms. Janelle Snarsky, Pastoral Assoc.
Res.: 8 Hawthorn Rd., 02184-1402. Tel: 781-843-1980; Fax: 781-843-7110. Web: www.stmparish.org.
Catechesis/Religious Program—Tel: 781-843-2142. Anne Vail, D.R.E.; Jerry Hubbard, D.R.E.

Bridgewater, Plymouth Co., St. Thomas Aquinas (1848) [CEM] Very Rev. Joseph K. Raeke; Rev. Carlos C. Kim, Parochial Vicar; Deacon Gerald P. Ryan. In Res., Rev. Edward J. McLaughlin (Retired).
Res.: 103 Center St., 02324-1397. Tel: 508-697-9528; Fax: 508-279-1859. Email: stthomasaquinas@comcast.net. Web: www.stthomasaquinas.com.
Catechesis/Religious Program—Tel: 508-697-3652; Fax: 508-697-8907. Ms. Francine Bell, D.R.E.

Brockton, Plymouth Co.

1—St. Casimir (1898), (Lithuanian), Unassigned.
Res.: 21 Sawtell Ave., 02302. Tel: 508-586-2226; Fax: 508-559-2761.

2—Christ the King (2004) Revs. David P. O'Donnell; Garcia Breneville (Haiti), Parochial Vicar; Sr. Alice M. Arsenault, S.U.S.C., Pastoral Assoc.; Deacon Philip H. LaFond.

Res.: 42 Wendell Ave., 02302-3122. Tel: 508-586-1575; Fax: 508-586-9393. Web: www.ctkp.org.
Catechesis/Religious Program—Judy A. Sullivan, D.R.E.; Joseph Sanon, D.R.E.
Convent—45 Erie Ave., 02302. Tel: 508-559-7642.

3—ST. COLMAN OF CLOYNE (2004), St. Colman of Cloyne, Brockton was suppressed. This parish's records are located at Christ the King, Brockton.

4—ST. EDITH STEIN (2003) Revs. Brian P. Smith, Team Ministry; Brian L. Flynn, Team Ministry; Sisters Eugenia DaSilva, F.I.C., Pastoral Assoc.; Djai, Pastoral Assoc.
Res.: 71 E. Main St., 02301-2461. Tel: 508-586-6491; Fax: 508-587-1796. Email: saintedithstein@gmail.com. Web: www.stedithsteinparish.org.
Catechesis/Religious Program—Tel: 508-588-7032. Mary Ann Yezukevich, D.R.E.

5—ST. EDWARD (1897), St. Edward, Brockton was suppressed. This parish's records are located at St. Edith Stein, Brockton.

6—ST. MARGARET (1902), St. Margaret, Brockton was suppressed. This parish's records are located at Our Lady of Lourdes, Brockton.

7—OUR LADY OF LOURDES (1931) Very Rev. Francis J. Cloherty; Ms. Jeanne Lafond, Pastoral Assoc.
Res.: 439 West St., 02301-4803. Tel: 508-586-4715; Fax: 508-584-6257. Email: our.lourdes@comcast.net. Web: www.ourladyoflourdes-brockton.com.
Catechesis/Religious Program—Tel: 508-588-1484; Fax: 508-584-6257. Sr. Marie Madigan, M.H.S.H., D.R.E.

8—OUR LADY OF OSTROBRAMA (1914), Our Lady of Ostrobrama, Brockton was suppressed. This parish's records are located at St. Edith Stein, Brockton.

9—ST. PATRICK (1856) Rev. Jose M. Abalon (NEW).
Res.: 335 Main St., 02301-5396. Tel: 508-586-4840; Fax: 508-941-0639. Email: stpatrickbrockton@yahoo.com.

10—SACRED HEART (1891), Sacred Heart, Brockton was suppressed. This parish's records are located at Christ the King, Brockton.

BROOKLINE, NORFOLK CO.

1—ST. AIDAN (1911), St. Aidan, Brookline was suppressed. This parish's records are located at St. Mary of the Assumption, Brookline.

2—INFANT JESUS (1938), Infant Jesus, Brookline was suppressed. This parish's records are located at St. Mary of the Assumption, Brookline.

3—INFANT JESUS-ST. LAWRENCE (Chestnut Hill) (1999), Infant Jesus-St. Lawrence, Brookline was suppressed. This parish's records are located at St. Mary of the Assumption, Brookline.

4—ST. LAWRENCE (1898), St. Lawrence, Brookline was suppressed. This parish's records are located at St. Mary of the Assumption, Brookline.

5—ST. MARY OF THE ASSUMPTION (1852) Revs. Brian M. Clary; Robert J. Congdon, Parochial Vicar. In Res., Revs. Richard J. Butler (Retired); Sebastian Musa (Nigeria); Bruce N. Teague (SPR).
Res.: 5 Linden Pl., 02445-7311. Tel: 617-734-0444; Fax: 617-734-3001. Web: www.stmarybrookline.com.
School—67 Harvard St., 02445. Tel: 617-566-7184. Maureen Jutras, Prin.
Catechesis/Religious Program—Julianne J. Shanklis, D.R.E.

BURLINGTON, MIDDLESEX CO.

1—ST. MALACHY (1964) Rev. John M. Capuci; Mr. Ken Meltz, Pastoral Assoc.
Res.: 99 Bedford St., 01803. Tel: 781-272-5111; Fax: 781-270-9407. Email: office@saint-malachy.org. Web: www.saint-malachy.org.
Catechesis/Religious Program—Donald P. Nealon, D.R.E.; Susan Hurton, D.R.E.; Ms. Anna Molettieri, D.R.E.

2—ST. MARGARET (1945) Revs. Joseph P. Robinson; Harry J. Kaufman, Parochial Vicar; Deacon Richard F. Bilotta.
Res.: 111 Winn St., 01803. Tel: 781-272-3111; Fax: 781-272-9204. Email: tinapeg2@verizon.net. Web: www.saintmargaretschurch.net.
Catechesis/Religious Program—Tel: 781-935-7373. Mary Murgo, D.R.E.

CAMBRIDGE, MIDDLESEX CO.

1—ST. ANTHONY OF PADUA (1902), (Portuguese), Very Rev. Walter A. Carreiro; Rev. James M. Achadinha, Parochial Vicar. In Res., Rev. Cristiano G. Borro Barbosa (Brazil).
Res.: 400 Cardinal Medeiros Ave., 02141-1411. Tel: 617-547-5593; Fax: 617-547-1505. Email: stanthony.camb@verizon.net. Web: www.stanthony-cambridge.com.
Catechesis/Religious Program—Mariazinha Sousa, D.R.E.

2—BLESSED SACRAMENT (1905), Blessed Sacrament, Cambridge was suppressed. This parish's records are located at St. Mary of the Annunciation, Cambridge.

3—ST. FRANCIS OF ASSISI (1917), (Italian), Rev. Norbert DeAmato, O.F.M.; Ms. Joan DeGuglielmo, Pastoral Assoc.
Res.: 42 Sciarappa St., 02141. Tel: 617-876-6754; Fax: 617-876-6753. Email: st_francis_42@yahoo.com.

4—ST. HEDWIG (1907), St. Hedwig, Cambridge was suppressed. This parish's records are located at Archives, Boston.

5—IMMACULATE CONCEPTION (1910), (Lithuanian), Immaculate Conception, Cambridge was suppressed. This parish's records are located at Sacred Heart, Cambridge.

6—IMMACULATE CONCEPTION (1926), Immaculate Conception, Cambridge was suppressed. This parish's records are located at St. John the Evangelist, Cambridge.

7—ST. JOHN THE EVANGELIST (1893) Revs. Charles E. Collins; Garcia Breneville (Haiti), Parochial Vicar; Deacon Alfred J. Geneus. In Res., Revs. Robert E. Nee; Thomas L. Leclerc, M.S.
Res.: 2254 Massachusetts Ave., 02140-1837. Tel: 617-547-4880; Fax: 617-441-8028. Email: info@stjohncambridge.org. Web: www.stjohncambridge.org.
Catechesis/Religious Program—Maureen Megnia, D.R.E.

8—ST. MARY OF THE ANNUNCIATION (1867) Revs. Gabriel Troy; Alonso E. Macias (Mexico), Parochial Vicar; Deacon Stanley A. Straub.
Res.: 134 Norfolk St., 02139. Tel: 617-547-0120; Fax: 617-547-0232. Email: parishinfo@stmaryoftheannunciation.com. Web: www.stmaryoftheannunciation.com.
Catechesis/Religious Program—Tel: 617-547-0145. Maria Bermudez, D.R.E.

9—OUR LADY OF PITY (1892), Our Lady of Pity, Cambridge was suppressed. This parish's records are located at St. John the Evangelist, Cambridge.

10—ST. PATRICK (1908), St. Patrick, Cambridge was suppressed. This parish's records are located at Sacred Heart, Cambridge.

11—ST. PAUL (1875) Revs. Michael E. Drea; James W. Savage, Parochial Vicar. In Res., Revs. William F. Murphy; George S. Salzmann, O.S.F.S.
Res.: 29 Mt. Auburn St., 02138-6097. Tel: 617-491-8400; Fax: 617-354-7092. Email: info@stpaulparish.org. Web: www.stpaulparish.org.
School—Boston Archdiocesan Choir School, Tel: 617-868-8658. Jennine D. Zito, Prin.
Catechesis/Religious Program—Ms. Patty Lee, D.R.E.

12—ST. PETER (1848) Rev. Leonard F. O'Malley; Ms. Anna Molettieri, Pastoral Assoc.
Res.: 31 Buckingham St., 02138-2297. Tel: 617-547-4235; Fax: 617-547-1525. Email: office@stpetercamb.org. Web: www.stpetercamb.org.
School—96 Concord Ave., 02138. Tel: 617-547-0101. Mrs. Mary Jo Keaney, Prin. Sisters 5; Lay Teachers 7; Students 201.
Catechesis/Religious Program—Kathryn Smith, D.R.E.

13—SACRED HEART (1842) Rev. John P. Tackney.
Res.: 49 Sixth St., 02141-1594. Tel: 617-547-0399; Fax: 617-441-8648. Email: sacredheartofj@msn.com.
Catechesis/Religious Program—

CANTON, NORFOLK CO.

1—ST. GERARD MAJELLA (1960) Rev. John L. Sullivan; Ms. Ellie George, Pastoral Assoc.
Res.: 1860 Washington St., 02021. Tel: 781-828-3420; Fax: 781-828-2520. Email: welcome@saintgerard.org. Web: www.saintgerard.org.
Catechesis/Religious Program—Eleanor George, D.R.E.

2—ST. JOHN THE EVANGELIST (1861) Rev. Michael F. McLellan. In Res., Rev. Msgr. Charles J. Bourque (Retired); Rev. John F. Reardon.
Res.: 700 Washington St., 02021-3036. Tel: 781-828-0090; Fax: 781-828-2480. Web: www.stjohncanton.org.
School—696 Washington St., 02021-3036. Tel: 781-828-2130. Charlotte Kelly, Prin. Sisters 1; Lay Teachers 25; Students 261.
Catechesis/Religious Program—Tel: 781-828-5130. Mrs. Lorraine M. Wright, D.R.E.

CARLISLE, MIDDLESEX CO., ST. IRENE (1960) Revs. Thomas P. Donohoe; Romain Rurangirwa (Rowanda), Parochial Vicar; Deacons Dean C. Bulpett; Charles A. Ferraro.
Res.: 187 East St., 01741-1104. Tel: 978-369-3940; Fax: 978-287-1440. Email: stirene@comcast.net. Web: www.stirenes.org.
Catechesis/Religious Program—Georgia Winfrey, D.R.E.

CARVER, PLYMOUTH CO., OUR LADY OF LOURDES (1950) Rev. Anthony J. Medairos; Deacon Paul S. Jones.
Parish Office: 130 Main St., 02330-0068. Tel: 508-866-4000; Fax: 508-866-5588. Email: ololcarver@comcast.net. Web: www.ourladyoflourdescarver.parishesonline.com.
Catechesis/Religious Program—Tel: 508-866-9211. Linda Cedrone, D.R.E.

CHELMSFORD, MIDDLESEX CO.

1—ST. JOHN THE EVANGELIST (1893) Very Rev. Paul E. Ritt; Rev. William N. Ventura, Parochial Vicar. In Res., Rev. Francis B. Leonard (Retired).
Res.: 115 Middlesex St., 01863-2030. Tel: 978-251-8571; Fax: 978-251-7873. Email: sje.church@verizon.net. Web: www.parishesonline.com.
Catechesis/Religious Program—Tel: 978-251-4310. Ms. Debra Anderson, D.R.E.

2—ST. MARY (1931) Revs. Stephen S. Donohoe; William S. Dunn, Parochial Vicar; Deacon John E. Bortz.
Res.: 25 North Rd., 01824-2767. Tel: 978-256-2374; Fax: 978-256-0122. Web: www.saint-mary.org.
Catechesis/Religious Program—Ms. Heather Hannaway, D.R.E.

CHELSEA, SUFFOLK CO.

1—OUR LADY OF GRACE (1913) Very Rev. James J. Barry; Linda DeCristoforo, Pastoral Assoc.
Res.: 59 Nichols St., 02150-1225. Tel: 617-884-0030; Fax: 617-884-0957. Email: ologparish@comcast.net. Web: www.olgp.net.
Catechesis/Religious Program—Fax: 617-884-2482. Sr. Kathy Stark, D.R.E.

2—OUR LADY OF THE ASSUMPTION (1907), Our Lady of the Assumption, Chelsea was suppressed. This parish's records are located at Saint Rose of Lima, Chelsea.

3—ST. ROSE OF LIMA (1849) Revs. Terence J. Moran; Joseph P. Nam, C.M.C., Parochial Vicar; Succes Jeanty (Mexico), Parochial Vicar; Sr. Sergia Jimenez, Pastoral Assoc.; Deacons Luis F. Rivera; Alejandro Iraola.
Res.: 601 Broadway, 02150-2998. Tel: 617-889-2774; Fax: 617-889-2854. Email: strosechelsea@hotmail.com.
School—580 Broadway, 02150-2998. Tel: 617-884-2626. Mary Ann Babineau, Prin. Sisters 8; Lay Teachers 10; Students 423.
Catechesis/Religious Program—Marie Horgan, D.R.E. (English); Sor Ynocencia, D.R.E. (Spanish); Danha Nguyen, D.R.E. (Vietnamese).

4—ST. STANISLAUS (1905), (Polish), Rev. Andrew T. Grelak.
Res.: 163 Chestnut St., 02150. Tel: 617-889-0261; Fax: 617-466-2107. Email: stanislaus61@comcast.com.

COHASSET, NORFOLK CO., ST. ANTHONY OF PADUA (1886) Rev. John R. Mulvehill; Deacon Paul S. Rooney.
Res.: 129 S. Main St., 02025. Tel: 781-383-0219; Fax: 781-383-2988 (Rectory). Email: stanthonycoh@aol.com. Web: www.saintanthonycohasset.org.
Catechesis/Religious Program—Tel: 781-383-0630. Virginia Macleod, D.R.E.

CONCORD, MIDDLESEX CO.

1—ST. BERNARD (1863), St. Bernard, Concord was suppressed. This parish's records are located at Holy Family, Concord.

2—HOLY FAMILY (2004) Rev. Austin H. Fleming; Deacons Charles I. Clough; Gregory J. Burch; Sr. Rose Marie Lipke, C.D.P., Pastoral Assoc.
55 Church St., 01742.
Res.: 70 Monument Sq., 01742. Tel: 978-369-7442; Fax: 978-371-0853. Email: holyfamily@holyfamilyconcord.org. Web: www.holyfamilyconcord.org.
Catechesis/Religious Program—Sandra Meuller, D.R.E.; Helen Cushman, D.R.E.

3—OUR LADY HELP OF CHRISTIANS (1907), Our Lady Help of Christians, Concord was suppressed. This parish's records are located at Holy Family, Concord.

DANVERS, ESSEX CO.

1—ST. MARY OF THE ANNUNCIATION (1871) [CEM] Rev. Gerard L. Dorgan. In Res., Rev. Msgr. Frederick J. Murphy (Retired).
Res.: 24 Conant St., 01923-2968. Tel: 978-774-0340; Fax: 978-774-9407. Email: stmarydanvers@comcast.net. Web: www.stmarysdanvers.4lpi.com.
School—14 Otis St., 01923. Tel: 978-774-0307. Molly Kelley, Prin.
Catechesis/Religious Program—Tel: 978-774-8605. John J. Dillon, D.R.E.; Judy DiGennaro, D.R.E.

2—ST. RICHARD OF CHICHESTER (1963) Rev. Bruce G. Flannagan; Deacon Edward P. Elibero.
Res.: 90 Forest St., 01923-1806. Tel: 978-774-7575; Fax: 978-774-9543. Web: www.stricharddanvers.org.
School—St. Mary of the Annunciation School, 20 Otis St., 01923-1806. Tel: 978-774-0307. Molly Kelley, Prin.
Catechesis/Religious Program—Doreen Verda, D.R.E.

DEDHAM, NORFOLK CO.

1—ST. MARY (1866) [CEM] Revs. William G. Williams; William P. Lohan, Parochial Vicar; Deacon Louis W. Sheedy; Sr. Barbara Lavin, O.P., Pastoral

Assoc. In Res., Rev. Joseph F. Mozer Jr.
Res.: 420 High St., 02026-2892. Tel: 781-326-0550; Fax: 781-326-1809. Email: secretary@stmaryonline.net. Web: www.stmaryonline.net.
Catechesis/Religious Program—Tel: 781-329-5488. Sr. Anne Michael Hannigan, S.N.D., D.R.E.
2—ST. SUSANNA (1960) Rev. Stephen S. Josoma; Deacon Laurence J. Bloom.
Res.: 262 Needham St., 02026-7009. Tel: 781-329-9575; Fax: 781-329-5966. Email: saintsusanna@hotmail.com. Web: www.saintsusanna.org.
Catechesis/Religious Program—Nancy Leoncini, D.R.E.

DOVER, NORFOLK CO., MOST PRECIOUS BLOOD (1959) Very Rev. John J. Grimes.
30 Centre St., 02030-0812. Tel: 508-785-0305; Fax: 508-785-0432. Email: mpb.dover@verizon.net. Web: www.mostpreciousbloodchurch.org.
Catechesis/Religious Program—Tel: 508-785-9909 (Grades 6-12); 508-785-1217. Ann Carroll, D.R.E. (Grades 1-5); Regina O'Connor, D.R.E. (Grades 6-12).

DRACUT, MIDDLESEX CO.
1—ST. FRANCIS OF ASSISI (1963) Revs. Robert L. Connors; Christopher J. Casey, Parochial Vicar; Deacon John C. Hunt; Ms. Kathleen Long, Pastoral Assoc. Tel: 978-453-4460.
P.O. Box 609, 01826.
Parish Office: 115 Wheeler Rd., 01826-4254. Tel: 978-452-6611; Fax: 978-452-0772. Web: www.saintfrancis.net.
Catechesis/Religious Program—
2—STE. MARGUERITE D'YOUVILLE (2001) Revs. Robert L. Connors; Christopher J. Casey, Parochial Vicar; Deacon Everett F. Penney; Joan Donnelly, Pastoral Assoc.; Paul Duquette, Pastoral Assoc. In Res., Rev. James D. Lyons (Retired).
Res.: 1340 Lakeview Ave., 01826-3499. Tel: 978-957-0322; Fax: 978-957-5266. Email: stmar@comcast.net. Web: www.stmar.org.
School—77 Boisvert St., Lowell, 01850. Tel: 978-458-7594. Sr. Irene Martineau, S.A.S.V., Prin.
Convent—85 Boisvert St., Lowell, 01850. Tel: 978-454-5742.
3—ST. MARY OF THE ASSUMPTION (1909), St. Mary of the Assumption, Dracut was suppressed. This parish's records are located at St. Marguerite d'Youville, Dracut.
4—ST. THERESE (1927), St. Therese, Dracut was suppressed. This parish's records are located at St. Marguerite d'Youville, Dracut.

DUXBURY, PLYMOUTH CO., HOLY FAMILY (1945) Very Rev. Bryan K. Parrish; Rev. Sean M. Maher, Parochial Vicar; Deacons Arthur J. Keefe; Daniel R. Burns.
Church: 601 Tremont St., 02332-4450. Tel: 781-934-5055; Fax: 781-934-5796. Email: office@holyfamilyduxbury.org. Web: www.holyfamilyduxbury.org.
Catechesis/Religious Program—Tel: 781-934-6839. Mrs. Catherine Kelleher, D.R.E.

EAST BRIDGEWATER, PLYMOUTH CO., ST. JOHN THE EVANGELIST (1903) Rev. Walter F. Keymont.
Res.: 210 Central St., 02333-1998. Tel: 508-378-4207; Fax: 508-378-7317. Email: stjohnebridge@comcast.net. Web: www.geocities.com/stjohnseb.
Catechesis/Religious Program—Tel: 508-378-1521. Mrs. Nancy Smith, D.R.E. (Pre-K-K); Richard Grasso, D.R.E. (Gr. 1); Pam LeBlanc, D.R.E. (Gr. 2); Carolyn Sullivan, D.R.E. (Gr. 8-11).

ESSEX, ESSEX CO., ST. JOHN THE BAPTIST (1931) Rev. John W. Gentleman, Admin.
P.O. Box 986, 01929.
Res.: 52 Main St., 01929. Tel: 978-768-6284; Fax: 978-526-4335.
Catechesis/Religious Program—Valerie Shippen, D.R.E.

EVERETT, MIDDLESEX CO.
1—ST. ANTHONY OF PADUA (1927), (Italian), Revs. Dominic Rodighiero, C.S.; Lino Ayala Garcia, C.S., Parochial Vicar; Deacon Thomas W. Marchant.
Res.: 38 Oakes St., 02149. Tel: 617-387-0310; Fax: 617-387-1229.
School—54 Oakes St., 02149. Tel: 617-389-2448. Maria Giggie, Prin. Sisters 2; Lay Teachers 8; Students 213.
Catechesis/Religious Program—Doris DiTullio, D.R.E. (Gr. 1-6 English). Tel: 617-387-4806; Maria Sentance, D.R.E. (Gr. 7-10 English); Maybell Montano, D.R.E. (Spanish).
2—IMMACULATE CONCEPTION (1885) Rev. Gerald J. Osterman; Marie Philomene Pean, Pastoral Assoc.
Res.: 489 Broadway, 02149-3603. Tel: 617-389-5660; Fax: 617-389-2456. Email: iceverett@comcast.net. Web: www.parishesonline.com/iceverett.
Catechesis/Religious Program—Janine Keller, D.R.E. (Gr. 3-5). Tel: 617-710-4963; Richard Randazzo, D.R.E. (Gr. 6-10); Fran Foley, D.R.E. (Gr. 1 & 2).
3—ST. JOSEPH (1912), St. Joseph, Everett was suppressed. This parish's records are located at Immaculate Conception, Everett.
4—ST. THERESE (1927), St. Therese, Everett was suppressed. This parish's records are located at Immaculate Conception, Everett.

FOXBOROUGH, NORFOLK CO., ST. MARY (1859) Revs. Stephen J. Madden; Jason M. Makos, Parochial Vicar.
Res.: 83 Central St., 02035. Tel: 508-543-7726; Fax: 508-543-7728. Email: st.mary@foxboro.comcastbiz.net. Web: www.stmarysfoxboro.org.
Catechesis/Religious Program—Tel: 508-543-4577. Geraldine Saegh, D.R.E.; Catherine Briggs, D.R.E.; Elaine L'Etoile, D.R.E.

FRAMINGHAM, MIDDLESEX CO.
1—ST. BRIDGET (1878) Rev. Msgr. Francis V. Strahan; Ms. Elizabeth Mingolelli, Pastoral Assoc.; Ms. Barbara Conlin, Pastoral Assoc.
Res.: 15 Wheeler Ave., 01702-2902. Tel: 508-875-5959; Fax: 508-875-1270. Email: strahan@stbridgetparish.org. Web: www.stbridgetparish.org.
School—832 Worcester Rd., 01702. Tel: 508-875-0181. Roseanne Mungovan, Prin. Lay Teachers 19; Students 344.
Catechesis/Religious Program—Gail Barbato, D.R.E. (Gr. K-5); Marguerite Tibbert, D.R.E. (Gr. 6-10).
2—ST. GEORGE (1847) Revs. John M. Rowan; Benjamin T. LeTran, Parochial Vicar; Sr. Ann Marie McAndrews, S.N.D., Pastoral Assoc.
Res.: 74 School St., 01701. Tel: 508-877-5130; Fax: 508-877-3080. Web: www.churchofstgeorge.org.
Catechesis/Religious Program—Paula Dolliver, D.R.E.; Leslee Willitts, D.R.E.
3—ST. JEREMIAH (1958), St. Jeremiah, Framingham was suppressed. This parish's records are located at St. George, Framingham.
4—ST. STEPHEN (1883) [CEM] Revs. Francisco J. Anzoategui, Team Ministry; Albert H. Stankard, Team Ministry; Mr. Enrique Mendez, Pastoral Assoc.; Deacons Pedro L. Torres; Alfredo Nieves.
Res.: 221 Concord St., 01702. Tel: 508-875-4788; Fax: 508-875-2577. Email: ststephenchurch1@verizon.net.
Catechesis/Religious Program—James J. Drummey, D.R.E.; Maria Nieves, D.R.E. Students 300.
5—ST. TARCISIUS (1907), (Italian), [CEM] Revs. Rinaldo Vecchiato, C.S.; Heitor Castoldi, C.S., Parochial Vicar; Deacons Manoel de Souza (Brazil); Edwin J. Robinson.
35 Cedar St., 01702-6925.
Res.: 562 Waverly St., 01702-6925. Tel: 508-875-8623; Fax: 508-875-6358. Email: sttarcis@aol.com.
School—560 Waverly St., 01702. Tel: 508-872-8188. Mary Ellen Wyman, Prin.
Catechesis/Religious Program—Marie Jutkiewicz, D.R.E.; Peter DeFazio, D.R.E.

FRANKLIN, NORFOLK CO., ST. MARY (1877) [CEM] Revs. Brian F. Manning; Frank D. Campo, Parochial Vicar; Ms. Nan Rafter, Pastoral Assoc.
Res.: One Church Sq., 02038-1896. Tel: 508-528-0020; Fax: 508-528-1641. Email: parishpublishing@stmarysfranklin.org. Web: www.stmarysfranklin.org.
Catechesis/Religious Program—Isabel Coyne, D.R.E.; Karen Ackles, D.R.E.

GEORGETOWN, ESSEX CO., ST. MARY (2006) Very Rev. James M. Carroll.
P.O. Box 396, 01833.
Res.: 94 Andover St., 01833-0396. Tel: 978-352-2024; Fax: 978-352-5513. Email: rectory@parishmail.com. Web: www.saintmaryparish.org.
Catechesis/Religious Program—Tel: 978-352-6540. Mary Williams, D.R.E.

GLOUCESTER, ESSEX CO.
1—ST. ANN (1855), St. Ann, Gloucester was suppressed. This parish's records are located at Holy Family, Gloucester.
2—HOLY FAMILY (2005) Revs. Timothy A. Harrison, Team Ministry; Ronald J. Gariboldi, Team Ministry; John J. Walsh, S.J., Parochial Vicar; Deacons Daniel A. Dunn; William F.X. Kane; Anna Matturro, Pastoral Assoc.
Res.: 60 Prospect St., 01930. Tel: 978-281-4820; Fax: 978-281-4964. Email: info@holyfamilycapeann.org. Web: www.holyfamilycapeann.org.
School—St. Ann Junior High, Tel: 978-283-3455. Sr. Judith O'Brien, I.H.M.M., Prin.
Catechesis/Religious Program—Dawn Alves, D.R.E.; Ms. Kathleen McCabe, D.R.E.
3—OUR LADY OF GOOD VOYAGE (1889), (Portuguese), Rev. Richard A. Uftring, Admin.
Res.: 142 Prospect St., 01930-3714. Tel: 978-283-1490; Fax: 978-283-0787. Email: olgv@comcast.net.
Catechesis/Religious Program—Tel: 978-283-8597. Sisters Mitrina, C.S.J., D.R.E.; Sebastian, C.S.J., D.R.E.
4—ST. PETER (1928), St. Peter, Gloucester was suppressed. This parish's records are located at Holy Family, Gloucester.
5—SACRED HEART (1946), Sacred Heart, Gloucester was suppressed. This parish's records are located at Holy Family, Gloucester.

GROTON, MIDDLESEX CO.
1—ST. JAMES (1945), St. James the Apostle, Groton was suppressed. This parish's records are located at Sacred Heart-St. James, Groton.
2—SACRED HEART, Sacred Heart, Groton was suppressed. This parish's records are located at Sacred Heart-St. James, Groton.
3—SACRED HEART-ST. JAMES (2003) Merged with St. Joseph in Pepperell to form Our Lady of Grace, Pepperell.

GROVELAND, ESSEX CO., ST. PATRICK (1946), St. Patrick, Groveland was suppressed. This parish's records are located at Sacred Hearts, Haverhill.

HALIFAX, PLYMOUTH CO., OUR LADY OF THE LAKE (1945) Rev. Stephen M. Healy.
P.O. Box 35, Monponsett, 02350-0035.
Res.: 580 Monponsett St., 02338-0035. Tel: 781-293-7971; Fax: 781-293-7969.
Catechesis/Religious Program—Tel: 781-294-4571. Patsy Gillespie, D.R.E.; Carolyn Sullivan, D.R.E.

HAMILTON, ESSEX CO., ST. PAUL (1922) Rev. Louis D. Bourgeois; Deacon James V. Manzi; Ms. Mary Elizabeth Reilly, Pastoral Assoc.
Res.: 50 Union St., 01982. Tel: 978-468-2337; Fax: 978-468-6538. Email: stpaulsparish@comcast.net. Web: churchofsaintpaul.net.
Catechesis/Religious Program—Tel: 978-468-3617. Jeanne Abbott, D.R.E.

HANOVER, PLYMOUTH CO., ST. MARY OF THE SACRED HEART (1907) Revs. Christopher J. Hickey; Ted K. Kofitse (Ghana), Parochial Vicar; Deacon Christopher P. Reilly. In Res., Rev. Martin P. Connor (Retired).
Res.: 392 Hanover St., 02339. Tel: 781-826-4303; Fax: 781-826-5203. Email: stm@stmaryshanover.com. Web: www.st.marysmass.org.
Catechesis/Religious Program—Tel: 781-826-2351; Fax: 781-829-9271. Kathy Gallo, D.R.E.

HANSON, PLYMOUTH CO., ST. JOSEPH THE WORKER (1956) Rev. John M. Hannon; Deacon John F. Alexander.
Res.: One Maquan St., 02341-1714. Tel: 781-293-3581; Fax: 781-294-1052. Email: j.worker@comcast.net. Web: www.stjosephtheworker.org.
Catechesis/Religious Program—Robin Muise, D.R.E.; Kevin Mossman, D.R.E.; Mary Lewek, D.R.E.

HAVERHILL, ESSEX CO.
1—ALL SAINTS (1998) Revs. Dennis T. Nason; Michael K. Harvey, Parochial Vicar. In Res., Rev. Arnold E. Kelley (Retired).
Res.: 120 Bellevue Ave., 01832. Tel: 978-372-7721; Fax: 978-372-2085. Email: aspsec@verizon.net.
School—St. Joseph, 56 Oak Ter., 01832. Tel: 978-521-4256. Carol J. Simone, Prin.
Catechesis/Religious Program—Tel: 978-373-5473. Maureen Cartier, D.R.E.
St. Joseph's Early Childhood Ed. Center—100 Bellevue Ave., 01832. Tel: 978-372-0111.
2—ST. GEORGE (1961), St. George, Haverhill was suppressed. This parish's records are located at All Saints, Haverhill.
3—ST. JAMES (1859) Rev. Robert W. Murray; Deacon Jose N. Agudelo; Senior Deacon Leo A. Martin.
Res.: 6 Cottage St., 01830-4920. Tel: 978-372-8537; Fax: 978-373-1505. Email: stjamesrcc@hotmail.com. Web: stjameshaverhill.net.
Catechesis/Religious Program—Larry N. Webster, D.R.E.
4—ST. JOHN THE BAPTIST (1955) Rev. Keith P. LeBlanc; Deacon Thomas A. Anthony.
Res.: 110 Lincoln Ave., 01830. Tel: 978-372-2780; Fax: 978-469-0947. Email: stjohn@parishmail.com. Web: www.stjohnhaverhill.org.
5—ST. JOSEPH (1876), St. Joseph, Haverhill was suppressed. This parish's records are located at All Saints, Haverhill.
6—ST. MICHAEL (1910), St. Michael, Haverhill was suppressed. This parish's records are located at All Saints, Haverhill.
7—ST. RITA (1932), St. Rita, Haverhill was suppressed. This parish's records are located at All Saints, Haverhill.
8—SACRED HEARTS (2007) Rev. Robert W. Conole.
48 S. Chestnut St., 01835.
Res.: 6 Carleton Ave., 01835. Tel: 978-373-1281; Fax: 978-374-3043. Web: www.sacredheartsparish-.com.

School—31 S. Chestnut St., 01835. Tel: 978-372-5451. Kathleen Blain, Prin. Sisters 1; Lay Teachers 9; Students 247.
Catechesis/Religious Program—Bridget Lacefield, D.R.E.

HINGHAM, PLYMOUTH CO.

1—ST. PAUL (1871) [CEM] Very Rev. James F. Rafferty; Rev. John A. Currie, Parochial Vicar; Ms. Patricia Mikus, Pastoral Assoc.
Res.: 147 North St., 02043-3995. Tel: 781-749-0587; Fax: 781-749-8053. Web: www.stpaulhingham.net.
School—18 Fearing Rd., 02043. Tel: 781-749-2407. Bro. Richard J. Lunny, C.F.X., Prin. Lay Teachers 9; Students 253; Religious 1.
Catechesis/Religious Program—Tel: 781-749-5568. Judy Tetreault-Murphy, D.R.E.

2—RESURRECTION OF OUR LORD AND SAVIOR JESUS CHRIST (1957) Rev. Kenneth B. Quinn.
Res.: 1057 Main St., 02043-3995. Tel: 781-749-3577; Fax: 781-740-0689. Email: resparish@comcast.net.
Catechesis/Religious Program—Janet Hickey, D.R.E.

HOLBROOK, NORFOLK CO., ST. JOSEPH (1887) Rev. Edward M. Riley; Sr. Catherine Joseph McDonough, D.C., Pastoral Assoc. In Res., Rev. Matthew M. Williams.
Res.: 153 S. Franklin St., 02343. Tel: 781-767-0605; Fax: 781-767-5225. Email: bulletin.sjp@comcast.net. Web: www.stjosephholbrook.org.
School—143 S. Franklin St., 02343. Tel: 781-767-1544. Anne F. Clough, Prin. Sisters 2; Lay Teachers 14; Students 290.
Catechesis/Religious Program—Tel: 781-767-0536. Maura Burke, D.R.E.
Convent—143 S. Franklin St., 02343. Tel: 781-767-4641.

HOLLISTON, MIDDLESEX CO., ST. MARY (1870) [CEM] Rev. Mark J. Coiro; Deacons Martin E. Breinlinger; Philip M. Caruso.
Res.: 8 Church St., 01746. Tel: 508-429-4427; Fax: 508-429-3324. Email: st.marys2@verizon.net. Web: www.stmarysholliston.com.
Catechesis/Religious Program—Tel: 508-429-6076. Andrea DeMayo, D.R.E.

HOPKINTON, MIDDLESEX CO., ST. JOHN THE EVANGELIST (1866) [CEM] Revs. Paul T. Clifford; Shawn P. Carey, Parochial Vicar; Deacon Michael M. Mott; Ms. Marie Buckley, Pastoral Assoc.
Res.: 20 Church St., 01748-1836. Tel: 508-435-3313; Fax: 508-435-5651. Email: stjohnshopkinton@verizon.net. Web: www.stjohnshopkinton.com.
Catechesis/Religious Program—Tel: 508-435-3313, Ext. 208. Carol Zani, D.R.E.; Ken Lysik, D.R.E.; Elaine Mitsock, D.R.E.

HUDSON, MIDDLESEX CO.

1—CHRIST THE KING (1927), Christ the King, Hudson was suppressed. This parish's records are located at St. Michael, Hudson.

2—ST. MICHAEL (1870) [CEM] Rev. Ronald G. Calhoun; Deacon Daniel F. Crimmins; Ms. Carmen Giombetti, Pastoral Assoc.
Res.: 21 Manning St., 01749-2315. Tel: 978-562-2552; Fax: 978-568-1761. Email: parish@stmikes.org. Web: www.stmikes.org.
School—198 Main St., 01749. Tel: 978-562-2917. Patricia E. Delaney, Prin. Lay Teachers 18; Students 201.
High School—Hudson Catholic High School, 198 Main St., 01749. Tel: 978-562-6701. Caroline P. Flynn, Prin. Lay Teachers 19; Students 201.
Catechesis/Religious Program—Tel: 978-562-7174. Ms. Karen Levelle, D.R.E.

HULL, PLYMOUTH CO., ST. MARY OF THE ASSUMPTION (1938) Rev. Timothy E. Kearney.
Res.: 208 Samoset Ave., 02045-0565. Tel: 781-925-0680; Fax: 781-925-0685. Web: www.stmaryhull.com.
Catechesis/Religious Program—Lisa H. Scarry, D.R.E.

IPSWICH, ESSEX CO.

1—ST. JOSEPH (1889), St. Joseph, Ipswich was suppressed. This parish's records are located at Our Lady of Hope, Ipswich.

2—OUR LADY OF HOPE (1997) Rev. John G. Kiley; Deacon Carl M. Roberts; Ms. Elisa St. Clair, Pastoral Assoc. Tel: 978-356-2522.
Res.: One Pineswamp Rd., 01938-2922. Tel: 978-356-3944; Fax: 978-356-9592. Email: rectory@ipswichcatholics.org. Web: www.ipswichcatholics.org.
Catechesis/Religious Program—Tel: 978-356-2522. Nancy Salah, D.R.E.

3—SACRED HEART (1908), Sacred Heart, Ipswich was suppressed. This parish's records are located at Our Lady of Hope, Ipswich.

4—ST. STANISLAUS (1910), St. Stanislaus, Ipswich was suppressed. This parish's records are located at Our Lady of Hope, Ipswich.

KINGSTON, PLYMOUTH CO., ST. JOSEPH (1908) [CEM] Rev. Charles J. Higgins; Deacon William V. Nagle.
270 Main St., 02364-1922.
Res.: 268 Main St., 02364-1922. Tel: 781-585-6679; Fax: 781-645-1337. Email: stjosephkingstonma@comcast.net. Web: www.stjosephkingston.com.
Catechesis/Religious Program—Tel: 781-585-6372. Margart M. Hall, D.R.E.; Ms. Ann M. Cussen, D.R.E.

LAKEVILLE, PLYMOUTH CO., SAINTS MARTHA AND MARY (1958) Rev. Francis E. Daley; Deacon Richard J. Brennan.
Res.: 354 Bedford St., 02347-2107. Tel: 508-947-2107; Fax: 508-947-6543. Email: parish@saintsmarthaandmary.com. Web: www.saintsmarthaandmary.com.
Catechesis/Religious Program—Sr. Rachel Labonville, C.S.C., D.R.E.

LAWRENCE, ESSEX CO.

1—ST. ANNE, St. Anne, Lawrence was suppressed. This parish's records are located at St. Patrick, Lawrence.

2—ASSUMPTION OF THE BLESSED VIRGIN, Assumption of the Blessed Virgin, Lawrence was suppressed. This parish's records are located at St. Mary of the Assumption, Lawrence.

3—ASUNCION DE LA VIRGEN MARIA (1993), (Hispanic), Asuncion de la Virgen Maria, Lawrence was suppressed. This parish's records are located at St. Mary of the Assumption, Lawrence.

4—ST. AUGUSTINE (1935), St. Augustine, Lawrence was suppressed. This parish's records are located at Our Lady of Good Counsel, Methuen.

5—CORPUS CHRISTI (2004) Rev. Francis X. Mawn; Deacon Julio C. Vargas.
Res.: 35 Essex St., 01840. Tel: 978-685-1711; Fax: 978-691-5927. Email: pastor@corpuschristilawrence.org. Web: www.corpuschristilawrence.org.
Catechesis/Religious Program—Mary Crow, D.R.E.

6—ST. FRANCIS (1903), St. Francis, Lawrence was suppressed. This parish's records are located at Corpus Christi, Lawrence.

7—HOLY ROSARY (1904), Holy Rosary, Lawrence was suppressed. This parish's records are located at Corpus Christi, Lawrence.

8—HOLY TRINITY (1905), Holy Trinity, Lawrence was suppressed. This parish's records are located at Corpus Christi, Lawrence.

9—IMMACULATE CONCEPTION, Immaculate Conception, Lawrence was suppressed. This parish's records are located at St. Mary of the Assumption, Lawrence.

10—ST. LAURENCE O'TOOLE, St. Laurence O'Toole, Lawrence was suppressed. This parish's records are located at St. Mary of the Assumption, Lawrence.

11—ST. MARY, St. Mary, Lawrence was suppressed. This parish's records are located at St. Mary of the Assumption, Lawrence.

12—ST. MARY OF THE ASSUMPTION (2004) Revs. Jorge A. Reyes, O.S.A.; Liam T. O'Doherty, O.S.A., Parochial Vicar; Deacons Jesus Castillo; Alvaro Arsenio Frias (Democratic Republic of Congo).
205 Hampshire St., 01841.
Res.: 300 Haverhill St., 01840. Tel: 978-685-1111; Fax: 978-686-5555. Web: www.stmaryassumption-lawrence.org.
School—301 Haverhill St., 01840. Tel: 978-685-2091. Vina Troianello, Prin. Sisters 2; Lay Teachers 8; Students 171.
Catechesis/Religious Program—Felix Duran, D.R.E.

13—ST. MARY-IMMACULATE CONCEPTION, St. Mary-Immaculate Conception, Lawrence was suppressed. This parish's records are located at St. Mary of the Assumption, Lawrence.

14—ST. PATRICK (1872) [CEM] Revs. Paul B. O'Brien; Paul G. McManus, Parochial Vicar; Deacon Paul V. Specht.
Res.: 118 S. Broadway, 01843-1427. Tel: 978-683-9416; Fax: 978-681-5808. Web: www.saintpatrickparish.com.
School—101 Parker St., 01843. Tel: 978-683-5822. Sr. Lucy Veilleux, S.C.I.M., Prin. Sisters 8; Lay Teachers 17; Students 500.
Catechesis/Religious Program—Ms. Diane Jarvis, D.R.E.

15—SS. PETER AND PAUL (1907), SS. Peter and Paul, Lawrence was suppressed. This parish's records are located at Corpus Christi, Lawrence.

16—SACRED HEART (1905), Sacred Heart, Lawrence was suppressed. This parish's records are located at St. Patrick, Lawrence.

LEXINGTON, MIDDLESEX CO.

1—ST. BRIGID (1848) Revs. Arnold F. Colletti; William P. Smith, O.M.I., Parochial Vicar; Ms. Beverly Goode, Pastoral Assoc.; Ms. Mary Peterson, Pastoral Assoc.
Res.: 2001 Massachusetts Ave., 02421-4812. Tel: 781-862-0335; Fax: 781-862-1409. Email: shepherd@lexingtoncatholic.org. Web: www.lexingtoncatholic.org.
Catechesis/Religious Program—George Begin, D.R.E. (Gr. 1-8). Tel: 781-862-8724; Megan Chenaille, D.R.E. (Gr. 9-12).

2—SACRED HEART (1931) Rev. Arnold F. Coletti; Ms. Beverly Goode, Pastoral Assoc.; Ms. Mary Peterson, Pastoral Assoc.
Res.: 2001 Massachusetts Ave., 02421-4812. Tel: 781-862-4646. Email: shepherd@lexingtoncatholic.org. Web: www.lexingtoncatholic.org.
Catechesis/Religious Program—Tel: 781-861-8385, Ext. 19. George Begin, D.R.E.

LINCOLN, MIDDLESEX CO., ST. JOSEPH (1946), St. Joseph, Lincoln was suppressed. This parish's records are located at St. Julia, Weston.

LITTLETON, MIDDLESEX CO., ST. ANNE (1945) Rev. Richard L. Casey, Temporary Admin.; Deacon Brian H. Laws.
Res.: 75 King St., 01460-1528. Tel: 978-486-4100; Fax: 978-952-6303. Email: stannes.rectory@verizon.net. Web: www.rc.net/boston/stanne.
Catechesis/Religious Program—Jacquelyn Butterfield, D.R.E.; Michelle Hatch, D.R.E.

LOWELL, MIDDLESEX CO.

1—ST. ANTHONY OF PADUA (1901), (Portuguese), Rev. Charles J. Hughes, Admin.; Mr. Victor Melo, Pastoral Assoc.
Res.: 893 Central St., 01852-3407. Tel: 978-452-1506; Fax: 978-458-9662. Email: st.anthony@comcast.net. Web: www.stanthony.portoinc.com.

2—HOLY FAMILY (2003) Rev. Donald G. Lozier, O.M.I.; Sr. Joan Gregoire, S.N.D., Pastoral Assoc. In Res., Rev. Norman E. Parent, O.M.I.
Res.: 122 Andrews St., 01852-5006. Tel: 978-453-2134; Fax: 978-453-0933. Email: holyfamilylowell@yahoo.com.
Catechesis/Religious Program—Richard Ouellette, D.R.E.

3—HOLY TRINITY (1904), (Polish), [CEM] Rev. Msgr. Stanislaw Kempa; Deacon Stephen M. Papik.
Res.: 340 High St., 01852-2760. Tel: 978-452-2564; Fax: 978-452-4679. Web: www.holytrinitylowell.org.
Catechesis/Religious Program—Robert Mullin, D.R.E.

4—IMMACULATE CONCEPTION (1869) Rev. Nicholas A. Sannella; Ms. Claire Couillard, Pastoral Assoc.
Res.: 3 Fayette St., 01852. Tel: 978-458-1474; Fax: 978-446-0790. Email: iclowell@yahoo.com.
School—218 E. Merrimack St., 01852. Tel: 978-454-5339. Jean B. Murphy, Prin. Sisters 1; Lay Teachers 8; Students 175.
Catechesis/Religious Program—Katherine Gendron, D.R.E.; Susan Hurton, D.R.E.

5—ST. JEAN BAPTISTE, St. Jean Baptist, Lowell was suppressed. This parish's records are located at St. Marguerite d'Youville, Dracut.

6—SAINT JEANNE D'ARC (1922), Saint Jeanne d'Arc, Lowell was suppressed. This parish's records are located at St. Rita, Lowell.

7—ST. JOSEPH (1908), St. Joseph, Lowell was suppressed. This parish's records are located at Immaculate Conception, Lowell.

8—ST. LOUIS DE FRANCE (1904), St. Louis de France, Lowell was suppressed. This parish's records are located at St. Marguerite d'Youville, Dracut.

9—ST. MARGARET (1910) [CEM] Rev. Raymond P. Benoit, Admin.; Deacon Barry V. Lloyd.
Res.: 374 Stevens St., 01851. Tel: 978-454-5143; Fax: 978-458-8472. Email: dmcandrews@parishmail.com. Web: www.stmargaretlowell.org.
School—486 Stevens St., 01851. Tel: 978-453-8491. Sr. Loretta Fleming, S.N.D., Prin. Sisters 1; Lay Teachers 19; Students 382.
Catechesis/Religious Program—Tel: 978-459-4481. Paula Nalavich, D.R.E.; Pamela Quinn, D.R.E.

10—ST. MARIE (1931), St. Marie, Lowell was suppressed. This parish's records are located at Holy Family, Lowell.

11—ST. MICHAEL (1883) Revs. Albert L. Capone; Thomas P. Rossi, Parochial Vicar; Michael Ngei Komu (Kenya), Parochial Vicar; Lisa K. Crowley, Pastoral Assoc.; Deacon Roland E. Leduc.
Res.: 543 Bridge St., 01850-2098. Tel: 978-459-0713; Fax: 978-453-1123. Email: stmichaels@comcast.net. Web: www.saint-michael.com.
School—21 Sixth St., 01850. Tel: 978-453-9511. Mary Frances Chisholm, Prin. Lay Teachers 26; Students 392.
Catechesis/Religious Program—Tel: 978-458-1617. Nicole Walsh, D.R.E.; Jean Haumann, D.R.E.

12—NOTRE DAME DE LOURDES (1908), Notre Dame de Lourdes, Lowell was suppressed. This parish's records are located at St. Margaret, Lowell.

13—NUESTRA SENORA DEL CARMEN (1990), Nuestra Senora del Carmen, Lowell was suppressed. This parish's records are located at St. Patrick, Lowell.

14—ST. PATRICK (1831) Revs. James E. Taggart, O.M.I.; Daniel Barron, O.M.V., Parochial Vicar; Paul Ouellette, O.M.I., Parochial Vicar; Sr. Angela

Zapata, M.S.S., Pastoral Assoc.; Deacon Peter An Ros.
Res.: 282 Suffolk St., 01854-4297. Tel: 978-459-0561; Fax: 978-446-0266. Email: stpatricklowell@comcast.net. Web: www.stpatricklowell.org.
Catechesis/Religious Program— Sr. Luzelana Vera, M.S.S., D.R.E.

15—ST. PETER (1841), St. Peter, Lowell was suppressed. This parish's records are located at Holy Family, Lowell.

16—ST. RITA (1910) Very Rev. Daniel D. Magni; Deacons Robert W. Dzuris; Donald W. Webster. In Res., Very Rev. Arthur M. Coyle.
Res.: 158 Mammoth Rd., 01854-2619. Tel: 978-452-4812; Fax: 978-459-8969. Email: saintritalowell01854@yahoo.com. Web: www.parishesonline.com.
School—St. Jeanne d'Arc, 68 Dracut St., 01854. Tel: 978-453-4114. Sr. Precille Malo, Prin.
Catechesis/Religious Program—Gail Irish, D.R.E.

17—SACRED HEART (1884), Sacred Heart, Lowell was suppressed. This parish's records are located at Holy Family, Lowell.

LYNN, ESSEX CO.

1—ST. FRANCIS OF ASSISI, St. Francis of Assisi, Lynn was suppressed. This parish's records are located at Holy Family, Lynn.

2—HOLY FAMILY (1922), (Italian), Rev. Gregory Mercurio; Deacon John M. Bresnahan.
Res.: 26 Bessom St., 01902. Tel: 781-599-7200; Fax: 781-599-2202. Web: holyfamilychurchlynn.net.
Catechesis/Religious Program—Tel: 781-596-2390; Fax: 781-599-2202. Catherine M. Raymond, D.R.E.

3—ST. JOHN THE BAPTIST (1886), St. John the Baptist, Lynn was suppressed. This parish's records are located at St. Mary, Lynn.

4—ST. JOSEPH (1874) Revs. James E. Gaudreau; Victor D. Marino Barragan (Brazil), Parochial Vicar; Senior Deacons Finley H. Chisholm; Lawrence R. McManus.
Res.: 40 Green St., 01902-2905. Tel: 781-599-7040; Fax: 781-598-7439.
Convent—43 Green St., 01902. Tel: 781-581-7848. Sisters of St. Joseph 2.

5—ST. MARY (1862) Rev. Msgr. Paul V. Garrity; Revs. Michael M. Ferraro, Parochial Vicar; Gabriel Loremus (Haiti), Parochial Vicar; Ms. Jaye Russo, Pastoral Assoc. Tel: 781-599-2275; Deacon Timothy F. Dempsey.
Res.: 8 S. Common St., 01902-4489. Tel: 781-598-4907; Fax: 781-599-2088. Email: rectory@saintmaryslynn.org. Web: www.saintmaryslynn.org.
High School—35 Tremont St., 01902. Tel: 781-595-7885. Carl DiMaiti, Prin. Lay Teachers 30; Students 650.

6—ST. MICHAEL (1906), (Polish), St. Michael, Lynn was suppressed. This parish's records are located at Sacred Heart, Lynn.

7—ST. PATRICK (1906), St. Patrick, Lynn was suppressed. This parish's records are located at St. Mary, Lynn.

8—ST. PIUS FIFTH (1912) Revs. Cornelius J. Mullaney, Team Ministry; Joseph M. Rossi, Team Ministry; Sr. Patricia Shea, S.N.D., Pastoral Assoc.
Res.: 215 Maple St., 01904-2799. Tel: 781-595-7487; Fax: 781-595-7270. Email: officeadministrator@stpiusvlynn.org. Web: www.stpiusvlynn.org.
School—28 Bowler St., 01904. Tel: 781-593-8292. Paul Maestranzi, Prin. Sisters 3; Lay Teachers 25; Students 511.
Catechesis/Religious Program—Tel: 781-581-3503; Fax: 781-595-7270. Deborah E. Bartlett, D.R.E.

9—SACRED HEART (1894) Rev. Mark G. Derrane; Ms. Frances Taylor, Pastoral Assoc. Tel: 781-592-1963; Senior Deacon John W. Hardy; Deacon Richard P. Field Jr.
Res.: 571 Boston St., 01905-2160. Tel: 781-593-8047; Fax: 781-599-4040. Email: parishsecretary@sacredheartlynn.org. Web: www.sacredheartlynn.org.
School—581 Boston St., 01905-2160. Tel: 781-592-7581. Joanne Eagan, Prin. Sisters 1; Lay Teachers 8; Students 261.
Catechesis/Religious Program—Tel: 781-592-1963.

LYNNFIELD, ESSEX CO.

1—ST. MARIA GORETTI (1960) Rev. Thomas J. Powers.
Res.: 112 Chestnut St., 01940-2405. Tel: 781-334-2367; Fax: 781-334-9819. Email: office@stmaria.org. Web: www.stmaria.org.
Catechesis/Religious Program—Hazel Kochocki, D.R.E.

2—OUR LADY OF THE ASSUMPTION (1937) Very Rev. John E. Farrell; Rev. Linus Mendis (Sri Lanka), Parochial Vicar; Deacon Paul A. Dow.
Res.: 17 Grove St., 01940. Tel: 781-598-4313; Fax: 781-598-0055.
School—34 Grove St., 01940. Tel: 781-599-4422. Dr. Joan Shea-Desmond, Prin. Sisters 2; Lay Teachers 16; Students 457.
Catechesis/Religious Program—Judith Dixon, D.R.E.

MALDEN, MIDDLESEX CO.

1—IMMACULATE CONCEPTION (1854) Very Rev. Richard J. Mehm; Rev. Tamiru F. Atraga, Parochial Vicar; Deacon Mark E. Rumley. In Res., Revs. James B. Canniff (Retired); John U. Paris; Richard T. Bakker, S.M.A.
Res.: 10 Fellsway E., 02148-5313. Tel: 781-324-4941; Fax: 781-397-8571. Web: www.icmalden.com.
Catechesis/Religious Program—Tel: 781-324-5518. Sr. Margo Shea, C.S.J., D.R.E.

2—ST. JOSEPH (1902) Rev. William J. Minigan; Very Rev. John F. Mulloy, Parochial Vicar.
Res.: 790 Salem St., 02148. Tel: 781-324-0402; Fax: 781-324-1790. Email: stjosephs2@comcast.net. Web: www.stjosephparishmalden.com.
Catechesis/Religious Program—Tel: 781-324-2444. David Wilcox, D.R.E.

3—ST. PETER (1972), St. Peter, Malden was suppressed. This parish's records are located at Immaculate Conception, Malden.

4—SACRED HEARTS (1890) Rev. Daniel J. Hickey.
Res.: 297 Main St., 02148-7414. Tel: 781-324-0728; Fax: 781-324-2714. Email: sh.parish@verizon.net. Web: www.sacredheartsparish.org.
School—30 Irving St., 02148. Tel: 781-324-6584. Susan M. Degnan, Prin. Lay Teachers 20; Students 400.
Catechesis/Religious Program—Susan Evans, D.R.E.

MANCHESTER BY THE SEA, ESSEX CO., SACRED HEART (1905) Rev. John W. Gentleman, Admin.; Ms. Jean Fecteau, Pastoral Assoc.
Res.: 62 School St., 01944-1342. Tel: 978-526-1263; Fax: 978-526-4335. Web: www.sacredheartmanchesterparishonline.com.
Catechesis/Religious Program—Valerie Shippen, D.R.E.

MARBLEHEAD, ESSEX CO., OUR LADY, STAR OF THE SEA (1859) Rev. Michael L. Steele; Deacon John E. Whipple.
Res.: 85 Atlantic Ave., 01945. Tel: 781-631-0086; Fax: 781-631-5668. Email: sosrectory@verizon.net. Web: www.staroftheseamarblehead.org.
Catechesis/Religious Program—Tel: 781-631-8340. Jude Odimone-Milan, D.R.E. (Gr. 1-4); Helen Haas, D.R.E. (Gr. 5-8).

MARLBOROUGH, MIDDLESEX CO.

1—ST. ANN (1921), St. Ann, Marlborough was suppressed. This parish's records are located at Immaculate Conception, Marlborough.

2—IMMACULATE CONCEPTION (1854) Revs. Michael W. MacEwen; Israel J. Rodriguez, Parochial Vicar; Ignacio D. Berrio (Colombia), Parochial Vicar; Deacon Robert I. Hoaglund.
Res.: 17 Washington Ct., 01752. Tel: 508-485-0016; Fax: 508-480-9644. Email: icmarlboro42@verizon.net. Web: www.icmarlboro.org.
School—25 Washington Ct., 01752. Tel: 508-460-3401. Martha McCook, Prin. Lay Teachers 14; Students 257.
Catechesis/Religious Program—Tel: 508-481-7535. Jennifer McKiernan, D.R.E.
Mission—St. Ann

3—ST. MARY (1870), St. Mary, Marlborough was suppressed. This parish's records are located at Immaculate Conception, Marlborough.

4—ST. MATTHIAS (1963) Rev. Francis P. O'Brien; Deacon Douglas P. Peltak.
Res.: 409 Hemenway St., 01752-6710. Tel: 508-460-9255; Fax: 508-480-8801. Email: admin@stmattpar.org. Web: www.stmattpar.org.
Catechesis/Religious Program—Karen McNamara, D.R.E.

MARSHFIELD, PLYMOUTH CO.

1—ST. ANN BY THE SEA (1945) Rev. John F. Carmichael; Mr. Paul Curtin, Pastoral Assoc.
Res.: 591 Ocean St., 02050. Tel: 781-834-4953; Fax: 781-834-7472. Email: info@stanns.net. Web: www.stanns.net.
Catechesis/Religious Program—Tel: 781-834-8223. Martha McLaughlin, D.R.E.

2—ST. CHRISTINE (1945) Rev. Thomas J. Walsh; Mary Doolan, Pastoral Assoc.; Doretha Gurry, Pastoral Assoc.; Deacon Paul F. Bankowski.
Res.: 1295 Main St., 02050-2029. Tel: 781-834-6003; Fax: 781-834-0671. Email: stchristinespsh@aol.com. Web: saintchristines.org.
Catechesis/Religious Program—Tel: 781-837-0088. Jean Godin, D.R.E.
Mission—St. Theresa's, Plymouth Co.

3—OUR LADY OF THE ASSUMPTION (1949) Rev. Mark E. Ballard.
Box 368, Green Harbor, 02041-0368.
Res.: 40 Canal St., 02050. Tel: 781-834-6252; Fax: 781-834-8338. Email: assumchrch@verizon.net. Web: www.assumptionparish.com.
Catechesis/Religious Program—Tel: 781-837-3662; Fax: 781-834-5694. Mary Forrester, D.R.E.

MAYNARD, MIDDLESEX CO.

1—ST. BRIDGET (1881) [CEM] Revs. John P. Prusaitis; Jean P. Aubin, Parochial Vicar; Deacon John W. Pepi.
Res.: One Percival St., 01754. Tel: 978-897-2171; Fax: 978-897-5358. Web: www.saintbridgetmaynard.com.
Catechesis/Religious Program—Tel: 978-897-4612. Joan Ferguson, D.R.E.

2—ST. CASIMIR (1912), St. Casimir, Maynard was suppressed. This parish's records are located at St. Bridget, Maynard.

MEDFIELD, NORFOLK CO., ST. EDWARD THE CONFESSOR (1892) Rev. Leroy E. Owens; Deacon Frederick B. Horgan.
Res.: 133 Spring St., 02052-2513. Tel: 508-359-2633; Fax: 508-359-1846. Email: mail@stedward-ma.org. Web: www.steward-ma.org.
Catechesis/Religious Program—Tel: 508-359-5853. Terry Ferraris, D.R.E.

MEDFORD, MIDDLESEX CO.

1—ST. CLEMENT (1912) Revs. Dennis A. Dever; Ixon Chateau, Parochial Vicar.
Res.: 71 Warner St., 02155. Tel: 781-396-3922; Fax: 781-396-2506.
School—589 Boston Ave., 02155. Tel: 781-396-3488. Robert G. Chevrier, Prin. Sisters of St. Joseph 2; Lay Teachers 17; Students 240.
High School—579 Boston Ave., 02155. Tel: 781-393-5600. Robert G. Chevrier, Prin. Sisters 2; Lay Teachers 3; Students 150.
Catechesis/Religious Program—Tel: 781-396-3322. Carla Garofalo, D.R.E.

2—ST. FRANCIS OF ASSISI (1921) Rev. Joseph R. Foster; Deacon Robert F. Breen.
Res.: 441 Fellsway W., 02155. Tel: 781-396-3400; Fax: 781-396-3254. Email: saintfrancischurch@comcast.net. Web: www.stfrancismedford.com.
School—One Saint Clare Rd., 02155. Tel: 781-395-9170. MaryGrace DiMartino, Prin. Lay Teachers 24; Students 255.
Catechesis/Religious Program—Tel: 781-395-4042; Fax: 781-306-0044. Margaret Aranyosi, D.R.E.

3—ST. JAMES (1919), St. James, Medford was suppressed. This parish's records are located at St. Joseph, Medford.

4—ST. JOSEPH (1883) Revs. Patrick J. McLaughlin, Admin.; Joseph Diem, Parochial Vicar.
Res.: 114 High St., 02155-3882. Tel: 781-396-0423; Fax: 781-391-2919. Email: stjosephparishmedfordma@msn.com. Web: www.stjoesmedford.org.
School—132 High St., 02155. Tel: 781-396-3636. Sr. Maureen Joseph Hunt, Prin. Sisters 5; Lay Teachers 14; Students 342.
Catechesis/Religious Program—Tel: 781-395-1784. Phyllis Patten, D.R.E.
Convent—2520 Mystic Valley Pkwy., 02155. Tel: 781-396-5670.

5—ST. RAPHAEL (1905) Revs. Kevin G. Toomey; Robert J. Cullen, Parochial Vicar.
Res.: 38 Boston Ave., 02155. Tel: 781-488-5444; Fax: 781-483-3375. Web: www.saintraphaelparish.org.
School—516 High St., 02155. Tel: 781-483-3373. Jean B. Murphy, Prin. Lay Teachers 19; Students 399.
Catechesis/Religious Program—Tel: 781-483-1139. Dr. Ginny McCabe, D.R.E.

6—SACRED HEART (1937), Sacred Heart, Medford was suppressed. This parish's records are located at St. Clement, Somerville.

MEDWAY, NORFOLK CO., ST. JOSEPH (1885) Rev. Msgr. Timothy J. Moran; Rev. Joseph T. MacCarthy, Parochial Vicar.
Res.: 2 Barber St., 02053. Tel: 508-533-6500; Fax: 508-533-1236.
Catechesis/Religious Program—145 Holliston St., 02053-1954. Tel: 508-533-7771; Fax: 508-533-0604. Sharon Moore, D.R.E.

MELROSE, MIDDLESEX CO.

1—INCARNATION OF OUR LORD AND SAVIOR JESUS CHRIST (1958) Rev. James A. Field; Linda Swett, Pastoral Assoc.
Res.: 429 Upham St., 02176. Tel: 781-662-8844; Fax: 781-662-9340. Email: l.rectory@comcast.net. Web: www.incarnationmelrose.org.
Catechesis/Religious Program—Linda Swett, D.R.E.

2—ST. MARY OF THE ANNUNCIATION (1894) Revs. John M. Sullivan; William R. Carroll, Parochial Vicar; Sr. Mary Samson, S.H.C.J., Pastoral Assoc. In Res., Rev. Msgr. Alfonso G. Palladino (Retired).
Res.: 46 Myrtle St., 02176-3827. Tel: 781-665-0152; Fax: 781-665-2750. Web: www.stmarysmelrose.org.
School—Myrtle & Grove St., 02176. Tel: 781-665-5037. Cynthia Boyle, Prin. Lay Teachers 27; Students 405.
Catechesis/Religious Program—9 Herbert St., 02176. Tel: 781-665-3707. Sheila Hurley, D.R.E.

MERRIMAC, ESSEX CO.
1—HOLY REDEEMER (2006) Rev. Edward F. Sherry. Mailing Address: 4 Green St., 01860.
Res.: 46 Maple St., West Newbury, 01985-1921. Tel: 978-346-8604; Fax: 978-346-9970. Email: nativityparish@verizon.net.
Catechesis/Religious Program—Doreen O'Leary, D.R.E.
2—NATIVITY (1891), Nativity, Merrimac was suppressed. This parish's records are located at Holy Redeemer, Merrimac.
METHUEN, ESSEX CO.
1—ST. LUCY (1958) Rev. Thomas E. Keyes; Sr. Rina Brunetti, P.M., Pastoral Assoc.
Res.: 254 Merrimack St., 01844. Tel: 978-686-3311; Fax: 978-686-5343. Email: stlucy254@yahoo.com. Web: www.stlucymethuen:4lpi.com.
Catechesis/Religious Program—Tel: 978-794-0383. Kevin Fitzgerald, D.R.E.
2—ST. MONICA (1917) Revs. Patrick S. Armano; David W. Gunter, Parochial Vicar; Deacons John B. Pierce; Andrew J. Goldy. In Res., Rev. Marc J. Bishop.
Res.: 214 Lawrence St., 01844-3852. Tel: 978-683-1193; Fax: 978-686-0249. Email: stmonica@parishmail.com.
School—212 Lawrence St., 01844. Tel: 978-686-1801. Beth Ingeneri, Prin. Sisters 4; Lay Teachers 12; Students 522.
Catechesis/Religious Program—Tel: 978-686-9573; Fax: 978-738-8898. Claire Tebeau, D.R.E. (Gr. K-5); Laurene Costello, D.R.E. (Gr. 6-8); Wendy Adams, D.R.E. (Gr. 9-10).
Convent—212 Lawrence St., 01844. Tel: 978-682-2448.
3—OUR LADY OF GOOD COUNSEL (2000) Rev. Marc J. Bishop; Deacon Steven J. Murphy.
Res.: 22 Plymouth St., 01844-4299. Tel: 978-686-3984; Fax: 978-686-8300. Email: olgcparish@comcast.net. Web: www.olgcparish.com.
School—526 Lowell St., Lawrence, 01841. Tel: 978-682-9761. Maureen Cocchiaro, Prin. Sisters 1; Lay Teachers 9; Students 206.
Catechesis/Religious Program—Tel: 978-686-3985; Fax: 978-686-8300. Mark Friedrich, D.R.E.; Mark Houle, D.R.E.
4—OUR LADY OF MOUNT CARMEL (1937), Our Lady of Mount Carmel, Methuen was suppressed. This parish's records are located at St. Monica, Methuen.
5—ST. THERESA (1936), St. Theresa, Methuen was suppressed. This parish's records are located at Our Lady of Good Counsel, Methuen.
MIDDLEBOROUGH, PLYMOUTH CO., SACRED HEART (1885) Revs. Richard P. Crowley; Jason W. Worthley, Parochial Vicar; Ms. Holly Clark, Pastoral Assoc.; Deacon George M. Gabriel. In Res., Rev. Daniel J. Crowley (Retired).
Res.: 340 Center St., 02346-2102. Tel: 508-947-0444; Fax: 508-947-4333. Email: info@sacredheartstrose.org. Web: www.sacredheartstrose.org.
Catechesis/Religious Program—M. Judith West, D.R.E. Tel: 508-947-2050; Fax: 508-947-2364; Michelle Sylvie, D.R.E. Tel: 508-923-1151; Lori Handerhan, D.R.E.
MIDDLETON, ESSEX CO., ST. AGNES (1945) Rev. Michael A. Hobson; Deacon John W. Wise.
Res.: 22 Boston St., 01949-2199. Tel: 978-774-1958; Fax: 978-774-1964. Email: stagnes@parishmail.com. Web: www.saintagnesparish.parishesonline.com.
Catechesis/Religious Program—Tel: 978-777-3404. Sr. Mildred Rothwell, O.S.F., D.R.E.
MILLIS, NORFOLK CO., ST. THOMAS THE APOSTLE (1937) Rev. Henry G. Chambers.
Res.: 111 Exchange St., 02054-1273. Tel: 508-376-2621; Fax: 508-376-4308. Email: stthomasmillis@comcast.net.
Catechesis/Religious Program—Helen Boucher, D.R.E.; Annmarie Fontecchio, D.R.E.
MILTON, NORFOLK CO.
1—ST. AGATHA (1922) Revs. Peter J. Casey; Robert A. Poitras, Parochial Vicar; Mary Gallagher, Pastoral Assoc.; Deacon Daniel F. Sullivan. In Res., Revs. Robert J. Butler (Retired); Robert J. Deehan.
Res.: 432 Adams St., 02186-4399. Tel: 617-698-2439; Fax: 617-698-1517. Email: rectory@stagathaparish.org. Web: www.stagathaparish.org.
School—440 Adams St., 02186. Tel: 617-696-3548. Maureen C. Simmons, Prin. Sisters 2; Lay Teachers 15; Students 377.
Catechesis/Religious Program—Sr. Susan Czaplick, S.S.N.D., D.R.E.
2—ST. ELIZABETH (1946) Rev. Aidan J. Walsh.
Res.: 350 Reedsdale Rd., 02186-3999. Tel: 617-696-6688; Fax: 617-698-4864. Email: office@stelizabethmilton.org. Web: www.stelizabethmilton.org.
Catechesis/Religious Program—Tel: 617-698-5763. Sr. Mary K. Walsh, C.S.T., D.R.E.
3—ST. MARY OF THE HILLS (1931) Rev. Arthur J. Wright; Harold J. Feldmann, Pastoral Assoc. In Res., Rev. Thomas J. Naughton (Retired).
Res.: 29 St. Mary's Rd., 02186-2024. Tel: 617-696-0120; Fax: 617-696-7044. Email: smhrectory@aol.com. Web: www.saintmaryofthehills.org.
School—250 Brook Rd., 02186. Tel: 617-698-2464. Mrs. Andrea Tavaska, Prin. Sisters 2; Lay Teachers 14; Students 307.
Catechesis/Religious Program—Tel: 617-696-6117. Madeline Feldmann, D.R.E.
4—ST. PIUS TENTH (1954) Rev. Peter P. Nolan, C.S.Sp., Admin.
Res.: 865 Brush Hill Rd., 02186-1299. Tel: 617-333-0401; Fax: 617-364-2590. Email: piusx.miltonma@verizon.net.
Catechesis/Religious Program—Sheila Farley, D.R.E.
NAHANT, ESSEX CO., ST. THOMAS AQUINAS (1902) Rev. Philip M. Conroy, Admin. (Retired).
Res.: 248 Nahant Rd., 01908-1340. Tel: 781-581-0023; Fax: 781-598-8860. Email: secretarystthomasnahant@comcast.net. Web: www.stthomasnahant.com.
Catechesis/Religious Program—Tel: 781-595-7942. Kathy Marini, D.R.E.
NATICK, MIDDLESEX CO.
1—ST. LINUS (1950) Rev. Msgr. J. Robert Giggi; Donna McIntosh, Pastoral Assoc.; Deacon Herbert C. Hanson.
Res.: 119 Hartford St., 01760. Tel: 508-653-5505; Fax: 508-655-4577. Web: www.stlinusparish.com.
Catechesis/Religious Program—Tel: 508-653-6005. Cynthia Giardina, D.R.E.; Laura McLarnon, D.R.E.
2—ST. PATRICK (1858) Revs. Brian R. Kiely; David C. Goodrow, Parochial Vicar. In Res., Most Rev. Walter J. Edyvean.
Res.: 44 E. Central St., 01760. Tel: 508-653-1093; Fax: 508-650-2922. Email: stpatsparish@comcast.net. Web: www.stpatsnatick.org.
Catechesis/Religious Program—Lisa Correia, D.R.E.
3—SACRED HEART (1891), Sacred Heart, Natick was suppressed. This parish's records are located at St. Patrick, Natick.
NEEDHAM, NORFOLK CO.
1—ST. BARTHOLOMEW (1952) Rev. Philip E. McGaugh; Ms. Barbara Dury, Pastoral Assoc. In Res., Rev. Thomas J. Stanton.
Res.: 1180 Greendale Ave., 02492-4706. Tel: 781-444-3434; Fax: 781-449-7550. Email: stbarthomew@comcast.net. Web: www.stbartholomew-needham.org.
Catechesis/Religious Program—Tel: 781-444-4343. Melisa Hughes, D.R.E.
2—ST. JOSEPH (1917) Revs. J. Michael Lawlor; Paul V. Sullivan, Parochial Vicar. In Res., Rev. Msgr. Francis J. McGann (Retired).
Res.: 1382 Highland Ave., 02492-2694. Tel: 781-444-0245; Fax: 781-444-7713. Web: www.stjoes.com.
School—Elementary School, 90 Pickering St., 02492. Tel: 781-444-4459. Paul G. Kelly, Prin. Lay Teachers 34; Students 440.
NEWBURYPORT, ESSEX CO.
1—IMMACULATE CONCEPTION (1848) Revs. Marc A. Piche; James T. Kelly, Parochial Vicar; Ms. Marin Fortune, Pastoral Assoc. Tel: 978-234-7405; Deacon Richard Siebert.
42 Green St., 01950-2502. In Res., Revs. Paul W. Berube (Retired); James M. Broderick (Retired).
Res.: 7 Court St., 01950-2502. Tel: 978-462-2724; Fax: 978-234-7399. Web: www.newburyportcatholic.org.
School—One Washington St., 01950. Tel: 978-465-7780. Mary Reardon, Prin. Sisters 2; Lay Teachers 7; Students 198.
Catechesis/Religious Program—Tel: 978-234-7420; Fax: 978-234-7399.
Mission—St. James Plum Island.
2—ST. LOUIS DE GONZAGUE (1902), (French), St. Louis de Gonzague, Newburyport was suppressed. This parish's records are located at Immaculate Conception, Newburyport.
NEWTON, MIDDLESEX CO.
1—ST. BERNARD (1876), St. Bernard, Newton was suppressed. This parish's records are located at Corpus Christi-St. Bernard, Newton.
2—CORPUS CHRISTI (1922), Corpus Christi, Newton was suppressed. This parish's records are located at Corpus Christi-St. Bernard, Newton.
3—CORPUS CHRISTI - ST. BERNARD (2006) Rev. Frank J. Silva; Thomas F. Griffin, Pastoral Assoc.; Deacon Daniel C. Nelson. In Res., Revs. Francis M. Conroy (Retired); Stephen M. Boyle.
Res.: 1529 Washington St., 02465. Tel: 617-244-0608; Fax: 617-969-1025. Email: info@ccsbparish.org. Web: www.ccsbparish.org.
Catechesis/Religious Program—Maureen Connell, D.R.E.
4—ST. IGNATIUS LOYOLA (1926) Revs. Robert F. VerEecke, S.J.; J. Allan Loftus, S.J., Parochial Vicar; Kenneth G. Loftus, S.J., Parochial Vicar; Sr. Diane Vallerio, O.S.F., Pastoral Assoc.
Res.: 28 Commonwealth Ave., 02465. Tel: 617-552-6100; Fax: 617-552-6101. Email: ignatius@bc.edu. Web: www.bc.edu/st-ignatius.
Catechesis/Religious Program—Melisa Melnyk, D.R.E.
5—ST. JOHN THE EVANGELIST (1911), St. John the Evangelist, Newton was suppressed. This parish's records are located at Our Lady Help of Christians, Newton.
6—MARY IMMACULATE OF LOURDES (1870) Rev. Charles J. Higgins.
Res.: 270 Elliot St., 02464. Tel: 617-244-0558; Fax: 617-965-4815. Email: miol@parishmail.com. Web: www.maryimmaculatenewton.org.
Catechesis/Religious Program—Jean Johnson, D.R.E.
7—OUR LADY HELP OF CHRISTIANS (1878) Rev. John E. Sassani; Rev. Msgr. Dennis F. Sheehan, Parochial Vicar; Ms. Jennifer Sues-Vassel, Pastoral Assoc.; Deacon William B. Koffel.
Res.: 573 Washington St., 02458-1494. Tel: 617-527-7560; Fax: 617-527-1338. Email: welcome@ourladys.com. Web: www.ourladys.com.
High School—Trinity Catholic High School, 575 Washington St., 02458-1494. Tel: 617-244-1841. Kelly Surapeneni, Prin. Sisters 2; Lay Teachers 10; Students 152.
Catechesis/Religious Program—Rosemary Seibold, D.R.E.; Kara O'Malley, D.R.E. Students 363.
8—ST. PHILIP NERI (1934), St. Philip Neri was suppressed. This parish's records are located at Sacred Heart Parish, Newton.
9—SACRED HEART (1890) Revs. John J. Connelly; Jeremy P. Saint Martin, Parochial Vicar; Ms. Winifred Murphy, Pastoral Assoc. Tel: 617-969-4021. In Res., Rev. Robert P. Imbelli (NY).
Res.: 1321 Centre St., 02459-2466. Tel: 617-969-2248; Fax: 617-965-7515. Email: parish@sacredheart.ws. Web: www.sacredheart.ws;deafcatholic.org.
Catechesis/Religious Program—Michelle Solomon, D.R.E.
NORFOLK, NORFOLK CO., ST. JUDE (1949) Rev. Msgr. Peter V. Conley; Deacon David R. Ghioni.
P.O. Box 305, 02056-0305. In Res., Rev. Robert Rivard, F.M.S.I.
Res.: 86 Main St., 02056. Tel: 508-528-0170; Fax: 508-528-1860. Email: stjudenorfolk@comcast.net. Web: www.stjudenorfolk.org.
Catechesis/Religious Program—Tel: 508-528-1470. Terry Ferraris, D.R.E.
NORTH ANDOVER, ESSEX CO., ST. MICHAEL (1900) Very Rev. John W. Delaney, Team Ministry; Revs. George G. Hogan, Team Ministry; Paul T. Keyes, Team Ministry; Ms. Mary Alice Rock, Pastoral Assoc.
Res.: 196 Main St., 01845-2598. Tel: 978-686-4050; Fax: 978-686-5408. Email: st-michael@comcast.net. Web: www.saint-michael.org.
School—80 Maple Ave., 01845. Tel: 978-688-9181. Susan Reidy, Prin. Sisters 1; Lay Teachers 21; Students 525.
Catechesis/Religious Program—Tel: 978-682-9484. Maryann Marinelli, D.R.E.; Ms. Mary Alice Rock, D.R.E.
NORTH READING, MIDDLESEX CO., ST. THERESA OF LISIEUX (1945) Revs. Thomas M. Gillespie; Thomas J. Reilly, Parochial Vicar; Deacon Alfred O. Balestracci; Mary Ann Thomas, Pastoral Assoc.
Res.: 63 Winter St., 01864-2282. Tel: 978-664-3412; Fax: 978-276-0034. Email: sttheresa@parishmail.com.
Catechesis/Religious Program—Tel: 978-664-2962. Paula L. Colpitts, D.R.E.; Nancy Cirone, D.R.E.
NORWELL, PLYMOUTH CO., ST. HELEN MOTHER OF THE EMPEROR CONSTANTINE (1950) Rev. Thomas H. Maguire.
Res.: 383 Washington St., 02061. Tel: 781-659-2993; Fax: 781-659-7861. Email: sthelenrectory@aol.com. Web: www.sthelenchurchnorwell.org.
Catechesis/Religious Program—Mary Nedder, D.R.E.; Kathleen Mogayzel, C.R.E.
NORWOOD, NORFOLK CO.
1—ST. CATHERINE OF SIENA (1890) Rev. Msgr. Cornelius M. McRae; Rev. Anthony V. Luongo, Parochial Vicar; Deacon John A. Brent. In Res., Rev. Msgr. Paul T. Ryan (Retired).
Res.: 547 Washington St., 02062-0547. Tel: 781-762-6080; Fax: 781-255-9312. Email: parish@stcatherinenorwood.org. Web: www.stcatherinenorwood.org.
School—249 Nahatan St., 02062. Tel: 781-769-5354. Gretchen Hawley, Prin. Sisters 1; Lay Teachers 40; Students 472.
Catechesis/Religious Program—Frank Connell, D.R.E. Tel: 781-254-5087; Marybeth McDonough, D.R.E. Students 759.

2—ST. GEORGE (1912), St. George, Norwood was suppressed. This parish's records are located at St. Catherine of Siena, Norwood.
3—ST. PETER (1918), St. Peter, Norwood was suppressed. This parish's records are located at Archives, Boston.
4—ST. TIMOTHY (1963) Rev. John P. Culloty. In Res., Rev. George F. Emerson (Retired).
Res.: 650 Nichols St., 02062-1099. Tel: 781-769-2522; Fax: 781-769-9362. Email: sttim@sttim.net. Web: www.sttim.net.
Catechesis/Religious Program—Tel: 781-762-4868. Judith Miley, D.R.E.; Frank Connell, Dir. Faith Formation.

PEABODY, ESSEX CO.
1—ST. ADELAIDE (1962) Revs. Raymond Van De Moortell, Team Ministry; David C. Lewis, Team Ministry.
Res.: 17 Bow St., 01960-3427. Tel: 978-535-1985; Fax: 978-535-4845. Email: saintadelaide@verizon.net. Web: www.stadelaidereligiouseducation.com.
Catechesis/Religious Program—712 Lowell St., 01960. Tel: 978-535-5376. Angela Federico, D.R.E.
2—ST. ANN (1937) Rev. Charles R. Stanley; Deacon Richard W. Cordeau.
Res.: 136 Lynn St., 01960-6432. Tel: 978-531-1480; Fax: 978-531-6683. Web: www.catholic-church.org/st-ann-peabody.
Catechesis/Religious Program—Tel: 978-531-5791. Ellen Fitzgerald, D.R.E.
3—ST. JOHN THE BAPTIST (1871) Revs. John E. MacInnis; Paul F. Coughlin, Parochial Vicar. In Res., Rev. Msgr. Francis G. O'Sullivan (Retired).
Res.: 17 Chestnut St., 01960-5429. Tel: 978-531-0002; Fax: 978-531-5199. Email: parishcenter@stjohnspeabody.com. Web: www.stjohnspeabody.com.
School—19 Chestnut St., 01960-5429. Tel: 978-531-0444. Maureen J. Kelleher, Prin. Sisters 2; Lay Teachers 20; Students 510.
Catechesis/Religious Program—Tel: 978-532-1586. Karen E. Hinton, D.R.E.
4—ST. JOSEPH (1927), St. Joseph, Peabody was suppressed. This parish's records are located at Archives, Boston.
5—OUR LADY OF FATIMA (1965), (Portuguese), Rev. Richard T. Burton, Admin.; Bro. Thomas Petitte, F.M.S., Pastoral Assoc.
Res.: One Margin St., 01960-1999. Tel: 978-532-0272; Fax: 978-977-2991. Email: ourladyoffatima@verizon.net. Web: www.rc.net/boston/fatima.
Catechesis/Religious Program—Ms. Frances Taylor, D.R.E.

PEMBROKE, PLYMOUTH CO., ST. THECLA (1964) Rev. Joseph S. McCarthy (Retired); Deacon John A. Sullivan.
P.O. Box 587, 02358-0587.
Res.: 145 Washington St., 02359. Tel: 781-826-9786; Fax: 781-826-3484. Email: sttheclaparish@msn.com. Web: www.stthecla.org.
Catechesis/Religious Program—Tel: 781-826-8042. Mary K. Doller, D.R.E.

PEPPERELL, MIDDLESEX CO.
1—ST. JOSEPH (1870) Merged with Sacred Heart-St. James in Groton to form Our Lady of Grace, Pepperell.
2—OUR LADY OF GRACE (2009) Rev. Paul L. Ring; Deacon Michael J. Markham; Ms. Jeanne S. DiPietro, Pastoral Assoc.
28 Tarbell St., 01463. Tel: 978-433-5737; Fax: 978-433-9566. Email: stjoseph@sjpp.org. Web: www.sjpp.org.

PLAINVILLE, NORFOLK CO., ST. MARTHA (1953) Rev. J. Garret Thomson; Deacon Bertrand H. Guerin.
P.O. Box 1745, 02762.
Res.: 219 South St., 02762. Tel: 508-699-8543; Fax: 508-699-6677. Email: stmarthaoffice@gmail.com. Web: www.saintmarthaschurch.org.
Catechesis/Religious Program—Sharon Guerin, D.R.E.

PLYMOUTH, PLYMOUTH CO.
1—BLESSED KATERI TEKAKWITHA (1982) Rev. James E. Braley; Senior Deacon Edward F. Creutz; Deacon James F. Greer.
Res.: 126 S. Meadow Rd., 02360. Tel: 508-747-1568; Fax: 508-747-0616. Email: office@blessedkateri.com. Web: www.blessedkateri.com.
Catechesis/Religious Program—Tel: 508-747-1568. Joyce Hokanson, D.R.E.
2—ST. BONAVENTURE (1950) Rev. Kenneth C. Overbeck; Sr. Jeremy Horgan, C.S.J., Pastoral Assoc.
Box 996, Manomet, 02345-0996.
Res.: 807 State Rd., Manomet, 02345-0996. Tel: 508-224-3636; Fax: 508-224-5889. Email: stbonaventure@parishmail.com. Web: www.catholic-church.org/stbonaventure.
Church: 799 State Rd., 02362.
Catechesis/Religious Program—Tel: 508-224-3636. Rachel Patnaude, D.R.E.
Mission—St. Catherine's Chapel 95 White Horse Rd., White Horse Beach, 02381.
3—ST. MARY (1915) Rev. John P. Kearns; Deacons Eugene V. Stenstrom; Thomas D. Edmonds. In Res., Rev. Paul F. Bailey (Retired).
Res.: 313 Court St., 02360-4336. Tel: 508-746-0426; Fax: 508-747-5886. Web: www.stmarysplymouth.org.
Catechesis/Religious Program—Kathleen Liolios, D.R.E.
4—ST. PETER (1876) Rev. Robert T. Milling, Admin.; Deacon John A. Hulme.
10 Memorial Dr., 02360.
Res.: 81 Court St., 02360. Tel: 508-746-0663; Fax: 508-747-1071. Email: stpeterparish@comcast.net. Web: www.stpetersplymouth.com.
Catechesis/Religious Program—Tel: 508-746-8268. Elizabeth Adey, D.R.E.

QUINCY, NORFOLK CO.
1—ST. ANN (1922) Revs. John J. Ronaghan; Thomas C. Boudreau, Parochial Vicar; Sr. Patricia Boyle, C.S.J., Pastoral Assoc.; Deacon Joseph E. MacDonald. In Res., Rev. Thomas C. Foley (Retired).
Res.: 757 Hancock St., 02170. Tel: 617-479-5400; Fax: 617-479-0955. Email: stannquincy@comcast.net.
School—One St. Ann Rd., 02170. Tel: 617-471-9071. Sr. Catherine Lee, S.C.N., Prin. Sisters 3; Lay Teachers 26; Students 355.
Catechesis/Religious Program—One St. Ann Rd., 02170. Tel: 617-479-2385. Nancy White, D.R.E.; Joseph DelRosso, D.R.E.
2—ST. BONIFACE (1956), St. Boniface, Quincy was suppressed. This parish's records are located at Holy Trinity, Quincy.
3—ST. ELIZABETH ANN SETON (2001), St. Elizabeth Ann Seton, Quincy was suppressed. This parish's records are located at Holy Trinity, Quincy.
4—HOLY TRINITY (2005) Rev. William J. English; Deacons John R. Menz; William F. Maloney.
Rectory—227 Sea St., 02169. Tel: 617-479-9200; Fax: 617-479-5766. Email: sueattrinity@verizon.net.
Catechesis/Religious Program—Denise Gleason, D.R.E.
5—ST. JOHN THE BAPTIST (1863) Revs. Richard E. Cannon; Mark D. Barr, Parochial Vicar; Deacon Paul A. Lewis. In Res., Very Rev. Thomas S. Foley.
Res.: 21 Gay St., 02169-6602. Tel: 617-773-1021; Fax: 617-773-5608. Email: stjohns@stjohnsquincy.org. Web: www.stjohnsquincy.org.
Catechesis/Religious Program—Ms. Joanne Curry, D.R.E.
6—ST. JOSEPH (1917) Rev. Vincent P. Doolan; Senior Deacon John F. Jennette; Deacon Leo J. Donoghue.
Res.: 556 Washington St., 02169-7216. Tel: 617-472-6321; Fax: 617-471-8849. Email: stjoesquincy@comcast.net. Web: www.stjosephsquincy.com.
Catechesis/Religious Program—550 Washington St., 02169-7216. Ellen Curran, D.R.E.
7—ST. MARY (1840) Rev. David P. Callahan. In Res., Rev. F. Dominic Menna (Retired).
Res.: 115 Crescent St., 02169-4040. Tel: 617-773-0120; Fax: 617-786-9199.
School—121 Crescent St., 02169-4040. Tel: 617-773-5237. Catherine Cameron, Prin. Lay Teachers 10; Students 226.
Catechesis/Religious Program—Tel: 617-773-0515. Ellen March, D.R.E.; Margaret L. Donaher, D.R.E.
8—MOST BLESSED SACRAMENT (1915), Most Blessed Sacrament, Quincy was suppressed. This parish's records are located at Holy Trinity, Quincy.
9—OUR LADY OF GOOD COUNSEL (1938), Our Lady of Good Counsel, Quincy was suppressed. This parish's records are located at Holy Trinity, Quincy.
10—SACRED HEART (1903) Revs. John W. O'Brien; James J. McGowan, Parochial Vicar; Senior Deacon John D. Salenius. In Res., Rev. William T. Kelly.
Res.: 386 Hancock St., 02171-2414. Tel: 617-328-8666; Fax: 617-773-2522. Email: office@sacredheartquincy.org. Web: www.sacredheartquincy.org.
School—(Grades K-8), 370 Hancock St., 02171-2414. Tel: 617-328-3830. Katherine Hunter, Prin. Sisters 5; Lay Teachers 16; Students 479.
Catechesis/Religious Program—Marjory O'Day, D.R.E.
11—STAR OF THE SEA (1945), Star of the Sea, Quincy was suppressed. This parish's records are located at Sacred Heart, Quincy.

RANDOLPH, NORFOLK CO.
1—ST. BERNADETTE (1937) Rev. Linh T. Nguyen; Sr. Ann Shea, D.C., Pastoral Assoc.; Senior Deacon John J. Ego; Deacon Thomas P. Burke.
Res.: 1026 N. Main St., 02368. Tel: 781-963-1327; Fax: 781-963-0198. Email: stbernadetteparish@comcast.net. Web: www.stbernadetterandolph.com.
Catechesis/Religious Program—Laura Donovan, D.R.E.; Sandy Messia, D.R.E.; Jen Rajani, D.R.E.
2—ST. MARY (1851) Revs. Ronald D. Coyne; Garrett J. Barry, Parochial Vicar.
22 Seton Way, 02368. In Res., Rev. Vincent R. Maffei (Retired).
Res.: 211 N. Main St., 02368. Tel: 781-963-4141; Fax: 781-963-0884. Email: stmary@stmaryrandolph.org. Web: www.stmaryrandolph.org.
Catechesis/Religious Program—Tel: 781-961-5009. Patricia O'Connor, D.R.E.

READING, MIDDLESEX CO.
1—ST. AGNES (1904) Revs. Stephen B. Rock; Edward T. Malone, Parochial Vicar.
Res.: 186 Woburn St., 01867-3599. Tel: 781-944-0490. Email: saint.agnes@st-agnes-reading.org. Web: www.st-agnes-reading.org.
Catechesis/Religious Program—Tel: 781-944-4552; Fax: 781-944-4403. Eileen A. McGrath, D.R.E.
2—ST. ATHANASIUS (1961) Rev. William T. Kremmell; Deacon Neil J. Sumner; Dorothy Parker, Pastoral Assoc.
Rectory—300 Haverhill St., 01867-1810. Tel: 781-944-0330; Fax: 781-944-1266. Email: stathanasius@parishmail.com. Web: www.rc.net/boston/stathanasius.
Catechesis/Religious Program—Nancy McAllister, D.R.E.; Jennifer Campagna, D.R.E.

REVERE, SUFFOLK CO.
1—ST. ANTHONY OF PADUA (2001) Revs. R. Michael Guarino; George J. Butera, Parochial Vicar; Udayakumar Xavariapitchai (India), Parochial Vicar; Deacon Joseph A. Belmonte.
Res.: 250 Revere St., 02151-4618. Tel: 781-289-1234; Fax: 781-289-6394. Web: www.saintanthonysrevere.org.
Catechesis/Religious Program—Mary Belliveau, D.R.E.
2—IMMACULATE CONCEPTION (1888) Revs. George L. Szal, S.M.; Carlos F. Flor (NEW), Parochial Vicar.
Res.: 22 Lowe St., 02151. Tel: 781-289-0735; Fax: 781-286-1124. Email: icrevere@comcast.net.
School—125 Winthrop Ave., 02151. Tel: 781-284-0519. Josephine Felice, Prin. Sisters 1; Lay Teachers 10; Students 269.
Catechesis/Religious Program—Tel: 781-289-8126.
3—ST. JOHN VIANNEY (1950), St. John Vianney, Revere was suppressed. This parish's records are located at St. Anthony of Padua Revere.
4—ST. MARY OF THE ASSUMPTION (1947) Rev. Paul J. Aveni.
Res.: 670 Washington Ave., 02151. Tel: 781-284-5252; Fax: 781-284-5801. Email: stmaryrevere@verizon.net.
Catechesis/Religious Program—Irene Hunt, D.R.E.
5—OUR LADY OF LOURDES (1905), Our Lady of Lourdes, Revere was suppressed. This parish's records are located at Immaculate Conception, Revere.
6—ST. THERESA (1937), St. Theresa, Revere was suppressed. This parish's records are located at St. Anthony of Padua, Revere.

ROCHESTER, PLYMOUTH CO., ST. ROSE OF LIMA (1980), St. Rose of Lima, Rochester was suppressed. This parish's records are located at Sacred Heart, Middleborough.

ROCKLAND, PLYMOUTH CO., HOLY FAMILY (1882) [CEM] Revs. James F. Hickey; James O'Driscoll, Parochial Vicar; Darci Donizetti da Silva (Brazil), Parochial Vicar; Sr. Anne Conway, C.S.J., Pastoral Assoc.; Ms. Teresa D. Smith, Pastoral Assoc.
Res.: 403 Union St., 02370-1799. Tel: 781-878-0160; Fax: 781-871-6389. Web: www.holyfamilyrockland.org.
School—6 Del Prete Ave., 02370. Tel: 781-878-1154. Ann Marie Manning, Prin. Religious 3; Lay Teachers 14; Students 315.
Catechesis/Religious Program—Tel: 781-871-1244. Helen Ulich, D.R.E.

ROCKPORT, ESSEX CO., ST. JOACHIM (1849), St. Joachim, Rockport was suppressed. This parish's records are located at Holy Family, Gloucester.

ROWLEY, ESSEX CO., ST. MARY (1945), St. Mary, Rowley was suppressed. This parish's records are located at St. Mary, Georgetown.

SALEM, ESSEX CO.
1—ST. ANNE (1901), (French), Rev. George J. Dufour.
Res.: 290 Jefferson Ave., 01970-2895. Tel: 978-744-1930; Fax: 978-745-1190. Email: stannesalem@aol.com. Web: www.stannesalem.com.
Catechesis/Religious Program—Tel: 978-745-8915. Karen Moran, D.R.E.
2—IMMACULATE CONCEPTION (1826) Rev. Timothy J. Murphy; Mary Louise Daly, Pastoral Assoc.; Deacon Pablo Morel. In Res., Rev. Edward M. Keohan (Retired).
Res.: 30 Union St., 01970-3709. Tel: 978-745-6303; Fax: 978-744-4382. Email: office@icsalem.com. Web: www.icsalem.com.
Catechesis/Religious Program—
3—ST. JAMES (1850) Rev. John E. Sheridan; Ms. Andre Schwartz, Pastoral Assoc.; Senior Deacon Norman P. LaPointe. In Res., Revs. Lawrence J. Rondeau (Retired); Robert G. Labrie.

Res.: 161 Federal St., 01970-3297. Tel: 978-745-9060; Fax: 978-745-0561. Email: stjamessalem@aol.com. Web: www.stjamessalem.homestead.com.
School—160 Federal St., 01970. Tel: 978-744-4773. LouAnn Melino, Prin.
Catechesis/Religious Program—Tel: 978-744-2230. Diane Santos, D.R.E.
4—ST. JOHN THE BAPTIST (1903), (Polish), Rev. Msgr. Stanislaw Parfienczyk.
Res.: 28 St. Peter St., 01970. Tel: 978-744-1278; Fax: 978-744-2093.
Catechesis/Religious Program—Teresa Prochorska, D.R.E.
5—ST. JOSEPH (1873), St. Joseph, Salem was suppressed. This parish's records are located at St. James, Salem.
6—ST. MARY (1918), St. Mary, Salem was suppressed. This parish's records are located at Immaculate Conception, Salem.
7—ST. THOMAS THE APOSTLE (1927) Rev. Richard T. Burton; Bro. Thomas Petitte, F.M.S., Pastoral Assoc.
Res.: One Margin St., Peabody, 01960-1999. Tel: 978-531-0224; Fax: 978-531-6517. Email: stthomas344p@comcast.net. Web: www.stthomasparish.net.
Catechesis/Religious Program—Nancy O'Brine, D.R.E.
SALISBURY, ESSEX CO., STAR OF THE SEA (1947) Rev. Thomas B. Morgan.
Res.: 18 Beach Rd., 01952-2007. Tel: 978-465-3334; Fax: 978-465-5524. Email: starsea11@verizon.net.
SAUGUS, ESSEX CO.
1—BLESSED SACRAMENT (1917) Revs. George E. Morin, Team Ministry; Daniel P. McCoy, Team Ministry; Deacon Francis M. Gaffney.
Res.: 14 Summer St., 01906-2139. Tel: 781-233-2497. Web: www.blessedsacramentparish.org.
Catechesis/Religious Program—Tel: 781-231-3699. Donna G. Zinna, D.R.E.
2—ST. MARGARET (1949) Revs. George E. Morin, Team Ministry; Daniel P. McCoy, Team Ministry.
Res.: 431 Lincoln Ave., 01906-3917. Tel: 781-233-1040; Fax: 781-233-7135. Web: www.stmargaretssaugus.org.
Catechesis/Religious Program—Carol Nadeau, D.R.E.
SCITUATE, PLYMOUTH CO.
1—ST. FRANCES XAVIER CABRINI (1960), St. Frances Xavier Cabrini, Scituate was suppressed. This parish's records are located at St. Mary of the Nativity, Scituate.
2—ST. MARY OF THE NATIVITY (1921) Revs. Kenneth V. Cannon; Matthew J. Westcott, Parochial Vicar; Deacon Martin W. Henry; Ms. Jane Kuklis, Pastoral Assoc.
Res.: One Kent St., 02066-4215. Tel: 781-545-3335; Fax: 781-544-3678. Email: Akeefe@stmaryscituate.org. Web: www.stmaryscituate.org.
Catechesis/Religious Program—Fax: 781-544-3678. Rosemary Lonborg, D.R.E. (Grades K-5); Ms. Jane Kuklis, D.R.E. (Grades 6-10).
SHARON, NORFOLK CO., OUR LADY OF SORROWS (1906) Rev. Scott A. Euvrard; Deacon Michael A. Iwanowicz.
Res.: 59 Cottage St., 02067-2132. Tel: 781-784-2265; Fax: 781-784-2540. Web: www.ourladyofsorrows.net.
Catechesis/Religious Program—Tel: 781-784-5091. Tami C. Ellis, D.R.E.
SHERBORN, MIDDLESEX CO., ST. THERESA OF LISIEUX (1945) Rev. Brian E. Mahoney; Elizabeth Yon, Pastoral Assoc.
P.O.Box 176, 01770.
Res.: 35 S. Main St., 01770. Tel: 508-653-6253; Fax: 508-651-1318. Email: fr.brian@st-theresa.sherborn.org. Web: www.st-theresa.sherborn.org.
Catechesis/Religious Program—Regina O'Connor, D.R.E.
SHIRLEY, MIDDLESEX CO., ST. ANTHONY OF PADUA (1905) [CEM] Rev. Edmond M. Derosier; Senior Deacon Raymond A. Gagnon; Sr. Joan Guertin, S.U.S.C., Pastoral Assoc.
P.O. Box 595, 01464.
Res.: 14 Phoenix St., 01464. Tel: 978-425-4588; Fax: 978-425-2033. Web: stanthonychurchshirley.org.
Catechesis/Religious Program—Tel: 978-425-0980. Donna Vaira, D.R.E.
SOMERVILLE, MIDDLESEX CO.
1—ST. ANN (1881) Revs. Brian J. McHugh; Thomas B. Corcoran, Parochial Vicar.
50 Thurston St., 02145.
Rectory—179 Summer St., 02143-2501. Tel: 617-625-1904; Fax: 617-625-7043. Email: parish@stannsomerville.org. Web: www.stannsomerville.org.
2—ST. ANTHONY OF PADUA (1915), (Italian), Rev. Moacir Balen, C.S.; Deacon Pedro M. Rodrigues.
Res.: 12 Properzi Way, 02143-3226. Tel: 617-625-4530; Fax: 617-625-2457. Email: stanthonysomer@aol.com.
Catechesis/Religious Program—
3—ST. BENEDICT (1911) Rev. Robert J. Carr; William Jackson, Pastoral Assoc. Tel: 857-204-8332.
Res.: 25 Arlington St., 02145-3235. Tel: 617-625-0029; Fax: 866-571-8983. Email: stbenedictsomerville@hotmail.com. Web: www.stbenedictsomerville.com.
Catechesis/Religious Program—Tel: 617-825-4333. Daisy Gomez, D.R.E. Tel: 617-825-4333.
4—ST. CATHERINE OF GENOA (1891) Revs. Brian J. McHugh; Thomas B. Corcoran, Parochial Vicar.
Res.: 179 Summer St., 02143-2501. Tel: 617-666-2087; Fax: 617-666-5470. Email: parishsec@stcofg.com. Web: www.stcatherinesomerville.com.
School—192 Summer St., 02143-2501. Tel: 617-666-9116. Marian Burns, Prin. Sisters 2; Lay Teachers 9; Students 225.
Catechesis/Religious Program—
5—ST. JOSEPH (1869) Revs. Henry J. Jennings; Charles Madi-Okin, Parochial Vicar; Sr. Marie Saint Joseph Santry, S.N.D., Pastoral Assoc.
Res.: 264 Washington St., 02143-3313. Tel: 617-666-4140; Fax: 617-628-0557. Email: stjoe1869@verizon.net.
Catechesis/Religious Program—John J. Piantedosi, D.R.E.
6—ST. POLYCARP (1927), St. Polycarp, Somerville was suppressed. This parish's records are located at St. Ann, Somerville.
STONEHAM, MIDDLESEX CO., ST. PATRICK (1868) Revs. William T. Schmidt; Mario J. Orrigo, Parochial Vicar; Sr. Marylou A. Cassidy, C.S.J., Pastoral Assoc.; Deacons J. Robert Turner; Cyril T. O'Neil.
Res.: 9 Pomeworth St., 02180-2025. Tel: 781-438-0960; Fax: 781-438-6809. Email: stpatstone@aol.com. Web: www.catholic-church.org/st-patricks.
School—20 Pleasant St., 02180. Tel: 781-438-2593. Arthur Swanson, Prin. Lay Teachers 10; Students 223.
Catechesis/Religious Program—Tel: 781-438-1093. Marie Kopf, D.R.E.
STOUGHTON, NORFOLK CO.
1—IMMACULATE CONCEPTION (1872) Revs. Joseph P. McDermott; Roberto F. deRezende (Brazil), Parochial Vicar.
Res.: 122 Canton St., 02072-2204. Tel: 781-344-2073; Fax: 781-344-2979. Email: immaculateconception@verizon.net.
Catechesis/Religious Program—Tel: 781-341-0611. Alice Bachant, D.R.E.
2—ST. JAMES (1962) Rev. John E. Kelly.
Res.: 560 Page St., 02072. Tel: 781-344-9121; Fax: 781-341-9323. Email: saintjamesstoughton@comcast.net.
Catechesis/Religious Program—Tel: 781-297-7582. Mrs. Mary Ann Caldwell, D.R.E.
3—OUR LADY OF THE ROSARY (1958), Our Lady of the Rosary, Stoughton was suppressed. This parish's records are located at St. James, Stoughton.
STOW, MIDDLESEX CO., ST. ISIDORE (1961) Rev. David A. Doucet; Deacons Charles A. Cornell; Robert F. Brady.
Res.: 429 Great Rd., 01775-1101. Tel: 978-897-2710; Fax: 978-461-0577. Email: info@stisidorestow.org. Web: www.stisidorestow.org.
Catechesis/Religious Program—Tel: 978-897-9790. Nancy Dome, D.R.E.
SUDBURY, MIDDLESEX CO.
1—ST. ANSELM (1963), St. Anselm, Sudbury was suppressed. This parish's records are located at Our Lady of Fatima, Sudbury.
2—OUR LADY OF FATIMA (1955) Very Rev. Michael J. Bova Conti; Deacon John D. Nicholson; Ms. Christine Dunn, Pastoral Assoc.
Res.: 160 Concord Rd., 01776-2353. Tel: 978-443-2647; Fax: 978-443-6264. Email: psecretary@fatimasudbury.org. Web: www.fatimasudbury.org.
Catechesis/Religious Program—Tel: 978-443-9166. Susan Murphy, D.R.E.
SWAMPSCOTT, ESSEX CO., ST. JOHN THE EVANGELIST (1905) Rev. Thomas S. Rafferty; Deacon Andrew J. Acampora.
Res.: 174 Humphrey St., 01907-2512. Tel: 781-593-2544; Fax: 781-593-3616. Email: stjohnsswampscott@gmail.com. Web: www.stjohnswampscott.com.
Catechesis/Religious Program—Tel: 781-599-4711. Mr. A. Joseph Hunt, D.R.E.
TEWKSBURY, MIDDLESEX CO., ST. WILLIAM (1935) Revs. John W. Hanley, O.M.I.; Daniel Nassaney, O.M.I., Parochial Vicar; John J. Hogan, O.M.I., Parochial Vicar; Deacons William R. Emerson; Gerard J. Hardy. In Res., Rev. J. George Croft, O.M.I.
Res.: 1351 Main St., 01876-2039. Tel: 978-851-7331; Fax: 978-858-0544. Email: stwilliamsrectory@comcast.net. Web: www.home.catholicweb.com/stwilliams.
Catechesis/Religious Program—Deborah M. Albano, D.R.E.
TOPSFIELD, ESSEX CO., ST. ROSE OF LIMA (1945) Very Rev. Mark A. Mahoney.
Res.: 17 Prospect St., 01983-0458. Tel: 978-887-5505; Fax: 978-887-8201.
Catechesis/Religious Program—Tel: 978-882-0882. Mary I. Connor, D.R.E.; Kathleen A. Yanchus, D.R.E.
TOWNSEND, MIDDLESEX CO., ST. JOHN THE EVANGELIST (1945) Rev. Shawn W. Allen; Edward Kelly, Pastoral Assoc.
Res.: One School St., 01469-0533. Tel: 978-597-2291; Fax: 978-597-3401. Email: saintjohns@comcast.net. Web: www.stjohnsoftownsend.com.
Catechesis/Religious Program—Tel: 978-597-2183. Kathleen Twombly, D.R.E.
TYNGSBOROUGH, MIDDLESEX CO., ST. MARY MAGDALEN (2004) Rev. Ronald L. Saint Pierre.
P.O. Box 100, 01879.
Res.: 93 Lakeview Ave., 01879. Tel: 978-649-7315; Fax: 978-649-3796. Email: saintmarymagdalen@verizon.net. Web: www.stmarymagdalenparish.com.
Catechesis/Religious Program—Cathy Kennedy, D.R.E.
WAKEFIELD, MIDDLESEX CO.
1—ST. FLORENCE (1947) Rev. Vincent J. Gianni; Deacon William E. Kerns.
Res.: 49 Butler Ave., 01880. Tel: 781-245-2711; Fax: 781-245-4512. Email: stflo@comcast.net. Web: www.stflorence.org.
Catechesis/Religious Program—Deanna Kerns, D.R.E.
2—ST. JOSEPH (1854) Rev. Ronald A. Barker.
Res.: 173 Albion St., 01880-3224. Tel: 781-245-5770; Fax: 781-246-2423. Email: office@stjosephwakefield.org. Web: www.stjosephwakefield.org.
School—15 Gould St., 01880-2700. Tel: 781-245-2081. Ms. Maria Morris, Prin. Sisters 1; Lay Teachers 15; Students 235.
Catechesis/Religious Program—Tel: 781-245-1930. Molly DiTonno, D.R.E.
3—MOST BLESSED SACRAMENT (1931) Rev. William D. Coughlin; Deacon Frank A. Valeri.
Res.: 11 Grove St., 01880-4222. Tel: 781-245-2080; Fax: 781-245-7981. Email: mbsparish1@aol.com. Web: www.nexteon.com/mbsparish.
Catechesis/Religious Program—Tel: 781-245-4669; 781-245-3414. Christine Carlson, D.R.E.; Laurine Kohler, D.R.E.
WALPOLE, NORFOLK CO.
1—BLESSED SACRAMENT (1874) Revs. Timothy J. Kelleher, Team Ministry; Emile R. Boutin, Team Ministry; Deacon Reynold G. Spadoni; Marie A. Martin, Pastoral Assoc.; William Dittrich, Pastoral Assoc.
10 Diamond St., 02081-3408.
Res.: 796 East St., 02081. Tel: 508-668-4700 (Parish); Fax: 508-668-3554 (Parish). Web: www.blessedsacrament.org.
School—808 East St., 02081. Tel: 508-668-2336. Russ W. Wilson, Prin. Lay Teachers 30; Students 440.
Catechesis/Religious Program—
Convent—808 East St., 02081. Tel: 508-668-6693.
2—ST. MARY (1931) Rev. Donald R. Delay.
P.O. Box 131, 02032-0131.
Res.: 176 Washington St., 02032-0131. Tel: 508-668-4974; Fax: 508-668-3083. Email: stmarys176@msn.com.
Catechesis/Religious Program—Tel: 508-668-6853. Thomas Connor, D.R.E.; Judith Connor, D.R.E.
WALTHAM, MIDDLESEX CO.
1—ST. CHARLES BORROMEO (1909) Rev. Rodney J. Copp.
Res.: 51 Hall St., 02453-5299. Tel: 781-893-0330; Fax: 781-893-2060. Email: stcharleswaltham@yahoo.com. Web: www.stcharleswaltham4lpi.com.
Catechesis/Religious Program—Tel: 781-893-1438. Carol A. Gill, D.R.E.
2—ST. JOSEPH (1894), St. Joseph, Waltham was suppressed. This parish's records are located at St. Mary Waltham.
3—ST. JUDE (1949) Rev. William T. Leonard; Deacon Alfred E. Santosuosso.
Res.: 147-R Main St., 02453-6622. Tel: 781-893-3100; Fax: 781-893-2424. Email: stjude1@comcast.net.
School—175 Main St., 02453-6622. Tel: 781-899-3644. Sr. Katherine Martin, S.N.D., Prin. Sisters 2; Lay Teachers 8; Students 199.
Catechesis/Religious Program—Tel: 781-891-5718. Barbara A. Keville, D.R.E.
4—ST. MARY (1839) Rev. Michael L. Nolan; Deacon Eduardo R. Mora. In Res., Rev. Daniel F. Hennessey.
Res.: 133 School St., 02451-4599. Tel: 781-891-1730; Fax: 781-642-0604.

Email: stmarychurch@earthlink.net. Web: www.rc.net/boston/stmary.
Catechesis/Religious Program—Tel: 781-893-0917. Marjorie Harris, D.R.E.
5—OUR LADY, COMFORTER OF THE AFFLICTED (1930) Rev. James M. DiPerri; Deacon Robert N. Johnson. 920-R Trapelo Rd., 02452-4841.
Res.: 857 Trapelo Rd., 02452-4841. Tel: 781-894-3481; Fax: 781-894-0021. Web: www.olca.org.
School—920 Trapelo Rd., 02452-4841. Tel: 781-899-0353. Chandra Mino, Prin. Lay Teachers 8; Students 180.
6—SACRED HEART (1922), (Italian), Rev. Dennis Wheatley, O.F.M.; Friar Damian J. Johnson, O.F.M., Pastoral Assoc.
Res.: 311 River St., 02453. Tel: 781-899-0469; Fax: 781-899-0081. Email: sacredheart311@aol.com. Web: www.sacredheart311.org.
Catechesis/Religious Program—Tel: 781-893-8461. Bernadette Scalese, D.R.E.
WATERTOWN, MIDDLESEX CO.
1—ST. PATRICK (1847) Revs. Raymond P. Kiley, Admin.; Paul Muyimbwa (Uganda), Parochial Vicar. 26R Chestnut St., 02472-2339.
Res.: 25 Chestnut St., 02472-2337. Tel: 617-926-9680; Fax: 617-926-3715. Email: parishoffice@stpatswatertown.org. Web: www.stpatswatertown.org.
Catechesis/Religious Program—Tel: 617-926-3441; Fax: 617-926-3715. Sandy Clancy, D.R.E.
2—SACRED HEART (1893) Rev. Joseph L. Curran; Sr. Mary Claire Kirkpatrick, O.P., Pastoral Assoc. In Res., Revs. John J. Stagnaro; Richard G. Curran.
Res.: 770 Mt. Auburn St., 02472-1567. Tel: 617-924-9110; Fax: 617-926-3341.
Catechesis/Religious Program—Judy Gilreath, D.R.E.
3—ST. THERESA OF THE CHILD JESUS (1927), St. Theresa of the Child Jesus, Watertown was suppressed. This parish's records are located at St. Patrick, Watertown.
WAYLAND, MIDDLESEX CO.
1—ST. ANN (1945) Very Rev. James J. Laughlin; Sr. Roberta Rzeznik, S.N.D., Pastoral Assoc.
Res.: 124 Cochituate Rd., 01778-2610. Tel: 508-358-2985; Fax: 508-358-3415. Email: parish@saintann.org. Web: www.saintann.org.
Catechesis/Religious Program—Jane Asber, D.R.E. Tel: 508-358-2985, Ext. 13.
2—ST. ZEPHERIN (1889) Very Rev. James J. Laughlin; Marjory O'Day, Pastoral Assoc.
Res.: 124 Cochituate Rd., 01778-2610. Tel: 508-653-8013; Fax: 508-655-6948. Email: stzepherin@comcast.net. Web: www.stzepherin.org.
Catechesis/Religious Program—Sr. Frances Thomas, D.R.E.
WELLESLEY, NORFOLK CO.
1—ST. JAMES THE GREAT (1947), St. James the Great, Wellesley was suppressed. This parish's records are located at St. Paul, Wellesley.
2—ST. JOHN THE EVANGELIST (1890) Very Rev. Thomas F. Powers; Deacon Thomas A. Smith; Sr. Evelyn Ronan, S.N.D., Pastoral Assoc. In Res., Rev. J. Bryan Hehir.
Res.: 9 Glen Rd., 02481-1600. Tel: 781-235-0045; Fax: 781-235-6990. Email: st-johns@comcast.net. Web: www.stjohnwellesley.org.
School—9 Ledyard St., 02481. Tel: 781-235-0300. Carol Roncari, Prin. Sisters 2; Lay Teachers 5; Students 187.
Catechesis/Religious Program—Tel: 781-235-5337. Linda Messore, D.R.E.; Jane Leonard, D.R.E.; Christine Tierney, D.R.E.
3—ST. PAUL (1922) Very Rev. Richard W. Fitzgerald; Rev. Mark J. Riley, Parochial Vicar; Deacon Paul M. Cloonan. In Res., Rev. Msgr. Joseph G. Lind (Retired).
Res.: 502 Washington St., 02482-5907. Tel: 781-235-1060; Fax: 781-235-4620. Email: stpauloffice1@verizon.net. Web: www.stpaulwellesley.com.
School—10 Atwood St., 02482. Tel: 781-235-1510. Karen McLaughlin, Prin. Sisters 1; Lay Teachers 7; Students 184.
Catechesis/Religious Program—Tel: 781-235-5012. Kathleen Curley, D.R.E.
WEST BRIDGEWATER, PLYMOUTH CO., ST. ANN (1938) Rev. Edward C. McDonagh.
Box 427, 02379-0427.
Res.: 103 N. Main St., 02379-0427. Tel: 508-586-4880; Fax: 508-586-3876. Email: stanns@comcast.net. Web: stannwb.com.
Catechesis/Religious Program—Maria Lallemand, D.R.E.
WEST NEWBURY, ESSEX CO., ST. ANN (1945), St. Ann, West Newbury was suppressed. This parish's records are located at Holy Redeemer, Merrimac.
WESTFORD, MIDDLESEX CO., ST. CATHERINE OF ALEXANDRIA (1922) [CEM] Revs. Peter F. Quinn; David P. White, Parochial Vicar; Majorie Hicks, Pastoral Assoc.; Deacon Richard T. Joy.
Res.: 107 N. Main St., 01886. Tel: 978-692-6353; Fax: 978-392-0644. Web: www.westford.com/stcatherines.
Catechesis/Religious Program—Diahne Goodwin, D.R.E.
WESTON, MIDDLESEX CO., ST. JULIA (1919) Revs. George P. Evans; Joseph M. Hennessey, Parochial Vicar; Susan Bayard, Pastoral Assoc.
Res.: 374 Boston Post Rd., 02493-1581. Tel: 781-899-2611; Fax: 781-899-8046. Email: stjulia@stjulia.org. Web: www.stjulia.org.
Catechesis/Religious Program—Tel: 781-899-2611. Sr. Marie LaBollita, S.C., D.R.E.
Mission—St. Joseph 142 Lincoln Rd., Lincoln, Middlesex Co. 01773.
WESTWOOD, NORFOLK CO.
1—ST. DENIS (1949) Rev. James G. Burke. In Res., Rev. William C. Burckhart (Retired).
Res.: 157 Washington St., 02090-1336. Tel: 781-326-5858; Fax: 781-326-1232. Web: www.stdeniswestwood.com.
Catechesis/Religious Program—Mary Campion, D.R.E.; Kathleen A. Burton, D.R.E.
2—ST. MARGARET MARY (1931) Rev. Christopher J. Coyne; Deacon Joseph E. Holderried; Ms. Dorothy R. Ruggiero, Pastoral Assoc.
Box 386, 02090-0386.
Res.: 845 High St., 02090-0386. Tel: 781-326-1071; Fax: 781-329-1879. Email: info@stmmparish.org. Web: www.saintmmparish.org.
Catechesis/Religious Program—Karlene Duffy, D.R.E.
WEYMOUTH, NORFOLK CO.
1—ST. ALBERT THE GREAT (1950) Rev. Paul R. Soper.
Res.: 1130 Washington St., 02189-1932. Tel: 781-337-8778; Fax: 781-335-5850. Email: parishoffice1130@verizon.net. Web: www.atgweymouth.org.
Catechesis/Religious Program—John J. Hammel, D.R.E.
2—ST. FRANCIS XAVIER (1859) [CEM] Revs. Eugene P. Sullivan; Richard S. DeVeer, Parochial Vicar; Deacon Joseph A. Canova. In Res., Rev. Charles J. Murphy.
Res.: 261 Pleasant St., 02190. Tel: 781-337-2171; Fax: 781-331-4192. Email: sfxprsh@aol.com. Web: www.stfrancisxavier.org.
School—234 Pleasant St., 02190. Tel: 781-335-6868. Sr. Teresa Vesey, C.S.J., Prin. Religious 1; Lay Teachers 18; Students 471.
Catechesis/Religious Program—Marjorie Kearney, D.R.E.; Barbara Spink, D.R.E.
3—IMMACULATE CONCEPTION (1871) Rev. William F. Salmon; Deacons Francis J. Corbett; Stephen M. Buttrick.
Res.: 1199 Commercial St., 02189. Tel: 781-337-0380; Fax: 781-340-3979. Email: icwey@comcast.net. Web: www.catholic-church.org/icweymouth.
Catechesis/Religious Program—Tel: 781-337-3024. Ruthann Sinibaldi, D.R.E. Tel: 781-335-3902.
4—ST. JEROME (1928) Rev. Robert M. Blaney; Deacon Joseph V. Vitello. In Res., Most Rev. John A. Dooher; Rev. Msgr. Peter T. Martocchio (Retired).
Res.: 632 Bridge St., 02191. Tel: 781-335-2038; Fax: 781-340-7165. Email: stjeromeparish@comcast.net. Web: www.saintjeromeparish.org.
School—598 Bridge St., 02191. Tel: 781-335-1235. Kathleen Shea, Prin. Sisters 1; Lay Teachers 9; Students 234.
Catechesis/Religious Program—Tel: 781-335-2786. Sr. Barbara Joyce, C.S.J., D.R.E.
5—SACRED HEART (1871) Very Rev. Daniel J. Riley; Rev. Joseph M. Mazzone, Parochial Vicar; Senior Deacon Henry M. Welch; Deacon Kenneth N. Ryan.
Res.: 55 Commercial St., 02188-2604. Tel: 781-337-6333; Fax: 781-337-9192. Email: p.heart@comcast.net. Web: www.sacredheartweymouth.org.
School—75 Commercial St., 02188-2604. Tel: 781-335-6010. Mary R. Ferrucci, Prin. Sisters 2; Lay Teachers 7; Students 165.
Catechesis/Religious Program—Jean Duke, D.R.E.; Susan McLeod, D.R.E.
WHITMAN, PLYMOUTH CO., HOLY GHOST (1897) Rev. John T. Swencki; Deacon Joseph T. Nickley.
Res.: 518 Washington St., 02382. Tel: 781-447-4421; Fax: 781-447-1375. Email: hgpwhitman@aol.com.
Catechesis/Religious Program—Tel: 781-447-3135. Ann Lawrence, D.R.E.
WILMINGTON, MIDDLESEX CO.
1—ST. DOROTHY (1954) Rev. Kevin P. Horrigan.
Res.: 11 Harnden St., 01887-3519. Tel: 978-658-3550; Fax: 978-658-2008. Web: www.saintdorothys.2om.com.
Catechesis/Religious Program—Mary E. Medeiros, D.R.E.
2—ST. THOMAS OF VILLANOVA (1919) Revs. Phillip B. Earley Esq.; Paul G. Flammia, Parochial Vicar; Deacons Clifford D. King; Joseph M. Fagan Jr.
Res.: 126 Middlesex Ave., 01887-2723. Tel: 978-658-4665; Fax: 978-658-4670. Web: www.stthomasvillanova.com.
Catechesis/Religious Program—Marilyn Mandosa, D.R.E.
WINCHESTER, MIDDLESEX CO.
1—ST. EULALIA (1966) Very Rev. Thomas F. Nestor; Ms. Moira Brady, Pastoral Assoc.
Res.: 38 Ridge St., 01890-3633. Tel: 781-729-8220; Fax: 781-729-0919. Email: steulalia@verizon.net. Web: www.steulalia.org.
Catechesis/Religious Program—Barbara Penkala, D.R.E.; Donna DiFonzo, D.R.E.
2—IMMACULATE CONCEPTION (1931), Immaculate Conception, Winchester was suppressed. This parish's records are located at St. Mary, Winchester.
3—ST. MARY (1876) Revs. Richard C. Messina; Richard C. Beaulieu, Parochial Vicar; Sr. Patricia Burke, S.M.S.M., Pastoral Assoc.; Salvatore Caraviello, Pastoral Assoc.
Res.: 158 Washington St., 01890. Tel: 781-729-0055; Fax: 781-721-6542. Email: stmarywinchester@comcast.net. Web: www.stmary-winchester.org.
School—162 Washington St., 01890-2173. Tel: 781-729-5515. Steven B. Ultrino, Prin. Lay Teachers 20; Students 198.
Catechesis/Religious Program—Tel: 781-729-1965.
WINTHROP, SUFFOLK CO.
1—HOLY ROSARY (1953) Rev. Thomas A. DiLorenzo, Admin.
Rectory—993 Shirley St., 02152-2535. Tel: 617-846-1210; Fax: 617-539-4402. Web: www.holyrosaryparish.net.
Church: 1015 Shirley St., 02152-2535.
Catechesis/Religious Program—Deborah Tewksbury, D.R.E.
2—ST. JOHN THE EVANGELIST (1907) Rev. Charles E. Bourke; Sr. Jane Iannaccone, S.P., Pastoral Assoc.
Res.: 320 Winthrop St., 02152-3127. Tel: 617-846-7400; Fax: 617-539-0627. Web: www.stjohnswinthrop.org.
Catechesis/Religious Program—Tel: 617-846-3100. Geraldine Butters, D.R.E.
WOBURN, MIDDLESEX CO.
1—ST. ANTHONY OF PADUA (1945) Revs. Richard J. Shmaruk; John R. Carroll, Parochial Vicar.
Rectory—80 Elm St., 01801-1855. Tel: 781-933-1323; Fax: 781-937-3233. Email: st_anthony_parish@verizon.net.
Catechesis/Religious Program—Sandra Strong, D.R.E.
2—ST. BARBARA (1954) Revs. Vincent P. Mellone; Gerard E. Reid (Jamaica), Parochial Vicar; Deacon James V. Kerrigan.
Res.: 138 Cambridge Rd., 01801-4772. Tel: 781-933-4130; Fax: 781-932-2536.
Catechesis/Religious Program—Tel: 781-935-0529. Barbara Jeannotte, D.R.E.
3—ST. CHARLES BORROMEO (1862) Revs. Timothy J. Shea; Arthur T. MacKay, Parochial Vicar; Deacons Philip P. Hardcastle; Manuel A. Rosario. In Res., Rev. Patrick J. Kelly (Retired).
Res.: 280 Main St., 01801. Tel: 781-933-0300; Fax: 781-932-7581. Web: www.saintcharleschurch.net.
School—Tel: 781-935-4635. Rita Masotta, Prin. Lay Teachers 25; Students 350.
Catechesis/Religious Program—Cliff Garvey, D.R.E.
4—ST. JOSEPH (1906) Rev. Harold E. LeBlanc.
Res.: 22 Central St., 01801-4616. Tel: 781-938-0473; Fax: 781-938-7818.
Catechesis/Religious Program—Tel: 781-937-6392. Donna Ingham, D.R.E.
WRENTHAM, NORFOLK CO., ST. MARY (1928) Rev. George C. Hines; Deacon Kenneth W. Oles.
Res.: 130 South St., 02093-0326. Tel: 508-384-3373; Fax: 508-384-5747. Email: stmary414@verizon.net. Web: stmaryswrentham.org.
Catechesis/Religious Program—Tel: 508-384-7922. Roberta Oles, D.R.E.

Absent on Leave. For contact information please call or write: Clergy Personnel Office, 66 Brooks Dr., Braintree, MA 02184-3839; Tel: 617-779-3685:
Revs.—
Antonellis, Joseph A.
Shoemaker, David A.
Sullivan, William M.

Awaiting Assignment. For contact information please call or write Clergy Personnel Office, 66 Brooks Dr., Braintree, MA 02184-3839; Tel. 617-779-3685:
Revs.—
Gillespie, Jerome F.
Jacques, Roger N.

Emergency Response Group. For contact information please call or write: Clergy Personnel Office 66 Brooks Dr., Braintree, MA 02184-3839; Tel: 617-779-3685:
Revs.—
Bouton, Thomas F.

Casey, Richard L.
Conway, Richard C.
Gianni, Vincent J.
Kelly, Thomas P.
Kiley, Raymond P.
Tighe, Leonard J.

Priests Pursuing Higher Studies. For contact information please call or write: Clergy Personnel Office, 66 Brooks Dr., Braintree, MA 02184-3839; Tel: 617-779-3685:
Rev.—
Borek, Derek J., M.Div., S.T.L.

Health Leave. For contact information please call or write: Clergy Personnel Office, 66 Brooks Dr., Braintree, MA 02184-3839; Tel: 617-779-3685:
Revs.—
Ajemian, David J.
Butera, George J.
Curley, Terence P.
Jacques, Roger N.
Keenan, Alexander J.
Keville, Joseph F.
Malloy, Stephen J.
McCarthy, Sean M.
Obayashi, Hal N.
Thuma, Clifton M.

Military & VA Chaplains. For contact information please call or write: Clergy Personnel Office, 66 Brooks Dr., Braintree, MA 02184-3839; Tel: 617-779-3685:
Revs.—
Butler, Timothy A.
Cuddy, William F.
Deeley, Kevin J.
Devine, William D.
Doyle, Michael J.
Hurley, Paul K.
Kennedy, William M.
Linehan, Stephen J.
McCabe, Edward D.
Monagle, Robert J.
Nichols, Henry P.
Raux, Redmond P.
Yanju, Henry M.

On Duty Outside the Archdiocese. For contact information please call or write: Clergy Personnel Office, 66 Brooks Dr., Braintree, MA 02184-3839; Tel: 617-779-3685:
Rev. Msgrs.—
Abruzzese, John A.
Deeley, Robert P., V.F., J.C.D.
Groden, Michael F.
McInerny, Paul B.
Russell, Paul F.
Revs.—
Donahue, Richard T.
Driscoll, Joseph J.
Galvin, John P., D.Th.
McLaughlin, John R.
McNeil, John R. (Retired)
Pucciarelli, George W.
Sullivan, Robert E.

Permanent Disability. For contact information please call or write: Clergy Personnel Office, 66 Brooks Dr., Braintree, MA 02184-3839; Tele: 617-799-3685:
Revs.—
Best, Russell W.
Buntel, Richard A.
Carroll, Edward G.
Curran, Thomas M.
Driscoll, Nicholas J.
Fraser, Gerald C.
Gomes, Ronald A.
McGrade, Kevin M.
McNulty, Martin J.
Moran, James F.
Nee, Robert E.
Scanlan, William A.

Senior Priests. For contact information please call or write: Clergy Personnel Office, 66 Brooks Dr., Braintree, MA 02184-3839; 617-779-3685:
Rev. Msgrs.—
Abucewicz, John A. (Retired), Box 363, Durham, NH 03824-0363.
Alves, Joseph T. (Retired), 60 William Cardinal O'Connell Way, Boston, 02114-2729.
Bourque, Charles J., V.F. (Retired), 700 Washington St., Canton, 02021-3036.
Boyle, Robert J. (Retired), 60 William Cardinal O'Connell Way, Boston, 02114-2729.
Brady, Roger J. (Retired), 81 Hartwell Rd., Bedford, 01730-2408.
Connell, Andrew F. (Retired), 275 Flaggler Dr., Box 756, Marshfield, 02050-0756.
Contons, Albert J. (Retired), P.O. Box 1025, Humarock, 02047-1025.
Coppenrath, Leonard A. (Retired), 1573 Cambridge St., Cambridge, 02138-4370.
Daly, Thomas J. (Retired), 60 William Cardinal O'Connell Way, Boston, 02114-2729.
Fichtner, Robert C. (Retired), 24 Beal Rd., Waltham, 02453-6644.
Finnegan, Thomas J. (Retired), P.O. Box 461, E Falmouth, 02536-0461.
Forster, William J. (Retired), 36 Glover Dr., Revere, 02151-4915.
Glynn, William F. (Retired), 290 Kingstown Way, Unit 228, Duxbury, 02332-4640.
Lind, Joseph G. (Retired), 502 Washington St., Wellesley, 02482-5907.
Martocchio, Peter T. (Retired), 632 Bridge St., Weymouth, 02191-1845.
McDonough, John P. (Retired), One Pond St., Apt. 4H, Winthrop, 02152-1080.
McGann, Francis J. (Retired), 1382 Highland Ave., Needham, 02492-2614.
McGrath, Laurence W., M.Div., M.A., M.S. (Retired), 34 Bunerk Hill Rd., Auburn, NH 03032-3528.
McManus, Paul J. (Retired), 1573 Cambridge St., Cambridge, 02138-4370.
McNamara, Eugene P. (Retired), 1573 Cambridge St., Cambridge, 02138-4370.
Murphy, Frederick J. (Retired), 24 Conant St., Danvers, 01923-2988.
O'Sullivan, Francis G. (Retired), 17 Chestnut St., Peabody, 01960-6498.
Palladino, Alfonso G. (Retired), 46 Myrtle St., Melrose, 02176-3827.
Roche, William H. (Retired), 60 William Cardinal O'Connell Way, Boston, 02114-2729.
Ryan, Paul T. (Retired), 547 Washington St., Norwood, 02062-0547.
Tierney, James E. (Retired), 60 William Cardinal O'Connell Way, Boston, 02114-2729.
Very Rev.—
Condon, Edwin D. (Retired), 225 Lincoln St., Unit E2, Duxbury, 02332-3627.
Revs.—
Ahearn, Richard F. (Retired), 1573 Cambridge St., Cambridge, 02138-4370.
Anderson, William R. (Retired), 76 Allendale Rd., Newport, VT 05855-9557.
Andrade, Antonio L. (Retired), 9 Brigham Cr., Apt. 6, Hudson, 01749-2449.
Bailey, Paul F. (Retired), 313 Court St., Plymouth, 02360-4336.
Barry, Gerard B. (Retired), 60 William Cardinal O'Connell Way, Boston, 02114-2729.
Bartley, David J. (Retired), 190 Bridge St., Apt. 3202, Salem, 01970-7409.
Beksha, Francis W. (Retired), 6 Cassidy Ln., Medway, 02053-1235.
Bergeron, Robert E. (Retired), 60 William Cardinal O'Connel Way, Boston, 02114-2729.
Bertelli, Ameilio James (Retired), 4 Payson St., Lexington, 02421-7924.
Berube, Paul W. (Retired), 42 Green St., Newburyport, 01950-2647.
Billicky, Louis S. (Retired), 24 Rickey Dr., Maynard, 01754-1052.
Blute, Robert H. (Retired), 60 William Cardinal O'Connell Way, Boston, 02114-2729.
Boivin, Henry P. (Retired), 660 Union St., Unit 3D, 02184-4130.
Bourgault, Ronald L. (Retired), 100 Salisbury Rd., Franklin, NH 03235-2501.
Brady, Richard J. (Retired), 863 Central St., Framingham, 01701-4892.
Brennan, Gerard M. (Retired), 60 William Cardinal O'Connell Way, Boston, 02114-2729.
Brennan, James F. (Retired), 60 William Cardinal O'Connell Way, Boston, 02114-2729.
Broderick, James M. (Retired), 42 Green St., Newburyport, 01950-2647.
Brown, Arthur A. (Retired), 45 Clipper Ln., Box 625, Falmouth, 02540.
Browne, Robert M. (Retired), 2 Park Ln., Gloucester, 01930-3924.
Brudzynski, Peter F. (Retired), 316 Angelico Dr., Nokomis, FL 34275-7446.
Buckley, Thomas W. (Retired), 198 Centre St., Abington, 02351-2208.
Burckhart, William C. (Retired), 157 Washington St., Westwood, 02090-1336.
Burns, John F. (Retired), 60 William Cardinal O'Connell Way, Boston, 02114-2729.
Butler, Allan L. W. (Retired), 27 Vaughan Ave., Whitman, 02382-1307.
Butler, James P. (Retired), 11 Courtney St. (#8), Fall River, 02720-6740.
Butler, Richard J. (Retired), 5 Linden Pl., Brookline, 02445-7801.
Butler, Robert J. (Retired), 432 Adams St., Milton, 02186-4399.
Byrne, Joseph F. (Retired), 41 Cooper Rd., Falmouth, 02540.
Calter, Arthur M. (Retired), 60 William Cardinal O'Connell Way, Boston, 02114-2729.
Campbell, William W. (Retired), 117 Heather Ln., N Falmouth, 02556.
Canniff, James B. (Retired), 10 Fellsway E., Malden, 02148-5313.
Carrigg, William J. (Retired), Cranberry Village, 27 Adams Cir., Carver, 02330-1611.
Carroll, John P. (Retired), 66 Brooks Dr., 02184-3839.
Chaisson, John C. (Retired), 38 Windsor Rd., Beverly, 01915-2626.
Chase, Francis G. (Retired), 34 Governor Bradford Ln., Box 1132, W Falmouth, 02574-1132.
Clifford, Donald P. (Retired), 125 Lakeview Blvd., Plymouth, 02360.
Clougherty, Paul L. (Retired), 2969 Flint Dr., S., Clearwater, FL 33759-2577.
Connolly, John G. (Retired), 36 Belmont Rd., Apt. E22, West Harwich, 02671-1357.
Connor, Martin P., S.T.L. (Retired), 392 Hanover St., Hanover, 02339.
Conroy, Francis M. (Retired), 1529 Washington St., Newton, 02465.
Conroy, Philip M. (Retired), 66 Brooks Dr., 02184-3839.
Cormier, Leo G. (Retired), 90 Flower Ln., Dracut, 01826-4650.
Cormier, Roger C. (Retired), 45 S. Meadow Village, Unit 5, Carver, 02330-1802.
Costello, Robert B. (Retired), P.O. Box 92, Nahant, 01908-0092.
Cowhig, Edward D. (Retired), P.O. Box 154, Greenbush, 02040-0154.
Craig, Richard J. (Retired), 209 E. Side Dr., Box 310, Alton Bay, NH 03810-0310.
Crowley, Daniel J. (Retired), 340 Center St., Middleboro, 02346-2102.
Cunney, Henry M. (Retired), 1008 Paradise Rd., Unit 1B, Swampscott, 01907-1303.
Curran, Paul E. (Retired), 60 William Cardinal O'Connell Way, Boston, 02114-2729.
Curtin, Eugene P. (Retired), 60 William Cardinal O'Connell Way, Boston, 02114-2729.
Curtin, James F. (Retired), 60 William Cardinal O'Connell Way, Boston, 02114-2729.
Daily, Vincent E. (Retired), 1573 Cambridge St., Cambridge, 02138-4370.
Daniele, Anthony J. (Retired), 444 Centre St., Milton, 02186-4198.
Darcy, James F. (Retired), 60 William Cardinal O'Connell Way, Boston, 02114-2729.
DeAdder, James W., S.T.D., Ph.D., J.C.D. (Retired), 60 William Cardinal O'Connell Way, Boston, 02114-2729.
Degnan, James F. (Retired), 60 William Cardinal O'Connell Way, Boston, 02114-2729.
DePietro, Arthur J. (Retired), 45 School St., Quincy, 02169-6664.
Desmond, Hubert E. (Retired), 51 Broad Reach, Apt. M56A, Weymouth, 02191-2266.
Desrosiers, Philip J. (Retired), P.O. Box 8149, Lynn, 01904-0149.
Doherty, Henry F. (Retired), 12 Sachem Village Rd., P.O. Box 31, West Dennis, 02670-0031.
Doherty, Robert J. (Retired), 13991 Amarilis Ct., Fort Pierce, FL 34951-4201.
Donovan, John L. (Retired), 60 William Cardinal O'Connell Way, Boston, 02114-2729.
Doyle, John L. (Retired), 83 Long Ave., Framingham, 01702-5735.
Drennan, Lawrence J. (Retired), 61 Broad Reach, T81B, Weymouth, 02191-2288.
Driscoll, Arthur J. (Retired), 57 Sylvan St., Unit 7A, Danvers, 01923-2747.
Driscoll, Richard A. (Retired), 69 Washington St., Apt. 11, Topsfield, 01983-1743.
DuFour, Louis C. (Retired), P.O. Box 731, Seabrook, NH 03874-0731.
Emerson, George F. (Retired), 650 Nichols St., Norwood, 02062-1099.
Fagan, Joseph K., M.Div. (Retired), 60 William Cardinal O'Connell Way, Boston, 02114-2729.
Fahey, James L. (Retired), 35 Sawyer Rd., Hampstead, NH 03841.
Fallon, John F. (Retired), 60 William Cardinal O'Connell Way, Boston, 02114-2729.
Fallon, John J. (Retired), 60 William Cardinal O'Connell Way, Boston, 02114-2729.
Ferreira, Jose S. (Retired), 6 McDewell Ave., Apt. 8, Danvers, 01923-3340.
Fitzpatrick, John P. (Retired), P.O. Box 130, Bennington, NH 03442-0130.
Fleming, Thomas J. (Retired), 60 William Cardinal O'Connell Way, Boston, 02114-2729.
Flynn, Arthur C. (Retired), 45 Folly Pond Rd., Apt. 24, Beverly, 01915-5384.
Flynn, George R. (Retired), Apartado 18-0825, Lima, Peru.

Flynn, John H. (Retired), 863 Central St., Framingham, 01701.
Foley, Thomas C. (Retired), 757 Hancock St., Quincy, 02170-2722.
Francis, Paul R. (Retired), 60 William Cardinal O'Connell Way, Boston, 02114-2729.
Franz, Paul R. (Retired), 19877 N. Emmerson Dr., Maricopa, AZ 85239-9400.
Gallagher, Edward L. (Retired), 10036 Connell Rd., San Diego, CA 92131-1430.
Gallagher, Francis L. (Retired), 863 Central St., Framingham, 01701-4972.
Gallagher, John E. (Retired), P.O. Box 465, Farmington, ME 04938-0465.
Garrity, Francis D. (Retired), 22 Weatherly Dr., Salem, 01970-6647.
Gaudet, Joseph A. (Retired), 39 Revere St., Everett, 02149-3524.
Geary, Edward P. (Retired), 61 Adamson St., Boston, 02134-1321.
Gillis, Edward F. (Retired), 204 Linden Ponds Way, WC612, Hingham, 02043-3779.
Girardin, Peter T. (Retired), 2616 Fenwood Rd., Houston, TX 77005-3436.
Goss, Francis G. (Retired), 171 Chestnut St., Apt. 1, Foxboro, 02035-1528.
Gosselin, Richard R. (Retired), 3 Hudson St., Apt. 3, Methuen, 01844.
Goulet, Raymond O. (Retired), 31 Simpson Rd., Marlborough, 01752-1532.
Grant, Frederick A. (Retired), 1006 Essex Village, Lynnfield, 01940-1273.
Guerrette, William J. (Retired), P.O. Box 2, Rumney, NH 03266-0002.
Haley, William J. (Retired), 9 Island View Rd., Hull, 02045-2916.
Harrington, James J. (Retired), 2 Raymond St., Manchester, 01944-1613.
Harrington, Richard L. (Retired), 60 William Cardinal O'Connell Way, Boston, 02114-2729.
Hegarty, Daniel P. (Retired), 14 Falmouth Rd., Newton, 02465-1119.
Hickey, Gerald J. (Retired), P.O. Box 141, Scituate, 02066-0141.
Hughes, Albert C. (Retired), 16C Rose Kennedy Ln., Apt. C, Framingham, 01702-2389.
Janiunas, Albin F. (Retired), 19 Maple Ave., Cambridge, 02139-1115.
Kane, Joseph M. (Retired), 60 William Cardinal O'Connell Way, Boston, 02114-2729.
Keane, John F. (Retired), 7 Bay Rd., P.O. Box 372, West Yarmouth, 02673-5803.
Keane, Thomas F. (Retired), 60 William Cardinal O'Connell Way, Boston, 02114-2729.
Kelleher, Robert N. (Retired), 67 Atlantic Rd., Gloucester, 01930-3241.
Kelley, Arnold E. (Retired), 120 Bellevue Ave., Haverhill, 01832.
Kelley, Laurence E. (Retired), 22 Elm St., Scituate, 02066-4009.
Kelly, John P. (Retired), 186 Highland Ave., Somerville, 02143.
Kelly, Patrick J. (Retired), 280 Main St., Woburn, 01801-5094.
Kenneally, William F. (Retired), 60 William Cardinal O'Connell Way, Boston, 02114-2729.
Keohan, Edward M. (Retired), 15 Hawthorne Blvd., Salem, 01970-3709.
King, Edward L. (Retired), 180 Water St., Haverhill, 01830.
King, Philip J. (Retired), 1573 Cambridge St., Cambridge, 02138-4370.
Kinsella, Charles R. (Retired), c/o Dr. Eric Champy, 21 Montrose Ave., Lawrence, 01843-3307.
Kirke, Eugene K. (Retired), 24 Clark St., Boston, 02109-1127.
Koen, Stephen A. (Retired), 3 Indian Mound Ln., Falmouth, 02540.
Lanergan, James F. (Retired), P.O. Box 547, Manomet, 02345-0547.
LaRaia, Joseph P. (Retired), 243 Franklin Rd., Box 297, Salisbury, NH 03268.
Lawson, Harold F. (Retired), 60 William Cardinal O'Connell Way, Boston, 02114-2729.
Leonard, Clyde A. (Retired), 176 Texas St., Marshfield, 02050-4612.
Leonard, Francis B. (Retired), 115 Middlesex St., Chelmsford, 01824.
Leonard, John F. (Retired), 43 Hill St., Newburyport, 01950-3952.
Lizio, John R. (Retired), 933 Central St., Framingham, 01701-4872.
Logue, Charles D. (Retired), 44 Ethelma Rd., Chatham, 02633-1508.
Lucey, William F. (Retired), 106 Church St., Boston, 02132-1052.
Lukas, Joseph S. (Retired), 1200 Liberty St., 02184-8212.
Lynch, Leo X. (Retired), 60 William Cardinal O'Connell Way, Boston, 02114-2729.
Lyons, James D. (Retired), 1340 Lakeview Ave., Dracut, 01826-3499.
MacDonald, Paul V. (Retired), 90 Oakmere St., Boston, 02132-5531.
MacKenzie, William M. (Retired), 115 Eagle Dr., Rochester, NH 03868.
Maffei, Vincent R. (Retired), 211 N. Main St., Randolph, 02368-1745.
Manning, Joseph H. (Retired), 379 Old Craigville Rd. W., Box 536, Hyannis Port, 02647-0536.
Mansfield, John L. (Retired), 60 William Cardinal O'Connell Way, Boston, 02114-2729.
Martel, Leo E. (Retired), 32 Kings Dr., Raymond, NH 03077-2682.
Martin, Jon C. (Retired), 96 Damsite Rd., Center Barnstead, NH 03225.
Martin, Joseph I. (Retired), 24 Clark St., Boston, 02109-1127.
Martineau, Laurier J. (Retired), 60 William Cardinal O'Connell Way, Boston, 02114-2729.
McAskill, Kenneth F. (Retired), 1573 Cambridge St., Cambridge, 02138-4370.
McAuliffe, Robert J. (Retired), 60 William Cardinal O'Connell Way, Boston, 02112-2729.
McConnell, William J. (Retired), 60 William Cardinal O'Connell Way, Boston, 02114-2729.
McCormick, John J. (Retired), One Grace Ave., Billerica, 01821-2504.
McCune, James L. (Retired), 60 William Cardinal O'Connell Way, Boston, 02114-2729.
McElroy, John W. (Retired), 6 Lakeview Ln., Palm Coast, FL 32137-1490.
McGlone, Joseph F. (Retired), 22 Fuller St., Box 58, Carver, 02330-0058.
McGowan, Frederick R. (Retired), 2C Greenleaf Park, Merrimac, 01860-1833.
McLaughlin, Edward J. (Retired), 103 Center St., Bridgewater, 02324-1397.
McLaughlin, Richard P. (Retired), 14 Boston Ave., Somerville, 02144-2302.
McPartland, Paul G. (Retired), 50 Monument Ave., Boston, 02129-3324.
McQuade, Richard E. (Retired), 10 Buttonwood Ln., Scituate, 02066-1107.
Meade, Maurice P. (Retired), 411 Franklin St., #201, Cambridge, 02139.
Medeiros, Antonio S. (Retired), 131 Winston St., Acushnet, 02745.
Menna, F. Dominic (Retired), 95 Crescent St., Quincy, 02169-4040.
Meskell, David B. (Retired), 30 Cambridge St., Winchester, 01890-3730.
Moran, Richard S. (Retired), 23 Spruce St., Malden, 02148-4416.
Morris, John S. (Retired), 505 Mill St., #269, Worcester, 01602-2482.
Mottau, Robert S. (Retired), 20 Devens St., Apt. 404, Boston, 02129-3725.
Moynihan, T. Joseph (Retired), 151 Coolidge Ave., #610, Watertown, 02472-2867.
Mulligan, Paul F. (Retired), 60 William Cardinal O'Connell Way, Boston, 02114-2729.
Murphy, David C. (Retired), 223 Avenida Baja, San Clemente, CA 92672-2466.
Murphy, H. Joseph (Retired), 42 Melody Ln., Waltham, 02454.
Murray, John A. (Retired), 53 George St., Watertown, 02472-3343.
Murray, Thomas F. (Retired), 37 Gia Ln., Mashpee, 02649-3755.
Naughton, Thomas J. (Retired), 29 St. Mary's Rd., Milton, 02186-2022.
Nichols, John J. (Retired), Capella South 1104, Goat Island, Newport, RI 02840-1582.
Noonan, Mark L., Ph.D. (Retired), 78 Bucks Creek Rd., Chatham, 02633.
O'Brien, Frederick W. (Retired), 60 William Cardinal O'Connell Way, Boston, 02114-2729.
O'Connor, Maurice J. (Retired), 750 Whittenton St., Unit 723, Taunton, 02780-1353.
O'Connor, William B. (Retired), 129 Ash St., Stoughton, 02072-3521.
O'Connor, William J. (Retired), P.O. Box 414, Marshfield, 02050-0414.
O'Donnell, John F. (Retired), 61 Williams Way, Goffstown, NH 03045-6615.
O'Hara, Francis A. (Retired), 257 Acapesket Rd., East Falmouth, 02536-6021.
O'Leary, Arthur P. (Retired), 1416 Yorktown Ct., Melbourne, FL 32940-6829.
O'Meara, Gerard J. (Retired), 24 Clark St., Boston, 02109-1127.
O'Regan, Hugh H., V.F. (Retired), 101 Seth Parker Rd., Centerville, 02632-2166.
O'Rourke, James J. (Retired), 321 Market St., Boston, 02135-2199.
Oliviera, Joel D. (Retired), 155 Fort St., East Providence, RI 02914-5139.
Pashby, John J. (Retired), 24 Clark St., Boston, 02109-1127.
Pearsall, William T. (Retired), 60 William Cardinal O'Connell Way, Boston, 02114-2729.
Perron, Richard J. (Retired), 419 Lafayette St., Salem, 01970-5337.
Phinn, Paul A. (Retired), 265 Walker St., Box 331, Falmouth, 02541-0331.
Pied, Wilfrid L. (Retired), 60 William Cardinal O'Connell Way, Boston, 02114-2729.
Poirier, Vincent J. (Retired), 206 Linden Ponds Way, OW614, Hingham, 02043-3767.
Pollis, Robert G. (Retired), 60 William Cardinal O'Connell Way, Boston, 02114-2729.
Power, James F. (Retired), 66 Brooks Dr., 02184-3839.
Pratt, Lawrence E. (Retired), 112 Old Wharf Rd, E-3, Dennis Port, 02639-2230.
Regan, Francis A. (Retired), 863 Central St., Framingham, 01701-4892.
Regan, Michael J. (Retired), 60 William Cardinal O'Connell Way, Boston, 02114-2729.
Reilly, Thomas J. (Retired), 26 Centerville Way, Plymouth, 02360.
Riley, James H. (Retired), 66 Emerald Dr., Lynn, 01904-1255.
Rondeau, Lawrence J. (Retired), 161 Federal St., Salem, 01970-3297.
Rothwell, Joseph T. (Retired), 130 Dorchester St., Boston, 02127-2699.
Rouse, C. Paul (Retired), P.O. Box 347, Boston, 02127-0003.
Ruggeri, Joseph A. (Retired), 224 Grosbeak Ln., Naples, FL 34114-3013.
Sallese, Albert J. (Retired), 1158 Main St., Bellingham, 02019-1597.
Santerre, Richard R. (Retired), 1573 Cambridge St., Cambridge, 02138-4370.
Schatzel, John E. (Retired), P.O. Box 601, Bryantville, 02327-0601.
Serena, Edward T. (Retired), 40 South Meadow Village, Unit 6, Carver, 02330-1802.
Shea, John J. (Retired), 500 Ocean St., Marshfield, 02050-5007.
Sheehan, Daniel J. (Retired), 841 E. Broadway, Boston, 02127-2397.
Sheehy, Charles I. (Retired), 60 William Cardinal O'Connell Way, Boston, 02114-2729.
Smyth, Joseph P. (Retired), 46 Laurel Ct., Nashua, NH 03062-4461.
Soucy, Robert P. (Retired), 112 Old Wharf Rd., E-3, Dennis Port, 02639-2230.
Sullivan, E. Paul (Retired), 822 Orleans Rd., Harwich, 02645-3037.
Sullivan, James L. (Retired), 6333 Rancho Mission Dr., San Diego, CA 92108-1099.
Sullivan, Lawrence F. (Retired), 102 Brooksby Village Dr., Apt. 3, Peabody, 01960.
Svirskas, Joseph J. (Retired), 3 Pleasant Ave., South Hamilton, 01982-1752.
Sweeney, Frederick E. (Retired), 49 Ocean Ave., Box 1111, York, ME 03909-1111.
Thomas, Robert W. (Retired), 3115 Corrib Dr., Tallahassee, FL 32309-3307.
Toomey, John M. (Retired), 60 William Cardinal O'Connell Way, Boston, 02112-2729.
Vartzelis, George D. (Retired), 1573 Cambridge St., Cambridge, 02138-4370.
Verrill, O. Wendell, V.F. (Retired), 91 Wompatuck Rd., Hingham, 02043-1175.
Von Euw, Vincent P. (Retired), 130 Dorchester St., Boston, 02127-2642.
Waldron, Robert J. (Retired), 75 Chase St., Box 77, West Harwich, 02671-0077.
Wasnewski, Richard P. (Retired), 46 Village St., Medway, 02053-1048.
Weber, Charles P. (Retired), 385 Heath Rd., Sanbornville, NH 03872-4112.
Wetterholm, Lawrence E. (Retired), 60 William Cardinal O'Connell Way, Boston, 02114-2729.
Wyndham, Thomas F. (Retired), 9 Settlers Ter., Box 801, Eastham, 02642-0801.

Society of St. James the Apostle. For contact information please call or write: Society of Saint James the Apostle, 24 Clark St., Boston, MA 02109-1127; Tel: 617-742-4715:

Revs.—
De Angelis, Mark J.
McCarthy, Jeremiah J.
O'Sullivan, Raymond S.
Oates, Thomas F.
Tynan, Desmond A.

Unassigned. For contact information please call or write: Clergy Personnel Office, 66 Brooks Dr., Braintree, MA 02184-3839; Tel: 617-779-3685:

Revs.—
Clark, James B.
Cordery, Robert J.
Curran, Richard G.
McNamara, Michael J.
Picardi, John M.
Randone, Michael C.
Sullivan, Robert J.

Tighe, Leonard J.
Twomey, Daniel F.

Permanent Deacons:
Acampora, Andrew J., St. John the Evangelist, Swampscott
Agudelo, Jose N., St. James, Haverhill
Alexander, John F., St. Joseph the Worker, Hanson
Anthony, Thomas A., St. John the Baptist, Haverhill
Arsenault, Joseph G., St. Francis of Assisi, Braintree
Balestracci, Alfred O., St. Theresa of Lisieux, North Reading
Bankowski, Paul F., St. Christine, Marshfield
Beatrice, Lee A., (Unassigned)
Belmonte, Joseph A., St. Anthony of Padua, Revere
Bilotta, Richard F., St. Margaret, Burlington
Biron, R. Donald, (Lend Lease)
Bloom, Laurence J., St. Susanna, Dedham
Bortz, John E., Saint Mary, Chelmsford
Bower, Charles H., Sacred Heart, Middleborough
Boyle, John F., St. Joseph, Holbrook
Brady, Robert F., St. Isidore, Stow
Breen, Robert F., St. Francis of Assisi, Medford
Breinlinger, Martin E., St. Mary's, Holliston
Brennan, Richard J., Sts. Martha and Mary, Lakeville
Brent, John A., St. Catherine of Siena, Norwood
Bresnahan, John M., Holy Family, Lynn
Bulpett, Dean C., St. Irene, Carlisle
Burch, Gregory J., Holy Family, Concord
Burke, Thomas P., St. Bernadette, Randolph
Burns, Daniel R., Formation Dir., Office for Permanent Diaconate
Buttrick, Stephen M., Immaculate Conception, Weymouth
Cabral, John F., (Unassigned)
Cabrera, Crescencio A., (Lend Lease)
Camacho, Teodoro, (Lend Lease)
Canova, Joseph A., St. Francis Xavier, Weymouth
Carey, John J., (Lend Lease)
Caruso, Philip M., St. Mary, Holliston
Casillas, Luis R., (Lend Lease)
Castillo, Jesus, St. Mary of the Assumption, Lawrence
Cavanaugh, Michael J., St. Clare, Braintree
Cloonan, Paul M., St. Paul, Wellesley
Clough, Charles I., Holy Family, Concord
Constantino, Anthony J., Sacred Heart, East Boston
Corbett, Francis J., Immaculate Conception, Weymouth
Cordeau, Richard W., St. Ann, Peabody
Cornell, Charles A., St. Isidore, Stowe
Crimmins, Daniel F., St. Anne, Littleton
Delio, Richard P., (Unassigned)
Dello Russo, Francis B., St. Patrick, Stoneham
Dempsey, Timothy F., St. Mary, Lynn
DiBello, Phillip T., St. Theresa of Lisieux, Billerica
Donoghue, Leo J., St. Joseph, Quincy
Doucette, Raymond E., Holy Family, Amesbury
Dow, Paul A., Our Lady of the Assumption, Lynnfield
Dunn, Daniel A., Holy Family, Gloucester
Dzuris, Robert W., St. Rita, Lowell
Eames, James H., St. Mary, Randolph
Elibero, Edward P., St. Richard of Chichester, Danvers
Fagan, Joseph M., Jr., St. Thomas of Villanova, Wilmington
Farguheson, Wood Rowe, St. Joseph, Salem
Fenton, Jack H., (Lend Lease)
Ferraro, Charles A., St. Irene, Carlisle
Ferrazzi, Charles J., (Unassigned)
Field, Richard P., Jr., (Unassigned)
Fitzgerald, Brendan A., (Unassigned)
Fonseca, Marcio O., St. Ambrose, Dorchester
Gabriel, George M., Sacred Heart, Middleborough
Gaffney, Francis M., Blessed Sacrament, Saugus
Gagne, Ronald D., (Unassigned)
Gallant, Robert J., (Leave of Absence)
Gardyna, Henry A., (Health Leave)
Gaudreau, Robert J., (Unassigned)
Geneus, Alfred J., Saint John the Evangelist, Cambridge; Haitian Community
Ghioni, David R., St. Jude, Norfolk
Goldy, Andrew J., (Health Leave)
Greer, James F., Blessed Kateri Tekakwitha, Plymouth
Grimley, Edward J., (Lend Lease)
Guerin, Bertrand H., St. Martha, Plainville
Guerrini, Patrick E., Asst. Dir., Office for Permanent Diaconate
Hanson, Herbert C., St. Linus, Natick
Hardcastle, Philip P., St. Charles Borromeo, Woburn
Hardin, Howard P., (Unassigned)
Hardy, Gerard J., St. William, Tewksbury
Henry, Martin W., St. Mary of the Nativity, Scituate
Herrera, Luciano, Our Lady of Lourdes, Jamaica Plain
Hickey, C. Michael, (Unassigned)
Hidalgo, Nelson J., St. Joseph, Lynn
Hoaglund, Robert I., (Unassigned)
Holderried, Joseph E., St. Margaret Mary, Westwood
Horgan, Frederick B., St. Edward the Confessor, Medfield
Hulme, John A., St. Peter, Plymouth
Hunt, John C., St. Francis of Assisi, Dracut
Hwang, Augustine J., Sacred Heart, Newton
Iraola, Alejandro, St. Rose of Lima, Chelsea
Iwanowicz, Michael A., Our Lady of Sorrows, Sharon
Johnson, Robert N., Our Lady Comforter of the Afflicted, Waltham
Jones, Paul S., Our Lady of Lourdes, Carver
Joy, Richard T., St. Catherine of Alexandria, Westford
Kane, William F.X., Holy Family, Gloucester
Keefe, Arthur J., Holy Family, Duxbury
Kerns, William E., St. Florence, Wakefield
Kerrigan, James V., St. Barbara, Woburn
King, Clifford D., St. Thomas, Wilmington
Koffel, William B., Our Lady Help of Christians, Newton
Kramich, Robert A., Holy Family, Gloucester
L'ltalien, George G., (Unassigned)
LaFond, Philip H., Christ the King, Brockton
LaTorre, Pedro, (Unassigned)
Laws, Brian H., St. Anne, Littleton
Leduc, Roland E., St. Michael, Lowell
Lewis, Paul A., St. John the Baptist, Quincy
Lloyd, Barry V., St. Margaret, Lowell
MacDonald, Joseph E., St. Benedict, Somerville
Maloney, William F., Holy Trinity, Quincy
Manzi, James A., St. Paul, Hamilton
Markham, Michael J., Our Lady of Grace, Pepperell
Martinez, Orlando, (Unassigned)
Martino, Richard C., (Lend Lease)
McCarthy, Daniel E., (Unassigned)
McCarty, William J., (Lend Lease)
McGuffie, Jacques A., St. Patrick, Roxbury
McHugh, Francis W., Most Holy Redeemer, East Boston
McHugh, John W., St. Katherine Drexel, Roxbury
McLaughlin, James V., St. Briget, Abington
McLaughlin, Richard B., Hanscom AFB, Bedford
Menendez, Silvio J., (Lend Lease)
Menz, John R., Holy Trinity, Quincy
Mesa, Ricardo M., Cathedral of the Holy Cross, Boston
Messina, Joseph M., St. Timothy, Westwood
Miles, Walter J., (Unassigned)
Mills, Chester P., (Unassigned)
Montes, Eddy M., (Health Leave)
Mora, Eduardo R., St. Mary, Waltham
Morel, Pablo, St. Joseph, Lynn
Morey, Russell W., (Unassigned)
Mott, Michael M., St. John the Evangelist, Hopkinton
Murphy, Steven J., (Health Leave)
Nagle, William V., St. Joseph, Kingston
Naveo, Jose D., (Unassigned)
Nelson, Daniel C., Corpus Christi-Saint Bernard, Newton
Nguyen, Hon H., St. Ambrose, Dorchester
Nicholson, John D., Our Lady of Fatima, Sudbury
Nickley, Joseph T., Jr., Holy Ghost, Whitman
Nieves, Alfredo, St. Stephen, Framingham
O'Neil, Cyril T., St. Patrick, Stoneham
Oles, Kenneth W., St. Mary, Wrentham
Ortiz, Jesus M., Our Lady of Lourdes, Jamaica Plain
Papik, Stephen M., Holy Trinity, Lowell
Patino, Jorge A., (Unassigned)
Patrick, Alexander J., (Unassigned)
Peltak, Douglas P., St. Matthias, Marlborough
Penney, Everett F., St. Marguerite D'Youville, Dracut
Pepi, John W., St. Bridget, Maynard
Perea, Antonio M., Most Holy Redeemer, East Boston
Perez, Jose, (Unassigned)
Pierce, John B., St. Monica, Methuen
Quiles, Francisco M., (Lend Lease)
Radford, Richard F., (Lend Lease)
Ramrath, Joseph R., (Unassigned)
Reilly, Christopher P., St. Mary of the Sacred Heart, Hanover
Rivera, Luis F., St. Rose of Lima, Chelsea
Rivera, Valentin, St. John the Baptist, Peabody
Rivero, Victor R., Most Holy Redeemer, East Boston
Rizzuto, Anthony P., (Unassigned)
Roberts, Carl M., Our Lady of Hope, Ipswich
Robinson, Edwin J., St. Tarcisius, Framingham
Rodrigues, Pedro M., St. Anthony of Padua, Somerville
Rodriguez, Diego N., (Lend Lease)
Rogers, Arthur F., Jr., Prison Ministry
Rooney, Paul S., St. Anthony of Padua, Cohasset
Ros, Peter An, St. Patrick, Lowell
Rosario, Manuel A., St. Charles Borromeo, Woburn
Rumley, Mark E., Immaculate Conception, Malden
Ryan, Gerald P., St. Thomas Aquinas, Bridgewater
Ryan, Kenneth N., Sacred Heart, Weymouth
Saint Hilaire, Norman R., (Unassigned)
Saint Sauveur, Guy C., St. Michael, Bedford
Santosuosso, Alfred E., St. Jude, Waltham
Shanahan, Allan R., St. Mary, Billerica
Sheedy, Louis W., St. Mary, Dedham
Shrader, David J., (Lend Lease)
Sicuso, Anthony C., (Leave of Absence)
Siebert, Richard, Immaculate Conception, Newburyport
Smith, Thomas A., St. John the Evangelist, Wellesley
Spadoni, Reynold G., Blessed Sacrament, Walpole
Specht, Paul V., St. Patrick, Lawrence
Spiri, Guy J., St. Stephen, Framingham
Stenstrom, Eugene V., St. Mary, Plymouth
Straub, Stanley A., St. Mary of the Annunciation, Cambridge
Sullivan, Charles E., Office of the Regional Bishop-South
Sullivan, Daniel F., St. Agatha, Milton
Sullivan, John A., St. Thecla Parish, Pembroke
Sumner, Neil J., St. Athanasius, Reading
Taylor, Carroll H., Prison Ministry
Theriault, James G., St. Mary of the Assumption, Hull
Torres, Pedro L., St. Stephen, Framingham
Tremblay, Francis R., St. Timothy, Norwood
Turner, J. Robert, St. Patrick, Stoneham
Valeri, Frank A., Most Blessed Sacrament, Wakefield
Vandi, Dennis, (Unassigned)
Vargas, Julio C., Corpus Christi, Lawrence
Velasquez, Edin, Most Holy Redeemer, East Boston
Vitale, Paul D., (Lend Lease)
Vitello, Joseph V., St. Jerome, Weymouth
Webb, Charles P., St. Thomas More, Braintree
Wheeler, Raymond A., (Lend Lease)
Whipple, John E., Our Lady, Star of the Sea, Marblehead
Wildes, William H., (Lend Lease)
Wise, John W., St. Agnes, Middleton

Senior Deacons:
Senior Deacons—
Abercrombie, J. Scott
Alence, Robert W.
Alicea, Francisco
Amerault, Robert P.
Bubello, Charles M.
Callahan, James C.
Capomaccio, John J.
Chisholm, Finley H.
Connor, John P.
Counihan, Eugene A.
Creutz, Edward F.
Crump, James M.
D'Ambrosio, Francis D.
Delaney, Joseph L.
Ego, John J.
Gagnon, Raymond A.
Guerrios, Francisco
Hackett, Robert T.
Hanlon, Thomas H.
Hardy, John W.
Heffernan, Francis X.
Jennette, John F.
Juliano, Anthony J.
Kaelin, Gerard J.
LaBrache, Leo F.
Lacey, Neil F.
LaPointe, Norman P.
Lauture, Albert
Leavitt, James P.
MacDonald, Joseph P.
MacKinnon, William J.
Mannion, John J., Prison Ministry
Marchant, Thomas W.
Markey, Paul G.
Martin, Leo A.
McManus, Lawrence R.
Murphy, Alfred L.
Pugsley, Stanley G.
Quigley, Edward M.
Quiles, Jesus M.
Salenius, John D.
Sanchez, Tomas E.
Watson, John W.
Welch, Henry M.
Yanikoski, Florian F.

INSTITUTIONS LOCATED IN THE ARCHDIOCESE

[A] SEMINARIES, ARCHDIOCESAN

BOSTON. *St. John Seminary* (1884) 127 Lake St., Brighton, 02135. Tel: 617-254-2610; Fax: 617-787-2336. Web: www.sjs.edu. Revs. Arthur L. Kennedy, Ph.D., Rector; Raymond Van De Moortell, Th.M., M.Div., Ph.D., M.L.I.S., Librarian; Joseph F. Scorzello, M.Div., S.T.L., Ph.D.; Stephen E. Salocks, S.S.L., M.Div., Dean, Faculty; Romanus Cessario, O.P., S.T.D., S.T.L.; Peter P. Gojuk, O.M.V., Coord., Spiritual Dir.; Philip E. Merdinger, M.A., Spiritual Dir.; Christopher K. O'Connor, M.Div., M.A., Ph.L, Vice Rector; Michael B. Medas, M.S.W., Dir. Supervised Ministries; Robert W. Oliver, J.C.D., S.T.D.; Rev. Msgr. James P. Moroney, B.A., S.T.L.; Rev. Derek J. Borek, M.Div., S.T.L., Dean of Students; Kathleen Heck, B.A., J.D., Dir. Communications & Devel.; Dr. J. David Franks, Ph.D., Prof.; Sr. Mary Veronica Sabelli, R.S.M., Ph.D., Prof.; Mrs. Aldona Lingertat, Ph.D., Dir. Master of Arts in Ministry; Dr. J. David Franks, Ph.D., Co-Assoc. Dir. Master of Arts in Ministry; Dr. Angela Franks, Co-Assoc. Dir. Master of Arts in Ministry; Sr. Mary Cora Uryase, R.S.M., Ph.D.; Dr. Janet Hunt. Priests 21; Sisters 2; Lay Teachers 14; Students 180; Total Enrollment 180.

WESTON. *Blessed John XXIII National Seminary* (1964) 558 South Ave., 02493. Tel: 781-899-5500; Fax: 781-899-9057. Email: seminary@blessedjohnxxiii.edu. Web: www.blessedjohnxxiii.edu. Very Rev. Peter J. Uglietto, M.Div., S.T.L., S.T.D., Rector & Pres.; Revs. James M. DiPerri, M.A., M.Div., J.C.L.; Paul E. Fitzpatrick, S.M., S.T.L., S.T.D.; John J. Moriarty, S.J.; Joseph K. Fagan, M.Div. (Retired); Gregory J. Hoppough, C.S.S., M.Div., S.T.L., S.T.D., M.A.; Thomas F. Schmitt, S.T.L., Dean of Students; Paul E. Miceli; William B. Palardy, Ph.D., Academic Dean; Leo M. Manglaviti, S.J.; Dr. Anthony W. Keaty; Dr. Leonard Maluf, S.T.D.; Sr. Jacqueline Miller, S.S.A., Librarian. A Major National Seminary open to men over thirty studying for the diocesan and religious priesthood. Priests 9; Lay Teachers 2; Students 65.

[B] SEMINARIES, RELIGIOUS OR SCHOLASTICATES

BOSTON. *Oblate Provincialate*, 2 Ipswich St., 02215-3607. Tel: 617-536-4141; Fax: 617-536-7016. Email: omv.office@verizon.net. Web: www.omvusa.org. Rev. William M. Brown, O.M.V., Prov.; Bro. Luigi Falbo, O.M.V., Treas. St. Ignatius Province of the Oblates of the Virgin Mary, Inc.
Priests of the Province on Special Assignment: Philippines: Revs. Lino Estadilla, O.M.V.; Thomas Kleinschmidt, O.M.V.; Gregory Short, O.M.V.; Mark Yavarone, O.M.V. (Philippines).

Our Lady of Grace Seminary, 1105 Boylston St., 02215-3604. Tel: 617-266-5999; Fax: 617-247-7576. Web: www.omvusa.org. Revs. Daniel Barron, O.M.V., Rector; David N. Beauregard, O.M.V., Dean of Studies; Timothy M. Gallagher, O.M.V., Formation Staff; Gregory Staab, O.M.V., Formation Staff; Peter Grover, O.M.V., Vocation Dir.; Peter P. Gojuk, O.M.V., Formation Staff. St. Ignatius Province of the Oblates of the Virgin Mary, Inc. Priests 6; Lay Teachers 2; Students 10.

CHESTNUT HILL. *The Ecclesiastical Faculty at Boston College* (known as Weston Jesuit, an academic department within the Boston College School of Theology and Ministry), 140 Commonwealth Ave., 02467. Tel: 617-552-6501; Fax: 617-552-0811. Email: stm@bc.edu. Web: www.bc.edu/stm. Revs. William P. Leahy, S.J., Ph.D., Pres.; Richard J. Clifford, S.J., Dean. Priests 12; Sisters 1; Lay Teachers 5; Students 133.

Redemptoris Mater Archdiocesan Missionary House of Formation, 774 Boylston St., 02467-2501. Tel: 617-879-9813; 617-879-9814; Fax: 617-879-0170. Revs. Antonio Medeiros, Rector; Roderick A. Crispo, O.F.M., Spiritual Dir.

DANVERS. *Xavier Center* House of Formation., 21 Spring St., 01923. Tel: 978-777-1326. Bro. John D. Hamilton, C.F.X., Dir. Xaverian Brothers, USA. Brothers Professed 4.

FRAMINGHAM. *Sylva Maria* (1952) 567 Salem End Rd., 01702-5599. Tel: 508-879-6711; Fax: 508-879-7667. Email: sonsboston@verizon.net. Web: www.sonsofmary.com. Revs. Robert Rivard, F.M.S.I.; John Wallace, F.M.S.I. House and Novitiate of the Sons of Mary, Health of the Sick. Priests 4; Brothers 4.
Council: Revs. John Murphy, F.M.S.I., Coord.; John Coss, F.M.S.I., Councilor; Bro. Kevin Courtney, F.M.S.I., Councilor.

[C] COLLEGES AND UNIVERSITIES

BOSTON. *Caritas Laboure College, Inc.* (1892) 2120 Dorchester Ave., 02124. Tel: 617-296-8300; Fax: 617-296-7947. Web: www.laboure.edu. Joseph W. Mc Nabb, Ph.D., Pres.; Andrew Calo, Librarian. Two year college for nursing and allied health. Member of Caritas Christi Health Care System. Priests 1; Lay Teachers 75; Students 578; Total Enrollment 680.

Emmanuel College, 400 The Fenway, 02115. Tel: 617-735-9715; Fax: 617-735-9877. Email: hatten@emmanuel.edu. Web: www.emmanuel.edu. Sr. Janet Eisner, S.N.D., Ph.D., Pres. Sisters of Notre Dame de Namur; Rev. Stephen Bayle, Co-Dir. Campus Ministry; Sr. Margaret Cummins, S.N.D., Dir. Campus Ministry. Priests 1; Sisters 3; Lay Teachers 49; Students 1,856.

CHESTNUT HILL. **Boston College* (1863) (Coed), 02467. Tel: 617-552-8000. Web: www.bc.edu. Rev. William P. Leahy, S.J., Ph.D., Pres.; Cutberto Garza, Ph.D., Provost; Thomas Wall, Univ. Librarian. Priests 33; Sisters 5; Lay Teachers 726; Students 14,796.

College of Arts and Sciences (1863) Tel: 617-552-2393; Fax: 617-552-1383. David Quigley, Ph.D., Dean. Students 6,137.

Summer Session Tel: 617-552-3900; Fax: 617-552-3199. Rev. James A. Woods, S.J., Dean. Students 3,431.

Graduate School of Arts and Sciences (1925) Tel: 617-552-3268; Fax: 617-552-3700. David Quigley, Ph.D., Dean. Students 912.

School of Law (1929) Tel: 617-552-4340; Fax: 617-552-2851. John H. Garvey Esq., J.D., Dean. Students 827.

Woods College of Advancing Studies (1929) Tel: 617-552-3900; Fax: 617-552-3199. Rev. James A. Woods, S.J., Dean. Students 810.

Graduate School of Social Work (1936) Tel: 617-552-4020; Fax: 617-552-2374. Alberto Godenzi, Ph.D., Dean. Students 526.

Carroll School of Management (1938) Tel: 617-552-8420; Fax: 617-552-2593. Andrew C. Boynton, Ph.D., Dean. Students 1,970.

Carroll Graduate School of Management (1957) Tel: 617-552-8420; Fax: 617-552-2593. Andrew C. Boynton, Ph.D., Dean. Students 889.

Connell School of Nursing (1947) Tel: 617-552-4250; Fax: 617-552-0745. Susan Gennaro, D.S.N., Dean. Students 399.

Lynch School of Education (1952) Tel: 617-552-4200; Fax: 617-552-0812. Rev. Joseph M. O'Keefe, S.J., Dean. Students 665.

Connell Graduate School of Nursing (1994) Tel: 617-552-4250; Fax: 617-552-0745. Susan Gennaro, D.S.N., Dean. Students 330.

Lynch Graduate School of Education (1994) Tel: 617-552-4200; Fax: 617-552-0812. Rev. Joseph M. O'Keefe, S.J., Dean. Students 1,021.

The School of Theology and Ministry (2008) Tel: 617-552-6501; Fax: 617-552-0811. Rev. Richard J. Clifford, S.J., Dean. Students 310.

NORTH ANDOVER. *Merrimack College*, 315 Turnpike St., 01845-5800. Tel: 978-837-5000; Fax: 978-837-5222. Web: www.merrimack.edu. Ronald O. Champagne, Pres.; Michael Bell, Interim Provost; Joseph Kelley, Vice Pres. Institutional Advancement; Mary Lou Retelle, Vice Pres. Enrollment Mgmt.; Frederick Quivey, Vice Pres. & CFO; Revs. Kevin F. Dwyer, O.S.A., Prof. & Subprior - Austin House, Res.: Austin House, 111 Peters St., 01845. Tel: 978-682-7986; Fax: 978-682-2567; James Wenzel, O.S.A., Dir. Augustinian Ctr., Res.: St. Ambrose Friary, 196 Elm St., Andover, 01810. Tel: 978-475-8485; Fax: 978-409-1072; Shawn DeVeau, Dean of Students; Sr. Mary Ellen Dow, S.N.D., Dir. Campus Ministry. Priests 6; Lay Teachers 139; Students (Full-Time) 1,826; Continuing Education 139.

Our Mother of Good Counsel Monastery (1947) Tel: 978-837-5213; Fax: 978-837-5269. In Res. Revs. William T. Garland, O.S.A., Prior & Community Treas.- Austin House, Res.: Austin House, 111 Peters St., 01845. Tel: 978-682-7986; Fax: 978-682-2567; Edward J. Enright, O.S.A., Prof.; Raymond F. Dlugos, O.S.A., Vice Pres. Mission & Ministry; William F. Waters, O.S.A., Campus Min.

SWAMPSCOTT. *Marian Court College*, Little's Point Rd., 01907. Tel: 781-595-6768; Fax: 781-595-3560. Email: info@mariancourt.edu. Web: www.mariancourt.edu. Dr. Ghazi Darkazalli, Ph.D., Pres. & C.E.O.; James Chatterton, CPA, C.F.O.; Greg Lamontagne, Ph.D., Dean Academic Affairs, Faculty & Student Svcs.; Gretchen Manning, Vice Pres. Inst. Advancement & Enrollment. Sisters 1; Lay Teachers 20; Lay Staff 25; Students 300.

WESTON. *Regis College* (1927) 235 Wellesley St., 02493-1571. Tel: 781-768-7000; Fax: 781-768-8339. Email: postmaster@regiscollege.edu. Web: www.regiscollege.edu. Mary Jane England, M.D., Pres.; Sr. Rosemary Mulvihill, R.S.M., Campus Min.; Lynn Triplett, Librarian Dir. Sisters of St. Joseph 7; Lay Teachers 169; Students 2,093.

[D] HIGH SCHOOLS, PRIVATE

BOSTON. *Boston College High School*, 150 Morrissey Blvd., Dorchester, 02125. Tel: 617-929-9495; Fax: 617-929-9459. Email: rperry@sjnen.org. Web: www.bchigh.edu/. Revs. Ronald V. Perry, S.J., Rector; Joseph T. Bennett, S.J. Tel: 617-929-9482; Herbert J. Cleary, S.J.; Robert R. Dorin, S.J.; Jon D. Fuller, S.J.; William J. Hamilton, S.J. Tel: 617-929-9478; James J. Hederman, S.J.; James J. Hosie, S.J. Tel: 617-929-9488; Gerard R. McKeon, S.J.; James W. O'Neil, S.J. Tel: 617-929-9452; Bros. Paul J. Geysen, S.J.; Cornelius C. Murphy, S.J. Tel: 617-929-9414; Donald J. Murray, S.J. Tel: 617-436-3900; Michael J. Rogers, S.J. Priests 10; Brothers 3; Scholastics 1; Sisters 1; Lay Teachers 128; Students 1,578.

Cathedral High School, Inc., 74 Union Park St., 02118. Tel: 617-542-2325; Fax: 617-542-1745. Web: www.cathedral.mec.edu. Christol Murch, Chief Admin. & Contact Person. Brothers 1; Sisters 6; Lay Teachers 18; Staff 7; Students 270.

Catholic Memorial School, (Grades 7-12), (Boys), 235 Baker St., West Roxbury, 02132-4395. Web: www.catholicmemorial.org. Paul E. Sheff, Pres.; Richard F. Chisholm, Prin. Congregation of Christian Brothers. Brothers 4; Lay Teachers 63; Boys 800.

Mount Saint Joseph Academy, 617 Cambridge St., 02134-2460. Tel: 617-254-8383 (School Office); 617-783-4747 (Guidance Office); Fax: 617-254-0240. Email: kathleen.fraser@mountsaintjosephacademy.org. Web: www.mountsaintjosephacademy.org. Kathleen Fraser, Prin.; Linda Walkins, Librarian. Sponsored by Sisters of St. Joseph of Boston. Sisters 3; Lay Teachers 22; Girls 240.

BRAINTREE. *Archbishop Williams High School, Inc.* (1949) 80 Independence Ave., 02184. Tel: 781-843-3636; Fax: 781-843-3782. Email: mlsadowski@awhs.org. Web: www.awhs.org. Mary Louise Sadowski, Prin.; Dr. Carmen Mariano, Pres.; Joanna Sands, Librarian. Sisters 1; Teachers 42.

BROCKTON. *Cardinal Spellman High School, Inc.* (1958) 738 Court St., 02302. Tel: 508-583-6875; Fax: 508-580-1977. Email: cshs@spellman.pvt.k12.ma.us. Web: www.spellman.com. John F. McEwan, Ed.D., Pres., Chief Admin. & Contact Person; Dorothy Lynch, Prin.; Diane McDonough, Librarian. Sisters of St. Joseph. Brothers 1; Sisters 1; Lay Teachers 48; Students 690.

CAMBRIDGE. *Matignon High School, Inc.*, 1 Matignon Rd., 02140. Tel: 617-876-1212; Fax: 617-661-3905. Web: www.matignon-hs.org. Thomas F. Galligani, Headmaster; Joseph DiSarcina, Prin.; Ms. Mary Croxen, Librarian. College Preparatory. Religious 1; Lay Staff 40; Students 380.

North Cambridge Catholic High School, Inc., 40 Norris St., 02140. Tel: 617-876-6068; Fax: 617-576-1898. Email: rmccarthy@northcambridgecatholic.org. Web: northcambridgecatholic.org. Robert J. McCarthy, Pres.; Rev. Jose Medina, F.S.C.B., Prin. Priests 2; Brothers 1; Sisters 1; Lay Teachers 16; Students 286.

DANVERS. *St. John's Preparatory School* (1907) 01923. Tel: 978-774-1050; Fax: 978-774-5069. Email: sshannon@stjohnsprep.org. Web: www.stjohnsprep.org. Albert J. Shannon, Ph.D., Headmaster; Edward Hardiman, Prin. Day Students. Brothers 5; Lay Teachers 104; Boys 1,260.

DEDHAM. *Ursuline Academy* (1946) (Grades 7-12), 85 Lowder St., 02026-4299. Tel: 781-326-6161; Fax: 781-326-4898. Email: ursuline@ursulineacademy.net. Web: www.ursulineacademy.net. Mrs. Rosann Whiting, Pres.; Mrs. Mary Jo Keaney, Prin.; Amity Johnson, Librarian. Operated by Ursuline Convent. Ursuline Nuns. College Prep School for Girls. Sisters 7; Lay Teachers 32; Total Staff 63; Girls 388.

EVERETT. *Pope John XXIII High School, Inc.* (1966) 888 Broadway, 02149. Tel: 617-389-0240; Fax: 617-389-2201. Email: info@popejohnhs.org. Web: www.popejohnhs.org. Kathleen Donovan, Pres.; Mary Ann DiMarco, Prin.; Maria Touet, Librarian. Lay Teachers 18; Students 250.

FRAMINGHAM. *Marian High School, Inc.*, 273 Union Ave., 01702. Tel: 508-875-7646; Fax: 508-875-0838. Email: mbaril@marianhigh.org. Web: www.marianhigh.org. Sr. Catherine Clifford, C.S.J., Prin. & Chief Admin.

Sisters 1; Lay Teachers 23; Students 262.

HINGHAM. *Notre Dame Academy* (1853) 1073 Main St., 02043. Tel: 781-749-5930; Fax: 781-749-8366. Email: president@ndahingham.com. Web: www.ndahingham.com. Sr. Barbara Barry, S.N.D., Pres.; Kathleen Colin, Prin.; Patricia Bologna, Librarian. Girls 600; Lay Teachers 55; Sisters 5; Total Staff 100.

KINGSTON. *Sacred Heart High School*, 399 Bishops Hwy., 02364-2098. Tel: 781-585-7511; Fax: 781-585-7063; 781-585-1249. Email: info@sacredheartkingston.com. Web: www.sacredheartkingston.com. Mr. John Enos III, Prin.; Mrs. Marilyn Rennie-Stanton, Asst. Prin. Academics; Mrs. Anne Marie League, Asst. Prin., Student Svcs & Dir. Intermediate School. Sisters 8; Lay Teachers 49; Students 470.

LAWRENCE. *Central Catholic High School of Lawrence, Inc.*, 300 Hampshire St., 01841. Tel: 978-682-0260; Fax: 978-685-2707. Email: ddefillippo@centralcatholic.net. Web: www.centralcatholic.net. Bro. Thomas P. Long, F.M.S., Pres.; David M. DeFillippo, Prin.; Kristina Keleher, Librarian. Conducted by the Marist Brothers of the Schools. Religious 8; Lay Teachers 94; Students 1,340.

Notre Dame High School of Lawrence, Inc. (2004) 301 Haverhill St., 01840. Tel: 978-689-8222; Fax: 978-689-8728. Sr. Mary Murphy, S.N.D., Ph.D., Pres.; Dr. Thomas Ryan, Prin.; Sr. Maggy Lindgren, S.N.D., Dir. of Curriculum. Sisters 5; Lay Teachers 16; Students 245.

LOWELL. *Lowell Catholic High School, Inc.*, 530 Stevens St., 01851. Tel: 978-452-1794. Email: ed2000@tiac.net. Mr. Edward J. Quinn, Prin. Sisters 2; Lay Teachers 18; Students 280.

MALDEN. *Malden Catholic High School*, 99 Crystal St., 02148. Tel: 781-322-3098; Fax: 781-397-0573. Email: tyrrelle@maldencatholic.org. Web: www.maldencatholic.org. Thomas P. Arria Jr., Headmaster. Xaverian Brothers. Brothers 10; Lay Teachers 45; Boys 700.

METHUEN. *Presentation of Mary Academy* (1958) 209 Lawrence St., 01844. Tel: 978-682-9391; Fax: 978-975-3595. Web: www.pmamethuen.org. Sr. Susan Frederick, P.M., Pres.; Rose Maria Redman, Prin.; Maureen Waterworth, Librarian. Sisters of the Presentation of Mary. Sisters 4; Lay Teachers 21; Total Staff 31; Girls 200.

MILTON. *Fontbonne Academy* (1954) 930 Brook Rd., 02186. Tel: 617-696-3241; Fax: 617-696-7688. Web: www.fontbonneacademy.org. Mary Ellen Barnes, Prin.; Anne Malone, Ph.D., Pres.; Florence Lathrop, Librarian. Sisters of St. Joseph 14; Lay Teachers 50; Students 515.

NEEDHAM. *St. Sebastian's School, Inc.*, (Grades 7-12), 1191 Greendale Ave., 02492. Tel: 617-449-5200; Fax: 617-449-5630. Web: www.stsebs.org. Mr. William L. Burke III, Headmaster; Revs. John F. Arens; John U. Paris. Priests 2; Lay Teachers 59; Boys 365.

NEWTON. *Country Day School of the Sacred Heart*, (Grades 5-12), 785 Centre St., 02158. Tel: 617-244-4246; Fax: 617-965-5313. Email: alazure@newtoncountryday.org. Web: www.newtoncountryday.org. Sr. Barbara Rogers, R.S.C.J., Prin.

Boston Academy of the Sacred Heart Religious of the Sacred Heart 1; Lay Teachers 70; Girls 380.

Mount Alvernia High School, (Grades 7-12), 790 Centre St., 02458. Tel: 617-964-4766 (Convent); 617-969-2260 (School); Fax: 617-969-4246. Email: MAHSinfo@mountalverniahs.org. Web: mountalverniahs.org. Mrs. Kathleen Kent, Head of School; Susan Riley, Devel. Dir.; Susan Akie, Librarian. Missionary Franciscan Sisters of the Immaculate Conception. Sisters 3; Lay Teachers 22; Total Staff 40; Girls 252.

PEABODY. *Bishop Fenwick High School, Inc* (1959) 99 Margin St., 01960. Tel: 978-587-8300; Fax: 978-587-8309. Email: bfhs@fenwick.org. Web: www.fenwick.org. Sr. Catherine Fleming, S.N.D., Prin., Chief Admin. & Contact Person; Alison Connelly, Librarian. Sisters 3; Lay Teachers 53; Students 613.

READING. *Austin Preparatory School*, (Grades 6-12), 101 Willow St., 01867. Tel: 781-944-4900; Fax: 781-944-7530. Email: pmoran@austinprepschool.org. Web: www.austinprepschool.org. Mr. Paul J. Moran, Headmaster; Rev. Kenneth Healey, S.M.; James Morris; Jay Zimmerman, Librarian. Priests 2; Sisters 1; Lay Teachers 61; Administrators 10; Students 730.

TYNGSBOROUGH. *Academy of Notre Dame* (1854) 01879. Tel: 978-649-7611; Fax: 978-649-2909. Web: www.ndatyngsboro.org. Sr. Patricia Conner, S.N.D., Prin.; Kathy Arsneault, Librarian. Sisters of Notre Dame de Namur 1; Faculty 27; Girls 174; Lay Teachers 26; Religious 1.

WESTWOOD. *Xaverian Brothers High School* (1963) 800 Clapboardtree St., 02090. Tel: 781-326-6392; Fax: 781-320-0458. Email: admin@xbhs.com. Web: www.xbhs.com. Bro. Daniel Skala, C.F.X., Headmaster; Domenic Lalli, Prin. Xaverian Brothers. Brothers 4; Lay Teachers 77; Boys 1,000.

[E] ELEMENTARY SCHOOLS, ARCHDIOCESAN

DANVERS. *St. Mary of the Annunciation School*, 14 Otis St., 01923. Tel: 978-774-0307; Fax: 978-750-4852. Email: mkelley@stmaryschooldanvers.org. Web: stmaryschooldanvers.org. Molly Kelley, Prin. (Grades PreK-8 & Extended Day Care). Sisters of Notre Dame de Namur 1; Lay Teachers 25; Students 500.

[F] MONTESSORI SCHOOLS

HAVERHILL. *The Merrimack Montessori School*, 55 Saltonstall Rd., 01830. Tel: 978-374-6103; Fax: 978-469-0730. Email: mmsronni@aol.com. Web: www.merrimackmontessori.org. Ronni George, Head of School. (For boys and girls aged 3-6) Lay Teachers 14; Students 131.

MARLBOROUGH. *St. Anne Montessori School* (1964) 720 Boston Post Rd. E., 01752. Tel: 508-597-1416. Web: www.stannemontessori.org. Kathleen Finn, Dir. (For boys and girls aged 3-6) Religious 2; Lay Teachers 4; Students 72.

NEWTON. *Walnut Park Montessori School*, 47 Walnut Park, 02458. Tel: 617-969-9208; Fax: 617-969-6408. Email: walnutpk@gis.net. Web: www.walnutparkmontessori.org. Ms. Mary Rockett, Head of School; Sr. Alice Mary Brady, C.S.J., Librarian. Religious 5; Lay Teachers 14; Students 127.

WENHAM. *Notre Dame Children's Class* (1967) 74 Grapevine Rd., 01984. Tel: 508-468-1340; Fax: 508-468-0166. Email: notredcc@aol.com. Web: sndden.org/ndcc. Sisters Barbara Beauchamp, S.N.D., Dir.; Susan Raymo, S.N.D., Co-Dir. Religious 2; Lay Teachers 3; Primary Class 20; Preschool 48.

[G] ELEMENTARY SCHOOLS, PRIVATE

BOSTON. *St. Columbkille School, Inc.*, 25 Arlington St., 02135. Mary E. Battles, Prin.

Mother Caroline Academy (1993) 515 Blue Hill Ave., Dorchester, 02121. Tel: 617-427-1177; Fax: 617-427-7788. Email: info@mcaec.org. Web: www.mcaec.org. Ingrid Tucker, Pres.; Dr. Shirley Grover, Librarian.

Mother Caroline Academy for Girls, Inc. Sisters 1; Lay Teachers 10; Students 60.

Nativity Preparatory School, (Grades 5-8), 30 Raynor Cir., Roxbury, 02120. Tel: 617-442-1993; Fax: 617-541-4148. Email: hicks@bchigh.edu. Web: www.nativityboston.org. Revs. William F. Campbell, S.J., Exec. Dir.; Alfred J. Hicks, S.J., Prin.; Simon E. Smith, S.J.

Nativity-Boston, Inc., A Jesuit Middle School. Priests 3; Brothers 1; Lay Teachers 12; Boys 65.

BRAINTREE. *Cardinal Cushing Centers*, 85 Washington St., 02184. Tel: 617-848-6250; Fax: 617-848-0640. Email: PLarson@Coletta.org. Web: www.Coletta.org.

St. Coletta's and Cardinal Cushing Schools of MA, Inc., Day School for multiple handicapped, developmentally delayed children, ages 4-22 years. Lay Teachers 9; Students 33.

BROCKTON. *Trinity Catholic Academy, Inc.*, 37 Erie Ave., 02302. Tel: 508-583-6237. Mr. Anthony Luizzi, Reg. Dir.

DORCHESTER. *Pope John Paul II Catholic Academy Inc.*, 2214 Dorchester Ave., 02124. Tel: 617-265-0019; Fax: 617-298-2926. Russ W. Wilson, Regional Dir. Religious 2; Lay Teachers 77.

GROTON. *Country Day School of the Holy Union* (1949) 14 Main St., 01450. Tel: 978-448-5646; Fax: 978-448-2392. Email: cdsgroton@yahoo.com. Web: www.cdsgroton.org. Sr. Yvette Ladurantaye, S.U.S.C., Prin. Holy Union Sisters 1; Lay Teachers 21; Students 230.

HANOVER. *Cardinal Cushing Centers, Inc.*, 400 Washington St., 02339. Tel: 781-826-6371; Fax: 781-826-1559. Email: skozaryn@coletta.org. Lawrence Sauer, Exec. Dir., Hanover; Pat Larson, Exec. Dir., Braintree; Jean Rogers, Exec. Dir. Adult Svcs. Lay Staff 450; Students 163.

St. Coletta and Cardinal Cushing Schools of Massachusetts, Inc., 400 Washington St., 02339. Lay Teachers 1; Lay Staff 16; Students 20.

KINGSTON. *Sacred Heart Elementary School* (Day School), 329 Bishops Hwy., 02364. Tel: 617-585-2114; Fax: 617-585-6993. Sr. Ann Therese Connolly, C.D.P., Prin. (Grades 1-6). Sisters of Divine Providence 6; Lay Teachers 21; Students 430.

Sacred Heart Pre-Primary School, 363 Bishops Hwy., 02364-2035. Tel: 781-585-3545; Fax: 781-422-5224. Sr. Angela Provost, C.D.P., Dir. Religious 1; Lay Teachers 3; Students 64.

LAWRENCE. *Blessed Stephen Bellesini, O.S.A., Academy, Inc.* (2002) 94 Bradford St., 01840-1003. Tel: 978-989-0004; Fax: 978-989-9404. Email: office@bellesiniacademy.org. Web: www.bellesiniacademy.org. Ms. Julie DiFilippo, Exec. Dir. Total Staff 8; Students 60.

LOWELL. *Franco-American Private School* (1908) 357 Pawtucket St., 01854. Tel: 978-458-0308; Fax: 978-458-0308. Email: faslowell@comcast.net. Web: www.francoamericanschool.org. Sisters Lorraine Richard, S.C.Q., Prin.; Jane Holland, S.C.Q., Asst. Prin. Religious 2; Lay Teachers 17; Students 250.

MARLBOROUGH. *Our Lady Thrift Shop* (1973) 197 Pleasant St., 01752. Tel: 508-485-0740; Fax: 508-481-0663. Email: chretienne@verizon.net. Sr. Ida M. Devoe, S.S.Ch., Officer of the Board. Religious 5.

NEWTON. *Jackson School Elementary*, (Grades K-6), 200 Jackson Rd., 02458-1428. Tel: 617-969-1537; Fax: 617-244-8596. Email: info@jacksonschool.org. Web: www.jacksonschool.org. Mrs. Susan G. Niden, Prin. Sisters 9; Lay Teachers 22; Staff 5; Students 255.

Jackson Walnut Park Educational Collaborative, Inc., (Grades PreSchool-6), 47 Walnut Park St., 02458. Tel: 617-686-0105; 617-969-9208; Fax: 617-969-6908. Email: victoria.londergan@cojboston.org. Web: www.jacksonschool.org. Victoria N. Londergan, Pres.; Mrs. Susan G. Niden, Prin. (Elementary); Mary Reckett, Prin. (Pre-School); Sr. Diane Neumyer, C.S.J., Librarian. Sisters (Jackson) 8; Lay Teachers (Jackson) 17; Sisters (Walnut Park) 4; Lay Teachers (Walnut Park) 19.

Mount Alvernia Academy, 20 Manet Rd., Chestnut Hill, 02467. Tel: 617-527-7540; Fax: 617-527-7995. Email: jtsullivan@mtalverniaacad.org. Web: www.mtalverniaacad.org. Joan T. Sullivan, Prin. Sisters 1; Lay Teachers 26; Students 341; Personnel 49.

TYNGSBOROUGH. *Academy of Notre Dame at Tyngsboro*, 180 Middlesex Rd., 01879. Tel: 978-649-7611; Fax: 978-649-2909. Email: mduke@ndatyngsboro.org. Web: www.ndatyngsboro.org. Sr. Mary Duke, S.N.D., Prin.; Kathy Smith, Librarian. Sisters of Notre Dame de Namur 2; Lay Teachers 26; Students 435.

[H] SPECIAL SCHOOLS

METHUEN. *St. Ann's Home Special Needs School*, 100 A. Haverhill St., 01844. Tel: 978-682-5276; Fax: 978-688-4932. Email: dgrandbois@st.annshome.org. Web: www.st.annshome.org. Mr. Denis Grandbois, Exec. Dir. Ungraded special needs school for emotionally disturbed and behaviorally disordered children. Lay Teachers 38; Psychotherapists 20; Counselors 120; Administrators 11; Staff 23; Residential Students 103; Day Students 68; Bed Capacity 130; Total Staff 250.

PEABODY. *Holy Childhood Nursery & Kindergarten* (1854) 5 Wheatland St., 01960. Tel: 978-531-4733; Fax: 978-531-2468. Email: carmelite@verizon.net. Web: www.carmelitepreschool.com. Sr. Kathleen A. Bettencourt, O.Carm., Coord. & Co-Dir. Sisters 5; Lay Teachers 6; Students 90.

WATERTOWN. *Rosary Academy Learning Center* (1981) 2 Rosary Dr., 02472. Tel: 617-923-1935; Fax: 617-923-2993. Email: ralc1@verizon.net. Web: www.rosaryacademy.net. Sr. Judith Ward, S.N.D., Dir. Sisters of St. Dominic (St. Catharine, KY)., Preschool & Day Care. Sisters 1; Lay Teachers 8; Students 54.

[I] CATHOLIC CHARITIES

BOSTON. *Catholic Charitable Bureau of the Archdiocese of Boston, Inc.* (1903) Central Office, 75 Kneeland St., 8th Fl., 02111-1931. Tel: 617-482-5440; Fax: 617-451-0337. Email: info@ccab.org. Web: www.ccab.org. Ms. Tiziana Dearing, Pres. Social Service Agency Total Clients Served (Across Eastern Massachusetts) 200,000.

El Centro Del Cardenal/Catholic Charities, 76 Union Park St., 02118. Tel: 617-542-9292; Fax: 617-542-6912. Ms. Elisabeth Zweig-Snippe, Contact Person.

DORCHESTER. *Yawky Center for Early Ed & Care Catholic Charities*, 185 Columbia Rd., 02121. Tel: 617-506-6930; Fax: 617-929-0453. Email: esther_garcia@ccab.org. Web: www.ccab.org. Sr. Esther Garcia, S.A., Asst. Dir. Community Based Agency of the Catholic Charitable Bureau of the Archdiocese of Boston, Inc.; Day Care. Franciscan Sisters of the Atonement 2.

[J] FAMILY COUNSELING AND GUIDANCE CENTERS

BROCKTON. *Catholic Charities South* A Division of Catholic Charities, 686 N. Main St., 02301. Tel: 508-587-0815; Fax: 508-580-0837. Email: lisa_lodge@ccab.org. Web: ccab.org.
Local Clinics:
North Shore-Danvers, 140 Commonwealth Ave., Ste. 202, Danvers, 01923. Tel: 978-774-6820; Fax: 978-777-4242.
Brockton, 686 N. Main St., 02301. Tel: 508-587-0815; Fax: 508-580-0837.

[K] SOCIETY OF ST. VINCENT DE PAUL

STOUGHTON. *Society of St. Vincent DePaul, Central Office*, 18 Canton St., 02072. Tel: 781-344-3100; Fax: 781-341-4560. Email: ejresnick@svdpboston.com. Web: svdpboston.com. Paul MacNeil, Exec. Dir.

[L] CHILD CARE AGENCIES

BOSTON. *Nazareth Child Care Center*, 19 St. Joseph St., Jamaica Plain, 02130. Tel: 617-522-4040; Fax: 617-983-0460. Email: pam-penton@ccab.org. Pamela J. Penton, Dir.
Catholic Charities dba Nazareth Child Care Center Capacity 83; Total Staff 18.
Nazareth Residence for Mothers and Children, 91 Regent St., Roxbury, 02119. Tel: 617-541-0100; Fax: 617-541-8781. Email: nazareth_residence@ccab.org. Sr. Mary Farren, R.G.S., Program Dir. Home for homeless mothers and children who are HIV positive. Capacity 8; Total Staff 10; Total in Residence 22.

METHUEN. *St. Ann's Home, Inc.*, 100A Haverhill St., 01844. Tel: 978-682-5276; Fax: 978-688-4932. Email: dgrandbois@st.annshome.org. Web: www.st.annshome.org. Mr. Denis Grandbois, Exec. Dir.; Mrs. Sharon Cutter, Business Mgr. Total in Residence 105; Day Students 66; Total Staff 245; School Children 145.
Residential Treatment Center Tel: 978-692-5276; Fax: 978-688-4932. Children 165.

[M] GUIDANCE CENTERS

BOSTON. *St. Mary's Women and Children's Center* (1993) 90 Cushing Ave., 02125. Tel: 617-436-8600; Fax: 617-288-8961. Email: jbeckler@smwcc.org. Web: www.smwcc.org. Ms. Judith Beckler, Pres. Provides residential, education and training programs for women and children who are homeless or living in poverty. Patients Assisted Annually 250; Total Staff 100.
Salesian Boys & Girls Club (Central Unit), 150 Byron St., 02128. Tel: 617-567-6626; Fax: 617-568-3851. Email: sbgclub@juno.com. Web: www.salesianclub.com. Salesians of St. John Bosco. Total Assisted 1,750; Total Staff 16.
Orient Heights Unit, 145-150 Bryon St., 02128. Tel: 617-567-6626. Rev. John Nazzaro, S.D.B., Exec. Dir., Club Admin. & Rector Salesian Staff: Revs. William Ferruzzi, S.D.B.; Richard Putnam, S.D.B.; Richard Cressman, S.D.B.; Bro. Alfred Flatoff, S.D.B.

BRAINTREE. *Life Resources, Inc.*, 100 River Rd., 02184. Tel: 781-849-7751; Fax: 781-849-7754. Web: www.liferesourcesinc.org. Ms. Lynne Marie Bielecki, Pres.
Life Resources/Alpha-Omega, 140 Adams St., 02184. Tel: 781-848-5510; Fax: 781-380-7565. Web: www.liferesourcesinc.org. A long term residence for 20 adolescent boys.

BROCKTON. *Phaneuf Youth Treatment Center*, 104 Market St., 02301. Tel: 508-584-0500. Short term residence for 16 adolescent males.

LAKEVILLE. *Bishop Joseph John Ruocco House*, 22 Highland Rd., 02347. Tel: 508-947-2823; Fax: 508-947-0305. Web: liferesourcesinc.org. Short term residence for 16 female adolescents. To provide comprehensive life skill services to residents and their families.

[N] INFORMATION - CONFERENCE CENTERS

BOSTON. *Paulist Center*, 5 Park St., 02108. Tel: 617-742-4460; Fax: 617-720-5756. Email: fiveparkst@aol.com. Web: www.paulistboston.com. Rev. Paul D. Huesing, C.S.P., Ph.D., Dir.; Susan Rutkowski, M.Div., Pastoral Min., Family Rel. Educ. & Social Justice; Patricia Simpson, M.Div., Admin.; Michael Kurley, Pastoral Min., Liturgy & Music.

BROCKTON. *Chapel of Our Savior-Catholic Pastoral and Information Center* (1961) 475 Westgate Dr., 02301-1819. Tel: 508-583-8357; Fax: 508-586-5510. Revs. Gerald DiGiralamo, S.A., Dir.; Henry Mair, S.A.; Norman Boyd, S.A.; Malcolm Martin, S.A. (Retired); Bros. Thomas Banacki, S.A.; Louis Marek, S.A.; Savio McNeice, S.A. Priests 4; Brothers 3.

[O] GENERAL HOSPITALS

BOSTON. *Caritas Carney Hospital, Inc.*, 2100 Dorchester Ave., 02124-5666. Tel: 617-723-1100. Mr. Wilson D. Rogers Jr., Esq., Contact Person.
Caritas St. Elizabeth's Medical Center of Boston, Inc., 736 Cambridge St., Brighton, 02135. Tel: 617-789-3000; Fax: 617-789-3007. Email: shagop@aol.com. Web: www.cchcs.org. Dr. Ralph de la Torre, M.D., CEO, Caritas Christi; Mr. John J. Holiver, Pres., St. Elizabeth; Revs. Robert J. Caprio, O.F.M., Dir. Spiritual Care Dept.; Charles E. Salamone; Sr. Mary Anne Gallagher, O.S.F.; Rev. Anselm Nwagbara (Nigeria); Sisters Shirley Nugent, S.C.N.; Mary Olsen, C.S.J.; Timothy Duff; Martha Sullivan; Ms. Cheryl Amrich. Priests 3; Total Staff 10; Bed Capacity 350; Bassinets (NICU level 3) 20; Nursery Beds 30; Patients Assisted Annually 118,223.

BROCKTON. *Caritas Good Samaritan Medical Center, Inc.*, 235 N. Pearl St., 02401. Tel: 508-427-3000; 508-427-3151; 508-427-2602. Mr. Steven R. Gordon, Pres.; Rev. Richard W. Visbisky, Chap. & Dir. of Pastoral Care; Pauline Heal, (Congregational). A Caritas family hospital. Total Assisted 193,388; Total Staff 1,302; Sisters of Charity of Nazareth 1; Sisters of Jesus Crucified and the Sorrowful Mother 1; Holy Union Sisters 1.
Caritas Good Samaritan Cancer Center, Inc.
Caritas Good Samaritan Occupational Health Services, Inc.

LOWELL. *Saints Memorial Health System, Inc.*, One Hospital Dr., 01852. Tel: 978-458-1411; Fax: 978-458-8369. Email: info@stmmc.org. Web: www.saints-memorial.org. Thom Clark, Pres. & CEO. Sisters of Charity of Ottawa. Bed Capacity 218; Total Assisted 214,000; Total Staff 1,352.

METHUEN. *Caritas Holy Family Hospital, Inc.* (1984) 70 East St., 01844-4597. Tel: 978-687-0151; Fax: 978-688-7689. Web: www.holyfamilyhosp.org. Lester Schindel, Pres. & CEO; Rev. Richard O'Brien, Chap. Affiliating Hospital for: St. Anselm's Collegiate School of Nursing; Northern Essex Community College; UMass, Lowell; Salem State College; New Hampshire Technical School; Massachusetts Bay Community College; Northeastern University; Rivier College; Greater Lawrence Vocational School. Bed Capacity 222; Bassinets 28; Patients Assisted Annually 230,000; Total Staff 1,575; Priests 1.
Caritas Holy Family Hospital Auxiliary (1947) 70 East St., 01844-4597. Tel: 978-687-0156, Ext. 2301; Fax: 978-688-7689.
Caritas Holy Family Hospital Men's Guild (1950) 70 East St., 01844-4597. Tel: 978-687-0156, Ext. 2362; Fax: 978-688-7689.

[P] SPECIAL HOSPITALS

BOSTON. *Franciscan Hospital for Children*, 30 Warren St., Brighton, 02135. Tel: 617-254-3800; Fax: 617-779-1119. Email: fch@fhfc.org. Web: www.fhfc.org. Mr. Paul Della Rocco, Pres. & CEO. General Pediatrics, Rehabilitation, Special Education, Mental Health Services & Home Care. Bed Capacity 100; Number under care 59,000; Day Program 90; Total Staff 650.

[Q] SOCIAL SERVICES

BOSTON. *Chinese Catholic Pastoral Center*, 78 Tyler St., 02111-1831. Tel: 617-482-2949; Fax: 617-482-2949.
Little Sisters of the Assumption, Family Health Service, Inc. (1981) (Project Hope), 500 Dudley St., 02119. Tel: 617-442-1880; Fax: 617-238-0473. Email: mleonard@prohope.org. Web: www.prohope.org. Project Hope is a multi-service agency at the forefront of efforts in Boston to move families beyond homelessness and poverty. It provides low-income women with children with access to education, jobs, housing and emergency services; fosters their personal transformation; and works for broader systems charge. Total Assisted 1,000; Total Staff 54; Sisters 4.

CAMBRIDGE. **Helping Hands of St. Marguerite, Inc.*, 799 Concord Ave., 02138. Tel: 617-492-1023; Fax: 617-492-1025. Email: ddougherty@helpinghands-homecare.org. Web: www.helpinghands-homecare.org. Daniel Dougherty, Exec. Dir. Covenant Health Systems, Lexington, MA., Personal care, housekeeping and companion services to individuals and families in their own homes, in assisted living residences or in retirement communities.

LAWRENCE. **M.I. Adult Day Health Center, Inc.*, 189 Maple St., 01841. Tel: 978-682-6321; Fax: 978-975-0050. Email: barbara_grant@mihcs.com. Web: www.mihcs.com. Barbara Grant, Pres. & CEO. Sisters of Charity of Montreal (Grey Nuns)., Adult day health care for senior citizens; also, bilingual/bicultural (Spanish) adult day health care. Total in Residence 70; Total Staff 12.
**M.I. Transportation, Inc.*, 189 Maple St., 01841. Tel: 978-682-7575; Fax: 978-691-5374. Email: barabar_grant@mihcs.com. Web: www.mihcs.com. Covenant Health Systems. Total Assisted 75; Total Staff 5.
**Mary Immaculate Adult Day Health Center, Inc.*, 189 Maple St., 01841. Tel: 978-685-6321; Fax: 978-975-0050. Email: barbaragrant@mihcs.com. Web: www.mihcs.com. Barbara Grant, Pres. Covenant Health Systems, Lexington, MA

[R] PROTECTIVE INSTITUTIONS

BOSTON. *St. Mary's Women and Infants Center*, 90 Cushing Ave., 02125. Center for pregnant women.; (See Guidance Centers for more information.)

[S] HOMES FOR AGED-RESIDENTS & NURSING

BOSTON. *Don Orione Nursing Home*, 111 Orient Ave., East Boston, 02128-1006. Tel: 617-569-2100; Fax: 617-561-1138. Email: donorione@aol.com. Revs. Mario Guarino, F.D.P.; Rocco Crescenzi, F.D.P.; Gino Marchesani, F.D.P.; Marcelo Boschi, F.D.P.; Claudio Peters, F.D.P. Sons of Divine Providence (Don Orione Fathers) 5; Guests 190; Total Assisted 185; Total Staff 230.
Marian Manor (1954) 130 Dorchester St., South Boston, 02127. Tel: 617-268-3333; Fax: 617-268-4589. Email: joe@marianmanor.org. Web: www.marianmanor.org. Sr. Mark Louis, Admin.; Rev. Herbert J. Cleary, S.J., Chap. Priests 1; Carmelite Sisters for the Aged and Infirm 10; Total Staff 520; Guests 366.

BROCKTON. *St. Joseph Manor Health Care Inc.* (1965) 215 Thatcher St., 02302. Tel: 508-583-5834; Fax: 508-583-8551. Email: ademinico@sjmbrockton.org. Web: www.sjmbrockton.org. Ms. Anne M. DeMinico, CEO & Admin. A member of Covenant Health Systems, Lexington, MA. Sisters of Jesus Crucified and the Sorrowful Mother 5; Residents 118; Total Staff 202.
Adult Day Health Center Tel: 508-583-8313; Fax: 508-588-7384. Total Assisted Per Day 60; Total Staff 12.

CAMBRIDGE. *Sancta Maria Nursing Facility* (1948) 799 Concord Ave., 02138. Tel: 617-868-2200; Fax: 617-864-2801. Sr. Mary Mark, D.M., Admin. Daughters of Mary of the Immaculate Conception., An affiliate of Covenant. Sisters 4; Residents 141; Bed Capacity 141; Total Staff 217.
**Youville Hospital & Rehabilitation Center, Inc.*, 1575 Cambridge St., 02138-4398. Tel: 617-876-4344; Fax: 617-547-5501. Email: leaheyd@youville.org. Web: www.youville.org. Mr. Daniel Leahey, Pres. & CEO; Mr. Robert Short, Sr. Dir., Mission & Pastoral Care; Rev. Martin Okwir (Uganda), Chap.; Bruce Aguilar, Chap.; Janice Matter, Chap. Covenant Health Systems, Lexington, MA. Priests 1; Bed Capacity 180; Patients Assisted Annually 2,340; Total Staff 650.
**Youville House, Inc.*, 1573 Cambridge St., 02138-4398. Tel: 617-491-1234; Fax: 617-491-8838. Email: joannecparsons@youvillehouse.org. Web: www.youvillehouse.com. Joanne C. Parsons, CEO. Covenant Health Systems, Lexington, MA., Youville House is an assisted living facility housing retired priests from the Archdiocese of Boston and elders from the community. Total in Residence 100; Total Apartments 95; Residents Assisted Annually 120; Total Staff 85.

FRAMINGHAM. *Carmel Terrace* (1995) 933 Central St., 01701. Tel: 508-788-8000; Fax: 508-626-1603. Web: www.carmelterrace.org. Sr. Jeanette DiLindsay, O.Carm., Dir. Carmelite Sisters for the Aged and Infirm 2; Apartments for Assisted Living of the Elderly 69; Total Assisted 75; Total Staff 38.
St. Patrick's Manor, Inc., 863 Central St., 01701. Tel: 508-879-8000; Fax: 508-626-1604. Web: www.stpatricksmanor.org. Sr. Maureen McDonough, O.Carm., Admin. Carmelite Sisters for the Aged and Infirm 30; Total Staff 460.

IPSWICH. *St. Julie Billiart Residential Care Center, Inc.* (2002) 30 Jeffreys Neck Rd., 01938. Tel: 978-356-4381; Fax: 978-356-1380. Email: lee.pakstis@sndden.org. Lee Pakstis, Admin. Total Staff 45; Bed Capacity 54; Total Assisted Annually 58.

LAWRENCE. *M.I. Residential Community II, Inc.*, 191 Maple St., 01841. Tel: 978-685-6321; Fax: 978-975-0050. Email: barbara_grant@mihcs.com. Web: www.mihcs.com. Barbara Grant, Pres. & CEO. Covenant Health Systems, Lexington, MA., Covenant Health Systems; Independent & assisted living for Elderly and Handicapped. Units 106; Total in Residence 120; Total Staff 35.
M.I. Residential Community III, Inc., 191 Maple St., 01841. Tel: 978-685-6321; Fax: 978-975-0050. Email: barbara_grant@mihcs.com. Web: www.mihcs.com. Barbara Grant, Pres. & CEO. Covenant Health Systems, Lexington, MA., Independent & assisted living for Elderly and Handicapped. Units 88; Total in Residence 95; Total Staff 35.

M.I. Residential Community, Inc., 189 Maple St., 01841. Tel: 978-685-6321; Fax: 978-975-0050. Email: barbara_grant@mihcs.com. Web: www.mihcs.com. Barbara Grant, Pres. & CEO. Convenant Health Systems., Covenant Health Systems.; "Marguerite's House" Assisted Living Facility-106 Units. Units 106; Total in Residence 121; Total Staff 35.

Mary Immaculate Nursing Restorative Center, 172 Lawrence St., 01841. Tel: 978-685-6321; Fax: 978-975-0050. Email: barbara_grant@mihcs.com. Web: www.mihcs.com. Barbara Grant, Pres. & CEO. Convenant Health Systems, Lexington, MA., Multi-level Skilled Nursing Facility; Member of Covenant Health Systems, Lexington, MA. Unit of Mary Immaculate Health Care Services. Residents 250; Total Staff 300.

MI Management, Inc., 172 Lawrence St., 01841. Tel: 978-685-6321; Fax: 978-975-0050. Email: barbara_grant@mihcs.com. Web: www.mihcs.com. Barbara Grant, Pres. & CEO. Convenant Health Systems, Lexington, MA., Management company for all Mary Immaculate Facilities.

LEXINGTON. *Youville Place, Inc.* (1997) 10 Pelham Rd., 02421-8408. Tel: 781-861-3535; Fax: 781-862-4289. Email: joannecparsons@youvillehouse.org. Web: youvilleplace.org. Joanne C. Parsons, CEO. Covenant Health Systems., Assisted Living Facility.

LOWELL. *D'Youville Senior Care, Inc.*, 981 Varnum Ave., 01854. Tel: 978-569-1000; Fax: 978-453-3561. Email: nprendergast@dyouville.org. Web: www.dyouville.org. Ms. Naomi M. Prendergast, CEO; Deacon John Aliskevicz. Sisters of Charity of Ottawa (Grey Nuns of the Cross). Sisters 5; Deacons 1; Total Assisted 208; Total Staff 350; Adult Day Health Care Capacity 23; Total Staff 6.

MARLBOROUGH. *Marie Esther Health Center, Inc.* (1993) 720 Boston Post Rd. E., 01752. Tel: 508-485-3791; 508-460-1951; Fax: 508-229-2294. Email: ecaron@sistersofsaintanne.org. Total Assisted 72; Total Staff 58.

SOMERVILLE. *Jeanne Jugan Pavilion*, 190 Highland Ave., 02143. Tel: 617-776-4420; Fax: 617-623-0707. Email: smmothersuperior@littlesistersofthepoor.org. 186 Highland Ave., 02143. Apartments for the Elderly 27; Residents 29; Total Staff 1.

Jeanne Jugan Residence, 186 Highland Ave., 02143. Tel: 617-776-4420; Fax: 617-623-0707. Email: smmothersuperior@littlesistersofthepoor.org. Little Sisters of the Poor 14; Residents 84; Senior Citizen Total in Residence 84; Total Staff 105.

WALTHAM. *Maristhill Nursing and Rehabilitation Center* (1969) 66 Newton St., 02453-6063. Tel: 781-893-0240; Fax: 781-894-6330. Email: cfenn@maristhill.org. Web: www.maristhill.org. Ms. Carolyn Fenn, Pres./CEO. Covenant Health Systems, Lexington, MA.

[T] PERSONAL PRELATURES

CAMBRIDGE. *Opus Dei, Prelature of the Holy Cross and Opus Dei*, 25 Follen St., 02138. Tel: 617-354-3204; Fax: 617-868-0349. Web: www.opusdei.org. Revs. Thomas J. Lamb; David J. Cavanagh.

NEWTON. *Prelature of the Holy Cross and Opus Dei*, 481 Hammond St., 02167. Tel: 617-738-7348; Fax: 617-739-6001. Web: www.opusdei.org. Revs. Jose P. Ruisanchez; Richard W. Rieman; Salvador S. Vahi.

[U] MONASTERIES AND RESIDENCES OF PRIESTS AND BROTHERS

BOSTON. *Assumptionist Center* (1989) 330 Market St., 02135. Tel: 617-783-0400; Fax: 617-783-8030. Email: despinosa@assumptio.org. Web: www.assumption.us. Revs. Donald Espinosa, A.A., Provincial Treas.; Claude Grenache, A.A., B.A., S.T.B., S.T.L., Campus Minister, Bentley/Supr.; Vincent Machozi, A.A.; Roland Guilmain, A.A. Total in Residence 11.

Assumption Guild, Inc.: Rev. Donald Espinosa, A.A. *Assumption Guild*, 330 Market St., Brighton, 02135. Tel: 617-783-0495; Fax: 617-783-8030. Email: assumptionguild@yahoo.com. Web: masscardsaa-.com. Rev. Gerard Messier, A.A., Hospital Chap.

Serving Abroad: Revs. Gary Perron, A.A., Parroquia Emperatrix de America, Mercaderes 99, 03900 Mexico D.F., Mexico. Tel: 525-593-2002; Fax: 525-651-2000; Leo Brassard, A.A., Haktari Songdang, 600-2 Hakgyio-Ri Hakgyio-Myon, Hamp Yong-Gun, Jeollan Amdo 525-812 Korea, South. Tel: 011-061-323-1337; Fax: 011-061-323-1337; Richard Brunelle, A.A., Novice Master, Austin House, P.O. Box 13230, Arusha, Tanzania. Tel: 011-255-57-2443; Luc Martel, A.A., Prov. Treas., Assumptionist Community, P.O. Box 58488, Nairobi 0200 Kenya. Tel: 011-254-2-567-698; Fax: 011-254-2-570-303; Very Rev. Richard Lamoureux, A.A., Supr. General, Padri Assunzionisti, Via San Piov 55, Rome 00165 Italy.

St. Bonaventure Friary, Franciscan Friars, 284 Foster St., 02135. Tel: 617-254-2447. Email: stbonafriary@aol.com. Rev. Francis Walter, O.F.M., Guardian and Novice Master; Bros. Mark Brown, O.F.M., Formation Staff; Juan Luis Rivera, O.F.M., Novice; Justin Morrisette, O.F.M., Novice. Priests 1; Total Staff 2.

Carmelite Monastery (1942) 166 Foster St., 02135-3902. Tel: 617-787-5056; Fax: 617-783-1396. Revs. Salvatore Sciurba, O.C.D., Prior; Kevin Culligan, O.C.D., B.A., M.A., M.S., Ph.D.; Terrence Dougherty, O.C.D.; Paul Fohlin, O.C.D.; Bro. Charles F. Gamen, O.C.D.; Revs. Bonaventure Lussier, O.C.D.; George Mangiaracina, O.C.D.; Lawrence F. Sullivan, O.C.D.; Bro. Augustine Wharf, O.C.D. Discalced Carmelite Friars. Priests 10; Brothers 1; Total in Residence 11.

St. Christopher Friary, 18 N. Bennet St., 02113. Tel: 617-742-4190; Fax: 617-742-1676. Revs. Brennan R. Egan, O.F.M., Ph.D., Health Care Dir.; Michael Bercik, O.F.M.; Kieran Monahan, O.F.M.; Richard Passeri, O.F.M. (Retired); Aubert Marie Picardi, O.F.M.; Berard Tufo, O.F.M. (Retired); Bro. James T. Welch, O.F.M. Brothers 1; Priests 8.

St. Francis of Assisi Friary (2008) (The Province of St. Mary of the Capuchin Order, White Plains, NY), 46 Brookside Ave., Jamaica Plain, 02130-2370. Tel: 617-522-6469. Web: www.capuchin.org. Rev. Brendan P. Buckley, O.F.M.Cap., Pastor & Guardian; Bro. James M. Peterson, O.F.M.Cap., J.D., J.C.L., Vicar; Revs. John Rathschmidt, O.F.M.Cap., Ph.D., Dir. of Formation; David Couturier, O.F.M.Cap., Ph.D., D.Min. Student Friars 3.

Little Brothers of St. Francis, 785-789 Parker St., 02120. Tel: 617-442-2556. Web: www.littlebrothersofstfrancis.org. Bro. Anthony Joseph Dusza, L.B.S.F., Servant General.

Little Brothers of St. Francis Franciscan Fraternity of Peace and Love, Inc., Regional Fraternity and Novitiate. Brothers 7.

Loyola House, 300 Newbury St., 02115-2801. Tel: 617-424-0155; Fax: 617-424-0155. Revs. James F. Walsh, S.J., Supr.; Charles B. Connolly, S.J.; James M. Keegan, S.J.; Frederic A. Maples, S.J.; Robert G. McMillan, S.J., Treas.; Bruce T. Morrill, S.J.; Francis J. Moy, S.J.; Richard H. Roos, S.J., Min.; James M. Shaughnessy, S.J.; John P. Spencer, S.J.; Richard J. Stanley, S.J.; George P. Winchester, S.J.; Dennis J. Yesalonia, S.J. The Society of Jesus. Priests 13; Total in Residence 13.

Marist Fathers and Brothers Provincial House (1924) 27 Isabella St., 02116-5216. Tel: 617-426-5297; 617-426-4448; Fax: 617-848-3767. Email: smboston@conversent.net. Web: users.aol.com/rlajoie/marists.htm. Very Rev. Roland Lajoie, S.M., Prov.; Rev. Raymond E. Coolong, S.M., Vicar Prov. Brothers 5; Priests 56.

Marist Fathers Lourdes Residence, 698 Beacon St., 02215. Tel: 617-262-2271. Revs. Gerard Caron, S.M., Dir.; Marcel Lajoie, S.M. Priests 2.

Marist Fathers of Our Lady of Victories (Boston Prov.) (1884) 27 Isabella St., 02116. Tel: 617-426-4448; Fax: 617-426-1884. Email: olvboston@yahoo.com. Web: olvboston.tripod.com. Revs. Roger Bourgea, S.M., Chap., Boston Medical Center; Lucien Chasse, S.M.; Gerard Demers, S.M., Supr.; John Granato, S.M., Parochial Vicar; Clifton Moors, S.M. (Retired); Armand Robichaud, S.M., S.T.L.; Jose Ronaipe; William Rowland, S.M.; Edward Sheehan, S.M.; Bro. James Dvorak, S.M. Priests 9; Brothers 1; Sisters 5.

Paulist Fathers Residence, 5 Park St., 02108-4897. Tel: 617-742-4460; Fax: 617-723-2170. Email: pdhcsp@yahoo.com. Web: www.paulistboston.com; www.paulistnewengland.org. Revs. Paul D. Huesing, C.S.P., Ph.D., Dir. & Supr.; Robert W. Baer, C.S.P.; Wilfred A. Brimley, C.S.P., Senior Ministry Status; Robert S. Rivers, C.S.P., S.T.L., Dir. Paulist New England Outreach. Total in Residence 4; Total Staff 17.

The Salesian Community (1945) 145 Byron St., 02128. Tel: 617-569-6551; 617-569-6645; Fax: 617-568-3851. Email: salesians@comcast.net. Web: www.salesiansociety.org. Total Assisted 2,000.

San Lorenzo Friary (2002) (The Province of St. Mary of the Capuchin Order, White Plains, New York), 15 Montebello Rd., Jamaica Plain, 02130-2352. Tel: 617-983-1919; 617-983-3692; Fax: 617-983-0515. Email: yakiecap@yahoo.com. Web: www.capuchin.org. Bro. Joseph Yakimovich, O.F.M.Cap., B.S., M.S., Guardian; Rev. Martin Curtin, O.F.M.Cap., M.Div., Vicar & Dir., Formation. Student Friars 11.

The Society of Jesus of New England-Provincial Offices (1926) 85 School St., Watertown, 02472-4251. Tel: 617-607-2800; Fax: 617-607-2888. Email: nenprvsj@sjnen.org. Web: www.sjnen.org. P.O. Box 9199, Watertown, 02471-9199. Very Rev. Myles N. Sheehan, S.J., Prov.; Revs. John Higgins, S.J., Exec. Asst.; John T. Butler, S.J., Vocation Dir.; Robert J. Daly, S.J., Asst. for Higher Educ.; Thomas J. Feely, S.J., Asst. for Formation; Michael D. Linden, S.J., Asst. for Intl., Pastoral, & Social Ministries; James M. Shaughnessy, S.J., Liaison for Hospital Chaplaincy Ministry; Dennis J. Yesalonia, S.J., Treas.

Priests of Province on Special Assignment: Revs. Albert A. Agresti, S.J.; Ronald J. Amiot, S.J.; Robert J. Araujo, S.J.; John J. Begley, S.J.; I. Michael Bellafiore, S.J.; Richard D. Bertrand, S.J.; B. Jeffrey Blangiardi, S.J.; Richard P. Boyle, S.J.; Robert J. Braunreuther, S.J.; Scott N. Brodeur, S.J.; Joseph J. Bruce, S.J.; Mark J. Burke, S.J.; Paul E. Carrier, S.J.; Gregory C. Chisholm, S.J.; Thomas F. Clark, S.J.; Brian J. Conley, S.J.; Michael J. Connolly, S.J.; John T. Crabb, S.J.; John R. d'Anjou, S.J.; Terrence P. Devino, S.J.; Andrew N. Downing, S.J.; Theodore A. Dziak, S.J.; Gerald F. Finnegan, S.J.; Thomas J. Fitzpatrick, S.J.; Anthony J. Forte, S.J.; Andrew J. Garavel, S.J.; John F. Gavin, S.J.; Francois Gick, S.J.; David H. Gill, S.J.; Julio Giulietti, S.J.; Richard K. Gross, S.J.; William J. Hamilton, S.J.; Robert M. Hanlon, S.J.; G. Simon Harak, S.J.; Charles J. Healey, S.J.; Daniel P. Jamros, S.J.; John W. Keegan, S.J.; Charles F. Kelley, S.J.; Brian F. Linnane, S.J.; Daniel J. Lusch, S.J.; Leo M. Manglaviti, S.J.; Frederic A. Maples, S.J.; James J. Martin, S.J.; Richard B. McCafferty, S.J.; Frederick G. McLeod, S.J.; Ronald A. Mercier, S.J.; John W. Michalowski, S.J.; Matthew S. Monnig, S.J.; John J. Moriarty, S.J.; Francis J. Moy, S.J.; Thomas R. E. Murphy, S.J.; James C. O'Brien, S.J.; Joseph R. Palmisano, S.J.; Arthur H. Pare, S.J.; Normand A. Pepin, S.J.; James F.X. Pratt, S.J.; Robert F. Regan, S.J.; Very Rev. Thomas J. Regan, S.J.; Revs. Stephen J. Sanford, S.J.; Solomon I. Sara, S.J.; Joseph J. Schad, S.J.; Very Rev. Myles N. Sheehan, S.J.; Revs. John R. Siberski, S.J.; Edward J. Small, S.J.; Lawrence C. Smith, S.J.; Walter J. Smith, S.J.; John E. Surette, S.J.; Robert F. Taft, S.J.; Luis A. Tampe, S.J.; David O. Travers, S.J.; James F. Walsh, S.J.; Terrance G. Walsh, S.J.; Robert L. Keane, S.J., Chap.; John C. Monahan, S.J., Chap.

The Society of St. James the Apostle, Inc., 24 Clark St., 02109. Tel: 617-742-4715; Fax: 617-723-7389. Email: info@socstjames.com. Web: socstjames.com. Rev. Kevin Hays, Dir. Founded by His Eminence Richard Cardinal Cushing, in 1958 to recruit Diocesan Priest volunteers for South America. See American Foreign Missions section for Diocesan Priests serving in Latin America. In Res. Rev. Patrick Universal.

ANDOVER. *St. Francis Friary*, 459 River Rd., 01810. Tel: 978-851-3391; Fax: 978-858-0675. Email: franretc@aol.com. Web: www.franrcent.org. Bro. Robert Artman, O.F.M., Guardian. Order of Friars Minor. Total in Residence 7.

Community: Revs. John C. DiMauro, O.F.M.; Robert J. Caprio, O.F.M.; Bro. Charles Trebino, O.F.M.; Revs. Richard Donovan, O.F.M.; Roland Petinge, O.F.M.

BRIGHTON. *Divine Word Missionaries* (1875) 9 Olive St., #3, 02135. Tel: 617-202-5675; Fax: 617-202-5674. Revs. Donald Skerry, S.V.D., Rel. Supr.; Kenneth Feehan, S.V.D., Asst. Mission Dir. Divine Word Missionaries.

Priests of the Assumption, Inc., 330 Market St., 02135. Tel: 617-783-0400; Fax: 617-783-8030.

BROCKTON. *Chapel of Our Savior* (1961) 475 Westgate Dr., 02301-1819. Tel: 508-583-8357; Fax: 508-586-5510. Revs. Gerald DiGiralamo, S.A., Dir.; Henry Mair, S.A.; Malcolm Martin, S.A. (Retired); Norman Boyd, S.A.; Bros. Savio McNeice, S.A.; Louis Marek, S.A.; Thomas Banacki, S.A. Franciscan Friars of the Atonement. Priests 4; Brothers 3.

CAMBRIDGE. *Weston Jesuit Community*, 20 Sumner Rd., 02138. Tel: 617-547-3742; Fax: 617-868-8714. Priests 41; Brothers 2; Scholastics 23. *Claver House*, 7 Kirkland Rd., 02138-3012. Tel: 617-661-4155. Revs. Richard J. Clifford, S.J., Dean - Boston College School of Theology & Ministry; Christopher Frechette, S.J., Faculty - Boston College School of Theology & Ministry; John Karuvelil, S.J., Doctoral Student -Boston College School of Theology & Ministry; Rene Mario Micallef, S.J., Doctoral Student - Boston College School of Theology & Ministry. *Faber House*, 42 Kirkland St., 02138-2031. Tel: 617-497-5564. Revs. Arnel Aquino, S.J.; Cristian Del Campo, S.J.; Kenneth J. Hughes, S.J., Spiritual Dir. - Boston College School of Theology & Ministry; William L. Mulligan, S.J., Chap.; Bradley M. Schaeffer, S.J., Rector - Weston Jesuit Community; Balint Nagy, S.J. *Hopkins House*, 40 Kirkland St., 02138-2031. Tel: 617-868-6568. Revs. Jose Alexander Badiola, S.J.; Peter Pojol,

S.J.; Thomas D. Stegman, S.J., Faculty - Boston College School of Theology & Ministry; Edward V. Vacek, S.J., Faculty - Boston College School of Theology & Ministry; Gonzalo Villagran, S.J., Doctoral Student - Boston College School of Theology & Ministry; Arsene Brice Bado, S.J.; R. Benjamin Osborne, S.J. *Jogues House*, 12 Linnaean St., 02138-1613. Tel: 617-547-0931. Revs. Daniel J. Harrington, S.J., Faculty - Boston College School of Theology & Ministry; Rodrigo Esteban Zarazaga, S.J. *La Farge House*, 6 Sumner Rd., 02138-3015. Tel: 617-547-5310. Revs. Francis X. Clooney, S.J.; Germano Cord Neto, S.J.; John R. Sachs, S.J., Faculty - Boston College School of Theology & Ministry; Cyprian Tellis, S.J. *Rahner House*, 66 Oxford St., 02138-1940. Tel: 617-876-1233. Revs. Thomas Massaro, S.J., Faculty - Boston College School of Theology & Ministry; Francisco Jimenez Buendia; Fidele Ingiyimbere, S.J.; Pascal Rumb Musans, S.J. *St. Edmund's House*, 15 Avon St., 02138-1507. Tel: 617-492-3908. Revs. John Baldovin, S.J., Faculty - Boston College School of Theology & Ministry; Brian Banda, S.J.; Pierluigi DeLucia, S.J.; Christopher Hadley, S.J. *Zipoli House*, 10 Martin St., 02138. Tel: 617-491-2155. Revs. Vicente Chong, S.J.; James A. Gillon, S.J., Minister - Weston Jesuit Community; Henri Elphege Quenum, S.J.; Martin Sebo, S.J.

COHASSET. *Bellarmine House*, 150 Howard Gleason Rd., 02025. Tel: 781-383-0723; Fax: 781-383-3164. Rev. Michael F. Ford, S.J., Admin. (Summer Res. for Jesuits of New England Prov.).

DANVERS. *Xavier Center* (1975) 21 Spring St., 01923. Tel: 978-777-1326. Bro. John D. Hamilton, C.F.X., Dir. of Formation, House of Formation. Xaverian Brothers, U.S.A. Brothers Professed 4.

DEDHAM. *African Mission House* Society of African Missions, Inc., 337 Common St., 02026-4030. Tel: 781-326-3288; 781-326-4670; Fax: 781-326-7627. Email: smausa-d@ix.netcom.com. Web: www.smafathers.org. Revs. Ulick Bourke, S.M.A.; Anthony Fevlo, S.M.A.; Hugh Lagan, S.M.A. Priests 1.

DUXBURY. *Society of the Divine Word*, 121 Parks St., P.O. Box M, 02331-0614. Tel: 781-585-2460; Fax: 781-585-3770. Email: miramarma@aol.com. Web: www.miramarretreat.org. Bro. Donald Champagne, S.V.D., Dir., Rector; Revs. John J. Bergin, S.V.D.; Joseph Connolly, S.V.D.; John Farley, S.V.D.; Thomas Griffith, S.V.D.; James Heiar, S.V.D.; Robert M. Jones, S.V.D.; Robert Mallonee, S.V.D.; Thomas Umbras, S.V.D. Priests 8; Brothers 1; Total Staff 26.

HINGHAM. *Glastonbury Abbey* (1954) 16 Hull St., 02043. Tel: 781-749-2155; Fax: 781-749-6236. Email: office@glastonburyabbey.org. Web: www.glastonburyabbey.org. Revs. Mark F. Serna, O.S.B., Admin.; Nicholas J. Morcone, O.S.B.; Very Rev. Timothy J. Joyce, Prior; Revs. Andrew M. Quillen; John P. Kelleher, O.S.B.; Gerald T. Leibenguth, O.S.B.; Thomas J. O'Connor, Vocation Dir.; Bros. David K. Coakley, O.S.B., Music Dir.; James Crowley, O.S.B.; Daniel F. Walters, O.S.B., Conference Center Dir. Benedictine Monks., Benedictine Monastery. Priests 7; Brothers 3; Retreat House Capacity 32; Conference Center Capacity 180.

HOLLISTON. *Xaverian Missionaries*, 101 Summer St., P.O. Box 5857, 01746-5857. Tel: 508-429-2144; Fax: 508-429-4793. Email: pino_ma@hotmail.com. Web: www.xaviermissionaries.org. Revs. Giuseppe Matteucig, S.X., Supr.; Francis Signorelli, S.X.; Robert S. Maloney, S.X.; Gerard Furlan, S.X.; Tony B. Lalli, S.X. Priests 5.

LAWRENCE. *Franciscans of Primitive Observance*, 30 Trinity St., 01841. Revs. Peter Giroux, F.P.O.; Benedict Grant, F.P.O.; Andrew F. Beauregard, F.P.O.; Joseph Paul Medio, F.P.O.; John Maria Sweeney, F.P.O.; Bros. Pio Anthony Butti, F.P.O.; Sean Patrick Hurley, F.P.O.; Michael Francis Sheehan, F.P.O.; Lawrence Mary Stamm, F.P.O.; Felix Mary Waldren, F.P.O.; James Magdalen Wartman, F.P.O. Co-Redemptrix Friary.

Marist Brothers, 26 Leeds Ter., 01843. Tel: 978-686-7411. Bros. Kenneth Hogan, F.M.S.; Jerry Dowsky, F.M.S.; John Kachinsky, F.M.S.; Thomas P. Long, F.M.S. Brothers 4.

Marist Brothers Residence, 12 Sheridan St., 01841. Tel: 508-682-1163. Bros. William Lambert, F.M.S., Dir.; C. Vincent Dinnean, F.M.S.; Ernest Beland, F.M.S.; Richard Carey, F.M.S. Brothers 4.

LEXINGTON. *Priestly Fraternity of the Missionaries of St. Charles Borromeo, Inc.*, 21 Follen Rd., 02421-5921. Tel: 617-304-4324; 781-538-6181. Web: www.fraternityofsaintcharles.org. Rev. Antonio Lopez, F.S.C.B., Contact Person.

LOWELL. *Missionary Oblates of Mary Immaculate*, 27 Kirk St., 01852-1004. Tel: 978-937-9594; Fax: 978-458-3603. Email: garin.residence@juno.com; andregarinresidence@yahoo.com. *Andre Garin Retirement Residence* Tel: 978-937-9594; Fax: 978-458-3603. Email: garin.residence@juno.com. Bro. Charles Gilbert, O.M.I., Dir. Tel: 978-441-1245; Revs. Roland Couture, Asst. Dir.; Adhemar Deveau, O.M.I.; Donald G. Lozier, O.M.I.; Bros. Richard Cote, O.M.I.; Thomas Cruise, O.M.I.

Missionary Oblates of Mary Immaculate (1847) *Northeast / Southeast Area Office*, 60 Wyman St., 01852-2841. Tel: 978-458-9912; Fax: 978-458-7274. Email: suds@omiusa.org. Web: www.omiusa.org. Revs. Richard M. Sudlik, O.M.I., Area Councillor; George Brown, O.M.I.; Norman Comtois, O.M.I., Retreat Center; Wilfred Harvey, O.M.I., Pastoral School Chap.; John King, O.M.I., Hermitage; Roland St. Pierre, O.M.I. (Retired); William Sheehan, O.M.I., Preacher, Spiritual Dir.; Andre Tanguay, O.M.I. (Retired); Louis J. Villarreal, O.M.I., Preaher. Priests 103; Brothers 11; Total Staff 1; Total in Residence 8; Total Membership 113. *St. Eugene House (Residence)* (1995) 285 Andover St., 01852-1438. Tel: 978-441-0649; Fax: 978-454-0677. Revs. Charles Breault, O.M.I.; Herve Gagnon, O.M.I. (Retired); Dwight Hoeberechts, O.M.I., Dir. Oblate Vocation Office for Northeast/Southeast Areas; William Martin, O.M.I.; Richard M. Sudlik, O.M.I., Area Councillor; Lucien A. Sawyer, O.M.I., Chap.; William Sheehan, O.M.I., Supr.; Bro. Augustin Cote, O.M.I., Dir. Oblate Foreign Mission Office. *Oblate Foreign Mission Office, Northeast*, 60 Wyman St., 01852-2841. Tel: 978-458-4380; Fax: 978-458-7274. Email: oblate_missions_lowell@juno.com. Bro. Augustin Cote, O.M.I., Dir. *Oblate Vocation Office, Northeast / Southeast*, 60 Wyman St., 01852-2841. Tel: 978-458-9912; Fax: 978-458-7274. Email: flyingpadre1997@yahoo.com. Rev. Dwight Hoeberechts, O.M.I., Dir.

LYNN. *Franciscan Community (Province of Immaculate Conception)*, 38 Michigan Ave., 01902. Tel: 617-592-7396; Fax: 617-593-8805. Revs. Alphonse Ferreira, O.F.M., Procurator & Guardian; Bede Ferrara, O.F.M. *"The Listening Place" (Counseling Center)*, 36 Michigan Ave., 01902. Tel: 781-592-7396; Fax: 781-593-8805. Rev. Alphonse Ferreira, O.F.M., Dir.; Sr. Jane Hogan, O.S.F., Assoc. Dir.

MILTON. *Oblate Residence (St. Joseph House)*, 65 Fr. Carney Dr., 02186-4206. Tel: 617-698-6785; Fax: 617-698-7621. Web: www.omvusa.org. Revs. Dennis Brown, O.M.V.; John Ferrara, O.M.V.; Robert Lowrey, O.M.V.; Craig McMahon, O.M.V.; James Montanaro, O.M.V.; David Nicgorski, O.M.V.; David Yankauskas, O.M.V.; Bro. Joseph O'Connor, O.M.V. Congregation of the Oblates of the Virgin Mary. Priests 7; Brothers 1.

NEWTON. *The Jesuit Community at Boston College* (1863) 02467. Tel: 617-552-8200; Fax: 617-552-2380. Web: www.bc.edu/sj/. Very Rev. Myles N. Sheehan, S.J., Prov.; Revs. T. Frank Kennedy, S.J., Rector; Michael F. Ford, S.J., Asst. Rector & Admin.; Francis R. Herrmann, S.J., Asst. Rector; Edward M. O'Flaherty, S.J., Treas.; Joseph M. O'Keefe, S.J., Dean; James A. Woods, S.J., Dean; Stanislaus Alla, S.J.; Joseph A. Appleyard, S.J.; Nicholas Austin, S.J.; Albertus Bagus Laksana, S.J.; Casey C. Beaumier, S.J.; James W. Bernauer, S.J.; Richard Blake, S.J.; Michael Boughton, S.J.; James F. Bresnahan, S.J.; James T. Bretzke, S.J.; Emmanuel Bueya, S.J.; John Butler, S.J.; Lucas Chan, S.J.; Sammy Chong, S.J.; Jeremy Clarke, S.J.; Christopher S. Collins, S.J.; James J. Conn, S.J.; James Conroy, S.J.; Robert J. Daly, S.J.; Richard A. Deshaies, S.J.; Trung Hoa Dinh, S.J.; George Drury, S.J.; Joseph P. Duffy, S.J.; Harvey D. Egan, S.J.; Frederick Enman, S.J.; Michael A. Fahey, S.J.; Robert Farrell, S.J.; Joseph F. X. Flanagan, S.J.; James Fleming, S.J.; Gary Gurtler, S.J.; Raymond G. Helmick, S.J.; Juan Carlos Henriquez, S.J.; John Higgins, S.J.; Kenneth Himes, O.F.M.; David Hollenbach, S.J.; Jiang Joseph, S.J.; Gregory Kalscheur, S.J.; James Keenan, S.J.; Thomas J. Kenny, S.J.; Kevin Kersten, S.J.; Philip Kiley, S.J.; William P. Leahy, S.J., Ph.D., Pres.; Joseph Lehman, T.O.R.; John Allan Loftus, S.J.; Kenneth G. Loftus, S.J.; Donald A. MacMillan, S.J.; Arthur R. Madigan, S.J.; Bienvenu Mayemba, S.J.; Richard A. McGowan, S.J.; John P. McIntyre, S.J.; Paul McNellis, S.J.; William W. Meissner, S.J.; Paul A. Messer, S.J.; Misael Meza, S.J.; J. Donald Monan, S.J.; John P. Murray, S.J.; William B. Neenan, S.J.; Gerard C. O'Brien, S.J.; Taegon-Seil Oh, S.J.; Cyril Opeil, S.J.; John Paris, S.J.; Frank J. Parker, S.J.; Roy Pereira, S.J.; Darlusz Piorkowski, S.J.; Donald J. Plocke, S.J.; William J. Richardson, S.J.; M. Ross Romero, S.J.; William C. Russell, S.J.; Stephen Schloesser, S.J.; Francis A. Sullivan, S.J.; Tone Svetelj, S.J. (Slovenia); Ronald K. Tacelli, S.J.; Thomas Tjaya, S.J. (Indonesia); Robert F. VerEecke, S.J.; Andrea Vicini, S.J.; Quyen Kim Vu, S.J.; John C. Wronski, S.J.

PEABODY. *Our Lady of the Scapular Priory* (1970) 4 Wheatland St., 01960. Tel: 978-532-2891; Fax: 978-532-1040. Revs. Herbert J. Jones, O.Carm., Chapel Dir.; Felix Prior, O.Carm.; Mario Lopez, O.Carm.; Bro. Damien Chong, O.Carm. Priests 5; Brothers 1.

SOMERVILLE. *Brotherhood of Hope* (1980) 194 Summer St., 02143-2525. Tel: 617-623-9592; Fax: 617-625-1837. Email: bohinfo@brohope.net. Web: www.brotherhoodofhope.org. Brothers 5; Brothers Elsewhere 10; Priests 3; Total in Residence 8.

TEWKSBURY. *Oblate World/Missionary Association of Mary Immaculate*, 486 Chandler St., 01876-0680. Tel: 978-858-0434; Fax: 978-858-3661. Email: oblateworld@omires.com. Rev. Richard M. Sudlik, O.M.I., Editor & Dir.

WALTHAM. *Bertoni Hall - Formation House* Bertoni Hall, 554 Lexington, 02452-3097. Tel: 781-209-3100. Web: www.stigmatines.com. Revs. Joseph Henchey, C.S.S., Senior Priest; Nicholas Spagnolo, C.S.S.

Stigmatine Fathers & Brothers Provincial House, 554 Lexington St., 02452. Tel: 718-209-3100; Fax: 781-894-9785. Web: www.stigmatines.com. Revs. Gregory J. Hoppough, C.S.S., M.Div., S.T.L., S.T.D., M.A., Prof. Blessed John XXIII Sem.; Peter Piamote Chinnacode, C.S.S. (Thailand); Charles Dolan, C.S.S. (Thailand); Richard Woodarek, C.S.S. (Thailand); Robert Masciocchi, C.S.S. Total Staff 4.

WESTON. *Campion Health Center, Inc.*, 319 Concord Rd., 02493-1398. Tel: 781-788-6800; Fax: 781-894-5864. *Covenant Health Systems*, 420 Bedford St., Lexington, 02420. Revs. Paul D. Holland, S.J., Rector; Ronald E. Wozniak, S.J., Min.; Dudley R. C. Adams, S.J.; Francis R. Allen, S.J.; Joseph F. Brennan, S.J.; Albert A. Cardoni, S.J.; Joseph H. Casey, S.J.; Richard T. Cleary, S.J.; James M. Collins, S.J.; William J. Connolly, S.J.; Lawrence E. Corcoran, S.J.; Charles G. Crowley, S.J.; William J. Cullen, S.J.; Stephen F. Dawber, S.J.; Neil F. Decker, S.J.; Alfred R. Desautels, S.J.; John F. Devane, S.J.; William G. Devine, S.J.; Joseph D. Devlin, S.J.; James J. Dressman, S.J.; George A. Duffy, S.J.; Joseph G. Fennell, S.J.; Thomas J. Gallagher, S.J.; Paul P. Gilmartin, S.J.; John B. Handrahan, S.J.; Edward J. Hanrahan, S.J.; Philip K. Harrigan, S.J.; John J. Karwin, S.J.; John B. Kerdiejus, S.J.; Donald L. Larkin, S.J.; Joseph R. Laughlin, S.J.; Robert E. Lindsay, S.J.; Paul T. Lucey, S.J.; James B. Malley, S.J.; John J. Mandile, S.J.; Stanley B. Marrow, S.J.; Martin F. McCarthy, S.J.; Paul T. McCarty, S.J.; J. Joseph McGrath, S.J.; Joseph B. McHugh, S.J.; James F. Morgan, S.J.; Francis J. Nicholson, S.J.; Francis J. O'Neill, S.J.; Lawrence J. O'Toole, S.J.; Joseph A. Paquet, S.J.; Ernest F. Passero, S.J.; Anthony R. Picariello, S.J.; William J. Raftery, S.J.; Richard W. Rousseau, S.J.; Patrick J. Ryan, S.J.; Francis X. Sarjeant, S.J.; James W. Skehan, S.J.; Wilfrid J. Vigeant, S.J.; Bros. Edward P. Babinski, S.J.; Vincent M. Brennan, S.J.; H. Francis Cluff, S.J.; Edward L. Niziolek, S.J.; Italo A. Parnoff, S.J. Priests 54; Brothers 5; Total in Community 59.

Campion Jesuit Community, 319 Concord Rd., 02493. Tel: 781-788-6800; Fax: 781-894-5864. Revs. Paul D. Holland, S.J., Rector; Ronald E. Wozniak, S.J., Min.; James R. Mattaliano, S.J., Dir., Renewal Ctr.; William A. Barry, S.J.; Harry J. Cain, S.J.; Ned H. Cassem, S.J.; John T. Crabb, S.J.; Robert G. Doherty, S.J.; William B. Foley, S.J.; Robert G. Gilroy, S.J.; Edward F. Howard, S.J.; John W. Howard, S.J.; William D. Ibach, S.J.; Paul C. Kenney, S.J.; Michael D. Linden, S.J.; Joseph B. McHugh, S.J.; Francis J. McManus, S.J.; Leo M. Manglaviti, S.J.; John J. Moriarty, S.J.; George B. Murray, S.J.; Joseph V. Owens, S.J.; Robert V. Paskey, S.J.; James F. Talbot, S.J.; Thomas Vallamattam, S.J.; E. Corbett Walsh, S.J.; John J. Walsh, S.J.; Kevin R. White, S.J.; George T. Williams, S.J.; Alfred O. Winshman, S.J.; Bros. Theodore C. Bender, S.J.; Calvin A. Clarke, S.J. *Campion Residence & Renewal Center, Inc.* Priests 28; Brothers 2; Total Staff 30.

[V] CONVENTS AND RESIDENCES FOR SISTERS

BOSTON. *The Congregation of the Sisters of Our Lady of Mercy*, 241 Neponset Ave., 02122. Tel: 617-288-1202; Fax: 617-288-1177. Email: mercy@sisterfaustina.org. Web: www.sisterfaustina.org. Sr. M. Saula Firer, Local Supr. Professed Sisters 8.

Daughters of St. Paul Inc. (1915) 50 St. Paul's Ave., 02130-3491. Tel: 617-522-8911; Fax: 617-524-8648. Email: usaprov@paulinemedia.org. Web: www.pauline.org.

Daughters of St. Paul, Inc. Novitiate,

Provincialate Headquarters, and Publishing House for U.S. Prov. Community 7; Perpetually Professed Sisters 58; Novices 2.

Pauline Book & Media Center (1988) 885 Providence Hwy., Dedham, 02026. Tel: 781-326-5385; Fax: 781-461-1013.

Franciscan Missionary Sisters for Africa (1957) (USA Headquarters and only house.), 172 Foster St., Box 35095, Brighton, 02135. Tel: 617-254-4343; Fax: 617-787-8007. Email: brightonsisters172@yahoo.com; connorju46@yahoo.com. Web: www.members.aol.com/sisters172/fmsa.html. Serving in Uganda, Kenya, Zambia, Zimbabwe, and South Africa. Completely a Missionary congregation. Sisters 7.

Franciscan Monastery of St. Clare, The (1906) 920 Centre St., 02130. Tel: 617-524-1760; Fax: 617-983-5205. Email: bostonpoorclares@yahoo.com. Web: www.StAnthonyShrine.org/PoorClares. Sr. Clare Frances McAvoy, O.S.C., Abbess. Franciscan Poor Clare Nuns., Solemn Vows. Cloistered Solemnly Professed 18; Extern Sisters 2.

Little Sisters of the Assumption Convent (1947) 65 Magnolia St., 02125. Tel: 617-442-9411. Email: mleonard@prohope.org. Web: www.littlesisters.org.

Little Sisters of the Assumption

Missionary Sisters of St. Columban, 73 Mapleton St., 02135. Tel: 617-782-5683; Fax: 617-789-3569. Email: columbansbrighton@verizon.net. Web: columbansistersusa.com. Sr. Margaret Holleran, S.C.C., U.S. Area Coord.

Missionary Sisters of Saint Columban Professed Sisters 8.

Monastery of Discalced Carmelites (1890) 61 Mt. Pleasant Ave., 02119. Tel: 617-442-1411; Fax: 617-442-0203. Email: bostoncarmel@juno.com. Web: www.carmelitesofboston.org. Sr. Eileen Mary, O.C.D., Prioress. Cloistered. Professed 10; Novices 1.

Motherhouse of the Sisters of St. Joseph of Boston (1873) 631 Cambridge St., 02135. Tel: 617-783-9090; Fax: 617-783-8246. Email: bostoncsj@csjboston.org. Web: www.csjboston.org. Admin. Offices - 637 Cambridge St. Total in Residence 82.

Sister Disciples of the Divine Master (1924) Convent and Eucharistic Center, 43 West St., 02111. Tel: 482-682-0978; 482-423-2629; Fax: 482-682-3779. Email: sddmboston@aol.com. Web: www.pddm.us. Sr. Josephine Fallon, Supr. Sisters 12.

Sisters of Notre Dame de Namur (Boston Province Offices), 351 Broadway, Everett, 02149-3425. Tel: 617-387-2500; Fax: 617-387-1303. Email: boadministrator@sndden.org. Web: www.sndden.org/boston. Total in Community 206. Provincial Team: Sisters Rosemary Crowley, S.N.D.deN., Prov. Admin.; Evelyn McKenna, S.N.D.deN., Prov. Admin.; Patricia McSharry, S.N.D.deN., Prov. Admin.; Anne M. Donovan, S.N.D.deN., Treas.

Sisters of the Eucharistic Heart of Jesus, St. Patrick's Convent, 115 Mt. Pleasant Ave., 02110. Tel: 617-427-0985; Cell: 617-767-9097. Email: ehjsistersboston@verizon.net; ehisistersboston@netzero.net; convewuche@yahoo.com. Web: www.ehjsrsboston.org.

Sisters of the Good Shepherd, 35 Tyndale St., 02131. Tel: 617-469-2492; Fax: 617-469-9857. Email: smhrgs@verizon.net. Sisters 3.

ANDOVER. *Monastery of St. Clare*, 445 River Rd., 01810-4213. Tel: 978-683-7599; Fax: 978-683-6085. Sr. Therese Marie Lacroix, O.S.C., Abbess. Poor Clare Nuns. Cloistered Solemnly Professed 12; Extern Perpetually Professed 3; In Perpetual Vows 1; Extern in Temporary Vows 1.

BELMONT. *US Federation of Sisters of St. Joseph*, 11 Davis St., 02478-5029. Tel: 617-484-1801. Email: cssjfedkathy@aol.com. Web: www.sistersofsaintjosephfederation.org. Sr. Kathleen McCluskey, C.S.J., Exec. Dir.

BRIGHTON. *Franciscan Missionaries of Mary* (1990) 284 Foster St., Boston, 02135. Tel: 617-787-1505; Fax: 617-787-1982. Email: nkloanfmm@yahoo.com. Sr. Lois A. Pereira, F.M.M., Prov.

(1990) 3305 Wallace Ave., Bronx, NY 10467-6599. Tel: 718-547-4693; Fax: 718-547-4607. Sr. Lois A. Pereira, F.M.M., Prov.

BROCKTON. *Our Lady of Sorrows Convent*, 261 Thatcher St., 02302-3997. Tel: 508-588-5070; Fax: 508-580-6770. Email: mjv@cjcbrockton.org. Web: www.cjcbrockton.org. Sr. Mary Valliere, C.J.C., Gen. Supr. Poor Sisters of Jesus Crucified and the Sorrowful Mother. Sisters 25.

CAMBRIDGE. *Sancta Maria Convent*, 799 Concord Ave., 02138. Tel: 617-868-2200, Ext. 2950 (Convent); 617-868-2200, Ext. 2100 (Office); Fax: 617-864-2801.

CHELSEA. *Don Guanella Center, Inc., Daughters of St. Mary of Providence* (1982) 37 Nichols St., 02150. Tel: 617-889-0179; Fax: 617-889-3363. Email: dgcenter.chelsea2@verizon.net. Web: www.donguanellacenter.com. Sr. Rhonda Brown, D.S.M.P., Dir. of Center. Family Support Respite for Developmentally Handicapped Women (ages 18 & older). Sisters 2; Families 70; Total Staff 12.

DANVERS. *Discalced Carmelite Monastery* (1958) 15 Mt. Carmel Rd., 01923-3796. Tel: 978-774-3008; Fax: 978-774-7409. Sr. Anne of the Mother of God, O.C.D., Prioress. Total in Residence 16.

DEDHAM. *Ursuline Convent, Inc.*, 65 Lowder St., 02026-4205. Tel: 781-326-3158; Fax: 781-326-4428. Email: nestabeaudoin@verizon.net. Sr. Mercedes Videira, O.S.U., Prioress. Sisters 7.

Ursuline Provincialate (1947) 45 Lowder St., 02026-4200. Tel: 781-326-7296; Fax: 781-326-7296. Email: provosu@verizon.net. Sr. Angela Krippendorf, O.S.U., Prov. Ursulines of the Roman Union, Northeastern Province 30.

DORCHESTER. *Franciscan Sisters of the Atonement*, 651 Adamst St., 02122. Tel: 617-740-0614; Fax: 617-740-0603.

IPSWICH. *Sisters of Notre Dame de Namur Generalate Office*, 30 Jeffrey's Neck Rd., 01938. Tel: 978-356-2159; Fax: 978-356-1034. Email: connell@sndden.org. Web: www.sndden.org. Sr. Lorraine Connell, S.N.D.deN., Gen. Treas.

Casa Generalizia di Suore di Nostra Signora di Namur, Via Raffaello Sardiello, 20, Rome 00165 Italy. Tel: 39-06-6641-8704; Fax: 39-06-6641-8709. Sr. Teresita Weind, S.N.D.deN., Gen. Moderator. (Generalate)

The Sisters of Notre Dame de Namur Congregational Mission Office, Inc., 30 Jeffrey's Neck Rd., 01938. Tel: 978-356-2159; Fax: 978-356-1034.

Sisters of Notre Dame de Namur (Provincial Residence) (1804) 30 Jeffreys Neck Rd., 01938-1308. Tel: 978-380-1372; Fax: 978-356-9759. Email: mary.farren@sndden.org. Web: www.sndden.org. Sisters 76; Total Staff 62. Provincial Leadership Team: Sisters Mary M. Farren, S.N.D.deN., Prov. Admin.; Mary Boretti, S.N.D.deN., Prov. & Admin.; Andrea Walsh, S.N.D.deN., Prov. & Admin.

KINGSTON. *Congregation of the Sisters of Divine Providence* (1851) Providence House, 363 Bishops Hwy., 02364. Tel: 781-585-7707; Fax: 781-582-1596. Email: cdpward@comcast.net. Sr. Claudia Ward, C.D.P., Area Asst.

LEXINGTON. *Congregation of Armenian Catholic Sisters of Immaculate Conception, Inc.*, 6 Eliot Rd., 02173. Tel: 781-863-5962; Fax: 781-862-8479. Sisters 3.

Grey Nuns Area Offices, 10 Pelham Rd., Ste. 1000, 02421-8499. Tel: 781-674-7401; Fax: 781-861-9641. Email: srjuneketterer@sgmlex.org. Web: www.grey-nuns. Headquarters (U.S.A. Region) of the Sisters of Charity of Montreal. "Grey Nuns".

General Administration, 138 Rue Saint-Pierre, Montreal QC H2Y 2L7 Canada. Tel: 514-842-9411; Fax: 514-842-7855. Sr. June Ketterer, S.G.M., Area Coord. Sisters 3.

LOWELL. *St. Joseph Provincial House*, 559 Fletcher St., 01854-3434. Tel: 978-458-4472; Fax: 978-441-1452. Email: prleblanc2@comcast.net. Web: www.soeursdelachariteottowa.com. Sr. Pauline LeBlanc, S.C.O., Prov. Supr. Sisters of Charity of Ottawa (Grey Nuns of the Cross); D'Youville Senior Care Center, Lowell; Saints Medical Center, Lowell. Sisters 24.

MARLBOROUGH. *Sisters of St. Anne, Provincialate* (1850) 720 Boston Post Rd. E., 01752. Tel: 508-481-4934; Fax: 508-481-4939. Email: srybellerose@yahoo.com. Web: www.ssacong.org. Headquarters of American Province. Sisters 115.

Community of the Sisters of Saint Anne Tel: 508-481-4934; Fax: 508-481-4939. *St. Anne Convent*, 720 Boston Post Rd. E., 01752. Tel: 508-485-3791; Fax: 508-481-4939. Sisters 58.

Sisters of St. Chretienne (1807) 197 Pleasant St., 01752-1169. Tel: 508-485-0740; Fax: 508-481-0663. Email: chretienne@verizon.net. Web: www.sistersofstchretienne.org. Sr. Jeannette Desorcy, S.S.Ch., Local Coord. House of Retirement. Sisters 30.

Sisters of St. Chretienne, 207 Pleasant St., 01752-1169. Tel: 508-229-3505; Fax: 508-481-0663.

Sisters of the Good Shepherd, 406 Hemenway St., 01752. Tel: 508-485-8610; Fax: 508-460-6372. Sr. Theresa Marie O'Leary, Contact Person & Pastoral Care. Sisters 29.

METHUEN. *Presentation of Mary*, 209 Lawrence St., 01844. Tel: 978-687-1369; Fax: 978-975-1998. Email: prov.methuen@verizon.net. Web: www.presmarymethuen.org. Sr. Cecile Plasse, P.M., Prov. Supr. Presentation of Mary Academy. Sisters 103; Total in Residence 77.

MILTON. *Holy Union Sisters* (1826) *Province Office*, 444 Centre St., P.O. Box 410, 02186-0006. Tel: 617-696-8765; Fax: 617-696-8571. Web: www.holyunionsisters.org. Sisters Mary Catherine Burns, S.U.S.C., Province Mission Team; Paula Coelho, S.U.S.C., Province Mission Team; Maryellen Ryan, S.U.S.C., Province Mission Team.

NEWTON. *Immaculate Conception Provincialate* (1873) 790 Centre St., 02458-2530. Tel: 617-527-1004; Fax: 617-527-2528. Email: mfic@mficusa.org. Web: www.mficusa.org. Missionary Franciscan Sisters of the Immaculate Conception. Total in Residence 3; Total Staff 4.

Mt. Alvernia Convent (1873) 790 Centre St., 02458-2530. Tel: 617-969-4766; Fax: 617-527-2528. Email: mtalverniaconvent@comcast.net. Web: www.mficusa.org. Sisters 22; Staff 3.

SOMERVILLE. *Medical Missionaries of Mary, Inc.* (1937) 179 Highland Ave., 02143. Tel: 617-666-3223; Fax: 617-666-1877. Email: mmmsomerville@comcast.net. Web: www.mmmusa.org. Medical Missionaries of Mary Motherhouse, Beechgrove, Drogheda, Ireland. Professed Sisters 10.

WAKEFIELD. *Mother Saint Joseph House*, 7 Emerson St., 01880. Tel: 781-246-2194, Ext. 12; Fax: 781-224-0644. Email: rosemary.crowley@sndden.org. Sisters Rosemary Crowley, S.N.D.deN., Pres.; Marna Rogers, S.N.D.deN., Community Coord. Sponsored by the Sisters of Notre Dame de Namur (Boston). Sisters 15; Staff 20.

WALTHAM. *Marist Missionary Sisters*

Missionary Sisters of the Society of Mary, Inc., S.M.S.M. Provincial Offices, 349 Grove St., 02453-6018. Tel: 781-893-0149; Fax: 781-899-6838. Email: maristsmsm@aol.com. Web: www.maristmissionarysmsm.org. *Residence for Senior Sisters*, 62 Newton St., 02453-6058. Tel: 781-893-3960. Sisters 30.

Marillac Residence, 125 Oakland St., Wellesley, 02481-5338. Sisters 17.

Bethany Health Care Centre, 97 Bethany Rd., Framingham, 01702-7296. Tel: 508-872-6750. Sisters 3.

Maristhill Nursing Home, 66 Newton St., 02453-6058. Sisters 4.

Other Local Communities: 21 Beech St., Belmont, 02478-1299. Tel: 617-489-3587. Sisters 5. 4 Craig St., Framingham, 01701-7664. Tel: 508-877-7371. Sisters 3. 357 Grove St., 02453-6018. Tel: 781-899-3839. Sisters 6. 88 Lexington St., 02452. Sisters 3.

Religious of Christian Education, Inc., 68 Lafayette St., Apt. A, 02453-6829. Tel: 781-899-6292; Fax: 781-899-6293. Email: yvettetrce@aol.com. Sr. Yvette Rivard, R.C.E., Contact Person.

Sisters of the Good Shepherd, 83-85 Lake St., 02451. Tel: 781-891-7688; Fax: 617-471-6622. Email: elishmcpar@aol.com. Sr. Elish McPartland, Contact Person.

WATERTOWN. *Rosary Manor*, One Rosary Dr., 02472. Tel: 617-924-1717; Fax: 617-924-8118. Email: rosmanor@juno.com. Sr. Mary Elizabeth Thompson, O.P., Coord. Total in Residence 19; Total Staff 1.

WELLESLEY. *Marillac Residence, Inc.*, 125 Oakland St., Wellesley Hills, 02481-5338. Tel: 781-997-1165; Fax: 781-237-8152. Email: crowleyk28@aol.com. Web: www.schalifax.ca. Sr. Kathleen Crowley, S.C. Sisters of Charity (Halifax).

Mount St. Vincent Retirement Community, 125 Oakland St., Wellesley Hills, 02481-5338. Tel: 781-997-1165; Fax: 781-237-8152. Email: crowleyk28@aol.com. Web: www.schalifax.com. Sisters Eleanor Ballantine, S.C., Community Leadership Team. Tel: 781-997-1165; Fax: 781-237-8152; Kathleen Crowley, S.C., Community Leadership Team. Tel: 781-997-1165; Fax: 791-237-8152; Maureen Murphy, S.C., Community Leadership Team. Tel: 781-997-1165; Fax: 781-237-8152. Sisters of Charity (Halifax).

Sisters of Charity (Halifax) Supporting Corporation (1977) 125 Oakland St., 02481-5338. Tel: 781-997-1126; Fax: 781-235-8065. Sr. Donna Geernaert, Congregational Leader.

WELLESLEY HILLS. *Elizabeth Seton Residence, Inc.*, 125 Oakland St., 02481. Tel: 781-237-2161; Fax: 781-431-2589. Email: eseton@schalifax.org. Web: www.Elizabethseton.org. Ms. Phyllis A. Tedesco, Admin. Sisters of Charity of St. Vincent de Paul, Halifax, Nova Scotia, Canada., 84 Bed Skilled Nursing & Rehab Facility. Medicare-Medicaid Certified.

Sisters of Charity (Halifax) (1849) (Boston Office), 125 Oakland St., 02481. Tel: 781-997-1355; Fax: 781-997-1358. Email: smclaughlin@schalifax.ca; aregan@schalifax.ca. Web: www.schalifax.ca. Sisters Sally McLaughlin, S.C.H., Congregational Councilor; Ann Regan, Congregational Councilor; Marjory Gallagher, Congregational Councillor & Sec.

Sisters of Charity (Halifax) Corporate Mission, Inc., 125 Oakland St., 02481. Tel: 781-997-1100. Email: dgeernaert@schalifax.ca. Web: www.schalifax.ca. Sr. Donna Geernaert, Congregational Leader.

WRENTHAM. *St. Chretienne Provincialate* (1807) 297 Arnold St., 02093-1798. Tel: 508-384-7841; 508-384-8066; Fax: 508-384-3170. Email: ssch@tiac.net. Web: sistersofstchretienne.org. Sisters of St. Chretienne. Sisters 3; Total in Residence 3.

Mount St. Mary's Abbey (1949) 300 Arnold St., 02093. Tel: 508-528-1282; Fax: 508-528-5360. Email: sisters@msmabbey.org. Web: www.msmabbey.org. Sr. Maureen McCabe, O.C.S.O., Abbess.

The Cistercians of the Strict Observance in Massachusetts, Inc. The Cistercian Nuns of the Strict Observance (Trappistines). Professed Sisters 42; Total in Residence 45.

[W] RETREAT HOUSES

ANDOVER. *Franciscan Center - Retreat House*, 459 River Rd., 01810. Tel: 978-851-3391; Fax: 978-858-0675. Email: franretc@aol.com. Web: www.franrcent.org. Bro. Robert Artman, O.F.M., Guardian & Dir. Retreats; Revs. Richard Donovan, O.F.M., Asst. Dir. Retreats; John C. DiMauro, O.F.M., Retreat Team; Robert J. Caprio, O.F.M., Chap., St. Elizabeth Hospital; Bro. Charles Trebino, O.F.M., Retreat Team; Rev. Roland Petinge, O.F.M. Order of Friars Minor. Total in Residence 6; Total Staff 2.

COHASSET. *St. Joseph Retreat Center*, 339 Jerusalem Rd., 02025. Tel: 781-383-6024; 781-383-6029. Email: retreat.center@csjboston.org. Web: www.csjretreatcenter.org. Sr. Joan M. McCarthy, C.S.J., Co-Dir.; Eileen Moran, Co-Dir.; Sr. Joan Duffy, C.S.J., Asst. Program Coord.; Jean Martin, Admin. Asst. Sisters of St. Joseph 2.

DUXBURY. *Miramar Retreat Center*, 121 Parks St., P.O. Box M, 02331-0614. Tel: 781-585-2460; Fax: 781-585-3770. Email: miramarma@aol.com. Web: www.miramarretreat.org. Bro. Donald Champagne, S.V.D., Dir., Rector. Total in Residence 11; Total Staff 28.

FRAMINGHAM. *The Marist House*, 518 Pleasant St., 01701. Tel: 508-879-1620; Fax: 508-879-1132. Email: director@themarists.org. Web: themarists.org. Revs. Raymond E. Coolong, S.M., Supr. & Dir.; Robert E. Champagne, S.M.; Joseph S. Chasse, S.M. (Retired); Raymond A. Fournier, S.M. (Retired); Walter Gaudreau, S.M.; Robert Graham, S.M.; Adrien O. Pelletier, S.M. (Retired); Bros. Roland Bernier, S.M., (Retired); Leonard Haley, S.M. Total in Residence 9; Total Staff 3.

GLOUCESTER. *Eastern Point Retreat House*, Gonzaga, 37 Niles Pond Rd., 01930. Tel: 978-283-0013; Fax: 978-282-1989. Email: office@easternpoint.org. Web: www.easternpoint.org. Revs. James P. Carr, S.J., Dir.; Joseph McHugh, S.J.; Richard J. Stanley, S.J.; Paul M. Sullivan, S.J.; Sr. Madeline Tiberii, S.S.J. Priests 4; Sisters 1; Total Staff 5.

SCITUATE. *Foyer of Charity* (1977) 74 Hollett St., 02066. Tel: 781-545-1080; Fax: 240-332-5826. Email: info@foyerofcharity.com. Web: www.foyerofcharity.com. Rev. Matthew Bradley, Dir. Total in Residence 1; Total Staff 6.

WALTHAM. *Espousal Retreat House and Conference Center*, 554 Lexington St., 02452. Tel: 781-209-3120; Fax: 781-893-0291. Email: espousaladmin@gmail.com. Web: www.espousal.org. Rev. Robert Masciocchi, C.S.S., Dir. Stigmatine Fathers and Brothers., Weekend and Weekly Retreats, Days-Evenings of Recollection. Total in Residence 2; Total Staff 10.

WESTON. *Campion Renewal Center* (1975) 319 Concord Rd., 02493-1398. Tel: 781-419-1337; Fax: 781-894-5864. Email: acopponi@campioncenter.org. Web: www.campioncenter.org. Revs. James R. Mattaliano, S.J., Dir.; James R. Mattaliano, S.J., Staff Member. Total in Residence 2; Total Staff 2.

[X] RETIREMENT RESIDENCES FOR PRIESTS AND BROTHERS

BOSTON. *Saint Anthony Residence*, 103 Arch St., 02110-1102. Tel: 617-542-6454; Fax: 617-778-5882. Revs. Bernardine Kessing, O.F.M. (Retired); Callistus Bamberg, O.F.M. (Retired); Leo Clifford, O.F.M. (Retired); Thomas R. Hartle, O.F.M.; Vianney Devlin, O.F.M., Vicar (Retired); Stephen Doyle, O.F.M. (Retired); Carmel F. Miotke, O.F.M. (Retired); Kenan Morris, O.F.M. (Retired); Reginald Redlon, O.F.M. (Retired); Cyril Seaman, O.F.M. (Retired); Bros. William G. Fitzgerald, O.F.M., Guardian/Dir.; Albert Aldrich, O.F.M., (Retired); Nathnael Necaster, O.F.M., (Retired); Brian J. Hart, O.F.M. (For Retired Franciscan Friars.) Priests 11; Brothers 4; Retired 14; Total in Residence 15.

Regina Cleri Residence, 60 William Cardinal O'Connell Way, 02114. Tel: 617-523-1861; Fax: 617-720-0585. Email: sgust@reginacleri.org. Mr. Stephen J. Gust, Exec. Dir. Residence for Retired Archdiocesan Priests. Priests 57; Sisters 3.

TEWKSBURY. *Immaculate Heart of Mary Residence*, 486 Chandler St., 01876-2899. Tel: 978-851-7258; Fax: 978-851-0952. Email: tmohan@omires.com. Revs. T. Francis Bagan, O.M.I.; Charles Beausoleil, O.M.I.; Marcel Bolduc, O.M.I.; Richard Bolduc, O.M.I.; Chester J. Cappucci, O.M.I.; Raymond Crowe, O.M.I.; Lawrence Deery, O.M.I.; Francis Demers, O.M.I.; Michael J. Devaney, O.M.I.; Gerald Flater, O.M.I.; James Flavin, O.M.I.; Francis X. Gorham, O.M.I.; Richard Harr, O.M.I.; Patrick F. Healy, O.M.I.; Andre Houle, O.M.I.; Albert P. Martineau, O.M.I.; Richard McAlear, O.M.I.; John F. Mc Hugh, O.M.I.; William McSweeney, O.M.I.; Francis Ouellette, O.M.I.; Joseph A. Ryan, O.M.I.; William P. Smith, O.M.I.; Raymond Steen, O.M.I.; Bros. Robert Dutil, O.M.I.; Joseph Gagne, O.M.I.; James H. Lucas, O.M.I.; Lorenzo Williams, O.M.I. Priests 24; Brothers 4.

WALTHAM. *Stigmatine Fathers and Brothers*, St. Joseph's Hall, 554 Lexington St., 02452. Tel: 781-209-3100; Fax: 781-209-3070. Web: www.stigmatines.com. Revs. Gregory J. Hoppough, C.S.S., M.Div., S.T.L., S.T.D., M.A., Prof., Blessed John XXIII Sem.; Joseph M. Connolly, C.S.S. (Retired); James Cunningham, C.S.S. (Retired); Leonard Fereochia, C.S.S. (Retired); James E. Flanagan, C.S.S. (Retired); Henry Linse, C.S.S. (Retired); David F. Gallagher, C.S.S. (Retired). Priests 6.

[Y] RESIDENCES FOR MEN AND WOMEN

BOSTON. *St. Helena House*, 89 Union Park St., 02118. Tel: 617-426-2922; Fax: 617-542-3460. James A. Smith, Property Mgr. Seniors, low income & disabled persons. Residents 99.

Our Lady's Guild House - Residence for Women, 20 Charlesgate W., 02215. Tel: 617-536-3000; Fax: 617-536-8508. Andrea Beall, Admin. Daughters of Mary of the Immaculate Conception 1; Residents 126.

BRIGHTON. *Archdiocesan Central High Schools, Inc.*, 66 Brooks Dr., 02184-3839. Tel: 617-746-5855; Fax: 617-782-0213. His Eminence Sean Cardinal O'Malley, O.F.M.Cap.

[Z] PUBLIC ORATORIES AND CHAPELS

BOSTON. *St. Anthony Shrine* 100 Arch St., 02110. Tel: 617-542-6440; Fax: 617-542-4225. Email: info@StAnthonyShrine.org. Web: www.StAnthonyShrine.org. Revs. David Convertino, O.F.M., Guardian & Exec. Dir.; Raphael Bonanno, O.F.M.; Brennan Connelly, O.F.M.; Charles Finnegan, O.F.M.; Richard C. Flaherty, O.F.M.; Fergus Healey, O.F.M.; John P. Hogan, O.F.M.; Barry J. Langley, O.F.M.; Paul Lostritto, O.F.M.; Hugh Macsherry, O.F.M.; Raymond Mann, O.F.M.; Myron McCormick, O.F.M.; Donan McGovern, O.F.M.; Francis McHugh, O.F.M.; Emeric Meier, O.F.M.; Philip O'Shea, O.F.M.; Gene Pistacchio, O.F.M.; Flavian A. Walsh, O.F.M.; Bros. Gregory Day, O.F.M.; Thomas Donovan, O.F.M.; Dominic Finneran, O.F.M.; Justus Frazier, O.F.M.; John Jaskowiak, O.F.M.; Gary Maciag, O.F.M.; John Maganzini, O.F.M.; Thomas McGowan, O.F.M.; Daniel Murray, O.F.M. Priests 18; Brothers 9.

Chapel of Our Lady of Lourdes 698 Beacon St., 02215. Tel: 617-536-2761. Marist Fathers. Priests 2.

Marist Fathers Residence Tel: 617-262-2271. Revs. Gerard Caron, S.M., Dir.; Marcel Lajoie, S.M.

Chapel of the Holy Spirit Paulist Center, 5 Park St., 02108. Tel: 617-742-4460; Fax: 617-720-5756. Email: fiveparkst@aol.com. Web: www.paulist.org/boston. Rev. Paul D. Huesing, C.S.P., Ph.D., Dir.; Patricia Simpson, M.Div., Admin.; Susan Rutkowski, M.Div., Pastoral Min., Family Religious Educ. & Social Justice; Michael Kurley, Pastoral Min. Liturgy & Music. Paulist Fathers.

St. Clement Archdiocesan Eucharistic Shrine 1105 Boylston St., 02215. Tel: 617-266-5999; Fax: 617-247-7576. Email: petergrover@juno.com. Web: www.omvusa.org. Revs. Peter Grover, O.M.V., Dir. of Shrine; David N. Beauregard, O.M.V. St. Ignatius Province of the Oblates of the Virgin Mary. Priests 2.

St. Francis Chapel Prudential Center Plaza, 800 Boylston St., #1001, 02199. Tel: 617-437-7117; Fax: 617-437-8420. Email: st.francis@chapel.as. Web: www.stfrancischapel.org. Revs. John Wykes, O.M.V., Dir.; Dennis Brown, O.M.V.; Robert Lowrey, O.M.V.; David Yankauskas, O.M.V.; Craig MacMahon, O.M.V.; Gregory Staab, O.M.V. St. Ignatius Province of the Oblates of the Virgin Mary. Priests 6.

Madonna Queen Shrine 111 Orient Ave., 02128. Tel: 617-569-2100; Fax: 617-569-8701. Email: dofathers@aol.com. Rev. Marcelo Boschi, F.D.P., Rector. Don Orione Fathers.

Our Lady of the Airways Chapel First Floor, Tower Bldg., Logan International Airport, 02128. Tel: 617-567-2800; Fax: 617-569-6950. Email: fatherrichard@assport.com. Rev. Richard A. Uftring.

BROCKTON. *Chapel of Our Saviour* 475 Westgate Dr., 02301-1819. Tel: 508-583-8357; Fax: 508-586-5510. Revs. Gerald DiGiralamo, S.A., Dir.; Norman Boyd, S.A.; Henry Mair, S.A.; Malcolm Martin, S.A. (Retired); Bros. Thomas Banacki, S.A.; Louis Marek, S.A.; Savio McNiece, S.A. Priests 4; Brothers 3.

HOLLISTON. *Our Lady of Fatima Shrine* 101 Summer St., P.O. Box 5857, 01746-5857. Tel: 508-429-2144; Fax: 508-429-4793. Email: holliston.sx@gmail.com. Web: www.xaviermissionaries.org. Rev. Francis Signorelli, S.X. Xaverian Missionaries.

LOWELL. *St. Joseph the Worker Shrine* 37 Lee St., 01852-1103. Tel: 978-458-6346; 978-459-9522; 800-287-9522 (Gift Shop); Fax: 978-441-0963; 978-323-0763 (Gift Shop). Email: info@stjosephshrine.org. Web: www.stjosephshrine.org.

St. Joseph the Worker Residence, 37 Lee St., 01852-1103. Tel: 978-454-6004. Revs. John Cox, O.M.I., Dir.; Charles Beausoleil, O.M.I.; John Morin, O.M.I.; Albert P. Martineau, O.M.I.; Norman E. Parent, O.M.I.

PEABODY. *St. Theresa Carmelite Chapel* North Shore Mall, 01960. Tel: 978-531-6145; Fax: 978-531-1359. Email: hjones@carmelnet.org. Revs. Herbert J. Jones, O.Carm., Prior & Dir.; Mario Lopez, O.Carm.; Felix Prior, O.Carm.; Bro. Damien Chong, O.Carm. Priests 5; Brothers 1.

[AA] CAMPUS MINISTRY

BOSTON. *The Catholic Center at Boston University* 211 Bay State Rd., 02215. Tel: 617-353-3632; Fax: 617-358-2049. Email: catholic@bu.edu. Web: www.bu.edu/CATHOLIC. Rev. Paul D. Helfrich, B.H.; Bros. Patrick Reilly, B.H.; Samuel Gunn, B.H.; Sr. Olga Yaqob.

Emmanuel College Campus Ministry (1919) 400 The Fenway, 02115. Tel: 617-735-9703. Web: emmanuel.edu. Sr. Margaret Cummins, S.N.D.

University of Massachusetts at Boston Campus Ministry

Harbor Campus, Dorchester, 02125. Tel: 617-287-5839. Email: maggie.cahill@umb.edu.

BRIDGEWATER. *Bridgewater State College Catholic Center* 122 Park Ave., 02325. Tel: 508-531-1346; Fax: 508-531-6188. Email: mnolan@bridgew.edu. Web: www.bridgew.edu/depts/cathcntr/. Rev. Michael Nolan, Campus Min.

CAMBRIDGE. *Harvard Catholic Student Center* 29 Mount Auburn St., 02138. Tel: 617-868-6585; Fax: 617-354-7092. Email: mdrea@stpaulparish.org. Web: www.stpaulparish.org. Revs. Michael E. Drea, Senior Chap.; George S. Salzmann, O.S.F.S., Chap.; William F. Murphy, M.Div., Undergrad Chaplain.

Massachusetts Institute of Technology Catholic Community 40 Massachusetts Ave., W-11, 02139. Tel: 617-253-2981; Fax: 617-253-3260. Email: catholic@mit.edu. Web: www.web.mit.edu/tcc/. Rev. Richard F. Clancy; Cyndi Aimo. Total Staff 2.

FRAMINGHAM. *Framingham State College Campus Ministry* 100 State St., 01701. Tel: 508-626-4610; Fax: 508-626-4939. Email: pgojuk@frc.mass.edu. Ms. Hai Ok Hwang, M.Div., Chap.

LOWELL. *The Catholic Center U Mass, Lowell* 52 Colonial Ave., 01854. Tel: 978-454-0151. Email: Catholic_Center@uml.edu; Kenneth_Apuzzo@uml.edu. Web: www.uml.edu/student-services/ministry/catholic/. Bro. Kenneth Apuzzo, Campus Min. Total in Residence 4; Total Staff 1.

MEDFORD. *Tufts Interfaith Center Tufts University Catholic Chaplaincy* 58 Winthrop St., 02155-5300. Tel: 781-391-7272. Email: ann.penick@tufts.edu. Web: www.tuftslife.edu. Ms. Ann Penick, M.A., NCC, Catholic Chap. Total Staff 1; Total Assisted Annually 2,800.

NEWTON. *Boston College Campus Ministry* 140 Commonwealth Ave., Chestnut Hill, 02467. Tel: 617-552-3475; Fax: 617-552-3044. Email: ministry@bc.edu. Web: www.bc.edu/ministry. Total in Residence 6; Total Staff 14.

McElroy 233, Chestnut Hill, 02467. Tel: 617-552-3475; Fax: 617-552-3044. Email: ministry@bc.edu. Web: www.bc.edu/ministry.

NORTH ANDOVER. *Merrimack College Campus Ministry Center* 315 Turnpike St., 01845. Tel: 978-837-5450; Fax: 978-837-5004. Sr. Mary Ellen Dow, S.N.D., Dir.; Rev. William F. Waters, O.S.A., Campus Min.; Ms. Peggy Agolino Schumann, Campus Min. Priests 1; Total Assisted 2,000; Total Staff 5.

SALEM. *Salem State College, Catholic Campus Ministry* 352 Lafayette St., 01970. Tel: 978-542-6074; Fax: 978-744-2757. Email: gmckeon@salemstate.edu. Rev. Gerard R. McKeon, S.J.

WALTHAM. *Bentley University Spiritual Life Center* (1917) 175 Forest St., 02452-4705. Tel: 781-891-2754; Fax: 781-891-2839. Email: cgrenache@bentley.edu. Web: www.bentley.edu. Rev. Claude Grenache, A.A., B.A., S.T.B., S.T.L., Dir. Spiritual Life Center Catholic Chap.

Brandeis University Catholic Chaplaincy Mail stop 205, P.O. Box 549110, 02454-9110. Tel: 781-736-3574; Fax: 781-736-3577. Email: cuenin@brandeis.edu. Rev. Walter H. Cuenin.

WELLESLEY. *Babson College Campus Ministry* 9 Glen Rd., 02181. Tel: 617-235-1200. Sr. Frances Sheehey, O.S.F., Campus Coord.

Wellesley College Campus Ministry 02481. Tel: 781-283-2688; Fax: 781-283-3676. Email: ncorcora@wellesley.edu. Sr. Nancy Corcoran, C.S.J., Dir. Catholic Min.

WESTON. *Regis College Office of Campus Ministry* 235 Wellesley St., 02493. Tel: 781-768-7027; 781-768-7028; 781-768-7029; Fax: 781-768-8339. Email: ministry@regiscollege.edu. Web: www.regiscollege.edu. Sr. Rosemary Mulvihill, R.S.M., Dir.; Rev. Paul E. Kilroy, Chap.

[BB] FOUNDATIONS, FUNDS & TRUSTS

BOSTON. *Chancery Office*, 66 Brooks Dr., 02184-3839. Tel: 617-254-0100; Fax: 617-783-4564. Web: www.rcab.org. Also see Miscellaneous Section for additional listings.

The Cardinal Medeiros Trust Tel: 617-254-0100.

Cardinal Cushing General Hospital Foundation, Brockton

The Carney Hospital Foundation, Inc., 2100 Dorchester Ave., 02124. Tel: 617-296-1788. J. Barry Driscoll, Pres.; Paul J. Kingston, Vice Pres.; Daniel J. McDevitt, Sec.; William F. Henderson, Exec. Dir. (Formerly The New Caritas Christi Hospital, Inc.)

The Catholic Cemetery Association Perpetual Care Trust, 66 Brooks Dr., 02184-3839.

**Catholic Schools Foundation, Inc.* Tel: 617-254-0100; Fax: 617-783-6366. (Formerly St. Anthony's Scholarship Fund, Inc.).

Clergy Benefit Trust Tel: 617-254-0100; Fax: 617-783-2947.

Clergy Fund Society Tel: 617-254-0100; Fax: 617-783-2947.

Clergy Medical-Hospitalization Trust Tel: 617-254-0100; Fax: 617-783-2947.

Archdiocese of Boston Clergy Retirement/Disability Trust Tel: 617-254-0100; Fax: 617-783-2947.

Family Counseling Endowment Fund, Inc., 141 Tremont St., 02111. Tel: 617-482-4355.

Marist Capital Trust Fund

c/o Financial Admin., The Missionary Sisters of the Society of Mary, Inc., 349 Grove St., Waltham, 02154. Tel: 617-893-0149. Sr. Virginia Fornasa, S.M.S.M., Trustee; John E. McCormack.

Metropolitan Boston Dialysis Center, Inc., 736 Cambridge St., Brighton, 02135.

Mission Promotion Missionary Sisters of the Society of Mary.

c/o Mission Promoter, 349 Grove St., Waltham, 02453. Tel: 781-893-0149.

Roman Catholic Archdiocese of Boston Health Benefit Trust Tel: 617-746-5680; Fax: 617-783-4564. Mr. James M. Walsh, Admin.

Roman Catholic Archdiocese of Boston Insurance Trust Tel: 617-746-5640; Fax: 617-783-4564. Mr. James M. Walsh, Admin. Benefit Office.

Roman Catholic Archdiocese of Boston Pension Trust Tel: 617-746-5640; Fax: 617-746-4564. Mr. James M. Walsh, Admin. Benefit Office.

Roman Catholic Archdiocese of Boston Long Term Disability Trust Tel: 617-746-5640; Fax: 617-783-4564. Mr. James M. Walsh, Admin.

Roman Catholic Archdiocese of Boston Common Investment Fund Tel: 617-746-5680; Fax: 617-783-4564.

Roman Catholic Archdiocese of Boston Fixed Income Investment Fund Tel: 617-746-5680; Fax: 617-783-4564.

St. Charles Borromeo Educational Foundation, Inc.

Sacred Heart Trust Fund, c/o Society of Jesus, Trustee, 761 Harrison Ave., 02118. Tel: 617-536-5604. Bro. H. Francis Cluff, S.J.

St. Elizabeth's Hospital Foundation, Inc., 159 Washington St., Brighton, 02135.

Caritas Holy Family Hospital Foundation, Inc.

Catholic Foundation of the Archdiocese of Boston, 66 Brooks Dr., 02184-3839. Tel: 617-746-5621; Fax: 617-783-6366. Mr. James Mooney, Pres.

The Xaverian Brothers Northeastern Community Support Charitable Trust Fund, 704 Brush Hill Rd., Milton, 02186.

Benefit Trust for Non-Incardinated Priests Tel: 617-254-0100; Fax: 617-783-2947.

Benefit Trust for Non-Incardinated Priest Duly Assigned for Service in the Archdiocese of Boston

St. Mary's High School Foundation, Inc., 66 Brooks Dr., 02184-3839. Tel: 617-746-5680. David W. Smith, Contact Person.

Clergy Assistance Trust, 66 Brooks Dr., 02184-3839. Tel: 617-746-5615; Fax: 617-783-2947.

Massachusetts Catholic Self-Insurance Group, Inc., 66 Brooks Dr., 02184-3839. Tel: 617-746-5740; Fax: 517-746-5421. Email: Joseph_McEnness@rcab.org. Mr. Joseph F. McEnness, Admin.; Timothy McCrystal, Esq., Counsel.
Board of Directors: Rev. Charles J. Higgins, Clerk; James P. McDonough, Pres.; Mr. James M. Walsh, Treas.; Mr. Robert Guyon; Mr. Joseph P. Welch; Mr. John Shuman; Sr. Joan Duffy, C.S.J.

FRAMINGHAM. *Senior Religious Trust Fund of Marist Fathers of Boston*, 518 Pleasant St., 01701-2898. Tel: 508-879-7223; Fax: 508-879-0719.

IPSWICH. *Blin Charitable Trust* (1995) 30 Jeffrey's Neck Rd., 01938. Tel: 978-380-1372; Fax: 978-356-9759. Email: mary.farren@sndden.org. Web: www.sndden.org. Sisters of Notre Dame de Namur.

LEXINGTON. *Providentia Prima Trust*, 420 Bedford St.,Ste. 100, 02420. Tel: 781-862-1634; Fax: 781-862-5477. Email: john_ahle@covenanths.org. John Ahle, CFO/Treas. Covenant Health Systems.

LOWELL. *D'Youville Senior Care Foundation, Inc.*, 981 Varnum Ave., 01854. Tel: 978-569-1000; Fax: 978-569-1070. Email: lcoulture@dyouville.org. Web: dyouville.org.

Saints Memorial Medical Center Foundation, P.O. Box 367, 01853-0367. Tel: 978-934-8334; Fax: 978-934-8479. Email: fund.kec@tmmc.org. Web: www.saints-memorial.org. Thom Clark, Pres. & CEO; Kevin E. Coughlin, Vice Pres.; D. Harold Sullivan, Chm.

METHUEN. *Caritas Holy Family Hospital Foundation, Inc.*, 70 East St., 01844-4597. Tel: 978-687-0151; Fax: 978-688-7689. Email: nmallen@cchcs.org. Web: www.holyfamilyhosp.org. Mrs. Noreen V. Mallen, Exec. Dir.

NEEDHAM. *St. Joseph Parish School Fund, Inc., Needham*, 1382 Highland Ave., 02492. Tel: 781-444-0245; Fax: 781-444-7713. John Brennan, Treas.

[CC] MISCELLANEOUS

BOSTON. *Caritas Christi Retirement Plan and Trust*, 66 Brooks Dr., 02184-3839. Tel: 617-746-5857; Fax: 617-783-0736. James M. Walsh, Plan Admin.; Mary T. Regan, Plan Mgr.
Governing Board: His Eminence Sean Cardinal O'Malley, O.F.M.Cap.; Very Revs. Joseph K. Raeke, V.F.; Richard M. Erikson, V.G.; Bro. James M. Peterson, O.F.M.Cap., J.D., J.C.L.; Mr. Robert Guyon; Mr. David Woonton; James P. McDonough; Jonathan A. Noonan; Joseph Maher Esq.; Mark Rich; Joseph P. Welch.

Caritas Christi-A Catholic Health Care System, 736 Cambridge St., 02135. Tel: 617-789-2500; Fax: 617-789-2124. Web: www.caritaschristi.org. Dr. Ralph de la Torre, M.D., Pres. & CEO. Caritas Christi, Boston; Cardinal Cushing General Hospital Foundation, Inc., Brockton; Caritas Carney Hospital Foundation, Inc., Boston; Caritas Carney Hospital, Inc., Boston, Caritas Carney Medical Group, Inc., Boston*; Caritas Christi Network Services, Inc.; Caritas Christi Diagnostic Support Services, Inc., Boston*; Caritas Christi Network Services, Inc., Boston; Caritas Christi Physician Network, Inc., Boston*; Caritas Christi Support Services, Inc., Boston; Caritas Excell Clinical Laboratories, Inc., Boston*; Caritas Good Samaritan Cancer Center, Inc.; Caritas Good Samaritan Hospice, Inc., Boston; Caritas Good Samaritan Medical Center, Inc., Brockton, MA*; Caritas Good Samaritan Medical Practice Corporation, Brockton*; Caritas Good Samaritan Occupational Health Services, Inc., Brockton*; Caritas Holy Family Hospital Foundation, Inc., Methuen; Caritas Holy Family Hospital, Inc., Methuen; Caritas Home Care, Inc., Boston*; Laboure College, Inc., Boston; Caritas Norwood Hospital, Inc., Norwood; Caritas Por Cristo, Inc., Boston*; Caritas Southwood Hospital, Inc., Norfolk; Caritas St. Elizabeth's Hospital Foundation, Inc., Boston; Caritas St. Elizabeth's Medical Center of Boston, Inc., Boston; Caritas St. Elizabeth's Realty Corp., Boston*; Caritas St. John of God Hospital, Inc., Boston; Caritas St. Joseph Nursing Care Center, Inc., Boston; Caritas Valley Regional Health System, Inc., Methuen; Caritas Valley Regional Medical Services Corporation, Methuen; Caritas Valley Regional Support Services, Inc., Methuen; Greater Lawrence Mental Health Center, Inc., Lawrence; Neponset Valley Hospice, Inc., Norwood*; Norfolk-Bristol Homemaker Services, Inc., Norwood*; NVHS Coverage Associates, Inc., Norwood*; NVHS Management Services, Inc., Norwood*; Caritas Christi Retirement Plan and Trust, Boston; Caritas Medical Trust; Caritas Holy Family Hospital Auxiliary, Methuen; Caritas Holy Family Hospital Men's Guild, Methuen.

Caritas Good Samaritan Hospice, Inc., 310 Allston St., 02135. Tel: 617-566-6242; Fax: 617-566-3055. Web: caritaschristi.org. Mr. Leo P. Smith, L.I.C.S.W., Exec. Dir. & Contact Person.

The Catholic Lawyers Guild of the Archdiocese of Boston, Inc., One Lewis Wharf, 02110. Tel: 617-722-8175; Fax: 617-723-1180. Hon. Joseph R. Nolan, Pres.

Corporation for the Sponsored Ministries of the Sisters of St. Joseph of Boston (2000) 637 Cambridge St., 02135-2800. Tel: 617-746-2190; Fax: 617-746-2194. Email: suzanne.kearney@csjboston.org. Web: www.csjboston.org. Suzanne M. Kearney, Exec. Dir.

CSJ Ministries Connection, Inc. (2004) 637 Cambridge St., 02135-2800. Tel: 617-746-2191; Fax: 617-746-2194. Email: margaret.joyce@csjboston.org. Web: www.csjboston.org. Sr. Margaret Joyce, C.S.J., Admin. Coord.

Equestrian Order of the Holy Sepulchre of Jerusalem (1099)

Northeastern Lieutenancy, c/o Rev. Jonathan Gaspar, Pastoral Ctr., 66 Brooks Dr., 02184-3839.

The Fund for Catholic Schools, Inc. dba Campaign for Catholic Schools 143 Newbury St., Fl 3, 02116. Tel: 617-262-5600; Fax: 617-262-5601. Email: campaignforcatholicschools@rcab.org. Web: campaignforcatholicschools.org. Kathleen Driscoll, Pres.; Mary Myers, Vice Pres.

**KOLBE Association, Inc.*, 66 Brooks Dr., 02184-3839. Tel: 617-746-5425. Email: rev.michael.medas@sjs.edu. His Eminence Sean Cardinal O'Malley, O.F.M.Cap., Episcopal Moderator; Rev. Michael B. Medas, M.S.W., Exec. Dir.

Lanteri Charitable Trust, 1105 Boylston St., 02215-3660. Tel: 617-536-4141; Fax: 617-536-7016. Email: wbrownomv@aol.com. Laurence Flynn, Admin.

League of Catholic Women of the Archdiocese of Boston, St. Mary of the Sacred Heart, 392 Hanover St., Hanover, 02339. Tel: 781-826-4303. Mrs. John F. O'Donoghue Jr., Pres.; Rev. Martin P. Connor, S.T.L., Spiritual Dir. (Retired).

Lourdes Bureau, 698 Beacon St., 02215. Tel: 617-536-2761. Marist Fathers., Official Representatives in America for the Shrine of Lourdes, France.

Medaille Corporation, 637 Cambridge St., 02135. Tel: 617-783-9090; Fax: 617-783-8246. Email: bostoncsj@csjboston.org. Web: www.csjboston.org. Sisters Mary L. Murphy, C.S.J., Pres.; Maureen Doherty, C.S.J., Treas.

Most Holy Name of Jesus Federation of Poor Clare Monasteries in the Eastern Region of the United States (1959) Monastery of Saint Clare, 920 Centre St., 02130. Tel: 617-524-1760; Fax: 617-983-5205. Email: bostonpoorclares@yahoo.com. Sr. Clare Frances McAvoy, O.S.C., Pres. Solemn Vows 124; Simple Professed 8.

National Catholic Bioethics Center, 100 Cambridge St., 20th Fl., Ste. 2000, 02114. Email: postmaster@NCBCenter.org. Web: www.NCBCenter.org. Dr. John M. Haas, Ph.D., S.T.L., K.M., Pres. Tel: 215-877-2660; Donald J. Powers, Vice Pres. Finance. Tel: 401-289-0680; Mark E. Bradford, Exec. Vice Pres. Tel: 215-871-2009.

PACE - Parents Alliance for Catholic Education, 14 Beacon St., Ste. 102, 02108. Tel: 617-723-9890; Fax: 617-723-9892. Email: fkalisz@paceorg.net. Web: www.paceorg.net. Frederick M. Kalisz Jr., Exec. Dir.

Pontifical Association of the Holy Childhood, Pontifical Society for the Propagation of the Faith & Pontifical Society of St. Peter the Apostle, Mailing Address: P.O. Box 120138, 02112-0138. Tel: 617-542-1776; Fax: 617-542-1778. Email: info@propfaithatboston.org. Office: 66 Brooks Dr., 02184. Rev. Thomas A. Kopp, Archdiocesan Dir. Total Staff 10.

Sancta Maria House, Inc (1972) 11 Waltham St., 02118-2162. Tel: 617-423-4366. Rev. Msgr. William H. Roche, Pres. (Retired).

St. Vincent Pallotti Center for Apostolic Development of Boston, Inc., 66 Brooks Dr., 02184-3839. Tel: 617-783-3924. Email: VolService@aol.com. Web: www.pallotticenterboston.org.

**Women Affirming Life, Inc.*, P.O. Box 35532, 02135. Tel: 617-254-2277; Fax: 617-254-2299. Email: mail@affirmlife.com. Web: www.affirmlife.com. Frances X. Hogan, Pres.

ARLINGTON. *Fidelity House*, 25 Medford St., 02474-3105. Tel: 781-648-2005; Fax: 781-648-4604. Email: Fidelityhouse@rcn.com. Web: www.fidelityhouse.org. Edward F. Woods, Dir. Purpose: A community center sponsored by the Saint Agnes Parish providing quality services primarily for youth development with flexible and diverse services for people of all ages.

BRIGHTON. *The Literacy Connection* (1987) 637 Cambridge St., 02135. Tel: 617-746-2100; Fax: 617-783-8246. Sr. Patricia Andrews, C.S.J., Dir.

CAMBRIDGE. *North Cambridge Catholic Corporate Work Study Program, Inc.*, 40 Norris St., 02140. Tel: 617-876-6068; Fax: 617-576-1898. Web: northcambridgecatholic.org. Robert J. McCarthy, Pres. Total Assisted 286; Total Staff 10.

**The Youville House, Inc.*, 1575 Cambridge St., 02138-4398. Tel: 617-876-4344. Email: leaheyd@youville.org. Web: www.youville.org. Mr. T. Richard Quigley, Pres. & CEO; Ms. Marsha V. Whelan, Vice Pres. Mission Integration; Revs. William L. Mulligan, S.J., Chap.; Jennifer Casstevens, Chap.; Ms. Patricia Kennedy, Dir. of Pastoral Care Svcs. & Chap.; Elizabeth Walsh, Chap. Member of Youville Lifecare, Inc. Priests 1; Sisters of Charity (Grey Nuns) 3; Assisted Living Units 95.

**Youville Lifecare, Inc.* (1895) 1575 Cambridge St., 02138-4398. Tel: 617-876-4344; Fax: 617-547-5501. Email: leaheyd@youville.org. Web: www.youville.org. Mr. Daniel Leahey, Pres. & CEO. Covenant Health Systems, Lexington, MA

FRAMINGHAM. *Bethany Health Care Center, Inc.*, 97 Bethany Rd., 01702-7237. Tel: 508-872-6750; Fax: 508-875-5425. Email: jacquelyn.mccarthy@csjboston.org. Web: www.bethanyhealthcare.org. Sr. Jacquelyn McCarthy, C.S.J., CEO & Admin. Congregation of Sisters of St. Joseph of Boston., Skilled Nursing Facility. Residential Living Bed Capacity 169.

Bethany Hill School, Inc., 89 Bethany Rd., 01702. Tel: 508-875-1117; Fax: 508-875-2288. Email: dakcsj@aol.com. Sponsored by the Sisters of St. Joseph of Boston., 41 units of educational housing for low-income people with a variety of needs.

IPSWICH. *Cuvilly Arts and Earth Center, Inc.* (1983) 10 Jeffrey Neck Rd., 01938. Tel: 508-356-4288. Email: cuvilly@verizon.net. Web: cuvilly.org. Sr. Patricia Rolinger, S.N.D.deN., M.A., Exec. Dir. Total Assisted 100; Total Staff 12.

LAWRENCE. **Greater Lawrence Mental Health Center, Inc.*, 30 General St., 01841. Tel: 978-683-3128; Fax: 978-686-7856. Jeffrey Fox, Exec. Dir.

Notre Dame Education Center (1992) (Adult Literacy), 354 Merrimack St., Ste. 210, 01843. Tel: 978-682-6441; Fax: 978-974-9840. Email: executivedirector@ndeclawrence.com. Sr. Eileen T. Burns, S.N.D.deN., Exec. Dir. Sisters of Notre Dame de Namur., ESOL, Citizenship, LEAD, Computer, Spanish, Nursing Assistant Program, GED. Sisters 2; Adults 450; Total Staff 10.

Notre Dame High School Corporate Internship Program, Inc. (2004) 207 Hampshire St., 01841. Tel: 978-689-8222; Fax: 978-689-8728. Sr. Mary Murphy, S.N.D., Ph.D., Pres.

LEXINGTON. *Covenant Health Systems, Inc.*, 420 Bedford St., Ste. 100, 02420. Tel: 781-862-1634; Fax: 781-862-5477. Email: info@covenanths.org. Web: www.covenanths.org. David R. Lincoln, Pres. & CEO. Sponsored organizations: Youville Hospital and Rehabilitation Center, Cambridge, MA; Youville House Assisted Living Residence, Cambridge, MA; St. Joseph Healthcare, Nashua, NH; St. Mary's Health Care System, Lewiston, ME; St. Mary's Regional Medical Center, Lewiston, ME; Mary Immaculate Health/Care Services, Lawrence, MA; Maristhill Nursing Home, Waltham, MA; St. Joseph Manor Health Care, Brockton, MA; Fanny Allen Corp., Colchester, VT; St. Mary Health Care Center, Worcester, MA; St. Andre Healthcare Facility, Biddeford, ME: St. Mary's Villa Nursing Home, Moscow, PA; St. Mary's Villa Personal Care Residence, Moscow, PA; Youville Place Assisted Living Residence, Lexington, MA; Affiliate organizations: Sancta Maria Nursing Facility, Cambridge, MA; Mont Marie Health Care Center, Holyoke, MA; Bethany Health Care Center, Framingham, MA; D'Youville Senior Care Center, Lowell, MA; Notre Dame duLac, Worcester, MA; Notre Dame Long Term Care Center, Worcester, MA; Matulaitis Nursing Home, Putnam, CT; St. Joseph Healthcare, Bangor, ME.

LOWELL. *Saints Memorial Special Service, Inc.*, Saints Medical Center, One Hospital Dr., 01852. Tel: 978-458-1411. Email: sguimond@saintsmedicalcenter.com. Web: www.saintsmedicalcenter.com. Mr. Stephen Guimond, CFO.

MALDEN. *The Catholic Cemetery Association of the Archdiocese of Boston, Inc.*, 175 Broadway, 02148. Tel: 781-322-6300; Fax: 781-322-3801. Email: dina_currier@rcab.org. Web: www.ccemetery.org. Robert Visconti, Exec. Dir; David W. Smith, Sec.

METHUEN. *Caritas Holy Family Hospital Men's Guild* (1950) 70 East St., 01844-4597. Tel: 978-687-0156, Ext. 2362; Fax: 978-688-7689. Web: www.holyfamilyhosp.org. Lester Schindel, Pres. & CEO.

Caritas Valley Regional Health System, Inc. (1945) 70 East St., 01844-4597. Tel: 978-687-0151; Fax: 978-688-7689. Web: www.holyfamilyhosp.org.

Caritas Holy Family Hospital, Inc. (1984) Tel: 978-687-0151; Fax: 978-688-7689.

Caritas Holy Family Hospital Auxiliary (1947) Tel: 978-687-0156, Ext. 2301; Fax: 978-688-7689.

Caritas Holy Family Hospital Men's Guild (1950) Tel: 978-687-0156, Ext. 2362; Fax: 978-688-7689.

Caritas Holy Family Hospital Foundation, Inc. (1987) Tel: 978-687-0156, Ext. 2104; Fax: 978-688-7689.

Caritas Valley Regional Support Services, Inc. (1984) Tel: 978-687-0151; Fax: 978-688-7689.

Caritas Valley Regional Medical Services Corporation (1995) 70 East St., 01844. Tel: 978-687-0151; Fax: 978-682-9908.

Caritas Valley Regional Ventures, Inc.

Greater Lawrence Mental Health Center, Inc.

NEEDHAM. *St. Sebastian's School Fund, Inc.*, 1191 Greendale Ave., 02492. Tel: 781-449-5200. John J. Doherty, Contact Person & Business Mgr.

NEWTON. *Catholic Purchasing Services, Inc.* (1985) 580 Washington St., 02458. Tel: 617-965-4343; Fax: 617-965-5430. Email: RJW@catholicpurchasing.org. Web: catholicpurchasing.org. Mr. Richard J. Wasilauskas, Pres.

QUINCY. *The Good Shepherd: Maria Droste Services*, 1354 Hancock St., Ste. 209, 02169. Tel: 617-471-5686; Fax: 617-471-6622. Email: mariadroste@verizon.net. Sr. Lorraine Bernier, R.G.S.

Madonna Hall Total Staff 6; Volunteers 16; Total Assisted 290.

SCITUATE. *Mass Times Trust dba Masstimes.org* 91 Surfside Rd., 02066. Mr. Robert A. Hummel, Trustee.

WALTHAM. **Marist Missionary Sisters Senior Religious Trust*, 349 Grove St., 02453. Tel: 781-893-0149; Fax: 781-899-6838. Email: maristsmsm@aol.com. Web: www.maristmissionarysmsm.org.

RELIGIOUS INSTITUTES OF MEN REPRESENTED IN THE ARCHDIOCESE

For further details refer to the corresponding bracketed number in the Religious Institutes of Men or Women section.

[0130]—*Assumptionists*—A.A.
[1040]—*The Augustinians* (Villanova, PA)—O.S.A.
[0200]—*Benedictine Monks*—O.S.B.
[1350]—*Brothers of St. Francis Xavier*—C.F.X.
[0330]—*Brothers of the Christian Schools* (Long Island, New England Provs.)—F.S.C.
[0470]—*The Capuchin Friars* (Prov. of Mary)—O.F.M.Cap.
[0270]—*Carmelite Fathers & Brothers* (Prov. of Most Pure Heart of Mary)—O.Carm.
[0310]—*Congregation of Christian Brothers* (Eastern Prov.)—C.F.C.
[1210]—*Congregation of the Missionaries of St. Charles*—C.S.
[1000]—*Congregation of the Passion* (St. Paul of the Cross Prov.)—C.P.
[1140]—*Congregation of the Sacred Hearts of Jesus and Mary*—SS.CC.
[0480]—*Conventual Franciscans* (Buffalo, NY)—O.F.M.Conv.
[0260]—*Discalced Carmelite Friars*—O.C.D.
[0520]—*Franciscan Friars* (Assumption of B.V.M., Holy Name, Immaculate Conception Provs.)—O.F.M.
[0530]—*Franciscan Friars of the Atonement*—S.A.
[0670]—*Hospitaller Brothers of St. John of God*—O.H.
[0690]—*Jesuit Fathers and Brother* (New England Prov.)—S.J.
[0770]—*The Marist Brothers* (Poughkeepsie, NY)—F.M.S.
[0780]—*Marist Fathers* (Boston Prov.)—S.M.
[0800]—*Maryknoll*—M.M.
[]—*Mekhitarist Fathers*—C.M.V.D.
[0720]—*The Missionaries of Our Lady of La Salette* (Eastern Prov.)—M.S.
[0910]—*Oblates of Mary Immaculate* (Eastern, St. John the Baptist Provs.)—O.M.I.
[0430]—*Order of Preachers-Dominicans* (Prov. of St. Joseph)—O.P.
[1030]—*Paulist Fathers*—C.S.P.
[0610]—*Priests of the Congregation of Holy Cross* (Eastern Prov.)—C.S.C.
[1070]—*Redemptorist Fathers* (Baltimore Prov.)—C.SS.R.
[1190]—*Salesians of Don Bosco* (Prov. of St. Philip)—S.D.B.
[0110]—*Society of African Missions*—S.M.A.
[0420]—*Society of Divine Word* (Sacred Heart Prov.)—S.V.D.
[0850]—*Society of Missionaries of Africa*—M.Afr.
[0370]—*Society of St. Columban* (American Region)—S.S.C.
[0410]—*Sons of Divine Providence*—F.D.P.
[1270]—*Sons of Mary Missionary Society*—F.M.S.I.
[1280]—*Stigmatine Fathers and Brothers* (Rome, Italy)—C.S.S.
[1360]—*Xaverian Missionary Fathers*—S.X.

RELIGIOUS INSTITUTES OF WOMEN REPRESENTED IN THE ARCHDIOCESE

[1810]—*Bernardine Franciscan Sisters*—O.S.F.
[0330]—*Carmelite Sisters for the Aged and Infirm*—O.Carm.
[0670]—*Cistercian Nuns of the Strict Observance*—O.C.S.O.
[0270]—*Congregation of Bon Secours*—C.B.S.
[3110]—*Congregation of Our Lady of the Retreat in the Cenacle*—R.C.
[]—*Congregation of the Armenian Catholic Sisters of the Immaculate Conception, Inc.*
[1920]—*Congregation of the Sisters of the Holy Cross*—C.S.C.
[0760]—*Daughters of Charity of St. Vincent de Paul*—D.C.
[0860]—*Daughters of Mary of the Immaculate Conception*—C.M.
[0420]—*Discalced Carmelite Nuns*—O.C.D.
[1070-03]—*Dominican Sisters*—O.P.
[1070-13]—*Dominican Sisters*—O.P.
[1115]—*Dominican Sisters of Peace*—O.P.
[1170]—*Felician Sisters*—C.S.S.F.
[1370]—*Franciscan Missionaries of Mary*—F.M.M.
[1320]—*Franciscan Missionary Sisters for Africa* (Co. Louth, Ireland)—O.S.F.
[1180]—*Franciscan Sisters of Allegany, New York*—O.S.F.
[1470]—*Franciscan Sisters of St. Joseph*—F.S.S.J.
[1840]—*Grey Nuns of the Sacred Heart*—G.N.S.H.
[2070]—*Holy Union Sisters*—S.U.S.C.
[0410]—*Institute of the Sisters of Our Lady of Mt. Carmel*—O.Carm.
[2290]—*Little Missionary Sisters of Charity*—L.M.S.C.
[2310]—*Little Sisters of the Assumption*—L.S.A.
[2320]—*Little Sisters of the Holy Family*—P.S.S.F.
[2340]—*Little Sisters of the Poor*—L.S.P.
[2420]—*Marist Missionary Sisters-Missionary Sisters of the Society of Mary*—S.M.S.M.
[2470]—*Maryknoll Sisters of St. Dominic*—M.M.
[2480]—*Medical Missionaries of Mary*—M.M.M.
[1360]—*Missionary Franciscan Sisters of the Immaculate Conception*—O.S.F.
[2790]—*Missionary Servants of the Most Blessed Trinity*—M.S.B.T.
[2880]—*Missionary Sisters of St. Columban*—S.S.C.
[2800]—*Missionary Sisters of the Most Sacred Heart of Jesus of Hiltrup*—M.S.C.
[3030]—*Oblates of the Most Holy Redeemer*—O.SS.R.
[3760]—*Order of St. Clare*—O.S.C.
[0950]—*Pious Society Daughters of St. Paul*—D.S.P.
[3240]—*Poor Sisters of Jesus Crucified and the Sorrowful Mother*—C.J.C.
[3410]—*Religious of Christian Education*—R.C.E.
[2070]—*Religious of the Holy Union of the Sacred Hearts*—S.U.S.C.
[2970]—*School Sisters of Notre Dame*—S.S.N.D.
[3550]—*Servants of the Immaculate Heart of Mary*—S.C.I.M.
[0980]—*Sisters Disciples of the Divine Master*—P.D.D.M.
[0490]—*Sisters of Charity of Montreal-Grey Nuns*—S.G.M.
[0500]—*Sisters of Charity of Nazareth*—S.C.N.
[0560]—*Sisters of Charity of Quebec-Grey Nuns*—S.C.Q.
[0590]—*Sisters of Charity of Saint Elizabeth, Convent Station*—S.C.
[0640]—*Sisters of Charity of St. Vincent de Paul, Halifax*—S.C.
[0540]—*Sisters of Charity, At Ottawa-Grey Nuns of the Cross*—S.C.O.
[0990]—*Sisters of Divine Providence*—C.D.P.
[2580]—*Sisters of Mercy of the Union in the United States of America*—R.S.M.
[3000]—*Sisters of Notre Dame de Namur*—S.N.D.deN.
[3360]—*Sisters of Providence of Saint Mary-Of-The-Woods, Indiana*—S.P.
[3950]—*Sisters of Saint Mary of Namur*—S.S.M.N.
[3720]—*Sisters of St. Anne*—S.S.A.
[3750]—*Sisters of St. Chretienne*—S.S.Ch.
[1650]—*Sisters of St. Francis of Philadelphia*—O.S.F.
[3830]—*Sisters of St. Joseph*—C.S.J.
[3815]—*Sisters of Ste. Jeanne D'Arc*—S.J.A.
[0150]—*Sisters of the Assumption B.V.*—S.A.S.V.
[1830]—*Sisters of the Good Shepherd*—R.G.S.
[3310]—*Sisters of the Presentation of Mary*—P.M.
[1490]—*Sisters of the Third Franciscan Order*—O.S.F.

[1705]—*Sisters of the Third Order of St. Francis of Assisi*—O.S.F.
[4060]—*Society of the Holy Child Jesus*—S.H.C.J.
[4070]—*Society of the Sacred Heart*—R.S.C.J.
[4110]—*Ursuline Nuns* (Eastern Prov.)—O.S.U.

ARCHDIOCESAN CEMETERIES

BOSTON. *Diocesan Office*, 175 Broadway, Malden, 02148.
ARLINGTON. *St. Paul*
BEVERLY. *St. Mary*
CAMBRIDGE. *North Cambridge Catholic*
CHARLESTOWN. *St. Francis de Sales*
HAVERHILL. *St. James, St. Joseph & St. Patrick*
LOWELL. *St. Patrick*
LYNN. *St. Mary, St. Joseph & St. Jean Baptiste*
MALDEN. *Holy Cross & St. Mary*
MARBLEHEAD. *Star of the Sea*
SALEM. *St. Mary*
SAXONVILLE. *St. George*
STONEHAM. *St. Patrick*
WALTHAM. *Calvary*
WATERTOWN. *Mount Auburn & St. Patrick*
WOBURN. *Calvary*

NECROLOGY

† Cunningham, Rev. Msgr. Richard G., (Retired)—Died Dec. 28, 2009
† McDonnell, Rev. Msgr. Thomas J., (Retired)—Died June 14, 2009
† Bolduc, Paul J., (Retired)—Died Dec. 29, 2009
† Burns, Dennis J., (Retired)—Died Aug. 25, 2009
† Conway, Thomas D., (Retired)—Died Oct. 25, 2009
† Duggan, Charles T., (Retired)—Died May 18, 2009
† Fratus, James F., (Retired)—Died April 8, 2009
† Gagnon, Adelard J., (Retired)—Died May 2, 2009
† Gibbons, James M., (Retired)—Died Aug. 21, 2009
† Gilmartin, Daniel J., (Retired)—Died Oct. 8, 2009
† Johnson, Harold J., (Retired)—Died Dec. 22, 2009
† Kelley, Paul G., (Retired)—Died Oct. 11, 2009
† Larner, James M.—Died Aug. 24, 2009
† McCarthy, William R., (Retired)—Died July 24, 2009
† McConville, Philip G., (Retired)—Died Nov. 13, 2009
† McCoy, Charles J., (Retired)—Died Nov. 30, 2009
† Moran, Daniel F., (Retired)—Died April 9, 2009
† O'Donohoe, James A., (Retired)—Died Oct. 27, 2009
† Slyva, Joseph W.—Died Feb. 20, 2009
† Tyrrell, Robert D., (Retired)—Died Feb. 15, 2009

An asterisk (*) denotes an organization that has established tax-exempt status directly with the IRS and is not covered by the USCCB Group Ruling.

Diocese of Bridgeport

(Dioecesis Bridgeportensis)

Most Reverend

WILLIAM E. LORI, S.T.D.

Bishop of Bridgeport; ordained May 14, 1977; appointed Titular Bishop of Bulla and Auxiliary of Washington April 20, 1995; appointed Bishop of Bridgeport January 23, 2001; installed March 19, 2001. *Office: 238 Jewett Ave., Bridgeport, CT 06606-2892.*

Chancery: The Catholic Center, 238 Jewett Ave., Bridgeport, CT 06606-2892. Tel: 203-372-4301; Fax: 203-371-8698.

Web: www.bridgeportdiocese.org

ESTABLISHED AUGUST 6, 1953.

Square Miles 633.

Corporate Title: The Bridgeport Roman Catholic Diocesan Corporation.

Comprises all of Fairfield County in the State of Connecticut.

For legal titles of parishes and diocesan institutions, consult the Chancery at The Catholic Center.

STATISTICAL OVERVIEW

Personnel	
Bishop	1
Priests: Diocesan Active in Diocese	163
Priests: Diocesan Active Outside Diocese	15
Priests: Diocesan in Foreign Missions	3
Priests: Retired, Sick or Absent	52
Number of Diocesan Priests	233
Religious Priests in Diocese	46
Total Priests in Diocese	279
Extern Priests in Diocese	27
Ordinations:	
Diocesan Priests	6
Transitional Deacons	3
Permanent Deacons in Diocese	112
Total Sisters	344
Parishes	
Parishes	87
With Resident Pastor:	
Resident Diocesan Priests	72
Resident Religious Priests	3
Without Resident Pastor:	
Administered by Priests	11
Administered by Deacons	1
Professional Ministry Personnel:	
Sisters	63
Lay Ministers	214
Welfare	
Catholic Hospitals	1
Total Assisted	206,000
Health Care Centers	2
Total Assisted	22,453
Homes for the Aged	15
Total Assisted	1,168
Day Care Centers	6
Total Assisted	230
Specialized Homes	18
Total Assisted	200
Special Centers for Social Services	9
Total Assisted	490,000
Educational	
Seminaries, Diocesan	1
Students from This Diocese	19
Diocesan Students in Other Seminaries	13
Total Seminarians	32
Colleges and Universities	3
Total Students	11,373
High Schools, Diocesan and Parish	5
Total Students	2,402
High Schools, Private	2
Total Students	1,218
Elementary Schools, Diocesan and Parish	33
Total Students	7,769
Elementary Schools, Private	1
Total Students	480
Non-residential Schools for the Disabled	2
Total Students	98
Catechesis/Religious Education:	
High School Students	2,245
Elementary Students	34,946
Total Students under Catholic Instruction	60,563
Teachers in the Diocese:	
Priests	15
Scholastics	2
Sisters	30
Lay Teachers	1,322
Vital Statistics	
Receptions into the Church:	
Infant Baptism Totals	4,217
Adult Baptism Totals	126
Received into Full Communion	564
First Communions	5,569
Confirmations	5,314
Marriages:	
Catholic	822
Interfaith	91
Total Marriages	913
Deaths	2,992
Total Catholic Population	401,136
Total Population	884,050

Former Bishops—His Eminence LAWRENCE J. CARDINAL SHEHAN, D.D., ord. Dec. 23, 1922; cons. Dec. 12, 1945 as Auxiliary Bishop of Baltimore; installed as first Bishop of Bridgeport, Dec. 1, 1953; transferred to Archdiocese of Baltimore, July 10, 1961; created Cardinal, Feb. 22, 1965; died Aug. 26, 1984; Most Revs. WALTER W. CURTIS, S.T.D., ord. Dec. 8, 1937; appt. Auxiliary Bishop of Newark and Titular Bishop of Bisica in Tunis; cons. Sept. 24, 1957; appt. Bishop of Bridgeport, Sept. 23, 1961; installed Nov. 20, 1961; retired June 28, 1988; died Oct. 18, 1997; EDWARD M. EGAN, J.C.D., ord. Dec. 15, 1957; appt. Titular Bishop of Allegheny and Auxiliary Bishop of New York, April 1, 1985; cons. May 22, 1985; appt. Bishop of Bridgeport, Nov. 8, 1988; installed Dec. 14, 1988; appt. Archbishop of New York, May 11, 2000; installed June 19, 2000; created Cardinal Feb. 21, 2001.

Vicars General—Rev. Msgrs. J. PETER CULLEN, P.A., V.G.; WILLIAM J. SCHEYD, P.A., V.G.; THOMAS J. DRISCOLL, P.A., V.G., 238 Jewett Ave., Bridgeport, 06606-2892.

Episcopal Vicar for Administration—Rev. Msgr. JERALD A. DOYLE, Ph.D., J.C.D.

Chancery—The Catholic Center, 238 Jewett Ave., Bridgeport, 06606-2892. Tel: 203-372-4301; Fax: 203-371-8698. Office Hours: Mon.-Fri. 8:30-4:30.

Chancellor—Mrs. NANCY B. MATTHEWS, Esq., Catholic Center, 238 Jewett Ave., Bridgeport, 06606-2892. Tel: 203-416-1356.

Secretary to the Bishop—Rev. JOSEPH A. MARCELLO.

Episcopal Vicar for Religious—Rev. Msgr. ERNEST T. ESPOSITO, D.Min.

Episcopal Vicar for Clergy—Rev. Msgr. KEVIN T. ROYAL, S.T.L., Dir.

Episcopal Vicar for Haitians—Rev. G. FRANTZ DESRUISSEAUX, J.C.L.

Episcopal Vicar for Hispanics—Rev. Msgr. ANICETO VILLAMIDE.

Chief Finance Officer—Mr. NORMAN R. WALKER, CFO.

Diocesan Tribunal—The Catholic Center, 238 Jewett Ave., Bridgeport, 06606-2892. Tel: 203-416-1423.

Judicial Vicar—Rev. Msgr. JERALD A. DOYLE, Ph.D., J.C.D.

Adjutant Judicial Vicar—Rev. Msgr. J. JAMES CUNEO, J.C.D.

Judges—Rev. Msgrs. WILLIAM A. GENUARIO, P.A., J.C.D. (Retired); THOMAS J. DRISCOLL, P.A., V.G.; Revs. MICHAEL A. BOCCACCIO; ROBERT V. BIROSCHAK, J.C.L.; JOSEPH K. PARAMPATH, J.C.D. (Retired); MICHAEL SKROGKY, J.C.D.; WILLIAM M. QUINLAN, J.C.L.; WILLIAM F. VERRILLI, J.C.L.

Defenders of the Bond—Revs. RICHARD F. FUTIE, J.C.D.; ALFRED F. PECARIC, S.T.L.

Promoter of Justice—Rev. G. FRANTZ DESRUISSEAUX, J.C.L.

Notaries—MARY A. MOLLOY; KERRY PERILLE.

Diocesan Legal Services—R. SCOTT BEACH, Esq., Day Pitney, LLP, One Canterbury Green, Stamford, 06901.

Diocesan Censors—Rev. Msgrs. LAURENCE R. BRONKIEWICZ, S.T.D.; THOMAS J. DRISCOLL, P.A., V.G.; CHRISTOPHER J. WALSH, Ph.D., S.T.D.

Diocesan Consultors—Rev. Msgrs. LAWRENCE J. CARROLL; J. PETER CULLEN, P.A., V.G.; LOUIS A. DEPROFIO, P.A. (Retired); THOMAS J. DRISCOLL, P.A., V.G.; Rev. THOMAS P. THORNE; Rev. Msgrs. WILLIAM J. SCHEYD, P.A., V.G.; WALTER C. ORLOWSKI; ANDREW G. VARGA; ANICETO VILLAMIDE; DARIUSZ J. ZIELONKA; JERALD A. DOYLE, Ph.D., J.C.D.

Presbyteral Council—Most Rev. WILLIAM E. LORI, S.T.D., Presider; Rev. Msgrs. WILLIAM J. SCHEYD, P.A., V.G., Vice Chm.; J. PETER CULLEN, P.A., V.G.; LOUIS A. DEPROFIO, P.A. (Retired); JERALD A. DOYLE, Ph.D., J.C.D.; ANICETO VILLAMIDE; KEVIN W. WALLIN; THOMAS J. DRISCOLL, P.A., V.G.; Revs. CYRUS BARTOLOME; ROBERT J. CROFUT; Rev. Msgr. KEVIN T. ROYAL, S.T.L.; Revs. ROBERT J. LEVENS, S.J.; PETER J. LYNCH; Rev. Msgr. WALTER C. ORLOWSKI; Revs. NICHOLAS S. PAVIA; RUSSELL AUGUSTINE; MICHAEL L. DUNN; J. BARRY FUREY; FRANCIS T. HOFFMANN; PAWEL HREBENKO; IAN JEREMIAH; JOSEPH A. MARCELLO; Rev. Msgrs. ERNEST T. ESPOSITO, D.Min.; LAWRENCE J. CARROLL; Rev. PAUL MURPHY; Rev. Msgr. MARTIN P. RYAN, D.Min.; Rev. THOMAS P. THORNE.

Finance Council—Most Rev. WILLIAM E. LORI, S.T.D.; Rev. Msgrs. WILLIAM J. SCHEYD, P.A., V.G.; J. PETER CULLEN, P.A., V.G.; THOMAS J. DRISCOLL, P.A., V.G.; Mrs. NANCY B. MATTHEWS, Esq.; Mr. NORMAN R. WALKER; Mr. DIGBY W. BARRIOS; Mr. WILLIAM H. BESGEN; Mr. MICHAEL F. HOBEN; Mr. MICHAEL O'ROURKE; Mr. BRIAN YOUNG; Mr. PHILLIP D. AMEEN; Mrs. ANNE O. MCCRORY; Mr. WILLIAM B. JAMES, C.F.A.; Mr. DENNIS NALLY; Mr. JOSEPH D. ROXE; Mr. WILLIAM J. TOTTEN.

Parochial Examiners—Rev. ROBERT J. CROFUT; Rev. Msgrs. WALTER C. ORLOWSKI; LAWRENCE J. CARROLL.

Territorial Vicars—Vicariate I (Stamford, Darien, Glenbrook, Greenwich, Byram, Riverside): Rev. FRANK T. HOFFMANN, St. Catherine of Siena Rectory, 4 Riverside Ave., Riverside, 06878. Tel: 203-637-3661. Vicariate II (Norwalk, New Canaan, Wilton, Weston, Westport): Rev. THOMAS P. THORNE, 98 Riverside Ave., Westport, 06880. Tel: 203-227-5161; Fax: 203-227-1206. Vicariate III (Fairfield, Easton, West Bridgeport): Rev. Msgr. LAWRENCE J. CARROLL, St. Pius Rectory, 834 Brookside Dr., Fairfield, 06430. Tel: 203-255-6134. Vicariate IV (East Bridgeport, Stratford, Trumbull, Monroe, Shelton): Rev. NICHOLAS S. PAVIA, St. Joseph Rectory, 50 Fairmont Pl., Shelton, 06484. Tel: 203-924-8611. Vicariate V (Bethel, Brookfield, Danbury, Georgetown, Newtown, New Fairfield, Redding, Ridgefield, Sherman): Rev. Msgr. MARTIN P. RYAN, D.Min., Mailing Address: St. Edward the Confessor Rectory, P.O. Box 8866, New Fairfield, 06812. Tel: 203-746-2200.

Office for Clergy Personnel—Rev. Msgrs. ERNEST T. ESPOSITO, D.Min., Episcopal Vicar for Rel.; KEVIN T. ROYAL, S.T.L., Episcopal Vicar for Clergy Personnel; Deacon ANTHONY J. DETJE, Asst. to Dir.

The Catholic Center—238 Jewett Ave., Bridgeport, 06606. Tel: 203-372-4301; Fax: 203-372-9835. Web: www.bridgeportdiocese.org.

Services-Business Office—The Catholic Center, 238 Jewett Ave., Bridgeport, 06606-2892. Mr. NORMAN R. WALKER, CFO; Ms. TERESA NUNES, Diocesan Financial Dir.; Deacon WILLIAM A. KONIERS, Financial Dir., Office of Parish Accounting Svcs. Tel: 203-416-1439; Fax: 203-371-0875. Email: wkoniers@diobpt.org; Mr. ROBERT LEBLANC, Dir. Property Mgmt. Tel: 203-416-1419.

Members of the Clergy Personnel Committee—Rev. Msgr. LAWRENCE J. CARROLL; Rev. J. BARRY FUREY; Rev. Msgr. KEVIN T. ROYAL, S.T.L.; Rev. DAVID W. BLANCHFIELD.

Office for the Continuing Education of Clergy—Rev. Msgr. KEVIN T. ROYAL, S.T.L.; Revs. DONALD A. GUGLIELMI, S.T.D.; MICHAEL K. JONES, S.T.D.

Office of Vocations—Rev. ROBERT M. KINNALLY, 238 Jewett Ave., Bridgeport, 06606. Tel: 203-416-1512; Fax: 203-612-9832. Email: frkinnally@diobpt.org. Assistant Vocation Directors: Revs. LEONEL S. MEDEIROS; JOSEPH A. MARCELLO.

Pastors' Vocation Advisory Board—Rev. Msgrs. J. PETER CULLEN, P.A., V.G.; THOMAS J. DRISCOLL, P.A., V.G.; WILLIAM J. SCHEYD, P.A., V.G.; Revs. LEONEL S. MEDEIROS; JOSEPH A. MARCELLO; GUSTAVO A. FALLA; STEPHEN J. GLEESON; NICHOLAS A. CIRILLO; MICHAEL K. JONES, S.T.D.; Rev. Msgrs. KEVIN T. ROYAL, S.T.L.; ANICETO VILLAMIDE; LAWRENCE J. CARROLL; Rev. SAMUEL V. SCOTT.

Office of the Permanent Diaconate—Deacons ANTHONY J. DETJE, Dir.; JOHN J. MORANSKI, Asst. Dir. Diaconate Formation.

Office for Ecumenical and Interreligious Affairs—Rev. SAMUEL V. SCOTT, Dir., St. John Fisher Residence, 894 Newfield Ave., Stamford, 06905-2518. Fax: 203-461-9876.

Diocesan Office of Divine Worship—VACANT.

Pastoral Services—Mr. DAMIEN O'CONNOR, The Catholic Center, 238 Jewett Ave., Bridgeport, 06606-2892. Tel: 203-416-1446; Fax: 203-373-1418. Email: doconnor@diobpt.org.

Family Life Ministry Diocesan Office—238 Jewett Ave., Bridgeport, 06606-2892. Tel: 203-416-1442; Fax: 203-371-8698. Rev. Msgr. ERNEST T. ESPOSITO, D.Min., Dir. Ministry Programs include Post Abortion Support and Pro-Life Ministry. Respect Life Ministry, Catholic Center, 238 Jewett Ave., Bridgeport, 06606-2892. Tel: 203-416-1440; Fax: 203-371-8698. Please call Mrs. Betty Ann Casaretti, Dir. Tel: 203-416-1442 for the following programs: Bereavement; Divorced and Separated; Marriage Preparation; Marriage Enrichment; Family Enrichment and Natural Family Planning.

Youth Ministry—Sr. ERIKA SCHEELJE. Tel: 203-416-1449. Email: srscheelje@diobpt.org.

Formation—VACANT, Dir.

Adult Formation—Ms. GINO DONNARUMMO. Tel: 203-416-1446. Email: gdonnarummo@diobpt.org.

Catholic Scouts—VACANT.

Bridgeport Diocesan Schools, Corp.—238 Jewett Ave., Bridgeport, 06606. Tel: 203-416-1375; Fax: 203-372-1961. Dr. MARGARET A. DAMES, Ed.D., Supt. Schools, 238 Jewett Ave., Bridgeport, 06606-2892. Tel: 203-416-1375; Fax: 203-372-1961. Email: mdames@diobpt.org; Mr. JOHN COOK, Deputy Supt. Schools. Tel: 203-416-1417; Sr. MARY GRACE WALSH, A.S.C.J., Deputy Supt. Schools. Tel: 203-416-1397; Mr. MARTIN TRISTINE, Dir. School Finance. Tel: 203-416-1377. Email: mtristine@diobpt.org; JENNIFER MITCHELL, Dir. Devel. & Communication. Tel: 203-416-1378.

Special Education—VACANT, Special Educ., The Catholic Center, 238 Jewett Ave., Bridgeport, 06606-2892. Tel: 203-416-1374; Fax: 203-372-1961; Sr. NANCY O'NEILL, C.N.D., Coord., Ministry to the Deaf. Tel: 203-416-1383; 203-372-4782 (TTY); Fax: 203-372-1961. Email: sroneill@diobpt.org.

Catholic Charities of Fairfield County, Inc.—Mr. ALBERT BARBER, Exec. Dir., Catholic Center, 238 Jewett Ave., Bridgeport, 06606-2892. Tel: 203-416-1307; 203-416-1333. Email: abarber@ccfc-ct.org.

Diocesan Offices and Directors

Ethnic and Cultural Services—Mr. MICHAEL TINTRUP, Sec., 238 Jewett Ave., Bridgeport, 06606-2892. Tel: 203-416-1305; Fax: 203-372-5045.

Aging, Diocesan Task Force—VACANT.

Archives—Deacon WILLIAM J. BISSENDEN, Archivist. Tel: 203-416-1354.

African Americans, Apostolate of—Rev. REGINALD NORMAN, The Catholic Center, 238 Jewett Ave., Bridgeport, 06606.

Catholic Lawyers—Rev. Msgr. J. JAMES CUNEO, J.C.D., Spiritual Moderator; LEOPOLD DEFUSCO, Esq., Coord., St. Thomas More Society of Fairfield Co., 238 Jewett Ave., Bridgeport, 06606-2892. Tel: 203-374-2590.

Catholic Physicians Guild—Dr. THOMAS G. FLYNN, Coord., 39 Old Studio Rd., New Canaan, 06840. Tel: 203-966-1959.

Catholic Women, Council of—Mrs. MARIE WALSH, 63 Glenbrook Rd,. Apt. 7A, Stamford, 06902. Tel: 203-358-8598. District Spiritual Directors: Rev. Msgr. ERNEST T. ESPOSITO, D.Min., (Bridgeport), Catholic Center, 238 Jewett Ave., Bridgeport, 06606. Tel: 203-416-1443; Fax: 203-371-8698; Rev. MARTIN S. IGOE, (Greenwich) (Retired), Sacred Heart Parish, 95 Henry St., Greenwich, 06830. Tel: 203-531-8730; Fax: 203-531-8794.

Cemeteries—RAY CAPO, Dir., 238 Jewett Ave., Bridgeport, 06606-2892. Tel: 203-416-1494; Fax: 203-374-7588. Email: rcapo@diobpt.org.

Communications—Mr. BRIAN D. WALLACE, Interim Dir., 238 Jewett Ave., Bridgeport, 06606-2892. Tel: 203-416-1464; Fax: 203-374-2044. Email: fcc@diobpt.org. Web: www.bridgeportdiocese.com; Rev. MARK CONNOLLY, Diocesan Dir., Radio & Television (Retired), Mailing Address: P.O. Box 7466, Greenwich, 06836. Tel: 203-316-9394.

Connecticut Catholic Conference—MICHAEL C. CULHANE, 134 Farmington Ave., Hartford, 06105. Tel: 203-524-7882.

Cursillos of Fairfield County, Inc.—Rev. Msgr. ANICETO VILLAMIDE, Advisor for Spanish Language, St. Peter Rectory, 695 Colorado Ave., Bridgeport, 06605. Tel: 203-366-5611.

Deaf, Apostolate for—Rev. PETER A. DEMARCO, Moderator (Retired), Res.: Catherine Dennis Keefe Queen of the Clergy, 274 Strawberry Hill Ave., Stamford, 06902. Tel: 203-358-9906. Email: pdem243377@aol.com.

Development, Office of—Mr. JEFF MACHI, Exec. Dir. Devel. Tel: 203-416-1324; KAREN GALLAGHER, Dir. Oper. Devel., 238 Jewett Ave., Bridgeport, 06606-2892. Tel: 203-416-1470.

Fairfield Foundation of the Diocese of Bridgeport, Inc.—MICHELLE JONES DELMHORST, Pres., 238 Jewett Ave., Bridgeport, 06606-2892. Tel: 203-416-1400.

Inner-City Foundation for Charity and Education—Rev. Msgr. KEVIN W. WALLIN, Exec. Dir.; Mr. RICHARD T. STONE, Dir., 238 Jewett Ave., Bridgeport, 06606-2892. Tel: 203-416-1363; Fax: 203-371-8698. Email: innercity.foundation@snet.net.

Catholic Ministry for the Elderly—VACANT.

Haitian American Catholic Center of Greater Stamford—Rev. JEAN-RONY PHILIPPE, 93 Hope St., Stamford, 06906. Tel: 203-406-0343; Fax: 203-406-0347.

Support Services, Office of—LOUISE STEWART-SPAGNUOLO, Dir., 238 Jewett Ave., Bridgeport, 06606-2892. Tel: 203-416-1402; Fax: 203-371-0875. Email: lsspagnuolo@diobpt.org.

Insurance Office—JOSEPH G. BURTON, Claims & Risk Mgr., Catholic Mutual Group, 238 Jewett Ave., Bridgeport, 06606. Tel: 203-416-1310; Fax: 203-371-6139. Email: jburton@catholicmutual.org.

Nurses, Council of Catholic—Rev. STEPHEN J. GLEESON, Dir., St. Stephen Rectory, 6949 Main St., Trumbull, 06611. Tel: 203-268-6217; Fax: 203-268-9861.

Official Newspapers— "The Fairfield County Catholic", (Biweekly) Most Rev. WILLIAM E. LORI, S.T.D., Publisher; Mr. BRIAN D. WALLACE, Interim Dir., 238 Jewett Ave., Bridgeport, 06606. Tel: 203-416-1464; Fax: 203-374-2044. Web: www.bridgeportdiocese.com; Mrs. PATRICIA HENNESSY, Asst. Editor. Tel: 203-416-1460; Fax: 203-374-2044. Email: phennessy@diobpt.org.

Pilgrimages, Office of Diocesan—Rev. Msgr. WILLIAM J. LOUGHLIN (Retired), Catherine Dennis Keefe Queen of the Clergy Retired Priests' Residence, 274 Strawberry Hill Ave., Stamford, 06902. Tel: 203-358-9906.

Pontifical Association of the Holy Childhood—Rev. FREDERICK L. SAVIANO, Dir., The Catholic Center, 238 Jewett Ave., Bridgeport, 06606-2892. Tel: 203-416-1447; Fax: 203-371-8698.

Portuguese-Speaking People, Apostolate for—VACANT.

Propagation of the Faith—Rev. FREDERICK L. SAVIANO, Dir., The Catholic Center, 238 Jewett Ave., Bridgeport, 06606-2892. Tel: 203-416-1447; Fax: 203-371-8698. Email: frsaviano@diobpt.org.

Boy Scouts and Girl Scouts—VACANT.

Retired Priests—Rev. Msgr. LOUIS A. DEPROFIO, P.A., Dir. (Retired); VICKEY HICKEY, Admin., The Catherine Dennis Keefe Queen of the Clergy Retired Priests' Residence, 274 Strawberry Hill Ave., Stamford, 06904. Tel: 203-358-9906; Fax: 203-358-9524.

Office of Safe Environments—Ms. ERIN NEIL, Dir., 238 Jewett Ave., Bridgeport, 06606. Tel: 203-416-1406. Email: eneil@diobpt.org.

Victims Assistance Coordinators—Mr. MICHAEL TINTRUP. Tel: 203-241-0987. Email: mtintrup@diobpt.org; Ms. ERIN NEIL, M.S.W., 238 Jewett Ave., Bridgeport, 06606. Tel: 203-650-3265. Email: eneil@diobpt.org.

CLERGY, PARISHES, MISSIONS AND PAROCHIAL SCHOOLS

CITY OF BRIDGEPORT

(FAIRFIELD COUNTY)

1—ST. AUGUSTINE CATHEDRAL (1842) Rev. Msgr. Kevin W. Wallin; Revs. Leonel S. Medeiros; Jhon Gomez; Deacon Santos Garcia. In Res., Rev. Ha Dang; Sr. Antoinette Mongkolrutana, S.L.C., Vietnamese Pastoral Assoc.
Res.: 359 Washington Ave., 06604. Tel: 203-368-6777; Fax: 203-368-6386.
See St. Augustine Cathedral, Bridgeport under Elementary Schools, Regional located in the Institution section.
Catechesis/Religious Program—Students 265.

2—ST. AMBROSE (1928) Rev. John Stronkowski; Deacon Kenneth J. Ruge. In Res., Rev. Churchill Penn.
Res.: 1596 Boston Ave., 06610. Tel: 203-333-1336; Fax: 203-330-9085. Email: stambrose@optonline.net.
See St. Ambrose, Bridgeport under Elementary Schools, Regional located in the Institution section.
Catechesis/Religious Program—Students 58.
Station—Bishop Curtis Homes 525 Palisade Ave. Tel: 203-366-4333.
Station—Success Park Success Ave.

3—ST. ANDREW (1961) Revs. Eugene R. Szantyr; Roy Henderson. In Res., Rev. William F. Verrilli.
Res.: 435 Anton St., 06606. Tel: 203-374-6171; Fax: 203-372-7709.
See St. Andrew, Bridgeport under Elementary Schools, Regional located in the Institution section.
Catechesis/Religious Program—Tel: 203-374-8118; Fax: 203-374-9450. Mr. Michael McNally, D.R.E. Students 235.

4—ST. ANN (1922) [CEM] Rev. Peter J. Towsley.
Res.: 481 Brewster St., 06605. Tel: 203-368-1607; Fax: 203-368-0859. Email: admin@stannblackrock.com. Web: www.stannblackrock.com.
See St. Ann, Bridgeport under Elementary Schools, Regional located in the Institution section.
Catechesis/Religious Program—Students 50.

5—ST. ANTHONY OF PADUA, Merged with St. Peter, Bridgeport. See separate listing.

6—BLESSED SACRAMENT (1917) Rev. Reginald D. Norman, Admin.; Deacons Ricardo Martinez; Donald P. Foust; Joseph Mihalek, Pastoral Assoc.
Res.: 275 Union Ave., 06607. Tel: 203-333-1202; Fax: 203-368-3502. Email: blessedsacramentrc@sbcglobal.net. Web: http://blessedsacramentrc.parishesonline.net.
Catechesis/Religious Program—Students 40.

7—ST. CHARLES BORROMEO (1902) Revs. Jean-Jacques Rousseau; Edicson Orozco; Rogerio Silva Perri; Sr. Antoinette Mongkolrutana, S.L.C., Laotian Pastoral Assoc. Tel: 203-333-0837.
Res.: 391 Ogden St., 06608. Tel: 203-333-2147; Fax: 203-330-8316.
Catechesis/Religious Program—Tel: 203-576-1629. Students 276.

8—SS. CYRIL AND METHODIUS (1907), (Slovak), Rev. Msgr. Joseph W. Pekar.

Res.: 79 Church St., 06608. Tel: 203-333-7003.

9—ST. GEORGE (1907), (Lithuanian), Revs. Julio Lopresti, I.V.E.; Gustavo Campo, I.V.E.
Res.: 443 Park Ave., 06604. Tel: 203-335-1797; Fax: 203-334-6359. Email: stgeorge.church@sbcglobal.net.
Catechesis/Religious Program—Tel: 203-330-8409. Email: c-damaris@sersdoras.org. Web: www.ss/musa.org. Sr. Maria DoDivino-Pranto, D.R.E. Students 145.

10—HOLY ROSARY (1903), (Italian), Deacon Donald P. Foust, Admin. In Res., Rev. John Punnakunnel (India) (Retired).
Res.: 365 E. Washington Ave., 06608. Tel: 203-334-2447; Fax: 203-335-5334.
Catechesis/Religious Program—Students 3.

11—ST. JOHN NEPOMUCENE, Closed. For inquiries for parish records contact Holy Name of Jesus, Stratford.

12—ST. JOSEPH'S, Closed. May 23, 1988. For inquiries for parish records contact St. Patrick, Bridgeport.

13—ST. MARY (1857), (Spanish), [CEM] Rev. Msgr. Matthew Bernelli.
Res.: 25 Sherman St., 06608. Tel: 203-334-8811; Fax: 203-334-8574. Email: stmarychurchbpt@optonline.net. Web: www.stmarychurchbridgeport.com.
Catechesis/Religious Program—Students 158.

14—ST. MICHAEL THE ARCHANGEL (1899), (Polish), [CEM] Rev. Stefan Morawski, O.F.M.Conv.
Res.: 310 Pulaski St., 06608. Tel: 203-334-1822; Fax: 203-696-0078. Web: www.smaparish.com.
Catechesis/Religious Program—Students 83.

15—OUR LADY OF FATIMA (1962), (Portuguese), Rev. Joseph De Brito Alves (Portugal), Admin.; Deacon Gabriel A. Pereira.
Res.: 429 Huntington Rd., 06608. Tel: 203-333-7575; Fax: 203-333-7575.
Catechesis/Religious Program—Tel: 203-929-1085. Students 122.

16—OUR LADY OF GOOD COUNSEL (1955) [CEM] Rev. Reginald D. Norman, Admin.
Res.: 163 Ortega Ave., 06606. Tel: 203-372-3533.
Catechesis/Religious Program— Noreen Franklin, D.R.E. Students 24.

17—ST. PATRICK CHURCH (1889) Rev. Norman J. Guilbert; Deacons William J. Bissenden; Alix Africot. In Res., Rev. Bernardo C. Rodriguez.
Res. & Business Office: 170 Thompson St., 06604-2816. Tel: 203-335-0106; Fax: 203-335-0107. Email: stpats@optonline.net. Web: www.stpatrickbridgeport.com.
Church: 851 North Ave., 06606.
Catechesis/Religious Program—Email: mgruce@optonline.net. Marcia Gruce, D.R.E. Students 63.
Station—Connecticut State Correctional Institution
Station—St. Vincent Medical Center, Tel: 203-576-6000.
Station—Northbridge Health Care Center, Tel: 203-336-0232.

18—ST. PETER (1900), (Spanish), [CEM] Rev. Msgr. Aniceto Villamide; Rev. Jose Rebaque, S.A.C., Temp. Parochial Vicar; Deacons Domingo Reveron; Luis Torres.
Res.: 695 Colorado Ave., 06605. Tel: 203-366-5611; Fax: 203-335-1924.
See St. Peter, Bridgeport under Elementary Schools, Regional located in the Institution section.
Catechesis/Religious Program—Tel: 203-334-5681; Fax: 203-333-1590. Sr. Aida Ramirez, M.S.S., D.R.E. Students 395.

19—ST. RAPHAEL (1925), (Italian), Revs. Alfonso Picone, Admin.; Grazioso Artuso; Giandomenico Flora, Parochial Vicar; Deacon Joseph Melita.
Res.: 162 Oak St., 06604. Tel: 203-333-3161; Fax: 203-368-1727.
See St. Raphael, Bridgeport under Elementary Schools, Regional located in the Institution section.
Catechesis/Religious Program—Students 95.
Convent—671 Oak St., 06604. Tel: 203-335-9817; Fax: 203-336-9205.
Chapel—St. Margaret's Shrine 2539 Park Ave., 06604. Tel: 203-368-4425.

OUTSIDE THE CITY OF BRIDGEPORT

BETHEL, FAIRFIELD CO., ST. MARY (1882) [CEM] Revs. Corey V. Piccinino; Cyrus Bartolome; Edward J. McAuley, (Diocese of Tororo); Deacons Michael Oles; John DeRoin.
Church & Office: 26 Dodgingtown Rd., 06801. Tel: 203-744-5777; Fax: 203-744-3740. Email: stmaryoffice@comcast.net. Web: www.stmarybethel.org.
See St. Mary, Danbury under Elementary Schools, Regional located in the Institution section.
Catechesis/Religious Program—24 Dodgingtown Rd., 06801. Tel: 203-743-4557. Email: meferri@aol.com. Mary Ferri, D.R.E. Students 747.
Convent—Tel: 203-743-6985.

BROOKFIELD, FAIRFIELD CO.

1—ST. JOSEPH (1941) Revs. George F. O'Neill; Henry Hoffmann, Parochial Vicar; Deacons William J. Shaughnessy; Peter J. Kuhn.
Res.: 163 Whisconier Rd., 06804. Tel: 203-775-1035; Fax: 203-775-1684. Web: www.stjosephbrookfield.com.
See St. Joseph, Brookfield under Elementary Schools, Regional located in the Institution section.
Catechesis/Religious Program—Tel: 203-775-1035. Andrea Woronick, D.R.E. Students 681.

2—ST. MARGUERITE BOURGEOYS (1982) [CEM] Revs. George S. Sankoorikal; Pawel Hrebenko; Deacons Richard A. Fenton; Anthony J. Detje.
Res.: 138 Candlewood Lake Rd., 06804. Tel: 203-775-5117; Fax: 203-775-9254.
Catechesis/Religious Program—Tel: 203-775-2644. Carole Harris, D.R.E. Students 366.

DANBURY, FAIRFIELD CO.

1—ST. GREGORY THE GREAT (1960) Revs. Angelo S. Arrando; Raymond M. Scherba; Deacons Robert Blankschen; William D. Murphy; Daniel N. Myott; Paul B. Pilkington.
Res.: 85 Great Plain Rd., 06811. Tel: 203-797-0222; Fax: 203-743-7049. Email: frarrando@aol.com. Web: www.danbury.org/stgreg.
See St. Gregory the Great, Danbury under Elementary Schools, Regional located in the Institution section.
Catechesis/Religious Program—Tel: 203-743-5168. Mrs. Mary Ann Hauser, D.R.E. Students 193.

2—IMMACULATE HEART OF MARY (1980), (Portuguese), [CEM] Rev. Antonio Carvalho de Azevedo, Admin.; Deacon Jose Rodrigues Cabral.
Res.: 149 Deer Hill Ave., 06811. Tel: 203-797-1821; Fax: 203-743-9146. Email: heartofmary@sbcglobal.net.
Catechesis/Religious Program— Helena Andrade, D.R.E. Students 112.

3—ST. JOSEPH (1905) Revs. Michael F. Dogali; David W. Franklin. In Res., Revs. Joseph Dasari (India); Raymond K. Petrucci.
Res.: 8 Robinson Ave., 06810. Tel: 203-748-8177; Fax: 203-748-2010. Web: www.stjosephsdanbury.com.
See St. Joseph, Danbury under Elementary Schools, Regional located in the Institution section.
Catechesis/Religious Program—Tel: 203-778-1920; Fax: 203-730-0026. Sherry Morris, D.R.E. Students 350.

4—OUR LADY OF GUADALUPE (1985), (Spanish), [CEM] Revs. Hector Leon; Jose Montoya (Colombia).
Res.: 29 Golden Hill Rd., 06811-4629. Tel: 203-743-1021; Fax: 203-798-8143.
Catechesis/Religious Program—Students 311.

5—ST. PETER (1851) [CEM] Rev. Gregg D. Mecca; Rev. Msgr. Pedro D. Diniz (Brazil), Ministry to Brazilian Community; Deacon John Buchholz. In Res., Revs. Paul F. Merry; M. Joseph Joaquin.
Res.: 104 Main St., 06810. Tel: 203-743-2707; Fax: 203-794-1928. Email: office@stpeterdanb.org. Web: www.stpeterdanb.org.
See St. Peter-Sacred Heart School, Danbury under Elementary Schools, Diocesan located in the Institution section.
Catechesis/Religious Program—Tel: 203-743-1048; Fax: 203-797-9471. Joanne Durkin, D.R.E. (K-8). Students 297.

6—SACRED HEART OF JESUS (1925) Rev. Dennis Mason, O.F.M.Conv.; Deacon John F. Esterheld. In Res., Rev. Michael Lasky, O.F.M.Conv.
Parish Center—46 Stone St., 06810.
Res.: 12 Cottage St., 06810. Tel: 203-748-9029; Fax: 203-748-9168. Email: sacred_heart@snet.net. Web: www.sacredhrtchurch.org.
See Sacred Heart, Danbury under Elementary Schools, Regional located in the Institution section.
Catechesis/Religious Program—Tel: 203-743-0689. Email: sh-dre@snet.net. Students 95.

DARIEN, FAIRFIELD CO.

1—ST. JOHN (1895) [CEM] Rev. Msgr. Frank C. McGrath; Rev. Francisco Gomez, Parochial Vicar; Deacons William K. Rowe; Wayne E. Malloy. In Res., Rev. Hernan D. Bohorquez.
Res.: 1986 Post Rd., 06820. Tel: 203-655-1145; Fax: 203-655-1048. Email: stjohn2@oponline.net. Web: www.stjohndarien.com.
Catechesis/Religious Program—Tel: 203-655-8020. Email: religiousedsj@optonline.net. John Cunningham, D.R.E. Students 600.

2—ST. THOMAS MORE (1966) Revs. J. Barry Furey; Robert J. Post; Deacon Roland Blier.
Res. & Parish Office: 374 Middlesex Rd., 06820. Tel: 203-655-3303; Fax: 203-655-6478. Email: stmdarienct@aol.com. Web: www.stmdarienct.org.
Catechesis/Religious Program—374 Middlesex Rd., 06820. Tel: 203-655-3077; Fax: 203-655-8901. Email: stmdariened@aol.com. Sandra Kluun, C.R.E. (Gr. 1-5); Mrs. Jeanne Bisson, D.R.E.; Janice Pataky, Youth Min. (Gr. 6-12); Maria Oliveira, Dir. PreSchool. Students 975.

EASTON, FAIRFIELD CO., NOTRE DAME (OF EASTON) (1956) [CEM] Rev. Msgr. Thomas J. Driscoll; Rev. Michael P. Lyons; Deacons Harold J. Lynch; Gerald F. Sabol.
Res.: 640 Morehouse Rd., 06612. Tel: 203-268-5838; Fax: 203-459-4940. Email: notredame@optonline.net. Web: www.notredameofeaston.org.
Church: 655 Morehouse Rd., 06612-1334.
Catechesis/Religious Program—Tel: 203-261-5596; Fax: 203-459-4940. Deacon Vincent J. Heidenreich, D.R.E. Students 456.

FAIRFIELD, FAIRFIELD CO.

1—ST. ANTHONY OF PADUA (1927) Rev. John P. Baran; Deacon Donald J. Ross.
Res.: 149 S. Pine Creek Rd., 06824. Tel: 203-259-0358; Fax: 203-259-5112.
Catechesis/Religious Program— Eleanor W. Sauers, D.R.E. Students 198.

2—ST. EMERY (1932), (Hungarian), (Franciscan), (United with St. Stephen's of Bridgeport 1897-1971) Rev. Louis M. Pintye, O.F.M.; Deacon Rudolph P. Trankovich.
Office/Friary: 838 King's Hwy. E., 06825-5418. Tel: 203-334-0312; Fax: 203-579-9423. Email: ssemerstep@aol.com. Web: www.stemerys.com.
Catechesis/Religious Program—Tel: 203-335-4854. Students 15.
Convent—Congregation of Notre Dame, 105 Biro St., 06825-5418. Tel: 203-334-3913. Congregation of Notre Dame 3.

3—HOLY CROSS (1913), (Slovenian), Rev. Alfred F. Pecaric.
Res.: 750 Tahmore Dr., 06825. Tel: 203-372-4595; Fax: 203-372-4668. Email: holy-cross-church@sbcglobal.net.
Catechesis/Religious Program—Tel: 203-373-0466. Students 35.

4—HOLY FAMILY (1938) Revs. Guido G. Montanaro; Edward J. Small, S.J.; Deacons Joseph De Biase; Stephen Sebestyen.
Res.: 700 Old Stratfield Rd., 06825. Tel: 203-336-1835; Fax: 203-336-0342.
See Holy Family, Fairfield under Elementary Schools, Regional located in the Institution section.
Catechesis/Religious Program—Tel: 203-336-1835; Fax: 203-336-0342. Students 210.

5—OUR LADY OF THE ASSUMPTION (1922) [CEM] Rev. Msgr. Blase M. Gintoli; Deacons Raymond J. Chervenak; Kevin Moore.
Res.: 545 Stratfield Rd., 06825. Tel: 203-333-9065; Fax: 203-333-2562. Email: ola.fairfield@svcglobal.net. Web: www.assumption-fairfield.org.
School—591 Stratfield Rd., 06825. Tel: 203-334-6271; Fax: 203-382-0399. Email: schoolbulldogs@aol.com. See separate listing under Elementary Schools in the Institution section.
Catechesis/Religious Program—Tel: 203-367-1108; Fax: 203-367-0927. Frank Macari, D.R.E.; Alice Kilcullen-McFarland, C.R.E. Students 415.
Parish Center—605 Stratfield Rd., 06825. Tel: 203-336-3419.

6—ST. PIUS X (1955) [CEM] Rev. Msgr. Lawrence J. Carroll; Rev. Samuel S. Kachuba. In Res., Rev. Msgr. Stanlislaus B. Rousseau (Retired).
Res.: 834 Brookside Dr., 06824. Tel: 203-255-6134; Fax: 203-255-5232. Email: jdonnelly@st-pius.org. Web: www.st-pius.org.
Catechesis/Religious Program—Tel: 203-259-4800; Fax: 203-255-5232. Email: dcamillo@st-pius.org. Diane Camillo, D.R.E.; Michael Lantowski, Dir. Music. Students 880.

7—ST. THOMAS AQUINAS (1876) [CEM] Revs. Victor T. Martin; Roger F. McDonough; Deacon Daniel Ianniello; Sr. Catherine Leonard, C.N.D., Pastoral Asst.
Res.: 1719 Post Rd., 06824. Tel: 203-255-1097; Fax: 203-256-8177. Email: stthoaq@aol.com.
See St. Thomas Aquinas, Fairfield under Elementary Schools, Regional located in the Institution section.
Catechesis/Religious Program—Tel: 203-255-1984; Fax: 203-256-9305. Email: stthoaqccd@aol.com. Sr. Monica Leonard, C.N.D., D.R.E. Students 988.

GEORGETOWN, FAIRFIELD CO., SACRED HEART (1881) Revs. David C. Leopold; Colin J. McKenna.
Res.: 30 Church St., Box 388, 06829. Tel: 203-544-8345. Email: sacredheartgtn@aol.com. Web: www.sacredheartct.org.
Catechesis/Religious Program—Tel: 203-544-8423. Email: sacredheart.rel.edu@sbcglobal.net. Students 290.

GREENWICH, FAIRFIELD CO.

1—ST. AGNES (1963) Rev. William F. Carey; Deacon John M. Linsenmeyer.
Res.: 247 Stanwich Rd., 06830. Tel: 203-869-5396; Fax: 203-625-0596. Email: stagnesgreenwich@aol.com. Web: www.stagnesre.org.
Catechesis/Religious Program—Students 40.

2—ST. MARY (1874) [CEM] Rev. Msgr. Francis C. Wissel; Revs. Rolando Torres; Richard J. Gemza; Deacon Paul Tupper.
Res.: 178 Greenwich Ave., 06830. Tel: 203-869-9393; Fax: 203-869-1032. Email: stmaryparish@verizon.net. Web: www.stmaryparishgreenwich.org.
Catechesis/Religious Program—Tel: 203-869-9250; Fax: 203-625-4760. Email: saintmre@verizon.net. Students 298.

3—ST. MICHAEL THE ARCHANGEL (1963) [CEM] Rev. Msgr. J. Peter Cullen; Revs. Ciprian Bejan (Romania); Shawn W. Cutler; Deacon Russell T. Rigg.
Res.: 469 North St., 06830. Tel: 203-869-5421; Fax: 203-869-0169.
Catechesis/Religious Program—Tel: 203-661-3088; Fax: 203-869-0169. Email: srceline@optonline.net. Sr. Celine M. Flynn, S.S.N.D., D.R.E. Students 630.
Mission—St. Timothy's, Fairfield Co. Tel: 203-869-5421; Fax: 203-869-0169.

4—ST. PAUL (1902) [CEM] Rev. Frank A. Winn.
Res.: 84 Sherwood Ave., 06831. Tel: 203-531-8741; Fax: 203-532-1414. Email: stpgreenwichct@aol.com. Web: www.stpaulgreenwich.org.
Catechesis/Religious Program—Tel: 203-531-4265. Rosie Pennella, D.R.E. Students 462.

5—ST. ROCH (1938) Very Rev. Canon Matthew Mauriello; Rev. Carlos Rodriques.
Res.: 10 St. Roch Ave., 06830-6234. Tel: 203-869-4176; Fax: 203-618-0341. Email: strochcatholic@verizon.net.
Catechesis/Religious Program—Jane Kowaleski, D.R.E. Students 128.

6—SACRED HEART (1890) [CEM] Rev. Bose Raja Selvaraj (India).
Res.: 95 Henry St., 06830. Tel: 203-531-8730; Fax: 203-531-8794. Email: sacredheartqrn@optonline.net.
Catechesis/Religious Program—Tel: 203-531-4772. Laurie Palastro, C.R.E. Students 100.

MONROE, FAIRFIELD CO., ST. JUDE (1973) Rev. Msgr. John B. Sabia; Rev. Joseph J. Karcsinski; Deacon John DiTaranto.
Res.: 707 Monroe Tpke., 06468. Tel: 203-261-6404; Fax: 203-261-7507. Email: parishoffice@saintjudechurch.net. Web: www.stjudechurch.net.
See St. Jude, Monroe under Elementary Schools, Regional located in the Institution section.
Catechesis/Religious Program—Tel: 203-261-6788. Mrs. Jean Paul, D.R.E. Students 1,777.

NEW CANAAN, FAIRFIELD CO., ST. ALOYSIUS (1896) Rev. Msgr. William J. Scheyd; Revs. William G. Carey; Ian Jeremiah; Deacons Louis F. Howe Sr.; Stephen W. Pond. In Res., Rev. Bernard A. Keefe (Retired).
Res.: 40 Maple St., 06840. Tel: 203-966-0020; Fax: 203-972-7691. Email: office@starcc.com. Web: www.starcc.com.
See St. Aloysius, New Canaan under Elementary Schools, Regional located in the Institution section.
Catechesis/Religious Program—Tel: 203-966-4555. Students 1,178.

NEW FAIRFIELD, FAIRFIELD CO., ST. EDWARD THE CONFESSOR (1954) Rev. Msgr. Martin P. Ryan; Revs. Joseph Cervero; Sebastine Ukwanda; Deacons David Vaughn; Frank Foyt.
Res.: 1 Gillotti Rd., P.O. Box 8866, 06812. Tel: 203-746-7298; Fax: 203-746-4856. Web: www.saintedwardchurch.org.
Catechesis/Religious Program—Tel: 203-746-4270. Kathryn LaRegina, C.R.E. Students 1,205.

NEWTOWN, FAIRFIELD CO., ST. ROSE OF LIMA (1859) [CEM] Rev. Msgr. Robert E. Weiss; Revs. Milan Dimic; Jose Ignacio A. Ortigas; Deacons Thomas F. Curran; Donald Naiman; Norman Roos; Daniel O'Connor.
Res.: 46 Church Hill Rd., 06470. Tel: 203-426-1014; Fax: 203-426-6222.
Catechesis/Religious Program—38 Church Hill Rd., 06470. Tel: 203-426-2333; Fax: 203-426-8074. Pam Arsenault, D.R.E. Students 1,659.

NORWALK, FAIRFIELD CO.

1—ST. JEROME (1960) [CEM] Revs. David W. Blanchfield; Joseph Palacino (Retired).
Church: 23 Half Mile Rd., 06851. Tel: 203-847-5349; Fax: 203-846-0238.
Catechesis/Religious Program—Tel: 203-846-2111. Email: reachstjerome@optonline.net. Web: www.stnorwalkst.org. Students 408.

2—ST. JOSEPH (South Norwalk) (1895) Rev. Gilbert P. D'Souza; Deacons William O. Murphy; Augustin Pierre-Louis. In Res., Revs. G. Frantz Desruisseaux; Paul Sankar.
Res.: 85 S. Main St., 06854. Tel: 203-838-4171; Fax: 203-899-0007. Email: stjosono@aol.com.
Catechesis/Religious Program—Tel: 203-866-1225. Mrs. Dora Deandrade, C.R.E. Students 294.
Convent—14 Chestnut St., 06854. Tel: 203-866-9452.

3—ST. LADISLAUS (1907), (Hungarian), [CEM] Rev. Michael J. Bachman. In Res., Rev. Stephen J. Balint.
Res.: 25 Cliff St., 06854. Tel: 203-866-1867; Fax: 203-866-7830.
Catechesis/Religious Program—Students 16.

4—ST. MARY (1848) [CEM] Revs. Greg J. Markey; Juan G. Pineda (Colombia); Richard G. Cipolla; Deacon Stephan A. Genovese. In Res., Rev. Paul N. Check.
Res.: 669 West Ave., 06850. Tel: 203-866-5546; Fax: 203-866-0464. Web: www.stmarynorwalk.net.
Catechesis/Religious Program—Tel: 203-866-7429; Fax: 203-866-0127. Mrs. Jacqueline Juhasz, D.R.E. Students 245.

5—ST. MATTHEW (1957) Rev. Msgr. Walter C. Orlowski; Rev. Tomi Thomas, I.M.S.; Deacon David M. Sochacki.
Res.: 216 Scribner Ave., 06854. Tel: 203-838-3788; Fax: 203-838-8195. Email: stmattparish@hotmail.com. Web: www.stmatthewnorwalk.com.
Catechesis/Religious Program—Tel: 203-838-0231; Fax: 203-838-4195. Laurie Fan, Coord. Rel. Formation; Michele Scholl, Coord. Rel. Formation; Frances Consiglio, Coord. Rel. Formation. Students 659.

6—ST. PHILIP (1964) Rev. Michael A. Boccaccio; Sr. Mary Ann McPartland, C.N.D., Pastoral Assoc.; Deacons Frank J. Chiappetta; Paul J. Reilly; John W. Mahon.
Res.: One Fr. Conlon Pl., 06851. Tel: 203-847-4549 (Office); Fax: 203-847-4148.
Catechesis/Religious Program—Tel: 203-847-4286. Mrs. Doris Chiappetta, Dir. Faith Formation. Students 230.

7—ST. THOMAS THE APOSTLE (1935) Revs. Robert J. Crofut; Sudhir D'Souza; Deacon Joseph Gagne.
Res.: 203 East Ave., 06855. Tel: 203-866-3141; Fax: 203-866-1219. Email: stthomasnorwalk@optonline.net.
Malta House—5 Prowitt St., 06855. Tel: 203-857-0088; Fax: 203-857-0018.
Catechesis/Religious Program—208 East Ave., 06855. Tel: 203-866-1189; Fax: 203-866-1219. Email: stthomasfuture@sbcglobal.net. Mrs. Patricia Postiglione, D.R.E. Students 354.

REDDING, FAIRFIELD CO., ST. PATRICK (1879), (Irish), Rev. Russell Augustine; Deacon William C. Timmel. In Res., Rev. Miroslav Stachurski.
Res.: 169 Black Rock Tpke., P.O. Box 119, Redding Ridge, 06876. Tel: 203-938-2253; Fax: 203-938-3396. Email: stpatrickreading@sbcglobal.net.
Catechesis/Religious Program—Tel: 203-938-2963. Email: rdaureli@sbcglobal.net. Annette O'Hara, C.R.E. Students 225.

RIDGEFIELD, FAIRFIELD CO.

1—ST. ELIZABETH SETON (1976) Rev. Joseph A. Prince; Deacon Robert Morris.
Res.: 520 Ridgebury Rd., 06877. Tel: 203-438-7292; Fax: 203-438-0600. Email: stsetonparish@comcast.net.
Catechesis/Religious Program—Tel: 203-438-9707; Fax: 203-438-7947. Gigi Pekala, C.R.E.; Marie Trebing, C.R.E. Students 502.

2—ST. MARY (1882) [CEM] Rev. Msgr. Laurence R. Bronkiewicz, Pastor; Revs. Mariusz Olbrys; Brian P. Gannon, Parochial Vicar; Deacons Robert A. Salvestrini; Henry Hein; Hans J. Gram.
Res.: 31 Bryon Ave., 06877. Tel: 203-438-6538; Fax: 203-438-4406. Web: www.smcr.org.
School—183 Highridge Ave., 06877. Tel: 203-438-7288; Fax: 203-431-8742. Email: brennane@diobptedu.org. Mr. Edward Brennan, Prin. See separate listing under Elementary Schools in the Institution Section.
Catechesis/Religious Program—Tel: 203-438-7335; Fax: 203-438-6876. Sr. Joan Brennan, D.R.E. Students 1,400.

RIVERSIDE, FAIRFIELD CO., ST. CATHERINE OF SIENA Rev. Msgr. Alan F. Detscher; Rev. Francis T. Hoffmann; Deacons Renato Berzolla; Robert Henrey; Vincent J. Heidenreich.
Res.: 4 Riverside Ave., 06878. Tel: 203-637-3661; Fax: 203-637-8934. Email: scsrectory@aol.com. Web: www.stcath.org.
Catechesis/Religious Program—6 Riverside Ave., 06878. Tel: 203-637-3661, Ext. 30; Fax: 203-637-2089. Marcella Abatemarco, D.R.E. Students 635.

SHELTON, FAIRFIELD CO.

1—ST. JOSEPH (1906) Rev. Msgr. Christopher J. Walsh; Revs. Nicholas S. Pavia; Marcel St. Jean, Parochial Vicar; Deacons Jeffrey J. Kingsley; Anthony Conti.
Res.: 50 Fairmont Pl., 06484. Tel: 203-924-8611; Fax: 203-924-9446. Email: stjoseph.rectory@snet.net. Web: www.sjcshelton.org.
See St. Joseph School, Shelton under Elementary Schools, Regional located in the Institution section.
Catechesis/Religious Program—Tel: 203-924-9677. Mrs. Patricia Heller, D.R.E. Students 420.
Convent—Apostles of the Sacred Heart of Jesus, 420 Coram Ave., 06484. Tel: 203-924-1449.

2—ST. LAWRENCE (1955) [CEM] Revs. Michael K. Jones; F. John Ringley; Peter K. Smolik; Deacons Joseph Filingeri; Frank J. Masso.
Res.: 505 Shelton Ave., 06484. Tel: 203-929-5355; Fax: 203-929-8939. Email: stlawrpar1@aol.com. Web: www.diobptstlawrenceparish.net.
School—Tel: 203-929-4422; Fax: 203-929-3669. Email: sis@snet.net. Martha Reitman, Prin. See separate listing located in Shelton under Elementary Schools in the Institution section.
Catechesis/Religious Program—Tel: 203-929-8421. Mrs. Barbara Pekar, D.R.E. Students 790.

3—ST. MARGARET MARY (1963) [CEM] Rev. Msgr. Thomas J. Whalen; Rev. Nello Barachini (Retired).
Res.: 380 Long Hill Ave., 06484. Tel: 203-924-4929; Fax: 203-924-1849.
Catechesis/Religious Program—Tel: 203-924-2679. Mrs. Carol D'Amico, D.R.E. Students 220.

SHERMAN, FAIRFIELD CO., HOLY TRINITY (1985) [CEM] Rev. Paul Murphy.
Res.: Rte. 37 & 39, P.O. Box 97, 06784. Tel: 860-354-1414; Fax: 860-355-9439.
Catechesis/Religious Program—Tel: 860-355-1483; Fax: 860-355-9439. Mrs. Michele Curnan, D.R.E. Students 243.

STAMFORD, FAIRFIELD CO.

1—THE BASILICA OF SAINT JOHN THE EVANGELIST (1854) [CEM] Rev. Msgr. Stephen M. Di Giovanni; Rev. Terrence P. Walsh, Parochial Vicar. In Res., Rev. Albert Audette (Retired).
Res.: 279 Atlantic St., 06901. Tel: 203-324-1553; Fax: 203-359-2660. Email: stjc@optonline.net. Web: stjohnsstamford.com.
Catechesis/Religious Program—Students 137.

2—ST. BENEDICT (1930), (Slovak), Merged with Our Lady of Montserrat, Stamford to form Saint Benedict and Our Lady of Montserrat, Stamford.

3—SAINT BENEDICT - OUR LADY OF MONTSERRAT (2000) [CEM] Revs. Gustavo A. Falla; Peter F. Lenox, Parochial Vicar.
Mailing Address: One St. Benedict Cir., 06902. Tel: 203-327-7250; 203-323-7379; Fax: 203-323-0798. Email: myparish@optonline.net.
Catechesis/Religious Program—Tel: 203-353-1733. Students 259.

4—ST. BRIDGET OF IRELAND (1963) Rev. Gill C. Babeu.
Res.: 278 Strawberry Hill Ave., 06902. Tel: 203-324-2910; Fax: 203-363-0135. Email: bridgetct@aol.com. Web: www.stbridgetofireland.org.
Catechesis/Religious Program—Tel: 203-357-8157. Beth Wilson-Jordan, D.R.E. Students 154.

5—ST. CECILIA (1926) [CEM] Rev. David J. Riley.
Res.: 1184 Newfield Ave., 06905-1496. Tel: 203-322-1562; Fax: 203-968-1550.
School—Tel: 203-322-6505; Fax: 203-322-6835. See separate listing under Elementary Schools in the Institution section.
Catechesis/Religious Program—Tel: 203-329-8783; Fax: 203-595-0519. Students 403.

6—ST. CLEMENT OF ROME (1928) Rev. Joseph J. Malloy.
Res.: 535 Fairfield Ave., 06902. Tel: 203-348-4206; Fax: 203-316-8131. Email: stclement@optonline.net.
Catechesis/Religious Program—Tel: 203-348-1233; Fax: 203-316-8131. JoAnn Tolla, D.R.E. Students 125.

7—ST. GABRIEL (1963) Rev. Cyprian P. LaPastina; Deacon Larry Buzzeo.
Res.: 914 Newfield Ave., 06905. Tel: 203-322-7426; Fax: 203-968-6266. Email: gab914@optonline.net.
See St. Gabriel, Stamford under Elementary Schools, Regional located in the Institution section.
Catechesis/Religious Program—Tel: 203-329-1978. Maryanne Didelot, Asst. D.R.E. Students 205.

8—HOLY NAME OF JESUS (1903), (Polish), Rev. Eugene Kotlinsky, C.M.
Res.: 4 Pulaski St., 06902. Tel: 203-323-4967; Fax: 203-327-2229.
Catechesis/Religious Program—Tel: 203-359-3618; Fax: 203-323-4546. Sr. Joanna McCloskey, S.M.M.I., D.R.E. Students 170.

9—HOLY SPIRIT (1962) [CEM] Rev. Robert J. Hyl; Deacon Paul J. Jennings.
Res.: 403 Scofieldtown Rd., 06903-4009. Tel: 203-322-3722; Fax: 203-322-0543. Email: holyspiritparish@aol.com.
See Holy Spirit, Stamford under Elementary Schools, Regional located in the Institution section.
Catechesis/Religious Program— Mrs. Judith Kavulich, D.R.E. Students 169.

10—ST. LEO (1960) [CEM] Revs. James D. Grosso; Leszek P. Szymaszek. In Res., Rev. William M. Quinlan.
Res.: 24 Roxbury Rd., 06902. Tel: 203-322-1669; 203-329-8884; Fax: 203-461-9761.
Catechesis/Religious Program—Tel: 203-348-0052; Fax: 203-357-9639. Mrs. Eileen Towne, D.R.E. Students 700.

11—ST. MARY (1907) [CEM] Revs. Arthur Mollenhauer, L.C.; John Jairo Perez, Parochial Vicar.

Res.: 566 Elm St., 06902. Tel: 203-324-7321; Fax: 203-323-9407. Email: stmarystamford@yahoo.com. Web: www.stmarystamford.org.
Catechesis/Religious Program—Tel: 203-348-5196; Fax: 203-323-9401. Phyllis Taylor, D.R.E. & Office Mgr. Students 185.

12—St. Maurice (1935) [CEM] Rev. Albert G. Pinciaro; Deacon Ralph Hammock. In Res., Rev. Ayub Mwampela.
Res.: 358 Glenbrook Rd., 06906-2198. Tel: 203-324-3434; Fax: 203-964-8023. Email: stmauricegb@optonline.net. Web: www.stmauricegb.org.
Catechesis/Religious Program—Tel: 203-348-8768; Fax: 203-964-8023. Email: stmauricedff@optonline.net. Mrs. Deborah Ruffin, D.R.E. Students 140.

13—Our Lady of Montserrat (1984), (Spanish), Merged with St. Benedict, Stamford to form Saint Benedict and Our Lady of Montserrat, Stamford.

14—Our Lady Star of the Sea (1964) Rev. Msgr. Edward R. Surwilo; Deacon Vincent Gauthier.
Res.: 1200 Shippan Ave., 06902. Tel: 203-324-4634; Fax: 203-348-9963. Web: ourladystaroftheseastamford.org.
See Our Lady Star of the Sea, Stamford under Elementary Schools, Regional located in the Institution section.
Catechesis/Religious Program—Dee Fumega, C.R.E. Students 27.
Convent—1216 Shippan Ave., 06902. Tel: 203-569-0310.

15—Sacred Heart (1920), (Italian), [CEM] Rev. Richard F. Futie. In Res., Rev. Carlos R. Rodrigues.
Res.: 37 Schuyler Ave., 06902. Tel: 203-324-9544; Fax: 203-324-9202.
Catechesis/Religious Program—Tel: 203-541-3977. Students 78.

Stratford, Fairfield Co.

1—Holy Name of Jesus (1923), (Slovak), Rev. Andrew G. Marus; Deacon Michael Saranich. In Res., Rev. Msgr. J. James Cuneo.
Res.: 1950 Barnum Ave., 06614. Tel: 203-375-5815; Fax: 203-375-5954.
School— See separate listing under Elementary Schools, Regional in the Institution section.
Catechesis/Religious Program—Tel: 203-378-7407. Sr. Madonna Figura, S.S.C.M., D.R.E. Students 190.
Convent—2 Mary Ave., 06614. Tel: 203-378-1203.

2—St. James (1886) Revs. Thomas F. Lynch; Robert A. Uzzilio; Bruce Roby; Deacons John Barton; Timothy Bolton; James Brown; Thomas Masaryk.
Res.: 2110 Main St., 06615. Tel: 203-375-5887; Fax: 203-378-1562. Web: www.stjamesstratford.com.
See St. James, Stratford under Elementary Schools, Regional located in the Institution section.
Catechesis/Religious Program—Liz O'Connell, Youth Min. Students 1,530.

3—St. Mark (1960) Revs. Donald A. Guglielmi; Martin P. deMayo; Birendra Soreng (India), Parochial Vicar; Deacons T. Emmet Murray; F. Paul Kurmay.
Res.: 500 Wigwam Ln., 06614. Tel: 203-377-0444; Fax: 203-386-8071. Web: www.stmarkstratford.com.
See St. Mark, Stratford under Elementary Schools, Regional located in the Institution section.
Catechesis/Religious Program—Tel: 203-377-3158. Mrs. Patricia Nettleton, D.R.E. Students 510.

4—Our Lady of Grace (1954) [CEM] Rev. Msgr. William F. Schultz; Rev. Walter J. Seekamp; Deacon Robert W. McLaughlin. In Res., Rev. Msgr. Jerald A. Doyle.
Res.: 497 Second Hill Ln., 06614-2595. Tel: 203-377-0928; Fax: 203-377-5235. Web: www.olgstratford.com.
Parish Center—345 Second Hill Ln., 06614-2595. Tel: 203-375-2005 (Hall and gym); 203-375-6610 (Preschool).
Catechesis/Religious Program—Tel: 203-375-6133. Mrs. Denise L. Bartelson, C.R.E.(Pre School Dir.). Students 266.

5—Our Lady of Peace (1948) Rev. Richard D. Murphy.
Office: 10 Ivy St., 06615. Tel: 203-377-4863; Fax: 203-378-5253. Email: ourlady@sbcglobal.net.
Res.: 230 Park Blvd., 06615.
Catechesis/Religious Program—Tel: 203-378-3053. Sr. Carolyn Stoe, S.S.N.D., D.R.E. Students 106.

Trumbull, Fairfield Co.

1—St. Catherine of Siena (1955) [CEM] Rev. Msgr. Richard J. Shea; Deacon William A. Koniers.
Res.: 200 Shelton Rd., 06611. Tel: 203-377-3133; Fax: 203-377-1023. Email: marymurphy@st.catherinetrumbull.com. Web: www.stcatherinetrumbull.com.
See St. Catherine of Siena, Trumbull under Elementary Schools, Regional located in the Institution section.
Catechesis/Religious Program—220 Shelton Rd., 06611. Tel: 203-377-3133, Ext. 22. Students 540.

2—Christ the King (1962) [CEM] Revs. Bernard M. Dolan; Lawrence F. Carew.
Res.: 4700 Madison Ave., 06611. Tel: 203-268-8695; Fax: 203-268-9265. Email: ctkparish@aol.com.
Catechesis/Religious Program—Tel: 203-261-2583. Students 382.

3—St. Stephen (1953) Revs. Stephen J. Gleeson; Sean R. Kulacz; Deacons Gary Carpenter; John S. Moranski. In Res., Rev. Msgr. Ernest T. Esposito.
Res.: 6948 Main St., 06611-1340. Tel: 203-268-6217; Fax: 203-268-9861. Email: ststephen@ststephentc.org. Web: www.ststephentc.org.
Catechesis/Religious Program—Tel: 203-268-6860. Liz Harakal, D.R.E. Students 544.

4—St. Theresa (1934) [CEM] Revs. Michael L. Dunn, Admin.; Michael F. Flynn, Parochial Vicar; Sr. Joan Flynn, R.S.M., Dir. Pastoral Min.; Deacon Salvatore Clarizio. In Res., Rev. Peter A. Cipriani.
Res.: 5301 Main St., 06611. Tel: 203-261-3676; Fax: 203-268-8723.
See St. Theresa, Trumbull under Elementary Schools located in the Institution section.
Catechesis/Religious Program—19 Rosemond Ter., 06611. Tel: 203-261-4706. Mrs. Denise Heady, D.R.E. Students 875.
Convent—

Weston, Fairfield Co., St. Francis of Assisi (1955) Rev. Msgr. Nicholas V. Grieco; Deacon Donald W. Brunetto. In Res., Rev. Frederick L. Saviano.
Res.: 35 Norfield Rd, P.O. Box 1025, 06883. Tel: 203-227-1341; Fax: 203-226-1154. Email: msgr@sfaparish.com. Web: www.sfaparish.com.
Catechesis/Religious Program—Tel: 203-226-9474. Email: jlacorte@sfaparish.com. Students 289.

Westport, Fairfield Co.

1—Church of the Assumption (1876) [CEM] Revs. Thomas P. Thorne; Lawrence A. Larson. In Res., Rev. Robert M. Kinnally.
Res.: 98 Riverside Ave., 06880. Tel: 203-227-5161; Fax: 203-227-1206. Web: www.assumption-westport.org.
Catechesis/Religious Program—Tel: 203-226-5448. Cathy Romano, D.R.E.; Frank Matto, Music Dir. Students 592.

2—St. Luke (1957) Rev. Msgr. Andrew G. Varga; Rev. Alfred A. Riendeau, Parochial Vicar; Sr. Maureen Fleming, S.S.N.D., Coord. Pastoral Outreach Activities; Deacons Brian J. Kelly; Lance C. Fredricks.
Res.: 84 Long Lots Rd., 06880. Tel: 203-227-7245; Fax: 203-226-8063. Web: www.stlukewestport.com.
Catechesis/Religious Program—49 N. Turkey Hill Rd., 06880. Tel: 203-226-0729; Fax: 203-226-5446. Deacon Lance C. Fredricks, D.R.E. Students 308.

Wilton, Fairfield Co., Our Lady of Fatima (1953) Revs. Michael C. Palmer; James C. Vattakunnel; Deacon Thomas J. McManus.
Res.: 229 Danbury Rd., 06897. Tel: 203-762-3928; Fax: 203-834-1261. Email: ourlady229@aol.com. Web: www.olfwilton.org.
See Our Lady of Fatima, Wilton under Elementary Schools, Regional located in the Institution section.
Catechesis/Religious Program—225 Danbury Rd., 06897. Tel: 203-762-9080. Email: angels225@aol.com. Web: www.olfreligiousedorg. Mrs. Kathleen Rooney, D.R.E. Students 1,074.

Chaplains of Public Institutions

Bridgeport. *Bridgeport Community Correctional Facility*, 1106 North Ave., 06604. Tel: 203-579-6131. Rev. Bernardo C. Rodriguez, Chap.
Bridgeport Health Care, 600 Bond St., 06610. Tel: 203-384-6400. Rev. George Maslar, O.F.M.Conv., Chap.
Bridgeport Hospital, 267 Grant St., 06610. Tel: 203-384-3311. Rev. Remigius Nwabichie.

Danbury. *Danbury Area Mental Health Authority*, 64 West St., 06810. Tel: 203-778-1640, Ext. 247. Vacant.
Danbury Hospital, 24 Hospital Ave., 06810. Tel: 203-797-7912. Rev. Raymond K. Petrucci, Chap.
Federal Correctional Institution 06811. Tel: 203-743-6471. Sr. Anne Marie Raftery, O.S.F., Dir. of Pastoral Care.

Greenwich. *Greenwich Hospital* 06830. Tel: 203-863-3000. Revs. Stephen J. DeLuca, Chap., Ayub Mwampela, Chap.

Norwalk. *Norwalk Hospital* 06856. Tel: 203-852-2000.

Stamford. *Stamford Hospital* 06902. Tel: 203-325-7584. Rev. Msgr. Peter P. Dora.

On Duty Outside the Diocese:
Rev. Msgrs.—
Green, Thomas J., J.C.D., Catholic University of America, Dept. of Canon Law, Washington, DC 20017.
Millea, William V., Via della Nocetta 63, Rome 00164 Italy.
Potter, Joseph D. (Retired)
Revs.—
Daigle, David, CHC, USN, LTJG Chap, Ch01, USS Iwo Jima (LHD-7), Fpo, AE 09574-1664.
Devore, Daniel B., 9 Arbor Club Dr., Ponte Vedra, FL 32082.
Lincon, Joseph, St. Anthony, 908 E. Olive St., Longview, TX 75601.
McCall, Edward
McDevitt, James A., St. John the Evangelist Rectory, 250 Twenty-first St., Brooklyn, NY 11215.
Posluszny, Francis, Parroquia San Juan Apostal, APTO 735, Chiclayo, Peru.
Powers, Thomas, North American College 00120 Vatican City State.
Smolko, John F. (Retired), 9808 Dale Dr., Upper Marlboro, MD 20772.
Talar, Charles J.T., 9845 Memorial Dr., Houston, TX 77024.
Tracy, David W., University of Chicago, The Divinity School, 1025 E. 58th St., Chicago, IL 60637.

Leave of Absence:
Revs.—
Bohorquez, Hernan D.
Gray, Brian M.
Gray, Sherman
Haber, Thomas N.
Huminski, Gregory J.
Madden, Michael J.
Morrissey, Robert
Moynihan, Michael, J.C.L.

Retired:
Rev. Msgrs.—
Birge, George D.
Caldas, Constantino R.
DeProfio, Louis A., P.A.
Genuario, William A., P.A., J.C.D.
Gilmartin, John E.
Hossan, John B.
Howley, Edward J.
Jazowski, John F.
Kohut, Joseph J.
Loughlin, William J.
Nagle, William A.
Potter, Joseph D.
Rousseau, Stanlislaus B.
Sanders, John C.
Scull, Edward J.
Watts, Roger J.
Revs.—
Audette, Albert
Barachini, Nello
Brady, Philip W.
Breen, James J.
Colohan, Edward A.
Connolly, Mark
Coyne, Edwin J.
DeMarco, Peter A.
Dennehy, Martin J.
Devore, Gerald T., 44 Haddon St., Apt. 3, 06605.
Dytkowski, Louis M.
Fernandez, Jose A.
Giuliani, John
Gregori, Emidio O.
Grise, Clifford J.
Hitchcock, Martin B.
Howell, David W.
Hribsek, Aloysius J.
Igoe, Martin S.
Joaquin, Joseph M.
Knurek, Dennis A.
Koziol, Stanley N.
Lalic, Paul
Maty, Robert J.
Monahan, Richard J.
Onze, Robert E.
Palacino, Joseph
Parampath, Joseph K., J.C.D.
Punnakunnel, John (India)
Saba, Joseph J.
Smolko, John F.
Szlezak, Emeric
Usenza, Robert J.
Watts, Albert W.
Wright, Addison G., S.S.

Permanent Deacons:
Africot, Alix, St. Patrick, Bridgeport
Barton, Jack, St. James, Stratford
Berzolla, Renato L., St. Catherine, Riverside
Bissenden, William J., St. Patrick, Bridgeport
Blankschen, Robert, St. Gregory, Danbury
Blier, Roland, St. Thomas More, Darien
Bolton, Timothy, St. James, Stratford
Brown, James, St. Lawrence, Huntington
Brunetto, Donald W., St. Francis, Weston
Buchholz, John, St. Mary, Bethel
Buzzeo, Michael L., St. Gabriel, Stamford
Cabral, Jose R., Immaculate Heart of Mary, Danbury

Carpenter, Gary E., St. Stephen, Trumbull
Chervenak, Raymond J., St. Ambrose, Bridgeport
Chiappetta, Frank, St. Philip, Norwalk
Clarizio, Salvatore, Ph.D., St. Theresa, Trumbull
Conti, Anthony, St. James, Stratford
Curran, Thomas F., St. Rose, Newtown
De Biase, Joseph, Holy Family, Fairfield
DeRoin, John, St. Mary, Bethel
Detje, Anthony, St. Marguerite Bourgeoys, Brookfield
DiTaranto, John, St. Jude, Monroe
Dwyer, F. Robert, (Retired)
Dzujna, Andrew W., St. Mark, Stratford
Esterheld, John, Sacred Heart, Danbury
Farley, Joseph J., (Retired)
Fenton, Richard A., St. Marguerite Bourgeoys, Brookfield
Filingeri, Joseph, St. Lawrence, Huntington
Finch, Dean W., St. Jerome, Norwalk
Foust, Donald P., Blessed Sacrament, Bridgeport; Holy Rosary, Bridgeport
Foyt, Frank, St. Edward the Confessor, New Fairfield
Fredricks, Lance C., St. Luke, Westport
Gagne, Joseph, St. Thomas the Apostle, Norwalk
Garcia, Santos, St. Augustine, Bridgeport
Gauthier, Vincent, Our Lady Star of the Sea, Stamford
Genovese, Stephan A., St. Mary, Norwalk
Gram, Hans J., St. Mary, Ridgefield
Grant, Terence J., St. Elizabeth Seton, Ridgefield
Hammock, Ralph, (Leave of Absence)
Heidenreich, Vincent J., St. Catherine, Riverside
Hein, Henry R., St. Mary, Ridgefield
Henrey, Robert, St. Catherine of Siena, Riverside
Herman, H. Paul, (Leave of Absence)
Howe, Louis F., St. Aloysius, New Canaan
Ianniello, Daniel, St. Thomas Aquinas, Fairfield
Jennings, Paul J., Holy Spirit, Stamford
Kelly, Brian J., Ph.D., St. Luke, Westport
Kingsley, Jeffrey J., St. Joseph, Shelton
Koniers, William A., St. Pius, Fairfield
Kovacs, Richard P.
Kuhn, Peter J., St. Joseph, Brookfield
Kurmay, Paul F., St. Mark, Stratford
Landry, Ronald, St. Catherine of Siena, Trumbull
Linsenmeyer, John M., St. Agnes, Greenwich
Lynch, Harold J., Notre Dame, Easton
Mahon, John W., St. Philip, Norwalk
Malloy, Wayne E., St. John, Darien
Martinez, Ricardo, Blessed Sacrament, Bridgeport
Masaryk, Thomas, St. James, Stratford
Masso, Frank J., St. Lawrence, Huntington
McLaughlin, Robert W., Our Lady of Grace, Stratford
McMarcus, Thomas J., Our Lady of Fatima, Wilton
Melita, Joseph, St. Raphael, Bridgeport
Moore, Kevin, Assumption, Fairfield
Moranski, John J., St. Stephens, Trumbull
Morris, Robert, St. Elizabeth Seton, Ridgefield
Murphy, William D., St. Gregory the Great, Danbury
Murphy, William O., St. Joseph, Norwalk
Murray, Emmet, St. Mark, Stratford
Myott, Daniel N., St. Gregory the Great, Danbury
Naiman, Donald, St. Rose, Newtown
O'Connor, Daniel, St. Rose, Newtown
Olavarria, Rinaldo, St. Mary, Bridgeport
Oles, Michael, St. Mary, Bethel
Pereira, Gabriel, Our Lady of Fatima, Bridgeport
Pierre-Louis, Augustin, St. Joseph, S. Norwalk
Pilkington, Paul B., St. Gregory, Danbury
Pond, Stephen W., St. Aloysius, New Canaan
Reilly, Paul, St. Philip, Norwalk
Reveron, Domingo, St. Peter, Bridgeport
Rigg, Russ, St. Michael the Archangel, Greenwich
Roos, Norman, St. Rose, Newtown
Ross, Donald J., St. Anthony of Padua, Fairfield
Rowan, Joseph L., St. Aloysius, New Canaan
Rowe, William K., (Retired), St. John, Darien
Ruge, Kenneth J., St. Ann, Bridgeport
Sabol, Gerald, Notre Dame, Easton
Salvestrini, Robert A., St. Mary, Ridgefield
Saranich, Michael, Holy Name, Stratford
Sebestyen, Stephen, Holy Family, Fairfield
Seith, Thomas K., (Retired)
Shaughnessy, William J., St. Joseph, Brookfield
Shine, Mark T., St. Matthew, Norwalk
Sochacki, David M., St. Matthew, Norwalk
Stroud, Kenneth, (Retired)
Sullivan, Timothy A., St. Joseph Manor, Trumbull
Timmel, William C., St. Patrick, Redding
Torres, Luis, St. Peter, Bridgeport
Tugman, John H., (On Duty Outside the Diocese)
Tupper, Paul, St. Mary, Greenwich
Vaughn, David J., St. Peter, Danbury
Volpe, James, (Retired)
Wolfer, Michael K., (Retired)

INSTITUTIONS LOCATED IN THE DIOCESE

[A] SEMINARIES, DIOCESAN

STAMFORD. *St. John Fisher Seminary Residence* (1989) 894 Newfield Ave., 06905. Tel: 203-322-5331; Fax: 203-461-9876. Email: info@hearthecall.org. Web: www.hearthecall.org. Revs. Samuel V. Scott, Rector; Nicholas A. Cirillo, Spiritual Dir.; Robert M. Kinnally. Priests 5; Deacons 1; Lay Teachers 4; Lay Staff 4.

[B] COLLEGES AND UNIVERSITIES

BRIDGEPORT. *St. Vincent's College* (1991) 75 Huntington St., 06606. Tel: 203-576-5318; Fax: 203-576-5893. Email: nmusante@stvincentscollege.edu. Web: www.stvincentscollege.edu. John K. Fisher, Ed.D., Pres. & CEO; Joanne R. Wolfertz, Ed.D., Vice Pres. Dean; Robert S. Trojanowski, M.B.A., J.D., CFO; Janice Faye, Dir. Admin. Svcs.; Joseph Macionus, M.P.A., Registrar; Anita K. McCain, Ed.D., Dean, Academic Svcs.; Joseph Marrone, M.S., Dir., Admissions. Lay Teachers 46; Students 510.

FAIRFIELD. **Fairfield University* (Coed), 1073 N. Benson Rd., 06824-5195. Tel: 203-254-4910; Fax: 203-254-4221. Web: www.fairfield.edu. Revs. Jeffrey P. von Arx, S.J., Ph.D., Pres.; Walter J. Conlan, S.J., Rector; James M. Bowler, S.J., Facilitator Catholic Jesuit Mission & Identity; Charles H. Allen, S.J., Exec. Asst. to Pres.; Gerald R. Blaszczak, S.J., Univ. Chap.; William H. Weitzer, Sr. Vice Pres.; Rev. Paul J. Fitzgerald, S.J., Sr. Vice Pres. Academic Affairs; Mr. Robert C. Russo, Univ. Registrar; Mr. Mark J. Guglielmoni, Dir. Human Resources; Dr. Norman A. Solomon, Dean Dolan School of Business; Dr. Jeanne M. Novotny, Dean School of Nursing; Dr. Robin Crabtree, Dean, Arts & Sciences; Dr. Evangelos Hadjimichael, Dean School of Engineering; Dr. Edna Wilson, Dean, University College; Susan Franzosa, Dean, Graduate School of Educ. & Allied Professions; Dr. M. Debnam Chappell, Dean, Freshmen; Judith M. Dobai, Assoc. Academic Vice Pres., Enrollment Mgmt.; Erin R. Chiaro, B.S., Dir. Financial Aid; Mr. James Estrada, Vice Pres. Information Svcs. & Univ. Librarian; Mr. Mark C. Reed, Vice Pres. Admin. Svcs. & Student Affairs; Mr. Thomas Pellegrino, Assoc. Vice Pres. & Dean, Students; Rama Sudhakar, Vice Pres. Mktg. & Communications; Mr. James D. Fitzpatrick, Asst. Vice Pres. Students Affairs Operations; Dr. Susan Birge, Asst. Vice Pres. & Dir., Counseling Svcs.; Larri W. Mazon, Dir. Inst. Diversity Initiative; Mr. Matthew Dinnan, Sr. Assoc. Dean, Students Activities; Rev. Michael J. Doody, S.J., Dir. Campus Ministry; Ms. Carolyn Rusiackas, Assoc. Univ. Chap.; Conor L. O'Kane, Assoc. Dir. Campus Ministry; Ms. Stephanie Frost, Vice Pres. Advancement; Ms. Janet Canepa, Dir. Alumni Rels.; David W. Frassinelli, Asst. Vice Pres. & Dir. Univ. Facilities Mgmt.; Michael T. Boyd, Assoc. Vice Pres. Individual Giving; Mr. William J. Lucas, Vice Pres. Finance & Admin. and Treas.; Mr. Michael S. Maccarone, Assoc. Vice Pres. Finance; Mr. Kenneth R. Fontaine, Controller; Revs. Francis T. Hannafey, S.J., Assoc. Prof., Religious Studies; Mark P. Scalese, S.J., M.F.A., Asst. Prof., New Media; James J. Mayzik, S.J., Dir. Media Ctr., Asst. Prof. New Media & Dir. Ignatian Res. College; Richard J. Ryscavage, S.J., Dir. for Center of Faith & Public Life; Fredy Cesar Maldonado, S.J., Asst. Prof. Modern Languages & Literature; Ms. Ann K. Stehney, Dir. Inst. Research. The Society of Jesus. College of Arts and Sciences; Dolan School of Business; University College; School of Nursing; School of Engineering; Graduate School of Education & Allied Professions; Graduate Program in Financial Management; Graduate Program in Nursing; Masters in Business Administration; Graduate Programs in Engineering and Masters in American Studies and Mathematics.; (See separate listing for Fairfield College Prep). Jesuits 13; Priests 13; Lay Teachers 248; Students 5,146; Personnel (not including faculty) 546.

**Sacred Heart University*, 5151 Park Ave., 06825-1000. Tel: 203-371-7999; Fax: 203-365-7652. Web: www.sacredheart.edu. Dr. Anthony J. Cernera, Pres.; Dr. Thomas Forget, Vice Pres. for Academic Affairs; Mr. James M. Barquinero, Vice Pres. Enrollment Planning & Student Affairs; Dr. Paul K. Madonna, Univ. Vice Pres.; Mr. Michael J. Kinney, Sr. Vice Pres. Finance & Admin. Coeducational and Comprehensive University. Courses offered year round, day & evening. Priests 2; Sisters 2; Lay Teachers 480; Students 5,800.

[C] HIGH SCHOOLS, DIOCESAN

BRIDGEPORT. *Kolbe-Cathedral High School* (1963) 33 Calhoun Pl., 06604. Tel: 203-335-2554; Fax: 203-335-2556. Email: cougars@kolbecaths.org. Web: www.kolbecaths.org. Mrs. Jo Anne Jakab, Prin.; Mr. Philip Broadhurst, Asst. Prin.; Mrs. Lisa Matson, Asst. Prin.; Rev. F. John Ringley, Spiritual Dir. Priests 1; Lay Teachers 23; Administrators 3; Students 312.

DANBURY. *Immaculate High School* (1962) 73 Southern Blvd., 06810. Tel: 203-744-1510; Fax: 203-744-1275. Email: ihsmail@immaculatehs.org. Web: www.immaculatehs.org. Kathleen Casey, Pres.; Mr. Dan Murphy, Prin.; Mrs. Mary Ann Foncello, Asst. Principal. Priests 1; Lay Teachers 32; Students 420.

FAIRFIELD. *Notre Dame Catholic High School*, 220 Jefferson St., 06825. Tel: 203-372-6521; Fax: 203-374-0387. Email: info@notredame.org. Web: www.notredame.org. Rev. William F. Sangiovanni, Prin.; Mr. Carl Philipp, Asst. Prin.; Mr. Christopher Cipriano, Asst. Prin.; Rev. Peter A. Cipriani, Chap.; Miss Jean Baranyor, Librarian. Priests 2; Lay Teachers 45; Students 555.

STAMFORD. *Trinity Catholic High School*, 926 Newfield Ave., 09605. Tel: 203-322-3401; Fax: 203-322-5330. Email: TCHS1@JUNO.COM. Web: www.trinitycatholic.org. Kevin Burke, Pres.; Kevin Sutton, Asst. Prin.; Mrs. Connie McGoldrick, Admissions Coord.; Rev. Nicholas A. Cirillo, Spiritual Dir.; Mr. Tracy Nichols, Athletic Dir.; Mrs. Diane Warzaha, Dean of Students; Mrs. Mary D'Aquila, Reach Out; Mrs. Lorraine Castelluccio, Librarian. (Formerly Stamford Catholic High School); Records for Central Catholic High School, Norwich, and St. Mary's High School, Greenwich, located at Trinity. Priests 1; Lay Teachers 42; Students 465.

TRUMBULL. *St. Joseph High School* (1962) 2320 Huntington Tpke., 06611-5099. Tel: 203-378-9378; Fax: 203-378-7306. Web: www.sjcadets.org. Mr. William J. Fitzgerald, Ph.D., M.Div., Pres.; Mr. Kenneth Mayo, Prin.; Mrs. Laurene Collins, Asst. Prin.; Mrs. Patricia Hayes, Ph.D., Asst. Prin.; Mrs. Suzanne Siano, Dir. Guidance; Rev. Christopher J. Samele; Mr. James Olayos, Esq., Dir. Athletics; Mr. Paul Bernetsky, Advancement Dir.; Mrs. Maureen Anderson, Coord. Student Activities; Mr. Martin Dempsey, Dean of Students; Mrs. Margaret Marino, Admissions Dir.; Sr. Florencia Silva, Dir. Campus Ministry; Mrs. Christine Woods, Registrar; Mrs. Joanne Rodgerson, Bursar; Mrs. Linda Batton, Dir. Finance; Mrs. Lynn Dalton-Mallon, Alumni Dir.; Mr. Brian Highland, Librarian. Priests 1; Sisters 2; Lay Teachers 61; Students 806.

[D] SPECIAL SCHOOLS, DIOCESAN

FAIRFIELD. *St. Catherine Academy*, (Grades K-12), 760 Tahmore Dr., 06825. Tel: 203-540-5381; Fax: 203-540-5383. Email: srmuldoon@diobpt.org. Web: www.stcatherineacademy.org. Helen Burland, Pres.; Sr. Marilyn Muldoon, O.S.U., Prin. & Admin. Sisters 4; Lay Teachers 2; Students 20.

[E] HIGH SCHOOLS, PRIVATE

FAIRFIELD. *Fairfield College Preparatory School* (1942) 1073 N. Benson Rd., 06824. Tel: 203-254-4200; Fax: 203-254-4108. Email: rperrotta@fairfieldprep.org. Web: www.fairfieldprep.org. Dr. Robert A. Perrotta, Ed.D., J.D., Prin.; Revs. John J. Hanwell, S.J., Pres. Fairfield Prep.; William J. Eagan, S.J., Chm. Theology Dept.; George A. Gallarelli, S.J., Guidance; Laurence D. Ryan, S.J., Chap.; Martin G. Shaughnessy, S.J., Theology Teacher; Robert J. Levens, S.J., Faculty & Alumni Chaplain; Ms. Sandra Stock, Librarian. Society of Jesus of New England., A preparatory day school for boys, established in 1942. Priests 6; Lay Teachers 77; Students 921.

GREENWICH

See Convent of the Sacred Heart, Greenwich under Elementary Schools, Private located in the Institution section.

[F] ELEMENTARY SCHOOLS DIOCESAN

BRIDGEPORT. *Cathedral Education Cluster*, The Catholic Center, 238 Jewett Ave., 06606. Tel: 203-416-1370; Fax: 203-372-0020. Email: rgaits@bcess.com. Web: www.cathedralcluster.org.

St. Ambrose (Grades PreK-8), 461 Mill Hill Ave., 06610. Tel: 203-368-2835; Fax: 203-366-0599. Mrs. Margaret Carabelli, Prin. Servants of the Immaculate of Mary 2; Lay Teachers 14; Students 245.

St. Andrew (Grades PreK-8), 395 Anton St., 06606. Tel: 203-373-1552; Fax: 203-373-0641. Mrs. Maria O'Neill, Prin. Lay Teachers 11; Students 235.

St. Ann (Grades PreK-8), 521 Brewster St., 06605. Tel: 203-334-5856; Fax: 203-333-8263. Mrs. Theresa Tillinger, Prin. Daughters of the Holy Spirit 1; Lay Teachers 11; Students 210.

St. Augustine Cathedral (Grades PreK-8), 63 Pequonnock St., 06604-3599. Tel: 203-366-6500; Fax: 203-362-2934. Mrs. Mary M. Daley, Prin. Lay Teachers 13; Students 223.

St. Peter (Grades K-8), 659 Beechwood Ave., 06605. Tel: 203-333-2048; Fax: 203-333-2878. Miss Suzanna Zello, Prin. Sisters of the Company of the Savior 2; Lay Teachers 7; Students 187.

St. Raphael (Grades PreK-8), 324 Frank St., 06604. Tel: 203-333-6818; Fax: 203-336-9205. Sr. Veronica A. Beato, A.S.C.J., Prin. Apostles of the Sacred Heart 3; Lay Teachers 11; Students 220.

DANBURY. *Bridgeport Diocesan Schools Corporation*, 238 Jewett Ave., 06606. Tel: 203-416-1380.

St. Gregory the Great (Grades K-8), 85 Great Plain Rd., 06811. Tel: 203-748-1217; Fax: 203-748-1217. Sr. Mary John O'Rourke, O.S.U., Prin. Lay Teachers 12; Students 288.

St. Joseph (Grades PreK-8), 370 Main St., 06810. Tel: 203-748-6615; Fax: 203-748-6508. Mrs. Gerianne O'Rourke, Prin. Lay Teachers 23; Students 330.

St. Peter-Sacred Heart School (Grades N-8), 98 Main St. & 17 Cottage St., 06810. Tel: 203-748-2895; Fax: 203-748-5684. Mrs. Mary McCormack, Prin. Lay Teachers 12; Students 173.

St. Joseph (Grades K-8), Rte. 133, Brookfield, 06804. Tel: 203-775-2774; Fax: 203-775-5810. Mrs. Rosemarie Forte, Prin. Lay Teachers 21; Students 176.

St. Rose (Grades K-8), 40 Church Hill Rd., Newtown, 06470. Tel: 203-426-5102; Fax: 203-426-5374. Mrs. Mary Maloney, Prin. Religious 2; Lay Teachers 27; Students 444.

FAIRFIELD. *Bridgeport Diocesan Schools Corporation*, 238 Jewett Ave., 06606. Tel: 203-416-1380.

Holy Family (Grades PreK-8), 140 Edison Ave., 06825. Tel: 203-367-5409; Fax: 203-335-7317. Web: www.holyfamilyffld.org. Mr. Larry Fitzgerald, Prin. Lay Teachers 18; Students 185.

Our Lady of the Assumption (Grades PreK-8), 591 Stratfield Rd., 06825. Tel: 203-334-6271; Fax: 203-334-1374. Web: www.assumptionschoolffld-.homestead.com. Ms. Gerri Desio, Prin. Lay Teachers 17; Students 195.

St. Thomas Aquinas (Grades PreK-8), 1719 Post Rd., 06824. Tel: 203-255-0556; Fax: 203-255-0596. Web: www.saintthomasaquinasschool.net. Ms. Patricia Brady, Prin. Lay Teachers 25; Students 398.

GREENWICH. *Bridgeport Diocesan Schools Corporation*, 238 Jewett Ave., 06606. Tel: 203-416-1380.

Greenwich Catholic School, 471 North St., 06830. Tel: 203-869-4000; Fax: 203-869-3405. Email: Greencath@aol.com; info@greenwichcatholicschool.org. Web: www.greenwichcatholicschool.org. Mrs. Mary Flume, Office Mgr.; Mrs. Pat Kopas, Prin.; Mrs. Johanna DaKan, Librarian. Lay Teachers 33; Students 394.

NORWALK. *Bridgeport Diocesan Schools Corporation*, 238 Jewett Ave., 06606. Tel: 203-416-1380.

All Saints Catholic Elementary School (Grades Day Care-8), 139 W. Rocks Rd., 06851. Tel: 203-847-3881; Fax: 203-847-8055. Mrs. Nancy Dibuono, Prin. Priests 1; Sisters 1; Lay Teachers 38; Students 754.

SHELTON. *Bridgeport Diocesan Schools Corporation*, 238 Jewett Ave., 06606. Tel: 203-416-1380.

St. Lawrence Rectory/Shelton Catholic Regional School (Grades K-8), 505 Shelton Ave., 06484. Tel: 203-929-4422; Fax: 203-877-4171. Email: rlaluna@diobpt.org. Martha Reitman, Prin.

St. Joseph (Grades PreK-8), 430 Coram Ave., 06484. Tel: 203-924-4669; Fax: 203-922-0161. Email: stjoseph.school@snet.net. Mrs. Arlene Clancy, Prin. Lay Teachers 16; Students 199.

St. Lawrence (Grades PreK-8), 503 Shelton Ave., 06484. Tel: 203-929-4422; Fax: 203-929-3669. Email: sls@snet.net. Web: www.diobptstlawrenceparish-.net. Martha Reitman, Prin. Sisters 1; Lay Teachers 18; Students 270.

STAMFORD. *Bridgeport Diocesan Schools Corporation*, 238 Jewett Ave., 06606. Tel: 203-416-1380.

St. Aloysius (Grades K-8), 33 South Ave., New Canaan, 06840. Tel: 203-966-0786; Fax: 203-972-6960. Email: dhoward@diobpt.org. Dr. Donald Howard, Prin. Lay Teachers 21; Students 191.

Holy Spirit (Grades PreK-5), 403 Scofieldtown Rd., 06903. Tel: 203-329-1623; Fax: 203-595-0858. Email: ptorchen@diobpt.org. Patricia Torchen, Prin. Lay Teachers 14; Students 118.

Our Lady Star of the Sea (Grades PreK-5), 1170 Shippan Ave., 06903. Tel: 203-348-1155; Fax: 203-324-6150. Email: gryan@diobpt.org. Mrs. Gail Ryan, Prin. Sisters 1; Lay Teachers 17; Students 139.

Sacred Heart (Grades PreK-8), One Schuyler Ave., 06902. Tel: 203-323-4844; Fax: 203-359-9859. Ms. Sherry Tarantino, Prin. Sisters 1; Lay Teachers 3; Students 43.

St. Cecilia (Grades PreK-5), 1186 Newfield Ave., 06903. Tel: 203-322-6505; Fax: 203-322-6835. Email: jborchetta@diobpt.org. Mrs. Joann Borchetta, Prin. Sisters 1; Lay Teachers 19; Students 296.

Trinity Catholic Middle School (Grades 6-8), 948 Newfield Ave., 06905. Tel: 203-322-7383; Fax: 203-322-4435. Email: rfox@diobpt.org. Mr. Richard Fox, Prin. Religious 1; Lay Teachers 21; Students 214.

STRATFORD. *Bridgeport Diocesan Schools Corporation*, 238 Jewett Ave., 06606. Tel: 203-416-1380.

St. James (Grades K-8), One Monument Pl., 06615. Tel: 203-375-5994; Fax: 203-380-0749. Mrs. Kathleen A. Lainey, Prin. Lay Teachers 30; Students 365.

St. Mark (Grades K-8), 500 Wigwam Ln., 06614. Tel: 203-375-4291; Fax: 203-375-4833. Mr. Gene Holmes, Prin. Lay Teachers 21; Students 187.

TRUMBULL. *Bridgeport Diocesan Schools Corporation*, 238 Jewett Ave., 06606. Tel: 203-416-1380.

St. Jude (Grades PreK-8), 707 Monroe Tpke., Monroe, 06468. Tel: 203-261-3619; Fax: 203-268-8748. Mrs. Linda Dunn, Prin. Lay Teachers 16; Students 186.

St. Catherine of Siena (Grades PreK-8), 190 Shelton Rd., 06611. Tel: 203-375-1947; Fax: 203-378-3935. Mrs. Beth Hamilton, Prin. Lay Teachers 20; Students 223.

St. Theresa (Grades PreK-8), 55 Rosemond Ter., 06611. Tel: 203-268-3236; Fax: 203-268-7966. Mr. Salvatore Vittoria, Prin. Lay Teachers 21; Students 240.

WILTON. *Bridgeport Diocesan Schools Corporation*, 238 Jewett Ave., 06606. Tel: 203-416-1380.

Our Lady of Fatima (Grades PreK-8), 225 Danbury Rd., 06897. Tel: 203-762-8100; Fax: 203-834-0614. Mr. Joseph Carmen, Prin. Lay Teachers 20; Students 192.

Saint Mary's (Grades K-7), 183 High Ridge Ave., Ridgefield, 06877. Tel: 203-438-7288; Fax: 203-431-8742. Mr. Edward Brennan, Prin. Lay Teachers 22; Students 220.

[G] ELEMENTARY SCHOOLS, PRIVATE

GREENWICH. *Convent of the Sacred Heart*, (Grades PreSchool-12), Day School for Girls, 1177 King St., 06831. Tel: 203-531-6500; Fax: 203-531-5206. Email: sacredheart@cshgreenwich.org. Web: www.cshgreenwich.org. Pamela Juan-Hayes, Headmistress; Sr. Maureen Wade, S.C., Librarian; Mrs. Jayne Collins, U.S. Head; Mr. David Olson, M.S. Head; Dr. Ann Marr, L.S. Head. Sisters 4; Lay Teachers 180; Students 777.

STAMFORD. *Villa Maria Education Center*, 161 Sky Meadow Dr., 06903. Tel: 203-322-5886; Fax: 203-322-0228. Email: scarol@villamariaedu.org. Web: villamariaedu.org. Sr. Carol Ann Nawracaj, O.S.F., Exec. Dir. & Prin.; Ilena Cassidy, Education Dir.; Wanda Serafino, Librarian. Bernardine Franciscan Sisters., School for Children with Learning Disabilities. Sisters 4; Lay Teachers 20; Students 76.

[H] CATHOLIC CHARITIES

BRIDGEPORT. *Catholic Charities*, Catholic Center, 238 Jewett Ave., 06606-2892. Tel: 203-416-1307; Fax: 203-372-5045. Email: abarber@ccfc-ct.org. Web: www.ccfc-ct.org. Mr. Albert Barber, Pres.

Family Directions, 238 Jewett Ave., 06606-2892. Tel: 203-416-1336; Fax: 203-373-0835. Email: azajac@ccfc-ct.org. Amy Zajac, Dir. Family Directions. Adoptions and Home Studies.

Catholic Charities, Bridgeport, 238 Jewett Ave., 06606-2892. Tel: 203-416-1318; Fax: 203-373-0835. Email: mtintrup@ccfc-cr.org. Mr. Michael Tintrup, Vice Pres.

Catholic Charities, Danbury, 30 Main St., Suite 503, Danbury, 06810. Tel: 203-743-4412; Fax: 203-744-3500. Email: emalgieri@ccfc-ct.org. Elaine Malgieri, M.S.W., L.C.S.W., District Dir.

Ways to Work Family Loan Program, 30 Main St., Ste. 503, Danbury, 06810. Tel: 203-743-4412; Fax: 203-744-3500. Email: emalgieri@ccfc-ct.org.

Catholic Charities, Norwalk, One Park St., P.O. Box 2025, Norwalk, 06851. Tel: 203-416-1318; Fax: 203-750-9651. Email: mtintrup@ccfc-ct.org. Mr. Michael Tintrup, Vice Pres.

Catholic Charities, Stamford, 30 Myano Ln., Ste. 12, Stamford, 06902. Tel: 203-416-1318; Fax: 203-323-1108. Email: mtintrup@ccfc-ct.org. Mr. Michael Tintrup, Vice Pres.

Catholic Campaign for Human Development, 238 Jewett Ave., 06606. Tel: 203-416-1320.

Room to Grow School Readiness, 208 East Ave., Norwalk, 06850. Tel: 203-855-0637; Fax: 203-831-8200. Email: nowens@ccfc-ct.org. Nancy Owens, Dir.

Houses of Hospitality:

New Covenant House of Hospitality, 90 Fairfield Ave., Stamford, 06904. Tel: 203-964-8228; Fax: 203-375-0314. Email: bjenkins@ccfc-ct.org. Brian Jenkins, Dir.

Thomas Merton Center, 43 Madison Ave., 06604. Tel: 203-367-9036; Fax: 203-367-8828. Email: mgrasso@ccfc-ct.org. Mark Grasso, Dir.

St. Stephen's Emergency Food Center, 43 Madison Ave., 06604. Tel: 203-394-6881.

NEW HEIGHTS, 66 West Street, Danbury, 06810. Tel: 203-794-0819; Fax: 203-731-3260. Email: cpeters@ccfc-ct.org. Camilla Peters, Dir.

Case Management Program, 24 Grassy Plain St., Bethel, 06801. Tel: 203-748-0848; Fax: 203-796-0046. Email: scole@ccfc-ct.org. Web: www.ccfc-ct.org. Sandy Cole, Vice Pres.

Homeless Outreach Team, 24 Grassy Plain St., Bethel, 06801. Tel: 203-748-0848; Fax: 203-796-0046. Email: mconderino@ccfc-ct.org. Web: www.ccfc-ct.org. Michelle Conderino, Dir.

Senior Nutrition Program, 30 Myano Ln., Stamford, 06902. Tel: 203-324-6175; Fax: 203-323-1108. Email: cphelps@ccfc-ct.org. Cindy Phelps, B.S., Dir.

Senior Neighborhood Support Services, 18 Quintard Ter., Stamford, 06901. Tel: 203-324-2404. Sandy Cole, Vice Pres.

Catholic Charities, 238 Jewett Ave., 06606. Tel: 203-416-1338. Email: dfrederick@ccfc-ct.org. Ms. Debra Frederick, COO.

Housing Services, Catholic Center, 238 Jewett Ave., 06606-2892. Tel: 203-416-1317. Email: lbrowngambino@ccfc-ct.org. Letticia Brown-Gambino, Dir.

Early Childhood Consultation Services, Catholic Center, 238 Jewett Ave., 06606. Tel: 203-416-1308.

Immigration Services, Catholic Center, 238 Jewett Ave., 06606. Tel: 203-416-1313. Email: mgrasso@ccfc-ct.org. Mark Grasso, Vice Pres.

[I] DAY NURSERIES

BRIDGEPORT. *Daughters of Charity of the Most Precious Blood Day Nursery* (1908) 1490 North Ave., 06604. Tel: 203-334-7000; Fax: 203-334-7000. Email: daughtersofcharity@yahoo.com. Sr. Theresa Tremblay, D.C.P.B., Dir. Sisters 2; Lay Staff 3.

STAMFORD. *Our Lady of Grace Day Nursery*, 635 Glenbrook Rd., 06906. Tel: 203-348-5531; Fax: 203-324-9638. Email: littleworkerposc@aol.com. Sr. Gesuina Gencarelli, P.O.S.C., Supr. Little Workers of the Sacred Hearts.

Stepping Stones Preschool, Inc., (Grades PreSchool-K), Sacred Heart Academy, 200 Strawberry Hill Ave., 06902. Tel: 203-323-3173; 203-323-7554; Fax: 203-975-7804. Sr. Jeanne Paulella, C.S.J., Dir. Sisters of Saint Joseph.

[J] GENERAL HOSPITALS

BRIDGEPORT. *St. Joseph Medical Center Foundation, Inc.*, Diocese of Bridgeport, 238 Jewett Ave., 06606-2852.

St. Vincent's Development Corporation, 2800 Main St., 06606. Tel: 203-576-5459; Fax: 203-576-5345. Web: www.stvincents.org. Anthony Milano, Chm.; Susan L. Davis, Pres. & CEO.

St. Vincent's Health Services Corporation, 2800 Main St., 06606. Tel: 203-576-5455; Fax: 203-576-5345. Web: www.stvincents.org. Ruben Rodriguez, Chm.; Susan L. Davis, Pres. & CEO. Bed Capacity 473; Total Assisted Annually 230,000; Total Staff 3,000.

St. Vincent's Medical Center, 2800 Main St., 06606. Tel: 203-576-6000; Fax: 203-576-5345. Web: www.stvincents.org. Ruben Rodriguez, Chm.; Susan L. Davis, CEO; John Glecker, Interim CFO; Revs. Daniel Kennelly; Anselm Nzekwe, Chap. Daughters of Charity of St. Vincent de Paul (Albany, NY). Bed Capacity 473; Total Assisted Annually 206,000; Total Staff 2,350.

St. Vincent's College Tel: 203-576-5578; Fax: 203-576-5893. Students 531.

Saint Vincent's Special Needs Center, Inc., 95 Merritt Blvd., Trumbull, 06611. Tel: 203-375-6400; Fax: 203-380-1190. Web: www.stvincentsspecialneed.org. Barry Buxbaum, Pres. & CEO. Staff 284; Total Assisted Annually 1,783.

Hall-Brooke Behavioral Health Services, 47 Long Lots Rd., Westport, 06880. Tel: 203-227-1251; Fax: 203-227-8616. Web: www.hallbrooke.org. James McCreath, Ph.D., Pres. & CEO. Total Staff 300; Bed Capacity 76; Total Assisted Annually 20,670.

St. Vincent's Medical Center Foundation, 2800 Main St., 06606. Tel: 203-576-5451; Fax: 203-576-5880. Email: rbianchi@svhs-ct.org. Mr. Anthony Vallilo, Chm.; Mr. Ronald J. Bianchi, Pres. & CEO. Bed Capacity 400; Total Assisted Annually 110,000; Total Staff 1,700.

[K] SPECIAL HOSPITALS

BRIDGEPORT. *Bridgeport Diocesan Health Care Corporation*, 238 Jewett Ave., 06606. Tel: 203-372-4301; Fax: 203-372-1817.

St. Camillus Home Foundation, Inc., 238 Jewett Ave., 06606. Tel: 203-416-1355.

The Pope John Paul II Foundation, Inc., 238 Jewett Ave., 06606. Tel: 203-416-1355.

DANBURY. *The Pope John Paul II Center for Health Care, Inc.*, 33 Lincoln Ave., 06810. Tel: 203-416-1355. Email: onedee98@aol.com. Sr. Frances Smalkowski, C.F.S.N., Co-Dir. Pastoral Care; Rev. Douglas Tufaro. Total Staff 198.

STAMFORD. *St. Camillus Health Center*, 494 Elm St., 06902. Tel: 203-325-0200; Fax: 203-353-0550. Web: www.stcamillushealth.org. Rev. Carlos R. Rodrigues, Chap. Total Staff 167.

St. Camillus Auxiliary Committee, 494 Elm St., 06902. Tel: 203-325-0200; Fax: 203-353-0550.

[L] HOMES FOR AGED

BRIDGEPORT. *Augustana Homes/Bishop Curtis Homes*, 525 Palisade Ave., 06610. Tel: 203-366-4333; Fax: 203-366-4756. Mr. Alan Regan, Regl. Vice Pres. (Winn Mgmt. Corp.); Mrs. Lillian Araujo, Site Mgr. Apartments 186; Total Staff 4.

Augustana Homes/Bishop Curtis Homes (1991) 280 Jewett Ave., 06606. Tel: 203-374-5346. Mr. Alan Regan, Regl. Vice Pres. (Winn Residential Corp.); Mrs. Nilda Alamo, Site Mgr.

Augustana Homes/Bishop Curtis Homes - East Bridgeport, 264 Union Ave., 06607-1895. Mr. Alan Regan, Regl. Vice Pres. (Winn Residential Corp.). Total Assisted 48; Total Staff 2.

Roncalli Apartments, 430 Grant St., 06610. Tel: 203-384-9984. Mariann Callahan, L.P.N., Admin. Affiliate of the Roncalli Institute, Supervised Apartments for the Elderly & Handicapped.

BETHEL. *Augustana Homes/Bishop Curtis Homes*, 28 & 101 Simeon Rd., 06801. Tel: 203-743-2508; Fax: 203-743-4570. Mr. Alan Regan, Regl. Vice Pres. (Winn Residential Corp.); Anne Dennis Tapia, Property Mgr. Total Staff 12; Total Assisted 143.

DANBURY. *Augustana Homes Bishop Curtis Homes - Danbury*, 88 Main St., 06810. Tel: 203-791-8510; Fax: 203-743-2352. Mr. Alan Regan, Regl. Vice Pres. (Winn Residential Corp.). Total Assisted 46; Total Staff 2.

FAIRFIELD. *Augustana Homes/Bishop Curtis Homes*, 1677 Post Rd., 06430. Mr. Alan Regan, Regl. Vice Pres. (Winn Residential Corp.).

RIVERSIDE. *Augustana Homes of Greenwich/Bishop Curtis Homes*, 1040 E. Putnam Ave., 06878. Tel: 203-637-8065; Fax: 203-637-7432. Mr. Alan Regan, Regl. Vice Pres. (Winn Residential Corp.). Total Assisted 33; Total Staff 2.

STAMFORD. *Augustana Homes/Bishop Curtis Homes - Glenbrook*, 352 Glenbrook Rd., 06906. Tel: 203-324-5881; Fax: 203-324-5881. Mr. Alan Regan, Regl. Vice Pres. (Winn Residential Corp.). Total Assisted 35; Total Staff 2.

TRUMBULL. *Carmel Ridge*, 6454 Main St., 06611. Tel: 203-261-2229. Mr. Peter Cady, Property Mgr.

St. Joseph's Housing Corporation, Teresian Towers & Carmel Ridge Estates, 6448 Main St., 06611. Tel: 203-261-2229. Mr. Peter Cady, Property Mgr.

St. Joseph's Manor, 6448 Main St., 06611. Tel: 203-268-6204; Fax: 203-268-5271. Web: www.harborsidehealthcare.com. Rev. Msgr. Ernest T. Esposito, D.Min., Chap.; Deacon Timothy A. Sullivan, Asst. Chap. Capacity 297; Total Staff 500.

[M] CONVALESCENT HOMES

NORWALK. *Notre Dame Convalescent Home* (1952) 76 W. Rocks Rd., 06851. Tel: 203-847-5893; Fax: 203-849-1959. Sr. Jean Marie Raymond, S.S.T.V., Supr.; Mr. Dana Paul, Admin.; Rev. Samuel Martis (India). Sisters of St. Thomas of Villanova. Sisters 3; Patients Assisted Annually 75; Total Staff 85.

[N] MONASTIC FOUNDATIONS

WEST REDDING. *The Benedictine Grange* (1977) 06896. Tel: 203-938-3689; Fax: 203-938-3689. Email: navj@optonline.net. Rev. John B. Giuliani.

[O] RESIDENCES OF PRIESTS AND BROTHERS

BRIDGEPORT. *Instituto Verbo Encarnado*, St. George Parish, 443 Park Ave., 06604-5493. Tel: 203-335-1797; Fax: 203-334-6359. Email: st_george_church@sbcglobal.net. Revs. Julio Lopresti, I.V.E.; Gustavo Campo, I.V.E.

Provincial Offices of the Priests and Brothers of Holy Cross, Eastern Province (Province of Our Lady of Holy Cross), 835 Clinton Ave., 06604. Tel: 203-367-7252; Fax: 203-366-7886. Email: tlooney@hcep.com. Web: www.stonehill.Edu.HolyCross. Revs. Thomas P. Looney, C.S.C., Prov.; George J. Lucas, C.S.C., Asst. Prov. & Vicar.

Congregation of Holy Cross - Eastern Province, Inc.

FAIRFIELD. *The Fairfield Jesuit Community-Fairfield University*, 86 Barlow Rd., 06824-5195. Tel: 203-256-1650; Fax: 203-255-5947. Web: www.faculty.fairfield.edu/jesuit. Revs. Jeffrey P. von Arx, S.J., Ph.D., Pres.; Charles H. Allen, S.J.; Gerald R. Blaszczak, S.J.; Gerhard H. Bowering, S.J. (Germany); James M. Bowler, S.J.; Vincent M. Burns, S.J.; Paul E. Carrier, S.J., (On Sabbatical); Walter J. Conlan, S.J., Rector; Michael J. Doody, S.J.; William J. Eagan, S.J.; John W. Elder, S.J. (Retired); Paul J. Fitzgerald, S.J.; George A. Gallarelli, S.J.; Francis T. Hannafey, S.J.; John J. Hanwell, S.J.; Robert J. Levens, S.J., Chap.; Fredy Cesar Maldonado, S.J.; James J. Mayzik, S.J.; Mr. Thomas M. Olson, S.J.; Revs. Walter R. Pelletier, S.J. (Retired); Laurence D. Ryan, S.J.; Richard J. Ryscavage, S.J.; Mark P. Scalese, S.J., M.F.A.; Martin G. Shaughnessy, S.J.; Edward J. Small, S.J.; Mr. Bret J. Stockdale, S.J.

STAMFORD. *The Catherine Dennis Keefe Queen of the Clergy Retired Priests' Residence*, 274 Strawberry Hill Ave., 06902. Tel: 203-358-9906; Fax: 203-358-9524. Rev. Msgrs. Louis A. DeProfio, P.A. (Retired); William A. Genuario, P.A., J.C.D. (Retired); John E. Gilmartin (Retired), 7 Wind Mill Rd., New Fairfield, 06812; Joseph J. Kohut (Retired); William J. Loughlin (Retired); Thaddeus F. Malanowski; William A. Nagle (Retired); John C. Sanders (Retired); Revs. James E. Breen (Retired); Nicholas J. Calabro (Retired); Edward A. Colohan (Retired); Peter A. DeMarco (Retired); Clifford J. Grise (Retired); Joseph K. Parampath, J.C.D. (Retired), P.O. Box 1025, Weston, 06883. Home for Retired Priests

[P] CONVENTS AND RESIDENCES FOR SISTERS

BRIDGEPORT. *Convent of Mary Immaculate, Missionary Sisters of the Blessed Sacrament and Mary Immaculate.* Prov. Headquarters., 1111 Wordin Ave., 06605. Tel: 203-334-5681; Fax: 203-333-1590. Email: misamie.ucarvistia@sbcglobal.net. Sr. Presencion Zabata, Prov. Assisting the Apostolate to Spanish-Speaking People. Sisters 5.

Daughters of Charity of the Most Precious Blood Convent, 1482 North Ave., 06604. Tel: 203-334-7000; Fax: 203-334-7000. Email: daughtersofcharity@yahoo.com. Web: www.dcmpb.org. Sr. Theresa Tremblay, D.C.P.B., Dir.

Institute Servants of the Lord and the Virgin of Matara (1988) 153 Linden Ave., 06604-5730. Tel: 203-330-8409; Fax: 203-334-6359. Email: c.damaris@servidoras.org. Web: www.servidoras.org. Sr. Myriam Altnah, S.S.V.M., Local Supr.

Missionaries of Charity, 599 Beechwood Ave., 06604. Tel: 203-336-5626. Sr. M. Regis Devasia, M.C., Contact Person.

Sisters of the Company of the Savior, 820 Clinton Ave., 06604. Tel: 203-368-1875; Fax: 203-368-1875. Sr. Constanza Lopez, Supr. Spanish-Speaking Apostolate.

GREENWICH. *Sacred Heart Convent*, 38 Gold St., 06830. Tel: 203-531-8547. Franciscan Sisters of the Atonement 4.

MONROE. *Sisters of the Holy Family of Nazareth, C.S.F.N.* (1875) 1428 Monroe Tpke., 06468. Tel: 203-268-6560; Fax: 203-261-0866. Web: www.nazarethcsfn.org. Rev. James J. Cole, Chap. Professed 48.

NORWALK. *Regional House of Sisters of St. Thomas of Villanova* (1948) 76 W. Rocks Rd., 06851. Tel: 203-847-2885; Fax: 203-847-3740. Email: sstv_usa@sbcglobal.net. Web: www.saintthomasofvillanova.com. Sr. Jean Marie Raymond, S.S.T.V., Supr. Notre Dame Convalescent Home. Professed 3.

RIDGEFIELD. *Provincial House, Congregation de Notre Dame*, 30 Highfield Rd., Wilton, 06897. Tel: 203-762-4300; Fax: 203-762-4319. Email: rhager@cnd-m.org. Sr. Mary Caplice, C.N.D., Prov. Leader.

STAMFORD. *Franciscan Sisters of the Immaculate Heart of Mary*, 1216 Shippan Ave., 06902-7425. Tel: 203-569-0310. Email: fihmstamford@yahoo.com. Sr. Franciscal Alphonse, F.I.H.M., Supr.

Heart of Mary Convent (Residence for Bernardine Sisters), 163 Sky Meadow Dr., 06903-3414. Tel: 203-322-5920; Fax: 203-322-5491. Email: HMCSTAM@aol.com. Sr. Maria Angela Kurczak, O.S.F., Local Min. Tel: 203-322-8721. Bernardine Sisters 11. In Res. Sisters Robertine Babula, O.S.F.; Dulceline Cieslukowski, O.S.F.; M. de Lourdes Okoniewski; M. Laetitia Okoniewski, O.S.F.; Joanne Helen Grejdus, O.S.F.; Jolancia Kozlinski, O.S.F.; Carol Ann Nawracaj, O.S.F.; Mary Cabrini Nowosielski, O.S.F.; Phyllis Marie Soja, O.S.F.; Mary Innocentia Spaniak, O.S.F.

Villa Maria Education Center, 161 Sky Meadow Dr., 06903. Tel: 203-322-5886; Fax: 203-322-0228. Sr. Carol Ann Nawracaj, O.S.F., Exec. Dir. School for children with learning disabilities (Grades 1-8). Sisters 4; Lay Teachers 23; Students 84.

Our Lady of Grace Convent, 635 Glenbrook Rd., 06906. Tel: 203-348-5531; Fax: 203-324-9638. Email: sgesuina@aol.com. Sr. Gesuina Gencarelli, P.O.S.C., Supr. Motherhouse and Novitiate of Little Workers of Sacred Hearts.

Sisters Minor of Mary Immaculate, 305 Washington Blvd., 06902. Tel: 203-323-4546. Sisters 2.

St. Francis Villa, 138 Brushy Hill Rd., Danbury, 06810. Tel: 203-744-8041; Fax: 203-744-8041. Sr. Donna Marie Shattell, S.M.M.I., Delegate. Sisters Minor of Mary Immaculate Custody House Sisters 2.

Villa Divino Amore Convent, Little Workers of the Sacred Hearts of Jesus & Mary, 117 Hope St., 06906. Tel: 203-324-2449. Sr. Giacinta Scaramuzzo, P.O.S.C., Supr.

Villa Maria Guadalupe Life Center, 159 Skymeadow Dr., 06903. Tel: 203-329-1492; Fax: 203-329-1495. Sr. Mary Grace, S.V., Supr. Beds for Retreat Center 80; Sisters in Residence 8.

STRATFORD. *Holy Spirit Convent, Daughters of the Holy Spirit* (1706) 1811 North Ave., 06614. Tel: 203-383-4377; Fax: 203-383-4377. Email: Daughters831@aol.com.

WILTON. *Lourdes Health Care Center, Inc.* (1973) 345 Belden Hill Rd., 06897-3898. Tel: 203-762-4135; Fax: 203-762-2144. Email: adm@lourdeswilton.org. Sr. Eileen Shea, S.S.N.D., Prov. Councilor; Rev. Thomas Elliot, C.S.C., Resident Chap.

School Sisters of Notre Dame Motherhouse (Northeastern Province) (1833) 345 Belden Hill Rd., 06897. Tel: 203-762-3318; Fax: 203-762-9434. Web: www.ssnd.org. Sr. Mary V. Maher, Prov. Supr.; Rev. Thomas Elliott, C.S.C. Tel: 203-762-3318. Priests 1; Professed 115.

[Q] SECULAR INSTITUTES

BRIDGEPORT. *The Society of Our Lady of the Way*, 584 Capitol Ave., Apt. 6, 06606. Tel: 203-579-4531. Miss Margaret Gould. A secular institute for women.

[R] FOUNDATIONS, TRUSTS AND FUNDS

BRIDGEPORT. *Fairfield Foundation of the Diocese of Bridgeport, Inc.*, 238 Jewett Ave., 06606-2892. Tel: 203-372-4301; Fax: 203-371-8698. Most Rev. William E. Lori, S.T.D., Pres.; Mrs. Nancy B. Matthews, Esq., Sec.

Inner-City Foundation For Charity & Education (1991) 238 Jewett Ave., 06606-2892. Tel: 203-416-1363; Fax: 203-372-0364. Email: info@innercity.foundation.org. Web: www.innercityfoundation.org. Rev. Msgr. Kevin W. Wallin, Exec. Dir.; Mr. Richard T. Stone, Dir.

[S] GUEST HOUSES

DARIEN. *Convent of St. Birgitta*, Vikingsborg, 4 Rukenhage Rd., 06820. Tel: 203-655-1068; Fax: 203-655-3496. Email: convent@birgittines-us.com; conventsb@optonline.net. Web: www.birgittines-us.com. Sr. M. Eunice Kulangrathottyil, O.SS.S., Supr.; Rev. Robert F. McCormick, Chap.

[T] HOUSES OF STUDIES

BRIDGEPORT. *St. Peter's Parish, St. Maximillian Kolbe House of Studies*, 535 Colorado Ave., 06605. Tel: 203-869-1032. Email: st.m.kolbe.house@snet.net. Rev. Msgr. Francis C. Wissel, Dir.

[U] RETREAT HOUSES

BRIDGEPORT. *Queen of Saints, The Catholic Center*, 238 Jewett Ave., 6606. Tel: 203-416-1403. Retreat Facility

The Urban Center of St. Charles Parish, 1279 E. Main St., 06608. Tel: 203-333-2147; Fax: 203-330-8316.

St. Charles Outreach Program Tel: 203-333-2147; Fax: 203-330-8316. Rev. Edicson Orozco, Admin.

DARIEN. *Convent of St. Birgitta*, 4 Runkenhage Rd., 06820. Tel: 203-655-1068; Fax: 203-655-3496. Email: convent@birgittines-us.com; conventsb@optonline.net. Web: www.birgittines-us.com. Sr. M. Eunice Kulangrathottyil, O.SS.S., Supr.

MONROE. *Marian Heights Convent*, 1428 Monroe Tpke., 06468. Tel: 203-268-6540; Fax: 203-261-0866. Web: www.nazarethcsfn.org. Sisters of the Holy Family of Nazareth

STAMFORD. *Villa Maria Guadalupe Retreat Center*, 159 Sky Meadow Dr., 06903. Tel: 203-329-1492; Fax: 203-329-1495. Web: sistersoflife.org. Sr. Dorothy Guadalupe Schuster, S.V., Supr. Owned by Sisters of Life Sisters of Life 8; Bed Capacity 60.

[V] CAMPUS MINISTRY

DANBURY. *Newman Center at Western CT State University* 7 Eighth Ave., 06810. Tel: 203-744-5846. Email: laskym@wcsu.edu. Rev. Michael Lasky, O.F.M.Conv., Chap.

FAIRFIELD. *Fairfield University* , (Fairfield), 1073 N. Benson Rd., 06824-5195. Tel: 203-254-4190; Fax: 203-254-4221. Ms. Ann K. Stehney, Dir. Inst. Research; Revs. Gerald R. Blaszczak, S.J., Univ. Chap.; Michael J. Doody, S.J., Dir. Campus Min.; Mrs. Carolyn M. Rusiackas, Assoc. Univ. Chap.; Conor L. O'Kane, Assoc. Dir. Campus Ministry; Wylie J. Smith, Asst. Univ. Chap.; Cristina Bowen, Campus Min.

[W] MISCELLANEOUS LISTINGS

BRIDGEPORT. *Blessed Brother Andre Charitable Trust*, 835 Clinton Ave., 06604. Tel: 203-367-7252; Fax: 203-366-7886. Email: tlooney@hcep.com; jlack@hcep.com.

Cardinal Shehan Center, Inc., 1494 Main St., 06604. Tel: 203-336-4468; Fax: 203-368-0901. Email: tjo@shehancenter.org. Web: shehancenter.org. Mr. Terry O'Connor, Exec. Dir.

Caroline House, Inc., 574 Stillman St., 06608. Tel: 203-334-0640; Fax: 203-334-0248. Email: thecarolinehouse@snet.net. Web: thecarolinehouse.org. Sr. Ann Moles, S.S.N.D., Exec. Dir.; Mary Ellen Gavin, Devel. Dir.

The Diocesan Cemetery Care Fund, Inc., 238 Jewett Ave., 06606. Tel: 203-416-1491.

Faith in the Future Fund, Inc., 238 Jewett Ave., 06606. Tel: 203-416-1472; Fax: 203-373-6890.

Hispanic Social Ministries of Fairfield County, Inc., 238 Jewett Ave., 06606-9990. Tel: 203-366-5611; Fax: 203-335-1924. Rev. Msgr. Aniceto Villamide, Contact Person.

**McGivney Community Center, Inc.*, Mailing Address: P.O. Box 5220, 06610-0220. 338 Stillman St., 06610-0220. Tel: 203-333-2789; Fax: 203-334-1933. Email: karenking@mcgivney.org. Web: www.mcgivney.org. Karen King, Exec. Dir.

Needle Fund, Inc., 238 Jewett Ave., 06606.

Saint Charles Brazilian Children, 238 Jewett Ave., 06606. Tel: 203-929-4798. Email: scbc1@sbcglobal.net.

DANBURY. *Magnificat, A Ministry to Catholic Women* (2003) 25 Maplewood Dr., 06811. Tel: 203-778-3950. Email: magnificatbpt@sbcglobal.net. Web: www.triumphantheart.org. Roxane Angotta, Coord. (Triumphant Heart of Mary Immaculate)

GREENWICH. *Clemons Productions, Inc.* (1981) (In association with That's The Spirit Productions, Inc.), P.O. Box 7466, 06836. Tel: 203-316-9394; Fax: 203-316-9396. Email: clemons10@aol.com. Web: www.spirituality.org. Rev. Mark Connolly, Pres. (Retired). Tel: 203-316-9394.

Spirituality For Today (1995) Tel: 203-316-9394; Fax: 203-316-9396.

Radio Program: Thoughts for the Week (1993) Tel: 203-316-9394; Fax: 203-316-9396. Web: www.spirituality.org.

NORWALK. *Malta House of Good Counsel*, 5 Prowitt St., 06855-1203. Tel: 203-857-0088; Fax: 203-857-0018. Email: maltahouse@aol.com.

RIVERSIDE. *The Mother Teresa of Calcutta Center*, P.O. Box 455, 06878. Tel: 203-637-7578. Email: tleogallagher@aol.com.

STAMFORD. *Haitian American Catholic Center* (2000) 93 Hope St., 06906. Tel: 203-406-0343; Fax: 203-406-0347. Rev. Jean-Rony Philippe.

RELIGIOUS INSTITUTES OF MEN REPRESENTED IN THE DIOCESE

For further details refer to the corresponding bracketed number in the Religious Institutes of Men or Women section.

[0470]—*The Capuchin Friars* (Prov. of St. Mary)—O.F.M.Cap.

[0520]—*Franciscan Friars* (Commissariat of St. Stephen)—O.F.M.

[0650]—*Holy Ghost Fathers* (Irish Prov.)—C.S.Sp.

[]—*Instituto Verbo Encarnado*—I.V.E.

[0690]—*Jesuit Fathers and Brothers* (New England Prov.)—S.J.

[0870]—*Montfort Missionaries* (Haitian Prov.)—S.M.M.

[0610]—*Priests of the Congregation of Holy Cross* (Prov. of Our Lady of Holy Cross)—C.S.C.

[]—*The Augustinians*—O.S.A.

RELIGIOUS INSTITUTES OF WOMEN REPRESENTED IN THE DIOCESE

[0130]—*Apostles of the Sacred Heart of Jesus*—A.S.C.J.

[1810]—*Bernardine Sisters of the Third Order of St. Francis*—O.S.F.

[0280]—*Brigittine Sisters*—O.SS.S.

[]—*The Community of the Mother of God of Tenderness*—C.M.G.T.

[0710]—*Company of the Saviour*—C.S.

[4030]—*Congregation of Sisters of St. Thomas of Villanova*—S.S.T.V.

[0760]—*Daughters of Charity of St. Vincent de Paul*—D.C.

[0740]—*Daughters of Charity of the Most Precious Blood*—D.C.P.B.

[0820]—*Daughters of the Holy Spirit*—D.H.S.

[]—*Dominican Sisters*—O.P.

[]—*Dominican Sisters of Hope* (New Burgh, NY)—O.P.

[1190]—*Franciscan Sisters of the Atonement*—S.A.

[]—*Franciscan Sisters of the Immaculate Heart of Mary*—F.I.H.M.

[2575]—*Institute of the Sisters of Mercy of the Americas*—R.S.M.

[]—*Institute Servants of the Lord and the Virgin of Matara*—S.S.V.M.

[2345]—*Little Workers of the Sacred Hearts of Jesus & Mary*—P.O.S.C.

[]—*Marian Community of Reconciliation*—M.C.R.

[]—*Missionaries of Charity*—M.C.

[]—*Missionary Franciscan Sisters of the Immaculate Conception*—M.F.I.C.

[]—*Missionary Sisters of the Blessed Sacrament and Mary Immaculate*—M.S.S.M.I.

[2780]—*Missionary Sisters of the Most Blessed Sacrament* (Spain)—M.SS.S.

[3430]—*Religious Teachers Filippini*—M.P.F.

[2970]—*School Sisters of Notre Dame*—S.S.N.D.

[]—*Sisters Minor of the Mary Immaculate*—S.M.M.I.

[]—*Sisters of Charity of St. Vincent de Paul of New York*—S.C.

[]—*Sisters of Life*—S.V.

[]—*Sisters of Love of the Holy Cross*—S.L.C.

[2990]—*Sisters of Notre Dame*—S.N.D.

[3000]—*Sisters of Notre Dame de Namur*—S.N.D.deN.

[3780]—*Sisters of Saints Cyril and Methodius*—SS.C.M.

[]—*Sisters of St. Joseph*—S.S.J.

[]—*Sisters of St. Joseph of Chambery*—C.S.J.

[]—*Sisters of St. Mary of Namur*—S.S.M.N.

[2980]—*Sisters of the Congregation de Notre Dame*—C.N.D.

[]—*Sisters of the Holy Cross*—C.S.C.

[1970]—*Sisters of the Holy Family of Nazareth*—C.S.F.N.

[2160]—*Sisters, Servants of the Immaculate Heart of Mary*—I.H.M.

[4070]—*Society of the Sacred Heart*—R.S.C.J.

[]—*Ursuline Nuns (Roman Union)*

[4130]—*Ursuline Sisters of the Congregation of Tildonk, Belgium*—O.S.U.C.

DIOCESAN CEMETERIES

DANBURY. *St. Peter's*, Lake Ave. Exit, 06810. Tel: 203-743-9626.

DARIEN. *St. John's*, 25 Camp Ave., 06820. Tel: 203-322-0455; Fax: 203-595-9243.

Queen of Peace, c/o St. John Cemetery, 25 Camp Ave., 06820. Tel: 203-322-0455; Fax: 203-595-9243.

GREENWICH. *St. Mary's*, 399 North St., 06830. Tel: 203-869-7026.

Putnam, 35 Parsonage Rd., 06830. Tel: 203-869-4828; Fax: 203-869-9246.

NEWTOWN. *Resurrection*, c/o Gate of Heaven Cemetery, 1056 Daniels Farm Rd., Trumbull, 06611. Tel: 203-268-5574.

NORWALK. *Assumption Green Farms*, Kings Hwy., c/o St. John Cemetery, 223 Richards Ave., 06850. Tel: 203-838-4271.

St. John's & St. Mary's, 223 Richards Ave., 06850. Tel: 203-838-4271.

STRATFORD. *St. Michael's*, 2205 Stratford Ave., 06615. Tel: 203-378-0404; Fax: 203-378-0313.

TRUMBULL. *Gate of Heaven*, 1056 Daniels Farms Rd., 06611. Tel: 203-268-5574; Fax: 203-268-2203.

NECROLOGY

† Horgan-Kung, Rev. Msgr. John V., (Retired)—Died Oct. 16, 2009

† Karl, Rev. Msgr. Edward B., (Retired)—Died Sept. 20, 2009

† McMahon, Rev. Msgr. Lawrence J., (Retired)—Died Dec. 15, 2009

† Fay, Michael Jude, (Leave of Absence)—Died Aug. 22, 2009

† Renda, Xavier F., (Retired)—Died June 22, 2009

† Russo, Alfred E., (Retired)—Died Dec. 14, 2009

An asterisk (*) denotes an organization that has established tax-exempt status directly with the IRS and is not covered by the USCCB Group Ruling.

Diocese of Brooklyn

(Dioecesis Bruklyniensis)

Most Reverend

THOMAS V. DAILY, D.D.

Retired Bishop of Brooklyn; ordained January 10, 1952; appointed Auxiliary to the Archbishop of Boston and Titular Bishop of Bladia December 31, 1974; consecrated February 11, 1975; appointed First Bishop of Palm Beach July 17, 1984; appointed Sixth Bishop of Brooklyn February 20, 1990; took possession April 16, 1990; installed April 18, 1990; retired August 1, 2003. *Mailing Address: 7200 Douglaston Pkwy., Douglaston, NY 11362.*

Most Reverend

JOSEPH M. SULLIVAN, M.S.W., M.P.A.

Retired Auxiliary Bishop of Brooklyn; ordained June 2, 1956; appointed Titular Bishop of Suliana October 7, 1980; episcopal ordination November 24, 1980; retired May 12, 2005. *Mailing Address: 378 Clermont Ave., Brooklyn, NY 11238.*

Most Reverend

RENE A. VALERO, M.S.W.

Retired Auxiliary Bishop of Brooklyn; priestly ordination June 2, 1956; appointed Titular Bishop of Vicus Turris October 7, 1980; episcopal ordination November 24, 1980; retired October 27, 2005. *Res.: 34-43 93rd St., Jackson Heights, NY 11372.*

Most Reverend

IGNATIUS A. CATANELLO, PH.D., V.E.

Twelfth Auxiliary Bishop of Brooklyn; ordained May 28, 1966; appointed Titular Bishop of Deulto June 28, 1994; episcopal ordination August 22, 1994. *Res.: 175-20 74th Ave., Flushing, NY 11366.*

Most Reverend

NICHOLAS DIMARZIO, PH.D., D.D.

Seventh Bishop of Brooklyn; ordained May 30, 1970; appointed Titular Bishop of Mauriana and Auxiliary Bishop of Newark September 10, 1996; consecrated October 31, 1996; appointed Bishop of Camden June 18, 1999; installed July 22, 1999; appointed Bishop of Brooklyn August 1, 2003; installed October 3, 2003. *Office: 310 Prospect Park W., Brooklyn, NY 11215.*

Chancery Office: 310 Prospect Park W., Brooklyn, NY 11215. Tel: 718-399-5990; Fax: 718-399-5934.

Email: curia@diobrook.org

Most Reverend

OCTAVIO CISNEROS, D.D., V.E.

Auxiliary Bishop of Brooklyn; ordained May 29, 1971; appointed Titular Bishop of Eanach Duin June 6, 2006; episcopal ordination August 22, 2006. *Mailing Address: Holy Child Jesus, 111-11 86th Ave., Richmond Hill, NY 11418-1613.*

Most Reverend

GUY SANSARICQ, D.D., V.E.

Auxiliary Bishop of Brooklyn; ordained June 29, 1960; appointed Titular Bishop of Glenndalocha June 6, 2006; episcopal ordination August 22, 2006. *Mailing Address: St. Gregory the Great, 224 Brooklyn Ave., Brooklyn, NY 11213-2505.*

Most Reverend

FRANK J. CAGGIANO, D.D., V.G.

Auxiliary Bishop of Brooklyn; ordained May 16, 1987; appointed Titular Bishop of Inis Cathaig June 6, 2006; episcopal ordination August 22, 2006. *Mailing Address: 310 Prospect Park W., Brooklyn, NY 11215.*

ESTABLISHED JULY 29, 1853.

Square Miles 179.

Comprises Kings and Queens Counties in the State of New York.

For legal titles of parishes and diocesan institutions consult the Chancery Office.

STATISTICAL OVERVIEW

Personnel	
Bishop	1
Auxiliary Bishops	4
Retired Bishops	3
Priests: Diocesan Active in Diocese	278
Priests: Diocesan Active Outside Diocese	19
Priests: Retired, Sick or Absent	228
Number of Diocesan Priests	525
Religious Priests in Diocese	174
Total Priests in Diocese	699
Extern Priests in Diocese	100
Ordinations:	
Diocesan Priests	3
Transitional Deacons	3
Permanent Deacons	20
Permanent Deacons in Diocese	159
Total Brothers	138
Total Sisters	868
Parishes	
Parishes	197
With Resident Pastor:	
Resident Diocesan Priests	162
Resident Religious Priests	22
Without Resident Pastor:	
Administered by Priests	6
Professional Ministry Personnel:	
Brothers	10
Sisters	110
Lay Ministers	376
Welfare	
Health Care Centers	10
Total Assisted	10,284
Homes for the Aged	5
Total Assisted	1,300
Residential Care of Children	1
Total Assisted	6,800
Day Care Centers	28
Total Assisted	5,403
Specialized Homes	30
Total Assisted	9,100
Special Centers for Social Services	90
Total Assisted	108,000
Residential Care of Disabled	74
Total Assisted	3,100
Other Institutions	2,697
Total Assisted	3,500
Educational	
Seminaries, Diocesan	1
Students from This Diocese	15
Students from Other Diocese	9
Diocesan Students in Other Seminaries	17
Seminaries, Religious	1
Students Religious	13
Total Seminarians	45
Colleges and Universities	3
Total Students	20,659
High Schools, Diocesan and Parish	4
Total Students	2,037
High Schools, Private	17
Total Students	14,362
Elementary Schools, Diocesan and Parish	104
Total Students	33,494
Elementary Schools, Private	3
Total Students	413
Non-residential Schools for the Disabled	2
Total Students	103
Catechesis/Religious Education:	
High School Students	3,727
Elementary Students	33,051
Total Students under Catholic Instruction	104,891
Teachers in the Diocese:	
Brothers	43
Sisters	117
Lay Teachers	2,864
Vital Statistics	
Receptions into the Church:	
Infant Baptism Totals	17,095
Minor Baptism Totals	1,037
Adult Baptism Totals	624
Received into Full Communion	828
First Communions	11,045
Confirmations	10,612
Marriages:	
Catholic	2,393
Interfaith	303
Total Marriages	2,696
Deaths	9,103
Total Catholic Population	1,440,000
Total Population	4,798,388

Former Bishops—Rt. Revs. JOHN LOUGHLIN, D.D., First Bishop of Brooklyn; ord. Oct. 18, 1840; cons. Oct. 30, 1853; died Dec. 28, 1891; CHARLES E. MCDONNELL, D.D., Second Bishop of Brooklyn; ord. May 19, 1878; cons. April 25, 1892; died Aug. 8, 1921; Most Revs. THOMAS E. MOLLOY, D.D., Third Bishop of Brooklyn; ord. Sept. 19, 1908; cons. Second Auxiliary Bishop of Brooklyn, Oct. 3, 1920; appt. Bishop of Brooklyn, Nov. 21, 1921; installed Feb. 15, 1922; died Nov. 26, 1956; BRYAN J. MCENTEGART, D.D., LL.D., Fourth Bishop of Brooklyn; ord. Sept. 8, 1917; appt. Bishop of Ogdensburg, June 5, 1943; cons. Aug. 3, 1943; appt. Rector of the Catholic University of America, Washington, DC, June 26, 1953; appt. Titular Bishop of Aradi, Aug. 19, 1953; appt. Bishop of Brooklyn, April 16, 1957; installed June 13, 1957; retired and appt. Titular Archbishop of Gabii, July 17, 1968; died Sept. 30, 1968; FRANCIS J. MUGAVERO, D.D., Fifth Bishop of Brooklyn; ord. May 18, 1940; Bishop of Brooklyn; appt. July 15, 1968; cons. Sept. 12, 1968; installed Sept. 12, 1968; retired Feb. 20, 1990; died July 12, 1991; THOMAS V. DAILY, D.D., ord. Jan. 10, 1952; appt. Auxiliary to the Archbishop of Boston and Titular Bishop of Bladia Dec. 31, 1974; cons. Feb. 11, 1975; appt. First Bishop of Palm Beach July 17, 1984; appt. Sixth Bishop of Brooklyn Feb. 20, 1990; took possession April 16, 1990; installed April 18, 1990; retired Aug. 1, 2003.

Central Offices—310 Prospect Park W., Brooklyn, 11215. Tel: 718-399-5900. Office Hours: Mon.-Fri. 8:30-5.

Vicar General and Moderator of the Curia—Most Rev. FRANK J. CAGGIANO, D.D., S.T.D., V.G., 310 Prospect Park W., Brooklyn, 11215. Tel: 718-399-5995; Fax: 718-399-5965.

Regional Bishop of Brooklyn—Most Rev. GUY SANSARICQ, D.D., St. Gregory the Great, 224 Brooklyn Ave., Brooklyn, 11213. Tel: 718-773-0100.

Regional Bishop of Queens—Most Rev. OCTAVIO CISNEROS, D.D., Immaculate Conception Center, 7200 Douglaston Pkwy., Douglaston, 11362.

Episcopal Vicars-Territorial—Brooklyn: Rev. Msgr. STEVEN A. FERRARI, V.E., Immaculate Heart of Mary, 2805 Fort Hamilton Pkwy., Brooklyn, 11218. Tel: 718-871-1310. Queens: Rev. Msgr. PAUL R. SANCHEZ, V.E., Resurrection-Ascension, 61-11 85th St., Rego Park, 11374. Tel: 718-424-5212.

Vicar for Black Catholic Concerns—Most Rev. GUY SANSARICQ, D.D., St. Gregory the Great, 224 Brooklyn Ave., Brooklyn, 11213.

Vicar for Canonical Affairs—Rev. Msgr. ANTHONY HERNANDEZ, 310 Prospect Park W., Brooklyn, 11215. Tel: 718-399-5990.

Secretariat for Financial Administration/Econome—Rev. Msgr. MICHAEL J. REID, Vicar.

Secretariat for Catholic Education and Formation—Sr. ANGELA GANNON, C.S.J., Sec.

Secretariat for Communications—Rev. Msgr. KIERAN E. HARRINGTON, V.E., Vicar.

Secretariat for Development—Rev. Msgr. JAMIE J. GIGANTIELLO, Vicar.

Secretariat for Human and Information Resources—Deacon EDWARD S. GAINE, Sec.

Human Resources Office—310 Prospect Park W., Brooklyn, 11215. Tel: 718-965-7300; Fax: 718-965-7363.

Secretariat for Pastoral Support—Very Rev. JOSEPH G. FONTI, S.T.L., Vicar.

Vicar for Clergy, Consecrated Life and Apostolic Organizations—Rev. Msgr. RAYMOND F. CHAPPETTO, Our Lady of the Snows, 258-15 80th Ave., Floral Park, 11004. Tel: 718-347-6070; Fax: 718-343-3221.

Special Assistant to Vicar for Clergy—Rev. RAYMOND RODEN.

Vicar for Higher Education—Rev. Msgr. JOHN STRYNKOWSKI, 250 Cathedral Pl., Brooklyn, 11201. Tel: 718-852-4002.

Vicar for Hispanic Concerns—Most Rev. OCTAVIO CISNEROS, D.D., Immaculate Conception Center, 7200 Douglaston Pkwy., Douglaston, 11362.

Vicar for Human Services—Rev. Msgr. ALFRED P. LOPINTO, V.E., St. Helen, 157-10 83rd St., Howard Beach, 11414. Tel: 718-738-1616.

Vicar for Migrant and Ethnic Apostolates—Rev. Msgr. RONALD T. MARINO, V.E., 1258 65th St., Brooklyn, 11219. Tel: 718-236-3000.

Finance Officer—Mr. JOHN BORGIA, CFO & Treas.; Mr. MARTIN J. MCMANUS, CPA, Comptroller. Tel: 718-965-7300, Ext. 1401; Fax: 718-965-7371.

Parish Services Corp.—Rev. Msgr. DAVID L. CASSATO, M.Div., M.S.Ed., Pres.; Mr. JOHN BORGIA, Vice Pres.; Rev. PATRICK J. WEST, Bd. of Dir.; Mr. MARTIN J. MCMANUS, CPA, Treas.; BRIAN T. COSGROVE, Sec., 310 Prospect Park W., Brooklyn, 11215. Tel: 718-965-7300; Fax: 718-965-7382.

Peter Turner Insurance Co.—7 Hanover Square, New York, 10004. Rev. CHRISTOPHER J. TURCZANY, Pres.; Mr. JOHN BORGIA, Exec. Vice Pres.; Mr. MARTIN J. MCMANUS, CPA, Treas.; BRIAN T. COSGROVE, Sec.; Rev. Msgrs. DAVID L. CASSATO, M.Div., M.S.Ed.; JOSEPH P. NAGLE; PETER V. KAIN; B. MCCOURT; Rev. PATRICK J. WEST; Mr. JOHN G. DOLAN; Ms. SUZANNE B. HOLOHAN.

Development Office—Tel: 718-965-7300; Fax: 718-965-7341.

Building and Property Administration—COLEEN CERIELLO; Mr. ROBERT DADONA. Tel: 718-965-7300; Fax: 718-965-7353.

Chancery Office—310 Prospect Park W., Brooklyn, 11215. Tel: 718-399-5990; Fax: 718-399-5934.

Chancellor—Rev. Msgr. ANTHONY HERNANDEZ.

Vice Chancellor—VACANT.

Assistant Chancellor—VACANT.

Diocesan Archivist—JOSEPH W. COEN, C.A., Mailing Address: 310 Prospect Park W., Brooklyn, 11215. Tel: 718-965-7300, Ext. 1001.

Censors of Books—Most Rev. FRANK J. CAGGIANO, D.D., S.T.D., V.G.; Rev. Msgr. PETER I. VACCARI, S.T.L.; Revs. BRYAN D. PATTERSON; JOHN P. CUSH, B.A., S.T.L., 310 Prospect Park W., Brooklyn, 11215.

Assistant to the Bishop—Deacon JAMIE VARELA. Tel: 718-399-5970; Fax: 718-399-5975.

Tribunal—7200 Douglaston Pkwy., Douglaston, 11362. Tel: 718-229-8131; Fax: 718-631-1339.

Officialis-Judicial Vicar—Rev. Msgr. STEVEN J. AGUGGIA, J.C.L.; Dr. GLENN CARROZZA, J.C.D., Dir.

Vice Officiale-Associate Judicial Vicar—Rev. THOMAS C. MACHALSKI, J.C.L.

Diocesan Judges—Rev. Msgrs. STEVEN J. AGUGGIA, J.C.L.; THOMAS F. DONOVAN (Retired); OTTO L. GARCIA, J.C.D., V.G.; Rev. JOSEPH R. GRIMALDI, J.C.L.; Rev. Msgr. RAYMOND W. KUTNER, J.C.D.; Rev. THOMAS C. MACHALSKI, M.S.Ed., J.C.L.; Rev. Msgr. JOSEPH C. MULQUEEN (Retired); Revs. WITOLD MROZIEWSKI, J.C.D.; REINALDO A. SALDARRIAGA, J.C.D.; Dr. GLEN CAROZZA, J.C.D.

Defenders of the Marriage Bond—Rev. Msgrs. JOHN J. BROWN, S.T.L., J.C.L.; ANDREW J. VACCARI, J.C.L.

Promoter of Justice—Rev. WILLIAM HOPPE, J.C.L.

Presiding Judge of the Appellate Court—Rev. Msgr. ROBERT THELEN.

Attorney and Counselor at Canon Law—Rev. WITOLD MROZIEWSKI, J.C.D.

Religious, Episcopal Delegate for—Sr. MARYANN SETON LOPICCOLO, S.C., 310 Prospect Park W., Brooklyn, 11215. Tel: 718-399-5900.

Office of Legislative Affairs—Rev. Msgr. KIERAN E. HARRINGTON, V.E.

Cemeteries—STEVEN COMANDO, Dir.

Education, Offices— (See Institutions located in the Diocese for details)

Diocesan Insurance Committee—310 Prospect Park W., Brooklyn, 11215. Tel: 718-965-7300; Fax: 718-965-7382. BRIAN T. COSGROVE, Dir. Insurance. Tel: 718-965-7300, Ext. 1351; Rev. CHRISTOPHER J. TURCZANY; Rev. Msgrs. DAVID L. CASSATO, M.Div., M.S.Ed.; JOSEPH P. NAGLE; PETER V. KAIN; B. MCCOURT; Rev. PATRICK J. WEST; GINA DAVI. Tel: 718-965-7300, Ext. 1352.

Mediation and Arbitration, Board of—Rev. Msgr. EDWARD B. SCHARFENBERGER, S.T.L., J.C.L., Exec. Sec., Mailing Address: 310 Prospect Park W., Brooklyn, 11215.

Ministerial Development Program—Very Rev. JOSEPH G. FONTI, S.T.L. Tel: 718-229-8001.

Newspaper "The Tablet"—ED WILKINSON, Editor, 310 Prospect Park W., P.O. Box 159013, Brooklyn, 11215-0013. Tel: 718-965-7300; Fax: 718-965-7339.

Office for Clergy Personnel—Deacon JULIO BARRENECHE, 310 Prospect Park W., Brooklyn, 11215. Tel: 718-399-5941; Fax: 718-399-7194.

Assignment Board—Most Rev. IGNATIUS CATANELLO, D.D., Ph.D., V.E.; Rev. Msgr. RONALD T. MARINO, V.E.; Deacon JULIO BARRENECHE; Rev. Msgrs. KEVIN B. NOONE, V.E.; JOHN W. MALONEY, V.E.; STEVEN A. FERRARI, V.E.; PAUL R. SANCHEZ, V.E.; Revs. MICHAEL A. CARRANO; PATRICK KEATING.

Mission Office—Rev. TERRENCE J. MULKERIN (Retired), Office, 310 Prospect Park W., Brooklyn, 11215. Tel: 718-965-7300.

Public Information Office—Rev. Msgr. KIERAN E. HARRINGTON, V.E., Dir., 310 Prospect Park W., Brooklyn, 11215. Tel: 718-399-5955; Fax: 718-399-5957.

Retirement Board (Priests)—Most Rev. IGNATIUS CATANELLO, D.D., Ph.D., V.E., Chm., Mailing Address: 7200 Douglaston Pkwy., Douglaston, 11362.

Victim Assistance Coordinator—Sr. ELLEN PATRICIA FINN, O.P., M.Ed., L.M.S.W. Tel: 718-722-6050. Email: srepfinn@ccbq.org.

Safe Environment, Office of—7200 Douglaston Pkwy., Douglaston, 11362. Tel: 718-281-9672; Fax: 718-281-9673.

Vocations, Office of—Revs. KEVIN J. SWEENEY, Dir.; KEVIN P. ABELS, B.A., M.Div., Assoc. Dir.

Consultative Bodies

Presbyteral Council—Most Revs. OCTAVIO CISNEROS, D.D.; GUY SANSARICQ, D.D.; Rev. Msgrs. PETER V. KAIN, Exec. Sec.; PAUL SANCHEZ; Most Revs. FRANK J. CAGGIANO, D.D., S.T.D., V.G.; IGNATIUS CATANELLO, D.D., Ph.D., V.E.; Revs. JAMES K. CUNNINGHAM; JAMES E. DEVLIN; JOSEPH R. GRIMALDI, J.C.L.; Rev. Msgrs. VINCENT F. FULLAM; JOSEPH A. NUGENT; PETER W. ZENDZIAN; Revs. THOMAS W. AHERN; RICHARD J. BEUTHER; WILLIAM KRLIS; THOMAS F. LEACH; PETER J. RAYDER; RICHARD J. AHLEMEYER; Rev. Msgrs. RAYMOND F. CHAPPETTO; STEVEN A. FERRARI, V.E.; Revs. GERALD J. FITZSIMMONS, S.M.M.; GORDON P. KUSI; CHRISTOPHER M. O'CONNOR; Rev. Msgrs. SEAN G. OGLE; ANTHONY HERNANDEZ; JOHN F. CASEY (Retired), 310 Prospect Park W., Brooklyn, 11215.

Diocesan Budget Committee—Rev. Msgr. MICHAEL J. REID.

Diocesan Consultors—Most Rev. FRANK J. CAGGIANO, D.D., S.T.D., V.G.; Rev. RICHARD J. BEUTHER; Rev. Msgr. RAYMOND F. CHAPPETTO; Rev. JAMES E. DEVLIN; Rev. Msgr. VINCENT FULLUM; Rev. JOSEPH R. GRIMALDI, J.C.L.; Rev. Msgrs. ANTHONY HERNANDEZ; PETER V. KAIN; Revs. WILLIAM KRLIS; CHRISTOPHER O'CONNOR; Rev. Msgr. MICHAEL J. REID, Exec. Sec.

Diocesan Finance Council—Rev. Msgr. MICHAEL J. REID.

Diocesan Diaconal Council—Deacons JOHN SUCICH, Chm.; ROBERT ZEUNER; RONALD RIZZUTTO; BRYAN AMORE; JULIO BARRENECHE; ARTHUR CUTTER; STANLEY J. GALAZIN; SAL LICATA; JAIME COBHAM; JOHN WARREN; JORGE A. GONZALEZ; MICHAEL W. VICINANZA.

Diocesan Pastoral Council—WILLIAM KEARNS, Pres.; Most Rev. FRANK J. CAGGIANO, D.D., S.T.D., V.G., Bishop's Liaison.

Commissions and Offices for Pastoral Services

Alcoholism Committee—Rev. Msgr. THOMAS M. HAGGERTY.

Art and Architecture Commission—Revs. FRANK C. TUMINO, Dir.; ROBERT B. ADAMO; ROBERT J. ARMATO; HILAIRE BELIZAIRE; VITO A. BUONANNO; Mr. GREGORY JACK, Office: Immaculate Conception Center, 7200 Douglaston Pkwy., Douglaston, 11362. Tel: 718-281-9612; Fax: 718-281-9613.

Catholic Charities—Mr. ROBERT SIEBEL, M.S.W., Exec. Dir., 191 Joralemon St., Brooklyn, 11201. Tel: 718-722-6000 (See Institutions located in the Diocese for details).

Catholic Migration and Refugee Office— (See Institutions located in the Diocese for details)

Catholic Migration Services, Inc.—Rev. Msgr. RONALD T. MARINO, V.E., Dir. Tel: 718-236-3000.

Chaplains and Uniformed Services, Official—Police Department: Rev. ROBERT J. ROMANO, M.Div.; Rev. Msgr. DAVID L. CASSATO, M.Div., M.S.Ed. Fire Department: Rev. Msgr. JOHN DELENDICK; Rev. JOSEPH M. HOFFMAN. Sanitation Department: Rev. Msgr. ROBERT J. THELEN. BMT Holy Name Society: Rev. Msgr. WILLIAM J. FLOOD (Retired).

Diocesan Liturgy Office—Rev. FRANK C. TUMINO, Exec. Sec., St. Thomas the Apostle, 87-19 88 Ave., Woodhaven, 11421. Tel: 718-847-1353; Fax: 718-849-3776.

Diocesan Real Estate Board—Rev. Msgrs. RAYMOND W. KUTNER, J.C.D., Chm.; JOHN DELENDICK; Revs. JOSEPH R. GRIMALDI, J.C.L.; WILLIAM F. KRLIS; Mr. KEVIN KEARNEY; COLEEN CERIELLO; COLLEEN LEFFERTS.

Diocesan Food Service—Mr. JAMES AUSTIN, Dir., 7200 Douglaston Pkwy., Douglaston, 11362. Tel: 718-229-8001, Ext. 531.

Diaconate Formation Office—Deacon JORGE A. GONZALEZ, Dir., 7200 Douglaston Pkwy., Douglaston, 11362. Tel: 718-281-9577.

Ecumenical and Interreligious Affairs, Diocesan Commission for—Rev. Msgr. GUY A. MASSIE, Exec. Sec.

Committee for Eastern Orthodox-Catholic Relations—Rev. Msgr. STEVEN J. AGUGGIA, J.C.L., Chm.

Committee for Catholic-Protestant Relations—Rev. Msgr. JOHN STRYNKOWSKI.

Committee for Catholic-Jewish Relations—Rev. Msgr. GUY A. MASSIE.

Catholic Muslim Dialogue—Rev. Msgr. GUY A. MASSIE, Chm.

Catholic Hindu/Buddhist Dialogue—Rev. ABRAHAM MATTHEW, Chm.

Home School Association—VACANT.

Liturgical Commission—Rev. FRANK C. TUMINO, Exec. Sec.; Mr. DAVE ALI; Revs. VITO A. BUONANNO; JOSEPH R. GIBINO, Ph.D.; Sr. MARY JANE KELLY, O.P.; Rev. Msgr. FERNANDO FERRARESE; Dr. JULIE UPTON, R.S.M., Office, 310 Prospect Park W., Brooklyn, 11215; Deacon JORGE A. GONZALEZ.

Office of Music Ministry—Immaculate Conception Center, 7200 Douglaston Pkwy., Douglaston, 11362. Tel: 718-281-9612; Fax: 718-281-9613.

Music Commission—Rev. FRANK C. TUMINO, Exec. Sec.; Mr. EMMANUEL BOLOGNA, Co Chm.; Ms. TERESA BRYANT; Mr. MICHAEL FONTANA; Ms. VANESSA GECEWICZ; Mr. STEVEN GIUSTO; MICHAEL KAMINSKI; Rev. ANDREW KLOCEK; Dr. MERRY NADDEO; Ms. JOSEPHINE SANGES; Mr. JOSEPH SMITH; Ms. JESSICA TRANZILLO, Immaculate Conception Center, 7200 Douglaston Pkwy., Douglaston, 11362. Tel: 718-281-9612; Fax: 718-281-9613.

Pastoral Care of the Sick Office— (See Institutions located in the Diocese for details)

Pastoral Communications, Office of—Mr. CHRISTOPHER QUINN, Gen. Mgr. TVC, 1712 10th Ave., Brooklyn, 11215. Tel: 718-499-9705 Legal Title: Trans Video Communications, Inc.

Pastoral Institute—Sr. ANGELA GANNON, C.S.J., Dir., 7200 Douglaston Pkwy., Douglaston, 11362. Tel: 718-631-4267.

Pilgrimage Office—Rev. GERARD J. SAUER, Dir., 7200 Douglaston Pkwy., Douglaston, 11362. Tel: 718-965-7313. Email: pilgrimages@rcdob.org.

Prison Ministries Office— (See listing under Catholic Charities)

Office of Faith Formation—Dr. PHILIP FRANCO, Dir., Immaculate Conception Center, 7200 Douglaston Pkwy., Douglaston, 11362. Tel: 718-281-9545.

Family Life Office—Mrs. ANA PUENTE, Dir., 7200 Douglaston Pkwy., Douglaston, 11362. Tel: 718-229-8001, Ext. 342.

Coordinator of Childhood Faith Formation—VACANT.

Coordinator of Adolescent and Young Adult Faith Formation—VACANT.

Coordinator of Adult Faith Formation—VACANT.

Coordinator of Catholic School Faith Formation and Catechist Formation—VACANT.

Coordinator of RCIA—Sr. ALICE MICHAEL, S.U.S.C.

Coordinator of Marriage and Family Ministry—Mrs. ANA PUENTE.

Coordinator of Respect Life Education—VACANT.

Pastoral Planning Office—Mr. ROBERT CHOINIERE, Dir., Mailing Address: 310 Prospect Park W., Brooklyn, 11215. Tel: 718-399-5900.

Apostolic Organizations

Catholic Youth Organization, Diocesan—Dr. JOSEPH CATANELLO, 90-39 189th St., 2nd Fl., Hollis, 11423. Tel: 718-464-5645; Fax: 718-464-0510.

Charismatic Groups, Catholic—

Charismatic Renewal (English-speaking) of the Diocese of Brooklyn—JOSEPHINE CACHIA, Dir.; JOSEPHINE MCNALLY, Sec., 240 Jay St., Brooklyn, 11201. Tel: 718-260-9111; Fax: 718-260-9121.

Renouveau Charismatique of the Diocese of Brooklyn— (serving the Haitian Charismatics of the Diocese) Rev. Msgr. JOSEPH P. MALAGRECA, Dir., 2530 Church Ave., Brooklyn, 11226. Tel: 718-469-5900; Fax: 718-469-5901.

Renovacion Carismatica of the Diocese of Brooklyn—(serving the Hispanic Charismatics of the Diocese) Rev. Msgr. JOSEPH P. MALAGRECA, Dir., 2530 Church Ave., Brooklyn, 11226. Tel: 718-469-5900; Fax: 718-469-5901.

Confraternity of the Guard of Honor and Confraternity of the Holy Hour—VACANT.

Confraternity of the Precious Blood—Rev. Msgr. AUSTIN P. BENNETT, J.C.D., P.A., Dir. (Retired), 5300 Fort Hamilton Pkwy., Brooklyn, 11219. Tel: 718-436-1120.

Courage Ministry—Rev. Msgr. WALTER C. MURPHY (Retired), Immaculate Conception Center, 7200 Douglaston Pkwy., Douglaston, 11362. Tel: 718-229-1748 (Hotline).

Guilds—

Accountants—Rev. Msgr. WALTER C. MURPHY, Dir. (Retired).

Catholic Cemetery Guild—Rev. Msgr. MICHAEL J. REID, Moderator.

Lawyers—Rev. Msgrs. EDWARD B. SCHARFENBERGER, S.T.L., J.C.L., Kings Co.; THOMAS F. DONOVAN, Queens Co. (Retired).

Physicians—VACANT.

Teachers—Rev. Msgr. THOMAS F. NOONAN, Dir. (Retired).

Holy Name Society—Rev. DENNIS J. FARRELL, Moderator.

Marriage Encounter—Coordinators: JOHN TORIO; TONI TORIO. Tel: 718-746-8979.

National Council of Catholic Women—CLAIRE DUNNE, Pres.

Legion of Mary—Rev. Msgrs. VINCENT F. FULLAM, Dir.; JOSEPH ROSA, Spanish Curia; Deacon JEAN BAPTISTE BOURSIQUOT, Haitian Curia; VACANT, Korean Curia; VACANT, Flushing Curia; Revs. CHARLES REPOLE, O.F.M.Cap., N.W. Queens Curia; JOSEPH MARRIN, C.Ss.R., Bay Ridge Curia, 82-00 35th Ave., Jackson Heights, 11372. Tel: 718-429-2333.

Nocturnal Adoration Society—Rev. JOHN MADURI.

St. John's Priests Relief Society—Rev. Msgr. GEORGE M. SCHUSTER, Pres. (Retired).

Apostleship of Prayer—Rev. Msgr. VINCENT A. KEANE (Retired).

CLERGY, PARISHES, MISSIONS AND PAROCHIAL SCHOOLS

CITY OF NEW YORK

BOROUGH OF BROOKLYN

1—ST. AGATHA'S (1912) Revs. Francisco J. Walker; Lewis H. Maynard (Retired); Thomas F. Vassalotti.
Res.: 702 48th St., 11220. Tel: 718-436-1080; Fax: 718-436-8870. Email: stagatha@aol.com.
School—736 48th St., 11220. Tel: 718-435-3137; Fax: 718-437-7505. Mrs. Eilleen Bubbico, Prin. Sisters of St. Joseph 1; Lay Teachers 12; Students 222.
Catechesis/Religious Program—Vincent Estevez, C.R.E. Students 227.

2—ST. AGNES (1878) Merged with Saint Peter-Paul-Our Lady of Pilar, Brooklyn to form Saint Paul and Saint Agnes, Brooklyn

3—ALL SAINTS (1867), (Spanish), Merged with Our Lady of Monserrate-St. Ambrose, Brooklyn to form All Saints, Brooklyn.

4—ALL SAINTS (2008) Rev. William Chacon (Costa Rica); Deacon Carlos A. Martinez. In Res., Revs. David P. Bertolotti; James O'Shea, C.P.; Kevin Dance, C.P.
Res.: 115 Throop Ave., 11206-4415. Tel: 718-388-1951; Fax: 718-388-7712.
Additional Worship Site:—
Our Lady of Montserrate Chapel—134 Vernon Ave., 11206-4415.
Catechesis/Religious Program—Awilda Martinez, C.R.E. (All Saints); Elsie Torres, C.R.E. (Our Lady of Montserrate Chapel).

5—ST. ALPHONSUS, Merged 1976. Records at St. Anthony of Padua-St. Alphonsus.

6—ST. AMBROSE, Merged 1978. Records at Our Lady of Monserrate-St. Ambrose.

7—ST. ANDREW THE APOSTLE (1971) Rev. Msgr. Guy A. Massie; Deacons Gregory Dixon; Bryan Amore.
Res.: 6713 Ridge Blvd., 11220. Tel: 718-680-1010; Fax: 718-680-3160. Email: standrew@att.net.
Catechesis/Religious Program—Tel: 718-836-4679; Fax: 718-680-3160. Christine Kemp, D.R.E. Students 256.

8—ST. ANN-ST. GEORGE (1860) Closed. For inquiries for parish records contact the chancery.

9—ANNUNCIATION OF THE BLESSED VIRGIN MARY (1863), (Lithuanian), Rev. Msgr. Joseph P. Calise, Admin.
Mailing Address: 275 N. Eighth St., 11211. Tel: 718-384-0223; Fax: 718-384-5838.
Church: 259 N. 5th St., 11211.
Catechesis/Religious Program— Aurea Guzman, D.R.E.

10—ST. ANSELM (1922) Rev. Msgr. John W. Maloney; Revs. Martin R. Kull; Michael L. Gelfant; Deacon Thomas Davis. Brooklyn, NY St. Anselm
Res.: 356 82nd St., 11209. Tel: 718-238-2900; Fax: 718-238-2902. Email: stanselmrectory@aol.com. Web: www.starcc.net.
School—365 83rd St., 11209. Tel: 718-745-7643; Fax: 718-745-0086. Mrs. Linda Addonisio, Prin. Sisters of Notre Dame 2; Lay Teachers 22; Students 439.
Catechesis/Religious Program—Tel: 718-745-0077. Sisters Anne Bernadette, M.S.B.T., C.R.E.; Regina Corde, O.P., Pastoral Ministry. Tel: 718-836-0780; Bro. Robert E. Duffy, O.S.F., Dir. Faith Formation. Students 133.
Missionary Cenacle—351 83rd St., 11209. Tel: 718-836-0957. Missionary Servants of the Most Blessed Trinity 2.

11—ST. ANTHONY OF PADUA-ST. ALPHONSUS (1856) Revs. Robert W. Czok; Dagoberto Noguera.
Res.: 862 Manhattan Ave., 11222. Tel: 718-383-3339; Fax: 718-383-6958. Email: ant862@aol.com.
Catechesis/Religious Program—Tel: 718-383-6935. Rose Accetta, D.R.E. Students 179.

12—ASSUMPTION OF THE BLESSED VIRGIN MARY (1842), (Lithuanian), Rev. James W. King; Gary Cushing, Pastoral Assoc. In Res., Rev. Peter Mahoney.
Res.: 64 Middagh St., 11201. Tel: 718-625-1161; Fax: 718-625-7223. Email: frjamesking@gmail.com. Web: www.assumptionparish.net.
Catechesis/Religious Program—Students 37.

13—ST. ATHANASIUS (1913) Rev. Msgr. David L. Cassato; Revs. Ronald M. D'Antonio; Gabriel Toro-Rivas; Deacon Dante Colandrea; John Fruner, Pastoral Assoc.
Res.: 2154 61st St., 11204. Tel: 718-236-0124; Fax: 718-236-4960. Email: stathanasiusny@aol.com. Web: www.stathanasiusny.tripod.com.
School—6120 Bay Pkwy., 11204. Tel: 718-236-4791; Fax: 718-621-1423. Email: sta.6120@aol.com. Mrs. Lorraine Garone-Tesoro, Prin. Lay Teachers 13; Students 318.
Catechesis/Religious Program—Tel: 718-331-8811; Fax: 718-331-2582. Mrs. Nicoletta Milo, Dir. Faith Formation. Students 425.
Convent—2201 62nd St., 11204. Tel: 718-236-2680.
Chapel—St. Augustine Yu Chin-gil Chapel 2115 61st St., 11204. Tel: 718-729-0132; Fax: 718-729-0132.

14—ST. AUGUSTINE (1870) Rev. Thomas W. Ahern; Deacon Joseph Bichotte. In Res., Revs. Agnelo Pinto, (St. Boniface, Winnipeg, Canada); Charles P. Keeney; Lucien Charlot (Retired).
Res.: 116 Sixth Ave., 11217. Tel: 718-783-3132; Fax: 718-638-4669. Email: staugustinerc@aol.com. Web: www.staugustineparkslope.org.
Catechesis/Religious Program—Sr. Ellen Glavey, R.S.M., C.R.E. Students 190.

15—ST. BARBARA (1893) Rev. Fulgencio Gutierrez.
Res.: 138 Bleecker St., 11221. Tel: 718-452-3660; Fax: 718-452-1279. Email: rec138@aol.com.
Catechesis/Religious Program—139 Menaham St., 11221. Tel: 718-453-1406. Carmen Morales, D.R.E.; Alberta Williams, D.R.E. Students 504.

16—ST. BENEDICT'S, Closed. For inquiries for parish records contact the chancery.

17—ST. BERNADETTE (1935) Rev. Msgr. Thomas G. Caserta; Revs. Joseph A. Gancila; Ponnachan Georgekutty; Deacon Anthony P. Martucci. In Res., Rev. Msgr. Cosmo G. Saporito, Pastor Emeritus (Retired).
Res.: 8201 13th Ave., 11228. Tel: 718-837-3400; Fax: 718-236-5883.
School—1313 83rd St., 11228. Tel: 718-236-1560; Fax: 718-236-3364. Sr. Joan DiRienzo, M.P.F., Prin. Sisters (Religious Teachers Filippini) 3; Lay Teachers 18; Students 397.
Catechesis/Religious Program—Tel: 718-232-7733. Students 188.

18—ST. BERNARD, Closed. For inquiries for parish records contact the chancery.

19—ST. BERNARD OF CLAIRVAUX Revs. Ralph J. Caputo; Winson Parekkat; Deacon Frank J. D'Accordo; Mr. James Millen, Music Dir.
Res.: 2055 E. 69th St., 11234. Tel: 718-763-5533; Fax: 718-763-0224. Email: ralphmystery@aol.com.
School—2031 E. 69th St., 11234. Tel: 718-241-6040; Fax: 718-241-7258. Kathleen Buscemi, Prin. Lay Teachers 13; Students 355.
Catechesis/Religious Program—Tel: 718-444-4674; Fax: 718-241-7258. Students 370.

20—ST. BLAISE, Merged with St. Francis of Assisi in 1980. Records at St. Francis of Assisi-St. Blaise.

21—BLESSED SACRAMENT (1891) Rev. Francis T. Shannon; Deacon William Contreras.
Res.: 198 Euclid Ave., 11208. Tel: 718-827-1200; Fax: 718-827-2422. Email: devinemaster2@aol.com.
School—187 Euclid Ave., 11208. Tel: 718-235-4863; Fax: 718-235-1132. Marylou Celmer, Prin. Lay Teachers 12; Students 267.
Catechesis/Religious Program—Tel: 718-277-3231; Fax: 718-277-3231. Sr. Patricia DeMarco, O.P., D.R.E. Students 432.

22—ST. BONIFACE (1854) Rev. Mark J. Lane, C.O.; Very Rev. Dennis M. Corrado, C.O., Provost, Brooklyn Oratory; Rev. Joel M. Warden, C.O.; Deacon William Powers; Christopher Smith, Business Mgr.; Dennis Delaney, Music Dir. In Res., Bro. James Simon, C.O., Dir. Devel.; Revs. Anthony Andreassi, C.O.; Michael J. Callaghan, C.O.
Res.: 109 Willoughby St., 11201. Tel: 718-875-2096; Fax: 718-875-4678. Email: info@oratory-church.org. Web: www.oratory-church.org.
Catechesis/Religious Program—Email: eileen.randig@oratory-church.org. Eileen Randig, D.R.E. Students 240.

23—ST. BRENDAN (1907) Rev. Frank W. Spacek; Rev. Msgr. Rocco D. Villani (Retired); Stephen Rzonca, Pastoral Assoc. In Res., Rev. Kevin P. Cavalluzzi.
Res.: 1525 E. 12th St., 11230. Tel: 718-339-2828; Fax: 718-339-5951. Email: stbrendanbklyn@yahoo.com.
Catechesis/Religious Program—Tel: 718-377-6932; Fax: 718-377-6374. Students 90.
Convent—1526 E. 13th St., 11230. Tel: 718-998-2032.

24—ST. BRIGID (1887) Rev. Msgr. James J. Kelly; Rev. John H. Wilkinson (Retired).
Res.: 409 Linden St., 11237. Tel: 718-821-1690; Fax: 718-386-4302.
School—438 Grove St. E., 11237. Tel: 718-821-1477; Fax: 718-821-1079. Shelia Gonzalez, Prin. Lay Teachers 11; Students 231.
Catechesis/Religious Program—Tel: 718-821-6401. Sr. Patricia Neary, O.P., D.R.E. Students 846.

25—ST. CASIMIR, (Polish), Merged with Our Lady of Czestochowa in 1980. Records at Our Lady of Czestochowa-St. Casimir.

26—ST. CATHARINE OF ALEXANDRIA (1902) Revs. Freddy Cintron; Francis Asagba; Deacon Gustavo Medina; Sr. Barbara Mullen, Pastoral Assoc. In Res., Revs. Dariusz Piotr Blicharz; Luis Martinez; Lukasz Pawel Trocha.
Res.: 1119 41st St., 11218. Tel: 718-436-5917; Fax: 718-871-5140.
Catechesis/Religious Program—Tel: 718-436-2471. Mrs. Grace Olavarria, D.R.E. Students 314.

27—THE CATHEDRAL-BASILICA OF ST. JAMES (Jay St. at Tillary) (1822) Rev. Msgr. John Strynkowski; Joseph B. Smith, Music Dir. In Res., Rev. Kevin P. Cavalluzzi.
Office: 240 Jay St., 11201. Fax: 718-852-9452. Email: secretary@brooklyncathedral.net. Web: www.brooklyncathedral.net.
Res.: 250 Cathedral Pl., 11201. Tel: 718-852-4002 (Office); 718-855-6390 (Rectory); Fax: 718-852-9452. Email: jjscath@mail.com.

28—ST. CATHERINE OF GENOA (1911) Revs. Charles Akoto Oduro (Ghana); Anthony Iroh (Nigeria).
Res.: 520 Linden Blvd., 11203. Tel: 718-282-7162; Fax: 718-282-5568. Email: stcatherineofgenoa@hotmail.com. Web: www.stcatherineofgenoachurchonline.com.
School—870 Albany Ave., 11203. Tel: 718-284-1050; Fax: 718-284-3461. Kathleen Trainor, Co-Prin.; Patricia Maio, Co-Prin. Lay Teachers 13; Students 270.
Catechesis/Religious Program—Tel: 718-469-7505. Marie Rose Terlonge, D.R.E. Students 44.

29—ST. CECILIA (1871) Rev. James J. Krische; Deacon Carlos Valderama. In Res., Revs. Richard E. Long; Matthew Ugwoji.
Res.: 84 Herbert St., 11222. Tel: 718-389-0010; Fax: 718-389-5090. Email: parish@stcecilia-bklyn.org. Web: www.stcecilia-bklyn.org.
Catechesis/Religious Program—1-15 Monitor St., 11222. Tel: 718-389-2546. Hugh Harvey, D.R.E. Students 46.

30—ST. CHARLES BORROMEO (1849) Rev. Edward P. Doran.

Res.: 21 Sidney Pl., 11201. Tel: 718-625-1177; Fax: 718-624-1627. Email: stcharlesbklyn@aol.com.
Catechesis/Religious Program—Students 46.

31—ST. COLUMBA (1967) Revs. Francis J. Hughes; Benedict Etafo; Peter Dery; Deacon Lawrence Coyle.
Res.: 2245 Kimball St., 11234. Tel: 718-338-6265; Fax: 718-377-6440.
Catechesis/Religious Program—Tel: 718-253-8840. Deacon Fred Ritchie, D.R.E. Students 173.

32—ST. COLUMBKILLE, Closed. Parochial records are located at SS. Cyril and Methodius. Became a mission in 1939.

33—SS. CYRIL AND METHODIUS (1917), (Polish), Revs. Tadeusz Maciejewski, C.M.; Joseph Wisniewski, C.M.
Res.: 150 Dupont St., 11222. Tel: 718-389-4424; Fax: 718-389-4191. Email: parish@cyrilandmethodius.org. Web: www.cyrilandmethodius.org.
Catechesis/Religious Program—Tel: 718-349-7732. Dariusz Karnicki, D.R.E. Students 146.

34—ST. DOMINIC (1972) Rev. John Tino; Deacons Carlo V. Mellace; Paul P. Morin.
Res.: 2001 Bay Ridge Pkwy., 11204. Tel: 718-259-4636; Fax: 718-259-3066. Email: stdom2001@gmail.com.
Catechesis/Religious Program—Tel: 718-621-0422. Maria Siragusa, D.R.E. Students 182.

35—ST. EDMUND (1922) Rev. Edward G. Brophy; Deacon Ronald Rizzuto. In Res., Rev. Msgr. Thomas F. Noonan, Pastor Emeritus (Retired); Rev. Anthony V. Dell'Anno (Retired).
Res.: 2450 Ocean Ave., 11229-3509. Tel: 718-743-0102; Fax: 718-891-7834.
School—1902 Avenue T, 11229. Tel: 718-648-9229. Jean McEvoy, Prin. Lay Teachers 12; Students 276.
High School—Denis Maloney Institute/St. Edmund Preparatory High School, 2474 Ocean Ave., 11229. Tel: 718-743-6100; Fax: 718-743-5243. Mr. John Lorenzetti, Prin.; Allison McGinnis, Asst. Prin.; Sr. Barbara Doyle, C.S.J., Campus Min. Sisters 2; Lay Teachers 44; Students 750.
Catechesis/Religious Program—Tel: 718-743-8107; Fax: 718-891-7834. Deacon Ronald Rizzuto, D.R.E. Students 75.

36—ST. EDWARD, Merged with St. Michael Archangel in 1942. St. Michael Archangel-St. Edward merged with Sacred Heart in 2008 to form Mary of Nazareth, Brooklyn.

37—ST. EPHREM (1921) Rev. Msgr. Peter V. Kain; Revs. Francis J. Labita (Retired); Theopnilos Joseph; Donald M. Berran (Retired); Deacons Wilfred N. Horne; Anthony Stucchio; Thomas Marchesiello, Music Dir.; Sisters Marie Antoinette Mannuzza, C.S.J., Dir. Outreach Prog.; Martha Ondreicka, O.P., Dir. Spirituality Ctr.; Michele James, Business Mgr.
Res.: 929 Bay Ridge Pkwy., 11228. Tel: 718-833-1010; Fax: 718-921-5232. Email: stephremrectory@aol.com.
School—7415 Ft. Hamilton Pkwy., 11228. Tel: 718-833-1440; Fax: 718-745-5301. Email: stephremschool@aol.com. Web: stephremsch.org. Annamarie Bartone, Prin. Servants of the Immaculate Heart of Mary 3; Lay Teachers 26; Students 365.
Catechesis/Religious Program—Tel: 718-745-7486; Fax: 718-745-2302. Email: stephremreled@verizon.net. Rita Lavin O'Connell, D.R.E. Students 183.
Convent—935 Bay Ridge Pkwy., 11228. Tel: 718-833-1555.

38—EPIPHANY (1905) Merged with SS. Peter and Paul, Brooklyn. For inquiries for parish records please see SS. Peter and Paul, Brooklyn.

39—ST. FINBAR (1880) Revs. James J. Mueller; Stanley Shinkut; Gary DiFranco, Music Dir.
Res.: 138 Bay 20th St., 11214. Tel: 718-236-3312; Fax: 718-236-3750.
Catechesis/Religious Program—Tel: 718-837-3935. Sr. Eileen Sweeney, O.S.F., D.R.E. Students 244.
Convent—131 Bay 19 St., 11214. Tel: 718-259-4439.

40—ST. FORTUNATA (1934) Rev. Vincent F. Miceli; Sr. Anna Calentano, C.S.J.B., Pastoral Assoc. In Res., Rev. Msgr. James W. Ryan, Pastor Emeritus (Retired).
Res.: 2609 Linden Blvd., 11208. Tel: 718-647-2632; Fax: 718-647-1321. Email: stfortunatachurch@netzero.net.
Catechesis/Religious Program—Sr. Loretta M. Florio, C.S.J.B., D.R.E. Students 133.

41—FOURTEEN HOLY MARTYRS, Merged with St. Martin of Tours in 1976. Records at St. Martin of Tours-Fourteen Holy Martyrs.

42—ST. FRANCES CABRINI (1963) Rev. Gaetano J. Sbordone.
Church, Office & Rectory: 1562 86th. St., 11228. Tel: 718-236-9165; Fax: 718-331-8139.
Catechesis/Religious Program—21 Bay 11th St., 11228. Tel: 718-232-4228. Sara Nespoli, Coord. Faith Formation. Students 127.

43—ST. FRANCES CABRINI CHAPEL, Closed. For inquiries for parish records please see Sacred Heart of Jesus and Mary and St. Stephen.

44—ST. FRANCES DE CHANTAL (1891) Revs. Canon Andrzej Kurowski, S.A.C.; Marian Wierzchowski, S.A.C.; Antoni Zemula, S.A.C.
Res.: 1273 58th St., 11219. Tel: 718-436-6407; Fax: 718-854-2761.
Catechesis/Religious Program—Lay Teachers 18; Students 385.

45—ST. FRANCIS IN THE FIELDS, Closed. For inquiries for parish records contact the chancery.

46—ST. FRANCIS OF ASSISI-ST. BLAISE (1898) Revs. Juan J. Gonzalez, S.M.; Philip Parent, S.M.
Res.: Tel: 718-756-2015; Fax: 718-756-1773. Email: sfa-stb@optonline.net.
Church: 319 Maple St., 11225.
School—400 Lincoln Rd., 11225. Tel: 718-778-3700; Fax: 718-778-7877. Email: office@sfabrooklyn.org. Web: www.sfabrooklyn.org. Sr. Theresa Scanlon, C.S.J., Prin. Sisters 2; Lay Teachers 13; Students 396.
Catechesis/Religious Program—335 Maple St., 11225. Tel: 718-778-1302. Ms. Myrmonde Dorismond, D.R.E. Students 72.

47—ST. FRANCIS OF PAOLA (1918), (Italian), Revs. Matteo Rizzo; Cosmas U. Ozuagu; Deacon John P. Orlandello.
Res.: 219 Conselyea St., 11211. Tel: 718-387-0256; Fax: 718-384-0068.
Catechesis/Religious Program— Suzanne O'Connor, D.R.E. Students 61.

48—ST. FRANCIS XAVIER (1886) Rev. William J. Rueger; Deacon James Ramos; Michael Kaminski, Music Dir.
Res.: 225 Sixth Ave., 11215. Tel: 718-638-1880; Fax: 718-638-2839. Email: franxrc@gmail.com. Web: www.stfxbrooklyn.org.
School—763 President St., 11215. Tel: 718-857-2559; Fax: 718-857-5391. Email: sfxparkslope@att.net. Web: www.sfxparkslope.com. Sr. Kathleen Sullivan, C.S.J., Prin. Sisters of St. Joseph 3; Lay Teachers 16; Students 269.
Catechesis/Religious Program—Tel: 718-857-2903. Email: hacreled@aol.com. Sr. Helene Conway, C.S.J., D.R.E. Students 205.

49—ST. GABRIEL THE ARCHANGEL (1901) Merged with Saint John Cantius, Brooklyn to form St. Mary, Mother of the Church, Brooklyn

50—ST. GEORGE, Closed. For inquiries for parish records contact the chancery.

51—GOOD SHEPHERD (1927) Revs. James E. Devlin; Michael J. McGee; Patrick J.T. Grace; John J. Reinhardt, Dir. Pastoral Care; Mr. Michael Fontana, Music Dir. In Res., Rev. Msgr. Thomas F. Brady (Retired); Rev. Anthony M. Ozele.
Res.: 1950 Batchelder St., 11229. Tel: 718-998-2800; Fax: 718-382-5428. Email: gsrcc@aol.com. Web: www.goodshepherdrcc.org.
School—1943 Brown St., 11229. Tel: 718-339-2745; Fax: 718-645-4513. Web: www.goodshepherdbklyn.org. Mr. Anthony Paparelli, Prin. Lay Teachers 17; Students 377.
Catechesis/Religious Program—Tel: 718-375-0899. Elvira Anselmo, D.R.E. Students 433.

52—ST. GREGORY THE GREAT (1905) Most Rev. Guy Sansaricq; Rev. Caleb A. Buchanan, Admin.; Deacons Roy N. George; Andres De Leon II. In Res., Rev. Brunache Michel Pierre.
Res.: 224 Brooklyn Ave., 11213-2505. Tel: 718-773-0100; Fax: 718-773-4198.
School—991 St. Johns Pl., 11213-2532. Tel: 718-774-3330; Fax: 718-774-3332. Rudolph Cyrus-Charles, Prin. Lay Teachers 11; Students 221.
Catechesis/Religious Program—Tel: 718-773-0100; Fax: 718-773-4198. Students 82.

53—GUARDIAN ANGEL (1885) Revs. Freddi A. Rosales; Andrzej Lukianiuk.
Res.: 2978 Ocean Pkwy., 11235. Tel: 718-266-1561; Fax: 718-372-1603. Email: gangelchurch@aol.com. Web: www.guardianangelchurch.com.
Catechesis/Religious Program—Tel: 718-372-1967. Olga Ortiz, D.R.E. Students 230.

54—HOLY CROSS (1848) Rev. Msgr. Joseph P. Malagreca; Revs. Pascal Louis; Donelson Thevenin.
Res.: 2530 Church Ave., 11226. Tel: 718-469-5900; Fax: 718-469-5901. Email: churchofholycross@hotmail.com.
Catechesis/Religious Program—Tel: 718-941-5066. Catherine Hayes, D.R.E. Students 140.

55—HOLY FAMILY (1880) Merged with St. Thomas Aquinas to form Holy Family-St. Thomas Aquinas. For inquiries and parish records see Holy Family-St. Thomas Aquinas.

56—HOLY FAMILY (1880) Revs. John J. Amann; Edward R. Kane; Jean Augustin Francois. In Res., Revs. John J. Gildea; Vitalis N. Opara (Nigeria).
Res.: 9719 Flatlands Ave., 11236. Tel: 718-257-4423; Fax: 718-257-4806.
Catechesis/Religious Program—Tel: 718-257-8016; Fax: 718-272-2279. Brendan Egonu, D.R.E. Students 188.

57—HOLY FAMILY (1905), (Slovak), Revs. Walter Thelapilly, C.M.I. (India); Winson Parekkat.
Res.: 21 Nassau Ave., 11222. Tel: 718-388-5145; Fax: 718-387-1877. Email: hfschurch@hotmail.com. Web: www.hfschurch.org.

58—HOLY FAMILY-SAINT THOMAS AQUINAS (2008) Revs. Jesus Cuadros; Ngozi Osuji; Deacon John A. Flannery. In Res., Rev. Msgr. Leo J. White (Retired).
Res.: 249 Ninth St., 11215. Tel: 718-768-9471; Fax: 718-789-3390. Web: www.stthomasaquinaschurch.org.
Additional Worship Site:—
Holy Family Church—205 14th St., 11215.
Catechesis/Religious Program—Sr. Doryne M. Bermoy, F.L.P., D.R.E. Students 152.

59—HOLY INNOCENTS (1910) Revs. Pascal Louis, Admin.; Rony Mendes.
Res.: 279 E. 17th St., 11226. Tel: 718-469-9500; Fax: 718-941-4931. Email: priest279@optonline.net.
Catechesis/Religious Program— Nancy Gerard, D.R.E. Students 297.

60—HOLY NAME (1878) Revs. Gary P. Rogers; Robert Ambalathingal, O.C.D.; Felix Quarshie; Deacons Abel Torres; Thomas J. Devaney. In Res., Rev. Msgr. Raphael Peprah; Revs. James H. Sweeney; Terrence J. Mulkerin (Retired).
Res.: 245 Prospect Park W., 11215. Tel: 718-768-3071; Fax: 718-369-2039. Web: www.holynamebrooklyn.org.
School—241 Prospect Park W., 11215. Tel: 718-768-7629; Fax: 718-768-3007. Web: www.hnjbklyn.org. Joan E. Caccamo, Prin. & D.R.E. Lay Teachers 10; Students 224.
Catechesis/Religious Program—241 Prospect Park W., 11215. Tel: 718-768-7629; Fax: 718-768-3007. Gloria V. Kreth, D.R.E. Students 90.

61—HOLY ROSARY (1889), (African American), Merged with Our Lady of Victory & St. Peter Claver, Brooklyn to form Saint Martin de Porres, Brooklyn

62—HOLY SPIRIT Rev. Heebong Nam; Deacon Wilfredo Hernandez. In Res., Rev. Angelo Gomes, S.F.X.
Res.: 1712 45th St., 11204. Tel: 718-436-5565; Fax: 718-436-5586. Email: holyspiritparishbp@hotmail.com.
Catechesis/Religious Program—Theresa Neri, C.R.E.; Olimpia Perez, C.R.E. Students 50.
Convent—1679 47th St., 11204.

63—ST. IGNATIUS (1908) Rev. Carlos Quijano, S.J., Admin.; Deacons Berthal Beaubrun; Jean-Baptiste Boursiquot; Dominic Russo, Music Dir.
Res.: 1101 Carroll St., 11225. Tel: 718-774-2102; Fax: 718-774-5821.
Catechesis/Religious Program— Lorraine Pierre, D.R.E. Students 150.

64—IMMACULATE CONCEPTION OF THE BLESSED VIRGIN MARY (1853) Closed. For inquiries and parish records, see Most Holy Trinity - St. Mary, Brooklyn.

65—IMMACULATE HEART OF MARY (1893) Rev. Robert B. Adamo; Sr. Mary Ann Ambrose, C.S.J., Pastoral Assoc.; Deacon James D. Noble. In Res., Rev. Msgr. Steven A. Ferrari; Rev. Russell Governale, O.F.M.Conv.
Res.: 2805 Ft. Hamilton Pkwy., 11218. Tel: 718-871-1310; Fax: 718-633-1866. Email: ihmoffice@verizon.net.
School—3002 Ft. Hamilton Pkwy., 11218. Tel: 718-438-7373; Fax: 718-853-5994. Web: www.ihmary-school.org. Ms. Maureen Rooney, Prin. Lay Teachers 12; Students 187.
Catechesis/Religious Program—Tel: 718-854-7326. Alice E. Leesha, D.R.E. Students 179.

66—ST. JEROME (1901) Revs. Jean-Miguel Aguste, Admin.; Hugues Berrette; Deacon Magloire Marcel.
Res.: 2900 Newkirk Ave., 11226. Tel: 718-462-0224; Fax: 718-462-7753. Email: stjerricc@netzero.com.
School—465 E. 29th St., 11226. Tel: 718-462-0211; Fax: 718-462-1828. Marie Clobette Jean-Louis, Prin. Lay Teachers 17; Students 313.
Catechesis/Religious Program—Paul Norman, D.R.E. Students 202.
Convent—455 E. 29th St., 11226. Tel: 718-856-3323.

67—ST. JOHN CANTIUS (1902) Merged with Saint Gabriel the Archangel, Brooklyn to form St. Mary Mother of the Church, Brooklyn (2007).

68—ST. JOHN THE BAPTIST (1868) Revs. Emmett J. Nolan, C.M.; Astor Rodgriguez, C.M.; Orlando D. Cardona, C.M.
Res.: 75 Lewis Ave., 11206. Tel: 718-455-6864; Fax: 718-452-3738. Email: jagostino@stjohnthebaptistrcc.org. Web: www.stjohnthebaptistrcc.org.
Additional Worship Site:—
Our Lady of Good Counsel—915 Putnam Ave., 11221.
School—82 Lewis Ave., 11206. Tel: 718-453-1000; Fax: 718-453-1000. Bruno Marchan, Prin. Lay Teachers 11; Students 229.

Catechesis/Religious Program—Eugenia Ortiz, D.R.E. Students 147.

69—ST. JOHN THE EVANGELIST (1849) Rev. Msgr. Thomas M. Haggerty; Rev. Johnson Chanassery, O.C.D. In Res., Rev. James McDevitt.
Res.: 250 21st St., 11215. Tel: 718-768-3751; Fax: 718-768-4689. Email: johnevangelist@verizon.net.
Catechesis/Religious Program—Students 97.

70—ST. JOHN'S CHAPEL, Closed. For inquiries for parish records please see Queen of all Saints Church.

71—ST. JOSEPH (1850) Rev. Msgr. Kieran E. Harrington, Admin.; Rev. Jorge Ortiz; Sr. Juliet Duruanyaoha, D.D.L., Pastoral Assoc. In Res., Bro. Vincenzo Cartilicchia.
Res.: 856 Pacific St., 11238. Tel: 718-783-4500; Fax: 718-398-2410.
Catechesis/Religious Program—Students 49.

72—ST. JOSEPH PATRON OF THE UNIVERSAL CHURCH (1921), (Scalabrini Fathers) Revs. Mariano Cisco; Jairo Ariel Alfonso, C.S.
Res.: 185 Suydam St., 11221. Tel: 718-386-0175; Fax: 718-484-3176. Email: marianocisco@hotmail.com.
School—St. Frances Cabrini, 181 Suydam St., 11221. Tel: 718-386-9277; Fax: 718-386-9064. Miss Maria Crifasi, Prin. Lay Teachers 12; Students 307.
Catechesis/Religious Program—Students 732.

73—ST. JUDE SHRINE CHURCH (1961) Rev. Msgr. John Delendick; Rev. Michael J. McHugh; Deacon Alejandro Alick.
Res.: 1677 Canarsie Rd., 11236. Tel: 718-763-6300; Fax: 718-531-9655.
School—Our Lady of Trust School-St. Jude Campus, 1696 Canarsie Rd., 11236. Tel: 718-241-6633. Robert Hughes, Prin. Lay Teachers 22; Students 288.
Catechesis/Religious Program—Tel: 718-241-4030. Ms. Helen Teifer, D.R.E. Students 162.

74—ST. LAURENCE (1964) Rev. Frank A. Black; Sr. Nora Lohan, M.F.I.C., Pastoral Assoc.; Bryan Rosenthal, Pastoral Assoc.; Jacob Schwendinger, Pastoral Assoc.
Res.: 1020 Van Siclen Ave., 11207. Tel: 718-649-0545; Fax: 718-649-1606. Email: stlaurence@worldnet.att.net. Web: www.stlaurencercchurch.com.
Catechesis/Religious Program—Email: judinawilson@att.net. Ms. Judina Wilson, D.R.E. Students 74.

75—ST. LEONARD OF PORT MAURICE, Closed. 1978. Records at St. Joseph, Patron of the Universal Church.

76—ST. LOUIS, Closed. Became a Mission of St. Lucy in 1939. Parochial records are at St. Lucy-St. Patrick's, 285 Willoughby Ave., 11205. Tel: 718-622-8748; Fax: 718-622-6330.

77—ST. LUCY-ST. PATRICK (1843) Rev. Stephen P. Lynch, Admin. In Res., Rev. Jose Ramon Burgos.
Res.: 285 Willoughby Ave., 11205. Tel: 718-622-8748; Fax: 718-622-6330. Email: fathlyn@aol.com.
Catechesis/Religious Program—Angelo Serrano, D.R.E. Students 92.

78—ST. MALACHY (1854) Merged with Saint Michael the Archangel, Brooklyn to form Saint Michael-Saint Malachy, Brooklyn

79—ST. MARGARET MARY (1920) Rev. Joseph R. Grimaldi, Admin.
215 Exeter St., 11235-3725. Tel: 718-743-1824; Fax: 718-934-8226. Email: stmarkrccbklyn@aol.com.

80—ST. MARK (1861) Revs. Joseph R. Grimaldi; Joseph Vella; Cyril F. Doody (Retired). In Res., Revs. Andrew Dunyo; Joseph P. Quigley.
Res.: 2609 E. 19th St., 11235. Tel: 718-891-3100; Fax: 718-891-9677. Email: stmarkrccbklyn@aol.com. Web: www.stmarkparish.org.
Church: Ocean Ave. & Ave. Z, 11235.
School—2602 E. 19th St., 11235. Tel: 718-332-9604; Fax: 718-332-3872. Email: stmarkschool9@hotmail.com. Web: www.stmarkschoolbklyn.org. Carol Donnelly, Prin. Religious 1; Lay Teachers 12; Students 639.
Catechesis/Religious Program—Tel: 718-769-6311. Joann Pino, D.R.E. Students 115.

81—SAINT MARTIN DE PORRES (2007) Rev. Msgr. Paul W. Jervis; Rev. Christopher L. Coleman.
Office: 583 Throop Ave., 11216.
Worship Sites:—
Our Lady of Victory—583 Throop Ave., 11216.
Holy Rosary—172 Bainbridge St., 11233.
St. Peter Claver—29 Peter Claver Pl., 11238.
Convent—Missionaries of Charity, 262 Macon St., 11216.
Convent—Daughters of Divine Love

82—ST. MARTIN OF TOURS-OUR LADY OF LOURDES (1906), (1872) Revs. John Jaime Tobon Arango; Pedro N. Ossa (Retired); Deacon Pedro V. Leon. In Res., Rev. Maximo Loez-Gambarte, Sch.P.
Res.: 1288 Hancock St., 11221. Tel: 718-443-8484; Fax: 718-443-2968. Email: smotchurch@optonline.net. Web: www.stmartinbrooklyn.parishesonline.com.
See St. Elizabeth Seton, Brooklyn under Consolidated Elementary Schools (Regional) located in the Institution section.
Catechesis/Religious Program—Mark Kruse, D.R.E. Held at St. Elizabeth Seton School (751 Knickerbocker Ave., Brooklyn, NY 11221). Students 268.
Chapel—Our Lady of Lourdes Chapel 89 Furman Ave., 11207.

83—ST. MARY MOTHER OF JESUS (1889) Rev. Msgrs. Andrew J. Vaccari; Rocco D. Villani, Pastor Emeritus (Retired); Rev. Reynolds Basilious, O.C.D. In Res., Rev. Benjamin Elias.
Res.: 2326 84th St., 11214. Tel: 718-372-4000; Fax: 718-372-4002. Email: smmj@broadview.net. Web: www.smmjparishesonline.com.
School—St. Mary Mother of Jesus-St. Frances Cabrini Academy, 8401 23rd Ave., 11214. Tel: 718-372-0025; Fax: 718-265-6498. Email: smmjbk@aol.com. Dr. Vincent Bellafiore, Prin. Lay Teachers 14; Students 288.
Catechesis/Religious Program—Tel: 718-449-8263; Fax: 718-265-6209. Students 198.

84—ST. MARY MOTHER OF THE CHURCH (2007) Revs. Jose A. Orellana, I.V.E.; Anthony Melendez, I.V.E.
Church: *St. Gabriel the Archangel*, 749 Linwood St., 11208. Tel: 718-257-0612; Fax: 718-257-5258. Email: par.mary.brooklyn@ive.org. Web: www.marymotherofthechurch.us.
Catechesis/Religious Program—666 Essex St., 11208. Tel: 718-649-0450; Fax: 718-649-0450. Sr. Maria Madre del Senor Zalazar, S.S.V.M., D.R.E.
Worship Site: *St. John Cantius*, 479 New Jersey Ave., 11207. Tel: 718-342-2679; Fax: 718-342-4878. Email: jcantius@aol.com.
Catechesis/Religious Program—Sr. Mary of the Angelus, S.S.V.M., C.R.E.

85—MARY OF NAZARETH (2008) Rev. Robert P. Vitaglione; Sr. Eileen Neary, R.S.M., Pastoral Assoc.
Res & Office: 41 Adelphia St., 11205. Tel: 718-625-5115; Fax: 718-625-2918.
Worship Sites:—
Sacred Heart—41 Adelphi St., 11205.
St. Edward—108 St. Edward's St., 11205.
Catechesis/Religious Program—Students 170.

86—ST. MARY OF THE ANGELS, (Lithuanian), Closed. For inquiries for parish records contact the chancery.

87—MARY QUEEN OF HEAVEN (1927) Rev. Msgr. Jamie J. Gigantiello; Rev. Ilyas Gill, O.F.M. (Pakistan); Sr. Joan J. Holmberg, S.C., Pastoral Assoc. In Res., Rev. Msgr. John A. Burns, Pastor Emeritus (Retired).
Res.: 1395 E. 56th St., 11234. Tel: 718-763-2330; Fax: 718-763-6592. Email: mqhchurch@aol.com. Web: www.mqhchurch.net.
School—1326 E. 57th St., 11234. Tel: 718-763-2360; Fax: 718-763-7540. Email: mqhsec@optonline.net. Sr. Donna Murphy, O.P., Prin. Lay Teachers 11; Students 338.
Catechesis/Religious Program—Tel: 718-763-2590. Mrs. Patricia McGrath, D.R.E. Students 111.
Convent—Sisters of St. Dominic, 1304 E. 57th St., 11234. Tel: 718-891-7451.

88—ST. MARY STAR OF THE SEA (1851) Rev. Christopher T. Cashman; Salvatore Mazzucco, Min. of Music & Environment.
Res.: 467 Court St., 11231. Tel: 718-625-2270; Fax: 718-624-9017. Email: smss1851@aol.com.
Catechesis/Religious Program—Tel: 718-625-1717.

89—ST. MATTHEW (1886) Revs. Andrew L. Struzzieri; Victor O. Ubaka; Deacons Florencio Cruz; Dennis A. DaCosta; James J. Lacy. In Res., Rev. Saint-Martin Estiverne.
Res.: 1123 Eastern Pkwy., 11213. Tel: 718-774-6747; Fax: 718-953-4895. Email: stmatthew1123@aol.com. Web: www.stmatthewromancatholicchurch.org.
Catechesis/Religious Program—1351 Lincoln Pl., 11213. Steven J. Horka, D.R.E. Students 428.

90—ST. MICHAEL (1860) Merged with Saint Malachy, Brooklyn to form Saint Michael-Saint Malachy, Brooklyn

91—ST. MICHAEL ARCHANGEL AND ST. EDWARD THE CONFESSOR (1891) Merged with Sacred Heart to form Mary of Nazareth, Brooklyn.

92—ST. MICHAEL - SAINT MALACHY (2007) Revs. Leonardo G. Lopez, I.V.E.; Gaston Giacinti, I.V.E.
Church: *St. Michael*, 284 Warwick St., 11207. Tel: 718-647-5900; Fax: 718-647-2384. Email: stmichael284@yahoo.com.
Worship Site:—
St. Malachy—207 Hendrix St., 11207.
Res.: 225 Jerome St., 11207. Tel: 718-647-1818.
Catechesis/Religious Program—Sr. Maria Virgo Offerens, D.R.E. Students 317.
School—237 Jerome St., 11207. Tel: 718-277-6766. Email: info@stmicheal-bklyn.org. Sr. Peggie Meritt, Prin. Sisters 1; Lay Teachers 13; Students 268.
Convent—129 Van Siclen Ave., 11207. Tel: 718-647-2751.

93—ST. MICHAEL (1870) Revs. Kevin J. Sweeney; Manuel Rodriguez; Deacon Julio C. Mejia. In Res., Rev. Msgr. Youssef Bochra Nasri.
Res.: 352 42nd St., 11232. Tel: 718-768-6065; Fax: 718-768-3336. Email: stmichaelarc42@verizon.net.
Catechesis/Religious Program—Tel: 718-788-3442. Ines Cordero, C.R.E. Students 350.

94—MOST HOLY TRINITY - SAINT MARY (1841) Revs. Santo Cricchio, O.F.M.Conv.; Timothy Dore, O.F.M-.Conv.; Dariusz Barna, O.F.M.Conv. (Poland).
Res.: 138 Montrose Ave., 11206. Tel: 718-384-0215; Fax: 718-384-3030. Email: mhtbrooklyn@yahoo.com. Web: www.mhtbrooklyn.org.
See Saints Joseph & Dominic Catholic Academy of Williamsburg under Consolidated Elementary Schools (Regional) located in the Institution section.
Catechesis/Religious Program—Tel: 718-486-6276. Sr. Karen Landermenn, O.P., C.R.E. Students 175.

95—MOST PRECIOUS BLOOD (1927) Revs. John Maduri; Joseph Attard. In Res., Rev. Joseph Rose.
Res.: 70 Bay 47th St., 11214. Tel: 718-372-8022; Fax: 718-996-6575.
Catechesis/Religious Program—Mary Ann Behan, D.R.E. Students 43.

96—NATIVITY OF OUR BLESSED LORD, Merged with St. Peter Claver in 1973. Records at St. Peter Claver Church.

97—ST. NICHOLAS (1865) Rev. Kenneth J. Grande.
Res.: 26 Olive St., 11211. Tel: 718-388-1420; Fax: 718-388-9516.
School—287 Powers St., 11211. Tel: 718-388-7992. Sr. Joan Losson, O.P., Prin. Lay Teachers 11; Students 223.
Catechesis/Religious Program—Amilia Castro, C.R.E. Students 78.
Convent—312 De Voe St., 11211.

98—OUR LADY HELP OF CHRISTIANS (1927) Rev. Peter J. Rayder.
Res.: 1315 E. 28th St., 11210. Tel: 718-338-5242; Fax: 718-258-5341.
See Midwood Catholic Academy, Brooklyn under Consolidated Elementary Schools (Regional) in the Institution Section.
Catechesis/Religious Program—Tel: 718-377-6932. Stephen Rzonca, Pastoral Assoc. Students 36.

99—OUR LADY OF ANGELS (1891) Rev. Msgr. Kevin B. Noone; Revs. Kenneth J. Calder (Retired); Richard Lewkiewicz; Deacon Ed Gaine; Gloria Florez, Spanish Ministry. In Res., Rev. Arputham Arulsamy.
Res.: 7320 Fourth Ave., 11209. Tel: 718-836-7200; Fax: 718-238-2466. Email: ola.bayridge@verizon.net.
School—Tel: 718-238-5045. Lay Teachers 17; Students 215.
Catechesis/Religious Program—Tel: 718-748-6553. Ann O'Brien, D.R.E. Students 202.

100—OUR LADY OF CHARITY (1903), (African American), Merged with St. Matthew, Brooklyn. For inquiries for parish records please see St. Matthew, Brooklyn.

101—OUR LADY OF CONSOLATION (1909), (Polish), Revs. Wlodzimierz R. Las, S.D.S. (Poland); Ludwik Kolodziej.
Res.: 184 Metropolitan Ave., 11211. Tel: 718-388-1942; Fax: 718-388-8993. Email: olconsolation@verizon.net. Web: www.mbpbrooklyn.com.
Catechesis/Religious Program—Students 121.

102—OUR LADY OF CZESTOCHOWA-ST. CASIMIR (1896), (Polish), Revs. Witold Mroziewski; Thomas Shepanzyk.
Res.: 183 25th St., 11232. Tel: 718-768-5724; Fax: 718-768-4996.
Catechesis/Religious Program—Students 305.

103—OUR LADY OF GOOD COUNSEL (1886) Merged with St. John the Baptist, Brooklyn. For inquiries for parish records please see St. John the Baptist, Brooklyn.

104—OUR LADY OF GRACE (1935), (Italian), Revs. Thomas F. Leach; Dominick F. Cutrone, Pastor Emeritus (Retired); Edward A. Cassar; Deacon Philip Siani; Annette Bonvino, Pastoral Assoc.
Res.: 430 Avenue W, 11223. Tel: 718-627-2020; Fax: 718-336-8033. Email: olgie430@aol.com. Web: www.ologchurch.com.
School—385 Avenue W, 11223. Tel: 718-375-2081; Fax: 718-376-7685. Email: olgie385@aol.com. Mrs. Joan McMaster, Prin. Lay Teachers 9; Students 308.
Catechesis/Religious Program—Tel: 718-375-0404. Phyllis Niwinski, D.R.E. Students 147.

105—OUR LADY OF GUADALUPE (1906), (Italian—Spanish), Rev. Msgr. Robert Romano; Revs. Francis Wright, C.S.Sp.; Colbert DaSilva, S.D.B.; John J. Granados; Deacon John J. LaGreca.
Res.: 7201 Fifteenth Ave., 11228. Tel: 718-236-8300; Fax: 718-236-8119. Email: churcholg@netscape.net.
School—1518 73rd St., 11228. Tel: 718-236-5587; Fax: 718-236-5587. Ms. Diana C. Meringolo, Prin. Sisters of St. Dominic 2; Sisters of St. Joseph 1; Lay Teachers 12; Students 400.

Catechesis/Religious Program—Tel: 718-331-4003. Students 157.

106—OUR LADY OF LORETO (1894) Merged with Our Lady of the Presentation.

107—OUR LADY OF LOURDES (1872) Merged with St. Martin of Tours, Brooklyn. For inquiries for parish records please see St. Martin of Tours, Brooklyn.

108—OUR LADY OF MERCY (1961) Rev. John J. Gildea. 9719 Flatlands Ave., 11212.
Office: 680 Mother Gaston Blvd., 11212. Tel: 718-346-3166; Fax: 718-346-5776. Email: jjgildea@verizon.net.
Catechesis/Religious Program—Sr. Bernadette Sassone, D.W., D.R.E. Students 145.

109—OUR LADY OF MERCY, Closed. in 1908. Second church at Schermerhorn & Bond closed April, Debevoise Place & DeKalb Ave. For inquiries for parish records contact the chancery.

110—OUR LADY OF MIRACLES (1936) Revs. Gerald Dumont; Calonge Lemaine; Giovanna Piccioli, A.O., Pastoral Assoc.; Deacon Ernst Paul; Patrick David, Music Dir. In Res., Rev. Francis J. Hughes.
Res.: 757 E. 86th St., 11236. Tel: 718-257-2400; Fax: 718-257-4634.
School—Our Lady of Trust School at Our Lady of Miracles Campus, 744 E. 87 St., 11236. Tel: 718-649-0271; Fax: 718-272-0442. Robert Hughes, Prin. Lay Teachers 22; Students 241.
Catechesis/Religious Program—Tel: 718-649-1006. Sr. Doryne M. Bermoy, F.L.P., D.R.E. Students 124.

111—OUR LADY OF MONSERRATE-ST. AMBROSE (1954) Merged with All Saints, Brooklyn.

112—OUR LADY OF MOUNT CARMEL SHRINE CHURCH (1887), (Italian), Rev. Msgr. Joseph P. Calise; Deacons Everett A. Deming, Pastoral Assoc.; Edward F. O'Connell; Giuditta Coccia, A.O., Pastoral Assoc. & Italian Apostolate. In Res., Revs. Michael O. Zunno, M.M.; Dominick Obelosi.
Res.: 275 N. Eighth St., 11211. Tel: 718-384-0223; Fax: 718-384-5838. Email: olmcn8th@yahoo.com. Web: www.olmcfeast.com.
School—Northside Catholic Academy at Mt. Carmel, 10 Withers St., 11211. Tel: 718-782-1110; Fax: 718-782-3344. Beverly D'Angelo, Prin.
Catechesis/Religious Program—Rosemarie Walsh, D.R.E. Students 181.

113—OUR LADY OF PEACE (1899), (Italian), Revs. John R. Scarangello, O.F.M.; Octavio Salinas, O.F.M. In Res., Revs. Bruno Ciardiello, O.F.M. (Retired); John Cassese, O.F.M.
Res.: 522 Carroll St., 11215. Tel: 718-624-5122; Fax: 718-852-6149. Email: olp1899@aol.com.
Catechesis/Religious Program— Lillian Flores, D.R.E. Students 130.
Convent—Hermanas Franciscanas de la Immaculada, 209 First St., 11215. Tel: 718-624-6720; Fax: 718-625-7657.

114—OUR LADY OF PERPETUAL HELP BASILICA (1893) Revs. Joseph Tizio, C.Ss.R.; Norman S. Bennett, C.Ss.R.; Peter Cao, C.Ss.R. (Vietnam); Luis A. Caro, C.Ss.R. (Chile); Ruskin Piedra, C.Ss.R.; Pierce Kenny, C.Ss.R.; John Hamrogue, C.Ss.R.; Francis Mulvaney; Sr. Lucille Aliperti, C.S.J., Dir. Adult Faith Formation; Deacons Abdon Mejia (Peru), Pastoral Assoc.; Jesus Soto, Pastoral Assoc. In Res., Revs. Sylvester E. Feeley, C.Ss.R.; John Gauci, C.Ss.R.; Thomas F. Hickey, C.Ss.R.; Thomas Maceda, C.Ss.R.
Res.: 526-59th St., 11220. Tel: 718-492-9200; Fax: 718-439-8528.
School—5902 6th Ave., 11220. Tel: 718-492-8067; Fax: 718-439-8081. Mr. Vincent Tannacore, Prin. Sisters 1; Lay Teachers 14; Students 240.
Catechesis/Religious Program—Tel: 718-439-4795. Maritza Mejia, D.R.E. Students 506.

115—OUR LADY OF REFUGE (1911) Revs. Michael A. Perry; Adrien Pierre, O.M.I.
Res.: 2020 Foster Ave., 11210. Tel: 718-434-2090; Fax: 718-859-7411. Email: olrefuge@aol.com.
Catechesis/Religious Program—Jennifer Baptiste, D.R.E. Students 295.

116—OUR LADY OF SOLACE (1900) Revs. Patrick J. West; Giovani Romero; Deacon Dan J. Marley.
Res.: 2866 W. 17th St., 11224. Tel: 718-266-1612; Fax: 718-946-3651. Email: pastor@olsbrooklyn.com. Web: www.olsbrooklyn.com.
Catechesis/Religious Program—Email: rec@olsbrooklyn.com. Mr. Augusto Lucero, D.R.E. Students 268.

117—OUR LADY OF SORROWS, Merged with St. Leonard in 1942. Parochial records are at St. Joseph Patron of the Universal Church.

118—OUR LADY OF THE PRESENTATION-OUR LADY OF LORETO (1887), (African American—Hispanic), Rev. James H. Sweeney; Deacons Jaime Landron, (Retired); Ricardo Reyes; Jaime Varela.
Res.: 1677 St. Marks Ave., 11233-4813. Tel: 718-345-2604; Fax: 718-345-4639. Email: nugejose@aol.com.
Additional Worship Site:—
Our Lady of Loreto—Church: 124 Sackman St., 11233.
Catechesis/Religious Program—Students 102.

119—OUR LADY OF THE ROSARY OF POMPEII (1900), (Hispanic), Revs. Frank Amato, S.A.C.; Bernard Carman.
Res.: 225 Seigel St., 11206. Tel: 718-497-0614; Fax: 718-366-3236.
Catechesis/Religious Program—Students 83.

120—OUR LADY OF VICTORY (1868) Merged with Holy Rosary & St. Peter Claver, Brooklyn to form Saint Martin de Porres, Brooklyn

121—ST. PATRICK (1849) Rev. Msgr. Joseph P. Nagle; Revs. Mark Simmons; Anthony Banye; Andre Bain; Deacons Charles Postler; John E. Hull; Sr. Jeanne Elaine Matullo, O.P., Pastoral Assoc. In Res., Rev. Thomas Anastasio (Retired).
Res.: 9511 Fourth Ave., 11209. Tel: 718-238-2600; Fax: 718-238-1508.
School—401 97th St., 11209. Tel: 718-833-0124; Fax: 718-238-6840. Mrs. Andrea D'Emic, Prin. Lay Teachers 13; Students 271.
Catechesis/Religious Program—Mrs. Nancy Lussier, D.R.E. Tel: 718-238-2600, Ext. 104. Students 210.

122—ST. PATRICK'S, Merged with St. Lucy's in 1974. Records at St. Lucy-St. Patrick's.

123—SAINT PAUL AND SAINT AGNES ROMAN CATHOLIC CHURCH (2007) Rev. Robert M. Powers, Admin.; Deacons Jaime Cobham; Louis Gonzalez.
Tel: 718-625-1717; Fax: 718-625-1929. Email: peterpaulagnes@aol.com.
Worship Sites:—
St. Agnes—433 Sackett St., 11231.
St. Paul—234 Congress St., 11201.
Catechesis/Religious Program—William Gorman, D.R.E. Students 73.

124—SS. PETER AND PAUL (1843) Rev. Richard J. Beuther.
Church: 82 S. 2nd St., 11211.
Res.: 71 S. Third St., 11211. Tel: 718-388-9576; Fax: 718-388-0714.
Additional Worship Site:—
Epiphany—Church: 96 S. 9th St., 11211.
Catechesis/Religious Program—Tel: 718-387-1041. Sr. Mother Maria Foy, S.S.V.M., D.R.E. Students 326.

125—ST. PETER CLAVER (1921) Merged with Our Lady of Victory & Holy Rosary, Brooklyn to form Saint Martin de Porres, Brooklyn

126—ST. PETER-ST. PAUL-OUR LADY OF PILAR (1836) Merged with Saint Agnes, Brooklyn to form Saint Paul and Saint Agnes, Brooklyn

127—QUEEN OF ALL SAINTS (1879) Rev. Joseph A. Ceriello; Sr. Aileen Halleran, S.C., Pastoral Assoc. In Res., Rev. Christopher L. Coleman.
Res.: 300 Vanderbilt Ave., 11205. Tel: 718-638-7625; 718-638-7626; Fax: 718-638-7393. Email: queenofallsaintsrc@verizon.net.
School—300 Vanderbilt Ave., 11205. Tel: 718-857-3114; Fax: 718-857-0632. Theresa Attianese, Prin. Lay Teachers 14; Students 233.
Catechesis/Religious Program—Ralphetta Moses, D.R.E. Students 75.

128—REGINA PACIS VOTIVE SHRINE (1951), For personnel see St. Rosalia., 1230 65th St., 11219. Tel: 718-236-0909; Fax: 718-236-5357. Email: rosalia1230@aol.com.

129—RESURRECTION (1924) Revs. Dennis J. Farrell; Edwin Okey Nwabugwu.
Res.: 2331 Gerritsen Ave., 11229. Tel: 718-743-7234; 718-743-7235; Fax: 718-743-0152.
Catechesis/Religious Program—2335 Gerritsen Ave., 11229. Tel: 718-891-0888. Mrs. Angela Parente, D.R.E. Students 237.

130—RESURRECTION CATHOLIC COPTIC CHAPEL (1985) Rev. Msgr. Youssef Bochra Nasri, (Coptic Catholic Patriarchate).
Mailing Address: 352 42nd St., 11232. Tel: 718-965-0422; Fax: 718-768-3336.
Church: 328 14th St., 11215. Tel: 718-499-6946.

131—ST. RITA (1913), (Spanish), Rev. Luis Fernando Laverde Saldarriaga (Colombia), Admin.; Deacons Marco Lopez; Ronald Ronacher; Andres DeLa Rosa.
Res.: 275 Shepherd Ave., 11208. Tel: 718-647-4910; Fax: 718-827-2767. Email: ritcon123@aol.com. Web: www.stritabrooklyn.com.
School—260 Shepherd Ave., 11208. Tel: 718-647-6040; Fax: 718-647-5298. William Geasor, Prin. Sisters 1; Lay Teachers 23; Students 493.
Catechesis/Religious Program—Mrs. Annemarie Ronacher, D.R.E. Students 175.

132—ST. ROCCO (1902) Rev. Msgr. Faustino Cordero.
Res.: 216 27th St., 11232. Tel: 718-768-9798; Fax: 718-768-7742. Email: strcchurch@aol.com. Web: www.saintrocco.com.
Catechesis/Religious Program— Karen Salinas-Reyes, D.R.E. Students 367.

133—ST. ROSALIA-REGINA PACIS (1904) Rev. Msgr. Ronald T. Marino; Rev. Vincentius Toan Do; Sr. Anna O'Brien, Pastoral Assoc.
Res.: 1230 65th St., 11219. Tel: 718-236-0909; Fax: 718-236-5357. Email: rosalia1230@aol.com.
Regina Center, Inc.—1258 65th St., 11219. Tel: 718-232-4340.
Catechesis/Religious Program—Tel: 718-236-0909, Ext. 40. Elizabeth Mathew, D.R.E. Students 147.
Mission—Regina Pacis Votive Shrine, Kings Co.

134—ST. ROSE OF LIMA (1870) Revs. Lukasz Pawel Trocha; Jose Lopez.
Res.: 269 Parkville Ave., 11230. Tel: 718-434-8040; Fax: 718-421-4223. Email: stroseoflimabkln@aol.com.
Catechesis/Religious Program—Sr. Maureen Sullivan, C.S.J., D.R.E. Students 128.
Convent—Sisters of St. Joseph, 250 Newkirk Ave., 11230. Tel: 718-859-5722.

135—SACRED HEART (1871) Merged with St. Michael Archangel and St. Edward the Confessor to form Mary of Nazareth, Brooklyn.

136—SACRED HEART CHAPEL (1996) Closed. For inquiries for parish records contact the Chancery.

137—SACRED HEART MISSION (1942) Closed. For inquiries for parish records contact the Chancery.

138—SACRED HEARTS OF JESUS AND MARY AND ST. STEPHEN (1866), (Italian), Revs. Anthony J. Sansone; Anthony Camora.
Res.: 108 Carroll St., 11231. Tel: 718-596-7750; Fax: 718-260-9233.
Church: Summit & Hicks Sts., 11231.
Catechesis/Religious Program—Tel: 718-596-0880. Sr. Rosalind Picciano, C.S.J., D.R.E. Students 98.

139—ST. SAVIOUR (1905) Revs. Daniel S. Murphy; Timothy P. Tighe, C.S.P.; Deacon William Williamsen. In Res., Rev. Robert Frueh.
Res.: 611 Eighth Ave., 11215. Tel: 718-768-4055; 718-768-7983; Fax: 718-768-4872. Email: saviourchurch@aol.com. Web: www.saintsaviourchurch.org.
School—701 Eighth Ave., 11215. Tel: 718-768-8000. Ms. Maura Lorenzen, Prin. Lay Teachers 17; Students 367.
High School—588 Sixth St., 11215. Tel: 718-768-4406; Fax: 718-369-2688. Sr. Valeria Belanger, S.S.N.D., Prin. Students 358.
Catechesis/Religious Program—Tel: 718-768-4055; Fax: 718-768-4872. Ms. Sue Walsh, D.R.E. Students 131.
Convent—590 6th St., 11215.

140—SS. SIMON AND JUDE (1897) Revs. Gregory A. Stankus; Matthew U. Obiekezie (Nigeria); Sr. Ann Elizabeth DiLiberti, O.P., Pastoral Assoc.
Res.: 185 Van Sicklen St., 11223. Tel: 718-375-9600; Fax: 718-375-6642. Email: rectoryssj@optonline.net.
Catechesis/Religious Program—294 Avenue T, 11223. Tel: 718-372-0733. Email: rel.ed@stsimonandjude.org. Sara Nespoli, Dir. Faith Formation. Students 177.

141—ST. STANISLAUS KOSTKA (1896), (Polish), Revs. Marek W. Sobczak, C.M.; Jan Urbaniak, C.M.; Jaroslaw Robert Lawrenz, C.M.; Jan Szylar, C.M.; Joseph Szpilski, C.M.
Res.: 607 Humboldt St., 11222. Tel: 718-388-0170; Fax: 718-384-5290. Web: www.ststanskostka.org.
School—12 Newel St., 11222. Tel: 718-383-1970; Fax: 718-383-1711. Web: www.ststansgreenpoint.org. Ms. Christina Cieloszczyk, Prin. Priests 5; Sisters of the Holy Family of Nazareth 5; Lay Teachers 12; Students 260.
Catechesis/Religious Program—Tel: 718-388-0170. Krzysztof Gospodarzec, D.R.E. Students 393.

142—ST. STANISLAUS MARTYR, Merged with Holy Family (14th St.) in 1979. Records at Holy Family, 14th St., between Sixth and Seventh Aves.

143—ST. STEPHEN, Merged with Sacred Hearts in 1941. Parochial records are at Sacred Hearts-St. Stephen Church, Carroll St.

144—ST. SYLVESTER (1923) Revs. Anthony F. Raso; James L. Hughes; Deacon Jose L. Oviedo. In Res., Rev. Dominic Oliagba.
Res.: 416 Grant Ave., 11208. Tel: 718-647-1995; Fax: 718-348-4035.
School—396 Grant Ave., 11208. Tel: 718-235-4729; Fax: 718-235-4729. Web: www.stsylvesterschool.org. Ana Maria Ricciardi, Prin. Lay Teachers 12; Students 330.
Catechesis/Religious Program— Carmen Perez, D.R.E. Students 182.

145—ST. TERESA OF AVILA (1874) Revs. Saint Charles Borno; Anthony Bature (Nigeria); Isaie Jean-Louis (Haiti).
Res.: 563 Sterling Pl., 11238. Tel: 718-622-6500; Fax: 718-622-2234.
Catechesis/Religious Program—Louis A. Maione, D.R.E. Students 42.

146—ST. THERESE OF LISIEUX (1926), (The Little Flower) Rev. Hilaire Belizaire; Deacons Mauclair Simon; Ronald Agnant. In Res., Rev. Lawrence Anare.
Res.: 1281 Troy Ave., 11203. Tel: 718-451-1500; Fax: 718-451-1502. Email: sttheresels@aol.com. Web: www.stthereseoflisieux.org.
School—4410 Avenue D, 11203. Tel: 718-629-9330;

Fax: 718-629-6854. Sr. Paulette Pollina, R.S.M., Prin. Sisters of Mercy 3; Lay Teachers 12; Students 260.
Catechesis/Religious Program—Tel: 718-451-1671; Fax: 718-451-1671. Frances McCormick, D.R.E. Students 105.

147—ST. THOMAS AQUINAS (1884) Merged with Holy Family to become Holy Family-St. Thomas Aquinas. For inquiries and parish records see Holy Family-St. Thomas Aquinas.

148—ST. THOMAS AQUINAS (1885) Revs. Thomas V. Doyle; Antonius P. Gopaul; Sr. Theresa Agliardi, R.S.M., Pastoral Assoc.
Res.: 1550 Hendrickson St., 11234. Tel: 718-253-4404.
Catechesis/Religious Program—Tel: 718-253-4404, Ext. 31; Fax: 718-338-7757. Sr. Denise Nolan, O.P., D.R.E. Students 208.

149—TRANSFIGURATION (1874) Rev. Msgr. Anthony Hernandez, Admin.; Deacon Jimmy Garcia.
Res.: 263 Marcy Ave., 11211. Tel: 718-388-8773; Fax: 718-388-8774.
Catechesis/Religious Program—Sr. Maryann Ricioppo, D.R.E. Students 119.
Southside Mission for Social Services—280 Marcy Ave., 11211. Tel: 718-388-3784. John Mulhern, Dir.

150—ST. VINCENT DE PAUL, Closed. For inquiries for parish records contact the chancery.

151—ST. VINCENT FERRER (1923) Rev. Msgr. Joseph A. Nugent; Mrs. Mary Anne Muller, Pastoral Assoc. In Res., Revs. Charles Akoto Oduro (Ghana); Edward Owusu-Ansah.
Res.: 1603 Brooklyn Ave., 11210-3495. Tel: 718-859-0041; 718-859-9009; Fax: 718-859-9032. Email: saintferrer@aol.com.
Church: E. 37th St. & Glenwood Rd., 11210.
Catechesis/Religious Program— Mrs. Mary Anne Muller, D.R.E. Students 168.

152—VISITATION OF THE BLESSED VIRGIN MARY (1854) Rev. Carlos D. Valencia.
Res.: 98 Richards St., 11231. Tel: 718-624-1572; Fax: 718-722-7748.
Catechesis/Religious Program—Milagros Almonte, D.R.E. Students 68.

*BOROUGH AND COUNTY OF QUEENS

1—ST. ADALBERT (1892), (Polish), Revs. Paul Miskiewicz, O.F.M.Conv.; Herman Czaster, O.F.M.-.Conv.; Miroslaw Podymniak, O.F.M.Conv. (Poland).
Res.: 52-29 83rd St., Elmhurst, 11373. Tel: 718-639-0212; Fax: 718-651-1705.
School—52-17 83rd St., Elmhurst, 11373. Tel: 718-424-2376; Fax: 718-639-0465. Sr. Kathleen Maciej, C.S.F.N., Prin. Sisters 3; Lay Teachers 21; Students 429.
Catechesis/Religious Program—Tel: 718-565-8227. Mary Anne Page, D.R.E. Students 302.
Office for Pastoral Care of the Sick—

2—ST. ALOYSIUS (1892) Revs. George Poltorek, S.A.C.; Marek Rudecki, S.A.C.; Deacon Fabio Flaim; Gisela Sterbenz, Sec. In Res., Rev. Alex Ramos, Chap.
Res.: 382 Onderdonk Ave., Ridgewood, 11385. Tel: 718-821-0231; Fax: 718-628-7304. Email: saloysius@nyc.rr.com.
Catechesis/Religious Program—Tel: 718-417-6327. Raymond Calcagno, D.R.E. Students 260.
Pastoral Care Office—Tel: 718-963-7689.

3—AMERICAN MARTYRS (1948) Rev. Frank L. Schwarz; Deacon Stanley J. Galazin. In Res., Rev. William Sweeney.
Res.: 79-43 Bell Blvd., Oakland Gardens, 11364. Tel: 718-464-4582; Fax: 718-464-5488. Email: americanmartyrs@aol.com.
Catechesis/Religious Program—Tel: 718-464-6411. Ms. Christine Rahner, D.R.E. Students 179.

4—ST. ANASTASIA (1915) Rev. Msgr. George J. Ryan; Revs. William A. McLaughlin; Chris Piasta, O.F.M.
Res.: 45-14 245th St., Douglaston, 11362. Tel: 718-631-4454; Fax: 718-631-1774. Email: info@stanastasia.info. Web: www.stanastasia.info.
Catechesis/Religious Program—Tel: 718-225-5191. Janine Kramer, D.R.E. Students 241.

5—ST. ANDREW AVELLINO Revs. Joseph T. Holcomb; John A. Gurrieri. In Res., Rev. Matthew J. Diamond (Retired).
Res.: 35-60 158th St., Flushing, 11358. Tel: 718-359-0417; Fax: 718-539-2830. Email: pastorsaa@aol.com.
School—35-50 158th St., Flushing, 11358. Tel: 718-359-7887; Fax: 718-359-2295. Debora A. Hanna, Prin. Lay Teachers 19; Students 341.
Catechesis/Religious Program—Tel: 718-445-7012. Mrs. Maria Tortorella, D.R.E. Students 196.

6—ST. ANN (1927) Revs. Edward M. Kachurka; Samuel Ebulley Afful (Ghana); Deacon Sal Licata. In Res., Rev. George A. Pfundstein (Retired).
Res.: 142-30 58th Ave., Flushing, 11355-5314. Tel: 718-886-3890; Fax: 718-358-4964. Email: stann.1@netzero.com.
Catechesis/Religious Program—142-25 58th Rd., Flushing, 11355. Tel: 718-359-8019. Sr. Patricia A. Anglin, O.P., Dir. Faith Formation. Students 67.

7—ST. ANTHONY OF PADUA (1937) Revs. William A. Smith; Christopher Ezeoke; Nelsa I. Elias, Pastoral Assoc.
Res.: 133-25 128th St., South Ozone Park, 11420-3303. Tel: 718-843-7410; 718-843-3356; Fax: 718-659-1478. Email: stanthonysoozpk@aol.com.
Catechesis/Religious Program—Students 76.

8—ASCENSION (1945) Revs. Jovito B. Carongay Jr.; Kyrian C. Echekwu.
Res.: 86-13 55th Ave., Elmhurst, 11373. Tel: 718-335-2626; Fax: 718-335-4181. Email: ascensionrc@aol.com.
Catechesis/Religious Program—Helen Collins, D.R.E. Students 157.

9—ST. BARTHOLOMEW (1706) Revs. Joseph M. Hoffman; Patrick Keating; Joyce Ellen Lubofsky, Pastoral Assoc.; Sr. Susan Sabol, C.S.J., Outreach Dir.
Res.: 43-22 Ithaca St., Elmhurst, 11373. Tel: 718-424-5400; Fax: 718-899-5257. Email: stbartrcch@aol.com.
School—44-15 Judge St., Elmhurst, 11373. Tel: 718-446-7575. Jeannette Boursiquot-Charles, Prin. Lay Teachers 11; Students 228.
Catechesis/Religious Program—44-15 Judge St., Elmhurst, 11373. Tel: 718-898-0096. Joyce Ellen Lubofsky, D.R.E. Students 339.

10—ST. BENEDICT JOSEPH LABRE (1892), (Spanish), Rev. Msgr. John H. O'Brien; Revs. Thomas R. Gilbert; Thomas Muthukatti (Retired); Deacon Manuel I. Martinez. In Res., Rev. Msgr. Cornelius T. Kneafsey (Retired).
Res.: 94-40 118th St., South Richmond Hill, 11419. Tel: 718-849-4048; Fax: 718-846-0732. Email: sbjl1892@nycrr.com.
Catechesis/Religious Program—Tel: 718-849-0246. Sr. Maria Rypkema, D.R.E. Students 154.

11—ST. BENEDICT, THE MOOR (1932), (African American), Merged with St. Bonaventure to form St. Bonaventure-St. Benedict the Moor RC Church.

12—BLESSED SACRAMENT (1929) Revs. Patrick G. Burns; Edward J. Smith; Richard Conlon; Robinson Sierra Quiroz, S.A. (Colombia); Edward J. Smith. In Res., Most Rev. Rene A. Valero.
Res.: 34-43 93rd St., Jackson Heights, 11372. Tel: 718-639-3888; Fax: 718-478-5536. Email: blessacjh@aol.com. Web: www.blessedsacramentqueensny.org.
Catechesis/Religious Program—93-15 35th Ave., Jackson Heights, 11372. Tel: 718-639-6159. Email: pcmny@yahoo.com. Sisters Lisbeth Pimentel Maya, P.C.M., D.R.E.; Neyda Maritza Eslava Grimaldos, P.C.M., D.R.E. Students 903.
Convent—93-11 35th Ave., Jackson Heights, 11372. Tel: 718-639-1545.

13—BLESSED TRINITY ROMAN CATHOLIC CHURCH (2008) Rev. Msgrs. Michael J. Curran; Ronald Newland; Revs. Michael C. Gribbon; Francis JoJo Obu-Mends; Deacons Bernard M. Deschler; Richard G. Lee; James F. Ruoff; Sr. Mary Beata, Music Dir. In Res., Rev. John F. Cullinane, P.E. (Retired).
Res.: 204-25 Rockaway Point Blvd., Rockaway Point, 11697. Tel: 718-634-6357; Fax: 718-634-6222. Email: stmste@aol.com.
Additional Worship Sites:—
St. Thomas More-St. Edmund—Church: 204-25 Rockaway Point Blvd., Rockaway Point, 11697.
St. Genevieve—Church: 6 Beach 178th St., Rockaway Point, 11697.
Catechesis/Religious Program—Betsy Heinlein, D.R.E. Students 248.

14—BLESSED VIRGIN MARY, HELP OF CHRISTIANS (1854) Revs. Noel Moynihan, C.S.Sp.; Edmund Brendan Duggan, C.S.Sp.; Andrew Joo; Sr. Mary Conroy, C.S.J., Pastoral Assoc.; Deacon Leopold Montes.
Res.: 70-31 48th Ave., Woodside, 11377. Tel: 718-672-4848; Fax: 718-457-4055. Email: bvmwoodside11377@aol.com.
Catechesis/Religious Program—Tel: 718-672-4784. Patricia Wise, D.R.E. Students 370.

15—ST. BONAVENTURE (1932) Merged with St. Benedict, the Moor to form St. Bonaventure-St. Benedict the Moor RC Church.

16—ST. BONAVENTURE-ST. BENEDICT THE MOOR RC CHURCH Rev. Gordon P. Kusi (Ghana); Deacon Pasqual Olivas.
Res.: 114-58 170th St., Jamaica, 11434. Tel: 718-526-0040; Fax: 718-526-4825.
Catechesis/Religious Program—Mrs. Angela Lewis, D.R.E. Students 95.

17—SAINT CAMILLUS-SAINT VIRGILIUS (1908) Revs. Richard J. Ahlemeyer; James M. Dunne, Pastor Emeritus (Retired); Sisters Joan Cahill, O.P., Pastoral Assoc.; Mary Rose Feeney, C.S.J., Pastoral Min.; Rosemary O'Connell, C.S.J., Pastoral Assoc.
Res.: 99-15 Rockaway Beach Blvd., Rockaway Beach, 11694. Tel: 718-634-8229; Fax: 718-634-8193. Email: stcamillusrc@aol.com.
Additional Worship Site:—
St. Virgilius—Church: 210 Noel Rd., Broad Channel, 11693. Tel: 718-634-5680; Fax: 718-424-1538.
School—St. Camillus, 185 Beach 99th St., Rockaway Beach, 11694. Tel: 718-634-5260; Fax: 718-634-8253. Sr. Agnes White, C.S.J., Prin. Sisters of St. Joseph 1; Lay Teachers 10; Students 173.
Catechesis/Religious Program—Tel: 718-634-8229 (St. Camillus); 718-634-6237 (St. Virgilius). Sr. Mary Ann Kollmer, O.P., D.R.E. Students 177.

18—ST. CATHERINE OF SIENNA (1920) Merged with St. Pascal Baylon, to form Our Lady of Light Roman Catholic Church.

19—CHRIST THE KING (1933) Rev. Jeffry T. Dillon; Deacon Winston M. Mayers; Mary Doyle, Pastoral Assoc. In Res., Rev. Francis LeMaire.
Res.: 145-39 Farmers Blvd., Springfield Gardens, 11434. Tel: 718-528-6010; Fax: 718-949-3255. Email: christthekingsg@aol.com.
Catechesis/Religious Program—Tel: 718-528-6010. Email: mdoylectk@verizon.net. Mary Doyle, D.R.E. Students 89.

20—ST. CLARE (1924) Revs. Kevin F. McBrien; Anthony Iroh (Nigeria).
Res.: 137-35 Brookville Blvd., Rosedale, 11422. Tel: 718-341-1018; Fax: 718-276-2001. Email: stclareqns@aol.com. Web: www.stclaregns.com.
School—137-25 Brookville Blvd., Rosedale, 11422. Tel: 718-528-7174; Fax: 718-528-4389. Email: stclareschool@nyc.rr.com. Web: www.stclarerosedale.com. Mary Basile, Prin. Lay Teachers 14; Students 361.
Catechesis/Religious Program—Tel: 718-527-6153. Lorena DeFilippis, D.R.E. Students 173.

21—ST. CLEMENT POPE (1908) Revs. Jeffry T. Dillon; Frederick Anawonah; Bro. Dennis Wermert, S.C., Pastoral Assoc.
Res.: 141-11 123rd Ave., South Ozone Park, 11436. Tel: 718-529-0273; Fax: 718-529-3089.
Catechesis/Religious Program—120-09 141st St., Jamaica, 11436. Tel: 718-641-1915; Fax: 718-738-0588. Sr. Patience Quayson, D.R.E. Students 67.

22—CORPUS CHRISTI (1937) Revs. Peter D. Gillen; Jose F. Herrera; Deacon Juan J. Zhagnay. In Res., Rev. John O'Neill, I.V.Dei.
Res.: 31-30 61st St., Woodside, 11377. Tel: 718-278-8114; Fax: 718-278-3619. Email: c.corpuschristi@verizon.net.
School—31-29 60th St., Woodside, 11377. Tel: 718-721-2484; Fax: 718-721-4579. Email: ccsprincipal01@nsm.com. Linda Parisi, Prin. Lay Teachers 13; Students 213.
Catechesis/Religious Program—Email: cc11414@optonline.net. Mr. Paul Canestro, C.R.E. Students 145.

23—ST. ELIZABETH (1873) Revs. Robert F. Barclay; Maurice Mmegbuadimma; Rafael Gomez (Colombia); Sr. Mary Jareth, R.S.M., Pastoral Assoc.; Deacon Manuel Rodriquez. In Res., Rev. Thomas D. Dolan (Retired).
Res.: 94-20 85th St., Ozone Park, 11416-1237. Tel: 718-296-4900; Fax: 718-296-1140.
School—94-01 85th St., Ozone Park, 11416. Tel: 718-641-6990; Fax: 718-323-5010. Web: www.teacherweb.com/ny/ses/11416. William Ferguson, Prin. Lay Teachers 14; Students 251.
Catechesis/Religious Program—Sr. Estela Arango, P.C.M., D.R.E. Students 166.

24—ST. FIDELIS (1856), (Irish—German), Revs. Arthur G. Minichello; Alfred Guthrie (Retired); Joseph Vu; Deacon John Reichert. In Res., Rev. Frank Mann.
Res.: 123-06 14th Ave., College Point, 11356. Tel: 718-445-6164; Fax: 718-445-1623.
School—124-06 14th Ave., College Point, 11356. Tel: 718-539-2628. Web: www.stfidelis.org. Ms. Diana Silvestri, Prin. Lay Teachers 13; Students 204.
Catechesis/Religious Program—Tel: 718-539-1249. Anna Klidas, D.R.E. & Dir. School Devel. Students 276.

25—ST. FRANCIS DE SALES (1906) Rev. Msgr. John J. Brown; Revs. Bryan J. Carney; John Wtulich; Deacon Vincent M. LaGamba.
Res.: 129-16 Rockaway Beach Blvd., Belle Harbor, 11694. Tel: 718-634-6464; Fax: 718-634-0716. Email: sfdsparish@aol.com. Web: www.stfrancisdesalesparish.org.
School—219 Beach 129th St., Belle Harbor, 11694. Tel: 718-634-2775; Fax: 718-634-6673. Sr. Patricia Chelius, C.S.J., Prin. Sisters of St. Joseph 3; Lay Teachers 25; Students 565.
Catechesis/Religious Program—Tel: 718-945-6911. Dr. Virginia Clark, D.R.E. Students 402.

26—ST. FRANCIS OF ASSISI (1930) Rev. Msgr. Ralph J. Maresca; Revs. Raphael Munkday-Kukana; Victor Mbanisi; Deacons Savior Hili; John R. Sucich.
Res.: 21-17 45 St., Astoria, 11105. Tel: 718-728-7801; Fax: 718-728-7853.
School—21-18 46th St., Astoria, 11105. Tel: 718-726-9405; Fax: 718-721-2577. Barbara McArdle, Prin. Lay Teachers 11; Students 316.
Catechesis/Religious Program—Tel: 718-278-0259. Carmen Macchio, D.R.E. Students 130.

27—ST. GABRIEL (1923) Revs. Gioacchino Basile; Celestine Anyanwu (Nigeria); Robert J. Sadlack.
Res.: 26-26 98th St., East Elmhurst, 11369.

Tel: 718-639-0474; Fax: 718-639-2810.
School—26-25 97th St., East Elmhurst, 11369. Tel: 718-426-7170; Fax: 718-426-1741. Bro. Edward Shields, F.S.C., Prin. Sisters 2; Brothers 3; Lay Teachers 13; Students 230.
Catechesis/Religious Program—Ms. Nelly Gitierrez, D.R.E. Students 115.

28—ST. GENEVIEVE, (German—Irish), Merged with St. Thomas More-St. Edmund to form Blessed Trinity Roman Catholic Church, Rockaway Point, NY. Records are at Blessed Trinity Roman Catholic Church.

29—ST. GERARD MAJELLA (1907) Rev. Josephjude C. Gannon; Deacons Guillermo Gomez; Joseph H. Dass.
Res.: 188-16 91st Ave., Hollis, 11423-2520. Tel: 718-468-6565; Fax: 718-468-3136. Email: stgerardm@verizon.net.
Catechesis/Religious Program—Tel: 718-468-1166, Ext. 22. Anne Coghlan, D.R.E. Students 155.

30—ST. GERTRUDE (1911) Merged with St. Mary Star of the Sea to form St. Mary Star of the Sea and St. Gertrude. Parish records at St. Mary Star of the Sea and St. Gertrude.

31—ST. GREGORY THE GREAT (1936) Revs. Joseph L. Cunningham; William R. Dulaney; Johnson Nedungadan, C.M. (India); Deacons Arthur Cutter; Robert Zeuner.
Res.: 242-20 88th Ave., Bellerose, 11426. Tel: 718-347-3707; Fax: 718-347-0583.
School—244-44 87th Ave., Bellerose, 11426. Tel: 718-343-5053; Fax: 718-347-1142. Ms. Joanne Aldorisio, Prin. Lay Teachers 17; Students 381.
Catechesis/Religious Program—Tel: 718-347-0525. Regina Joyce, D.R.E. Students 285.
Convent—88-19 Cross Island Pkwy., Bellerose, 11426. 242-11 88th Rd., Bellerose, 11426.

32—ST. HELEN (1960) Rev. Msgr. Alfred P. LoPinto; Rev. Robert E. Keighron; Sr. Hannah Marie Cox, P.B.V.M., Pastoral Assoc.; Deacons Armand D'Accordo; Richard E. Elrose. In Res., Rev. Msgr. Joseph C. Pfeiffer, Pastor Emeritus (Retired).
Res.: 157-10 83rd St., Howard Beach, 11414. Tel: 718-738-1616; Fax: 718-835-5144. Web: www.sthelen.org.
School—83-09 157th Ave., Howard Beach, 11414. Tel: 718-835-4155; Fax: 718-848-8722. Peter M. Doran, Prin. Religious 1; Lay Teachers 13; Students 253.
Catechesis/Religious Program—Tel: 718-835-6216. Ms. Sandra Pepitone, D.R.E. Students 243.

33—HOLY CHILD JESUS (1910) Most Rev. Octavio Cisneros; Revs. Thomas M. Catania; Francis A. Colamaria, Admin.; Reinaldo A. Saldarriaga; Deacons Dean Tully; Raul S. Elias.
Res.: 111-11 86th Ave., Richmond Hill, 11418. Tel: 718-847-1860; Fax: 718-847-2696. Email: hcjchurch@aol.com.
School—111-02 86th Ave., Richmond Hill, 11418. Tel: 718-849-3988; Fax: 718-850-2842. Martin C. Abruzzo, Prin. Lay Teachers 22; Students 441.
Catechesis/Religious Program—Tel: 718-805-5771. Students 220.

34—HOLY CROSS (1913), (Polish), Rev. Msgr. Peter W. Zendzian; Revs. Grzegorz Stasiak (Poland); Ryszard Koper (Poland).
Res.: 61-21 56th Rd., Maspeth, 11378-2498. Tel: 718-894-1387; Fax: 718-416-9245.
Catechesis/Religious Program—Mrs. Jolanta Neubauer, D.R.E. Students 333.

35—HOLY FAMILY (1940) Most Rev. Ignatius Catanello; Revs. Edward M. Keane, Pastor Emeritus (Retired); Casper J. Furnari; Deacon Joseph V. Catanello; Sr. Nora McNiff, Pastoral Assoc. In Res., Rev. Msgr. Joseph L. Stafford (Retired); Revs. Augustine C. Adams; Louis D. Aufiero (Retired).
Res.: 175-20 74th Ave., Flushing, 11366-1529. Tel: 718-969-2448; Fax: 718-591-6166. Web: www.hfsflushing.org.
School—74-15 175th St., Flushing, 11366. Tel: 718-969-2124; Fax: 718-380-2183. Mary Scheer, Prin. Sisters of St. Joseph 1; Lay Teachers 12; Students 294.
Catechesis/Religious Program—Tel: 718-591-6438. Barbara Makolin, D.R.E. Students 152.
Convent—175-11 75 Ave., Flushing, 11366.

36—HOLY TRINITY (1965) Revs. Joseph R. Gibino; James F. Fraser.
Res.: 14-51 143rd St., Whitestone, 11357. Tel: 718-746-7730; Fax: 718-767-1368. Email: holytrinityrcchurch@verizon.net. Web: www.holytrinityrcparish.org.
School—14-45 143rd St., Whitestone, 11357. Tel: 718-746-1479; Fax: 718-746-4793. Eleanor Menna, Prin. Lay Teachers 10; Students 295.
Catechesis/Religious Program—Email: holytrinityfaithformation@verizon.net. Donna Marie D. Spoto, Coord. Faith Formation. Students 149.

37—IMMACULATE CONCEPTION (1924) Revs. Jed Sumampong, C.P.; Theophane Cooney, C.P.; Lee Havey, C.P.; Salvatore Riccardi, C.P.; Sr. Karen Cavanagh, C.S.J., Pastoral Assoc.
Res.: 86-45 Edgerton Blvd., Jamaica, 11432. Tel: 718-739-0880; Fax: 718-657-0543. Email: ICCJamaica@aol.com.
School—179-14 Dalny Rd., Jamaica, 11432. Tel: 718-739-5933; Fax: 718-523-7436. Ms. Dorothea Breen, Prin. Sisters of St. Joseph 3; Lay Teachers 13; Students 263.
Catechesis/Religious Program—86-16 Midland Pkwy., Jamaica, 11432. Tel: 718-291-3080. Sr. Elizabeth Gildea, C.S.J., D.R.E. Students 221.

38—IMMACULATE CONCEPTION (1924) Rev. Msgr. Fernando Ferrarese; Revs. Joseph Gaspar D. Hugo (Philippines); Liju Augustine, C.M.I. In Res., Rev. Msgr. Charles P. Boccio, Pastor Emeritus (Retired); Rev. Allan Basilio (Philippines); Deacon Michael Bruno.
Res.: 21-47 29th St., Astoria, 11105. Tel: 718-728-1613; Fax: 718-956-9229. Email: icastoria@nyc.rr.com.
School—21-63 29th St., Astoria, 11105. Tel: 718-728-1969; Fax: 718-728-3374. Email: principal@icsastoria.org. Web: www.icsastoria.org. Eileen Harnischfeger, Prin. Sisters 1; Lay Teachers 19; Students 501.
Catechesis/Religious Program—Tel: 718-956-4494. Marylyn Crum, D.R.E. Students 327.
Convent—21-60 31st St., Long Island City, 11105. Fax: 718-959-9229.

39—INCARNATION (1927) Rev. John J. O'Connor; Deacons Francois Innocent; Franklin Munoz; Clemenceau Pierre-Antoine; Robinson Despeignes.
Res.: 89-43 Francis Lewis Blvd., Queens Village, 11427. Tel: 718-465-8534; Fax: 718-465-3834. Email: pastor@incrcc.org. Web: www.incrcc.org.
School—89-15 Francis Lewis Blvd., Queens Village, 11427. Tel: 718-465-5066; Fax: 718-464-4128. Email: principal@incrcc.org. Mrs. Satti Marchan, Prin. Sisters of St. Dominic (Amityville) 1; Lay Teachers 12; Students 315.
Catechesis/Religious Program—Mrs. Amalia Vais, C.R.E.; Ms. Lorraine Marrero, Youth Min. Coord. Students 168.

40—SS. JOACHIM AND ANNE (1896) Revs. Robert M. Robinson; Jean M. Delva. In Res., Very Rev. Jean-Pierre Ruiz.
Res.: 218-26 105th Ave., Queens Village, 11429. Tel: 718-465-0124; Fax: 718-479-3548.
School—218-19 105th Ave., Queens Village, 11429. Tel: 718-465-2230; Fax: 718-468-5698. Linda Freebes, Prin. Sisters of Notre Dame de Namur 1; Lay Teachers 25; Students 511.
Catechesis/Religious Program—Lisa Sampson, D.R.E. Students 326.

41—ST. JOAN OF ARC (1920) Rev. Msgr. Otto L. Garcia; Revs. Stephen Valdazo; Anthony Sikandar Chanan; William K. Aguzey; Deacon Jorge L. Castillo.
Res.: 82-00 35th Ave., Jackson Heights, 11372. Tel: 718-429-2333; Fax: 718-672-5881. Email: joanofarcqueens@aol.com.
School—35-27 82nd St., Jackson Heights, 11372. Tel: 718-639-9020; Fax: 718-639-5428. Email: sjaschool@juno.com. Web: www.sjaschoolny.com. John Fruner, Prin. Lay Teachers 20; Students 553.
Catechesis/Religious Program—Tel: 718-478-5593; Fax: 718-651-8485. Email: sjareled@netzero.com. Noemi Fitzgerald, D.R.E. Students 559.

42—ST. JOHN VIANNEY (1967) Revs. Antonius Ho, C.S.J.B. (Taiwan), Temp. Admin.; Victor Cao, C.S.J.B.; Deacon John McGreevey; Sr. Monica Gan, C.S.T., Pastoral Assoc. In Res., Revs. Hugo Bedoya (Retired); Edward Zhang, C.S.J.B.
Res.: 140-10 34th Ave., Flushing, 11354. Tel: 718-762-7920; Fax: 718-460-8032. Email: stjv@aol.com.
Catechesis/Religious Program—Tel: 718-961-5092. Eileen Nesi, D.R.E. Students 154.

43—ST. JOSAPHAT (1910), (Polish), Rev. Thomas C. Machalski. In Res., Rev. James J. Meszaros (Retired).
Res.: 34-32 210th St., Bayside, 11361. Tel: 718-229-1663; Fax: 718-229-8018.
Catechesis/Religious Program—Barbara Lougo, C.R.E. Students 49.

44—ST. JOSEPH (1904), (Polish), Rev. Richard P. Zuk, Admin.; Deacon Arthur Cutter, Business Mgr.
Parish Office/Parish House: 108-43 Sutphin Blvd., Jamaica, 11435-5445. Tel: 718-739-4781; Fax: 718-658-5447.
Catechesis/Religious Program—Students 13.

45—ST. JOSEPH (1877) Revs. John P. Harrington; Robert J. Armato; William C. Farrugia; Lawrence Gellel, S.J.; Andrzej Klocek; Deacon Felipe J. Alvarez. In Res., Rev. William C. Farrugia.
Res.: 43-19 30th Ave., Astoria, 11103. Tel: 718-278-1611; Fax: 718-956-3589. Email: stjos11103@aol.com.
School—28-46 44th St., Astoria, 11103. Tel: 718-728-0724; Fax: 718-728-6142. Web: www.stjosephsch.org. Luke Nawrocki, Prin. Sisters of St. Dominic 1; Lay Teachers 23; Students 477.
Catechesis/Religious Program—Tel: 718-545-7338. Email: sjreled@gmail.com. Loretta Rosas, C.R.E. Students 311.

46—ST. KEVIN (1926) Rev. Msgr. D. Joseph Finnerty; Rev. Louis J. DeGaetano; Deacon Julio Barreneche; Mr. Thomas Sexton, Music Dir. In Res., Rev. Michael Parisi (Retired).
Res.: 45-21 194th St., Flushing, 11358. Tel: 718-357-8888; Fax: 718-357-3671.
School—45-50 195th St., Flushing, 11358. Tel: 718-357-8110; Fax: 718-357-2519. Sue Ann Roye, Prin.; Mr. John Gillooly, Dir. Bldgs. & Grounds. Lay Teachers 11; Students 250.
Catechesis/Religious Program—Tel: 718-357-5317. Mrs. Laura Stroligo, Rel. Educ. Office Coord. Students 190.

47—ST. LEO (1903), (Hispanic—Italian), Revs. William M. Hoppe; Joaquin Suran (Retired); Diego Villegas.
Res.: 104-05 49th Ave., Corona, 11368. Tel: 718-592-7569; Fax: 718-271-6726. Email: saintleo@earthlink.net.
School—104-19 49th Ave., Corona, 11368. Tel: 718-592-7050; Fax: 718-592-0787. Mrs. Maureen Blaine, Prin. Lay Teachers 18; Students 385.
Catechesis/Religious Program—Tel: 718-699-8565. Elizabeth Graff, D.R.E. Students 325.
Mission—Our Lady of Mount Carmel Corona. 103-56 52nd Ave., Corona, Queens Co. 11368. Tel: 718-592-7569.

48—ST. LUKE (1870) Rev. Msgr. John C. Tosi; Revs. David J. Dettmer; Vincent G. Chirichella; Sr. Catherine T. Reilly, O.P., Pastoral Assoc.
Res.: 16-34 Clintonville St., Whitestone, 11357. Tel: 718-746-8102; Fax: 718-746-3589.
School—16-01 150th Pl., Whitestone, 11357. Tel: 718-746-3833; Fax: 718-747-2101. Mrs. Barbara Reiter, Prin. Lay Teachers 19; Students 452.
Catechesis/Religious Program—Tel: 718-746-3409. Sr. Katherine Burke, C.S.J., D.R.E. Students 484.

49—ST. MARGARET (1860) Rev. Msgr. Steven J. Aguggia; Revs. William A. With; Joseph F. Wilson; Sr. Bridget Olwell, O.S.U., Pastoral Assoc. In Res., Rev. Msgr. Nicholas W. Sivillo (Retired).
Res.: 66-05 79th Pl., Middle Village, 11379. Tel: 718-326-1911; Fax: 718-326-1883. Email: rectory@stmargaretparish.com. Web: www.stmargaretparish.com.
School—66-10 80th St., Middle Village, 11379. Tel: 718-326-0922. Sr. Rena Perrone, O.P., Prin. Sisters of St. Dominic 1; Lay Teachers 15; Students 345.
Catechesis/Religious Program—Tel: 718-381-4048. Marie Vella, D.R.E. Students 337.

50—ST. MARGARET MARY (1961) Merged with Our Lady of Mount Carmel in 2007. Parish records at Our Lady of Mount Carmel.

51—ST. MARY (1868) Rev. Ralph Barile.
Res.: 10-08 49th Ave., Long Island City, 11101. Tel: 718-786-0705; Fax: 718-482-7115. Email: stmarylic@aol.com.
Catechesis/Religious Program—Students 25.

52—ST. MARY GATE OF HEAVEN (1904) Rev. Gerald J. Fitzsimmons, S.M.M.; Very Rev. Matthew J. Considine, S.M.M.; Rev. Hugh Gillespie; Bro. Paul Llorens, S.M.M.; Deacons Richard Gilligan; Timothy McBride; Ramon Cruz; Frances Franzke, Business Mgr.
Res.: 101-25 104th St., Ozone Park, 11416. Tel: 718-847-5957; Fax: 718-846-6489. Email: information@smghparish.org. Web: www.smghparish.org.
School—104-06 101st Ave., Ozone Park, 11416. Tel: 718-846-0689; Fax: 718-846-1059. Patrick Scannell, Prin. Sisters 1; Lay Teachers 21; Students 568.
Catechesis/Religious Program—Tel: 718-849-9329. Ann Farrell, D.R.E. Students 245.

53—ST. MARY MAGDALENE (1913) Revs. Jeffry T. Dillon; John Manso-Hamilton (Ghana); Deacon Lee C. Williams; Sr. Maryellen Kane, C.S.J., Parish Life Coord.; Mary Harris, Pastoral Assoc.
Res.: 218-12 136th Ave., Springfield Gardens, 11413. Tel: 718-949-4311; Fax: 718-528-7208.
Catechesis/Religious Program—Students 115.

54—ST. MARY STAR OF THE SEA (1857) [CEM] Merged with St. Gertrude to form St. Mary Star of the Sea and St. Gertrude.

55—ST. MARY STAR OF THE SEA AND ST. GERTRUDE (2008) Revs. James K. Cunnigham; Jean Y. Pierre; Maria Christina Beyra, Pastoral Assoc.; Deacons Antonio Bobadilla; Michael C. Moss; Adalberto Montero. In Res., Revs. Augustine Emeh (Nigeria); Charles H. White (Retired).
Res.: 1920 New Haven Ave., Far Rockaway, 11691. Tel: 718-327-1133; Fax: 718-327-3276.
Additional Worship Site:—
St. Gertrude—Church: 336 Beach 38th St., Far Rockaway, 11691.
School—595 Beach 19th St., Far Rockaway, 11691. Tel: 718-327-2242; Fax: 718-327-0797. Angela Brucia, Prin. Priests 2; Lay Teachers 13; Students 260.

Catechesis/Religious Program—Maria Christina Beyra, D.R.E. Students 327.

56—MARY'S NATIVITY (1926) Revs. James T. Rooney; Anacleto Acebias. In Res., Rev. Thaddeus J. Abraham; Rev. Msgr. Edward J. Bottino, Pastor Emeritus (Retired); Rev. Joseph F. Wiseman (Retired).
Res.: 46-02 Parsons Blvd., Flushing, 11355. Tel: 718-359-5996; Fax: 718-939-6737. Email: marysnativity@aol.com. Web: www.marysnativitychurch.com.
Church & Convent: Jasmine Ave. & Parsons Blvd., Flushing, 11355. Tel: 718-445-7180.
Catechesis/Religious Program—Email: marysnativityccd@verizon.net. Mrs. Barbara Devito, D.R.E. Students 108.

57—ST. MATTHIAS (1908) Rev. Msgr. Edward B. Scharfenberger; Revs. Richard J. Bretone; Wladyslaw Z. Kubrak; Silvaster Sarihadduk; Deacon John Sands.
Res.: 58-15 Catalpa Ave., Ridgewood, 11385. Tel: 718-821-6447; 718-821-6448; 718-821-6449; Fax: 718-821-6876.
School—58-25 Catalpa Ave., Ridgewood, 11385. Tel: 718-381-8003; Fax: 718-381-5319. Miss Barbara Wehnes. School Sisters of Notre Dame 6; Lay Teachers 21; Students 405.
Catechesis/Religious Program—Tel: 718-386-1077; Fax: 718-821-6876. Mrs. Carol M. Powell, D.R.E. Students 373.

58—ST. MEL (1941) Revs. Christopher J. Turczany; Italo Barozzi. In Res., Bro. Lawrence Larmann, O.S.F.
Res.: 28-20 154th St., Flushing, 11354. Tel: 718-886-0201; 718-886-0881; Fax: 718-886-0882.
School—154-24 26th Ave., Flushing, 11354. Tel: 718-539-8211. Mrs. Diane Competello, Prin. Sisters 3; Lay Teachers 21; Students 396.
Catechesis/Religious Program—Tel: 718-461-9840; Fax: 718-886-0882. Students 188.

59—ST. MICHAEL (1833) Rev. Msgr. Edward V. Wetterer; Revs. Jorge L Dinguis; Juan Pablo Florez; Reinaldo A. Saldarriaga; Leonard Ugbor; Sr. Maureen Jessnik, Pastoral Asst.
Res.: 136-76 41st Ave., Flushing, 11355. Tel: 718-961-0295; Fax: 718-961-1403. Email: stmicheal1833@aol.com. Web: www.stmichaelflushingonline.org.
School—136-58 41st Ave., Flushing, 11355. Tel: 718-961-0246. Email: rogonesms@aol.com. Mrs. Maureen Rogone, Prin. Sisters of St. Joseph 1; Daughters of Mary Mother of Mercy 2; Sisters of St. Dominic 1; Lay Teachers 11; Students 188.
Catechesis/Religious Program—138-25 Barclay Ave., Flushing, 11355. Tel: 718-961-0312. Luz May, Rel. Educ. Coord. Students 369.

60—ST. MONICA, (Jamaica), Closed. For inquiries for parish records contact the chancery.

61—MOST PRECIOUS BLOOD (1922) Revs. William F. Krlis; James A. Hughes; Ellis Tommaseo (Italy); James Rodriguez, Parochial Vicar; Deacon Giacomo Panessa.
Res.: 32-23 36th St., Long Island City, 11106. Tel: 718-278-3337; Fax: 718-278-4354.
School—32-52 37th St., Long Island City, 11103. Tel: 718-278-4081; Fax: 718-278-3089. Barbara DeMaio, Prin. Sisters of St. Joseph 2; Lay Teachers 20; Students 401.
Catechesis/Religious Program—Tel: 718-721-9850.
Convent—32-16 36th St., Long Island City, 11106. Tel: 718-278-4706.

62—NATIVITY OF THE BLESSED VIRGIN MARY (1925) Revs. Paul C. Palmiotto; Angelo B. Pezzullo (Retired); Andrezej Salwowski; Paul M. Gyamfi; Deacon Edward J. Guster Jr. In Res., Rev. James H. Sweeney.
Res.: 101-41 91st St., Ozone Park, 11416-2227. Tel: 718-845-3691; Fax: 718-845-8978.
Catechesis/Religious Program—101-41 91st St., Ozone Park, 11416. Tel: 718-461-9840. Liz Perretta, D.R.E. Students 350.

63—ST. NICHOLAS OF TOLENTINE (1916) Revs. Thomas G. Pettei, Admin.; Abraham P. Mathew; Anthony Nzegwu (Nigeria).
Res.: 150-75 Goethals Ave., Jamaica, 11432. Tel: 718-969-3226; Fax: 718-380-0345. Web: www.stnicholasoftolentine.org.
School—80-22 Parsons Blvd., Jamaica, 11432. Tel: 718-380-1900; Fax: 718-591-6977. Anne Badalamenti, Prin. Sisters of Charity (Halifax) 1; Lay Teachers 17; Students 352.
Catechesis/Religious Program—150-85 Goethals Ave., Jamaica, 11432. Tel: 718-591-6536. Monica Gonzalez, C.R.E. Students 254.

64—OUR LADY OF CHINA CHAPEL (1978) Attended by St. John Vianney, Flushing Rev. Edward Zhang, C.S.J.B.; Sr. Monica Gan, C.S.T., Pastoral Assoc.
Office: 54-09 92nd St., Elmhurst, 11373. Tel: 718-699-1929; Fax: 718-592-5981. Email: olcny@msn.com. Web: olc.faithweb.com.
School—Ming Yuan Chinese School, 54-17 90th St., Elmhurst, 11373. Tel: 718-271-3944. 6201 8th Ave., 11219. Tel: 718-439-3656. Bro. Peter Li, C.S.J.B., Prin.
Catechesis/Religious Program—Tel: 718-961-5092; Fax: 718-460-8032. Students 31.

65—OUR LADY OF FATIMA (1948) Rev. Msgrs. Michael J. Brennan; John E. Mahoney; Revs. Yovanny Acosta; Eugene F. Donnelly (Retired). In Res., Rev. Msgr. Edward J. Breen, Pastor Emeritus (Retired); Revs. James Fedigan; Patrick J. Frawley.
Res.: 25-02 80th St., Jackson Heights, 11370. Tel: 718-899-2801; Fax: 718-429-6404. Email: olfatima11370@msn.com. Web: www.olfparish.catholicweb.com.
School—25-38 80th St., Jackson Heights, 11370. Tel: 718-429-7031; Fax: 718-899-2811. Mrs. Cassie Zelic, Prin. Lay Teachers 26; Students 625.
Catechesis/Religious Program—25-56 80th St. Tel: 718-457-3457. Patricia Anton, D.R.E. Students 166.
Convent—25-56 80th St., Jackson Heights, 11370. Tel: 718-747-3457.

66—OUR LADY OF GRACE (1924) Rev. Anthony M. Rucando. In Res., Rev. Marc E. Swartvagher.
Res.: 100-05 159th Ave., Howard Beach, 11414. Tel: 718-843-6218; Fax: 718-738-8208.
Catechesis/Religious Program—Tel: 718-835-2165; Fax: 718-835-4524. Sr. Ann Martha, O.P., D.R.E. Students 315.

67—OUR LADY OF HOPE (1960) Revs. Michael A. Carrano; Arthur A. Candreva, I.V.Dei; Deacon Robert F. Lavanco.
Res.: 61-27 71st St., Middle Village, 11379. Tel: 718-429-5438; Fax: 718-429-2764. Email: olhrectory@aol.com.
School—61-21 71st St., Middle Village, 11379. Tel: 718-458-3535. Mrs. Michelle Krebs, Prin. Sisters 4; Lay Teachers 27; Students 594.
Catechesis/Religious Program—Tel: 718-335-8394. Karen Colletti, D.R.E. Students 200.

68—OUR LADY OF LIGHT ROMAN CATHOLIC CHURCH (2008) Rev. William G. Smith; Rev. Msgrs. Robert R. McCourt, Pastor Emeritus (Retired); Francis Yaw Tawiah; Deacons Albert Saldana; Luis C. Taylor; Freddy Torres; Yvonne C. Knight, Music Min.; Florence McKinley, Music Min.; Jeffrey Hicks, Youth Min.
Res.: 118-22 Riverton St., St. Albans, 11412. Tel: 718-528-1220; Fax: 718-528-7907.
Rectory—112-43 198th St., St. Albans, 11412. Tel: 718-468-3511; Fax: 718-479-2303.
Additional Worship Sites:—
St. Catherine of Sienna—Church: 118-22 Riverton St., St. Albans, 11412.
St. Pascal Baylon—Church: 112-43 198th St., St. Albans, 11412.
Catechesis/Religious Program—Mary Harris, D.R.E.; Sr. Mary Jane Rolston, O.P., D.R.E. Students 122.

69—OUR LADY OF LOURDES (1924) Rev. Msgr. Robert J. Pawson; Rev. Michael G. Tedone. In Res., Rev. Msgr. John F. Casey (Retired); Revs. Amaricho Checon, S.J.; Cuong M. Pham; Deacons Richard Moreno; Walter C. Zimmermann.
Res.: 92-96 220th St., Queens Village, 11428. Tel: 718-479-5111; Fax: 718-479-0826.
School—92-80 220th St., Queens Village, 11428. Tel: 718-464-1480; Fax: 718-740-4091. Web: www.ollqv.org. Sr. Josephine Barbiere, C.S.J., Prin. Lay Teachers 19; Students 388.
Catechesis/Religious Program—Tel: 718-740-4090. Joanne Russo, D.R.E. Students 330.

70—OUR LADY OF MERCY (1930) Rev. Msgr. John A. McGuirl; Revs. John J. Cremins; Christopher Okorie (Nigeria); Deacon Edward Smolinski. In Res., Rev. Msgr. Gerald J. Langelier, Pastor Emeritus (Retired); Rev. August J. Iantosca, Chap. Creedmoor Psychiatric Ctr.
Res.: 70-01 Kessel St., Forest Hills, 11375. Tel: 718-268-6143; Fax: 718-544-3764. Email: office@mercyhills.org. Web: www.mercyhills.org.
School—70-25 Kessel St., Forest Hills, 11375. Tel: 718-793-2086; Fax: 718-897-2144. Email: principal@mercyhills.org. Linda Dougherty, Prin. Josephites 1; Sisters Servants of the Immaculate Heart of Mary 1; Lay Teachers 24; Students 375.
Catechesis/Religious Program—70-20 Juno St., Forest Hills, 11375. Tel: 718-261-6285. Web: www.olm-religioused.com. Sr. Ann Barbara DeSiano, I.H.M., D.R.E. Students 120.

71—OUR LADY OF MOUNT CARMEL (1841) Rev. Msgr. Sean G. Ogle; Revs. Joseph Pham; Vitus H. Nguyen, C.S.J.B. In Res., Revs. Edmund P. Brady (Retired); Richard J. Bretone; Raymond Roden.
Res.: 23-25 Newtown Ave., Long Island City, 11102. Tel: 718-278-1834; Fax: 718-278-0998. Email: church@mountcarmelastoria.org. Web: www.mountcarmelastoria.org.
Additional Worship Site:—
St. Margaret Mary—Church: 9-18 27th Ave., Long Island City, 11102.
Catechesis/Religious Program—Fax: 718-278-0998. Zilia Hirsch, D.R.E. Students 221.

72—OUR LADY OF PERPETUAL HELP (1923) Revs. Vincent M. Daly; John G. Garkowski; Sr. Margaret Sweeney, C.S.J., Pastoral Assoc. In Res., Revs. Donald M. Berran (Retired); Michael Walsh.
Res.: 111-50 115th St., South Ozone Park, 11420. Tel: 718-843-1212; Fax: 718-843-3554. Email: olphchurchqns@hotmail.com.
School—111-10 115th St., South Ozone Park, 11420. Tel: 718-843-4184; Fax: 718-843-6838. Mrs. Frances DeLuca, Prin. Religious 1; Lay Teachers 37; Students 613.
Catechesis/Religious Program—Tel: 718-641-6165. Sr. Maria Pilar, O.P., D.R.E. Students 141.

73—OUR LADY OF SORROWS (1876) Revs. Thomas J. Healy; Manuel Ros (Retired); James A. Kuroly; Deacons Francisco J. Tineo; Daniel Magana.
Res.: 104-11 37th Ave., Corona, 11368. Tel: 718-424-7554; Fax: 718-424-4910. Email: olsrectory@nyc.rr.com.
School—35-34 105th St., Corona, 11368. Tel: 718-426-5517; Fax: 718-651-5682. Email: khanrahan@olscorona.org. Sr. Katherine Hanrahan, C.S.J., Prin. Sisters of St. Joseph 1; Lay Teachers 11; Students 278.
Catechesis/Religious Program—Tel: 718-651-5682. Email: olsccd@aol.com. Aurora De La Cruz, D.R.E. Students 1,303.

74—OUR LADY OF THE ANGELUS (1938) Revs. John Mendonca; Daniel Ayala; Deacons Edwin Cancel; Julio C. Murillo. In Res., Revs. Daniel G. Keohane (Retired); Jose Cadusale (Philippines).
Res.: 63-63 98th St., Rego Park, 11374. Tel: 718-897-4444; Fax: 718-897-1453. Email: pola@nyc.rr.com. Web: www.ola63.org.
School—98-05 63rd. Dr., Rego Park, 11374. Tel: 718-896-7220; Fax: 718-896-5723. Email: joan7armstrong@yahoo.com. Web: www.ourladyoftheangelus.com. Joan M. Armstrong, Prin. Lay Teachers 12; Students 248.
Catechesis/Religious Program—Tel: 718-896-4388. Sr. Jo Ann Schwarz, S.C., D.R.E. Students 150.

75—OUR LADY OF THE BLESSED SACRAMENT (1930) Revs. Robert J. Whelan; Thomas G. D'Albro; George Bourbeau, Youth Min. In Res., Rev. Michael Udoh; Rev. Msgr. William J. Flood (Retired).
Res.: 34-24 203rd St., Bayside, 11361. Tel: 718-229-5929; Fax: 718-229-3354.
School—34-45 202nd St., Bayside, 11361. Tel: 718-229-4434; Fax: 718-229-5820. Joan Kane, Prin. Sisters 1; Lay Teachers 23; Students 405.
Catechesis/Religious Program—Tel: 718-225-6179. Sr. Carla Lorenz, P.B.V.M., D.R.E. Students 212.

76—OUR LADY OF THE CENACLE (1922) Revs. Robert P. Morales; Adnel T. Burgos; Deacon Eduardo Sencion. In Res., Rev. Pablo Sans (Retired).
Res.: 136-06 87th Ave., Richmond Hill, 11418. Tel: 718-291-2540; Fax: 718-291-6211.
Catechesis/Religious Program—Marlene Stafford, D.R.E. Students 151.

77—OUR LADY OF THE MIRACULOUS MEDAL (1917) Rev. Msgrs. Edward A. Ryan; Anthony Danna. In Res., Rev. Msgr. George M. Schuster, Pastor Emeritus (Retired).
Res.: 62-81 60th Pl., Ridgewood, 11385. Tel: 718-366-3360; Fax: 718-456-0564. Email: olmm11385@aol.com. Web: www.ourladymm.com.
Catechesis/Religious Program—Tel: 718-456-3275. Mary Macchiaroli, D.R.E. Students 250.

78—OUR LADY OF THE SKIES CHAPEL (1955) Rev. Gerard T. Walker, Admin. & Chap.
Kennedy International Airport Terminal: JFK International Airport, Terminal 4, Jamaica, 11430. Tel: 718-656-5348; Fax: 718-656-8162. Web: www.jfkchapel.org. Email: alice@jfkchapel.org.

79—OUR LADY OF THE SNOWS (1948) Rev. Msgr. Raymond F. Chappetto; Rev. Patrick H. O. Longalong, Parochial Vicar; Deacons Henry J. Smith; Matthew Oellinger; Steven Borheck. In Res., Rev. Hyacinth I. Ikemelu (Nigeria).
Res.: 258-15 80th Ave., Floral Park, 11004. Tel: 718-347-6070; Fax: 718-343-3221. Email: church@olsnows.org. Web: www.olsnows.org.
School—79-33 258th St., Floral Park, 11004. Tel: 718-343-1346; Fax: 718-343-7303. Web: www.ourladyofsnowsschool.org. Sr. Roberta Oberle, C.S.J., Prin. Lay Teachers 23; Students 496.
Catechesis/Religious Program—Tel: 718-347-3511. Email: rel.ed@olsnows.org. Regina Moreno, D.R.E. Students 297.

80—OUR LADY, QUEEN OF MARTYRS (1917) Rev. Msgr. Joseph A. Funaro; Rev. Francis J. Passenant; Deacon Gregory Kandra. In Res., Rev. Msgr. Michael J. Dempsey (Retired); Rev. Jan Czudek.
Res.: 110-06 Queens Blvd., Forest Hills, 11375. Tel: 718-268-6251; Fax: 718-793-2584. Email: info@ourladyqueenofmartyrs.org. Web: www.ourladyqueenofmartyrs.org.
School—72-55 Austin St., Forest Hills, 11375. Tel: 718-263-2622; Fax: 718-263-0063. Email: olqmschool@aol.com. Web: www.olqmschool.com.

Mrs. Ann Zuscalag, Prin. Sisters 1; Lay Teachers 13; Students 326.
Catechesis/Religious Program—Tel: 718-263-0907. Email: olqmreled@verizon.net. Students 204.

81—ST. PANCRAS (1904) Rev. Vincent Gallo (Retired); Deacon James E. Maloney.
Res.: 72-22 68th St., Glendale, 11385. Tel: 718-821-2323; Fax: 718-417-8021. Email: stpancrasparish@aol.com. Web: www.saintpancras.org.
School—68-20 Myrtle Ave., Glendale, 11385. Tel: 718-821-6721; Fax: 718-418-8991. Mr. Philip Ciani, Prin. Lay Teachers 15; Students 301.
Catechesis/Religious Program—Tel: 718-479-0590. Email: fotopeg@aol.com. Margaret Walter, D.R.E. Students 247.
Convent—72-21 68th St., 72-25 68th St., Glendale, 11385.

82—ST. PASCAL BAYLON (1930), (African American), Merged with St. Catherine of Sienna to form Our Lady of Light Roman Catholic Church.

83—ST. PATRICK (1869) Rev. Alexander G. Abugel; Deacon Carlos A. Trochez. In Res., Revs. Charles F. Gilley, I.V.Dei.; Phil James Laquindanum (Philippines).
Res.: 39-38 29th St., Long Island City, 11101. Tel: 718-729-6060; Fax: 718-729-1276. Email: stpatparishlic@earthlink.net.
Catechesis/Religious Program—Tel: 718-937-1239; Fax: 718-706-0565. Sr. Flora Marinelli, C.S.J., D.R.E. Students 124.

84—ST. PAUL CHONG HA-SANG ROMAN CATHOLIC CHAPEL (2006), (Korean), Revs. Gabriel Lee; Eun Seok Son; John Dea Ha Kim; Deacon Paul M. Chin. Office: 32-15 Parsons Blvd., Flushing, 11354. Tel: 718-321-7676; Fax: 718-321-7005.
Catechesis/Religious Program—Rev. Joseph R. Veneroso, M.M., D.R.E. Students 389.
Convent—Olivetan Benedictine Sisters, 32-15 Parsons Blvd., Flushing, 11354.

85—ST. PAUL THE APOSTLE (1964) Rev. Darrell Da Costa. In Res., Rev. Jose Sanchez (Philippines).
Res. & Office: 98-16 55 Ave., Corona, 11368. Tel: 718-271-1000; Fax: 718-760-3496.
Catechesis/Religious Program—Students 343.

86—ST. PIUS V (1908) Rev. Luiz Antonio DeAguiar (Brazil).
Res.: 106-12 Liverpool St., Jamaica, 11435. Tel: 718-739-3731; Fax: 718-739-7086. Email: stpiusvjamaica@aol.com.
Catechesis/Religious Program—Students 159.

87—ST. PIUS X (1960) Rev. Msgr. Thomas A. Graham; Revs. Joachim Fernando (Sri Lanka) (Retired); George E. Gorap; Christopher C. Odina; Louis N. Uzoh.
Res.: 148-10 249th St., Rosedale, 11422. Tel: 718-525-9099; Fax: 718-276-2467. Email: stpiusxrestore@aol.com.
Catechesis/Religious Program—Marilyne Jean, D.R.E. Students 52.

88—PRESENTATION OF THE BLESSED VIRGIN MARY (1886) Revs. Christopher O'Connor; Domingo Collado; Deacon Jose Armanso Lizama.
Res.: 88-19 Parsons Blvd., Jamaica, 11432. Tel: 718-739-0241; Fax: 718-739-2753. Email: pbvmchurch@msn.com.
Providence House III—159-23 89th Ave., Jamaica, 11432. Tel: 718-739-1348.
Youth Ministry Office—88-13 Parsons Blvd., Jamaica, 11432. Tel: 718-739-2003; Fax: 718-526-8153.
Catechesis/Religious Program—Mr. Eric Velazquez-Sanchez, Dir.Youth Min. Students 584.

89—QUEEN OF ANGELS (1953) Revs. Brian P. Dowd; Michael Mulvihill, C.S.Sp.; Juan Fuentes, Music Min.
Res.: 44-04 Skillman Ave., Long Island City, 11104. Tel: 718-392-0011; 718-392-0012; Fax: 718-472-2625.
Catechesis/Religious Program—Tel: 718-937-5174. Students 126.

90—QUEEN OF PEACE (1939) Rev. James Tighe; Mercedes Lopez, Admin. Asst.
Res.: 141-36 77th Ave., Flushing, 11367. Tel: 718-380-5031; Fax: 718-969-2025. Email: queenofpeacerectory@verizon.net.
Catechesis/Religious Program—Gregory J. Bizzoco Jr., D.R.E. Students 101.
Convent—Tel: 718-380-4293.

91—ST. RAPHAEL (1868) Rev. Jerome Jecewicz.
Res.: 35-20 Greenpoint Ave., Long Island City, 11101. Tel: 718-729-8957; Fax: 718-729-5238. Web: www.straphaelsparish.com.
School—48-25 37th St., Long Island City, 11101. Tel: 718-784-0482; Fax: 718-482-0214. Web: www-.straphaelschoollic.com. Sr. Maureen Ahlemeyer, P.B.V.M., Prin. Sisters of the Presentation 1; Lay Teachers 10; Students 212.
Catechesis/Religious Program—Monica Gonzalez, D.R.E. Students 105.

92—RESURRECTION-ASCENSION (1926) Rev. Msgr. Vincent F. Fullam; Rev. Salvatore Amato. In Res., Rev. Msgrs. Joseph P. Bynon (Retired); Paul R. Sanchez.
Res.: 61-11 85th St., Rego Park, 11374. Tel: 718-424-5212; Fax: 718-639-8679.
School—85-25 61st Rd., Rego Park, 11374. Tel: 718-426-4963; Fax: 718-426-0940. Joann Heppt, Prin. Lay Teachers 13; Students 265.
Catechesis/Religious Program—Tel: 718-533-7898. Students 123.

93—ST. RITA (1900) Revs. Philip J. Pizzo; Jose Carlos Da Silva; Sr. M. Erlinda Pimo, I.S.S.M., Pastoral Assoc. In Res., Rev. Sylvester C. Ileka.
Res.: 36-25 11th St., Long Island City, 11106. Tel: 718-361-1884; Fax: 718-786-4573. Web: www.stritalic.org.
Catechesis/Religious Program—Tel: 718-361-1884; Fax: 718-786-4573. Aida Alvarez, D.R.E. Students 252.

94—ST. ROBERT BELLARMINE (1939) Rev. Msgr. Martin T. Geraghty; Revs. Godofredo Felicitas (Philippines); Andrew M. Kim; Deacon Andrew Ciccaroni. In Res., Rev. Henry A. Lang (Retired).
Res.: 56-15 213th St., Bayside, 11364. Tel: 718-229-6465; Fax: 718-229-8126.
School—56-10 214th St., Bayside, 11364. Tel: 718-225-8795; Fax: 718-423-5612. Ms. Angela Fazio, Prin. Sisters 1; Lay Teachers 10; Students 203.
Catechesis/Religious Program—Tel: 718-225-3181. Students 173.

95—ST. ROSE OF LIMA (1886) Rev. Msgr. James F. Spengler; Rev. Andrzej Lukianiuk; Deacon Patrick Logue.
Res.: 130 Beach 84th St., Rockaway Beach, 11693. Tel: 718-634-7394; Fax: 718-634-6591. Web: www.stroseoflimarb.org.
School—154 Beach 84th St., Rockaway Beach, 11693. Tel: 718-474-7079; Fax: 718-634-0524. Mrs. Theresa Andersen, Prin. Sisters 4; Lay Teachers 22; Students 398.
Catechesis/Religious Program—Tel: 718-945-4850. Email: job616@aol.com. Students 107.

96—SACRED HEART Revs. Bryan D. Patterson; Felix Akpabio (Nigeria); Bony Monastere; Deacons Paul Dorsinville; Roy Dudley; Francois G. Cajoux; Sr. Carmele Nerette, F.D.M., Pastoral Assoc. In Res., Rev. Joseph M. Nolan (Retired).
Res.: 115-58 222nd St., Cambria Heights, 11411. Tel: 718-528-0577; Fax: 718-341-0253. Email: shcambria@aol.com.
School—115-50 221st St., Cambria Heights, 11411. Tel: 718-527-0123; Fax: 718-527-1204. Email: sacredheartch@gmail.com. Mrs. Yvonne-Therese Russell Smith, Prin. Lay Teachers 16; Students 365.
Catechesis/Religious Program—Students 90.

97—SACRED HEART (1931) Revs. John J. Fullum; Joseph A. Pfaff; Sr. Margaret Mary Raibaldi, C.S.J., Pastoral Assoc.; Deacon Peter Stamm; Mr. Charles Nicholson, Mus. Dir. In Res., Revs. Romano Zanon; Biju Mathew, C.M.I. (India).
Res.: 83-17 78th Ave., East Glendale, 11385. Tel: 718-821-6434; Fax: 718-497-2881. Email: sacredheartglendale@earthlink.net.
School—84-05 78th Ave., East Glendale, 11385. Tel: 718-456-6636; Fax: 718-456-0286. Ms. Joanne Gangi, Prin. Grey Nuns of the Sacred Heart 1; Lay Teachers 13; Students 305.
Catechesis/Religious Program—Tel: 718-386-5616. Mrs. Laura Ciraolo, D.R.E. Students 350.

98—SACRED HEART OF JESUS (1878) Revs. Thomas F. Brosnan; Joseph Aboagye-Tawiah; Peter Lim Chan-Yong; Deacon William McNamara; Sr. Kathleen Masterson, R.S.M., Pastoral Min.
Res.: 215-35 38th Ave., Bayside, 11361. Tel: 718-428-2200; Fax: 718-428-5840. Web: www.sacredheartbayside.net.
School—216-33 38th Ave., Bayside, 11361. Tel: 718-631-4804; Fax: 718-631-5738. Mr. Dennis J. Farrell, Prin. Lay Teachers 21; Students 554.
Catechesis/Religious Program—Tel: 718-631-1307. Mrs. Georgette Lyons, D.R.E. Students 243.

99—ST. SEBASTIAN (1894) Rev. Msgr. Michael J. Hardiman; Revs. Michael J. McHugh; Gerard J. Sauer; Joy Alookaran (India); Sabino Estrada (Retired); Deacons Stephen Damato; Richard Perez; Ms. Sally Williams, Dir. Outreach; Mr. Harry Connor, Dir. Parish Center. In Res., Rev. Daniel Suh.
Res.: 39-63 57th St., Woodside, 11377. Tel: 718-429-4442; Fax: 718-429-7581. Email: administration@stsebastianwoodside.org. Web: www.stsebastianwoodside.org.
School—39-68 58th St., Woodside, 11377. Tel: 718-429-1982; Fax: 718-446-7225. Mrs. JoAnn Dolan, Prin. Sisters of Charity (Halifax) 1; Lay Teachers 20; Students 436.
Catechesis/Religious Program—39-66 58th St., Woodside, 11377. Tel: 718-899-3341. Ms. Sonia Casanova, D.R.E. Students 454.

100—ST. STANISLAUS BISHOP AND MARTYR (1923), (Polish), Revs. Paul C. Palmiotto; Andrezej Salwowski.
Res.: 88-10 102nd Ave., Ozone Park, 11416. Tel: 718-845-6206; Fax: 718-843-6408. Web: www.st-stanislaus.com.
Catechesis/Religious Program—Liz Perretta, D.R.E. Students 55.

101—ST. STANISLAUS KOSTKA (1872) Revs. Paul A. Wood; Joseph Palackal, C.M.I. (India); Deacon David J. Ciorciari. In Res., Rev. Justo Beltran Regado.
Res.: 57-15 61st St., Maspeth, 11378-2713. Tel: 718-326-2185; Fax: 718-416-2108. Email: ststanislauskostka@catholicweb.com.
School—61-17 Grand Ave., Maspeth, 11378. Tel: 718-326-1585; Fax: 718-326-1745. Web: www.ststans-school.org. Sr. Rose Torma, C.S.J., Prin. Lay Teachers 12; Students 239.
Catechesis/Religious Program—Diane Allison, Dir. Childhood Faith Formation (Grades K-8). Students 137.

102—ST. TERESA (1928) Rev. Msgr. Denis M. Herron; Deacons Martin Soraire; Roberto Abundo. In Res., Rev. Msgr. Perfecto Vasquez.
Res.: 50-20 45th St., Woodside, 11377. Tel: 718-784-2123; Fax: 718-706-6797.
Catechesis/Religious Program—Tel: 718-937-4819. Sr. Mary Jane Kelly, O.P., D.R.E. Students 337.

103—ST. TERESA OF AVILA (1929) Rev. Richard Hoare; Deacon Louis Panico; Ruth Meletiche, Dir. Community Svcs.
Res.: 109-26 130th St., South Ozone Park, 11420. Tel: 718-529-3587; Fax: 718-529-0324.
School—Tel: 718-641-1316; Fax: 718-843-0769. Ms. Loretta Rybacki, Prin. Lay Teachers 11; Students 309.
Catechesis/Religious Program—Tel: 718-641-5710. Douglas M. Blaine, D.R.E. Students 108.

104—ST. THOMAS APOSTLE (1910) Revs. Frank C. Tumino; John Francis; Rafael Gomez (Colombia); Deacon Jose A. Contreras.
Res.: 87-19 88th Ave., Woodhaven, 11421. Tel: 718-847-1353; Fax: 718-849-3776. Email: staadmin@nyc.rr.com. Web: www.stawoodhaven.org.
School—87-49 87th St., Woodhaven, 11421. Tel: 718-847-3904; Fax: 718-847-3513. Cathleen Quinn, Prin. Sisters 1; Lay Teachers 15; Students 231.
Catechesis/Religious Program—Tel: 718-441-8409. Sr. Helene Jakubowski, R.S.M., D.R.E. Students 215.

105—ST. THOMAS MORE-ST. EDMUND (1937) Merged with St. Genevieve to form Blessed Trinity Roman Catholic Church, Rockaway Point, NY. Records are at Blessed Trinity Roman Catholic Church.

106—TRANSFIGURATION (1908), (Lithuanian), Revs. Paul A. Wood; Vytautas Volertas; Deacons William Oggeri; Arthur J. Griffin.
Res.: 64-14 Clinton Ave., Maspeth, 11378. Tel: 718-326-2236; Fax: 718-326-2249. Email: transfiguration@catholicweb.com. Web: transfiguration.catholicweb.com.
Catechesis/Religious Program—Diane Allison, Dir. Childhood Faith Formation (Grades K-8). Students 67.

107—ST. VIRGILIUS (1914) Merged with St. Camillus in 2008 to form St. Camillus-St. Virgilius.

Chaplains of Public Institutions

BROOKLYN. *Bernard Fineson Development Center*. Vacant.
Beth Israel Medical Center/Kings Hgwy. Elaine Chan.
Metropolitan Detention Center. Rev. James McDevitt.
Brookdale Hospital Medical Center. Angela DiPaola.
Brooklyn Development Center. Vacant.
The Brooklyn Hospital. Rev. John O'Leary.
Coney Island Hospital. Rev. Joseph P. Quigley.
Downstate Medical Center. Vacant.
Kings County Hospital Center. Rev. Souvenir Jean Paul, S.M.
Kingsboro Psychiatric Center. Rev. Robert Frueh, M.S.
Long Island College Hospital. Has an interfaith Chap.
Lutheran Medical Center. Sr. Mary Ellen Vesey, C.S.J.
Maimonides Medical Center of Brooklyn. Deacon Thomas J. Devaney, Chap.
Methodist Hospital. Sr. Therese Marie Camardella, C.S.J.
Veterans Administration Medical Center. Rev. Thomas Mullin.
Victory Memorial Hospital. Vacant.
Woodhull Medical & Mental Health Center. Revs. Justo Beltran (Philippines), David P. Bertolotti.
Wyckoff Heights Hospital. Rev. Francisco J. Ares.

QUEENS. *Creedmoor Psychiatric Center*. Revs. Paul Chenot, C.P., August J. Iantosca.
Elmhurst General Hospital. Rev. Alan Briceland, S.J.
Flushing Hospital and Medical Center. Rev. Thaddeus J. Abraham.
Jamaica Hospital - Trump Pavilion. Rev. James Nunes, M.S.

St. John's Episcopal Hospital. Rev. Augustine Emeh (Nigeria).
Long Island Jewish Hospital. Sr. Faustina Quayson, H.H.C.J., Rev. Hyacinth I. Ikemelu (Nigeria).
The Mount Sinai Hospital of Queens. Rev. Sylvester C. Ileka.
N.Y. Hospital Medical Center of Queens. Sr. Rosarine Quinn, C.S.J.
Peninsula Hospital Center. Rev. Augustine Emeh (Nigeria).
Queens Hospital Center--Pastoral Care Office. Rev. Jose Cadusale (Philippines).
Queensboro Correctional Facility. Deacon Frank A. DeTucci.
Veterans Affairs Extended Care Center, St. Albans, NY. Rev. Andrew Sioleti, O.F.M. Conv.

Special Assignment:
Rev. Msgr.—
Reilly, Philip J., Chap., Monastery of the Precious Blood (Retired), 5400 Ft. Hamilton Pkwy., 11219.
Rev.—
Camora, Antonio, Chap., Apostleship of the Sea

Military Chaplains:
Revs.—
Finley, James F., US Navy, Command Chap., US Marine Corps. Air Station, Box 99100, Yuma, AZ 85369-9100.
Hirten, Timothy J., US Airforce Base, 97 AMW HC (Bldg. 301), 306 F Ave., Altus Afb, OK 73523.

Released from Diocesan Assignment:
Rev. Msgrs.—
Harris, Robert M., M.S.W., M.Phil., M.A., St. Vincent's Residence, 66 Boerum Pl., 11201.
Maksymowicz, John H., Apostolic Nunciature, 3339 Massachusetts Ave., N.W., Washington, DC 20008.
Marchese, Richard E., Apostolic Nunciature, 3339 Massachusetts Ave., N.W., Washington, DC 20008.
Sarno, Robert J., Congregation for the Causes of Saints, Piazza Pio XII, 10 00120 Vatican City State.
Sherman, Anthony F., USCCB, 3211 4th St., Washington, DC 20017.
Vaccari, Peter I., S.T.L., Immaculate Conception Seminary, W. Neck Rd., Lloyd Harbor, Huntington, 11743.
Very Rev.—
Ruiz, Jean-Pierre, S.T.D., SS. Joachim & Anne, 218-26 105th Ave., Queens Village, 11429.
Revs.—
Bellantonio, Albert, P.O. Box 382, Tannersville, PA 18372.
Bordeleau, Beau-Pierre G., 512 W. River Rd., Apt. 219, Hooksett, NH 03106.
Buonanno, Vito A., Basilica of the National Shrine of the Immaculate Conception, 400 Michigan Ave. N.E., Washington, DC 20017.
Caccavale, Charles, Seminary of the Immaculate Conception, Huntington, 11743.
Costello, John J., Dir. Pastoral Formation, Pontifical North American College 00120 Vatican City State.
DeSanctis, Peter A., Our Lady of the Isle Church, 5 Prospect Ave., P.O. Box 3027, Shelter Island Heights, 11965.
Fermeglia, Charles, Most Holy Redeemer, 100 Diamond St., San Francisco, CA 94114.
Frawley, Patrick J., Fidelis Care, 95-25 Queens Blvd., Rego Park, 11374.
Himes, Michael J., Dept. of Theology, Boston College, Chestnut Hill, MA 02167-3806.
Lauder, Robert E., Bishop Mugavero Residence, 7200 Douglaston Pkwy., Douglaston, 11362.
Massa, James, USCCB, 3211 Fourth St., N.E., Washington, DC 20017.
Musumeci, James S., 222 E. 19th St. (7F), New York, 10003.
Penta, Leo J., Catholic University of Applied Sciences, Kopenicker Allee 39-57, Berlin, Germany.
Vesey, John E., Northeastern University, Foreign Affairs Office, Shenyang 110004 China.

Graduate Studies:
Revs.—
Champoli, Daniel
Mucci, Robert V.
Pham, Cuong M.
Purpura, Peter J.
Suh, Daniel
Swartvagher, Marc E., S.T.L.

On Leave/Unassigned:
Revs.—
Boyd, James A.
Brown, Charles L.
Bukofsky, James W.
Capolarello, Salvatore
Collins, Robert
Ercolano, Anthony S.
Espinal, David
Espinosa, David F.
Greene, Michael M.
Guiry, Robert W.
Hand, Kenneth J.
Hannan, James G.
Hauser, John G.
Javier, Nazareno
Klein, Dennis D. (Retired)
Lazar, John E.
Lynch, Michael, S.T.L.
Mathew, Abraham P.
McHugh, Michael J.
Miller, John C.
Miller, Joseph A.
Pasciuto, Joseph C.
Perez, Jose
Piro, Gerald J.
Reynolds, James J.
Sobiech, Slawomir
Steinhauser, Michael G.
Stewart, Edward R.
Tivenan, John J.
Wulinski, Stanley F.

Retired:
Rev. Msgrs.—
Adessa, Dominick J., 16 Orient Ct., Ridge, 11961.
Angles, Sebastian, 2601 Muscatello St., Orlando, FL 32821.
Arella, Gerard J., Bishop Mugavero Residence, 7200 Douglaston Pkwy., Douglaston, 11362.
Basler, Howard B., 156-06 46th Ave., Flushing, 11355.
Bednartz, August C., 130 Arcadia Walk, Rockaway Point, 11697.
Bennett, Austin P., J.C.D., P.A., 378 Clermont Ave., 11238.
Boccio, Charles P., 336 N. Birch Rd., #7A, Fort Lauderdale, FL 33304.
Bottino, Edward J., Mary's Nativity, 46-02 Parsons Blvd., Flushing, 11355.
Brady, Thomas F., Good Shepherd, 1950 Batchelder St., 11229.
Breen, Edward J., Our Lady of Fatima, 25-02 80 St., Jackson Heights, 11370.
Burns, John A., 1395 E. 56th St., 11234.
Bynon, Joseph P., Bishop Mugavero Residence, 7200 Dougluston Pkwy., Douglaston, 11362.
Cantley, Michael J., Bishop Mugavero Residence, 7200 Douglaston Pkwy., Douglaston, 11362.
Casey, John F., Our Lady of Lourdes, 150-75 Goethals Ave., Jamaica, 11432.
Collini, Celsus O., 141-36 77th Ave., Kew Gardens Hills, 11367.
Cooney, James J., B.A., M.A., Cathedral Preparatory Seminary, 56-25 92nd St., Elmhurst, 11373.
Deas, George T., Bishop Mugavero Residence, 7200 Douglaston Pkwy., Little Neck, 11362.
Dietz, Conrad R. (RVC), Bishop Mugavero Residence, 7200 Douglaston Pkwy., Douglaston, 11362.
Donovan, Thomas F., Bishop Mugavero Residence, 7200 Douglaston Pkwy., Douglaston, 11362.
Dunn, Richard F., Bishop Mugavero Residence, 7200 Douglaston Pkwy., Douglaston, 11362.
Ecker, Robert J., 300 Second St., Coronado, CA 92118.
Feldhaus, Eugene A., Bishop Magavero Residence, 7200 Douglaston Pkwy., Douglaston, 11362.
Flanagan, Thomas J., P.O. Box 804, Hampton Bays, 11946.
Flood, William J., Our Lady of the Blessed Sacrament, 34-24 203rd St., Bayside, 11361.
Foley, Matthew F., P.O. Box 91T, Bethel, 12720.
Gotimer, James E., 43-22 Ithaca St., Elmhurst, 11373.
Gradilone, Thomas J., Bishop Mugavero Residence, 7200 Douglaston Pkwy., Little Neck, 11362.
Hartmann, John F., 51 Bradley Rd., Madison, CT 06443.
Hinch, Lawrence E., Bishop Mugavero Residence, 7200 Douglaston Pkwy., Douglaston, 11362.
Hunt, James A., Roman Catholic Church-Presbytery, Dennery Box 40, Saint Lucia.
Keane, Vincent A., 341 Highland Blvd., 11207.
Kelly, Raymond J., S.T.L., Bishop Mugavero Residence, 7200 Douglaston Pkwy., Douglaston, 11362.
Keppler, John F., Bishop Mugavero Residence, 7200 Douglaston Pkwy., Douglaston, 11362.
King, James P., Bishop Mugavero Residence, 7200 Douglaston Pkwy., Little Neck, 11362.
Kneafsey, Cornelius T., St. Benedict Joseph Labre, 94-40 118 St., South Richmond Hill, 11419.
Langelier, Gerald J., Our Lady of Mercy, 70-01 Kessel St., Forest Hills, 11375.
McCourt, Robert R., Our Lady of the Light, 118-22 Riverton St., St. Albans, 11412.
Mulqueen, Joseph C., St. Mary, 10-08 49 Ave., Long Island City, 11101.
Murphy, Walter C., Bishop Mugavero Residence, 7200 Douglaston Pkwy., Douglaston, 11362.
Noonan, Thomas F., St. Edmund, 2460 Ocean Ave., 11229.
O'Toole, Patrick F., 13105 S.W. 16 Ct., Apt. L413, Pembroke Pines, FL 33027.
O'Toole, Patrick F., 13105 S.W. 16 Ct., Apt. L413, Pembroke Pines, FL 33027.
Pfeiffer, Joseph C., 157-10 83rd St., Howard Beach, 11414. 157-10 83rd St., Howard Beach, 11414.
Phillips, Michael J., St. Anselm, 356 82nd St., 11209.
Powis, John J., 138 Bleeker St., 11221.
Reilly, Philip J., Monastery of the Precious Blood, 5400 Fort Hamilton Pkwy., 11219.
Rodgers, William J., Queen of Peace Residence, 110-30 221st St., Queens Village, 11429.
Ryan, James W., 2609 Linden Blvd., 11208.
Saporito, Cosmo G., St. Bernadette, 6309 N.W. 23rd St., Boca Raton, FL 33434.
Schuster, George M., Our Lady of the Miraculous Medal, 62-81 60th Pl., Ridgewood, 11385.
Sivillo, Nicholas W., St. Margaret, 66-05 79th Pl., Middle Village, 11379.
Stafford, Joseph L., Holy Family, 175-20 74 Ave., Flushing, 11366.
Vazquez, Perfecto, St. Teresa, 50-20 45th St., Woodside, 11377.
Villani, Rocco D., St. Brendan, 1525 East 12th St., 11230.
Waldron, John E., Bishop Mugavero Residence, 7200 Douglaston Pkwy., Douglaston, 11362.
White, Leo J., St. George's Cathedral, Westminster Bridge Rd., London SW1 7HY England.
Zeni, Dino M., Bishop Mugavero Residence, 7200 Douglaston Pkwy., Douglaston, 11362.
Revs.—
Anastasio, Thomas, St. Patrick, 9511 Fourth Ave., 11209.
Aufiero, Louis D., Holy Family Church, 175-20 74th Ave., Flushing, 11366.
Badia, Leonard F., Ph.D., 4810 N.W. 4th St., Apt. C, Delray Beach, FL 33445.
Bedoya, Hugo, St. John Vianney, 140-10 34th Ave., Flushing, 11354.
Berran, Donald M., Our Lady Queen of Martyrs Residence, 109-04 72nd Rd., Forest Hills, 11375.
Blauvelt, Robert, Bishop Mugavero Residence, 7200 Douglaston Pkwy., Douglaston, 11362.
Borzaga, Rinaldo, Manhattan College, Riverdale, 10471.
Boyle, Victor J., 15 Mackay Pl., Apt. 5E, 11209.
Brady, Edmund P., Our Lady of Mount Carmel, 23-25 Newtown Ave., Astoria, 11102.
Byrne, Hugh A., Bishop Mugavero Residence, 7200 Douglaston Pkwy., Douglaston, 11362.
Byrnes, Francis J., Bishop Mugavero Residence, 7200 Douglaston Pkwy., Douglaston, 11362.
Byrnes, John W., Bishop Mugavero Residence, 7200 Douglaston Pkwy., Douglaston, 11362.
Calder, Kenneth J., Our Lady of Angels, 7320 Fourth Ave., 11209.
Casey, Anthony C., Queen of Peace Residence, 110-30 221st St., Queens Village, 11429.
Cestaro, Joseph A., 111 W. 71st St., Apt. 11B, New York, 10023.
Charlot, Lucien, St. Augustine, 116 Sixth Ave., 11217.
Cheng, Thomas, J.C.D., M.A., Ozanam Hall, 42-41 201 St., Bayside, 11361.
Costello, Coleman J., Bishop Mugavero Residence, 7200 Douglaston Pkwy., Douglaston, 11362.
Cowan, George R., Bishop Mugavero Residence, 7200 Douglaston Pkwy., Douglaston, 11362.
Coyle, Eugene P., 7200 Douglaston Pkwy., Douglaston, 11362.
Cullinane, John F., P.E., Blessed Trinity, 204-25 Rockaway Point Blvd., Rockaway Point, 11697.
Cutrone, Dominick F., Our Lady of Grace, 430 Ave. W., 11223.
De Laura, Felice J., 81-23 189th St., Jamaica, 11423.
Dell'Anno, Anthony V., St. Edmund, 2060 Ocean Ave., 11229.
Denzer, Joseph W., Bishop Mugavero Residence, 7200 Douglaston Pkwy., Douglaston, 11362.
Devine, James T., 103-00 Shore Front Pkwy., Apt. 12R, Rockaway Park, 11694.
Diamond, Matthew J., St. Andrew Avellino, 35-60 158th St., Flushing, 11358.
Diffley, Patrick J., 8000 Shore Front Pkwy., Apt. 6B, Rockaway Beach, 11693.
Dolan, Joseph, Bishop Mugavero Residence, 7200 Douglaston Pkwy., Douglaston, 11362.
Dolan, Thomas D., 94-20 85th St., Ozone Park, 11416.
Donnelly, Eugene F., 25-02 80th St., Jackson Heights, 11370.
Doody, Cyril F., 27 Parkway Dr., Sag Harbor, 11963.

Dunne, James M., St. Camillus-St. Virgilius, 99-15 Rockaway Beach Blvd., Rockaway Beach, 11693.
Duran, Ernesto, Santa Beatriz 269, Apt. 503, Santiago 9, Chile.
Early, William F., 53-91 Outlook Point, San Diego, CA 92124.
Estrada, Sabino, 39-76 57th St., #3D, Woodside, 11377.
Fernando, Joachim (Sri Lanka), St. Pius X, 148-10 249 St., Rosedale, 11422.
Gallo, Vincent, 32 Beac 219th St., Breezy Point, 11697.
Grzelak, Thaddeus A.
Guarracino, Ralph, Mount Saint Mary Cemetery, 172-00 Booth Memorial Ave., Flushing, 11365.
Gural, Marion A., 123 Henry Rd., Southampton, 11968.
Guthrie, Alfred, St. Fidelis, 123-06 14th Ave., College Point, 11356.
Harth, Charles F., Queen of Peace Residence, 110-30 221 St., Queens Village, 11429.
Heffernan, James F., 146 Swan Lake, Poughkeepsie, 12605.
Keane, Edward M., 12534 Jasmine Dr., Fort Myers, FL 33908.
Kehoe, Charles B., Rose Garden Villa, Unit 202, 5510 S.W. 4th Pl., Cape Coral, FL 33914.
Kelly, Thomas F., Van Dyk Manor, 42 Mountain Ave., Montclair, NJ 07042.
Kennedy, Louis J., Bishop Mugavero Residence, 7200 Douglaston Pkwy., Douglaston, 11362.
Keohane, Daniel G., Our Lady of the Angelus, 63-63 98th St., Rego Park, 11374.
Kiernan, Edward J., 43 Highland Rd., Southampton, 11968.
Kirby, Martin F., M.A., Bishop Mugavero Residence, 7200 Douglaston Pkwy., Douglaston, 11362.
Kirrane, James A., Chapin Home for the Aging, 165-01 Chapin Pkwy., Jamaica, 11432.
Labita, Francis J., Our Lady Queen of Martyrs, 109-04 72nd Rd., Forest Hills, 11375.
Lang, Henry A., 56-15 213th St., Bayside Hills, 11364.
Leone, James M., 126 Laurelton Dr., P.O. Box 426, Mastic Beach, 11951.
Lutjen, George J., 71-08 72nd Pl., Glendale, 11385.
Lynch, Francis, Our Lady of Mt. Carmel, 23-25 Newtown Ave., Astoria, 11361.
Maloney, John P., 209-10 41st Ave., Apt. 2R, Bayside, 11361.
Mariano, John M., 1620 S. Ocean Blvd., Apt. 9N, Pompano Beach, FL 33062.
Matonti, Charles J., St. Columba, 2245 Kimball St., 11234.
Maynard, Lewis H., St. Agatha, 702 48th St., 11220.
McGovern, Eugene F., Bishop Mugavero Residence, 7200 Douglaston Pkwy., Douglaston, 11362.
McShane, John A., 7200 Douglaston Pkwy., Douglaston, 11362.
Meszaros, James J., St. Josaphat, 34-32 210th St., Bayside, 11361.
Mitchell, Walter A., St. Margaret Mary, 215 Exeter St., 11235.
Mulkerin, Terrence J., Holy Name of Jesus, 245 Prospect Park W., 11215.
Muthukatti, Thomas, St. Benedict Joseph Labre Church, 94-40 118th St., South Richmond Hill, 11419.
Nadine, Jerome E., 720 Kenney Way, Las Vegas, NV 89134.
Newell, John J., 94 Rose Ave., Floral Park, 11001.
Nolan, Joseph M., 115-58 222nd St., Cambria Heights, 11411.
O'Donoghue, Kevin J., Bishop Mugavero Residence, 7200 Douglaston Pkwy., Douglaston, 11362.
Ossa, Pedro N., St. Martin of Tours, 1288 Hancock St., 11221.
Parisi, Michael R., St. Kevin, 45-21 194th St., Flushing, 11358.
Pezzullo, Angelo B., Nativity of the Blessed Virgin Mary, 101-41 91st St., Ozone Park, 11416.
Pfundstein, George A., St. Ann, 142-30 58th Ave., Flushing, 11355.
Pomilio, Matthew J., 175-20 Wexford Ter., Jamaica, 11432.
Richards, Edward W., Bishop Mugavero Residence, 7200 Douglaston Pkwy., Douglaston, 11362.
Ros, Manuel, Our Lady of Sorrows, 104-11 37th Ave., Corona, 11368.
Sabatos, Daniel C., 7 Henry St., Bellows Falls, VT 05101.
Salerno, Emilio J., 118 Lake Emerald Dr. #104, Oakland Park, FL 33309.
Sans, Pablo, 136-06 87th Ave., Richmond Hill, 11416.
Schmidt, Jerome J., Bishop Mugavero Residence, 7200 Douglaston Pkwy., Douglaston, 11362.
Schmidt, Raymond F., 507 Barberry Ln., New Windsor, 12553.
Sheridan, Matthew W., Bishop Mugavero Residence, 7200 Douglaston Pkwy., Douglaston, 11362.
Smith, LeRoy J., P.O. Box 23, Old Chatham, 12136.
Sommermeyer, Gary H., 622 A. Heritage Village, Southbury, CT 06488.
Suran, Joaquin, St. Leo, 104-05 49th Ave., Flushing, 11368.
Termine, Vincent J., 3736 Bayview Ave., 11224.
Varano, Andrew R., 1238 Avenue V., 11229.
Vendetti, Michael A., 94-26 Sutter Ave., Ozone Park, 11417.
Verrengio, Rocco F., P.O. Box 61321, Staten Island, 10306.
Visich, Eduard C., 5510 N. Ocean Dr., Singer Island, FL 33404.
Vivona, Anthony, 388 Avenue S Apt. 2F, 11223-2955.
Wei, Luke, 2886 Fernley Dr. E., West Palm Beach, FL 33415.
Weiscopf, Daniel J., St. Mary Star of Sea & St. Gertrude, 1920 New Haven Ave., Far Rockaway, 11691.
White, Charles H., St. Mary Star of the Sea, 1920 New Haven Ave., Far Rockaway, 11691.
Wilkinson, John H., St. Brigid, 409 Linden St., 11237.
Wiseman, Joseph F., 46-02 Parsons Blvd., Flushing, 11355.
Zaccagnigno, Raffaele, Via Federico Paolini 115, Scala D. int. 11, 00122 Ostia Lido, Rome, Italy.
Zanon, Romano A., Sacred Heart, 83-17 78th Ave., Glendale, 11385.

Permanent Deacons:
Abundo, Roberto S., St. Teresa, Woodside
Agnant, Ronald Y., St. Therese of Lisieux, Brooklyn
Aigbojie, Edward A., St. Martin Porres, Brooklyn
Alayu, Perlito B., Diocese of Orlando
Alick, Alejandro, St. Jude, Brooklyn
Almodovar, Ismael, Diocese of Orlando
Alvarado, Jorge L., Our Lady of Perpetual Help, South Ozone Park
Alvarez, Felipe J., St. Joseph, Long Island City
Alvia, Humberto R., (Diocese of Venice)
Amore, Bryan J., St. Andrew Apostle, Brooklyn
Arcand, Dennis A., Diocese of Savannah
Aris, Anthony J., (Inactive)
Baez, Angel, (Inactive)
Barahona, Manuel S., Our Lady of Mount Carmel, Astoria
Barber, Christopher E., St. Clare, Rosedale
Barreneche, Julio C., St. Kevin, Flushing
Beaubrun, Berthal, St. Ignatius, Brooklyn
Bichotte, Joseph, St. Augustine, Brooklyn
Bobadilla, Antonio, St. Mary Star of the Sea, Far Rockaway
Borheck, Steven J., Our Lady of the Snows, N. Floral Park
Boursiquot, Jean B., (Retired)
Brainerd, Michael J., St. Margaret, Middle Village
Branch, LeRoy P., St. Paul & St. Agnes, Brooklyn
Breviario, Alexander, Our Lady of Grace, Howard Beach
Bugay, Josefino Y., (Inactive)
Caceres, Ycelso, (Inactive)
Cajiao, Henry, Diocese of St. Petersburg
Cajoux, Francois G., Sacred Heart Cambria Hts.
Calvo, Juan, (Retired)
Campisi, Joseph, (Retired)
Cancel, Edwin, Our Lady of the Angelus, Rego Park
Carattini, Juan M., (Leave of Absence)
Cardona, Ramon, Diocese of Mayaguez, PR
Casares, Gabriel, (Leave of Absence)
Castillo, Jorge L., St. Joan of Arc, Jackson Heights
Catanello, Joseph V., Holy Family, Flushing
Cederroth, Charles J., Diocese of Trenton
Cepin, Concepcion, St. Joseph Patron, Brooklyn
Chin, Paul M., St. Paul Chong Ha-Sang Chapel, Flushing
Ciccaroni, Andrew, St. Robert Bellarmine, Bayside
Ciorciari, David J., St. Stanislaus Kostka, Maspeth
Cobham, Jaime A., St. Paul & St. Agnes, Brooklyn
Coffey, John P., (Inactive)
Colandrea, Dante, St. Athanasius, Brooklyn
Colon, Rafael, (Inactive)
Contreras, Jose A., St. Thomas the Apostle, Woodhaven
Contreras, William de Jesus, Blessed Sacrament, Brooklyn
Coyle, Lawrence J., St. Columba, Brooklyn
Cruz, Florencio, St. Matthew, Brooklyn, Chap. Mary Immaculate Hosp., Jamaica
Cruz, Rafael, Archdiocese of Miami
Cruz, Ramon, St. Mary Gate of Heaven, Ozone Park
Cutter, Arthur, St. Gregory the Great, Bellerose
D'Accordo, Armand C., St. Helen, Howard Beach
D'Accordo, Frank J., Saint Bernard, Brooklyn
Da Costa, Dennis A., (Retired)
Damato, Stephen T., St. Sebastian, Woodside
Daniel, Gordon V., (Inactive)
Dass, Joseph H., St. Gerard Majella, Hollis
Davis, Thomas G., St. Anselm, Brooklyn
De Tucci, Frank A., Catholic Charities Office for Prison Ministry and Our Lady of Mt. Carmel, Astoria
DeBiase, Vincent, (Retired)
DeLeon, Andres, Our Lady of Mount Carmel, Brooklyn
DeMichele, Frank, St. Bernadette, Brooklyn
Deming, Everett A., (Retired)
Dennehy, John P., (Inactive)
Denzler, Joseph C., Our Lady of Lourdes, Queens Village
Deschler, Bernard M., (Retired)
Despeignes, Robinson, Incarnation, Queens Village
Devaney, Thomas J., Holy Name of Jesus, Brooklyn
Diaz, Rafael, (Retired)
Diaz, Ramon G., Immaculate Conception, Jamaica
Dixon, Gregory D., St. Andrew the Apostle, Brooklyn
Dolan, John G., St. Rosalia-Regina Pacis, Brooklyn
Donnelly, Daniel P., St. Fidelis, College Point
Dorsinville, Paul C., Sacred Heart, Cambria Heights
Dudley, Roy A., (Retired)
Duncan, Isaac, (Inactive)
Dupuy, Eulogio S., (Retired)
Duran, Fausto, P.D., St. Barbara, Brooklyn
Duran, Juan R., Archdiocese of Minneapolis
Elias, Raul S., Holy Child Jesus, Richmond Hill
Elijio, Victorino P., Our Lady of Mercy, Brooklyn
Elrose, Richard E., St. Helen, Howard Beach
Espinal, Luis J., (Diocese of Camden)
Favale, Anthony, St. Finbar, Brooklyn
Felix, Antoine, (Inactive)
Fernandez, Jose M., Queen of Peace, Kew Gardens Hills
Fernandez, Justo I., (Inactive)
Flaim, Fabio, (Retired)
Flannery, John A., (Retired)
Francis, John J., (Retired)
Gaine, Edward S., Our Lady of Angels, Brooklyn
Galazin, Stanley J., American Martyrs, Bayside, Dir. Immaculate Conception Center, Douglaston
Garamella, Robert, Diocese of Rockville Centre
Garcia, Jimmy, Our Lady of the Cenacle, Richmond Hill
George, Roy N., (Inactive)
Germain, Moliere, (Retired)
Gilligan, Richard J., St. Mary Gate of Heaven, Ozone Park
Gomez, Guillermo D., St. Gerard Majella, Hollis
Gonzales, Rafael, Diocese of Orlando
Gonzalez, Jorge A., Dir. Diaconate Formation Office
Gonzalez, Louis A., St. Paul & St. Agnes, Brooklyn
Gordon, Daniel, (Inactive)
Griffin, Arthur J., Transfiguration, Maspeth
Guster, Edward J., Jr., Nativity of the Blessed Virgin Mary, Ozone Park
Hernandez, Rafael, Diocese of Orlando
Hernandez, Wilfredo, Holy Spirit, Brooklyn
Hili, Saviour, St. Francis of Assisi, Long Island City
Horne, Wilfred N., St. Ephrem, Brooklyn
Huckemeyer, Edward J., (On Leave)
Hull, John E., St. Patrick, Brooklyn
Hynes, James R., Our Lady of the Miraculous Medal, Ridgewood
Innocent, Francois, (Retired)
Kandra, Gregory, Our Lady Queen of Martyrs, Forest Hills
Kennedy, James F., Diocese of St. Petersburg, FL
Knight, Lionel A., St. Nicholas of Tolentine, Jamaica
Krebs, Jerome H., (Retired)
Lacy, James J., St. Matthew, Brooklyn
LaGamba, Vincent M., St. Francis De Sales, Belle Harbor
LaGreca, John J., Our Lady of Guadalupe, Brooklyn
Landron, Jaime, (Retired)
Lavanco, Robert F., Our Lady of Hope, Middle Village
Lee, Richard G., (Retired)
Leon, Pedro V., St. Martin of Tours, Brooklyn
Licata, Salvatore V., (Retired)
Lima, Ramon, St. Raphael, Long Island City
Lizama, Jose Armanso, Presentation of the Blessed Virgin Mary, Jamaica
Logue, Patrick J., St. Rose of Lima, Rockaway Beech
Lonergan, Robert P., St. Andrew Avellino, Flushing
Lopez, Eduvigis, (Inactive)
Lopez, Hiram, Archdiocese of New York
Lopez, Marco V., St. Rita, Brooklyn
Magana, Daniel, Our Lady of Sorrows, Corona
Maldonado, Andres, Diocese of Ponce, PR
Malone, William F., Diocese of Trenton, NJ
Maloney, James E., St. Pancras, Glendale
Marcel, Magloire, St. Jerome, Brooklyn
Marchello, Andrew A., (Retired)
Marley, Daniel J., Our Lady of Solace, Brooklyn
Marte, Rafael, St. Mary Mother of the Church, Brooklyn
Martinez, Carlos A., All Saints, Brooklyn

Martinez, German, Transfiguration, Brooklyn
Martinez, Manuel I., St. Benedict Joseph Labre, Richmond Hill
Martucci, Anthony P., St. Bernadette, Brooklyn
Mateo, Francis G., St. Finbar, Brooklyn
Mayers, Winston M., (Retired)
Mazza, Nicholas, (Retired)
McBride, Timothy, St. Mary Gate of Heaven, Ozone Park
McGreevey, John F., (Retired), St. John Vianney, Flushing
McGuire, Joseph P., (Retired)
McNamara, William, Sacred Heart, Bayside
Medina, Gustavo, St. Catharine of Alexandria, Brooklyn
Mejia, Abdon (Peru), (Retired)
Mejia, Julio C., St. Michael, Brooklyn
Mejia, Rafael A., Diocese of Orlando
Mellace, Carlo V., St. Dominic, Brooklyn
Miller, Leon F., (Diocese of San Jose, CA)
Miranda, Osborne, St. Fortunata, Brooklyn
Montalvo, Hector, (Inactive)
Montero, Adalberto, St. Mary Star of Sea & St. Gertrude, Far Rockaway
Montes, Leopoldo R, Blessed Virgin Mary Help of Christians, Woodside
Morales, Julio A., Diocese of Orlando
Moreno, Ricardo, Our Lady of Lourdes, Queens Village
Morin, Paul P., St. Dominic, Brooklyn
Moss, Michael C., St. Mary Star of the Sea, Far Rockaway
Mule, Lawrence C., St. Matthias, Ridgewood
Munoz, Franklin G., Incarnation, Queens Village
Murillo, Julio C., Our Lady of Angelus, Rego Park
Murphy, John J., (Retired)
Noble, James D., Immaculate Heart of Mary, Brooklyn
O'Connell, Edward F., Our Lady of Mount Carmel, Brooklyn
Occhiuto, Joseph J., (Inactive)
Oellinger, Matthew J., Our Lady of the Snows, North Floral Park
Oggeri, William, (Retired)
Olivas, Pascual B., St. Bonaventure, Jamaica
Orlandello, John P., St. Francis of Paola, Brooklyn
Oviedo, Jose L., St. Sylvester, Brooklyn
Panessa, Giacomo, Most Precious Blood, Astoria
Panico, Louis J., St. Teresa of Avila, South Ozone Park
Park, Julio, (Retired)
Park, Kyuchon J., (Inactive)
Pascal, Orlando, Archdiocese of NY
Paul, Ernst, Our Lady of Miracles, Brooklyn
Pavlyshin, Peter, (Diocese of Venice)
Perez, Richard, (Retired)
Pierre-Antoine, Clemenceau, Incarnation, Queens Village
Pons, Ramon C., St. Rosalia-Regina Pacis, Brooklyn
Postler, Charles A., St. Patrick, Brooklyn
Pouso, Roberto J., (Inactive)
Rameau, Jean J., St. Therese of Lisieux, Brooklyn
Ramirez, Manuel, (Inactive)
Ramos, James, (Inactive)
Ramos, Jose A., (Diocese of Orlando)
Reichert, John P., St. Fidelis, College Point
Reyes, Ricardo, Our Lady of the Presentation, Brooklyn
Ritchie, Frederick V., St. Columba, Brooklyn
Rivera, Angel R., St. Benedict Joseph Labre, Richmond Hill
Rivera, Hector R., Archdiocese of San Juan, PR
Rizzo, Giovanni A., (Retired)
Rizzuto, Ronald, St. Edmund, Brooklyn
Roberts, Lionel V., Diocese of St. Petersburg, FL
Rodriguez, Daniel R., Immaculate Conception, Jamaica
Rodriguez, Manuel L., St. Elizabeth, Ozone Park
Roman, Luis A., SS. Peter & Paul, Brooklyn
Ronacher, Ronald M., St. Rita, Brooklyn
Rosa, Andres, St. Rita, Brooklyn
Rosario, Israel, Transfiguration, Brooklyn
Ruiz, José D., Diocese of Ponce, PR
Ruoff, James F., Blessed Trinity, Rockaway Point
Russo, Anthony J., (Retired)
Ryan, Kevin F., (Retired)
Saldana, Albert, Our Lady of Light, St. Albans
Sampson, Harold S., St. Rose of Lima, Rockaway Beach
Sands, John E., St. Matthias, Ridgewood
Sawney, Ira, Florida
Sclafani, Leonard A., Holy Trinity, Whitestone
Sencion, Eduardo, Our Lady of the Cenacle, Richmond Hill
Siani, Philip J., Our Lady of Grace, Brooklyn
Siavichay, Ruben G., St. Anthony of Padua, South Ozone Park
Simon, Mauclair, St. Therese of Lisieux, Brooklyn
Sinisi, Henry C., (On Leave)
Smith, Charles J., Diocese of Trenton
Smith, Henry J., (Retired)
Smith, Nathaniel J., St. Clement Pope, South Ozone Park
Smith, Ramon, (On Leave)
Smolinski, Edward A., (Retired)
Soraire, Martin D., St. Teresa, Woodside
Soto, Jesus, Our Lady of Perpetual Help, Brooklyn
Stamm, Peter, Sacred Heart, Glendale
Stucchio, Anthony, St. Ephrem, Brooklyn
Sucich, John R., St. Francis of Assisi, Long Island City
Svebel, Harry A., (Retired)
Taylor, Luis C., Our Lady of Light, St. Albans
Thompson, Balfour A., St. Martin de Porres, Brooklyn
Tierney, John A., Diocese of Albany
Tineo, Jose F., Our Lady of Sorrows, Corona
Tokarcsik, George M., Pennsylvania
Torres, Abel, Holy Name, Brooklyn
Torres, Freddy, Our Lady of Light, St. Albans
Trochez, Carlos A., Corpus Christi, Woodside
Troy, Michael J., Help of Christians, Brooklyn
Tully, Dean T., Holy Child Jesus, Richmond Hill
Uzoigwe, Okafor C., St. Fortunata, Brooklyn
Valderrana, Carlos, St. Cecilia, Brooklyn
Valle Valle, Esteban, Archdiocese of San Juan, PR
Van de Ven, Theodore, Diocese of Rockville Centre
Van Wassenhove, Raymond J., Diocese of Peoria
Varela, Jamie, (Assistant to the Bishop), Our Lady of the Presentation & Our Lady of Loreto, Brooklyn
Vargas, Juan R., (Diocese of Orlando)
Vicinanza, Michael W., (Dean of Diaconate Formation), Immaculate Conception, Douglaston
Warren, John, Our Lady of the Snows, Floral Park
Williams, Lee C., (Retired)
Williamsen, William, (Retired)
Yepes, Elias H., St. Michael, Flushing
Zeuner, Robert J., St. Gregory the Great, Bellerose
Zhagnay, Juan J., Corpus Christi, Woodside
Zimmermann, Walter C., (Retired)

INSTITUTIONS LOCATED IN THE DIOCESE

[A] PASTORAL CENTERS

DOUGLASTON. *Immaculate Conception Center* (1968) 7200 Douglaston Pkwy., 11362-1997. Tel: 718-281-9526; Fax: 718-229-2658. Email: sgalazin@iccdob.org. Web: www.iccdouglaston.org. Deacon Stanley J. Galazin, Dir.; Mr. Howard Maresca, Asst. Dir. Bldg. Svcs. & Maintenance.

[B] SEMINARIES, DIOCESAN

DOUGLASTON. *Cathedral Seminary Residence of the Immaculate Conception*, 7200 Douglaston Pkwy., 11362. Tel: 718-229-8001; Fax: 718-281-9536. Rev. Msgrs. Robert J. Thelen, Rector; Conrad R. Dietz (RVC), Philosophy Prof. (Retired); Revs. Fred Marano, B.A., M.A., Spiritual Dir.; Marc E. Swartvagher, S.T.L., Academic Dean, Philosophy Prof.; Rev. Msgr. John E. Waldron, Adjunct Spiritual Dir. (Retired); Very Rev. Joseph G. Fonti, S.T.L., Assoc. Spiritual Dir.; Dr. Glenn Carrozza, J.C.D., Adjunct Prof. in Canon Law. Residence for college level and post college level candidates for Priesthood. Priests 4; Lay Teachers 3; Seminarians 28.

ELMHURST. *Cathedral Preparatory Seminary of the Immaculate Conception*, 56-25 92nd St., 11373. Tel: 718-592-6800; Fax: 718-592-5574. Email: frmarano@cathedralprepseminary.com. Revs. Fred Marano, B.A., M.A., Rector & Prin.; John P. Cush, B.A., S.T.L., Spiritual Dir. & Dir. Recruitment; Rev. Msgr. James J. Cooney, B.A., M.A., Asst. Spiritual Dir. (Retired); Rev. Kevin P. Abels, B.A., M.Div., Assoc. Vocation Dir. & Catholic High Schools Liaison. Priests 4; Sisters 1; Lay Teachers 14; Seminarians 163.

[C] SEMINARIES, RELIGIOUS

BRONX. *St. Alphonsus Formation Residence, Redemptorist Formation Residence Immaculate Conception Rectory*, 389 E. 150th St., 10455-2796. Tel: 718-292-6970. Email: safrny@yahoo.com. Web: www.redemptorists.net. Revs. Patrick A. Keyes, C.Ss.R., Rector & Dir. of Formation; Tat Hoang, C.Ss.R., Denver Province Co-Vocation Dir.; Bro. Larry Lujan, C.Ss.R., Denver Province Co-Vocation Dir. Priests 7; Brothers 3; Students 13. In Res. Revs. Alex Ortiz, C.Ss.R.; Richard Schiblin, C.Ss.R.

[D] COLLEGES AND UNIVERSITIES

BROOKLYN. **St. Francis College*, 180 Remsen St., 11201. Tel: 718-489-5309; Fax: 718-624-6692. Web: www.stfranciscollege.edu. Brendan J. Dugan, Pres.; James Smith, Librarian. Brothers 4; Sisters 1; Students 2,511; Total Staff 80.

**St. Joseph's College*, 245 Clinton Ave., 11205. Tel: 718-940-5300; Fax: 718-636-7245. Email: fburns@sjcny.edu. Web: www.sjcny.edu. Under supervision of Board of Trustees. Priests 1; Sisters 4; Lay Teachers 47; Students 1,359; Total Staff 51.

Branch Campus, 155 W. Roe Blvd., Patchoque, 11772. Tel: 631-687-5100; Fax: 631-654-1782. Web: www.sjcny.edu. Sisters Elizabeth A. Hill, C.S.J., M.A., J.D., Pres.; Mary Florence Burns, C.S.J., Ph.D., Asst. to Pres.; Nancy J. Connors, M.S., Vice Pres. Institute Advancement; John Roth, M.B.A., CFO; Joseph Spadaro, M.A., M.S., CIO; Sisters Loretta McGrann, C.S.J., Ph.D., Provost; Margaret Buckley, C.S.J., Ed.D., Academic Dean, School of Arts & Sciences, Brooklyn Campus; Katerina Andriotis-Baitinger, Ph.D., Academic Dean, School of Arts & Sciences, Patchogue Campus; Thomas G. Travis, Ph.D., Vice Pres. & Dean, School of Professional Graduate Educ.; William Meng, Ph.D., Dir., McEntegart Library. Priests 1; Sisters 15; Lay Teachers 152; Students 4,365.

QUEENS. *St. John's University* (1870) 8000 Utopia Pkwy., 11439. Tel: 718-990-6161; Fax: 718-990-5723. Email: admhelp@stjohns.edu. Web: www.stjohns.edu. Rev. Donald J. Harrington, C.M., B.A., M.Div., Th. M., Pres. Sponsored by the Vincentian Priests and Brothers Eastern Province of the Congregation of the Mission. Priests 7; Sisters 2; Lay Teachers 687; Queens Campus Enrollment 17,135; Total Enrollment (Undergraduate and Graduate of Queens, Staten Island Campuses and Rome) 20,109.

Officers of Administration: Dr. James P. Pellow, Exec. Vice Pres. & COO; Dr. Julia A. Upton, R.S.M., Provost; Dr. Tony H. Bonaparte, Ph.D., Special Asst. to Pres.; Rev. Patrick J. Griffin, C.M., B.S., M.Div., Th.M, M.A., Ph.D., Exec. Vice Pres. Mission & Branch Campuses; Cecilia S. Chang, Ed.D., Vice Pres. Intl. Rels.; John P. Connolly Jr., Vice Pres. & Dir. Oakdale Location; Michael A. Simons, Dean Law School; Dr. Jeffrey Fagen, Dean, St. John's College; Dr. Dorothy E. Habben, Ph.D., Vice Pres. & Univ. Sec.; Mary Harper Hagan, Senior Vice Pres. Human Resources & Strategic Planning IR; Dr. Steven D. Papamarcos, Dean, Tobin College of Business; Thomas Lawrence, Vice Pres. Public Safety; Dr. Kathleen Voute MacDonald, Dean, College of Professional Studies; Rev. James J. Maher, C.M., B.A., M.Div., D.Min., Vice Pres. Student Affairs & Exec. Dir.-VISA; Dr. Robert Mangione, Dean, College of Pharmacy & Allied Health Professions; Dr. Jerrold Ross, Dean, School of Educ.; Joseph A. Sciame, Vice Pres. Community Rels.; Robert Wile, Vice Pres., Chief of Staff to Pres., & Chief Advancement Officer; Dr. Andre McKenzie, Vice Pres. Academic Support Svcs; Jacqueline Travisano, Assoc. Vice Pres. & Acting Chief Fin. Officer; Anthony R. Pacheco, Vice Pres. & Chief of Staff; Dr. Clover Hall, Vice Pres. Inst. Research & Academic Planning; Theresa Maylone, Univ. Librarian.

Bread & Life Soup Kitchen, 75 Lewis Ave., 11206. Tel: 718-574-0058. Larry Gile, Dir.; Rev. James J. Maher, C.M., B.A., M.Div., D.Min., Pres.

[E] CAMPUS MINISTRY

Campus Ministers and Ministry Centers 250 Cathedral Pl., 11201. Tel: 718-852-4002. Rev. Msgr. John Strynkowski, Vicar Higher Educ.; Revs. Richard E. Long. Tel: 718-434-1900 Brooklyn College; Paul A. Wood. Tel: 718-793-3130 Queens College; Stephen P. Lynch, Pratt Institute of Technology; Charles P. Keeney. Tel: 718-488-3359 Long Island University; Bro. Thomas Grady, O.S.F. Tel: 718-489-5345 St. Francis College; Revs. Michael G. Tedone. Tel: 718-423-0002 Queensborough Community College; James Mahar St. John's University; Sr. Susan Wilcox, C.S.J., St. Joseph X College; Revs. Kevin P. Cavalluzzi. Tel: 718-522-2105 Polytechnic University & NY Technical College; Martin Esguerra-Lopez, Id.M. Tel: 718-361-1884 La Guardia Community College; York College. Legal Titles & Corporations: Newman Apostolate, Inc.

[F] CATHOLIC EDUCATION OFFICES

BROOKLYN. *Office of Faith Formation*, 7200 Douglaston Pkwy., Douglaston, 11362. Tel: 718-281-9544. Email: pfranco@rcdob.org. Web: www.dioceseofbrooklyn.org/OFF. Dr. Philip Franco, Diocesan Dir. Tel: 718-281-9545; Sr. Alice Michael, S.U.S.C., Coord. Childhood Faith Formation. Tel: 718-281-9583; Mrs. Ana Puente,

Coord. Marriage & Family Ministry. Tel: 718-281-9543; Mrs. Mayra Reyes, Admin. Asst. Tel: 718-281-9544; Ms. Iris Flores, Pre-Cana Registration Sec. Tel: 718-281-9540.

DOUGLASTON. *Office of the Superintendent of Schools*, 7200 Douglaston Pkwy., 11362. Tel: 718-281-9650. Web: www.dioceseofbrooklyn.org/catholic-ed. Thomas Chadzutko, Ed.D., Supt. Priests 14; Brothers 43; Sisters 117; Lay Teachers 2,864; Total Enrollment 48,269.

Diocese of Brooklyn Education Offices Legal Titles & Corporations: Department of Education, Diocese of Brooklyn; Henry M. Hald High School Association; Saint John's Preparatory School, Brooklyn.

[G] HIGH SCHOOLS, DIOCESAN

BROOKLYN. *Bishop Loughlin Memorial High School*, 357 Clermont Ave., 11238. Tel: 718-857-2700; Fax: 718-398-4227. Email: dcronin@blmhs.org. Web: www.bishoploughlin.org. Bro. Dennis Cronin, F.S.C., Pres.; James Dorney, Prin.; Nancy McKeever, Asst. Prin.; Nicole Maxwell, Dean; John Flack, Dean. (Coed); Legal Corp.: Henry M. Hald Assoc. Brothers of the Christian Schools 4; Sisters 2; Lay Teachers 50; Students 876.

[H] HIGH SCHOOLS, PRIVATE

BROOKLYN. *Bishop Ford Central Catholic High School*, 500 19th St., 11215. Tel: 718-360-2500; Fax: 718-360-2595. Email: brancato11@aol.com. Web: www.bishopfordhs.org. Mr. Raymond P. Nash, Pres.; Mr. Frank V. Brancato, Prin.; Mr. Rocco V. Grella, Asst. Prin.; Mr. Sam Sued, Asst. Prin.; Mrs. Marta Gut, Librarian. (Coed) Brothers 4; Sisters 4; Lay Teachers 63; Students 1,000.

Bishop Kearney High School, 2202 60th St., 11204-2599. Tel: 718-236-6363; Fax: 718-236-7784. Email: thomasine@bishopkearneyhs.org. Web: www.bishopkearneyhs.org. Sisters Thomasine Stagnitta, C.S.J., Prin.; Barbara Lynch, C.S.J., Librarian. (Girls) Priests 1; Sisters of St. Joseph (Brentwood Community) 20; Lay Teachers 35; Students 674.

Catherine McAuley, 710 E. 37th St., 11203. Tel: 718-462-7282; Fax: 718-462-7284. Sr. Margaret Dempsey, R.S.M., Pres.; Ms. Peggy Lake, Co-Prin.; Ms. Josephine Valente, Co-Prin.; Ms. Eileen Gallo, Librarian. (Girls) Sisters of Mercy 3; Lay Teachers 15; Students 200.

Fontbonne Hall Academy, 9901 Shore Rd., 11209. Tel: 718-748-2244; Fax: 718-745-3841. Email: crepeau@fontbonne.org. Web: www.fontbonne.org. Sisters Dolores F. Crepeau, C.S.J., Prin.; Margaret Kelly, C.S.J., Librarian. (Girls) Sisters of St. Joseph (Brentwood Community) 8; Lay Teachers 38; Students 540.

St. Joseph, 80 Willoughby St., 11201-5265. Tel: 718-624-3618; Fax: 718-624-2792. Email: admin@sjhsbridge.org. Web: www.sjhsbridge.org. Sr. Joan Gallagher, C.S.J., Prin.; Mrs. Miranda Cruz, Librarian. (Girls) Sisters of St. Joseph (Brentwood Community) 7; Other Religious 2; Lay Teachers 27; Students 280.

Lourdes Academy Cristo Rey, 11 DeSales Pl., 11207. Tel: 718-455-3555; Fax: 718-455-3556. Robert Catell, Bd. Chm.; Maureen Reiser, Pres.; Roger Diaz, Dir. Corp. Work Study; Marie Bathemy-Larotte, Dir. Admissions; Cheryl Malcovso, Prin.; Keisha Baptiste, Dean. Lay Teachers 7.

Nazareth Regional, 475 E. 57th St., 11203. Tel: 718-763-1100, Ext. 229; Fax: 718-629-5382. Web: www.nazarethrhs.org. Barbara Gil, Prin.; Kristine Liberto, Librarian. (Coed) Brothers 1; Lay Teachers 25; Students 460.

Xaverian, 7100 Shore Rd., 11209. Tel: 718-836-7100; Fax: 718-836-7114. Email: ralesi@xaverian.org. Web: www.xaverian.org. Mr. Robert Alesi, Pres.; Deacon Kevin McCormack, Prin.; Mr. Michael Wilson, Dean Students; Mr. Robert Oliva, Dir. of Alumni Affairs; Ms. Vincenza Milkie, Librarian; Ms. Maria Rodriguez, Dir. Guidance; Ms. Sandra Mummolo, Dean Faculty. (Boys) Priests 1; Xaverian Brothers 3; Deacons 2; Lay Teachers 113; Students 1,369.

Queens

ASTORIA

St. John Preparatory School (1870) 21-21 Crescent St., 11105-3398. Tel: 718-721-7200; Fax: 718-545-9385. Web: www.stjohnsprepschool.org. Mr. William A. Higgins, B.A., M.A., M.S., Prin.; Revs. James Rodriguez, Chap.; Peter Ngyen, C.S.J.B., Chap.; Valerie Bove, Librarian. (Coed) Priests 2; Sisters 3; Lay Teachers 55; Students 1,000.

BRIARWOOD

Archbishop Molloy, 83-53 Manton St., 11435. Tel: 718-441-2100; Fax: 718-849-8251. Email: president@molloyhs.org. Web: www.molloyhs.org. John P. Sherry, Pres.; Bro. Thomas Schady, F.M.S., Prin. (Coed) Brothers 14; Sisters 2; Lay Teachers 68; Students 1,530.

COLLEGE POINT

St. Agnes Academic, 13-20 124 St., 11356-1814. Tel: 718-353-6276; Fax: 718-353-6068. Email: jmartin@stagneshs.org. Web: stagneshs.org. Sr. Joan Martin, O.P., Prin.; Mrs. Darlene O'Neill-Gerasoulis, Librarian. (Girls) Sisters of St. Dominic (Amityville) 11; Lay Teachers 22; Students 321.

EAST ELMHURST

Monsignor McClancy (1956) 71-06 31st Ave., 11370. Tel: 718-898-3800; Fax: 718-898-3929. Bro. Joseph Holthaus, S.C., Pres.; Mr. James P. Carey, Prin. (Boys) Priests 1; Brothers 12; Sisters 1; Lay Teachers 30; Boys 539.

FLUSHING

Holy Cross High School (1955) 26-20 Francis Lewis Blvd., 11358. Tel: 718-886-7250; Fax: 718-886-7257. Email: info@holycrosshs.org. Web: www.holycrosshs.org. Bro. Stephen LaMendola, C.S.C., Pres.; Mr. Joseph Giannuzzi, Prin.; Mrs. Denise Fox, Librarian. (Boys) Brothers of Holy Cross 7; Lay Teachers 55; Students 890.

FRESH MEADOWS

St. Francis Preparatory School, 6100 Francis Lewis Blvd., 11365. Tel: 718-423-8810; Fax: 718-224-2108. Email: 21stcentury@sfponline.org. Web: www.sfponline.org. Bro. Leonard Conway, O.S.F., Prin.; Rev. William F. Sweeney, Chap.; Mr. Frank Trubiano, Librarian. (Coed) Priests 1; Franciscan Brothers 6; Sisters 8; Lay Teachers 143; Students 2,653; Personnel 31.

JAMAICA ESTATES

The Mary Louis Academy (College Preparatory), 176-21 Wexford Ter., 11432. Tel: 718-297-2120; Fax: 718-739-0037. Web: www.tmla.org. Sr. Kathleen McKinney, C.S.J., Prin.; Mrs. Marie Whelan, Librarian. (Girls) Sisters of St. Joseph (Brentwood Community) 20; Lay Teachers 67; Students 944.

MIDDLE VILLAGE

Christ the King Regional High School, 68-02 Metropolitan Ave., 11379. Tel: 718-366-7400; Fax: 718-366-1165. Email: info@ctkrhs.org. Web: www.ctkrhs.org. Michael W. Michel, Pres.; Peter J. Mannarino, Prin.; Veronica Arbitello, Asst. Prin.; Maria Spagnuolo-Cordoba, Asst. Prin.; Rebecca Tibbetts, Asst. Prin.; Carolann Timpone, Asst. Prin.; Mr. Steven Giusto, Dir. Admissions; Marie Weisner, Librarian. (Coed) Sisters 1; Lay Teachers 51; Students 1,100.

ROCKAWAY PARK

Stella Maris High School, Beach 112th St., 11694. Tel: 718-634-4994; Fax: 718-634-5267. Email: gmartinez@stellamarishigh.org. Web: www.stellamarishs.org. Miss Geri Martinez, Prin. Tel: 718-634-4994; Fax: 718-634-5267. (Girls) Sisters of St. Joseph (Brentwood) 7; Brothers 1; Lay Teachers 35; Students 300.

[I] HIGH SCHOOLS PAROCHIAL

BROOKLYN. *Denis Maloney Institute/St. Edmund Preparatory High School*, 2474 Ocean Ave., 11229. Tel: 718-743-6100; Fax: 718-743-5243. Email: principal@stedmundprep.org. Web: www.stedmundprep.org. Mr. John P. Lorenzetti, Prin.; Kevin Raphael, Asst. Prin. (Coed) Sisters 1; Lay Teachers 45; Students 753.

St. Saviour High School, 588 6th St., 11215. Tel: 718-768-4406; Fax: 718-369-2688. Email: belanger.sv@stsaviour.org. Web: www.stsaviour.org. Sisters Valeria Belanger, S.S.N.D., Prin.; Mary Peter Colantuoni, S.S.N.D., Librarian; Mrs. Margaret Bernstein, Asst. Prin. (Girls) Priests 1; Sisters 3; Lay Teachers 31; Students 268.

[J] SPECIAL SCHOOLS

BROOKLYN. *St. Catherine Laboure Special Education Program*, Dept. of Educ., 21 Bay 11th St., 11228. Tel: 718-256-2605; Fax: 718-449-1607. Web: www.dioceseofbrooklyn.org. Mr. William E. Slow, Assoc. Supt. Program for mentally challenged students ages 5-21 and learning disabled students grades 6-8. Lay Teachers and Staff 45; Students 95.

St. Francis de Sales School for the Deaf (1960) 260 Eastern Pkwy., 11225. Tel: 718-636-4573; Fax: 718-636-4577. Email: school@sfdesales.org. Web: www.sfdesales.org. Edward McCormack, M.A., Supt. Infant through Elementary Grades (8th Grade). Sisters 2; Lay Teachers 39; Students 100.

St. Francis De Sales School for the Deaf Development Fund, 260 Eastern Pkwy., 11225. Tel: 718-636-4573; Fax: 718-636-4577. Email: school@sfdesales.org.

Ryken Educational Center, Inc., 7100 Shore Rd., 11209. Tel: 718-836-7100; Fax: 718-836-7714. Email: sferrara@xaverian.org. Dr. Carol Trasborg, Pres.

SPRINGFIELD GARDENS. *Martin de Porres School*, 136-25 218th St., 11413-2226. Tel: 718-525-3414; Fax: 718-525-0982. Email: mdpschool@metrocon.com. Web: www.mdp.org. Bro. Raymond R. Blixt, F.S.C., M.A., Exec. Dir.; Mr. Eon Parks, Prin. Specialized day school for emotionally challenged children, ages 6-21. Brothers 5; Administrators 15; Teachers 45; Asst. Teachers 45; Classroom Aides 45; Residential Case Workers 24; Counselors 35; Support Personnel 40; Total Staff 250; Capacity 480.

Additional Sites:

Martin de Porres High School, 147-65 249th St., Rosedale, 11422. Tel: 718-525-5550; Fax: 718-525-5440. Ms. Karel Lancaster, Prin.

Martin de Porres Academy for Career Development, 621 Elmont Rd., Elmont, 11003. Tel: 516-616-0580; Fax: 516-616-0582. Mr. David Robinson, Prin.

Martin de Porres Group Residence, 101-25 104th St., Ozone Park, 11416. Tel: 718-850-0191; Fax: 718-850-0192. Mr. Alan Karpf, Residence Dir. Day & residential school for emotionally challenged youth.

[K] ELEMENTARY SCHOOLS PRIVATE

BROOKLYN. *Brooklyn Jesuit Prep* (2003) 560 Sterling Pl., 11238. Tel: 718-638-5884; Fax: 718-638-5284. Web: www.nynativity.org. Rev. Jack Podsiadlo, S.J., Pres.; Emily Seelaus, Prin.; Ms. Patricia Gauvey, Librarian. Priests 2; Lay Teachers 9; Students 74.

Visitation Academy, 8902 Ridge Blvd., 11209. Tel: 718-680-9452; Fax: 718-680-4441. Email: dobsc261@impresso.com. Web: www.visitationacademy.net. Sr. Mary Pauline Baulis, V.H.M., R.N., Supr. & Pres.; Mrs. Arlene Figaro, Prin. Sisters of the Visitation 5; Lay Teachers 13; Girls 179.

[L] CONSOLIDATED ELEMENTARY SCHOOLS (REGIONAL)

BROOKLYN. *St. Elizabeth Seton*, 751 Knickerbocker Ave., 11221. Tel: 718-386-4050; Fax: 718-386-1565. Email: dobsc137@connectinc.com. Louise McNamara, Prin. Consolidated from Fourteen Holy Martyrs and St. Martin of Tours Lay Teachers 14; Students 179.

St. Frances Cabrini School, 181 Suydam St., 11221. Tel: 718-386-9277; Fax: 718-386-9064. Email: mariacrifasi@aol.com. Miss Maria Crifasi, Prin. Lay Teachers 12; Students 307.

Saints Joseph & Dominic Catholic Academy of Williamsburg, 140 Montrose Ave., 11206. Tel: 718-384-1101; Fax: 718-384-6567. Email: ssjdacademy@ssjda.org. Evette Ngadi, Prin. Lay Teachers 11; Students 277.

St. Michael (1864) 237 Jerome St., 11207. Tel: 718-277-6766; Fax: 718-348-0513. Email: info@stmichael-bklyn.org. Sr. Margaret Merritt, O.P., Prin. Sisters 1; Lay Teachers 13; Students 268.

Midwood Catholic Academy, 1501 Hendrickson St., 11234. Tel: 718-377-1800; Fax: 718-377-6374. Web: www.midwoodcatholicacademy.org. Mrs. Elena Heimbach, Prin. Lay Teachers 13; Students 369.

OZONE PARK. *Divine Mercy Catholic Academy*, 101-60 92nd St., 11416. Tel: 718-845-3074; 718-845-3188; Fax: 718-845-5068; 718-835-9447. Web: www.dmcacademy.com. Sr. Francis Marie Wystepek, C.S.F.N., Prin.; Ms. Linda Coyne, Librarian. Elementary Campus N-5; Middle School Campus 6-8.

[M] CATHOLIC CHARITIES

BROOKLYN. *Catholic Charities*, Central Office, 191 Joralemon St., 11201. Tel: 718-722-6000; Fax: 718-722-6096. Email: lhunte@ccbq.org. Web: www.ccbq.org. Most Rev. Nicholas A. DiMarzio, Ph.D., D.D.; Rev. Msgr. Alfred P. LoPinto, V.E., Episcopal Vicar for Human Svcs.; Mr. Robert Siebel, M.S.W., CEO; Sr. Ellen Patricia Finn, O.P., M.Ed., L.M.S.W., Deputy Exec. Dir.; Alan Wolinetz, C.F.O.; Emmie Glynn Ryan, Esq., Dir. Legal Affairs & Chief Compliance Officer; Thaddeus B. Taberski, M.S.W., M.B.A., Exec. Dir. Catholic Charities Neighborhood Services, Inc.; Donna Corrado, Exec. Sec. & COO-Catholic Charities Neighborhood Services, Inc.; Gladys Rodriguez, C.S.W., Vice Pres. Family Svcs.; Robert Marquez, Vice Pres. Early Childhood Svcs.; Janice Aris, Vice Pres. Developmental Disabilities; Patricia Bowles, Vice Pres. Behavioral Svcs., Chief Privacy Officer; Judith Kleve, Vice Pres. Svcs. for Older Adults; Mary O'Reilly, Admin. Family Svcs.; Rev. Peter Mahoney, Assoc. Dir. Evaluation; Anne Fitzgerald, Ph.D., Dir. Quality Assurance; Barbara Conley, M.S.W., Planning & Child Welfare Liaison; John Tynan, M.U.P., Dir. Housing Devel.; Nina Valmonte, Dir. Parish & Community Svcs. and Campaign for Human Devel.; Jacqueline Gibbons, Dir. Human Resources; Patrick Mahon, Dir. Computer Svcs.; Catherine Nicolini, Ph.D., Dir. Training; Richard Abrahamsen, Controller; Frank Paterno, Chief Information Officer & Chief Security Officer;

Sr. Ellen Patricia Finn, O.P., M.Ed., L.M.S.W., Pres. Tel: 718-722-6050.

Parish & Community Outreach & Services, 191 Joralemon St., 7th Fl., 11201. Tel: 718-722-6115. Nina Valmonte, Assoc. Dir. The Catholic Charities Community Centers provide outreach to and support for parishes and communities, direct social services, and open the door to the Catholic Charities network of programs & services. Direct Services: emergency food; limited financial assistance; support groups; GED/English as a Second Language; advocacy for public benefits; case management; immigration informatioin & referral; and employment counseling. Outreach: parish/cluster pastoral planning; sharing Catholic Social Teaching; community organizing; and leadership development.

Brooklyn East Community Center, 191 Joralemon St., 11201. Tel: 718-722-6001; Fax: 718-722-6254. Erin Carman, Community Center Dir.; Cristina Grisham, Community Project Dir. Tel: 718-722-6109. Caseworkers are out-stationed in various neighborhoods in Brooklyn East. Call for the nearest mobile site.

Brooklyn West Community Center, 191 Joralemon St., 1st Fl., 11201. Tel: 718-722-6001; Fax: 718-722-6254. Erin Carman, Community Center Dir.; Sara Suman, Community Project Dir. Tel: 718-722-6046.

Our Lady of Angels Human Service Center, 336 73rd St., 11209. Tel: 718-680-6344; Fax: 718-680-0331.

Queens North Community Center, 23-40 Astoria Blvd., Astoria, 11102. Tel: 718-726-9790; Fax: 718-728-8817. Debbie Hampson, Community Center Dir.; Josefa Castro, Community Project Dir.

Queens South Community Center, 90-39 189th St., Hollis, 11423. Tel: 718-217-1238; Fax: 718-479-8791. Debbie Hampson, Community Center Dir.; Jason Soto, Community Project Dir.

Rockaway Food Pantry, 307 Beach 37th St., Far Rockaway, 11691. Tel: 718-217-1238.

Advocate for Persons with Disabilities Services, 191 Joralemon St., 7th Fl., 11201. Tel: 718-722-6232. Rev. James P. Bradley, Program Coord.

Bereavement Services, 191 Joralemon St., 7th Fl., 11201. Tel: 718-722-6214. Ingrid Seunarine, Dir. Co-sponsored by Catholic Charities, Catholic Cemeteries, Catholic Cemeteries Guild and St. Vincent de Paul Society.

Deafness Services, 191 Joralemon St., 7th Fl., 11201. Tel: 718-722-6216; Teletype: 718-722-6226.

Restorative Justice, 191 Joralemon St., 7th Fl., 11201. Tel: 718-722-6113.

Services for Pregnant Women, 191 Joralemon St., 7th Fl., 11201. Tel: 718-722-6121; 718-725-7800 24-Hour Emergency Helpline.

St. Fidelis Mother and Child Residence Tel: 718-353-4749. JoAnn Lynch, Residence Mgr.

Comprehensive Human Services:

Catholic Charities Neighborhood Services, Inc., 191 Joralemon St., 11201. Tel: 718-722-6000; Fax: 718-722-6096. Mr. Robert Siebel, M.S.W., CEO; Donna Corrado, Exec. Sec. & COO; Thaddeus B. Taberski, M.S.W., M.B.A., Exec. Dir.; Mr. Thomas DeStefano, MSW, LIHD, Pres. of Board; Mary Ann Dantuono Esq., Vice Pres.

CCNS - Older Adult Services:

Alzheimers Adult Day Care, 157-16 65th Ave., Flushing, 11357. Tel: 718-358-3541; Fax: 718-961-4712. Judith Kleve, Vice Pres. Tel: 718-722-6095.

Bayside Senior Center and Bayside Senior Center Transportation Program, 221-15 Horace Harding Expwy., Bayside, 11364. Tel: 718-225-1144; Fax: 718-229-7320.

South Brooklyn Alzheimer's Adult Care Program, 5201 Avenue H., 11234. Tel: 718-241-7711; 718-241-1936.

Benson Ridge Senior Services Assistance Center, 6825 5th Ave., 11220. Tel: 718-236-3205; Fax: 718-837-1957.

Hillcrest Senior Center, 168-01B Hillside Ave., Jamaica, 11432. Tel: 718-297-7171; Fax: 718-657-2247.

Pete McGuinness Senior Center, 715 Leonard St., 11222. Tel: 718-383-1940; Fax: 718-383-1960.

Northside Senior Center, 179 N. 6th St., 11211. Tel: 718-387-2316; Fax: 718-387-3235.

The Bay Senior Center, 3643 Nostrand Ave., 11230. Tel: 718-648-2053; Fax: 718-648-7213.

Catherine Sheridan Senior Center, 35-24 83rd St., Jackson Heights, 11372. Tel: 718-458-4600; Fax: 718-458-5665.

Glenwood Senior Center, 5701 Avenue H, 11234. Tel: 718-241-7711; Fax: 718-241-1936.

Narrows at the Lodge, 7711 18th Ave., 11214. Tel: 718-621-1081; Fax: 718-621-1407.

Narrows Senior Center, 1230 63rd St, 11219. Tel: 718-232-3211; Fax: 718-232-0512.

Ozone Park Senior Center, 103-02 101st Ave., Ozone Park, 11416. Tel: 718-847-2100; Fax: 718-847-2166.

Project Independence, 183-16 Jamaica Ave., Hollis, 11423. Tel: 718-217-0126; Fax: 718-217-0495.

Peter J. Della Monica Center for Seniors, 23-56 Broadway, Astoria, 11106. Tel: 718-626-1500; Fax: 718-278-4432.

Richmond Hill Senior Center, 87-25 118th St., Richmond Hill, 11418. Tel: 718-846-2877; Fax: 718-847-9089.

Seaside Senior Center, 90-01 Rockaway Beach Blvd., Rockaway Beach, 11693. Tel: 718-634-4047; Fax: 718-634-6853.

Sheepshead Bay Supportive Services (NORC), 3677 Nostrand Ave. #3-A, 11229. Tel: 718-769-3579; Fax: 718-769-4155.

Southwest Queens Senior Services, 186-16 Jamaica Ave., 2nd Fl., Hollis, 11423. Tel: 718-217-0126; Fax: 718-217-0495.

Steinway Senior Center, 20-43 Steinway St., Astoria, 11105. Tel: 718-728-8472; Fax: 718-278-5301.

St. Charles Jubilee Senior Center, 55 Pierrepont St., 11201. Tel: 718-855-0326; Fax: 718-852-5415.

St. Louis Senior Center, 230 Kingston Ave., 11213. Tel: 718-771-7945; Fax: 718-467-2524.

St. Mary's Senior Center, 10-15 49th Ave., Long Island City, 11101. Tel: 718-729-2688; Fax: 718-729-5377.

Wakefield Senior Center, 135-45 Lefferts Blvd., South Ozone Park, 11420. Tel: 718-641-0454; Fax: 718-641-2418.

Woodhaven Senior Center, 87-25 118th St., Richmond Hill, 11418. Tel: 718-847-9200; Fax: 718-805-9496.

CCNS Home Delivered Meals Program, 103-02 101st Ave., Ozone Park, 11416. Tel: 718-847-2168; Fax: 718-847-2166.

CCNS NE Queens Home Delivered Meals Program, 168-01B Hillside Ave., Jamaica, 11432. Tel: 718-357-4903; Fax: 718-357-5731.

Northeast Queens Friendly Visiting Program, c/o Hillcrest Senior Center, 168-01 Hillside Ave., Jamaica, 11432. Tel: 718-357-4903; Fax: 718-357-5731.

CCNS - Child Care & Head Start Programs:

Coney Island Child Care Center, 2757 W. 33rd St., 11224. Tel: 718-946-8759; Fax: 718-266-6879.

Farragut Child Care Center, 32 Navy St., 11201. Tel: 718-875-7555; Fax: 718-596-9649.

J. Di Marco Child Care Center, 36-49 11th St., Long Island City, 11106. Tel: 718-786-1166; Fax: 718-706-7198.

Joseph Di Marco Family Day Care, 36-49 11th St., Long Island City, 11106. Tel: 718-786-7309; Fax: 718-786-7044.

J.F. Kennedy Child Care Center, 103-15 Farragut Rd., 11236. Tel: 718-272-8751; Fax: 718-272-6035.

Msgr. Andrew Landi Daycare, 21-20 35th Ave., Long Island City, 11106. Tel: 718-784-2856; Fax: 718-784-9612.

John Oravecz Child Care Center, 25 Nassau Ave., 11222. Tel: 718-782-2727; Fax: 718-782-5166.

R.F. Kennedy Child Care Center, 741 Flushing Ave., 11206. Tel: 718-782-0766; Fax: 718-782-0767.

Vincent J. Caristo Child Care Center, 5901 13th Ave., 11219. Tel: 718-853-8300; Fax: 718-871-8186.

De Paul Head Start, 231 E. 17th St., 11226. Tel: 718-693-5488; Fax: 718-693-5509.

Madeline Jones Head Start, 3415 Neptune Ave., 11224. Tel: 718-266-5962; Fax: 718-266-5891.

Padre Kennedy Head Start, 288 Berry St., 11211. Tel: 718-387-3679; Fax: 718-599-3319.

St. Joseph's Head Start, 300 Vernon Ave., 11206. Tel: 718-455-5900; Fax: 718-455-7513.

Sunset Park Head Start, 4222 4th Ave., 11232. Tel: 718-768-1012; Fax: 718-768-1607.

Sunset Park Family Day Care, 4222 4th Ave., 11232. Tel: 718-788-3035; Fax: 718-788-4056.

St. Margaret Mary Head Start, 9-16 27th Ave., Astoria, 11102. Tel: 718-721-8065; Fax: 718-721-7454.

Therese Cervini Head Start and Annex, 35-34 105th St., Corona, 11368. Tel: 718-478-2169; Fax: 718-478-3993.

Therese Cervini Family Day Care, 35-33 104th St., 3rd Fl., Corona, 11368. Tel: 718-334-0806; Fax: 718-334-0809.

St. Malachy Child Development Center, 220 Hendrix St., 11207. Tel: 718-647-1015; Fax: 718-647-1042.

St. Malachy Head Start, 220 Hendrix St., 11207. Tel: 718-647-0966; Fax: 718-647-1042.

Colin Newell Head Start, 161-06 89th Ave., Jamaica, 11432. Tel: 718-523-1888; Fax: 718-523-2354.

Caritas Training Center, 191 Joralemon St., 13th Fl., 11201. Tel: 718-722-6032; Fax: 718-722-6031.

CCNS - Behavioral Health Services: Patricia Bowles, Vice Pres. Tel: 718-722-6146; Fax: 718-722-6062; Ellen Wagman, Assoc. Dir.

Casa Betsaida, 267 Hewes St., 11211. Tel: 718-218-7890; Fax: 718-218-8264.

Brooklyn Community Living Program, 1900B Ralph Ave., 11234. Tel: 718-253-1366; Fax: 718-253-4890.

Central Brooklyn Supported Housing, 1900B Ralph Ave., 11234. Tel: 718-253-1366; Fax: 718-253-4893.

Brooklyn Supported Housing, 1900B Ralph Ave., 11234. Tel: 718-253-1366; Fax: 718-253-4893.

Corona - Elmhurst Guidance Center, 37-22 82 St., 2nd Fl., Jackson Heights, 11372. Tel: 718-779-1600; Fax: 718-803-0895.

Corona Elmhurst - CDT, 37-22 82 St., Jackson Heights, 11372. Tel: 718-779-1600; Fax: 718-396-6189.

Flatbush Addiction Treatment Center, 1463 Flatbush Ave., 11210. Tel: 718-951-9009; Fax: 718-951-9719.

Bohan-Denton Flatlands Guidance Center, 2037 Utica Ave., 11234. Tel: 718-377-5755; Fax: 718-377-0752.

Glendale Mental Health Clinic, 67-29 Myrtle Ave., 2nd Fl., Glendale, 11385. Tel: 718-456-7001; Fax: 718-456-9470.

Jamaica Continuing Day Treatment, 165-15 88th Ave., Jamaica, 11432. Tel: 718-291-4848; Fax: 718-291-5485.

Partnership of Hope, Intensive Case Management, 29 Chapel St., Ste. 901, 11201. Tel: 718-398-0153; Fax: 718-623-2531.

Bethlehem/Blended Case Management, 29 Chapel St., Ste. 901, 11201. Tel: 718-398-0153; Fax: 718-623-2531.

Queen Community Living Program, 35-24 83rd St., Jackson Heights, 11372. Tel: 718-639-0700; Fax: 718-639-7684.

Queens Supported Housing, 35-24 83rd St., Jackson Heights, 11372. Tel: 718-639-0700; Fax: 718-639-7684.

Rockaway Psychosocial Club/Freedom Club, 13-29 Beach Channel Dr., Far Rockaway, 11691. Tel: 718-337-0509; Fax: 718-868-2059.

Rockaway Community Life Skills/MICA Services Program, 13-29 Beach Channel Dr., Far Rockaway, 11691. Tel: 718-337-6850; Fax: 718-868-3782.

Street 2 Home Brooklyn/Queens, 179 N. 6th St., 11211. Tel: 718-360-8000; Fax: 718-360-8005.

Rockaway Mental Health Clinic, 13-29 Beach Channel Dr., Far Rockaway, 11691. Tel: 718-337-6800; Fax: 718-337-0940.

Woodside Health Clinic, 61-20 Woodside Ave., Woodside, 11377. Tel: 718-779-1234; Fax: 718-779-7775.

Mercy Gardens SRO, 249 Classon Ave., 11205. Tel: 718-399-8141; Fax: 718-399-3208.

The Open Door Club, 2037 Utica Ave., 11234. Tel: 718-377-7757; Fax: 718-951-1318.

Monica House, 161-01 89th Ave., Jamaica, 11432. Tel: 718-262-8190; Fax: 718-739-4331.

Queens Case Management, 165-15 88th Ave., Jamaica, 11432. Tel: 718-725-1120; Fax: 718-291-5485.

Woodside Mobile Outreach Team, 61-20 Woodside Ave., Woodside, 11377. Tel: 718-779-1234; Fax: 718-779-7775.

World of Work - Queens, 37-22 82nd St., Jackson Heights, 11372. Tel: 718-779-1600; Fax: 718-396-6189.

World of Work, 2037 Utica Ave., 11234. Tel: 718-758-9491; Fax: 718-758-9497.

Circle of Hope, 2520 Flatbush Ave., Ste. 10, 11234. Tel: 718-338-4716; Fax: 718-338-5383.

Peer Advocacy Program, 13-29 Beach Channel Dr., Far Rockaway, 11691. Tel: 718-337-0504; Fax: 718-868-2059.

CCNS - Services for People with Developmental Disabilities: Janice Aris, Vice Pres. Tel: 718-722-6081.

Peter J. Connolly Residence, 15 Willow St., 11201. Tel: 718-625-5590; Fax: 718-625-4856.

Adessa House, 101-38 92 St., Ozone Park, 11416. Tel: 718-848-1940; Fax: 718-323-1250.

Alhambra Day Services, 11-29 Catherine St., 11211. Tel: 718-388-5900; Fax: 718-388-3927.

Caldwell Home, 121-01 116th Ave., South Ozone Park, 11420. Tel: 718-845-1200; Fax: 718-323-1267.

Carmel Residence, 277 N. 8th St., 11211. Tel: 718-388-6109; Fax: 718-599-6519.

Cribbin House, 218-20 104th Ave., Queens Village, 11429. Tel: 718-776-4190; Fax: 718-464-4849.

Dawson Manor IRA, 94-17 84th St., Ozone Park, 11416. Tel: 718-296-1172; Fax: 718-296-1247.

Donald Savio Residence, 104-22 48th Ave., Corona, 11368. Tel: 718-699-7800; Fax: 718-699-3773.

James Fitzpatrick Residence, 240 McKinley Ave., 11208. Tel: 718-647-7070; Fax: 718-647-6458.

Garfield Manor, 305 Garfield Pl., 11215. Tel: 718-622-2100; Fax: 718-622-3850.

Golden Residence, 225 Brooklyn Ave., 11213. Tel: 718-953-4444; Fax: 718-953-0622.

Graci Residence, 132-14 90th St., Ozone Park, 11417. Tel: 718-848-1970; Fax: 718-323-7349.

Home & Community Based Services, 168-01B Hillside Ave., Jamaica, 11432. Tel: 718-943-7713; Fax: 718-943-7716.

Helen Owen Carey Residence, 174 Java St., 11222. Tel: 718-383-2451; Fax: 718-383-1488.

McLees House, 112-16 200th St., St. Albans, 11412. Tel: 718-217-0285; Fax: 718-217-9491.

Mugavero Manor, 145-16 Farmers Blvd., Springfield Gardens, 11434. Tel: 718-712-9054; Fax: 718-723-2877.
Mulrooney Manor, 479 E. 29th St., 11226. Tel: 718-287-7553; Fax: 718-826-2519.
Senior F.U.N., 415 Bleeker St., 11237. Tel: 718-417-5316; Fax: 718-417-5317.
Jeanne Noel Hower Manor, 156 Midwood St., 11225. Tel: 718-282-8045; Fax: 718-469-2874.
Mary Wayrick Residence, 90-37 189th St., Hollis, 11423. Tel: 718-464-4090; 718-464-0962 (TTY); Fax: 718-468-8919.
Straus Residence, 3730 Shore Pkwy., 11233. Tel: 718-769-8836; Fax: 718-368-0418.
Mullaney Apts., 4301 8th Ave., 11232. Tel: 718-437-4285; Fax: 718-854-5945.
CCNS - Services for Persons Living with AIDS:
Circle of Hope Brooklyn and Queens, 2520 Flatbush Ave., Ste. 10, 11234. Tel: 718-338-4716; Fax: 718-338-5383.
CCNS - Family Services: Gladys Rodriguez, Vice Pres. Tel: 718-722-6185.
Housing Development and Management Services Catholic Charities:
Catholic Charities Progress of Peoples Development Corporation Tel: 718-722-6041; Fax: 718-722-6045. John Tynan, M.U.P., Dir.
Progress of Peoples Management Corporation Tel: 718-722-6138; Fax: 718-722-6134. Thomas Catlaw, Dir.; Alla Eleon, Controller.
Housing Corporations:
Bellerose Senior HDFC, Inc., 191 Joralemon St., 11201. Tel: 718-479-4739; Fax: 718-479-6612.
Bethlehem Community HDFC Inc., 191 Joralemon St., 11201. Tel: 718-722-6000; Fax: 718-722-6045.
Bishop Boardman Senior HDFC, 191 Joralemon St., 11201. Tel: 718-965-4444; Fax: 718-965-3577.
Bishop Francis J. Mugavero Senior HDFC, 191 Joralemon St., 11201. Tel: 718-643-6490; Fax: 718-643-6492.
Casa Betsaida HDFC, 191 Joralemon St., 11201. Tel: 718-722-6000.
Catherine Sheridan HDFC, Inc., 191 Joralemon St., 11201. Tel: 718-274-7200; Fax: 718-274-2333.
St. Teresa of Avila Senior HDFC, 191 Joralemon St., 11201. Tel: 718-722-6000.
Sr. Lucian Senior HDFC, 191 Joralemon St., 11201. Tel: 718-417-4102; Fax: 718-381-9407.
Caring Communities Associates HDFC, Inc., 191 Joralemon St., 11201. Tel: 718-857-2266; Fax: 718-857-5866.
Mary Star of the Sea Senior HFDC, 191 Joralemon St., 11201. Tel: 718-858-7263; Fax: 718-858-7265.
Pierrepont HDFC, 191 Joralemon St., 11201. Tel: 718-722-6000; Fax: 718-722-6096.
Mary Immaculate, Inc., 191 Joralemon St., 11201. Tel: 718-722-6000; Fax: 718-722-6096.
Mary Immaculate HDFC, Inc., 191 Joralemon St., 11201. Tel: 718-722-6000; Fax: 718-722-6096.
Mount Carmel Senior HDFC, 191 Joralemon St., 11201. Tel: 718-722-6000; Fax: 718-722-6045.
Pope John Paul II Senior HDFC, 191 Joralemon St., 11201. Tel: 718-748-2882; Fax: 718-748-4425.
Pierrepont House for the Elderly, Inc., 191 Joralemon St., 11201. Tel: 718-852-3390; Fax: 718-852-3352.
Queens Rehab Corp., 191 Joralemon St., 11201. Tel: 718-722-6000; Fax: 718-722-6045.
St. Brendan Senior HDFC, 191 Joralemon St., 11201. Tel: 718-645-7113; Fax: 718-645-7180.
St. Lucy/St.Patrick HDFC, 191 Joralemon St., 11201. Tel: 718-722-6000; Fax: 718-722-6045.
Msgr. John P. O'Brien Senior HDFC, 191 Joralemon St., 11201. Tel: 718-972-4556; Fax: 718-972-9265.
St. Paul the Apostle Senior HDFC, 191 Joralemon St., 11201. Tel: 718-722-6000; Fax: 718-722-6045.
Sunset Park HFDC, Inc., 191 Joralemon St., 11201. Tel: 718-438-1119; Fax: 718-871-2407.
Msgr. Thomas Campbell Senior HDFC, 191 Joralemon St., 11201. Tel: 718-545-0816; Fax: 718-545-0817.
Families Together HDFC, Inc., 191 Joralemon St., 11201. Tel: 718-722-6000; Fax: 718-722-6045.
Msgr. Edward T. Burke Senior HDFC, 191 Joralemon St., 11201. Tel: 718-859-9248; Fax: 718-859-3314.
Holy Spirit Senior HDFC, 191 Joralemon St., 11201. Tel: 718-854-0050; Fax: 718-854-8521.
The Msgr. Joseph F. Stedman Residence HDFC, 191 Joralemon St., 11201. Tel: 718-722-6000; Fax: 718-722-6134.
161-01 89th Avenue Corp., 191 Joralemon St., 11201. Tel: 718-262-8190; Fax: 718-739-4331.
101-105 South Eighth Street Apartments Housing Development Fund Corporation, 191 Joralemon St., 11201. Tel: 718-722-6000; Fax: 718-722-6096.
176 South Eighth Street Apartments Housing Development Fund Corporation, 191 Joralemon St., 11201. Tel: 718-722-6000; Fax: 718-722-6096.
72 Lewis Avenue, Apartments Housing Development Fund Corporation, 191 Joralemon St., 11201.
Our Lady of Fatima Apartments HDFC, Inc., 191 Joralemon St., 11201. Tel: 718-507-1933; Fax: 718-507-1214.
The David Minkin Residence HDFC, Inc., 191 Joralemon St., 11201. Tel: 718-438-7997; Fax: 718-438-0052.
Emmaus of the Diocese of Brooklyn, Inc., 191 Joralemon St., 11201. Tel: 718-722-6000; Fax: 718-722-6096.
St. Pius V Senior HDFC, 191 Joralemon St., 11201. Tel: 718-722-6000; Fax: 718-722-6045.
Affiliated Agencies:
Ss. Joachim & Anne Residence, 2720 Surf Ave., 11224. Tel: 718-714-4800; Fax: 718-714-0874.
Anthonian Hall, Inc. Tel: 718-722-6000; Fax: 718-722-6096. Sr. Ellen Patricia Finn, O.P., M.Ed., L.M.S.W., Treas.; Most Rev. Joseph M. Sullivan, D.D., M.S.W., M.P.A., V.E., Treas. (Retired).
Catholic Guild for the Blind, Diocese of Brooklyn, Inc., 191 Joralemon St., 11201. Tel: 718-722-6000; Fax: 718-722-6096.
Catholic Youth Organization, 191 Joralemon St., 11201. Tel: 718-722-6074; Fax: 718-722-6233.
Mary's Hall, Inc., 191 Joralemon St., 11201. Tel: 718-722-6000; Fax: 718-722-6096. Most Rev. Joseph M. Sullivan, D.D., M.S.W., M.P.A., V.E., Pres. (Retired).
Family Home Care Services:
Care at Home for the Diocese of Brooklyn, Inc., 269 37th St., 11232-2409. Tel: 718-907-4711; Fax: 718-965-7010.
Family Home Care Services of Brooklyn and Queens, Inc., 241 37 St., 11232. Tel: 718-832-0550; Fax: 718-907-8750.
Child Welfare Programs:
Office of Child Welfare, 191 Joralemon St., 11201. Tel: 718-722-6091.
Catholic Child Care Society, 191 Joralemon St., 11201. Tel: 718-722-6091.
HeartShare Human Services of NY, 12 Metro Tech Center, 11201. Tel: 718-422-4200. William R. Garinello, Pres./CEO. Tel: 718-522-4506; Carol Smith-Njiri, Senior Vice Pres. Tel: 718-422-4216. Diocese of Brooklyn (formerly Catholic Guardian Society/Diocese of Brooklyn).
Little Flower Children's Services of New York, Corporate Office: 186 Joralemon St., 11201. Tel: 718-875-3500. Long Island Office: N. Wading River Rd., Wading River, 11792. Tel: 516-929-6200. Queens Office: 89-12 162nd St., Queens, 11439. Tel: 718-526-9150. Grace LoGrande, LMSW, Exec. Dir.
Mercy Home for Children, 243 Prospect Park W., 11215. Tel: 718-832-1075. Sr. Catherine Crumlish, R.S.M., Exec. Dir.
MercyFirst, Long Island Office: 525 Convent Rd., Syosset, 11791. Tel: 516-921-0808. Brooklyn Office: 6301 12th Ave., 11219. Gerard McCaffery, Exec. Officer.
Providence House, Inc. (1979) *Administrative Office*, 703 Lexington Ave., 11221. Tel: 718-455-0197; Fax: 718-455-0692. Web: www.providencehouse.org. Sr. Janet Kinney, C.S.J., Exec. Dir.
Providence House 1 (1979) 2518 Church Ave., 11226. Tel: 718-284-6688; Fax: 718-284-4890.
Providence House 2 (1982) 388 Prospect Ave., 11215. Tel: 718-369-9140; Fax: 718-369-9158.
Providence House 3 (1983) 159-23 89th Ave., Jamaica, 11432. Tel: 718-739-1348; Fax: 718-526-6315.
Providence House 4 (1986) 89 Sickles Ave., New Rochelle, 10801. Tel: 914-632-4177; Fax: 914-235-5766.
Providence House 5 (1986) 396 Lincoln Rd., 11225. Tel: 718-778-1310; Fax: 718-493-5932.
Providence House 6 (1988) 2876 W. 17 St., 11224. Tel: 718-996-3386.
Providence House 7, 701 Lexington Ave., 11221. Tel: 718-574-6847; Fax: 718-455-0457.
Permanent Housing (1995) 85 & 87 Sickles Ave., New Rochelle, 10801.
SCO Family of Services, 1 Alexander Pl., Glen Cove, 11542. Tel: 561-671-1253; 718-895-8670 (Tie Line); 718-935-9466 (Brooklyn); 718-526-7533 (Queens); Fax: 516-671-2899. Robert J. McMahon, Exec. Dir.
Madonna Heights Services, 151 Burr Ln., P.O. Box 8020, Dix Hills, 11746. Tel: 516-643-8800; Fax: 516-491-4440.
St. John's Residence & School for Boys, 144 Beach 111th St., Rockaway Park, 11694. Tel: 718-945-2800. Bro. Thomas N. Trager, S.M., Exec. Dir.; Rev. Paul J. Landolfi, S.M., Chap.
St. Vincent's Services, Inc., 66 Boerum Pl., 11201. Tel: 718-522-3700. Rev. Msgr. Robert M. Harris, M.S.W., M.Phil., M.A., Pres./CEO; Henry J. Ford, Vice Pres.
Other Affiliated Agencies:
Ecclesial Consultants, Inc., 191 Joralemon St., 11201. Tel: 718-722-6000; Fax: 718-722-6096. Most Rev. Joseph M. Sullivan, D.D., M.S.W., M.P.A., V.E., Dir. (Retired); Rev. Msgrs. Emmet Fagan (RVC), Dir.; Charles J. Fahey (SY), Dir. A management service for Church agencies and organizations.
Ferrini Welfare League, 98-21 101 Ave., Ozone Park, 11416. Tel: 718-845-0539.
Italian Board of Guardians, 7808 18 Ave., 11214. Tel: 718-232-4242; Fax: 718-232-6402. Rev. Msgr. Fernando Ferrarese, Moderator; Maria Patalano, Exec. Dir.; Mrs. Beatrice Rizzo, Exec. Sec.
Society of St. Vincent de Paul in Diocese of Brooklyn, Central Office, 191 Joralemon St., 11201. Tel: 718-625-1400; Fax: 718-625-1421. Most Rev. Thomas V. Daily, D.D., Spiritual Advisor; Mr. Joseph Martino, Pres.
District Council of Kings, 191 Joralemon St., 11201. Tel: 718-625-1400; Fax: 718-625-1421. Rev. Msgr. Raymond J. Kelly, S.T.L., Spiritual Advisor (Retired); Mr. Carlos Harris, Pres.
District Council of Queens, 191 Joralemon St., 11201. Tel: 718-625-1400; Fax: 718-625-1421. Mr. Vito Buccaria, Pres.
Family Services:
East New York/Brownsville Support Center, 1165 Rockaway Ave., 11236. Tel: 718-385-2043; Fax: 718-385-2179.
Project Bridge, 52 Wilson Ave., 11237. Tel: 718-628-1905; Fax: 718-628-3783.
CSP Community of Caring Consortium and Adolescent Pregnancy Prevention Service (APPS), 52 Wilson Ave., 11237. Tel: 718-628-1905; Fax: 718-628-3783. Mark Payne, Project Mgr. (CO, 1, 4, 5)
Refugee Resettlement Program, 191 Joralemon St., 11201. Tel: 718-722-6017; Fax: 718-722-6073.
Volunteer Services, 191 Joralemon St., 11201. Tel: 718-722-6118; Fax: 718-722-6233.
After School Plus Program at P.S. 50, 143-26 101st Ave., Jamaica, 11435. Tel: 718-526-5336, Ext. 407; Fax: 718-526-7261.
Queens Commodity Supplemental Food Program, 89-56 162nd St., Jamaica, 11432. Tel: 718-523-2220; Fax: 718-523-2333.
Jamaica Family and Youth Center, 87-80 Merrick Blvd., Jamaica, 11432. Tel: 718-526-5151; Fax: 718-526-6776.
Homebase Homeless Prevention/Division, 87-80 Merrick Blvd., Jamaica, 11432. Tel: 718-674-1000; Fax: 718-674-1008.
After School Program and OST at P.S. 106 (CD4), 1314 Putnam Ave., 11221. Tel: 718-574-0260; Fax: 718-574-1054.
Safe Alternatives for Family Enrichment (SAFE) at I.S. 349 (CD4), 35 Starr St., 11211. Tel: 718-366-0409; Fax: 718-821-1332.

[N] SPECIAL CARE FACILITIES

BROOKLYN. **Bishop Francis J. Mugavero Center for Geriatric Care, Inc.*, 155 Dean St., 11217. Tel: 718-694-6700; Fax: 718-694-6710. Paul Rosenfeld, Exec. Dir. Continuing Care; Ida Santos, Licensed Admin. Affiliated with St. Vincents Catholic Medical Center. Bed Capacity 288; Total Staff 310.
St. Jerome's Health Services Corp. dba Holy Family Home 1740 84th St., 11214. Tel: 718-232-3666; Fax: 718-259-9180. Sr. Teresita R. Samson, S.F.P., Dir. Pastoral Care Dept.; Lisa Schiano-Denis, Dir. & Admin. Affiliated with Saint Vincent Catholic Medical Centers of New York. Bed Capacity 200; Total Staff 266.

[O] CHILD CARE AGENCIES

BROOKLYN. *St. Francis Home for Boys*, 132 Eagle St., 11222. Tel: 718-383-9870; Fax: 718-349-1558. Email: yth2000ny@aol.com. Web: www.youth2000ny.com. Rev. Benedict J. Groeschel, C.F.R., Exec. Dir.; Mr. Joseph Campo, Dir. Residents 7.
Good Shepherd Services, 441 Fourth Ave., 11215. Tel: 718-788-0666; Fax: 718-965-0365. Email: plomonaco@goodshepherd.org. Web: www.GoodShepherds.org. Sr. Paulette LoMonaco, R.G.S., Exec. Dir. Provides a comprehensive range of neighborhood family services to individuals & youth from the South Brooklyn community. Services include educational support, counseling, after school programs, a domestic violence shelter, crisis intervention, & advocacy services to children & families.
HeartShare Human Services of New York, Roman Catholic Diocese of Brooklyn, 12 Metro Tech Center, 29th Fl., 11201. Tel: 718-422-4200; Fax: 718-522-4506. Email: info@heartshare.org. Web: www.heartshare.org. William R. Guarinello, M.S., Pres. & CEO. Children and Family Services: Foster Boarding Home Program, Adoption Program, Family Services Centers, School-Based Beacon Program, Youth Services, Services for People with HIV/AIDS. Programs for the Developmentally Disabled: Group Homes, Supportive Apartments, Preschool Program (Early Childhood Centers), School Age Program, Respite & Recreation Program, Day Services/Day Habilitation Programs, Case Management,

Family Support Services
Children and Family Services:
Adoption & Foster Care Services-Brooklyn Office, 191 Joralemon St., 6th Fl., 11201. Tel: 718-422-4216; Fax: 718-422-4229.
Adoption & Foster Care Services-Queens Office, 90-04 161st St., Jamaica, 11432. Tel: 718-739-5000; Fax: 718-739-6828.
Family Service Centers:
Bensonhurst-Bay Ridge Kiwanis Club Family Services, 138 Bay 20th St., 11214. Tel: 718-234-1717; Fax: 718-331-1541.
East Brooklyn Family Services, 3005 Glenwood Rd., 11210. Tel: 718-434-7900; Fax: 718-434-6715.
South Brooklyn Family Services, 266 Court St., 11201. Tel: 718-855-7766; Fax: 718-855-7999.
Family Services at P.S. 288, 2865 W. 19th St., 11224. Tel: 718-372-0580; Fax: 718-372-0634.
School-Based Beacon Programs:
McKinley Beacon Program-I.S. 259, 7301 Fort Hamilton Pkwy., 11228. Tel: 718-836-3620; Fax: 718-836-3683.
Beacon Program at P.S. 288, 2950 W. 25th St., 11224. Tel: 718-714-0103; Fax: 718-714-6738.
Youth Services/Summer Camps:
PS 102 One World After School Program, 211 72nd St., 11209. Tel: 718-567-2365; Fax: 718-567-2367.
Services for People with HIV/AIDS:
Community Follow-Up Program, 2865 W. 19th St., 11224. Tel: 718-372-0580; Fax: 718-372-0634.
Residential Housing Program, 1069 Liberty Ave., 11208. Tel: 718-647-0118; Fax: 718-323-4113.
Developmental Disabilities Services:
12 Metro Tech Center, 29th Fl., 11201. Tel: 718-422-3306; 718-422-3304; Fax: 718-422-3324.
Adult Day Habilitation Services:
Bay Ridge Day Habilitation Program, 347 74th St., 2nd Fl., 11209. Tel: 718-745-7117; Fax: 718-745-3741.
Brooklyn Day Habilitation Program, 177 Livingston Ave., 2nd Fl., 11201. Tel: 718-237-4063; Fax: 718-797-2059.
Queens Day Habilitation Program, 61-58 Springfield Blvd., Bayside, 11364. Tel: 718-281-0480; Fax: 718-281-0478.
Francis Aiello Day Habilitation Program, 163 MacDonough St., 11216. Tel: 718-443-5071; Fax: 718-443-5741.
Harry Hoffman Day Habilitation Program, 62-10 Northern Blvd., Woodside, 11377. Tel: 718-899-2752; Fax: 718-899-9365.
Eileen and William Lavin Day Habilitation Program, 347 74th St., 11209. Tel: 718-745-7117; Fax: 718-745-3741.
Partnering with Autistic Citizens (PACT) Day Habilitation Program, 177 Livingston Ave., 2nd Fl., 11201. Tel: 718-237-4063; Fax: 718-797-2059.
Union Turnpike Day Habilitation Program, 159-05 Union Tpke., Fresh Meadows, 11366. Tel: 718-969-0419; Fax: 718-969-0983.
Staten Island PACT Day Habilitation Program, 930 Willowbrook Rd., Bldg. 41A, Rm. 10, Staten Island, 10314. Tel: 917-648-4649.
Kaleidoscope Day Services Program, 177 Livingston St., 2nd Fl., 11201. Tel: 718-797-2020.
Early Childhood Services:
Angels on the Bay Early Childhood Evaluation Center, 162-30 Cross Bay Blvd., Howard Beach, 11414. Tel: 718-323-2877; Fax: 718-323-2897.
Governor Mario and Matilda Raffa Cuomo First Step Early Childhood Center, 115-15 101st. Ave., Richmond Hill, 11419. Tel: 718-441-5333; Fax: 718-805-0657.
Lefferts/Liberty Kiwanis First Step Early Childhood Center, 82-12 151st Ave., Howard Beach, 11414. Tel: 718-848-0300; Fax: 718-835-2862.
Dolly and Frank Russo, Sr. First Step Early Childhood Center, 118-01/03 101st Ave., Richmond Hill, 11419. Tel: 718-805-7117; Fax: 718-805-7124.
Heart Share First Step Early Childhood Center, 1825 Bath Ave., 11214. Tel: 718-238-4637; Fax: 718-238-9584.
Family Support Services Programs:
Family Support Services Program, 12 Metro Tech Center, 29th Fl., 11201. Tel: 718-422-3271; Fax: 718-855-5821.
School Age Program, The Heart Share School, 1825 Bath Ave., 11214. Tel: 718-621-1614; Fax: 718-621-1649.
Supported Apartment Program:
12 Metro Tech Center, 29th Fl., 11201. Tel: 718-422-4200; Fax: 718-422-3324.
Marian and Anthony Attardi Residence
Thomas J. Cuite Residence
James and Kathleen Buckley Residence
Clermont Residence
Clinton Residence
Doonan-Drake Residence
Antonetta Ferraro Residence
Msgr. Thomas G. Hagerty Residence
Hart Street Residence
Carol and James Scibelli Residence
Maureen Moore Residence
Lillian and John Sharkey, Sr. Residence
Helen and John Sharkey Residence
Rita P. Short Residence
35th Ave. Residence, 172-07 35th Ave., Flushing, 11358. Tel: 718-961-7673; Fax: 718-961-7753.
Clare and Frank Torre Residence
Dr. Catherine White Residence
Maureen and Vincent Curatola Residence
Josephine and Joseph Abatemarco Residence
Lydia and Napoleon Giannattasio Residence
Ann and Charles Subbiondo Residence
Affiliate Programs:
Heartshare Wellness Ltd., 177 Livingston Ave. Cellar Level, 11201. Tel: 718-855-7707; Fax: 718-855-7717.
Energy Programs, 12 Metro Tech Center, 29th Fl., 11201. Tel: 718-422-4211; Fax: 718-522-4506.
The Heart Share School, 1825 Bath Ave., 11214. Tel: 718-621-1614; Fax: 718-621-1649.

Little Flower Children and Family Services, 186 Joralemon St., 11201-4326. Tel: 718-875-3500; Fax: 718-260-8863. Email: stupph@lfchild.org. Web: www.LittleFlowerNY.org. Hon. Herbert W. Stupp, CEO; Grace LoGrande, LMSW, Exec. Dir.; Sr. Agnes Palczynski, C.S.F.N., Sister Supr.; George Grigg, Prin. Foster Care, Adoption & Post Adoption Services, Services for Adult MR/DD clients; Residential Treatment Center, U.F.S.D., & Family Day Care at Wading River, NY; Teen Mothers & Infants in Foster Homes. Lay Teachers 25.

Mercy Home for Children (1865) 243 Prospect Park W., 11215. Tel: 718-832-1075; Fax: 718-832-7612. Email: info@mercyhomeny.org. Web: www.mercyhomeny.org. Sr. Catherine Crumlish, R.S.M. Under the sponsorship of the Sisters of Mercy.; Six Intermediate Care Facilities (Residences & 5 Individual Residential Alternatives) for adolescents & adults who are developmentally disabled: Visitation Residence; Harold Warren Residence; de Porres Residence; Littlejohn Residence; Santulli Residence; Kevin Keating Residence; Chrys Residence; Gail Addeo Residence; Rev. Michael J. McGivney Residence; Augusta Residence & Frank's Residence. Three all day Saturday Recreation Programs, for adolescents and adults with developmental disabilities and autistic children, we offer MSC Services for families and the individuals. Four all day recreational respite programs need of supportive services. In Home Respite Services; James P. Slattery, CPA, Creative Arts Program, Mercy-Mitsui USA & Co. Creative Arts Program. Sisters 5; Total Staff 281; Residents 104; Saturday Programs 36; MSC Families 50; Saturday Creative Arts Center 60; In Home Respite 5.

MercyFirst, 6301 12th Ave., 11219. Tel: 718-232-1500; Fax: 718-232-0331. Web: www.mercyfirst.org. Gerard McCaffery, CEO. Residential services provided in campus and group home settings, including diagnostic/group emergency foster care, non-secure detention, hard to place (JD and clinically intensive), abuse treatment and prevention, mother/child, and OMH programs.; Foster Boarding Home/Adoption, Aftercare and Preventive Services programs provide services in Nassau, Queens and Brooklyn. Children in Care 3,891; Bed Capacity 193; Total Staff 615.
Residential Programs:
McAuley Residence for Mother and Child (Agency Operated Boarding Home), Tel: 718-469-0360; Fax: 718-940-0406.
Manning Residence for Mother and Child (Agency Operated Boarding Home), Tel: 718-641-4301.
Virginia Group Residence for Mother and Child Tel: 718-369-3812; Fax: 718-369-5891.
Preventive Programs:
Montague Center, 186 Montague St., 11201. Tel: 718-624-2100; Fax: 718-624-7740.
Gerard C. Durr Center, 333 Avenue X, 11223. Tel: 718-375-7444; Fax: 718-375-2444.
South Ozone Park Center, 115-01 Lefferts Blvd., South Ozone Park, 11420. Tel: 718-848-1532; Fax: 718-848-9032.
Rockaway Center, 230 Beach 102 St., Ste. 1-A, Rockaway Park, 11694. Tel: 718-318-6167; Fax: 718-634-6691.

St. Vincent's Services, Inc. (1869) (Formerly St. Vincent's Home for Boys and St. Vincent's Hall, Inc.), 66 Boerum Pl., 11201. Tel: 718-522-3700; Fax: 718-875-8536. Web: www.svs.org. Rev. Msgr. Robert M. Harris, M.S.W., M.Phil., M.A., Pres. & CEO. Services includes: Family Foster Boarding Homes & Adoption and Post Adoption Services, Pediatric AIDS Program, Specialized Preventive Program for Medically Fragile Children, Primary Care Medical Clinic for children and adolescents, Group Foster Home Services, Residences for the Developmentally Disabled, NYS Licensed Alcohol and Substance Abuse Outpatient Treatment Program for youth and adults, NYS Licensed Outpatient Mental Health Clinics for children, adolescents and adults. Sisters 3; Priests 2; Employees 470.
Office Program Centers:
66 Boerum Pl., 11201.
205 Montague St., 11201.
333 Atlantic Ave., 11201.
1310 Rockaway Pkwy. (Canarsie), 11236.
89-31 161st St., Jamaica, 11432.
56 Bay St., Staten Island, 10301.
148 Bay St., Staten Island, 10301.

GLEN COVE. *SCO Family of Services*, 1 Alexander Pl., 11542. Tel: 516-671-1253; 718-895-2555; Fax: 516-671-2899. Email: bmcmahon@sco.org. Web: www.sco.org. Robert J. McMahon, Exec. Dir.; Mary Hall, Dir. of Intake and Placement. Residential Treatment Center for the profoundly & severely mentally retarded, Intermediate Care Facilities, Group Homes for Adolescent Teenage Boys and Girls, Teen Mother-Child Residence Program, Homeless Program for Teenage RS, Preventive Programs (3), EFBH Network, Supervised Independent Living Apartments, Therapeutic Foster Boarding Homes, Residential Treatment Facility, Article 81/89 Schools (4), Foster Care, Adoption Homeless Shelters (4), Single Stop, Beacon Programs, After School Programs, Employment and Education Services, Nurse Family Partnership and Parent Child Home Programs, Crisis Respite, Home & Community Based Waiver Services, Madonna Heights Services, Family Dynamics, Center for Family Life. Children 5,000.

ROCKAWAY PARK. *St. John's Residence for Boys, Inc.*, 144-Beach 111 St., 11694. Tel: 718-945-2800, Ext. 200; Fax: 718-945-4662. Email: stjohnsresidence@aol.com. Bro. Thomas N. Trager, S.M., Exec. Dir. Conducted by the Brothers of Society of Mary (Marianists). Residential care for adolescent boys. Diagnostic Reception Centers, Non-Secure Detention/Independent Living Program. Brothers 5; Residents 57.

[P] GROUP HOMES FOR RETARDED CHILDREN

SPRINGFIELD GARDENS. *Martin De Porres Group Homes* (1974) 136-25 218th St., 11413. Tel: 718-527-0606; Fax: 718-723-1528. Email: phiro@nyc.rr.com. Web: mdp.org. Bro. Philip Rofrano, F.S.C., L.C.S.W., Exec. Dir. Bed Capacity 15; Total Assisted Annually 26; Total Staff 17.

[Q] RESIDENCES FOR THE AGED

BROOKLYN. *SS. Joachim & Anne Residence, Inc. dba Saints Joachim + Anne Nursing and Rehabilitation Center* 2720 Surf Ave., 11224. Tel: 718-714-4800; Fax: 718-266-1743. Claude Ritman, Exec. Dir. Bed Capacity 200; Total Assisted Annually 68,542; Total Staff 300.

BAYSIDE. *Ozanam Hall of Queens Nursing Home, Inc.* (1971) 42-41 201st St., 11361. Tel: 718-423-2000; Fax: 718-224-7598. Email: jcraymond@ozanamhall.org. Web: www.ozanamhall.org. Sr. M. Joseph Catherine Raymond, O.Carm., Admin.; Rev. James M. Kelly, C.M., M.A., Chap. Carmelite Sisters for the Aged and Infirm. Sisters 17; Residents 432; Bed Capacity 432; Total Assisted Annually 1,025; Total Staff 648.

QUEENS VILLAGE. *Queen of Peace Residence* (1869) 110-30 221st St., 11429. Tel: 718-464-1800; Fax: 347-626-2181. Sr. Margaret Charles Hogarty, L.S.P., Supr.; Rev. Msgr. William J. Rodgers, Chap. (Retired).
Home for the Aged, Little Sisters of the Poor Sisters 20; Bed Capacity 80; Total Assisted Annually 80; Total Staff 110. In Res. Revs. John W. Byrnes (Retired); Anthony C. Casey (Retired); Charles F. Harth (Retired); Charles Repole, O.F.M.Cap.

[R] SETTLEMENT ASSOCIATIONS

GLENDALE. *Catholic Kolping Society*, 65-04 Myrtle Ave., 11385. Tel: 718-456-7727. Evelyn H. Blatz, Pres.
Catholic Kolping Society (Katholischer Gesellen Verein) of Brooklyn, Inc.

[S] CATHOLIC MIGRATION AND REFUGEE OFFICES

BROOKLYN. *Catholic Migration & Refugee Office* (1971) 1258 65th St., 11219. Tel: 718-236-3000; Fax: 718-256-9707. Web: www.catholicmigration.org.
Apostolate Coordinators.
Arabic Speaking Apostolate (2003) Tel: 718-965-0422. Rev. Msgr. Youssef Bochra Nasri, Coord.
Brazilian Apostolate Tel: 718-361-1884; Fax: 718-786-4573. Rev. Jose Carlos Da Silva, Coord.

Chinese Apostolate-Queens Tel: 718-961-0714; Fax: 718-460-8032. Rev. Antonius Ho, C.S.J.B. (Taiwan), Coord.

Chinese Apostolate-Brooklyn Rev. Vincentius Toan Do, Asst. Tel: 718-236-0909; Fax: 718-236-5357.

Czech/Slovak Apostolate Tel: 718-268-6251; Fax: 718-793-2584. Rev. Jan Czudek, Coord.

Croatian Apostolate Tel: 718-278-3337; Fax: 718-278-4354. Rev. Ellis Tommaseo (Italy), Coord.

Filipino Apostolate Tel: 718-229-6465; Fax: 718-229-8126; 718-743-0152. Rev. Godofredo Felicitas (Philippines), Coord.

Ghanaian Apostolate Tel: 718-282-7162; Fax: 718-282-5568. Rev. Charles Akoto Oduro (Ghana), Coord.

Haitian Apostolate Tel: 718-469-5900; Fax: 718-469-5901 1. Rev. Donelson Thevenin, Coord.

Indian Latin Rite Apostolate Tel: 718-768-3071; Fax: 718-369-2039. Rev. Robert Ambalathingal, O.C.D.

Indonesian Apostolate Tel: 516-764-0048; Fax: 516-282-2525. Rev. Ignatius Hadimulia Sasmita, S.J.

Irish Apostolate Tel: 718-672-4848; Fax: 718-457-4055. Rev. Edmund Brendan Duggan, C.S.Sp., Coord.

Italian Apostolate Tel: 347-545-0549; Fax: 718-326-1883. Deacon Vincent M. LaGamba, Coord.

Korean Apostolate Tel: 718-436-5565; Fax: 718-436-5586. Rev. Heebong Nam, Coord.

Lithuanian Tel: 718-326-2236; Fax: 718-326-2249. Rev. Vytautas Volertas, Coord.

Nigerian Apostolate Tel: 718-969-3226; Fax: 718-380-0345. Rev. Anthony Nzegwu (Nigeria).

Pakistani Apostolate Tel: 718-763-2330; Fax: 718-763-6592. Rev. Ilyas Gill, O.F.M. (Pakistan), Coord.

Polish Apostolate Tel: 718-768-5724; Fax: 718-768-4996. Rev. Witold Mroziewski, J.C.D., Coord.

Russian Apostolate Tel: 718-456-7011. Rt. Rev. Roman V. Russo, Coord.

Vietnamese Apostolate Tel: 718-278-1834; Fax: 718-278-0998. Rev. Peter H. Nguyen, Coord.

West Indian Apostolate Tel: 718-773-0100; Fax: 718-773-4198. Rev. Caleb A. Buchanan, Coord.

Apostleship of the Sea Tel: 718-596-7750; Fax: 718-260-9233. Rev. Antonio Camora.

Resources, Inc., 1258 65th St., 11219. Tel: 718-236-3000; Fax: 718-256-9707. Edward Dominguez, Dir.; Michael Campo, Mgr. Maintenance Dept.; Mr. James Casale, Business Devel.

Catholic Immigrant Ministries, Inc., 1258 65th St., 11219. Tel: 718-236-3000; Fax: 718-256-9707. Edward Dominguez, Exec. Dir.

Catholic Migration Services, Inc., 1258 65th St., 11219. Tel: 718-236-3000; Fax: 718-256-9707. Edward Dominguez, Exec. Dir.

[T] MONASTERIES AND RESIDENCES OF PRIESTS AND BROTHERS

BROOKLYN. *Brothers of the Christian Schools*, 1214-1216 Beverley Rd., 11218. Tel: 718-857-4311; Fax: 718-857-7576. Bros. Peter Bonventre, F.S.C.; David Carroll, F.S.C.; Ralph Darmento, F.S.C.; Robert Ferguson, F.S.C.; Richard Grieco, F.S.C.; William Kemmerer, F.S.C.; Michael McLoughlin, F.S.C.; Philip Zeller, F.S.C. Brothers 8.

Carmelites of Mary Immaculate, Inc., 21 Nassau Ave., 11222. Tel: 718-388-4866; Fax: 718-387-1877. Email: cmiusa@hotmail.com. Web: www.cmiusa.org. Revs. Walter Thelapilly, C.M.I., Coord. Gen. & Procurator for Missions; L.F. Jose, Provincial Coord., 1006 St. Elizabeth St., St. Martinville, LA 70582.

Curial Residence, 378 Clermont Ave., 11238. Tel: 718-638-0697. Most Rev. Joseph M. Sullivan, D.D., M.S.W., M.P.A., V.E. (Retired); Rev. Msgr. Austin P. Bennett, J.C.D., P.A. (Retired).

St. Francis Monastery-Generalate Offices of Franciscan Brothers, 135 Remsen St., 11201-4212. Tel: 718-858-8217; Fax: 718-858-8306. Email: generalate@gmail.com. Web: www.franciscanbrothers.org. Bros. William Boslet, O.S.F., M.A., Supr. Gen.; Thomas Grady, O.S.F., 1st Councilor; Gabriel O'Brien, O.S.F., 2nd Councilor; Joshua Di Mauro, O.S.F., 3rd Councilor; Richard Contino, O.S.F., 4th Councilor. Brothers 78.

St. John the Baptist Rectory (1868) 75 Lewis Ave., 11206. Tel: 718-455-6864; Fax: 718-452-3738. Web: www.stjohnthebaptistrcc.org. Revs. Emmett J. Nolan, C.M., Pastor; Astor Rodriguez, C.M., Parochial Vicar; Orlando D. Cardona, C.M., Parochial Vicar.

St. Michael's Friary, 225 Jerome St., 11207. Tel: 718-827-6990; Fax: 718-827-5789. Email: stmarypostulancy@gmail.com. Bro. Celestino Arias, O.F.M.Cap., Guardian & Co-Dir. Capuchian Postulancy Program; Revs. Michael Greco, O.F.M.Cap., Co-Dir. Capuchian Postulancy Program; James Gavin, O.F.M.Cap. Priests 2; Postulants 3.

Oratory of Saint Philip Neri, Congregation Pontifical Rite (1988) 109 Willoughby St., 11201. Tel: 718-875-2096; Fax: 718-875-4678. Email: philipneri@aol.com. Web: Brooklyn-oratory.org. Very Rev. Dennis M. Corrado, C.O., Provost; Revs. Mark J. Lane, C.O.; Joel M. Warden, C.O.; Anthony Andreassi, C.O.; Michael J. Callaghan, C.O.; Bro. James Simon, C.O. Priests 5; Brothers 1.

Redemptorist Fathers of New York, Inc.-Baltimore Province (1969) 7509 Shore Rd., 11209. Tel: 718-833-1900; Fax: 718-630-5666. Web: www.redemptorists.net. Very Rev. Patrick F. Woods, C.Ss.R., Prov. Supr.; Revs. Lawrence E. Lover, C.Ss.R., J.C.D., Cannon Lawyer; Joseph F. Jones, C.Ss.R., Supr. & Rector; Carl W. Hoegerl, C.Ss.R., Prov. Archivist; Robert M. Pagliari, Asst. Procurator & Sec. to Province; Edmund Faliskie, C.Ss.R., Prov. Consultor & Procurator. Provincial Residence for Redemptorist Fathers and Brothers Priests 10.

ASTORIA. *Our Lady of China Chapel*, 54-09 92nd St., Elmhurst, 11373. Tel: 718-699-1929; Fax: 718-460-8032. Email: olcny@msn.com. Web: olc.faithweb.com. Revs. Antonius Ho, C.S.J.B. (Taiwan), Dir.; Dehua Zhang, C.S.J.B., Assoc.

DOUGLASTON. *Bishop Mugavero Residence*, 7200 Douglaston Pkwy., 11362. Tel: 718-229-8001, Ext. 411; Fax: 718-428-3070. Email: moellinger@rcdob.org. Deacon Matthew Oellinger, Coord., Office of Sr. Priests In Res. Most Rev. Thomas V. Daily, D.D. (Retired); Rev. Msgrs. Gerard Arella (Retired); Joseph P. Bynon (Retired); Michael J. Cantley (Retired); George T. Deas (Retired); Conrad R. Dietz (RVC) (Retired); Thomas F. Donovan (Retired); Richard F. Dunn (Retired); Eugene A. Feldhaus (Retired); Thomas J. Gradilone (Retired); Lawrence E. Hinch (Retired); Vincent A. Keane (Retired); Raymond J. Kelly, S.T.L. (Retired); John F. Keppler (Retired); James P. King (Retired); Walter C. Murphy (Retired); Dino M. Zeni (Retired); Revs. Robert Blauvelt (Retired); Hugh A. Byrne (Retired); Coleman J. Costello (Retired); George R. Cowan (Retired); Eugene P. Coyle (Retired); Joseph W. Denzer (Retired); James T. Devine (Retired); Louis J. Kennedy (Retired); Daniel G. Keohane (Retired); Martin F. Kirby, M.A. (Retired); Eugene McGovern (Retired); John A. McShane (Retired); Kevin J. O'Donoghue (Retired); James J. Reynolds; Edward W. Richards (Retired); Jerome J. Schmidt (Retired); Matthew W. Sheridan (Retired).

ELMHURST. *Congregation of St. John the Baptist of China*, 54-17 90th St., 11373. Tel: 718-271-3944; Fax: 718-271-3215. Email: csjbny@catholic.org. Web: csjb.faithweb.com. Revs. Antonius Ho, C.S.J.B. (Taiwan), Regl. Supr.; Dehua Zhang, C.S.J.B.; Victor Cao, C.S.J.B.; Ambrose Khong, C.S.J.B. Priests 4; Brothers 2.

JAMAICA. *Saint Charles House of Studies*, 168-41 84th Ave., 11432. Tel: 718-351-8808; Fax: 718-667-4598. Rev. Matthew Didone, C.S., Prov. Supr.

Immaculate Conception Monastery (1936) 86-45 Edgerton Blvd., 11432. Tel: 718-739-6502; Fax: 718-739-7770. Email: pgrace@cpprov.org. Web: www.icmonastery.org. Revs. Peter Grace, C.P., Rector; Richard A. Nalepa, C.P., Vice-Rector; Quentin Amrhein, C.P. (Retired); Lawrence Bellew, C.P., Confessor; Jerome Bracken, C.P., Seminary Prof.; Michael Brennan, C.P., Confessor; Alberto Cabrera, C.P., Hispanic Min.; Paul Chenot, C.P., Chap.; Christopher Cleary, C.P., Asst. Dir. Retreat House; Theophane Cooney, C.P., Asst. Pastor; Neil Davin, C.P., Officialis; Daniel Free, C.P. (Retired); Henry Free, C.P. (Retired); Mario Gallipoli, C.P., Mission Preacher; Thomas Griffiths, C.P., Confessor; Joseph D. Guzinski, C.P., Confraternity Dir.; Stephen Haslach, C.P., Confessor; Angelo Iacovone, C.P. (Retired); Thomas Joyce, C.P., Confessor; Owen Lally, C.P., Charismatic Min.; Richard Leary, C.P. (Retired); John Michael Lee, C.P., Dir. Retreat House; Malachy McGill, C.P. (Retired); Gerard A. Orlando, C.P. (Retired); Dominic Papa, Preaching Office; Kenan Peters, C.P., Mission Preacher; Isaias Powers, C.P. (Retired); Salvatore Riccardi, C.P., Asst. Pastor; John Chrysostom Ryan, C.P. (Retired); Lawrence Rywalt, C.P., Gen. Sec.; Richard Scheiner, C.P., Confessor; Roy Srampical, C.P., Prof.; Jed Sumampong, C.P.; Theodore Walsh, C.P., Mission Preacher; Bros. Anselm Catalucci, C.P., (Retired); Philip Maggiulli, C.P., (Retired); Kenneth Pughe, C.P., (Retired); Angelo Sena, C.P., Receptionist. Priests 40; Brothers 3.

Passionist Benefactor's Society Tel: 718-739-9337; Fax: 718-206-9284. Email: pgrace@cpprov.org. Web: www.icmonastery.org.

St. Vincent's House, 84-15 Kendrick Pl., 11432. Tel: 718-990-7900; Fax: 718-990-7933. Email: mckennaj@stjohns.edu. Revs. John H. McKenna, C.M., B.A., M.A., S.T.D., Supr.; Kevin G. Creagh, C.M.; Joseph V. Daly, C.M., B.A., M.A., M.S.; Patrick J. Griffin, C.M., B.S., M.Div., Th.M, M.A., Ph.D.; Donald J. Harrington, C.M., B.A., M.Div., Th. M.; John A. Kettleberger, C.M., Th.M.; James J. Maher, C.M., B.A., M.Div., D.Min.; Michael D. Whalen, C.M., B.A., M.Div., Th.M., M.A., S.T.L., S.T.D. Vincentian Fathers.

Vincentian Residence (1958) St. John's University, 8000 Utopia Pkwy., 11439. Tel: 718-990-6744; Fax: 718-990-5724. Email: freundj@cmglobal.org. Revs. John B. Freund, C.M., Supr.; Tri Minh Duong, C.M., B.A., M.Div., M.A., Asst. Supr. & Campus Min.; Henry M. Bradbury, C.M., B.A., S.T.L., General Min.; Michael J. Callaghan, C.M., Ph.D., B.A., M.Div., M.A.T., Assoc. Prof. English; Dang Kim Doai; James F. Dorr, C.M., Chap.; Patrick S. Flanagan, C.M., B.S., M.Div., Local Procurator & Asst. Prof. Theology & Religious Studies; Peter D. Goldbach, C.M., B.A., S.T.L. (Retired); Walter F. Graham, C.M., M.A. (Retired); Evaristus A. Igwe, C.M.; James M. Kelly, C.M., M.A., Chap. Ozanam Nursing Home; Sheng Jiao Lin; Bro. Adam Budzyna, C.M.

JAMAICA ESTATES. *Paulist Fathers - Generalate*, 86-11 Midland Pkwy., 11432. Tel: 718-291-5995; Fax: 718-291-6646. Email: jfdcsp1@cs.com. Web: www.paulist.org. Revs. John F. Duffy, C.S.P., Pres.; Francis P. DeSiano, C.S.P., First Consultor; James W. Moran, C.S.P., Vice Pres.

LONG ISLAND CITY. *Holy Ghost Fathers of Ireland*, 48-49 37th St., 11101. Tel: 718-729-5273; Fax: 718-729-6949. Email: tbasquel@aol.com. Web: www.irishspiritans.ie. Very Rev. Thomas Basquel, C.S.Sp., Prov. Delegate; Revs. James Delaney, C.S.Sp. (Retired); Noel P. O'Meara, C.S.Sp.; Jerry Kirwin, C.S.Sp., Bursar.

OZONE PARK. *Montfort Missionaries Provincialate (Missionaries of the Company of Mary)* (1705) 101-18 104th St., 11416. Tel: 718-849-5885; Fax: 718-849-7518. Email: montfort.secretariat@gmail.com. Web: montfortmissionaries.com. Very Rev. Matthew J. Considine, S.M.M.; Rev. Richard Schebera, S.M.M. Priests 8.

Priests of Province Serving Abroad: Revs. John Breslin, S.M.M.; Peter D'Abele, S.M.M., Chontales, Nicaragua; Donald LaSalle, S.M.M., Generalate, Rome, Italy; Alonzo Lazo, S.M.M., Chontales, Nicaragua; Harry Flores Morales, S.M.M., Chontales, Nicaragua; Thomas D. Poth, S.M.M., Chontales, Nicaragua; Delegation Supr.

QUEENS VILLAGE. *DePaul Residence*, 80-14 217th St., 11427. Tel: 718-766-7344; Fax: 718-468-2903. Revs. Stephen C. Bicsko, C.M.; Michael J. Cummins, C.M.; Richard J. Devine, C.M.; Joseph P. Foley, C.M.

ROCKAWAY PARK. *Franciscan Missionary Brothers of North America New York*, 99-07 Rockaway Beach Blvd., 11694. Tel: 718-634-6476; Fax: 718-634-5833. Email: franciscanbi@netzero.net. Bro. Jose Valliara, C.M.S.F., Supr. General.

SOUTH OZONE PARK. *Sacred Heart Provincialate* (NY Province), 141-11 123 Ave., 11436-1426. Tel: 718-322-3309; Fax: 718-529-6004. Email: nyprovince@verizon.net. Bro. Joseph Rocco, S.C., Prov. Brothers 3.

SPRINGFIELD GARDENS. *Martin De Porres Brothers Community*, 136-01 219th St., 11413. Tel: 718-525-3414; Fax: 718-525-0982. Email: rrbfsc@mdp.org. Web: www.mdp.org. Bros. Raymond R. Blixt, F.S.C., M.A., Exec. Dir. Martin de Porres School; Philip Rofrano, F.S.C., L.C.S.W., Exec. Martin de Porres Group; Kevin Finn, F.S.C., M.A., Dir. of Community. Brothers 3.

[U] CONVENTS AND RESIDENCES FOR SISTERS

BROOKLYN. *The Congregation of the Daughters of Mary, Brooklyn*, 332 E. 32nd St., 11226. Tel: 718-856-3323; Fax: 718-703-0980. Sr. Marcelle Fils-aime, Vice Chm.

Discalced Carmelite Nuns (2004) 361 Highland Blvd., 11207. Tel: 718-235-0422; Fax: 718-235-0035.

Franciscan Sisters of the Poor, Congregational Office, 133 Remsen St., 11201. Tel: 718-643-1919; Fax: 718-643-9710. Email: sfp@franciscansisters.org. Web: www.franciscansisters.org. Sr. Tiziana Merletti, S.F.P., Congregation Min.

Missionaries of Charity, Contemplative/Our Lady of Lourdes Convent (1982) 34 Aberdeen St., 11207. Tel: 718-443-2868. Sisters 12.

Monastery of the Sisters Adorers of the Precious Blood, 5400 Ft. Hamilton Pkwy., 11219. Tel: 718-438-6371; Fax: 718-438-6381. Rev. Msgrs. Austin P. Bennett, J.C.D., P.A., Exec. Dir. Confraternity of the Precious Blood (Retired); Philip J. Reilly, Chap. (Retired). Sisters 6.

Sisters of Mercy of the Americas, Mid-Atlantic Community (1855) 273 Willoughby Ave.,

11205-1487. Tel: 718-622-5840; Fax: 718-398-7866. Web: www.mercymidatlantic.org. Sr. Christine McCann, R.S.M., Pres. Sisters 1,071.

Sisters of the Good Shepherd, 348 Ninth St., 11215. Tel: 718-499-9212. Sisters 2.

Provincial Office, 25-30 21st Ave., Astoria, 11105. Tel: 718-278-1155. Sr. Ellen Kelly, Prov. Officer.

Sisters of the Visitation of Brooklyn, NY (1855) 8902 Ridge Blvd., 11209. Tel: 718-745-5151; Fax: 718-745-3680. Email: srp2srr@aol.com. Web: www.visitationsisters.org/mona/bro_main.asp. Sr. Mary Pauline Baulis, V.H.M., R.N., Supr. Professed Sisters 19.

ASTORIA. *Provincialate of the Sisters of the Good Shepherd* (1834) 25-30 21st Ave., 11105. Tel: 718-278-1155; Fax: 718-278-1158. Email: ekelly@nygoodsheperd.org. Web: goodshepherdsistersna.com. Sr. Ellen Kelly, Prov.; Zenovia Jackson, Prov. Sec.

Sisters of the Good Shepherd, Province of New York

Sisters of the Good Shepherd, 61-03 56th Ave., Maspeth, 11378. Tel: 718-418-0280; Fax: 718-418-0282. Sisters 6.

JAMAICA. *The Congregation of the Sisters of Jesus the Savior*, 171-17 110th Ave., 11433. Tel: 718-526-0973; Fax: 718-526-0973. Sisters Mary Fidelis Ezemaduka, S.J.S., Regional Coord.; Maria Gemma Njeze, S.J.S., Community Supr.; Christiana Nwachukwu, S.J.S., Bursar.

Ursuline Provincial Administration Office, Glengarda, 81-15 Utopia Pkwy., 11432-1308. Tel: 718-591-0681; Fax: 718-969-4275. Email: mbarrett@tildonkursuline.org. Web: www.tildonkursuline.org. Sr. Mairead M. Barrett, O.S.U., Prov. Supr.

QUEENS VILLAGE. *St. Ann's Novitiate, Little Sisters of the Poor* (1902) 110-39 Springfield Blvd., P.O. Box 280356, 11428. Tel: 718-464-4920; Fax: 718-479-3126. Email: nvmothersuperior@littlesistersofthepoor.org. Web: www.littlesistersofthepoor.org. Sr. Mary Richard, L.S.P., Supr. & Mistress of Novices; Rev. Msgr. James Pereda, C.R.C., Chap. Sisters 6; Novices 8; Postulants 5.

Little Sisters of the Poor, Provincial Residence, 110-30 221st St., 11429. Tel: 718-464-1800; Fax: 347-626-2181. Email: provincialbklyn@littlesistersofthepoor.org. Web: www.littlesistersofthepoor.org. Sr. Margaret Regina Halloran, L.S.P., Prov. Sisters 150.

RIDGEWOOD. *Convent of the Sisters of Mary Reparatrix*, 62-67 60 Pl., 11385. Tel: 718-456-4242; 718-386-1107 (Altar Bread Department); Fax: 718-386-2254. Email: smrny@att.net. Web: www.smr.org. Sr. Pat Mullen, S.M.R., Local Leader. Sisters 2.

ROCKAWAY PARK. *Stella Maris Convent, Sisters of St. Joseph* 11694-2497. Tel: 718-634-1886.

[V] EVANGELIZATION AND RENEWAL CENTERS

BROOKLYN. *Grassroots Renewal Project, Inc.*, 119 Eagle St., 11222. Rev. Glenn Sudano, C.F.R., Pres.

Ss. Peter and Paul Spirituality Center Brooklyn Campus, 118 Congress St., 11201. Tel: 718-624-5670; Fax: 718-624-5806. Very Rev. Joseph G. Fonti, S.T.L., Dir.; Rev. Msgr. Perfecto Vasquez; Deacons Francis G. Mateo; Jimmy Garcia.

DOUGLASTON. *Ss. Peter and Paul Spirituality Center Queens Campus* (Queens Campus), Immaculate Conception Ctr., 7200 Douglaston Pkwy, 11362. Tel: 718-281-9491; Fax: 718-352-2490. Very Rev. Joseph G. Fonti, S.T.L., Dir.

JAMAICA. *Bishop Molloy Retreat House* (1924) 86-45 Edgerton Blvd., 11432. Tel: 718-739-1229; Fax: 718-739-3421. Web: www.bishopmolloy.org. Revs. John Michael Lee, C.P., Retreat Dir.; Christopher Cleary, C.P., Assoc. Passionist Fathers.

[W] SECULAR INSTITUTES

BROOKLYN. *The Institute of the Apostolic Oblates* (1950) 730 E. 87th St., 11236. Tel: 718-649-0324; Fax: 718-272-5012. Email: apostolicoblates@verizon.net. Web: www.prosanctity.org. Giovanna Piccioli, A.O., Local Moderator.

FOREST HILLS. *Asociacion Misioneros Contemplativos Laicos* (Lay Association of Contemplative Missionaries), 3543 84th St., Apt. 308, Jackson Heights, 11372. Tel: 718-592-5458; Fax: 718-592-5458. Antonio Alvarez, Representative; Ana Luisa Ortega, Treas.

[X] MISCELLANEOUS LISTINGS

BROOKLYN. *Aid to the Church in Need, Inc.*, 725 Leonard St., 3rd Fl., 11222-0384. Tel: 718-609-0939; Fax: 718-609-0938. Web: www.churchinneed.org.

Alive in Hope Foundation of the Diocese of Brooklyn (1998) 310 Prospect Park West, 11215. Tel: 718-965-7375; Fax: 718-965-7341. Email: info@aliveinhope.org. Web: www.aliveinhopefoundation.org.

Casa Betsaida Housing Development Fund Corp., 191 Joralemon St., 11201. Tel: 718-722-6086. Jeanne M. Diulio, Asst. Dir., Office of Legal Affairs.

Casa Betsaida-Home for people with AIDS, 267 Hewes St., 11211. Tel: 718-218-7890; Fax: 718-218-8264. Email: cbetsaidainc@aol.com. Rev. Msgr. Anthony Hernandez, Chm. Bd. Total Staff 16; Total Assisted 67.

The Cathedral Club of Brooklyn, P.O. Box 315, 11209-0315. Tel: 718-809-2440; Fax: 718-680-0655. Web: www.cathedralclubbrooklyn.org. James B. McHugh, Pres.

Churches United Corp., 280 Marcy Ave., 11211. Tel: 718-388-3774; Fax: 718-388-3784. Web: churchesunitedcorp.org.

Compostela Fund of the Roman Catholic Diocese of Brooklyn (2002) 310 Prospect Park W., 11215. Tel: 718-965-7300; Fax: 718-965-7311. Email: mreid@diobrook.org. Rev. Msgr. Michael J. Reid, Vicar for Financial Admin.

**Federation of Oases of Koinonia John the Baptist*, 205 14th St., 11215.

Franciscan Brothers Charitable Trust (1999) 135 Remsen St., 11201. Tel: 718-858-8217; Fax: 718-858-8306. Email: generalate@gmail.com. Web: www.francisanbrothers.org. Richard T. Arkwright, Trustee; Robert Schaefer, Trustee; Michael Henning, Trustee.

Franciscan Sisters of the Poor Charitable Trust, 133 Remsen St., 11201. Tel: 718-643-1919; Fax: 718-643-9710. Email: sfp@franciscansisters.org. Web: www.franciscansisters.org. Sr. Tiziana Merletti, S.F.P., Congregation Min.

Franciscan Sisters of the Poor Communities, Inc., 133 Remsen St., 11201.

The Futures in Education Foundation, Inc., 310 Prospect Park W., 11215. Tel: 718-965-7340; Fax: 718-965-7341. Email: futuresinfo@dioceseofbrooklyn.org. Web: www.dioceseofbrooklyn.org/futures.

Good Shepherd Charitable Trust, 310 Prospect Park W., 11215.

HeartShare Human Services of NY - Clermont Residence, 26 Clermont Ave., 11205. Tel: 718-834-9317; Fax: 718-834-9364. Miss Sharon Bewry, Resident Mgr. Residence for Developmentally Disabled Adults.

St. John Vianney Fund Charitable Trust, 310 Prospect Park West, 11215.

St. John's Bread & Life Program, Inc., 795 Lexington Ave., 11221. Tel: 718-443-2240; Fax: 718-455-7796. Mr. Anthony Butler, Exec. Dir.; Sr. Kathleen Byrne, S.C., Mobile Soup Kitchen Dir.; Yemi Oyename, Dir. Food Svcs. (Soup Kitchen, Employment Counseling, HIV/AIDS Support Group/Food Pantry, Counseling, Referrals and Advocacy)

Juan Neumann Center (Immigration Services), 550 59th St., 11220. Tel: 718-439-8160; Fax: 718-439-8685.

**The Maura Clarke Ita Ford Center* (1993) 138 Bleecker St., 11221. Tel: 718-573-8631; Fax: 718-602-3487. Email: mcifcenter@verizon.net. Web: mauraclarke-itafordcenter.org. Janet Henriquez, Dir.

Mercy Home Foundation, 243 Prospect Park W., 11215. Tel: 718-832-1075; Fax: 718-832-7612. Sr. Virginia Farnan, Contact Person.

Mercy Medical Mission (Sisters of Mercy Mid-Atlantic Community), 273 Willoughby Ave., 11205.

National Center of the Haitian Apostolate, 332 E. 32nd St., 11226. Tel: 718-856-3323; Fax: 718-703-0980. Web: snaa.org. Most Rev. Guy Sansaricq, Exec. Dir.

Pro Sanctity Movement (1947) 730 E. 87th St., 11236. Tel: 718-649-0324; Fax: 718-272-5012. Email: prosanctitynewyork@verizon.net. Web: www.nyprosanctity.org. Angela DiPaola, Dir.; Rev. Msgr. Steven J. Aguggia, J.C.L., Spiritual Advisor.

The Roman Catholic Pontifical Lay Association Memores Domini, 218 76th St., 11209. Tel: 718-833-3992. Email: asala218@gmail.com.

Men's House (1993) 218 76 St., 11209. Tel: 718-833-3992. Email: cvath@earthlink.net. Christopher H. Vath, Head of the House.

Women's House (1993) 10 Kraft Ave., Bronxville, 10708. Tel: 916-395-0019. Email: mariacerny@yahoo.com. Maria Ceruti, Head of the House.

Ryken Educational Center, Inc., 7100 Shore Rd., 11209. Tel: 718-836-7100. Email: sferrara@xaverian.org. Dr. Salvatore Ferrara, Pres.

Society of the Immaculate Conception of Brooklyn (Missionary Society), 310 Prospect Park W., 11215. Tel: 718-965-7326; Fax: 718-965-7325. Email: tmulkerin@rcdob.org. Rev. Terrence J. Mulkerin, Exec. Dir. (Retired). (Missionary Society)

St. Mary's Supportive Housing Development Fund Corp., 1534 Prospect Pl., 11213. Tel: 718-818-5055. Email: mditommaso@svcmcny.org. Marianne DiTommaso, Asst. Sec., Bd. Dirs. HDFC.

St. Theresa of Avila Senior Housing Development Fund Corporation, 191 Joralemon St., 11201. Tel: 718-722-6086. Jeanne M. Diulio, Asst. Dir., Office of Legal Affairs.

ASTORIA. *Flowers With Care/Catholic Charities Neighborhood Services, Diocese of Brooklyn, Inc.*, 23-40 Astoria Blvd., 11102. Tel: 718-726-9790; Fax: 718-728-8817. Email: fwcareyscc@yahoo.com. Catherine Nicolini, Ph.D., Exec. Dir.

Flowers with Care Youth Services GED Program, NYCALI, Out of School Youth (OSY) & 21st Century After School Program, 23-40 Astoria Blvd., 11102. Tel: 718-726-9790; Fax: 718-728-8817.

Youth Employment Program: L.I.F.E. (Looking Into Future Employment), 200 Gold St., 11201. Tel: 718-875-8801; Fax: 718-875-4367.

Big Brothers/Big Sisters, 200 Gold St., 11201. Tel: 718-875-8801; Fax: 718-875-4367.

Choosing Abstinence with Peers (CAPS), 200 Gold St., 11201. Tel: 718-875-8801; Fax: 718-875-4367.

Healthy Families, 200 Gold St., 11201. Tel: 718-875-8801; Fax: 718-875-4367.

Man-Up Fatherhood Program, 200 Gold St., 11201. Tel: 718-875-8801; Fax: 718-875-4367.

Northwest Brooklyn Parenting Project: Reaching Families One Parent at a Time, 200 Gold St., 11201. Tel: 718-875-8801; Fax: 718-875-4367.

Redford Hills The Children's Center, 247 Harris Rd., Bedford Hills, 10507. Tel: 914-241-3100, Ext. 4050; Fax: 914-248-7588.

Redford Hills Teen Program, 247 Harris Rd., Bedford Hills, 10507. Tel: 917-241-3100; Fax: 914-248-7588.

Brighter Tomorrows - 21st Century at St. John the Baptist, 82 Lewis Ave., 11206. Tel: 718-453-1000; Fax: 718-453-1860.

Good Shepherd Volunteers, 25-30 21st Ave., 11105. Tel: 718-943-7489; Fax: 718-777-1928.

HandCrafting Justice, Inc. (1997) 25-30 21st Ave., 11105. Tel: 718-204-0909; Fax: 718-777-1928. Email: hcj@handcraftingjustice.org. Web: www.handcraftingjustice.org. Sr. Maureen McGowan, R.G.S., Prog. Dir.

BAYSIDE. *Ozanam Geriatric Foundation* (1997) 42-41 201 St., 11361. Tel: 718-971-2020; Fax: 718-971-2025. Email: godonovan@ozanamhall.org. Web: www.ozanamhall.org.

BRIARWOOD. *Archbishop Molloy High School Charitable Trust*, 85-53 Manton St., 11435. Tel: 718-441-9210; Fax: 718-846-3202.

FLUSHING. **Women Helping Women* (1981) P.O. Box 580086, 11358-0086. Tel: 718-539-9111; Fax: 718-961-3322. Email: whwcol@earthlink.net.

HOLLIS HILLS. *Glencara, Inc.* (1996) 86-05 218th St., 11427. Tel: 718-454-9804; Fax: 718-454-9806. Email: sfoley@nyc.rr.com. Sisters Sean Foley, R.S.M., Pres.; Kathleen Quinn, R.S.M., Vice Pres.; Francene Horan, R.S.M., Sec.; Eileen Trainor, 2nd Vice Pres.; Regina Williams, Treas.

JACKSON HEIGHTS. **Eternal Flame of Hope Ministries, Inc.*, c/o Rev. Richard J. Bretone, 74-18 Ditmars Blvd., 11370. Tel: 718-274-4919. Rev. Richard J. Bretone, Spiritual Dir.

Preachers of Christ and Mary, 93-11 35th Ave., 11372. Tel: 718-779-4134.

JAMAICA. *Immaculata Hall Housing Development Fund Corporation*, 149-29 90th Ave., 11432. Tel: 718-818-5055. Email: Mditommaso@svcmcny.org. Marianne DiTommaso, Dir.

LONG ISLAND CITY. *Hour Children* (1995) 36-11A 12th St., 11106. Tel: 718-443-4724; Fax: 718-433-4728. Email: hourchildren@verizon.net. Web: www.hourchildren.org. Sr. Teresa Fitzgerald, C.S.J., Exec. Dir. Families Capacity 50; Total Staff 35; Total Assisted Annually (Includes work inside prisons) 1,100; Volunteers 60.

World Compassion Link, P.O. Box 4279, 11104-9808. Tel: 201-395-0710; Fax: 201-395-0710. Email: omearanoel@gmail.com. Web: worldcompassionlink.org. 48-49 37th St., 11101. Rev. Noel P. O'Meara, C.S.Sp., Pres.; Very Rev. Thomas Basquel, C.S.Sp., Vice Pres.; Rev. James Delaney, C.S.Sp., Dir. Devel. & Treas. (Retired).

MIDDLE VILLAGE. *National Italian Apostolate Conference* (1968) 66-05 79th Pl., 11379. Tel: 718-326-1911; Fax: 718-326-1883. Email: niac.america@gmail.com. Rev. Msgr. Steven J. Aguggia, J.C.L., Exec. Dir.

QUEENS. *Focolare Movement*

REGO PARK. *Lifeway Network, Inc.*, 85-10 61st Rd., 11374. Tel: 718-779-8075; Fax: 718-651-5645.

RIDGEWOOD. *Friends of RADIO MARIA, Inc.* (1992) 70-05 Fresh Pond Rd., 11385. Tel: 718-417-0550; Fax: 718-417-5188.

Email: info.nyi@radiomaria.org. Web: www.radiomaria.org. Rev. Walter Tonelotto, C.S., Dir.

ROCKAWAY PARK. *Franciscan Missionary Brothers of North America, NY* (1901) 99-07 Rockaway Beach Blvd., 11694. Tel: 718-634-6476; Fax: 718-634-5833. Email: franciscanbi@netzero.net. Bro. Joseph Karimalayil, C.M.S.F., Ph.D., Pres. & Supr. General.

WOODHAVEN. *School Sisters of Notre Dame Educational Center*, 87-04 88th Ave., 11421. Tel: 718-738-0588; Fax: 718-322-5515. Email: ssndec@aol.com. Sr. Catherine Feeney, S.S.N.D., Exec. Dir. Staff 5; Total Assisted 80.

RELIGIOUS INSTITUTES OF MEN REPRESENTED IN THE DIOCESE

For further details refer to the corresponding bracketed number in the Religious Institutes of Men or Women section.

[1350]—*Brothers of St. Francis Xavier* (Sacred Heart Prov.)—C.F.X.
[0330]—*Brothers of the Christian Schools*—F.S.C.
[0600]—*Brothers of the Congregation of Holy Cross*—C.S.C.
[1100]—*Brothers of the Sacred Heart*—S.C.
[0470]—*The Capuchin Friars* (Prov. of St. Mary)—O.F.M.Cap.
[0275]—*Carmelites of Mary Immaculate*—C.M.I.
[]—*Congregation of St. John the Baptist of China, Inc.*—C.S.J.B.
[1330]—*Congregation of the Mission* (Eastern, New England, Spanish Provs.)—C.M.
[1330]—*Congregation of the Mission - Philadelphia (Vincentians)*—C.M.
[1330]—*Congregation of the Mission (Vincentian Fathers)*—C.M.
[1210]—*Congregation of the Missionaries of St. Charles*—C.S.
[]—*Congregation of the Missionary Brothers of St. Francis of Assisi*—C.M.S.F.
[1000]—*Congregation of the Passion* (Prov. of St. Paul of the Cross)—C.P.
[0480]—*Conventual Franciscans* (Polish Prov.)—O.F.M.Conv
[0490]—*Franciscan Brothers of Brooklyn*—O.S.F.
[0520]—*Franciscan Friars* (Immaculate Conception Prov.; Lithuanian Vicariate)—O.F.M.
[0650]—*Holy Ghost Fathers*—C.S.Sp.
[]—*Institute of the Incarnate Word*—I.V.E.
[0690]—*Jesuit Fathers and Brothers* (New York Prov.)—S.J.
[0770]—*The Marist Brothers*—F.M.S.
[0780]—*The Marist Fathers*—S.M.
[0870]—*Montfort Missionaries (Missionaries of the Company of Mary)*—S.M.M.
[1330]—*New England Province of the Congregation of the Mission (Vincentian)*—C.M.
[0950]—*Oratorians* (Brooklyn)—C.O.
[0520]—*Order of St. Francis (Lithuanian)*—O.F.M.
[0990]—*Pallottine*—S.A.C.
[]—*Pallottine* (Polish Prov.)—S.A.C.
[1030]—*Paulist Fathers*—C.S.P.
[1070]—*The Redemptorists*—C.SS.R.
[1200]—*Salvatorian Fathers*—S.D.S.
[1210]—*Scalabrini Fathers (The Pious Society for the Missionaries of St. Charles)*—C.S.S.J.
[0690]—*Society of Jesus*—S.J.
[0760]—*Society of Mary (Marianists)* (New York Prov.)—S.M.
[0990]—*Society of the Catholic Apostolate*—S.A.C.
[1200]—*Society of the Divine Savior*—S.D.S.
[1350]—*Xaverian Brothers U.S.A., Inc.*—C.F.X.

RELIGIOUS INSTITUTES OF WOMEN REPRESENTED IN THE DIOCESE

[0340]—*Carmelite Sisters of Charity*—C.C.V.
[0330]—*Carmelite Sisters of the Aged and Infirm*—O.Carm.
[2980]—*Congregation of Notre Dame*—C.N.D.
[2950]—*Congregation of Notre Dame de Sion*—N.D.S.
[]—*Congregation of Olivetan Benedictine Sisters* (Korea)—O.S.B.
[2230]—*Congregation of the Infant Jesus*—C.I.J.
[3832]—*Congregation of the Sisters of St. Joseph*—C.S.J.
[0760]—*Daughters of Charity of St. Vincent de Paul*—D.C.
[]—*Daughters of Divine Love*—D.D.L.
[]—*Daughters of Mary*—F.de.M.
[]—*Daughters of Mary Mother of Mercy*—D.M.M.M.
[0960]—*Daughters of Wisdom*—D.W.
[0420]—*Discalced Carmelite Nuns*—O.C.D.
[1070-11]—*Dominican Congregation of Our Lady of the Rosary (Sparkill Dominicans)*—O.P.
[1070-05]—*Dominican Sisters* (Amityville, NY)—O.P.
[1105]—*Dominican Sisters of Hope*—O.P.
[1115]—*Dominican Sisters of Peace*—O.P.
[1400]—*Franciscan Missionary Sisters of the Sacred Heart*—F.M.S.C.
[1190]—*Franciscan Sisters of the Atonement*—S.A.
[]—*Franciscan Sisters of the Immaculate (Honduras)*—H.F.I.
[1440]—*Franciscan Sisters of the Poor*—S.F.P.
[1840]—*Grey Nuns of the Sacred Heart*—G.N.S.H.
[]—*Handmaids of the Divine Redeemer* (Ghana)—H.D.R.
[]—*Handmaids of the Holy Child Jesus* (Nigeria)—H.H.C.J.
[]—*Hermanas Franciscanos de la Immaculata*—H.F.I.
[]—*Hermanas Predicadoras de Cristo y Maria* (Columbia)—P.C.M.
[2070]—*Holy Union Sisters*—S.U.S.C.
[]—*Idente Missionaries*—M.Id
[2340]—*Little Sisters of the Poor*—L.S.P.
[2470]—*Maryknoll Sisters of St Dominic*—M.M.
[2710]—*Missionaries of Charity*—M.C.
[2710]—*Missionaries of Charity (Contemplative)*—M.C.
[]—*Missionary Congregation Sisters Servants of the Holy Spirit*—S.Sp.S.
[2790]—*Missionary Servants of the Most Blessed Trinity*—M.S.B.T.
[]—*Missionary Sisters of the Immaculate Conception*—M.F.I.C.
[]—*Missionary Sisters of the Precious Blood* (Canada)—C.P.S.
[4190]—*Order of Visitation*—V.H.M.
[3160]—*Parish Visitors of Mary Immaculate*—P.V.M.I.
[2070]—*Religious of the Holy Union of the Sacred Hearts*—S.U.S.C.
[3465]—*Religious of the Sacred Heart of Mary*—R.S.H.M.
[3430]—*Religious Teachers Filippini*—M.P.F.
[2970]—*School Sisters of Notre Dame*—S.S.N.D.
[]—*Servants of the Lord and the Virgin of Matara* (Argentina)—S.S.V.M.
[0110]—*Sisters Adorers of the Most Precious Blood*—A.P.B.
[0650]—*Sisters of Charity of St. Vincent de Paul of New York*—S.C.
[0640]—*Sisters of Charity of St. Vincent de Paul, Halifax*—S.C.
[]—*Sisters of Jesus the Savior* (Nigeria)—S.J.S.
[]—*Sisters of Mary Immaculate* (Kenya)—S.M.I.
[2575]—*Sisters of Mercy of the Americas* (Mid-Atlantic Community)—R.S.M.
[2990]—*Sisters of Notre Dame*—S.N.D.
[3000]—*Sisters of Notre Dame de Namur*—S.N.D.deN.
[2670]—*Sisters of Our Lady of Mercy*—S.O.L.M.
[3820]—*Sisters of St. John the Baptist*—C.S.J.B.
[3830-05]—*Sisters of St. Joseph*—C.S.J.
[3830-01]—*Sisters of St. Joseph of Boston*—C.S.J.
[1830]—*Sisters of the Good Shepherd*—R.G.S.
[1970]—*Sisters of the Holy Family of Nazareth* (Immaculate Heart of Mary Prov.)—C.S.F.N.
[]—*Sisters of the Immaculate Heart of Mary* Kongmoon, China—I.H.M.
[]—*Sisters of the Korean Martyrs*—S.B.K.M.
[3320]—*Sisters of the Presentation of the B.V.M.* (Newburgh)—P.B.V.M.
[2160]—*Sisters, Servants of the Immaculate Heart of Mary*—I.H.M.
[2460]—*Society of Mary Reparatrix*—S.M.R.
[4130]—*Ursuline Sisters of the Congregation of Tildonk, Belgium*—O.S.U.
[4190]—*Visitation Nuns*—V.H.M.

CATHOLIC CEMETERIES

MIDDLE VILLAGE. *Saint John's Cemetery* Operating: St. Johns's Cemetery (Middle Village); Holy Cross Cemetery (Brooklyn); Mount St. Mary Cemetery (Flushing); St. Charles/Resurrection Cemetery (Farmingdale), 80-01 Metropolitan Ave., 11379. Tel: 718-894-4888; Fax: 718-326-2033. Web: www.ccbklyn.org. Steven Comando, Exec. Dir.

PARISH CEMETERIES

BROOKLYN. *Trinity*, Tel: 718-894-4888. Most Holy Trinity Parish, Brooklyn.

AMITYVILLE. *Most Holy Trinity* Most Holy Trinity Parish, Brooklyn.

ROCKAWAY. *St. Mary Star of the Sea Cemetery*, Far Rockaway, 11691. Tel: 718-894-4888.

NECROLOGY

† Demski, Rev. Msgr. Arthur A., (Retired)—Died Dec. 10, 2009
† Grace, Rev. Msgr. James P., Queens, NY St. Andrew Avellino—Died March 3, 2009
† Hendel, Rev. Msgr. Thomas W. J., (Retired)—Died Jan. 6, 2009
† Mulhall, Rev. Msgr. Francis X., (Retired)—Died Sept. 23, 2009
† Rau, Rev. Msgr. Raymond F., (Retired)—Died Sept. 20, 2009
† Brady, Coman V., Brooklyn, NY St. Vincent Ferrer—Died July 20, 2009
† Buetow, Harold A., (Retired)—Died Oct. 17, 2009
† Culkin, Henry M., (Retired)—Died Aug. 2, 2009
† D'Amato, James J., (Retired)—Died Jan. 30, 2009
† Heffernan, Thomas A., (Retired)—Died Aug. 6, 2009
† Keane, Joseph P., (Retired)—Died June 10, 2009
† Longres, Joaquin S., (Retired)—Died Feb. 11, 2009
† Lyons, Thomas J., (Retired)—Died Jan. 22, 2009
† Marron, James F., Rosedale, NY St. Pius X—Died March 16, 2009
† Teahan, Timothy J., (Retired)—Died Oct. 3, 2009
† Vogel, Charles P., Brooklyn, NY St. Sylvester—Died Feb. 10, 2009

An asterisk (*) denotes an organization that has established tax-exempt status directly with the IRS and is not covered by the USCCB Group Ruling.

Diocese of Brownsville

(Dioecesis Brownsvillensis)

Most Reverend

DANIEL E. FLORES

Bishop of Brownsville; ordained January 30, 1988; appointed Auxiliary Bishop of Detroit and Titular Bishop of Cozyla October 28, 2006; consecrated November 29, 2006; appointed Bishop of Brownsville December 9, 2009; installed February 2, 2010. *Mailing Address: P.O. Box 2279, Brownsville, TX 78522-2279.*

Most Reverend

RAYMUNDO J. PEÑA, D.D.

Retired Bishop of Brownsville; ordained May 25, 1957; appointed Titular Bishop of Trisipa and Auxiliary of San Antonio October 16, 1976; consecrated December 13, 1976; appointed Bishop of El Paso April 29, 1980; installed June 18, 1980; appointed Bishop of Brownsville May 23, 1995; installed August 6, 1995; retired December 9, 2009. *Mailing Address: P.O. Box 2279, Brownsville, TX 78522-2279.*

ESTABLISHED JULY 10, 1965.

Square Miles 4,226.

Comprises the four Counties of Cameron, Hidalgo, Starr and Willacy in the State of Texas.

For legal titles of parishes and diocesan institutions, consult the Catholic Pastoral Center.

Catholic Pastoral Center: 1910 University Blvd., P.O. Box 2279, Brownsville, TX 78522-2279. Tel: 956-542-2501; Fax: 956-542-6751.

Web: www.cdob.org

Email: cdob@cdob.org

STATISTICAL OVERVIEW

Personnel	
Bishop	1
Retired Bishops	1
Priests: Diocesan Active in Diocese	70
Priests: Diocesan Active Outside Diocese	3
Priests: Retired, Sick or Absent	11
Number of Diocesan Priests	84
Religious Priests in Diocese	38
Total Priests in Diocese	122
Extern Priests in Diocese	9
Ordinations:	
Diocesan Priests	2
Transitional Deacons	1
Permanent Deacons in Diocese	69
Total Brothers	20
Total Sisters	13
Parishes	
Parishes	69
With Resident Pastor:	
Resident Diocesan Priests	48
Resident Religious Priests	20
Without Resident Pastor:	
Administered by Priests	1
Missions	45
Pastoral Centers	2
New Parishes Created	1
Professional Ministry Personnel:	
Brothers	5
Sisters	11
Lay Ministers	80
Welfare	
Health Care Centers	3
Total Assisted	5,486
Homes for the Aged	2
Total Assisted	226
Day Care Centers	1
Total Assisted	38
Special Centers for Social Services	6
Total Assisted	23,287
Other Institutions	4
Total Assisted	8,251
Educational	
Seminaries, Diocesan	1
Students from This Diocese	4
Diocesan Students in Other Seminaries	17
Total Seminarians	21
High Schools, Private	3
Total Students	949
Elementary Schools, Diocesan and Parish	8
Total Students	2,193
Elementary Schools, Private	3
Total Students	932
Catechesis/Religious Education:	
High School Students	9,018
Elementary Students	29,980
Total Students under Catholic Instruction	43,093
Teachers in the Diocese:	
Priests	1
Brothers	7
Sisters	10
Lay Teachers	274
Vital Statistics	
Receptions into the Church:	
Infant Baptism Totals	8,681
Minor Baptism Totals	756
Adult Baptism Totals	170
Received into Full Communion	804
First Communions	7,023
Confirmations	3,700
Marriages:	
Catholic	1,088
Interfaith	102
Total Marriages	1,190
Deaths	2,778
Total Catholic Population	1,021,861
Total Population	1,202,189

Former Prelates—Rt. Revs. DOMINIC MANUCY, Titular Bishop of Delma and Vicar Apostolic of Brownsville; cons. Dec. 8, 1874; transferred to Mobile, March 9, 1884; reappointed to Vicariate Apostolic of Brownsville, Feb. 1, 1885; died Dec. 4, 1885; PETER VERDAGUER, Titular Bishop of Aulon and Vicar Apostolic of Brownsville; cons. Nov. 9, 1890; died Oct. 26, 1911; CLAUDE JAILLET, O.P., Administrator of Vicariate Apostolic of Brownsville, 1911-1913.

Former Bishops—Most Rev. ADOLPH MARX, D.D., J.C.D., first Bishop of Brownsville, ord. May 2, 1940; appt. Titular Bishop of Citrus and Auxiliary Bishop of Corpus Christi, July 6, 1956; cons. Oct. 9, 1956; appt. first Bishop of Brownsville, July 19, 1965; installed Sept. 2, 1965; died in Cologne, Germany Nov. 1, 1965; His Eminence HUMBERTO CARDINAL MEDEIROS, D.D., second Bishop of Brownsville, appt. April 14, 1966; cons. June 9, 1966; installed Bishop of Brownsville, June 29, 1966; appt. Archbishop of Boston, Sept. 8, 1970; installed Archbishop of Boston, Oct. 7, 1970; created Cardinal, March 5, 1973; died Sept. 17, 1983; Most Revs. JOHN J. FITZPATRICK, D.D., third Bishop of Brownsville, ord. Dec. 13, 1942; appt. Auxiliary Bishop of Miami, June 24, 1968; cons. Aug. 28, 1968; appt. Bishop of Brownsville, April 27, 1971; installed May 27, 1971; retired Nov. 30, 1991; died July 15, 2006; ENRIQUE SAN PEDRO, S.J., S.T.D., S.S.L., fourth Bishop of Brownsville, ord. March 18, 1957; appt. Auxiliary Bishop of Galveston-Houston April 1, 1986; cons. June 29, 1986; appt. Coadjutor Bishop of Brownsville, Aug. 13, 1991; installed Sept. 26, 1991; succeeded to the See, Nov. 30, 1991; died July 17, 1994; RAYMUNDO J. PENA, D.D., fifth Bishop of Brownsville, ord. May 25, 1957; appt. Titular Bishop of Trisipa and Auxiliary of San Antonio Oct. 16, 1976; cons. Dec. 13, 1976; appt. Bishop of El Paso April 29, 1980; installed June 18, 1980; appt. Bishop of Brownsville May 23, 1995; installed Aug. 6, 1995; retired Dec. 9, 2009.

Office of the Bishop—Most Rev. DANIEL E. FLORES, 1910 University Blvd., P.O. Box 2279, Brownsville, 78522-2279. Tel: 956-550-1510; Fax: 956-550-1565. Email: bishopflores@cdob.org.

Vicar General—Rev. Msgr. ROBERT E. MAHER, V.G. Email: rmaher@cdob.org; Rev. THOMAS LUCZAK, O.F.M., V.G., Office, 700 Virgen de San Juan Blvd., San Juan, 78589. Tel: 956-781-5323; Fax: 956-784-5081. St. Joseph Parish, 122 W. Fay, Edinburg, 78539. Tel: 956-383-3728; Fax: 956-383-8630. Email: stjo-edinburg@sbcglobal.net.

Deans/Deaneries—St. John: Rev. Msgr. HEBERTO M. DIAZ JR. Tel: 956-542-2501. St. James: Rev. ISAAC EMEKA ERONDU. Tel: 956-399-2865. St. Paul: Rev. GABRIEL I. EZEH. Tel: 956-797-2666. St. Matthew: Rev. PATRICK K. SEITZ. Tel: 956-968-7471. St. Philip: Rev. Msgr. GUSTAVO BARRERA. Tel: 956-686-0251. St. Peter: Rev. EUSEBIO MARTINEZ. Tel: 956-383-5472. St. Andrew: Rev. CRAIG G. CAROLAN. Tel: 956-580-4551.

Development Office—Mr. JESSE SALINAS, Dir., 1910 University Blvd., P.O. Box 2279, Brownsville, 78522-2279. Tel: 956-542-2501; Fax: 956-542-6751. Email: jsalinas@cdob.org.

Stewardship Office—VACANT, Dir.

Judicial Department and Diocesan Tribunal—Rev. Msgr. LUIS JAVIER GARCIA, J.C.L., Judicial Vicar.

Email: lgarcia@cdob.org; Ms. ANNITA GONZALEZ, Ecclesiastical Notary & Advocate Coord., Main Address: 1910 University Blvd., P.O. Box 2279, Brownsville, 78522-2279. Tel: 956-542-2501. Mailing and Physical Address: San Juan Office, 700 N. Virgen de San Juan Blvd., San Juan, 78589. Tel: 956-784-5070; Fax: 956-784-5087. Email: agonzalez@cdob.org.

Presiding Judge—Rev. Msgr. LUIS JAVIER GARCIA, J.C.L.

Promoter of Justice—Rev. Msgr. GUSTAVO BARRERA.

Procurators and Advocates—Ms. ANNITA GONZALEZ, Coord.

Court Expert—Sr. NORMA PIMENTEL, M.J., L.P.C.

Associate Judges—Revs. A. OLIVER ANGEL, J.C.L.; THOMAS G. KULLECK.

Canonical Assistance—Revs. JOSE RENE ANGEL, J.C.L.; A. OLIVER ANGEL, J.C.L.; Rev. Msgr. LUIS JAVIER GARCIA, J.C.L.

Defenders of the Bond—Rev. Msgr. GUSTAVO BARRERA, First Instance. Email: gcbarrera@rgv.rr.com; Revs. RICARDO GARCIA, J.C.L., First Instance. Email: frricardo@rgv.rr.com; JOSE RENE ANGEL, J.C.L., Second Instance.

Office of the Chancellor—1910 University Blvd., P.O. Box 2279, Brownsville, 78522-2279. Tel: 956-542-2501; Fax: 956-542-6751. Rev. Msgr. HEBERTO M. DIAZ JR., Chancellor. Email: hdiaz@cdob.org; Rev. THOMAS G. KULLECK, Historical Archivist. Email: tkulleck@cdob.org.

Moderator of the Curia/Brownsville/San Juan—Rev. Msgr. HEBERTO M. DIAZ JR., 1910 University Blvd., P.O. Box 2279, Brownsville, 78522-2279. Tel: 956-542-2501; Fax: 956-542-6751. Email: hdiaz@cdob.org.

Pastoral Life and Planning Office—Mr. LUIS ZUNIGA, Dir. Tel: 956-542-2501, Ext. 356. Email: lzuniga@cdob.org.

Diocesan Relations—700 N. Virgen de San Juan Blvd., San Juan, 78589. Tel: 956-781-5323; Fax: 956-784-5082. Mrs. BRENDA NETTLES RIOJAS, Dir. Email: bnrpr@cdob.org.

Fiscal Office—1910 University Blvd., P.O. Box 2279, Brownsville, 78522-2279. Tel: 956-542-2501, Ext. 336; Fax: 956-550-1563. Mr. JACK GRAHAM, Comptroller. Email: jgraham@cdob.org.

Information Technology—1910 University Blvd., P.O. Box 2279, Brownsville, 78522-2279. Tel: 956-542-2501, Ext. 340; Fax: 956-542-6751. *700 N. Virgen de San Juan Blvd., San Juan, 78589.* Tel: 956-784-5004; Fax: 956-784-5097. Mr. ALBERTO ZAVALA, Dir. Tel: 956-550-1540. Email: azavala@cdob.org.

Human Resources Office—1910 University Blvd., P.O. Box 2279, Brownsville, 78522-2279. Tel: 956-542-2501, Ext. 345; Fax: 956-550-1561. Mrs. GENOVEVA TREVINO, Dir. Email: gtrevino@cdob.org.

Insurance and Pensions—1910 University Blvd., P.O. Box 2279, Brownsville, 78522-2279. Tel: 956-542-2501, Ext. 357; Fax: 956-550-1586. Mrs. PATRICIA GOMEZ, Insurance Admin. Tel: 956-550-1557. Email: pgomez@cdob.org.

Building/Property/Construction Management—700 N. Virgen de San Juan Blvd., San Juan, 78589. Tel: 956-781-5323; Fax: 956-784-5096. Mr. JAVIER SOLIS, Dir. Email: jsolis@cdob.org.

Vicar for Priests—Rev. JOSE M. VILLALON JR., 901 N. Texas Blvd., Weslaco, 78596. Tel: 956-968-2691.

Office of Permanent Deacons—Rev. Msgr. LUIS JAVIER GARCIA, J.C.L., Facilitator. Email: lgarcia@cdob.org; Main Address: 1910 University Blvd., P.O. Box 2279, Brownsville, 78522. Tel: 956-542-2501. Mailing & Physical Address: 700 N. Virgen de San Juan Blvd., San Juan, 78589. Tel: 956-784-5070.

Vicar for Religious—Rev. Msgr. LOUIS L. BRUM, 2201 Martin Ave., McAllen, 78503. Tel: 956-631-5295; Fax: 956-631-5460; Sr. NORMA PIMENTEL, M.J., L.P.C., Asst. Tel: 956-702-4088; Fax: 956-782-0418.

Campaign for Human Development—Rev. Msgr. HEBERTO M. DIAZ JR., 1910 University Blvd., P.O. Box 2279, Brownsville, 78522-2279. Tel: 956-542-2501; Fax: 956-542-6751.

Catholic Relief Services—Rev. EDUARDO ORTEGA, 400 N. Virgen de San Juan Blvd., San Juan, 78589. Tel: 956-787-0033; Fax: 956-787-2908.

Immigration Counseling Services—700 N. Virgen de San Juan Blvd., San Juan, 78589. Tel: 956-784-5057; Fax: 956-784-5096. Mrs. SANTA ACUNA, Coord. Email: sacuna@cdob.org.

Division for Education and Formation—Tel: 956-787-8571; Fax: 956-784-5081.

Coordinator—VACANT.

Media Resource/Library Director—Sr. MAUREEN CROSBY, S.S.D. Tel: 956-787-8571. Email: mcrosby@cdob.org.

San Juan Diego Lay Ministry Institute—Rev. GREGORY T. LABUS, Dir. Tel: 956-784-5011; Fax: 956-784-5086. Email: glabus@cdob.org.

Catholic Schools Office—700 N. Virgen de San Juan Blvd., San Juan, 78589-3042. Tel: 956-781-5323. Mrs. LISETTE ALLEN, Supt. Email: lallen@cdob.org.

Family Life Office—700 N. Virgen de San Juan Blvd., San Juan, 78589-3042. Tel: 956-781-5323. Mrs. LYDIA PESINA, Dir. Email: lpesina@cdob.org; Mrs. MARY MAGDALINE VALLE, Assoc. Dir. Email: mvalle@cdob.org.

Office of Catechesis—700 N. Virgen de San Juan Blvd., San Juan, 78589-3042. Tel: 956-784-5040. Mr. OSCAR DAYAON, Dir. Email: odayaon@cdob.org.

Division for Health Care Ministries—

Coordinator—Rev. EDOUARD ATANGANA, S.T.L., 700 N. Virgen de San Juan Blvd., San Juan, 78589. Tel: 956-784-5007; Fax: 956-784-5088.

Respect for Life Ministry—Sr. NANCY BOUSHEY, O.S.B., Mailing Address: P.O. Box 1501, Rio Grande City, 78582. Tel: 956-486-2680.

Email: sanbenito@granderiver.net.

Diocesan Attorney—Mr. DAVID GARZA, 680 E. St. Charles, Brownsville, 78520. Tel: 956-541-4914; Fax: 956-542-7403.

Presbyteral Council—Revs. RICARDO GARCIA, J.C.L., Health Care Commission; GREGORY T. LABUS, Liturgy & Worship Commission; PATRICK K. SEITZ, Marriage & Family Life Commission; RUBEN DELGADO, Educ. & Formation Commission; EDUARDO VILLA, Evangelization Commission; CRAIG G. CAROLAN, Peace & Justice Commission; ESTEBAN HERNANDEZ, Youth & Young Adults Ministry Commission; EDOUARD ATANGANA, S.T.L., Catholic Charities Commission; ROBERT CHARLTON, SS.CC., Clergy & Life Ministry Commission; Rev. Msgrs. ROBERT E. MAHER, V.G., Communications Commission; HEBERTO M. DIAZ JR., Basilica Commission; Rev. THOMAS LUCZAK, O.F.M., V.G., Parish Needs Commission; Rev. Msgr. GUSTAVO BARRERA, Vocations & Seminarians Commission.

Catholic Foundation of the Rio Grande Valley Board—Most Rev. RAYMUNDO J. PENA, D.D.; Mr. ALONZO BELTRAN; Rev. Msgr. HEBERTO M. DIAZ JR.; Mr. JACK GRAHAM; Ms. DELIA CHAVEZ; Mr. ANTONIO M. ARTEAGA, C.F.P., C.T.F.A.; Mr. JOE D. TREVINO; Mr. RICK FLORES.

College of Consultors—Revs. PATRICK K. SEITZ; CRAIG G. CAROLAN; RUBEN DELGADO; Rev. Msgrs. HEBERTO M. DIAZ JR.; GUSTAVO BARRERA; ROBERT E. MAHER, V.G.

Diocesan Finance Council—Most Rev. RAYMUNDO J. PENA, D.D.; Ms. LILY G. DE LA ROSA; Mr. NOE GARZA; Rev. Msgr. GUSTAVO BARRERA; Mr. BOB ELLIOT; Mr. RUBEN BOSQUEZ; Dr. CHARLES ELLARD; Mr. H. HUGH EMERSON; Ms. EDNA MARTINEZ; Rev. Msgr. ROBERT E. MAHER, V.G.

Parish Priests Consultors and Priests' Personnel Board—Rev. Msgr. GUSTAVO BARRERA; Revs. THOMAS L. PINCELLI; JORGE A. GOMEZ; IGNACIO TAPIA; EDUARDO VILLA.

Office for Propagation of the Faith—Rev. Msgr. LUIS JAVIER GARCIA, J.C.L., Main Address: P.O. Box 2279, Brownsville, 78522-2279. Tel: 956-542-2501. Email: lgarcia@cdob.org; Mailing & Physical Address: 700 N. Virgen de San Juan Blvd., San Juan, 78589. Tel: 956-784-5070; Fax: 956-784-5087.

Office for the Church in Latin America—Rev. Msgr. LUIS JAVIER GARCIA, J.C.L., Main Address: 1910 University Blvd., Brownsville, 78520. Tel: 956-542-2501. Email: lgarcia@cdob.org; Mailing & Physical Address: 700 N. Virgen de San Juan Blvd., San Juan, 78589. Tel: 956-784-5070; Fax: 956-784-5087.

Victim Assistance and Safe Environment Coordinator—Mr. WALTER LUKASZEK, L.M.S.W., I.P.R. Tel: 956-784-5066; Cell: 956-457-0010. Email: wlukaszek@cdob.org; walukaszek@gmail.com.

CLERGY, PARISHES, MISSIONS AND PAROCHIAL SCHOOLS

CITY OF BROWNSVILLE

(CAMERON COUNTY)

1—IMMACULATE CONCEPTION CATHEDRAL (1849) Rev. Michael Amesse, O.M.I., Rector; Deacons Roberto Cano; Paul McArdle. In Res., Revs. Armand Matthews, O.M.I.; Pasquale Lanese, O.M.I. (Retired).
Res.: 1218 E. Jefferson St., P.O. Box 311, 78522. Tel: 956-546-3178; Fax: 956-546-1284.
Catechesis/Religious Program—Mrs. Alondra Guerrero, D.R.E. Students 199.
Mission—St. Thomas 155 E. Jefferson St., Cameron Co. 78520.
Mission—Sacred Heart 602 E. Elizabeth St., Cameron Co. 78520.

2—CHRIST THE KING (1953) Rev. George Kerketta.
2255 Southmost Rd., 78521. Tel: 956-546-1982; Fax: 956-546-7120.
Catechesis/Religious Program—Tel: 956-546-5147. Mrs. Elva Reyes, D.R.E. Students 454.
Mission—San Juan Diego de Guadalupe Valle Escondido 4180 S. Browne, Cameron Co. 78521.

3—CHURCH OF THE GOOD SHEPHERD (1968) Rev. Mario A. Castro; Deacon Alvino C. Olvera.
Res.: 2645 Tulipan, 78521. Tel: 956-542-5142; Fax: 956-542-5278.
Catechesis/Religious Program—Mrs. Arabella Garcia, D.R.E. Students 617.

4—ST. EUGENE DE MAZENOD (1996) Rev. Timothy W. Paulsen, O.M.I.
Res.: 5409 Austin Rd., 78521. Tel: 956-831-9923; Fax: 956-831-3110. Email: frtimpaulsenomi@aol.com.
Catechesis/Religious Program—Ms. Hipolita Vela, C.R.E., (Grades 1-6); Ms. Belinda Rodriguez, C.R.E., (Grades 7-12). Students 305.

5—HOLY FAMILY (1966) Rev. Salvador Ramirez.
Mailing Address: 2405 E. Tyler, 78520. Email: rans2531@gmail.com.
Church: 2308 E. Tyler, 78520. Tel: 956-546-6975; Fax: 956-550-8884.
Catechesis/Religious Program—Tel: 956-574-9873. Miss Marysol Longoria, D.R.E. Students 317.

6—ST. JOSEPH (1953) Rev. Gerald W. Frank; Deacon Francisco Garza.
Res. & Mailing Address: 555 W. St. Francis St., 78520. Tel: 956-542-2709; Fax: 956-546-5162.
Catechesis/Religious Program—Tel: 956-546-4894. Mrs. Sandra Huerta, D.R.E. Students 359.

7—ST. LUKE (1974) Rev. Msgr. Heberto M. Diaz Jr.; Rev. Juan Pablo Robles; Deacons George Terrazas; Andres Munoz, (Retired).
Res.: 2800 Rockwell Dr., 78521. Tel: 956-541-1480; Fax: 956-542-8043. Email: saint-luke@cdob.org.
School—(Grades PreK-6), 2850 Price Rd., 78521. Tel: 956-544-7982; Fax: 956-544-4874. Web: stlukecatholicchurch.com. Mrs. Ana E. Gomez, Prin. Lay Teachers 18; Students 271.
Catechesis/Religious Program—Mrs. Helen Vargas, D.R.E. Students 586.

8—MARY, MOTHER OF THE CHURCH (1967) Rev. Ricardo Garcia; Deacons Gilbert Borja, (Retired); John P. Kinch; Heriberto Solis; Heriberto Trevino, (Retired); Juan Pablo Navarro.
Res.: 1904 Barnard Rd., 78520-8247. Tel: 956-541-1799; Fax: 956-546-1589.
School—(Grades PreK-6), 1300 Los Ebanos Blvd., 78520. Tel: 956-546-1805; Fax: 956-546-0787. Mr. Juan Barreda, Prin.; Mrs. Margaret Van Nostrand, Librarian. Religious 1; Lay Teachers 25; Students 433.
Catechesis/Religious Program—Mrs. Betty Bonnet, D.R.E. Students 671.

9—OUR LADY OF GOOD COUNSEL (1966) Rev. Lawrence J. Klein; Deacon Enrique Saldana.
1055 Military Hwy., 78520. Tel: 956-541-8341; Fax: 956-548-0229.
Catechesis/Religious Program—Rosario Figueroa, D.R.E. Students 477.

10—OUR LADY OF GUADALUPE (1928) Rev. Francisco Acosta; Deacon Bruno Cedillo.
Mailing Address: P.O. Box 4900, 78523.
Res.: 1200 E. Lincoln St., 78521. Tel: 956-542-4823; Fax: 956-542-5944.
Catechesis/Religious Program—Tel: 956-542-3619. Sr. Arminda Rangel, M.J., D.R.E. Students 282.

11—THE PARISH OF THE LORD OF DIVINE MERCY (2005) Rev. Rodolfo Franco.
Office & Rectory: 1350 Northridge Rd., 78526. Tel: 956-544-2112; Fax: 956-544-2208.
Catechesis/Religious Program—Students 620.
Mission—San Pedro 7602 Old Military Rd., San Pedro, Cameron Co. Tel: 956-542-2596; Fax: 956-546-8080. Mailing Address: P.O. Box 1658, Olmito, 78575. Rev. Hector Cruz, S.M.
Mission—Our Heavenly Father 9178 Tomas Cortez Jr. St., Olmito, Cameron Co. 78575. Tel: 956-350-5190; Fax: 956-350-5207. Mailing Address: P.O. Box 249, Olmito, 78575. Rev. Hector Cruz, S.M.

12—SAN FELIPE DE JESUS (1996) Revs. Hector Cruz, S.M.; Alejandro Francisco Flores, Parochial Vicar; Joel Grissom, S.M., Parochial Vicar.
Mailing Address: P.O. Box 8093, 78526-8093.
Res.: 2511 Dennis, 78526. Tel: 956-982-2007; Fax: 956-541-4177.
Catechesis/Religious Program—Tel: 956-982-2035. Ms. Dominga Torres, C.R.E. Students 367.

OUTSIDE THE CITY OF BROWNSVILLE

ALAMO, HIDALGO CO., RESURRECTION (1926), (Formerly St. Joseph/Our Lady of Fatima) Rev. Emmanuel Bialoncik, O.F.M.
Res.: 312 N. 9th St., 78516. Tel: 956-787-2963; Fax: 956-787-6788.

Catechesis/Religious Program—Ms. Erica Vargas, D.R.E. Students 2,114.

ALTON, HIDALGO CO., SAN MARTIN DE PORRES (1967) Rev. Julian Becerril, O.de.M.
Mailing Address: 106 S. Alton Blvd., PMB 9023, 78572.
Res.: 621 W. Main St., 78572.
Catechesis/Religious Program—Tel: 956-585-3125. Students 798.
Mission—Capilla Santa Cecilia Monte Cristo, Hidalgo Co., TX.
Mission—Centro Catolico San Juan Diego El Flaco, Hidalgo Co., TX.

DONNA, HIDALGO CO., ST. JOSEPH (1928) Revs. Alberto T. Trevino Jr., M.S.F.; James Lienert, M.S.F.; Camillo Botello, M.S.F.; Deacons Eduardo Ovalle; Juan Barbosa.
Res.: 306 S. D Salinas Blvd., 78537. Tel: 956-464-3331; Fax: 956-464-6808.
Catechesis/Religious Program—Tel: 956-464-3472; Fax: 956-464-7373. Mrs. Liza G. Tobias, D.R.E. Students 799.
Mission—Christ the King 1/2 Mile S. FM 493, Colonia Nueva, Hidalgo Co.

EDCOUCH, HIDALGO CO., ST. THERESA OF THE INFANT JESUS (1948) Rev. Ernesto Magallon.
Res.: 200 P. Salazar, P.O. Box 307, 78538. Tel: 956-262-1347; Fax: 956-262-1348.
Catechesis/Religious Program—Mr. Luis Carlos, D.R.E. Students 395.
Mission—Our Lady of Guadalupe 200 N. Laurel, La Villa, Hidalgo Co. 78562.

EDINBURG, HIDALGO CO.

1—HOLY FAMILY (1967) Rev. Eusebio Martinez; Deacon Ruben Lopez.
Res.: 1302 E. Champion, 78539-4864. Tel: 956-383-5472; Fax: 956-383-5034.
Catechesis/Religious Program—Tel: 956-383-4593. Ms. Susie de la Garza, C.R.E. Students 514.

2—ST. JOSEPH (1948) Rev. Msgr. Robert E. Maher; Deacon Irineo Gonzalez Jr.
Res.: 122 W. Fay St., 78539. Tel: 956-383-3728; Fax: 956-383-8630. Email: stjoseph-edinburg@catholic.org.
School—(Grades PreK-8), 119 W. Fay St., 78539. Tel: 956-383-3957; Fax: 956-318-0681. Web: stjoseph-edinburg.org. Sr. Kathleen Murray, D.C., Prin.; Ms. Lupita Davila, Librarian. Lay Teachers 28; Students 282.
Catechesis/Religious Program—Mrs. Ann Ameling, D.R.E. Students 708.

3—SACRED HEART (1927) Revs. Robert Charlton, SS.CC.; Emilio Vega-Garcia, SS.CC.; Deacons Jose Solis; Gilberto Lopez. In Res., Rev. Alfredo Garcia, SS.CC.
Res.: 215 N. 16th Ave., 78541. Tel: 956-383-3253; Fax: 956-383-7311. Email: sacredheartedg@sbcglobal.net.
Catechesis/Religious Program—Tel: 956-383-4631. Mrs. Nidia Perez, D.R.E. Students 1,035.
Mission—Capilla de San Jose 4101 Flores St., Hidalgo Co. 78541. Ms. Susan Mercado, D.R.E.

ELSA, HIDALGO CO., SACRED HEART (1948) Revs. Ruben Delgado; Mishael J. Koday.
Res.: 1100 N. Broadway, P.O. Box 6, 78543. Tel: 956-262-1406; Fax: 956-262-4265.
Catechesis/Religious Program—Ms. Maria E. Martinez, D.R.E. Students 727.
Mission—Christ the King Monte Alto, Hidalgo Co. 78538.
Mission—Holy Cross Catechetical Center, Mile 15

ESCOBARES, STARR CO., SACRED HEART (1967) Rev. Jean Olivier M. Sambu; Deacon Rodolfo C. Salinas.
Mailing Address: P.O. Box 1180, Roma, 78584.
Res.: 4987 Old Escobares Hwy. 83, Roma, 78584. Tel: 956-849-1741; Fax: 956-847-1502.
Catechesis/Religious Program—Mr. Rolando Munoz, D.R.E. Students 224.
Mission—Santa Rosa de Lima 7 Miles of Roma, Rosita, Starr Co.
Mission—Our Lady of Guadalupe FM 649, 13 Miles N., El Sauz, Starr Co.

GRULLA, STARR CO., HOLY FAMILY (1967) Rev. Terrence Gorski, O.F.M.; Deacon Benito Saenz.
Mailing Address: P.O. Box 67, 78548.
Res.: 107 W. Private Lazaro Solis St., 78548. Tel: 956-487-3365; Fax: 956-487-4727.
Catechesis/Religious Program—Ms. Maria Guzman, D.R.E.; Ms. Martina Garcia, C.R.E.; Ms. Irma Garcia, C.R.E. Students 370.
Mission—Cristo Rey N. FM 2360, Cristo Rey, Starr Co.
Mission—Our Lady of the Peace FM 1430, La Casita, Starr Co.

HARLINGEN, CAMERON CO.

1—ST. ANTHONY (1940) Rev. Thomas L. Pincelli. In Res., Rev. Thomas G. Kulleck.
Res.: 209 S. 10th, 78550. Tel: 956-428-6111; Fax: 956-428-4276. Email: stanthonychurch2@aol.com.
School—(Grades PreK-8), 1015 E. Harrison St., 78550. Tel: 956-423-2486; Fax: 956-412-0084. Mrs. Esther Flores, Prin.; Mrs. Belinda Casarez, Librarian. Lay Teachers 16; Students 229.
Catechesis/Religious Program—Tel: 956-428-2476; Fax: 956-425-8969. Mrs. Mary Kyser, D.R.E. Students 702.

2—IMMACULATE HEART OF MARY (1927) Rev. Msgr. Pedro Briseno; Rev. Eduardo Gomez; Deacon Jesus H. Reyes.
Res.: 412 S. C St., 78550. Tel: 956-423-0855; Fax: 956-421-1071. Email: immaculateheartofmary@hotmail.com. Web: heartofmarytexas.org.
Catechesis/Religious Program—Students 490.

3—OUR LADY OF THE ASSUMPTION (1958) Rev. Horacio Chavarria; Deacon Juan Valenzuela.
1313 W. Buchanan St., 78550. Tel: 956-423-4670; Fax: 956-423-5970.
Catechesis/Religious Program—Tel: 956-423-1765. Ms. Yzenia Huerta, D.R.E. Students 1,260.
Mission—San Felipe 1706 Rangerville Rd., San Felipe, Cameron Co. 77473.

4—QUEEN OF PEACE (1967) Revs. William T. Penderghest, SS.CC.; Alphonsus McHugh, SS.CC.; Deacon Genaro Ibarra.
Res.: 1509 New Combes Hwy., 78550. Tel: 956-423-6341; Fax: 956-423-2864. Email: qp_secretary@rgv.rr.com; queen-of-peace@cdob.org.
Catechesis/Religious Program—Tel: 956-425-2830. Ms. Maria T. Hernandez, D.R.E. Students 416.

HIDALGO, HIDALGO CO., SACRED HEART (1967) Rev. Mario Alberto Aviles, C.O.
Res.: 308 E. Camelia St., P.O. Box 579, 78557. Tel: 956-843-2463; Fax: 956-843-2187.
Catechesis/Religious Program—Mrs. Elisa Garza, D.R.E. Students 502.

LA FERIA, CAMERON CO., ST. FRANCIS XAVIER (1930) Rev. Gabriel I. Ezeh; Deacon Hugo De la Cruz.
Res.: 500 S. Canal St., P.O. Box 116, 78559. Tel: 956-797-2666; Fax: 956-797-3387. Email: stfrancislaferia@aol.com.
Catechesis/Religious Program—Tel: 956-797-5568. Mrs. San Juana Betancourt, D.R.E. Students 605.

LA JOYA, HIDALGO CO., OUR LADY, QUEEN OF ANGELS (1960) Revs. Fernando Gonzalez; Juan Pablo Davalos; Deacon Alberto X. Chapa.
Res.: 916 S. Leo Ave., 78560. Tel: 956-585-5223; Fax: 956-585-4878.
Catechesis/Religious Program—Rosie Gonzalez, D.R.E. Students 566.
Mission—St. Mary Magdalene Abram, Hidalgo Co.
Mission—St. Anthony Penitas, Hidalgo Co.
Mission—St. Michael Los Ebanos, Hidalgo Co.
Mission—St. William Sullivan City, Hidalgo Co.

LOS FRESNOS, CAMERON CO., ST. CECILIA (1964) Rev. Esteban Hernandez; Deacon Augusto Chapa Jr.
Res.: 606 W. Ocean Blvd., 78566. Tel: 956-233-5619; Fax: 956-233-5565.
Catechesis/Religious Program—Tel: 956-233-5213. Mrs. Letty Villarreal, D.R.E. Students 534.

LYFORD, WILLACY CO., PRINCE OF PEACE (1967) Rev. Aglayde Rafael Vega.
Res.: 8413 Park Ave., P.O. Box 460, 78569. Tel: 956-347-3580; Fax: 956-347-3649.
Catechesis/Religious Program—Students 185.
Mission—Santa Monica FM 1018 & 1420, Santa Monica, Willacy Co.
Mission—St. Martin 345 Martin Cavazos St., P.O. Box 247, Sebastian, Willacy Co. 78594.

MCALLEN, HIDALGO CO.

1—HOLY SPIRIT (1981) Rev. Msgr. Louis L. Brum; Deacons Carlos S. Trevino; Alvin H. Gerbermann.
Res.: 2201 Martin Ave., 78504. Tel: 956-631-5295; Fax: 956-631-5460.
Catechesis/Religious Program—Tel: 956-664-2518. Students 1,251.

2—ST. JOSEPH THE WORKER (1967) Rev. Alfonso M. Guevara; Deacon Alejandro Gamboa.
Office: 2315 Ithaca St., 78501. Tel: 956-682-1351; Fax: 956-618-3317.
Church: 900 S. 23rd St., 78501.
Catechesis/Religious Program—Tel: 956-686-6871. Students 885.

3—SAINT JUAN DIEGO CUAUHTLATOATZIN (2002) Rev. Carlos Zuniga; Deacon Salvador Rojas.
3309 Helena Ave., 78503.
Office: 3408 Idela Ave., 78503. Tel: 965-682-5155; Fax: 956-682-5472. Email: sjdparish2002@aol.com.
Catechesis/Religious Program—Mr. Noe Cortina, Youth Min.; Ms. Mercedes Medina, D.R.E. Students 592.

4—OUR LADY OF PERPETUAL HELP (1967) Rev. Msgr. Juan Nicolau; Deacon Agapito L. Cantu. In Res., Rev. Raymond Nwachukwu.
Res.: 2209 Kendlewood Ave., 78501. Tel: 956-682-4238; Fax: 956-682-0289. Email: olph2209@yahoo.com.
Catechesis/Religious Program—Tel: 956-682-3663. Mrs. Michelle Lee Reyes, C.R.E. Students 840.

5—OUR LADY OF SORROWS (1941) Rev. Msgr. Gustavo Barrera; Revs. Juan Rogelio Gutierrez; Hyo-Geun Park (Korean Community); Deacon John Schwarz.
Res.: 1108 W. Hackberry St., 78501-4370. Tel: 956-686-0251; Fax: 956-686-0322. Email: parish@oladyofsorrows.org. Web: www.oladyofsorrows.org.
School—(Grades PreK-8), 1100 Gumwood, 78501. Tel: 956-686-3651; Fax: 956-686-1996. Frederico Valle, Prin.; Patrick O'Keefe, Asst. Prin.; Patricia Espinosa, Librarian Mgr. Religious 1; Lay Teachers 31; Students 583.
Catechesis/Religious Program—Mrs. Janie Barragan, D.R.E.; Ms. Letty Huggins, D.R.E. Students 1,030.

6—SACRED HEART (1917) Rev. Thomas Luczak, O.F.M.; Deacon Jose Luis Mendoza. In Res., Bro. Mario Nagy, O.F.M.
Res.: 306 S. 15th St., P.O. Box 370, 78505-0370. Tel: 956-686-7711; Fax: 956-686-2028.
Catechesis/Religious Program—Ms. Sandra Kent, D.R.E. Students 397.

MCCOOK, HIDALGO CO., IMMACULATE CONCEPTION (1950) Rev. Jose Rene Angel.
28212 FM 2058, Edinburg, 78541. Tel: 956-842-3663.

MERCEDES, HIDALGO CO.

1—OUR LADY OF MERCY (1909) Rev. Gregory T. Labus; Deacon Roberto Cantu.
Res.: 322 S. Vermont Ave., P.O. Box 805, 78570. Tel: 956-565-1141; Fax: 956-565-1640.
Catechesis/Religious Program—Students 236.

2—SACRED HEART CHURCH (1969) Rev. Celso Tabalanza, C.I.C.M.
920 Anacuitas, 78570. Tel: 956-565-0271; Fax: 956-565-0272.
Res.: 600 N. Washington, 78570.
Catechesis/Religious Program—Miss Maria Celeste Garcia, D.R.E. Students 695.

MISSION, HIDALGO CO.

1—OUR LADY OF GUADALUPE (1899) [CEM] Revs. Roy Lee Snipes, O.M.I.; James Pfeifer, O.M.I.; Deacon Guillermo "Bill" Castaneda Jr.
Res.: 620 Dunlap St., P.O. Box 1047, 78572-1047. Tel: 956-585-2623; Fax: 956-584-5856. Email: olgparish@sbcglobal.net. Web: olgmissiontexas.org.
Catechesis/Religious Program—Tel: 956-585-1376. Sr. Maria Guadalupe Cortes, M.C.P., D.R.E. Students 1,411.
Chapel—La Lomita

2—OUR LADY OF ST. JOHN OF THE FIELDS (1967) Rev. Francisco Castillo; Deacons Daniel Zamora; Pedro Requenez.
Res.: 1052 Washington St., 78572. Tel: 956-585-2325; Fax: 956-585-7270.
Catechesis/Religious Program—Tel: 956-581-1289. Mrs. Ana Maria Middlebrook, D.R.E. Students 467.

3—OUR LADY OF THE HOLY ROSARY (1968) Rev. Ariel O. Angel; Deacon Eduardo Reyna.
Res.: 923 Matamoros St., P.O. Box 1439, 78572. Tel: 956-581-2193; Fax: 956-581-1906.
Catechesis/Religious Program—Mrs. Olga Gomez, D.R.E. Students 380.

4—ST. PAUL (1915) Rev. Gregory M. Kuczmanski; Deacon Robert Ledesma.
Res.: 1119 Francisco Ave., 78572. Tel: 956-585-2701; Fax: 956-581-4801.
Catechesis/Religious Program—Tel: 956-585-2486. Mrs. Cindy Schaefer, D.R.E. Students 721.

5—SAN CRISTOBAL MAGALLANES & COMPANIONS (2004) Rev. Craig G. Carolan.
Mailing Address: 3805 Plantation Blvd., Ste. 5, 78572. Tel: 956-580-4551; Fax: 956-519-3537. Email: sancristobalmagallanes@gmail.com.
Catechesis/Religious Program—Ms. Maria Guadalupe Segura, D.R.E. Students 275.
Mission—Our Lady of Fatima 6634 El Camino Real, Hidalgo Co. 78572.
Mission—Our Lady of Lourdes 2 1/2 Miles S. Conway, Hidalgo Co. 78572.

PHARR, HIDALGO CO.

1—ST. ANNE, MOTHER OF MARY (1973) Rev. Genaro Henriquez.
801 E. Juarez, 78577. Tel: 956-787-8122.
Res.: 309 N. First, 78577. Tel: 956-783-7787; Fax: 956-787-8272.
Catechesis/Religious Program—Tel: 956-787-5139. Janie Leal, C.R.E. Students 377.

2—ST. FRANCES XAVIER CABRINI (1999) Revs. Edouard Atangana; Miguel Angel Ortega, Parochial Vicar; Deacon Jesus Antonio Osorio.
Mailing Address: P.O. Box 8538, Hidalgo, 78557-8538. Tel: 956-787-3554; Fax: 956-283-1354. Email: st-frances-cabrini@cdob.org. Web: madrecabrini.org.
Church: 8001 S. Cage Blvd., 78577.
Catechesis/Religious Program—Ms. Alicia Monica Islas, D.R.E. Students 589.

3—ST. JUDE THADDEUS (1951) Very Rev. Leo Francis Daniels, C.O.; Revs. Jose E. Losoya, C.O.; Jose Juan Ortiz, C.O.
Res.: 505 S. Ironwood, P.O. Box 1688, 78577-1630. Tel: 956-781-2489; Fax: 956-783-4614.

School—Oratory Academy School of St. Philip Neri, (Grades PreK-8), 1407 W. Moore Rd., 78577. Tel: 956-781-3056; Fax: 956-702-3047. Rev. Mario Alberto Aviles, C.O., Prin.; Mrs. G. Yvonne Perez, Pres.; Revs. Jose E. Losoya, C.O., Asst. Prin.; Jose Juan Ortiz, C.O., Librarian. Religious Teachers 4; Lay Teachers 47; Students 542.
School—Oratory School - Athenaeum for University Preparation, 1407 W. Moore Rd., 78577. Revs. Mario Alberto Aviles, C.O., Prin.; Jose E. Losoya, C.O., Vice Prin.; Jose Juan Ortiz, C.O., Librarian. Religious Teachers 4; Lay Teachers 14; Students 162.
Catechesis/Religious Program—Tel: 956-781-3521. Mrs. Sochil J. Duran, D.R.E. Students 402.

4—St. Margaret Mary (1927) Rev. Martin de la Cruz; Deacon Pedro F. Sanchez.
Res.: 122 W. Hawk Ave., 78577. Tel: 956-787-8563; Fax: 956-702-4509.
Catechesis/Religious Program—Tel: 956-787-0832; Fax: 956-787-5385. Students 458.

Port Isabel, Cameron Co., Our Lady Star of the Sea (1927) Rev. Gerard Barrett, O.M.I. In Res., Rev. Harry Schuckenbrock, O.M.I.
Res.: 705 S. Longoria St., 78578. Tel: 956-943-1297; Fax: 956-943-1422.
Catechesis/Religious Program—Tel: 956-943-6392. Mrs. Rosa Gonzalez, D.R.E. Students 467.
Mission—Laguna Heights Chapel Garfield St., Laguna Heights, Cameron Co. 78578.

Progreso, Hidalgo Co., Holy Spirit (1969) Rev. Thomas Matondo, C.I.C.M.; Deacon Salvador G. Saldivar.
Res.: 210 Watts Ave., P.O. Box 216, 78579. Tel: 956-565-6856; Fax: 956-565-3462.
Catechesis/Religious Program—Tel: 956-565-1572. Mrs. Yolanda Mora, D.R.E. Students 370.
Mission—St. Margaret Ann Military Hwy. 281, Santa Maria, Cameron Co. 78592.
Mission—Cristo Rey Military Hwy. 281, Bluetown, Cameron Co. 78592.

Ranchito, Cameron Co., St. Ignatius (1967) Rev. Albert Lelo-Luemba, C.I.C.M.
24380 W. U.S. Hwy. 281, San Benito, 78586. Tel: 956-399-2022; Fax: 956-399-1213.
Catechesis/Religious Program—Ms. Maria Valdez, D.R.E. Students 461.
Mission—Our Lady of Lourdes La Paloma, Cameron Co.
Mission—Sacred Heart Las Rucias, Cameron Co.

Raymondville, Willacy Co.
1—St. Anthony (1907) Rev. Juan Victor Heredia.
Res.: 464 S. First St., 78580. Tel: 956-690-4078; Fax: 956-690-4078.
2—Our Lady of Guadalupe (1927) Revs. Frank A. Wittouck, S.C.J.; Richard MacDonald, S.C.J.; Deacon Juan Francisco Gonzalez.
Res.: 693 N. Third St., 78580. Tel: 956-689-2408; Fax: 956-689-1687.
Catechesis/Religious Program—Miss Margaret Lopez, D.R.E. Students 664.
Mission—St. Patrick 1 Mile S. of 186 on Hwy. 1015, Lasara, Willacy Co. 78561.
Mission—St. Frances Xavier Cabrini 215 N. Couch St., Hargill, Hidalgo Co. 78549.
Mission—St. Anne, Mother of Mary Corner of 1st & Paloma, San Perlita, Hidalgo Co. 78590.

Rio Grande City, Starr Co.
1—Immaculate Conception (1880) [CEM] Rev. Amador Garza.
Res.: 101 E. Third St., P.O. Box 1, 78582. Tel: 956-487-2317; Fax: 956-488-8133.
School—(Grades PreK-8), 305 N. Britton Ave., 78582. Tel: 956-487-2558; Fax: 956-487-6478. Mrs. Rubirita Urbina, Prin.; Ms. Donis Garza, Librarian. Religious 2; Lay Teachers 14; Students 238.
Catechesis/Religious Program—Sr. Beatriz Martinez, S.S.N.D., D.R.E. Students 500.
Mission—Sacred Heart Old US Hwy. 83, Los Garcias Ranch, Starr Co.
2—St. Paul the Apostle Parish (2009) Rev. Eduardo Villa.
P.O. Box 269, Garciasville, 78547. Tel: 956-488-8349; Fax: 956-488-8085.

Rio Hondo, Cameron Co., St. Helen (1943) Rev. Felix A. Cazares; Deacon Jose Guerra.
Res.: 228 Huisache, P.O. Box 451, 78583. Tel: 956-748-2327; Fax: 956-748-0089. Email: saint-helen@cdob.org.
Catechesis/Religious Program—Virginia Salinas, C.R.E. Students 231.
Mission—St. Vincent de Paul 2513 Lozano Rd., Lozano, Cameron Co. 78568.

Roma, Starr Co., Our Lady of Refuge (1853) Rev. Richard Philion, O.M.I.
Res.: 4 St. Eugene de Mazenod Ave., P.O. Box 156, 78584. Tel: 956-849-1455; Fax: 956-849-2257.
Catechesis/Religious Program—Tel: 956-849-7155. Mrs. Maria Teresa Garcia, D.R.E. Students 570.
Mission—Holy Trinity 14 Miles S. FM 2098, Falcon Heights, Starr Co. Tel: 956-848-5882.
Mission—St. Joseph Iglesia St., Salineno, Starr Co. 78585. Tel: 956-848-5814.
Mission—Holy Family 202 S. Francesca Ave., Los Saenz, Starr Co. 78584. Tel: 956-849-3375.
Mission—Lamb of God Church St., Fronton, Starr Co. 78584. Tel: 956-849-2199.

San Benito, Cameron Co.
1—St. Benedict (1912) Rev. Ignacio Luna; Deacon Manuel Sanchez.
Res.: 351 S. Bowie, P.O. Box 1780, 78586. Tel: 956-399-2353; Fax: 956-399-5701.
Catechesis/Religious Program—Tel: 956-399-5975. Students 505.
2—Our Lady, Queen of the Universe (1960) Rev. Isaac Emeka Erondu; Deacon Margarito Briones.
Res.: 121 Garrison Dr., 78586. Tel: 956-399-2865; Fax: 956-399-2045.
Church: 1425 N. Sam Houston, 78586.
Catechesis/Religious Program—Miss Estefana Garcia, D.R.E. Students 313.
Mission—St. Joseph 1001 W. Hwy. 77, Cameron Co. 78586. Tel: 956-399-2615.
3—St. Theresa (1954) Rev. Samuel Arizpe; Deacon Benito Flores.
Res.: 1300 Combes St., P.O. Box 1839, 78586. Tel: 956-399-3247; Fax: 956-276-0142.
Catechesis/Religious Program—Ms. Estela de la Fuente, D.R.E. Students 662.

San Carlos, Hidalgo Co., St. Joseph the Worker (1970) Rev. Jose Luis Garcia; Deacon Hector Perez.
Res.: 8310 Highland Ave., Edinburg, 78541. Tel: 956-383-5880; Fax: 956-383-0420.
Catechesis/Religious Program—Tel: 956-381-1888. Students 620.
Mission—St. Anne San Manuel 22 Miles N. 281, San Manuel, Hidalgo Co.
Mission—St. Theresa Faysville Faysville, Hidalgo Co. Deacon Mariano Jurado.

San Isidro, Starr Co., St. Isidore (1964) Rev. Jose Rene Angel.
5160 FM 1017, P.O. Box 60, 78588. Tel: 956-481-3392; Fax: 956-481-3869.
Catechesis/Religious Program—Mrs. Manuelita Olivarez, D.R.E. Students 86.

San Juan, Hidalgo Co.
1—Basilica of Our Lady of San Juan del Valle-National Shrine Revs. Eduardo Ortega, Rector; Francisco J. Solis, Asst. to Rector; Mr. Esteban Martinez, Admin.; Deacons Julio Castilleja; Jesus P. Galvan.
Res.: 400 Virgen de San Juan Blvd., 78589. Tel: 956-787-0033; Fax: 956-787-2908.
2—St. John the Baptist (1949) Rev. Rufino Carlos Nava, O.M.I.; Deacon Rene Villalon Sr.
Mailing Address: 216 W. First St., P.O. Box 1269, 78589. Tel: 956-783-1196; Fax: 956-702-7447. Email: sjtbchurch@sbcglobal.net. Web: www.sanjuanparish.org. In Res., Rev. Gerald McGovern, O.M.I. (Retired).
Catechesis/Religious Program—Tel: 956-783-1068. Ms. Rebecca Huerta, D.R.E. Students 1,493.
Mission—Immaculate Conception 3.5 miles N. I Rd., Lopezville, Hidalgo Co.

Santa Rosa, Cameron Co., St. Mary (1967) Rev. Oscar O. Siordia.
Res.: 101 San Antonio Ave., P.O. Box 365, 78593. Tel: 956-636-1211; Fax: 956-636-2941.
Catechesis/Religious Program—Mrs. Rosie Aguilar, D.R.E. Students 150.

Weslaco, Hidalgo Co.
1—St. Joan of Arc (1929) Rev. Lee DaCosta.
Res.: 109 S. Illinois Ave., 78596. Tel: 956-968-3670; Fax: 956-968-1872.
Catechesis/Religious Program—Tel: 956-968-6812. Mrs. Rosa Ochoa, D.R.E. Students 466.
2—St. Pius X (1955) Rev. Patrick K. Seitz; Deacon Jesus Aguayo.
Res.: 600 S. Oklahoma Ave., 78596. Tel: 956-968-7471; Fax: 956-969-3040.
Catechesis/Religious Program—Tel: 956-968-0317. Mr. John Trevino, D.R.E. Students 744.
3—San Martin de Porres (1967) Rev. Jose M. Villalon Jr.; Deacons Juan Delgado; Jose G. Garza.
Res.: 901 N. Texas Blvd., 78596. Tel: 956-968-2691; Fax: 956-968-1473.
School—(Grades PreK-3), 905 N. Texas Blvd., 78596. Tel: 956-973-8642; Fax: 956-973-0522. Sr. Helen Rottier, C.S.J., Prin.; Ms. Adelina Olivo, Librarian. Religious 1; Lay Teachers 5; Students 75.
Catechesis/Religious Program—Tel: 956-968-1979. Ms. Maria Luisa Villanueva, D.R.E. Students 1,492.
Mission—St. Jude Chapel, Hidalgo Co.
Mission—Nuestra Senora de Guadalupe Corpus Christi Dr., Expressway Heights, Hidalgo Co.

Chaplains of Public Institutions

Brownsville. *Jail Ministry*, 955 W. Price Rd., 78520. Tel: 956-541-0220. Mr. Jaime Gomez, Coord., Mr. Victor Villegas, Jail Min.
Valley Baptist Health Systems-Brownsville, 1040 W. Jefferson St., 78520. Tel: 956-698-4452. Rev. Michael Gnanaraj. Email: ranjithagmich@yahoo.com, Sr. Gloria Morales, M.J., Chap. Email: gloria.morales@valleybaptist.net.
Valley Regional Medical Center, 100 Alton Gloor Blvd., Unit A, 78526. Tel: 956-350-7124. Sr. Esther Rodriguez, O.P. Email: esther.rodriguez@hcahealthcare.com.

Edinburg. *Doctor's Hospital at Renaissance*, 5501 S. McColl Rd., 78539. Tel: 956-661-7100. Rev. Rigobert Poulang Mot, Rev. Msgr. Agostinho S. Pacheco (Retired), Sisters Therese Ann Ridge, I.W.B.S. Email: zonestar44@hotmail.com, Mary Lucy Ugo, D.D.L. Email: Lugo@dhr-rgv.com, Mr. Ray Flores. Email: rayflores57@yahoo.com, Mr. Carlos Salinas. Email: ca.salinas@dhr-rgv.com, Ms. Mary Carmen Thomas. Email: mcstivalet@aol.com.
Edinburg Regional Hospital, 1102 W. Trenton Rd., 78539. Tel: 956-388-6634. Sr. Aurora P. Sibug Realubit, O.S.B.

Harlingen. *Harlingen Medical Center*, 5501 S. Expressway 77, 78550. Tel: 956-365-1844. Rev. Emmanuel Kwofie.
Jail Ministry, 412 S. "C" St., 78550. Tel: 956-423-0855. Rev. George Gonzalez, Chap.
Valley Baptist Health System-Harlingen, 2101 Pease St., 78550. Tel: 956-389-1194. Mr. Lawrence Reeve. Email: lorenzolupe@yahoo.com.

McAllen. *McAllen Heart Hospital*, 1900 S. "D" St., 78503. Tel: 956-994-2107. Ms. Melida Salinas. Email: melida.salinas@uhsrgv.com.
McAllen Medical Hospital, 301 W. Expwy. 83, 78503. Tel: 956-632-4388. Deacon Larry Hildebrand. Email: larryhildebrand@att.net, Rev. Joseph Ayissi Nkoumu.
Rio Grande Regional Hospital, 101 E. Ridge Rd., 78503. Tel: 956-632-6616. Sr. Julia Billiart Maris Nkchi Onunkwo. Email: JuliaOnunkwo@hcahealthcare.com, Rev. Franklin N. Epie.

Mission. *Mission Hospital*, 900 S. Bryan Rd., 78572. Tel: 956-323-1273. Mr. Jerry Garcia, Chap. Email: gegarcia@missionrmc.org.

Rio Grande City. *Starr County Memorial Hospital*, P.O. Box 78, 78582. Tel: 956-487-5561, Ext. 2206. Rev. Larry Wieseler (CR) (Retired). Email: lawieseler@hotmail.com.

San Juan. *San Juan Nursing Home*, P.O. Box 1238, 78589. Tel: 956-787-1771. Ms. Josefina Suarez, Chap. Email: sjnhfina@yahoo.com.

Weslaco. *Knapp Medical Center*, P.O. Box 1110, 78596. Tel: 956-968-4564. Vacant.

On Assignment Outside the Diocese:
Revs.—
Figueroa, Honecimo
Lopez, Lionel
Mestas, Leonard J., St. Joseph the Worker Church, 10816 Mount View Ave., Loma Linda, CA 92354.

Retired:
Rev. Msgrs.—
DaVola, F. Robert, 1503 Evergreen Ter., Mission, 78572.
Doherty, Patrick J., P.O. Box 747, San Juan, 78589.
Pacheco, Agostinho S., P.O. Box 5548, Mcallen, 78502.
Revs.—
Azcoiti, Vicente, P.O. Box 747, San Juan, 78589.
Cabanas, Jaime, P.O. Box 747, San Juan, 78589.
Clancy, Frank, S.C.J., R.R. 2, P.O. Box 788, Raymondville, 78580.
Escobedo, Armando, 615 Palo Blanco Ave., Mission, 78572.
Felion, Jerome (CR), 4130 S. Alameda St., Corpus Christi, 78411.
Gomez, Frank, 4130 S. Alameda, Corpus Christi, 78411.
Lanese, Pasquale, O.M.I., P.O. Box 311, 78522. Tel: 956-546-3178
Mateos, Tomas, S.F.O., P.O. Box 747, San Juan, 78589.
O'Malley, John A., P.O. Box 747, San Juan, 78589. Tel: 956-783-1013
Ortiz, Benedicto, 625 W. Fronton St., 78520.

Permanent Deacons:
Aguayo, Jesus, St. Pius X, Weslaco
Barbosa, Juan, St. Joseph, Donna
Borja, Gilberto, (Retired)
Briones, Margarito, (Retired)
Cano, Roberto, Immaculate Conception Cathedral, Brownsville
Cantu, Agapito L., Our Lady of Perpetual Help, McAllen
Cantu, Roberto, Our Lady of Mercy, Mercedes
Castaneda, Guillermo "Bill", Jr., Our Lady of Guadalupe, Mission

Castilleja, Julio, Basilica of Our Lady of San Juan del Valle-National Shrine
Castro, Jose R., (Retired)
Cedillo, Bruno, Our Lady of Guadalupe, Brownsville
Chapa, Alberto X., Our Lady, Queen of Angels, La Joya
Chapa, Augusto, Jr., St. Cecilia, Los Fresnos
Crixell, Alfred V., (Retired), (Inactive)
De la Cruz, Hugo, St. Francis Xavier, La Feria
Delgado, Juan, San Martin de Porres, Weslaco
Diaz, Inocencio, (Inactive)
Flores, Alejandro, (Retired)
Flores, Benito, St. Theresa, San Benito
Galvan, Jesus P., Basilica of Our Lady of San Juan del Valle National-Shrine, San Juan
Gamboa, Alejandro, St. Joseph the Worker, McAllen
Garcia, Ismael, St. Paul, Mission
Garza, Francisco, St. Joseph, Brownsville
Garza, Jose G., San Martin de Porres, Weslaco
Gerbermann, Alvin H., Holy Spirit, McAllen
Gonzales, Ignacio R., (Retired), (Inactive)
Gonzalez, Irineo, Jr., St. Joseph, Edinburg
Gonzalez, Juan F., Our Lady of Guadalupe, Raymondville
Gonzalez, Leopoldo, (Retired), (Inactive)
Guerra, Jose, St. Helen, Rio Hondo
Hildebrand, Larry, South Texas Health System, Mission
Ibarra, Genaro, Queen of Peace, Harlingen
Jurado, Mariano, St. Joseph the Worker, San Carlos
Kinch, John P., Mary, Mother of the Church, Brownsville
Leal, Ramon G., (Retired), (Inactive)
Ledesma, Robert, St. Paul, Mission
Lopez, Gilberto, Sacred Heart, Edinburg
Lopez, Ruben, Holy Family, Edinburg
McArdle, Paul, Immaculate Conception Cathedral, Brownsville
Mendoza, Jose Luis, Sacred Heart, McAllen
Munoz, Andres, (Retired)
Navarro, Juan Pablo, Mary, Mother of the Church, Brownsville
Oden, Louis, (Retired), (Inactive)
Olvera, Alvino C., Good Shepherd, Brownsville
Osorio, Jesus Antonio, St. Frances Xavier, La Feria
Ovalle, Eduardo, (Retired)
Perez, Gilberto, St. Theresa of the Infant Jesus, Edcouch
Perez, Hector, St. Joseph the Worker, San Carlos
Requenez, Pedro, Our Lady of St. John of the Fields, Mission
Reyes, Jesus H., Immaculate Heart of Mary, Harlingen
Reyna, Eduardo, Our Lady of the Holy Rosary, Mission
Rodriguez, Arturo, (Retired)
Rojas, Salvador, St. Juan Diego Cuauhtlatoatzin, McAllen
Saenz, Benito, Jr., Holy Family, Grulla
Saldana, Enrique, Our Lady of Good Counsel, Brownsville
Saldivar, Salvador G., Holy Spirit, Progreso
Salinas, Rodolfo C., Sacred Heart, Escobares
Sanchez, Manuel, St. Benedict, San Benito
Sanchez, Pedro F., St. Margaret Mary, Pharr
Schwarz, John, Our Lady of Sorrows, McAllen
Solis, Heriberto, Mary, Mother of the Church, Brownsville
Solis, Jose, Sacred Heart, Edinburg
Terrazas, George, St. Luke, Brownsville
Trevino, Carlos S., Holy Spirit, McAllen
Trevino, Felipe, (Retired)
Trevino, Heriberto, Mary, Mother of the Church, Brownsville
Valenzuela, Juan, Our Lady of the Assumption, Harlingen
Villalon, Rene, Sr., St. John the Baptist, McAllen
Zamora, Daniel, Our Lady of St. John of the Fields, Mission

INSTITUTIONS LOCATED IN THE DIOCESE

[A] SEMINARIES

MISSION. *The Saint Joseph and Saint Peter Seminary*, 5208 S. 494 Hwy., 78572. Tel: 956-585-7078; Fax: 956-424-9851. Mailing Address: P.O. Box 3888, 78573. Rev. Msgr. Luis Javier Garcia, J.C.L., Rector; Sr. Helena Nunes, Language Instructor; Revs. Ignacio Tapia, Vocations Dir./Dean of Men & Academics, 700 N. Virgen de San Juan Blvd., San Juan, 78589. Tel: 956-781-5323; Eduardo Villa, Spiritual Dir.; Martin de la Cruz, Philosophy Prof.; Jorge A. Gomez, Asst. Spiritual Dir.; Alfonso M. Guevara, Asst. Spiritual Dir.; Mrs. Dora Dovalina, Choir Dir. & Teacher; Mr. Oscar Dayon, Music Teacher.

[B] HIGH SCHOOLS, PRIVATE

BROWNSVILLE. *St. Joseph Academy*, (Grades 7-12), 101 St. Joseph Dr., 78520. Tel: 956-542-3581; Fax: 956-542-4748. Email: president@sja.us. Web: www.sja.us. Dr. Robert Brescia, Pres.; Ms. Lucy A. Williams, Prin. Marist Brothers, United States Religious 7; Lay Teachers 56; Students 794.

EDINBURG. *San Juan Diego Catholic Regional High School*, 1122 Pecan Blvd., Ste. B, P.O. Box 2347, Mcallen, 78502. Tel: 956-287-3260; Fax: 956-992-0306. Web: sanjuandiegohs.org. Sisters Marcella Ewers, D.C., Admin. & Develop. Dir.; Julie Sullivan, High School Project Coord.

PHARR. *Oratory Athenaeum for University Preparation*, 1407 W. Moore Rd., 78577. Tel: 956-781-3056; Fax: 956-702-3047. Email: maviles@mail.oratoryschools.org; yperez@mail.oratoryschools.org. Web: www.oratoryschools.org. Very Rev. Leo Francis Daniels, C.O., Rector; Rev. Mario Alberto Aviles, C.O., Prin.; Mrs. G. Yvonne Perez, Pres.; Revs. Jose E. Losoya, C.O., Vice Prin.; Jose Juan Ortiz, C.O., Librarian. Religious 4; Lay Teachers 14; Students 162.

[C] JUNIOR AND ELEMENTARY SCHOOLS, PRIVATE

BROWNSVILLE. *Guadalupe Regional Middle School*, (Grades 6-8), 1214 E. Lincoln St., 78521. Tel: 956-504-5568; Fax: 956-504-9393. Email: guadalupe678@gmail.com; leosheafms@yahoo.com. Web: guadalupe.schoolfusion.us. Mr. Michael Motyl, Prin.; Bro. Leo Shea, F.M.S., Pres.; Ms. Emily Lefler, Librarian. Religious 3; Lay Teachers 7; Students 82.

Incarnate Word Academy, (Grades PreK-8), (Convent Academy of the Incarnate Word), 244 Resaca Blvd., 78520. Tel: 956-546-4486; Fax: 956-504-3960. Web: www.iw-academy.org. Ms. Christina Moreno, Prin. (6-8); Sisters Marilyn Springs, I.W.B.S., Prin., (PreK-5); Irma Gonzalez, I.W.B.S., Campus Dir.; Mrs. Eva Cuellar, Librarian; Miss Magda Garza, Devel. Dir. Sisters of the Incarnate Word and Blessed Sacrament. Religious 3; Lay Teachers 27; Students 303.

St. Luke School, (Grades PreK-6), 2850 E. Price Rd., 78521. Tel: 956-544-7982; Fax: 956-544-4874. Email: slschool@sbcglobal.net. Web: www.stlukecatholicschool.com. Mrs. Ana E. Gomez, Prin.; Ms. Patty Garza, Librarian. Lay Teachers 19; Students 288.

St. Mary Catholic School, (Grades PreK-6), 1300 Los Ebanos Blvd., 78520. Tel: 956-546-1805; Fax: 956-546-0787. Email: jfaulk@stmarys-cs.org. Web: stmarys-cs.org. Mr. Juan Barreda, Prin.; Mrs. Margaret Van Nostrand, Librarian. Religious 1; Lay Teachers 28; Students 435.

EDINBURG. *St. Joseph School*, (Grades PreK-8), 119 W. Fay, 78539. Tel: 956-383-3957; Fax: 956-318-0681. Email: kmurray@stjoseph-edinburg.org. Web: www.stjoseph-edinburg.org. Sr. Kathleen Murray, D.C., Prin.; Ms. Lupita Davila, Librarian. Religious 1; Lay Teachers 28; Students 282.

HARLINGEN. *St. Anthony School*, (Grades PreK-8), 1015 E. Harrison, 78550. Tel: 956-423-2486; Fax: 956-412-0084. Email: saintanthonyeagles@yahoo.com. Web: www.saintanthonyeagles.com. Mrs. Esther Flores, Prin.; Mrs. Belinda Casarez, Librarian. Lay Teachers 16; Students 229.

MCALLEN. *Our Lady of Sorrows School*, (Grades PreK-8), 1100 Gumwood, 78501. Tel: 956-686-3651; Fax: 956-686-1996. Email: fvalle@olssnet.org. Web: www.olschool.org. Mr. Fred Valle, Prin.; Patrick O'Keefe, Asst. Prin.; Patricia Espinosa, Librarian. Religious 1; Lay Teachers 31; Students 590.

MISSION. *Our Lady of Guadalupe School*, (Grades PreK-4), 611 N. Dunlap, 78572. Tel: 956-585-6445; Fax: 956-584-3055. Email: olgprincipal@sbcglobal.net. Sr. Cynthia Mello, S.S.D., Prin.; Ms. Mary Lovig, Librarian. Religious 2; Lay Teachers 5; Students 86.

PHARR. *Oratory Academy School of St. Philip Neri*, (Grades PreK-8), 1407 W. Moore Rd., 78577. Tel: 956-781-3056; Fax: 956-702-3047. Email: maviles@mail.oratoryschools.org. Very Rev. Leo Francis Daniels, C.O., Rector; Revs. Mario Alberto Aviles, C.O., Prin.; Jose E. Losoya, C.O., Vice Prin.; Mrs. G. Yvonne Perez, Pres.; Rev. Jose Juan Ortiz, C.O., Librarian. Religious 4; Lay Teachers 47; Students 542.

RIO GRANDE CITY. *Immaculate Conception School*, (Grades PreK-8), 305 N. Britton Ave., 78582. Tel: 956-487-2558; Fax: 956-487-6478. Mrs. Rubirita Urbina, Prin.; Ms. Donis Garza, Librarian. Religious 2; Lay Teachers 14; Students 238.

WESLACO. *San Martin de Porres School*, (Grades PreK-3), 905 N. Texas Blvd., 78596. Tel: 956-973-8642; Fax: 956-973-0522. Sr. Helen Rottier, C.S.J., Prin.; Ms. Adelina Olivo, Librarian. Religious 1; Lay Teachers 7; Students 77.

[D] CATHOLIC CHARITIES OF THE RIO GRANDE VALLEY

BROWNSVILLE. *Catholic Charities of the Rio Grande Valley Brownsville Office*, 955 W. Price Rd., 78520. Tel: 956-541-0220; Fax: 956-544-7580.

SAN JUAN. *Catholic Charities of the Rio Grande Valley San Juan Main Office*, 700 N. Virgen de San Juan Blvd., 78589. Tel: 956-702-4088; Fax: 956-782-0418. Email: npimentel@cdob.org. Mailing Address: P.O. Box 1306, 78589.

Catholic Charities of the Rio Grande Valley Executive Board: Most Rev. Raymundo J. Pena, D.D.; Rev. Msgrs. Robert E. Maher, V.G.; Heberto M. Diaz Jr. Board of Directors: Terry Avalos; Karina Cardoza; Silvia Castillo; Terri Drefke; Eddie Garza; Miguel Angel Robledo.

[E] HOMES FOR THE AGED

BROWNSVILLE. *Mother of Perpetual Help Nursing Home, Inc.*, 519 E. Madison St., 78520. Tel: 956-546-6745; Fax: 956-546-0711. Mr. Robert Avila, Admin. Owner: Sisters of the Holy Spirit and Mary Immaculate.; Chapel attended from Immaculate Conception Cathedral. Bed Capacity 46.

SAN JUAN. *San Juan Nursing Home, Inc.*, 300 N. Nebraska Ave., 78589. Tel: 956-787-1771; Fax: 956-787-8091. Most Rev. Raymundo J. Pena, D.D.; Mr. Patrick Eronini, Admin. Bed Capacity 111. Board of Directors: Mr. Ricardo Martinez, Pres.; Mr. Eduardo Vela; Mr. Crawford Higgins; Hermila Anzaldua; Rev. Edouard Atangana, S.T.L., Ex-Officio; Mr. Patrick Eronini, Ex Officio.

[F] RESIDENCES FOR PRIESTS AND BROTHERS

BROWNSVILLE. *Congregation of Christian Brothers* Our Lady of Guadalupe, Regional Middle School., 1214 E. Lincoln St., 78521. Tel: 956-986-0614; Fax: 956-504-9393. Brothers 3.

Marist Brothers, 32995 Henderson Rd., Los Fresnos, 78566. Tel: 956-233-6829. Bros. Francis Garza, Dir.; Paul U. Phillipp; Frances Klug; Thomas J. Lee; Leo Shea; John A. Allen; Summer Herrick. Brothers 7.

Marist Brothers, 1780 Westminster Rd., 78521. Tel: 956-504-6532. Bros. George Dicarluccio, F.M.S.; Richard Sharpe, F.M.S.; Norbert Rodrigue, F.M.S. Brothers 3.

PHARR. *Pharr Oratory of St. Philip Neri of Pontifical Right*, P.O. Box 1698, 78577. Tel: 956-843-8217; Fax: 956-843-2946. Very Rev. Leo Francis Daniels, C.O., Provost; Revs. Jose E. Losoya, C.O., Sec.; Mario Alberto Aviles, C.O., Vicar & Treas.; Jose Juan Ortiz, C.O.

RAYMONDVILLE. *Priests of the Sacred Heart*, Rte. 2, Box 788, 78580. Tel: 956-689-6428; Fax: 956-689-3583. Priests 3.

[G] CONVENTS AND RESIDENCES FOR SISTERS

BROWNSVILLE. *Dominican Sisters of Charity of the Presentation*, 934 W. St. Charles St., 78520. Tel: 956-542-7225. Sisters 4.

Missionaries of Jesus, 1501 W. Adams, 78520. Tel: 956-542-2180. Sisters 4.

Sisters of the Holy Spirit and Mary Immaculate, 519 E. Madison, 78520. Tel: 956-546-2414.

ALAMO. *Monastery of Saint Joseph and Saint Rita of the Capuchin Sisters of St. Clare*, 725 E. Bowie St., 78516. Tel: 956-781-1044. Sisters Martha Alicia Garcia Torres, Abbess; Beatriz Ayala Juarez, Treas.; Luz Maria Leyva Duarte, Sec. & Counselor; Martha Leticia Camarillo Meza, Mistress of Novices. Sisters 7.

EDINBURG. *Incarnate Word and Blessed Sacrament*, 609 Baltic Ave., 78539. Tel: 956-383-6870. P.O. Box 2063, 78540. Sisters 2.

Misioneras Eucaristicas Franciscanas, 311 W. Fay St., 78539. Tel: 956-292-0691.

PALMVIEW. *Daughters of Mary Mother of Mercy*, 237 S. Green Rd., 78573. Tel: 956-867-0993. Sisters 5.

PENITAS. *Missionary Sisters of the Immaculate Heart of Mary*, P.O. Box 1017, 78576. Tel: 956-580-9726; 956-585-5488; Fax: 956-519-9123. Email: icmtx@juno.com. 17617 Sabal Palm Dr., 78576. Sisters 5.

PROGRESO. *Sisters of St. Dorothy*, P.O. Box 147, 78579. Tel: 956-565-9430. Sisters 4.

RIO GRANDE CITY. *Benedictine Sisters of the Good Shepherd*, P.O. Box 1501, 78582. Tel: 956-486-2680; Fax: 956-486-2680. Email: francesosb@gmail.com. Sisters 3.

SAN JUAN. *Missionaries of Jesus*, 700 N. Oblate Dr., 78589. Tel: 956-781-9292. Sisters 2.

[H] RETREAT HOUSES

SAN JUAN. *St. Eugene de Mazenod Christian Renewal Center*, P.O. Box 747, 78589. Tel: 956-787-0033; Fax: 956-787-2908.

[I] BASILICA

SAN JUAN. *The Basilica of Our Lady of San Juan del Valle-National Shrine*, 400 N. Virgen de San Juan Blvd., 78589. Tel: 956-787-0033; Fax: 956-787-2908. Rev. Eduardo Ortega, Rector; Mr. Esteban Martinez, Admin.; Rev. Francisco J. Solis, Asst. to Rector; Deacons Julio Castilleja; Jesus P. Galvan.

San Juan Pilgrim House/Hotel Tel: 956-787-0033, Ext. 223. Mrs. Petra Ruiz, Mgr.

Religious Gift & Book Store Tel: 956-787-0033, Ext. 265. Ms. Frances Silva, Mgr.

[J] CAMPUS MINISTRY

BROWNSVILLE. *Youth & Young Adult Ministry/University of Texas at Brownsville-Texas Southmost College* 1910 University Blvd., 78520. Tel: 956-541-9697; Fax: 956-542-6751. Web: www.cdob.org; www.utbcatholics.org. Hilda Escandon, Campus Min.

EDINBURG. *Youth & Young Adult Ministry/University of Texas Pan American* 1615 W. Kuhn St., 78541. Tel: 956-383-0133; Fax: 956-387-0738. Mr. Miguel Santos, Campus Min.

[K] MISCELLANEOUS

BROWNSVILLE. *Asociacion Nacional de Sacerdotes Hispanos* (1990) P.O. Box 2279, 78522-2279. Tel: 956-542-2501; Fax: 956-542-6751. Email: info@ansh.org. Web: www.ansh.org. Rev. Msgr. Heberto M. Diaz Jr., Pres.; Revs. Claudio Diaz, Vice Pres., 3525 S. Lake Park Ave., Chicago, IL 60653. Tel: 312-534-1080; Jhon Guarnizo, Sec., P.O. Box 908, Crescent City, FL 32112. Tel: 386-698-2055; Manuel La Rosa-Lopez, Treas., 410 Clay St., Richmond, 77469. Tel: 281-723-3589.

**Bishop Enrique San Pedro Ozanam Center, Inc.*, 656 N. Minnesota Ave., 78521. Tel: 956-831-6331; Fax: 956-831-8577. Victor Maldonado, Dir.

Catholic Foundation of the Rio Grande Valley, 1910 University Blvd., 78520-4998. Tel: 956-542-2501; Fax: 956-542-6751. Rev. Msgr. Heberto M. Diaz Jr., Vice Chm. & Contact Person.

The Guadalupe Regional Middle School Endowment, 1214 Lincoln St., 78521. Tel: 956-504-5568. Sr. Mary Ann Korczynski, I.W.B.S., Chm.

The St. Joseph Academy Endowment, 101 St. Joseph Dr., 78520. Tel: 956-542-4748. Email: richard@sja.us. Bro. Richard Sharpe, F.M.S., Contact Person.

Movimiento Familiar Cristiano/Federacion Este, 109 Lucylle Ln., 78520. Tel: 956-589-2491.

Texas Historical Preservation Foundation, P.O. Box 2279, 78522-2279. Tel: 956-542-2501; Fax: 956-542-6751. Mr. Jack Graham, Contact Person.

Villa Maria Language Institute, 224 Resaca Blvd., 78520. Tel: 956-546-7196; Fax: 956-546-1731. Sr. Irma Gonzalez, I.W.B.S., Dir.

ALAMO. *ARISE-South Tower*, 330 W. San Bernardino, P.O. Box 778, 78516. Tel: 956-783-8517; Fax: 956-783-5498. Ms. Lourdes Mendoza, Pres.

ARISE Support Center, 1417 S. Tower Rd., P.O. Box 778, 78516. Tel: 956-783-6959; Fax: 956-783-0274. Email: arisesotex@rgv.rr.com. Web: www.arisesotex.org. Ms. Virginia Santana, Pres. *ARISE Support Center*

EDINBURG. *ARISE-Muñiz*, 3917 Jam Sq., 78539. Tel: 956-782-4041; Fax: 956-782-6430. Ms. Andrea Olvera, Pres.

Catholic Engaged Encounter, 1304 W. Russell Rd., 78541. Tel: 956-381-1135. Email: zamco52@hotmail.com.

Movimiento Familiar Cristiano: Federacion Oeste, 102 Delia Dr., 78539. Tel: 956-207-7795.

HARLINGEN. *Encuentro Matrimonial/East*, 514 N. K., 78550. Tel: 956-428-5370. Mr. Manuel Lugo, Contact Person; Mrs. Gabriela Lugo, Contact Person.

**Guadalupe Health Center*, 310 N. Eye St., 78550. Tel: 956-440-8776; Fax: 956-440-8265. Mr. Rolando Martinez, Exec. Dir.

**Proyecto Juan Diego, Inc.*, 1906 Susan Ave., 78550-2744. Tel: 956-542-2334; 956-542-2488; Fax: 956-542-5055. Email: mewers@cdob.org. Sisters Phylis Peters, D.C., Exec. Dir.; Marcella Ewers, D.C., Chairperson.

**RGV Educational Broadcasting, Inc.*, P.O. Box 2147, 78551. Tel: 956-421-4111; Fax: 956-421-4150. Email: pbriseno@aol.com. Web: www.kmbh.org. Rev. Msgr. Pedro Briseno, Gen. Mgr. & Pres.

Worldwide Marriage Encounter, 1642 Hamilton, 78550. Tel: 956-536-8284. Email: robleandsons@sbcglobal.net.

LA JOYA. *Boy Scouts*, 916 S. Leo Ave., 78560. Tel: 956-585-5223. Rev. Juan Pablo Davalos.

MCALLEN. *Comfort House Services, Inc.*, 617 Dallas Ave., 78501. Tel: 956-687-7367; Fax: 956-630-6423. Email: chsi@att.net. Ms. Maria Botello, Admin. AIDS Education & Outreach; Palliative Care to the Terminally Ill. Bed Capacity 10.

MERCEDES. *La Merced Charitable Trust*, 413 S. Virginia, 78570. Tel: 956-565-2622; Fax: 956-565-4185. Email: rmedrano@cdob.org.
Housing Board: Mr. Roel A. Rodriguez, Trustee; Mr. Alfredo Huerta, Trustee; Mr. Robert A. Calvillo, Trustee; Mr. Jose Luis Gonzalez, Trustee; Ms. Estella L. Trevino, Trustee.

MISSION. *El Rosario Charitable Trust*, 119 Retama, 78572. Tel: 956-585-5051; Fax: 956-585-9938. Email: rmedrano@cdob.org.

Fraternity of Our Lady of Guadalupe Secular Franciscan Order, 1-3/4 Miles West on 7 Mile Line, 78574. Tel: 956-519-9504; Fax: 956-580-4944. 2600 W. Mile 7 Rd., 78574. Rev. Tomas Mateos, Spiritual Asst.

PHARR. *ARISE-Las Milpas*, 125 E. Denny, 78577. Tel: 956-783-9293; Fax: 956-783-2099. Ms. Andrea Olvera, Pres.

Encuentro Matrimonial: West, 413 E. Arapano Ave., 78577. Tel: 956-655-1713. Mr. Felipe Teyer, Contact Person; Mrs. Leticia Tyer, Contact Person.

SAN BENITO. *La Posada Providencia*, 1610 Marydale Rd., 78586. Tel: 956-399-3826; Fax: 956-399-2898. Email: cdplaposada@sbcglobal.net. Web: www.lppshelter.org. Sisters Zita Telkamp, C.D.P., Dir.; Therese Cunningham, S.H.Sp., Mentor/ESL Teacher. (A program of Providence Ministry Corp.) A not for-profit transitional & emergency shelter for homeless men, women and children with minimal income.

WESLACO. *Natural Family Planning*, 600 S. Oklahoma Ave., 78596. Tel: 956-969-3079; 956-968-7142.

RELIGIOUS INSTITUTES OF MEN REPRESENTED IN THE DIOCESE

For further details refer to the corresponding bracketed number in the Religious Institutes of Men or Women section.

[0310]—*Congregation of Christian Brothers*—C.F.C.

[0630]—*Congregation of the Missionaries of the Holy Family*—M.S.F.

[1130]—*Congregation of the Priests of the Sacred Heart*—S.C.J.

[1140]—*Fathers of the Sacred Hearts*—SS.CC.

[0410]—*Franciscans-Assumption BVM Province*—O.F.M.

[0770]—*The Marist Brothers*—F.M.S.

[0780]—*Marist Priests and Brothers of the Society of Mary*—S.M.

[0370]—*Missionary Society of St. Columban*—S.S.C.

[0860]—*Missionhurst Congregation of the Immaculate Heart of Mary*—C.I.C.M.

[0910]—*Oblates of Mary Immaculate*—O.M.I.

[0950]—*Oratorians of St. Philip Neri*—C.O.

[]—*Orden de la Merced*—O.de.M.

RELIGIOUS INSTITUTES OF WOMEN REPRESENTED IN THE DIOCESE

[]—*Benedictine Sisters of the Good Shepherd (Monastery)*—O.S.B.

[0990]—*Congregation of Divine Providence*—C.D.P.

[0470]—*Congregation of the Sisters of Charity of the Incarnate Word, Houston, Texas*—C.C.V.I.

[1920]—*Congregation of the Sisters of the Holy Cross*—C.S.C.

[0760]—*Daughters of Charity of St. Vincent de Paul*—D.C.

[0793]—*Daughters of Divine Love*—D.D.L.

[]—*Daughters of Mary Mother of Mercy*—D.M.M.M.

[1115]—*Dominican Sisters of Peace*—O.P.

[1070-19]—*Dominican Sisters, Congregation of the Sacred Heart* (Houston)—O.P.

[1415]—*Franciscan Sisters of Mary*—F.S.M.

[]—*Franciscan Sisters of Little Falls, Minnesota*

[]—*Hermana de Jesus*—H.J.

[1150]—*Misioneras Eucaristicas Franciscanas*—M.E.F.

[2690]—*Missionary Catechists of Divine Providence*—M.C.D.P.

[]—*Missionary Sisters of Jesus*—M.J.

[2750]—*Missionary Sisters of the Immaculate Heart of Mary*—I.C.M.

[]—*Missioneras Catequistas de los Pobres*—M.C.P.

[]—*Missioneras del Espiritu Santo Y la Sagrada Familia*—M.E.S.S.F.

[]—*Order of St. Clare Capuchins*—O.S.C.Cap.

[2970]—*School Sisters of Notre Dame* (Prov. of Dallas)—S.S.N.D.

[]—*Sisters for a Christian Community*—S.F.C.C.

[]—*Sisters of Charity*—S.C.

[2575]—*Sisters of Mercy of the Americas* (St. Louis, MO; Cincinnati, OH; Silver Spring, MO)—R.S.M.

[0230]—*Sisters of St. Benedict of Crookston*—O.S.B.

[3790]—*Sisters of St. Dorothy*—S.S.D.

[1705]—*Sisters of St. Francis of Assisi*—O.S.F.

[3840]—*Sisters of St. Joseph of Carondelet* (St. Paul & St. Louis Provs.)—C.S.J.

[]—*Sisters of the Franciscan Order*—S.F.O.

[2050]—*Sisters of the Holy Spirit and Mary Immaculate*—S.H.Sp.

[2205]—*Sisters of the Incarnate Word and Blessed Sacrament*—I.W.B.S.

[3320]—*Sisters of the Presentation of the Blessed Virgin Mary*—P.B.V.M.

[3670]—*Sisters of the Sacred Heart of Jesus of St. Jacut*—S.S.C.J.

[4120-04]—*Ursuline Nuns of the Congregation of Parish* (Cleveland, OH)—O.S.U.

NECROLOGY

† Meyers, Frederick, Edinburg, TX Sacred Heart—Died Aug. 30, 2008

† Wichmann, Edward W., (Retired)—Died June 28, 2009

An asterisk (*) denotes an organization that has established tax-exempt status directly with the IRS and is not covered by the USCCB Group Ruling.

Diocese of Buffalo

(Dioecesis Buffalensis)

Most Reverend

EDWARD U. KMIEC, D.D., S.T.L.

Bishop of Buffalo ordained December 20, 1961; appointed Titular Bishop of Simidicca and Auxiliary Bishop of Trenton August 26, 1982; consecrated November 3, 1982; appointed Bishop of Nashville October 13, 1992; installed December 3, 1992; appointed Bishop of Buffalo August 12, 2004; installed October 28, 2004. *Res.: 77 Oakland Pl., Buffalo, NY 14222-1241.*

Chancery Office: 795 Main St., Buffalo, NY 14203. Tel: 716-847-5500; Fax: 716-847-5557.

Web: www.buffalodiocese.org

Email: dob@buffalodiocese.org

Most Reverend

BERNARD J. McLAUGHLIN, D.D., V.G.

Retired Auxiliary Bishop of Buffalo; ordained December 21, 1935; appointed Auxiliary Bishop of Buffalo and Titular Bishop of Mottola December 28, 1968; consecrated January 6, 1969; retired January 15, 1988. *Res.: 204 Knoche Rd., Tonawanda, NY 14150.*

Most Reverend

EDWARD M. GROSZ, D.D.

Auxiliary Bishop of Buffalo; ordained May 29, 1971; appointed November 22, 1989; consecrated February 2, 1990. *Res.: St. Stanislaus Parish, 123 Townsend St., Buffalo, NY 14212-1299.*

ESTABLISHED APRIL 23, 1847

Square Miles 6,357.

Incorporated under the laws of the State of New York October 30th, 1897. Re-incorporated by special act passed April 5, 1951, Chapter 568 of the laws of 1951.

Corporate Title: The Diocese of Buffalo, N.Y.

Comprises the Counties of Erie, Niagara, Genesee, Orleans, Chautauqua, Wyoming, Cattaraugus and Allegany in the State of New York.

For legal titles of parishes and diocesan institutions, consult the Chancery Office.

STATISTICAL OVERVIEW

Personnel	
Bishop	1
Auxiliary Bishops	1
Retired Bishops	2
Priests: Diocesan Active in Diocese	199
Priests: Diocesan Active Outside Diocese	9
Priests: Retired, Sick or Absent	126
Number of Diocesan Priests	334
Religious Priests in Diocese	115
Total Priests in Diocese	449
Extern Priests in Diocese	7
Ordinations:	
Diocesan Priests	2
Transitional Deacons	1
Permanent Deacons	9
Permanent Deacons in Diocese	125
Total Brothers	42
Total Sisters	964
Parishes	
Parishes	171
With Resident Pastor:	
Resident Diocesan Priests	138
Resident Religious Priests	12
Without Resident Pastor:	
Administered by Priests	16
Administered by Deacons	3
Administered by Religious Women	1
Administered by Pastoral Teams, etc.	1
Missions	1
Pastoral Centers	2
New Parishes Created	6
Closed Parishes	15
Professional Ministry Personnel:	
Brothers	1
Sisters	40
Lay Ministers	121
Welfare	
Catholic Hospitals	4
Total Assisted	1,451,025
Health Care Centers	1
Total Assisted	960
Homes for the Aged	9
Total Assisted	3,447
Day Care Centers	3
Total Assisted	206
Specialized Homes	3
Total Assisted	5,241
Special Centers for Social Services	5
Total Assisted	259,503
Residential Care of Disabled	8
Total Assisted	49
Other Institutions	1
Total Assisted	9,039
Educational	
Seminaries, Diocesan	1
Students from This Diocese	15
Students from Other Diocese	1
Diocesan Students in Other Seminaries	3
Seminaries, Religious	1
Students Religious	2
Total Seminarians	20
Colleges and Universities	7
Total Students	17,201
High Schools, Private	15
Total Students	5,221
Elementary Schools, Diocesan and Parish	55
Total Students	11,976
Elementary Schools, Private	3
Total Students	689
Non-residential Schools for the Disabled	1
Total Students	399
Catechesis/Religious Education:	
High School Students	9,051
Elementary Students	26,688
Total Students under Catholic Instruction	71,245
Teachers in the Diocese:	
Priests	37
Brothers	24
Sisters	90
Lay Teachers	2,527
Vital Statistics	
Receptions into the Church:	
Infant Baptism Totals	4,110
Minor Baptism Totals	165
Adult Baptism Totals	132
Received into Full Communion	224
First Communions	5,201
Confirmations	5,167
Marriages:	
Catholic	1,048
Interfaith	467
Total Marriages	1,515
Deaths	6,217
Total Catholic Population	656,760
Total Population	1,529,043

Former Bishops—Rt. Revs. JOHN TIMON, C.M., D.D., ord. Sept. 23, 1826; cons. Oct. 17, 1847; died April 16, 1867; STEPHEN V. RYAN, C.M., D.D., ord. June 24, 1849; cons. Nov. 8, 1868; died April 10, 1896; JAMES EDWARD QUIGLEY, D.D., ord. April 13, 1879; cons. Bishop of Buffalo, Feb. 24, 1897; promoted to the Archdiocese of Chicago, Feb. 19, 1903; died July 10, 1915; CHARLES HENRY COLTON, D.D., ord. June 10, 1876; cons. Aug. 24, 1903; died May 9, 1915; His Eminence DENNIS CARDINAL DOUGHERTY, D.D., ord. May 31, 1890; cons. Bishop of Nueva Segovia, June 14, 1903; transferred to the Diocese of Jaro, April 19, 1908; transferred to the Diocese of Buffalo, Dec. 6, 1915; promoted to Archdiocese of Philadelphia, May 1, 1918; created Cardinal, March 7, 1921; died May 31, 1951; Most Revs. WILLIAM TURNER, D.D., ord. Aug. 13, 1893; cons. March 30, 1919; died July 10, 1936; JOHN A. DUFFY, D.D., ord. June 13, 1908; cons. Bishop of Syracuse, June 29, 1933; transferred to the Diocese of Buffalo, April 14, 1937; died Sept. 27, 1944; His Eminence JOHN CARDINAL O'HARA, C.S.C., ord. Sept. 9, 1916; appt. Military Delegate of the Armed Forces and Titular Bishop of Mylasa, Dec. 11, 1939; cons. Jan. 15, 1940; transferred to Buffalo, March 10, 1945; installed May 8, 1945; promoted to the Archdiocese of Philadelphia, Nov. 23, 1951; created Cardinal, Dec. 15, 1958; died Aug. 28, 1960; Most Revs. JOSEPH A. BURKE, D.D., ord. Aug. 3, 1912; cons. Titular Bishop of Vita and Auxiliary, June 29, 1943; promoted to the See, Feb. 9, 1952; died Oct. 16, 1962; JAMES A. MCNULTY, D.D., ord. July 12, 1925; cons. Oct. 7, 1947; Titular Bishop of Methone and Auxiliary Bishop of Newark, NJ; appt. Bishop of Paterson, NJ April 9, 1953; transferred to Buffalo, Feb. 12, 1963; died Sept. 4, 1972; EDWARD D. HEAD, D.D., ord. Jan. 27, 1945; appt. Titular Bishop of Ardstratha and Auxiliary of New York, Jan. 27, 1970; cons. March 19, 1970; appt. Bishop of Buffalo, Jan. 17, 1973; installed March 19, 1973; retired June 12, 1995; died March 29, 2005; HENRY J. MANSELL, D.D., ord. Dec. 19, 1962; appt. Titular Bishop of Marazane and Auxiliary of New York Nov. 24, 1992; ord. Jan. 6, 1993; appt. Bishop of Buffalo April 18, 1995; installed June 12, 1995; promoted to Archbishop of Hartford Oct. 20, 2003.

Vicars General—Most Rev. EDWARD M. GROSZ, D.D., V.G.; Rev. Msgr. DAVID S. SLUBECKY, J.C.L., S.T.L., V.G.

Chancery Office—795 Main St., Buffalo, 14203. Tel: 716-847-5500; Fax: 716-847-5557. Email: dob@buffalodiocese.org. Office Hours: Mon.-Fri. 9-4:30.

Moderator of the Curia—Rev. Msgr. DAVID S. SLUBECKY, J.C.L., S.T.L., V.G.

Chancellor—Rev. Msgr. PAUL A. LITWIN, J.C.L.

Secretary to Diocesan Bishop and Vice Chancellor—Rev. Msgr. DAVID G. LIPUMA.

Diocesan Tribunal—795 Main St., Buffalo, 14203. Tel: 716-847-8769; Fax: 716-847-8772. Email: tribunal@buffalodiocese.org. Send all rogatory commissions to the Tribunal.

Judicial Vicar—Rev. Msgr. SALVATORE MANGANELLO, J.C.L., S.T.L.

Adjunct Judicial Vicar—Rev. PAUL P. SABO.

Defenders of the Bond—Revs. EDWARD R. CZARNECKI; FRANCIS X. MAZUR; GREGORY M. FAULHABER, S.T.D.; DENNIS A. FRONCZAK.

Advocates—Deacon DANIEL E. BRICK ESQ.; Revs. RICHARD S. DIGIULIO; ROBERT W. VOGT (Retired).

Promoter of Justice—Rev. Msgr. W. JEROME SULLIVAN, J.C.D.

Judges—Rev. JAMES M. AUGUSTYN (Retired); Rev. Msgr. VINCENT J. BECKER; Rev. JOSEPH KLOS, J.C.L.; Rev. Msgr. SALVATORE MANGANELLO, J.C.L., S.T.L.; Revs. HENRY A. ORSZULAK; PAUL P. SABO.

Notaries—NICOLE BALL; LUCILLE BUCZEK.

Consultors, College of—Most Rev. EDWARD M. GROSZ, D.D., V.G.; Rev. Msgrs. DAVID S. SLUBECKY, J.C.L., S.T.L., V.G.; JAMES E. WALL; W. JEROME SULLIVAN, J.C.D.; ROBERT E. ZAPFEL, S.T.D.; Revs. PETER J. DRILLING, Th.D.; JACOB C. LEDWON; PETER J. KARALUS; RONALD W. SAMS, S.J.; Rev. Msgr. JOSEPH J. SICARI.

Council of Priests—Most Revs. EDWARD U. KMIEC, D.D., S.T.L.; EDWARD M. GROSZ, D.D., V.G.; Rev. Msgr. DAVID S. SLUBECKY, J.C.L., S.T.L., V.G.; Revs. MICHAEL H. BURZYNSKI; DENNIS A. FRONCZAK; STEVEN G. FRENIER, O.F.M.Conv.; PETER J. DRILLING, Th.D.; JAMES G. JUDGE; PETER J. KARALUS; JOSEPH F. KOZLOWSKI; Rev. Msgr. SALVATORE MANGANELLO, J.C.L., S.T.L.; Revs. JOSEPH S. ROGLIANO; IVAN R. TRUJILLO; WILLIAM R. TUYN; JAMES VACCO, O.F.M., M.A.; JOSEPH A. ZALACCA; Rev. Msgr. ROBERT E. ZAPFEL, S.T.D.; Revs. MATTHEW J. ZIRNHELD; DENNIS J. MANCUSO; RONALD W. SAMS, S.J.; JOSEPH D. PORPIGLIA; GREGORY M. FAULHABER, S.T.D.; Rev. Msgr. GERARD L. GREEN (Retired); Rev. JACOB C. LEDWON; Rev. Msgrs. JOSEPH J. SICARI; W. JEROME SULLIVAN, J.C.D.; JAMES E. WALL.

Finance Council—Most Revs. EDWARD U. KMIEC, D.D., S.T.L.; EDWARD M. GROSZ, D.D., V.G.; Rev. Msgrs. PAUL J.E. BURKARD; ANGELO M. CALIGIURI (Retired); JAMES F. CAMPBELL; Mr. GEORGE J. EBERL; Rev. Msgr. FREDERICK D. LEISING; Rev. JOHN R. GAGLIONE; Rev. Msgr. WILLIAM J. GALLAGHER; Rev. CZESLAW M. KRYSA; Rev. Msgr. THOMAS F. MALONEY; Rev. FABIAN J. MARYANSKI; Mr. CHARLES A. MENDOLERA, Ex Officio; Rev. Msgr. J. THOMAS MORAN; Mr. PATRICK F. REILLY; Rev. Msgr. DAVID S. SLUBECKY, J.C.L., S.T.L., V.G., Chm.; Mr. STEVEN D. TIMMEL, Ex Officio; Rev. MARK J. WOLSKI; Rev. Msgrs. ROBERT E. ZAPFEL, S.T.D.; PAUL A. LITWIN, J.C.L.; Mr. JOSEPH F. KAPSIAK; Mr. DAVID ROGERS; Mr. JAY MCWATTERS, CPA.

Vicariates—

Vicars—Revs. ROBERT L. GEBHARD JR., Northwest-Central Buffalo; FABIAN J. MARYANSKI, Southeast Buffalo; Rev. Msgr. ROBERT E. ZAPFEL, S.T.D., Northern Erie; Rev. THOMAS J. QUINLIVAN, Eastern Erie; Rev. Msgrs. PAUL J.E. BURKARD, Southern Erie; VINCENT J. BECKER, Allegany; Revs. PETER J. KARALUS, Tri-County; GREGORY J. DOBSON, Southern Cattaraugus; DENNIS G. RITER, Chautauqua; ARTHUR E. MATTULKE, Genesee-Wyoming; ROBERT S. HUGHSON, Western Niagara; RICHARD A. CSIZMAR, Eastern Niagara-Orleans.

The Diocese of Buffalo, N.Y.— A corporation under the laws of the State of New York. Most Revs. EDWARD U. KMIEC, D.D., S.T.L., Pres.; EDWARD M. GROSZ, D.D., V.G., Vice Pres.; Rev. Msgrs. DAVID S. SLUBECKY, J.C.L., S.T.L., V.G., Vice Pres.; PAUL A. LITWIN, J.C.L., Sec.

Diocesan Offices and Directors

All offices are located at: 795 Main St., Buffalo, NY 14203. Tel: 716-847-8700; Fax: 716-847-5557 (Unless otherwise noted).

Apostleship of Prayer—Rev. RICHARD M. I. POBLOCKI, Dir., 20 Peoria Ave., Cheektowaga, 14206.

Apostleship of the Sea—Rev. Msgr. JOHN I. DUCETTE, Dir. (Retired), Res.: Sheehan Residence, 330 Linwood Ave., Buffalo, 14209.

Archives—Sr. ANN LOUISE HENTGES, S.S.M.N. Tel: 716-847-5500.

Bishop's Committee for Christian Home and Family—Moderators: Deacon THOMAS SCHULTZ; GINI SCHULTZ. Tel: 716-847-2210.

Boy Scouts—Rev. MICHAEL J. PUTICH, O.F.M. Tel: 716-823-2358; Mr. JAMES S. SMYCZYNSKI, Committee Chm.

Buildings and Properties—MICHAEL J. SULLIVAN, Dir. Tel: 716-847-8750; Fax: 716-847-8756.

Camp Turner—JOHN MANN, Steward, 9150 Asp Rd. #3, Salamanca, 14779. Tel: 716-354-4555; Fax: 716-354-2055. Email: campturner@gmail.com.

Catechumenate Office—Mrs. JUDITH WAGGONER, Dir. Tel: 716-847-5546; Fax: 716-847-5593.

Catholic Charities—Rev. Msgr. JOSEPH J. SICARI, Dir. & Pres.; DENNIS C. WALCZYK, CEO, 741 Delaware Ave., Buffalo, 14209. Tel: 716-218-1400; Fax: 716-856-2005.

Catholic Charities Appeal—Rev. Msgr. JOSEPH J. SICARI, Dir., Office: 741 Delaware Ave., Buffalo, 14209. Tel: 716-218-1400.

Daybreak TV Productions—CLAIRE RUNG, Exec. Producer. Tel: 716-847-8734.

Catholic Relief Services—741 Delaware Ave., Buffalo, 14209. Tel: 716-856-4494.

Chautauqua Catholic Community, Chautauqua Institution—Rev. TODD M. REMICK, Spiritual Dir. & Diocesan Liaison.

Council of Catholic Men—Rev. PAUL P. SABO, Moderator.

Council of Catholic Women—Mrs. BERNICE S. DINSMORE, Exec. Sec.

Cemeteries—CARMEN A. COLAO, Dir., Mt. Olivet Cemetery, 4000 Elmwood Ave., Kenmore, 14217. Tel: 716-873-6500; Fax: 716-873-3247.

Censors--Board of Diocesan Censors of Books and Vigilance for the Faith—Rev. Msgrs. SAMUEL J. FAIOLA, S.T.D. (Retired); THOMAS E. CRANE (Retired).

Charismatic Renewal Program—Rev. RICHARD S. DIGIULIO, Dir.

Clergy Personnel Board—Rev. JAMES A. WALTER, Coord. Tel: 716-847-5537; Rev. Msgrs. RUPERT A. WRIGHT (Retired); JAMES G. KELLY; Revs. RICHARD A. CSIZMAR; THOMAS J. QUINLIVAN; RONALD P. SAJDAK.

Communications—KEVIN A. KEENAN, Dir. Tel: 716-847-8719; Fax: 716-847-8722.

Diocesan Directory—GREGG PRINCE. Tel: 716-847-8719.

Public Relations, Assistant Director for Communications—KRISTINA M. CONNELL. Tel: 716-847-8749.

Assistant Director of Communications for Radio—GREGG PRINCE. Tel: 716-847-8744.

Computer Services (Diocesan)—JAMES C. KAVANAGH, Dir. Tel: 716-847-5500.

Continuing Education for Clergy—Co-Directors: Rev. Msgrs. JAMES E. WALL; RICHARD W. SIEPKA, M.A., S.T.L.

Cursillo Movement—Deacon RICHARD F. MACKIEWICZ, Spiritual Dir. Tel: 716-652-3972; Mr. DONALD APPENHEIMER, Lay Dir.

Deaf—Rev. CONRAD P. STACHOWIAK, Chap., 130 Como Park Blvd., South Cheektowaga, 14227.

Advancement Office—DAVID KERSTEN, Exec. Dir., The Foundation of the Roman Catholic Diocese of Buffalo and Diocesan Advancement. Tel: 716-847-8370; THERESE BIANCHI, Assoc. Dir. Advancement.

Due Process—Rev. Msgr. SALVATORE MANGANELLO, J.C.L., S.T.L., Chm., Catholic Center. Tel: 716-847-8769; Fax: 716-847-8772.

Ecumenism—Rev. FRANCIS X. MAZUR, Diocesan Liaison.

Catholic Education—Mrs. CAROL A. KOSTYNIAK, Sec. Educ., 795 Main St., Buffalo, 14203-1250. Tel: 716-847-5520; Fax: 716-847-5593; ROSEMARY J. HENRY, Ph.D., Supt. Catholic Schools. Tel: 716-847-5512; Mrs. ELIZABETH SCHANBACHER, Asst. Supt., Educational Technology. Tel: 716-847-5512; Mrs. PATRICIA TRIMPER, Asst. Supt., Curriculum, Instruction & Assessment. Tel: 716-847-5517; Mr. THOMAS E. PETERS, Asst. Supt. Govt. Programs. Tel: 716-847-5511; BARBARA MAROTTO, Professional Devel. Coord. Tel: 716-847-5507; Mr. BRIAN KISZEWSKI, Dir. Athletics. Tel: 716-866-5081; KARIN KRASEVAC-LENZ, Dir. Catholic Alumni Partnership. Tel: 716-847-8372.

Eucharistic Adoration—Deacon JOHN T. SETERA. Tel: 716-847-5548.

Evangelization Commission—Rev. DANIEL J. PALYS, Chm., 5271 Clinton St., Elma, 14059. Tel: 716-668-4017.

Family Life—Directors: Deacon THOMAS SCHULTZ; GINI SCHULTZ. Tel: 716-847-2210; Fax: 716-847-2206.

Finance Office—Mr. STEVEN D. TIMMEL. Tel: 716-847-5500; Fax: 716-847-5557.

Guild for the Blind, Inc.—Office: 741 Delaware Ave., Buffalo, 14209. Tel: 716-218-1400, Ext. 205.

Bishop's Representative for Health Care—Rev. Msgr. ROBERT E. ZAPFEL, S.T.D. Tel: 716-835-8905.

Office of Cultural Diversity—Mrs. MILAGROS RAMOS, Dir. Tel: 716-847-2217; Fax: 716-847-2206.

Holy Name Society—Rev. PAUL P. SABO, Moderator; RAYMOND ZIENTARA, Exec. Dir. Diocesan Union of Holy Name Societies. Tel: 716-847-2202.

Hospital Chaplains—Rev. RICHARD H. AUGUSTYN, Dir. Hospital Ministry, 100 High St., Buffalo, 14203. Tel: 716-859-5600.

Human Resources—Sr. SHAWN CZYZYCKI, C.S.S.F., Dir. Tel: 716-847-8376.

Insurance Services—JOHN SCHOLL, Dir. Tel: 716-847-8394; Fax: 716-847-5538.

Internal Audit—BRUCE C. EVERT, Dir. Tel: 716-847-5500. Email: audit@buffalodiocese.org.

Legion of Mary—Rev. DAVID W. BIALKOWSKI, Spiritual Dir. Tel: 716-847-5545.

Lifelong Faith Formation—Mrs. MARY BETH COATES, M.S., MAPM, Diocesan Dir. Lifelong Faith Formation. Tel: 716-847-5505; Ms. ELAINE DANKOWSKI, Assoc. Dir. Sacramental Catechesis. Tel: 716-847-5516; Mrs. SHARON URBANIAK, Assoc. Dir. People with Special Needs. Tel: 716-847-5514; Mr. CHRISTOPHER HANLEY, Assoc. Dir. Adult & Intergenerational Catechesis. Tel: 716-847-5521; Sr. JULIE UHRICH, O.S.F., Regl. Dir., Allegany, Southern Cattaraugus and Southern Chautauqua Counties; Cuba, NY. Tel: 585-968-5776.

Liturgical Commission—KAREN L. PODD, Chm.

Newman Club Chaplains—Rev. PATRICK J. ZENGIERSKI, Ph.D., Mailing Address: Vicar Campus Ministry and Newman Club Centers, 1219 Elmwood Ave., Buffalo, 14222. Tel: 716-882-1080.

Newspaper— "Western New York Catholic" KEVIN A. KEENAN, Editor in Chief. Tel: 716-847-8719; RICK FRANUSIAK, Mng. Editor. Tel: 716-849-8738; Fax: 716-847-8722.

Parish Life—Mrs. KATHLEEN B. HEFFERN, M.A.T., Dir. Tel: 716-847-5531; Fax: 716-847-2206. Email: parish-life@buffalodiocese.org; Mr. DENNIS G. MAHANEY, Assoc. Dir. Tel: 716-847-8393.

Pastoral Council—Mr. EDWARD RESKA, Exec. Chm.

Peace and Justice (Diocesan Commission)—Rev. RONALD P. SAJDAK, 26 Wyoming Ave., Buffalo, 14215.

Permanent Diaconate—Deacons THADDEUS P. MAY, Dir., Christ the King Seminary, 711 Knox Rd., P.O. Box 607, East Aurora, 14052. Tel: 716-652-4308; GREGORY L. FEARY, Dir. Formation. Tel: 716-681-3484.

Priests, Vicar for—Rev. Msgr. JAMES E. WALL, 711 Knox Rd., P.O. Box 607, East Aurora, 14052-0607. Tel: 716-652-5047.

Pro-Life Activities—Mr. DENIS COAKLEY, Coord. Tel: 716-847-2205; Fax: 716-847-2206. Email: prolifeoffice@buffalodiocese.org.

Propagation of the Faith—Rev. Msgr. JOSEPH J. SICARI, Dir., 741 Delaware Ave., Buffalo, 14209. Tel: 716-856-4494.

Purchasing (Diocesan)—CHARLES MUSSEN. Tel: 716-847-8711; Fax: 716-847-8702. Email: dpd@buffalodiocese.org.

Research and Planning—Sr. REGINA MURPHY, S.S.M.N. Tel: 716-847-5539; Fax: 716-847-5593. Email: rmurphy@buffalodiocese.org.

Safe Environment—DONALD R. BLOWEY JR., Prog. Dir. Tel: 716-847-5532; Fax: 716-847-5593.

Worship, Office Of—Rev. CZESLAW M. KRYSA, Dir. Tel: 716-847-5545; Fax: 716-847-2206; ALAN D. LUKAS, M.Mus., Dir. Music, Mailing Address: Christ the King Seminary, P.O. Box 607, East Aurora, 14052-0607. Tel: 716-652-6565; Fax: 716-652-8903.

Vicar for Religious—Sr. JEAN THOMPSON, O.S.F., Vicar. Tel: 716-847-5529.

Victim Assistance Coordinator—MARY ANN C. DEIBEL-BRAUN, L.C.S.W. Tel: 716-895-3010. Email: maryann.deibel-braun@ccwny.org.

Vocations—Rev. WALTER J. SZCZESNY, M.Div., Dir. Tel: 716-847-5535; Fax: 716-847-2206. Email: vocations@buffalodiocese.org.

Youth and Young Adult Ministry—KATHRYN M. GOLLER, Dir. Tel: 716-847-8789; Fax: 716-847-8797. Email: youth@buffalodiocese.org.

CLERGY, PARISHES, MISSIONS AND PAROCHIAL SCHOOLS

CITY OF BUFFALO

(ERIE COUNTY)

1—ST. JOSEPH'S CATHEDRAL (1851) Rev. Msgr. James F. Campbell, Rector. In Res., Rev. Msgr. David S. Slubecky.
Res.: 50 Franklin St., 14202. Tel: 716-854-5855; Fax: 716-854-5861.
See Catholic Academy of West Buffalo, Buffalo under Regional and Consolidated Elementary Schools located in the Institution section.

2—ST. ADALBERT (1886), (Polish), [CEM] Rev. Thaddeus Nicholas Bocianowski.
Res.: 212 Stanislaus St., 14212. Tel: 716-895-8091; Fax: 716-895-8773.
Catechesis / Religious Program—130 Kosciuszko St., 14212. Tel: 716-894-8366. Students 31.

3—ST. AGATHA (1921), (Canonically merged with St. Ambrose) Rev. Msgr. David M. Lee.
Office: 54 Alamo Pl., 14220. Tel: 716-822-2668; Fax: 716-828-1405. Email: stagathabuffalo@aol.com.
See South Buffalo Catholic School under Regional and Consolidated Elementary Schools located in the Institution section.
Catechesis / Religious Program—Students 65.

4—ALL SAINTS (1911) Rev. Msgr. Albert W. Clody.
Res.: 127 Chadduck Ave., 14207-1531. Tel: 716-875-8183; Fax: 716-875-6597.
Catechesis / Religious Program—Ronald Szczerbiak, D.R.E. Students 106.

5—ST. AMBROSE (1930), (Canonically merged with St. Agatha) Rev. Msgr. David M. Lee.
Res.: 65 Ridgewood Rd., 14220. Tel: 716-822-5962; Fax: 716-822-0966.
See South Buffalo Catholic School under Regional & Consolidated Elementary schools.
Catechesis / Religious Program—Tel: 716-826-4125. Ms. Denise McKenzie, D.R.E. Students 297.

6—ST. ANTHONY OF PADUA (1891), (Italian), Rev. Secondo Casarotto, C.S.
Res.: 160 Court St., 14202. Tel: 716-854-2563; Fax: 716-854-2564.
See Catholic Academy of West Buffalo, Buffalo under Regional and Consolidated Elementary Schools located in the Institution section.

7—ASSUMPTION (1888) [CEM] Rev. Richard Jedrzejewski. In Res., Rev. Msgr. John M. Ryan (Retired); Rev. Thomas P. Taton.
Res.: 435 Amherst St., 14207. Tel: 716-875-7626; Fax: 716-447-1027. Email: blackrockrcc@broadviewnet.net. Web: www.broadviewnet.net/assumption.
School—Our Lady of Black Rock Regional, (Grades K-8), 16 Peter St., 14207. Tel: 716-873-7497; Fax: 716-447-9926. Email: olbrschool@yahoo.com. Mrs. Julie Watroba, Prin. Students 98.
See Our Lady of Black Rock, Buffalo under Regional and Consolidated Elementary Schools located in the Institution section.
Catechesis / Religious Program—Tel: 716-873-7187. Mary Lou Wyrobek, D.R.E. Students 80.

8—ST. BERNARD (1906), (Linked with St. Casimir) Revs. Gary J. Szczepankiewicz; Francis J. Chmielewski, Sr. Parochial Vicar.
Res.: 414 S. Ogden, 14206. Tel: 716-822-8856; Fax: 716-822-7799. Email: stbernardchurch@adelphia.com.
Catechesis / Religious Program—St. Casimir Center, 1813 Clinton St., 14206. Students 122.

9—BLESSED SACRAMENT (1887) Rev. Paul R. Bossi. In Res., Most Rev. Edward M. Grosz.
Res.: 1035 Delaware Ave., 14209-1605. Tel: 716-884-0053; Fax: 716-884-2279. Email: frpaulb@blsacbflo.org. Web: www.blsacbflo.org.
See Catholic Academy of West Buffalo, Buffalo under Regional and Consolidated Elementary Schools located in the Institution section.
Catechesis / Religious Program—Students 62.

10—BLESSED TRINITY (1906) Rev. George L. Reger.
Res.: 317 Leroy Ave., 14214. Tel: 716-833-0301; Fax: 716-834-4711. Email: blessedtrinitychurch@gmail.com.
See Catholic Central School, Buffalo under Regional and Consolidated Elementary Schools located in the Institution section.
Catechesis / Religious Program—Students 14.

11—ST. CASIMIR (1890), (Polish), (Linked with St. Bernard Parish) Revs. Gary J. Szczepankiewicz; Francis J. Chmielewski, Sr. Parochial Vicar.
Res.: 414 S. Ogden St., 14206. Tel: 716-822-8856; Fax: 716-822-7799.
Catechesis / Religious Program—1833 Clinton St., 14206. Tel: 716-826-9338. Twinned with St. Bernard. Students 122.

12—ST. CLARE (2007) Rev. Michael J. Putich, O.F.M.; Bro. Maurice V. Swartout, O.F.M., Pastoral Assoc.
Res.: 193 Elk St., 14210-1499. Tel: 716-823-2358; Fax: 716-826-2168. Email: stclareparish@gmail.com.
Catechesis / Religious Program—Students 112.

13—SS. COLUMBA-BRIGID (1888) Rev. Roy T. Herberger. Tel: 716-852-2076; Deacon Mark F. Nowak.
Res.: 418 N. Division St., 14204. Tel: 716-852-3331; Fax: 716-852-3331.
See Catholic Central School, Buffalo under Regional and Consolidated Elementary Schools located in the Institution section.

14—CORONATION OF THE BLESSED VIRGIN MARY (1950), (Vietnamese), Rev. Andrew Tu Minh Nguyen; Deacon Robert W. Badaszewski.
Res.: 348 Dewitt St., 14213. Tel: 716-882-2650.
See Our Lady of Black Rock, Buffalo under Regional and Consolidated Elementary Schools located in the Institution section.
Catechesis / Religious Program—Tel: 716-882-6360. Mr. Frank Antonnucci, D.R.E. Students 78.

15—CORPUS CHRISTI (1898), (Polish), Revs. Anselm Chalupka, O.S.P.P.E.; Mateusz Wydmanski, O.S.P.P.E.
Res.: 199 Clark St., 14212-1407. Tel: 716-896-1050; Fax: 716-896-1595. Email: anzelm@czestochowa.us. Web: www.corpuschristi.buffalo.org.
Catechesis / Religious Program—Students 9.

16—HOLY ANGELS (1852) Revs. James M. Fee, O.M.I.; Porfirio Garcia-Rodriguez, O.M.I., Parochial Vicar. In Res., Revs. Ronald F. LaFramboise, O.M.I.; Daniel F. O'Leary, O.M.I.; Stephen Vasek, O.M.I.; Arthur King, O.M.I.
Res.: 348 Porter Ave., 14201. Tel: 716-885-3767; Fax: 716-882-8211. Email: holyangelschurchbuffalo@yahoo.com.
See Catholic Academy of West Buffalo, Buffalo under Regional and Consolidated Elementary Schools located in the Institution section.
Catechesis / Religious Program—Students 47.

17—HOLY CROSS (1914) Rev. Msgr. David M. Gallivan. In Res., Rev. Paul Ladda (Tanzania).
Res.: 345 Seventh St., 14201. Tel: 716-847-6930; Fax: 716-847-6934. Email: rectory@holycrossbuffalo.org. Web: www.holycrossbuffalo.org.
See Catholic Academy of West Buffalo, Buffalo under Regional and Consolidated Elementary Schools located in the Institution section.
Catechesis / Religious Program—Jodi Miller, D.R.E. Students 110.

18—HOLY FAMILY (1902) Deacons David R. Velasquez, Temp. Pastoral Admin.; Robert A. Dobmeier.
Res.: 1885 S. Park Ave., 14220. Tel: 716-822-0308; Fax: 716-826-6018. Email: hfamchurch@verizon.net. Web: www.holyfamily-buffalo.org.
See South Buffalo Catholic School under Regional and Consolidated Elementary Schools located in the Institution section.
Catechesis / Religious Program—Students 30.

19—HOLY SPIRIT (1910) Rev. Joseph D. Wolf; Sr. Katherine Marie Bogner, S.S.M.N., Pastoral Assoc. Parish Center: 85 Dakota Ave., 14216. Tel: 716-875-9478.
Res.: 91 Dakota Ave., 14216. Tel: 716-875-8102; Fax: 716-875-4186.
Catechesis / Religious Program—Tel: 716-875-9478. Ms. Karen Adamski, D.R.E. Students 72.

20—IMMACULATE HEART OF MARY (1946) Rev. Richard H. Augustyn.
Res.: 381 Edison St., 14215. Tel: 716-894-6953; Fax: 716-892-1370.

21—ST. JOHN KANTY (1892), (Polish), (Linked with St. Stanislaus) Rev. Thaddeus Nicholas Bocianowski. In Res., Rev. Anthony Lutostanski (Retired).
Office: 101 Swinburne St., 14212. Tel: 716-893-0412; Fax: 716-893-9864. Email: stjohnkanty121212@roadrunner.com.
Res.: 123 Townsend St., 14212.
Catechesis / Religious Program—Students 12.

22—ST. JOHN THE EVANGELIST (1906), Linked with St. Teresa Parish. Rev. James T. Bartnik (Retired); Rev. Msgr. Fred R. Voorhes, Temp. Admin.
Res. & Parish Office: 1974 Seneca St., 14210-2396. Tel: 716-822-0608; Fax: 716-826-3795. Email: stjohn14210@yahoo.com.
Catechesis / Religious Program—Tel: 716-825-1252. Students 75.

23—ST. JOSEPH-UNIVERSITY (1850) Rev. Jacob C. Ledwon; Sr. Jeremy Midura, C.S.S.F., Pastoral Assoc.; Patricia Bubar Spear, Pastoral Assoc.; Deacons Thaddeus V. Pijacki; Paul C. Emerson.
Res.: 3269 Main St., 14214. Tel: 716-833-0298; Fax: 716-833-7339. Email: ledwon@acsu.buffalo.com. Web: www.stjosephbuffalo.com.
School—(Grades PreK-8), 3275 Main St., 14214. Tel: 716-835-7395; Fax: 716-833-6550. Web: www.sjsbuffalo.org. Sr. M. Fredrica Polanski, C.S.S.F., Prin.; Marie Clark, Librarian. Sisters of St. Francis of Penance and Christian Charity 1; Lay Teachers 17; Students 222.
Catechesis / Religious Program—Tel: 716-837-2971. Email: ebssmn@juno.com. Sr. Elizabeth Buchala, S.S.M.N., D.R.E. Students 375.

24—ST. KATHARINE DREXEL (2007) Rev. James M. Monaco.
Res.: 118 Schiller St., 14206. Tel: 716-895-6813; Fax: 716-891-4609.
Catechesis / Religious Program—Students 98.

25—ST. LAWRENCE (1929) Deacons Paul F. Weisenburger, Co-Pastoral Admin.; Joseph A. Pasquella; Mary Weisenburger, Co-Pastoral Admin. In Res., Rev. Joseph F. Moreno.
Res.: 1520 E. Delavan Ave., 14215. Tel: 716-892-2471; Fax: 716-892-1315. Email: stlawrencechurch@verizon.net. Web: www.stlawrencebuffalo.org.
Catechesis / Religious Program—Students 30.

26—ST. LOUIS (1829) Rev. Msgr. Salvatore Manganello.
Res.: 35 Edward St., 14202. Tel: 716-852-6040; Fax: 716-853-9225. Email: stlouischurch@verizon.net. Web: www.stlouisrc.bfn.org.
See Catholic Academy of West Buffalo, Buffalo under Regional and Consolidated Elementary Schools located in the Institution section.
Catechesis / Religious Program—Students 70.

27—ST. MARGARET (1916) Rev. Msgr. James G. Kelly; Deacon Terrance P. Harter.
Res.: 1395 Hertel Ave., 14216. Tel: 716-876-5318; Fax: 716-875-9068.
School—(Grades PreK-8) Tel: 716-876-8885; Fax: 716-876-7553. Mrs. Toni Marie DiLeo, Prin. Lay Teachers 14; Students 157.
Catechesis / Religious Program—Tel: 716-876-6122. Students 72.

28—ST. MARK (1908) Rev. Msgr. Francis Braun.
Res.: 401 Woodward Ave., 14214. Tel: 716-836-1600; Fax: 716-836-1611.
School—(Grades K-8) Tel: 716-836-1191; Fax: 716-836-0391. Sr. Jeanne Eberle, S.S.J., Prin. Sisters of St. Joseph 2; Lay Teachers 20; Students 315.
Catechesis / Religious Program—Students 64.
Convent—223 Summit Ave., 14214. Tel: 716-837-9055.

29—ST. MARTIN (1926), (Linked with St. Thomas Aquinas) Revs. James G. Judge; Arthur J. Smith, Sr. Parochial Vicar; Deacons Lawrence D. Eschbach; John H. Burke.
Res.: 1140 Abbott Rd., 14220. Tel: 716-823-7077; Fax: 716-995-0300. Email: stmartinoftours@stmartinoftours.net. Web: www.stmartinoftours.org.
See South Buffalo Catholic School, Buffalo under Regional and Consolidated Elementary Schools located in the Institution section.
Catechesis / Religious Program—Joint program with St. Thomas Aquinas Parish. Students 210.

30—ST. MARTIN DE PORRES (1993), (African American), Rev. Ronald P. Sajdak; Deacon Ronald Walker; Sr. Philip Marie, S.S.J., Pastoral Assoc.; Joan Ersing, Pastoral Assoc.
Office: 555 Northampton St., 14208. Tel: 716-883-7729; Fax: 716-886-4101.
See Catholic Central School, Buffalo under Regional and Consolidated Elementary Schools located in the Institution section.
Catechesis / Religious Program—Students 55.

31—ST. MICHAEL (1851) Revs. Ronald W. Sams, S.J.; Francis J. Staebell, S.J.; John G. Sturm, S.J.; Joseph R. Spellerberg, S.J.; Richard J. Hoar, S.J.; H. James Roleke, S.J.; James A. Catalano, S.J.; John G. Marzolf, S.J.; Bro. James Dennehy, S.J. In Res., Rev. John J. Mattimore, S.J.
Res.: 651 Washington St., 14203. Tel: 716-854-6726; Fax: 716-854-4616. Email: rsams@roadrunner.com.
See Catholic Academy of West Buffalo, Buffalo under Regional and Consolidated Elementary Schools located in the Institution section.

32—OUR LADY OF HOPE (2008) Rev. George Kirwin, O.M.I.; Ronald Thaler, Pastoral Assoc.
Res.: 18 Greenwood Pl., 14213. Tel: 716-885-2469; Fax: 716-885-3385.
Church: Lafayette Ave. & Grant St., 14213.
See Catholic Academy of West Buffalo, Buffalo under Regional and Consolidated Elementary Schools located in the Institution section.
Catechesis / Religious Program—Tel: 716-882-6360. Frank Antonucci, C.R.E. Students 52.

33—OUR LADY OF PERPETUAL HELP (1897) Rev. Donald J. Lutz.
Res.: 115 O'Connell Ave., 14204. Tel: 716-852-2671; Fax: 716-852-2672.
Catechesis / Religious Program—Students 50.

34—ST. ROSE OF LIMA (1925) Rev. Patrick H. Elis, Admin.
Res.: 500 Parker Ave., 14216. Tel: 716-834-6688; Fax: 716-834-6689. Email: strose@roadrunner.com. Web: www.stroselima.net.
Catechesis / Religious Program—Tel: 716-833-4100. Mrs. Mary Frances Mc Crorey, D.R.E. Students 89.

35—St. Stanislaus (1873), (Polish), [CEM], (Linked with St. John Kanty) Rev. Thaddeus Nicholas Bocianowski.
Res.: 123 Townsend St., 14212. Tel: 716-854-5511; Fax: 716-854-0170. Email: ststansbm@adelphia.net. Web: www.ststanislauschurch.com.
Catechesis/Religious Program—

36—St. Teresa (1897) Rev. James B. Cunningham.
Church, Res. & Office: 1974 Seneca St., 14210-2396. Tel: 716-822-0608; Fax: 716-826-3795. Email: teresa14210@yahoo.com.
See South Buffalo Catholic School, Buffalo under Regional and Consolidated Elementary Schools location in the Institution section.
Catechesis/Religious Program—Tel: 716-822-1660. Students 125.

37—St. Thomas Aquinas (1920), (Linked with St. Martin) Revs. James G. Judge; Arthur J. Smith, Sr. Parochial Vicar.
Res.: 450 Abbott Rd., 14220-1796. Tel: 716-822-1250; Fax: 716-822-2594.
See South Buffalo Catholic School, Buffalo under Regional and Consolidated Elementary Schools located in the Institution section.
Catechesis/Religious Program—Tel: 716-826-0888; Fax: 716-824-2539. Students 176.

OUTSIDE THE CITY OF BUFFALO

Akron, Erie Co., St. Teresa of Avila (1859) [CEM] Rev. Msgr. Robert J. Williamson.
Res.: 5771 Buell St., P.O. Box 168, 14001. Tel: 716-542-9103; Fax: 716-542-2444. Email: stteresaofakron@verizon.net. Web: www.stteresasofakron.com.
Catechesis/Religious Program—Tel: 716-542-9717; Fax: 716-542-2444. Sr. Mary Ruth Warejko, C.S.S.F., D.R.E. Students 234.

Albion, Orleans Co., Holy Family (2008) [CEM] Rev. Richard A. Csizmar; Deacon James L. Collichio.
Res.: 106 S. Main St., 14411. Tel: 585-589-4243; Fax: 585-589-0734.
Catechesis/Religious Program—Tel: 585-589-5236. Miss Nancy J. Sedita, D.R.E. Students 225.
Oratory—St. Mary Assumption (1891) 47 Brown St., 14411.

Alden, Erie Co., St. John the Baptist (1850) [CEM] Rev. James D. Ciupek; Deacon Richard J. Mahaney; Sr. Ellen McCarthy, S.S.J., Pastoral Assoc.
Res.: 2021 Sandridge Rd., 14004. Tel: 716-937-6959; Fax: 716-937-0075. Web: www.stjohnalden.com.
School—(Grades PreK-8) Tel: 716-937-9483; Fax: 716-937-9794. Email: stjohnschool@stjohnsalden.com. Ms. Marilynn Camp, Prin. Lay Teachers 15; Students 156.
Catechesis/Religious Program—Tel: 716-937-3448. Email: reled@stjohnalden.com. Margaret McCartin Orcutt, Catechetical Leader. Students 394.

Allegany, Cattaraugus Co., St. Bonaventure (1854) Rev. Richard Husted, O.F.M.; Peggy Reitz, Pastoral Assoc.
Res.: 95 E. Main St., 14706. Tel: 716-373-1330; Fax: 716-373-4220. Email: pegstbonas@yahoo.com. Web: www.stbonasparish.org.
See Southern Tier Catholic, Olean under Regional and Consolidated Elementary Schools located in the Institution section.
Catechesis/Religious Program—Holly Keenan, D.R.E. Students 282.
Oratory—St. John the Baptist S. Nine Mile Rd., Vandalia, Cattaraugus Co. 14706.

Alfred/Almond, Allegany Co., SS. Brendan and Jude (1992), (Linked with Blessed Sacrament, Andover) Rev. Sean E. DiMaria; Mr. Chris Yarnal, Campus Min.
St. Brendan Oratory & Res.: 11 S. Main St., Box G, Almond, 14804. Tel: 607-276-5304.
Catechesis/Religious Program—Students 54.
Chapel—St. Jude Parish Office: Lower College Dr., 14802. Tel: 607-587-9411; Fax: 607-587-9431. Email: stjude.alfred@gmail.com. Web: www.ssbjparish.net.

Amherst, Erie Co.

1—St. Gregory the Great (1958) Revs. Joseph C. Gatto; Francis Lombardo, O.F.M.Conv.; Paul S. Salemi; Deacons Kevin J. Smith; John D. Leardon; Michael G. Bochiechio; Daniel U. Golinski.
Res.: 260 St. Gregory Ct., Williamsville, 14221-2635. Tel: 716-688-5678; Fax: 716-688-5679; Fax: 716-688-2315. Email: saintgregs@yahoo.com. Web: www.stgregs.org.
School—(Grades K-8), 250 St. Gregory Ct., Williamsville, 14221. Tel: 716-688-5323; Fax: 716-688-6629. Mrs. Patricia Freund, Prin. Sisters 1; Lay Teachers 44; Students 644.
Catechesis/Religious Program—Tel: 716-688-5760; Fax: 716-639-8251. Mrs. Joan Rischmiller, D.R.E. Students 1,210.

2—St. Leo the Great (1953) Rev. Msgr. Robert E. Zapfel; David Ehrke, Business Mgr.
Res.: 885 Sweet Home Rd., 14226. Tel: 716-835-8905; Fax: 716-835-8997. Email: office@stleothegreatamherst.com. Web: stleothegreatamherst.com.
School—(Grades PreK-8) Tel: 716-832-6340. Mrs. Carolyn Kraus, Prin. Lay Teachers 17; Students 200.
Catechesis/Religious Program—Tel: 716-833-8359. Mary Beth Lalka, D.R.E. Students 235.

Andover, Allegany Co., Blessed Sacrament (1855) [CEM], Linked with SS. Brendan & Jude Parish, Alfred/Almond. Rev. Sean E. DiMaria.
Res.: 11 S. Main St., Box G, Almond, 14804. Tel: 607-276-5304; Fax: 607-587-9431. Email: fathersean1@gmail.com.
Catechesis/Religious Program—Students 23.

Angola, Erie Co., Most Precious Blood (1871) [CEM] Rev. Matt Mieczyslaw Nycz.
Res.: 22 Prospect St., 14006. Tel: 716-549-0420; Fax: 716-549-0425. Email: rectory@mpbangola.org. Web: www.mpbangola.org.
Catechesis/Religious Program—Students 150.

Arcade, Wyoming Co., St. Mary (2007) [CEM], Parish with two sites: St. Mary, Arcade; St. Mary, East Arcade. Rev. Joseph A. Gullo.
Office & Res.: 417 Main St., 14009-1195. Tel: 585-492-5330; Fax: 585-492-1047. E. Arcade Site: 6785 E. Arcade Rd., 14009-9617.
See St. Aloysius Regional School, Springville under Regional and Consolidated Elementary Schools located in the Institution section.
Catechesis/Religious Program—Students 93.

Athol Springs, Erie Co., St. Francis of Assisi (1929) Rev. Steven G. Frenier, O.F.M.Conv.; Deacon Robert T. Ciezki. In Res., Rev. Mark David Skura, O.F.M.Conv.
Res.: S-4263 St. Francis Dr., 14010. Tel: 716-627-2710; Fax: 716-627-5263.
Catechesis/Religious Program—Tel: 716-627-3357. Annette Breen, D.R.E. Students 379.

Attica, Wyoming Co., SS. Joachim & Anne (2008) [CEM] Rev. Karl E. Loeb.
Res.: 50 East Ave., 14011. Tel: 585-591-1228; Fax: 585-591-1614. Email: esaintvincentd@rochester.rr.com.
Varysburg Site: 2311 Attica Rd., Varysburg, 14167.
Catechesis/Religious Program—Tel: 585-591-8611. Email: sbeck3@verizon.net. Scott Beck, C.R.E. (Attica); Paula Beck, C.R.E. (Attica); Don Gregoire, C.R.E. (Varysburg). Students 185.

Barker, Niagara Co., Our Lady of the Lake (2009) [CEM], Parish with two sites: Barker; Lyndonville. Rev. James F. Hassett.
Office & Res.: 1726 Quaker Rd., 14012. Tel: 716-795-9991; Fax: 716-795-3919. Email: st.patrickschurch@mail.com.
Lyndonville Site: 38 Lake Ave., Lyndonville, 14098.
Catechesis/Religious Program—Tel: 716-795-3459. Students 126.

Batavia, Genesee Co.

1—Ascension (2008), (Polish), [CEM] Rev. Eugene S. Slomba.
Res.: 15 Sumner St., 14020. Tel: 585-343-1796; Fax: 585-343-0919.
St. Anthony Site: 122 Liberty St., 14020.
Catechesis/Religious Program—Students 88.

2—Resurrection (2008) [CEM] Revs. Ivan R. Trujillo; Robert E. Waters, Sr. Parochial Vicar; Deacon John J. Stone.
Res.: 303 E. Main St., 14020. Tel: 585-343-5800; Fax: 585-345-9525. Email: ivantrujillo1@rochester.rr.com.
St. Mary's site: 18 Elliott St., 14020.
School—St. Joseph School, (Grades PreK-8), 2 Summit St., 14020. Tel: 585-343-6154; Fax: 585-343-8911. Web: sjsbatavia.org. Mrs. Karen Green, Prin. Lay Teachers 20; Students 281.
Catechesis/Religious Program—Sr. M. Francine Fasano, R.S.M., D.R.E.; Linda Pembrook, D.R.E. Students 127.

Belfast, Allegany Co., St. Patrick (1859) [CEM], (Linked with St. Patrick, Fillmore) Rev. Dennis J. Mancuso.
Res. & Mailing Address: 109 W. Main St., P.O. Box 198, Fillmore, 14735.
Church: 31 E. Hughes St., 14711. Tel: 585-567-2282; Fax: 585-567-4172.
Catechesis/Religious Program—Students 59.

Belmont, Allegany Co., Holy Family of Jesus, Mary & Joseph (1861) Deacon Frank W. Pasquale, Pastoral Admin.; Rev. Jerome M. Dissek, Sacramental Min.
Office: 5 Milton St., 14813. Tel: 585-268-7272; Fax: 585-268-9128.
Catechesis/Religious Program—Students 36.
Oratory—St. Joseph (1844) Cottage Bridge Rd., Scio, Allegany Co. 14880. Tel: 585-268-7272; Fax: 585-268-7272.

Bemus Point, Chautauqua Co., St. Mary of Lourdes (2008) Rev. Todd M. Remick.
Bemus Point Site: 41 Main St., P.O. Box 500, 14712. Tel: 716-386-2400; Fax: 716-386-5562.
Mayville Site: 24 E. Chautauqua St., Mayville, 14757.
See Catholic Academy of the Holy Family, Jamestown under Regional and Consolidated Elementary Schools located in the Institution section.
Catechesis/Religious Program—Tracy Nelson, D.R.E. Students 78.

Bergen, Genesee Co., St. Brigid (1861) [CEM], (Linked with Our Lady of Mercy, LeRoy) Rev. Michael R. Rock, O.de.M.
Res.: 44 Lake St., LeRoy, 14482. Tel: 585-768-6543; Fax: 585-768-7093.
Church: 18 Gibson St., 14416.
Catechesis/Religious Program— Twinned with Our Lady of Mercy, LeRoy.

Blasdell, Erie Co., Our Mother of Good Counsel (1905) Revs. Lawrence E. Burns; Edward R. Czarnecki.
Res.: 3688 S. Park Ave., 14219. Tel: 716-822-2630; Fax: 716-821-5980.
Catechesis/Religious Program—Alice Appenheimer, D.R.E. Students 183.

Blossom, Erie Co., St. Gabriel (1925) Revs. Daniel J. Palys; John J. Mitka, Senior Parochial Vicar; Sr. Joseph Marie Marczak, C.S.S.F., Pastoral Assoc.; Ann Bauman, Pastoral Assoc.; Deacon Samuel G. Puleo.
Res.: 5271 Clinton St., Elma, 14059-7617. Tel: 716-668-4017; Fax: 716-656-0616. Email: stgabriel5271@roadrunner.com. Web: www.stgabes.net.
Catechesis/Religious Program—Tel: 716-668-2070. Email: bloom@stgabes.net. Paul J. Bloom, D.R.E. Students 1,671.

Bolivar, Allegany Co., St. Mary (1903) [CEM] Deacon Frank W. Pasquale, Pastoral Admin.; Rev. Msgr. Vincent J. Becker, Sacramental Min.
Church: 111 Wellsville St., 14715. Tel: 585-928-1024; Fax: 585-928-1024. Email: qualery1@yahoo.com.
Catechesis/Religious Program—Mary Snyder, D.R.E. Students 37.

Boston, Erie Co., St. John the Baptist (1869) [CEM] Rev. Robert J. Hora.
Res.: 6895 Boston Cross Rd., 14025-9601. Tel: 716-941-3549; Fax: 716-941-3030. Email: rjhora@roadrunner.com.
Catechesis/Religious Program—Tel: 716-941-6363. Students 206.
Oratory—St. Mary 8175 E. Eden Rd., East Eden, Erie Co. 14057.

Bowmansville, Erie Co., Sacred Heart (1920) [CEM] Rev. A. Mark Illig.
Res.: 5337 Genesee St., 14026-1098. Tel: 716-683-2375; Fax: 716-683-0412. Email: sheartshrine@aol.com. Web: www.catholicweb.com.
Catechesis/Religious Program—Tel: 585-894-0154. Students 159.

Canaseraga, Allegany Co., St. Mary (1855) [CEM] Rev. John J. Cullen.
Mailing Address: P.O. Box 189, 14822. Tel: 607-545-8601.
Catechesis/Religious Program—Students 17.

Cattaraugus, Cattaraugus Co., St. Mary (1863), (Linked with St. Joseph, Gowanda) Revs. Daniel P. Walsh; Joseph F. Moreno, Sacramental Min.; Deacon Fred Johnson, Pastoral Assoc.
Res.: 36 Washington St., 14719. Tel: 716-257-9351. Email: stmaryscatt@adelphia.net.
Catechesis/Religious Program—Students 34.

Cheektowaga, Erie Co.

1—St. Aloysius Gonzaga (1940) Rev. Msgr. Peter J. Popadick. In Res., Rev. James R. Bastian.
Res.: 157 Cleveland Dr., 14215. Tel: 716-833-1715; Fax: 716-837-5703. Email: stalschurch@aol.com.
Catechesis/Religious Program—Tel: 716-836-9657. Students 95.
Convent—130 Highview Rd., 14215. Tel: 716-834-1889. Email: stalscon@yahoo.com.

2—Infant of Prague (1946) Rev. Raymond G. Corbin. In Res., Rev. Msgr. W. Jerome Sullivan.
Res.: 921 Cleveland Dr., 14225. Tel: 716-634-3660; Fax: 716-634-3661. Email: infantofpragueparish@roadrunner.com. Web: www.iopparish.org.
Catechesis/Religious Program—Sr. M. Antonita Sikorski, C.S.S.F., D.R.E. Students 151.

3—St. John Gualbert (1917), (Polish), Rev. David W. Bialkowski; Deacon Edward S. Walek. In Res., Rev. Patrick Gardocki, O.F.M. (Poland).
Res.: 83 Gualbert Ave., 14211. Tel: 716-892-5746; Fax: 716-897-3906.
Catechesis/Religious Program—Tel: 716-897-2619. Mrs. Karen Pszczolkowski, Assoc. D.R.E.; Lea Bethge, Assoc. D.R.E. Students 45.

4—St. Josaphat (1906), (Polish), Rev. Richard M. I. Poblocki.
Res.: 20 Peoria Ave., 14206. Tel: 716-893-1086; Fax: 716-893-1099. Email: sjrectory@roadrunner.com. Web: www.st-josaphat.com.
Catechesis/Religious Program—Tel: 716-896-5007; Fax: 716-893-0118. Students 90.

5—OUR LADY HELP OF CHRISTIANS (1890) [CEM], (National Historic Site) Rev. Richard A. Jesionowski.
Res.: 4125 Union Rd., 14225. Tel: 716-634-3420; 716-634-3428; Fax: 716-634-3464.
See Mary Queen of Angels School, Cheektowaga under Regional and Consolidated Elementary Schools located in the Institution section.
Catechesis/Religious Program—Tel: 716-632-3532. Denise Seeley, D.R.E. Students 185.

6—OUR LADY OF CZESTOCHOWA (1922), (Polish), Rev. Harry F. Szczesniak.
Res.: 23 Willowlawn Pkwy., 14206. Tel: 716-822-5590; Fax: 716-822-5597.
Catechesis/Religious Program—Tel: 716-826-3497. Students 35.

7—ST. PHILIP THE APOSTLE (1967) Revs. David J. Borowiak; Robert Marino; Deacon Walter N. Fudala.
Res.: 950 Losson Rd., 14227. Tel: 716-668-8370; Fax: 716-668-3824. Email: loaves@roadrunner.com.
Catechesis/Religious Program—Tel: 716-668-3344. Mary Ann Mercurio, D.R.E.; Judy Kogut, D.R.E. Students 714.

8—QUEEN OF MARTYRS (1946) Rev. Louis S. Klein. In Res., Rev. John J. Sardina.
Res.: 180 George Urban Blvd., 14225-3095. Tel: 716-892-1746; Fax: 716-892-3005.
See Mary Queen of Angels School, Cheektowaga under Regional and Consolidated Elementary Schools located in the Institution section.
Catechesis/Religious Program—Tel: 716-895-2162. Rita Sandage, D.R.E. Students 206.

9—RESURRECTION (1944) Rev. Conrad P. Stachowiak.
Res.: 130 Como Park Blvd., 14227. Tel: 716-683-3712; Fax: 716-685-4487.
Catechesis/Religious Program—Students 140.

CLARENCE, ERIE CO., OUR LADY OF PEACE (1922) Rev. Thomas D. Doyle.
Res.: 10950 Main St., 14031. Tel: 716-759-8554; Fax: 716-759-8537. Email: olpclarence@roadrunner.com. Web: www.olpclarence.com.
Catechesis/Religious Program—Students 434.

CORFU, GENESEE CO., ST. MAXIMILIAN KOLBE PARISH (2009) [CEM], Parish with two sites: Corfu; East Pembroke. Rev. Robert J. Orlowski.
Office & Res.: 18 W. Main St., P.O. Box 278, 14036. Tel: 585-599-4833; Fax: 585-599-2833. Email: stfranciscorfu@yahoo.com.
East Pembroke Site: P.O. Box 219, East Pembroke, 14056. Tel: 585-762-9006; Fax: 585-762-9036.
Catechesis/Religious Program—Students 65.

CUBA, ALLEGANY CO., OUR LADY OF THE ANGELS (1850) [CEM] Rev. Jerome M. Dissek.
Res.: 50 South St., 14727. Tel: 585-968-2885; Fax: 585-968-0123. Email: ourlady@localnet.net.
See Southern Tier Catholic, Olean under Regional and Consolidated Elementary Schools located in the Institution section.
Catechesis/Religious Program—Students 63.

DARIEN CENTER, GENESEE CO., IMMACULATE HEART OF MARY (2008) [CEM] Rev. Joseph A. Fiore. In Res., Rev. Walter L. Matuszak (Retired).
Office: 10675 Allegany Rd., 14040-9701. Tel: 585-547-3547; Fax: 585-547-3660.
Bennington Center Site: 1230 Clinton St., Attica, 14011. Tel: 585-591-0176; Fax: 585-591-4818.
See Genesee-Wyoming Catholic Central Consolidated School, Attica under Regional and Consolidated Elementary Schools located in the Institution section.

DEPEW, ERIE CO.

1—ST. AUGUSTINE (1909), (Polish), [CEM]

2—ST. BARNABAS (1960) Rev. Msgr. John W. Madsen; Deacon Thaddeus P. May. In Res., Rev. Robert G. Beiter (Retired).
Res.: 2049 George Urban Blvd., 14043. Tel: 716-685-2350; Fax: 716-685-8679.
Catechesis/Religious Program—2099 George Urban Blvd., 14043. Tel: 716-685-2000; Fax: 716-685-2350. Judith Major, D.R.E. Students 355.

3—ST. JAMES (1897/2009) Rev. Lawrence P. Damian.
Res.: 496 Terrace Blvd., 14043. Tel: 716-683-2746; Fax: 716-683-3121. Email: FRLPD@yahoo.com.
Catechesis/Religious Program—Janet Corda, D.R.E. Students 110.
Convent—Felician Nuns, 55 Westfield Ave., 14043. Tel: 716-685-1114.
Oratory—St. Augustine St. Augustine, 425 Penora St., 14043.

4—OUR LADY OF THE BLESSED SACRAMENT (1965) Rev. Bartholomew W. Lipiec; Deacon Timothy E. Chriswell.
Res.: 10 French Rd., 14043-2129. Tel: 716-684-6342; Fax: 716-684-1853. Email: olbsparish@juno.com. Web: www.olbsdepew.org.
School—(Grades K-8), 20 French Rd., 14043. Tel: 716-685-2544; Fax: 716-685-9103. Sr. M. Janita Krawczyk, C.S.S.F., Prin.; Mrs. Karen Bauer, Librarian. Felician Sisters 2; Lay Teachers 14; Students 194.
Catechesis/Religious Program—Tel: 716-685-2546. Sr. Catherine Taberski, S.S.M.N., D.R.E. Students 323.

DUNKIRK, CHAUTAUQUA CO.

1—BLESSED MARY ANGELA PARISH (2008), (Polish), [CEM], Parish with two sites. Rev. Thomas J. Wopperer, Temp. Admin. (Retired); Deacon Daniel H. Mackowiak; Sr. M. Rachel Mikolajczak, C.S.S.F., Pastoral Assoc.
Office: 295 Lake Shore Dr. E., 14048. Tel: 716-366-7266; Fax: 716-363-0031. Email: st.hyacinth@yahoo.com.
St. Hedwig Site: 324 Townsend St., 14048.
See Northern Chautauqua Catholic School under Regional & Consolidated Elementary Schools.
Catechesis/Religious Program—296 Lake Shore Dr. E., 14048. Tel: 716-366-5707; Fax: 716-363-0031. Students 120.

2—ST. ELIZABETH ANN SETON (1975) [CEM] Rev. Dennis G. Riter. In Res., Rev. Walter Werbicki.
Res.: 328 Washington Ave., 14048. Tel: 716-366-1750; Fax: 716-366-4398. Email: st.elizannseton@verizon.com.
See Northern Chautauqua Catholic, Dunkirk under Regional and Consolidated Elementary Schools located in the Institution section.
Catechesis/Religious Program—Tel: 716-366-2827. Wendy Kachermeyer, C.R.E. Students 95.

3—HOLY TRINITY (1908), (Italian), [CEM] Rev. David A. Bellittiere.
Res.: 1032 Central Ave., 14048. Tel: 716-366-2306; Fax: 716-366-4738. Email: frdavid@localnet.com. Web: www.holytrinitydunkirk.com.
See Northern Chautauqua Catholic, Dunkirk under Regional and Consolidated Elementary Schools located in the Institution section.
Catechesis/Religious Program—Tel: 716-366-0499. Roberta Coniglio, D.R.E.; Donna Seyedian, D.R.E. Students 110.

EAST AURORA, ERIE CO., IMMACULATE CONCEPTION (1901) [CEM] Rev. Robert W. Wardenski.
Res.: 520 Oakwood Ave., 14052. Tel: 716-652-6400; Fax: 716-652-7168.
School—(Grades K-8), 510 Oakwood Ave., 14052. Tel: 716-652-5855; Fax: 716-805-0192. Ms. Karen Adamski, Prin. Lay Teachers 16; Students 210.
Catechesis/Religious Program—Tel: 716-655-0067. Sr. Judith Beiswanger, O.S.F., D.R.E. Students 437.

EAST BETHANY, GENESEE CO., IMMACULATE CONCEPTION (1954), (Linked with St. Mary, Pavilion) Rev. Richard J. Cilano.
Parish Office: 5865 Ellicott St., 14054. Tel: 585-343-4537.
Catechesis/Religious Program—Fax: 585-344-0856. Mrs. Christine Bow, D.R.E. Students 43.

EDEN, ERIE CO., IMMACULATE CONCEPTION (1908) [CEM] Rev. Walter P. Grabowski.
Res.: 8791 S. Main St., 14057. Tel: 716-992-3933; Fax: 716-992-2201. Email: icceden@verizon.net. Web: www.icceden.org.
Catechesis/Religious Program—Tel: 716-992-3508. Email: iccreligioused@aol.com. Sharon Reed, D.R.E. Students 231.

EGGERTSVILLE, ERIE CO., ST. BENEDICT (1920) Revs. Joseph D. Porpiglia; Paul P. Sabo, Sr. Parochial Vicar; Deacon William J. Hynes. In Res., Rev. Joseph G. Fifagrowicz (Retired).
Res.: 1317 Eggert Rd., 14226. Tel: 716-834-1041; Fax: 716-835-5949. Email: frporpiglia@saintbenedicts.com. Web: www.saintbenedicts.com.
School—(Grades PreK-8), 3980 Main St., Amherst, 14226. Tel: 716-835-2518; Fax: 716-834-4932. Molly Halady, Prin. Lay Teachers 27; Students 199.
Catechesis/Religious Program—Tel: 716-836-6444. Sr. Virginia Judge, O.S.F., D.R.E. Students 385.

ELLICOTTVILLE, CATTARAUGUS CO., HOLY NAME OF MARY (1850) [CEM] Rev. Ronald B. Mierzwa.
Res.: 22 Jefferson St., P.O. Box 543, 14731. Tel: 716-699-2592; Fax: 716-699-8439.
Catechesis/Religious Program—Students 101.
Oratory—St. Pacificus Chapel Hill Rd., Humphrey, Cattaraugus Co. 14778.

ELMA, ERIE CO., ANNUNCIATION OF THE BLESSED VIRGIN MARY (1905) [CEM] Rev. Eugene P. Ulrich; Deacons Joseph P. Mercurio; James J. Jaworski; Dennis W. Kapsiak.
Res.: 7580 Clinton St., 14059. Tel: 716-683-5254; Fax: 716-681-5668.
School—(Grades PreK-8) Tel: 716-681-1327; Fax: 716-685-6380. Sr. Marilyn Ann Dudek, C.S.S.F., Prin. Lay Teachers 18; Students 91; Preschool Students 32.
Catechesis/Religious Program—Tel: 716-683-5515. Students 278.

FALCONER, CHAUTAUQUA CO., OUR LADY OF LORETO (1912), (Linked with St. Patrick, Randolph) Rev. Joseph J. Janaczek.
Res.: 309 W. Everett St., 14733. Tel: 716-665-4253; Fax: 716-664-9223.
See Holy Family Catholic School, Jamestown under Regional and Consolidated Elementary Schools located in the Institution section.
Catechesis/Religious Program—Tel: 716-665-3764. Mrs. Deborah C. Ognibene, C.R.E. Students 97.

FARNHAM, ERIE CO., ST. ANTHONY'S (1904) [CEM] Rev. James W. Fliss; Deacon Frank Polizzi.
Mailing Address: P.O. Box A-9, 14061.
Res.: 421 Commercial St., 14061. Tel: 716-549-1159.
Catechesis/Religious Program—Tel: 716-549-2867; Fax: 716-549-7742. Theresa L. White, D.R.E. Students 141.

FILLMORE, ALLEGANY CO., ST. PATRICK (1881) [CEM], (Linked with St. Patrick, Belfast) Rev. Dennis J. Mancuso.
Res.: 109 W. Main St., P.O. Box 198, 14735. Tel: 585-567-2282; Fax: 585-567-4172.
Catechesis/Religious Program—Students 24.

FRANKLINVILLE, CATTARAUGUS CO., ST. PHILOMENA (1906) [JC] Rev. Joseph A. Zalacca.
Res.: 26 N. Plymouth Ave., 14737. Tel: 716-676-3629; Fax: 716-676-2104.
Catechesis/Religious Program—Tel: 716-676-2123. Students 53.

FREDONIA, CHAUTAUQUA CO.

1—ST. ANTHONY (1905) Rev. Carlton J. Westfield.
Res.: 42 Orchard St., 14063. Tel: 716-679-4050; 716-679-4096 (Office); Fax: 716-672-8576 (Office); 716-679-0326 (Res.). Email: fr.westfield@yahoo.com.
Cassadaga Site: *Immaculate Conception*, 88 N. Main St., Cassadaga, 14718.
See Northern Chautauqua Catholic, Dunkirk under Regional and Consolidated Elementary Schools located in the Institution section.
Catechesis/Religious Program—Mrs. Barbara O'Connell, D.R.E. Students 325.

2—ST. JOSEPH (1899) Rev. Charles J. Zadora; Deacon Michael C. Lemieux.
Res.: 145 E. Main St., 14063. Tel: 716-679-4116; Fax: 716-679-1352 (1-5 P.M.).
See Northern Chautauqua Catholic, Dunkirk under Regional and Consolidated Elementary Schools located in the Institution section.
Catechesis/Religious Program—(Intergenerational - 100 households), Tel: 716-672-2647. Email: jbradley@stjosephfredonia.org.

FRENCH CREEK, CHAUTAUQUA CO., CHRIST OUR HOPE (2008) [CEM] Rev. Jozef Dudzik, Admin.
Church & Office: 1762 French Creek Mina Rd., Clymer, 14724-9660. Tel: 716-355-8891; Fax: 716-355-2576.
Sherman Site: 119 Miller St., Sherman, 14781.
See Holy Family Catholic School, Jamestown under Regional and Consolidated Elementary Schools located in the Institution section.
Catechesis/Religious Program—Lisa Lespada, D.R.E. Students 47.

GETZVILLE, ERIE CO., ST. PIUS X (1958) Rev. James C. O'Connor; Deacon Brian C. Walkowiak.
Res.: 1700 N. French Rd., P.O. Box 162, 14068-0162. Tel: 716-688-9143; Fax: 716-688-1203. Email: tkpiusx@aol.com. Web: www.stpiusxgetzville.org.
Catechesis/Religious Program—Tel: 716-688-5417. Students 411.

GOWANDA, ERIE CO., ST. JOSEPH (1898) [CEM], (Linked with St. Mary, Cattaraugus) Rev. Daniel P. Walsh.
Res.: 26 Erie Ave., 14070. Tel: 716-532-5100; Fax: 716-532-4096.
School—(Grades PreK-8) Tel: 716-532-2520; Fax: 716-532-4172. Mr. Patrick J. Brady, Prin. Lay Teachers 10; Students 80.
Catechesis/Religious Program—Tel: 716-257-5486. Wilma Parry, C.R.E. Students 90.

GRAND ISLAND, ERIE CO., ST. STEPHEN (1862) [CEM] Revs. Paul M. Nogaro; Lynn M. Shumway, Sr. Parochial Vicar.
Res.: 2100 Baseline Rd., 14072. Tel: 716-773-7647; Fax: 716-773-5792. Email: ststephenswny@roadrunner.com. Web: www.ststephenswny.com.
School—(Grades PreK-8), 2080 Baseline Rd., 14072. Tel: 716-773-4347; Fax: 716-773-1438. Email: school@ststephensgi.org. Web: www.ststephens-gi.org. Mrs. Donna Ende, Prin. Lay Teachers 22; Students 225.
Catechesis/Religious Program—Tel: 716-773-2002. Angela Diebold, D.R.E. Students 1,000.

HAMBURG, ERIE CO.

1—ST. MARY OF THE LAKE (1948) Rev. William R. Bigelow; Sr. Paula Zelazo, F.S.S.J., Pastoral Assoc.
Res.: 4857 Kennison Pkwy., 14075. Tel: 716-627-3123; Fax: 716-627-7062. Email: stmary@smolc.org.
Church: 54737 Lake Shore Rd., 14075.
School—(Grades PreK-8), 4737 Lake Shore Rd., 14075. Tel: 716-627-7700; Fax: 716-627-1255. Mrs. Kristine Hider, Prin. Franciscan Sisters of St. Joseph 1; Lay Teachers 19; Students 187.
Catechesis/Religious Program—Tel: 716-627-7150. Patricia Jerzewski, D.R.E. Students 386.

2—SS. PETER AND PAUL (1844) [CEM] Revs. Mark J. Wolski; James W. Kirkpatrick Jr.; Deacons Carlton

M. Koester; Roy P. Dibb.
Res.: 66 E. Main St., 14075. Tel: 716-649-2765; Fax: 716-649-5218. Web: www.sspeterandpaulhamburg.org.
School—(Grades PreK-8), 68 E. Main St., 14075. Tel: 716-649-7030. Mrs. Jenny Bainbridge, Prin. Lay Teachers 27; Students 313.
Catechesis/Religious Program—Tel: 716-649-0231. Mary Ann Senchyne, D.R.E. Students 715.

HARRIS HILL, ERIE CO., NATIVITY OF THE BLESSED VIRGIN MARY (1954) Rev. Msgr. Frederick D. Leising; Rev. John J. Leising, Sr. Parochial Vicar; Kathy Fonte, Pastoral Assoc.; Donald J. Ehrenreich, Business Mgr.
Res.: 4375 Harris Hill Rd., Williamsville, 14221. Tel: 716-632-8838; Fax: 716-632-7898. Email: pastor@nativityharrishill.org. Web: www.nativityharrishill.org.
School—(Grades PreK-8), 8550 Main St., Williamsville, 14221. Tel: 716-633-7441. Email: natofmary@yahoo.com. Web: www.nativityofmary-school.com. Mrs. Cherie M. Ansuini, Prin. Lay Teachers 17; Students 226.
Catechesis/Religious Program—8550 Main St., Williamsville, 14221. Tel: 716-634-3130. Email: nativityreligiouseducation2004@yahoo.com. Mrs. Mary Ann Hoag, D.R.E. Students 900.

HOLLAND, ERIE CO., ST. JOSEPH (1890) [CEM 2] Rev. Dennis A. Fronczak.
Res.: 46 N. Main St., 14080-9509. Tel: 716-537-9434; Fax: 716-537-9988. Email: stjholland@roadrunner.com. Web: www.stjholland.org.
Catechesis/Religious Program—Tel: 716-655-2841; Fax: 716-537-9988. Cheryl Zielen-Ersing, D.R.E. Students 192.

HOLLEY, ORLEANS CO., ST. MARY (1866) [CEM], Linked with St. Mark, Kendall. Rev. Joseph F. Kozlowski.
Res.: 11 S. Main St., 14470-1107. Tel: 585-638-6718; Fax: 585-638-3210. Email: smysmk@yahoo.com. Web: www.forministry.com/usnyrcathsmr1/.
Catechesis/Religious Program—Sr. Mary Anne Rapp, O.S.F., D.R.E. Students 93.

JAMESTOWN, CHAUTAUQUA CO.

1—HOLY APOSTLES (2008) [CEM 2] Rev. Dennis W. Mende.
Res.: 508 Cherry St., 14701. Tel: 716-664-5703; Fax: 716-664-5288. Email: sspp@netsync.net. Web: www.holyapostlesparish.org.
St. John Site: 270 Newton Ave., 14701.
See Holy Family Catholic School, Jamestown under Regional and Consolidated Elementary Schools located in the Institution section.
Catechesis/Religious Program—Tel: 716-484-8958; Fax: 716-484-8958. Students 190.

2—ST. JAMES (1910) [CEM] Rev. Darrell G. Duffy; Deacon Michael Lennon, Financial Admin.
Res.: 27 Allen St., 14701. Tel: 716-487-0125; Fax: 716-661-3677.
See Holy Family Catholic School, Jamestown under Regional and Consolidated Elementary Schools located in the Institution section.
Catechesis/Religious Program—Tel: 716-664-4237. Joanne Zdrojewski, C.R.E. Students 165.
Oratory—Our Lady of Victory 6 Institute St., Frewsburg, 14738.

KENDALL, ORLEANS CO., ST. MARK (1984) Attended by St. Mary, Holley. Rev. Joseph F. Kozlowski.
Office & Res.: 11 S. Main St., Holley, 14470-1107. Tel: 585-638-6718; Fax: 585-638-3210. Email: smysmk@yahoo.com. Web: www.forministry.com/usnyrcathsmcsm.
Catechesis/Religious Program—Tel: 585-659-8631. Sr. Mary Anne Rapp, O.S.F., D.R.E. Students 50.

KENMORE, ERIE CO.

1—ST. ANDREW (1944) Rev. Msgr. Richard W. Siepka; Rev. Robert A. Martin, Sr. Parochial Vicar; Deacon Stephen J. Swinarski; Theresa Bornholdt, Pastoral Assoc. In Res., Rev. Vincent J. Ferraro, Chap.
Res.: 1525 Sheridan Dr., 14217. Tel: 716-873-6716; Fax: 716-873-2214. Email: standrewkenmore@roadrunner.com. Web: www.standrewkenmore.com.
School—(Grades PreK-8), 1545 Sheridan Dr., 14217. Tel: 716-877-0422; Fax: 716-877-3973. Dennis Welka, Prin. Lay Teachers 34; Students 309.
Catechesis/Religious Program—Tel: 716-877-3034. Students 247.
Mission—St. Andrew Kim 9 O'Hara Rd., Tonawanda, Erie Co. 14150.

2—ST. JOHN THE BAPTIST (1836) [CEM] Revs. Michael J. Parker; David E. Tourville, Parochial Vicar.
Res.: 1085 Englewood Ave., 14223-1982. Tel: 716-873-1122; Fax: 716-873-3305.
School—(Grades PreK-8) Tel: 716-877-6401; Fax: 716-877-9139. Web: www.sjtbschool.com. Cynthia Jacobs, Prin. Lay Teachers 29; Students 295.
Catechesis/Religious Program—Tel: 716-877-0474. Catherine Salzman, D.R.E.; Andrea Cammarata, Youth Min. Students 334.

3—ST. PAUL (1897) Rev. Jay W. McGinnis; Deacon Richard Parker; Zachariah Presutti, Pastoral Assoc.
Res.: 33 Victoria Blvd., 14217. Tel: 716-875-2730; Fax: 716-874-3475.
School—(Grades PreK-8) Tel: 716-877-6308; Fax: 716-877-3874. Christopher Meagher, Prin. Lay Teachers 16; Students 110.
Catechesis/Religious Program—Tel: 716-873-9429. Students 317.

LACKAWANNA, ERIE CO.

1—ST. ANTHONY (1917) Sr. Barbara Riter, S.S.M.N., Pastoral Admin.; Deacon Michael D. Quinn.
Res.: 306 Ingham Ave., 14218-2511. Tel: 716-823-0782; Fax: 716-827-1381. Email: bizmgrstanthonys@roadrunner.com.
Catechesis/Religious Program—Tel: 716-827-8384. Students 45.

2—OUR LADY OF BISTRICA (1917), (Croatian), Rev. Christopher Coric, O.F.M.Conv. (Croatia).
Res.: 1619 Abbott Rd., 14218. Tel: 716-822-0818; Fax: 716-823-1553.
Catechesis/Religious Program—Students 58.

3—OUR LADY OF VICTORY NATIONAL SHRINE (1854) Rev. Msgr. Paul J.E. Burkard; Revs. Romulus Rosolowski, O.F.M.Conv.; Marko Ilnitskyi. In Res., Rev. Msgr. John H. Bugman (Retired).
Res.: 767 Ridge Rd., 14218. Tel: 716-828-9444; Fax: 716-828-9429. Email: olvrectory@olv-bvs.org. Web: ourladyofvictory.org.
School—(Grades PreK-8) Tel: 716-828-9434; Fax: 716-828-9383. Email: olv@adelphia.net. Sr. Ellen O'Keefe, Prin. Sisters 5; Lay Teachers 20; Students 282.
Catechesis/Religious Program—Tel: 716-828-9437. Email: religioused@olv-bvs.org. Carmel Zomeri, D.R.E. Students 264.

4—QUEEN OF ANGELS (2008), (Polish), Rev. John F. Kasprzak.
Res.: 144 Warsaw St., 14218. Tel: 716-826-0880; Fax: 716-828-1867.

LAKE VIEW, ERIE CO., OUR LADY OF PERPETUAL HELP (1922) Rev. Msgr. John W. Zeitler; Sr. Sharon Erickson, R.S.M., Pastoral Assoc.; Deacons Mark J. Hooper; Neal M. Linnan.
Res.: 2052 Lake View Ave., P.O. Box 115, 14085. Tel: 716-627-2910; Fax: 716-627-7972. Email: olphrectory@juno.com. Web: www.olphlakeview-.com.
See Southtowns Catholic, Lakeview under Regional and Consolidated Elementary Schools located in the Institution section.
Catechesis/Religious Program—Tel: 716-627-9397. Mrs. Barbara Manley, D.R.E. Students 372.

LAKEWOOD, CHAUTAUQUA CO., SACRED HEART (1912) [JC] Rev. Msgr. Joseph M. Dowdell.
Res.: 380 E. Fairmount Ave., 14750-2197. Tel: 716-763-2815; Fax: 716-763-5646. Email: sacredheart@sacredheartlakewood.com. Web: www.sacredheartlakewood.com.
Panama Site: P.O. Box 236, Panama, 14767.
See Holy Family Catholic School, Jamestown under Regional and Consolidated Elementary Schools located in the Institution section.
Catechesis/Religious Program—Marilyn Wozneak, Pastoral Assoc. & D.R.E. Students 248.

LANCASTER, ERIE CO.

1—ST. MARY OF THE ASSUMPTION (1850) [CEM] Rev. Paul W. Steller.
Res.: 1 St. Mary's Hill, 14086-2094. Tel: 716-683-6445; Fax: 716-684-8446.
School—(Grades PreK-8) Tel: 716-683-2112; Fax: 716-683-2134. Email: Janed@stmarysonthehill.org. Miss Jane Driscoll, Prin. Sisters of Third Order of St. Francis 1; Lay Teachers 24; Students 313.
Catechesis/Religious Program—Tel: 716-683-8564; Fax: 716-693-2134. Mrs. Elaine Driscoll, D.R.E. Students 506.

2—OUR LADY OF POMPEII (1909/2008) Rev. Leon J. Biernat; Sr. M. Joyce Frances King, C.S.S.F., Pastoral Assoc.; Deacons Gregory L. Feary; John P. Gaulin.
Res.: 158 Laverack Ave., 14086. Tel: 716-683-6522; Fax: 716-685-8066. Email: ladyofpompeii@yahoo.com. Web: olplancaster.catholicweb.com.
School—(Grades PreK-8) Tel: 716-684-4664; Fax: 716-684-4699. Mrs. Diane Liptak, Prin. Lay Teachers 17; Students 104.
Catechesis/Religious Program—Michael Denz, D.R.E. Students 232.

LANGFORD, ERIE CO., EPIPHANY OF OUR LORD (1851/2006) [CEM] Rev. Peter J. Karalus.
Res.: 10893 Sisson Hwy. (Langford), North Collins, 14111. Tel: 716-337-2686; Fax: 716-337-0028. Email: epiphany@hughes.net.
See St. Aloysius Regional School, Springville under Regional and Consolidated Elementary Schools located in the Institution section.
Catechesis/Religious Program—Tel: 716-337-2686, Ext. 6. Students 150.

LEROY, GENESEE CO., OUR LADY OF MERCY (2008) [CEM], (Linked with St. Brigid Parish, Bergen) Revs. Michael R. Rock, O.de.M.; Timothy Brady, O.de.M, Parochial Vicar; Deacon David C. Ehrhart.
Res.: 44 Lake St., 14482. Tel: 585-768-6543; Fax: 585-768-7093. Email: leroystpeter@aol.com. Web: www.stpetersleroy.com.
School—Holy Family School, (Grades K-8) Tel: 585-768-7390; Fax: 585-768-6680. Mr. Kevin Robertson, Prin. Lay Teachers 13; Students 135.
Catechesis/Religious Program—Tel: 585-768-6720. Students 340.
Oratory—St. Joseph 27 Lake St., 14482.

LEWISTON, NIAGARA CO., ST. PETER (1851) Rev. Sebastian C. Pierro; Sr. Marcia Ann Fiutko, F.S.S.J., Pastoral Assoc.
Res.: 620 Center St., 14092. Tel: 716-754-4118; Fax: 716-754-4120. Email: stpeterlewiston@wny.twcbc.com. Web: www.stpeterlewiston.net.
School—(Grades PreK-8), 140 N. 6th St., 14092. Tel: 716-754-4470; Fax: 716-754-0167. Web: www-.stpeterrc.org. Ms. Kami Halgash, Prin.; Mrs. Sandra Jordan, Librarian. Lay Teachers 20; Students 140.
Catechesis/Religious Program—Tel: 716-754-2812; Fax: 716-754-0167. Email: reled@adelphia.net. Students 280.
Convent—162 S. Seventh St., 14092. Tel: 716-754-4761.

LIMESTONE, CATTARAUGUS CO., ST. PATRICK (1875) [CEM], (Linked with Our Lady of Peace, Salamanca) Rev. F. Patrick Melfi; Deacon Michael L. Anderson.
Res.: 5823 Church St., 14753. Tel: 716-925-8596; Fax: 716-925-7319. Email: stpatrickslimestone@yahoo.com.
Catechesis/Religious Program—Students 13.

LOCKPORT, NIAGARA CO.

1—ALL SAINTS (2008) [CEM] Rev. Joseph E. Vatter; Deacon Donald R. Watkins Jr.; Sr. Rene Ruberto, S.S.M.N., Pastoral Assoc. In Res., Revs. Gerald L. Bartko, O.S.F.S.; Francis M. Schimscheiner, O.S.F.S.
Office: 76 Church St., 14094. Tel: 716-433-3707; Fax: 716-438-5608. Email: allsaintslockport@verizon.net. Web: www.all-saintslockport.org.
See DeSales Catholic School, Lockport under Regional and Consolidated Elementary Schools located in the Institution section.
Catechesis/Religious Program—Tel: 716-434-3194. Sally Sayward, D.R.E. Students 245.
Convent—138 N. Transit St., 14094. Tel: 716-433-9193.
Oratory—St. Joseph 391 Market St., 14094.

2—ST. JOHN THE BAPTIST (1834) Revs. James A. Waite; Joseph C. Dumphrey, O.S.F.S.
Res.: 168 Chestnut St., 14094. Tel: 716-433-8118; Fax: 716-433-3562. Web: stjohnslockport.org.
See DeSales Catholic School, Lockport under Regional and Consolidated Elementary Schools located in the Institution section.
Catechesis/Religious Program—Tel: 716-433-5792. Sally Sayward, D.R.E. Students 355.

3—ST. MARY (1859) [JC] Rev. Gary R. Kibler.
Res.: 5 Saxton St., 14094. Tel: 716-434-6316; Fax: 716-438-5495.
See DeSales Catholic School, Lockport under Regional and Consolidated Elementary Schools located in the Institution section.
Catechesis/Religious Program—Tel: 716-433-0340; Fax: 716-438-5495. Carol Costello, D.R.E. Students 139.

MEDINA, ORLEANS CO., HOLY TRINITY (2008) [CEM] Rev. Daniel J. Fawls.
Res.: 211 Eagle St., 14103. Tel: 585-798-0112; Fax: 585-798-2834.
Middleport Site: 21 Vernon St., Middleport, 14105.
Catechesis/Religious Program—Tel: 585-798-5399. Students 220.
Oratory—Sacred Heart 208 Ann St., 14103.

NEWFANE, NIAGARA CO., ST. BRENDAN ON THE LAKE (2008) [CEM] Rev. Robert A. Wozniak; Deacon David H. Harvey.
Res.: 3455 Ewings Rd., Box 87, 14108-0087. Tel: 716-778-9822; Fax: 716-778-8786. Email: office@stbrendanonthelake.org. Web: www.stbrendanonthelake.org.
Wilson Site: 359 Lake St., Wilson, 14172.
Catechesis/Religious Program—William Smith, C.R.E. Students 178.
Oratory—St. Charles Borromeo 5972 Main St., Olcott, 14126.

NIAGARA FALLS, NIAGARA CO.

1—DIVINE MERCY (2008) Rev. Jacek P. Mazur.
Res.: 2437 Niagara St., 14303. Tel: 716-285-3604; Fax: 716-282-2297.
Catechesis/Religious Program—Tel: 716-282-0919. Students 72.

2—HOLY FAMILY OF JESUS, MARY AND JOSEPH (2008), (Italian), [CEM] Rev. Duane R. Klizek; Sr. Regina

Ryan, R.S.M., Pastoral Assoc. In Res., Rev. Stewart M. Lindsay, O.S.F.S.
Office: 1413 Pine Ave., 14301. Tel: 877-864-7131 (Toll Free); 716-282-1379; Fax: 716-285-3704. Email: info@stjosephsrcchurch.org. Web: www.stjosephsrcchurch.org.
Res.: 2486 Grand Ave., 14301.
Catechesis/Religious Program—Tel: 716-283-8442. Mrs. Rae Pullo, D.R.E. Students 126.

3—ST. JOHN DE LA SALLE (1907) Rev. Slawomir Siok, S.A.C.; Deacon David P. Slish, Pastoral Assoc.
Office & Res.: 8477 Buffalo Ave., 14304. Tel: 716-283-2238; Fax: 716-283-7973. Email: stjohndelasalle@juno.com. Web: www.stjohndelasalle.org.
Catechesis/Religious Program—Tel: 716-283-2238, Ext. 307. Students 200.

4—ST. MARY OF THE CATARACT (1847) Rev. Michael H. Burzynski. In Res., Rev. James J. Kasinski; Bro. Francis Murray, O.S.F.S.
Res.: 259 Fourth St., 14303. Tel: 716-282-0059; Fax: 716-282-3372. Email: stmaryniagara@aol.com. Web: stmaryofthecataract.com.
Catechesis/Religious Program—Students 110.

5—ST. RAPHAEL (2008) Rev. Ivan Skenderovic.
Res.: 3840 Macklem Ave., 14305. Tel: 716-282-5583; Fax: 716-282-0453. Email: st.raphael_parish@verizon.net.
Catechesis/Religious Program—Tel: 716-282-0795; Fax: 716-282-2447. Maria Gleason, C.R.E. Students 128.

6—ST. VINCENT DE PAUL (2008) Revs. Robert S. Hughson; James L. Fugle.
Res.: 1040 Cayuga Dr., 14304. Tel: 716-283-2715; Fax: 716-283-5635. Email: rsfh@roadrunner.com.
Church: 1055 N. Military Rd., 14304.
Church: 2748 Military Rd., 14304.
Catechesis/Religious Program—Tel: 716-297-5010. Students 185.

NORTH COLLINS, ERIE CO., HOLY SPIRIT (1951) [CEM 2] Rev. John S. Kwiecien.
Res.: 2017 Halley Rd., 14111. Tel: 716-337-2544; Fax: 716-337-3803. Email: hschurch@roadrunner.com.
Catechesis/Religious Program—Tel: 716-337-3701. Marge Awald, D.R.E. Students 90.

NORTH EVANS, ERIE CO., ST. VINCENT (1914) [CEM] Rev. William R. Tuyn.
Res.: 2050 S. Creek Rd., 14112. Tel: 716-627-3382; Fax: 716-627-3176.
See Southtowns Catholic, Lakeview under Regional and Consolidated Elementary Schools located in the Institution section.
Catechesis/Religious Program—Tel: 716-627-7673. Email: red@buffnet.net. Ann Kirkpatrick, D.R.E. Students 148.

NORTH TONAWANDA, NIAGARA CO.

1—ST. JUDE THE APOSTLE (2007) Rev. Edward F. Jost; Deacons Daniel E. Brick Esq.; Gary C. Terrana. In Res., Rev. Duane G. Fimbel.
Office: 1510 Kingston Ave., 14120. Tel: 716-694-0540; Fax: 716-694-8943. Email: stalbert@adelphia.net.
Catechesis/Religious Program—Tel: 716-694-4540. Students 560.

2—OUR LADY OF CZESTOCHOWA (1903), (Polish), Rev. Louis S. Dolinic; Deacon Paul J. Schnettler.
Res.: 64 Center Ave., 14120. Tel: 716-693-3822; Fax: 716-693-3882. Web: www.ntolc.org.
See North Tonawanda Catholic, North Tonawanda under Regional and Consolidated Elementary Schools located in the Institution section.
Catechesis/Religious Program—Tel: 716-693-3855. Students 192.

OAKFIELD, GENESEE CO., ST. PADRE PIO (2009) [CEM], Merged parish with two sites. Rev. Arthur E. Mattulke.
Res.: 56 Maple Ave., 14125. Tel: 585-948-5344; Fax: 585-948-8239. Email: office@padrepiony.org.
Elba Site: 65 S. Main St., Elba, 14058-0185. Tel: 716-757-6891; Fax: 716-757-2472.
Catechesis/Religious Program—Students 111.
Oratory—St. Patrick Lewiston Rd. at Knowlesville Rd., Wheatville, Genesee Co. 14013. Tel: 585-948-5344; Fax: 585-948-8239.

OLEAN, CATTARAUGUS CO.

1—ST. JOHN (1896) Rev. Edward J. Sheedy.
Res.: 931 N. Union St., 14760. Tel: 716-372-5313; Fax: 716-373-0919. Email: stjohnsofolean@verizon.net.
See Southern Tier Catholic, Olean under Regional and Consolidated Elementary Schools located in the Institution section.
Catechesis/Religious Program—Tel: 716-372-6633; Fax: 716-795-3919. Students 163.
Mission—Transfiguration 1102 Walnut St, Cattaraugus Co. 14760.

2—ST. MARY OF THE ANGELS (1876) Rev. Gregory J. Dobson; Deacon Richard F. Matthews. In Res., Rev. Barry J. Allaire.
Res.: 202 S. Union St., 14760. Tel: 716-372-4841; Fax: 716-372-5905. Email: ram@saintmaryoftheangels.org. Web: www.stmary-oftheangels.org.
See Southern Tier Catholic, Olean under Regional and Consolidated Elementary Schools located in the Institution section.
Catechesis/Religious Program—Tel: 716-373-1855. Sr. Regina G. Aman, C.R.E. Students 194.
Oratory—Oratory of the Sacred Heart 43 Maple Ave., Portville, 14770.

ORCHARD PARK, ERIE CO.

1—ST. BERNADETTE (1957) Revs. Paul D. Seil; Richard S. DiGiulio, Sr. Parochial Vicar; Deacons Edward R. Howard; Lawrence P. Markowski.
Res.: 5930 S. Abbott Rd., 14127-4516. Tel: 716-649-3090; Fax: 716-649-0211.
School—(Grades K-8) Tel: 716-649-3369. Sr. Diane Swanson, R.S.M., Prin. Lay Teachers 15; Students 197.
Catechesis/Religious Program—Tel: 716-648-1720. Georgette Jebb, D.R.E. Students 800.

2—ST. JOHN VIANNEY (1958) Rev. Msgr. William J. Gallagher.
Res.: 2950 Southwestern Blvd., 14127. Tel: 716-674-9133; Fax: 716-674-9134. Email: sjv2950@pcom.net.
School—(Grades PreK-8) Tel: 716-674-9232; Fax: 716-674-9248. Email: sjvoffice@stjohnvianney.com. Web: stjohnvianney.com. Mr. Christopher Hope, Prin.; Sr. Francianne Zielezinski, C.S.S.F., Librarian. Sisters 1; Lay Teachers 17; Students 183.
Catechesis/Religious Program—Tel: 716-674-9145. Christine Lawrence, D.R.E. Students 926.

3—NATIVITY OF OUR LORD (1908) [CEM] Revs. Bernard U. Nowak; Ryszard S. Biernat; Deacon Samuel G. Puleo.
Res.: 26 Thorn Ave., 14127. Tel: 716-662-9339; Fax: 716-662-2195.
School—(Grades PreK-8) Tel: 716-662-7572. Ruth Frost, Prin. Sisters of St. Francis of Penance and Christian Charity 1; Lay Teachers 22; Students 252.
Catechesis/Religious Program—Tel: 716-662-2169. Mary Barone, D.R.E. Students 639.

4—OUR LADY OF THE SACRED HEART (1920) Rev. Adolph M. Kowalczyk; Deacon William J. Walkowiak.
Res.: 3148 Abbott Rd., 14127. Tel: 716-824-2935; Fax: 716-827-7643. Email: rectory@olshop.org. Web: www.olshop.org.
School—(Grades PreK-8), 3144 Abbott Rd., 14127. Tel: 716-824-8208; Fax: 716-827-7643. Email: olshschool@aol.com. Web: www.ourladyofthesacred-heart.com. Christopher Gordon, Prin. Sisters of Mercy 1; Lay Teachers 18; Students 219.
Catechesis/Religious Program—Tel: 716-824-8209. Paula White, C.R.E.; Judy Quinn, C.R.E. Students 582.

PAVILION, GENESEE CO., ST. MARY (1865) [CEM], (Linked with Immaculate Conception, East Bethany) Rev. Richard J. Cilano.
Res.: 11095 Saint Mary St., P.O. Box 442, 14525. Tel: 585-584-3280; Fax: 585-584-8628. Email: stmarys@rochester.rr.com.
Catechesis/Religious Program—Students 20.

PENDLETON, NIAGARA CO., GOOD SHEPHERD (1847/2009) [CEM], Parish with two sites: Pendleton; Clarence. Rev. Daniel A. Young; Deacon Robert Bauer; Mrs. Peggy Mead, Pastoral Assoc.
Office & Res.: 5442 Tonawanda Creek Rd., North Tonawanda, 14120-9699. Tel: 716-625-8594; Fax: 716-625-8365.
Clarence Center Site: *St. Augustine Campus*, 8700 Goodrich Rd., Clarence Center, 14032.
Catechesis/Religious Program—Tel: 716-625-8817. Michele Ranke, C.R.E.; Rosemary Frost, C.R.E. Students 215.

PERRY, WYOMING CO., ST. ISIDORE (2008) [CEM] Rev. Richard W. Blazejewski; Deacon Daniel J. McGuire.
Res.: 8 Park St., 14530. Tel: 585-237-2625; Fax: 585-237-0150.
Catechesis/Religious Program—Students 56.

RANDOLPH, CATTARAUGUS CO., ST. PATRICK (1853) [CEM], (Linked with Our Lady of Loreto, Falconer) Rev. Joseph J. Janaczek.
Res.: 309 W. Everett St., Falconer, 14733. Tel: 716-665-4253; Fax: 716-664-9223.
See Catholic Academy of the Holy Family, Jamestown under Regional and Consolidated Elementary Schools located in the Institution section.
Catechesis/Religious Program—Students 55.

RANSOMVILLE, NIAGARA CO., IMMACULATE CONCEPTION (1891) Rev. Joseph P. Badding; Deacon Paul S. Stankiewicz.
Res.: 4671 Townline Rd., Rte. 429, 14131-9740. Tel: 716-731-4822; Fax: 716-731-4911.
Catechesis/Religious Program—Tel: 716-731-5387. Students 334.

RUSHFORD, ALLEGANY CO., ST. MARK (1948) Rev. Francis J. Jann (Retired).
Mailing Address: P.O. Box 37, 14777. Tel: 585-365-9977; Fax: 585-437-5532.
Res.: 7693 State Rte. 243, Caneadea, 14717. Fax: 585-437-5332.
Catechesis/Religious Program—Students 20.

SALAMANCA, CATTARAUGUS CO., OUR LADY OF PEACE (2007), (Linked with St. Patrick, Limestone) Rev. F. Patrick Melfi; Deacon Michael L. Anderson.
Res.: 79 River St., 14779-1414. Tel: 716-945-2666; Fax: 716-945-0676.
Catechesis/Religious Program—Students 72.

SANBORN, NIAGARA CO., HOLY FAMILY (1953), (Tuscarora Native Americans) Rev. Peter M. Calabrese, C.R.S.P.
Res.: 1023 Swan Rd., P.O. Box 167, Youngstown, 14174-0167. Tel: 716-754-7489; Fax: 716-754-9130. Email: pmccrsp@fatimashrine.com.
Church: 5180 Chew Rd., 14132. Tel: 716-523-9114.
Catechesis/Religious Program—Students 27.

SARDINIA, ERIE CO., ST. JUDE (1953) Rev. Alfons M. Osiander.
Res.: 12820 Genesee Rd., P.O. Box 267, 14134-0267. Tel: 716-496-7535; Fax: 716-496-7535.
See St. Aloysius Regional School, Springville under Regional and Consolidated Elementary Schools located in the Institution section.
Catechesis/Religious Program—Tel: 716-496-5419. Students 27.

SILVER CREEK, CHAUTAUQUA CO., OUR LADY OF MT. CARMEL (1882/2008) [CEM], Parish with two sites. Rev. Daniel F. Fiebelkorn.
Res.: 165 Central Ave., 14136. Tel: 716-934-2233; Fax: 716-934-6216.
Forestville Site: 11 Center St., Forestville, 14062.
See Northern Chautauqua Catholic, Dunkirk under Regional and Consolidated Elementary Schools located in the Institution section.
Catechesis/Religious Program—Tel: 716-934-4891. Students 155.

SLOAN, ERIE CO., ST. ANDREW (1915), (Polish), Rev. Fabian J. Maryanski.
Res.: 34 Francis Ave., 14212. Tel: 716-892-0425; Fax: 716-892-3092.
Catechesis/Religious Program—Sr. M. Therese Chmura, C.S.S.F., Dir. Faith Formation. Students 120.
Convent—Felician Sisters, 17 Gierlach St., 14212. Tel: 716-893-1007.

SNYDER, ERIE CO., CHRIST THE KING (1926) Rev. John R. Gaglione; Deacon Norman E. Foster. In Res., Rev. Msgr. Joseph J. Sicari.
Res.: 30 Lamarck Dr., 14226. Tel: 716-839-1430; Fax: 716-839-1433. Web: www.ctksnyder.com.
School—(Grades PreK-8), 2 Lamarck Dr., 14226. Tel: 716-839-0473; Fax: 716-568-8198. JoAnn Mikulec, Prin. Lay Teachers 21; Students 263.
Catechesis/Religious Program—Tel: 716-839-0946. Students 29.

SPRINGBROOK, ERIE CO., ST. VINCENT (1850) [CEM] Rev. James A. Walter; Deacons Richard F. Mackiewicz; Peter Walders.
Res.: 6441 Seneca St., P.O. Box 290, 14140. Tel: 716-652-3972; Fax: 716-655-3048. Web: www.stvincentsspringbrook.4lpi.com.
School—(Grades K-8) Tel: 716-652-8697. Mrs. Lisa Meegan, Prin.; Debbie Bank, Librarian. Lay Teachers 12; Students 170.
Catechesis/Religious Program—Tel: 716-652-7242. Cheryl Mackiewicz, D.R.E. Students 475.

SPRINGVILLE, ERIE CO., ST. ALOYSIUS (1853) [CEM], (Linked with St. John the Baptist, West Valley) Rev. Lawrence F. Cobel.
Res.: 190 Franklin St., 14141-1199. Tel: 716-592-2701; Fax: 716-592-4347.
See St. Aloysius Regional School, Springville under Regional and Consolidated Elementary Schools located in the Institution section.
Catechesis/Religious Program—Tel: 716-592-4869; Fax: 716-592-4869. Students 288.
Convent—Sisters of St. Francis, 71 W. Main St., 14141. Tel: 716-592-7601.

STRYKERSVILLE, WYOMING CO., ST. JOHN NEUMANN (2008) [CEM] Rev. Matthew J. Zirnheld.
Res.: 3854 Main St., P.O. Box 9, 14145-0009. Tel: 585-457-3222.
Sheldon Site: 991 Centerline Rd., 14145-9553. Tel: 585-457-9437; Fax: 585-535-0477.
Catechesis/Religious Program—Students 230.
Oratory—St. Patrick 1468 Main St., Java Center, 14082.

SWORMVILLE, ERIE CO., ST. MARY (1849) [CEM] Revs. Robert M. Yetter; Robert W. Zilliox, Parochial Vicar; Deacons Paul Snyder; Gary M. Hoover.
Res.: 6919 Transit Rd., Box 460, 14051. Tel: 716-688-9380; Fax: 716-688-6025. Email: stmaryswormville@roadrunner.com. Web: www.stmaryswormville.org.
School—(Grades PreK-8) Tel: 716-689-8424; Fax: 716-689-8424. Web: www.stmaryschoolswormville-.org. Sisters Sheila Anne Burke, O.S.F., Prin.; Suzanne Hitzges, O.S.F., Librarian. Sisters of the Third Order of St. Francis 2; Lay Teachers 15; Students 250.

Catechesis/Religious Program—Tel: 716-688-0599; Fax: 716-639-8891. Email: reled14051@roadrunner.com. Students 1,420.

TONAWANDA, ERIE CO.

1—ST. AMELIA (1953) Rev. Msgr. Thomas F. Maloney; Rev. Mark J. Noonan; Sr. Helen Buscarino, F.M.D.C., Pastoral Assoc.; Brian Ruh, Pastoral Assoc.; Judy Reitz, Pastoral Assoc. In Res., Rev. Donald L. Measer (Retired).
Res.: 210 St. Amelia Dr., 14150. Tel: 716-836-0011; Fax: 716-832-5439. Web: www.stamelia.com.
School—(Grades PreK-8), 2999 Eggert Rd., 14150. Tel: 716-836-2230; Fax: 716-832-9700. Email: office@stameliaschool.org. Web: www.stameliaschool.org. James Mule, Prin. Lay Teachers 32; Students 500.
Catechesis/Religious Program—Tel: 716-833-8647. Elaine Volker, C.R.E. Students 533.

2—ST. ANDREW KIM (1993), Mission for Korean Catholics. Rev. Jae Hun You (Korea, South), Admin.
Mailing Address: 9 O'Hara Rd., 14150. Tel: 716-693-7116; 716-693-1600; Fax: 716-693-7130. Email: jaehun.you@gmail.com. Web: www.bukoca.cyworld.com.
Catechesis/Religious Program—Students 24.

3—BLESSED SACRAMENT (1929) Rev. William J. Quinlivan; Sr. M. Lucette Kinecki, C.S.S.F., Pastoral Assoc. In Res., Rev. Msgr. Leo F. McCarthy (Retired).
Res.: 263 Claremont Ave., 14223. Tel: 716-834-4282; Fax: 716-834-9573. Web: www.blsacparish.org.
Catechesis/Religious Program—Tel: 716-832-6161. Josephine Palumbo, D.R.E. Students 216.

4—ST. CHRISTOPHER (1928) Rev. Charles E. Slisz; Deacons Francis A. Zwack; Matthew V. Skulicz; David P. McDermott; Thomas R. Healey.
Church & Parish Office: 2660 Niagara Falls Blvd., 14150-1499. Tel: 716-692-2660; Fax: 716-693-5639. Email: rectory@saintchris.org. Web: www.stchris.org.
Res. & Outreach: *St. Edmund*, 530 Ellicott Creek Rd., 14150.
School—(Grades PreK-8) Tel: 716-693-5604; Fax: 716-693-5127. Email: school@saintchris.org. Mrs. Elizabeth A. Philage, Prin. Lay Teachers 28; Students 514.
Catechesis/Religious Program—Tel: 716-694-4310. Email: reled@saintchris.org. Students 907.

5—ST. FRANCIS OF ASSISI (1852) [CEM] Rev. Michael G. Uebler.
Res.: 73 Adam St., 14150. Tel: 716-693-1150; Fax: 716-693-2025.
School—(Grades PreK-8) Tel: 716-692-7886. Mr. Paul Pinto, Prin. Lay Teachers 19; Students 146.
Catechesis/Religious Program—Tel: 716-694-5342. Students 154.

6—ST. TIMOTHY (1960) Rev. Dennis F. Fronckowiak; Deacon Gordon J. Steinagle.
Res.: 565 E. Park Dr., 14150. Tel: 716-875-9430; Fax: 716-931-5237. Email: sttimothyrcchurch@aol.com.
Catechesis/Religious Program—Students 286.

WARSAW, WYOMING CO., ST. MICHAEL (1858) [CEM] Rev. James W. Hartwell; Deacon John J. Kelly.
Res.: 171 N. Main St., 14569. Tel: 585-786-2400; Fax: 585-786-3977. Web: stmichaelswarsaw.com.
Catechesis/Religious Program—Students 110.

WELLSVILLE, ALLEGANY CO., IMMACULATE CONCEPTION (1850) [CEM], Providing Sacramental Ministry to St. Mary, Bolivar. Rev. Msgr. Vincent J. Becker.
Res.: 6 Maple Ave., 14895. Tel: 585-593-4834; Fax: 585-593-7167. Email: icclynv@roadrunner.com.
Immaculate Conception School of Allegany County. See Regional and Consolidated Schools located in the Institution section.
Catechesis/Religious Program—Tel: 585-593-4834. Mrs. Mary Ann Newark, D.R.E. Students 130.

WEST FALLS, ERIE CO., ST. GEORGE (Jewettville) (1942/2008) Rev. Pascal D. Ipolito.
Res.: 74 Old Glenwood Rd., 14170. Tel: 716-652-3153; Fax: 716-687-1336. Email: stgeorges@roadrunner.com.
Catechesis/Religious Program—Tel: 716-652-0126. Students 76.

WEST SENECA, ERIE CO.

1—BLESSED JOHN XXIII (2008) Rev. Dennis G. Wolf; Sr. M. Jeanne Thomas, R.S.M., Pastoral Assoc.
Office: 36 Flohr Ave., 14224. Tel: 716-823-1090; Fax: 716-825-4376.
Res.: One Arcade St., 14224.
Catechesis/Religious Program—Tel: 716-825-5053. Sharon Voigt, D.R.E. Students 209.

2—FOURTEEN HOLY HELPERS (1864) [CEM] Rev. Joseph S. Rogliano; Deacon Thomas E. Scherr. In Res., Rev. Robert M. Mock.
Res.: 1345 Indian Church Rd., 14224. Tel: 716-674-2374; Fax: 716-675-4864.
School—(Grades PreK-8) Tel: 716-674-1670. Joseph Duttweiler, Prin.; Mrs. Laura Kaplan, Librarian. Lay Teachers 16; Students 204.
Catechesis/Religious Program—Tel: 716-674-2180. Students 304.

3—QUEEN OF HEAVEN (1955) Revs. Thomas J. Quinlivan; David D Baker; Deacon John M. Ruh.
Res.: 4220 Seneca St., 14224. Tel: 716-674-3468; Fax: 716-674-3475.
School—(Grades PreK-8), 839 Mill Rd., 14224. Tel: 716-674-5206; Fax: 716-674-2793. Miss Barbara Ryan, Prin. Lay Teachers 24; Students 328.
Catechesis/Religious Program—Tel: 716-675-3714. Barbara Maloney, D.R.E.; Elaine Kishbaugh, C.R.E. Students 638.

WEST VALLEY, CATTARAUGUS CO., ST. JOHN THE BAPTIST (1904) [CEM], (Linked with St. Aloysius, Springville) Rev. Lawrence F. Cobel.
Res.: 5381 Depot St., P.O. Box 315, 14171-0315. Tel: 716-942-3259; Fax: 716-942-3259.
See St. Aloysius Regional School, Springville under Regional and Consolidated Elementary Schools located in the Institution section.
Catechesis/Religious Program—Tel: 716-942-6874. Janet Vant, D.R.E. Students 122.

WESTFIELD, CHAUTAUQUA CO., ST. DOMINIC (2008) [CEM 2] Rev. Marius Walter, O.S.B.; Deacon William J. Boneberg.
Office: 15 Union St., 14787-1494. Tel: 716-326-2816; Fax: 716-326-4863. Email: stdominic@fairpoint.net.
Brocton Site: 12 Central Ave., P.O. Box P, Brocton, 14716-0675.
Catechesis/Religious Program—Tel: 716-326-3003. Denise Johnson, C.R.E. Students 110.

WILLIAMSVILLE, ERIE CO., SS. PETER AND PAUL (1836) [CEM 2] Rev. Jerome E. Kopec; Deacon George L. Klein; Mr. Robert Grinewich, Pastoral Assoc.; Ann Marie MacIsaac, Pastoral Assoc.
Office: 17 Grove St., 14221.
Res.: 5480 Main St., 14221. Tel: 716-632-2559; Fax: 716-204-0329.
School—(Grades PreK-8) Tel: 716-632-6146. Mrs. Marianne Maines, Prin. Lay Teachers 27; Students 412.
Catechesis/Religious Program—Tel: 716-632-2678. Roberta Spencer, D.R.E.; Casey Hanley, Sacramental Coord. Students 375.

YOUNGSTOWN, NIAGARA CO., ST. BERNARD'S (1946) [CEM] Rev. Msgr. J. Thomas Moran.
Res.: 218 Hinman St., 14174. Tel: 716-745-7460; Fax: 716-745-1359.
Catechesis/Religious Program—Mrs. Donna Parent, D.R.E. Students 220.

Chaplains of Public Institutions

BUFFALO. *Buffalo Fire Department and Erie County Emergency Services*. Revs. Joseph Bayne, O.F.M.Conv., Arthur J. Smith, Asst. Chap.
Buffalo General Hospital. Revs. Patrick O. Fernandes, Richard H. Augustyn.
Buffalo Psychiatric Center, 400 Forest Ave., 14213. Vacant.
Erie County Holding Center. Deacon Thomas A. McDonnell.
Erie County Juvenile Detention Center. Deacon Frank J. Shaughnessey.
Erie County Medical Center. Rev. Francis X. Mazur.
Hope House. Deacon Terry P. Harter.
Millard Fillmore Hospital. Rev. Thomas P. Taton.
Roswell Park Memorial Institute. Rev. Raymond G. Corbin, Deacons Neal M. Linnan, Stephen J. Swinarski.
Sheehan Memorial Emergency Hospital. Rev. Roy T. Herberger.
Veterans Hospital. Revs. Christopher Coric, O.F.M-.Conv. (Croatia), Patrick Gardocki, O.F.M. (Poland), Michael J. Putich, O.F.M.
Women and Children's Hospital. Sr. Brenda Whelan, R.S.M., Deacon Gary P. Andelora.

ALBION. *Albion Correctional Facility*. Rev. Eugene S. Slomba. Tel: 585-343-1796.
Orleans Correction Facility. Rev. Eugene S. Slomba, Deacons Thomas Bringenberg Jr., Heinz H. Friedman, Chap.

ALDEN. *Erie County Correctional Facility*, 11581 Walden Ave., 14004. Tel: 716-937-9101. Rev. Robert Moreno (STF).
Erie County Home, 11580 Walden Ave., 14004. Tel: 716-937-5693. Rev. Robert Moreno (STF), Deacon Joseph A. Pasquella.
Wende Correctional Facility. Rev. Thomas D. Doyle, Chap., Deacons Gordon J. Steinagle, Timothy J. Maloney.

AMHERST. *Millard Fillmore Suburban Hospital*. Revs. Richard D. Bordonaro, Stepan Kuklich (STF), Chap., Deacons Paul L. Snyder III, Daniel U. Golinski.

ARCADE. *Pines Nursing Home*. Deacon Raymond H. Stahl.

ATTICA. *Attica Correctional Facility*. Rev. Ivan R. Trujillo, Sr. Rosalind Rosolowski, C.S.S.F.
Wyoming Correctional Facility. Deacon Brian C. Walkowiak.

BATAVIA. *Crossroads House*. Deacon David C. Ehrhart.
U.S. Department of Immigration & Naturalization Federal Detention Center. Rev. John J. Mattimore, S.J., Chap.
United Memorial Medical Center. Rev. Richard J. Cilano.

COLLINS. *Collins Correctional Facility*. Rev. John S. Kwiecien, Sr. Mary Lou Schnitzer, S.S.J., Deacons John H. Burke, Peter J. Walders.

CUBA. *Cuba Memorial Hospital and Adult Day Care Facility*. Deacon Michael R. Bray.

DUNKIRK. *Brooks Memorial Hospital*. Vacant.

GOWANDA. *Gowanda Correctional Facility*. Deacons Carlos W. Ramos, Timothy J. Maloney, Chap.
Tri-County Hospital. Deacon Frederick M. Johnson Jr.

LAKEVIEW. *Lakeview Shock Incarceration Correctional Facility*. Revs. Stepan Kuklich (STF), Walter Werbicki.

LANCASTER. *Elderwood Health Care*. Deacon Samuel G. Puleo.

NIAGARA FALLS. *Niagara Falls Memorial Medical Centers*. Rev. James J. Kasinski, Sacramental Min., Deacon Gary C. Terrana, Chap.

NORTH TONAWANDA. *DeGraff Memorial Hospital*, 1520 Kingston Ave., 14120. Tel: 716-694-4500. Rev. Duane G. Fimbel.

OLEAN. *Olean General Hospital*. Deacon Michael L. Anderson, Sr. Dana Hollis, O.S.F.

WESTFIELD. *Absolute Center for Nursing & Rehabilitation*. Deacon William J. Boneberg.

WEST SENECA. *WNY Children's Psychiatric Center*. Deacon Carlton M. Koester.

WILLIAMSVILLE. *Gateway - Longview Residence for Youth*. Deacon Michael G. Bochiechio.
Park Creek Senior Living Community. Rev. Frederick M. Hinton.

On Duty Outside the Diocese:
Revs.—
Furlong, Richard V., 17 Jethol Dr., Assonet, MA 02702.
Juran, Michael P., Diocese of St. Petersburg, FL
Nielsen, Kenneth M., Kentwood Village Apts., 246 Kentwood Blvd., Brook, NJ 08724.
Wild, Robert A., Madonna House, Combermere ON Canada.
Zaczynski, Piotr F., St. Joseph Parish, 606 E. Fourth St., Sault Sainte Marie, MI 49783.
Zuffoletto, Michael P., 3250 Catlin Ave., Ste. 112, Quantico, VA 22134.

Military Chaplains:
Revs.—
Glassmire, David R., USN, 314 N. Nevada St., Unit 12, Oceanside, CA 92054.
Kelly, John E., USN, CHC, NWS Charleston, Base Chapel, 2316 Redbank Rd., Ste. 100, Goose Creek, SC 29445.
Koester, Timothy J., NAVSTA Pearl Harbor, 800 Ticonderoga St., Pearl Harbor, HI 96860.

Absent on Leave:
Revs.—
Bagienski, Ronald A., (Med.)
Blesnuk, Donald J.
Budez, Jorge H.
Moss, Robert D., (Med.)
Swartz, Michael R.

Awaiting Assignment:
Rev. Msgr.—
Voorhes, Fred R.
Revs.—
Chimera, Angelo M.
O'Keefe, Patrick T.
Stelmach, Jerome J.
Venne, Samuel J.

Retired:
Rev. Msgrs.—
Ayoub, S. Paul, Bishop Head Residence, 10 Rosary Ave, Lackawanna, 14218.
Belzer, Paul J., 368 Everett Pl., Tonawanda, 14150.
Biniszkiewicz, Leonard E., 2417 Lake Rd., Ransomville, 14131.
Boruszewski, Joseph A., 29 Tamark Ct., Upper, Cheektowaga, 14227.
Bugman, John H., Our Lady of Victory, 767 Ridge Rd., Lackawanna, 14218-1697.
Cahill, Richard M., 1825 Alberta Dr., Clearwater, FL 33756.
Caligiuri, Angelo M., O'Hara Residence, 69 O'Hara Rd., Tonawanda, 14150-6224.
Caligiuri, Anthony J., O'Hara Residence, 69 O'Hara Rd., Tonawanda, 14150-6227.
Connelly, James N., O'Hara Residence, 69 O'Hara Rd., Apt. 3, Tonawanda, 14150-6227.
Crane, Thomas E., O'Hara Residence, 69 O'Hara Rd., Tonawanda, 14150-6227.

DelVecchio, Michael E., P.O. Box 22, Orchard Park, 14127.
Ducette, John I., Sheehan Residence, 330 Linwood Ave., 14209.
Engelhardt, Herbert G., 5539 Broadway, Apt. 155, Lancaster, 14086-2223.
Faiola, Samuel J., S.T.D., 72B Lexington Ct., Lockport, 14094-5365.
Fisher, Edward T., 42 Warburton Pl., Town Of Tonawanda, 14223.
Gill, Richard, 103 E. 7th St., Dunkirk, 14048-2650.
Golombek, Robert K., 800 W. Ferry St., 14222.
Green, Gerard L., 9686 Oak Grove Dr., Angola, 14006-8904.
Griffin, Charles T., O'Hara Residence, 69 O'Hara Rd., Tonawanda, 14150-6227.
Hammerl, Leo E., O'Hara Residence, 69 O'Hara Rd., Tonawanda, 14150-6227.
Higgins, Grant J., 170 Countryside Ln., Apt. #4, Orchard Park, 14127.
Jasinski, Anthony J., Bishop Head Residence, 10 Rosary Ave., Lackawanna, 14218.
Juenker, Paul R., O'Hara Residence, 69 O'Hara Rd., Tonawanda, 14150-6227.
Kopacz, Matthew S., 9993 Trevett Rd., Boston, 14025-9743.
Kozminski, Max M., 150 Brush Creek Rd., 14221-2743.
Lichtenthal, James J., 9335 SE 177th Simon's Ln., The Villages, FL 32162.
Lorenzetti, Dino J., O'Hara Residence, 69 O'Hara Rd., Tonawanda, 14150-6227.
Mack, Robert A., 105 Gardenwood Ln., Tonawanda, 14223.
McCarthy, Leo F., 263 Claremont Ave., Kenmore, 14223.
Myszka, Daniel J., 391 Bristol St., 14206-3721.
Neu, Leon M., Bishop Head Residence, 10 Rosary Ave., Lackawanna, 14218.
O'Neill, Kevin T., 1170 Indian Church Rd., West Seneca, 14224.
Ronald, Roy K., 200 Boncroft Dr., West Seneca, 14224-2829.
Ryan, John M., 435 Amherst St., 14207-2891.
Scanlan, Edward J., 4421 Lower River Rd., Stella Niagara, 14144.
Schwab, Robert C., Patio Apts., 2710 N. Forest, #137, Getzville, 14068.
Schwinger, William A., Mercy Skilled Nursing Home, 55 Melroy Ave. #415, Lackawanna, 14218.
Sciera, Ronald P., P.O. Box 553, 14240-0553.
Skupien, Francis M., Bishop Head Residence, 10 Rosary Ave., Lackawanna, 14218.
Sobierajski, Edward J., O'Hara Residence, 69 O'Hara Rd., Tonawanda, 14150-6299.
Sorci, Francis P., 34 Loch Lee, 14221-4934.
Stengel, Paul F., Bishop Head Residence, 10 Rosary Ave., Lackawanna, 14218.
Ulaszeski, Edward J., 2035 Bush Rd., Grand Island, 14072.
Wagner, Harold, Weinberg Campus, Dosberg Manor, 2700 N. Forest Rd., Apt. 125, Getzville, 14068.
Wangler, Donald R., 7360 Rochester Rd., Lockport, 14094-1626.
Wangler, William O., P.O. Box 38, Frewsburg, 14738.
Weldgen, Francis G., 6955 Maple Dr., Wheatfield, 14120.
Wendzikowski, Mecislaus S., 142 Phyllis Ave., 14215-2826.
Wetter, Richard L., O'Hara Residence, 69 O'Hara Rd., Tonawanda, 14150-6227.
Whitney, Paul J., 5B Lexington Ct., Lockport, 14094.
Wright, Rupert A., O'Hara Residence, 69 O'Hara Rd., Tonawanda, 14150.
Yiengst, George B., 73 Reiman St. - Upper, 14206.
Yunk, Michael J., 47 Linwood Ave., 14221-6501.

Revs.—
Amico, Charles R., Ph.D., S.T.D., Christ the King Seminary, P.O. Box 607, East Aurora, 14052-0607.
Augustyn, James M., Bishop Head Residence, 10 Rosary Ave., Lackawanna, 14218.
Bartnik, James T., Autumn View Health Care Facility, 4650 Southwestern Blvd., Hamburg, 14075.
Becker, Donald, 32 Green Meadow Dr., Orchard Park, 14127.
Beiter, Robert G., 2049 George Urban Blvd., Depew, 14043.
Biesinger, Robert J., Sheehan Residence, 330 Linwood Ave., 14209-1689.
Bosack, Albert J., Bishop Head Residence, 10 Rosary Ave., Lackawanna, 14218.
Carlo, Joseph C., 1317 Norwood Ave., Niagara Falls, 14305. P.O. Box 2927, Vero Beach, FL 32969.
Conoscenti, Frederick M., 169 Grand Oaks Way, Apt. 201, Naples, FL 34110.
Coveny, Richard C., Bishop Head Residence, 10 Rosary Ave., Lackawanna, 14218. (11/15-6/15): 1533 Tropic Terrace, North Fort Myers, FL 33903.
Cusimano, Salvatore J., O'Hara Residence, 69 O'Hara Rd., Tonawanda, 14150-6227.
Della Neve, Louis, 6A Lexington Ct., Lockport, 14094-5365.
Donohue, Raymond A.J., P.O. Box 24, Fredonia, 14063.
Dudek, Stanislaw, 26 Bowd P.D.E., P.O. Box 276, Wawell Heights, Labrador QLD 4215 Australia.
Enright, James C., 15 Clark St., Auburn, 13021.
Fafinski, Donald S., 137 Serval St., Dunkirk, 14048.
Faraci, Douglas F., 132 Wilmington Ave., Tonawanda, 14150.
Fifagrowicz, Joseph G., St. Benedict Parish, 1317 Eggert Rd., Eggertsville, 14226.
Fox, John J., P.O. Box 852, Amherst, 14226-1297.
Friel, Mark M., Sheehan Residence, 330 Linwood Ave., 14209-1689.
Gagliardo, Anthony F., 1301 Wynkoop Dr., Colorado Springs, CO 80909-3243.
Gresock, Thomas G., 749 Gilmore St., North Tonawanda, 14120.
Griffin, David G., 5904 Shoreham Dr., Lake View, 14085.
Grimmer, James A., Tonawanda Manor, 111 Ensminger Rd., #219, Tonawanda, 14150.
Haran, James E., St. Elizabeth Home, 5539 Broadway, Lancaster, 14086.
Hatrick, Brian M., 5114 Maple Grove Rd., Friendship, 14739.
Hogan, Francis T., P.O. Box 760, Melbourne, FL 32902-0760.
Ingalls, Fred D., c/o 795 Main St., 14203.
Jann, Francis J., P.O. Box 37, Rushford, 14777-0037.
Kasprzyk, James H., P.O. Box 2202, Blasdell, 14219-0402.
Kaukus, Edwin J., 3640 N.E. 16th Ave., Oakland Park, FL 33334.
Kemp, Thomas L., 58 Lake St., Le Roy, 14482.
Keppeler, Richard J., 1358 McKinley Pkwy., Lackawanna, 14218.
Kuhlmann, John L., 50 Fairmont St., Jamestown, 14701.
Lex, Henry V., Elderwood Village at Maplewood, 229 Bennett Rd., Cheektowaga, 14227.
Lutostanski, Anthony, 101 Swineburne St., 14212.
Mahar, Raymond J., Sheehan Residence, 330 Linwood Ave., 14209-1689.
Martlock, Loville N., P.O. Box 10, Jemez Springs, NM 87025-0010.
Massar, Richard A., Bishop Head Residence, 10 Rosary Ave., Lackawanna, 14218.
Matuszak, Walter L., 10675 Alleghany Rd, Darien Center, 14040.
McArtney, Robert J., 1358 McKinley Pkwy., Lackawanna, 14218.
McCarthy, Thomas J., 34 Birchwood Ave., Apt 6., West Seneca, 14224.
McGarry, William C., Our Lady of Peace Home, 5285 Lewiston Rd., Lewiston, 14092-1942.
McTigue, Norman P., 1088 Delaware Ave., #13B, 14209.
Measer, Donald L., St. Amelia, 210 St. Amelia Dr., Tonawanda, 14150-7126.
Mergenhagen, John J., P.O. Box 36, South Wales, 14139-0036.
Milby, Lawrence M., 24 Golden Sq., London, United Kingdom W1F9JR.
O'Hara, Michael D., 15 Clough Ave., Arcade, 14009.
Orsolits, Norbert F., P.O. Box 91, Springville, 14141.
Pavlock, Martin L., 247 State St., Jamestown, 14701.
Peter, David J., 2420 First St., Grand Island, 14072.
Rodriguez, Antonio L., Bishop Head Residence, 10 Rosary Ave., Lackawanna, 14218.
Rog, Theodore C., Bishop Head Residence, 10 Rosary Ave., Lackawanna, 14218.
Rossello, Nicholas A., 118 Old Niagara Rd., Apt. 3, Lockport, 14094-1520.
Russell, Raymond R., Sheehan Residence, 330 Linwood Ave., 14209-1689.
Schreck, Paul C., Sheehan Residence, 330 Linwood Ave., 14209.
Schroeder, Edward H., Apt. 3503, 4805 Transit Rd., Depew, 14043.
Siracuse, Guy F., Brothers of Mercy, 10570 Bergtold Rd., Clarence, 14031.
Sullivan, F. Norman, 8281 Lower East Hill Rd., Colden, 14033.
Uschold, Raymond F., Bishop Head Residence, 10 Rosary Ave., Lackawanna, 14218.
Vogt, Robert W., 229 Moulton Dr., Longs, SC 29568.
Werth, Charles M., 65-35 Yellowstone Blvd., Apt. 5G, Forest Hills, 11375.
Wood, Robert W., 127 W. Winspear, 14214.
Wopperer, Thomas J., 1 W. Beach Rd., Dunkirk, 14048.
Zancan, Robert D., PMB 205, 13680 Bear Valley Rd., E-4, Victorville, CA 92392.
Zmozynski, Francis J., Lancer Court Apartments, Apt. 600-A-4, Depew, 14043.

Permanent Deacons:
Amantia, Philip J., Sr.
Andelora, Gary P.
Anderson, Michael L.
Badaszewski, Robert W.
Barr, Joseph M.
Bauer, Robert A.
Bochiechio, Michael G.
Boneberg, William J.
Boyd, Jimmie L., Sr.
Bray, Michael R.
Brick, Daniel E., Esq.
Bringenberg, Thomas B.
Burke, John H.
Burns, Robert E.
Canzoneri, Michael J.
Carmody, Paul F.
Casey, Christopher T.
Chriswell, Timothy E.
Ciezki, Robert T.
Collichio, James L.
Comerford, Michael V., Jr.
Conroy, Dennis P.
Crimi, Victor P.
Darroch, Nelson
Dibb, Roy P.
Dobmeier, Robert A.
Ehrhart, David C.
Emerson, Paul C.
Eschbach, Lawrence D.
Eschrich, Paul C.
Feary, Gregory L., Jr.
Forcucci, Thomas M.
Foster, Norman E.
Fox, Albert F.
Friedman, Heinz H.
Fudala, Walter N.
Gaulin, John P.
Golinski, Daniel U.
Gomola, Michael A.
Griesbaum, Charles J., Jr.
Hart, Thomas J.
Harter, Terrance P.
Harvey, David H.
Healey, Thomas R.
Hooper, Mark J.
Hoover, Gary M.
Howard, Edward R.
Hynes, William J.
Jacobi, Robert J.
Jaworski, James J.
Jerome, David R.
Johnson, Frederick M., Jr.
Kapsiak, Dennis W.
Kelly, John J.
Klein, George L.
Koester, Carlton M.
Krahling, Francis R.
Leardon, John D.
Lemieux, Michael C.
Lennon, Michael
Licata, Thomas C.
Linnan, Neal M.
Mackiewicz, Richard F.
Mackowiak, Daniel H.
Mahaney, Richard J.
Maloney, Timothy J.
Marino, Benjamin R.
Markowski, Lawrence P.
Matthews, Richard F.
May, Thaddeus P.
McDermott, David P.
McDonnell, Thomas A.
McGuire, Daniel G.
McKeating, Michael P.
Meister, Alan A.
Mercurio, Joseph P.
Miranda, Roberto G.
Molnar, Alexander S.
Moscicki, Henry E.
Moses, Robert J.
Nowak, Mark F.
O'Connell, Edward G.
Parker, Richard W.
Pasquale, Francis W., Jr.
Pasquella, Joseph A.
Penksa, Daniel M.
Pijacki, Thaddeus V.
Polizzi, Frank
Puleo, Samuel G.
Quinn, Michael D.
Radlinski, Donald E.
Ramos, Carlos W.
Ruh, John M.
Scherr, Thomas E.
Schnettler, Paul J.

Schultz, Thomas E.
Setera, John T.
Shaughnessey, Frank J.
Skulicz, Matthew V.
Slish, David P.
Smith, Kevin J.
Snyder, Paul L., III
Stahl, Raymond H.
Stando, Matthew
Stankiewicz, Paul S.
Steffen, Franklyn C.
Steinagle, Gordon J.
Stone, John J.
Swinarski, Stephen J.
Terrana, Gary C.
Thomann, Bernard M.
Trzaska, James J.
Velasquez, David R.
Walders, Peter J.
Walek, Edward S.
Walker, Ronald
Walkowiak, Brian C.
Walkowiak, William J.
Watkins, Donald R., Jr.
Weisenburger, Paul F.
Wetter, Donald A.
Wick, John G.
Willis, William W.
Zielinski, John R.
Zwack, Francis A.

INSTITUTIONS LOCATED IN THE DIOCESE

[A] SEMINARIES

EAST AURORA. *Christ the King Seminary* (1857) *Graduate School of Theology*, 711 Knox Rd., P.O. Box 607, 14052. Tel: 716-652-8900; Fax: 716-652-8903. Email: cksacad@cks.edu. Web: www.cks.edu.
Interdiocesan Theologate. Owned and operated by the Diocese of Buffalo. Seminarians are assigned by the Bishop of any diocese for preparation for ordination to Priesthood.
Administration and Faculty: Revs. Peter J. Drilling, Th.D., Pres. & Rector; Gregory M. Faulhaber, S.T.D., Vice Rector; John P. Mack, Seminarian Formation Advisor; Richard A. Reina, M.Div., M.S.W., M.C.Sp., Dir. Spiritual Formation; Walter J. Szczesny, M.Div., Dir. Seminarians; Deacons Thaddeus P. May, Dir. Deacon Personnel; Gregory L. Feary, Dir. Diaconal Formation; Mr. Dennis Castillo, Ph.D., Academic Dean; Mr. Douglas George, M.A.P.M., Dir. Lay Formation; Mrs. Nancy Ehlers, Dir. Business Affairs; Mrs. Teresa Lubienecki, B.A., M.L.S., Dir. Library; Mr. Michael Sherry, Exec. Dir. Opers.
Faculty: Revs. Charles R. Amico, Ph.D., S.T.D. (Retired); Gregory M. Faulhaber, S.T.D.; Gabriel Scarfia, O.F.M., S.T.D.; Paul L. Varuvel, S.T.D.; Alan D. Lukas, M.Mus., Dir. of Music; Rev. Peter J. Drilling, Th.D.; Dennis Castillo, Ph.D.; Kathleen M. Castillo, M.A., Dir. Field Educ.; Sr. Marion Moeser, O.S.F., Ph.D.
Adjunct Faculty: Rev. Msgr. David M. Lee; Rev. Alfons M. Osiander, Th.D.; Rev. Msgr. Paul A. Litwin, J.C.L.; Revs. Czeslaw M. Krysa, S.L.D., M.Div.; Joseph F. Burke, S.J., Ph.D.; Joseph C. Gatto, S.T.D.; Rev. Msgr. Richard W. Siepka, M.A., S.T.L.; Rev. Paul W. Steller, M.A.

[B] SEMINARIES, RELIGIOUS

LEWISTON. *St. Anthony M. Zaccaria Seminary, The Barbabite Fathers of Lewiston, NY, Inc.*, 981 Swann Rd., P.O. Box 167, Youngstown, 14174-0167. Tel: 716-754-7448; Fax: 716-754-9130. Email: BarnabitesUSA@fatimashrine.com. Web: www.fatimashrine.com. Revs. Peter M. Calabrese, C.R.S.P., Chancellor & Supr.; Paul M. Keeling, C.R.S.P., Treas.; Julio M. Ciavaglia, C.R.S.P.; Richard M. Delzingaro, C.R.S.P., Librarian; Joseph M. Gariolo, C.R.S.P. Priests 5; Total Staff 6; Postulants 2.

[C] COLLEGES AND UNIVERSITIES

BUFFALO. *Canisius College* (1870) 2001 Main St., 14208-1098. Tel: 716-883-7000; Fax: 716-888-2525. Email: info@canisius.edu. Web: www.canisius.edu. Revs. Vincent M. Cooke, S.J., Pres.; John P. Bucki, S.J., Dir. Campus Ministry; Dr. Ellen O. Conley, Vice Pres. for Student Affairs; Mr. John J. Hurley, Vice Pres. for College Rels. and Sec. Bd. Trustees; Patrick E. Richey, Vice Pres., Business & Finance & Treas.; Dr. Scott Chadwick, Vice Pres. for Academic Affairs; Dr. Leonid Khinkis, Interim Dean College of Arts & Sciences; Dr. Antone F. Alber, Dean Wehle School of Business; Dr. Margaret C. McCarthy, Dean School of Educ. & Human Svcs.; Dr. Joel A. Cohen, Dir., Assoc. Vice Pres. for Library & Information Svcs. Priests 8; Lay Teachers 222; Total Enrollment 4,781.

**D'Youville College* (1908) 320 Porter Ave., 14201. Tel: 716-829-8000; Fax: 716-829-7780. Email: Brayjd@dyc.edu. Web: www.dyc.edu. Sr. Denise A. Roche, G.N.S.H., Ph.D., Pres.; Rev. Thomas Ribits, O.S.F.S., Dir. Campus Ministry; Rand Bellavia, Librarian. Grey Nuns of the Sacred Heart. Sisters 5; Lay Teachers 261; Total Staff 203; Students 2,986.

Trocaire College (1958) 360 Choate Ave., 14220. Tel: 716-826-1200; Fax: 716-828-6107. Email: hurleyp@trocaire.edu. Web: www.trocaire.edu. Paul B. Hurley Jr., Ph.D., Pres.; Thomas J. Mitchell, M.A., Vice Pres. Academic Affairs; Richard N. Bernecki, M.B.A., Vice Pres. Fin. & Admin.; Michael C. LaFever, Ed.D., Dean Prog. Devel. & Enrollment Mgmt.; Jeff Lesinski, M.B.A., Dean Educ. Tech.; Sr. Margaret Mary Gorman, R.S.M., M.S., Dean Student Affairs; Richard T. Linn, Ph.D., Dean Research, Assessment & Planning; John A. Vecchio, M.B.A., Vice Pres. Inst. Advancement; Maria Povlock, M.S., Dir. Admissions; Kathy Popielski, B.S., Dir. Communications; Judith K. Schwartz, M.L.S., Librarian; Rev. Robert M. Mock, Assoc. Dean, Academic Affairs; Sr. Sally Maloney, R.S.M., M.A., Dir. Mission Svc. A private career-oriented Catholic College established by the Sisters of Mercy in 1958. Priests 1; Sisters 7; Lay Teachers 138; Students 1,090; Total Staff 81.

Villa Maria College of Buffalo (1960) 240 Pine Ridge Rd., 14225-3999. Tel: 716-896-0700; 716-961-1805; Fax: 716-896-0705. Email: admissions@villa.edu. Web: www.villa.edu. Sr. Marcella Marie Garus, Pres.; Janet Reohr, Ed.D., Vice Pres. Academic Affairs; Sisters Mary De Angelis Nowak, Vice Pres. Business Affairs; Mary Marcine Borowiak, Vice Pres. Devel.; Mary Louis Rustowicz, Vice Pres. Student Affairs; Mary Anna Falbo, Dir. Library. Sisters 18; Lay Teachers 70; Students 503; Total Staff 127.

HAMBURG. *Hilbert College* (1957) 5200 S. Park Ave., 14075. Tel: 716-649-7900; Fax: 716-558-6380. Email: czane@hilbert.edu. Web: www.hilbert.edu/. Cynthia A. Zane, Ed.D. Lay Teachers 102; Students 997; Total Staff 150.

NIAGARA UNIVERSITY. *Niagara University* (1856) Lewiston Rd., 14109. Tel: 716-285-1212; Fax: 716-286-8355. Web: www.niagara.edu. Rev. Joseph L. Levesque, C.M., Pres.; Bonnie Rose, Ph.D., Exec. Vice Pres. & Vice Pres. Academic Affairs; Michael S. Jaszka, Vice Pres. for Admin.; Sheila L. Hausrath, M.S.Ed., Vice Pres. for Student Life; Donald P. Bielecki, Vice Pres. for Institutional Advancement; Judith A. Willard, Ph.D., Asst. to the Pres. for Planning; Nancy E. McGlen, Ph.D., Dean College of Arts & Sciences; Mark Wilson, Ph.D., Dean College of Business Admin.; Debra A. Colley, Ph.D., Dean College of Educ.; Michael J. Konopski, Dean of Enrollment Mgmt.; Gary Praetzel, Ph.D., Dean College of Hospitality & Tourism Mgmt.; Jon Jay Stockslader, Dir. Ctr. for Continuing & Community Educ.; Patricia G. Kinner, M.A., Dir. Academic Support; David M. Schoen, M.L.S., Dir. Library; Maureen Salfi, M.S.Ed., Dir. Financial Aid; John B. Stranges, Ph.D., Univ. Prof.; Mati Ortiz, Dir., Campus Activities; Joseph H. Cuda, M.A., Dean Student Affairs; Lori Soos, Dir. Health Svcs.; David Blackburn, Dir. Multicultural Student Affairs; Thomas J. McDermott, Dir. Counseling Svcs.; Kimberly J. Zukowski, M.S.Ed., Dir. Univ. Housing; Arthur Cardella, Dir. Alumni Rels.; Lisa McMahon, Acting Dir. Public Rels.; Robert Pfeil, Dir. Human Resources; Stephanie A. Cole, Esq., Gen. Counsel; Revs. Joseph G. Hubbert, C.M., Assoc. Prof. Rel. Studies & Supr. of Vincentian Community; Bruce J. Krause, C.M., Campus Min.; Stephen J. Denig, C.M., Assoc. Prof., Educ.; John T. Maher, C.M., Univ. Chap. & Dir. Campus Ministry; Thomas F. McKenna, C.M., Asst. to Pres., Mission Devel.; Bros. Martin J. Schneider, C.M., Coord. of Commencement & Asst. to Dir. of Theatre & Fine Arts; Augustine D. Towey, C.M., Dir. Emeritus of Niagara Univ. Theater. Priests 1; Sisters 1; Lay Teachers 150; Students 4,202.

ST. BONAVENTURE. *St. Bonaventure University* (1858) 3261 W. State Rd., Saint Bonaventure, 14778. Tel: 716-375-2000; Fax: 716-375-2055. Web: www.sbu.edu. Franciscan Friars, Province of the Holy Name, Order of Friars Minor., School of Arts and Sciences, School of Educ., School of Business, School of Journalism & Mass Communication; School of Franciscan Studies and the Franciscan Institute; Graduate Studies. Priests 12; Brothers 7; Sisters 4; Lay Teachers 205; Students 2,472.
Administration: Sr. Margaret Carney, O.S.F., S.T.D., Pres.; Michael J. Fischer, Vice Pres. Academic Affairs & Provost; Brenda McGee Snow, B.S., Senior Vice Pres. Finance & Admin.; Emily F. Sinsabaugh, Univ. Rels.; Peggy Y. Burke, Dean Graduate Studies; Eleanor Green, Ph.D., Dean School of Arts & Sciences; Rev. Michael F. Cusato, O.F.M., Ph.D., Dir. Franciscan Institute & Dean School of Franciscan Studies; John G. Watson, Dean School of Business; Peggy Y. Burke, Ed.D., Dean School of Educ.; Lee Coppola, J.D., Dean Russel J. Jandoli School of Journalism & Mass Communication; David DiMattio, Dean Clare College; James M. DiRisio, B.A., Dir. Admissions; Ann Lehman, M.B.A., Registrar & Dir. Inst. Research & Planning; Nichole J. Gonzalez, B.A., Dir. Residence Life; Joseph V. Flanagan, M.S., Dir. Alumni Svcs.; Anne Ciolek, Dir. Human Resources; Margaret T. Bryner, M.S., Dir. Higher Educ. Opportunities Prog. (HEOP); Jean T. Ehman, M.A., Dir. The Teaching & Learning Ctr.; Kimberly S. Young, Dir. Leadership Prog.; Alice F. Sayegh, M.S., Dir. Intl. Studies; Michael Hoffman, B.S., Exec. Dir. of Technology Svcs.; Paul J. Spaeth, M.L.S., M.A., Dir. Library; Constance F. Whitcomb, M.S.Ed., Dir. Career Devel.; Robert M. Donius, M.A., Vice Pres. Univ. Ministries.

Friar Community, 14778. Tel: 716-375-2416; Fax: 716-375-2424. Bros. F. Edward Coughlin, O.F.M., Ph.D., Vice Pres. Franciscan Mission; Christopher Coccia, O.F.M.; Robert Lentz, O.F.M., B.A.; David Haack, O.F.M., Ph.D.; Basil J. Valente, O.F.M., M.T.S.; Revs. David D. Blake, O.F.M., Ph.D.; Michael Blastic, O.F.M., Ph.D.; Xavier Seubert, O.F.M., S.T.D., Guardian; Michael D. Calabria, O.F.M., M.A., Vicar; Michael F. Cusato, O.F.M., Ph.D.; Robert Karris, O.F.M., Th.D.; Harry Monaco, O.F.M.; Peter Schneible, O.F.M., Ph.D.; James Vacco, O.F.M., M.A.; Allen Weber, O.F.M., Ph.D.

Holy Peace Friary, Mt. Irenaeus, West Clarksville, 14786-0100. Tel: 716-973-2470; Fax: 716-973-2400. Bros. Joseph A. Kotula, O.F.M., Ph.D.; Kevin Kriso, O.F.M; Revs. Daniel A. Hurley, O.F.M., M.A.; Louis M. McCormick, O.F.M., D.Min.; Daniel P. Riley, O.F.M., M.A., Guardian, Dir.; Robert Struzynski, O.F.M.

[D] HIGH SCHOOLS, PRIVATE

BUFFALO. *Bishop Timon-St. Jude High School* (1946) 601 McKinley Pkwy., 14220. Tel: 716-826-3610; Fax: 716-824-5833. Web: www.bishoptimon.com. Mr. Thomas J. Sullivan, Prin. Owned and operated by Bishop Timon Board of Trustees. Lay Teachers 28; Students 300; Total Staff 35.

Canisius High School (1870) 1180 Delaware Ave., 14209. Tel: 716-882-0466; Fax: 716-883-1870. Email: knight@canisiushigh.org. Web: www.canisiushigh.org. Mr. John M. Knight, Pres.; Mr. William J. Kopas, Prin.; Revs. Frederick G. Betti, S.J.; William J. McCurdy, S.J.; Michael A. Guzik, S.J.; John J. Ryan, S.J.; Eugene A. Zimpfer, S.J. Society of Jesus. Priests 5; Lay Teachers 64; Students 810; Total Staff 98.

Holy Angels Academy (1861) 24 Shoshone Dr., 14214-1097. Tel: 716-834-7120; Fax: 716-834-7128. Email: jkaczor@holyangelsacademy.org. Web: www.holyangelsacademy.org. Joan Thomas, Pres.; Julie A. Kaczor, Prin. Grey Nuns of the Sacred Heart 2; Lay Teachers 36; Religious 1; Students 249; Total Staff 50.

St. Joseph's Collegiate Institute (1861) 845 Kenmore Ave., 14223-3195. Tel: 716-874-4024; Fax: 716-874-4956. Email: rscott@sjci.com. Web: www.sjci.com. Robert T. Scott, A.F.S.C., Pres. & Prin.; Rev. James C. Croglio, Chap. of School and Brothers' Community; Bros. Christopher Belleman, F.S.C., Vice Prin. Student Affairs; Peter Henderson, F.S.C., Community Dir.; Joseph Reed, F.S.C.; Luke Wittmann, F.S.C.; Deacons Thaddeus V. Pijacki; Gregory L. Feary; William J. Hynes; William J. Walkowiak; Rev. James R. Bastian; Mrs. Elizabeth Kamke, Librarian. Brothers of the Christian Schools. (De La Salle Christian Brothers). Priests 2; Deacons 4; Brothers 4; Lay Teachers 43; Students 751; Total Staff 76.

Mt. Mercy Academy (1904) 88 Red Jacket Pkwy., 14220. Tel: 716-825-8796; Fax: 716-825-0976. Email: pgaske@mtmercy.org. Web: www.mtmercy.org. Sr. Mary Ellen Twist, R.S.M., Pres.; Mrs. Paulette Gaske, Prin.; Michele Kujawinski, Librarian. Sisters of Mercy. Students 294; Total Staff 53.

Nardin Academy High School (1857) 135 Cleveland Ave., 14222. Tel: 716-881-6262; Fax: 716-881-0086. Email: rreeder@nardin.org. Web: www.nardin.org. Mrs. Marsha Sullivan, Pres.; Rebecca R. Reeder, Prin.; Karen Roslowski, Librarian. Lay Teachers 47; Girls 461.

ATHOL SPRINGS. *St. Francis High School* (1927) 4129 Lake Shore Rd., 14010-0185. Tel: 716-627-1200; Fax: 716-627-4610. Email: frmichaels@stfrancishigh.org. Web: stfrancishigh.org. Rev. Michael Sajda, O.F.M.Conv., Pres.; Mr. Thomas Braunscheidel, Prin.; Revs. Joseph Bayne, O.F.M.Conv.; Aurelian W. Brzezniak, O.F.M.Conv.

(Retired); Innocent Kurkowski, O.F.M.Conv. (Retired); Francis Lombardo, O.F.M.Conv.; Justin Ross, O.F.M.Conv.; Mark David Skura, O.F.M.Conv.; Bros. Nicholas Romeo, O.F.M.Conv.; William Surdyka, O.F.M.Conv. St. Anthony Province of the Order of Friars Minor Conventual. Priests 7; Brothers 2; Lay Teachers 44; Total Staff 67; Students 508.

BATAVIA. *Notre Dame High School of Batavia*, 73 Union St., 14020. Tel: 585-343-2783; Fax: 585-343-7323. Email: ndhs@ndhsbatavia.com. Web: www.ndhsbatavia.com. Dr. Joseph Scanlan, Prin.; Mr. Mike Rapone, Asst. Prin. & Athletic Dir.; Miss Jennifer Kleparek, Librarian. Owned and operated by Notre Dame Board of Trustees. Lay Teachers 18; Students 185; Total Staff 25.

EGGERTSVILLE. *Buffalo Academy of the Sacred Heart*, 3860 Main St., 14226. Tel: 716-834-2101; Fax: 716-834-2944. Email: Info@sacredheartacademy.org. Web: www.sacredheartacademy.org. Jennifer Demert, Headmistress; Lynn Biniskiewicz, Librarian. Sisters of St. Francis of Penance and Christian Charity. Sisters 6; Lay Teachers 40; Students 396; Total Staff 78.

HAMBURG. *Immaculata Academy*, 5138 S. Park Ave., 14075. Tel: 716-649-6161; Fax: 716-646-1782. Email: mstahl@immaculataacademy.com. Sr. M. Paulette Tirone, F.S.S.J., Pres.; Mrs. Mary Lou Stahl, Prin.; Sr. Jane Muldoon, Librarian. Franciscan Sisters of St. Joseph. Sisters 4; Lay Teachers 26; Students 209; Total Staff 19.

KENMORE. *Mount St. Mary Academy* (1927) 3756 Delaware Ave., 14217. Tel: 716-877-1358; Fax: 716-877-0548. Email: driggie@mt-st-marys.org. Web: mt-st-marys.org. Mrs. Dawn M. Riggie, Prin.; Ms. Mary Jo Grundle, Librarian. Owned and operated by the Mt. St. Mary Academy Board of Trustees. Sisters 1; Lay Teachers 40; Girls 350.

LANCASTER. *St. Mary's High School*, 142 Laverack Ave., 14086. Tel: 716-683-4824; Fax: 716-683-4996. Email: lancer@smhlancers.org. Web: www.smhlancers.org. Rebecca L. Kranz, Prin.; Emily Sityar, Librarian. Owned and operated by St. Mary's Board of Trustees. Sisters 2; Lay Teachers 30; Students 340; Total Staff 55.

NIAGARA FALLS. *Niagara Catholic High School* (1975) 520-66th St., 14304. Tel: 716-283-8771; Fax: 716-283-8774. Email: rdifrancesco@niagaracatholic.org. Web: www.niagaracatholic.org. Robert M. DiFrancesco, Prin.; Rev. Gerald L. Bartko, O.S.F.S.; Deacon Daniel H. Mackowiak, Campus Min.; Ms. Karlen Chase, Librarian. Owned and operated by Niagara Catholic Board of Trustees. Priests 1; Deacons 1; Lay Teachers 15; Students 144.

OLEAN. *Archbishop Walsh High School*, 208 N. 24th St., 14760-1985. Tel: 716-372-8122; Fax: 716-372-6707. Email: archbishopwalsholean@yahoo.com. Web: www.mywalsh.com. Mr. Robert McFarland, Bd. Pres.; Mrs. Donna Sweet, Prin. Owned and operated by Archbishop Walsh Board of Trustees. Lay Teachers 11; Students 60; Total Staff 20.

TONAWANDA. *Cardinal O'Hara High School*, 39 O'Hara Rd., 14150. Tel: 716-695-2600; Fax: 716-692-8697. Email: mciurczak@cardinalohara.com. Web: www.cardinalohara.com. Matthew Ciurczak, Prin.; Janet Kindron, Librarian. Owned and operated by Cardinal O'Hara Board of Trustees. Lay Teachers 30; Students 248.

[E] ELEMENTARY SCHOOLS, PRIVATE

BUFFALO. *Nardin Academy* (1857) 135 Cleveland Ave., 14222. Tel: 716-881-6262; Fax: 716-881-4190. Email: msullivan@nardin.org. Web: www.nardin.org. Rebecca Reeder, High School Prin.; Margaret Abels, Elementary Prin.; Kristin Whitlock, Montessori Prin. (Montessori-Grade 12) Sisters 3; Lay Teachers 107; Students 926.

LEWISTON. *Sacred Heart Villa School*, (Grades PreK-5), 5269 Lewiston Rd., 14092. Tel: 716-284-8273; 716-285-9257 (school); Fax: 716-284-8273. Email: sacredhrtv@yahoo.com. Web: www.shvilla.org. Sr. Elizabeth Domin, S.S.H.J., Prin. Sisters 8; Lay Teachers 2; Students 45.

STELLA NIAGARA. *Stella Niagara Education Park*, (Grades PreK-8), 4421 Lower River Rd., 14144. Tel: 716-754-4314; Fax: 716-754-2964. Sr. Margaret Sullivan, O.S.F., Prin. Sisters of St. Francis of Penance and Christian Charity Sisters 4; Lay Teachers 22; Students 179.

[F] ELEMENTARY SCHOOLS, SPECIAL

BUFFALO. *Cantalician Center for Learning, Inc.* (1955) 3233 Main St., 14214. Tel: 716-833-5353; Fax: 716-833-0108. Email: tscofidio@cantalician.org. Web: www.cantalician.org. Terese M. Scofidio, Exec. Dir.; Anne Spisiak, Dir. Community Svcs.; Sr. Paul Marie Baczkowski, C.S.S.F., Dir. Educ. Program for the disabled: Infant, Toddler and Preschool; Elementary and Secondary. Workshop for adult individuals with disabilities, day treatment-lite program, & day habilitation for retired, disabled adults. Daycare. Sisters 2; Lay Staff 247; Students 411; Total Staff 249.

[G] REGIONAL AND CONSOLIDATED ELEMENTARY SCHOOLS

BUFFALO. *Catholic Academy of West Buffalo*, (Grades PreK-8), 1069 Delaware Ave., 14209. Tel: 716-885-6111; Fax: 716-885-6452. Email: gglenn@cawb.org. Sr. Gail Glenn, S.S.J., Prin.; Mrs. Geraldine Kizielewicz, Assoc. Prin.; Christine Traum, Librarian. Sisters 2; Lay Teachers 16; Students 212; Total Staff 24.

Catholic Central School, (Grades 6-8), St. Monica Campus: 201 Winston Rd., Cheektowaga, 14215. Tel: 716-852-6854; Fax: 716-852-8410. Email: es88@buffalodiocese.org. St. Augustine Campus: 21 Davison St., 14215. Tel: 716-836-5188; Fax: 716-836-5188. Rev. James F. Joyce, S.J., Canonical Admin.; Nancy M. Langer, Pres.; Rev. Edward J. Durkin, S.J., Prin. & Dir. St. Augustine Scholars Prog.; Ms. Laura Derigo, Dir. St. Monica Scholars Prog. Priests 1; Sisters 1; Lay Teachers 7; Students 88; Total Staff 14.

Our Lady of Black Rock, (Grades K-8), 16 Peter St., 14207. Tel: 716-873-7497; Fax: 716-447-9926. Email: es15@buffalodiocese.org. Mrs. Julie Watroba, Prin.; Sharon Leising, Librarian. Lay Teachers 15; Students 98; Total Staff 18.

South Buffalo Catholic School, (Grades PreK-8), A regional school with three sites: Trinity Catholic Academy 16 Hayden St., Buffalo; Notre Dame Academy, 1125 Abbott Rd., Buffalo, NY; and Ambrose Catholic Academy, 260 Okell St., Buffalo, NY., 16 Hayden St., 14210. Tel: 716-822-4546; Fax: 716-822-2576. Laura Kazmierczak, Prin. Ambrose Catholic Academy; Kimberly Suminski, Prin. Notre Dame Academy; Dolores C. Oakes, Prin. Trinity Academy; Rev. Msgr. David M. Lee, Canonical Admin. Lay Teachers 50; Students 729.

CHEEKTOWAGA. *Mary Queen of Angels Catholic School* (2003) (Grades PreK-8), 170 Rosewood Ter., 14225. Tel: 716-895-6280; Fax: 716-895-6359. Email: maryqueenofangels@catholic.org. Web: www.mqangels.com. MaryAlice Bagwell, Prin.; Rev. Msgr. Kevin T. O'Neill, Canonical Admin. (Retired). (Regional School) Lay Teachers 19; Students 186.

DUNKIRK. *Northern Chautauqua Catholic School* (1989) (Grades PreK-8), 336 Washington Ave., 14048. Tel: 716-366-0630; Fax: 716-366-5101. Email: es37@buffalodio.org. Kathy Y. Moser, Prin. Lay Teachers 17; Students 176; Total Staff 25.

JAMESTOWN. *Catholic Academy of the Holy Family* (1887) (Grades PreK-8), 1135 N. Main St., 14701-3199. Tel: 716-483-3245; Fax: 716-483-3245. Email: es47@buffalodiocese.org. Web: www.holyfamilyjamestown.org. Mr. Samuel Pellerito, Prin.; Rev. Dennis W. Mende, Canonical Admin.; Paula Slagle, Librarian. Lay Teachers 15; Students 118; Total Staff 27.

LAKE VIEW. *Southtowns Catholic*, (Grades PreK-8), 2052 Lakeview Rd., Box 86, 14085. Tel: 716-627-5011; Fax: 716-627-5335. Email: jmacdonald@southtownscatholic.org. Web: www.southtownscatholic.org. Judith M. MacDonald, Prin. Lay Teachers 21; Students 231; Total Staff 31.

LOCKPORT. *DeSales Catholic School*, (Grades PreK-8), 6914 Chestnut School, 14094. Tel: 716-433-6422; Fax: 716-434-4002. Email: desalesp@desalescatholicschool.org. Web: www.desalescatholicschool.org. Mr. Michael P. Powers, Prin. Sisters 1; Lay Teachers 32; Students 438; Total Staff 43.

NIAGARA FALLS. *Catholic Academy of Niagara Falls* (Two sites) Rev. Stephen J. Denig, C.M., Canonical Admin.

St. Dominic Savio Middle School Campus (Grades 6-8), 504 66th St., 14303. Tel: 716-215-1461; Fax: 716-215-1465. Email: es62@buffalodiocese.org. Rose Mary Buscaglia, Prin. Lay Teachers 12; Students 130.

Catholic Academy of Niagara Falls Elementary Campus (Grades PreK-5), 1055 N. Military Rd., 14304. Tel: 716-283-1455; Fax: 716-283-1355. Mrs. Jeannine M. Fortunate, Prin. Lay Teachers 20; Students 215.

NORTH TONAWANDA. *North Tonawanda Catholic School*, (Grades K-8), 75 Keil St., 14120. Tel: 716-693-2828; Fax: 716-693-0169. Email: office@ntcatholic.org. Web: www.ntcatholic.org. Mrs. Martha J. Eadie, Supervising Prin.; Mrs. Nancy Kindred, Asst. Prin. & Devel. Dir.; Rev. Louis S. Dolinic, Canonical Admin. Sisters 1; Lay Teachers 15; Total Staff 23; Students 91.

OLEAN. *Southern Tier Catholic School*, (Grades PreK-8), 206 N. 24th St., 14760. Tel: 716-372-2891; Fax: 716-373-1175. Web: www.wnystcs.info. Daniel McCarthy, Prin.; Rev. Gregory J. Dobson, Canonical Admin.; Bonnie Hadley, Librarian. Lay Teachers 16; Students 140; Total Staff 25.

SPRINGVILLE. *St. Aloysius Regional School*, (Grades K-8), 186 Franklin St., 14141-1112. Tel: 716-592-7002; Fax: 716-592-7002. Email: stalsschool@aol.com. Web: www.staloysiusregional.com. Bonnie Renzi, Prin.; Kathy Walker, Librarian. Lay Teachers 14; Students 98.

WELLSVILLE. *Immaculate Conception School of Allegany County*, 24 Maple Ave., 14895. Tel: 585-593-5840; Fax: 585-593-5846. Email: es80@buffalodiocese.org. Web: www.icc-ics.com. Charles E. Cutler, Prin. Sisters of Mercy 1; Lay Teachers 16; Students 138.

[H] CATHOLIC CHARITIES

BUFFALO. *The Catholic Charities of the Diocese of Buffalo* (1923) 741 Delaware Ave., 14209. Tel: 716-218-1400; Fax: 716-856-2005. Serving the eight counties of Western New York.

Appeal Administration and Publicity Offices Rev. Msgr. Joseph J. Sicari, Pres. & Dir.

Agency Administration Dennis C. Walczyk, CEO.

Delta Development of Western New York, Inc. Tel: 716-847-1635; Fax: 716-856-7201. Bernadette Harlan, Dir. See separate listing in the Miscellaneous section.

The Msgr. Carr Institute, 76 W. Humboldt Pkwy., 14214. Tel: 716-835-9745; Fax: 716-835-6785. See separate listing in the Miscellaneous section.

[I] ORPHANAGES AND INFANT HOMES

BUFFALO. *German Roman Catholic Orphan Home*, 795 Main St., 14203. Inactive.

[J] PROTECTIVE INSTITUTES

BUFFALO. *St. Adalbert's Response to Love Center, Inc.*, 130 Kosciuszko St., 14212. Tel: 716-894-7030; Fax: 716-891-5474. Web: www.responsetolovecenter.org. Sr. Mary Johnice Rzadkiewicz, C.S.S.F., Dir. Total Assisted Annually 992.

The Franciscan Center, Inc., 1910 Seneca St., 14210-1842. Tel: 716-822-8017; Fax: 716-822-8537. Web: www.franciscancenterinc.org. Rev. Joseph Bayne, O.F.M.Conv., Exec. Dir. Transitional Shelters for Adolescent Males 16-20: Transitional Indep. Living Program, Supported Residence. Total Assisted 387; Total Staff 12.

LACKAWANNA. *Baker Victory Services* (1851) (formerly known as Baker Hall, Our Lady of Victory Infant Home, St. Joseph Orphanage and St. John's Protectory), 780 Ridge Rd., 14218. Tel: 716-828-9500; 888-287-1160; Fax: 716-828-9526. Email: baker@buffnet.net. Web: www.bakervictoryservices.org. Rev. Msgr. Paul J.E. Burkard, Pres. of Board; James J. Casion, CEO; Alan Nelson, Vice Pres. Admin. Svcs. Bakery Victory Services assists children, adults and families in need through preventative, outpatient, educational, and residential programs, including international and domestic adoptions, foster care, early childhood education, and a dental clinic, as well as programs for individuals with developmental disabilities and young people who are emotionally, behaviorally, or mentally challenged. Staff 875; Total Assisted 31,018.

Family Pointe Development & Evaluation Center Tel: 716-828-7700; Fax: 716-828-9545. Web: www-.bakervictoryservices.org. Early Identification of delays in ages birth to five.

Baker Victory Healthcare Center Tel: 716-828-9334; Fax: 716-828-9355. Web: www.bakervictoryservice-s.org.

Child Pro/Monarch Child Pro at Monarch Academy, Tel: 716-822-4782; Fax: 716-825-5765. Web: www.childpro.net.

[K] GENERAL HOSPITALS

BUFFALO. *Catholic Health System, Inc.* (1998) *Seton Professional Bldg.*, 2121 Main St., Ste. 300, 14214. Tel: 716-862-2400; Fax: 716-862-2468. Email: webmaster@WNYCHS.org. Web: www.chsbuffalo.org. Joseph D. McDonald, Pres. & CEO. Bed Capacity 891; Patients Assisted Annually 1,514,232; Total Staff 8,250.

McAuley Mercy Corporation, 2121 Main St., Ste. 300, 14214. Sr. Sally Maloney, R.S.M., M.A., Chairperson. A holding company for Mercy Home Care of Western New York. Sponsored by the Catholic Health System, Inc.

Mercy Hospital (1904) 565 Abbott Rd., 14220. Tel: 716-826-7000; Fax: 716-828-2700. Email: JPD@chsbuffalo.org. *c/o Catholic Health System*, 2121 Main St., Ste. 300, 14214. Mr. C. J. Urlaub, Pres. & CEO; Mary Beth Farruggio, Nursing Svcs. Sponsored by the Catholic Health System, Inc. Sisters of Mercy 4; Patients Assisted Annually 390,626; Outpatients 368,426; Admissions 22,200; Bed Capacity 326; Total Staff 1,883.

Sisters Hospital Foundation, Inc., 2130 Main St., 14214. Tel: 716-862-1990; Fax: 716-835-8643. Email: jsnyder@chsbuffalo.org. Web: www.sistershospitalfoundation.org. *c/o Catholic Health System*, 2121 Main St., Ste. 300, 14214. Julie R. Snyder, Exec. Dir.

Sisters of Charity Hospital of Buffalo, NY (1849) 2157 Main St., 14214. Tel: 716-862-1000; Fax: 716-862-1899. Email: pbergman@chsbuffalo.org. Web: www.chsbuffalo.org. *c/o Catholic Health Systems*, 2121 Main St., Ste. 300, 14214. Peter U. Bergmann, Pres. & CEO. Sponsored by the Catholic Health System, Inc. Daughters of Charity of St. Vincent de Paul 10; Bed Capacity 413; Patients Assisted Annually 648,760; Total Staff 1,638.

St. Joseph Campus, 2605 Harlem Rd., 14225.

CHEEKTOWAGA. *McAuley-Seton Home Care* (1988) 14 Appletree Business Park, 14227. Tel: 716-685-4870; Fax: 716-651-9613. Email: jmarkiew@chsbuffalo.org. *c/o Catholic Health Systems*, 2121 Main St., Ste. 300, 14214. Joyce Markiewicz, Pres. & CEO. Patients Assisted Annually 9,039; Staff 269; Home Care 1,365; Staff 195; Long Term Hospital Patients 361; Staff 11.

KENMORE. *Kenmore Mercy Foundation Inc.* (1980) 2950 Elmwood Ave., 14217. Tel: 716-447-6204; Fax: 716-447-6052. Email: smcdonou@chsbuffalo.org. Web: www.kenmoremercyfoundation.org. *c/o Catholic Health Systems*, 2121 Main St., Ste. 300, 14214. Shari McDonough, Exec. Dir.

Kenmore Mercy Hospital, 2950 Elmwood Ave., 14217. Tel: 716-447-6100; Fax: 716-447-6090. *c/o Catholic Health Systems*, 2121 Main St., Ste. 300, 14214. James M. Millard, Pres. & CEO; Rev. Vincent J. Ferraro, Chap. Sponsored by the Catholic Health System, Inc. Bed Capacity 184; Total Staff 851; Outpatient Visits 148,847; Admissions 7,605.

LEWISTON. *Mount St. Mary's Hospital of Niagara Falls*, 5300 Military Rd., 14092-1997. Tel: 716-297-4800; Fax: 716-298-2333 (Gen.); 716-298-2001 (Pres.). Web: www.msmh.org. Judith A. Maness, Pres. & CEO; Rev. Stewart M. Lindsay, O.S.F.S., Chap.; Sisters Grace Marie Dunn, D.C., Vice Pres. for Mission; Margaret Tuley, D.C., Board Pres.; Jeraldine Fritz, D.C., Chap.; Diane Louttit, D.C., Chap.; Christine Steigerwald, O.S.F., Chap. Ascension Health, St. Louis, MO. Capacity 175; Patients Assisted Annually 140,829; Total Staff 844.

[L] HEALTH CARE FACILITIES

BUFFALO. *St. Francis of Buffalo, Inc.* Formerly known as St. Francis Hospital., 34 Benwood Ave., 14214. Tel: 716-862-2500; Fax: 716-862-2505. Email: dcrispel@chsbuffalo.org. c/o Catholic Health Systems, 2121 Main St., Ste. 300, 14214. Darlene Jones Crispell, Admin.; Rev. Msgr. Robert E. Zapfel, S.T.D., Chap.; Sr. Mary Powers, D.C., Chap. Sisters of St. Francis 1; Total Assisted 290; Total Staff 243.

LOCKPORT. *Niagara Homemaker Services, Inc. dba Mercy Home Care of Western New York* 111 Main St., 14094. Tel: 716-282-0091. c/o Catholic Health System, 2121 Main St., Ste. 300, 14214.

[M] HOMES FOR AGED

BATAVIA. *St. Luke Manor*, c/o Catholic Health System, 121 Main St., Ste. 300, 14214.

CLARENCE. *Brothers of Mercy Housing Co., Inc.*, 10500 Bergtold Rd., 14031. Tel: 716-759-2122; Fax: 716-759-8030. Email: len@brothersofmercy.org. Web: www.brothersofmercy.org. Leonard Krufka, Admin.; Bro. Jude Holzfoerster, F.M.M., Pres. Apartments 100; Total in Residence 100; Total Staff 6.

Brothers of Mercy Nursing & Rehabilitation Center, 10570 Bergtold Rd., 14031. Tel: 716-759-6985; Fax: 716-759-6223. Email: valerie@brothersofmercy.org. Web: www.brothersofmercy.org. Ms. Valerie Kane, Admin.; Bro. Jude Holzfoerster, F.M.M., Pres.; Rev. John J. Sardina, Chap. Bed Capacity 240; Total Assisted Annually 960; Staff 500. In Res. Bro. Fidelis Verrall, F.M.M.

Brothers of Mercy Sacred Heart Home, Inc., 4520 Ransom Rd., 14031. Tel: 716-759-2644; Fax: 716-759-6433. Email: marion@brothersofmercy.org. Web: www.brothersofmercy.org. Marion Hummell, Admin.; Bro. Jude Holzfoerster, F.M.M., Pres. of Bd.; Rev. John J. Sardina, Chap. Total Assisted Annually 106; Total Staff 50.

DUNKIRK. *St. Vincent's Home for the Aged*, 319 Washington Ave., 14048. Tel: 716-366-2066; Fax: 716-366-0545. Email: dsmith@chsbuffalo.org. *c/o Catholic Health Systems*, 2121 Main St., Ste. 300, 14214. Deborah A. Smith, Admin. Residents 40; Total Staff 25.

KENMORE. *McAuley Residence*, 1503 Military Rd., 14217. Tel: 716-447-6600; Fax: 716-447-6620. Email: tkristal@chsbuffalo.org. *c/o Catholic Health Systems*, 2121 Main St., Ste. 300, 14214. Tova Kristal, Admin. Residential Health Care Facility; Sponsored by the Catholic Health System, Inc. Bed Capacity 160; Total Assisted 1,030; Total Staff 254.

LANCASTER. *St. Elizabeth's Home* (1958) 5539 Broadway, 14086. Tel: 716-683-5150; Fax: 716-683-4049. Email: bsiener@chsbuffalo.org. *c/o Catholic Health Systems*, 2121 Main St., Ste. 300, 14214. Bartholomew J. Siener, Admin. Felician Sisters 2; Residents 117; Total Assisted 213; Total Staff 54.

LEWISTON. *Our Lady of Peace, Inc. dba Our Lady of Peace Nursing Care Residence* 5285 Lewiston Rd., 14092. Tel: 716-298-2900; Fax: 716-298-2800. Ronald F. Zito, Exec. Dir.; Sisters Margaret Tuley, D.C., Chairperson; Eleanor Marie Shea, D.C., Chap. Total Assisted Annually 600.

LOCKPORT. *St. Clare Manor*, c/o Catholic Health System, 2121 Main St., Ste. 300, 14214.

NIAGARA FALLS. *St. Mary Manor*, c/o Catholic Health System, 2121 Main St., Ste. 300, 14214.

OLEAN. *S. Joseph Manor*, c/o Cahtolic Health System, 2121 Main St., Ste. 300, 14214.

ORCHARD PARK. *Father Baker Manor* (1994) 6400 Powers Rd., 14127. Tel: 716-667-0001; Fax: 716-667-0028. Email: sguenthe@chsbuffalo.org. Web: www.chsbuffalo.org. *c/o Catholic Health Systems*, 2121 Main St., Ste. 300, 14214. Michael E. McRae, Admin. Nursing facility sponsored by the Catholic Health System, Inc. Bed Capacity 160; Total Assisted 700; Total Staff 300.

SILVER CREEK. *St. Columbans on the Lake, Home for the Aged* (1970) 2546 Lake Rd., 14136. Tel: 716-934-4515; Fax: 716-934-3919. Web: www.stcolumbanshome.org. Sr. Corona Colleary, S.S.C., Admin. Bed Capacity 50; Columban Sisters 11; Total Staff 36; Total Assisted Annually 175. In Res. Most Rev. James Michaels, S.S.C. (Retired); Revs. Peter J. Cronin, S.S.C.; Thomas M. Walsh, S.S.C.

WILLIAMSVILLE. *St. Francis of Williamsville*, 147 Reist St., 14221. Tel: 716-633-5400; Fax: 716-663-6404. Email: cyouknut@chsbuffalo.org. Web: www.chsbuffalo.org. *c/o Catholic Health Systems*, 2121 Main St., Ste. 300, 14214. Charlene Youknut, Admin.

St. Francis of Williamsville, Skilled Nursing Facility Residents 142; Total Assisted 286; Total Staff 215.

[N] DAY CARE CENTERS

BUFFALO. *Holy Innocents Day Care Center*, 128 Wilson St., 14212. Tel: 716-896-6386; Fax: 716-896-0662. Email: debbie.coyne@ccwny.org. Web: www.ccwny.org. Mrs. Deborah L. Coyne, Dir. Day care for children age 6 weeks to 12 yrs. Children 90; Total Staff 17.

[O] MONASTERIES AND RESIDENCES OF PRIESTS AND BROTHERS

BUFFALO. *Bishop's Residence*, 77 Oakland Pl., 14222-2041. Tel: 716-883-7707; Fax: 716-883-7702. Most Rev. Edward U. Kmiec, D.D., S.T.L.; Rev. Msgrs. David G. LiPuma, Bishop Sec. & Vice Chancellor; Paul A. Litwin, J.C.L., Chancellor.

Canisius Jesuit Community Inc., 2001 Main St., 14208. Tel: 716-883-7000; Fax: 716-886-6506. Email: tunneym@canisius.edu. Web: www.canisius.edu. Revs. Michael F. Tunney, S.J., Rector; Michael J. Agliardo, S.J.; Frederick G. Betti, S.J.; Joseph E. Billotti, S.J.; John P. Bucki, S.J.; Joseph F. Burke, S.J., Ph.D.; Thomas A. Colgan, S.J.; Vincent M. Cooke, S.J.; Paul J. Dugan, S.J.; Edward J. Durkin, S.J.; Michael A. Guzik, S.J.; Robert A. Haus, S.J. (Retired); Daniel P. Jamros, S.J.; Frank LaRocca, S.J.; Daniel J. Lusch, S.J.; Patrick J. Lynch, S.J.; William J. McCurdy, S.J.; Vincent M. McNally, S.J. (Retired); Martin X. Moleski, S.J.; Paul W. Nochelski, S.J.; Michael H. Pastizzo, S.J.; James M. Pribek, S.J.; George A. Restrepo, S.J.; John J. Ryan, S.J.; David F. White, S.J.; Eugene A. Zimpfer, S.J.

The Canisius Jesuit Community, Inc.

The Eudists - Congregation of Jesus and Mary (1642) 1088 Delaware Ave., Apt. 9G, 14209. Tel: 716-886-4594. Rev. Robert J. Perelli, C.J.M., D.Min. Total in Residence 1.

Maryknoll House; Maryknoll Fathers & Brothers, 127 Chadduck Ave., 14207. Tel: 716-875-0005; Fax: 716-875-2322. Email: buffalo@maryknoll.org. Web: www.maryknoll.org. Mr. Paul Bork, Dir. Total in Residence 1; Total Staff 2.

St. Patrick Friary, 102 Seymour St., 14210. Tel: 716-856-5790; Fax: 716-856-4019. Rev. Francis Pompei, O.F.M., Guardian; Bros. Timothy S. Dauenhauer, O.F.M.; Vianney Justin, O.F.M.; Michael G. Oberst, O.F.M.; Maurice V. Swartout, O.F.M.

Sheehan Residence for Priests Residence for retired priests., 330 Linwood Ave., 14209-1689. Tel: 716-884-9679; Fax: 716-881-3268. Sr. Virginia Balk, O.S.F., Admin.; Rev. Msgr. John I. Ducette (Retired); Revs. Robert J. Biesinger (Retired); Mark M. Friel (Retired); Raymond J. Mahar (Retired); Raymond R. Russell (Retired); Paul C. Schreck (Retired).

ATHOL SPRINGS. *St. Francis of Assisi Friary* (1927) 4129 Lake Shore Rd., 14010-0185. Tel: 716-627-5762; Fax: 716-627-4610. Email: frmichaels@stfrancishigh.org. Web: www.stfrancishigh.org. Revs. Joseph Bayne, O.F.M.Conv.; Aurelian W. Brzezniak, O.F.M.Conv. (Retired); Charles Jagodzinski, O.F.M.Conv.; Michael Sajda, O.F.M.Conv., Guardian & Pres.; Francis Lombardo, O.F.M.Conv.; Innocent Kurkowski, O.F.M.Conv. (Retired); Justin Ross, O.F.M.Conv.; Bros. Nicholas Romeo, O.F.M.Conv.; William Surdyka, O.F.M.Conv. Faculty Residence for St. Francis High School Priests 7; Brothers 2; Total in Residence 9.

St. Maximilian Kolbe Friary, 4263 St. Francis Dr., P.O. Box 182, 14010. Tel: 716-627-2710; Fax: 716-627-5263. Email: frdaniel@localnet.com. Bro. Daniel Geary, O.F.M.Conv., Guardian; Revs. Steven G. Frenier, O.F.M.Conv., Vicar; Ronald Sermak, O.F.M.Conv.; Marcel Sokalski, O.F.M.Conv. Priests 3; Brothers 1; Total in Residence 4.

CLARENCE. *Regional Motherhouse of Brothers of Mercy*, 4520 Ransom Rd., 14031. Tel: 716-759-8341; Fax: 716-759-7243. Email: jude@brothersofmercy.org. Web: www.brothersofmercy.org. Bro. Jude Holzfoerster, F.M.M., Regl. Supr.; Rev. John J. Sardina, Chap.

Brothers of Mercy, Inc. Brothers 12.

LACKAWANNA. *Bishop Head Residence* (2002) 10 Rosary Ave., 14218. Tel: 716-824-4644; Fax: 716-824-4844. Sr. Marguerite Gendreau, S.S.M.N., Admin.; Rev. Msgrs. S. Paul Ayoub (Retired); Anthony J. Jasinski (Retired); Leon M. Neu (Retired); Kevin T. O'Neill (Retired); Francis M. Skupien (Retired); Paul F. Stengel (Retired); Revs. Albert J. Bosack (Retired); Richard C. Coveny (Retired); Richard A. Massar (Retired); L. Antonio Rodriguez (Retired); Theodore C. Rog (Retired); Raymond F. Uschold (Retired).

LEROY. *Order of the BVM of Mercy/Mercedarian Friars*, Mercygrove, 7758 E. Main Rd., 14482-9701. Tel: 585-768-7110; Fax: 585-768-4803. Web: www.orderofmercy.org. Revs. Eugene Costa, O.de.M., Novice Master; Michael R. Rock, O.de.M., Pastor Our Lady of Mercy & St. Brigid; Timothy Brady, O.de.M, Local Supr. & Parochial Vicar; Bro. Matthew J. Levis, O.de.M., Pastoral Assoc. United States headquarters for the community. Novitiate formation community. Total in Community: Professed Religious 4.

St. Raymond Nonnatus Novitiate (1948) Order of the BVM of Mercy.; Residence for religious serving Our Lady of Mercy and St. Brigid Parishes., Mercygrove, 7758 E. Main Rd., 14482-9701. Tel: 585-768-7110; Fax: 585-768-4803. Web: www.orderofmercy.org. Revs. Eugene Costa, O.de.M., Novice Master; Timothy Brady, O.de.M, Supr. & Parochial Vicar; Michael R. Rock, O.de.M.; Bro. Matthew J. Levis, O.de.M., Pastoral Assoc.

NIAGARA UNIVERSITY. *Vincentian Community at Niagara University*, Vincentian Residence, 14109-2209. Tel: 716-286-8110; Fax: 716-286-8766. Email: jhubbert@niagara.edu. Bros. Martin J. Schneider, C.M.; Augustine D. Towey, C.M.; Revs. Stephen J. Denig, C.M.; Joseph G. Hubbert, C.M., Supr.; Bruce J. Krause, C.M.; Joseph L. Levesque, C.M.; John T. Maher, C.M.; Thomas F. McKenna, C.M. Total in Residence 8.

NORTH TONAWANDA. *Society of the Catholic Apostolate, Infant Jesus Delegature*, 3452 Niagara Falls Blvd., P.O. Box 563, 14120-0563. Tel: 716-694-4313; Fax: 716-743-5430. Revs. John Posiewala, S.A.C., Supr. & Prov. Delegate; Severyn J. Koszyk, S.A.C.; George C. Maj, S.A.C.

ST. BONAVENTURE. *St. Bonaventure Friary* (1856) 14778. Tel: 716-375-2416; Fax: 716-375-2424. Email: skellogg@sbu.edu. Web: www.sbu.edu. Revs. Michael Blastic, O.F.M., Ph.D.; David D. Blake, O.F.M., Ph.D.; Michael D. Calabria, O.F.M., M.A., Vicar; Michael F. Cusato, O.F.M., Ph.D.; Robert Karris, O.F.M., Th.D.; Harry Monaco, O.F.M.; Peter Schneible, O.F.M., Ph.D.; Xavier Seubert, O.F.M., S.T.D., Guardian; James Vacco, O.F.M., M.A.; Allen Weber, O.F.M., Ph.D.; Bros. Christopher Coccia, O.F.M., Vicar; F. Edward Coughlin, O.F.M., Ph.D.; David Haack, O.F.M., Ph.D.; Robert Lentz, O.F.M., B.A.; Basil J. Valente, O.F.M., M.T.S. Fathers 10; Brothers 5.

TONAWANDA. *O'Hara Residence* (1995) 69 O'Hara Rd., 14150-6227. Tel: 716-743-0037; Fax: 716-743-8772. Rev. Msgrs. Angelo M. Caligiuri (Retired); Anthony J. Caligiuri (Retired); James N. Connelly (Retired); Thomas E. Crane (Retired); Rev. Salvatore J. Cusimano (Retired); Rev. Msgrs. Charles T. Griffin (Retired); Leo E. Hammerl (Retired); Paul R. Juenker (Retired); Dino J. Lorenzetti (Retired); Edward J. Sobierajski (Retired); Richard L. Wetter (Retired); Rupert A. Wright (Retired). Total in Residence 13; Total Staff 7.

WILLIAMSVILLE. *Consolata Fathers*, 35 Brompton Rd., P.O. Box 570, 14221. Tel: 716-634-5678; 716-634-3793. Revs. John N. Reuther, I.M.C., Admin.; Robert Rezac, I.M.C., Supr.; James Kingori, I.M.C. (Kenya).

[P] CONVENTS AND RESIDENCES FOR SISTERS

BUFFALO. *Discalced Carmelite Monastery of St. Teresa of the Child Jesus* (1920) 75 Carmel Rd., 14214. Tel: 716-837-6499; Fax: 716-837-3517. Sr. Mother Miriam of Jesus, O.C.D., Prioress. Cloistered Professed Sisters 11; Extern Professed Sisters 2; Novices 1.

Holy Name Province - Provincial Motherhouse Tel: 716-754-4312, Ext. 9777; Fax: 716-754-7657. Email: office@franciscans-stella-niagara.org. Web: www.franciscans-stella-niagara.org.

Sisters of St. Francis of Holy Name Province, Inc., 4421 Lower River Rd., Stella Niagara, 14144-1001. Tel: 716-754-4312, Ext. 9777; Fax: 716-754-7657. Email: office@franciscans-stella-niagara.org. Sr. Dorothy Mueller, O.S.F., Prov. Min.

Center of Renewal, Inc., 4421 Lower River Rd., Stella Niagara, 14144. Tel: 716-754-7376; Fax: 716-754-1223. Email: hospitality@center-of-renewal.org. Web: www.center-of-renewal.org. Sr. Dorothy Mueller, O.S.F., Prov. Min.

Francis Center, 335 24th St., Niagara Falls, 14303. Tel: 716-234-2050; Fax: 716-282-3783. Email: bneumeister14301@yahoo.com. Sr. Dorothy Mueller, O.S.F., Prov. Min.

Stella Niagara Education Park, Inc., 4421 Lower River Rd., Stella Niagara, 14144. Tel: 716-754-4314; Fax: 716-754-2964. Email: snepoffice@yahoo.com. Web: www.stellaniagara.org. Sr. Dorothy Mueller, O.S.F., Prov. Min.

The Stella Niagara Education Park Endowment Foundation, 4421 Lower River Rd., Stella Niagara, 14144. Tel: 716-754-4314; Fax: 716-754-2964. Email: snepoffice@yahoo.com. Web: www.stellaniagara.org. Sr. Dorothy Mueller, O.S.F., Prov. Min.

The Sisters of St. Francis Retirement Fund, 4421 Lower River Rd., Stella Niagara, 14144. Tel: 716-754-4312, Ext. 9727; Fax: 716-754-7657. Email: serbacki@franciscans-stella-niagara.org. Sr. Dorothy Mueller, O.S.F., Prov. Min.

The Providence Fund, 4421 Lower River Rd., Stella Niagara, 14144. Tel: 716-754-4312; Fax: 716-754-7657. Sr. Dorothy Mueller, O.S.F., Prov. Min.

Buffalo Academy of the Sacred Heart, Inc., 3860 Main St., 14226-3398. Tel: 716-834-2101; Fax: 716-834-2944. Email: jdemert@sacredheartacademy.org. Web: www.sacredheartacademy.org.

Immaculate Heart of Mary and Convent (1900) Villa Maria, 600 Doat St., 14211. Tel: 716-892-4141; Fax: 716-892-4177. Email: ihmcon@feliciansisters.org. Web: www.feliciansisters.org. Sisters M. Charlene Nowak, C.S.S.F., M.A.T., Co-Min.; M. Kevin Szeluga, C.S.S.F., Co-Min. Felician Sisters 160.

Monastery of Our Lady of the Rosary (1905) 335 Doat St., 14211-2199. Tel: 716-892-0066; Fax: 716-892-8846. Email: mgemma@opnuns.org. Sr. Mother Mary Gemma, O.P., Prioress; Rev. Jacob Restrick, O.P., Chap.

Dominican Nuns of the Perpetual Rosary, Buffalo, NY Professed Nuns 24; Postulants 1.

Sisters of Mercy of the Americas-New York, Pennsylvania, Pacific West Community, Inc., 625 Abbott Rd., 14220. Tel: 716-826-5051; Fax: 716-826-1518. Email: nhoff@mercynyppaw.org. Web: www.mercynyppaw.org. Sr. Nancy Hoff, R.S.M., Pres. Vowed Members 490; Associates 394.

Mercy Center, Residence for Sisters: 625 Abbott Rd., 14220. Tel: 716-825-5531; Fax: 716-826-1518.

Sisters of Social Service of the Diocese of Buffalo, Inc. (1923) 296 Summit Ave., 14214-1936. Tel: 716-834-0197; Fax: 716-834-6168. Email: sssbuf@verizon.net. Web: www.sistersofsocialservicebuffalo.org. Sr. Teresina Joo, S.S.S., District Moderator. Sisters 4.

Other Convents:

Generalate, Bathori Laszlo u 10, Budapest H-1029 Hungary. Tel: 011-361-275-7057; Fax: 011-361-391-6229. Email: sss.gen@hcbc.hu. Sr. Agnes Pataki, S.S.S., Gen. Moderator.

Sara House, 42 Linden Ave., 14214. Tel: 716-836-0685. Sisters 3.

Bethany House, 152 Kinsey Ave., Kenmore, 14217. Tel: 716-873-6179. Sisters 1.

Sisters of St. Mary of Namur (1819) St. Mary Center, St. Mary Center, 241 Lafayette Ave., 14213. Tel: 716-884-8221; Fax: 716-884-6598. Email: ssmnprov@verizon.net. Web: www.ssmn.us. Sisters Caroline Smith, S.S.M.N., Prov. Supr.; Marian Baumler, S.S.M.N., Prov. Councillor. Provincial House of the Sisters of St. Mary of Namur. Professed Sisters 87.

Annunciation Convent, 245 Lafayette Ave., 14213.

Sisters of St. Mary, 160 Lovering Ave., 14216.

Sisters of St. Mary, 165 University Ave., 14214.

Sisters of St. Mary, 8691 Supervisor Ave., Colden, 14033.

Sisters of St. Mary, 3100 Elmwood Ave., Kenmore, 14217.

Sisters of St. Mary, 83 LaSalle Ave., Kenmore, 14217.

Sisters of St. Mary, 104 Garden St., Lockport, 14094.

Sisters of St. Mary, 2484 River Rd., Niagara Falls, 14304.

ALLEGANY. *Franciscan Sisters of Allegany, New York, Inc.* (1859) 115 E. Main St., 14706. Tel: 716-373-0200; Fax: 716-372-5774. Email: fsa@fsallegany.org. Web: www.alleganyfranciscans.org. Sr. M. Avril Chin Fatt, O.S.F., Congregational Min.

St. Elizabeth Motherhouse (1859) 115 E. Main St., 14706. Tel: 716-373-0200; Fax: 716-372-5774. Email: fsa@fsallegany.org. Web: www.alleganyfranciscans.org. Sisters M. Avril Chin Fatt, O.S.F., Congregational Min. & Pres.; Jean Hayes, O.S.F., Local Min. Sisters 88.

CLARENCE. *Congregation of the Sisters of St. Joseph Generalate*, Administrative Offices, 10324 Main St., 14031. Tel: 716-759-6454; Fax: 716-759-6415. Email: buffssj@aol.com. Web: www.ssjbuffalo.org. Sr. Jean Marie Zirnheld, S.S.J., Pres. Professed Sisters 97.

Sisters of St. Joseph, Clarence Residence, 4975 Strickler Rd., 14031. Tel: 716-759-6893; Fax: 716-759-2488. Email: ssjbuffalo@msn.com. Sr. Ruth Haselbauer, Coord. Total in Residence 41; Total Staff 41.

HAMBURG. *Immaculate Conception Convent*, 5286 S. Park Ave., 14075. Tel: 716-649-1205; Fax: 716-649-5958. Web: www.franciscansistersofstjoseph.org. Rev. Mark David Skura, O.F.M.Conv., Chap.; Sr. Judith Elaine Salzman, F.S.S.J., Gen. Min. Motherhouse of the Franciscan Sisters of St. Joseph Sisters in Residence 63; Sisters in Congregation 100.

Union of Our Lady of Charity (1855) *U.S. Province*, 3800 Howard Rd., 14075. Tel: 716-648-4988; Fax: 716-648-3062. Email: altarbread@verizon.net. Sr. Rosemary Toth, Local Supr. Sisters 7.

LEROY. *Sisters of Our Lady of Mercy (SOLM) (Mercedarians)* (1864) 27 Lake St., 14482. Tel: 585-768-8053. Email: Mercy@Rochester.rr.com. Sr. Rosaria Savarimuthu, S.O.L.M., Supr. Sisters 3.

LEWISTON. *Sisters of the Sacred Heart of Jesus (S.S.H.J.)*, Sacred Heart Villa School & Convent, 5269 Lewiston Rd., 14092. Tel: 716-284-8273; Fax: 716-284-8273. Email: sacredhrtv@yahoo.com. Sr. M. Terenzia Guidice, S.S.H.J., Supr. Sisters 10.

SILVER CREEK. *Missionary Sisters of St. Columban, St. Columban's on the Lake* (1924) 2546 Lake Rd., 14136. Tel: 716-934-4515; Fax: 716-934-3919. Email: sisters@stcolumbanshome.org. Web: www.columbansisters.org. Sr. Corona Colleary, S.S.C., U.S. Area Coord. Professed Sisters 11.

WEST SENECA. *Sisters of Charity of St. Vincent de Paul of Zagreb, Croatia*, 171 Knox Ave., 14224. Tel: 716-825-5859; 716-822-6841; Fax: 716-822-6841. Email: milosrdnice@roadrunner.com. Sr. Stella Simetich, V.Z., Supr.

Sisters of Charity of St. Vincent de Paul of Zagreb, Croatia - U.S.A. Delegacy Headquarters Professed Sisters 9.

WILLIAMSVILLE. *Sisters of St. Francis of the Neumann Communities, Western New York Region, St. Mary of the Angels Convent*, P.O. Box 275, 14231. Tel: 716-632-2155; Fax: 716-632-0339. Sisters Roberta Smith, O.S.F., Gen. Councilor; Beatrice Leising, O.S.F., Regl. Co-Min. Professed Sisters in the Region 105.

[Q] RETREAT HOUSES

DERBY. *St. Columban Center* (1947) 795 Main St., 14203. 6892 Lake Shore Rd., P.O. Box 816, 14047-0816.

WEST CLARKSVILLE. *Mount Irenaeus, Franciscan Mountain Retreat & Holy Peace Friary* (1982) P.O. Box 100, 14786. Tel: 585-973-2470; Fax: 585-973-2400. Email: mmarc@sbu.edu. Web: www.mounti.com. Revs. Daniel P. Riley, O.F.M., M.A., Pres. & Guardian; Daniel A. Hurley, O.F.M., M.A.; Bro. Joseph A. Kotula, O.F.M., Ph.D., Vicar; Revs. Louis M. McCormick, O.F.M., D.Min.; Robert Struzynski, O.F.M.; Bro. Kevin Kriso, O.F.M. Order of Friars Minor Holy Name Province. Total in Residence 6.

[R] CAMPUS MINISTRY AND NEWMAN CENTERS

BUFFALO. *Buffalo State College* 1219 Elmwood Ave., 14222. Tel: 716-882-1080; Fax: 716-882-6914. Email: bscnewmancenter@yahoo.com. Web: www.buffalostate.edu/newmanct. Rev. Patrick J. Zengierski, Ph.D., Dir. & Vicar Campus Ministry; Sr. Candice Tucci, O.S.F., Campus Min.; William Vaughan, Campus Min.; Dayana Castillo, Peer Min.; Jessica Hall, Peer Min.; Kara Lindbloom, Peer Min.; Alesandra Mercedes, Peer Min.; William Sanchez, Peer Min.; Henry Zomerfeld.

Trocaire College 360 Choate Ave., 14220. Tel: 716-827-2489; Fax: 716-825-0416. Sr. Marie Andre Main, R.S.M., Dir.

Villa Maria College 240 Pine Ridge Rd., 14225. Tel: 716-896-0700; Fax: 716-896-0705. Web: www.villa.edu. Frank Antonucci, Dir.

ALFRED. *Alfred University and Alfred State College Campus Ministry* Lower College Dr., P.O. Box 1154, 14802. Tel: 607-587-9411; Fax: 607-587-9431. Email: stjude.alfred@gmail.com. Mr. Chris Yarnal, Dir. Campus Ministry.

Canisius College, Campus Ministry Office 2001 Main St., 14208. Tel: 716-888-2420; Fax: 716-888-3144. Email: campmin@canisius.edu. Web: www.canisus.edu/camp-minist/. Revs. John P. Bucki, S.J., Dir.; Thomas A. Colgan, S.J., Assoc. Campus Minister; Ms. Luanne Firestone, Assoc. Campus Min.; Ms. Susan Fischer, Assoc. Campus Min.; Ms. Sarah Signorino, Assoc. Campus Min.; Mr. Joseph VanVolkenburg, Assoc. Campus Min.

D'Youville College 320 Porter Ave., 14201. Tel: 716-829-7672; Fax: 716-829-7760. Rev. Thomas Ribits, O.S.F.S., Dir. of Campus Min.; Rev. Jan Mahle.

Hilbert College, Campus Ministry Office 5200 S. Park Ave., Hamburg, 14075. Tel: 716-649-7900; Fax: 716-649-0702. Deacon Dennis P. Conroy.

Niagara University Campus Ministry, P.O. Box 2016, Niagara University, 14109. Tel: 716-286-8400; Fax: 716-286-8477. Email: ministry@niagara.edu. Web: www.niagara.edu/ministry. Revs. John T. Maher, C.M., Dir. Campus Ministry; Bruce J. Krause, C.M., Campus Min.; Ms. Monica Saltarelli, Campus Min.

State University College at Fredonia 222 Temple St., Fredonia, 14063. Tel: 716-679-4686; Fax: 716-679-3486. Nathan Kropp, M.S., M.A., Dir. Campus Ministry.

State University of New York at Buffalo (Main St. South Campus) St. Joseph University Parish, 3269 Main St., 14214. Tel: 716-833-0298; Fax: 716-833-7339. Web: www.newman.buffalo.edu. Rev. Jacob C. Ledwon, Dir.; Mr. Michael Hayes, Campus Min.

AMHERST. *State University of New York at Buffalo (North Campus) Newman Center* 495 Skinnersville Rd., 14228. Tel: 716-636-7495; Fax: 716-568-0692. Email: prspat@buffalo.edu. Web: www.newman.buffalo.edu. Rev. Msgr. J. Patrick Keleher, Dir.; Ms. Katy Koch, Campus Min.; David Greenman, Devel.

ST. BONAVENTURE. *St. Bonaventure University* P.O. Box AR, 14778. Tel: 716-375-2600; Fax: 716-375-2618. Robert M. Donius, M.A., Vice Pres. Univ. Ministries; Rev. Daniel A. Hurley, O.F.M., M.A.; Rev. Daniel McKee; Revs. Daniel P. Riley, O.F.M., M.A.; Robert Struzynski, O.F.M.; Bro. Joseph A. Kotula, O.F.M., Ph.D.; Mrs. Della Moore; Mr. Trevor Thompson.

[S] CAMPS AND COMMUNITY CENTERS

ANGOLA. *St. Vincent de Paul Camp* Tel: 716-549-2950; Fax: 716-882-3556. Email: info@svdpwny.org. Web: www.SVDPWNY.org. Mailing Address: 1298 Main St., 14209. Tel: 716-882-3360; Fax: 716-882-3556. (Camp for needy boys and girls).

SALAMANCA. *Camp Turner* (Coed)., Office: P.O. Box 264, 14779. Tel: 716-354-4555; Fax: 716-354-2055. Email: Director@CampTurner.com. Web: www.campturner.com. John Mann, Dir.

[T] MISCELLANEOUS

BUFFALO. *Catholic Communications of Western New York, Inc.*, 795 Main St., 14203. Tel: 716-847-8719; Fax: 716-847-8722. Email: comm@buffalodiocese.org. Catholic Communications of Western New York produces and distributes Catholic print and electronic programs.

Catholic Health System Program of All-Inclusive Care for the Elderly, Inc. (CHS PACE), Seton Professional Building, 2121 Main St., Ste. 300, 14214. Thomas Schifferli, Pres.

Catholic Union Store (1899) 795 Main St., 14203. Tel: 716-847-8715; Fax: 716-847-8702. Email: cus@buffalodiocese.org.

Chestnut Ridge Medical Supplies, Inc. dba Catholic Health Infusion Pharmacy 5539 Broadway, Lancaster, 14086. *c/o Catholic Health Systems,* 2121 Main St., Ste. 300, 14214. A Catholic Health System organization.

St. Clare Apartments Housing Development Fund Company, Inc. Low income housing for the elderly age 62 and over., c/o Delta Development of Western New York, 525 Washington St., 14203. Tel: 716-847-1635; Fax: 716-856-7201. Email: bernadette.harlan@ccwny.org. Web: www.deltadevelopmentwny.com. Bernadette Harlan, Exec. Dir. Residents 39; Staff 3.

Delta Development of Western New York, Inc., c/o Delta Development of WNY, Inc., 525 Washington St., 14203. Tel: 716-847-1635; Fax: 716-856-7201. Bernadette Harlan, Exec. Dir.; Rev. Msgr. Joseph J. Sicari, Pres., Catholic Charities. Staff 5.

50-60 Kosciuzko Street Housing Development Fund Company, Inc. Special Purpose Housing for the chronically mentally ill., *c/o Delta Development of WNY, Inc.,* 525 Washington St., 14203. Tel: 716-847-1635; Fax: 716-856-7201. Email: bernadette.harlan@ccwny.org. Web: www.deltadevelopmentwny.com. Bernadette Harlan, Exec. Dir. Residents 5; Staff 2.

The Foundation of the Roman Catholic Diocese of Buffalo, NY, Inc., 795 Main St., 14203-1250. Tel: 716-847-8370; Fax: 716-847-5557. Email: devoffice@buffalodiocese.org. Web: www.FRCDB.org. David Kersten, Exec. Dir.

Franciscan Mystery Players, Inc., 102 Seymour St., 14210. Tel: 315-415-3739. Web: www.mysteryplay.org. Rev. Francis Pompei, O.F.M., Dir.

Gerard Place Housing Development Fund Company, Inc., 2515 Bailey Ave., 14215. Tel: 716-897-9948; Fax: 716-897-9953. Email: gerardhdfc@aol.com. Web: www.gerardplace.org. David Zapfel, M.S., Dir.

Immaculate Heart of Mary Home for Children, Inc. (1896) 600 Doat St., 14211. Tel: 716-892-4141; Fax: 716-892-4177. Web: www.feliciansisters.org.

St. Joseph Investment Fund, Inc., 795 Main St., 14203. Tel: 716-856-5500. Email: dslubecky@buffalodiocese.org. Rev. Msgr. David S. Slubecky, J.C.L., S.T.L., V.G., Pres.

Kolping Catholic Young Men's Association of Buffalo, NY dba Kolping Society of Buffalo 1145 Cleveland Dr., 14225. Tel: 716-632-7360. Willi Evelt, Pres.

La Casa De Los Tainos Housing Development Fund Company, Inc., c/o Delta Development of WNY, Inc., 525 Washington St., 14203. Tel: 716-847-1635; Fax: 716-856-7201. Email: bernadette.harlan@ccwny.org. Web: www.deltadevelopmentwny.com. Bernadette Harlan, Exec. Dir. Low income housing for the elderly age 62 & over. Residents 49; Staff 2.

Monsignor Adamski Village Housing Development Fund Company, Inc., 123 Townsend St., 14212. Tel: 716-854-5510; Fax: 716-854-0170.

Monsignor Adamski Village, Inc., 855 Williams St., 14206. 123 Townsend St., 14212. Facility for elderly and handicapped persons of low income.

The Monsignor Carr Institute, 76 W. Humboldt Pkwy., 14214. Tel: 716-835-9745; Fax: 716-835-6785. Web: www.ccwny.org. Brian T. O'Herron, M.Ed., M.B.A., Dir. Msgr. Carr Institute; Bruce Pace, Ph.D., Dir. Children's Mental Health Clinics. Licensed outpatient mental health and substance abuse treatment, community outreach team, senior advocacy and socialization, marriage counseling, school-based drug prevention, adult psychosocial club, abstinence until marriage education, creative arts studio. Also licensed outpatient mental health children's clinics serving seriously emotionally disturbed children and providing collateral services for families. Children's clinics in Niagara Falls, North Tonawanda and Lockport. Total Assisted 14,364; Total Staff 100.

Monsignor Kirby Apartments Housing Development Fund Company, Inc., c/o Delta Development of WNY, Inc., 525 Washington St., 14203. Tel: 716-847-1635, Ext. 3029; Fax: 716-856-7201. Email: bernadette.harlan@ccwny.org. Web: www.deltadevelopmentwny.com. Bernadette Harlan, Exec. Dir. Low income housing for the elderly age 62 and over. Total in Residence 39; Total Staff 2.

Mount St. Mary's Housing Development Fund Company, Inc., c/o Delta Development of WNY, Inc., 525 Washington St., 14203. Tel: 716-847-1635; Fax: 716-856-7201. Email: bernadette.harlan@ccwny.org. Web: www.deltadevelopmentwny.com. Bernadette Harlan, Exec. Dir. Total in Residence 39; Staff 2.

Msgr. Gambino Tower, Ltd. dba Santa Maria Towers c/o Delta Development of WNY, Inc., 525 Washington St., 14203. Tel: 716-847-1635; Fax: 716-856-7201. Email: bernadette.harlan@ccwny.org. Web: www.deltadevelopmentwny.com. Bernadette Harlan, Exec. Dir. Housing for mobility impaired and elderly of low income. Total in Residence 114; Staff 5.

Nazareth Nursing Home, 291 North St., 14201. *c/o Catholic Health Systems,* 2121 Main St., Ste. 300, 14214.

NyPPaW Fides, Inc., 625 Abbott Rd., 14220. Tel: 716-826-5051. Sr. Jo Anne Courneen, R.S.M., Chair.

158 Chenango Street Housing Development Fund Company, Inc. dba St. John Bosco Apartments c/o Delta Development of WNY, Inc., 525 Washington St., 14203. Tel: 716-847-1635; Fax: 716-856-7201. Email: bernadette.harlan@ccwny.org. Web: www.deltadevelopmentwny.com. Bernadette Harlan, Exec. Dir. Low income housing for the elderly age 62 and over. Staff 3; Residents 12.

Our Lady of Victory Community Housing Development Organization, Inc., c/o Catholic Health Systems, 2121 Main St., Ste. 300, 14214. Tel: 716-923-4802; Fax: 716-604-1805. Email: agb@chsbuffalo.org. Christine J. Kluckhohn, Pres.

Our Lady of Victory Renaissance Corporation, c/o Catholic Health Systems, 2121 Main St., Ste. 300, 14214. Tel: 716-923-4802; Fax: 716-604-1805. Email: agb@chsbuffalo.org. Christine J. Kluckhohn, Pres., OLV Renaissance.

Our Mother of Good Counsel Housing Development Fund Co., Inc., c/o Delta Development of WNY, Inc., 525 Washington St., 14203. Tel: 716-847-1635; Fax: 716-856-7201. Email: bernadette.harlan@ccwny.org. Web: www.deltadevelopmentwny.com. Bernadette Harlan, Exec. Dir. Housing for mobility impaired & elderly of low income. Total in Residence 39; Total Staff 2.

St. Rita's Home, Inc. (1940) 600 Doat St., 14211. Tel: 716-892-4141; Fax: 716-892-4177. Web: www.feliciansisters.org.

Salesian Studios, 152 Plymouth Ave., 14201-1214. Tel: 716-886-6597. Rev. Thomas Ribits, O.S.F.S.

Timon Towers Housing Development Fund Company, Inc., c/o Delta Development of WNY, Inc., 525 Washington St., 14203. Tel: 716-847-1635; Fax: 716-856-7201. Email: bernadette.harlan@ccwny.org. Web: deltadevelopmentwny.com. Bernadette Harlan, Exec. Dir. Low income housing for the mobility impaired and elderly. Total Staff 5; Total in Residence 124.

St. Timothy's Park Villa Housing Development Fund Company, Inc., c/o Delta Development of WNY, Inc., 525 Washington St., 14203. Tel: 716-847-1635; Fax: 716-856-7201. Email: bernadette.harlan@ccwny.org. Web: www.deltadevelopmentwny.com. Bernadette Harlan, Exec. Dir. Low income housing for the elderly age 62 and over. Total in Residence 49; Total Staff 2.

Western New York Catholic Healthcare Corporation, 2121 Main St., Ste. 300, 14214.

Wheatfield Housing Development Fund Company, Inc., c/o Delta Development of WNY, Inc., 525 Washington St., 14203. Tel: 716-847-1635; Fax: 716-856-7201. Email: bernadette.harlan@ccwny.org. Web: www.deltadevelopmentwny.com. Bernadette Harlan, Exec. Dir. Low income housing for the elderly age 62 and over. Apartments 49; Staff 2.

ALLEGANY. *Canticle Farm, Inc.,* 115 E. Main St., 14706. Tel: 716-373-0200; Fax: 716-373-3554. Email: canticleoffice@yahoo.com. Kristine Later, Bd. Chairperson; Sr. Joyce Ramage, O.S.F., Pres.

Dr. Lyle F. Renodin Foundation, Inc., 115 E. Main St., 14706. Tel: 716-373-0200; Fax: 716-372-5774. Web: www.alleganyfranciscans.org. Gail Sweitzer, Pres.

St. Elizabeth Mission Society, Inc. (1947) 115 E. Main St., 14706. Tel: 716-373-1130; Fax: 716-373-9324. Email: stelizmission@fsallegany.org. Web: www.stelizabethmissionsociety.com. Sr. M. Chris Doherty, O.S.F., Dir.

AMHERST. *Victorious Missionaries,* 911B Robin Rd., 14228. Tel: 716-639-7542. Miss Carol A. Buchla, Pres. A spiritual and social movement for the handicapped and chronically ill.

ATHOL SPRINGS. *Fr. Justin Rosary Hour,* 4190 St. Francis Dr., P.O. Box 454, 14010. Tel: 716-627-3861; Fax: 716-926-8501. Email: info@rosaryhour.net. Web: www.rosaryhour.net. Bro. Daniel Geary, O.F.M.Conv., Exec. Dir.; Jerry Kornowicz, Office Mgr. A prayer and catechetical program in Polish and English aired over various radio stations and internet, conducted by St. Anthony of Padua Province of the Order of Friars Minor Conventual. Priests 1; Brothers 1; Lay Staff 5; Total Staff 7.

KENMORE. *Catholic Cemeteries of the Roman Catholic Diocese of Buffalo, Inc.,* 4000 Elmwood Ave., 14217. Tel: 716-873-6500; Fax: 716-873-3247. Email: ccolao@buffalodiocese.org. Web: www.buffalocatholiccemeteries.org. Carmen A. Colao, Dir. Cemeteries: Assumption, Grand Island; Gate of Heaven, Niagara Falls; Holy Cross, Lackawanna; Holy Sepulchre, Cheektowaga; Mount Olivet, Kenmore; Queen of Heaven, Lockport.

K M H Homes, INC., 1503 Military Rd., 14217. Tel: 716-447-6600. *c/o Catholic Health Systems,* 2121 Main St., Ste. 300, 14214. Christine J. Kluckhohn, CEO & Pres., Continuing Care. A holding company of the Catholic Health System.

LACKAWANNA. *Mother of Divine Grace Housing Development Fund Company, Inc.* (1991) 780 Ridge Rd., 14218. Tel: 716-828-9500; Fax: 716-828-9526. Email: baker@buffnet.net. Web: www.bakervictoryservices.org. James J. Casion, CEO. Sponsored by Baker Victory Services., Purpose: To provide housing for persons of low income, particularly handicapped mentally retarded and developmentally disabled adults. Total in Residence 10; Total Staff 11.

Nativity Housing Development Fund Company, Inc. (1992) 780 Ridge Rd., 14218. Tel: 716-828-9500; Fax: 716-828-9526. Email: baker@buffnet.net. Web: www.bakervictoryservices.org. James J. Casion, CEO. Sponsored by Baker Victory Services., Purpose: To provide housing for persons of low income, particularly handicapped mentally retarded and developmentally disabled adults. Total in Residence 8; Total Staff 9.

Our Lady of Peace Housing Development Fund Company, Inc. (2000) 780 Ridge Rd., 14218. Tel: 716-828-9500; Fax: 716-828-9526. Email: baker@buffnet.net. Web: www.bakervictoryservices.org. James J. Casion, CEO. Sponsored by Baker Victory Services., Purpose: To provide housing for persons of low income, particularly handicapped mentally retarded and developmentally disabled adults. Total in Residence 6; Total Staff 10.

Our Lady of Victory Homes of Charity (1851) 780 Ridge Rd., 14218. Tel: 716-828-9648; Fax: 716-828-9643. Email: baker@buffnet.net. Web: www.OurLadyofVictory.org.

Our Lady of Victory Homes of Charity

Society for the Protection of Destitute Roman Catholic Children at Buffalo, NY

Father Baker's, (Formerly Association of Our Lady of Victory); Includes the following Institutions: Baker Victory Services 716-828-9500 or 1-888-287-1160 (Formerly Baker Hall, Our Lady of Victory Infant Home, St. Joseph Orphanage and St. John's Protectory). Total Assisted Annually 4,824; Total Staff 100.

LEWISTON. *Basilica of the National Shrine of Our Lady of Fatima, Inc.* 1023 Swann Rd., P.O. Box 167, Youngstown, 14174-0167. Tel: 716-754-7489; Fax: 716-754-9130. Email: office@fatimashrine.com. Web: www.fatimashrine.com. Revs. Julio M. Ciavaglia, C.R.S.P., Rector & Shrine Dir.; Paul M. Keeling, C.R.S.P., Assoc. Dir. & Treas.; Peter M. Calabrese, C.R.S.P., Assoc. Dir.; Richard M. Delzingaro, C.R.S.P. Priests 3; Total Staff 18.

NIAGARA UNIVERSITY. *Our Lady of Angels Association* (1918) P.O. Box 1918, 14109-1918. Tel: 716-754-0035; Fax: 716-754-0137. Email: novena@niagara.edu. Web: www.ourladyofangels.net. Deborah Korzak, Dir. of Devel. Development Office for the Congregation of the Mission, Eastern Province. Total Staff 6.

NORTH TONAWANDA. *Shrine of the Infant Jesus* 3452 Niagara Falls Blvd., P.O. Box 563, 14120-0563. Tel: 716-694-4313; Fax: 716-743-5430. Administered by the Pallottine Fathers.

STELLA NIAGARA. *DeSales Resources and Ministries, Inc.* (1980) 4421 Lower River Rd., 14144-1001. Tel: 716-754-4948; 800-782-2270; Fax: 716-754-4948. Email: desales@desalesresource.org. Web: www.desalesresource.org. Rev. John Graden, O.S.F.S., Dir.; Joanne Kinney, Admin.; Laura Imerese, Business Mgr. Total Staff 3.

WILLIAMSVILLE. *Holy Family Home, c/o Sisters of St. Francis,* P.O. Box 275, 14231. Web: www.sosf.org.

St. Francis Asylum Corporation of the City of Buffalo, Sisters of St. Francis, P.O. Box 275, 14231. Web: www.sosf.org.

[U] CLOSED AND MERGED PARISHES

BUFFALO. *St. Agnes* (1883) Closed in merger to form St. Katharine Drexel Parish. Records at St. Katharine Drexel Parish.

St. Ann Merged into SS. Columba-Brigid Parish. Currently a temporary second site for SS. Columba-Brigid. Records at SS. Columba-Brigid.

Annunciation Name changed when merged with Nativity and Our Lady of Loretto Parishes to form Our Lady of Hope Parish at the Annunciation site. Records at Our Lady of Hope.

St. Bartholomew Closed in merger with Blessed Trinity Parish. Records at the Catholic Center, 795 Main St., Buffalo, NY 14203. Tel: 716-847-5567.

St. Benedict the Moor Closed in merger to form St. Martin de Porres Parish. Records at the Catholic Center, 795 Main St. Buffalo, NY 14203. Tel: 716-847-5567.

St. Boniface Closed in merger to form St. Martin de Porres Parish. Records at the Catholic Center, 795 Main St. Buffalo, NY 14203. Tel: 716-847-5567.

St. Brigid Closed in merger with St. Columba Parish to form SS. Columba-Brigid Parish. Records at SS. Columba-Brigid Parish.

St. Elizabeth of Hungary (1906) Closed in merger with Assumption Parish. Records at Assumption Parish.

St. Florian (1917) Closed in a merger with All Saints Parish. Records at All Saints Parish.

St. Francis of Assisi Name changed when merged with St. Agnes and Visitation of the B.V.M. parishes to form St. Katharine Drexel Parish at the St. Francis of Assisi site. Records at St. Katharine Drexel Parish.

St. Francis Xavier (1849) Closed in a merger with Assumption Parish. Records at Assumption Parish.

St. Gerard (1902) Closed in merger with Blessed Trinity Parish. Records at Blessed Trinity Parish.

Holy Apostles SS. Peter and Paul (1909) Closed in merger to form St. Clare Parish. Records at St. Clare Parish.

Holy Name of Jesus Closed. Merged into St. John Gualbert Parish. Records at St. John Gualbert Parish.

Immaculate Conception (1849) Closed when merged into Holy Cross Parish. Records at Holy Cross Parish.

Immaculate Heart of Mary (1946) Closed in merger with St. Aloysius Gonzaga Parish, Cheektogawa. Records at St. Aloysius Gonzaga.

St. James (1916) Closed in merger with Blessed Trinity Parish. Records at Blessed Trinity Parish.

St. Joachim Closed. Records at the Catholic Center, 795 Main St. Buffalo, NY 14203. Tel: 716-847-5567.

St. John the Baptist (1867) Closed. Records at Assumption Parish.

St. John the Evangelist (1906) Closed in merger with St. Theresa Parish. Records at St. Theresa.

St. Luke Closed. Records at the Catholic Center, 795 Main St. Buffalo NY 14203. Tel: 716-847-5567.

St. Mary of Sorrows (1872) Closed & merged into SS Columba-Brigid Parish. Records at SS. Columba-Brigid Parish.

St. Matthew Closed in a merger to form St. Martin de Porres Parish. Records at the Catholic Center, 795 Main St. Buffalo, NY 14203. Tel: 716-847-5567.

St. Monica Closed. Records at the Catholic Center, 795 Main St. Buffalo, NY 14203. Tel: 716-847-5567.

The Nativity of the Blessed Virgin (1898) Closed in merger with Annunciation and Our Lady of Loretto parishes to form Our Lady of Hope Parish. Records at Our Lady of Hope.

Our Lady of Loretto (1940) Closed in merger with Annunciation and Nativity parishes to form Our Lady of Hope Parish. Records at Our Lady of Hope.

Our Lady of Lourdes Closed in merger to form St. Martin de Porres Parish. Records at the Catholic Center, 795 Main St. Buffalo, NY 14203. Tel: 716-847-5567.

Precious Blood (1899) Closed in merger to form St. Clare Parish. Records at St. Clare Parish.

Queen of Peace (1920) Closed. Merged into St. John Gualbert Parish. Records at St. John Gualbert Parish.

Queen of the Most Holy Rosary Closed. Records at the Catholic Center 795 Main St. Buffalo, NY 14203. Tel: 716-847-5567.

SS. Rita & Patrick (1854) Closed in merger to form St. Clare Parish. Records at St. Clare Parish.

St. Stephen Name changed when merged with SS. Rita and Patrick, Holy Apostles, SS. Peter & Paul, St. Valentine and Precious Blood Parishes to form St. Clare Parish at the St. Stephen site. Records at St. Clare Parish.

Transfiguration Closed. Records at the Catholic Center, 795 Main St. Buffalo, NY 14203. Tel: 716-847-5567.

St. Valentine (1920) Closed in merger to form St. Clare Parish. Records at St. Clare Parish.

St. Vincent de Paul Closed. Merged into Blessed Trinity Parish. Records at the Catholic Center, 795 Main St. Buffalo, NY 14203. Tel: 716-847-5567.

The Visitation of the B.V.M. (1898) Closed in merger to form St. Katharine Drexel Parish. Records at St. Katharine Drexel Parish.

ALBION. *St. Joseph* Name changed when merged with St. Mary Assumption to form Holy Family Parish. Records at Holy Family.

St. Mary Assumption (1891) Merged with St. Joseph Parish to form Holy Family Parish at the St. Joseph site. St. Mary Assumption became an oratory of Holy Family Parish. Records at Holy Family Parish.

ANGELICA. *Sacred Heart* (1848) Closed in merger to form Holy Family of Jesus, Mary & Joseph Parish in Belmont. Records at Holy Family of Jesus, Mary & Joseph Parish.

ARCADE. *SS. Peter & Paul* Name changed when merged with St. Mary, East Arcade and Blessed Sacrament, Delevan to form St. Mary Parish in Arcade and using both the Arcade and East Arcade sites. Records at St. Mary Parish, Arcade.

ATTICA. *St. Vincent de Paul* Name changed when merged with St. Joseph Parish in Varysburg to form SS. Joachim & Anne Parish using both the Attica and Varysburg sites. Parish records at SS. Joachim and Anne Parish in Attica.

BARKER. *St. Patrick* (1865) Name changed with merged with St. Joseph Parish, Lyndonville, to form Our Lady of the Lake Parish. Both the Barker and Lyndonville sites are used. Records at Our Lady of the Lake, Barker.

BATAVIA. *St. Anthony* (1908) Merged with Sacred Heart Parish to form Ascension Parish using both sites. Records at Ascension Parish.

St. Joseph Name changed when merged with St. Mary to form Resurrection Parish using both sites. Records at Resurrection Parish.

St. Mary (1906) Merged with St. Joseph to form Resurrection Parish using both sites. Records at Resurrection Parish.

Sacred Heart Named changed when merged with St. Anthony Parish to form Ascension Parish using both sites. Records at Ascension Parish.

BELMONT. *St. Mary* Named changed when merged with St. Joseph, Scio and Sacred Heart, Angelica to form Holy Family of Jesus, Mary & Joseph at the Belmont site. Records at Holy Family of Jesus, Mary & Joseph.

BEMUS POINT. *Our Lady of Lourdes* Named changed when merged with St. Mary, Mayville to form St. Mary of Lourdes Parish using both sites. Records at St. Mary of Lourdes, Bemus Point.

BENNINGTON CENTER. *Sacred Heart of Jesus* (1872) Merged with Our Lady of Good Counsel, Darien Center to form Immaculate Heart of Mary Parish using both sites. Records at Immaculate Heart of Mary, Bennington Center.

BLISS. *St. Joseph* (1907) Closed in merger to form St. Isidore Parish, Perry & Silver Springs. Records at St. Isidore Parish, Perry.

BRANT. *Our Lady of Mt. Carmel* (1906) Closed in merger with St. Anthony, Farnham. Records at St. Anthony, Farnham.

BROCTON. *St. Patrick* (1922) Merged with St. James Major, Westfield and St. Thomas More, Ripley to form St. Dominic Parish using the Westfield and Brocton sites. Records at St. Dominic, Brocton.

CASSADAGA. *Immaculate Conception* Merged with St. Anthony, Fredonia using both sites. Records at St. Anthony, Fredonia.

CHEEKTOWAGA. *Most Holy Redeemer* (1913) Closed in merger with St. Lawrence Parish, Buffalo. Records at St. Lawrence Parish.

Mother of Divine Grace (1946) Closed in merger with Infant of Prague, Cheektowaga. Records at Infant of Prague.

CHERRY CREEK. *St. Elizabeth* Closed. Records at the Catholic Center, 795 Main St. Buffalo, NY 14203. Tel: 716-847-5567.

CLARENCE CENTER. *St. Augustine* (1949) Merged with Good Shepherd, Pendleton, using both sites. Records at Good Shepherd, Pendleton.

COLDEN. *Our Lady of the Sacred Heart* (1912) Closed in merger with St. George Parish, West Falls. Records at St. George, West Falls.

COLLINS CENTER. *St. Frances Cabrini* (1955) Closed in merger to form Epiphany of Our Lord Parish, Langford. Records at Epiphany of Our Lord Parish.

CORFU. *St. Francis of Assisi* (1898) Name changed when merged with Holy Name of Mary, East Pembroke, to form St. Maximilian Kolbe Parish, using both sites. Records at St. Maximilian Kolbe, Corfu.

CRITTENDEN. *St. Patrick* (1857) Closed in merger with St. Francis of Assisi, Corfu. Records at St. Francis of Assisi, Corfu.

DARIEN CENTER. *Our Lady of Good Counsel* (1911) Name changed when merged with Sacred Heart of Jesus, Bennington Center to become Immaculate Heart of Mary using both sites. Records at Immaculate Heart of Mary, Darien Center.

DAYTON. *St. Paul of the Cross* Closed. Records at St. Joseph Parish, Gowanda.

DELEVAN. *Blessed Sacrament* (1947) Closed in merger to form St. Mary Parish, Arcade. Records at St. Mary Parish, Arcade.

DEPEW. *St. Augustine* (1909) Merged with St. James, Depew, and became an oratory of that parish. Records at St. James, Depew.

SS. Peter and Paul (1896) Closed in merger with Our Lady of Pompeii, Lancaster. Records at Our Lady of Pompeii, Lancaster.

DUNKIRK. *St. Hedwig* (1902) Merged with St. Hyacinth Parish to form Blessed Mary Angela Parish, but using both sites. Records at Blessed Mary Angela Parish, St. Hyacinth site.

St. Hyacinth (1875) Name changed when merged with St. Hedwig to form Blessed Mary Angela Parish, but using both sites. Records at Blessed Mary Angela Parish, St. Hyacinth site.

EAST ARCADE. *St. Mary's* (1846) Merged with SS. Peter & Paul, Arcade to form St. Mary Parish, Arcade using both sites. Records at St. Mary, Arcade.

EAST BENNINGTON. *Our Lady Help of Christians* Closed in merger with Darien Center. Records at Immaculate Heart of Mary, Bennington Center.

EAST EDEN. *St. Mary* (1835) Merged with St. John the Baptist Parish, Boston. St. Mary Church became an oratory of St. John the Baptist. Records at St. John the Baptist.

EAST OTTO. *St. Isidore* Closed in merger with St. Mary Cattaraugus. Records at St. Mary Cattaraugus.

EAST PEMBROKE. *Holy Name of Mary* (1868) Merged with St. Francis of Assisi, Corfu, to form St. Maximilian Kolbe Parish, using both sites. Records at Oakfield site.

EDEN. *St. Mary of Immaculate Conception* (1858) Closed in merger to form Epiphany of Our Lord Parish, Langford. Records at Epiphany of Our Lord.

ELBA. *Our Lady of Fatima* (1947) Merged with St. Cecilia, Oakfield, to form St. Padre Pio Parish using both sites. Records at St. Padre Pio, Oakfield.

FORESTVILLE. *St. Rose of Lima* (1850) Merged with Our Lady of Mt. Carmel, Silver Creek. Both sites are used. Records at Our Lady of Mt. Carmel, Forestville site.

FRENCH CREEK. *St. Matthias* Name changed when merged with St. Isaac Jogues, Sherman to form Christ Our Hope Parish using both sites. Records at the French Creek site.

FREWSBURG. *Our Lady of Victory* (1950) Merged into St. James Parish, Jamestown. The church became an oratory of St. James Parish. Records at St. James, Jamestown.

GASPORT. *St. Mary* (1968) Closed in merger with St. John Parish in Lockport. Records at St. John Parish.

HINSDALE. *St. Helen* (1947) Closed in merger with St. John Parish in Olean. Records at St. John Parish, Olean.

HULBERTON. *St. Rocco* Closed. Records at St. Mary, Holley.

HUMPHREY. *St. Pacificus* (1855) Merged with Holy Name of Mary, Ellicottville. Records at Holy Name of Mary, Ellicottville.

JAMESTOWN. *St. John* Merged with SS. Peter & Paul to form Holy Apostles Parish using both sites. Records at Holy Apostles, SS. Peter & Paul site.

SS. Peter & Paul Name changed when merged with St. John to form Holy Apostles Parish. Records at Holy Apostles, SS. Peter & Paul site.

JAVA CENTER. *St. Patrick* (1838) Merged with parishes in Sheldon, Strykersville & North Java to form St. John Neumann Parish. St. Patrick church became an oratory of St. John Neumann. Records at St. John Neumann, Strykersville.

KNAPP CREEK. *Sacred Heart, Mission of St. Bonaventure Parish Allegany* Closed. Records at St. Mary of the Angels, Olean.

LACKAWANNA. *Assumption* (1918) Closed. Records at the Catholic Center, 795 Main St. Buffalo, NY 14203. Tel: 716-847-5567.

St. Barbara (1903) Closed in merger to form Queen of Angels Parish. Records at Queen of Angels.

St. Hyacinth (1910) Closed in merger to form Queen of Angels Parish. Records at Queen of Angels.

St. Michael the Archangel Name changed when merged with St. Barbara, St. Hyacinth & Our Lady of Grace (Woodlawn) parishes to form Queen of Angels Parish at St. Michael's site. Records at Queen of Angels.

Queen of All Saints (1949) Closed in merger with St. Anthony Parish. Records at St. Anthony, Lackawanna.

LANGFORD. *St. Martin* Name changed when merged with parishes in New Oregon and Collins Center to form Epiphany of Our Lord Parish at the Langford site. Records at Epiphany of Our Lord.

LE ROY. *St. Joseph* (1907) Merged with St. Peter Parish & St. Anthony, Lime Rock to form Our Lady of Mercy Parish. St. Joseph Church is an oratory of Our Lady of Mercy; records at Our Lady of Mercy.

St. Peter Name changed when merged with St. Joseph, LeRoy & St. Anthony in Lime Rock to form Our Lady of Mercy Parish at St. Peter's site. Records at Our Lady of Mercy.

LIME ROCK. *St. Anthony* (1907) Merged with St. Joseph & St. Peter parishes in LeRoy to form Our Lady of Mercy Parish. Records at Our Lady of Mercy.

LITTLE VALLEY. *St. Mary* (1874) Closed in merger with St. Mary, Cattaraugus. Records at St. Mary, Cattaraugus.

LOCKPORT. *St. Anthony* (1928) Closed in merger to form All Saints Parish, Lockport. Records at All Saints, Lockport.

St. Joseph (1912) Merged with St. Anthony & St. Patrick parishes to form All Saints Parish and became an oratory of All Saints. Records at All Saints.

St. Patrick Name changed when merged with St. Anthony & St. Joseph parishes to form All Saints Parish at the St. Patrick site. Records at All Saints.

LYNDONVILLE. *St. Joseph* (1962) Merged with St. Patrick, Barker, to form Our Lady of the Lake Parish, using both the Barker and Lyndonville sites. Records at Our Lady of the Lake, Barker.

MACHIAS. *Holy Family* (1948) Closed in merger with St. Philomena, Franklinville. Records at St. Philomena Franklinville.

MAYVILLE. *St. Mary* (1925) Merged with Our Lady of Lourdes, Bemus Point to form St. Mary of Lourdes Parish using both sites. Records at St. Mary of Lourdes, Mayville.

MEDINA. *St. Mary* Name changed when merged with Sacred Heart, Medina & St. Stephen, Middleport to form Holy Trinity Parish using the St. Mary & St. Stephen sites. Records at Holy Trinity, Medina.

Sacred Heart (1910) Merged with St. Mary, Medina & St. Stephen, Middleport to become Holy Trinity Parish. Temporarily an oratory of Holy Trinity. Records at Holy Trinity, Medina.

MIDDLEPORT. *St. Stephen* (1854) Merged with St. Mary & Sacred Heart, Medina to form Holy Trinity Parish using the St. Mary & St. Stephen sites. Records at Holy Trinity, Medina.

NEWFANE. *St. Bridget* Name changed when merged with Our Lady of the Rosary, Wilson & St. Charles Borromeo, Olcott to form St. Brendan on the Lake Parish using the Newfane and Wilson sites. Records at St. Brendan on the Lake, Newfane.

NIAGARA FALLS. *Prince of Peace* Name changed when merged with St. Leo Parish to form St. Vincent de Paul Parish using both sites. Records at St. Vincent de Paul.

St. Charles Borromeo (1970) Closed in merger with St. John de LaSalle Parish. Records at St. John de LaSalle.

St. George (1915) Closed in merger to form Divine Mercy Parish. Records at Divine Mercy.

Holy Trinity (1902) Closed in merger to form Divine Mercy Parish. Records at Divine Mercy.

St. Joseph Name changed when merged with Our Lady of Mt. Carmel to form Holy Family of Jesus, Mary & Joseph Parish using both sites. Records at Holy Family of Jesus, Mary & Joseph, St. Joseph site.

St. Leo (1957) Merged with Prince of Peace to form St. Vincent de Paul Parish using both sites. Records at St. Vincent de Paul.

Our Lady of Lebanon (1914) Closed in merger to form Divine Mercy Parish. Records at Divine Mercy.

Our Lady of Mount Carmel (1949) Merged with St. Joseph Parish to form Holy Family of Jesus, Mary & Joseph Parish using both sites. Records at Holy Family of Jesus, Mary & Joseph, St. Joseph site.

Our Lady of the Rosary (1906) Closed in merger to form Divine Mercy Parish. Records at Divine Mercy.

Sacred Heart (1854) Closed when merged with St. Teresa Parish to form St. Raphael Parish. Records at St. Raphael.

St. Stanislaus Kostka Name changed when merged with four other parishes to form Divine Mercy Parish at the St. Stanislaus site. Records at Divine Mercy.

St. Teresa of the Infant Jesus Name changed when merged with Sacred Heart Parish to form St. Raphael Parish at the St. Teresa site. Records at St. Raphael.

NORTH JAVA. *St. Nicholas* (1890) Closed in merger to form St. John Neumann Parish. Records at St. John Neumann, Strykersville.

NORTH TONAWANDA. *St. Albert the Great* Name changed when merged with Ascension Parish to form St. Jude the Apostle Parish. Records at St. Jude the Apostle.

Ascension (1887) Closed in merger to form St. Jude the Apostle Parish. Records at St. Jude the Apostle.

St. Joseph (1947) Closed in merger with Our Lady of Czestochowa Parish. Records at Our Lady of Czestochowa.

OAKFIELD. *St. Cecilia* (1906) Name changed when merged with Our Lady of Fatima, Elba, to form St. Padre Pio Parish. Both sites used. Records at St. Padre Pio, Oakfield.

OLCOTT. *St. Charles Borromeo* (1912) Merged with parishes in Wilson & Newfane to form St. Brendan on the Lake Parish. Summer oratory of St. Brendan on the Lake. Records at St. Brendan on the Lake, Newfane.

OLEAN. *Transfiguration* (1902) Merged with St. Helen, Hinsdale, and St. John, Olean, at St. John's site. Became an oratory of St. John. Records at St. John, Olean.

PANAMA. *Our Lady of the Snows* (1946) Merged into Sacred Heart Parish, Lakewood but Panama site is still used. Records at Sacred Heart, Lakewood.

PERRY. *St. Joseph* Name changed when merged with St. Stanislaus, Perry, St. Mary, Silver Springs & St. Joseph, Bliss to form St. Isidore Parish using the St. Joseph, Perry & St. Mary, Silver Springs sites. Records at St. Isidore, Perry.

St. Stanislaus Kostka (1910) Closed in merger to form St. Isidore Parish. Records at St. Isidore, Perry.

PERRYSBURG. *St. Joan of Arc* (1950) Closed in merger with St. Joseph, Gowanda. Records at St. Joseph, Gowanda.

PORTAGEVILLE. *Assumption B.V.M.* (1849) Closed in merger with St. Mary, Silver Springs. Records at St. Isidore, Perry.

PORTVILLE. *Sacred Heart* (1909) Merged with St. Mary of the Angels, Olean and became an oratory. Records at St. Mary of the Angels, Olean.

RIPLEY. *St. Thomas More* (1941) Closed in merger to form St. Dominic Parish, Westfield. Records at St. Dominic, Westfield.

SALAMANCA. *Holy Cross* Name changed when merged with St. Patrick to form Our Lady of Peace Parish temporarily using both sites. Records at Our Lady of Peace, Holy Cross site.

St. Patrick (1868) Merged with Holy Cross to form Our Lady of Peace Parish. Records at Our Lady of Peace.

SCIO. *St. Joseph* (1844) Merged with two other parishes to form Holy Family of Jesus, Mary & Joseph Parish, Belmont. Oratory of Holy Family of Jesus, Mary & Joseph, Belmont. Records at Holy Family of Jesus, Mary & Joseph, Belmont.

SHELDON. *St. Cecilia* (1848) Merged with parishes in Strykersville, North Java & Java Center to form St. John Neumann Parish using the Sheldon & Strykersville sites. Records at St. John Neumann, Strykersville.

SHERIDAN. *St. John Bosco* (1949) Closed in merger with Our Lady of Mt. Carmel, Silver Creek. Records at Our Lady of Mt. Carmel.

SHERMAN. *St. Isaac Jogues* (1947) Merged with St. Matthias, French Creek to form Christ Our Hope Parish using both sites. Records at Christ Our Hope, French Creek.

SILVER SPRINGS. *St. Mary* (1892) Merged with parishes in Perry & Bliss to form St. Isidore Parish using both the Perry & Silver Springs sites. Records at St. Isidore, Perry.

SINCLAIRVILLE. *St. John the Evangelist* (1940) Closed in merger with Immaculate Conception, Cassadaga. Records at St. Anthony Parish, Fredonia.

SOUTH BYRON. *St. Michael* (1892) Closed in merger with St. Brigid, Bergen. Records at Our Lady of Mercy, LeRoy.

SOUTH DAYTON. *St. John Fisher* (1946) Closed in merger with St. Joseph Parish, Gowanda. Records at St. Joseph, Gowanda.

STRYKERSVILLE. *St. Mary, Queen of the Rosary* Name changed when merged with parishes in Sheldon, North Java & Java Center to form St. John Neumann Parish using the Sheldon & Strykersville sites. Records at St. John Neumann, Strykersville.

TONAWANDA. *St. Edmund* (1965) Closed as a worship site in merger with St. Christopher Parish, Tonawanda. Site used for outreach ministry. Records at St. Christopher Parish.

VANDALIA. *St. John the Baptist* (1900) Merged with St. Bonaventure Parish, Allegany & became an oratory of St. Bonaventure. Records at St. Bonaventure, Allegany.

VARYSBURG. *St. Joseph* (1910) Merged with St. Vincent de Paul, Attica to form SS. Joachim & Anne Parish using both the Attica & Varysburg sites. Parish records at SS. Joachim & Anne Parish, Attica.

WEST SENECA. *St. Bonaventure* (1918) Closed in merger with St. William to form Blessed John XXIII Parish. Records at Blessed John XXIII Parish, West Seneca.

St. Catherine of Siena (1967) Closed in merger with Queen of Heaven Parish, West Seneca. Records at Queen of Heaven.

St. William Name changed when merged with St. Bonaventure Parish to form Blessed John XXIII Parish at St. William's site. Records at Blessed John XXIII Parish, West Seneca.

WESTFIELD. *St. James Major* Name changed when merged with churches in Brocton & Ripley to form St. Dominic Parish, Westfield. Records at St. Dominic.

WHEATVILLE. *St. Patrick* (1882) Merged into St. Cecilia, Oakfield and became an oratory of St. Cecilia. Records at St. Cecilia.

WHITESVILLE. *St. John of the Cross* (1949) Closed in merger with Immaculate Conception, Wellsville. Records at Immaculate Conception.

WILSON. *Our Lady of the Rosary* (1920) Merged with St. Brigid, Newfane & St. Charles Borromeo, Olcott to form St. Brendan on the Lake Parish using the Newfane & Wilson sites. Records at St. Brendan on the Lake, Newfane.

WOODLAWN. *Our Lady of Grace* (1940) Closed in merger to form Queen of Angels Parish, Lackawanna. Records at Queen of Angels.

RELIGIOUS INSTITUTES OF MEN REPRESENTED IN THE DIOCESE

For further details refer to the corresponding bracketed number in the Religious Institutes of Men or Women section.

[0200]—*Benedictine Monks*—O.S.B.
[0810]—*Brothers of Mercy*—F.M.M.
[0330]—*Brothers of the Christian Schools* (District of Eastern N. America.)—F.S.C.
[0160]—*Clerics Regular of St. Paul*—C.R.S.P.
[1330]—*Congregation of the Mission* (Eastern Prov.)—C.M.
[0390]—*Consolata Missionaries*—I.M.C.
[0480]—*Conventual Franciscans* (St. Anthony of Padua)—O.F.M.Conv.
[0450]—*The Eudists - Congregation of Jesus and Mary*—C.J.M.
[0520]—*Franciscan Friars* (Holy Name Prov.)—O.F.M.
[0690]—*Jesuit Fathers and Brothers* (New York Prov.)—S.J.
[0800]—*Maryknoll* (Buffalo)—M.M.
[0850]—*Missionaries of Africa*—M.Afr.
[1210]—*Missionaries of St. Charles-Scalabrinians*—C.S.
[0910]—*Oblates of Mary Immaculate* (Eastern Prov.)—O.M.I.
[0920]—*Oblates of St. Francis De Sales*—O.S.F.S.
[0970]—*Order of Our Lady of Mercy* (Le Roy)—O.deM.
[0430]—*Order of Preachers-Dominicans* (Prov. of St. Joseph)—O.P.
[1010]—*Pauline Fathers*—O.S.P.P.E.
[0370]—*Society of St. Columban*—S.S.C.
[0990]—*Society of the Catholic Apostolate* (Christ the King Prov.)—S.A.C.
[0560]—*Third Order Regular of St. Francis*—T.O.R.

RELIGIOUS INSTITUTES OF WOMEN REPRESENTED IN THE DIOCESE

[]—*Catechetical Sisters of Arogymatha - The Society of Sisters of Our Lady of Good Health*—C.S.A.
[]—*Christ the Light Sisters (Christu Jyothi Sisters)*—C.J.S.
[0760]—*Daughters of Charity of St. Vincent de Paul*—D.C.
[]—*Daughters of Mary Mother of Mercy*—D.M.M.M.
[]—*Daughters of Our Lady of the Holy Rosary* (Vietnam)—F.M.S.R.
[]—*Daughters of Our Lady of the Visitation* (Vietnam)—F.M.V.
[]—*Daughters of St. Francis of Assisi* (South Africa)—F.S.F.
[0420]—*Discalced Carmelite Nuns*—O.C.D.
[1050]—*Dominican Contemplative Sisters*—O.P.
[1170]—*Felician Sisters*—C.S.S.F.
[1180]—*Franciscan Sisters of Allegany, New York*—O.S.F.
[1470]—*Franciscan Sisters of St. Joseph*—F.S.S.J.
[1280]—*Franciscan Sisters of the Immaculate Conception*—O.S.F.
[1840]—*Grey Nuns of the Sacred Heart*—G.N.S.H.
[]—*Immaculate Heart Sisters of Africa*—I.H.S.A.

[2575]—*Institute of the Sisters of Mercy of the Americas*—R.S.M.
[2480]—*Medical Missionaries of Mary*—M.M.M.
[2830]—*Missionary Sisters of Our Lady of Mercy*—M.O.M.
[2880]—*Missionary Sisters of St. Columban*—S.S.C.
[3040]—*Oblate Sisters of Providence*—O.S.P.
[]—*Servants of Mary the Queen* (Zimbabwe)—A.M.R.
[0630]—*Sisters of Charity of St. Vincent de Paul of Zagreb*—V.Z.
[3000]—*Sisters of Notre Dame de Namur* (Ohio Prov.)—S.N.D.deN.
[2670]—*Sisters of Our Lady of Mercy (Mercedarians)*—S.O.L.M.
[3950]—*Sisters of Saint Mary of Namur*—S.S.M.N.
[4090]—*Sisters of Social Service*—S.S.S.
[1630]—*Sisters of St. Francis of Penance and Christian Charity*—O.S.F.
[1805]—*Sisters of St. Francis of the Neumann Communities*—O.S.F.
[1660]—*Sisters of St. Francis of the Providence of God*—O.S.F.
[3830-06]—*Sisters of St. Joseph* (Buffalo, NY)—S.S.J.
[3830-13]—*Sisters of St. Joseph* (Baden, Pa)—C.S.J.
[3658]—*Sisters of the Sacred Heart of Jesus*—S.S.H.J.
[]—*Union of Our Lady of Charity*—O.L.C.

NECROLOGY

† Berg, Rev. Msgr. S. Theodore, (Retired)—Died April 16, 2009
† Kempczynski, Rev. Msgr. John, (Retired)—Died Jan. 25, 2009
† Letourneau, Rev. Msgr. Paul R., (Retired)—Died Oct. 23, 2009
† Nugent, Rev. Msgr. Richard T., (Retired)—Died Oct. 16, 2009
† Smiraldo, Rev. Msgr. Onofrio R., (Retired)—Died May 15, 2009
† Weimer, Rev. Msgr. John C., (Retired)—Died Oct. 1, 2009
† Zak, Rev. Msgr. Casimir A., (Retired)—Died July 22, 2009
† Fitzgerald, Donald J., (Retired)—Died Sept. 1, 2009
† Fitzgerald, James E., (Retired)—Died Dec. 13, 2009
† Meurder, Edward E., (Retired)—Died Jan. 13, 2009
† Nowak, Stanley F., (Retired)—Died July 15, 2009
† Nuwer, Harold M., (Retired)—Died May 28, 2009
† Sokolowski, Bernard T., (Retired)—Died March 8, 2009
† Vallone, Louis A., (Retired)—Died April 5, 2009

An asterisk (*) denotes an organization that has established tax-exempt status directly with the IRS and is not covered by the USCCB Group Ruling.

Diocese of Burlington

(Dioecesis Burlingtonensis)

Most Reverend

SALVATORE R. MATANO, D.D., S.T.L., J.C.D.

Bishop of Burlington; ordained December 17, 1971; appointed Coadjutor Bishop of Burlington March 3, 2005; ordained April 19, 2005; succeeded November 9, 2005. *Mailing Address: 351 North Ave., P.O. Box 489, Burlington, VT 05402-0489.*

Chancery Office: 351 North Ave., P.O. Box 489, Burlington, VT 05402-0489. Tel: 802-658-6110; Fax: 802-658-0436.

Web: www.vermontcatholic.org

Most Reverend

KENNETH A. ANGELL, D.D.

Bishop Emeritus of Burlington; ordained May 26, 1956; appointed Auxiliary Bishop of Providence August 9, 1974; consecrated October 7, 1974; transferred to Bishop of Burlington October 6, 1992; installed November 9, 1992; retired November 9, 2005. *Mailing Address: 351 North Ave., P.O. Box 489, Burlington, VT 05402-0489.* Fax: 802-658-0436.

ESTABLISHED JULY 29, 1853.

Square Miles 9,135.

Comprises the State of Vermont.

For legal titles of parishes and diocesan institutions, consult the Chancery Office.

STATISTICAL OVERVIEW

Personnel	
Bishop	1
Retired Bishops	1
Priests: Diocesan Active in Diocese	57
Priests: Diocesan Active Outside Diocese	1
Priests: Retired, Sick or Absent	47
Number of Diocesan Priests	105
Religious Priests in Diocese	37
Total Priests in Diocese	142
Extern Priests in Diocese	15
Ordinations:	
Diocesan Priests	4
Transitional Deacons	1
Permanent Deacons	2
Permanent Deacons in Diocese	50
Total Brothers	22
Total Sisters	121
Parishes	
Parishes	77
With Resident Pastor:	
Resident Diocesan Priests	55
Resident Religious Priests	11
Without Resident Pastor:	
Administered by Priests	11
Missions	37
Pastoral Centers	1
New Parishes Created	2
Closed Parishes	3
Professional Ministry Personnel:	
Sisters	6
Lay Ministers	13
Welfare	
Homes for the Aged	4
Total Assisted	175
Special Centers for Social Services	1
Total Assisted	10,364
Educational	
Diocesan Students in Other Seminaries	10
Total Seminarians	10
Colleges and Universities	2
Total Students	2,924
High Schools, Diocesan and Parish	2
Total Students	451
Elementary Schools, Diocesan and Parish	10
Total Students	1,393
Elementary Schools, Private	2
Total Students	477
Catechesis/Religious Education:	
High School Students	1,713
Elementary Students	5,041
Total Students under Catholic Instruction	12,009
Teachers in the Diocese:	
Priests	1
Lay Teachers	398
Vital Statistics	
Receptions into the Church:	
Infant Baptism Totals	870
Minor Baptism Totals	82
Adult Baptism Totals	64
Received into Full Communion	121
First Communions	999
Confirmations	897
Marriages:	
Catholic	276
Interfaith	130
Total Marriages	406
Deaths	1,383
Total Catholic Population	118,000
Total Population	623,000

Former Bishops—Rt. Revs. LOUIS DE GOESBRIAND, D.D., ord. July 13, 1840; cons. Oct. 30, 1853; died Nov. 3, 1899; JOHN S. MICHAUD, D.D., ord. June 7, 1873; cons. Coadjutor Bishop with right of succession June 29, 1892; succeeded to Nov. 3, 1899; died Dec. 22, 1908; Most Revs. JOSEPH J. RICE, D.D., ord. Sept. 29, 1894; cons. April 14, 1910; died April 1, 1938; MATTHEW F. BRADY, D.D., ord. June 10, 1916; cons. Oct. 26, 1938; transferred to Manchester, NH, Nov. 11, 1944; died Sept. 20, 1959; EDWARD F. RYAN, D.D., ord. Aug. 10, 1905; cons. Jan. 3, 1945; died Nov. 3, 1956; ROBERT F. JOYCE, D.D., ord. May 26, 1923; cons. Auxiliary Bishop Oct. 28, 1954; installed Diocesan Bishop Feb. 26, 1957; retired Jan. 24, 1972; died Sept. 2, 1990; JOHN A. MARSHALL, D.D., ord. Dec. 19, 1953; cons. and installed Jan. 25, 1972; transferred to Springfield, MA, Dec. 27, 1991; died July 3, 1994; KENNETH A. ANGELL, D.D., ord. May 26, 1956; appt. Auxiliary Bishop of Providence Aug. 9, 1974; cons. Oct. 7, 1974; transferred to Bishop of Burlington Oct. 6, 1992; installed Nov. 9, 1992; retired Nov. 9, 2005.

Vicars General—Rev. Msgrs. JOHN J. MCDERMOTT, V.G., J.C.L., Vicar Gen. & Chancellor; PETER A. ROUTHIER, V.G., Vicar Gen., 351 North Ave., P.O. Box 489, Burlington, 05402-0489. Tel: 802-658-6110; Fax: 802-658-0436.

Vicar for Clergy—Rev. Msgr. RICHARD G. LAVALLEY, St. Francis Xavier Parish, 3 St. Peter St., Winooski, 05404.

Chancery Office—Rev. Msgr. JOHN J. MCDERMOTT, V.G., J.C.L., Chancellor; Rev. DANIEL E. WHITE, Moderator of the Curia & Vice Chancellor, 351 North Ave., P.O. Box 489, Burlington, 05402-0489. Tel: 802-658-6110; Fax: 802-658-0436 Office Hours: Mon.-Fri. 9-12 & 1-5.

Finance Office—Mr. MARTIN A. HOAK, Diocesan Finance Officer, 351 North Ave., P.O. Box 489, Burlington, 05402-0489. Tel: 802-658-6110; Fax: 802-658-6113.

Secretary to the Most Rev. Bishop—Rev. DANIEL E. WHITE, 351 North Ave., P.O. Box 489, Burlington, 05402-0489. Tel: 802-658-6110.

Office of the Tribunal—351 North Ave., P.O. Box 489, Burlington, 05402-0489. Tel: 802-658-6110; Fax: 802-658-0436.

Judicial Vicar—Rev. DANIEL J. JORDAN, J.C.L.

Case Director—Ms. SUSAN MIELNICZUK.

Judges—Rev. Msgr. JOHN R. MCSWEENEY, J.C.L. (Retired); Revs. THOMAS V. MATTISON, J.C.L.; DANIEL J. JORDAN, J.C.L.; JOHN MAHONEY JR., J.C.L.

Promoter of Justice—Rev. Msgr. JOHN J. MCDERMOTT, V.G., J.C.L.

Defenders of the Bond—Revs. ROGER L. CHARBONNEAU; JOHN G. FELTZ; Rev. Msgr. JOHN J. MCDERMOTT, V.G., J.C.L.

Advocate—Rev. Msgr. PETER A. ROUTHIER, V.G.

Notaries—Revs. ROGER L. CHARBONNEAU; JOHN G. FELTZ; Ms. SUSAN MIELNICZUK.

Diocesan Administrative Board—Most Rev. SALVATORE R. MATANO, D.D., S.T.L., J.C.D., Pres.; Rev. Msgr. JOHN J. MCDERMOTT, V.G., J.C.L.; Mrs. JEANNINE COUILLARD; Mr. MICHAEL J. MITIGUY; Rev. Msgrs. PETER A. ROUTHIER, V.G., Clerk; REID C. MAYO (Retired); Mr. SCOTT BEAUDIN; Mr. MARTIN A. HOAK, Finance Officer & D.A.B. Consultant.

Diocesan Consultors—Rev. Msgrs. JOHN R. MCSWEENEY, J.C.L. (Retired); PETER A. ROUTHIER, V.G.; JOHN J. MCDERMOTT, V.G., J.C.L.; Revs. JUSTIN J. BAKER; DANIEL E. WHITE; MICHAEL W. DEFORGE; BENEDICT C. KIELY.

Deans—Rev. Msgr. RICHARD G. LAVALLEY; Revs. JEROME MERCURE; PIERRE A. LAVALLEE; DANIEL E. WHITE; PATRICK J. FORMAN; JUSTIN J. BAKER; THOMAS L. MOSHER; JAMES T. PRESKENIS, C.S.C.; MAURICE J. ROY; MICHAEL W. DEFORGE; LANCE W. HARLOW.

Canon 1742 Panel of Pastors—Rev. Msgrs. REID C. MAYO (Retired); THOMAS J. BALL; Revs. MICHAEL W. DEFORGE; JAY C. HASKIN, M.Ch.A.; JEROME MERCURE; JAMES T. PRESKENIS, C.S.C.; DANIEL J. RUPP; MAURICE J. ROY; YVON J. ROYER.

Diocesan Offices and Directors

Apostolate for the Handicapped—Office of Catholic Formation, Special Needs Ministry, 351 North

Ave., P.O. Box 489, Burlington, 05402-0489. Tel: 802-658-6110.

Development Office—Mr. RICHARD A. FISCHER, 351 North Ave., P.O. Box 489, Burlington, 05402-0489. Tel: 802-658-6110.

The Blue Army (World Apostolate of Fatima)—DIANA CHARBONEAU, Pres., 1234 North Ave., Burlington, 05408. Tel: 802-734-1048.

Catholic Committee on Scouting—NORBERT VOGEL, Treas., 205 Biscayne Heights, Colchester, 05446. Tel: 802-862-1756. Email: norb_vogl@hotmail.com; DAVID ELY, Chm., 175 Elmwood Ave., Burlington, 05401. Tel: 802-862-5109.

Building Commission—Chancery Office: 351 North Ave., P.O. Box 489, Burlington, 05402-0489. Tel: 802-658-6110.

Vermont Catholic Charities, Inc.—Mr. LAWRENCE ASSELL, Exec. Dir., Central Office, 351 North Ave., P.O. Box 489, Burlington, 05402-0489. Tel: 802-658-6110; Fax: 802-860-0451. Rutland Office, 24 Center St., Rutland, 05701. Tel: 802-773-3379; Fax: 802-773-7550.

Campaign for Human Development—VACANT, 351 North Ave., P.O. Box 489, Burlington, 05402-0489. Tel: 802-658-6110; Fax: 802-860-0451.

Catholic Daughters of The Americas—Rev. PATRICK J. FORMAN, Chap., St. John the Evangelist Parish, 49 Winter St., St. Johnsbury, 05819-2144. Tel: 802-748-8129.

Catholic Relief Services—VACANT, 351 North Ave., P.O. Box 489, Burlington, 05402-0489. Tel: 802-658-6110; Fax: 802-860-0451.

Catholic Golden Age—Rev. SEAN P. DOWLING, Christ the King/St. Anthony Parish, 136 Locust St., Burlington, 05401. Tel: 802-862-5784.

Censor Librorum—Rev. RICHARD L. VANDERWEEL, S.S.E., 351 North Ave., P.O. Box 489, Burlington, 05402-0489. Tel: 802-658-6110.

Charismatic Renewal—Rev. LANCE W. HARLOW, St. Charles Parish, 31 Cherry Hill, Bellows Falls, 05101. Tel: 802-463-3128; Deacon DANIEL PUDVAH, 12 Edgewood Ave., Barre, 05641. Tel: 802-479-9407.

Superintendent of Catholic Schools—Ms. MONA FAULKNER, Office of Catholic Schools, 351 North Ave., P.O. Box 489, Burlington, 05402-0489. Tel: 802-658-6110.

Diocesan Archives—Rev. Msgr. JOHN J. MCDERMOTT, V.G., J.C.L., 351 North Ave., P.O. Box 489, Burlington, 05402-0489. Tel: 802-658-6110.

Diocesan Coordinator of the Vietnamese Ministry—Rev. DANIEL E. WHITE, The Catholic Center at U.V.M., 390 S. Prospect St., Redstone Campus, Burlington, 05401. Tel: 802-862-8403.

Office of Communications—Rev. DANIEL E. WHITE, 351 North Ave., P.O. Box 489, Burlington, 05402-0489. Tel: 802-658-6110.

Daughters of Isabella—Rev. YVON J. ROYER, Chap., St. Peter Parish, 85 S. Maple St., Vergennes, 05491-0324. Tel: 802-877-2367.

Diocesan Cemetery—Resurrection Park, South Burlington, 05403. Mr. PETER WELLS, Insurance and Facilities Office, 351 North Ave., P.O. Box 489, Burlington, 05402-0489. Tel: 802-658-6110; Mr. PATRICK JENNINGS, Chm., 45 Morrill Dr., Burlington, 05401. Tel: 802-864-5071.

Diocesan Finance Council—Ex Officio Members: Most Rev. SALVATORE R. MATANO, D.D., S.T.L., J.C.D., Chm.; Rev. Msgr. PETER A. ROUTHIER, V.G. Board Members: WILLIAM E. BOND; MAYNARD MCLAUGHLIN; Mr. MARK KELLEY, Bishop's Delegate; Rev. BRIAN J. CUMMINGS, S.S.E.; Mr. J. PAUL GIULIANI, Esq.; Mrs. KATHRYN A. WESTOVER; Mr. MICHAEL HENRY. Consultants: Rev. DANIEL E. WHITE; Mr. MARTIN A. HOAK, Finance Officer.

Diocesan Director of Facilities and Insurance—Mr. PETER WELLS, 351 North Ave., P.O. Box 489, Burlington, 05402-0489. Tel: 802-658-6110.

Diocesan Director of Human Resources—Ms. EILEEN O'ROURKE, 351 North Ave., P.O. Box 489, Burlington, 05402-0489. Tel: 802-658-6110.

Ecumenical Commission—Rev. Msgr. PETER A. ROUTHIER, V.G.; Mr. JAMES G. CASE, 1818 Richmond Rd., Hinesburg, 05461.

Diocesan Board of Catholic Education—Contact: Office of Catholic Schools, 351 North Ave., P.O. Box 489, Burlington, 05402. Tel: 802-658-6110.

Evangelization—VACANT.

Office of Marriage, Family Life/Respect Life—Mrs. CARRIE HANDY, Mailing Address: 351 North Ave., Ste. 312, P.O. Box 989, Burlington, 05402-0989. Tel: 802-658-6111.

Engaged Encounter—Rev. PATRICK J. FORMAN, St. John the Evangelist Parish, 49 Winter St., Saint Johnsbury, 05819. Tel: 802-748-8129.

Liturgical Commission—Rev. Msgr. PETER A. ROUTHIER, V.G., 351 North Ave., P.O. Box 489, Burlington, 05402-0489. Tel: 802-658-6110.

House of Discernment—Rev. JON-DANIEL SCHNOBRICH, Dir., The Catholic Center at UVM, 390 S. Prospect St., Redstone Campus, Burlington, 05401. Tel: 802-862-8403; Fax: 802-865-9480.

Knights of Columbus—Rev. KARL A. HAHR, All Saints Rectory, 152 Main St., Richford, 05476.

Leap—Rev. MARCEL R. RAINVILLE, S.S.E., St. Michael's College, Winooski Park, Colchester, 05439. Tel: 802-654-2332.

Marriage Encounter, Vermont—DAVID ERKSON; JENNIE ERKSON, 2115 Jericho Rd., Richmond, 05477. Tel: 800-434-4218. Email: erksonmevt@comcast.net.

Diocesan Master of Ceremonies—Rev. DANIEL E. WHITE, 351 North Ave., P.O. Box 489, Burlington, 05402-0489. Tel: 802-658-6110; Fax: 802-658-0436.

Office of Continuing Education for Clergy—Rev. BENEDICT C. KIELY, Dir., Mailing Address: Blessed Sacrament Parish, P.O. Box 27, Stowe, 05672. Tel: 802-253-7536; Fax: 802-253-4445.

Office of Safe Environment Programs—Mr. KEVIN P. SCULLY, Dir.; JEANNE MITIGUY BRUNO, Programs Devel. Admin.

The Review Board—Dr. WILLIAM CUNNINGHAM, Chm.; GAIL ENGELS; Rev. Msgr. JOHN J. MCDERMOTT, V.G., J.C.L.; Rev. JAMES T. PRESKENIS, C.S.C.; THERESE CORSONES, J.D.; DALE STAFFORD, M.D.; MARY FRAN STAFFORD. Ex Officio/Consultant: Rev. Msgr. PETER A. ROUTHIER, V.G.; Mr. KEVIN P. SCULLY.

Victim's Advocacy Committee—BEATRICE M. WELLS, M.S.W.; Rev. Msgr. PETER A. ROUTHIER, V.G.; Mr. KEVIN P. SCULLY.

National Shrine of the Immaculate Conception, Washington—Rev. ROGER L. CHARBONNEAU, Holy Cross Rectory, 416 Church Rd., Colchester, 05446. Tel: 802-863-3002.

Office of Catholic Formation—Mrs. DOROTHY BAREWICZ, Dir., 351 North Ave., P.O. Box 489, Burlington, 05402-0489.

Youth Ministry Coordinator—VACANT.

Office of Diocesan Pastoral Planning—Rev. Msgr. JOHN J. MCDERMOTT, V.G., J.C.L., Dir., Mailing Address: 351 North Ave., P.O. Box 489, Burlington, 05402-0489. Tel: 802-658-6110.

Office of Permanent Diaconate Ministry—Rev. DANIEL E. WHITE, Spiritual Dir., 390 S. Prospect St., Burlington, 05401; Deacon THOMAS F. COONEY, Dir., 592 Cole Hill Rd., Morrisville, 05661. Tel: 802-888-2452. Email: cooneyfamily2@myfairpoint.net.

Institute for Catholic Enrichment and Lay Apostolate Formation—Rev. Msgr. JOHN J. MCDERMOTT, V.G., J.C.L., Dir.; Mrs. DOROTHY BAREWICZ, Asst. Dir., Mailing Address: 351 North Ave., P.O. Box 489, Burlington, 05402-0489. Tel: 802-658-6110.

Diocesan Presbyteral Council—Members Ex Officio: Most Rev. SALVATORE R. MATANO, D.D., S.T.L., J.C.D., Bishop of Burlington; Rev. Msgrs. PETER A. ROUTHIER, V.G.; JOHN J. MCDERMOTT, V.G., J.C.L., Chancellor; Rev. DANIEL E. WHITE, Moderator of the Curia & Vice Chancellor. Elected Members: Rev. Msgr. REID C. MAYO (Retired); Revs. PATRICK J. FORMAN; THOMAS L. MOSHER; JUSTIN J. BAKER; LANCE W. HARLOW; DANIEL J. JORDAN, J.C.L.; CHARLES H. RANGES, S.S.E.; LEOPOLD J. BILODEAU; BERNARD E. GAUDREAU; DANIEL J. RUPP; JAY C. HASKIN, M.Ch.A.; WILLIAM R. BEAUDIN; THOMAS V. MATTISON, J.C.L.

Magazine— "Vermont Catholic" Most Rev. SALVATORE R. MATANO, D.D., S.T.L., J.C.D., Publisher; Mrs. PATRICIA GORE, Editor, Editorial & Business Office, 351 North Ave., P.O. Box 489, Burlington, 05402-0489. Tel: 802-658-6110; Fax: 802-658-3866.

Priests' Benefit Fund—Rev. MICHAEL E. AUGUSTINOWITZ, Chm., 351 North Ave., P.O. Box 489, Burlington, 05402-0489. Tel: 802-658-6110.

Prison Ministry—Deacon DENNIS MOORE, 351 North Ave., P.O. Box 489, Burlington, 05402-0489. Tel: 802-658-6110.

Propagation of the Faith—Rev. ROGER L. CHARBONNEAU, Dir., 351 North Ave., P.O. Box 489, Burlington, 05402-0489. Tel: 802-658-6110.

Office of Catholic Schools—Ms. MONA FAULKNER, Supt. of Schools; Mrs. MARY BETH DAVIDSON, Asst. to Supt., 351 North Ave., P.O. Box 489, Burlington, 05402-0489. Tel: 802-658-6110; Fax: 802-658-0436.

Vermont Cursillo—Ms. JUDY HUSSEY, 1847 River Rd., Orleans, 05860. Tel: 802-899-2518.

Vocations and Seminarians—Rev. DANIEL E. WHITE, Dir., 351 North Ave., P.O. Box 489, Burlington, 05402. Tel: 802-658-6110; Fax: 802-658-0436.

CLERGY, PARISHES, MISSIONS AND PAROCHIAL SCHOOLS

CITY OF BURLINGTON

(CHITTENDEN COUNTY)

1—CATHEDRAL OF THE IMMACULATE CONCEPTION (1830) Rev. Msgr. Thomas J. Ball, Rector; Deacon William Glinka.
Res.: 20 Pine St., 05401. Tel: 802-658-4333.
Catechesis/Religious Program—Tel: 802-862-3258. Michelle La Croix, D.R.E. Students 20.

2—CHRIST THE KING-ST. ANTHONY (2007), Parish includes Christ the King, Burlington & St. Anthony, Burlington. Revs. Daniel J. Rupp; Sean P. Dowling; Ronald Camet; Deacons Timm Taylor; Louis A. Meunier.
Res.: 136 Locust St., 05401-4849. Tel: 802-862-5784; Fax: 802-651-3021.
School—(Grades PreK-8) Tel: 802-862-6696; Fax: 802-658-6553. Ms. Paulette Thibault, Prin.; Aida Cadrecha, Librarian. Lay Teachers 17; Students 244.
Catechesis/Religious Program—Students 94.

3—ST. JOSEPH'S CO-CATHEDRAL (1850) [CEM] Rev. Msgr. Peter A. Routhier, Rector; Rev. Dallas T. St. Peter. In Res., Rev. Daniel E. White.
Res.: 85 Elmwood Ave., 05401. Tel: 802-863-2388; Fax: 802-863-2380.
School—(Grades PreK-8) Tel: 802-864-5623; Fax: 802-860-2627. Mrs. Evelyn Rogerson, Prin. Lay Teachers 10; Students 74.
Catechesis/Religious Program—Tel: 802-862-0512. Monica Morano-Aurigemma, D.R.E. Students 33.

4—ST. MARK'S (1940) Rev. William P. Giroux; Deacon Timothy Gibbo.
Res.: 1251 North Ave., 05408. Tel: 802-864-7686; Fax: 802-651-9391.
Catechesis/Religious Program—Sr. Helen Hadcock, S.A., D.R.E. Students 111.
Convent—Franciscan Sisters of the Atonement, 21 Dodds Ct., 05408. Tel: 802-862-8288.

OUTSIDE THE CITY OF BURLINGTON

ALBURGH, GRAND ISLE CO., ST. AMADEUS (1886) [CEM 2] Rev. Lawrence P. Ridgley, Admin.; Deacon Alan Vincelette.
Res.: P.O. Box 49, 05440. Tel: 802-796-3481; Fax: 802-796-3481.
Catechesis/Religious Program—Carol Cleland, D.R.E. Students 48.
Mission—St. Joseph Isle La Motte, Grand Isle Co.

ARLINGTON, BENNINGTON CO., ST. MARGARET MARY (1946) [CEM] Closed. See Christ Our Savior Parish, Manchester Center.

BARRE, WASHINGTON CO., ST. MONICA (1892) Revs. Leopold J. Bilodeau; Emmanuel Ajanma; Paul Sackevich; Deacons David Bisson; Daniel Pudvah.
Res.: 79 Summer St., 05641. Tel: 802-479-3253; Fax: 802-479-3154.
School—Central Vermont Catholic School - St. Monica Campus, (Grades PreK-8) Tel: 802-476-5015; Fax: 802-476-0861. Ms. Patricia M. O'Mahoney, Prin. Lay Teachers 18; Students 146.
Catechesis/Religious Program—Tel: 802-476-4020; Fax: 802-479-3154. Marybeth Hebert, D.R.E. Students 212.

BARTON, ORLEANS CO., MOST HOLY TRINITY (2003), Parish includes St. Paul, Barton, St. Theresa, Orleans & St. John Vianney, Irasburg. Rev. Sixmund Nyabenda, Admin.
Res.: 85 St. Paul Ln., 05822. Tel: 802-525-3711; Fax: 802-525-1292.
School—St. Paul School, (Grades K-8) Tel: 802-525-6578; Fax: 802-525-3869. Mr. Peter T. Close, Prin. Lay Teachers 7; Students 87.
Catechesis/Religious Program—Students 54.

BELLOWS FALLS, WINDHAM CO., ST. CHARLES (1871) [CEM] Rev. Lance W. Harlow.
Res.: 31 Cherry Hill St., 05101. Tel: 802-463-3128; Fax: 802-463-8179. Email: 1wharlow@sover.net.
Catechesis/Religious Program—Students 50.

BENNINGTON, BENNINGTON CO., SACRED HEART ST. FRANCIS DE SALES (1995) Revs. James T. Preskenis, C.S.C.; Vincent J. Coppola, C.S.C.
Parish Office—238 W. Main St., 05201. Tel: 802-442-3141; Fax: 802-442-3142.
School—The School of Sacred Heart St. Francis de Sales, (Grades PreK-8), 307 School St., 05201. Tel: 802-442-2446; Fax: 802-442-3584. Mr. David B. Estes, Prin.; Marcia Hendery, Librarian; Kathy Murphy, Librarian. Lay Teachers 11; Students 163.
Catechesis/Religious Program—Tel: 802-447-0223. Janet Lucy, D.R.E. Students 160.
Mission—Our Lady of Lourdes North Pownal, Bennington Co.

BETHEL, WINDSOR CO., ST. ANTHONY (1912) Rev. Kenneth Ekekwe, Admin.
Res.: 221 Church St., P.O. Box 63, 05032. Tel: 802-234-9916; Fax: 802-234-9020.
Catechesis/Religious Program—Tel: 802-234-9522. Rosemary Brown, D.R.E. Students 25.
Mission—St. Elizabeth Rochester, Windsor Co.

BRADFORD, ORANGE CO., OUR LADY OF PERPETUAL HELP (1945) Rev. Donald J. Roy; Deacon Kelly Fitzpatrick.
Res.: 113 Upper Plain, 05033. Tel: 802-222-5268.
Catechesis/Religious Program—Students 45.
Mission—St. Francis of Assisi Norwich, Windsor Co.
Mission—St. Eugene Wells River, Orange Co.
Mission—Our Lady of Light South Strafford, Orange Co.

BRANDON, RUTLAND CO., ST. MARY'S (1867) [CEM 2] Rev. Albert G. Baltz; Deacon Gary Griffin.
Res.: 38 Carver St., 05733. Tel: 802-247-6351; Fax: 802-247-6396.
Catechesis/Religious Program—Students 45.
Mission—St. Agnes Leicester, Addison Co.

BRATTLEBORO, WINDHAM CO., ST. MICHAEL (1855) [CEM] Rev. Richard C. O'Donnell.
Res.: 47 Walnut St., 05301. Tel: 802-257-5101; Fax: 802-257-5102.
School—(Grades PreK-8) Tel: 802-254-5666; Fax: 802-254-5229. Mrs. Elaine Beam, Prin. Lay Teachers 16; Students 74.
Catechesis/Religious Program—Students 140.

BRISTOL, ADDISON CO., ST. AMBROSE (1893) [CEM] Rev. Pierre A. LaVallee.
Res.: 11 School St., 05443. Tel: 802-453-2488; Fax: 802-453-7712.
Catechesis/Religious Program—Students 67.

CAMBRIDGE, LAMOILLE CO., ST. MARY (1914) Rev. Charles R. Danielson.
312 N. Main St., P.O. Box 129, 05444. Tel: 802-644-5073; Fax: 802-644-2546.
Catechesis/Religious Program—Students 25.

CANAAN, ESSEX CO., ASSUMPTION OF THE BLESSED VIRGIN MARY (1950) [CEM] Closed. For inquiries into sacramental records contact St. Albert Parish P.O. Box 176, Beecher Falls, VT 05902.

CASTLETON, RUTLAND CO., ST. JOHN THE BAPTIST (1899) Rev. Henry P. Furman.
Res.: P.O. Box 128, 05735. Tel: 802-468-5706; Fax: 802-468-2777.
Catechesis/Religious Program—Tel: 802-468-2155. Luis Bauzo, D.R.E. Students 25.

CHARLOTTE, CHITTENDEN CO., OUR LADY OF MOUNT CARMEL (1858) [CEM] Rev. David G. Cray, S.S.E.
Res.: 2894 Spear St., P.O. Box 158, 05445. Tel: 802-425-2637; Fax: 802-425-2671.
Catechesis/Religious Program—Students 112.

CHESTER, WINDSOR CO., ST. JOSEPH (1946) Rev. James E. Zuccaro, Admin.
Res.: 96 S. Main St., P.O. Box 1129, 05143. Tel: 802-875-2610; Fax: 802-875-2745.
Catechesis/Religious Program—Students 30.
Station—St. Joseph Chapel Londonderry.

COLCHESTER, CHITTENDEN CO.
1—HOLY CROSS (1950) [CEM] Rev. Roger L. Charbonneau; Deacon Ivan O. Hawk III.
Res.: 416 Church Rd., 05446. Tel: 802-863-3002; Fax: 802-862-5687.
Catechesis/Religious Program—Peggy Hawk, D.R.E. Students 165.
2—OUR LADY OF GRACE (1966) Rev. Jay C. Haskin.
Res.: 800 Main St., 05446. Tel: 802-878-5987; Fax: 802-878-9308.
Catechesis/Religious Program—Students 157.

DERBY LINE, ORLEANS CO., ST. EDWARD (1946) [CEM] Rev. Michael Reardon, S.D.V.; Deacon John P.E. Gratton.
Res.: 250 Main St., P.O. Box 397, 05830. Tel: 802-873-3522; Fax: 802-873-3299.
St. Edward's Pre-School—Tel: 802-873-4570; Fax: 802-334-8877. Theresa Forbes, Dir. Lay Teachers 4; Students 20.
Catechesis/Religious Program—Students 133.
Mission—St. Benedict Labre West Charleston, Orleans Co.

EAST DORSET, BENNINGTON CO., ST. JEROME (1868) Closed. See Christ Our Savior, Manchester Center.

ENOSBURG FALLS, FRANKLIN CO., ST. JOHN THE BAPTIST (1874) [CEM] Rev. Daniel J. Jordan.
Res.: P.O. Box 563, 05450. Tel: 802-933-4464; Fax: 802-933-4225.
Catechesis/Religious Program—Students 100.

ESSEX CENTER, CHITTENDEN CO., ST. PIUS X (1957) Rev. Richard W. Tinney; Deacon Gerald Scilla.
Res.: 20 Jericho Rd., Essex Junction, 05452-2707. Tel: 802-878-5997; Fax: 802-878-7793.
Catechesis/Religious Program—Tel: 802-878-1182. Michelle Scilla, D.R.E.; Andrew Coulter, D.R.E. Students 267.

ESSEX JUNCTION, CHITTENDEN CO., HOLY FAMILY-ST. LAWRENCE (2006) [CEM], Parish includes Holy Family, Essex Junction & St. Lawrence, Essex Junction. Rev. Charles H. Ranges, S.S.E.
Res.: 4 Prospect St., 05452. Tel: 802-878-5331; Fax: 802-878-5332.
Catechesis/Religious Program—Tel: 802-878-5331, Ext. 202. John McMahon, D.R.E. Students 210.

FAIRFAX, FRANKLIN CO., ST. LUKE (1943) [CEM] Revs. John G. Feltz; Julian Asucan; Deacon Stephen J. Ratte.
Res.: 17 Huntville Rd., P.O. Box 7, 05454-0007. Tel: 802-849-6205; Fax: 802-849-6078.
Catechesis/Religious Program—Students 119.

FAIRFIELD, FRANKLIN CO., ST. PATRICK (1858) [CEM] Rev. Leonidas B. Laroche; Deacon Gabriel Liegey Jr.
Res.: 116 Church Rd., P.O. Box 18, 05455. Tel: 802-827-3203; Fax: 802-827-9940.
Catechesis/Religious Program—Students 65.
Mission—St. Anthony-St. George East Fairfield, Franklin Co.

FAIR HAVEN, RUTLAND CO., OUR LADY OF SEVEN DOLORS (1866) [CEM] Rev. James A. Lawrence, Admin.
Res.: 10 Washington St., 05743. Tel: 802-265-3135.
Catechesis/Religious Program—Tel: 802-265-8045. Jane Schraff, D.R.E. Students 75.
Mission—St. Matthew of Avalon West Castleton, Rutland Co.
Mission—St. Frances Cabrini West Pawlet, Rutland Co. 05775.

GRANITEVILLE, WASHINGTON CO., ST. SYLVESTER (1895) [CEM] Revs. Leopold J. Bilodeau, Admin.; Andrzej Bednarowicz, Parochial Vicar.
Res.: 217 Church Hill Rd., 05654. Tel: 802-476-3913.
Catechesis/Religious Program—Students 32.
Mission—St. Cecilia & St. Frances Cabrini East Barre, Washington Co.

HARDWICK, CALEDONIA CO., MARY QUEEN OF ALL SAINTS PARISH (1902) [CEM 2], St. Norbert, Hardwick; St. Michael, Greensboro Bend & Our Lady of Fatima, Craftsbury were suppressed. Mary Queen of All Saints was erected. Parish includes St. Norbert, Hardwick; St. Michael, Greensboro Bend & Our Lady of Fatima, Craftsbury. Rev. Peter P. O'Leary.
Res.: 193 S. Main St., 05843. Tel: 802-472-5544; Fax: 802-472-5543.
Catechesis/Religious Program—Students 69.

HINESBURG, CHITTENDEN CO., ST. JUDE THE APOSTLE (1946) Rev. David G. Cray, S.S.E.
Res.: 10759 Rte. 116, P.O. Box 69, 05461-0069. Tel: 802-482-2290; Fax: 802-482-5263.
Catechesis/Religious Program—Students 147.

ISLAND POND, ESSEX CO., ST. JAMES THE GREATER (1871) [CEM] Rev. Francis E. Connors.
Res.: 146 Middle St., P.O. Box 407, 05846. Tel: 802-723-4312.
Catechesis/Religious Program—Students 12.
Mission—St. Bernard Norton, Essex Co.

LUDLOW, WINDSOR CO., ANNUNCIATION OF THE BLESSED VIRGIN MARY (1885) Rev. Romanus Igweonu.
Res.: 7 Depot St., 05149. Tel: 802-228-3451; Fax: 802-228-7012.
Catechesis/Religious Program—Students 58.
Mission—Holy Name of Mary Proctorsville, Windsor Co.

LYNDONVILLE, CALEDONIA CO., ST. ELIZABETH (1891) [CEM] Revs. Patrick J. Forman; Dwight Baker; Deacons Alfred Toborg; David Baker.
Rectory—St. John the Evangelist Rectory, 49 Winter St., Saint Johnsbury, 05819. Tel: 802-748-8129; Fax: 802-748-8120.
Catechesis/Religious Program—Students 75.
Mission—Our Lady Queen of Peace Danville, Caledonia Co.

MANCHESTER CENTER, BENNINGTON CO., CHRIST OUR SAVIOR PARISH (1896), St. Paul, Manchester Center; St. Jerome, East Dorset & Holy Trinity, Danby were suppressed. Christ Our Savior was erected. Parish includes St. Paul, Manchester Center & St. Margaret Mary, Arlington. Rev. Thomas V. Mattison.
Res.: 398 Bonnet St., 05255. Tel: 802-362-1380; Fax: 802-366-1168.
Catechesis/Religious Program—Students 126.

MIDDLEBURY, ADDISON CO., ASSUMPTION OF THE BLESSED VIRGIN MARY (1855) [CEM] Revs. William R. Beaudin; Brian J. O'Donnell.
Res.: 326 College St., 05753. Tel: 802-388-2943; 802-388-4444; Fax: 802-388-1349.
School—St. Mary's, (Grades PreK-6), 86 Shannon St., 05753. Tel: 802-388-8392. Ms. Monique Almquist, Prin. Lay Teachers 8; Students 75.
Catechesis/Religious Program—Students 165.
Mission—St. Bernadette/St. Genevieve Shoreham, Addison Co.

MIDDLETOWN SPRINGS, RUTLAND CO., ST. ANNE (1963) Rev. Adam J. Krempa.
Res.: P.O. Box 1098, 05757.
Catechesis/Religious Program—Students 5.

MILTON, CHITTENDEN CO., ST. ANN (1866) [CEM] Rev. John G. Feltz; Deacon Paul Garrow.
Res.: 41 Main St., P.O. Box 1, 05468. Tel: 802-893-2487; Fax: 802-893-3701.
Catechesis/Religious Program—Lori Daudelin, D.R.E. Students 212.

MONTPELIER, WASHINGTON CO., ST. AUGUSTINE (1850) [CEM] Rev. Michael E. Augustinowitz; Deacons Regis E. Cummings; Walter Brenneman Jr.; Gesualdo Schneider.
Res.: 16 Barre St., 05602. Tel: 802-223-5285; Fax: 802-223-3621.
Catechesis/Religious Program—Students 136.
Mission—North American Martyrs (1963) Marshfield, Washington Co.

MORRISVILLE, LAMOILLE CO., THE PARISH OF THE HOLY NAME OF JESUS (2008) [CEM], Parish includes Holy Cross, Morrisville, St. Gabriel, Eden, St. Theresa, Hyde Park & St. John the Apostle, Johnson. Rev. Francis R. Prive, Admin.; Deacon Thomas F. Cooney.
Res.: P.O. Box 339, 05661. Tel: 802-888-3318; Fax: 802-888-6177.
Catechesis/Religious Program—Students 49.

NEWPORT, ORLEANS CO., ST. MARY STAR OF THE SEA (1873) [CEM] Rev. Michael Reardon, S.D.V.
Res.: 191 Clermont Ter., 05855. Tel: 802-334-5066; Fax: 802-334-5067.
Catechesis/Religious Program—Tel: 802-334-6240. Dennis De La Bruere, D.R.E.; Aline De La Bruere, D.R.E. Students 104.

NORTH BENNINGTON, BENNINGTON CO., ST. JOHN THE BAPTIST (1885) [CEM] Rev. Patrick Walsh, C.S.C.; Deacon David O'Brien.
Res.: 3-5 Houghton St., P.O. Box 219, 05257. Tel: 802-447-7504; Fax: 802-442-6620.
Catechesis/Religious Program—Eileen M. Flynn, D.R.E. Students 65.

NORTH TROY, ORLEANS CO., ST. VINCENT DE PAUL (1939) [CEM] Rev. Henry Mlinganisa, Admin.
Res.: P.O. Box 109, Troy, 05868. Tel: 802-988-2608; Fax: 802-988-2608.
Catechesis/Religious Program—Students 19.

NORTHFIELD, WASHINGTON CO., ST. JOHN THE EVANGELIST (1865) [CEM] Rev. Kevin E. Rooney.
Res.: 206 Vine St., 05663. Tel: 802-485-8313; Fax: 802-485-3043.
Catechesis/Religious Program—Students 55.
Mission—St. Edward Williamstown, Orange Co.

ORLEANS, ORLEANS CO., ST. THERESA OF CHILD JESUS (1942) [CEM 2] Closed. See Most Holy Trinity Parish.

ORWELL, ADDISON CO., ST. PAUL (1886) [CEM] Rev. Henry P. Furman.
Res.: c/o P.O. Box 128, Castleton, 05735-0128. Tel: 802-468-2777.
Catechesis/Religious Program—Tel: 802-948-2408. Students 18.

PITTSFORD, RUTLAND CO., ST. ALPHONSUS LIGUORI (1893) [CEM] Rev. Joseph Romano.
Res.: 2918 U.S. Rte. 7, 05763-9499. Tel: 802-483-2301; Fax: 802-483-2136.
Catechesis/Religious Program—Lisa Adamsen, D.R.E. Students 72.
Mission—St. Robert Chittenden, Rutland Co.

POULTNEY, RUTLAND CO., ST. RAPHAEL (1884) [CEM] Rev. Adam J. Krempa.
Res.: 21 E. Main St., 05764-1107. Tel: 802-287-5703.
Catechesis/Religious Program—Students 31.

PROCTOR, RUTLAND CO., ST. DOMINIC (1888) [CEM] Rev. Theodosius Corley, O.F.M.Cap.
Church: 45 South St., 05765.
Catechesis/Religious Program—Marie Baccei, D.R.E. Students 32.

PUTNEY, WINDHAM CO., OUR LADY OF MERCY (1931) Rev. Frederick E. McLachlan, S.S.E.; Deacons Jerome Driscoll; Richard Anderberg. In Res., Rev. Francis X. McMahon, S.S.E. (Retired).
Res.: 52 Old Depot Rd., P.O. Box 246, 05346. Tel: 802-387-5861; Fax: 802-387-2154.
Catechesis/Religious Program—Students 31.
Mission—St. Edmund of Canterbury Saxtons River, Windham Co.
Mission—Chapel of the Snows Stratton Mountain, Windham Co.
Mission—Our Lady of the Valley Townshend, Windham Co.

RANDOLPH, ORANGE CO., OUR LADY OF THE ANGELS (2008) Rev. John M. Milanese.
Res.: 43 Hebard Hill Rd., P.O. Box 428, 05060. Tel: 802-728-5251; Fax: 802-728-9922.
Catechesis/Religious Program—Students 16.

READSBORO, BENNINGTON CO., ST. JOACHIM (1895) Rev. Vincent J. Coppola, C.S.C., Admin.
Res.: P.O. Box 158, 05350-9738. Tel: 802-423-5267; Fax: 802-423-5267.
Catechesis/Religious Program—Students 40.
Mission—St. John Bosco Stamford, Bennington Co.

RICHFORD, FRANKLIN CO., ALL SAINTS (1899) [CEM] Rev. Karl A. Hahr; Deacons Clifford Chagnon; Jon Ramey.
Res.: 152 Main St., 05476. Tel: 802-848-7741; Fax: 802-848-3150.
Catechesis/Religious Program—Students 66.
Mission—Our Lady of Lourdes East Berkshire, Franklin Co.
Mission—St. Isidore Montgomery Center, Franklin Co.

RICHMOND, CHITTENDEN CO., OUR LADY OF THE HOLY ROSARY (1860) [CEM 2] Rev. Donald J. Ravey.
Res.: 64 W. Main St., P.O. Box 243, 05477. Tel:

802-434-2521.
Catechesis/Religious Program—Jill Danilich, D.R.E. Students 97.

RUTLAND, RUTLAND CO.
1—CHRIST THE KING (1907) Revs. Justin J. Baker; Sebastian Madike; Timothy Naples.
Res.: 66 S. Main St., 05701. Tel: 802-773-6820; Fax: 802-773-6820 Ext. 136.
Catechesis/Religious Program—Students 127.
2—IMMACULATE HEART OF MARY (1869) [CEM] Rev. Remigius Bukuru Ntahondi.
Res.: 18 Lincoln Ave., 05701. Tel: 802-775-0846; Fax: 802-775-9640.
Catechesis/Religious Program—Tel: 802-775-0845. Cindy Tuomisto, D.R.E. Students 158.
3—ST. PETER (1855) [CEM] Rev. Theodosius Corley, O.F.M.Cap. In Res., Revs. Raynold Thibodeau, O.F.M.Cap.; Richard Crawley, O.F.M.Cap.
Res.: 134 Convent Ave., 05701. Tel: 802-775-1994; Fax: 802-775-0178.
Catechesis/Religious Program—Students 11.

ST. ALBANS, FRANKLIN CO.
1—HOLY ANGELS (1872) [CEM] Revs. Maurice J. Roy; Daniel Lokanga; Deacon Duane Langlois.
Res.: 246 Lake St., 05478. Tel: 802-524-2585; Fax: 802-524-2586.
Catechesis/Religious Program—Students 190.
Mission—Ascension Georgia, Franklin Co.
2—IMMACULATE CONCEPTION (1847) [CEM] Rev. Wilfred Andre Houle; Deacon Gabriel Gagne.
Res.: 45 Fairfield St., 05478. Tel: 802-527-7775; Fax: 802-527-1667.
Catechesis/Religious Program—Tel: 802-524-9416. Kathy Rogers, C.R.E. (Grades 1-8); Bart Tatro, C.R.E. (Grades 9-12). Students 115.

ST. JOHNSBURY, CALEDONIA CO., ST. JOHN THE EVANGELIST (1896) [CEM] Revs. Patrick J. Forman; Dwight Baker; Deacons Bruce Burk; Raymond J. Desilets; Bernier L. Mayo; Peter Gummere; David Baker.
Res.: 49 Winter St., 05819. Tel: 802-748-8129; Fax: 802-748-8120.
Catechesis/Religious Program—506 Summer St., 05819. Tel: 802-748-9256 (PreK-8). Marie Hagan, D.R.E. (PreK-8); Debra Priest, D.R.E. (High School). Students 125.
Mission—St. Leo Lunenburg, Orleans Co.

SHELBURNE, CHITTENDEN CO., ST. CATHERINE OF SIENA (1906) [CEM] Rev. Michael W. DeForge.
Res.: 72 Church St., P.O. Box 70, 05482. Tel: 802-985-2373; Fax: 802-985-9181. Email: info@shelburnecatholic.org.
Catechesis/Religious Program—Marie Cookson, D.R.E. Students 168.

SHELDON SPRINGS, FRANKLIN CO., ST. ANTHONY (1906) [CEM 2] Rev. Bernard J. Bechard, S.S.E.
Res.: 102 Shawville Rd., P.O. Box 97, 05485-0097.
Catechesis/Religious Program—Students 21.
Mission—St. Mary [CEM] 145 Square Rd., Franklin, Franklin Co. 05457.

SOUTH BURLINGTON, CHITTENDEN CO., ST. JOHN VIANNEY (1940) Rev. Bernard E. Gaudreau; Deacons Joseph Lane; Anthony Previti; Christopher Keough. In Res., Rev. Timothy Sullivan.
Res.: 160 Hinesburg Rd., 05403. Tel: 802-864-4166; Fax: 802-863-6065.
Catechesis/Religious Program—Tel: 802-864-4166, Ext. 204. Patricia Soychak, D.R.E. Students 235.

SOUTH HERO, GRAND ISLE CO., ST. ROSE OF LIMA (1895) Rev. Lawrence P. Ridgley.
Res.: 501 Rte. 2, 05486. Tel: 802-372-4092; Fax: 802-372-4770.
Catechesis/Religious Program—Students 47.
Mission—St. Joseph Grand Isle, Grand Isle Co.

SPRINGFIELD, WINDSOR CO., MATERNITY OF THE BLESSED VIRGIN MARY (1900) [CEM] Rev. Peter Y. Williams.
Res.: 40 Summer St., 05156. Tel: 802-885-3400; Fax: 802-885-2250.
Catechesis/Religious Program—Eileen Kendall, C.R.E. Students 50.

STOWE, LAMOILLE CO., BLESSED SACRAMENT (1954) Rev. Benedict C. Kiely.
Res.: 728 Mountain Rd., P.O. Box 27, 05672. Tel: 802-253-7536; Fax: 802-253-4445.
Catechesis/Religious Program—Tel: 802-253-7536, Ext. 13. Victoria Colyer, D.R.E. Students 73.

SWANTON, FRANKLIN CO., NATIVITY OF THE BLESSED VIRGIN MARY-ST. LOUIS (2008) [CEM], Parish includes Nativity of the Blessed Virgin Mary, Swanton & St. Louis, Highgate Center. Rev. Thomas D. Nadeau, Admin.
Res.: 65 Canada St., 05488. Tel: 802-868-4517; 802-868-4262; Fax: 802-868-9202.
Catechesis/Religious Program—Students 194.

TROY, ORLEANS CO., SACRED HEART OF JESUS (1931) [CEM] Rev. Henry Mlinganisa.
Res.: P.O. Box 109, 05868. Tel: 802-988-2608; Fax: 802-988-2608.
Catechesis/Religious Program—Pauline Couture, D.R.E. Tel: 802-744-2733; Cheryl Clarke, D.R.E. Tel: 802-744-9935. Students 38.
Mission—St. Ignatius Loyola Lowell, Orleans Co.

UNDERHILL CENTER, CHITTENDEN CO., ST. THOMAS (1856) [CEM 3] Rev. Charles R. Danielson; Deacon Peter Brooks.
Res.: 6 Green St., P.O. Box 3, 05490-0003. Tel: 802-899-4632; Fax: 802-899-5120.
Catechesis/Religious Program—Tel: 802-899-4770. Suzanne Widlicka, D.R.E. Students 92.

VERGENNES, ADDISON CO., ST. PETER (1881) [CEM] Rev. Yvon J. Royer.
Res.: 85 S. Maple St., P.O. Box 324, 05491-0924. Tel: 802-877-2367; Fax: 802-877-1063.
Catechesis/Religious Program—Kathleen Krayewsky, D.R.E. Students 52.

WALLINGFORD, RUTLAND CO., ST. PATRICK (1910) [CEM] Revs. Justin J. Baker; Timothy Naples; Sebastian Modike.
Res.: 218 N. Main St., P.O. Box 99, 05773-0099. Tel: 802-446-2161.
Catechesis/Religious Program—Students 31.

WATERBURY, WASHINGTON CO., ST. ANDREW (1869) [CEM] Rev. Jerome Mercure.
Res.: 109 S. Main St., 05676. Tel: 802-244-7734; Fax: 802-244-7934.
Catechesis/Religious Program—Dianne Bilodeau, D.R.E. Students 136.
Mission—Our Lady of the Snows Waitsfield, Washington Co.
Mission—St. Patrick Moretown, Washington Co.

WEST RUTLAND, RUTLAND CO.
1—ST. BRIDGET (1857) [CEM 2] Rev. Barry C. Meehan, S.J., Admin.
Res.: 28 Church St., 05777. Tel: 802-438-2490.
Catechesis/Religious Program— Lisa Harvey, D.R.E. Students 49.
2—ST. STANISLAUS KOSTKA (1904), (Polish), [CEM] Rev. Msgr. Frank S. Warzocha.
Res.: 23 Barnes St., 05777. Tel: 802-438-5671.
Catechesis/Religious Program—Students 12.

WHITE RIVER JUNCTION, WINDSOR CO., ST. ANTHONY (1869) [CEM 2] Revs. Kenneth Thibodeau, S.M.; Kenneth Ridgeway, S.M.; Deacon John P. Guarino.
Res.: 15 Church St., 05001. Tel: 802-295-2225; Fax: 802-296-6008.
Religious Education Center—53 Church St., 05001. Tel: 802-295-6607.
Catechesis/Religious Program—Roisin Viens, D.R.E.; Eileen Urquhart, D.R.E.; Kelli Kehoe, D.R.E.; Dorothy Moffitt, D.R.E. Students 70.

WILLISTON, CHITTENDEN CO., IMMACULATE HEART OF MARY (1951) Rev. Donald J. Ravey.
Res.: 7417 Williston Rd., P.O. Box 1047, 05495. Tel: 802-878-4513.
Catechesis/Religious Program—Students 186.

WILMINGTON, WINDHAM CO., OUR LADY OF FATIMA (1959) Rev. Vincent Onunkwo, Admin.
Res.: 96 E. Main St., P.O. Box 188, 05363. Tel: 802-464-7329; Fax: 802-464-9483.
Catechesis/Religious Program—Students 35.

WINDSOR, WINDSOR CO., ST. FRANCIS OF ASSISI (1886) [CEM] Rev. Rene Butler, M.S. In Res., Rev. Paul Belhumeur, M.S.
Res.: 30 Union St., P.O. Box 46, 05089. Tel: 802-674-2157; Fax: 802-674-9416.
Catechesis/Religious Program—Joyce K. Corbin, D.R.E. Students 72.

WINOOSKI, CHITTENDEN CO.
1—ST. FRANCIS XAVIER (1868) [CEM] Rev. Msgr. Richard G. LaValley; Deacon John F. Place. In Res., Rev. Bernard W. Bourgeois.
Res.: 3 St. Peter St., Ste. 2, 05404. Tel: 802-655-2290; Fax: 802-655-3036.
School—(Grades PreK-8) Tel: 802-655-2600; Fax: 802-655-3096. Mr. Jesse Gaudette, Prin.; Mr. Eric Becker, Vice Prin.; Kathryn LaVigne, Admin. Sisters 1; Lay Teachers 16; Students 151.
Catechesis/Religious Program—Students 119.
Convent—Our Lady of Providence, Tel: 802-655-2395; Fax: 802-655-3888.
St. Vincent de Paul Center—Tel: 802-655-3006.
Extension Program—Tel: 802-655-4660.
2—ST. STEPHEN (1882) [CEM] Rev. Msgr. Wendell H. Searles, Admin. (Retired).
Res.: 115 Barlow St., 05404. Tel: 802-655-0318; Fax: 802-655-4779.
Catechesis/Religious Program—Jeffrey Badillo, D.R.E. Students 20.

WOODSTOCK, WINDSOR CO., OUR LADY OF THE SNOWS (1894) Rev. Thomas L. Mosher.
Res.: 7 South St., P.O. Box 397, 05091-0397. Tel: 802-457-2322; Fax: 802-457-5805.
Catechesis/Religious Program—Deborah Greenan, D.R.E. Students 64.
Mission—Our Lady of the Mountains Killington, Rutland Co.

Chaplains of Public Institutions

BURLINGTON. *Fletcher Allen Health Care* 05401. Tel: 802-656-2770. Revs. John Nwagbaraocha, D.S., Fidelis Agughara, Timothy Sullivan.

WATERBURY. *State Hospital*. Rev. Jerome Mercure.

WHITE RIVER JUNCTION. *Veterans Administration Hospital*. Rev. Joseph L. O'Keefe.

On Duty Outside the Diocese:
Rev.—
Dowd, Barry G., Mary Queen of the Universe Shrine, 8300 Vineland Ave., Orlando, FL 32821.

Retired:
Rev. Msgrs.—
Gelineau, Edward J., Starr Farm Nursing Home, 98 Starr Farm Rd., 05408.
Mayo, Reid C., 265 Morrison Rd., Barre, 05641.
McSweeney, John R., J.C.L., 125 Kennedy Dr., Unit #36, South Burlington, 05403. Tel: 802-863-6017
Rivard, Roland J., 50 Winding Brook Dr., South Burlington, 05403.
Revs.—
Beauregard, James E., Birchwood Terrace Healthcare, 43 Starr Farm Rd., 05408.
Branon, Philip J., St. Albans Healthcare & Rehab Center, 596 Sheldon Rd., Saint Albans, 05478.
Chant, William S., P.O. Box 3192, 05408-0031.
Davignon, Charles P., 62 Davingnon Ln., Brownington, 05860.
Depeaux, Bernard F., J.C.L., 351 North Ave., P.O. Box 489, 05402-0489. Tel: 802-658-6110
Dupuis, George H., Loretto Home, 59 Meadow St., Rutland, 05701.
Hart, Edward J., Burlington Health and Rehabilitation, 300 Pearl St., 05401.
Herbert, John J., The Loretto Home, 59 Meadow St., Rutland, 05701. Tel: 802-773-8840
Holland, Francis M., Our Lady of Providence Convent, 47 W. Spring St., Winooski, 05404.
Kennedy-Warley, David G., 17028 N. Pinion Ln., Sun City, AZ 85373.
LaFlamme, Julien J., 239 Rte. 67 W., North Bennington, 05257. Tel: 802-442-9974
LaMothe, Philip R., 386 Stephenson Rd., Apt. 1, Lowell, 05847.
Laplante, Jean-Paul, 64 N. Elm St., St. Albans, 05478.
Lively, Joseph A., 257 Peacham Pond Rd., Marshfield, 05658. Tel: 802-426-3847
McCarthy, Joseph, Starr Farm Nursing Home, 98 Starr Farm Rd., 05408.
Morgan, William P., 2609 Roy Mountain Rd., P.O. Box 76, Barnet, 05821. Tel: 802-633-2870
Pray, Joseph N., P.O. Box 85, Castleton, 05735. Tel: 802-273-2621
Ragis, Gerald, 2215 The Terraces, Shelburne, 05482. Tel: 802-985-0707
Rousseau, Peter A., The Arbors, 687 Harbor Rd., Shelburne, 05482.
Shea, James M., 792 Capri Isles Blvd., Venice, FL 34292. Tel: 941-416-2455
Vignoe, Joseph M., 109 Preston Ln., P.O. Box 532, Bomoseen, 05732. Tel: 802-468-5349
Von Fauer, Stephen C., Mary Theotokos Center, P.O. Box 88, West Burke, 05871. Tel: 802-467-1132
Whalen, John, 201 River Rd., Westmoreland, NH 03467-4410.
Whalen, Robert B., P.O. Box 59, Poultney, 05764. Tel: 802-287-9758

Permanent Deacons:
Anderberg, Richard, Our Lady of the Valley, Townshend
Baker, David, St. John the Evangelist, St. Johnsbury
Bisson, David, St. Monica, Barre
Blicharz, John, Bellows Falls
Brenneman, Walter, St. Augustine, Montpelier
Brooks, Peter T., St. Thomas, Underhill Ctr.
Brown, William J., III
Burk, Bruce, St. John, St. Johnsbury
Chagnon, Clifford, All Saints, Richford
Cooney, Thomas F., Holy Cross, Morrisville
Cummings, Regis E., St. Augustine, Montpelier
Desilets, Raymond J., St. John, St. Johnsbury
Driscoll, Jerome, Chapel of the Snows, Stratton Mountain
Fitzpatrick, Kelly, Our Lady of Perpetual Help, Bradford
Gagne, Gabriel, St. Mary; St. Albans
Garrow, Paul, St. Ann, Milton
Gibbo, Timothy, St. Mark, Burlington
Glinka, William, Cathedral of the Immaculate Conception, Burlington
Gratton, John P.E., St. Benedict, West Charleston
Griffin, Gary, St. Mary, Brandon
Guarino, John P., St. Anthony, White River Junction
Gummere, Peter, St. John the Evangelist, St. Johnsbury
Hawk, Ivan O., III, Holy Cross, Colchester
Keough, Christopher, St. John Vianney, South Burlington
Krawczyk, Eugene, (Outside the Diocese)

Lane, Joseph W., Sr., St. John Vianney, South Burlington
Langlois, Duane, Holy Angels, St. Albans
Liegey, Gabriel M., Jr., St. Patrick, Fairfield
Lissandrello, Paul (On Duty Outside the Diocese)
Mayo, Bernier L., St. John, St. Johnsbury
Mello, Paul (On Duty Outside the Diocese)
Meunier, Louis A., St. Anthony and Christ the King, Burlington
Moore, Dennis, Ascension, Georgia
Moran, Robert J., St. Anne, Middletown Springs
O'Brien, David, St. John the Baptist, North Bennington
Perkins, Richard, St. Frances Cabrini, West Pawlet
Place, John F., St. Francis Xavier, Winooski
Previti, Anthony, St. John Vianney, South Burlington
Pudvah, Daniel, St. Monica, Barre
Ramey, Jon, St. Isidore, Montgomery Center
Ratte, Stephen J., St. Luke, Fairfax
Rixon, John, St. Mary, St. Albans
Rock, James E., (On Duty Outside the Diocese)
Schneider, Gesualdo, St. Augustine, Montpelier
Scilla, Gerald, St. Pius X, Essex Ctr.
Taylor, Timm, St. Anthony; Christ the King, Burlington
Toborg, Alfred, St. Elizabeth, Lyndonville
Vincelette, Alan, St. Amadeus, Alburg

INSTITUTIONS LOCATED IN THE DIOCESE

[A] COLLEGES AND UNIVERSITIES

COLCHESTER. *St. Michael's College*, One Winooski Park, 05439. Tel: 802-654-2000; 802-654-2476; Fax: 802-654-2780. Web: www.smcvt.edu. Dr. John J. Neuhauser, Pres.; Mr. Joseph P. Garrity, Chm. of the Bd.; Ms. Lisa Powlison, Asst. to Pres.; Ms. Marilyn Cormier, Dir. Community Rels.; Dr. Karen A. Talentino, Vice Pres. Academic Affairs; Mr. Michael D. Samara, Vice Pres. Student Affairs; Mr. Patrick Gallivan, Vice Pres. Institutional Advancement; Rev. Brian J. Cummings, S.S.E., Dir. Campus Ministry; Mr. Jerry E. Flanagan, Vice Pres. Enrollment & Mktg.; Mr. John D. Sheehey, Registrar; Dr. Edward Mahoney, Dir. Graduate Theology & Pastoral Ministry Prog.; Jerome P. Monachino, Dir., Liturgical Music; Michael J. New, Vice Pres. Human Resources; Revs. Raymond J. Doherty, S.S.E., Campus Min.; Richard N. Berube, S.S.E., Local Supr.; Joseph M. McLaughlin, S.S.E., Prof.; John K. Payne, Dir. Library & Information Svcs. Priests 1; Lay Teachers 150; Students 2,500.

RUTLAND. **College of St. Joseph in Vermont*, 71 Clement Rd., 05701-3899. Tel: 802-773-5900; Fax: 802-776-5258. Email: fmiglorie@csj.edu. Web: www.csj.edu. Dr. Frank G. Miglorie Jr., Pres.; Doreen McCullough, Librarian. Lay Teachers 13; Students 424.

[B] CENTRAL HIGH SCHOOLS, DIOCESAN AND PAROCHIAL

RUTLAND. *Mount St. Joseph Academy - Rutland Catholic Schools*, 127 Convent Ave., 05701. Tel: 802-775-0151; Fax: 802-775-0424. Email: principal@msjvermont.org. Web: www.msjvermont.org. Mr. Paolo Zancanaro, Prin.; Lorin Gides, Guidance Dir.; Julie Reynolds, Admissions Dir.; Donna Butman, Librarian; Rev. Timothy Naples, Chap. Sisters of St. Joseph. Priests 1; Lay Teachers 15; Students 86.

SOUTH BURLINGTON. *Rice Memorial High School*, 99 Proctor Ave., 05403. Tel: 802-862-6521; Fax: 802-864-9931. Email: bourgeois@ricehs.org. Web: www.ricehs.org. Rev. Bernard W. Bourgeois, Prin.; Brian Ricca, Assoc. Prin. for Academics; Christian Frenette, Dean of Students; Ann Kenney, Librarian. Priests 2; Lay Teachers 35; Students 365.

[C] ELEMENTARY SCHOOLS, PAROCHIAL

BURLINGTON. *Christ The King*, (Grades PreSchool-8), 136 Locust St., 05401. Tel: 802-862-6696; Fax: 802-658-6553. Web: www.christthekingburlington.org. Ms. Paulette Thibault, Prin.; Aida Cadrecha, Librarian. Lay Teachers 20; Students 244.

St. Joseph, (Grades PreK-8), 20 Allen St., 05401. Tel: 802-864-5623; Fax: 802-860-2627. Email: sjsoffice@comcast.net. Web: www.stjosephvermont.com. Mrs. Evelyn Rogerson, Prin. Lay Teachers 10; Students 74.

Mater Christi School, (Grades PreK-8), 50 Mansfield Ave., 05401. Tel: 802-658-3992; Fax: 802-863-1196. Email: bbroomhall@mcschool.org. Web: www.mcschool.org. Mrs. Beverly Broomhall, Prin.; Linda Audette, Librarian; Kathy Duggan, Librarian. Sisters 1; Lay Teachers 32; Students 341.

BARRE. *Central Vermont Catholic School (St. Monica Campus)*, (Grades PreK-8), 79 Summer St., 05641. Tel: 802-476-5015; Fax: 802-476-0861. Email: pattiecvcs@yahoo.com. Ms. Patricia M. O'Mahoney, Prin.; Gwen Minoli, Librarian. Lay Teachers 11; Students 146.

BARTON. *St. Paul's*, (Grades PreK-8), 54 Eastern Ave., 05822. Tel: 802-525-6578; Fax: 802-525-3869. Email: stpaulcatholicschool@yahoo.com. Mr. Peter T. Close, Prin. Lay Teachers 6; Students 89.

BENNINGTON. *The School of Sacred Heart St. Francis de Sales*, (Grades PreK-8), 307 School St., 05201. Tel: 802-442-2446; Fax: 802-442-2344. Email: estesdb@comcast.net. Web: www.sacredheartbennington.org. Mr. David B. Estes, Prin.; Marcia Hendery, Librarian; Kathy Murphy, Librarian. Lay Teachers 10; Students 163.

BRATTLEBORO. *St. Michael School*, (Grades PreSchool-8), 48 Walnut St., 05301. Tel: 802-254-6320; Fax: 802-254-5229. Email: principal@smsvt.info. Mrs. Elaine Beam, Prin.; Melissa Worden, Librarian. Lay Teachers 6; Students 70.

MIDDLEBURY. *St. Mary School*, (Grades PreK-6), 86 Shannon St., 05753. Tel: 802-388-8392; Fax: 802-388-8392. Email: moniquealmquist@saintmarysvt.org. Ms. Monique Almquist, Prin. Lay Teachers 13; Students 75.

MORRISVILLE. *Bishop John A. Marshall School*, (Grades PreK-8), 680 La Porte Rd., 05661. Tel: 802-888-4758; Fax: 802-888-3137. Email: cwilson@bjams.org. Web: www.bjams.org. Mrs. Carrie Wilson, Prin.; Jennifer Wileman, Librarian. Lay Teachers 19; Students 136.

RUTLAND. *Christ the King - Rutland Catholic Schools*, (Grades PreK-8), 60 S. Main St., 05701. Tel: 802-773-0500; Fax: 802-773-0554. Email: cwincowski@cksrutland.org. Web: www.cksrutland.com. Mrs. Carol H. Wincowski, Prin.; Lila Millard, Librarian. Sisters 1; Lay Teachers 14; Students 190.

ST. JOHNSBURY. *Good Shepherd School*, (Grades PreK-8), 121 Maple St., 05819. Tel: 802-751-8223; Fax: 802-751-8111. Email: khaskins@gscsvt.org. Mrs. Karen Haskins, Prin. Lay Teachers 10; Students 165.

WINOOSKI. *St. Francis Xavier*, (Grades PreK-8), 5 St. Peter St., 05404. Tel: 802-655-2600; Fax: 802-655-3096. Email: gaudette_stfrancis@yahoo.com. Web: www.SFXWinooski.org. Mr. Jesse Gaudette, Prin.; Mr. Eric Becker, Vice Prin.; Kathryn LaVigne, Admin. & Dir. Early Educ.; Mrs. Kathleen Finn, Librarian. Sisters 1; Lay Teachers 21; Students 162.

[D] HOMES FOR AGED

BURLINGTON. *St. Joseph/Kervick Home*, 243 N. Prospect St., 05401. Tel: 802-864-0264; Fax: 802-864-5640. Mr. Lawrence Assell, Dir.; David Anderson, Admin.; Rev. Fidelis Agughara, Chap. Managed by Vermont Catholic Charities. Guests 40.

DERBY LINE. *Michaud/Kervick Home*, 47 Herrick Rd., 05830. Tel: 802-873-3152; Fax: 802-873-9206. Email: mmmanor@comcast.net. Web: www.vermontcatholic.org. Mr. Lawrence Assell, Dir.; Ward Nolan, Admin. Managed by Vermont Catholic Charities. Guests 29.

RUTLAND. *St. Joseph/Kervick Residence*, 131 Convent Ave., 05701. Tel: 802-775-5133; Fax: 802-747-0167. Barbara Mucha, R.N., Admin.; Mr. Lawrence Assell, Dir.; Rev. John W. Hamilton, Resident Chap. (Retired). Managed by Vermont Catholic Charities. Guests 51.

Loretto/Kervick Home, 59 Meadow St., 05701. Tel: 802-773-8840; Fax: 802-773-9638. Email: lhometc@sover.net. Barbara Mucha, R.N., Admin.; Mr. Lawrence Assell, Dir.; Rev. John J. Herbert, Resident Chap. (Retired). Managed by Vermont Catholic Charities. Guests 55.

[E] MONASTERIES AND RESIDENCES OF PRIESTS AND BROTHERS

ARLINGTON. *Carthusian Foundation in America, Inc., Charterhouse of the Transfiguration*, 1084 Ave Maria Way, 05250. Tel: 802-362-2550; Fax: 802-362-3584. Email: carthusians_in_america@chartreuse.info. Web: transfiguration.chartreux.org. Revs. Johan de Bruijn, O.Cart. (Holland), Librarian; Philip Dahl, O.Cart. (Norway), Sacristan; Lorenzo Maria Tolentino de la Rosa Jr., O.Cart. (Philippines), Prior; Mary Joseph Kim, O.Cart. (Korea, South), Novice Master. Carthusian Foundation, Association Fraternelle Romande. Choir Monks: Solemn Professed 4; Converse Brothers: Solemn Professed 4; Choir Monks: Simple Professed 1; Converse Brothers: Simple Professed 1; Perpetual Donates 1; Novices 1; Aspirant 1; Postulants 2.

COLCHESTER. *Society of St. Edmund* (Edmundite Generalate), 270 Winooski Park, 05439. Tel: 802-654-3400; Fax: 802-654-3409. Email: generalate@aol.com. Web: www.sse.org. Very Rev. Michael P. Cronogue, S.S.E., Supr. Gen.; Revs. Edward J. Dubriske, S.S.E. (Venezuela); Philippe Simonnet, S.S.E. (France). Central Offices, Society of Saint Edmund. *Society of St. Edmund*, P.O. Box 272, 05439. Tel: 802-654-2000; Fax: 802-654-3409. Revs. Richard N. Berube, S.S.E., Supr.; Paul E. Couture, S.S.E.; Brian J. Cummings, S.S.E.; Raymond J. Doherty, S.S.E.; Joseph M. McLaughlin, S.S.E.; Richard L. Vanderweel, S.S.E.; John T. Scully, S.S.E.; David Theroux, S.S.E.; Bro. Thomas Berube, S.S.E. (Edmundite Community at St. Michael's College) *Edmundnite House of Formation*, 25 Milham Ct., South Burlington, 05403. Tel: 802-497-0893; Fax: 802-654-3409. Revs. Marcel R. Rainville, S.S.E., Dir. Formation; Stanley Deresienski, S.S.E. Residents 4.

WESTON. *Priory of Benedictine Monks*, 58 Priory Hill Rd., 05161-6400. Tel: 802-824-5409; Fax: 802-824-3573. Email: brothers@westonpriory.org. Web: www.westonpriory.org. Very Rev. Richard Iaquinto, O.S.B., Prior; Revs. Peter Claude Anctil, O.S.B.; Robert J. Kiernan, O.S.B.; Mark Ronald Nicolosi, O.S.B.; John Hammond, O.S.B. Priests 5; Brothers 9.

[F] CONVENTS AND RESIDENCES OF SISTERS

BURLINGTON. *Franciscan Sisters of the Atonement Convent*, 21 Dodds Ct., 05401. Tel: 802-862-8288. Sr. Helen Hadcock, S.A. Sisters 2.

Sisters of Mercy of the Americas-Northeast Community, 100 Mansfield Ave., 05401. Tel: 802-863-6835; Fax: 802-863-1486. Email: rsmvermont@hotmail.com. Sr. Marianne Read, R.S.M., M.Ed., C.A.E.S., Life & Ministry Admin. Residence for Sisters and Life Ministry Office. Sisters 30.

LOWELL. *The Carmelite Nuns of Vermont, Inc., St. Joseph's Carmelite Community*, 386 Stephenson Rd., 05847. Tel: 802-744-2346. Sr. Diane Gauthier, O.C.D., Contact Person. Sisters 5.

NEWPORT. *Sacred Heart Convent* (Daughters of Charity of the Sacred Heart), 119 Clermont Ter., 05855. Tel: 802-334-7058. Sisters 3.

RUTLAND. *Congregation of the Sisters of St. Joseph of Springfield, MA*, 15 Clement Rd., 05701.

WESTFIELD. *Monastery of the Immaculate Heart of Mary*, 4103 VT Rte. 100, 05874. Tel: 802-744-6525; Fax: 802-744-6236. Sisters Laurence A. M. Couture, O.S.B., Prioress; Maria-Magdalen Grumm, O.S.B., Subprioress & Novice Mistress; Rev. Dom Lawrence Brown, O.S.B., Resident Chap., Monk of Clear Creek, OK. Benedictine Cloistered Nuns, Congregation of Solesmes. Professed Nuns 11; Temporary Professed 1; Postulants 1; Novices 2.

WINOOSKI. *Missionary Sisters of Our Lady of Africa (M.S.O.L.A.)*, 47 W. Spring St., 05404. Tel: 802-655-4003; Fax: 802-655-1830. Email: m.heintz@verizon.net. Sr. Marie Heintz, Contact Person. Sisters 7.

Religious Hospitallers of St. Joseph (1636) 47 W. Spring St., 05404-1319. Tel: 802-655-1160; Fax: 802-654-3976. Sr. Adrienne Desjardins, R.H.S.J., Supr. Sisters 8.

Sisters of Providence, 47 W. Spring St., 05404. Tel: 802-655-2395; Fax: 802-655-3888. Email: olopr@aol.com. Sr. Carmen Proulx, S.P., Supr. Sisters 23.

[G] NEWMAN CENTERS

BURLINGTON. *University of Vermont-The Catholic Center at UVM* 390 S. Prospect St., Redstone Campus, 05401. Tel: 802-862-8403; Fax: 802-865-9480. Email: catholiccenteruvm@gmail.com. Web: www.uvmcatholic.com. Rev. Jon-Daniel Schnobrich, Dir. In Res. Rev. Msgr. John J. McDermott, V.G., J.C.L.

Castleton State College St. John Rectory, P.O. Box 128, Castleton, 05735. Tel: 802-468-5706; Fax: 802-468-2777. Rev. Henry P. Furman, Chap.

Goddard College (Plainfield) Attended by St. Augustine, 16 Barre St., Montpelier, 05602. Tel: 802-223-5285; Fax: 802-223-3621. Rev. Michael E. Augustinowitz.

Green Mountain College St. Raphael Rectory, Main St., Poultney, 05764. Tel: 802-287-5703. Rev. Adam J. Krempa.

Johnson State College (Johnson) P.O. Box 339, Morrisville, 05661. Tel: 802-888-3318; Fax: 802-888-6177. Attended by Holy Cross, Morrisville

Lyndon State College Lyndonville, 05851. Tel: 802-626-5267; Fax: 802-656-3324.

Middlebury College St. Mary Rectory, 326 College St., Middlebury, 05753. Tel: 802-388-2943; Fax: 802-388-6023. Rev. William R. Beaudin.

Norwich Newman Apostolate Norwich University, Northfield, 05663. Tel: 802-862-8403; Fax: 802-865-9480. Rev. Msgr. Richard G. LaValley, Co-Chap.; Rev. Michael W. DeForge, Co-Chap.

Vermont Technical College Sts. Donatian and Rogatian Rectory, 25 S. Pleasant St., Randolph, 05060. Tel: 802-728-3227; Fax: 802-728-3570. Rev. John M. Milanese, Chap.

[H] MISCELLANEOUS

BURLINGTON. *Institute for Spiritual Development, Inc.*, 100 Mansfield Ave., 05401. Tel: 802-862-2202; Fax: 802-843-1486. Email: claireboissy@hotmail.com. Web: www.spiritvt.org. Sr. Claire Boissy, R.S.M., Admin. Coord.

Mercy Connections, Inc., 346 Shelburne Rd., 05401. Tel: 802-846-7062; Fax: 802-846-7237. Email: bferries@mercyconnections.org. Web: www.mercyconnections.org. Betsy Ferries, Exec. Dir.

Mercy Investment Program, Inc., Sisters of Mercy of the Americas, 100 Mansfield Ave., 05401. Tel: 802-863-6835; Fax: 802-863-1486. Sisters Catherine McGroarty, R.S.M., (Merion, PA); Barbara Wheeley, R.S.M., (Belmont, NC); Ellen Kurtz, R.S.M., (Cumberland, RI); Nancy Hoff, R.S.M., (Buffalo, NY); Norita Cooney, R.S.M., (Omaha, NE); Linda Werthman, R.S.M., (Silver Spring, MD). MIP Members & Regional Communities.

BENSON. *Lumen Christi Retreat House*, 56 Howard Hill Rd., P.O. Box 300, 05731. Tel: 802-537-4531. Sr. Ellen Kurtz, R.S.M., Pres. Reservations for retreat call Tel: 802-846-7084

BRATTLEBORO. *Neringa, Inc.*, 600 Liberty Hwy., Putnam, CT 06260. Tel: 978-582-5592. Email: dainora@neringa.org. Web: www.neringa.org. Dainora Kupcinskas, Asst. Exec. Dir.

COLCHESTER. *Fanny Allen Corporation*, 101 College Pkwy., 05446. Tel: 781-862-1634. Sponsored by Covenant Health Systems, Lexington, MA.

Fanny Allen Holdings, Inc., 790 College Pkwy., 05446. Tel: 802-847-6448; Fax: 802-847-6434. Email: irene.duchesneau@vtmednet.org. Sr. Irene Duchesneau, R.H.S.J., Exec. Dir. Fanny Allen Holdings, Inc. oversees property that it owns in Colchester, Vermont, leases to Fletcher Allen Health Care for use as a hospital and seeks to promote its Catholic identity. Fanny Allen Corporation operates a Community Fund that supports charitable organizations serving the poor, the sick and the most vulnerable.

ISLE LA MOTTE. *St. Anne's Shrine* 05463. Tel: 802-928-3362; Fax: 802-928-3305. Email: fstanne@aol.com. Web: www.saintannesshrine.org. Rev. Brian J. Cummings, S.S.E., Spiritual Dir. Conducted by Fathers of Society of St. Edmund; Open May 15-Oct. 15.

RANDOLPH. *Prelature of the Holy Cross and Opus Dei*, Wynnview Center, R.D. 1, Sunset Hill, 05060. Tel: 802-728-5414; Fax: 802-728-3334. Web: www.opusdei.org.

RELIGIOUS INSTITUTES OF MEN REPRESENTED IN THE DIOCESE

For further details refer to the corresponding bracketed number in the Religious Institutes of Men or Women section.

[0200]—*Benedictine Monks*—O.S.B.
[]—*Capuchin Friars of North America*—O.F.M., Cap.
[0780]—*Marist Fathers*—S.M.
[0720]—*The Missionaries of Our Lady of La Salette* (Prov. of the Immaculate Heart of Mary)—M.S.
[0280]—*Order of Carthusians*—O.Cart.
[0610]—*Priests of the Congregation of Holy Cross* (Eastern Prov.)—C.S.C.
[]—*Society of Jesus*—S.J.
[0440]—*Society of Saint Edmund*—S.S.E.

RELIGIOUS INSTITUTES OF WOMEN REPRESENTED IN THE DIOCESE

[0170]—*Benedictine Cloistered Nuns of the Congregation of Solesmes*—O.S.B.
[0750]—*Daughters of the Charity of the Sacred Heart of Jesus*—F.C.S.C.J.
[0820]—*Daughters of the Holy Spirit*—D.H.S.
[0420]—*Discalced Carmelite Nuns*—O.C.D.
[1190]—*Franciscan Sisters of the Atonement*—S.A.
[2820]—*Missionary Sisters of Our Lady of Africa*—M.S.O.L.A.
[3440]—*Religious Hospitallers of Saint Joseph*—R.H.S.J.
[1930]—*Sisters of Holy Cross*—C.S.C.
[2575]—*Sisters of Mercy*—R.S.M.
[3000]—*Sisters of Notre Dame de Namur*—S.N.D.deN.
[3350]—*Sisters of Providence*—S.P.
[3830-07]—*Sisters of St. Joseph (Springfield, MA)*—S.S.J.

DIOCESAN CEMETERIES

SOUTH BURLINGTON. *Resurrection Park Cemetery*, P.O. Box 489, 05402-0489. Mr. Peter Wells, Dir. Facilities & Insurance.

NECROLOGY

† Demasi, Michael A., (Retired)—Died May 19, 2009
† McKnight, Robert J., (Retired)—Died June 29, 2009

An asterisk (*) denotes an organization that has established tax-exempt status directly with the IRS and is not covered by the USCCB Group Ruling.

Diocese of Camden

(Dioecesis Camdensis)

Most Reverend

JOSEPH A. GALANTE, D.D., J.C.D.

Bishop of Camden; ordained May 16, 1964; appointed Titular Bishop of Equilum and Auxiliary Bishop of San Antonio October 13, 1992; consecrated December 11, 1992; appointed Bishop of Beaumont April 5, 1994; installed Bishop of Beaumont May 9, 1994; appointed Coadjutor Bishop of Dallas November 23, 1999; installed January 14, 2000; appointed Bishop of Camden March 23, 2004; installed April 30, 2004.

Chancery Office: Camden Diocesan Center, 631 Market St., P.O. Box 708, Camden, NJ 08101. Tel: 856-756-7900; Fax: 856-963-2655.

ESTABLISHED DECEMBER 9, 1937.

Square Miles 2,691.

Legal Corporate Title: "The Diocese of Camden, New Jersey."

Comprises six Counties in the State of New Jersey--viz., Atlantic, Camden, Cape May, Cumberland, Gloucester and Salem.

For legal titles of parishes and diocesan institutions, consult the Chancery Office.

STATISTICAL OVERVIEW

Personnel	
Bishop	1
Priests: Diocesan Active in Diocese	128
Priests: Diocesan Active Outside Diocese	46
Priests: Diocesan in Foreign Missions	4
Priests: Retired, Sick or Absent	111
Number of Diocesan Priests	289
Religious Priests in Diocese	36
Total Priests in Diocese	325
Extern Priests in Diocese	26
Ordinations:	
Diocesan Priests	1
Transitional Deacons	4
Permanent Deacons in Diocese	152
Total Brothers	12
Total Sisters	286
Parishes	
Parishes	125
With Resident Pastor:	
Resident Diocesan Priests	119
Resident Religious Priests	5
Without Resident Pastor:	
Administered by Priests	1
Missions	7
Pastoral Centers	30
Professional Ministry Personnel:	
Brothers	12
Sisters	286
Welfare	
Catholic Hospitals	1
Total Assisted	309,187
Health Care Centers	2
Total Assisted	19,304
Homes for the Aged	6
Total Assisted	1,616
Day Care Centers	2
Total Assisted	215
Specialized Homes	1
Total Assisted	899
Special Centers for Social Services	1
Total Assisted	5,588
Residential Care of Disabled	1
Total Assisted	625
Other Institutions	1
Total Assisted	6,334
Educational	
Diocesan Students in Other Seminaries	12
Total Seminarians	12
High Schools, Diocesan and Parish	7
Total Students	6,400
High Schools, Private	3
Total Students	1,385
Elementary Schools, Diocesan and Parish	39
Total Students	10,003
Elementary Schools, Private	1
Total Students	46
Non-residential Schools for the Disabled	2
Total Students	974
Catechesis/Religious Education:	
High School Students	1,400
Elementary Students	28,184
Total Students under Catholic Instruction	48,404
Teachers in the Diocese:	
Priests	8
Brothers	6
Sisters	40
Lay Teachers	1,038
Vital Statistics	
Receptions into the Church:	
Infant Baptism Totals	5,640
Minor Baptism Totals	452
Received into Full Communion	393
First Communions	5,370
Confirmations	5,260
Marriages:	
Catholic	958
Interfaith	454
Total Marriages	1,412
Deaths	3,846
Total Catholic Population	500,326
Total Population	1,610,641

Former Bishops—Most Revs. BARTHOLOMEW J. EUSTACE, S.T.D., First Bishop of Camden; consecrated March 25, 1938; died Dec. 11, 1956; JUSTIN J. MCCARTHY, S.T.D., LL.D., Second Bishop of Camden; cons. June 17, 1954; appt. to Camden, Jan. 27, 1957; died Dec. 26, 1959; CELESTINE J. DAMIANO, D.D., Third Bishop of Camden; cons. Feb. 11, 1953; transferred to Camden, Jan. 24, 1960, with the personal title of Archbishop; died Oct. 2, 1967; GEORGE H. GUILFOYLE, D.D., J.D., ord. March 25, 1944; appt. Titular Bishop of Marazanae and Auxiliary Bishop of New York, Oct. 17, 1964; cons. Nov. 30, 1964; appt. Fourth Bishop of Camden, Jan. 2, 1968; installed March 4, 1968; retired May 22, 1989; died June 11, 1991; JAMES T. MCHUGH, S.T.D., ord. May 25, 1957; appt. Titular Bishop of Morosbisdo and Auxiliary Bishop of Newark, Nov. 20, 1987; cons. Jan. 25 1988; appt. Fifth Bishop of Camden, May 13, 1989; installed June 20, 1989; appt. Coadjutor Bishop of Rockville Centre, Dec. 7, 1998; installed Third Diocesan Bishop, Jan. 4, 2000; died Dec. 10, 2000; NICHOLAS A. DIMARZIO, Ph.D., D.D., ord. May 30, 1970; appt. Titular Bishop of Mauriana and Auxiliary Bishop of Newark, Sept. 10, 1996; cons. Oct. 31, 1996; appt. Sixth Bishop of Camden June 8, 1999; installed July 22, 1999; appt. Bishop of Brooklyn, Aug. 1, 2003; installed Oct. 3, 2003.

Diocesan Offices

Camden Diocesan Center—631 Market St., Camden, 08102. Tel: 856-756-7900; Fax: 856-963-2655. Some offices are listed at separate locations.

The Diocese of Camden— A corporation under the laws of the State of New Jersey.

Officers—Most Rev. JOSEPH ANTHONY GALANTE, D.D., J.C.D., Pres.; Rev. Msgr. ROGER E. MCGRATH, Ph.D., Vice Pres.; Very Rev. DAVID J. KLEIN, J.C.L.

Diocesan Bishop—Most Rev. JOSEPH ANTHONY GALANTE, D.D., J.C.D., 631 Market St., Camden, 08102. Tel: 856-583-2808; Fax: 856-963-5777. Email: jgalante@camdendiocese.org.

Vicars General—Rev. Msgrs. JOHN H. BURTON, V.G., St. Isidore, 1655 Magnolia Rd., Vineland, 08360. Tel: 856-691-9077; Fax: 856-692-3305; ROBERT T. MCDERMOTT, V.G., Saint Joseph Pro-Cathedral, 2907 Federal St., Camden, 08102. Tel: 856-964-2776; Fax: 856-964-0044; ROGER E. MCGRATH, Ph.D., Vicar Gen. & Moderator of the Curia, 631 Market St., Camden, 08102. Tel: 856-583-2802; Fax: 856-338-0376.

Chancellor—Very Rev. DAVID J. KLEIN, J.C.L., 631 Market St., Camden, 08102. Tel: 856-583-2803; Fax: 856-338-0376.

Vice Chancellor—CATHERINE C. DARCY, J.C.D., 631 Market St., Camden, 08102. Tel: 856-583-2811; Fax: 856-338-0376.

Assistant Chancellor for Marriage Preparation—Deacon ROBERT WILLSON, 631 Market St., Camden, 08102. Tel: 856-583-2810; Fax: 856-338-0376.

Judicial Vicar—Very Rev. DAVID J. KLEIN, J.C.L., 631 Market St., Camden, 08102. Tel: 856-583-6162; Fax: 856-756-0113.

Vicar for Clergy—Rev. TERRY M. ODIEN, 631 Market St., Camden, 08101. Tel: 856-583-2854; Fax: 856-966-5957.

Vicar for Hispanics—Rev. Msgr. VICTOR S. MURO, Divine Mercy Parish, 23 W. Chestnut Ave., Vineland, 08360. Tel: 856-691-9181; Fax: 856-794-9029.

Delegate for Men Religious—Bro. THOMAS OSORIO, O.H., Saint John of God Monastery, 1145 Delsea Dr., Westville Grove, 08093. Tel: 856-848-4700, Ext. 1163; Fax: 856-848-2154.

Delegate for Temporalities—WILLIAM J. MURRAY, 631 Market St., Camden, 08102. Tel: 856-583-2828; Fax: 856-963-2655.

Delegate for Women Religious—Sr. MARIAN D. FRANTZ, I.H.M., St. Pius X Retreat House, 1840 Peter Cheeseman Rd., Blackwood, 08012. Tel: 856-227-1436; Fax: 856-227-2907.

Delegate of Lifelong Faith Formation—Sr. ROSEANN QUINN, S.S.J., 631 Market St., Camden, 08102. Tel: 856-583-6124; Fax: 856-225-0096.

Delegate for Inter-Parochial Affairs—Rev. Msgr. WILLIAM A. HODGE, V.F., St. Nicholas of Tolentine, 1409 Pacific Ave., Atlantic City, 08401. Tel: 609-344-1040; Fax: 609-344-3103.

Deaneries and Vicars Forane—

Camden City Deanery—Rev. Msgr. ROBERT T. MCDERMOTT, V.G., St. Joseph Pro-Cathedral, 2907 Federal St., Camden, 08105. Tel: 856-964-2776; Fax: 856-964-0044.

Camden West Deanery—Rev. Msgr. ANTHONY J. MANUPPELLA, V.F., St. Peter, 43 W. Maple Ave., Merchantville, 08109. Tel: 856-663-1373; Fax: 856-488-0647.

Camden Central Deanery—Rev. Msgr. WILLIAM P. BRENNAN, V.F., Christ the King, 200 Windsor Ave., Haddonfield, 08033. Tel: 856-429-1600;

Fax: 856-429-2734.
Camden South Deanery—Rev. RAYMOND P. GORMLEY, V.F., St. Teresa, 13 E. Evesham Rd., Runnemede, 08078. Tel: 856-939-1681; Fax: 856-939-3878.
Camden-Gloucester Deanery—Rev. Msgr. JAMES R. TRACY, Ph.D., V.F., St. Charles Borromeo, 176 Stagecoach Rd., Sicklerville, 08081. Tel: 856-629-0411; Fax: 856-629-0412.
Southwest Deanery—Rev. PAUL D. HARTE, V.F., Corpus Christi, 369 Georgetown Rd., Carney's Point, 08069. Tel: 856-299-3833; Fax: 856-299-3834.
Gloucester County Deanery—Rev. JOSEPH J. ADAMSON, V.F., Our Lady Queen of Peace, 161 Pitman Ave., Pitman, 08071. Tel: 856-589-5673; Fax: 856-589-0102.
Cumberland Deanery—Rev. Msgr. JOHN H. BURTON, V.G., St. Isidore, 1655 Magnolia Rd., Vineland, 08360. Tel: 856-691-9077; Fax: 856-692-3305.
Cape May Deanery—Rev. JOSEPH A. PERREAULT, V.F., St. Joseph, 126 44th St., Sea Isle City, 08243. Tel: 609-263-8696; Fax: 609-263-7884.
Atlantic South Deanery—Rev. JOSEPH LUONG T. PHAM, Our Lady, Star of the Sea, 2651 Atlantic Ave., Atlantic City, 08401. Tel: 609-345-1878; Fax: 609-348-0248.
Atlantic North Deanery—Rev. JOSEF A. WAGENHOFFER, V.F., St. Joseph, 606 Shore Rd., Somers Point, 08244. Tel: 609-927-3568; Fax: 609-653-8707.
Central Deanery—Rev. THOMAS S. DONIO, V.F., St. Martin de Porres, 129 Park Ave., Hammonton, 08037. Tel: 609-561-4322; Fax: 609-561-4433.

Diocesan Tribunal

Diocesan Tribunal—15 N. 7th St., Camden, 08102. Tel: 856-583-6162; Fax: 856-756-0113.
Judicial Vicar—Very Rev. DAVID J. KLEIN, J.C.L. Tel: 856-583-6162.
Adjutant Judicial Vicars—Rev. Msgr. DOMINIC J. BOTTINO, J.C.L.; Revs. FRANCIS P. GAFFNEY, J.C.L.; EDWARD J. LIPINSKI; JOSEPH A. SALERNO, J.C.L.
Judges—Rev. Msgrs. EDWARD D. ALLEYNE (Retired); DOMINIC J. BOTTINO, J.C.L.; Rev. FRANCIS P. GAFFNEY, J.C.L.; Rev. Msgr. PETER M. JOYCE, J.C.L.; Very Rev. DAVID J. KLEIN, J.C.L.; Revs. EDWARD J. LIPINSKI; JOSEPH A. SALERNO, J.C.L.; CATHERINE C. DARCY, J.C.D.
Defenders of the Bond—Deacon W. LEO MCBLAIN; Rev. Msgr. THOMAS F. SHARKEY, J.C.D. (Retired); Rev. ROBERT J. KANTZ, J.C.L.
Procurator-Advocate—Rev. CHRISTOPHER V. RUGGLES, J.C.L.
Auditors—Rev. WALTER A. NORRIS, Esq.; Deacon FELIX MIRANDA.
Notaries—DIANE GABLE; Mrs. CATHERINE GOLDY; Mrs. RANDEE HAYDEN.
Councils—
Presbyteral Council—
Appointed Members—Rev. Msgrs. JOSEPH V. DIMAURO; ANTHONY J. MANUPPELLA, V.F.; Revs. THOMAS A. NEWTON; JOHN J. VIGNONE.
Elected Members—
Representatives by Ordination Seniority—Revs. PAUL D. HARTE; JOSEPH P. CAPELLA; JAMES A. CASADIA.
Representative for Retired Priests—Rev. Msgr. HARRY J. JORDAN (Retired).
Representatives by Deaneries—Rev. Msgr. MICHAEL J. DOYLE, Camden City; Rev. JAMES O. DABROWSKI, Camden West; Rev. Msgr. THOMAS J. MORGAN, V.G., Camden Central; Revs. RAYMOND P. GORMLEY, V.F., Camden South; JOSEPH J. ADAMSON, V.F., Camden-Gloucester; DAVID A. GROVER, Southwest; JOSEPH T. SZOLACK, M.Div., Gloucester; PETER M. SAPORITO, Cumberland; Rev. Msgrs. JOHN T. FREY, Cape May; WILLIAM A. HODGE, V.F., Atlantic South; Revs. PERRY A. CHERUBINI, Atlantic North; EDWARD F. NAMIOTKA, Central.
International Priests Representatives—Revs. STEEPHAN CHELLAN; COSME R. DE LA PENA; SANJAI DEVIS, V.C.; CESAR REBOLLEDO RAMIREZ.
Ex Officio Members—Rev. Msgr. JOHN H. BURTON, V.G.; Very Rev. DAVID J. KLEIN, J.C.L.; Rev. Msgrs. ROBERT T. MCDERMOTT, V.G.; ROGER E. MCGRATH, Ph.D.; Revs. TERRY M. ODIEN; MATTHEW J. HILLYARD, O.S.F.S.
Priests Personnel Board—Ex Officio Members: Rev. Msgr. JOHN H. BURTON, V.G.; Very Rev. DAVID J. KLEIN, J.C.L.; Rev. Msgrs. ROBERT T. MCDERMOTT, V.G.; ROGER E. MCGRATH, Ph.D.; VICTOR S. MURO; Rev. TERRY M. ODIEN. Elected Members: Revs. PERRY A. CHERUBINI; JOHN A. DELDUCA; THOMAS R. KIELY; MARK R. CAVAGNARO; THOMAS A. NEWTON; JOSEPH T. SZOLACK, M.Div.
Continuing Education & Spiritual Formation of Priests (CESF)—Revs. JOHN E. BRUNI; JOHN C. COUGHLIN, O.F.M.; ANTHONY R. DIBARDINO, Chm.; THOMAS S. DONIO, V.F.; MICHAEL J. GOYETTE; ARIEL HERNANDEZ; ROBERT E. HUGHES; ALLEN B. LOVELL; GERARD C. MARABLE; WILLIAM F. MOORE. Ex Officio Members: Rev. Msgr. JOHN H. BURTON, V.G.; Very Rev. DAVID J. KLEIN, J.C.L.; Rev. Msgrs. ROBERT T. MCDERMOTT, V.G.; ROGER E. MCGRATH, Ph.D.; Rev. TERRY M. ODIEN.
Advanced Studies for Priests—Rev. TERRY M. ODIEN, Vicar. Tel: 856-583-2854.
Liaison with Retired Priests—Rev. ROBERT V. SMITH (Retired). Tel: 856-751-2010.
Delegate for Men Religious—Bro. THOMAS OSORIO, O.H., St. John of God Monastery, 1145 Delsea Dr., Westville Grove, 08093. Tel: 856-227-1436, Ext. 21.
Permanent Diaconate—Deacon LEO MCBLAIN. Tel: 856-583-2857.
Clergy Health Panel—Rev. JOSEPH J. ADAMSON, V.F., Chm. Members: Rev. Msgr. ANDREW E. MARTIN; Revs. THOMAS A. NEWTON; JOSEPH D. WALLACE; Dr. DOUGLAS CRAWFORD; Dr. JOSEPH W. SOKOLOWSKI.
Office of Vocations—Tel: 856-583-6170; Fax: 856-583-1046. Rev. THOMAS R. KIELY, Dir.; Rev. Msgr. ROGER E. MCGRATH, Ph.D., Dir. Seminarians.
Vocation Advisory Board—Revs. CHRISTOPHER T. BAKEY; THOMAS J. BARCELLONA; JAMES J. DURKIN; Very Rev. DAVID J. KLEIN, J.C.L.; Rev. Msgr. ROGER E. MCGRATH, Ph.D.; Revs. WILLIAM F. MOORE; JOSEPH LUONG T. PHAM; JOSEPH T. SZOLACK; Deacon JOSEPH B. CHANDLER; Mr. REGGIE BECKETT; Mrs. CLARE MCNAMEE; Dr. WILLIAM F. RANIERI; Rev. Msgr. THOMAS J. MORGAN, V.G., Consultant.
Amicus—Rev. Msgr. JOHN T. FREY, Chap. Tel: 856-547-0564.
Friends of the Sacred Heart—Rev. Msgr. CHARLES P. BARTH, Chap. (Retired). Tel: 609-561-3313.
Serra Clubs International— District 35: Mr. THOMAS HALPIN, Governor. Tel: 609-822-6361; Mr. DICK INGAGLIO, Prog. Dir. Tel: 609-390-0670; Rev. ROBERT J. GREGORIO, S.T.D., Chap. Atlantic County East: Mr. THOMAS HALPIN, Pres. Tel: 609-822-6361. Cape May County: Mr. JOHN PARIS, Pres.
Diocesan Historian—Rev. JAMES F. BETZ.
College of Consultors—Rev. Msgr. ROGER E. MCGRATH, Ph.D., Exec. Sec.; Very Rev. DAVID J. KLEIN, J.C.L.; Rev. Msgrs. JOHN H. BURTON, V.G.; WILLIAM P. BRENNAN, V.F.; JOSEPH V. DIMAURO; ROBERT T. MCDERMOTT, V.G.; THOMAS J. MCINTYRE; THOMAS J. MORGAN, V.G.; WILLIAM QUINN; RUSSELL L. ROCK; JAMES R. TRACY, Ph.D., V.F. Consultants: Revs. JOSEPH P. CAPELLA; PERRY A. CHERUBINI; PAUL D. HARTE; ROBERT E. HUGHES; Rev. Msgr. ANTHONY J. MANUPPELLA, V.F.; Revs. THOMAS A. NEWTON; JOSEPH AN NGUYEN; TERRY M. ODIEN; JOHN J. VIGNONE.
Diocesan Finance Council—Rev. Msgr. WILLIAM A. HODGE, V.F.; JOHN FINLEY; THOMAS GRANITE; Mr. JAMES F. MCHALE; ED RADETICH.
Information Technology Services—JOSEPH D. TORRIERI JR., Dir. Tel: 856-583-2888.
Office of Propagation of the Faith and Diocesan Missions—Rev. GEORGE C. SEITER, Dir. Tel: 856-583-2859; Fax: 856-338-0826.
Campaign for Human Development—Rev. KENNETH P. HALLAHAN, Coord.
Office of Development—JAMES LANAHAN, Dir. Tel: 856-583-6134; Fax: 856-338-0766.
House of Charity-Bishop's Annual Appeal—MARIANN GETTINGS, Dir. Tel: 856-583-6128.
Planned Giving—JAMES LANAHAN. Tel: 856-583-6134.
Office of Stewardship—RUSSELL DAVIS, Dir. Tel: 856-583-6102.
South Jersey Scholarship Fund—JAMES LANAHAN. Tel: 856-583-6134.
Major Gifts—HEATHER CAPPUCCIO, Dir. Tel: 856-583-6161.
Communications and Community Relations—
Office of Communications—ANDREW J. WALTON, Dir. Tel: 856-583-2851; Fax: 856-338-0826; MARIA D'ANTONIO, Asst. Tel: 856-583-2853; NICOLE JACOB, Webmaster. Tel: 856-583-2852.
Diocesan Newspaper— "The Catholic Star Herald" *Mailing Address: 15 N. 7th St., Camden, 08102.* Tel: 856-583-6198; Fax: 856-756-7938. ANDREW J. WALTON, Assoc. Publisher. Tel: 856-583-2851; CARL D. PETERS, Mng. Editor. Tel: 856-583-6147; CYNTHIA E. SOPER, Business Mgr. Tel: 856-583-6142; PAUL J. WORTHINGTON, Advertising Mgr. Tel: 856-583-6166.
Office of Community Relations—Rev. Msgr. MICHAEL T. MANNION, S.T.L., Dir., 4824 Camden Ave., Pennsauken, 08110.
Cemeteries—ROBERT GUERRIERI, Dir. Tel: 856-583-2850.
Facilities—ART BASCIANO, E.A.I.A., Diocesan Architect & Dir. Tel: 856-583-2844; THOMAS BECHARD, Diocesan Engineer. Tel: 856-583-2845; AKEMI R. KURODA, R.A. Tel: 856-583-2846; JOSEPH MARTIN, Diocesan Center. Cell: 856-278-4686; Tel: 856-583-2870; STEVEN TRAENKNER. Tel: 856-583-6176; Cell: 609-320-3522.
Administrative and Financial Services—
Diocesan Finance Officer & Bishop's Delegate for Temporalities—WILLIAM J. MURRAY. Tel: 856-583-2828.
Temporal Services—Mr. LAWRENCE J. READER, Exec. Dir. Tel: 856-583-4121.
Financial Services—EDWARD J. LOCASALE, CPA, Dir. Tel: 856-583-2822; Fax: 856-963-2655.
Diocesan Liability Insurance Program—CATHY JAMES. Tel: 856-583-2871.
Diocesan Self-Insurance Plan (DSIP) & Pension Funds—WILLIAM J. MURRAY. Tel: 856-583-2828.
Budgeting—CAROLYN THOMPSON, Dir. Tel: 856-583-2825; MICHAEL R. PORTER, Analyst. Tel: 856-583-2832.
Comptrollers—LISA M. CILIBERTO, CPA, Comptroller. Tel: 856-583-2827; MARIE E. PELUSO, Asst. Comptroller. Tel: 856-583-2823.
Coordinator for Parish Review and Support—THOMAS J. ARDECKI. Tel: 856-583-2830.
Human Resources—JOHN RAFTERY, Dir. Tel: 856-583-2867; JOSEPH P. HIGGINS, Assoc. Dir. Tel: 856-583-2868; CANDY NEWHOUSE, Health Insurance. Tel: 856-583-2313.
Office of Pastoral Planning—Sr. ANTOINE LAWLOR, I.H.M., Dir. Pastoral Priorities. Tel: 856-583-2842; LAWRENCE FARMER, Dir. Mergers. Tel: 856-583-2840; LISA WATSON, Asst. Tel: 856-583-2843.
Real Estate—KENNETH MCILVAINE, Consultant. Tel: 856-583-2867.
Safe Environment for Children, Youth and Adults—ROD J. HERRERA, L.C.S.W., Dir. Tel: 856-583-6114; Fax: 856-583-1045.
Safe Environment Training (CAP)—Tel: 856-583-6165.
Victim Assistance Coordinator—BARBARA ANN GONDEK, L.C.S.W. Tel: 856-524-4552.
Catholic Schools—
Executive Director, Catholic Schools—NICHOLAS REGINA. Tel: 856-583-6175; Fax: 856-756-0225.
Superintendent of Schools—MARY P. BOYLE, M.Ed. Tel: 856-583-6103.
Assistant Superintendents of Schools—Sr. ROSE DIFLURI, I.H.M. Tel: 856-583-6110; Mrs. PATRICIA MUNYAN. Tel: 856-583-6107.
Special Education—EILEEN MURTHA, M.A. Tel: 856-583-6108.
Parent-Teachers Association—Rev. Msgr. JAMES P. CURRAN, Moderator. Tel: 856-456-0052; PATRICIA WIRBICK, Pres. Tel: 856-456-4839.

Lifelong Formation

Diocesan Delegate for Lifelong Formation—Sr. ROSEANN QUINN, S.S.J. Tel: 856-583-6124; Fax: 856-225-0096; KEVIN O'CONNOR, Assoc. Dir. Tel: 856-583-6122; Sr. SONIA AVI, I.H.M., Assoc. Dir. Tel: 856-583-6113.
Black Catholic Ministry—CAROLYN C. JENKINS, Dir. Tel: 856-583-6136; Fax: 856-756-0297.
Hispanic Ministry—Sisters KATHLEEN BROWN, I.H.M., Dir. Tel: 856-583-6112; Fax: 856-756-0297; SONIA AVI, I.H.M., Assoc. Dir. Tel: 856-583-6113.
Ethnic Ministries—Rev. JOSEPH LUONG T. PHAM. Tel: 609-345-1878.
Ministry with the Deaf and Persons with Disabilities—Sr. BERNADETTE MCMENAMIN, S.S.J., Dir.; Rev. BRIAN E. O'NEILL. Tel: 856-583-6111; Fax: 856-756-0297.
Faith and Family Life Formation—Sr. KATHLEEN BURTON, S.S.J., Dir. Tel: 856-583-6131; Fax: 856-964-3401; MARY LOU HUGHES, Assoc. Dir. Faith Formation. Tel: 856-583-6132; LINDA K. ROBINSON, Assoc. Dir. Family Life Formation. Tel: 856-583-6116.
Bereavement Ministry—Tel: 856-583-6118.
Family Ministries—MARY ANN CHEZIK, Ph.D., Coord. Tel: 856-583-6117.
Marriage Preparation—LINDA K. ROBINSON. Tel: 856-583-6116.
Natural Family Planning—LINDA K. ROBINSON. Tel: 856-583-6116.
Project Rachael—STEPHANIE CLAUDY, Outreach Coord. Tel: 856-583-6129; Fax: 856-964-3401.
Separated and Divorced Ministry—Mrs. CAROL A. JENNINGS, Coord. Tel: 856-583-6118.
Senior Ministries—LINDA K. ROBINSON, Assoc. Dir. Family Life. Tel: 856-583-6116; Fax: 856-964-3401.
Religious Education/Faith Formation—Sr. KATHLEEN BURTON, S.S.J., Dir. Tel: 856-583-6131; Fax: 856-541-9644.
Evangelization—ANDRES ARANGO, Dir. Tel: 856-583-2876; Fax: 856-583-2879.
Lay Ministry Formation—KEVIN CONNOR. Tel: 856-583-6122; Fax: 856-225-0096.
Youth Ministries—JOSEPH ZAGARELLA, Dir. Tel: 856-583-2877; Fax: 856-583-2879.

Young Adult Ministries—ANDRES ARANGO, Dir. Tel: 856-583-2876; Fax: 856-583-2879.
Scouting—ANSON WAGER, Chm. Tel: 856-547-3197.
Campus Ministries—ANDRES ARANGO, Dir. Tel: 856-583-2876; Fax: 856-583-2879.
Rutgers University—Rev. MICHAEL J. MCCUE, O.S.F.S., Campus Min. Tel: 856-964-1580; Fax: 856-757-0438.
Rowan University—ANN POLO, Dir. Tel: 856-881-2554; Fax: 856-881-4183; LOIS DARK, Asst. Dir. Tel: 856-881-3474.
Richard Stockton College of New Jersey—Rev. GRACE MANANO, Campus Min. Tel: 609-652-0230; Fax: 609-804-9135.
Life and Justice Ministries—LAWRENCE M. DIPAUL, Dir. Tel: 856-583-2874.
Worship and Christian Initiation—STEPHEN F. OBARSKI, Dir. Tel: 856-583-2865; Fax: 856-338-0826; TRUDY CRANSTON, Assoc. Dir. Tel: 856-583-2864.
School of Liturgy—TRUDY CRANSTON, Dir. Tel: 856-583-2864.
Liturgical Commission—Rev. Msgr. JOHN H. BURTON, V.G., Chm. Tel: 856-691-9077.
Liturgical Art and Architectural Commission—Rev. Msgr. JOHN H. BURTON, V.G., Chm.; Rev. ROBERT E. HUGHES; STEPHEN F. OBARSKI.
St. Pius X Spiritual Life Center—1840 Peter Cheeseman Rd., Blackwood, 08012. Tel: 856-227-1436; Fax: 856-227-2907. Rev. FRANCIS W. DANELLA, O.S.F.S., Dir., 1840 Peter Cheeseman Rd., Blackwood, 08012. Tel: 856-227-1436.
Charismatic Renewal—Deacon JOSEPH A. GAROZZO, Diocesan Liaison. Tel: 856-467-0792.
English Cursillo—Rev. Msgr. JOHN T. FREY, Spiritual Dir. Tel: 609-967-3746; Fax: 609-967-8172; Deacon JOSEPH A. GAROZZO, Asst. Dir. Tel: 856-467-0792.
Ecumenical and Inter-Religious Affairs—Rev. JOSEPH D. WALLACE, Coord. Tel: 609-522-4114.

CLERGY, PARISHES, MISSIONS AND PAROCHIAL SCHOOLS

CITY OF CAMDEN

(CAMDEN COUNTY)

1—THE CHURCH OF THE IMMACULATE CONCEPTION, CAMDEN, N.J. (1864) [CEM] Revs. Matthew J. Hillyard, O.S.F.S., Rector; Michael J. McCue, O.S.F.S.; Deacons James Hogan. Tel: 856-225-1077; E. Michael Henry. In Res., Rev. Francis J. Blood, O.S.F.S.
Res.: 642 Market St., 08102. Tel: 856-964-1580; Fax: 856-757-0438.

2—ST. ANTHONY OF PADUA ROMAN CATHOLIC CHURCH, CAMDEN, N.J. (1945), (Hispanic), Revs. William J. Weiksnar, O.F.M.; John C. Coughlin, O.F.M.; Bros. Gerald Hudson, O.F.M.; John Quinn, O.F.M.
Res.: 2818 River Ave., 08105. Tel: 856-963-5884; Fax: 856-635-1286. Web: www.stanthonycamden.org.
School—(Grades K-8) Tel: 856-966-6791; Fax: 856-966-1616. Anna Mae Muryasz, Prin. Lay Teachers 11; Students 156.
Catechesis/Religious Program—Tel: 856-541-5025. Students 115.

3—ST. BARTHOLOMEW'S R.C. CHURCH, CAMDEN, N.J. (1940), (African American), Rev. Gerard C. Marable.
Res.: 751 Kaighns Ave., 08103. Tel: 856-365-0573; Fax: 856-365-0744.
Catechesis/Religious Program—Students 39.

4—THE CHURCH OF ST. JOAN OF ARC, WEST COLLINGSWOOD, N.J. (1920) Revs. Gerard C. Marable; Rico Ducle; Deacon Thomas E. Jennings. In Res., Revs. Gerard C. Marable; Patrick Sieber, O.F.M.
Res.: 3107 Alabama Rd., 08104. Tel: 856-962-8642; Fax: 856-962-7123. Email: arcmail@joanofarcchurch.org. Web: www.joanofarcchurch.org.
Catechesis/Religious Program—Students 85.

5—THE CHURCH OF SACRED HEART (1885), Records for St. George kept at Sacred Heart, Camden. Records for Sts. Peter and Paul kept at the Cathedral of the Immaculate Conception, Camden. Records for St. John the Baptist kept at St. Joseph Pro-Cathedral, Camden. Rev. Msgr. Michael J. Doyle; Deacon Felix Tito Miranda.
Res.: 1739 Ferry Ave., 08104. Tel: 856-966-6700; Fax: 856-756-0102.
School—(Grades K-8), Fourth & Jaspers Sts., 08104. Tel: 856-963-1341; Fax: 856-963-3551. Miss Janet Williams, Prin. Lay Teachers 12; Students 245.
Catechesis/Religious Program—Students 180.

6—THE CHURCH OF THE HOLY NAME, CAMDEN, N.J. (1913), (Hispanic), Revs. Matthew J. Hillyard, O.S.F.S.; Thomas M. Gavin, S.J.
Res.: 522 State St., 08102-1919. Tel: 856-963-1621; Fax: 856-338-0793.
School—(Grades K-8) Tel: 856-365-7930; Fax: 856-365-8041. Mrs. Patricia Quinter, Prin. Lay Teachers 9; Students 138.
Catechesis/Religious Program—Students 145.

7—ST. JOSEPH CATHOLIC CHURCH, EAST CAMDEN, N.J. (PRO-CATHEDRAL) (1893) Rev. Msgr. Robert T. McDermott; Revs. Joel Arciga Camarillo; Albert E. Harshaw; Deacon Luis J. Espinal; Sr. Margaret Mary Schmicker, O.S.F., Pastoral Min.; John Klein, Business Admin.; Mr. Michael Giansiracusa, Dir., Romero Ctr.; Kristen Prinn, Dir. Youth Ministry.
Res.: 2907 Federal St., 08105. Tel: 856-964-2776; Fax: 856-964-0044. Email: bmcder@comcast.net. Web: www.sjprocathedral.org.
School—(Grades K-8) Tel: 856-964-4336; Fax: 856-964-1080. Mrs. Frances Montgomery, Prin.; Jeanne Thorpe, Librarian. Lay Teachers 18; Students 263.
St. Joseph Child Development Center, Inc.—17 Church St., 08105. Tel: 856-963-9202; Fax: 856-963-8940. Betty Mitchell, Dir. Children 75.
Catechesis/Religious Program—Tel: 856-541-4944, Ext. 502. Berta Machado, C.R.E. Tel: 856-541-4944, Ext. 502. Students 207.

8—ST. JOSEPH'S CATHOLIC CHURCH, CAMDEN, N.J. (1892), (Polish), [CEM] Rev. Pawel Kryszkiewicz.
Res.: 1010 Liberty St., 08104. Tel: 856-963-1285; Fax: 856-963-2466. Web: www.stjoenj.net.

9—OUR LADY OF MOUNT CARMEL, CAMDEN, N.J./ CHURCH OF OUR LADY OF FATIMA, CAMDEN, N.J., (Hispanic—Italian), Rev. Matthew J. Hillyard, O.S.F.S.; Deacon Aladino Velez.
Res.: 832 S. 4th St., 08103. Tel: 856-541-7618; Fax: 856-541-2835. Email: ourladyofmtcarmelfatima@netscape.com.
Catechesis/Religious Program—Students 80.

OUTSIDE THE CITY OF CAMDEN

ABSECON, ATLANTIC CO., CHURCH OF SAINT ELIZABETH ANN SETON, ABSECON, N.J. (1975) Revs. Perry A. Cherubini; Cosme R. de la Pena; Deacons Joseph Becker; William Peters.
Res.: 591 New Jersey Ave., 08201. Tel: 609-641-1480; Fax: 609-641-7396.
See Assumption Regional School, Galloway under Regional Schools, Elementary located in the Institution section.
Catechesis/Religious Program—Tel: 609-641-7043; Fax: 609-641-5709. Students 520.
Mission—St. Andrew Kim Korean Catholic Mission, Inc. 702 S. New Rd., 08201. Rev. Sung Heum (John) Kim, Admin.

ATCO, CAMDEN CO., THE CHURCH OF THE ASSUMPTION, ATCO, N.J. (1947) Rev. James A. Casadia; Deacon Charles McAleer.
Res.: 318 Carl Hasselhan Dr., 08004. Tel: 856-753-4161; Fax: 856-753-7917.
School—(Grades PreK-8), 2131 Cooper Rd., 08004. Tel: 856-767-0569; Fax: 856-753-7917. Mr. Paul Ricci, Prin. Tel: 856-767-0569; Fax: 856-768-8910. Lay Teachers 11; Students 212.
Catechesis/Religious Program—Tel: 856-767-3414. Students 512.

ATLANTIC CITY, ATLANTIC CO.

1—CHURCH OF ST. NICHOLAS, ATLANTIC CITY, N.J. (1855) Rev. Msgr. William A. Hodge; Rev. Joseph V. Jurkowski. In Res., Rev. Robert B. Matysik.
Res.: 1409 Pacific Ave., 08401. Tel: 609-344-1040; Fax: 609-344-7975.
Catechesis/Religious Program—Students 8.

2—THE CHURCH OF THE HOLY SPIRIT, ATLANTIC CITY, N.J. (1908) Closed. For requests for ecclesiastical documents please refer to St. Nicholas of Tolentine, Atlantic City. Very Rev. David J. Klein.

3—ST. MICHAEL'S CHURCH, ATLANTIC CITY, N.J. (1904), (Italian), Rev. Joseph Luong T. Pham, Admin.
Res.: 10 N. Mississippi Ave., 08401. Tel: 609-344-8536; Fax: 609-344-5304.

4—ST. MONICA'S CATHOLIC CHURCH, ATLANTIC CITY, N.J. (1925) Rev. Paul C. Wise, Admin.; Deacon Angel Ramos Vega.
Res.: 108 N. Pennsylvania Ave., 08401. Tel: 609-345-1786; Fax: 609-344-5090.
Catechesis/Religious Program—Students 35.

5—OUR LADY, STAR OF THE SEA, ATLANTIC CITY, N.J. (1894) Revs. Joseph Luong T. Pham; Jaime E. Hostios; Deacon Luis E. Correa.
Res.: 2651 Atlantic Ave., 08401. Tel: 609-345-1878; Fax: 609-348-0248. Email: olss2651@aol.com. Web: www.olssparish.com.
School—(Grades PreK-8), 15 N. California Ave., 08401. Tel: 609-345-0648; Fax: 609-344-6735. Sr. Mary Shamus Zehrer, R.S.M., Prin. & Supr. Sisters 4; Lay Teachers 8; Students 191.
Catechesis/Religious Program—Tel: 609-340-0116. Students 305.
Convent—Sisters of Mercy, 15 N. California Ave., 08401. Tel: 609-347-0434.

AUDUBON, CAMDEN CO., CHURCH OF THE HOLY MATERNITY, AUDUBON, NJ (1957) Revs. Robert J. Dunphy; Michael P. Hegarty; Deacon George R. Liss.
Res.: 431 W. Nicholson Rd., 08106. Tel: 856-547-0444; Fax: 856-547-0045.
Catechesis/Religious Program—Students 123.

AVALON, CAPE MAY CO., THE CHURCH OF MARIS STELLA, AVALON, N.J. (1961) Rev. Msgr. John T. Frey.
Res.: 5012 Dune Dr., 08202. Tel: 609-967-3746; Fax: 609-967-8172. Email: marisstella@comcast.net.
See Bishop McHugh Regional School, Cape May Court House under Regional Schools, Elementary located in the Institution section.
Catechesis/Religious Program—Tel: 609-967-3017. Students 44.

BARRINGTON, CAMDEN CO., CHURCH OF ST. FRANCIS DE SALES, BARRINGTON, N.J. (1955) Revs. Edward J. Maher; Charles J. Colozzi.
Res.: 199 Willmont Ave., 08007. Tel: 856-547-2313; Fax: 856-547-8225. Email: stfdesales@comcast.net.
Catechesis/Religious Program—Students 197.
Convent—424 Browning Rd., Bellmawr, 08031. Tel: 856-931-8973. Daughters of Our Lady of the Sacred Heart

BELLMAWR, CAMDEN CO.

1—THE CHURCH OF MARY, MOTHER OF THE CHURCH, BELLMAWR, N.J. (1965) Rev. Glenn Hartman.
Res.: 20 Braisington Ave., 08031. Tel: 856-931-0204; Fax: 856-933-5120. Web: www.marymotherofthechurch.org.
See Our Lady of the Sacred Heart Regional School, Barrington, under Regional Schools, Elementary located in the Institution section.
Catechesis/Religious Program—Students 76.

2—THE CHURCH OF THE ANNUNCIATION BVM, BELLMAWR, N.J. (1951) Rev. James O. Dabrowski; Deacon Gerard V. DeMuro.
Res.: 601 W. Browning Rd., 08031. Tel: 856-931-6307; Fax: 856-931-0155. Email: annun.church@comcast.net.
Catechesis/Religious Program—Tel: 856-931-8590. Students 207.
Convent—603 W. Browning Rd., 08031. Tel: 856-931-7192. Sisters Servants of Immaculate Heart of Mary
Mission—Mater Ecclesiae Church 261 Cross Keys Rd., Berlin, Camden Co. 08009. Tel: 856-753-3408; Fax: 856-753-2671. Email: rector@matereccIesiae.org. Web: www.matereccIesiae.org. Rev. Robert C. Pasley, Rector.

BERLIN, CAMDEN CO.

1—CHURCH OF OUR LADY OF MOUNT CARMEL, BERLIN, N.J. (1903) [CEM] Merged with St. Edward Parish, Pine Hill to form Saint Simon Stock Parish, Berlin.

2—SAINT SIMON STOCK PARISH, BERLIN, N.J. (2009) [CEM] Revs. Joseph R. Ferrara; Jose Manjakunnel; Deacons Joseph Beebe; John D. Rich Jr.
Res.: 178 W. White Horse Pike, 08009-2023. Tel: 856-767-2563; Fax: 856-767-8791. Email: www.olmcweb@catholic.org. Web: www.stsimonstock.net.
See Our Lady of Mt. Carmel, Berlin under Regional Schools, Elementary located in the Institution section.
Catechesis/Religious Program—Tel: 856-767-1537; Fax: 856-767-3304. Students 305.
Convent—1 Maple Ave., 08009. Tel: 856-767-2115. Religious Sisters of Mercy of the Americas

BLACKWOOD, CAMDEN CO.

1—ST. AGNES' CHURCH, BLACKWOOD TERRACE, N.J. (1946) Revs. Mark R. Cavagnaro; Nicholas Dudo; Kenneth P. Hallahan; John A. DelDuca; Deacons John Werner; Michael J. Harkins.
Res.: 701 Little Gloucester Rd., 08012. Tel: 856-228-4331; Fax: 856-227-0743.
See Our Lady of Hope Regional School, Blackwood under Regional Schools, Elementary located in the Institution section.
Catechesis/Religious Program—Tel: 856-227-0555. Students 800.

2—THE R.C. CHURCH OF ST. JUDE, GLOUCESTER TOWNSHIP, N.J. (1961) Revs. Daniel M. Rocco; Joseph P. Varghese, V.C.; Deacon William Drum, (Retired).
Res.: 402 S. Black Horse Pike, 08012. Tel: 856-227-0572; Fax: 856-227-1276.
See Our Lady of Hope Regional School, Blackwood under Regional Schools, Elementary located in the Institution section.
Catechesis/Religious Program—Tel: 856-227-8558. Students 217.

BLUE ANCHOR, CAMDEN CO., PARISH OF BLESSED JOHN THE TWENTY-THIRD, BLUE ANCHOR, N.J. (1925), (Italian), [CEM] Revs. Hugh J. Bradley; Joachim Oforchukwu, C.S.Sp. (Nigeria).
Res.: 250 S. Rte. 73, 08037-2317. Tel: 609-561-6116; Fax: 866-825-4766. Email: parishbj23@verizon.net. Web: www.blessedjohn23.org.
St. Lucy—(1925) Church: 08037.
Sacred Heart—(1904) Church: Cedar Brook, 08018.

See St. Joseph School, Hammonton, under Regional Schools, Elementary located in the Institution section.
Catechesis/Religious Program—Students 100.
BRIDGETON, CUMBERLAND CO.
1—THE CHURCH OF ST. TERESA AVILA, BRIDGETON, N.J. (1961) Rev. Ariel Hernandez; Deacon William Johnson.
Res.: 46 Central Ave., 08302. Tel: 856-455-2323; Fax: 856-455-7291. Email: stteresa@comcast.net.
Catechesis/Religious Program—Students 118.
2—THE CHURCH OF THE IMMACULATE CONCEPTION, BRIDGETON, N.J. (1874) [CEM] Revs. Ariel Hernandez, Admin.; Daniel A. DiNardo; William Kelly, O.Praem.; Deacons C. J. Achee; Carmen Bischer.
Res.: 312 N. Pearl St., 08302. Tel: 856-451-0254; Fax: 856-451-7842.
Catechesis/Religious Program—Students 340.
Convent—54 North St., 08302. Tel: 856-455-9960. Missionary Daughters of the Most Pure Virgin Mary
BRIGANTINE, ATLANTIC CO., ST. THOMAS' CATHOLIC CHURCH, BRIGANTINE, N.J. (1958) Rev. Alfred Mungujakisa; Deacon Leonard W. Long.
Res.: 331 8th St. S., 08203. Tel: 609-266-2123; Fax: 609-266-6416.
Catechesis/Religious Program—Tel: 609-266-3154. Students 300.
Convent—4101 Brigantine Ave., 08203. Tel: 609-266-4153. Sisters of St. Joseph of Chestnut Hill
BROOKLAWN, CAMDEN CO., ST. MAURICE'S CHURCH, BROOKLAWN, N.J. (1955) Rev. Frederick G. Link.
Res.: 401 Community Rd., 08030. Tel: 856-456-9039; Fax: 856-456-0161. Email: stmaurice@verizon.net.
Catechesis/Religious Program—
BUENA BOROUGH, ATLANTIC CO., QUEEN OF ANGELS PARISH, BUENA BOROUGH, N.J. (2001) [CEM] Revs. Edward F. Namiotka; John E. Bruni; Sigfrido Troche, M.SS.CC.
Res.: 202 N.W. Blvd., Landisville, 08326. Tel: 856-697-1450; Fax: 856-697-6996. Email: queenofangelsrcc@aol.com. Churches,
Our Lady of Victories, Landisville—
St. Michael, Minotola—
See Notre Dame Regional School, Newfield under Regional Schools, Elementary located in the Institution section.
Catechesis/Religious Program—Tel: 856-697-6320. Students 175.
Shrine—St. Padre Pio Shrine
CAPE MAY COURT HOUSE, CAPE MAY CO., THE CHURCH OF OUR LADY OF THE ANGELS, CAPE MAY COURT HOUSE, N.J. (1956) Revs. John A. O'Leary; Stephen J. Rapposelli; Deacons Ralph A. Catanese; George M. Ferland, (Retired). In Res., Rev. Anthony Savari Muthu.
Res.: 106 Mechanic St., 08210. Tel: 609-465-5245. Email: office@ourladyoftheangels.net. Web: www.ourladyoftheangels.net.
Parish Center: 35 Mechanic St., 08210. Tel: 609-465-5432; Fax: 609-465-7647.
See Bishop McHugh Regional School, Cape May Court House under Regional Schools, Elementary located in the Institution section.
Catechesis/Religious Program—Students 210.
CAPE MAY, CAPE MAY CO., THE CHURCH OF OUR LADY STAR OF THE SEA, CAPE MAY (1878) [CEM] Rev. Msgr. Thomas J. McIntyre; Bro. Robert Carson, S.J. In Res., Rev. Msgr. Timothy A. Ryan (Retired).
Res.: 525 Washington St., 08204. Tel: 609-884-5311; Fax: 609-884-0162. Web: www.ladystarofthesea.org.
See Our Lady, Star of the Sea Regional School, Cape May under Regional Schools, Elementary located in the Institution section.
Catechesis/Religious Program—Tel: 609-884-4437; Fax: 609-898-4253. Students 38.
Convent—516 Lafayette St., 08204. Tel: 609-884-7736. Sisters of St. Joseph of Chestnut Hill
Chapel—Cape May Point, St. Agnes, (Summer)
CARNEYS POINT, SALEM CO., THE CHURCH OF CORPUS CHRISTI, CARNEYS POINT, N.J. (1966) Rev. Paul D. Harte.
Res.: 369 Georgetown Rd., 08069. Tel: 856-299-3833; Fax: 856-299-3887. Email: corpuschrist@comcast.net.
School—Bishop Guilfoyle Regional Catholic School, Carney's Point., (Grades PreK-8) Tel: 856-299-0400; Fax: 856-299-6556. Mrs. Kathryn Chestnut, Prin.; Nessa Oswald, Librarian.
Catechesis/Religious Program—Students 122.
CEDARVILLE, CUMBERLAND CO., ST. MICHAEL'S ROMAN CATHOLIC CHURCH (1942) Rev. Ariel Hernandez, Res.: 312 N. Pearl St., Bridgeton, 08302. Tel: 856-451-0254.
Rectory—367 Main St., P.O. Box 327, 08311. Tel: 856-447-3480; Fax: 856-447-3480.
Catechesis/Religious Program—Students 12.
Mission—St. Anthony (1913) 1560 Main St., Port Norris, Cumberland Co. 08349.
Station—NJ State Medium Security Prison, Bayside Prison Rte. 47, Leesburg, 08327. Tel: 856-785-0040, Ext. 5458.
Station—Ancora Bayside Prison Winslow Twp.
CHERRY HILL, CAMDEN CO.
1—THE CATHOLIC COMMUNITY OF CHRIST OUR LIGHT, CHERRY HILL, N.J. (2009), Merger of The Church of St. Peter Celestine, Delaware Township, N.J. & Church of the Queen of Heaven, Erlton, N.J. Rev. Thomas A. Newton; Deacons W. Leo McBlain; Joseph F. Seaman. In Res., Rev. Terry M. Odien.
Rectory—402 Kings Hwy. N., 08034-1091. Tel: 856-667-2440; Fax: 856-482-0332. Churches,
Saint Peter Celestine, Cherry Hill—
Queen of Heaven, Cherry Hill—
School—Resurrection Catholic School, Tel: 856-667-3034; Fax: 856-667-9160. Mrs. Camille Forrest, Prin.
Convent—402A N. Kings Hwy., 08034. Tel: 856-667-0395.
2—THE CHURCH OF ST. PETER CELESTINE, DELAWARE TOWNSHIP, N.J. (1961) Merged with Church of the Queen of Heaven, Erlton, N.J. to form The Catholic Community of Christ Our Light, Cherry Hill, N.J.
3—THE CHURCH OF ST. PIUS X, DELAWARE TOWNSHIP, N.J. (1961) Merged with The Church of the Holy Rosary, Ashland, N.J., Cherry Hill to form Holy Eucharist Parish, Cherry Hill, N.J.
4—THE CHURCH OF THE HOLY ROSARY, ASHLAND, N.J. (1958) Merged with The Church of St. Pius X, Delaware Township, N.J. to form Holy Eucharist Parish, Cherry Hill, N.J.
5—CHURCH OF THE QUEEN OF HEAVEN, ERLTON, N.J. (1955) Merged with The Church of St. Peter, Celestine, Delaware Township, N.J. to form The Catholic Community of Christ Our Light, Cherry Hill, N.J.
6—THE CHURCH OF ST. THOMAS MORE, CHERRY HILL, NEW JERSEY (1968) Rev. Msgr. Thomas J. Morgan; Deacon John H. Harrington Jr.; Rev. George Donkor Tang.
Res.: 1439 Springdale Rd., 08003. Tel: 856-424-3212; Fax: 856-424-2411. Email: sthomasmore@comcast.net. Web: www.stthomasmorenj.org.
Catechesis/Religious Program—Students 169.
7—HOLY EUCHARIST PARISH, CHERRY HILL, N.J. (2009) Revs. George C. Seiter; Michael J. Coffey, Senior Priest; Deacons Anthony D. Malatesta; Peter J. Powell.
Res.: 344 Kresson Rd., 08034. Tel: 856-429-1330; Fax: 856-429-8679.
St. Pius X, Cherry Hill—Church:
See Christ the King Regional School, Haddonfield under Regional Schools, Elementary located in the Institution section.
Catechesis/Religious Program—Tel: 856-428-9207. Students 520.
Mission—St. Yi Yun Il John Korean Catholic Mission 99 Burnt Mill Rd., Camden Co. 08003. Tel: 856-427-4229. Rev. Sung Heum (John) Kim, Admin.; Deacon Paul Lee.
8—ST. MARY'S R.C. CHURCH, DELAWARE TOWNSHIP, N.J. (1961) Revs. John C. Killeen; Christopher V. Ruggles; Deacon Michael L. Welsh; Ms. Kathleen G. Rando, Pastoral Assoc.
Res.: 2001 Springdale Rd., 08003. Tel: 856-424-1454; Fax: 856-424-8270. Email: stmarycherryhill@verizon.net. Web: www.stmaryofcherryhill.org.
Catechesis/Religious Program—Tel: 856-424-2679. Students 494.
CLAYTON, GLOUCESTER CO., ST. CATHERINE'S ROMAN CATHOLIC CHURCH, CLAYTON, N.J. (1943) Rev. Jaromir Michalak; Deacon Matthew J. Hanrahan.
Res.: 49 W. North St., 08312. Tel: 856-881-9155; Fax: 856-881-9166. Email: st.cath@comcast.net. Web: catherineofsiena.com.
School—St. Michael the Archangel Regional School, (Grades PreK-8), 51 W. North St., 08312. Tel: 856-881-0067; Fax: 856-881-4064. Miss Janice Bruni, Prin. Lay Teachers 25; Students 310.
Catechesis/Religious Program—Students 400.
COLLINGS LAKES, ATLANTIC CO., CHURCH OF OUR LADY OF THE LAKES, COLLINGS LAKES, N.J. (1976) Rev. John A. Cavagnaro.
Res.: 19 Malaga Rd., 08094. Tel: 609-561-8313; Fax: 609-561-8374.
See Notre Dame Regional School, Newfield under Regional Schools, Elementary located in the Institution section.
Catechesis/Religious Program—Students 112.
COLLINGSWOOD, CAMDEN CO., ST. JOHN'S CATHOLIC CHURCH, COLLINGSWOOD, N.J. (1919) Rev. Msgr. Martin J. Mannion; Rev. Anthony L. Minniti.
Res.: 809 Park Ave., 08108. Tel: 856-858-0298; Fax: 856-858-2796. Web: www.stjohn-colls.org.
School—Good Shepherd Regional School, (Grades PreSchool-8), 100 Lees Ave., 08108. Tel: 856-858-1562; Fax: 856-858-2943. Mr. Donald W. Garecht, Prin. Lay Teachers 14; Students 183.
Catechesis/Religious Program—Students 140.
DELAIR, CAMDEN CO., ST. VERONICA'S R.C. CHURCH, TOWNSHIP OF PENNSAUKEN, NEW JERSEY (1961) Merged with St. Cecilia Church, North Merchantville, N.J. & St. Edward's R.C. Church, Pine Hill, New Jersey to form Mary, Queen of All Saints, Pennsauken, N.J.
DEPTFORD, GLOUCESTER CO., THE CHURCH OF ST. JOHN VIANNEY, GLOUCESTER COUNTY, N.J. (1971) Merged with St. Margaret's Church, Woodbury Heights, N.J. to form Infant Jesus Parish, Woodbury Heights, N.J.
EGG HARBOR CITY, ATLANTIC CO., ST. NICHOLAS' CHURCH, EGG HARBOR CITY (1864) Revs. Michael J. Matveenko; Ronald S. Falotico; Grace Manano; Deacon Michael H. Guerrieri.
Res.: 525 St. Louis Ave., 08215-2224. Tel: 609-965-0350; Fax: 609-804-1313. Email: stnicholaschurch@comcast.net. Web: stnicholashc.org.
School—Assumption Regional Catholic School, Pitney Rd., Galloway, 08205. Tel: 609-652-7134. Mrs. Antonia Taylor, Prin. Lay Teachers 15; Students 250.
Catechesis/Religious Program—Tel: 609-965-0720. Students 197.
EGG HARBOR TOWNSHIP, ATLANTIC CO., THE CHURCH OF SAINT KATHARINE DREXEL, MCKEE CITY, NEW JERSEY (2000) Rev. John J. Vignone.
6075 W. Jersey Ave., 08234. Tel: 609-645-7313; Fax: 609-645-9680. Email: office@skd-parish.org. Web: www.skd-parish.org.
Catechesis/Religious Program—Students 500.
ELMER, SALEM CO., ST. ANN'S CATHOLIC CHURCH, ELMER, N.J. (1961) Rev. Edward M. Friel; Deacon Robert M. Fanelli.
Res.: 115 Broad St., 08318. Tel: 856-358-3106; Fax: 856-358-3117. Email: stannelmer@yahoo.com. Web: www.churchofstann.net.
See Notre Dame Regional School, Newfield under Regional Schools, Elementary located in the Institution section.
Catechesis/Religious Program—Students 65.
FRANKLINVILLE, GLOUCESTER CO., R.C. CHURCH OF THE NATIVITY, FRANKLINVILLE, N.J. (1961) Rev. Jaromir Michalak; Deacon John J. Luko Jr.
Res.: 2677 Delsea Dr., 08322. Tel: 856-694-2349; Fax: 856-694-4131. Email: churchofthenativity@verizon.net.
See St. Michael the Archangel Regional School, Clayton under St. Catherine's Roman Catholic Church, Clayton, N.J.
Catechesis/Religious Program—Students 216.
GALLOWAY, ATLANTIC CO., THE CHURCH OF THE ASSUMPTION (1938) Revs. Michael J. Matveenko; Yvans Jazon; Senior Deacon James J. Teeney; Deacon Charles A. Tobin.
Res.: 146 S. Pitney Rd., Bldg. 1, 08205. Tel: 609-652-0008; Fax: 609-652-0883.
See Assumption Regional School, Galloway under Regional Schools, Elementary located in the Institution section.
Catechesis/Religious Program—Tel: 609-965-7368. Students 524.
GIBBSBORO, CAMDEN CO., ST. ANDREW THE APOSTLE'S R.C. CHURCH, GIBBSBORO, N.J. (1963) Rev. Msgr. Ciaran P. OMearain; Revs. Howard E. Muhlbaier; Allen B. Lovell; Deacon Vincent A. Okoro.
Res.: 120 United States Ave., 08026. Tel: 856-784-3878; Fax: 856-435-7508. Email: andrewapos@aol.com. Web: www.standrewsrc.com.
See Our Lady of Mt. Carmel, Berlin under Regional Schools, Elementary located in the Institution section.
Catechesis/Religious Program—Tel: 856-783-0550. Students 713.
GIBBSTOWN, GLOUCESTER CO., ST. MICHAEL'S CHURCH, GIBBSTOWN, N.J. (1940) Revs. David A. Grover; Francis P. Gaffney; Deacons James Kiley; Robert Willson.
Res.: 313 Memorial Ave., 08027. Tel: 856-423-0007; Fax: 856-423-1445. Email: stmichaelsparish@comcast.net.
See Guardian Angels Regional School, Gibbstown under Regional Schools, Elementary located in the Institution section.
Catechesis/Religious Program—Tel: 856-423-9337. Students 180.
Convent—320 Memorial Ave., 08027. Tel: 856-423-8680; Fax: 856-423-8681. Franciscan Missionary Sisters of the Infant Jesus
GLASSBORO, GLOUCESTER CO.
1—ST. BRIDGET'S CATHOLIC CHURCH, GLASSBORO, N.J. (1887), (Italian), [CEM] Revs. Matthew Weber; Fabio Jose Fernandez; Deacon Joseph W. Loungo.
Res.: 125 Church St., 08028. Tel: 856-881-2753; Fax: 856-881-9697. Email: bridget125@comcast.net.
See St. Michael the Archangel Regional School, under St. Catherine's Roman Catholic Church, Clayton, N.J.

Catechesis/Religious Program—Tel: 856-694-2349. Students 110.
Convent—206 Ellis St., 08028. Tel: 856-881-4604. Franciscan Missionary Sisters of the Immaculate Heart of Mary

2—THE CHURCH OF OUR LADY OF LOURDES, GLASSBORO, N.J. (1966) Revs. Vincent G. Carpinelli; Robert J. D'Imperio; Deacons Nicholas Mortelliti; Michael J. Carter.
Res.: 500 Greentree Rd., 08028. Tel: 856-881-0909; Fax: 856-881-5457. Email: ourladyoflourdes@mycomcast.com. Web: www.churchofourladyoflourdes.org.
See St. Bridget Regional School, Glassboro under Regional Schools, Elementary located in the Institution section.
Catechesis/Religious Program—Tel: 856-881-1552. Students 441.

GLOUCESTER, CAMDEN CO., ST. MARY'S CHURCH, GLOUCESTER (1848) [CEM] Rev. Msgr. James P. Curran (RIC); Rev. Steephan Chellan; Deacon Frank Crosson.
Res.: 426 Monmouth St., 08030. Tel: 856-456-0052; Fax: 856-456-1837. Email: stmaryrectory@comcast.net. Web: www.stmarysgloucester.org.
School—(Grades PreK-8), 340 Cumberland St., 08030. Tel: 856-456-0913; Fax: 856-456-7382. Mrs. Gail Corey, Prin.; Sr. Maureen Cooper, O.P., Librarian. Lay Teachers 13; Students 219.
Catechesis/Religious Program—Students 133.
Convent—820 Hudson Ave., 08030. Tel: 856-456-0071. Dominican Sisters of Hope

HADDON HEIGHTS, CAMDEN CO., CHURCH OF ST. ROSE, HADDON HEIGHTS, N.J. (1896) Revs. E. Joseph Byerley; Thanh Q. Pham; Deacons Douglas R. Crawford; Brian T. Ayscue. In Res., Rev. Alfred J. Hewett (Retired).
Res.: 300 Kings Hwy., 08035-1397. Tel: 856-547-0564; Fax: 856-547-7311. Email: strosenj@yahoo.com. Web: www.strosenj.com.
School—(Grades K-8) Tel: 856-546-6166; Fax: 856-546-6601. Email: stroseprincipal@yahoo.com. Steven Hogan, Prin.; Marguerite Crowell, Librarian. Dominican Sisters of Hope 1; Lay Teachers 21; Students 425.
Catechesis/Religious Program—Tel: 856-546-0564, Ext. 103; Fax: 856-547-7311. Students 418.

HADDON TOWNSHIP, CAMDEN CO., THE CHURCH OF ST. VINCENT PALLOTTI, HADDON TOWNSHIP, N.J. (1963) Rev. Msgr. Louis A. Marucci; Deacon Emil Ralbusky. In Res., Rev. Msgr. Eugene J. Fitzsimmons (Retired).
Res.: 901 Hopkins Rd., Ste. A, Haddonfield, 08033. Tel: 856-858-1313; 856-858-1314; Fax: 856-869-9010. Web: www.svpchurch.org.
Catechesis/Religious Program—Students 218.

HADDONFIELD, CAMDEN CO., CHURCH OF CHRIST THE KING, HADDONFIELD, N.J. (1927) Rev. Msgrs. William P. Brennan; Roger E. McGrath; Rev. George Punnolil; Deacons Nicholas A. Danze; Thomas J. Hafner.
Res.: 200 Windsor Ave., 08033. Tel: 856-429-1600; Fax: 856-429-2734. Email: ckp@christ-the-king-parish.org. Web: www.christ-the-king-parish.org.
See Christ the King Regional School, Haddonfield under Regional Schools, Elementary located in the Institution section.
Catechesis/Religious Program—Students 530.

HAMMONTON, ATLANTIC CO.

1—ST. ANTHONY OF PADUA ROMAN CATHOLIC CHURCH, HAMMONTON, N.J. (1964) Rev. Carmel F. Polidano. In Res., Rev. Msgr. Charles P. Barth (Retired).
Res.: 285 Rte. 206, 08037-8925. Tel: 609-561-3313; Fax: 609-567-7764. Web: www.stanthonyofpadua.org.
See St. Joseph School, Hammonton, under Regional Schools, Elementary located in the Institution section.
Catechesis/Religious Program—Students 102.

2—ST. JOSEPH'S CHURCH, HAMMONTON, N.J. (1886) [CEM] Revs. Carmen A. Carlone; Ronald S. Falotico; Deacon Ismael Perez Tavarez.
Res.: 226 French St., 08037. Tel: 609-561-0180; Fax: 609-561-6808.
See St. Joseph Regional School, Hammonton, under Regional Schools, Elementary located in the Institution section.
Catechesis/Religious Program—Students 200.
Convent—219 N. Third St., 08037. Tel: 609-561-0347. Religious Teachers Filippini

3—ST. MARTIN DE PORRES ROMAN CATHOLIC CHURCH, HAMMONTON, N.J. (1962) Revs. Thomas S. Donio; Charles Conaty; Deacon George R. VanLeer.
Res.: 129 Park Ave., 08037. Tel: 609-561-4322; Fax: 609-561-4433. Email: st.martindeporres@comcast.net.
See St. Joseph School, Hammonton, under Regional Schools, Elementary located in the Institution section.
Catechesis/Religious Program—Students 426.

LINDENWOLD, CAMDEN CO.

1—CHURCH OF ST. LAWRENCE, LAUREL SPRINGS, N.J. (1896) Merged with The R.C. Church of St. Luke, Stratford, N.J. & Our Lady of Grace, R.C. Church, Somerdale, New Jersey to form Our Lady of Guadalupe, Lindenwold.

2—OUR LADY OF GUADALUPE PARISH, LINDENWOLD, N.J. (2009) Revs. Joseph A. Capella; Jeffrey T. Cesarone, O.Praem. In Res., Rev. Wilson Kidangan Paulose.
Rectory—Res.: 100 South Ave., 08021-1696. Tel: 856-627-2222; 856-627-7522; Fax: 856-627-8210.
Churches,
St. Lawrence, Lindenwold—
St. Luke, Stratford—
Our Lady of Grace—
School—John Paul II Regional School, 55 Warwick Rd., Stratford, 08084. Tel: 856-783-3088; Fax: 856-783-9302. Mrs. Helen Persing, Prin.
Catechesis/Religious Program—Tel: 856-346-0902. Students 305.

LINWOOD, ATLANTIC CO., THE CHURCH OF OUR LADY OF SORROWS, LINWOOD, N.J. (1965) Rev. Malcolm MacLeod, M.SS.CC.
Res.: 724 Maple, 08221. Tel: 609-927-1154; Fax: 609-927-0398. Email: ourladyofsorrowslinwoodnj@verizon.net. Web: www.ourladyofsorrows.us/.
Catechesis/Religious Program—Tel: 609-927-0121. Students 489.

LONGPORT, ATLANTIC CO., CHURCH OF THE EPIPHANY, LONGPORT, N.J. (1954) Rev. Joseph F. Ganiel, Admin.
Res.: 2801 Ventnor Ave., 08403. Tel: 609-822-8940; Fax: 609-822-1050. Email: ecl2801@comcast.net. Web: www.epiphany-longportnj.org.
See Holy Family Regional School, Ventnor under St. James Catholic Church, Ventnor, N.J.
Catechesis/Religious Program—Students 30.

MAGNOLIA, CAMDEN CO., ST. GREGORY'S CHURCH, MAGNOLIA, N.J. (1955) Rev. Jason T. Rocks; Deacon Leonard P. Carlucci.
Res.: 340 E. Evesham Ave., 08049. Tel: 856-784-4090; Fax: 856-784-6371. Email: stg340@comcast.net. Web: www.stgregorynj.com.
See John Paul II Regional School, Stratford under R.C. Church of St. Luke, Stratford, N.J.
Catechesis/Religious Program—230 E. Evesham Ave., 08049. Tel: 856-784-6608. Students 58.
Convent—230 E. Evesham Ave., 08049.

MALAGA, GLOUCESTER CO., ST. MARY'S ROMAN CATHOLIC CHURCH OF MALAGA, N.J. (1961) Rev. Edward F. Namiotka.
Res.: 2565 Old Dutch Mill Rd., P.O. Box 780, 08328. Tel: 856-694-2576; Fax: 856-694-4636. Email: stmaryreco7@comcast.net. Web: www.stmarymalaga.com.
See Notre Dame Regional School, Newfield under Regional Schools, Elementary located in the Institution section.
Catechesis/Religious Program—Students 65.

MANTUA, GLOUCESTER CO., R.C. CHURCH OF THE INCARNATION, TOWNSHIP OF MANTUA, NEW JERSEY (1956) Revs. Kenneth J. Johnston; Michael M. Romano; Deacons Thomas F. O'Brien; John Schiavo; Joseph J. Izzo.
Res.: 234 Shadow Pl., 08051. Tel: 856-468-1314; Fax: 856-468-4886.
See St. Margaret School, Woodbury Heights under Regional Schools, Elementary located in the Institution section.
Catechesis/Religious Program—Tel: 856-468-7566. Students 1,100.

MARGATE, ATLANTIC CO., CHURCH OF THE BLESSED SACRAMENT, MARGATE CITY, NEW JERSEY (1945) Rev. James P. Rush; Deacon Mark J. Gallagher.
Res.: 11 N. Kenyon Ave., 08402. Tel: 609-822-7105; Fax: 609-822-3817. Email: bsrectory@yahoo.com. Web: www.bsrcc.org.
See Holy Family Regional School, Ventnor under St. James Catholic Church, Ventnor, N.J.
Catechesis/Religious Program—Tel: 609-822-7105. Students 360.

MARMORA, CAPE MAY CO., CHURCH OF THE RESURRECTION, MARMORA, N.J. (1975) Revs. Robert J. Gregorio; David Michael; Jose Ainikkal, C.M.I.
Res.: 200 W. Tuckahoe Rd., 08223. Tel: 609-390-0664; Fax: 609-390-8717.
School—Bishop McHugh Regional School, Cape May Court House, (Grades K-8) Tel: 609-624-1900; Fax: 609-624-9696.
See Bishop McHugh Regional School, Cape May Court House under Regional Schools, Elementary located in the Institution section.
Catechesis/Religious Program—Tel: 609-390-2203. Students 415.

MAYS LANDING, ATLANTIC CO., CHURCH OF ST. VINCENT DE PAUL, MAYS LANDING, N.J. (1906) [CEM] Rev. Edward F. Heintzelman; Very Rev. Anthony Patrizio; Deacon Richard Wigglesworth.
Res.: 114 Rte. 50, 08330. Tel: 609-625-2124; Fax: 609-625-8718. Web: www.vincentdepaul.org/index.ofm.
School—(Grades PreK-8), 5809 E. Main St., 08330. Tel: 609-625-1565; Fax: 609-625-4703. Email: pirolli@svdprs.com. Web: www.svdprs.com. Miss Linda Pirolli, Prin. Lay Teachers 14; Students 212.
Catechesis/Religious Program—5809 Main St., 08330. Tel: 609-625-1567. Students 351.
Convent—Sisters of St. Joseph of Chestnut Hill, 5807 Main St., 08330. Tel: 609-625-1566.
Mission—St. Bernard [CEM] Pennsylvania Ave., Dorothy, Atlantic Co.

MERCHANTVILLE, CAMDEN CO., ST. PETER'S CATHOLIC CHURCH, MERCHANTVILLE, N.J. (1903) Rev. Msgr. Anthony J. Manuppella; Revs. Allain B. Caparas; David V. Minniti (Retired); Deacon Joseph P. McHugh.
Res.: 43 W. Maple Ave., 08109. Tel: 856-663-1373; Fax: 856-488-0647. Web: www.stpeterrcc.com.
School—(Grades PreK-8) Tel: 856-665-5789; Fax: 856-665-4943. Maureen D. Lesniak, Prin. Lay Teachers 22; Students 312.
Catechesis/Religious Program—Tel: 856-663-4490. Sheila O'Boyle, C.R.E. Students 275.
Convent—55 W. Maple Ave., 08109. Tel: 856-662-0473. Religious Teachers Filippini

MILLVILLE, CUMBERLAND CO.

1—THE CHURCH OF ST. JOHN BOSCO, MILLVILLE, N.J. (1966) Rev. William C. Pierce. In Res., Rev. Sergio Bicomong.
Res.: 2 Hillcrest Ave., 08332. Tel: 856-825-1513; Fax: 856-765-9489. Email: heavensjb@comcast.net.

2—THE CHURCH OF SAINT MARY MAGDALEN, MILLVILLE (1864) [CEM] Rev. Paul A. Olszewski; Deacon Hipolito Lagares. In Res., Revs. Joseph A. Salerno; Cesar A. Rebolledo Ramiriz, O.F.M.
Res.: 621 Dock St., 08332. Tel: 856-825-0021; Fax: 856-825-4338.
School—(Grades K-8), 7 W. Powell St., 08332. Tel: 856-825-3600; Fax: 856-825-9119. Email: advancement@smmrs.org. Web: www.smmrs.org. Sr. Rosa Maria Ojeda, Prin. Sisters 2; Lay Teachers 17; Students 189.
Catechesis/Religious Program—Tel: 609-617-5461. Sr. Rafaela Valdez, Supr. Students 100.
Convent—Missionary Daughters of the Most Pure Virgin Mary, 3 W. Powell St., 08332. Tel: 856-327-2235. Sr. Armida Fabela, M.D.P.V.M., Supr.

MOUNT EPHRAIM, CAMDEN CO., CHURCH OF THE SACRED HEART, MT. EPHRAIM, N.J. (1939) Rev. Robert J. Dunphy; Deacon William Norquist.
Res.: 11 N. Black Horse Pike, 08059. Tel: 856-931-1441; Fax: 856-931-9433.
Catechesis/Religious Program—Tel: 856-931-9444. Students 177.

MULLICA HILL, GLOUCESTER CO., CHURCH OF THE HOLY NAME OF JESUS, MULLICA HILL, N.J. (1901) [CEM] Revs. Anthony R. DiBardino; Jerry Gomez.
Res.: 17 Earlington Ave., 08062. Tel: 856-478-2294; Fax: 856-478-4120. Email: office@holynameofjesus.org. Web: www.holynameofjesus.org.
Catechesis/Religious Program—Tel: 856-478-9694. Email: religious@holynameofjesus.org. Students 1,000.

NATIONAL PARK, GLOUCESTER CO., ST. MATTHEW'S CATHOLIC CHURCH, NATIONAL PARK, N.J. (1915) Rev. Walter Norris; Deacon William J. Rumaker, (Retired).
Res.: 307 Wesley Ave., P.O. Box 38, 08063. Tel: 856-845-2523; Fax: 856-251-0822. Email: st.matts@comcast.net. Web: www.mattsnp.org.
Catechesis/Religious Program—Tel: 856-845-2523; Fax: 856-251-0822.
Convent—Hessian Ave., Verga, 08093. Tel: 856-845-7203; Fax: 856-853-7771.

NEWFIELD, GLOUCESTER CO., ST. ROSE'S CATHOLIC CHURCH (1922) Rev. John Joseph Tumosa; Deacon Anthony M. Jadick.
Res.: 104 Catawba Ave., 08344. Tel: 856-697-3232; Fax: 856-697-1455. Email: stroseoflima@comcast.net. Web: www.strosenewfield.net.
See Notre Dame Regional School, Newfield under Regional Schools, Elementary located in the Institution section.
Catechesis/Religious Program—108 Church St., 08344. Tel: 856-697-0155, Ext. 5; Fax: 856-697-5114. Students 65.

NORTH CAPE MAY, CAPE MAY CO., THE CHURCH OF ST. JOHN OF GOD, NORTH CAPE MAY, N.J. (1966) Rev. Ernest R. Soprano.
Res.: 680 Town Bank Rd., 08204. Tel: 609-884-1656; Fax: 609-898-0673.
Catechesis/Religious Program—Students 193.

NORTHFIELD, ATLANTIC CO., THE CHURCH OF ST. BERNADETTE, NORTHFIELD, N.J. (1966) Rev. Patrick J. Brady; Deacon George Del Rossi.
Res.: 1421 New Rd., 08225. Tel: 609-646-5611; Fax: 609-484-8345. Email: stbernadette@comcast.net.
See Holy Family Regional School, Ventnor under

St. James Catholic Church, Ventnor, N.J.
Catechesis/Religious Program—Tel: 609-484-0249. Students 320.

OAKLYN, CAMDEN CO., ST. ALOYSIUS CATHOLIC CHURCH, OAKLYN, N.J. (1935) Rev. Msgr. Leonard G. Scott; Deacons Michael F. Scott; Timothy M. Sullivan. In Res., Rev. Andzej C. Kielkowski, S.D.S.
Res.: 37 W. Haddon Ave., 08107. Tel: 856-854-2352; Fax: 856-854-4189.
See Good Shepherd Regional School, Collingswood under Regional Schools, Elementary located in the Institution section.
Catechesis/Religious Program—Students 76.

OCEAN CITY, CAPE MAY CO.

1—ST. AUGUSTINE'S CATHOLIC CHURCH, OCEAN CITY, N.J. (1894) Revs. Michael P. Rush; Alvaro Diaz; Deacon Joseph P. Orlando.
Res.: 1310 Ocean Ave., 08226. Tel: 609-399-0648; Fax: 609-399-0063.
Catechesis/Religious Program—Tel: 609-399-2316. Students 125.

2—THE CHURCH OF ST. FRANCES CABRINI, OCEAN CITY, N.J. (1966) Rev. Edward R. Kolla, Admin.; Deacon Vincent E. Trainer.
Res.: 114 Atlantic Ave., 08226. Tel: 609-399-4776; Fax: 609-391-9412. Web: www.stfrancesoc.org.
Catechesis/Religious Program—Tel: 609-399-2643. Students 140.
Convent—712 2nd St., 08226. Tel: 609-398-6713. Sisters of Christian Charity

3—THE CHURCH OF OUR LADY OF GOOD COUNSEL, OCEAN CITY, N.J. (1961) Rev. Massimo S. Fasciglione, Admin.
Res.: 3948 Central Ave., 08226. Tel: 609-399-2085; 609-398-3654 (Office); Fax: 609-399-3761.
Catechesis/Religious Program—Sr. Elizabeth Mercer, D.R.E. Students 25.

PAULSBORO, GLOUCESTER CO., ST. JOHN'S CHURCH, PAULSBORO, N.J. (1904) Rev. David A. Grover, Admin.; Deacons Joseph Lopes; John D. Colanero.
Res.: 647 Beacon Ave., 08066. Tel: 856-423-0086; Fax: 856-423-0123.
Catechesis/Religious Program—St. Michael, Gibbstown, Tel: 856-423-0007. Students 180.

PENNS GROVE, SALEM CO., ST. JAMES' CHURCH, PENNSGROVE, N.J. (1901) Revs. Paul D. Harte; Rene L. Canales.
Office: 369 Georgetown Rd., Carneys Point, 08069. Tel: 856-299-3833; Fax: 856-299-3834. Email: corpuschrist@comcast.net.
Church: 114 State St., 08069.
Catechesis/Religious Program—Students 122.

PENNSAUKEN, CAMDEN CO.

1—ST. CECILIA'S CHURCH, NORTH MERCHANTVILLE, N.J. (1939) Merged with St. Veronica's R.C. Church, Township of Pennsauken, New Jersey & St. Edward's R.C. Church, Pine Hill, New Jersey to form Mary, Queen of All Saints, Pennsauken, N.J.

2—MARY, QUEEN OF ALL SAINTS, PENNSAUKEN, N.J. (2009) Rev. William F. Moore; Rev. Msgr. Michael T. Mannion; Deacon Miguel A. Rivera Sr.
Rectory—4824 Camden Ave., 08110-1921. Tel: 856-662-2723; Fax: 856-486-2089. Web: www.stceciliapennsauken.org. Churches,
Saint Cecilia, Pennsauken—
Saint Veronica, Delair—
Little Angels Child Care Center—48th St. & Camden Ave., 08110. Tel: 856-662-9228. Vickie Caracciolo, Dir.
School—St. Cecilia School, (Grades PreK-8), 4851 Camden Ave., 08110. Tel: 856-662-0149; Fax: 856-662-7460. Email: stceciliaschool@yahoo.com. Mr. Ernest Benson, Prin.; Mrs. Denise Carpenter, Librarian. Lay Teachers 17; Students 243.
Catechesis/Religious Program—Monica Smith, D.R.E. Students 74.

3—ST. STEPHEN'S R.C. CHURCH, PENNSAUKEN TOWNSHIP, N.J. (1952) Revs. Vincent Orum; Thomas R. Kiely; Deacon Ernest Picknally.
Res.: 6306 Browning Rd., 08109. Tel: 856-662-9338; Fax: 856-662-4679.
School—(Grades PreK-8) Tel: 856-662-5935; Fax: 856-662-6128. Email: principal@ststephenspennsauken.com. Web: www.ststephenspennsauken.com. Mrs. Patricia Higgins, Prin. Lay Teachers 16; Students 248.
Catechesis/Religious Program—Students 38.
Convent—6300 Browning Rd., 08109. Tel: 856-665-5227. Sisters of St. Joseph of Chestnut Hill

PENNSVILLE, SALEM CO., CHURCH OF THE QUEEN OF THE APOSTLES, PENNSVILLE, N.J. (1955) Rev. Dennis W. Bajkowski.
Res.: 391 S. Broadway, 08070. Tel: 856-678-5400; Fax: 856-678-4153.
School—Bishop Guilfoyle Regional School, Carneys Point, Tel: 856-299-0400. Mrs. Kathryn Chesnut, Prin.
Catechesis/Religious Program—Students 150.

PINE HILL, CAMDEN CO., ST. EDWARD'S R.C. CHURCH, PINE HILL, NEW JERSEY (1953) Merged with St. Cecilia's Church, North Merchantville, N.J. & St. Veronica's R.C. Church, Township of Pennsauken, New Jersey to form Mary Queen of All Saints, Pennsuken, N.J.

PITMAN, GLOUCESTER CO., OUR LADY QUEEN OF PEACE R.C. CHURCH, PITMAN N.J. (1940) Revs. Joseph J. Adamson; Robert J. Fritz; Deacon Philip E. Giordano.
Res.: 161 Pitman Ave., 08071. Tel: 856-589-5673; Fax: 856-589-0102.
See St. Michael the Archangel Regional School, Clayton under St. Catherine's Roman Catholic Church, Clayton, N.J.
Catechesis/Religious Program—Judy O'Donnell, C.R.E. Students 216.

PLEASANTVILLE, ATLANTIC CO., ST. PETER'S CATHOLIC CHURCH, PLEASANTVILLE, N.J. (1896) Rev. Patrick J. Brady; Deacon Richard S. Maxwell. In Res., Rev. Aland Jean, C.I.C.M.
Res.: 25 W. Black Horse Pike, 08232. Tel: 609-641-0285; Fax: 609-641-0385. Email: stpeterpville@comcast.net.
Catechesis/Religious Program—c/o St. Bernadette Parish, 1421 New Rd., Northfield, 08225. Students 92.

ROSENHAYN, CUMBERLAND CO., ST. MARY'S CHURCH, ROSENHAYN, N.J. (1914) [CEM] Rev. Edward F. Sobolewski; Deacons Christopher D. Nichols; Donald W. Rogozenski. In Res., Rev. Sebastian V. Annino.
Res.: Morton Ave., P.O. Box 376, 08352-0376. Tel: 856-451-8763; Fax: 856-453-8831.
See Mary Magdelen Regional School, Millville under Regional Schools, Elementary located in the Institution section.
Catechesis/Religious Program—Students 190.

RUNNEMEDE, CAMDEN CO.

1—CHURCH OF ST. MARIA GORETTI, RUNNEMEDE, N.J. (1965) Rev. Msgr. Russell L. Rock.
Res.: 321 Orchard Ave., 08078. Tel: 856-933-0037; Fax: 856-933-0036.
Catechesis/Religious Program—Tel: 856-939-3311. Students 82.

2—CHURCH OF ST. TERESA OF THE INFANT JESUS, RUNNEMEDE, N.J. (1927) Revs. Raymond P. Gormley; Edward T. O'Donnell, S.J.; Deacon A. Kenneth Bandiera.
Res.: 13 E. Evesham Rd., 08078. Tel: 856-939-1681; Fax: 856-939-3878. Email: stteresaparish@comcast.net. Web: www.stteresaparish.net.
See St. Teresa School, Runnemede under Regional Schools, Elementary located in the Institution section.
Catechesis/Religious Program—Tel: 856-939-0592. Students 288.
Convent—42 Ardmore Ave., 08078. Tel: 856-939-5508. Sisters, Servants of the Immaculate Heart of Mary

SALEM, SALEM CO., ST. MARY'S CATHOLIC CHURCH, SALEM (1848) [CEM] Rev. James F. Barry; Sr. Carol Adams, C.S.J.P., Pastoral Assoc.
Res.: 25 Oak St., 08079. Tel: 856-935-0288; Fax: 856-935-8778. Web: www.stmarysalem.4lpi.com.
Catechesis/Religious Program—Tel: 856-935-0660. Students 96.
Convent—177 Cook St., 08079. Tel: 856-935-2298. Sisters of St. Joseph of Peace

SEA ISLE CITY, CAPE MAY CO., ST. JOSEPH'S CATHOLIC CHURCH, SEA ISLE CITY, N.J. (1884) Rev. Joseph A. Perreault; Deacon Liam C. O'Clishim.
Res.: 126-44th St., 08243. Tel: 609-263-8696; Fax: 609-263-7884. Email: stjoseph1884@yahoo.com. Web: www.home.catholicweb.com/st.joesic/.
Catechesis/Religious Program—Tel: 609-263-2087. Students 105.
Convent—132 44th St., 08243. Tel: 609-263-6228. Sisters of Mercy of the Americas

SEWELL, GLOUCESTER CO., CHURCH OF THE HOLY FAMILY, WASHINGTON TOWNSHIP (1974) Revs. Robert E. Hughes; Sanjai Devis, V.C.
Res.: 226 Hurffville Rd., 08080. Tel: 856-228-1616; Fax: 856-228-6332. Email: office@churchoftheholyfamily.org. Web: www.churchoftheholyfamily.org.
See Our Lady of Hope Regional School, Blackwood under Regional Schools, Elementary located in the Institution section.
Catechesis/Religious Program—Tel: 856-228-2215; Fax: 856-401-1817. Students 1,101.

SICKLERVILLE, CAMDEN CO.

1—THE CHURCH OF ST. CHARLES BORROMEO, WASHINGTON TOWNSHIP, N.J. (1965) Rev. Msgr. James R. Tracy; Rev. John M. Stabeno; Mrs. Mary Ann Exler, Pastoral Assoc.; Deacons Joseph B. Chandler; Joseph Buccilli, Business Mgr.
Res.: 176 Stagecoach Rd., 08081. Tel: 856-629-0411; Fax: 856-629-9109. Email: parishcentersch@comcast.net. Web: www.saint-charles-borromeo.org.
See Our Lady of Hope Regional School, Blackwood under Regional Schools, Elementary located in the Institution section.
Catechesis/Religious Program—Tel: 856-228-5694. Mrs. Mary Ann Exler, D.R.E. Students 916.

2—CHURCH OF ST. JOHN NEUMANN, SICKLERVILLE, N.J. (1977) Merged with St. Mary's Church, Williamstown, N.J. to form Our Lady of Peace Parish, Monroe Township, NJ.

SOMERDALE, CAMDEN CO., OUR LADY OF GRACE, R.C. CHURCH, SOMERDALE, NEW JERSEY (1954) Merged with Church of St. Lawrence, Laurel Springs, N.J. & The R.C. Church of St. Luke, Stratford, N.J. to form Our Lady of Guadalupe Parish, Lindenwold.

SOMERS POINT, ATLANTIC CO., ST. JOSEPH'S CHURCH, SOMERS POINT, N.J. (1946) Rev. Josef A. Wagenhoffer.
Res.: 606 Shore Rd., 08244. Tel: 609-927-3568; Fax: 609-653-8707.
School—St. Joseph Regional School, (Grades PreK-8) Tel: 609-927-2228; Fax: 609-927-7834. Sr. Frances Kane, S.S.J., Prin.; Mrs. Jan Hutton, Librarian. Regionalized with Our Lady of Sorrows Parish, Linwood; St. Augustine, St. Frances Cabrini, & Our Lady of Good Council, Ocean City. Sisters 6; Lay Teachers 24; Students 505.
Catechesis/Religious Program—Tel: 609-927-3302. Students 450.
Convent—Sisters of St. Joseph of Chestnut Hill, 580 Shore Rd., 08244. Tel: 609-926-9127.

STONE HARBOR, CAPE MAY CO., ST. PAUL'S CHURCH, STONE HARBOR, N.J. (1911) Rev. Msgr. John T. Frey; Deacon William Lauth.
Res.: 9910 Third Ave., 08247. Tel: 609-368-3091; Fax: 609-368-2775.
See Bishop McHugh Regional School, Cape May Court House under Regional Schools, Elementary located in the Institution section.
Catechesis/Religious Program—5012 Dune Dr., Avalon, 08202. Tel: 609-967-3746; Fax: 609-967-8172. Students 26.

STRATFORD, CAMDEN CO., THE R.C. CHURCH OF ST. LUKE, STRATFORD, N.J. (1961) Merged with Church of St. Lawrence, Laurel Springs, N.J. & Our Lady of Grace, R.C. Church, Somerdale, New Jersey to form Our Lady of Guadalupe, Lindenwold.

SWEDESBORO, GLOUCESTER CO., ST. JOSEPH'S CHURCH, SWEDESBOROUGH (1854) [CEM 2] Rev. Steven V. Pinzon; Deacons Pablo Berrios; Joseph A. Garozzo.
Res.: 140 N. Broad St., 08085. Tel: 856-467-0037; Fax: 856-467-0038. Web: www.sjcswedesboro.org.
School—Bishop Guilfoyle Regional School, (Grades K-8), 350 Georgetown Rd., Carneys Point, 08069. Mrs. Kathryn Chestnut, Prin.
Catechesis/Religious Program—Students 680.

TURNERSVILLE, CAMDEN CO., THE CHURCH OF SAINTS PETER AND PAUL, WASHINGTON TOWNSHIP, N.J. (1973) Revs. Edward J. Lipinski; Danilo Quiray; Calogero N. LaVerde; Deacons John A. Contino; Eugene L. McLeer, (Retired).
Res.: 362 Ganttown Rd., P.O. Box 1022, 08012. Tel: 856-589-3366; Fax: 856-256-1964. Email: sspp.fin@verizon.net. Web: www.peterandpaulchurch.org.
See Our Lady of Hope Regional School, Blackwood under Regional Schools, Elementary located in the Institution section.

VENTNOR, ATLANTIC CO., ST. JAMES CATHOLIC CHURCH, VENTNOR, N.J. (1922) Revs. Joseph F. Ganiel; Krzysztof Wtorek; Deacon Agatino A. Garufi.
Res.: 6415 Atlantic Ave., 08406. Tel: 609-822-2176; Fax: 609-487-8137.
School—Holy Family Regional School, (Grades PreK-8), 30 S. Portland Ave., Ventnor City, 08406. Tel: 609-822-2234; Fax: 609-822-7941. Web: www.hfrsvnj.org. Sr. Lydia Etter, O.S.F., Prin. Sisters 3; Lay Teachers 8; Students 145.
Catechesis/Religious Program—Students 95.
Convent—Oblates of St. Francis (Glen Riddle, PA), 30 S. Portland, 08406. Tel: 609-487-8110.

VILLAS, CAPE MAY CO., ST. RAYMOND'S CATHOLIC CHURCH, WILDWOOD VILLAS, N.J. (1937) Rev. William S. Vandegrift.
Res.: 25 E. Hudson Ave., 08251. Tel: 609-886-5366; Fax: 609-886-9415.
Catechesis/Religious Program—Tel: 609-886-7640. Students 105.
Convent—25 E. Ocean Ave., 08251. Tel: 609-886-8335. IHM

VINELAND, CUMBERLAND CO.

1—THE CATHOLIC CHURCH OF THE SACRED HEART, VINELAND, N.J. (1874), (Italian), [CEM] Rev. Msgr. John H. Burton; Revs. Robert Ngageno; John P. Ward; Deacons Richard Sampson; Frank Guaracini Jr.
Res.: 1010 Landis Ave., 08360. Tel: 856-691-0420; Fax: 856-691-1516. Email: sacredheartchurch@verizon.net.
See Bishop Schad Regional School, Vineland under Regional Schools, Elementary located in the Institution section.
Catechesis/Religious Program—922 E. Landis Ave. Tel: 856-696-0325. Students 115.

2—THE CHURCH OF ST. FRANCIS OF ASSISI, VINELAND, N.J. (1961) Merged with The Parish of the

Immaculate Heart of Mary, La Parroquia Del Inmaculado Corazon De Maria, Vineland, New Jersey to form Divine Mercy, Vineland, N.J.

3—THE CHURCH OF SAINT ISIDORE THE FARMER, VINELAND, N.J. (1962) Rev. Msgr. John H. Burton; Rev. Lawrence E. Polansky; Sr. Catherine Kane, O.S.F., Pastoral Assoc.; Deacons Robert Andreacchio; William J. Deliberis.
Res.: 1655 Magnolia Rd., 08361-6598. Tel: 856-691-9077; Fax: 856-692-3305. Email: isidore@comcast.net. Web: www.stisidorethefarmer-.org.
See Bishop Schad Regional School, Vineland under Regional Schools, Elementary located in the Institution section.
Catechesis/Religious Program—Tel: 856-563-0482; Fax: 856-692-3305. Anita MacDonald, C.R.E. Students 200.

4—DIVINE MERCY, VINELAND, N.J. (2009) Rev. Msgrs. Victor S. Muro; Dominic J. Bottino; Deacons Charles J. Girard; Thomas S. Moleski; Joseph A. Perella. In Res., Rev. Jones Kukatla.
Rectory—23 W. Chestnut Ave., 08360-5303. Tel: 856-691-9181; Fax: 856-794-9029.
Catechesis/Religious Program—Tel: 856-691-9181, Ext. 13. Students 340.
Convent—Daughters of Mercy, Tel: 856-691-8129.
Pope John Paul II Retreat Center—Tel: 856-691-2299; Fax: 856-691-5522.

5—ST. MARY'S (1887) [CEM] Merged with Our Lady of Pompeii to form St. Padre Pio Parish, Vineland, N.J.

6—OUR LADY OF POMPEII (1909) Merged with St. Mary's to form St. Padre Pio Parish, Vineland, N.J.

7—ST. PADRE PIO PARISH, VINELAND, N.J. (2003) Revs. Peter M. Saporito; Jerold G. Anthony.
Rectory—4680 Dante Ave., 08360-6810. Tel: 856-691-7526; Fax: 856-692-2686.
Church: *St. Mary's*, 736 S. Union Rd., 08360. Tel: 856-691-9721.
Church: *Our Lady of Pompeii*, 4680 Dante Ave., 08361.
School—St. Mary Regional School, (Grades PreK-8), 735 S. Union Rd., 08360. Tel: 856-692-8537; Fax: 856-692-5034. Sr. Margaret Curcio, D.M., Prin.; Lori Yeager, Librarian.
Catechesis/Religious Program—Students 170.

8—THE PARISH OF THE IMMACULATE HEART OF MARY, LA PARROQUIA DEL INMACULADO CORAZON DE MARIA, VINELAND, NEW JERSEY, Merged with The Church of St. Francis of Assisi, Vineland, N.J. to form Divine Mercy, Vineland, N.J.

WATERFORD, CAMDEN CO., ST. ANTHONY'S CHURCH, WATERFORD, N.J. (1966) Rev. Piotr Szamocki; Deacon Nicholas P. Ludovich.
Res.: 436 Pennington Ave., 08089. Tel: 856-767-7535; Fax: 856-767-7372. Email: stanthonywfd@comcast.net.
See St. Joseph School, Hammonton, under Regional Schools, Elementary located in the Institution section.
Catechesis/Religious Program—c/o Assumption Church, 318 Carl Hasselman Dr., Atco, 08004. Students 89.

WEST COLLINGSWOOD, CAMDEN CO., CHURCH OF THE TRANSFIGURATION, WEST COLLINGSWOOD, N.J. (1950) Revs. Richard J. Lodge; Mike Steve Ezeatu; Deacon William C. Robinson.
Res.: 445 White Horse Pike, 08107. Tel: 856-854-0364; Fax: 856-869-5129. Web: www.transfigurationparish.org.
Catechesis/Religious Program—Students 36.

WESTMONT, CAMDEN CO., THE CHURCH OF THE HOLY SAVIOUR, WESTMONT, N.J. (1928) Revs. Edward M. Friel, Admin.; Bruno Dongo, A.J.; Deacon James H. Rocks.
Res.: 50 Emerald Ave., 08108. Tel: 856-854-0022; Fax: 856-854-5741. Email: holysaviourchurch@comcast.net. Web: www.holysaviourchurch.org.
Catechesis/Religious Program—Tel: 856-854-1516. Students 297.
Convent—30 Emerald Ave., 08108. Tel: 856-858-2638. Franciscan Missionary Sisters of the Immaculate Heart of Mary

WESTVILLE GROVE, GLOUCESTER CO., CHURCH OF THE MOST HOLY REDEEMER, WESTVILLE GROVE, N.J. (1958) Rev. Robert J. Kantz, Admin.; Deacon Vincent Latini.
Res.: 1219 Delsea Dr., 08093. Tel: 856-848-6779; Fax: 856-848-6208.
School—Holy Trinity Regional School, (Grades PreK-8), 1215 Delsea Dr., 08093. Tel: 856-848-6826; Fax: 856-251-0344. Mrs. Patricia Mancuso, Prin. Lay Teachers 17; Students 278.

WESTVILLE, GLOUCESTER CO., ST. ANNE'S CHURCH, WESTVILLE, N.J. (1921) Rev. Frederick G. Link.
Res.: 213 Woodbine Ave., 08093. Tel: 856-456-4136; Fax: 856-456-7502. Email: secretary@stanneschurch.com.
School—Holy Trinity Regional School, Westville Grove, (Grades PreK-8) Tel: 856-848-6826; Fax: 856-251-0344. See separate listing.
Catechesis/Religious Program—Tel: 856-456-8713; Fax: 856-456-7502. Students 88.

WILDWOOD CREST, CAPE MAY CO., THE CHURCH OF THE ASSUMPTION B.V.M., WILDWOOD CREST, N.J. (1961) Merged with St. Ann's Church, Holly Beach, N.J. to form Notre Dame de la Mer Parish, Wildwood, N.J.

WILDWOOD, CAPE MAY CO.

1—ST. ANN'S CHURCH, HOLLY BEACH, N.J. (1895) Merged with The Church of the Assumption of the B.V.M., Wildwood Crest, N.J. to form Notre Dame de la Mer Parish, Wildwood, N.J.

2—NOTRE DAME DE LA MER PARISH, WILDWOOD, N.J., 2900 Pacific Ave., 08260-4943.

WILLIAMSTOWN, GLOUCESTER CO., ST. MARY'S CHURCH, WILLIAMSTOWN, N.J. (1906) [CEM] Merged with Church of St. John Neumann, Sicklerville, N.J. to form Our Lady of Peace Parish, Monroe Township, NJ.
Our Lady of Peace Parish, Monroe Township, N.J.— (2009)Revs. Cadmus D. Mazzarella; Victorino B. Coronado, C.I.C.M.; Christopher M. Markellos; Deacons John J. Leyden, (Retired); John Kacy; Michael McDonaugh; Albert A. LaMonaca Jr.
Rectory—32 Carrol Ave., 08094-1713. Tel: 856-629-6142; Fax: 856-875-2097. Email: olopp@olopp.org. Web: www.olopp.org.
Rectory—640 S. Main St., 08094. Tel: 856-262-1358. Churches,
Saint Mary, Williamstown—
Saint John Neumann, Sicklerville—
School—32A Carrol Ave., 08094. Tel: 856-629-6190; Fax: 856-728-1437. Miss Judith McBride, Prin. Lay Teachers 35; Students 572.
Catechesis/Religious Program—Tel: 856-629-0614. Students 1,030.

WOODBINE, CAPE MAY CO., ST. CASIMIR'S R.C. CHURCH, WOODBINE, N.J. (1939) [CEM] Revs. Christopher T. Bakey; Jose Ainikkal, C.M.I.; Deacon Gary F. Tankard.
Res.: 304 Clay St., P.O. Box 533, 08270. Tel: 609-861-3771; Fax: 609-861-7112. Email: stcasimir@comcast.net. Web: www.stcasimirwoodbine.4lpi.com/.
See Bishop McHugh Regional School, Cape May Court House under Regional Schools, Elementary located in the Institution section.
Catechesis/Religious Program—Tel: 609-861-3771. Students 64.
Mission—St. Elizabeth [CEM] Rte. 47, Goshen, Cape May Co. 08218. Tel: 609-861-5218.

WOODBURY HEIGHTS, GLOUCESTER CO.

1—INFANT JESUS PARISH, WOODBURY HEIGHTS, N.J., 334 Beech Ave., 08097-1317.

2—ST. MARGARET'S CHURCH, WOODBURY HEIGHTS, N.J. (1961) Merged with The Church of St. John Vianney, Gloucester County, N.J., Deptford to form Infant Jesus Parish, Woodbury Heights, N.J.

WOODBURY, GLOUCESTER CO., ST. PATRICK'S CHURCH, WOODBURY (1877) Rev. Msgr. Joseph V. DiMauro; Revs. Thomas S. Capperella; John Onyenanu Ekeocha; Melchoir Chetty; Deacons David Murnane; Albert J. Riviello; Paul M. Parchinski.
Res.: 64 Cooper St., 08096. Tel: 856-845-0123; Fax: 856-845-7409.
Catechesis/Religious Program—211 Cooper St., 08096. Tel: 856-853-6681. Students 600.

WOODLYNNE, CAMDEN CO., THE IMMACULATE HEART OF MARY, WOODLYNNE, N.J. (1949), (Vietnamese), Rev. Joseph An Nguyen; Deacon Kim T. Nguyen.
Res.: 201 Cooper Ave., 08107. Tel: 856-962-8610; Fax: 856-962-9438. Email: ihmvietmy@yahoo.com.
Catechesis/Religious Program—Students 142.

WOODSTOWN, SALEM CO., ST. JOSEPH'S CATHOLIC CHURCH, WOODSTOWN, N.J. (1895) [CEM] Revs. Anthony R. DiBardino; John P. Picinic, S.A.C.
Res.: 51 Broad St., 08098. Tel: 856-769-0004; Fax: 856-769-9904. Email: stjoewdtn@verizon.net.
Catechesis/Religious Program—Students 220.

Chaplains of Public Institutions

ANCORA. *New Jersey State Psychiatric Hospital*, Tel: 609-561-1700. Rev. Joachim Oforchukwu, C.S.Sp. (Nigeria), Chap.

BRIDGETON. *Southwoods State Prison, Immaculate Conception*, 08302. Rev. Robert P. Weber, Ph.D., Chap. (Retired).

CAPE MAY. *United States Coast Guard, Command Chaplain's Office*, 1 Munro Ave., 08204-5001. Tel: 609-898-6974. Rev. Miles J. Barrett.

DELMONT. *Southern State Correctional Facility*, Tel: 856-785-1300, Ext. 6389. Rev. Robert P. Weber, Ph.D. (Retired).

FAIRTON. *Federal Correctional Institution*, P.O. Box 280, 08320. Tel: 856-227-1436. Rev. Sergio Bicomong, Chap.

LAKELAND. *Camden County Hospital at Lakeland*, St. Joseph's Chapel, Blackwood Post Office, 08012. Tel: 856-227-3000, Ext. 444. Rev. Jose Kadukunnel Alexander, C.M.I., Chap.

LEESBURG. *New Jersey State Medium Security Prison* 08327. Tel: 856-785-0040. Rev. William James Bleiler (Retired).

VINELAND. *Vineland State School*.
Chaplaincy, St. Isidore, 08362. Tel: 856-691-9077.

WOODBINE. *State Colony*.
Chaplaincy, *St. Casimir's Church*, 304 Clay St., 08270. Tel: 609-861-3771.

On Duty Outside the Diocese:

Rev. Msgrs.—
Checchio, James F., Pontifical North American College 00120 Vatican City State.
Daiber, Sean J., Central Mailing Address, Paroguia de Sao Jose Rua 90 N. 40, Setor Sul, Caiza Postal 716, 74,000 Goiania Goias, Brazil. Brazilian Missions
Pokusa, Joseph W., J.C.D., Apostolic Nunciature, 3339 Massachusetts Ave. N.W., Washington, DC 20008. Tel: 202-333-7121

Revs.—
Amabile, Patsy L., Our Lady of Lourdes, Islip, NY 11751.
Bartoloma, James L., Casa Santa Maria, Rome, Italy.
Betz, James F., CMR 419, Box 444, Apo, AE 09102.
Guasp Santos, Walter, Parroquia San Jose Obrero, 632 Ramos Antonini E. Tuque, Ponce, PR 00716. Tel: 787-843-9072
Hubbs, Timothy L., Chap. (Major), 1117 Will Way, Clarksville, TN 37043.
Kocik, Francis W., 19 Hawley St., Binghamton, NY 13901.
McLaughlin, Peter A., St. Michael, 19 N. Palafax St., P.O. Box 12423, Pensacola, FL 32582. Tel: 850-438-4985
Nwoga, Laserian, 10 ABW/HC, 5134 Cathedral Dr., Ste. 100, U S A F Academy, CO 80840-2700.
Orsi, Michael P., Ave Maria School of Law, 1025 Commons Cir., Naples, FL 34119.
Rossi, John A., St. Joseph Ukrainian Seminary, 201 Taylor St., N.E., Washington, DC 20017.
Sinatra, Robert L., Casa Santa Maria, Rome, Italy.

On Sick Leave:

Rev.—
Trinh, Paul H.

On Leave of Absence:

Revs.—
Conners, John P.
Delaney, John C.
Goyette, Michael J.
Idler, Peter M.
McLaverty, Albert J.
Melendez, Daniel J.
Pham, Joseph Luong
Tabone, Marcel M.
Witcoskie, Stanley L.

Retired:

Rev. Msgrs.—
Alleyne, Edward D., Sacred Heart Residence for Priests, 200 St. Mary's Dr., Cherry Hill, 08003-5217. Tel: 856-449-7503
Barth, Charles P., St. Anthony of Padua, 285 Rte. 206, Hammonton, 08037. Tel: 609-561-3313
Budney, David F., 315 Ryder Cup Cir., Unit 106, St. Augustine, FL 32092. Tel: 904-940-3390
Carr, James A., Sacred Heart Residence for Priests, 200 St. Mary's Dr., Cherry Hill, 08003.
Casey, John H., 104 Wood Ln., Sparta, TN 38583.
Chiarilli, Patrick S., Clayton Mews, 865 N. Delsea Dr., Box 102, Clayton, 08312.
Clarke, John A., 112 Franklin Dr., Mullica Hill, 08062. Tel: 856-371-1933
Coyne, Michael J., P.O. Box 95, Leeds Point, 08220.
Fitzsimmons, Eugene J., J.C.D., P.O. Box 116, Sea Isle City, 08243.
Fitzsimmons, Thomas B., Saint Ann, 2900 Pacific Ave., Wildwood, 08260-4943. Tel: 609-522-5583
Flaherty, J. Francis, Villa Rafaella, 917 S. Main St., Pleasantville, 08232. Tel: 609-645-9300
Flynn, Thomas M., Sacred Heart Residence, 200 St. Mary's Dr., Cherry Hill, 08003. Tel: 856-751-8109
Gallagher, John Gerald, Blessed Sacrament, 15 Shea Pl., New Rochelle, NY 10801. Tel: 904-823-0975
Graham, William P., V.F., 414 Erie Ave., Carney's Point, 08069. Tel: 856-534-7976
Herron, Joseph P., P.O. Box 615, Longport, 08403.
Jordan, Harry J., Sacred Heart Residence, 200 St. Mary's Dr., Cherry Hill, 08003. Tel: 856-874-1959
Joynes, Joseph P., Sacred Heart Residence, 200 St. Mary Dr., Cherry Hill, 08003. Tel: 856-751-1966
Kennedy, Edward J., St. Mary's Catholic Home, 210 St. Mary's Dr., Cherry Hill, 08003.

Kernan, Eugene J., 91 Geneva Ave., Westmont, 08108.
Kloskowski, Stanley E., c/o 27 Fleetwood Dr., Hamilton Square, 08690.
O'Connor, Paul, 23 N. Wissahickan Ave., Ventnor, 08406.
O'Leary, Cornelius P., 25098 Jaclyn Ave., Moreno Valley, CA 92557-5703. Tel: 909-242-6939
O'Neill, Felix M., 717 S. Columbus Blvd., Apt. 518, Philadelphia, PA 19147. Tel: 215-925-7001
Poyatt, William F., St. Mary's Catholic Home, 210 St. Mary's Dr., Cherry Hill, 08003. Tel: 856-547-2313
Ryan, Timothy A., Our Lady Star of the Sea, 525 Washington St., Cape May, 08204-1427. Tel: 609-884-5311
Sharkey, Thomas F., J.C.D., 3 Catherine Pl., Northfield, 08225.
Sprecace, Francis A., 856 Palermo Rd., St. Augustine, FL 32086.
Storlein, Joseph G., 97 Hobart Ave., Absecon, 08201.

Revs.—
Anderson, Arthur T., Sacred Heart Residence for Priests, 200 St. Mary's Dr., Cherry Hill, 08003.
Battisti, Lewis A., V.F., Garden Lake Park #128, 1402 S. Rte. #9, Cape May Court House, 08210.
Bean, Charles S., Saint Mary's Catholic Home, 210 St. Mary's Dr., Cherry Hill, 08003-2517. Tel: 856-791-2010
Beebe, David E., Country Club Estates, 248 Rte. 40, A-8, Newfield, 08344. Tel: 856-358-0262
Bleiler, William James, Saint Michael, P.O. Box 327, Cedarville, 08311. Tel: 856-447-3480
Bober, Marjan L., 791 Burman Ln., N.E., Palm Bay, FL 32905.
Bolcar, Andrew J., Sacred Heart Residence for Priests, 200 St. Mary's Dr., Cherry Hill, 08003-2517. Tel: 856-424-2035
Bourke, John F., 4 Twig Ct., Willingboro, 08046. Tel: 609-871-3890
Burns, Joseph, St. Mary's Home, 210 St. Mary Dr., Cherry Hill, 08003.
Cairone, A. Robert, Sacred Heart Residence, 200 St. Mary's Dr., Cherry Hill, 08003.
Carey, Stephen, Templetuohy, Thurles, County Tipperary, Ireland.
Collins, William F., 216 Leeds Ave., Bellmawr, 08031.
Dante, Neal F., 5001 Pleasant Mill Rd., Hammonton, 08037. Tel: 609-965-0464
Eckert, William F., 181 Elm St., Pittsfield, MA 01201.
Fleming, John M., 161 Kamal Pkwy., Cape Coral, FL 33904. Tel: 609-369-6324
Forbes, Richard L., Sacred Heart North, 250 St. Mary's Dr., Cherry Hill, 08003. Tel: 609-425-8653
Gannon, Bernard J., Sacred Heart South, 230 St. Mary's Dr., Cherry Hill, 08003. Tel: 856-424-2035
Gomes, Robert M., 1023 McTavish Way, Palm Harbor, FL 34684.
Gramigna, Francis J., 1015 Black Horse Pike #51, Egg Harbor Twp., 08046. Tel: 609-871-3890
Hart, William H., Sacred Heart Residence, 200 St. Mary Dr., Cherry Hill, 08003.
Hayden, Joseph M., 2354 Mulligan Dr., Lakeland, FL 33810. Tel: 863-815-2541; 863-604-0272
Hewett, Alfred J., St. Rose of Lima, 300 Kings Hwy., Haddon Heights, 08035-1397. Tel: 609-547-0564
Hope, Abbott J., Sacred Heart Residence for Priests, 200 St. Mary's Dr., Cherry Hill, 08003. Tel: 856-489-8483
Jones, J. Overton, 447 N. Tennessee Ave., Atlantic City, 08401.
Karczewski, Julian A., Our Lady's Multi-Care Center, 1100 Clematis Ctr., Pleasantville, 08232.
Kolton, Stanislaus J., 117 Brown Ave., Spring Lake, 07762-1017. Tel: 908-449-6364
Kunzman, Richard T., 1910 N.W. Second Pl., Cape Coral, FL 33993. Tel: 239-458-7959
Lambert, Cornelius F., Maris Stella, 5012 Dune Dr., Avalon, 08202. Tel: 609-967-3345
Lavin, Wayne Patrick, Sacred Heart Residence, 200 St. Mary's Dr., Cherry Hill, 08003.
Longo, Robert, O.F.M.Cap., 1762 Crown Point Rd., Apt. 674, Thorofare, 08086. Tel: 856-848-2422
Lyons, Edward D., 1402 Massachusetts Ave., Somers Point, 08244. Tel: 609-927-1669
McBride, Henry J., Sacred Heart Residence, 200 St. Mary's Dr., Cherry Hill, 08003.
McCabe, Patrick A., 10 S. Wrenn Pl., Foxfire Village, NC 27281.
Meaney, Brendan J., Sacred Heart Residence, 200 St. Mary's Dr., Cherry Hill, 08003.
Messina, Joseph, 1209 Burrough's Mill Cir., Cherry Hill, 08002.
Minniti, David V., Saint Peter, 43 W. Maple Ave., Merchantville, 08109-5141. Tel: 856-663-1373
Orsini, Joseph E., 42 W. 50th St., Bayonne, 07002.
Ploude, Thomas E., Summer Fields, 511 Shadow Creek Ln., Williamstown, 08094.
Plummer, James, 216 N. Jerome Ave., Margate, 08402.
Romanowski, Jerome C., 168 Ellmtowne Blvd., Hammonton, 08037. Tel: 609-870-6073
Rosinski, Edward B., 39 Central Ave., Audubon, 08106.
Rush, Joseph E., 178 Berlin Rd., Gibbsboro, 08026.
Ryan, William F., 1401 S. Rte. 9, Lot 50, Cape May Court House, 08210.
Selleck, John P., St. Dominic Rectory, 5012 Whitaker St., Panama City, FL 32404.
Smith, Robert V., Sacred Heart Residence, 200 St. Mary Dr., Cherry Hill, 08003. Tel: 856-751-1951
Sommers, Edward P., 105 Whitman Ave., Stratford, 08084.
Stoegbauer, Carlton C., Sacred Heart Residence, 200 St. Mary Dr., Cherry Hill, 08003.
Stout, O. Hugh, Sacred Heart Residence, 200 St. Mary Dr., Cherry Hill, 08003. Tel: 856-751-2010
Sugrue, John F., Villa Rafaello, 917 S. Main St., Pleasantville, 08232.
Sullivan, Brendan V., 217 W. Ridgewood Dr., Northfield, 08225.
Tovar, Ireneo Lopez, 121 Country Club Dr., Tower II, Apt. 403, Lake Placid, FL 33852.
Tracey, Thomas S., 21217 N. St., Rehoboth Beach, DE 19971. Tel: 302-227-3063
Voltaggio, Fred, 303 W. Beach Ave., Brigantine, 08203. Tel: 609-923-9649
Wade, Edward C., Queen of Peace, 3011 Telephone Rd., Houston, TX 77023.
Weber, Robert P., Ph.D., 824 Stokes Ave., Collingswood, 08108. Tel: 856-513-5085
Yori, Robert O., 13 W. 4th St., Hazleton, PA 18201. Tel: 570-454-3476

Permanent Deacons:
Achee, C. J.
Andreacchio, Robert A.
Ayscue, Brian T.
Bandiera, A. Kenneth
Becker, Joseph F.
Beebe, Joseph F.
Berrios, Pablo
Berstecher, John L.
Bischer, Carmen M.
Buccilli, Joseph C.
Carlucci, Leonard P.
Carson, Robert L., S.J.
Carter, Michael J.
Cassidy, Joseph P., (Retired)
Catanese, Ralph A.
Cerullo, Francis A.
Chandler, Joseph B.
Colanero, John D.
Como, Anthony C., (Retired)
Contino, John A.
Correa, Luis E.
Costello, Joseph A., (Retired)
Crawford, Douglas R.
Crosson, Francis W.
Cruz, Jose M.
D'Ariano, Michael A.
Danze, Nicholas A.
Del Rossi, George C.
Deliberis, William J.
DeMuro, Gerard V.
Drum, William J., (Retired)
Ellis, Raymond V.
Engel, Francis J., (Retired)
Espinal, Luis J.
Fanelli, Robert M.
Ferland, George M., (Retired)
Ferrario, Raymond C., (Retired)
Gallagher, Mark J.
Gallimore, John R., (Retired)
Ganci, Joseph A., (Retired)
Garozzo, Joseph A.
Garufi, Agatino A., (Senior)
Giordano, Philip E.
Girard, Charles J.
Guaracini, Frank, Jr.
Guerrieri, Michael H.
Hafner, Thomas J.
Hanrahan, Matthew J.
Harkins, Michael J.
Harrington, John H., Jr.
Henry, E. Michael
Hogan, James N.
Iannuzzi, William P., (Retired)
Izzo, Joseph J.
Jablonowski, Gerard J.
Jadick, Anthony M.
Jennings, Thomas E.
Johnson, William G.
Kacy, John J.
Kearney, J. Brian, (Retired)
Kenney, Robert M.
Kiley, James W., (Senior)
Lagares, Hipolito
LaMonaca, Albert A., Jr.
Latini, Vincent
Lauth, William
Lee, Paul K.
Leyden, John J., (Retired)
Liss, George R.
Long, Leonard W.
Lopes, Joseph S.
Loungo, Joseph W.
Ludovich, Nicholas P.
Luko, John J., Jr.
Malatesta, Anthony D.
Maxwell, Richard S.
McAleer, Charles L., Sr.
McBlain, W. Leo
McCarthy, Richard F., (Retired)
McDonaugh, Michael L.
McHugh, Joseph P.
McLeer, Eugene L., (Retired)
Miranda, Felix Tito
Moleski, Thomas S.
Mortelliti, Nicholas V.
Murnane, David W.
Nasuti, Samuel S., Jr.
Nguyen, Kim T.
Nichols, Christopher D.
Norquist, William V.
O'Brien, Thomas F.
O'Clishim, Liam C.
Okoro, Vincent A.
Olesiewicz, Ronald J.
Orlando, Joseph P.
Parchinski, Paul M.
Pepe, Frank J., (Retired)
Perella, Joseph A.
Peters, William L.
Peterson, George J.
Picknally, Ernest F.
Pierce, Joseph R.
Porowicz, Alfred T., (Retired)
Powell, Peter J.
Quiles, Bernardino S., (Senior)
Radziak, Raymond R.
Ralbusky, Emil A.
Ramos Vega, Angel R.
Reiss, Charles C., (Retired)
Rich, John D., Jr.
Rivera, Miguel A., Sr.
Riviello, Albert J.
Robinson, William C.
Rocks, James H.
Rogozenski, Donald W.
Rumaker, William J., (Retired)
Sampson, Richard T.
Schiavo, John A.
Scott, Michael F.
Seaman, Joseph F.
Sullivan, Timothy M.
Tankard, Gary F.
Tavarez, Ismael P.
Tobin, Charles A.
Trainer, Vincent E.
Van Leer, George R.
Velez, Aladino
Watts, William L., (Retired)
Welsh, Michael L.
Werner, John F.
Wigglesworth, Richard J.
Willson, Robert F.
Teeney, James J., (Senior)

INSTITUTIONS LOCATED IN THE DIOCESE

[A] HIGH SCHOOLS, DIOCESAN

ABSECON. *Holy Spirit High School, Absecon, N.J.*, 500 South New Rd., 08201. Tel: 609-646-3000; Fax: 609-646-1770. Email: holyspirithighschool@yahoo.com. Web: www.holyspirithighschool.com. Miss Susan W. Dennen, Prin.; Mrs. Joann Malecki, Librarian. Sisters of Mercy 1; Priests 1; Lay Teachers 45; Students 780.

CHERRY HILL. *Camden Catholic High School, Cherry Hill, N.J.* (1887) 300 Cuthbert Rd., 08002. Tel: 856-663-2247; Fax: 856-661-0632. Email: camdencatholic@aol.com. Web: www.camdencatholic.org. Rev. Msgr. Andrew E. Martin, Pres.; Mr. Thomas J. Kiely, Prin.; Lindsey Perry, Librarian. Priests 3; Sisters of Mercy 1; Lay Teachers 60; Students 902; Staff 16.

HADDONFIELD. *Paul VI High School, Haddon Township, N.J.* (1966) 901 Hopkins Rd., Ste. B, 08033. Tel: 856-858-4900; Fax: 856-858-6832. Email: principal@pvihs.org. Web: pvihs.org. Rev. Robert E. Hughes, Pres.; Sr. Marianne McCann,

M.P.F., Prin.; Rev. Michael M. Romano; Mrs. Michelle Anastasia, Librarian. Priests 2; Religious Teachers Filippini 3; Franciscan Missionary Sisters 1; Lay Teachers 70; Students 1,192.

HAMMONTON. *St. Joseph High School Hammonton, NJ, Inc.*, 328 Vine St., 08037. Tel: 609-561-8700; Fax: 609-561-8701. Mrs. Lynn Domenico, Prin. Religious 3; Lay Teachers 41; Students 420.

[B] HIGH SCHOOLS, PAROCHIAL

GLOUCESTER. *Gloucester Catholic High School, Inc.*, 333 Ridgeway St., 08030. Tel: 856-456-4400; Fax: 856-456-0506. Email: Pmurphy@gchsrams.org. Web: www.gchsrams.org. Mr. John T. Colman, Prin.; Katharine Coughlin, Librarian. Priests 1; Lay Teachers 42; Students 730.

NORTH WILDWOOD. *Wildwood Catholic High School*, 1500 Central Ave., 08260. Tel: 609-522-7257; Fax: 609-522-2453. Web: wildwoodcatholic.org. Mr. Richard J. Turco, Prin.; Mr. Frank Smith, Vice Prin.; Bro. Robert Carson, S.J., Asst. Prin. Brothers 1; Lay Teachers 19; Students 230.

VINELAND. *Sacred Heart High School* (1927) 15 N. East Ave., 08360. Tel: 856-691-4491; Fax: 856-563-1644. Web: www.shhslions.com. Rev. Edward F. Namiotka, Pres.; Mrs. Diane Tucker, Prin. Priests 1; Lay Teachers 24; Students 287.

[C] HIGH SCHOOLS, PRIVATE

NEWFIELD. *Our Lady of Mercy Academy* (1962) 1001 Main Rd., 08344. Tel: 856-697-2008; Fax: 856-697-2887. Email: srgrace@olmanj.org. Web: www.olmanj.org. Sr. Grace Marie, D.M., Prin. Daughters of Our Lady of Mercy. Sisters 2; Lay Teachers 21; Students 187.

PENNSAUKEN. *Bishop Eustace Prep School* (1954) 5552 Rte. 70, 08109-4798. Tel: 856-662-2160, Ext. 211; Fax: 856-662-0802. Web: www.eustace.org. Rev. Robert Nolan, S.A.C.; Bro. James Beamesderfer, S.A.C., Headmaster & Local Community Supr.; Mr. Cyril J. Bleistine, Prin.; A. Nancy Croce, Librarian. Society of the Catholic Apostolate, Province of the Immaculate Conception. Priests 1; Brothers 1; Lay Teachers 70; Students 789.

RICHLAND. *St. Augustine Preparatory School*, 611 N. Cedar Ave., P.O. Box 279, 08350. Tel: 856-697-2600; 856-697-2612 (Monastery); Fax: 856-697-8389. Email: fr.galetto@hermits.com. Web: www.hermits.com. Revs. Paul W. Galetto, O.S.A., O.S.A., Pres.; Ronald A. Hamaday, O.S.A.; Francis J. Horn, O.S.A., J.C.D., Headmaster; Bro. David Graber, M.SS.CC.; Rev. Msgr. Peter M. Joyce, J.C.L.; Revs. Kevin J. Hollis, O.S.A.; Stephen M. Curry, O.S.A.; Francis X. Devlin, O.S.A. Order of St. Augustine, Province of St. Thomas of Villanova. Priests 3; Brothers 1; Lay Teachers 47; Students 692.

[D] ELEMENTARY SCHOOLS, PRIVATE

CAMDEN. **San Miguel School, Inc.* (1997) (Grades 6-8), 836 S. 4th St., 08103. Tel: 856-342-6707; Fax: 856-342-6708. Email: president@sanmiguelcamden.org. Web: www.sanmiguelcamden.org. Bro. Joseph Juliano, F.S.C., Pres.; James Horan, Prin.; Bro. Steven Casale, F.S.C., Librarian. De La Salle Christian Brothers 2; Lay Teachers 7; Students 40.

[E] REGIONAL SCHOOLS, ELEMENTARY

BERLIN. *Our Lady of Mt. Carmel*, (Grades PreK-8), One Cedar Ave., 08009. Tel: 856-767-1751; Fax: 856-767-1293. Email: olm@hotmail.net. Web: www.olmcparish.net. Sr. Mary Ellen Tucker, O.S.F., Prin. Serving Our Lady of Mt. Carmel, Berlin and St. Andrew, Gibbsboro. Sisters of Mercy (U.S. Province) 1; Lay Teachers 18; Students 342.

BLACKWOOD. *Our Lady of Hope Regional School*, (Grades PreK-8), 420 S. Black Horse Pike, 08012. Tel: 856-227-4442; 856-227-8558; Fax: 856-401-1622. Email: ourladyofhope@snip.net. Web: www.ourladyofhopecatholicschool.org. Sr. Paula Marie Randow, O.S.F., Prin.; Mr. John T. Cafagna, Asst. Prin.; Marge Rocco, Librarian. Serving St. Jude, Blackwood; SS. Peter & Paul, St. Charles Borromeo, & Holy Family, Washington Township, St. Agnes, Blackwood. Franciscan Sisters 1; Lay Teachers 26; Students 486.

CAPE MAY. *Our Lady, Star of the Sea Regional School*, (Grades PreK-8), 520 Lafayette St., 08204. Tel: 609-884-4437; Fax: 609-898-4253. Email: dollinger@capemayschools.com. Mrs. Donna DiPasquale, Prin. Serving Our Lady, Star of the Sea, Cape May. Sisters of St. Joseph 1; Lay Teachers 14; Students 180.

CAPE MAY COURT HOUSE. *The Bishop James T. McHugh Regional School, Inc.*, (Grades PreK-8), 2221 Rte. 9 N, 08210. Tel: 609-624-1900; Fax: 609-624-9696. Ms. Barbara Byrne, Prin.; Ruth Gensel, Librarian. Lay Teachers 21; Students 276.

CARNEYS POINT. *The Bishop George H. Guilfoyle Regional Grammar School, Inc.*, (Grades PreK-8), 350 Georgetown Rd., 08069. Tel: 856-299-0400; Fax: 856-299-6556. Email: principal@bgres.org. Web: www.bgrcs.org. Mrs. Kathryn Chesnut, Prin. Serving parishes of: Corpus Christi, Carney's Point; Queen of Apostles, Pennsville; St. Mary, Salem; St. James, Penns Grove; St. Joseph, Woodstown; St. Joseph, Swedesboro. Lay Teachers 11; Students 162.

COLLINGSWOOD. *Good Shepherd Regional School*, (Grades PreK-8), 100 Lees Ave., 08108. Tel: 856-858-1562; Fax: 856-858-2943. Email: goodshepherdprincipal@comcast.net. Web: www.goodshepherdcollingswood.org. Mr. Donald W. Garecht, Prin. Serving St. John, Collingswood; St. Aloysius, Oaklyn; Transfiguration, W. Collingswood; Holy Saviour, Westmont; St. Vincent Pallotti, Haddon Township. Lay Teachers 12; Students 140; PreK 48.

GALLOWAY. *Assumption Regional School*, (Grades PreK-8), 146 S. Pitney Rd., 08205. Tel: 609-652-7134; Fax: 609-652-2544. Email: mschurtz@aresgalloway.org. Web: www.arcsgalloway.org. Mary Ellen Schurtz, Prin. Serving Assumption, Pomona; St. Elizabeth Ann Seton, Absecon; St. Thomas, Brigantine. Lay Teachers 21; Students 335.

GIBBSTOWN. *Guardian Angels Regional School*Sr. Jerilyn Einstein, F.M.I.J., Prin. Sisters 3; Lay Teachers 11; Students 234.

Gibbstown Campus (Grades PreK-3), 150 S. School St., 08027. Tel: 856-423-9440; Fax: 856-423-9441. Email: gars@comcast.net.

Paulsboro Campus (Grades 4-8), 717 Beacon Ave., Paulsboro, 08066. Tel: 856-423-9401.

HADDONFIELD. *Christ the King Regional School*, (Grades PreK-8), 164 Hopkins Ave., 08033. Tel: 856-429-2084; Fax: 856-429-4959. Email: ccerullo@ckrs.org. Web: www.ckrs.org. Dr. Claudio Cerullo, Prin.; Mary Stiltz, Librarian. Serving Christ the King, Haddonfield; St. Pius X, Cherry Hill. Lay Teachers 27; Students 329.

HAMMONTON. *St. Joseph Regional Elementary School*, (Grades PreK-8), 133 N. 3rd St., 08037. Tel: 609-704-2400; Fax: 609-561-4940. Web: www.stjosephprek8.org. Sr. Helen Sanchez, M.P.F., Prin. Serving St. Joseph, St. Martin de Porres, St. Anthony of Padua, Hammonton; St. Anthony, Waterford; Blessed John XXIII, Blue Anchor. Religious Teachers Filippini 2; Lay Teachers 24; Students 363.

NEWFIELD. *Notre Dame Regional School, Inc.*, (Grades PreK-3), 108 Church St., 08344. Tel: 856-697-0155 (Newfield, Grades PK3-4); 856-697-3456 (Landisville, Grades 5-8); Fax: 856-697-5114; 856-697-8540. Email: notredameregional@comcast.net. Web: www.ndschool.org. Dr. Mary Alimenti, Prin.; Lucille Doyle, Librarian. Serving Queen of Angels, Landisville; Our Lady of the Lakes, Collings Lakes; St. Rose, Newfield; St. Mary, Malaga; St. Ann, Elmer. Lay Teachers 18; Students 175.

RUNNEMEDE. *St. Teresa School*, (Grades K-8), 27 E. Evesham Rd., 08078. Tel: 856-939-0333; Fax: 856-939-1204. Email: schooloffice@stteresa.xohost.com. Web: www.stteresaparish.net. Sr. Patricia Scanlon, I.H.M., Prin. Serving St. Teresa & St. Maria Goretti, Runnemede. Sisters Servants of the Immaculate Heart of Mary 3; Lay Teachers 12; Students 140.
18 Ardmore Rd., 08078.

VINELAND. *Bishop Schad Regional School*, (Grades K-8), 922 E. Landis Ave., 08360. Tel: 856-691-4490; Fax: 856-691-5579. Email: mainofc@bsrschool.org. Web: www.bsrschool.org. Dr. Patrice DeMartino, Prin.; Terry Smith, Librarian. Serving Sacred Heart, St. Isidore; St. Francis, Immaculate Heart of Mary Lay Teachers 25; Students 334.

St. Mary's Regional School, (Grades PreK-8), 735 Union Rd., 08360. Tel: 856-692-8537; Fax: 856-692-5034. Email: mainoffice@smrschool.org. Web: www.smrschool.org. Sr. Margaret Curcio, D.M., Prin.; Lori Yeager, Librarian. Serving St. Padre Pio, East Vineland. Daughters of Our Lady of Mercy 2; Lay Teachers 23; Students 304.

WOODBURY HEIGHTS. *St. Margaret Regional School* (1963) 773 Third St., 08097. Tel: 856-845-5200; Fax: 856-845-2405. Email: principal@stmargarets-rs.org. Web: www.stmargarets-rs.org. Sisters Michele DeGregorio, F.M.I.J., Prin.; Gloria Louise Levari, F.M.I.J., Supr. Serving St. Margaret, Woodbury Heights; Incarnation, Mantua. Sisters 4; Lay Teachers 18; Students 563.

[F] SCHOOLS FOR SPECIAL CHILDREN

WESTVILLE GROVE. *Archbishop Damiano School/St. John of God Community Services* (1965) 1145 Delsea Dr., 08093. Tel: 856-848-4700; Fax: 856-848-3965. Ms. Muncie Buckalew, Exec. Dir. Brothers 3; Sisters 1; Lay Teachers 77; Students 615; Total Staff 250.

[G] CATHOLIC FOUNDATIONS

CAMDEN. *Diocese of Camden Trusts, Inc.* (2001) 631 Market St., 08102. Martin F. McKernan Jr., Esq., Contact Person. Priests 2; Lay Staff 1.

Francis, Elizabeth and Edward Roger Welsh Scholarship Trust, 631 Market St., 08102. Tel: 856-583-2835; Fax: 856-963-2655. Rev. Msgr. Roger E. McGrath, Ph.D., Advisory Committee Chair.

The Frank J. and Rosina W. Suttill Catholic Foundation, 631 Market St., 08102. Tel: 856-583-2806. Rev. Msgr. Roger E. McGrath, Ph.D.

The Sharkey Family Charitable Trust, 631 Market St., 08102. Tel: 856-583-2802. Rev. Msgr. Roger E. McGrath, Ph.D., Treas.

The Tuition Assistance Fund, Inc., 631 Market St., 08102. Tel: 856-583-2835; Fax: 856-963-2655. Email: bpastore@camdendiocese.org. Betty Pastore, Admin.

[H] GENERAL HOSPITALS

CAMDEN. *Our Lady of Lourdes Health Care Services, Inc.*, 1600 Haddon Ave., 08103. Tel: 856-757-3500; Fax: 856-757-3611. Web: www.lourdesnet.org. Alexander J. Hatala, Pres. & CEO. Bed Capacity 641; Total Staff 2,552; Patients Assisted Annually 301,060.

Our Lady of Lourdes Medical Center (Formerly Our Lady of Lourdes Hospital)(Parent Corporation: Our Lady of Lourdes Health Care Services, Inc.), 1600 Haddon Ave., 08103. Tel: 856-757-3500; Fax: 856-757-3611. Franciscan Sisters of Allegany.

Our Lady of Lourdes Health Foundation, Inc., 1600 Haddon Ave., 08103. Tel: 856-382-1802; Fax: 856-382-1782.

Lourdes Cardiovascular Foundation, Inc., 1600 Haddon Ave., 08103. Tel: 856-482-4950; Fax: 856-482-4960.

Osborn Family Health Center Inc., 1600 Haddon Ave., 08103. Tel: 856-757-3700; Fax: 856-365-7972.

Our Lady of Lourdes School of Nursing, 1600 Haddon Ave., 08103. Tel: 856-757-3629; Fax: 856-757-3758. Web: www.lourdesnursingschool.org.

Our Lady of Lourdes Medical Center Auxiliary, 1600 Haddon Ave., 08103. Tel: 856-382-1795; Fax: 856-382-1782.

Lourdes Ancillary Services, Inc., 1600 Haddon Ave., 08103. Tel: 856-757-3500; Fax: 856-757-3611.

[I] NURSING HOMES

CHERRY HILL. *St. Mary's Catholic Home, Cherry Hill, N.J.* (1952) 210 St. Mary's Dr., 08003. Tel: 856-874-5300; Fax: 856-424-5143. Email: sr.beatrix.wieczorek@camdendiocese.org. Sr. M. Beatrix Wieczorek, R.N., L.N.H.A., Admin.; Rev. James J. Durkin, Chap. Little Servant Sisters of the Immaculate Conception. Sisters 4; Total Staff 250; Total Assisted Annually 250.

NEWFIELD. *The Mater Dei Nursing Home, Newfield, New Jersey* (1967) 176 Rte. 40, 08344. Tel: 856-358-2061; Fax: 856-358-0403. Sr. Anne Ebersold, M.S.C., L.N.H.A., Admin.; Rev. Sebastian V. Annino, Chap. Marianites of Holy Cross. Marianites of the Holy Cross 1; Sisters of Mary Immaculate 3; Bed Capacity 64; Total Staff 104; Total Assisted Annually 97.

PLEASANTVILLE. *Our Lady's Residence, Pleasantville, N.J. dba Our Lady's Multi-Care Center, Inc.* 1100 Clematis Ave., 08232. Tel: 609-646-2450; Fax: 609-646-7569. Anna Tosti, L.N.H.A., Admin.; Sr. Normita Nunez, H.S.M., Supr.; Rev. John Perdue, M.SS.CC., Chap. Hospitaler Sisters of Mercy. Sisters 4; Bed Capacity 214; Patients Assisted Annually 214; Total Staff 240.

Villa Raffaella, 917 S. Main St., 08232. Tel: 609-645-9300; Fax: 609-645-9600. Senior Assisted Living Community, Hospitaler Sisters of Mercy. Total Staff 15; Bed Capacity 40.

VINELAND. *Bishop McCarthy Residence*, 1045 E. Chestnut Ave., 08360. Tel: 856-692-2850; Fax: 856-696-5770. Email: sr.lucia.maroor@camdendiocese.org. Sr. Lucia Maroor, L.N.H.A., Admin.; Rev. Jones Kukatla, Chap. Hospitaler Sisters of Mercy. Sisters 4; Bed Capacity 182; Patients Assisted Annually 315.

[J] HOME CARE

EGG HARBOR TOWNSHIP. *Holy Redeemer Home Care*, 6550 Delilah Rd., Ste. 501, 08234. Tel: 609-625-2200; Fax: 609-625-2992. A subsidiary of Holy Redeemer Health System, Inc.

SWAINTON. *Holy Redeemer Home Care*, 1801 Rte. 9 N., Cape May Court House, 08210. Tel: 609-465-2082; 800-745-4693; Fax: 609-463-6121. Web: www.holyredeemer.com. Donald Friel, Exec. Vice Pres. Sponsor: Sisters of the Holy Redeemer, C.S.R., A subsidiary of the Holy Redeemer, C.S.R.;

A Medicare Certified Home Health Agency serving patients in their own homes. A Medicare Certified Hospice Program providing services for terminally ill patients and their families.

Atlantic County Office, 6550 Delilah Rd., Ste. 501, Egg Harbor Township, 08234. Tel: 609-625-2200; 800-788-3029; Fax: 609-625-2992.

[K] HOUSING FOR AGED

CAPE MAY. *Victorian Towers, Inc.* (1973) 608 Washington St., 08204. Tel: 609-884-5883; Fax: 609-884-5625.

CHERRY HILL. *The Manor at St. Mary's* (1991) 220 St. Mary's Dr., 08003. Tel: 856-424-5128; Fax: 856-874-5363. Sr. Zdzislawa Krukowska, L.S.I.C., Admin. Total in Residence 92; Total Staff 60.

Marian Residence, 1000 Cropwell Rd., 08003. Tel: 856-424-1131; Fax: 856-424-5333. Little Sister Servants of the Immaculate Conception Total in Residence 5; Total Staff 2.

Village Apartments of Cherry Hill, NJ, Inc., 212 Lourdes Ct., 08003. Tel: 856-424-7913; Fax: 856-424-9211. Email: terry.mosteig@camdendiocese.org. Total in Residence 168; Total Staff 8.

NORTH CAPE MAY. *Haven House at St. John of God, Inc.*, 676 Townbank Rd., 08204. Tel: 609-884-4548; Fax: 609-884-4316. Email: havenhouse@camdendiocese.org. Curtis H. Johnson Jr., Sec. & Contact Person.

PENNSAUKEN. *Stonegate at St. Stephen, Inc.*, 5101 Stonegate Dr., Ste. 100, 08109. Tel: 856-486-7877; Fax: 856-486-1771. Curtis H. Johnston Jr., Sec. & Contact Person.

[L] CHILD CARE CENTERS

CAMDEN. *St. Joseph's Child Development Center, Inc.*, 17 Church St., 08105. Tel: 856-963-9202; Fax: 856-963-8940. Email: stjosephcdc@yahoo.com. Betty Mitchell, Dir.; John Klein, Admin. Staff 13; Children 75.

CHERRY HILL. *Blessed Edmund Early Childhood Education Center* (1996) 1000 Cropwell Rd., 08003. Tel: 856-424-3063; Fax: 856-424-3063. Sr. M. Elizabeth Potuczko, Dir. Sisters 6; Lay Teachers 5; Children 149.

[M] MONASTERIES AND RESIDENCES OF PRIESTS AND BROTHERS

CAMDEN. *Dominican Sisters of the Perpetual Rosary Chaplain's Residence*, 1500 Haddon Ave., 08103. Tel: 856-635-1179. Rev. Anthony I. Cataudo, O.P., Chap. Tel: 856-365-4427; Sr. Immaculate Heart, O.P., Prioress.

BLACKWOOD. *Bishop's Residence*, Marywood, 1600 Peter Cheeseman Rd., 08012. Tel: 856-227-7565; Fax: 856-228-6082. In Res. Most Rev. Joseph A. Galante, D.D., J.C.D.; Rev. Francis W. Danella, O.S.F.S.; Very Rev. David J. Klein, J.C.L.

CHERRY HILL. *Sacred Heart Residence for Priests, Inc.*, 200 St. Mary's Dr., 08003. Tel: 856-751-2010; Fax: 856-489-8999. Rev. Msgr. Harry J. Jordan, Dir. (Retired). *Sacred Heart North*, 250 St. Mary's Dr., 08003. Tel: 856-424-1741; Fax: 856-424-2896. Rev. Msgr. Harry J. Jordan, Dir. (Retired). *Sacred Heart South*, 230 St. Mary Dr., 08003. Tel: 856-424-2035. Rev. Msgr. Harry J. Jordan, Dir. (Retired).

LINWOOD. *Villa Pieta. Missionaries of the Sacred Hearts of Jesus & Mary*, 2249 Shore Rd., P.O. Box 189, 08221. Tel: 609-927-5600; Fax: 609-927-5262. Email: mssccusa@aol.com. Revs. Malcolm MacLeod, M.SS.CC., Rector; Frederick Clement, M.SS.CC.; Peter DiTomasso, M.SS.CC.; Robert McDade, M.SS.CC.; John Perdue, M.SS.CC., Vice Rector; Bro. David Graber, M.SS.CC.

MARGATE. *Franciscan Friary* Holy Name Province., 118 S. Mansfield Ave., 08402-2516. Tel: 609-822-9552; Fax: 609-822-0601. Email: margate1@comcast.net. Rev. Bernard Splawski, O.F.M. Total Staff 2.

OCEAN CITY. *Augustinian Friars*, St. Rita of Cascia Cottage, 823 5th St., 08226. Tel: 609-398-1299; Fax: 609-398-1229. Rev. Joseph S. Mostardi, O.S.A., Guestmaster. Tel: 610-574-3544.

Ocean Rest Summer School and Retreat House, 3045 Central Ave., 08226. Tel: 609-399-6480; Fax: 609-398-7520. 444-A Rte. 35 S., Eatontown, 07724. Tel: 732-380-7926; Fax: 732-380-7937. Bro. Edward Hofmann, F.S.C., Dir. Brothers of Christian Schools Summer School and Retreat House.

WESTVILLE GROVE. *Hospitaller Order of St. John of God* (1965) 1145 Delsea Dr., 08093. Tel: 856-848-4700; Fax: 856-848-7305. Email: malachyoh@msn.com. Web: www.sjogbrothers.com. Bro. Malachy Brannigan, O.H., Prior. Brothers 3.

[N] CONVENTS AND RESIDENCES FOR SISTERS

CAMDEN. *Monastery of the Dominican Nuns of the Perpetual Rosary*, 1500 Haddon Ave., 08103. Tel: 856-342-8340. Sr. Mary Of The Immaculate Heart, O.P., Prioress; Rev. Anthony I. Cataudo, O.P., Chap. Sisters 6.

ATLANTIC CITY. *St. John's Retreat House*, 128 S. Dover Ave., 08401. Tel: 609-317-4399; Fax: 609-317-4399. Sr. Maria Silvia Giraldo, Supvr. Little Servant Sisters of the Immaculate Conception. Sisters 2.

BLACKWOOD. *Sisters of St. Joseph - Joseph House*, 1840 Peter Cheeseman Rd., 08012. Tel: 856-227-1436; Fax: 856-227-2907. Email: stpiusxrh@camdendiocese.org. Sisters 4.

CHERRY HILL. *Franciscan Missionary Sisters of the Infant Jesus, Inc.*, U.S. Province and Novitiate: 1215 Kresson Rd., 08003. Tel: 856-428-8834; Fax: 856-428-5599. Email: fmijusdel@yahoo.com. Sr. Angela Pia Camillotti, F.M.I.J., Delegate Supr. Sisters 18.

Little Servant Sisters of the Immaculate Conception (1942) Provincialate and Novitiate., 1000 Cropwell Rd., 08003. Tel: 856-424-1962; Fax: 856-424-5333. Email: lsic.prov.@verizon.net. Web: www.littleservantsisters.com. Sr. Jadwiga Cierpinska, L.S.I.C., Prov. Professed Sisters 25; Novices 1.

ELMER. *The Sisters of Mary Immaculate of Nyeri, Inc.*, 400 State St., 08318. Tel: 856-358-4030; Fax: 856-358-8496. Email: smi21sep1999@yahoo.com. Sr. Bernadette Gachiri, S.M.I., Pres. & Contact Person.

HADDONFIELD. *St. Mary of the Angels Convent*, 134 Kings Hwy. W., 08033. Tel: 856-428-0824. Franciscan Sisters of Allegany. Sisters 4.

NEWFIELD. *Villa Rossello* Provincial House and Novitiate of Daughters of Our Lady of Mercy., 1009 Main Rd., 08344. Tel: 856-697-2983; Fax: 856-697-8595. Email: dmnewfield@yahoo.com. Sr. Daniel Marie, D.M., Prov. Sisters 20.

PLEASANTVILLE. *Hospitaler Sisters of Mercy Novitiate*, 915 S. Main St., 08232. Tel: 609-272-7659; Fax: 609-645-9600. Email: villaraffaella@msn.com.

Hospitaler Sisters of Mercy Convent, 909 S. Main St., 08232. Tel: 609-677-1407; Fax: 609-645-9600. Sisters 8.

Hospitaler Sisters of Mercy - Our Lady's Residence Convent, 1100 Clematis Ave., 08232. Tel: 609-272-0672. Sisters 4.

SEA ISLE CITY. *The Sisters of St. Francis of Philadelphia*, 55th & Landis Ave., 08243. Tel: 610-558-7676; Fax: 610-558-6122. Email: roconnor@osfphila.org. Web: www.osfphila.org.

STONE HARBOR. *Villa Maria by the Sea* (1937) 11101 First Ave., 08247. Tel: 609-368-3621; 609-368-5290; Fax: 609-368-0315. Summer retreat house for Sisters Servants of the Immaculate Heart of Mary. (Immaculata, PA)

VENTNOR. *The Benedictine Sisters of Elizabeth, NJ*, 114 S. Troy Ave., 08406. Tel: 609-823-9843.

Holy Family, Seaside Convent, 496 Western Hwy., Blauvelt, NY 10913. Tel: 609-822-5127; Fax: 845-359-5773. Email: phowell@blauvelt.org. Sisters of St. Dominic (Blauvelt, NY).

VINELAND. *Bishop McCarthy Residence Convent*, 1045 E. Chestnut Ave., 08360. Tel: 856-691-0740; Fax: 856-696-5770. Email: hsm856@aol.com. Sr. Lucia Maroor, L.N.H.A., Supr. Hospitaler Sisters of Mercy 5.

[O] RETREAT HOUSES

BLACKWOOD. *St. Pius X Retreat House*, 1840 Peter Cheeseman Rd., 08012. Tel: 856-227-1436; Fax: 856-227-2907.

CAPE MAY POINT. *Marianist Family Retreat Center*, 417 Yale Ave., Box 488, 08212-0488. Tel: 609-884-3829; Fax: 609-884-0545. Email: mfrc@capemaymarianists.org. Web: www.capemaymarianists.org. Rev. Theodore Cassidy, S.M., Chap.; Mr. Anthony Fucci, Center Dir.; Bros. Albert Koch, S.M., (Retired); Edward Unferdorfer, S.M., (Retired).

VINELAND. *Pope John Paul II Retreat Center*, 414 S. 8th St., 08360. Tel: 853-692-8992. Email: sccpjIIrc@aol.com. Rev. Msgr. Victor S. Muro, Dir.

[P] APOSTOLIC CENTERS

CAMDEN. *Padre Pio Shrine, Buena Borough, N.J., Inc.*, 401 N. Harding Hwy., Box 203, Landisville, 08326-0203. Rev. Allain B. Caparas, Contact Person. Tel: 856-663-1373.

BERLIN. *Mater Ecclesiae Mission* 261 Cross Keys Rd., 08009-9431. Tel: 856-753-3408; Fax: 856-753-2671. Email: rector@materecclesiae.org. Web: www.materecclesiae.org. Rev. Robert C. Pasley, Rector.

DEPTFORD. **Collegium Center for Faith and Culture*, 2901 Good Intent Rd., 08096. Tel: 856-904-1834; Fax: 856-228-1823. Email: info@collegiumcenter.org. Web: www.collegiumcenter.org. Mailing Address: P.O. Box 5526, 08096. Rev. Timothy E. Byerley, Dir.

[Q] FAMILY SERVICES AND COMMUNITY CENTERS OF CATHOLIC CHARITIES

CAMDEN. *Catholic Charities, Diocese of Camden, Inc.* Administrative Office, 1845 Haddon Ave., 08103. Tel: 856-342-4100; Fax: 856-342-4180. Web: www.catholiccharitiescamden.org. Kevin H. Hickey, Exec. Dir., Catholic Charities.

Catholic Charities - Camden County, 1845 Haddon Ave., 08104. Tel: 856-342-4100; Fax: 856-342-4180. Cereida Medina, Coord.

Catholic Charities - Atlantic County, 9 N. Georgia Ave., Atlantic City, 08401. Tel: 609-345-3448; Fax: 609-345-7180. Sr. Grace Nolan, R.S.M., B.S., Co-ord.

Catholic Charities - Cape May County, Village Shoppes, 1304 Rte. 47 S., Rio Grande, 08242. Tel: 609-886-2662; Fax: 609-886-3583. Cheryl King May, Coord.

Catholic Charities - Cumberland County, 810 Montrose St., Vineland, 08360. Tel: 856-691-1841; Fax: 856-692-6575. John Desparrois, CSW, Coord.

Catholic Charities - Salem County, 114 State St., Penns Grove, 08069. Tel: 856-299-1296; Fax: 856-299-4010. John Desparrois, CSW, Coord.

Catholic Charities - Gloucester County, 1200 N. Delsea Dr., Ste. One, Westville, 08093. Tel: 856-845-9200; Fax: 856-845-8905. Evelyn Cruz, Coord.

Counseling Center - Cumberland, 810 Montrose St., Vineland, 08360. Tel: 856-691-6084; Fax: 856-691-6179.

Counseling Center - Atlantic, 9 N. Georgia Ave., Atlantic City, 08401. Tel: 609-345-3448; Fax: 609-345-7180.

Counseling Center - Cape May, Village Shoppes, 1304 Rte. 47 S., Rio Grande, 08242. Tel: 609-886-2662; Fax: 609-886-3583.

Counseling Center - Camden, 1845 Haddon Ave., 08103. Tel: 866-682-2166; Fax: 856-342-4180. Sylvia Loumeau, L.C.S.W., Dir.

Counseling Center - Gloucester, 1200 Delsea Dr., Ste. One, Westville Grove, 08093. Tel: 856-845-9200; Fax: 856-845-8905. Sylvia Loumeau, L.C.S.W., Dir.

Guadalupe Family Services Inc., 509 State St., 08102. Tel: 856-365-8081; Fax: 856-365-8247. Sr. Helen Cole, S.S.J., L.C.S.W., Dir.

Catholic Social Services, Diocese of Camden, 1845 Haddon Ave., 08103. Tel: 856-342-4100; Fax: 856-342-4180.

[R] CAMPUS MINISTRIES

CAMDEN. *Rutgers University* c/o 642 Market St., 08102. Tel: 215-582-1666. Email: dsw@oblates.org. Rev. Michael J. McCue, O.S.F.S., Chap.

GLASSBORO. *Rowan University* Newman Center, 1 Redmond Ave., 08028. Tel: 856-881-5642; Fax: 856-881-4183. Ann Polo, Dir.

POMONA. *Richard Stockton College of New Jersey* (1969) Jim Leeds Rd., 08240. Tel: 609-652-0230; Fax: 609-804-9135. Neil Babcox, Dir.; Rev. Grace Manano, Chap.

Catholic Campus Ministry Center at Stockton P.O. Box 1003, 08240. Tel: 609-804-0200; Fax: 609-804-9135.

[S] MEDICAL CLINICS

CAMDEN. *St. John the Baptist Pre-Natal Clinic, Incorporated* (1969) 6th St. & Erie St., 08102. Tel: 856-757-9540; Fax: 856-757-9541. Patricia A. Chico, L.P.N., B.A., Admin. Patients Assisted Annually 1,750.

Saint Luke's Catholic Medical Services, Inc., 511 State St., 08102. Tel: 856-365-4642; Fax: 856-365-0539. Email: jennifer.dyer@camdendiocese.org. Lesly A. D'Ambola, D.O., Medical Dir. Patients Assisted Annually 5,000; Total Staff 7.

[T] LEGAL SERVICES

CAMDEN. **Camden Center for Law and Social Justice, Inc.* (1994) 509 State St., 08102. Tel: 856-342-4160; Fax: 856-541-8826. Email: jdecristofaro@cclsj.org. Jeffrey S. DeCristofaro, Esq., Dir. Clients Assisted Annually 6,000; Total Staff 9.

Camden Center for Law and Social Justice, Inc. Immigration Services & Legal Assistance to the Poor, 126 N. Broadway, 08103. Tel: 856-583-2950; Fax: 856-583-2955. 509 State St., 08103. Tel: 856-966-8896; Fax: 856-583-2955. 9 N. Georgia Ave., Atlantic City, 08401. Tel: 609-348-2111; Fax: 609-348-4125.

[U] FOOD CENTERS

CAMDEN. **The Cathedral Soup Kitchen, Inc.*, 1514 Federal St., 08105. Tel: 856-964-6771 (Office); Fax: 856-964-6772. Web: www.cathedralkitchen.org. Thomas Bergbauer Jr., Pres. Bd. Dirs.; Karen Talarico, Exec. Dir. Total Assisted 90,000; Total Staff 9.

[V] MISCELLANEOUS

CAMDEN. *The Diocesan Housing Services Corporation of The Diocese of Camden, Incorporated*, 1845 Haddon Ave., 08103. Tel: 856-342-4125; Fax: 856-342-4172. Email: diocesanhousing@camdendiocese.org. Curtis H. Johnson Jr., Exec. Dir.

**Hopeworks N Camden, Inc.*, 543 State St., 08102. Tel: 856-365-4673; Fax: 856-365-8734. Email: info@hopeworks.org. Web: www.hopeworks.org. Rev. Jeffrey Putthoff, S.J., Exec. Dir.

Life at Lourdes, Inc., 1600 Haddon Ave., 08103. Alexander J. Hatala, Pres. & CEO. Parent Corp: Our Lady of Lourdes Health Care System, Inc.

Lourdes Dialysis at Innova, Inc., 1600 Haddon Ave., 08103. Alexander J. Hatala, Pres. & CEO. Parent Corp: Our Lady of Lourdes Health Care System, Inc.

Village at St. Peter's Inc., 1845 Haddon Ave., 08103. Curtis H. Johnson Jr., Sec.

CHERRY HILL. *St. Mary's Auxiliary, Inc.*, 210 St. Mary's Dr., 08003. Tel: 856-874-5300. Catherine A. Michon, M.D., Contact Person.

HAINESPORT. *Domicilium Corporation (Davenport Village)*, 301 Davenport Ave., 08060. Tel: 609-702-0138; Fax: 609-702-5817. Email: Davenport@Pennrose.com.

NORTH CAPE MAY. *Christ Child Society, Cape May County Chapter*, P.O. Box 882, 08204. Tel: 609-602-7682. Jean Murphy, Contact Person.

RELIGIOUS INSTITUTES OF MEN REPRESENTED IN THE DIOCESE

For further details refer to the corresponding bracketed number in the Religious Institutes of Men or Women section.

[]—*Apostles of Jesus Missionaries* (East Africa)—A.J.
[0140]—*The Augustinians* (Province of St. Thomas of Villanova, Villanova, PA)—O.S.A.
[0330]—*Brothers of the Christian Schools*—F.S.C.
[0275]—*Carmelites of Mary Immaculate*—C.M.I.
[0650]—*Congregation of the Holy Ghost*—C.S.Sp.
[0520]—*Franciscan Friars* (Prov. of the Most Holy Name of Jesus)—O.F.M.
[0670]—*Hospitaller Brothers of St. John of God*—O.H.
[0690]—*Jesuit Fathers and Brothers*—S.J.
[1120]—*Missionaries of the Sacred Hearts of Jesus and Mary*—M.SS.CC.
[0860]—*Missionary Congregation of the Immaculate Heart of Mary*—C.I.C.M.
[]—*Norbertines*—O.Praem.
[0920]—*Oblates of St. Francis De Sales* (Wilmington-Philadelphia)—O.S.F.S.
[0430]—*Order of Preachers-Dominicans* (St. Joseph Prov., New York)—O.P.
[1190]—*Salesians of St. John Bosco*—S.D.B.
[0760]—*Society of Mary*—S.M.
[0990]—*Society of the Catholic Apostolate*—S.A.C.
[1200]—*Society of the Divine Saviour*—S.D.S.
[]—*Vincentian Congregation* (India)—V.C.

RELIGIOUS INSTITUTES OF WOMEN REPRESENTED IN THE DIOCESE

[2410]—*Congregation of the Marianites of Holy Cross*—M.S.C.
[0890]—*Daughters of Our Lady of Mercy*—D.M.
[0900]—*Daughters of Our Lady of the Sacred Heart*—F.D.N.S.C.
[1105]—*Dominican Sisters of Hope*—O.P.
[1050]—*Dominican Sisters of the Perpetual Rosary (contemplative)*—O.P.
[]—*Franciscan Missionaries Sisters of the Immaculate Heart of Mary*—F.M.I.H.M.
[1365]—*Franciscan Missionary Sisters of the Infant Jesus*—F.M.I.J.
[1180]—*Franciscan Sisters of Allegany, New York*—O.S.F.
[]—*Hospitaler Sisters of Mercy* (Pleasantville, NJ)—H.S.M.
[2300]—*Little Servant Sisters of the Immaculate Conception*—L.S.I.C.
[2490]—*Medical Mission Sisters*—M.M.S.
[2717]—*Missionary Daughters of the Most Pure Virgin Mary*—M.D.P.V.M.
[2575]—*Religious Sisters of Mercy of the Americas* (Merion, PA)—R.S.M.
[2575]—*Religious Sisters of Mercy of the Americas* (New Jersey)—R.S.M.
[3430]—*Religious Teachers Filippini* (Morristown, NJ)—M.P.F.
[0600]—*Sisters of Charity of St. Joan of Antida*—S.C.S.J.A.
[0660]—*Sisters of Christian Charity*—S.C.C.
[]—*Sisters of Mary Immaculate of Nyeri, Kenya*—S.M.I.
[1490]—*Sisters of Saint Francis of the Neumann Communities*
[3893]—*Sisters of Saint Joseph of Chestnut Hill, Philadelphia*—S.S.J.
[1650]—*Sisters of St. Francis of Philadelphia*—O.S.F.
[3890]—*Sisters of St. Joseph of Peace*—C.S.J.P.
[2170]—*Sisters, Servants of the Immaculate Heart of Mary* (Immaculata)—I.H.M.
[2160]—*Sisters, Servants of the Immaculate Heart of Mary* (Scranton)—I.H.M.

CEMETERIES

Camden Diocesan Center, 631 Market St., P.O. Box 708, 08102. Robert Guerrieri, Dir. Tel: 856-583-2849.

ATLANTIC COUNTY

DOROTHY
St. Bernard Cemetery Tel: 609-625-2124. (St. Vincent de Paul, Mays Landing)

HAMMONTON
Holy Sepulchre Cemetery Tel: 609-561-0180. (St. Joseph's)

LANDISVILLE
Our Lady of Victories Cemetery Tel: 856-691-1290 (Call Sacred Heart Cemetery).

MAYS LANDING
Holy Cross Cemetery & Mausoleum, Rte. 40, 08330. Tel: 609-625-2123.

PLEASANT MILLS
Our Lady of the Assumption Cemetery Closed, (Call Holycross Cemetery, Mays Landing, 609-625-2123)

CAMDEN COUNTY

BELLMAWR
St. Mary's Cemetery & Mausoleum Tel: 856-931-1570.

BERLIN
Gate of Heaven Cemetery Tel: 856-767-3354.

CEDARBROOK
Sacred Heart Cemetery Tel: 609-561-6116. (St. Lucy, Blue Anchor)

CHEWS LANDING
St. Joseph's Cemetery (St. Joseph, Camden), Tel: 856-228-7588.

CHERRY HILL
Calvary Cemetery & Mausoleum Tel: 856-663-3345.

CAPE MAY COUNTY

COLD SPRINGS
St. Mary's Cemetery & Mausoleum Tel: 609-884-3614.

GOSHEN
St. Elizabeth's Cemetery Tel: 609-884-3614.

WOODBINE
St. Casimir's Cemetery Tel: 609-884-3614.

CUMBERLAND COUNTY

BRIDGETON
St. Mary's Cemetery Tel: 856-451-0254. (Immaculate Conception)

EAST VINELAND
St. Mary's Cemetery Tel: 856-691-7526. (Padre Pio)
Our Lady of Pompeii Cemetery Tel: 856-691-7526. (Padre Pio)

MILLVILLE
Holy Cross Cemetery Tel: 856-825-0021. (St. Mary Magdalen)

ROSENHAYN
St. Mary's Cemetery Tel: 856-451-8763. (St. Mary)

VINELAND
Sacred Heart Cemetery & Mausoleum Tel: 856-691-1290.

GLOUCESTER COUNTY

GLASSBORO
St. Bridget's Cemetery Tel: 856-881-2753. (St. Bridget Church)

MULLICA HILL
Holy Name Cemetery Tel: 856-478-2294. (Holy Name Church)

NEWFIELD
All Saints Cemetery Tel: 856-697-1098.

SWEDESBORO
St. Joseph's Cemetery Tel: 856-467-0037.

WILLIAMSTOWN
St. Mary's Cemetery Tel: 856-767-3354.

SALEM COUNTY

SALEM
St. Mary's Cemetery Tel: 856-935-0288. (St. Mary's Church)

WOODSTOWN
St. Joseph's Cemetery Tel: 856-769-0004. (St. Joseph Church)

NECROLOGY

† Hewitt, Rev. Msgr. Bernard P., (Retired)—Died Nov. 6, 2009
† Tierney, Rev. Msgr. Patrick M., (Retired)—Died June 13, 2009
† Burns, Thomas, (Retired)—Died June 11, 2009
† Newton, John G., (Retired)—Died Feb. 6, 2009

An asterisk (*) denotes an organization that has established tax-exempt status directly with the IRS and is not covered by the USCCB Group Ruling.

Diocese of Charleston

(Dioecesis Carolopolitana)

Most Reverend

ROBERT E. GUGLIELMONE

Bishop of Charleston; ordained April 8, 1978; appointed Bishop of Charleston January 24, 2009; installed March 25, 2009. *Office: 119 Broad St., P.O. Box 818, Charleston, SC 29402.*

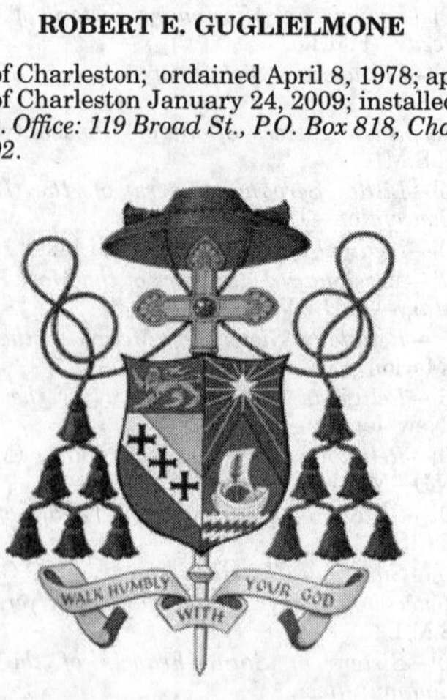

Most Reverend

DAVID B. THOMPSON, D.D., J.C.L.

Retired Bishop of Charleston; ordained May 27, 1950; appointed Coadjutor Bishop of Charleston April 22, 1989; ordained May 24, 1989; succeeded to Bishop of Charleston February 22, 1990; retired July 13, 1999. *Res.: 4479 Downing Pl., Mount Pleasant, SC 29466.* Tel: 843-971-2810.

ESTABLISHED JULY 11, 1820.

Square Miles 31,055.

Comprises the State of South Carolina.

For legal titles of parishes and diocesan institutions, consult the Chancery Office.

Chancery Office: 119 Broad St., P.O. Box 818, Charleston, SC 29402. Tel: 843-853-2130; Fax: 843-724-6387.

Web: www.catholic-doc.org

Email: andrea@catholic-doc.org

STATISTICAL OVERVIEW

Personnel	
Bishop	1
Retired Bishops	1
Priests: Diocesan Active in Diocese	53
Priests: Diocesan Active Outside Diocese	6
Priests: Retired, Sick or Absent	22
Number of Diocesan Priests	81
Religious Priests in Diocese	38
Total Priests in Diocese	119
Extern Priests in Diocese	36
Ordinations:	
Diocesan Priests	1
Transitional Deacons	3
Permanent Deacons in Diocese	103
Total Brothers	23
Total Sisters	136
Parishes	
Parishes	92
With Resident Pastor:	
Resident Diocesan Priests	37
Resident Religious Priests	8
Without Resident Pastor:	
Administered by Priests	42
Administered by Deacons	2
Administered by Professed Religious Men	2
Administered by Religious Women	1
Missions	24
Pastoral Centers	1
Professional Ministry Personnel:	
Brothers	144
Sisters	29
Lay Ministers	71
Welfare	
Catholic Hospitals	3
Total Assisted	296,399
Homes for the Aged	1
Total Assisted	25
Special Centers for Social Services	8
Total Assisted	43,131
Educational	
Diocesan Students in Other Seminaries	12
Total Seminarians	12
High Schools, Diocesan and Parish	2
Total Students	1,182
High Schools, Private	2
Total Students	582
Elementary Schools, Diocesan and Parish	28
Total Students	5,598
Catechesis/Religious Education:	
High School Students	2,502
Elementary Students	10,393
Total Students under Catholic Instruction	20,269
Teachers in the Diocese:	
Priests	2
Brothers	1
Sisters	22
Lay Teachers	700
Vital Statistics	
Receptions into the Church:	
Infant Baptism Totals	3,324
Minor Baptism Totals	317
Adult Baptism Totals	201
Received into Full Communion	404
First Communions	3,057
Confirmations	2,304
Marriages:	
Catholic	407
Interfaith	275
Total Marriages	682
Deaths	1,186
Total Catholic Population	184,728
Total Population	4,394,300

Former Bishops—Rt. Revs. JOHN ENGLAND, D.D., first Bishop; cons. Sept. 21, 1820; died April 11, 1842; WILLIAM CLANCY, D.D., cons. Dec. 21, 1834, Coadjutor; made Vicar-Apostolic of British Guiana, April 12, 1837; died June 19, 1847; IGNATIUS A. REYNOLDS, D.D., second Bishop; cons. March 19, 1844; died March 6, 1855; PATRICK N. LYNCH, D.D., third Bishop; cons. March 14, 1858; died Feb. 26, 1882; HENRY P. NORTHROP, D.D., fourth Bishop; consecrated Titular-Bishop of Rosalia and Vicar-Apostolic of North Carolina, Jan. 8, 1882; transferred to Charleston, by brief dated Jan. 27, 1883; died June 7, 1916; WILLIAM T. RUSSELL, D.D., fifth Bishop; cons. March 15, 1917; died March 18, 1927; Most Revs. EMMET M. WALSH, D.D., sixth Bishop; cons. Sept. 8, 1927; transferred to Youngstown, Ohio, as Coadjutor Bishop, Sept. 8, 1949; JOHN J. RUSSELL, D.D., seventh Bishop; cons. March 14, 1950; transferred to Bishop of Richmond, July 10, 1958; PAUL J. HALLINAN, D.D., eighth Bishop; cons. Oct. 28, 1958; transferred to Archbishop of Atlanta, Feb. 21, 1962; FRANCIS F. REH, S.T.L., J.C.D. (Retired), ninth Bishop; cons. June 29, 1962; appt. Titular Bishop of Macriana in Mauretania and Rector of North American College, Rome, Italy, Sept. 5, 1964; transferred to Saginaw, Dec. 18, 1968; installed Feb. 26, 1969; retired April 29, 1980; ERNEST L. UNTERKOEFLER, D.D., J.C.D., S.T.L., tenth Bishop; ord. May 18, 1944; appt. Titular Bishop of Latopolis and Auxiliary Bishop of Richmond, Dec. 13, 1961; cons. Feb. 22, 1962; appt. Bishop of Charleston, Dec. 12, 1964; resigned Feb. 22, 1990; died Jan. 4, 1993; DAVID B. THOMPSON, D.D., J.C.L. (Retired), eleventh Bishop; ord. May 27, 1950; appt. Coadjutor Bishop of Charleston April 22, 1989; ord. May 24, 1989; succeeded to Bishop of Charleston Feb. 22, 1990; retired July 13, 1999; ROBERT J. BAKER, twelfth Bishop; ord. March 21, 1970; appt. Bishop of Charleston July 13, 1999; cons. Sept. 29, 1999; appt. Bishop of Birmingham Aug. 14, 2007; installed Oct. 2, 2007.

Vicar General's Office—Rev. Msgr. MARTIN T. LAUGHLIN, P.A., Vicar Gen. Tel: 843-853-2130, Ext. 207. Email: mlaughlin@catholic-doc.org; LARRY PAPINEAU, Administrative Asst., 119 Broad St., Charleston, 29402. Tel: 843-853-2130, Ext. 208. Email: lpapineau@catholic-doc.org.

Chancellor—Rev. EDWARD W. FITZGERALD, J.C.L. (Pro Tem) 119 Broad St., P.O. Box 818, Charleston, 29402. Tel: 843-853-2130, Ext. 201. Email: efitzgerald@catholic-doc.org; ANDREA A. CRAWFORD, Chancery Coord. & Administrative Asst. to the Office of Matrimonial Concerns. Tel: 843-853-2130, Ext. 202. Email: andrea@catholic-doc.org.

Vice-Chancellor—Rev. DAVID A. RUNNION (Pro Tem).

Chancery West—1662 Ingram Rd., Charleston, 29407. Tel: 843-402-9115; Fax: 843-402-9071; 843-402-7724 (Christian Formation and The Office of Research and Planning).

Diocesan Web Page—Web: www.catholic-doc.org.

Archives—BRIAN P. FAHEY, M.L.I.S., Archivist. Tel: 843-577-1017; Fax: 843-724-6387. Email: bfahey@catholic-doc.org; JENNIFER E. NEAL, M.A., Archives Technician. Tel: 843-724-8372. Email: jneal@catholic-doc.org.

Bishop's Office—JOSEPH OHENS, Exec. Asst. to Bishop. Tel: 843-853-2130; Rev. TITUS FULCHER, Asst. to Bishop for Special Admin. Affairs. Email: frtitus@catholic-doc.org; ANDREA A. CRAWFORD, Chancery Coord. Tel: 843-853-2130, Ext. 202. Email: andrea@catholic-doc.org; JOHN ALEXANDER, Correspondence Specialist. Tel: 843-853-2130, Ext. 205. Email: jalexander@catholic-doc.org; ANDREW HAWKINS. Tel: 843-853-2130, Ext. 201. Email: ahawkins@catholic-doc.org.

Office of Finance—Mr. JOHN L. BARKER, CFO. Tel: 843-402-9115, Ext. 11. Email: jbarker@catholic-doc.org; CRISTINA G. NATIVIDAD, Exec.

Administrative Asst. to CFO. Tel: 843-402-9115, Ext. 30. Email: cnatividad@catholic-doc.org; DEBBIE TOMAK, Clerk Asst. Tel: 843-402-9115, Ext. 12. Email: dtomak@catholic-doc.org; BERNADETTE W. FARETRA, Exec. Financial Analyst. Tel: 843-402-9115, Ext. 13. Email: bernadette@catholic-doc.org; PAT SULLIVAN, Payroll & Accounts Payable. Tel: 843-402-9115, Ext. 31. Email: psullivan@catholic-doc.org; TERRI BRISSON, Dir. Financial Svcs. Tel: 843-402-9115, Ext. 37. Email: tbrisson@catholic-doc.org; JUN ZHANG, Sr. Accountant. Tel: 843-402-9115, Ext. 85; Fax: 843-402-9071 (Chancery West). Email: junzhang@catholic-doc.org; JOYCE KIERNAN, Financial Analyst. Tel: 843-402-9115, Ext. 48. Email: jkiernan@catholic-doc.org; DEBBIE CARDENAS, Staff Accountant & Financial Analyst. Tel: 843-402-9115, Ext. 33. Email: dcardenas@catholic-doc.org; TAMRA BOWMAN, Accounting Technician. Tel: 843-402-9115, Ext. 42. Email: tbowman@catholic-doc.org; BARBIE BIANCHI, Accounting Technician. Tel: 843-402-9115, Ext. 34. Email: bbianchi@catholic-doc.org.

Campus Ministry— (See Christian Formation)

Canonical Consultant—Rev. Msgr. THOMAS X. HOFMANN, J.C.L. Tel: 843-724-8363.

Carter-May Home—JANINE BAUDER, Admin., 1660 Ingram Rd., Charleston, 29407. Tel: 843-556-8314 (Main); 843-402-5460 (Office); Fax: 843-556-6879.

Office of Computer Services—MARK T. HOUPT, Dir. Tel: 843-402-9115, Ext. 24. Email: mthoupt@catholic-doc.org; JON OMAN, Systems Analyst/Information Project Specialist. Tel: 843-402-9115, Ext. 25. Email: joman@catholic-doc.org; LINDA COLLINS, Accounting/Computer Specialist. Tel: 843-402-9115, Ext. 49. Email: lcollins@catholic-doc.org.

Continuing Education for Priests—Rev. Msgr. EDWARD D. LOFTON, 11001 Dorchester Rd., Summerville, 29485. Tel: 843-875-5002; Fax: 843-875-4884.

Office of Tribunal—Mailing Address: P.O. Box 818, Charleston, 29402. Tel: 843-724-8363. Rev. Msgrs. CHARLES H. ROWLAND, P.A., J.C.L., Judicial Vicar; THOMAS X. HOFMANN, J.C.L., Adjutant Judicial Vicar; MARY E. MCKENZIE, Dir. Tribunal; LUCINDA BRYAN, Procurator & Advocate; MEG WALTER, Procurator & Advocate; Deacons THOMAS J. BARONOWSKI, Procurator & Advocate; J. WESCOAT SANDLIN, Esq., Procurator & Advocate; JOAN MARIE DOWD, Procurator & Advocate; CHARLES WUJCIK, Ecclesiastical Notary; MARIA WERSINGER GALLEGO, Hispanic Desk Case Analyst. Phone inquiries are accepted from 10:30-11:30 am & 1:30-4 pm. All petitions for a sanatio, declarations of invalidity, and other questions related to divorced persons should be sent to the Office of Tribunal. All other prenuptial matters, requests for dispensations and permissions should be sent to the: Office for Matrimonial Concerns and Dispensations, P.O. Box 818, Charleston, SC 29402. Tel: 843-853-2130, ext. 202.

Judges—Rev. Msgr. JOSEPH R. ROTH, D.D., P.A.; Most Rev. DAVID B. THOMPSON, D.D., J.C.L. (Retired); MARY E. MCKENZIE.

Defenders of the Bond—Rev. C. THOMAS MILES; Sisters CHRISTINA MURPHY, S.N.D.deN.; SANDRA MAKOWSKI, S.S.M.N., J.C.L.

Promoter of Justice—VACANT, All petitions for a sanatio, declarations of nullity, and other questions related to divorced persons should be sent to the Office of the Tribunal. (All other prenuptial matters, requests for dispensations and permissions should be sent to the Office for Matrimonial Concerns and Dispensations, P.O. Box 818, Charleston, SC 29402. Tel: 843-853-2130, ext. 202).

College of Consultors—Rev. Msgrs. MARTIN T. LAUGHLIN, P.A.; JOSEPH R. ROTH, D.D., P.A.; STEVEN L. BROVEY, V.F.; Rev. EDWARD W. FITZGERALD, J.C.L.; Rev. Msgr. JOSEPH F. HANLEY JR., V.F.; Very Revs. KARL J. ROESCH, O.S.B., V.F.; PAUL M. WILLIAMS, O.F.M., V.F.; Rev. Msgrs. E. CHRISTOPHER LATHEM; CHARLES H. ROWLAND, P.A., J.C.L.; Revs. RICHARD HARRIS; MICHAEL J. OENBRINK, V.F.

Deans—Rev. Msgr. JOSEPH F. HANLEY, V.F., Coastal Deanery. Tel: 843-556-0801; Fax: 843-556-2851. Email: blessac@bellsouth.net; Rev. MICHAEL J. OENBRINK, V.F., Lowcountry Deanery (Pro Tem). Tel: 843-815-3100; Fax: 843-815-3150. Email: gw@sgg.cc; Very Revs. PAUL M. WILLIAMS, O.F.M., V.F., Midlands Deanery. Tel: 803-254-6862; Fax: 803-799-4720. Email: pw4ofm@aol.com; KARL J. ROESCH, O.S.B., V.F., Pee Dee Deanery (Pro Tem). Tel: 843-332-7773; Fax: 843-332-2812. Email: stmary2@earthlink.net; Rev. Msgr. STEVEN L. BROVEY, V.F., Piedmont Deanery. Tel: 864-268-4352; Fax: 864-322-2239. Email: taylorspop@juno.com.

Family Life Services—Rev. JAMES L. LEBLANC, Dir., Mailing Address: P.O. Box 438, Aiken, 29802-0438. Tel: 803-649-4777; Fax: 803-642-6421; KATHY SCHMUGGE, Asst. Dir., 2879 Hwy. 160 W., PMB #4336, Fort Mill, 29708. Tel: 803-547-5063. Email: kschmugge@catholic-doc.org; CHRISTY BROWN, Post Abortion Ministry Coord.

Finance Council—Rev. Msgrs. MARTIN T. LAUGHLIN, P.A.; JOSEPH R. ROTH, D.D., P.A.; Mr. JOHN L. BARKER, CFO; BERNADETTE W. FARETRA; JOSEPH GRIFFITH SR., K.S.G.; JAY KEENAN; CHRISTINA MYERS; ESTHER TECKLENBURG; JOHN WARD; WILLIAM C. ROBINSON; DANIEL P. FANNING; EUGENE J. ZURLO; WILLIAM CONDY; DARRYL REYNA; PERRY KEITH WARING.

Office of Ethnic Ministries—Ms. KATHLEEN MERRITT, Dir., 204 Douthit St., A1, Greenville, 29601. Tel: 864-242-2233, Ext. 214; Fax: 864-331-2631. Email: kathleen@catholic-doc.org; CONNIE BRUSHABER, Administrative Asst. Tel: 864-242-2233, Ext. 209. Email: cbrushaber@catholic-doc.org.

Administrator for African-American Catholics—Very Rev. PAUL M. WILLIAMS, O.F.M., V.F., 2229 Hampton St., Columbia, 29204. Tel: 803-254-6862. Email: pw4ofm@aol.com.

Vicar for Hispanic Ministry—Rev. FILEMON JUYA, Mailing Address: 3504 Devine St., P.O. Box 290515, Columbia, 29229-0009. Tel: 803-779-7584; 803-788-1246. Email: fileajuyab@aol.com.

Administrator for Vietnamese Ministry—Rev. DAC T. TRAN, O.F.M., 3710 Augusta Rd., P.O. Box 8396, Greenville, 29604. Tel: 864-422-1648. Email: dacofm@yahoo.com.

Office of Hispanic Ministries—Rev. FILEMON JUYA, Vicar for Hispanic Ministries, The Croghan Center, 2700 Ashland Rd., Columbia, 29210. Tel: 803-740-6249. Email: fileajuyab@aol.com.

Bishop's Missionary Support Committee—Rev. Msgr. EDWARD D. LOFTON, Mailing Address: St. Theresa the Little Flower, 11001 Dorchester Rd., Summerville, 29485.

Building & Renovation Commission—Rev. Msgrs. MARTIN T. LAUGHLIN, P.A., Chm.; CHESTER M. MOCZYDLOWSKI; STEVEN L. BROVEY, V.F.; Mr. JOHN L. BARKER; Deacon JOSEPH CAHILL; Revs. RICHARD D. HARRIS; ROBERT F. HIGGINS; ROSS KUYKENDALL; LISA RAWLINS; JIM POSDA; WILLIAM ROBERTS; FRANK SZEWCZAK; MATTHEW DWYER; CRISTINA G. NATIVIDAD, Sec.

Catholic Charities—

Main Office—Deacon ED PEITLER, Ph.D., Dir., 1662 Ingram Rd., Charleston, 29407. Tel: 843-402-9115, Ext. 14. Email: epeitler@catholic-doc.org; JENNIFER ELKINS, Coord. Tel: 843-402-9115, Ext. 15. Email: jelkins@catholic-doc.org; JOAN KEBER, Billing Clerk/Administrative Asst. Tel: 843-402-9115, Ext. 16. Email: jkeber@catholic-doc.org.

Counseling Services—MARA CALDERON, Ph.D. Tel: 843-402-9115, Ext. 17 Services in English and Spanish.

Elderly Services—JANINE BAUDER, Admin., Carter May Home/St. Joseph Residence, 1660 Ingram Rd., Charleston, 29407. Tel: 843-556-8314; Fax: 843-556-6879.

Coastal Deanery—HELEN O'LEARY, Regl. Coord., St. John Church, 3921 St. John's Ave., North Charleston, 29405. Tel: 843-308-9361; Fax: 843-744-2792. Email: holeary@catholic-doc.org.

Immigration Services—EMILY GUERRERO, Immigration Svcs. Supvr., 1145 Six Mile Rd., Mount Pleasant, 29466. Tel: 843-388-0089; Fax: 843-849-0943. Email: eguerrero@catholic-doc.org.

Lowcountry Deanery—Deacon JAMES P. HYLAND, Regl. Coord. & Coord. Jail and Prison Ministry, St. Peter's Church, 70 Lady's Island Pkwy., Beaufort, 29907. Tel: 843-522-6518; Fax: 843-522-0667. Email: jhyland@catholic-doc.org.

Midlands Deanery—MARY GOHEAN, Regl. Coord., Mailing Address: P.O. Box 7245, Columbia, 29202. Tel: 803-254-9776; Fax: 803-252-7605. Email: mgohean@catholic-doc.org.

Pee Dee Deanery—DARYL KANGARLOO, Regl. Coord. & Senior Care Mgmt. Coord., 537-B Hwy. 90, Conway, 29526. Tel: 843-234-1999; Fax: 843-234-3132. Email: dkangarloo@catholic-doc.org.

Piedmont Deanery—Deacon GABRIEL CUERVO, Regl. Coord. & Coord. Hispanic Outreach, Mailing Address: 204 Douthit St., Ste. A1, Greenville, 29601. Tel: 864-242-2233, Ext. 206; Fax: 864-242-1387. Email: gcuervo@catholic-doc.org.

Catholic Women, Council of—Rev. WILLIAM F. PENTIS, C.O., Moderator, Mailing Address: P.O. Box 11586, Rock Hill, 29731. Tel: 803-327-2097.

Cemeteries—WARREN STUCKEY, Dir. Cemeteries, Holy Cross Cemetery; PAMELA PAQUETTE, Administrative Asst., Holy Cross Cemetery. Tel: 843-795-2111; Fax: 843-402-9071. Email: holycros@dycon.com; JIMMY LYLES, Supvr., St. Lawrence Cemetery. Tel: 843-723-8228.

Charismatic Renewals and Prayer Groups—Deacon JACK L. CROCKER, D.D.S., Diocesan Liaison, 107 Arbor End Rd., Lexington, 29072. Tel: 803-356-3042. Email: jackrocker3@windstream.com.

Chief Financial Officer—Mr. JOHN L. BARKER. Tel: 843-402-9115, Ext. 12. Email: jbarker@catholic-doc.org. (Chancery West).

Divine Worship & Sacraments, Administrator for—Rev. Msgr. STEVEN L. BROVEY, V.F. Email: padre.slb@princeofpeacetaylors.org; BEBE NORRIS, Administrative Asst., 1209 Brushy Creek Rd., Taylors, 29687-4103. Tel: 864-268-4352; Fax: 864-322-2239. Email: bebe.norris@princeofpeacetaylors.org.

Catholic Schools Office—Sr. JULIA HUTCHISON, S.N.D., Supt. Catholic Schools. Email: jhutchison@catholic-doc.org; Mrs. SANDRA LEATHERWOOD, Asst. to Supt. of Schools. Email: sleatherwood@catholic-doc.org; KIMBERLY HOPKINS, Coord. Tel: 843-402-9115, Ext. 19. Email: khopkins@catholic-doc.org.

Catechesis & Christian Initiation for Parishes and Schools—Sr. PAMELA SMITH, S.S.C.M., Dir. Tel: 843-402-9115, Ext. 35. Email: psmith@catholic-doc.org; CATHY ROCHE, Administrative Asst. Tel: 843-402-9115, Ext. 18. Email: cathy@catholic-doc.org.

Youth & Young Adults Ministry Office—JERRY WHITE, Dir. Tel: 843-402-9115, Ext. 38; Fax: 843-402-7724. Email: jerry@catholic-doc.org. (Chancery West); Deacon JAMES R. MOORE, Assoc. Dir. Young Adult Ministry. Tel: 843-670-2586. Email: jmoore@catholic-doc.org; RHINA MEDINA, Assoc. Dir. Hispanic Youth Ministry, The Croghan Center, 2700 Ashland Rd., Columbia, 29210. Tel: 803-445-1942. Email: rmedina@catholic-doc.org; AMANDA SUMERSETT, Administrative Asst. Tel: 843-402-9115, Ext. 20. Email: asumersett@catholic-doc.org.

Campus Ministry—Dr. JANE LAMARCHE, Dir. Campus Ministry, MSC 58 The Citadel, 171 Moultrie St., Charleston, 29409. Tel: 843-953-7692.

Holy Childhood Association—Rev. Msgr. EDWARD D. LOFTON, Dir., Mailing Address: St. Theresa, The Little Flower, 11001 Dorchester Rd., Summerville, 29485. Tel: 843-875-5002; Fax: 843-875-4884.

Human Resources—MARY LOUISE HUDSON, Dir. Tel: 843-402-9115, Ext. 21. Email: mlhudson@catholic-doc.org; RIITTA WIDELSKI, Sr. Generalist & Benefits Specialist. Tel: 843-402-9115, Ext. 56. Email: rwidelski@catholic-doc.org. (Chancery West); JESSICA HOBBS, Administrative Asst. Tel: 843-402-9115, Ext. 47. Email: jhobbs@catholic-doc.org.

Insurance—TRACY BATES, Claims/Risk Mgr., Catholic Mutual, 901 Island Park Dr., Ste. 205, Charleston, 29492. Tel: 843-884-9696; Fax: 843-884-9979. Email: tracy@catholic-doc.org; CINDY ACUFF, Asst. Tel: 843-884-9776.

Investment Council—Rev. Msgrs. MARTIN T. LAUGHLIN, P.A.; JOSEPH R. ROTH, D.D., P.A.; Mr. JOHN L. BARKER; SCOTT CRACRAFT; BERNADETTE W. FARETRA; JAY KEENAN; JOHN WARD; WILLIAM C. ROBINSON.

Marian Programs—Rev. STANLEY SMOLENSKI, S.P.M.A., Dir., 300 Ashton Ave., Kingstree, 29556. Tel: 843-355-3527.

Diocesan Master of Ceremonies—Rev. BRYAN P. BABICK, Christ Our King, 1149 Russell Dr., Mount Pleasant, 29464. Tel: 843-884-5587; Fax: 843-884-7086.

Ministry for People with Disabilities—Office of Social Ministry. Tel: 843-402-9115, Ext. 15; Fax: 843-402-9071 (Chancery West).

Newspaper— "The Catholic Miscellany" Tel: 843-724-8375. DEIRDRE C. MAYS, Editor. Tel: 843-853-6385. Email: editor@catholic-doc.org; AMY WISE TAYLOR, Reporter & Staff Writer. Tel: 843-853-6302. Email: ataylor@catholic-doc.org; ANNE E. CLARK, Graphic Designer. Tel: 843-724-6383. Email: aclark@catholic-doc.org; STEPHANIE D. PAETSCH, Circulation Coord. Tel: 843-724-8375; Fax: 843-724-8368. Email: stevie@catholic-doc.org; CHRISTINA LEE KNAUSS, Reporter & Staff Writer. Tel: 803-238-7610. Email: cknauss@catholic-doc.org.

Office of Child Protective Services—Rev. TITUS FULCHER, Dir., 119 Broad St., Charleston, 29402. Tel: 843-853-2130, Ext. 209. Email: frtitus@catholic-doc.org; BONNIE SIGERS, Safe Environment Mgr. Tel: 843-853-2130, Ext. 210. Email: bsigers@catholic-doc.org; NANCY FERRIGAN, Screening Svcs. Coord. Tel: 843-853-2130, Ext. 206. Email: nferrigan@catholic-doc.org; JENNA WEBB, Admin. Asst. & The Office of Child Protection Svcs. Tel: 843-853-2130, Ext. 216. Email: jwebb@catholic-doc.org.

Office of Prayer & Worship—Rev. Msgr. STEVEN L. BROVEY, V.F., 1209 Brushy Creek Rd., Taylors, 29687. Tel: 864-268-4352.

Propagation of the Faith—Rev. Msgr. EDWARD D. LOFTON, Dir.; HELEN MONIZ, Coord., 11001 Dorchester Rd., Summerville, 29485. Tel: 843-875-5002; Fax: 843-875-4884. Email: propagation@sttheresachurch.com.

Office of Publications and Information—DEIRDRE C. MAYS, Dir., 119 Broad St., Charleston, 29402. Tel:

843-724-8375. Email: editor@catholic-doc.org; ANNE E. CLARK, Publications Assoc. Email: aclark@catholic-doc.org; STEPHANIE D. PAETSCH, Admin. Asst. Tel: 843-724-8375; Fax: 843-724-8368. Email: stevie@catholic-doc.org.

Respect Life— (Please see Catholic Charities Regional Offices)

Vocations—Rev. RICHARD D. HARRIS, Admin. Email: vocationsharris@aol.com; Deacon JOSEPH F. CAHILL, Dir. Tel: 843-402-9115, Ext. 54. Email: joe@catholic-doc.org; JESSICA HOBBS, Administrative Asst. Tel: 843-402-9115, Ext. 22; 800-660-4102; Fax: 843-402-9071. Email: jhobbs@catholic-doc.org. (Chancery West).

Bishop's Missionary League—Mailing Address: P.O. Box 818, Charleston, 29402. Tel: 843-853-2130, Ext. 0.

Cursillo Movement—BRIAN PUSATARI, Lay Dir.; Rev. HAYDEN J. VAVEREK, Spiritual Advisor.

Diaconate, Office of—Rev. Msgr. JOSEPH R. ROTH, D.D., P.A. Tel: 843-402-9115, Ext. 18. Email: jrr@catholic-doc.org; CATHY ROCHE, Administrative Asst., 1662 Ingram Rd., Charleston, 29407. Tel: 843-402-9115, Ext. 18. Email: cathy@catholic-doc.org.

Campaign for Human Development—Office of Social Ministry. Tel: 843-402-9115, Ext. 15; Fax: 843-402-9071. (Chancery West)

Office of Stewardship & Mission Advancement—MATTHEW DWYER, Dir. Stewardship & Devel. Tel: 843-853-2130, Ext. 211. Email: mdwyer@catholic-doc.org; LILIA CORREA, Annual Appeal Administrative Asst. Tel: 843-853-2130, Ext. 212. Email: lilia@catholic-doc.org; EDRINA S. HAMILTON, Admin. Asst. Tel: 843-853-2130, Ext. 211. Email: edrina@catholic-doc.org.

Personnel Committee—Rev. Msgrs. E. CHRISTOPHER LATHEM, Chm.; MARTIN T. LAUGHLIN, P.A.; JOSEPH R. ROTH, D.D., P.A.; Rev. FILEMON JUYA; Very Rev. PAUL M. WILLIAMS, O.F.M., V.F.; Revs. RICHARD HARRIS; MICHAEL J. OENBRINK, V.F.; Rev. Msgrs. STEVEN L. BROVEY, V.F.; JOSEPH F. HANLEY, V.F.; Very Rev. KARL ROESCH, O.S.B., V.F.

Priests' Retirement—Mailing Address: P.O. Box 818, Charleston, 29402. Tel: 843-853-2130, Ext. 206.

Scouting Programs—Rev. DAVID MICHAEL, Boy Scout Chap., St. Andrew Catholic Church, 168 Madison St., Barnwell, 29812. Tel: 803-259-7593.

Sites & Boundaries Committee—Rev. Msgr. MARTIN T. LAUGHLIN, P.A.; Mr. JOHN L. BARKER. Email: jbarker@catholic-doc.org. (West Chancery); LISA RAWLINS. Email: rawlins@catholic-doc.org.

Office of Research and Planning—LISA M. RAWLINS, Dir. Tel: 843-402-9115, Ext. 43. Email: rawlins@catholic-doc.org; HEATHER CLARK, Admin. Asst. Tel: 843-402-9115, Ext. 44; Fax: 843-402-7724. Email: hclark@catholic-doc.org.

Vietnamese Apostolate— (See Office of Ethnic Ministries)

African-American Catholics— (See Office of Ethnic Ministries)

Administrator for Ecumenical & Interreligious Affairs—Rev. C. ALEXANDER MCDONALD; MELISSA WALKER, Admin., Mailing Address: P.O. Box 247, Chapin, 29036. Tel: 803-345-7407. Email: mwalker@catholic-doc.org.

Education, Dept. of— (See Christian Formation)

Hispanic Ministry— (See Office of Ethnic Ministries)

Office of Black Catholic Ministry— (See Office of Ethnic Ministries)

Vicar for Clergy—Rev. Msgr. E. CHRISTOPHER LATHEM. Email: clathem@sc.rr.com; LARRY PAPINEAU, Coord. Tel: 843-853-2130, Ext. 208; Fax: 843-958-2162. Email: lpapineau@catholic-doc.org.

Victim Assistance Coordinator—LUISA STOREN, 886 Johnnie Dodds Blvd., Mount Pleasant, 29464. Tel: 843-856-0748; 800-921-8122 (Toll Free); Fax: 843-856-0753; 800-923-8122 (Toll Free).

Vocations Board—Rev. RICHARD HARRIS, Admin.; Rev. Msgrs. MARTIN T. LAUGHLIN, P.A.; JOSEPH R. ROTH, D.D., P.A.; EDWARD D. LOFTON; Revs. JEFFREY KIRBY; MICHAEL J. OENBRINK, V.F.; TEOFILO TRUJILLO; Deacon JOSEPH F. CAHILL; Sr. JULIENNE GUY, O.S.U.; Deacon ED PEITLER, Ph.D.; M. TODD CRUMP; ROBERT BOLCHOZ; A. PETER SHAHID JR.

Volunteers, Office of—Deacon JEROME P. REMKIEWICZ, Diocesan Volunteer Prog. Admin., 34 Wentworth St., Charleston, 29401. Tel: 843-723-5758; Fax: 843-723-5760.

Youth Ministry— (See Christian Formation)

Office of Ongoing Formation for Recently Ordained Clergy—Rev. Msgr. MARTIN T. LAUGHLIN, P.A., Dir.; Rev. TITUS FULCHER, Admin.

Office of Media Relations—STEPHEN GAJDOSIK, Media Rels. Officer, 119 Broad St., Charleston, 29401. Tel: 843-853-2130, Ext. 218.

CLERGY, PARISHES, MISSIONS AND PAROCHIAL SCHOOLS

GREATER CHARLESTON

(CHARLESTON COUNTY)

1—CATHEDRAL OF ST. JOHN THE BAPTIST (1821) Revs. Gregory B. Wilson, Rector (Pro. Tem.); Jeremi Wodecki, Parochial Vicar; Deacons Charles Olimpio; Jerome P. Remkiewicz.
Mailing & Res. Address: 120 Broad St., 29401. Tel: 843-937-8504 (Res.); 843-724-8395; Fax: 843-724-6386 (Parish). Email: cathedral@charlestoncatholiccathedral.org. Web: www.catholic-doc.org/cathedral.
See Charleston Catholic School, Charleston under Sacred Heart, Charleston for details.
Catechesis/Religious Program—Students 126.

2—ST. BENEDICT (1999) Rev. Msgr. Chester M. Moczydlowski.
Church: 3850 Bessmer Rd., Ste. 120, Mount Pleasant, 29466. Tel: 843-216-0039; Fax: 843-971-6789. Email: stbenedictparish@aol.com. Web: www.stbenedictparish.org.
Catechesis/Religious Program—Students 250.

3—BLESSED SACRAMENT (1944) Rev. Msgr. Joseph F. Hanley Jr.; Deacon James R. Moore.
Res.: 9 St. Teresa Dr., 29407. Tel: 843-556-0801; Fax: 843-556-2851. Email: blesssac@bellsouth.net. Web: www.blsac.org.
School—(Grades K-8), 7 St. Teresa Dr., 29407. Tel: 843-766-2128; Fax: 843-766-2154. Email: chabless@bellsouth.net. Web: www.scbss.org. Roseann Tracy, Interim Prin.; Bonnie Perry, Librarian. Lay Teachers 26; Students 409.
Catechesis/Religious Program—Students 152.
Convent—O Moore Dr., 29407. Tel: 843-766-5120.

4—CHRIST OUR KING (1971) Rev. Msgr. James A. Carter; Rev. Bryan P. Babick, Parochial Vicar; Deacons Joseph Cahill; Andre Guillet.
1149 Russell Dr., Mount Pleasant, 29464. Tel: 843-884-5587; Fax: 843-884-7086. Web: www.christourking.com.
School—Christ Our King-Stella Maris School, (Grades K-8), 1183 Russell Dr., Mount Pleasant, 29464. Tel: 843-884-4721; Fax: 843-971-7850. Web: www.coksm.org. Jean Moschella, Prin. Lay Teachers 41; Students 650.
Catechesis/Religious Program—Students 356.

5—CHURCH OF CHRIST THE DIVINE TEACHER (1968) Rev. Dennis B. Willey; Deacon Peter Curcio.
Mailing Address: *The Catholic Chaplaincy to the Citadel*, The Citadel, MSC 58, 29409-0058. Tel: 843-953-7692; 843-953-7693; Fax: 843-953-4811. Email: willeyd1@citadel.edu. Web: www.citadel.edu/catholic.

6—CHURCH OF THE HOLY SPIRIT (1938) [CEM] Rev. Msgr. Charles H. Rowland; Rev. Jose Gabrie Rodriguez Cruz, Parochial Vicar.
Mailing Address: P.O. Box 719, Johns Island, 29457. Tel: 843-768-0357; Fax: 843-768-0751. Email: hschrch@bellsouth.net. Web: www.holyspiritjohnsisland.com. 3871 Betsy Kerrison Pkwy., Johns Island, 29457.

7—CHURCH OF THE NATIVITY (1959) Rev. S. Thomas Kingsley, Admin.
1061 Folly Rd., 29412. Tel: 843-795-3821; Fax: 843-795-2714. Email: nativityc@bellsouth.net.
School—(Grades K-8), 1125 Pittsford Cir., 29412. Tel: 843-795-3975; Fax: 843-795-7575. Email: mary_nativity@bellsouth.net. Ms. Patti Dukes, Prin.; Paula Hart, Librarian. Lay Teachers 14; Students 148.
Catechesis/Religious Program—Mrs. Mary L. Smith, D.R.E. Students 97.

8—DIVINE REDEEMER (1956) Rev. Edward W. Fitzgerald; Deacon Donald R. Dashnaw.
Office & Mailing Address: 1106 Fort Dr., Hanahan, 29410-2053. Tel: 843-553-0340; Fax: 843-533-0346. Email: divineredeemer@bellsouth.net. Web: www.divineredeemerchurch.org.
School—(Grades K-8), 1104 Fort Dr., Hanahan, 29410-2053. Tel: 843-553-1521; Fax: 843-553-7109. Email: secretary@divineredeemerschool.com. Web: www.divineredeemerschool.com. Jean Steinhoff, Prin.; Pat Swain, Librarian. Lay Teachers 17; Students 155.
Catechesis/Religious Program—Students 58.

9—ST. JOHN (1929) Rev. Msgr. Joseph F. Hanley Jr., Mod./Canonical Pastor; Bro. Edward E. Bergeron, C.F.C., Parish Life Facilitator.
Mailing Address: 3921 St. John's Ave., North Charleston, 29405-7158. Tel: 843-744-6201; Fax: 843-744-2792. Email: parishoffice@saintjohncatholicsc.org. Web: www.saintjohncatholicsc.org.
School—(Grades K-8) Tel: 843-744-3901; Fax: 843-744-3689. Email: schooloffice@saintjohncatholicsc.org. Ms. Carole Anne White, Prin. Lay Teachers 11; Students 58.
Catechesis/Religious Program— Sr. Leonie Marie Maigret, S.N.D., D.R.E. Students 10.

10—ST. JOSEPH (1966) Rev. Gabriel J. Smith.
Mailing Address & Res.: 1695 Wallenberg Blvd., 29407. Tel: 843-566-4611; Fax: 843-566-4612. Email: info@saintjosephchas.com. Web: www.saintjosephchas.com.
Catechesis/Religious Program—Students 68.

11—ST. JOSEPH'S, Closed. For inquiries for parish records please contact Diocesan Archive, P.O. Box 818, Charleston, SC 29402. Tel: 843-724-8372.

12—ST. MARY OF THE ANNUNCIATION (1789) [CEM] Rev. Gregory B. Wilson, Admin.; Deacon Jerome P. Remkiewicz.
89 Hasell St., 29401. Tel: 843-722-7696; Fax: 843-577-5036. Email: stmarys1789@bellsouth.net. Web: www.catholic-doc.org/saintmarys/.
Catechesis/Religious Program—Students 53.

13—OUR LADY OF MERCY (1928), (African American), Rev. Henry N. Kulah (Ghana), Admin.
Mailing Address: c/o St. Patrick, P.O. Box 20726, 29413.
Res.: 77 America St., 29403. Tel: 843-723-6066; Fax: 843-853-8114.
See Charleston Catholic School, Charleston under Sacred Heart, Charleston for details.
Catechesis/Religious Program—

14—ST. PATRICK (1837), (African American), [CEM] Rev. Henry N. Kulah (Ghana), Admin.
Res.: 134 St. Phillip St., P.O. Box 20726, 29413. Tel: 843-723-6066; Fax: 843-853-8114. Email: stpat@bellsouth.net.
See Charleston Catholic School, Charleston under Sacred Heart, Charleston for details.
Catechesis/Religious Program—

15—ST. PETER'S, Closed. For inquiries for parish records contact St. Patrick, P.O. Box 20726, Charleston, SC 29413.

16—SACRED HEART (1920) Rev. Dennis B. Willey.
Office: 888 King St., 29403-4139. Tel: 843-722-7018; Fax: 843-579-9604. Email: sacredheartchas@aol.com.
School—Charleston Catholic School, (Grades K-8), 888-A King St., 29403-4139. Tel: 843-577-4495; Fax: 843-577-6916. Web: www.charlestoncatholic.com. Fred S. McKay Jr., Prin.; Ms. Elizabeth Halberstadt, Librarian. Lay Teachers 21; Students 200; Religious 2.

17—STELLA MARIS (1845) Rev. Msgr. Lawrence B. McInerny; Rev. Richard Tomlinson; Deacons Walter S. Pezanowski; Gerald W. Grismore; R. Michael Osbourne.
Mailing Address: P.O. Box 280, Sullivan's Island, 29482.
1204 Middle St., Sullivan's Island, 29482. Tel: 843-883-3108 (Office); 843-883-9158 (Rectory); Fax: 843-883-3160. Web: www.catholic-doc.org/stellamaris.
Catechesis/Religious Program—Christian Formation/CCD, Tel: 843-883-9040. Students 213.

18—ST. THOMAS THE APOSTLE (1966) Rev. Andrew Riley, Admin.; Deacon Frank T. Petrusak.
Res.: 6650 Dorchester Rd., North Charleston, 29418. Tel: 843-552-2223; 843-552-9045. Web: www.catholic-doc.org/stthomas.
Catechesis/Religious Program—Students 159.

OUTSIDE OF THE CITY OF CHARLESTON

ABBEVILLE, ABBEVILLE CO., SACRED HEART (1885) Rev. Allam Marreddy (India), Admin.
Mailing Address: P.O. Box 812, 29620.
206 N. Main St., 29620. Tel: 864-366-5150; Fax: 864-366-5150. Email: sacredheart@wctel.net.
Catechesis/Religious Program—Students 4.
Mission—Good Shepherd P.O. Box 1468, McCormick, McCormick Co. 29835. Tel: 843-852-4722; Fax: 843-852-4722.
Station—McCormick Correctional Institution McCormick.

AIKEN, AIKEN CO.

1—ST. GERARD (1943) Rev. Anthony Batung (Ghana), Admin.
Res.: 640 Edrie St., N.E., 29801. Tel: 803-649-3030; Fax: 803-649-3030. Email: stgerardscatholi@bellsouth.net.
School—(Grades K-8), See St. Mary Help of Christians Catholic School, Aiken, under St. Mary Help of Christians for details.
Catechesis/Religious Program—

2—ST. MARY, HELP OF CHRISTIANS (1853) [CEM] Revs. James L. LeBlanc; Agustin Torm, Parochial Vicar; Deacon Robert A. Pierce; Rev. Robert J. Waters (SC).
Mailing Address: P.O. Box 438, 29802.
203 Park Ave. S.E., 29802. Tel: 803-649-4777; Fax: 803-642-6421. Email: stmaryaikn@aol.com. Web: www.stmarys-aiken.org.
School—(Grades K-8), 118 York St., 29801. Tel: 803-649-2071; Fax: 803-643-0092. Email: office@stmaryhoc.net. Web: smhoc.info. Marguerite

B. Wertz, Prin. Lay Teachers 26; Students 358.
Catechesis/Religious Program—Students 358.

ANDERSON, ANDERSON CO.

1—ST. JOSEPH (1868) Rev. Hayden J. Vaverek.
Office: 1200 Cornelia Rd., 29621-3344. Tel: 864-225-5341; Fax: 864-225-6432.
School—(Grades K-5), 1200 Cornelia Rd., 29621. Mary Ann Wheeler, Prin.; Francene Galbally, Librarian. Lay Teachers 11; Students 85.
Catechesis/Religious Program—Students 198.

2—ST. MARY OF THE ANGELS (1943) Rev. Aubrey McNeil, O.F.M.
Res. & Mailing Address: 1821 White St., 29624. Tel: 864-226-8621; Fax: 864-226-2536.
Catechesis/Religious Program—Tel: 864-226-3881. Students 67.

BARNWELL, BARNWELL CO., ST. ANDREW (1831) Rev. David Michael, Admin.
Mailing Address: 168 Madison St., 29812. Tel: 803-259-7593.
Church: 110 Madison St., 29812.
Catechesis/Religious Program—Dana Depew, D.R.E. Students 15.
Mission—Sacred Heart Blackville, Barnwell Co.
Mission—St. Theresa Springfield, Orangeburg Co.

BATESBURG-LEESVILLE, LEXINGTON CO., ST. JOHN OF THE CROSS (1959) Revs. Robert J. Sayer, Admin.; Filemon Juya (Colombia), Parochial Vicar; Jose Orlando Cheverria Jimenez (Colombia).
Res.: 320 W. Columbia Ave., P.O. Box 2279, 29070-2279. Tel: 803-532-1208; Fax: 803-532-1208.
Catechesis/Religious Program—Tel: 803-532-6777. Email: jhaden2@sc.rr.com. Students 117.

BEAUFORT, BEAUFORT CO., ST. PETER (1846) [CEM] Rev. Timothy D. Tebalt.
Church: 70 Lady's Island Dr., 29907. Tel: 843-522-9555; Fax: 843-522-0667. Email: stpeters@stpeters-church.org. Web: www.stpeters-church.org.
School—(Grades K-8) Tel: 843-522-2163; Fax: 843-522-6513. Email: stpetersschool@stpeters-church.org. Web: www.stpeters-church.org/school. Christopher A. Trott, Prin. Sisters 1; Lay Teachers 15; Students 154.
Catechesis/Religious Program—Students 139.
Mission—Holy Cross St. Helena Island, Beaufort Co. Tel: 843-838-2195.

BLUFFTON, BEAUFORT CO., ST. GREGORY THE GREAT (1960) [CEM] Rev. Ronald R. Cellini; Deacons Gregory W. Sams; Dennis Burkett; Walt Hollis; Richard D'Angelo; James Graham.
Mailing Address: 333 Fording Island Rd., 29909. Tel: 843-815-3100; Fax: 843-815-3150. Email: lc@sgg.cc. Web: www.sgg.cc.
Res.: 232 Pinckney Colony Rd., 29909. Tel: 843-757-5558.
School—(Grades PreK-7), 323 Fording Island Rd., 29909. Tel: 843-815-9988; Fax: 843-815-6137. Sr. Canice Adams, SS.C.M., Prin.; Ms. Ann Caruso, Librarian.
Catechesis/Religious Program—Students 298.
Chapel—St. Andrew 220 Pinckney Colony Rd., 29909. Tel: 843-757-6057.

BLYTHEWOOD, RICHLAND CO., TRANSFIGURATION (1998) Rev. Bernardino S. Yebra (Philippines), Admin.
Office & Mailing Address: 9720 Wilson Blvd., 29016. Tel: 803-735-0512; Fax: 803-735-1742. Email: transfiguration@bellsouth.net. Web: www.catholic-doc.org/transfiguration.
Catechesis/Religious Program—Students 99.
Mission—St. Theresa 321 Bypass, P.O. Box 1004, Winnsboro, Fairfield Co. 29180.

CAMDEN, KERSHAW CO., OUR LADY OF PERPETUAL HELP (1914) Revs. Francis J. Travis; Jose Rodolfo Lache Avila (Colombia), Parochial Vicar.
1709 Lyttleton St., 29020. Tel: 803-432-6131; Fax: 803-432-3440. Email: olph@bellsouth.net. Web: ourlady.catholicweb.com.
Catechesis/Religious Program—Tel: 803-432-8808. Students 172.

CHAPIN, LEXINGTON CO., OUR LADY OF THE LAKE (1989) [CEM] Rev. Andrew J. Vollkommer; Deacons Joseph P. Biviano; Charles LaRosa; Gregory Weigold.
Mailing Address: 195 Amicks Ferry Rd., P.O. Box 549, 29036. Tel: 803-345-3962; Fax: 803-345-8933. Email: andrewjv@logicsouth.com. Web: www.ollchapin.org.
Res.: 2 Oak Stand Ct., Irmo, 29063. Tel: 803-781-8767.
Catechesis/Religious Program—Students 360.

CHERAW, CHESTERFIELD CO., ST. PETER (1842) [CEM] Rev. John Paul Pentareddy, P.V., Admin.
Parish & Mailing Address: 602 Market St., P.O. Box 905, 29520. Tel: 843-537-7351; 843-287-2702 (Rectory Phone); Fax: 843-537-7351. Email: stpeterscatholic@bellsouth.net.
Catechesis/Religious Program—
Mission—St. Denis Bennettsville, Marlboro Co.
Mission—St. Ernest [CEM] Pageland, Chesterfield Co.

CHESTER, CHESTER CO., ST. JOSEPH (1854) Rev. David A. Runnion, Admin.
110 West End, P.O. Box 869, 29706. Tel: 803-377-4695; Fax: 803-581-7848. Email: stjoseph@truvista.net.
Catechesis/Religious Program—Students 10.

CLEMSON, PICKENS CO., ST. ANDREW (1935) Revs. C. Alexander McDonald; Emmanuel Andinam (Nigeria).
200 Edgewood Ave., P.O. Box 112, 29633. Tel: 864-654-1757; Fax: 864-654-2950.
Catechesis/Religious Program—Attended by St. Paul's & St. Andrew Students 365.
Mission—St. Paul the Apostle 170 Bountyland Rd., Seneca, Oconee Co. 29672. Tel: 864-882-8551; 864-882-7115 (Hispanic Ministry).
Mission—St. Francis of Assisi 103 W. Mauldin St., Walhalla, Oconee Co. 29691. Tel: 864-638-2984.
Station—Campus Ministry-Clemson University, Tel: 864-654-7804.

COLUMBIA, LEXINGTON CO., OUR LADY OF THE HILLS (1972) Revs. D. Anthony Droze; Jose Rodolfo Lache Avila (Colombia), Parochial Vicar; Sr. Christina Murphy, S.N.D.deN., Pastoral Assoc.; Deacons Charles R. DiRusso; Dennis N. Jones; Stephen Burdick.
Mailing Address: 120 Marydale Ln., 29210. Email: oloh@sc.rr.com. Web: www.ourladyofthehillssc.org.
Catechesis/Religious Program—Students 341.

COLUMBIA, RICHLAND CO.

1—GOOD SHEPHERD (1984) Rev. William D. Ladkau.
Mailing Address: P.O. Box 1298, 29202. Tel: 803-765-1334; Fax: 803-765-2208.
809 Calhoun, 29202.
Res.: 1625 Granby Rd., Cayce, 29033.
Catechesis/Religious Program—

2—ST. JOHN NEUMANN (1977) Rev. Frederick F. Masad.
Mailing Address: P.O. Box 23689, 29224.
100 Polo Rd., 29223. Tel: 803-788-0811; Fax: 803-788-1501. Email: marshas@sc.rr.com. Web: www.stjohnneumannsc.com.
School—(Grades K-6), 721 Polo Rd., 29223. Tel: 803-788-1367; Fax: 803-788-7330. Web: www.sjn-catholic.com. Barbara Cole, Prin.; Ms. Karen Zimmerman, Librarian. Lay Teachers 33; Students 358.
Catechesis/Religious Program— Mrs. Cherie Smith, D.R.E. Students 249.

3—ST. JOSEPH (1948) Rev. Richard D. Harris; Deacon Charles P. Poole Jr.
Office: 3512 Devine St., 29205. Tel: 803-254-7646; Fax: 803-799-7607. Email: stjoedoc@aol.com. Web: www.stjosephcolumbia.org.
Rectory—136 High Hampton, 29209. Tel: 803-776-7610.
Church: 3600 Devine St., 29205.
School—(Grades K-6), 3700 Devine St., 29205. Tel: 803-254-6736; Fax: 803-540-1913. Web: www.stjos-devine.com. Ms. Roselyn Tindall, Prin.; Nick Cole, Librarian. Ursuline Nuns of the Congregation of Paris 1; Lay Teachers 16; Students 314.
Catechesis/Religious Program—Tel: 803-540-1906. Students 204.

4—SAINT MARTIN DE PORRES (1935) Very Rev. Paul M. Williams, O.F.M.; Deacons Carl Johnson; Henry L. Fulmer, O.F.M.
2229 Hampton St., 29204. Tel: 803-254-6862; Fax: 803-799-4720. Email: deporres@yahoo.com.
Rectory—2505 Treeside Dr., 29204. Tel: 803-376-6027. Email: pw4ofm@aol.com. Web: stmartinofcolumbia.org.
School—(Grades K-6), 2225 Hampton Rd., 29204. Tel: 803-254-5477; Fax: 803-254-7335. Web: www-.saintmartindeporres.org. Sr. Roberta Fulton, S.S.M.N., Prin. Lay Teachers 11; Students 85.
Catechesis/Religious Program—Students 76.
Station—Correctional Institutions in the Greater Columbia Area

5—ST. PETER (1824) [CEM 3] Rev. Msgr. Leigh A. Lehocky; Deacons Charles M. Easterling, Pastoral Assoc.; Ronald J. Anderson; John Stetar; David Thompson.
Mailing Address: P.O. Box 1896, 29202. Email: stpeters@visitstpeters.org. Web: www.visitstpeters.org.
Res.: 2125 Raven Tr., West Columbia, 29169. Tel: 803-791-0552.
Church: 1529 Assembly St., 29201. Tel: 803-779-0036; Fax: 803-799-2438.
School—(Grades K-6), 1035 Hampton St., 29201. Tel: 803-252-8285; Fax: 803-254-4736. Web: www.stpeters-catholic-school.org. Ms. Bonnie Bardin, Prin. Lay Teachers 18; Students 152.
Catechesis/Religious Program—Students 215.

CONWAY, HORRY CO., ST. JAMES (1945) Revs. Frederick LaBrecque; John E. Silver (OG) (Retired); Deacon Jeffrey P. Mevissen.
Church, Office & Mailing Address: 1071 Academy Dr., 29526. Tel: 843-347-5168; Fax: 843-347-1212. Email: stjames@stjamesconway.org. Web: stjamesconway.org.
Catechesis/Religious Program—Students 211.
Mission—Catholic Church of the Resurrection 204 Heritage Rd., Loris, Horry Co. 29569. Tel: 843-756-6168; Fax: 843-756-4197.

DILLON, DILLON CO., ST. LOUIS (1943) Rev. Marcian Thet-Kyaw (Burma), Admin.
Mailing Address: 607 N. 4th Ave., 29536.
Church: 207 E. Roosevelt St., 29536. Tel: 843-774-0255 (Office); Fax: 843-774-0255. Email: stlouiscatholicc@bellsouth.net.
Catechesis/Religious Program—Students 15.
Mission—Infant Jesus 4534 Hwy. 501 N., P.O. Box 520, Marion, Marion Co. 29571. Tel: 843-423-1823; Fax: 843-423-3987. Email: lauren.denitto@yahoo.com.

EDGEFIELD, EDGEFIELD CO., ST. MARY OF THE IMMACULATE CONCEPTION (1856) [CEM] Rev. Noel Tria (Philippines), Canonical Mod./Admin.; Deacon John P. Klein, Parish Life Facilitator.
Office: 302 Jeter St., 29824. Tel: 803-637-6248; Fax: 803-637-6241. Email: stmaryscc@bellsouth.net.
Church: 305 Buncombe St., 29824.
Catechesis/Religious Program—Students 17.

FLORENCE, FLORENCE CO.

1—ST. ANNE (1940) [JC] Rev. John M. Zimmerman, Admin.; Deacons James H. Johnson; Robert C. Gerald Jr.
113 S. Kemp St., 29506. Tel: 843-662-1736; 843-661-5012 (Church Office); Fax: 843-661-5012. Email: stanns@bellsouth.net.
Catechesis/Religious Program—Tel: 843-662-8727. Students 46.

2—ST. ANTHONY'S ALL SOULS MEMORIAL (1872) Rev. Arturo O. Dalupang (Philippines); Deacons Reginald A.T. Armstrong; Jeffery Pierfy.
Mailing Address: P.O. Box 5327, 29501.
Church: 2536 W. Hoffmeyer Rd., 29502. Tel: 843-665-5853 (Rectory); 843-662-5674; Fax: 843-662-4800. Email: art.dalupang@saintanthony.com. Web: www.saintanthony.com.
School—(Grades K-8) Tel: 843-662-1910; Fax: 843-662-5335. Email: stanthonyf10@aol.com. Ms. Phyllis Brandis, Prin.; Patty Long, Librarian. Priests 1; Lay Teachers 18; Students 147.
Catechesis/Religious Program—Students 253.

FOLLY BEACH, CHARLESTON CO., OUR LADY OF GOOD COUNSEL (1950) Rev. Jesuprathap Narichetti (India), Admin.
Mailing Address: P.O. Box 1257, 29439. Email: olgc@bellsouth.net. Web: www.olgc-follybeach.org.
56 Center St., 29439. Tel: 843-588-2336; Fax: 843-588-3478.
Catechesis/Religious Program—Students 50.

FORT MILL, YORK CO., ST. PHILIP NERI (1993) [CEM] Revs. John P. Giuliani, C.O.; Edward P. McDevitt, C.O., Parochial Vicar; Deacons Jon Dwyer; Steven Rhodes.
Church: 292 Munn Rd., 29715. Tel: 803-548-7282; Fax: 803-547-2999. Email: stphilipneri@comporium.net. Web: www.saintphilipneri.org.
Catechesis/Religious Program—Students 644.
Mission—Our Lady of Grace Indian Land, 29707.

GAFFNEY, CHEROKEE CO., SACRED HEART (1955) Rev. Michael F. McCafferty, Admin.
407 Grace St., 29340. Tel: 864-649-1280; Fax: 864-649-1281.
Catechesis/Religious Program—Students 66.

GARDEN CITY, HORRY CO., ST. MICHAEL (1975) Revs. Raymond J. Carlo; Andrew Trapp, Parochial Vicar; Deacons Donald C. Efken; Charlie Fiore; Robert Starr; Robert James.
572 Cypress Ave., 29576. Tel: 843-651-3737; Fax: 843-651-6316. Email: pastor@saintmichaelsc.org.
School—(Grades PreK-8) Tel: 843-651-6795; Fax: 843-651-6803. Mrs. Miriam James, Prin. Lay Teachers 17; Students 170.
Catechesis/Religious Program—Students 373.

GEORGETOWN, GEORGETOWN CO.

1—ST. CYPRIAN (1950), (African American—Hispanic), Rev. Ronald J. Farrell, Admin.; Sr. Susan Pugh, Parish Life Facilitator.
Center & Mailing Address: 1905 Front St., P.O. Box 2037, 29442. Tel: 843-546-1470; Fax: 843-527-2139. Email: stcyprian2@hotmail.com.
Catechesis/Religious Program—Students 34.

2—ST. MARY OUR LADY OF RANSOM (1899) [JC], (Our Lady of Ransom) Rev. Ronald J. Farrell, Admin.
Mailing Address: 317 Broad St., 29440. Tel: 843-546-7416; Fax: 843-546-7003. Email: smolor@sccc.tv. Web: www.stmaryourladyofransom.com.
Res.: 810 Highmarket St., 29440. Tel: 843-527-1087.
Catechesis/Religious Program—Students 56.

GLOVERVILLE, AIKEN CO., OUR LADY OF THE VALLEY (1954) Rev. Peter Clarke (Retired).
Mailing Address: P.O. Box 419, 29828. Tel: 803-593-2241; Fax: 803-593-2241. Email: olv@atlanticbbn.net.
2429 Augusta Rd., 29828.
Parish Community Center—Tel: 803-593-2623; Fax: 803-593-2678.
Catechesis/Religious Program—Students 39.

Convent—Horsecreek Valley Convent, P.O. Box 358, 29828. Tel: 803-593-9862. Daughters of Charity 4.

GOOSE CREEK, BERKELEY CO., IMMACULATE CONCEPTION (1976) Revs. Nicholas Capetola, C.R.M.; Nestor Abog, C.M.R., Parochial Vicar. In Res., Rev. Lilson Rodriguez, Vicar, Brazilians; Deacons Joseph A. Anonie; Daniel McNerny.
510 St. James Ave., 29445. Tel: 843-553-1386 (Rectory); 843-572-1270 (Office); Fax: 843-572-3128. Email: icgc@comcast.net.
Catechesis/Religious Program—Students 300.

GREENVILLE, GREENVILLE CO.

1—ST. ANTHONY OF PADUA (1939), (African American), Revs. Patrick Tuttle, O.F.M.; Raymond Selker, O.F.M., Parochial Vicar; Deacons Winston C. Wright; James Williams; Henry Dillard.
307 Gower St., 29611. Tel: 864-233-7717; Fax: 864-233-2852. Email: anthonyofm@yahoo.com. Web: www.newstanthony.com.
School—(Grades K-5), 309 Gower St., 29611. Tel: 864-271-0167; Fax: 864-271-2936. Sr. Catherine Noecker, O.S.F., Prin. Sisters of St. Francis of Williamsville 3; Lay Teachers 11; Students 93.
Catechesis/Religious Program—Students 103.

2—ST. MARY (1852) Rev. Jay Scott Newman; Deacons John Karandisevsky; George Tierney; Diego Ferro; John Heuser.
Mailing Address & Res.: 111 Hampton Ave., 29601. Tel: 864-271-8422; Fax: 864-370-9880. Web: www.stmarysgvl.org.
School—(Grades K-8), 101 Hampton Ave., 29601. Tel: 864-271-3870; Fax: 864-271-0159. Sr. Mary John Slonkosky, O.P., Prin. Dominicans 4; Lay Teachers 16; Students 296.
Catechesis/Religious Program—Students 243.

3—OUR LADY OF THE ROSARY (1952) Rev. Dac T. Tran, O.F.M., Admin.
3710 Augusta Rd., P.O. Box 8396, 29604. Tel: 864-422-1648; Fax: 864-277-5969. Email: church.office@ourladyoftherosary.net. Web: www.ourladyoftherosary.net.
School—(Grades K-8), 2 James Dr., 29605. Tel: 864-277-5350; Fax: 864-277-7745. Email: info@olrschool.net. Mr. John Harrington, Prin.; Robin Calamia, Librarian. Lay Teachers 15; Students 178.
Catechesis/Religious Program—Students 148.

GREENWOOD, GREENWOOD CO., OUR LADY OF LOURDES (1920) Rev. James M. Crowley.
Office & Mailing Address: 915 Mathis Rd., 29649. Tel: 864-223-8410; Fax: 864-223-7555. Email: pastor@olol.org. Web: www.olol.org.
Res.: 120 Colonial Dr., 29649. Tel: 864-223-3003.
Catechesis/Religious Program—Tel: 864-223-4406. Email: tomrel@embarqmail.com. Students 175.

GREER, GREENVILLE CO., BLESSED TRINITY (1974) Rev. Oscar Borda Rojas (Colombia), Admin.
901 River Rd., 29652-1371. Tel: 864-879-4261; Fax: 864-879-4261. Email: blessedtrinityca@bellsouth.net.
Catechesis/Religious Program—Students 227.

HARTSVILLE, DARLINGTON CO.

1—ST. JOSEPH'S, Closed. For inquiries for parish records contact St. Mary the Virgin Mother, 363 N. 5th St., Hartsville, SC 29550.

2—ST. MARY THE VIRGIN MOTHER (1941) Very Rev. Karl J. Roesch, O.S.B., Admin.; Deacon John S. Larkin.
Res.: 115 Church St., 29550. Tel: 843-332-7773; Fax: 843-332-2812. Email: stmary2@ymail.com.
Church: 363 N. 5th St., 29550.
Catechesis/Religious Program—Students 37.
Mission—St. Joseph the Worker 1308 N. Main St., Darlington, Darlington Co. 29540.

HILTON HEAD ISLAND, BEAUFORT CO.

1—ST. FRANCIS BY THE SEA (1984) [CEM] Revs. Michael J. Oenbrink; Christopher Smith, Parochial Vicar; Sr. Kathleen Kane, S.S.M.N., Pastoral Assoc.
Res.: 45 Beach City Rd., 29926-2423. Tel: 843-681-6350; Fax: 843-689-5502. Email: office@stfrancishhi.org. Web: www.stfrancishhi.org.
School—(Grades PreK-8) Tel: 843-681-6501; Fax: 843-689-3725. Web: www.sfcshhi.org. Mike Rockers, Prin. Lay Teachers 8; Students 232.
Catechesis/Religious Program—Tel: 843-681-6350, Ext. 248. Students 286.

2—HOLY FAMILY (1966) Rev. Robert E. Morey; Deacon John DeWolfe.
24 Pope Ave., 29928. Tel: 843-785-2895; Fax: 843-842-7494. Email: pastor@holyfamilyhhi.org. Web: www.holyfamilyhhi.org.
Catechesis/Religious Program—Email: education@holyfamily.hhi.org. Students 219.

JOANNA, LAURENS CO., ST. BONIFACE (1949) Rev. Francisco Cruz (Colombia), Admin.
Office: 403 N. Main St., P.O. Box 188, 29351. Tel: 864-697-6745; Fax: 864-697-6745.
Catechesis/Religious Program—Students 12.
Mission—Holy Spirit (1963) 1040 W. Main St., P.O. Box 864, Laurens, Laurens Co. 29360. Tel: 864-984-2880; Fax: 864-984-2880.

KINGSTREE, WILLIAMSBURG CO., ST. ANN (1947) Rev. Jeffrey A. Kendall; Deacon Harold Jackson.
Church & Mailing Address: 303 Main St., P.O. Box 529, 29556.
Center—908 Thorne Ave., 29556. Tel: 843-354-9415; Fax: 843-354-9093.
Res.: 120 Hirsch St., P.O. Box 529, Kingtree, 29556.
Catechesis/Religious Program—Students 16.
Convent—908 Thorne Ave., 29556. Felician Sisters 2.

LAKE CITY, FLORENCE CO., ST. PHILIP THE APOSTLE (1952) [JC] Rev. Jeffrey A. Kendall.
120 Westover St., P.O. Box 399, 29560. Tel: 843-394-8343.
Catechesis/Religious Program—Fax: 843-394-1814. Students 20.
Mission—St. Patrick the Apostle P.O. Box 399, Johnsonville, Florence Co. 29560.

LANCASTER, LANCASTER CO., ST. CATHERINE (1948) Rev. David A. Runnion, Admin.
720 W. Meeting St., 29720. Tel: 803-283-3362; Fax: 803-283-3363. Email: stcstm@comporium.net.
Catechesis/Religious Program—Students 38.
Mission—St. Michael 310 Chester Ave., Great Falls, Chester Co. 29055.

LEXINGTON, LEXINGTON CO., CORPUS CHRISTI (1977) Rev. Robert J. Sayer; Deacons Dale Palmer; Coleman T. Parks.
2350 Augusta Hwy., 29072. Tel: 803-359-4391; Fax: 803-359-8885. Web: www.catholic-doc.org/corpuschristi.
Catechesis/Religious Program—Students 426.

MAULDIN, GREENVILLE CO., ST. ELIZABETH ANN SETON (1972) Rev. Patrick E. Cooper; Deacon Richard J. Murtgaugh Jr.
P.O. Box 672, 29662-0672. 8 Gillin Dr., Simpsonville, 29680-6108. Tel: 864-963-3959; Fax: 864-967-9726. Email: steaseton@aol.com. Web: www.steaseton.org.
Res.: 117 Ivy Dr., Simpsonville, 29680-6124. Tel: 864-963-4892.
Catechesis/Religious Program—Students 177.

MONCKS CORNER, BERKELEY CO., ST. PHILIP BENIZI (1965) Rev. Edgardo Enverga, C.R.M., Admin.
1404 Old Hwy. 52 S., 29461. Tel: 843-761-3777; Fax: 843-761-0905. Email: diane@spbcc.org; mary@spbcc.org. Web: spbcc.org.
Catechesis/Religious Program—Students 80.
Mission—Our Lady of Peace 224 Murray's Ferry Rd., Bonneau, Berkeley Co. 29431.

MURPHY VILLAGE, EDGEFIELD CO., ST. EDWARD (1964) Rev. Cherian Thalakulam, C.M.I. (India).
Mailing Address: P.O. Box 6340, North Augusta, 29861.
1370 Edgefield Rd., North Augusta, 29860. Tel: 803-279-1837; Fax: 803-279-9655.
Catechesis/Religious Program—Students 159.

MYRTLE BEACH, HORRY CO., ST. ANDREW (1946) Rev. Msgr. Joseph R. Roth; Rev. Matthew Bulala, Parochial Vicar.
Parish Administration Office—3501 N. King Hwy. Ste. 102, 29577. Tel: 843-448-5930; Fax: 843-448-3947. Email: standrewmb@sc.rr.com. Web: standrewcatholicchurch.org.
Church: 503 37th Ave. N., 29577.
School—(Grades K-8), 3601 N. Kings Hwy., 29577. Tel: 843-448-6062; Fax: 843-626-8644. Email: mhalasz@standrewschoolmb.org. Mrs. Mary M. Halasz, Prin.; Cheryl Sedota, Librarian. Lay Teachers 16; Students 238.
Catechesis/Religious Program—Students 281.

NEWBERRY, NEWBERRY CO., ST. MARK (1956) [JC] Rev. Francisco Cruz (Colombia), Admin.; Deacon Gerald Loignon Jr.
928 Boundary St., 29108. Tel: 803-276-6446; Fax: 803-276-0856.
Catechesis/Religious Program—Students 72.

NORTH AUGUSTA, AIKEN CO., OUR LADY OF PEACE (1948) Rev. Timothy M. Lijewski; Deacon Bob Hookness.
856 Old Edgefield Rd., P.O. Box 6605, 29861-6605. Tel: 803-279-0315; Fax: 803-279-5247. Web: www.ourlady.ws.
School—(Grades K-8) Tel: 803-279-8396; Fax: 803-279-7167. Karen Wilcox, Prin.; Ms. Nancy Mack, Librarian. Lay Teachers 14; Students 119.
Catechesis/Religious Program—Students 185.

NORTH MYRTLE BEACH, HORRY CO., OUR LADY STAR OF THE SEA (1964) Revs. Robert F. Higgins, Admin.; Jacob Joseph, C.M.I., Parochial Vicar; Deacons Robert Tyson; Chester Gormon; Andrew Stoshak.
Office: 1100 Eighth Ave. N., 29582. Tel: 843-249-2356; Fax: 843-249-8514. Email: olss@sc.rr.com. Web: olssnmb.com.
Res.: 1010 8th Ave. N., 29582. Tel: 843-249-8049.
School—Holy Trinity Catholic School, 1760 Living Stones Ln., Longs, 29568. Tel: 843-390-4108; Fax: 843-390-4097. Email: htcs@sccoast.net. Web: www.holytrinitylongs.com. Colette Ott, Prin.
Catechesis/Religious Program—

ORANGEBURG, ORANGEBURG CO.

1—CHRIST THE KING, Closed. For inquiries for parish records contact Holy Trinity, 2202 Riverbank Dr., N.W. 29118-4044. Tel: 803-534-8177.

2—HOLY TRINITY (1917) Rev. Michael C. Okere (Nigeria), Admin.
Office: 2202 Riverbank Dr., 29118-4044. Tel: 803-534-8177; Fax: 802-535-0012. Email: holytrin@sc.rr.com. Web: www.masstransit.com/sc/trinity.
Catechesis/Religious Program—Students 66.
Mission—St. Mary Allendale, Barnwell Co.

PAWLEYS ISLAND, GEORGETOWN CO., PRECIOUS BLOOD OF CHRIST (1986) [CEM] Rev. Patrick J. Stenson, M.S.C., Admin.
Office: 1633 Waverly Rd., 29585. Tel: 843-237-3428; Fax: 843-237-2293. Web: www.pbocchurch.com.
Catechesis/Religious Program—Students 168.

PICKENS, PICKENS CO., HOLY CROSS (1965) Rev. Emmanuel Efiong (Nigeria).
Church: 558 Hampton Ave., 29671. Fax: 864-878-0028. Email: holycros@bellsouth.net.
Catechesis/Religious Program—Students 50.
Mission—St. Luke 4408 Hwy. 86, Easley, Anderson Co. 29642. Tel: 864-855-9039; Fax: 864-855-9038. Deacons Eugene Egendoerfer; Anthony J. Cassandra.

RIDGELAND, JASPER CO., ST. ANTHONY (1963) Rev. Gerald J. Lutz, Admin.; Deacon Robert E. Dotson.
Mailing Address: P.O. Box 548, 29936.
696 S. Jacob Smart Blvd., 29936. Tel: 843-726-3606; Fax: 843-726-3606.
Catechesis/Religious Program—Students 40.
Mission—St. Mary 703 5th St. E., Hampton, Hampton Co. 29924. Tel: 803-941-4019. In Res., Rev. Carl Bauer.
Mission—St. Anthony 1 Charles St., Hardeeville, Jasper Co. 29927. Tel: 843-784-2943. Rev. Francis J. Gillespie, Admin.; Deacon Albert Shito.

ROCK HILL, YORK CO.

1—ST. ANNE (1919) Rev. Adilso Coelho, C.O., Admin.; Very Rev. Joseph A. Wahl, C.O., Parochial Vicar; Deacons Ray Moore; Guillermo Nunez.
Office & Mailing Address: 1694 Bird St., 29730. Tel: 803-329-2662; Fax: 803-329-2190. Email: parishoffice@saintanne.com. Web: www.saintanne.com.
Res.: 434 Charlotte Ave., P.O. Box 11586, 29731. Tel: 803-327-2315.
School—(Grades K-8), 1698 Bird St., 29730. Tel: 803-324-4814; Fax: 803-324-0189. Mr. Anthony Perrini, Prin. Lay Teachers 27; Students 285.
Catechesis/Religious Program—Students 500.

2—ST. MARY (1946) Rev. David D. Valtierra, C.O., Canonical Pastor; Bro. David Boone, C.O., Parish Life Facilitator; Sr. Mary John Nguyen, F.M.S.R., Parish Life Facilitator.
Bannon Hall, 902 Crawford Ave., P.O. Box 11982, 29731. Tel: 803-329-1008; Fax: 803-329-3799. Email: stmary@comporium.net. Web: www.catholic-doc.org/stmaryrh/index.html.
Catechesis/Religious Program—Students 57.
Convent—916 Crawford Rd., 29730. Tel: 803-327-7450. Daughters of Our Lady of the Holy Rosary.
St. Martin de Porres Parish Center—911 Crawford Rd., 29730.

SANTEE, ORANGEBURG CO., ST. ANN (2004) Rev. David R. Whitman, Admin.; Deacon Robert C. Kronyak.
Mailing Address: P.O. Box 250, 29142.
Church: 2205 State Park Rd., 29142. Tel: 803-854-5075; Fax: 803-485-8592.
Catechesis/Religious Program—Students 8.

SIMPSONVILLE, GREENVILLE CO., ST. MARY MAGDALENE (1989) Revs. Teofilo Trujillo; James N. Dubrouillet, Parochial Vicar. In Res., Rev. Robert Falabella; Deacons Matthew A. Mannino; Gabriel Cuervo.
Church & Office: 2252 Woodruff Rd., 29681. Tel: 864-288-4884; Fax: 864-297-5804. Web: smmcc.org.
Catechesis/Religious Program—Tel: 864-288-4884, Ext. 205. Students 1,118.

SPARTANBURG, SPARTANBURG CO.

1—JESUS OUR RISEN SAVIOR (1978) Revs. Frank Palmieri, C.R.M., Admin.; Oscar Borda Rojas (Colombia); Teodoro Kalaw, C.R.M., Parochial Vicar; Deacons Robert M. Sturm, Parish Life Facilitator; Paul F. Shook.
2575 Reidville Rd., 29301. Tel: 864-576-1164; 864-574-8117 (Rectory); Fax: 864-576-0860. Web: www.jors.cc.
Catechesis/Religious Program—Nancy Cormack, D.R.E. Students 450.

2—ST. JOSEPH'S, Closed. For inquiries for parish records contact St. Paul the Apostle, Spartanburg.

3—ST. PAUL THE APOSTLE (1883) Revs. Timothy Gahan, Admin.; Michael F. McCafferty; Deacons Robert L. Mahaffey Jr.; Harry Pecko.
161 N. Dean St., 29302. Tel: 864-582-0674; Fax: 864-582-0716. Web: www.st-paultheapostle.org.
School—(Grades K-8), 152 Alabama St., 29302. Tel: 864-582-6645; Fax: 864-582-1225. Patricia Lanthier, Prin. Lay Teachers 18; Students 150.

Catechesis/Religious Program—Tel: 864-585-1858; Fax: 864-582-0716. Students 203.

SUMMERTON, CLARENDON CO., ST. MARY (1914) Rev. David R. Whitman, Admin.; Deacon Charles Michael Walsh.
12 N. Cantey St., P.O. Box 1110, 29148. Tel: 803-485-2925; Fax: 803-485-8592.
Catechesis/Religious Program—Tel: 803-478-4333.
Mission—Our Lady of Hope Mission 2451 Raccoon Rd., Manning, Clarendon Co. 29102.

SUMMERVILLE, DORCHESTER CO.

1—ST. JOHN THE BELOVED (1898) Rev. Msgr. E. Christopher Lathem; Deacons Michael P. O'Connor; J. Wescoat Sandlin.
28 Sumter Ave., 29483. Tel: 843-873-0631; Fax: 843-873-1431. Email: schurchrectory@sc.rr.com. Web: www.stjohnthebelovedcatholic.org.
School—Summerville Catholic School, (Grades K-8), 226 Black Oak Blvd., 29483. Tel: 843-873-9310; Fax: 843-873-5709. Lisa Tanner, Prin. Sisters 1; Lay Teachers 21; Students 265.
Catechesis/Religious Program—Students 230.

2—ST. THERESA THE LITTLE FLOWER (1984) Rev. Msgr. Edward D. Lofton; Deacons Shane Graham; Eugene Phillips.
11001 Dorchester Rd., 29485. Tel: 843-875-5002; 843-875-6911; Fax: 843-875-4884. Email: office@sttheresachurch.com.
Catechesis/Religious Program—Students 130.
Station—Charleston Detention Center

SUMTER, SUMTER CO.

1—ST. ANNE (1911) [CEM] Revs. Thomas Burke, C.Ss.R.; James Burke, C.Ss.R.; Deacons Billy J. Ellis; Michael Kulungowski.
216 E. Liberty St., 29150. Tel: 803-773-3524; Fax: 803-778-1644. Web: stannesumtersc.org.
School—(Grades K-8) Tel: 803-775-3632; Fax: 803-938-9074. Ms. Kristi Doyle, Prin. Lay Teachers 13; Students 180.
Catechesis/Religious Program—Tel: 803-755-0764. Students 100.

2—ST. JUDE (1939) Revs. Charles Donovan, C.Ss.R.; James Burke, C.Ss.R.; Deacon Lawrence Corum.
611 W. Oakland Ave., P.O. Box 1589, 29151. Tel: 803-773-9244; Fax: 803-775-6913. Email: stjudeschur@sc.rr.com. Web: stjudesumtersc.org.
Catechesis/Religious Program—Tel: 803-778-6404. Students 94.

TAYLORS, GREENVILLE CO., PRINCE OF PEACE (1975) Rev. Msgr. Steven L. Brovey; Deacons Gary Walczak; Bob Smith.
1209 Brushy Creek Rd., 29687-4103. Tel: 864-268-4352; Fax: 864-322-2239. Email: taylorspop@juno.com. Web: www.princeofpeacesc.org.
School—(Grades K-4) Tel: 864-331-2145; Fax: 864-331-2153. Dr. Michael Pennell, Prin. Child Development Center
Catechesis/Religious Program—Tel: 864-331-3919. Students 337.

UNION, UNION CO., ST. AUGUSTINE (1967) Rev. Michael F. McCafferty, Admin.; Deacon William Bower.
Mailing Address: P.O. Box 507, 29379. Tel: 864-427-7240; Fax: 864-427-7240.
103 E. South St., 29379.

WALTERBORO, COLLETON CO.

1—ST. ANTHONY (1917) [CEM] Rev. Donald S. Abbott, Admin.
925 S. Jefferies Blvd., 29488. Tel: 843-549-5230; Fax: 843-549-9176.
Catechesis/Religious Program—Students 53.
Mission—St. James the Greater [CEM] 3087 Ritter Rd., Colleton Co. 29488.

2—ST. JOSEPH, Closed. For inquiries for parish records contact St. Anthony.

WARD, SALUDA CO., ST. WILLIAM (1895) [CEM] Rev. Noel Tria (Philippines), Canonical Mod./Admin.; Deacon John P. Klein, Parish Life Facilitator.
1199 Ridge Spring Hwy., 29166. Tel: 864-445-7215; Fax: 864-445-1150. Email: stwill@pbtcomm.net.
Catechesis/Religious Program—Students 50.

YONGES ISLAND, CHARLESTON CO., ST. MARY (1911) Rev. Anthony Benjamine (India).
4255 State Hwy. 165, 29449. Tel: 843-889-8549; Fax: 843-889-8549.
Catechesis/Religious Program—Students 4.
Mission—SS. Frederick & Stephen P.O. Box 602, Edisto Island, Charleston Co. 29438. Tel: 843-869-0124; Fax: 843-869-0124.

YORK, YORK CO., DIVINE SAVIOUR (1938) Revs. Elbano Munoz, C.O., Admin.; William F. Pentis, C.O., Canonical Pastor; Deacon Melvin W. Carroll.
Mailing Address: P.O. Box 341, 29745. Email: divsaviour@comporium.net.
232 Herndon Ave., 29745. Tel: 803-684-3431; Fax: 803-684-3431.
Catechesis/Religious Program—Students 88.
Mission—All Saints P.O. Box 5443, Lake Wylie, York Co. 29710. Tel: 803-831-9095; Fax: 803-831-9096. Email: allsaintsparish@bellsouth.net. Web: www.allsaintscatholicmission.org.

Chaplains of Public Institutions

LEXINGTON. *Correctional Institutions in the Greater Columbia Area*, 4214 Grand St., 29203. Tel: 803-786-7177. Mr. Roland L. Thomas.

Graduate Studies:
Revs.—
Kirby, Jeffrey, Pontifical North American College, Rome
Miles, Thomas, St. Paul University, Ottawa, ON

Military Chaplains:
Revs.—
Linsky, Gary S., U.S. Air Force
Spencer, Robert A., U.S. Navy

Absent On Leave:
Very Rev.—
West, Gregory
Revs.—
Bush, Carson
Congro, Basil P.
Davino, Michael J.
Morrison, Thomas F.
Robinson, Ralph C.
Sorce, John J.
Watters, Timothy J.

Retired:
Most Rev.—
Thompson, David B., D.D., J.C.L.
Rev. Msgrs.—
Gorski, J. Donald, 43155 Portola Ave., SPC 120, Palm Desert, CA 92260-2547.
Simonin, John A., 826 N. Shem Dr., Mt. Pleasant, 29464-4009.
Revs.—
Cilwick, Theodore T., 1600 Ingram Rd., Apt. 101, 29407.
Clarke, Peter, S.T.D., North Augusta, 29861.
Day, Charles J.
Fix, Robert H., 1660 Ingram Rd., Columbia, 29205.
Kennedy, Ernest E.
Leonard, Eugene A., 347 W. Pointe, Spartanburg, 29301.
McCaffrey, Edmund M., Ph.D.
Parker, James
Riplog, Duane T., 298 Summerset Ln., Summerville, 29483-8338.
Seitz, Paul F.X.
Snopek, Charles J.
Ward, Jerome A., O.M.I., 5001 Bedfordshire Dr., Fort Worth, TX 76135.

Permanent Deacons:
Anderson, Ronald J., St. Peter, Columbia
Anonie, Joseph A., Immaculate Conception Church, Goose Creek
Armstrong, Reginald, St. Anthony, Florence
Arnold, Mark, (On Duty Outside the Diocese)
Baranoski, Thomas, St. Joseph, Charleston
Barlow, Robert, St. Andrew, Myrtle Beach
Beeler, Michael A., St. Peter, Beaufort
Biviano, Joseph P., Our Lady of the Lake Church, Chapin
Bower, William, St. Augustine, Union
Brown, John H., (Retired)
Burdick, Steve, Our Lady of the Hills, Columbia
Burkett, Dennis, St. Gregory the Great, Bluffton
Cahill, Joseph F., Christ Our King Church, Mount Pleasant
Campana, Richard, Sr., St. Andrew, Clemson; St. Francis Mission, Walhalla; St. Paul the Apostle Mission, Seneca
Cardenas, Mario, Holy Spirit, Johns Island
Carmody, Joseph E., (Retired)
Carroll, Melvin W., Divine Saviour, York
Cassandra, Anthony J., St. Luke, Easley
Collins, James, Church of the Resurrection, Loris
Corum, Lawrence, St. Jude, Sumter
Crocker, Jack L., D.D.S., Corpus Christi, Lexington
Cuervo, Gabriel, Blessed Trinity, Greer
Cuomo, Nicholas G., (Retired)
Curcio, Peter A., Christ the Divine Teacher, Charleston
D'Angelo, V. Richard, St. Gregory the Great, Bluffton
Dashnaw, Donald R., Ph.D., Ed.D., Divine Redeemer, Hanahan
Davis, Thomas E., (On Duty Outside the Diocese)
Delmonte, Richard, (Retired)
DeNitto, Donald, Church of the Infant Jesus, Marion
DeWolfe, John, Holy Family, Hilton Head
Dillard, Henry, St. Anthony of Padua, Greenville
DiRusso, Charles R., Our Lady of the Hills, Columbia
Dotson, Robert E., (Retired)
Drinkwater, Oscar, (Retired)
Dwyer, Jon E., St. Philip Neri, Fort Mill
Easterling, Charles M., St. Peter, Columbia
Efken, Donald C., St. Michael, Garden City
Egendoerfer, Eugene, St. Luke, Easley
Ellis, Billy J., St. Anne, Sumter
Ferland, George, St. Andrew, Myrtle Beach
Ferro, Diego, St. Mary, Greenville
Fiore, Charlie, St. Michael, Garden City
Gerald, Robert C., Jr., St. Anne, Florence
Gorman, Chester E., Our Lady of the Sea, North Myrtle Beach
Graham, James, St. Gregory the Great, Bluffton
Graham, Shane, St. Theresa the Little Flower, Summerville
Grismore, Gerald W., Stella Maris, Sullivan's Island
Guillet, Andre, Christ Our King, Mount Pleasant
Hand, Gerald, St. Francis by the Sea, Hilton Head
Hanvey, Samuel E., (Retired)
Heuser, John, St. Mary, Greenville
Hollis, Walter W., St. Gregory the Great, Bluffton
Hookness, Robert, Our Lady of Peace, North Augusta
Houle, Matthew, St. Francis by the Sea, Hilton Head Island
Hyland, James P., St. Peter, Beaufort
Jackson, Harold I., St. Ann, Kingstree
Jacobi, Robert, (Retired)
Johnson, James H., St. Ann, Florence
Johson, Carl, St. Martin de Porres, Columbia
Jones, Dennis N., Our Lady of the Hills, Columbia
Jones, Robert, St. Michael, Garden City
Karandisevsky, John F., (Retired)
Kemper, Joseph G., (Retired)
Klein, John P., St. William, Ward
Kronyak, Robert C., St. Ann, Holly Hill
Kulungowski, Michael, St. Anne, Sumter
La Rosa, P. Charles, Jr., Our Lady of the Lake, Chapin
LaCombe, William, St. Peter, Beaufort
Larkin, John S., St. Mary, the Virgin Mother, Hartsville
Loignon, Gerald, Jr., St. Mark, Newberry
Mahaffey, Robert L., Jr., St. Paul the Apostle, Spartanburg
Mahefky, Paul, St. Mary, Georgetown
Mannino, Matthew A., St. Mary Magdalene, Simpsonville
McDonald, Thomas F., (Retired)
McNerny, Daniel, Immaculate Conception, Goose Creek
Mevissen, Jeffrey P., St. James, Conway
Meyer, Philip M.
Moore, James R., Blessed Sacrament, Charleston
Moore, Oliver R., St. Anne, Rock Hill
Moynihan, Patrick, St. Andrew, Clemson; St. Paul the Apostle, Seneca; St. Francis, Walhalla
Murtgaugh, Richard J., Jr., St. Elizabeth Ann Seton, Mauldin
Nazzaro, Joseph J., St. Francis by the Sea, Hilton Head
Nunez, Guillermo, St. Anne, Rock Hill
Olimpio, Charles, Cathedral of St. John the Baptist, Charleston
Osbourne, R. Michael, Stella Maris, Sullivan's Island
Palmer, Orean D., Corpus Christi, Lexington
Parks, Coleman T., Corpus Christi, Lexington
Payne, Alfred, (On Duty Outside the Diocese)
Peacock, Terry, (On Duty Outside the Diocese)
Pecko, Harry, (Retired)
Peitler, Edward, St. Peter, Beaufort
Perham, Raymond, Our Lady of the Rosary, Greenville
Petrusak, Frank T., (Retired)
Pezanowski, Walter S., Stella Maris, Sullivan's Island
Phillips, Eugene, St. Theresa the Little Flower, Summerville
Pierce, Robert A., St. Mary Help of Christians, Aiken
Pierfy, Jeffery, St. Anthony, Florence
Poole, Charles P., Jr., (Retired)
Ramirez, Jorge V.
Remkiewicz, Jerome P., Cathedral of St. John the Baptist/St. Mary, Charleston
Rhodes, Steven, St. Philip Neri, Fort Mill
Richardson, David W. (NTN), Melkite Community
Roberts, Lawrence, Immaculate Conception, Goose Creek
Roseborough, Donald, (On Duty Outside the Diocese)
Sams, Gregory W., St. Gregory the Great, Bluffton
Sandlin, J. Wescoat, St. John the Beloved, Summerville
Sheehan, Patrick, St. Francis by the Sea, Hilton Head Island
Shito, Albert, St. Anthony, Hardesville
Shook, Paul F., (Retired)
Smith, Robert, Prince of Peace, Taylors
Starr, Robert, St. Michael, Garden City
Stetar, John, St. Peter, Columbia

Stoshak, Andrew, Our Lady Star of the Sea, North Myrtle Beach
Sturm, Robert M., Jesus, Our Risen Savior, Spartanburg
Thompson, David, St. Peter, Columbia
Tierney, George, St. Mary, Greenville
Traxler, Harold G., Jr., (Retired)
Tyson, Robert, Our Lady Star of the Sea, North Myrtle Beach
Walczak, Gary, Prince of Peace, Taylors
Walsh, Charles Michael, St. Mary; Our Lady of Hope, Manning
Waters, Robert J., Our Lady of the Valley, Gloverville
Weigold, Gregory, Our Lady of the Lake, Chapin
West, James L., (On Duty Outside the Diocese)
William, W. James, III, St. Anthony of Padua, Greenville
Wright, Winston C., St. Anthony of Padua, Greenville

INSTITUTIONS LOCATED IN THE DIOCESE

[A] HIGH SCHOOLS, DIOCESAN

CHARLESTON. *Bishop England High School*, 363 Seven Farms Dr., 29492-7534. Tel: 843-849-9599; Fax: 843-849-9221. Email: dheld@behs.com. Web: www.behs.com. Mr. David F. Held, Prin.; Cindi Haviland, Librarian. Lay Teachers 62; Students 730.

COLUMBIA. *Cardinal Newman School*, (Grades 7-12), 4701 Forest Dr., 29206. Tel: 803-782-2814; Fax: 803-782-9314. Email: jkasprowski@cnhs.org. Web: www.cnhs.org. Jacqualine Kasprowski, Prin.; Kathleen Cole, Librarian. Sisters 1; Lay Teachers 51; Students 455.

[B] HIGH SCHOOLS, PRIVATE

GREENVILLE. *St. Joseph's Catholic School* (1993) (Grades 6-12), 100 St. Joseph's Dr., 29607. Tel: 864-234-9009; Fax: 864-234-5516. Email: info@sjcatholicschool.org. Web: www.sjcatholicschool.org. Keith F. Kiser, Headmaster. Lay Teachers 47; Total Staff 69; Students 544.

SUMTER. *St. Francis Xavier High School* (1997) 15 School St., 29150. Tel: 803-773-0210; Fax: 803-775-0119. Email: sfxhs@sc.rr.com. Web: www.sfxhs.com. Susan Lavergne, Prin.; Ilknur Leverich, Librarian. Lay Teachers 8; Students 42.

[C] GENERAL HOSPITALS

CHARLESTON. *Bon Secours St. Francis Hospital* (1882) 2095 Henry Tecklenburg Dr., 29414. Tel: 843-402-1000; Fax: 843-402-1945. Email: allen.carroll@ropersaintfrancis.com. Web: www.ropersaintfrancis.com. Sr. Alice Talone, C.B.S., Pres., Sisters of Bon Secours USA; Mr. Allen P. Carroll, CEO; Robert Morris, Dir. Clinical Pastoral Educ. Sponsored by the Sisters of Bon Secours, Marriottsville, MD. Bed Capacity 204; Total Staff 1,058; Patients Assisted Annually 115,276.

GREENVILLE. *Bon Secours St. Francis Health System, Inc.*, One St. Francis Dr., 29601. Tel: 864-255-1000; Fax: 864-255-1137. Web: www.stfrancishealth.org.

St. Francis Hospital, Inc. Tel: 864-255-1000; Fax: 864-255-1137. John Shea, Interim CEO; Elizabeth Keith, Senior V.P. Mission. Sisters of Bon Secours 2; Bed Capacity 338; Total Staff 2,619; Patients Assisted Annually 181,123.

[D] HOMES FOR AGED

CHARLESTON. *Carter-May Home Assisted Living & St. Joseph Residence for Retired Priests*, 1660 Ingram Rd., 29407. Tel: 843-556-8314; Fax: 843-556-6879. Email: janine@catholic-doc.org. Mrs. Janine N. Bauder, Admin. Bed Capacity 25; Total Staff 20; Total Assisted Annually 25.

[E] MONASTERIES AND RESIDENCES OF PRIESTS AND BROTHERS

MONCKS CORNER. *Mepkin Abbey* (1949) (Trappist Monks), 1098 Mepkin Abbey Rd., 29461-4796. Tel: 843-761-8509; Fax: 843-761-6719. Email: community@mepkinabbey.org. Web: www.mepkinabbey.org. Rt. Revs. Stanislaus Gumula, O.C.S.O., Abbot; Christian Aidan Carr, O.C.S.O. (Retired); Revs. Kevin V. Walsh, O.C.S.O, Contact Person & Novice Dir.; Leonard A. Cunningham, O.C.S.O.; Aelred Hagan, O.C.S.O.; Guerric Frederick A. Heckel; Feliciano Manalili, O.C.S.O.; Richard G. McGuire, O.C.S.O.; Bros. Stephen Petronek, O.C.S.O.; John Corrigan, Cellarer. Professed Monks 16; Priests 8; Postulants 1; Novices 2; Total in Community 19.

ROCK HILL. *Oratory of St. Philip Neri, Congregation of the Oratory of Pontifical Rite*, 434 Charlotte Ave., P.O. Box 11586, 29731. Tel: 803-327-2097; Fax: 803-327-6264. Email: rhoratory@comporium.net. Web: www.rockhilloratory.org. P.O. Box 11586, 29731-1586. Tel: 803-327-2097; Fax: 803-327-6264. Very Rev. Joseph A. Wahl, C.O., S.T.D., Provost; Revs. William F. Pentis, C.O., Deputy; Edward P. McDevitt, C.O.; Bro. David Boone, C.O., Deputy; Revs. Robert S. Dell, C.O.; John P. Giuliani, C.O., Deputy; James Moran, C.O.; Halbert Weidner, C.O., Ph.D.; Clarence Edward Jones, C.O.; Joseph Francis Pearce, C.O.; David D. Valtierra, C.O., Vicar; Adilso Coelho, C.O.; Fabio Refosco, C.O., Treas.; Elbano Munoz, C.O. Fathers 13; Brothers 5; Seminarians 2.

[F] CONVENTS AND RESIDENCES FOR SISTERS

CHARLESTON. *Daughters of St. Paul Convent*, 243 King St., 29401. Tel: 843-577-0175; Fax: 843-577-9833. Email: charleston@pauline.org. Web: www.pauline.org. Sr. Jane Livingston, Local Supr. Sisters 4.

Sisters of Charity of Our Lady of Mercy (1829) 424 Ft. Johnson Rd., P.O. Box 12410, 29422. Tel: 843-795-6083; Fax: 843-795-6083. Email: olm@comcast.com. Sr. Bridget Sullivan, O.L.M., Gen. Supr. Tel: 843-795-2866. Professed Sisters in Community 21.

ST. HELENA ISLAND. *Franciscan Center*, 85 Mattis Rd., U.S. Hwy. 21, P.O. Box 682, 29920. Tel: 843-838-3924; Fax: 843-838-2152. Email: franctr@islc.net. Web: www.islc.net/~franctr. Sisters of St. Francis of Philadelphia, Glen Riddle-Aston, PA 2.

TRAVELERS REST. *Monastery of St. Clare*, 37 McCouley Rd., 29690. Tel: 864-834-8015; Fax: 864-834-5402. Email: oscgreenville@juno.com. Web: www.poorclaresc.com. Sr. Mary Connor, O.S.C., Abbess. Franciscan Poor Clare Nuns. Cloistered Nuns in Solemn Vows 15; Extern in Perpetual Vows 1; Novices 2.

[G] CATHOLIC CHARITIES

CHARLESTON. *Catholic Charities of the Diocese of Charleston*, 1662 Ingram Rd., 29407. Tel: 843-402-9115, Ext. 15; Fax: 843-402-9071. Email: epeitler@catholic-doc.org. Web: www.supportcatholiccharities.org. Deacon Ed Peitler, Ph.D., Dir.

Coastal Regional Office, 3921 St. John's Ave., North Charleston, 29405-7158. Tel: 843-308-9361; Fax: 843-308-9361. Email: holeary@catholic-doc.org. Helen O'Leary, Regl. Coord.

Midlands Regional Office, P.O. Box 7245, Columbia, 29202-7245. Tel: 803-254-9776; Fax: 803-252-7605. Email: mgohean@catholic-doc.org. Mary Gohean, Regl. Coord.

Pee Dee Regional Office, 407 Blossom St., P.O. Box 3091, Conway, 29528. Tel: 843-488-2112; Fax: 843-488-0658. Daryl Kangarloo, Regl. Coord.

Piedmont Regional Office, 204 Douthit St., Ste. A1, Greenville, 29601. Tel: 864-242-2233; Fax: 864-242-1387. Deacon Gabriel Cuervo, Regl. Coord.

Lowcounty Regional Office, 70 Lady's Island Dr., Beaufort, 29907. Tel: 843-522-6518; Fax: 843-379-5330. Deacon James P. Hyland, Regl. Coord.

Echo House-Inner City Apostolate (1967) 1911 Hackermann Ave., North Charleston, 29405. Tel: 843-554-7319; Fax: 843-225-8090.

[H] CAMPUS MINISTRIES

CHARLESTON. *Catholic Campus Ministry at the College of Charleston c/o St. Patrick*, 134 St. Phillip St., 29413. Tel: 843-937-5993; Fax: 843-881-7072. Email: cofcatholics@aol.com.

Charleston Southern University P.O. Box 118087, 29423-8087. Tel: 843-863-7081. Email: emcdermo@csuniv.edu. Rev. William F. Leonard; Dr. Eugene McDermott, Ph.D., Faculty Advisor.

The Citadel Office of the Catholic Chaplain, The Citadel, MSC 58, 29409-0058. Tel: 843-953-7692; Fax: 843-953-4811. Web: citadel.edu/catholic.

AIKEN. *University of South Carolina, Aiken Extension c/o St. Mary Help of Christians*, P.O. Box 438, 29802. Tel: 803-649-4777.

BEAUFORT. *University of South Carolina, Beaufort Extension St. Peter*, 70 Lady's Island Dr., 29907. Tel: 843-522-9555. Rev. Timothy D. Tebalt.

CLEMSON. *Clemson University, Southern Wesleyan University & TriCounty Technical College* P.O. Box 112, 29633. 209 Sloan St., 29633. Tel: 864-654-7804; 864-654-1757; 864-654-9670; Fax: 864-654-2950. Email: csa@clemson.edu. Web: www.clemson.edu/~csa. Revs. C. Alexander McDonald; Emmanuel Andinam (Nigeria), Campus Min.; Mr. Fred Mercadante, Campus Min.

Clemson University - Catholic Campus Ministry at St. Andrew's Church and the Catholic Student Association.

CLINTON. *Presbyterian College c/o St. Mark*, 928 Boundary St., Newberry, 29108. Tel: 803-276-6446; Fax: 803-276-0856.

COLUMBIA. *Allen University, Benedict College* c/o St. Martin de Porres Church, 2229 Hampton St., 29204. Tel: 803-254-6862; Fax: 803-799-4720. Email: deporres@yahoo.com. Very Rev. Paul M. Williams, O.F.M., V.F.

St. Thomas More Center 1610 Greene St., 29201. Tel: 803-799-5870; Fax: 803-765-0800. Email: stmcola@gmail.com. Web: www.stthomasmoreusc.org. Rev. Marcin Zahuta (Poland), Chap. & Campus Min.

CONWAY. *Coastal Carolina University Catholic Campus Ministry*, P.O. Box 261954, 29528. Tel: 843-349-2026; Fax: 843-349-2127.

FLORENCE. *Francis Marion University c/o St. Ann Church*, 113 S. Kemp St., 29506. Tel: 843-661-5012; Fax: 843-673-2680. Rev. John M. Zimmerman.

GAFFNEY. *Limestone College c/o Sacred Heart Church*, 407 Grace St., 29340. Tel: 864-649-1280; Fax: 864-649-1281. Email: sacredheartgaffney@charterinternet.com. Rev. Francisco Cruz (Colombia).

GREENVILLE. *Furman University Campus Ministry St. Mary's Catholic Church*, 111 Hampton Ave., 29601. Tel: 864-271-8422; Fax: 864-370-9880. Email: churchoffice@stmarysgvl.org. Web: www.stmarysgvl.org. Rev. Jay Scott Newman, J.C.L.; Dan Sloughter, Faculty Advisor. Students 300.

GREENWOOD. *Lander University c/o Our Lady of Lourdes*, 915 Mathis Rd., 29646. Tel: 864-223-8410; Fax: 864-223-7555. Email: frtebalt@olol.org. Rev. Timothy D. Tebalt.

HARTSVILLE. *Coker College c/o St. Mary the Virgin Mother*, 363 N. Fifth St., 29550. Tel: 843-332-7773; 843-332-3136; Fax: 843-332-2812. Email: stmary2@ymail.com. Very Rev. Karl J. Roesch, O.S.B., V.F.

ORANGEBURG. *South Carolina State University & Claflin College* P.O. Box 1691, 29116. Tel: 803-534-8177; Fax: 803-535-0012.

ROCK HILL. *Winthrop University, York Co. Tech Center c/o The Oratory of St. Philip Neri*, 434 Charlotte Ave., Box 11586, 29731. Tel: 803-327-6450; Fax: 803-327-6450. Email: valtiera@navacore.net. Rev. David D. Valtierra, C.O.

SPARTANBURG. *Converse College c/o St. Paul the Apostle*, 161 N. Dean St., 29302. Tel: 864-582-0674; Fax: 864-582-0716. Web: www.st-paultheapostle.org. Rev. Teodoro Kalaw, C.R.M.

Wofford College 429 N. Church St., 29303-3668. Tel: 864-597-4180. Mr. Doyle Boggs, Advisor.

[I] RETREAT CENTERS

EDISTO ISLAND. *Sea of Peace House of Prayer* (1995) 542 Palmetto Pointe Rd., 29438. Tel: 843-869-0513. Email: sharonculhane@bellsouth.net. Web: www.seaofpeacehouseofprayer.org.

[J] MISCELLANEOUS

CHARLESTON. *The Barry Charitable Trust*, 424 Ft. Johnson Rd., P.O. Box 12410, 29422. Tel: 843-795-2866; Fax: 843-795-6083.

Catholic Radio Association, 121 Broad St., 29401. Tel: 843-853-2300. Web: www.catholicradioassociation.org. Stephen Gajdosik, Pres.; Douglas Sherman, Chm.

Catholic Stewardship Charitable Trust of South Carolina, 1662 Ingram Rd., 29407.

Ladies of Charity of Sacred Heart Church, 888 King St., 29403-4138. Tel: 843-722-7018.

Our Lady of Mercy Community Outreach Services, Inc./Neighborhood House, 77 America St., 29403. Tel: 843-853-8329; Fax: 843-853-8329. Email: neighborhoodhse@bellsouth.net; srpat@bellsouth.net. Sponsored by the Sisters of Charity of Our Lady of Mercy. Total Assisted Annually 47,810.

Pauline Books & Media, 243 King St., 29401. Tel: 843-577-0175; Fax: 843-577-9833. Email: charleston@pauline.org. Web: www.pauline.org. Daughters of St. Paul.

AIKEN. *Society of St. Vincent de Paul*, 190 Hunting Hills Dr., 29803. Tel: 803-641-3875. Email: greg_flach@bellsouth.net. Greg Flach, Diocesan Council Pres.; Oren Guidry, Piedmont District Council Pres.; Donna Willis, Midlands District Council Pres.

BLUFFTON. *Divine Mercy Hermitage, Inc.*, 38 Huquenin Ln., 29909. Tel: 843-304-5569. Email: srmjj@msn.com. Elizabeth Menendez, Contact Person.

COLUMBIA. *Family Honor, Inc.* (1987) 2927 Devine St., Ste. 130, 29205. Tel: 803-929-0858; Fax: 803-771-2379. Email: famhonor@aol.com. Web: www.familyhonor.org. Brenda Cerkez, Exec. Dir.

Sisters of Charity Foundation of South Carolina, 2711 Middleburg Dr., Ste. 115, 29204-2413. Tel: 803-254-0230; Fax: 803-748-0444. Email: scfsc@sistersofcharitysc.com. Web: www.sistersofcharitysc.com.

Sisters of Charity Ministry Development Corporation, 2711 Middlebury Dr., Ste. 204, 29204-2413. Tel: 216-696-5560; Fax: 216-696-2204. Web: www.CSAHealthSystems.org. Sr. Judith Ann Karam, C.S.A., Pres. & CEO.

Sisters of Charity Providence Hospitals, 2435 Forest Dr., 29204. Tel: 803-256-5313; Fax: 803-296-5765. Email: George.Zara@providencehospitals.com.

GREENVILLE. *SFH, Inc.*, One St. Francis Dr., 29601. Tel: 864-255-1000; Fax: 864-255-1137. Web: www.stfrancishealth.org.

HILTON HEAD. *Nazareth Hermitage*, 21 Angel Wing Dr., Hilton Head Island, 29926. Tel: 843-681-2189; Fax: 843-682-2339. Doris Hadden, Contact Person.

JOHNS ISLAND. *Our Lady of Mercy Community Outreach Services, Inc.* (1989) 1684 Brownswood Rd., 29455. Tel: 843-559-4109; Fax: 843-559-8819. Email: olmoutreach@aol.com. Web: olmoutreach.org. P.O. Box 607, 29457. Tel: 843-559-4109; Fax: 843-558-8819. Sponsored by Sisters of Charity of Our Lady of Mercy. Total Staff 25; Outreach Center 9,693; Wellness Center 3,834.

KINGSTREE. *Shrine of Our Lady of South Carolina-Our Lady of Joyful Hope* 313 E. Main St., Hwy. 261, 29556. Tel: 843-355-3527. Email: frss@ftc-i.net. Web: www.ourladyofsouthcarolina.net. Mailing Address: 300 Ashton Ave., 29556-4036. Rev. Stanley Smolenski, S.P.M.A., Office of the Shrine Dir. Administered by the Diocese of Charleston, 330 Main St., Charleston, SC 29556.

MYRTLE BEACH. *Bishop Baker Catholic High School Association*, 3501 N. Kings Hwy., Ste. 102, 29577.

RELIGIOUS INSTITUTES OF MEN REPRESENTED IN THE DIOCESE

For further details refer to the corresponding bracketed number in the Religious Institutes of Men or Women section.

[0100]—*Adorno Fathers*—C.R.M.
[0200]—*Benedictines*—O.S.B.
[]—*Carmelites of Mary Immaculate*—C.M.I.
[0350]—*Cistercians Order of the Strict Observance-Trappist*—O.C.S.O.
[0310]—*Congregation of Christian Brothers*—C.F.C.
[]—*Congregation of Holy Cross*—C.S.C.
[]—*Dominicans*—O.P.
[0520]—*Franciscan Friars* (Prov. of the Most Holy Name)—O.F.M.
[0690]—*Jesuit Fathers and Brothers* (New Orleans; New England Provs.)—S.J.
[1110]—*Missionaries of the Sacred Heart*—M.S.C.
[0910]—*Oblates of Mary Immaculate* (Eastern American Prov.)—O.M.I.
[0950]—*Oratorians*—C.O.
[1070]—*Redemptorist Fathers* (Richmond Vice Prov.)—C.SS.R.

RELIGIOUS INSTITUTES OF WOMEN REPRESENTED IN THE DIOCESE

[0270]—*Congregation of Bon Secours*—C.B.S.
[1000]—*Congregation of Divine Providence* (KY)—C.D.P.
[1730]—*Congregation of the Sisters of the Third Order of St. Francis* (Oldenburg, IN)—O.S.F.
[0760]—*Daughters of Charity of St. Vincent de Paul*—D.C.
[0960]—*Daughters of Wisdom* (American Prov.)—D.W.
[1070-03]—*Dominican Sisters* (Sinsinawa, WI)—O.P.
[1070-04]—*Dominican Sisters* (San Rafael, CA)—O.P.
[]—*Dominican Sisters* (Nashville, TN)—O.P.
[]—*Dominican Sisters* (Ann Arbor, MI)—O.P.
[1070-11]—*Dominican Sisters* (Sparkill, NY)—O.P.
[1070-13]—*Dominican Sisters* (Adrian, MI)—O.P.
[1170]—*Felician Sisters*—C.S.S.F.
[1415]—*Franciscan Sisters of Mary*—F.S.M.
[1425]—*Franciscan Sisters of Peace*—F.S.P.
[1440]—*Franciscan Sisters of the Poor*—S.F.P.
[1360]—*Missionary Franciscan Sisters of the Immaculate Conception*—M.F.I.C.
[2790]—*Missionary Servants of the Most Blessed Trinity*—M.S.B.T.
[3760]—*Order of St. Clare*—O.S.C.
[0950]—*Pious Daughters of St. Paul*—F.S.P.
[2970]—*School Sisters of Notre Dame*—S.S.N.D.
[0500]—*Sisters of Charity of Nazareth*—S.C.N.
[0510]—*Sisters of Charity of Our Lady of Mercy*—O.L.M.
[0580]—*Sisters of Charity of St. Augustine*—C.S.A.
[2575]—*Sisters of Mercy of the Americas* (Chicago, IL; Pittsburgh, PA)—R.S.M.
[3000]—*Sisters of Notre Dame* (Baltimore, MD)—S.N.D.deN.
[2990]—*Sisters of Notre Dame* (Toledo, OH)—S.N.D.
[3950]—*Sisters of Saint Mary of Namur*—S.S.M.N.
[3780]—*Sisters of Saints Cyril and Methodius*—SS.C.M.
[1540]—*Sisters of St. Francis* (Clinton, IA)—O.S.F.
[1620]—*Sisters of St. Francis of Millvale, Pennsylvania*—O.S.F.
[1650]—*Sisters of St. Francis of Philadelphia*—O.S.F.
[1570]—*Sisters of St. Francis of the Holy Family*—O.S.F.
[1800]—*Sisters of St. Francis of the Third Order Regular* (Williamsville, New York)—O.S.F.
[3840]—*Sisters of St. Joseph of Carondelet* (Prov. of St. Louis)—C.S.J.
[2110]—*Sisters of the Humility of Mary*—H.M.
[]—*Sisters of the Sacred Heart of Jesus* (Mexico)—H.C.J.S.
[1720]—*Sisters of the Third Order of St. Francis of the Congregation of Our Lady of Lourdes* (Rochester)—O.S.F.
[1890]—*Society of Helpers*—H.H.S.
[4048]—*Society of Sisters Faithful Companions of Jesus*—F.C.J.
[4120-03]—*Ursuline Nuns, of the Congregation of Paris*—O.S.U.

DIOCESAN CEMETERIES

CHARLESTON. *St. Lawrence and Holy Cross*, 604 Ft. Johnson Rd., 29412. Tel: 843-795-2111. Mr. Warren R. Stuckey Jr., Dir.

NECROLOGY

† Bench, John F., (Retired)—Died June 6, 2009
† Burn, William C., (Retired)—Died May 29, 2009
† Ninedorf, Robert W., (Retired)—Died July 6, 2009

An asterisk (*) denotes an organization that has established tax-exempt status directly with the IRS and is not covered by the USCCB Group Ruling.

Diocese of Charlotte

(Dioecesis Carolinana)

CARITAS CHRISTI URGET NOS

Most Reverend

PETER J. JUGIS, J.C.D.

Bishop of Charlotte; ordained June 12, 1983; appointed Bishop of Charlotte August 1, 2003; episcopal ordination October 24, 2003.

Chancery: P.O. Box 36776, Charlotte, NC 28236. Tel: 704-370-6299; Fax: 704-370-3379.

Web: charlottediocese.org

Email: chancery@charlottediocese.org

ESTABLISHED JANUARY 12, 1972.

Square Miles 20,470.

Comprises the Counties of Alexander, Alleghany, Anson, Ashe, Avery, Buncombe, Burke, Cabarrus, Caldwell, Catawba, Cherokee, Clay, Cleveland, Davidson, Davie, Forsyth, Gaston, Graham, Guilford, Haywood, Henderson, Iredell, Jackson, Lincoln, Macon, Madison, McDowell, Mecklenberg, Mitchell, Montgomery, Polk, Randolph, Richmond, Rockingham, Rowan, Rutherford, Stanley, Stokes, Surry, Swain, Transylvania, Union, Watauga, Wilkes, Yadkin and Yancey in the State of North Carolina.

For legal titles of parishes and diocesan institutions, consult the Chancery.

STATISTICAL OVERVIEW

Personnel	
Bishop	1
Retired Bishops	1
Abbots	1
Retired Abbots	1
Priests: Diocesan Active in Diocese	72
Priests: Diocesan Active Outside Diocese	6
Priests: Retired, Sick or Absent	39
Number of Diocesan Priests	117
Religious Priests in Diocese	49
Total Priests in Diocese	166
Extern Priests in Diocese	4
Ordinations:	
Diocesan Priests	1
Transitional Deacons	2
Permanent Deacons in Diocese	96
Total Brothers	12
Total Sisters	122
Parishes	
Parishes	73
With Resident Pastor:	
Resident Diocesan Priests	57
Resident Religious Priests	16
Missions	19
Pastoral Centers	1
Professional Ministry Personnel:	
Brothers	3
Sisters	14
Lay Ministers	220
Welfare	
Health Care Centers	16
Total Assisted	67,000
Homes for the Aged	2
Total Assisted	174
Day Care Centers	13
Total Assisted	1,000
Specialized Homes	4
Total Assisted	503
Special Centers for Social Services	4
Total Assisted	24,079
Residential Care of Disabled	1
Total Assisted	125
Educational	
Diocesan Students in Other Seminaries	16
Total Seminarians	16
Colleges and Universities	1
Total Students	1,638
High Schools, Diocesan and Parish	2
Total Students	1,956
Elementary Schools, Diocesan and Parish	16
Total Students	5,738
Catechesis/Religious Education:	
High School Students	3,237
Elementary Students	15,173
Total Students under Catholic Instruction	27,758
Teachers in the Diocese:	
Priests	5
Brothers	3
Sisters	11
Lay Teachers	762
Vital Statistics	
Receptions into the Church:	
Infant Baptism Totals	3,462
Minor Baptism Totals	469
Adult Baptism Totals	235
Received into Full Communion	625
First Communions	5,465
Confirmations	3,457
Marriages:	
Catholic	575
Interfaith	231
Total Marriages	806
Deaths	1,172
Total Catholic Population	171,909
Total Population	4,792,483

Former Bishops—Most Revs. MICHAEL J. BEGLEY, D.D., ord. May 26, 1934; appt. Nov. 30, 1971; cons. first Bishop of Charlotte Jan. 12, 1972; retired 1984; died Feb. 9, 2002; JOHN F. DONOGHUE, D.D., ord. June 4, 1955; appt. Nov. 6, 1984; cons. Dec. 18, 1984; appt. Archbishop of Atlanta June 22, 1993; cons. Aug. 19, 1993; WILLIAM G. CURLIN, D.D. (Retired), ord. May 25, 1957; appt. Auxiliary Bishop of Washington Nov. 2, 1988; cons. Dec. 20, 1988; appt. Bishop of Charlotte, Feb. 22, 1994; installed April 13, 1994; retired Sept. 10, 2002.

Chancery—P.O. Box 36776, Charlotte, 28236. Tel: 704-370-6299; Fax: 704-370-3379.

Vicar General, Chancellor, and Moderator of the Curia—Rev. Msgr. MAURICIO W. WEST, P.O. Box 36776, Charlotte, 28236. Tel: 704-370-3326; Fax: 704-370-3379.

Vice Chancellor—Rev. Msgr. ANTHONY J. MARCACCIO, St. Pius Tenth Church, 2210 N. Elm St., Greensboro, 27408.

Chief Financial Officer—WILLIAM G. WELDON, 1123 S. Church St., Charlotte, 28203. Tel: 704-370-3313.

Controller—STELLA NELL, 1123 S. Church St., Charlotte, 28203. Tel: 704-370-3312.

Diocesan Properties and Risk Management—Deacon GUY A. PICHE, Dir., 1123 S. Church St., Charlotte, 28203. Tel: 704-370-3304.

Employee Benefits—TERRI WILHELM, 1123 S. Church St., Charlotte, 28203. Tel: 704-370-3338.

Diocesan Tribunal—1123 S. Church St., Charlotte, 28203. Tel: 704-370-3293. LISA D. SARVIS, Head Tribunal.

Judicial Vicar—Very Rev. JOHN T. PUTNAM, J.C.L.; JOY BARNES, S.I.M., Advocate; DEBBIE M. WRIGHT, Auditor; JACINTA LEWIS, Sec. & Notary.

Education—Very Rev. ROGER K. ARNSPARGER, V.F., Vicar, 1123 S. Church St., Charlotte, 28203. Tel: 704-370-3210; Fax: 704-370-3291.

Diocesan Consultors—Rev. Msgrs. MAURICIO W. WEST; ANTHONY J. MARCACCIO; RICHARD BELLOW; Very Revs. PAUL GARY; JOHN T. PUTNAM, J.C.L.; ROGER K. ARNSPARGER, V.F.

Office for Religious—Sr. M. TIMOTHY WARREN, R.S.M., 1123 S. Church St., Charlotte, 28203. Tel: 704-370-3213.

Diocesan Offices and Directors

Airport Chaplain—Deacon GEORGE A. SZALONY, 1123 S. Church St., Charlotte, 28203. Tel: 704-370-3344; Fax: 704-370-3378.

Archives—CYNTHIA BARNES, Dir., 1123 S. Church St., Charlotte, 28203. Tel: 704-370-3215; Fax: 704-370-3378.

Boy Scouts—Deacon JAMES R. JOHNSON, St. Charles Borromeo Church, 714 W. Union St., Morganton, 28655. Tel: 828-437-3461.

Campus Ministry—Ms. MARY WRIGHT, Dir., 1123 S. Church St., Charlotte, 28203. Tel: 704-370-3212; Fax: 704-370-3378.

Communications—DAVID HAINS, Dir., 1123 S. Church St., Charlotte, 28203. Tel: 704-370-3336; Fax: 704-370-3382.

Evangelization & Lay Ministry—Dr. FRANK VILLARONGA, Dir., 1123 S. Church St., Charlotte, 28203. Tel: 704-370-3274; Fax: 704-370-3291.

Office of Faith Formation—Very Rev. ROGER K. ARNSPARGER, V.F., Dir.; Dr. CRIS VILLAPANDO, Prog. Dir., 1123 S. Church St., Charlotte, 28203. Tel: 704-370-3246; Fax: 704-370-3378.

Youth Ministry—PAUL KOTLOWSKI, 1123 S. Church St., Charlotte, 28203. Tel: 704-370-3211.

Development—JAMES K. KELLEY, Dir.; BARBARA GADDY, Assoc. Dir., 1123 S. Church St., Charlotte, 28203. Tel: 704-370-3301; 704-370-3302; Fax: 704-370-3378.

Foundation of the Roman Catholic Diocese of Charlotte, Inc., The—JAMES KELLEY, Exec. Dir., 1123 S. Church St., Charlotte, 28203. Tel: 704-370-3301.

Hispanic Ministry—Sr. ANDREA INKROTT, O.S.F., Dir., 1123 S. Church St., Charlotte, 28203. Tel: 704-370-3269; Fax: 704-370-3291.

Hmong Ministry—Deacon PE NHIA CHA LEE, Coord., 1123 S. Church St., Charlotte, 28203. Tel: 828-584-6012.

Human Resources—TERRI WILHELM, Dir., 1123 S. Church St., Charlotte, 28203. Tel: 704-370-3338; 704-370-3339; Fax: 704-370-3378.

Korean Catholic Cultural Center—Revs. JAEHEE LEE, Dir., 7109 Robinson Church Rd., Charlotte, 28215. Tel: 704-531-8417; Fax: 704-531-1843; YOON JO PARK, 2516 Glen Meadow Dr., Greensboro, 27455. Tel: 336-282-8663.

African-American Ministry—Mrs. SANDRA P. MURDOCK, Dir., 1123 S. Church St., Charlotte, 28203. Tel: 704-370-3267; Fax: 704-370-3378.

Media Resource Center—Sr. PATRICIA DURBIN, R.S.M., 1123 S. Church St., Charlotte, 28203. Tel: 704-370-3242.

Cathedral Publishing Corporation—Mailing Address: P.O. Box 37267, Charlotte, 28237. Tel: 704-370-6299. *1123 S. Church St., Charlotte, 28203.* Tel: 704-370-3336.

Newspaper: "The Catholic News & Herald"—VACANT, Editor, Mailing Address: P.O. Box 37267, Charlotte, 28237. Tel: 704-370-3333; 704-370-3334; Fax: 704-370-3382.

Permanent Diaconate—Rev. Msgr. MAURICIO W. WEST, Coord.; Deacon LOUIS PAIS, Dir., Mailing Address: P.O. Box 36776, Charlotte, 28236. Tel: 704-370-6299; Fax: 704-370-3379.

Planning and Research—GEORGE COBB, OblSB, Dir., 1123 S. Church St., Charlotte, 28203. Tel: 704-370-3328; Fax: 704-370-3378.

Propagation of the Faith—Rev. MARK S. LAWLOR, 1123 S. Church St., Charlotte, 28203. Tel: 704-370-6299; Fax: 704-370-3378.

School—LINDA CHERRY, Supt.; JANICE RITTER, Asst. Supt., 1123 S. Church St., Charlotte, 28203. Tel: 704-370-3271; Fax: 704-370-3291.

Mecklenburg Area Catholic Schools—1123 S. Church St., Charlotte, 28203. Tel: 704-370-3270; Fax: 704-370-3291.

Prison Ministry— Contact Permanent Diaconate Office: *1123 S. Church St., Charlotte, 28203.* Tel: 704-370-3344; Fax: 704-370-3378.

Social Services—ELIZABETH THURBEE, A.C.S.W., Exec. Dir., 1123 S. Church St., Charlotte, 28203. Tel: 704-370-3228.

Campaign for Human Development—MARY JANE BRUTON, Prog. Dir., 1123 S. Church St., Charlotte, 28203. Tel: 704-370-3283; Fax: 704-370-3277.

Justice and Peace—JOSEPH PURELLO, Dir., 1123 S. Church St., Charlotte, 28203. Tel: 704-370-3225; Fax: 704-370-3277.

Victim Assistance Coordinator—DAVID W. HAROLD, A.C.S.W. Tel: 336-714-3202. Email: dwharold@charlottediocese.org.

Vietnamese Apostolate—4929 Sandy Porter Rd., Charlotte, 28273. Tel: 704-504-0907. Rev. PETER TAN VAN LE, Chap.

Vocations—Rev. CHRISTOPHER M. GOBER, 1123 S. Church St., Charlotte, 28203.

Worship—Dr. LARRY STRATEMEYER, St. Patrick Cathedral, 1621 Dilworth Rd., E., Charlotte, 28203. Tel: 704-334-2283; Fax: 704-377-6403.

CLERGY, PARISHES, MISSIONS AND PAROCHIAL SCHOOLS

CITY OF CHARLOTTE

(MECKLENBURG COUNTY)

1—ST. PATRICK CATHEDRAL (1939), (Phelan Memorial) Very Rev. Christopher A. Roux, Rector; Deacons Nicholas Fadero, (Retired); Carlos A. Medina Sr.
Res.: 1621 Dilworth Rd., E., 28203. Tel: 704-334-2283; Fax: 704-377-6403. Email: stpatrickcharlotte@charlottediocese.org. Web: www.stpatricks.org.
Catechesis/Religious Program—Tel: 704-334-2283, Ext. 427. Jonathan Garcis, D.R.E.; Quentin Salerno, Youth Min. Students 261.

2—ST. ANN (1955) Rev. Timothy S. Reid; Deacon George A. Szalony; Sr. Judy Monahan, S.S.J., Pastoral Assoc.
Church: 3635 Park Rd., 28209. Tel: 704-521-9589; Fax: 704-527-8671. Email: stanncharlotte@charlottediocese.org. Web: www.stannsparish.org.
Catechesis/Religious Program—Students 95.
Convent—3430 Willow Oak Rd., 28209. Tel: 704-523-0331.

3—ST. GABRIEL (1957) Revs. Francis J. O'Rourke (Retired); J. Patrick Cahill, Parochial Vicar; Deacons Bernard Wenning Jr., (Retired); Mark Diener; Curtiss Todd, (Retired); Robert Gettelfinger, (Retired); Guido Pozo.
Res.: 3016 Providence Rd., 28211. Tel: 704-364-5431; Fax: 704-362-5049. Email: StGabrielCharlotte@charlottediocese.org.
Catechesis/Religious Program—Tel: 704-366-2738. Susan Krasniewski, D.R.E. Tel: 704-362-5047, Ext. 271. Students 1,015.

4—ST. JOHN NEUMANN (1977) Rev. Patrick T. Hoare; Deacon John N. Parrish. In Res., Rev. Peter T. Pham.
Res.: 8451 Idlewild Rd., 28227. Tel: 704-536-6520; Fax: 704-536-3147. Email: stjohnneumanncharlotte@charlottediocese.org. Web: www.4sjnc.org.
Catechesis/Religious Program—Tel: 704-535-4197. Shannon Cutler, D.R.E. Students 399.

5—ST. JOSEPH CHURCH Rev. Peter Tan Van Le.
4929 Sandy Porter Rd., 28273. Tel: 704-504-0907. Email: stjosephcharlotte@charlottediocese.org.
Catechesis/Religious Program—Students 162.

6—ST. LUKE (1987) Very Rev. Paul Q. Gary; Sr. Veronica Grover, S.H.C.J., Pastoral Assoc.; Deacons Jeffrey S. Evers; Rafael J. Torres.
Office: 13700 Lawyers Rd., 28227. Tel: 704-545-1224; Fax: 704-545-7288. Email: stlukeminthill@charlottediocese.org. Web: www.stlukechurch.net.
Catechesis/Religious Program—Tel: 704-545-0065. Students 846.

7—ST. MATTHEW (1986) Rev. Msgr. John J. McSweeney; Rev. Patrick D. Toole, Parochial Vicar; Sisters Jeanne Marie Kienast, R.S.M., Pastoral Assoc.; Eileen C. McLoughlin, M.S.B.T., Pastoral Assoc.; Deacons James Hamrlik; William G. Griffin; Mark J. King. In Res., Rev. Eugene Schellberg.
Office: 8015 Ballantyne Commons Pkwy., 28277. Tel: 704-543-7677; Fax: 704-542-7244. Email: stmatthewcharlotte@charlottediocese.org. Web: www.stmatthewcatholic.org.
Catechesis/Religious Program—Tel: 704-541-8362; Fax: 704-542-7244. Patricia Tomlinson, D.R.E.; Katie Dunne, Youth Min. Students 4,465.

8—OUR LADY OF CONSOLATION (1955) Rev. Martin A. Schratz, O.F.M.Cap.; Deacon Charles Knight.
Mailing Address: 1224 Dearborn Ave., 28206-2491. Email: olccharlotte@charlottediocese.org. In Res., Bro. Lombardo D'Auria, O.F.M.Cap.
Church: 2301 Statesville Ave., 28206. Tel: 704-375-4339; Fax: 704-375-8039.
Catechesis/Religious Program—Students 77.
Mission—St. Helen 341 Dallas-Spencer Mountain Rd., Spencer Mountain, Gaston Co. 28059.

9—OUR LADY OF GUADALUPE CHURCH Revs. Vincent H. Finnerty, C.M.; Joseph Elzi, C.M., Parochial Vicar; Karina Romero, Business Mgr.; Haydee Garcia, Pastoral Assoc.
6212 Tuckaseegee Rd., 28214. Tel: 704-391-3732; Fax: 704-391-6594. Email: olgcharlotte@charlottediocese.org.
Catechesis/Religious Program—Juan Cajero, D.R.E. Students 510.

10—OUR LADY OF THE ASSUMPTION (1949) Rev. Philip J. Scarcella (MET); Deacons Stephen J. Horai, (Retired); Peter Duca; Kevin Williams; Luis Flores.
Res.: 4207 Shamrock Dr., 28215. Tel: 704-535-9965; 704-535-9970; Fax: 704-535-3621. Email: olacharlotte@charlottediocese.org. Web: www.rc.net/charlotte/ola/.
Catechesis/Religious Program—Tel: 704-535-3310. David S. Reiser, D.R.E. Students 602.

11—ST. PETER (1851) Revs. Patrick F. Earl; Thomas P. McDonnell, S.J. In Res., Rev. Vincent de P. Alagia, S.J.
Res.: 507 S. Tryon St., 28202. Tel: 704-372-6808; Fax: 704-358-0050. Email: stpetercharlotte@charlottediocese.org. Web: www.stpeterscatholic.org.
Catechesis/Religious Program—Tel: 704-332-2901. Students 136.

12—ST. THOMAS AQUINAS (1978) Revs. Remo DiSalvatore, O.F.M.Cap.; Stanley Kobel, O.F.M.-Cap.; Bro. Doug Soik, O.F.M.Cap.; Deacons Mark D. Nash; Brian P. McNulty.
Res.: 1400 Suther Rd., 28213. Tel: 704-549-1607; Fax: 704-549-1614. Email: stthomascharlotte@charlottediocese.org. Web: www.stacharlotte.com.
Catechesis/Religious Program—Tel: 704-549-5160; Fax: 704-503-5060. Sisters Angelita Codilla, O.P., D.R.E.; Felicidad Lala, O.P., Asst. D.R.E.; Michelle Hollis, Asst. D.R.E. Students 684.
Convent—1216 Ogden Pl., 28213. Tel: 704-503-4934.

13—ST. VINCENT DE PAUL (1965) Revs. Mark S. Lawlor; Richard DeClue; Deacons Gerald P. Hickey; John Kopfle.
Res.: 6828 Old Reid Rd., 28210. Tel: 704-554-7088; Fax: 704-554-0490. Email: stvincentcharlotte@charlottediocese.org. Web: stvincentdepaulchurch.com.
Catechesis/Religious Program—Tel: 704-554-1622. Aida Tamayo, C.R.E.; Ruben A. Tamayo, Youth Min. Students 509.

OUTSIDE THE CITY OF CHARLOTTE

ALBEMARLE, STANLY CO., OUR LADY OF THE ANNUNCIATION (1934) Rev. Peter L. Fitzgibbons.
Res.: 416 N. Second St., 28001. Tel: 704-982-2910; Fax: 704-982-0881. Email: olaalbemarle@charlottediocese.org.
Catechesis/Religious Program—Tel: 704-982-1048. Cyndi Norton, D.R.E. Students 126.

ANDREWS, CHEROKEE CO., HOLY REDEEMER (1962) Rev. Carl E. Kaltreider.
Res.: 214 Aquone Rd., 28901-9776. Tel: 828-321-4463. Email: holyredeemerandrews@charlottediocese.org.
Mission—Prince of Peace 704 Talluah Rd., Rte. #129 S., Robbinsville, Graham Co. 28771. Email: princeofpeacerobbinsville@charlottediocese.org.
Catechesis/Religious Program—Irene Weber, D.R.E. Students 30.

ARDEN, BUNCOMBE CO., ST. BARNABAS (1964) Rev. Adrian Porras; Deacons Michael L. Stout; Rudy J. Triana.
Mailing Address: P.O. Box 38, 28704. Tel: 828-684-6098; Fax: 828-684-6152. Email: stbarnabasarden@charlottediocese.org. Web: www.saintbarnabasarden.org.
Res.: 109 Crescent Hill Rd., 28704.
Catechesis/Religious Program—Miss Sheryl Peyton, D.R.E. Students 310.

ASHEBORO, RANDOLPH CO., ST. JOSEPH (1948) Rev. Christopher J. Davis.
512 W. Wainman Ave., 27203. Tel: 336-629-0221; Fax: 336-629-6968. Email: stjosephasheboro@charlottediocese.org. Web: www.stjoenc.org.
Res.: 308 S. Park St., 27203. Tel: 336-629-0450.
Catechesis/Religious Program—Students 214.

ASHEVILLE, BUNCOMBE CO.

1—BASILICA OF ST. LAWRENCE (1869) Very Rev. Wilbur N. Thomas, V.F.; Rev. C. Morris Boyd; LuWinn Rutherford, Pastoral Assoc.; Andrew Davis, Dir. Music Min.
Church Office: 97 Haywood St., 28801. Tel: 828-252-6042; Fax: 828-254-0414. Email: stlawrenceasheville@charlottediocese.org.
Catechesis/Religious Program—Mrs. Elizabeth Girton, D.R.E. Students 136.

2—ST. EUGENE (1957) Rev. Edward J. Sheridan (Retired); Deacon Michael Zboyovski Sr.
Office & Mailing Address: 72 Culvern St., 28804. Tel: 828-254-5193; Fax: 828-254-5797. Email: steugeneasheville@charlottediocese.org. Web: www.steugene.org.
Catechesis/Religious Program—Tracy Jedd, D.R.E. Students 200.

BELMONT, GASTON CO., QUEEN OF THE APOSTLES (1965) Rev. Francis T. Cancro; Sr. Bernadette McNamara, R.S.M., Pastoral Assoc.
Church: 503 N. Main St., 28012. Tel: 704-825-9600; Fax: 704-825-1413. Email: QofABelmont@charlottediocese.org. Web: www.queenoftheapostles.org.
Res.: 2121 Ferncliff Ln., Cramerton, 28012. Tel: 704-825-9907.
Catechesis/Religious Program—Tel: 704-825-9600, Ext. 26. Students 270.

BISCOE, MONTGOMERY CO., OUR LADY OF THE AMERICAS Rev. Ricardo Sanchez; Laura Lowder, Music Dir.
Mailing Address: P.O. Box 519, Candor, 27229. 298 Farmers Market Rd., 27209. Tel: 910-974-3051; Fax: 910-974-4156. Email: ourlady298@embargmail.com. Web: www.ourladyofamericas.org.
Catechesis/Religious Program—Mary Wallace, D.R.E.; Jorge Chavez, D.R.E. Students 43.

BOONE, WATAUGA CO., ST. ELIZABETH (1954) Rev. Joseph Mulligan.
Office & Mailing Address: 259 Pilgrim's Way, 28607. Tel: 828-264-8338; Fax: 828-262-3721. Email: stelizabethboone@charlottediocese.org. Web: www.stehc.org.
Res.: 333 Poplar Hill Dr., 28607. Tel: 828-264-4503.
Catechesis/Religious Program—Ellisa Miller, D.R.E Students 150.
Mission—Epiphany 163 Galax Ln., Blowing Rock, 28607.

BOONVILLE, YADKINVILLE CO., DIVINE REDEEMER (DIVINO REDENTOR) (2004) Rev. Jose Enrique Gonzalez-Gaytan; Deacon Michael Langsdorf.
Res.: 209 Lon Ave., 27011. Tel: 336-367-7067; Fax: 336-367-7954.
Catechesis/Religious Program— Aleksandra Banasik, D.R.E. Students 565.

BREVARD, TRANSYLVANIA CO., SACRED HEART (1949) Rev. Carl Del Giudice; Deacons John J. Burke Jr.; Patrick Crosby.
Res.: 100 Brian Berg Ln., 28712. Tel: 828-883-9572; Fax: 828-883-9587. Email: sacredheartbrevard@charlottediocese.org. Web: sacredheartcatholicchurchbrevardnc.org.
Catechesis/Religious Program— Myriam Gonzalez, D.R.E. Students 72.
Mission—St. Jude Sapphire, 28774. Tel: 828-743-5717. Email: stjudesapphirevalley@charlottediocese.org. P.O. Box 3126, Cashiers. Rev. Dean Cesa.

BRYSON CITY, SWAIN CO., ST. JOSEPH (1941) Rev. Shawn O'Neal.
Res.: P.O. Box 727, 28713. Tel: 828-488-6766; Fax: 828-488-0586. Email: stjosephbrysoncity@charlottediocese.org. Web: www.stjosephbryson.org.
Catechesis/Religious Program—Kathy Posey, D.R.E. Students 17.

Mission—Our Lady of Guadalupe 82 Lambert Branch Rd., Cherokee, Swain Co. 28719. Tel: 828-497-9755.

CANDLER, BUNCOMBE CO., ST. JOAN OF ARC (1928) Rev. Frank J. Seabo.
Church: 768 Ashbury Rd., 28715. Tel: 828-670-0051; Fax: 828-670-0052. Email: stjoanasheville@charlottediocese.org. Web: www.stjoanofarcasheville.catholicweb.com.
Catechesis/Religious Program—Students 54.

CLEMMONS, FORSYTH CO., HOLY FAMILY (1980) Very Rev. Michael J. Buttner; Rev. Tri Vinh Truong, Parochial Vicar; Deacon Gerard Schumacher, (Retired).
Office Address—P.O. Box 130, 27012. Tel: 336-778-0600. Email: holyfamilyclemmons@charlottediocese.org. Web: www.holyfamilyclemmons.com.
Res.: 2890 Knobb Hill Dr., 27012. Tel: 336-766-1882.
Church: 4820 Kinnamon Rd., Winston-Salem, 27103. Fax: 336-766-2918.
Catechesis/Religious Program—Tel: 336-766-0600, Ext. 214. Ms. Peggy Schumacher, D.R.E.; Dr. Nick Passero, Youth Min. Students 636.

CONCORD, CABARRUS CO., ST. JAMES (1869) Revs. J. Joseph Dionne, C.Ss.R.; Francis Ezaqnikatt, C.Ss.R.; Oscar E. Rojas Paniagua, C.Ss.R; Deacon J. Daniel Carl.
Mailing Address: P.O. Box 123, 28025-0123. Tel: 704-720-0600; Fax: 704-720-0610. Email: stjamesconcord@charlottediocese.org. In Res., Rev. Vang Cong Tran, C.Ss.R.
Res.: 139 Manor Ave. S.W., 28025. Tel: 704-720-0608.
Catechesis/Religious Program— Patti Andruzzi, D.R.E. Students 934.

DENVER, LINCOLN CO., HOLY SPIRIT (1988) Rev. Carmen Malacari; Deacon James Atkinson.
Church: 537 N. Hwy. 16, 28037-9235. Tel: 704-483-6448; Fax: 704-483-6898. Email: holyspiritdenver@charlottediocese.org. Web: www.holyspiritnc.org.
Res.: 6789 Hawks Nest Ln., Stanley, 28164. Tel: 704-820-0153.
Catechesis/Religious Program—Students 312.

EDEN, ROCKINGHAM CO., ST. JOSEPH OF THE HILLS (1938) Rev. Francis M. Cintula (Retired).
Res.: 316 Boone Rd., 27288. Tel: 336-623-2661. Email: stjosepheden@charlottediocese.org.
Catechesis/Religious Program—Tel: 336-573-8997. Students 48.

FOREST CITY, RUTHERFORD CO., IMMACULATE CONCEPTION (1950) Rev. Herbert Burke; Deacon Andrew Cilone.
Res.: 1024 W. Main St., 28043. Tel: 828-245-4017. Email: immconcepforestcity@charlottediocese.org.
Catechesis/Religious Program—Students 130.

FRANKLIN, MACON CO., ST. FRANCIS OF ASSISI (1953) Rev. Tien H. Duong.
Res.: 299 Maple St., 28734. Tel: 828-524-2289; Fax: 828-369-0809. Email: stfrancisfranklin@charlottediocese.org. Web: www.stfrancisofassisifranklin.org.
Catechesis/Religious Program—Tel: 828-369-8131. Fred Carl Stickney, D.R.E. Students 83.
Mission—Our Lady of the Mountains P.O. Box 2729, Highlands, Macon Co. 28741. Tel: 828-526-2418. Email: olmountainshighlands@charlottediocese.org. Web: www.ourladyofthemountains.net. Rev. Dean Cesa; Deacon Charles Heine.

GASTONIA, GASTON CO., ST. MICHAEL (1903) Very Rev. Roger K. Arnsparger; Deacons John P. Weisenhorn, (Retired); Arthur J. Kingsley.
Church: 708 St. Michael's Ln., 28052. Tel: 704-853-8808; 704-867-6212; Fax: 704-867-6379. Email: stmichaelgastonia@charlottediocese.org. Web: www.stmichaelsgastonia.org.
School—(Grades PreK-8) Tel: 704-865-4382; Fax: 704-864-5108. Web: www.smsgastonia.com. Joseph Puceta, Prin. Lay Teachers 19; Students 211.
Catechesis/Religious Program—Tel: 704-867-6212, Ext. 114. Students 124.

GREENSBORO, GUILFORD CO.

1—ST. BENEDICT (1901) Revs. James Duc H. Duong; M. David Boissey.
Res.: 109 W. Smith St., 27401. Tel: 336-272-0303. Email: stbenedictgreensboro@charlottediocese.org.
Catechesis/Religious Program—Students 48.

2—ST. MARY (1928) Revs. Michael Manh Nguyen, C.M.; John P. Timlin, C.M.; Deacons Vincent Shaw; Pierre M. K'Briuh.
Mailing Address: P.O. Box 21012, 2742.
Res.: 812 Duke St., 27401. Tel: 336-272-8650; Fax: 336-272-3594. Email: stmarygreensboro@charlottediocese.org. Web: www.stmarysgreensboro.org.
Catechesis/Religious Program—Josie Carter-Zieglar, D.R.E. Students 368.

3—OUR LADY OF GRACE (1952), (Ethel Clay Price Memorial) Revs. Fidel C. Melo; James Stuhrenberg; Deacons Timothy Rohan; Paul A. Teich, (Retired).
Mailing Address: 201 S. Chapman St., 27403-1611.
Res.: 207 S. Chapman St., 27403. Tel: 336-274-6520 (Office); 336-275-5376 (Rectory); Fax: 336-274-7326. Email: olggreensboro@charlottediocese.org. Web: www.olgchurch.org.
Church: 2205 W. Market St., 27403.
School—(Grades K-8) Tel: 336-275-1522; Fax: 336-279-8824. Email: olgsch@olgsch.org. Web: www.olgsch.org. Gary Gelo, Prin.; Shirley Kinlaw, Asst. Prin. Lay Teachers 27; Students 358.
Catechesis/Religious Program— James D. McCullough, D.R.E.; Graciela Flores, Hispanic D.R.E. Students 269.

4—ST. PAUL THE APOSTLE (1974) Revs. John A. Allen; Benjamin A. Roberts; Deacons Gordon L. Forester, (Retired); Larry Lisk.
Res.: 2715 Horsepen Creek Rd., 27410. Tel: 336-297-1971; 336-294-4696 (Office); Fax: 336-294-6149. Email: stpaulgreensboro@charlottediocese.org. Web: www.stpaulcc.org.
Catechesis/Religious Program— Jeannine Martin, D.R.E. Students 323.

5—ST. PIUS THE TENTH (1960) Rev. Msgr. Anthony J. Marcaccio; Mr. Tracy Earl Welliver, Pastoral Assoc.; Mrs. Patricia Spivey, Pastoral Assoc.; Mrs. Toni Redifer, Pastoral Coord.; Deacons Philip Cooper; William S. Shaw; Ronald F. Steinkamp.
Office: 220 State St., 27408. Tel: 336-272-4681; 336-272-8598; Fax: 336-274-8112. Email: stpiusgreensboro@charlottediocese.org. Web: www.stpiusxnc.com.
School—(Grades K-8), 2200 N. Elm St., 27408. Tel: 336-273-9865; Fax: 336-273-0199. Anne Knapke, Prin. Lay Teachers 29; Students 468.
Catechesis/Religious Program—Tel: 336-273-9860. Students 470.
Catholic Campus Connection (Thea House)—1009 Bluford St., 27401. Tel: 336-272-5868.

HAMLET, RICHMOND CO., ST. JAMES (1910) Rev. John F. Starczewski.
Mailing Address: P.O. Box 1208, 28345. Tel: 910-582-0207.
Catechesis/Religious Program—Email: stjameshamlet@charlottediocese.org. Cecilia Wilson, D.R.E. Students 55.
Mission—Sacred Heart 205 Rutherford St., Wadesboro, Anson Co. 28710.

HENDERSONVILLE, HENDERSON CO., IMMACULATE CONCEPTION (1912) Revs. Nicholas A. Mormando, O.F.M.Cap.; John Salvas, O.F.M.Cap.; Bro. Michael Molloy, O.F.M.Cap.; Alma Lopez, Pastoral Assoc.
Parish Office—208 7th Ave., W., 28791-3602. Tel: 828-693-6901; Fax: 828-697-1656. Email: ImmConcepHendersonville@charlottediocese.org.
Res.: 717 Buncombe St., 28791-3609. Tel: 828-692-0550.
School—Immaculata, (Grades K-8), 711 Buncombe St., 28791-3609. Tel: 828-693-3277; Fax: 828-696-3677. Carole Breerwood, Prin. Lay Teachers 18; Students 139.
Catechesis/Religious Program—Tel: 828-697-7420. Sandy Donecho, D.R.E. Students 306.

HICKORY, CATAWBA CO., ST. ALOYSIUS (1913) Revs. Robert M. Ferris; Jean-Pierre Swamunu Lhoposo, C.I.C.M.; Deacons Hugo L. May, (Retired); Thomas A. Rasmussen; Sr. Mary Norman, C.L.H.C., Pastoral Assoc.; Kathy Sucoop, Pastoral Assoc.
Res.: 862 1st St., N.E., 28601. Tel: 828-327-2341; Fax: 828-327-3376. Email: staloysiushickory@charlottediocese.org. Web: www.staloysiushickory.org.
Catechesis/Religious Program—Students 784.

HIGH POINT, GUILFORD CO.

1—CHRIST THE KING (1940) Rev. Philip Kollithanath.
Res.: 1505 E. Kivett Dr., 27260. Tel: 336-884-0244; Fax: 336-887-1200. Email: christkinghighpoint@charlottediocese.org.
Catechesis/Religious Program—Jill Frentz, D.R.E. Students 90.

2—IMMACULATE HEART OF MARY (1947) Revs. John Kelly, O.S.F.S.; Joseph C. Zuschmidt, O.S.F.S.; James F. Byrne, O.S.F.S.; Deacons Thomas Kak, (Retired); Walter Haarsgaard.
Mailing Address: 605 Barbee Ave., 27262. Email: ihmhighpoint@charlottediocese.org. Web: www.ihmchurch.org.
Church: 4145 Johnson St., 27265. Tel: 336-869-7739; Fax: 336-869-1059.
Res.: 3821 Oak Forest Dr., 27265. Tel: 336-886-4847.
School—(Grades K-8), 500 Montlieu Ave., 27262. Tel: 336-887-2613; Fax: 336-884-1849. Web: www.ihm-school.com. Wanda Garrett, Prin. Lay Teachers 23; Students 252.
Catechesis/Religious Program—Tel: 336-885-5210. Students 550.

HUNTERSVILLE, MECKLENBURG CO., ST. MARK (1997) Rev. Msgr. Richard Bellow; Rev. Brandon H. Jones, Parochial Vicar; Deacons Louis A. Pais; Ronald Sherwood; Robert Murphy.
Church: 14740 Stumptown Rd., 28078. Tel: 704-948-0231; Fax: 704-948-8018. Email: stmarkhuntersville@charlottediocese.org. Web: www.stmarknc.org.
Catechesis/Religious Program—Tel: 704-948-1306. Donna Smith, D.R.E. Students 1,205.

JEFFERSON, ASHE CO., ST. FRANCIS OF ASSISI (1962) Rev. Joseph Long Dinh.
Mailing Address: P.O. Box 1, 28640. Tel: 336-246-9151; Fax: 336-246-3141. Email: stfrancisjefferson@charlottediocese.org. Web: stfrancisofassisi-jefferson.org.
Catechesis/Religious Program—Patrick Hession, D.R.E. Students 79.
Mission—St. Frances of Rome 29 Highland Dr., Sparta, 28675. Tel: 336-372-8846.

KANNAPOLIS, CABARRUS CO., ST. JOSEPH CHURCH Rev. Alvaro A. Riquelme, C.Ss.R.; Deacon Myles Decker.
108 Saint Joseph St., 28081. Tel: 704-932-4607; Fax: 704-786-5412. Email: stjosephchurch@ctc.net. Web: www.stjosephcatholic.org.
Rectory—274 Spring St., Concord, 28026. Tel: 704-720-0549.
Catechesis/Religious Program—Students 175.

KERNERSVILLE, FORSYTH CO., HOLY CROSS (1973) Rev. Paul Dechant, O.S.F.S.; Deacons Eugene J. Gillis; Timothy Ritchie.
Res.: 616 S. Cherry St., 27284. Tel: 336-996-5109; Fax: 336-996-5669. Email: holycrosskernersville@charlottediocese.org. Web: www.holycrossnc.org.
Child Developmental Center—Tel: 336-996-5144; Fax: 336-996-5115. Cathie Reel, Dir.
Catechesis/Religious Program— Marie Kinney, D.R.E. Students 612.

LENOIR, CALDWELL CO., ST. FRANCIS OF ASSISI (1936) Rev. Julio Dominguez; Deacons A. Stephen Pickett; Ronald Caplette, (Retired).
Res.: 328-B Woodsway Ln., N.W., 28645-4356. Tel: 828-754-5281; Fax: 828-754-5281. Email: stfrancislenoir@charlottediocese.org. Web: www.stfrancislenoir.com.
Catechesis/Religious Program—Students 128.

LEXINGTON, DAVIDSON CO., OUR LADY OF THE ROSARY (1944) Rev. Albert J. Gondek, O.S.F.S.
Res.: 619 S. Main St., 27292-3238. Tel: 336-248-2463; Fax: 336-238-3241. Email: olrosarylexington@charlottediocese.org. Web: www.olr-nc.org.
Catechesis/Religious Program—Sr. Katherine Francis French, S.P., D.R.E. Students 177.

LINCOLNTON, LINCOLN CO., ST. DOROTHY (1944) Rev. Matthew R. Buettner.
Res.: 148 St. Dorothy Ln., 28092. Tel: 704-735-5575. Email: stdorothylincolnton@charlottediocese.org. Web: www.stdorothys.org.
Catechesis/Religious Program—Students 216.

MAGGIE VALLEY, HAYWOOD CO., ST. MARGARET OF SCOTLAND (1968) Rev. John T. Denny, O.S.A.; Deacon Gerald P. LaPointe; Bro. William C. Harkin, O.S.A., Pastoral Assoc.
Mailing Address: P.O. Box 1359, 28751-1359. Tel: 828-926-0106; Fax: 828-926-0855. In Res., Rev. P. Thomas Pohto, O.S.A.
Res.: 37 Murphy Dr., 28751. Tel: 828-926-0025. Email: stmargaretmaggievalley@charlottediocese.org. Web: www.catholicretreat.org/stmargaret.htm.
Catechesis/Religious Program—Betsy McLeod, D.R.E. Students 49.

MARS HILL, MADISON CO., ST. ANDREW THE APOSTLE (1985) Rev. Frederick H. Werth; Deacon Michael Leahy.
Mailing Address: P.O. Box 1406, 28754-1406. Tel: 828-689-3719; Fax: 828-689-3719. Email: standrewmarshill@charlottediocese.org.
Res. & Church: 149 Brook St., 28754.
Catechesis/Religious Program—Fax: 828-689-3719. Ann Stowe, D.R.E. Students 28.
Mission—Sacred Heart Burnsville, Madison Co. 28714. Email: sacredheartburnsville@charlottediocese.org.

MOCKSVILLE, DAVIE CO., ST. FRANCIS OF ASSISI (1958) Rev. Andrew Draper, T.O.R.; Deacon John O. Zimmerle.
Church: 862 Yadkinville Rd., 27028. Tel: 336-751-2973; Fax: 336-751-9929. Email: stfrancismocksville@charlottediocese.org. Web: www.stfrancismocksville.com.
Catechesis/Religious Program— Nancy Gerrety, D.R.E. Students 126.

MONROE, UNION CO., OUR LADY OF LOURDES (1945) Rev. Thomas Kessler; Deacons Jesus Reyes; Sidney Huff.
Res.: 725 Deese St., 28112. Tel: 704-289-2773; Fax: 704-283-7210. Email: ollourdesmonroe@charlottediocese.org. Web: www.rc.net/charlotte/oll.
Catechesis/Religious Program—Students 613.

MOORESVILLE, IREDELL CO., ST. THERESE (1946) Revs. Vincent C. Curtin, S.J.; Joseph B. Kappes, S.J.;

Donald M. Ward Jr., S.J.; Deacon John E. Sims. In Res., Rev. William J. Lynch, S.J.
Res.: 217 Brawley School Rd., 28117. Tel: 704-664-3992; Fax: 704-660-6321. Email: sttheresemooresville@charlottediocese.org. Web: www.sainttherese.net.
Catechesis/Religious Program—Tel: 704-664-7762; Fax: 704-664-2045. Students 1,197.

MORGANTON, BURKE CO., ST. CHARLES BORROMEO (1947) Very Rev. Kenneth L. Whittington; Deacons James R. Johnson; Pe nhia cha Lee; John Martino; Edward A. Konarski.
Res.: 728 W. Union St., 28655. Tel: 828-437-3108; Fax: 828-437-6262. Email: stcharlesmorganton@charlottediocese.org.
Catechesis/Religious Program— Terri Martino, D.R.E. Students 164.
Mission—Our Lady of the Angels P.O. Box 1006, Marion, 28752. 258 N. Garden St., Marion, McDowell Co. 28752. Tel: 828-652-8690. Email: olamarion@charlottediocese.org. Rev. Gnanapragasam Mariasoosai.

MOUNT AIRY, SURRY CO., HOLY ANGELS (1921) Rev. Eric Kowalski; Deacon Paul Liotard.
Res.: 1208 N. Main St., Mt. Airy, 27030. Tel: 336-786-8147. Email: holyangelsmountairy@charlottediocese.org.
Catechesis/Religious Program—Tel: 336-786-8315. Linda Gallasetti-Simmons, D.R.E. Students 151.

MURPHY, CHEROKEE CO., ST. WILLIAM (1952) Very Rev. George M. Kloster; Deacon Carl Hubbel.
Res.: 765 Andrews Rd., P.O. Box 546, 28906. Tel: 828-837-2000; Fax: 828-835-9889. Email: stwilliammurphy@charlottediocese.org. Web: www.st-william.net.
Catechesis/Religious Program— Michelle Calascione, D.R.E. Students 87.
Mission—Immaculate Heart of Mary U.S. Hwy. 64 W., Hayesville, Clay Co. 28906. Email: ihmhayesville@charlottediocese.org. Web: www.ihmhayesville.com. P.O. Box 546, 28906.

NEWTON, CATAWBA CO., ST. JOSEPH (1978) Rev. James M. Collins; Deacon Scott D. Gilfillan.
Church: 720 W. 13th St., 28658-3899. Tel: 828-464-9207; Fax: 828-464-9880. Email: stjosephnewton@charlottediocese.org.
Holy Family Parish Center—Tel: 828-465-2878.
Catechesis/Religious Program—Students 213.

NORTH WILKESBORO, ST. JOHN BAPTIST DE LASALLE (1952) Very Rev. John D. Hanic; Deacon Harold Markle, (Retired).
Res.: 275 C.C. Wright School Rd., 28659. Tel: 336-838-5562. Email: stjohnnwilkesboro@charlottediocese.org.
Catechesis/Religious Program—Tel: 336-670-2792. Students 75.
Mission—St. Stephen 101 Hawthorne, Elkin, Surry Co. 28621. Tel: 336-835-3007.

REIDSVILLE, ROCKINGHAM CO., HOLY INFANT (1961) Rev. Joseph W. Mack; Deacon Gerald W. Potkay.
Res.: 1042 Freeway Dr., P.O. Box 1197, 27323. Tel: 336-342-1448. Email: holyinfantreidsville@charlottediocese.org.
Catechesis/Religious Program—Students 106.

SALISBURY, ROWAN CO., SACRED HEART (1882) Very Rev. John T. Putnam; Rev. Nohe Torres; Deacon James Mazur; Sr. Mary Robert Williams, R.S.M., Pastoral Assoc. In Res., Rev. James A. Ebright, canonical studies at Catholic University of America.
Church Office: 375 Lumen Christie Ln., 28147. Tel: 704-633-0591; Fax: 704-647-0126. Email: sacredheartsalisbury@charlottediocese.org. Web: www.salisburycatholic.org.
School—(Grades K-8), 123 N. Ellis St., 28144. Tel: 704-633-2841; Fax: 704-633-6033. Sr. M. Anastacia Pagulayan, O.P., Prin. Religious 3; Lay Teachers 19; Students 188.
Catechesis/Religious Program—Students 330.
Convent—Dominican Sisters at St. Catherine of Siena, 425 W. Council St., 28144. Tel: 704-636-4070.

SHELBY, CLEVELAND CO., ST. MARY'S (1935) Rev. Michael T. Kottar.
Res.: 818 McGowan Rd., 28150. Tel: 704-487-7697; Fax: 704-487-0187. Email: stmaryshelby@charlottediocese.org. Web: stmaryshelbync.parishesonline.com.
Catechesis/Religious Program—Jean Judge, C.R.E. Students 175.
Mission—Christ the King 714 Stone St., Kings Mountain, Cleveland Co. 28086. Email: christkingkingsmountain@charlottediocese.org.

SPRUCE PINE, MITCHELL CO., ST. LUCIEN (1940) Rev. Christopher M. Gober.
Res.: 695 Summit Ave., P.O. Box 688, 28777. Tel: 828-765-2224; Fax: 828-765-2238. Email: stluciensprucepine@charlottediocese.org.
Mission—St. Bernadette P.O. Box 1252, Linville, Avery Co. 28646. Tel: 828-898-6900. Email: stbernadettelinville@charlottediocese.org. Web: www.stbernadettelinville.org. Rev. Christopher M. Gober.
Catechesis/Religious Program—Students 43.

STATESVILLE, IREDELL CO., ST. PHILIP THE APOSTLE (1898) Rev. Kurt M. Fohn; Deacons Charles Brantley, (Retired); Matthew Reilly.
Mailing Address: P.O. Box 882, 28687-0882.
Office: Tel: 704-872-2579; Fax: 704-872-2579. Email: stphillipstatesville@charlottediocese.org. Web: gaelicaine.org/saintphilip.
Res.: 525 Camden Dr., 28677. Tel: 704-873-8641.
Catechesis/Religious Program—Tel: 704-872-2579; Fax: 704-872-2579. Students 309.
Mission—Holy Trinity 1039 NC Hwy. 90 W., Taylorsville, Alexander Co. 28681. Tel: 828-632-8009; Fax: 828-632-8009. Email: holytrinitytaylorsville@charlottediocese.org. P.O. Box 882, 28687. Rev. James M. Byer.

SWANNANOA, BUNCOMBE CO., ST. MARGARET MARY (1936) Rev. Matthew Leonard; Deacon Ralph R. Eckoff, (Retired).
Office: Tel: 828-686-8833; Fax: 828-686-8832.
Res.: 102 Andrews Pl., 28778. Tel: 828-686-5300. Email: stmargaretswannanoa@charlottediocese.org. Web: www.stmargaretmarycatholic.org.
Catechesis/Religious Program— Bea Madden, D.R.E. Students 48.

SYLVA, JACKSON CO., ST. MARY (1955) Rev. W. Ray Williams.
Res.: 141 Dillsboro Rd., 28779. Tel: 828-586-9496. Email: stmarysylva@charlottediocese.org.
Catechesis/Religious Program— Isabella Harcourt, D.R.E. Students 49.

THOMASVILLE, DAVIDSON CO., OUR LADY OF THE HIGHWAYS (1953) Rev. James M. Turner, O.S.F.S.; Deacon Wayne Adams.
Res.: 943 Ball Park Rd., 27360. Tel: 336-475-2667; Fax: 336-476-3337. Email: olhighwaysthomasville@charlottediocese.org.
Catechesis/Religious Program—Students 312.

TRYON, POLK CO., ST. JOHN THE BAPTIST (1911) Rev. Patrick J. Winslow.
Mailing Address & Office: 180 Laurel Ave., 28782. Tel: 828-859-9574; Fax: 828-859-5932. Email: stjohntryon@charlottediocese.org.
Church: 120 Laurel Ave., 28782.
Catechesis/Religious Program—Tel: 828-859-5932. Theresa Finch, D.R.E. Students 92.

WAYNESVILLE, HAYWOOD CO., ST. JOHN THE EVANGELIST (1926) Rev. Lawrence M. LoMonaco.
Res.: 234 Church St., 28786. Tel: 828-456-6707; Fax: 828-456-4329. Email: stjohnwaynesville@charlottediocese.org. Web: webpages.charter.net/stjohnswnc.
Catechesis/Religious Program— Mary Finn, D.R.E. Students 113.
Mission—Immaculate Conception 42 Newfound Rd., Canton, Haywood Co. 28716.

WINSTON-SALEM, FORSYTH CO.

1—ST. BENEDICT THE MOOR (1940) Rev. Lawrence W. Heiney.
Res.: 1625 E. Twelfth St., 27101. Tel: 336-725-9200; Fax: 336-722-4264. Email: stbenedictwinstonsalem@charlottediocese.org.
Mission—Good Shepherd P.O. Box 1149, King, Stokes Co. 27021. Tel: 336-983-2680.
Catechesis/Religious Program—Tel: 336-725-1801; Fax: 336-725-1801. Students 128.

2—ST. LEO THE GREAT (1891) Revs. Brian J. Cook; H. Alejandro Ayala; Deacon Robert DeSautels.
Res.: 334 Springdale Ave., 27104. Tel: 336-724-5314. Email: stleowinstonsalem@charlottediocese.org. Web: www.st-leothegreatw-s.org.
Church: 335 Springdale Ave., 27104. Tel: 336-724-0561; Fax: 336-724-7036.
School—(Grades PreK-8), 333 Springdale Ave., 27104. Tel: 336-748-8252; Fax: 336-748-9005. Mrs. Georgette Schraeder, Prin. Sisters of St. Joseph 1; Lay Teachers 35; Students 284.
Catechesis/Religious Program—Tel: 336-724-0561. Lauren Gardner, D.R.E. Students 326.
Convent—1975 Georgia Ave., 27104. Tel: 336-723-3639.

3—OUR LADY OF MERCY (1954) Revs. William Robinson, O.F.M.Conv.; Mario Giuliano, O.F.M.Conv.; Deacon Joseph Schumacher, (Retired); Pat Hinton, Pastoral Assoc. In Res., Revs. Jude T. DeAngelo, O.F.M.Conv.; Conall McHugh, O.F.M.Conv.
Church & Friary: 1730 Link Rd., 27103. Tel: 336-722-7001; 336-724-6806; Fax: 336-722-0465. Email: olmwinstonsalem@charlottediocese.org. Web: www.olmnc.org.
School—(Grades K-8) Tel: 336-722-7204; Fax: 336-725-2294. Email: admin@ourladyofmercyschool.org. Web: www.ourladyofmercyschool.org. Sr. Geri Rogers, S.S.J., Prin. Sisters of St. Joseph 1; Lay Teachers 20; Students 212.
Catechesis/Religious Program—Tel: 336-722-7001, Ext. 26. Sr. Kathleen Ganiel, O.S.F., D.R.E. Students 467.
Convent—2141 New Castle Dr., 27103. Tel: 336-774-3956.
Mission—Our Lady of Fatima 211 W. 3rd St., Forsyth Co. 27101. Tel: 336-723-8238; Fax: 336-723-8290.

Special Assignment:
Rev. Msgr.—
West, Mauricio W., Vicar Gen. & Chancellor
Revs.—
Hoover, John P.
Roux, Christopher Alan

On Duty Outside the Diocese:
Revs.—
Brzoska, David
Choquet, Alexei H.
Osorio, Louis
Wilderotter, Paul C.

Graduate Studies:
Rev.—
DeClue, Richard

Military Chaplains:
Revs.—
Fitzgibbons, Peter L., U.S. Army
Klepacki, Michael S., U.S. Navy

Unassigned:
Revs.—
Hanson, Richard N.
Tarasi, Carlo D.

On Sabbatical:
Rev.—
Pagel, John M.

Absent On Leave:
Revs.—
Baker, Donald P.
DeAguilar, Arturo
Hanic, Jonathan
Kuhn, Dennis R.
Schneider, John
Tice, Cecil
Williamson, Thomas

Absent on Medical Leave:
Rev.—
Hokanson, Richard P.

Retired:
Most Rev.—
Curlin, William G., D.D., 3005 Markworth Ave., 28203.
Rev. Msgrs.—
Kerin, Joseph A., 2410 Old Steine Rd., Apt. 803, 28269.
Kovacic, Anthony, 411 Dogwood Ln., Belmont, 28012.
Showfety, Joseph, 7-A Fountain Manor Dr., Greensboro, 27405.
Walsh, Thomas R., 12 N. 6th St., Allegany, NY 14706.
Revs.—
Ayathupadam, Joseph, 114 White Branch Ct., Fort Mill, SC 29715.
Cahill, James, P.O. Box 1856, Sylva, 28779-1856.
Cintula, Francis M., 45 S.E. 13th St., A-1, Boca Raton, FL 33432.
Clements, Thomas P., P.O. Box 5086, Statesville, 28687.
Evans, William Morris, P.O. Box 665, Cashiers, 28717-0665.
Hawker, James, 133 Cmdr. Shae Blvd., Unit 807, Quincy, MA 02171.
Hoover, Conrad, D.Min., 1300 Reece Rd., Apt. 505, 28209.
Hourihan, Raymond B., 507 Fulton St., Elmira, NY 14904.
Kelleher, Joseph, 1525 Woods Rd., Apt. 101, 27106.
Kimbrough, Conrad, Taylor Village, 107 Penny Rd., Apt. 1022, High Point, 27260.
Latsko, Andrew, St. Mary of Providence Center, 227 Isabella Rd., Elverson, PA 19520.
Manley, Bernard A., Taylor Village, 107 Penny Rd., Apt. 1017, High Point, 27260.
McCue, Richard T., 50 Brookside Dr., Apt. D2, Exeter, NH 03833-1653.
Meehan, Gabriel, 805 Foxwood Ct. S.W., Lenoir, 28645.
Reese, Charles T., 800 Bay Dr., No. 25, Niceville, FL 32578.
Sheridan, Edward J., 6860 Greedy Hwy., Hickory, 28602.
Solari, James K., 109 Penny Rd., 219E, High Point, 27260.

Sullivan, D. Edward, Autumn House East, 2618 E. Market St., York, PA 17402-2411.
Tuller, John, St. Ann's House, 2161 Leonard St., N.W., Grand Rapids, MI 49504.
Waters, Joseph, Pennybyrn at Maryfield, 107 Penny Rd., Apt. 1020, High Point, 27260.

Permanent Deacons:
Adams, Wayne, Our Lady of the Highways, Thomasville
Atkinson, James, Holy Spirit, Denver
Boissey, David, St. Benedict, Greensboro
Brantley, Charles, (Retired), St. Philip the Apostle, Statesville
Burke, John J., Jr., Sacred Heart, Brevard
Caplette, Ronald, St. Francis of Assisi, Lenoir
Carl, Daniel, St. James, Concord
Cilone, Andrew, Immaculate Conception, Forest City
Cooper, Philip, St. Pius X, Greensboro
Crosby, Patrick, Sacred Heart, Brevard
Decker, Myles, St. Joseph, Kannapolis
DeSautels, Charles, St. Leo, Winston-Salem
Diener, Mark, St. Gabriel, Charlotte
Dotson, Robert E., (Living Outside of the Diocese)
Duca, Peter, Our Lady of the Assumption, Charlotte
Eckoff, Ralph R., (Retired), St. Margaret Mary, Swannanoa
Evers, Jeffrey S., St. Luke, Charlotte
Fadero, Nick, (Retired), St. Patrick Cathedral, Charlotte
Flores, Louis, Our Lady of the Assumption, Charlotte
Forester, Gordon L., (Retired), St. Paul the Apostle, Greensboro
Geoffroy, Roland, (Unassigned)
Gettlefinger, Robert, (Retired), St. Gabriel, Charlotte
Gilfillan, Scott D., St. Joseph, Newton
Gillis, Eugene J., Holy Cross, Kernersville
Haarsgard, Walter, Immaculate Heart of Mary, High Point
Hamrlik, James, St. Matthew, Charlotte
Harkin, William, St. Margaret, Maggie Valley
Haslett, Bruce H., (Living Outside of Diocese)
Heine, Charles, Our Lady of the Mountains, Highlands
Herman, Paul, St. Matthew, Charlotte
Hickey, Gerald P., (Retired), St. Vincent de Paul, Charlotte
Horai, Stephen J., (Retired), Our Lady of the Assumption, Charlotte
Hubbell, Carl, St. William, Murphy
Huff, Sidney, Our Lady of Lourdes, Monroe
Johnson, James R., St. Charles, Morganton
K'Briuh, Pierre M., St. Mary, Greensboro
Kak, Thomas, (Retired), Immaculate Heart of Mary, High Point
Killian, Philip, Jr., (Unassigned)
King, David E., Maryfield Pennybyrn
King, Mark J., St. Matthew, Charlotte
Kingsley, Arthur J., St. Michael, Gastonia
Knight, Charles, Our Lady of the Consolation, Charlotte
Konarski, Edward A., St. Charles Borromeo, Morganton
Kopfle, John, St. Vincent de Paul, Charlotte
La Pointe, Gerard P. St. Margaret, Maggie Valley
Langsdorf, Michael, Divine Redeemer, Boonville
Leahy, Michael, St. Andrew the Apostle, Mars Hill
Lee, Pe nhia cha, St. Charles Borromeo, Morganton
Liotard, Paul, Holy Angels, Mount Airy
Lisk, Larry, St. Paul the Apostle, Greensboro
Lyerly, R. Alexander, (Unassigned)
Mack, Joseph H., Jr., (Retired), (Living Outside Diocese)
Manning, Franklin L., Sr., (Retired)
Markle, Harold, (Retired), St. John Baptiste de la Salle, North Wilkesboro
Martino, John, St. Charles Borromeo, Morganton
May, Hugo L., (Retired), St. Aloysius, Hickory
Mazur, James, Sacred Heart, Salisbury
McNulty, Brian P., St. Thomas Aquinas, Charlotte
Medina, Carlos A., Sr., St. Patrick, Charlotte
Murphy, Robert, St. Mark, Huntersville
Nash, Mark D., St. Thomas Aquinas, Charlotte
O'Madigan, Dennis T., (Retired), (Unassigned)
Pais, Louis, St. Mark, Huntersville
Parrish, John N., St. John Neumann, Charlotte
Piche, Guy, Chap., Catholic Conference Center, Hickory; St. Helen, Spencer Mountain
Pickett, A. Stephen, St. Francis, Lenior
Potkay, Gerald, Holy Infant, Reidsville
Pozo, Guido, St. Gabriel, Charlotte
Rasmussen, Thomas, St. Aloysius, Hickory
Reilly, Matthew, St. Phillip The Apostle, Statesville
Reyes, Jesus, Our Lady of Lourdes, Monroe
Rinkus, Louis, (Retired), (Unassigned)
Ritchie, Timothy, Holy Cross, Keunersville
Rodriguez, Edwin, (Unassigned)
Rohan, Timothy, Our Lady of Grace, Greensboro
Schumacher, Gerard A., (Retired), Holy Family, Clemmons
Schumacher, Joseph N., (Retired), Our Lady of Mercy, Winston-Salem
Shaw, Vincent H., Jr., St. Mary, Greensboro
Shaw, William S., St. Pius Tenth, Greensboro
Sherwood, Ronald D., St. Mark, Huntersville
Sims, John E., St. Therese, Mooresville
Smith, Joseph T., (Retired), (Unassigned)
Steinkamp, Ronald F., St. Pius Tenth, Greensboro
Stout, Michael L., St. Barnabas, Arden
Szalony, George A., St. Ann, Charlotte
Teich, Paul A., (Retired), Our Lady of Grace, Greensboro
Todd, Curtiss, (Retired), St. Gabriel, Charlotte
Torres, Rafael J., St. Luke, Charlotte
Triana, Rudy J., St. Barnabas, Arden
Weisenhorn, John P., (Retired), St. Michael, Gastonia
Wenning, Bernard W., Jr., (Retired), St. Gabriel, Charlotte
Williams, Kevin, Our Lady of the Assumption, Charlotte
Zboyovski, Michael J., Sr., St. Eugene, Asheville
Zimmerle, John O., St. Francis of Assisi, Mocksville

INSTITUTIONS LOCATED IN THE DIOCESE

[A] COLLEGES AND UNIVERSITIES

BELMONT. **Belmont Abbey College*, 100 Belmont-Mount Holly Rd., 28012-1802. Tel: 704-825-6700; Fax: 704-825-6743. Email: donaldbeagle@bac.edu. Web: belmontabbeycollege.edu. Rt. Rev. Placid D. Solari, O.S.B., Chancellor; William Thierfelder, Ph.D., Pres.; Carson Daly, Ph.D., Academic Dean; Very Rev. David G. Brown, O.S.B., Registrar; Wayne Scroggins, Vice Pres. Admin. & Finance; Donald Beagle, Dir. Library. (Coed) Liberal Arts Senior College. Priests 1; Brothers 2; Sisters 2; Lay Teachers 69; Students 1,638.

The Ecumenical Institute of Wake Forest University and Belmont Abbey College Tel: 704-825-6748; Fax: 704-825-6743.

Sacred Heart College, 101 Mercy Dr., 28012-4805. Tel: 704-829-5100; Fax: 704-829-5137. Sr. Rosalind Picot, R.S.M., Pres. Sisters of Mercy., College ceased academic operation, effective August 1987. Corporation intact.

[B] HIGH SCHOOLS

KERNERSVILLE. *Bishop McGuinness Catholic High School*, 1725 N.C. Hwy. 66 S., 27284. Tel: 336-564-1010; Fax: 336-564-1060. Email: grepass@bmhs.us. Web: www.bmhs.us. George L. Repass, M.Ed., Prin.; Sr. Anne Thomas Taylor, Dean of Students; Lyndall Cantrell, Librarian. Sisters of St. Joseph 2; Lay Teachers 40; Students 553.

[C] ELEMENTARY SCHOOLS, INTERPAROCHIAL

ASHEVILLE. *Asheville Catholic School*, (Grades PreK-8), 12 Culvern St., 28804. Tel: 828-252-7896; Fax: 828-252-5708. Email: info@ashevillecatholic.org. Web: www.ashevillecatholic.org. Donna Gilson, Prin.; Shonra McManus, Librarian. Lay Teachers 18; Students 197.

[D] REGIONAL SCHOOLS

CHARLOTTE. *Mecklenburg Area Catholic Schools (M.A.C.S.)*, (Grades PreK-12), Catholic School System of Eight Schools., 1123 S. Church St., 28203. Tel: 704-370-3270; Fax: 704-370-3292. Web: www.charlottediocese.org/catholicschools. Linda Cherry, Supt.; Janice Ritter, Asst. Supt.

Charlotte Catholic High School (Bishop Hafey Memorial), 7702 Pineville-Matthews Rd., 28226. Tel: 704-543-1127; Fax: 704-543-1217. Web: www.gocougars.org. Gerald A. Healy, Prin.; Randy Belk, Dean of Students; Steve Carpenter, Asst. Prin.; Angela Montague, Asst. Prin.; Lyndall Cantrell, Librarian. Clergy 1; Lay Teachers 105; Students 1,403.

Charlotte Catholic High School Athletic Association Tel: 704-543-1127; Fax: 704-543-1217.

Charlotte Catholic High School Alumni Association Tel: 704-543-9118; Fax: 704-543-1217.

Charlotte Catholic High School Home School Association Tel: 704-543-1127; Fax: 704-543-1217.

Holy Trinity Middle School (Grades 6-8), 3100 Park Rd., 28209. Tel: 704-527-7822; Fax: 704-525-7288. Kevin Parks, Prin.; Sheena Zawistowicz, Dean of Students; Deb Robinson, Asst. Prin. Clergy 1; Lay Teachers 66; Students 921.

St. Matthew School (Grades 6-8), 11525 Elm Ln., 28277. Tel: 704-544-2070; Fax: 704-544-2184. Kevin O'Herron, Prin.; Kathy McKinney, Asst. Prin. Lay Teachers 40; Students 630.

Our Lady of the Assumption School (Grades PreK-5), 4225 Shamrock Dr., 28215. Tel: 704-531-0067; Fax: 704-531-7633. Allana Rue-Ram Kisoon, Prin.; Mary Leva, Asst. Prin. Lay Teachers 18; Students 114.

St. Ann School (Grades PreK-5), 600 Hillside Ave., 28209. Tel: 704-525-4938; Fax: 704-525-2640. Peggy Mazzola, Prin.; Lisa Horton, Asst. Prin. Lay Teachers 32; Students 156.

St. Gabriel School (Grades K-5), 3028 Providence Rd., 28211. Tel: 704-366-2409; Fax: 704-362-5063. Sharon Broxterman, Prin. Lay Teachers 40; Students 567.

St. Mark School (Grades K-7), 14750 Stumptown Rd., Huntersville, 28078. Tel: 704-766-5000; Fax: 704-875-6377. Debbie Butler, Prin.; Anne Fulmer, Asst. Prin. Lay Teachers 50; Students 714.

St. Patrick School (Grades K-5), 1125 Buchanan St., 28203. Tel: 704-333-3174; Fax: 704-333-3178. Debbie Mixer, Prin.; Kelly Parks, Asst. Prin. Lay Teachers 28; Students 327.

[E] GENERAL HOSPITALS

ASHEVILLE. *Sisters of Mercy Services Corporation*, 1201 Patton Ave., 28806. Tel: 828-281-1303; Fax: 828-254-4102. Email: laltsheler@somsc.org. Web: www.somsc.org. P.O. Box 16367, 28816-0367. Tim Johnston, Pres. & CEO.

Sisters of Mercy Urgent Care, Inc., 1201 Patton Ave., 28806-0367. Tel: 828-210-2121; Fax: 828-254-4102. Email: shana@urgentcares.org. P.O. Box 16367, 28816. Patients Assisted Annually 6,700; Total Staff 61.

[F] SPECIAL CARE FACILITIES

BELMONT. **Holy Angels Services, Inc.*, 6600 Wilkinson Blvd., 28012. Tel: 704-825-4161; Fax: 704-825-0553. Email: info@holyangelsnc.org. Web: www.holyangelsnc.org. Mailing Address: P.O. Box 710, 28012. Mrs. Regina P. Moody, M.Ed., Pres. & CEO. Residential and developmental programs and svcs. for children and adults with mental retardation and physical disabilities. Sisters of Mercy 2; Capacity (All Programs) 125.

Morrow Center (Children 0-20)

Little Angels Child Development Center On-site integrated day care.

Great Adventures Social Club Adults with mental retardation.

South Point Adult group home.

Lakewood Adult group home.

McAuley Residence ICF/MR Group Homes Bed Capacity 48.

Cherubs Cafe, Gifts & Candy Bouquets Tel: 704-825-0414; Fax: 704-825-0416. (Age 18+); Job coaching, work options.

Supported Living (Age 18+)

Camp Hope Recreational opportunities for individuals with developmental disabilities.

Carrabaun Adult group home.

Gary Home Adult group home. Total Assisted Annually 125.

[G] CATHOLIC SOCIAL SERVICES

CHARLOTTE. *Catholic Social Services of the Diocese of Charlotte, Inc.*, The Pastoral Center: 1123 S. Church St., 28203. Tel: 704-370-3228; Fax: 704-370-3298. Email: ekthurbee@Charlottediocese.org. Web: www.cssnc.org. Elizabeth K. Thurbee, M.S.W., A.C.S.W, Exec. Dir.; Gerard A. Carter, Assoc. Dir.

Area Offices:

Catholic Social Services-Western Regional Office, 50 Orange St., Asheville, 28801. Tel: 828-255-0146; Fax: 828-253-7339. Jacqueline Crombie, Dir.

Catholic Social Services-Charlotte Regional Office, 1123 S. Church St., 28203. Tel: 704-370-3262; Fax: 704-370-3377. Geri King, M.S.W., Dir.

Catholic Social Services-Piedmont and Triad Office, 627 W. Second St., Winston-Salem, 27101. Tel: 336-727-0705; Fax: 336-714-3232.

Catholic Social Services-Refugee Resettlement Office, 1123 S. Church St., 28203. Tel: 704-370-3262; Fax: 704-370-3377. Cira Ponce, Refugee Resettlement Dir.

Special Ministries:

CSS: Domestic Adoption Program of North & South Carolina Jeannie Beall, Prog. Dir. Tel: 828-255-0146, (Asheville); Tel: 336-714-3201, (Winston-Salem); Tel: 704-370-3232, Fax: 704-370-3377, (Charlotte).

Catholic Social Services-International Adoption Program, Asheville. Tel: 828-255-0146; 888-990-4199; Fax: 828-253-7339. Carol Meyerriecks, M.S.W., Prog. Dir. Int'l. Adoptions.

Catholic Social Services-Elder Ministry, 1123 S. Chruch St., 28203. Tel: 704-370-3220; 704-370-3228; Fax: 704-370-3377. Sandra Breakfield, Prog. Dir.

Catholic Social Services-Disaster Relief, 1123 S. Church St., 28203. Tel: 704-370-3250; Fax: 704-370-3377. Gerard A. Carter, Dir.

Catholic Social Services-Marriage Preparation Program Tel: 704-370-3228; Fax: 704-370-3377. Sherill Beason, Contact Person.

Catholic Social Services-Family Life Office, 1123 S. Church St., 28203. Tel: 704-370-3250; Fax: 704-370-3377. Gerard Carter, Dir.

Catholic Social Services-Youth Empowerment Services Contact Winston-Salem Office., 627 W. Second St., Winston-Salem, 27101. Tel: 336-725-4263; Fax: 336-714-3232. Katisha Blackwell, Dir., YESS.

Catholic Social Services-Latino Family Center, 210 Gatewood Ave., High Point, 27260. Tel: 336-884-5858; Fax: 336-884-9062.

Catholic Social Services-Immigration Services Contact Asheville, Winston-Salem, or Charlotte Offices., Tel: 828-255-0146 (Asheville); 336-727-0705 (Winston-Salem).

Catholic Social Services-Host Homes Contact Winston-Salem Office., 621 W. Second St., Winston-Salem, 27101. Tel: 336-725-4678; Fax: 336-727-9333. Dewey Haley, Prog. Dir.

Catholic Social Services-Natural Family Planning Contact the Diocesan Office., 1123 S. Church St., 28203. Tel: 704-370-3230; Fax: 704-370-3377. Batrice Adcock, Contact Person.

Office of Justice and Peace, 1123 S. Church St., 28203. Tel: 704-370-3225; Fax: 704-370-3377. Joseph Purello, Dir.

Catholic Campaign for Human Development Contact Office of Justice and Peace., Tel: 704-370-3234; Fax: 704-370-3377. Mary Jane Bruton, Prog. Dir.

Catholic Relief Services Contact Office of Justice and Peace., Tel: 704-370-3225; Fax: 704-370-3377. Joseph Purello, Diocesan Dir.

Operation Rice Bowl Contact Office of Justice and Peace., Tel: 704-370-3234; Fax: 704-370-3377. Mary Jane Bruton, Prog. Dir.

Catholic Social Services-Office of Economic Opportunity, 27 Hatchett St., Murphy, 28906. Tel: 828-835-3535; Fax: 828-835-9794. Claudie Burchfield, Prog. Dir.

Catholic Social Services-Pregnancy Support Services Contact the pregnancy support worker at any of the CSS offices., Tel: 888-789-4989; 704-370-3222 (Charlotte); 828-255-0146 (Asheville); 336-727-0705 (Winston); Fax: 704-370-3377 (Charlotte).

Catholic Social Services-Respect Life Program, 1123 S. Church St., 28203. Tel: 704-370-3229; Fax: 704-370-3377. Maggi Nadol, Prog. Dir.

[H] HOME HEALTH CARE

ROSMAN. **Frances Warde Health Service*, 9526 Rosman Hwy., 28772. Tel: 828-884-7990; Fax: 828-966-9609. Email: jdewarrsm@juno.com. Sisters Gretchen Hermanny, R.S.M., M.D., Medical Dir.; Carol Hoban, S.C., M.S.N., Nurse Practitioner; Jacqueline Dewar, R.S.M., Business Mgr. Sisters 3; Total Assisted 3,000; Staff 7.

[I] NURSING HOMES

HIGH POINT. *Maryfield Nursing Home*, 1315 Greensboro Rd., 27260. Tel: 336-821-4000; Fax: 336-886-4036. Email: sisterlucy@pbmccrc.com. Web: www.pennybyrnatmaryfield.com. Sr. Lucy Hennessy, S.M.G., Admin./Chm. of the Board. Poor Servants of the Mother of God 5; Bed Capacity 125; Cottages 49.

Pennybyrn at Maryfield Tel: 336-886-2444; Fax: 336-886-4036. Retirement Homes 49; Apartments 131.

[J] MONASTERIES AND RESIDENCES OF PRIESTS AND BROTHERS

BELMONT. *Belmont Abbey*, 100 Belmont-Mount Holly Rd., 28012-1802. Tel: 704-461-6675; Fax: 704-461-6242. Email: AbbotPlacid@bac.edu. Web: www.bac.edu/monastery. Rt. Revs. Placid D. Solari, O.S.B., Abbot; Oscar C. Burnett, O.S.B. (Retired); Very Rev. David G. Brown, O.S.B., Prior; Revs. Agostino Fernandez, O.S.B.; Matthew T. McSorley, O.S.B.; Kenneth A. Geyer, O.S.B.; David R. Kessinger, O.S.B.; Kieran A. Neilson, O.S.B.; Francis P. Forster, O.S.B.; Arthur J. Pendleton, O.S.B.; Christopher A. Kirchgessner, O.S.B.; Bros. Tobiah Abbott, O.S.B.; Elsas Correa-Torres, O.S.B.; Paul Shanley, O.S.B.; Edward Mancuso, O.S.B.; Emmanuel Slobodzian, O.S.B.; Anthony Swofford, O.S.B., Subprior; Andrew Spivey, O.S.B.

Southern Benedictine Society of North Carolina, Inc. Abbots 2; Monk Priests of Abbey 10; Priests in Residence 10; Brothers 7.

MOORESVILLE. *Jesuit Community*, 217 Brawley School Rd., 28117-9103. Tel: 704-664-3992; Fax: 704-660-6321. Email: vcurtin@gmail.com. Revs. Vincent de P. Alagia, S.J.; Vincent C. Curtin, S.J.; Joseph B. Kappes, S.J.; William J. Lynch, S.J.; Thomas P. McDonnell, S.J.; Francis X. Reese, S.J.; Joseph A. Sobierajski, S.J.; Donald M. Ward Jr., S.J.; Bro. Ricardo E. Greeley, S.J.

Jesuit Community in Western North Carolina

STONVILLE. *Franciscan Friary*, 477 Grogan Rd., Stoneville, 27048. Tel: 336-573-3751; Fax: 336-573-3752. Revs. Louis Canino, O.F.M., Dir.; John McDowell, O.F.M.

[K] CONVENTS AND RESIDENCES FOR SISTERS

CHARLOTTE. *Missionaries of Charity*, 1625 Glenn St., 28205. Tel: 704-531-2943. Ministry for poor. Sisters 4.

Sisters of Mercy of the Americas, South Central Community, Inc., Carmel House, 11427 Olde Turnbury Ct., 28277. Tel: 704-542-0951; Fax: 704-542-0951. Sisters Kathy Green, R.S.M., Pres.; Paulette Williams, R.S.M., Sec./Treas., Sisters of Mercy, N.C. Administration

ASHEVILLE. *Sisters of Mercy of the Americas, South Central Community, Inc.*, Sisters of Mercy Convent, 2 Sunset Walk, 28804. Tel: 828-232-0084. Email: smg@somsc.org. Web: www.urgentcares.org. Sisters 3; Health Care 2; Parish 1.

BELMONT. *Sisters of Mercy of the Americas, South Central Community, Inc.*, Sacred Heart Convent, 100 Mercy Dr., 28012-4805. Tel: 704-829-5260; Fax: 704-829-5267. Web: www.mercysc.org. Sr. Mary Andrew Ray, R.S.M., Coord. Connected with the Motherhouse are Holy Angels, Inc., the McAuley Center, House of Mercy, Inc., and Catherine's House, Inc. Sisters in Motherhouse 32.

Sisters of Mercy of the Americas, South Central Community, Inc., Mercy Administration Center: 101 Mercy Dr., 28012-2898. Tel: 704-829-5260; Fax: 704-829-5267.

HAMPTONVILLE. *Sisters of Mercy of the Americas, South Central Community, Inc., Well of Mercy*, 181 Mercy Ln., 27020-7199. Tel: 704-539-5449.

HIGH POINT. *Congregation of the Sisters of Charity of St. Vincent De Paul*, St. Vincent Convent, 1225 Elon Pl., 27263. Tel: 336-884-1442; Fax: 336-887-1200. Email: scvusa@triad.rr.com. Sr. Archana, S.C.V., Supr.

Poor Servants of the Mother of God Inc., 1315 Greensboro Rd., 27260. Tel: 336-821-4000; Fax: 336-886-4036. Email: sisterlucy@pbmccrc.com. Sr. Lucy Hennessy, S.M.G., Mission Leader.

MATTHEWS. *Sisters of Mercy of the Americas, South Central Community, Inc., Coolock House*, 1510 Kirkbridge Ct., 28105. Tel: 704-847-5363; Fax: 704-847-5363. Email: therese_galligan@yahoo.com. Parish and Bereavement Ministry. Sisters of Mercy of the Americas 2.

VALE. *Maryvale Motherhouse*, 2522 June Bug Rd., 28168. Tel: 704-276-2626; Fax: 704-276-2626. Sr. Mary Louis, Foundress and Supr. Congregation of Our Lady Help of the Clergy, (Maryvale Sisters). Parish ministry, day-care center, spiritual/retreat center. Sisters 5.

WINSTON-SALEM. *Sisters of St. Joseph of Chestnut Hill, PA, Our Lady of Mercy Convent*, 2141 New Castle Dr., 27103. Tel: 336-774-3956; Fax: 336-725-2294.

Sisters of St. Joseph of Chestnut Hill, PA, St. Leo Convent, 1975 Georgia Ave., 27104. Tel: 336-723-3639.

[L] CAMPUS MINISTRY CENTERS

CHARLOTTE. *Diocesan Office of Campus Ministry* Ms. Mary Wright, Dir.

University of North Carolina-Charlotte Catholic Campus Ministry House, 9408 Sandburg Ave., 28213-0565. Tel: 704-717-7104. Email: catholic@unec.edu.

University of North Carolina-Asheville/Mars Hill College Catholic Campus Ministry, UNC-Asheville, P.O. Box 8067, Asheville, 28814. Tel: 828-226-3809. Email: uncacatholic@aol.com. Gloria Schweizer, Catholic Campus Ministry.

Belmont Abbey College 100 Belmont-Mount Holly Rd., Belmont, 28012. Tel: 704-829-7196. Jenny Ryan, Dir. Campus Ministry. Email: jenniferryan@bac.edu; Charles Pobee-Mensah, Asst. Dir.

Appalachian State University 232 Faculty St., Boone, 28607. Tel: 828-264-7087; Fax: 828-262-0970. Erin Leonard, Catholic Campus Min.

Western Carolina University Catholic Student Center, P.O. Box 2766, Cullowhee, 28723-0364. Tel: 828-293-9374; Fax: 828-262-3721. Email: ccm@wcucatholic.org. Matthew Newsome, Catholic Campus Min.

Davidson College P.O. Box 7181, Davidson, 28035-7181. Tel: 704-894-2423. Email: kasoos@davidson.edu. Karen Soos, Catholic Campus Min. (Davidson)

NC Agricultural and Technical State University & Bennett College 1009 Bluford St., Greensboro, 27401. Tel: 336-272-5868. Email: theahouse@bellsouth.net. Alberta Hairston.

University of North Carolina-Greensboro, Greensboro College & Guilford College UNG-G ACM Center, P.O. Box 26170, Greensboro, 27402-6170. Tel: 336-334-4264; Fax: 336-334-4264. Email: ptdeloca@uncg.edu.

Wake Forest University and Winston-Salem University P.O. Box 7204, Reynolda Station, Winston-Salem, 27109. Tel: 336-758-5018; Fax: 336-758-4462. Julie McElmurry, Dir.; Rev. Jude T. DeAngelo, O.F.M-.Conv.

[M] RETREAT CENTERS

STONEVILLE. **St. Francis Springs Prayer Center*, 477 Grogan Rd., 27048. Tel: 336-573-3751; Fax: 336-573-3752. Email: fransprings@aol.com. Web: www.stfrancissprings.com. Revs. John McDowell, O.F.M., Dir.; Louis Canino, O.F.M.

[N] REFLECTION CENTERS

BELMONT. *The McAuley Center* Center for Adult Religious Education., 100 Mercy Dr., 28012. Tel: 704-829-5113; Fax: 704-829-5137. Sr. Mary Hugh Mauldin, R.S.M., Dir.

HAMPTONVILLE. *Well of Mercy Inc.*, 181 Mercy Ln., 27020. Tel: 704-539-5449; Fax: 704-539-4487. Email: mercy@yadtel.net. Sisters Brigid McCarthy, R.S.M., Co-Dir.; Donna Marie Vaillancourt, R.S.M., Co-Dir. Retreats and psycho-spiritual development programs.

MAGGIE VALLEY. *Living Waters Catholic Reflection Center*, 103 Living Waters Ln., 28751. Tel: 828-926-3833; Fax: 828-926-1997. Email: lwcrc@bellsouth.net. Web: www.catholicretreat.org. Bro. William C. Harkin, O.S.A., Dir. Retreats, days of recollection, and continuing educ.

[O] HISPANIC MINISTRY

CHARLOTTE. *Diocesan Hispanic Ministry*, 1123 S. Church St., 28203. Tel: 704-370-3269; Fax: 704-370-3291. Email: aminkrott@charlottediocese.org. Sr. Andrea Inkrott, O.S.F., Dir. Hispanic Ministry.

[P] CONFERENCE CENTERS

HICKORY. *Catholic Conference Center*, 1551 Trinity Ln., 28602-9049. Tel: 828-327-7441; 888-536-7441 (Toll Free); Fax: 828-327-0872. Email: info@catholicconference.org. Web: www.catholicconference.org. Deacon Guy A. Piche, Dir. & Chap.

[Q] MISCELLANEOUS

CHARLOTTE. *Catholic Diocese of Charlotte Housing Corp.*, 1123 S. Church St., 28203. Tel: 704-370-3248; Fax: 704-971-4312. Email: juwidelski@charlottediocese.org. Rev. Msgr. Mauricio W. West, Pres.; Elizabeth Thurbee, A.C.S.W., Vice Pres.; William G. Weldon, Treas.; Jerry Widelski, Dir. Provides housing facilities and services for individuals and families with special needs.

MACS Education Foundation, 1123 S. Church St., 28203. Tel: 704-370-3303; Fax: 704-370-3398. Web: www.charlottediocese.org.

**Room at the Inn, Inc.*, 3737 Weona Ave., 28209. Tel: 704-525-4673; Fax: 704-521-2751. Email: iroomattheinn@rati.org. Web: www.rati.org. Jeannie Wray, Exec. Dir. Room at the Inn-Charlotte, 3737 Weona Ave., Charlotte, NC 28209. Tel: 704-525-4673. Long-term maternity and aftercare services for single, pregnant women, with their babies.

**Seton Media House, Inc.*, 7421 Carmel Executive Park, Ste. 214, 28226. Tel: 704-544-2077; Fax: 704-542-0867. Email: setonhouse@aol.com. Richard G. Hoefling, Pres. & CEO; Stephen M. Wilfong, Exec. Dir. Purpose: Distribution of printed materials reflective of Catholic teaching to Catholic schools, and religious educ. programs at no cost to students, family or school.

Sisters of Mercy of North Carolina Foundation, Inc., 2115 Rexford Rd., Ste. 401, 28211. Tel: 704-366-0087; Fax: 704-366-8850. Web: www.somncfdn.org. Edward J. Schlicksup, Pres.; Sr. Mary Jerome Spradley, R.S.M., Bd. Chairperson.

ASHEVILLE. *Catherine McAuley Mercy Foundation, Inc.*, 1201 Patton Ave., 28806. Tel: 828-281-2598; Fax: 828-254-4102. Email: sharon@somsc.org. Mailing Address: P.O. Box 16367, 28816-0367.

BELMONT. **Catherine's House*, 400 Mercy Dr., P.O. Box 1633, 28012. Tel: 704-825-9599; Fax: 704-825-2734. Email: patsyfuller@catherineshouse.org. Web: www.catherineshouse.org. Karen Andrews, Pres. & CEO. Transitional housing for women and women with children who are homeless.

Holy Angels Foundation, Inc., 6600 Wilkinson Blvd., 28012. Mailing Address: P.O. Box 710, 28012.

House of Mercy, Inc., 701 Mercy Dr., 28012. Tel: 704-825-4711; Fax: 704-825-9976.

Email: hse4mercy@aol.com. Web: www.thehouseofmercy.org. P.O. Box 808, 28012. Stan Patterson, Pres. & CEO. Provides a home for persons living with AIDS in the advanced stages who have no other housing alternative in an 11 county region. Bed Capacity 6.

Mercy Community Housing North Carolina (MCHNC), 6531 Wilkinson Blvd., 28012. Tel: 404-873-3887; Fax: 877-693-2333. Email: pgrant@mercyhousing.org. Web: www.mercyhousing.org. Peter Walker, Pres.; Paula Grant, Vice Pres.

Mercy Housing, South East, Inc., 6531 Wilkinson Blvd., 28012. Tel: 404-873-3887; Fax: 877-693-2333. Email: pgrant@mercyhousing.org. Web: www.mercyhousing.org. Purpose: provide housing and supportive services to low income, special needs populations and seniors.

Mercy Place Belmont, 6531 Wilkinson Blvd., 28012. Tel: 404-873-3887; Fax: 877-698-2333. Peter Walker, Pres.; Paula Grant, Vice Pres.; Patricia O'Roark, Legal Affairs Mgr. Provides housing and support services for very low-income seniors.

Sisters of Mercy of the Americas, South Central Community, Inc., 101 Mercy Dr., 28012-2898. Tel: 704-829-5260; Fax: 704-829-5267. Email: support@mercysc.org. Web: www.mercysc.org. Sr. Kathy Green, R.S.M., Pres.

South Central FIDES, Inc., 101 Mercy Dr., 28012.

GREENSBORO. *Franciscan Center*, 233 N. Greene St., 27401. Tel: 336-273-2554; Fax: 336-273-2441. Email: fransprings@aol.com. Web: www.stfrancissprings.com. Rev. Louis Canino, O.F.M., Dir.

Society of St. Vincent De Paul, 201 S. Chapman St., 27403. Tel: 336-272-0336. Financial assistance, furniture and appliances.

KERNERSVILLE. *Triad Catholic Schools Foundation*, P.O. Box 2565, 27285-2565. Tel: 800-560-6311; 704-370-3303; Fax: 704-370-3398.

SALISBURY. *Cursillos in Christianity*, 218 W. Thomas St., 28144. Butch Mayer, Contact Person.

RELIGIOUS INSTITUTES OF MEN REPRESENTED IN THE DIOCESE

For further details refer to the corresponding bracketed number in the Religious Institutes of Men or Women section.

[0140]—*Augustinians* (Villanova, PA)—O.S.A.

[0200]—*Benedictine Monks* (Belmont, NC)—O.S.B.

[]—*Benedictine Monks* (St. Meinrad, IN)—O.S.B.

[0470]—*The Capuchin Friars Province of the Stigmata*—O.F.M.Cap.

[0860]—*Congregation of the Immaculate Heart of Mary*—C.I.C.M.

[1330]—*Congregation of the Mission* (Eastern Prov.)—C.M.

[0480]—*Conventual Franciscans* (Union City, NJ)—O.F.M.Conv

[0520]—*Franciscan Friars* (New York, NY)—O.F.M.

[0690]—*Jesuit Fathers and Brothers* (Maryland Prov.)—S.J.

[]—*Jesuit Fathers and Brothers* (Detroit Province)—S.J.

[0920]—*Oblates of St. Francis De Sales* (Wilmington-Philadelphia)—O.S.F.S.

[1070]—*Redemptorist Fathers* (Baltimore Prov.)—C.Ss.R.

[0560]—*Third Order Regular of St. Francis* (Pittsburgh, PA)—T.O.R.

RELIGIOUS INSTITUTES OF WOMEN REPRESENTED IN THE DIOCESE

[2980]—*Congregation de Notre Dame*—C.N.D.

[3080]—*Congregation of Our Lady, Help of the Clergy*—C.L.H.C.

[1110]—*Dominican Sisters of St. Catherine of Siena*—O.P.

[]—*Grey Nuns of the Sacred Heart*—C.N.S.H.

[2470]—*Maryknoll Sisters*—M.M.

[2710]—*Missionaries of Charity*—M.C.

[]—*Missionary Servants of the Most Blessed Trinity*—M.S.B.T.

[3640]—*Poor Servants of the Mother of God*—S.M.G.

[]—*School Sisters of Notre Dame*—S.S.N.D.

[]—*School Sisters of St. Francis* (Milwaukee, WI)—O.S.F.

[]—*Sisters of Charity* (Leavenworth, KS)—S.C.C.

[0590]—*Sisters of Charity of Saint Elizabeth, Convent Station*—S.C.

[]—*Sisters of Charity of Saint Vincent de Paul*—S.C.V.

[]—*Sisters of Mercy of the Americas* (South Central Community, Inc.)—R.S.M.

[]—*Sisters of Mercy of the Americas* (Mid-Atlantic Community)—R.S.M.

[]—*Sisters of Mercy of the Americas* (West Midwest Community)—R.S.M.

[]—*Sisters of Providence*—S.P.

[]—*Sisters of St. Joseph of Carondelet* (Rochester, MN)—C.S.J.

[]—*Sisters of St. Francis* (Tiffin, OH)—O.S.F.

[]—*Sisters of St. Francis* (Philadelphia, PA)—O.S.F.

[3893]—*Sisters of St. Joseph* (Chestnut Hill, PA)—S.S.J.

[4060]—*Society of the Holy Child Jesus* (Drexel Hill)—S.H.C.J.

NECROLOGY

(No Deaths)

An asterisk (*) denotes an organization that has established tax-exempt status directly with the IRS and is not covered by the USCCB Group Ruling.

Diocese of Cheyenne

(Dioecesis Cheyennensis)

Most Reverend

PAUL D. ETIENNE, D.D., S.T.L.

Bishop of Cheyenne; ordained June 27, 1992; appointed Bishop of Cheyenne October 19, 2009; episcopal ordination and installed December 9, 2009. *Res.: P.O. Box 1468, Cheyenne, WY 82003-1468.*

Most Reverend

JOSEPH HART, D.D.

Retired Bishop of Cheyenne; ordained May 1, 1956; appointed July 1, 1976; appointed Titular Bishop of Timida Regia; Episcopal Ordination August 31, 1976; installed June 12, 1978; retired September 26, 2001. *Res.: P.O. Box 1468, Cheyenne, WY 82003.*

ESTABLISHED AUGUST 2, 1887.

Square Miles 97,548.

Comprises the State of Wyoming and Yellowstone National Park.

For legal titles of parishes and diocesan institutions, consult the Chancery Office.

Chancery Office: 2121 Capitol Ave., P.O. Box 1468, Cheyenne, WY 82003-1468. Tel: 307-638-1530; Fax: 307-637-7936.

Web: www.dioceseofcheyenne.org

Email: dmcintyre@dioceseofcheyenne.org

STATISTICAL OVERVIEW

Personnel	
Bishop	1
Retired Bishops	1
Priests: Diocesan Active in Diocese	35
Priests: Diocesan Active Outside Diocese	1
Priests: Retired, Sick or Absent	16
Number of Diocesan Priests	52
Religious Priests in Diocese	9
Total Priests in Diocese	61
Extern Priests in Diocese	10
Ordinations:	
Diocesan Priests	1
Transitional Deacons	2
Permanent Deacons in Diocese	22
Total Sisters	16
Parishes	
Parishes	36
With Resident Pastor:	
Resident Diocesan Priests	26
Resident Religious Priests	5
Missions	36
Professional Ministry Personnel:	
Sisters	4
Lay Ministers	43
Welfare	
Homes for the Aged	2
Total Assisted	104
Residential Care of Children	1
Total Assisted	242
Special Centers for Social Services	4
Total Assisted	10,804
Educational	
Diocesan Students in Other Seminaries	10
Total Seminarians	10
Elementary Schools, Diocesan and Parish	7
Total Students	975
Catechesis/Religious Education:	
High School Students	811
Elementary Students	2,987
Total Students under Catholic Instruction	4,783
Teachers in the Diocese:	
Sisters	2
Lay Teachers	103
Vital Statistics	
Receptions into the Church:	
Infant Baptism Totals	926
Minor Baptism Totals	110
Adult Baptism Totals	127
Received into Full Communion	139
First Communions	982
Confirmations	818
Marriages:	
Catholic	167
Interfaith	134
Total Marriages	301
Deaths	578
Total Catholic Population	51,467
Total Population	532,000

Former Bishops—Rt. Revs. MAURICE F. BURKE, D.D., cons. Oct. 28, 1887; transferred to the See of St. Joseph, MO, June 19, 1893; died March 17, 1923; THOMAS M. LENIHAN, D.D., cons. Feb. 24, 1897; died Dec. 15, 1901; Most Revs. JAMES J. KEANE, D.D., cons. Bishop of Cheyenne Oct. 28, 1902; raised to the archiepiscopal dignity and transferred to Archdiocese of Dubuque, Aug. 11, 1911; died Aug. 2, 1929; PATRICK A. MCGOVERN, D.D., LL.D., ord. Aug. 18, 1895; assistant at the Pontifical Throne; appt. Jan. 19, 1912; cons. April 11, 1912; died Nov. 8, 1951; HUBERT M. NEWELL, D.D., LL.D., ord. June 15, 1930; appt. Coadjutor Aug. 2, 1947; cons. Sept. 24, 1947; succeeded to the See Nov. 8, 1951; retired Jan. 3, 1978; died Sept. 8, 1987; HUBERT JOSEPH HART, D.D., ord. May 1, 1956; appt. Titular Bishop of Timida Regia July 1, 1976; cons. Aug. 31, 1976; installed June 12, 1978; retired Sept. 26, 2001; DAVID L. RICKEN, D.D., J.C.L., ord. Sept. 12, 1980; appt. Coadjutor Bishop of Cheyenne Dec. 14, 1999; Episcopal Ordination Jan. 6, 2000; succeeded to See Sept. 26, 2001; installed Bishop of Green Bay Aug. 28, 2008.

Chancery Office—2121 Capitol Ave., P.O. Box 1468, Cheyenne, 82003-1468. Tel: 307-638-1530; Fax: 307-637-7936.

Chancellor—CAROL DELOIS, Mailing Address: P.O. Box 1468, Cheyenne, 82003-1468. Tel: 307-638-1530; Fax: 307-637-7936.

Judicial Vicar—Rev. THOMAS E. CRONKLETON JR., J.C.D., Mailing Address: P.O. Box 1468, Cheyenne, 82003-1468. Tel: 307-638-1530; 866-790-0014; Fax: 307-637-7936.

Adjutant Judicial Vicar—Rev. THOMAS R. KADERA, J.C.L., Mailing Address: P.O. Box 1468, Cheyenne, 82003-1468.

Vicar for Retired and Disabled Clergy—VACANT.

College of Consultors—Most Rev. PAUL D. ETIENNE, D.D., S.T.L.; Revs. MICHAEL CARR; THOMAS E. CRONKLETON JR., J.C.D.; ANDREW D. DUNCAN; Very Rev. CARL GALLINGER; Revs. JAMES HEISER; GLEN SZCZECHOWSKI.

Presbyteral Council—VACANT.

Vicars Forane—Very Revs. KEVIN A. KOCH, Casper Deanery; CARL GALLINGER, Cheyenne Deanery; SAMUEL HAYES, Rock Springs Deanery; CLIFFORD JACOBSON, Sheridan Deanery; VERNON F. CLARK, Thermopolis Deanery.

Finance Officer—Mr. JAMES T. DINNEEN, Mailing Address: P.O. Box 1468, Cheyenne, 82003-1468. Tel: 307-638-1530; Fax: 307-637-7936.

Finance Council—Ex Officios, Voting: Most Rev. PAUL D. ETIENNE, D.D., S.T.L.; Rev. GARY RUZICKA; The Honorable MIKE SULLIVAN; Mr. HOWARD BAKER. Ex Officios, Non-Voting: Revs. THOMAS E. CRONKLETON JR., J.C.D.; THOMAS OGG; Mr. JAMES T. DINNEEN. Appointed Members, Voting: JARED BLACK; WILLIAM DOWNES; FRANK ROTELLINI; CHUCK HARKINS, Chm.; LYNNE BOOMGAARDEN; BILL MANZER.

Diocesan Pastoral Council—VACANT.

Tribunal Office— All marriage correspondence are to be directed to: *Mailing Address: The Tribunal Office, P.O. Box 1468, Cheyenne, 82003-1468.* Tel: 307-638-1530; 866-790-0014; Fax: 307-637-7936.

Judicial Vicar—Rev. THOMAS E. CRONKLETON JR., J.C.D.

Adjutant Judicial Vicar—Rev. THOMAS R. KADERA, J.C.L.

Tribunal Case Instructor—CONNIE KASSAHN.

Bookkeeper/Secretary/Ecclesiastical Notary—LINDA ROBBINS.

Promoter of Justice—Rev. Msgr. CHARLES F. TAYLOR, J.C.D. (Retired).

Judges—Revs. MICHAEL CARR; THOMAS E. CRONKLETON JR., J.C.D.

Defenders of the Bond—Very Rev. SAMUEL HAYES; Rev. Msgr. CHARLES F. TAYLOR, J.C.D. (Retired); Very Rev. CARL GALLINGER; Rev. THOMAS R. KADERA, J.C.L.; DIANE L. BARR, J.C.D.; Revs. DAVID L. DEIBEL, J.D., J.C.L.; LOUIS A. SIRIANNI, J.C.L.

Advocates—SUSAN SIMON; BONNIE BAUMBERGER; Deacon EDWARD MCCARTHY; PAT MCCARTHY; DORENE MCINTYRE; Deacon KIM CARROLL; Revs. JAMES HEISER; RANDALL J. OSWALD.

Diocesan Administrative Offices and Boards

Development—VACANT, Dir.; TRISH SCHUMACHER, Exec. Asst., Mailing Address: P.O. Box 1468, Cheyenne, 82003-1468. Tel: 307-638-1530; 866-790-0014.

Education Office—DAVID JOHNSON, Supt. Catholic Schools, Mailing Address: P.O. Box 1468,

Cheyenne, 82003. Tel: 307-638-1530; Fax: 307-637-7936; Deacon VERNON DOBELMANN, Dir. Pastoral Ministries, Mailing Address: P.O. Box 1468, Cheyenne, 82003-1468. Tel: 307-638-1538; Fax: 307-637-7936; VACANT, Media Consultant, St. Rose of Lima, 605 E. 22nd Ave., Torrington, 82240. Tel: 307-532-5556; Fax: 307-534-2329.

Diocesan Schools Advisory Group—Most Rev. PAUL D. ETIENNE, D.D., S.T.L.; DAVID JOHNSON, Supt. Catholic Schools; Revs. CARL BEAVERS; ANDREW D. DUNCAN; THOMAS OGG; GARY RUZICKA; JAMES SCHUMACHER; LINDA MARCOS, Lead Teacher Holy Spirit School; Sr. FLORENCE MCMANAMEN, O.S.B., Prin. St. Margaret School; JANET MATERI, Prin. St. Mary's School; CYNDY NOVOTNY, Prin. St. Anthony Tri-Parish Catholic School; TOM WILHELM, Interim Prin. St. Laurence O'Toole School; COLLEEN MODEL, Prin. Holy Name School; LYNN GRASSEL, Prin. John Paul II School.

Director of Pastoral Ministries—Deacon VERNON DOBELMANN, Mailing Address: P.O. Box 1468, Cheyenne, 82003-1468. Tel: 307-638-1530; Fax: 307-637-7936.

Beginning Experience for Divorced or Widowed—CURTIS WEST, Mailing Address: P.O. Box 9953, Casper, 82609. Tel: 307-463-2677.

Bereavement Ministry—TERRY CASSIDY. Tel: 307-635-4965.

Divorced/Separated/Widowed Ministry—LINDA HURLESS. Tel: 307-265-3509.

Marriage Encounter—MIKE WINGERT; ANN WINGERT, 2005 Apache St., Cheyenne, 82009. Tel: 307-637-0441.

Natural Family Planning—Deacon VERNON DOBELMANN.

Rainbows for All God's Children—JULIE PETERSEN, 1334 Juniper Dr., Rock Springs, 82901. Tel: 307-362-7595.

Respect Life Catholic Pro-Life Ministry—Deacon VERNON DOBELMANN.

Retrouvaille, Ministry for Hurting Marriages—Deacon VERNON DOBELMANN.

Newspaper "Wyoming Catholic Register"—

Stewardship Committee—Most Rev. PAUL D. ETIENNE, D.D., S.T.L.; Deacon DOUGLAS VLCHEK; LEE BOSCH; Deacon KIM CARROLL; DORENE MCINTYRE; DONNA CUIN; D. J. CUNNINGHAM.

Vocation Office—Rev. RAY RODRIGUEZ, Dir., Mailing Address: St. Paul's Newman Center, 1800 E. Grand Ave., Laramie, 82070. Tel: 307-745-5461; Fax: 307-742-0521.

Youth Office—Deacon VERNON DOBELMANN, Mailing Address: P.O. Box 1468, Cheyenne, 82003-1468. Tel: 307-638-1530; Fax: 307-637-7936.

Other Diocesan Boards, Councils and Programs

Diocese of Cheyenne, Board of Directors—Most Rev. PAUL D. ETIENNE, D.D., S.T.L.; Rev. GARY RUZICKA; Mr. HOWARD BAKER; The Honorable MIKE SULLIVAN.

Bishop's Annual Campaign, "Bishop's Appeal"—Mr. JAMES T. DINNEEN, Mailing Address: P.O. Box 1468, Cheyenne, 82003-1468. Tel: 307-638-1530; Fax: 307-637-7936.

Boy Scouts—WILL HILL, 1025 Falls Court, Riverton, 82501. Tel: 307-332-2688.

Building Committee—Most Rev. PAUL D. ETIENNE, D.D., S.T.L.; ROGER BAALMAN, A.I.A., Chm.; Rev. GARY RUZICKA; BOB ADAMS; CAROL DELOIS; JOHN STEIL; HERBERT W. STOUGHTON, Ph.D.; Mr. JAMES T. DINNEEN, Sec.; Mr. GENE ROCCABRUNA, P.E.

Catholic Relief Services—

Clergy Continuing Education Grants—Very Rev. CLIFFORD JACOBSON, 1000 Butler Spaeth Rd., Gillette, 82716. Tel: 307-682-3319; Fax: 307-682-6386.

Confraternity of Christian Doctrine—Deacon VERNON DOBELMANN, Mailing Address: P.O. Box 1468, Cheyenne, 82003-1468. Tel: 307-638-1530.

Council of Religious—Sr. RUTH ANN HEHN, S.C.L.

Cursillo Board—VACANT.

Permanent Diaconate—Deacon KEN PITLICK, Interim Dir., 736 Houston, Newcastle, 82701.

Diaconate Program, Permanent—Deacon ROLLAND RABOIN, Mailing Address: 4525 Rd. 66, Torrington, 82240. Tel: 307-532-1571.

Ecumenism Commission—Rev. PETER JOHNSON, Chm.

Holy Child Pontifical Association—

Housing—JUNE THRONBURG, Admin., St. Anthony Manor, 211 E. 6th, Casper, 82601. Tel: 307-237-0843; Sr. RUTH ANN HEHN, S.C.L., Admin., Holy Trinity Manor, 2516 E. 18th St., Cheyenne, 82001. Tel: 307-778-8850.

Information Office—

June Priests' Retreat—Rev. GLEN SZCZECHOWSKI, Coord., Mailing Address: P.O. Box 818, Powell, 82435. Tel: 307-754-2480.

Liturgical Commission—Rev. GARY RUZICKA, Exec. Sec.

Propagation of the Faith—

Director of Pastoral Ministries—Deacon VERNON DOBELMANN, Mailing Address: P.O. Box 1468, Cheyenne, 82003-1468. Tel: 307-638-1530; Fax: 307-637-7936.

Rural Life Ministry—Rev. PETER JOHNSON, Dir., 532 N. Lobban Ave., Buffalo, 82834.

St. Joseph's Society for Priests (Clergy Mutual Benefit Society)—Most Rev. PAUL D. ETIENNE, D.D., S.T.L.; Revs. THOMAS OGG, Pres.; CARL BEAVERS; KARL MILLIS; WILLIAM HILL III; THOMAS E. CRONKLETON JR., J.C.D., Sec.; THOMAS R. KADERA, J.C.L.; Rev. Msgrs. EUGENE SULLIVAN (Retired); CHARLES F. TAYLOR, J.C.D. (Retired); Mr. LEO RILEY, Admin.

Retirees' Representative—Rev. Msgrs. CHARLES F. TAYLOR, J.C.D. (Retired); EUGENE SULLIVAN (Retired).

Victim Assistance Coordinator—Deacon ROLLAND RABOIN. Tel: 307-532-4586. Email: rraboin@vistabeam.com.

CLERGY, PARISHES, MISSIONS AND PAROCHIAL SCHOOLS

CITY OF CHEYENNE

(LARAMIE COUNTY)

1—ST. MARY'S CATHEDRAL (1868) [CEM] Revs. Gary Ruzicka; Steven Matthew Titus; Michael Adeniji; Deacons Al Lancaster; Vernon Dobelmann.
Mailing Address: P.O. Box 1268, 82003-1268. Tel: 307-635-9261; Fax: 307-635-5723. Web: www.stmarycathedral.com.
School—Janet Materi, Prin. Lay Teachers 19; Students 200.
Catechesis/Religious Program—Tel: 307-637-4009; 307-635-9261. Becky Hart, D.R.E. (Grades PreK-5); Vicki Yeoman, D.R.E. (Grades 6-8); Chris Martinez, Youth Dir. (Grades 9-12). Students 374.
St. Mary's Goods Bookstore—100 W. 21st St., 82001. Tel: 307-635-4228. Email: bookstore@stmarycathedral.com. Total Staff 1; Total Assisted 150.

2—HOLY TRINITY (1957) Rev. Thomas E. Cronkleton Jr.; Deacon David Zelenka. In Res., Rev. Msgr. William Delaney (Retired); Rev. James Doudican (Retired).
Res.: 1836 Hot Springs Ave., 82003-5337. Tel: 307-632-5872; Fax: 307-632-1810. Web: www.holytrinitycheyenne.org.
Catechesis/Religious Program—Lillian (Lee) Bosch, Dir. Adult Faith Formation/Stewardship; Cameron Smith, Dir. Youth Faith Formation. Students 319.

3—ST. JOSEPH'S (1929), (Hispanic), Rev. Raymond B. Moss; Deacon Patrick Bradley.
Mailing Address: P.O. Box 1141, 82003-1141. Tel: 307-634-4625; Fax: 307-635-4700.
Office: 314 E. Sixth St., 82007.
Res.: 515 House, 82007. Tel: 307-638-3133.
Church: 300 E. 6th St., 82007.
Catechesis/Religious Program—Tel: 307-634-4625, Ext. 103. Eva Estorga, D.R.E. Students 255.

OUTSIDE CITY OF CHEYENNE

BUFFALO, JOHNSON CO., ST. JOHN THE BAPTIST (1885), (Basque), Rev. Peter Johnson.
Res.: 532 N. Lobban, 82834. Tel: 307-684-7268; Fax: 307-684-5490. Email: frpete@bresnan.net.
Catechesis/Religious Program—Tel: 307-684-7440; Fax: 307-684-5490. Carol Gagliano, D.R.E. Students 90.
Mission—St. Mary Clearmont, Johnson Co. 82834.
Mission—St. Hubert Kaycee, Johnson Co. 82834.

CASPER, NATRONA CO.

1—ST. ANTHONY OF PADUA (1903) Very Rev. Kevin A. Koch; Rev. Philip Vaske, Parochial Vicar; Deacons Don Stewart; David Johnson.
Office: 604 S. Center, 82601. Tel: 307-266-2666; Fax: 307-266-4127. Email: shepherd@bresnan.net. Web: www.stanthonyscasper.org.
School—St. Anthony Tri-Parish School, 218 E. Seventh, 82601. Tel: 307-234-2873; Fax: 307-235-4946. Email: sasprincipal@bresnan.net. Web: www.stanthonytri-parishschool.net. Cyndy Novotny, Prin. Lay Teachers 24; Students (K-9) 176; Preschool 39.
Catechesis/Religious Program—Email: stanthonyRE@bresnan.net. Debbie Salazar, C.R.E.; Dean Menardi, Youth Min. Students 130.

2—OUR LADY OF FATIMA (1954) Rev. Robert L. Fox; Deacon Ed McCarthy.
Res.: 1401 CY Ave., 82604. Tel: 307-265-5586; Fax: 307-266-2958. Email: church@fatimaincasper.org.
Catechesis/Religious Program—Tel: 307-473-2076. Carol O'Hearn, C.R.E. Students 73.

3—SAINT PATRICK'S (1963), (Irish), Rev. August Koeune; Rev. Msgr. James O'Neill (Retired); Deacon Russ Humphreys.
Office: 400 Country Club Rd., Box 50397, 82605-0397. Tel: 307-235-5535; 307-266-2495; Fax: 307-237-7244. Web: www.stpatricks-casper.com.
Catechesis/Religious Program—Email: samsc@tribcsp.com. Sam Carrick, D.R.E. Students 191.

CODY, PARK CO., ST. ANTHONY (1942) Very Rev. Vernon F. Clark; Deacon Lee Pico.
Res.: 1333 Monument Dr., 82414-3406. Tel: 307-587-3388; Fax: 307-587-3383. Email: info@stanthonycody.org. Web: www.stanthonycody.org.
Catechesis/Religious Program—Tel: 307-587-2567; Fax: 307-587-3383. Rick Moser, D.R.E. Students 130.
Mission—Tel: 307-587-3388. Sunday Services at Old Faithful, Lake Lodge, Canyon, and Mammoth in summer only.
Mission—St. Therese 1406 State, Meeteetse, Park Co. 82433.

DOUGLAS, CONVERSE CO., ST. JAMES (1907) Rev. John Savio.
Mailing Address: P.O. Box 1500, 82633-1500. Tel: 307-358-2338; Fax: 307-358-8498. Email: stjames@communicomm.com.
Catechesis/Religious Program—Kathi Cox, D.R.E. Students 104.
Mission—Our Lady of Lourdes, . Tel: 307-358-2338.

EVANSTON, UINTA CO., ST. MARY MAGDALEN (1878) [JC] Rev. Jaime Bueno (Colombia).
Mailing Address: Box 163, 82931-0163. Tel: 307-789-2189; Fax: 307-789-2788. Email: stmmagdalen@msn.com.
Catechesis/Religious Program—Students 67.
Mission—St. Helen P.O. Box 183, Fort Bridger, Uinta Co. 82933. Tel: 307-782-6190.
Catechesis/Religious Program—Tel: 307-787-6590. Students 20.

GILLETTE, CAMPBELL CO., ST. MATTHEW'S (1926) [JC] Very Rev. Clifford Jacobson; Rev. William Hill III.
Res.: 1000 Butler Spaeth Rd., 82716. Tel: 307-682-3319; Fax: 307-682-6386. Email: stmatthews@stmatthewswy.org. Web: www.stmatthewswy.org.
School—John Paul II Catholic School, (Grades PreSchool-8) Tel: 307-686-4114; Fax: 307-682-6368. Web: www.johnpauliicatholicschool.com. Lynn Grassel, Prin. Lay Teachers 15; Students (K-8) 115; Students (Preschool) 110.
Catechesis/Religious Program—Students 230.
Mission—Blessed Sacrament 624 Wright Blvd., Wright, Campbell Co. 82732. Tel: 307-464-0809.
Mission—St. Patrick 216 N. Belle Fourche, Moorcroft, Crook Co. 82721. Tel: 307-756-9478.

GLENROCK, CONVERSE CO., ST. LOUIS (1920) [JC] Rev. George E. Von Kaenel, S.J.
Mailing Address: P.O. Box 27, 82637-0027. Tel: 307-436-9529. Email: chstlou@vcn.com.
Catechesis/Religious Program—Tel: 307-436-8347. Naomi Brungardt, C.R.E. Students 42.

GREEN RIVER, SWEETWATER CO., IMMACULATE CONCEPTION (1884) [JC] Rev. Thomas Sheridan; Deacon Wes Nash.
Mailing Address: P.O. Box 70, 82935-0070. Tel: 307-875-2441; Fax: 307-875-2184. Email: icc@wyoming.com.
Catechesis/Religious Program—Judy Philpot, D.R.E. Students 165.

GREYBULL, BIG HORN CO., SACRED HEART (1919) Rev. Michael Ehiemere.
Mailing Address: P.O. Box 231, 82426-0231. Tel: 307-765-2438; Fax: 307-765-2438. Email: shcg@tctwest.net.
Catechesis/Religious Program—Students 57.
Mission—St. Philip Ave. D, Basin, Big Horn Co. 82410. Fax: 307-765-2478.

GUERNSEY, PLATTE CO., ST. ANTHONY'S (1969) [JC 0] Rev. Felix S. Martinito Jr.
Res.: P.O. Box 430, 82214-0430. Tel: 307-836-2586. Email: stanthonyguernsey@embarqmail.com.
Catechesis/Religious Program—Lori Ibarra, D.R.E. Students 15.

JACKSON, TETON CO., OUR LADY OF THE MOUNTAINS (1955) [JC] Revs. Joseph Geders, C.M.; Florante E. Marcelo; Deacons Robert J. Miller; Doug Vlchek; Bill Hill.
Mailing Address: P.O. Box 992, 83001-0992. Tel: 307-733-2516; Fax: 307-739-1478. Email: olm@wyoming.com. Web: www.olmcatholic.org.
Catechesis/Religious Program—Tel: 307-733-7919. Email: chris.owens@wyoming.com. Students 180.
Mission—Holy Family P.O. Box 231, Afton, Lincoln Co. 83110. Tel: 307-886-0731. Web: www.holyfamilywy.org.
Chapel—Sacred Heart Chapel, (Grand Teton National Park)Web: www.olmcatholic.org.

KEMMERER, LINCOLN CO., ST. PATRICK'S (1901), (Italian—Slovak), [JC] Rev. Randall J. Oswald.

Mailing Address: Box 311, 83101-0311. Tel: 307-877-4573; Fax: 307-877-3354. Email: stpatricks@hamsfork.net.
Catechesis/Religious Program—Students 30.
Mission—St. Dominic
Mission—La Barge Catholic Community Center

LANDER, FREMONT CO., HOLY ROSARY (1882) [JC] Rev. David Erickson. In Res., Rev. Robert K.C. Siu (HON) (Retired).
Res.: 163 Leedy Rd., P.O. Box 1047, 82520-1047. Tel: 307-332-4952; Fax: 307-332-6141. Email: holyrosary@wyoming.com.
Catechesis/Religious Program—Tel: 307-332-4803. Michael Lewis, D.R.E. Students 83.
Mission—Ascension
Mission—St. Brendan Jeffrey City, Freemont Co.

LARAMIE, ALBANY CO.

1—ST. LAURENCE O'TOOLE (1872) [JC] Rev. James Schumacher; Deacons John Deti; Alfred Franco.
Mailing Address: 617 S. Fourth St., 82070-1045. Tel: 307-745-3115; Fax: 307-745-3131. Email: slotoole@qwest.net.
School—(Grades K-6), 608 S. Fourth St., 82070. Tel: 307-742-6363; Fax: 307-745-3131. Tom Wilhelm, Prin. Lay Teachers 6; Students 51.
Catechesis/Religious Program—Students 82.

2—ST. PAUL'S NEWMAN CENTER (1957) Very Rev. Carl Gallinger; Brian Neely, Dir. Campus Min.
Mailing Address: Parish, 1800 E. Grand Ave., 82070-4316. Tel: 307-745-5461; Fax: 307-742-0521. Email: newman@newmancenter.org. Web: www.newmancenter.org.
Catechesis/Religious Program—Students 75.

LOVELL, BIG HORN CO., ST. JOSEPH'S (1979) Rev. Eckley Macklin, S.O.L.T.
Church: 1141 Shoshone Ave., P.O. Box 185, 82431-0185. Tel: 307-548-2282; Fax: 307-548-2395. Email: stjoseph@tctwest.net.
Catechesis/Religious Program—Students 31.

LUSK, NIOBRARA CO., ST. LEO'S (1911), (German—Irish), [JC] Revs. Michael Carr; Raphael Chiaka (Nigeria), Parochial Admin.
Res.: 900 W. Fifth St., Box 959, 82225-0959. Tel: 307-334-2702; Fax: 307-334-3161. Email: stleochurch@gmail.com.
Catechesis/Religious Program—Kristi Hart, D.R.E. & Parish Sec. Students 23.

NEWCASTLE, WESTON CO., CORPUS CHRISTI (1890) [JC] Rev. Philip C. Wagner; Deacons Kenneth Pitlick, Pastoral Assoc. & Sec.; Peter Kim Carroll, Pastoral Assoc.
Res.: 19 W. Winthrop, 82701. Tel: 307-746-4219; Fax: 307-746-9909. Email: corpus@rtconnect.net.
Catechesis/Religious Program—Students 42.
Mission—St. Paul P.O. Box 28, Sundance, Crook Co. 82729. Tel: 307-283-2383; Fax: 307-283-2383. Rev. Peter James Maura.
Catechesis/Religious Program—Students 24.
Mission—St. Anthony P.O. Box 177, Upton, Weston Co. 82730.
Catechesis/Religious Program—Students 31.
Mission—St. Matthew's 26 Hunter, Hulett, Crook Co. 82720.
Catechesis/Religious Program—Students 26.

PINE BLUFFS, LARAMIE CO., ST. PAUL'S (1913) Rev. Killian Muli (Kenya).
Mailing Address: P.O. Box 97, 82082-0097.
Rectory—Res.: 307 Beech St., 82082-0097. Tel: 307-245-3761. Email: stpaulschurch@RTconnect.net.
Church: 501 E. 4th St., 82082.
Catechesis/Religious Program—Tel: 307-245-3304. Pam Miller, D.R.E. Students 29.
Mission—St. Joseph Albin, Laramie Co.
Mission—St. Peter 316 4th St., Carpenter, Laramie Co. 82054.

PINEDALE, SUBLETTE CO., OUR LADY OF PEACE (1940) Rev. Lucas K. Simango (Zambia); Deacon Daniel Kostelc.
Mailing Address: P.O. Box 70, 82941-0070. Tel: 307-367-2359; Fax: 307-367-3553.
Church: 112 S. Sublette, 82941.
Catechesis/Religious Program—Barbara Lauger, D.R.E. (K-12). Students 52.
Mission—St. Anne Big Piney, Sublette Co. 83113. Tel: 307-276-3227.

POWELL, PARK CO., ST. BARBARA (1910) Rev. Glen Szczechowski.
Res.: 115 E. Third, P.O. Box 818, 82435-0818. Tel: 307-754-2480; Fax: 307-754-5018. Email: stbarb@bresnan.net.
Catechesis/Religious Program—Tel: 307-754-3361. Tom Spiering, D.R.E.; Janet Spiering, D.R.E. Students 85.
Mission—Our Lady of the Valley P.O. Box 818, Clark, Park Co. 82435. Tel: 307-754-2480.

RAWLINS, CARBON CO., ST. JOSEPH'S (1867) [JC] Very Rev. Samuel Hayes; Deacon Jesus P. Juarez.
Mailing Address: P.O. Box 68, 82301-0068. Tel: 307-324-4631; Fax: 307-324-3288. Email: cachurcsaj@qwestoffice.net.
Catechesis/Religious Program—Tel: 307-324-4033. Dan Rehard, D.R.E.; Ellen Rehard, D.R.E. Students 110.
Mission—Our Lady of the Sage P.O. Box 116, Baggs, Carbon Co. 82321. Tel: 307-383-6100.

RIVERTON, FREMONT CO., ST. MARGARET'S (1908) Revs. Andrew D. Duncan; David H. Gau, S.J.
Res.: 622 E. Park, 82501. Tel: 307-856-3757; Fax: 307-856-8533. Email: stmargc@msn.com.
School—(Grades PreK-6), 220 N. 7th E., 82501. Tel: 307-856-5922. Sr. Florence McManamen, O.S.B., Prin. Lay Teachers 13; Students 111.
Catechesis/Religious Program—Tel: 307-856-1277. Cheryl Rodgers, D.R.E. Students 43.
Mission—St. Joseph 211 Wyoming St., Shoshoni, Fremont Co. 82649. Tel: 307-876-2760.
Mission—Our Lady of the Woods 4 S. Riverton St., P.O. Box 1134, Dubois, Fremont Co. 82513. Tel: 307-455-2533.
Mission—St. Edward Kinnear Rectory, 11350 US Hwy. 26, P.O. Box 34, Kinnear, Fremont Co. 82516. Tel: 307-856-5502.

ROCK SPRINGS, SWEETWATER CO.

1—SS. CYRIL AND METHODIUS (1910) Consolidated with Our Lady of Sorrows Church, Rock Springs to form Holy Spirit Catholic Community.

2—HOLY SPIRIT CATHOLIC COMMUNITY (1887) Revs. Carl Beavers; Jing Baldo (Philippines); Deacon Charles Lux.
Mailing Address: 116 Broadway, 82901. Tel: 307-362-2611; Fax: 307-382-4911. Email: info@theholyspiritparish.com.
Res.: 633 Bridger Ave., 82901. Tel: 307-362-3493.
School—Holy Spirit Catholic School, Tel: 307-362-6077; Fax: 307-362-2177. Email: hscsoffice@wyoming.com. Linda Marcos, Prin. Lay Teachers 7; Students 73.
Catechesis/Religious Program—Tel: 307-362-2611; Fax: 307-382-4911. Email: tamarakusler@theholyspiritparish.com. Students 197.
Mission—St. Vivian Superior, Sweetwater Co.
Mission—St. Anthony Wamsutter, Sweetwater Co.
Mission—St. Christopher Eden, Sweetwater Co. 82926.

3—OUR LADY OF SORROWS, Consolidated with SS. Cyril and Methodius to form Holy Spirit Catholic Community.

SAINT STEPHENS, FREMONT CO., ST. STEPHEN'S (1884), (Native American), [CEM], Indian Mission for the Shoshone and Arapaho Indians. St. Stephen's Indian Mission, Inc. Revs. Ronald S. Seminara, S.J.; J. Robert Hilbert, S.J.; Daniel J. Gannon, S.J.; Sisters Florence Petsch, O.S.F., Pastoral Assoc.; Teresa Frawley, O.S.F., Pastoral Assoc.; Monica Suhayda, C.S.J., Pastoral Assoc.
Mailing Address: 33 St. Stephens Rd., Box 250, 82524-0250. Tel: 307-856-5937; Fax: 307-856-3853. Email: ssimf@wyoming.com. Web: www.ssimf.com/.
Catechesis/Religious Program—Tel: 307-856-7806. Jean Watt, D.R.E. Students 44.
Mission—St. Joseph Box 8358, Ethete, Fremont Co. 82520. Tel: 307-332-4415.
Mission—Blessed Sacrament

SARATOGA, CARBON CO., ST. ANN'S (1957) Rev. Karl Millis.
Mailing Address: P.O. Box 667, 82331-0667. Tel: 307-326-5461; Fax: 307-326-5461 (Call first). Email: stanns@union-tel.com.
Catechesis/Religious Program—Tel: 307-326-8190. Marilyn Verplancke, D.R.E. Students 30.
Mission—St. Joseph Hanna, Carbon Co. 82327.

SHERIDAN, SHERIDAN CO., HOLY NAME (1885) [JC] Revs. Thomas Ogg; Ronald Stolcis; Robert Spaulding.
Mailing Address: 9 S. Connor, 82801. Tel: 307-672-2848; Fax: 307-672-5105. Email: holynamechurch@fiberpipe.net. Web: www.holynamesheridan.org.
School—121 S. Connor, 82801. Tel: 307-672-2021; Fax: 307-673-4474. Web: www.hncswy.org. Colleen Model, Prin. Lay Teachers 19; Students 100.
Catechesis/Religious Program—Tel: 307-672-2848, Ext. 17. Students 106.
Mission—Our Lady of the Pines 34 Wagon Box Rd., Story, Sheridan Co. 82842.
Mission—St. Edmund 310 Historic Hwy. 14, Ranchester, Sheridan Co. 82839.

THERMOPOLIS, HOT SPRINGS CO., ST. FRANCIS (1906) Rev. Hugo L. Blotsky, O.S.B.
Mailing Address: 815 Arapahoe, P.O. Box 272, 82443-0272. Tel: 307-864-2674. Email: stfrancis@rtconnect.net.
Catechesis/Religious Program—Fax: 307-864-2458. Sharon Cordingly, C.R.E.; Kent Cordingly, C.R.E. Students 44.

TORRINGTON, GOSHEN CO., ST. ROSE (1906) Rev. Michael Carr; Deacon Rolland Raboin.
Res.: 605 E. 22nd Ave., 82240. Tel: 307-532-5556; Fax: 307-534-2329. Email: strosetorrington@yahoo.com.
Catechesis/Religious Program—Tel: 307-532-3125. Patricia Amberg, D.R.E. Students 81.

WHEATLAND, PLATTE CO., ST. PATRICK'S (1891) [JC] Rev. Jan Santich.
Res.: 1009 Ninth St., 82201. Tel: 307-322-2070. Email: stpatrickchurch@qwestoffice.net. Web: www.dioceseofcheyenne.org/npar_st_patrick_wheatland.html.
Catechesis/Religious Program—Tel: 307-322-4213. Students 90.
Mission—Mary Queen of Heaven 401 5th St., Chugwater, Platte Co. 82201.

WORLAND, WASHAKIE CO., ST. MARY MAGDALEN (1949) [JC] Rev. James Heiser.
Mailing Address: 1099 Charles Ave., 82401-0901. Tel: 307-347-2820; Fax: 307-347-2450. Email: stmarym@rtconnect.net. Web: www.worland.com/magdalen.
Catechesis/Religious Program—Students 117.

Chaplains of Public Institutions

CHEYENNE. *U.S. Veterans Administration Hospital 1*, 90 MW/HC, F.E. Warren AFB, 82005. Rev. Thomas R. Kadera, J.C.L.

EVANSTON. *Wyoming State Hospital*. Vacant.

LUSK. *Wyoming Women's Center (Correctional Facility)*. Rev. Raphael Chiaka (Nigeria).

RAWLINS. *Wyoming State Penitentiary*, P.O. Box 468, 82301-0068. Tel: 307-324-4631. Rev. Karl Millis.

SHERIDAN. *U.S. Veterans Administration Hospital*. Vacant.

In Res.:

Revs.—

Schneider, Daniel Mary, M. Carm., Prior, Monks of the Most Blessed Virgin Mary of Mt. Carmel, 35 Rd. AFW, Powell, 82435.

Siu, Robert K.C. (HON) (Retired), Holy Rosary Church, P.O. Box 1047, Lander, 82520-1047.

Retired:

Rev. Msgrs.—

Delaney, William, 1836 Hot Springs Ave., 82001-5337.

O'Neill, James, P.O. Box 50397, Casper, 82605-0397. Tel: 307-235-5535

Sullivan, Eugene, 1416 Trent Ct., 82009.

Taylor, Charles F., J.C.D., P.O. Box 710, Kemmerer, 83101.

Revs.—

Chleborad, Gerald, 6388 S. Grape Ct., Centennial, CO 80121.

Cloonan, Dennis, 3654 Larkwood Ct., Boulder, CO 80304.

Colibraro, Daniel, P.O. Box 1368, Casper, 82602-1368.

Colibraro, Philip, P.O. Box 2025, Casper, 82602-2025.

Daley, Joseph A., 2919 Bass Ave., Cody, 82414.

Doudican, James, 1836 Hot Springs Ave., 82001-5337.

Fahey, Thomas C., Chap., Victory Noll Sisters, 1900 W. Park Dr., Box 109, Huntington, IN 46750.

Fraher, Joseph P., 412 Kearney St., Laramie, 82070.

Gianola, William, 650 Mooring Line Dr., Naples, FL 34102.

Murray, John, 604 S. Center, Casper, 82601.

Reid, Malcolm, 120 W. Pine St., Rawlins, 82301.

Wright, John A., 639 Ave. H #22, Powell, 82435.

Permanent Deacons:

Bradley, Patrick, UMC Chap.; St. Joseph, Cheyenne

Carroll, Kim, Corpus Christi, Newcastle

Deti, John, St. Laurence O'Toole, Laramie

Dobelmann, Vernon, St. Mary, Cheyenne (St. Mary's Cathedral)

Franco, Alfred, Immaculate Conception, Green River

Hill, Bill, Our Lady of the Mountains, Jackson

Hruska, Randy, Holy Family, Afton

Humphreys, Russ, St. Patrick's Church, Casper

Johnson, David, St. Anthony, Casper

Juarez, Jesus, St. Joseph, Rawlins

Kostelc, Daniel, Pinedale

Lancaster, Al, St. Mary's Cathedral, Cheyenne

Lux, Charles, Holy Spirit, Rock Springs

McCarthy, Ed, Our Lady of Fatima, Casper

Miller, Robert J., Our Lady of the Mountains, Jackson

Nash, Wes, Immaculate Conception, Green River

Pico, Lee, St. Anthony, Cody, Yellowstone National Park

Pitlick, Ken, Corpus Christi, Newcastle

Raboin, Rolland, St. Rose of Lima, Torrington

Stewart, Don, St. Anthony's Church, Casper

Vlchek, Douglas, Our Lady of the Mountains, Jackson

Zelenka, David, Holy Trinity, Cheyenne

INSTITUTIONS LOCATED IN THE DIOCESE

[A] PROTECTIVE INSTITUTIONS

TORRINGTON. *St. Joseph's Children's Home* (1930) Box 1117, 82240-1117. Tel: 307-532-4197; Fax: 307-532-8405. Email: bmayor@stjoseph-wy.org. Web: www.stjoseph-wy.org. Robert C. Mayor, Exec. Dir. Children 62; Total Staff 150; Total Assisted 242.

[B] COLLEGES AND UNIVERSITIES

LANDER. **Wyoming Catholic College*, P.O. Box 750, 82520. Tel: 307-332-2930; Fax: 307-332-2918. Email: info@wyomingcatholiccollege.com. Web: www.wyomingcatholiccollege.com. Rev. Robert W. Cook, Pres.; Mrs. Aileen Coccia, Librarian. Priests 2; Lay Teachers 12.

[C] HOUSING FOR THE ELDERLY (LOW INCOME)

CHEYENNE. *Holy Trinity Manor* (1989) 2516 E. 18th St., 82001. Tel: 307-778-8850; Fax: 307-778-8850. Email: rhehn@archdiocesanhousing.org; holytrinitymanor@archdiocesanhousing.org. Sr. Ruth Ann Hehn, S.C.L., Admin. & Site Mgr. Total Staff 1; Total in Residence 30; Total Assisted 43.

CASPER. *St. Anthony Manor* (1983) 211 E. Sixth St., 82601. Tel: 307-237-0843; Fax: 307-237-3516. Email: stanthonymanor@archdiocesanhousing.org. Very Rev. Kevin A. Koch; June Thronburg, Site Mgr. Total Staff 6; Total in Residence 64; Total Assisted Annually 61.

[D] MONASTERIES AND RESIDENCES FOR PRIESTS AND BROTHERS

SAINT STEPHENS. *St. Stephens Mission - Jesuit Community* (1884) 33 St. Stephens Rd., 82524. Tel: 307-856-7806; Fax: 307-856-3853. Email: seminara@wyoming.com. Revs. Ronald S. Seminara, S.J.; J. Robert Hilbert, S.J.; Daniel J. Gannon, S.J.; Sisters Florence Petsch, O.S.F., Pastoral Assoc.; Teresa Frawley, O.S.F., Pastoral Assoc.; Monica Suhayda, C.S.J., Pastoral Assoc. Total Staff 15.

POWELL. *Monks of the Most Blessed Virgin Mary of Mt. Carmel* (2004) 31 Road AFW, 82435. Tel: 307-645-3310; Fax: 307-645-3085. Web: www.carmelitemonks.org. Rev. Daniel Mary Schneider, M. Carm., Prior. Priests 1; Novices 6; Postulants 4; Temporary Vows 3; Perpetual Vows 3.

[E] CONVENTS AND RESIDENCES FOR SISTERS

DAYTON. *Benedictine Sisters of Perpetual Adoration, San Benito Monastery*, P.O. Box 510, 82836-0520. Tel: 307-655-9013. Email: sanbenito@vcn.com. Web: www.benedictinesisters.org/b6.html. Sr. Josetta Grant, O.S.B., Supr. Sisters 3.

[F] CAMPUS MINISTRY

CASPER. *St. Francis Newman Center* (1984) 1732 S. Elm St., 82601. Tel: 307-266-2666. 604 S. Center, 82601. Rev. Philip Vaske, Dir. Total Staff 4.

LARAMIE. *St. Paul's Newman Center, University Catholic Community (University of Wyoming)* 1800 E. Grand Ave., 82070-4316. Tel: 307-745-5461; Fax: 307-742-0521. Email: newman@newmancenter.org. Web: www.newmancenter.org. Very Rev. Carl Gallinger. Total Staff 8.

POWELL. *NorthWest College John Henry Newman Center, St. Barbara Church*, P.O. Box 818, 82435. Tel: 307-754-9220; Fax: 307-754-5018. Email: stbarb@bresnan.net. Rev. Glen Szczechowski; Malinda Hetzel, Coord. Attended by St. Barbara, Powell.

[G] MISCELLANEOUS LISTINGS

CHEYENNE. *Catholic Charities of Wyoming, Inc.*, P.O. Box 907, 82003. Tel: 307-637-0554; Fax: 307-632-2346. P.O. Box 1026, Torrington, 82240. Most Rev. Paul D. Etienne, D.D., S.T.L.; Mike Chadey, Bd. Member; Bill Sniffin, Bd. Member; Lynne Chadey, Bd. Member; Rev. Robert L. Fox, Bd. Member; Robert C. Mayor, Agency Dir.

Holy Trinity Youth Education Trust, c/o Fr. Thomas E. Cronkleton, 1836 Hot Springs Ave., 82001-5337. Tel: 307-632-5872; Fax: 307-632-1810.

Mall at St. Vincent DePaul (1998) *c/o St. Mary Cathedral*, P.O. Box 1268, 82003. Tel: 307-432-0253. Mary Genereux, Mgr. Total Staff 5; Total Assisted 885.

St. Mary's School Foundation, P.O. Box 1268, 82003. Tel: 307-635-9261; Fax: 307-635-5723. Email: gruzicka@stmarycathedral.com. Rev. Gary Ruzicka; Janet Materi, Prin.

The Wyoming Catholic Ministries Foundation, P.O. Box 227, 82003. Tel: 307-638-2558; Fax: 307-637-7936. Email: development@wyocmf.org. Board of Directors Most Rev. Paul D. Etienne, D.D., S.T.L., Diocesan Admin.; Ret. Major Gen. Charles Wing; Esther McGann; Matthew N. Potter, C.F.P.; Gay Woodhouse.

CASPER. *St. Anthony Tri-Parish School Foundation*, 218 E. 7th St., 82601. Tel: 307-234-2873; Fax: 307-235-4946. Email: sasprincipal@bresnan.net. Web: www.stanthonytri-parishschool.net. Very Rev. Kevin A. Koch; Cyndy Novotny, Prin.; Mary Doherty, Contact Person.

**Holy Cross Food Center, Inc.* (1982) 1030 N. Lincoln, 82601. Tel: 307-577-1041. Kitty Carr, Dir. Operated by Holy Cross Center, Inc. Total Staff 25; Total Assisted 9,502.

Knights of Columbus Charitable Trust for Seminarian Education and Priests' Retirement (1991) 604 S. Center, 82601. Tel: 307-266-2666. Email: dstewart@bresnan.net. Deacon Don Stewart, Chm. & Trustee.

**Mother Seton Housing, Inc.* (1989) 910 N. Durbin, P.O. Box 1557, 82602. Tel: 307-577-8026; Fax: 307-577-0125. Email: setonh@tribcsp.com. Pam Kozola, Exec. Dir. Emergency & Transitional Housing for Homeless Single Parents and Children.

Shelter, 324 E. H St., P.O. Box 1557, 82602. Tel: 307-577-8026; Fax: 307-577-0125. Total Assisted 60; Individuals 417.

St. Vincent De Paul Thrift Store (1965) 301 E. H St., 82601. Tel: 307-237-2607. Amanda Perrotta, Mgr.

LARAMIE. *St. Laurence School Foundation*, 608 S. 4th, 82070. Tel: 307-742-6363; Fax: 307-745-3131. Email: twilhelm@stlos.com. Web: stlos.com. Tom Wilhelm, Prin.; Rev. James Schumacher, Contact Person.

ROCK SPRINGS. *Rock Springs Catholic School Foundation*, 116 Broadway St., 82901. Tel: 307-362-2611; Fax: 307-382-4911. Email: patgreenlee@holyspiritparish.com. Rev. Carl Beavers; Linda Marcos, Prin.

SAINT STEPHENS. *St. Stephens Indian Mission Foundation* (1974) P.O. Box 278, St. Stephens, 82524-0278. Tel: 307-856-6797; Fax: 307-857-1802. Email: smif@wyoming.com. Rev. Ronald S. Seminara, S.J., Dir.

RELIGIOUS INSTITUTES OF MEN REPRESENTED IN THE DIOCESE

For further details refer to the corresponding bracketed number in the Religious Institutes of Men or Women section.

[0200]—*Benedictine Monks*—O.S.B.
[]—*Congregation of the Mission*—C.M.
[0690]—*Jesuit Fathers and Brothers Jesus*—S.J.
[]—*Monachi Carmelitarm*—M.Carm.
[0975]—*Society of Our Lady of the Most Holy Trinity*—S.O.L.T.

RELIGIOUS INSTITUTES OF WOMEN REPRESENTED IN THE DIOCESE

[0230]—*Benedictine Sisters of Pontifical Jurisdiction*—O.S.B.
[1070-03]—*Dominican Sisters* (Sinsinawa)—O.P.
[]—*Dominican Sisters of Hope*—O.P.
[3130]—*Our Lady of Victory Missionary Sisters*—O.L.V.M.
[1680]—*School Sisters of St. Francis* (Milwaukee, WI)—O.S.F.
[0480]—*Sisters of Charity of Leavenworth, Kansas*—S.C.L.
[1650]—*Sisters of St. Francis of Philadelphia*—O.S.F.
[3830]—*Sisters of St. Joseph*—C.S.J.

DIOCESAN CEMETERIES

CHEYENNE. *Olivet Cemetery* Rev. Gary Ruzicka.

NECROLOGY

† Shea, Patrick, (Retired)—Died Nov. 15, 2009

An asterisk (*) denotes an organization that has established tax-exempt status directly with the IRS and is not covered by the USCCB Group Ruling.

Archdiocese of Chicago

(Archidioecesis Chicagiensis)

Most Reverend

TIMOTHY J. LYNE

Retired Auxiliary Bishop of Chicago; ordained May 1, 1943; appointed Auxiliary Bishop of Chicago and Titular Bishop of Vamalla October 31, 1983; consecrated December 13, 1983; retired January 24, 1995. *Res.: Holy Name Cathedral, 730 N. Wabash, Chicago, IL 60611.* Tel: 312-787-8040; Fax: 312-787-9113.

Most Reverend

THAD J. JAKUBOWSKI

Retired Auxiliary Bishop of Chicago; ordained May 3, 1950; appointed Auxiliary Bishop of Chicago and Titular Bishop of Plestia February 16, 1988; consecrated April 11, 1988; retired January 24, 2003. *Res.: 6002 W. Berteau Ave., Chicago, IL 60634-1630.* Tel: 773-202-7720; Fax: 773-202-7725.

Most Reverend

JOHN R. GORMAN

Retired Auxiliary Bishop of Chicago and Titular Bishop of Catula; ordained May 1, 1952; appointed February 16, 1988; consecrated April 11, 1988; retired January 24, 2003. *Res.: Our Lady of the Woods, 10731 W. 131st St., Orland Park, IL 60462.* Tel: 708-361-4754.

Most Reverend

RAYMOND E. GOEDERT

Retired Auxiliary Bishop of Chicago; ordained May 1, 1952; appointed Auxiliary Bishop of Chicago and Titular Bishop of Tamazeni July 8, 1991; consecrated August 29, 1991; retired January 24, 2003. *Res.: 1555 N. State Pkwy., Chicago, IL 60610.* Tel: 312-534-8271.

Most Reverend

GEORGE J. RASSAS

Auxiliary Bishop of Chicago; ordained May 2, 1968; appointed Auxiliary Bishop of Chicago and Titular Bishop of Reperi December 1, 2005; consecrated February 2, 2006. *Mailing Address: 200 N. Milwaukee Ave., Ste. 200, Libertyville, IL 60048-2250.* Tel: 847-549-0160; Fax: 847-549-0163.

His Eminence

FRANCIS CARDINAL GEORGE, O.M.I., PH.D., S.T.D.

Archbishop of Chicago; Profession of Perpetual Vows September 8, 1961; ordained December 21, 1963; appointed Bishop of Yakima July 10, 1990; Episcopal Ordination and Installation September 21, 1990; appointed Archbishop of Portland in Oregon April 30, 1996; installed May 27, 1996; appointed Archbishop of Chicago April 8, 1997; installed May 7, 1997; created Cardinal Priest February 21, 1998. *Res.: 1555 N. State Pkwy., Chicago, IL 60610.*

Archbishop Quigley Center & Cardinal Meyer Center: P.O. Box 1979, Chicago, IL 60690-1979. Tel: 312-534-8200.

Web: www.archchicago.org

Most Reverend

FRANCIS J. KANE

Auxiliary Bishop of Chicago; ordained May 14, 1969; appointed Auxiliary Bishop of Chicago and Titular Bishop of Sault Sainte Marie in Michigan January 24, 2003; consecrated March 19, 2003. *Mailing Address: 1641 W. Diversey Pkwy., Chicago, IL 60614.* Tel: 773-388-8670; Fax: 773-388-8676.

Most Reverend

JOHN R. MANZ

Auxiliary Bishop of Chicago; ordained May 12, 1971; appointed Auxiliary Bishop of Chicago and Titular Bishop of Mulia January 13, 1996; consecrated March 5, 1996. *Mailing Address: 1820 S. Leavitt St., Chicago, IL 60608.* Tel: 312-243-4655; Fax: 312-243-4970.

Most Reverend

JOSEPH N. PERRY

Auxiliary Bishop of Chicago; ordained May 24, 1975; appointed Auxiliary Bishop of Chicago and Titular Bishop of Lead May 5, 1998; consecrated June 29, 1998. *Mailing Address: P.O. Box 733, South Holland, IL 60473-0733.* Tel: 708-339-2474; Fax: 708-339-2477.

Most Reverend

THOMAS J. PAPROCKI

Auxiliary Bishop of Chicago; ordained May 10, 1978; appointed Auxiliary Bishop of Chicago and Titular Bishop of Vulturara January 24, 2003; consecrated March 19, 2003. *Mailing Address: 1400 S. Austin Blvd., Cicero, IL 60804.* Tel: 708-329-4040; Fax: 708-222-8854.

Most Reverend

GUSTAVO GARCIA-SILLER, M.SP.S.

Auxiliary Bishop of Chicago; ordained June 22, 1984; appointed Auxiliary Bishop of Chicago and Titular Bishop of Esco January 24, 2003; consecrated March 19, 2003. *Mailing Address: 2330 W. 118th St., Chicago, IL 60643.* Tel: 773-779-8440; Fax: 773-779-8469.

ESTABLISHED NOVEMBER 28, 1843; CREATED 1880.

Square Miles 1,411.

Comprises the Counties of Cook and Lake in the State of Illinois.

Legal Title: The Catholic Bishop of Chicago, a Corporation Sole.
For legal titles of institutions, consult The Pastoral Center.

STATISTICAL OVERVIEW

Personnel	
Cardinals	1
Auxiliary Bishops	6
Retired Bishops	4
Priests: Diocesan Active in Diocese	531
Priests: Diocesan Active Outside Diocese	28
Priests: Diocesan in Foreign Missions	3
Priests: Retired, Sick or Absent	245
Number of Diocesan Priests	807
Religious Priests in Diocese	787
Total Priests in Diocese	1,594
Extern Priests in Diocese	163
Ordinations:	
Diocesan Priests	9
Religious Priests	7
Transitional Deacons	11
Permanent Deacons	15
Permanent Deacons in Diocese	643
Total Brothers	269
Total Sisters	1,966
Parishes	
Parishes	357
With Resident Pastor:	
Resident Diocesan Priests	274
Resident Religious Priests	53
Without Resident Pastor:	
Administered by Priests	30
Missions	11
Pastoral Centers	8
New Parishes Created	1
Closed Parishes	3
Professional Ministry Personnel:	
Brothers	10
Sisters	71
Lay Ministers	521
Welfare	
Catholic Hospitals	19
Total Assisted	3,026,299
Health Care Centers	2
Total Assisted	17,157
Homes for the Aged	45
Total Assisted	6,655
Residential Care of Children	2
Total Assisted	2,959
Day Care Centers	33
Total Assisted	1,802
Specialized Homes	6
Total Assisted	484
Special Centers for Social Services	100
Total Assisted	716,648
Residential Care of Disabled	6
Total Assisted	1,330
Other Institutions	5
Total Assisted	962
Educational	
Seminaries, Diocesan	2
Students from This Diocese	95
Students from Other Diocese	122
Diocesan Students in Other Seminaries	2
Seminaries, Religious	1
Students Religious	106
Total Seminarians	203
Colleges and Universities	6
Total Students	51,175
High Schools, Diocesan and Parish	7
Total Students	1,380
High Schools, Private	33
Total Students	24,953
Elementary Schools, Diocesan and Parish	206
Total Students	60,730
Elementary Schools, Private	9
Total Students	2,065
Non-residential Schools for the Disabled	5
Total Students	450
Catechesis/Religious Education:	
High School Students	8,118
Elementary Students	88,176
Total Students under Catholic Instruction	237,250
Teachers in the Diocese:	
Priests	27
Brothers	32
Sisters	113
Lay Teachers	5,517
Vital Statistics	
Receptions into the Church:	
Infant Baptism Totals	35,151
Adult Baptism Totals	1,630
Received into Full Communion	1,028
First Communions	27,273
Confirmations	21,379
Marriages:	
Catholic	5,408
Interfaith	1,111
Total Marriages	6,519
Deaths	13,235
Total Catholic Population	2,338,000
Total Population	5,989,502

Former Bishops—Rt. Revs. WILLIAM QUARTER, D.D., cons. March 10, 1844; died April 10, 1848; JAMES O. VAN DE VELDE, D.D., cons. Feb. 11, 1849; transferred to Natchez, July 29, 1853; died Nov. 13, 1855; ANTHONY O'REGAN, D.D., cons. July 25, 1854; resigned 1858; died Nov., 1866; JAMES DUGGAN, D.D., cons. Bishop of Antigone, and Coadjutor to the Archbishop of St. Louis, May 1, 1857; transferred to Chicago, Jan. 21, 1859; hospitalized, 1869; died March 27, 1899; THOMAS FOLEY, D.D., Coadjutor-Bishop and Administrator of the diocese; cons. Bishop of Pergamus, Feb. 27, 1870; died Feb. 19, 1879; Most Revs. PATRICK A. FEEHAN, D.D., First Archbishop of Chicago; cons. Bishop of Nashville, Nov. 1, 1865; promoted to Chicago, Sept. 10, 1880; died July 12, 1902; JAMES EDWARD QUIGLEY, D.D., Archbishop of Chicago; ord. April 12, 1879; cons. Bishop of Buffalo, Feb. 24, 1897; promoted to Archbishop of Chicago, Jan. 8, 1903; died July 10, 1915; His Eminence GEORGE CARDINAL MUNDELEIN, Archbishop of Chicago; ord. June 8, 1895; cons. Titular Bishop of Loryma and Auxiliary Bishop of Brooklyn, Sept. 21, 1909; promoted to the See of Chicago, Dec. 9, 1915; created Cardinal Priest, March 24, 1924; died Oct. 2, 1939; SAMUEL CARDINAL STRITCH, Archbishop of Chicago; ord. May 21, 1910; appt. Bishop of Toledo, Aug. 10, 1921; promoted to Archbishop of Milwaukee, Aug. 26, 1930; transferred to Archbishop of Chicago, Dec. 27, 1939; created Cardinal Priest Feb. 18, 1946; elevated to the Roman Curia, Sacred Congregation for the Propagation of the Faith, March 1, 1958; died in Rome, May 27, 1958; ALBERT CARDINAL MEYER, Archbishop of Chicago; ord. July 11, 1926; appt. Bishop of Superior, Feb. 18, 1946; promoted to Archbishop of Milwaukee, July 21, 1953; transferred to Archbishop of Chicago, Sept. 19, 1958; created Cardinal Priest, Dec. 24, 1959; died April 9, 1965; JOHN CARDINAL CODY, S.T.D., D.D., Archbishop of Chicago; ord. Dec. 8, 1931; appt. Auxiliary Bishop of St. Louis, May 14, 1947; cons. July 2, 1947; promoted to Coadjutor of St. Joseph, Jan. 27, 1954; transferred to Kansas City-St. Joseph, Aug. 29, 1956; promoted to Coadjutor Archbishop of New Orleans, Aug. 14, 1961; acceded to the See of New Orleans, Nov. 8, 1964; transferred to the Archdiocese of Chicago, June 16, 1965; created Cardinal Priest in the Consistory, June 26, 1967; died April 25, 1982; JOSEPH CARDINAL BERNARDIN, D.D., Archbishop of Chicago; ord. April 26, 1952; appt. Auxiliary Bishop of Atlanta, March 9, 1966; cons. April 26, 1966; appt. Archbishop of Cincinnati, Nov. 21, 1972; appt. Archbishop of Chicago, July 10, 1982; installed Aug. 25, 1982; created Cardinal Priest, Feb. 2, 1983; died Nov. 14, 1996.

Vicar General—Very Rev. JOHN F. CANARY.

Episcopal Vicars—Most Revs. GEORGE J. RASSAS, Vicariate I (Deaneries A, B, C, D, E, F); FRANCIS J. KANE, Vicariate II (Deaneries A, B, C, D, E, F); JOHN R. MANZ, Vicariate III (Deaneries A, B, D, E); THOMAS J. PAPROCKI, Vicariate IV (Deaneries A, B, C, D, E); GUSTAVO GARCIA-SILLER, M.Sp.S., Vicariate V (Deaneries A, BE, BW, C, D, E); JOSEPH N. PERRY, Vicariate VI (Deaneries A, B, C, D).

Deans—Revs. RONALD J. LEWINSKI, Deanery I-A; PATRICK G. CECIL, Deanery I-B; MICHAEL G. MCGOVERN, Deanery I-C; EDWARD R. FIALKOWSKI, Deanery I-D; ROBERT F. TONELLI, Deanery I-E; BERNARD J. PIETRZAK, Deanery I-F; MICHAEL A. WULSCH, Deanery II-A; JAMES L. BARRETT, Deanery II-B; JAMES T. KACZOROWSKI, Deanery II-C; DANIEL G. MAYALL, Deanery II-D; RONALD N. KALAS, Deanery II-E (Retired); KENNETH A. BUDZIKOWSKI, Deanery II-F; MICHAL OSUCH, C.R., Deanery III-A; NICHOLAS R. DESMOND, Deanery III-B; LAWRENCE R. DOWLING, Deanery III-D; DONALD J. NEVINS, Deanery III-E; PAUL G. SEAMAN, Deanery IV-A; CLAUDIO HOLZER, C.S., Deanery IV-B; MARK A. BARTOSIC, Deanery IV-C; ANDREW P. WYPYCH, Deanery IV-D; ROBERT J. CLARK, Deanery IV-D; THOMAS E. CIMA, Deanery V-A; ANTHONY B. PIZZO, O.S.A., Deanery V-B Midway-East; THADDEUS J. BOJCZUK, Deanery V-B Midway-West; THOMAS P. CONDE, M.Div., S.T.B., M.B.A., Deanery V-C; WILLIAM T. CORCORAN, Ph.D., Deanery V-D; EDWARD F. UPTON, Deanery V-E; DAVID A. JONES, Deanery VI-A; JAMES E. FLYNN, Deanery VI-B; CARL J. QUEBEDEAUX, C.M.F., Deanery VI-C; MICHAEL A. NACIUS, Deanery VI-D.

College of Consultors—Revs. JEREMIAH M. BOLAND; JOHN W. CLEMENS; JOHN COLLINS; Rev. Msgr. ROBERT J. DEMPSEY; Revs. LAWRENCE R. DOWLING; EDWARD R. FIALKOWSKI; DAVID A. JONES; PATRICK R. LAGGES, J.C.D.; EDWARD M. MIKOLAJCZYK; PATRICK J. POLLARD; FRANCIS ROG, C.R.; LAWRENCE J. SULLIVAN.

Presbyteral Council—Revs. EDWARD M. MIKOLAJCZYK, Chm.; LAWRENCE J. SULLIVAN, Vice Chm.; MICHAEL P. KNOTEK, Treas.; LOUIS J. TYLKA, Sec.

Administrative Council—Very Rev. JOHN F. CANARY; Mr. JIMMY M. LAGO; Most Revs. GEORGE J. RASSAS; FRANCIS J. KANE; JOHN R. MANZ; JOSEPH N. PERRY; THOMAS J. PAPROCKI; GUSTAVO GARCIA-SILLER, M.Sp.S.; Revs. THOMAS A. BAIMA, M.B.A., S.T.D.; MICHAEL M. BOLAND; Mr. RAYMOND P. COUGHLIN; Ms. COLLEEN H. DOLAN; Dr. CAROL L. FOWLER; Rev. RICHARD P. HYNES; Mr. KEVIN J. MARZALIK; Sr. MARY PAUL MCCAUGHEY, O.P.

Finance Council—Vice Chairmen: Very Rev. JOHN F. CANARY; Mr. JAMES M. DENNY; Mr. JIMMY M. LAGO. Members: Mr. WILLIAM L. BAX; Mr. JOHN BRENNAN; Miss EILEEN T. CORCORAN; Mr. JOHN W. CROGHAN; Mr. GENO FERNANDEZ; Mr. DONALD GOSS; Mr. RICHARD J. GUZIOR; Mr. H. PATRICK HACKETT JR.; Mr. ANDREW J. MCKENNA SR.; Mr. JAMES J. MCNULTY; Mr. KENNETH MEYER; Revs. MARTIN E. O'DONOVAN; MICHAEL D. PLACE, S.T.D.; Rev. Msgr. R. GEORGE SARAUSKAS; Mr. TIMOTHY SULLIVAN; Mr. SCOTT C. SWANSON; Mr. FIDELIS N. UMEH; Mr. EDWARD J. WEHMER; Rev. RUFUS J. WHITLEY, O.M.I.

Pastoral Council—Mr. STEPHEN KUBICZKY, Chm.; Ms. MARYANN RUSSO, Vice Chm.

Women's Committee—Ms. JAN PETERS, Chm.; Ms. BETSY BOCCIO-HUNT, Vice Chm.; Ms. RITA KATTNER, Dir., Office for Councils. Tel: 773-534-8364.

Consejo Pastoral Arquidiocesano Hispano - Americano—Mr. JAIME BASCUNAN, M.S., Chm.; Rev. CLAUDIO DIAZ JR., Exec. Dir. Tel: 312-534-1080; Most Rev. GUSTAVO GARCIA-SILLER, M.Sp.S., Archbishop's Delegate. Tel: 773-779-8440.

Provincial Offices

Catholic Conference of Illinois—ROBERT F. GILLIGAN, 65 E. Wacker Pl., Ste. 1620, Chicago, 60601. Tel: 312-368-1066; Fax: 321-368-1090. Web: catholicconferenceofillinois.org.

Provincial Court of Appeals—Rev. JOHN P. LUCAS, 20 N. Wacker Dr., Ste. 3420, Chicago, 60606. Tel: 312-553-4080; Fax: 312-553-4085. Email: johnplucas43@yahoo.com.

Archdiocesan Offices

Archdiocesan Departments can be contacted through the Archbishop Quigley Center, 835 N. Rush St., Chicago, IL 60611-2030 or the Cardinal Meyer Center, 3525 S. Lake Park Ave., Chicago, IL 60653-1402 (street & package delivery addresses). Address all mail to P.O. Box 1979, Chicago, IL 60690-1979. Tel: 312-534-8200.

Office of the Archbishop—Rev. DANIEL A. FLENS, Priest Sec. to the Archbishop. Tel: 312-534-8219; Mrs. MARIE FELLER-KNOLL, Special Asst. Tel: 312-534-8299; Mrs. MARY HALLAN FIORITO, Exec. Asst. Tel: 312-534-8211; Rev. RAYMOND C. BAUMHART, S.J., Personal Consultant to the Cardinal. Tel: 773-508-2004.

The Chancery— See Office of the Chancellor.

The Metropolitan Tribunal— See Office for Canonical Services.

Vicar General

Vicar General—Very Rev. JOHN F. CANARY, Archbishop Quigley Center, 835 N. Rush St., Chicago, 60611-2030. Tel: 312-534-8271.

Vicar for Priests—Revs. JOHN COLLINS; VINCENT F. COSTELLO, 980 N. Michigan Ave., Ste. #1525, Chicago, 60611. Tel: 312-642-1837; Fax: 312-642-4933.

Commission on the Mission and Life of Diocesan Priests—Rev. VINCENT F. COSTELLO, Chm., 980 N. Michigan Ave., Ste. #1525, Chicago, 60611. Tel: 312-642-1837.

Diocesan Priests' Placement Board—Revs. JAMES J. DONOVAN JR., Exec. Sec. Tel: 312-534-5270; Fax: 312-534-5281; ROBERT L. TUZIK, Special Consultant. Tel: 312-534-5278.

Archbishop's Delegate for Extern and International Priests—Rev. JEREMIAH M. BOLAND, Archbishop's Delegate. Tel: 312-534-5237; Fax: 312-534-5381.

Mundelein Seminary/University of St. Mary of the Lake—Very Rev. DENNIS J. LYLE, S.T.D., Rector & Pres.; Revs. THOMAS A. BAIMA, M.B.A., S.T.D., Provost; RAYMOND J. WEBB, S.T.L., Ph.D., Academic Dean; KEVIN J. FEENEY, M.A.S., D.Min. (Cand.), Dean of Formation, 1000 E. Maple Ave., Mundelein, 60060. Tel: 847-566-6401.

St. Joseph College Seminary at Loyola University—Very Rev. JAMES PRESTA, S.T.L., S.T.D., Rector & Pres., 6551 N. Sheridan Rd., Chicago, 60626. Tel: 773-973-9700.

Bishop Abramowicz Seminary—Very Rev. MAREK KASPERCZUK, Rector, 750 N. Wabash Ave., Chicago, 60611-2514. Tel: 312-915-0598; 312-640-1065; Fax: 312-640-1066.

Casa Jesus—Very Rev. OCTAVIO MUNOZ, Rector, 750 N. Wabash, Chicago, 60611-2514. Tel: 312-640-1065; Fax: 312-640-1066.

The Tuite Program at St. Joseph College Seminary—Very Rev. JAMES PRESTA, S.T.L., S.T.D., Dir., 6551 N. Sheridan Rd., Chicago, 60626. Tel: 773-973-9700; Fax: 773-973-9758.

Archdiocesan Vocations—Rev. JOSEPH T. NOONAN, B.A., CPA, M.Div., Dir. Tel: 312-534-8298; Fax: 312-867-0357. Email: vocations@usml.edu Insearch Program. Web: www.chicagopriest.org.

Chaplaincies/Chaplain Affairs—Very Rev. JOHN F. CANARY, Liaison. Tel: 312-534-8271.

Chicago Airports Catholic Chaplaincy—Rev. MICHAEL G. ZANIOLO, S.T.L., C.A.C., Chap., Mailing Address: P.O. Box 66353, Chicago, 60666-0353. Tel: 773-686-2636; Fax: 773-686-0130. Email: ordchapel@aol.com. Web: www.airportchapels.org.

Fire Department Chaplain—Rev. THOMAS A. MULCRONE, Chap., 1140 W. Jackson Blvd., Chicago, 60607. Tel: 312-738-9246.

Police Department Chaplain—Rev. THOMAS R. NANGLE, Dir., 1140 W. Jackson Blvd., Chicago, 60607. Tel: 312-738-7588; Fax: 312-738-2825.

Ecumenical and Interreligious Affairs, Office for—Sisters JOAN MCGUIRE, O.P., Dir. Tel: 312-534-5325; MARY ELLEN COOMBE, N.D.S., Assoc. Dir. Tel: 312-534-5324.

Institute for Catholic Jewish Education—Sr. MARY ELLEN COOMBE, N.D.S., Dir. Tel: 312-251-8800, Ext. 316.

Office of the Chancellor

Chancellor—Mr. JIMMY M. LAGO, Archbishop Quigley Center, 835 N. Rush St., Chicago, 60611-2030. Tel: 312-534-8220; Fax: 312-534-5381.

Department Directors—Rev. RICHARD P. HYNES, Evangelization, Catechesis & Worship; Mr. RAYMOND P. COUGHLIN, Stewardship & Devel.; Rev. MICHAEL M. BOLAND, Human Svcs.; Mr. KEVIN J. MARZALIK, Financial Svcs.; Ms. COLLEEN H. DOLAN, Communication & Pub. Rels.; Dr. CAROL L. FOWLER, Personnel Svcs.; Sr. MARY PAUL MCCAUGHEY, O.P., Catholic Schools.

Racial Justice—Sr. ANITA P. BAIRD, D.H.M., Dir.; Ms. ALICIA JUAREZ, Assoc. Dir., Cardinal Meyer Center, 3525 S. Lake Park Ave., Chicago, 60616. Tel: 312-534-8336.

Legal Services—Mr. JOHN C. O'MALLEY, Dir. Tel: 312-534-5379.

Information Technology—Ms. ELLEN M. ANDERSON, Dir. Tel: 312-534-5330; Fax: 312-534-5346; Mr. GANG CHEN, Mgr. Applications Svcs. Tel: 312-534-8331; Fax: 312-534-5346; Mr. HUGH O'NEILL, Mgr. Technical Svcs. Tel: 312-534-5249; Fax: 312-534-5346.

Research & Planning—Ms. JEAN WELTER, Dir. Tel: 312-534-8345; Fax: 312-534-8766.

Archives and Records—Mr. JOHN J. TREANOR, Vice Chancellor Archives & Records, 711 W. Monroe St., Chicago, 60661. Tel: 312-831-0711; Fax: 312-831-0610.

Office of Canonical Services

Canonical Services—Rev. DANIEL A. SMILANIC, J.C.D., Vicar, Archbishop Quigley Center, 835 N. Rush St., Chicago, 60611-2030. Tel: 312-534-8250. Associate Vicars: Revs. RICHARD B. SAUDIS. Tel: 312-534-8382; WILLIAM H. WOESTMAN, O.M.I., J.C.D. Tel: 312-534-8362; Deacon DANIEL G. WELTER, J.D., Actuarius. Tel: 312-534-8283. Email: dwelter@archchicago.org; SUZETTE CASH, Administrative Asst. Tel: 312-534-8207; Fax: 312-534-8314.

Metropolitan Tribunal

Metropolitan Tribunal—Tel: 312-534-8280; Fax: 312-534-8314.

Judicial Vicar—Rev. MICHAEL A. HACK, J.C.D. Tel: 312-534-8255. Email: tribunal@archchicago.org.

Adjutant Judicial Vicar—Rev. DANIEL A. SMILANIC, J.C.D. Tel: 312-534-8206.

Applications Coordinator—GLENDA MCFADDEN. Tel: 312-534-8253.

Promoter of Justice—Rev. WILLIAM H. WOESTMAN, O.M.I., J.C.D.

Judges—Rev. MICHAEL A. HACK, J.C.D.; Sr. JOYCE HOBEN, S.N.D.; Revs. JOHN M. GRIFFITHS, J.C.D.; JOHN C. HERGENROTHER; PATRICK R. LAGGES, J.C.D.; DANIEL A. SMILANIC, J.C.D.; WOJCIECH A. MARAT; DAVID M. HYNOUS, O.P.; MICHAEL BRADLEY, J.C.L.; ALEC J. WOLFF; Sr. CHRISTINE KUB, O.P., J.C.L.; MONICA MAVRIC DE BELTRAMI, Esq.; Mr. RAPHAEL FRACKIEWICZ, J.C.D.

Defenders of the Bond—Revs. WILLIAM H. WOESTMAN, O.M.I., J.C.D.; RIGOBERTO GAMEZ, J.C.D.; Mr.

OLEGARIO CASTILLO, J.C.L.; Ms. RENATA BABICZ, J.U.D.

Delegate of the Archbishop for Privilege Cases—Rev. JOSEPH C. MOL.

Auditors—Ms. SUSAN MILLER; Sr. BARBARA KOSINSKA, M.Ch.R.

Advocates—Revs. JOSEPH C. MOL; MACIEJ GALLE; Sr. DIONETTE WERNER, C.S.S.F.; LUIS FLORES, J.C.L.

Department of Evangelization, Catechesis and Worship

Department of Evangelization, Catechesis and Worship—Rev. RICHARD P. HYNES, Dir., Cardinal Meyer Center, 3525 S. Lake Park Ave., Chicago, 60653-1402. Tel: 312-534-8388; Mr. ROBERT BENNETT, Prog. Asst. Tel: 312-534-8385; Ms. PATTY MONTES, Sec. Tel: 312-534-8389; Fax: 312-534-3856. Web: www.archchicago.org/decw.

Office for Catechesis and Youth Ministry—MARIA H. "MARUJA" SEDANO, Dir.; Sr. JUDITH DIETERLE, S.S.L., Assoc. Dir. Tel: 312-534-3700; Fax: 312-534-3801. Web: www.catechesis-chicago.org. Catechetical Ministry Coordinators: ELZBIETA WOJTAS; JUAN CARLOS FARIAS-GONZALES; NELLY LORENZO; KRISTEN HEMPSTEAD MCGANN; BRIGID WOLFF.

Vicariate Catechetical Coordinators—

Vicariate I—PAT REDINGTON.

Vicariate II—THOMAS MCLAUGHLIN.

Vicariate III—LIBIA PAEZ-HOWARD.

Vicariate IV—FRANK KOOB.

Vicariate V—CATHY WALZ.

Vicariate VI—LOIS DEFELICE.

Vicariate Youth Coordinators—

Vicariate I—JOANNE WALCZYNSKI Web: www.catechesis-chicago.org.

Vicariate II—DARIUS VILLALOBOS.

Vicariate III—JESUS "CHUY" DELEON.

Vicariate IV—THOMAS HOWARD.

Vicariate V—MARIA "COOKY" PEREZ-ERACI.

Vicariate VI—TIFFANY SWANN-COVINGTON.

Polish Youth Ministry—JACEK CHABA.

Jegen Center for Catechetical Media & Research—Sr. JUDITH DIETERLE, S.S.L., Coord. Tel: 312-534-3700; Fax: 312-534-3801. Web: www.jegen.org.

Special Religious Education (SPRED)—Rev. JAMES H. MCCARTHY, Dir. Emeritus (Retired), 2956 S. Lowe, Chicago, 60616. Tel: 312-842-1039; Fax: 312-842-4449; Sisters MARY THERESE HARRINGTON, S.H.; SUSANNE GALLAGHER, S.P.

Office for Evangelization—VACANT, Dir. Tel: 312-534-5353; Ms. NANCY POLACEK, Coord. Catholics Come Home. Tel: 312-534-5316; Mr. DOUGLAS STEARNS, Coord. Parish Evangelization. Tel: 312-534-5288.

Family Ministries—Mr. FRANCIS P. HANNIGAN, Dir. Associate Directors: VALENTIN ARAYA; ELSIE RADTKE. Tel: 312-534-8351; Fax: 312-534-3858. Web: www.familyministries.org.

Marriage Preparation—Mr. FRANCIS P. HANNIGAN. Tel: 312-534-8340.

Marriage Education—Mr. FRANCIS P. HANNIGAN. Tel: 312-534-8340.

Annulment Support Ministry—ELSIE RADTKE. Tel: 312-534-8391.

Hispanic Family Ministries—VALENTIN ARAYA, Contact. Tel: 312-534-8240.

Natural Family Planning—MARIA GARCIA, Contact. Tel: 312-534-5298 (Spanish); 312-534-8273 (English).

Divorce Ministry—ELSIE RADTKE. Tel: 312-534-8353.

Divine Worship, Office for—Mr. TODD WILLIAMSON, Dir.; Ms. MARGIE GUADAGNO, Administrative Asst.; Mr. JOSE CASTILLO, Dir. Hispanic Programming; Sr. RENE SIMONELIC, O.S.F., Dir. Gen. Programming; Ms. JACKIE MOYENO, Prog. Assoc.; Rev. ROBERT L. TUZIK, Special Project Coord.; Ms. ANNA BELLE O'SHEA, Dir. Liturgies & Music. Tel: 312-534-5153; Fax: 312-534-5158. Web: www.odw.org.

Young Adult Ministry/Singles—Rev. JOHN C. CUSICK, Dir.; Dr. KATHERINE F. DEVRIES, Assoc. Dir., 711 W. Monroe St., Chicago, 60661. Tel: 312-466-9473; Fax: 312-466-9474. Web: www.yamchicago.org.

Office for Peace & Justice—Mr. NICHOLAS C. LUND-MOLFESE, M.A., J.D., Dir. Tel: 312-534-5383; Fax: 312-787-1554.

Catholic Campaign for Human Development—Mr. REY FLORES.

Office of Immigrant Affairs and Immigration Education—Ms. ELENA SEGURA, Dir.

St. Toribio Immigrant Center—MARCO LOPEZ, Dir., 2434 S. California Ave., Chicago, 60608. Tel: 773-376-1276; Fax: 773-376-9678.

Catholic Relief Services—Ms. ADRIENNE CURRY.

Parish Sharing Program—Mr. REY FLORES.

Catholic Missions Office, Propagation of the Faith, Holy Childhood Association—Sr. MADGE KARECKI, S.S.J.-T.O.S.F., Dir. Tel: 312-534-3318.

Respect Life/Pro-Life Office—MARY-LOUISE KUREY, Dir. Tel: 312-534-5355; Fax: 312-534-1554.

Project Rachel—Tel: 312-337-1962; 800-456-4673 (800-456-HOPE).

Chastity Education Initiative—Tel: 312-534-5355.

Jail Ministry/Kolbe House—Rev. ARTURO PEREZ-RODRIGUEZ, Dir., 2434 S. California, Chicago, 60608. Tel: 773-247-0070; Fax: 773-247-0665.

Councils, The Archdiocesan Office for—Ms. RITA KATTNER, Dir.

Parish Pastoral Councils—Ms. RITA KATTNER, Dir. Tel: 312-534-8364; Fax: 312-534-3883.

Christ Renews His Parish—Ms. RITA KATTNER, Spiritual Dir. Tel: 312-534-8364.

Amate House/Young Adult Volunteer Program—Deacon JOHN LUCAS JR., Exec. Dir., 3600 S. Seeley, Chicago, 60609. Tel: 773-376-2445. Web: www.amatehouse.org.

Ethnic Offices—MARY NORFLEET-JOHNSON, Dir., Office for Black Catholics. Tel: 312-534-8377; Fax: 312-534-5207; Mrs. TERESITA L. NUVAL, Dir., Office for Asian Catholics. Tel: 312-534-8305; Fax: 312-534-5207; Revs. CASIMIR GARBACZ, S.V.D., Dir., Office for European Catholics. Tel: 312-534-8352; Fax: 312-534-5207; CLAUDIO DIAZ JR., Dir., Office for Hispanic Catholics. Tel: 312-534-1080; Fax: 312-534-3459.

Vicariate Hispanic Coordinators—

Vicariate I—GRACIELA CONTRERAS, 200 N. Milwaukee Ave., Ste. 212, Libertyville, 60048. Tel: 847-549-0164.

Vicariate V—PETER DUCTRAM, 2330 W. 118th St., Chicago, 60643. Tel: 773-881-2100.

Centro Espiritu Santo - Vicariate V—PETER DUCTRAM, Dir., 2330 W. 118th St., Chicago, 60643. Tel: 773-881-2100; Fax: 773-779-8469.

Vicariate VI—CARLOS SALMERON, 16160 Seton Rd., South Holland, 60473. Tel: 708-339-5044.

Hispanic Young Adult Ministry—Mr. JORGE RIVERA, 1838 S. Throop St., Chicago, 60608. Tel: 312-534-1080.

Ethnic Apostolates—

Anawim Center (Native American Apostolate)—Sr. PATRICIA ANN MULKEY, Anawin Center, 4750 N. Sheridan Rd., Chicago, 60640-7512. Tel: 773-561-6155.

Haitian Catholic Apostolate—7851 S. Jeffery Blvd., Chicago, 60649. Tel: 773-721-6365.

Indochinese Catholic Center—Rev. PETER HUNG, Dir. (Retired), 4827 N. Kenmore, Chicago, 60640. Tel: 773-784-1932.

Archdiocesan Council of Catholic Women (ACCW)—SHIRLEY HERMES, Pres. Tel: 312-534-8325.

Archdiocesan Council of Catholic Men—Rev. JOHN C. CUSICK, 711 W. Monroe St., Chicago, 60661. Tel: 312-466-9473; Fax: 312-466-9474.

Department of Stewardship and Development

Department of Stewardship and Development—Mr. RAYMOND P. COUGHLIN, Dir., Archbishop Quigley Center, 835 N. Rush St., Chicago, 60611-2030. Tel: 312-534-7910; Ms. PATRICIA A. CONDON, Senior Administrative Asst. Tel: 312-534-7935; Fax: 312-534-7354.

Vicariate Stewardship Coordinators—Mr. MICHAEL J. GLEASON. Tel: 312-534-7830; Ms. LEA DECANAY. Tel: 312-534-7713.

Development Services—Ms. BARBARA SHEA COLLINS. Tel: 312-534-7944.

Wills, Trusts, Estates & Planned Giving/Annuities—Mr. RICHARD S. GOODE, Dir. Tel: 312-534-7848.

Major Gifts—Mr. PETER CULLEN-CONWAY, Dir. Tel: 312-534-7929.

Major Gifts Officer, Catholic Schools—Mr. WILLIAM BOOTH. Tel: 312-534-8486.

Benefactor Relations Coordinator—Ms. MARY ANN PERROTTI. Tel: 312-534-7928.

Department of Human Services

Director—Rev. MICHAEL M. BOLAND, 721 N. LaSalle St., Chicago, 60654-3574. Tel: 312-655-7460; Fax: 312-655-0219.

Catholic Charities of Chicago—Rev. MICHAEL M. BOLAND, Admin., Pres. & CEO; Mr. J. ANTONIO FERNANDEZ, Sr. Vice Pres. Oper.; Ms. CYNTHIA D. SMETANA, CFO; Ms. KATHY DONAHUE, Sr. Vice Pres. Programs. Associate Administrators: Revs. RICHARD E. BULWITH; ROGER J. COUGHLIN (Retired); RICHARD JAKUBIK; GERARD KELLY; CHARLES T. RUBEY (Retired); WAYNE F. WATTS; Deacon MANUEL DORANTES, 721 N. LaSalle St., Chicago, 60654-3574. Tel: 312-655-7000 Central Intake Phone; 800-244-0505 (Refer to Catholic Charities section under the Institutions located in the Archdiocese for further listings).

Maternity Fund—Rev. ROGER J. COUGHLIN (Retired), 721 N. LaSalle St., Chicago, 60654-3574. Tel: 312-655-7596.

Office for Persons with Disabilities—Rev. CHARLES T. RUBEY, Dir. (Retired), 721 N. LaSalle St., Chicago, 60654-3574. Tel: 312-655-7280.

Catholic Office of the Deaf—Rev. JOSEPH A. MULCRONE, Dir.; Ms. MARGARET SWATEK, D.R.E., Cardinal Meyer Center, 3525 S. Lake Park Ave., Chicago, 60653-1402. Tel: 312-534-7899; 312-534-8368 TTY; Fax: 312-534-0394. Email: cathdeafch@archchicago.org. Web: www.deafchurchicago.parishesonline.com.

Health/Hospital Affairs—Most Rev. THOMAS J. PAPROCKI, Cardinal's Liaison, Vicariate IV Office, 1400 S. Austin Blvd., Cicero, 60804. Tel: 708-329-4040; Fax: 708-222-8854; Revs. WILLIAM P. GROGAN, Cardinal's Delegate for Hospitals. Tel: 312-534-8339; MICHAEL M. BOLAND, Cardinal's Delegate for Nursing Homes & Senior Svcs. Tel: 312-655-7460; Fax: 312-655-0219.

Bio Ethics Commission—Rev. WILLIAM P. GROGAN, Recording Sec. Tel: 312-534-8339.

Mercy Home for Boys and Girls—Revs. JAMES J. CLOSE, Pres. Emeritus (Retired); SCOTT DONAHUE, Pres., 1140 W. Jackson, Chicago, 60607. Tel: 312-738-9240.

Office for Persons with Disabilities—Rev. CHARLES T. RUBEY (Retired), 721 N. LaSalle St., Chicago, 60654-3574. Tel: 312-655-7280.

Department of Financial Services

Director—Mr. KEVIN J. MARZALIK, Archbishop Quigley Center, 835 N. Rush St., Chicago, 60611-2030. Tel: 312-534-8218.

Facilities and Construction—Mr. C. GREGORY VEITH, Mgr. Tel: 312-534-8342.

Controller's Operations—Ms. SUSAN LORENZ, Controller. Tel: 312-534-5266.

Risk Management - Property & Casualty—Mr. DON TURLEK, Mgr. Tel: 312-534-8295; Fax: 312-534-8302.

Real Estate—Ms. MAUREEN O'BRIEN, Mgr. Tel: 312-534-8221.

Parish Operations—TAFFIE IWANICKI, Mgr. Tel: 312-534-5312.

Vicariate I—DENNIS ROBAK. Tel: 312-534-5364. Vicariate Office. Tel: 847-549-0165.

Vicariate II—GENE MYERS. Tel: 312-534-5321. Vicariate Office. Tel: 773-388-8673.

Vicariate III—JESSE ESTRADA. Tel: 312-534-5323. Vicariate Office. Tel: 312-243-1135.

Vicariate IV—PATRICIA POMYKALSKI. Tel: 312-534-5384. Vicariate Office. Tel: 708-329-4050.

Vicariate V—ERICH BANGERT. Tel: 312-534-5318. Vicariate Office. Tel: 773-239-4559.

Vicariate VI—PAMELA GUTTER. Tel: 312-534-5342. Vicariate Office. Tel: 708-333-6132.

Catholic Cemeteries—Rev. PATRICK J. POLLARD, Dir.; Mr. ROMAN SZABELSKI, Exec. Dir., 1400 S. Wolf Rd., Hillside, 60162. Tel: 708-449-6100; Fax: 708-449-3419.

Bereavement Ministry—MARTHA BURKE TRESSLER. Tel: 708-423-0471.

Department of Communications and Public Relations

Department of Communications and Public Relations—Ms. COLLEEN H. DOLAN, Dir., Archbishop Quigley Center, 835 N. Rush St., Chicago, 60611-2030. Tel: 312-534-8289; Fax: 312-534-5306.

Office of Media Relations—Ms. SUSAN BURRITT, Dir. Communications. Tel: 312-534-8233.

Office of Radio & Television—Mr. JIM DISCH, Dir. Tel: 312-534-8277.

School Marketing and Communications—RYAN BLACKBURN, Dir. Tel: 312-534-5334; Fax: 312-534-5295.

New World Publications—DAWN VIDMAR, Gen. Mgr., Cardinal Meyer Center, 3525 S. Lake Park Ave., Chicago, 60653-1402. Tel: 312-534-7777; Fax: 312-534-7310.

The Catholic New World—JOYCE DURIGA, Editor. Tel: 312-534-7577.

Hispanic Communications—ALEJANDRO CASTILLO, Dir. Tel: 312-534-7880; Fax: 312-534-7310.

Chicago Catolico—ALEJANDRO CASTILLO, Gen. Mgr. Tel: 312-534-7880.

KATOLIK— The Polish language newspaper of the Archdiocese. ALICIJA POZYWIO, News Editor. Tel: 312-534-7294.

Department of Personnel Services

Director—Dr. CAROL FOWLER, Archbishop Quigley Center, 835 N. Rush St., Chicago, 60611-2030. Tel: 312-534-8349.

Human Resources—FRED VAN DEN HENDE, Mgr. Tel: 312-534-5352.

Lay Ecclesial Ministry, Office for—CAROL A. WALTERS, Dir. Tel: 312-534-5263; Fax: 312-534-5281. Web: www.archchicago.org/about_us/employment.shtm Job listing.

Office of Conciliation—RALPH BONACCORSI, Exec. Dir. Email: concil@archchicago.org.

Office of Ministerial Evaluation—KATHLEEN LEGGDAS, Dir. Tel: 312-534-5265; Fax: 312-534-5281.

Religious, Office for—Sisters JOAN MCGLINCHEY, M.S.C., Dir. Tel: 312-534-8360; KATHLEEN MCNULTY, O.S.F., Asst. Dir. Tel: 312-534-3877; MARGARET COLEMAN, O.S.F., Retirement Collection. Tel: 312-534-8234.

Priests' Retirement and Mutual Aid Association (PRMAA)—Mr. ALEX BECKER, Exec. Dir., 4951 Harrrison St., Hillside, 60162. Tel: 708-449-8026; Fax: 708-449-8148.

Vicar for Senior Priests—Most Revs. TIMOTHY J. LYNE, Co-Vicar (Retired). Tel: 312-787-8040; Fax: 312-787-9113; THAD J. JAKUBOWSKI, D.D., Co-Vicar. Tel: 773-202-7720; Fax: 773-202-7725; Rev. JOHN A. KUZINSKAS, Asst. Vicar (Retired).

Vicar for the Diaconate Community—Rev. MICHAEL P. AHLSTROM, 816 Marengo, Forest Park, 60130. Tel: 708-366-8900; Fax: 708-366-8968; Deacons DENNIS L. COLGAN, Assoc. Dir. Diaconate Community; ENRIQUE ALONSO, Assoc. Dir. Hispanic Diaconate Community.

Office for Protection of Children and Youth—Ms. JAN SLATTERY, Dir., 737 N. Michigan Ave., Ste. 900, Chicago, 60611-2956. Tel: 312-751-5319; Fax: 312-751-8307.

Victim Assistance Coordinator—MATT HUNNICUTT, Dir. Tel: 312-751-8267; Fax: 312-751-8307. Email: mhunnicutt@archchicago.org.

Child Abuse Investigations and Review—Ms. LEAH R. MCCLUSKEY, Dir. Tel: 312-751-5205; Fax: 312-751-5279. Email: lmccluskey@archchicago.org.

Safe Environment—VACANT, Dir. Tel: 312-751-5238; Fax: 312-751-5307.

Cardinal Stritch Retreat House—Deacon RICHARD F. HUDZIK, Dir., 1300 Stritch Dr., P.O. Box 455, Mundelein, 60060-0455. Tel: 847-566-6060; Fax: 847-566-6082.

Department of Catholic Schools

Department of Catholic Schools—Sr. MARY PAUL MCCAUGHEY, O.P., Supt., Archbishop Quigley Center, 835 N. Rush St., Chicago, 60611-2030. Tel: 312-534-5210; Fax: 312-534-5392; JAMES QUAID, Ph.D., Assoc. Supt. Tel: 312-534-5255.

Other Archdiocesan Agencies

Personal Consultant to the Cardinal—Rev. RAYMOND C. BAUMHART, S.J., Sullivan Center, 6339 N. Sheridan Rd., Rm. 264, Chicago, 60660. Tel: 773-508-2004; Fax: 773-508-2098. Email: rbaumha@luc.edu.

Food Service Professionals, Archdiocese—Mr. JOHN KOUBEK, Dir., 5150 Northwest Hwy., Chicago, 60638. Tel: 773-385-5100; Fax: 773-385-6025. Web: www.fspro.com.

Liturgy Training Publications (LTP)—JOHN A. THOMAS, Dir., 3943 S. Racine Ave., Chicago, 60690. Tel: 773-486-8970; Fax: 773-486-7094. Orders: Tel: 800-933-2800; Fax: 800-933-7094. Email: orders@ltp.org; DEANNA KEEFE, Mktg. & Sales Fulfillment Mgr. Email: dkeefe@ltp.org. Web: www.ltp.org.

CLERGY, PARISHES, MISSIONS AND PAROCHIAL SCHOOLS

CITY OF CHICAGO

(COOK COUNTY)

1—HOLY NAME CATHEDRAL (1849) Revs. Daniel G. Mayall, Rector & Pastor of Parish; John Boivin; Matthew Ross Compton; Deacons Michael McCloskey; Stan Strom; Mrs. Ann Klocke, Pastoral Assoc.; Ms. Pat Still, Pastoral Asst.; Mary Ann Hoban, Coord. of Ministry of Care; H. Ricardo Ramirez, Dir. Music; Mr. David C. Jonies, Assoc. Dir. Music; Mr. Andrew Skura, Comptroller; Ms. Jamie Sanchez, Bulletin Editor; Mr. Joseph A. Konen, Stewardship Dir.; Mr. Alex Lucio, Stewardship Coord. In Res., Most Rev. Timothy J. Lyne, Pastor Emeritus & Auxiliary Bishop of Chicago (Retired); Revs. Michael M. Boland; William J. Moriarity; Eugene F. Durkin (Retired); Louis J. Cameli; Joseph T. Noonan; William H. Woestman, O.M.I.
Rectory—830 N. Wabash Ave., 60611. Tel: 312-787-8040; Fax: 312-787-9113. Web: www.holynamecathedral.org.
Cardinal's Residence—1555 N. State Pkwy., 60610. His Eminence Francis Cardinal George, O.M.I., Archbishop of Chicago; Most Rev. Raymond E. Goedert, Auxiliary Bishop (Retired); Very Rev. John F. Canary, Vicar Gen.; Rev. Daniel A. Flens, Sec. to the Archbishop.
Seminary Formation House-Casa Jesus—750 N. Wabash, 60611. Tel: 312-640-1065. Rev. Alejandro Garrido; Very Rev. Octavio Munoz, Rector.
Seminary Formation House-Bishop Abramowicz Seminary—Tel: 312-915-0598; Fax: 312-640-1066. Very Rev. Marek Kasperczuk (Poland), Rector.
Catechesis/Religious Program—Tel: 312-787-8040. Ms. Sharon Kinsley, D.R.E. Students 120.
Convent—Oblate Sisters of Jesus the Priest, 740 N. Wabash Ave., 60611. Tel: 312-787-8040; Fax: 312-787-9113.

2—ST. ADALBERT Rev. Michael S. Michelini; Deacons Joseph Mally; Oscar Gonzalez; Juan Dominguez. In Res., Rev. Antoni Bradlo, C.Ss.R.
Res.: 1650 W. 17th St., 60608-0194. Tel: 312-226-0340; Fax: 312-266-0194.
Catechesis/Religious Program—Students 265.

3—ST. ADRIAN Rev. Thomas J. Mescall.
Res.: 7000 S. Fairfield Ave., 60629. Tel: 773-434-3223; Fax: 773-434-6380. Email: stadrian@archchicago.org.
Church: 70th and S. Washtenaw Ave., 60619.
Catechesis/Religious Program—Students 125.

4—ST. AGATHA Revs. Lawrence R. Dowling; Thomas P. Walsh; Deacon Gregory Shumpert.
Res.: 3147 W. Douglas Blvd., 60623. Tel: 773-522-3050; Fax: 773-522-3842.
School—Saint Agatha Catholic Academy, (Preschool-3rd Grade Campus): 3151 W. Douglas Blvd., 60623-1898. Tel: 773-762-1809; Fax: 773-762-9781. (4th-8th Grade Campus): 3800 W. Lexington St., 60624-3648. Tel: 773-638-6555; Fax: 773-638-0070. Lay Teachers 10; Students 200.

5—ST. AGNES OF BOHEMIA Revs. Donald J. Nevins; Rene Mena-Beltran; Martin D. Ibarra; Sisters Fatima Prieto, CCD Coord.; Bertha Lopez, Human Services; Deacon Angel Favila.
Res.: 2651 S. Central Park Ave., 60623. Tel: 773-522-0142; Fax: 773-522-0172. Email: stagnes-central@archchicago.org. Web: www.stagnesofbohemia.org.
School—2643 S. Central Park Ave., 60623. Tel: 773-522-0143; Fax: 773-522-0132. Lay Teachers 26; Students 465.
Catechesis/Religious Program—Tel: 773-277-5446. Students 724.
Convent—Misioneras de San Pio X, 2658 S. Central Park Ave., 60623. Tel: 773-762-3229.

6—ST. AILBE Revs. Lawrence M. Duris; Andrew Charles Smith Jr.; Deacon Bruce T. McElrath.
Res.: 9015 S. Harper Ave., 60619. Tel: 773-374-2345; Fax: 773-374-7096. Email: stailbe@aol.com.
School—9037 S. Harper Ave., 60619. Tel: 773-734-1386; Fax: 773-734-1440. Stephanie Clausell, Prin. Lay Teachers 15; Students 200.
Catechesis/Religious Program—Students 205.

7—ALL SAINTS-ST. ANTHONY Rev. John W. Parker; Deacons Peter Liberti; Duke Vemich; Saul Vazquez.
Res.: 518 W. 28th Pl., 60616. Tel: 312-842-2744; Fax: 312-842-2791.
See Bridgeport Catholic Academy, Chicago under Consolidated Elementary Schools, located in the Institution section.
Catechesis/Religious Program—Students 160.

8—ST. ALOYSIUS Rev. Nicholas R. Desmond; Deacons Adolfo Lopez; Dennis Ramos; Jose Alvarez; Ramon Navarro.
Res.: 2300 W. Le Moyne St., 60622. Tel: 773-278-4808; Fax: 773-278-4898. Email: parish@staloysiusparish.org. Web: www.staloysiusparish.org.
Catechesis/Religious Program—Students 147.

9—ST. ALPHONSUS, (German), Rev. James F. Hurlbert.
Res.: 1429 W. Wellington Ave., 60657. Tel: 773-525-0709; Fax: 773-525-3238. Email: stalparish@aol.com. Web: www.stalphonsuschgo.org.
School—Alphonsus Academy and Center for the Arts, Tel: 773-348-4629; Fax: 773-348-4829. Students 300.
Catechesis/Religious Program—Students 90.

10—ST. AMBROSE Revs. Freddy Washington, C.S.Sp.; Edmond Aristil, C.S.Sp. (Haiti).
Res.: *Congregation of the Holy Ghost (Spiritans)*, 1012 E. 47th St., 60653. Tel: 773-624-3695; Fax: 773-624-3697. Email: ambrose47@aol.com.

11—ST. ANDREW Revs. Sergio Romo; John A. Farry, Pastor Emeritus (Retired); Protasio Ndereba (Kenya).
Res.: 3546 N. Paulina St., 60657. Tel: 773-525-3016; Fax: 773-525-4124. Web: www.saintandrewchicago.com.
School—1710 W. Addison, 60613. Tel: 773-248-2500; Fax: 773-248-2709. Lay Teachers 30; Students 398.
Catechesis/Religious Program—Students 100.

12—ST. ANGELA, Closed. Consult Archives and Records Center for parish and school records.

13—ST. ANN Rev. Felipe Vaglienty; Deacons Rodrigo Silva; Jesus Blanco.
Res.: 1840 S. Leavitt St., 60608. Tel: 312-733-7486; Fax: 312-733-5681.
School—2211 W. 18th Pl., 60608. Tel: 312-829-4153. Sr. Michael Marie Franzak, Prin. Lay Teachers 8; Students 300.
Catechesis/Religious Program—Students 120.

14—ANNUNCIATA Revs. Paul M. Cullen, O.S.M.; Dennis Kriz, O.S.M.; Bro. Brian Fitzpatrick, O.S.M., Pastoral Min.; Mr. Mike Schnabel, Business Mgr. In Res., Rev. Conrad M. Borntrager, O.S.M.
Res.: 11128 S. Avenue G, 60617. Tel: 773-221-1040; Fax: 773-221-1556. Email: annunciata@archchicago.org. Web: www.annunciataonline.com.
School—3750 E. 112th St., 60617. Tel: 773-375-5711; Fax: 773-375-5704. Lay Teachers 10; Students 180.
Catechesis/Religious Program—Students 190.

15—ST. ANSELM Revs. Abelardo Gabriel, S.V.D., Admin.; Bernard Espiritu, S.V.D.; Bros. Steven Wang, S.V.D.; Paul Thuong Chi Hoang, S.V.D. In Res., Rev. Donald J. Ehr, S.V.D.
Res.: 6045 S. Michigan Ave., 60637. Tel: 773-493-5959; Fax: 773-363-1887.
Catechesis/Religious Program—Students 37.

16—ST. ANTHONY OF PADUA Rev. Mark J. Krylowicz; Deacons Edward Ryan; Juan Morales. In Res., Rev. Ronald L. Kondziolka.
Res.: 11533 S. Prairie Ave., 60628. Tel: 773-468-1200; Fax: 773-468-1922. Email: saintanthony@ameritech.net.
Catechesis/Religious Program—Students 109.

17—ASSUMPTION Rev. Arturo Perez Rodriguez.
Res.: 2434 S. California Ave., 60608. Tel: 773-247-6644; Fax: 773-247-0665.
Convent—2831 W. 24th St. Blvd., 60623. Tel: 773-247-1100.
Kolbe House—Web: www.kolbehouseministry.org. Rev. Arturo Perez-Rodriguez, Dir. Catholic Prison Ministry.
Catechesis/Religious Program—Students 181.

18—ASSUMPTION OF THE B.V.M./ST. CATHERINE OF GENOA, Closed. Consult Archives and Records Center for parish and school records.

19—ASSUMPTION OF THE BLESSED VIRGIN MARY Rev. Joseph Chamblain, O.S.M. In Res., Revs. John M. Pawlikowski, O.S.M.; David M. Brown, O.S.M.; Damian M. Charbonneau, O.S.M.; Michael Doyle, O.S.M.
Res.: 323 W. Illinois St., 60654-7812. Tel: 312-644-0036; Fax: 312-644-1838. Email: parishoffice@assumption-chgo.org.

20—ST. BARBARA Revs. Dennis A. Ziomek, Admin.; Francis Li.
Res.: 2859 S. Throop St., 60608. Tel: 312-842-7979; Fax: 312-842-7978. Email: stbarbara@stbarbarachicago.org. Web: www.stbarbarachicago.org.
School—Tel: 312-326-6243; Fax: 312-842-7960. Lay Teachers 12; Students 170.
Catechesis/Religious Program—Students 5.

21—ST. BARNABAS Revs. William E. Malloy; Gene F. Smith; Deacons James Temple; William Sullivan; James L. Conway; Andrew Neu; Ms. Kitty T. Ryan, Pastoral Assoc. & Liturgy Dir. In Res., Revs. James J. Donovan Jr.; Anthony M. Leahy (Retired).
Res.: 10134 S. Longwood Dr., 60643. Tel: 773-779-1166; Fax: 773-445-9671. Web: www.stbarnabasparish.org.
School—10121 S. Longwood Dr., 60643. Tel: 773-445-7711; Fax: 773-445-9815. Lay Teachers 29; Students 425.
Catechesis/Religious Program—Tel: 773-445-3450. Students 189.

22—ST. BARTHOLOMEW Revs. Jason A. Malave; Tirso S. Villaverde; Mr. Jesus Flores, Lay Min.; Mrs. Leonor Navarro, Lay Min.; Mrs. Nancy Kleiber, Lay Min.; Mr. Faustino Santiago, Lay Min.; Ms. Cyndee Zbtlut, Music Dir. In Res., Revs. Eduardo Pinzon, S.J. (Retired); Michael A. Goergen (Retired).
Res.: 4949 W. Patterson Ave., 60641. Tel: 773-286-7871; Fax: 773-286-4808. Web: www.stbartholomew.net.
School—4941 W. Patterson Ave., 60641. Tel: 773-282-9373; Fax: 773-282-4757. Mr. Martin Graham-McHugh, Prin. Lay Teachers 14; Students 249.
Catechesis/Religious Program—Maria Arrez, C.R.E. Students 337.

23—ST. BASIL/VISITATION Rev. Marco Cardenas, C.M.F., Admin.
Res.: 843 W. Garfield Blvd., 60621. Tel: 773-846-3570; Fax: 773-783-3348. Email: basvis@aol.com.
School—Visitation School, 900 W. Garfield Blvd., 60609. Tel: 733-373-5200; Fax: 733-373-5201. Sisters 5; Lay Teachers 14; Students 260.
Catechesis/Religious Program—Students 14.

24—ST. BEDE THE VENERABLE Revs. William J. Stenzel; Jose de Jesus Medina; Juan Carlos Arrieta Correa.
Res.: 8200 S. Kostner Ave., 60652. Tel: 773-884-2000; Fax: 773-582-0026. Web: www.stbedechicago.org.
School—4440 W. 83rd St., 60652. Tel: 773-884-2020; Fax: 773-582-3366. Lay Teachers 28; Students 590.
Catechesis/Religious Program—Tel: 773-884-2038; Fax: 773-884-2037. Students 300.

25—St. Benedict Rev. Robert W. Beaven; Deacon Philip Bertolani.
Res.: 2215 W. Irving Park Rd., 60618. Tel: 773-588-6484; Fax: 773-588-4927. Email: sbparish@stben.com. Web: www.stbenedict.com.
School—3920 N. Leavitt St., 60618. Tel: 773-463-6797; Fax: 773-463-0782. Lay Teachers 17; Students 300.
High School—3900 N. Leavitt St., 60618. Tel: 773-539-0066; Fax: 773-539-3397. Sisters 2; Lay Teachers 22; Students 185.
Catechesis / Religious Program—Students 150.

26—St. Benedict the African (East) Rev. David A. Jones; Sisters Mary Pokorny, Pastoral Min.; Joanne Delehanty, Pastoral Min.
Res.: 340 W. 66th St., 60621. Tel: 773-873-4464; Fax: 773-873-1992.
School—Academy of St. Benedict the African Total Students for 2 Sites 200.
Stewart Site—6547 S. Stewart, 60636. Tel: 773-994-6100.
Catechesis / Religious Program—Students 75.

27—St. Benedict the African (West) Very Rev. Paul De Porres Whittington, O.P.; Deacon Louis Constanopolis. In Res., Rev. John Bosco Mujuni (Uganda).
Res.: 1818 W. 71st St., 60636. Tel: 773-925-2535; Fax: 773-925-7071.
School—Academy of St. Benedict the African
Laflin Site—6020 S. Laflin St., 60636. Tel: 773-776-3316; Fax: 773-776-3715.
Stewart Site—6547 S. Stewart St., 60636. Tel: 773-994-6100; Fax: 773-994-1433.
Catechesis / Religious Program—Students 138.

28—Blessed Alojzije Stepinac Croatian Mission Rev. Ivica Majstorovic, O.F.M., Admin. (Independent Mission)
Res.: 6346 N. Ridge, 60660. Tel: 773-262-0535; Fax: 773-262-4603. Email: bastepinacchicago@sbcglobal.net.
Catechesis / Religious Program—Suzana Culjak, D.R.E. Students 36.

29—Blessed Sacrament Revs. Thomas Smithson, S.S.S.; Michael J. Boehm; Deacons Dismas Fernandez; Rudolf Hess; Rafael Pineda. In Res., Revs. Juancho D. Ramos, S.S.S.; Rudsend Paragas, S.S.S.; Richard O'Donnell, S.S.S.; Bros. John Christman, S.S.S.; Anthony Marshall, S.S.S.; Peter Harley, S.S.S.
Office: 3528 S. Hermitage Ave., 60609-1217. Tel: 773-847-3357; Fax: 773-847-3804.
Catechesis / Religious Program—

30—Blessed Sacrament-Millard, Closed. Consult Archives and Records Center for parish and school records.

31—St. Bonaventure, Closed. Consult Archives and Records Center for parish and school records. See Section W-Miscellaneous for oratory listing.

32—St. Bride Rev. Robert J. Roll.
Res.: 7811 S. Coles Ave., 60649. Tel: 773-731-8822; Fax: 773-721-0673. Email: stbride@archchicago.org. Web: www.st-bride.org.
Catechesis / Religious Program—Carole Palmore, D.R.E. Students 25.

33—St. Bronislava Rev. Ricardo Castillo.
Res.: 8708 S. Colfax Ave., 60617. Tel: 773-734-0776; Fax: 773-734-1429. Email: jesusp@saintbronislava.com.
Catechesis / Religious Program—Students 135.

34—St. Bruno Rev. Anthony Bury; Deacon Sal Villa. In Res., Revs. Emil Cudak (Poland); Bruno Janik (Retired).
Res.: 4751 S. Harding Ave., 60632. Tel: 773-523-3467; Fax: 773-523-4253. Email: stbruno@comcast.net. Web: www.stbrunochicago.org.
School—4839 S. Harding Ave., 60632. Tel: 773-847-0697; Fax: 773-847-1620. Lay Teachers 14; Students 250.
Catechesis / Religious Program—Students 100.

35—St. Cajetan Rev. Frank A. Kurucz.
Parish Center Office—2445 W. 112th St., 60655. Tel: 773-474-7800; Fax: 773-474-7878.
Res.: 11234 S. Artesian Ave., 60655. Tel: 773-238-4100.
School—2447 W. 112th St., 60655. Tel: 773-233-8844. Lay Teachers 22; Students 389.
Catechesis / Religious Program—Students 160.

36—St. Camillus Revs. Waclaw L. Lech, O.C.D.; Michael G. Veneklase, O.C.D.
Res.: 5426 S. Lockwood Ave., 60638. Tel: 773-767-8183; Fax: 773-284-3812.
Catechesis / Religious Program—Students 545.

37—Christ the King Rev. Thomas P. Conde. In Res., Rev. Michael J. Adams (Retired).
Res.: 9235 S. Hamilton Ave., 60643-6360. Tel: 773-238-4877; Fax: 773-238-4963. Web: www.ckchicago.org.
School—9240 S. Hoyne Ave., 60643-6303. Tel: 773-779-3329; Fax: 773-779-3390. Lay Teachers 24; Students 312.
Catechesis / Religious Program—Mrs. Irene Friend, D.R.E. Students 90.

38—Christ the Redeemer Byzantine Bielarusian, Closed. Consult Archives and Records Center for parish records.

39—St. Christina Revs. Lawrence J. Sullivan; Andrzej Bartos (Poland); Karol Tybor; Thomas J. Purtell (Retired); Deacons Thomas Ryan; Stanley Rakauskas.
Res.: 11005 S. Homan Ave., 60655. Tel: 773-779-7181; Fax: 773-238-2942.
School—3333 W. 110th St., 60655. Tel: 773-445-2969; Fax: 773-445-0444. Lay Teachers 30; Students 629.
Catechesis / Religious Program—3333 W. 110th St., 60655. Tel: 773-445-2969; Fax: 773-445-0444. Students 403.

40—St. Clare of Montefalco Rev. Michael Sullivan, O.F.M.Cap.
Res.: 5443 S. Washtenaw Ave., 60632. Tel: 773-436-4422; Fax: 773-476-1888. Email: st.clare@sbcglobal.net.
Catechesis / Religious Program—Tel: 773-434-5599. Students 207.

41—St. Clement Revs. Kenneth C. Simpson; Ramil E. Fajardo. In Res., Rev. Vincent F. Costello.
Res.: 642 W. Deming Pl., 60614. Tel: 773-281-0371; Fax: 773-281-2509. Email: feedback@stclementchurch.org. Web: www.stclementchurch.org.
School—2524 N. Orchard St., 60614. Tel: 773-348-8212; Fax: 773-348-4712. Mrs. Anne Rog, Prin. Lay Teachers 36; Students 447.
Catechesis / Religious Program—Tel: 773-281-0371, Ext. 14. Students 160.

42—St. Clotilde Revs. John B. Atoyebi; Michael Ajiboye, (Extern); Raymond Adebowale (Nigeria).
Res.: 8430 Calumet Ave., 60619. Tel: 773-874-1022; Fax: 773-874-1736.
Catechesis / Religious Program—Sr. Theresa Ocloo, E.H.J., D.R.E.

43—St. Columba Rev. James F. Nallen.
Res.: 13323 S. Greenbay Ave., 60633. Tel: 773-646-2660; Fax: 773-646-6821.

44—St. Columbanus Rev. Matthew S. Eyerman; Deacon William McKinnis. In Res., Rev. Philip Mensah (Ghana).
Res.: 331 E. 71st St., 60619. Tel: 773-224-1022; Fax: 773-224-1477.
School—7120 S. Calumet, 60619. Tel: 773-224-3811; Fax: 773-224-3810. Lay Teachers 25; Students 300.
Catechesis / Religious Program—Students 35.

45—St. Constance (1916) Revs. Thaddeus Dzieszko; Robert Lojek; Maciej Galle; Deacons Ted Lisowski, Pastoral Assoc.; George Gniech, Pastoral Assoc. In Res., Rev. Wladyslaw Podeszwik (Poland) (Retired).
Res.: 5843 W. Strong St., 60630. Tel: 773-545-8581; Fax: 773-545-0227. Email: church@stconstance.org. Web: www.stconstance.org.
School—5841 W. Strong St., 60630. Tel: 773-283-2311; Fax: 773-283-3515. Lay Teachers 13; Students 137.
Catechesis / Religious Program— 81 English; 351 Polish. Students 432.

46—St. Cornelius Revs. Daniel R. Fallon; Joseph M. Wilk; Deacons Carl D. Olson; Edward Condon.
Res.: 5205 N. Lieb Ave., 60630. Tel: 773-283-5222; Fax: 773-283-8484.
School—Tel: 773-283-2192; Fax: 773-283-1377. Lay Teachers 21; Students 350.
Catechesis / Religious Program—Students 100.

47—Corpus Christi Rev. Raphael Ezeh, M.S.P.
Corpus Christi Friary—4920 King Dr., 60615-2306. Tel: 773-285-7720; Fax: 773-285-2572.
Catechesis / Religious Program—Students 20.

48—St. Daniel the Prophet Revs. John T. Noga; Gerald K. O'Reilly; Slawomir Kurc (Poland); Deacon Richard Voytas. In Res., Revs. John M. Cassidy (Retired); Francis P. Cassidy (Retired).
Parish Office & Res.: 5300 S. Natoma Ave., 60638. Tel: 773-586-1223; Fax: 773-583-1238. Email: stdaniel1@attglobal.net.
School—Tel: 773-586-1225; Fax: 773-586-1232. Lay Teachers 30; Students 647.
Catechesis / Religious Program—Tel: 773-586-0660. Students 150.

49—St. Denis Rev. Theodore L. Ostrowski; Sr. Norine Burns, O.P., Pastoral Assoc.; Deacons Thomas Ewers; Thomas Solon.
Res.: 8301 S. St. Louis Ave., 60652. Tel: 773-434-3313; Fax: 773-776-3922. Email: stdenis@archchicago.org.
Catechesis / Religious Program—Students 120.

50—St. Dorothy Rev. Robert J. Miller; Deacons Roscoe Dixon; Wallace Harris.
Res.: 450 E. 78th St., 60619. Tel: 773-651-7000; Fax: 773-651-0969.
School—7740 S. Eberhart Ave., 60619. Tel: 773-783-0555; Fax: 773-783-3736. Sisters of the Presentation of the Blessed Virgin Mary 1; Lay Teachers 15; Students 263.
Catechesis / Religious Program—Tel: 773-651-7000; Fax: 773-651-0969. Students 75.

51—St. Edward Rev. Edward A. Carlson. In Res., Revs. Joseph C. Taylor (Retired); Tomy Vadakevattukula, M.S.T. (India).
Res.: 4350 W. Sunnyside Ave., 60630-4146. Tel: 773-545-6496; Fax: 773-545-1136.
School—4343 W. Sunnyside Ave., 60630-4146. Tel: 773-736-9133; Fax: 773-736-9280. Dominican Sisters (Springfield, IL) 4; Lay Teachers 20; Students 350.
Catechesis / Religious Program—Students 148.

52—St. Elizabeth Rev. Richard Andrus, S.V.D.
Res.: 50 E. 41st St., 60653. Tel: 773-373-8638; Fax: 773-268-2640. Email: stelizabethchicago@sbcglobal.net.
School—4052 S. Wabash, 60653. Tel: 773-548-4100; Fax: 773-373-8642. Sisters 2; Lay Teachers 9; Students 231.
Catechesis / Religious Program—Students 231.
Convent—4117 S. Michigan, 60653. Tel: 773-373-8630.

53—Epiphany Rev. Daniel Long.
Res.: 2524 S. Keeler Ave., 60623. Tel: 773-521-1112; Fax: 773-521-4394. Web: www.epiphanychicago.org.
School—4223 W. 25th St., 60623. Tel: 773-762-1542. Lay Teachers 13; Students 164.
Catechesis / Religious Program—Students 223.

54—St. Ethelreda, Closed. Consult Archives and Records Center for parish records. (See St. Kilian parish for school information).

55—St. Eugene Revs. George Koeune; Philip J. Grib, S.J.; Jerome Twarog; Deacons Gerard Kwasegroch; Edward O'Leary.
Res.: 7958 W. Foster Ave., 60656-1651. Tel: 773-775-6659; Fax: 773-775-2832. Email: churchoffice@st-eugene.org. Web: www.st-eugene.org.
School—7930 W. Foster Ave., 60656-1651. Tel: 773-763-2235; Fax: 773-763-2775. Lay Teachers 22; Students 328.
Catechesis / Religious Program—Students 148.

56—St. Felicitas Rev. Gregory A. Rom; Sr. Kathleen Smith, Pastoral Assoc.; Deacon John Cook. In Res., Res.: 1526 E. 84th St., 60619. Tel: 773-734-2300; Fax: 773-731-5381.
Catechesis / Religious Program—Students 20.

57—St. Ferdinand Revs. Zdzislaw J. Torba; Tomasz Sztandera (Poland); Robert M. Pajor; Deacons Irwin Hotcaveg; Ron Weiner; Mr. Marcin Wojtulewicz, Fin. Mgr.
Res.: 5900 W. Barry Ave., 60634. Tel: 773-622-5900; Fax: 773-622-5903. Web: www.saintferdinand.org.
High School—Notre Dame High School, 3000 N. Mango Ave., 60634. Tel: 773-622-9494; Fax: 773-622-8511. Email: kjones@ndhs4girls.org. Web: www.ndhs4girls.org. Mrs. Kathryn Piper, Prin.; Ms. Kelly Jones, Pres.; Mr. Jorge Mora, Info Tech Mgr. Sisters of Notre Dame de Namur. Lay Teachers 21; Girls 250.
School—3131 N. Mason Ave., 60634. Tel: 773-622-3022; Fax: 773-622-2807. Dr. Lucine Mastalerz, Prin. Lay Teachers 18; Students 281.
Catechesis / Religious Program—Tel: 773-622-5900, Ext. 366. Dr. Lucine Mastalerz, D.R.E. Students 848.
Convent—5936 W. Barry Ave., 60634. Tel: 773-889-7979. Missionary Sisters of Christ the King for Polonia 4.

58—St. Fidelis, Closed. Consult Archives and Records Center for parish and school records.

59—Five Holy Martyrs Revs. Wojciech Baryski, S.Ch.; Robert Wojslaw, S.Ch. In Res., Rev. Rafal Dygula, S.Ch.
Res.: 4327 S. Richmond St., 60632. Tel: 773-254-3636; Fax: 773-254-3609. Email: fiveholymartyrs@yahoo.com.
School—Pope John Paul II School, Five Holy Martyrs Campus, 4325 S. Richmond St., 60632. Tel: 773-523-6161; Fax: 773-254-9194. Lay Teachers 13; Students 190.
Catechesis / Religious Program—Students 84.

60—St. Florian Rev. James A. Mezydlo.
Res.: 13145 S. Houston Ave., 60633. Tel: 773-646-4877; Fax: 773-646-5965. Email: stflorian@archchicago.org. Web: florian.hegewisch.net.
School—13110 S. Baltimore Ave., 60633. Tel: 773-646-2868; Fax: 773-646-2891. Lay Teachers 10; Students 125.
Catechesis / Religious Program—Students 85.

61—St. Francis Borgia Revs. Andrew P. Wypych; Piotr Gnoinski; Deacons Robert Cnota; Casimir Fronczek; Ralph Hinch; William Lehman, (Retired). In Res., Rev. Joseph A. Mulcrone.
Res.: 8033 W. Addison St., 60634. Tel: 773-625-1118; Fax: 773-625-1110. Web: www.stfrancisborgiachicago.org.
School—Tel: 773-589-1000; Fax: 773-589-0781. Lay Teachers 14; Students 304.
Catechesis / Religious Program—Tel: 773-625-1705; Fax: 773-625-1774. Students 136.

Convent—3521 N. Panama St., 60634. Tel: 773-625-8063.

62—ST. FRANCIS DE SALES Most Rev. Joseph N. Perry, Admin.; Rev. Clement Oyafemi (Nigeria).
Res.: 10201 S. Ewing Ave., 60617. Tel: 773-734-1383; Fax: 773-734-3022.

63—ST. FRANCIS OF ASSISI, (Hispanic), Revs. Francisco Liporace, I.V.E.; Ruben Rios, I.V.E., Parochial Vicar; Deacons J. Zeferino Ochoa; Manuel Rodriguez; Pedro Sedano.
Res.: 813 W. Roosevelt Rd., 60608. Tel: 312-226-7575; Fax: 312-226-6283.
Catechesis/Religious Program—Tel: 312-226-7575; Fax: 312-226-6283. Students 570.

64—ST. FRANCIS OF ASSISI/OUR LADY OF THE ANGELS Rev. Lawrence M. Choate, O.S.M., Admin.; Deacon Sabino Sanchez.
Res.: 932 N. Kostner, 60651. Tel: 773-235-3132; Fax: 773-486-7726.
Catechesis/Religious Program—Students 150.
Catechesis/Religious Program—Javier Castillo, D.R.E. Students 250.

65—ST. GABRIEL Rev. James E. Merold. In Res., Rev. Richard C. Creagh.
Res.: 4522 S. Wallace St., 60609. Tel: 773-268-9595; Fax: 773-268-9586. Email: saintgabes@saintgabes.com. Web: www.saintgabes.com.
Church: 45th St. & Lowe Ave., 60609. Fax: 773-268-9568.
School—607 W. 45th St., 60609. Tel: 773-268-6636; Fax: 773-268-2501. Lay Teachers 11; Students 160.
Catechesis/Religious Program—Students 90.

66—ST. GALL Revs. Gary M. Graf; Armando Morales-Martinez; Deacons Michael Slajchert; Albert Herrera; John Bumbul. In Res., Rev. Robert L. Tuzik.
Res.: 5511 S. Sawyer Ave., 60629. Tel: 773-737-3113; Fax: 773-737-0272.
School—5515 S. Sawyer Ave., 60629. Tel: 773-737-3454. Lay Teachers 13; Students 327.
Catechesis/Religious Program—Students 350.

67—ST. GELASIUS, Closed. Consult Archives and Records Center for parish and school records.

68—ST. GENEVIEVE Revs. Salvador Den Hallegado; Joaquin Garcia-Valencia (Mexico); Sr. Jean Michael Rafferty, S.P., Pastoral Assoc.; Deacon Benito Centeno.
Res.: 4835 W. Altgeld St., 60639. Tel: 773-237-3011; Fax: 773-237-3043.
School—4854 W. Montana St., 60639. Tel: 773-237-7131; Fax: 773-237-7265. Lay Teachers 17; Students 297.
Catechesis/Religious Program—Tel: 773-637-6086; Fax: 773-237-3043. Students 326.

69—ST. GEORGE, (Slovenian), Most Rev. Joseph N. Perry, Admin.; Rev. Phillip C. Kiley.
Res.: 9546 S. Ewing Ave., 60617. Tel: 773-734-0554; Fax: 773-734-3327.
Catechesis/Religious Program—Tel: 773-734-1383. Students 225.

70—ST. GERTRUDE Rev. Dominic J. Grassi; Dr. Peter Buttitta, Dir. Ministries. In Res., Rev. Michael J. Bradley.
Res.: 1420 W. Granville Ave., 60660. Tel: 773-764-3621; Fax: 773-761-4164. Email: stgertrude1420@sbcglobal.net. Web: www.stgertrudechicago.org.
School—Northside Catholic Academy, 6216 N. Glenwood Ave., 60660. Tel: 773-743-6277; Fax: 773-743-6174. Lay Teachers 22; Students 450.
Catechesis/Religious Program—Students 75.

71—GOOD SHEPHERD Revs. Marco A. Mercado; Benjamin Arevalos Lupercia. In Res., Most Rev. John R. Manz.
Res.: 2719 S. Kolin Ave., 60623. Tel: 773-762-2322; Fax: 773-762-4885.
Catechesis/Religious Program—Students 390.

72—ST. GREGORY, THE GREAT Revs. Paul H. Wachdorf; Brian J. Fischer; Sr. Barbara Quinn, S.N.D.deN., Pastoral Assoc.; Scott Snider, Pastoral Assoc. In Res., Rev. John P. Moulder.
Office: 5545 N. Paulina St., 60640.
Res.: 1634 W. Gregory St., 60640. Tel: 773-561-3546; Fax: 773-728-3827. Email: info@stgregory.net. Web: www.stgregory.net.
High School—1677 W. Bryn Mawr Ave., 60660. Tel: 773-907-2100; Fax: 773-907-2120. Lay Teachers 17; Students 200.
Catechesis/Religious Program—Students 85.

73—ST. HEDWIG Revs. Stanislaw Jankowski, C.R.; Tomasz Wojciechowski, C.R. In Res., Revs. Walter Wilczek, C.R. (Retired); Eugene Szarek, C.R.; Deacons Gilberto Cintron; Wilmer Rodriguez; Daniel Cabrera.
Res.: 2226 N. Hoyne Ave., 60647. Tel: 773-486-1660; Fax: 773-486-1684. Email: sthedwig@sbcglobal.net. Web: www.sthedwigrcchurch-bucktown.org.
Catechesis/Religious Program—Students 70.

74—ST. HELEN Revs. Waldemar Stawiarski; Jan Bukowski, COr (Poland).
Res.: 2315 W. Augusta Blvd., 60622. Tel: 773-235-3575; Fax: 773-235-3810. Email: sthelen@archchicago.org. Web: www.sthelenparish.net.
School—2347 W. Augusta Blvd., 60622. Tel: 773-486-1055. Lay Teachers 24; Students 285.
Catechesis/Religious Program—Fax: 773-235-3810. Students 10.

75—ST. HELENA Revs. Thomas J. Kaminski; Francis Diyaolu (Nigeria); Deacons Daniel Sutton; Tommy West; Clayton Kort.
Res.: 10121 S. Parnell Ave., 60628. Tel: 773-779-2243; Fax: 773-779-2749.
School—10115 S. Parnell Ave., 60628. Tel: 773-238-5432; Fax: 773-238-6026. Lay Teachers 11; Students 242.
Catechesis/Religious Program—Students 247.

76—ST. HENRY Rev. Dominic Vinh Van Ha; Deacons Frank G. Duffy; Duc Nguyen; Neba Ambe.
Res.: 6335 N. Hoyne Ave., 60659. Tel: 773-764-7413; Fax: 773-764-5994.

77—ST. HILARY Revs. William A. Eddy; Arthur J. Olsen; Deacon Donald Wehling.
Res.: 5600 N. Fairfield Ave., 60659. Tel: 773-561-3474; Fax: 773-561-1129.
School—5614 N. Fairfield Ave., 60659. Tel: 773-561-5885; Fax: 773-561-6409. Lay Teachers 22; Students 370.
Catechesis/Religious Program—Students 80.

78—HOLY ANGELS Rev. John B. Atoyebi; Deacon Leroy Gill Jr.
Res.: 615 E. Oakwood Blvd., 60653. Tel: 773-624-5375; Fax: 773-624-8393. Email: holyangelschurch@comcast.net. Web: www.holyangels.com.
School—750 E. 40th St., 60653. Tel: 772-624-0727; Fax: 773-538-9683. Priests 2; Sisters 3; Lay Teachers 22; Students 300.
Catechesis/Religious Program—Sr. Theresa Ocloo, E.H.J., D.R.E.

79—HOLY CROSS/IMMACULATE HEART OF MARY Revs. Bruce L. Wellems, C.M.F.; George Ruffolo, C.M.F.; Mark J. Brummel, C.M.F.; Manuel Villalobos, C.M.F.
Res.: 4557 S. Wood St., 60609. Tel: 773-376-3900; Fax: 773-376-8929. Email: hcihm@claret.org. Web: www.hcihm.org.
Catechesis/Religious Program—Students 791.

80—HOLY FAMILY Rev. Jeremiah M. Boland, Admin.; Deacon Rudolph Kotleba, (Retired).
Res.: 1080 W. Roosevelt Rd., 60608. Tel: 312-492-8442; Fax: 312-492-8430. Web: www.holyfamilychurchchicago.org.
Catechesis/Religious Program—Students 30.

81—HOLY INNOCENTS Rev. Philip E. Cyscon; Very Rev. Marek Kasperczuk (Poland).
Res.: 743 N. Armour St., 60622. Tel: 312-666-3675; Fax: 312-666-0714. Email: holyinnocents743@aol.com.
Catechesis/Religious Program—1448 W. Superior St., 60622. Tel: 312-243-9887; Fax: 312-243-4524. Students 225.
Bishop Abramowicz Seminary—1447 W. Superior St., 60622. Tel: 312-455-0598.

82—HOLY NAME OF MARY Revs. James F. Flynn; Thadeo Mgimba; Mary Johnson, Pastoral Assoc.
Res.: 11159 S. Loomis St., 60643. Tel: 773-238-6800; Fax: 773-238-7304.
Mission—Sacred Heart 11652 S. Church St., Cook Co. 60643. Tel: 773-233-3955.
Catechesis/Religious Program—Students 48.

83—HOLY ROSARY Rev. Michael V. Kalck; Deacon Jorge Rozo. In Res., Most Rev. Lawrence Sabatini, C.S.
Res.: 612 N. Western Ave., 60612. Tel: 773-278-4820; Fax: 773-278-3770. Web: www.holyrosaryonwesternave.org.
Catechesis/Religious Program—Students 78.

84—HOLY ROSARY-113TH, Closed. Consult Archives and Records Center for parish and school records.

85—HOLY TRINITY, (Croatian), Closed. For inquiries for parish records contact Archives and Records Center.

86—HOLY TRINITY MISSION, (Polish), Revs. Andrzej Maslejak, S.Ch.; Hubert Zasacla, S.Ch.; Robert Nalepka, S.Ch.
Res.: 1118 N. Noble St., 60642. Tel: 773-489-4140; Fax: 773-489-5918. Email: parafia@trojcowo.com. Web: www.trojcowo.com.
Catechesis/Religious Program—Students 400.

87—ST. HYACINTH BASILICA Revs. Michal Osuch, C.R.; Francis Rog, C.R.; Marion Wroblewski, C.R.; Adam Piasecki, C.R. (Poland); Stanislaw Lasota, C.R. (Poland); Deacon Frank Girjatowicz.
Res.: 3636 W. Wolfram St., 60618. Tel: 773-342-3636; Fax: 773-342-3638. Web: www.sthyacinthbasilica.org.
School—3640 W. Wolfram St., 60618. Tel: 773-342-7550; Fax: 773-384-0581. Lay Teachers 8; Students 120.
Catechesis/Religious Program—Students 650.

88—ST. IGNATIUS Rev. Joseph M. Jackson. In Res., Revs. William P. Grogan; Jackson Colon; Patrick J. McAteer, S.J.; Elias Kinoti, (Extern, Meru, Kenya).
Res.: 6559 N. Glenwood Ave., 60626. Tel: 773-764-5936; Fax: 773-764-4360.
Catechesis/Religious Program—Students 95.

89—IMMACULATE CONCEPTION Revs. Eric Meyer, C.P.; Ronan Newbold, C.P.; Deacon Richard Moritz; Sr. Judy David, S.S.J.-T.O.S.F., Pastoral Assoc.
Res.: 7211 W. Talcott Ave., 60631. Tel: 773-775-3833; Fax: 773-631-1024. Web: www.icparish.net.
School—7263 W. Talcott Ave., 60631. Tel: 773-775-0545; Fax: 773-775-3822. Bernadette Felicione, Prin. Lay Teachers 36; Students 440.
Catechesis/Religious Program—Tel: 773-775-0545, Ext. 216. Students 215.

90—IMMACULATE CONCEPTION, (Lithuanian), Revs. Thomas R. Koys; Stephen F. Lesniewski; Edward J. Maxa (Retired); Jaunius Kelpsas (Lithuania); Deacons Vincente Estrada; Roberto Rivas.
Res.: 2745 W. 44th St., 60632-1999. Tel: 773-523-1402; Fax: 773-523-8465. Email: ftkoys@aol.com. Web: www.icchurch-chicgo.org.
See Pope John Paul II School, Five Holy Martyrs Campus under Five Holy Martyrs, Chicago.
Catechesis/Religious Program—Students 300.

91—IMMACULATE CONCEPTION OF THE BLESSED VIRGIN MARY Revs. Patrick J. Lee; Ronald Galt (Scotland).
Res.: 1431 N. North Park Ave., 60610. Tel: 312-944-1230; Fax: 312-944-0673. Web: sjicparish.org.
Catechesis/Religious Program—Mrs. Alice Doering, D.R.E. Students 365.

92—IMMACULATE CONCEPTION OF THE BLESSED VIRGIN MARY Rev. Ricardo Castillo.
Parish Office and Rectory—2944 E. 88th St., 60617. Tel: 773-768-2100.
Church: 88th & Commercial Ave., 60617.
School—8739 S. Exchange, 60617. Tel: 773-375-4674. Sr. Claudia Carrillo, Prin. Students 180.
Catechesis/Religious Program—Tel: 773-221-1423. Jose Delgadillo, D.R.E. Students 125.

93—IMMACULATE HEART OF MARY Rev. James A. Heneghan; Deacon David Reyes.
Res.: 3834 N. Spaulding, 60618. Tel: 773-478-1157; Fax: 773-267-6884. Email: FatherJim_ihm@comcast.net. Web: ihm.archchicago.org.
Catechesis/Religious Program—Tel: 773-478-1157, Ext. 16. Students 117.

94—IMMACULATE HEART OF MARY VICARIATE, Closed. See Holy Cross/Immaculate Heart of Mary.

95—SAINT ITA Revs. David P. Pavlik; Daniel J. Cassidy; Khue Vu (Vietnam).
Res.: 1220 W. Catalpa Ave., 60640. Tel: 773-561-5343; Fax: 773-561-5609. Email: stita@archchicago.org.
School—Northside Catholic Academy, 5525 N. Magnolia Ave., 60640. Tel: 773-271-2008; Fax: 773-271-3101. Email: dsullivan@ncaweb.org. Web: www.northsidecatholic.org. Lay Teachers 38; Students 443.
Catechesis/Religious Program—Students 267.

96—ST. JAMES Rev. Edward Linton, O.S.B.
Res.: 2942 S. Wabash Ave., 60616. Tel: 312-842-1919; Fax: 312-842-3612. Email: info@stjamesonwabash.com. Web: www.stjamesonwabash.com.
Catechesis/Religious Program—Students 5.

97—ST. JAMES Revs. Wojciech Kwiecien; John L. Wodniak, Pastor Emeritus (Retired); Jose Antonio Murcia Abellan (Poland) (Poland); Krzysztof Pankanin (Poland) (Extern).
Res.: 5730 W. Fullerton Ave., 60639. Tel: 773-237-1474; Fax: 773-237-1546.
Catechesis/Religious Program—Tel: 773-237-1474; Fax: 773-237-1546. Students 200.
Convent—2441 N. Menard Ave., 60639. Tel: 773-637-9187. Missionary Sisters of Christ the King for Polonia 2.

98—ST. JANE DE CHANTAL Rev. Thomas C. McNeff; Deacon Ron Morowczynski.
Res.: 5252 S. Austin Ave., 60638. Tel: 773-767-2411; Fax: 773-767-2769.
School—5201 S. McVicker Ave., 60638. Tel: 773-767-1130; Fax: 772-767-1387. Lay Teachers 13; Students 265.
Catechesis/Religious Program—Students 82.

99—ST. JEROME Revs. Jeremy Thomas; Norman H. Moran-Rosero; Deacons Fritz Jean-Pierre; Raymond Ward, (Retired); Elisco Ramos; Francisco Marin.
Res.: 1709 W. Lunt Ave., 60626. Tel: 773-262-3170; Fax: 773-262-2834. Email: stjerome-lunt@archchicago.org.
Catechesis/Religious Program—1706 W. Morse Ave., 60626. Tel: 773-262-9880; Fax: 773-262-2834. Students 358.

100—ST. JEROME, (Croatian), Revs. Jozo Grbes, O.F.M.; Ivan M. Strmecki, O.F.M.
Res.: 2823 S. Princeton Ave., Cardinal Stepinac Way, 60616. Tel: 312-842-1871; Fax: 312-842-6427. Email: grbes@aol.com. Web:

www.stjeromecroatian.org.
School—2801 S. Princeton Ave., 60616. Tel: 312-842-7668; Fax: 312-842-6427. Lay Teachers 19; Students 225.
Catechesis/Religious Program—2716 S. Princeton Ave., 60616. Tel: 312-842-4077. Students 43.

101—ST. JOACHIM Rev. Robert J. Gilbert.
Res.: 700 E. 91st St., 60619. Tel: 773-488-4488; Fax: 773-994-8945. Email: stjoachim@sbcglobal.net.

102—ST. JOHN BERCHMANS Rev. Wayne F. Watts; Deacons Jorge Cabrera; Guillermo Mendizabal. In Res., Rev. A. Paul Reicher (Retired).
Res.: 2517 W. Logan Blvd., 60647. Tel: 773-486-4300; Fax: 773-252-5346. Email: info@stjohnberchmans.org. Web: www.stjohnberchmans.org.
School—2509 W. Logan Blvd., 60647. Tel: 773-486-1334; Fax: 773-486-1782. Lay Teachers 24; Students 227.
Catechesis/Religious Program—Students 112.

103—ST. JOHN BOSCO Revs. Timothy Zak, S.D.B.; Gregory Fishel, S.D.B.; Oswaldo Guillen, S.D.B. (Venezuela); Louis Aineto, S.D.B.; Bro. Charles Thenier, S.D.B.; Deacon Ronald Swiatek.
Res.: 2250 N. McVicker Ave., 60639. Tel: 773-622-4620; Fax: 773-622-5040.
Catechesis/Religious Program—2310 N. McVicker Ave., 60639. Tel: 773-836-2413. Sr. Lourdes Ramirez, D.R.E. Students 700.

104—ST. JOHN CANTIUS Revs. C. Frank Phillips, C.R.; Albert Tremari, S.J.C.; James Isaacson, S.J.C.; Scott Haynes, S.J.C.; Brendan Gibson, S.J.C.; Bartholomew Juncer, S.J.C.
Res.: 825 N. Carpenter St., 60622. Tel: 312-243-7373; Fax: 312-243-4545. Web: www.societycantius.org.

105—ST. JOHN DE LA SALLE Rev. Michael P. Knotek.
Res.: 10205 King Dr., 60628. Tel: 773-785-2022.
School—St. John de la Salle Catholic Academy, Tel: 773-785-2331. Mr. Charles Carroll, Prin. Lay Teachers 12; Students 280.
Catechesis/Religious Program—Students 8.

106—ST. JOHN FISHER Revs. Robert J. Kyfes; Thomas J. Purtell, Pastor Emeritus (Retired); Marion Soprych; Deacons Raymond Reilly; Thomas Siska; Robert Carroll. In Res., Rev. Wojciech A. Marat (Poland).
Res.: 10234 S. Washtenaw Ave., 60655. Tel: 773-445-6565; Fax: 773-445-1644.
School—10200 S. Washtenaw Ave., 60655. Tel: 773-445-4737; Fax: 773-233-3012. Sisters of St. Joseph (LaGrange, IL) 1; Lay Teachers 36; Students 690.
Catechesis/Religious Program—Tel: 773-238-1851. Students 100.

107—ST. JOSAPHAT Revs. Richard J. Prendergast; Michael A. Gabriel; Deacon Daniel G. Welter; Dr. Margaret Hanrahan, Pastoral Assoc.
Res.: 2311 N. Southport Ave., 60614. Tel: 773-327-8955; Fax: 773-327-2047. Email: mail@stjosaphatparish.org. Web: www.stjosaphatparish.org.
School—2245 N. Southport Ave., 60614. Tel: 773-549-0909; Fax: 773-549-3127. Lay Teachers 29; Students 330.
Catechesis/Religious Program—Students 75.

108—ST. JOSEPH Rev. Patrick J. Lee; Deacon Donald Palmer. In Res., Rev. Ronald Galt (Scotland).
Res.: 1107 N. Orleans St., 60610. Tel: 312-787-7174; Fax: 312-787-9825. Web: www.sjicparish.org.
Catechesis/Religious Program—Students 68.

109—ST. JOSEPH Rev. Hugo Leon Londono, M.S.C.
Res.: 4821 S. Hermitage Ave., 60609. Tel: 773-254-2366; Fax: 773-254-2640.
Catechesis/Religious Program—Students 390.

110—ST. JULIANA Revs. Stephen F. Kanonik; Philip J. Dressler, Pastor Emeritus (Retired); Donald J. Ahearn, Pastor Emeritus (Retired); Ms. Pam Francisco, Pastoral Assoc. & D.R.E.; Deacons Robert Ryan; Edward Dolan.
Office: 7200 N. Osceola, 60631. Tel: 773-631-4127; Fax: 773-631-4150.
Res.: 7158 N. Osceola Ave., 60631. Tel: 773-631-4386; Fax: 773-631-4150.
School—7400 W. Touhy, 60631. Tel: 773-631-2256. Lay Teachers 35; Students 554.
Catechesis/Religious Program—Students 325.

111—ST. KEVIN Rev. Pedro Campos.
Res.: 10509 S. Torrence Ave., 60617. Tel: 773-721-2563; Fax: 773-721-2208.
Catechesis/Religious Program—Tel: 708-862-1087; Fax: 773-721-2563. Students 175.

112—ST. KILIAN Revs. William E. Vanecko; Leo Tinkatumire, (Extern, Mbarara, Nigeria); Deacon Warren Allen.
Res.: 8725 S. May St., 60620. Tel: 773-651-4000; Fax: 773-651-5876.
School—St. Ethelreda, 8734 S. Paulina St., 60620. Tel: 773-238-1757; Fax: 773-238-6059. Lay Teachers 12; Students 220.
Catechesis/Religious Program—Students 20.

113—ST. LADISLAUS Revs. Jan F. Kaplan; Jan Mucha (Poland).
Res.: 5345 W. Roscoe St., 60641. Tel: 773-725-2300; Fax: 773-725-6042. Email: stladislaus@sbcglobal.net. Web: www.stladislauschurch.org.
School—3330 N. Lockwood Ave., 60641. Tel: 773-545-5600; Fax: 773-545-5676. Sisters of the Holy Family of Nazareth (Des Plaines, IL) 2; Lay Teachers 13; Students 215.
Catechesis/Religious Program—Tel: 773-545-5809; Fax: 773-545-4340. Students 180.
Convent—5330 W. Henderson St., 60641. Tel: 773-545-1811; Fax: 773-545-4340.

114—ST. LAURENCE, Closed. Consult Archives and Records Center for parish and school records.

115—ST. LEO THE GREAT, Closed. Consult Archives and Records Center for parish and school records.

116—ST. MALACHY Revs. George Roy, O.M.I.; George Knab, O.M.I.; Deacons Mario Avila; David Castaneda; Dexter Watson; John D. Burt, (Retired).
Res.: 2248 W. Washington Blvd., 60612. Tel: 312-733-1068; Fax: 312-491-9164. Email: stmalachy@sbcglobal.net.
School—2252 W. Washington Blvd., 60612. Tel: 312-733-2252; Fax: 312-733-5703. Sisters 1; Lay Teachers 12; Students 250.
Catechesis/Religious Program—Students 250.
Chapel—Precious Blood 2411 W. Congress Pkwy., 60612. Tel: 312-733-5371; Fax: 312-733-1285.

117—ST. MARGARET MARY Rev. James L. Barrett. In Res., Revs. Donatus Chukwu (Nigeria); Harold B. Murphy (Retired).
Res.: 2324 W. Chase Ave., 60645. Tel: 773-764-0615; Fax: 773-764-0641.
School—Tel: 773-764-0641; Fax: 773-764-1095. Lay Teachers 27; Students 186.
Catechesis/Religious Program—Students 39.

118—ST. MARGARET OF SCOTLAND Revs. Daniel J. Mallette (Retired); Claude Souffrant, S.J.
Res.: 9837 S. Throop St., 60643. Tel: 773-779-5151; Fax: 773-779-6198.
School—9833 S. Throop St., 60643. Tel: 773-238-1088; Fax: 773-238-1049. School Sisters of Notre Dame 2; Lay Teachers 25; Students 260.
Shelter—St. Margaret of Scotland-Heartland. Tel: 773-371-2500; Fax: 773-371-2515. Students 35.
Catechesis/Religious Program—Students 55.

119—ST. MARK Rev. Elmer Romero; Deacons Jorge Gutierrez; Antonio Villalobos; Antonio Navarro; Kenneth Velasquez, Pastoral Assoc. In Res., Most Rev. Enrique Rivera Hernandez (Puerto Rico).
Res.: 1048 N. Campbell Ave., 60622. Tel: 773-342-1516; Fax: 773-342-1372. Email: stmarkparish@comcast.net.
Catechesis/Religious Program—Maria Garcia, C.R.E.

120—ST. MARTIN DE PORRES Revs. Peter Premarini, M.C.C.J.; Maurizio Binaghi, M.C.C.J.; Michele Stragapede, M.C.C.J.; Deacon Anthony Llorens.
Res.: 5112 W. Washington Blvd., 60644. Tel: 773-287-0206; Fax: 773-261-2344.

121—ST. MARY MAGDALENE Revs. Freddy Washington, C.S.Sp.; Edmond Aristil, C.S.Sp. (Haiti); Deacon Juan J. Gomez. In Res. Congregation of the Holy Ghost (Spiritans), Revs. James C. Okoye, C.S.Sp.; Bernard A. Kelly, C.S.Sp.; Brandon Nguyen, C.S.Sp.
Res.: 8426 S. Marquette Ave., 60617. Tel: 773-768-1700; Fax: 773-734-8518.
Catechesis/Religious Program—Students 30.

122—ST. MARY OF PERPETUAL HELP Rev. Donald R. Craig.
Res.: 1039 W. 32nd St., 60608. Tel: 773-927-6646; Fax: 773-523-4565. Email: stmaryph@aol.com.
Catechesis/Religious Program—Students 56.

123—ST. MARY OF THE ANGELS Revs. Hilary F. Mahaney; Joseph P. Landauer. In Res., Rev. Charles M. Ferrer.
Res.: 1850 N. Hermitage Ave., 60622. Tel: 773-278-2644; Fax: 773-278-8904. Email: info@stmaryoftheangels.net. Web: www.stmaryoftheangels.net.
School—1810 N. Hermitage Ave., 60622. Tel: 773-486-0119; Fax: 773-486-0996. Sisters of the Resurrection (Chicago, IL) 1; Lay Teachers 12; Students 119.
Catechesis/Religious Program—Students 105.

124—ST. MARY OF THE ASSUMPTION Rev. John L. Harvey.
Res.: 310 E. 137th St., 60827-1896. Tel: 773-568-1611; Fax: 773-568-6268. Email: stmary-assumption@earthlink.net.
Catechesis/Religious Program—Students 43.

125—ST. MARY OF THE LAKE Rev. James J. Kastigar; Deacons Paul Spalla; John Navolio; Ubaldo Munoz, Pastoral Assoc. In Res., Revs. Daniel J. Collins (Retired); Richard O'Nyamwaro, A.J.
Res.: 4200 N. Sheridan Rd., 60613. Tel: 773-472-3711; Fax: 773-327-2899. Web: www.smolchicago.com.
School—1026 W. Buena Ave., 60613. Tel: 773-281-0018; Fax: 773-281-0112. Lay Teachers 11; Students 285.
Catechesis/Religious Program—Students 59.

126—ST. MARY OF THE WOODS Revs. Gregory Sakowicz; Kurt D. Boras; Leo T. Mahon, Pastor Emeritus (Retired); Deacon William Mages; Marcia Mahoney, Pastoral Assoc. & D.R.E. In Res., Revs. Thomas F. Maher (Retired); Donald J. Headley (Retired).
Res.: 7033 N. Moselle Ave., 60646. Tel: 773-763-0206; Fax: 773-763-4968. Email: smowparish@sbcglobal.net. Web: www.smow.org.
School—Tel: 773-763-7577; Fax: 773-763-4293. Lay Teachers 28; Students 448.
Catechesis/Religious Program—Students 230.

127—ST. MARY, STAR OF THE SEA Revs. John J. McDonnell; James D. Beath; Deacons Jesse Navarro; Jesus Ochoa; Gregory Serratore. In Res., Rev. Charles Balskus (Retired).
Res.: 6435 S. Kilbourn Ave., 60629. Tel: 773-767-1246; Fax: 773-735-3894. Email: stmary-sea@archchicago.org. Web: stmarystarofthesea.archchicago.org.
School—6424 S. Kenneth Ave., 60629. Tel: 773-767-6160. Lay Teachers 19; Students 319.
Catechesis/Religious Program—Tel: 773-767-7078; Fax: 773-767-7077. Students 284.

128—MATERNITY OF THE BLESSED VIRGIN MARY Revs. Thomas Pelton; Manuel G. Padilla; Deacons Jorge Garcia; Felipe Gonzalez; Floro Hita; Milton Rodriguez; Jose Vazquez.
Res.: 3647 W. North Ave., 60647. Tel: 773-772-9401; Fax: 773-772-7454.
School—1537 N. Lawndale Ave., 60651. Tel: 773-227-1140; Fax: 773-227-2939. Lay Teachers 10; Students 215.
Catechesis/Religious Program—Students 263.

129—ST. MATTHIAS Revs. John J. Sanaghan, Admin.; Francis A. Cimarrusti (Retired); Deacon D.J. Shinkle.
Res.: 2310 W. Ainslie St., 60625. Tel: 773-506-2191; Fax: 773-506-2418.
School—4910 N. Claremont Ave., 60625. Tel: 773-784-0999; Fax: 773-784-3601. Lay Teachers 13; Students 260.
Catechesis/Religious Program—5044 N. Rockwell. Students 138.

130—ST. MAURICE, Closed. Consult Archives and Records Center for parish and school records.

131—ST. MICHAEL ARCHANGEL, (Italian), Closed. Consult Archives and Records Center for parish records.

132—ST. MICHAEL IN OLD TOWN Revs. Richard Thibodeau, C.Ss.R.; Thomas Donaldson, C.Ss.R.; Kenneth Sedlak, C.Ss.R.; Joseph J. Morin, C.Ss.R. In Res., Revs. John Paul Andree, C.Ss.R.; John Dowd, C.Ss.R. (Retired); Anthony Judge, C.Ss.R.; Edward Wilhelm, C.Ss.R. (Retired); Arturo Uribe, C.Ss.R.; John Kuehner, C.Ss.R.; Gan Nguyen, C.Ss.R.
Res.: 1633 N. Cleveland Ave., 60614. Tel: 312-642-2498; Fax: 312-642-9283. Email: stmichael@st-mikes.org. Web: www.st-mikes.org.
Catechesis/Religious Program—Tel: 312-943-4767. Mrs. Mary Catherine Meek, D.R.E. Students 70.

133—ST. MICHAEL THE ARCHANGEL Revs. Robert R. Perez; Guido Gutierrez. In Res., Rev. John S. Breslin.
Res.: 8237 S. Shore Dr., 60617. Tel: 773-734-4921; Fax: 773-734-8723. Email: info@stmichaelchicago.org. Web: www.stmichaelchicago.org.
School—8231 S. Shore Dr., 60617. Tel: 773-221-0212; Fax: 773-734-8732. Barbara C. Lee, Prin. Lay Teachers 14; Students 214.
Catechesis/Religious Program—Students 49.

134—ST. MICHAEL THE ARCHANGEL, (Slovak), Revs. Thomas E. Cima; John E. Tilford; Bro. Alfred J. Marshall, F.S.C., Pastoral Assoc.
Res.: 4821 S. Damen Ave., 60609. Tel: 773-523-1248; Fax: 773-523-0955. Email: sma48@ameritech.net.
Catechesis/Religious Program—Students 250.

135—ST. MONICA Revs. Theodore J. Schmitt; Andrew Izyk; Deacons Ken Jenney, Pastoral Assoc.; Ron Gronek. In Res., Revs. William M. Holbrook (Retired); James J. O'Brien (Retired).
Office: 5136 N. Nottingham Ave., 60656. Tel: 773-763-1661; Fax: 773-763-4917.
Res.: 5135 N. Mont Clare Ave., 60656.
School—Tel: 773-631-7880; Fax: 773-631-3266. Raymond Coleman, Prin.; Christopher Haruska, Asst. Prin. Lay Teachers 17; Students 400.
Catechesis/Religious Program—Tel: 773-631-7810; Fax: 773-763-4917. Students 180.

136—NATIVITY OF OUR LORD Rev. Daniel J. Brandt; Deacons Francis Henry; Erik Zeimys. In Res., Revs. Michael Flynn, O.Carm.; Richard P. Hynes.
Res.: 653 W. 37th St., 60609. Tel: 773-927-6263; Fax: 773-847-0600. Email: fatherdan@nativitybridgeport.org. Web: www.nativitybridgeport.org.

See Bridgeport Catholic Academy, Chicago under Consolidated Elementary Schools, located in the Institution section.
Catechesis/Religious Program—Students 420.

137—NATIVITY OF THE BLESSED VIRGIN MARY Rev. Anthony L. Markus.
Res.: 6812 S. Washtenaw Ave., 60629. Tel: 773-776-4600; Fax: 773-776-0677.
School—6820 S. Washtenaw Ave., 60629. Tel: 773-476-0571; Fax: 773-476-0065. Lay Teachers 14; Students 92.
Convent—6804 S. Washtenaw Ave., 60629. Tel: 773-476-5135.

138—ST. NICHOLAS OF TOLENTINE Rev. Jose Sequeira; Deacon Pablo Perez.
Res.: 3721 W. 62nd St., 60629. Tel: 773-735-1121; Fax: 773-735-1135. Email: stnicholas-tolentine@archchicago.org. Web: www.stnicksparish.org.
School—3743 W. 62nd St., 60629. Tel: 773-735-0772; Fax: 773-735-5414. Lay Teachers 12; Students 230.
Catechesis/Religious Program—Tel: 773-284-2635. Students 415.

139—NOTRE DAME DE CHICAGO Revs. Patrick J. Pollard; JoAndre Beltran; Megan Mio, Pastoral Assoc. In Res., Revs. Dennis R. Karamitis, S.J.; Michael A. Hack; Robert L. Tuzik.
Res.: 1335 W. Harrison St., 60607-3318. Tel: 312-243-7400; Fax: 312-243-7614. Email: nddechgo@aol.com. Web: www.nddc.archchicago.org.
Catechesis/Religious Program—Students 100.

140—OLD ST. MARY Revs. Michael J. Kallock, C.S.P.; Robert M. Cary, C.S.P.; Richard Sparks, C.S.P.; Deacon Timothy Donovan.
Res.: 1500 S. Michigan, 60605. Tel: 312-922-3444; Fax: 312-922-3447. Web: www.oldstmarys.com.
School—1532 S. Michigan Ave., 60605. Tel: 312-386-1560; Fax: 312-386-1560. Students 173.
Catechesis/Religious Program—Students 50.

141—OLD ST. PATRICK Revs. John J. Wall; John C. Cusick; Thomas J. Hurley.
Res.: 700 W. Adams St., 60661. Tel: 312-648-1021; Fax: 312-648-9025. Web: www.oldstpats.org.
Shrine—Shrine of Our Lady of Pompeii, Tel: 312-421-3757; Fax: 312-421-3756.

142—OUR LADY GATE OF HEAVEN Rev. Mel Hermanns, O.F.M.Cap.
Res.: 2338 E. 99th St., 60617. Tel: 773-375-3059; Fax: 773-375-3046. Email: OL-GateOfHeaven@archchicago.org.
Catechesis/Religious Program—Students 23.

143—OUR LADY HELP OF CHRISTIANS, Closed. Consult Archives and Records Center for parish and school records.

144—OUR LADY OF AGLONA, (Latvian), Closed. Consult Archives and Records Center for mission records.

145—OUR LADY OF FATIMA Rev. Nester Saenz (Peru).
Res.: 2751 W. 38th Pl., 60632. Tel: 773-927-2421; Fax: 773-247-1737. Email: ol-fatima@archchicago.org.
Catechesis/Religious Program—Sr. Martin Atilano, C.R.E. Students 300.

146—OUR LADY OF GOOD COUNSEL, Closed. Consult Archives and Records Center for parish and school records.

147—OUR LADY OF GRACE Rev. George L. Schopp; Sr. Florence Norton, S.P., Pastoral Assoc.; Deacons James Kwasigroch; Enrique Alonso; Ernesto Robles; Juan Ramirez. In Res., Rev. Lawrence E. Gorski.
Res.: 2455 N. Hamlin Ave., 60647. Tel: 773-772-5900; Fax: 773-276-4469.
School—2446 N. Ridgeway Ave., 60647. Tel: 773-342-0170; Fax: 773-342-5305. Dominican Sisters (Springfield, IL) 7; Lay Teachers 12; Students 175.
Catechesis/Religious Program—Students 375.

148—OUR LADY OF GUADALUPE Revs. Carl J. Quebedeaux, C.M.F.; Raymond E. O'Connor, C.M.F.; Thomas Moran, C.M.F.; Deacon Raul Nunez. In Res., Revs. Severino Lopez, C.M.F.; Richard Farrell, C.M.F.
Res.: 3200 E. 91st, 60617. Tel: 773-768-0793; Fax: 773-768-3245. Email: olg@claretians.org.
School—9050 S. Burley, 60617. Tel: 773-768-0999; Fax: 773-768-0529. Lay Teachers 16; Students 242.
Shrine—National Shrine of St. Jude, Tel: 312-236-7782; Fax: 312-236-7230. (Claretian Missionaries)
Catechesis/Religious Program—9049 S. Brandon, 60617. Tel: 773-734-0605. Students 370.

149—OUR LADY OF LOURDES Revs. Michael J. Shanahan; Diego F. Cadavid; Deacon Daniel Patino. In Res., Rev. Richard E. Bulwith.
Res.: 4640 N. Ashland Ave., 60640. Tel: 773-561-2141; Fax: 773-561-9853. Email: ol-lourdes-ashland@archchicago.org. Web: www.ololchicago.parishesonline.com.
Catechesis/Religious Program—Students 250.

150—OUR LADY OF LOURDES, Closed. Consult Archives and Records Center for parish and school records.

151—OUR LADY OF MERCY Revs. Joseph P. Tito; Noel B. Reyes; Deacons Manuel R. Del Llano; Robert Janega; Aurelio Garcia; Ms. Theresita Perez, Dir. Evangelization & Formation.
Res.: 4432 N. Troy St., 60625. Tel: 773-588-2620; Fax: 773-866-1838. Email: ol-mercy@archchicago.org. Web: www.olmchicago.com.
Catechesis/Religious Program—4414 N. Troy St. (2nd door bell), 60625. Tel: 773-588-1637; Fax: 773-588-1638. Students 650.

152—OUR LADY OF MOUNT CARMEL Revs. Thomas E. Srenn; Thomas J. Campana; Deacons Edmund Gronkiewicz; Thomas Lambert; Richard Johnson. Office: 708 W. Belmont, 60657.
Res.: 690 W. Belmont, 60657. Tel: 773-525-0453; Fax: 773-525-9438. Email: olmcinfo@aol.com. Web: www.mt-carmel.org.
School—720 W. Belmont Ave., 60657. Tel: 773-525-8779; Fax: 773-525-7810. Lay Teachers 12; Students 225.
Catechesis/Religious Program—Students 64.

153—OUR LADY OF PEACE Rev. Mark Kalema.
Res.: 7851 S. Jeffery Blvd., 60649. Tel: 773-768-0105; Fax: 773-721-3835.
Catechesis/Religious Program—Students 40.

154—OUR LADY OF POMPEII, See separate listing. See Old St. Patrick, Shrine of Our Lady of Pompeii

155—OUR LADY OF SORROWS, BASILICA OF Rev. Christopher M. Krymski, O.S.M.; Deacons Joseph Lewis; Alfred Bouey; Davis Fair. In Res., Rev. Vidal M. Martinez, O.S.M.
Res.: 3121 W. Jackson Blvd., 60612. Tel: 773-638-0159; Fax: 773-638-3036. Email: olsparish@olsparish-chicago.org. Web: www.ols-chicago.org.
Catechesis/Religious Program—Students 22.

156—OUR LADY OF TEPEYAC Rev. Rigoberto Gamez-Alfonso (Colombia); Maria Brito-Ramos, Pastoral Assoc.; Deacon Ramon Echevarria.
Res.: 2226 S. Whipple St., 60623. Tel: 773-521-8400; Fax: 773-521-4890.
School—2235 S. Albany, 60623. Tel: 773-522-0024; Fax: 773-522-4577. Lay Teachers 13; Students 228.
High School—2228 S. Whipple St., 60623. Tel: 773-522-0023; Fax: 773-522-0508. Sisters 1; Lay Teachers 15; Students 176.
Catechesis/Religious Program—Tel: 773-277-0320. Students 632.

157—OUR LADY OF THE SNOWS
Res.: 4858 S. Leamington Ave., 60638. Tel: 773-582-2266; Fax: 773-582-3363.
School—4810 S. Leamington Ave., 60638. Tel: 773-735-4810; Fax: 773-582-3363. Lay Teachers 11; Students 250.
Catechesis/Religious Program—Tel: 773-582-4904. Students 101.

158—OUR LADY OF VICTORY Revs. Christopher E. Doering; Eugene R. Winkowski; Deacons Robert Leck; Michael Ahern. In Res., Rev. Abraham M. Jacob (SYM).
Res.: 5212 W. Agatite Ave., 60630. Tel: 773-286-2950; Fax: 773-286-8579. Web: www.olvchicago.org.
School—4434 N. Laramie, 60630. Tel: 773-283-2229; Fax: 773-283-0842. Mrs. John Kasel, Prin. Students 202.
Catechesis/Religious Program—Mary Beth Frystak, D.R.E. Students 105.

159—OUR LADY, MOTHER OF THE CHURCH Rev. Richard J. Klajbor.
Res.: 8747 W. Lawrence Ave., 60656. Tel: 773-625-3369; Fax: 773-625-0226.
Catechesis/Religious Program—Jackie Froehlich, D.R.E.

160—ST. PANCRATIUS Rev. Bronislaus Chmiel.
Res.: 4025 S. Sacramento Ave., 60632. Tel: 773-523-5666; Fax: 773-523-3115.

161—ST. PASCAL Revs. Paul G. Seaman; Pawel Zemczak; Deacons Eugene Dorgan; Thomas Stubstad. In Res., Rev. Thomas M. Dore (Retired).
Res.: 3935 N. Melvina Ave., 60634. Tel: 773-725-7641; Fax: 773-725-9368. Email: StPascal@archchicago.org. Web: www.stpascal.org.
School—6143 W. Irving Park Rd., 60634. Tel: 773-736-8806; Fax: 773-725-3461. Lay Teachers 14; Students 205.
Ciezadlo Center—3954 N. Meade Ave., 60634. Tel: 773-545-9453.
Catechesis/Religious Program—Tel: 773-725-7641, Ext. 22. Students 96.

162—ST. PAUL Rev. Michael P. Enright.
Res.: 2127 W. 22nd Pl., 60608. Tel: 773-847-7622; Fax: 773-847-8687.
School—2114 W. 22nd Pl., 60608. Tel: 773-847-6078. Sisters 3; Lay Teachers 13; Students 270.
Catechesis/Religious Program—Students 110.

163—SS. PETER AND PAUL Rev. Pascal Bigirimana, Admin. (Extern). In Res., Rev. Honoratus Canute Mwageni (Rwanda).
Res.: 12433 S. Halsted St., 60628. Tel: 773-785-1200.

164—SS. PETER AND PAUL, Closed. Consult Archives and Records Center for parish and school records.

165—ST. PETER CANISIUS, Closed. Consult Archives and Records Center for parish and school records.

166—ST. PETER'S Rev. Kurt Hartrich, O.F.M.
St. Peter's Friary—110 W. Madison St., 60602. Tel: 312-372-5111; Fax: 312-853-2361. Email: stpeter-madison@archchicago.org. Web: stpetersloop.org. (For complete listing of residents see Section N Residences of Priests and Brothers.) Priests 14; Brothers 6.

167—ST. PHILIP NERI Rev. Thomas G. Belanger; Deacon Willie Cooper; Odessa Foster, Pastoral Assoc. In Res., Most Rev. Joseph N. Perry; Rev. William H. Sheridan (Retired).
Res.: 2132 E. 72nd St., 60649. Tel: 773-363-1700; Fax: 773-363-1718.
School—2110 E. 72nd St., 60649. Tel: 773-288-1138; Fax: 773-288-8252. Lay Teachers 7; Students 88.
Catechesis/Religious Program—Lay Teachers 32.

168—ST. PHILOMENA Rev. Jesus Puentes (Colombia), Admin.; Deacons Francisco Ramos; Israel Valentin; Edwin Martinez; Benjamin Diaz.
Res.: 1921 N. Kedvale Ave., 60639. Tel: 773-489-1100; Fax: 773-489-1088.
Catechesis/Religious Program—Tel: 773-342-3462. Students 471.

169—ST. PIUS V Revs. Matthias R. Mueller, O.P.; Brendan A. Curran, O.P.
Office: 1919 S. Ashland Ave., 60608. Tel: 312-226-6161. Web: www.stpiusvparish.org.
Res.: 1914 S. Ashland Ave., 60608. Tel: 312-829-1931; Fax: 312-226-7265.
School—1919 S. Ashland Ave., 60608. Tel: 312-226-1590. Mrs. Nancy Nasko, Prin. Lay Teachers 13; Students 268.
Shrine—Shrine of St. Jude Thaddeus, Tel: 312-226-0020; Fax: 312-226-6440. Web: www.shrineofsaint-jude.com.

170—PRECIOUS BLOOD, Closed. Consult Archives and Records Center for parish and school records.

171—PRESENTATION, Closed. Consult Archives and Records Center for parish and school records.

172—ST. PRISCILLA Revs. Idzi Stacherczak; Joseph Vadakumcherry; Gregory W. Warmuz, O.Cist.; Deacon Fred Spitzerri.
Res.: 6949 W. Addison St., 60634. Tel: 773-545-8840; Fax: 773-545-8919.
Catechesis/Religious Program—Tel: 773-685-3785. Students 321.

173—ST. PROCOPIUS Revs. Timothy A. Howe, S.J.; Michael T. Conley, S.J.; Eric Knapp, S.J.; James Collins, S.J. In Res., Rev. John P. Foley, S.J.
Res.: 1641 S. Allport St., 60608. Tel: 312-226-7887; Fax: 312-226-0812.
School—Tel: 312-421-5135; Fax: 312-492-8368. Lay Teachers 10; Students 243.
Catechesis/Religious Program—Students 250.

174—PROVIDENCE OF GOD Revs. Rigoberto Gamez-Alfonso (Colombia), Admin.; Rodrigo Pena-Jimenez (Colombia). In Res., Rev. Claudio Diaz Jr.
Res.: 717 W. 18th St., 60616. Tel: 312-226-2929; Fax: 312-226-3694. Email: providence@archchicago.org. Web: www.providenceofgod.com.
Catechesis/Religious Program—1814 S. Union, 60616. Students 137.

175—QUEEN OF ALL SAINTS BASILICA Revs. Wayne F. Prist; Arek Falana; John Trout, S.P.S.; Deacons Michael Monnelly; William Malloy; Sr. Ann Kathleen McDonnell, B.V.M., Pastoral Assoc. In Res., Revs. Richard Conyers, C.S.C.; Edward D. Grace.
Res.: 6280 N. Sauganash Ave., 60646. Tel: 773-736-6060; Fax: 773-736-6099. Web: qasparish.org.
School—Tel: 773-736-0567. Sisters 3; Lay Teachers 33; Students 600.
Catechesis/Religious Program—Students 237.

176—QUEEN OF ANGELS Revs. James T. Kaczorowski; Thomas E. Lamping; Deacon Bienvenido Nieves. In Res., Rev. John M. Griffiths.
Parish Office—4412 N. Western Ave., 60625. Tel: 773-539-7510; Fax: 773-539-3408. Email: parish@queenofangelschicago.org. Web: parish.queenofangelschicago.org.
Res.: 2330 W. Sunnyside Ave., 60625.
School—4520 N. Western Ave., 60625. Tel: 773-769-4211; Fax: 773-769-4289. Lay Teachers 23; Students 340.
Catechesis/Religious Program—Students 150.

177—QUEEN OF THE UNIVERSE Rev. Victor Zuniga, M.S.P.; Victor Manuel Correa-Roballo (Colombia); Deacon Marcial Herrera.
Res.: 7114 S. Hamlin Ave., 60629. Tel: 773-582-4662; Fax: 773-581-3313. Email: q.universe@sbcglobal.net.
School—7130 S. Hamlin Ave., 60629. Tel: 773-582-4266; Fax: 773-585-7254. Lay Teachers 13; Students 274.

Catechesis/Religious Program—Students 218.

178—ST. RENE GOUPIL Rev. Thomas R. Kasputis; Deacon Salvatore Lema.
Res.: 6949 W. 63rd Pl., 60638. Tel: 773-229-8523; Fax: 773-229-1252. Email: strenec6949@earthlink.net. Web: www.strenegoupilchicago.com.
School—6340 S. New England Ave., 60638. Tel: 773-586-4414; Fax: 773-586-3747. Marlene DeSantis, Prin. Lay Teachers 13; Students 247.
Catechesis/Religious Program—Students 87.

179—RESURRECTION Revs. Paul J. Kalchik; Thomas A. Tivy (Retired); Fernando Zuleta; Deacons Paul Bovyn; George Fuller, (Retired); Uriol Rodriguez; Efrain Lopez; Juan Gonzalez; Francisco Rivera.
Business Office—3043 N. Francisco Ave., 60618. Tel: 773-478-9705; Fax: 773-478-1387.
Res.: 2840 W. Nelson St., 60618. Tel: 773-478-1441.
Catechesis/Religious Program—Students 225.

180—ST. RICHARD Rev. Thomas A. Bernas.
Office: 5030 S. Kostner Ave., 60632.
Res.: 5032 S. Kostner Ave., 60632. Tel: 773-585-1221; Fax: 773-585-4959.
School—5025 S. Kenneth Ave., 60632. Tel: 773-582-8083; Fax: 773-582-8330. Lay Teachers 16; Students 305.
Catechesis/Religious Program—Students 150.

181—ST. RITA OF CASCIA Revs. Anthony B. Pizzo, O.S.A.; Carlos Urbina, O.S.A.; Deacon Francisco Torres; Jenny Meehan, Pastoral Assoc. In Res., Very Rev. William E. Lego, O.S.A.; Rev. Bernard Danber, O.S.A.; Bro. Mark Emken, O.S.A.
Res.: 6243 S. Fairfield Ave., 60629. Tel: 773-434-9600; Fax: 773-434-9668. Email: ritaparishosa@ameritech.net.
Catechesis/Religious Program—Students 298.

182—ST. ROBERT BELLARMINE Revs. Neil E. Fackler; Frank J. Burek. In Res., Rev. L. Scott Donahue.
Res.: 4646 N. Austin Ave., 60630. Tel: 773-777-2666; Fax: 773-777-2770. Web: www.srb-chicago.org.
School—6036 W. Eastwood Ave., 60630. Tel: 773-725-5133; Fax: 773-777-2770. Sisters 5; Lay Teachers 15; Students 230.
Catechesis/Religious Program—Tel: 773-286-0956. Students 200.

183—ST. ROMAN Rev. Walter Yepes.
Res.: 2311 S. Washtenaw Ave., 60608. Tel: 773-247-6645; Fax: 773-927-1610.
Catechesis/Religious Program—Students 384.

184—ST. SABINA Rev. Michael L. Pfleger.
Res.: 1210 W. 78th Pl., 60620. Tel: 773-483-4300; Fax: 773-483-7583.
School—7801 S. Throop St., 60620. Tel: 773-483-5000; Fax: 773-483-7583. Dominican Sisters (Sinsinawa, WI) 1; Sisters (Congregation of Mother of Carmel) 3; Lay Teachers 20; Students 348.
Catechesis/Religious Program—Students 201.

185—SACRED HEART, (Croatian), Rev. Stephen Bedenikovic, O.F.M.
Res.: 2864 E. 96th St., 60617. Tel: 773-768-1423; Fax: 773-768-3750.
School—2906 E. 96th St., 60617. Tel: 773-773-3728; Fax: 773-768-5034. School Sisters of St. Francis 3; Lay Teachers 9; Students 155.
Catechesis/Religious Program—Students 26.

186—SACRED HEART MISSION OF HOLY NAME OF MARY Rev. James F. Flynn.
Res.: 11652 S. Church St., 60643. Tel: 773-233-3955.
Catechesis/Religious Program—Students 36.

187—SANTA LUCIA-SANTA MARIA INCORONATA Rev. Nicholas A. Marro, C.S.
Res.: 3022 S. Wells St., 60616. Tel: 312-842-6115; Fax: 312-842-0103. Email: bersantalucia@hotmail.com.
School—3017 S. Wells St., 60616. Tel: 312-326-1839; Fax: 312-326-1945. Geraldine Maratea, Prin. Lay Teachers 12; Students 182.
Catechesis/Religious Program—Students 56.

188—SANTA MARIA ADDOLORATA Rev. Vincent Gennardo, C.S.; Deacons Arthur DeLuna; James Cozzo Jr.; Luis Perez.
Res.: 528 N. Ada St., 60642. Tel: 312-421-3122; Fax: 312-421-4814. Email: santamariaaddolorata@yahoo.com.
Catechesis/Religious Program—Students 220.

189—ST. SIMON THE APOSTLE Rev. Francis Q. Kub; Laura L. Zbella, Pastoral Assoc.
Res.: 5157 S. California Ave., 60632. Tel: 773-436-1045; Fax: 773-436-4684. Email: stsimonchurch@comcast.net. Web: www.stsimontheapostle.org.
Catechesis/Religious Program—Students 378.

190—ST. STANISLAUS KOSTKA, (Polish—Spanish), Revs. Anthony Bus, C.R.; Eduardo Garcia-Ferrer (Extern); Edmund Jastrzebski, C.R.; Deacons Nicolas Flores; Miguel Garcia.
Res.: 1351 W. Evergreen Ave., 60622. Tel: 773-278-2470; Fax: 773-278-2471.
School—1255 N. Noble St., 60622. Tel: 773-278-4560; Fax: 773-278-9097. Sisters 1; Lay Teachers 12; Students 220.
Catechesis/Religious Program—Students 119.

191—ST. STANISLAUS, BISHOP AND MARTYR Revs. Anthony Dziorek, C.R.; Richard Balazs, C.R.; Deacons Zygfryd Oborski; Mitchell Szady.
Res.: 5352 W. Belden Ave., 60639. Tel: 773-237-5800; Fax: 773-237-7029.
Catechesis/Religious Program—Students 38.

192—ST. STEPHEN, KING OF HUNGARY Rev. Nicholas R. Desmond, Admin.
Office: 2915 W. Palmer St., 60647.
Res.: 2015 W. Augusta Blvd., 60622. Tel: 773-486-1896; Fax: 773-486-1902.
Catechesis/Religious Program—Students 7.

193—ST. SYLVESTER Revs. Paul Stein; Jose Maria Garcia; Deacons Sigifredo Ortiz; Emiliano Rodriguez; Santos Soto; Carlos Soria.
Res.: 2157 N. Humboldt Blvd., 60647. Tel: 773-235-3646; Fax: 773-489-0974.
School—3027 W. Palmer Blvd., 60647. Tel: 773-772-5222; Fax: 773-722-0352. Lay Teachers 15; Students 231.
Catechesis/Religious Program—Tel: 773-772-9082. Students 370.

194—ST. SYMPHOROSA AND SEVEN SONS Revs. Thaddeus J. Bojczuk; Francis N. Maniola, Pastor Emeritus (Retired); Norman J. Trela; K. Joseph Kunnathukizhakethil, S.D.B. (India).
Res.: 6135 S. Austin Ave., 60638. Tel: 773-767-1523; Fax: 773-767-6135.
School—6125 S. Austin Ave., 60638. Tel: 773-585-6888; 773-585-6804; Fax: 773-585-8411. Lay Teachers 18; Students 315.
Catechesis/Religious Program—Students 247.

195—ST. TARCISSUS Revs. Daniel P. McCarthy; Krzysztof D. Ciaston; Edmond Aristil, C.S.Sp. (Haiti); Michael Leonard (Ireland); Deacon Gregory M. Bzdon.
Res.: 6020 W. Ardmore Ave., 60646. Tel: 773-763-8228; Fax: 773-774-8461. Email: mail_sttars@sbcglobal.net. Web: www.sttars.org.
School—6040 W. Ardmore Ave., 60646. Tel: 773-763-7080; Fax: 773-775-3593. Lay Teachers 20; Students 392.
Catechesis/Religious Program—Students 110.

196—ST. TERESA OF AVILA Rev. Frank J. Latzko; Deacon Hector Rivera.
Parish Office: 1930 N. Kenmore, 60614-4139. Tel: 773-528-6650; Fax: 773-871-6766. Email: secretary@stteresaparish.org. Web: www.st-teresa.net.
Cardinal Bernardin Early Childhood Center—1651 W. Diversey Pkwy., 60614. Tel: 773-975-6330; Fax: 773-975-6339. Web: www.cbecc.org. Sr. Barbara Jean Ciszek, C.S.J., Prin.
Catechesis/Religious Program—Students 136.

197—ST. THADDEUS Rev. Frank M. Sasso; Deacon Jimmie Flewellen.
Res.: 9540 S. Harvard Ave., 60628. Tel: 773-568-7077; Fax: 773-928-5447.
Catechesis/Religious Program—Students 12.

198—ST. THECLA Revs. Kenneth A. Budzikowski; Pawel Komperda; Deacons John Rottman; Robert Cnota; Steven Wagner.
Res.: 6725 W. Devon Ave., 60631. Tel: 773-792-3077; Fax: 773-792-3820. Web: www.saintthecla.org.
School—6323 N. Newcastle Ave., 60631. Tel: 773-763-3380; Fax: 773-763-6151. Lay Teachers 18; Students 250.
Catechesis/Religious Program—Students 130.

199—ST. THERESE CATHOLIC CHINESE CHURCH Rev. Michael Davitti, S.X. In Res., Rev. Aniello Salicone, S.X.
Res.: 218 W. Alexander St., 60616. Tel: 312-842-6777; Fax: 312-567-1389.
School—247 W. 23rd St., 60616. Tel: 312-326-2837; Fax: 312-326-6068. Sisters 4; Lay Teachers 14; Students 296.
Catechesis/Religious Program—Students 254.

200—ST. THOMAS APOSTLE Revs. Michael Mulhall, O.Carm.; Kevin McBrien, O.Carm.
Res.: 5472 S. Kimbark Ave., 60615. Tel: 773-324-2626; Fax: 773-753-7415. Web: www.stahydepark.org.
School—5467 S. Woodlawn Ave., 60615. Tel: 773-667-1142; Fax: 773-753-7434. Lay Teachers 20; Students 200.
Catechesis/Religious Program—Students 120.

201—ST. THOMAS MORE Revs. Charles V. Fanelli; Michael E. Flynn. In Res., Revs. John P. Frawley (Retired); John F. McGrath (Retired).
Res.: 2825 W. 81st St., 60652. Tel: 773-436-4444; Fax: 773-778-9087. Email: stmrc@comcast.net.
Convent—8120 S. California, 60652. Tel: 773-737-9440. Congregation of the Mother of Carmel 6; Sinsinwa Dominicans 1.
Catechesis/Religious Program—Students 17.

202—ST. THOMAS OF CANTERBURY Rev. Daniel F. Costello; Deacon Orlando Perez. In Res., Rev. Trinh Peter Hung, Senior Priest.
Res.: 4827 N. Kenmore Ave., 60640. Tel: 773-878-5507.
School—Tel: 773-271-8655; Fax: 773-271-1624. Lay Teachers 13; Students 270.
Catechesis/Religious Program—

203—ST. TIMOTHY Rev. Peter Fernandes, S.F.X. (India).
Res.: 6326 N. Washtenaw Ave., 60659. Tel: 773-262-6600; 773-262-6665; Fax: 773-262-9214.
Catechesis/Religious Program—Fax: 773-262-9214. Students 50.

204—TRANSFIGURATION OF OUR LORD Revs. Terence M. Keehan; John J. Rudnik (Retired). In Res., Rev. Robert A. Florido (Philippines).
Res.: 2609 W. Carmen Ave., 60625. Tel: 773-561-7953; Fax: 773-561-7635. Email: transofourlordcc@aol.com. Web: www.stmatthias-transfiguration.com.

205—ST. TURIBIUS Revs. Ralph H. Zwirn; Libardo Ladino Diaz (Colombia).
Res.: 5646 S. Karlov Ave., 60629. Tel: 773-581-2730; Fax: 773-581-5396.
School—4120 W. 57th St., 60629. Tel: 773-585-5150; Fax: 773-585-5328. Felician Sisters 3; Lay Teachers 12; Students 215.
Catechesis/Religious Program—Sr. Mary Beth Bromer, C.S.S.F., D.R.E. Students 230.

206—ST. VIATOR Rev. Charles G. Bolser, C.S.V.
Res.: 4170 W. Addison St., 60641. Tel: 773-286-4040; Fax: 773-286-4122.
School—4140 W. Addison St., 60641. Tel: 773-545-2173; Fax: 773-794-1697. Lay Teachers 18; Students 221.
Catechesis/Religious Program—Students 95.

207—ST. VINCENT DE PAUL Rev. Christopher S. Robinson, C.M.
Res.: 1010 W. Webster Ave., 60614. Tel: 773-325-8610; Fax: 773-325-8626. Email: info@stvdep.org. Web: www.stvdep.org.

208—ST. WALTER Rev. Peter J. Heidenrich; Deacon James Deiters.
Res.: 11722 S. Oakley Ave., 60643. Tel: 773-779-1515; Fax: 773-779-0381. Email: stwalterchgo@aol.com. Web: www.stwalter.com.
School—11741 S. Western Ave., 60643. Tel: 773-445-8850; Fax: 773-445-0277. Sisters 3; Lay Teachers 9; Students 213.
Catechesis/Religious Program—Students 58.

209—ST. WENCESLAUS Rev. Jacek Praski, C.R. In Res., Rev. John H. Nowak, C.R.
Res.: 3400 N. Monticello Ave., 60618. Tel: 773-588-1135; Fax: 773-588-3735.
Catechesis/Religious Program—Students 258.

210—ST. WILLIAM Revs. William J. Hastings; Michael G. Scherschel; Deacons Dennis Colgan; Edward Simola.
Res.: 2600 N. Sayre Ave., 60707. Tel: 773-637-6565; Fax: 773-637-7042. Email: stwilliam@archchicago.org. Web: www.stwilliamelmwoodpark.parishesonline.com.
School—2559 N. Sayre Ave., 60707. Tel: 773-637-5130; Fax: 773-745-4208. Lay Teachers 13; Students 169.
Catechesis/Religious Program—Students 100.

OUTSIDE THE CITY OF CHICAGO

ALSIP, COOK CO., ST. TERRENCE Rev. Edward J. Barrett.
Res.: 4300 W. 119th Pl., 60803. Tel: 708-597-0970; Fax: 708-597-9118. Email: stterrence@comcast.net. Web: www.stterrence.org.
Catechesis/Religious Program—Tel: 708-597-0754. Students 409.

ANTIOCH, LAKE CO.

1—ST. PETER Revs. Michael F. McMahon; Dean F. Semmer; Deacons Robert A. Gagnon; Paul M. Neurauter; Scott McIntosh; Jonathan Thompson.
Res.: 557 W. Lake St., 60002. Tel: 847-395-0274; Fax: 847-395-4553. Email: administration@stpeterantioch.org. Web: www.stpeterantioch.org.
School—900 St. Peter St., 60002. Tel: 847-395-0037; Fax: 847-395-2532. Lay Teachers 15; Students 220.
Catechesis/Religious Program—559 Elizabeth, 60002. Tel: 847-395-0246; Fax: 847-395-2532. Students 567.

2—ST. RAPHAEL THE ARCHANGEL Revs. John A. Jamnicky; Ronald C. Lewandowski, Senior Priest (Retired).
2101 E. Rte. 173, 60002. Tel: 847-395-3474; Fax: 847-395-3552. Email: rectory@straphaelcatholic.org. Web: www.straphaelcatholic.org.
Catechesis/Religious Program—Students 165.

ARGO, COOK CO., ST. BLASE Revs. Michael L. Zoufal; Ryszard Czerniak, S.Ch.; Jorge L. Estrada.
Res.: 6101 S. 75th Ave., 60501. Tel: 708-458-0007; Fax: 708-458-0276. Email: stblase@archchicago.org.
Catechesis/Religious Program—Tel: 708-458-0246 (Spanish & English); 708-458-8772 (Polish); Fax: 708-458-8554 (Spanish & English); 708-458-9560 (Polish). Students 1,181.

ARLINGTON HEIGHTS, COOK CO.

1—ST. EDNA Revs. Jerome J. Jacob; Diego Berrio; Deacons Raymond J. Graffia Jr.; James Gaughan;

James Pauwels. In Res., Revs. John J. Hurley, Pastor Emeritus (Retired); Eugene J. Faucher (Retired).
Res.: 2525 N. Arlington Heights Rd., 60004. Tel: 847-398-3362; Fax: 847-394-5226. Email: parishmanager@stedna.org. Web: www.stedna.org.
Catechesis/Religious Program—Students 490.

2—ST. JAMES Revs. William J. Zavaski; Krzysztof A. Kulig; Joji Thanugundla (India); Deacons Louis Lekan, (Retired); Matt Hennessy; Paul Schmidt; Pierce Sheehan; Tom Morgan; Matt Hahn; William Reinert; Thomas Westerkamp; Marianne Dilsner, Pastoral Assoc.
Office: 820 N. Arlington Heights Rd., 60004. Tel: 224-345-7200; Fax: 224-345-7220. Email: parishoffice@stjamesah.org. Web: www.stjamesah.org.
School—Tel: 224-345-7145; Fax: 224-345-7140. Lay Teachers 27; Students 527.
Catechesis/Religious Program—Melody Devine, D.R.E. Students 850.

3—MISSION SAN JUAN DIEGO Rev. Juan Bosco Jimenez Garcia, S.D.B.
Res.: 2323 North Wilke Rd., 60004. Tel: 847-590-9332; Fax: 847-590-9333.
Catechesis/Religious Program—Students 400.

4—OUR LADY OF THE WAYSIDE Revs. Edward R. Fialkowski; Patrick M. Wangai; Deacons Thomas Corcoran; Donald Grossnickle; Brendan Foley; Donna Cunningham, Pastoral Assoc. In Res., Rev. Daniel J. Brady (Retired).
Res.: 432 W. Park St., 60005. Tel: 847-253-5353; Fax: 847-253-7175. Web: www.olwparish.org.
School—Tel: 847-253-0050; Fax: 847-253-0543. Lay Teachers 60; Students 710.
Catechesis/Religious Program—432 S. Mitchell, 60005. Tel: 847-398-5011; Fax: 847-253-0050. Students 525.

BARRINGTON, LAKE CO., ST. ANNE Revs. Bernard J. Pietrzak; Thomas Bishop; Fred Licciardi, C.PP.S.; Joseph Anthony Rex Pillai, C.Ss.R. (Sri Lanka); Deacons Richard Seveska; James Crane; Robert Powers; Sr. Lauretta Leipzig, Pastoral Assoc.
Res.: 120 N. Ela St., 60010. Tel: 847-382-5300; Fax: 847-382-5363.
School—319 E. Franklin St., 60010. Tel: 847-381-0311; Fax: 847-381-0384. School Sisters of St. Francis 6; Lay Teachers 30; Students 600.
Catechesis/Religious Program—Students 779.

BARTLETT, COOK CO., ST. PETER DAMIAN Rev. Walter J. Takuski.
Res.: 109 S. Crest Ave., 60103. Tel: 630-837-5411; Fax: 630-837-9424. Email: info@stpeterdamian.org. Web: www.stpeterdamian.org.
Catechesis/Religious Program—Tel: 630-830-2295. Students 712.

BELLWOOD, COOK CO., ST. SIMEON Rev. Kombo L. Peshu. In Res., Revs. Joseph Ekpo; Stanislaus K. Fernando (India).
Res.: 430 Bohland Ave., 60104. Tel: 708-547-6868; Fax: 708-547-7075.
Catechesis/Religious Program—Students 58.

BERWYN, COOK CO.

1—ST. LEONARD Revs. Thomas W. McQuaid; Khue Vu (Vietnam); Deacons Joel Chrastka; Peter Morrissey; Jose Cisneros; Frank Mamolella.
Res.: 3318 S. Clarence Ave., 60402. Tel: 708-484-0015; Fax: 708-484-6982.
School—3322 S. Clarence Ave., 60402. Tel: 708-749-3666; Fax: 708-749-7981. Lay Teachers 13; Students 292.
Catechesis/Religious Program—Tel: 708-795-5919. Students 160.

2—ST. MARY OF CELLE Rev. William J. Clavey.
Res.: 1428 Wesley Ave., 60402. Tel: 708-788-0876; Fax: 708-788-0242. Email: smcrectory@sbcglobal.net. Web: www.stmaryofcelle.org.
Catechesis/Religious Program—Tel: 708-795-6460; Fax: 708-749-2120. Students 285.

3—ST. ODILO Revs. Anthony J. Brankin; Juan C. Gavancho. In Res., Revs. Richard B. Saudis; Thomas J. Kaveney (Retired).
Res.: 2244 East Ave., 60402. Tel: 708-484-2161; Fax: 708-788-0565. Web: www.saintodilo.org.
School—2301 S. Clarence Ave., 60402. Tel: 708-484-0755; Fax: 708-484-0088. William Donegan, Prin. Sisters of Charity B.V.M. 2; Lay Teachers 15; Students 220.
Catechesis/Religious Program—Students 126.
Shrine—Poor Souls, Tel: 708-484-2161; Fax: 708-788-0565.

BLUE ISLAND, COOK CO.

1—ST. BENEDICT Revs. Ismael Sandoval-Manzo; Wayne A. Svida; Augustine Madafa R. Mahonge; Deacons Juan Limon; Abundio Valadez; Dan Carroll.
Res.: 2339 York St., 60406. Tel: 708-385-8510; Fax: 708-371-2631.
School—2324 New St., 60406. Tel: 708-385-2016; Fax: 708-385-4490. Lay Teachers 14; Students 235.
Catechesis/Religious Program—Students 220.
Mission—St. Peter Claver 14125 Claire Blvd., Robbins, Cook Co. 60472. Tel: 708-389-2434; Fax: 708-389-2434.

2—ST. DONATUS Revs. Gerardo DeTomasi, M.C.C.J.; Paul J. Ewers, M.C.C.J. In Res., Rev. Hugo Riva, M.C.C.J.
Res.: 1939 Union St., 60406. Tel: 708-385-2890; Fax: 708-385-4708.
Catechesis/Religious Program—12905 Division St., 60406. Tel: 708-388-7886. Students 250.

3—ST. ISIDORE Most Rev. Joseph N. Perry, Admin.; Revs. Eze Venantius Umunnakwe, C.S.Sp. (Extern); Casimir Eke, C.S.Sp. (Extern).
Res.: 1811 W. Burr Oak Ave., 60406. Tel: 708-388-0807; Fax: 708-388-5077.

BRIDGEVIEW, COOK CO., ST. FABIAN Revs. Peter J. Cyscon; Jan Bukowski, COr (Poland); Jerzy Matuscak, C.R.; Deacons Charles Tipperreiter; Kevin O'Donnell; Ronald Zielinski.
Res.: 8300 S. Thomas Ave., 60455. Tel: 708-599-1110; Fax: 708-599-0673. Email: stfabian65@sbcglobal.net. Web: www.saint-fabian.org.
Catechesis/Religious Program—7450 83rd St., 60455. Tel: 708-458-6150; Fax: 708-458-2398. Students 1,300.

BROOKFIELD, COOK CO.

1—ST. BARBARA Rev. Robert G. Casey; Sr. Margaret Halligan, C.S.J., Pastoral Assoc.; Deacons John Debnar; Dave Brencic; Kevin Reynolds; Miguel Luevano. In Res., Rev. Michael P. Ahlstrom.
Res.: 4008 Prairie Ave., 60513. Tel: 708-485-2900; Fax: 708-387-0103. Email: stbarbara-prairie@archdiocese.org. Web: www.stbarbaraparish.com.
School—8900 Windemere Ave., 60513. Tel: 708-485-0806; Fax: 708-485-2343. Lay Teachers 13; Students 144.
Catechesis/Religious Program—Tel: 708-485-4610. Students 190.

2—CZECH MISSION OF SAINTS CYRIL AND METHODIUS Rev. Dusan Hladik (Czech Republic).
Res.: 9415 Rochester Ave., 60513. Tel: 708-656-7472; Cell: 708-533-1050; Fax: 708-656-7472. Web: www.velehradchicago.home.comcast.net.
Catechesis/Religious Program—

BUFFALO GROVE, LAKE CO., ST. MARY, [CEM] Revs. Marc W. Reszel; Denis Carneiro (India); John Trout, S.P.S.; Deacons Eugene Kukla, Senior Deacon; Gary Long, Senior Deacon; William J. Krueger, Senior Deacon.
Res.: 10 N. Buffalo Grove Rd., 60089. Tel: 847-541-1450; Fax: 847-541-2443. Web: www.stmarybg.org.
School—50 N. Buffalo Grove Rd., 60089. Tel: 847-459-6270; Fax: 847-537-2810. Lay Teachers 30; Students 344.
Catechesis/Religious Program—Tel: 847-537-9423; Fax: 847-808-0548. Students 656.

BURBANK, COOK CO., ST. ALBERT THE GREAT Revs. Richard Milek, Admin.; Robert A. Stepek, (On Leave); Mariusz Nawalaniec (Poland); Robert Marchwiany; Deacon Irvin Bryce.
Res.: 5555 W. State Rd., 60459. Tel: 708-423-0321; Fax: 708-425-4329.
School—5535 W. State Rd., 60459. Tel: 708-424-7757. Lay Teachers 14; Students 222.
Catechesis/Religious Program—Tel: 708-636-0406. Students 250.

BURNHAM, COOK CO., MOTHER OF GOD Rev. Edmund F. Guz, Pastor Emeritus (Retired).
Res.: 14207 S. Green Bay Ave., 60633. Tel: 708-862-8777; Fax: 708-891-1349.

CALUMET CITY, COOK CO.

1—ST. ANDREW THE APOSTLE Rev. Martin E. Michniewicz; Deacon Robert Banet.
Res.: 768 Lincoln Ave., 60409. Tel: 708-862-4165; Fax: 708-862-4124. Email: a.rectory@comcast.net. Web: www.saintandrewparish.com.
School—Christ Our Savior East Campus, Inter-parish school serving St. Andrew, Our Lady of Knock, St. Victor, Holy Ghost, St. Jude and Queen of Apostles, 320 156th St., 60409. Tel: 708-862-4143; Fax: 708-862-4148.
Catechesis/Religious Program—Tel: 708-862-4165. Students 75.

2—OUR LADY OF KNOCK Revs. Patrick M. Lyons; Donald J. Fenske, Pastor Emeritus (Retired); Sr. Alban Hermes, O.P., Pastoral Assoc.; Deacons Edward Ryan; Thomas Knetl.
Res.: 501 163rd St., 60409. Tel: 708-862-3011; Fax: 708-862-9618.
School—Christ Our Savior, (Inter-Parish School), Tel: 708-333-8173; Fax: 708-339-3336. Web: www.christoursaviorcatholicschool.org.
Catechesis/Religious Program—Tel: 708-868-1711. Students 70.

3—ST. VICTOR Rev. Leonard A. Dubi; Deacon Dan Ragonese.
Res.: 553 Hirsch Ave., 60409. Tel: 708-891-8920; Fax: 708-891-8929. Email: stvictorcc@sbcglobal.net. Web: www.stvictorcc.org.
School—Christ Our Savior, (Inter-Parish School), Tel: 708-333-8173; Fax: 708-333-3247.
Catechesis/Religious Program—Students 135.

CALUMET PARK, COOK CO., SEVEN HOLY FOUNDERS Most Rev. Joseph N. Perry, Admin.; Rev. Pius E. Kokose, C.S.Sp. (Ghana).
Res.: 12400 S. Ada St., 60827. Tel: 708-385-8459; Fax: 708-385-2143.
Catechesis/Religious Program—Tel: 708-385-8498. Students 40.

CHICAGO HEIGHTS, COOK CO.

1—ST. AGNES Revs. John S. Siemianowski; Juan Pablo Avila-Ibarra; Deacons Thomas Nowak; David Brothers; Charlene Klabacha, Pastoral Assoc.; Karen Zerante, Devel. Dir.; Carl Opat, Liturgy & Music Dir.
Res.: 1501 Chicago Rd., 60411. Tel: 708-709-2694; Fax: 708-709-2693. Web: www.stagnes-parish.org.
School—Lay Teachers 18; Students 300.
Catechesis/Religious Program—Students 145.

2—ST. KIERAN Rev. Joseph T. Cook; Deacons Eugene La Belle; David Dutko.
Res.: 724 W. 195th St., 60411. Tel: 708-755-0074; Fax: 708-754-2246. Web: www.stkieranchurch.org.
School—700 W. 195th St., 60411. Tel: 708-754-8999; Fax: 708-754-9007. Lay Teachers 11; Students 115.
Catechesis/Religious Program—Tel: 708-754-0484; Fax: 708-754-0484. Students 77.

3—ST. PAUL Revs. John S. Siemianowski; Juan Pablo Avila-Ibarra; Deacons Juan L. Garza; Joseph Kudra.
Res.: 206 E. 25th St., 60411. Tel: 708-754-3120; Fax: 708-754-0076.
Catechesis/Religious Program—Tel: 708-754-7720. Students 500.

CHICAGO RIDGE, COOK CO., OUR LADY OF THE RIDGE Revs. Wayne A. Svida; George O. Omwando; Deacons Terris Albano; Edwin Hill; John Orzechowski; Robert Landuyt.
Res.: 10811 S. Ridgeland Ave., 60415. Tel: 708-425-3800; Fax: 708-425-2792.
School—10859 S. Ridgeland Ave., 60415. Tel: 708-424-4409. Lay Teachers 9; Students 168.
Catechesis/Religious Program—Tel: 708-424-4949. Students 262.

CICERO, COOK CO.

1—ST. ANTHONY OF PADUA Rev. Sergio Solis; Deacons Alfonso Salgado; Claude Hensley; Gilberto Mercado.
Res.: 1515 S. 50th Ave., 60804. Tel: 708-652-0231; Fax: 708-652-0228.
St. Anthony Center—1510 S. 49th Ct., 60804. Tel: 708-652-0231; Fax: 708-652-0228.
Catechesis/Religious Program—Students 446.

2—ST. FRANCES OF ROME Revs. Mark A. Bartosic; Cliff Ermatinger, L.C.; Deacon Javier Pineda. In Res., Most Rev. Thomas J. Paprocki; Rev. Wilfred Bwezani Phiri.
Res.: 1428 S. 59th Ct., 60804. Tel: 708-652-2140; Fax: 708-652-6513.
School—1401 S. Austin Blvd., 60804. Tel: 708-652-2277. Web: www.sfr-school.org. Lay Teachers 12; Students 255.
Catechesis/Religious Program—Tel: 708-656-8632. Students 329.

3—ST. MARY OF CZESTOCHOWA, (Polish—Spanish), Revs. Radoslaw Jaszczuk, C.Ss.R.; Waldemar Wieladek, C.Ss.R.; Zbigniew Pienkos, C.Ss.R.; Dariusz Grzegorz Pabis, C.Ss.R.
Res.: 3010 S. 48th Ct., 60804. Tel: 708-652-0948; Fax: 708-652-0646. Email: parish@stmaryofczestochowa.org. Web: stmaryofczestochowa.org.
Catechesis/Religious Program—Tel: 708-652-0948; Fax: 708-652-0646. Students 170.

4—MARY, QUEEN OF HEAVEN Revs. Esequiel Sanchez; Hugo Morales; Deacon Armando Herrera.
Res.: 5300 W. 24th St., 60804. Tel: 708-863-6608; Fax: 708-863-2349.
Catechesis/Religious Program—Students 326.

5—OUR LADY OF CHARITY Rev. Mark A. Bartosic; Deacon Antonio Ponce.
Res.: 3600 57th Ct., 60804-4235. Tel: 708-863-1207; Fax: 708-863-1209. Email: office@olc-church.org.
School—3620 57th Ct., 60804. Tel: 708-652-0262; Fax: 708-652-0601. Web: www.olc-school.org. Lay Teachers 10; Students 200.
Catechesis/Religious Program—Students 253.

6—OUR LADY OF THE MOUNT Rev. Lawrence E. Collins; Deacons Robert E. Devereux; Antonio Llano.
Res.: 2414 S. 61st Ave., 60804. Tel: 708-652-2791; Fax: 708-863-6014.
Catechesis/Religious Program—Students 372.

COUNTRY CLUB HILLS, COOK CO., ST. EMERIC Rev. Martin T. Marren; Deacons James Detloff, (Retired); Philip DuBrownik.
Res.: 4330 W. 180th St., 60478. Tel: 708-798-0757; Fax: 708-798-0799. Email: stemeric@comcast.net. Web: stemeric-countryclubhills.e-paluch.com.
Catechesis/Religious Program—Tel: 708-799-4430; Fax: 708-798-0799. Students 80.

DEERFIELD, LAKE CO., HOLY CROSS Rev. Harold B. Stanger; Deacons Edward Melton; Kevin Garvey; Mary Ann Spina, Pastoral Assoc.; Paul D. Schmidt, Business Mgr.; Kathleen Jeffers, Music Dir. In Res., Rev. Dennis Stafford.
Res.: 724 Elder Ln., 60015. Tel: 847-945-0430; Fax: 847-945-7651. Web: www.holycrossparish.net.
School—720 Elder Ln., 60015. Tel: 847-945-0135; Fax: 847-945-0705. Dr. Jack Sloan, Prin. Lay Teachers 24; Students 301.
Catechesis/Religious Program—Tel: 847-945-0581; Fax: 847-945-0582. Stacey Sus, D.R.E. Students 312.

DES PLAINES, COOK CO.
1—ST. MARY Revs. Gene J. Dyer; Charles H. Schlax; Martin E. Bedoya.
Res.: 794 Pearson St., 60016. Tel: 847-824-8144; Fax: 847-824-3906. Email: stmary-pearson@archchicago.org. Web: www.stmary-dp.org.
School—Our Lady of Destiny, 1880 Ash St., 60018. Tel: 847-827-2900. Linda Chorazy, Prin. Lay Teachers 15; Students 197.
Catechesis/Religious Program—Tel: 847-298-1435; Fax: 847-824-3906. Students 587.
2—ST. PAUL CHONG HASANG Rev. Simeon Ho Chan Cha (Korea, South), Dir.
Res.: 725 Dursey Ln., 60016. Tel: 847-699-6334; Fax: 847-699-1281. Email: stpaul-mission@archchicago.org. Web: www.stpaulchong.org.
Catechesis/Religious Program—Students 195.
3—ST. STEPHEN PROTOMARTYR Revs. Gerald E. Rogala; Flavio V. Gonzalez; Deacons Donald J. Telposky; Anthony Towey; William H. Warmouth.
1267 Everett Ave., 60018-2398. Tel: 847-824-2026; Fax: 847-824-3842. Email: ststephen@sbcglobal.net. Web: www.ststephen-desplaines.org. In Res., Rev. Michael G. Zaniolo.
School—Our Lady of Destiny, 1880 Ash St., 60018-2343. Tel: 847-827-2900; Fax: 847-827-0475. Lay Teachers 14; Students 171.
Catechesis/Religious Program—Tel: 847-297-3844; Fax: 847-824-3842. Students 85.
4—ST. ZACHARY Revs. John S. Plotkowski; David R. Straub; Anthony C. Puchenski; Deacons Peter N. Lagges, (Retired); John J. Smith; Sam Pincich. In Res., Rev. Lawrence F. Springer (Retired).
Res.: 567 W. Algonquin Rd., 60016. Tel: 847-956-7020; Fax: 847-981-1148. Email: zacharyoffice@aol.com. Web: www.saintzachary.org.
School—Tel: 847-437-4022. Lay Teachers 13; Students 177.
Catechesis/Religious Program—Tel: 847-956-1175. Students 315.

ELK GROVE VILLAGE, COOK CO.
1—ST. JULIAN EYMARD Rev. Leon J. Rezula.
Res.: 601 Biesterfield Rd., 60007. Tel: 847-956-0130; Fax: 847-956-0189.
Catechesis/Religious Program—Tel: 847-593-8938. Students 750.
2—QUEEN OF THE ROSARY Rev. Edward Pelrine; Deacon Ted Czarnecki. In Res., Rev. Robert L. Ebrom.
Res.: 750 Elk Grove Blvd., 60007. Tel: 847-437-0403; Fax: 847-437-8461. Email: sqrm59@comcast.net. Web: www.qotr.org.
School—690 Elk Grove Blvd., 60007. Tel: 847-437-3322; Fax: 847-437-3290. Lay Teachers 19; Students 315.
Catechesis/Religious Program—680 Elk Grove Blvd., 60007. Tel: 847-437-3346; Fax: 847-431-8961. Students 650.

ELMWOOD PARK, COOK CO., ST. CELESTINE Rev. Jeffrey S. Grob; Deacon Michael DeLarco. In Res., Rev. Bernard C. White (Retired).
Res.: 3020 N. 76th Ct., 60707. Tel: 708-453-2555; Fax: 708-462-0560. Web: www.stcelestine.org.
School—3017 N. 77th Ave., 60707. Tel: 708-453-8234; Fax: 708-452-0237. Lay Teachers 22; Students 475.
Catechesis/Religious Program—Students 237.

EVANSTON, COOK CO.
1—ST. ATHANASIUS Revs. Thomas A. Libera; Richard E. Sztorc; Deacon Richard S. Jay.
Res.: 1615 Lincoln St., 60201. Tel: 847-328-1430; Fax: 847-328-1809. Web: www.stathanasius-evanston.org.
School—2510 Ashland Ave., 60201. Tel: 847-864-2650; Fax: 847-475-7385. Lay Teachers 31; Students 350.
Catechesis/Religious Program—Students 160.
2—ST. MARY Revs. Michael J. Solazzo; Antony A. Joseph; Deacon Dennis R. Robak. In Res., Rev. Anselm Russell, O.S.B.
Parish Center—Res.: 1012 Lake St., 60201. Tel: 847-864-0333; Fax: 847-864-0354. Email: stmary1012@aol.com. Web: www.stmaryparish-evanston.org.
School—Tel: 847-475-5678; Fax: 847-475-5683. Consolidated with St. Nicholas Parish to form Pope John XXIII School. See St. Nicholas for further details.
Catechesis/Religious Program—Students 126.
3—ST. NICHOLAS Rev. William Tkachuk; Deacon Mario Tamayo; Suzanne Lefevre, Business Mgr.; Mr. David Philippart, Liturgy Director.
Res.: 806 Ridge Ave., 60202. Tel: 847-864-1185; Fax: 847-864-7810. Email: stnicks@nickchurch.org. Web: www.nickchurch.org.
School—1120 Washington, 60202. Tel: 847-475-5678; Fax: 847-475-5683. Mrs. Rosalie Musiala, Prin. Consolidated with St. Mary Parish to form Pope John XXIII School. Lay Teachers 28; Students 316.
Catechesis/Religious Program—Students 364.

EVERGREEN PARK, COOK CO.
1—ST. BERNADETTE Rev. Gary M. Miller.
Res.: 9343 Francisco Ave., 60805. Tel: 708-422-8995; Fax: 708-422-8699. Web: stbernardettechurch.org.
School—9311 S. Francisco Ave., 60805. Tel: 708-422-6429; Fax: 708-422-6484. Dominican Sisters (Springfield, IL) 1; Lay Teachers 11; Students 133.
Catechesis/Religious Program—Tel: 708-425-7697. Students 143.
2—MOST HOLY REDEEMER Revs. James M. Hyland; Joseph B. Ruiz (Retired); Matthew Nemchausky; Deacon Alfred Antonsen. In Res., Rev. Albert R. Adamich (Retired).
Res.: 9525 S. Lawndale Ave., 60805. Tel: 708-425-5354; Fax: 708-346-8182. Web: www.mostholyredeemer.org.
School—9535 S. Millard Ave., 60805. Tel: 708-422-8280; Fax: 708-422-4193. Lay Teachers 28; Students 439.
Catechesis/Religious Program—Tel: 708-346-8185. Students 380.
3—QUEEN OF MARTYRS Rev. Edward M. Mikolajczyk.
Res.: 10233 S. Central Park, 60805-3799. Tel: 708-423-8110; Fax: 708-423-7372.
School—3550 W. 103rd St., 60655. Tel: 708-422-1540; Fax: 708-422-1811. Lay Teachers 25; Students 499.
Catechesis/Religious Program—Tel: 708-422-1647. Students 153.

FLOSSMOOR, COOK CO., INFANT JESUS OF PRAGUE Revs. Michael A. Nacius, Admin.; Michael F. Wheaton; John J. Doyle; Deacon George Brooks.
Res.: 1131 Douglas Ave., 60422. Tel: 708-799-5400.
School—1101 Douglas Ave., 60422. Lay Teachers 22; Students 500.

FOREST PARK, COOK CO., ST. BERNARDINE Rev. George Velloorattil; Deacons John Walters; Loretto J. Madonia. In Res., Revs. Francis J. Grady, S.S.C.; Abraham Kaduthodil.
Res.: 7246 Harrison St., 60130. Tel: 708-366-0839; Fax: 708-366-3136. Email: saintbernardine@juno.com. Web: www.stbern.com.
School—815 Elgin Ave., 60130. Tel: 708-366-6890; Fax: 708-366-8015. Lay Teachers 16; Students 140.
Catechesis/Religious Program—Tel: 708-366-3553. Students 120.

FRANKLIN PARK, COOK CO., ST. GERTRUDE Revs. Eryk Czarnicki (Poland); Aldo Pozza, M.C.C.J.; Enrique Francisco Lozada (Mexico); Fabio Venturini (NEW); Deacons Robert Murphy; Lorenzo Chaidez.
Res.: 9613 Schiller Blvd., 60131. Tel: 847-455-1100; Fax: 847-455-1209.
Catechesis/Religious Program—9617 Schiller Blvd., 60131. Tel: 847-455-5810. Students 235.

GLENVIEW, COOK CO.
1—ST. CATHERINE LABOURE Revs. Paul Maina Waithaka; Alfredo J. Salera; Deacons Ray Gavin; Frank Beil.
Res.: 3535 Thornwood Ave., 60026. Tel: 847-729-1414; Fax: 847-729-5184. Email: sc13535@att.net. Web: www.stcatherinelaboure.com.
School—3425 Thornwood Ave., 60026. Tel: 847-724-2240; Fax: 847-724-5805. Lay Teachers 32; Students 325.
Catechesis/Religious Program—Students 280.
2—OUR LADY OF PERPETUAL HELP Revs. Thomas E. Hickey; Jacek A. Jura; Patrick Tyrrell, S.J. (Ireland); Robeth Molina-Torres; Deacons James Revord; David Kalina.
Res.: 1775 Grove St., 60025. Tel: 847-729-1525; Fax: 847-729-0623. Email: OL-Help@archchicago.org. Web: www.olphglenview.org.
School—1123 Church St., 60025. Tel: 847-724-6990; Fax: 847-724-7025. School Sisters of St. Francis 3; Lay Teachers 74; Students 950.
Catechesis/Religious Program—Tel: 847-998-5289; Fax: 847-729-6194. Students 1,057.

GLENWOOD, COOK CO., ST. JOHN Rev. John J. Sullivan; Jamae Myers, Pastoral Assoc.
Res.: 301 S. Cottage Grove Ave., 60425. Tel: 708-758-5098; Fax: 708-758-0408. Web: www.rc.net/chicago/stjohn.
Catechesis/Religious Program—Students 125.

GRAYSLAKE, LAKE CO., ST. GILBERT Revs. Eugene J. Nowak; Samson Ngatia Mukundi; Deacon Richard Globis.
Res.: 301 E. Belvidere Rd., 60030. Tel: 847-223-4731; Fax: 847-223-5840. Web: www.stgilbert.org.
School—231 E. Belvidere Rd., 60030. Tel: 847-223-8600. Gloria Petraitis, Prin. Lay Teachers 34; Students 680.
Catechesis/Religious Program—Tel: 847-223-3071; Fax: 847-223-6545. Students 678.

GURNEE, LAKE CO., ST. PAUL THE APOSTLE Revs. Farrell J. Kane, O.Carm.; Raymond Clennon, O.Carm.; Deacons Michael Penich; Mark J. Purdome.
Res.: 6401 Gages Lake Rd., 60031. Tel: 847-918-0600; Fax: 847-918-0640. Email: stpaultheapostle@sbcglobal.net. Web: www.stpaul-gurnee.com.
Catechesis/Religious Program—Tel: 847-816-8677; Fax: 847-918-0640. Students 1,892.

HANOVER PARK, COOK CO., ST. ANSGAR Rev. Xamie M. Reyes; Deacons Oscar Monterroso; Ronald Weber; John Szarek.
Res.: 2040 Laurel Ave., 60133. Tel: 630-837-5553; Fax: 630-837-9847. Email: ansgar@sbcglobal.net.
Catechesis/Religious Program—Students 400.

HARVEY, COOK CO.
1—ASCENSION-ST. SUSANNA Revs. Joseph W. Altman; Michael Oduor Sande; Deacons Thomas R. Carvlin; Henry Burke Jr.
Res.: 15234 Myrtle Ave., 60426. Tel: 708-333-0931; Fax: 708-333-3281. Email: pastor@ascstsus.org.
Catechesis/Religious Program—Students 20.
2—ST. JOHN THE BAPTIST, (Polish), Rev. Edward Romanski (Poland), Admin.
Res.: 15746 Union Ave., 60426. Tel: 708-333-0184; Fax: 708-333-0861.
Catechesis/Religious Program—Students 90.

HARWOOD HEIGHTS, NORRIDGE, COOK CO., ST. ROSALIE Revs. Jaroslaw Cendrowicz, O.S.P.P.E.; Jerzy Maj, O.S.P.P.E.; Rafal Walczyk, O.S.P.P.E.
Res.: 4401 N. Oak Park Ave., Harwood Heights-Norridge, 60706. Tel: 708-867-8817; Fax: 708-867-8615.
Catechesis/Religious Program—6750 W. Montrose, Harwood Hts., 60706. Tel: 708-867-4588; Fax: 708-867-0774. Students 174.

HAZEL CREST, COOK CO., ST. ANNE Rev. Kevin M. Birmingham; Deacons John Leonas, (Retired); Herman Benthey; Steven Moore; William Churilla.
Res.: 16802 S. Lincoln St., 60429. Tel: 708-355-1792; Fax: 708-335-1953. Web: www.saintanne.cc.
Early Learning Center—(Grades PreK-Day Care), 16777 Dixie Hwy., 60429. Tel: 708-335-4831. Students 82.
Catechesis/Religious Program—Tel: 708-335-2286. Students 60.

HICKORY HILLS, COOK CO., ST. PATRICIA Revs. Marcel J. Pasciak; Darrio L. Boscutti; Michael Owen; Deacons Charles Keegan; Norbert Weitendorf. In Res., Rev. Joseph C. Mol.
Res.: 9050 S. 86th Ave., 60457. Tel: 708-598-5222; Fax: 708-598-5280.
School—9000 S. 86th Ave., 60457. Tel: 708-598-8200; Fax: 708-598-8233. Sisters of the Holy Family of Nazareth (Des Plaines, IL) 1; Lay Teachers 15; Students 350.
Catechesis/Religious Program—Tel: 708-599-1221; Fax: 708-598-8233. Students 430.

HIGHLAND PARK, LAKE CO., IMMACULATE CONCEPTION Rev. Phillip F. Cioffi; Deacons Louis Vignocchi; Luis Lara; Stewart Adams; Dr. Bradley R. Nitschke, Music Min.; Deacon Robert Ochsner, Business Mgr.; Jim Walsh, Youth Min. In Res., Rev. Alec J. Wolff.
Res.: 770 Deerfield Rd., 60035. Tel: 847-433-0130; Fax: 847-433-0669. Email: parishinfo@icparish.org. Web: www.icparish.org.
Catechesis/Religious Program—Tel: 847-433-2224. Students 160.

HIGHWOOD, LAKE CO., ST. JAMES Revs. Thomas F. Baldonieri; James F. O'Malley, Pastor Emeritus (Retired); Phillip F. Cioffi; Deacons Bruno Pagliai; James Gallagher; Ellsworth Cordesman; Roger Mullaney. In Res., Rev. John E. Mulvihill.
Res.: 134 North Ave., 60040. Tel: 847-433-1494; Fax: 847-433-2011.
School—140 North Ave., 60040. Tel: 847-432-2277; Fax: 847-432-1321. Web: www.stjamesschoolhwd.org. Lay Teachers 18; Students 185.
Catechesis/Religious Program—Tel: 847-432-2570. Mrs. Judy Cullen, D.R.E. Students 180.

HILLSIDE, COOK CO., ST. DOMITILLA Revs. Timothy R. Fiala; Peter Galek; Robert J. Botthof, O.P.; Deacons Angelo Marotto; Kenneth Bell.
Res.: 4940 Washington St., 60162. Tel: 708-449-8430; Fax: 708-449-2009.
School—601 Hillside Ave., 60162. Tel: 708-449-7420. Sisters 3; Lay Teachers 10; Students 300.
Catechesis/Religious Program—Tel: 708-449-1558. Students 130.

HOFFMAN ESTATES, COOK CO., ST. HUBERT Rev. Robert C. Rizzo; Deacons Richard Lawson; Thomas Hayden; Steven Baldasti; Allen Tatara.

Res.: 729 Grand Canyon St., 60169. Tel: 847-885-7700; Fax: 847-885-4631.
School—255 Flagstaff Ln., 60169. Tel: 847-885-7702; Fax: 847-885-0604. Lay Teachers 30; Students 538.
Catechesis/Religious Program—Tel: 847-855-7703. Students 455.

HOMETOWN, COOK CO., OUR LADY OF LORETTO Rev. Thomas S. Cabala.
Res.: 8925 S. Kostner Ave., 60456. Tel: 708-424-7471; Fax: 708-424-7588. Web: ourladyloretto.com.
Catechesis/Religious Program—Tel: 708-499-0832. Students 125.

HOMEWOOD, COOK CO., ST. JOSEPH Revs. Richard J. Kozak; Daniel Jarosewic; Deacons Jack O'Leary; George Maddock; Daniel Dietsch.
Res.: 17951 Dixie Hwy., 60430. Tel: 708-798-0622; Fax: 708-798-6137. Web: www.parishofstjoseph-homewood.org.
School—17949 Dixie Hwy., 60430. Tel: 708-798-0467; Fax: 708-957-5659. Lay Teachers 11; Students 222.
Catechesis/Religious Program—Tel: 708-798-6311. Patricia Hoffman, D.R.E. Students 295.

INDIAN CREEK, LAKE CO., ST. MARY OF VERNON Revs. Joseph C. Curtis; Eduardo Martinez-Solis; Deacons Mark R. Zwolski; James Wogan; Philip Pagnotta Jr.; John Glenn; Maureen Evers, Pastoral Assoc.
Res.: 236 U.S. Hwy. 45, 60061. Tel: 847-362-1005; Fax: 847-362-6375. Email: smv@maryofvernon.org. Web: www.maryofvernon.org.
Catechesis/Religious Program—Tel: 847-362-0653. Students 675.

INGLESIDE, LAKE CO., ST. BEDE Rev. Timothy J. Fairman; Deacons John McMahon; James Devine; Lawrence Spohr. In Res., Rev. Robert J. Fitzpatrick, Pastor Emeritus (Retired).
Res.: 36455 N. Wilson Rd., 60041. Tel: 847-587-2251; Fax: 847-973-1765. Web: www.stbedechurch.com.
School—36399 N. Wilson Rd., 60041. Tel: 847-587-5541; Fax: 847-587-2713. Lay Teachers 17; Students 257.
Catechesis/Religious Program—Tel: 847-587-2301. Students 250.

INVERNESS, COOK CO., HOLY FAMILY Rev. Terence M. Keehan; Dawn Mayer, Pastoral Assoc.
Res.: 2515 W. Palatine Rd., 60067. Tel: 847-359-0042; Fax: 847-359-0639. Email: staff@holyfamilyparish.org. Web: www.holyfamilyparish.org.
School—Holy Family Catholic Academy
Catechesis/Religious Program—Tel: 847-359-0572. Students 1,700.

LA GRANGE, COOK CO.

1—ST. CLETUS Revs. Robert J. Clark; Charles G. Gallagher, Pastor Emeritus (Retired); Edgar Rodriguez; Charles W. Watkins; Deacon Jesus Casas.
Res.: 600 W. 55th St., 60525. Tel: 708-352-6209; Fax: 708-352-6774.
School—700 W. 55th St., 60525. Tel: 708-352-4820; Fax: 708-352-0788. Lay Teachers 30; Students 446.
Catechesis/Religious Program—Tel: 708-352-2383. Students 652.

2—ST. FRANCIS XAVIER Revs. John R. Hoffman; Robert A. Bacchi; Stanislaw Kuca; Susan D. Matthews, Pastoral Assoc.; Allen Sterwalt, Music Dir.; Deacon Andrew Allison.
Res.: 124 N. Spring Ave., 60525. Tel: 708-352-0168; Fax: 708-352-4904. Email: SFXinLG@sfx-lg.org. Web: www.sfx-lg.org.
School—145 N. Waiola Ave., 60525. Tel: 708-352-2175; Fax: 708-352-2057. Lay Teachers 56; Students 686.
Catechesis/Religious Program—Tel: 708-352-4555. Terri Simeoni, D.R.E. Students 1,185.

LA GRANGE PARK, COOK CO., ST. LOUISE DE MARILLAC Revs. Fred W. Tomzik; Joseph J. Wojcik; Deacon Michael McLynn.
Res.: 1144 Harrison Ave., 60526. Tel: 708-352-7388; Fax: 708-352-0714. Email: parishoffice@stlouisedemarillac.com. Web: www.stlouisedemarillac.com.
School—Tel: 708-352-2202; Fax: 708-352-6654. Lay Teachers 14; Students 175.
Youth Ministry—1144 Harrison Ave., 60526. Tel: 708-352-7388; Fax: 708-352-0714.
Catechesis/Religious Program—1125 Harrison Ave., 60526. Tel: 708-482-8814. Students 264.

LAKE FOREST, LAKE CO.

1—ST. MARY Revs. Michael G. McGovern; Donald C. Woznicki; Deacons James L. Kenney; Joseph G. Krakora. In Res., Rev. Stephen E. Grunow.
Res.: 175 E. Illinois Rd., 60045. Tel: 847-234-0205; Fax: 847-234-9860. Email: information@churchofstmary.org. Web: www.churchofstmary.org.
School—185 E. Illinois Rd., 60045. Tel: 847-234-0371; Fax: 847-234-9593. Lay Teachers 57; Students 560.
Catechesis/Religious Program—Tel: 847-234-0090; Fax: 847-234-2755. Students 680.

2—ST. PATRICK Rev. Laurence J. Dunn.
Res.: 991 S. Waukegan Rd., 60045. Tel: 847-234-1401; Fax: 847-234-1433. Web: www.stpatrick-lakeforest.org.
Catechesis/Religious Program—Tel: 847-234-2179; Fax: 847-234-2313. Students 611.

LAKE VILLA, LAKE CO., PRINCE OF PEACE Revs. Richard M. Yanos; David R. Straub; Deacons Timothy Leonard; Jeff Barton; Joseph LaFleur; Christopher Savage; Jim Minor. In Res., Rev. Daniel F. Sullivan (Retired).
Res.: 135 S. Milwaukee Ave., 60046. Tel: 847-356-7915; Fax: 847-265-1678. Web: www.princeofpeacelv.org.
School—Tel: 847-356-6111; Fax: 847-356-6121. Lay Teachers 14; Students 262.
Catechesis/Religious Program—Tel: 847-356-5850; Fax: 847-265-1678. Students 558.

LAKE ZURICH, LAKE CO., ST. FRANCIS DE SALES Rev. David Ryan; Deacon Robert Arvidson.
Res. & Rectory: 227 & Main St., 60047.
Church: 135 S. Buesching Rd., 60047. Tel: 847-438-6622; Fax: 847-438-6638. Web: www.stfrancislz.org.
School—11 S. Buesching Rd., 60047. Tel: 847-438-7921; Fax: 847-438-7114. Roy Rash, Prin.; Sr. Michael Marie, C.S.F.N., Asst. Prin. Lay Teachers 36; Students 505.
Catechesis/Religious Program—Tel: 847-726-4850; Fax: 847-438-7114. Kathy Brady-Murfin, D.R.E. Students 1,318.

LANSING, COOK CO., ST. ANN Rev. Fred C. Pesek.
Parish Office—3010 Ridge Rd., 60438. Tel: 708-895-6700; Fax: 708-895-6877. Email: stannch@comcast.net.
Res.: 3026 Ridge Rd., 60438. Tel: 708-895-6700; Fax: 708-895-6877.
School—3014 Ridge Rd., 60438. Tel: 708-895-1661; Fax: 708-865-6923. Lay Teachers 16; Students 289.
Catechesis/Religious Program—Tel: 708-895-5970. Students 16.

LEMONT, COOK CO.

1—ST. ALPHONSUS Rev. Brian Ardagh.
Res.: 210 E. Logan, 60439. Tel: 630-257-2414; Fax: 630-257-2476. Email: stals-lemont@comcast.net. Web: www.st-als.org.
School—St. Alphonsus-St. Patrick Consolidated, (Grades K-8), Admin. Office: 20 W. 145 Davey Rd., 60439. Tel: 630-783-2220. Sisters 1; Lay Teachers 19; Students 338.
Catechesis/Religious Program—Tel: 630-257-2371; Fax: 630-257-2381. Students 400.

2—BLESSED JURGIS MATULAITIS MISSION Rev. Antanas Saulaitis, S.J. In Res., Rev. Msgr. Ignatius L. Urbonas (GRY) (Retired).
Lithuanian Catholic Mission—14915-127th St., Unit 101, 60439. Tel: 630-257-5613; Fax: 630-257-5695. Email: matulaitismission@sbcglobal.net. Web: www.matulaitismission.com.
Catechesis/Religious Program—Students 500.

3—SS. CYRIL AND METHODIUS Revs. Lawrence M. Lisowski; Marcin Szczypula; Deacon Norbert Lesnieski, (Retired).
Res.: 608 Sobieski St., 60439. Tel: 630-257-2776; Fax: 630-257-9372. Email: rectory@stcyril.org. Web: www.stcyril.org.
School—607 Sobieski St., 60439. Tel: 630-257-6488; Fax: 630-257-6465. Lay Teachers 18; Students 480.
Catechesis/Religious Program—Tel: 630-257-9314; Fax: 630-257-5806. Students 600.

4—ST. JAMES AT SAG BRIDGE, [CEM] Rev. Edward D. Gleeson; Pamela Stafford, Music Min.
Res.: 10600 South Archer Ave., 60439-9344. Tel: 630-257-7000; Fax: 630-257-7912.
Catechesis/Religious Program—Students 65.

5—ST. PATRICK Rev. Michael J. Cronin; Deacon Joseph Winblad.
Res.: 200 Illinois St., 60439. Tel: 630-257-6134; Fax: 630-257-0401. Email: stpatricklemont@sbcglobal.net.
School—St. Alphonsus-St. Patrick Consolidated, (Grades PreK-8), Admin. Office: 20 W. 145 Davey Rd., 60439. Tel: 630-783-2220; Fax: 630-783-2230. Lay Teachers 14; Students 239.
Catechesis/Religious Program—Tel: 630-257-8012; Fax: 630-257-0401. Students 223.

6—SLOVENIAN CATHOLIC MISSION, (Dedicated to Bl. A.M. Slomsek) Rev. Metod Ogorevc, O.F.M.; Deacon John Vidmar.
Res.: 14246 Main St., P.O. Box 608, 60439-0608. Tel: 630-257-2068; Fax: 630-257-2359.

LIBERTYVILLE, LAKE CO., ST. JOSEPH Revs. John E. Hennessey; Kenneth Kiepura; Valerian Laini; Deacons Robert E. Matthews; Dan Simmet; David Tiemeier; George Kashmar.
Res.: 121 E. Maple Ave., 60048. Tel: 847-362-2073; Fax: 847-362-6821. Email: info@stjoseph-libertyville.org. Web: www.stjoseph-libertyville.org.
School—221 Park Pl., 60048. Tel: 847-362-0730; Fax: 847-362-8130. Lay Teachers 20; Students 520.
Catechesis/Religious Program—116 Hurlburt Ct., 60048. Tel: 847-362-5797; Fax: 847-362-6821. Students 1,219.

LYONS, COOK CO., ST. HUGH Rev. Robert J. Burnell.
Res.: 7939 W. 43rd St., 60534. Tel: 708-447-3108; Fax: 708-447-9870. Email: sthughlyon@sbcglobal.net.
Catechesis/Religious Program—Tel: 708-447-5711. Students 50.

MARKHAM, COOK CO., ST. GERARD MAJELLA Rev. Joseph W. Altman, Admin.
Res.: 16130 Clifton Park, 60426. Tel: 708-331-8400; Fax: 708-596-0770.
Catechesis/Religious Program—Students 48.

MATTESON, COOK CO., ST. LAWRENCE O'TOOLE Rev. Michael Novick; Deacons Rossini Alcos; John Rangel; Edward Winter.
Res.: 4101 St. Lawrence Ave., 60443. Tel: 708-748-6090; Fax: 708-748-4055. Web: www.slotoole.org.
School—Tel: 708-748-6090; Fax: 708-747-4099. Lay Teachers 15; Students 270.
Catechesis/Religious Program—Tel: 708-748-6090. Students 100.

MAYWOOD, COOK CO.

1—ST. EULALIA Rev. Jose del Carmen Mendez; Deacons Giulio Camerini; George Lambert, (Retired). In Res., Rev. Benjamin Chinnappan (India) (MO).
Res.: 1851 S. 9th Ave., 60153. Tel: 708-343-6120.

2—ST. JAMES, Closed. Consult Archives and Records Center for parish and school records.

MELROSE PARK, COOK CO.

1—ST. CHARLES BORROMEO Revs. Claudio Holzer, C.S.; Leandro Fossa, C.S.; Deacons Freddy Palacios; Giulio Camerini.
Res.: 1637 N. 37th Ave., 60160. Tel: 708-343-7646; Fax: 708-343-3527.
Catechesis/Religious Program—Modesta Soto-Martinez, D.R.E.

2—OUR LADY OF MOUNT CARMEL, (Italian), Revs. Claudio Holzer, C.S.; Mauro Lazzarato, C.S.; Jesus Olivars, C.S. In Res., Rev. Agostino Lovatin, C.S.
Res.: 1101 N. 23rd Ave., 60160. Tel: 708-344-4140; Fax: 708-344-0902. Email: olmc@aol.com.
Catechesis/Religious Program—Ceci Diaz, D.R.E. Students 350.

3—SACRED HEART Rev. Erwin J. Friedl; Deacons Raymond Behrendt; Norberto Ojeda; Michael K. Barnish. In Res., Rev. Benedict Ezeoke (Nigeria).
Res.: 819 N. 16th Ave., 60160. Tel: 708-344-0757; Fax: 708-344-5906. Email: parish@shsparish.org. Web: www.shsparish.org.
School—815 N. 16th Ave., 60160. Tel: 708-681-0240; Fax: 708-681-0454. Sisters of the Third Order of St. Francis of the Holy Family 1; Lay Teachers 10; Students 140.
Catechesis/Religious Program—Students 200.
Convent—1503 W. Rice St., 60160. Tel: 708-344-6940.

MIDLOTHIAN, COOK CO., ST. CHRISTOPHER Revs. Mark J. Walter; Laurent Mhagama; Deacons Joseph Brady, Pastoral Assoc. (Retired); Michael Smith.
Res.: 4130 W. 147th St., 60445. Tel: 708-388-8190; Fax: 708-388-0072. Email: stchris@stchristopherparish.com. Web: www.stchristopherparish.com.
School—14611 S. Keeler Ave., 60445. Tel: 708-385-8776; Fax: 708-385-8102. Sisters 1; Lay Teachers 16; Students 208.
Catechesis/Religious Program—Tel: 708-388-4040. Students 194.

MORTON GROVE, COOK CO., ST. MARTHA Rev. Dennis B. O'Neill; Deacons Bernard Berquist, (Retired); Peter Meehan.
Res.: 8523 Georgiana Ave., 60053. Tel: 847-965-0262; Fax: 847-965-2535. Email: stmarthachurch@yahoo.com. Web: www.saintmarthachurch.org.
Catechesis/Religious Program—Tel: 847-965-6861. Students 161.

MT. PROSPECT, COOK CO.

1—ST. CECILIA Rev. Michael A. Olivero.
Res.: 700 S. Meier Rd., 60056. Tel: 847-437-6208; Fax: 847-437-2520. Email: stcecilia@archchicago.org. Web: www.stceciliamtprospect.org.
Catechesis/Religious Program—Tel: 847-437-6310; Fax: 847-437-5730. Students 200.

2—ST. EMILY Revs. Ronald W. Navoy; Stephen Newton, C.S.C.; Jacek Dada (Poland); Deacon Bill DiCanio; Gail Goleas, Pastoral Assoc.; Barbara Stempien, Business Mgr.; Charlotte Schiller, Music Dir.; Gregg Belgard, Youth Min. In Res., Rev. John W. Roller (Retired).
Office: 1400 E. Central Rd., 60056.
Res.: 101 N. Horner Ln., 60056. Tel: 847-824-5049; Fax: 847-297-0358. Web: www.stemily.org.
School—1400 E. Central Rd., 60056. Tel: 847-296-3490; Fax: 847-296-1155. Sisters of the Holy Family of Nazareth 1; Lay Teachers 29; Students 336.
Catechesis/Religious Program—Tel: 847-299-5865. Students 466.

3—St. Raymond de Penafort Revs. Steven G. Dombrowski; Rodolfo Gaytan Ramirez; Nhat Hong Le (Vietnam); Sr. Dee Peppard, Pastoral Assoc.; Deacon John Lorbach. In Res.,
Res.: 301 S. Ioka St., 60056. Tel: 847-253-8600; Fax: 847-253-0023. Email: pmc@st-raymond.org. Web: www.st-raymond.org.
School—300 S. Elmhurst Ave., 60056. Tel: 847-253-8555; Fax: 847-253-8939. Lay Teachers 32; Students 537.
Catechesis/Religious Program—Tel: 847-253-8600, Ext. 150. Students 813.

4—St. Thomas a Becket Rev. Edward B. Panek. In Res., Rev. Peter B. McQuinn.
Res.: 1321 Burning Bush Ln., 60056. Tel: 847-827-9220; Fax: 847-827-0370.
Catechesis/Religious Program—Tel: 847-296-9051. Students 142.

Mundelein, Lake Co.

1—St. Mary of the Annunciation (Fremont Center) Revs. Ronald J. Lewinski; Robert Fedek; Deacons Robert A. Poletto; Michael O'Malley.
Res.: 22333 W. Erhart Rd., 60060. Tel: 847-223-0010; Fax: 847-223-5960. Email: parishes@stmaryfc.org. Web: www.stmaryfc.org.
School—22277 W. Erhart Rd., 60060. Tel: 847-223-4021; Fax: 847-223-3489. Lay Teachers 13; Students 187.
Catechesis/Religious Program—Tel: 847-223-0011. Students 575.

2—Santa Maria Del Popolo Rev. David Arcila, O.C.D., Admin.; Deacons John Simmons; Dave Auld; Efrain Flores; Felipe Vasquez.
Res.: 116 N. Lake St., 60060. Tel: 847-949-8300; Fax: 847-949-2339. Web: www.smdpparish.org.
School—126 N. Lake St., 60060. Tel: 847-990-6866; Fax: 847-566-1096. Lay Teachers 24; Students 158.
Catechesis/Religious Program—Tel: 847-990-6865. Students 480.
Convent—133 N. Lincoln Ave., 60060. Tel: 847-566-7343.

Niles, Cook Co.

1—St. Isaac Jogues Rev. Andrew E. Luczak; Deacons Frederick W. Ray, (Retired); Robert C. O'Keefe; Paul Stanton; Rod Ranola.
Res.: 8149 Golf Rd., 60714. Tel: 847-967-1060; Fax: 847-967-1070.
Catechesis/Religious Program—Tel: 847-966-1180; Fax: 847-966-0159. Students 343.

2—St. John Brebeuf Revs. Thomas P. May; Jacek A. Jura; Krzysztof Janczak; Andrzej Nowicki; Deacons John Perkowitz, (Retired); Thomas Paluch, Pastoral Assoc.; Lawrence Skaja.
Res.: 8307 N. Harlem Ave., 60714. Tel: 847-966-8145; Fax: 847-966-0014.
School—8301 Harlem Ave., 60714. Tel: 847-966-3266; Fax: 847-966-5351. Sisters 2; Lay Teachers 16; Students 465.
Catechesis/Religious Program—Tel: 847-966-3269. Students 340.

3—Our Lady of Ransom Revs. Thomas M. Enright; Christopher M. Gustafson; Deacons Robert Crandall, (Retired); Charles O'Donnell; James Fruge.
Ministry Center—8624 W. Normal, 60714. Tel: 847-823-2550; Fax: 847-823-4291. Web: www.olransom.org.
Catechesis/Religious Program—Tel: 847-696-2994. Students 190.

Norridge, Cook Co., Divine Savior Rev. Richard J. LoBianco.
Res.: 7740 W. Montrose, 60706. Tel: 708-456-9000; Fax: 708-456-7838. Email: dsavior@aol.com. Web: www.divinesaviornorridge.com.
School—Academy of St. Priscilla at Divine Savior, (Grades PreK-2) Tel: 708-452-0323; Fax: 708-452-0494. Email: elem.acadpriscilla@archchicago.org. Web: www.stpriscillaacademy.org.
Catechesis/Religious Program—Students 230.

North Chicago, Lake Co., Queen of Peace, Merged with Holy Family, Waukegan & Immaculate Conception B.V.M. to form Most Blessed Trinity, Waukegan.

North Riverside, Cook Co., Mater Christi Rev. Louis J. Tylka; Deacon Ronald Pilarski.
Res.: 2431 S. 10th Ave., 60546. Tel: 708-442-5611; Fax: 708-442-1306. Web: www.materchristichurch.com.
Catechesis/Religious Program—Students 115.
Shrine—Mother of Mothers

Northbrook, Cook Co.

1—St. Norbert Revs. Robert P. Heinz; William J. Vollmer. In Res., Revs. Richard J. Mueller (Retired); Richard J. Valker (Retired).
Res.: 1809 Walters Ave., 60062. Tel: 847-272-7090; Fax: 847-272-7771. Email: rectory@stnorbertparish.org. Web: www.stnorbertparish.org.
School—1817 Walters Ave., 60062. Tel: 847-272-0051; Fax: 847-272-5274. Robert Loranger, Prin. Lay Teachers 29; Students 309.
Catechesis/Religious Program—Tel: 847-272-3086; Fax: 847-513-6761. Students 579.

2—Our Lady of the Brook Revs. Thomas A. Moran; Joseph Sellas (India); Deacons Dennis F. McAllister; Perry Duderstadt. In Res., Rev. Lawrence Yawe Mudduse (Uganda).
Res.: 3700 W. Dundee Rd., 60062. Tel: 847-272-5686; Fax: 847-498-0899. Email: rectory@olbparish.org. Web: www.olbparish.org.
Catechesis/Religious Program—Tel: 847-272-5131; Fax: 847-498-0899. Justin Huyck, C.R.E. Students 223.

Northfield, Cook Co., St. Philip the Apostle Rev. Msgr. Robert J. Dempsey. In Res., Rev. George W. Klein (Retired).
Res.: 1962 Old Willow Rd., 60093. Tel: 847-446-8383; Fax: 847-446-8338. Email: spapnf@sbcglobal.net. Web: www.stphilipparish.org.
Catechesis/Religious Program—1962 Old Willow Rd., 60093. Tel: 847-446-8390. Students 142.

Northlake, Cook Co., St. John Vianney, Cure of Ars Revs. Thomas Refermat; Dwight Campbell (PEO); Benjamin Reese (PEO); Cruz Buitrago Salvador, (Extern); Deacons John Zurawski; James Sinacore.
Res.: 46 N. Wolf Rd., 60164. Tel: 708-562-0500; Fax: 708-562-1824. Email: sjvchurch@comcast.net. Web: www.freewebs.com/sjvchurch.
School—27 N. Lavergne Ave., 60164. Tel: 708-562-1466; Fax: 708-562-0142. Lay Teachers 11; Students 180.
Catechesis/Religious Program—Tel: 708-562-1466, Ext. 120. Students 192.

Oak Forest, Cook Co., St. Damian Revs. Michael G. Meany; Phi Nguyen; Deacons Len Steinbeigle, (Retired); Thomas Hipelius; William Stearns; John Rex. In Res., Rev. Francis G. Scanlan (Retired).
Office: 5250 W. 155th St., 60452. Email: stdamian@hotmail.com.
Res.: 5220 W. 155th St., 60452. Tel: 708-687-1370; Fax: 708-687-1377.
School—5300 W. 155th St., 60452. Tel: 708-687-4230; Fax: 708-687-8347. Chad Prosen, Prin. Lay Teachers 20; Students 600.
Catechesis/Religious Program—Tel: 708-687-7788; Fax: 708-687-1735. Students 650.

Oak Lawn, Cook Co.

1—St. Catherine of Alexandria Revs. Patrick J. Henry; William J. Lion, Pastor Emeritus (Retired); William M. McFarlane; Sr. Mary Cullen, O.P., Pastoral Assoc.; Deacon Richard Feltes.
Res.: 4100 W. 107th St., 60453. Tel: 708-425-2850; Fax: 708-425-2313.
School—10621 S. Kedvale Ave., 60453. Tel: 708-425-5547; Fax: 708-425-3701. Lay Teachers 22; Students 584.
Catechesis/Religious Program—Tel: 708-425-5747; Fax: 708-425-3701. Students 184.

2—St. Gerald Rev. Lawrence J. Malcolm.
Parish Office—9310 S. 55th Ct., 60453. Tel: 708-422-0234; Fax: 708-422-0822. Web: www.stgerald.com.
Res.: 9349 S. Central Ave., 60453. Tel: 708-422-0234; Fax: 708-422-0822.
School—9320 S. 55th Ct., 60453. Tel: 708-422-0121; Fax: 708-422-9216. Lay Teachers 21; Students 366.
Catechesis/Religious Program—Tel: 708-423-0458. Students 200.

3—St. Germaine Revs. Michael J. Furlan; William O. Goedert, Pastor Emeritus (Retired); Andrzej Bartosz (Poland); Deacons John Flanagan; Donald Daum; John L. Malone; Everett Helmer.
Res.: 9711 S. Kolin, 60453. Tel: 708-636-5060; Fax: 708-636-8007.
School—9735 S. Kolin, 60453. Tel: 708-425-6063. Lay Teachers 18; Students 390.

4—St. Linus Revs. William T. Corcoran; Marcin J. Bulinski; Deacon Edward Gadomski. In Res., Rev. Orlando Martins (Portugal).
Res.: 10300 S. Lawler Ave., 60453. Tel: 708-422-2400; Fax: 708-422-2707. Web: www.saintlinusreligiouseducation.org.
School—10400 S. Lawler Ave., 60453. Tel: 708-425-1656; Fax: 708-425-1802. Lay Teachers 22; Students 378.
Catechesis/Religious Program—Tel: 708-636-4373. Students 189.

5—St. Louis De Montfort Revs. Mark P. Canavan; Daniel W. Tomich; Deacons Michael Karnoski; William Sullivan.
Res.: 8808 S. Ridgeland, 60453. Tel: 708-599-5300; Fax: 708-599-2678. Email: stlouismonfort@archchicago.org. Web: www.sldmchurch.com.
School—Tel: 708-599-5781; Fax: 708-599-5782. Lay Teachers 11; Students 250.
Catechesis/Religious Program—8840 S. Ridgeland, 60453. Tel: 708-591-5787. Students 215.

Oak Park, Cook Co.

1—Ascension Rev. Lawrence R. McNally; Deacons Roger Vandervest; Lendell Richardson.
Parish Office: 808 S. East Ave., 60304. Tel: 708-848-2703; Fax: 708-848-2773. Email: ascensionchurch@comcast.net. Web: www.ascensionchurch.com.
School—601 Van Buren, 60304. Tel: 708-386-7282; Fax: 708-524-4796. Lay Teachers 26; Students 494.
Catechesis/Religious Program—Tel: 708-848-3099. Students 365.

2—St. Catherine of Siena-St. Lucy Revs. Daniel Whiteside; John J. Carolan, Pastor Emeritus (Retired); James Hargadon, Pastoral Assoc.
Res.: 38 N. Austin Blvd., 60302. Tel: 708-386-8077; Fax: 708-386-5190.
School—27 Washington Blvd., 60302. Tel: 708-386-5286; Fax: 708-386-7328. Sr. Marion Cypser, R.S.M., Prin. Sisters of Mercy 1; Lay Teachers 12; Students 200.
Catechesis/Religious Program—Students 290.

3—St. Edmund Rev. John W. McGivern; Sr. Madeleva Deegan, R.S.M., Pastoral Assoc.; Deacons James Przepasniak; Edward P. DeLorenzo. In Res., Rev. John P. Lucas.
Res.: 188 S. Oak Park Ave., 60302. Tel: 708-848-4417; Fax: 708-848-0049.
School—200 S. Oak Park Ave., 60302. Tel: 708-386-5131; Fax: 708-386-5616. Lay Teachers 14; Students 250.
Catechesis/Religious Program—Tel: 708-848-7220. Students 260.

4—St. Giles Revs. Carl Morello; Thomas M. Dore, Pastor Emeritus (Retired); James P. Hearne; Deacon John A. Henricks. In Res., Rev. Edward P. Salmon (Retired).
Office: 1025 Columbian Ave., 60302. Tel: 708-383-3430; Fax: 708-383-8644. Email: stgiles@stgilesparish.org. Web: www.stgilesparish.org.
Res.: 1045 Columbian Ave., 60302.
School—1034 Linden Ave., 60302. Tel: 708-383-6279; Fax: 708-383-9952. Lay Teachers 35; Students 407; PreK 58.
Catechesis/Religious Program—Tel: 708-383-4185; Fax: 708-383-8669. Students 356.

Orland Hills, Cook Co., St. Elizabeth Seton Revs. Richard M. Homa; Brian T. Welter; Deacon Frank Gildea. In Res., Rev. William B. Gubbins (Retired).
Res.: 9300 W. 167th St., 60477. Tel: 708-403-0101; Fax: 708-403-0105. Web: www.steseton.com.
School—Cardinal Joseph Bernardin, 9250 W. 167th St., 60477. Tel: 708-403-6525; Fax: 708-403-8621. Mary Iannueilli, Prin. Inter-Parish School serving St. Elizabeth Seton, St. Francis of Assisi, St. Julie Billiart and St. Stephen, Deacon and Martyr.
Catechesis/Religious Program—Tel: 708-403-0101; Fax: 708-403-9810. Students 1,121.

Orland Park, Cook Co.

1—St. Francis of Assisi Revs. Edward F. Upton; John Zurek; Deacons Joseph Truesdale; Daniel Carroll.
Res.: 15050 S. Wolf Rd., 60467. Tel: 708-460-0042; Fax: 708-460-0136. Email: parishoffice@assisiparish.org. Web: www.assisiparish.org.
Catechesis/Religious Program—15010 S. Wolf Rd., 60467. Tel: 708-460-0155; Fax: 708-460-5086. Students 1,300.

2—St. Michael Revs. Paul Burak; Michael G. Foley; Adan Sandoval; Sr. Marietta Umlor, C.S.C., Pastoral Assoc.; Deacons Michael McDonough; Thomas Bartholomew; Tony Cocco; Jim Janicek. In Res., Rev. William J. Finnegan (Retired).
Res.: 14310 Highland Ave., 60462. Tel: 708-349-0903; Fax: 708-349-6015. Email: info@saintmike.com. Web: www.saintmike.com.
School—14355 Highland Ave., 60462. Tel: 708-349-0068; Fax: 708-349-2658. Sisters 1; Lay Teachers 30; Students 600.
Catechesis/Religious Program—14345 Highland Ave., 60462. Tel: 708-349-0769; Fax: 708-873-4643. Students 467.

3—Our Lady of the Woods Rev. Michael W. O'Connell; Deacon John Macarol. In Res., Most Rev. John R. Gorman, Emeritus Auxiliary Bishop (Retired).
Res.: 10731 W. 131st St., 60462. Tel: 708-361-4754; Fax: 708-361-5965. Email: olwparish@aol.com. Web: www.ourladyofthewoods.org.
Catechesis/Religious Program—Tel: 708-361-9435. Students 701.

Palatine, Cook Co.

1—St. Theresa Revs. Richard M. Zborowski; Grzegorz P. Gorczyca; Andrew Beltowski (Poland); Deacons Stephen Norys; Richard Pizzato; Lou Riccio; Gail McCusker, Business Mgr.; Bob Moffet, Dir. Music. In Res., Rev. Paul F. Rosemeyer (Retired).
Res.: 455 N. Benton, 60067. Tel: 847-358-7760; Fax: 847-202-8941. Web: www.sttheresachurch.org.
Church: 465 N. Benton, 60067. Tel: 847-358-7760.
Pauline Center/Ministry Center—455 N. Benton, 60067. Tel: 847-359-2846.
School—445 N. Benton, 60067. Tel: 847-359-1820; Fax: 847-705-2084. Lay Teachers 40; Students 618.

Catechesis/Religious Program—Tel: 847-358-2846. Elizabeth Vogt, D.R.E. Students 632.

2—ST. THOMAS OF VILLANOVA Revs. Thomas R. Rzepiela; Ryszard Gron (Poland); Deacons Edward Kaczmarek; Thomas J. Maloney; Thomas Dunne; Len Marturano; Richard Willer; Mark Duffey; William Karstenson; John Breit. In Res., Rev. Raymond A. Yadron, Pastor Emeritus (Retired).

Office: 1201 E. Anderson Dr., 60074. Tel: 847-358-6999; Fax: 847-934-4919. Email: stovparish@stov.org. Web: www.stov.org.

School—1141 E. Anderson Dr., 60074. Tel: 847-358-2110; Fax: 847-776-1435. Lay Teachers 14; Students 200.

Catechesis/Religious Program—Tel: 847-358-2386. Students 695.

PALOS HEIGHTS, COOK CO.

1—ST. ALEXANDER Revs. Edward J. Cronin; Patrick J. O'Neill.

Res.: 7025 W. 126th St., 60463. Tel: 708-448-4861; Fax: 708-448-0039. Email: alchurch1@comcast.net. Web: www.saintalsparish.org.

School—126th St. at 71st Ave., 60463. Tel: 708-448-0408; Fax: 708-448-5947. Lay Teachers 30; Students 445.

Catechesis/Religious Program—Tel: 708-448-6624. Students 435.

2—INCARNATION Revs. Ronald J. Mass; William Wilkosz; Deacon James Langwell; Kathryn L. McNicholas, Pastoral Assoc. In Res., Rev. Edward J. McLaughlin (Retired).

Res.: 5757 W. 127th St., 60463. Tel: 708-597-3180; Fax: 708-597-2452. Email: church@incarnationcatholic.com. Web: www.incarnationcatholic.com.

School—Tel: 708-385-6250; Fax: 708-597-0588. Lay Teachers 16; Students 229.

Catechesis/Religious Program—Tel: 708-388-4004; Fax: 708-597-0588. Students 230.

PALOS HILLS, COOK CO., SACRED HEART Revs. Patrick M. Tucker; Robert F. McGinnity, Pastor Emeritus (Retired); Grzegorz Wojcik; Deacon Richard Werner. In Res., Rev. Robert G. Herne (Retired).

Res.: 8245 W. 111th St., 60465. Tel: 708-974-3336; Fax: 708-974-3556.

Catechesis/Religious Program—Tel: 708-974-3900; Fax: 708-974-3922. Students 300.

PARK FOREST, COOK CO., ST. IRENAEUS

Res.: 78 Cherry St., 60466. Tel: 708-748-6891; Fax: 708-748-7998.

Catechesis/Religious Program—Tel: 708-748-7997.

PARK RIDGE, COOK CO.

1—MARY, SEAT OF WISDOM Revs. Gerald T. Gunderson; Ronald N. Kalas, Pastor Emeritus (Retired). In Res., Rev. Theodore Stone (Retired).

Res.: 920 Granville Ave., 60068. Tel: 847-825-3153; Fax: 847-825-3484. Email: mswrectory@maryseatofwisdom.org. Web: www.mswparish.org.

School—1352 S. Cumberland, 60068. Tel: 847-825-2500; Fax: 847-825-1943. Lay Teachers 36; Students 482.

Catechesis/Religious Program—Tel: 847-825-8763; Fax: 847-825-8658. Students 420.

2—ST. PAUL OF THE CROSS Revs. Britto Berchmans; John P. Chrzan; Charles E. Musula; Deacons Aloysius J. Memmel; Robert T. Bulger. In Res., Rev. Daniel A. Smilanic.

Res.: 320 S. Washington St., 60068. Tel: 847-825-7605; Fax: 847-825-5186. Web: www.spc-parish.net.

School—140 S. Northwest Hwy., 60068. Tel: 847-825-6366; Fax: 847-825-2466. Lay Teachers 42; Students 696.

Catechesis/Religious Program—215 S. Ridge Ter., 60068. Tel: 847-692-2758. Students 1,319.

POSEN, COOK CO., ST. STANISLAUS BISHOP AND MARTYR Rev. Paul Maina Waithaka; Deacon Daniel Dutkiewicz.

Res.: 14414 McKinley Ave., 60469. Tel: 708-597-4910; Fax: 708-597-4841.

Catechesis/Religious Program—Students 35.

PROSPECT HEIGHTS, COOK CO., ST. ALPHONSUS LIGUORI Revs. Curtis Lambert; John W. Hurley; Deacons Norbert Ciesil; Calvin Blickle Jr.

Res.: 411 N. Wheeling Rd., 60070. Tel: 847-255-7452; Fax: 847-255-7520. Email: saintalphonsus@hotmail.com. Web: www.saintalphonsus.com.

School—Tel: 847-255-5538. Lay Teachers 21; Students 300.

Catechesis/Religious Program—Tel: 847-255-9490. Students 260.

RIVER FOREST, COOK CO.

1—ST. LUKE Revs. Kenneth J. Fischer; Leroy A. Wickowski; Deacons Terrance Norton; John O'Neill; Paul Faherty; Robert Slobig.

Res.: 528 Lathrop Ave., 60305-1835. Tel: 708-771-8250; Fax: 708-771-8809. Email: stlukeparish@earthlink.net. Web: www.stlukeparish.org.

School—519 Ashland Ave., 60305-1824. Tel: 708-366-8587; Fax: 708-366-3831. Lay Teachers 25; Students 316.

Catechesis/Religious Program—Tel: 708-771-5959; Fax: 708-771-5960. Students 270.

2—ST. VINCENT FERRER Revs. Herbert C. Hayek, O.P.; Dennis C. Woerter, O.P.; Michael G. Kyte, O.P.; Deacons John Gaughan; Robert C. Sassetti; Jerome J. Trakszelis. In Res., Revs. John J. O'Malley, O.P.; Kevin O'Rourke, O.P.; Kevin R. Fane, O.P.; Peter J. Hereley, O.P.; Albert G. Judy, O.P.; Michael A. Garcia, O.P.; Andrew M. McAlpin, O.P.

Res.: 1530 Jackson Ave., 60305. Tel: 708-366-7090; Fax: 708-366-7092. Web: www.svfparish.org.

Church: 1530 Jackson Ave., 60305.

School—1515 Lathrop Ave., 60305. Tel: 708-771-5905; Fax: 708-771-7114. Lay Teachers 20; Students 277.

Catechesis/Religious Program—1527 Lathrop, 60305. Tel: 708-366-7090, Ext. 144. Students 127.

RIVER GROVE, COOK CO., ST. CYPRIAN Rev. Eugene W. Gratkowski; Deacons James Platt; Gerald Zych.

Res.: 2601 Clinton St., 60171. Tel: 708-453-4800; Fax: 708-453-6141. Email: stcyprianchurch@netzero.net. Web: www.stcyprian.org.

School—2561 Clinton St., 60171. Tel: 708-453-6300; Fax: 708-453-6141. Religious 1; Lay Teachers 10; Students 147.

Catechesis/Religious Program—Tel: 708-453-5719; Fax: 708-453-6141. Students 119.

RIVERDALE, COOK CO., QUEEN OF APOSTLES Rev. John L. Harvey; Deacon Gerald Hahn.

Res.: 207 W. 145th St., 60827. Tel: 708-849-4901; Fax: 708-849-5903. Email: qofa207@att.net.

School—Christ Our Savior, (Inter-Parish School), Tel: 708-333-8173. Web: www.christoursaviorcatholicschool.org.

RIVERSIDE, COOK CO., ST. MARY Rev. Msgr. R. George Sarauskas; Rev. Michal Lewon; Sr. Margaret Sannasardo, B.V.M., Pastoral Assoc.

Res.: 126 Herrick Rd., 60546. Tel: 708-447-1020; Fax: 708-447-3309. Email: maryriver@stmaryriverside.org. Web: www.stmaryriverside.org.

School—97 Herrick Rd., 60546. Tel: 708-442-5747; Fax: 708-442-0125. Sisters 2; Lay Teachers 29; Students 436.

Catechesis/Religious Program—Tel: 708-447-6812. Students 425.

ROLLING MEADOWS, COOK CO., ST. COLETTE Rev. Dennis M. Zalecki; Deacons John Connor; Eddies Ortiz.

Res.: 3900 S. Meadow Dr., 60008. Tel: 847-394-8100; Fax: 847-394-8102.

School—Tel: 847-392-4098; Fax: 847-392-8155. Lay Teachers 14; Students 217.

Catechesis/Religious Program—Tel: 847-394-0274. Students 413.

ROSEMONT-DES PLAINES, COOK CO., OUR LADY OF HOPE Revs. John W. Clemens; William D. Mannion, Pastor Emeritus (Retired); Thomas E. Schwab, Pastor Emeritus (Retired); Deacon James J. Ernst. In Res., Rev. Msgr. Kenneth Velo.

Res.: 9711 W. Devon Ave., 60018. Tel: 847-825-4673; Fax: 847-825-4631.

Catechesis/Religious Program—Students 202.

ROUND LAKE, LAKE CO., ST. JOSEPH Revs. Timothy J. O'Malley; Donald J. Lund; David Galeana; Deacons David Bresemann; Eusebio Moreno; Joel Ruiz.

Res.: 114 N. Lincoln Ave., 60073. Tel: 847-546-3610; Fax: 847-546-3449. Web: www.stjosephrl.org.

School—118 N. Lincoln Ave., 60073. Tel: 847-546-1720. Lay Teachers 18; Students 235.

Catechesis/Religious Program—Tel: 847-546-3554. Diane Raihle, D.R.E. Students 600.

SAUK VILLAGE, COOK CO., ST. JAMES Revs. David B. Krolczyk; David J. Simonetti.

Res.: 22400 S. Torrence Ave., 60411-5144. Tel: 708-757-2170; Fax: 708-757-2176.

Catechesis/Religious Program—Tel: 708-757-2174; Fax: 708-757-2176. Students 215.

Convent—21903 Orion St., 60411. Tel: 708-758-5431.

SCHAUMBURG, COOK CO.

1—CHURCH OF THE HOLY SPIRIT Rev. John W. Dearhammer; Deacons Raymond Doud; Lowell Taylor, (Retired); Timothy Kryszak Sr.; Luis Trevino; Wayne Beyer; Mario Contreras; Mike Enger; Sung Han; Xavier Carrera.

Res.: 1451 W. Bode Rd., 60194. Tel: 847-882-7580; Fax: 847-882-1845. Email: pastor@churchoftheholyspirit.org. Web: www.churchoftheholyspirit.org.

Catechesis/Religious Program—Tel: 847-882-7584. Students 1,004.

2—ST. MARCELLINE Rev. Denis Condon; Deacons Joe Garcia; Thomas LaMantia; Michael Filipucci; Paul Migala; Don Maiers.

Res.: 822 Springinsguth Rd., 60193. Tel: 847-524-4429; Fax: 847-524-4597. Email: stmarcelline@stmarcelline.com. Web: www.stmarcelline.com.

Catechesis/Religious Program—Students 386.

3—ST. MATTHEW Rev. Joseph Glab, C.R.; Deacons Thomas Duszynski; Lawrence J. Smith.

Res.: 1001 E. Schaumburg Rd., 60194. Tel: 847-891-1220; Fax: 847-891-3140. Web: www.saintmatthewparish.org.

Catechesis/Religious Program—1005 Schaumburg Rd., 60194. Tel: 847-891-8408; Fax: 847-891-4291. Students 581.

SCHILLER PARK, COOK CO.

1—ST. BEATRICE Revs. Robert Schultz; Raymond P. Devereux (Retired); John J. Bresnahan (Retired).

Res.: 4157 Atlantic Ave., 60176. Tel: 847-678-0138; Fax: 847-678-3974.

Catechesis/Religious Program—Students 113.

2—ST. MARIA GORETTI Rev. James F. Blazek.

Res.: 3929 N. Wehrman Ave., 60176. Tel: 847-678-3988; Fax: 847-678-3901.

School—Tel: 847-678-2560; Fax: 847-678-2919. Lay Teachers 13; Students 255.

Catechesis/Religious Program—Students 80.

SKOKIE, COOK CO.

1—ST. JOAN OF ARC Rev. James P. Kehoe.

Res.: 9248 N. Lawndale Ave., Evanston, 60203-1509. Tel: 847-673-0409; Fax: 847-673-9626. Email: sja60203@aol.com. Web: www.saintjoanofarc.net.

School—Tel: 847-679-0660; Fax: 847-673-0689. Lay Teachers 18; Students 210.

Catechesis/Religious Program—Students 95.

2—ST. LAMBERT Revs. Richard T. Simon; Ronald S. Plomillo (Philippines); Deacon John C. O'Leary.

Res.: 8148 Karlov Ave., 60076. Tel: 847-673-5090; Fax: 847-677-5135. Email: saintlambert@aol.com. Web: www.stlambert.org.

Catechesis/Religious Program—Tel: 847-329-1201. Students 142.

3—ST. PETER Revs. Michael A. Wulsch; Luke E. Winkelmann; Deacon James Wills. In Res., Rev. Thomas A. Baima.

Res.: 8116 Niles Center Rd., 60077. Tel: 847-673-1492; Fax: 847-673-6979.

School—8140 Niles Center Rd., 60077. Tel: 847-673-0918; Fax: 847-673-6469. Lay Teachers 20; Students 172.

Catechesis/Religious Program—Tel: 847-679-1202; Fax: 847-673-6469. Students 230.

SOUTH HOLLAND, COOK CO.

1—HOLY GHOST Rev. Anthony M. Talarico; Deacon James Renwick.

Res.: 700 E. 170th St., 60473. Tel: 708-333-7011; Fax: 708-333-1996.

School—Christ Our Savior, (Inter-Parish School), Tel: 708-333-8173.

Catechesis/Religious Program—Tel: 708-333-7011. Students 28.

2—ST. JUDE THE APOSTLE Revs. Ignatius I. Anaele; John J. Powers, Pastor Emeritus (Retired); Deacons Herbert Drazba; Arthur Nylen; Mel Stasinski; Timothy Springer.

Res.: 880 E. 154th St., 60473. Tel: 708-333-3550; Fax: 708-339-3336. Email: apostljude@aol.com. Web: www.stjudetheapostle.org.

School—Christ Our Savior West Campus, Inter-Parish school serving St. Andrew, Our Lady of Knock, St. Victor, Holy Ghost, St. Jude and Queen of Apostles., 900 E. 154th St., 60473-1106. Tel: 708-333-8173.

Catechesis/Religious Program—Tel: 708-225-1180. Students 30.

STICKNEY, COOK CO., ST. PIUS X Rev. Neil Van Dyke; Deacons Marvin Kocar; Russell Ramirez.

Res.: 4314 S. Oak Park Ave., 60402. Tel: 708-484-7951; Fax: 708-749-8518. Email: spxparish@aol.com.

Catechesis/Religious Program—4300 S. Oak Park Ave., 60402. Tel: 708-788-6090. Students 123.

STREAMWOOD, COOK CO., ST. JOHN THE EVANGELIST Revs. Robert F. Tonelli; Benedykt M. Pazdan; Deacons Earl Dahl; James Furey; Robert DeFiore; Larry Rybicki.

Res.: 540 S. Park Blvd., 60107. Tel: 630-837-6500; Fax: 630-483-3153.

School—513 Parkside Cir., 60107. Fax: 630-289-3026. Lay Teachers 13; Students 193.

Catechesis/Religious Program—Tel: 630-837-1060; Fax: 630-289-3026. Students 462.

SUMMIT, COOK CO., ST. JOSEPH Revs. Robert Stuglik; Henry Pozdol, Pastor Emeritus (Retired); Thomas E. Lamping; Deacons Ben Michalowski; Richard Tryjfaczkam; Raymundo Diaz DeLeon.

Res.: 7240 W. 57th St., 60501. Tel: 708-458-0501.

School—5641 S. 73rd Ave., 60501. Tel: 708-458-2927. Lay Teachers 12; Students 248.

Catechesis/Religious Program—Students 110.

TINLEY PARK, COOK CO.

1—ST. GEORGE Revs. Kenneth J. Fleck; William J. Curran; Deacons Paul Gilbert; Dominick Dattoli; John Ficker; Joseph Panek. In Res., Revs. Blaise Coelho; Eugene Rybansky (Extern, Nitra, Slovakia).

Res.: 6707 W. 175th St., 60477. Tel: 708-532-2243;

Fax: 708-532-2055. Web: www.stgeorge60477.org.
School—6700 W. 176th St., 60477. Tel: 708-522-2626; Fax: 708-532-2025. Mantellate Sisters 2; Felician Sisters 1; Lay Teachers 22; Students 380.
Catechesis/Religious Program—Tel: 708-532-8211. Nancy Bishop, CRE. Students 400.

2—SAINT JULIE BILLIART Revs. Steven M. Lanza; Artur Sowa; Deacons Michael Kiley; Richard Miska, Business Mgr.; Gael Gensler, Pastoral Assoc.; Deanne Tumpich, Music Dir.; Sheila Pluchar, Youth Min.; Mary Alice Roth, Liturgy Director.
Res.: 7399 W. 159th St., 60477. Tel: 708-429-6767; Fax: 708-429-6788. Web: www.stjulie.org.
Catechesis/Religious Program—Tel: 708-429-1044. Patricia Kmak, D.R.E. Students 850.

3—ST. STEPHEN, DEACON AND MARTYR Revs. James Finno; Grzegorz Warmuz; Deacons Joseph Stalcup Sr.; Kenneth Zawadzki; William Engler; Charles McFarland; Peter Van Merkestyn; William Schultz.
Res.: 17500 S. 84th Ave., 60487. Tel: 708-342-2400; Fax: 708-342-1545. Email: karen@ststephentinley.com. Web: www.ststephentinley.com.
Catechesis/Religious Program—Students 1,445.

VOLO, LAKE CO., ST. PETER Revs. Dennis Kolinski, S.J.C.; Anthony Rice, S.J.C.
Res.: 27570 Volo Village Rd., 60073. Tel: 815-385-5496. Email: stpetervolo@juno.com. Web: www.stpetervolo.org.
Catechesis/Religious Program—Students 204.

WADSWORTH, LAKE CO., ST. PATRICK Revs. Patrick G. Cecil; George J. Dyer, Pastor Emeritus (Retired); Deacons John Richardson, (Retired); Louis Abboud; Phillip Fragassi; Edward Tomkowiak; David Egan; David Wagner; Dennis Brown, Pastoral Assoc.; Bernie Oberdick, Music Dir.; Amanda Spreigel, Liturgy Dir.
Res.: 15000 Wadsworth Rd., 60083. Tel: 847-244-4161; Fax: 847-336-0630. Web: www.stpatrickwadsworth.org.
School—15020 Wadsworth Rd., 60083. Tel: 847-623-8446; Fax: 847-623-3119. Marcella Bosnak, Prin. Lay Teachers 26; Students 674.
Catechesis/Religious Program—Tel: 847-236-9131; Fax: 847-336-0630. John Devine, Youth Min. Students 335.

WAUCONDA, LAKE CO., TRANSFIGURATION Revs. Ronald J. Gollatz; Krzysztof Paluch; Deacons Marion Omiatek; Feliks Pezowicz; Jose Mancilla; Marilyn Omiatek, Pastoral Min.; Josette Pezowicz, Pastoral Min.; Tomasa Mancilla, Pastoral Min.
Res.: 316 W. Mill St., 60084. Tel: 847-526-2400; Fax: 847-526-2961. Email: parish@transfig-wauconda.org. Web: www.transfig-wauconda.org.
School—Tel: 847-526-6311; Fax: 847-526-4637. Lay Teachers 18; Students 228.
Catechesis/Religious Program—Tel: 847-526-6400. Students 528.

WAUKEGAN, LAKE CO.

1—ST. ANASTASIA Rev. Aloysius Funtila.
Res.: 624 Douglas Ave., 60085. Tel: 847-623-2875; Fax: 847-623-4882.
School—Tel: 847-623-8320; Fax: 847-623-0556. Lay Teachers 19; Students 305.
Catechesis/Religious Program—Students 110.

2—ST. BARTHOLOMEW, Merged with St. Joseph. See Holy Family for details.

3—ST. DISMAS Rev. Patrick J. Rugen; Deacon Anthony Sacramento.
Res.: 2600 Sunset Ave., 60087. Tel: 847-623-5050; Fax: 847-623-5292. Web: www.stdismasparish.net.
Catechesis/Religious Program—2226 McAree Rd., 60087. Tel: 847-244-9510. Students 160.

4—HOLY FAMILY, Merged with Immaculate Conception B.V.M., Waukegan to form Most Blessed Trinity, Waukegan.

5—IMMACULATE CONCEPTION B.V.M., Merged with Holy Family, Waukegan to form Most Blessed Trinity, Waukegan.

6—ST. JOSEPH, Merged with St. Bartholomew, Waukegan. See Holy Family for details.

7—MOST BLESSED TRINITY Revs. Gary M. Graf; Nestor Torres (Colombia); Deacons Edward Scarbalis, (Retired); Angel Velazquez; Marcellino Hernandez; Dennis Mudd.
450 Keller Ave., 60085-5030.
School—Academy of Our Lady, 510 Grand Ave., 60085. Tel: 847-623-4110; Fax: 847-599-0477. Lay Teachers 16; Students 17.
Catechesis/Religious Program—Students 272.

WESTCHESTER, COOK CO.

1—DIVINE INFANT Revs. Michael J. Wanda; Gerald P. Joyce, Pastor Emeritus (Retired); Thomas Winikates.
Res.: 1601 Newcastle Ave., 60154. Tel: 708-865-8071; Fax: 708-865-8032.
School—Tel: 708-865-0122; Fax: 708-865-9495. Lay Teachers 14; Students 184.
Catechesis/Religious Program—Students 160.

2—DIVINE PROVIDENCE Revs. Thomas E. Unz; John C. Rosemeyer, Pastor Emeritus (Retired); Mr. Marco Matonich, Pastoral Assoc.; Deacons Frank DeVita, (Retired); Jerry Fox; Edward DeLorenzo.
Res.: 2550 S. Mayfair Ave., 60154. Tel: 708-562-3364; Fax: 708-562-3134. Email: pastor@dprov.org. Web: www.dprov.org.
School—2500 S. Mayfair Ave., 60154. Tel: 708-562-2258; Fax: 708-562-9171. Lay Teachers 13; Students 184.
Catechesis/Religious Program—Tel: 708-562-3422; Fax: 708-562-3134. Students 140.

WESTERN SPRINGS, COOK CO., ST. JOHN OF THE CROSS Revs. David P. Dowdle; Kenneth J. Baker; Darrio L. Boscutti; Deacons Thomas McGorey; Joseph Pepitone; John E. Schopp IV. In Res., Rev. Deusdedit Byomuhangi (Extern).
Res.: 5005 Wolf Rd., 60558. Tel: 708-246-4404; Fax: 708-246-4566.
School—705 51st St., 60558. Tel: 708-246-4454; Fax: 708-246-9010. Lay Teachers 40; Students 686.
Catechesis/Religious Program—51st St. & Wolf Rd., 60558. Tel: 708-246-6760; Fax: 708-246-9010. Students 1,320.

WHEELING, COOK CO., ST. JOSEPH THE WORKER Revs. Michael J. Bonner, S.V.D.; Jerzy Gawlik, S.V.D.; Paul Cuong Hung Nguyen, S.V.D.; Deacons Perry Duderstadt; Steve Stecker.
Res.: 181 W. Dundee Rd., 60090. Tel: 847-537-2740; Fax: 847-537-7914.
Polska Parafialna Szkola Im. Juliusza Slowackiego, NFP—Web: www.juliuszlowacki.com.
Catechesis/Religious Program—Tel: 847-537-4182. Students 800.

WILLOW SPRINGS, COOK CO., OUR LADY, MOTHER OF THE CHURCH POLISH MISSION Revs. John Muc, O.Cist., Dir.; Michael Blicharski, O.Cist.; Filip Krzemien, O.Cist.; Ludwik Zyla, O.Cist.
Mailing Address: Box 334, Argo, 60501.
Church: 116 Hilton St., 60480-0479. Tel: 708-467-0436; Fax: 708-467-0479. Email: cistercianfathers@yahoo.com.
Catechesis/Religious Program—Students 300.

WILMETTE, COOK CO.

1—ST. FRANCIS XAVIER Revs. William J. Sheridan; Edward F. Harnett, Pastor Emeritus (Retired); Przemyslaw Wojcik; Sr. Joyce Shanabarger, O.S.F., Pastoral Assoc.; Dr. Patty Jane Pelton, Pastoral Assoc.; Deacon Robert Kerls. In Res., Rev. Richard Jakubik.
Office: 524 Ninth St., 60091-2714. Tel: 847-256-4250; Fax: 847-256-4254. Email: sfxparish@comcast.net. Web: www.sfxparish.org.
School—808 Linden Ave., 60091-2714. Tel: 847-256-0644; Fax: 847-256-0753. Daniel G. McKenna, Prin. Lay Teachers 28; Students 275.
Catechesis/Religious Program—Tel: 847-251-6730; Fax: 847-256-4254. Sr. Mary Ann Casey, O.P., Dir. PREP Prog. Students 493.

2—ST. JOSEPH Revs. John E. Pollard; Henry C. Kricek. In Res., Revs. Thomas M. Powers (Retired); Albano Fernandes, (Extern, Goa).
Res.: 1747 Lake Ave., 60091. Tel: 847-251-0771; Fax: 847-251-5715.
School—1740 Lake Ave., 60091. Tel: 847-256-7870. Ronald Berger, Prin. Lay Teachers 30; Students 366.
Catechesis/Religious Program—Tel: 847-851-3734. Ms. Dana McKenna, D.R.E. Students 365.

WINNETKA, COOK CO.

1—SS. FAITH, HOPE AND CHARITY Revs. Martin E. O'Donovan; Kenneth J. Anderson; Joseph Nam H. Dao; Paul G. Stemn; Deacons Michael Cavanaugh; Barry Schliesmann; Susan Martin, Pastoral Assoc. In Res., Rev. William J. Flaherty (Retired).
Res.: 191 Linden St., 60093. Tel: 847-446-7646; Fax: 847-446-7630. Web: www.faithhope.org.
School—180 Ridge Ave., 60093. Tel: 847-446-0031; Fax: 847-446-9064. Sisters 1; Lay Teachers 36; Students 363.
Catechesis/Religious Program—200 Ridge Rd., 60093. Tel: 847-446-1828; Fax: 847-446-2145. Students 550.

2—SACRED HEART Revs. Robert J. Heidenreich; Avitus L. Rukuratwa; Deacons Michael McNulty; John Fay.
Res.: 1077 Tower Rd., 60093. Tel: 847-446-0856; Fax: 847-501-5311. Email: sh@shparish.com. Web: www.shparish.com.
Parish Center—1090 Gage St., 60093. Tel: 847-446-0856.
School—1095 Gage St., 60093. Tel: 847-446-0005. Lay Teachers 26; Students 279.
Catechesis/Religious Program—Tel: 847-446-6535; Fax: 847-446-1969. Students 635.

ZION-BEACH PARK, LAKE CO., OUR LADY OF HUMILITY Revs. Thomas Hoffman; Jan Krutewicz; Deacons James Askew; Max Jinkens; Michael Mercure; Robert Ochsner.
Res.: 10655 W. Wadsworth Rd., 60099-3558. Tel: 847-872-8778; Fax: 847-872-8780. Email: olhch@yahoo.com. Web: ourladyofhumility.org.
School—10601 Wadsworth Rd., 60099. Tel: 847-746-3722; Fax: 847-731-2870. Patrick Browne, Prin. Lay Teachers 13; Students 259.
Catechesis/Religious Program—Tel: 847-746-3744; Fax: 847-872-8780. Students 590.

Syro-Malabar Rite

BELLWOOD, COOK CO., SYRO-MALABAR CATHOLIC MISSION OF THE ARCHDIOCESE OF CHICAGO, See separate listing. Under the Diocese of St. Thomas Syro-Malabar.

CHICAGO, COOK CO., KNANITE SYRO-MALABAR CATHOLIC MISSION OF THE ARCHDIOCESE OF CHICAGO, See separate listing. Under the Diocese of St. Thomas Syro-Malabar.

Malankara Rite

CHICAGO, COOK CO., SYRO-MALANKARA CATHOLIC MISSION OF THE ARCHDIOCESE OF CHICAGO
Divine Liturgy-Ascension Church—1208 Ashland Ave., Evanston, 60202. Tel: 847-332-1794; Fax: 847-424-0889. Rev. Saji George Mukkoot, Dir. In Res., Rev. Thomas Kuttiyanickal, S.A.C.

Chaplains of Public Institutions

CHICAGO. *Chicago Airports Catholic Chaplaincy*, P.O. Box 66353, 60666. Rev. Michael G. Zaniolo, S.T.L., C.A.C.
Hines V.A. Hospital. Revs. James Burnett (DAV), Benjamin Chinnappan (India) (MO), Terry L. Langford.
John H. Stroger, Jr. Hospital of Cook County, Tel: 312-864-1246. Revs. Eugene J. Nevins, S.J., Dir., James Chambers, S.J., Robert E. Finn, S.J., Sr. Marie Louise Jilk, S.Sp.S.

NORTH CHICAGO. *Veterans Affairs Medical Center*. Rev. William F. Vander Heyden (GB).

OAK FOREST. *Oak Forest Hospital*, 4700 W. 159th St., 60452. Tel: 708-687-2035. Rev. Wayne H. Wurst.

On Duty Outside the Archdiocese:
Rev. Msgrs.—
Dobes, George E., J.C.L., 3370 S. 2nd St., Arlington, VA 22204-1709.
Trisco, Robert F., Hist.Eccl.D. (Retired), Curley Hall, Catholic University of America, Washington, DC 20064.
Revs.—
Brankin, Patrick M., St. Theresa, P.O. Box 297, Collinsville, OK 74021-0297.
Coughlin, Daniel P., Office of the Chaplain, U.S. House of Representatives, H B 25 The Capitol, Washington, DC 20515.
Kiley, J. Cletus, Pres. & CEO, Faith & Politics Institute, 110 Maryland Ave., N.E., Ste. 504, Washington, DC 20002.
Lorenz, Matthais E., 5531 E. Lake Dr., #31C, Lisle, 60532.

Military Chaplains:
Revs.—
Barkemeyer, John F., c/o Mr. & Mrs. Barkemeyer, 120 Fourth St., Wilmette, 60091.
Carlson, Kenneth F., M.Div., c/o 10830 S. Oak, Chicago Ridge, 60415.
Falkenthal, Thomas W., Apostleship/Seaport Everglades, 1835 N.E. Miami Gardens Dr., #294, P.O. Box 55001, North Miami Beach, FL 33179.
Foley, Matthew E., 1 Inje St., Fort Bragg, NC 28307.
Greschel, Mark, 3731 Laguna Vista Dr., #2, Fayetteville, NC 28311.
Hannigan, John T., 1306 Kings Crest Dr., Stafford, VA 22554-7728.
Joslyn, James W., Quarters D Mustin Rd., NAS, Jacksonville, FL 32212.
Keener, Robert J., 126 Westerfield Pl., Great Lakes, 60030.
Kloak, David G., COMPACFLT/CODE NO1C, 250 Makalapa Dr., Pearl Harbor, HI 96860-3131.
Nguyen, Hoang H., 5692A Ft. Write Oval, Fairchild Air Force Base, WA 99011.
Simpson, Brian L., Chaplain Box 100, USS Tarawa Lha 1, Fpo, AP 96622-1600.
Stake, Ronald P., Nsa Bahrain, Psc 451, Box 90, Fpo, AE 09834-0050.

Missionary Work:
Revs.—
Cleary, Philip C., 5503 Danbury Cir., Lake In The Hills, 60156.
Hays, Kevin W., Missionary Society of St. James the Apostle, 24 Clark St., Boston, MA 02109.
Hicks, Ronald A., B.A., M.Div., Nuestros Pequenos Hermanos, APDO Postal #450, Santa Ana, El Salvador.

Other Assignments:
Revs.—
Alcantara, Miguel B., Abby Manor, 7450 Waukegan Ave., #209, Niles, 60714.
Becker, Charles P., P.O. Box 633, Wauconda, 60084.

Behnke, Robert C., 980 N. Michigan Ave., Ste. 1525, 60611.
Bennett, Joseph R., 980 N. Michigan Ave., Ste. 1525, 60611.
Boyle, John T., St. Benedict Home, 6930 W. Touhy Ave., Niles, 60714.
Buck, Daniel P., P.O. Box 455, Mundelein, 60060.
Coleman, Robert P., 5802 Bullock Freeway, C1-9-292, Laredo, TX 78041.
Delgado, Jose A., 980 N. Michigan Ave., Ste. 1525, 60611.
Egan, Gerard P., Hancock Bldg., 175 E. Delaware, Apt. 4810, 60611.
Galivan, James F., 1039 W. 32nd St., 60608.
Gilligan, Michael J., Ph.D., San Rocco Oratory of St. Agnes, 315 E. 22nd St & San Rocco Pl., Chicago Hts., 60411.
Grzela, Marek B., 980 N. Michigan Ave., Ste. 1525, 60611.
Henseler, Philip E., Holy Family Villa, 12220 S. Will-Cook Rd., Orland Park, 60462-4898.
Hergenrother, John C., W7585 Ethelyn Dr., Delavan, WI 53115-2698.
Heyd, James F., Priests for Life, Maryville, 1150 N. River Rd., Des Plaines, 60016.
Keehan, John J., P.O. Box 455, Mundelein, 60060.
Killeen, William E., 72 Lake Ln., Fox Lake, 60020.
Kleiber, Kenneth R., 15202 N. 40th St., #223-2, Phoenix, AZ 85032-4652.
Kobus, John J., St. Andrew Life Center, 7000 N. Newark Ave., Niles, 60714.
LaChance, Charles P., 810 W. Montrose Ave., 60613.
Laz, Medard P., P.O. Box 300415, 60630.
Lefebure, Leo D., Our Lady of Victory, 4835 MacArthur Blvd. N.W., Washington, DC 20007.
Lewanski, Gary J., 3525 W. 55th Pl., 60629.
Lisowski, Brian A., 3322 N. Avers Ave., 60618.
Lupton, Brendan P., Mundelein Seminary, 1000 E. Maple Ave., Mundelein, 60060.
Marin, Moises, 980 N. Michigan Ave., Ste. 1525, 60611.
McKenna, Edward J., P.O. Box 648, Beverly Shores, IN 46301-0648.
McNalis, John P., 3219 W. Dickens, 60647.
Munoz-Capetillo, Octavio, Casa Jesus, 750 N. Wabash, 60611.
Nangle, Thomas R., Police Chaplaincy, 1140 W. Jackson, 60607.
Nguyen, Joseph Thai, 7800 Carousel Ln., Richmond, VA 23294.
Nguyen, Phien T., St. Callistus, 12921 Lewis St., Garden Grove, CA 92840.
Parrish, L. Jerome, c/o 2610 E. 78th St., 60649.
Patte, Steven W., 980 N. Michigan Ave., #1525, 60611.
Price, John R., 6054 W. 64th Place, 60638.
Quinlan, James V., 3050 N.E. 47th Ct., Fort Lauderdale, FL 33308.
Ramon-Jimenez, Edilberto, 980 N. Michigan Ave., Ste. 1525, 60611.
Robinson, John A., P.O. Box 455, Mundelein, 60060.
Sanchez-Espinoza, Juan, 980 N. Michigan Ave., Ste. 1525, 60611.
Spiess, Kevin J., 980 N. Michigan Ave., Ste. 1525, 60611.
Stefanski, Gery W., 902 Oakton, Unit 1A, Evanston, 60202.
Strus, Walter A., 1039 W. 32nd St., 60608.
Szabelski, Joseph R. (Retired), Queen of Peace Retirement Center, 24955 N. Hwy. 12, Lake Zurich, 60047.
Tillrock, Raymond J., 5346 S. Cornell, Apt. 201, 60615.
Vitro, Thomas J., P.O. Box 932, Lake Geneva, WI 53147.
Yakaitis, Michael T., 980 N. Michigan Ave., Ste. 1525, 60611.
Zimmer, William E., 5758 W. Potomoac Ave., 60651-1132.

Retired:
Rev. Msgr.—
Mroczkowski, Joseph J., 1501 Hoffman St., Hammond, IN 46327.
Revs.—
Adamich, Albert R., Most Holy Redeemer, 9525 S. Lawndale Ave., Evergreen Park, 60042.
Adams, Michael J., Christ the King, 9235 S. Hamilton Ave., 60620.
Ahearn, Donald J., St. Juliana, 7142 N. Osceola, 60063.
Anglim, Ronald H., 7231 S. Wolf Rd. F6, Indian Head Park, 60525.
Auer, Joseph E., Bishop Lyne Home, 12210 S. Will-Cook Rd., Palos Park, 60464-7332.
Baldwin, John F., CHC, USN, 5100 Marine Dr., #27-M, 60640.
Balskus, Charles, St. Mary, Star of the Sea, 6435 S. Kilbourn Ave., 60629-5599.
Banzin, Robert S., 5100 Marine Dr., #13 M, 60640.
Bonin, Harold A., St. Jerome, 1709 W. Lunt Ave., 60623-3212.
Borowczyk, Martin R., St. Benedict Home, 6930 W. Touhy Ave., Niles, 60714.
Bowler, Michael J., 3211 S. Racine Ave., 1st Fl. Front, 60608.
Bowman, R. Peter, Resurrection Life Center, 7370 W. Talcott Ave., 60631.
Brady, Daniel J., 432 W. Park St., Arlington Heights, 60005.
Bresnahan, John J., 1675 Mill St., Apt. 504, Des Plaines, 60018.
Broccolo, Gerard T., 1011 S. Valentia St., #135, Denver, CO 80231.
Burke, William A., Bishop Lyn Home, 12230 S. Will-Cook Rd., Palos Park, 60464.
Caplis, Roger J., P.O. Box 656, Williams Bay, WI 53191-0656.
Carolan, John J., St. Catherine of Siena-St. Lucy, 38 N. Austin Blvd., Oak Park, 60302.
Carroll, Gilbert A., Resurrection Life Center, 7370 W. Talcott Ave., 60631.
Cassidy, Francis P., St. Daniel, 5330 S. Nashville, 60638.
Cassidy, John M., St. Daniel, 5330 S. Nashville, 60638.
Cerny, George F., Holy Family Villa, 12220 S. Will-Cook Rd., Orland Park, 60462-4898.
Chen, Anthony K., St. M G Nursing Home, 103 Fang An Rd., Chiayi 600, Taiwan.
Cimarrusti, Francis A., St. Matthias, 2310 W. Ainslie St., 60625.
Clements, George H., 10226 S. Trumbull St., Evergreen Park, 60805.
Close, James J., 1140 W. Jackson Blvd., 60607.
Colleran, James A., 8627 Wapalo Rd., Marshall, IN 47859.
Collins, Daniel J., 4200 N. Sheridan Rd., 60613.
Corbo, Alfred P., 321 Bryn Mawr, Itasca, 60143.
Corcoran, Edward G., P.O. Box 28232, San Diego, CA 92128.
Costello, William J., 632 Pinehurst Ct., Twin Lakes, WI 53181.
Coughlin, Roger J., 721 N. LaSalle St., 60610.
Cowell, Raymond, Paraoquia Nuest, Sen De Fatima, El Pari Casilla 919, Santa Cruz, Bolivia.
Cross, Robert A., 700 Ashland, River Forest, 60305.
Czajka, Norman M., Resurrection Life Center, 7370 W. Talcott, 60631.
Darow, Robert G., 5901 N. Sauganash Ln., 60646.
Dempsey, Richard J., 11022 S. Fairfield Ave., 60655.
Devereux, Raymond P., St. Beatrice, 4157 Atlantic Ave., Schiller Park, 60176.
Devine, William J., P.O. Box 53, Worth, 60482.
Dewes, John W., St. Anne, 120 N. Ela St., Barrington, 60010.
Dolciamore, John V., J.C.L., S.T.L., University of St. Mary of the Lake, 1000 E. Maple Ave., Mundelein, 60060-1174.
Donohue, John J., 282 Woodstone Cir., Buffalo Grove, 60089-6701.
Dore, Thomas M., St. Pascal, 3935 N. Melvina Ave., 60634-2527.
Dovick, Robert E., Alvernia Manor, 13950 Main St., Lemont, 60439.
Dressler, Philip J., 7142 N. Osceola Ave., 60631.
Dufficy, Edward C., St. Benedict Home, 6930 Touhy, Niles, 60714.
Duffy, Donald J., Resurrection Life Center, 7370 W. Talcott, 60631.
Duggan, J. Edward, Bishop Lyne Residence, 12230 S. Will-Cook Rd., Palos Park, 60464.
Durkin, Eugene F., Holy Name Cathedral, 730 N. Wabash Ave., 60611.
Dyer, George J., 890 Audubon Way Bw-T12, Lincolnshire, 60069.
Enright, John P., 1801 W. 35th St., #1217, Oakbrook, 60521.
Farry, John A., St. Andrew, 3546 N. Paulina St., 60657.
Faucher, Eugene J., St. Edna, 2525 N. Arlington Heights Rd., Arlington Heights, 60004.
Felczak, Leonard J., 4325 S. Spaulding, 60632.
Feller, Richard J., 1201 Bonita, Park Ridge, 60068.
Fenske, Donald J., Our Lady of Knock, 501 163rd St., Calumet City, 60409.
Ferrigan, Robert E., 1340 N. Dearborn, Unit 17A, 60610.
Finnegan, John P., 660 Chandler Rd., Gurnee, 60031.
Finnegan, William J., 14327 Highland Ave., Orland Park, 60462.
Fitzpatrick, Edmund J., 444 Fullerton, #1604, 60614.
Fitzpatrick, Robert J., St. Bede Parish, 36455 N. Wilson Rd., Ingleside, 60041-9609.
Flaherty, William J., 191 Linden St., Winnetka, 60093-3832.
Flavin, John E., Our Lady of Perpetual Help, 1775 Grove St., Glenview, 60025.
Frawley, John P., 2825 W. 81st St., 60652-2722.
Gallagher, Charles G., St. Cletus, 600 W. 55th St., La Grange, 60525.
Gallagher, James R., 2108 S. Scoville, Berwyn, 60402.
Gerrity, Raymond J., 917 S. 8th Ave., #2, LaGrange, 60525.
Goedert, William O., St. Germaine, 4240 W. 98th St., Oak Lawn, 60453.
Goergen, Michael A., 4949 W. Patterson Ave., 60641.
Grace, James N., 1833 E. Wildberry Dr., Glenview, 60025.
Grace, John J., St. Benedict Home, 6930 Touhy, Niles, 60714.
Greeley, Andrew M., N.O.R.C., 1155 E. 60th St., 60637.
Gubbins, William B., 9440 Seton Pl., Orland Park, 60459.
Guz, Edmund F., 14207 S. Green Bay Rd., 60633.
Hanley, Lawrence F., 7112 Concord Cir., Fox Lake, 60020.
Harnett, Edward F., St. Francis Xavier, 524 Ninth St., Wilmette, 60091.
Headley, Donald J., St. Mary of the Woods, 7033 N. Moselle Ave., 60646.
Healy, Thomas I., St. Bonaventure Oratory, 1641 W. Diversey Pkwy., 60614.
Hefferan, John E., Bishop Lyne Home, 12210 S. Will-Cook Rd., Palos Park, 60464.
Herne, Robert G., Sacred Heart Parish, 8245 W. 111th St., Palos Hills, 60465.
Hung, Peter, St. Thomas of Canterbury, 4827 N. Kenmore Ave., 60634-2527.
Huppenbauer, Walter E., St. Joseph's Home, 80 Northwest Hwy., Palatine, 60067.
Hurley, John J., St. Edna, 2525 N. Arlington Hts. Rd., Arlington Hts., 60004.
Huske, Leonard G., 347 Daffodil Ln., Matteson, 60443.
Ivers, Victor J., St. Benedict Home, 6930 W. Touhy Ave., Niles, 60714.
Jabusch, Willard F., 5040 Warren St., Apt. 404, Skokie, 60077.
Janik, Bruno, Ul. Cegielniana 18/E/24, Rzeow 35-068 Poland.
Jasinski, Raymond J., Rosary Hill Nursing Home, 9000 W. 81st St., Justice, 60458.
Joyce, Gerald P., Divine Infant, 1601 Newcastle Ave., Westchester, 60154.
Kalas, Ronald N., 7258 W. Gregory, 60656.
Kane, George J., 1700 Cambourne, Schaumburg, 60194.
Kash, Robert J., Bishop Lyne Home, 12230 S. Will-Cook Rd., Palos Park, 60464.
Kastigar, John J., 1774 Lexington Dr., Sierra Vista, AZ 85635.
Kauzlarich, John J., Bishop Lyne Home, 12230 S. Will-Cook Rd., Palos Park, 60464.
Kaveney, Thomas J., St. Odilo, 2244 S. East Ave., Berwyn, 60402.
Kelly, Charles F., Holy Family Villa, 12220 S. Will-Cook Rd., Palos Park, 60464-7332.
Kelly, William J., c/o Jones, 3332 S. 59th Ave., Cicero, 60650.
Kenneally, William G., 10427 S. Hoyne, 60643.
Kinn, James W., 6318 243rd Ct., Salem, WI 53168.
Kissane, Maurice J., 21663 Howell Dr., Cassopolis, MI 49031.
Klein, George W., St. Philip the Apostle, 1962 Old Willow Rd., Northfield, 60093.
Knittel, Kilian J., P.O. Box 9408, Michigan City, IN 46361.
Kouba, Charles J., St. Benedict Home, 6930 W. Touhy Ave., Niles, 60714.
Krebs, John F., St. Benedict Life Center, 6930 W. Touhy Ave., Niles, 60714.
Kuzinskas, John A., Holy Family Villa, 12220 S. Will-Cook Rd., Palos Park, 60464-7332.
Laske, Kenneth S., 4032 W. Nelson St., 60641.
Lee, Joseph, 6157 N. Leavitt St., 60659.
Lewandowski, Ronald C., 24961 87th St., #3, Salem, WI 53168.
Lion, William J., Catherine of Alexandria, 4100 W. 107th St., Oak Lawn, 60453.
Lisowski, William J., 15714 Old Orchard Ct., Orland Park, 60462.
Lynch, Joseph P., 14130 Green Valley Dr., Orland Park, 60462.
Lyons, Leo J., 14226-84th Ave., Orland Park, 60462.
Lyons, William J., Bishop Lyne Home, 12230 S. Will-Cook Rd., Palos Park, 60464.
Maddock, Laurence F., S.T.L., St. Joseph Seminary College at Loyola University, 6551 N. Sheridan Rd., 60626.
Maginot, Richard J., St. Benedict Home, 6930 W. Touhy Ave., W4, Niles, 60714.
Maher, Byron G., Springbrook Village, 1101 S. Pine St., Apt. 106, Burlington, WI 53105.
Maher, Thomas F., St. Mary of the Woods, 7033 N.

Moselle Ave., 60646.
Mahon, Leo T., St. Mary of the Woods, 7033 N. Moselle Ave., 60646.
Mair, Robert G., c/o Thomas Place, 2200 Patriot Blvd., Glenview, 60026.
Mallette, Daniel J., St. Margaret of Scotland, 9837 S. Throop St., 60643.
Maloney, Edward J., 7417 Channahon Ct., Fox Lake, 60020.
Maniola, Francis N., 6135 S. Austin, 60638.
Mannion, William D., 5100 N. Marine Dr., #15A, 60640.
Maraczewski, Edward S., 1516 E. Lowden Ln., Mount Prospect, 60056.
Marszalek, Paul B., Bishop Lyne Residence, 12230 S. Will-Cook Rd., Palos Park, 60464-7332.
Martin, Richard J., 10806 S. Trumbull, 60655.
Maxa, Edward J., 2745 W. 44th St., 60632-1999.
McCarthy, James H., SPRED, 2953 S. Lowe Ave., 60616.
McCarthy, Terrence A., 1301 N. Western Ave., #320, Lake Forest, 60045.
McCarthy, Warren J., 1080 W. Irving Park Rd., Roselle, 60172.
McDonald, Matthew D., Resurrection Life Center, 7370 W. Talcott Ave., Rm. 139, 60631.
McDonnell, Joseph F., 17 W. 706 Butterfield Rd., Oakbrook Terrace, 60181.
McGinnity, Robert F., Sacred Heart, 8245 W. 111th St., Palos Hills, 60465.
McGlinn, Robert J., St. Hyacinth, 1414 W. Becher St., Milwaukee, WI 53215.
McGrath, John F., St. Thomas More, 2825 W. 81st St., 60652.
McHugh, Thomas J., St. Benedict Home, 6930 W. Touhy Ave., Niles, 60714.
McKenna, George P., Bishop Lyne Home, 12230 S. Will-Cook Rd., Palos Park, 60464.
McLaughlin, Edward J., Incarnation, 5757 W. 127th St., Palos Heights, 60463.
McNamara, John P., Bishop Lyne Home, 12230 S. Will-Cook Rd., Palos Park, 60464.
McNulty, William J., 1433 Perry St., #402, Des Plaines, 60016.
Meyer, Charles R., M.A., S.T.D., Mundelein Seminary, University of St. Mary of the Lake, Mundelein, 60060.
Meyr, Herbert J., 1706 N. Broadway, Melrose Park, 60130.
Mikolaitis, Vito E., Bishop Lyne Home, 12230 Will-Cook Rd., Palos Park, 60464.
Militello, Cosmo F., St. Benedict Home, 6930 W. Touhy Ave., Niles, 60714.
Millea, Thomas V., P.O. Box 48623, Niles, 60714.
Moriarty, James F., Bishop Lyne Home, 12230 Will-Cook Rd., Palos Park, 60464.
Mueller, Richard J., 1809 Walters Ave., Northbrook, 60062.
Mulcahy, Gerald F., 8225 Concord Ln., Apt. C, Justice, 60458.
Mulvihill, David J., J.C.D., Ph.D., St. Benedict Nurs & Rehab, 6930 W. Touhy Ave., Rm. 21, Niles, 60714-4522.
Murphy, Harold B., St. Margaret Mary, 2324 W. Chase Ave., 60645.
Murphy, James P., St. Barbara, 4008 Prairie Ave., Brookfield, 60513.
Murray, John W., 1804 N. Riverwoods Dr., Melrose Park, 60160.
Nemecek, Cyril, 2333 S. 8th Ave., North Riverside, 60546.
Nicola, John J., Belle Meade, 400 Waters Dr., Apt. D1-13, Southern Pines, NC 28387.
Novak, Robert J., Addolorata Villa, 553 McHenry Rd., Apt. 271, Wheeling, 60090.
O'Brien, James J., St. Monica, 5136 N. Nottingham Ave., 60656-3696.
O'Brien, John E., Bishop Lyne Home, 12230 Will-Cook Rd., Palos Park, 60464-7332.
O'Brien, Joseph J., 300 N. State St., #2627, 60610.
O'Connor, James T., 447 N. Dover Ave., LaGrange Park, 60526.
O'Donnell, Richard J., 3528 S. Hermitage, 60609.
O'Malley, James F., St. James, 134 North Ave., Highwood, 60040-1522.
O'Malley, Patrick J., M.A., S.T.L., Mundelein Seminary, 1000 E. Maple, Mundelein, 60060.
O'Mara, William T., 9765 Cambridge Cir., Mokena, 60448.
Oldershaw, Robert H., 2244 Sherman Ave., Evanston, 60201.
Ouletta, James F., N2020 County Rd. H., S., Lot 206, Lake Geneva, WI 53147.
Pacocha, Edwin D., 2712 N. Western Ave., 60647.
Pastick, Joseph A., 4939 Floramar Ter., #608, New Port Richey, FL 34652-3310.
Paurazas, Peter P., Maria H.S. Convent, 6727 S. California Ave., 60629.
Peng, John B., c/o Stephanie Leung, 6833 N. Minnetonka, 60646.
Powers, John J., St. Jude the Apostle, 880 E. 154th St., South Holland, 60473.
Powers, Thomas M., St. Benedict Nurs and Rehab Center, 6930 W. Touhy Ave., Niles, 60714.
Pozdol, Henry, Bishop Lyne Residence, 12230 S. Will-Cook Rd., Apt. 107, Palos Park, 60464-7332.
Purtell, Thomas J., St. John Fisher, 10234 S. Washtenaw, 60655.
Reicher, A. Paul, St. John Berchmans, 2517 W. Logan Blvd., 60647.
Riley, Dennis S., 7801 S. Ingleside Ave., 60619-3215.
Roache, James P., P.O. Box 58, Lyons, WI 53148-0058.
Rochford, John J., Bishop Lyne Home, 12230 S. Will-Cook Rd., Palos Park, 60464.
Rodell, Jeremiah J., Devonshire, 1700 Robin Ln., Apt. 424, Lisle, 60532.
Roller, John W., 1400 E. Central Rd., Mount Prospect, 60056.
Rosemeyer, John C., 2550 Mayfair Ave., Westchester, 60154.
Rosemeyer, Paul F., St. Theresa, 467 Benton, Palatine, 60067.
Rudcki, Stanley R., 7712 W. Oak Ridge Ct., #2B, Palos Heights, 60463.
Rudnik, John J., Transfiguration, 2609 W. Carmen Ave., 60625.
Ruiz, Joseph B., Holy Redeemer, 9525 S. Lawndale Ave., Evergreen Park, 60805.
Ryan, John M., 26 N. Pistakee Lake Rd., #2A, Fox Lake, 60020.
Salmon, Edward P., 1045 Columbian Ave., Oak Park, 60302.
Sayers, James M., 155 Vintage Cir., Apt. 204, Naples, FL 34119.
Scanlan, Francis G., St. Damian, 5220 W. 155th St., 60452.
Scarlata, Ronald E., 1577 W. Cadillac Cir., Romeoville, 60446.
Schouten, Francis L., 3755 W. 112th Pl., 60655.
Schroeder, Richard F., 7216 Oxford Cir., Fox Lake, 60020.
Schwab, Thomas E., 9711 W. Devon Ave., Rosemont, 60018.
Seitz, Joseph W., 9131 S. Sacramento, Evergreen Park, 60805.
Shannon, Richard J., 709 79th St., Unit 107, Darien, 60561.
Sheridan, William H., 2132 E. 72nd St., 60649.
Skriba, Raymond F., P.O. Box 455, Mundelein, 60060.
Springer, Lawrence F., 567 W. Algonquin Rd., Des Plaines, 60016.
Stockus, Edward S., 10508 S. Keeler, Oak Lawn, 60453.
Stone, Theodore, 355 S. Crescent, Park Ridge, 60068.
Strand, Ralph S., P.O. Box 455, Mundelein, 60060.
Sullivan, Daniel F., 129 E. Mill St., Apt. 203, Wauconda, 60084.
Sullivan, Daniel J., 3217 W. 184th St., Homewood, 60430.
Szabelski, Joseph R., Queen of Peace Retirement Ctr., 24955 N. Hwy. 12, Lake Zurich, 60047.
Tapper, John W., Mayslake Village, 1725 35th St., #2231, Oak Brook, 60523.
Taylor, Joseph C., 4350 W. Sunnyside Ave., 60630.
Thinnes, John M., 2200 Patriot Blvd., Unit 330, Glenview, 60026.
Thomas, Joseph S., P.O. Box 455, Mundelein, 60060.
Tivy, Thomas A., Resurrection Parish, 2840 W. Nelson, 60618.
Tlapa, Richard J., 6350 S. Taft Ave., Merrillville, IN 46410.
Tuite, Howard A., 700 S. Paulina, #922, 60612.
Vader, Anthony J., Holy Family Villa, 12220 S. Will-Cook Rd., Palos Park, 60464.
Valker, Richard J., St. Norbert, 1809 Walters Ave., Northbrook, 60062.
Vita, Mariano L., 2949 Glacier Tr., Porter, IN 46304.
Wagner, Leon R., 2435 Seabrook Island Rd., John Island, SC 29455.
Walsh, Michael J., Bishop Lyne Home, 12230 S. Will-Cook Rd., Palos Park, 60464.
Weber, Gerard P., Our Lady of Grace, 5011 White Oak Ave., Encino, CA 91436. St. John of God Rtr. and Care Ctr., 2458 S. St. Andrews Pl., #320, Los Angeles, CA 90018.
Welsh, William P., 8340 Callie Ave., #314, Morton Grove, 60053.
White, Bernard C., 3020 N. 76th Ct., Elmwood Park, 60707.
Winters, Martin N., Benedictine Monastery of Our Lady of Sorrows, 5800 W. 147th St., 60452.
Wodniak, John L., 5730 W. Fullerton, 60639.
Wojcik, Richard J., S.T.L., M.C.G., Mundelein Seminary of the University of St. Mary of the Lake, 1000 E. Maple, Mundelein, 60060.
Yadron, Raymond A., 1152 E. Anderson Dr., Palatine, 60074.
Zake, Louis J., Ph.D., 15157 S. Hollyhock Ct., Orland Park, 60462. 310 S. Michigan Ave., Unit 704, 60604.

Permanent Deacons:
Abboud, Louis, St. Patrick, Wadsworth
Adams, Stewart, Immaculate Conception, Highland Park
Aguilar, Ruben, St. Adrian, Chicago
Ahern, Michael, Our Lady of Victory
Albano, Terris, Our Lady of the Ridge, Chicago Ridge
Alcos, Rossini, St. Lawrence O'Toole, Matteson
Allen, Warren, St. Kilian, Chicago
Allison, Andrew, St. Francis, LaGrange
Alonso, Enrique, Our Lady of Grace, Chicago, Office of the Diaconate
Alvarez, Ignacio, St. Gall, Chicago
Alvarez, Jose, St. Aloysius, Chicago
Ambe, Neba, St. Henry, Chicago
Amberg, John, (Retired), Frankfort, IL
Annoreno, August, Our Lady Mother of the Church, Chicago
Antiss, Robert S., Hoffman Estates, IL
Antonsen, Larry, Most Holy Redeemer, Evergreen Park
Arndt, John, (Retired), Evanston, IL
Arvidson, Robert, St. Francis de Sales, Lake Zurich
Askew, James, Our Lady of Humility, Beach Park/Zion
Auld, David D., Santa Maria del Popolo, Mundelein
Avila, Mario, St. Malachy, Chicago
Ayala, Efrain, (Retired), Downers Grove, IL
Baldasti, Steven, St. Hubert, Hoffman Estates
Banet, Robert, St. Andrew the Apostle, Calumet City
Barker, William, Sacred Heart, Palos Hills
Barnish, Michael K., Sacred Heart, Melrose Park
Bartholomew, Thomas, St. Michael, Orland Park
Barton, Jeffrey, Prince of Peace, Lake Villa
Bartos, Gregory, St. George, Tinley Park
Battisto, John, Our Lady of Mount Carmel, Melrose Park
Baum, Richard, Cary, IL
Behrendt, Raymond J., Sacred Heart, Melrose Park
Beierwaltes, Andrew J., St. John Brebeuf, Niles
Beil, Frank, St. Catherine Laboure, Glenview
Belanger, James, (Retired), Mount Prospect, IL
Bell, Kenneth, St. Domitilla, Hillside
Benthey, Herman, St. Anne, Hazel Crest
Bergquist, Bernard, (Retired), Morton Grove, IL
Bertolani, Philip, St. Benedict, Chicago
Beyer, Wayne, Church of Holy Spirit, Schaumburg
Blais, Emile, (Retired)
Blanco, Jesus, St. Ann
Blickle, Calvin, Jr., St. Alphonsus Ligouri, Prospect Heights
Bohannon, Morris E., (Retired), Creve Coeur, MO
Boharic, Robert, St. Mary, Riverside
Boppart, Irwin, Queen of Peace, North Chciago
Borha, George, St. Thomas More, Chicago
Both, Melvyn, St. Cecilia, Mount Prospect
Bouey, Alfred, Our Lady of Sorrows Basilica
Bovyn, Paul, Resurrection, Chicago
Brady, Joseph, St. Christopher, Midlothian
Brauch, Robert, St. Anne, Barrington
Breit, John, St. Thomas of Villanova, Palatine
Brencic, David, St. Barbara, Brookfield
Bresemann, David, St. Joseph, Round Lake
Bretz, Michael, St. Mary, Des Plaines
Brezinski, David, St. John the Evangelist, Streamwood
Brooks, George, Flossmoor, IL
Brothers, David, St. Agnes, Chicago Heights
Brown, Dennis G., St. Patrick, Wadsworth
Bryce, Irvin, St. Albert the Great, Burbank
Buissereth, Rameau, Haitian Catholic Apostolate, Chicago
Bulger, Robert, St. Paul of the Cross, Park Ridge
Bumbul, John, St. Gall, Chicago
Burke, Henry, Ascension/St. Susanna, Harvey
Burns, James, St. Donatus, Blue Island
Burt, John D., (Retired), Chicago, IL
Bzdon, Gregory M., St. Tarcissus, Chicago
Cabrera, Daniel, St. Hedwig
Cabrera, Jorge, St. John Berchmans, Chicago
Camerini, Guilio, St. Eulalia, Maywood
Carerra, Xavier, Holy Spirit, Schaumburg
Carrillo, Martin, St. Joseph, (Hermitage Ave.)
Carrizales, Maximiliano, Providence of God, Chicago
Carroll, Daniel, Orland Park, IL
Carroll, James, (Retired), Holy Cross, Deerfield
Carroll, Robert O., Jr., St. John Fisher, Chicago
Carter, Jeremy N., St. Patrick, Wadsworth
Carvlin, Thomas, Ascension/St. Susanna, Harvey
Casas, Jesus, St. Anthony, Cicero
Cascino, Joseph, Jr., Huntley, IL
Castaneda, David, St. Malachy, Chicago
Cavanaugh, Michael, Ss. Faith, Hope and Charity, Winnetka

Centeno, Benito, (Retired), Pompano Beach, FL
Cervantes, Leopoldo, St. James (Fullerton), Chicago
Chairez, Victor, St. Simeon, Bellwood
Chausse, Joseph, (Retired), St. Francis Borgis; Center for the Deaf, Chicago
Chavez, Abraham, Immaculate Conception, 88th, Chicago
Chrastka, Joel, St. Leonard, Berwyn
Christensen, Thomas, St. Turibius, Chicago
Churilla, William, St. Anne, Hazelcrest
Chyba, Lawrence J., St. Bruno
Ciesil, Norbert, St. Alphonsus, Prospect Heights
Cintron, Gilberto, St. Hedwig, Chicago
Cisneros, Jose, St. Leonard, Berwyn
Cnota, Robert, St. Thecla, Chicago
Cocco, Anthony, St. Michael, Orland Park
Coffey, Thomas W., St. Mary, Riverside
Coleman, Alfred, II, St. Basil/Visitation, Chicago
Colgan, Dennis L., St. William; Office of the Diaconate, Chicago
Collins, Terrence, St. James (Wabash), Chicago
Condill, James, St. Anne, Barrington
Condon, Edward, St. Cornelius, Chicago
Connor, John, (Retired), St. Colette, Rolling Meadows
Contanopolis, Louis, Chicago, IL
Contreras, Mario, Church of the Holy Spirit, Schaumburg
Conway, James, St. Barnabas, Chicago
Conway, William, (Retired), Chicago, IL
Cook, John, St. Felicitas
Cooper, Willie, (Retired), Chicago, IL
Corcoran, Thomas, Our Lady of the Wayside, Arlington Heights
Cordesman, Ellsworth, (Retired), Immaculate Conception, Highland Park
Cornejo, Salvador, (Retired), Chicago, IL
Cozzo, James, Santa Maria Addolorata
Crandall, Robert, (Retired), Our Lady of Ransom, Niles
Crane, Walter James, (Retired), St. Ann, Barrington
Crespo, Feliciano, St. Wencelaus, Chicago
Cunalata, Oswaldo, (Retired), Wooddale, IL
Czarnecki, Thaddeus, Queen of the Rosary, Elk Grove Village
Dahl, Earl, St. John the Evangelist, Streamwood
Dahn, James C., Our Lady, Mother of the Church, Chicago
Dattoli, Dominick, St. George, Tinley Park
Daum, Donald, (Retired), St. Germaine, Oak Lawn
Davis, James, (Retired), St. Martin de Porres, Chicago
Deabel, Raymond, St. James Hospital, Chicago Heights
Debnar, John, (Retired), St. Barbara, Brookfield
DeFiore, Robert, St. John the Evangelist, Streamwood
DeFrank, Frank, (Retired), Sta. Maria del Popolo, Mundelein
Deiters, James, St. Walter, Chicago
Del Llano, Manuel, Our Lady of Mercy, Chicago
DeLarco, Michael, St. Celestine, Elmwood Park
Delgado, Antonio, St. Genevieve, Chicago
DeLorenzo, Edward, Oratorian Community, Divine Providence, Westchester
DeLuna, Arthur, Sta. Maria Addolorata, Chicago
Detloff, James, St. Emeric, Country Club Hills
Devereux, Robert, Our Lady of the Mount, Cicero
Devine, James, St. Bede, Ingleside
DeVita, Frank, (Retired), Divine Providence, Westchester
Diaz, Benjamin, St. Philomena, Chicago
Diaz De Leon, Raymundo, St. Joseph, Summit
DiCanio, Vito W., St. Emily, Mt. Prospect
Dietsch, Daniel, St. Joseph, Homewood
Disparte, Philip, O'Hare Airport Chapel
Dixon, Roscoe B., St. Benedict, Blue Island
Dolan, Edward, St. Juliana, Chicago
Dominguez, Juan
Donovan, Timothy, Old St. Mary's, Chicago
Dorgan, Eugene J., St. Pascal, Chicago
Doud, Raymond, Church of the Holy Spirit, Schaumburg
Drazba, Herbert, St. Jude the Apostle, South Holland
Dubrownik, Phillip, St. Emeric, Country Club Hills
Duderstadt, Peery, Our Lady of the Brook, Northbrook
Duffey, Mark, St. Thomas of Villanova, Palatine
Dulen, John, (Retired), Niles Buffalo Grove, IL
Dunne, Thomas, St. Thomas of Villanova, Palatine
Duszynski, Thomas, St. Matthew, Schaumburg
Dutkiewicz, Daniel, (Retired), St. Stanislaus and Martyr, Posen
Dutko, David, St. Kieran, Chicago Heights
Dwyer, James T., (Retired), Fox Lake, IL
Dwyer, Thomas M., St. Edmund, Oak Park
Echevarria, Ramon, Our Lady of Tepeyac, Chicago
Egan, David, St. Patrick, Wadsworth
Ende, Gilbert, (Lemont Nursing Home)
Enger, Michael, Church of the Holy Spirit, Schaumburg
Engler, William, St. Stephen, Deacon & Martyr, Tinley Park
Ernst, James, Our Lady of Hope, Rosemont
Esposito, Robert, St. Peter Damian, Bartlett
Estrada, Jose M., Our Lady of Guadalupe, Chicago
Ewers, Thomas, St. Denis, Chicago
Faherty, Paul, St. Luke, River Forest
Fair, Davis, Our Lady of Sorrows Basilica, Chicago
Favila, Angel, St. Agnes of Bohemia, Chicago
Fay, John, Sacred Heart, Winnetka
Feltes, Richard, St. Catherine of Alexandria, Oak Lawn
Fernandez, Dismas, St. Maurice, Chicago
Ficker, John, St. George, Tinley Park
Filipucci, Michael, St. Marcelline, Schaumburg
Fitterer, George, (Retired), Evergreen, CO
Flaherty, George, St. Francis DeSales, Lake Zurich
Flanagan, John, St. Germaine, Oak Lawn
Flewellen, James, (Retired), St. Thaddeus, Chicago
Flores, Nicolas, St. Stanislaus Kostka, Chicago
Flores-Zamora, Efrain, (Retired), Santa Maria del Popolo, Mundelein
Foley, Brendan, Our Lady of the Wayside, Arlington Heights
Foti, Francisco, Our Lady of the Snows, Chicago
Fox, Gerald, (Retired), Divine Providence, Westchester
Fragassi, Phillip, St. Patrick, Wadsworth
Fronczek, Casimir, St. Francis Borgia Deaf Center, Chicago
Fruge, James, Immaculate Conception, Highland Park
Furey, James P., St. John the Evangelist, Streamwood
Gadomski, Edward, St. Linus, Oak Lawn
Gagnon, Robert, St. Peter, Antioch
Gallagher, James, (Retired), St. James, Highwood
Garcia, Aurelio, Our Lady of Mercy, Chicago
Garcia, Joe, St. Marcelline, Schaumburg
Garcia, Jorge, Maternity BVM, Chicago
Garcia, Miguel, St. Stanislaus Kostka, Chicago
Garvey, Kevin, Holy Cross, Deerfield
Garza, Juan L., St. Paul, Chicago Heights
Gaughan, James, St. Edna, Arlington Hts.
Gaughan, John, St. Vincent Ferrer, River Forest
Gavin, Raymond, St. Catherine Laboure, Glenview
Gianatasio, Philip, St. Mary of Celle, Berwyn
Gilbert, Paul, St. George, Tinley Park
Gildea, Francis, St. Elizabeth Seton, Orland Park
Gill, Leroy, Jr., Holy Angels, Chicago
Girjatowicz, Frank, Hoffman Estates, IL
Glenn, John, St. Mary of Vernon, Indian Creek
Globis, Richard J., St. Gilbert, Grayslake
Gniech, George, St. Constance, Chicago
Gomez, Juan J., St. Mary Magdalene, Chicago
Gonzalez, Felipe, Maternity, B.V.M., Chicago
Gonzalez, Juan, Resurrection, Chicago
Gonzalez, Oscar, St. Adalbert, Chicago
Graham, William, St. Cecilia, Mount Prospect
Gronek, Ronald, St. Monica, Chicago
Gronkiewicz, Edmund, Our Lady of Mount Carmel, Chicago
Grossnickle, Donald R., Our Lady of the Wayside, Arlington Heights
Gutierrez, Jorge, St. Mark, Chicago
Guzman, Paul, St. John Cantius, Chicago
Hahn, Gerald E., Queen of Apostles, Riverdale
Hahn, Matthew, St. Mary, Buffalo Grove
Han, Sung, Church of the Holy Spirit, Schaumburg
Harris, Wallace, St. Dorothy, Chicago
Hayden, Thomas L., St. Hubert, Hoffman Estates
Helmer, Everett, (Retired), St. Germaine, Oak Lawn
Hennessy, Matthew, St. James, Arlington Heights
Henricks, John, St. Giles, Oak Park
Henry, Francis, Nativity of Our Lord, Chicago
Hensley, Claude, St. Anthony, Cicero
Hernandez, Marcelino, Holy Family, Waukegan
Herrera, Albert, St. Gall, Chicago
Herrera, Armando, Mary Queen of Heaven, Chicago
Herrera, Marcial, Queen of the Universe, Chicago
Hess, Rudolf, Our Lady of Good Counsel
Hill, Edwin, Our Lady of the Ridge, Chicago Ridge
Hill, Kevin D., St. John Brebeuf, Niles
Hinch, Ralph, St. Francis Borgia Deaf Center, Chicago
Hipelius, Thomas, St. Damian, Oak Forest
Hita, Floro, Maternity BVM, Chicago
Horton, James, St. Alexander, Palos Heights
Hotcaveg, Irwin E., St. Ferdinand, Chicago
Howard, Samuel E., Infant Jesus of Prague, Flossmoor
Huber, Charles, St. Francis Borgia, Chicago
Hudzik, Richard F., St. Maria Goretti, Schiller Park
Hyde, Thomas, St. Symphorosa, Chicago
Janega, Robert, Our Lady of Mercy
Janicek, James, St. Michael, Orland Park
Jannotta, Anthony, St. Thomas Becket, Mt. Prospect
Jay, Richard, (Retired), St. Athanasius, Evanston
Jean-Pierre, Fritz, St. Jerome, Chicago
Jeffrey, August, (Retired), Divine Savior, Norridge
Jenney, Kenneth, Jr., St. Monica, Chicago
Jinkens, Max R., Our Lady of Humility, Zion
Johnson, Richard, Our Lady of Mount Carmel, Chicago
Joynt, William, (Retired), Elgin, IL
Kaczmarek, Edward, St. Thomas of Villanova, Palatine
Kalina, David J., Our Lady of Perpetual Help, Glenview
Kalivoda, Bill, Addolorata Villa, Wheeling
Kancler, Lawrence, B.S., M.S., St. Alexius Medical Center
Karnoski, Michael, St. Louis de Montfort, Oak Lawn
Karstenson, William, St.Thomas of Villanova, Palatine
Kashmar, George, St. Joseph, Libertyville
Kasimatis, Jerome, (Retired), Holy Cross, Deerfield
Keating, Timothy, St. Alexander, Palos Heights
Keegan, Charles, St. Patricia, Hickory Hills
Kenney, James, St. Mary, Lake Forest
Kerls, Robert, St. Francis Xavier, Wilmette
Kiley, Michael E., St. Julie Billart, Tinley Park
Knetl, Thomas, Our Lady of Knock, Calumet City
Kocar, Marvin, St. Pius X, Stickney
Kort, Clayton, St. Helena of the Cross, Chicago
Kotleba, Rudolf, Holy Family, Chicago
Kowalski, David J., St. Louise de Marillac, LaGrange Park
Krakora, Joseph, St. Mary, Lake Forest
Krueger, William J., St. Mary, Buffalo Grove
Kudra, Joseph, St. Paul, Chicago, Heights
Kukla, Eugene, St. Mary, Buffalo Grove
Kush, Michael G., (Retired), Deltona, FL
Kwasigroch, James, Our Lady of Grace, Chicago
La Belle, Eugene, St. Kieran, Chicago Heights
LaCoursiere, Victor, St. Jerome, Chicago
LaFleur, Joseph, Prince of Peace, Lake Villa
Lagges, Peter, St. Zachary, Des Plaines
LaMantia, Thomas, St. Marcelline Schaumburg
Lambert, George, (Retired), St. Eulalia, Maywood
Lambert, Thomas, Our Lady of Mt. Carmel, Chicago
Landuyt, Robert, Our Lady of the Ridge, Chicago Ridge
Langwell, James E., Incarnation, Palos Heights
Lara, Luis, Immaculate Conception, Highland Park
Lawson, Richard, St. Hubert, Hoffman Estates
Leck, Robert, (Retired), Our Lady of Victory, Chicago
Lehman, William B., St. Francis Borgia, Chicago
Lekan, Louis, (Retired), St. James, Arlington Heights
Lema, Salvatore, St. Rene Goupil, Chicago
Leonard, Timothy, Prince of Peace, Lake Villa
Leonas, John, St. Anne, Hazel Crest
Lesnieski, Norbert, SS. Cyril & Methodius, Lemont
Liberti, Peter, All Saints-St. Anthony, Chicago
Lilly, Leroy, (Retired), St. Simeon, Bellwood
Limon, Juan, St. Benedict, Blue Island
Lisowski, Thaddeus, St. Constance, Chicago
Llorens, Anthony, St. Martin de Porres, Chicago
Loman, Raymond, St. Patrick, Lake Forest
Long, Gary, St. Mary, Buffalo Grove
Lopez, Adolfo, St. Aloysius, Chicago
Lopez, Efrain, Resurrection, Chicago
Lopez, Sergio, St. Simeon, Bellwood
Lorbach, John, St. Raymond de Penafort, Mt. Prospect
Lubben, William, St. Julie Billiart, Tinley Park
Lucas, John, Jr., St. Patrick, Lake Forest
Luevano, Miguel, St. Barbara, Brookfield
Macarol, John, Our Lady of the Woods, Orland Park
Maddock, George, St. Joseph, Homewood
Madonia, Loretto, St. Bernardine, Forest Park
Mages, William, St. Mary of the Woods, Chicago
Maiers, Donald R., St. Marcelline, Schaumburg
Maldonado, Meliquides, (Retired), St. Mark, Chicago
Malloy, William, Queen of All Saints Basilica
Malone, Jack, St. Germaine, Oak Lawn
Maloney, Thomas J., St. Thomas of Villanova, Palatine
Mamolella, Frank, St. Leonard, Berwyn
Mancilla-Martinez, Jose, Transfiguration, Wauconda
Manning, Peter, St. Joseph, Summit
Marin, Francisco, St. Jerome, Chicago
Marotto, Angelo, (Retired), St. Domitilla, Hillside
Marquez, J. Frank, (Retired), St. Pascal, Chicago
Marrero, Jose, (Retired), St. Roman, Chicago
Marszalek, Theodore D., Our Lady, Mother of the Church, Chicago
Marturano, Leonard, St. Thomas of Villanova, Palatine

Matthews, Robert, St. Joseph, Libertyville
Maune, William, (Retired), St. Irenaeus, Park Forest
McAllister, Dennis F., Our Lady of the Brook, Northbrook
McCloskey, Michael, Holy Name Cathedral, Chicago
McDonnell, Joseph, St. Irenaeus, Park Forest
McDonough, Michael, St. Michael, Orland Park
McElrath, Bruce, St. Ailbe, Chicago
McFarland, Charles, St. Stephen, Deacon and Martyr, Tinley Park
McGorey, Thomas, St. John of the Cross, Western Springs
McGuire, Terrence, St. Alphonsus, Lemont
McIntosh, Scott, St. Peter, Antioch
McKinnis, William, St. Columbanus, Chicago
McLynn, Michael, St. Louis de Marillac, La Grange Park
McMahon, John, St. Bede, Ingleside
McNulty, Michael, Sacred Heart, Winnetka
Meehan, Peter, St. Martha, Morton Grove
Meehan, Thomas, (Retired), Our Lady of Loretto, Hometown
Melton, Edward, Holy Cross, Deerfield
Memmel, Aloysius, St. Paul of the Cross, Park Ridge
Mendez, Genaro, St. Anastasia, Waukegan
Mendieta, Raul, (Retired), Chicago
Mendizabal, Guillermo, St. John Berchmans, Chicago
Mercado, Gilberto, St. Anthony of Padua, Cicero
Merced, Rolando, Transfiguration of Our Lord
Mercure, Michael, Our Lady of Humility, Zion-Beach Park
Metallo, Arthur, St. Francis Hospital, Evanston
Miarka, Gary, St. Turibius, Chicago
Michalowski, Benedict, St. Joseph, Summit
Migala, Paul, St. Marcelline, Schaumberg
Minor, James R., Prince of Peace, Lake Villa
Miska, Richard, St. Terrence, Alsip
Monica, Robert, (Retired), Chicago
Monnelly, Michael, Queen of All Saints, Chicago
Monterroso, Oscar, St. Ansgar, Hanover Park
Moore, Steven, (Retired), St. Anne, Hazel Crest
Mora, Raul, St. Ignatius, Chicago
Moran, Charles, (Retired), St. John the Evangelist, Streamwood
Moreno, Eusebio, St. Joseph, Round Lake
Morgan, Thomas, St. James, Arlington Heights
Moritz, Richard H., Immaculate Conception (Talcott Rd.)
Morowczynski, Romuald, St. Jane de Chantal, Chicago
Morrissey, Henry, St. Leonard, Berwyn
Mudd, Dennis, Holy Family, Waukegan
Mullaney, Roger, St. James, Highwood
Munda, Gary, Sr., Queen of Peace, North Chicago
Munoz, Romeo, (Retired), Calumet City, IL
Munoz, Ubaldo, St. Mary of the Lake
Murphy, Robert, St. Gertrude, Franklin Park
Murray, Michael, (Retired), Our Lady of the Brook, Northbrook
Navarro, Antonio, St. Mark, Chicago
Navarro, Jesse, St. Mary, Star of the Sea, Chicago
Navarro, Ramon, St. Aloysius, Chicago
Neiman, Harold, St. Sabina, Chicago
Neu, Andrew, St. Barnabas
Neurauter, Paul, St. Peter, Antioch
Newhall, Redondo, (Retired), St. Cajetan, Chicago
Newton, Robert, St. Peter Damian, Bartlett
Nguyen, Duc Van, St. Henry, Chicago
Nieves, Bienvenido, Queen of Angels, Chicago
Nimietz, James, (Retired), Chicago, IL
Nolan, John, St. Julian Eymard, Elk Grove Park
Norton, Terrence, St. Luke, River Forest
Norys, Stephen, St. Theresa, Palatine
Nowak, Thomas, St. Agnes, Chicago Heights
Nunez, Raul, Our Lady of Guadalupe, Chicago
Nylen, Arthur A., St. Jude the Apostle, South Holland
O'Donnell, Charles, Our Lady of Ransom, Niles
O'Donnell, Kevin, St. Fabian, Bridgeview
O'Keefe, Robert C., St. Isaac Jogues, Niles
O'Leary, Edward, St. Eugene, Chicago
O'Leary, John A., St. Joseph, Homewood
O'Leary, John C., St. Lambert, Skokie
O'Malley, James, (Retired), Chicago Airports Catholic Chaplaincy
O'Malley, Michael, St. Mary of the Annunciation, Mundelein
O'Neill, John, St. Luke, River Forest
Oborski, Zygfryd, (Retired), St. Stanislaus Bishop & Martyr, Chicago
Ochoa, J. Zeferino, St. Francis of Assisi, Chicago
Ochoa, Jesus, St. Rita, Chicago
Ochsner, Robert, Our Lady of Humility, Beach Park & Zion
Ojeda, Norberto, Sacred Heart, Melrose Park
Olson, Carl, St. Cornelius, Chicago
Omiatek, Marion, Transfiguration, Wauconda
Ontiveros, Philip, St. Julian Eymard, Elk Grove Village
Ortega, Ignacio, (Retired), Fondulac, IL
Ortiz, Eddies, St. Colette, Rolling Meadows
Ortiz, Sigifredo, St. Sylvester, Chicago
Orzechowski, John, Our Lady of the Ridge, Chicago Ridge
Pagliai, Bruno, St. James, Highwood
Pagnotta, Philip, Jr., St. Mary of Vernon, Indian Creek
Palacios, Freddy, Our Lady of Mount Carmel, Melrose Park
Palmer, Donald, St. Joseph (Orleans St.), Chicago
Palmer, Lawrence, Actadena, CA
Panek, Joseph, St. George, Tinley Park
Paskauskas, Vitas, Nativity, B.V.M.
Patino, Daniel, Our Lady of Lourdes
Pauwels, James, St. Edna, Arlington Heights
Pena, Leonardo, Area Hispanic Ministry
Penich, Michael, Jr., St. Paul the Apostle, Gurnee
Pepitone, Joe, St. John of the Cross, Western Springs
Perez, Carlos, (Retired), Chicago, IL
Perez, Luis, Santa Maria Addolorata, Chicago
Perez, Miguel, St. Pius V., Chicago
Perez, Orlando, St. Thomas of Canterbury, Chicago
Perez, Pablo, St. Nicholas of Tolentine, Chicago
Perkowitz, John, (Retired), St. John Brebeuf, Niles
Peters, Bruce, St. Dismas, Waukegan
Peterson, George A., (Retired), Prospect Heights, IL
Pezowicz, Feliks, Transfiguration, Wauconda
Pilarski, Ronald, Mater Christi, North Riverside
Pincich, Samuel, St. Zachary, Des Plaines
Pineda, Javier, St. Frances of Rome, Cicero
Pineda, Rafael, St. Maurice, Chicago
Pizzato, Richard, St. Theresa, Palatine
Platt, James, St. Cyprian, River Grove
Pluchar, Edward, St. Julie Billiart, Tinley Park
Poletto, Robert, St. Mary, Fremont Center, Mundelein
Ponce, Antonio, Our Lady of Charity, Cicero
Porter, John, St. Joseph's Home for the Elderly, Palatine
Pouncy, William, St. Martin de Porres, Chicago
Powers, Robert, St. Anne, Barrington
Principe, Michael, St. Gertrude, Schiller Park
Puhala, Robert A., St. Philip, Northfield
Purdome, Mark J., St. Paul the Apostle, Gurnee
Quackenbush, Edward, (Retired), St. Bede, Ingleside
Ragonese, Dan, St. Victor, Calumet City
Rakauskas, Stanley, St. Christina, Chicago
Ramirez, Juan, St. Bartholomew, Chicago
Ramirez, Rosalio, St. Pius X, Stickney
Ramos, Dennis, St. Aloysius, Chicago
Ramos, Eliseo, St. Jerome
Ramos, Francisco, St. Philomena, Chicago
Rangel, John, St. Lawrence O'Toole, Matteson
Ranola, Rodrigo, St. Isaac Jogues, Niles
Reilly, Raymond, St. John Fisher, Chicago
Reinert, William, St. James, Arlington Heights
Reinhart, James, St. Linus, Oak Lawn
Renwick, James, Holy Ghost, South Holland
Revering, Roman, (Retired), St. Luke School
Revord, James, Our Lady of Perpetual Help, Glenview
Rex, John, St. Damian, Oak Forest
Reyes, David, Immaculate Heart of Mary
Reynolds, Kevin, St. Barbara, Brookfield
Riccio, Louis, St. Theresa, Palatine
Richardson, John, St. Patrick, Wadsworth
Richardson, Lendell, Ascension, Oak Park
Richardson, Leonard M., St. Sabina, Chicago
Riffner, Joseph, (Retired), St. Alphonsus, Chicago
Rios, Jamie, St. Wenceslaus, Chicago
Rittenhouse, Daniel, St. Alphonsus, Lemont
Rivas, Roberto, Immaculate Conception, Chicago
Rivera, Francisco, Resurrection, Chicago
Rivera, Hector, St. Teresa of Avila, Chicago
Robak, Dennis R., St. Mary, Evanston
Robles, Ernesto, Our Lady of Grace, Chicago
Roccasalva, Joseph, St. Cajetan, Chicago
Rodriguez, Antonio, St. Viator, Chicago
Rodriguez, Candelario, St. Procopius, Chicago
Rodriguez, Emiliano, (Retired), Chicago, IL
Rodriguez, Manuel, (Retired), St. Francis of Assisi, Chicago
Rodriguez, Milton, Maternity of B.V.M., Chicago
Rodriguez, Uriol, Resurrection, Chicago
Rodriguez, Wilmer, St. Hedwig
Romano, Francisco, (Retired), Chicago, IL
Romano, Michael, St. Joseph Hospital, Chicago
Rottman, John, St. Thecla
Rozo, Jorge, Holy Rosary, Chicago
Rueth, William, St. Hugh, Lyons
Ruiz, Joel, St. Joseph, Round Lake
Ruiz, Victor, St. Dismas, Waukegan
Ryan, Edward, Our Lady of Knock, Calumet City
Ryan, Robert E., Sr., St. Juliana, Chicago
Ryan, Thomas, St. Christina, Chicago
Rybicki, Lawrence, St. John the Evangelist, Streamwood
Rynkiewicz, Stephen I.
Sacramento, Anthony, St. Dismas, Waukegan
Sanchez, Sabino, St. Francis and Our Lady of the Angels, Chicago
Sanchez, Salvador, St. James, Fullerton Ave., Chicago
Sandoval, Jose M., Immaculate Conception
Sanford, James, St. Emily, Mount Prospect
Santos, Antero, St. Colette, Rolling Meadows
Sanzone, Michael, St. Paul the Apostle, Gurnee
Sassetti, Robert C., St. Vincent Ferrer, River Forest
Sattler, David, St. Peter Damian, Bartlett
Savage, Christopher, Prince of Peace, Lake Villa
Scarbalis, Edward, Holy Family, Waukegan
Schiltz, James, St. Constance, Chicago
Schliesmann, Barry, SS. Faith, Hope and Charity, Winnetka
Schmidt, Paul, St. James, Arlington Heights
Schopp, John E., IV, St. John of the Cross, Western Springs
Schultz, Ronald, (Retired), St. Victor, Calumet City
Schultz, William, St. Stephen, Deacon and Martyr, Tinley Park
Schumacher, Lawrence R., St. Theresa, Palatine
Sedano, Pedro, St. Francis of Assisi, Chicago
Sedivy, Alan, Our Lady of Perpetual Help, Glenview
Seitz, John, (Retired), Knoxville, TN
Serratore, Gregory, St. Mary Star of Sea, Chicago
Seveska, Richard, St. Anne, Barrington
Sheehan, Patrick P., St. James, Arlington Heights
Shinkle, Derald, St. Joseph, Wilmette
Shumpert, Gregory, St. Agatha
Silva, Rodrigo, St. Ann, Chicago
Simmet, Daniel, St. Mary of the Annunciation, Mundelein
Simmons, John, Santa Maria del Popolo, Mundelein
Simola, Edward, St. William, Chicago
Sinacore, James M., St. John Vianney, Northlake
Siranovic, Joseph, St. Domitilla, Hillside
Siska, Thomas, St. John Fisher, Chicago
Skaja, Lawrence, St. John Brebeuf, Niles
Slajchert, Michael, St. Gall, Chicago
Slobig, Robert, St. Luke, River Forest
Smith, John J., St. Zachary, Des Plaines
Smith, Lawrence J., St. Matthew, Schaumburg
Smith, Michael E., St. Christopher, Midlothian
Solon, Thomas, St. Denis, Chicago
Soria, Carlos, (Retired), St. Sylvester, Chicago
Soto, Rogelio, St. Ignatius, Chicago
Soto, Santos, St. Sylvester, Chicago
Spalla, Paul, St. Mary-of-the-Lake, Chicago
Spitizzeri, Fred, (Retired), St. Priscilla, Chicago
Spohr, Lawrence, St. Bede, Ingleside
Springer, Timothy, St. Jude the Apostle, South Holland
Stalcup, Joseph, Sr., St. Stephen, Tinley Park
Stanton, Paul, St. Isaac Jogues, Niles
Stasinski, Melvin, St. Jude the Apostle, South Holland
Stearns, William, St. Damian, Oak Forest
Stecker, Stephen, St. Joseph the Worker, Wheeling
Steinbeigle, Francis, St. Damian, Oak Forest
Strom, Stanley, Holy Name Cathedral, Chicago
Stubstad, Thomas, St. Pascal, Chicago
Sullivan, Dwight, St. Eulalia, Maywood
Sullivan, William, St. Barnabas, Chicago
Sullivan, William, St. Louis de Montfort, Oak Lawn
Sutton, Daniel, (Retired), Oak Lawn, IL
Swiatek, Ronald, St. John Bosco, Chicago
Swiech, Edward, (Retired), Lake Zurich, IL
Szady, Mitchell, (Retired), St. Stanislaus B & M, Chicago
Szarek, John, St. Ansgar, Hanover Park
Tamayo, Mario, St. Nicholas, Evanston
Tatara, Allen, St. Hubert, Hoffman Estates
Taylor, Lowell, (Retired), Church of the Holy Spirit, Schaumburg
Telle, Paul, Holy Family, Waukegan
Telposky, Donald, (Retired), St. Stephen, Des Plaines
Temple, James, St. Barnabas, Chicago
Thompson, Johnathan, St. Peter, Antioch
Tiemeier, David, St. Joseph, Libertyville
Tipperreiter, Charles, St. Fabian, Bridgeview
Tomkowiak, Edward, St. Patrick, Wadsworth
Torres, Francisco, St. Rita of Cascia
Towey, Anthony, St. Stephen Protomartyr, Des Plaines
Trakszelis, Jerome J., St. Vincent Ferrer, River Forest
Trevino, Luis, Chicago-O'Hare International Airport
Truesdale, Joseph, St. Francis of Assisi, Orland Park
Tryjefaczek, Richard, St. Joseph, Summit
Tylutki, Glenn, St. Mary of the Angels, Chicago
Uroza, Jose, (Retired), Schiller Park, IL
Vaeth, Dean G., St. Vincent de Paul, Chicago

Valadez, Abundio, St. Benedict, Blue Island
Valadez, Asuncion, St. Mary of Celle, Berwyn
Valencia, Juan, Epiphany, Chicago
Valentin, Jose, (Retired), Buffalo Grove
Valle, Miguel Angel, St. Genevieve, Chicago
Van Merkestyn, Peter, St. Stephen, Deacon and Martyr, Tinley Park
Vandervest, Roger, Ascension, Oak Park
Vargas, Miguel, Mision San Juan Diego, Arlington Heights
Vazquez, Gilberto, Santa Maria Del Popolo, Mundelein
Vazquez, Jose, Maternity B.V.M., Chicago
Vazquez, Saul, All Saints-St. Anthony
Velasco, Benito, (Retired), Joliet, IL
Vellurattil, Matthew, St. Ladislaus
Vemich, Duke, All Saints-St. Anthony, Chicago
Vidmar, John, Bl. A.M. Slomsek Slovenian Catholic Mission, Lemont
Vignocchi, Louis, Immaculate Conception, Highland Park
Villa, Salvatore, St. Bruno, Chicago
Villalobos, Antonio, St. Mark, Chicago
Villasenor, Faustino, St. Mary, Des Plaines
Virruso, Christopher, Our Lady, Mother of the Church, Chicago
Voytas, Richard, St. Daniel the Prophet, Chicago
Wagner, David, St. Patrick, Wadsworth
Wagner, Steve J., St. Thecla, Chicago
Walsh, Joseph A., Ascension, Oak Park
Walters, John, St. Bernardine, Forest Park
Ward, Raymond, (Retired), Queen of All Saints, Chicago
Warfield, Richard, Little Company of Mary Hospital
Warmouth, William H., St. Stephen Protomartyr, Des Plaines
Wasielak, Peter G., Tucson, AZ
Watson, Dexter, St. Malachy, Chicago
Wegner, Albin J., Jr., St. Michael, Chicago
Wehling, Donald, St. Hilary, Chicago
Weiner, Ronald, St. Ferdinand, Chicago
Weitendorf, Norbert, St. Patricia, Hickory Hills
Welter, Daniel G., J.D., St. Josaphat, Chicago
Werner, Richard, Sacred Heart, Palos Hills
White, Philip, St. Eulalia, Maywood
Wilkinson, John, St. James at Sag Bridge, Lemont
Willer, Richard, St. Thomas of Villanova, Palatine
Wills, James, St. Peter, Skokie
Winblad, Joseph, St. Patrick, Lemont
Winter, Edward, St. Lawrence O'Toole, Matteson
Wogan, James, St. Mary of Vernon, Indian Creek
Wundsam, Michael E., St. Zachary, Des Plaines
Zadruzny, Wieslaw, (Retired), St. Pancratius, Chicago
Zanardo, Ronald, (Retired), St. Lawrence O'Toole, Matteson
Zaragoza, Luis, Mission San Juan Diego, Arlington Heights
Zawadzki, Kenneth, St. Stephen, Deacon & Martyr, Tinley Park
Zeimys, Erik, Nativity of Our Lord, Chicago
Zeller, John, St. Marcelline, Schaumburg
Zielinski, Ronald, St. Fabian, Bridgeview
Zima, Robert, (Retired), Lake in the Hills
Zimmerman, Edward, (Retired), Springhill, FL
Zurawski, John, St. John Vianney, Northlake
Zwolski, Mark, St. Mary of Vernon, Mundelein
Zych, Gerald, St. Cyprian, River Grove

INSTITUTIONS LOCATED IN THE ARCHDIOCESE

[A] SEMINARIES, ARCHDIOCESAN

CHICAGO. *St. Joseph College Seminary*, The Seminary College at Loyola University, 6551 N. Sheridan Rd., 60626. Tel: 773-973-9700; Fax: 773-973-9718. Email: jpresta@luc.edu. Web: www.stjoseph.luc.edu. Priests 5; Lay Teachers 6; Enrollment 32.

Seminary Administration: Very Rev. James Presta, S.T.L., S.T.D., Rector-Pres.; Revs. Peter Snieg Jr., S.T.L., Vice Rector & Dean, Formation; Laurence F. Maddock, S.T.L., Spiritual Dir. (Retired); Duy Cao, D.Min. (Cand.), Dir. Liturgy; David J. Stagaman, S.J., Academic Dean; Gerald G. Walsh, M.Div., Asst. Vocation Dir.

Full-Time Faculty: Mr. John A. Houlihan, M.A., M.S., J.D., Dir. Information Technologies; Mrs. Maria Anabella Mora, M.A., Academic Admin., Spanish; Very Rev. James Presta, S.T.L., S.T.D., Theology.

Part-Time Faculty: Rev. Britto Berchmans, Ph.D., Communications; Dr. Brian DuSell, D.M.A., Music Instructor; Revs. Timothy R. Fiala, S.T.L., Theology; Henry C. Kricek, M.A., S.T.L., Philosophy; Dr. William Joseph Napiwocki, Ph.D., Latin Instructor.
Administrative Staff: Mrs. Yuvanka Zavala-Juarez, B.A., Fin. Aid Admin., Human Resources Mgr., Student Business Mgr.; Ms. Pamela Ferrarini, Quigley Alumni Office; Ms. Carol Mackie, Accounts Mgr.; Ms. Diana Kozojed, Dir., Institutional Advancement Office; Ms. Mary Katherine Minogue, Office of Institutional Advancement; Ms. Debra Puce, Grant Writer; Mrs. Sally Walsh, Sec. to the Rector; Sr. Vivian Johnson, B.S., Receptionist.

MUNDELEIN. *University of St. Mary of the Lake/ Mundelein Seminary*, 1000 E. Maple Ave., 60060-1174. Tel: 847-566-6401; Fax: 847-566-7330. Email: rector@usml.edu. Web: www.usml.edu. Priests 32; Sisters 1; Lay Teachers 9; Students 185.

Administration: Very Rev. Dennis J. Lyle, S.T.D., Rector, Pres.; Revs. August J. Belauskas, M.A., S.T.L., Vice Rector; Thomas A. Baima, M.B.A., S.T.D., Vice Pres. & Provost; Raymond J. Webb, S.T.L., Ph.D., Vice Pres. & Academic Dean; Kevin J. Feeney, M.A.S., D.Min. (Cand.), Vice Pres. & Dean of Formation; John G. Lodge, S.S.L., S.T.D., Pres., Ecclesiastical Faculty; Martin Zielinski, M.Div., Ph.D., Vice Pres. Ongoing Formation; Mr. John Lehocky, C.P.A., M.B.A., Vice Pres. Finance; Mr. Stanley C. Rys, M.B.A., Vice Pres. Facilities; Mr. Mark J. Teresi, CFRE, Vice Pres. Institutional Advancement; Rev. Robert Fedek, Canonical Recorder.

Faculty: Revs. Peter Damian Akpunonu, S.S.L., S.T.D., Prof., (Extern); Thomas A. Baima, M.B.A., S.T.D., Prof.; Martin Barnum, D.Min., Assoc. Dean of Formation; Dr. Melanie Barrett, S.T.L., Ph.D., S.T.D. (Cand.), Asst. Prof; Revs. Robert E. Barron, M.A. (Phil.), S.T.D., Prof.; August J. Belauskas, M.A., S.T.L., Assoc. Dean of Formation; Jacque B. Beltran, S.T.B., D.Min. (Cand.), Assoc. Dean of Formation; Patrick J. Boyle, S.J., M.A., Ph.L., S.T.L., Ph.D., Assoc. Prof.; Ms. Linda Cerabona, M.A., Dir. of Music; Revs. Christopher Ciomek, D.Min. (Cand.), Assoc. Dean of Formation; Emery de Gaal, Dipl. Theol., Ph.D., Chairperson & Assoc. Prof, (Extern); John T. Dillon, S.J., M.A., M.Ed., Spiritual Dir.; John V. Dolciamore, J.C.L., S.T.L., Professor Emeritus (Retired); Mr. Thomas Dougherty, B.A., Dir., ESL; Revs. Kevin J. Feeney, M.A.S., D.Min. (Cand.), Dean of Formation; Thomas R. Franzman, Chief Campaign & Stewardship Officer; Michael J.K. Fuller, S.T.D. (RCK), Chairperson & Asst. Prof.; W. Scott Hebden, S.T.D., Asst. Prof.; Philip Timko, O.S.B., Paluch Prof. Theology; Lawrence R. Hennessey, M.A., S.T.L., Ph.D., Prof.; Dr. Paul Hilliard, Ph.D., Asst. Prof.; Revs. Ronald T. Kunkel, S.T.D. (Cand.), Instructor; John G. Lodge, S.S.L., S.T.D., Assoc. Prof.; Very Rev. Dennis J. Lyle, S.T.D., Assoc. Prof.; Rev. Douglas A. Martis, Ph.D., S.T.D., Dir. & Assoc. Prof.; Dr. Christopher McAtee, D.Min., Asst. Academic Dean; Rev. James P. McIlhone, S.T.L., Ph.D., Chairperson, Assoc. Academic Dean & Prof.; Dr. Denis R. McNamara, Ph.D., Asst. Dir., Liturgical Institute; Rev. Charles R. Meyer, M.A., S.T.D., Prof. Emeritus (Retired); Sr. Kathleen Mulchay, S.S.C.M., M.Ed., M.A.P.S., Assoc. Dean of Formation; Dr. Elizabeth Nagel, S.S.D., Prof.; Rev. Edward T. Oakes, S.J., Ph.D., Assoc. Prof.; Ms. Lorraine Olley, M.A.Div., M.A.L.S., Library Dir.; Revs. Patrick J. O'Malley, M.A., S.T.L., Spiritual Dir. (Retired); Alberto Rojas, M.Div., D.Min. (Cand.), Assoc. Dean Formation; Robert L. Schoenstene, M.A., S.S.L. (JOL), Asst. Prof.; Daniel S. Siwek, S.T.L., Instructor; John S. Szmyd, M.Div., S.T.B., Assoc. Dean of Formation & Dir. of Liturgy; Raymond J. Webb, S.T.L., Ph.D., Prof., Dir. Pastoral Internships; Mrs. Kathleen Wiskus, M.A., D.Min., Assoc. Dean of Formation; Revs. Richard J. Wojcik, S.T.L., M.C.G., Prof. Emeritus (Retired); Martin Zielinski, M.Div., Ph.D., Assoc. Prof.

Convent Tel: 847-970-4827; Fax: 847-566-7330. Sr. Doris Monter, Supr. Oblate Sisters of Jesus the Priest 4.

The Liturgical Institute, 1000 E. Maple Ave., 60060. Tel: 847-837-4542; Fax: 847-837-4545. Web: www.liturgicalinstitute.org. Rev. Douglas A. Martis, Ph.D., S.T.D., Dir.; Dr. Denis R. McNamara, Ph.D., Asst. Dir.

Ministerial and Continuing Education, 1000 E. Maple Ave., 60060-1174. Tel: 847-970-4860; Fax: 847-970-4818. Rev. Thomas A. Baima, M.B.A., S.T.D., Cardinal's Liaison.

Diaconate Formation Program, 1000 E. Maple Ave., 60060-1174. Tel: 847-837-4563; Fax: 847-837-4565. Deacon Robert A. Puhala, Dir.; Rev. Dennis Stafford, Dir. Spiritual Formation; Anne Chrzan, Assoc. Dir.

Instituto De Liderazgo Pastoral (Hispanic Programs for Lay Ministry and Permanent Diaconate), 1000 E. Maple Ave., 60060-1174. Tel: 847-837-4556; Fax: 847-837-4565. Mr. Jaime Bascunan, M.S., Dir.; Rev. Carlos Monsalve, O.C.D. (Colombia), Dir. Spiritual Formation; Sr. Marguerite Bukowska, Assoc. Dir. Instituto de Liderazgo Pastoral.

Lay Ministry Formation Programs, 1000 E. Maple Ave., 60060-1174. Tel: 847-837-4550; Fax: 847-837-4565. Graziano Marcheschi, Dir.

Conference Center, 1000 E. Maple Ave., 60060-1174. Tel: 847-837-4505; Fax: 847-837-4505. Rev. Thomas A. Baima, M.B.A., S.T.D., Dir.; Carol Rose, Mgr. Guest Svcs.; Richard Arnold, Mgr. Event Planning.

Ongoing Formation, 1000 E. Maple Ave., 60060-1174. Tel: 847-837-4558; Fax: 847-837-4565. Rev. Martin Zielinski, M.Div., Ph.D., Dir.; Ms. Lorraine Olley, M.A.Div., M.A.L.S., Library Dir.

[B] SEMINARIES, RELIGIOUS OR SCHOLASTICATES

CHICAGO. *The Catholic Theological Union at Chicago*, 5401 S. Cornell Ave., 60615. Tel: 773-371-5400; Fax: 773-324-8490. Email: presoffice@ctu.edu. Web: www.ctu.edu. Major Seminary. Serving the following: Franciscans, Servites, Passionists, Augustinians, Norbertines, Society of the Divine Word, Missionaries of the Precious Blood, Claretians, Crosier Fathers, Spiritans, Sacred Heart Missionaries, Viatorians, Comboni Missionaries, Franciscans Capuchins, Sacred Heart Fathers and Brothers, Congregation of the Blessed Sacrament, Columban Missionaries, Redemptorist Fathers, Oblates of Mary Immaculate, Xaverian Missionaries, Maryknoll Missionaries, Conventual Franciscans, Oratorians, Scalabrinians, Discalced Carmelites, Vincentians Priests 15; Sisters 7; Lay Teachers 7; Lay Administrators 14; Non-Catholic Clergy 2; Students 508.

Administration: Revs. Donald Senior, C.P., S.T.D., Pres.; Gary L. Riebe-Estrella, S.V.D., Vice Pres. & Academic Dean; Mr. Michael W. Connors, C.P.A., Vice Pres. Admin. & Finance; Ms. Anne Marie Tirpak, Dir. Devel.; Ms. Kathy Van Duser, Dir. Admissions & Recruitment; Ms. Vanessa White, M.T.S., Dir. Augustus Tolton Prog.; Ms. Sheila McLaughlin, Dir. Bernardin Center; Sr. Maria Hughes, A.S.C., Dir. Institute for Rel. Formation; Rev. Terrence M. Johnson, Dir. Hesburgh Center, Continuing Formation in Min.; Mrs. Maria de Jesus Lemus, Registrar; Carlos Salmeron, Dir. Romero Prog.; Sr. Barbara Blesse, O.P., Dir. Israel Study Prog.; Ms. Keiren O'Kelly, Dir. Continuing Education and Extension Education; Mr. Terrence Stadler, Dir. Emmaus Prog.; Mr. Brian Murphy, Vice Pres. External Rels.; Ms. Elizabeth White, Dir. Public Information & Media Rels.

Faculty: Mr. Michel Andraos, Ph.D., Assoc. Prof. Cross Cultural Ministry; Mr. Scott C. Alexander, Ph.D., Assoc. Prof of Islam & Dir. Catholic Muslim-Studies; Rev. Claude-Marie Barbour, S.T.D., Prof. World Mission; Sr. Dianne Bergant, C.S.A., Ph.D., Prof. Old Testament Studies; Rev. Stephen B. Bevans, S.V.D., Prof. Mission & Culture; Sisters Barbara Bowe, R.S.C.J., Th.D., M.Div., Dir. M.Div. Program & Prof. Biblical Studies; Laurie A. Brink, O.P., Asst. Prof. of Biblical Studies; Carmen Nanko-Fernandez, Dir. Field Educ. & Asst. Prof. Pastoral Ministry; Sr. Eleanor Doidge, L.O.B., D.Min., Dir., M.A.P.S. Prog. & Assoc. Prof. Cross Cultural Ministry; Mr. Edmund Kee-Fook Chia, Ph.D., Asst. Prof. Doctrinal Theology; Mr. Richard E. McCarron, Ph.D., Assoc. Prof. Liturgy; Revs. Richard Fragomeni, Ph.D., Assoc. Prof. Liturgy & Preaching; Edward Foley, O.F.M.Cap., D. Min. Dir. & Prof. Liturgy & Music; Archimede Fornasari, M.C.C.J., Ph.D., Senior Research Fellow, Ethics; Ms. Mary Frohlich, Ph.D., Assoc. Prof. Spirituality & Dir. M.A. Prog.; Revs. Anthony Gittins, C.S.Sp., Ph.D., Prof. Catholic Missiology; vanThanh Nguyen, S.V.D., Asst. Prof. New Testament; James C. Okoye, C.S.Sp., Prof. of Biblical Studies; Gilbert Ostdiek, O.F.M., S.T.D., Prof. of Liturgy; John M. Pawlikowski, O.S.M., Ph.D., Dir. Catholic-Jewish Studies, Prof. of Ethics; Sisters Barbara Reid, O.P., Ph.D., Prof. New Testament Studies; Dawn Nothwehr, O.S.F., Ph.D., Assoc. Prof. of Ethics; Revs. Gary L. Riebe-Estrella, S.V.D., Vice Pres. & Academic Dean, Assoc. Prof Practical Theology & Hispanic Ministry; Robin Ryan, C.P., Ph.D., Dir. Catholics on Call & Assoc. Prof. Systematic Theology; Robert Schreiter, C.PP.S., Th.D., Prof. Systematic Theology; Roger P. Schroeder, S.V.D., Prof. Cross-Cultural Ministry; Donald Senior, C.P., S.T.D., Pres. & Prof. of New Testament Studies; Gilberto Cavazos-Gonzales, O.F.M., S.L.T., Assoc. Prof. Spirituality; Rabbi David Sandmel, Ph.D., Crown-Ryan Chair, Assoc. Prof., Jewish Studies; Eileen Crowley, Ph.D., Asst. Prof., Word & Worship; Amanda Quantz, Ph.D., Asst. Prof., History of World Christianity; C. Vanessa White, Asst. Prof. Spirituality & Dir. Augustus Tolton Prog.

[C] COLLEGES AND UNIVERSITIES

CHICAGO. *De Paul University*, One E. Jackson Blvd., 60604. Tel: 312-362-8000; Fax: 312-362-6606. Web: www.depaul.edu. Revs. Dennis H. Holtschneider, C.M., Pres.; John T. Richardson, C.M., Chancellor;

Edward R. Udovic, C.M., Senior Exec. Univ. Mission, Sec.; Dr. Helmut P. Epp, Provost; Mr. Robert L. Kozoman, Exec. Vice Pres. Sponsored by the Congregation of the Mission (Vincentian Fathers and Brothers)., Campuses: Downtown, Lincoln Park, Oak Forest, O'Hare, Naperville, Rolling Meadows. Faculty 825; University Staff 1,377; Students 24,352.

Administrative Officers of the University: Mr. Jose D. Padilla, Vice Pres. and General Counsel; Mr. Jeff Bethke, Treas.; Mr. James R. Doyle, Vice Pres. Student Affairs; Ms. Bonnie Hirsch, Vice Pres. Finance; Mr. Robert Janis, Vice Pres. Facilities Operations; Dr. David Kalsbeek, Senior Vice Pres. Enrollment Mgmt. & Mktg.; Mr. Robert McCormick, Dir. Information Svcs.; Mr. William Seithel, Vice Pres. Human Resources; Ms. Jay Braatz, Senior Exec., Presidential Opers.; Ms. Mary C. Finger, Senior Vice Pres., Advancement; Mr. David Lively, Vice Pres. Devel.; Mr. J. D. Bindenagel, Vice Pres. Community, Government & Intl. Affairs; Ms. Elizabeth Ortiz, Vice Pres. Institutional Diversity & Equity; Mrs. Patricia O'Donoghue, Vice Pres. Alumni Engagement & Outreach; Ms. Cheryl Procter-Rogers, Vice Pres. Public Rels. & Communications; Rev. Edward R. Udovic, C.M., Sr. Exec. Univ. Mission & Vice Pres. Teaching & Learning Resources.

College of Liberal Arts and Sciences, 990 W. Fullerton Ave., Ste. 4200, 60614. Tel: 773-325-7310; Fax: 773-325-7304. Dr. Charles S. Suchar, Dean.

College of Law, 931 Lewis Center, 25 E. Jackson Blvd., 60604. Tel: 312-362-8701; Fax: 312-362-5826. Hon. Warren Wolfson, Interim Dean.

College of Commerce, Kellstadt Graduate School of Business, 7103 DePaul Center, One E. Jackson Blvd., 60604. Tel: 312-362-6783; Fax: 312-362-6677. Dr. Ray Whittington, Dean.

College of Communication, 14 E. Jackson Blvd., Ste. 1800, 60604. Dr. Jacqueline Taylor, Dean.

School of Music, 200 Music Bldg., 804 W. Belden, 60614. Tel: 773-325-7260; Fax: 773-325-7263. Dr. Donald E. Casey, Dean.

School for New Learning, 212 Lewis Center, 25 E. Jackson Blvd., 60604. Tel: 312-362-8001; Fax: 312-362-8809. Dr. Marisa Alicea, Interim Dean.

College of Computing and Digital Media, CDM Center 401, 243 S. Wabash Ave., 60604-2302. Tel: 312-362-8381; Fax: 312-362-6116. Dr. David Miller, Dean.

The Theatre School, 214 Theatre School Bldg., 2135 N. Kenmore Ave., 60614. Tel: 773-325-7917; Fax: 773-325-7920. Mr. John Culbert, Dean.

School of Education, 458 Schmitt Academic Center, 60614. Tel: 773-325-7740; Fax: 773-325-7713. Dr. Paul Zionts, Dean.

Jesuit Community at Loyola University Chicago, 6324 N. Kenmore, 60660. Tel: 773-508-8800; Fax: 773-508-2098. Web: www.luc.edu. Revs. Paul Tango Abomo, S.J.; Robert J. Araujo, S.J.; Raymond C. Baumhart, S.J.; Peter J. Bernardi, S.J.; Robert L. Bireley, S.J.; Mark G. Bosco, S.J.; Marco Bran-Flores, S.J.; Robert J. Braunreuther, S.J.; Pawel W. Brozyniak, S.J.; William E. Creed, S.J.; John D. Cunningham, S.J.; Justin Daffron, S.J.; John T. Dillon, S.J., M.A., M.Ed.; Patrick Dorsey, S.J.; Keith J. Esenther, S.J.; Michael J. Garanzini, S.J.; David A. Godleski, S.J., Acting Rector; Daniel F. Hartnett, S.J.; Brendan Horan, S.J.; Steven F. Hurd, S.J.; Charles Jurgensmeier, S.J.; John J. Kilgallen, S.J.; Steven E. Kimmons, S.J.; Stephen T. Krupa, S.J.; Tuan Le, S.J.; Mark J. Link, S.J.; Patrick J. McAteer, S.J.; John M. McManamon, S.J.; Keith F. Muccino, S.J.; Paul R. Mueller, S.J.; Kafarhire Murhula, S.J.; James G. Murphy, S.J.; John J. O'Callaghan, S.J.; Thomas E. Oguagua, S.J.; Peter Otieno Omollo, S.J.; T. Jerome Overbeck, S.J.; Sajeev Painunkal, S.J.; Eduardo Pinzon Umana, S.J.; Lawrence Reuter, S.J.; Donald F. Rowe, S.J.; J. Michael Sparough, S.J.; David J. Stagaman, S.J.; Martin J. Schreiber, S.J.; Arturas Sederevicius, S.J.; Christoph Soyer, S.J.; John E. Surette, S.J.; Robert J. Thesing, S.J.; Thomas H. Tobin, S.J.; Deepak Toppo, S.J.

The Jesuit Community Corporation at Loyola University Priests 40.

**Loyola University-Chicago*, 6631 N. Sheridan Rd., 60660. Tel: 312-915-6000; 773-274-3000; Fax: 312-915-8501. Web: www.luc.edu.

Loyola University of Chicago, Illinois Total University Enrollment 15,879; Total Full-Time Faculty 1,394; Total Staff 1,521.

President's Office, 820 N. Michigan Ave., 60611. Tel: 312-915-6400; Fax: 312-915-6414. Web: www.luc.edu. Michael R. Quinlan, Bd. Chm.; Rev. Michael J. Garanzini, S.J., Pres.; Dr. Paul K. Whelton, M.D., M.Sc., Pres. & CEO, Loyola Univ. Medical Center; Mr. Jonathan Heintzelman, Vice Pres. Advancement; Dr. Robert Kelly, Vice Pres. Student Devel.; Dr. John Hardt, Asst. to the Pres. Mission & Identity; Prof. Christine M. Wiseman, J.D., Provost; Mr. Philip D. Hale, Vice Pres., Public Affairs; Mr. Phil Kosiba, Vice Pres., Facilities; Mr. Tom Kelly, Vice Pres. Human Resources; Dr. Richard S. Hurst, Dir. Inst. Research; Mr. Paul Roberts, Assoc. Provost Enrollment Mgmt., Graduate & Professional Enrollment Mgmt.; Ms. Lori Greene, Dir. Undergraduate Admissions; Mr. Eric Weems, Dir. Student Financial Assistance; Ms. Claire Korinek, Dir. Registration & Records; Ms. Diane Hullinger, Asst. Dir. Registration and Records; Mr. Warren Hale, Dir. Residence Life; Dr. Robert Seal, Dean of Libraries; Ms. Kelly M. Shannon, Vice Pres. University Mktg. & Communications; Mr. Eugene Grotbeck, University Controller; Mr. William Laird, Vice Pres. Finance & CFO; Mr. Wayne Magdziarz, Vice Pres. & Chief of Staff; Mrs. Ellen Kane Munro, Vice Pres. & Gen. Counsel.

The following are the Schools and Colleges which compose the University:

The College of Arts and Sciences (1870) 6525 N. Sheridan Rd., 60626. Tel: 773-508-3500; Fax: 773-508-3514. Dr. Francis Fennell, Dean.

The School of Law (1908) 25 E. Pearson St., 60611. Tel: 312-915-7120; Fax: 312-915-7201. David Yellen, Dean.

The Stritch School of Medicine (1909) 2160 S. First Ave., Maywood, 60153. Tel: 708-216-3223; Fax: 708-216-4305. Dr. Richard Gamelli, Dean.

School of Social Work (1914) 820 N. Michigan Ave., 60611. Tel: 312-915-7005; Fax: 312-915-7645. Dr. Jack Wall, Dean.

School of Professional Studies, 820 N. Michigan Ave., 60611. Tel: 312-915-6501; Fax: 312-915-6508. Dr. Jeffrey Rosen, Dean.

The School of Business Administration (1922) 820 N. Michigan Ave., 60611. Tel: 312-915-6113; Fax: 312-915-6118. Mr. Abol Jalilvand, Dean.

The Graduate School (1926) 6525 N. Sheridan Rd., 60626. Tel: 773-508-3396; Fax: 773-508-2460. Dr. Samuel Attoh, Dean.

The School of Nursing (1935) 6525 N. Sheridan Rd., 60626. Tel: 773-508-3249; Fax: 773-508-3241. Dr. Vicki Keough, Dean.

The School of Education (1969) 820 N. Michigan Ave., 60611. Tel: 312-915-6800; Fax: 312-915-6660. Dr. David Prasse, Dean.

School of Communication (2008) 820 N. Michigan Ave., 60611. Tel: 312-915-6548; Fax: 312-915-8593. Dr. Donald Heider, Dean.

St. Joseph's Seminary, 6551 N. Sheridan Rd., 60626. Tel: 773-973-9700; Fax: 773-973-9718. Rev. David J. Stagaman, S.J., Academic Dean.

Saint Xavier University, 3700 W. 103rd St., 60655-3105. Tel: 773-298-3000; Fax: 773-779-9061. Web: www.sxu.edu. Judith A. Dwyer, Ph.D., Pres.; Mark A. Vargas, Librarian. Sponsorship: Institute of the Sisters of Mercy of the Americas., Campus locations: Chicago, Orland Park & Chicago Bar Association. Priests 2; Sisters 5; Faculty 187; Staff 480; Students 5,680.

Administrative Officers of the University: Rev. Francis S. Tebbe, O.F.M., D.Min., Vice Pres., Office of the Pres. & Sec. of the Corporation; Angela Durante, Ph.D., Provost; Steven J. Murphy, Ed.D., Vice Pres., University Advancement; John P. Pelrine Jr., M.P.S., Vice Pres., Student Affairs; Robert C. Tenczar Jr., B.A., Vice Pres., University Rels.; Kathleen Carlson, Ph.D., Vice Pres., University Research, Planning & Assessment; Calvin J. Williams, M.L.S., Vice Pres., Information Resources & Technologies; Sr. Susan M. Sanders, R.S.M., Ph.D., Vice Pres., University Mission & Heritage; Susan Landy Piros, M.B.A., Vice Pres., Business & Finance.

College of Arts and Sciences Tel: 773-298-3091; Fax: 773-298-3872. Kathleen Alaimo, Ph.D., Dean.

School of Nursing Tel: 773-298-3701; Fax: 773-298-3704. Kay Thurn, Psy.D., R.N., Interim Dean.

Graham School of Management Tel: 773-298-3600; Fax: 773-298-3610. James D. Brodzinski, Ph.D., Dean.

School of Education Tel: 773-298-3200; Fax: 773-298-3201. S. Beverly Gulley, Ph.D., Dean.

School for Continuing and Professional Studies Tel: 708-802-6205; Fax: 708-802-6202. Leslie M. Petty, Ed.D., Dean.

The Bishop John R. Gorman Institute Tel: 708-802-6200; Fax: 708-802-6202.

RIVER FOREST. *Dominican University (Formerly Rosary College)*, 7900 W. Division St., 60305. Tel: 708-366-2490; Fax: 708-524-5990. Email: webmaster@email.dom.edu. Web: www.dom.edu. Dr. Donna M. Carroll, Pres.; Sr. Elwyn McHale, O.P., Prioress; Dr. Norman Carroll, Provost.

Dominican University Dominican Sisters of Sinsinawa, WI. Priests 1; Sisters 5; Lay Teachers 91; Total Enrollment 2,900.

Rosary College of Arts and Sciences at Dominican University Tel: 708-524-6816; Fax: 708-524-5990. Dr. Jeffrey Carlson, Dean.

School of Business Tel: 708-524-6826; Fax: 708-524-6939. Dr. Molly Burke, Dean.

School of Education Tel: 708-524-6830; Fax: 708-524-6665. Sr. Colleen McNicholas, Dean.

Graduate School of Library and Information Science Tel: 708-524-6472; Fax: 708-524-6657. Dr. Prudence Dalrymple, Dean.

Graduate School of Social Work Tel: 708-366-3463; Fax: 708-366-3446. Dr. Vimala Pillari, Dean.

Institute for Adult Learning Tel: 708-714-9125; Fax: 708-714-9126. Bryan Watkins, Exec. Dir.

[D] HIGH SCHOOLS, PRIVATE

CHICAGO. *Brother Rice High School*, 10001 S. Pulaski Rd., 60655-3356. Tel: 773-429-4300; Fax: 773-779-5239. Email: kwalczak@brrice.org. Web: www.brrice.org. Bro. Karl J. Walczak, C.F.C., Pres.; Mr. James P. Antos, Prin.; Ms. Beverly Buciak, Librarian. Congregation of Christian Brothers. Priests 1; Brothers 8; Lay Teachers 62; Students 1,027.

Christ the King Jesuit College Preparatory School, 5088 W. Jackson Blvd., 60644. Tel: 773-261-7505; Fax: 773-261-7507. Email: cdevron@ctkjesuit.org. Web: www.ctkjesuit.org. Rev. Christopher Devron, S.J., Pres.; Brendan Conroy, Prin. Participant in the Cristo Rey Work/Study Program, Inc. Priests 1; Sisters 1; Lay Teachers 11; Students 165.

Cristo Rey Jesuit High School, Inc., 1852 W. 22nd Pl., 60608. Tel: 773-890-6800; Fax: 773-890-6801. Email: jgartland@cristorey.net. Web: www.cristorey.net. Rev. James G. Gartland, S.J., Pres.; Patricia Garrity, Prin.; Diane Madrid-Limon, Librarian. Priests 2; Sisters 1; Brothers 1; Scholastics 2; Lay Teachers 26; Students 535.

Cristo Rey Work / Study Program, Inc., 1852 W. 22nd Pl., 60608. Tel: 773-890-6800; Fax: 773-890-6880. Carlos De La Rosa, Dir.

De La Salle Institute

De La Salle Institute Brothers of the Christian Schools.

Institute Campus for Young Men, 3455 S. Wabash Ave., 60616. Tel: 312-842-7355; Fax: 312-842-4142. Email: webmaster@dls.org. Web: www.dls.org. Rev. Paul M. Novak, O.S.M., Pres.; Mr. James Krygier, Prin. Brothers 2; Lay Teachers 55; Students 713.

Lourdes Hall Campus for Young Women, 1040 W. 32nd Pl., 60608. Tel: 773-650-6800; Fax: 773-650-9722. Email: webmaster@dls.org. Web: www.dls.org. Rev. Paul M. Novak, O.S.M., Pres.; Ms. Diane Brown, Prin.; Sr. Josita Krzeminski, Campus Min.; Mrs. Patricia Kozubowski, Librarian.

St. Francis de Sales High School, 10155 S. Ewing Ave., 60617. Tel: 773-731-7272; Fax: 773-731-7888. Email: info@sfdshs.org. Web: www.sfdshs.org. Mary Kay Ramirez, Prin. Lay Teachers 22; Students 310.

Gordon Tech High School, 3633 N. California Ave., 60618-4602. Tel: 773-539-3600; Fax: 773-539-9158. Email: ehowe@gordontech.org. Web: www.gordontech.org. Revs. Joseph Malczyk, C.R.; Donald Zinn, C.R.; Bro. Ed Jaszkowski, C.R.; Daniel Antosz, Prin.; Mr. John Muellner, Librarian. Priests 2; Brothers 1; Lay Teachers 32; Students 496. In Res. Revs. Martin Bratek, C.R.; Edward Jaskula, C.R.; Joseph Korabik, C.R.

**Hales Franciscan High School, Inc.*, 4930 Cottage Grove Ave., 60615. Tel: 773-285-8400; Fax: 773-285-7025. Robert Anderson, Pres.; Ms. Avis Wright, Acting Prin.; Friar Johnpaul Cafiero, O.F.M., D.Min., M.A., M.Div., Dir. Campus Ministry; Revs. Phil D. Hogan, O.F.M., Coord. Student Activities & Special Programs; David Rodriguez, O.F.M., M.F.A., Fine Arts & Theology Chair; Bro. Fred Smith, O.F.M., Mgr. Bookstore. Priests 3; Brothers 1; Lay Teachers 28; Students 400.

Hales Services, Inc., 4930 S. Cottage Grove, 60615. Tel: 773-285-8400, Ext. 255; Fax: 773-285-7025. Sylvia Lottie, Dir.

Holy Trinity High School, 1443 W. Division St., 60622. Tel: 773-278-4212; Fax: 773-278-0144. Email: cszumilas@holytrinity-hs.org. Web: www.holytrinity-hs.org. Mr. Timothy Bopp, Pres.; Ms. Charlene Szumiles, Prin.; Ms. Lynne Wexler, Librarian. Brothers of Holy Cross. Priests 2; Sisters 2; Lay Teachers 29; Students 418.

St. Ignatius College Prep, 1076 W. Roosevelt Rd., 60608-1594. Tel: 312-421-5900; Fax: 312-421-7124. Email: brian.paulson@ignatius.org. Web: www.ignatius.org. Revs. Brian G. Paulson, S.J., Pres.; Patrick A. Fairbanks, S.J., Rector; Dr. Catherine A. Karl, Ph.D., Prin.; Revs. Richard W. Anderson, S.J., Faculty Chap.; Joseph T. Brennan, S.J.; Ross Pribyl, S.J.; James S. Vorwoldt, S.J.; Ms. Carla Hickey, Librarian. Priests 3; Sisters 1; Lay Teachers 99; Students 1,360.

St. Ignatius Jesuit Community, 1025 W. Taylor, 60607. Tel: 312-829-2297; Fax: 312-829-9552.

Revs. Patrick A. Fairbanks, S.J., Rector; Joseph T. Brennan, S.J., High School Counselor; Louis E. Busemeyer, S.J., Assoc. Pastor; James Chambers, S.J., Hospital Chap.; John P. Coakley, S.J., Hospital Chap.; James J. Creighton, S.J., Hospital Chap.; John R. Crocker, S.J., Retreat Dir.; Philip J. Grib, S.J., Assoc. Pastor; Robert I. Grib, S.J., Assoc. Pastor; Eugene J. Nevins, S.J., Hospital Chap.; Brian G. Paulson, S.J., Pres.; Ross Pribyl, S.J., High School English Teacher; James F. Vorwoldt, S.J., High School Art Teacher. Priests 16.

Josephinum Academy, 1501 N. Oakley Blvd., 60622. Tel: 773-276-1261; Fax: 773-292-3963. Email: martha.roughan@josephinum.org. Web: www.josephinum.org. Sr. Martha Roughan, R.S.C.J., Prin.; Nancy Rowley, Librarian.

Josephinum, Inc., Middle School and High School (Grades 6-12) Sisters 3; Lay Teachers 19; Girls 150.

Leo High School, 7901 S. Sangamon, 60620. Tel: 773-224-9600; Fax: 773-224-3856. Email: admin@leohighschool.org. Web: www.leohighschool.org. Mr. Robert W. Foster, Pres.; Mr. Peter W. Doyle, Prin. Boys 322.

Maria High School (Formerly St. Casimir Academy), 6727 S. California Ave., 60629. Tel: 773-925-8686; Fax: 773-925-8885. Email: maria-hs@archchicago.org. Web: www.mariahighschool.org. Wendy Lynn, Pres.; Margaret Hayes, Prin.; Pamela Hovan, Librarian. Sisters of St. Casimir. Sisters 2; Lay Teachers 21; Students 252.

Marist High School, 4200 W. 115th St., 60655-4306. Tel: 773-881-5300; Fax: 773-881-0595. Email: laurencell.karen@marist.net. Web: www.marist.net. Bro. Patrick McNamara, F.M.S., Pres.; Larry N. Tucker, Prin. Brothers 5; Sisters 1; Lay Teachers 113; Students 1,797.

Marist Brothers Tel: 773-881-5300; Fax: 773-881-0595. Bro. Richard J. Carey, F.M.S., Pres.; Larry N. Tucker, Prin.

Mother McAuley Liberal Arts High School, 3737 W. 99th St., 60655. Tel: 773-881-6500; Fax: 773-881-6562. Email: cmelone@mothermcauley.org. Web: www.mothermcauley.org. Dr. Christine M. Melone, Pres. & Prin.; Ms. Patricia McGreal, Librarian. Sisters of Mercy. Sisters 3; Lay Teachers 91; Students 1,408.

Mt. Carmel High School, 6410 S. Dante Ave., 60637. Tel: 773-324-1020; Fax: 773-324-9235. Email: cmarkelz@mchs.org. Web: www.mchs.org. Carmelites.

Res.: 6401 S. Harper Ave., 60638. Revs. Benjamin Aguilar, O.Carm.; Carl J. Markelz, O.Carm., Prin.; Daniel Carroll, O.Carm. (Retired); Mark Kwiecien, O.Carm.; Peter McGarry, O.Carm. Carmelites in Residence 5; Lay Teachers 65; Students 850.

St. Patrick High School, 5900 W. Belmont Ave., 60634. Tel: 773-282-8844; Fax: 773-282-2361. Web: www.stpatrick.org. Bro. Konrad Diebold, F.S.C., Pres.; Dr. Joseph Schmidt, Prin.; Mr. Jeffrey Troxell, Asst. Prin.; Ms. Marilyn Wenzel, Librarian.

St. Patrick High School Brothers of the Christian Schools. Brothers 3; Lay Teachers 70; Students 850.

Resurrection High School, 7500 W. Talcott Ave., 60631. Tel: 773-775-6616; Fax: 773-775-0611. Email: hs.resurrection@archchicago.org. Web: www.reshs.org. Dr. Lynne Saccaro, Pres. & Prin.; Ms. Mary Klemundt, Librarian. Sisters of the Resurrection. Sisters 3; Lay Teachers 50; Girls 700.

St. Rita of Cascia High School, 7740 S. Western Ave., 60620. Tel: 773-925-6600; Fax: 773-925-2451. Email: strita@stritahs.com. Web: www.stritahs.com. Rev. Thomas R. McCarthy, O.S.A., Pres.; Mrs. Sally Deenihan, Prin.; Mrs. Robyn Kurnat, Librarian.

St. Rita of Cascia High School Corporation, (See Section N for Monastery listing) Priests 4; Brothers 3; Sisters 3; Lay Teachers 45; Students 731.

St. Rita of Cascia High School Foundation, 7740 S. Western Ave., 60620. Tel: 773-925-6600; Fax: 773-925-2451. Email: mgallagher@stritahs.com. Mike Gallagher, Dir. Office of Institutional Advancement.

St. Rita of Cascia High School Facilities, Inc., 7740 S. Western Ave., 60620. Tel: 773-925-6600; Fax: 773-925-2451.

St. Scholastica Academy, 7416 N. Ridge Blvd., 60645. Tel: 773-764-5715; Fax: 773-764-0304. Web: www.scholastica.us. Loretta A. Namovic, Pres.; Mr. Ronald Hoover, Prin.; Mr. Russell Kracke, Librarian. Sisters 4; Lay Teachers 29; Students 250.

Convent, 7430 N. Ridge Blvd., 60645. Tel: 773-764-2413; Fax: 773-761-5131.

ARLINGTON HEIGHTS. *St. Viator High School*, 1213 E. Oakton St., 60004. Tel: 847-392-4050; Fax: 847-392-8305. Email: megan@saintviator.com. Web: www.saintviator.com. Revs. Robert M. Egan, C.S.V., Pres.; Corey D. Brost, C.S.V.; Daniel R. Hall, C.S.V.; Arnold E. Perham, C.S.V.; John E. Van Wiel, C.S.V.; Bros. James E. Leonard, C.S.V.; Rob Robertson, C.S.V.; Daniel J. Tripamer, C.S.V.; Eileen Manno, Prin.; Cheryl Quinn, Librarian. Clerics of St. Viator. Priests 5; Brothers 3; Lay Teachers 89; Students 1,058.

BURBANK. *St. Laurence High School, Inc.*, 5556 W. 77th St., 60459. Tel: 708-458-6900; Fax: 708-458-6908. Email: vikings@stlaurence.com. Web: www.stlaurence.com. Thomas J. Ondria, Pres.; James C. Muting Jr., Prin.; Laura Baldwin, Librarian. Congregation of Christian Brothers. Priests 1; Brothers 3; Lay Teachers 43; Students 687.

Queen of Peace High School (Girls)., 7659 S. Linder Ave., 60459. Tel: 708-458-7600; Fax: 708-458-5734. Email: info@queenofpeacehs.org. Web: www.queenofpeacehs.org. Dr. Kathleen Hanlon, Ph.D., Pres./Prin.; Ms. Stacy Kolack, Asst. Prin. Student Life; Ms. Natalie Formica, Asst. Prin. Student Svcs.; Ms. Barbara Smith, Asst. Prin. & Dir. Technology Integration. Lay Teachers 47; Students 500.

CHICAGO HEIGHTS. *Marian Catholic High School*, 700 Ashland Ave., 60411. Tel: 708-755-7565; Fax: 708-756-9758. Email: mchsinfo@marianchs.com. Web: www.marianchs.com. Sisters Judine Hilbing, O.P., Pres.; Kathleen Anne Tait, O.P., Prin.; Mrs. Susan Silander, Librarian. Dominican Sisters (Springfield, IL). Sisters 13; Lay Teachers 85; Students 1,505.

LAGRANGE PARK. *Nazareth Academy*, 1209 W. Ogden Ave., La Grange Park, 60526. Tel: 708-354-0061; Fax: 708-354-0109. Email: dvondrasek@nazarethacademy.com. Web: www.nazarethacademy.com. Ms. Deborah Vondrasek, Prin.; Mr. Dennis Moran, Pres.; Vera Beggs, Librarian. Congregation of St. Joseph. Sisters 2; Lay Teachers 47; Students 787.

LAKE FOREST. *Woodlands Academy of the Sacred Heart*, 760 E. Westleigh Rd., 60045-3298. Tel: 847-234-4300; Fax: 847-234-4348. Email: admission@woodlandsacademy.org. Web: www.woodlandsacademy.org. Mr. Gerald Grossman, Head of School; Ms. Madonna L. Edmunds, Prin.; Ms. Ellen Hines, Librarian. Religious of Sacred Heart. Sisters 1; Lay Teachers 24; Students 173.

LEMONT. *Mt. Assisi Academy*, 13860 Main St., 60439. Tel: 630-257-7844; Fax: 630-257-6362. Sr. Mary Francis Werner, O.S.F. Sisters of St. Francis of Christ the King. Sisters 5; Lay Teachers 30; Students 219.

MUNDELEIN. *Carmel Catholic High School*, One Carmel Pkwy., 60060. Tel: 847-566-3000; Fax: 847-566-8465. Email: (name)@carmelhs.org. Web: www.carmelhs.org. Judith Mucheck, Ph.D., Pres.; Lynne Strutzel, M.A., Prin.; Jay Hoffmann, Chm. Bd. Dirs. Sisters 2; Lay Teachers 80; Students 1,410.

NILES. *Notre Dame College Prep.* (Boys), 7655 Dempster St., 60714. Tel: 847-965-2900; Fax: 847-965-2975. Web: www.nddons.org. Revs. John P. Smyth, Pres.; Raymond F. Klees, Exec. Vice Pres.; Mr. Joseph Gurdak, Exec. Chair; Mr. Charles McNulty, CFO; Mr. Daniel Tully, Prin.; Mr. Scott L. Dutton, Asst. Prin. Academics; Mr. Timothy M. Jarotkiewicz, Asst. Prin. Student Life; Mr. Richard Balentine, Dir. Campus Ministry; Ms. MaryAnn Malartsik, Business Mgr.; Mr. Michael Hennessey, Dir. Athletics; Rev. Richard Conyers, C.S.C.; Mrs. Veronica Price, Librarian. Priests 3; Sisters 1; Lay Teachers 56; Students 830.

OAK PARK. *Fenwick High School*, 505 Washington Blvd., 60302. Tel: 708-386-0127; Fax: 708-386-3052. Email: admin@fenwickfriars.com. Web: www.fenwickfriars.com. Rev. Richard C. LaPata, O.P., Assoc. Dir. Devel. & Alumni; Dr. James Quaid, Prin.; Revs. William J. Bernacki, O.P.; Joseph Ekpo; DePorres C. Durham, O.P., Pres.; Michael A. Winkels, O.P.; Bros. Gabriel J. Dault, O.P.; R. Douglas-Adam Greer, O.P.; Andrew McAlpin, O.P.; Ms. Mary Pat Ryan, Librarian. Dominican Order. Dominican Order Priests 3; Dominican Brothers 2; Diocesan Priests 1; Lay Teachers 81; Students 1,177.

RIVER FOREST. *Trinity High School*, 7574 W. Division St., 60305. Tel: 708-771-8383; Fax: 708-488-2014. Web: www.trinityhs.org. Sr. Michelle Germanson, O.P., Pres.; Antonia C. Bouillette, Prin. Dominican Sisters (Sinsinawa, WI). Sisters 1; Lay Teachers 38; Students 521.

RIVER GROVE. *Guerin College Preparatory High School*, 8001 Belmont Ave., 60171. Tel: 708-453-6233; Fax: 708-453-6296. Email: nnolan@guerinprep.org. Web: www.guerinprep.org. Sr. Nancy Nolan, S.P., Pres.; Mrs. Bonnie Brown, Prin.; Bro. John Ptaszek, C.S.C., Librarian. Sisters of Providence. Sisters 9; Lay Teachers 61; Students 700.

SOUTH HOLLAND. *Seton Academy*, 16100 Seton Dr., 60473-1899. Tel: 708-333-6300; Fax: 708-333-1534. Email: seton@seton-academy.org. Web: www.seton-academy.org. Richard Hussmann, Pres.; Norma Guzman, Prin.; Earl McKay, Dean; Elizabeth Starczewski, Campus Min. Lay Teachers 20; Students 300.

WAUKEGAN. *St. Martin de Porres High School*, 515 S. Martin Luther King Jr. Ave., 60085. Tel: 847-623-5500; Fax: 847-623-5604. Email: grattin@smdpwaukegan.org. Web: www.smdpwaukegan.org. Mr. George Rattin, Pres.; Mr. Michael Odiotti, Prin.; Sr. Judy Seiberlich, O.P., Asst. Prin.; Arthur Jones, Dean Students.

SMDP Work Study, Inc., 501 S. Martin Luther King Jr. Ave., 60085. Tel: 847-244-6895; Fax: 847-244-8237. Email: jmaloney@smdpwaukegan.org. Web: www.smdpwaukegan.org.

WESTCHESTER. *St. Joseph High School*, 10900 W. Cermak Rd., 60154-4299. Tel: 708-562-4433; Fax: 708-562-4459. Email: dkiel@stjoeshs.org. Web: stjoeshs.org. Mr. David McCreery, Pres.; Ms. Donna Keil, Prin. Brothers of the Christian Schools. Lay Teachers 48; Students 850.

WILMETTE. *Loyola Academy*, 1100 Laramie Ave., 60091-1021. Tel: 847-256-1100; Fax: 847-251-4031. Web: www.goramblers.org. Revs. Patrick E. McGrath, S.J., Pres.; Richard H. McGurn, S.J., Rector; Mr. Patrick Mahoney, Athletic Dir.; Ms. Mary MacLean Kearney, Ed.D., Dean of Academics; Ms. Margaret Culhane, Dean of Students; Mr. David McNulty, D.C., Vice Prin. & Pres. Academic & Student Affairs; Mr. Terence K. Brennan, Vice Pres. & CFO; Rev. Paul J. Faulstich, S.J., Registrar; Geryl Cerney, Controller. Priests 9; Brothers 1; Lay Teachers 180; Students 2,000.

Regina Dominican High School, 701 Locust Rd., 60091. Tel: 847-256-7660; Fax: 847-256-3726. Email: mpachucki@rdhs.org. Web: www.rdhs.org. Sr. Mary Margaret Pachucki, O.P., Pres.; Kathy Rzany, Prin. Sisters of St. Dominic (Adrian, MI)., (Catholic School for Women) Sisters 7; Lay Teachers 29; Students 356.

[E] ELEMENTARY SCHOOLS, PRIVATE

CHICAGO. *Chicago Jesuit Academy, at Resurrection Campus*, 5058 W. Jackson Blvd., 60644-4324. Tel: 773-638-6103; Fax: 773-638-6107. Email: info@cjacademy.org. Web: www.cjacademy.org. Revs. Richard H. McGurn, S.J., Jesuit Dir.; Richard L. Millbourn, S.J., Jesuit Dir.; Patrick E. McGrath, S.J., Jesuit Dir.; Matthew Lynch, Pres.; Dr. Kevin Zajdel, Prin.; Mr. David Diehl, Dean, Students; Ms. Catherine Cassidy, Vice Pres. Operations & Devel. Operated by the Chicago Province of the Society of Jesus. Full-scholarship, college-prep Roman Catholic, Jesuit middle school for boys of modest economic backgrounds from Chicago's west side; serving 80, 5th, 6th, 7th & 8th grade boys; 12-student learning groups; extended academic day; 11-month school year; prepares young men for success in the college-prep high schools, universities and community leadership; high school scholarship support available for alumni. Total Staff 17; Total Assisted Annually 80.

The Frances Xavier Warde School, 120 S. Des Plaines St., 60661-3515. Tel: 312-466-0700; Fax: 312-466-0711. Email: fxw@fxw.org. Web: www.fxw.org. Ms. Mary Reiling, Head of School; Mrs. Erin Horne, Prin., Old St. Patrick Campus (Grades K-3); D. Michael Veitch, Prin. Holy Name Campus (Grades 4-8). Lay Teachers 80; Students 815.

Sacred Heart Schools (Academy of the Sacred Heart for Girls, Hardey Prep. for Boys), (Grades K-8), 6250 N. Sheridan Rd., 60660-1730. Tel: 773-262-4446; Fax: 773-262-6178. Email: sacred.heart@shschicago.org. Web: www.shschicago.org. Mr. Nat Wilburn, Head Schools; Mrs. Mary Ann Ligon, Head of Lower School, (Grades 3-5); Mrs. Christine Elliott, Head of Middle School, (Grades 6-8); Ms. Meg Steele, Head of Primary School, (Grades K-2); Mrs. Jean Brunder, Library Media Specialist. Religious of the Sacred Heart. Lay Teachers 80; Students 680.

San Miguel Febres Cordero School, Inc., 1949 W. 48th St., 60609-4145. Tel: 773-890-0233 (Administrative Office); Fax: 773-890-0250 (Administrative Office). Email: info@sanmiguelchicago.org. Web: www.sanmiguelchicago.org. Bro. Edwin Dupre, F.S.C.; Michael Anderer-McClelland, Pres. & Exec. Dir.; Caprice Smalley, Prin. Gary Comer Campus; Kate Seche, Co-Prin. Back of the Yards Campus;

Ted Smith, Co-Prin. Back of the Yards Campus. Operated by DeLaSalle Christian Brothers. Gratuitous Catholic Middle School with two campuses for at risk youth; adult education (ESL, financial mgmt., and computer skills); after school and evening youth development programs, ages 11-18; parenting skills classes. Mentoring, tutoring retreat opportunities, and support to graduates who study in high school. Total Staff 53; Total Assisted Annually 1,481.

LEMONT. *Everest Academy of Lemont, Inc.*, 14911 127th St., 60439. Tel: 630-243-1995; Fax: 630-243-1988. Email: mbrackett@wpasite.com. Web: www.whitepinesacademy.org. Rev. Jose F. Ortega, L.C., Sec. & Treas. Total Staff 16; Priests 2; Lay Teachers 14; Total Assisted Annually 58.

[F] CONSOLIDATED ELEMENTARY SCHOOLS

CHICAGO. *Bridgeport Catholic Academy*, 3700 S. Lowe, 60609. Tel: 773-376-6223. Mrs. Lillian Buckley, Prin. Serving the following parishes: All Saints-St. Anthony (518 W. 28th Pl.); Nativity of Our Lord (653 W. 37th St.). Lay Teachers 10; Students 200.

[G] CATHOLIC CHARITIES

CHICAGO. *Catholic Charities of the Archdiocese of Chicago-Archdiocesan Offices*, 721 N. LaSalle St., 60654. Tel: 312-655-7000; Fax: 312-655-0219. Web: catholiccharities.net. Rev. Michael M. Boland, Pres. & CEO; Mr. J. Antonio Fernandez, Sr. Vice Pres. Operations; Rev. Charles T. Rubey, Assoc. Dir. Programs (Retired); Ms. Kathy Donahue, Sr. Vice Pres. Programs; Cynthia Smetana, CFO; Revs. Roger J. Coughlin, Assoc. Admin. (Retired); Richard E. Bulwith, Assoc. Admin.; Gerard P. Kelly, C.M., Staff Chap.; Francis A. Cimarrusti (Retired); Charles T. Rubey (Retired); Wayne F. Watts, Assoc. Admin. Administers charitable activities of the Archdiocese.

Administration:

Civic and Public Affairs, 721 N. LaSalle St., 60654. Tel: 312-655-7908; Fax: 312-655-0219. John Ryan, Chief of Staff.

Development, 721 LaSalle St., 60654. Tel: 312-655-7289; Fax: 312-655-0605. Judith M. Silekis, Dir.

Facilities Operations, 721 N. LaSalle St., 60654. Tel: 312-655-7435; Fax: 312-266-7146. Sandra DeSico, Dir.

Finance, 721 N. LaSalle St., 60654. Tel: 312-655-7326; Fax: 312-266-4276. Elida Hernandez, Dir.

Human Resources, 721 N. LaSalle St., 60654. Tel: 312-651-2077; Fax: 312-831-1321. Ed Guerrero, Dir.

Advocacy Services, 721 N. LaSalle, 60654. Tel: 312-655-7314; Fax: 312-266-6556. Laurie Barretto, Dir.

Legal and Compliance Services, 721 N. LaSalle, 60654. Tel: 312-655-7538; Fax: 312-654-0849. Michele Bianchi, Sr. Vice Pres.

Board Relations, 721 N. LaSalle St., 60654. Tel: 312-655-7171; Fax: 312-930-0425. Anne Grosklaus, Dir.

Communications, 721 N. LaSalle St., 60654. Tel: 312-655-7010; Fax: 312-930-0425. Kristin Ortman, Dir.

Research and Quality Improvement, 721 N. LaSalle, 60654. Tel: 312-655-7592; Fax: 312-266-2142.

Veterans Affairs, 651 W. Lake St., 60661. Tel: 312-655-7138; Fax: 312-648-1034. Rodney Bowling, Dir.

Cook County Regional Services:

Chicago Services, 721 N. LaSalle St., 60654. Tel: 312-655-7298; Fax: 312-948-6974. Arlene Jackson-Ervin, Regl. Svcs. Rep.

North Suburban Services, 1717 Rand Rd., Des Plaines, 60016. Tel: 847-376-2100; Fax: 847-390-8214. Mary Beth Hartmann, Regl. Svcs. Rep.

Northwest Suburban Services, 1717 Rand Rd., Des Plaines, 60016. Tel: 847-376-2100; Fax: 847-390-8214. Glenn Van Cura, Regl. Svcs. Rep.

South Suburban Services, 16100 Seton Dr., South Holland, 60473. Tel: 708-333-8379, Ext. 222; Fax: 708-333-9519. Frederick Shannon, Regl. Svc. Rep.

Southwest Suburban Services, 7000 W. 111th St., Worth, 60482. Tel: 708-586-1355; Fax: 708-430-0502. Jeff Sims, Regl. Svc. Rep.

West Suburban Services, 1400 S. Austin Blvd., Cicero, 60804. Tel: 708-329-4022; Fax: 708-222-1491. Dalia Rocotello, Regl. Svc. Rep.

Lake County Regional Services:

Joseph Cardinal Bernardin Center for Lake County Services, 671 S. Lewis Ave., Waukegan, 60085. Tel: 847-782-4000; Fax: 847-782-1040. Teresa Denny, Community Liaison & Business Mgr.

Division of Community Development and Outreach Services:

Division Office, 721 N. La Salle, 60654. Tel: 312-655-7508; Fax: 312-642-9716. Angel Gutierrez, Vice Pres.

Commodity and Food Supplemental Program (CFSP), 4940 W. Flournoy, 60644. Tel: 773-378-6643; Fax: 773-261-0536. Eliu Irizarry, Prog. Dir.

Mother and Child Food and Nutrition Program (MAC), 4940 W. Flournoy, 60644. Tel: 773-378-3127; Fax: 773-261-0536. Eliu Irizarry, Prog. Dir.

Mother and Child Food and Nutrition (MAC) Warehouse, 1965 W. Pershing Rd., 60608. Tel: 773-523-0299. Emil Atoyebi, Program Dir.

Women Infant Children Food Centers Program, 4624 W. Diversey, 60639. Tel: 312-951-7672; Fax: 773-205-1271. William Abi Rached, Program Dir. WIC Food Centers: 416 E. 43rd St., Chicago, IL 60653; 6202 S. Halsted St., Chicago, IL 60621; 2310 W. Roosevelt Rd., Chicago, IL 60608; 5332 S. Western, Chicago, IL 60609; 3110 W. Armitage, Chicago, IL 60647; 4500 W. Chicago Ave., Chicago, IL 60651 WIC Warehouse; 1643 W. Cermak Rd., Chicago, IL 60608; 1734 W. Chicago Ave., Chicago, IL 60622; 3932 W. Madison St., Chicago, IL 60624; 5125 W. Chicago, Chicago, IL 60651; 1802 E. 71st St., Chicago IL 60649; 11255 S. Michigan Ave., Chicago, IL 60628; 4622 W. Diversey Ave., Chicago, IL 60639; 8959 S. Commercial Ave., Chicago, IL 60617; 2400 S. Kedzie Ave., Chicago, IL 60623 and 1106 W. 79th St., Chicago, IL 60620.

Division of Family and Parish Support Services:

Division Office, 651 W. Lake St., 60661. Tel: 312-655-7305; Fax: 312-648-1034. Veronica Glodowski, Vice Pres.; Bob Haennicke, Assoc. Mgr.; Eileen Higgins, Assoc. Mgr.

Addiction Consultation and Educational Services, 651 W. Lake St., 60661. Tel: 312-655-7453. Mary Ellen Flynn, Prog. Dir.

Casa Catalina, 4533-37 S. Ashland Ave., 60609. Tel: 312-655-7299.

Central Information and Referral Services, 651 W. Lake St., 60661. Tel: 312-655-7700; Fax: 312-655-0678. Maureen Flamm, Prog. Dir.

Central States Institute of Addiction, 651 W. Lake St., 60661. Tel: 312-655-7530; Fax: 312-266-9027. Kevin J. Doyle, Dept. Dir.

Community Family Service Center, 1100 S. May, 60607. Tel: 312-733-5661, Ext. 1467; Fax: 312-733-5211. Sandra Villwocks, Prog. Dir.

Cooke's Manor Transitional Housing For Men, Bldg. 14 Hines VA Campus, 5th Ave. & Roosevelt Rd., Hines, 60141. Tel: 708-273-6627; Fax: 708-343-4469. Rev. Richard E. Bulwith, Chap.; Rodney Bowling, Dir.

Emergency Assistance Department, 721 N. LaSalle St., 60654. Tel: 312-655-7500; Fax: 312-654-9861. Christene Dykes-Sorrells, Prog. Dir.

Community Casework and Counseling, 641 W. Lake St., 60661. Tel: 312-655-7299; Fax: 312-879-0208. Pam Davis, Dept. Dir.

Forever Free, 6212 S. Sangamon, 60621. Tel: 773-374-8165; Fax: 773-548-4522. Sharon Love Williams, Prog. Dir. Tel: 773-548-9500; Fax: 773-548-4522; Mary Kelly, Prog. Dir.

Archdiocesan AIDS Ministry Office, 651 W. Lake St., 60661. Tel: 312-948-6500; Fax: 312-879-0208. Patricia Drott, Program Dir.

Holbrook Center for Counseling and Psychotherapy, 641 W. Lake St., 60661. Tel: 312-655-7719; Fax: 312-655-0678. Linda Hoag, Program Dir.

Lake County HIV/AIDS Case Management, 671 S. Lewis, Waukegan, 60085. Tel: 847-782-4144; Fax: 847-782-4133. John Turner, Program Dir.

Immigration & Naturalization Services, 651 W. Lake St., 60661. Tel: 312-382-2707; Fax: 312-427-3130. Nancy Gavilanes, Prog. Dir.

Refugee Resettlement Program, 651 W. Lake St., 60661. Tel: 312-655-7856; Fax: 312-879-0208. Elmida Kulovic, Prog. Dir.

LOSS (Loving Outreach to Survivors of Suicide), 651 W. Lake St., 60661. Tel: 312-655-7283; Fax: 312-559-1530. Bruce Engle, Coord.

Joseph Cardinal Bernardin Family Shelter Program, 651 W. Lake St., 60661. Tel: 312-655-7700; Fax: 773-483-5301. Jackie Huckabee, Dept. Dir.

St. Francis de Paula Interim Housing, 7811 S. Ellis, 60619. Tel: 773-487-8615; Fax: 773-651-0582. Jean Stratton, Supvr.

St. Susanna Shelter Apartments, 14926 S. Honore, Harvey, 60426. Tel: 708-331-8211; Fax: 708-339-4398. Derrolyn Steele, Supvr.

Madonna House, 1114 W. Grace St. Tel: 773-327-1605; Fax: 773-248-1497. Mary Fuqua, Admin.

New Hope Apartments, 651 W. Lake St., 60661. Tel: 312-651-2007; Fax: 312-906-8265. Eileen Higgins, Dept. Dir.

Lake County Samaritan House, 671 S. Lewis Ave., Waukegan, 60085. Tel: 847-782-4000; Fax: 847-782-4133. Joyce Molett, Supvr.

North/Northwest Suburban Family Shelter Program, 1717 N. Rand Rd., Des Plaines, 60016. Tel: 847-376-2100; Fax: 847-390-8214. Millicent Ntiamoah, Dir.

Homelessness Prevention Call Center, 721 N. LaSalle St., 60610. Tel: 312-698-5070; Fax: 312-655-0678. Sandra Murray, Program Dir.

Legal Assistance, 651 W. Lake St., 60610. Tel: 312-948-6983; Fax: 312-475-9039.

Streets to Home, 651 W. Lake St., 60661. Tel: 312-655-7554; Fax: 312-879-0208. Jackie Huckabee, Program Dir.

Division of Child, Youth and Family Services:

Division Office, 651 W. Lake St., 60661. Tel: 312-655-7646; Fax: 312-879-0293. Laura Rios, Vice Pres.

Chicago Lawn Childhood Center, 3001 W. 59th St., 60629. Tel: 773-925-1085; Fax: 773-925-1170.

Childhood Development Programs, Day Care/Head Start, 721 N. LaSalle St., 60610. Tel: 312-655-7875; Fax: 312-255-0068.

Child Welfare Counseling and Therapeutic Services, 651 W. Lake, 60661. Tel: 312-655-7191; Fax: 312-236-5384. Asela Paredes, Dept. Dir.

Cordi-Marian Childhood Center, 1100 S. May St., 60607. Tel: 312-666-3787; Fax: 312-666-3562.

Grace Mission Childhood Center, 5332 S. Western Ave., 60609. Tel: 773-476-1990; Fax: 773-476-2421.

Our Lady of Lourdes Childhood Center, 1449 S. Keeler, 60623. Tel: 773-521-3126; Fax: 773-522-3753.

Intact Family Services, 651 W. Lake St., 60661. Tel: 312-655-7601; Fax: 773-292-5713. Laura Rios, Div. Mgr.

Maternity/Adoption Services, 651 W. Lake St., 60661. Tel: 312-655-7071; Fax: 312-236-5384. Norene Chesebro, Dept. Dir.

Jadonal E. Ford Center for Adolescent Parenting, 11255 S. Michigan Ave., 60628. Tel: 773-995-1737; Fax: 773-995-0125. Velma Brown-Walker, Dir.

Children & Adolescent Parent Program, 651 W. Lake St., 60661. Tel: 312-655-7222; Fax: 312-236-5384. James Scherrer, Ph.D., Dept. Dir.

Arts of Living Institute, 651 W. Lake St., 60661. Tel: 312-948-6003; Fax: 312-236-5384. Alice Wyatt, Prog. Dir.

Our Lady of Tepeyac Head Start, 2414 S. Albany, 60623. Tel: 773-277-5888; Fax: 773-522-3403.

St. Blase Childhood Center, 7438 W. 61st Pl., Summit, 60501. Tel: 708-496-1193; Fax: 708-496-1246.

St. John of God, 5114 S. Elizabeth, 60609. Tel: 773-446-6242; Fax: 773-446-6227.

St. Joseph Childhood Center, 4800 S. Paulina, 60609. Tel: 773-927-2524; Fax: 773-927-2122.

St. Mary of Celle, 1428 S. Wesley Ave., Berwyn, 60402. Tel: 312-655-8492.

Division of Residential Housing:

Division Office, 721 N. LaSalle St., 60654. Tel: 312-655-7490; Fax: 312-944-1550. Email: wdarcy@catholiccharities.net. William G. D'Arcy, Vice Pres.; Gracia Shiffrin, Assoc. Mgr.; Elaine Layden, Assoc. Mgr.

Catholic Charities Housing Development Corporation, 721 N. LaSalle, 60654. Tel: 312-655-7975; Fax: 312-337-8793. William D'Arcy, COO.

Ailbe Assisted Housing Corporation
Ailbe Senior Housing Corporation
Bernardin Senior Housing Corporation
Brendan Senior Housing Corporation
Cortland Manor Development Association
Frances Senior Housing Corporation
Goedert Senior Housing Corporation
Lawrence Senior Housing Corporation
Hayes Senior Housing Corporation
St. Leo Assisted Housing Corporation, NFP
St. Leo Development Association
Matthew Senior Housing Corporation
North Center Senior Housing, NFP
Northlake Senior Housing, NFP
Palos Park Senior Housing Corporation
St. Peter Claver Senior Housing Corporation
Roseland Senior Housing Corporation
Sabina Senior Housing Corporation
Tolton Senior Housing Corporation

Affordable Housing Institutions:

Bishop Goedert Residence, Bldg. 53, Hines VA Campus, Hines, 60141. Tel: 708-273-6600; Fax: 708-273-6609.

Cooke's Manor, Bldg. 14, Hines VA Campus, 5th Ave. & Roosevelt Rd., Hines, 60164. Tel: 708-343-2873; Fax: 708-343-4469.

Hayes Manor, 1211 W. Marquette Rd., 60636. Tel: 773-873-7400; Fax: 773-873-1709.

Matthew Manor, 271 N. Albany Ave., 60612. Tel: 773-533-0001; Fax: 773-533-0622.

Ozanam Village, 271 N. Albany Ave., 60612. Tel: 773-533-0001; Fax: 773-533-0622.

Roseland Manor, 11717 S. State St., 60628. Tel: 773-995-9000; Fax: 773-995-1310.

St. Peter Claver Courts, 14115 St. Claire Blvd., Robbins, 60472. Tel: 708-389-1570; Fax: 708-389-1571.

St. Ailbe Faith Apartments, 1244 E. 93rd St., 60619. Tel: 773-721-0903; Fax: 773-721-0920.

St. Ailbe Love Apts., 9240 S. Kimbark, 60615. Tel: 773-721-0903; Fax: 773-721-0920.

St. Ailbe Hope Apts., 9101-9103 S. Harper, 60615. Tel: 773-721-0903.

St. Brendan Apts., 6718 S. Racine, 60636. Tel: 773-846-8600; Fax: 773-846-0531.
St. Francis of Assisi Residence, 12218 S. Will-Cook Rd., Palos Park, 60464. Tel: 630-343-1880.
St. Leo Residence for Veterans, 7750 S. Emerald, 60620. Tel: 773-651-9950; Fax: 773-651-9970.
St. Sabina Elders Village, 1222 W. 79th St., 60620. Tel: 773-994-7850; Fax: 773-994-7945.
St. Theodore Apts., 6209 S. Paulina St., 60636. Tel: 773-776-0200; Fax: 773-846-8600.
Tolton Manor, 6345 S. Stewart, 60621. Tel: 773-783-7800; Fax: 773-783-6362.
Frances Manor, 1270 E. Golf Rd., Des Plaines, 60016. Tel: 847-390-1270; Fax: 847-390-9331.
Lawrence Manor, 21425 Southwick, Matteson, 60443. Tel: 708-481-1200; Fax: 708-481-3168.
Bernardin Manor, 1700 Memorial Dr., Calumet City, 60409. Tel: 708-832-1700; Fax: 708-832-9160.
Donald W. Kent Residence, 100 S. Wolf Rd., Northlake, 60164. Tel: 708-409-4710; Fax: 708-409-4712.
St. Vincent de Paul Residence, 4040 N. Oakley St., 60618. Tel: 312-655-7440.
Pope John Paul II Residence, 7747 S. Emerald Ave., 60620. Tel: 773-651-9950; Fax: 773-651-9970.

Division of Senior Social Services:

Division Office, 721 N. La Salle Dr., 60654. Tel: 312-655-7572; Fax: 312-640-1587. Wendy S. Siefert, Div. Mgr.; Dorothy Russell, Vice Pres.
Northeast/Northwest Chicago Case Management Services, 3125 N. Knox, 60641. Tel: 773-583-9224; Fax: 773-583-2373. Dorothy Russell, Assoc. Mgr.
South Suburban Senior Services and Senior Activity Center, 15300 S. Lexington, Harvey, 60426. Tel: 708-596-2222; Fax: 708-596-6329. Margaret Latham, Dept. Dir.
Lake County Senior Case Management Services, 116 N. Lincoln, Round Lake, 60073. Tel: 847-546-5733; Fax: 847-546-7114. Carol Lentz-Headley, Dept. Dir.
Lake County Senior Community Services & Nutrition Program Sites, 671 S. Lewis Ave., Waukegan, 60085. Tel: 847-782-4267; Fax: 847-782-4296. Carol Lentz-Headley, Dept. Dir.
Lake County Senior Nutrition Program Sites:
Round Lake Latino Site, 116 N. Lincoln, Round Lake, 60073. Tel: 847-740-6714.
Grayslake Senior Center, 50 Library Ln., Grayslake, 60030. Tel: 847-543-1041.
Good Shepherd Manor, 445 E. Main St., Barrington, 60010. Tel: 847-381-5030.
Barrington Area Council on Aging, 235 Lion Dr., Barrington, 60010.
North Suburban Meals on Wheels, 1700 E. Lake St., Glenview, 60025. Tel: 847-729-1300, Ext. 230.
Antioch/Lake Villa Meals on Wheels, 1625 Deep Lake Rd., Lake Villa, 60046.
Park Place, 414 S. Lewis Ave., Waukegan, 60085. Tel: 847-740-6714.
The Avalon Family Restaurant, 4821 Grand Ave., Gurnee, 60031.
Dino's Den Restaurant, 88 E. Grand Ave., Fox Lake, 60020. Tel: 847-587-6604.
Northwest Suburban Senior Services, 1801 W. Central, Arlington Heights, 60005. Tel: 847-797-5321; Fax: 847-253-9597. Ms. Cindy Gunderson, Prog. Dir.
Accolade Adult Day Care, 112 S. Humphrey, Oak Park, 60302-2704. Tel: 708-445-1300; Fax: 708-445-9595. Denise Smith, Site Dir.
Ada S. Niles Adult Day Care, 6717 S. Elizabeth, 60639. Tel: 773-488-5400; Fax: 773-488-5878. Delizza Russell, Site Dir.
St. Ailbe Adult Day Care, 9249 S. Avalon, 60619. Tel: 773-721-0177; Fax: 773-721-1228. Charlyne McFarland, Site Dir.
Ada S. Niles Senior Center and Adult Day Care Services, 653 W. 63rd St., 60621. Tel: 312-745-3307; Fax: 312-745-3330. Denise King, Senior Center Dir.
Senior Aides Employment Program Tel: 773-874-2400; Fax: 773-488-5878. Paris Brewer, Supr.
Catholic Home Care, Inc., 721 N. La Salle St., 60654. Tel: 312-655-7415; Fax: 312-337-2705. Greta Brown, Dept. Dir.

Senior Care Institutions:

Holy Family Villa, 12220 S. Will-Cook Rd., Palos Park, 60464-7332. Tel: 630-257-2291; Fax: 630-257-2334. Roberta Magurany, Admin.
Bishop T.J. Lyne Residence for Retired Priests, 12230 South Will-Cook Rd., Palos Park, 60464-7332. Tel: 630-257-9510; Fax: 630-257-2334. Roberta Magurany, Contact Person.

Supportive Housing:

Bishop Edwin M. Conway Residence, 1900 N. Karlov Ave., 60639. Tel: 773-252-8578; Fax: 773-525-9946. Maureen Scholle, Dir.

Non-Division Listing:

Christ Child Society of Chicago, 1616 Sheridan Rd., Wilmette, 60091. Tel: 847-251-9253. Mrs. Jane Helmer, Contact Person.
Keenager News, 721 N. LaSalle St., 60654. Tel: 312-948-7672; Fax: 312-930-0425. Sheila Haennicke, Editor.
Mission of the Holy Cross, 721 N. LaSalle St., 60654. Tel: 312-655-7000; Fax: 312-655-0219. Rev. Michael M. Boland.
Options for Housing, Inc. f/k/a Shelter for the Homeless, Inc., 721 N. LaSalle St., 60610. Tel: 312-655-7305. Ms. Kathy Donahue, Contact Person.
St. Josephs Carondelet Child Center, 721 N. LaSalle St., 60654.
Society of St. Vincent De Paul of Chicago, 651 N. Lake St., 60661. Tel: 312-655-7181; Fax: 312-454-0101. Web: www.svdpchicago.org. Claudia Pieske, Exec. Dir.; Mrs. Mary Van Wazer, Pres.

Affiliated Agencies:

Maryville Academy, 1150 N. River Rd., Des Plaines, 60016. Tel: 847-824-6126; Fax: 847-824-7190. Sr. Catherine M. Ryan, O.S.F., Exec. Dir.
Mercy Home for Boys & Girls, 1140 W. Jackson Blvd., 60607. Tel: 312-738-7590; Fax: 312-738-0484. Rev. Scott Donahue, Pres.
Misericordia Home, Heart of Mercy Village, Marian Center, 6900 N. Ridge, 60660. Tel: 773-973-6300; Fax: 773-973-5214. Sr. Rosemary Connelly, R.S.M., Exec. Dir.
St. Coletta's of Illinois, 18350 Crossing Dr., Tinley Park, 60477. Tel: 708-342-5200; Fax: 708-342-2579. Wayne A. Kottmeyer, Exec. Dir.

[H] RESIDENTIAL CHILD-YOUTH CARE

CHICAGO. *Mission of Our Lady of Mercy-Mercy Home for Boys and Girls*, 1140 W. Jackson Blvd., 60607. Tel: 312-738-7560; Fax: 312-738-0484. Email: info@mercyhome.org. Web: www.mercyhome.org. Revs. James J. Close, Pres. Emeritus (Retired); L. Scott Donahue, Pres. & CEO; Cheryl Murphy, CFO, Vice Pres. Facilities & Human Resources; Tom Gilardi, Vice Pres. Youth Programs; Juan Medina, Vice Pres. The Academy; Mark Mroz, Vice Pres. Agency Advancement; Mimi LeClair, Vice Pres. Devel.; Tim Henry, Vice Pres. Information Systems & Quality Improvement; Tom Scheffers, Mgr. Mission Press & Facilities. Total Staff 289; Religious 6; Youths 400.

DES PLAINES. *Maryville Academy*, 1150 N. River Rd., 60016. Tel: 847-294-1999; Fax: 847-824-7277. Web: www.maryvilleacademy.org. Sr. Catherine M. Ryan, O.S.F., Exec. Dir.; Cheryl M. Heyden, Asst. Exec. Dir.
Maryville Academy Patients Assisted Annually 2,559.
Casa Imani Parenting Teen Program, 951 W. Bartlett Rd., Bartlett, 60103. Tel: 630-736-7480; Fax: 630-736-7485. Sandra Braine, Prog. Dir.
Children's HealthCare Center, 4015 N. Oak Park Ave., 60634. Tel: 773-205-3600; Fax: 773-205-3630. Mary Argol, Prog. Dir.
Crisis Nursery, 4015 N. Oak Park Ave., 60634. Tel: 773-205-3600; Fax: 773-205-3633. Amy Kendal-Lynch, Prog. Dir.
Eisenburg Campus, 951 W. Bartlett Rd., Bartlett, 60103. Tel: 630-736-7450; Fax: 630-736-7485. Marsha Koen, Dir.; Dr. Rocco Cimmarusti, Prog. Dir.
Farm Campus for Young Women Tel: 815-599-3800; Fax: 815-599-3805. Katie Dill, Prog. Dir.
Fatherhood Initiative Program Tel: 847-294-1987. Don Pettway, Dir.
Madden Shelter, 1658 W. Grand Ave., 60622. Tel: 312-491-3500; Fax: 312-491-3501. Fred Smith, Prog. Dir.
Maryville CYO, 1658 W. Grand Ave., 60622. Tel: 312-491-3500; Fax: 312-491-3501. Kimberly Williams, Prog. Coord.
Maryville Jen School Tel: 847-390-3020; Fax: 847-294-1738. Dr. Craig Maki, Educ. Dir.
Saint George Homes Tel: 847-294-1721; Fax: 847-294-1916. Marsha Koen, Dir.; Dr. Rocco Cimmarusti, Clinical Dir.
Scott Nolan Acute Psychiatric Hospital, 555 Wilson Ln., 60016. Tel: 847-768-5430; Fax: 847-768-5478. Teresa Maganzini, Hospital Admin.
Child and Family Behavioral Health Center, 555 Wilson Ln., 60016. Tel: 847-390-3000; Fax: 847-294-2788. Teresa Maganzini, Admin.
Scott Nolan Mental Illness/Substance Abuse Program Tel: 847-768-5430; Fax: 847-768-5478. Mary Pernaccairo, Prog. Dir.
Scott Nolan Residential Treatment Center, 555 Wilson Ln., 60016. Tel: 847-768-5430; Fax: 847-768-5478. Jason Evans, Prog. Dir.

[I] DAY NURSERIES, SETTLEMENTS AND SOCIAL CENTERS

CHICAGO. **Claver House of Renewal, Inc.*, 8514 S. Avalon St., 60619. Tel: 773-731-3294. Edward Chatman, Pres. Food pantry, soup kitchen, homebound senior citizen care, after-school youth recreational programs; mentoring; tutoring and scholarship assistance to elementary and high school graduates continuing studies at Catholic educational institutions. Outreach to the homeless: clothing, toys and basic toiletries for local shelters.
Marillac Social Center, 212 S. Francisco Ave., 60612. Tel: 773-722-7440; Fax: 773-722-1469. Web: Marillachouse.org. Sr. Catherine Mary Norris, D.C., CEO. Day care for children ages 15 months to 12 years; Recreation programs for ages 6 to 19 years; emergency assistance food for poor families; child abuse and neglect treatment; counseling svcs.; programs for pregnant & parenting teens and their babies; home bound elderly; svcs. for teenage mothers. Day Care Capacity 250.
**Port Ministries*, 5013 S. Hermitage Ave., 60609. Tel: 773-778-5955; Fax: 773-778-2451. Email: port532857@aol.com. Web: www.portministries.org. Rev. Augustin Milon, O.F.M., Founder & Pres. A Franciscan outreach to the poor and homeless; mobile soup kitchen, family transitional shelter, GED, ESL, family svcs., neighborhood gym and free clinic. Total Staff 30; Total Assisted Annually 3,000.
St. Rose Center, 4911 S. Hoyne Ave., 60609. Tel: 773-436-1433; Fax: 773-436-2280. Email: strosecenter@aol.com. Web: www.strosecenter.org. Sr. Theresa Tamburo, D.S.M.P., Admin. Day Training Program for Developmentally Impaired young adults. Sisters 2; Q.M.R.P. 2; Developmental Support Person (DSP's) 6; Work Activity Director 1; Job Coach 1; Bookkeeper 1; Secretary 1; Capacity 50.
St. Vincent de Paul Center, 2145 N. Halsted St., 60614. Tel: 312-943-6776; Fax: 312-943-2257. Email: bwinters@svdpc.org. Bart Winters, CEO. Day care for children 3 months to 13 years; family social svcs; early childhood education; pre-school and afterschool programs; family social services.; Provides case management, counseling, and emergency relief for senior citizens. Intergenerational living quarters for 16 seniors (low income) and 5 young adults. Outreach to the homeless in the form of case management and other concrete services. Daughters of Charity 5; Capacity 468.

[J] HOSPITALS

CHICAGO. *St. Anthony Hospital* Ascension Health & Missionary Sisters of the Sacred Heart of Jesus., 2875 W. 19th St., 60623. Tel: 773-484-1000. Mr. Peter Fazio, Bd. Chm.; Mr. Guy Medaglia, Interim CEO; Sr. Benigna Morais, M.S.C., Chap.; Revs. Paschalis Agu (Africa); Benedict Ezeoke (Nigeria); David Petraitis, O.S.A.
Catholic Health Partners Services Total Staff 880; Total Nursing Beds 20; Total Licensed Beds 166; Patients Assisted Annually 101,018.
St. Bernard Hospital & Health Care Center, 326 W. 64th St., 60621. Tel: 773-962-3900; Fax: 773-873-8247. Email: elizvs@aol.com. Web: stbernardhospital.com. Sisters Janet Wahleithner, R.H.S.J., Supr.; Elizabeth Van Straten, R.H.S.J., Pres. & CEO; Janet Wahleithmer, R.H.S.J., Dir. Pastoral Care Dept.
St. Bernard Hospital Religious Hospitallers of St. Joseph. Sisters 2; Bed Capacity 226; Patients Assisted Annually 120,000.
Holy Cross Hospital, 2701 W. 68th St., 60629. Tel: 773-884-9000. Web: www.holycrosshospital.org. Wayne M. Lerner, D.P.H., F.A.C.H.E., Pres. & CEO; Sr. Dolores Cavalli, O.P., Chap.; Revs. Bernard R. Danber, O.S.A., Chap.; Thomas Griffin, O.S.A., Chap.; Sr. Agnes Chapp, Patient Visitor.
Holy Cross Hospital Sisters of St. Casimir of Chicago. Sisters 5; Licensed Beds 305; Patients Assisted Annually 180,000; Total Staff 1,080.
Holy Cross Hospital and Sisters of St. Casimir Foundation
Saint Joseph Hospital, 2900 N. Lake Shore Dr., 60657. Tel: 773-665-3000; Fax: 773-665-4859. Web: www.sjh.reshealth.org. Sandra Bennett Bruce, Pres.; Ron Struxness, Group Vice Pres., Exec. Vice Pres. & CEO; Revs. Theodore Ploplis, Coord. Spiritual Svcs.; Donatus Chukwu (Nigeria); Richard O'Nyamwaro, A.J.; Deacon Michael Romano, Chap.; Sr. Alverda Bonifas, O.P., Chap.; Rabbi Norm Lewison. Sponsored by Sisters of the Holy Family of Nazareth & Sisters of the Resurrection., An Affiliate of Resurrection Health Care. Bassinets 31; Bed Capacity 402; Patients Assisted Annually 190,924.
Saints Mary and Elizabeth Medical Center, 2233 W. Division, 60622. Tel: 312-770-2000; Fax: 312-770-2392. Web: www.smemc.reshealth.org. Sandra Bennett Bruce, Pres.; Margaret McDermott, Exec. Vice Pres. & CEO; Isidro Gallegos Rodriguez, Coord., Spiritual Svcs.; Most Rev. Enrique Rivera Hernandez (Puerto Rico), Chap.; Revs. William G. Hubmann, C.PP.S., Chap.; Ihor Koshyk, Chap.; Skariya Poulose, M.S.T., Chap.; Daniel R. Steiner, Chap.; Sr. Blanche Zalewski, C.S.F.N., Chap.; Michael Doyle, Chap.; William F. Kramer, Chap.

Sponsored by Sisters of the Holy Family of Nazareth & Sisters of the Resurrection., An Affiliate of Resurrection Health Care. Bed Capacity-Saint Mary Campus 325; Bed Capacity-Saint Elizabeth Campus 251; Patients Assisted Annually 93,958; Total Staff 2,115.

Mercy Hospital and Medical Center, 2525 S. Michigan Ave., 60616-2477. Tel: 312-567-2100; Fax: 312-567-6575. Web: www.mercy-chicago.org. Sr. Sheila Lyne, R.S.M., Pres. & CEO. Tel: 312-567-2580; Fax: 312-567-6575; Rev. Martin J. Hebda, Vice Pres., Spirituality & Mission. Tel: 312-567-2045; Fax: 312-328-7741. Sisters 5; Bed Capacity 479; Staffed Beds 305; Patients Assisted Annually 338,019.

Affiliates:

Mercy Health System of Chicago

Mercy Family Health Center

Mercy Services Corp.

Mercy Foundation, Inc.

Mercy Health System of Chicago Liability Self-Insurance Trust

Mercy Medical at Dearborn Station (Outpatient Physician Offices), 47 W. Polk St., 60605. Tel: 312-922-3011.

Mercy Works at Dearborn Station, 47 W. Polk St., 60605. Tel: 312-922-3011; Fax: 312-922-5860.

Mercy Medical in Chinatown (Outpatient Physician Offices), 2347 S. Wentworth, 60616. Tel: 312-842-0100.

Mercy Medical on Pulaski (Outpatient Satellite Facility), 5525 S. Pulaski Rd., 60629. Tel: 773-585-1955; 773-284-5268.

Mercy Works on Pulaski, 5635 S. Pulaski Rd., 60629. Tel: 773-284-5278; Fax: 773-585-0395.

Mercy Medical on Michigan, 2930 S. Michigan Ave., 60616. Tel: 312-808-0400.

Mercy Works on Ashland, 3316 S. Ashland, 60608. Tel: 773-254-2133.

Mercy Medical in Chatham, 8541 S. State St., 60619. Tel: 773-994-2300.

**Our Lady of the Resurrection Medical Center*, 5645 W. Addison, 60634. Tel: 773-282-7000; Fax: 773-794-7671. Web: www.olr.reshealth.org. Sandra Bennett Bruce, Pres.; Ivette Estrada, Exec. Vice Pres. & CEO; Mr. Robert Shuford, Coord., Spiritual Svcs.; Revs. Abraham M. Jacob (SYM), Chap.; Tomy Vadakevattukula, M.S.T. (India), Chap.; Sisters Sebastiana Filip, C.F.S.N., Chap.; Mary Hedwig Kuczynski, C.R., Chap.; Kathleen Ponce, Chap. Sponsored by Sisters of the Holy Family of Nazareth & Sisters of the Resurrection., An Affiliate of Resurrection Health Care. Bed Capacity 264; Patients Assisted Annually 186,187.

Resurrection Medical Center, 7435 Talcott Ave., 60631. Tel: 773-774-8000; Fax: 773-990-7626. Web: www.reshealth.org. Sandra Bennett Bruce, Pres.; Sr. Donna Marie, C.R., Exec. Vice Pres. & CEO; James Croegaert, Coord., Spiritual Svcs.; Revs. Mykola Buryadnyk, Chap.; Kevin R. Fane, O.P., Chap.; Saji Mukkoot, Chap.; Jerome Onwughalu, C.S.Sp., Chap.; Sr. Francisa Witkowska, C.S.F.N., Chap.; Mr. Habteghabr Anisera, Chap.; Ann Moran, Chap.; Michael Doyle, Chap.; S. Bonaventure Kusek, Sacristan. Sponsored by Sisters of the Holy Family of Nazareth & Sisters of the Resurrection., An Affiliate of Resurrection Health Care. Bed Capacity 449; Patients Assisted Annually 222,077; Student Nurses affiliated with Nurses-Triton College 40; Student Nurses, Oakton Community College 20; Chicago Board of Education 12.

CHICAGO HEIGHTS. *St. James Hospital and Health Centers*, 1423 Chicago Rd., 60411. Tel: 708-756-1000; Fax: 708-756-6863. Web: www.stjameshospital.org. 20201 S. Crawford Ave., Olympia Fields, 60461. Tel: 708-747-4000; Fax: 708-503-3270. Mr. Seth C.R. Warren, Pres. & CEO; Sr. M. Madonna Rougeau, O.S.F., Vice Pres. Mission Integration; Rev. Ronald L. Kondziolka, Chap.

Sisters of St. Francis Health Services, Inc. Sisters 4; Bed Capacity 562; Patients Assisted Annually 163,229; Total Staff 2,000.

St. James Community Foundation, 1423 Chicago Rd., 60411. Tel: 708-756-1000; Fax: 708-756-1000. Email: tom.senesac@ssfhs.org. Thomas W. Senesac, Treas.

Alverno Clinical Laboratories, 1423 Chicago Rd., 60411. Tel: 708-756-1000; Fax: 708-756-6863. Email: tom.senesac@ssfhs.org. Thomas W. Senesac, Vice Pres.

DES PLAINES. *Holy Family Medical Center*, 100 N. River Rd., 60016. Tel: 847-297-1800; Fax: 847-297-1863. Web: www.reshealth.org. Sandra Bennett Bruce, Pres.; John Baird, Exec. Vice Pres. & CEO; Bro. Kenney Gorman, C.F.X., Coord. Spiritual Svcs.; Revs. Stepan Kostiuk (STN), Chap.; Haldane Mysliwiec, Chap.; Mr. Richard Nash, Chap.; Sr. Bridget Zanin, M.S.C., Chap. Sponsored by Sisters of the Holy Family of Nazareth & Sisters of the Resurrection., An Affiliate of Resurrection Health Care. Bed Capacity 252; Patients Assisted Annually 98,233.

ELK GROVE VILLAGE. *Alexian Brothers Medical Center*, 800 Biesterfield Rd., 60007-3392. Tel: 847-437-5500; Fax: 847-981-5774. Email: werrbacj@alexian.net. Web: www.alexian.org. John Werrbach, Pres. & CEO; Beth Collier, Chap.; James Gullickson, Chap.; Phyllis Harman, Chap.; Larry Kancler, Chap.; Rosemary A. Kimpel, Chap.; Sandy Reback, Chap.; Dave Sattler, Chap.; Revs. Binu Kuriachen, Chap.; Matthew Varkey, Chap.; William E. Veith, Chap. Congregation of Alexian Brothers, Immaculate Conception Province., Parent Institution: Alexian Brothers Hospital Network Licensed Beds 387; Lay Staff 3,121; Patients Assisted Annually 386,210.

EVANSTON. *Saint Francis Hospital*, 355 Ridge Ave., 60202. Tel: 847-316-4000; Fax: 847-316-7733. Web: www.sfh.reshealth.org. Sandra Bennett Bruce, Pres.; Jeffrey Murphy, Exec. Vice Pres. & CEO; Anne Murphy, Coord. Spiritual Svcs.; Revs. Thomas Kuttiyanickal, S.A.C., Chap.; Tomy Vadakevattukula, M.S.T. (India), Chap.; Eoli Roselada, O.F.M., Chap.; Rabbi Ilene Melemad, Chap. Sponsored by Sisters of the Holy Family of Nazareth & Sisters of the Resurrection., An Affiliate of Resurrection Health Care. Bed Capacity 375; Patients Assisted Annually 200,000.

EVERGREEN PARK. *Little Company of Mary Hospital and Health Care Centers*, 2800 W. 95th St., 60805. Tel: 708-422-6200; Fax: 708-425-9756. Web: www.lcmh.org. Sr. Kathleen McIntyre, L.C.M., Bd. Chm.; Dennis Reilly, Pres.; Mary Jo Quick, Vice Pres. Mission & Spirituality; Revs. James R. Gallagher, Chap. (Retired); James Thompson, O.S.A., Chap.; Bro. Brian Boyle, Chap.; Carol Ehler, Chap.; Deacon Rick Feltes, Chap.; Sisters Christa Henrich, S.L.W., Chap.; Margaret Nyangreli, Chap.; Margaret Schneider, Chap.; Joellyn Skrip; Deacon Richard Warfield, Mgr. Pastoral Care.

The Little Company of Mary Hospital and Health Care Centers Sisters of the Little Company of Mary 23; Bed Capacity 294; Bassinets 24; Patients Assisted Annually 267,790.

Affiliates:

Little Company of Mary Auxiliary, 2800 W. 95th St., 60805. Tel: 708-229-5447.

Little Company of Mary Affiliated Services, Inc., 2800 W. 95th St., 60805. Tel: 708-422-6200, Ext. 5100; Fax: 708-425-9369.

Palos Office Center, 12450 S. Harlem, Palos Heights, 60463. Tel: 708-448-1207; Fax: 708-361-8049.

Oak Lawn Care Station, 5660 W. 95th St., Oak Lawn, 60453. Tel: 708-499-2273; Fax: 708-857-3705.

Burbank Office Building, 4901 W. 79th St., Burbank, 60459. Tel: 708-424-2273; Fax: 708-857-3713.

Mary Potter Pavilion, 2850 W. 95th St., 60805. Tel: 708-229-5148.

Little Company of Mary Hospital Foundation, 2800 W. 95th St., 60805. Tel: 708-229-5022; Fax: 708-229-6525. Mary Jo May, Exec. Dir.

Little Company of Mary Health Systems of Evergreen Park, 2800 W. 95th St., 60805. Tel: 708-422-6200, Ext. 5004. Dennis Reilly, Pres.

HOFFMAN ESTATES. *Alexian Brothers Behavioral Health Hospital*, 1650 Moon Lake Blvd., 60169. Tel: 847-882-1600; Fax: 847-755-8060. Web: www.abbhh.org. Francine McGouey, CEO & COO; Stan Kedzior, Dir. Mission Integration. Congregation of Alexian Brothers, Immaculate Conception Province. Licensed Beds 137; Patients Assisted Annually 20,102.

Parents:

Alexian Brothers Health System Tel: 847-385-7147; Fax: 847-483-7036.

Alexian Brothers Hospital Network Tel: 847-385-7147; Fax: 847-483-7036.

St. Alexius Medical Center, 1555 Barrington Rd., 60169. Tel: 847-843-2000; Fax: 847-490-2570. Web: www.stalexius.org. Edward M. Goldberg, Pres. & CEO; Stan Kedzior, Regl. Dir. Mission Integration; Sisters Laura Mankivsky, M.Div., Staff Chap.; N. Noemia Silva, Staff Chap.; Revs. Domingo Hurtado-Badillo, Chap.; Tom Thomas, Chap.; Mrs. Betty Skonieczny, Coord. Chaplains. Congregation of Alexian Brothers, Immaculate Conception Province. Brothers 1; Licensed Beds 339; Lay Staff 2,114; Patients Assisted Annually 266,120.

Parent Institutions:

Alexian Brothers Health System Tel: 847-385-7147; Fax: 847-483-7036.

Alexian Brothers Hospital Network Tel: 847-385-7147; Fax: 847-483-7036.

MAYWOOD. **Loyola University Medical Center aka Foster G. McGaw Hospital* 2160 S. First Ave., 60153. Tel: 708-216-9000. Web: loyolamedicine.org. Dr. Paul K. Whelton, M.D., M.Sc., Pres. & CEO; Sharon O'Keefe, B.S., R.N., M.S., Pres., LUH; Rev. Lawrence Reuter, S.J., Vice Pres., Mission & Ministry; Mr. Charles E. Reiter III, Sr. Vice Pres., Gen. Counsel & Sec.; Marie Coglianese, M.P.S., Dir. Pastoral Care & Educ.; Revs. John P. Coakley, S.J.; Ronald Galt (Scotland); Tuan Le, S.J.; Mr. Jerry Kaelin, M.Div., M.A., Chap. SIT Supvr., CPE Mgr.; Rev. James J. Creighton, S.J., CPE Supvr.; Rev. Monica Isaac, M.Div.; Deacon Albin Wegner; Ms. Kathleen Brannigan, M.T.S.; Mr. Matthew Eaton, M.Div.; Mr. John Garrity, M.S.W., J.D.; Mr. John Grubba, M.Div., M.A.; Sisters Fran Glowinski, O.S.F.; Cyrilla Zarek, O.P., M.A.; Mrs. Ruth Jandeska, M.Div.; Rev. Lee Smits, M.Div. Bed Capacity 568; Total Staff 6,000; Patients Assisted Annually 70,000.

MELROSE PARK. **Westlake Community Hospital*, 1225 Lake St., 60160. Tel: 708-681-3000; Fax: 708-938-4672. Web: www.reshealth.org. Sandra Bennett Bruce, Pres.; M. Patricia Shehorn, Exec. Vice Pres. & CEO; Mr. Conceicao Mesquita, Coord. Spiritual Svcs.; Rev. Peter Kunnalakatt (India), Chap.; Sr. Mary Dominic Russell, C.R., Chap.; Chad Leonard, Chap.; Rev. Janet Lundblad, Chap., (Evangelical Covenant Minister). Sponsored by Sisters of the Holy Family of Nazareth & Sisters of the Resurrection., An Affiliate of Resurrection Health Care.; Student Nurses affiliated with Nurses-Triton College, Student Nurses, Elmhurst College Licensed Bed Capacity 225; Total Assisted Annually 8,833; Total Staff 1,025.

OAK PARK. *Rush Oak Park Hospital*, 520 S. Maple Ave., 60304. Tel: 708-383-9300; Fax: 708-660-6658. Mr. Bruce M. Elegant, Pres. & CEO; Aoife Lee, Dir. Spiritual Care & Mission; Ian C. Burch, Chap.; Sylvia Fromme, Chap.

Rush Oak Park Hospital Wheaton Franciscan Sisters. Bed Capacity 177; Total Staff 804; Patients Assisted Annually 99,877.

Oak Park Hospital Endowment Fund Affiliate.

**West Suburban Medical Center*, 3 Erie Ct., 60302. Tel: 703-383-6200; Fax: 708-383-3159. Web: www.reshealth.org. Sandra Bennett Bruce, Pres.; Mr. Jay Kreuzer, Exec. Vice Pres. & CEO; Mr. Conceicao Mesquita, Coord. Spiritual Svcs.; Rev. Christopher Anumata, Chap.; Sr. Sandi Sosnowski, C.S.F.N., Chap.; David Beleckis, Chap.; Sharon Lund, Chap. Sponsored by Sisters of the Holy Family of Nazareth & Sisters of the Resurrection., An Affiliate of Resurrection Health Care. Total Staff 1,450; Bed Capacity 287; Total Assisted Annually 75,000.

West Suburban College of Nursing Tel: 708-763-6530; Fax: 708-763-1531. Email: admissions@wcn.edu. Web: www.wscn.edu. Rebecca Jones, D.N.Sc., R.N., C.N.A.A., B.C., Chancellor. Accredited by the Commission on Collegiate Nursing Education, Higher Learning Commission, a member of North Central Association of Colleges and Schools and approved by the Illinois Department of Financial and Professional Regulation. Degrees Offered: Bachelor of Science in Nursing (BSN), Master of Science in Nursing (MSN). Students 209.

[K] HEALTH CARE CENTERS

CHICAGO. *St. Basil Health Service - Free People's Clinic*, 1850 W. Garfield, 60609. Tel: 773-436-4758; Fax: 773-436-2749. Patients Assisted Annually 5,000.

BROADVIEW. **Proviso Family Services, Inc. dba Resurrection Behavioral Health, d.b.a. ProCare Centers* 1820 S. 25th Ave., 60160. Tel: 708-681-2324; Fax: 708-681-1289. Web: www.reshealth.org. Sandra Bennett Bruce, Pres.; Mr. Frank C. Perham, Vice Pres., Behavioral Health. Sponsored by the Sisters of the Holy Family of Nazareth & Sisters of the Resurrection., An Affiliate of Resurrection Health Care. Patients Assisted Annually 20,000.

[L] PROTECTIVE INSTITUTIONS

CHICAGO. *House of the Good Shepherd*, 1114 W. Grace St., 60613. Tel: 773-935-3434; Fax: 773-935-3523.

House of the Good Shepherd Sisters of The Good Shepherd., Shelter for abused women with children. Sisters 4; Capacity (Families) 14; Total Staff 30.

**L'Arche Chicago*, 1049 S. Austin Blvd., 60644. Tel: 773-287-8249; Fax: 708-863-1273 (Call first). Email: larchechicago@sbcglobal.net. Web: www.larchechicago.org. Alexandra Conroy, Community Leader & Dir. A Christian Community concerned with life sharing between persons with a developmental disability and persons who assist them.

St. Mary of Providence, 4200 N. Austin Ave., 60634. Tel: 773-545-8300; Fax: 773-545-8035. Email: SrRitaB@sbcglobal.net. Sr. Rita Butler, Dir.; Darlene Zdanowski, Admin.; Rev. Thomas A. Mulcrone, Chap.

Daughters of St. Mary of Providence Operated by the Daughters of St. Mary of Providence., Developmental training and residential care of developmentally disabled adults. Sisters 8; Total Staff 150; Total Assisted Annually 110.

Misericordia/Heart of Mercy Center, 6300 N. Ridge, 60660-1017. Tel: 773-973-6300; Fax: 773-973-5214. Web: www.misericordia.com. Sr. Rosemary Connelly, R.S.M., Exec. Dir.; Rev. John J. Clair, Asst. Exec. Dir. Children and adults with developmental disabilities. Priests 1; Sisters 13; Total Staff 1,020; Bed Capacity 550; Total Assisted Annually 550.

BARTLETT. *Bartlett Learning Center*, 801 W. Bartlett Rd., 60103. Tel: 630-289-4221; Fax: 630-289-4390. Anne M. Craig, Prin.

Barlett Learning Center, Inc. dba Clarewoods Academy and Cupertino Home. Sponsored by the Sisters of St. Joseph, Third Order of St. Francis., Operates Bartlett Learning Center Day School Program and the Cupertino Home, Warrenville, IL. Day School program serves developmentally delayed and multiple handicapped individuals ages 3 to 21. Day School Program accepts youth identified LD, BD, EMH, TMH, and TBI Speech/Language Impaired, Autistic. Community Integrated Living Arrangement Serves developmentally delayed gentlemen ages 18 to 45. Sisters 5; Lay Staff 100; Patients Assisted Annually 140.

LAKE ZURICH. *Mt. St. Joseph Home*, 24955 North Hwy. 12, 60047. Tel: 847-438-5050; Fax: 847-438-6313. Email: msjlz@aol.com. Sr. Gertrude Barbera, D.S.M.P., Exec. Dir.; Rev. Aloysius Romanski, O.F.M.Conv., Chap. Operated by the Daughters of St. Mary of Providence., Intermediate care for developmentally disabled women. Sisters 5; Total Staff 140; Total Assisted Annually 130.

RIVER FOREST. *Big Sisters*, P.O. Box 5728, 60305. Tel: 708-488-8893. Web: bigsistersofchicago.org. Mrs. Elizabeth J. Brennan, Pres.; Mrs. Mary Alice Jovan, Past Pres. & Recording Sec.

TINLEY PARK. *St. Coletta's of Illinois, Inc.*, 18350 Crossing Dr., 60487. Tel: 708-342-5200; Fax: 708-342-2579. Web: www.stcolettas.com. Wayne A. Kottmeyer, Exec. Dir. Sponsored by the Sisters of St. Francis of Assisi. Residential care, education, job training & job placement for developmentally disabled children and adults. Capacity 187; Total Assisted Annually 400; Total Staff 320.

Divisions:

Lt. Joseph P. Kennedy Jr. School, Tinley Park Tel: 708-342-5200; Fax: 708-342-2579.

Vocational Job Training Center, Tinley Park Tel: 708-342-5200; Fax: 708-342-2579.

St. Coletta's of Illinois Foundation Tel: 708-342-5246; Fax: 708-342-2579. Email: bsiwinski@stcolettail.org. Affiliate.

[M] SENIOR CARE INSTITUTIONS

CHICAGO. *Cortland Manor Retirement Home*, 1900 N. Karlov, 60639. Tel: 773-235-3670. Maureen Scholle, Admin. Catholic Charities Housing Development Corporation. Capacity 48.

Franciscan Communities dba St. Joseph Village of Chicago 4021 W. Belmont Ave., 60641. Tel: 773-328-5500; 800-524-6126. Email: sla@franciscancommunities.com. Web: www.stjosephvillageofchicago.com. Lora Ann Slawinski, Admin.; Rev. John H. Nowak, C.R., Chap. Sisters 8; Licensed Beds 94.

Jugan Terrace, 2300 N. Racine, 60614. Tel: 773-935-9600; Fax: 773-935-9614. Email: mschicago@littlesistersofthepoor.org.

Little Sisters of the Poor of Chicago, Inc. Senior Housing Apts. 50.

Little Sisters of the Poor Center for the Aging, 2325 N. Lakewood Ave., 60614. Tel: 773-935-9600; Fax: 773-935-9614. Sr. Patricia Metzgar, L.S.P., Supr.

Little Sisters of the Poor of Chicago, Inc., Intermediate and skilled care facility. Sisters 13; Residents 76; Bed Capacity 76; Staff 110.

Resurrection Life Center, 7370 W. Talcott Ave., 60631. Tel: 773-594-7400; Fax: 773-594-7402. Web: www.seniors.reshealth.org. Sandra Bennett Bruce, Pres.; Nancy Razo, Admin.; Leszek Baczkura, Coord. Spiritual Svcs.; Rev. Robert Bovenzi, C.P., Chap.; Sisters M. Leonette Klafeta, C.R., Chap.; Elaine Skrzypczynski, C.S.F.N., Chap. A division of Resurrection Senior Services.; Skilled intermediate and sheltered nursing care. Bed Capacity 162.

Resurrection Retirement Community, 7262 W. Peterson Ave., 60631. Tel: 773-792-7930; Fax: 773-792-8316. Web: www.reshealth.org. Sandra Bennett Bruce, Pres.; Sr. Kathleen Ann Stadler, C.S.F.N., Exec. Dir.; Leszek Baczkura, Coord., Spiritual Svcs.; Lawrence Valentine, Chap. A division of Resurrection Health Care managed by Resurrection Senior Services Independent Living Apartments 435; Assisted Living Apartments 37; Total Staff 102; Total Assisted Annually 600.

DES PLAINES. *Holy Family Nursing and Rehabilitation Center*, 2380 Dempster, 60016. Tel: 847-296-3335; Fax: 847-296-2027. Web: www.seniors.reshealth.org. Sandra Bennett Bruce, Pres.; Anthony Madl, Admin.; Leszek Baczkura, Coord. Spiritual Svcs. Sponsored by Sisters of the Holy Family of Nazareth and Sisters of the Resurrection., A division of Resurrection Senior Services; Intermediate and Skilled Nursing Facility. Licensed Bed Capacity 251.

Nazarethville, 300 N. River Rd., 60016. Tel: 847-297-5900; Fax: 847-297-0504. Web: www.nazarethville.com. Sr. M. Lucille Madura, C.S.F.N., Admin. Sponsored by the Sisters of the Holy Family of Nazareth. Total Assisted Annually 30,295. In Res. Rev. John Stephen, C.R.

EVANSTON. *Saint Francis Nursing and Rehabilitation Center*, 500 Ashbury Ave., 60202. Tel: 847-316-3320; Fax: 847-316-3337. Web: www.seniors.reshealth.org. Sandra Bennett Bruce, Pres.; Michael Kaplan, Admin.; Leszek Baczkura, Coord. Spiritual Svcs.; Lauren Ivory, Chap. Sponsored by Sisters of the Holy Family of Nazareth and Sisters of the Resurrection., A division of Resurrection Senior Services; Comprehensive nursing, rehabilitation and social services. Bed Capacity 127.

GLENVIEW. *Maryhaven Nursing and Rehabilitation Center*, 1700 East Lake Ave., 60025. Tel: 847-729-1300; Fax: 847-729-9620. Web: www.seniors.reshealth.org. Sandra Bennett Bruce, Pres.; Sara Szumski, Admin.; Leszek Baczkura, Coord. Spiritual Svcs.; Michael Stacy, Chap. Sponsored by Sisters of the Holy Family of Nazareth and Sisters of the Resurrection., A division of Resurrection Senior Services; Home for Aged, intermediate and skilled care facilities, Medicare, Therapy. Capacity 135.

JUSTICE. *Rosary Hill Home*, 9000 W. 81st St., 60458. Tel: 708-458-3040; Fax: 708-458-7230. Email: rosaryhill@sbcglobal.net. Web: www.sistersop.org. Sr. M. Natalie, O.P., Admin.; Rev. Raymond J. Jasinski (Retired). Operated by the Dominican Sisters of the Immaculate Conception. Sisters 10; Bed Capacity 60; Number under care 60.

LAGRANGE PARK. *Bethlehem Woods Retirement Community*, 1571 Ogden Ave., La Grange Park, 60526. Tel: 708-579-3663; Fax: 708-579-7159. Web: www.seniors.reshealth.org. Sandra Bennett Bruce, Pres.; Mary Jester, Exec. Dir.; Leszek Baczkura, Coord. Spiritual Svcs.; Timothy John Doody, Chap. Sponsored by Sisters of the Holy Family of Nazareth and Sisters of the Resurrection., A division of Resurrection Health Care managed by Resurrection Senior Services. Independent living apartments and Licensed assisted living apartments. Residents 316; Bed Capacity 334; Total Staff 100.

LEMONT. *Alvernia Manor Senior Living*, 13950 Main St., 60439. Tel: 630-257-7721; Fax: 630-257-0338. Email: info@alverniamanor.org. Web: www.alverniamanor.org. Sr. Cynthia Drozd, O.S.F., Admin. Sponsored by The School Sisters of St. Francis of Christ the King. Residents 50.

Franciscan Village, 1270 Franciscan Dr., 60439. Tel: 630-243-3400; Fax: 630-257-5823. Email: rcoon@franciscancommunities.com. Web: www.franciscancommunities.com. Robert E. Coon, Exec. Dir. Sponsored by the Franciscan Sisters of Chicago., Continuing Care Retirement Community. Independent Living 187; Assisted Living 30; Nursing Home 127; Total Staff 207.

NILES. *Saint Andrew Life Center*, 7000 N. Newark Ave., 60714-4497. Tel: 847-647-8332; Fax: 847-647-7073. Web: www.seniors.reshealth.org. Sandra Bennett Bruce, Pres.; Ms. Anne Berg, Exec. Dir.; Leszek Baczkura, Coord. Spiritual Svcs.; Rev. Stepan Kostiuk (STN), Chap.; Sr. Kathryn Wojcik, C.R., Chap. Sponsored by Sisters of the Holy Family of Nazareth and Sisters of the Resurrection., A division of Resurrection Senior Services.; Independent living apartments, Licensed assisted living apartments and Intermediate Nursing Care. Number Under Care 164.

Saint Benedict Nursing and Rehabilitation Center, 6930 W. Touhy Ave., 60714. Tel: 847-647-0003; Fax: 847-647-1936. Web: www.seniors.reshealth.org. Sandra Bennett Bruce, Pres.; Peter E. Goschy, Admin.; Leszek Baczkura, Coord. Spiritual Svcs.; Deacon Ed O'Leary, Chap. Sponsored by Sisters of the Holy Family of Nazareth and Sisters of the Resurrection., A division of Resurrection Senior Services. Residents 99.

NORTHLAKE. *Casa San Carlo Retirement Community*, 420 N. Wolf Rd., 60164. Tel: 708-562-4300; Fax: 708-492-3526. Web: www.seniors.reshealth.org. Sandra Bennett Bruce, Pres.; Sr. M. Elizabeth Trembczynski, C.S.F.N., Exec. Dir.; Leszek Baczkura, Coord., Spiritual Svcs.; Timothy John Doody, Chap. Sponsored by Sisters of the Holy Family of Nazareth and Sisters of the Resurrection., A division of Resurrection Health Care managed by Resurrection Senior Services.; Independent living apartments Residents 175; Bed Capacity 182; Total Staff 54.

Villa Scalabrini Nursing and Rehabilitation Center, 480 N. Wolf Rd., 60164-1667. Tel: 708-562-0040; Fax: 708-562-5180. Web: www.seniors.reshealth.org. Sandra Bennett Bruce, Pres.; Jim Kouzios, Admin.; Bro. Kenney Gorman, C.F.X., Coord. Spiritual Svcs.; Sisters Maria Cigolini, M.S.C.S., Chap.; Ruth Marostica, M.S.C.S., Chap.; Rev. Abraham Kaduthodil. Sponsored by Sisters of the Holy Family of Nazareth and Sisters of the Resurrection., A division of Resurrection Senior Services.; Skilled and intermediate nursing care Residents 259.

PALATINE. *St. Joseph's Home for the Elderly*, 80 W. Northwest Hwy., 60067. Tel: 847-358-5700; Fax: 847-358-5763. Email: mspalatine@littlesistersofthepoor.org. Sr. Maureen Weiss, Supr.; Most Rev. Andrew J. McDonald, D.D., J.C.D. (Retired).

Little Sisters of the Poor of Palatine, Inc. Operated by the Little Sisters of the Poor. Sisters 15; Total Assisted Annually 103; Bed Capacity 101; Total Staff 111.

PALOS PARK. *Holy Family Villa*, 12220 S. Will-Cook Rd., 60464. Tel: 630-257-2291; Fax: 630-257-2334. Email: hfv12375@aol.com. Roberta Magurany, Admin. Catholic Charities, Archdiocese of Chicago. Sisters 2; Residents 99; Bed Capacity 99; Total Assisted 142; Total Staff 120.

PARK RIDGE. *Resurrection Nursing and Rehabilitation Center*, 1001 N. Greenwood, 60068. Tel: 847-692-5600; Fax: 847-692-2305. Web: www.seniors.reshealth.org. Sandra Bennett Bruce, Pres.; Tony Madl, Admin.; Bro. Kenney Gorman, C.F.X., Coord. Spiritual Svcs.; Rev. Stepan Kostiuk (STN), Chap.; Sisters Rita Mary Ganser, C.R., Chap.; Fidelis Rolfes, S.L.W., Chap.; Dominic Doherty, Chap. Sponsored by Sisters of the Holy Family of Nazareth and Sisters of the Resurrection., A division of Resurrection Senior Services. Skilled Care Bed Capacity 295.

WHEELING. **Addolorata Villa*, 555 McHenry Rd., 60090-3899. Tel: 847-537-2900; Fax: 847-215-5805. Email: nhusaib@franciscancommunities.com. Web: www.franciscancommunities.com. Mr. Lawrence D. Carlson, Exec. Dir.; Ms. Dawn Cohn, Dir. Campus Oper.; Madelyn Seckler, Dir. Residential Svcs.; Mr. David A. Matenear, M.Div., Pastoral Care Coord.; Rev. Nicolas F. Husain, Dir. Mission Integration & Pastoral Care; Ms. Carol Jagielinik, Chap.; Deacon Bill Kalivoda, Chap. Sponsored by the Franciscan Sisters of Chicago, a continuing care retirement community. Sisters (Servants of Mary) 9; Skilled 88; Intermediate 10; Sheltered 31; Assisted Living 39; Assisted Living - Memory Lane 22; Independent Living Apartments 100.

[N] MONASTERIES AND RESIDENCES OF PRIESTS AND BROTHERS

CHICAGO. *St. Augustine Friary*, 5413 S. Cornell Ave., 60615. Tel: 773-358-6500, Ext. 402. Email: veraosa@mac.com. Revs. Gary Rye, O.S.A., Prior; Philip C. Cook, O.S.A., Treas.; Luis A. Vera, O.S.A., Formation Dir.

Carmelite Priory of St. Cyril, 6401 S. Harper Ave., 60637. Tel: 773-684-0112; Fax: 773-684-4713. Web: www.mchs.org. Rev. Daniel Carroll, O.Carm. (Retired).

Residing here are all the priests who teach at Mt. Carmel High School: Revs. Carl J. Markelz, O.Carm., Prin.; Peter McGarry, O.Carm.; Benjamin Aguilar, O.Carm.; Michael Kwiecien, O.Carm.

Chicago Province of the Society of Jesus-Provincial Office, 2050 N. Clark St., 60614. Tel: 773-975-6363; Fax: 773-975-0230. Email: chgprov@jesuits-chi.org. Web: www.jesuits-chi.org. Revs. Timothy P. Resicki, S.J., Prov.; Richard L. Millbourn, S.J., Socius; James S. Prehn, S.J., Asst. Secondary Education; Paul V. Robb, S.J., Asst. Treas.; Theodore G. Munoz, S.J., Asst. for Business & Finance; Paul J. Faulstich, S.J., Asst. Records & Res.; Patrick A. Fairbanks, S.J., Asst. for Vocation Promotion; Raymond P. Guiao, S.J., Asst. Formation.

Jesuits Serving Abroad: Revs. Richard J. Baumann, S.J., Zimbabwe; Philip J. Chmielewski, S.J., Beijing, China; Kevin H. Flaherty, S.J., Peru; Robert J. Geisinger, S.J., Rome; Jeffrey L. Klaiber, S.J., Peru; Lewis C. Murtaugh, S.J., Peru; Peter P. Nguyen, S.J., Toronto, Canada; James M. O'Leary, S.J.,

Spain; Charles Rodrigues, S.J., India; John R. Sima, S.J., Peru; William J. Spine, Rome.
Residing elsewhere in the U.S.: Revs. Robert E. Beckman, S.J., Clarkston, MI; Michael Brophy, S.J., Clarkston, MI; Matthew T. Gamber, S.J., Weston, MA; J. Timothy Hipskind, S.J., Weston, MA; Bernard F. McAniff, S.J., Weston, MA; Henry T. Chamberlain, S.J., Cincinnati, OH; David G. DeMarco, S.J., Berkley, MI; Andrew N. Downing, S.J., South Bend, IN; William L. Verbryke, S.J., Berkley, MI; Paul B. Macke, S.J., Washington, DC; David V. Meconi, S.J., St. Louis, MO; James M. McCann, S.J., Washington, DC; Paul J. Nienaber, S.J., Winona, MN; William P. O'Brien, S.J., St. Louis, MO; Robert J. Ochs, S.J., El Cerrito, CA; Frank M. Oppenheim, S.J., Clarkston, MI; Mitchell C. Pacwa, S.J., Birmingham, AL; John F. Pennington, S.J., Clarkston, MI; Denis A. Dirscherl, S.J., Fairborn, OH; Bradley M. Schaeffer, S.J., Cambridge, MA; James A. Stoeger, S.J., Washington, DC; Thomas W. Florek, S.J., South Bend, IN; Michael W. Cooper, S.J., Safety Harbor, FL; Brian E. Daley, S.J., South Bend, IN; Lester E. Love, S.J., Oakland, CA; John S. Thiede, S.J., South Bend, IN. *Clark Street Jesuit Residence*, 2050 N. Clark St., 60614. Tel: 773-935-3947; Fax: 773-975-0230. Revs. John F. Costello, S.J.; Paul Campbell, S.J.; Michael E. Dorrler, S.J.; Raymond P. Guiao, S.J.; Richard L. Millbourn, S.J.; Very Rev. Edward W. Schmidt, S.J. Priests 7. *Woodlawn Jesuit Community*, 5554 S. Woodlawn, 60637. Tel: 773-667-1395; Fax: 773-667-2089. Revs. Robert E. Finn, S.J.; Paul V. Mankowski, S.J.; Anthony Canoll, S.J.; George A. Lane, S.J.; Paul V. Robb, S.J.; James W. Schulz, S.J.; Robert T. Sears, S.J.; Bro. Anthony R. Kreutzjans, S.J. Priests 7.

St. Clare Friary, 3407 S. Archer Ave., 60608-6817. Tel: 773-890-1238; Fax: 773-847-7409. Web: www.capuchinfranciscans.org. Revs. Mark Joseph Costello, O.F.M.Cap., Dir. Post-Novitiate Formation; William Cieslak, O.F.M.Cap., Devel.; John Holly, O.F.M.Cap., Local Min. & Dir. Vocations; Peter Kutch, O.F.M.Cap., Local Vicar, Asst. Dir. Post-Novitiate Formation; Bros. Jerome Johnson, O.F.M.Cap., Asst. Dir. Vocations; Todd Wieschowski, O.F.M.Cap., Temporary Professed; David Hirt, O.F.M.Cap., Temporary Professed; Zoilo Garibay, O.F.M.Cap., R.N., B.S.N., Temporary Professed.

Claretian Missionaries, St. Jude League, Inc., 205 W. Monroe, 60606. Tel: 312-236-7782; Fax: 312-236-7230. Web: www.claretians.org. Revs. John Molyneux, C.M.F., Dir.; Mark J. Brummel, C.M.F., Dir. Editorial Offices: "U.S. Catholic" and other Claretian Publications.

Columban Fathers Mission Center, 6449 N. Magnolia Ave., 60626. Tel: 773-274-9111; Fax: 773-274-9053. Revs. Thomas G. Glennon, S.S.C.; Charles Duster, S.S.C.

Columban Fathers Theologate, 5103 S. Ellis Ave., 60615. Tel: 773-955-0660; Fax: 773-955-0805. Revs. Timothy Mulroy, S.S.C., Rector; Leo Distor, S.S.C., Vice Rector. Priests 2; Seminarians 14.

Comboni Missionaries Theologate (M.C.C.J.), Verona Fathers, 5512 Hyde Park Blvd., 60637. Tel: 773-667-8920. Email: chicombtheo@ameritech.net. Revs. David Bohnsack, M.C.C.J.; Archimede Fornasari, M.C.C.J., Ph.D.; Mario Malacrida, M.C.C.J. (Italy). Theology Students 2.

Congregation of Christian Brothers, Brother Rice Community, 10001 S. Pulaski Rd., 60655. Tel: 773-429-4300. Bros. Robert McGovern, C.F.C., Community Leader; Eugene O. Carty, C.F.C.; Robert E. Beckstrom, C.F.C.; Thomas J. Collins, C.F.C.; George G. Gremley, C.F.C.; Charles E. Joyce, C.F.C.; Patrick B. Martin, C.F.C.; Paul Ickes, C.F.C.; John Toole, C.F.C.; Patrick T. Varilla, C.F.C. Brothers 10.

Congregation of Marian Fathers of the Immaculate Conception, 6336 S. Kilbourn Ave., 60629-5588. Tel: 773-767-1687 (Religious House); 773-582-8191 (Fr. Petraitis); Fax: 773-582-8961 (Fr. Petraitis). Web: www.marians.org. Revs. Donald S. Petraitis, M.I.C., Rector; Jonas Duoba, M.I.C. (Retired); Victor Rimselis, M.I.C. (Retired). Priests 3.

Conventual Franciscans of St. Bonaventure Province, 6107 N. Kenmore Ave., 60660. Tel: 773-274-7681; Fax: 773-274-9751. Very Rev. Patrick Greenough, O.F.M.Conv., Min. Prov.
The Conventual Franciscans of Saint Bonaventure Province Corporation
The Conventual Franciscans of Saint Bonaventure Province Charitable Continuing Care Trust Fund
Franciscan Friars Educational Corporation
St. Hedwig Cemetery and Mausoleum Corporation
Franciscan Friars Retirement Corporation Sacred Heart Friary, 6107 N. Kenmore Ave., 60660. Tel: 773-764-8811. Bros. Joseph Graff; George Searles, Treas.; Joseph Wood, O.F.M.Conv., Vocation Dir. & Formation Dir.
Assigned but serving elsewhere: Revs. Francis Kiley, O.F.M.Conv., St. Michael's, 13270 Maple Dr., St. Louis, MO 63127; Aloysius Romanowski, O.F.M-.Conv., Mount St. Joseph Institute - Chaplaincy, 24955 North Hwy. 12, Lake Zurich, 60047-9752; Bernard Geiger, O.F.M.Conv., Apostolate for Family Consecration, 3375 County Rd. 36, Bloomingdale, OH 43910-7903.
Friars of the Province Serving Abroad: Revs. John Calgaro, O.F.M.Conv. (Mexico); Abraham Crisostomo, O.F.M.Conv. (Mexico); Bros. Paschal Metzger, O.F.M.Conv. (Mexico); Stanley Zabkiewicz, O.F.M.Conv. (Zambia).

Croatian Franciscan Custody of the Holy Family, 4851 S. Drexel Blvd., 60615. Tel: 773-536-0552; Fax: 773-536-2094. Email: custody@sbcglobal.net. Web: www.croatianfranciscans.org. Rev. Marko Puljic, O.F.M., Custos, Croatia Franciscan Custody of the Holy Family. *St. Anthony's Friary*, 4848 S. Ellis Ave., 60615. Tel: 773-373-3463. Revs. Josip N. Galic, O.F.M., Guardian; Jerome Kucan, O.F.M. (Retired); Vjekoslav Bambir, O.F.M.; Timothy Majic, O.F.M.; Theodore Benkovic, O.F.M.; Bruno Raspudic, O.F.M.; Ljubo Krasic, O.F.M., Vicar; Philip Pavich, O.F.M.

Croatian Franciscan Fathers, 6346 N. Ridge, 60660. Tel: 773-262-0535; Fax: 773-262-4603. Email: bastepinacchicago@sbcglobal.net. Rev. Ivica Majstorovic, O.F.M., Croatian Catholic Mission Blessed Alojzije Stepinac.

Crosier Community of Chicago, 5401 S. Cornell Ave., 60615. Tel: 773-684-6975; Fax: 773-684-8357. Rev. Thomas Enneking, O.S.C.; Bro. David Donnay, O.S.C.

DePaul Vincentian Residence, 2233 N. Kenmore Ave., 60614-3594. Tel: 773-325-8700; Fax: 773-325-8719. Rev. John E. Rybolt, C.M., Supr.; Mr. Michael Walsh, Treas. Congregation of the Mission, Society of Priests.
Members of the Vincentian Community (Congregation of the Mission-Western Province): Bros. Paul P. Joseph, C.M.; Leo F. Keigher, C.M.; Revs. Kevin S. Collins, C.M.; John Era, C.M.; Daniel Hasso, C.M., (Ethiopia Province); Dennis H. Holtschneider, C.M., (Eastern Province); Ronald J. Hoye, C.M.; Jaroslav Jasso, C.M., (Ukraine Province); John P. Minogue, C.M.; Firmin Mola Mbalo, C.M., (Toulouse Province); Jose Nazhianpara, C.M., (North India Province); Donald Ours, C.M.; Robert R. Rohrich, C.M.; Charles F. Shelby, C.M.; Paul Sisul, C.M.; Edward J. Tomasiewicz, C.M.

Discalced Carmelite Friars, 5345 S. University Ave., 60615-5103. Tel: 773-324-8613; Fax: 773-752-6594. Bro. Michael Stoegbauer, O.C.D. Brothers 1.

Divine Word Theologate, 5342 S. University, 60615-5106. Tel: 773-288-2777 (office); 773-288-7923 (residence); Fax: 773-288-6307. Email: theologate@aol.com. Revs. Stanley Uroda, S.V.D., Rector; Quang Duc Dinh, S.V.D., Dir. Formation; vanThanh Nguyen, S.V.D., Admonitor; Roger P. Schroeder, S.V.D.; Bro. Michael Decker, S.V.D., Vice Rector & Dir. Brother Formation. Priests 8; Brothers 4; Students 29.

Edward McGuinn, S.V.D. Residence, 5045 S. Ellis Ave., 60615-2711. Tel: 773-538-0431. Revs. Stephen B. Bevans, S.V.D.; Gary L. Riebe-Estrella, S.V.D.; Mark Schramm, S.V.D.

Angels Studio, 701 W. Jackson Blvd., Ste. 111, 60661. Tel: 312-234-9838; Fax: 312-583-9561; 312-234-9839. Rev. Derek Simons, S.V.D.

Dominican Community, 1914 S. Ashland Ave., 60608. Tel: 312-829-1931; Fax: 312-226-6119. Email: bcurran@stpiusvparish.org. Revs. Charles W. Dahm, O.P.; Matthias R. Mueller, O.P.; Brendan A. Curran, O.P.

Dominicans (Provincial Office), St. Pius V. Priory, 1909 S. Ashland Ave., 60608. Tel: 312-243-0011; Fax: 312-829-8471. Email: provincial@domecentral.org. Web: www.op.org/domcentral.
Dominicans, Province of St. Albert the Great, U.S.A. (Central Dominican Province) Provincial Office Tel: 312-666-3244; Fax: 312-829-8471. Email: domcenprov@dominicans.org.
Provincial Staff: Very Rev. Michael A. Mascari, O.P., Prior Prov.; Revs. Robert J. Botthof, O.P., Dir. Shrine of St. Jude; Donald J. Goergen, O.P., Promoter of Social Justice; John J. Meany, O.P., Syndic & Vicar Prov.; Andrew-Carl Wisdon, O.P., Dir. Vocations & Vocational Support; Jay Harrington, O.P., Regent of Studies; Jerome M. Walsh, O.P., Promoter of Dominican Laity; Bro. Edward J. Van Merriemboer, O.P., Vicar for Ministry & Corporate Sec. *St. Pius V Priory* Tel: 312-226-0074; Fax: 312-226-6199. Very Rev. Michael A. Mascari, O.P., Prior Prov.; Revs. Robert L. Barry, O.P.; William J. Bernacki, O.P.; John Vincent Blake, O.P.; Robert J. Botthof, O.P.; Roderick M. Brown, O.P.; Gerard B. Cleator, O.P.; Francis R. Crowe, O.P.; John R. Dolehide, O.P.; Rapael A. Fabish, O.P.; John M. Gambro, O.P.; Robert A. Goedert, O.P.; Wilfred G. Hoff, O.P.; David M. Hynous, O.P.; James M. Karepin, O.P.; Lawrence T. Kearney, O.P.; Robert Kilbridge, O.P.; Giles R. Klapperich, O.P.; John J. Meany, O.P.; Gregory J. Moore, O.P.; Thomas A. Morrison, O.P.; Walter T. O'Connell, O.P.; Mark Paraday, O.P.; Andrew-Carl Wisdon, O.P.; Bros. Carlos Griego, O.P.; Reginald W. Neu, O.P.; Michael McGovern, O.P.
Spirituality Today Journal, Inc.; Shrine of St. Jude Thaddeus; Society for Vocational Support, Inc.; St. Dominic Mission Society; Dominican Social Action Fund; Dominican Laity; The Bolivian Trust of the Dominicans; Office for Mission Advancement
Assigned but Serving Elsewhere: Revs. Richard de Ranitz, O.P.; Thomas P. Doyle, O.P.; Francis X. Dyer, O.P.; John C. Fabian, O.P.; Daniel W. Morrissey, O.P.; Frank M. Nouza, O.P.
Priests of the Province Serving Abroad: Revs. Eric deWasseige, O.P., Bolivia; Joseph P. Kenny, O.P., Nigeria; Peter Otillio, O.P., Nigeria; Justus M. Pokrzewinski, O.P., Nigeria; Edward H. Riley, O.P., Nigeria; Edward Ruane, O.P., Italy; Lewis M. Shea, O.P., Kenya; Gilbert J. Thesing, O.P., Nigeria; Benedict T. Viviano, O.P., Switzerland; Bro. Stephen D. Lucas, O.P., Nigeria.

Franciscan House of Studies, 6107 N. Kenmore Ave., 60660. Tel: 773-764-8811; Fax: 773-274-9751. Bro. Joseph Wood, O.F.M.Conv., Formation Dir. A Formation House of Conventual Franciscan Friars.

Holy Evangelists Friary Order of Friars Minor., 4513 N. Ashland Blvd., 60651-5401. Tel: 773-878-3723; Fax: 773-878-1382. Email: rfpawell@aol.com. Friar Johnpaul Cafiero, O.F.M., D.Min., M.A., M.Div.; Revs. Robert Pawell, M.Div.; Eulogio Roselada, M.Div. Priests 3.

Holy Name Friary, Assumption BVM Province, 3800 W. Peterson Ave., 60659-3116. Tel: 773-539-4042; Fax: 773-539-9553. Revs. Lawrence Janowski, O.F.M., Guardian; Faculty, Loyola Univ.; Nathan Jaskulski, O.F.M., Chap., Felician Sisters; Hugh Zurat, O.F.M., Chap., Felician Sisters; Camillus Janas, O.F.M.

Holy Spirit Friary, Order of Friars Minor, 5225 S. Greenwood Ave., 60615-4335. Tel: 773-753-1920. Revs. Gilberto Cavazos-Gonzales, O.F.M., S.L.T., Faculty, Catholic Theological Union; Albert Haase, O.F.M., Staff, Mayslake Ministries; Phil D. Hogan, O.F.M., Faculty, Hales Franciscan High School; Gilbert Ostdiek, O.F.M., S.T.D., Faculty, Catholic Theological Union; Charles E. Payne, O.F.M., Ph.D., Adjunct Faculty, Catholic Theological Union; Bro. Charles Reid, O.F.M., Theological Student; Rev. David Rodriguez, O.F.M., M.F.A., Faculty, St. Rita of Cascia High School.

Institute of Christ the King Sovereign Priest, 6415 S. Woodlawn Ave., 60637-3817. Tel: 773-363-7409; Fax: 773-363-7824. Email: info@institute-christ-king.org. Web: www.institute-christ-king.org. Very Rev. Msgr. R. Michael Schmitz; Rev. Matthew L. Talarico, Vice Rector. *Shrine of Christ the King Sovereign Priest* Church: *St. Clara*, 64th and Woodlawn. Res.: *Priory of the Infant Jesus*.

St. John Stone Friary, 1165 E. 54th Pl., 60615-5109. Tel: 773-684-6510; Fax: 773-684-9830. Web: www.midwestaugustinians.org. Revs. James Thompson, O.S.A., Prior; David Petraitis, O.S.A.; Reinhard J. Sternemann, O.S.A., Treas.; John Szura, O.S.A.; James R. Halstead, O.S.A.

St. Joseph Interprovincial Post-Novitiate Formation House (A Franciscan House of the Sacred Heart Province), 5495 S. Hyde Park Blvd., 60615. Tel: 773-363-0072; Fax: 773-363-0076. Revs. Mark Soehner, O.F.M., Guardian & Formation Staff; Ed Shea, O.F.M., Vicar Formation Staff; Bernard Kennedy, O.F.M., Formation Dir.; Daniel Sulmosy, O.F.M., Prof. Medicine & Ethics, University of Chicago. Professed 15.

Korean Catholic Center, 4115 N. Kedvale, 60641. Tel: 773-283-3979. Rev. John Smith, S.S.C., Dir.

Lithuanian American Jesuits (Della Strada Residence and Lithuanian Youth Center), 2345 W. 56th St., 60636. Tel: 773-737-8400.
Jesuit Fathers of Della Strada Inc. Baltic Jesuits Advancement Office, 12690 Archer Ave., Lemont, 60439-6732. Tel: 630-243-6234. Email: lithjesuit@hotmail.com. Revs. Gediminas Kijauskas, S.J., Pres.; Antanas Grazulis, S.J., Sec.; Antanas Saulaitis, S.J., Chap. Dir. *Blessed Jurgis Matulaitis Mission*, 14911 E. 127th St., Lemont, 60439. Tel: 630-257-5613. Priests 3. *Lithuanian Youth Center Inc.*, 5620 S. Claremont Ave., 60636. Tel: 773-778-7500.

Marist Brothers, Monastery Community, 4200 W. 115th St., 60655. Tel: 773-881-6380; Fax: 773-881-0595. Email: kmoran@marist.net. Web: www.marist.net. Bros. Gerard Brown; Kevin Moran, Dir.; Julian Roy; Paul Forgues; Richard Grenier; Christopher Shannon.

Marist Brothers, St. Ann Residence, 10114 S. Leavitt, 60643. Tel: 773-239-4116. Bros. Vito

Aresto, Dir.; Stephen Synan; Hugh Turley, F.M.S.; Henry Hammer; Brendan Brennan.

Maryknoll Fathers & Brothers, 5128 S. Hyde Park Blvd., 60615-4217. Tel: 773-493-3367; Fax: 773-493-3427. Email: chicago@maryknoll.org. Web: society.maryknoll.org. Mr. Gregory Darr, Regnl. Dir.; Mr. Jay Weingarten, Major Gift Officer; Revs. Herman W. Cisek, M.M.; William J. Donnelly, M.M.; John W. Eybel, M.M.; Bros. Joseph Bruener, M.M.; Adrian R. Mazuchowski, M.M.

Legal Title: The Catholic Foreign Mission Society of America

Miguel Pro Jesuit Community, 1611 S. Allport St., 60608. Tel: 312-226-6496; Fax: 312-226-2915. Revs. Michael T. Conley, S.J.; Christopher J. Denron, S.J., Pres. Christ the King Jesuit College Preparatory School; John P. Foley, S.J., Chm. Cristo Rey Network; James G. Gartland, S.J., Pres. Cristo Rey Jesuit High School; Timothy A. Howe, S.J.; Sean A. O'Sullivan, S.J. (Ireland), Local Supr., Dir. Counseling, Cristo Rey Jesuit High School; Bro. David L. Henderson, S.J.

Monastery of the Holy Cross, 3111 S. Aberdeen St., 60608-6503. Tel: 773-927-7424; Fax: 773-927-5734. Email: porter@chicagomonk.org. Web: www.chicagomonk.org. Revs. Peter Funk, O.S.B., Prior; Thomas-Benedict Baxter, O.S.B., (On Leave); Brendan D. Creeden, O.S.B., Sub Prior; Edward J. Glanzmann, O.S.B., Novice Master, Guest Master; Bros. Antonio Bravo, O.S.B., Hospitality; Ignatius Isaac, O.S.B., Oblate Dir. & Librarian. Benedictine Monks (Subiaco Congregation). Novices 1.

St. Monica Monastery, 4445 W. 64th St., 60629-5547. Tel: 773-581-5360; Fax: 773-581-7405. Revs. L. Dudley Day, O.S.A.; Erwin J. Dodge, O.S.A.; Daniel J. Hartigan, O.S.A. Tel: 773-585-0629; Ronald E. Scheible, O.S.A. Priests 4.

The Oblate House of Theology, 5535 S. Kenwood Ave., 60637. Tel: 773-493-8917. Rev. Gregory T. Cholewa, O.M.I., Caretaker.

Order of Friar Servants of Mary (Servites) United States of America Province, Inc., Servite Provincial Center, 3121 W. Jackson Blvd., 60612-2729. Tel: 773-533-0360; Fax: 773-533-8307. Email: michaelcallary@servitesUSA.org. Web: www.servite.org. Very Rev. John M. Fontana, O.S.M., Prior Prov.; Revs. Frank M. Falco, O.S.M., Prov. Councilor; Gerald M. Horan, O.S.M., Prov. Councilor; Michael M. Pontarelli, O.S.M., Prov. Counselor & Prov. Vocation Team Coord.; Luke M. Stano, O.S.M., Asst. Prov.; Bro. Edmund Baran, O.S.M., Prov. Treas.; Rev. Lawrence M. Choate, O.S.M., Prov. Treas. Elect; Bro. Michael M. Callary, O.S.M., Prov. & Corp. Sec. Mission Procurator; Revs. Conrad M. Borntrager, O.S.M., Prov. Archivist & Historian; Christopher M. Krymski, O.S.M., Dir. National Shrine of St. Peregrine O.S.M.; Robert M. Warsey, O.S.M., Dir. National Shrine of Our Lady of Sorrows & Dir. Marian Center; Vidal M. Martinez, O.S.M., Natl. Asst. for Servite Secular Order; John M. Topper, O.S.M., Dir., National Shrine of Our Sorrowful Mother "The Grotto", Portland, OR. Priests 71; Brothers 12; Temporary Professed 3; Novices 2.

Servite Vocation Team Coordinator, 31520 Camino Capistrano, San Juan Capistrano, CA 92675. Tel: 714-322-5862; Fax: 773-533-8307. Email: ciaopadre@hotmail.com. Web: www.servite.org. Rev. Michael M. Pontarelli, O.S.M., Prov. Vocation Team Coord. *Servite Secular Order*, 3121 W. Jackson Blvd., 60612-2729. Tel: 773-638-5800, Ext. 48; Fax: 773-533-8307. Email: osmsecular@aol.com. Web: www.servite.org. Rev. Vidal M. Martinez, O.S.M., National Asst. Servite Secular Order. *Servite Marian Center*, 3121 W. Jackson Blvd., 60612-2729. Tel: 773-638-5800, Ext. 37; Fax: 773-533-8307. Email: rjwarseyosm@aol.com. Web: www.servite.org. Rev. Robert M. Warsey, O.S.M., Dir. *National Shrine of Our Lady of Sorrows*, 3121 W. Jackson Blvd., 60612-2729. Tel: 773-638-0159, Ext. 102. Email: rjwarseyosm@aol.com. Web: www.ols-chicago.org. Rev. Robert M. Warsey, O.S.M., Dir. *National Shrine of St. Peregrine, O.S.M.*, 3121 W. Jackson Blvd., 60612-2729. Tel: 773-638-0189, Ext. 100. Email: chrisart77@aol.com. Web: www.servite.org. Rev. Christopher M. Krymski, O.S.M., Dir. *Annunciata Priory*, 11128 S. Avenue G, 60617. Tel: 773-221-1043; Fax: 773-221-1556. Bro. Brian M. Fitzpatrick, O.S.M.; Revs. Conrad M. Borntrager, O.S.M.; Paul M. Cullen, O.S.M.; Dennis Kriz, O.S.M. *Assumption Priory*, 323 W. Illinois St., 60610. Tel: 312-644-0036; Fax: 312-644-1838. Revs. David M. Brown, O.S.M.; Joseph M. Chamblain, O.S.M.; Damian M. Charbonneau, O.S.M.; Lawrence Michael Doyle, O.S.M.; John M. Pawlikowski, O.S.M., Ph.D. *Servants of Mary (Servite) Development Office*, 1439 S. Harlem Ave., Berwyn, 60402. Tel: 708-795-8885; Fax: 708-795-8892. Email: lchoate@servitedevelopment.org. Web: www.servite.org. Rev. Lawrence M. Choate, O.S.M., Dir., Devel. Office & Prov. Sacristan.

Members of the Province Located Elsewhere in the Archdiocese of Chicago and Other Locations in the U.S.: Revs. Robert M. Anderson, O.S.M., Sanctuary of Our Sorrowful Mother, Portland, OR; Richard R. Boyle, O.S.M., St. Anne's Parish, Union City, CA; Joseph M. Carbone, O.S.M., Our Lady of Mount Carmel Priory, Denver, CO; Joseph M. Cheah, O.S.M., St. Ann Church, Avon, CT; Thomas M. Crotty, O.S.M., Seven Holy Founders Priory, Anaheim, CA; Patrick M. Donovan, O.S.M., St. Juliana Falconieri Priory, Fullerton, CA; Donald Duplessis, O.S.M., Servite Residence, Fullerton, CA; Frank M. Falco, O.S.M., St. Juliana Falconieri Priory, Fullerton, CA; Carl M. Feil, O.S.M., Our Lady of Lourdes, Melbourne, FL; Very Rev. John M. Fontana, O.S.M., Servite Residence, Chicago, IL; Revs. Mark M. Franceschini, O.S.M., Our Lady of Mount Carmel Priory, Denver, CO; David M. Gallegos, O.S.M., St. Philip Benizi Priory, Buena Park, CA; Donald M. Gantley, O.S.M.; Anthony M. Gaydos, O.S.M., St. Marie du Lac Parish, Ironton, MO; Paul M. Gins, O.S.M., St. Juliana Falconieri Parish, Fullerton, CA; Thomas M. Greaney, O.S.M.; Hugh Guentner, O.S.M., St. Patrick Parish, Vail, CO; Michael M. Guimon, O.S.M., Paolo Sarpi Priory, Berkeley, CA; Thomas M. Heskin, O.S.M.; Gerald M. Horan, O.S.M., St. Philip Benizi Priory, Buena Park, CA; Ignatius M. Kissel, O.S.M., Sanctuary of Our Sorrowful Mother, Portland, OR; Bruce M. Klikunas, O.S.M., Paolo Sarpi Priory, Berkeley, CA; Damian M. Kobus, O.S.M., Sanctuary of Our Sorrowful Mother, Portland, OR; Timothy M. Kremen, O.S.M., Our Lady of Mount Carmel Priory, Denver, CO; Manuel Maya-Chavez, O.S.M., St. Ignatius Priory, El Paso, TX; Perry M. McCoy, O.S.M., Seven Holy Founders Priory, Anaheim, CA; Philip M. McGlynn, O.S.M., Servite Residence, Chicago, IL; Paul M. Novak, O.S.M., Servite Residence, Chicago, IL; Anthony M. O'Connell, O.S.M., Servite Residence, Chicago, IL; Edward M. Penonzek, O.S.M., Seven Holy Founders Priory, Anaheim, CA; Justin M. Pisciotta, O.S.M., St. Philip Benizi Priory, Buena Park, CA; Michael M. Pontarelli, O.S.M., Mission San Juan Capistrano, San Juan Capistrano, CA; Gabriel M. Ramacciotti, O.S.M., Our Lady of Mount Carmel Priory, Denver, CO; Peter M. Rookey, O.S.M.; Stephen M. Ryan, O.S.M., Our Lady of Perpetual Help, Cotton Grove, OR; Philip M. Scherer, O.S.M., Servite Residence, Hazel Crest, IL; Donald M. Siple, O.S.M., Seven Holy Founders Priory, Affton, MO; John M. Topper, O.S.M., The Sanctuary of Our Sorrowful Mother, Portland, OR; Lawrence M. Walling, O.S.M., Servite Residence, Denver, CO; Robert M. Warsey, O.S.M.; Gabriel M. Weber, O.S.M., Our Lady of Mount Carmel Priory, Denver, CO; Bros. Gregory M. Atherton, O.S.M., The Sanctuary of Our Sorrowful Mother, Portland, OR; Edmund M. Baran, O.S.M.; Michael M. Callary, O.S.M., Servite Residence, Chicago, IL; Robert M. Fandel, O.S.M.; Joseph Fundak, O.S.M.; Joel A. Lechner, O.S.M., Seven Holy Founders Priory, Affton, MO; Bonfilius M. McGovern, O.S.M.; Christopher Moran, O.S.M., Seven Holy Founders Priory, Anaheim, CA; Arnaldo M. Sanchez, O.S.M., Seven Holy Founders Priory, Affton, MO.

Members of the Province Serving Abroad: Revs. Oscar M. Aguilera Acosta, O.S.M., Tuart Hill, Australia; Patrick M. Boyle, O.S.M., Tuart Hill, Australia; Frank M. Christie, O.S.M., Tuart Hill, Australia; Declan M. Doherty, O.S.M., Kwazulu-Natal, Republic of South Africa; Sean M. Lennon, O.S.M., Benburb, Ireland; Mel M. Loftus, O.S.M., Kwazulu-Natal, Republic of South Africa; Myles M. Lynch, O.S.M., Parkville, Australia; Liam M. Mackle, O.S.M., Parkville, Australia; Carlo M. Marchetti, O.S.M., Tuart Hill, Australia; Mafanisa Mthembu, O.S.M., Kwazulu-Natal, Republic of South Africa; Thulani Ntsele, O.S.M., Kwazulu-Natal, Republic of South Africa; Christopher M. Ross, O.S.M., Tuart Hill, Australia; Eugene M. Smith, O.S.M., Convento San Marcello, Rome, Italy; Leo M. Spicer, O.S.M., Rome, Italy; Charles M. Toland, O.S.M., Kwazulu-Natal, Republic of South Africa; Robert M. Zivkovic, O.S.M., Tuart Hill, Australia; Bro. Stephen M. Barker, O.S.M., Tuart Hill, Australia.

Passionist Community-CTU, 5417 S. Cornell Ave., 60615. Tel: 773-324-2704; Fax: 773-324-2557. Email: smacdonald@passionist.org. Revs. Sebastian MacDonald, C.P., S.T.D., Supr.; Kenneth O'Malley, C.P., Ph.D., CTU Archivist; Robin Ryan, C.P., Ph.D., CTU Faculty; Donald Senior, C.P., S.T.D., Pres., CTU; Paul Zilonka, C.P., S.S.L., S.T.D., Formation Dir.; Bros. Hugo Esparza, C.P., Scholastic; Ian Gayle, C.P., Scholastic; Alfredo Ocampo, C.P., Scholastic; Jamie Parisi, C.P.; Michael Rowe, C.P., Scholastic.

Congregation of the Passion: St. Vincent Strambi Community Priests 5; Scholastics 4.

Passionist Community-Immaculate Conception Monastery, 5700 N. Harlem Ave., 60631-2342. Tel: 773-631-1686; Fax: 773-631-1705. Email: cusackf@passionist.org. Web: www.passionist.org. Rev. Francis Cusack, C.P., Supr.; Very Rev. Donald Webber, C.P., Prov. Supr.; Revs. Louis Doherty, C.P.; Christopher Gibson, C.P., Dir. Recruitment (Vocations); Michael Higgins, C.P.; E. John Hilgert, C.P.; James Strommer, C.P., Dir. Vocation Office; Francis X. Keenan, C.P., Chap., Lutheran General Hospital; Eric Meyer, C.P., Pastor, Immaculate Conception Parish; Ronan Newbold, C.P., Assoc. Pastor, Immaculate Conception Parish; Bros. Kevin O'Malley, C.P.; Raymond Sanchez, C.P.

Congregation of the Passion: Immaculate Conception Community Priests 15; Brothers 2.

Passionist Provincial Office, 5700 N. Harlem Ave., 60631-2342. Tel: 773-631-6336; Fax: 773-631-8059. Email: passdw@aol.com. Web: www.passionist.org. Very Rev. Donald Webber, C.P., Prov.; Revs. James Strommer, C.P., Asst. Prov. & Consultor; Joseph Moons, C.P., Consultor; John Schork, C.P., Consultor; Philip Paxton, C.P., Consultor.

Congregation of the Passion: Holy Cross Province

Special Assignment: Revs. Richard Johnson, C.P., 20120 N. Key Dr., Boca Raton, FL 33498. Tel: 451-470-5828; Robert Coward, C.P., Curia Generalizia Dei Passionisti, Piazza SS. Giovanni e Paolo 13, Rome 00184 Italy. Tel: 011-39-06-772-711; Fax: 011-39-06-700-8454. Email: rcoward@passionist.org; John B. Ormechea, C.P., Dei Passionisti, Piazza SS. Giovanni e Paolo 13, Rome 00184 Italy. Tel: 001-39-6-072-711; Fax: 001-39-06-700-8454; John P. Day, C.P., Holy Martyrs of Japan, 8244 Highway AE, Sullivan, MO 63080. Tel: 573-627-3378; Fax: 573-627-3387. Email: jpday@passionist.org; Louis Doherty, C.P., RR#2, Box 36, Pierce City, MO 65723. Tel: 417-476-2281; Joseph Van Leeuwen, C.P., Ashram J.X.P., Pallichal Rd. - Palluruthy, Kerala 682-006 India. Tel: 001-91-0484-223-1309; Fax: 011-91-0484-222-3652. Email: juanleeuwen@passionist.org; Bro. James Griffin, C.P., 35090 W. Eight Mile Rd., #6, Farmington Hills, MI 48335. Tel: 901-321-3964; Fax: 901-321-3505.

Provincial Offices: *Stauros U.S.A.*, 5700 N. Harlem, 60631-2342. Tel: 773-484-0581; Fax: 773-631-8059. Email: stauros@stauros.org. Web: www.stauros.org. Deacon Donald Grossnickle, Exec. Dir. *Passionist Missions of India*, 5700 N. Harlem Ave., 60631. Tel: 773-631-6336; Fax: 773-631-8059. Email: arthurcp@passionist.org. Rev. Arthur Carrillo, C.P., Procurator. *Congregation of the Passion*, 5700 N. Harlem Ave., 60631. Tel: 773-631-6336; Fax: 773-631-8059. *Passionist Missions, Inc.*, 5700 N. Harlem Ave., 60631. Tel: 847-518-8844; Fax: 847-518-0461. Rev. Arthur Carrillo, C.P., Mission Appeals, 23335 Schoolcraft St., Detroit, MI 48223-2405. Tel: 313-531-0562; Fax: 313-535-8468. *Province Development Office*, 5700 N. Harlem Ave., 60631-2342. Tel: 847-518-8844; Fax: 847-518-0461. Mr. Keith Zekind, Exec. Dir. *Planned Giving*, 5700 N. Harlem Ave., 60631-2342. Tel: 847-518-8844; Fax: 847-518-0461. Mr. Patrick Quinn, Dir. Planned Giving. *Passionist Communications*, 5700 N. Harlem Ave., 60631-2342. Tel: 847-518-8844; Fax: 847-518-0461. Nancy Nickel, Dir. Communications. *Province Finance Office*, 5700 N. Harlem Ave., 60631-2342. Tel: 773-631-6336; Fax: 773-631-8059. Mr. Keith Zekind, Dir. Finance; Mrs. Susan Arvanitis, Controller; Rev. Michael Hoolahan, C.P., Province Treas. *Passionist Archives*, 5700 N. Harlem Ave., 60631-2342. Tel: 773-631-1686; Fax: 773-631-1705. Mr. Damian Schaab, Archivist.

St. Patrick's Missionary Society, 1347 W. Granville Ave., 60660-1910. Tel: 773-973-3737; Fax: 773-973-6049. Email: spfil@stpatrickfathers.com. Web: spms.org. Revs. Karl Langsdorf, S.P.S., Supr.; Michael Conroy.

St. Peter's Friary, 110 W. Madison St., 60602-4196. Tel: 312-372-5111; Fax: 312-853-2361. Web: www.stpetersloop.org. Revs. William Burton, O.F.M.; Elric Sampson; Lawrence Janezic, O.F.M.; Bro. Fred Smith, O.F.M.; Rev. Wenceslaus Church; Bro. Sammy Danna; Revs. Thomas Ess; Charles Faso; Robert Hutmacher; Robert Karris, O.F.M.; Bros. Clarence Klingert; Thomas Krull; William Lanning; Revs. Paul LaChance; George Musial; Glenn Phillips; Bros. Duncanh Pham; Herbert Rempe, Business Mgr.; Javier Ruiz-Cadena; Raymond Shuhert; Thinh Van Tran; Revs. Michael Luke Ubben; Arthur Anderson; Aex Assuncao DaSilva, O.F.M., Studies; Mario DiCicco, O.F.M., Pres. & Prof. Franciscan School of Theology, Berkeley, CA; Vaughn Fayle, O.F.M., D.Phil., Prof. Catholic Theological Union; Bro. Leo Geurts, O.F.M., Front Office, Book Store; Revs. Kurt Hartrich, O.F.M.; James A. Hoffman, O.F.M., Confessor, Franciscan Outreach Ministry; Bros. Gary Jerhia, O.F.M., Music Ministry; Edward

McKenzie, O.F.M., Theological Studies at Catholic Theological Union; Joseph Middleton, O.F.M., Front Office, Guest Master; Rev. James Perluzzi, O.F.M., Guardian, Confessor. Order of Friars Minor.

Premonstratensian Fathers and Brothers (Norbertines), 4841 S. Woodlawn Ave., 60615. Tel: 773-548-8020; Fax: 773-548-8023. Web: www.norbertines.org. Rev. David Komatz, O.Praem, House Supr.; Bro. Terrence Lauerman, O.Praem. Holy Spirit House of Studies. Priests 1; Brothers 1; Students 3.

Priests of the Sacred Heart, 1421 E. 53rd St., 60615-4501. Tel: 773-363-1326; Fax: 773-363-1442. Rev. Vien Nguyen, S.C.J., Formation Dir.; Bro. Duane Lemke, S.C.J., College Prog. Formation Dir. SCJ College Program. Priests 4; Brothers 2; Scholastics 4; College Candidates 8. *SCJ Novitiate* Tel: 773-363-1326; Fax: 773-363-1442. Revs. John Czyzynski, S.C.J., Novice Dir.; Robert W. Bossie, S.C.J. *SCJ Theology Program* Tel: 773-752-2325; Fax: 773-363-1442. Bro. Peter Mankins, S.C.J., Treas.

Provincial Office of the Congregation of the Resurrection, 7050 N. Oakley Ave., 60645-3426. Tel: 773-465-8320; Fax: 773-465-8314. Very Rev. Michael Danek, C.R., Prov. Supr.; Rev. Dennis Sanders, C.R.

Weber High School, Inc., Tel: 773-465-8320

Weber Endowment Fund, Tel: 773-465-8320

Priests serving abroad: Very Rev. Norbert W. Raszeja, C.R., Supr. Gen., Curia Generalate, Via San Sebastianello 11, Rome 00187 Italy. Tel: 011-39-06-679-5908; Fax: 011-39-06-678-4397; Rev. Steven Bartczyszyn, C.R., Procurator & Sec., Curia Generalate, Via San Sebastianello 11, Rome 00187 Italy. Tel: 011-39-06-679-5908; Fax: 011-39-06-678-4397.

Priests serving elsewhere: Revs. Richard Grek, C.R., Resurrection Parish, 3601 N. California Ave., 60618; Dennis Sanders, C.R., Resident, 7050 N. Oakley Ave., 60645-3426. Tel: 773-465-8406; Fax: 773-465-8314; Jerzy Zieba, C.R., St. John the Evangelist Parish, 1008 Fortune Ave., Panama City, FL 32401. Tel: 850-763-1821; Fax: 850-784-1739; Gerald Watt, C.R., St. John the Baptist Parish, 2302 W. Church St., Johnsburg, 60050. Tel: 815-385-1477; Fax: 815-363-3333; James Gibson, C.R., St. Joseph Parish, 17080 Arrow Blvd., Fontana, CA 92335-3807. Tel: 909-822-0566; 909-822-0567; Fax: 909-829-1739; Tomasz Wojciechowski, C.R., St. Hedwig Parish, 2226 N. Hoyne, 60622; Bro. William Hallas, C.R., Devel. Dir. & Prov. Treas., Archbishop Weber House, 7050 N. Oakley Ave., 60645-3426. Tel: 773-465-8320; Fax: 773-465-8314.

The Redemptorist Fathers of Chicago, 1633 N. Cleveland Ave., 60614. Tel: 312-642-2498; Fax: 312-642-9283. Email: stmichael-cleveland@archchicago.org. Web: www.st-mikes.org. Revs. Richard Thibodeau, C.Ss.R., Pastor, St. Michael in Old Town; Kenneth Sedlak, C.Ss.R.; Thomas Donaldson, C.Ss.R., Assoc. Pastor, St. Michael in Old Town; Edward Wilhelm, C.Ss.R. (Retired); John Paul Andree, C.Ss.R., Mission Team; John Dowd, C.Ss.R. (Retired); Joseph J. Morin, C.Ss.R., Local Supr., Assoc. Pastor, St. Michael in Old Town; John Kuehner, C.Ss.R., Mission Team; Anthony Judge, C.Ss.R., Mission Team; Arturo Uribe, C.Ss.R., Mission Team Coord.; Gan Nguyen, C.Ss.R., Mission Team.

Redemptorist Theology Residence, 1027 E. Hyde Park Blvd., 60615-2807. Tel: 773-363-2094; Fax: 773-363-2095. Email: jkevin61@aol.com. Revs. John K. Schmidt, C.Ss.R., Formation Dir. & Supr.; J. Robert Fenili, C.Ss.R., Vicar Supr.; John P. Fahey-Guerra, C.Ss.R., Co-Dir. Formation Prog.; Bros. Bruce Davidson, C.Ss.R.; Ted Dorcey, C.Ss.R.; Fawaz Kako, C.Ss.R.; Thanh Nguyen, C.Ss.R.; Landon Cao, C.Ss.R. Priests 4; Students 4.

Assigned to Community, Living in Rome: Rev. Stephen Rehrauer, C.Ss.R.

Assigned to Community, Living in Manila, Philippines: Bro. Eugene Batungbacal, C.Ss.R.

St. Rita Monastery, 7740 S. Western Ave., 60620-5867. Tel: 773-476-3879; Fax: 773-925-2451. Revs. Wes E. Benak, O.S.A.; Bernard R. Danber, O.S.A., Prior; Thomas R. McCarthy, O.S.A.; Walter F. McNicholas, O.S.A.; Bros. John M. Hibbard, O.S.A.; Gary L. Hresil, O.S.A. (See High Schools, Private)

Sacred Heart Mission House, 4105 N. Avers Ave., 60618. Tel: 773-588-7476; Fax: 773-588-6517. Email: polmes@jezuicichicago.org. Web: www.jezuicichicago.org. Revs. Stanislaw Czarnecki, S.J., Supr. & Pres., Editor, The Messenger of The Sacred Heart in Polish language; Miroslaw Bozek, S.J. (Poland); Wieslaw Faron, S.J.; Piotr Kochanowicz, S.J., Treas.; Tadeusz Kukulka, S.J.; Bro. Adam Laska, S.J. *The Polish Messenger of The Sacred Heart, Inc.* Priests 5; Brothers 1. *Jesuit Millennium Center*, 5835 W. Irving Park Rd., 60634. Tel: 773-777-7000; Fax: 773-427-0126. Email: agendajom@yahoo.com. *Jan Beyzym Society, Inc.*, 4105 N. Avers Ave., 60618. Tel: 773-588-7476; Fax: 773-588-6517. Rev. Stanislaw Czarnecki, S.J. (Polish Jesuit Foreign Missions)

Scalabrini House of Theology, 5121 S. University Ave., 60615. Tel: 773-684-5230; 773-684-1706; Fax: 773-684-5240. Email: scalajmr@hotmail.com. Revs. Jesus Reyes, C.S., Rector; Mauro Lazzarato, C.S., Animator; Gino Dalpiaz, C.S., Spiritual Dir. Priests 2; Students 8.

Viatorian Residence, 1201 W. Belden, 60614. Email: d.p.houde@sbcglobal.net. Web: www.viatorians.com. Revs. Thomas G. Kass, C.S.V. Tel: 773-871-6342; Kenneth R. Morris, C.S.V. Tel: 773-871-6279; C. Gregory Jones, C.S.V. Tel: 773-871-6245; Thomas E. Long, C.S.V. Tel: 773-883-1003; John E. Eck, C.S.V.; Bro. Donald P. Houde, C.S.V. Tel: 773-871-6523. Priests 5; Brothers 1.

Vincentian Community, Congregation of the Mission, Western Province, 2210-12 N. Racine Ave., 60614. Tel: 773-325-8761; Fax: 773-348-4802. Revs. Guillermo Campuzano, C.M.; Thomas Croak, C.M.; Patrick V. Harrity, C.M.; Gerard P. Kelly, C.M.; Robert Lucas, C.M.; J. Patrick Murphy, C.M.; James Murphy, C.M.; Christopher S. Robinson, C.M.; Edward R. Udovic, C.M., Supr.; Bro. Mark Elder, C.M.

Xaverian Missionaries (S.X.), 1347 E. Hyde Park Blvd., 60615-2924. Tel: 773-643-5745; Fax: 773-643-6907. Email: kaskampascox@yahoo.com. Web: www.xaviermissionaries.org. Rev. Pascal Kasanziki, S.X., Rector.

ARLINGTON HEIGHTS. *Congregation of Alexian Brothers Immaculate Conception Province, Inc.*, 3040 W. Salt Creek Ln., 60005. Tel: 847-385-7147; Fax: 847-483-7036. Web: www.alexianbrothers.org.

Provincial Councilors: Bros. Theodore Loucks, C.F.A.; James Classon, C.F.A.; John Howard, C.F.A.; Lawrence Krueger, C.F.A., Treas. & Asst. Sec.; Richard Lowe, C.F.A. *Brothers of St. Alexius Health and Welfare Fund, Inc.* Tel: 847-385-7147; Fax: 847-483-7036.

Viatorian Province Center-Clerics of St. Viator, 1212 E. Euclid Ave., 60004-5799. Tel: 847-398-1354; Fax: 847-637-2145. Email: tvonbehren@viatorians.com. Web: www.viatorians.com. Very Rev. Thomas R. von Behren, C.S.V.; Revs. George J. Auger, C.S.V.; Robert R. Cooney, C.S.V.; James F. Crilly, C.S.V., 4219 Pinecrest Cir. E., Las Vegas, NV 89121; Robert E. Erickson, C.S.V.; Donald J. Fitzsimmons, C.S.V.; Charles L. Maranto, C.S.V.; William C. Mayer, C.S.V.; John W. Milton, C.S.V.; Arnold E. Perham, C.S.V.; John E. Van Wiel, C.S.V.; Francis P. White, C.S.V.; Thomas F. Wise, C.S.V.; Deacon Dale A. Barth, C.S.V.; Bros. Carlos Ernesto Florez, C.S.V.; Michael T. Gosch, C.S.V., Asst. Provincial; Leo V. Ryan, C.S.V.

Priests & Brothers of the Province Serving Abroad: Very Rev. Mark R. Francis, C.S.V., Supr. Gen., Chierici di San Viatore, Casella Postale 10793, Rome 00144 Italy. Tel: 011-39-06-529-1603; Fax: 011-39-06-529-4076; Revs. Alejandro Adame, C.S.V., Clerigos de San Viator, Apartado Aereo 140011 (Centro Chia), Bogota D.C., Colombia. Tel: 011-571-862-7060; Carlos Luis Claro, C.S.V., Clerigos de San Viator, Apartado Aereo 140011 (Centro Chia), Bogota D.C., Colombia. Tel: 011-571-862-7060; Brian G. Cooper, C.S.V., Catholic Mission Corozal, P.O. Box 34, Corozal Town, Belize. Tel: 011-501-422-2018; Fax: 011-501-422-2845; Christopher J. Glancy, C.S.V.; Pedro E. Herrera, C.S.V., Clergios de San Viator, Apartado Aereo 120060, Bogota, D.C., Colombia. Tel: 011-571-676-0296; Luis E. Lopez, C.S.V., Clergios de San Viator, Apartado Aero 120060, Bogota D.C., Colombia. Tel: 011-571-676-0296; Jose Felipe Montes, C.S.V., Parroquia San Juan Maria Vianney, Transversal 18B #187-31 (Barrio Verbenal), Bogota, D.C., Colombia. Tel: 011-571-677-5915; John A. Pisors, C.S.V., Clergios de San Viator, Apartado Aereo 140011 (Centro Chia), Bogota D.C., Colombia. Tel: 011-571-862-7060; Rafael Sanabria, C.S.V., Parroquia San Juan Maria Vianney, Transversal 18B #187-31 (Barrio Verbenal), Bogota D.C., Colombia. Tel: 011-571-677-5915; Edgar Suarez, C.S.V., Parroquia San Basilio Magno, Calle 80A #101-37 (Barrio Bochica), Bogota D.C., Colombia. Tel: 011-571-229-2248; Albeyro Vanegas, C.S.V., Clerigos de San Viator, Calle 61 #4-49 (Chapinero Alto), Bogota D.C., Colombia. Tel: 011-571-255-2947; Bros. Fredy Contreras, C.S.V., Clerigos de San Viator, Calle 61 #4-49 (Chapinero Alto), Bogota, D.C., Colombia. Tel: 011-571-255-2947; Frank H. Enciso, C.S.V., Parroquia San Basilio Magno, Calle 80A #101-37 (Barrio Bochica), Bogota D.C., Colombia. Tel: 011-571-229-2248; John R. Eustice, C.S.V.; Gustavo C. Lopez, C.S.V., Clerigos de San Viator, Apartade Aereo 120060, Bogota D.C., Colombia. Tel: 011-571-676-0296; Edwin J. Ruiz, C.S.V.; Fredy L. Santos, C.S.V., Parroquia San Juan Maria Vianney, Transversal 18B #187-31 (Barrio Verbenal), Bogota D.C., Colombia. Tel: 011-571-677-5915; Daniel M. Villalobos, C.S.V.

Priests & Brothers Serving Elsewhere In The Archdiocese of Chicago: Revs. Charles G. Bolser, C.S.V.; Corey D. Brost, C.S.V.; William Carpenter, C.S.V.; John E. Eck, C.S.V.; Robert M. Egan, C.S.V.; Daniel B. Hall, C.S.V.; Bro. Donald P. Houde, C.S.V.; Revs. C. Gregory Jones, C.S.V.; Thomas G. Kass, C.S.V.; Bro. James E. Lewnard, C.S.V.; Rev. Thomas E. Long, C.S.V.; Bro. Moises L. Mesh, C.S.V.; Rev. Kenneth R. Morris, C.S.V.; Bro. Jason P. Nesbit, C.S.V.; Revs. John C. Puisis, C.S.V.; Hugh W. Robbins, C.S.V.; Bros. Rob Robertson, C.S.V.; Daniel J. Tripamer, C.S.V.

Priests & Brothers Serving Elsewhere In U.S.A.: Revs. Daniel R. Belanger, C.S.V.; Victor E. Bertrand, C.S.V., 4801 N. Hills Blvd., Apt. 1106, North Little Rock, AR 72116; Philip E. Kendall, C.S.V., 1900 N. 70th St., Kansas City, KS 66102; Edward Anderson, C.S.V., 4219 Pinecrest Cir. E., Las Vegas, NV 89121; Patrick J. Durkin, C.S.V., 4219 Pinecrest Cir. E., Las Vegas, NV 89121; John N. Peeters, C.S.V., 428 S. Indiana Ave., Kankakee, 60901; Donald R. Wehnert, C.S.V., 428 S. Indiana Ave., Kankakee, 60901; Robert T. Bolser, C.S.V., 2736 Legend Hollow Ct., Henderson, NV 89074; Michael P. Keliher, C.S.V., 2736 Legend Hollow Ct., Henderson, NV 89074; Patrick W. Render, C.S.V., 2736 Legend Hollow Ct., Henderson, NV 89074; Bros. John J. Dodd, C.S.V., 5710 E. Tropicana Ave., #2040, Las Vegas, NV 89122; Patrick T. Drohan, C.S.V., Villa Desderata, 3015 N. Bayview Ln., McHenry, 60051; Revs. James F. Fanale, C.S.V., 230 N. Sixth Ave., P.O. Box 470, Saint Anne, 60964; William F. Haesaert, C.S.V., 2461 E. Flamingo Rd., Las Vegas, NV 89121; Bro. Michael A. Rice, C.S.V., 2461 E. Flamingo Rd., Las Vegas, NV 89121; Revs. Richard A. Rinn, C.S.V., 2461 E. Flamingo Rd., Las Vegas, NV 89121; Donald W. Huntimer, C.S.V., 800 N. County Club Rd., Tucson, AZ 85716; Thomas G. Langenfeld, C.S.V., 1932 Heritage Oaks, Las Vegas, NV 89119; Simon P. Lefebvre, C.S.V., P.O. Box 515, Aguanga, CA 92536; Lawrence D. Lentz, C.S.V., 336 Cathedral Way, Las Vegas, NV 89109; John E. Linnan, C.S.V., 445 Briarcliff Ln., Apt. 5, Bourbonnais, 60914; James E. Michaletz, C.S.V., 308 E. Marsile St., Bourbonnais, 60914; Richard J. Pighini, C.S.V., 308 E. Marsile St., Bourbonnais, 60914; Daniel J. Mirabelli, C.S.V., 1303 40th St., Rock Island, 61201; Daniel T. Nolan, C.S.V., University of Notre Dame, 120 Keenan Hall, Notre Dame, IN 46556-0366; John M. Palmer, C.S.V., 1861 Portsmouth Dr., Lisle, 60532; Erwin M. Savela, C.S.V., 1601 Barton Rd., Apt. 1206, Redlands, CA 92373; Alan M. Syslo, C.S.V., 3785 Viking Garden Cir., Las Vegas, NV 89121; Eugene J. Weitzel, C.S.V., 318 W. 6th St., Beardstown, 62618; Kenneth E. Yarno, C.S.V., 5272 E. 5000 North Rd., Bourbonnais, 60914.

BLUE ISLAND. *Marist Brothers*, 12212 Irving Ave., 60406. Tel: 708-385-1488. Bros. Patrick McNamara, F.M.S.; Patrick McNulty, F.M.S.; James McKnight, F.M.S.

BURBANK. *Congregation of Christian Brothers dba Christian Brothers of Ireland, Inc.* 5550 W. 87th St., 60459-2914. Tel: 773-429-5343; Fax: 773-429-4381. Bro. George G. Gremley, C.F.C.

CICERO. *San Damiano Friary Order of Friars Minor*, 4856 W. 29th St., 60804-3611. Tel: 708-656-1022. Revs. Gerald Bleem, O.F.M.; Paul Gallagher, O.F.M.; Lawrence Jagdfeld, O.F.M.; Bro. Christopher Neuman, O.F.M.

COUNTRYSIDE. *St. Gratian Friary, Franciscan Friars*, 5536 S. Edgewood Ln., 60525-3426. Tel: 708-482-4546; Fax: 708-482-8676. Email: stgratian@aol.com. Revs. James Walton, O.F.M.; Benet Fonck, O.F.M.; Dennis Koopman, O.F.M., Guardian; Kieran Kemner, O.F.M.; Albert Haase, O.F.M.; Bro. Leon Beranek, O.F.M. Priests 5; Brothers 1.

EVANSTON. *Canisius House*, 201 Dempster St., 60201-4704. Tel: 847-475-1825; Fax: 847-475-1869. Revs. Daniel L. Flaherty, S.J., Acting Supr.; Gene D. Phillips, S.J.; Theodore G. Munz, S.J.; James S. Prehn, S.J.; Timothy P. Kejicki, S.J.

GLENVIEW. *The Redemptorists of Glenview, Illinois* North American Redemptorist Novitiate, 1111 N. Milwaukee Ave., P.O. Box 6, 60025. Tel: 847-724-0425; Fax: 847-724-8953. Revs. Gary Lauenstein, C.Ss.R., Novice Dir.; Ramon Dompke, C.Ss.R., Treas.; Henry Novak, C.Ss.R.; Raymond Corriveau, C.Ss.R., Asst. Novice Dir.; Kevin Fraher, C.Ss.R., Missionary; Bros. Daniel Hall, C.Ss.R.; Daniel Korn, C.Ss.R., Local Supr.

HILLSIDE. *Legion of Christ*, 601 N. Hillside Ave., 60162. Tel: 630-248-5287. Email: chicago@legionaries.org. Revs. Andre LaSana, L.C., Supr.;

Jason Brooks, L.C., Vice Rector; Bros. Pedro Miranda, L.C.; Marcin Ubas, L.C.; Juan Carlos Vazquez, L.C.; Revs. Jacob Dumont, L.C.; Matthew Kaderabek, L.C.

LA GRANGE PARK. *Comboni Missionaries*, 1615 E. 31st St., 60526-1377. Tel: 708-354-1999; Fax: 708-354-2006. Email: cmcoffice@sbcglobal.net. Web: www.combonimissionaries.org; www.laymission-comboni.org. Revs. Dennis Conway, M.C.C.J., Supr.; Angel Camorlinga, M.C.C.J., Ministry; Abil Nairki Modi, M.C.C.J., Ministry.

LEMONT. *The Slovene Franciscan Fathers, Order of Friars Minor, Commissariat of the Holy Cross*, 14246 Main St., P.O. Box 608, 60439. Tel: 630-257-2494; Fax: 630-257-6432. Revs. Blase Chemazar, O.F.M., Pres.; Metod Ogorevc, O.F.M., Guardian; Bernardin Susnik, O.F.M.; Martin Stepanich, O.F.M.; Athanasius Lovrencic, O.F.M. Priests 5.

**Slovenian Catholic Center*, 14252 Main St., P.O. Box 634, 60439. Tel: 708-204-4390. Email: john.vidmar@synovate.com. Web: www.slovenian-center.org. Deacon John Vidmar, Bd. Member.

LIBERTYVILLE. *Marytown, Our Lady of Fatima Friary*, 1600 W. Park Ave., 60048-2593. Tel: 847-367-7800; Fax: 847-367-7831. Email: frstephen@marytown.com. Web: www.marytown.com; www.consecration.com. Bro. Augustine Kelly, O.F.M.Conv., Vicar; Revs. Stephen McKinley, O.F.M.Conv., Rector & Vicar Prov., J.I. Editorial Office for Immaculata Magazine & Prow Books; Edmond Des Forges, O.F.M.Conv.; Anthony Fox, O.F.M.Conv. *Conventual Franciscan Friars of Marytown* Tel: 847-367-7800; Fax: 847-367-7831. *National Shrine of St. Maximilian Kolbe* Tel: 847-367-7800; Fax: 847-367-7831. Conventual Franciscan Friars 13.

MATTESON. *Austin Friary*, 5245 Stoneridge Ct., 60443-2269. Tel: 708-747-2732; Fax: 708-747-3549. Revs. G. Jerome Knies, O.S.A., Vicar Prov.; Terry A. Deffenbaugh, O.S.A., Prior; Bros. David W. Adelsbach, O.S.A.; Thomas P. Taylor, O.S.A. Priests 2; Brothers 2.

OAK PARK. *Claretian Missionaries USA Eastern Province*, 400 N. Euclid, 60302. Tel: 708-848-2076; Fax: 312-236-7756. Email: usaeastprov@claretians.org. Web: www.claretians.org. Very Rev. Eddie De Leon, C.M.F., Prov. Supr.; Revs. Wayne Barron, C.M.F.; Thomas Brummel, C.M.F.; Richard Farrell, C.M.F.; Raymond E. O'Connor, C.M.F.; Joseph Peplansky, C.M.F.; Ronald Stua, C.M.F., Supr.; Bro. Richard Wilga, C.M.F. Priests 27; Scholastics 14; Brothers 4.

Claretian Formation Houses:

Claret House, 5540 S. Everett, 60637. Tel: 773-493-8119; Fax: 773-493-8411. Email: joycet@claretians.org. Revs. Theodore Cirone, C.M.F.; Wayne Schimmelmann, C.M.F.; Ronald Stua, C.M.F.; Bro. Oscar Mendoza, C.M.F.

Barbastro House (Claretian Candidate House), 5533 S. Sawyer, 60629. Tel: 773-737-2070. Email: joycet@claretians.org. Revs. Thomas Joyce, C.M.F., Supr.; Brian Culley, C.M.F., Dir.

Priests and Brothers living elsewhere in the Archdiocese of Chicago: Revs. Marco Cardenas, C.M.F.; Severino Lopez, C.M.F.; Bro. Thomas Haerle, C.M.F.; Revs. Allan Fredrick Sahuc, C.M.F.; Mark J. Brummel, C.M.F., Supr.; Carl J. Quebedeaux, C.M.F.; Bruce L. Wellems, C.M.F.; Thomas Moran, C.M.F.; Manuel Villalobos, C.M.F.; Ferdinand Okorie, C.M.F.; George Ruffolo, C.M.F.; Jose Marino Novoa, C.M.F.; Hector Navalo, C.M.F.; Richard White, C.M.F.; Bro. Manuel Benavides, C.M.F.; Rev. Francesco Iacona, C.M.F.

Priests living elsewhere: Revs. James F. Maloney, C.M.F., Marian Village, 15555 Mount Carmel Dr., Homer Glen, 60491. Tel: 708-226-3780; Fax: 708-226-3781; Richard Bartlett, C.M.F., Resurrection Life Center, 7370 W. Talcott, 60631; Stephen Keusenkothen, C.M.F., 400 N. Euclid Ave., 60302. Tel: 312-544-8163. *Claretian Missionaries Community Support Trust*, 400 N. Euclid Ave., 60302. Tel: 708-848-2076; Fax: 708-848-2069. Very Rev. Eddie De Leon, C.M.F., Pres.; Revs. Mark J. Brummel, C.M.F., Treas.; Carl J. Quebedeaux, C.M.F., Sec.; Ronald Stua, C.M.F.; Bruce L. Wellems, C.M.F.

Dominican Community of St. Martin de Porres, 204 S. Humphrey, 60302. Tel: 708-848-4271. Email: stmartin@dominicans.org. Web: www.dominicans.org; www.digitalfriars.net. Revs. Michael A. Winkels, O.P.; James Marchionda, O.P.; Bro. Gabriel Dault, O.P.

Missionaries of Saint Charles, Provincial Residence, 546 N. East Ave., 60302. Tel: 708-386-4430; Fax: 708-386-4457. Web: www.scalabrinians.org. Rev. Adilso Luiz Balen, C.S., Prov.

Fathers of St. Charles Scalabrini Development Office, 546 N. East Ave., 60302. Tel: 708-848-1616; Fax: 708-848-2525. Rev. Aldo Vendramin, C.S., Dir. *Scalabrinians Community Support Corporation, Oak Park* Tel: 708-386-4430; Fax: 708-386-4457. *Scalabrinians Community Formation Corporation, Oak Park* Tel: 708-386-4430; Fax: 708-386-4457.

OLYMPIA FIELDS. *The Augustinians-Provincialate*, Tolentine Center, 20300 Governors Hwy., 60461-1081. Tel: 708-748-9500; Fax: 708-481-2090. Email: secretary@midwestaugustinians.org. Web: www.midwestaugustinians.org. Very Rev. William E. Lego, O.S.A., Prior Prov.; Bro. Thomas Taylor, O.S.A., Prov. Sec.; Revs. Thomas R. McCarthy, O.S.A., Vocation Dir. Tel: 773-776-3044; G. Jerome Knies, O.S.A., Vicar Prov. & Personnel Dir.; Michael J. Slattery, O.S.A., Province Treas.

Tolentine Monastery at Tolentine Center, 20300 Governors Hwy., 60461. Tel: 708-748-9500; Fax: 708-481-2090; 708-748-0018. Web: www.midwestaugustinians.org. Very Rev. Robert F. Prevost, O.S.A., Prior Gen., Curia Agostiniana, Rome; Rev. Thomas L. Osborne, O.S.A., Prior; Most Rev. John C. McNabb, O.S.A., Prior Prov.; Revs. Edward Andrews, O.S.A.; Alfred M. Burke, O.S.A.; John J. Flaherty, O.S.A.; James Friedel, O.S.A.; John R. Gavin, O.S.A.; Christopher K. Howe, O.S.A.; Edwin Kuczynski, O.S.A.; Francis X. Lawlor, O.S.A.; Michael J. O'Connor, O.S.A.; John T. Shirley, O.S.A.; Christopher C. Steinle, O.S.A.; John P. Tasto, O.S.A.; Ronald R. Turcich, O.S.A.; John van der Beek, O.S.A.; Bros. John Patrick Currier, O.S.A.; Angelo Sturn, O.S.A.; Lawrence Sparacino, O.S.A.

RIVER FOREST. *St. Thomas Aquinas Priory*, 7200 Division St., 60305. Tel: 708-771-3030; Fax: 708-714-9002. Revs. Thomas F. O'Meara, O.P., Prior; Bede R. Jagoe, O.P., Lector; Richard C. LaPata, O.P.; Jordan A. McGrath, O.P., Subprior; Richard J. Woods, O.P.; DePorres C. Durham, O.P.; Alfred A. Lopez, O.P.; Bros. Edward van Merrienboer, O.P.; Douglas Greer, O.P. Legal Subsidiaries and holdings: The Priory Press, 2005 S. Ashland Ave., Chicago, IL 60608. Tel: 312-243-0011; Fax: 312-829-8471. President: Rev. William J. Bernacki, O.P., '56, theology texts for high schools. Priests 7; Brothers 1; Deacons 1.

Living elsewhere: Bro. Joseph Kilikevich, O.P.

TECHNY. *Divine Word Residence*, 1901 Waukegan Rd., P.O. Box 6000, 60082-6000. Tel: 847-412-1100; Fax: 847-753-7456. Email: rector@techny.org. Web: www.divineword.org. Revs. James Braband, S.V.D., Rector; George Artis, S.V.D.; James Artzer, S.V.D.; Lukas Batmomolin, S.V.D.; Charles Boykins, S.V.D.; Joseph Bugner, S.V.D.; Most Rev. John Bukovsky, S.V.D. (Retired), (Retired Archbishop and Papal Nuncio); Revs. Lloyd Cunningham, S.V.D.; John Donaghey, S.V.D.; Felix Eckerman, S.V.D.; Bernard Fisher, S.V.D.; Sunny Francis, S.V.D.; Dariusz Garbaciak, S.V.D.; Kazimierz Garbacz, S.V.D.; Gilbert Gawlik, S.V.D.; Elzear Gehlen, S.V.D.; Joseph Guidry, S.V.D.; Raymond Guidry, S.V.D.; William Halvey, S.V.D.; Anthony Hemphill, S.V.D.; Edward Herberger, S.V.D.; Janusz Horowski; Most Rev. Raymond Kalisz, S.V.D. (Retired), (Retired Bishop of Wewak, Papua New Guinea); Revs. Francis J. Kamp, S.V.D.; Robert Kelly, S.V.D.; John Kersten, S.V.D.; Arnold Lang, S.V.D.; August Langenkamp, S.V.D.; William Liebert, S.V.D. (Retired); Paschal LoBianco, S.V.D.; Adam MacDonald, S.V.D., Vice Rector; John McSherry, S.V.D.; Robert Myers, S.V.D.; Tan Viet Nguyen, S.V.D.; Edward Norton, S.V.D.; Raymond Quetchenbach, S.V.D.; Alexander Rodlach, S.V.D.; Charles Scanlon, S.V.D.; Charles Schneider, S.V.D.; William Seifert, S.V.D.; Peter Silvester, S.V.D.; Francis Theriault, S.V.D.; Eric Vargas, S.V.D.; Richard Vaz, S.V.D.; Very Rev. Mark Weber, S.V.D., Prov.; Rev. Jerome Ziliak, S.V.D.; Bros. Raymond Albers, S.V.D.; Rodney Bowers, S.V.D.; Joachim Brignac, S.V.D.; Rene Gawlik, S.V.D.; Patrick Hegarty, S.V.D.; Daniel Holman, S.V.D.; Herman Thomas Joseph, S.V.D.; Brian McLauchlin, S.V.D.; Dennis Newton, S.V.D.; Gerard Pashia, S.V.D.; Cyril Schroeder, S.V.D.; Kenneth Valois, S.V.D.; Robert Zalikowski, S.V.D.; Mathew Zemel, S.V.D.

Divine Word Techny Community Corporation, (Formerly Divine Word Seminary-St. Mary's Mission House) Retired Archbishop 1; Retired Bishop 1; Priests 44; Brothers 14.

Society of the Divine Word, Provincial Headquarters-Chicago Prov. (Province of Saint Joseph Freinademetz, S.V.D.), 1985 Waukegan Rd., P.O. Box 6038, 60082-6038. Tel: 847-272-2700; Fax: 847-272-2517. Email: provincial@uscsvd.org. Web: www.divineword.org. Very Rev. Mark Weber, S.V.D., Prov.; Revs. Thomas Ascheman, S.V.D., Vice Prov.; Dariusz Garbaciak, S.V.D., Treas.; James Braband, S.V.D., Sec. Education, Recruitment & Formation. *Vocation Office* Tel: 800-553-3321; Fax: 563-876-5515. Email: svdvocations@dwci.edu. Web: www.svdvocations.org. Mr. Len Uhal, National Dir. *Blessed Arnold Charitable Trust*, 1985 Waukegan Rd., P.O. Box 6067, 60082-6067. Tel: 847-272-2700; Fax: 847-753-7464. Email: dgarbaciak@uscsvd.org. Web: www.divineword.org. Rev. Dariusz Garbaciak, S.V.D., Sec. *DWTCRE Charitable Trust*, 1901 Waukegan Rd., 60082. Tel: 847-272-2700; Fax: 847-753-7464. Email: dgarbaciak@uscsvd.org. Web: www.divineword.org. Rev. Dariusz Garbaciak, S.V.D., Sec. *Divine Word Funds, Inc. S.V.D. Funds, Inc.*, P.O. Box 6067, 60082-6067. Tel: 847-272-2700; Fax: 847-753-7464. Email: dgarbaciak@uscsvd.org. Web: www.annunitysvd.org. Very Rev. Mark Weber, S.V.D., Pres.; Rev. Dariusz Garbaciak, S.V.D., Treas. *Divine Word Novitiate*, 1940 Waukegan Rd., 60082-6000. Tel: 847-412-1444; Fax: 847-753-7456. Bro. Rodney Bowers, S.V.D., Novice Dir.; Rev. William Seifert, S.V.D., Assoc. Novice Dir. Novices 4.

WILLOW SPRINGS. *Cistercian Fathers, Our Lady Mother of the Church Polish Mission*, 116 Hilton St., 60480-1697. Tel: 708-467-0436; Fax: 708-467-0479. Email: cistercianfathers@yahoo.com. Box 334, Argo, 60501. Revs. Michael Blicharski, O.Cist.; Filip Krzemien, O.Cist.; John Muc, O.Cist.; Ludwik Zyla, O.Cist.

Cistercian Fathers, Our Lady Mother of the Church., Cistercian Priory dependant monastery of the Abbey in Szczyrzyc, Poland (Polish Congregation) est. 1982. Priests 4.

[O] CONVENTS AND RESIDENCES FOR SISTERS

CHICAGO. *Benedictine Sisters of Chicago*, St. Scholastica Monastery, 7430 N. Ridge Blvd., 60645. Tel: 773-764-2413; Fax: 773-761-5131. Email: prioress@osbchicago.org. Web: www.osbchicago.org. Sr. Patricia Crowley, O.S.B., Prioress. Sisters 51.

Congregation of the Albertine Sisters, 1550 N. Astor, 60610. Tel: 312-642-5838. Sr. Domicela Pekala, Contact Person.

Daughters of Divine Love Congregation, 2601 N. Sayre Ave., 60707. Tel: 773-622-2434 (office); 773-622-3758 (convent); Fax: 773-622-2499. Email: ddloveus@aol.com. Sr. Mary Thecla Akubue, D.D.L., Regl. Supr. A Pontifical Religious Institute.

Daughters of St. Mary of Providence, Provincialate: 4200 N. Austin Ave., 60634-1615. Tel: 773-205-1313; Fax: 773-205-1316. Email: dsmpchi@sbcglobal.net. Web: www.dsmpic.org. Sr. Patricia McCafferty, Prov.

Daughters of St. Paul, 172 N. Michigan, 60601. Tel: 312-346-4902 (convent); 312-346-4228 (center); Fax: 312-346-2587. Email: chicago@pauline.org. Web: www.pauline.org. Sr. Helen Rita Lane, F.S.P., Supr. Sisters 5.

St. Elizabeth Convent, 1356 N. Claremont Ave., 60622. Sr. Bonnie Boilini, P.H.J.C., Contact Person. Poor Handmaids of Jesus Christ.

Little Sisters of Jesus, 1529 S. Sawyer St., 60623. Tel: 773-277-5061. Email: littlesrs.chg@juno.com. Web: www.rc.net/org/littlesisters. Sisters 3.

Little Sisters of the Poor, The, 2325 N. Lakewood Ave., 60614. Tel: 773-935-9600; Fax: 773-935-9614. Sr. Patricia Metzgar, L.S.P., Supr.

Little Sisters of the Poor of Chicago, Inc. Sisters 13.

Medical Missionaries of Mary, 3410 W. 60th Pl., 60629. Tel: 773-737-3458; Fax: 773-737-4582. Email: mmmchi@sbcglobal.net. Web: www.mmmusa.org. Sisters 4.

Mercy Convent, 10044 S. Central Park, 60655. Tel: 773-238-4887; Fax: 773-238-0024. Sr. Ann Sullivan, R.S.M., Admin. Sisters 30.

Missionaries of Charity, 2325 W. 24th Pl., 60608. Tel: 773-847-8771. Sr. M. Janita, M.C., Local Supr. Sisters 6.

Missionary Sisters of Christ the King, 4910 N. Menard Ave., 60630. Tel: 773-481-1831; Fax: 773-545-4171. Sr. Ewa Biniek, M.Ch.R., Supr. 1118 N. Noble St., 60622. Tel: 773-489-0714. Sr. Gertruda Szymanska, M.Ch.R., Supr. 5936 W. Barry Ave., 60634-5130. Tel: 773-889-7979. Sr. Genowefa Potaczala, M.Ch.R., Supr. 2441 N. Menard Ave., 60639-2334. Tel: 773-637-9187. Sr. Marta Cichon, M.Ch.R., Supr. 3651 W. George St., 60618. Tel: 773-395-3520. Sr. Dorota Domin, M.Ch.R., Supr. 6101 S. 75th Ave., Summit, 60501. Tel: 708-458-8556. Sr. Renata Bochenek, M.Ch.R., Supr.

Missionary Sisters of the Sacred Heart, 434 W. Deming Pl., 60614. Tel: 773-883-7302; Fax: 773-525-0513. Sr. Joaquina Costa, M.S.C., Treas.

Mother of Good Counsel Provincialate, 3800 W. Peterson Ave., 60659-3116. Tel: 773-463-3020; Fax: 773-463-3567. Email: cssf@felicianschicago.org. Web: www.felicianschicago.org. Sr. Mary Andrea Chudzik, C.S.S.F., Prov. Min.; Revs. Nathan Jaskulski, O.F.M.; Lawrence Jankowski, O.F.M.; Hugh Zurat, O.S.B.

The Felician Sisters of the United States of America, Incorporated, Chicago Province, Provincialate of the Felician Sisters: Mother of Good Counsel Convent; Our Lady of the Angels Convent; Archives; (*) Felician Services, Inc. Professed Sisters 148.

Felician Volunteers in Mission, Inc.

North American Province of the Congregation of Our Lady of the Cenacle, Inc., 513 W. Fullerton Pkwy., 60614-6428. Tel: 773-528-6300; Fax: 773-549-0554. Email: cenacleprovincialate@usa.net. Web: www.cenaclesisters.org. Sr. Evelyn Jegen, R.C., Prov. Professed Sisters 117.

Cenacle Sisters, 513 W. Fullerton Pkwy., 60614-6428. Tel: 773-528-6300; Fax: 773-528-2456. Email: csisters@cenaclechicago.org. Web: www.cenaclesisters.org. Sr. Helen Donahue, R.C., Coord. Professed Sisters 23.

Queen of the Resurrection House of Prayer, 7430 W. Talcott Ave., 60631. Sr. M. Therese Yokiel, Supr. Sisters 23.

Religious Hospitallers of St. Joseph of Delaware, Inc., 326 W. 64th St., 60621. Tel: 773-962-3900; Fax: 773-873-8247. Email: elizvs@aol.com. Sr. Janet Wahleither, R.H.S.J., Local Contact.

Sisters of Charity of Seton Hill Generalate, Seton House International, 4933 W. Patterson Ave., 60641-3512. Tel: 773-205-1822; Fax: 773-205-1855. Email: marlenemondalek@hotmail.com. Sr. Marlene Mondalek, S.C., Gen. Supr. Seton House International

Sisters of Mercy of the Americas West Midwest Community, Inc., 10024 S. Central Park, 60655-3132. Tel: 773-779-6011; Fax: 773-779-6094. Email: info@mercywmw.org. Web: www.mercywestmidwest.org. Sr. Norita Cooney, R.S.M., Pres. Sisters 4.

Sisters of Mercy of the Americas, Regional Community of Chicago Charitable Trust Tel: 773-779-6011; Fax: 773-779-6094.

Sisters of Our Lady of LaSalette, 4220 N. Sheridan Rd., 60613. Tel: 773-248-4047. Email: marijosnds@starpower.com; sr_emie@yahoo.com. Sisters Josephine S. Valenton, S.N.D.S., U.S.A. Mission in Charge; Emelita S. Sobrepena, S.N.D.S., Local Supr. Sisters (Chicago Community) 2; Sisters (Miami, FL Community) 3; Sisters (Virginia Community) 3.

Sisters of St. Casimir, Motherhouse and Novitiate, 2601 W. Marquette Rd., 60629-1817. Tel: 773-776-1324; Fax: 773-776-8755. Web: www.ssc2601.com. Sr. M. Immacula Wendt, S.S.C., Gen. Supr. Sisters 90.

Sisters of the Good Shepherd, 1114 W. Grace St., 60613. Tel: 773-935-3434; Fax: 773-935-3523. Sr. Dorothy Renckens, R.G.S., Coord. Sisters 4.

Sisters of the Holy Cross, 7422 N. Harlem, 60631-4409. Tel: 773-774-5449.

Other Residences: *Sisters of the Holy Cross*, 9964 W. 153rd St., Orland Park, 60462. Tel: 708-403-5134.

Sisters of the Resurrection Provincial House and Novitiate, 7432 Talcott Ave., 60631. Tel: 773-792-6363; Fax: 773-792-9590. Sr. Virginia Ann Wanzek, C.R., Prov. Supr.

Sisters of the Resurrection Congregation of the Sisters of the Resurrection, Chicago Province., Attended by Passionist Fathers. Sisters 46.

Society of Helpers (1956) Provincial Office, 4721 J S. Woodlawn, 60615. Tel: 773-548-5026; Fax: 773-548-5026. Email: memooresh@sbcglobal.net. Sr. Mary Ellen Moore, Prov. Professed Sisters 30.

Other residences:

Society of Helpers, 2043 N. Humboldt Blvd., 1st Fl., 60647. Tel: 773-342-8832. *Society of Helpers*, 2043 N. Humboldt Blvd., 2nd Fl., 60647. Tel: 773-384-7707. *Society of Helpers*, 4721 J S. Woodlawn, 60615. Tel: 773-548-5026; Fax: 773-548-5026. *Society of Helpers*, 4541 S. Wood, 60609. Tel: 773-807-8561; Fax: 773-376-8929. *Society of Helpers*, 2258 S. Marshall Blvd., 60623. Tel: 773-522-9160; Fax: 773-522-9161.

Wright Hall-Sisters of Charity B.V.M., 6364 Sheridan Rd., 60660-1726. Tel: 773-761-7550; Fax: 773-761-4341. Email: sisters@wrighthall.org. Sr. Mary Donahey, B.V.M., Treas. Professed Sisters B.V.M. 40.

ARLINGTON HEIGHTS. *Missionaries of the Sacred Heart of Jesus and Our Lady of Guadalupe M.S.C.Gpe.*, 1212 E. Euclid Ave., 60004. Tel: 847-255-5616.

Sisters of the Living Word, 800 N. Fernandez Ave. B, 60004-5336. Tel: 847-577-5972; Fax: 847-577-5980. Email: slw@slw.org. Web: www.slw.org. Sr. Barbara Mass, S.L.W., Center Admin. Sisters 69.

BARTLETT. *Immaculata Congregational Home*, 801 W. Bartlett Rd., 60103-4401. Tel: 630-837-4061; Fax: 630-837-0052. Email: ssj801@sbcglobal.net. Sr. Patricia Schafke, S.S.J.-T.O.S.F., Coord. Congregational Home of the Sisters of St. Joseph, T.O.S.F. Sisters in Residence 19.

BERWYN. *Poor Handmaids of Jesus Christ*, 1916 S. Clarence Ave., 60402. Tel: 708-749-0125. Email: jiffert@sbcglobal.net. Sisters 2.

BLUE ISLAND. *Mother of Sorrows Convent*, 13811 S. Western Ave., 60406. Tel: 708-385-2103; Fax: 708-824-0688. Sr. M. Eleanor Carella, O.S.M., Regl. Supr.

Mantellate Sisters Servants of Mary, Motherhouse of the Servants of Mary. Sisters 13.

DES PLAINES. *Monastery of Discalced Carmelites*, 1101 N. River Rd., 60016. Tel: 847-298-4241; Fax: 847-298-4242. Sr. Anne of Jesus, O.C.D., Prioress. Attended by priests of the Archdiocese.

Sisters of the Holy Family of Nazareth, Holy Family Province, 310 N. River Rd., 60016. Tel: 847-298-6760; Fax: 847-803-1941. Email: skiepura@nazarethcsfn.org. Web: www.nazarethcsfn.org. Sr. Sally Marie Kiepura, C.S.F.N., Prov. Supr. Professed Sisters 358.

EVERGREEN PARK. *American Province of Little Company of Mary Sisters* (Little Company of Mary Sisters), 9350 S. California, 60805. Tel: 708-422-0130; Fax: 708-422-2212. Email: kmcintyre@lcmh.org. Web: www.lcmglobal.org. Sr. Kathleen McIntyre, L.C.M., Prov. Leader. Charitable Trust: American Province of Little Company of Mary Sisters Charitable Trust. Total in Community 22.

HOFFMAN ESTATES. *Poor Handmaids of Jesus Christ, Annunciation Convent*, 1480 Ashley Rd., 60169-4818. Tel: 847-519-1384; Fax: 847-885-2757. Email: phjcashley@aol.com. Web: www.poorhandmaids.org.

JUSTICE. *Immaculate Conception Prov. House and Novitiate of the Dominican Sisters*, 9000 W. 81st St., 60458. Tel: 708-458-3040; Fax: 708-458-7230. Email: rosaryhill@sbcglobal.net. Web: www.sistersop.org. Sr. Natalie, O.P., Prov. Vicar. Sisters 39.

LA GRANGE PARK. *Adrian Dominican Sisters, Dominican Midwest Mission Chapter*, 1515 W. Ogden Ave., 60526-1721. Tel: 708-482-5047; Fax: 708-354-9573. Email: pdulka@adriandominicans.org. Web: www.adriandominicans.org. Sr. Patricia Ann Dulka, O.P., Chapter Prioress.

Sisters of St. Joseph of La Grange, 1515 W. Ogden Ave., 60526. Tel: 708-354-9200; Fax: 708-354-9573. Email: joursler@csjoseph.org. Web: csjoseph.org. Sr. Nancy Conway, C.S.J., Pres.

Nazareth Academy, Sisters of St. Joseph Charitable Trust. Sponsored ministries include secondary education, Christ in the Wilderness (retreat center), School on Wheels, an adult literacy program, The Well (spirituality center) and Taller de Jose (outreach program). Total in Community 81.

LAKE VILLA. *Handmaids of the Precious Blood*, 724 W. Petite Lake Rd., 60046-9619. Tel: 847-356-7729; Fax: 847-356-7729. Sr. Mary Genevieve, H.P.B., Prioress. Sisters 3.

LEMONT. *Franciscan Sisters of Chicago, General Administration Building*, 11500 Theresa Dr., 60439-2727. Tel: 630-243-3600; Fax: 630-243-3576. Email: dcollins@chicagofranciscans.com. Web: www.chicagofranciscans.org. Sr. Diane Marie Collins, Gen. Min.

Franciscan Sisters of Chicago Sisters 52; Professed Sisters 52.

Mount Assisi Convent, Sisters of St. Francis of Christ the King, 13900 Main St., 60439-9736. Tel: 630-257-7495; Fax: 630-257-2618. Email: lemont_prov@sbcglobal.net. Sr. M. Patricia Kolenda, S.S.F.C.R., Prov. Supr. Sisters 47.

Our Lady of Victory Convent, 11400 Theresa Dr., 60439-2728. Tel: 630-243-3600; Fax: 630-243-3601. Email: dcollins@chicagofranciscans.com. Web: www.chicagofranciscans.org. Sr. Diane Marie Collins, Gen. Min. General Motherhouse and Novitiate of the Franciscan Sisters of Chicago.

MELROSE PARK. *Missionary Sisters of St. Charles Borromeo* Provincialate, Novitiate and Bishop Scalabrini Community., 1414 N. 37th Ave., 60160. Tel: 708-343-2162; Fax: 708-343-6452. Email: provincialmscs@sbcglobal.net. Web: www.scalabrinian.org. Sisters Marciana Zambiasi, M.S.C.S., Prov. Supr.; Marissonia Daltoe, M.S.C.S., First Councilor & Treas.; Gloria Rosetto, M.S.C.S., Councilor; Maruja Padre Juan, M.S.C.S.; Elizabeth Pedemal, M.S.C.S., Councilor & Sec. Missionary Sisters of St. Charles Borromeo (Scalabrinians). Sisters 65.

NORRIDGE. *School Sisters of Notre Dame*, 4425 N. Ozanam Ave., 60206. Tel: 708-583-2402; Fax: 708-583-2409. Email: kcornell@amssnd.org. Web: www.ssnd.org. Professed Sisters 82.

OAK FOREST. *Missionary Sisters of St. Benedict of Illinois, Inc.*, 5900 W. 147th St., 60452. Tel: 708-535-9623; Fax: 708-535-3625. Email: missionarysis@aol.com. Sr. Assumpta Wrobel, Supr. In Res. Rev. Martin N. Winters (Retired).

OAK PARK. *Daughters of the Heart of Mary*, 140 N. Euclid Ave., #401, 60302-1684. Tel: 708-386-0190; Fax: 708-383-1327. Email: ephpheta@sbcglobal.net. Web: www.dhmna.org. Sr. Anita P. Baird, D.H.M., Supr.

Ephpheta Center Sisters 3.

PALOS PARK. *Poor Clare Monastery of the Immaculate Conception of Illinois*, 12210 S. Will Cook Rd., 60464-7332. Tel: 708-361-1810; Fax: 708-361-1816. Web: www.chicagopoorclares.org. Sr. M. Teresita, P.C.C., Abbess.

TECHNY. *Provincial House of the Missionary Sisters Servants of the Holy Spirit*, 319 Waukegan Rd., P.O. Box 6026, 60082-6026. Tel: 847-441-0126; Fax: 847-441-5587. Email: provinceleader@live.com. Sr. Carol Welp, S.Sp.S., Prov. Supr. Professed Sisters 70.

Arnold Janssen Foundation

Helena Stollenwerk Foundation

WAUKEGAN. *Franciscan Missionaries of Mary*, 726 S. Lincoln Ave., 60085. Tel: 847-662-8439. Email: waukfmm@aol.com. Web: www.fmmusa.org. Sr. Malgorzata Bukowska, F.M.M., Coord. Sisters 4.

WILMETTE. *Maria Immaculata Convent-The Province Center* The Society of the Sisters of Christian Charity, Corporation of Mallinckrodt College of the North Shore, 2041 Elmwood Ave., 60091-1431. Tel: 847-920-9341; Fax: 847-920-9346. Email: srjanice@sccwilmette.org. Web: www.sccwilmette.org. Sr. Janice Boyer, S.C.C., Prov. Supr. Sisters 5.

Sacred Heart Convent, 2221 Elmwood Ave., 60091-1435. Tel: 847-251-3770; Fax: 847-251-8040. Sr. Harriette Stieber, S.C.C., Supr. A home for aged and infirm Sisters of Christian Charity. Motherhouse in Wilmette, Illinois. Sisters in Residence 50.

[P] PIOUS UNIONS AND OTHER SOCIETIES

CHICAGO. **Canons Regular of Saint John Cantius*, 825 N. Carpenter St., 60642-5499. Tel: 312-243-7373; Fax: 312-243-4545. Email: pastor@cantius.org. Web: www.canons-regular.org. Revs. C. Frank Phillips, C.R., Moderator; James Isaacson, S.J.C.; Dennis Kolinski, S.J.C.; Albert Tremari, S.J.C.; Brendan Gibson, S.J.C.; Scott Haynes, S.J.C.; Bartholomew Juncer, S.J.C.; Anthony Rice, S.J.C. A public diocesan association of the Christian Faithful. Priests 8; Brothers 2; Seminarians 5; Novices 7; Juniors 4.

LIBERTYVILLE. *Marytown, U.S. National Center of the Militia of the Immaculata Movement*, Shrine of St. Maximilian Kolbe, 1600 W. Park Ave., 60048-2593. Tel: 847-367-7800; Fax: 847-367-7831. Email: frstephen@marytown.com. Web: www.marytown.com. Very Rev. Patrick Greenough, O.F.M.Conv., Min. Prov. & National Dir. M.I. International Latin name: Militia Immaculatae (M.I.).; An association of clergy, religious and laity dedicated to Catholic evangelization, founded 1917 in Rome by St. Maximilian Kolbe.

[Q] VISITING AND NURSING OF THE SICK IN THEIR HOMES

CHICAGO. *Catholic Home Care*, 721 N. LaSalle St., 60610. Tel: 312-655-7415. Home health agency, Medicare certified, JCAHO accredited, providing health care to individuals in their homes in Cook and Lake Counties.

Catholic Home Care Home Services, 721 N. LaSalle St., 60610. Tel: 312-655-7415. Home health agency, private duty, JCAHO accredited

MORTON GROVE. **Resurrection Home Health Services*, 5747 W. Dempster St., Ste. B, 60053-3061. Tel: 877-742-7447 (toll free); Fax: 847-568-8537. Web: www.reshealth.org. Sandra Bennett Bruce, Pres.; Mrs. Marie Cleary-Fishman, Senior Vice Pres., Performance Distinction & Home Health Svcs. Sponsored by Sisters of the Holy Family of Nazareth & Sisters of the Resurrection., An Affiliate of Resurrection Health Care. Patients Assisted Annually 72,795.

[R] SOCIETIES, CLUBS AND RESIDENCES

CHICAGO. *Kolping Center*, 5826 N. Elston, 60646. Tel: 773-792-2190; Fax: 773-792-0062. Email: chicagokolping@aol.com. Web: www.kolping.org. Rev. Paul Cao, Praeses. The Catholic Kolping Society of Chicago.

VERNON HILLS. *Equestrian Order of the Holy Sepulchre of Jerusalem* North Central Lieutenancy, 202 Annapolis Dr., 60061. Tel: 815-244-9397. Email: jwrapp@grics.net. Web: www.holysepulchre.net. H.E. John W. Rapp, KC*HS; Sir Thomas Mulligan, KGCHS, Treas.; Sir Charles H. Foos, KC*HS, Sec.

[S] RETREAT HOUSES

CHICAGO. *Ascension Guest House*, 3111 S. Aberdeen St., 60608. Tel: 773-927-7424; 888-539-4261 (toll free); Fax: 773-927-5734. Email: porter@chicagomonk.org. Web: www.chicagomonk.org.

Cenacle Retreat and Conference Center, 513 Fullerton Pkwy., 60614. Tel: 773-528-6300; Fax: 773-528-0361. Email: crcc@cenaclechicago.org; ministryoffice@cenaclechicago.org (ministry office); prayercardoffice@cenaclechicago.org (prayer enrollment office). Web: www.cenaclechicago.org. Mr. Robert J. Raccuglia, Dir.

Focolare Movement-Mariapolis Center, 5001 S. Greenwood Ave., 60615. Tel: 773-285-2746; Fax: 773-536-5054. Email: midwest.focolare@sbcglobal.net. Web: www.focolare.us. Daytime Capacity 60; Overnight Capacity 30.

BARRINGTON. *Jesuit Retreat League of Chicago aka Bellamine Jesuit Retreat House* 420 W. County Line Rd., 60010. Tel: 847-381-1261; Fax: 847-381-4695. Email: bellarmine@bellarminehall.org. Web: www.bellarminehall.org. Jesuit Retreat House serving laity (High School, College & Adults), priests and religious. Overnight Capacity 72.

The Jesuit Retreat League of Chicago Tel: 847-381-1261; Fax: 847-381-4695. Revs. Mark W. Andrews, S.J., Supr. & Acting Dir.; Robert S. Flack, S.J.; James P. Gschwend, S.J.

DES PLAINES. *Cabrini Retreat Center* (Formerly St. Frances Cabrini Retreat House), 9430 Golf Rd., 60016. Tel: 847-297-6530; Fax: 847-297-6544. Email: info@cabrinicenter.org. Web: www.cabrinicenter.org. Nancy A. Golen, Dir.; Sr. Grace Waters, M.S.C., Mission Integration Dir.; Christy Salazar, Assoc. Dir. Retreats for youth, laity, religious and immigrants. Sponsored by the Missionary Sisters of the Sacred Heart of Jesus. Sisters 2.

LEMONT. *St. Mary's Retreat House*, 14230 Main St., P.O. Box 608, 60439. Tel: 630-257-5102; Fax: 630-257-6432. Rev. Blase Chemazar, O.F.M., Dir.

MUNDELEIN. *Cardinal Stritch Retreat House*, 1300 Stritch Dr., P.O. Box 455, 60060-0455. Tel: 847-566-6060; Fax: 847-566-6082. Email: stritch@archchicago.org. Web: www.stritchretreat.org. Deacon Richard F. Hudzik, Dir.; Ms. Eva Schopper, Office Mgr. Serves the clergy, Catholic laity and ministers of Chicago and Region VII. Retreatants during year 1,600.

TECHNY. *Techny Towers Retreat and Conference Center (Divine Word International)*, 2001 Waukegan Rd., P.O. Box 176, 60082-0176. Tel: 847-272-1100; Fax: 847-272-9363. Email: info@technytowers.org. Web: www.technytowers.org. Catherine M. Collins, Exec. Dir.; Erin Brown, Conference Mgr. A full-service conference facility used by parish groups, religious communities, nonprofit organizations and schools. Accommodations for 250 (daytime) and 125 (overnight). Chapel seats 750.

[T] NATIONAL INSTITUTIONS

CHICAGO. *Catholic Church Extension Society aka Catholic Extension* 150 S. Wacker Dr., 20th Fl., 60606-4200. Tel: 800-842-7804; Fax: 312-236-5276. Email: info@catholicextension.org. Web: www.catholicextension.org. His Eminence Francis Cardinal George, O.M.I., Ph.D., S.T.D., Chancellor; Most Rev. William R. Houck, D.D., Pres. Emeritus (Retired); Rev. John J. Wall, Pres.; Ms. Julie Turley, Vice Pres. Devel.; Tom Gordon, COO; Mr. Kevin P. McGowan, CFO.

The Catholic Church Extension Society of the United States of America

**Catholic Guild for the Blind*, 180 N. Michigan Ave., Ste. 1700, 60601-7463. Tel: 312-236-8569; Fax: 312-236-8128. Email: guild@guildfortheblind.org. Web: www.guildfortheblind.org. Mr. David J. Tabak, Exec. Dir. Provides devotional services including large print Mass, library, scholarships for Catholic Students; the liturgy of the Hours in large print or audio cassette; the sacramental rites in large print; and large print Bibles.

Catholic Kolping Society of America-National Endowment Fund, 5826 N. Elston Ave., 60646-5544. Tel: 877-659-7237; Fax: 973-478-8049. Email: patfarkas@optonline.net. Web: www.Kopling.org. Lisa Brinkmann, Treas.

Catholic League for Religious Assistance to Poland, Headquarters, 6002 W. Berteau Ave., 60634-1630. Tel: 773-202-7720; Fax: 773-202-7725. Most Rev. Thad J. Jakubowski, D.D., Exec. Dir.; Rev. Thaddeus Dzieszko, Asst. Dir.

Catholic League for Religious Assistance to Poland Center for the Study of Religious Life, 5401 S. Cornell Ave., 60615-5698. Tel: 773-752-2720; Fax: 773-752-2723. Email: csrl@religious-life.org. Web: www.religious-life.org. Sr. Mary Charlotte Chandler, R.S.C.J., Dir. Sponsored by the Conference of Major Superiors of Men, the Leadership Conference of Women Religious and Catholic Theological Union at Chicago to conduct interdisciplinary and intercultural reflection on U.S. religious life and serve as a resource to religious leadership.

Jan Beyzym Society, Inc., 4105 N. Avers Ave., 60618. Tel: 773-588-7476; Fax: 773-588-6517. Email: polmes@jezuicichicago.org. Web: www.jezuicichicago.org. Polish Jesuits Foreign Missions.

Lumen Christi Institute, 5735 S. University Ave., 60637-1507. Tel: 773-955-5887; Fax: 773-955-5233. Email: info@lumenchristi.org. Web: www.lumenchristi.org. Organized by Catholic scholars at the University of Chicago in 1997, The Lumen Christi Institute promotes Catholic thought and culture among students and faculty at the University of Chicago through lectures, courses, conferences and other programs. It also sponsors a national Catholic Scholars Program that works with faculty from across the nation in fields such as law, theology, philosophy and science and religion to renew Catholic thought and mentor the next generation of college teachers.

**The National Center for the Laity*, P.O. Box 291102, 60629. Tel: 773-776-9036; Fax: 773-776-9036. Email: wdroel@cs.com. Web: www.catholiclabor.org/ncl.htm. Mr. Vaile Scott, Pres. Founded in 1977, the NCL is dedicated to advancing a key insight of Vatican II: that the church is the people of God in service to the modern world. NCL publishes a newsletter, INITIATIVES, hosts conferences and retreats and maintains a speakers' bureau.

National Coalition for Church Vocations, 5401 S. Cornell, 2nd Fl., 60615. Tel: 773-955-5453; Fax: 773-363-5530. Email: nccvvocations@gmail.com. Web: www.nccv-vocations.org. Sr. Diane Poplawski, O.P., Exec. Dir.

National Organization for Continuing Education of Roman Catholic Clergy, Inc., 333 N. Michigan Ave., Ste. 1205, 60601. Tel: 312-781-9450; Fax: 312-442-9709. Email: nocercc@nocercc.org. Web: www.nocercc.org. Rev. Norbert J. Maduzia Jr., D.Min. (GAL), Pres.; Mr. James H. Alphen, Exec. Dir. An association of dioceses and religious communities supporting continuing formation for priests. Founded in 1973, membership includes over 170 Roman Catholic dioceses and religious provinces in the United States and 50 other organizations and individuals around the world. Professional services offered include an annual convention, regional meetings, specialized workshops, a quarterly newsletter, practical resources in diverse media, and individual consultation.

National Religious Vocation Conference, 5401 S. Cornell, Ste. 207, 60615. Tel: 773-363-5454; Fax: 773-363-5530. Email: NRVC@nrvc.net. Web: www.nrvc.net. Bro. Paul Bednarczyk, C.S.C., Exec. Dir. A professional organization of women and men committed to vocation awareness, invitation and discernment to consecrated life as brothers, sisters and priests. In an inclusive and collaborative style we present religious life as a viable option for today's church.

Radio Maryja, P.O. Box 39565, 60639-0595. Tel: 773-385-8472; Fax: 773-385-5631. Email: admin@radiomaryjachicago.org. Web: www.radiomaryja.pl; www.radiomaryjachicago.org. 6965 W. Belmont Ave., 60634. Redemptorist religious radio.

ARLINGTON HEIGHTS. *Foundation For Children In Need*, 800 N. Pine Ave., 60004. Tel: 847-670-1145. Email: tomchitta@hotmail.com. Web: www.fcnindia.org. Tom Chitta, Pres. FCN is a Catholic lay organization established to reach out to the neediest in the rural villages of India. The main focus is to provide sponsorship help for education adn health care for the poor.

**Friends of the Orphans*, 85 W. Algonquin Rd., Ste. 395, 60005. Tel: 847-690-1700; Fax: 847-690-1701. Email: info@friendsoftheorphans.org. Web: www.friendsoftheorphans.org. Paula Garcia, Nat'l. Office Mgr. Dedicated to improving the lives of orphaned, abandoned and disadvantaged children through the support of the Nuestros Pequenos Hermanos (NPH) network of orphanages in Latin America and the Caribbean.

EVANSTON. **Solidarity Bridge, Inc.*, 1577 Florence Ave., 60201. Tel: 847-328-7748; Fax: 547-328-6860. Email: solidbridge@aol.com. Web: www.solidaritybridge.org. Juan L. Hinojosa, Exec. Dir. Provides short term international mission opportunities utilizing secular callings as vehicles of service to the poor in partnership with local counterparts in Bolivia through the Chicago Catholic Medical Mission, the Chicago Catholic Enterprise Mission and the Chicago Catholic Education Mission

GLENVIEW. **Coalition in Support of Ecclesia Dei, Ltd.*, P.O. Box 2071, 60025-6071. Tel: 847-724-7151; Fax: 847-724-7158. Email: ecclesiadei@sbcglobal.net. Web: www.ecclesiadei.org. Mary M. Kraychy, Pres. & Exec. Dir. The Coalition assists priests, seminarians and laity in the implementation of Pope Benedict XVI's Summorum Pontificum, providing Latin-English Booklet Missals and other inspirational/educational materials (electronic media DVD's/videos) and printed material, eg. Atlar Cards).

GURNEE. **Caritas For Children, Inc.*, 5250 Grand Ave., PMB 105, 60031-1877. Tel: 888-227-4827; Fax: 414-771-3528. Email: cthoar@caritasforchildren.org. Web: www.caritasforchildren.org. Christopher T. Hoar, Contact Person. A private juridic person in the Archdiocese of Chicago, Caritas for Children promotes and supports inter-country adoptions from Poland through Catholic Charities of Chicago and provides financial assistance for the health, education and general welfare of orphaned and other disadvantaged children located worldwide under a variety of Child-Sponsorship programs in partnership with the services of Catholic Religious communities.

LA GRANGE PARK. *Dominican Leadership Conference*, 1515 W. Ogden Ave., 60526-1721. Tel: 708-482-5033. Email: dlc@domlife.org. Web: www.domlife.org/dlc. Sr. Mary Ellen O'Grady, O.P., Exec. Dir.

Dominican Leadership Conference of Dominican Men and Women Religious in the United States of America

LIBERTYVILLE. **Institute on Religious Life*, P.O. Box 7500, 60048-7500. Tel: 847-573-8975; Fax: 847-573-8960. Email: IRLstaff@religiouslife.com. Web: www.religiouslife.com. Rev. Thomas Nelson, O.Praem., Nat'l. Dir.; Michael D. Wick, Exec. Dir.; M. Kathleen O'Brien, Dir. Operations. IRL promotes and supports the growth, development, and renewal of the consecrated life-particularly vowed religious life-as a gift to the Church and an evangelical witness to the world.

RIVER FOREST. **American Friends of the Ecole Biblique*, 1530 Jackson Ave., 60305. Tel: 708-366-7090. Email: ecolebibli@aol.com. Web: www.op.org/op/ebaf/index-eng.htm. Rev. Peter J. Hereley, O.P., Pres.; Judy Valentine Gerth, Mng. Dir. Tel: 847-475-4114. Organized to raise funds in the U.S. to support the work of the Ecole Biblique et Archeologique Francaise de Jerusalem and promote the dissemination of biblical scholarship and archeological research through newsletters, receptions, and seminars with biblical scholars.

TECHNY. *Divine Word Missionaries, Inc.*, 1835 Waukegan Rd., Box 6099, 60082-6099. Tel: 847-272-7600; Fax: 847-272-8572. Email: info@svdmissions.org. Web: www.svdmissions.org. Bro. Dennis Newton, S.V.D., Pres.; Rev. Richard Vaz, S.V.D., Supr. Delegate; Mr. David Gallagher, Treas.

S.V.D., Catholic Universities, Inc.

[U] MINISTRY IN HIGHER EDUCATION

CHICAGO. *Campus Ministries*, 835 N. Rush St., 60611. Tel: 312-534-8271.

Non-Catholic Institutions:

Northwestern University, Sheil Center 2110 N. Sheridan Rd., Evanston, 60201. Tel: 847-328-4648; Fax: 847-328-4660. Rev. John F. Kartje, Dir. & Chap.

University of Chicago Calvert House 5735 S. University Ave., 60637. Tel: 773-288-2311; Fax: 773-288-1124. Web: www.calvert.uchicago.edu. Rev. Patrick Lagges, Chap. & Dir.

University of Illinois at Chicago - John Paul II Newman Center 700 S. Morgan St., 60607-3429. Tel: 312-226-1880; Fax: 312-226-2361. Web: www.jp2newman.com. Revs. Patrick M. Marshall, Chap. & Exec. Dir.; Steven Bauer, Assoc. Chap.

[V] PERSONAL PRELATURE

CHICAGO. *Midtown Residence* Prelature of the Holy Cross and Opus Dei, 1825 N. Wood St., 60622. Tel: 773-292-5450; 773-292-0660; Fax: 773-292-0996. Web: www.opusdei.org. Revs. Charles M. Ferrer; Joseph P. Landauer; Hilary F. Mahaney; James Socias.

Northview University Center Prelature of the Holy Cross and Opus Dei, 7225 N. Greenview Ave., 60626. Tel: 773-465-3468; Fax: 773-465-1195. Web: www.opusdei.org. Rev. Paul Grant.

Prelature of the Holy Cross and Opus Dei, 5800 N. Keating Ave., 60646. Tel: 773-283-5800; Fax: 773-202-8179. Web: www.opusdei.org. Very Rev. Peter V. Armenio, B.S., Ph.D., Vicar for the Midwest; Revs. Frank J. Hoffman; F. Javier del Castillo; Edward G. Maristany. Office of the Vicar for the Midwest.

OAK PARK. *Oak Park Study Center* Prelature of the Holy Cross and Opus Dei, 831 S. Euclid Ave., 60304. Tel: 708-383-0928; Fax: 708-386-2612.

Web: www.oakparkstudy.org. Revs. Richard L. Schendt; Martin John Miller.

[W] MISCELLANEOUS LISTINGS

CHICAGO. **Aid for Women, Inc.*, 8 S. Michigan Ave., Ste. 1100, 60603-3311. Tel: 312-621-1101; Fax: 312-621-1972. Email: info@aidforwomen.org. Web: www.aidforwomen.org. Susan Barrett, Exec. Dir. Dedicated to upholding the principles of Humanae Vitae and Evangelium Vitae, the organization maintains a crisis center where any pregnant woman will find help and encouragement to choose life for her unborn child through pregnancy testing, confidential counseling and referral to community resources. Long-term support is also available through a one-to-one mentoring program and other services.

Alexian Brothers Bonaventure House, 825 W. Wellington Ave., 60657. Tel: 773-327-9921; Fax: 773-327-9113. Email: information@abam.org. Web: www.abam.org. Michelle Wetzel, CEO. Congregation of Alexian Brothers, Immaculate Conception Province., Housing and supportive services for otherwise homeless persons with AIDS.

The Aquin Guild, c/o Office for Catechesis & Youth Ministry, Cardinal Meyer Center, 3525 S. Lake Park Ave., 60653-1402. Tel: 312-534-3700; Fax: 312-534-3801. Rev. John W. Clemens, Dir. Provides spiritual direction to Catholics engaged in public and parochial education.

Aquinas Literacy Center (ESL), 3540 S. Hermitage, 60609. Tel: 773-927-0512; Fax: 773-927-8980. Email: aquinaslit@aol.com. Web: www.aquinasliteracycenter.org. Alison Altmeyer, Exec. Dir.

**Bethany Trust Fund*, Brown Brothers Harriman Trust Company, N.A., 150 S. Wacker Dr., Ste. 3250, 60606. Tel: 312-781-7140.

The Bolivian Trust of the Dominicans, 1909 S. Ashland Ave., 60608-2994. Tel: 312-666-3244; Fax: 312-829-8471. Rev. John J. Meany, O.P.

St. Bonaventure Oratory, Res.: 1641 W. Diversey Pkwy., 60614. Tel: 773-281-6588; Fax: 773-388-8676. Email: stbonaventure@archchicago.org. Rev. Thomas I. Healy (Retired).

**Brother David Darst Center for Justice and Peace, Spirituality and Education*, 2834 S. Normal Ave., 60616. Tel: 312-225-3099; Fax: 312-842-4178. Email: darst-center@sbcglobal.net. Web: www.brdaviddarstcenter.org. Melinda Rueden, Exec. Dir.

Catholic Conference of Illinois, 65 E. Wacker Pl., Ste. 1620, 60601. Tel: 312-368-1066; Fax: 312-368-1090. Email: rfgcci@aol.com. Web: www.catholicconferenceofillinois.org. Mr. Robert Gilligan, Exec. Dir.

The Catholic Education Institute, P.O. Box 597524, 60659. Tel: 718-823-8565. Email: johnpiderit@msn.com. Web: www.catholicexcellence.org. Rev. John J. Piderit, S.J., Pres.

Catholic Health Partners Services, 2875 W. 19th St., 60623. Tel: 773-484-4300; Fax: 773-521-7902. Web: www.saintanthonyhospital.org. Sponsored by Ascension Health and the Missionary Sisters of the Sacred Heart of Jesus to operate St. Anthony Hospital.

St. Anthony Health Affiliates, 2875 W. 19th St., 60623. Tel: 773-484-4300; Fax: 773-521-7902.

The Catholic New World, 3525 S. Lake Park Ave., 60616. Tel: 312-534-7777; Fax: 312-534-7350. Email: mail@catholicnewworld.com. Web: www.catholicnewworld.com. Ms. Colleen H. Dolan, Dir. Communications & Public Rels.; Dawn Vidmar, Gen. Mgr.; Joyce Duriga, Editor; Ann DeFrisco, Office Mgr. Publishers of The Catholic New World; Chicago Catolico; Katolik; and the Archdiocesan Directory.

Catholic Office of the Deaf, 3525 S. Lake Park Ave., 60616. Tel: 312-534-7899 (Voice); 312-751-8368 (TDD); Fax: 312-534-0394. Email: cathdeafch@archchicago.org. Web: www.deafchurchchicago.parishesonline.com. Rev. Joseph A. Mulcrone, Dir.

**Central American Martyrs Center (Su Casa Catholic Worker Community)*, 5045 S. Laflin, 60609. Tel: 773-376-9263; Fax: 773-376-9241. Email: sucasacw@gmail.com. Web: www.sucasacw.org. Bro. Denis Murphy, F.S.C.; Sr. Mary Davis, I.H.M.; Chantal de Alcuaz.

Charis Ministries, 1400 Devon Ave., Box 415, 60660. Tel: 773-508-3237; Fax: 773-508-2844. Email: charis@charisministries.org. Web: www.charisministries.org. Provides opportunities for spiritual growth utilizing the gifts of Ignatian Spirituality for adults in their 20s and 30s.

Chicago Airports Catholic Chaplaincy, P.O. Box 66353, 60666-0353. Tel: 773-686-2636; Fax: 773-686-0130. Email: ordchapel@aol.com. Web: www.airportchapels.org. Rev. Michael G. Zaniolo, S.T.L., C.A.C., Chap.

Claret Center, 5536 S. Everett, 60637. Tel: 773-643-6259; Fax: 773-643-6929. Email: claret_center@claret.org. Web: www.claret.org. Pauline LaMothe, O.P., Admin. Resources for Counseling and Spiritual Direction.

Claretian Associates, Inc., 9108 S. Brandon Ave., 60617. Tel: 773-734-9181; Fax: 773-734-9221. Email: angelah@claretianassociates.org. Web: www.claretianassociates.org. Angela Hurlock, Exec. Dir. Organization to provide affordable housing and encourage neighborhood improvement in South Chicago.

Claretian Volunteers and Lay Missionaries, 205 W. Monroe St., 60606. Tel: 312-236-7782, Ext. 479; Fax: 312-236-7756. Email: volunteers@claretians.org. Web: www.claretianvolunteers.org. Deana Brewer, Dir.

Court of Appeals-Province of Chicago, 20 N. Wacker Dr., Ste. 3420, 60606. Tel: 312-553-4080; Fax: 312-553-4085. Email: johnplucas43@yahoo.com. Rev. John P. Lucas, Judicial Vicar. The Court of Second Instance in matrimonial cases for the Tribunals of the Province of Chicago.

**Cristo Rey Network*, 14 E. Jackson Blvd., Ste. 1200, 60604. Tel: 312-784-7200; Fax: 312-784-7201. Email: rbirdsell@cristoreynetwork.org. Web: www.cristoreynetwork.org. Rev. John P. Foley, S.J., Exec. Chm.; Rob Birdsell, Pres.; Rob Cummings, Vice Pres. Advancement. The Cristo Rey Network supports and helps establish Catholic high schools where students work to earn tuition and gain business experience. Each school is modeled after Cristo Rey Jesuit High School of Chicago.

Daughters of Charity Ministries of Chicago, Inc., 30 N. LaSalle St., Ste. 4100, 60602. Tel: 312-422-9140; Fax: 312-621-0297. Email: dancoyne@okeefe-law.com. Daniel W. Coyne, Registered Agent.

**DeSales Charitable Trust*, Brown Brothers Harriman Trust Company, N.A., 150 S. Wacker Dr., Ste. 3250, 60606. Tel: 312-781-7140.

**Dominican Volunteers USA*, P.O. Box 891121, 60608. Tel: 708-524-5984; 708-524-5985. Email: dominicanvolunteers@gmail.com. Web: www.dvusa.org. Audry Butler, B.A., Exec. Dir. Dominican Volunteers USA provides full-time volunteer opportunities for lay people. Volunteers live and work with Dominican (Order of Preachers) ministries and communities across the United States, serving those who are in most need.

**Felician Services, Inc.*, 3800 W. Peterson Ave., 60659-3116. Tel: 773-463-3806; Fax: 773-463-2059. Sr. Mary Clarette Stryzewski, C.S.S.F., Pres. & CEO.

Felician Volunteers in Mission, Inc., 3800 W. Peterson Ave., 60659. Tel: 773-463-3732. Sr. M. Andrea Chudzik, Pres.

Focolare Movement, P.O. Box 53426, 60653. Tel: 773-536-7873; Fax: 773-536-5054. Email: midwest.focolare@sbcglobal.net. Web: www.focolare.us. Work of Mary founded in Trent, Italy in 1943. International headquarters are in Rome, Italy; national formation center in New York.

Women, 5017 S. Greenwood Ave., 60615. Tel: 773-536-7873; Fax: 773-536-5054. Ms. Paloma Cabetas, Co-Dir.

Men, 7018 W. 34th St., Berwyn, 60402. Tel: 708-484-9771; Fax: 708-484-4998. Mr. Marco Desalvo, Co-Dir.

Franciscan Friars Retirement Corporation, 6107 Kenmore Ave., 60660-2797. Tel: 773-274-7681; Fax: 773-274-9751.

Franciscan Outreach Association, 1645 W. LeMoyne St., 60622. Tel: 773-278-6724; Fax: 773-278-7120. Web: www.franoutreach.org. Diana Faust, Exec. Dir.; Christine Curran, Dir. Mission & Volunteers. Owns & operates: Marquard Center (dining room for the homeless), Franciscan House of Mary & Joseph (shelter) and a Case Management Program for the homeless in Chicago.

General Assistance, Inc. aka Daughters of Charity International Project Services 30 N. LaSalle St., Ste. 4100, 60602. Tel: 312-422-9140; Fax: 312-621-0297. Email: dancoyne@okeefe-law.com. Daniel W. Coyne, Contact Person. Support organization for the Daughters of Charity.

**Hermitage Charitable Trust*, Brown Brothers Harriman Trust Company, N.A., 150 S. Wacker Dr., Ste. 3250, 60606. Tel: 312-781-7140.

Holy Family Church, Inc., 2050 N. Clark St., 60614. Tel: 773-975-6363; Fax: 773-975-0230. Email: treasurer@jesuits-chgdet.org.

Holy Rosary, 352 E. 113th St., 60628. Rev. Mark J. Krylowicz.

Ignatian Spirituality Project, 6214 N. Glenwood Ave., Second Fl., Ste. 3, 60660. Tel: 773-465-8699. Email: info@ignatianspiritualityproject.org. Web: www.ignatianspiritualityproject.org. The project works with the homeless through retreats and spiritual companionship in the belief that by claiming their spiritual life they can recover from addiction and other problems associated with homelessness

Ignatius Productions, Inc., 2050 N. Clark St., 60614. Tel: 773-975-6363; Fax: 773-975-0230. Web: www.fathermitchpacwa.org.

Illinois Catholic Health Association, 65 E. Wacker Pl., Ste. 1620, 60601. Tel: 312-368-0011; Fax: 312-368-1701. Email: pcacchione@il-cha.org. Web: www.il-cha.org. Patrick J. Cacchione, Exec. Dir.

The Illinois Patrons of the Arts in the Vatican Museums, c/o Thomas Stack, 100 W. Madison, 16th Fl., 60603. Tel: 312-624-8667. Email: AD612@aol.com. His Eminence Francis Cardinal George, O.M.I., Ph.D., S.T.D., Chm.; Anne Shea, Pres.

Institute for Spiritual Leadership, 5401 S. Cornell, 60615. Tel: 773-752-5962; Fax: 773-752-5964. Email: islusa@aol.com. Web: www.spiritleader.org. Lucy Abott-Tucker, Co-Dir.; David Schimmel, Co-Dir. Education Center for Spiritual Direction and Renewal.

Intercommunity Housing Corporation, c/o Edward T. Joyce & Associates, 11 S. LaSalle St., Ste. 1600, 60603. Tel: 312-641-2600. Email: ejoyce@joycelaw.com. David E. Myles, Pres.; Edward T. Joyce, Sec. The Intercommunity Housing Corporation promotes the development and establishment of affordable residential retirement housing for religious, clergy and laity; a design for 21st century living.

Italian Catholic Federation, 2825 W. 81st St., 60652. Tel: 773-436-4444; Fax: 773-778-9087. Email: info@icf.org. Web: www.icf.org. Rev. Charles V. Fanelli, Chap.

Jesuit International Missions, Inc., 2050 N. Clark St., 60614. Tel: 773-975-6870; Fax: 773-975-0230. Email: treasurer@jesuits-chi.org. Rev. Richard L. Millbourn, S.J., Asst. for Intl. Ministry.

Jesuit Seminary Association, 2050 N. Clark St., 60614. Tel: 773-975-6363; Fax: 773-975-0230. Web: www.jesuits-chi.org.

St. Joseph Services, Inc., 30 N. LaSalle St., Ste. 4100, 60602. Tel: 312-422-9140. Email: dancoyne@okeefe-law.com. Daniel W. Coyne, Registered Agent. Supports the mission of the Daughters of Charity to serve the poor.

Kolbe House, 2434 S. California Ave., 60608. Tel: 773-247-0070; Fax: 773-247-0665. Email: khjailmin@aol.com. Revs. David A. Kelly, C.PP.S.; Arturo Perez-Rodriguez, Dir.; Deacons Pablo Perez, Jail Chap.; John Richardson. Catholic jail ministry.

Loyola Press, 3441 N. Ashland Ave., 60657. Tel: 773-281-1818; Fax: 773-281-0555. Email: lane@loyolapress.com. Web: www.loyolapress.com. Rev. George A. Lane, S.J., Pres.

Marist Volunteer Program, 4200 W. 115th St., 60655-4306. Tel: 773-881-5343; Fax: 773-881-3667. Email: maristvolunteerprogram@yahoo.com. Bro. Hugh Turley, F.M.S., Contact Person.

Martin de Porres House, 3322 Washington Blvd., 60624. Tel: 773-826-9336. Margaret Brooks, Pres.; Cathryn Peters, Vice Pres.; Claire Cummings, Sec.

Medical Missionaries of Mary, Inc., Mission Development Office, 4425 W. 63rd St., Ste. 100, 60629-5530. Tel: 773-735-3712; Fax: 773-735-4661. Email: development@mmmusa.org. Web: www.mmmusa.org. Sr. Mary Ann MacRae, M.M.M., Devel. Dir.

Miles Jesu, P.O. Box 267989, 60626. Tel: 773-262-0861; Fax: 773-267-1093. Email: administration@milesjesu.com. Web: www.milesjesu.com.

Men's Formation Center, 1128 W. Morse Ave., 60626. Tel: 773-262-0861; Fax: 773-262-1093. Mr. Scott Ferrer, M.J., Vocation Dir.; Rev. Christopher Foeckler, M.J., Formation Dir.

Women's Formation Center, 1126 W. Morse Ave., 60626. Tel: 773-262-1253; Fax: 773-262-1093. Maire Duggan, M.J., Vocation Dir.

Mother Cabrini League, 434 W. Deming Pl., 60614. Tel: 773-388-7329; Fax: 773-525-0513. Sr. Joaquina Costa, M.S.C., Dir.; Joyce Bandera, Office Supvr. The purpose of the League is to spread devotion to St. Frances Xavier Cabrini.

Mundelein College, Office of the General Counsel of Loyola University-Chicago, 820 N. Michigan Ave., 60611. Tel: 312-915-6195. Email: emunro@luc.edu. Web: www.luc.edu. 6525 N. Sheridan Rd., 60626. Tel: 773-508-3029; Fax: 312-915-6208. Mr. Wayne Magdziarz, Pres. & Chm. Bd. Trustees; Ms. Ellen Kane Munro, Sec.; Philip R. Kosiba, Vice Pres. & Treas.

Oblates for International Pastoral aka Oblate International Pastoral Investment Trust 161 N. Clark St., Ste. 4700, 60601. Email: whitley@omigen.org. Revs. Marcel Dumais, O.M.I.; Rufus J. Whitley, O.M.I.; William Morell, O.M.I.; Joseph Hitpas, O.M.I.

Office for Mission Advancement Dominicans: Province of St. Albert the Great., 1909 S. Ashland Ave., 60608. Tel: 312-226-0020; Fax: 312-226-6440. Email: dominicans@preachers.org. Web: www.op.org.

Order of Friar Servants of Mary United States of America Province, Inc., 3121 W. Jackson Blvd., 60612. Tel: 773-533-0360; Fax: 773-533-8307. Email: bromikeosm@hotmail.com. Web: www.servite.org. The Order of Friar Servants of Mary-U.S.A. Province, Inc, Chicago, IL.

Pathways to Hope, Inc., 205 W. Monroe St., 60606. Tel: 312-223-1085; 866-784-5900; Fax: 312-223-0947. Web: www.pathwaystohope.com. Jennifer Reed, L.C.P.C., Exec. Dir. Pathways to Hope, established by 15 male Roman Catholic religious communities in the Midwest, provides a compassionate and appropriate pastoral response to victims of sexual misconduct by their members.

The Peace Corner, Incorporated, P.O. Box 440113, 60644. Tel: 773-261-5330; Fax: 773-261-1523. Email: thepeacecorner@yahoo.com. Web: www.thepeacecorner.org. Revs. Mario Malacrida, M.C.C.J. (Italy), Pres. & Exec. Dir.; Dennis Conway, M.C.C.J., Vice Pres. & Sec.; Peter Ciuciulla, M.C.C.J., Treas. A ministry of the Comboni Missionaries of the Heart of Jesus, Inc., The Peace Corner is a youth center in the Austin neighborhood of Chicago (5014 W. Madison Ave.) serving youth in need with no distinction of faith, race and background. The Peace Corner offers a safe and caring environment for youth while providing tutoring, computer classes, GED preparation, legal counseling, job training, support groups and recreational activities.

Precious Blood Ministry of Reconciliation, P.O. Box 09379, 60609-0379. Tel: 773-579-0781; Fax: 773-579-0782. Email: nojail@aol.com. Revs. David A. Kelly, C.PP.S., Exec. Dir.; Dennis Kinderman, C.PP.S.; William Nordenbrock, C.PP.S.; Sr. Mary Louise Degenhart, A.S.C. A ministry of the Cincinnati and Kansas City provinces of the Missionaries of the Precious Blood that responds to violence and conflict in the Back of the Yards neighborhood of Chicago (5114 S. Elizabeth St.) and fosters renewal of the church through reconciliation programs, retreats and training workshops for church communities.

Resurrection Health Care, 7435 W. Talcott Ave., 60631. Tel: 773-774-8000; Fax: 773-792-9926. Web: www.reshealth.org. Sandra Bennett Bruce, Pres. & CEO; Sr. Clara Frances Kusek, C.R., Exec. Vice Pres., Mission; Deacon Robert Bulger, Mission Senior Vice Pres.; Sr. Paracleta Amrich, S.S.C.M., Dir. Clinical Pastoral Educ. The Sisters of the Holy Family of Nazareth and the Sisters of the Resurrection co-sponsor Holy Family Medical Center, Our Lady of the Resurrection Medical Center, Resurrection Medical Center, Saint Francis Hospital (Evanston), Saint Joseph Hospital, Saints Mary and Elizabeth Medical Center, Westlake Hospital and West Suburban Medical Center in addition to other legal corporations listed below.

Other members of Resurrection Health Care:

**Proviso Family Services, Inc. dba Resurrection Behavioral Health, d.b.a. ProCare Centers* Tel: 708-681-2324; Fax: 708-681-1289.

Resurrection Development Foundation Tel: 847-813-3477; Fax: 847-813-3482.

**Partners Home Care Foundation dba Resurrection Home Health Foundation* Tel: 847-568-8536; Fax: 847-568-8537.

**Resurrection Home Health Foundation*, 7000 N. Newark, Ste. 144, Niles, 60714. Tel: 847-647-2383; Fax: 847-647-2762.

**Resurrection Home Health Services* Tel: 847-568-8536; Fax: 847-568-8537.

Resurrection Senior Services Tel: 847-813-3176; Fax: 847-813-3876.

Resurrection Services Tel: 773-774-8000; Fax: 773-792-9926.

Retirement Plan of the Order of Friar Servants of Mary-U.S.A. Province, Inc., 3121 W. Jackson Blvd., 60612. Tel: 773-533-0360; Fax: 773-533-8307. Email: bromikeosm@hotmail.com. Web: www.servite.org.

S.F.V., Inc., 1645 W. LeMoyne St., 60622. Tel: 773-278-6724; Fax: 773-278-7021. Rev. Kurt Hartrich, O.F.M., Pres. Sponsor corporation of St. Francis Village (a retirement village) in Crowley, TX.

Serra International, 70 E. Lake St., Ste. 1210, 60601. Tel: 312-419-7411; 800-488-4008 (toll free); Fax: 312-419-8077; 800-377-7877 (toll free). Email: serra@serra.org. Web: www.serra.org. Mr. John W. Woodward, Exec. Dir., Serra International & Serra International Foundation.

USA Council of Serra International Tel: 312-201-6549; 888-777-6681 (toll free); Fax: 312-201-6548; 888-777-6803 (toll free). Email: serraus@serraus.org. Web: www.serraus.org. Mr. E.V. Verbeke, Exec. Dir.

**Society of Friends of the John Paul II Foundation*, P.O. Box 34618, 60634. Email: mskawski@earthlink.net.

**Society of Jesus Worldwide*, 2050 N. Clark St., 60614. Tel: 773-975-6363; Fax: 773-975-0230.

St. Thomas Aquinas Foundation (STAF) (St. Albert the Great Prov.), 1909 S. Ashland Ave., 60608-2994. Tel: 312-666-3244; Fax: 312-829-8471. Very Rev. Michael A. Mascari, O.P., Sec. & Treas.

United Stand Family Center, 3731 W. 62nd St., 60629. Tel: 773-585-4499. Sr. Kim Mis, C.S.S.F., Exec. Dir. Education, Prevention, Problem Identification, Consultation, and Intervention with Children and Families. Total Staff 55.

Villa Guadalupe Senior Services Corporation, 3201 E. 91st St., 60617. Tel: 773-933-0344; Fax: 773-933-0827. Angela Hurlock, Exec. Dir.; Rev. Mark J. Brummel, C.M.F., Treas. Organization to provide affordable housing and related services for Senior Citizens in South Chicago.

Westcourt Corporation, 9757 S. Seeley Ave., 60643-1639. Tel: 773-429-5343; Fax: 773-429-4381. Bro. George G. Gremley, C.F.C.

Zaccheus House (2002) 12242 S. Parnell, 60628. Tel: 773-568-7822; Fax: 773-287-1258. Web: www.zacchaeushouse.org. Most Rev. Joseph N. Perry, Moderator. A ministry of Deacons offering hospitality and life skills education to men in transition to stability in their lives.

ARLINGTON HEIGHTS. **Alexian Brothers Center for Mental Health*, 3350 W. Salt Creek Ln., Ste. 114, 60005. Tel: 847-952-7460; Fax: 847-222-1754. Web: www.alexiancenter.org. Mr. Scott Burgess, Vice Pres. Opers. Congregation of Alexian Brothers, Immaculate Conception Province.

Alexian Brothers Community Services, 3040 W. Salt Creek Ln., 60005. Tel: 847-385-7147; Fax: 847-483-7036. Web: www.alexianbrothers.org. Alexian Brothers Community Services (Programs for the care of the elderly) in Chattanooga, TN.

Alexian Brothers Health System dba Alexian Brothers Foundation 3040 W. Salt Creek Ln., 60005. Tel: 847-385-7147; Fax: 847-483-7036. Web: www.alexianbrothers.org. Congregation of Alexian Brothers, Immaculate Conception Province.

**Alexian Brothers Health System, Inc. Investment Trust*, 3040 W. Salt Creek Ln., 60005. Tel: 847-385-7147; Fax: 847-483-7036. Web: www.alexianbrothers.org.

Alexian Brothers of America, Inc., 3040 W. Salt Creek Ln., 60005. Tel: 847-385-7147; Fax: 847-483-7036. Web: www.alexianbrothers.org. Congregation of Alexian Brothers, Immaculate Conception Province.

Alexian Brothers Senior Ministries, 3040 W. Salt Creek Ln., 60005. Tel: 847-385-7147; Fax: 847-483-7036. Web: www.alexianbrothers.org. Congregation of Alexian Brothers, Immaculate Conception Province.

**Chicago Catholic Healthcare System, Inc.*, 3040 W. Salt Creek Ln., 60005. Tel: 847-385-7147; Fax: 847-483-7036. Web: www.alexianbrothers.org. Congregation of Alexian Brothers, Immaculate Conception Province.

Living Word Charitable Trust, 800 N. Fernandez Ave.-B, 60004-5336. Tel: 847-577-5972; Fax: 847-577-5980. Email: slw@slw.org. Web: slw.org. Michael Gibbs, Trustee.

BLUE ISLAND. *St. Francis Hospital and Health Center*, 12935 S. Gregory St., 60406.

DES PLAINS. *Maryville-Our Lady of Guadalupe Chapel*, 1150 N. River Rd., Des Plaines, 60016. Tel: 847-294-1806; Fax: 847-294-1841. Email: ol-guadalupe-cerrito@archchicago.org. Web: www.maryville.org. Rev. Miguel Angel Martinez, Chap.

Sisters of the Holy Family of Nazareth - U.S.A., Inc., 310 N. River Rd., Des Plaines, 60016. Tel: 847-298-6760; Fax: 847-803-1941. Email: skiepura@nazarethcsfn.org.

EVERGREEN PARK. *American Province of Little Company of Mary Sisters Charitable Trust*, 9350 S. California, 60805. Tel: 708-422-0130; Fax: 708-422-2212. Email: kmcintyre@lcmh.org. Web: www.lcmglobal.org.

Network for Mercy Education, 9318 S. Kedzie Ave., Ste. 1, 60805. Tel: 708-229-1630. Web: www.netmercyed.org.

GLENVIEW. *Redemptorist Fathers of St. Alphonsus Parish of Chicago, c/o Redemptorists of Glenview, Illinois*, 1111 N. Milwaukee Ave., P.O. Box 6, 60025. Tel: 847-724-0425; Fax: 847-724-8953.

The Redemptorists of Blessed Sacrament, c/o Redemptorists of Glenview Illinois, 1111 N. Milwaukee Ave., P.O. Box 6, 60025. Tel: 847-724-0425; Fax: 847-724-8953.

Villa Redeemer, c/o Redemptorists of Glenview, Illinois, 1111 N. Milwaukee Ave., P.O. Box 6, 60025. Tel: 847-724-0425; Fax: 847-724-8953.

GURNEE. *Assisi Homes of Gurnee, Inc.*, 3495 W. Grand Ave., 60031. Tel: 847-336-4428; Fax: 847-336-3778. Web: www.wfhealthcare.org. Units 60.

HOMEWOOD. **The Clare at Water Tower*, 1055 W. 175th St., Ste. 202, 60430. Tel: 708-647-6500.

Franciscan Communities, 1055 W. 175th St., Ste. 202, 60430. Tel: 708-647-6500; Fax: 708-647-6982.

**Franciscan Communities St. Mary of the Woods, Inc.*, 1055 W. 175th St., Suite 202, 60430. Tel: 708-647-6500. Web: www.franciscancommunities.org.

Franciscan Community Benefit Services, 1055 W. 175th St., Ste. 202, 60430. Tel: 708-647-3127; Fax: 708-647-6982. Email: jsisler@franciscanservices.com. Web: www.madonnafoundation4girls.org. Janet Sisler, Pres. Sponsored by the Franciscan Sisters of Chicago., A charitable foundation focused on the ministry of the Franciscan Sisters of Chicago and increasing access to Catholic high schools by young women in urban areas through scholarships and program enhancement.

JUSTICE. **Pope John Paul II Eucharistic Adoration Association, Inc.*, 9000 W. 81st. St., 60458. Tel: 708-728-0840; Fax: 708-728-0840. Email: pjp2ea@sbcglobal.net. Web: www.pj2ea.org. Charles Smith, Treas.

LAGRANGE PARK. **Joyful Again*, P.O. Box 1365, La Grange Park, 60526-9465. Tel: 708-354-7211. Email: joyfulagain@att.net. Web: www.joyfulagain.org. Rev. Medard P. Laz, Exec. Dir.; Charlotte Hrubes, Dir. Support program for widowed men and women.

Sisters of St. Joseph of LaGrange Charitable Trust, 1515 W. Ogden Ave., La Grange Park, 60526-2721. Tel: 708-354-9200; Fax: 708-354-9573. Email: gsbr@juno.com.

LAKE FOREST. *Barat Education Foundation*, P.O. Box 457, 60045. Tel: 847-501-1726; Fax: 847-234-4628. Email: alumni@thebaratfoundation.org. Web: www.thebaratfoundation.org. Maureen Ryan, Exec. Dir.

**New Ethos*, 825 S. Waukegan Rd. A8 #225, 60045. Tel: 312-208-8777. Email: frdon@new-ethos.org. Web: www.new-ethos.org. Rev. Donald C. Woznicki, Exec. Dir. Collaborates with the Entertainment Industry to bring the Catholic consumer true, good & beautiful entertainment.

MELROSE PARK. **Dominican Literacy Center (ESL)*, 1503 Rice St., 60160. Tel: 708-338-0659; Fax: 708-338-0659. Email: jcurranx@yahoo.com. Sr. Judith Curran, O.P., Dir.

MUNDELEIN. *Civitas Dei Foundation*, 1000 E. Maple Ave., 60060. Tel: 847-566-6401. Rev. Lawrence R. Hennessey, M.A., S.T.L., Ph.D. The Journal is named Chicago Studies.

Foundation for Adult Catechetical Teaching Aids, 22333 W. Erhart Rd., 60060. Tel: 847-223-0010; Fax: 847-223-5960. Revs. Ronald J. Lewinski, Pres.; Donald Senior, C.P., S.T.D., Treas.

NORTHLAKE. *Scalabrini Village*, 420-480 N. Wolf Rd., 60164. Tel: 708-562-0040; Fax: 708-562-5180.

RIVER FOREST. **Education and Intervention, Inc. dba ICAP (Inter Congregational Addictions Program)* 7777 W. Lake St., 60305-1734. Tel: 708-488-9770; Fax: 708-488-9774. Email: icapsrs@sbcglobal.net. Sisters Letitia Close, Pres. & Exec. Dir.; Mary Gene Kinney, B.V.M., Master Addictions Counselor (M.A.C.).

Education and Intervention, Inc., National and International network for women religious recovering in 12 step programs; services of intervention, referral, follow-up and education to communities of women religious.

ROLLING MEADOWS. *Rainbows for All God's Children, Inc.*, 2100 Golf Rd., Suite 370, 60008. Tel: 800-266-3206; Fax: 847-952-1774. Email: info@rainbows.org. Web: www.rainbows.org. Mrs. Suzy Yehl Marta, Founder & Pres.

SOUTH HOLLAND. **American Catholic Press*, 16565 S. State St., 60473. Tel: 708-331-5485; Fax: 708-331-5484. Email: acp@acpress.org. Web: www.americancatholicpress.org. Rev. Michael J. Gilligan, Ph.D., Exec. Dir. Founded in 1967, ACP makes available resources on liturgy and liturgical music, especially for parishes and dioceses. ACP was incorporated as a nonprofit organization in 1972.

TECHNY. *Blessed Arnold Religious Charitable Trust*, 1985 Waukegan Rd., P.O. Box 6067, 60082-6067. Tel: 847-272-2700; Fax: 847-753-7464. Email: dgarbaciak@uscsvd.org. Web: www.divineword.org. Society of the Divine Word.

Divine Word Techny Community Corporation dba Divine Word Seminary/Divine Word Residence f/k/a DWTCRE Charitable Trusts 1901 Waukegan Rd., 60082. Tel: 847-272-2700; Fax: 847-753-7464. Email: tlc1670@uscsvd.org. Web: www.divineword.org. Revs. James Braband, S.V.D., Trustee; Dariusz Garbaciak, S.V.D., Sec.

WAUKEGAN. *Alexian Brothers The Harbor*, 826 North Ave., 60085. Tel: 847-782-8015; Fax: 847-782-0822. Email: information@abam.org. Web: www.abam.org. Michelle Wetzel, CEO. Congregation of Alexian Brothers, Immaculate Conception Province., Operated by Alexian Brothers Bonaventure House, Inc.; Residences for persons with AIDS.

WILMETTE. *Loyola Recreational Facility Corp.*, 1100 Laramie, 60091-1021. Tel: 847-256-1100; Fax: 847-251-4031. Web: www.gorambiers.org. Rev. Patrick E. McGrath, S.J.

Musica Pacis, Office of the Treasurer, P.O. Box 969, 60091-0969. Tel: 708-624-2559. Email: musicapacis@attglobal.net. Revs. Willard F. Jabusch, Pres. (Retired); Alec J. Wolff, Treas.

[X] CLOSED INSTITUTIONS

CHICAGO. *Archdiocese of Chicago's Joseph Cardinal Bernardin Archives and Records Center*, 711 W. Monroe St., 60661. Tel: 312-831-0711; Fax: 312-831-0610. Email: info@archchicago.org. Web: archives.archchicago.org. The following parish, school or institution records may be found at the above address unless otherwise indicated. Notations to sacramental records of closed parishes held by the Archives and Records Center should be directed to the Archives and Records Center and should specify the name of the parish. The location of records periodically changes. Inquiries for records of parishes, schools or institutions not on this list should be directed to the above address.

Academy of St. Benedict the African (May St.)
Academy of St. Benedict the African (Honore St.), 6547 S. Stewart Ave., 60621. Tel: 773-994-6100.
Academy of the Immaculate Conception (Unknown)
Academy of the Sacred Heart, 6250 N. Sheridan Rd., 60660. Tel: 773-262-4446. Sacred Heart Schools
Academy of Our Lady aka Longwood Academy
Academy of Our Lady of Mount Carmel (Unknown) Became school for Our Lady of Mount Carmel.
Academy of St. Joseph (Unknown)
Academy of St. Scholastica Renamed St. Scholastica Academy
Academy of the Holy Child St. Anastasia School
St. Adalbert School and Commercial High School
St. Adrian School
St. Agatha Academy (Unknown)
St. Agatha School
Blessed Agnes Commercial High School and School, St. Agnes of Bohemia School, 2643 S. Central Park, 60623. Tel: 773-522-0143.
Blessed Agnes of Bohemia Church, St. Agnes of Bohemia Parish, 2643 S. Central Park, 60623. Tel: 773-522-0143.
St. Agnes Academy (Unknown)
St. Agnes Parish (39th St.) (Pershing Rd.)
St. Agnes School (39th St.)
St. Agnes High School (Unknown)
St. Albertus Academy (Waukegan) (Unknown)
Alexine Learning Center School
All Saints Parish (State St.)
All Saints School (State St.)
All Saints Parish (Wallace St.)
All Saints School (Wallace St.)
All Saints / St. Anthony School (Wallace)
St. Aloysius School
St. Aloysius Commercial High School (Boys) (Unknown)
St. Aloysius High School (Boys) (Unknown)
St. Alphonsus School (Wellington) Renamed St. Alphonsus Academy and Center for the Arts
St. Alphonsus School (Lemont), St. Alphonsus/St. Patrick School, 205 Cass St., Lemont, 60439. Tel: 630-257-2380; Fax: 630-257-4648.
St. Alphonsus Commercial High School (Chicago)
St. Alphonsus Commercial High School (Lemont) (Unknown)
Alvernia Conservatory of Music (Unknown)
Alvernia High School
St. Ambrose High School (Unknown)
St. Ambrose School (47th St.)
St. Ambrose Parish (117th St.) See St. Louis de France Parish (117th St.)
St. Andrew High School
St. Andrew Mission (Wadsworth), St. Patrick Parish, 15000 Wadsworth Rd., Wadsworth, 60083. Tel: 847-244-4161; Fax: 847-336-0630.
St. Andrew The Apostle School (Calumet City)
Angel Guardian Croatian Catholic Mission 6346 N. Ridge Ave., 60660. Tel: 773-262-0535; Fax: 773-262-4603. renamed Blessed Alojzije Stepinac Croatian Catholic Mission
Angel Guardian Orphanage
St. Angela Parish
St. Angela Academy (Unknown)
St. Ann Parish (Chicago Heights)
St. Ann School (Chicago Heights)
St. Ann High School (Leavitt St.)
St. Anne Hospital, Saint Elizabeth Campus, Saints Mary and Elizabeth Medical Center, 1431 N. Claremont Ave., 60622. Tel: 773-278-2000.
St. Anne's School of Nursing, Ancilla College, 9601 Union Rd., Plymouth, IN 46563. Tel: 574-936-8898; 866-262-4552 (Toll Free).
St. Anne Parish (Garfield Blvd.)
St. Anne School (Garfield Blvd.)
St. Anne School (Hazel Crest)
St. Anne Parish (Waukegan), Immaculate Conception, 508 Grand Ave., Waukegan, 60085. Tel: 847-336-3684; Fax: 847-336-9040.
St. Anne Mission Chapel , (Richton), St. Liborius Parish, 71 W. 35th St., Steger, 60475. Tel: 708-754-1363.
Annunciation Parish (Wabansia)
Annunciation School (Wabansia)
St. Anselm School
St. Anthony of Padua Parish (24th Pl.)
St. Anthony of Padua School (24th Pl.)
St. Anthony School (Cicero)
St. Anthony High School & Commercial High School (24th Pl.)
St. Anthony School (Prairie)
Aquinas Catholic High School
Aquinas Dominican High School
Aquinas High School
Archbishop Quigley Preparatory Seminary
Ascension Parish (Harvey), at Ascension-St. Susanna Parish, 15234 Myrtle Ave., Harvey, 60426-3194. Tel: 708-333-0931; Fax: 708-333-3281.
Ascension School (Harvey)
Ascension-St. Susanna School (Harvey)
Ascension of Our Lord Parish (Evanston)
Ascension of Our Lord School (Evanston)
Assumption School (24th St.)
Assumption Parish (Marshfield Ave.)
Assumption School (Marshfield Ave.)
Assumption BVM Parish (123rd St.)
Assumption BVM School (123rd St.)
Assumption School (Illinois St.) (Unknown)
Assumption / St. Catherine of Genoa School and Parish
St. Attracta Parish (Cicero)
St. Attracta School (Cicero)
St. Attracta-St. Valentine Church (Cicero)
St. Augustine Parish (S. Laflin)
St. Augustine School & High School
St. Beatrice School
Barat College (Lake Forest), De Paul University, 1 E. Jackson Blvd., 60604. Tel: 312-362-8850.
St. Barbara High School
St. Bartholomew Parish (Waukegan)
St. Bartholomew School (Waukegan)
St. Basil Parish, St. Basil/Visitation Parish 5443 S. Honore, 60609.
St. Basil Parish (Ukrainian Rite), St. Michael Parish (Ukrainian Rite), 12205 S. Parnell, 60628. Tel: 773-291-0168.
St. Basil School
Bellarmine School of Theology, Loyola University of Chicago, Dean of Students of the Graduate School, 820 N. Michigan Ave., 60611.
St. Benedict High School (Coed 1919-1939) (Unknown)
St. Bernard Parish (65th St.)
St. Bernard School
Bishop Quarter Boarding School for Motherless Boys
Bishop Quarter Junior Military School aka Bishop Quarter School for Little Boys
St. Blase School (Argo)
Blessed Sacrament Parish (Millard St.)
Blessed Sacrament School (Millard St.)
Blessed Sacrament / Our Lady of Lourdes School
SS. Benedict and Scholastica Academy St. Scholastica Academy
St. Bonaventure Parish, St. Alphonsus Parish, 1429 W. Wellington Ave., 60657-4121. Tel: 773-525-0709.
St. Bonaventure School (Diversey)
St. Boniface Parish (N. Noble)
St. Boniface School (N. Noble)
St. Boniface High School (Unknown)
St. Brendan Parish (Racine)
St. Brendan School (Racine)
St. Bride School
St. Bridget Parish
St. Bridget School & High School
Bridgeport Industrial School for Boys See Illinois Industrial School for Boys
Bridgeport Catholic Academy Middle School (St. Mary of Perpetual Help Campus)
Bridgeport Catholic Academy North Campus (All Saints/St. Anthony Campus)
Bridgeport Catholic Academy South Campus (Nativity of Our Lord Campus) open, Pre-2002
St. Bronislava School
Brother Candidates High School (Techny), Box 107, East Troy, WI 53120. Tel: 414-642-3300.
Cabrini Green Alternative High School
Cabrini Hospital Sacramental records - St. Anthony Hospital (Chicago); Medical records - St. Anthony Hospital
St. Callistus Parish
St. Callistus School
St. Camillus School
Cardinal Stritch High School
Carmel High School, Carmel High School, One Carmel Pkwy., Mundelein, 60060-2499. Tel: 847-566-3000. (Boys and Girls)
St. Carthage Parish (73rd St.)
St. Carthage School
St. Casimir Academy, Maria High School, 6727 S. California Ave., 60629-1887. Tel: 773-925-8686.
St. Casimir Parish (Chicago Heights)
St. Casimir School (Chicago Heights)
St. Casimir Parish (Whipple St.)
St. Casimir School (Whipple St.)
St. Casimir High School, Our Lady of Tepeyac High School, 2228 S. Whipple St., 60623. Tel: 773-522-0023; Fax: 773-522-0508. (Whipple St.)
St. Catherine Academy (See Siena High School)
St. Catherine High School (See Siena High School)
Cathedral College
Cathedral High School
Chrysalis Program
Corpus Christi School
St. Catherine of Genoa Parish
St. Catherine of Genoa School
St. Catherine of Siena Parish (Oak Park), Sacramental Records: St. Catherine/St. Lucy Parish, 38 N. Austin Blvd., Oak Park, 60302. Tel: 708-386-8077; Fax: 708-386-5190.
St. Catherine of Siena School (Oak Park), School Records: St. Catherine/St. Lucy School, 27 W. Washington Blvd., Oak Park, 60302. Tel: 708-386-5286.
St. Cecilia Parish (Wells St.)
St. Cecilia School (Wells St.)
St. Charles Borromeo Parish (Hoyne Ave.)
St. Charles Borromeo School (Hoyne Ave.)
St. Charles Borromeo School (Melrose Park)
St. Charles Lwanga Parish (W. Garfield)
St. Charles Lwanga School (W. Garfield)
Christ the Redeemer Church (Byzantine Rite)
St. Clara Parish (Woodlawn Ave.)
St. Clara School (Woodlawn)
St. Clara-St. Cyril Parish (S. Woodlawn)
St. Clara-St. Cyril School
St. Clare of Montefalco School
St. Clement High School
St. Clotilde School
St. Columba Academy (Unknown)
St. Columba School (134th St.)
St. Columbanus High School (Unknown)
St. Columbkille Parish (Paulina)
St. Columbkille School & Commercial High School
St. Columbkille High School, Mother Guerin Convent, 8001 Belmont Ave., River Grove, 60171. Tel: 708-453-6233. (Girls)
Columbus Hospital Sacramental Records - Archives, Medical Records - St. Anthony Hospital
Columbus Hospital School of Nursing
St. Constance High School
Convent of the Holy Child Renamed Holy Child High School
Convent of the Sacred Heart (Chicago), Sacred Heart Schools, 6250 N. Sheridan Rd., 60660. Tel: 773-262-4446.
Convent of the Sacred Heart High School (Lake Forest), Woodlands Academy of the Sacred Heart, 760 E. Westleigh Rd., Lake Forest, 60045-3298. Tel: 847-234-4300.
Cook County Hospital (Sacramental Records)
Corpus Christi High School, Hales Franciscan High School, 4930 S. Cottage Grove, 60615. Tel: 773-285-8400.
Cuneo Hospital Medical Records - St. Anthony Hospital; Sacramental-Archives
St. Cyril College, Mt. Carmel High School.
St. Cyril Parish (Dante Ave.)
St. Cyril School
Ss. Cyril & Methodius Church & School (Hermitage Ave.)
Ss. Cyril & Methodius Church & School (Walton St.)
St. David School
St. David Parish
De Lourdes College (Des Plaines), Holy Family College, Registrar's Office, Grant Ave. & Frankford Ave., Philadelphia, PA 19114. Tel: 215-637-4851.
St. Denis School
DePaul Academy & DePaul University Academy, DePaul University, Registrar's Office, 243 S. Wabash, 60604. Tel: 312-341-8610.
DePaul High School (Unknown)
DePaul University Loop High School (Unknown)
St. Dionysius Parish (Cicero)
St. Dionysius School (Cicero)
Divine Savior School
St. Dionysius High School (Cicero)
St. Dominic Parish (Locust)
St. Dominic School & High School
St. Donatus School (Blue Island)

St. Elizabeth High School (41st St.) Pre-1924 - Records Unknown; Post-1924 at Archives
St. Emeric Church (Washtenaw Ave.), St. Stephen King of Hungary Parish, 2015 W. Augusta Blvd., 60622-4947. Tel: 773-486-1896; Fax: 773-486-1902.
St. Emeric School (County Club Hills)
Englewood Catholic Academy (Honore St.)
Englewood Catholic Academy (Laflin St.)
Englewood Catholic Academy (May St.)
Englewood Catholic Academy (Princeton St.)
Ephpheta School for the Deaf
St. Ethelreda Parish
St. Eulalia School (Open pre-1989)
Felician College
St. Felicitas High School (Unknown)
St. Felicitas School
St. Fidelis Parish, St. Aloysius Parish, 2300 W. LeMoyne St., 60622-1979. Tel: 773-278-4808.
St. Fidelis School (N. Washtenaw)
St. Finbarr Parish
St. Finbarr High School and School (Unknown)
Five Holy Martyrs School
St. Florian Commerical High School (Unknown)
St. Florian Mission , (52nd & Archer), St. Camillus, 5426 S. Lockwood Ave., 60638. Tel: 773-767-8183.
Ford City Catholic Center
Fournier Institute, DePaul University, Registrar's Office, 243 S. Wabash, 60604. Tel: 312-341-8610.
Fornier Institute Viatorian Preparatory (Lemont), Viatorian Archives, Arlington Heights, 60006.
St. Frances Xavier Cabrini Parish (Lexington St.)
St. Frances Xavier Cabrini School (Lexington St.)
St. Frances Xavier Cabrini School of Nursing
St. Francis Xavier Commercial High School (Unknown)
St. Francis de Paula Parish
St. Frances de Paula School (S. Ellis)
St. Francis de Sales School
St. Francis of Assisi Church (Kostner Ave.), St. Francis of Assisi/Our Lady of the Angels Parish, 3808 W. Iowa St., 60651. Tel: 773-235-3132; Fax: 773-486-7726.
St. Francis of Assisi High School (Unknown)
St. Francis of Assisi School (Kostner Ave.)
St. Francis of Assisi School (Roosevelt Ave.)
St. Francis Xavier Parish (Nelson), Resurrection Parish, 2840 W. Nelson, 60618-7012. Tel: 773-478-9705; Fax: 773-478-1387.
St. Francis Xavier School (Nelson)
St. Gabriel Commercial High School St. Gabriel School
St. Gabriel School (open) Records (1941-1965) at Archives
Garfield Alternative High School
St. Gelasius Parish and School
St. George Parish (Wentworth Ave.)
St. George School & Commercial High School (Lituanica Ave.)
St. George School (Wentworth Ave.)
St. George Parish (Lituanica Ave.)
St. George School (Ewing St.)
St. George High School (Evanston)
St. Gerald High School (Oak Lawn) (Unknown)
St. Gerard Majella School (Markham)
St. Gertrude High School (Oak Lawn) (Unknown)
St. Gertrude School (Chicago)
St. Gertrude School (Franklin Park)
Good Counsel High School
Good Shepherd Chapel (Illinois Technical School for the Colored Girls).
Good Shepherd School
St. Gregory the Great School
Hardey Preparatory, Sacred Heart Schools, 6250 N. Sheridan Rd., 60660. Tel: 773-262-4446.
Heart of Mary High School
St. Hedwig Mission St. John Berchmans Parish, 2517 W. Logan Blvd., 60647. Tel: 773-486-4300; Fax: 773-252-5346. (Washtenaw Ave.)
St. Hedwig Orphanage (Niles)
St. Hedwig School
St. Henry School
St. Henry Commercial High School
Holy Child High School (Waukegan), St. Anastasia School, 629 Glen Flora, Waukegan, 60685. Tel: 847-623-8320; Fax: 847-623-4882.
Holy Cross Parish (65th St.)
Holy Cross School (65th St.)
Holy Cross School (Wood St.)
Holy Cross Parish (46th St.)
Holy Cross High School (River Grove) Records at Guerin College Preparatory High School (River Grove)
Holy Family Parish (North Chicago)
Holy Family High School (Unknown)
Holy Family School (North Chicago)
Holy Family School (May St.)
Holy Family Academy (Division St.)
Holy Family Extension High School (Des Plaines), Sisters of Holy Family of Nazareth, Provincial Archives, 310 N. River Rd., Des Plaines, 60016. Tel: 847-298-6760.
Holy Family Orphanage (Unknown)
Holy Ghost Parish & School
Holy Ghost Academy (Techny), Convent of the Holy Spirit (Techny).
Holy Ghost School (South Holland)
Holy Guardian Angel Parish (Arthington/Cabrini)
Holy Guardian Angel School
Holy Innocents School
Holy Name Cathedral School
Holy Name Cathedral High School
Holy Name High School
Holy Name of Mary Mission , (Church St.) Renamed Sacred Heart Mission (Church St.)
Holy Name of Mary School
Holy Rosary Commercial High School (North Chicago) (Unknown)
Holy Rosary Slovak Parish (108th St.)
Holy Rosary Slovak School (108th St.)
Holy Rosary Parish and School (113th St.)
Holy Rosary Parish (North Chicago)
Holy Rosary School (North Chicago)
Holy Rosary School (Western Ave.)
Holy Trinity Parish, Holy Trinity Polish Mission, 1118 N. Noble St., 60622-4015. Tel: 773-489-4140; Fax: 773-489-5918.
Holy Trinity School (Noble St.)
Holy Trinity Parish (Wolcott)
Holy Trinity Parish (Throop)
Holy Trinity School (Throop)
Holy Trinity School (Wolcott)
Holy Trinity School (Taylor, Deaf Children)
House of the Good Shepherd
St. Hugh School (Lyons)
St. Hyacinth Mission , (Spaulding), St. Hyacinth Basilica Parish, 3636 N. Wolfram, 60618. Tel: 773-342-3636; Fax: 773-342-3638.
St. Ignatius College, St. Ignatius College Prep., 1073 W. Roosevelt Rd., 60608. Tel: 312-421-5900.
St. Ignatius School
Illinois Industrial School for Boys (Unknown)
Illinois Technical School for Colored Girls
Illinois Industrial School for Girls (Unknown)
Immaculata High School
Immaculate Conception School (Exchange Ave.; Open, 1884-1984 only)
Immaculate Conception Commercial High School (Aberdeen St.)
Immaculate Conception-St. Bridget School
Immaculate Conception Parish (Aberdeen St.)
Immaculate Conception School (Aberdeen St.)
Immaculate Conception School (44th St.)
Immaculate Conception School (Waukegan)
Immaculate Conception School (Highland Park)
Immaculate Conception School (North Park Ave.; Open, 1868-1986 only)
Immaculate Conception (Highland Park); (Unknown)
Immaculate Conception Parish (Buffalo Grove) St. Mary Parish (Buffalo Grove)
Immaculate Heart of Mary High School (Westchester)
Immaculate Heart of Mary School (Spaulding Ave.)
Immaculate Heart of Mary Vicariate (Ashland)
Industrial and Manual Labor School (Unknown)
Institute of Our Lady of the Sacred Heart Renamed Academy of Our Lady (Longwood Academy)
St. Irenaeus School (Park Forest)
St. Isaac Jogues School (Niles)
St. Isidore the Farmer School (Blue Island)
St. Ita High School (Unknown)
St. Ita School
St. James Academy (Lemont) (Unknown)
St. James Parish (Strassburg or New Strassburg) (Unknown)
St. James School (Wabash Ave.)
St. James Parish & School (Maywood)
St. James Parish (Mundelein or Fremont Center), St. Mary of the Annunciation Parish, 22333 W. Erhart Rd., Mundelein, 60060. Tel: 847-223-0010; Fax: 847-223-5960.
St. James Commercial (Maywood); (Unknown)
St. James School (Fullerton and Menard)
St. James School (Sauk Village)
St. James High School (Wabash) (Unknown)
St. Jarlath Parish (Jackson)
St. Jarlath School (Jackson)
St. Jean Baptiste Church (33rd Pl.)
St. Jerome School (Lunt)
Jesuit School of Theology, 820 N. Michigan Ave., 60611. Loyola University of Chicago, Office of the Dean of Graduate School.
Jesus, Our Brother School
St. Joachim School
St. John Bosco School
Old St. John Parish (18th St.)
Old St. John School, Christian Brothers University, 2455 Avery Ave., Memphis, TN 38112.
St. John Cantius Commercial High School (Unknown)
St. John Cantius School
St. John Chrysostom Parish and School (Bellwood)
St. John Chrysostom School (Bellwood)
St. John De La Salle School Renamed St. John De La Salle Academy of Fine Arts
St. John Nepomucene Church & School
St. John of God Parish & School (S. Throop)
St. John the Baptist Parish (50th Pl.)
St. John the Baptist Church (Burley Ave.)
St. John the Baptist School (50th Pl.)
St. John the Baptist School (Harvey)
St. Josaphat Commerical High School
St. Josaphat School (Open pre 1961)
St. Josaphat Parish Orphanage (Unknown)
St. Joseph Bohemian Orphanage, Maryville Academy, 1150 N. River Rd., Des Plaines, 60016. Tel: 708-824-6126; Fax: 847-824-7277. (Lisle)
St. Joseph Commercial Business College (Waukegan)
St. Joseph Orphanage (Lisle); See St. Joseph Bohemian Orphanage (Lisle)
St. Joseph School (Wilmette); (Pre-1986 only at Archives)
St. Joseph the Worker School
St. Joseph High School (Hermitage)
St. Joseph's Institute
St. Joseph Parish (17th Pl.)
St. Joseph School (17th Pl.) (Unknown)
St. Joseph Parish and School (38th Pl.) (See St. Joseph and St. Anne Parish)
St. Joseph School (Orleans)
St. Joseph School (Hermitage)
St. Joseph Commercial High School (Hermitage); Unknown
St. Joseph Parish (Chicago Heights)
St. Joseph School (Chicago Hts.)
St. Joseph Parish (Saginaw St.)
St. Joseph School (Saginaw St.)
St. Joseph's Orphan Asylum (35th St.)
St. Joseph Orphanage for Boys (destroyed by fire, post-1859 in archives)
St. Joseph Parish Orphanage (Unknown)
St. Joseph Provident Orphanage
St. Joseph Military Academy (See St. Joseph's Institute)
St. Joseph Academy (LaGrange Park) (See St. Joseph's Institute)
St. Joseph Commercial High School (Waukegan); (Unknown)
St. Joseph & SS. Joseph & Bartholomew Parish (Waukegan)
SS. Joseph & Bartholomew Parish Renamed Holy Family Parish (Waukegan)
St. Joseph School (Waukegan)
St. Joseph & St. Anne Parish, Our Lady of Fatima Parish, 2751 W. 38th Pl., 60632-1686. Tel: 773-927-2421; Fax: 773-247-1737. (First Register at the Archives)
St. Joseph & St. Anne Commercial High School and School (Unknown)
St. Joseph Mission , (13th St.)
St. Joseph Mission School , (13th St.)
St. Joseph Servite Seminary (Elgin-St. Charles), Provincial Archives, Servite Provincial Center, 3121 W. Jackson Blvd., 60612. Tel: 773-533-0360.
St. Joseph's Academy Renamed St. Scholastica Academy
St. Joseph's Carondelet Child Center
St. Joseph's Home for the Friendless
St. Joseph Technical High School (Techny), Divine Word Missionaries, East Troy, WI 53120.
St. Josaphat Commercial High School (Hermitage)
Josephinum High School renamed Josephinum Academy
St. Jude the Apostle School (South Holland)
St. Justin Martyr Parish (71st St.)
St. Justin Martyr School
St. Kevin School, 10509 S. Torrence, 60617. Tel: 773-721-2563. St. Kevin Parish.
St. Kilian School
Lake Shore Catholic Academy (Waukegan & North Chicago)
St. Lambert School (Skokie)
St. Laurence School and Parish
St. Leo High School, Mother Guerin Convent, 8001 Belmont Ave., River Grove, 60171. Tel: 708-453-6233.
St. Leo the Great School and Parish
St. Leonard Commercial High School (Berwyn), St. Leonard School, 3322 S. Clarence, Berwyn, 60402. Tel: 708-749-1989; Fax: 708-749-7981.
Lewis Memorial Maternity Hospital
Little Flower Parish & School see St. Therese of the Infant Jesus School
Little Flower High School
Longwood Academy see Academy of Our Lady
Loretto Academy (Adams St., 1864-1871) (Unknown)
Loretto Academy (Woodlawn)
Loretto Academy (Englewood)
Loretto Adult Center (Englewood), Kennedy King College, 6800 S. Wentworth, 60621.
Loretto Extension Service (Unknown)
Loretto High School (Englewood)

St. Louis de France Parish (117th St.)
St. Louis de France School (117th St.)
St. Louis Parish (Polk St.)
St. Louis School (Polk St.) (Unknown)
St. Louis Academy
Lourdes High School Records located at De LaSalle Institute, 3455 S. Wabash, 60616. Tel: 312-842-7355; Fax: 312-842-5640.
Loyola Academy (Chicago), 1100 N. Laramie Ave., Wilmette, 60091. Tel: 847-256-1100. Moved to Loyola Academy.
St. Lucy Parish, St. Catherine-St. Lucy Parish, 38 N. Austin Blvd., Oak Park, 60302. Tel: 708-386-8077; Fax: 708-386-5190.
St. Lucy School
St. Ludmilla Parish
St. Ludmilla School
St. Louise Marillac High School
Madonna High School
St. Malachy High School, St. Malachy School, 2252 W. Washington, 60612. Tel: 312-733-2252; Fax: 312-733-5703.
Mallinckrodt High School
Mallinckrodt College (Wilmette)
St. Margaret's Home & Hospital (Unknown)
Marian School for Deaf (Unknown)
Maria Immaculata Academy (Wilmette)
St. Mark School (Cortez St.)
St. Mark the Evangelist School
Marquette Institute (Clark St.)
St. Martha School (Morton Grove)
St. Martin Parish (Princeton St.)
St. Martin de Porres Academy
St. Martin de Porres School (Jackson Blvd.)
St. Martin School & Commercial High School (Princeton)
St. Mary Academy (Libertyville) (Unknown)
St. Mary Commercial High School (Mundelein) (Unknown)
St. Mary High School (Lake Forest) (Unknown)
St. Mary High School (Highland Park) (Unknown)
St. Mary High School (Grenshaw)
St. Mary School (Des Plaines)
St. Mary School (Evanston)
St. Mary School (Riverside) (Open) (1948-1995 at Archives)
St. Mary Parish (Lemont), St Patrick Parish, 200 Illinois St., Lemont, 60439. Tel: 708-257-6134; Fax: 630-257-0401.
St. Mary Parish (Waukegan), Immaculate Conception Parish, 508 Grand Ave., Waukegan, 60085. Tel: 847-336-3684; Fax: 847-336-9040.
St. Mary Center for Learning (Grenshaw)
St. Mary Alternative High School (Grenshaw) Records to 1976 at Archives. Records after 1976 or from the night school at, *Harold Washington College*, 30 E. Lake St., 60601. Tel: 312-553-6065.
St. Mary Parish and St. Mary's Mission St. Mary (Seeley); St. Mary's Mission (90th St.); (Byzantine Rite), *Annunciation Byzantine*, 14610 Will-Cook Rd., Lockport, 60441-9212. Tel: 708-645-0214.
St. Mary Magdalen School
St. Mary of Celle School (Berwyn)
St. Mary of the Assumption School (137th St.)
St. Mary of the Lake Parish (1870-1928, Ingleside); Renamed St. Bede Parish (Ingleside)
St. Mary of the Lake High School (1844-1867); Unknown, assumed destroyed
St. Mary of Mt. Carmel Parish (Hermitage St.)
St. Mary of Mt. Carmel School (Hermitage)
St. Mary of Nazareth School (Harvey)
St. Mary of Perpetual Help School, Bridgeport Catholic Academy, 3700 S. Lowe, 60609-6507. Tel: 773-376-6223; Fax: 773-376-3864.
St. Mary of Perpetual Help High School
St. Mary of the Woods Parish (Highland Park), Immaculate Conception Parish, 700 W. Deerfield Rd., Highland Park, 60035. Tel: 847-433-0130; Fax: 847-433-0669.
St. Mary Mission Seminary (Techny), Catholic Theological Union, 5401 S. Cornell, 60615-5698. Tel: 773-324-8000.
St. Mary Orphanage for Girls (Destroyed in fire, some records exist in St. Joseph Orphanage registers)
Mary, Queen of Heaven School (Cicero)
St. Mary's Training School, Maryville Academy, 1150 N. River Rd., Des Plaines, 60016. Tel: 847-824-6126; Fax: 847-824-7277. Several intake registers are at the archives.
St. Mary's School of Nursing (Des Plaines), Holy Family College, Registrar's Office, Grant Ave. & Frankford Ave., Philadelphia, PA 19114. Tel: 215-637-4851.
St. Mary's Academy, Christian Brothers University, 2455 Avery Ave., Memphis, TN 38112.
St. Mary's High School (Des Plaines) (Unknown)
St. Mary's Select School, Sisters of the Holy Cross, Notre Dame, IN 46556.
St. Mary's Seminary (Unknown)
Marywood High School (Evanston), *Mother Guerin Convent*, 8001 Belmont Ave., River Grove, 60171. Tel: 773-625-3278; 708-453-6233.
Mater Christi School
Mater Dolorosa Seminary (Hillside), 3121 W. Jackson Blvd., 60612. See Servite Seminary, Servite Provincial Archives.
Maternity B.V.M. Mission (92nd) Renamed St. Ailbe Parish.
St. Matthew Parish (Walnut St.)
St. Matthew Commercial High School (Unknown)
St. Matthew School (Walnut St.)
St. Matthias School
St. Maurice Parish Renamed Blessed Sacrament (Hoyne Ave.)
St. Maurice School
McKinley Park Catholic School
St. Mel Parish & St. Mel-Holy Ghost Parish
St. Mel & St. Mel-Holy Ghost School
St. Mel High School (Up to 1969)
Mendel High School
Mercy High School
Mercy Mission High School
St. Michael School (Cleveland & Hudson) (1918-1949 only)
St. Michael Central High School (Cleveland & Hudson)
St. Michael School (South Shore Dr.); (Open); Pre-1949 only at Archives.
St. Michael Parish (Wabansia St.)
St. Michael School (Wabansia St.)
St. Michael Parish (24th Pl.)
St. Michael School (24th Pl.)
St. Michael the Archangel Parish (Bellwood); Renamed St. Simeon Parish (Bellwood)
St. Michael the Archangel School
St. Michael the Archangel Commercial High School (Unknown)
St. Michael Commercial High School (South Shore Dr.)
Misericordia Hospital, Client Records & Adoption Placements: *Catholic Charities*, 651 N. LaSalle, 60611. Tel: 312-655-7073; Fax: 312-236-5172. Sacramental Records in registers of St. Agnes Parish, 39th St. and Catholic Charities.
Mission of the Holy Ghost , (Northbrook), St. Norbert Parish, 1809 Walters Ave., Northbrook, 60062. Tel: 847-272-7090; Fax: 847-272-7771.
St. Monica Parish (36th St.)
St. Monica School (36th St.) (Unknown)
St. Monica Mission (Harwood Heights); Renamed St. Rosalie Parish (Harwood Heights)
Monastery of Mt. St. Phillip Servite Novitiate, Provincial Archives, Servite Provincial Center, 3121 W. Jackson Blvd., 60612. Tel: 773-533-0360. (Granville, WI)
Montay College
Mother Theodore Guerin High School (River Grove), at Guerin College Preparatory High School, 8001 W. Belmont, River Grove, 60171. Tel: 708-453-6233; Fax: 708-453-6296.
Mother of God Parish (Waukegan)
Mother of God School & High School (Waukegan)
Mother of Sorrows Grade and High School (Blue Island)
Mount Carmel Academy (Unknown)
Mount Carmel Academy (Girls); (Part of St. Patrick Academy in Chicago, later Des Plaines), *Mother McAuley High School*, 3737 W. 99th St., 60642. Tel: 773-881-6522.
Mount Carmel School (Chicago Heights) (Served St. Rocco)
Mundelein College, Office of Registration & Records, 820 N. Michigan Ave., Room 504, 60611. Tel: 312-915-7221. Loyola University
Mundelein Cathedral High School
Mundelein High School
Mundelein Seminary See University of St. Mary of the Lake (Mundelein)
Municipal Tuberculosis Sanitarium (Sacred Heart Chapel)
Nativity of Our Lord High School (Unknown)
Nativity of Our Lord School & Commercial High School
Nativity BVM Parish (Paulina St.) (Ukranian Rite: Moved to Palos Park)
Nazareth Academy (LaGrange) Renamed Our Lady of Bethlehem Academy.
St. Nicholas School (Evanston)
St. Nicholas Parish (State St.)
St. Nicholas School (State St.)
Niles College at St. Joseph Seminary, Loyola University Chicago.
Northside Catholic Academy (St. Henry Campus); (Records split between two remaining campuses), *St. Gertrude Campus*, 6216 N. Glenwood Ave., 60660. Tel: 773-743-6277. *St. Ita Campus*, 5525 N. Magnolia Ave., 60640-1306. Tel: 773-271-2008.
Notre Dame Academy (Unknown)
Notre Dame de Chicago School
Our Lady of Aglona, St. Aloysius Parish, 2300 W. LeMoyne St., 60622-1799.
Our Lady of Bethlehem Academy
Our Lady of Fatima Mission , (Christina Ave.), St. Hyacinth Basilica Parish, 3636 N. Wolfram, 60618. Tel: 773-342-3636; Fax: 773-342-3638.
Our Lady of Fatima School (39th/Pershing Rd.)
Our Lady of the Gardens Parish
Our Lady Gate of Heaven School
Our Lady of Good Counsel Parish (Western Ave.)
Our Lady of Good Counsel School (Western Ave.)
Our Lady of the Good Counsel Parish (Hermitage Ave.), Blessed Sacrament, 3615 S. Hoyne Ave., 60609. Tel: 773-847-3357.
Our Lady of Good Counsel School (Hermitage Ave.)
Our Lady of Guadalupe Chapel Holy Cross-Immaculate Heart of Mary Parish, 4541 S. Wood St., 60609. Tel: 773-376-3900; Fax: 773-376-8929.
Our Lady Help of Christians Parish
Our Lady Help of Christians School
Our Lady of Hope School (Des Plaines)
Our Lady of Hungary Parish (93rd St.)
Our Lady of Hungary School (93rd St.)
Our Lady of Knock School (Calumet City)
Our Lady of Loretto School (Hometown)
Our Lady of Lourdes School (Ashland Ave.)
Our Lady of Lourdes Commercial High School (Keeler St.)
Our Lady of Lourdes Parish (Keeler St.)
Our Lady of Lourdes School (Keeler St.)
Our Lady of Lourdes High School (Ashland Ave.); (Unknown)
Our Lady of Mercy Commercial High School (Unknown)
Our Lady of Mercy School
Our Lady of the Miraculous Medal Parish (Langley Ave.); Renamed Our Lady of the Gardens Parish
Our Lady of the Mount School (Cicero)
Our Lady of Mt. Carmel School (Melrose Park)
Our Lady of Peace School
Our Lady of Perpetual Help Vicariate (13th St.)
Our Lady of Perpetual Help Vicariate School (13th St.)
Our Lady of Providence Academy (Records destroyed in flood)
Our Lady of Ransom School
Our Lady of Solace Parish (Sangamon)
Our Lady of Solace School (Sangamon)
Our Lady of Sorrows High School (1887-1897), Mother Guerin Convent, River Grove, 60171.
Our Lady of Sorrows School
Our Lady of Sorrows Seminary, Servite Provincial Archives, 3121 W. Jackson, 60612. Tel: 773-638-0159; Fax: 773-638-3036.
Our Lady of the Angels Parish, St. Francis of Assisi/Our Lady of the Angels Parish, 3808 W. Iowa St., 60651. Tel: 773-235-3132; Fax: 773-486-7726.
Our Lady of Angels School
Our Lady of the Cross Mission Chapel St. Margaret Mary Parish, 2324 W. Chase, 60645. Tel: 773-764-0615; Fax: 773-764-0941.
Our Lady of Pompeii School
Our Lady of Pompeii Parish
Our Lady of Victory High School (Unknown)
Our Lady of Vilna Parish (23rd St.)
Our Lady of Vilna School (23rd St.), St. Paul/Our Lady of Vilna School, 2114 W. 22nd Pl., 60608. Tel: 773-847-6078; Fax: 773-847-2118.
Our Lady of the West Side School Renamed St. Agatha Catholic Academy
St. Pancratius School
St. Patrick Academy (Chicago, later Des Plaines) (Girls), *Mother McAuley High School*, 3737 W. 99th St., 60608. Tel: 773-881-6522.
St. Patrick High School (Belmont Ave.)
St. Patrick School (Adams St.) (pre 1967, post 1967 at Frances Xavier Ward School)
St. Patrick School (Lemont), St. Alphonsus-St. Patrick School, 205 Cass St., Lemont, 60439. Tel: 630-257-2380.
St. Patrick Parish (Commercial Ave.)
St. Patrick School (Commercial Ave.)
St. Patrick Academy (Boys); at St. Patrick High School (Belmont Ave.)
St. Patrick High School (Boys, Adams St.); at St. Patrick High School (Belmont Ave.)
St. Patrick High School (Adams St.) (Girls)
St. Patrick High School (Commercial Ave.) (Unknown)
St. Paul School (Chicago Heights); (Unknown)
St. Paul School (22nd St.), St. Paul/Our Lady of Vilna School (22nd St.), 2114 W. 22nd Pl., 60608. Tel: 773-847-6078; Fax: 773-847-2118.
St. Paul Commercial High School (Unknown)
St. Paul High School (Midway)
St. Paul Parish (12th St.) (Records destroyed in 1871 fire)
St. Paul Select School (Unknown)
St. Paul's Home for Working Boys (Renamed Mercy Mission)
St. Peter School (Volo), St. Peter Parish, 27551 W. Hwy. 120, Round Lake, 60073. Tel: 815-385-5496;

Fax: 631-514-4647.
St. Peter School (Madison) (Unknown)
St. Peter Canisius Parish, St. Francis of Assisi/Our Lady of the Angels Parish, 932 N. Kostner, 60651. Tel: 773-235-3132; Fax: 773-486-7726.
St. Peter Canisius School
St. Peter Commercial High School (Skokie) (Unknown)
SS. Peter and Paul Parish (Exchange St.)
SS. Peter and Paul School (Exchange St.)
St. Peter & Paul School (Halsted St.)
SS. Peter and Paul Parish (Paulina St.), Blessed Sacrament Parish, 3615 S. Hoyne Ave., 60609. Tel: 773-847-3357.
Ss. Peter & Paul School (Paulina St.)
SS. Peter & Paul Parish (Libertyville), St. Joseph Parish, 121 E. Maple, Libertyville, 60048. Tel: 847-362-2073; Fax: 847-362-6821.
SS. Peter & Paul High School (Exchange Ave.)
St. Peter & Paul Church (Central Park Ave.); (Byzantine Rite), St. Nicholas Parish (Byzantine Rite), 8103 Columbia Ave., Munster, IN 46321-1802. Tel: 219-838-9380.
St. Philip Benizi Parish (Maypole St.) (later named St. Mel Parish)
St. Philip Benizi Parish (Maypole St.) (Unknown)
St. Philip Benizi Parish (Oak St.)
St. Philip Benizi School (Oak St.)
St. Philip Evening School (Unknown)
St. Philip Basilica High School
St. Philip the Apostle School (Northfield)
St. Philomena School
St. Philomena Commercial High School
St. Pius V Commercial High School, St. Pius V School, 1919 S. Ashland, 60608. Tel: 312-226-1590; Fax: 312-226-7265.
St. Pius X School (Stickney)
Precious Blood School
Presentation Parish
Presentation School
Presentation-Precious Blood Unit School, 2401 W. Congress, 60612. Tel: 773-421-6157. St. Agatha Catholic Academy.
St. Procopius College Academy (Chicago); Renamed St. Procopius College Academy (Lisle)
St. Procopius School (open) (pre 1983)
St. Procopius High School
Providence Academy & High School (pre-1970), Guerin College Preparatory High School, 8001 Belmont Ave., River Grove, 60171. Tel: 312-625-3278.
Providence of God School and Commercial High School
Providence-St. Mel High School, 119 S. Central Park Blvd., 60624. Tel: 773-722-4600.
Queen of Angels High School (Unknown)
Queen of Apostles School (Riverdale)
Quigley Preparatory Seminary North
Quigley Preparatory Seminary South
Quigley Preparatory Seminary
St. Raphael Parish (60th St.)
St. Raphael School (60th St.)
Resurrection Catholic Academy (Barry Ave.)
Resurrection Parish and School (Jackson Blvd.)
St. Rita College, St. Rita High School, 7740 S. Western Ave., 60620. Tel: 773-925-6600.
St. Rita of Cascia School
St. Rocco Parish (Chicago Heights) (For school records, see Mt. Carmel School.)
St. Roman School
St. Rosalie School (Harwood Heights)
Rosary House High School (River Forest), 7574 W. Division St., River Forest, 60305. Tel: 708-771-8383. Trinity High School.
Rosary College, Dominican University, 7900 W. Division St., River Forest, 60305. Tel: 708-366-2490.
St. Rose of Lima Parish (W. 48th St.)
St. Rose of Lima School
Sacred Heart Parish (19th St.)
Sacred Heart School & High School (19th St.)
Sacred Heart Parish (May St.)
Sacred Heart School & High School (May St.)
Sacred Heart Parish (Oakley Blvd.)
Sacred Heart School (Oakley Blvd.)
Sacred Heart High School (Oakley) (Unknown)
Sacred Heart (Church St.), Sacred Heart Mission, 11652 S. Church St., 60643. Tel: 773-233-3955.
Sacred Heart of Jesus Parish (46th St.)
Sacred Heart of Jesus School (46th St.)
Sacred Heart of Jesus High School (46th St.)
Sacred Heart of Mary High School (Arlington Heights), St. Viator High School, 1213 E. Oakton St., Arlington Heights, 60004. Tel: 847-392-4050.
Sacred Heart Seminary (Melrose Park) (Stone Park), Scalabrini Mission Center, 3800 W. Division St., Stone Park, 60165. Tel: 708-345-8270.
St. Salomea Parish (S. Indiana)
St. Salomea School (S. Indiana)
San Callisto Mission
San Marcello Mission (Evergreen), Immaculate Conception Parish, 1415 N. North Park, 60610. Tel: 312-944-1230; Fax: 312-944-0673.
Santa Lucia Mission , Sacramental Records:, Santa Lucia-Santa Maria Incoronata Parish, 3022 S. Wells, 60616. Tel: 312-842-6115; Fax: 312-842-0103.
Santa Lucia, 3017 S. Wells, 60616. Tel: 312-326-1839; Fax: 312-842-0103. (School Records)
Santa Maria Addolorata School
Santa Maria Incoronata Parish, Santa Lucia-Santa Maria Incoronata Parish, 3022 S. Wells, 60616. Tel: 312-842-6115; Fax: 312-842-0103. Sacramental Records:
Santa Lucia, 3017 S. Wells, 60616. Tel: 312-326-1839; Fax: 312-842-0103. (School Records)
Santa Teresita Vicariate (Palatine), Mision San Juan Diego, 35 W. Wood St., Palatine, 60067. Tel: 847-358-6337; Fax: 847-202-4603.
St. Scholastica High School Renamed St. Scholastica Academy.
St. Sebastian Parish (W. Wellington)
St. Sebastian School & High School
Servite Seminary (Hillside), Provincial Archives, Servite Provincial Center, 3121 W. Jackson Blvd., 60612. Tel: 773-533-0360.
Seven Holy Founders School (Calumet Park)
Sheil Institute
Siena High School, Mother McAuley High School, 3737 W. 99th St., 60642. Tel: 773-881-6522.
St. Simeon School (Bellwood)
St. Simon the Apostle School
St. Stanislaus Bishop and Martyr School (Lorel Ave.)
St. Stanislaus Bishop and Martyr School (Posen)
St. Stanislaus College, Gordon Technical High School, 3633 N. California, 60618. Tel: 773-539-3600.
St. Stanislaus Kostka High School, St. Stanislaus Kostka Elementary, 1255 N. Noble, 60622. Tel: 773-278-4560; Fax: 773-278-2471.
St. Stanislaus Parish and School (19th, renamed Sacred Heart)
St. Stephen School (22nd Pl.)
St. Stephen Protomartyr School (Des Plaines)
St. Stephen Parish (22nd Pl.)
Old St. Stephen Parish (Ohio St.)
Old St. Stephen School (Ohio St.)
St. Susanna Parish (Harvey), Ascension-St. Susanna Parish, 15234 Myrtle, Harvey, 60426-3194. Tel: 708-333-0931.
St. Susanna School (Harvey)
St. Sylvester Commercial High School
St. Thaddeus School
St. Theodore Parish (S. Paulina)
St. Theodore School
St. Teresa of Avila School
St. Therese of the Infant Jesus Parish (Wood St.)
St. Therese of the Infant Jesus School
St. Thomas Aquinas (Washington Blvd.) (Church and School)
St. Thomas More School
St. Thomas Mission , (River Forest), St. Luke Parish, 528 Lathrop, River Forest, 60305. Tel: 708-771-8250; Fax: 708-771-8809.
St. Thomas the Apostle High School, St. Thomas the Apostle School, 5467 S. Woodlawn, 60615. Tel: 773-667-1142; Fax: 773-753-7434.
St. Timothy School
Transfiguration of Our Lord School
Unity Catholic High School
Unity High School
University of St. Mary of the Lake (Chicago, 1844-1866) (Unknown, assumed destroyed)
St. Valentine Parish (Cicero)
St. Valentine School (Cicero)
St. Veronica Parish, Resurrection Parish, 2840 W. Nelson, 60618. Tel: 773-478-9705.
St. Veronica School (Whipple St.)
St. Viator High School (Addison) (Unknown)
Viatorian Preparatory School (Lemont) See Fournier Institute, Viatorian Preparatory School (Lemont)
St. Victor High School (Calumet City) (Unknown)
Villa Nazareth High School (Des Plaines)
St. Vincent de Paul School
St. Vincent de Paul Academy & St. Vincent Academy (Girls) (See DePaul High School)
St. Vincent de Paul High School Seminary (Lemont), *Vincentians Academic Archives*, 2233 N. Kenmore St., 60614. Tel: 312-362-8042.
St. Vincent Orphanage / St. Vincent Infant Hospital / St. Vincent Infant Asylum Client & School Records: Catholic Charities, Division of Services for Children and Youth, 651 N. LaSalle, Chicago, IL 60611. Tel: 312-655-7073; Sacramental Records: Holy Name Cathedral, 730 N. Wabash, Chicago, IL 60611 Tel: 312-787-8040 Fax: 312-787-9113
St. Vincent Ferrer Orphanage (Unknown)
St. Vincent Infant Hospital School of Child Care, St. Vincent de Paul Center, 2145 N. Halsted, 60614. Tel: 312-943-6776.
Visitation Parish (Garfield Blvd.), *St. Basil-Visitation Parish*, 5443 S. Honore, 60609. Tel: 773-625-6311; Fax: 773-783-3348.
Visitation Academy (Evanston) See Marywood High School. (Records destroyed in flood.)
Visitation High School
St. Vitus Parish
St. Vitus School
Weber High School, Gordon Technical High School, 3633 N. California Ave., 60618. Tel: 773-539-3600.
St. Wenceslaus School (Monticello St.)
St. Wenceslaus Parish (DeKoven St.)
St. Wenceslaus School (DeKoven St.) (Unknown)
St. Willibrord Parish (114th St.)
St. Willibrord School (114th St.)
Willibrord Catholic High School
St. Willibrord High School
St. Xavier Academy, Mother McAuley High School, 3737 W. 99th St., 60655. Tel: 773-881-6500.
Young Ladies' Seminary of the Sacred Heart Renamed Woodlands Academy of the Sacred Heart (Lake Forest)

RELIGIOUS INSTITUTES OF MEN REPRESENTED IN THE ARCHDIOCESE

For further details refer to the corresponding bracketed number in the Religious Institutes of Men or Women section.

[0120]—*Alexian Brothers*—C.F.A.
[0140]—*The Augustinians* Chicago—O.S.A.
[0200]—*Benedictine Monks*—O.S.B.
[0330]—*Brothers of the Christian Schools (Midwest Province)* (Burr Ridge, IL)—F.S.C.
[0600]—*Brothers of the Congregation of Holy Cross*—C.S.C.
[0900]—*Canons Regular of Premontre* (U.S. Circary)—O.Praem.
[]—*Canons Regular of St. John Cantius*—S.J.C.
[0400]—*Canons Regular of the Order of the Holy Cross* (Prov. of St. Odilia, Minneapolis, MN)—O.S.C.
[0470]—*The Capuchin Friars*—O.F.M.Cap.
[0270]—*Carmelite Fathers & Brothers* (Most Pure Heart of Mary)—O.Carm.
[0340]—*Cistercian Fathers* (Polish Congr.)—O.Cist.
[0360]—*Claretian Missionaries*—C.M.F.
[1320]—*Clerics of St. Viator* (Chicago, IL)—C.S.V.
[0380]—*Comboni Missionaries of the Heart of Jesus-Verona*—M.C.C.J.
[0310]—*Congregation of Christian Brothers*—C.F.C.
[0750]—*Congregation of Marianhill Missionaries*—C.M.M.
[0220]—*Congregation of the Blessed Sacrament* (Rome, Italy)—S.S.S.
[]—*Congregation of the Holy Spirit* (Eastern Prov.)—C.S.Sp.
[1330]—*Congregation of the Mission* (Western Prov.)—C.M.
[1210]—*Congregation of the Missionaries of St. Charles* (Western Prov.)—C.S.
[1000]—*Congregation of the Passion* (Western Prov.)—C.P.
[1130]—*Congregation of the Priests of the Sacred Heart*—S.C.J.
[1080]—*Congregation of the Resurrection* (Chicago Prov.)—C.R.
[0480]—*Conventual Franciscans* (St. Bonaventure, Our Lady of Consolation Provs.)—O.F.M.Conv.
[0260]—*Discalced Carmelite Friars*—O.C.D.
[0520]—*Franciscan Friars* (Sacred Heart, Assumption of B.V.M. Provs.; Commissariats of the Holy Cross, Holy Family)—O.F.M.
[0690]—*Jesuit Fathers and Brothers* (Chicago, Polish, Lithuanian Provs.)—S.J.
[0730]—*Legionnaires of Christ*—L.C.
[0740]—*Marian Fathers*—M.I.C.
[0770]—*The Marist Brothers*—F.M.S.
[0780]—*Marist Fathers*—S.M.
[0800]—*Maryknoll*—M.M.
[0830]—*Mill Hill Missionaries*—M.H.M.
[0860]—*Missionhurst Congregation of the Immaculate Heart of Mary*—C.I.C.M.
[0910]—*Oblates of Mary Immaculate*—O.M.I.
[0430]—*Order of Preachers-Dominicans*—O.P.
[1030]—*Paulist Fathers* (New York Prov.)—C.S.P.
[0610]—*Priests of the Congregation of Holy Cross* (Notre Dame, IN)—C.S.C.
[1070]—*Redemptorist Fathers* (Denver)—C.SS.R.
[1190]—*Salesians of Don Bosco*—S.D.B.
[1220]—*Servants of Charity*—S.C.
[1240]—*Servites* (Chicago, IL)—O.S.M.
[1260]—*Society of Christ*—S.Ch.
[0760]—*Society of Mary*—S.M.
[0370]—*Society of St. Columban*—S.S.C.
[1200]—*Society of the Divine Savior*—S.D.S.
[0420]—*Society of the Divine Word*—S.V.D.
[1060]—*Society of the Precious Blood* (Kansas City Prov.)—C.PP.S.

[1170]—*St. Patrick Missionary Society*—S.P.S.
[1360]—*Xaverian Missionary Fathers*—S.X.

RELIGIOUS INSTITUTES OF WOMEN REPRESENTED IN THE ARCHDIOCESE

[0100]—*Adorers of the Blood of Christ*—A.S.C.
[0230]—*Benedictine Sisters of Pontifical Jurisdiction* (Chicago, IL; Duluth, MN)—O.S.B.
[0690]—*Comboni Missionary Sisters*—C.M.S.
[3110]—*Congregation of Our Lady of the Retreat in the Cenacle*—R.C.
[1860]—*Congregation of the Handmaids of the Precious Blood*—H.P.B.
[2100]—*Congregation of the Humility of Mary*—C.H.M.
[]—*Congregation of the Mother of Carmel*—C.M.C.
[0460]—*Congregation of the Sisters of Charity of the Incarnate Word*—C.C.V.I.
[3710]—*Congregation of the Sisters of Saint Agnes*—C.S.A.
[3832]—*Congregation of the Sisters of St. Joseph*—C.S.J.
[1920]—*Congregation of the Sisters of the Holy Cross*—C.S.C.
[1780]—*Congregation of the Sisters of the Third Order of St. Francis of Perpetual Adoration*—F.S.P.A.
[1710]—*Congregation of the Third Order of St. Francis of Mary Immaculate, Joliet, IL*—O.S.F.
[1730]—*Congregation of the Third Order of St. Francis, Oldenburg, IN*—O.S.F.
[0760]—*Daughters of Charity of St. Vincent de Paul*—D.C.
[0793]—*Daughters of Divine Love*—D.D.L.
[0940]—*Daughters of St. Mary of Providence*—D.S.M.P.
[0810]—*Daughters of the Heart of Mary*—D.H.M.
[0420]—*Discalced Carmelite Nuns*—O.C.D.
[1070-03]—*Dominican Sisters*—O.P.
[1070-07]—*Dominican Sisters*—O.P.
[1070-27]—*Dominican Sisters*—O.P.
[1070-13]—*Dominican Sisters*—O.P.
[1070-10]—*Dominican Sisters*—O.P.
[1115]—*Dominican Sisters of Peace*—O.P.
[1170]—*Felician Sisters*—C.S.S.F.
[1370]—*Franciscan Missionaries of Mary*—F.M.M.
[1210]—*Franciscan Sisters of Chicago*—O.S.F.
[1230]—*Franciscan Sisters of Christian Charity*—O.S.F.
[1310]—*Franciscan Sisters of Little Falls, Minnesota*—O.S.F.
[1415]—*Franciscan Sisters of Mary*—F.S.M.
[1430]—*Franciscan Sisters of Our Lady of Perpetual Help*—O.S.F.
[1450]—*Franciscan Sisters of the Sacred Heart*—O.S.F.
[1240]—*Franciscan Sisters, Daughters of the Sacred Hearts of Jesus and Mary*—O.S.F.
[2370]—*Institute of the Blessed Virgin Mary (Loretto Sisters)*—I.B.V.M.
[2330]—*Little Sisters of Jesus*—L.S.J.
[2320]—*Little Sisters of the Holy Family*—P.S.S.F.
[2340]—*Little Sisters of the Poor*—L.S.P.
[3570]—*Mantellate Sisters, Servants of Mary of Blue Island*—O.S.M.
[2420]—*Marist Missionary Sisters*—S.M.S.M.
[2430]—*Marist Sisters Congregation of Mary*—S.M.
[2470]—*Maryknoll Sisters of St. Dominic*—M.M.
[2480]—*Medical Missionaries of Mary*—M.M.M.
[2680]—*Misericordia Sisters*—S.M.
[2710]—*Missionaries of Charity*—M.C.
[2865]—*Missionaries of the Sacred Heart of Jesus and Our Lady of Guadalupe*—M.S.C.Gpe.
[2790]—*Missionary Servants of the Most Blessed Trinity*—M.S.B.T.
[2715]—*Missionary Sisters of Christ the King for Polonia*—M.CHR.
[2900]—*Missionary Sisters of St. Charles Borromeo*—M.S.C.S.
[3990]—*Missionary Sisters of St. Peter Claver*—S.S.P.C.
[2860]—*Missionary Sisters of the Sacred Heart*—M.S.C.
[3530]—*Missionary Sisters Servants of the Holy Spirit*—S.Sp.S.
[]—*Oblate Sisters of Jesus the Priest*—O.J.S.
[3040]—*Oblate Sisters of Providence*—O.S.P.
[3130]—*Our Lady of Victory Missionary Sisters*—O.L.V.M.
[0950]—*Pious Society Daughters of St. Paul*—F.S.P.
[3230]—*Poor Handmaids of Jesus Christ*—P.H.J.C.
[3440]—*Religious Hospitallers of Saint Joseph*—R.H.S.J.
[2970]—*School Sisters of Notre Dame*—S.S.N.D.
[1680]—*School Sisters of St. Francis*—O.S.F.
[3590]—*Servants of Mary (Servite Sisters)*—O.S.M.
[3520]—*Servants of the Holy Heart of Mary*—S.S.C.M.
[0440]—*Sisters of Charity of Cincinnati, Ohio*—S.C.
[0570]—*Sisters of Charity of Seton Hill, Greensburg, Pennsylvania*—S.C.
[0630]—*Sisters of Charity of St. Vincent de Paul*—S.V.Z.
[0430]—*Sisters of Charity of the Blessed Virgin Mary*—B.V.M.
[0660]—*Sisters of Christian Charity*—S.C.C.
[0990]—*Sisters of Divine Providence*—C.D.P.
[2360]—*Sisters of Loretto at the Foot of the Cross*—S.L.
[2575]—*Sisters of Mercy of the Americas* (Chicago, IL)—R.S.M.
[3000]—*Sisters of Notre Dame de Namur*—S.N.D.deN.
[3080]—*Sisters of Our Lady Christian Doctrine*—R.C.D.
[3350]—*Sisters of Providence*—S.P.
[3360]—*Sisters of Providence of Saint Mary-of-the-Woods, IN*—S.P.
[1620]—*Sisters of Saint Francis of Millvale, Pennsylvania*—O.S.F.
[1540]—*Sisters of Saint Francis, Clinton, Iowa*—O.S.F.
[3780]—*Sisters of Saints Cyril and Methodius*—SS.C.M.
[3740]—*Sisters of St. Casimir*—S.S.C.
[1520]—*Sisters of St. Francis of Christ the King*—O.S.F.
[1640]—*Sisters of St. Francis of Perpetual Adoration*—O.S.F.
[1570]—*Sisters of St. Francis of the Holy Family*—O.S.F.
[1800]—*Sisters of St. Francis of the Third Order Regular*—O.S.F.
[3830-15]—*Sisters of St. Joseph*—C.S.J.
[3840]—*Sisters of St. Joseph of Carondelet*—C.S.J.
[3930]—*Sisters of St. Joseph of the Third Order of St. Francis*—S.S.J.-T.O.S.F.
[0260]—*Sisters of the Blessed Sacrament for Indians and Colored People*—S.B.S.
[2980]—*Sisters of the Congregation de Notre Dame*—C.N.D.
[1030]—*Sisters of the Divine Savior*—S.D.S.
[1830]—*Sisters of the Good Shepherd*—R.G.S.
[1970]—*Sisters of the Holy Family of Nazareth*—C.S.F.N.
[2140]—*Sisters of the Immaculate Conception of the Blessed Virgin Mary* (Lithuanian)
[2270]—*Sisters of the Little Company of Mary*—L.C.M.
[2350]—*Sisters of the Living Word*—S.L.W.
[3320]—*Sisters of the Presentation of the B.V.M*—P.B.V.M.
[3480]—*Sisters of the Resurrection*—C.R.
[1705]—*Sisters of the Third Order of St. Francis of Assisi*—O.S.F.
[1720]—*Sisters of the Third Order of St. Francis of the Congregation of Our Lady of Lourdes*—O.S.F.
[2150]—*Sisters, Servants of the Immaculate Heart of Mary*—I.H.M.
[1890]—*Society of Helpers*—H.H.S.
[4060]—*Society of the Holy Child Jesus*—S.H.C.J.
[4070]—*Society of the Sacred Heart*—R.S.C.J.

ARCHDIOCESAN CEMETERIES

CHICAGO. *Central Office*, Catholic Cemeteries: 1400 S. Wolf Rd., Hillside, 60162-2197. Tel: 708-449-6100; Fax: 708-449-3419. Web: www.cathcemchgo.org. Rev. Patrick J. Pollard, Archdiocesan Dir.; Mr. Roman Szabelski, Exec. Dir.
St. Boniface
St. Casimir
St. Henry
Mt. Olivet

CALUMET CITY. *Holy Cross*
CRESTWOOD. *St. Benedict*
DES PLAINES. *All Saints*
EVANSTON. *Calvary*
EVERGREEN PARK. *St. Mary*
FOX LAKE. *St. Bede*
FREMONT CENTER. *St. Mary*
GLENWOOD. *Assumption*
HIGHLAND PARK. *St. Mary*
HILLSIDE. *Mt. Carmel*
Our Lady of Sorrows
Queen of Heaven
JUSTICE. *Resurrection*
LAKE FOREST. *St. Mary*
LEMONT. *St. Alphonsus*
SS. Cyril & Methodius
St. James, Sag Bridge
St. Patrick
LIBERTYVILLE. *Ascension*
NILES. *St. Adalbert*
Maryhill
NORTHBROOK. *Sacred Heart*
OAK FOREST. *St. Gabriel*
ORLAND PARK. *St. Michael*
PALATINE. *St. Michael the Archangel*
PARK FOREST. *St. Anne*
RIVER GROVE. *St. Joseph*
ROSENCRANS. *St. Patrick*
ROUND LAKE. *St. Joseph*
SAUK VILLAGE. *St. James*
SKOKIE. *St. Peter*
STEGER. *Calvary*
VOLO. *St. Peter*
WAUCONDA. *Transfiguration*
WAUKEGAN. *St. Mary*
WEST LAKE FOREST. *St. Patrick*
WILMETTE. *St. Joseph*
WORTH. *Holy Sepulchre*

NECROLOGY

† Cardiff, Rev. Msgr. John I., Oak Lawn, IL St. Linus—Died Oct. 3, 2009
† Ciemiega, Ernest D., (Retired)—Died March 27, 2009
† Gruchot, Stanley J., (Retired)—Died Nov. 12, 2009
† Jenks, Francis C., (Retired)—Died July 16, 2009
† Kaucky, Francis M., (Retired)—Died Aug. 18, 2009
† Lambert, Rollins E., (Retired)—Died Jan. 25, 2009
† Mollan, Ralph R., (Retired)—Died April 14, 2009
† Murphy, William P., Evergreen Park, Queen of Martyrs—Died May 22, 2009
† O'Sullivan, Daniel J., Park Forest, IL St. Irenaeus—Died Dec. 15, 2008
† Orozco, Raphael R., (Retired)—Died Dec. 21, 2008
† Siedlecki, Edmund J., (Retired)—Died Sept. 27, 2009
† White, William J., Oak Lawn, IL St. Gerald—Died Dec. 31, 2008

An asterisk (*) denotes an organization that has established tax-exempt status directly with the IRS and is not covered by the USCCB Group Ruling.

Archdiocese of Cincinnati

(Archidioecesis Cincinnatensis)

Most Reverend

DENNIS M. SCHNURR, J.C.D., D.D.

Archbishop of Cincinnati; ordained July 20, 1974; appointed Bishop of Duluth January 18, 2001; ordained April 2, 2001; appointed Coadjutor Archbishop of Cincinnati October 17, 2008; installed December 7, 2008; Succeeded to the See December 21, 2009. *Office: 100 E. Eighth St., Cincinnati, OH 45202-2129.*

Most Reverend

DANIEL E. PILARCZYK, S.T.D., PH.D., D.D.

Archbishop Emeritus of Cincinnati; ordained December 20, 1959; appointed Titular Bishop of Hodelm and Auxiliary Bishop of Cincinnati November 12, 1974; consecrated December 20, 1974; appointed Archbishop of Cincinnati November 2, 1982; installed December 20, 1982; retired December 21, 2009. *Office: 100 E. Eighth St., Cincinnati, OH 45202-2129.*

Archdiocesan Offices: 100 E. Eighth St., Cincinnati, OH 45202-2129. Tel: 513-421-3131; Fax: 513-421-6225.

Web: www.catholiccincinnati.org

Square Miles 8,543.

Erected Diocese June 19, 1821; Archdiocese July 19, 1850.

Comprises that part of the State of Ohio lying south of 40 degrees, 41 minutes, being the 19 Counties south of the northern line of Mercer, Auglaize, and Logan, all west of the eastern line of Logan, Champaign, Clark, Greene, Clinton, Highland and Adams Counties.

For legal titles of parishes and archdiocesan institutions, consult the Chancery Office.

STATISTICAL OVERVIEW

Personnel	
Archbishops	1
Retired Archbishops	1
Priests: Diocesan Active in Diocese	190
Priests: Diocesan Active Outside Diocese	4
Priests: Retired, Sick or Absent	86
Number of Diocesan Priests	280
Religious Priests in Diocese	213
Total Priests in Diocese	493
Extern Priests in Diocese	23
Ordinations:	
Diocesan Priests	7
Transitional Deacons	2
Permanent Deacons in Diocese	176
Total Brothers	121
Total Sisters	925
Parishes	
Parishes	218
With Resident Pastor:	
Resident Diocesan Priests	143
Resident Religious Priests	19
Without Resident Pastor:	
Administered by Priests	52
Administered by Deacons	1
Administered by Religious Women	1
Administered by Lay People	2
Closed Parishes	2
Professional Ministry Personnel:	
Brothers	6
Sisters	34
Lay Ministers	330
Welfare	
Catholic Hospitals	9
Total Assisted	1,577,130
Homes for the Aged	13
Total Assisted	3,273
Residential Care of Children	1
Total Assisted	1,269
Day Care Centers	1
Total Assisted	267
Special Centers for Social Services	4
Total Assisted	36,308
Residential Care of Disabled	1
Total Assisted	35
Other Institutions	5
Total Assisted	23,450
Educational	
Seminaries, Diocesan	1
Students from This Diocese	21
Students from Other Diocese	15
Diocesan Students in Other Seminaries	5
Total Seminarians	26
Colleges and Universities	4
Total Students	20,450
High Schools, Diocesan and Parish	18
Total Students	10,359
High Schools, Private	4
Total Students	3,317
Elementary Schools, Diocesan and Parish	88
Total Students	29,337
Elementary Schools, Private	6
Total Students	1,844
Non-residential Schools for the Disabled	1
Total Students	97
Catechesis/Religious Education:	
High School Students	5,356
Elementary Students	27,472
Total Students under Catholic Instruction	98,258
Teachers in the Diocese:	
Priests	12
Brothers	9
Sisters	41
Lay Teachers	2,217
Vital Statistics	
Receptions into the Church:	
Infant Baptism Totals	5,955
Minor Baptism Totals	388
Adult Baptism Totals	471
Received into Full Communion	731
First Communions	7,135
Confirmations	7,336
Marriages:	
Catholic	1,284
Interfaith	741
Total Marriages	2,025
Deaths	4,719
Total Catholic Population	468,204
Total Population	3,023,332

Former Bishops—Rt. Rev. EDWARD D. FENWICK, O.P., D.D., ord. Feb. 23, 1793; cons. Jan. 13, 1822; died Sept. 26, 1832; Most Revs. JOHN BAPTIST PURCELL, D.D., ord. May 20, 1826; cons. Oct. 13, 1833; appt. Archbishop, July 19, 1850; died July 4, 1883; WILLIAM HENRY ELDER, D.D., cons. Bishop of Natchez May 3, 1857; appt. Titular Bishop of Avar, and Coadjutor to the Archbishop of Cincinnati cum jure successionis, Jan. 30, 1880; succeeded to the See of Cincinnati, July 4, 1883; died Oct. 31, 1904; HENRY K. MOELLER, D.D., cons. Bishop of Columbus, Aug. 25, 1900; promoted to Archiepiscopal See of Areopolis and made Coadjutor to the Most Rev. William Henry Elder cum jure successionis, April 27, 1903; succeeded to the See of Cincinnati, Oct. 31, 1904; died Jan. 5, 1925; JOHN T. MCNICHOLAS, O.P., S.T.M., cons. Bishop of Duluth, MN Sept. 8, 1918; promoted to Archiepiscopal See of Cincinnati, July 8, 1925; appt. Assistant at the Pontifical Throne, Feb. 18, 1923; died April 22, 1950; KARL J. ALTER, D.D., LL.D., cons. Bishop of Toledo, June 17, 1931; appt. Assistant to the Pontifical Throne, May 30, 1950; elevated to Archbishop of Cincinnati, June 21, 1950; retired July 23, 1969; died Aug. 23, 1977; PAUL F. LEIBOLD, D.D., J.C.D., appt. Titular Bishop of Trebenna and Auxiliary of Cincinnati, April 10, 1958; cons. June 17, 1958; installed as Bishop of Evansville, June 15, 1966; transferred to Archdiocese of Cincinnati, July 23, 1969; installed Oct. 2, 1969; died June 1, 1972; His Eminence JOSEPH CARDINAL BERNARDIN, D.D., appt. Titular Bishop of Lugura and Auxiliary Bishop of Atlanta, March 9, 1966; cons. April 26, 1966; appt. Archbishop of Cincinnati, Nov. 21, 1972; installed Dec. 19, 1972; appt. Archbishop of Chicago, July 10, 1982; installed Aug. 25, 1982; created Cardinal Priest, Feb. 2, 1983; died Nov. 14, 1996; Most Rev. DANIEL E. PILARCZYK, S.T.D., Ph.D., D.D., ord. Dec. 20, 1959; appt. Titular Bishop of Hodelm and Auxiliary Bishop of Cincinnati Nov. 12, 1974; cons. Dec. 20, 1974; appt. Archbishop of Cincinnati Nov. 2, 1982; installed Dec. 20, 1982; retired Dec. 21, 2009.

Vicar General—Most Rev. DENNIS M. SCHNURR, J.C.D., D.D.; Rev. JOSEPH R. BINZER, J.C.L.

Archdiocesan Department Directors—Ms. KATHLEEN DONNELLAN, Dir., Community Svcs.; Bro. JOSEPH KAMIS, S.M., Dir., Educational Svcs.; Rev. JOSEPH R. BINZER, J.C.L., Dir., Exec. Svcs.; Mr. RICHARD KELLY, Dir., Financial Svcs.; Most Rev. DENNIS M. SCHNURR, J.C.D., D.D., Dir., Pastoral Svcs.; MICHAEL VANDERBURGH, Dir. Stewardship Svcs.

Presbyteral Council—Ex Officio Members: Most Revs. DANIEL E. PILARCZYK, S.T.D., Ph.D., D.D.; DENNIS M. SCHNURR, J.C.D., D.D.; Revs. JOSEPH R. BINZER, J.C.L.; MARK J. BURGER; GEOFFREY D. DREW; JOHN J. MATTSCHECK (Retired); JOHN E. WALL (Retired); JAMES J. WALSH. Priest Councilors: Revs. ANTHONY E. CUTCHER; RICHARD FRIEBEL, C.PP.S.; TERENCE J. HAMILTON; EDWARD M. JACH, S.M.; J. DENNIS JASPERS; TIMOTHY S. KALLAHER; HAROLD W. KIST; ERIC J. KNAPP, S.J.; CARL J. LANGENDERFER, O.F.M.; MICHAEL U. PUCKE; THOMAS W. SCHMIDT; JAMES SHAPPELLE; STEVEN L. SHOUP; WILLIAM C. WAGNER; LEONARD C. WENKE.

Vicarri Foranei (Deans)—Revs. JOSEPH A. ROBINSON, Cathedral Deanery; MARK J. BURGER, St. Andrew

Deanery; LEONARD C. WENKE, St. Francis de Sales Deanery; JAMES J. WALSH, St. Lawrence Deanery; GEORGE JACQUEMIN, St. Margaret Mary Deanery; TIMOTHY S. BUNCH, Hamilton Deanery; WILLIAM C. WAGNER, St. Martin Deanery; DAVID E. BRINKMOELLER, Dayton Deanery; DENNIS J. CAYLOR, J.C.L., Springfield Deanery; STEVEN L. SHOUP, Sidney Deanery; JAMES C. SEIBERT, C.PP.S., St. Mary's Deanery.

Consultors—Revs. JOSEPH R. BINZER, J.C.L.; MARK J. BURGER; ANTHONY E. CUTCHER; GEOFFREY D. DREW; HAROLD W. KIST; JOHN J. MATTSCHECK (Retired); MICHAEL U. PUCKE; JAMES SHAPPELLE; STEVEN L. SHOUP; WILLIAM C. WAGNER; JOHN E. WALL (Retired); JAMES J. WALSH.

Archdiocesan Offices

Unless otherwise indicated, all Archdiocesan Offices and Directors are located at: *100 E. Eighth St., Cincinnati, 45202*. Tel: 513-421-3131; Fax: 513-421-6225.

Office of the Archbishop—LINDA CHOUTEAU, Exec. Sec. to the Archbishop.

Office of Mediation—JOSEPH B. CROWE, Admin. Tel: 513-421-3131, Ext. 408.

Department of Executive Services

Director—Rev. JOSEPH R. BINZER, J.C.L.

Chancery—

Chancellor—Rev. JOSEPH R. BINZER, J.C.L.

Vice Chancellor—VACANT.

Assistant Chancellor—Rev. THOMAS A. SNODGRASS, J.C.L.

Archivist—DON H. BUSKE (Special Address & Phone No. for Historical Archives Only), 212 E. Eighth St., Cincinnati, 45202. Tel: 513-621-2086.

Imprimatur Censors—Revs. CHRISTOPHER R. ARMSTRONG, J.C.D., St. Antonius, 1500 Linneman Rd., Cincinnati, 45238. Tel: 513-922-5400; EARL K. FERNANDES, S.T.D., Mt. St. Mary Seminary, 6616 Beechmont Ave., Cincinnati, 45230. Tel: 513-233-4245; RICHARD L. KLUG, S.T.L. (Retired), 3776 Francis Ave., Cincinnati, 45211. Tel: 513-662-3049; DONALD G. MCCARTHY (Retired), St. Ignatius Loyola, 5222 N. Bend Rd., Cincinnati, 45247. Tel: 513-661-6565; GILES H. PATER (Retired), 1435 Meadowbright, Cincinnati, 45230. Tel: 513-233-0066; MICHAEL PUCKE, St. Julie Billiart, 224 Dayton St., Hamilton, 45011. Tel: 513-863-1040; TIMOTHY P. SCHEHR, Ph.D., Mt. St. Mary Seminary, 6616 Beechmont Ave., Cincinnati, 45230. Tel: 513-231-6139; ROBERT A. STRICKER (Retired), 5560 Kirby Ave., Cincinnati, 45239. Tel: 513-541-5560; FRANCIS W. VOELLMECKE, Ph.D., Mt. St. Mary's Seminary, 6616 Beechmont Ave., Cincinnati, 45230. Tel: 513-231-2223; RICHARD W. WALLING Coldwater Cluster (St. Anthony, St. Anthony; St. Mary, Philothea; and Holy Trinity, Coldwater) 116 E. Main St., Coldwater, 45828. Tel: 419-678-4802; JOHN E. WESSLING (Retired), 10095 Wayside Dr., #259, Cincinnati, 45241. Tel: 513-779-5350; DAVID L. ZINK, Saint Nicholas Parish, P.O. Box 9, Osgood, 45351. Tel: 419-582-2531; JEFFREY M. KEMPER, Ph.D., St. John the Baptist, 110 N. Hill St., Harrison, 45030. Tel: 513-367-9086; MICHAEL A. SEGER, S.T.D., Mt. St. Mary's Seminary, 6616 Beechmont Ave., Cincinnati, 45230. Tel: 513-231-2223.

Communications Office—DAN ANDRIACCO, Dir.

Newspaper--"The Catholic Telegraph"—Most Rev. DANIEL E. PILARCZYK, S.T.D., Ph.D., D.D., Publisher.

Office of Religious—Sr. MARY GARKE, C.PP.S., Dir.

Permanent Diaconate Office—BERNARD J. MERSMANN.

Victim Assistance Coordinator—Sr. MARY GARKE, C.PP.S. Tel: 513-421-3131, Ext. 2865. Email: mgarke@catholiccincinnati.org.

Tribunal-Archdiocese of Cincinnati—Tel: 513-421-3131; Fax: 513-723-1035.

Director—Sr. VICTORIA VONDENBERGER, R.S.M., J.C.L.

Judicial Vicar—Rev. MANUEL VIERA, O.F.M., J.C.L.

Adjutant Judicial Vicars—Revs. STEVEN J. ANGI, J.C.L.; EDWIN F. GEARHART, J.C.L.; BARRY M. WINDHOLTZ, J.C.L.

Judges—Rev. CHRISTOPHER R. ARMSTRONG, J.C.D.; Deacon MICHAEL A. ASCOLESE; Revs. MICHAEL D. BEATTY; JOSEPH R. BINZER, J.C.L.; JAMES A. BRAMLAGE; Deacon STEVEN R. BROWN, J.C.L.; Revs. DAVID E. FAY; JOHN P. FISCHER; GERALD R. HAEMMERLE, M.A.; TIMOTHY S. KALLAHER; RAYMOND C. KELLERMAN; RICHARD L. KLUG, S.T.L. (Retired); FRANCIS G. LAMMEIER (Retired); NORMAN W. LANGENBRUNNER; THOMAS C. NOLKER; ROBERT A. OBERMEYER; R. MARC SHERLOCK; TERRANCE W. SMITH; THOMAS A. SNODGRASS, J.C.L.; LARRY R. THARP; FRANCIS W. VOELLMECKE, Ph.D.; JOHN R. WHITE, J.C.L.

Defenders of the Bond—Rev. DENNIS J. CAYLOR, J.C.L.; Sr. VICTORIA VONDENBERGER, R.S.M., J.C.L.; Rev. WILLIAM H. WYSONG, J.C.L.

Promoter of Justice—Sr. VICTORIA VONDENBERGER, R.S.M., J.C.L.

Assessors—Mrs. KELLY M. TERRY; Miss CHRISTINE GATELY.

Auditors—Mrs. CANDY L. ENGELKE; Mrs. AMI R. QUINN.

Vocations Office—Rev. KYLE E. SCHNIPPEL, Dir.; Mr. WAYNE TOPP, Asst. Dir.

Department of Community Services

Director—Ms. KATHLEEN DONNELLAN.

Archdiocesan Office of Catholic Charities—Ms. KATHLEEN DONNELLAN, Dir.

Catholic Residential Services of Archdiocese of Cincinnati with People with Mental Retardation—100 E. Eighth St., Cincinnati, 45202. Tel: 513-784-0400; Fax: 513-333-3172. Co Directors: AMY LINZ; PEGGY FRYER.

Catholic Charities of Southwestern Ohio—Ms. KATHLEEN DONNELLAN, Exec. Dir. Tel: 513-241-7745.

Hamilton Office—SHELLY WALLPE, Regl. Dir., 140 N. Fifth St., Hamilton, 45011. Tel: 513-863-6129.

Springfield Office—KEITH WILLIAMSON, Regl. Dir., 701 E. Columbia St., Springfield, 45504. Tel: 937-325-8715.

Catholic Social Services of Miami Valley—LAURA ROESCH, Exec. Dir., 922 W. Riverview Dr., Dayton, 45407. Tel: 937-223-7217.

Rural Life Conference—266 Bainbridge St., Dayton, 45402. Tel: 937-224-3026.

Catholic Social Action—ANTHONY STIERITZ, Dir., 100 E. 8th St., Cincinnati, 45202. Tel: 513-421-3131. Dayton Office: PAM LONG, 266 Bainbridge St., Dayton, 45402. Tel: 937-224-3026.

Department of Educational Services

Director—Bro. JOSEPH KAMIS, S.M.

School Office—Bro. JOSEPH KAMIS, S.M., Supt., Archdiocesan Schools, 100 E. Eighth St., Cincinnati, 45202. Tel: 513-421-3131; Dr. LAURA MEIBERS, Deputy Supt., Archdiocesan Schools Office, 266 Bainbridge St., Dayton, 45402. Tel: 937-223-5151.

Office of Evangelization and Catechesis—KENNETH GLEASON, Archdiocesan Dir., 100 E. Eighth St., Cincinnati, 45202. Tel: 513-421-3131; DAVID RILEY, Regl. Dir., Dayton Office of Evangelization and Catechesis, 226 Bainbridge St., Dayton, 45402. Tel: 937-223-4075; JANE PIERRON, Regl. Dir., Sidney Office of Evangelization and Catechesis, 119 E. Water St., Sidney, 45365. Tel: 937-498-1192.

Department of Financial Services

Chief Financial Officer—Mr. RICHARD KELLY.

Controller—STEPHEN E. BURGER.

Assistant Directors—ANNIE LIPPS, Asst. Dir. & Payroll Mgr.; ANNE MORROW.

Director of Benefits and Risk Management—BARBARA A. WALSH.

Cemeteries—GARY RAFFEL, Dir., 100 E. 8th St., Cincinnati, 45202. Tel: 513-421-3131.

Office of Property Management-Central Services—GARY RAFFEL, Dir.

Office of Human Resources—BILL HANCOCK, Dir.

Planning and Research—VACANT.

Department of Pastoral Services

Director—Most Rev. DENNIS M. SCHNURR, J.C.D., D.D.

Campus Ministry—Dr. JANE STEINHAUSER, Dir., 444 W. Third St., Dayton, 45402. (See Special Listing: Campus Ministry).

African American Catholic Ministries—Deacon ROYCE E. WINTERS, Dir.

Ecumenical and Interfaith Relations—LOUISE VERA, Prog. Coord.

Family Life—Deacon JAMES A. MERRITT, Dir. Dayton: NOREEN WENDELN, 266 Bainbridge St., Dayton, 45402. Tel: 937-222-0227. Northern Area: VELMA JEAN BORGERT, 119 E. Water St., Sidney, 45365. Tel: 937-492-4449.

Missions—

Pontifical Mission Aid Societies—Most Rev. DENNIS M. SCHNURR, J.C.D., D.D.

Missions Office—Dr. MIKE GABLE, Dir.

Pastoral Council Secretariat—Rev. RAYMOND E. LARGER, Exec. Sec.

Priestly Formation—Rev. THOMAS P. DIFOLCO, Dir.

Priests' Personnel Director—Rev. LEONARD C. WENKE, Dir.

Hispanic Catholic Ministry, Dayton—Sr. MARIA FRANCINE STACY, S.N.D., Holy Family/Nazareth Center, 2725 E. 5th St., Dayton, 45403. Tel: 937-258-1309.

Archdiocesan Office of Hispanic Ministry—Rev. WILLIAM J. JANSEN, M.C.C.J., Dir., 115 W. Seymour Ave., Cincinnati, 45216. Tel: 513-948-1760.

Worship—Ms. KAREN KANE, Dir.

Youth and Young Adult—Mr. SEAN REYNOLDS, Dir., 100 E. Eighth St., Cincinnati, 45202. Tel: 513-421-3131; TIMOTHY E. COLBERT, Regl. Dir., Dayton & Northern Area: 266 Bainbridge St., Dayton, 45402. Tel: 937-223-1001.

CLERGY, PARISHES, MISSIONS AND PAROCHIAL SCHOOLS

GREATER CINCINNATI

(HAMILTON COUNTY)

1—ST. PETER IN CHAINS CATHEDRAL (1822) Rev. James A. Bramlage; Deacon David Klingshirn. In Res., Revs. Thomas A. Snodgrass; Raymond E. Larger.
Res.: 325 W. Eighth St., 45202. Tel: 513-421-5355; Fax: 513-241-9517. Email: info@stpeterinchainscathedral.org. Web: www.stpeterinchainscathedral.org.
Church: Tel: 513-421-5354.

2—ST. AGNES (Bond Hill) (1892), (African American), Rev. Thomas P. DiFolco; Deacon Royce Winters, Pastoral Admin.; Patrick Lesher, Business Mgr.
Res.: 1619 California Ave., 45237. Tel: 513-242-4747; Fax: 513-641-3983. Email: church@stagnes.cc. Web: stagnes.cc.
Catechesis/Religious Program—Students 22.

3—ALL SAINTS (Kenwood) (1948) Rev. J. Dennis Jaspers; Deacon Amado Lim, Pastoral Assoc.; Robert Leever, Asst. Pastoral Assoc.; Marianna Kuhn, Business Mgr.; Ron Miller, Music Dir.
Res.: 8939 Montgomery Rd., 45236. Tel: 513-792-4600; Fax: 513-792-4730. Web: www.allsaints.cc.
School—(Grades K-8) Tel: 513-792-4732; Fax: 513-792-7990. Mrs. Mary E. Stratford, Prin.; Christine Toogood, Librarian. Lay Teachers 29; Students 453.
Catechesis/Religious Program—Tel: 513-792-4603; Fax: 513-792-4730. Ginny Rush, Dir. Faith Formation; Micki Harrell, Dir. Devel. Students 180.

4—ST. ALOYSIUS GONZAGA (Bridgetown) (1866) Rev. W. Michael Hay; Deacon Jerry Schneider.
Res.: 4366 Bridgetown Rd., 45211. Tel: 513-574-4840; Fax: 513-574-4402. Email: staloysius5@fuse.net. Web: saintals.org.
School—(Grades K-8), 4390 Bridgetown Rd., 45211. Tel: 513-574-4035; Fax: 513-574-5421. James Leisring, Prin. Lay Teachers 14; Students 194.
Catechesis/Religious Program—Tel: 513-574-4840; Fax: 513-574-4402. Students 67.

5—ST. ALOYSIUS-ON-THE-OHIO (1873) Rev. Richard E. Dressman; Deacon Luis Riva Saleta.
Res.: 134 Whipple St., 45233. Tel: 513-941-3445; Fax: 513-941-2257. Web: www.saoto.org.
School—(Grades PreK-8), 6207 Portage, 45233. Tel: 513-941-7831; Fax: 513-941-5418. Edward Jung, Prin.; Jean Hoferer, Librarian. Lay Teachers 13; Students 122.
Catechesis/Religious Program—Tel: 513-941-3445; Fax: 513-941-2257. Students 15.

6—ST. ANDREW (1874), (African American), Revs. Jerry Steinbrunner, C.PP.S.; William H. Cross, Sacramental Min.; John W. Jones, Business Mgr.; Gloria Turnbow, Youth Min. Coord.
3401 Reading Rd., P.O. Box 29064, 45229. Tel: 513-281-7504; Fax: 513-281-3096. Email: standrew@fuse.net.
Catechesis/Religious Program—Nancy Ertel, D.R.E. Students 17.

7—ST. ANN (Groesbeck) (1953) Rev. Thomas J. Dennemann; Deacon John M. Quattrone. In Res., Revs. Shawn R. Landenwitch, Faculty, LaSalle High School; Anthony Muller.
Res.: 2900 Galbraith Rd., 45239. Tel: 513-521-8440; Fax: 513-521-7221. Email: info@saintannparish.org. Web: www.saintannparish.org.
See Our Lady of Grace, Cincinnati under Consolidated Elementary Schools located in the Institution section.
Catechesis/Religious Program—Tel: 513-729-2810. Web: www.saintannparish.org/ReligiousEd/religious_education.htm. Diane C. Ferrier, D.R.E. Students 106.

8—ANNUNCIATION OF THE BLESSED VIRGIN MARY (1910) Rev. Todd Grogan.
Res.: 3547 Clifton Ave., 45220. Tel: 513-861-1295, Fax: 513-861-6789. Web: www.annunciationbvmparish.org.
School—(Grades K-8), 3545 Clifton Ave., 45220. Tel: 513-221-1230; Fax: 513-281-8009. Ms. Cindy Hardesty, Prin. Lay Teachers 14; Students 147.
Catechesis/Religious Program—Tel: 513-861-1295. Students 30.

9—ST. ANTHONY (Madisonville) (1858) [CEM] Rev. Leonard C. Wenke; Sr. Carol Leveque, S.C., Pastoral Assoc.

Res.: 6104 Desmond St., 45227. Tel: 513-271-0920; Fax: 513-271-6630. Email: office@stanthonychurch.net. Web: www.stanthonychurch.net.
Catechesis/Religious Program—Tel: 513-271-0920; Fax: 513-271-6630. Sr. Roseann Klosterman, C.S.J., Dir. Faith Formation. Students 51.

10—St. Antoninus (1944) Revs. Christopher R. Armstrong; Lawrence J. Mick (Retired); Deacon Robert J. Schroeder, Pastoral Assoc.
Res.: 1500 Linneman Rd., 45238. Tel: 513-922-5400; Fax: 513-451-5871. Email: saintantoninus@fuse.net. Web: www.saintantoninus.org.
School—(Grades K-8), 5425 Julmar Dr., 45238. Tel: 513-922-2500; Fax: 513-922-5519. Jack Corey, Prin.; Marilyn Ruther, Librarian. Lay Teachers 26; Students 470.
Catechesis/Religious Program—Tel: 513-922-4759. Students 35.

11—Assumption of the Blessed Virgin Mary (Walnut Hills) (1872) Rev. Thomas Bokenkotter.
Res.: 2622 Gilbert Ave., 45206. Tel: 513-961-3242; 513-271-0016.

12—St. Bartholomew (1961) Rev. Patrick J. Welsh; Deacon Michael A. Ascolese; Sr. Ruth Kluemper, Pastoral Assoc.; Paul Bresciani, Pastoral Assoc. Music & Liturgy; Suzanne Engel, Pastoral Assoc. Sacraments & Youth; John Finn, Business Mgr.
Res.: 9375 Winton Rd., 45231. Tel: 513-522-3680; Fax: 513-728-3141.
See St. John Paul II Catholic, Cincinnati under Consolidated Elementary Schools located in the Institution section.
Catechesis/Religious Program—Tel: 513-728-3146, Ext. 105; Fax: 513-728-3141. Students 52.

13—St. Bernard (1919) Rev. James Shappelle.
Res.: 740 Circle Ave., 45232. Tel: 513-541-3732; Fax: 513-541-0362. Email: stbernardwp@fuse.net.
Catechesis/Religious Program— Twinned with Mother of Christ. Students 8.

14—St. Bernard (Taylor's Creek) (1867) [CEM] Rev. Donald L. Siciliano.
Res.: 7130 Harrison Rd., 45247. Tel: 513-353-4207; Fax: 513-353-9600. Email: stbernard@cinci.rr.com. Web: www.stbernardtc.catholicweb.com.
School—(Grades K-8), 7115 Springdale Rd., 45247. Tel: 513-353-4224; Fax: 513-353-3958. Web: www.stbernardtc.org. Jane Acra, Prin. Lay Teachers 10; Students 169.
Catechesis/Religious Program—Students 25.

15—St. Boniface (1863) Rev. Joseph A. Robinson; Deacon Jerry Yetter; Carol Roosa, Pastoral Admin.
Res.: 1750 Chase Ave., 45223. Tel: 513-541-1563; Fax: 513-541-1514. Email: stboniface@cinci.rr.com. Web: www.stbonifacecincinnati.com.
See St. Boniface School, Cincinnati under Consolidated Elementary Schools located in the Institution section.
Catechesis/Religious Program—Students 8.

16—St. Catharine of Siena (1903) Rev. Anthony M. Dattilo; Therese Bower Hibdon, Pastoral Min.
Res.: 2848 Fischer Pl., 45211. Tel: 513-661-0651; Fax: 513-661-0652. Web: stcatharinesiena.org.
School—(Grades K-8), 3324 Wunder Ave., 45211. Tel: 513-481-7683; Fax: 513-481-9438. Mary Ann Bernier, Prin. Lay Teachers 10; Students 185.
Catechesis/Religious Program—Students 8.

17—St. Cecilia (Oakley) (1908) Rev. Jamie Weber; Deacon John Slattery. In Res., Rev. Elmer W. Smith (Retired).
Res.: 3105 Madison Rd., 45209. Tel: 513-871-5757; Fax: 513-533-6066. Email: fr.jamie@stceciliacincinnati.org. Web: stceciliacincinnati.org.
School—(Grades K-8), 4115 Taylor Ave., 45209. Tel: 513-533-6060; Fax: 513-533-6068. Ms. Lori Heffner, Prin. Lay Teachers 12; Students 180.
Catechesis/Religious Program—Julie Althaver, D.R.E. Students 48.
Parish Center—4030 Gilmore Ave., 45209.

18—Church of the Assumption (Mount Healthy) (1854) [CEM] Rev. William M. Kennedy; Deacons Richard J. Reder; Robert A. Staab Jr.
Res.: 7711 Joseph St., 45231. Tel: 513-521-7274; Fax: 513-521-3728. Email: rectory@assumptionmthealthy.org. Web: www.assumptionmthealthy.org.
See Our Lady of Grace, Cincinnati under Consolidated Elementary Schools located in the Institution section.
Catechesis/Religious Program—Tel: 513-728-4941. Sr. Marietta Sharkey, O.S.F., D.R.E. Students 61.

19—St. Clare (College Hill) (1908) Rev. George Jacquemin. In Res., Rev. Robert J. Hater (Retired).
See John Paul II Catholic, Cincinnati under Consolidated Elementary Schools located in the Institution section.
Res.: 1443 Cedar Ave., 45224. Tel: 513-541-2100; Fax: 513-541-2101. Email: stclare@one.com. Web: www.saintclareparish.org.
Catechesis/Religious Program—Students 30.

20—St. Clement (St. Bernard) (1850) Revs. Fred Link, O.F.M.; Louis Bartko, O.F.M.; Bro. Joel Soldenski, O.F.M., Pastoral Assoc.; Deacon John P. Gerke; Marty Cunningham, Music Min.
St. Clement Friary: 4536 Vine St., 45217. Tel: 513-641-3176 (Church); 513-641-2257 (Friary); Fax: 513-641-2262 (Friary); 513-641-0149 (Church Office).
School—(Grades PreK-8), 4534 Vine St., 45217. Tel: 513-641-2137; Fax: 513-242-6036. Web: www.stcschool.org. Ms. Linda Westendorf, Prin. Tel: 513-641-2137, Ext. 802. Sisters 1; Lay Teachers 13; Students 212.
Catechesis/Religious Program—1619 California Ave., 45237. Tel: 513-641-2137, Ext. 808; Fax: 513-641-0149. Lawrence Ungerer, D.R.E. Students 219.

21—Corpus Christi (1958) Rev. James W. Meade; Deacon John Corson, Pastoral Assoc.; Pam McLaughlin, Pastoral Assoc.; William Marshall, Pastoral Assoc.; Deacon Larry H. Day. In Res., Rev. Robert B. Buening (Retired).
Res.: 2014 Springdale Rd., 45231. Tel: 513-825-0618; Fax: 513-825-0182. Email: info@corpuschristicommunity.org. Web: corpuschristicommunity.org.
See St. John the Baptist Catholic School, Cincinnati under Consolidated Elementary Schools in the institution section.
Catechesis/Religious Program—Tel: 513-825-0182. Students 110.

22—St. Dominic (Delhi Hills) (1933) Revs. Jim J. Walsh; Chris Lack; Deacon Mark A. Bardonaro.
Res.: 4551 Delhi Pike, 45238. Tel: 513-471-7741; Fax: 513-471-0363. Email: parishoffice@stdominicdelhi.org. Web: www.stdominicdelhi.org.
School—(Grades K-8), 371 Pedretti Ave., 45238. Tel: 513-251-1276; Fax: 513-251-6428. William S. Cavanaugh, Prin. Lay Teachers 28; Students 510.
Catechesis/Religious Program—Tel: 513-471-7741, Ext. 481. Email: aandriaccos@stdominicdelhi.org. Students 98.

23—St. Francis de Sales (1849) [CEM], Collaborative cluster - see St. Robert, Bellarmine. Revs. Edward M. Jach, S.M.; John Manahan, S.M.
Res.: 1600 Madison Rd., 45206. Tel: 513-961-1945; Fax: 513-221-4907.
School—(Grades K-8) Tel: 513-961-1953; Fax: 513-961-2900. William Shula, Prin. Brothers 1; Lay Teachers 11; Students 210.
Catechesis/Religious Program— Collaborative Cluster, see St. Robert Bellarmine.

24—St. Francis Seraph (1859) Rev. Greg Friedman; Bro. Timothy Sucher, O.F.M., Admin.
St. Francis Friary: 1615 Vine St., 45202. Tel: 513-535-2719; Fax: 513-421-9672. Web: stfrancisseraph.org.
School—(Grades K-8), 14 E. Liberty St., 45202. Tel: 513-721-7778; Fax: 513-721-5445. Web: stfrancisseraph.org/School/school.html. Ms. Wanda W. Hill, Prin. Sisters 1; Lay Teachers 12; Students 146.
Catechesis/Religious Program—Students 2.

25—St. Francis Xavier (1819) Revs. Eric J. Knapp, S.J.; Cyril W. Whitaker; John P. Murphy, S.J.; M. Joseph Casey, S.J.
Res.: 607 Sycamore St., 45202. Tel: 513-721-4045; Fax: 513-723-0451. Email: stxavier1@fuse.net. Web: www.stxchurch.org.

26—St. Gabriel (Glendale) (1857) Rev. David E. Fay; Deacons Herman H. Bryant; Gerald A. Flamm.
Res.: 48 W. Sharon Ave., 45246. Tel: 513-771-4700; Fax: 513-612-4545. Email: gabrielglendale@fuse.net.
See St. Gabriel Consolidated School, Cincinnati under Consolidated Elementary Schools located in the Institution section.
Catechesis/Religious Program—Fax: 513-621-4545. Rose Voulgarakis, D.R.E. Students 31.

27—St. Gertrude (Madeira) (1923) Revs. Darren Pierre, O.P.; Walter C. Wagner, O.P., Novice Master; Michael Mary Dosch, O.P.; Charles A. Farrell, O.P.; Joseph Clement Burns, O.P.; George Schommer, O.P.; Kenneth Andrew Hofer, O.P.
Res.: 7630 Shawnee Run Rd., 45243. Tel: 513-561-5954; Fax: 513-527-3971. Web: www.stgertrude.org.
School—(Grades PreK-8), 6543 Miami Ave., 45243. Tel: 513-561-8020; Fax: 513-561-7184. Web: www.stgertrudesch.org. Sr. Mary Sheila, O.P., Prin.; Patricia Lacker, Librarian. Dominican Sisters (Nashville, TN) 4; Lay Teachers 22; Students 445.
Catechesis/Religious Program—Tel: 513-561-8369; Fax: 513-561-8369. Students 540.

28—Good Shepherd (1973) Revs. Robert E. Schmitz; Terrance W. Smith, Parochial Vicar; Deacons Richard W. Gallenstein, Pastoral Min.; Max Schellman, Human Resources Min.; James Jones; Stephen P. Lindner, Dir. Liturgical Ministries; Patricia Lindner, Dir. Communications; Donna Krabbe, Dir. Educ. & Formation; Teri Cunningham, Dir. Stewardship; Rick Hagee, Dir. Music Ministry; Dan Parker, Dir. Facilities; Mark Westendorf, Coord. Outreach Ministries.
Res.: 8815 E. Kemper Rd., 45249. Tel: 513-489-8815; Fax: 513-489-8521. Email: gs.info@goodshepherd.org. Web: www.good-shepherd.org.
Catechesis/Religious Program—Sharon Mattfeld, Co-Admin. Faith Formation (K-6); Jeffrey Davis, Coord. Youth & Young Adult Ministries. Students 601.

29—Guardian Angels (Mt. Washington) (1892) [CEM] Rev. Thomas M. King; Deacons Rick Novick; Robert Fey; David Meyer.
Res.: 6531 Beechmont Ave., 45230. Tel: 513-231-7440; Fax: 513-624-3145. Email: office@gaparish.org. Web: www.gaparish.org.
School—(Grades K-8), 6539 Beechmont Ave., 45230. Tel: 513-624-3141; Fax: 513-624-3150. Web: www.gaschool.org. William Kenney, Prin.; Mrs. Karen Lavelle, Librarian. Lay Teachers 40; Students 560.
Catechesis/Religious Program—Tel: 513-624-3146. Students 260.

30—Holy Cross-Immaculata (Mount Adams) (1859) Rev. Martin O. Moran III (HBG); Bill Frantz, Pastoral Admin.; Deacon Mark Desmond.
Res.: 30 Guido St., 45202. Tel: 513-721-6544; Fax: 513-721-6177. Email: holymac30@fuse.net. Web: www.hciparish.org.
Catechesis/Religious Program—

31—Holy Family (Price Hill) (1883), Includes the consolidation of Our Lady of Grace, Our Lady of Perpetual Help Parishes, Blessed Sacrament and St. Michael. Rev. James G. Kiffmeyer.
Parish Office—3006 W. 8th St., 45205. Tel: 513-921-7527; Fax: 513-921-6033. Email: holyfamily@fuse.net. Web: www.holyfamilycincinnati.com.
Res.: 814 Hawthorne Ave., 45205. Tel: 513-921-7527; Fax: 513-921-6033.
School—(Grades K-8), 3001 Price Ave., 45205. Tel: 513-921-8483; Fax: 513-921-2460. Web: www.hfschool.org. Sr. Brenda Busch, S.C., Prin. Sisters 4; Lay Teachers 19; Students 155.
Catechesis/Religious Program—Students 220.

32—Holy Name (1904) Rev. Alan Hirt, O.F.M.; Sr. Mary Gallagher, S.C., Pastoral Admin.
Res.: 2448 Auburn Ave., 45219. Tel: 513-721-5608; Fax: 513-721-5608 (call first).
Catechesis/Religious Program—Students 18.

33—Holy Trinity Church (Norwood) (1994) Rev. Raymond C. Kellerman.
Res.: 2420 Drex Ave., 45212. Tel: 513-366-4400; Fax: 513-366-4404. Email: holytrinity1@fuse.net. Web: www.holytrinitynorwood.org.
See St. Nicholas Academy, Cincinnati under Consolidated Elementary Schools in the institution section.
Catechesis/Religious Program—Tel: 513-791-3238; Fax: 513-686-2720. Twinned with St. John the Evangelist, Cincinnati. Students 14.

34—St. Ignatius of Loyola (Monfort Heights) (1946) Revs. Peter T. St. George; Donald G. McCarthy (Retired); John E. Wall (Retired); Deacon Anthony Gagliarducci; Frank Posinski, Business Mgr.; Sisters Lucy Zientek, C.D.P., Pastoral Assoc.; Patty Stretch, Music Min.
Res.: 5222 North Bend Rd., 45247. Tel: 513-661-6565; Fax: 513-389-3241. Email: office@sainti.org. Web: www.sainti.org.
School—(Grades K-8) Tel: 513-389-3242; Fax: 513-389-3255. Timothy Reilly, Prin. Lay Teachers 44; Students 998.
Catechesis/Religious Program—Tel: 513-389-3247. Kris Schoettmer, D.R.E. Students 140.

35—Immaculate Heart of Mary (Forestville) (1944) Revs. Thomas W. Kreidler; Robert F. Hadden, Parochial Vicar; Mr. Sean Ater, Pastoral Assoc.; Deacons Bill Mullaney; Dave Shea; Dave Shaffer.
Res.: 7820 Beechmont Ave., 45255. Tel: 513-388-4466; Fax: 513-388-4097. Email: parish@ihom.org. Web: www.ihom.org.
School—(Grades 1-8), 7800 Beechmont Ave., 45255. Tel: 513-388-4086; Fax: 513-388-3026. Email: school@ihom.org. Web: www.ihomschool.org. Mrs. Mary Hedger, Co-Prin.; Mrs. Nancy Goebel, Co-Prin. Brothers 1; Lay Teachers 37; Students 650.
Catechesis/Religious Program—Tel: 513-388-4093; Fax: 513-388-4097. Email: formation@ihom.org. Mr. Patrick Reis, Youth Min. Students 670.

36—St. James of the Valley (Wyoming) (1886) Rev. Jack W. Wehman; Deacon Conrad C. Kolis; Scott C. Dover, Business Mgr.
Res.: 411 Springfield Pk., Wyoming, 45215. Tel: 513-948-1218; Fax: 513-948-1225. Email: sdover@stjamesotv.org. Web: www.stjamesotv.com.
School—(Grades K-8) Tel: 513-821-9054; Fax: 513-821-9556. Email: mrosemond@stjamesvalley.org. Web: www.stjamesvalley.org. Miss Marianne Rosemond, Prin.; Mrs. Rosie Eiser, Librarian. Lay Teachers 14; Students 184.

Catechesis/Religious Program—Mrs. Angela Glassmeyer, D.R.E. Students 170.

37—ST. JAMES THE GREATER (White Oak) (1843) [CEM] Revs. Thomas C. Nolker; Martin E. Bachman, Parochial Vicar; Deacons Tim A. Crooker; Paul Kluener.
Res.: 3565 Hubble Rd., 45247. Tel: 513-741-5300; Fax: 513-741-5302. Email: info@stjameswhiteoak.com. Web: www.stjameswhiteoak.com.
School—(Grades K-8), 6111 Cheviot Rd., 45247. Tel: 513-741-5333; Fax: 513-741-5312. Web: www-.stjameswo.org. Donna Beebe, Prin. Sisters 1; Lay Teachers 39; Students 801.
Catechesis/Religious Program—Tel: 513-741-5335; Fax: 513-741-5302. Students 58.

38—ST. JEROME (1863) Rev. Carl J. Wollering.
Church: 131 Rohde St., 45230-7115.
Res.: 5858 Kellogg Ave., 45230-7115. Tel: 513-231-7042; Fax: 513-231-7042 (Call First). Web: www.st-jerome-cinci.org.
Catechesis/Religious Program—Guardian Angels, 6531 Beechmont Ave., 45230. Tel: 513-624-3146; Fax: 513-624-3145. Students 11.

39—ST. JOHN FISHER (Newtown) (1947) Rev. Steven P. Walter; Aimee Baer, Pastoral Assoc.
Office: 3227 Church St., 45244. Tel: 513-561-9431; Fax: 513-561-7513. Email: stjohnfisher@juno.com. Web: www.sjfchurch.org.
Catechesis/Religious Program—Students 183.

40—ST. JOHN NEUMANN (Springfield Township) (1978) Rev. Steven J. Kolde; Deacons John R. Gobbi, Pastoral Assoc.; Patrick A. Palumbo, Pastoral Assoc.; Ronald H. Risch, Pastoral Assoc.
Res.: 12191 Mill Rd., 45240. Tel: 513-742-0953; Fax: 513-742-5875.
See St. John the Baptist Catholic School, Cincinnati under Consolidated Elementary Schools located in the Institution section.
Catechesis/Religious Program—Tel: 513-742-0953; Fax: 513-742-5875. Students 135.

41—ST. JOHN THE BAPTIST (Dry Ridge) (1860) [CEM] Rev. Timothy S. Kallaher.
Res.: 5361 Dry Ridge Rd., 45252. Tel: 513-385-8010; Fax: 513-385-8080. Email: pastor@stjohns-dr.org. Web: www.stjohns-dr.org.
See St. John the Baptist Catholic School, Cincinnati under Consolidated Schools in the Institution section.
Catechesis/Religious Program—Students 90.

42—ST. JOHN THE BAPTIST (Harrison) (1851) [CEM] Revs. Jeffrey M. Kemper; Edward J. Shine (Retired); William J. Dorrmann (Retired); Deacon Donald J. Meyer Jr.
Res.: 110 N. Hill St., Harrison, 45030. Tel: 513-367-9086; Fax: 513-367-6864. Email: parishoffice@sjbharrisonparish.org. Web: www.sjbharrisonparish.org.
School—(Grades K-8) Tel: 513-367-6826; Fax: 513-367-6864. Web: sjbharrison.org. Carey Owens, Prin.; Julia Koors, Librarian. Lay Teachers 21; Students 308.
Catechesis/Religious Program—Tel: 513-367-9878. Students 265.

43—ST. JOHN THE EVANGELIST (1891) Revs. Thomas Espelage; Dale C. Peterka.
Res.: 7121 Plainfield Rd., 45236. Tel: 513-791-3238; Fax: 513-686-2720. Web: www.stjohndp.org.
See St. Nicholas Academy, Cincinnati under Consolidated Schools in the Institution section.
Catechesis/Religious Program—Laura E. Davis, Pastoral Min. Students 68.

44—ST. JOSEPH (1846), (African American), Rev. Reynaldo S. Taylor; Deacon Raphael Simmons; Wylie G. Howell, Pastoral Assoc.; William Jefferson, Business Mgr.
Res.: 224 E. 8th St., Ste. 307, 45202. Tel: 513-284-4201.
Church & Mailing Address: 745 Ezzard Charles Dr., 45203. Tel: 513-381-4526; Fax: 513-381-5244. Email: stjosephchurch@fuse.net. Web: www.stjoseph-catholicchurch.org.
School—(Grades K-8) Tel: 513-381-2126; Fax: 513-381-6513. Dionne Thompson, Prin.; Maureen Lechleiter, Librarian. Lay Teachers 13; Students 170.
Catechesis/Religious Program—Tel: 513-381-4526, Ext. 16. Sr. Rachel Richards, S.F.C.C., D.R.E. Students 35.

45—ST. JUDE THE APOSTLE (1956) Rev. Eric A. Bowman; Deacon James Sunderman, Pastoral Assoc.
Res.: 5924 Bridgetown Rd., 45248. Tel: 513-574-1230; Fax: 513-598-2109. Email: stjude@fuse.net. Web: www.stjudebridgetown.org.
School—5940 Bridgetown Rd., 45248. Tel: 513-598-2100; Fax: 513-598-2118. Robert Huber, Prin. Lay Teachers 32; Students 499.
Catechesis/Religious Program—Tel: 513-598-2100, Ext. 30; Fax: 513-598-2109. Students 106.

46—ST. LAWRENCE (Price Hill) (1868) Rev. Mark T. Watkins; Sr. Helen Julia Hahn, S.C., Pastoral Assoc.
Res.: 3680 Warsaw Ave., 45205. Tel: 513-921-0328; Fax: 513-921-5108. Web: www.stlawrenceparish.org.
School—(Grades PreSchool-8), 1020 Carson Ave., 45205. Tel: 513-921-4996. Mrs. Alma Lee Joesting, Prin. Lay Teachers 25; Students 267.
Catechesis/Religious Program—Students 288.

47—ST. LEO THE GREAT (1886) Rev. James R. Schutte.
Mailing Address: 2573 St. Leo Pl., 45225-1960. Tel: 513-921-1044; Fax: 513-921-8048.
See St. Boniface School, Cincinnati under Consolidated Elementary Schools located in the Institution section.
Catechesis/Religious Program—Students 50.
Chapel—San Antonio di Padova 1950 Queen City Ave., 45214.

48—ST. LOUIS (1870), (German), Rev. Joseph R. Binzer.
Res.: 29 E. Eighth St., 45202-2086. Tel: 513-263-6621; Fax: 513-263-6624. Web: stlouischurchcincinnati.org.

49—ST. MARGARET - ST. JOHN PARISH (2008) Rev. David Lemkuhl; Mark Friedman, Pastoral Assoc.
Mailing Address: 4100 Watterson St., 45227. Tel: 513-271-0856; Fax: 513-271-1513. Email: smcoffice@fuse.net; sjvoffice@fuse.net. In Res., Rev. William H. Cross.
Res. & Church: 4448 Berwick St., 45227. Tel: 513-271-1968.
Worship Sites:—
St. Margaret of Cortona Church—Church: 6000 Murray Rd., 45227.
St. John Vianney Church—Church: 4448 Berwick St., 45227.
School—Prince of Peace, (Grades K-8), 6000 Murray Rd., 45227. Tel: 513-271-8288; Fax: 513-272-1740. Web: www.princeofpeacecincinnati.org. Mr. Frank Barlag, Prin. Lay Teachers 14; Students 143.
Catechesis/Religious Program—Students 48.

50—ST. MARGARET MARY (North College Hill) (1920) Rev. Jerome J. Gardner; Deacon Raymond S. Burger.
Res.: 1830 W. Galbraith Rd., 45239. Tel: 513-521-7387; Fax: 513-521-7388. Email: mmason@zoomtown.com. Web: www.stmargaret-maryparish.org.
See Our Lady of Grace, Cincinnati under Consolidated Elementary Schools located in the Institution section.
Catechesis/Religious Program—Tel: 513-729-0222. Mrs. Wilma McGlasson, D.R.E. Students 72.

51—ST. MARK THE EVANGELIST (1905) Rev. Jerry Steinbrunner, C.PP.S.; Bro. Hugh Henderson, C.PP.S., Pastoral Assoc.
Res.: 3500 Montgomery Rd., 45207. Tel: 513-961-0472; Fax: 513-961-0492. Email: st.mark@fuse.net. Web: www.stmarkcatholic.com.
Catechesis/Religious Program—Nancy Ertel, D.R.E. Students 15.

52—ST. MARTIN DE PORRES (Lincoln Heights) (1935), (African American), Rev. Thomas P. DiFolco.
Res.: 9927 Wayne Ave., 45215. Tel: 513-554-4010; Fax: 513-554-4191.
See St. Gabriel Consolidated School, Cincinnati under Consolidated Elementary Schools located in the Institution section.
Catechesis/Religious Program—Mary E. Lear, D.R.E. Students 8.

53—ST. MARTIN OF TOURS (Cheviot) (1911) Rev. Terence J. Hamilton.
Res.: 3720 St. Martin Pl., 45211. Tel: 513-661-2000; Fax: 513-661-1432.
School—(Grades K-8), 3729 Harding Ave., 45211. Tel: 513-661-7609; Fax: 513-661-8102. Mrs. Patricia Dieckman, Prin. Lay Teachers 14; Students 223.
Catechesis/Religious Program—Students 35.

54—ST. MARY (Hyde Park) (1898) Rev. Kenneth E. Schartz; Deacon John D. Thamann; Ms. Mary Anne Bressler, Pastoral Assoc.; Mrs. Emily Besl Henry, Pastoral Assoc.; Mr. Keith Pfaller, Pastoral Assoc.; Ms. Margaret Shank, Pastoral Assoc.; Mrs. Maggi Hunt, Pastoral Assoc.
Res.: 2853 Erie Ave., 45208. Tel: 513-321-1207; Fax: 513-533-5518. Email: parish@saintmaryhydepark.org. Web: www.saintmaryhydepark.org.
School—(Grades K-8), 2845 Erie Ave., 45208. Tel: 513-321-0703; Fax: 513-533-5517. Web: www.smshp.com. Mrs. Suzanne McBrayer, Prin. Lay Teachers 24; Students 528.
Catechesis/Religious Program—Tel: 513-321-0703; Fax: 513-533-5518. Students 325.

55—ST. MATTHIAS (Forest Park) (1967) Revs. David E. Fay; Paul A. Bader (Retired); Deacon Raymond George.
Res.: 1050 W. Kemper Rd., 45240. Tel: 513-851-1930; Fax: 513-589-3850.
Catechesis/Religious Program—Tel: 513-851-1930, Ext. 14; Fax: 513-589-3850. Students 14.

56—ST. MICHAEL (1919) Rev. John P. Fischer; Deacon Kenneth J. Dehanes Sr., Pastoral Assoc.; Brian Bisig, Dir. Music; Scott Hungler, Business Mgr.
Res.: 11144 Spinner Ave., 45241. Tel: 513-563-6377; Fax: 513-554-3543. Web: www.saintmichaelchurch.net.
School—(Grades K-8), 11136 Oak St., 45241. Tel: 513-554-3555; Fax: 513-554-3551. Jody Farrell, Prin. Lay Teachers 22; Students 413.
Catechesis/Religious Program—Tel: 513-563-6377, Ext. 303. Lori Anne Fothergill, Dir. Faith Formation (Youth). Students 136.

57—ST. MONICA-ST. GEORGE PARISH NEWMAN CENTER (1993) Revs. Alan Hirt, O.F.M.; Thomas Speier, O.F.M.
328 W. McMillan St., 45219.
Res.: 533 Howell Ave., 45220. Tel: 513-381-6400; Fax: 513-381-2540. Email: st.monica-st.george@fuse.net. Web: home.fuse.net/stmonica-stgeorge.
Church: Tel: 513-381-6400.
Catechesis/Religious Program—Students 75.

58—MOTHER OF CHRIST (1946), (African American), Rev. James Shappelle; Jodie A. Bender, Pastoral Admin.
Church: 5301 Winneste Ave., 45232. Tel: 513-242-0164 (Church); 513-541-3732 (Res); Fax: 513-242-0164 (Church); 513-541-0362 (Res). Email: mocaoc@aol.com. Web: www.motherofchrist.homestead.com.
Catechesis/Religious Program—Students 32.

59—NATIVITY OF OUR LORD (Pleasant Ridge) (1917) Rev. Paul F. DeLuca.
Res.: 5935 Pandora Ave., 45213-2017. Tel: 513-531-3164; Fax: 513-458-6761. Web: www.nativity-cincinnati.org.
School—(Grades K-8), 5936 Ridge Ave., 45213-1699. Tel: 513-458-6767; Fax: 513-458-6769. Robert C. Herring, Prin. Lay Teachers 20; Students 408.
Catechesis/Religious Program—Students 27.

60—OLD ST. MARY (1842) Revs. Martin O. Moran III; Lawrence Juarez.
Res.: 123 E. 13th St., 45202. Tel: 513-721-2988; Fax: 513-721-0436. Web: www.oldstmarys.org.
Catechesis/Religious Program—Students 0.

61—OUR LADY OF LOURDES (Westwood) (1927) Rev. David A. Sunberg; Deacon Thomas E. Westerfield; Sr. Carla Murar, O.S.U., Pastoral Assoc.; James G. Frede, Parish Admin. In Res., Rev. Kyle E. Schnippel.
Res.: 2832 Rosebud Dr., 45238. Tel: 513-922-0715; 513-347-2641 (Res.); Fax: 513-347-2644. Email: parish@lourdes.org. Web: www.lourdes.org.
School—(Grades K-8), 5835 Glenway Ave., 45238. Tel: 513-347-2660; Fax: 513-347-2663. Ms. Aimee Ellmaker, Prin. Lay Teachers 20; Students 383.
Catechesis/Religious Program—Tel: 513-347-2646. Carol Greulich, D.R.E. Students 89.

62—OUR LADY OF THE ROSARY (Greenhills) (1938) Rev. Peter Helmlinger; Deacon Walter A. Hucke Jr.; Katherine A. Klich, Pastoral Assoc.
Res.: 17 Farragut Rd., 45218. Tel: 513-825-8626; Fax: 513-825-2783. Email: bcrowley@olr.net. Web: www.olr.net.
See John Paul II Catholic, Cincinnati under Consolidated Elementary Schools located in the Institution section.
Catechesis/Religious Program—Tel: 513-825-8626, Ext. 321. Mr. David Nissen, D.R.E. Students 150.

63—OUR LADY OF THE SACRED HEART (Reading) (1874) Rev. Ronald Williams; Quint Robinson, Business Mgr.
Res.: 177 Siebenthaler Ave., 45215. Tel: 513-733-4950; Fax: 513-733-0973. Email: olsh@fuse.net.
School—(Grades K-8), 170 Siebenthaler Ave., 45215. Tel: 513-733-5225; Fax: 513-733-0186. Web: olshschool.net. JoAnne Fischesser, Prin. Lay Teachers 12; Students 168.
Catechesis/Religious Program—Students 95.

64—OUR LADY OF THE VISITATION (Mack) (1947) Rev. William J. Kramer; Sr. Marla Gipson, C.PP.S., Pastoral Assoc.; Bill Tonnis, Youth & Pastoral Min.; Carolyn Witterstaetter, Music Min.; Diane Williams, Business Mgr.
Res.: 3172 South Rd., 45248. Tel: 513-922-2056; Fax: 513-347-2238. Email: olvisititation@olvisitation.net. Web: www.olvisitation.org.
School—3180 South Rd., 45248. Tel: 513-347-2222; Fax: 513-347-2225. Mr. Terry P. Chapman, Prin. Sisters 1; Lay Teachers 40; Students 858.
Catechesis/Religious Program—Tel: 513-347-2228; Fax: 513-347-2225. Sr. Mary Tewes, O.S.B., D.R.E. Students 125.

65—OUR LADY OF VICTORY (Delhi Hills) (1842) [CEM] Revs. James G. Reutter; George R. Schmitz; Deacon Charles Jenkins.
Res.: 810 Neeb Rd., 45233. Tel: 513-922-4460; Fax: 513-922-5476. Web: www.olv.org.
School—(Grades K-8), 808 Neeb Rd., 45233. Tel: 513-347-2072; Fax: 513-922-5476. Ms. Kathy Kane, Prin.; Mrs. Mary Brigham, Librarian. Lay Teachers 35; Students 583.
Catechesis/Religious Program—Tel: 513-347-2071;

Fax: 513-922-5476. Mrs. Doris Steidle, D.R.E. Students 82.

66—OUR LORD, CHRIST THE KING (Mt. Lookout) (1926) Revs. Robert A. Obermeyer; Godfred Boachie-Yiadom; Deacon Donald Gloeckler.
Res.: 3223 Linwood Ave., 45226. Tel: 513-321-4121; Fax: 513-871-3978. Email: parish@ourlordchristtheking.org. Web: www.ourlordchristtheking.org.
School—Cardinal Pacelli, (Grades PreK-8), 927 Ellison, 45226. Tel: 513-321-1048; Fax: 513-533-6118. Web: ww.carinalpacelli.org. Kim Roy, Prin. Lay Teachers 25; Students 393.
Catechesis/Religious Program—Students 60.

67—OUR MOTHER OF SORROWS (Roselawn) (1941) Closed. For inquiries for parish records, contact Nativity of Our Lord, Cincinnati.

68—STS. PETER AND PAUL (Reading) (1850) [CEM] Rev. David G. Howard; Deacon Tom Lynd; Mrs. Beth Pettigrew, Pastoral Assoc.
330 W. Vine St., Reading, 45215. Tel: 513-554-1010; Fax: 513-554-0190. In Res., Rev. John P. Heim, S.J.
Catechesis/Religious Program—Email: ppanzecal@fuse.net. Web: saintspeterandpaulreading.com. Students 73.

69—RESURRECTION OF OUR LORD (1919) Rev. Robert L. Keller.
Res.: 1744 Iliff Ave., 45205-1018. Tel: 513-471-2700; Fax: 513-471-2703.
School—(Grades K-8), 1740 Iliff Ave., 45205-1018. Tel: 513-471-6600; 513-471-6620; Fax: 513-471-2610. Kathleen Sparks, Prin. Sisters 2; Lay Teachers 11; Students 175.
Catechesis/Religious Program—

70—ST. ROBERT BELLARMINE (1927) Revs. Richard W. Bollman, S.J.; Kent A. Beausoleil, S.J.; Jeff Campbell, Dir. Social Mission. Tel: 513-745-1908; Scott Buzza, Dir. Music Min. Tel: 513-745-3270; Sue Antoinette, Dir. Youth Min. Tel: 513-745-4224; Karen Brandstetter, Pastoral Assoc. Tel: 513-745-3349.
Xavier University: 3800 Victory Pkwy., 45207-2211. Tel: 513-745-3398; Fax: 513-745-2031. Web: www.bellarminechapel.org.
Catechesis/Religious Program—Tel: 513-745-3317. James Crosby, D.R.E. Students 105.

71—ST. ROSE OF LIMA (1867) Rev. Barry M. Windholtz.
Res.: 2501 Riverside Dr., 45202. Tel: 513-871-1162; Fax: 513-871-2851.

72—SACRED HEART (1870), (Italian), Revs. Mario Rauzi, C.S.; Vincent Cutrara, C.S.
Res.: 2733 Massachusetts Ave., 45225. Tel: 513-541-4654; Fax: 513-541-4662. Email: sacredheartcamp@yahoo.com.
See Corryville Catholic Elementary School, Cincinnati under Consolidated Elementary Schools located in the Institution section.

73—ST. SAVIOUR (Blue Ash) (1947) Rev. Patrick H. Crone; Deacon Jerome Cain.
Res.: 4136 Myrtle Ave., 45236. Tel: 513-791-9004; Fax: 513-791-6530.
Catechesis/Religious Program—Tel: 513-791-0119. Students 73.

74—ST. SIMON THE APOSTLE (1966) Rev. Michael D. Beatty.
Res.: 825 Pontius Rd., 45233. Tel: 513-941-3656; Fax: 513-941-1562. Email: stsimon@isoc.net. Web: www.stsimonparish.org.
Catechesis/Religious Program—Beth Schumacher, D.R.E. Students 190.

75—ST. STEPHEN (1867) Revs. Robert A. Obermeyer, Canonical Pastor; Stanley H. Neiheisel (Retired); Beth Worland, Pastoral Admin.
Res.: 320 Donham Ave., 45226. Tel: 513-871-3373. Email: bethststephen@fuse.net.

76—ST. TERESA OF AVILA (1916) Rev. Thomas L. Bolte; Deacons Michael Davenport; Gregg Rose. In Res., Rev. George R. Schmitz.
Res.: 1175 Overlook Ave., 45238. Tel: 513-921-9200; Fax: 513-921-0307. Email: stteresa@fuse.net. Web: www.stteresa-avila.org.
School—(Grades K-8), 1194 Rulison Ave., 45238. Tel: 513-471-4530; Fax: 513-471-1254. Email: vogt_s@stteresa.net. Web: www.stteresa.net. Mrs. Sharon Willmes, Prin.; Mrs. Judy Honkomp, Librarian; Mrs. Chris Artmayer, Librarian. Lay Teachers 23; Students 304.
Catechesis/Religious Program—Tel: 513-921-9200, Ext. 117. Web: www.stteresa-avila.org. Michelle Thoman, C.R.E. Students 80.

77—ST. THERESE, THE LITTLE FLOWER (Mt. Airy) (1926) Revs. Robert W. Goebel; Robert A. Stricker (Retired).
Res.: 5560 Kirby Ave., 45239. Tel: 513-541-5560; Fax: 513-681-2631. Email: janlf@zoomtown.com. Web: www.littleflower-church.org.
See Our Lady of Grace, Cincinnati under Consolidated Elementary Schools located in the Institution section.
Catechesis/Religious Program—Tel: 513-541-5560. Sr. Francis Margaret Maag, C.D.P., D.R.E. Students 16.

78—ST. VINCENT DE PAUL (1861) Rev. Donald R. Rettig.
Res.: 4026 River Rd., 45204. Tel: 513-451-5714; Fax: 513-451-3830. Email: svdpcin@hotmail.com.

79—ST. VINCENT FERRER (Kenwood) (1946) Rev. George C. Kunkel.
Res.: 7754 Montgomery Rd., 45236. Tel: 513-791-9030; Fax: 513-791-7405. Web: www.svfchurch.org.
School—(Grades K-8) Tel: 513-791-6320; Fax: 513-791-3332. Email: doug.alpiger@svf-school.org. Douglas Alpiger, Prin. Lay Teachers 17; Students 195.
Catechesis/Religious Program—Tel: 513-791-6321; Fax: 513-791-7405. Karen McMichael, Dir. Faith Formation. Students 100.

80—ST. VIVIAN (1943) Rev. Paul L. Gebhardt; Kathleen Rothschild, Business Mgr.; Lynne Morris, Dir. Devel.; Deacon Larry Maag; Tim McManus, Dir. Liturgy & Music; Jeanne Schaefer, Dir. Youth Ministry & Lay Pastoral Min.
Res.: 7600 Winton Rd., 45224. Tel: 513-728-4331; Fax: 513-728-4335. Email: rectory@stvivian.org. Web: www.stvivian.org.
School—(Grades PreSchool-8), 885 Denier Pl., 45224. Tel: 513-522-6858; Fax: 513-728-4336. Email: steve.zinser@stvivianschool.org. Web: www.stvivianschool.org. Steve Zinser, Prin.; Mary Hanson, Librarian. Lay Teachers 27; Students 384.
Catechesis/Religious Program—Tel: 513-728-4339; Fax: 513-728-4335. Jodie A. Bender, D.R.E. Students 35.

81—ST. WILLIAM (1909) Rev. Andrew J. Umberg; Deacons George Bruce; Thomas Faeth. In Res., Rev. Paul L. Rehling (Retired).
Res.: 4108 W. Eighth St., 45205. Tel: 513-921-0247; Fax: 513-921-2810. Email: info@saintwilliam.com. Web: www.saintwilliam.com.
School—(Grades K-8), 4125 St. William Ave., 45205. Tel: 513-471-2989; Fax: 513-471-8226. Ms. Catie Blum, Prin. Sisters 1; Lay Teachers 23; Students 274.

OUTSIDE THE CITY OF CINCINNATI

AMELIA, CLERMONT CO., ST. BERNADETTE'S (1944) Rev. William R. Stockelman.
Res.: 1479 Locust Lake Rd., 45102-1798. Tel: 513-753-5566; Fax: 513-753-7664. Email: stbernadetteamelia@fuse.net. Web: www.stbernadetteamelia.org.
School—(Grades K-8), 1453 Locust Lake Rd., 45102-1703. Tel: 513-753-4744; Fax: 513-753-9018. Mr. Thomas Salerno, Prin. Lay Teachers 13; Students 145.
Catechesis/Religious Program—Tel: 513-753-4243. Elizabeth Himes, D.R.E. Students 65.

ARNHEIM, BROWN CO., ST. MARY (1837) [CEM] Rev. Dohrman W. Byers; Marilyn Fryer, Pastoral Assoc.
Res.: 6647 Van Buren St., Georgetown, 45121. Tel: 937-446-2555; Fax: 937-446-2555. Email: stmaryarnheim@hughes.net.
Catechesis/Religious Program—Tel: 937-446-1854. Linda Mulaney, D.R.E. Combined with St. Elizabeth, Sardinia, OH Students 65.

BATAVIA, CLERMONT CO., HOLY TRINITY (1906) Rev. Bryan T. Reif; Deacon James Hennessey.
Res.: 140 N. 6th St., 45103. Tel: 513-732-2024; Fax: 513-732-0049. Email: alleluia@fuse.net.
Catechesis/Religious Program—Tel: 513-732-2024, Ext. 13. Students 49.

BEAVERCREEK, GREENE CO., ST. LUKE (1955) Rev. Terrance L. Schneider; Deacon Gerry Dupree.
Res.: 1440 N. Fairfield Rd., 45432. Tel: 937-426-1733; Fax: 937-426-3965. Email: stluke@saintlukeparish.org. Web: www.saintlukeparish.org.
School—(Grades K-8), 1442 N. Fairfield Rd., 45432. Tel: 937-426-1733; Fax: 937-426-6435. Email: suttond@stluke.cnd.pvt.k12.oh.us. Web: www.stluke.cnd.pvt.k12.oh.us. Mrs. Leslie Vondrell, Prin. Lay Teachers 22; Students 444.
Catechesis/Religious Program—1444 N. Fairfield Rd., 45432. Fax: 937-426-4385. Students 264.

BELLEFONTAINE, LOGAN CO., ST. PATRICK (1852) [CEM] Rev. Patrick L. Sheridan; Deacons Harold Dipple; Robert A. Crook.
Res.: 328 E. Patterson Ave., 43311. Tel: 937-592-1656; Fax: 937-592-0971. Web: www.catholicbellefontaine.org.
Catechesis/Religious Program—316 E. Patterson Rd., 43311. Students 208.

BETHEL, CLERMONT CO., ST. MARY (1941) Rev. Michael F. Leshney; Deacon Jerry Etienne.
Res. & Mailing Address: 1192 Bethel-New Richmond Rd., New Richmond, 45157.
Church: 3398 S.R. 125, 45106. Tel: 513-734-4041; Fax: 513-734-3588. Email: michaelleshney@fuse.net. Web: www.stmary-bethel.org.
Catechesis/Religious Program—Tel: 513-734-3676; Fax: 513-734-3588. Students 156.

BOTKINS, SHELBY CO., IMMACULATE CONCEPTION (1865), (German), [CEM] Revs. Patrick L. Sloneker; Matthew K. Lee, Parochial Vicar.
Res.: 116 N. Mill St., P.O. Box 519, 45306. Tel: 937-693-2561; Fax: 937-693-2561.
Church: N. Main & Walnut Sts., 45306.
Catechesis/Religious Program—Students 267.

BRADFORD, MIAMI CO., IMMACULATE CONCEPTION (1875) [JC] Rev. James L. Simons.
Res.: 6925 W. U.S. Rte. 36, Covington, 45318. Tel: 937-473-2970. Email: icinbraford@woh.rr.com.
Church: 5874 N. Buckneck Rd., R.R. 2, 45308. Tel: 937-448-6220; Fax: 937-473-2476.
Catechesis/Religious Program—Tel: 937-448-6220. Students 42.

BURKETTSVILLE, MERCER CO., ST. BERNARD (1874), (St. Henry Cluster) Revs. Thomas Hemm, C.PP.S.; Benedict Magabe, C.PP.S.
Mailing Address: 272 E. Main St., Box 350, Saint Henry, 45883. Web: www.sthenrycluster.com.
Church: 71 W. Main St., 45310. Tel: 419-678-4118; Fax: 419-678-8285.
St. Henry Catechetical Center—Tel: 419-678-3811. See St. Henry, St. Henry for details.
Catechesis/Religious Program—Students 127.

CAMDEN, PREBLE CO., ST. MARY (1942) Revs. Francis Tandoh, C.S.Sp., Admin.; Joshua Elvis Otusafo, C.S.Sp.
Res.: 130 Gramont Ave., P.O. Box 17219, Dayton, 45417. Tel: 937-268-2747.
Church: 7721 N. Main St., P.O. Box 28, 45311. Tel: 937-452-3352.
Catechesis/Religious Program—Students 35.

CARTHAGENA, MERCER CO., ST. ALOYSIUS (1865), (German), [CEM], (St. Henry Cluster) Revs. Thomas Hemm, C.PP.S.; Benedict Magabe, C.PP.S.
Mailing Address: P.O. Box 350, St. Henry, 45883. Tel: 419-678-4118. Web: www.sthenrycluster.com.
Res.: 1509 Cranberry Rd., St. Henry, 45883. Tel: 419-925-4776; Fax: 419-678-8285. Email: tomhemm@hotmail.com.
Church: 6036 State Rte. 274, 45822.
St. Henry Catechetical Center— For details call Tel: 419-678-3811.
Catechesis/Religious Program—Catherine Wenning, D.R.E. Students 35.

CASSELLA, MERCER CO., NATIVITY OF THE BLESSED VIRGIN MARY (1847) [CEM], (Marion Cluster) Rev. Eugene H. Schnipke, C.PP.S.
7428 State Rte. 119, Maria Stein, 45860. Tel: 419-925-4775; Fax: 419-925-1745. Email: marioncathcom@gmail.com. Web: www.marioncatholiccommunity.org.
Catechesis/Religious Program—Tel: 419-925-4017. Katie Dippold, C.R.E. Students 83.

CELINA, MERCER CO., IMMACULATE CONCEPTION OF THE BLESSED VIRGIN MARY (1864), (German), [CEM] Revs. Thomas Brenberger, C.PP.S.; Richard R. Riedel, C.PP.S.
Res.: 229 W. Anthony St., 45822. Tel: 419-586-6648; Fax: 419-586-6649.
School—(Grades PreK-6), 200 W. Wayne St., 45822-1469. Tel: 419-586-2379; Fax: 419-586-6649. Ms. Kathryn Mescher, Prin. Sisters of the Precious Blood 1; Lay Teachers 14; Students 126.
Catechesis/Religious Program—Wayne & Walnut Sts., 45822. Tel: 419-586-2370; Fax: 419-586-6649. Students 340.

CENTERVILLE, MONTGOMERY CO.

1—ST. FRANCIS OF ASSISI (1969) Rev. Thomas W. Schmidt; Deacons Mark Stasiak, Business Mgr.; Jack Pitts; Joyce Connell, Parish Sec.; Frances Obringer, Sec.
Res.: 6245 Wilmington Pike, 45459. Tel: 937-433-1013; Fax: 937-433-1699. Web: www.sfacc.org.
Catechesis/Religious Program—Tel: 937-433-0128; Fax: 937-433-1699. Mary Ellen Singer, D.R.E. Students 418.

2—INCARNATION (1945) Revs. Lawrence E. Mierenfeld; Ryan Thomas Ruiz, Parochial Vicar; Deacons Robert Zinck; Roger E. Duffy; Tim Niesel, Pastoral Assoc.; Marilyn Porcino, Pastoral Assoc.
Res.: 55 Williamsburg Ln., 45459. Tel: 937-433-1188; Fax: 937-433-3263. Web: www.incarnation-parish.com.
School—45 Williamsburg Ln., 45459. Tel: 937-433-1051; Fax: 937-433-9796. Web: www.incarnation-school.com. Cheryl Reichel, Prin. Lay Teachers 48; Students 853.
Catechesis/Religious Program—Tel: 937-433-3377; Fax: 937-433-3263. Paula Weckesser, C.R.E.; Daniel Dunn, Youth & Young Adult Ministry. Students 767.

COLDWATER, MERCER CO., HOLY TRINITY (1867) [CEM], (Coldwater Cluster) Revs. Richard W. Walling; Barry J. Stechschulte, Parochial Vicar; Deacons Virgil Lochtefeld; Thomas Huff.
Mailing Address: P.O. Box 107, 45828. Email: cwcluster@coldwatercluster.org. Web: www.coldwatercluster.org.
Res.: 116 E. Main St., P.O. Box 107, 45828. Tel: 419-678-4802; Fax: 419-678-4803.
Catechesis/Religious Program—110 N. Second St.,

45828. Tel: 419-678-3328. Charmaine Bettinger, D.R.E. Students 1,059.

COVINGTON, MIAMI CO., ST. TERESA OF THE INFANT JESUS (1950), (German—French), [JC] Rev. James L. Simons.
Res.: 6925 W. U.S. 36, 45318. Tel: 937-473-2970; Fax: 937-473-2476. Email: stteresaij@woh.rr.com.
Catechesis/Religious Program—Tel: 937-473-2970; Fax: 937-473-2476. Mrs. Elaine Christian, D.R.E. Students 70.

CRANBERRY PRAIRIE, MERCER CO., ST. FRANCIS (1858), (German), [CEM], (St. Henry Cluster) Revs. Thomas Hemm, C.PP.S.; Benedict Magabe, C.PP.S.
Mailing Address: P.O. Box 350, St. Henry, 45883. Web: www.sthenrycluster.com.
Church & Res.: 1509 Cranberry Rd., St. Henry, 45883. Tel: 419-678-4118 (Church); 419-925-4776; Fax: 419-678-8285. Email: tomhemm@hotmail.com.
St. Henry Catechetical Center—Catherine Wenning, D.R.E. See St. Henry, St. Henry for details. Tel: 419-678-3811. E-mail: sthenryccd@bright.net Students 28.

DAYTON, GREENE CO., QUEEN OF APOSTLES (1973) Rev. Thomas A. Schroer, S.M., Priest Coord.; Deacon Greg Cecere, Pastoral Assoc.
Church: 4400 Shakertown Rd., 45430-1057. Tel: 937-429-0510; Fax: 937-429-0510. Email: qacohio@sbcglobal.net. Web: www.qac-ohio.org.
Catechesis/Religious Program— Maggie Atkinson, D.R.E. Students 69.

DAYTON, MONTGOMERY CO.

1—ST. ADALBERT (1903), (Polish), Rev. Michael J. Holloran; Anne Rusen, Pastoral Min.
Office: 22 Notre Dame Ave., 45404. Tel: 937-228-8802.
Catechesis/Religious Program— Joint program with Holy Cross, Our Lady of the Rosary, and St. Stephen.

2—ST. ALBERT THE GREAT (1939) Rev. Thomas E. Meyer; Deacon Jeffrey Hall Sr. In Res., Rev. David J. Endres, Faculty, Fenwick High School.
Res.: 3033 Far Hills Ave., 45429. Tel: 937-293-1191; Fax: 937-293-1848. Email: parish@stalbertthegreat.net. Web: www.stalbertthegreat.net.
School—(Grades PreK-8) Tel: 937-293-9452; Fax: 937-293-1848. Email: npsamkirry@mdeca.org. Web: www.stalbertthegreat.net. Mr. Mike Kirry, Prin. Lay Teachers 31; Students 415.
Catechesis/Religious Program—104 Dorothy Ln., Kettering, 45429. Tel: 937-298-2402; Fax: 937-293-1848. Jean Carr, C.R.E. Students 330.

3—ST. ANTHONY OF PADUA (1913) Rev. Christopher C. Coleman; Janet Gaier, Pastoral Assoc.; Madelon Kinzig, Music Dir.; Sidney Gnann, Business Mgr.
Res.: 830 Bowen St., 45410. Tel: 937-253-9132; Fax: 937-253-6658. Email: stabmanager@bizwoh.rr.com.
School—(Grades K-8) Tel: 937-253-6251; Fax: 937-253-1541. David Bogle, Prin.; Sarah Jones, Librarian. Lay Teachers 10; Students 180.
Catechesis/Religious Program—

4—ASCENSION (1955) Rev. Christopher J. Worland; Sr. Agnes Kramer, C.D.P., Pastoral Assoc.; Deacon Victor B. Hildebrand, Pastoral Assoc.; Tom Platfoot, Business Mgr.
Res.: 2025 Woodman Dr., Kettering, 45420. Tel: 937-253-5171; Fax: 937-253-0886.
School—(Grades K-8), 2001 Woodman Dr., Kettering, 45420. Tel: 937-254-5411; Fax: 937-254-1150. Brent Devitt, Prin.; Sherry Smith, Librarian. Lay Teachers 23; Students 373.
Catechesis/Religious Program—Tel: 937-254-0622. Sue Graham, D.R.E. Students 335.

5—ST. BENEDICT THE MOOR (2005), (African American), Revs. Francis Tandoh, C.S.Sp.; Joshua Elvis Otusafo, C.S.Sp.; Deacon Jacob Jernigan.
Rectory—130 Gramont Ave., P.O. Box 17219, 45417. Tel: 937-268-2747.
Office: 519 Liscum Dr., P.O. Box 17219, 45417. Tel: 937-268-6697 Office; Fax: 937-268-6698 Office. Email: sajares@yahoo.com. Web: www.unitedinhope.com.
See Mary Queen of Peace, Dayton under Consolidated Elementary Schools located in the Institution section.
Catechesis/Religious Program—Students 15.

6—ST. CHARLES BORROMEO (Kettering) (1962) Revs. Gerald R. Haemmerle; Ronald C. Haft, Parochial Vicar; Deacons Leonard Baltes; Robert Collins; Brenda Tibbits, Pastoral Assoc.
Res.: 4440 Andrea, 45429.
Church: 4500 Ackerman Rd., 45429. Tel: 937-434-6081; Fax: 937-434-6251. Web: www.stcharles-kettering.org.
School—(Grades K-8), 4600 Ackerman Blvd., 45429. Tel: 937-434-4933; Fax: 937-434-6692. Mrs. Fran Moore, Prin. Lay Teachers 26; Students 427.
Catechesis/Religious Program—Tel: 937-434-9272. Tim Clarke, Dir. Faith Formation. Students 210.

7—CORPUS CHRISTI (1911) Rev. Del Staigers; Deacons Tom Platfoot; Skip Royer; Denny Bensman, Pastoral Admin. Business; Ritter Werner, Dir. Music; Jennifer Melke, Lay Ecclesial Min. Evangelization; Marie Brose, Outreach Min.; Cindy Rogerson, Dir. Food Pantry; Charlie Helldoerfer, Dir. Stewardship & Devel.; Jennie Freiberger, Communications Coord.; Mary Bartley, Bookkeeper; Bob Erli, Dir., Facilities; Wanda Hollinger, Office Mgr.
Res., Mailing Address & Parish Office: 220 W. Siebenthaler Ave., 45405. Tel: 937-274-2107. Email: info@corpusmercymartyrs.org. Web: www.corpusmercymartyrs.org.
Church: 527 Forest Ave., 45405.
See Mary Queen of Peace, Dayton under Consolidated Elementary Schools located in the Institution section.
Catechesis/Religious Program—Tel: 937-277-2092. Sr. Angela Jarboe, O.S.B., Lay Ecclesial Min. Faith Formation.

8—EMMANUEL (1837) Rev. Lee L. Sciarrotta, S.M.
Res.: 149 Franklin St., 45402. Tel: 937-228-2013; Fax: 937-228-5354. Email: parishoffice@emmanuelcatholic.com. Web: www.emmanuelcatholic.com.
Catechesis/Religious Program—Email: jpoppdre@gmail.com. Students 51.

9—ST. HELEN (1953) Revs. David E. Brinkmoeller; Satish Antony Joseph; Mary Heider, Pastoral Assoc. Liturgy & Stewardship; Deacons Susano Mascorro; Ralph O'Bleness.
Res.: 605 Granville Pl., 45431. Tel: 937-254-6233; Fax: 937-256-6117. Email: office@sthelenparish.org. Web: www.sthelenparish.org.
School—(Grades K-8) Tel: 937-256-1761; Fax: 937-254-4614. Ms. Barbara Markus, Prin.; Jackie Skiple, Librarian. Lay Teachers 22; Students 352.
Catechesis/Religious Program—Tel: 937-256-8815. Joan Torres, Dir. Faith Formation (Adult); Peggy Brun, Dir. Faith Formation (Youth). Students 152.

10—ST. HENRY (1960) Revs. Thomas M. Shearer; Ronald P. Combs; Deacon Michael Mahoney; Mary Ehret, Pastoral Assoc.
Mailing Address & Church: 6696 Springboro Rd., 45449. Tel: 937-434-9231; Fax: 937-434-6798. Email: sthenrysec@woh.rr.com. Web: www.sthenryparish.com.
Res.: 6340 Blossom Park Dr., West Carrollton, 45449-3021. Email: sthenrysec@woh.rr.com. Web: www.sthenryparish.com.
See Bishop Leibold School, Dayton under Consolidated Elementary Schools located in the Institution section.
Catechesis/Religious Program—Students 360.

11—HOLY ANGELS (1902) Rev. Daniel J. Meyer; Sr. Annette Grisley, O.S.F., Pastoral Assoc.
Parish Office—1322 Brown St., 45409. Tel: 937-229-5911; Fax: 937-229-5919. Email: dorankas@holyangels.cc. Web: www.holyangels.cc.
Church: Brown & L Sts., 45409.
School—(Grades PreK-8) Tel: 937-229-5959; Fax: 937-229-5960. Email: bauerbej@holyangels.cc. Rob Fortener, Prin. Lay Teachers 22; Students 340.
Catechesis/Religious Program—Tel: 937-229-5916. Jeanne Fairbanks, D.R.E. Students 211.

12—HOLY CROSS (1914), (Lithuanian), Rev. Michael J. Holloran.
22 Notre Dame Ave., 45404. Tel: 937-228-8902.
Catechesis/Religious Program—Tel: 937-228-8802; Fax: 937-443-0969. Students 3.

13—HOLY FAMILY (1905) Rev. Francis Tandoh, C.S.Sp.; Kathy Shirley, Pastoral Assoc.; Jim Buerschen, Business Mgr.
Mailing Address & Office: 310 Allen St., 45410. Tel: 937-256-5633; Fax: 937-256-7138. Email: hfsmchurches@sbcglobal.net. Web: www.hfandsmchurches.org.
Church: 140 S. Findlay St., 45403.
See Mary Queen of Peace, Dayton under Consolidated Elementary Schools located in the Institution section.
Catechesis/Religious Program— Please call office for information.

14—HOLY TRINITY (1860) [JC] Rev. Richard Friebel, C.PP.S.; Deacon George Zvonar; Mary C. Wlodarski, Pastoral Assoc.; Judith L. Trick, Business Mgr.
Parish Office: 272 Bainbridge St., 45402. Tel: 937-228-1223; Fax: 937-445-0232. Web: holytrinityofdayton.org.
Catechesis/Religious Program—Students 54.

15—ST. JOSEPH (1847) Rev. John Mencsik, C.PP.S.
Res.: 411 E. Second St., 45402. Tel: 937-228-9272; 937-228-9522; Fax: 937-228-6144. Email: stjosephday@sbcglobal.net.

16—ST. MARY'S (1859) Rev. Francis Tandoh, C.S.Sp.; Deacon William Saluke; Kathy Shirley, Pastoral Assoc.; Jim Buerschen, Business Mgr.
Rectory & Office: 310 Allen St., 45410. Tel: 937-256-5633; Fax: 937-256-7138. Email: hfsmchurches@sbcglobal.net. Web: www.hfandsmchurches.org.
See Mary Queen of Peace, Dayton under Consolidated Elementary Schools located in the Institution section.
Catechesis/Religious Program—Tel: 937-222-1600. Please contact parish office for more information.

17—OUR LADY OF MERCY (1928) Rev. Del Staigers; Deacons Tom Platfoot; Skip Royer; Denny Bensman, Pastoral Admin. Business; Ritter Werner, Dir. Music; Jennifer Melke, Lay Ecclesial Min. Evangelization; Marie Brose, Outreach Min.; Cindy Rogerson, Dir. Food Pantry; Charlie Helldoerfer, Dir. Stewardship & Devel.; Mary Bartley, Bookkeeper; Jennie Freiberger, Communications Coord.; Bob Erli, Dir. Facilities; Wanda Hollinger, Office Mgr.
Res.: 220 W. Siebenthaler Ave., 45405. Tel: 937-274-2107; Fax: 937-274-4363. Email: info@corpusmercymartyrs.org. Web: www.corpusmercymartyrs.org.
See Mary Queen of Peace Catholic School, Dayton under Consolidated Elementary Schools in the Institution section.
Catechesis/Religious Program—Sr. Angela Jarboe, O.S.B., Lay Ecclesial Min. Faith Formation.

18—OUR LADY OF THE IMMACULATE CONCEPTION (1938) Revs. David E. Brinkmoeller; Satish Antony Joseph.
Res.: 2300 S. Smithville Rd., 45420. Tel: 937-252-9919; Fax: 937-252-1992. Web: www.icparishdayton.org.
School—(Grades K-8), 2268 S. Smithville Rd., 45420. Tel: 937-253-8831; Fax: 937-252-8832. Mrs. Karyn J. Hecker, Prin. Lay Teachers 12; Students 216.
Catechesis/Religious Program—Students 42.

19—OUR LADY OF THE ROSARY (1887) Rev. Michael J. Holloran; Deacon Henry B. Beck.
Res.: 22 Notre Dame Ave., 45404. Tel: 937-228-8802; Fax: 937-443-0969. Email: olrdayton@aol.com. Web: www.olrdayton.com.
School—(Grades K-8), 40 Notre Dame Ave., 45404. Tel: 937-222-7231; Fax: 937-222-7393. Web: www.olr.com. Gregg Marino, Prin. Lay Teachers 11; Students 204.
Catechesis/Religious Program— Joint program with Holy Cross, Our Lady of the Rosary, and St. Stephen & St. Peter. Please see St. Peter, Huber Heights. Students 15.

20—ST. PETER (Huber Heights) (1959) Revs. Earl Francis Simone; Patrick M. McMullen, Parochial Vicar; Bro. Tim Cahill, C.PP.S.; Deacons Allen K. Miller; Norbert Nagy; John E. Gould; Timothy J. Harris; Russell O. Baldwin; Ms. Joy Blaul, Dir. School of Religion.
Res.: 6161 Chambersburg Rd., 45424. Tel: 937-233-1503; Fax: 937-237-3523. Email: bulletin@saintpeterparish.org. Web: www.saintpeterparish.org.
School—(Grades PreK-8) Tel: 937-233-8710; Fax: 937-237-3974. Email: npstpeter@mdeca.org. Feliza Poling, Prin. Lay Teachers 42; Students 834.
Catechesis/Religious Program—Tel: 937-237-3516; Fax: 937-233-5717. Ms. Joy Blaul, D.R.E. Students 250.

21—PRECIOUS BLOOD (1948) Revs. William O'Donnell, C.PP.S.; Edward Pratt; Deacon Richard Janowiecki; Joseph Hurr, Business Mgr.
Res.: 4961 Salem Ave., 45416. Tel: 937-276-5954; Fax: 937-276-5956. Email: parishoffice@preciousbloodchurch.org. Web: www.preciousbloodchurch.org.
School—(Grades K-8), 4870 Denlinger Rd., 45426. Tel: 937-277-2291; Fax: 937-277-2217. Web: www-.preciousbloodschool.org. Dan Mecoli, Prin.; Kay Feldmann, Librarian. Lay Teachers 20; Students 322.
Pre-School—1995 Shiloh Springs Rd., 45426. Tel: 937-854-7173; Fax: 937-854-8052.
Catechesis/Religious Program—Tel: 937-276-5954; Fax: 937-276-5955. Kristi Gaston, Coord. Children's Faith Formation; Benjamin Darnell, Youth Min. Students 140.

22—QUEEN OF MARTYRS (Northridge) (1948) Rev. Del Staigers; Deacons Tom Platfoot; Skip Royer; Denny Bensman, Pastoral Admin. Business; Ritter Werner, Dir. Music; Jennifer Melke, Lay Ecclesial Min. Evangelization; Marie Brose, Outreach Min.; Cindy Rogerson, Dir. Food Pantry; Charlie Helldoerfer, Dir. Stewardship & Devel.; Mary Bartley, Bookkeeper; Jennie Freiberger, Communications Coord.; Bob Erli, Dir. Facilities; Wanda Hollinger, Office Mgr.
Mailing Address, Res. & Church Office: 220 W. Siebenthaler Ave., 45405-2240. Tel: 937-274-2107; Fax: 937-274-4363.
Church: 4144 Cedar Ridge Rd., 45414.
See Mary Queen of Peace, Dayton under Consolidated Elementary Schools located in the Institution section.
Catechesis/Religious Program—Tel: 937-277-2092.

23—ST. RITA (1922) Revs. William O'Donnell, C.PP.S.; Edward Pratt, Parochial Vicar; Matt Ruttle, Pastoral Assoc.; Deacon James C. Olinger.
Res.: 5401 N. Main St., 45415. Tel: 937-278-5815;

Fax: 937-275-3302. Web: www.stritadayton.org.
School—(Grades K-8), 251 Erdiel Dr., 45415. Tel: 937-277-8978; Fax: 937-277-8979. Veronica Murphy, Prin. Lay Teachers 13; Students 195.
Catechesis/Religious Program—Deacon Charles O. Wright, D.R.E. Students 26.

24—ST. STEPHEN (North Dayton) (1906), (Hungarian), Rev. Michael J. Holloran.
Parish Office—22 Notre Dame Ave., 45404-1924. Tel: 937-228-8802; Fax: 937-443-0969.
Church: 1114 Troy St., 45404.
Catechesis/Religious Program—Refer to St. Adalbert, Dayton., Tel: 937-228-8604.

EATON, PREBLE CO., VISITATION OF THE BLESSED VIRGIN MARY (1853) Rev. J. Thomas Fitzsimmons.
Res.: 407 E. Main St., 45320. Tel: 937-456-3380; Fax: 937-456-3380. Email: church@visitationstjohn.com.
Catechesis/Religious Program—Tel: 937-456-3395. Email: ccdvisitation@msn.com. Sharon Stump, D.R.E.; Kimberly Leach, Youth Min. Students 125.

EGYPT, AUGLAIZE CO., ST. JOSEPH (1852) [CEM], Clustered with St. Augustine, Minster. Rev. Rick Nieberding, C.PP.S.
Res.: 02441 SR 364, 45865. Tel: 419-628-2614; Fax: 419-628-1078.
Catechesis/Religious Program—Tel: 419-628-3434. Clustered with St. Augustine, Minster. Students 57.

ENGLEWOOD, MONTGOMERY CO., ST. PAUL (1972) Rev. Kenneth R. Baker; Deacon Joseph Subler.
Res.: 1000 W. Wenger Rd., 45322. Tel: 937-836-7535; Fax: 937-836-1130. Web: www.stpaulenglewood.org.
Catechesis/Religious Program—Liza Peters, D.R.E. Students 108.

FAIRBORN, GREENE CO., MARY HELP OF CHRISTIANS (1862) [CEM] Rev. Charles F. Lang; Deacon Max Roadruck; Bill Fortener, Pastoral Assoc.
Res.: 954 N. Maple Ave., 45324-5498. Tel: 937-878-8353; Fax: 937-879-8800. Web: www.mhcparish.com.
Catechesis/Religious Program—Tel: 937-878-7325; Fax: 937-879-8800. Molly Hynes Collinsworth, D.R.E. Students 86.

FAIRFIELD, BUTLER CO., SACRED HEART OF JESUS (1957) Rev. Larry R. Tharp.
Church: 400 Nilles Rd., 45014. Tel: 513-858-4210; Fax: 513-858-4211. Web: www.sacredheart-fairfield.org.
Res.: 5202 Mississippi Dr., 45014. Tel: 513-863-5318; Fax: 513-863-5318.
School—Tel: 513-858-4215; Fax: 513-858-4218. Joseph Nagle, Prin. Lay Teachers 21; Students 419.
Catechesis/Religious Program—Tel: 513-858-4213; Fax: 513-858-4211. Students 209.

FAYETTEVILLE, BROWN CO., ST. ANGELA MERICI (2003) Rev. Henry F. Albietz.
130 Stone Alley, P.O. Box 279, 45118. Tel: 513-875-5020; Fax: 513-875-5022. Email: stangelamericiparish@cinci.rr.com. Web: www.home.catholicweb.com/stangelamerici.
Catechesis/Religious Program—130 Stone Alley, P.O. Box 279, 45118. Tel: 513-875-5020; Fax: 513-875-5022. Email: stangelamericiparish@cinci.rr.com. Web: home.catholicweb.com/stangelamerici. Students 124.
Chapel—St. Patrick Chapel 45118.
Chapel—St. Martin Chapel 45118.

FORT LORAMIE, SHELBY CO., ST. MICHAEL (1838) [CEM] [JC 3] Rev. Steven L. Shoup; Ann Bollheimer, Pastoral Assoc.; Rose Meyer, Pastoral Assoc.; Kevin Musser, Youth Min. Coord.
Res.: 33 Elm St., P.O. Box 7, 45845. Tel: 937-295-3001. Email: steves@nflregion.org. Web: www.nflregion.org.
Catechesis/Religious Program—Tel: 937-295-2179; Fax: 937-295-3349. Diane Seger, D.R.E.; Kate Boeke, D.R.E. Students 614.

FORT RECOVERY, MERCER CO.

1—MARY HELP OF CHRISTIANS (1881) [CEM], (Fort Recovery Cluster) Revs. Thomas E. Dorn; Charles F. Mullen, C.PP.S.; Deacon John Parker.
Mailing Address: 403 Sharpsburg Rd., 45846.
Res.: 417 Meiring Rd., 45846. Tel: 419-375-2603. Email: maryhelpccc@bright.net. Web: www.fortrecoverycatholicparishes.com.
Catechesis/Religious Program—Tel: 419-375-4153; Fax: 419-375-4154. Students 283.

2—ST. PETER (1860), (German), [CEM], (Fort Recovery Cluster) Rev. Thomas E. Dorn.
Mailing Address: 403 Sharpsburg Rd., 45846.
Church: 1477 Philothea Rd., 45846. Tel: 419-375-4153; Fax: 419-375-4154. Email: maryhelpccc@bright.net. Web: www.fortrecoverycatholicparishes.com.
Catechesis/Religious Program—Virginia Fortkamp, D.R.E. Twinned with St. Joseph Parish, St. Joseph. Students 249.

FRANKLIN, WARREN CO., ST. MARY (1867) Rev. James J. Manning; Deacon Stephen Bermick III.
Church: 115 S. Main St., 45005. Tel: 937-746-5404; Fax: 937-746-5470. Email: stmaryfranklin@sbcglobal.net. Web: www.stmaryfranklin.org.
Catechesis/Religious Program—Tel: 937-746-1404. Students 316.

FRENCHTOWN, DARKE CO., HOLY FAMILY (1846) [CEM] Rev. David P. Vincent; Deacon Jack Borgerding.
Res.: 14 E. Wood St., Versailles, 45380-1440. Tel: 937-526-4945; Fax: 937-526-4893. Web: www.stdenishf.org.
Catechesis/Religious Program—Tel: 937-526-3957. Linda Meyer, C.R.E. Students 89.

FRYBURG, AUGLAIZE CO., ST. JOHN (1850), (German), [CEM 2] Rev. Oscar H. Seger; Deacon Nicholas Jurosic.
Res.: 11319 Van Buren St., Wapakoneta, 45895-8467. Tel: 419-738-6043; Fax: 419-738-4364.
Catechesis/Religious Program—Tel: 419-738-6268. Ann Limbert, D.R.E. Students 55.

GEORGETOWN, BROWN CO., ST. GEORGE (1902) Rev. Dohrman W. Byers; Joan St. Clair, Pastoral Assoc.; Susan Caproni, Business Mgr.
Parish Office & Mailing Address: 16 N. 4th St., Ripley, 45167. Tel: 937-392-1116; Fax: 937-392-1699. Email: stsmichael-george@sbcglobal.net. Web: www.stgeorge.homestead.com.
Church: 509 E. State St. & Elm St., 45121.
Catechesis/Religious Program—Tel: 937-378-6453. Joan St. Clair, D.R.E. Students 19.

GERMANTOWN, MONTGOMERY CO., ST. AUGUSTINE (1941) Revs. Francis Tandoh, C.S.Sp.; Joshua Otusafo, C.SS.P., Sacramental Min.
Res.: 130 Gramont Ave., Dayton, 45417. Tel: 937-268-2747; Fax: 937-268-6698. Email: info@unitedinhope.org.
Church: 6939 Weaver Rd., 45327-9378. Tel: 937-855-2289; Fax: 937-855-2289.
Catechesis/Religious Program—Tel: 937-855-2289. Students 117.

GLYNWOOD, AUGLAIZE CO., ST. PATRICK (1857), (Irish), [CEM] Rev. Oscar H. Seger.
Church: 06959 Glynwood Rd., St. Marys, 45885. Tel: 419-738-6043; Fax: 419-738-4364.
Catechesis/Religious Program—Tel: 419-394-8458. Margaret Oen, D.R.E. Students 45.

GREENFIELD, HIGHLAND CO., ST. BENIGNUS (1856) [CEM] Rev. Michael A. Paraniuk; Ann Marie Gunderman, Business Mgr.
Res.: 218 S. Second St., P.O. Box 399, 45123. Tel: 937-981-2785; Fax: 937-981-4483. Web: stbenignus.org.
Catechesis/Religious Program—Tel: 937-981-4483. Katie Paugh, C.R.E. Students 70.

GREENVILLE, DARKE CO., ST. MARY (1853) [CEM] Rev. John R. White.
Res.: 233 W. 3rd St., 45331. Tel: 937-548-1616; Fax: 937-548-0352. Email: stmjc@bizwoh.rr.com. Web: www.stmarysgreenville.org.
School—(Grades PreK-8), 238 W. 3rd St., 45331. Tel: 937-548-2345; Fax: 937-548-0878. Email: chrisdetling@swohio.twcbc.com. Vernon Rosenbeck, Prin. Lay Teachers 10; Students 94.
Catechesis/Religious Program—Email: stmak@bizwoh.rr.com. Students 102.

HAMILTON, BUTLER CO.

1—ST. ANN (1909) Rev. Stephen J. Mondiek; Deacon George Schmidl.
Res.: 171 Washington St., 45011. Tel: 513-863-1424. Church & Mailing Address: 646 Clinton Ave., 45015. Tel: 513-863-4963; Fax: 513-863-4963. Email: slmcabee@gmail.com. Web: www.stanncc.org.
School—(Grades K-8), 3064 Pleasant Ave., 45015. Tel: 513-863-0604. Web: www.stannhamilton.net. Mrs. Donna L. Weber, Prin. Lay Teachers 9; Students 150.
Catechesis/Religious Program—Tel: 513-863-4963. Students 30.

2—ST. JOSEPH (1867), (German), Revs. Stephen J. Mondiek; James H. Elsbernd, Sacramental Min.
Res. and Mailing Address: 171 Washington St., 45011. Tel: 513-863-1424; Fax: 513-863-1451. Email: jhaubner@sjcshamilton.org.
School—(Grades K-8), 925 Second St., 45011. Tel: 513-863-8758; Fax: 513-863-5772. Web: www.sjcshamilton.org. J. William Hicks, Prin. Lay Teachers 10; Students 210.
Catechesis/Religious Program—Students 3.

3—ST. JULIE BILLIART (1989) [CEM 2], (This parish is the successor in interest to St. Mary, St. Stephen and St. Veronica parishes, formerly located in Hamilton, OH.) Rev. Michael U. Pucke; Sr. Andre Burkhart, O.S.F., Pastoral Assoc.; Deacons William B. Renneker, Pastoral Assoc.; Thomas Strodtbeck; Mrs. Betty Meiner, Business Mgr.
Church: 224 Dayton St., 45011-1634. Tel: 513-863-1040; Fax: 513-863-1132. Email: sjbparish@stjulie.net.
Catechesis/Religious Program—Mrs. Alison Smith, C.R.E. Students 87.

4—ST. PETER IN CHAINS (1894), (German), Rev. Timothy S. Bunch.
Res.: 471 Ridgelawn Ave., 45013. Tel: 513-863-9115; Fax: 513-863-1257. Email: parishoffice@stpeterinchains.org. Web: www.stpeterinchains.org.
Church: 382 Liberty Ave., 45013.
School—(Grades K-8), 451 Ridgelawn Ave., 45013. Tel: 513-863-0685; Fax: 513-863-1859. Email: schooloffice@stpeterinchains.org. Charlotte Sharon, Prin. Lay Teachers 20; Students 257.
Catechesis/Religious Program—Tel: 513-863-3344. Email: valeriust@stpeterinchains.org. Students 64.

HILLSBORO, HIGHLAND CO., ST. MARY (1853) [CEM] Rev. Michael A. Paraniuk; Deacon Leonard Parker.
Res.: 212 S. High St., 45133-1445. Tel: 937-393-1742; Fax: 937-393-1742. Email: edbourdase@yahoo.com. Web: stmaryhillsboro.org.
School—(Grades PreSchool-5) Tel: 937-840-9932; Fax: 937-840-9932. Email: sschool35@cinci.rr.com. Mary Stanforth, Prin. Lay Teachers 3; Students 55.
Catechesis/Religious Program—Email: stmarydrem@cinci.rr.com. Michelle Salyer, C.R.E. Students 70.

JAMESTOWN, GREENE CO., ST. AUGUSTINE (1870) Rev. John E. Krumm.
Res.: 16 Lucerne, Dayton, 45410. Tel: 937-907-9355.
Church: 44 E. Washington St., P.O. Box 189, 45335. Tel: 937-675-2601.
Catechesis/Religious Program—Gabrielle Bradds, D.R.E. Students 35.

LEBANON, WARREN CO., ST. FRANCIS DE SALES (1883) Rev. Bernard J. Weldishofer; Deacon Herschel Steward; Susan Olsen, Business Mgr.
Parish Office: 20-A DeSales Ave., 45036. Tel: 513-932-2601; Fax: 513-932-9144. Web: stfrancisdesales-lebanon.org.
Res.: 15 DeSales Ave., 45036. Tel: 513-933-0708.
Oratory— 20 DeSales Ave., 45036. Tel: 513-932-6501; Fax: 513-932-9919. Mr. Paul McLaughlin, Prin. Lay Teachers 12; Students 216.
Catechesis/Religious Program—Tel: 513-932-2601. Mike Kletzly, D.R.E.; Patrica Metzger, Music Min. Students 219.

LIBERTY TOWNSHIP, BUTLER CO., ST. MAXIMILIAN KOLBE (1989) Revs. Geoffrey D. Drew; Thomas H. McCarthy, Parochial Vicar; Deacon Jeffrey Merrell.
Church & Mailing: 5720 Hamilton-Mason Rd., 45011. Tel: 513-777-4322; Fax: 513-777-7264. Email: web@saint-max.org. Web: www.saint-max.org.
Res.: 7168 St. Albans Way, Liberty Twp., 45011.
See St. Gabriel Consolidated School, Cincinnati under Consolidated Elementary Schools located in the Institution section.
Catechesis/Religious Program—Students 1,387.

LOVELAND, CLERMONT CO., ST. COLUMBAN (1859) Rev. Lawrence R. Tensi; Deacons Joseph Coll; James Miller; Edward Reising; Gerard J. Sasson; Harry Walker.
Office & Mailing Address: 894 Oakland Rd., 45140. Tel: 513-683-0105; Fax: 513-683-1389. Email: frontdesk@stcolumban.org. Web: www.stcolumban.org.
Res.: 885 Oakland Rd., 45140. Tel: 513-677-8084.
School—(Grades K-8), 896 Oakland Rd., 45140. Fax: 513-683-7904. Web: www.saintcolumbanschool.org. Mrs. Jo Rhoten, Prin. Sisters 1; Lay Teachers 29; Students 693.
Catechesis/Religious Program—Tel: 513-683-0105; Fax: 513-683-1389. Students 491.
Convent—Sisters of Notre Dame, (Covington, KY), 896 Oakland Rd., 45140. Tel: 513-683-0255.

MARIA STEIN, MERCER CO.

1—ST. JOHN THE BAPTIST (1836) [CEM], (Marion Cluster) Rev. Eugene H. Schnipke, C.PP.S.; Deacon Omer Bertke.
Marion Catholic Community Office: 7428 State Rte. 119, 45860. Tel: 419-925-4775; Fax: 419-925-1745. Email: marioncathcom@gmail.com. Web: www.marioncatholiccommunity.org.
Res.: 8533 State Rte. 119, 45860. Tel: 419-925-4522.
Catechesis/Religious Program—Tel: 419-925-6200; 419-925-4822. Julie Brunswick, D.R.E.; Angie Bertke, D.R.E. Students 313.

2—MOST PRECIOUS BLOOD (1903), (German), [CEM], (Marion Cluster) Rev. Eugene H. Schnipke, C.PP.S.
Office: *Marion Catholic Community Office*, 7428 State Rte. 119, 45860. Tel: 419-925-4775; Fax: 419-925-1745. Email: marioncathcom@gmail.com. Web: www.marioncatholiccommunity.org.
Res.: 8533 State Rte. 119, 45860. Tel: 419-925-4522.
Church: 35 S. Maple St., Box 26, Chickasaw, 45826-0026.
Catechesis/Religious Program—Mary Bruns, C.R.E. Students 116.

MASON, WARREN CO., ST. SUSANNA (1938) Revs. Robert J. Farrell; Anthony G. Tozzi, Parochial Vicar; Deacons James A. Merritt; Daniel L. Rader; Karen Gottschall, Pastoral Assoc.; Chris Kreger, Pastoral Assoc.; Charlotte McManis, Business Mgr.
Mailing Address: 305 Fourth Ave., 45040. Tel: 513-398-3821; Fax: 513-398-2254. Email: stsusanna@stsusanna.org. Web: www.stsusanna.org.

Church: 616 Reading Rd., 45040.
School—500 Reading Rd., 45040. Tel: 513-398-3821; Fax: 513-398-1657. Kevan Hartman, Prin. Lay Teachers 35; Students 620.
Catechesis/Religious Program—Tel: 513-398-3821. Students 1,297.

MCCARTYVILLE, SHELBY CO., SACRED HEART OF JESUS (1882) Rev. John W. Tonkin; Deacon Paul Luthman.
Res. & Mailing Address: 9333 State Rte. 119 W., Anna, 45302-9520. Tel: 937-394-3823; 419-628-2502; Fax: 937-394-2723. Email: Sachrt@bright.net.
Catechesis/Religious Program—Barbara Riethman, C.R.E. Students 479.

MECHANICSBURG, CHAMPAIGN CO., ST. MICHAEL'S (1865) Rev. Lawrence M. Gearhart, Admin.
Res.: 40 Walnut St., 43044. Tel: 937-834-2664. Web: wwwchampaigncatholic.org.
Catechesis/Religious Program—Students 42.

MIAMISBURG, MONTGOMERY CO., OUR LADY OF GOOD HOPE (1852) [CEM] Rev. Thomas A. Nevels; Deacon Richard Martin.
Res.: 6 S. Third St., 45342. Tel: 937-866-1432; Fax: 937-859-5035. Email: olgh2@sbcglobal.net. Web: www.olghchurch.org.
See Bishop Leibold School, Dayton under Consolidated Elementary Schools located in the Institution section.
Catechesis/Religious Program—Tel: 937-866-1492; Fax: 937-859-5035. Email: olghreled@catholicweb.com. Students 135.

MIDDLETOWN, BUTLER CO., HOLY FAMILY (1991) [JC], (This parish is the successor in interest to Holy Trinity, St. John the Baptist and St. Mary parishes, formerly located in Middletown, OH) Rev. John R. Civille; Sr. Jean Sora, O.S.F., Pastoral Assoc.; Deacons William Krumm; Thomas Coyle.
Office: 201 Clark St., 45042. Tel: 513-422-0602; Fax: 513-424-7416. Web: www.holyfamilymiddletown.com.
See John XIII Catholic Elementary School under Consolidated Elementary Schools located in the Institution section.
Catechesis/Religious Program—Tel: 513-422-0602; Fax: 513-424-7416. Students 140.

MILFORD, CLERMONT CO., ST. ANDREW (1854) [CEM] Rev. Robert C. Waller; Deacon Timothy Schutte.
Res.: 552 Main St., 45150. Tel: 513-831-3353; Fax: 513-831-6597. Email: standy@cinci.rr.com. Web: www.standrew-milford.org.
School—St. Andrew-St. Elizabeth Seton, (Grades K-8), 555 Main St., 45150. Tel: 513-831-5277; Fax: 513-831-8436. Mr. Thomas Devolve, Prin. Consolidated. Lay Teachers 35; Students 516.
Catechesis/Religious Program—Tel: 513-831-3812; Fax: 513-831-6597. Barbara Aluotto, D.R.E. Students 200.

MILLVILLE, BUTLER CO., QUEEN OF PEACE (1941) Rev. Jeffery W. Bacon; Deacon Michael E. Mignery.
Res.: 2550 Millville Ave., Hamilton, 45013. Tel: 513-863-4344; Fax: 513-863-4364. Email: parishoffice@qpchurch.org. Web: www-queenofpeachchurch.net.
School—(Grades PreK-8) Tel: 513-863-8705; Fax: 513-863-4310. Susan Schnell, Prin. Lay Teachers 15; Students 229.
Catechesis/Religious Program—Fax: 513-863-4364. Mary Ann Estridge, C.R.E. Students 94.

MINSTER, AUGLAIZE CO., ST. AUGUSTINE (1832), (German), [CEM] Rev. Rick Nieberding, C.PP.S.; Deacons John J. Schmiesing; Hal Belcher; Roger L. Klosterman.
Res.: 48 N. Hanover St., P.O. Box 93, 45865. Tel: 419-628-2614; Fax: 419-628-1078. Email: info@staugie.com. Web: www.staugie.com.
Catechesis/Religious Program—89 N. Lincoln St., P.O. Box 93, 45865. Tel: 419-628-3434; Fax: 419-628-3584. Email: augreled@staugie.com. Jane Boeke, D.R.E. Students 680.

MONROE, BUTLER CO., OUR LADY OF SORROWS (1883) Rev. Terence A. Meehan (Retired); Deacon Daniel Thomas; Corinne Butera, Pastoral Assoc.
Mailing Address: 330 Lebanon St., 45050. Web: www.olsmonroe.parishesonline.com.
Res.: 416 Lebanon St., 45050. Tel: 513-539-8383; Fax: 513-539-0443.
Catechesis/Religious Program—330 Lebanon St., 45050. Tel: 513-539-8061; Fax: 513-539-0443. Email: bheing@cinci.rr.com. Students 147.

MONTEZUMA, MERCER CO., OUR LADY OF GUADALUPE (1904) [CEM] Rev. James H. Dugal, C.PP.S.
Res.: 6701 State Rte. 219, P.O. Box 69, 45866. Tel: 419-268-2312; Fax: 419-268-1602.
Catechesis/Religious Program—Tel: 419-268-2312. Ruth Wynk, C.R.E. Students 99.

MORROW, WARREN CO., ST. PHILIP THE APOSTLE (1965) [CEM] Rev. Ronald J. Piepmeyer.
Res.: 824 E. U.S. 22-3, 45152-9690.
Church: 944 E. U.S. 22-3, 45152-9690. Tel: 513-899-3601; Fax: 513-899-3785. Email: frronstphilip@earthlink.net. Web: www.stphilipmorrow.org.
Catechesis/Religious Program—Tel: 513-899-3601; Fax: 513-899-3601. Sr. Janet Schneider, C.D.P., C.R.E. Students 149.

MOUNT CARMEL, CLERMONT CO., ST. VERONICA (1949) Revs. Michael T. Flaherty; Francis W. Voellmecke; Deacons Walter Srode; R. Daniel Murphy.
Res.: 4470 Hall St., 45244. Tel: 513-528-1622; Fax: 513-528-1622. Email: office@stveronica.org. Web: www.stveronica.org.
Church: 4473 Mt. Carmel-Tobasco Rd., 45244.
School—(Grades K-8), 4475 Mt. Carmel-Tobasco Rd., 45244. Tel: 513-528-0442; Fax: 513-528-0513. Email: school@stveronica.org. Gina Code, Prin.; Lisa Gnotek, Librarian. Sisters 1; Lay Teachers 22; Students 476.
Catechesis/Religious Program—Tel: 513-528-8723. Students 149.

MOUNT ORAB, BROWN CO., ST. MICHAEL (1944) Rev. Henry F. Albietz; Marilyn Fryer, Pastoral Assoc.
Res. & Offices: 130 Stone Alley, P.O. Box 279, Fayetteville, 45118. Tel: 513-875-5020; Fax: 513-875-5022. Email: stangelamericiparish@cinci.rr.com.
Church: 220 S. High St., 45154.
Catechesis/Religious Program—Tel: 937-446-1854; 937-446-2555. Linda Mulvaney, C.R.E. Students 36.

MOUNT REPOSE, CLERMONT CO., ST. ELIZABETH ANN SETON (1976) Rev. Michael L. Cordier; Deacon Steve Brown.
Res.: 5890 Buckwheat Rd., Milford, 45150. Tel: 513-575-0119; Fax: 513-575-0957. Email: easeton@cinci.rr.com. Web: www.setonmilford.org.
School—(Grades K-8), 5900 Buckwheat Rd., Milford, 45150. Tel: 513-575-0093; Fax: 513-575-1078. Mr. Thomas Devolve, Prin. Lay Teachers 21; Students 328.
Preschool—Tel: 513-575-9900; Fax: 513-575-1078. Mrs. Terri Imming, Dir. Lay Teachers 8; Students 118.
Catechesis/Religious Program—Tel: 513-575-0119; Fax: 513-575-0957. Patricia Norris, D.R.E. Students 278.

NEW BREMEN, AUGLAIZE CO., HOLY REDEEMER (1948) Rev. Thomas M. Mannebach; Deacon Gregory Bornhorst.
Church: 120 S. Eastmoor Dr., P.O. Box 67, 45869. Tel: 419-629-2543; Fax: 419-629-2543. Email: holyredeemer@nktelco.net. Web: www.holyredeemercatholicchurch.org.
Catechesis/Religious Program—Students 370.

NEW CARLISLE, CLARK CO., SACRED HEART (1950) Rev. Michael L. Bidwell; Deacon Robert Kozlowski.
Res.: 476 N. Scott St., 45344. Tel: 937-845-3121; Fax: 937-846-1223. Email: shsaintsnc@aol.com. Web: home.catholicweb.com/sacredsaints.
Catechesis/Religious Program—Tel: 937-845-1373. Melissa Elleman, C.R.E. Students 213.

NEW PARIS, PREBLE CO., ST. JOHN THE EVANGELIST (1870) [CEM] Rev. J. Thomas Fitzsimmons.
Res. & Mailing Address: 407 E. Main St., Eaton, 45320. Tel: 937-456-3380; Fax: 937-456-3380.
Church: N. Spring St., 45347.
Catechesis/Religious Program—Students 8.

NEW RICHMOND, CLERMONT CO., ST. PETER (1850) [CEM] Rev. Michael F. Leshney; Deacon Ronald L. Stang.
Res.: 1192 Bethel-New Richmond Rd., 45157. Tel: 513-553-3267; Fax: 513-553-4321. Email: michaelleshney@fuse.net. Web: www.stpeter-newrichmond.org.
Catechesis/Religious Program— Tina Conners, D.R.E. Students 65.

NEWPORT, SHELBY CO., SS. PETER AND PAUL (1856) [CEM] Rev. Steven L. Shoup.
Res.: 6788 State Rte. 66, P.O. Box 199, Fort Loramie, 45845. Tel: 937-295-2891; Fax: 937-295-3349. Email: bettyanne@nflregion.org. Web: www.nflregion.org.
Catechesis/Religious Program—Tel: 937-295-2536. Lisa Monnin, C.R.E. Students 82.

NORTH LEWISBURG, CHAMPAIGN CO., IMMACULATE CONCEPTION (1869) Rev. Lawrence M. Gearhart.
Res. & Mailing Address: 40 Walnut St., Mechanicsburg, 43044. Tel: 937-834-2664. Web: www.champaigncatholic.org.
Church: Corner of Elm & Winder Sts., 43060.
Catechesis/Religious Program—Students 8.

NORTH BEND, HAMILTON CO., ST. JOSEPH (1860) Rev. Michael A. Savino.
Mailing Address: P.O. Box 219, 45052. Email: stjosephnorthbend@roadrunner.com. Web: www.stjosephnorthbend.com.
Church: 25 E. Harrison Ave., 45052. Tel: 513-941-3661; Fax: 513-941-8559.
Res.: 3700 Chestnut Park, Cleves, 45002. Tel: 513-467-0450.
Catechesis/Religious Program—Mary Jo Ressel, D.R.E. Students 125.

NORTH STAR, DARKE CO., ST. LOUIS (1891) [CEM] Rev. David L. Zink.
Parish Office—P.O. Box 9, Osgood, 45351. Tel: 419-582-2531; Fax: 419-582-2015.
Church: 15 Star Rd., 45350.
Catechesis/Religious Program—Linda Wehrkamp, D.R.E. Students 173.

OSGOOD, DARKE CO., ST. NICHOLAS (1909) [CEM] Rev. David L. Zink.
Office: 128 Church St., P.O. Box 9, 45351. Tel: 419-582-2531; Fax: 419-582-2015.
Catechesis/Religious Program—Linda Kuether, D.R.E. Students 248.

OWENSVILLE, CLERMONT CO., ST. LOUIS (1856) [CEM] Rev. Gerard P. Hiland.
Res.: 210 N. Broadway, 45160. Tel: 513-732-0649; 513-732-2218 (office); Fax: 513-732-2368. Email: fatherhiland@aol.com. Web: www.stlparish.org.
School—(Grades PreK-8), 250 N. Broadway, 45160. Tel: 513-732-0636. Mrs. Margaret Noonan Hunsberger, Prin. Lay Teachers 12; Students 174.
Catechesis/Religious Program—Students 53.

OXFORD, BUTLER CO., ST. MARY CHURCH AND CATHOLIC CAMPUS MINISTRY (Miami U.) (1853) [CEM] Rev. Jeffrey P. Silver; Roberta L. Kinne, Pastoral Assoc.; Kimberly Wagner, Campus Min.; Ryan Leep, Music Dir.; Pam Burk, Business Mgr.; Tara Nixon, Sec.
Res.: 111 E. High St., 45056. Tel: 513-523-2153; Fax: 513-523-0559. Email: info@stmaryoxfordohio.org. Web: www.stmaryoxfordohio.org.
Catechesis/Religious Program—Michael Puglielli, D.R.E. Students 150.

PEEBLES, ADAMS CO., ST. MARY QUEEN OF HEAVEN (1952), (Vicariate) Rev. Theodore C. Kosse.
Office & Mailing Address: *Holy Trinity*, 612 E. Mulberry St., West Union, 45693. Tel: 937-544-2757; Fax: 937-544-1430.
Church: 205 Wendall Ave., 45660.
Catechesis/Religious Program—Tel: 937-446-9294. Students 12.

PHILOTHEA, MERCER CO., ST. MARY (1851), (German), [CEM], (Coldwater Cluster) Revs. Richard W. Walling; Barry J. Stechschulte, Parochial Vicar.
Mailing Address: P.O. Box 107, Coldwater, 45828.
Res.: 116 E. Main St., P.O. Box 107, Coldwater, 45828. Tel: 419-678-4802; Fax: 419-678-4803. Email: coldwatercluster@bright.net. Web: www.coldwatercluster.org.
Catechesis/Religious Program—Sue Homan, D.R.E. Students 80.

PIQUA, MIAMI CO.
1—ST. BONIFACE (1855) Revs. Martin E. Fox; Angelo C. Caserta (Retired). Tel: 937-778-9526.
310 S. Downing St., 45356.
Res.: 528 Broadway, 45356. Tel: 937-773-0075. Web: www.stbonifacepiqua.org.
See Piqua Catholic School, Piqua under Consolidated Elementary Schools located in the Institution section.
Catechesis/Religious Program—Tel: 937-773-1656; Fax: 937-773-2665. Email: religioused@stbonifacepiqua.org. Students 85.
2—ST. MARY (1843) Revs. Martin E. Fox; Thomas J. Grilliot, Parochial Vicar; Sr. Joan Clare Stewart, S.C., Pastoral Assoc.; Jon Paul Hebert, Youth Min.
Mailing Address & Parish Offices: 310 S. Downing St., 45356.
Res. & Church: 528 Broadway, 45356. Tel: 937-773-1327; Fax: 937-773-2665.
See Piqua Catholic School, Piqua under Consolidated Elementary Schools located in the Institution section.
Catechesis/Religious Program— Jon Paul Hebert, C.R.E. Students 38.

RHINE, SHELBY CO., ST. LAWRENCE (1856), (German), [CEM] Revs. Patrick L. Sloneker; Matthew K. Lee, Parochial Vicar; Deacon Terrell Coleman.
Mailing Address & Parish Office: P.O. Box 519, Botkins, 45306.
Res.: 16053 Botkins Rd., P.O. Box 519, Botkins, 45306. Tel: 937-693-2561; Fax: 937-693-2561.
Catechesis/Religious Program—Tel: 937-693-2571. Students 102.

RIPLEY, BROWN CO., ST. MICHAEL THE ARCHANGEL (1840) Rev. Dohrman W. Byers; Maureen Harvey, Pastoral Assoc. & Rel. Educ.; Susan Caproni, Business Mgr.
Church & Parish Office: 16 N. Fourth St., 45167. Tel: 937-392-1116 (Office Sec.); 937-392-1840 (Bus. Mgr.); Fax: 937-392-1699. Email: stsmichael-george@sbcglobal.net. Web: www.stmichael.homestead.com.
School—(Grades PreK-8) Tel: 937-392-4202; Fax: 937-392-4248. Web: www.stmichaelcatholic-school.org. Sr. Carol Ann Mause, O.S.F., Prin.; Melody Kokensparger, Librarian. Lay Teachers 10; Students 80.
Catechesis/Religious Program—Tel: 937-392-1335. Students 14.

ROCKFORD, MERCER CO., ST. TERESA (1936) Rev. Thomas Brenberger, C.PP.S.
Church: 4227 State Rte. 707, P.O. Box 445, 45882. Tel: 419-363-2633; Fax: 419-363-2633. Email:

stteresachurch@bright.net.
Catechesis/Religious Program— Annie Ford, C.R.E. Students 80.

RUSSELLS POINT, LOGAN CO., ST. MARY OF THE WOODS (1927) Rev. Harold W. Kist.
Mailing Address: P.O. Box 329, 43348-0329.
Res.: 464 Madison Ave., P.O. Box 329, 43348. Tel: 937-843-3127; Fax: 937-843-3866. Email: stmarwds@bright.net. Web: saintmaryofthewoods.com.
Catechesis/Religious Program—Tel: 937-843-4227. Dona Fischer. Students 150.
Mission—St. George Chapel Marianists of Ohio 9636 Lake Shore Dr., E., Huntsville, Logan Co. 43324. Tel: 937-842-4902.

RUSSIA, SHELBY CO., ST. REMY (1846) [CEM] Rev. Frank G. Amberger.
Res.: 108 E. Main St., 45363-9701. Tel: 937-526-3437; Fax: 937-526-5326. Email: stremy@roadrunner.com. Web: www.stremychurch.com.
Catechesis/Religious Program—Tel: 937-526-3437; Fax: 937-526-5326. Email: stremydre@roadrunner.com. Karen Rosenbeck, C.R.E. Students 354.

ST. ANTHONY, MERCER CO., ST. ANTHONY (1852), (German), [CEM], (Coldwater Cluster) Revs. Richard W. Walling; Barry J. Stechschulte, Parochial Vicar.
Mailing Address: P.O. Box 107, Coldwater, 45828. Tel: 419-678-4802; Fax: 419-678-4803.
Church: 471 St. Anthony Rd., Fort Recovery, 45846-9404.
Catechesis/Religious Program—Tel: 419-375-3013. Cindy Muhlenkamp, D.R.E. Students 98.

ST. HENRY, MERCER CO., ST. HENRY (1839) [CEM], (St. Henry Cluster) Revs. Thomas Hemm, C.PP.S.; Benedict Magabe, C.PP.S.; Deacons Jerry Buschur; Randy Balster.
Res.: 1509 Cranberry Rd., Cranberry, 45883. Tel: 419-925-4776.
Church: 272 E. Main St., Box 350, 45883. Tel: 419-678-4118; Fax: 419-678-8285. Email: shclusteroffice@hotmail.com. Web: www.sthenrycluster.com.
Inter-parish Center—162 S. Walnut, 45883. Tel: 419-678-3811; Fax: 419-678-8285.
Catechesis/Religious Program—Tel: 419-678-3811. Email: sthenryccd@bright.net. Catherine Wenning, D.R.E. Students 876.

ST. JOSEPH, MERCER CO., ST. JOSEPH (1839), (German), [CEM], (Fort Recovery Cluster) Rev. Thomas E. Dorn.
Mailing Address: 403 Sharpsburg Rd., Fort Recovery, 45846. Tel: 419-375-4153. Email: maryhelpccc@bright.net. Web: www.fortrecoverycatholicparishes.com.
Church: 1689 St. Joseph Rd., Fort Recovery, 45846. Fax: 419-375-4154.
Catechesis/Religious Program—Virginia Fortkamp, D.R.E. Twinned with St. Peter Parish, St. Peter. Students 249.

ST. MARYS, AUGLAIZE CO., HOLY ROSARY (1852) [CEM] Rev. Anthony E. Cutcher.
Res.: 511 E. Spring St., 45885. Tel: 419-394-5050; Fax: 419-394-0184. Email: holyrosary@bright.net. Web: www.holyrosarychurch.us.
School—(Grades PreK-8) Tel: 419-394-5291. Web: www.holyrosaryschool.us. Lora Krugh, Prin. Lay Teachers 11; Students 140.
Catechesis/Religious Program—Email: mielkecrew@yahoo.com. Nan Mielke, C.R.E. Students 136.

ST. PARIS, CHAMPAIGN CO., SACRED HEART (ST. PARIS) (1868) Rev. Gregory J. Konerman.
Res.: 231 Washington Ave., Urbana, 43078-1728. Tel: 937-653-1375; Fax: 937-653-1383. Email: stmary@ctcn.net. Web: www.champaigncatholic.org.
Church: 121 E. Walnut St., 43072.
Catechesis/Religious Program—Tel: 937-653-1375. Twinned with St. Mary, Urbana. Students 5.

ST. ROSE, MERCER CO., ST. ROSE (1839), (German), [CEM], (Marion Cluster) Rev. Eugene H. Schnipke, C.PP.S.
Marion Catholic Community Office: 7428 State Rte. 119, Maria Stein, 45860. Tel: 419-925-4775; Fax: 419-925-1745. Email: marioncathcom@gmail.com. Web: www.marioncatholiccommunity.org.
Res.: 8533 State Rte. 119, Maria Stein, 45860. Tel: 419-925-4522.
Catechesis/Religious Program—Tel: 419-925-4641. Mary Jane Meier, D.R.E. Students 84.

ST. SEBASTIAN, MERCER CO., ST. SEBASTIAN (1852), (German), [CEM], (Marion Cluster) Rev. Eugene H. Schnipke, C.PP.S.
Mailing Address: 7428 State Rte. 119, Maria Stein, 45860. Tel: 419-925-4775. Email: marioncathcom@gmail.com. Web: www.marioncatholiccommunity.org.
Church: 3280 Co. Rd. 716-A, Celina, 45822.
Catechesis/Religious Program—Becky Kunkler, D.R.E. Students 47.

ST. WENDELIN, MERCER CO., ST. WENDELIN (1856) [CEM], (St. Henry Cluster) Revs. Thomas Hemm, C.PP.S.; Benedict Magabe, C.PP.S.
Mailing Address: 272 E. Main St., Box 350, Saint Henry, 45883. Tel: 419-678-4118; Fax: 419-678-8285. Email: tomhemm@hotmail.com. Web: www.sthenrycluster.com.
Res.: 1509 Cranberry Rd., Saint Henry, 45883. Tel: 419-925-4776.
Church: 2980 Ft. Recovery-Minster Rd., St. Henry, 45833.
Catechesis/Religious Program—Tel: 419-678-3811. Email: sthenryccd@bright.net. Students 30.

SARDINIA, BROWN CO., ST. ELIZABETH PARISH (1955) Closed. For inquiries for parish records, contact St. Mary, Arnheim.

SHANDON, BUTLER CO., ST. ALOYSIUS (1867) [CEM] Rev. Raymond J. Leurck; Joan Mills, Lay Pastoral Min.; Deacon Bill Brunsman.
Res.: 5484 Cinti Brookville Rd., 45063. Tel: 513-738-1014; Fax: 513-738-2084.
Church: 3350 Chapel Rd., P.O. Box 95, 45063. Tel: 513-738-1014.
Catechesis/Religious Program—Tel: 513-738-4641. Students 150.

SHARPSBURG, MERCER CO., ST. PAUL (1868) [CEM], (Fort Recovery Cluster) Revs. Thomas E. Dorn; Charles F. Mullen, C.PP.S.
Mailing Address: 403 Sharpsburg Rd., Fort Recovery, 45846. Tel: 419-375-4153. Email: maryhelpccc@bright.net. Web: www.fortrecoverycatholicparishes.com.
Res.: 517 Meiring Rd., Fort Recovery, 45846. Tel: 419-375-2603; Fax: 419-375-9413.
Catechesis/Religious Program—Tel: 419-375-2308. Helen Lefevre, D.R.E. Students 156.

SIDNEY, SHELBY CO., HOLY ANGELS (1848) Revs. Daniel J. Schmitmeyer; Jason Edward Bedel, Parochial Vicar; Deacons Philip Myers; John Holthaus, Pastoral Assoc.
Res.: 324 S. Ohio Ave., 45365-3012. Tel: 937-498-2307; Fax: 937-498-2308. Email: info@holyangelssidney.com. Web: www.holyangelssidney.com.
School—(Grades K-8), 120 E. Water St., 45365-3199. Tel: 937-492-9293; Fax: 937-492-8578. Email: info@holyangelscatholic.com. Web: www.holyangelscatholic.com. Hal Belcher, Prin.; Jill Heitmeyer, Librarian. Lay Teachers 20; Students 271.
Catechesis/Religious Program—c/o Office 121 E. Water St., 45365-3199. Tel: 937-498-0433; Fax: 937-498-1448. Email: hareligioused@hotmail.com. Susan Anderson, C.R.E. Students 239.

SOUTH CHARLESTON, CLARK CO., ST. CHARLES BORROMEO (1866) [CEM] Rev. Anthony J. Geraci; Deacon Paul E. Richardson.
31 S. Chillicothe St., P.O. Box F, 45368-0806. Tel: 937-462-8971; Fax: 937-462-9184. Web: www.charlesborromeo.com.
Rectory—St. Paul Rectory, Res.: 308 Phillips St., Yellow Springs, 45387-1724. Tel: 937-767-7450; Fax: 937-767-7465. Email: stpauloffice@woh.rr.com.
Catechesis/Religious Program—Fax: 937-462-9184. Students 19.

SPRINGFIELD, CLARK CO.

1—ST. BERNARD (1860), (German), [CEM] Rev. Paul F. Hurst.
Res.: 910 Lagonda Ave., 45503. Tel: 937-322-5243; Fax: 937-322-3788.
School—Catholic Central Elementary, (Grades PreK-6), *Central Offices*, 1817 N. Limestone St., 45503-2696. Tel: 937-399-5451; Fax: 937-342-0042. Ms. Mary Callahan, Prin.; Laura Watkins, Librarian; Molly Mann, Librarian. Lay Teachers 14; Students 201.
Catechesis/Religious Program—Tel: 937-324-2870; Fax: 937-322-3788. Trish Evans, C.R.E. Students 64.

2—ST. JOSEPH (1882) Rev. Dennis J. Caylor; Deacons John R. Collins; Norman G. Horstman.
Res.: 802 Kenton St., 45505.
Church Mailing Address: 225 E. High St., 45505. Tel: 937-323-7523; Fax: 937-324-1512. Web: www.josephraphael.org.
See Catholic Central Elementary School, Springfield under St. Bernard, Springfield for details.
Catechesis/Religious Program— Twinned with St. Raphael, Springfield. Students 34.

3—ST. RAPHAEL (1849) Rev. Dennis J. Caylor; Deacons John R. Collins; Norman G. Horstmann.
Res.: 802 Kenton St., 45505. Tel: 937-323-7097.
Church: 225 E. High St., 45505. Tel: 937-323-7523; Fax: 937-324-1512. Web: www.josephraphael.org.
See Catholic Central Elementary School, Springfield under St. Bernard, Springfield for details.
Catechesis/Religious Program—Tel: 937-323-7523. Twinned with St. Joseph, Springfield. Students 168.

4—ST. TERESA OF THE CHILD JESUS (1931) Rev. Edwin F. Gearhart.
Res.: 137 Floral Ave., 45504.
Church: 1827 N. Limestone St., 45503. Tel: 937-342-8861; Fax: 937-399-6971. Email: stteresa.church@bizwoh.rr.com.
School—Catholic Central Elementary School, (Grades PreK-6) Tel: 937-399-5451; Fax: 937-342-0042. Ms. Mary Callahan, Prin.; Laura Watkins, Librarian.
Catechesis/Religious Program—Tel: 937-342-8861, Ext. 16; Fax: 937-399-6971. Melanie Oliver, C.R.E. Students 76.

STONELICK, CLERMONT CO., ST. PHILOMENA (1837) [CEM] Rev. Gerard P. Hiland.
Res.: 210 N. Broadway, Box 85, Owensville, 45160. Tel: 513-732-2218; Fax: 513-732-2368. Email: fatherhiland@aol.com.

TIPP CITY, MIAMI CO., ST. JOHN THE BAPTIST (1858) [CEM] Rev. R. Marc Sherlock.
Res.: 753 S. Hyatt St., 45371-1255. Tel: 937-667-3419; Fax: 937-667-9267. Email: ermahagan@woh.rr.com. Web: www.stjohnthebaptist.cc.
Catechesis/Religious Program—Tel: 937-667-3419. Daniel L. Thomas, D.R.E. Students 315.

TRENTON, BUTLER CO., HOLY NAME (1871) [CEM] Rev. George W. Klein; Deacon William Martin.
Res.: 222 Hamilton Ave., 45067. Tel: 513-988-6335; Fax: 513-998-9900.
Catechesis/Religious Program—Tel: 513-988-9348. Students 79.

TROY, MIAMI CO., ST. PATRICK (1857) Revs. James S. Duell; Joseph F. Kozar, S.M.; Deacons John Carlin; Robert Knight.
Res.: 409 E. Main St., 45373. Tel: 937-335-2833; Fax: 937-335-1453. Email: stpatofficemgr@woh.rr.com. Web: www.stpattroy.org.
School—(Grades PreK-6), 420 E. Water St., 45373. Tel: 937-339-3705; Fax: 937-339-1158. Mr. Robert Barrett, Prin. Lay Teachers 7; Students 142.
Catechesis/Religious Program—409 E. Main St., 45373. Students 300.

TWENTY MILE STAND, WARREN CO., ST. MARGARET OF YORK (1984) Rev. Jan Kevin Schmidt; Deacon Raymond Kroger.
Res.: 9483 Columbia Rd., Loveland, 45140. Tel: 513-683-7100; Fax: 513-683-7101. Email: feedback@stmargaretofyork.org. Web: www.stmargaretofyork.org.
School—(Grades K-8), 9495 Columbia Rd., Loveland, 45140. Tel: 513-683-9793; Fax: 513-683-8949. Email: info@smoyschool.com. Web: st-margaret-york.cnd.pvt.k12.oh.us. Mrs. Bernadine Stone, Educ. Admin. Team; Mrs. Nancy Shula, Educ. Admin.Team. Lay Teachers 27; Students 690.
Catechesis/Religious Program—Tel: 513-683-7100, Ext. 206. Email: susangravely@stmargaretofyork.org. Susan Gravely, D.R.E. Students 557.

URBANA, CHAMPAIGN CO., ST. MARY (1853) Rev. Gregory J. Konerman; Deacon Earl Rogers Jr.
Res.: 231 Washington Ave., 43078. Tel: 937-653-1375; Fax: 937-653-1383. Email: stmary@ctcn.net. Web: www.champaigncatholic.org.
School—Catholic Central Elementary School, (Grades K-6), *Administrative Offices*, 1827 N. Limestone St., Springfield, 45503. Tel: 937-399-5451; Fax: 937-342-0042. Ms. Mary Callahan, Prin.
Catechesis/Religious Program—Students 56.

VANDALIA, MONTGOMERY CO., ST. CHRISTOPHER (1957) Rev. Francis J. Keferl; Deacon Charles O. Wright; Joan Dunn, Pastoral Assoc.
Res.: 435 E. National Rd., 45377. Tel: 937-898-3542; Fax: 937-898-1017. Email: christophervandalia@catholicweb.com. Web: www.stchristopheronline.com.
School—(Grades K-8), 405 E. National Rd., 45377. Tel: 937-898-5104; Fax: 937-454-4790. Email: spk@stchris.cnd.pvt.k12.oh.us. Web: saintchrisschool.org. Sr. Patricia Kremer, Prin.; Sue Shira, Librarian. Lay Teachers 23; Students 389.
Catechesis/Religious Program—Email: lslattery@catholicweb.com. Students 342.

VERSAILLES, DARKE CO., ST. DENIS (1839) [CEM] Rev. David P. Vincent; Deacon Jack Borgerding.
Res.: 14 E. Wood St., 45380. Tel: 937-526-4945; Fax: 937-526-4893. Email: dvincent@bright.net. Web: www.stdenishf.org.
Catechesis/Religious Program—Tel: 937-526-3957. Linda Meyer, C.R.E. Students 562.

WAPAKONETA, AUGLAIZE CO., ST. JOSEPH (1839) [CEM] Revs. Patrick L. Sloneker; Matthew K. Lee, Parochial Vicar; Deacon Richard L. Westbay.
Office & Mailing Address: 309 S. Perry St., 45895. Tel: 419-738-2115; Fax: 419-738-4525. Email: stjoe@bright.net. Web: www.wapakstjoe.org.
Church: 101 W. Pearl St., 45895.
School—(Grades PreK-8), 1101 Lincoln Ave., 45895. Tel: 419-738-3311; Fax: 419-738-7706. Ronald Fahncke, Prin. Lay Teachers 5; Students 50.
Catechesis/Religious Program—Tel: 419-738-2115; Fax: 419-738-4525. Students 300.

WAYNESVILLE, WARREN CO., ST. AUGUSTINE (1876) [JC] Rev. Raymond Kammerer.
Res.: 5715 Lytle Rd., 45068. Tel: 513-897-2821; Fax: 513-897-2821.
Catechesis/Religious Program—Tel: 937-299-2772. Pat Ebright, D.R.E. Students 75.

WEST CHESTER, BUTLER CO., ST. JOHN (1880) Revs. Mark J. Burger; Don J. West; Deacon Gerald L. Barney.
Res.: 9080 Cincinnati-Dayton Rd., 45069. Tel: 513-777-6433; Fax: 513-777-9741. Email: info@stjohnwc.org. Web: www.stjohnwc.org.
See St. Gabriel Consolidated School, Cincinnati under Consolidated Elementary Schools located in the Institution section.
Catechesis/Religious Program—Tel: 513-755-4974. Students 300.

WEST MILTON, MIAMI CO., TRANSFIGURATION (1950) Rev. John D. MacQuarrie.
Res.: 972 S. Miami St., 45383. Tel: 937-698-4520; Fax: 937-698-4500. Email: transcathch@woh.rr.com. Web: www.transcatholic.com.
Catechesis/Religious Program—Students 183.

WEST UNION, ADAMS CO., HOLY TRINITY (1950) Rev. Theodore C. Kosse.
Res.: 612 E. Mulberry St., 45693. Tel: 937-544-2757; Fax: 937-544-1430.
Catechesis/Religious Program—Tel: 937-544-7637. Email: maryann.welling@holytrinity-ac.org. Students 48.

WILLIAMSBURG, CLERMONT CO., ST. ANN (1947) Rev. Bryan T. Reif.
Res. & Mailing Address: 140 N. Sixth St., Batavia, 45103. Tel: 513-732-2024; Fax: 513-732-0049. Email: alleluia@fuse.net.
Church: 370 S. 5th St., 45176. Tel: 513-724-7684.
Catechesis/Religious Program—Cynthia Barno, D.R.E. Students 31.

WILMINGTON, CLINTON CO., ST. COLUMBKILLE (1866) Rev. James M. Wedig; Deacons Robert G. Baker; Robert E. Meyer.
Res.: 73 N. Mulberry St., 45177-2277. Tel: 937-382-2236; Fax: 937-382-3234. Email: saintcolumbkille@yahoo.com. Web: www.stcolumbkille.org.
Catechesis/Religious Program—Tel: 937-382-1596. Students 249.

WITHAMSVILLE, CLERMONT CO., ST. THOMAS MORE (1940) Rev. William C. Wagner; Deacons John J. Convery, Pastoral Assoc.; Frederick J. Haas; Michael T. Thomas, Pastoral Assoc.
Res.: 800 Ohio Pike, 45245-2299. Tel: 513-752-2080 (Office); 513-753-2553 (Pastor); Fax: 513-753-2542. Email: stm@sttm.org. Web: www.sttm.org.
School—(Grades K-8), 788 Ohio Pike, 45245-2156. Tel: 513-753-2540, Ext. 122; Fax: 513-753-2554. Email: principal@sttm.org. Web: www.sttm-school.org. Mrs. Peggy Fischer, Prin. Lay Teachers 17; Students 297.
Catechesis/Religious Program—Tel: 513-753-2548; Fax: 513-753-2542. Mrs. Becky Ready, D.R.E. Students 145.

XENIA, GREENE CO., ST. BRIGID (1849) [CEM] Rev. John E. Krumm; Deacons Dennis Kall; Nicholas V. Kostic Jr.
Church & Mailing Address: 258 Purcell Dr., 45385. Tel: 937-372-3193; Fax: 937-374-3622.
Res.: 16 Lucerne Ave., Dayton, 45410. Tel: 937-258-1598.
School—(Grades PreK-8), 312 Fairground Rd., 45385. Tel: 937-372-3222. Patricia Harner, Prin. Lay Teachers 12; Students 196.
Catechesis/Religious Program—Tel: 937-372-3222. Students 108.

YELLOW SPRINGS, GREENE CO., ST. PAUL (1856) [CEM] Rev. Anthony J. Geraci; Deacon Paul E. Richardson.
Church & Mailing Address: 308 Phillips St., 45387. Tel: 937-767-7450; Fax: 937-767-7465. Email: stpauloffice@woh.rr.com. Web: www.stpaulchurchyso.org.
Catechesis/Religious Program—Email: stpauldre@woh.rr.com. Carole Grady, D.R.E. Students 100.

Closed and Merged Parishes

GREATER CINCINNATI
1—ST. ALOYSIUS CHURCH (Elmwood Place) Closed. For inquiries for parish records, contact St. Clement, (St. Bernard).
2—ST. BONAVENTURE (1869) Closed. For inquiries for parish records, contact St. Leo, Cincinnati.
3—ST. CHARLES BORROMEO CHURCH (Carthage) Closed. For inquiries for parish records, contact St. James of the Valley, (Wyoming).
4—COMMUNITY OF HOPE, Closed. For inquiries for parish records contact the chancery.
5—ST. ELIZABETH CHURCH (Norwood) Merged with St. Matthew Church, Norwood and Sts. Peter & Paul Church, Norwood to form Holy Trinity Church, Norwood. Records at Holy Trinity Church.
6—ST. GEORGE PARISH & NEWMAN CENTER, Closed. For inquiries for parish records contact St. Monica-St. George Newman Center.
7—HOLY ANGELS (1859) Merged with St. Francis de Sales, Cincinnati. Records at St. Francis de Sales.
8—ST. JOHN VIANNEY (Madison Pl.) (1949) Merged with St. Margaret of Cortona Parish, Cincinnati to form St. Margaret-St. John Parish, Cincinnati.
9—ST. MARGARET OF CORTONA (Madisonville) (1921) Merged with St. John Vianney Parish, Cincinnati to form St. Margaret-St. John Parish, Cincinnati.
10—ST. MATTHEW CHURCH (Norwood) Merged with St. Elizabeth Church, Norwood and Sts. Peter & Paul Church, Norwood to form Holy Trinity Church, Norwood. Records at Holy Trinity Church.
11—ST. MICHAEL CHURCH (LOWER PRICE HILL), Closed. For inquiries for parish records, contact Holy Family Parish, (Price Hill).
12—OUR LADY OF GRACE (Price Hill) Consolidated with Holy Family Parish. Records at Holy Family.
13—OUR LADY OF LORETTO (LINWOOD), Merged with St. Margaret of Cortona, Madisonville. Records with St. Margaret of Cortona.
14—OUR LADY OF PERPETUAL HELP (Sedamsville) Consolidated with Holy Family Parish, Price Hill. Records at Holy Family Parish.
15—OUR LADY OF PRESENTATION (ENGLISH WOODS), Closed. For inquiries for parish records contact St. Leo the Great, Cincinnati.
16—ST. PATRICK (Northside) Merged with St. Boniface, Cincinnati. See listing for details. Records at St. Boniface (Northside).
17—STS. PETER AND PAUL CHURCH (Norwood) Merged with St. Elizabeth Church, Norwood and St. Matthew Church, Norwood to form Holy Trinity Church, Norwood. Records at Holy Trinity Church.
18—ST. PIUS CHURCH (CUMMINSVILLE), Closed. For inquiries for parish records, contact St. Joseph Parish, Ezzard Charles Dr.
19—ST. RICHARD OF CHICHESTER (College Hill) Merged with St. Therese, the Little Flower, Cincinnati. See listing for details. Records at St. Therese, the Little Flower.
20—SAN ANTONIO DI PADOVA (FAIRMOUNT), (Italian), Refer to St. Leo for records.
21—ST. THOMAS AQUINAS (NORTH AVONDALE), Closed. For inquiries for parish records, contact St. Clement, St. Bernard.

BLANCHESTER, CLINTON CO., HOLY NAME (1853) Closed. For inquiries for parish records, see St. Columbille, Wilmington.
BLUE CREEK, ADAMS CO., ST. JOSEPH, Closed. For inquiries for parish records contact Holy Trinity, West Union.
DAYTON, MONTGOMERY CO.
1—ST. AGNES (1915) Closed. For Sacramental records, please see Corpus Christi, Dayton.
2—ASSUMPTION (1949) Merged with Our Lady of Mercy, Dayton.
3—ST. JAMES (1919) Closed. For Sacramental records, please see St. Benedict the Moor, Dayton.
4—SACRED HEART, Closed. For inquiries for parish records contact Emmanuel, Dayton.
FAYETTEVILLE, BROWN CO., ST. PATRICK (1837) [CEM] Closed. For inquiries for parish records, see St. Angela Merici, Fayetteville.
FELICITY, CLERMONT CO., OUR MOTHER OF GOOD COUNSEL, Closed. For inquiries for parish records please see St. Mary Church, Bethel.
HAMILTON, BUTLER CO.
1—ST. MARY, Merged now known as St. Julie Billiart. Records St. Julie Billiart, Hamilton.
2—ST. STEPHEN, Merged now known as St. Julie Billiart. Records St. Julie Billiart, Hamilton.
3—ST. VERONICA, Merged now known as St. Julie Billiart. Records St. Julie Billiart, Hamilton.
MANCHESTER, ADAMS CO., ST. MARY OF THE ASSUMPTION (1878) Closed. For inquiries for parish records please contact Holy Trinity, West Union.
SAINT MARTIN, BROWN CO., SAINT MARTIN (1830) [CEM] Closed. For inquiries for parish records, see St. Angela Merici, Fayetteville.
MIDDLETOWN, BUTLER CO.
1—HOLY TRINITY, Merged now known as Holy Family.
2—ST. JOHN THE BAPTIST, Merged now known as Holy Family.
3—ST. MARY, Merged now known as Holy Family.
NEW MIAMI, BUTLER CO., ST. LAWRENCE, Closed. For inquiries for parish records please see St. Julie Billiart, Hamilton.
NEW VIENNA, CLINTON CO., ST. MICHAEL (1874) Closed. For inquiries for parish records contact St. Benignus, Greenfield.
ST. PATRICK, SHELBY CO., ST. PATRICK, Closed. For inquiries for parish records contact St. Michael, Fort Loramie.
SPRINGFIELD, CLARK, CO., ST. MARY (1921) Closed. For inquiries for parish records please see St. Raphael, Springfield.
VERA CRUZ, BROWN CO., HOLY GHOST (VICARIATE), Closed. For inquiries for parish records contact St. Angela Merici, Fayetteville.

On Special and Archdiocesan Assignment:
Revs.—
Breaker, Donald J., P.O. Box 627, Fort Leonard Wood, MO 65473.
Elsbernd, James H., 6678 Paisley Dr., 45236.
Fecko, Leonard J., 2497 Riverside Dr., 45202.
Heis, Clarence G., 1140 Clifton Hills Dr., 45220.
Kindel, Joseph C., 6245 Wilmington Pike, Centerville, 45459.
Kroeger, John, 409 Elizabeth St., 45203.
Mick, Lawrence E., 3103 Observation Trail, Dayton, 45449. Tel: 937-434-4689
Peterka, Dale C., 7121 Plainfield Rd., 45236. Tel: 513-791-3238
Ruwe, Paul A., 2969 Otis Ave., Bronx, NY 10465.
Schmieder, Mark C., 1413 Garden Pl., 45246. Tel: 513-771-1877

On Duty Outside the Archdiocese:
Revs.—
McGuire, Frederick J., Blessed Trinity, 1600 54th Ave., St. Petersburg, FL 33712.
Nguyen, Linh N., St. Martha Church, 3702 Woodland Hills Dr., Kingwood, TX 77339.
Schmitmeyer, James M., P.O. Box 96, Quitaque, TX 79255.

Medical Leave of Absence:
Rev.—
Gaeke, Thomas M., 4578 Swigart Rd., Dayton, 45440.

Priests On Administrative Leave:
Revs.—
Cooper, Ronald C.
Feldhaus, Thomas F.
Kuhn, Thomas A.
Pater, Daniel R.
Reilly, David F.

Priests On Personal Leave:
Revs.—
Do, Tuan Anh
Fulmer, Jeffrey M.

Priests Commended to a Life of Prayer and Penance:
Revs.—
Hopp, Thomas R.
Massarella, Francis A. (Retired)

Retired:
Revs.—
Aichele, Raymond P., 2472 Picnic Woods, Lawrenceburg, IN 47025. Tel: 812-637-2490
Allison, Joseph C., 6019 Woodford Ct., #3, 45213. Tel: 513-731-5273
Axe, Thomas R., 2324 Madison Rd., 45208.
Bader, Paul A., 1044 W. Kemper Rd., 45240.
Beckman, Joseph F., 6616 Beechmont Ave., 45230. Tel: 513-624-0554
Bensman, Gerald E., S.T.L., 3505 Calumet Rd. #5A, Ludlow Falls, 45339. Tel: 937-719-3917
Bensman, John L., 2860 U.S. Rte. 127, Carthagena, 45822. Tel: 419-925-4516
Birarelli, Carl A., 3618 Prado Dr., Sarasota, FL 34235. Tel: 941-355-5246
Boeke, Anselm F., 2860 U.S. Rte. 127, Carthagena, 45822. Tel: 419-925-4516
Bruemmer, Joseph A., 5440 Moeller Ave., 45212. Tel: 513-351-4661
Bruening, Bernard H., 415 S. Heinke Rd., Miamisburg, 45342. Tel: 937-866-1550
Bruening, Joseph B., 5900 Delhi Rd., Mount Saint Joseph, 45051. Tel: 513-347-5311
Buening, Robert B., Corpus Christi, 2014 Springdale Rd., 45231. Tel: 513-825-0618
Byrne, James O., 2860 U.S. Rte. 127, Carthagena, 45822. Tel: 419-925-4516
Caserta, Angelo C., P.O. Box 1636, Piqua, 45356. Tel: 937-778-9526
Caserta, Charles W., 133 Douglas Dr., Lewisburg, 45338. Tel: 937-272-6761
Collins, James R., 19 Woodview Ct., 45246. Tel: 513-648-9659
Dettenwanger, Dennis, 135 Garfield Pl., #617, 45202.
Dorrmann, William J., 110 N. Hill St., Harrison, 45030. Tel: 513-367-1588
Emerick, Stephen J., 5371 S. Milford Rd. Room 86E, Milford, 45150. Tel: 513-248-8002
Evers, Gerard A., 1960 Madison Rd. #112, 45206. Tel: 513-487-3512
Gerdes, Harry J., Bayley Place, 928 Bayley Place Dr., 45233. Tel: 513-347-5647
Goetz, Joseph W., 1528 Turnberry Village Dr., Dayton, 45458. Tel: 937-432-6589
Guntzelman, Louis J., P.O. Box 428541, 45242.
Hackman, Marvin R., 121 Dover Rd., Springfield, 45504. Tel: 937-390-0925

Hater, Robert J., 1443 Cedar Ave., 45224. Tel: 513-541-4611
Henz, Kenneth W., 1805 John Glenn Rd., Dayton, 45420. Tel: 937-253-2829
Hohlmayer, Louis R., 3505 Calumet Rd., #1A, Ludlow Falls, 45339. Tel: 937-698-6757
Hoying, Leo A., 2860 US Rte. 127 #120, Celina, 45822-9533. Tel: 419-925-4516
Hussey, Edmund M., 3714 Falls Circle Dr., Hilliard, 43026. Tel: 614-771-2736
Keller, Neil J., 836 N. Hill Ln., 45224. Tel: 513-522-5578
Klug, Richard L., S.T.L., 3776 Francis Ave., 45211. Tel: 513-622-3049
Kummer, John R., 3505 Calumet Rd. #3B, Ludlow Falls, 45339. Tel: 937-698-5019
Lammeier, Francis G., 12120 Regency Run Ct. #7, 45240. Tel: 513-742-9982
Langenbrunner, Norman, 7864 Gapstow Bridge, 45231. Tel: 513-376-8191
Lutmer, Joseph H., 6940 Miami Hills Dr., 45234. Tel: 513-793-9937
Macpherson, Walter, 4830 Salem Ave. #1, Dayton, 45416.
Mattscheck, John J., 3468 Robb Ave., 45211. Tel: 513-389-9366
Mauntel, Robert J., 19 Mohave Dr., Sardinia, 45171. Tel: 937-446-3491
McCarthy, Donald G., 5222 N. Bend Rd., 45247. Tel: 513-661-6565
Meehan, Terence A., 3171 Bridget St., Dayton, 45418.
Meyer, Harry J., 4010 Townsely Dr., Loveland, 45140. Tel: 513-697-1048
Mick, Lawrence J., 1500 Linneman Rd., 45238. Tel: 513-922-5400
Miller, Francis J., 4988 Lord Alfred Ct., 45241-2196. Tel: 513-247-0966
Monnin, Robert J., 546 Unger Ave., Englewood, 45322. Tel: 937-540-1074
Mueller, Eugene J., 3055 Inwood Dr., 45241. Tel: 513-769-4908
Neiheisel, Stanley H., 320 Donham St., 45226.
Nguyen, Huan Tien, 314 Township Ave., 45216. Tel: 513-225-8221
Niehaus, Francis H., P.O. Box 727, Florence, KY 41022.
Niemeier, Dennis A., 1521 Nature Trail Way, 45231. Tel: 513-648-0976
O'Connor, James J., 319 Mulberry Pl., Sidney, 45365. Tel: 937-492-9577
Pater, Giles H., 1435 Meadowbright, 45230. Tel: 513-233-0066
Perin, Glen W., 3505 Calumet Rd., #1-B, Ludlow Falls, 45339. Tel: 937-698-6713
Porter, John E., 3505 Calumet Rd., #3A, Ludlow Falls, 45339. Tel: 937-698-5989
Raudabaugh, Joseph R., 3505 Calumet Rd. #4B, Ludlow Falls, 45339. Tel: 937-698-4821
Rehling, Paul L., 135 Garfield Pl., #517, 45202. Tel: 513-921-6739
Robisch, David C., 3 Sheldon Close, 45227. Tel: 513-271-4246
Rohrkemper, Charles, 2860 U.S. Rte. 127, Carthagena, 45822. Tel: 937-925-4516
Rudemiller, Edward L., 990 Bayley Pl., 45233. Tel: 513-347-5599
Seher, Philip O., 5536 Palisades Dr., 45238.
Shelander, Donald E., P.O. Box 11469, 45211.
Shine, Edward J., 212 George St., Harrison, 45030.
Smith, Elmer W., 3105 Madison Rd., 45209. Tel: 513-871-5757
Stricker, Robert A., 5560 Kirby Rd., 45239. Tel: 513-541-5560
Thomas, William V., 3505 Calumet Rd., #4A, Ludlow Falls, 45339. Tel: 937-698-5960
Thorsen, Robert J., 4580 E. Galbraith Rd., 45236. Tel: 513-745-9600
Trick, James F., 2860 Rte. 127, Carthagena, 45822-9591. Tel: 419-925-4516
Trippel, Edward G., 476 Riddle Rd., #612, 45220. Tel: 513-281-8001
Vonderhaar, Eugene F., 10560 Blocker Rd., Bradford, 45308.
Wall, John E., 5222 N. Bend Rd., 45247. Tel: 513-661-6565
Wessling, John E., 10095 Wayside Dr., #259, 45241. Tel: 513-779-5350
Westerhoff, Ralph A., 843 Neeb Rd. #1, 45233. Tel: 513-921-2021
Wilker, Ronald H., 7001 Cottonwood Rd., Celina, 45822. Tel: 419-268-2842
Witsken, Gary J., 5848 Bayou Ct., 45248. Tel: 513-347-0134
Wolfer, Robert R., c/o 230 Cloverhill Ter., 45238.

Permanent Deacons:
Ascolese, Michael A., St. Bartholomew, Cincinnati
Aufderheide, William, (Retired)
Baker, Robert, St. Columbkille, Wilmington
Baldwin, Russell O., St. Peter, Huber Heights
Balster, Randolph L., St. Henry Cluster Parishes
Baltes, Leonard W., (Retired)
Bardonaro, Mark A., St. Dominic, Cincinnati
Barney, Gerald L., St. John, West Chester
Beck, Henry B., Our Lady of the Rosary, Dayton
Belcher, Halver L., St. Augustine, Minster
Bermick, Stephen, III, St. Mary, Franklin
Bertke, Omer H., St. John the Baptist, Maria Stein
Borgerding, Jonathan P., St. Denis, Versailles; Holy Family, Frenchtown
Bornhorst, Gregory A., Holy Redeemer, New Bremen
Brodeur, Wilfred J., (Retired)
Brown, Steven R., J.C.L., St. Elizabeth Ann Seton, Milford
Bruce, George R., St. William, Cincinnati
Brunsman, Willard, St. Aloysius, Shandon
Bryant, Herman, St. Gabriel, Cincinnati
Burger, Raymond S., St. Margaret Mary, Cincinnati
Buschur, Jerome L., St. Henry, St. Henry
Cain, Jerome, St. Saviour, Cincinnati (Blue Ash)
Camele, David G., (Retired)
Carlin, John K., St. Patrick, Troy
Cecere, Gregory, Queen of Apostles, Dayton
Cohen, Kim, St. Thomas More, Sarasota, FL
Coleman, Terrell, St. Lawrence, Rhine; Immaculate Conception, Botkins
Coll, Joseph J., St. Columban, Loveland
Collins, John R., St. Joseph & St. Raphael, Springfield
Collins, Robert, St. Charles Borromeo, Kettering
Convery, John J., St. Thomas More, Withamsville
Corson, John, Corpus Christi, New Burlington
Couzins, Jerome, (Unassigned)
Coyle, Thomas J., Holy Family, Middletown
Crook, Robert A., St. Patrick, Bellefontaine
Crooker, Timothy, St. James the Greater, White Oak
Davenport, Michael D., (Retired)
Dawson, David A., (Unassigned)
Day, Larry H., Corpus Christi, New Burlington
Deardorff, Roy L., (Retired)
Dehanes, Kenneth J., Sr., St. Michael, Sharonville
Desmond, Mark, Holy Cross-Immaculata, Cincinnati
Dipple, Harold I., St. Patrick, Bellefontaine
Duffy, Roger E., Church of the Incarnation, Centerville
Dupree, Gerald M., St. Luke, Beavercreek
Edwards, Dennis, St. Mark, Cincinnati
Etienne, Jerald F., St. Mary, Bethel
Faeth, Thomas J., St. William, Cincinnati
Fey, Robert, Guardian Angels, Cincinnati
Fischesser, Elmer, Mercy Hospital, Fairfield
Flamm, Gerald A., St. Gabriel, Glendale
Gagliarducci, Anthony, St. Ignatius, Monfort Heights
Gallenstein, Richard W., Good Shepherd, Cincinnati
George, Raymond W., St. Matthias, Cincinnati
Geraci, James L., (Retired)
Gerke, John P., St. Clement, St. Bernard
Glassmeyer, Robert A., (Retired)
Gloeckler, Donald, Our Lord Christ the King, Cincinnati
Glynn, John T., (Retired)
Gobbi, John R., St. John Neumann, Cincinnati
Gould, John E., St. Peter, Huber Heights
Grismer, Raymond L., (Retired)
Haas, Frederick J., St. Thomas More, Withamsville
Hall, Jeffrey, Sr., St. Albert the Great, Kettering
Harris, Timothy J., St. Peter, Huber Heights
Hennessey, James F., Holy Trinity, Batavia
Hildebrand, Victor B., Ascension, Kettering
Holthaus, John G., Holy Angels, Sidney
Horstman, Norman G., St. Raphael & St. Joseph, Springfield
Hucke, Walter A., Jr., Our Lady of the Rosary, Greenhills
Huff, Thomas, Holy Trinity, Coldwater
Janowiecki, Richard J., Precious Blood, Dayton
Jenkins, Charles J., Our Lady of Victory, Cincinnati
Jernigan, Jacob, (Retired)
Jones, James E., Good Shepherd, Cincinnati
Jurosic, Nicholas T., St. John Fryberg; St. Patrick, Glynwood
Kall, Dennis, St. Brigid, Xenia
Keller, David R., (Leave of Absence)
Klingshirn, David, Cathedral of St. Peter in Chains, Cincinnati
Klosterman, Roger L., St. Augustine, Minster
Kluener, Paul, St. James, White Oak
Knight, Michael R., St. Patrick, Troy
Kolis, Conrad C., St. James of the Valley, Wyoming
Kostic, Nicholas V., Jr., St. Brigid, Xenia
Kowalski, James, (Retired)
Kozlowski, Robert R., Sacred Heart, New Carlisle
Kraus, Daniel E., Ascension, Kettering
Kroger, Raymond, St. Margaret of York, Twenty Mile Stand
Krumm, William T., Holy Family, Middletown
Leibold, Paul F., St. Mary, Hillsboro
Lim, Amado L., All Saints, Cincinnati
Lochtefeld, Virgil V., Holy Trinity, Coldwater
Luthman, Paul, Sacred Heart, McCartyville
Lynd, Thomas, Sts. Peter & Paul, Reading
Maag, Lawrence A., St. Vivian, Cincinnati
Mahoney, Michael, St. Henry, Dayton
Martin, Richaed W., Our Lady of Good Hope, Miamisburg
Martin, William, (Unassigned)
Mascorro, Susano, St. Helen, Dayton
Merrell, Jeffrey, St. Maximillian Kolbe, Liberty Township
Merritt, James A., St. Susanna, Mason
Meyer, David, Guardian Angels, Cincinnati
Meyer, Donald J., Jr., St. John the Baptist, Harrison
Meyer, Robert E., St. Columbkille, Wilmington
Mignery, Michael E., Queen of Peace, Millville
Miller, Allen K., (Retired)
Miller, James A., St. Columban, Loveland
Mullaney, William M., Immaculate Heart of Mary, Cincinnati
Murphy, Daniel R., St. Veronica, Cincinnati
Myers, Philip B., Holy Angels, Sidney
Nagy, Norbert, St. Peter, Huber Heights
Novick, Rick, Guardian Angels, Cincinnati
Obleness, Ralph F., St. Helen, Dayton
Olinger, James C., St. Rita, Dayton
Palumbo, Patrick A., St. John Neumann, Cincinnati
Parker, John G., Mary, Help of Christians, Fort Recovery
Parker, Leonard B., St. Mary, Hillsboro
Perry, Robert W., Our Lady, Queen of Peace, Wright Patterson Air Force Base
Petrie, William J., (Retired)
Pitts, Joseph L., Jr., St. Francis of Assisi, Centerville
Platfoot, Thomas F., Our Lady of Mercy, Queen of Martyrs, & Corpus Christi, Dayton
Quattrone, John M., St. Ann, Groesbeck
Rader, Daniel L., St. Susanna, Mason
Reder, Richard J., Assumption, Mt. Healthy
Reising, Edward B., St. Columban, Loveland
Renneker, William B., St. Julie Billiart, Hamilton
Richardson, Paul E., St. Paul, Yellow Springs
Risch, Ronald H., St. John Neumann, Cincinnati
Riva-Saleta, Luis O., St. Aloysius on-the-Ohio, Cincinnati
Roadruck, Max, Mary Help of Christians, Fairborn
Rogers, Earl, St. Mary, Urbana
Rose, Gregory L., St. Teresa of Avila, Cincinnati
Royer, Milton W., Queen of Martyrs, Our Lady of Mercy, & Corpus Christi, Dayton
Saluke, William M., St. Mary, Dayton
Sasson, Gerard J., St. Columban, Loveland
Schellman, Leon, Good Shepherd, Cincinnati
Schmidl, George L., St. Ann, Hamilton
Schmidt, Joseph Ted, (Retired)
Schmiesing, John J., St. Augustine, Minster
Schneider, Jerry R., St. Aloysius Gonzaga, Cincinnati
Schroeder, Robert J., St. Antoninus, Cincinnati
Schutte, Timothy, St. Andrew, Milford
Shaffer, David, Immaculate Heart of Mary, Anderson
Shea, David J., Immaculate Heart of Mary, Cincinnati
Simmons, Raphael, St. Joseph, Cincinnati
Slattery, John M., (Unassigned)
Sonnenberg, James J., (Retired)
Srode, Walter, St. Veronica, Mt. Carmel
Staab, Robert A., Jr., Assumption, Mt. Healthy
Stang, Ronald L., St. Peter, New Richmond
Stasiak, Mark, St. Francis of Assisi, Centerville
Steward, Herschel R., St. Francis De Sales, Lebanon
Strodtbeck, Thomas M., St. Julie Billiart, Hamilton
Subler, Joseph, St. Paul, Englewood
Sunderman, James P., St. Jude the Apostle, Cincinnati
Thamann, John D., St. Mary, Cincinnati
Thomas, Dan, Our Lady of Sorrows, Monroe
Thomas, Michael T., St. Thomas More, Withamsville
Vilaboy, Manuel D., (Retired)
Wagner, Francis X., St. Michael, Cincinnati
Walker, Harry S., St. Columban, Loveland
Wersching, J. Phillip, (Retired)
Westbay, Richard L., St. Joseph, Wapakoneta
Westerfield, Thomas E., Our Lady of Lourdes, Cincinnati
Winters, Royce E., St. Agnes, Cincinnati
Woeste, James H., St. Elizabeth Seton, Rockford, IL
Wright, Charles O., St. Christopher, Vandalia
Yetter, Jerry J., St. Boniface, Cincinnati
Zinck, Robert C., Jr., Incarnation, Centerville
Zvonar, George J., Holy Trinity, Dayton

INSTITUTIONS LOCATED IN THE ARCHDIOCESE

[A] THE ATHENAEUM OF OHIO

CINCINNATI. *The Athenaeum of Ohio* (1829) Mt. St. Mary's Seminary, 6616 Beechmont Ave., 45230. Tel: 513-231-2223; Fax: 513-231-3254. Email: ath@athenaeum.edu. Web: www.athenaeum.edu. Most Rev. Daniel E. Pilarczyk, S.T.D., Ph.D., D.D., Archbishop of Cincinnati, Chancellor, Chm. of Bd. of Trustees; Revs. Edward P. Smith, M.A., Pres. & Rector; Earl K. Fernandes, S.T.D., Dean, Mt. St. Mary's Seminary; Dr. Terrance Callan, Ph.D., Dean, Athenaeum; Mr. Dennis K. Eagan, B.B.A., Vice Pres., Finance Admin. Incorporated March 24, 1928 by the State of Ohio and presently has three divisions: Mt. St. Mary's Seminary of the West; the Lay Pastoral Ministry Program and the Special Studies Division.

Lay Pastoral Ministry Program, 6616 Beechmont Ave., 45230. Tel: 513-231-1200; Fax: 513-231-3254. Dr. Susan McGurgan, M.A.R., Dir.; Sr. Nancy McMullen, C.PP.S., Prog. Coord.; Mr. Thomas Giordano, M.Div., Assoc. Dir.; Janice VonHandorf, M.A.P.M., Assoc. Dir. Special Studies Division: Dr. Terrance Callan, Ph.D., Dean; Rev. Benedict O'Cinnsealaigh, S.T.D., Dir. Permanent Deacon Program; Ms. Tracy Koenig, M.A., M.L.S., Librarian.

The St. Gregory Seminary Trust, 100 E. Eighth St., 45202.

[B] SEMINARIES

CINCINNATI. *Mt. St. Mary's Seminary of the West* (1829) (Diocesan), 6616 Beechmont Ave., 45230. Tel: 513-231-2223; Fax: 513-231-3254. Email: ath@mtsm.org. Web: www.athenaeum.edu. Rev. Edward P. Smith, M.A., Rector; Dr. Terrance Callan, Ph.D., Athenaeum Academic Dean; Revs. Earl K. Fernandes, S.T.D., Seminary Dean; Michael W. Davis, M.Ed. Admin. (MIA), Spiritual Dir.; Ken Morman, S.S.L. (TOL), Dean of Students; Mr. Thomas Giordano, M.Div., Dir. of Pastoral Internship; Rev. Benedict O'Cinnsealaigh, S.T.D., Dir. of Formation; Michael E. Sweeney, M.A., Registrar; Mr. Dennis K. Eagan, B.B.A., Vice Pres., Finance & Admin.; Mr. Kevin Prendergast, Dir. Pastoral Counseling Degree; Mr. James W. Jackson, B.A., Dir. Devel. Major seminary for students in Theology. Priests 17; Sisters 3; Lay Teachers 30; Seminarians 36; Students 198. In Res. Revs. Joseph F. Beckman (Retired); Anthony M. Brausch, Ph.L.; Michael W. Davis, M.Ed. Admin. (MIA); Earl K. Fernandes, S.T.D.; J. Robert Jack, M.A.; Benedict O'Cinnsealaigh, S.T.D.; Theodore Ross, S.J., S.T.L.; Timothy P. Schehr, Ph.D.; Michael A. Seger, S.T.D.; Edward P. Smith, M.A.; Ken Morman, S.S.L. (TOL); Francis W. Voellmecke, Ph.D.

Non-Resident Faculty: Sr. Betty Jane Lillie, Ph.D.; Dr. Terrance Callan, Ph.D.; Mr. Anthony Dicello, M.M.; Ms. Tracy Koenig, M.A., M.L.S., Librarian; Mr. Kevin Prendergast; Mr. Dennis K. Eagan, B.B.A.; Mr. James W. Jackson, B.A.; Deacon Dave Shea, D.Min.; Dr. John Gutting, Ph.D.

[C] NOVITIATES AND HOUSES OF STUDY

CINCINNATI. *St. Anthony Shrine, Franciscan Postulancy* (1888) St. John the Baptist Province, 5000 Colerain Ave., 45223-1213. Tel: 513-541-2146; Fax: 513-541-9347. Revs. Kenan Freson, O.F.M., Liaison Sponsored Ministries; Carl J. Langenderfer, O.F.M., Dir. of Postulants & Vicar; Frank Geers, O.F.M., Assoc. Dir. of Postulants; Daniel Kroger, O.F.M., CEO-St. Anthony Messenger Press.; Frank Jasper, O.F.M., Vicar Prov.; Joseph Ricchini, O.F.M., Spiritual Dir.; Humbert Moster, O.F.M., Sacramental Min. for St. Peter/St. Mary of the Rock, IN; Bonaventure Bai, O.F.M., Chap. Mercy Hospital, Mt. Airy Campus; Bros. Gabriel Balassone, O.F.M., Porter; Scott Obrecht, O.F.M., (On Sabbatical); Gene Mayer, O.F.M., Guardian, Sec. of the Prov.; Brian Maloney, O.F.M., Dir. Friar Works (Devel.) Office. Priests 8; Brothers 4; Postulants 3.

Dominican Novitiate, 7630 Shawnee Run Rd., 45243. Tel: 513-527-3972; Fax: 513-527-3973. Email: wcw93@mac.com. Web: www.op-stjoseph.org. Rev. Walter C. Wagner, O.P., Novice Master & Contact Person. Novices 11.

DAYTON. *Marianist Novitiate*, 4435 E. Patterson Rd., 45430-1095. Tel: 937-426-5721; Fax: 937-429-4686. Rev. Michael Lisbeth, S.M., Dir. of Novices; Bro. Michael O'Grady, S.M., Asst. Dir. of Novices. Priests 2; Brothers 7; Novices 2.

[D] COLLEGES AND UNIVERSITIES

CINCINNATI. *College of Mount St. Joseph* (1920) 5701 Delhi Rd., 45233-1670. Tel: 513-244-4200; Fax: 513-244-4654. Email: petra_hofstedt@mail.msj.edu. Web: www.msj.edu. Mr. Tony Aretz, Ph.D., Pres.; Anne Marie Wagner, Chief Fin. Officer; Alan deCourcy, Chief Academic Officer; Keith Weber, Chief Information Officer; Douglas Frizzell, Dean of Students; Paul Jenkins, Dir., Library Svcs.; Kathleen Lundrigan, Dir. Mktg. Coed. Chartered by the State of Ohio. Priests 1; Sisters 4; Lay Teachers 227; Students 2,324; Total Staff 241.

Xavier University (1831) 3800 Victory Pkwy., 45207. Tel: 513-745-3000; Fax: 513-745-4223. Email: vezina@xavier.edu. Web: www.xu.edu. Revs. Michael J. Graham, S.J., Pres.; Richard W. Bollman, S.J., Pastor & Rector, Bellarmine Chapel; Dr. James Snodgrass III, Assoc. Dean College of Arts & Sciences; Dr. Debra Mooney, Assoc. Vice Pres. Mission & Identity; Dr. Hema Krishnan, Assoc. Dean Williams College of Business; Mr. Allen Cole, Registrar; Dr. Roger A. Fortin, Academic Vice Pres. & Provost; Dr. Mark Meyers, Dean College of Social Sciences, Health & Educ.; Robert Hill, Assoc. Vice Pres. Mktg. & Printing Svcs.; Maribeth Amyot, Vice Pres. Fin. Admin.; Dr. John F. Kucia, Admin. Vice Pres.; Dr. Ali Malekzadeh, Dean Williams College of Business; Mr. Gary R. Massa, Vice Pres. Univ. Rels.; Mr. David Dodd, Vice Pres. Information Resources & CIO; Dr. Kathleen Simons, Assoc. Provost Student Life & Leadership; Jackie Vezina, Contact Person; Dr. Janice Walker, Dean College of Arts & Sciences; Sheila Doran, Acting Dean Center Adult and Part-time Students; Robert Cotter, Assoc. Vice Pres. Information Resources & Dir. Discovery Svcs. College of Arts & Sciences Enrollment 1,983; Williams College of Business Undergraduates 1,025; College of Social Sciences Enrollment 1,075; Center for Adults & Part-time Students Enrollment 145; Graduate Program Enrollment 2,738; Permanent Staff: Priests 14; Sisters 2; Faculty (Full-Time): Priests 4; Lay Teachers 312.

DAYTON. *The University of Dayton* (1850) (Coed), 300 College Park Ave., 45469-1660. Tel: 937-229-1000; Fax: 937-229-4000. Web: www.udayton.edu. Dr. Daniel J. Curran, Ph.D., Pres.; David J. O'Brien, Ph.D., Univ. Prof. Faith & Culture; Joseph E. Saliba, Ph.D., Provost (Interim); Prof. Joseph Untener, M.S., BME, Assoc. Provost, Faculty & Administrative Affairs; Mr. Thomas E. Burkhardt, B.S., M.S., Vice Pres. for Finance Affairs & Admin. Svcs.; Timothy J. Wabler, B.S.B., Vice Pres. & Dir. of Athletics; Sr. Annette T. Schmelling, R.S.C.J., Vice Pres. Student Devel. & Dean of Students; Rev. Paul M. Marshall, S.M., M.Div., Rector; Mr. S. Ted Bucaro, B.A., M.A., Govt. & Regl. Rels. Dir.; Ms. Lynnette Heard, B.A., M.A., Exec. Dir. Pres. Office; Beth Keyes, Asst. Vice Pres. Facilities Mgmt; Mr. Thomas J. Westendorf, B.S., MBA, Asst. Vice Pres. & Registrar; J. Kathy McEuen Harmon, B.F.A., Exec. Dir. Fin. Aid; Joyce Carter, B.A., Vice Pres. Human Resources; Michael McCabe, Ph.D., Vice Pres. & Exec. Dir. Research Inst.; Deborah A. Read, Vice Pres. Univ. Advancement; Sundar Kumarasamy, Vice Pres. Enrollment Mgmt.; Dr. Deborah J. Bickford, Ph.D., Assoc. Provost Academic Affairs & Learning Initiatives; Dr. Thomas D. Skill, Ph.D., Assoc. Provost & Chief Information Officer; Ms. Lisa Risimiller, B.A., M.P.A., Dir. Women's Center; Revs. Norbert C. Burns, S.M.; Gerald T. Chinchar, S.M., D.Min.; Christopher W. Conlon, S.M.; Eugene Contadino, S.M., B.A., M.A., Ph.D.; Francois Rossier, S.M.; Joseph F. Kozar, S.M., Ph.D.; Paul M. Marshall, S.M., M.Div.; Paul F. Vieson, S.M.; Joseph P. Tedesco, S.M.; Thomas A. Thompson, S.M.; John S. Putka, S.M., Ph.D.; Bertrand A. Buby, S.M., Ph.D.; John A. McGrath; Johann B.G. Roten, S.M., S.T.D.; Joseph D. Massucci; Christopher T. Wittmann, S.M., Dir. Campus Min.; James Schimelpfening, S.M., D.Min.; Bros. Philip T. Aaron, S.M., Ph.D.; William M. Fackovec, S.M., M. S.L.S.; Thomas Farnsworth, S.M.; Raymond L. Fitz, S.M., Ph.D.; Victor M. Forlani, S.M., M.B.A., D.B.A.; Darwin Joseph George, S.M.; Robert H. Hughes, S.M.; Daniel L. Klco, S.M., M.S.; M. Gary Marcinowski, S.M., M.F.A. ; Thomas E. Oldenski, S.M.; Ronald Overman, S.M.; Thomas J. Pieper, S.M.; Thomas Wendorf, S.M., Ph.D.; Edward E. Zamierowski, S.M.; Sisters Jean Frisk, I.S.S.M., M.A., S.T.L.; Leanne Jablonski, F.M.I.; Linda Lee Jackson, O.P.; Laura M. Leming, F.M.I., Ph.D.; Alice Ann O'Neill, S.C., D.M.A.; Danielle M. Peters, I.S.S.M., S.T.L.; Kathleen A. Rossman, O.S.F.; Dennis Tisler; Nicole D. Trahan, F.M.I.; Pamela L. Thimmes, O.S.F., Ph.D.; Judith G. Martin, S.S.J., Ph.D.; Angela Ann Zukowski, M.H.S.H., D.Min.; Mary Louise Foley, F.M.I. Society of Mary (Marianists). Priests 3; Brothers 6; Sisters 2; Lay Teachers 463; Students 10,909.

College of Arts and Sciences (1882) Tel: 937-229-2611; Fax: 937-229-2615. Dr. Paul H. Benson, Ph.D., Dean; Donald L. Pair, Ph.D., Assoc. Dean for Integrated Learning & Curriculum; Dr. Mary J. Brown, Ph.D., Assoc. Dean for Fin. Information & Data Analysis; Donald J. Polzella, Ph.D., Assoc. Dean for Faculty Devel. & Graduate Prog. Professors 279; Students 3,407.

Graduate School Tel: 937-229-2390; Fax: 937-229-4545. Dr. Thomas F. Eggemeier, Ph.D., Dean of Graduate School; Dr. Edward F. Mykytka, Ph.D., Assoc. Dean Graduate School.

School of Business Administration (1921) Tel: 937-229-3731; Fax: 937-229-3301. Dr. Matthew D. Shank, Ph.D., Dean; Dr. Elizabeth F. Gustafson, Ph.D., Assoc. Dean; Dr. Paul D. Sweeney, Ph.D., Assoc. Dean. Professors 60; Students 1,767.

School of Education (1920) Tel: 937-229-3146; Fax: 937-229-3199. Dr. Thomas J. Lasley, Ph.D., Dean; Dr. C. Daniel Raisch, Ph.D., Assoc. Dean Admin.; Dr. H. Roberta Weaver, Ed.D., Assoc. Dean Community Outreach. Professors 49; Students 3,053.

School of Engineering (1910) 45469. Tel: 937-229-2736; Fax: 937-229-2756. Dr. Tony E. Saliba, Ph.D., Dean; Dr. Malcolm W. Daniels, Ph.D., Assoc. Dean. Professors 60; Students 1,949.

School of Law (1974) Tel: 937-229-3211; Fax: 937-229-4769. Lisa A. Kloppenberg, J.D., Dean; Richard D. Perna, J.D., Assoc. Dean for Academic Affairs. Professors 27; Students 503.

Libraries and Information Technologies Tel: 937-229-4265.

The Marian Library/International Marian Research Institute (IMRI) (1943) Tel: 937-229-4124; Fax: 937-229-4258. Revs. Johann B.G. Roten, S.M., S.T.D., Dir. International Marian Research Inst.; Thomas A. Thompson, S.M., Dir. & Curator, Marian Library.

Institute for Pastoral Initiatives (1971) Tel: 937-229-3126; Fax: 937-229-3130. Sr. Angela Ann Zukowski, M.H.S.H., D.Min., Dir.; Kathleen M. Webb, M.L.S., Dean of Libraries; Fred W. Jenkins, Ph.D., Assoc. Dean of Libraries, Collections Opers.

University of Dayton (1850) 45469-1390. Tel: 937-229-4214.

SAINT MARTIN. *Chatfield College* (1971) Brown County Ursulines, 20918 State Rte. 251, St. Martin, 45118. Tel: 513-875-3344; Fax: 513-875-3912. Email: john.tafaro@chatfield.edu. Web: www.chatfield.edu. John P. Tafaro, Pres.; Dolores Berish, Librarian. Faculty 2; Adjunct Faculty 51; Staff 21; Students 251.

[E] HIGH SCHOOLS, INTER-PAROCHIAL

CINCINNATI. *Elder High School* (1922) 3900 Vincent Ave., 45205-1699. Tel: 513-921-3744; Fax: 513-921-8123. Email: otten.t@elderhs.org. Web: www.elderhs.org. Tom Otten, Prin. & Contact Person; Rev. Donald R. Rettig. Priests 1; Lay Teachers 60; Students 899.

LaSalle High School (1960) 3091 N. Bend Rd., 45239-7696. Tel: 513-741-3000; Fax: 513-741-2666. Web: www.cincinnatilasalle.net/. Mr. Thomas Luebbe, Prin.; Jacob McCullough, Librarian & Media Center Specialist. Priests 1; Lay Teachers 62; Students 758.

McAuley High School, 6000 Oakwood Ave., 45224. Tel: 513-681-1800; Fax: 513-681-1802. Email: sucherc@mcauleyhs.net. Web: www.mcauleyhs.net. Mrs. Cheryl A. Sucher, Pres. & Contact Person; Mr. Christopher Pastura, Prin.; Mrs. Connie Kampschmidt, Asst. Prin.; Mrs. Kelly Grote, Asst. Prin.; Mrs. Becky Reilly, Librarian. Sisters of Mercy 2; Lay Teachers 59; Girls 720.

McNicholas High School, 6536 Beechmont Ave., 45230. Tel: 513-231-3500; Fax: 513-231-1351. Email: gsaelens@mcnhs.org. Web: www.mcnhs.org. Gregory R. Saelens, Prin.; Kathy Bollmer, Librarian. Lay Teachers 61; Students 710.

Moeller High School (1959) 9001 Montgomery Rd., 45242. Tel: 513-791-1680; Fax: 513-792-3343. Email: bbalbach@moeller.org. Web: www.moeller.org. Mr. Blane Collison, Prin.; William J. Balbach, Treas. & Contact Person. Sisters of Mercy 1; Marianist Brothers 3; Lay Teachers 55; Students 920.

Mother of Mercy High School, 3036 Werk Rd., 45211. Tel: 513-661-2740; Fax: 513-661-1842. Email: merkle_n@motherofmercy.org. Web: www.motherofmercy.org. Sr. Nancy Merkle, R.S.M., Prin. Sisters of Mercy 1; Lay Teachers 50; Girls 500.

Mt. Notre Dame High School, 711 E. Columbia Ave., 45215. Tel: 513-821-3044; Fax: 513-821-6068. Web: www.mndhs.org. Sr. Rita Sturwold, S.N.D.deN., Pres.; Mrs. Maureen Baldock, Prin. Sisters 4; Lay Teachers 70; Girls 751.

Purcell Marian High School (East Walnut Hills), 2935 Hackberry St., 45206. Tel: 513-751-1230;

Fax: 513-751-1395. Web: www.purcellmarian.org. Al Early, Pres.; Robert Obert, Bus. Mgr.; Bro. Ray Dominguez, S.M., Dir. Ministry; Paul Ramstetter, Prin.; Ms. Allison Nunery, Librarian. Priests 1; Brothers 2; Sisters 2; Lay Teachers 29; Students 410.

Roger Bacon High School (1928) 4320 Vine St., 45217. Tel: 513-641-1300; Fax: 513-641-0498. Email: wfarris@rogerbacon.org. Web: www.rogerbacon.org. Rick Stollmann, Prin.; Amy M. Wilson, Contact Person; Rev. William Farris, O.F.M., Pres.; Bro. Christopher Cahill, O.F.M., Computer Network Coord. Teacher; Rev. Mark J. Hudak, O.F.M., Teacher; Brandon Cowans, Dir. Retention Recruitment; Donna Briggs, Media Specialist. Franciscan Friars of the Cincinnati Province of St. John the Baptist. Priests 2; Brothers 1; Lay Teachers 40; Students 500.

Seton High School (Price Hill), 3901 Glenway Ave., 45205. Tel: 513-471-2600; Fax: 513-471-0529. Email: gibbonss@setoncincinnati.org. Web: www.setoncincinnati.org. Sr. Patricia Cruise, S.C., Pres.; Ms. Susan M. Gibbons, Prin.; Ms. Roberta Riser-Jennings, Vice Pres. Inst. Devel.; Mrs. Donna Brigger, Assoc. Prin.; Marianne Ridiman, Dir. Admissions; Mrs. Janice Linz, Campus Min.; Ms. Monica Williams-Mitchell, Librarian. Sisters of Charity of Cincinnati 4; Lay Teachers 37; Students 539.

DAYTON. *Archbishop Alter High School* (1962) 940 E. David Rd., Kettering, 45429. Tel: 937-434-4434; Fax: 937-434-0507. Email: alter@alterhighschool.org. Web: www.alterhighschool.org. Mrs. Nicole Brainard, Prin.; Mrs. Pat Brown, Librarian. Priests 1; Sisters 1; Lay Teachers 54; Students 668.

Carroll High School (1961) 4524 Linden Ave., 45432. Tel: 937-253-8188; Fax: 937-258-7001. Email: jsens@carrollhs.org. Web: www.carrollhs.org. Mr. Joseph R. Sens, Prin.; Ms. Patricia Spencer, Librarian. Sisters 1; Lay Teachers 61; Students 910.

Chaminade Julienne High School, 505 S. Ludlow St., 45402. Tel: 937-461-3740; Fax: 937-461-6256. Web: www.cjeagles.org. Mr. Dan Meixner, Pres.; Mr. John Marshall, Prin.; Jason Unger, Asst. Prin.; John W. Brothers, Dir. Fin. & Accounting; Mrs. Kelli Kinnear, Dir. Campus Ministry; Gina Harrington, Librarian. Conducted by the Society of Mary (Marianists) and Sisters of Notre Dame de Namur. Lay Teachers 55; Students 708.

HAMILTON. *Stephen T. Badin High School* (1966) 571 New London Rd., 45013. Tel: 513-863-3993; Fax: 513-785-2844. Email: fmargello@mail.badinhs.org. Web: badinhs.org. Mr. Frank Margello, Prin.; Mrs. Linda Weathers, Librarian. Lay Teachers 44; Total Staff 65; Students 501.

MIDDLETOWN. *Bishop Fenwick High School*, 4855 State Rte. 122, Franklin, 45005. Tel: 513-423-0723; Fax: 513-420-8690. Web: www.fenwickfalcons.org. Mr. Michael Miller, Prin.; Kathleen Griffith, Librarian. Priests 1; Sisters 1; Deacons 1; Lay Teachers 32; Students 548.

SIDNEY. *Lehman Catholic High School* (1970) 2400 St. Mary's Ave., 45365. Tel: 937-498-1161; Fax: 937-492-9877. Email: m.barhorst@lehmancatholic.com. Web: www.lehmancatholic.com. Mr. Michael Barhorst, Pres.; Denise Stauffer, Prin.; Kathleen Jordan, Librarian. Priests 2; Sisters 1; Lay Teachers 20; Students 229.

SPRINGFIELD. *Catholic Central Jr./Sr. High School*, (Grades 7-12), 1200 E. High St., 45505-1124. Tel: 937-325-9204; Fax: 937-328-7426. Email: dperin@ccirish.org. Web: www.ccirish.org. Steve DeWitt, Junior High Admin.; Kenith Britt, Pres.; Mr. David Perin, Prin.; Mrs. Bonny Bowlus, Librarian. Lay Teachers 28; Students 364.

[F] HIGH SCHOOLS, PRIVATE

CINCINNATI. *The Summit Country Day School*, (Grades PreK-12), Please see The Summit Country Day school located under Elementary Schools, Private., 2161 Grandin Rd., 45208-3300. Tel: 513-871-4700; Fax: 513-533-5373. Web: www.summitcds.org. Mr. Jerry Jellig, Head of School. Priests 1; Support Staff 93; Lay Teachers 115; Students 1,103.

St. Ursula Academy, 1339 E. McMillan St., 45206. Tel: 513-961-3410; Fax: 513-961-3856. Email: jwimberg@saintursula.org. Web: www.saintursula.org. Judith A. Wimberg, Pres.; Judy O'Donnell, Prin.; Jill Herald, Librarian. Lay Teachers 59; Girls 669.

Ursuline Academy of Cincinnati (1896) Senior High School., 5535 Pfeiffer Rd., 45242. Tel: 513-791-5791; Fax: 513-791-3170. Email: pwilson@ursulineacademy.org. Web: www.ursulineacademy.org. Rev. John E. Wessling (Retired); Sharon Redmond, Pres.; Adele Iwanusa, Prin.; Thomas Barhorst, Asst. Prin.; Ms. Mary Bender, Asst. Prin.; Julie Burwrinkel, Librarian. Ursuline Sisters of Brown Co. Saint Martin, OH. Priests 1; Sisters 1; Lay Teachers 69; Girls 700.

St. Xavier High School, 600 N. Bend Rd., 45224. Tel: 513-761-7600; Fax: 513-842-1610. Web: www.stxavier.org. Mr. David B. Mueller, Prin.; Rev. Timothy A. Howe, S.J., Pres.; Mr. William Sandquist Jr., Asst. Prin.; Revs. Edward L. Pigott, S.J., Rector; Dennis P. Ahern, S.J., Alumni Chap.; Francis J. Daly, S.J., Adult Faith Coord.; Mr. Dan Hogan, Chief Information Officer; Julie Conlon, Librarian. Priests 4; Sisters 1; Lay Teachers 120; Students 1,550.

[G] CONSOLIDATED ELEMENTARY SCHOOLS

CINCINNATI. *St. Boniface School* (1867) (Grades K-8), 4305 Pitts Ave., 45223. Tel: 513-541-5122; Fax: 513-541-3939. Email: gorman_a@stbonnie.org. Web: stbonifacecincinnati.com. Sr. Ann Gorman, R.S.M., Prin. & Contact Person; Mrs. Diane Stroud, B.A., M.A., Librarian. Serving the parishes of St. Boniface, St. Leo and Mother of Christ, Cincinnati. Sisters 4; Lay Teachers 15; Students 182.

Corryville Catholic Elementary School, (Grades PreSchool-8), 108 Calhoun St., 45219. Tel: 513-281-4856; Fax: 513-281-6497. Email: smith-ma@corryvillecatholic.org. Sr. Marie Smith, S.N.D.deN., Prin. & Contact Person. Consolidated school serving the parishes of Holy Name, St. Andrew, Assumption, Sacred Heart and Monica-St. George. Sisters 3; Lay Teachers 10; Students 175.

St. Gabriel Consolidated School, (Grades K-8), 18 W. Sharon Ave., 45246. Tel: 513-771-5220; Fax: 513-771-5133. Email: j.epplen@stgabeschool.org. Web: www.st.gabeschool.org. Joseph Epplen, Prin. & Contact Person. Consolidated school serving the parishes of St. Gabriel, Glendale; St. John, West Chester; St. Martin de Porres, Lincoln Heights; St. Matthias, Forest Park; St. Maximilian Kolbe, West Chester. Lay Teachers 22; Students 389.

John Paul II Catholic School (1980) (Grades K-8), 9375 Winton Rd., 45231. Tel: 513-521-0860; Fax: 513-728-3110. Email: nroach@jpiics.org. Web: www.jpiics.org. Mrs. Leanora Roach, Prin.; Mrs. Teri Mauntel, Asst. Prin.; Mrs. Nancy Acciani, Librarian. Lay Teachers 28; Students 482.

St. John the Baptist Catholic School, (Grades PreK-8), 5375 Dry Ridge Rd., 45252. Tel: 513-385-7970; Fax: 513-699-6964. Mr. Richard Harrmann, Prin. Teachers 23; Students 513.

St. Nicholas Academy, (Grades PreK-8), 7131 Plainfield Rd., 45236. Tel: 513-686-2727; Fax: 513-686-2729. Web: stnacademy.org. Gerard Myers, Prin.; Mrs. Jeane Perry, Librarian. An interparish elementary school sponsored by St. John the Evangelist, Deer Park and Holy Trinity Norwood parishes. Lay Teachers 17; Students 263.

Our Lady of Grace, (Grades K-8), 2940 W. Galbraith Rd., 45239. Tel: 513-931-3070; Fax: 513-931-3071. Mike Johnson, Prin.; Pam Ceddia, Librarian. Serving the parishes of St. Ann (Groesbeck), Church of the Assumption (Mount Healthy), St. Margaret Mary (North College Hill) & St. Therese, the Little Flower (Mt. Airy). Teachers 34; Students 691.

DAYTON. *Bishop Leibold School*, (Grades PreK-8)Web: www.bishopleiboldschool.com. Mr. Paul Beyerle, Prin. Consolidated school of St. Henry, Dayton and Our Lady of Good Hope, Miamisburg. Lay Teachers 35; Students 523.

West Campus (Grades PreK-3), 24 S. Third St., Miamisburg, 45342. Tel: 937-866-3021; Fax: 937-866-5680. Mr. Paul Beyerle, Prin.; Julie Wehner, Sec. (West Campus).

East Campus (Grades 4-8), 6666 Springboro Rd., 45449. Tel: 937-434-9343; Fax: 937-436-3048. Mr. Paul Beyerle, Prin.; Laura Eiken, Sec. (East Campus).

Mary Queen of Peace Catholic School, (Grades PreK-8), Central Offices: 224 Squirrel Rd., 45405. Tel: 937-222-1600; Fax: 937-222-1604. Gramont Campus: 138 Gramont Ave., 45417. Tel: 937-268-6391; Fax: 937-268-9775. Web: www.maryqueenofpeace.us. Homewood Campus: 200 Homewood Ave., 45405. Tel: 937-228-3091; Fax: 937-449-2440. Ms. Kathleen Driesen, Prin., Homewood Campus; Ms. Debra Johnson, Prin., Gramont Campus. Regional School for St. Benedict the Moor, Corpus Christi, Holy Family, St. Mary, Our Lady of Mercy and Queen of Martyrs. Lay Teachers 33; Students 505.

HAMILTON. *St. Joseph Consolidated School*, (Grades K-8), 925 S. Second St., 45011. Tel: 513-863-8758; Fax: 513-863-5772. Email: info@sjcshamilton.org. Web: www.sjcshamilton.org. J. William Hicks, Prin.; Theresa Stenger, Contact Person. Serving the parishes of St. Aloysius, Shandon and St. Joseph, Hamilton. Lay Teachers 11; Students 215; Total Staff 15.

MIDDLETOWN. *John XXIII Catholic School*, (Grades PreK-8), 3806 Manchester Rd., 45042. Tel: 513-424-1196; Fax: 513-420-8480. Web: john23middletown.org. Brenda Neu, Prin.; Mrs. Janet Lucas, Asst. Prin.; Mrs. Janet Zappia, Librarian. Serving the parishes of Holy Family, Middletown; St. Mary, Franklin; Holy Name, Trenton; Our Lady of Sorrows, Monroe. Lay Teachers 28; Students 450.

PIQUA. *Piqua Catholic School*, (Grades K-8) Sisters Mary Alice Haithcoat, Prin.; Mary Alice Haithcoat, Contact Person. Serving the parishes of St. Boniface and St. Mary.

North St. Campus (Grades 4-8), 503 W. North St., 45356. Tel: 937-773-1564; Fax: 937-773-0380. Email: haithcoatm@piquacatholic.org. Web: www.piqua-catholic.org. Anthony Frierott, Prin.; Karen Lachiewicz, Librarian.

Downing St. Campus (Grades K-3), 218 S. Downing St., 45356. Tel: 937-773-3876; Fax: 937-773-5875. Sr. Mary Alice Haithcoat, Prin.; Linda Lange, Contact Person; Gail Breisch, Bookkeeper; Karen Lachiewicz, Librarian. Sisters 1; Lay Teachers 15; Students 223.

[H] ELEMENTARY SCHOOLS, PRIVATE

CINCINNATI. **Queen of Angels Montessori School*, (Grades PreK-8), 4460 Berwick St., 45227. Tel: 513-271-4171; Fax: 513-271-4680. Web: www.qams.org. Daniel Teller, Prin. Students 197.

The Summit Country Day School (1890) (Grades PreK-12), 2161 Grandin Rd., 45208-3300. Tel: 513-871-4700; Fax: 513-533-5373. Email: summitinfo@summitcds.org. Web: www.summitcds.org. Jerry Jellig, Head of School; Marianne Cramer, Librarian. Priests 1; Lay Teachers 115; Support Staff 84; Students 1,087.

St. Ursula Villa, (Grades PreK-8), 3660 Vineyard Pl., 45226. Tel: 513-871-7218; Fax: 513-871-0082. Web: www.stursulavilla.org. Mrs. Sally Hicks, Prin. & Contact Person; Susan Hall, Librarian. Sisters 1; Lay Teachers 39; Students 494.

LIBERTY TOWNSHIP. *Mother Teresa Catholic Elementary School* (1998) (Grades K-8), 6085 Jackie Dr., 45044-9426. Tel: 513-779-6585; Fax: 513-779-6468. Email: sranne@mtces.org. Web: www.mtces.org. Kelli Kurtz, School Bd. Chm.; Noel Balster, Devel. Dir.; Sr. Anne Mary Schulz, C.PP.S., Prin.; Mr. Alex Schuster, Asst. Prin.; Debi Marklay, Librarian. Sisters 1; Lay Teachers 18; Students 422.

[I] CHILD CARE INSTITUTIONS

CINCINNATI. *St. Joseph Infant and Maternity Home dba St. Joseph Home of Cincinnati* (1876) 10722 Wyscarver Rd., 45241. Tel: 513-563-2520; Fax: 513-563-1958. Email: marianne@sjh-cincy.com. Web: www.sjh-cincy.com. Sr. Marianne Van Vurst, S.C., Pres. & CEO & Contact Person. Sisters of Charity of Cincinnati, OH. Respite Beds 8; Residential 48.

St. Joseph Orphanage (1829) 5400 Edalbert Dr., 45239-7695. Tel: 513-741-3100; Fax: 513-741-5686. Email: info@sjokids.org. Web: wwwsjokids.org. Robert J. Wehr, Ph.D., Exec. Dir. Archdiocesan Children's Residential Center. Lay Teachers 8.

Family Ties of Northern Kentucky, 3027 Dixie Hwy., Ste. 109A, Edgewood, KY 41017. Tel: 859-647-7220; Fax: 859-647-8814. Robert J. Wehr, Ph.D., Exec. Dir. Total Staff 5; Total Served 30.

A.C.T. Child Case Management, 5400 Edalbert Dr., 45239. Tel: 513-385-1900; Fax: 513-245-7970. Robert J. Wehr, Ph.D., Exec. Dir. Employees 47; Children Served 450.

St. Joseph Villa, 5400 Edalbert Dr., 45239. Tel: 513-741-3100; Fax: 513-741-5686. Residential Treatment and Education and Day Treatment and Foster Care Service for Children 6-18. Total Staff 90; Total Assisted 400.

Altercrest, 274 Sutton Rd., 45230. Tel: 513-231-5010; Fax: 513-231-8651. Robert J. Wehr, Ph.D., Exec. Dir.; Joseph Cassiere, Assoc. Exec. Dir. Residential Treatment and Education, Outpatient and Day Treatment Services for Boys ages 12-18. Total Staff 55; Total Assisted Annually 250.

C.A.R.E. Child Case Management, 282 N. Fair Ave., Hamilton, 45011. Tel: 513-887-2100; Fax: 513-887-2101. Robert J. Wehr, Ph.D., Exec. Dir. Total Staff 21; Children Served 300.

Dayton Foster Care, 3131 S. Dixie Dr., Ste. 220, Moraine, 45439. Tel: 937-643-0398; Fax: 937-643-9961. Total Staff 12; Total Assisted 75.

[J] SPECIAL SCHOOLS

CINCINNATI. *St. Rita School for the Deaf* (1915) (Grades PreK-12), 1720 Glendale-Milford Rd., 45215. Tel: 513-771-7600; Fax: 513-326-8264. Email: gernst@srsdeaf.org. Web: www.srsdeaf.org. Mr. Gregroy R. Ernst, Exec. Dir.; Rev. William H. Wysong, J.C.L. Residential and day school for deaf and hard of hearing children. Franciscan Sisters of Mary 1; Lay Teachers 29; High School Students 32; Elementary Students 64; Preschool 86.

[K] GENERAL HOSPITALS

CINCINNATI. *Good Samaritan Hospital*, Mailing Address: 619 Oak St., 3 S., 45206. Tel: 513-569-6739; Fax: 513-569-6358. 375 Dixmyth Ave., 45220. Tel: 513-862-1400; Fax: 513-862-1190. Web: www.trihealth.com. Mr. John Prout, Pres. & CEO; David Dornheggen, COO; Rev. Gerald R. Niklas, Chap. Tel: 513-862-2281; Fax: 513-862-7050. Catholic Health Initiative (CHI). Bassinets 69; Bed Capacity 592; Patients Assisted Annually 215,000; Total Staff 3,500.

Registered Training College of Nursing Tel: 513-862-2631; Fax: 513-862-3572. Students 305.

Mercy Hospital Anderson, 7500 State Rd., 45255. Tel: 513-624-4500; Fax: 513-624-3299. Web: www.e-mercy.com. Patrica A. Schroer, Pres. Sisters of Mercy. Bed Capacity 226; Patients Assisted Annually 189,859; Total Staff 1,102.

Mercy Hospitals West dba Mercy Franciscan Hospital-Western Hills 3131 Queen City Ave., 45238. Tel: 513-389-5000; Fax: 513-389-9141. Web: www.e-mercy.com. Patrick Kowalski, Pres.; Don Rohling, Senior Vice Pres. Mission Integration; Sr. Adrienne Colson, O.P., Chap.; Ms. Alberta Utrup, Chap.; Deacon Ted Jancha, D.Min., Chap. A member of the Mercy Health Partners. Sisters 1; Bed Capacity 241; Patients Assisted Annually 140,221; Total Staff 931.

Mercy Hospitals West dba Mercy Franciscan Hospital Mt. Airy 2446 Kipling Ave., 45239. Tel: 513-853-5000; Fax: 513-853-9141. Web: www.e-mercy.com. Paul Hiltz, Pres. & CEO; Don Rohling, Senior Vice Pres. Mission Integration. A member of the Mercy Health Partners. Bed Capacity 277; Patients Assisted Annually 98,677; Total Staff 925.

BATAVIA. *The Sisters of Mercy Of Clermont County, Ohio dba Mercy Hospital Clermont* 3000 Hospital Dr., 45103. Tel: 513-732-8200; Fax: 513-732-8537. Web: www.e-mercy.com. Gayle H. Heintzelman, Interim Pres. & CEO; Don Rohling, Senior Vice Pres. Mission Integration; Irene Behling, Dir. Mission Svcs.; Kay O'Rourke. Bed Capacity 166; Patients Assisted Annually 119,403; Total Staff 699.

DAYTON. *Good Samaritan Hospital* (1932) 2222 Philadelphia Dr., 45406. Tel: 937-278-2612. Web: www.goodsamdayton.org. Mr. Mark Shaker, Pres. & CEO. Affiliate with Catholic Health Initiative. Bed Capacity 560; Patients Assisted Annually 300,000; Total Staff 3,400.

FAIRFIELD. *Sisters of Mercy of Hamilton Ohio dba Mercy Hospital Fairfield* 3000 Mack Rd., 45014. Tel: 513-870-7000; Fax: 513-870-7065. Web: www.e-mercy.com. Thomas S. Urban, Pres. & CEO; Sr. Sharon Wiedmar, R.S.M., Dir. Mission Svcs. Bed Capacity 209; Total Assisted Annually 205,617; Total Staff 1,296.

[L] HEALTH CARE SYSTEMS

CINCINNATI. *Catholic Healthcare Partners*, 615 Elsinore Pl., 45202. Tel: 513-639-2800; Fax: 513-639-2700. Web: www.health-partners.org. Mr. Michael Connelly, Pres. & CEO. 32 hospitals, 30 acute care, 1 long-term acute care, and 1 specialty, 14 long-term care facilities, HUD: 15 facilities, 611 units; low-income tax credit housing: 2 facilities, 180 units, 6,692 licensed hospital beds, Total Staff 36,721 (Total System). Catholic Healthcare Partners is co-sponsored by the Sisters of Mercy, South Central Community; Sisters of Mercy, Mid-Atlantic Community; Covenant Health Systems, Sisters of the Humility of Mary, Franciscan Sisters of the Poor. Bed Capacity 4,897; Total Assisted Annually 5,273,525.

Mercy Health Partners of Southwest Ohio dba Mercy Health Partners 4600 McAuley Pl. 6th Fl., 45242. Tel: 513-981-6000; Fax: 513-981-6133. Web: www.mercy.health-partners.org. James E. May, Pres. & CEO. Total Staff 475.

DAYTON. *Dayton Heart Institute*, 2200 Philadelphia Dr., Ste. 510, 45406. Tel: 937-279-8660; Fax: 937-567-4130. Web: daytonheartinstitute.org. Mr. Josh Lader, Exec. Dir.

Samaritan Health Partners, 2222 Philadelphia Dr., 45406. Tel: 937-278-2612. Web: www.goodsamdayton.org. Affiliate of Catholic Health Initiative.

SPRINGFIELD. *Community Mercy Health Partners*, One S. Limestone St., Ste.700, P.O. Box 688, 45501-0688. Tel: 937-328-7000; Fax: 937-328-8006. Web: www.communitymercy.org. Mark Wiener, Pres. & CEO.

Mercy Memorial Hospital, 904 Scioto St., Urbana, 43078. Tel: 937-484-6112; Fax: 937-484-6105. Bed Capacity 25; Staff 125; Total Assisted Annually 56,201.

Springfield Regional Medical Center (1950) 2615 E. High St., 45505. Tel: 937-325-0531; Fax: 937-328-9760. Bed Capacity 277; Staff 1,557; Total Assisted Annually 252,152.

Mercy St. John's Center, 100 W. McCreight Ave., 45504. Tel: 937-399-9910; Fax: 937-399-9449. Day care center for adults. Four Levels of Care: 1. Adult Day (Petticrew Ctr.); 2. High Functioning Unit (The Gardens); 3. Intermediate Unit (The Bridge); 4. End Stage (The Rainbow). Skilled & intermediate long-term care facility for all ages, Alzheimer's unit, ventilator unit. Bed Capacity 125; Staff 143; Total Assisted Annually 472.

Oakwood Village, 1500 Villa Rd., 45503. Tel: 937-390-9000; Fax: 937-390-9333. Web: www.oakwoodvillage.com. Jamie J. Houseman, Admin. Total Assisted Annually 326; Bed Capacity 247; Total Staff 141.

Mercy McAuley Center, 906 Scioto St., Urbana, 43078. Tel: 937-653-5432; Fax: 937-652-2072. Mark Wiener, Regl. Pres. & CEO. Residents 129; Bed Capacity 129; Total Staff 134; Total Assisted Annually 221.

Mercy Siena Woods, 6125 N. Main St., Dayton, 45415. Retirement Community, nonsectarian. A member of Catholic Healthcare Partners. Specialized Alzheimer's Center, Skilled Nursing Center. Assisted living and Independent Cottages. Sponsored by the Religious Sisters of Mercy since 1943. Sisters 2; Bed Capacity 99; Total Assisted Annually 179; Total Staff 121.

Mercy Siena Gardens, 6105 N. Main St., Dayton, 45415. Tel: 937-279-6879; Fax: 937-279-6885. Web: www.mercysiena.com. Bed Capacity 55; Total Staff 27; Total Assisted Annually 30.

[M] SENIOR RESIDENCES

CINCINNATI. *Archbishop Leibold Home for the Aged*, 476 Riddle Rd., 45220-2493. Tel: 513-281-8001; Fax: 513-281-4943. Email: mscincinnati@littlesistersofthepoor.org. Rev. Cyprian Berens, O.F.M., Chap. (Retired); Sr. Cecilia Sartorius, Supr. The Little Sisters of the Poor. Sisters 10; Residents 95; Total Staff 120; Bed Capacity 95; Total Assisted 110.

St. Margaret Hall, 1960 Madison Rd., 45206-1896. Tel: 513-751-5880; Fax: 513-751-9813. Email: srnorah@stmargarethall.com. Web: www.stmargarethall.com. Sr. Norah Michael, O.Carm., Admin. & Contact Person. Carmelite Sisters for the Aged and Infirm 6; Residents 135; Total Staff 210.

Mercy Franciscan Senior Health and Housing Services Inc. dba Mercy St. Theresa Center 7010 Rowan Hill Dr., 45227. Tel: 513-271-7010; Fax: 513-527-0143. Web: www.e-mercy.com. Brian E. Forschner, Ph.D., Pres.; Debbie Welker, Exec. Dir.; Deacon Jerry Schneider. Bed Capacity 174; Residents 163; Total Assisted 302; Total Staff 161.

Mercy Franciscan Senior Health and Housing Services, Inc. dba Mercy Franciscan Terrace 100 Compton Rd., 45215. Tel: 513-761-9036; Fax: 513-761-5199. Web: www.e-mercy.com. Brian E. Forschner, Ph.D., Pres. & Exec. Dir.; Joan Owens, Pastoral Care. Licensed Beds 148; Total Assisted 323; Total Staff 187; Residents 155.

Mercy Franciscan Senior Health and Housing Services, Inc. dba Mercy Franciscan at West Park 2950 West Park Dr., 45238. Tel: 513-451-8900; Fax: 513-451-3728. Web: www.e-mercy.com. Brian E. Forschner, Ph.D., Pres.; Kendra Couch, Exec. Dir. Bed Capacity 326; Total Assisted Annually 346; Total Staff 285.

Sisters of Charity Senior Care Corp. dba Bayley Place 990 Bayley Place Dr., 45233. Tel: 513-347-5500; Fax: 513-347-5553. Email: bayleyplace@srcharitycinti.org. Web: www.bayleyplace.org. Adrienne Walsh, Pres. & CEO. Also includes Eldermount Adult Day Program and The Village at Bayley Place. Total Assisted Living 85; Independent Cottages 78; Health Care 110; Licensed Nursing 110; Total Staff 292.

CENTERVILLE. **St. Leonard*, 8100 Clyo Rd., 45458. Tel: 937-433-0480; Fax: 937-439-7165. Web: www.stleonard.net. Timothy C. Dressman, Exec. Dir. & Contact Person; Rev. Loren Connell, O.F.M., Chap. A facility of the Franciscan Services Corporation, sponsored by the Sisters of St. Francis, Sylvania, OH. A residence for Senior Citizens. Residents 700; Total Staff 360; Bed Capacity 663.

DAYTON. *Mercy Siena Springs I* (1984) 6215 N. Main St., 45415. Tel: 937-279-6114; Fax: 937-279-6870. Sponsored by the Sisters of Mercy., Apartments, Independent Living for the Elderly. Residents 45; Total Staff 2.

Mercy Siena Springs II (2001) 6217 N. Main St., 45415. Tel: 937-279-6114; Fax: 937-279-6870. Residents 34.

HAMILTON. *Mercy Franciscan Senior Health and Housing Services, Inc. dba Mercy Franciscan at Schroder* 1302 Millville Ave., 45013. Tel: 513-867-4100; Fax: 513-867-1415. Web: www.e-mercy.com. Brian E. Forschner, Ph.D., Pres.; Marcie Calvert, Exec. Dir. A Facility of the Mercy Health Partners. Sponsored by the Catholic Healthcare Partners. Premier short-term rehabilitation program. Bed Capacity 135; Total Assisted 307; Total Staff 162.

[N] MONASTERIES AND RESIDENCES OF PRIESTS AND BROTHERS

CINCINNATI. *The Catholic Foreign Mission Society of America, Inc.*, 6930 Greenfield Dr., 45224-1626. Tel: 513-681-7888. Email: mklcin@maryknoll.org. Web: www.maryknoll.org. Revs. Leslie F. Blowers, M.M., Regl. Dir.; Peter L. Chabot, M.M. Maryknoll Fathers.

St. Clare Friary, 5831 Saranac Ave., 45224. Tel: 513-541-0488; Fax: 513-541-2424. Revs. Patrick McCloskey, O.F.M.; David Kohut, O.F.M.; Bro. Robert Lucero, O.F.M.

Claver Jesuit Community (2000) 3731 Borden Ave., 45223-2310. Tel: 513-542-2312; Fax: 513-542-0889. Email: claver@fuse.net. Web: home.fuse.net/claver. Revs. James A. Hasse, S.J., Supr.; Joseph D. Folzenlogen, S.J., Dir.; J. Timothy Hipskind, S.J.; Louis J. Lipps, S.J. Priests 4. *Claver Jesuit Ministry*, 3838 Llewellyn Ave., 45223-2352. Tel: 513-681-8500; Fax: 513-681-4503. Email: clavermin@fuse.net. Web: home.fuse.net/clavermin.

St. Clement Friary (1850) 4536 Vine St., 45217. Tel: 513-641-2257; Fax: 513-641-2262. Email: vincedel@franciscan.org. Revs. Fred Link, O.F.M., Pastor; Louis Bartko, O.F.M.; Joel Byrne, O.F.M. (Retired); William Farris, O.F.M., Pres., Roger Bacon High School; Howard Hudepohl, O.F.M., Chap., Mercy Franciscan Terrrace; Bros. Conrad F. Rebmann, O.F.M., (Retired); Louis Lamping, O.F.M., (Retired); Joseph Haley, O.F.M., Fraternal Svc.; David W. Crank, Dir. of Office of Senior Friars; Bernard Jennings, O.F.M., (Retired); Kenneth Beetz, O.F.M., Maintenance; Joel Soldenski, O.F.M., (Retired); Stephen Richter, O.F.M., (Retired); Kevin Schroder, O.F.M., St. Anthony Messenger; Vincent Delorenzo, O.F.M., Mission Office; Christopher Meyer, O.F.M., Studies. St. John the Baptist Province. Residence for Retired Friars, Pastor of St. Clement Parish and other Friars. Priests 5; Brothers 11.

Comboni Missionaries (Verona Fathers)-Comboni Mission Center, 1318 Nagel Rd., 45255-3120. Tel: 513-474-4997; Fax: 513-474-0382. Email: info@combonimissionaries.org. Web: www.combonimissionaries.org. Revs. Louis Gasparini, M.C.C.J., Prov. Tel: 513-474-3818; Peter Ciuciulla, M.C.C.J., Dir. of Mission Office; Peter Ciuciulla, M.C.C.J., Prov. Treas.; Mario Ongaro, M.C.C.J. (Retired); Paul Donohue, M.C.C.J., Public Rels.; Cindy Browne, Mgr. & Editor, CPN Newsletter; Mgr., Justice & Peace Resource Ctr.; Jeanie Stephens, Devel. Dir.; Revs. Kenneth Gerth, M.C.C.J.; William J. Jansen, M.C.C.J.; Ms. Mary Bertolini, Dir. Communications. Houses Comboni Missionaries of the Heart of Jesus, Inc., The Offices of the Province of North America, including the Office of the Provincial. Priests 8.

De Sales Crossings Marianist Community, 1600 Madison Rd., 45206-1815. Tel: 513-961-1945; Fax: 513-221-4907. Bros. Giancarlo Bonutti, S.M.; Ray Dominguez, S.M.; Joseph H. Kamis, S.M., Dir. of Community; Brandon Paluch, (Aspirant); Robert A. Politi, S.M.; Robert N. Wiethorn, S.M.; William I. Grundish, S.M.; Revs. Edward M. Jach, S.M.; John Manahan, S.M. Priests 2; Brothers 6; Aspirant 1.

Faber Jesuit Community, 790 Clinton Springs Ave., 45229. Tel: 513-961-7700; Fax: 513-569-4587. Email: faberjs@cinci.rr.com. Revs. J. Peter Carey, S.J.; John M. Ferone, S.J., Supr.; Robert J. Hagee, S.J.; Charles A. Hofmann, S.J.; Harold Sommer, S.J.; Peter Sharkey, S.J.; John Beckman, S.J. 3771 MacNicholas, 45236. Tel: 513-984-2547. Rev. Robert J. Ross, S.J. 6818 Buckingham Pl., 45227. Bros. Donald H. Bengert, S.J.; John P. Martin, S.J.; Michael J. O'Grady, S.J.; Robert W. Schneider, S.J. Priests 10; Brothers 3.

St. Francis Seraph Friary, 1615 Vine St., 45202-6400. Tel: 513-721-4700; Fax: 513-421-9672. Email: sjbsec@franciscan.com. Web: www.franciscan.org. Revs. Donald A. Miller, O.F.M., Ph.D., Vocation Dir.; Hilarion Kistner, O.F.M., Educ. Homily Helps, Assoc. Chap, The Christ Hospital; Jeffrey Scheeler, O.F.M., Prov. Min.; Mr. David O'Brien, CFO; Revs. Page Polk, O.F.M., Dir. Ongoing Formation; Gregory Friedman, O.F.M., Pastor, St. Francis Seraph; Peter Paul James, O.F.M. (Retired); Simeon Cleves, O.F.M., Chap., Christ Hospital; Thomas Speier, O.F.M., Part-time Assoc. at St. Monica - St. George Parish and Newman Ctr.; Part-time

Word Ministry; Manuel Viera, O.F.M., J.C.L., Arch Judical Vicar, Latino Ministry; Damian Cesanek, O.F.M., Sacramental Ministry, Asst. Chap. at Christ Hospital, Cincinnati; Frank Jasper, O.F.M., Prov. Vicar/Treas.; Sr. Donna Graham, O.S.F., Office of Justice, Peace and Integrity of Creation; Ms. Toni Cashnelli, Dir. Communications; Bros. Gene Mayer, O.F.M., Prov. Sec.; Daniel Barrett, O.F.M., Parochial & Fraternal Assistance; John Carey, O.F.M., Assoc., Mission Office; David Crank, O.F.M., Office for Senior Friars; Timothy Sucher, O.F.M., Guardian, Pastoral Assoc.; Chris Cahill, O.F.M., Instructor, Roger Bacon High School; John Barker, O.F.M., Graduate Studies; Brian Maloney, O.F.M., Dir. Friar Works/Franciscan Min. & Mission; Vincent Delorenzo, O.F.M., Dir. Franciscan Mission Office. Provincial Headquarters of the Province of St. John the Baptist of the Order of Friars Minor. Priests 8; Brothers 5.

Friars of the Province Serving Abroad: Revs. Harold Geers, O.F.M., 69 San Pedro Bautista St., San Francisco del Monte, 1104 Quezon City, Philippines. Tel: 011-63-02-373-2973; Fax: 011-63-02-373-2972; James M. Bok, O.F.M.; Joseph Hund, O.F.M.; Bros. Philip Wilhelm, O.F.M., Sanctuario de San Antonio, Forbes Park, Makati, P.O. Box 3215 MCC, Metro Manila 1299 Philippines. Tel: 011-63-02-843-8830; Fax: 011-63-02-843-9223; Roger Covero, O.F.M., Balay Piksalabukan Friary, Josefina St., Zamboanga del Sur, Philippines; Louis Zant, O.F.M., St. Joseph Friary, P.O. Box 66, Savanna-la-mar, Westmoreland. Tel: 876-955-2648; Thomas Gerchak, O.F.M.

Friars on Special Assignment in the U.S.A.: Revs. Arthur Espelage, O.F.M., J.C.D., Marriage Tribunal, Diocese of Venice, FL; Matthias Crehan, O.F.M., Chap., Veteran's Affairs Med. Ctr., Phoenix, AZ; Robert Bruno, O.F.M., Senior Staff Chap./USAF Academy; Francis S. Tebbe, O.F.M., Vice Pres./Corp. Sec. for Xavier Univ., Chicago, IL; Jeremy Harrington, O.F.M., (On Special Assignment) Commissary & Guardian Franciscans for the Holy Land); Charles Smiech, O.F.M., Retreat Ministry; Duane Stenzel, O.F.M., Priest-Dir. Radio Maria; Rock Travnikar, O.F.M., Coord. Pastoral Svcs. for Rocky Creek Village, FL; Dennis Bosse, O.F.M., Chap./Campus Min. Marian Univ., IN; Valentine Young, O.F.M., Sacramental Ministry, Latin Mass Community, KY; Francis Wendling, O.F.M., Prayer Ministry, MO; Loren Connell, O.F.M., Chap. St. Leonard Senior Community, OH; Paul Walsman, O.F.M., Preaching, Food for the Poor, FL; Bros. Andrew Stettler, O.F.M., Studies; Cletus Riederer, O.F.M., Christian Svc. Prog., LA; Giovanni Ried, O.F.M., Christian Svc. Prog., LA; Josef Anderlohr, O.F.M., Prayer Ministry.

Friars in Retirement Homes in the Archdiocese of Cincinnati: Revs. Cyprian Berens, O.F.M., Chap. (Retired), Archbishop Leibold Home for the Aged, 476 Riddle Rd., 45220-2493. Tel: 513-281-8001; Fax: 513-281-4943; John Boehman, O.F.M. (Retired); Marne Breckensiek, O.F.M. (Retired); Curt Lanzrath, O.F.M. (Retired); Theobald Hattrup, O.F.M. (Retired), Archbishop Leibold Home for the Aged, 476 Riddle Rd., 45220-2493. Tel: 513-281-8001; Fax: 513-281-4943; Nicholas Lohkamp, O.F.M. (Retired); Noel William, O.F.M. (Retired), Archbishop Leibold Home for the Aged, 476 Riddle Rd., 45220-2493. Tel: 513-281-8001; Fax: 513-281-4943; Valens J. Waldschmidt, O.F.M. (Retired), Archbishop Leibold Home for the Aged, 476 Riddle Rd., 45220-2493. Tel: 513-281-8001; Fax: 513-281-4943; Gil Wohler, O.F.M.; Justus Wirth, O.F.M.; Bro. Donald Rewers, O.F.M.

St. Gertrude Priory, 7630 Shawnee Run Rd., 45243. Tel: 513-561-5954; Fax: 513-527-3971. Web: www.stgertrude.org. Revs. Walter C. Wagner, O.P., Novice Master; Darren Pierre, O.P., Prior & Pastor; Joseph Clement Burns, O.P.; George Schommer, O.P., Assoc.; Charles A. Farrell, O.P.; Kenneth Andrew Hofer, O.P., House of Assignment: St. Gertrude Priory - Studying at Notre Dame Univ.; Michael Mary Dosch, O.P., Assoc.

Headquarters of Glenmary Home Missioners (1939) P.O. Box 465618, 45246-5618. Tel: 513-874-8900; Fax: 513-874-1690. Email: info@glenmary.org. Web: www.glenmary.org. Also known as The Home Missioners of America. 4119 Glenmary Trace, Fairfield, 45014. Tel: 513-874-8900; Fax: 513-874-1690. Revs. Dan Dorsey, G.H.M., Pres.; Dominic R. Duggins, G.H.M., 1st Vice Pres. & Dir. of Devel.; Mike Kerin, G.H.M., 2nd Vice Pres. & Dir. of Educ.; Steve Pawelk, G.H.M., Dir. of Vocations; Francois Pellissier, G.H.M., Major Gifts Officer; Bros. Dennis Craig, G.H.M., Co-Dir. Senior & Disabled Members; Ken Woods, G.H.M., Co-Dir. Senior & Disabled Members.

Senior Members: Revs. Ed Gorny, G.H.M. (Retired); Robert Dalton, G.H.M. (Retired); Laurence Goulding, G.H.M. (Retired); August Guppenberger (Retired); Del Holmes, G.H.M. (Retired); Charles Hughes, G.H.M. (Retired); James Kelly, G.H.M. (Retired); Richard Kreimer, G.H.M. (Retired); Fid Levri, G.H.M. (Retired); George Mathis, G.H.M. (Retired); John Otterbacher, G.H.M. (Retired); Gerald Peterson, G.H.M. (Retired); Robert Rademacher, G.H.M. (Retired); Frank Ruff, G.H.M. (Retired); Francis Schenk, G.H.M. (Retired); Leo Schloemer, G.H.M. (Retired); Wil Steinbacher, G.H.M. (Retired); Bros. Robert Hoffman, G.H.M., (Retired); Thomas Kelly, G.H.M., (Retired); Terry O'Rourke, G.H.M., (Retired); Bernie Stern, G.H.M., (Retired).

Jesuit Community at Xavier University, Jesuit Community Residence, 3844 Victory Pkwy., 45207. Tel: 513-745-3591; Fax: 513-745-3858. Revs. Kent A. Beausoleil, S.J., Asst. Pastor, Bellarmine Chapel; Campus Min., Xavier Univ.; Joseph A. Bracken, S.J.; Albert J. Bischoff, S.J.; Richard W. Bollman, S.J., Parish Priest, Bellarmine Chapel; Robert Bueter, S.J., Adjunct Prof. & Assoc. Dir. of Center for Catholic Educ.; Bro. Darrell J. Burns, S.J., Mission & Identity, Activities Coord.; Revs. Eugene Carmichael, S.J.; Michael J. Graham, S.J.; Robert E. Hurd, S.J.; Thomas P. Kennealy, S.J.; J. Leo Klein, S.J.; John J. LaRocca, S.J., Rector; Theodore C. Thepe, S.J.; Benjamin J. Urmston, S.J.; Joseph Wagner, S.J.; George B. Wilson, S.J. Members of the Jesuit Community (Society of Jesus, S.J.). Priests 16; Brothers 1.

Jesuit Community at St. Xavier High School, Jesuit Community, 7361 View Pl., 45224. Tel: 513-761-5522; Fax: 513-761-0514. Revs. Dennis P. Ahern, S.J.; Glen Chun, S.J.; Francis J. Daly, S.J.; Timothy A. Howe, S.J.; Edward L. Pigott, S.J., Rector; John P. Heim, S.J.

St. John the Baptist Friary, 10722 Wyscarver Rd., 45241-3803. Tel: 513-769-1613; Fax: 513-769-1650. Email: jvv@fuse.net. Revs. Paul Desch, O.F.M.; Bruno Kremp, O.F.M.; Bill Reichel, O.F.M.; James VanVurst, O.F.M., Local Min.; Anthony Walter, O.F.M.; Warren Zeisler, O.F.M.; Bros. Martin Humphreys, O.F.M., (Retired); Dominic Lococo, O.F.M., Vicar; Allan Schmitz, O.F.M.

Marianist Community (1959) 9025 Montgomery Rd., 45242-7711. Tel: 513-793-7119; Fax: 513-792-3343. Email: rflaherty@moeller.org. Web: www.moeller.org. Bro. Robert M. Flaherty, S.M., Dir.; Rev. Lawrence L. Schoettelkotte, S.M. Priests 1; Brothers 5.

Marianist Community, 1514 Elm St., #11, 45202. Tel: 513-687-5561. Bros. J. Mitchell Schweickart, S.M.; Michael Murphy, S.M. Brothers 3.

Pleasant Street Friary (1969) 1723 Pleasant St., 45202-6413. Tel: 513-621-0599; Fax: 513-621-0599. Email: gregf@americancatholic.org. Revs. Gregory Friedman, O.F.M.; Mark J. Hudak, O.F.M.; Daniel J. Anderson, O.F.M.; Jack R. Wintz, O.F.M.; Murray L. Bodo, O.F.M. In Res. Rev. John Quigley, O.F.M.

CARTHAGENA. *St. Charles*, Society of the Precious Blood: 2860 U.S. Rte. 127, 45822. Tel: 419-925-4516; Fax: 419-925-4800. Web: ma.noacsc.org/stcharl. Revs. James C. Seibert, C.PP.S., Dir.; Norbert Adelman, C.PP.S (Retired); George Albers, C.PP.S. (Retired); John Behen, C.PP.S. (Retired); Thomas Beischel, C.PP.S. (Retired); John L. Bensman (Retired); Anselm F. Boeke (Retired); Joseph Brown, C.PP.S. (Retired); James O. Byrne (Retired); Harry M. Cavanaugh, C.PP.S. (Retired); Robert Conway, C.PP.S. (Retired); Lawrence Cyr, C.PP.S. (Retired); Bernard Diekhoff, C.PP.S. (Retired); Cornelius Fenton, C.PP.S. (Retired); Albert Fey, C.PP.S. (Retired); George Fey, C.PP.S. (Retired); Henry Frantz, C.PP.S. (Retired); Dominic Gerlach, C.PP.S. (Retired); Leonard Goettemoeller, C.PP.S (Retired); Lawrence Heiman, C.PP.S. (Retired); Alvin Herber, C.PP.S. (Retired); John Herber, C.PP.S.; John Hoying, C.PP.S. (Retired); Leo A. Hoying (Retired); Vincent Hoying, C.PP.S. (Retired); William Hoying, C.PP.S. (Retired); Alphonse Jungwirth, C.PP.S. (Retired); Leonard A. Kistler, C.PP.S. (Retired); Gerold Koller, C.PP.S. (Retired); William Kramer, C.PP.S. (Retired); Frederick Lang, C.PP.S. (Retired); Rev. Msgr. Vincent L. Lengerich (GRY) (Retired); Revs. James McCabe, C.PP.S. (Retired); Edward McCarthy, C.PP.S. (Retired); James Miller, C.PP.S., C.PP.S. (Retired); Bernard Mullen, C.PP.S. (Retired); Alfred Naseman, C.PP.S., Retreat & Renewal; Louis Osterhage, C.PP.S. (Retired); Daniel Raible, C.PP.S. (Retired); Ernest W. Ranly, C.PP.S. (Retired); Albert Reed, C.PP.S. (Retired); Robert Reinhart, C.PP.S. (Retired); Charles Rohrkemper (Retired); Louis Schmit, C.PP.S. (Retired); Kenneth J. Schroeder, C.PP.S.; Raymond Schultheis, C.PP.S. (Retired); Emil Schuwey, C.PP.S. (Retired); John Spatt, C.PP.S. (Retired); Marvin J. Steffes, C.PP.S., O.D. (Retired); James F. Trick (Retired); Paul W. Wohlwend, C.PP.S. (Retired); John Zvijak, C.PP.S.; Bro. Jude Brown, C.PP.S., Librarian. Priests 52; Brothers 9.

DAYTON. *Marianist Community*, 100 Chambers St., 45409. Tel: 937-627-8998. Revs. Christopher W. Conlon, S.M., Dir.; Eugene Contadino, S.M., B.A., M.A., Ph.D.; Bros. Philip Aaron, S.M.; M. Gary Marcinowski, S.M., M.F.A. ; Thomas E. Oldenski, S.M. Priests 2; Brothers 3. *Marianist Community*, 149 Franklin St., 45402-2598. Tel: 937-228-2013; Fax: 937-228-5354. Rev. Lee L. Sciarrotta, S.M., Dir. Priests 1; Brothers 2. *Marianist Community*, Meyer Hall, 4435 E. Patterson Rd., 45430-1095. Tel: 937-426-7852; Fax: 937-426-7858. Rev. James Schimelpfening, S.M., D.Min.; Bros. A. Joseph Barrish, S.M.; Joseph Mariscalco, S.M.; Donald Neff, S.M.; Donald Smith, S.M., Dir.; Jeffrey Sullivan, S.M. Priests 1; Brothers 5. *Marianist Community, Novitiate*, 4435 E. Patterson Rd., 45430-1095. Tel: 937-426-5721; Fax: 937-429-4686. Rev. Michael Lisbeth, S.M., Dir. & Master of Novices; Bros. Michael O'Grady, S.M., Asst. Novice Master; Basant Kujur; John Lember, S.M.; Claude Gerard Sery; John Somerville, S.M.; Donald Geiger, S.M., Ph.D.; Thomas Wendorf, S.M., Ph.D. Priests 1; Brothers 5. *Marianist Community*, 141 Washington St., 45402-2530. Tel: 937-224-9978. Rev. John A. McGrath; Bros. James Brown, S.M.; Bernard Hartman, S.M.; Kenneth Sommer; Victor M. Forlani, S.M., M.B.A., D.B.A.; Edward E. Zamierowski, S.M., Dir. Priests 3; Brothers 4. *Marianist Community*, 312 Stonemill Rd., 45409-2543. Tel: 937-627-1553. Revs. Gerald T. Chinchar, S.M., D.Min.; Paul M. Marshall, S.M., M.Div., Dir.; Bertrand A. Buby, S.M., Ph.D.; Bros. Eugene Adingra, S.M.; Raymond Fitz, S.M.; Daniel L. Klco, S.M., M.S. Priests 3; Brothers 3. *Marianist Community*, 121 Sawmill Rd., 45409-2524. Tel: 937-222-4928. Rev. Norbert C. Burns, S.M.; Bros. James Facette; Alex J. Tuss, S.M., Ph.D., Dir.; Lawrence Cada, S.M.; Raymond Martin, S.M. Priests 1; Brothers 4. *Marianist Community*, 1903 Trinity Ave., 45409-2445. Tel: 937-293-9744. Revs. Christopher T. Wittmann, S.M.; Francois Rossier, S.M.; Bros. Thomas Giardino, S.M., Dir.; Timothy Mazundah; Abraham Mewezino, S.M.; Robert Hughs, S.M. Priests 2; Brothers 4.

Marianist Community, Alumni Hall, University of Dayton, 45469-0300. Revs. Paul F. Vieson, S.M.; Robert E. Hughes, S.M.; Joseph F. Kozar, S.M., Ph.D.; Johann B.G. Roten, S.M., S.T.D.; Joseph P. Tedesco, S.M., Dir.; Thomas A. Thompson, S.M.; Bros. William Callahan, S.M.; William Fackovec, S.M.; Charles Gausling, S.M.; Ronald Overman, S.M.; David Schmitz, S.M.; Daniel R. Stupka, S.M.; Louis Fournier, S.M. Priests 7; Brothers 8. *Mercy Siena Gardens*, 6105 N. Main St., 45415-3110. Revs. Francis J. Kenney, S.M. Tel: 937-275-4257; Thomas A. Schoen, S.M., M.Div. Tel: 937-274-9673; Thomas Stanley, S.M. Tel: 937-274-9673; James R. McKay, S.M.; Robert Backherns, S.M.; Bros. Francis Deibel. Tel: 937-279-9803; Donald L. Fahrig, S.M. Tel: 937-279-9243; Robert Johns, S.M.; Francis Smith, S.M.; Paul Merland. Tel: 937-274-7810; Paul Quinn. Tel: 937-274-9597; Charles Roggemann. Tel: 937-274-9643; Donald Schaaf. Tel: 937-275-4257. Priests 5; Brothers 9. *Mercy Siena Woods, Nursing Care*, 6125 N. Main St., 45415-3110. Revs. Cyril G. Middendorf, S.M.; Eldon Reichert. Tel: 937-278-8211, Ext. 6421; Bro. Donald Winfree. Tel: 937-278-8211, Ext. 6405. Priests 2; Brothers 2. *Mercy Siena Support Community*, Old Dublin Ct., 45415-3194. Tel: 937-274-4626. Revs. Nicholas Rufo; Thomas A. Schroer, S.M., Dir.; Bro. Kenneth Thompson, S.M. *Mercy Siena Village*, 6045 N. Main St., 45415. Tel: 937-238-4323. Bro. Bernard Zalewski, S.M. *Marianist Community*, 301 Kiefaber St., 45409. Tel: 937-627-8091. Bros. Sean Downing, S.M.; Thomas J. Pieper, S.M., Dir.; Charles Wanda, S.M. Brothers 3. *Marianist Network for the Arts* Tel: 937-320-5450; Fax: 937-429-3195. Religious 3; Total Staff 3. *North American Center for Marianist Studies* Tel: 937-429-2521; Fax: 937-429-3195. Religious 2; Total Staff 9. *Marianist Mission*, 119 Franklin St., 45402-2599. Tel: 937-222-4641; 800-348-4732; Fax: 937-222-3038. Religious 5; Total Staff 62. *Marianist Environmental Education Center* Tel: 937-429-3582; Fax: 937-429-3195. Religious 2; Total Staff 6.

Provincial Office of the Cincinnati Province of the Society of the Precious Blood, 431 E. Second St., 45402-1764. Tel: 937-228-9263; Fax: 937-228-6878. Email: prodirsec@cpps-preciousblood.org. Web: www.cpps-preciousblood.org. Very Rev. Angelo Anthony, C.PP.S., Prov. Dir.; Bro. Joseph J. Fisher, C.PP.S., Treas.; Revs. Kenneth Schnipke, C.PP.S., Dir. Vocations. Tel: 937-228-6224; Larry J. Hemmelgarn, C.PP.S., Prov. Sec.; Benjamin Berinti, C.PP.S., Retreat & Renewal; Benedict Magabe, C.PP.S., Parish Assignment;

Alfons Minja, C.PP.S., Parish Assignment; Jayababu Nuthulapati, C.PP.S.; Kenneth G. Alt, C.PP.S.; Andrew O'Reilly, C.PP.S., Sabbatical Year; Clarence Williams, C.PP.S., Admin.; Bros. James Ballmann, C.PP.S.; Benjamin Basile, C.PP.S.; Terrence Nufer, C.PP.S.; Jerry Schwieterman, C.PP.S.; Antonio Sison, C.PP.S., Teaching.

Members of the Provincial Council: Revs. Kenneth Schnipke, C.PP.S., Vice Prov.; Kenneth J. Schroeder, C.PP.S., 5th Councilor; Thomas Hemm, C.PP.S., 2nd Councilor; Larry J. Hemmelgarn, C.PP.S., 1st Councilor; Clarence Williams, C.PP.S., 3rd Councilor; Bro. Joseph J. Fisher, C.PP.S., 4th Councilor, Provincial House.

Military: Rev. John S. Srode, C.PP.S., PSC 41 Box 3003, Apo, AE 09464-2801.

Priests of the Province Serving Abroad: Very Rev. Barry J. Fischer, C.PP.S., Mod. Gen., Viale di Porta Ardeatina, 66, Rome 1-00154 Italy. Tel: 011-39-06-574-1656; Fax: 011-39-06-574-2874.

Foreign Mission: Revs. William J. Beuth, C.PP.S., Parroguia Sangre de Cristo, Apartado Postal 2483, 01901 Guatemala City, Guatemala. Tel: 011-502-6640-2600; Fax: 011-502-6640-2686; Joseph F. Deardorff, C.PP.S., Nuestra Senora de la Luz, Apartado 2348, Lima, 100, Peru. Tel: 011-51-1-536-4592; Fax: 011-51-1-537-5107; Gerald G. Dreiling, C.PP.S., Apartado 07-0148, Lima 07, Peru. Tel: 011-51-1-539-5285; Fax: 011-51-1-546-0285; Edgar Jutte, C.PP.S., Iglesia Del Sagrado Corazon de Jesus, Calzada San Lorenzo 749, Col San Juan Xalpa, Iztapalapa 09850DF Mexico. Tel: 011-525-55-614-9022; John F. Falter, C.PP.S., Parroguia Sangre de Cristo, Casilla 194, Purranque, Chile. Tel: 011-56-64-351-340; James E. Gaynor, C.PP.S., San Francisco de Borja, Apartado Aereo, 85182, Carrera, 20 N. 52-23, Bogata, D.C., Colombia. Tel: 011-57-1-345-8466; Fax: 011-57-1-346-6388; James W. Bender, C.PP.S., Parroquia Cristo Rey, Apartado 36, La Oroya, Peru. Tel: 011-51-1-64-39-1675; Fax: 011-51-1-64-39-1675; Donald J. Thieman, C.PP.S., N.S. de la P. Sangre, Casilla 163 Correo 55, Santiago, Chile. Tel: 011-56-2-274-4584; Fax: 011-56-2-341-4279.

In Residences Not Listed Elsewhere: Revs. James E. Franck, C.PP.S., 5788 Thornton Ave., Newark, CA 94560. Tel: 510-797-0241; John Franck, C.PP.S, 2625 Vermont Ave., Los Angeles, CA 90007. Tel: 323-731-2464; Fax: 323-731-6186; Jerard Raj Irudayanathan Irudaya, C.PP.S; Jeffrey R. Keyes, C.PP.S., 5788 Thornton Ave., Newark, CA 94560. Tel: 510-797-0241; Ernest Krantz, C.PP.S., 3950 Columbia Ave., Columbia, PA 17512. Tel: 219-922-2859; Paul Aumen, C.PP.S., 315 Brick Ln., New Oxford, PA 17350-9050. Tel: 717-624-2562; John Bolan, C.PP.S., 16359 Emerald Dr., Middleburg Heights, 44130. Tel: 440-526-3030, Ext. 6265; David A. Kelly, C.PP.S., 4835 S. Marshfeld Ave., 2nd Fl., Chicago, IL 60609. Tel: 773-927-1664; Dennis Kinderman, C.PP.S., 1936 W. 48th St. - Rear, P.O. Box 09379, Chicago, IL 60609. Tel: 773-579-0781; Fax: 773-579-0782; Fred Licciardi, C.PP.S., 120 N. Ela St., Barrington, IL 60010. Tel: 847-382-5300; Fax: 847-382-5363; Stephen Dos Santos, C.PP.S., 2625 Vermont Ave., Los Angeles, CA 90007. Tel: 323-731-2464, Ext. 112; Dennis Chriszt, C.PP.S., 5332 S. Woodlawn Ave., Apt. 3, Chicago, IL 60615. Tel: 773-218-7249; Donald Davison, C.PP.S., 2222 E. Third St., Bloomington, IN 47401-5305. Tel: 812-336-6846; Robert Hunt, C.PP.S., 14037 Fairway Island Dr., Apt. 226, Orlando, FL 32837-5250. Tel: 407-251-0909; Edward Joyce, C.PP.S., 22866 Montalvo Rd., Laguna Niguel, CA 92677-2740. Tel: 714-493-2800; Jeffrey Kirch, C.PP.S., Chicago, IL; William Nordenbrock, C.PP.S., P.O. Box 09379, Chicago, IL 60609-0379. Tel: 773-579-0781; Fax: 773-579-0782; Mark Peres, C.PP.S., Chicago, IL; Joseph Rodak, C.PP.S., Our Lady of Good Counsel Church, 4423 Pearl St., Cleveland, 44109-4266. Tel: 216-749-2324; Fax: 216-741-7183; Leon Flaherty, C.PP.S., 1410 Baxter Ave., Superior, WI 54880. Tel: 715-392-8511; Eugene H. Schnipke, C.PP.S., Marion Catholic Community, 7428 SR 119, Maria Stein, 45860; Alphonse Spilly, C.PP.S., 652 Stewart Ct., Whiting, IN 46394-1464. Tel: 219-473-4351; Jerome P. Stack, C.PP.S., Whiting, IN; Michael Winkowski, C.PP.S., 8046 Shady Dr., Walkerton, IN 46574. Tel: 574-586-7408; Bros. Brian Boyle, C.PP.S., 5332 S. Woodlawn, Apt. 3, Chicago, IL 60615. Tel: 773-752-0672; Fax: 773-752-0676; Timothy Cahill, C.PP.S., 1114 Troy St., 45404-2719. Tel: 973-223-8306; Nicholas Renner, C.PP.S; Matthew Schaefer, C.PP.S; Jerome Schulte, C.PP.S., 4880 Denlinger Rd., 45426-2012. Tel: 937-278-3265.

HAMILTON. *St. Francis Friary*, 723 Main St., 45013-2548. Tel: 513-330-6906. Email: b.francesco@cinci.rr.com. Bros. Howard Parent, C.F.P.; Julian Lane, C.F.P. Brothers of the Poor of St. Francis. Res.: 7831 Ayerdayl Ln., 45255. Tel: 513-231-5970; 513-924-0111 (Mon. & Wed.).

HUNTSVILLE. *St. George Chapel of Marianist Community* (1953) 9636 Lakeshore Dr., E., 43324-9520. Tel: 937-842-4902. Email: pbredus@yahoo.com. Bros. Paul F. Bredestege, S.M., Dir. & Contact Person; William A. Deanhofer, S.M.; Rev. James A. Russell, S.M. Priests 1; Brothers 2.

[O] CONVENTS AND RESIDENCES FOR SISTERS

CINCINNATI. *St. Clare Convent, Franciscan Sisters of the Poor* U.S. Area Office Franciscan Sisters of the Poor, 60 Compton Rd., 45215. Tel: 513-761-9040; Fax: 513-761-6703. Email: sfpusarea@fuse.net. Web: www.franciscansisters.org. Sisters Joanne Schuster, S.F.P., Congregation Councilor & Contact Person; Mary Lawrence Vandenburg, S.F.P., Community Min. Sisters 20.

Convent of St. Dominic, 4027 Fawnhill Ln., 45205. Tel: 513-621-5899. Email: gaia916@juno.com. Dominican Sisters of Hope 2.

Franciscan Monastery of St. Clare (Poor Clares) (1990) 1505 Miles Rd., 45231-2427. Tel: 513-825-7177; Fax: 513-825-4071. Email: contactsisters@fuse.net. Web: www.poorclarescincinnati.org. Sr. Ann Bartko, O.S.C., Abbess. Sisters 9.

McAuley Convent (1964) 1768 Cedar Ave., 45224-2802. Tel: 513-681-2100; Fax: 513-354-5051. Sisters of Mercy 31.

Provincial House, Health Center of Sisters of Notre Dame de Namur, 699 E. Columbia Ave., 45215-3945. Tel: 513-821-7448; Fax: 513-821-7476. Web: www.sndohio.org. Sisters Marilyn Kerber, S.N.D.deN., Prov.; Elizabeth Marie Bowyer, S.N.D.deN., Local Mod.; Donna Wisowaty, S.N.D.deN., Admin. Sisters 80.

Sisters of Charity of Cincinnati, Ohio (1952) 5900 Delhi Rd., 45051. Tel: 513-347-5201; Fax: 513-347-5228. Email: barbara.hagedorn@srcharitycinti.org. Web: www.srcharitycinti.org. Sr. Barbara Hagedorn, S.C., Pres. Sisters in Congregation 455; Sisters in Archdiocese 330.

Ursulines of Cincinnati (1910) 1339 E. McMillan St., 45206-2164. Tel: 513-961-3410, Ext. 139; Fax: 513-872-7177. Email: ursofcinti@juno.com. Ursuline Sisters., Sisters of this community sponsor one high school, one elementary school, counseling, social service, communications, adult education and parish work. Sisters 14.

DAYTON. *Sisters of the Precious Blood Generalate* (1834) 4000 Denlinger Rd., 45426. Tel: 937-837-3302; Fax: 937-837-8825. Email: sisters@preciousbloodsistersdayton.org. Web: www.preciousbloodsistersdayton.org. Sisters Florence Seifert, C.PP.S., Pres.; Jeanette Buehler, C.PP.S., Vice Pres. & Councilor & Sec.; Marita Beumer, C.PP.S., Councilor; Edna Hess, C.PP.S., Councilor & Treas.; Madonna Ratermann, C.PP.S., Councilor; Noreen Jutte, C.PP.S., Archivist.

Sisters of the Precious Blood, Salem Heights Convent, 4960 Salem Ave., 45416-1797. Tel: 937-278-0871; Fax: 937-278-8722. Email: reslife@preciousbloodsistersdayton.org. Web: www.bright.net/~cppsnews. Barbara De Los Santos, Admin.; Sr. Beverly Bodnar, C.PP.S., Asst. Admin. Resident Life & Contact Person. Sisters 50.

SAINT MARTIN. *Ursulines of Brown County* (1845) Ursuline Center, 20860 State Rte. 251, St. Martin, 45118-9705. Tel: 513-875-2020, Ext. 27; Fax: 513-875-2311. Email: phoman@tds.net. Web: www.ursulinesofbc.org. Sr. Patricia Homan, O.S.U., Congregational Min. Ursuline Order, Congregation of Paris. Sisters 31.

[P] RESIDENCES FOR ADULTS AND YOUTHS

CINCINNATI. *Friars Club*, 1615 Vine St., 45202. Tel: 513-381-5432; Fax: 513-381-7909. Email: atimmons@friarsclubinc.org. Web: www.friarsclubinc.org. Michael L. Besl, Board Chair; Annie Timmons, Exec. Dir.

[Q] RETREAT HOUSES, CONFERENCE AND RENEWAL CENTERS

DAYTON. *Bergamo Center for Lifelong Learning* (1967) 4400 Shakertown Rd., 45430-1075. Tel: 937-426-2363; Fax: 937-426-1090. Email: info@bergamocenter.org. Web: www.bergamocenter.org. Mr. Dick Flack, Exec. Dir.; Kevin Kozlowski, Dir. Youth Programs; Barbara Kozlowski, Prog. Dir.; Patricia O'Grady, Dir. Conference Svcs. & Guest Rels.

MILFORD. *Jesuit Spiritual Center at Milford*, 5361 S. Milford Rd., 45150-9746. Tel: 513-248-3500; Fax: 513-248-3503. Email: rreder@jesuitspiritualcenter.com. Web: www.jesuitspiritualcenter.com. Revs. George W. Traub, S.J.; Henry Chamberlain, S.J.; Richard P. Reder, Exec. Dir. & Contact Person; Jennifer Verkamp, Chm. Bd.

[R] CAMPUS MINISTRY AND NEWMAN CENTERS

CINCINNATI. *College of Mt. St. Joseph Campus Ministry* (1920) 5701 Delhi Rd., 45233-1670. Tel: 513-244-4844; Fax: 513-244-4594. Email: andrea_stiles@mail.msj.edu. Web: www.msj.edu. Andrea Stiles, Dir. Campus Ministry; Kate Welsh, Campus Min.

University of Cincinnati Newman Center 328 W. McMillan St., 45219-1224. Tel: 513-381-6400; Fax: 513-381-2540. Email: smsgnewman@gmail.com. Web: www.smsgonline.com. Revs. Alan Hirt, O.F.M.; Thomas Speier, O.F.M.; Sr. Leslie Keener, C.D.P., Campus Min.; Mrs. Jill Kreinbrink, Music Min.; Ms. Linda Martin, Business Mgr.; Ms. Ann Boltz, Pastoral Assoc.; Michael Schreiner, Campus Min.

Xavier University Campus Ministry 3800 Victory Pkwy., 45207-2411. Tel: 513-745-3567; Fax: 513-745-1959. Email: minning@xavier.edu. Web: www.xavier.edu/campus_ministry. Mr. Joseph P. Shadle, Dir.; Rev. Kent A. Beausoleil, S.J., Campus Min.; Mr. Scot Buzza, Coord. Liturgical Music; Ms. Katie Minning, Sec.; Mr. Tim Dunn, Campus Min.; Rev. Albert J. Bischoff, S.J., Campus Min.; Mrs. Kelly Albainy-Jenei, Campus Min.; Ms. Deanna Martin, Assoc. Dir.

DAYTON. *Sinclair Community College Campus Ministry* 444 W. Third St., 45402. Tel: 937-512-2768. Email: jane.steinhauser@sinclair.edu. Web: www.sinclaircampusministry.org. Dr. V. Jane Steinhauser, Archdiocesan Dir. of Campus Ministry.

University of Dayton Campus Ministry 45469-0408. Tel: 937-229-3339; Fax: 937-229-2035. Email: campus-ministry@udayton.edu. Web: www.ministry.udayton.edu. Revs. Christopher T. Wittmann, S.M., Dir. Tel: 937-229-3339; Gerald T. Chinchar, S.M., D.Min., Campus Min. Catechetical Prog. & Priest On Call. Tel: 937-229-2725; Sisters Mary Louise Foley, F.M.I., Campus Min. for Law School & Faculty/Staff. Tel: 937-229-2093; Nicole D. Trahan, F.M.I., Residence Hall Campus Min. Marycrest; Kathleen Rossman, O.S.F., Campus Min. Sophomore/VWK. Tel: 937-229-4587; Bro. Thomas Pieper, S.M., Campus Min. Stuart Hall/Marianist Hall. Tel: 937-229-2211; Nick Cardilino, Assoc. Dir. Campus Ministry, Dir. Center of Social Concern & Coord. Community Outreach & Svc. Clubs. Tel: 937-229-2576; Sue Terbay, Sec. Center of Social Concern. Tel: 937-229-2524; Bridget Ebbert, Campus Min., Sophomore/South Quad/Founders. Tel: 937-229-1754; Terri Lauer, Admin. Sec. to Campus Min. Tel: 937-229-3339; Mary Niebler, Assoc. Dir. of C.S.C. & Coord. of Cross Cultural Immersions. Tel: 937-229-2012; Kelly Bohrer, Coord. for Community Outreach & Svc. Clubs; Mr. James Pera, Campus Min. Liturgical Music. Tel: 937-229-2019; Emily Strand, B.A., Asst. to Dir., Campus Min. Liturgies; Crystal Caruanna Sullivan, Asst. Dir. Campus Ministry, Dir. Residence Life Ministry & Admin. Grad. Asst. Prog. Tel: 937-229-2574; Sr. Linda Lee Jackson, O.P., Neighborhood Faith Communities Coord. Tel: 937-229-3570; Rev. James Schimelpfening, S.M., D.Min., Pastoral Min./Retreats; Kathy Sales, Sacristan Immaculate Conception Chapel; Rev. LaKendra Hardware, Campus Min. Interdenominational Min. & Marianist Hall; David Conard, Dir. Retreats & Faith Communities. Tel: 937-229-2010; Allison Leigh, Faith Communities Coord. & Campus Min. Retreats; Teri Dickison, Asst. to Dir. Campus Min.

FAIRBORN. *Catholic Campus Ministry* (1968) 3650 Colonel Glenn Hwy., 45324-2096. Tel: 937-426-1836; Fax: 937-426-3490. Email: edward.burns@wright.edu. Web: www.raidercatholics.com. Rev. Edward M. Burns, Dir. Catholic Campus Ministry; Ms. Joan Marquis, Campus Min.

OXFORD. *Miami University Catholic Campus Ministry* 111 E. High St., 45056. Tel: 513-523-2153; Fax: 513-523-0559. Email: info@stmaryoxfordohio.org. Web: www.stmaryoxfordohio.org. Rev. Jeffrey P. Silver; Roberta L. Kinne, Pastoral Assoc.; Michael Puglielli, D.R.E.; Kimberly Wagner, Campus Min.; Ryan Leep, Music Dir.; Pam Burk, Business Mgr.

WILMINGTON. *Wilmington College Campus Ministry* 73 N. Mulberry St., 45177. Tel: 937-382-2236; Fax: 937-382-3234. Email: saintcolumbkille@yahoo.com. Web: www.stcolumbkille.org. Rev. James M. Wedig. Pastoral care available through St. Columbkille Parish.

[S] COMMUNITY CENTERS

CINCINNATI. *Healthy Moms & Babes, Inc.* (1985) 2270 Banning Rd., Ste. 200, 45239. Tel: 513-591-5600; Fax: 513-591-5604. Email: director@healthymomsandbabes.org. Web: www.healthymomsandbabes.org. Kathleen Brogle,

M.S.W., Pres. & CEO. Annual Participants 4,000; Staff 20.

Mercy Franciscan Social Ministries, Inc. dba Mercy Franciscan at St. John 1800 Logan St., 45202. Tel: 513-981-5800; Fax: 513-981-5899. Web: www.e-mercy.com. Ericka Copeland, Exec. Dir. Provides emergency assistance, temporary shelter for families, job training classes, shared housing for seniors, a senior center and program for male responsibility. Total Staff 28.

HAMILTON. *Mercy Franciscan at St. Raphael, Inc.*, 610 High St., 45011. Tel: 513-603-8222; Fax: 513-893-1814. Email: camorris@health-partners.org. Web: www.e-mercy.com. Don Rohling, Senior Vice Pres. Mission Integration; Carrie Morris, M.R.C., L.S.W., Exec. Dir. Total Assisted 18,708; Total Staff 12.

[T] FOUNDATIONS AND ENDOWMENTS

CINCINNATI. *Community Support Charitable Trust* (1987) 1615 Vine St., 45202. Tel: 513-721-4700; Fax: 513-287-8488. David P. O'Brien, Admin.; Revs. Kenan Freson, O.F.M., Trustee; Jeremy Harrington, O.F.M., Trustee; Bro. Vincent Delorenzo, O.F.M., Trustee.

Community Support Charitable Trust for the Province of St. John the Baptist of the Order of Friars Minor

Friars Club Foundation, Inc., 1615 Vine St., 45202. Tel: 513-721-4700; Fax: 513-287-8488. Mr. Thomas Klinedinst Jr., Trustee & Pres.; Mr. David O'Brien, Trustee & Treas.; Mr. John O'Connor, Vice Pres., Sec. & Trustee.

Good Samaritan Hospital Foundation of Cincinnati, Inc., 375 Dixmyth Ave., 45220-2489. Tel: 513-862-3786; Fax: 513-862-1355. Email: mary_rafferty@trihealth.com. Web: www.gshfoundation.com. Mary L. Rafferty, Contact Person.

Mercy Health Partners of Southwest Ohio Foundation, 4600 Mc Auley Pl., 6th Fl., 45242. Tel: 513-981-6329; Fax: 513-981-6104. Web: www.e-mercy.com. Todd E. Lindley, Pres. A Subsidiary of Mercy Health Partners of Southwest Ohio. Total Staff 9.

Roger Bacon High School Endowment, 4320 Vine St., 45217. Tel: 513-641-1300; Fax: 513-641-0498. Email: wfarris@rogerbacon.org. Web: www.rogerbacon.org. Rev. William Farris, O.F.M., Pres. & Contact Person; Mr. Rick Sollmann, Prin.

SC Ministry Foundation, Inc. (1986) 345 Neeb Rd., 45233. Tel: 513-347-1122; Fax: 513-347-1017. Email: dsmiley@scministryfdn.org. Web: www.scministryfdn.org. Sr. Sally Duffy, S.C., Pres. & Exec. Dir.

Sisters of Charity of Cincinnati-Charitable Trust (1988) 5900 Delhi Rd., 45051. Tel: 513-347-5201; Fax: 513-347-5228. Email: barbara.hagedorn@srcharitycinti.org. Web: www.srcharitycinti.org. Sr. Barbara Hagedorn, S.C., Pres. A designated trust fund to primarily support older and infirmed members of the congregation.

Sisters of Notre Dame De Namur, Ohio Province, Charitable Trust, 701 E. Columbia Ave., 45215-3999. Tel: 513-761-7636; Fax: 513-761-6159. Email: ohprovoff@ohsnd.org. Web: www.sndohio.org. Sr. Marilyn Kerber, S.N.D.deN., Canonical Representative; Virginia Chasteen, Contact Person.

The Summit Country Day School Foundation (1994) 2161 Grandin Rd., 45208. Tel: 513-871-4700; Fax: 513-871-6558. Email: paulin_d@summitcds.org. George Thurner, Pres.; Tom Theobald, Chm.; David Paulin, Sec. & Treas.

Ursulines of Cincinnati, Ohio Charitable Trust, 1339 E. McMillan St., 45206-2164. Tel: 513-961-3410, Ext. 139; Fax: 513-872-7177. Email: ursofcinti@juno.com. Sr. Mary Jerome Buchert, O.S.U.

DAYTON. *Community Support Charitable Trust* (1994) 431 E. Second St., 45402. Tel: 937-228-9263; Fax: 937-228-6878. Revs. Kenneth F. Pleiman, C.PP.S., Trustee; Thomas Brenberger, C.PP.S., Chm. & Trustee; Scott T. Kramer, C.PP.S., Trustee; Bros. Joseph J. Fisher, C.PP.S., Admin. & Trustee; Thomas R. Bohman, C.PP.S., Trustee; Mr. John York, Trustee.

**Samaritan Health Foundation* (1973) 2222 Philadelphia Dr., 45406. Tel: 937-278-5770; Fax: 937-278-5140. Email: ktormey@shp-dayton.org. Web: www.samaritanhealthfoundation.org. J. Kay Tormey, Pres. & Exec. Dir. Affiliate of Catholic Health Initiatives and Samaritan Health Partners.

FAIRFIELD. *Glenmary Home Missioners Charitable Trust*, 4119 Glenmary Trace, 45014. Tel: 513-874-8900; Fax: 513-874-1690. Revs. Dominic R. Duggins, G.H.M., Sec. & Trustee; James Kelly, G.H.M., Trustee (Retired); Bro. Jack Henn, Trustee; Teresa Heckenmueller, Trustee; John Monroe, Trustee.

[U] MISCELLANEOUS LISTINGS

CINCINNATI. *St. Andrew Kim Korean Catholic Community* (1980) 3171 Struble Rd., 45251. Tel: 513-322-3183; Fax: 513-322-3183. Email: ckckimoh@gmail.com. Web: www.cincinnatikoreancatholic.org. Revs. Huengwoo Lee, Chap. & Admin.; Andrew Lee Gil-Sang, Pastoral Council.

St. Anthony Messenger (1893) 28 W. Liberty St., 45202. Tel: 513-241-5615; Fax: 513-241-0399. Email: st.anthony@americancatholic.org. Web: www.americancatholic.org. Thomas A. Shumate, Contact Person; Rev. Daniel Kroger, O.F.M. Operated by the St. John the Baptist Province of the Franciscan Friars.

St. Anthony Messenger Press and Franciscan Communications, 28 W. Liberty St., 45202. Tel: 513-241-5615; Fax: 513-241-0399. Email: stanthony@americancatholic.org. Web: www.americancatholic.org. Thomas A. Shumate, Contact Person; Rev. Daniel Kroger, O.F.M.

Catholic Alumni Club (Cincinnati Chapter), 3332 Alamo #9, 45209.

Catholic Cursillo of Cincinnati (1962) P.O. Box 317655, 45231. Tel: 513-931-7382. Email: tperazzo@cinci.rr.com. Web: www.cincinnati-cursillo.org. Mrs. Mary Ott, Lay Dir. Tel: 937-323-5409; Deacon William Krumm, Spiritual Advisor.

Catholic Healthcare Partners Housing Development, 615 Elsinore Pl., 45202. Tel: 513-639-2800; Fax: 513-639-2810. Web: www.health-partners.org. Scott Schitter, Dir.

Cincinnati Catholic Women's Association (1917) 958 Marion Ave., 45229. Tel: 513-961-3566. Web: cincinnaticatholicwomen.org. Pauline Fitzgerald, Pres.

The Comboni Lay Missionaries Association, 1318 Nagel Rd., 45255-3120. Tel: 513-474-4997; Fax: 513-474-0382. Email: info@laymission-comboni.org. Web: www.combonimissionaries.org; www.laymission-comboni.org. Mr. Thomas Drexler, Pres.; Mr. Chuck Carey, Vice Pres.; Mr. Paul Wheeler, Dir.; Ms. JoAnne Harbert, Assoc. Dir.; Ms. Opal Easter-Smith, Treas.; Mrs. Gisela Grundges-Andraos, Sec.

The Comboni Missionaries Auxiliary, Inc., 1318 Nagel Rd., 45255-3120. Tel: 513-474-4997; Fax: 513-474-0382. Email: info@combonimissionaries.org. Web: www.combonimissionaries.org. Marie Rose Obert, Pres.; Olga Baldwin, Vice Pres.; Jo DeSalvo, Sec.; Velma Bishak, Treas.; Rev. Paul Donohue, M.C.C.J., Spiritual Advisor.

Concerned Catholics for Gay/Lesbian Inclusion - Within Archdiocese of Cincinnati (1998) 328 W. McMillan St., 45219-1224. Tel: 513-729-0451; Fax: 513-381-2540. Email: jacintadoyle@fuse.net. Sr. Jacinta Doyle, F.S.P., Contact Person.

**The Couple to Couple League International* (1971) P.O. Box 111184, 45211. 4290 Delhi Pk., 45238. Tel: 513-471-2000; Fax: 513-557-2449. Email: ccli@ccli.org. Web: www.ccli.org. Michael D. Manhart, Ph.D., Exec. Dir.

St. Dymphna Ministry, c/o Summit Behavioral Healthcare, 1101 Summit Rd., 45237. Tel: 513-948-3600. Res.: 476 Riddle Rd., 45220. Tel: 513-961-4422. Rev. Valens J. Waldschmidt, O.F.M. (Retired).

Franciscan Central Purchasing (1965) St. Clement Friary, 4536 Vine St., 45217. Tel: 513-641-2257; Fax: 513-641-2262. Rev. Maynard Tetreault, O.F.M., Dir.

Franciscan Missionary Union, 1615 Vine St., 45202. Tel: 513-721-4700, Ext. 3222; Fax: 513-421-9672. Email: missionoffice@franciscan.org. Web: www.franciscan.org. Bro. Vincent Delorenzo, O.F.M., Exec. Dir.; Marilyn Wilson, Sec. & Contact Person.

Franciscans Network, 4820 Glenway Ave., 45238. Tel: 513-238-3214. Email: franciscansnetwork@cinci.rr.com. Web: www.franciscansnetwork.org. Ms. Diane H. Laake, Contact Person; Revs. John Quigley, O.F.M., Bd. of Trustees; Murray L. Bodo, O.F.M., Bd. of Trustees; Alan Hartman, S.F.O., Bd. of Trustees.

Good Samaritan College of Nursing and Health Science, 375 Dixmyth Ave., 45220. Tel: 513-862-2631; Fax: 513-862-3572. Email: morey.cohen@email.gscollege.edu. Web: www.trihealth.com; www.gscollege.edu. Morris Cohen, Pres.; Donna S. Nienaber, Sec.

Hispanic Ministry Office at St. Charles Borromeo, Archdiocese of Cincinnati, 115 W. Seymour Ave., 45216. Tel: 513-948-1760; Fax: 513-948-1823. Email: hispanicministry@catholiccincinnati.org. Web: www.archdiocese-cinti.org. Rev. William J. Jansen, M.C.C.J., Dir.

Jesuit Development Office, 607 Sycamore St., 45202. Tel: 513-751-6688; Fax: 513-723-0451. Email: mmaxwell@jesuits-chi.org. Web: www.jesuits-chi.org. Mark E. Maxwell, Dir.

Legion of Mary, 3105 Madison Rd., 45209. Tel: 513-871-5757; Fax: 513-533-6066. Email: schurch3@cinci.rr.com. Web: stceciliacincinnati.org/home. Rev. Elmer W. Smith, Spiritual Dir. (Retired).

Living Monuments of Reparation, P.O. Box 29372, 45229. Tel: 248-620-2542; Fax: 248-625-3526. Rev. Herbert J. Raterman, S.J., Dir.

Marian Center of Cincinnati, 5365 Cleves Warsaw, 45238. Tel: 513-922-1250; Fax: 859-441-0641. Mr. Robert E. Hater, Lay Dir.

Mercy Franciscan Social Ministries, Inc. dba Franciscan Home Development 4600 McAuley Pl., 6th Fl., 45242. Tel: 513-981-6000; Fax: 513-981-6133. Web: www.e-mercy.com. Kenneth C. Page, Pres. A member of Mercy Health Partners; Provides housing to over 270 persons in over 201 residential units.

**Mercy Neighborhood Ministries, Inc.*, 1602 Madison Rd., 45206. Tel: 513-751-2500; Fax: 513-221-5498. Web: www.mercyneighborhoodministries.org. Suzanne M. Kathman, Exec. Dir.

Ministers of Service, 745 Ezzard Charles, 45203. Tel: 513-381-0630; Fax: 513-742-9096. Email: church3824@cs.com. Mr. Jack D. McWilliams, Dir. The Ministers of Service Program, which began in 1979, provides training in urban ministry, primarily but not exclusively for African American laypersons. The Ministers of Service Program focuses on parish/community ministry to prepare laypersons to take active roles in church ministry.

**Natural Family Planning International Inc.*, Mailing Address: P.O. Box 11216, 45211. 2911 Werk Rd., 45211-7018. Tel: 513-661-7396; Fax: 513-661-7396. Web: www.nfpandmore.org. Mr. John F. Kippley, Pres.

New Jerusalem Community, 745 Derby Ave., 45232. Tel: 513-541-4748; Fax: 513-541-4748. Email: njcommunity@juno.com. Mary Heimert, Leadership Council; Debby Carrico, Leadership Council; Barb Gutting, Admin. & Coord. Community Life.

**Presentation Ministries, Inc.*, 3230 McHenry Ave., 45211. Tel: 513-662-5378. Email: pubsandtapes@presentationministries.com. Web: www.presentationministries.com. Deacon George Schmidl, Pres. & Contact Person.

**Ruah Woods*, 6675 Wesselman Rd., 45248. Tel: 513-407-8672; Fax: 513-417-8955. Web: www.ruahwoods.org. Leslie Kuhlman, Exec. Dir.

Secular Franciscan Order, 4012 Ryland, Springfield, 45503. Tel: 513-522-7430. Email: annekena@aol.com. Steve White, S.F.O. Formation Dir., (Cincinnati, OH); Rosemary Menetrey, S.F.O. Regl. Min., 13 N. Cresent Ave., Fort Thomas, KY 41075. Tel: 859-781-5196; Marilyn Anneken, S.F.O. Councilor, 4331 Erryn Ln., St. Bernard, 45217. Tel: 513-641-1210. Holy Trinity Regional Fraternity, Inc.; Founded by St. Francis of Assisi before A.D. 1215.

Seton Family Center, 712 Purcell Ave., 45205. Tel: 513-471-9169; Fax: 513-471-9159. Email: setonfam@aol.com. Web: www.setonfamilycenter.org. Sr. Jacqueline Kowalski, S.C., Foundress; Dr. Helmut R. Roehrig, Pres. Exec. Dir.; Richard P. Meder, Bd. Chair; Sr. Mary Jo Gasdorf, S.C., Vice Chair. Sponsored by: Sisters of Charity of Mt. St. Joseph., Purpose: Individual and Family Therapy, Children's Play Therapy and Diagnostic Services.

Su Casa Hispanic Center, 100 E. 8th St., 45202. Tel: 513-761-1588; Fax: 513-761-9538. Email: galvarez@catholiccharitiesswo.org. Web: www.catholiccharitiesswo.org. Giovanna Alvarez, Dir. A program of Catholic Charities.

Ursuline Education Services, 5535 Pfeiffer Rd., 45242. Tel: 513-686-7524. Email: phoman@ursulineacademy.org. Web: www.ursuline-education.com. Sisters Patricia Homan, O.S.U., Exec. Dir.; Patricia Homan, O.S.U., Representative. U.E.S. is a service to all Ursuline Schools.

Vietnamese Catholic Community of Our Lady of Lavang, 314 Township Ave., 45216. Tel: 513-242-2933. Rev. Dominic Nguyen, Chap. & Contact Person.

St. Xavier Church Property Corporation, 607 Sycamore St., 45202. Tel: 513-721-4045; Fax: 513-723-0451. Rev. Eric J. Knapp, S.J., Contact Person & Trustee; Very Rev. Timothy P. Kesicki, S.J., Pres.

CARTHAGENA. *The Society of the Precious Blood Senior Housing Corporation*, 2860 U.S. Rte. 127, 45822. Tel: 419-925-4516; Fax: 419-925-4800. Email: frjseibert@hotmail.com. Rev. James C. Seibert, C.PP.S., Pres. & Contact Person.

CENTERVILLE. *St. Leonard Faith Community*, 8100 Clyo Rd., 45458. Tel: 937-435-3626; Fax: 937-435-3626. Email: faithcomm4@sbcglobal.net. Web: www.stleonardfaithcommunity.com. Rev. Loren Connell, O.F.M., Moderator/Chap.; Deacon William Krumm.

St. Leonard Foundation, 8100 Clyo Rd., 45458. Tel: 937-436-6382; Fax: 937-439-7165. Web: www.stleonard.net. Jill Harris, Pres. & Contact Person.

DAYTON. *Catholic Alumni Club (Dayton Chapter)*, P.O. Box 3612, 45401-3612. Tel: 937-252-7035. Email: jwildenj516@yahoo.com. Jennifer Gladski, Contact Person; Rev. Daniel J. Meyer, Chap., 218 K St., 45409.

Catholic Vietnamese Community of Dayton, 217 W. Fourth St., 45402. Tel: 937-224-3904. Email: sacredheartdayton@yahoo.com. Rev. Hung M. Tran, Chap. & Admin.

Samaritan Behavioral Health, Inc. (2002) 601 Edwin C. Moses Blvd. 4th Fl., 45417. Tel: 937-276-8333; Fax: 937-276-8336. Email: smcgatha@shp-dayton.org. Web: www.sbhihelp.org. Sue McGatha, Pres. & CEO. Samaritan Behavioral Health, Inc. is a community-based provider of mental health and drug and alcohol services.

FAIRBORN. *National Diaconate Institute for Continuing Education, Inc.*, 330 Chatham Dr., 45324. Tel: 937-879-5332. Web: www.ndice.org. Max J. Roadruck Jr., Past Pres.

MARIA STEIN. *Maria Stein Center Shrine of the Holy Relics* (1846) 2291 St. Johns Rd., 45860. Tel: 419-925-4532; Fax: 513-925-5044. Email: director@mariasteincenter.org. Web: www.mariasteincenter.org. Sr. Barbara Ann Hoying, C.PP.S., Dir. Includes The National Marian Shrine of the Holy Relics, The Heritage Museum, and The Pilgrim Gift Shop.

MOUNT SAINT JOSEPH. *Archivists for Congregations of Women Religious, ACWR National Office*, 5900 Delhi Rd., Mount St. Joseph, 45051. Tel: 513-347-4080. Email: acwr@juno.com. Web: www.archivistsacwr.org. Purpose: Professional Preservation of the archives of Roman Catholic women religious congregations and collaboration with historians in making known the lives and works of women religious.

NEW RICHMOND. **Embrace the Children*, 3056 Twin Ridge Rd., 45157. Tel: 513-388-9115.

RELIGIOUS INSTITUTES OF MEN REPRESENTED IN THE ARCHDIOCESE

For further details refer to the corresponding bracketed number in the Religious Institutes of Men or Women section.

[0460]—*Brothers of the Poor of St. Francis*—C.F.P.
[0380]—*Comboni Missionaries of the Heart of Jesus (Verona)*—M.C.C.J.
[0650]—*Congregation of the Holy Spirit* (Eastern Province)—C.S.Sp.
[0520]—*Franciscan Friars* (Province of St. John the Baptist, Cincinnati and Province of Our Lady of Guadalupe, Albuquerque)—O.F.M.
[0570]—*Glenmary Home Missioners*—G.H.M.
[0690]—*Jesuit Fathers and Brothers* (Chicago Province)—S.J.
[0800]—*Maryknoll*—M.M.
[1210]—*Missionaries of St. Charles (Scalabrinians)*—C.S.
[0430]—*Order of Preachers (Dominicans)* (St. Joseph Province)—O.P.
[0760]—*Society of Mary (Marianists)* (United States Province)—S.M.
[1060]—*Society of the Precious Blood* (Cincinnati Province)—C.PP.S

RELIGIOUS INSTITUTES OF WOMEN REPRESENTED IN THE ARCHDIOCESE

[0230]—*Benedictine Sisters of Pontifical Jurisdiction* (Beech Grove, IN; Villa Hills, KY)—O.S.B.
[0330]—*Carmelite Sisters for the Aged and Infirm*—O.Carm.
[1000]—*Congregation of Divine Providence of Kentucky*—C.D.P.
[0870]—*Congregation of the Daughters of Mary Immaculate (Marianist Sisters)*—F.M.I.
[3832]—*Congregation of the Sisters of St. Joseph*—C.S.J.
[1920]—*Congregation of the Sisters of the Holy Cross*—C.S.C.
[1730]—*Congregation of the Sisters of the Third Order of St. Francis, Oldenburg, IN*—O.S.F.
[1710]—*Congregation of the Third Order of St. Francis of Mary Immaculate, Joliet, IL*—O.S.F.
[1070-07]—*Dominican Sisters* (Adrian, MI)—O.P.
[1070-16]—*Dominican Sisters* (Nashville, TN)—O.P.
[1070-17]—*Dominican Sisters* (Elkins Park, PA)—O.P.
[1070-15]—*Dominican Sisters of Hope*—O.P.
[1070-13]—*Dominican Sisters of Peace* (Columbus, OH)—O.P.
[1115]—*Dominican Sisters of Peace*—O.P.
[1415]—*Franciscan Sisters of Mary*—F.S.M.
[1430]—*Franciscan Sisters of Our Lady Perpetual Help* (St. Louis, MO)—O.S.F.
[1440]—*Franciscan Sisters of the Poor*—S.F.P.
[2340]—*Little Sisters of the Poor*—L.S.P.
[2470]—*Maryknoll Sisters of St. Dominic*—M.M.
[2720]—*Mission Helpers of the Sacred Heart*—M.H.S.H.
[3760]—*Order of St. Clare-Poor Clares*—O.S.C.
[3230]—*Poor Handmaids of Jesus Christ*—P.H.J.C.
[0440]—*Sisters of Charity of Cincinnati, Ohio*—S.C.
[0500]—*Sisters of Charity of Nazareth* (KY)—S.C.N.
[0570]—*Sisters of Charity of Seton Hill, Greensburg, Pennsylvania*—S.C.
[1710]—*Sisters of St. Francis of Mary Immaculate* (Joliet, IL)—O.S.F.
[2575]—*Sisters of Mercy of the Americas* (South Central Community, Belmont, NC)—R.S.M.
[2630]—*Sisters of Mercy of the Holy Cross*—S.C.S.C.
[2990]—*Sisters of Notre Dame* (Covington Prov.)—S.N.D.
[3000]—*Sisters of Notre Dame de Namur*—S.N.D.deN.
[3360]—*Sisters of Providence of Saint Mary-of-the-Woods, Indiana*—S.P.
[1530]—*Sisters of St Francis of the Congregation of Our Lady of Lourdes* (Sylvania, OH)—O.S.F.
[1630]—*Sisters of St. Francis of Penance and Christian Charity, Stella Niagara, NY*—O.S.F.
[1720]—*Sisters of St. Francis of Rochester, MN*—O.S.F.
[3840]—*Sisters of St. Joseph of Carondolet* (Latham, NY)—C.S.J.
[2110]—*Sisters of the Humility of Mary*—H.M.
[3260]—*Sisters of the Precious Blood* (Dayton, OH)—C.PP.S.
[2150]—*Sisters, Servants of the Immaculate Heart of Mary*—I.H.M.
[2560]—*Society of Mary Reparatrix*—S.M.R.
[4120]—*Ursuline Nuns of the Congregation of Paris* (Saint Martin)—O.S.U.
[4120-01]—*Ursuline Nuns of the Congregation of Paris* (Cincinnati, OH)—O.S.U.
[4120-03]—*Ursuline Nuns of the Congregation of Paris* (Louisville, KY)—O.S.U.

CEMETERIES

CINCINNATI. *Calvary*, 1721 Duck Creek Rd., 45207. Tel: 513-961-2179; Fax: 513-961-0062. Ronald Hilland, Supt.

Gate of Heaven, 11000 Montgomery Rd., 45242. Tel: 513-489-0300; Fax: 513-489-1817. Gary Raffel, Dir.; Paula Rooks, Supt.; Vickie Fisher, Sales & Family Svcs. Mgr.

St. John, 3819 W. 8th St., 45205. Tel: 513-242-4191. 4423 Vine St., 45217. Tel: 513-242-4191. Stephen E. Bittner, Pres.

St. Joseph, 3819 W. 8th St., 45205. Tel: 513-557-2306, Ext. 19; Fax: 513-557-2310. Stephen E. Bittner, Pres.

St. Joseph New, 4500 Foley Rd., 45238. Tel: 513-251-3110; Fax: 513-251-1075. Rob Winter, Gen. Mgr.

St. Mary, 701 Ross Ave., 45217. Tel: 513-242-4191. 3819 W. 8th St., 45205. Stephen E. Bittner, Pres.

DAYTON. *The Calvary Cemetery Association*, 1625 Calvary Dr., 45409. Tel: 937-293-1221; Fax: 937-293-7316. Janet Baughman, Office Mgr.

SPRINGFIELD. *Calvary*, 3155 E. Possum Rd., 45502. Tel: 937-323-7474. James P. Matthews, Supt.

NECROLOGY

✠ Moeddel, Most Rev. Carl K., Retired Auxiliary Bishop of Cincinnati—Died Aug. 25, 2009
† Andres, Joseph P., (Retired)—Died Feb. 2, 2009
† Ballman, Thomas J., (Retired)—Died March 1, 2009
† Behler, Donald A., (Retired)—Died June 17, 2009
† Bertke, Erwin J., (Retired)—Died Dec. 1, 2009
† Kelley, David J., (Administrative Leave)—Died June 6, 2009
† Wiemeyer, Raymond G., (Retired)—Died Oct. 14, 2009

An asterisk (*) denotes an organization that has established tax-exempt status directly with the IRS and is not covered by the USCCB Group Ruling.

Diocese of Cleveland

(Dioecesis Clevelandensis)

Most Reverend

RICHARD GERARD LENNON

Bishop of Cleveland; ordained priest May 19, 1973; appointed Titular Bishop of Sufes and Auxiliary Bishop of Boston June 29, 2001; ordained September 14, 2001; appointed Bishop of Cleveland April 4, 2006; installed May 15, 2006. *Office: 1404 E. Ninth St., Cleveland, OH 44114.* Tel: 216-696-6525; 800-869-6525 (Ohio only); Fax: 216-696-6547.

Cathedral Square Plaza: 1404 E. Ninth St., Cleveland, OH 44114. Tel: 216-696-6525; 800-869-6525 (Ohio only); Fax: 216-621-7332.

Web: www.dioceseofcleveland.org

Email: chancellor@dioceseofcleveland.org

Most Reverend

ANTHONY M. PILLA, D.D., M.A.

Retired Bishop of Cleveland; ordained May 23, 1959; appointed Auxiliary and Titular Bishop of Scardona June 30, 1979; consecrated August 1, 1979; named Apostolic Administrator of Cleveland July 29, 1980; appointed Bishop of Cleveland November 18, 1980; installed January 6, 1981; retired May15, 2006. *Office: 28700 Euclid Ave., Wickliffe, OH 44092.* Tel: 440-943-7600; Fax: 440-943-2428.

Most Reverend

A. EDWARD PEVEC, PH.D.

Retired Auxiliary Bishop of Cleveland; ordained April 29, 1950; appointed Auxiliary and Titular Bishop of Mercia April 13, 1982; consecrated July 2, 1982; retired September 1, 2002. *Office: Center for Pastoral Leadership, 28700 Euclid Ave., Wickliffe, OH 44092.* Tel: 216-944-1400; Fax: 440-943-7673.

Most Reverend

A. JAMES QUINN, J.C.D., J.D.

Retired Auxiliary Bishop of Cleveland; ordained May 24, 1958; appointed Auxiliary and Titular Bishop of Socia October 14, 1983; consecrated December 5, 1983; retired June 14, 2008. *Office: 2345 Bassett Rd., Westlake, OH 44145.* Tel: 440-250-9271; Fax: 440-835-5895.

Most Reverend

ROGER W. GRIES, O.S.B.

Auxiliary Bishop of Cleveland; ordained May 16, 1963; appointed Auxiliary and Titular Bishop of Presidio April 3, 2001; consecrated June 7, 2001. *Office: 1230 Ansel Rd., Cleveland, OH 44109.* Tel: 216-721-0676; Fax: 216-721-0903.

ESTABLISHED APRIL 23, 1847.

Square Miles 3,414.

Comprises, since July 22, 1943, eight counties in the north-central part of the State of Ohio, namely Ashland, Cuyahoga, Geauga, Lake, Lorain, Medina, Summit and Wayne Counties.

For legal titles of parishes and diocesan institutions, consult the Chancery Office.

STATISTICAL OVERVIEW

Personnel	
Bishop	1
Auxiliary Bishops	1
Retired Bishops	3
Abbots	1
Retired Abbots	1
Priests: Diocesan Active in Diocese	270
Priests: Diocesan Active Outside Diocese	7
Priests: Diocesan in Foreign Missions	4
Priests: Retired, Sick or Absent	124
Number of Diocesan Priests	405
Religious Priests in Diocese	101
Total Priests in Diocese	506
Extern Priests in Diocese	23
Ordinations:	
Diocesan Priests	5
Religious Priests	2
Transitional Deacons	2
Permanent Deacons	9
Permanent Deacons in Diocese	210
Total Brothers	58
Total Sisters	1,073
Parishes	
Parishes	201
With Resident Pastor:	
Resident Diocesan Priests	178
Resident Religious Priests	13
Without Resident Pastor:	
Administered by Priests	6
Administered by Deacons	1
Administered by Professed Religious Men	1
Administered by Religious Women	2
Missions	1
Pastoral Centers	2
New Parishes Created	8
Closed Parishes	31
Professional Ministry Personnel:	
Brothers	6
Sisters	84
Lay Ministers	173
Welfare	
Catholic Hospitals	3
Total Assisted	413,766
Health Care Centers	1
Total Assisted	259
Homes for the Aged	24
Total Assisted	5,116
Residential Care of Children	1
Total Assisted	355
Day Care Centers	9
Total Assisted	906
Specialized Homes	6
Total Assisted	939
Special Centers for Social Services	22
Total Assisted	292,821
Residential Care of Disabled	2
Total Assisted	237
Other Institutions	3
Total Assisted	42,807
Educational	
Seminaries, Diocesan	2
Students from This Diocese	52
Students from Other Diocese	2
Students Religious	13
Total Seminarians	65
Colleges and Universities	3
Total Students	7,154
High Schools, Diocesan and Parish	6
Total Students	3,216
High Schools, Private	16
Total Students	10,262
Elementary Schools, Diocesan and Parish	98
Total Students	33,493
Elementary Schools, Private	9
Total Students	2,453
Non-residential Schools for the Disabled	1
Total Students	107
Catechesis/Religious Education:	
High School Students	4,926
Elementary Students	38,991
Total Students under Catholic Instruction	100,667
Teachers in the Diocese:	
Priests	19
Brothers	20
Sisters	112
Lay Teachers	3,261
Vital Statistics	
Receptions into the Church:	
Infant Baptism Totals	7,009
Adult Baptism Totals	694
Received into Full Communion	573
First Communions	9,139
Confirmations	9,045
Marriages:	
Catholic	1,749
Interfaith	843
Total Marriages	2,592
Deaths	7,655
Total Catholic Population	744,000
Total Population	2,855,767

Former Bishops—Rt. Revs. AMADEUS RAPPE, D.D., ord. March 14, 1829; cons. Oct. 10, 1847; resigned July 29, 1870; died Sept 8, 1877; RICHARD GILMOUR, D.D., ord. Aug. 30, 1852; cons. April 14, 1872; died April 13, 1891; IGNATIUS F. HORSTMANN, D.D., ord. June 10, 1865; cons. Feb. 25, 1892; died May 13, 1908; JOHN P. FARRELLY, D.D., ord. May 22, 1880; cons. May 1, 1909; died Feb. 12, 1921; Most Revs. JOSEPH SCHREMBS, S.T.D., Archbishop-Bishop of Cleveland; cons. Feb. 22, 1911; transferred to the See of Cleveland, June 16, 1921; installed Sept. 8, 1921; appt. Archbishop, March 25, 1939; died November 2, 1945; EDWARD F. HOBAN, S.T.D., Ph.D., L.L.D., Archbishop-Bishop of Cleveland; cons. Dec. 21, 1921; transferred to Cleveland as Coadjutor Bishop "cum jure successionis" Nov. 14, 1942; succeeded to See of Cleveland, Nov. 2, 1945; appt. Archbishop, July 23, 1951; died Sept. 22, 1966; CLARENCE G. ISSENMANN, S.T.D., cons. May 25, 1954; transferred to Cleveland as Coadjutor Bishop "cum jure successionis" and Titular Bishop of Filaca. Ap-Adm. Oct. 7, 1964; succeeded to See of Cleveland, Sept. 22, 1966; retired June 5, 1974; died July 27, 1982; JAMES A. HICKEY, S.T.D., J.C.D., cons. April 14, 1967; appt. Bishop of Cleveland, June 5, 1974; installed July 16, 1974; appt. Archbishop of Washington, DC June 17, 1980; created Cardinal by Pope John Paul II in the consistory on June 28, 1988; retired Nov. 21, 2000; died Oct. 24, 2004; ANTHONY M. PILLA, ord. May 23, 1959; appt. Auxiliary and Titular Bishop of Scardona June 30, 1979; cons. Aug. 1, 1979; named Apostolic Administrator of Cleveland July 29, 1980; appt. Bishop of Cleveland Nov. 18, 1980; installed Jan. 6, 1981.

Vicars General—Most Revs. A. JAMES QUINN, J.C.D., J.D., V.G. (Retired), 2500 Elyria Ave., Lorain, 44055. Tel: 440-244-2120; 216-579-0326 (Cleveland Line); ROGER W. GRIES, O.S.B., D.D., M.Ed., St. Andrew, 5135 Superior Ave., Cleveland, 44103-1239. Tel: 216-361-0873; ANTHONY M. PILLA, D.D., M.A., (Bishop Emeritus) (Retired), Center for Pastoral Ministry, 28700 Euclid Ave., Wickliffe, 44092. Tel: 440-943-3928; A. EDWARD PEVEC, Ph.D. (Retired), Center for Pastoral Leadership, 28700 Euclid Ave., Wickliffe, 44092. Tel: 440-944-1400; Rev. RALPH E. WIATROWSKI, J.C.D., 1027 Superior Ave., Cleveland, 44114.

Tel: 216-696-6525, Ext. 2080.

College of Consultors—Most Rev. ROGER W. GRIES, O.S.B., D.D., M.Ed.; Revs. JOHN M. KUMSE; JOHN E. MANNING, M.A., M.Div.; THOMAS V. O'DONNELL; JOHN R. OLSAVSKY, J.C.L. (Retired); Most Rev. A. JAMES QUINN, J.C.D., J.D., V.G. (Retired); Revs. PAUL J. ROSING, M.Div.; ROBERT J. SANSON, J.C.D.; JOHN G. VRANA; KENNETH J. WOLNOWSKI (Retired).

Presbyteral Council—Most Rev. RICHARD G. LENNON, D.D., M.A., M.Th., Pres.; Revs. WALTER H. JENNE, Moderator; ALBERT A. KRUPP; ERIC ORZECH; THOMAS J. BEHREND; DAVID BLINE; WILLIAM G. BOUHALL; MARK A. DINARDO; Rt. Rev. CHRISTOPHER SCHWARTZ, O.S.B.; Rev. RICHARD S. RASCH, O.de.M.; Most Rev. ROGER W. GRIES, O.S.B., D.D., M.Ed. (ex officio); Revs. VINCENT J. HAWK; ROBERT J. JASNEY; JOSEPH H. CALLAHAN; EDWARD T. ESTOK, M.A., M.Div.; JOHN R. OLSAVSKY, J.C.L. (Retired); WALTER J. HYCLAK; ROBERT H. JACKSON; JOHN P. SINGLER; LORN J. SNOW, S.J.; JOHN T. MCDONOUGH (Retired); JOSEPH R. MAMICH; MARTIN F. POLITO; DONALD P. OLEKSIAK (ex officio); THOMAS W. TIFFT, Ph.D. (ex officio); PAUL J. ROSING, M.Div.; JOHN G. VRANA. Presbyteral Conveners: Revs. THOMAS J. BEHREND; WILLIAM G. BOUHALL; MARK A. DINARDO; VINCENT J. HAWK; ROBERT H. JACKSON; ERIC ORZECH; ALBERT A. KRUPP; MARTIN F. POLITO; LORN J. SNOW, S.J.; JOSEPH R. MAMICH; ROBERT J. JASANY; JOHN P. SINGLER; WALTER H. JENNE.

Diocesan Finance Council—RICHARD MARSH, Chm.; ANGELA CARLIN; SEAN HENNESSY; KAREN KLEINHENZ; DOMINIC OZANNE; THOMAS J. PERCIAK; JOSEPH SCAMINACE; ANTHONY LANG; WILLIAM J. REIDY; MARIA COYNE; ROBERT TRACZ; PATRICK MCMAHON.

Diocesan Pastoral Council—Most Rev. RICHARD G. LENNON, D.D., M.A., M.Th.; MARY D. HORVATH, Chm.; DANIEL W. VANEK, Vice Chm.; RICHARD S. KRIVANKA, Exec. Sec.

Conference of Religious Leadership—Sisters CECILIA LIBERATORE, S.N.D., Chm., 13000 Auburn Rd., Chardon, 44024-9331. Tel: 440-286-7101; M. ROCHELLE GUERTAL, O.SS.T., Treas., 21281 Chardon Rd., Euclid, 44117-1591. Tel: 216-481-8232.

Diocese of Cleveland—Cathedral Square Plaza, 1404 E. Ninth St., Cleveland, 44114.

All Diocesan Offices are in the Cathedral Square Plaza at 1404 E. Ninth St. and may be reached at: Tel: 216-696-6525; 800-869-6525 (Ohio only); Fax: 216-781-8243.

Address dispensations and all business communication to the Chancery Office.

Chancellor—Sr. THERESE GUERIN SULLIVAN, S.P., J.C.L., Office: Cathedral Square Plaza. Fax: 216-621-7332.

Assistant Chancellors—Rev. THEODORE MARSZAL, S.T.D. Office: Cathedral Square Plaza; Sr. LAURA BOUHALL, O.S.U. Office: Cathedral Square Plaza.

Administrative Assistant to the Bishop—Rev. THEODORE MARSZAL, S.T.D., Office: 1404 E. Ninth St., 6th Fl., Cleveland, 44114.

Stewardship Office—1404 E. Ninth St., 8th Fl., Cleveland, 44114. Tel: 216-696-6525, Ext. 2120. Mrs. MARY PAT FREY, Dir.

Office of Worship—1404 E. Ninth St., 6th Fl., Cleveland, 44114. Tel: 216-696-6525, Ext. 4120. Ms. CHRISTINA RONZIO, Dir.

Tribunal—Office: 1404 E. Ninth St., Ste. 700, Cleveland, 44114-2555. Tel: 216-696-6525; 800-869-6525 (Ohio only); 800-676-4431 (Outside Ohio); Fax: 216-696-3226.

Judicial Vicar—Rev. GARY D. YANUS, J.C.D.

Adjunct Judicial Vicars—Revs. WILLIAM M. JERSE, J.C.L.; LAWRENCE JURCAK, J.C.L.; CHARLES F. STREBLER, J.C.L.

Judges—Deacon LOUIS G. PECEK, Ph.D.; Sr. MARY ANN ANDREWS, C.S.A., J.C.L.; Ms. LYNETTE TAIT, J.C.L.; Rev. ROBERT M. WENDELKEN, D.Min. (Retired); Sr. THERESE GUERIN SULLIVAN, S.P., J.C.L.

Defenders of the Bond—Rev. JOSEPH A. BACEVICE, M.Div.; Sr. CHRISTINE M. RODY, S.C., J.C.L.

Judges in Second Instance—Revs. MIRKO HLADNI, J.C.L.; EDWARD J. LUCA, J.C.D. (Retired); JOHN R. OLSAVSKY, J.C.L. (Retired); WILLIAM P. O'NEILL, J.C.L.; ROBERT F. PFEIFFER, J.C.L. (Retired); ROBERT J. SANSON, J.C.D.; DAVID J. WALKOWIAK, J.C.D.; EDWARD F. WEIST, J.C.D.; RALPH E. WIATROWSKI, J.C.D.

Associate Judges—Deacon JAMES L. AGRIPPE, (Retired); Revs. CHARLES T. DIEDRICK, M.A.; JEROME J. DUKE; JOHN R. HENGLE; EDWARD J. KORDAS; ALLAN R. LAUBENTHAL, S.T.D. (Retired); JOHN E. MANNING, M.A., M.Div.; LAWRENCE N. MARTELLO, M.A., M.Div.; THOMAS W. MCCANN; PAUL J. ROSING, M.Div.; THOMAS R. SMITH, M.Div.; DONALD E. SNYDER, M.Div.; CHARLES J. STOLLENWERK, M.Div.; ALBERT J. TESEK (Retired); A. JONATHAN ZINGALES, J.C.L.

Auditors/Assessors—Ms. ALICE HINKEL; Deacon THOMAS B. DAW; Rev. DAVID R. TRASK; Mrs. ELAINE T. SHAWHAN; Mrs. PATRICIA DAW; Mr. CARL A. CALDWELL, M.A.

Procurators—Ms. ALICE HINKEL; Deacon DAVID PECOT; Ms. GAYLE CILIMBURG.

Promoters of Justice—Sr. CHRISTINE RODY, S.C., J.C.L.; Rev. MARK Q. FEDOR, J.C.D.

Ecclesiastical Notaries—Notary Publics: Mrs. LEE ANN CALVERT; Mrs. AMANDA L. HOCKENBERRY; Mrs. TERESA LUIKART.

Translators—Revs. EDWARD T. ESTOK JR., M.A., M.Div.; BEDE KOTLINSKI, O.S.B.; AUGUSTINE PHAM VAN LAN; JOHN F. WESSEL (Retired); MICHAEL J. TROHA; RICHARD BONA.

Director of Facilities—WILLIAM R. HUDSON, Cathedral Square Plaza, 6th Fl.

Archivist—Sr. THERESE GUERIN SULLIVAN, S.P., J.C.L.; CHRISTINE L. KROSEL, Archival Research Dir.; PHILIP HAAS, Archives Admin., Cathedral Square Plaza, 4th Fl.

Office of Mediation—Sr. DONNA MIKULA, O.S.U., Cathedral Square Plaza. Tel: 216-696-6525; 800-869-6525.

Catholic Cemeteries Association—ANDREJ N. LAH, Pres., 10000 Miles Ave., Cleveland, 44105. Tel: 216-641-7575.

The Catholic Diocese of Cleveland Foundation—Mr. PATRICK J. GRACE, Exec. Dir., 1404 E. 9th St., 8th Fl., Cleveland, 44114-1722. Tel: 216-696-6525, Ext. 5750; Fax: 216-348-0740.

Callistian Guild—Mailing Address: P.O. Box 605125, Cleveland, 44105. Tel: 216-641-7575.

Central Purchasing—JAMES P. TERESI, Dir., 9000 Town Centre Dr., Broadview Heights, 44147. Tel: 440-717-9700.

Communications Department—ROBERT D. TAYEK, Dir., Media & Pub. Rel., Chancery Building. Tel: 216-696-6525, Ext. 4460.

"Catholic Universe Bulletin"—Most Rev. RICHARD G. LENNON, D.D., M.A., M.Th., Publisher; JOSEPH M. POLITO, Assoc. Publisher & CEO, 1404 E. Ninth St., 6th Fl. Tel: 216-696-6525, Ext. 5870.

Catholic Universe Bulletin Publishing Company, Inc.—JOSEPH M. POLITO, CEO, 1404 E. 9th St., 6th Fl. Tel: 216-696-6525, Ext. 5870.

Diocesan Pastoral Planning Office—RICHARD S. KRIVANKA, Dir.; DAVID DE LAMBO, Ph.D., Assoc. Dir.; ANN MARIE PERKINS, Office Coord., Office: Tel: 216-696-6525, Ext. 4210.

Mission Office, Society for the Propagation of the Faith—Rev. R. STEPHEN VELLENGA, Dir., Office: 1404 E. 9th St., Cleveland, 44114. Tel: 216-696-6525, Ext. 4240.

Pontifical Programs— Society for the Propagation of the Faith; Society of St. Peter the Apostle; Missionary Union of the Clergy; Holy Childhood Assoc.

National Programs— Latin-American Program; Lay Mission Volunteers

Diocesan Programs— Missionary Cooperation Plan; St. Francis Xavier Mission Assoc.; Cleveland Diocesan Mission, C.A.

National Shrine of Immaculate Conception— Washington, DC. Sr. THERESE GUERIN SULLIVAN, S.P., J.C.L., Chancellor, Cathedral Square Plaza, 6th Fl.

Finance Office—JOHN R. MAIMONE, Finance Officer; GERALD ARNOLD, Controller, 1404 E. 9th St., 8th Fl., Cleveland, 44114.

Diocesan Legal Office—Bro. PATRICK T. SHEA, O.F.M., Gen. Counsel, 1404 E. 9th St., 7th Fl., Ste. 701, Cleveland, 44114.

Diocesan Building Commission—KEVIN T. BURKE, Coord., 1404 E. 9th St., 7th Fl., Cleveland, 44114.

Property/Casualty Office—KATHLEEN PIERCE, Dir., 1404 E. 9th St., 8th Fl., Cleveland, 44114.

DISC: Diocesan Insurance Service Committee—J. THOMAS HANNON, 1404 E. 9th St., 8th Fl., Cleveland, 44114.

Benefit Plans - Health Benefits, Group Life, and Pension—PALMIRA JURAS, 1404 E. 9th St., 8th Fl., Cleveland, 44114.

Human Resources Office—DONNA B. SPEAGLE, 1404 E. 9th St., 8th Fl., Cleveland, 44114.

Workers' Compensation Office—KATHLEEN PIERCE, 1404 E. 9th St., 8th Fl., Cleveland, 44114.

Secretariat for Education and Catechesis

Secretary for Education/Superintendent—MARGARET LYONS. Tel: 216-696-6525, Ext. 1022.

Secretary for Catechetical Services—Mr. WILLIAM B. MILLER, 1404 E. 9th St., Cleveland, 44114. Tel: 216-696-6525, Ext. 2880.

Departments—

Buildings and Grounds—DANIEL BRODNIK, Dir., 1404 E. 9th St., Cleveland, 44114. Tel: 216-696-6525, Ext. 3790.

Catholic Education Endowment Trust—JAN RAVAS, 1404 E. 9th St., Cleveland, 44114. Tel: 216-696-6525, Ext. 2830.

Office of Catechetical Services—Mr. WILLIAM B. MILLER, Dir., 1404 E. 9th St., Cleveland, 44114. Tel: 216-696-6525, Ext. 2880.

Newman Campus Ministry—Mr. WILLIAM B. MILLER, Dir., 1404 E. 9th St., Cleveland, 44114. Tel: 216-696-6525, Ext. 2880.

Ministers—Rev. NORMAN K. DOUGLAS, Akron University. Tel: 330-376-3585; JOHN SZARWARK, Akron University. Tel: 216-696-6525, Ext. 3000; TONY VENTO, Case Western Reserve University. Tel: 216-421-9614, Ext. 302; Rev. VINCENT J. HAWK, Ashland University. Tel: 419-994-4396; KAREN HAHN, College of Wooster. Tel: 330-287-3000, Ext. 4504; DEBBIE DACONE, Oberlin College. Tel: 440-775-5190; MINDY KUSHLAK, Baldwin Wallace College. Tel: 440-243-4955; GREGORY STEVENS, Cleveland State University. Tel: 216-398-7156; KIRSTEN KOLAJA, Baldwin Wallace College. Tel: 440-243-4955.

Catechetical Consultants—DENISE SMITHBERGER, Southern Area Office, 1558 Creighton Ave., Akron, 44310. Tel: 330-773-7621; PATRICIA FLAHERTY, Southern Area Office, 1558 Creighton Ave., Akron, 44310. Tel: 330-773-7621; MARY LOU NECKEL-JAMES, 1404 E. 9th St., Cleveland, 44114. Tel: 216-696-6525, Ext. 1028.

Media Consultant—JEFF STUTZMAN, 1404 E. 9th St., Cleveland, 44114. Tel: 216-696-6525, Ext. 4330.

Office of Catholic Education—MARGARET LYONS, Sec. Educ./Supt., 1404 E. 9th St., Cleveland, 44114. Tel: 216-696-6525, Ext. 1022.

Educational Services—KATHLEEN O'BRIEN, Dir., 1404 E. Ninth St., Cleveland, 44114. Tel: 216-696-6525, Ext. 1148.

Assistant Superintendents—FRANK M. KUHAR, Eastern Area, 1404 E. Ninth St., Cleveland, 44114. Tel: 216-696-6525, Ext. 1280; ANNE MARIE WOYMA, Western Area, 1404 E. Ninth St., Cleveland, 44114. Tel: 216-696-6525, Ext. 1890; MICHELLE C. KROLL, Southern Area, 1404 E. Ninth St., Cleveland, 44114. Tel: 216-696-6525, Ext. 1290.

Elementary Schools/Accreditation—ANNE MARIE WOYMA, Asst. Supt. Elementary Schools, 1404 E. 9th St., Cleveland, 44114. Tel: 216-696-6525, Ext. 1890.

Special Projects/Voucher Programs—JUDY NAKASIAN, Coord., 1404 E. 9th St., Cleveland, 44114. Tel: 216-696-6525, Ext. 3250.

Catholic Parent Teacher League—MICHELLE C. KROLL, Liaison, 1404 E. Ninth St., Cleveland, 44114. Tel: 216-696-6525, Ext. 1290; CYNTHIA S. PALUS, Pres. Tel: 216-466-4400; MARILYN HEIDELMAN, Corresponding Sec. Tel: 440-835-2744.

Finance—JOHN R. AHERN, Dir., 1404 E. 9th St., Cleveland, 44114. Tel: 216-696-6525, Ext. 5310.

Secondary Schools—WAYNE UEHLEIN, Assoc. Supt., 1404 E. 9th St., Cleveland, 44114. Tel: 216-696-6525, Ext. 2450.

Government Programs—MICHAEL VOINOVICH, Dir., 1404 E. 9th St., Cleveland, 44114. Tel: 216-696-6525, Ext. 3350.

Teacher Personnel Services—MELISSA HOKANSON, Dir., 1404 E. 9th St., Cleveland, 44114. Tel: 216-696-6525, Ext. 3360.

Nutrition Services/Summer Food Program—EDWARD MOREL, Dir., 1404 E. 9th St., Cleveland, 44114. Tel: 216-696-6525, Ext. 3110.

Curriculum—Dr. RUTHANN HEINTSCHEL, Coord., 1404 E. 9th St., Cleveland, 44114. Tel: 216-696-6525, Ext. 3240.

Educational Technology—DOLORES BRUNO, 1404 E. 9th St., Cleveland, 44114. Tel: 216-696-6525, Ext. 8990.

Technology—ANDREW BENTON, Dir., 1404 E. 9th St., Cleveland, 44114. Tel: 216-696-6525, Ext. 3200.

Mandated Services—Consultants: JOHN KASTELIC, Representative. Tel: 216-696-6525, Ext. 3770; PAMELA OUZTS, Coord., 1404 E. 9th St., Cleveland, 44114. Tel: 216-696-6525, Ext. 5140.

Secretariat for Parish Life

Secretary—Sr. RITA MARY HARWOOD, S.N.D., 1404 E. 9th St., 3rd Fl., Cleveland, 44114. Tel: 216-696-6525, Ext. 3500.

African Ministry—Sr. RITA MARY HARWOOD, S.N.D. Tel: 216-696-6525, Ext. 3500.

Apostleship of the Sea Chaplain for the Diocese of Cleveland (Port Chaplain)—Sr. RITA MARY HARWOOD, S.N.D., Interim. Tel: 216-696-6525, Ext. 3500.

Asian Ministry—Sr. RITA MARY HARWOOD, S.N.D. Tel: 216-696-6525, Ext. 3500.

Blue Army of Our Lady of Fatima—Marian Center, 6626 Pearl Rd., Parma Heights, 44130-3808. Tel: 440-888-8553.

Catholic Renewal Ministries—Rev. ROBERT J. FRANCO, 35777 Center Ridge Rd., North Ridgeville, 44039-3097. Tel: 440-327-2201. Bishop's Delegate, Presentation House, 28706 Euclid Ave., #4, Wickliffe, 44092. Tel: 440-944-9445.

Central City Ministry with Poor—Rev. JAMES P. O'DONNELL, 2186 E. 35th St., Cleveland, 44115. Tel: 216-566-0531.

Cleveland Diocesan Council, NCCW—EVELYN MCCUSKER, Pres.; Rev. RALPH HUDAK, Moderator, 6700 Lansing Ave., Cleveland, 44105-3797. Tel: 216-341-2734, Ext. 5110.

Diocesan Interfaith Commission—Rev. JOSEPH T. HILINSKI, Delegate. Tel: 216-696-6525, Ext. 5110.

Enthronement of the Sacred Heart—Diocesan Center, St. John Cathedral Rectory, 1007 Superior Ave., Cleveland, 44114. MARLENE R. PALUMBO, Sec. & Treas. Tel: 216-447-9375.

Ethnic Ministries— For the Pastoral Care of Migrants and Refugees and for any ethnic communities not listed below, please contact Sr. Rita Mary Harwood, S.N.D., The Parish Life Office. Tel: 216-696-6525, Ext. 3500.

Diocesan Hispanic Office—MISAEL MAYORGA, Dir., 1404 E. 9th St., Cleveland, 44114. Tel: 216-696-6525, Ext. 4300.

Korean Catholic Apostolate—Rev. CHANG SU O, St. Andrew Kim (Korean Pastoral Center), 2310 W. 14th St., Cleveland, 44113. Tel: 216-861-4630.

Native American Ministry—Sr. RITA MARY HARWOOD, S.N.D., Dir., 1404 E. 9th St., Cleveland, 44114. Tel: 216-696-6525, Ext. 3500.

Office of Ministry to African American Catholics—VANESSA GRIFFIN CAMPBELL, Dir. Tel: 216-696-6525, Ext. 3020.

Philippine-American Ministry—Rev. RODEL ANGELES, Dir., 1007 Superior Ave., Cleveland, 44114. Tel: 216-771-6666.

Vietnamese-American Apostolate—Rev. AUGUSTINE PHAM VAN LAN, Dir., 3545 W. 54th St., Cleveland, 44102. Tel: 216-961-2713, Ext. 2540.

Office of Evangelization—Sr. MARGARET MACH, S.C., Dir. Tel: 216-696-6525, Ext. 2540.

Holy Name Societies, Cleveland Diocesan Union—Rev. THOMAS A. HAREN, Spiritual Dir., 13623 Rockside Rd., Garfield Heights, 44125-5197. Tel: 216-662-8685.

Pastoral Ministry Office—Ms. KATHLEEN HAASE-FALBO, Dir., Center for Pastoral Leadership, 28700 Euclid Ave., Wickliffe, 44092. Tel: 440-943-7669.

Office for Women in Church and Society—LEANNE MAHOVLIC, Dir., 1404 E. 9th St., Cleveland, 44114. Tel: 216-696-6525, Ext. 3070.

Secretariat for Clergy and Religious

Secretary—Rev. LAWRENCE JURCAK, J.C.L., Sec. & Vicar for Clergy & Relg., 1404 E. 9th St., 2nd Fl., Cleveland, 44114.

Borromeo Seminary— See Seminaries.

Clergy Personnel Board—Rev. DONALD P. OLEKSIAK, Dir., 1404 E. 9th St., 2nd Fl., Cleveland, 44114.

Continuing Education for Formation of Ministers—Rev. JOSEPH T. HILINSKI, Dir.; Deacon PAUL KIPSFTUHL; KATHEE STERBENZ.

Diaconate Office—Deacon KENNETH PIECHOWSKI, Dir., The Center for Pastoral Leadership, 28700 Euclid Ave., Wickliffe, 44092; Rev. ANTHONY J. SCHUERGER, Special Dir. for the Re-establishment of the Permanent Diaconate Prog., St. Malachi Parish, 2459 Washington Ave., Cleveland, 44133-2380.

Retirement Board—Revs. JOHN T. CARLIN, St. Charles Borromeo, 5891 Ridge Rd., Parma, 44129-3642. Tel: 440-884-3030; THOMAS L. WEBER, Recording Sec., St. Bernadette, 2256 Clague Rd., Westlake, 44145. Tel: 440-734-1300.

St. Mary Seminary— See Seminaries.

Senior Priests—Rev. LAWRENCE JURCAK, J.C.L., Delegate, 1404 E. 9th St., 2nd Fl., Cleveland, 44114.

Vocations Office—Rev. MICHAEL K. GURNICK, M.A., M.Div.

Avilas of the Diocese of Cleveland—Mrs. MARIE BECKER, 20790 Lake Rd., Rocky River, 44116.

Parents of Priests—DONALD TRASK, Pres., 1404 E. 9th St., 2nd Fl., Cleveland, 44114.

Catholic Charities Health and Human Services

Catholic Charities Health and Human Services—J. THOMAS MULLEN, Pres. & CEO. Tel: 216-334-2901.

Catholic Charities Annual Appeal—Mr. PATRICK J. GRACE, 1404 E. Ninth St., 8th Fl., Cleveland, 44114. Tel: 216-696-6525, Ext. 5750; Fax: 216-348-0740.

Catholic Charities Parish Services—Executive Directors: TERRENCE FLANAGAN; JOHN P. KLEE, 7911 Detroit Ave., Cleveland, 44102. Tel: 216-334-2959; Fax: 216-334-2983.

Special Ministry to the Aged—6804 Lansing Ave., Cleveland, 44105-1521. Tel: 216-441-5402; Fax: 216-441-4510. Sr. ANNA KASZUBA, S.S.M.I., Dir.

Pro Life Office—PEGGY GEROVAC, Dir., 7911 Detroit Ave., Cleveland, 44102. Tel: 216-334-2965; Fax: 216-334-2976.

Office of Ministry for Persons with Disabilities—Rev. JOSEPH D. MCNULTY, Exec. Dir., St. Augustine Church, 2486 W. 14th St., Cleveland, 44113. Tel: 216-781-5530; Fax: 216-781-1124.

Marriage and Family Office—WILLIAM BOOMER, Dir., 7911 Detroit Ave., Cleveland, 44102. Tel: 216-334-2971.

Youth and Young Adult Ministry and CYO Office—GREG MOSER, Dir., 7911 Detroit Ave., Cleveland, 44102. Tel: 216-334-1261, Ext. 32.

Migration and Refugee Services—TOM MROSKO, Dir., 7800 Detroit Ave., Cleveland, 44102. Tel: 216-939-3731.

Catholic Charities Services Corporation—7911 Detroit Ave., Cleveland, 44102. THOMAS W. WOLL, Exec. Dir. Tel: 440-843-5501; Fax: 440-843-1627; MICHAEL HAGGERTY, Asst. Exec. Dir. Tel: 440-843-5514; Fax: 440-845-5910.

Catholic Charities Community Services—BERNADETTE WASHINGTON, Exec. Dir., 7911 Detroit Ave., Cleveland, 44102. Tel: 216-334-2937; Fax: 216-334-2907.

Disabilities Services—DENNIS MCNULTY, Senior Dir. Tel: 440-334-2962. OLA/St. Joseph Center, 2346 W. 14th St., Cleveland, 44113. Tel: 216-621-3451.

Emergency Assistance Services—GAYLE DOUCETTE, Dir., 1736 Superior Ave., Cleveland, 44114. Tel: 216-781-8262.

Older Adult Services—DAVE MODARSKY, Senior Dir., 7800 Detroit Ave., Cleveland, 44102. Tel: 216-939-3703; Fax: 216-631-3654.

Pastoral Care Services—Rev. KENNETH F. WALLACE, 7911 Detroit Ave., Cleveland, 44102. Tel: 216-587-8377.

Catholic Charities Facilities Corp.—7911 Detroit Ave., Cleveland, 44102. LAWRENCE E. MURTAUGH, Admin. Tel: 216-334-2949; Fax: 216-334-2907; CAROLYN SCHUEMANN, Dir. Finance. Tel: 216-334-2950; Fax: 216-334-2907.

Catholic Charities Housing Corporation—7911 Detroit Ave., Cleveland, 44102. MARYELLEN STAAB, Dir. Tel: 216-334-2954.

Catholic Charities Corporation—JOHN P. KLEE, Exec. Dir., 7911 Detroit Ave., Cleveland, 44102. Tel: 216-334-2959; Fax: 216-334-2983.

Diocesan Social Action Office—THOMAS J. ALLIO, Exec. Dir., 7800 Detroit Ave., Cleveland, 44102. Tel: 216-939-3851; Fax: 216-939-3850.

Commission on Catholic Community Action—VACANT, 7800 Detroit Ave., Cleveland, 44102. Tel: 216-939-3839; Fax: 216-939-3850.

Catholic Action Commission of Lorain County—SHARON KLEPPEL, Dir., 2500 Elyria Ave., Lorain, 44055. Tel: 216-244-6037; Fax: 216-899-1122.

Catholic Commission of Lake and Geauga Counties—JEROME WALCOTT, 28700 Euclid Ave., Wickliffe, 44092. Tel: 440-943-7608.

Catholic Commission (Summit County)—THOMAS J. ALLIO, Dir., 795 Russell Ave., Akron, 44307. Tel: 330-535-2787; Fax: 330-535-9040.

Catholic Commission of Wayne, Ashland and Medina Counties—PATRICK O'BRYAN, Dir., 521 Beall Ave., P.O. Box 15, Wooster, 44691. Tel: 330-263-6176; Fax: 330-262-4633.

Campaign for Human Development—Deacon JUAN ORTIZ, Coord., 2500 Elyria Ave., Lorain, 44055. Tel: 440-245-5043.

Catholic Relief Services—Deacon JUAN ORTIZ, Dir., 2500 Elyria Ave., Lorain, 44055. Tel: 440-245-5043.

Bishop William M. Cosgrove Family Center—1736 Superior Ave., Cleveland, 44114. Tel: 216-781-8262; Fax: 216-566-9161. NICOLE EVANS, Prog. Dir.

CYO and Community Services of Summit County—DONALD P. FINN, Exec. Dir., 812 Biruta St., Akron, 44307. Tel: 330-762-2961; Fax: 330-762-2001. Camp Christopher, Ira & Hametown Rd., Bath, 44210. Tel: 800-CYO-CAMP; Fax: 330-762-2001.

Rose-Mary, The Johanna Grasselli Rehabilitation and Education Center—Ms. PATRICIA A. COLOMBO, Exec. Dir., 19350 Euclid Ave., Cleveland, 44102. Tel: 216-634-7400; Fax: 216-634-7483.

St. Augustine Corporation—Mr. PATRICK GAREAU, Exec. Dir., 7801 Detroit Ave., Cleveland, 44102. Tel: 216-634-7400; Fax: 216-634-7483.

The Society of St. Vincent de Paul—Cathedral Square Plaza, 1404 E. 9th St., Cleveland, 44114. Tel: 216-696-6525, Ext. 3150.

Catholic Lawyers' Guild of Cleveland— The Catholic Diocese of Cleveland Foundation.

Catholic Lawyers' Guild of Cleveland Endowment Trust— The Catholic Diocese of Cleveland Foundation.

Victim Assistance Coordinator—Sr. LAURA BOUHALL, O.S.U. Tel: 216-696-6525, Ext. 2060. Email: lbouhall@dioceseofcleveland.org.

CLERGY, PARISHES, MISSIONS AND PAROCHIAL SCHOOLS

CITY OF CLEVELAND

(CUYAHOGA COUNTY)

1—CATHEDRAL OF ST. JOHN THE EVANGELIST (1848) Revs. Theodore Marszal; Rodel Angeles; Deacon John P. Sferry Sr., Pastoral Assoc. In Res., Revs. Lawrence Jurcak; Charles F. Strebler, Tribunal - Judical Vicar.
Res.: 1007 Superior Ave., N.E., 44114-2582. Tel: 216-771-6666; Fax: 216-781-5646.
Church: E. 9th St. & Superior Ave., N.E., 44114.
Catechesis/Religious Program—Students 6.

2—ST. ADALBERT (1883) Rev. Kenneth F. Pleiman, C.PP.S.; Bro. Thomas R. Bohman, C.PP.S., Pastoral Assoc.
Res.: 2347 E. 83rd St., 44104-2198. Tel: 216-881-7647; Fax: 216-881-7670.
School—2345 E. 83rd St., 44104. Tel: 216-881-6250; Fax: 216-881-9030. Paul Mattis, Prin. Religious 1; Lay Teachers 11; Students 181.
Catechesis/Religious Program—Students 25.

3—ST. AGNES - OUR LADY OF FATIMA (1980) Rev. Robert Marva, O.F.M.Cap.
Res.: 6800 Lexington Ave., 44103-3297. Tel: 216-391-1655 (Office); Fax: 216-391-7919.
Church: 6800 Lexington Ave., 44103. Tel: 216-391-1655.
School—St. Thomas Aquinas School, 9101 Superior Ave., 44106. Tel: 216-421-4668; Fax: 216-721-8444. Sr. Michelle Kelly, S.N.D., Prin. Religious 2; Lay Teachers 14; Students 238.
Catechesis/Religious Program—Students 69.

4—ST. ALOYSIUS - ST. AGATHA (1975) Bro. Paul Hoffman, S.M., Parish Life Coord.; Rev. William Behringer, S.M., Parochial Vicar; Deacon James Paul Jr. In Res., Bros. Robert Dzubinski, S.M.; George Kemmett, S.M.
Res.: 10932 St. Clair Ave., 44108-1939. Tel: 216-451-3262; 216-451-3263; Fax: 216-268-3830.
School—640 Lakeview Rd., N.E., 44108. Tel: 216-451-2050; Fax: 216-541-1601. Sr. Sandra Sabo, S.S.J.-T.O.S.F., Prin. Sisters 4; Lay Teachers 8; Students 125.
School—St. Joseph School, Tel: 216-451-2143; Fax: 216-451-8832. Sandra Dixon, Prin. Sisters 6; Lay Teachers 8; Students 177.
Catechesis/Religious Program—Students 25.

5—ST. ANDREW (1906), (Slovak), Closed. For inquiries for parish records, contact the Archives, Diocese of Cleveland.

6—ST. ANDREW KIM PASTORAL CENTER (1988), (Korean), Rev. Chang Su O, Admin.; Deacon Charles C. Shin.
Res.: 2310 W. 14th St., 44113-3613. Tel: 216-861-4630; Fax: 216-241-6366.
Catechesis/Religious Program—Students 31.

7—ANNUNCIATION (1924) Rev. Timothy M. Daw, Presbyteral Moderator; Sisters Janet Bednar, C.S.J., Parish Life Coord.; Marilyn Nickol, C.S.J., Pastoral Assoc.; Linda Francl, C.S.J., Pastoral Assoc.
Res.: 4697 W. 130th St., 44135-3798. Tel: 216-671-2015; Fax: 216-941-1014.
Catechesis/Religious Program—Students 14.

8—ASCENSION (1946) Rev. Joseph J. Fortuna; Ms. Laurel S. Jurecki, Pastoral Assoc.; Mrs. Kathleen Corbett, Pastoral Assoc.; Deacon John A. Koch Jr., Pastoral Assoc.
Res.: 14040 Puritas Ave., 44135-2822. Tel: 216-671-5890; 216-671-5891; 216-671-2189; Fax: 216-671-2320.
See West Park Catholic Academy under Elementary Schools Parochial & Diocesan located in the Institution section.
Catechesis/Religious Program—Students 34.

9—ST. AUGUSTINE (1860) Rev. Joseph D. McNulty; Sr. Corita Ambro, C.S.J., Pastoral Assoc.; Deacons John M. Rivera, Pastoral Assoc.; Louis Woyton, Pastoral Assoc.; Mary Smith, Pastoral Assoc.; Mary Ellen Czelusniak, Pastoral Assoc.
Res.: 2486 W. 14th St., 44113-4449. Tel: 216-781-5530 (Voice & TTY); 216-781-5880 (Voice & TTY); Fax: 216-781-1124.
Catechesis/Religious Program—Mrs. Kathleen Ulintz, D.R.E. Students 407.
Convent—2432 W. 14th St., 44113. Tel: 216-579-1306.

10—St. Barbara (1905), (Polish), Revs. Lucjan Stokowski, Admin.; Chester C. Cudnik, Pastor Emeritus (Retired).
Res.: 1505 Denison Ave., 44109-2890. Tel: 216-741-2067.
Catechesis/Religious Program—
Convent—3855 W. 16th St., 44109. Tel: 216-661-0547.

11—St. Benedict, Closed. For inquiries for parish records contact the chancery.

12—Blessed Sacrament (1903) Rev. Matthew A. Ischay.
Res.: P.O. Box 602776, 44102. Tel: 216-741-8338; Fax: 216-741-9397.
Catechesis/Religious Program—Students 11.

13—St. Boniface (1903) Rev. Augustine Pham Van Lan.
Res.: 3545 W. 54th St., 44102. Tel: 216-961-2713; 216-961-2714; Fax: 216-961-1859.
See Metro Catholic School, Cleveland under Elementary Schools, Parochial and Diocesan located in the Institution section.
Catechesis/Religious Program—Students 50.
Convent—3588 W. 52nd St., 44102. Tel: 216-961-0669.

14—St. Casimir (1891), (Polish), Closed. For inquiries for parish records contact the chancery.

15—St. Casimir (2009) Rev. Joseph A. Bacevice.
18022 Neff Rd., 44119-2644. Tel: 216-531-4263; Fax: 216-531-8441.

16—St. Catherine (1898) Closed. For inquiries for parish records, contact the Archives, Diocese of Cleveland.

17—St. Cecilia (1915) Rev. Daniel L. Begin; Deacon Hardin M. Martin.
Res.: 3476 E. 152nd St., 44120-4272. Tel: 216-921-3310; 216-921-3311; Fax: 216-921-2932.
Church: Kinsman Rd. & E. 152nd St., 44120.
Catechesis/Religious Program—Students 54.

18—St. Colman (1880) Rev. Robert T. Begin; Eileen Kelly, Pastoral Assoc.; Sisters Wilma Apack, C.S.J., Pastoral Assoc.; Audrey Koch, C.S.J., Pastoral Assoc.; Ann Kilbane, C.S.J., Pastoral Assoc.; Deacons William H. Corrigan; William E. Schill.
Res.: 2027 W. 65th St., 44102-4394. Tel: 216-651-0550; 216-939-9139; Fax: 216-651-1663.
Catechesis/Religious Program—Students 14.
Convent—2007 W. 65th St., 44102.

19—Community of St. Malachi (1975) Closed. For inquiries for parish records contact St. Malachi, Cleveland.; (Personal Parish)

20—Conversion of St. Paul (1931) Rev. William Wiethorn, O.F.M.Cap., Admin. In Res., Revs. Andrew Hohman, O.F.M.Cap.; Robert Marva, O.F.M-.Cap.; Bro. Walter Robb, O.F.M.Cap.
Res.: 4120 Euclid Ave., 44103-3728. Tel: 216-431-8854; 216-431-8855; Fax: 216-361-1951. Connected with the monastery of the Poor Clares of Perpetual Adoration.
Catechesis/Religious Program—
Convent—4108 Euclid Ave., 44103-3728. Tel: 216-361-0783.

21—Corpus Christi (1935) Rev. Russell P. Lowe; Deacon David J. Lundeen.
Res.: 5204 Northcliff Ave., 44144-4065. Tel: 216-351-8738; 216-351-8739; Fax: 216-741-5620.
Catechesis/Religious Program—Students 15.

22—Cristo Rey, Capilla De (1983), (Hispanic), Closed. For inquiries for parish records contact La Sagrada Familia.

23—St. Elizabeth of Hungary (1892), (Hungarian), Rev. Andras Antal, Admin.
Mailing Address: P.O. Box 20175, 44104-0175. Tel: 216-231-0325; Fax: 216-421-0461.
Church: 9016 Buckeye Rd., 44104.
Catechesis/Religious Program—Students 13.

24—St. Emeric (1904 & Territorial 1964), (Magyar), Rev. Sandor Siklodi, Admin.
Res.: 1860 W. 22nd St., 44113-3185. Tel: 216-861-1937.

25—Epiphany (1944) Closed. For inquiries for parish records contact the chancery.

26—St. Francis (1887) Closed. For inquiries for parish records contact the chancery.

27—St. George (1895), (Lithuanian), Closed. For inquiries for parish records contact St. Casimir, Cleveland.

28—St. Henry (1946) Closed. For inquiries for parish records, contact the Archives, Diocese of Cleveland.

29—Holy Family (1911) Closed. For inquiries for parish records contact the chancery.

30—Holy Name (1854) Rev. Thomas V. O'Donnell. In Res., Rev. Edward M. Czech (Retired).
Res.: 8328 Broadway Ave., S.E., 44105-3931. Tel: 216-271-4242; 216-271-4243; 216-271-6995; Fax: 216-271-0886.
School—Tel: 216-341-0084; Fax: 216-341-1122. Penelope Lins, Prin. Lay Teachers 13; Students 168.
Catechesis/Religious Program—Students 11.

31—Holy Redeemer (1924), (Italian), Rev. Martin F. Polito; Sr. Carmen Hocevar, O.S.U., Pastoral Assoc. In Res., Rev. Carl L. D'Agostino (Retired).
Res.: 15712 Kipling Ave., 44110-3104. Tel: 216-531-3313; 216-531-3338; Fax: 216-531-4717.
Catechesis/Religious Program—Students 14.
Convent—924 Ruple Rd., 44110. Tel: 216-481-2740.

32—Holy Rosary (1892), (Italian), Rev. Philip G. Racco; Deacon Bruce J. Battista; Sr. Mary Ann Isabella, S.N.D., Pastoral Assoc.; Anne DeMarco, Pastoral Assoc. In Res., Rev. Christopher H. Weber.
Res.: 12021 Mayfield Rd., 44106-1996. Tel: 216-421-2995; 216-421-2996; Fax: 216-421-2258.
Catechesis/Religious Program—Students 145.

33—Holy Trinity - St. Edward (1975) Closed. For inquiries for parish records contact the chancery.

34—St. Hyacinth (1906), (Polish), Closed. For inquiries for parish records contact the chancery.

35—St. Ignatius of Antioch (1902) Rev. James R. McGonegal; Sr. Dianne Piunno, S.N.D., Pastoral Assoc. In Res., Rev. Gary D. Yanus.
Res.: 10205 Lorain Ave., 44111-5470. Tel: 216-251-0300; Fax: 216-251-0302.
School—Tel: 216-671-0535; Fax: 216-671-0536. Margaret Ricksecker, Prin. Lay Teachers 21; Students 347.
Catechesis/Religious Program—Students 360.

36—Immaculate Conception (1865) Revs. Frank G. Godic; Albert J. Mackert, Pastor Emeritus (Retired). In Res., Rev. John J. Hayes (Retired).
Res.: 4129 Superior Ave., 44103-1179. Tel: 216-431-5900; Fax: 216-431-0463.
School—Tel: 216-361-1883; Fax: 216-881-4274. Miss Rosemary DiPietro, Prin. Religious 1; Lay Teachers 11; Students 115.
Catechesis/Religious Program—Students 5.

37—Immaculate Heart of Mary (1894), (Polish), [CEM] Revs. Ralph Hudak; Andrew Knapik, Parochial Vicar.
Res.: 6700 Lansing Ave., 44105-3797. Tel: 216-341-2734; 216-341-2735; Fax: 216-341-7200.
Catechesis/Religious Program—Students 23.
Convent—6804 Lansing Ave., 44105. Tel: 216-641-7121.

38—St. Jerome (1919) Rev. Anthony Cassese, Admin.; Deacon Peter Travalik.
Res.: 15000 Lake Shore Blvd., 44110-1298. Tel: 216-481-8200; Fax: 216-481-6459.
School—15100 Lake Shore Blvd., 44110. Tel: 216-486-3587; Fax: 216-486-4288. Mrs. Susan Coan, Prin. Religious 2; Lay Teachers 12; Students 158.
Catechesis/Religious Program—
Convent—15025 Ridpath Ave., 44110. Tel: 216-531-6118.

39—St. John Cantius (1898), (Polish), Revs. Lucjan Stokowski; Ralph A. Bodziony, Pastor Emeritus (Retired).
Res.: 906 College Ave., S.W., 44113-4494. Tel: 216-781-9095; Fax: 216-696-6065.
Catechesis/Religious Program—Students 4.

40—St. John Nepomucene (1902), (Bohemian), Rev. Robert J. Jasany; Barbara Weglewski, Pastoral Assoc.
Res.: 3785 Independence Rd., 44105-3357. Tel: 216-641-8444; 216-641-8445; Fax: 216-641-8824.
Church: Fleet Ave. & E. 50th St., 44105. Tel: 216-641-8444.
School—3777 Independence Rd., 44105. Tel: 216-341-1347; Fax: 216-341-4466. Mrs. Roswitha Wunker, Prin. Lay Teachers 13; Students 140.
Catechesis/Religious Program—Students 20.
Convent—Tel: 216-341-6393.

41—St. Josaphat (1908) Closed. For inquiries for parish records contact the chancery.

42—St. Joseph (Woodland) Closed. For inquiries for parish records contact the chancery.

43—St. Joseph (Collinwood) (1877) Closed. For inquiries for parish records contact St. Aloysius, Cleveland.

44—St. Lawrence (1901), (Slovenian), Revs. Dominic Mondzelewski, O.S.B., Admin.; Anthony Rebol, Pastor Emeritus, (On Administrative Leave).
Res.: 3547 E. 80th St., 44105-1521. Tel: 216-341-3886; Fax: 216-341-0886.
Church: 3532 E. 81st St., 44105.
Catechesis/Religious Program—
Convent—3551 E. 80th St., 44105. Tel: 216-341-1235.

45—St. Leo the Great (1948) Revs. Russell P. Lowe; Joseph P. O'Donnell, Parochial Vicar. In Res., Rev. James J. Vesely (Retired).
Res.: 4940 Broadview Rd., 44109-5799. Tel: 216-661-1006; 216-661-1007; 216-661-1008; Fax: 216-661-0887.
School—4900 Broadview Rd., 44109. Tel: 216-661-2120; Fax: 216-661-7125. Diane Weiss, Prin. Lay Teachers 18; Students 314.
Catechesis/Religious Program—Students 176.

46—St. Malachi (1865) Closed. For inquiries for parish records contact St. Malachi, Cleveland.

47—St. Malachi (2009) Revs. Anthony J. Schuerger; Paul J. Hritz, Pastor Emeritus (Retired); Mary Jane Treichel, Pastoral Assoc.; Sr. M. Francis Borgia Allwine, O.S.U., Pastoral Assoc.
Res.: 2459 Washington Ave., 44113-2380. Tel: 216-861-5343; 216-861-5344; Fax: 216-861-5340.
School—*Urban Community School*, 4909 Lorain Ave., 44102. Tel: 216-939-8330; Fax: 216-939-8360. Pamela Delly, Dir. (Intermediate Level) (See St. Wendelin listing for Primary Level) Sisters 3; Lay Teachers 23; Students 463.
Convent—2456 Vermont Ave., 44113. Tel: 216-781-3481.

48—St. Mark (1945) Revs. John P. Miceli; Anthony J. Muzic, Pastor Emeritus (Retired); Deacons Howard Masony; David J. Lundeen; Mrs. Donna M. Wimbiscus, Pastoral Assoc.; Mrs. Linda Cap, Pastoral Assoc.
Res.: 15800 Montrose Ave., 44111-1084. Tel: 216-226-7577; Fax: 216-521-0371.
School—15724 Montrose Ave., 44111. Tel: 216-521-4115; Fax: 216-221-8664. Dr. Marilyn Kurnath, Prin. Lay Teachers 23; Students 432.
Catechesis/Religious Program—Students 219.

49—St. Mary (1905), (Slovenian), Rev. John M. Kumse; Deacon David S. Kushner. In Res., Rev. Stephen M. Spisak; Deacon David S. Kushner.
Res.: 15519 Holmes Ave., 44110-2497. Tel: 216-761-7740; 216-761-1837; Fax: 216-761-6673.
School—716 E. 156th St., 44110. Tel: 216-451-1717; Fax: 216-451-7911. Luis Pla, Prin. Religious 1; Lay Teachers 11; Students 139.
Catechesis/Religious Program—Students 34.

50—St. Mary of Czestochowa (1913), (Polish), Closed. For inquiries for parish records contact the chancery.

51—St. Mel (1945) Rev. Mark Q. Fedor.
Res.: 14436 Triskett Rd., 44111-2263. Tel: 216-941-4313; 216-941-4314; Fax: 216-941-1093.
Catechesis/Religious Program—Students 27.
Convent—Tel: 216-941-6589.

52—St. Michael the Archangel (1882) Revs. James H. McCreight; Dennis R. O'Grady, Pastor Emeritus (Retired); Sr. Mary Reean Coyne, S.N.D., Pastoral Assoc.; Deacons Gonzalo Lopez; Edgar Sanchez; Miguel Figueroa.
Res.: 3114 Scranton Rd., 44109-1689. Tel: 216-861-6297; 216-621-3847 (Spanish).
See Metro Catholic School, Cleveland under Elementary Schools, Parochial and Diocesan located in the Institution section.
Catechesis/Religious Program—Students 104.

53—Nativity of the Blessed Virgin Mary, Closed. For inquiries for parish records contact the chancery.

54—Our Lady of Angels (1922) Rev. John J. Cregan; Deacon Thomas J. Senn.
Res.: 3644 Rocky River Dr., 44111-3998. Tel: 216-252-2332; Fax: 216-252-2383.
School—Tel: 216-251-6841; Fax: 216-251-7831. Miss Kathleen A. Lynch, Prin. Lay Teachers 26; Students 431.

55—Our Lady of Good Counsel (1873) Revs. Leroy Moreeuw, C.PP.S.; Ralph Verdi, C.PP.S., Parochial Vicar; Deacon Patrick F. Berigan. In Res., Rev. Joseph Rodak, C.PP.S.
Res.: 4423 Pearl Rd., S.W., 44109-4266. Tel: 216-749-2323; 216-749-2324; Fax: 216-741-7183.
School—4419 Pearl Rd., 44109-4265. Tel: 216-741-3685; Fax: 216-741-7183. Mrs. Jennifer Berardinelli, Prin. Lay Teachers 14; Students 190.
Catechesis/Religious Program—Students 42.

56—Our Lady of Lourdes (1883), (Bohemian), Rev. Joseph H. Callahan; Diana Llipfird, Pastoral Assoc.
Res.: 3395 E. 53rd St., 44127-1692. Tel: 216-641-2829; 216-641-2830; Fax: 216-641-0043.
Church: E. 53rd St. & Hamm Ave., 44127-1692.
Convent—3401 E. 53rd St., 44127.
Catechesis/Religious Program—Students 6.

57—Our Lady of Mercy (1922), (Slovak), Rev. Joseph T. Hilinski. In Res., Rev. Arthur Snedeker.
Res.: 2425 W. 11th St., 44113-4496. Tel: 216-781-8277 (Parish House); 216-781-7928 (Laheta Hall); Fax: 216-781-7928.
Catechesis/Religious Program—

58—Our Lady of Mount Carmel (East) (1936), (Italian), Officially closed as a parish on July 29, 1990, however, still in existence as an Oratory. Mrs. Rose Marie Criniti, Admin.
Res.: 2615 Martin Luther King Blvd., 44104-2553. Tel: 216-421-0140; Fax: 440-877-9883.
Oratory— 11501 Mount Carmel Rd., 44104.

59—Our Lady of Mount Carmel (West) (1926), (Italian), Revs. Richard S. Rasch, O.de.M.; Anthony M. Fortunato, O.de.M., Parochial Vicar; Michael Donovan, O.de.M., Parochial Vicar; Jerome P. Laubacker, O.de.M.
Res.: 6928 Detroit Ave., 44102-3093. Tel: 216-651-5043; 216-651-2547; Fax: 216-651-6641.
School—1355 W. 70th St., 44102. Tel: 216-281-7146; Fax: 216-281-6651. Sr. Rosario Vega, H.M.S.S.,

Prin. Sisters of Most Holy Trinity 3; Lay Teachers 16; Students 256.
Catechesis/Religious Program—Students 279.
Convent—1355 W. 70th St., 44102. Tel: 216-281-9304.

60—OUR LADY OF PEACE (1919) Rev. Gary Chmura; Deacon William E. Dirk; Sr. Margaret Ann Kelley, O.S.U., Pastoral Assoc.; Mrs. Nancy McIntosh, Pastoral Assoc.
Res.: 12503 Buckingham Ave., 44120-1498. Tel: 216-421-4211; 216-421-4212; Fax: 216-421-1612.
Church: Shaker Blvd. & E. 126th St., 44120.
Catechesis/Religious Program—Students 51.

61—OUR LADY OF PERPETUAL HELP (1929), (Lithuanian), Closed. For inquiries for parish records contact St. Casimir, Cleveland.

62—ST. PATRICK (1853) Rev. Mark A. DiNardo; Mary Jane Treichel, Pastoral Assoc.; Deacon William Merriman.
Res.: 3602 Bridge Ave., 44113-3314. Tel: 216-631-6872; 216-631-6873; 216-631-6874; Fax: 216-631-0267.
School—Urban Community School, Tel: 216-939-8330; Fax: 216-939-0240. See St. Malachi listing.
Catechesis/Religious Program—Students 55.

63—ST. PATRICK (West Park) (1848) [CEM] Revs. Thomas J. Hagedorn; Edward J. Janoch; Deacons Richard C. Beercheck; William Staab. In Res., Revs. Joseph C. Pednekar, M.S.F.S.; Edward N. Schwet.
Res.: 4427 Rocky River Dr., 44135-2551. Tel: 216-251-8286; 216-251-8287; Fax: 216-251-8555.
See West Park Catholic Academy under Elementary Schools Parochial & Diocesan located in the Institution section.
Catechesis/Religious Program—Students 40.
Convent—17712 Puritas Ave., 44135. Tel: 216-941-1088.

64—ST. PAUL (1902), (Croatian), Revs. Mirko Hladni; Zvonko Blasko.
Res.: 1369 E. 40th St., 44103-1194. Tel: 216-431-1895; Fax: 216-431-1128.
Catechesis/Religious Program—Students 104.

65—ST. PETER (1853), (German), Rev. Robert J. Marrone.
Res.: 1533 E. 17th St., 44114. Tel: 216-861-1798; Fax: 216-861-1799.
Catechesis/Religious Program—Students 39.

66—SS. PHILIP AND JAMES (1950) Rev. Joseph R. Spolny, Admin.
Res.: 10812 Adeline Rd., 44111-4806. Tel: 216-941-6808; 216-941-6809; Fax: 216-941-3808.
Church: 3727 Bosworth Rd., 44111.

67—ST. PHILIP NERI (1914) Closed. For inquiries for parish records, contact the Archives, Diocese of Cleveland.

68—ST. PROCOP (1872), (Bohemian), Closed. For inquiries for parish records contact the chancery.

69—ST. ROCCO (1922), (Italian), Very Rev. Michael Contardi, O.de.M.; Revs. Paschal Rosca, O.de.M.; Paul J. Pietrzyk, O.de.M. In Res., Bro. Richard Henry, O.de.M.
Res.: 3205 Fulton Rd., 44109-1495. Tel: 216-961-8331; Fax: 216-961-1845.
School—Tel: 216-961-8557; Fax: 216-961-1112. Sr. Judith Wulk, O.SS.T., Prin. Sisters of Most Holy Trinity 4; Lay Teachers 9; Students 201.
Catechesis/Religious Program—Students 74.
Convent—Tel: 216-961-2378.

70—ST. ROSE OF LIMA (1899) Revs. Robert Sieg, O.F.M., Admin.; William Rooney, O.F.M.; Walter Dolan, O.F.M.; Bro. Michael Ward, O.F.M.
Res.: 11411 Detroit Ave., 44102-2399. Tel: 216-521-0133; Fax: 216-521-1306.
Church: Detroit Ave. & W. 114th St., 44102.
Catechesis/Religious Program—Students 7.
Convent—1418 W. 114th St., 44102.

71—SACRED HEART OF JESUS (1888), (Polish), Rev. Joseph S. Mecir.
Res.: 6916 Krakow Ave., 44105-5737. Tel: 216-341-2828; 216-341-8525; Fax: 216-271-6287.
Church: E. 71st & Kazimier Ave., 44105.

72—SAGRADA FAMILIA (1997), (Hispanic), Rev. Robert J. Reidy; Deacons Ceferino Medina; Epifanio Torres; Victor Colon; Ignacio Miranda; Frederick Simon; Marilyn Hernandez, Pastoral Assoc.
Church: 7719 Detroit Ave., 44102-2811. Tel: 216-631-6817; 216-631-2888; 216-631-2889; Fax: 216-631-3305.
Catechesis/Religious Program—Students 184.

73—SAN JUAN BAUTISTA (1975), (Spanish), Closed. For inquiries for Parish Records contact La Sagrada Familia.

74—ST. STANISLAUS (1873), (Polish), Revs. Michael Surafka, O.F.M., Admin.; Placyd Kon, O.F.M.; Leonard Stunek, O.F.M. In Res., Bros. David Kelly, O.F.M.; Justin Kwietniewski, O.F.M.
Res.: 3649 E. 65th St., 44105-1293. Tel: 216-341-9091; Fax: 216-341-2688.
Church: Forman Ave. & E. 65th St., 44105.
School—6615 Forman Ave., 44105. Tel: 216-883-3307; Fax: 216-883-0514. Mrs. Deborah Martin, Prin. Sisters 1; Lay Teachers 15; Students 260.
Catechesis/Religious Program—Students 244.
Convent—6615 Forman Ave., 44105. Tel: 216-341-0934.

75—ST. STEPHEN (1869), (German), Rev. S. Michael Franz; Deacon Moises Cruz.
Res.: 1930 W. 54th St., 44102-3298. Tel: 216-631-5633; Fax: 216-631-5634.
See Metro Catholic School, Cleveland under Elementary Schools, Parochial and Diocesan located in the Institution section.
Catechesis/Religious Program—Students 16.
Convent—1891 W. 57th St., 44102. Tel: 216-631-0754.

76—ST. THOMAS AQUINAS, Closed. For inquiries for parish records contact the chancery.

77—TRANSFIGURATION (1943) Closed. For inquiries for parish records contact the chancery.

78—ST. VINCENT DE PAUL (1922) Revs. John E. Manning; Michael D. Ausperk; Deacon Kenneth J. Hill.
Res.: 13400 Lorain Ave., 44111-3470. Tel: 216-252-2626; Fax: 216-252-6993.
Church: Lorain Ave. & Berea Rd., 44111.
School—13442 Lorain Ave., 44111. Tel: 216-251-3932; Fax: 216-251-0455. Thomas Norton, Prin. Lay Teachers 13; Students 180.
Catechesis/Religious Program—Students 28.

79—ST. VITUS (1893), (Slovenian), Rev. Joseph P. Boznar; Sr. Mary Avsec, S.N.D., Pastoral Assoc. In Res., Rev. Victor J. Cimperman (Retired).
Res.: 6019 Lausche Ave., 44103-1455. Tel: 216-361-1444; 216-361-1445; Fax: 216-361-1445.
Catechesis/Religious Program—Students 5.

80—ST. WENDELIN (1903), (Slovak), Rev. Jerome M. Lajack; Deacon James J. Armstrong.
Res.: 2281 Columbus Rd., 44113-4230. Tel: 216-861-1141; Fax: 216-861-1141.
School—Urban Community School, 4909 Lorain Ave., 44102. Tel: 216-939-8330; Fax: 216-939-8360. Pam Delly, Prin. (Primary and Junior High) (See St. Malachi listing for Intermediate Level)
Catechesis/Religious Program—Students 19.
Convent—2259 Columbus Rd., 44113. Tel: 216-241-1773.

OUTSIDE THE CITY OF CLEVELAND

AKRON, SUMMIT CO.

1—ANNUNCIATION (1907) Closed. For inquiries for parish records contact Visitation of Mary, Akron.

2—ST. ANTHONY OF PADUA (1933), (Italian), Rev. James V. Ragnoni.
Res.: 83 Mosser Pl., 44310-3184. Tel: 330-762-7277; Fax: 330-762-2229.
School—80 E. York St., 44310. Tel: 330-253-6918. Sr. Elizabeth Szilvasi, M.P.F., Prin. Religious 3; Lay Teachers 8; Students 170.
Catechesis/Religious Program—Students 203.
Convent—93 Mosser Pl., 44310. Tel: 216-376-1735.

3—ST. BERNARD (1861) [CEM] Rev. Clyde K. Foster, Admin.; Deacon Ramon J. DiMascio; Sr. Catherine Walsh, C.S.A., Pastoral Assoc. In Res., Revs. Norman K. Douglas; Wilhelm Malasi (Tanzania); Bernard E. Okafor (Nigeria).
Res.: 44 University Ave., 44308-1609. Tel: 330-253-5161; 330-253-5162; 330-253-5265; 330-253-5364; Fax: 330-253-6949.
Catechesis/Religious Program—Students 103.

4—BLESSED TRINITY (2009) Rev. Joseph A. Warner; Sr. Mercia Madigan, O.S.U., Pastoral Min.
300 E. Tallmadge Ave., 44310-2399. Tel: 330-376-5144; Fax: 440-376-5311.

5—CHRIST THE KING (1935) Closed. For inquiries for parish records contact Blessed Trinity, Akron.

6—ST. FRANCIS DE SALES (1948) Revs. G. David Bline; James R. Schleicher, Pastor Emeritus (Retired); Anthony J. Suso, Parochial Vicar; Deacons Richard C. Butz; Raymond S. Herrick.
Res.: 4019 Manchester Rd., 44319-2193. Tel: 330-644-2225; 330-644-2226; Fax: 330-644-2225.
School—4009 Manchester Rd., 44319. Tel: 330-644-0638; Fax: 330-644-2663. Sherry Parrish, Prin. Sisters Servants of the Immaculate Heart of Mary 1; Lay Teachers 22; Students 315.
Catechesis/Religious Program—Students 246.

7—ST. HEDWIG (1912), (Polish), Closed. For inquiries for parish records contact the chancery.

8—ST. HILARY (1958) Revs. Steven K. Brunovsky; Gordon A. Yahner, Pastor Emeritus (Retired); Joseph A. Warner; Sr. Marlene LoGrasso, O.S.U., Pastoral Assoc.; Mrs. Patricia Schnee, Pastoral Assoc.
Res.: 615 Moorfield Rd., Fairlawn, 44333-4236. Tel: 330-867-1055; Fax: 330-869-2312.
Church: 2750 W. Market St., Fairlawn, 44333-4236.
School—645 Moorfield Rd., Fairlawn, 44333. Tel: 330-867-8720; Fax: 330-867-5081. Dr. Patricia Nugent, Prin. Religious 1; Lay Teachers 37; Students 670.
Catechesis/Religious Program—Students 1,097.

9—IMMACULATE CONCEPTION (1923) Rev. Michael B. Smith; Melissa Keegan, Pastoral Assoc. In Res., Rev. Samuel R. Ciccolini.
Res.: 2101 17th St., S.W., 44314-2315. Tel: 330-753-8429; Fax: 330-753-7440.
Church: 2100 16th St., S.W., 44314.
Catechesis/Religious Program—Students 21.

10—ST. JOHN THE BAPTIST (1907), (Slovak), Closed. For inquiries for parish records contact St. John of the Cross, Euclid.

11—ST. MARTHA (1919) Closed. For inquiries for parish records contact Blessed Trinity, Akron.

12—ST. MARY (1887) Rev. Edward A. Burba; Deacon Frederick Browne.
Res.: 750 S. Main St., 44311-1094. Tel: 330-762-9247; Fax: 330-252-1768.
School—Tel: 330-253-1233; Fax: 330-253-1472. Mr. David Csank, Prin. Lay Teachers 13; Students 197.
Catechesis/Religious Program—Students 12.

13—ST. MATTHEW (1943) Revs. Michael G. Williamson; Thomas A. McGovern, Pastor Emeritus (Retired); Ann Polack, Pastoral Assoc.
Res.: 2603 Benton St., 44312-1694. Tel: 330-733-9944; Fax: 330-733-9424.
Church: Berne & Woolf St., 44312.
School—2580 Benton St., 44312. Tel: 330-784-1711; Fax: 330-733-1004. James King, Prin. Lay Teachers 19; Students 322.
Catechesis/Religious Program—Students 190.

14—NATIVITY OF THE LORD JESUS (1977) Rev. David J. Halaiko; Deacon Dennis L. Smith; Rosemary Frey, Pastoral Assoc.
Res.: 2425 Myersville Rd., 44312-4951. Tel: 330-699-5086; Fax: 330-699-4299.
Catechesis/Religious Program—Students 141.

15—ST. PAUL (1919) Revs. Ralph W. Thomas; John M. Jenkins, Pastor Emeritus (Retired); Therese Nesline, Pastoral Assoc.; Deacon Francis R. Lonteen, (Retired).
Res.: 433 Mission Dr., 44301-2798. Tel: 330-724-1263; Fax: 330-724-7680.
School—1580 Brown St., 44301-2798. Tel: 330-724-1253; Fax: 330-724-1127. Mr. Robert Brodbeck, Prin. Lay Teachers 15; Students 228.
Catechesis/Religious Program—Students 86.

16—ST. PETER (1917) Closed. For inquiries for parish records contact St. Mary Parish, Akron.

17—SACRED HEART OF JESUS (1915), (Hungarian), Rev. Robert E. Clancy, Admin.
Res.: 212 E. Voris St., 44311-1508. Tel: 330-434-4348.
Church: 734 Grant St., 44311.
Catechesis/Religious Program—

18—ST. SEBASTIAN (1928) Revs. John A. Valencheck, Admin.; William D. Karg, Pastor Emeritus (Retired); John T. McDonough, Pastor Emeritus (Retired); Matthew E. Pfeiffer, Parochial Vicar; Deacon Terry W. Peacock.
Res.: 476 Mull Ave., 44320-1299. Tel: 330-836-2233; Fax: 330-836-2235.
School—500 Mull Ave., 44320. Tel: 330-836-9107; Fax: 330-836-7690. Mr. Howard J. Sheetz, Prin. Lay Teachers 28; Students 445.
Catechesis/Religious Program—Students 70.

19—ST. VINCENT (1837) [CEM] Rev. Joseph H. Kraker. In Res., Revs. Gordon A. Yahner (Retired); David L. McCafferty (Retired).
Res.: 164 W. Market St., 44303-2373. Tel: 330-535-3135; Fax: 330-535-4160.
Church: W. Market St. & Maple St., 44303.
School—17 S. Maple St., 44303. Tel: 330-762-5912; Fax: 330-535-2515. James Tawney, Prin. Lay Teachers 21; Students 225.
Catechesis/Religious Program—Students 70.

20—VISITATION OF MARY (2009) Rev. A. Jonathan Zingales; Deacon James A. White; Diana Herhold, Pastoral Min.
87 Broad St., 44305. Tel: 330-535-4141; Fax: 330-475-0054.

AMHERST, LORAIN CO., ST. JOSEPH (1864) [CEM] Revs. Lawrence N. Martello; James F. Mazanec; Maria Maldonado, Pastoral Assoc.; Deacons Daniel Hancock; Paul Heise. In Res., Rev. Denis L. St. Marie (Retired).
Res.: 200 St. Joseph Dr., 44001-1663. Tel: 440-988-2848; 440-988-2849; Fax: 440-984-2301.
School—175 St. Joseph Dr., 44001. Tel: 440-988-4244; Fax: 440-988-5249. Mrs. Karen Casper-Linn, Prin. Lay Teachers 17; Students 245.
Catechesis/Religious Program—Students 431.
Convent—151 St. Joseph Dr., 44001. Tel: 440-988-2621.

ASHLAND, ASHLAND CO., ST. EDWARD (1853) [JC] Rev. James M. Cassidy; Deacons James A. Kaniecki; Joseph P. Dietz.
Res.: 501 Cottage St., 44805-2167. Tel: 419-289-7224; Fax: 419-289-0515.
Administration Center—149 Pleasant St., 44805.
School—433 Cottage St., 44805. Tel: 419-289-7456; Fax: 419-289-9474. Suellen Valentine, Prin. Lay Teachers 16; Students 149.
Catechesis/Religious Program—Students 96.

AVON, LORAIN CO.

1—HOLY TRINITY (1833) [CEM] Revs. John A. Misenko; John J. Gorski, Pastor Emeritus (Retired); Deacon John F. Cullinane; Roger Camp, Pastoral Assoc.
Res.: 33601 Detroit Rd., 44011-1999. Tel: 440-937-5363; Fax: 440-937-5128.
School—2610 Nagel Rd., 44011. Tel: 440-937-6420; Fax: 440-937-1029. Mary Marunowski, Prin. Lay Teachers 21; Students 513.
Catechesis/Religious Program—Students 592.
Convent—2620 Nagel Rd., 44011. Tel: 440-937-5005.

2—ST. MARY OF THE IMMACULATE CONCEPTION (1841) [CEM] Revs. C. Thomas Cleaton; Arthur B. Egan, Pastor Emeritus (Retired).
Res.: 2640 Stoney Ridge Rd., 44011-1899. Tel: 440-934-4212; Fax: 440-934-0507.
School—2680 Stoney Ridge Rd., 44011-1899. Tel: 440-934-6246; Fax: 440-934-6250. John Stipek, Prin. Sisters of Notre Dame 2; Lay Teachers 14; Students 192.
Catechesis/Religious Program—Students 289.
Convent—2680 Stoney Ridge Rd., 44011. Tel: 440-934-5173.

AVON LAKE, LORAIN CO.

1—HOLY SPIRIT (1965) Rev. James H. Beatty; Patricia A. Kassay, Pastoral Assoc.; Deacon Robert K. Walling.
Res.: 410 Lear Rd., 44012-2004. Tel: 440-933-3777; 440-871-8157 (Cleveland Line); Fax: 440-871-8157.
Catechesis/Religious Program—Tel: 440-933-8818. Students 576.

2—ST. JOSEPH (1949) Rev. Timothy J. O'Connor.
Res.: 32929 Lake Rd., 44012-1497. Tel: 440-933-3152; 440-933-4022; Fax: 440-933-8919.
School—Tel: 440-933-6233; Fax: 440-933-2463. Mrs. Patricia Vaccaro, Prin. Lay Teachers 22; Students 324.
Catechesis/Religious Program—Students 253.
Convent—32911 Lake Rd., 44012. Tel: 216-933-5769.

BARBERTON, SUMMIT CO.

1—ST. AUGUSTINE (1898) Revs. David J. Majikas; Joseph G. Workman, Parochial Vicar; Karen Bellett, Pastoral Assoc.; Deacons Robin Adair; Harold R. Krause.
Res.: 204 Sixth St., N.W., 44203-2198. Tel: 330-745-0011; Fax: 330-745-0012.
Church: Corner of Sixth St., N.W. & Lake Ave., 44203.
School—195 Seventh St., N.W., 44203. Tel: 330-753-6435; Fax: 330-753-4095. Elaine Faessel, Prin. Lay Teachers 17; Students 215.
Catechesis/Religious Program—Students 129.

2—SS. CYRIL AND METHODIUS (1906), (Slovak), Closed. For inquiries for parish records contact the chancery.

3—HOLY TRINITY (1911), (Magyar), Closed. For inquiries for parish records contact the chancery.

4—ST. MARY'S (1912), (Polish), Closed. For inquiries for parish records contact the chancery.

5—PRINCE OF PEACE Revs. Robert H. Jackson; Albert A. Kunkel, Pastor Emeritus; Deacon Robert A. Youngblood; Lawrence G. Lauter, Pastoral Assoc.
Res.: 1263 Shannon Ave., 44203-6792. Tel: 330-825-9543; Fax: 330-706-1437.
Catechesis/Religious Program—Students 276.

6—SACRED HEART (1916), (Slovenian), Closed. For inquiries for parish records contact the chancery.

BAY VILLAGE, CUYAHOGA CO., ST. RAPHAEL (1946) Revs. Timothy W. Gareau; Nelson J. Callahan, Pastor Emeritus (Retired); Steven H. Breck, Parochial Vicar; Deacon Larry D. Gregg; Terri Telepak, Pastoral Assoc.
Res.: 525 Dover Center Rd., 44140-2366. Tel: 440-871-1100; Fax: 440-899-2911.
School—Tel: 440-871-6760; Fax: 440-871-1358. Ann Miller, Prin. Lay Teachers 37; Students 757.
Catechesis/Religious Program—Students 741.

BEDFORD, CUYAHOGA CO.

1—ST. MARY (1910) Closed. For inquiries for parish records contact the chancery.

2—OUR LADY OF HOPE (2009) Rev. John J. Wright; Deacon Daniel C. Terrion; Sr. Irene Mraz, V.S.C., Pastoral Min.
400 Center Rd., 44146-2296. Tel: 400-232-8166; Fax: 440-786-9929. In Res., Rev. Robert Nyeko Oboi.

3—ST. PIUS X (1952) Closed. For inquiries for parish records contact Our Lady of Hope, Bedford.

BEDFORD HEIGHTS, CUYAHOGA CO., HOLY TRINITY (1965) Closed. For inquiries for parish records contact Holy Trinity, Bedford Heights.

BEREA, CUYAHOGA CO.

1—ST. ADALBERT (1873), (Polish), [CEM] Revs. Barry T. Gearing, Admin.; Gerald J. Keller, Pastor Emeritus (Retired); Deacon Edmund A. Gardias; Sr. Marilyn Sabatino, S.N.D., Pastoral Assoc.
Res.: 66 Adalbert St., 44017-1799. Tel: 440-234-6830; Fax: 440-234-2588.
School—Academy of St. Adalbert, 56 Adalbert St., 44017. Tel: 440-234-5529; Fax: 440-234-2881. Mrs. Martha K. Jacobs, Prin. Lay Teachers 11; Students 144.
Catechesis/Religious Program—Students 142.
Convent—24 Adalbert St., 44017. Tel: 440-234-1096.

2—ST. MARY (1852) [CEM] Rev. George A. Vrabel.
Res.: 250 Kraft St., 44017-1449. Tel: 440-243-3877; 440-243-3878; Fax: 440-891-9417.
School—265 Baker St., 44017-1515. Tel: 440-243-4555; Fax: 440-243-6214. Mary Whelan, Prin. Lay Teachers 27; Students 489.
Catechesis/Religious Program—Students 346.

BRECKSVILLE, CUYAHOGA CO., ST. BASIL THE GREAT (1960) Revs. Walter H. Jenne; Douglas T. Brown; Deacon Louis M. Primozic; Sr. Judith Wood, S.S.J.-T.O.S.F., Pastoral Assoc.; Deacon David Pecot; Mrs. Robin Youngs, Pastoral Assoc.
Res.: 8700 Brecksville Rd., 44141-1999. Tel: 440-526-1686; 440-526-1687; Fax: 440-526-2373.
Catechesis/Religious Program—Tel: 440-526-3520; 440-526-3587. Students 800.
Convent—6901 Mill Rd., 44141. Tel: 440-526-2850.

BROADVIEW HEIGHTS, CUYAHOGA CO., ASSUMPTION (1857) Revs. Justin Drywal, O.S.B.; Paschal Petcavage, O.S.B.; Kenneth J. Katricak, O.S.B., Parochial Vicar; Deacons Robert C. Bubnick Sr.; Francis B. Wilson.
Res.: 9183 Broadview Rd., 44147-2596. Tel: 440-526-1177; 440-526-1178; Fax: 440-526-2838.
School—Tel: 440-526-4877; Fax: 440-526-3752. Donna Sejba, Prin. Sisters of Incarnate Word 1; Lay Teachers 19; Students 338.
Catechesis/Religious Program—Students 292.
Convent—9139 Broadview Rd., 44147. Tel: 216-526-4069.

BROOK PARK, CUYAHOGA CO.

1—ASSUMPTION OF MARY (1860) [CEM] Rev. James R. Stenger, Admin. In Res., Rev. John G. Crawford (Retired); Deacon Francis B. Wilson.
Res.: 5445 Smith Rd., 44142-2077. Tel: 216-267-0630; Fax: 216-267-3064.
Church: 5555 Smith Rd., 44142. Tel: 216-267-1775.
Catechesis/Religious Program—Fax: 216-267-0665. Students 42.

2—ST. PETER THE APOSTLE (1968) Rev. James R. Stenger; Deacon John R. Zdolshek; Sr. Therese Horan, O.S.U., Pastoral Assoc.; Elaine Gaughan, Pastoral Assoc. In Res., Rev. Dismas Boeff, O.S.B.
Res.: 6455 Engle Rd., 44142-3503. Tel: 216-433-1440; 216-433-1441; Fax: 216-433-1434.
Catechesis/Religious Program—Students 248.

BROOKLYN, CUYAHOGA CO., ST. THOMAS MORE (1946) Revs. William G. Bouhall; James J. Vesely, Pastor Emeritus (Retired); Sr. Elaine Theresa Burrows, S.I.W., Pastoral Assoc.; Deacons Martin A. Thiel; Charles W. Zawadzki.
Res.: 4170 N. Amber Dr., 44144-1399. Tel: 216-749-0414; 216-749-0415; Fax: 216-749-1001.
School—4180 N. Amber Dr., 44144. Tel: 216-749-1660; Fax: 216-398-4265. Mrs. Jennifer Francis, Prin. Lay Teachers 21; Students 317.
Catechesis/Religious Program—Students 158.

BRUNSWICK, MEDINA CO.

1—ST. AMBROSE (1957) Revs. Robert G. Stec; Gregory J. Olszewski; Sr. Donna Marie Bradesca, O.S.U., Pastoral Assoc.; Deacons Clement J. Belter; Thomas J. Sheridan; Gary R. Tomazic.
Res.: 929 Pearl Rd., 44212-2597. Tel: 330-225-3116; Fax: 330-220-1748.
School—923 Pearl Rd., 44212. Tel: 330-225-2116; Fax: 330-225-5425. Christine Bopp, Prin. Lay Teachers 24; Students 514.
Catechesis/Religious Program—Students 1,479.

2—ST. COLETTE (1977) Revs. William R. Krizner; Thomas G. Montavon, Pastor Emeritus (Retired); Arthur A. Bacher, Senior Priest (Retired).
Res.: 330 W. 130th St., 44212-2309. Tel: 330-273-5500; Fax: 330-225-7909.
Catechesis/Religious Program—Students 276.

CHAGRIN FALLS, CUYAHOGA CO.

1—HOLY ANGELS (1977) Rev. Daniel F. Schlegel, Admin.; Sr. Susan Javorek, S.N.D., Pastoral Assoc.; Deacons Stephen L. Yates; Vincent L. Belsito.
Mailing Address: 18205 Chillicothe Rd., 44023-4879.
Res.: 8390 Stoney Brook Dr., 44023-4879. Fax: 440-708-0787.
Church: 18046 Chillicothe Rd., 44023-4879. Tel: 440-708-0000.
Catechesis/Religious Program—Tel: 440-708-0808. Students 1,035.

2—ST. JOAN OF ARC (1948) Revs. David J. Walkowiak; John J. Kinkopf, Pastor Emeritus (Retired); John R. Olsavsky, Pastor Emeritus (Retired); Thomas J. Pajik; Sr. Ann Marie Kanusek, S.N.D., Pastoral Assoc.; Deacons Jeffrey Dunlop; Dennis A. Guritza.
Res.: 496 E. Washington St., 44022-2999. Tel: 440-247-7183; Fax: 440-247-2327.
School—498 E. Washington St., 44022-2998. Tel: 440-247-6530; Fax: 440-247-2045. Shelley DiBacco, Prin. Lay Teachers 16; Students 197.
Catechesis/Religious Program—Tel: 440-247-3606. Students 424.
Convent—456 E. Washington St., 44022. Tel: 440-247-4419.

CHARDON, GEAUGA CO., ST. MARY (1909) Revs. Thomas C. Gilles; Timothy D. Kalista; Carol Burtnett, Pastoral Assoc.; Deacons Lawrence Boehnlein; Thomas J. Peshek.
Res.: 401 North St., 44024-1087. Tel: 440-285-7051; Fax: 440-286-3886.
School—Tel: 440-286-3590; Fax: 440-285-2818. Sr. Mary Sandra Nativio, S.N.D., Prin. Sisters of Notre Dame 1; Lay Teachers 20; Students 325.
Catechesis/Religious Program—Students 556.
Convent—315 North St., 44024. Tel: 440-286-5641.

CHESTERLAND, GEAUGA CO., ST. ANSELM (1961) Rev. Thomas M. Sweany; Deacon Donald E. Sill; Jean Fitzgerald, Pastoral Assoc.
Res.: 12969 Chillicothe Rd., 44026-3115. Tel: 440-729-9575; Fax: 440-729-9103.
Church: 13013 Chillicothe Rd., 44026.
School—Tel: 440-729-7806; Fax: 440-729-3524. Miss Joan Agresta, Prin. Lay Teachers 19; Students 270.
Catechesis/Religious Program—Students 405.
Convent—13055 Chillicothe Rd., 44026. Tel: 440-729-0292.

CHIPPEWA LAKE, MEDINA CO., JESUS DIVINE REDEEMER (1976) Attended by Our Lady Help of Christians, Litchfield., 44215.

CLEVELAND HEIGHTS, CUYAHOGA CO.

1—ST. ANN (1915) Closed. For inquiries for parish records contact Communion of Saints Parish, Cleveland Heights.

2—COMMUNION OF SAINTS PARISH Revs. James E. Singler; Deogratias M. Ruwaainenyi; Ms. Renee Barber, Pastoral Assoc.
Res.: 2175 Coventry Rd., 44118-2898. Tel: 216-321-0024; Fax: 216-321-7702.
Worship Site at St. Philomena—13824 Euclid Ave., East Cleveland, 44112.
School—2160 Stillman Rd., 44118. Tel: 216-932-4177; Fax: 216-932-7439. Meg Cosgriff, Prin. Lay Teachers 22; Students 280.
Catechesis/Religious Program—Students 74.

3—ST. LOUIS (1947) Closed. For inquiries for parish records contact Communion of Saints Parish, Cleveland Heights.

CLINTON, SUMMIT CO., ST. GEORGE (1908) Closed. For inquiries for parish records, contact SS. Peter & Paul Parish, Doylestown, OH.

COLUMBIA STATION, LORAIN CO., ST. ELIZABETH ANN SETON (1976) Rev. Charles J. Ryba.
Mailing Address: 25777 Royalton Rd., P.O. Box 968, 44028-0968.
Res.: 25777 Royalton Rd., 44028-0968. Tel: 440-236-5095; Fax: 440-236-5804.
Church: 25801 Royalton Rd., 44028.
Catechesis/Religious Program—Tel: 440-236-3711. Students 153.

CONCORD TWP., LAKE CO., ST. GABRIEL (1966) Revs. Frederick F. Pausche; John M. Pfeifer; Robert J. Kropac; Deacons Ronald Adkins; Daniel P. Clavin; Robert Gegic; Carolyn Jablonski, Pastoral Assoc.; Joanne Spiek, Pastoral Assoc.; Paul Kelly, Pastoral Assoc.
Res.: 9925 Johnnycake Ridge Rd., 44060-6294. Tel: 440-352-8282; 440-953-3867 (Cleveland); Fax: 440-354-7558.
School—9935 Johnnycake Ridge Rd., 44060. Tel: 440-352-6169; Fax: 440-639-0143. Donna Lee Becka, Prin. Lay Teachers 37; Students 903.
Catechesis/Religious Program—Students 608.
Convent—9918 Johnnycake Ridge Rd., 44060. Tel: 440-354-7553.

COPLEY, SUMMIT CO., GUARDIAN ANGELS (1964) Rev. James F. Kramer; Rev. Msgr. Robert C. Wolff, Pastor Emeritus (Retired); Sr. Angela Nihill, O.S.U., Pastoral Assoc.
Church & Res.: 1686 Cleveland-Massillon Rd., 44321-1976. Tel: 330-666-1373; Fax: 330-666-8189.
Catechesis/Religious Program—Students 170.

CUYAHOGA FALLS, SUMMIT CO.

1—ST. EUGENE (1963) Rev. Neil A. Crosby; Sr. Marie Ellen Kuhel, O.S.U., Pastoral Assoc.
Res.: 1821 Munroe Falls Ave., 44221-3699. Tel: 330-923-5244; Fax: 330-923-8436.
Catechesis/Religious Program—Students 180.

2—IMMACULATE HEART OF MARY (1952) Revs. Thomas W. McCann; John R. Rathfon, Pastor Emeritus (Retired); Deacons J. David Seal; P. Hoefler; William J. Yoho Jr. In Res., Revs. Robert E. Pahler (Retired); Joseph C. Weigard (Retired).
Res.: 1905 Portage Tr., 44223-1792. Tel: 330-929-8361; 330-929-8362; 330-929-8399; Fax: 330-929-8496.
School—2859 Lillis Dr., 44223. Tel: 330-923-1220; Fax: 330-929-4373. Robert Hardesty, Prin. Lay Teachers 25; Students 415.
Catechesis/Religious Program—Students 269.

3—ST. JOSEPH (1831) Rev. James J. Marsick; Deacon Robert Kochanski. In Res., Rev. David J. McCarthy (Retired).
Res.: 215 Falls Ave., 44221-3999. Tel: 330-928-2173; Fax: 330-928-3082.
Church: 1761 Second St., 44221.
School—1909 Third St., 44221-3894. Tel: 330-928-2151; Fax: 330-928-3139. Robert Kochanski, Prin. Deacons 1; Lay Teachers 24; Students 332.
Catechesis/Religious Program—Students 43.

DOYLESTOWN, WAYNE CO., SS. PETER AND PAUL (1827) [CEM] [JC] Revs. Robert E. Stein; David J. McCarthy, Pastor Emeritus (Retired); Deacon Dale A. Youngblood.
Res.: 161 W. Clinton St., 44230-1297. Tel: 330-658-2145.
School—169 W. Clinton St., 44230. Tel: 330-658-2804; Fax: 330-658-2287. Katherine Yaussy, Prin. Lay Teachers 15; Students 154.
Catechesis/Religious Program—Students 155.

EAST CLEVELAND, CUYAHOGA CO.
1—CHRIST THE KING (1928) Closed. For inquiries for parish records contact Communion of Saints Parish, Cleveland Heights.
2—ST. PHILOMENA (1902) Closed. For inquiries for parish records contact Communion of Saints Parish, Cleveland Heights.

EASTLAKE, LAKE CO., ST. JUSTIN MARTYR (1962) Rev. Kevin M. Liebhardt.
Mailing Address: 35781 Stevens Blvd., 44095-5095. Tel: 440-946-1177; Fax: 440-946-9126.
Administration Center—Tel: 440-946-1177.
Res.: 35701 Stevens Blvd., 44095.
See St. Mary Magdalene-St. Justin Martyr under Elementary Schools Parochial & Diocesan located in the Institution section.
Catechesis/Religious Program—Students 240.
Convent—35711 Stevens Blvd., 44095. Tel: 440-946-1013.

ELYRIA, LORAIN CO.
1—ST. AGNES (1914) Rev. Albert A. Krupp; Deacon Bruce H. Tennant; Sr. Jennifer Kramer, S.N.D., Pastoral Assoc.
611 Lake Ave., 44035-3541. Tel: 440-322-5622; Fax: 440-322-0231.
Catechesis/Religious Program—Tel: 440-366-5999. Students 57.
2—HOLY CROSS (1922), (Polish), Closed. For inquiries for parish records contact the chancery.
3—ST. JUDE (1943) Rev. Frank P. Kosem; Sr. Margaret Marszal, H.M., Pastoral Assoc.; Deacons Patrick J. Humphrey; Frank J. O'Connell; Susan Kuchenbecker, Pastoral Assoc.
Res.: 590 Poplar St., 44035-3999. Tel: 440-366-5711; Fax: 440-366-1916.
School—594 Poplar St., 44035. Tel: 440-366-1681; Fax: 440-366-6238. Rozann Swanson, Prin. Lay Teachers 21; Students 400.
Catechesis/Religious Program—Students 189.
Convent—342 Longford, 44035. Tel: 440-366-1551.
4—ST. MARY (1845) [CEM] Revs. Charles T. Diedrick, Admin.; Joseph C. Weigand, Pastor Emeritus (Retired); Sr. Mary Dorothy Tecca, C.S.A., Pastoral Assoc.; Deacons Frank A. Humphrey III; Edward R. Dillon.
Res.: 320 Middle Ave., 44035-5796. Tel: 440-323-5539; Fax: 440-322-2329.
School—237 Fourth St., 44035. Tel: 440-322-2808; Fax: 440-322-1423. Sheila Mannix, Prin. Lay Teachers 14; Students 207.
Catechesis/Religious Program—Tel: 440-322-3054. Students 135.
Convent—235 Fourth St., 44035-5796. Tel: 440-322-1423.
5—SACRED HEART OF JESUS (1922), (Hungarian), Closed. For inquiries for parish records contact the chancery.

ELYRIA TOWNSHIP, LORAIN CO., ST. VINCENT DE PAUL (1949) Revs. James R. Ols; William J. Kitt, Pastor Emeritus (Retired); Deacons John K. Slatcoff; Edgar Gonzalez.
Res.: 41295 N. Ridge Rd., 44035-1098. Tel: 440-324-4212; 440-277-5285; Fax: 440-324-2892.
Catechesis/Religious Program—Students 135.

EUCLID, CUYAHOGA CO.
1—ST. CHRISTINE (1925) Rev. John P. McNulty, Admin. In Res., Rev. Joseph A. Goebel (Retired).
Res.: 840 E. 222nd St., 44123-3317. Tel: 216-261-1410; 216-261-6383; Fax: 216-261-9039.
Catechesis/Religious Program—Students 37.
2—ST. FELICITAS (1950) Closed. For inquiries for parish records contact St. John of the Cross, Euclid.
3—HOLY CROSS (1924) Rev. John P. McNulty; Sr. Kathleen Flannery, O.S.U., Pastoral Assoc.; Deacon Jerome B. Vrabel, Pastoral Assoc. In Res., Rev. John M. Jenkins (Retired).
Res.: 19951 Lake Shore Blvd., 44123-1066. Tel: 216-486-0850; 216-486-0853; Fax: 216-486-0851.
Church: Lake Shore Blvd. & E. 200th St., 44119.
School—175 E. 200th St., 44119. Tel: 216-481-6824; Fax: 216-481-9841. Patricia Patterson, Prin. Ursuline Nuns of Cleveland 1; Lay Teachers 23; Students 395.
Catechesis/Religious Program—Students 96.
Convent—177 E. 201st St., 44123. Tel: 216-486-0088.
4—ST. JOHN OF THE CROSS (2009) Rev. Salvatore M. Ruggeri; Deacon Thomas B. deHaas Jr.; Lisa Radey, Pastoral Min.
140 Richmond Rd., 44143-1299. Tel: 216-289-0770; Fax: 216-289-0740.
5—ST. PAUL (1860) [CEM] Closed. For inquiries for parish records contact St. John of the Cross, Euclid.
6—SS. ROBERT & WILLIAM (2009) Rev. John D. Betters; Sr. Irene Charette, O.S.U., Pastoral Min.
367 E. 260th St., 44132-1495. Tel: 216-731-1515; Fax: 216-731-7611. In Res., Rev. Jerome A. Lukachinsky (Retired).
7—ST. ROBERT BELLARMINE (1950) Closed. For inquiries for parish records contact SS. Robert & William, Euclid.
8—ST. WILLIAM (1946) Closed. For inquiries for parish records contact SS. Robert & William, Euclid.

FAIRPORT HARBOR, LAKE CO., ST. ANTHONY OF PADUA (1887) Rev. Peter M. Mihalic; Shanon Sterringer, Pastoral Assoc.; Sr. Maria Marcela Machicote, S.N.D., Pastoral Assoc.; Deacon John T. Wenzel.
Res.: 316 Fifth St., 44077-5696. Tel: 440-354-4525; Fax: 440-354-8313.
Catechesis/Religious Program—Students 146.

FAIRVIEW PARK, CUYAHOGA CO., ST. ANGELA MERICI (1923) Revs. Michael J. Lanning; Gregory F. Schaut, Parochial Vicar; Deacons James L. Agrippe, (Retired); J. Kevin McKenna.
Res.: 20970 Lorain Rd., 44126-2096. Tel: 440-333-2133; Fax: 440-333-8061.
School—20830 Lorain Rd., 44126. Tel: 440-333-2126; Fax: 440-333-8480. Denise Modic Urban, Prin. Lay Teachers 23; Students 540.
Catechesis/Religious Program—Tel: 216-333-2133. Students 590.

GARFIELD HEIGHTS, CUYAHOGA CO.
1—HOLY SPIRIT PARISH (2008) Rev. Philip J. Bernier, O.F.M.Cap.; Sr. Kathleen McCafferty, S.N.D., Pastoral Assoc.; Deacons Shelby Friend; Ronald R. James.
4341 E. 131st St., 44105-5563. Tel: 216-581-0981; 216-581-0982; Fax: 216-581-8222.
See Archbishop James P. Lyke Elementary School, Cleveland under Elementary Schools, Parochial and Diocesan located in the Institution section.
Catechesis/Religious Program—Students 50.
2—ST. MONICA (1952) Revs. Thomas A. Haren; Dennis J. Kristancic; Deacon Ralph W. Netzband. In Res., Rev. Thomas G. Montavon (Retired).
Res.: 13623 Rockside Rd., 44125-5197. Tel: 216-662-8685; 216-662-8686; 216-662-8687; 216-662-8625; Fax: 216-662-1245.
School—13633 Rockside Rd., 44125. Tel: 216-662-9380; Fax: 216-662-3137. Ruth Downey, Prin. Sisters of St. Joseph Third Order of St. Francis 1; Lay Teachers 21; Students 369.
Catechesis/Religious Program—Students 144.
Convent—Tel: 216-581-0810.
3—SS. PETER AND PAUL (1927), (Polish), Rev. Michael A. Matusz; Deacon William R. Starkey. In Res., Rev. Donald P. Oleksiak.
Res.: 4750 Turney Rd., 44125-1448. Tel: 216-429-1515; 216-429-1516; Fax: 216-429-1889.
See John Paul II Academy, Garfield Heights under Elementary Schools, Parochial and Diocesan in the Institution Section.
Catechesis/Religious Program—Students 76.
Convent—Tel: 216-429-2666.
4—ST. THERESE (1927) Revs. Daniel R. Fickes, Admin.; Norman A. Gajdzinski, Pastor Emeritus (Retired); Neil G. Walters.
Res.: 5276 E. 105th St., 44125-2698. Tel: 216-581-2852; 216-581-2853; Fax: 216-581-5091.
See John Paul II Academy, Garfield Heights under Elementary Schools, Parochial and Diocesan in the Institution Section.
Catechesis/Religious Program—Students 135.
5—ST. TIMOTHY (1923) Closed. For inquiries for parish records, contact the Archives, Diocese of Cleveland.

GATES MILLS, CUYAHOGA CO., ST. FRANCIS OF ASSISI (1943) Revs. James L. Caddy; Sylvester W. Fridrich, Pastor Emeritus (Retired); Gary J. Malin; Deacons Leo F. McNulty; William T. Elwood; Maureen Dowd, Pastoral Assoc.
Res.: 6850 Mayfield Rd., 44040-9635. Tel: 440-461-0066; Fax: 440-461-9053.
School—Tel: 440-442-7450; Fax: 440-446-1132. Adrienne Publicover, Prin. Religious 1; Lay Teachers 26; Students 468.
Catechesis/Religious Program—Students 263.

GRAFTON, LORAIN CO.
1—ASSUMPTION (1894), (Polish), Closed. For inquiries for parish records contact the chancery.
2—IMMACULATE CONCEPTION (1835) [CEM] Closed. For inquiries for parish records contact the chancery.
3—OUR LADY QUEEN OF PEACE PARISH Rev. John P. Seabold; Sr. Kathleen Knechtges, S.N.D., Pastoral Assoc.
1033 Elm St., 44044-1449. Tel: 440-926-2364; 440-926-1053; Fax: 440-926-3783.
Catechesis/Religious Program—Mr. Al DiVencenzo, D.R.E.; Robin Duplaga, D.R.E.; Nancy Johnson, D.R.E. Students 366.

HIGHLAND HEIGHTS, CUYAHOGA CO., ST. PASCHAL BAYLON (1953) Revs. John Thomas Lane, S.S.S.; William Fickel, S.S.S., Parochial Vicar; Roger Bourgeois, S.S.S.; Paul Bernier, S.S.S., Parochial Vicar; Mrs. Annette Cicatelli, Pastoral Assoc.; Deacons Robert J. Bowers; Joseph Bourgeois. In Res., Rev. William T. Young, S.S.S.
Res.: 5384 Wilson Mills Rd., 44143-3092. Tel: 440-442-3410; Fax: 440-442-2001.
School—5360 Wilson Mills Rd., 44143. Tel: 440-442-6766; Fax: 440-446-9037. Mr. John V. Bednar, Prin. Lay Teachers 29; Students 514.
Catechesis/Religious Program—Students 288.

HINCKLEY, MEDINA CO., OUR LADY OF GRACE (1965) Rev. William P. O'Neill. In Res., Rev. John T. McDonough (Retired).
Res.: 1088 Ridge Rd., 44233-9602. Tel: 330-278-4121; Fax: 330-278-2849.
Catechesis/Religious Program—Students 319.

HUDSON, SUMMIT CO., ST. MARY (1860) [CEM] Revs. Edward J. Kordas; John D. Betters; Sr. Barbara Einloth, S.C., Pastoral Assoc.; Deacon Carl H. Winterich; Rose Gordyan, Pastoral Assoc.
Res.: 340 N. Main St., 44236-2242. Tel: 330-653-8118; Fax: 330-463-5759.
Church: 340 N. Main St., 44236.
Catechesis/Religious Program—Students 1,455.

INDEPENDENCE, CUYAHOGA CO., ST. MICHAEL (1851) [CEM] Revs. Peter Colletti; Carl L. D'Agostino, Pastor Emeritus (Retired); Janice M. Wisnieski, Pastoral Assoc.; Deacon James Vincent. In Res., Rev. Douglas T. Makowski (Retired).
Res.: 6912 Chestnut Rd., 44131-3399. Tel: 216-524-1394; 216-524-1395; Fax: 216-328-8537.
Church: Brecksville Rd., 44131.
School—6906 Chestnut Rd., 44131. Tel: 216-524-6405; Fax: 216-524-7538. Michelle Nowakowski, Prin. Lay Teachers 24; Students 417.
Catechesis/Religious Program—Tel: 216-447-4406. Students 343.
Convent—6800 Chestnut Rd., 44131-3399. Tel: 216-447-4406.

KIRTLAND, LAKE CO., DIVINE WORD (1977) Rev. David G. Woost; Ms. Jan Geho, Pastoral Assoc.; Deacon Carl M. Varga. In Res., Rev. John J. Juhas (Retired).
Res.: 8100 Eagle Rd., 44094-9714. Tel: 440-256-1412; 440-256-1413; 440-256-1417; Fax: 440-256-4929.
Peaceful Children Montessori—Tel: 440-256-1976; Fax: 440-256-4370. Susan Lowe, Prin. Lay Teachers 8; Students 79.
Catechesis/Religious Program—Students 198.

LAKEWOOD, CUYAHOGA CO.
1—ST. CLEMENT (1922) Revs. David A. Novak; Alfred H. Winters, Pastor Emeritus (Retired); Sr. Kathryn Thomas, C.S.J., Pastoral Assoc.
Res.: 2022 Lincoln Ave., 44107-6099. Tel: 216-226-5116; Fax: 216-226-5117.
Church: Madison & Lincoln Aves., 44107.
See Lakewood Catholic Academy, Lakewood under Elementary Schools Parochial and Diocesan in the Institution Section.
Catechesis/Religious Program—Students 61.
Convent—14505 Madison Ave., 44107.
2—SS. CYRIL AND METHODIUS (1902), (Slovak), Revs. Jerome J. Duke; Richard J. Ondreyka, M.S., Pastor Emeritus (Retired).
Res.: 12608 Madison Ave., 44107-4997. Tel: 216-521-7288; 216-521-9091; Fax: 216-521-7005.
Church: Madison Ave. & Lakewood Ave., 44107.
School—1639 Alameda Ave., 44107-4997. Tel: 216-221-9409; Fax: 216-221-8516. William Bistak, Prin. Lay Teachers 12; Students 108.
Catechesis/Religious Program—Tel: 216-221-9402. Students 67.
Convent—1635 Alameda Ave., 44107. Tel: 216-221-3164.
3—ST. HEDWIG (1905), (Polish), Rev. Donald P. Oleksiak, Admin.
Res.: 12903 Madison Ave., 44107-4939. Tel: 216-521-5086; Fax: 216-521-4463.
Church: 12905 Madison Ave., 44107-4939.
4—ST. JAMES (1908) Revs. John J. Weigand; James T. Klein, Parochial Vicar; Deacons James R. Stewart; Danny Beyan; Ann Gilbert, Pastoral Assoc.
Res.: 17514 Detroit Ave., 44107-3498. Tel: 216-221-0233; Fax: 216-221-2431.
Church: Detroit & Granger Ave., 44107.

See Lakewood Catholic Academy, Lakewood under the Elementary Schools, Parochial and Diocesan in the Institution Section.
Catechesis/Religious Program—Students 126.

5—ST. LUKE (1922) Rev. Francis P. Walsh; Marilyn Streeter, Pastoral Assoc.; Deacon David A. Streeter.
Res.: 1212 Bunts Rd., 44107-2699. Tel: 216-521-0184; 216-521-0185; 216-521-0186; Fax: 216-521-9360.
See Lakewood Catholic Academy, Lakewood under the Elementary Schools, Parochial and Diocesan in the Institution Section.
Catechesis/Religious Program—Students 127.

LITCHFIELD, MEDINA CO., OUR LADY HELP OF CHRISTIANS PARISH (1976) Rev. Ronald J. Bryda, Coord. Pastoral Team; Deacon Michael F. Jervis Sr.; Rev. Edward F. Weist, Pastoral Team; Sandra J. Lynn, Pastoral Team.
Administration Center—9608 Norwalk Rd., 44253-9598. Tel: 330-722-1180; 330-273-1500 (Cleveland); Fax: 330-723-5891.
Catechesis/Religious Program—Students 157.
Convent—9608 Norwalk Rd., 44253.
Mission—Jesus the Christ Child, Medina Co.
Mission—Jesus Divine Redeemer Chippewa Lake, Medina Co.
Mission—Jesus the Good Shepherd 356 N. Main St., Nova-Savannah, Medina Co.
Mission—Jesus Emmanuel 60 High St., Seville-Creston, Medina Co.
Mission—Jesus Our Savior Spencer, Medina Co.
Mission—Jesus Our Teacher Lodi, Medina Co.

LODI, MEDINA CO., JESUS OUR TEACHER (1976) Attended by Our Lady Help of Christians, Litchfield., 44254.

LORAIN, LORAIN CO.

1—ST. ANTHONY OF PADUA (1923) Rev. Joseph West, O.F.M.Conv. In Res., Revs. Charles Henkle, O.F.M.-.Conv.; Edmund Goldbach, O.F.M.Conv.
Res.: 1305 E. Erie Ave., 44052-2299. Tel: 440-288-0106; 440-288-0107; Fax: 440-288-0143.
School—1339 E. Erie Ave., 44052. Tel: 440-288-2155; Fax: 440-288-2159. Daniel Humphrey, Prin. Lay Teachers 19; Students 255.
Catechesis/Religious Program—Students 72.

2—SS. CYRIL AND METHODIUS (1905), (Slovenian), Closed. For inquiries for parish records contact St. John, Lorain.

3—HOLY TRINITY (1906), (Slovak), Closed. For inquiries for parish records contact Mary Mother of God, Lorain.

4—ST. JOHN THE BAPTIST (1900) Revs. Thomas R. Smith; Thomas V. Rath, Pastor Emeritus (Retired).
Res.: 2143 Homewood Dr., 44055-2799. Tel: 440-277-7266.
Catechesis/Religious Program—Students 38.

5—ST. JOSEPH (1896), (German), Rev. James P. Schmitz, Presbyteral Moderator; Deacon Luis Maldonado, Parish Life Coord.
Res.: 317 W. 15th St., 44052-3488. Tel: 440-244-2179; Fax: 440-244-3036.
Church: Reid Ave. & 15th St., 44052.
Catechesis/Religious Program—Students 16.

6—ST. LADISLAUS (1890), (Hungarian), Closed. For inquiries for parish records contact the chancery.

7—ST. MARY (1873) Closed. For inquiries for parish records contact Mary Mother of God, Lorain.

8—MARY MOTHER OF GOD (2009) Rev. Daniel O. Divis; Mrs. Patricia Shullick, Pastoral Min.
309 Seventh St., 44052-1879. Tel: 440-245-5283; Fax: 440-246-0804.

9—NATIVITY OF THE BLESSED VIRGIN MARY (1898), (Polish), Rev. Robert J. Glepko; Deacon Robert J. Dybo.
Res.: 418 W. 15th St., 44052-3597. Tel: 440-244-9090; Fax: 440-244-0421.
Church: 1454 Lexington Ave., 44052.
Catechesis/Religious Program—Students 38.

10—ST. PETER (1909) Revs. Craig M. Hovanec; Kenneth J. Wolnowski, Pastor Emeritus (Retired); Charles Henkle, O.F.M.Conv.; Deacon Jay R. Ogan.
Res.: 3655 Oberlin Ave., 44053-2759. Tel: 440-282-9103; 440-282-8104; Fax: 440-282-9490.
School—3601 Oberlin Ave., 44053. Tel: 440-282-9909; Fax: 440-282-9320. Ms. Emily Fabanich, Prin. Lay Teachers 22; Students 440.
Catechesis/Religious Program—Students 229.
Convent—3651 Oberlin Ave., 44053. Tel: 440-282-2378.

11—SACRED HEART CHAPEL (1952), (Hispanic), Rev. William A. Thaden; Sr. Catherine McConnell, H.M., Pastoral Assoc.; Deacons Tomas Badillo, (Retired); Jose A. Flores; Carlos Rivera, (Retired); Jose A. DeGracia; Juan Ortiz.
Mailing Address: 4301 Pearl Ave., 44055-2634.
Res.: 3921 Seneca Ave., 44055. Tel: 440-277-7231; 440-277-7232; Fax: 440-277-4886.
Church: 4301 Pearl Ave., 44055.
Catechesis/Religious Program—Students 170.

12—ST. STANISLAUS (1908), (Polish), Closed. For inquiries for parish records contact the chancery.

13—ST. VITUS (1922), (Croatian), Revs. Simon J. Nekic; Thomas R. Smith, Admin.
Res.: 1785 E. 32nd St., 44055-1721. Tel: 440-277-8210.
Catechesis/Religious Program—

LOUDONVILLE, ASHLAND CO., ST. PETER (1870) [CEM] Rev. Vincent J. Hawk.
Res.: 132 N. Wood St., 44842-1235. Tel: 419-994-4396; Fax: 419-994-5263.
Catechesis/Religious Program—Tel: 419-994-3329. Students 28.

LYNDHURST, CUYAHOGA CO., ST. CLARE (1944) Rev. Stanley J. Klasinski; Mrs. Lori Mascia, Pastoral Assoc.; Deacon Ross C. DeJohn Sr. In Res., Rev. Robert M. Wendelken (Retired).
Res.: 5659 Mayfield Rd., 44124-2981. Tel: 440-449-4242; Fax: 440-646-9648.
School—5655 Mayfield Rd., 44124. Fax: 440-449-1497. Frank Przybojewski, Prin. Lay Teachers 16; Students 239.
Catechesis/Religious Program—Students 325.

MACEDONIA, SUMMIT CO., OUR LADY OF GUADALUPE (1967) Revs. David R. Trask; Lloyd J. Boymer, Pastor Emeritus (Retired); Deacon David Govern; Mrs. Nancy Freibott, Pastoral Assoc.
Res.: 9080 Shepard Rd., 44056-1450. Tel: 330-468-2194; Fax: 330-468-2196.
Catechesis/Religious Program—Students 237.

MADISON, LAKE CO., IMMACULATE CONCEPTION (1863) Rev. Sean J. Donnelly; Deacons Thomas G. Hupertz; Kenneth C. Meade; Richard F. Kuhlman. In Res., Rev. Wilfred T. Smith (Retired).
Res.: 2846 Hubbard Rd., 44057-2934. Tel: 440-428-5164; 440-428-3988; Fax: 440-428-3075.
Catechesis/Religious Program—Students 254.

MAPLE HEIGHTS, CUYAHOGA CO.

1—ST. MARTIN OF TOURS (1960) [CEM] Rev. Luigi C. Miola; Deacon Thaddeus C. Bizon Jr.
Res.: 14600 Turney Rd., 44137-4788. Tel: 216-475-4300; 216-475-4301; Fax: 216-475-8242.
School—Tel: 216-475-3633; Fax: 216-475-2484. Mrs. Kathy Krupar, Prin. Lay Teachers 11; Students 134.
Catechesis/Religious Program—Students 78.

2—ST. WENCESLAS (1923) Closed. For inquiries for parish records contact the chancery.

MEDINA, MEDINA CO.

1—ST. FRANCIS XAVIER (1860) [CEM] Revs. Anthony F. Sejba; A. Robert Lorkowski; Zachary M. Kawalec; Deacons Joseph E. Loutzenhiser; James T. Schlund; Daniel E. Norris; Paul Kipfstuhl.
Res.: 606 E. Washington St., 44256-2183. Tel: 330-725-4968; Fax: 330-723-6234.
Church: 600 E. Washington St., 44256.
School—612 E. Washington St., 44256. Tel: 330-725-3345; Fax: 330-721-8626. Sandra Bevec, Prin. Lay Teachers 30; Students 433.
Catechesis/Religious Program—Tel: 330-722-7700. Students 796.

2—HOLY MARTYRS (1980) Revs. Stephen J. Dohner; Robert F. Pfeiffer, Pastor Emeritus (Retired); Deacon Alfred J. Koch; Robin Hawkins, Pastoral Assoc.; Suzanne Kozub, Pastoral Assoc.; Janet Payton, Pastoral Assoc.
Res.: 3100 S. Weymouth Rd., 44256-9207. Tel: 330-722-6633; 330-273-1188 (Cleveland); Fax: 330-725-2193.
Catechesis/Religious Program—Students 778.

MENTOR, LAKE CO.

1—ST. BEDE THE VENERABLE (1964) Rev. Timothy J. Plavec; Mrs. Karen J. Roman, Pastoral Assoc.; Deacons Robert P. Ulman, Pastoral Assoc.; Kenneth Knight, Pastoral Assoc.
Res.: 9114 Lake Shore Blvd., 44060-1697. Tel: 440-257-5544; 440-257-5545; Fax: 440-257-2318.
Catechesis/Religious Program—Tel: 440-257-6988. Students 391.

2—ST. JOHN VIANNEY (1969) Revs. Thomas W. Johns; Jared P. Orndorff; John C. Retar; Deacon Wayne W. Snyder; Mary Kovach, Pastoral Assoc. In Res., Rev. Robert W. Kline, Pastor Emeritus (Retired).
7575 Bellflower Rd., 44060-3948. Tel: 440-943-3445 (Cleveland); 440-255-0600; Fax: 440-255-6482.
See All Saints of St. John Vianney School, Wickliffe under Elementary Schools, Parochial and Diocesan located in the Institution section.
Catechesis/Religious Program—Tel: 440-255-7266. Students 1,063.

3—ST. MARY OF THE ASSUMPTION (1857) Revs. Thomas G. Elsasser; Wilfred T. Smith, Pastor Emeritus (Retired); Deacons Joseph R. Kovitch; William A. Brys; Raymond C. Beebe, (Retired).
Res.: 8560 Mentor Ave., 44060-5853. Tel: 440-255-3404; 440-255-3405; 440-942-1774 (Cleveland); Fax: 440-255-4194.
School—8540 Mentor Ave., 44060. Tel: 440-255-9781; Fax: 440-974-8107. Mrs. Candice Konicki, Prin. Lay Teachers 30; Students 570.
Catechesis/Religious Program—Students 210.

MIDDLEBURG HEIGHTS, CUYAHOGA CO., ST. BARTHOLOMEW (1956) Revs. Leonard M. Bacik; William M. Jerse, Parochial Vicar; Deacon Robert G. Sabol.
Res.: 14865 E. Bagley Rd., 44130-5502. Tel: 440-842-5400; Fax: 440-842-2691.
School—Academy of St. Bartholomew, 14875 E. Bagley Rd., 44130-5502. Tel: 440-845-6660; Fax: 440-845-6672. Elizabeth Palascak, Prin. Sisters 1; Lay Teachers 23; Students 465.
Catechesis/Religious Program—Students 298.

MIDDLEFIELD, GEAUGA CO., ST. LUCY (1958) Revs. John T. Burkley; Harry S. Winca, Pastor Emeritus (Retired); Deacons Gregory C. Frania; Donald W. Lobdell, Pastoral Min.
Church & Mailing Address: 16280 Kinsman Rd., 44062-9405. Tel: 440-632-5824; 440-548-8091; Fax: 440-548-2221.
Catechesis/Religious Program—Students 67.

NEWBURY, GEAUGA CO., ST. HELEN (1949) Rev. James G. McPhillips; Deacons Willard Payne; Lawrence Somrack; Mary Weber, Pastoral Assoc.
Res.: 12060 Kinsman Rd., 44065-9678. Tel: 440-564-5805; 440-338-3358 (Cleveland); Fax: 440-564-7367.
School—Tel: 440-564-7125. Sr. Christin Alfieri, S.N.D., Prin. Sisters of Notre Dame 1; Lay Teachers 15; Students 270.
Catechesis/Religious Program—Students 286.

NORTH OLMSTED, CUYAHOGA CO.

1—ST. BRENDAN (1964) Revs. Thomas G. Woost; Cornelius J. Murray, Pastor Emeritus (Retired); Cirilo A. Nacorda, Parochial Vicar; Deacon Stanley J. Fulton; Sr. Judy Friedel, Pastoral Assoc. In Res., Rev. William Severt.
Church & Mailing Address: 4242 Brendan Ln., 44070-2999.
Res.: 3920 Brendan Ln., 44070. Tel: 440-777-7222; Fax: 440-779-7997.
School—Tel: 440-777-8433; Fax: 440-779-7997. Miss Julie Onacila, Prin. Lay Teachers 15; Students 173.
Catechesis/Religious Program—Students 187.

2—ST. CLARENCE (1978) Rev. Neil P. Kookoothe, Admin.; Deacon Wayne A. Bosau. In Res., Rev. Thomas A. Flynn, Pastor Emeritus (Retired).
Res.: 30106 Lorain Rd., 44070-3986. Tel: 440-734-2414; Fax: 440-734-4255.
Catechesis/Religious Program—Students 464.
Convent—30072 Lorain Rd., 44070. Tel: 440-777-5258.

3—ST. RICHARD (1950) Rev. Charles J. Stollenwerk; Deacon Gregory F. Noveske; Sr. M. Jerome Fitzgerald, S.I.W., Pastoral Assoc.; Mrs. Mary Ogan, Pastoral Assoc.; Mrs. Kathleen Huber, Pastoral Assoc.
Res.: 26855 Lorain Rd., 44070-3260. Tel: 440-777-5050; 440-777-5051; 440-777-5052; Fax: 440-777-3577.
School—Tel: 440-777-2922; Fax: 440-777-7374. Mr. Michael Cappabianca, Prin. Lay Teachers 26; Students 391.
Catechesis/Religious Program—Students 120.
Convent—5053 Whitethorn Ave., 44070. Tel: 440-777-2168.

NORTH RIDGEVILLE, LORAIN CO.

1—ST. JULIE BILLIART (1978) [JC] Rev. Richard A. Gonser; Deacons John M. Rivera; Kenneth A. DeLuca. In Res., Rev. Elmer E. Marquard.
Res.: 5545 Opal Dr., 44039-2025. Tel: 440-327-1978; 440-327-1979; Fax: 440-327-1994.
Church: 5500 Lear Nagle Rd., 44039.
Catechesis/Religious Program—Students 205.

2—ST. PETER (1875) [CEM] Revs. Robert J. Franco; Douglas Koesel, Parochial Vicar; Deacon Donald M. Jankowski; Cheryle Koberna, Pastoral Assoc.
Res.: 35777 Center Ridge Rd., 44039-3097. Tel: 440-327-2201; Fax: 440-327-2204.
School—35749 Center Ridge Rd., 44039. Tel: 440-327-3212; Fax: 440-327-6843. Sr. Mary Patricia Vovk, S.N.D., Prin. Sisters of Notre Dame 2; Lay Teachers 14; Students 289.
Catechesis/Religious Program—Students 416.
Convent—7209 Wil-Lou Ln. Tel: 440-327-8713.

NORTH ROYALTON, CUYAHOGA CO., ST. ALBERT THE GREAT (1959) Revs. Edward T. Estok Jr.; John L. Viall, Pastor Emeritus (Retired); Thomas E. Stock; Richard Bona. In Res., Rev. Albert J. Tesek (Retired); Laura Kuhn, Pastoral Assoc.
Res.: 6667 Wallings Rd., 44133-3067. Tel: 440-237-6760; 440-237-6761; Fax: 440-237-5945.
School—Tel: 440-237-1032; Fax: 440-237-3308. Mr. Thomas Brownfield, Prin. Lay Teachers 34; Students 773.
Catechesis/Religious Program—Students 829.

NORTHFIELD, SUMMIT CO., ST. BARNABAS (1956) Revs. Ralph E. Wiatrowski; Michael J. Denk; Robert Wenz; Deacon Gerald Butler.
Res.: 9451 Brandywine Rd., 44067-2484. Tel: 330-467-7959; 330-467-7941; 330-467-2348; Fax: 330-467-6424.
School—9200 Olde Eight Rd., 44067. Tel: 330-467-7921; Fax: 330-468-1926. Mrs. Kimberly A. Browning, Prin. Lay Teachers 37; Students 752.
Catechesis/Religious Program—Students 885.

NORTON, SUMMIT CO., ST. ANDREW THE APOSTLE (1951) Rev. James G. Maloney; Deacon Gregory A. Wunderle.
Res. & Church: 4022 Johnson Rd., 44203-5998. Tel: 330-825-2617; Fax: 330-825-5309.
Catechesis/Religious Program—Tel: 330-825-8264. Students 74.

OBERLIN, LORAIN CO., SACRED HEART (1880) Revs. Robert J. Cole, Admin.; William Padavick, Pastor Emeritus (Retired).
Res.: 410 W. Lorain St., 44074-1002. Tel: 440-774-6791; 440-774-1337; Fax: 440-775-1306.
Catechesis/Religious Program—Students 49.

OLMSTED FALLS, CUYAHOGA CO., ST. MARY OF THE FALLS (1854) [CEM] Revs. Walter J. Hyclak; Sean P. Ralph; Deacons Richard Mueller; Thomas Daw; P. Robert Martin; Mary Frances Ehlinger, Pastoral Assoc.; Judy Stasenko, Pastoral Assoc.
Res.: 25615 Bagley Rd., 44138-1915. Tel: 440-235-2222; 440-235-2223; Fax: 440-235-2937.
School—8262 Columbia Rd., 44138-2242. Tel: 440-235-4580; Fax: 440-235-6833. Sandra Isabella, Prin. Lay Teachers 16; Students 231.
Catechesis/Religious Program—Tel: 440-235-2808. Students 625.

ORANGE VILLAGE, CUYAHOGA CO., ST. MARGARET OF HUNGARY (1921), (Hungarian), Closed. For inquiries for parish records contact the chancery.

ORRVILLE, WAYNE CO., ST. AGNES (1879) Rev. Ronald J. Turek, Admin.; Deacon Steven K. Knox.
Res.: 541 Spring St., 44667-2414. Tel: 330-682-3606; 330-682-2611.
Church: E. Oak St. & Lake St., 44667.
Catechesis/Religious Program—Students 104.

PAINESVILLE, LAKE CO., ST. MARY (1848) [CEM] Revs. R. Stephen Vellenga; Michael P. McCandless; Deacon Thomas B. deHaas Jr.
Res.: 242 N. State St., 44077-4095. Tel: 440-354-4381; 440-354-4382; Fax: 440-354-9174.
Catechesis/Religious Program—Students 503.
Convent—339 Erie St., 44077-4095. Tel: 440-354-3762.

PARKMAN, GEAUGA CO., ST. EDWARD (1928) Revs. John T. Burkley; Harry S. Winca, Pastor Emeritus (Retired); Deacons Gregory C. Frania; Donald W. Lobdell.
Res.: P.O. Box 709, 44080-0709. Tel: 440-548-8091; 440-548-3812; Fax: 440-548-2221.
Church: 16150 Center St., 44080.
Catechesis/Religious Program—Students 69.

PARMA, CUYAHOGA CO.

1—ST. ANTHONY OF PADUA (1959) Revs. Dale W. Staysniak; Rodney A. Kreidler; Deacon Russell J. Glorioso, Pastoral Assoc.; Sr. Kathryn Mary O'Brien, O.S.U., Pastoral Assoc. In Res., Rev. Clement Metzger, S.J.
Res.: 6750 State Rd., 44134-4518. Tel: 440-842-2666; 440-842-2667; 440-842-2668; Fax: 440-845-9549.
School—6800 State Rd., 44134-4632. Tel: 440-845-3444; Fax: 440-884-4548. Sr. Roberta Goebel, O.S.U., Prin. Religious 1; Lay Teachers 20; Students 332.
Catechesis/Religious Program—Students 399.
Convent—6834 State Rd., 44134. Tel: 440-842-2211.

2—ST. BRIDGET (1956) Revs. Robert W. Wisniewski; Lawrence J. Bayer, Pastor Emeritus (Retired); Steven Malec, Pastoral Assoc. In Res., Rev. James R. Semonin.
Res.: 5620 Hauserman Rd., 44130-1698. Tel: 440-886-4434; 440-886-4435; Fax: 440-886-4431.
School—Tel: 440-886-1468; Fax: 440-886-5121. Thomas Norton, Prin. Lay Teachers 14; Students 294.
Catechesis/Religious Program—Students 318.
Convent—

3—ST. CHARLES BORROMEO (1923) Revs. John T. Carlin; Edward F. Suszynski Jr., Parochial Vicar; Edwin M. Leonard; Daniel J. Reed; Deacons John A. Talerico; Daniel M. Galla; Sr. Denise Marie Vlna, O.S.U., Pastoral Assoc.
Res.: 5891 Ridge Rd., 44129-3642. Tel: 440-884-3030; 440-884-3031; 440-884-3232; Fax: 440-884-5326.
School—7107 Wilber Ave., 44129-3445. Tel: 440-886-5546; Fax: 440-886-1163. Mrs. Eileen Updegrove, Prin. Ursuline Nuns of Cleveland 1; Lay Teachers 26; Students 583.
Catechesis/Religious Program—Students 313.
Convent—6818 Charles Ave., 44129. Tel: 440-886-0390.

4—ST. COLUMBKILLE (1956) Revs. Neil D. O'Connor; William E. Browne, Parochial Vicar; Kevin E. Estabrook; Joseph Previte; Deacons Edward A. Telepak; Paul C. Kutolowski.
Res.: 6740 Broadview Rd., 44134-4898. Tel: 216-524-1987; 216-524-1988; Fax: 216-524-9146.
School—6740 Broadview Rd., 44134-4899. Tel: 216-524-4816; Fax: 216-524-4153. Miss Rita Klement, Prin. Religious 1; Lay Teachers 24; Students 453.
Catechesis/Religious Program—Students 465.

5—ST. FRANCIS DE SALES (1931) Rev. Mark J. Peyton; Deacon Robert J. Piskach. In Res., Rev. John G. Crawford (Retired).
Res.: 3434 George Ave., 44134-2904. Tel: 440-884-2319; 440-884-2320; 440-884-2321; Fax: 440-884-1661.
Church: State & Snow Rd., 44134.
School—3421 Snow Rd., 44134-2596. Tel: 440-884-2340; Fax: 440-884-8211. Anne Sweeney, Prin. Lay Teachers 13; Students 166.
Catechesis/Religious Program—Students 104.
Convent—3425 Snow Rd., 44134. Tel: 440-884-7242.

6—HOLY FAMILY (1872) [CEM] Revs. Richard A. Evans, Admin.; Joseph R. Brankatelli; Daniel P. Redmond; Deacons Joseph P. Litke; Charles E. Tweddell.
Res.: 7367 York Rd., 44130-5162. Tel: 440-842-5533; Fax: 440-842-3090; 440-842-3141.
School—Tel: 440-842-7785; Fax: 440-842-3634. Mrs. Mary Ann Murnyack, Prin. Lay Teachers 19; Students 277.
Catechesis/Religious Program—Students 215.

7—ST. JOHN BOSCO (1963) Revs. David D. Liberatore; William A. Smith; Deacon Roger Polefko.
Res.: 6480 Pearl Rd., Parma Heights, 44130-2997. Tel: 440-886-3500; 440-886-3501; 440-886-3502; Fax: 440-886-0966.
Catechesis/Religious Program—Students 149.
Convent—12213 Denver Dr., 44130. Tel: 216-267-0133.

8—ST. MATTHIAS (1980) Rev. Raymond A. Sutter; Deacons Kenneth A. Golonka; Lindley W. Pennypacker; Ann Clark, Pastoral Assoc.; Dianne Laheta, Pastoral Assoc. In Res., Rev. Phillip P. Pritt (Retired).
Res.: 1200 W. Sprague Rd., 44134-6801. Tel: 440-888-8220; 440-888-8221; Fax: 440-888-8146.
Catechesis/Religious Program—Students 211.

PENINSULA, SUMMIT CO., MOTHER OF SORROWS (1882) Rev. John D. Terzano.
Res.: 6034 S. Locust St., 44264-9726. Tel: 330-657-2631; 330-657-2075; Fax: 330-657-2423.
Catechesis/Religious Program—Students 119.

PERRY, LAKE CO., ST. CYPRIAN (1968) Revs. Jerzy Kusy, Admin.; James J. Patton, Pastor Emeritus (Retired); Deacons Andrew Novak; James F. Daley Jr.
Res.: 4223 Middle Ridge Rd., 44081-9794. Tel: 440-259-2344; Fax: 440-259-2255.
Catechesis/Religious Program—Students 357.

RICHFIELD, SUMMIT CO., ST. VICTOR (1964) Revs. Allen F. Corrigan; Arthur A. Bacher, Pastor Emeritus (Retired).
Church & Res.: 3435 Everett Rd., 44286-0461. Tel: 330-659-6591; 330-659-6321; 330-659-3398; Fax: 330-659-3618.
Catechesis/Religious Program—Students 314.

RITTMAN, WAYNE CO., ST. ANNE (1855) [CEM] Revs. Phillip P. Pritt, Pastor Emeritus (Retired); Stephen P. Moran, Presbyteral Moderator; Sr. Joan Rader, O.P., Parish Life Coord.
Res.: 139 S. First St., 44270-1492. Tel: 330-927-2941; Fax: 330-927-3002.
Church: E. Ohio & S. First St., 44270.
Catechesis/Religious Program—Students 7.

ROCKY RIVER, CUYAHOGA CO., ST. CHRISTOPHER (1922) Revs. John C. Chlebo; John T. Ostrowski; Timothy M. Daw; Deacon John F. Downey; Mrs. Marianne Betters, Pastoral Assoc.; Ms. Gayle Cilimburg, Pastoral Assoc.; Laura Peltz, Pastoral Assoc.
Res.: 20141 Detroit Rd., 44116-2420. Tel: 440-331-4255; 440-331-4256; Fax: 440-331-3885.
School—1610 Lakeview Ave., 44116-2409. Tel: 440-331-3075; Fax: 440-331-0674. Joyce M. Needham, Prin. Lay Teachers 26; Students 496.
Catechesis/Religious Program—Tel: 440-331-6226. Students 568.

SEVILLE-CRESTON, MEDINA-WOOSTER COUNTIES, JESUS EMMANUEL (1976) Attended by Our Lady Help of Christians, Litchfield.

SHAKER HEIGHTS, CUYAHOGA CO., ST. DOMINIC (1945) Rev. Thomas G. Fanta; Deacon Robert Matoney Jr.; Bonnie Stein, Pastoral Assoc.; Nick Borchers, Pastoral Assoc.; Sr. Kathleen Glavich, S.N.D., Pastoral Assoc.
Res.: 3450 Norwood Rd., 44122-4967. Tel: 216-991-1444; 216-991-1445; Fax: 216-491-0190.
Church: 19000 Van Aken Blvd., 44122.
School—3455 Norwood Rd., 44122-4901. Tel: 216-561-4400; Fax: 216-561-1573. Kathleen H. Cherney, Prin. Lay Teachers 17; Students 172.
Catechesis/Religious Program—Students 411.

SHEFFIELD, LORAIN CO., ST. TERESA OF AVILA (1845) [CEM] Revs. Edward J. Smith; Edward J. Luca, Pastor Emeritus (Retired).
Church: 1878 Abbe Rd., 44054-2322. Tel: 440-934-4227; Fax: 440-934-4500.
Catechesis/Religious Program—Students 36.

SHEFFIELD LAKE, LORAIN CO., ST. THOMAS THE APOSTLE (1962) Rev. Stephen L. Shields.
Res.: 521 Harris Rd., 44054-1409. Tel: 440-949-7744; Fax: 440-949-8611.
Catechesis/Religious Program—Students 90.
Convent—37954 French Creek Rd., 44054. Tel: 440-934-6964.

SOLON, CUYAHOGA CO.

1—RESURRECTION OF OUR LORD (1971) Revs. J. Mark Hobson, Coord., Pastoral Team; Louis J. Trivison, Pastor Emeritus (Retired); Ms. Elisabeth Frey, Pastoral Team; Theresa Battaglia, Pastoral Team.
Res. & Church: 32001 Cannon Rd., 44139-1699. Tel: 440-248-0980; 440-248-0981; Fax: 440-248-0992.
Catechesis/Religious Program—Students 294.

2—ST. RITA (1929) Revs. Richard Burchell; Robert M. Wendelken, Pastor Emeritus (Retired); Stephen A. Flynn; Mrs. Joan Heacox, Pastoral Assoc.; Deacon Robert Anderson; Mr. Albert E. Leko, Pastoral Assoc.
Res.: 32820 Baldwin Rd., 44139-4098. Tel: 440-248-1350; Fax: 440-248-2094.
School—33200 Baldwin Rd., 44139. Fax: 440-248-9442. Mary Petelin, Prin. Lay Teachers 25; Students 482.
Catechesis/Religious Program—Students 448.

SOUTH AMHERST, LORAIN CO., NATIVITY OF BLESSED VIRGIN MARY (1933) Revs. Lawrence N. Martello, Admin.; Denis L. St. Marie, Pastor Emeritus (Retired). In Res., Rev. John M. Tezie (Retired).
Res.: 333 S. Lake St., 44001-2013. Tel: 440-986-7011; Fax: 440-986-7012.
Catechesis/Religious Program—Students 49.

SOUTH EUCLID, CUYAHOGA CO.

1—ST. GREGORY THE GREAT (1922) Revs. David R. Ireland; Edward T. Holland, Parochial Vicar. In Res., Deacon David N. Chordas.
Res.: 1545 S. Green Rd., 44121-4085. Tel: 216-382-7601; 216-382-7602; 216-382-7603; Fax: 216-382-4992.
School—4478 Rushton Rd., 44121-4084. Tel: 216-381-0363; Fax: 216-382-7561. Mr. Peter Wilson, Prin. Ursuline Sisters 1; Lay Teachers 24; Students 422.
Catechesis/Religious Program—Students 66.

2—ST. MARGARET MARY (1948) Revs. Richard E. Hudak; Thomas J. Lusoski, Pastor Emeritus (Retired).
Res.: 4217 Bluestone Rd., 44121-3427. Tel: 216-382-4114; 216-382-4115; Fax: 216-381-8730.
Catechesis/Religious Program—Tel: 216-382-4272. Students 10.
Convent—4215 Bluestone Rd., 44121. Tel: 216-381-8787.

SPENCER, MEDINA CO., JESUS OUR SAVIOR (1976) Attended by Our Lady Help of Christians, Litchfield.

STOW, SUMMIT CO., HOLY FAMILY (1946) Revs. Paul J. Rosing, Admin.; Patrick J. Shields; Joseph R. Mamich; Deacons Louis C. Dobos; Philip P. Kamlowsky; Joan Skalak, Pastoral Assoc.
Res.: 3450 Sycamore Dr., 44224-3999. Tel: 330-688-6411; Fax: 330-689-0186.
Church: 3179 Kent Rd., 44224. Tel: 330-688-6412.
School—3163 Kent Rd., 44224. Tel: 330-688-3816; Fax: 330-688-3474. Mrs. Sharon Fournier, Prin. Lay Teachers 29; Students 562.
Catechesis/Religious Program—Students 412.

STRONGSVILLE, CUYAHOGA CO.

1—ST. JOHN NEUMANN (1977) Revs. Robert J. Kraig; Russell G. Rauscher; Sr. Patricia Sylvester, S.N.D., Pastoral Assoc.; Deacons Thomas Grasson; Kenneth J. Piechowski; Mrs. Sandy Zorn, Pastoral Assoc.
Res.: 16271 Pearl Rd., 44136-6095. Tel: 440-238-1770; 440-238-1771; Fax: 440-238-2030.
See SS. Joseph & John Interparochial, Strongsville under St. Joseph, Strongsville.
Catechesis/Religious Program—Students 906.

2—ST. JOSEPH (1946) Revs. Robert J. Sanson; Kevin C. Shemuga, Parochial Vicar; Deacons Pete Moore; Robert Lester.
Res.: 12700 Pearl Rd., 44136-3484. Tel: 440-238-5555; 440-238-5556; 440-238-1038; Fax: 440-238-1059.
School—SS. Joseph and John Interparochial, 12580 Pearl Rd., 44136-3422. Tel: 440-238-4877; Fax: 440-238-8745. Mrs. Darlene Thomas, Prin. Sisters of St. Joseph 1; Lay Teachers 32; Students 725.
Catechesis/Religious Program—Tel: 440-238-5231. Students 561.
Convent—12600 Pearl Rd., 44136. Tel: 440-238-6352.

TALLMADGE, SUMMIT CO., OUR LADY OF VICTORY (1944) Rev. John R. Hengle; Diane Hardick, Pastoral Assoc.
Mailing Address: *Administration Center*, 73 North Ave., 44278-1996. Tel: 330-633-3637; 330-633-3672; Fax: 330-633-6978.
Rectory—55 North Ave., 44278.
Church: 105 North Ave., 44278.
Catechesis/Religious Program—Students 368.

THOMPSON, GEAUGA CO., ST. PATRICK (1854) [CEM] Rev. Paul F. Smith; Deacons Phillip P. Kraynik; James T. Martin; Robert F. Schwartz; Debra S. McCready, Pastoral Assoc.
Res.: 16550 Rock Creek Rd., Rte. 166, 44086-8753. Tel: 440-298-1327; Fax: 440-298-1846.
Catechesis/Religious Program—Students 85.

TWINSBURG, SUMMIT CO., SS. COSMAS AND DAMIAN (1963) Revs. John P. Singler; Robert E. Friedel, Pastor Emeritus (Retired); Deacon Edward J. Chernick.
Res.: 10419 Ravenna Rd., 44087-1726. Tel: 330-425-8141; 330-425-8142; Fax: 330-405-2947.
Church: 10439 Ravenna Rd., 44087-1726.
Catechesis/Religious Program—Students 380.

UNIONTOWN, SUMMIT CO., QUEEN OF HEAVEN (1964) Revs. David R. Durkee; Robert E. Pahler, Pastor Emeritus (Retired); Thomas P. Kowatch; Deacon Robert Bender.
Res.: 1800 Steese Rd., 44685-9555. Tel: 330-896-2345; Fax: 330-896-8882.
Catechesis/Religious Program—Students 616.

UNIVERSITY HEIGHTS, CUYAHOGA CO., GESU (1926) Revs. Lorn J. Snow, S.J.; Paul D. Panaretos, S.J.; Bro. Denis Weber, S.J., Pastoral Assoc.; Deacon James K. O'Donnell; Meg Madrigal Wilson, Pastoral Assoc.
Res.: 2470 Miramar Blvd., 44118-3896. Tel: 216-932-0616; 216-932-0617; 216-932-0618; Fax: 216-932-0731.
Church: 2490 Miramar Blvd., 44118.
School—2450 Miramar Blvd., 44118. Tel: 216-932-0620; Fax: 216-932-8326. Sr. Linda Martin, O.S.U., Prin. Ursuline Sisters 1; Lay Teachers 39; Students 778.
Catechesis/Religious Program—Students 239.
Convent—4070 Meadowbrook Blvd., 44118. Tel: 216-932-1660.

VALLEY CITY, MEDINA CO., ST. MARTIN OF TOURS (1840) [CEM] Rev. Thomas R. Dunphy.
Res.: 1824 Station Rd., 44280-9522. Tel: 330-483-3808; Fax: 330-483-3848.
Catechesis/Religious Program—Tel: 330-483-5925. Students 251.

WADSWORTH, MEDINA CO., SACRED HEART OF JESUS (1866) [JC] Revs. Joseph L. Labak; Joseph G. Workman, Admin.; Deacons Roger N. Klaas; Richard Michney.
Res.: 260 Broad St., 44281-2113. Tel: 330-336-3049; Fax: 330-336-0143.
School—110 Humbolt Ave., 44281. Tel: 330-334-6272; Fax: 330-334-3236. Mrs. Tracy Arnone, Prin. Lay Teachers 18; Students 299.
Catechesis/Religious Program—Students 381.
Convent—268 Broad St., 44281. Tel: 330-334-5063.

WARRENSVILLE HEIGHTS, CUYAHOGA CO., ST. JUDE (1945) Closed. For inquiries for parish records contact the chancery.

WELLINGTON, LORAIN CO., ST. PATRICK (1851) Rev. James J. Reymann.
Res.: 512 N. Main St., 44090-1198. Tel: 440-647-4375; Fax: 440-647-4675.
Catechesis/Religious Program—Students 259.

WEST SALEM, WAYNE CO., ST. STEPHEN (1952) Revs. James P. Schmitz; Carl A. Uhler, Pastor Emeritus; Deacon Peter J. Foradori.
Res.: 44 Britton St., 44287-9318. Tel: 419-853-4946; Fax: 419-853-7037.
Catechesis/Religious Program—Students 90.

WESTLAKE, CUYAHOGA, CO.
1—ST. BERNADETTE (1950) Revs. Thomas L. Weber; Eric Orzech, Admin.; Deacon Joseph E. McGraw; Sr. Margaret O'Brien, O.S.U., Pastoral Assoc.
Res.: 2256 Clague Rd., 44145-4328. Tel: 440-734-1300; 440-734-1301; 440-734-1302; 440-734-3220; Fax: 440-734-1584.
School—2300 Clague Rd., 44145. Tel: 440-734-7717; Fax: 440-734-9198. Helen D. Bykowski, Prin. Religious 1; Lay Teachers 24; Students 319.
Catechesis/Religious Program—Students 287.
2—ST. LADISLAS (1973) Revs. Donald E. Snyder; John G. Vrana, Admin.; Mary Ellen Downs, Pastoral Assoc. In Res., Most Rev. A. James Quinn (Retired).
Res. & Church Address: 2345 Bassett Rd., 44145-2999. Tel: 440-835-2300; Fax: 440-835-5895.
Catechesis/Religious Program—Students 222.

WICKLIFFE, LAKE CO., OUR LADY OF MOUNT CARMEL (1921) Revs. Thomas J. Behrend, Admin.; David L. McCafferty, Pastor Emeritus (Retired); Andrew B. Turner; John J. Sullivan, Parochial Vicar; Deacon John W. Strmac. In Res., Revs. David G. Baugh (Retired); Stephen J. Kaminski.
Res.: 1730 Mount Carmel Dr., 44092-1835. Tel: 440-585-0700; Fax: 440-585-0870.
Church: 29850 Euclid Ave., 44092.
School—29840 Euclid Ave., 44092. Tel: 440-585-0800; Fax: 440-585-9391. Rose Witmer, Prin. Lay Teachers 18; Students 278.
Catechesis/Religious Program—Students 192.

WILLOUGHBY, LAKE CO., IMMACULATE CONCEPTION (1866) Revs. Michael J. Troha; Francis D. Curran, Pastor Emeritus (Retired); Louis A. Pizmoht; Deacons Edward J. Feldkamp, (Retired); Paul J. Hlabse Sr.
Res.: 37935 Wright St., 44094-5899. Tel: 440-942-4500; Fax: 440-942-1540.
School—37940 Euclid Ave., 44094-5997. Tel: 440-942-2121; Fax: 440-942-6766. Miss Kathleen Hrutkay, Prin. Lay Teachers 15; Students 207.
Catechesis/Religious Program—Students 187.

WILLOUGHBY HILLS, LAKE CO., ST. NOEL (1980) Rev. George Smiga; Deacon David T. Nethery; Alice M. Hinkel, Pastoral Assoc.; Anthony Camino, Pastoral Assoc.
Res.: 35200 Chardon Rd., 44094-9193. Tel: 440-946-0887; Fax: 440-946-4331.
Catechesis/Religious Program—Mrs. Marianne Slattery, D.R.E. Students 334.

WILLOWICK, LAKE CO., ST. MARY MAGDALENE (1949) Revs. Ronald Wearsch, Pastoral Team; Theodore Lucas, Coord. Pastoral Team; Deacon Carl Toomey, Pastoral Team; Darlene Bednarz, Pastoral Team.
Res.: 460 E. 321 St., 44095-3581. Tel: 440-943-2133; Fax: 440-943-3780.
Church: 32114 Vine St., 44095.
See St. Mary Magdalene-St. Justin Martyr Elementary School, Inc. under Elementary Schools Parochial and Diocesan in the Institution Section.
Catechesis/Religious Program—Tel: 440-944-2523. Students 332.

WOOSTER, WAYNE CO., ST. MARY OF THE IMMACULATE CONCEPTION (1846) [CEM] Revs. Stephen P. Moran; John J. Mueller, Pastor Emeritus (Retired); Christopher J. Trenta, Parochial Vicar; Deacons Bernard E. Hosfeld; Edward Souza; Mrs. Jacquelynn Lee, Pastoral Assoc.
Res.: 527 Beall Ave., P.O. Box 109, 44691-0109. Tel: 330-264-8824; 330-264-8822; Fax: 330-262-4633.
Church: 527 Beall Ave., 44691.
School—515 E. Bowman St., 44691. Tel: 330-262-8671; Fax: 330-262-0967. Richard Carestia, Prin. Lay Teachers 14; Students 205.
Catechesis/Religious Program—Students 265.

Cleveland Diocesan Mission

EL SALVADOR, C.A. *Casa Parroquial Inmaculada Concepcion*. Rev. Msgr. Richard C. Antall, Rev. Paul E. Schindler. La Libertad Dept. La Libertad El Salvador, Central America.
Casa Parroquial San Pedro Teotepeque. Revs. Mark R. Riley, Michael J. Stalla. La Libertad El Salvador, Central America.
Casa Parroquial Santo Domingo. Sr. Rose Elizabeth Terrell, O.S.U. Chiltiupan, La Libertad El Salvador, Central America.
Cathedral Square Plaza, 1404 E. 9th St., 44114. Tel: 216-696-6525, Ext. 4240. Rev. R. Stephen Vellenga, Dir. Society Propagation Faith.

Chaplains of Public Institutions

CLEVELAND. *Cleveland Clinic Foundation*. Revs. William T. Young, S.S.S. Tel: 440-442-6311, Joseph S. Mecir. Tel: 216-341-2828.
Cleveland House of Correction. Vacant.
Cuyahoga County Detention Home. Rev. James P. O'Donnell. Tel: 216-566-9953.
Cuyahoga County Jail. Rev. Neil G. Walters. Tel: 440-238-1770, Deacon Martin Thiel. Tel: 216-351-8802.
Cuyahoga Hills Boys School. Vacant.
Euclid Hospital. Rev. John M. Jenkins (Retired). Tel: 216-486-0850.
Fairview General Hospital. Rev. Edward N. Schwet, St. Angela Merici. Tel: 440-333-2133.
Grace Hospital 44105. Attended from St. Augustine, Tel: 216-781-5530.
Health Hill Hospital for Children. Attended from St. Andrew Abbey, Tel: 216-721-5300.
Hillcrest Hospital. Attended from St. Francis of Assisi, Tel: 216-461-0066.
Huron Road Hospital. Attended from St. Philomena, Tel: 216-541-3540.
Kaiser Foundation Hospital. Attended from St. Bridget, Tel: 216-886-4434.
Lakewood Hospital. Rev. Nicodemus Urassa, A.J. Tel: 440-842-1436.
Lutheran Medical Center. Rev. Paul Pietrzyk, O.de.M. Tel: 216-961-8331.
Metro Health Medical Center & Rehabilitation Center. Rev. Arthur Snedeker, Chap. Tel: 216-781-8277. (Hospital)
Metzenbaum Children's Center. Attended from St. Augustine, Tel: 216-781-5330.
Northcoast Behavioral Healthcare System North Campus. Rev. Gary Chmura. Tel: 216-421-4211.
Northeast Pre Release Center. Rev. James P. O'Donnell. Tel: 216-566-9953.
Parma Community Hospital. Rev. James R. Semonin. Tel: 216-843-8781.
Rainbow Hospital. (See University Hospitals)
Richmond Heights Hospital. Attended from St. Felicitas, Tel: 216-289-0770.
South Pointe Hospital. Attended from Pastoral Care Office, Tel: 216-491-7924.
SouthWest General Hospital. Rev. Dismas Boeff, O.S.B. Tel: 216-433-0696.
University Hospitals. Rev. William H. Severt. Tel: 440-716-8591.
University Hospitals Bedford Medical Center. Attended from St. Pius X. Tel: 440-232-8166.
Veterans Administration Hospitals, Brecksville V.A., 1000 Brecksville Rd., 44141. Tel: 440-526-3030, Ext. 6268. Revs. John Milewski. Tel: 216-736-3079, Maurice D'Souza, C.S.C. Tel: 216-712-6506, Lowell G. Neuzil. Tel: 216-721-5300.
Cleveland V.A., 10701 East Blvd., 44106. Tel: 216-791-3800, Ext. 305. Rev. John Milewski. Tel: 216-736-3079.

AKRON. *Akron City Hospital*. Attended from Annunciation Parish; Tel: 330-535-4141
Akron General Hospital. Rev. Robert E. Clancy. Tel: 330-434-4348.
Edwin C. Shaw Hospital. Attended from Nativity of the Lord Jesus, Tel: 440-669-5086.
Summit County Jail. Deacon Daniel Matusicky. Tel: 330-724-8043.

AMHERST. *The Hospital of Orthopedics and Special Services*. Attended from St. Joseph, Tel: 440-988-2848.

APPLE CREEK. *Apple Creek State Institute*, Tel: 216-696-6525, Ext. 2700. Apostolate for Persons with Developmental Disabilities.

ASHLAND. *Ashland County Jail*. Attended from St. Edward, Tel: 419-289-7224.
Samaritan Hospital. Attended from St. Edward, Tel: 419-289-7224.

AVON. *Our Lady of the Wayside*. Rev. Robert T. Begin. Tel: 216-651-0550.

BARBERTON. *Barberton Citizens Hospitals*. Attended from St. Augustine, Tel: 330-745-0011.

CHAGRIN FALLS. *Windsor Hospital*. Attended from St. Joan of Arc, Tel: 440-247-7183.

CHARDON. *Geauga Community Hospital*. Attended from St. Helen, Newbury, Tel: 440-564-5805; (Cleveland) Tel: 440-338-3358.
Geauga County Jail. Deacon Frederick Giel. Tel: 440-834-8055.

CONCORD. *Tri Point Medical Center*. Rev. Stephen J. Kaminski. Tel: 440-585-0700. A Lake Health Hospital.

CUYAHOGA FALLS. *Fallsview Mental Health Center*. Attended from St. Eugene, Tel: 330-923-5244.
General Hospital. Attended from St. Joseph, Tel: 330-928-2173.

ELYRIA. *Elyria Memorial Hospital*. Sr. Joan Tomchey, O.S.U., Chap., Pastoral Care. Tel: 440-329-7680.

GRAFTON. *Grafton Correctional Institution*. Rev. Charles J. Ryba. Tel: 440-236-5095, Deacon John Rivera. Tel: 440-327-4426.

HUDSON. *Youth Development Center*. Attended from St. Andrew Abbey, Tel: 216-721-5300.

LODI. *Lodi Hospital*. Attended from Our Lady Help of Christians, Tel: 330-722-1180; 330-273-1500 (Cleveland).

LORAIN. *Lorain Correctional Institution*. Rev. Charles J. Ryba. Tel: 440-236-5095.

LOUDONVILLE. *Kettering Hospital*. Attended from St. Peter, Tel: 419-994-4396.

MEDINA. *Medina Community Hospital*. Attended from St. Francis Xavier, Tel: 330-725-4968.
Medina County Jail. Deacon Daniel Norris. Tel: 330-725-4968.

NORTHFIELD. *Northcoast Behavioral Healthcare System South* 44067. Rev. Gary Chmura. Tel: 216-421-4211.

OBERLIN. *Allen Memorial Hospital*. Attended from Sacred Heart, Tel: 330-774-6791.

ORRVILLE. *Dunlap Memorial Hospital*. Attended from St. Agnes, Tel: 330-682-3606.

PAINESVILLE. *Lake County Jail*. Attended from St. Mary Parish.

SMITHVILLE. *Boys Village of Ohio*. Attended from St. Mary, Wooster, Tel: 330-264-8824.

WADSWORTH. *Wadsworth Health Care Center*. Attended from Sacred Heart of Jesus, Tel: 330-336-3049.
Wadsworth-Rittman Hospital. Attended from Sacred Heart of Jesus, Tel: 330-336-3049.

WILLOUGHBY. *Lake Health Hospital, Willoughby Campus*. Rev. Stephen J. Kaminski. Tel: 440-585-0700.

WOOSTER. *Wayne County Jail*. Attended from St. Mary of the Immaculate Conception, Tel: 330-264-8824.
Wooster Community Hospital. Attended from St. Mary, Tel: 330-264-8824.

Released from Diocesan Assignment:
Revs.—
Conroy, Kevin M., Maryknoll Fathers & Brothers, Maryknoll, NY 10545.
Dickenson, William R.

Patrick, William J., St. Jude Hospital & Rehabilitation Center, 3733 N. Harbor #15, Fullerton, CA 92835.

Military Chaplains:
Revs.—
Buckon, Neal J.
Glaros, Matthew J.
Sheil, James

Absent on Leave:
Revs.—
Baranek, Raymond
Conway, Neil (Retired)
Dimengo, Michael
Kondik, Curtis L.
Proehl, Douglas
Weaver, Jeffrey

Absent on Sick Leave:
Revs.—
Lajack, Edward F.
Ocilka, John A.
Spisak, Stephen M.
Winkel, Thomas J.

Administrative Leave:
Revs.—
Banner, Russell
Brodnick, Joseph
Labbe, Joseph P.
Lieberth, Joseph
McBride, Daniel
Rebol, Anthony
Seminatore, Joseph
Viall, James A.
Weber, David

Life of Prayer and Penance:
Revs.—
Bruening, Allen
Lang, Joseph
Rupp, Edward F.

Retired:
Most Revs.—
Pevec, A. Edward, Ph.D. , Center for Pastoral Leadership, 28700 Euclid Ave., Wickliffe, 44092.
Pilla, Anthony M., D.D., M.A., Center for Pastoral Leadership, 28700 Euclid Ave., Wickliffe, 44092.
Quinn, A. James, J.C.D., J.D., V.G., 2345 Bassett Rd., Westlake, 44145.
Rev. Msgrs.—
Telesz, Leo, 5713 Frances Ave., 44127-1233.
Wolff, Robert C., 4516 Rex Lake Dr., Akron, 44319.
Revs.—
Bacher, Arthur A., 5269 Mill Creek Blvd., Brunswick Hills, 44212.
Baugh, David G., 1730 Mt. Carmel Dr., Wickliffe, 44092.
Bayer, Lawrence J., 13372 Olympus Way, Strongsville, 44149.
Becherer, James R., 4963 E. Lake Rd., Sheffield Lake, 44054.
Berardi, James J., 366 Aquaduct St., Akron, 44303-1958.
Bodziony, Ralph A., 5159 Everett Rd., Richfield, 44286.
Boymer, Lloyd J., St. Augustine Manor, 7801 Detroit Ave., 44102.
Bryk, John J., 351 Falling Leaf, Seven Hills, 44131.
Burge, Robert
Callahan, Nelson J., 12550 Lake Rd., Apt. 1309, Lakewood, 44107.
Cappelletti, Joseph, 7054 Austin Point Dr., Concord, 44077.
Cimperman, Victor J., 6114 Lausche Ave., Apt. 311, 44103.
Ciprian, Carl A., 6618 Pearl Rd., Parma Heights, 44130.
Colletta, Ralph V., P.O. Box 605, Bath, 44210-0605.
Cozzens, Donald, 20700 N. Park Blvd., University Hts, 44118.
Crawford, John G., 5445 Smith Rd., Brookpark, 44142-2077.
Cudnik, Chester C., 886 Eastlawn Dr., Highland Hts., 44143.
Curran, Francis D., Regina Health Care Center, 5232 Broadview Rd., Richfield, 44286-9205.
D'Agostino, Carl L., 15712 Kipling Ave., 44110-3104.
Dyrcz, Michael S., 111525 Thwing Rd., Chardon, 44024.
Egan, Arthur B., 800 Brick Mill Run #519, Westlake, 44145.
Flynn, Thomas A., St. Clarence, 30106 Lorain Rd., North Olmsted, 44070-3986.
Fridrich, Sylvester W., 33882 Maple Ridge Blvd., Avon, 44011.
Friedel, Robert E., 2943 Country Club Ln., Twinsburg, 44087.
Gajdzinski, Norman A., 20341 Brookstone Tr., Middleburg Heights, 44130.
Gallagher, Thomas J., Village of St. Edward, 3125 Smith Rd., Apt. 403, Fairlawn, 44333.
Goebel, Joseph A., St. Christine, 840 E. 222nd St., Euclid, 44123-3317.
Gorski, John J., 615 N.E. 12th Ave., Apt. 207, Fort Lauderdale, FL 33304-2841. (May-June): 2820 N. Bay Dr., Apt. P-9, Westlake, 44145-6020.
Hayes, John J., 4129 Superior Ave., 44103.
Hepner, Ernest C., 101 Single Tree Ln., Aiken, SC 29803.
Horley, Ray J., 4291 Richmond Rd., Warrensville Heights, 44122.
Hritz, Paul J., 10210 Granger Rd., #381, Garfield Heights, 44125.
Jenkins, John M., Holy Cross Church, 19951 Lake Shore Blvd., Euclid, 44119-1066.
Juhas, John J., 8100 Eagle Rd., Kirtland, 44094-9714.
Karg, William D., 7337 Trailside Dr., Unit B, Northfield, 44067.
Keller, Gerald J., 33896 Maple Ridge Rd., Avon, 44011.
Kinkopf, John J., Divine Word, 8100 Eagle Rd., Kirtland, 44094.
Kitt, William J., Grattan Park, Mountbellow, County Galway, Ireland.
Kline, John J., 33803 Electric Blvd., Apt. E-6, Avon Lake, 44012.
Kline, Robert W., St. John Vianney, 7575 Bellflower Rd, Mentor, 44060.
Krajnik, Paul A., 7821 Lake Rd., 44102.
Kunkle, Albert A., 39 N. Portage Path, Akron, 44303.
Labella, Robert, 1255 Richmond Rd., Lyndhurst, 44124.
Laubenthal, Allan R., S.T.D., Center for Pastoral Leadership, 28700 Euclid Ave., Wickliffe, 44092.
Lee, William J., S.S., 601 Maiden Choice Ln., Baltimore, MD 21228-3698.
Luca, Edward J., J.C.D., 1535 Elmwood Ave., Lakewood, 44107.
Lukachinsky, Jerome A., 367 E. 260th St., Euclid, 44132.
Lusoski, Thomas J., 21108 Franklin Rd., Maple Hts., 44137.
Mackert, Albert J., 13719 Tartan Dr., Sun City West, AZ 85375. Winter Months, 3644 Rocky River Dr., 44111.
Mahoney, Thomas D., 15555 Hillard Rd., #805, Lakewood, 44107.
Makowski, Douglas T., 6912 Chestnut Rd., Independence, 44131.
McCafferty, David L., 164 W. Market St., Akron, 44303-2395.
McCarthy, David J., 215 Falls Ave., Cuyahoga Falls, 44221.
McDonough, John T., 1088 Ridge Rd., Hinckley, 44233.
McGovern, Thomas A., 1986 Village Pkwy., Tallmadge, 44278-3036.
McShane, Patrick E., 10 Linda Ln. #4-2, Dorchester, MA 02125.
Montavon, Thomas G., 13623 Rockside Rd., Garfield Heights, 44125-5197.
Mueller, John J., 533 1/2 Berlin Rd., Apt. 8, Huron, 44839-1920.
Mulica, James
Mulvanity, Francis C., 37934 Brown Ave., Willoughby, 44094-5835.
Murphy, John F., 28700 Euclid Ave., Wickliffe, 44092-2585.
Murray, Cornelius J., 1742 Wagar Rd., Apt 211, Rocky River, 44116-2367.
Muzic, Anthony J., 6170 Thunderbird Dr., Mentor, 44060.
O'Grady, Dennis R., 7096 Pearl Rd., Parma Heights, 44130.
Olsavsky, John R., J.C.L., 215 Village Dr., Seven Hills, 44131-5713.
Ondreyka, Richard J., M.S., P.O. Box 1132, Norton, 44203.
Padavick, William B., 7948 E. Bay Shore Rd., #34, Marblehead, 43440.
Pahler, Robert E., 1905 Portage Tr., Cuyahoga Falls, 44223-1792.
Patton, James J., 6421 Lake Rd. W., Madison, 44051.
Pfeiffer, Robert F., J.C.L., 2114 Industry Rd., Atwater, 44201-9354.
Piskura, Joseph, 29050 Detroit Rd., Apt. 329, Westlake, 44145.
Pritt, Phillip P., St. Matthias, 1200 W. Sprague Rd., Parma, 44134-6801.
Rath, Thomas V., 5171 Riverstyx Rd., Medina, 44256.
Rathfon, John R., 3428 E. Prescott Cir., Cuyahoga Falls, 44223-1792.
Rosko, Ladislaus
Schleicher, James R., 4019 Manchester Rd., Akron, 44319-2193.
Schorr, James D., 3275 5th Ave., #304, San Diego, CA 92103-5729.
Sciarrotta, Paul J., 13000 Auburn Rd., Chardon, 44024-9331.
Sheehan, Thomas W.
Silva, David E., 2899 E. Ridgewood Dr., Seven Hills, 44131.
Smith, Wilfred T., 2846 Hubbard Rd., Madison, 44057-2998.
St. Marie, Denis L., 200 St. Joseph Dr., Amherst, 44001-1663.
Swirski, Thaddeus M., 476 Mull Ave., Akron, 44320.
Szudarek, Ronald J., 4880 E. 96th St., Garfield Heights, 44125.
Tesek, Albert J., Royalton Woods, 14277 State Rd., North Royalton, 44133.
Tezie, John M., 333 South Lake St., South Amherst, 44001. (Dec.-June): 4550 Pinebrook Cr., Apt. 105, Bradenton, FL 34209.
Tomicky, Ronald
Trivison, Louis J., 283 Union St., Bedford, 44146.
Valley, John, P.O. Box 5302, Willowick, 44095-5302.
Van Bergen, Francis G., 111 E. 291st St., Wickliffe, 44092.
Vesely, James J., 4940 Broadview Rd., 44109-5799.
Viall, John L., 12195 Pheasant Run, North Royalton, 44133.
Weigand, Joseph C., 1905 Portage Tr., Cuyahoga Falls, 44223.
Wendelken, Robert M., D.Min., St. Clare, 5659 Mayfield Rd., Lyndhurst, 44124-2915.
Wessel, John F., 2451 Crimson Dr., Westlake, 44145.
Winca, Harry S., 1620 Windrow La., Broadview Heights, 44147.
Winters, Alfred H., 12550 Lake Ave., #1403, Lakewood, 44107.
Wolnowski, Kenneth J., 3850 Galt Ocean Dr., Unit 504, Fort Lauderdale, FL 33308.
Wysocki, Paul, 8274 Kellogesville/Stanhope Rd., Williamsfield, 44093.
Yahner, Gordon A., 164 W. Market St., Akron, 44303.

Permanent Deacons:
Adair, Robin, St. Augustine, Barberton
Adkins, Ronald M., St. Gabriel, Concord Township
Agrippe, James L., (Retired)
Anderson, Robert C., St. Rita, Solon
Armstrong, James J., St. Wendelin, Cleveland
Bacik, Dale A., Apollo Beach, FL
Badillo, Tomas, Sacred Heart Chapel, Lorain
Battista, Bruce J., Holy Rosary, Cleveland
Beebe, Raymond C., (Retired)
Beercheck, Richard C., St. Patrick, (Rocky River), Cleveland
Belsito, Vincent L., Holy Angels, Chagrin Falls
Belter, Clement J., St. Ambrose, Brunswick
Bender, Robert C., Queen of Heaven, Green
Berigan, Patrick F., Our Lady of Good Counsel, Cleveland
Bizon, Thaddeus C., Jr., St. Martin of Tours, Maple Heights
Boehnlein, Lawrence A., St. Mary, Chardon
Bosau, Wayne A., St. Clarence, North Olmsted
Bowers, Robert J., St. Paschal Baylon, Highland Heights
Broering, J. Harry, Jr., (Retired)
Bryan, Daniel L., St. James, Lakewood
Brys, William A., St. Mary of the Assumption, Mentor
Bubnick, Robert C., Sr., Apostolate for the Mentally Retarded, Assumption, Broadview Heights
Buda, John M., (Retired)
Burke, John Jr., Commerce, GA
Butkovic, Donald P., (Retired)
Butz, Richard C., St. Francis de Sales, Akron
Cermak, Lawrence, (Leave of Absence)
Chernick, Edward J., SS. Cosmas & Damian, Twinsburg
Chordas, David N., St. Gergory the Great, South Euclid
Clavin, Daniel P., St. Gabriel, Concord
Colon, Victor R., Sagrada Familia, Cleveland
Corrigan, William H., St. Colman, Cleveland
Croniger, James D., (Retired)
Cruz, Moises, St. Stephen, Cleveland
Daley, James F., Jr., St. Cyprian, Perry
Daull, Raymond L., St. Ann, Cleveland Hts.
Daw, Thomas B., St. Mary of the Falls, Olmsted Falls, Diocesan Tribunal
DeGracia, Jose A., Sacred Heart Chapel, Lorain
DeHaas, Thomas B., Jr., St. Mary, Painesville
DeJohn, Ross C., Sr., St. Clare, Lyndhurst
DeLuca, Kenneth A., St. Julie Billiart, North Ridgeville
Di Mascio, Ramon J., St. Bernard, Akron
Dietz, Joseph P., St. Edward, Ashland

Dillon, Edward R., St. Mary, Elyria
Dirk, William E., Our Lady of Peace, Cleveland; St. Luke Hospital
Dobos, Louis C., Holy Family, Stow
Doerpers, Charles B.
Donlin, William A., (Retired)
Dunlop, Jeffrey F., St. Joan of Arc, Chagrin Falls
Dybo, Robert J., Nativity of the Blessed Virgin Mary, Lorain
Elwood, William T., St. Francis of Assisi, Gates Mills; Youth & Family Ministry, Eastern Region
Feldkamp, Edward J., (Retired)
Figueroa, Miguel A., St. Michael, Cleveland
Flores, Jose A., Sacred Heart Chapel, Lorain
Foradori, Peter J., St. Stephen, West Salem
Frania, Gregory C., St. Lucy Mission, Middlefield; St. Edward, Parkman
Friend, Shelby, Holy Spirit, Garfield Heights
Fulton, Stanley J., St. Brendan, North Olmstead
Galla, Daniel M., St. Charles Borromeo, Parma
Gardias, Edmund A., St. Adalbert, Berea
Giel, Frederick F., The Villages, FL
Glorioso, Russell J., St. Anthony of Padua, Parma
Golonka, Kenneth A., St. Matthias, Parma
Gonzalez, Edgar, St. Vincent de Paul, Elyria
Govern, David, Our Lady of Guadalupe, Macedonia
Grasson, Thomas J., St. John Neumann, Strongsville
Gregg, Larry D., St. Raphael, Bay Village
Grgic, Robert H., St. Gabriel, Concord Township
Guritza, Dennis A., St. Joan of Arc, Chagrin Falls
Hancock, Daniel J., St. Joseph, Amherst
Heise, Paul R., St. Joseph, Amherst
Herrick, Raymond S., St. Francis de Sales, Akron
Hill, Kenneth J., St. Vincent de Paul, Cleveland
Hinderscheid, Lee F., Brooksville, FL
Hlabse, Paul J., Immaculate Conception, Willoughby
Hoefler, Gregory P., Immaculate Heart of Mary, Cuyahoga Falls
Hosfeld, Bernard E., St. Mary of the Immaculate Conception, Wooster
Humphrey, Frank A., III, St. Mary, Elyria
Humphrey, Patrick J., St. Jude, Elyria
Hupertz, Thomas G., Immaculate Conception, Madison
James, Ronald R., Holy Spirits, Garfield Hts.
Jankowski, Donald M., Dir. Pastoral Care, St. Mary of the Woods, Avon; St. Peter, North Ridgeville
Jarosh, Rudolph, Jr., (Retired)
Jervis, Michael F., Our Lady Help of Christians, Litchfield
Johnson, Joseph W., (Retired)
Kamlowsky, Philip P., Holy Family, Stow
Kaniecki, James A., St. Edward, Ashland
Kipfstuhl, Paul J., St. Francis Xavier, Medina; Associate Dir., Office of Continuing Education for Ministers
Klaas, Roger N., Sacred Heart, Wadsworth
Knight, Kenneth, St. Bede the Venerable, Mentor
Knox, Steven K., St. Agnes, Orrville
Koch, Alfred J., Holy Martyrs, Medina
Koch, John A., Ascension, Cleveland
Kochanski, Robert M., St. Joseph, Cuyahoga Falls
Kovitch, Joseph R., St. Mary, Mentor
Kraynik, Phillip P., St. Patrick, Thompson
Krupp, Ralph J., (Retired)
Kuhlman, Richard F., Immaculate Conception, Madison
Kushner, David S., St. Mary, Collinwood
Kutolowski, Paul C., St. Columbkille, Parma
Leisure, Gregory A., St. John Vianney, Mentor
Lester, Robert J., St. Joseph, Strongville, Diaconate Staff
Litke, Joseph P., Holy Family, Parma
Lobdell, Donald W., (Retired)
LoCascio, Phillip A., Scottsdale, AZ
Lonteen, Francis R., (Retired)
Lopez, Gonzalo, St. Michael the Archangel, Cleveland
Loutzenhiser, Joseph E., St. Francis Xavier, Medina
Lozada, Frank, St. Francis, Cleveland
Lundeen, David J., St. Mark, Cleveland
Malcolm, Billy J., (Retired), Randleman, NC
Maldonado, Louis, St. Joseph Lorain
Malec, George P., St. Cyprian, Perry
Martin, Hardin M., Epiphany, Cleveland
Martin, James T., St. Patrick, Thompson
Martin, P. Robert, St. Mary of the Falls, Olmsted Falls
Masony, Howard J., St. Mark, Cleveland
Matoney, Robert, Jr., St. Dominic, Shaker Heights
Matusicky, Daniel J., (Retired)
McCarthy, Edward J., Jr., Naples, FL
McGraw, Joseph E., St. Bernadette, Westlake
McKenna, J. Kevin, St. Angela Merici, Fairview
McNulty, Leo F., St. Francis of Assisi, Gates Mills
Meade, Kenneth C., Immaculate Conception, Madison
Medina, Ceferino, Sagrada Familia, Cleveland
Merriman, William C., St. Patrick, Cleveland
Michney, Richard, Sacred Heart of Jesus, Wadsworth
Miranda, Ignacio, Sagrada Familia, Cleveland
Mueller, Richard A., St. Mary of the Falls, Olmstead Falls
Nethery, David T., St. Noel, Willoughby
Netzband, Ralph W., St. Monica, Garfield Heights
Norris, Daniel F., St. Francis Xavier, Medina.
Novak, Andrew J., St. Cyprian, Perry
Noveske, Gregory F., St. Richard, North Olmsted
O'Connell, Frank J., St. Jude, Elyria
O'Donnell, James K., Gesu, University Heights
Ogan, Jay R., St. Peter, Lorain
Ortiz, Juan, Sacred Heart Chapel, Lorain
Paul, James, Jr., St. Aloysius-St. Agatha, Cleveland
Payne, Willard C., St. Helen, Newbury
Peacock, Terry W., St. Sebastian, Akron
Pecek, Louis G., Ph.D., (Retired)
Pecot, David E., (Retired)
Pennypacker, Lindley W., St. Matthias, Parma
Perkowski, Gregory A., (On Leave of Absence)
Peshek, Thomas J., St. Mary, Chardon
Piechowski, Kenneth J., Dir. Diaconate; St. John Neumann, Strongsville
Piskach, Robert J., St. Francis de Sales, Parma
Polefko, Roger F., St. John Bosco, Parma Heights
Primozic, Louis M., St. Basil the Great, Brecksville
Quiles, Rafael, (Retired)
Ramos, Jose L., (On Leave of Absence)
Reiland, George J., Jr., (Retired)
Rivera, Carlos, (Retired)
Rivera, John M., St. Augustine, Cleveland; St. Julie Billiart, North Ridgeville
Sabol, Robert G., St. Bartholomew, Middleburg Heights
Sanchez, Reinaldo, St. Michael the Archangel, Cleveland
Schill, William E., St. Colman, Cleveland
Schwartz, Robert F., St. Patrick, Thompson
Seal, J. David, Immaculate Heart of Mary, Cuyahoga Falls
Senn, Thomas J., Our Lady of Angels, Cleveland
Sferry, John P., Sr., Cathedral of St. John the Evangelist, Cleveland
Sheridan, Thomas, St. Ambrose, Brunswick
Sherman, Homer L., St. Clarence, North Olmsted
Shin, Charles C., St. Andrew Kim Pastoral Center, Cleveland
Sill, Donald E., St. Anselm, Chesterland
Simon, Frederick F., Sagrada Familia, Cleveland
Skrha, Joseph W.
Slatcoff, John K., St. Vincent De Paul, Elyria Township
Smallhoover, James A., East Troy, WI
Smith, Dennis L., Nativity of the Lord Jesus, Akron
Snyder, Wayne W., St. John Vianney, Mentor
Somrack, Lawrence A., St. Helen, Newbury
Staab, William M., St. Patrick, Cleveland
Starkey, William R., Holy Trinity, Bedford Heights
Stewart, James R., St. James, Lakewood
Stokes, Troy F.
Streeter, David A., St. Luke, Lakewood; Representative, Deacon Clergy Personnel Bd.
Strmac, John W., Our Lady of Mount Carmel, Wickliffe
Talerico, John A., St. Charles Borromeo, Parma
Tatulinski, Frank E., (On Leave of Absence)
Telepak, Edward A., St. Columbkille, Parma
Tennant, Bruce H., St. Agnes, Elyria
Terrion, Daniel C., St. Pius X, Bedford
Thiel, Martin A., St. Thomas More, Brooklyn
Tomazic, Gary R., St. Ambrose, Brunswick
Toomey, Carl M., St. Mary Magdalene, Willowick
Torres, Epifanio, Sagrada Familia, Cleveland
Travalik, Peter M., St. Jerome, Cleveland
Tweddell, Charles E., Holy Family, Parma
Ulman, Robert P., St. Bede the Venerable, Mentor
Varga, Carl M., Divine Word, Kirtland
Vincent, James C., St. Michael, Independence
Volek, Ronald J., Seiverville, TN
Vrabel, Jerome B., Holy Cross, Euclid
Waken, Thomas J., Lexington, Kentucky
Walling, Robert K., Holy Spirit, Avon
Weglicki, Frank L., Jr., St. Ambrose, Brunswick
Wenzel, John T., St. Anthony of Padua, Fairport Harbor
Wilson, Francis B., Assumption of Mary, Brook Park
Winterich, Carl H., St. Mary, Hudson
Woods, Richard E., St. Louis, Cleveland Heights
Woyton, Louis M., St. Augustine, Cleveland
Wunderle, Gregory A., St. Andrew the Apostle, Norton
Yates, Stephen L., Holy Angels, Bainbridge
Yoho, William J., Jr., Immaculate Heart of Mary, Cuyahoga Falls
Youngblood, Dale A., S.S. Peter and Paul, Doylestown
Youngblood, Robert A., Prince of Peace, Norton; Representative, Deacon Clergy Personnel Bd.
Zawadzki, Charles W., St. Thomas More, Cleveland
Zdolshek, John R., St. Peter the Apostle, Brookpark

INSTITUTIONS LOCATED IN THE DIOCESE

[A] SEMINARIES, DIOCESAN

WICKLIFFE. *Borromeo Seminary* (1954) 28700 Euclid Ave., 44092-2585. Tel: 440-943-7600; Fax: 440-943-7577. Email: tmd@dioceseofcleveland.org. Web: www.borromeoseminary.org. Very Rev. Thomas M. Dragga, D.Min., Pres. & Rector; Revs. Michael G. Woost, S.T.L., Liturgy Dir.; Michael K. Gurnick, M.A., M.Div., Vocation Dir.; Michael Joyce, O.F.M.Cap., Formation Advisor; John F. Loya, M.Div., M.A., Spiritual Dir.; Bro. Charles McElroy, O.F.M.Cap., Rel. Studies; Mr. Philip J. Guban, B.A., Treas.; Revs. Donald Dunson, Formation Advisor; Robert L. McCreary, O.F.M.Cap., Formation Advisor; John F. Murphy, Formation Advisor (Retired); Damian J. Ference, M.A., Ph.L., Teacher, Philosophy; Most Rev. Anthony M. Pilla, D.D., M.A., Religious Studies; Dr. Chad A. Engelland, Ph.D., Lay Teacher-Philosophy; Dr. Ed Kaczuk, M.M., Music Dir.; Ray Leopold, M.Lit., Tutor; William Tighe, B.S., Athletic Dir. Priests 10; Brothers 1; Lay Teachers 4; Seminarians 35.

St. Mary Seminary and Graduate School of Theology (1948) (Our Lady of the Lake) , 28700 Euclid Ave., 44092-2585. Tel: 440-943-7600; Fax: 440-943-7577. Email: twt@dioceseofcleveland.org. Web: stmarysem.edu. Revs. Thomas W. Tifft, Ph.D., Pres./Rector; Mark A. Latcovich, Ph.D., Vice Pres.-Vice Rector, Academic Dean; Mrs. Paulette M. Begin, B.A., Registrar; Revs. Gerald J. Bednar, Ph.D.; Donald Dunson; Very Rev. Thomas M. Dragga, D.Min.; Revs. Mark L. Hollis, M.Div., Spiritual Dir.; Joseph M. Koopman, S.T.D.; Michael G. Woost, S.T.L.; Lorenzo Tosco, S.S.D., S.S.L.; Sr. Mary McCormick, O.S.U., Ph.D.; Dr. Edward J. Kaczuk, M.M.; Mr. Alan K. Rome, M.L.S., Librarian; Mr. Philip J. Guban, B.A., Treas. Priests 9; Sisters 1; Adjunct Faculty 10; Students for Priesthood, Diocesan 30; Religious 2; Permanent Diaconate 10; Other 103.

[B] COLLEGES AND UNIVERSITIES

CLEVELAND. *Notre Dame College* (1922) 4545 College Rd., South Euclid, 44121. Tel: 216-381-1680; Fax: 216-381-3802. Email: mkovach@ndc.edu. Web: www.notredamecollege.edu. Andrew P. Roth, Ph.D., Pres.; Deborah Sheren, Chief Information Officer; Karen Zoller, Dir. Clara Fritzsche Library. Priests 1; Sisters of Notre Dame 7; Lay Teachers 52; Total Staff 183; Students 1,926.

Ursuline College (1871) 2550 Lander Rd., Pepper Pike, 44124. Tel: 440-449-4200; Fax: 440-646-8102. Web: www.ursuline.edu. Sr. Diana Stano, O.S.U., Ph.D., Pres.; JoAnne Podis, Ph.D., Vice Pres. Academic Affairs; David Steiner, Vice Pres. & CFO; Deanne Hurley, Vice Pres. Student Affairs; Sisters Anna Margaret Gilbride, O.S.U., Ph.D., Asst. to the Pres.; Patricia McCaffrey, O.S.U., Ed.D., Vice Pres. Enrollment Mgmt.; June Gracyk, Vice Pres. Facilities Mgmt.; Kevin Gladstone, Vice. Pres. Inst. Advancement; Betsey Belkin, Dir., Library. Ursuline Sisters of Cleveland 18; Other Religious Sisters 1; Lay Professors 76; Students 1,515; Total Staff 211.

UNIVERSITY HEIGHTS. *John Carroll Jesuit Community* (1886) 2520 Miramar Blvd., 44118-3821. Tel: 216-397-1886; Fax: 216-397-4228. Email: jesuits@jcu.edu. Web: www.jcu.edu. Revs. Robert J. Niehoff, S.J., Pres.; William M. Bichl, S.J.; Casimir R. Bukala, S.J.; John E. Dister, S.J.; Harry J. Gensler, S.J.; Paul D. Panaretos, S.J.; Francis X. Ryan, S.J.; Gerald J. Sabo, S.J., Rector & Librarian; Thomas L. Schubeck, S.J.; Lorn J. Snow, S.J.; Ernest G. Spittler, S.J.; Mr. Jayme C. Stayer, S.J.; Bro. Denis Weber, S.J.; Rev. W. Jared Wicks, S.J. Jesuit Priests 12; Jesuit Brothers 1; Jesuit Scholastic Regents 1; Total Enrollment 4,101.

John Carroll University (1886) 20700 N. Park Blvd., 44118. Tel: 216-397-1886; Fax: 216-397-4256. Web: www.jcu.edu. Rev. Robert J Niehoff, S.J., Pres.; Jonathan Smith, Vice Pres. & Exec. Asst. to Pres.; Mark D. McCarthy, Vice Pres. Student Affairs; Ms. Doreen Riley, Vice Pres., Univ. Advancement; Mr. Richard F. Mausser, Vice Pres. Finance;

Dr. John T. Day, Academic Vice Pres.; Dr. James H. Krukones, Assoc. Academic Vice Pres.; Dr. Nicholas Santilli, Assoc. Academic Vice Pres. Planning & Assessment; Dr. Lauren Bowen, Assoc. Academic Vice Pres. Programs & Diversity; Steven P. Vitatoe, Exec. Dir. Enrollment; Mr. Brian Williams, Vice Pres. for Enrollment; Mr. Thomas Fanning, Dir. Recruitment & Admission; Dr. Karen Schuele, Acting Dean Boler School of Business; Dr. Beth Martin, Interim Dean College of Arts & Sciences; Dr. Sherri Crahen, Dean of Students; Dr. Peter Kvidera, Assoc. Dean College of Arts & Sciences; Dr. Mindy Peden, Assoc. Dean Student Svcs. & Advising; Dr. James Martin, Assoc. Dean Boler School of Business; Dr. Mark Storz, Assoc. Dean Graduate Studies; Dr. Jeanne M. Somers, Dir., Grasselli Library. Priests 6; Lay Faculty 206; Students 3,713; Total Staff 561.

[C] HIGH SCHOOLS, DIOCESAN

CLEVELAND. *Cleveland Central Catholic High School* (1968) 6550 Baxter Ave., 44105. Tel: 216-441-4700; Fax: 216-441-8353. Email: kertle@centralcatholichs.org. Web: www.centralcatholichs.org. Karl Ertle, Pres. Prin.; Karen Kilbane, Librarian. Sisters of Notre Dame 3; Lay Teachers 41; Students 536.

**St. Martin de Porres High School* (2003) 6111 Lausche Ave., 44103. Tel: 216-881-1689; Fax: 216-881-8303. Email: rclark@stmdphs.org. Mary Ann Vogel, Prin.; Richard Clark, Contact Person. Sisters 1; Lay Teachers 25.

Villa Angela-St. Joseph High School (1990) 18491 Lake Shore Blvd., 44119. Tel: 216-481-8414; Fax: 216-486-1035. Email: jroccosalva@vasj.com. Web: www.VASJ.com. Brian R. Menard, Pres.; Janice T. Roccosalva, Prin. Marianist Brothers 2; Ursuline Nuns 2; Lay Teachers 29; Students 395.

BEDFORD. *St. Peter Chanel High School*, 480 Northfield Rd., 44146. Tel: 440-232-5900; Fax: 440-232-9283. Email: mberlec@stpeterchanel.com. Web: www.stpeterchanel.com. Sr. Maria Berlec, O.S.U., Pres. & Prin.; Victoria Karakasis, Librarian. Sisters 1; Lay Teachers 20; Students 300.

ELYRIA. *Elyria Catholic High School* (1948) (Coed), 725 Gulf Rd., 44035. Tel: 440-365-1821; Fax: 440-365-7536. Web: www.elyriacatholic.com. Mr. Andrew G. Krakowaik, M.A., Pres.; Mrs. Amy Butler, Prin.; Ms. Kristen Frey, Librarian. Serving Elyria, Avon, Sheffield, North Ridgeville, Grafton, Oberlin, Amherst, Lorain, Avon Lake, Columbia Station, LaGrandge, Litchfield, Medina, N. Olmsted, New London, Olmsted Falls, Valley City, Vermilion, Wakeman, Wellington and Westlake. Deacons 1; Lay Teachers 31; Students 520.

MENTOR. *Lake Catholic High* (1970) 6733 Reynolds Rd., 44060. Tel: 440-951-0077; Fax: 440-974-9087. Web: www.lakecatholic.org. Rick Koenig, Prin.; Mr. Sal Miroglotta, Pres.; Sarah Goodman, Librarian. Ursuline Sisters of Cleveland (O.S.U.) 2; Lay Teachers 50; Students 791.

PARMA HEIGHTS. *Holy Name High School* (Coed), 6000 Queens Hwy., 44130. Tel: 440-886-0300; Fax: 440-886-1267. Email: bfarmer@schoolone.com. Web: www.holynamehs.com. Benjamin B. Farmer, Pres. & Prin.; Sr. Paula Greggila, Librarian. Sisters 2; Lay Teachers 42; Administration 3; Students 694.

[D] HIGH SCHOOLS, PRIVATE

CLEVELAND. *Benedictine High School*, 2900 Martin Luther King Dr., 44104-4898. Tel: 216-421-2080; Fax: 216-421-1100; 216-421-0107. Email: cbhs@cbhs.net. Web: www.cbhs.net. Rt. Rev. Christopher Schwartz, O.S.B., Chancellor; Mr. Joseph Gressock, Prin.; Rev. Gerard Gonda, O.S.B., Pres.; Mr. Thomas Erzen, Asst. Prin.; Mr. Anthony Russ, Athletic Dir.; Revs. Michael Brunovsky, O.S.B., Academic Dean; Timothy Buyansky, O.S.B., Librarian; Very Rev. Gary Hoover, O.S.B., Dir. Spiritual Life; Revs. Bede Kotlinski, O.S.B.; Anselm Zupka, O.S.B.; Bro. Patrick Ryan, O.S.B.; Mr. Ronald Samnik, Dir. Business Operations. Priests 7; Brothers 1; Lay Teachers 27; Students 400.

St. Edward High School (Boys), 13500 Detroit Ave., Lakewood, 44107. Tel: 216-221-3776; Fax: 216-221-4609. Email: bpgraham@sehs.net. Web: www.sehs.net. Bro. Peter Graham, C.S.C., Pres.; Eugene W. Boyer, Ed.S., Prin. Priests 2; Brothers 5; Lay Teachers 58; Students 830; Total Staff 100.

St. Ignatius High School (1886) 2926 Carroll Ave., 44113. Tel: 216-281-5392; Fax: 216-281-5393. 1911 W. 30th St., 44113. Tel: 216-651-0222; Fax: 216-651-6313. Web: www.ignatius.edu. Rev. John F. Libens, S.J., Dean of Teachers; Peter H. Corrigan Jr., Prin.; Revs. Karl Bonk, S.J.; Francis E. Canfield, S.J., Counselor; James V. Lewis, S.J.; Clement Metzger, S.J.; William Murphy, S.J., Pres.; Lawrence M. Ober, S.J.; Bernard J. Streicher, S.J.; Kenneth A. Styles, S.J.; Michael A. Vincent, S.J.; Robert J. Welsh, S.J., Rector, St. Martin de Porres High School; Bro. Michael L. Nusbaum, S.J., Min. & Asst. to Rector; Mr. Patrick J. Gilday, S.J.; Mr. Michael Singhurst, S.J. Priests 12; Lay Teachers 97; Students 1,435.

St. Joseph Academy (1890) 3430 Rocky River Dr., 44111. Tel: 216-251-6788; Fax: 216-251-5809. Web: www.sja1890.org. Mary Ann Corrigan-Davis, Pres.; Audrey Menard, Prin.; Rebecca Synk, Librarian. Lay Teachers 58; Students 645; Total Staff 91.

Magnificat High School (Girls), 20770 Hilliard Blvd., 44116. Tel: 440-331-1572; Fax: 440-331-7257. Email: scasmith@magnificaths.org. Web: www.magnificaths.org. Sr. Carol Anne Smith, H.M., Pres. & Prin. Sisters 2; Lay Teachers 65; Students 800.

Regina High School (Girls), 1857 S. Green Rd., 44121. Tel: 216-382-2110; Fax: 216-382-3555. Email: gormanm@reginahigh.com. Web: www.reginahigh.com. Sr. Margaret M. Gorman, S.N.D., Prin.; Carol Braden, Librarian. Sisters of Notre Dame. Sisters 5; Lay Teachers 25; Students 230.

**St. Martin de Porres High School Work Study Program* (2004) 6111 Lausche Ave., 44103. Tel: 216-881-1689; Fax: 216-881-8303. Email: tbennett@stmdphs.org. Thomas M. Bennett Jr., Pres.

AKRON. *Archbishop Hoban High School* (Coed), One Holy Cross Blvd., 44306. Tel: 330-773-6658; Fax: 330-773-9100. Email: beitingm@hoban.org. Web: www.hoban.org. Bro. Kenneth Haders, C.S.C., Pres.; Dr. Mary Anne Beiting, Prin.; Mrs. Tina Braman, Librarian. Brothers of Holy Cross. Sisters 1; Brothers 7; Lay Teachers 54; Students 874.

Our Lady of the Elms School, (Grades 7-12), 1375 W. Exchange St., 44313-7697. Tel: 330-867-0880; Fax: 330-864-6488. Web: www.theelms.org. Lisa Massello, Prin.; Tim DeFrange, Librarian. Please see complete listing under Secondary Schools. Sisters 1; Deacons 1; Lay Teachers 26; Students 200.

St. Vincent-St. Mary High School, 15 N. Maple St., 44303. Tel: 330-253-9113; Fax: 330-996-0020. Email: webmaster@stvm.com. Web: www.stvm.com. David V. Rathz, Headmaster; Joanne Wiseman, Dir. of Admissions; Stella Weigand, Controller; Burke Stephens, Dean of Students; Ken McDonald, Campus Min.; Pamela Godshalk, Librarian. Lay Teachers 49; Students 687.

CHARDON. *Notre Dame-Cathedral Latin School*, 13000 Auburn Rd., 44024. Tel: 440-286-6226; 888-214-8108 (toll free); Fax: 440-286-7199. Email: ndcl@ndcl.org. Web: www.ndcl.org. Sr. Jacquelyn Gusdane, S.N.D., Pres.; Mr. Joseph A. Waler, M.A., M.Ed., Prin. Sisters of Notre Dame. Sisters 6; Lay Teachers 61; Students 745.

CLEVELAND HEIGHTS. *Beaumont School*, 3301 N. Park Blvd., 44118. Tel: 216-321-2954; Fax: 216-321-3947. Email: Info@beaumontschool.org. Web: www.beaumontschool.org. Sr. Gretchen Rodenfels, O.S.U., Pres.; Mrs. Margaret Connell, Prin.; Mrs. Marie Engstrom, Librarian. Ursuline Sisters. Sisters 8; Lay Teachers 40; Students 436.

CUYAHOGA FALLS. *Walsh Jesuit High School*, 4550 Wyoga Lake Rd., 44224. Tel: 330-929-4205; 800-686-4694 (Cleveland); Fax: 330-929-9749. Web: www.walshjesuit.org. Rev. Michael J. Marco, S.J., Pres.; Mark Hassman, Prin.; Revs. Emmett P. Holmes, S.J.; James J. King, S.J.; Donald J. Petkash, S.J., Religious Supr.; Timothy J. Shepard; John V. White, S.J.; Nancy Heil, Librarian. Religious 2; Priests 6; Lay Teachers 68; Students 931.

GARFIELD HEIGHTS. *Trinity High School*, 12425 Granger, 44125. Tel: 216-581-1644; Fax: 216-581-9348. Email: cfritsch@ths.org. Web: www.ths.org. Sr. Shawn Lee, S.S.J.-T.O.S.F., Pres.; Thomas M. Maher, Ph.D., Exec. Prin.; Mr. Daniel J. Thomeier, Business Mgr.; Ms. Carla E. Fritsch, Prin.; Mrs. Linda Bacho, Asst. Prin.; Mr. William Svoboda, Asst. Prin. Sisters of St. Joseph of the Third Order of St. Francis. Sisters of St. Joseph 4; Lay Teachers 42; Students 370.

GATES MILLS. *Gilmour Academy*, (Grades PreK-12), Private., 34001 Cedar Rd., 44040-9356. Tel: 440-442-1104; Fax: 440-473-8010. Email: laveller@gilmour.org. Web: www.gilmour.org. Mr. Murlan J. Murphy Jr., Chm., Bd. of Trustees; Bro. Robert Lavelle, C.S.C., Headmaster; Todd R. Sweda, Asst. Headmaster; J. Brian Horgan, Dir. of Upper School; Yvonne Saunders, Dir. Middle School & Asst. Dir. Upper School; Dr. Monica Veto, Dir. of Lower School; Rev. John Blazek, C.S.C., Campus Min.; Lynn Hammond, Library Mgr. Congregation of Holy Cross., Day and Resident College Preparatory School. Priests 1; Brothers 6; Sisters 2; Lay Teachers 76; Students 714; Residents 52.

PARMA. *Padua Franciscan High School* (1961) 6740 State Rd., 44134. Tel: 440-845-2444; Fax: 440-845-5710. Email: padua@paduafranciscan.com. Web: www.paduafranciscan.com. Rev. Theodore Haag, O.F.M., Pres.; Gerald R. Jindra, Vice Pres. for Inst. Advancement; David G. Stec, Prin.; Robert Grgic, Campus Minister; Bro. Tom Carroll, O.F.M., Academic Dean; Linda George, Librarian. Priests 1; Sisters 1; Brothers 2; Lay Teachers 63; Students 870.

[E] ELEMENTARY SCHOOLS

CLEVELAND. *Villa Montessori Center* (1995) 5620 Broadway Ave., 44127. Tel: 216-641-4770; Fax: 216-641-4771. Email: villageecc@aol.com. Web: www.villamontessoricenter.org. Sr. Marie Veres, H.M., Pres. & Prin.

AKRON. *North Akron Catholic School* (2003) 1570 Creighton Ave., 44310. Tel: 330-633-1383; Fax: 330-633-4512. Email: northakron@leeca.org. Web: www.nacs.k12.oh.us. Christine Lackney, Prin.; Robin Spano, Librarian. Lay Teachers 9.

Business Office: 300 E. Tallmadge Ave., 44310. Tel: 330-376-5144; Fax: 330-376-5311.

Our Lady of the Elms School, (Grades PreK-6), 1290 W. Market St., 44313-7108. Tel: 330-864-7210; Fax: 330-867-1262. Email: mreichart@theelms.org. Web: www.theelms.org. Marie Reichart, Prin. Lay Teachers 18; Students 170.

CHARDON. *Notre Dame Elementary School* (1957) 13000 Auburn Rd., 44024. Tel: 440-279-1127; Fax: 440-286-1235. Email: bdoering@ndec.org. Web: www.notredameelementary.org. Barbara Doering, Prin.; Mrs. Sabrina Mysyk, Librarian; Mrs. Katherine Mullinger, Librarian. Sisters of Notre Dame 5; Lay Teachers 21; Students 433.

Notre Dame PreSchool (2000) 13000 Auburn Rd., 44024. Tel: 440-286-7101, Ext. 5920; Fax: 440-286-9364. Email: mfriel@ndec.org. Sr. Margaret Friel, S.N.D., Dir.; Barbara Doering, Prin. Sisters of Notre Dame 1; Lay Teachers 2; Aides 2; Students 52.

HUDSON. *Seton Catholic School* (1997) 6923 Stow Rd., 44236. Tel: 330-342-4200; Fax: 330-342-4276. Email: selnerh@setoncatholicschool.org. Web: www.setoncatholicschool.org. Mr. Harry L. Selner Jr., Prin.; Michael Boehringer, Chm., Bd. Directors; Evelyn Kremyar, Librarian. Sisters 1; Lay Teachers 27; Students 410.

KIRTLAND. *Peaceful Children Montessori School* (1994) 8100 Eagle Rd., 44094. Tel: 440-256-1976; Fax: 440-256-4370. Email: pcmschool@roadrunner.com. Web: peacefulchildrenmontessori.org. Jennifer Massiello, Prin. Lay Teachers 10; Total Enrollment 80; Total Staff 20.

PARMA HEIGHTS. *Incarnate Word Academy* (1930) 6620 Pearl Rd., 44130. Tel: 440-842-6818; Fax: 440-888-1377. Email: jcicerchi_iwa@yahoo.com. Web: incarnatewordacademy.org. Mrs. Janette Cicerchi, Prin.; Rev. Carl A. Ciprian, Chap. (Retired). Sisters 4; Lay Teachers 24; Students 467.

[F] ELEMENTARY SCHOOLS, PAROCHIAL AND DIOCESAN

CLEVELAND. *Archbishop James P. Lyke Elementary School* St. Henry, St. Timothy, and Our Lady of Peace schools consolidated to form Archbishop James P. Lyke School., 18230 Harvard Ave., 44128. Tel: 216-991-9644; Fax: 216-991-9470. Email: lykesthenry@leeca.org. Web: www.archbishoplykeschool.org. Sr. Brigetta Waldron, O.S.U., Dir. Sisters 1; Lay Teachers 34; Students 454.

Archbishop Lyke School-St. Henry (Grades K-4), 18230 Harvard Ave., 44128. Tel: 216-991-9644; Fax: 216-991-9470. Email: lykesthenry@leeca.org. Web: www.archbishoplykeschool.org. Ms. Mary Pat Hable, Prin.; Sr. Mary Beth Daly, S.N.D., Asst. Prin. Students 189.

Archbishop Lyke School-St. Timothy (Grades 5-8), 4351 E. 131st St., Garfield Heights, 44105. Tel: 216-581-3517; Fax: 216-581-6204. Email: lykesttimothy@leeca.org. Web: www.archbishoplykeschool.org. Mrs. Margarete W. Smith, Prin. Students 170.

Archbishop Lyke School-Our Lady of Peace (Grades K-8), 12406 Buckingham Ave., 44120. Tel: 216-795-7161; Fax: 216-795-7370. Email: olpeace@leeca.org. Web: www.archbishoplykeschool.org. William DiBacco, Prin. Students 95.

St. Francis School, 7206 Myron Ave., 44103. Tel: 216-361-4858; Fax: 216-361-1673. Sr. Karen Sommerville, S.N.D., Prin. Sisters of Notre Dame 2; Lay Teachers 12; Students 200.

Metro Catholic School (1988) Tel: 216-281-4044; Fax: 216-634-2853. Email: metro@leeca.net. Web: www.metrocatholic.org. Sr. Anne Maline, S.N.D., Dir.; Colleen Gotta, Librarian. Sisters of Notre Dame 17; Ursuline Nuns 2; Lay Teachers 33; (K-8) 550; Preschool 36.

St. Stephen Bldg. (Grade 5-8), 1910 W. 54th St., 44102. Tel: 216-281-4044; Fax: 216-634-2853. Email: metro@leeca.net. Web: www.metrocatholic.org. Robert Finkovich, Prin.

St. Michael Bldg. (Grades 2-4), 1910 W. 54th St., 44102. Tel: 216-281-4044; Fax: 216-634-2853. Email: metro@leeca.net. Web: www.metrocatholic.org. Sr. Karen Bohan, O.S.U., Prin.

St. Boniface Bldg. (PreK-1), 3555 W. 54th St., 44102. Tel: 216-631-5733; Fax: 216-634-2853. Email: metro@leeca.net. Web: www.metrocatholic.org. Patricia Scholl, Prin.

Urban Community School, 4909 Lorain Ave., 44102. Tel: 216-939-8441; Fax: 216-939-8198. Email: mdoyle2401@aol.com. Sr. Maureen Doyle, O.S.U., Dir.; Pam Delly, Prin.; Victoria Wagner, Librarian. Ursuline Nuns of Cleveland 3; Lay Teachers 24; Students 427.

West Park Catholic Academy, (Grades K-8), 17720 Puritas Ave., 44135. Tel: 216-671-7900; Fax: 216-671-5277. Email: westpark@leeca.org. Annemarie Rajnicek, Prin. Lay Teachers 20.

BEDFORD. *Holy Spirit Academy*, 370 Center Rd., 44146. Tel: 440-232-1531; Fax: 440-232-1534. Email: holyspirit@leeca.org. Web: www.hsabedford.org. Mrs. Sharon Vejdovec, Prin.; Mrs. Debbie Sigmund, Sec.; Mrs. Jean Oulton, Librarian. Lay Teachers 10.

EASTLAKE. *St. Mary Magdalene-St. Justin Martyr School, Inc.*, 35741 Stevens Blvd., 44095. Tel: 440-946-5414; Fax: 440-946-2074. Web: www.stjustin.net. Rev. Kevin M. Liebhardt, Pres.; Sr. Mary Quinlan, S.N.D., Prin. Lay Teachers 17.

GARFIELD HEIGHTS. *John Paul II Academy*, (Grades PreK-8), 10608 Penfield Ave., 44125. Tel: 216-581-3080; Fax: 216-581-3031. Sr. Helene Skrzyniarz, S.S.J.-T.O.S.F., Prin.; Mrs. Linda Borowy, Librarian. Sisters 1; Lay Teachers 16; Students 279.

LAKEWOOD. *Lakewood Catholic Academy* (includes Holy Family Learning Center), 14808 Lake Ave., 44107. Tel: 216-521-0559; Fax: 216-521-0515. Email: info@lakewoodcatholicacademy.com. Web: www.lakewoodcatholicacademy.com. Maureen Arbeznik, Prin.; Molly Spellacy, Librarian. Lay Teachers 40.

WICKLIFFE. *All Saints of St. John Vianney School* (1977) (Grades PreSchool-8), 28702 Euclid Ave., 44092. Tel: 216-943-1395; Fax: 216-943-4468. Email: allsaints@oh.rr.com. Web: www.allsaintssjv.org. Mrs. Rosemary Wilson, Prin.; Mrs. Paula Kirchner, Librarian. Sisters 1; Lay Teachers 20; Students 314.

[G] SPECIAL SCHOOLS AND CENTERS For Exceptional Children

CLEVELAND

Julie Billiart School (1954) 4982 Clubside Rd., Lyndhurst, 44124-2596. Tel: 216-381-1191; Fax: 216-381-2216. Email: aloporto@jbschool.org. Web: www.juliebilliartschool.org. Sr. Agnesmarie, S.N.D., Pres. Non-graded school for children having learning problems. Sisters 7; Lay Teachers 18; Students 110.

[H] PRESCHOOL AND DAY CARE CENTERS

CLEVELAND. *Catholic Charities Community Services/ Head Start* (1964) 7911 Detroit Ave., 44102. Tel: 216-334-2942; Fax: 216-334-2948. Email: mcurry@clevelandcatholiccharities.org. Michelle Curry, Dir. Lay Teachers 48; Children 870.

GARFIELD HEIGHTS. *Marymount Child Care Center* (1991) 12215 Granger Rd., 44125. Tel: 216-581-3540; Fax: 216-518-2188. Email: marymountcare@aol.com. Sr. Dorothy Ann Krolikowski, S.S.J.-T.O.S.F., Dir. Sisters 1; Total Staff 13; Total Assisted Annually 120.

LAKEWOOD. *Holy Family Learning Center*, 14808 Lake Ave., 44107. Tel: 216-521-4352; Fax: 216-521-0515. Email: hflcsko@yahoo.com. Web: www.lakewoodcatholicacademy.com/holyfamily. Sr. Kathleen Ogrin, O.S.U., Dir. Total Assisted 106.

[I] GENERAL HOSPITALS (For information on other Catholic related hospitals please contact the Chancery Office.)

CLEVELAND

St. John Hospital, 2351 E. 22nd St., 44115. Tel: 216-696-5560; Fax: 216-696-2204. Web: www.sistersofcharityhealth.org. Sisters Mary Patricia Barrett, C.S.A., Chm. Bd. Directors; Judith Ann Karam, C.S.A., Pres. & CEO.

Marymount Hospital, Inc., 12300 McCracken Rd., Garfield Heights, 44125. Tel: 216-587-8080; Fax: 216-587-8212. Email: dkilarski@marymount.org. Web: www.marymount.org. Mr. David J. Kilarski, Pres. & CEO; Rev. Kenneth F. Wallace, Priest Chap.; Sisters Betty Gulick, S.S.J.-T.O.S.F., Dir. Pastoral Care; Jo Ann Poplar, S.S.J.-T.O.S.F., Staff Chap.; Ms. Janet Elaine McDonald, Staff Chap. Sisters of St. Joseph of the Third Order of St. Francis 4; Bed Capacity 322; Bassinets 18; Patients Assisted Annually 161,602; Total Staff 1,371.

OBERLIN

Allen Community Hospital (1892) *Community Health Partners Regional Medical Center*, 200 W. Lorain St., 44074. Tel: 440-775-1211; Fax: 440-775-9147. Web: www.community-health-partners.com. Sue Bowers, Pres. Bed Capacity 25; Patients Assisted Annually 12,000; Total Staff 200.

[J] TRAINING SCHOOLS FOR NURSES

CLEVELAND. *Marymount School of Practical Nursing* (1952) 12300 McCracken Rd., Garfield Heights, 44125. Tel: 216-587-8160; Fax: 216-587-8632. Email: acarlucci@marymount.org. Web: www.marymount.org. Students 35.

[K] SPECIAL HOSPITALS

EUCLID. *Rose Mary, The Johanna Grasselli Rehabilitation and Education Center*, 19350 Euclid Ave., 44117. Tel: 216-481-4823; Fax: 216-481-4154. Web: rose-marycenter.com. Ms. Patricia A. Colombo, Exec. Dir. Children 42; Residents 93; Bed Capacity 93; Total Assisted Annually 155; Total Staff 250.

PARMA. *Holy Family Home and Hospice* (1956) 6707 State Rd., 44134. Tel: 440-888-7722; Fax: 440-866-6040. Email: info@holyfamilyhome.com. Web: www.holyfamilyhome.com. Rev. Simon Kimaryo, Chap.

Holy Family Home, Inpatient and community-based end of life care. Sisters 4; Total Staff 95; Bed Capacity 30; Patients Assisted Annually 250.

[L] PROTECTIVE INSTITUTIONS

CLEVELAND. *Catholic Charities Early Learning Center at the Quadrangle*, 2302 Community College Ave., 44115. Tel: 216-589-9750; Fax: 216-589-9702. Janet Lucha, Day Care Admin. Day Care program sponsored by Catholic Charities Services Corp. Funded by United Way Catholic Charities & County Vouchers. Students 85; Total Assisted Annually 150; Total Staff 15.

PARMA. *CCSC/Parmadale* (1925) 6753 State Rd., 44134. Tel: 440-845-7700; Fax: 440-845-5910. Email: pdale@clevelandcatholiccharities.org. Web: www.clevelandcatholiccharities.org. Thomas Woll, Exec. Dir. Specialized Residential Services; Intensive Treatment Services; Chemical Dependency Treatment; Community Flexible Clinical Response; Specialized Foster Care; Whole Family Treatment; In-Home Services; Outpatient Services; Training and Consultation Services; and Volunteer Program; Adoption Services; Head Start. Capacity 96; Children in Foster Care 100; Total Assisted Annually 1,500; Total Staff 207.

[M] HOMES FOR AGED

CLEVELAND. *St. Augustine Manor*, 7801 Detroit Ave., 44102. Tel: 216-634-7400; Fax: 216-634-7483. Email: pgareau@st-aug.org. Web: www.staugustinemanor.org. Carmen Naso, Chm., Bd. of Trustees; Mr. Patrick Gareau, Pres. & CEO. Affiliated with Catholic Charities. Provider of rehabilitation services, subacute care, skilled nursing, assisted living, hospice care and child day care. Bed Capacity 358; Patients Assisted Annually 755; Total in Residence 340; Total Staff 480.

Coterie of St. Augustine Manor, The, 7801 Detroit Ave., 44102. Tel: 216-634-7400; Fax: 216-634-7483. Mrs. Margaret Lynch, Pres. (Operates the Coterie Boutique)

Jennings Center for Older Adults (1942) 10204 Granger Rd., 44125. Tel: 216-581-2900; Fax: 216-581-4505. Email: martha.kutik@jenningscenter.org. Web: www.jenningscenter.org. Mrs. Martha M. Kutik, Pres. & CEO; Rev. Kestutis Zemaitis (Lithuania), Chap. Tel: 216-581-2900. Continuum of Services Campus for older adults, including long term care facility, independent and assisted living apartments, an adult day center, and intergenerational child day care center for 75 children. Under the sponsorship of the Sisters of the Holy Spirit. Sisters 7; Residents 174; Total Assisted Annually 351; Total Staff 300; Number of Suites: One-bedroom 52; Number of Suites: Two-bedroom 2.

Jennings Hall Skilled Nursing Facility Tel: 216-581-2900; Fax: 216-581-4505. Email: admissions@jenningscenter.org. Web: www.jenningscenter.org. Skilled Nursing Facility Bed Capacity 174.

Jennings Manor Housing Corporation (1998) Tel: 216-581-2900; Fax: 216-581-4505. Email: admissions@jenningscenter.org. Web: www.jenningscenter.org. Apartment Bldg.-HUD 202 Supportive Housing for Older Adults Apartments 61; HUD 202.

Holy Spirit Villas (1998) Tel: 216-581-2900; Fax: 216-581-4505. Email: admissions@jenningscenter.org. Web: www.jenningscenter.org. Independent Housing Units 10.

St. Agnes Terrace Apartments Independent Housing, Tel: 216-581-2900; Fax: 216-581-4505. Email: admissions@jenningscenter.org. Web: www.jenningscenter.org. Apartments 42.

Eva L. Bruening Adult Day Center (2003) Tel: 216-581-2900; Fax: 216-581-4505. Email: admissions@jenningscenter.org. Web: www.jenningscenter.org. Clients Per Day Capacity 50.

The Learning Circle Child Day Care Center (1999) Tel: 216-581-2900. Email: marketing@jenningscenter.org. Web: www.jenningscenter.org. Infant to before and after school care. Capacity 75.

Little Sisters of the Poor dba Sts. Mary and Joseph Home for the Aged 4291 Richmond Rd., 44122-6199. Tel: 216-464-1222; Fax: 216-464-8435. Email: mscleveland@littlesistersofthepoor.org. Web: www.littlesistersofthepoor.org. Sr. Ann Marguerite. Little Sisters of the Poor. Sisters 10; Association Members 40; Nursing 62; Independent Living 22; Bed Capacity 93; Residential Care Beds 32; Total Assisted Annually 150; Total Staff 150. In Res. Revs. Ray J. Horley, Chap. (Retired); Leonard P. Kellermann, S.M.

Mount St. Joseph, 21800 Chardon Rd., 44117. Tel: 216-531-7426; Fax: 216-531-4033. Sr. M. Raphael Gregg, NHA. Conducted by Sisters of St. Joseph of St. Mark - Mount St. Joseph. Sisters 8; Bed Capacity 100; Residents 100; Total Assisted Annually 182; Total Staff 151.

AKRON. *Francesca Residence*, 39 N. Portage Path, 44303. Tel: 330-867-6334; Fax: 330-867-6334. Email: martinovich00@hotmail.com. Sr. M. Martin Green, F.D.C., Admin.; Rev. Albert A. Kunkel, Chap. Daughters of Divine Charity 6; Total Assisted Annually 30; Total in Residence 24; Total Staff 6.

BEDFORD. *Light of Hearts Villa, Inc.*, 283 Union St., 44146. Tel: 440-232-1991; Fax: 440-232-1782. Email: information@lightofheartsvilla.org. Web: www.lightofheartsvilla.org. Michael DeLuca, Interim Exec. Dir. Total in Residence 109; Total Assisted 84; Total Staff 56.

FAIRLAWN. *St. Edward Home dba The Village at St. Edward Nursing Care and Assisted Living* (1964) 3131 Smith Rd., 44333. Tel: 330-666-1183; Fax: 330-666-2721. Email: jhennelly@vased.org. Web: www.vased.org. John J. Hennelly, Pres. & CEO; Rev. James F. Flood, Chap. Sisters 3; Nursing Care Residents 81; Assisted Living Residents 90; Total Staff 153.

St. Edward Home dba The Village at St. Edward Independent Living (1990) 3125 Smith Rd., 44333. Tel: 330-668-2828; Fax: 330-666-6636. Web: www.vased.org. John J. Hennelly, Pres. & CEO; Rev. James F. Flood, Chap. Total in Residence 77; Total Staff 41.

GARFIELD HEIGHTS. *Village at Marymount*, 5200 Marymount Village Dr., 44125. Tel: 216-332-1100; Fax: 216-332-1619. Email: jmyers@marymount.org. Web: www.villageatmarymount.org. Mr. Jeffry Myers, Pres.; Sr. Betty Gulick, S.S.J.-T.O.S.F., Dir. Mission Svcs.; Revs. Kenneth F. Wallace, Priest Chap.; George Jaskulski, O.F.M., Priest Chap. Village at Marymount provides comprehensive health care services in response to the needs of the local community by leasing and operating health care facilities and services, including Marymount Place, a 104-unit Senior Living Community for the Well-Elderly/Assisted Living and Villa St. Joseph, a 114-bed long-term facility and operates Clare Hall, a 28-bed Medicaid Licensed Nursing Home, under an Operating Agreement with Marymount Health Care Systems within the philosophy and objectives of the Sisters of St. Joseph of the Third Order of St. Francis. Bed Capacity 246; Total Assisted Annually 1,251; Total Staff 201.

PARMA. *Mount Alverna Village*, 6765 State Rd., 44134. Tel: 440-843-7800; Fax: 440-843-7107. Web: www.franciscancommunities.com/facilities/mtalverna. Patrick M. Welsh, Exec. Dir. Capacity 183; Residents 153; Total Assisted 183; Total Staff 253; Assisted Living 30.

RICHFIELD. *Regina Health Center* (1992) 5232 Broadview Rd., 44286-9608. Tel: 330-659-4161; Fax: 330-659-5113. Email: bflannery@reginahealthcenter.org. Sr. Miriam Erb, C.S.A., Congregational Leader; Brian J. Flannery, Admin. Sponsored by Sisters of Charity of St. Augustine. Nursing Home Beds 101; Assisted Living Units 54; Total in Residence 140; Total Assisted 41; Total Staff 210.

[N] MONASTERIES AND RESIDENCES OF PRIESTS AND BROTHERS

CLEVELAND. *Benedictine Order of Cleveland*, St. Andrew Abbey, 10510 Buckeye Rd., 44104. Tel: 216-721-5300; Fax: 216-721-1253. Email: abbotchristopher@cbhs.net. Web: www.bocohio.org. Most Rev. Roger W. Gries, O.S.B., D.D., M.Ed., Auxiliary Bishop of Cleveland. Priests 18; Brothers 12. 5135 Superior Ave., 44103. Tel: 216-361-0873; Fax: 216-361-0877. Rt. Rev. Clement Zeleznik, O.S.B. (Retired); Rev. Bede Kotlinski, O.S.B.; Very Rev. Albert Marflak, O.S.B., Subprior; Revs. Joachim Pastirik, O.S.B.; Gerard Gonda, O.S.B., Pres. Benedictine High School; Timothy Buyansky, O.S.B.; Dominic Mondzelewski, O.S.B.; Placid Pientek, O.S.B.; Very Rev. Gary Hoover, O.S.B., Prior; Revs. Paschal Petcavage, O.S.B., Assoc. Pastor of Assumption; Justin Dyrwal, O.S.B., Pastor of Assumption. Assumption Church: 9183 Broadview Rd., Broadview Heights, 44147. Tel: 440-526-1177; Fax: 440-526-2838.

Other Assignments: Rev. Anthony J. Ozimek, O.S.B., St. Vincent Hospital, Billings, MT 59107-5200. Tel: 406-657-7000; Rt. Rev. Christopher Schwartz, O.S.B., Abbot, Incarnate Word Academy, 6634 Pearl Rd., 44130-3898. Tel: 440-886-6996; Revs. Michael Brunovsky, O.S.B., Novice Master, St. Andrew, 5135 Superior Ave., 44130. Tel: 216-431-2057; Dismas Boeff, O.S.B., Chap., Southwest General Hospital, St. Peter, 6455 Engle Rd., 44142. Tel: 216-433-1440; Fax: 216-433-1434; Kenneth J. Katricak, O.S.B., Assoc. Pastor, Assumption, St. Andrew Abbey, 2900 M.L. King Dr., 44104. Tel: 216-721-5300; Anselm Zupka, O.S.B.

Congregation of the Blessed Sacrament, 5384 Wilson Mills Rd., 44143-3092. Tel: 440-442-3410; Fax: 440-442-2001. Web: blessedsacrament.com. Very Rev. Norman B. Pelletier, S.S.S., Prov. Supr.; Revs. John Thomas Lane, S.S.S., Pastor; William Fickel, S.S.S., Supr.; Roger Bourgeois, S.S.S.; Michael Noreika, S.S.S.; William T. Young, S.S.S.; Paul Bernier, S.S.S.; Julian Rousseau, S.S.S.; Lito Hitosis, S.S.S.; Deacon Joseph Bourgeois; Bros. Eugene Blee, S.S.S.; Gerard Hickey, S.S.S.; Gary L. Laverdiere, S.S.S.; Allen Boeckman, S.S.S. Priests 9; Deacons 1; Brothers 4. *Regina Health Center*, 5232 Broadview Rd., Richfield, 44286-9608. Tel: 330-659-4161. Rev. George Evans, S.S.S.; Bro. Thomas F. Flanagan, S.S.S.; Revs. Edmund J. Slattery, S.S.S.; Raymond Dubois, S.S.S.; Bro. David Phelan, S.S.S. Priests 3; Brothers 2. *Pine Valley Nursing Home*, 4360 Brecksville Rd., Richfield, 44286. Tel: 330-659-6166; Fax: 330-659-3676.

Congregation of the Blessed Sacrament Provincial House, 5384 Wilson Mills Rd., Highland Heights, 44143-3092. Tel: 440-442-6311; Fax: 440-442-4752. Web: www.blessedsacrament.com. Very Rev. Norman B. Pelletier, S.S.S., Prov. Supr. Province of St. Ann.

Priests Serving Outside Country: Rev. Ralph Roberts, S.S.S., Parrocchia S. Marco Evangelista, Via Del Modiano 1/1, Trieste 34148 Italy. Tel: 011-39-040-941218; Fax: 011-39-040-938-1987.

Priests attached to Provincialate: Revs. Andrew Beaudoin, S.S.S., 11487 Kerridale Ave., Spring Hill, FL 34608-3111. Tel: 352-686-8078; Edward Roberts, S.S.S., 36 Monument Sq., Apt. 4, Charlestown, MA 02129-3429. Tel: 617-241-9121; John Kamas, S.S.S., St. Francis DeSales, 135 E. 96th St., New York, NY 10128-3503. Tel: 212-289-1742; Dennis Ruane, S.S.S., Congregation of the Blessed Sacrament, P.O. Box 16289, Salt Lake City, UT 84116-0289. Tel: 801-495-3691; Joseph Thai Minh Tran, S.S.S., St. Charles Borromeo Church, 1818 Coal Pl. S.E., Albuquerque, NM 87106-4025; George Evans, S.S.S., Regina Health Center, 5232 Broadview Rd., Richfield, 44286-9608. Tel: 330-659-4161; Edmund J. Slattery, S.S.S., Regina Health Center, 5232 Broadview Rd., Richfield, 44286-9608. Tel: 330-659-4161; Raymond Dubois, S.S.S., Regina Health Center, 5232 Broadview Rd., Richfield, 44286-9608. Tel: 330-659-4161.

Marianist Community, 18340 Marcella Rd., 44119-2622. Tel: 216-481-1007; Fax: 216-486-1035. Email: jdempsey@vasj.com. Bro. John P. Dempsey, S.M., Dir.; Rev. George J. Abmayr, S.M., Chap.; Bros. William G. Halloway, S.M.; David F. Murphy, S.M.; Joseph A. Scheible, S.M. Priests 1; Brothers 5.

Maryknoll Fathers & Brothers (1911) 10309 Edgewater Dr., 44102. Tel: 216-651-2121; Fax: 216-651-8242. Email: mklcleve@aol.com. Web: www.maryknoll.org. Rev. James H. Huvane, M.M., Dir. Total in Residence 1; Total Staff 1.

Mercedarians (1218) 6928 Detroit Ave., 44102-3093. Tel: 216-651-5043; Fax: 216-651-6641. Email: mtcarmel@megsinet.net. Web: www.massintransit.com; www.olmccleveland.com; orderofmercy.org. Order of the B.V.M. of Mercy. Priests 4; Mercedarian Sisters (H.M.S.S.) 3; Total Staff 35. In Res. Revs. Richard S. Rasch, O.de.M., Vicar Provincial & Pastor; Jerome P. Laubacker, O.de.M.; Anthony M. Fortunato, O.de.M., Rectory Supr. & Asst. Pastor; Michael Donovan, O.de.M., Teacher.

St. Paul Friary, 4120 Euclid Ave., 44103. Tel: 216-431-8854; Fax: 216-361-1951. Email: Stpaulshrine@sbcglobal.net. Web: www.saintpaulshrine.com. Revs. Andrew Hohman, O.F.M.Cap.; Philip J. Bernier, O.F.M.Cap.; Robert Marva, O.F.M.Cap.; William Wiethorn, O.F.M.Cap.; Bro. Walter Robb, O.F.M.Cap. Priests 4; Brothers 1.

St. Agnes-Our Lady of Fatima, 6800 Lexington Ave., 44103. Tel: 216-391-1655; Fax: 216-391-7919. Rev. Robert Marva, O.F.M.Cap. Capuchin Franciscan Friars

St. Stanislaus Friary (1906) 3649 E. 65th St., 44105-1293. Tel: 216-341-9091; Fax: 216-341-2688. Email: ststans@ameritech.net. Web: www.ststanislaus.org. Revs. Michael Surufka, O.F.M.; Leonard Stunek, O.F.M., Guardian; Placyd Kon, O.F.M. The Franciscan Friars, Province of the Assumption of the Blessed Virgin., (Please see St. Stanislaus, Cleveland in the parish section for additional information.) *Marymount Convent*, Garfield Heights, 44125. Tel: 216-587-8376. Rev. George Jaskulski, O.F.M., Chap.

AVON. *Congregation of St. Joseph* (1873) 4076 Case Rd., 44011. Tel: 440-934-6270; Fax: 440-934-6270. Email: avon@murialdo.org. Web: www.murialdo.org. Revs. Lawrence Tosco, C.S.J., Formation Dir. & Local Supr.; Gaetano Menegatto, C.S.J. Fathers and Brothers of St. Joseph. Priests 2; Candidates 1; Temporary Professed 2.

BROOKLYN. *St. Anthony of Padua Friary* (1960) 4185 Brookway Ln., 44144. Tel: 216-661-7138; Fax: 216-845-5710. Revs. Walter Dolan, O.F.M., Guardian; Theodore Haag, O.F.M.; James Kelly, O.F.M.; James McManamon, O.F.M.; William Rooney, O.F.M.; Bros. Thomas Carroll, O.F.M., Vicar; Patrick T. Shea, O.F.M.; Michael Ward, O.F.M. Priests 5; Brothers 3.

[O] CONVENTS AND RESIDENCES FOR SISTERS

CLEVELAND. *Carmel of the Holy Family* (1923) 3176 Fairmount Blvd., 44118-4199. Tel: 216-321-6568; Fax: 216-321-1904. Email: sisters@clevelandcarmel.org. Web: www.clevelandcarmel.org. Sr. Annamae Dannes, O.C.D., Prioress. Discalced Carmelite Nuns. Professed Nuns 13.

Congregation of the Sisters of St. Joseph, Inc. dba Congregation of St. Joseph Cleveland Center, 3430 Rocky River Dr., 44111-2997. Tel: 216-252-0440; Fax: 216-941-3430. Web: www.csjoseph.org. Marlene Lee, Center Admin. Sisters 803.

Monastery of the Poor Clares (1877) Poor Clare Nuns (Colettine), 3501 Rocky River Dr., 44111-2998. Tel: 216-941-2821; Fax: 216-941-9298. Web: www.poorclarecolettines-cleveland.org. Observing the Primitive Rule of St. Clare (strictly cloistered, solemn vows). Perpetual exposition of the Blessed Sacrament. Cloistered Nuns 16; Extern Sisters 2.

Motherhouse and Novitiate of the Sisters of the Holy Spirit (1932) 10102 Granger Rd., 44125. Tel: 216-581-2941; Fax: 216-581-1207. Email: sister.mary.assumpta@jenningscenter.org. Sr. Patricia Raelene Peters, C.S.Sp., Supr. Gen. Professed Sisters 11.

Motherhouse and Novitiate of the Ursuline Sisters (1850) 2600 Lander Rd., 44124. Tel: 440-449-1200; Fax: 440-449-3588. Email: azawada@ursulinesisters.org. Web: www.ursulinesisters.org. Sisters Angelita Zawada, O.S.U., Pres.; Angelita Zawada, O.S.U., Pres.

The Ursuline Academy of Cleveland Professed Nuns 195.

Poor Clares of Perpetual Adoration, 4108 Euclid Ave., 44103. Tel: 216-361-0783; Fax: 216-361-0979. Email: angelspcpa@sbcglobal.net. Web: thepoorclares.com. Sr. Mary James, P.C.P.A., Supr. Monastery adjoins Conversion of St. Paul Church, where they maintain Perpetual Adoration. Cloistered Sisters 20.

Provincial House of Sisters of the Most Holy Trinity, 21281 Chardon Rd., 44117. Tel: 216-481-8232; Fax: 216-481-6577. Email: osst@srstrinity.com. Web: www.srstrinity.com. Sr. M. Rochelle Guental, O.S.S.T., Regl. Delegate. Attended from Center for Pastoral Leadership. Sisters 22; Total in Residence 14.

Sisters of St. Joseph of St. Mark General Motherhouse and Novitiate of Sisters of St. Joseph of St. Mark-Generalate, Diocese of Cleveland, 21800 Chardon Rd., 44117-2199. Tel: 216-531-7426; Fax: 216-383-0511. Email: sr_mpaschal_msj@yahoo.com. Sr. M. Therese Trunk, Gen. Supr. Sisters 9.

AKRON. *Dominican Sisters of Peace* (1929) Our Lady of the Elms Convent, 1230 W. Market St., 44313-7108. Tel: 330-836-4908; Fax: 330-836-5913. Email: srpeace@oppeace.org. Web: www.oppeace.org. Sr. Mary Noel, O.P., Mission Group Coord. Sisters in Congregation 638; Sisters in Diocese 68.

Provincial Motherhouse and Novitiate of the Daughters of Divine Charity (1950) 39 N. Portage Path, 44303-1183. Tel: 330-867-4960; Fax: 330-867-6334. Email: ddcakron@ameritech.net. Sr. Mary Coffelt, F.D.C., Prov. Supr.; Rev. Albert A. Kunkel, Chap. Tel: 330-867-2618. Sisters 17.

BEDFORD. *Sisters of Charity* (1852) Villa San Bernardo, 1160 Broadway, 44146-4523. Tel: 440-232-4755; Fax: 440-232-7832. Email: marie.tessmer@srcharitycinti.org. Web: www.srcharitycinti.org. Sisters Marie Tessmer, S.C., Dir. Sisters' Svcs.; Janet Gildea, Dir. Vocations. Sisters 13.

CHARDON. *Provincial House of the Sisters of Notre Dame, Juniorate, Novitiate* (1874) Notre Dame Education Center, 13000 Auburn Rd., 44024. Tel: 440-286-7101; Fax: 440-286-3377. Email: cliberatore@ndec.org. Web: www.sndchardon.org. Rev. Paul J. Sciarrotta, Chap. (Retired). Sisters 348.

GARFIELD HEIGHTS. *Marymount Congregational Home* (1926) 12215 Granger Rd., 44125. Tel: 216-581-3535; Fax: 216-518-2187. Email: sisterjoyce@marymount-ch.org. Web: www.ssj-tosf.org. Sr. Joyce Hollkamp, S.S.J.-T.O.S.F., Business & Facilities Coord.; Rev. George Jaskulski, O.F.M., Chap. & Contact Person. Residence of the Sisters of St. Joseph, Third Order of St. Francis. Sisters 26; Priests 1; Lay Staff 2.

PARMA HEIGHTS. *Sisters of the Incarnate Word and Blessed Sacrament* (1625) 6618 Pearl Rd., 44130-3808. Tel: 440-886-6440; Fax: 440-842-6391. Email: smrksiw@yahoo.com. Sr. Mary Rose Kocab, S.I.W., Congregational Leader.

Sisters of the Incarnate Word and Blessed Sacrament Final Professed Sisters 25.

6634 Pearl Rd., 44130-3808. Tel: 440-886-6996. In Res. Rev. Carl A. Ciprian (Retired).

RICHFIELD. *Mount Augustine, Motherhouse of the Sisters of Charity of St. Augustine* (1851) 5232 Broadview Rd., 44286-9608. Tel: 330-659-5100; Fax: 330-659-3899. Email: sme@srsofcharity.org. Web: www.srsofcharity.org. Sr. Miriam Erb, C.S.A., Congregational Leader. Final Professed Sisters 58.

Regina Health Center (1993) Tel: 330-659-4161; Fax: 330-659-5113. Religious Congregations 22; Total Assisted Care 54; Skilled Nursing Beds 101.

[P] SECULAR INSTITUTES

CLEVELAND HEIGHTS. *Society of Our Lady of the Way* (1936) c/o Mary Ann Tady, 1064 Oxford Rd., 44121. Tel: 216-381-5502. Email: matslow@aol.com. Web: www.secularinstitutes.org; www.saecimds.com. Secular Institute for Single Women.

[Q] HOMES FOR WOMEN

AKRON. *Leonora Hall* (1946) 39 N. Portage Path, 44303. Tel: 330-867-1752; Fax: 330-867-6334. Sr. M. Antoinette, F.D.C., Exec. Dir. Lenora Hall Residence "is a Home Away From Home" for Women who are working, going to school or unable to live independently. Semi-independent/supported living services are also provided for women with mild/moderate mental retardation/developmental disabilities in collaboration with Summit County Board of MR/DD. Daughters of Divine Charity 2; Residents 10; Personnel 4.

[R] LAY ASSOCIATIONS

CLEVELAND. *Community of Little Brothers and Sisters of the Eucharist, Inc.* (1977) 2186 East 35th St., 44115-3039. Tel: 216-566-0531; 216-566-9953; Fax: 216-566-0531. Email: littlesismaggie@gmail.com. Rev. James P. O'Donnell, Dir.

Society of St. Vincent de Paul, Diocesan Council, Cathedral Square Plaza, 1404 E. 9th St., 3rd Fl., 44114. Tel: 216-696-6525, Ext. 3150; Fax: 216-861-3200. Frank J. Fearon, Pres.; Lawrence Lauter, A.C.S.W, L.I.S.W., M.Div., Exec. Dir.

Akron District Council, 127 Marwyck Dr., Northfield, 44067. Tel: 330-476-5762. Cathie Perusek, Pres.

[S] RETREAT HOUSES

CLEVELAND. *Jesuit Retreat House* (1898) 5629 State Rd., 44134. Tel: 440-884-9300; Fax: 440-885-1055. Email: jrhcleve@att.net. Web: www.jrh-cleveland.org. Sr. Mary Ann Flannery, S.C., Dir.

AVON. *St. Leonard Youth Retreat Center* (1998) 4076 Case Rd., 44011. Tel: 440-934-6735; Fax: 440-934-6270. Web: www.stleonardyrc.com. Molly Smith, Dir.

BEDFORD. *Poustinia*, 1160 Broadway, 44146-4523. Tel: 440-232-4755; Fax: 440-232-7832. Email: marie.tessmer@srcharitycinti.org. Web: srcharitycinti.org. Judy Kendrick, Contact Person. Sisters of Charity of Cincinnati, OH.

[T] SOCIAL SERVICE AGENCIES AND INSTITUTIONS

For information call Catholic Information and Referral Services (CIRS) Tel: 216-696-HELP (4357).

CLEVELAND

Bishop William M. Cosgrove Center (1994) 1736 Superior Ave., 44114. Tel: 216-781-8262; Fax: 216-566-9161. Email: nxevans@clevelandcatholiccharities.org. Nicole Evans, Prog. Dir. Total Assisted 22,000; Total Staff 6.

Catholic Charities Community Services Corporation, 7911 Detroit Ave., 44102. Tel: 216-334-2931; Fax: 216-334-2907. Email: cmhorne@clevelandcatholiccharities.org. Web: www.clevelandcatholiccharities.org.

Catholic Charities Community Services of Medina County, 740 E. Washington St., Medina, 44256. Tel: 330-723-9615 (Medina); Fax: 330-764-8795 (Medina). Web: www.clevelandcatholiccharities.org. Timothy Putka, Dir.

Catholic Charities Community Services of Geauga County, 10771 Mayfield Rd., 44024-9323. Tel: 800-242-9755; Fax: 440-285-4909. Web: www.clevelandcatholiccharities.org. James Clements, Dir.

Catholic Charities Community Services of Lake County, 8 N. State St., Suite 455, Painesville, 44077-3954. Tel: 440-946-7264; Fax: 440-953-1608. Web: www.clevelandcatholiccharities.org. James Clements, Dir.

Catholic Charities Community Services of Lorain County, 628 Poplar St., Elyria, 44035. Tel: 440-366-1106; 877-566-1106; Fax: 440-366-5645. Kathleen Marsh, Dir.

St. Phillip Neri Family Center, 799 E. 82nd St., 44103. Tel: 216-391-4415. Phyllis Price, Dir.

Employment & Training Services - Midtown Professional Center, 3135 Euclid Ave., Room 101, 44115-2507. Tel: 216-426-9870; Fax: 216-426-9932. Vanessa Lee, Dir.

Fatima Family Center, 6600 Lexington Ave., 44103. Tel: 216-391-0505; Fax: 216-391-1118. LaJean Ray, Dir.

Head Start, 7911 Detroit Ave., 44102-2815. Tel: 440-334-2942; Fax: 440-334-2948. Michelle Curry, Dir.

Hispanic Senior Center, 7800 Detroit Ave., 44102. Tel: 216-939-3714; Fax: 216-631-3654. Nilda Ramos, Prog. Dir.

St. Martin de Porres Family Center, 1264 E. 123rd St., 44108-4042. Tel: 216-268-3909; Fax: 216-268-0207. Kevin Hodges, Dir.

Catholic Charities Community Services Early Learning Centers

Arbor Park, 3750 Fleming Ave., 44115. Tel: 216-431-4818; Fax: 216-431-4255. Allison DiCenzi, Center Admin.

Fatima Early Learning Center, 6600 Lexington Ave., 44103. Tel: 216-391-5375; Fax: 216-391-1118. Melissa Gibson, Center Admin.

Early Learning Center at the Quadrangle, 2302 Community College, 44115. Tel: 216-589-9750; Fax: 216-589-9702. Janet Lucha, Center Admin.

Catholic Charities Community Services of Ashland County, 1260 S. Center St., Ashland, 44805-2000. Tel: 419-289-1903; Fax: 419-281-8342. Bob Hurdle, Dir.

Catholic Charities Community Services of Wayne County, 521 Beall Ave., Wooster, 44691-3523. Tel: 330-262-7836; Fax: 330-262-2867. Bob Hurdle, Dir.

Catholic Charities Community Services Corporation, 7911 Detroit Ave., 44102. Tel: 216-334-2931; Fax: 216-334-2907.

Catholic Charities Community Services of Geauga County, 10771 Mayfield Rd., Chardon, 44024. Tel: 440-285-3537; 800-242-9755; Fax: 440-285-4909. James Clements, Dir. Outpatient counseling for families and individuals. Substance abuse counseling. Parenting programs. Services for the elderly. Services to strengthen and enrich the valued relationships of families and individuals for effective and healthy living. Employment programs for youth, young adults and adults.

Catholic Charities Community Services of Medina County, 740 E. Washington St., Medina, 44256-2136. Tel: 330-723-9615; Fax: 330-764-8795. Email: medina@clevelandcatholiccharities.org. Timothy J. Putka, M.S., Dir. Provides counseling, casework, and family life education in Medina County.
Medina. Tel: 330-723-9615; Fax: 330-764-8795.
Brunswick-Cleveland. Tel: 330-225-7100.
Wadsworth-Akron. Tel: 330-336-6657.

Catholic Charities Corporation (1919) 7911 Detroit Ave., 44102. Tel: 216-334-2959; 216-334-2900; Fax: 216-334-2983. Email: JPKlee@clevelandcatholiccharities.org. Web: www.ClevelandCatholicCharities.org. John P. Klee, Exec. Dir.

Catholic Charities Facilities Corporation (CCFC), 7911 Detroit Ave., 44102. Tel: 216-334-2949; Fax: 216-334-2907. Email: lxmurtaugh@clevelandcatholiccharities.org. Lawrence E. Murtaugh, Exec. Dir.

Catholic Charities Health and Human Services, 7911 Detroit Ave., 44102. Tel: 216-334-2901; Fax: 216-334-2907. Email: jtmullen@clevelandcatholiccharities.org. Web: www.clevelandcatholiccharities.org. J. Thomas Mullen, Pres. & CEO; Wayne Peel, CFO; Lisa Black, General Counsel; Patricia Holian, Exec. Vice Pres.

Catholic Charities Services Corporation, 6753 State Rd., 44134. Tel: 440-843-5501; Fax: 440-843-1627. Email: txwoll@clevelandcatholiccharities.org. Web: www.clevelandcatholiccharities.org. Thomas W. Woll, Exec. Dir. Tel: 216-696-6525, Ext. 416; Michael Haggerty, Asst. Exec. Dir.; A.M. Chip Bonsutto, Ed.D., Asst. Exec. Dir. Catholic Charities Services Corporation is part of the health and human services delivery system of the Diocese. Utilizing a holistic approach to healing, the system focuses on meeting the behavioral health needs of children and families in Cuyahoga County.

Chemical Dependency Services - Midtown Professional Center, 3135 Euclid Ave., Room 202, 44115-2507. Tel: 216-391-2030; Fax: 216-391-8946. Maureen Dee, Asst. Exec. Dir., Chemical Dependency Svcs.

Catholic Charities Services of Cuyahoga County, 6753 State Rd., Parma, 44134. Tel: 440-843-5501; Fax: 440-843-1627. Email: towers@clevelandcatholiccharities.org. Web: www.clevelandcatholiccharities.org. Thomas W. Woll, Exec. Dir. A multi-function social service agency which offers social service programs. Individual, family, and group counseling; marital counseling, psychiatric consultations; and outpatient psychiatric services for children, youth, and adults. Chemical dependency assessments and outpatient counseling for youth and families having alcohol and other drug-related problems. Bilingual services for Hispanic youth and families.

LaProvidencia Family Center, 2012 W. 25th St., 44113. Tel: 216-696-2089. Ramonita Johnson, Dir.

Matt Talbot Inn, 2270 Professor Ave., 44113-4489. Tel: 216-781-0288. Terry Morris, Dir.

Matt Talbot for Women, 2351 E. 22nd St., 44115. Tel: 216-592-2800. Colleen McKenna, Dir.

St. Malachi Center, Inc., 2416 Superior Viaduct, 44113. Tel: 216-771-3036; Fax: 216-771-3659. Email: st_malachi@ameritech.net. Web: www.stmalachi-center.org. Total Assisted 100 per day (Center); 20 per Monday (Health Services) 120; Total Staff 10.

Malachi House, Inc., 2810 Clinton Ave., 44113. Tel: 216-621-8831; Fax: 216-621-8841. Email: secretary@malachihouse.org. Web: www.malachihouse.org. Malachi House provides unskilled, family-like care to the dying poor without cost. Serves individuals who need an available caregiver, who have limited or no financial resources and are in need of special home care in the final stages of life. A trained staff and volunteers provide spiritual, emotional and physical support with the assistance of a hospice team. Acceptable only if care is manageable in a home setting. Handicapped access. Total Assisted Annually 110; Total Staff 25.

AKRON

Catholic Social Services of Summit County, Inc. (1920) 640 N. Main St., 44310-3098. Tel: 330-762-7481; Fax: 330-762-7484. Email: sglucas@clevelandcatholiccharities.org. Web: www.cssc.org. Patrick A. McGrath, M.S.S.W., Exec. Dir. Service sites throughout Summit County. Total Assisted 24,488; Total Staff 28.

CYO and Community Services (1936) 812 Biruta St., 44307-1104. Tel: 330-762-2961; Fax: 330-762-2001. Email: dpfinn@clevelandcatholiccharities.org. Web: www.akroncyo.org.
CYO Adult Day Services:
812 Biruta St., 44307. Tel: 330-762-2000; Fax: 330-762-2001. Email: dpfinn@clevelandcatholiccharities.org. Donald P. Finn, Exec. Dir. Total Assisted Annually (Adult Day Services) 206; Total Staff (Adult Day Services) 19.

Interval Brotherhood Home Alcohol-Drug Rehabilitation Center (1970) 3445 S. Main St., 44319. Tel: 330-644-4095; Fax: 330-645-2031. Email: sam@ibh.org. Web: www.ibh.org. Rev. Samuel R. Ciccolini, Dir. Bed Capacity 110; Total in Residential Treatment 430; Total Assisted Annually 435; Total Staff 96.

**St. Patrick Manor, Inc. c/o Humility of Mary Housing, Inc.*, 3250 W. Market St., Ste. 204, 44333. Tel: 330-384-1555; Fax: 330-384-2144. Email: kradigan@hmhousing.org. Web: www.hmhousing.org. Richard Donahue, Chm.; Patricia Lindley, Sec. Units (Independent Living) 50; Total Staff 2.

ELYRIA

Catholic Charities Community Services of Lorain County, 628 Poplar St., 44035. Tel: 440-366-1106; Fax: 440-366-5645. Kathleen Marsh, Dir.

Catholic Charities Family Center, 203 Eighth St., Lorain, 44052. Tel: 440-244-9915; Fax: 440-245-1057.

GARFIELD HEIGHTS

Brendan Manor, Inc., 13401 Cranwood Dr., 44105. Tel: 216-475-5230; Fax: 216-475-5852. Email: dlkalchert@hotmail.com. Diane Kalchert, Exec. Dir. Licensed nonprofit, nondenominational adult group home for chronically ill adults. Bed Capacity 16; Total Assisted Annually 20; Total Staff 9.

NORTHFIELD

St. Barnabas Villa, Inc. (1985) 9234 Olde Eight Rd., 44067. Tel: 330-467-3758; Fax: 330-908-1186. Anita Bartel, Mgr. A shared living facility for 11 people over 60 years of age. Bed Capacity 11; Total in Residence 11; Total Staff 16.

PAINESVILLE

Catholic Charities Community Services of Lake County, Mailing Address: 8 N. State St., 44077. Tel: 440-946-7264. James Clements, Dir. Mental Health Services.

[U] SHRINES

CLEVELAND. *Our Lady of Lourdes Shrine* , Euclid, (U.S. Rtes. 20 & 6). Administered by the Sisters of the Most Holy Trinity., 21281 Chardon Rd., 44117. Tel: 216-481-8232; Fax: 216-481-6577. Email: osst@srstrinity.com. Web: www.srstrinity.com. Sr. M. Rochelle Guertal, O.SS.T., Regnl. Supr. Total in Residence 14.

BEDFORD. *Our Lady of Levocha Shrine* , (Ohio Rte. 14). Administered by the Sisters of Charity (S.C.), 1160 Broadway, 44146-4523. Tel: 440-232-4755; Fax: 440-232-7832. Email: marie.tessmer@srcharitycinti.org. Web: www.srcharitycinti.org. Sr. Marie Tessmer, S.C., Contact Person.

GARFIELD HEIGHTS. *Our Lady of Czestochowa Shrine* , (Ohio Rte. 17). Administered by the Sisters of St. Joseph Third Order of St. Francis (S.S.J.-T.O.S.F.), 12215 Granger Rd., 44125. Tel: 216-581-3535; Fax: 216-518-2187. Sr. Joyce Hollkamp, S.S.J.-T.O.S.F., Business & Facilities Coord.

PARMA HEIGHTS. *Queen of the Holy Rosary Shrine* , (U.S. Rte. 42). Administered by the Sisters of the Incarnate Word and Blessed Sacrament (S.I.W.), 6618 Pearl Rd., 44130-3808. Tel: 440-886-6440; Fax: 440-842-6391. Email: smrksiw@yahoo.com. Sr. Mary Rose Kocab, S.I.W., Congregational Leader.

[V] MINISTRY TO THE SPANISH SPEAKING

CLEVELAND. *Office of Hispanic Ministry*, Diocese of Cleveland, 1404 E. 9th St., 44114. Tel: 216-696-6525, Ext. 2530; Fax: 216-861-3200. Email: mmayorga@dioceseofcleveland.org. Web: www.dioceseofcleveland.org/hispanicministry. Misael Mayorga, Dir.

Hispanic Parishes: Iglesia La Sagrada Familia, 7719 Detroit Ave., 44102. Tel: 216-631-6817; Fax: 216-631-3305. Rev. Robert J. Reidy.

Sacred Heart Chapel 4301 Pearl Ave., Lorain, 44055. Tel: 440-277-7231; 440-277-7232; Fax: 440-277-4886. Email: sagrada1997@att.net. Rev. William A. Thaden, Admin.

Parishes with Ministry to Spanish Speaking: St. Bernard, 47 University Ave., Akron, 44308. Tel: 330-253-5161; Fax: 330-253-6949. Rev. Clyde K. Foster.

St. Michael, 3114 Scranton Rd., 44109. Tel: 216-861-6297; Fax: 216-696-9351. Rev. James H. McCreight.

St. Mary's - Painesville, 242 N. State St., Painesville, 44077. Tel: 440-354-4381; Fax: 440-354-9174. Rev. R. Stephen Vellenga.

Our Lady of Lourdes, 3395 E. 53rd St., 44127. Tel: 216-641-2829 (Rectory & Office); Fax: 216-641-0043. Email: info@ourladyoflourdes-cle.org. Web: www.ourladyoflourdes-cle.org. Rev. Joseph Callahan.

St. Mary of the Immaculate Conception, 527 Beall Ave., P.O. Box 109, Wooster, 44691. Tel: 330-264-8824; 330-264-8822; Fax: 330-262-4633. Email: stmarywoost@embarqmail.com. Revs. Stephen P. Moran; Christopher J. Trenta; Judith Caraballo-Arzuaga, Dir. Latino Ministry, (Wayne, Ashland & Medina Districts).

[W] NEWMAN CENTERS

CLEVELAND. *Office of Newman Catholic Campus Ministry* 1404 E. 9th St., 44114. Tel: 216-696-6525, Ext. 2880; Fax: 216-696-6206. Web: www.oce-ocs.org/ocs. Mr. William B. Miller, Sec. Catechetical Svcs. Total Staff 9; Newman Centers 7.

Case-Western Reserve University Tel: 216-421-9614, Ext. 302; Fax: 216-791-2228. Tony Vento, Campus Min., 11205 Euclid Ave., 44106. Tel: 216-421-9614, Ext. 302; Fax: 216-791-2228.

University of Akron Newman Center, 44 University Ave., Akron, 44308. Tel: 330-253-6949; 216-696-6525, Ext. 3000; Fax: 216-696-8646. John Szarwark, Campus Min. (Akron)

Baldwin-Wallace College Newman Center 170 E. Center St., Berea, 44017. Tel: 216-243-4955; Fax: 216-243-0354. Mindy Kushlak, Campus Min.; Kirsten Vilinsky, Campus Min. (Berea)

Oberlin College Office of Religious & Spiritual Life, 135 W. Lorain St., Oberlin, 44074. Tel: 440-775-5190; Fax: 440-775-6896. Email: ddacone@dioceseofcleveland.org. Debbie Dacone, Campus Min. (Oberlin)

The College of Wooster 1473 Beall Ave., Wooster, 44691. Tel: 330-287-3000, Ext. 4504; Fax: 330-263-2534. Email: khahn@dioceseofcleveland.org. Web: www.dioceseofcleveland.org. Karen Hahn, Campus Min. (Wooster)

University of Ashland 132 N. Wood St., Loudonville, 44842. Tel: 419-994-4396. Rev. Vincent J. Hawk, Campus Min.

Cleveland State University 1512 Lorimer Rd., Parma, 44129. Tel: 216-398-7156. Greg Stevens, Campus Min.

[X] ENDOWMENT TRUSTS

CLEVELAND. *The Benedictine High School Endowment Trust* (2001) 2900 Martin Luther King Jr. Dr., 44104. Tel: 216-721-5300, Ext. 207; Fax: 216-721-1253. Email: abbotchristopher@cbhs.net. Web: www.cbhs.net. Rt. Rev. Christopher Schwartz, O.S.B., Bd. Chm.

St. John Cathedral Endowment Trust, 1007 Superior Ave. E., 44114-2582. Tel: 216-771-6666; Fax: 216-781-5646. Email: stjohns@dioceseofcleveland.org. Web: www.saintjohncathedral.com. Revs. Theodore Marszal, S.T.D.; Rodel Angeles, Parochial Vicar; Deacon John P. Sferry Sr., Pastoral Assoc.

Poor Clares Perpetual Adoration Foundation of Cleveland, Ohio, 19000 Lake Rd., Ste. 209, 44116. Tel: 440-331-2811.

Sisters of Saint Joseph Community Support Charitable Trust, 3430 Rocky River Dr., 44111-2997. Tel: 216-252-0440; Fax: 216-941-3430. Email: nconway@csjoseph.org. Web: www.csjoseph.org. Sr. Jeanne Cmolik, C.S.J., Contact Person.

The Thomas C. and Sandra S. Sullivan Foundation, 1404 E. 9th St., 8th Fl., 44114. Tel: 216-696-6525, Ext. 4200; Fax: 216-348-0740. Email: lgannon@cdcf.org. Web: www.cdcf.org. Mr. Patrick J. Grace, Exec. Dir.; Terri Preskar, Relationship Mgr.

Villa Angela - St. Joseph High School Education Endowment Trust (1990) 18491 Lake Shore Blvd., 44119. Tel: 216-481-8414; Fax: 216-486-1035. Email: bmenard@vasj.com. Web: www.vasj.com.

AKRON. *The Daughters of Divine Charity, St. Mary Province, Charitable Trust*, 39 N. Portage Path, 44303-1183. Tel: 330-867-4960; Fax: 330-867-6334. Email: gaburick@ameritech.net.

Our Lady of the Elms-Sisters of St. Dominic Foundation (1989) 1230 W. Market St., 44313-7108. Tel: 330-836-4908; Fax: 330-836-5913. Email: lamert@akrondominicans.org. Web: www.akrondominicans.org.

St. Vincent-St. Mary High School Endowment Trust (1983) 15 N. Maple St., 44303. Tel: 330-253-9113; Fax: 330-996-0000. Web: www.stvm.com. David V. Rathz, Headmaster.

CHARDON. *The Sisters of Notre Dame Charitable Trust*, 13000 Auburn Rd., 44024. Tel: 440-286-7101; Fax: 440-286-3377. Email: cliberatore@ndec.org. Web: www.snd1.org; www.sndchardon.org. Sr. Mary Cecilia Liberatore, S.N.D., Chm.

FAIRLAWN. **St. Hilary Parish Foundation*, 2750 W. Market St., 44333. Tel: 330-867-1055; Fax: 330-869-2312. Mr. Edward F. Carter, Pres.

MENTOR. *St. Mary of the Assumption Parish Endowment Trust* (1857) 8560 Mentor Ave., 44060-5853. Tel: 440-255-3404; Fax: 440-255-4194. Email: tgelsass@ameritech.net. Web: www.stmarysmentor.org. Priests 1.

PARMA HEIGHTS. *Incarnate Word Academy Student and Faculty Advancement Endowment (IWA Endowment)* (2002) 6620 Pearl Rd., 44130. Tel: 440-842-6818, Ext. 3104; Fax: 440-888-1377. Email: info@incarnatewordacademy.org. Web: www.incarnatewordacademy.com. Sr. Eileen Fitzgerald, S.I.W.

Incarnate Word Endowment Trust (1986) 6618 Pearl Rd., 44130-3808. Tel: 440-886-6440; Fax: 440-842-6391. Email: smrksiw@yahoo.com. Sr. Mary Rose Kocab, S.I.W., Congregational Leader.

ROCKY RIVER. *Friends of the Poor Clares Foundation*, 19000 Lake Rd., # 209, 44116. Tel: 440-331-2811. Thomas J. Kelley, Pres. & Treas.

SEVEN HILLS. *Sisters Servants of Mary Immaculate Endowment Fund in Memory of Sr. Amelia Kuska* (2000) 285 Panorama Dr., 44131. Tel: 216-441-5402; Fax: 216-441-4510. Email: ssmiendowment@hotmail.com. Web: www.ssmiendowment.org. Sr. Cecilia A. Sambor, S.S.M.I., Pres.

SHAKER HEIGHTS. *St. Dominic Endowment Fund* (2003) 3450 Norwood Rd., 44122. Tel: 216-991-1444; Fax: 216-491-0190. Email: kmqua@yahoo.com. Web: www.stdominicchurch.net. Rev. Thomas G. Fanta, Pres.

WELLINGTON. *St. Patrick Church Endowment Trust* (1990) 512 N. Main St., 44090. Tel: 440-647-4375; Fax: 440-647-4675. Email: stpatrickwellington@alltel.net.

WOOSTER. *St. Mary of the Immaculate Conception Elementary Day School Endowment Trust* (1990) 527 Beall Ave., P.O. Box 109, 44691. Tel: 330-264-8824; Fax: 330-262-4633. Email: stmarychurch@embarqmail.com. Web: stmarywooster.org.

[Y] MISCELLANEOUS

CLEVELAND. **St. Augustine Services Corporation*, 7801 Detroit Ave., 44102. Tel: 216-634-7400; Fax: 216-634-7483. Email: pgareau@st-aug.org. Mr. Patrick Gareau, Pres. Total Staff 15.

Catholic Charities Housing Corporation (CCHC), 7911 Detroit Ave., 44102. Tel: 216-334-2954; Fax: 216-334-2907. Email: lxmurtaugh@clevelandcatholiccharities.org. J. Thomas Mullen, Pres.; Lawrence E. Murtaugh, Vice Pres.; Maryellen Staab, Dir.

Catholic Community Connection, 2351 E. 22nd St., 44115. Tel: 216-875-4613; Fax: 216-696-2204. Email: lcalabrese@sistersofcharityhealth.org. Leonard M. Calabrese, Pres.

Catholic Ministry of Health Care Professionals, 2351 E. 22nd St., 44115. Tel: 216-363-2674; Fax: 216-363-3334.

Cleveland Slovenian Community Center, 15519 Holmes Ave., 44110-2497. Tel: 216-761-7740; Fax: 216-761-6673. Email: johnkumse@yahoo.com. Rev. John M. Kumse.

COAR Peace Mission, Inc. (1980) 4395 Rocky River Dr., 44135-2569. Tel: 216-252-5572; Fax: 216-252-5573. Email: coarpm@sbcglobal.net. Web: www.coarpeacemission.org. Mary Stevenson, Exec. Dir. Total Staff 100; Total Assisted 900.

COAR Children's Village Tel: 011-2-314-0824. Sr. Maria Isaura Arauz Quijano, Dir. (Zaragoza, El Salvador, C.A.); Comunidad Oscar Arnulfo Romero (COAR) provides housing, education and health care for orphaned, abandoned and street children in Zaragoza, El Salvador, Central America. The Children's Village can house up to 120 children under the supervision and guidance of a house-mother in fifteen home-like cottages. The COAR school provides a kindergarten to grade twelve school education to about 800 children from Zaragoza and neighboring villages. State approved vocational training is offered to high school students. The Santa Teresita Clinic, a quality medical clinic in an area with little other access to health care, serves the health and dental needs of up to 25-50 patients (adults and children) weekly. The Archdiocese of San Salvador through its Caritas ministries administers COAR Children's Village. The COAR Peace Mission in Cleveland, OH is the support and development office for the Children's Village in El Salvador. COAR was founded in August 1980 by Rev. Ken Myers, a priest of the Cleveland Diocese.

Congregation of the Sisters of St. Joseph Ministries, Inc., 3430 Rocky River Rd., 44111-2997.

CSA Health Network, 2351 East 22nd St., 44115. Tel: 216-659-5560; Fax: 216-696-2204. Web: www.sistersofcharityhealth.org. Sr. Judith Ann Karam, C.S.A., Pres. & CEO. Serves as the general partner to the joint venture ownership of Catholic healthcare providers.

**CSA St. John Ministries fka St. John West Shore Hospital*, 2351 E. 22nd St., 44115. Tel: 888-223-1816; Fax: 216-696-2204. Web: www.sistersofcharityhealth.org. Sr. Judith Ann Karam, C.S.A., Pres. & CEO.

CSA St. Vincent Charity Ministries fka St. Vincent Charity Hospital, 2351 E. 22nd St., 44115. Tel: 888-223-1816; Fax: 216-696-2204. Web: www.sistersofcharityhealth.org. Sr. Judith Ann Karam, C.S.A., Pres. & CEO.

First Friday Club of Cleveland, Inc., 1404 E. Ninth St., Ste. 100, 44114. Tel: 440-390-0172. Email: ffcofccleveland@sbcglobal.net. Gregory Szuter, Trustee; Nancy Walsh, Sec.

Healing Prayer Institute, P.O. Box 200404, 44120. Email: info@healingprayerinstitute.com. Web: www.healingprayerinstitute.com. Judith Pamula, Board Member.

L'Arche, Cleveland (1975) P.O. Box 20450, 44120. Tel: 216-721-2614; Fax: 216-229-2311. Email: office@larchecleveland.org. Web: www.larchecleveland.org. An ecumenical community providing homes for adults with developmental disabilities. Residents 14; Total Staff 30.

Ministering Together, 2351 E. 22nd St., 44115. Tel: 216-377-4358; Fax: 216-696-2204. Email: sgaughan@sistersofcharityhealth.org.

Ninth Street CDC, 1404 E. Ninth St., 8th Fl., 44114-1722. Tel: 216-696-6525; Fax: 216-696-8084. John R. Maimone, Pres.

Pulaski Franciscan Community Development Corp. (2001) 3649 E. 65th St., 44105. Tel: 216-341-9091; Fax: 216-341-2688. Email: pfcdc@sbcglobal.net. Rev. Michael Surufka, O.F.M., Pres.

River's Edge A Place for Reflection and Action, 3430 Rocky River Dr., 44111. Tel: 216-688-1111. Email: rita@riversedgecleveland.com. Web: www.riversedgecleveland.com. Sr. Rita Petruziello, C.S.J., Exec. Dir.

Sisters of Charity Foundation of Cleveland (1996) 1228 Euclid Ave., Ste. 330, 44115. Tel: 216-241-9300; Fax: 216-241-9345. Web: www.socfdncleveland.org. Susanna H. Krey, Pres.

Sisters of Charity of St. Augustine Health System, 2351 E. 22nd St., 44115. Tel: 216-696-5560; Fax: 216-696-2204. Web: www.sistersofcharityhealth.org. Sr. Judith Ann Karam, C.S.A., Pres. & CEO. Serves as the Member of foundations and health and human service corporations sponsored by the Sisters of Charity of St. Augustine, Richfield, OH. Serves as one of two members of the joint venture corporation operating St. John West Shore Hospital and St. Vincent Charity Hospital.

The Sisters of St. Joseph, 3430 Rocky River Dr., 44111-2997. Tel: 216-252-0440; Fax: 216-941-3430.

**St. Vitus Development Corporation* (2000) 6019 Lausche Ave., 44103. Tel: 216-361-1444; Fax: 216-361-1445. Email: skuhar@hotmail.com. Stane Kuhar, Sec. & Contact Person; Rev. Joseph P. Boznar, Pres.; Joseph V. Hocevar, Treas.

AKRON. *First Friday Club of Greater Akron* (2000) 795 Russell Ave., 44307. Tel: 330-535-7668; Fax: 330-535-9040. Email: ffcofga@neo.rr.com. Web: www.firstfridayclubofgreaterakron.org. Linda Tucci Teodosio, Pres.

H M Housing Development Corporation, 3250 W. Market St., Ste. 204, 44333. Tel: 330-384-1555; Fax: 330-384-2144. Email: kradigan@hmhousing.org. Web: www.hmhousing.org. Dana Murphy, Prog. Dir.; Sharon Kleppel, Chairperson.

H.M. Life Opportunity Services (1987) 1815 W. Market St. #102, 44313. Tel: 330-376-5600; Fax: 330-376-2277. Email: hmlife@hmlife.org.

Central Office, 1815 W. Market St. #102, 44313. Tel: 330-376-5600; Fax: 330-376-2277. Web: www.hm-housing.org.

Humility of Mary Housing, Inc., 3250 W. Market St., Ste. 204, 44333. Tel: 330-384-1555; Fax: 330-384-2144. Email: kradigan@hmhousing.org. Web: www.hmhousing.org. Kenneth W. Radigan, Pres. Affordable housing and housing related services for low and moderate income individuals. Total Assisted 450; Total Staff 11.

CHARDON. *Christ Child Society-Geauga Chapter*, P.O. Box 1133, 44024. Tel: 440-729-0536. Judy Benda, Pres.; Eileen Zavarella, Pres.

COPLEY. *Faith and Light U.S.A., Inc.*, 1518 Sunside Dr., P.O. Box 4049, 44321. Tel: 330-666-6816. Email: kirtbromley@yahoo.com. Web: www.faithandlightusa.org. W. Kirt Bromley, Contact Person.

GARFIELD HEIGHTS. *Jennings Manor Housing Corporation* (1996) 10204 Granger Rd., 44125. Tel: 216-581-2900; Fax: 216-581-4505. Email: marketing@jenningscenter.org. Web: www.jenningscenter.org. Mrs. Martha M. Kutik, Pres. & CEO; Allison Salopeck, Admin. & COO; Jane Carbeck, Housing Dir. 61 unit apartment building - HUD 202 Supportive Housing for Older Adults.

Marymount Health Care Systems, 12300 McCracken Rd., 44125. Tel: 216-587-8080; Fax: 216-587-8212. Email: dkilarski@marymount.org. Mr. David J. Kilarski, Pres. Provides comprehensive health and human services in response to the needs of the local community by owning, leasing and operating health care facilities and services consistent with the philosophy and objectives of the Roman Catholic religious congregation known as the Sisters of St. Joseph of the Third Order of St. Francis.

MHCS Real Estate Holding Company, 12300 McCracken Rd., 44125-2975. Tel: 216-587-8080; Fax: 216-587-8212. Email: dkilarski@marymount.org. Mr. David J. Kilarski, Pres. To assist in the provision of comprehensive health care services by acquiring, holding, owning, and leasing real estate (and interests therein) and health care facilities, including but not limited to leasing such as real estate and facilities to

Marymount Hospital, consistent with the philosophy and objectives of the Roman Catholic Church as promulgated by the National Conference of Catholic Bishops and the local Ordinary. Holds the Title to Marymount Hospital as a part of the Marymount Health Care Systems Special Member responsibility.

HUDSON. **Laurel Lake Retirement Community, Inc.* (1989) 200 Laurel Lake Dr., 44236. Tel: 330-650-0681; Fax: 330-655-1700. Email: info@laurellake.org. Web: www.laurellake.org. David Oster, Exec. Dir. Independent Living Residents 350; Assisted Living Residents 60; Skilled Nursing Residents 75; Total Staff 250.

KIRTLAND. *St. Philip Neri/Divine Word Church in the City Partnership Inc.* (1914) 8100 Eagle Rd., 44094. Tel: 440-256-1412; Fax: 440-256-4929. Email: spncarl@sbcglobal.net. Rev. David G. Woost, Pastor, Divine Word, Kirtland. (Partnership 1993) Total Staff 8.

LORAIN. *Community Health Partners Regional Health System*, 3700 Kolbe Rd., 44053. Tel: 440-960-3295; Fax: 440-960-4630. Email: ed.oley@health-partners.org. Edwin Oley, Pres. Total Assisted 240,164.

First Friday Forum of Lorain County, 2500 Elyria Ave., 44055. Tel: 440-244-0643. Email: ffflorain@gmail.com. Sharon Kleppel, Pres.

PAINESVILLE. *Christ Child Society of the Western Reserve*, 1515-R Mentor Ave., 44077. Tel: 440-352-8773. Jan Janos, Pres.

**Retrouvaille of Cleveland, Inc.*, 575 Southington Blvd., 44077-2858. Tel: 440-357-6580. Web: retrouvailleofcleveland.catholicweb.com.

PARMA. **Christ Child Society of Cleveland* (1916) 6753 State Rd., 44134. Tel: 440-843-1632; Fax: 440-843-1632 (call first). Email: christchildcleveland@yahoo.com. Web: www.christchildsocietycleveland.org. Mrs. Jean A. Canestraro, Pres. & Contact.

Society of St. Joseph the Worker (1979) 7033 State Rd., 44134-4952. Tel: 440-888-4872; Fax: 440-888-6825. Email: bsjw@msn.com. Web: www.bsjw.org. Lawrence R. Verbiar, Dir.

PEPPER PIKE. *Ursuline Child Care/Learning Center, Ursuline Educational Center*, 2600 Lander Rd., 44124. Tel: 440-449-1200, Ext. 280. Email: uil@ursulinesisters.org. Sr. Angelita Zawada, O.S.U., Dir. Sisters 18.

ROCKY RIVER. *Heartbeats* (1991) 20015 Detroit Rd., 44116. Tel: 440-356-8601; Fax: 440-356-8078. Email: heartbt@en.com. Web: www.heartbeatscatalog.org. Sr. Jo Marie Chrosniak, H.M., Dir.

SOLON. *The O'Neill Brothers Foundation*, 30000 Aurora Rd., Suite 250, 44139. Tel: 440-248-2027; Fax: 440-248-2153. Email: lstopar@aol.com. Mr. Robert K. Healey, Pres.

WESTLAKE. *The Center for Learning* (1970) Editorial/Administrative Office, 24600 Detroit Rd., Ste. 201, 44145. Tel: 440-250-9341; Fax: 440-250-9715. Web: www.centerforlearning.org. Melanie Wall, Pres. & CEO. Educational Publisher of values-based curriculum: Religion for Catholic schools and parishes; English/Language Arts, Social Studies, and Novel/Drama Curriculum Units for all schools.; Owned and operated by the Sisters of Humility of Mary. Directed by an Ecumenical Lay Board.

Customer Service Office, 2105 Evergreen Rd., P.O. Box 910, Villa Maria, PA 16155. Tel: 800-767-9090; 724-964-8083; Fax: 888-767-8080. Web: www.centerforlearning.org.

UHHS/CSAHS - Cuyahoga, Inc. (1999) 29000 Center Ridge Rd., 44145. Tel: 440-835-8000; Fax: 440-827-5015.

WICKLIFFE. *Center for Pastoral Leadership Services, Inc.* (1991) 28700 Euclid Ave., 44092-2585. Tel: 440-943-7600; Fax: 440-943-7577. Email: pguban@dioceseofcleveland.org. Very Rev. Thomas M. Dragga, D.Min., CEO; Mr. Philip J. Guban, B.A., COO.

RELIGIOUS INSTITUTES OF MEN REPRESENTED IN THE DIOCESE

For further details refer to the corresponding bracketed number in the Religious Institutes of Men or Women section.

[]—*Apostles of Jesus* (Karen, Kenya)—A.J.
[0200]—*Benedictine Monks* (St. Andrew Abbey)—O.S.B.
[0600]—*Brothers of the Congregation of Holy Cross* (Midwest Prov.)—C.S.C.
[0470]—*The Capuchin Friars*—O.F.M.Cap.
[1150]—*Congregation of St. Joseph*—C.S.J.
[0220]—*Congregation of the Blessed Sacrament*—S.S.S.
[0520]—*Franciscan Friars* (Provs. of Our Lady of Consolation & Assumption)—O.F.M.
[0480]—*Franciscan Friars (Conv.)*—O.F.M.Conv.
[0690]—*Jesuit Fathers and Brothers* (Maryland Prov.)—S.J.
[0690]—*Jesuit Fathers and Brothers (Society of Mary)* (Detroit Prov.)—S.J.
[0800]—*Maryknoll*—M.M.
[]—*Missionaries of St. Francis de Sales*—M.S.F.S.
[0970]—*Order of Our Lady of Mercy*—O.de.M.
[0610]—*Priests of the Congregation of the Holy Cross* (Indiana Prov.)—C.S.C.
[0760]—*Society of Mary-Marianists* (Dayton, OH)—S.M.
[1060]—*Society of the Precious Blood* (Cincinnati Prov.)—C.PP.S.

RELIGIOUS INSTITUTES OF WOMEN REPRESENTED IN THE DIOCESE

[0230]—*Benedictine Sisters of Pontifical Jurisdiction* (Erie, PA)—O.S.B.
[3832]—*Congregation of the Sisters of St. Joseph*—C.S.J.
[1710]—*Congregation of the Third Order of St. Francis of Mary Immaculate, Joliet, IL*—O.S.F.
[0790]—*Daughters of Divine Charity*—F.D.C.
[0420]—*Discalced Carmelite Nuns*—O.C.D.
[1070-14]—*Dominican Sisters* (Adrian, MI)—O.P.
[1115]—*Dominican Sisters of Peace*—O.P.
[1210]—*Franciscan Sisters of Chicago*—O.S.F.
[2340]—*Little Sisters of the Poor*—P.S.D.P.
[]—*Mercedarian Sisters of the Blessed Sacrament*—H.M.S.S.
[3760]—*Order of St. Clare-Poor Clare Colettine Nuns*—P.C.C.
[3210]—*Poor Clares of Perpetual Adoration*—P.C.P.A.
[3420]—*Religious of the Eucharist*—R.E.
[3430]—*Religious Teachers Filippini*—M.P.F.
[0440]—*Sisters of Charity of Cincinnati, Ohio*—S.C.
[0570]—*Sisters of Charity of Seton Hill*—S.C.
[0580]—*Sisters of Charity of St. Augustine*—C.S.A.
[0990]—*Sisters of Divine Providence*—C.D.P.
[2580]—*Sisters of Mercy of the Americas* (South Central)—R.S.M.
[2990]—*Sisters of Notre Dame* (Cleveland)—S.N.D.
[]—*Sisters of Notre Dame* (Toledo)—S.N.D.
[3360]—*Sisters of Providence*—S.P.
[1530]—*Sisters of St. Francis* (Sylvania)—O.S.F.
[]—*Sisters of St. Francis of Neuman Community*—O.S.F.
[3910]—*Sisters of St. Joseph of St. Mark* (Cleveland)—S.J.S.M.
[]—*Sisters of St. Joseph of St. Mark* (Louisville)—S.J.S.M.
[3930]—*Sisters of St. Joseph of the Third Order of St. Francis*—S.S.J.-T.O.S.F.
[]—*Sisters of the Good Shepherd* (St. Louis)—O.S.U.
[1970]—*Sisters of the Holy Family of Nazareth*—C.S.F.N.
[2030]—*Sisters of the Holy Spirit*—C.S.Sp.
[2110]—*Sisters of the Humility of Mary*—H.M.
[2210]—*Sisters of the Incarnate Word and Blessed Sacrament*—S.I.W.
[2350]—*Sisters of the Living Word*—S.L.W.
[2060]—*Sisters of the Most Holy Trinity*—O.SS.T.
[3260]—*Sisters of the Precious Blood* (Dayton, Ohio)—C.PP.S.
[3620]—*Sisters, Servants of Mary Immaculate*—S.S.M.I.
[2150]—*Sisters, Servants of the Immaculate Heart of Mary*—I.H.M.
[]—*Social Mission Sisters*—S.M.
[4120-04]—*Ursuline Nuns of the Congregation of Paris* (Cleveland)—O.S.U.
[4120-07]—*Ursuline Nuns of the Congregation of Paris* (Youngstown)—O.S.U.

DIOCESAN CEMETERIES

CLEVELAND. *Assumption of Mary Cemetery*, Mailing Address: *Calvary Cemetery*, 10000 Miles Ave., 44105.

Calvary Cemetery, 10000 Miles Ave., 44105.

St. John Cemetery, Mailing Address: *Calvary Cemetery*, 10000 Miles Ave., 44105.

St. Joseph Cemetery, Mailing Address: 10000 Miles Ave., 44105. 7916 Woodland Ave, 44104.

St. Mary Cemetery, Mailing Address: 10000 Miles Ave., 44105.

Holy Cross Cemetery, Mailing Address: 10000 Miles Ave., 44105.

Elmhurst Park Cemetery, Mailing Address: 10000 Miles Ave., 44105. (Non-Sectarian)

St. Mary of the Falls Cemetery, Mailing Address: 10000 Miles Ave., 44105.

Holy Trinity Cemetery, Mailing Address: 10000 Miles Ave., 44105.

Holy Trinity Cemetery, Mailing Address: 10000 Miles Ave., 44105.

St. Joseph Cemetery, Mailing Address: 10000 Miles Ave., 44105.

Holy Cross Cemetery, Mailing Address: 10000 Miles Ave., 44105.

St. Mary Cemetery, Mailing Address: 10000 Miles Ave., 44105.

St. Mary Cemetery, Mailing Address: 10000 Miles Ave., 44105.

Calvary Cemetery, Mailing Address: 10000 Miles Ave., 44105.

All Saints Cemetery, Mailing Address: 10000 Miles Ave., 44105.

Resurrection Cemetery, Mailing Address: 10000 Miles Ave., 44105.

CHARDON. *All Souls Cemetery*, Mailing Address: 10000 Miles Ave., 44105. 10366 Chardon Rd., P.O. Box 11, 44024.

NECROLOGY

† Bonnell, Robert A., Oberlin, OH Sacred Heart—Died March 5, 2009
† Fallon, David F., Cleveland, OH Sagrada Familia—Died May 1, 2009
† Johnson, William J., (Retired)—Died Jan. 6, 2009
† Klamet, Frank X., (Released from Diocesan Assignment)—Died April 19, 2009
† McMahon, Joseph W., (Retired)—Died Sept. 6, 2009
† Prendergast, Edward F., Rocky River, OH St. Christopher—Died Dec. 14, 2008
† Vieweg, Robert R., (Retired)—Died July 16, 2009
† Zepp, Anthony W., Garfield Hts., OH SS. Peter & Paul—Died April 27, 2009

An asterisk (*) denotes an organization that has established tax-exempt status directly with the IRS and is not covered by the USCCB Group Ruling.

Diocese of Colorado Springs

Most Reverend

RICHARD C. HANIFEN, D.D., J.C.L.

Bishop Emeritus of Colorado Springs; ordained June 6, 1959; appointed Titular Bishop of Abercorn and Auxiliary of Denver July 6, 1974; consecrated September 20, 1974; appointed First Bishop of Colorado Springs November 10, 1983; installed January 30, 1984; retired January 30, 2003. *Office: 228 N. Cascade Ave., Colorado Springs, CO 80903-1498.*

Most Reverend

MICHAEL J. SHERIDAN

Bishop of Colorado Springs; ordained May 29, 1971; appointed Titular Bishop of Tibiuca and Auxiliary Bishop of Saint Louis July 9, 1997; ordained September 3, 1997; appointed Coadjutor Bishop of Colorado Springs December 4, 2001; succeeded to the See January 30, 2003.

VIRTUS IN INFIRMITATE PERFICITUR

Diocesan Offices: 228 N. Cascade Ave., Colorado Springs, CO 80903-1498. Tel: 719-636-2345; Fax: 719-636-1216.

ESTABLISHED AND CREATED A DIOCESE JANUARY 30, 1984.

Square Miles 15,493.

Comprising the Counties of Chaffee, Cheyenne, Douglas, Elbert, El Paso, Kit Carson, Lake, Lincoln, Park and Teller.

For legal titles of parishes and diocesan institutions, consult the Diocesan Offices.

STATISTICAL OVERVIEW

Personnel	
Bishop	1
Retired Bishops	1
Priests: Diocesan Active in Diocese	23
Priests: Diocesan Active Outside Diocese	3
Priests: Retired, Sick or Absent	10
Number of Diocesan Priests	36
Religious Priests in Diocese	18
Total Priests in Diocese	54
Extern Priests in Diocese	13
Permanent Deacons in Diocese	38
Total Brothers	4
Total Sisters	112
Parishes	
Parishes	37
With Resident Pastor:	
Resident Diocesan Priests	25
Resident Religious Priests	5
Without Resident Pastor:	
Administered by Priests	4
Administered by Deacons	2
Administered by Lay People	1
Missions	5
Pastoral Centers	1
Professional Ministry Personnel:	
Brothers	1
Lay Ministers	77
Welfare	
Catholic Hospitals	2
Total Assisted	350,528
Health Care Centers	3
Total Assisted	1,809
Homes for the Aged	3
Total Assisted	1,809
Special Centers for Social Services	1
Total Assisted	75,000
Educational	
Diocesan Students in Other Seminaries	11
Students Religious	4
Total Seminarians	15
High Schools, Private	1
Total Students	346
Elementary Schools, Diocesan and Parish	5
Total Students	1,418
Catechesis/Religious Education:	
High School Students	2,701
Elementary Students	6,151
Total Students under Catholic Instruction	10,631
Teachers in the Diocese:	
Lay Teachers	118
Vital Statistics	
Receptions into the Church:	
Infant Baptism Totals	1,348
Minor Baptism Totals	95
Adult Baptism Totals	103
Received into Full Communion	154
First Communions	1,512
Confirmations	1,268
Marriages:	
Catholic	125
Interfaith	83
Total Marriages	208
Deaths	480
Total Catholic Population	82,540
Total Population	978,124

Former Bishops—Most Rev. RICHARD C. HANIFEN, D.D., J.C.L. (Retired), ord. June 6, 1959; appt. Titular Bishop of Abercorn and Auxiliary of Denver July 6, 1974; cons. Sept. 20, 1974; appt. first Bishop of Colorado Springs Nov. 10, 1983; installed Jan. 30, 1984; retired Jan. 30, 2003.

Diocesan Offices—228 N. Cascade Ave., Colorado Springs, 80903-1498. Tel: 719-636-2345; Fax: 719-636-1216. Office Hours: Mon.-Fri. 8-5.

Vicar General—Rev. Msgr. ROBERT E. JAEGER, V.G.

Vicar for Clergy—Rev. Msgr. ROBERT E. JAEGER, V.G.

Vicar for Hispanic Ministry—Rev. FRANCISCO J. QUEZADA.

Vicar for Religious—Rev. Msgr. RICARDO CORONADO-ARRASCUE, J.C.D.

Judicial Vicar and Chancellor—Rev. Msgr. RICARDO CORONADO-ARRASCUE, J.C.D.

Vice Chancellor—Rev. JAMES M. WILLIAMS.

Presbyteral Council—Most Rev. MICHAEL J. SHERIDAN, S.T.D.; Rev. Msgrs. ROBERT E. JAEGER, V.G.; RICARDO CORONADO-ARRASCUE, J.C.D.; Revs. ROBERT L. EPPING, C.S.C., V.F.; GEORGE V. FAGAN, J.C.L., V.F.; STEPHEN J. PARLET; KENNETH PRZYBYLA; FRANCISCO J. QUEZADA; MARK ZACKER.

College of Consultors—Most Rev. MICHAEL J. SHERIDAN, S.T.D.; Rev. Msgr. ROBERT E. JAEGER, V.G.; Revs. ROBERT L. EPPING, C.S.C., V.F.; ROBERT NEWBURY; KENNETH PRZYBYLA; FRANCISCO J. QUEZADA; MARK ZACKER.

Vicars Forane—Revs. ROBERT L. EPPING, C.S.C., V.F.; GEORGE V. FAGAN, J.C.L., V.F.; PAUL F. WICKER, V.F.; DONALD P. BROWNSTEIN, V.F.; AUGUST STEWART, V.F.

Deaneries—Metro-North Deanery (Colorado Springs): Rev. PAUL F. WICKER, V.F., Vicar. Metro-South Deanery (Colorado Springs): Rev. ROBERT L. EPPING, C.S.C., V.F., Vicar. Eastern Deanery: Rev. GEORGE V. FAGAN, J.C.L., V.F., Vicar. Northern Deanery: Rev. DONALD P. BROWNSTEIN, V.F., Vicar. Western Deanery: Rev. AUGUST STEWART, V.F., Vicar.

Diocesan Tribunal

Diocesan Tribunal—228 N. Cascade Ave., Colorado Springs, 80903. Tel: 719-636-2345.

Judicial Vicar—Rev. Msgr. RICARDO CORONADO-ARRASCUE, J.C.D.

Defender of the Bond—Rev. GEORGE V. FAGAN, J.C.L., V.F.

Judicial Auditor and Assessor—ANTHONY ST. LOUIS-SANCHEZ. Tel: 719-636-2345. Email: anthony@diocs.org.

Tribunal Secretary and Assistant to the Judicial Vicar and Ecclesiastical Notary—MARIA MAGALONG. Tel: 719-636-2345. Email: mmagalong@diocs.org.

Ecclesiastical Archivist and Ecclesiastical Notary—FAVIOLA O. TINSLEY. Tel: 719-636-2345. Email: ftinsley@diocs.org.

Advocates— Appointed individually for particular cases

Diocese of Colorado Springs, a Colorado Corporation Sole

Diocesan Offices and Ministries

Unless otherwise indicated offices and ministries are located in the Pastoral Center, 228 N. Cascade Ave., Colorado Springs, CO 80903. Tel. 719-636-2345. Web: www.diocs.org

Office of the Bishop—

Bishop—Most Rev. MICHAEL J. SHERIDAN, S.T.D. Tel: 719-636-2345.

Vicar General—Rev. Msgr. ROBERT E. JAEGER, V.G. Tel: 719-636-2345.

General Counsel and Chief of Staff—DOUGLAS M. FLINN, Esq. Tel: 719-636-2345. Email: dflinn@diocs.org.

Executive Assistant to the Bishop and Director of the Propagation of the Faith—ESPERANZA A. GRIFFITH. Tel: 719-636-2345. Email: egriffith@diocs.org.

Diocesan Senior Staff—

Vicar General—Rev. Msgr. ROBERT E. JAEGER, V.G. Tel: 719-636-2345.

Judicial Vicar and Chancellor—Rev. Msgr. RICARDO CORONADO-ARRASCUE, J.C.D. Tel: 719-636-2345.

Finance Officer—ROBERT G. DOERFLER JR. Tel: 719-636-2345. Email: rgdoerfler@diocs.org.

General Counsel and Chief of Staff—DOUGLAS M. FLINN, Esq. Tel: 719-636-2345. Email: dflinn@diocs.org.

President and CEO of Catholic Charities—JASON CHRISTENSEN. Tel: 719-636-2345. Email: jchristensen@ccharitiescs.org.

Diocesan Offices and Ministries—

Catholic Charismatic Renewal Services—Deacon CHARLES MATZKER, Liaison. Tel: 719-597-4249; Fax: 719-591-1816. Email: freshfire@q.com;

deaconchuck@holyapostlescc.org; CCRS c/o Holy Apostles Catholic Church, 4925 N. Carefree Cir., Colorado Springs, 80917.

Chancellor—

Chancellor and Judicial Vicar—Rev. Msgr. RICARDO CORONADO-ARRASCUE, J.C.D. Tel: 719-636-2345. *Vice Chancellor*, Rev. JAMES M. WILLIAMS. Tel: 719-636-2345. Email: vocations@diocs.org. *Assistant to the Chancellor*, FAVIOLA O. TINSLEY. Tel: 719-636-2345. Email: ftinsley@diocs.org.

The Colorado Catholic Herald—WILLIAM HOWARD, Editor. Email: editor@diocs.org; JAMES MYERS, Asst. Editor & Business Mgr. Tel: 719-636-2345. Email: jmyers@diocs.org.

Colorado Springs Council of Black Catholics—JULIA HYPOLITE, Pres. Tel: 719-574-8420. Email: anjuli_007@yahoo.com.

Colorado Springs Diocesan Council of Catholic Women—LALA MARTINEZ, Coord. Tel: 719-574-7403. Email: lita80916@yahoo.com.

Diaconate—Deacon PATRICK J. BIDON, Dir. Tel: 719-473-4633. Email: pat@diocs.org.

Finance Office—ROBERT G. DOERFLER JR., Dir. Tel: 719-636-2345. Email: rgdoerfler@diocs.org.

Director of Accounting—JERI THEIME. Tel: 719-636-2345. Email: jthieme@diocs.org.

Director of Properties and Construction—JANIS BALENTINE. Tel: 719-636-2345. Email: janisbalentine@diocs.org.

Benefits Clerk—KAREN SALAMON. Tel: 719-636-2345. Email: ksalamon@diocs.org.

Hispanic Ministry—Revs. FRANCISCO J. QUEZADA, Vicar. Tel: 719-636-2345. Email: fjquezada@diocs.org; JOHN TOEPFER, O.F.M.Cap. Tel: 719-473-4633. Email: fjtoepfer@diocs.org.

Human Resources—TERRI SOTOR, Dir. Tel: 719-636-2345. Email: tsotor@diocs.org.

Jail Ministry—Deacon PATRICK J. BIDON, Dir. Tel: 719-473-4633. Email: pat@diocs.org.

Mission Effectiveness—EDWARD GAFFNEY, Dir. Tel: 719-636-2345. Email: edgaffney@diocs.org.

Stewardship and Development—ROBERT C. FAUGHNAN, Dir. Tel: 719-636-2345. Email: rob@diocs.org.

Total Catholic Education—

Director and Superintendent of Catholic Schools—MICHELLE MAHER. Tel: 719-636-2345. Email: michelle@diocs.org. *Associate Director of Youth and Young Adult Ministries*, KATHY BULL. Tel: 719-636-2345. Email: kbull@diocs.org. *College Campus Ministry Coordinator*, VALERIE VELA. Tel: 719-636-2345. Email: valerie@diocs.org.

Office of Marriage and Family Life Coordinators—CHRISTIAN MEERT; CHRISTINE MEERT. Tel: 719-471-9702. Email: christian@cmeert.com.

Traumatic Brain Injury Ministry—Deacon PATRICK JONES, Coord. Email: lamontglen@mac.com.

Victim Assistance—BARBARA MAHONEY, Coord. Tel: 719-633-8182.

Vocations—Rev. JAMES M. WILLIAMS, Dir. Tel: 719-636-2345. Email: vocations@diocs.org.

CLERGY, PARISHES, MISSIONS AND PAROCHIAL SCHOOLS

CITY OF COLORADO SPRINGS

(COUNTY OF EL PASO)

1—ST. MARY CATHEDRAL (1887) Revs. Francisco J. Quezada; John Toepfer, O.F.M.Cap.; Deacons Patrick J. Bidon; Mark Griffith; Frank J. Ricotta Jr. Mailing Address: 22 W. Kiowa St., 80903.
Office: 15 W. Bijou St., 80903. Tel: 719-473-4633; Fax: 719-473-5248. Email: staff@stmaryscathedral.org. Web: www.stmaryscathedral.org.
Catechesis/Religious Program—Kerry Susser, D.R.E.; Terrie Hernandez, C.R.E. Students 425.

2—ST. ANDREW KIM QUASI PARISH (1981), (Korean), Rev. Dong-Ho Chae.
Office: 4515 E. Pikes Peak Ave., 80916. Tel: 719-638-0100; 719-638-0105 (Rectory); Fax: 719-638-0101.
Catechesis/Religious Program—Helen Hwang, D.R.E. Students 39.

3—CORPUS CHRISTI (1916) Rev. Mark Zacker; Deacons Benedict Cruise; Edward DeMattee.
Res.: 2313 Wood Ave., 80907. Tel: 719-633-1457; Fax: 719-473-7567. Email: parish@corpuschristicos.org. Web: corpuschristicos.org.
School—2410 N. Cascade Ave., 80907. Tel: 719-632-5092; Fax: 719-578-9124. Carol Johnson, Prin. Lay Teachers 24; Students 240.
Catechesis/Religious Program—Tel: 719-633-1457, Ext. 15. Gary Niemerg, D.R.E. Students 128.

4—DIVINE REDEEMER (1950) [JC] Rev. James J. Klein; Deacon Ray Milberg.
Parish Office—926 Farragut, 80909. Tel: 719-633-5559; Fax: 719-234-0358. Email: jklein@divineredeemer.net. Web: www.divineredeemer.net.
School—901 N. Logan, 80909. Tel: 719-471-7771; Fax: 719-234-0300. Email: jrigg@divineredeemer.net. Web: www.divineredeemer.net/school. Jim Rigg, Prin. Lay Teachers 22; Students 283.
Catechesis/Religious Program—Tel: 719-234-0342. Email: btittle@divineredeemer.net. Bernadette Tittle, D.R.E. Students 160.

5—ST. FRANCIS OF ASSISI (1981) Rev. John P. Cousins, O.F.M.Cap.; Deacon Michael Ciletti.
Office: 2650 Parish View, 80919. Tel: 719-599-5031; Fax: 719-599-3360. Email: parish@stfrancis.org.
Catechesis/Religious Program—Terri Kowalczyk, D.R.E. Students 276.

6—ST. GABRIEL THE ARCHANGEL (1998) Revs. C. Robert Manning (STL); Rafael Torres-Rico, Parochial Vicar; Deacon Kenneth Huard.
Office: 8755 Scarborough, 80920. Tel: 719-528-8407; Fax: 719-598-1696. Email: office@saintgabriel.net. Web: www.saintgabriel.net.
Catechesis/Religious Program—Students 501.

7—HOLY APOSTLES (1973) Revs. Paul F. Wicker; Kirk Slattery, Parochial Vicar; Deacons Michael Leverington; Charles Matzker; David Geislinger.
Res.: 4925 N. Carefree Cir., 80917. Tel: 719-597-4249; Fax: 719-591-1816. Email: haccoffice@holyapostlescc.org. Web: www.holyapostlescc.org.
Preschool—4925 N. Carefree Cir., 80917. Tel: 719-591-1566; Fax: 719-591-1816. Email: leslie@holyapostlescc.org. Web: www.holyapostle-spreschool.com. Leslie Versace, Dir. Lay Teachers 12; Students 118.
Catechesis/Religious Program—Tel: 719-597-4249. Email: msuperata@holyapostlescc.org. Mary Superata, D.R.E. Students 371.

8—HOLY TRINITY (1959) Rev. James M. Williams; Deacons David Geislinger; Philip Harrington.
Office: 3122 Poinsetta Dr., 80907. Tel: 719-633-2132; Fax: 719-633-0975. Email: holytrinitycatholicparish@comcast.net. Web: www.holytrinitycs.com.
Catechesis/Religious Program—Students 95.

9—ST. JOSEPH'S (Southgate) (1968) Revs. Gregory Golyzniak; Francis Maher (Retired); Deacon Ernest Romero; Randall Brungardt, Pastoral Assoc.
Res.: 1830 S. Corona Ave., 80905. Tel: 719-632-9903; Fax: 719-632-9170.
Catechesis/Religious Program—Tel: 719-635-3166. Students 286.

10—OUR LADY OF GUADALUPE (1948), (Hispanic), Rev. Alfredo Garcia (COL).
Res.: 2715 E. Pikes Peak, 80909. Tel: 719-633-7204; Fax: 719-630-3184. Email: olgassist@olgcos.org.
Catechesis/Religious Program—Students 345.

11—OUR LADY OF THE PINES-BLACK FOREST (1965) Deacon David Camous, Parish Dir.; Rev. Michael Butler, Sacramental Min.; Deacons Gene Eastham; Robert Broussard; David Evanitz.
Res.: 11020 Teachout Rd., 80908. Tel: 719-495-2351; Fax: 719-495-9062. Email: olp_blackforest@qwestoffice.net. Web: www.ourladyofthepines.org.
Catechesis/Religious Program—Vickie Welsh, D.R.E. Students 440.

12—ST. PATRICK (1981) Rev. Lawrence T. Solan; Deacons Richard Brown; Richard Antinora; Becky Gaughan, Dir. Liturgy & Music; Scarlet Tubridy, Bus. Admin.
Office: 6455 Brook Park Dr., 80918. Tel: 719-598-3595; Fax: 719-599-5741. Email: stpatscs@stpatscs.org. Web: www.stpatscs.org.
Catechesis/Religious Program—Angelita M. Dykes, Dir. Faith Formation; Eric Siverts, Dir. Adult Faith Formation; Donna Gaffney, Coord. Children's Faith Formation; Nate Rose, Coord. Youth & Young Adult Min. Students 710.

13—SAINT PAUL (1925) Rev. Msgr. Robert E. Jaeger; Rev. Andrzej Szczesnawicz; Deacons Richard J. Bowles; Michael Bowen.
Office: 9 El Pomar Rd., 80906. Tel: 719-471-9700; Fax: 719-471-3009. Email: stpaul@stpaulcos.org. Web: stpaulcos.org.
School—Pauline Memorial Catholic School, Tel: 719-632-1846; Fax: 719-632-0495. Stephanie Burke, Prin. Lay Teachers 15; Students 160.
Catechesis/Religious Program—Students 310.

14—SACRED HEART (1891) Revs. Robert L. Epping, C.S.C.; Vincent A. Kuna, C.S.C.
Office: 2021 W. Pikes Peak Ave., 80904. Tel: 719-633-8711; Fax: 719-633-1859. Email: tricommunity@qwestoffice.net. Web: tricommunity.org.
Catechesis/Religious Program—Email: vamorykuna@qwestoffice.net. Sr. Patricia King, F.M.A., D.R.E.; Sue Gerlach, Liturgy Director; Rob Plush, Dir. Youth Ministry. Students 177.
Mission—Our Lady of Perpetual Help 218 Ruxton Ave., Manitou Springs, El Paso Co. 80829.
Mission—Holy Rosary 4435 Holiday Tr., Cascade, El Paso Co. 80809.

15—THE VIETNAMESE HOLY MARTYRS PARISH (1993), (Vietnamese), [CEM] Rev. Joseph P. Minh Vu.
Church: 1133 N. Wahsatch Ave., 80903. Tel: 719-635-0679.
Catechesis/Religious Program—Students 40.

OUTSIDE THE CITY OF COLORADO SPRINGS

BAILEY, PARK CO., ST. MARY OF THE ROCKIES (1990) Rev. Kizito Osudibia.
Res.: 224 Buggy Whip Rd., P.O. Box 319, 80421-8319. Tel: 303-838-2375; Fax: 303-838-2375. Email: stmaryrockies@evcohs.com. Web: www.stmaryrockies.org.
Catechesis/Religious Program—Students 16.

BUENA VISTA, CHAFFEE CO., ST. ROSE OF LIMA (1880) Rev. Stephen J. Parlet; Deacon Richard Willburn.
Res.: 118 S. Gunnison, P.O. Box 458, 81211. Tel: 719-395-8424; Fax: 719-395-8424. Email: stroseoffice@rockmountains.net.
Catechesis/Religious Program—Students 71.
Mission—St. Joseph 5th & Castello, Fairplay, Park Co. 80440. Tel: 719-395-8424. (Send all correspondence to Buena Vista address.)

BURLINGTON, KIT CARSON CO., ST. CATHERINE OF SIENA (1916) Rev. Ernest W. Bond.
Res. & Mailing Address: P.O. Box 266, Stratton, 80836. Tel: 719-348-5336; Fax: 719-348-4601.
Church: 450 3rd St., P.O. Box 38, 80807. Tel: 719-346-7156; Fax: 719-346-7172. Email: strattonstcharles@yahoo.com.
Catechesis/Religious Program—Students 61.

CALHAN, EL PASO CO., ST. MICHAEL'S (1905) Rev. Paul F. Wicker; Tony Rawe, Admin. & Contact Person.
Res.: 574 8th St., Box 199, 80808. Tel: 719-347-2290; Fax: 719-347-2848.
Catechesis/Religious Program—Students 37.

CASTLE ROCK, DOUGLAS CO., ST. FRANCIS OF ASSISI (1888) Rev. Bradford Noonan; Deacon Thomas F. Liotta.
Res.: 2746 Fifth St., 80104. Tel: 303-688-3025; Fax: 303-688-4016. Web: www.stfranciscr.org.
Catechesis/Religious Program—Students 873.

CHEYENNE WELLS, CHEYENNE CO., SACRED HEART (1912) Rev. Kirk Slattery.
Res.: 105 W. 5th N., 80810. Tel: 719-767-5272.
Mission—St. Augustine (1918) P.O. Box 82, Kit Carson, Cheyenne Co. 80825. Tel: 719-962-3552.
Catechesis/Religious Program—Students 29.

ELIZABETH, ELBERT CO., OUR LADY OF THE VISITATION Rev. Brian Quinn Mohan.
34201 County Rd. 33, P.O. Box 1689, 80107. Tel: 303-646-4964; Fax: 303-646-9811. Email: olvoffice@avemariaonline.org. Web: www.ourladyofthevisitation.org.
Catechesis/Religious Program—Students 163.

FALCON, EL PASO CO., ST. BENEDICT QUASI-PARISH (2005) Deacon Lynn Sherman.
11625 Falcon Hwy., 80831. Tel: 719-495-1426. Email: stbeninfo@qwestoffice.net. Web: stbenedictfalcon.org.
Catechesis/Religious Program—Harriet Bauer, D.R.E. Students 90.

FOUNTAIN, EL PASO CO., ST. JOSEPH (1936) Merged with Holy Family, Security to St. Dominic, Security.

HIGHLANDS RANCH, DOUGLAS CO.

1—ST. MARK CATHOLIC CHURCH (2000) Rev. John Auer; Deacon Garrett Christnacht.
Mailing Address: 9905 Foothills Canyon Blvd., 80129. Tel: 720-348-9700; Fax: 720-344-6847. Web: www.stmarkhighlandsranch.org.
Catechesis/Religious Program—Students 600.

2—PAX CHRISTI CATHOLIC CHURCH (1988) Rev. Kenneth Przybyla.
Office: 5761 McArthur Ranch Rd., Littleton, 80124. Tel: 303-799-1036; Fax: 303-799-1072. Email: pastor@paxchristi.org. Web: www.paxchristi.org.
Catechesis/Religious Program—Sue Giudici, D.R.E. Students 751.

LEADVILLE, LAKE CO., HOLY FAMILY PARISH (1878) [CEM] [JC] Rev. August Stewart.
Office: 609 Poplar St., 80461. Tel: 719-486-1382; Fax: 719-486-3930. Email: himtnchurch@hotmail.com.
Res.: 424 W. 2nd, 80461.
Catechesis/Religious Program—Students 49.

LIMON, LINCOLN CO., OUR LADY OF VICTORY (1925) Rev. George V. Fagan.
Res.: 425 H Ave., P.O. Box 790, 80828. Tel: 719-775-2118.
Catechesis/Religious Program—Limon & Missions, Fax: 719-775-9406. Students 60.
Mission—St. Anthony of Padua 133 Fifth St., P.O. Box 275, Hugo, Lincoln Co. 80821. (Send all correspondence to Limon address.)
Mission—St. Mary [CEM] Flagler, Kit Carson Co.

80815. (Send all correspondence to Limon address.)

MONUMENT, EL PASO CO., ST. PETER (1911) Rev. Jeffrey A. Schneibel, C.S.C.; Deacon Michael Balchus.
Mailing Address: P.O. Box 827, 80132. Tel: 719-481-3511; Fax: 719-481-9606. Web: www.petertherock.org.
Res.: 55 N. Jefferson, 80132. Tel: 719-481-3511; Fax: 719-481-9606.
School—(Grades PreSchool-5) Tel: 719-481-1855; Fax: 719-955-0509. Kimberly Schindler, Prin.; Terri Mahon, Librarian. Teachers & Aides 20; Students 124.
Catechesis/Religious Program—Donna Hessel, Catechetical Leader. Students 280.

PARKER, DOUGLAS CO., AVE MARIA (1983) Revs. Donald P. Brownstein; Robert G. Newbury Jr., Parochial Vicar; Deacon Timothy "Tim" Walsh.
Res.: 9056 E. Parker Rd., 80138-7209. Tel: 303-841-3750; Fax: 303-841-2412. Web: www.avemariaonline.org.
School—(2000)Tel: 720-842-5400; Fax: 720-842-5402. Web: www.aveangels.org. Mrs. Theresa Loiselle, Prin. Lay Teachers 24; Students 460.
Catechesis/Religious Program—Lynne K. Lane, D.R.E.; David Hall, C.R.E. Students 1,016.

SALIDA, CHAFFEE CO., ST. JOSEPH (1907) Rev. Bogdan Siewiera (Poland). In Res., Rev. Anthony C. Uhl, Chap. Colorado Dept. of Corrections (Retired).
Res.: 320 E. 5th St., P.O. Box 847, 81201. Tel: 719-539-6419; Fax: 719-539-7127. Email: stjoseph@salida.net.
Catechesis/Religious Program—Students 40.

SECURITY, EL PASO CO.
1—ST. DOMINIC (2008) Rev. Lawrence W. Carmody; Deacons Albert E. Kimminau; Robert Cole.
Res.: 565 Marquette Dr., 80911. Tel: 719-392-7653; Fax: 719-392-1651. Email: st.dominic@pcisys.net. Web: www.coloradostdominic.org.
Catechesis/Religious Program—Cathy Jane King, D.R.E. Students 475.
2—HOLY FAMILY (1957) Merged with St. Joseph, Fountain to form St. Dominic, Security.
3—IMMACULATE CONCEPTION PARISH (2006) Rev. Stephane Dupre, F.S.S.P.
626 Aspen Dr., 80911. Mailing Address: P.O. Box 5211, 80931-5211. Tel: 719-382-0121.
Catechesis/Religious Program—

STRATTON, KIT CARSON CO., ST. CHARLES BORROMEO (1910) Rev. Ernest W. Bond.
Res.: 513 Colorado Ave., P.O. Box 266, 80836. Fax: 719-348-4601. Email: strattonstcharles@yahoo.com.
Church: P.O. Box 266, 80836. Tel: 719-348-5336.
Catechesis/Religious Program—Students 65.

WOODLAND PARK, TELLER CO., OUR LADY OF THE WOODS (1954), (Teller Co. Catholic Community) Rev. Donald W. Dilg, C.S.C., Parish Admin.; Deacons Anthony McKee; Patrick Jones.
Office: 116 S. West St., P.O. Box 5590, 80866-5590. Tel: 719-687-9345; Fax: 719-687-0893.
Catechesis/Religious Program—Students 143.
Mission—St. Peter's 3rd & Golden, Cripple Creek, Teller Co. 80813. (Send all correspondence to Woodland Park address.)
Mission—St. Victor's 2nd & Portland, Victor, Teller Co. 80860. (Send all correspondence to Woodland Park address.)

On Duty Outside Diocese:
Revs.—
Grabrian, Dennis, 7172 Regional St., PMB 434, Dublin, CA 94568.
Jenson, Jens-Peter, Jr., St. Augustine Cathedral Parish, 192 S. Stone Ave., Tucson, AZ 85701.
Ponce, James, Graduate Degree Canon Law; Pontifical North American College, Rome (Casa Santa Maria)

Retired:
Most Rev.—
Hanifen, Richard C., D.D., J.C.L., 228 N. Cascade Ave., 80903.
Rev. Msgrs.—
Dunn, Donald F., 411 Lakewood Cir., # A-8-7, 80910.
Slattery, John F., 7665 Assisi Heights, 80919-3836.
Revs.—
Battiato, Patrick, P.O. Box 5402, 80931.
Bruggeman, Gerald H., Chap., 23 E. Van Buren, 80907.
Gagliardo, Anthony (STF), 1301 Wyncoop Dr., 80909.
Halloran, James F., Medallion, 1719 E. Bijou St., #601, 80909.
Halloran, Joseph H., Fountain Terrace Apartments, 3211 E. Fountain Blvd., #103, 80910.
Krenzke, John W., 2626 Osceola St., Apt. 912 W., Denver, 80212.
Maher, Francis (JOL), 965-B Tenderfoot Hill Rd., 80906.
Myers, Rawley J., 26 W. Taylor, Apt. 1, 80907.
Smigiel, Walter J. (PBL), 3517 Atlantic Dr., 80910.
Stahl, Allen M. (ORL), P.O. Box 12610, 80902.
Uhl, Anthony C., P.O. Box 847, Salida, 81201.
Vollmer, William C., 35 Tilly Ln., Castle Rock, 80104.

Permanent Deacons:
Antinora, Richard, St. Patrick, Colorado Springs
Balchus, Michael, St. Peter Parish, Monument
Bidon, Patrick J., Dir. Office of the Diaconate & Coord. Jail Ministry, St. Mary's Cathedral, Colorado Springs
Bowen, Michael, M.D., St. Paul, Colorado Springs
Bowles, Richard, St. Paul, Colorado Springs; Fort Carson, Colorado Springs
Broussard, Robert, Our Lady of the Pines, Colorado Springs
Brown, Richard, St. Patrick, Colorado Springs
Camous, Dave, Our Lady of the Pines, Colorado Springs
Christnacht, Garrett, St. Mark, Highlands Ranch
Ciletti, Michael, Natl. Chap., St. Francis of Assisi, Colorado Springs; Faith and Light, USA
Cruise, Benedict, (Retired), Colorado Springs
DeMattee, Edward, Corpus Christi, Colorado Springs
Eastham, Eugene S., Our Lady of the Pines, Colorado Springs
Eberwein, Roger, (Retired), Colorado Springs
Evanitz, David, Our Lady of the Pines, Colorado Springs
Geislinger, David, Holy Apostles, Colorado Springs
Griffith, Mark, St. Mary's Cathedral, Colorado Springs
Huard, Kenneth, St. Gabriel the Archangel, Colorado Springs
Huber, Robert A., (Retired)
Jones, Patrick, Our Lady of the Woods, Woodland Park; Coord. Traumatic Brain Injury Ministry
Kimminau, Albert E., St. Dominic, Security
Kuss, Leroy, Hospice Min., Hospice, Colorado Springs
Leverington, Michael, Holy Apostles, Colorado Springs
Linehan, George D., Jr., (Retired), Parker
Liotta, Thomas F., St. Francis of Assisi, Castle Rock
Matzker, Charles, Contact Person for Catholic Charismatic Renewal Svcs., Holy Apostles Church, Colorado Springs
McKee, Anthony, Our Lady of the Woods, Woodland Park
McLean, Arthur J., (Retired), Colorado Springs
Milberg, Raymond, Divine Redeemer, Colorado Springs
Moss, Charles J., (Serving in North Carolina)
Ricotta, Frank J., Jr., St. Mary's Cathedral, Colorado Springs
Romero, Ernest, St. Joseph, Colorado Springs
Sherman, Lynn, Parish Dir., St. Benedict's, Falcon
Sherpa, Lee, (Retired), Colorado Springs
Specht, Charles W., (Retired), Colorado Springs
Toner, James, (Serving in Connecticut)
Waller, Robert L., (Serving Archdiocese Military Services, USA)
Walsh, Timothy "Tim", Ave Maria, Parker
Willburn, Richard, St. Rose of Lima, Buena Vista

INSTITUTIONS LOCATED IN THE DIOCESE

[A] HIGH SCHOOLS

COLORADO SPRINGS. **St. Mary's High School*, 2501 E. Yampa, 80909. Tel: 719-635-7540; Fax: 719-471-7623. Email: rcross@smhscs.org. Web: www.smhscs.org. Ms. Karen Levi, Contact Person; John D. McCord, Prin.; Robyn Cross, Admissions. Lay Teachers 31; Students 396.

[B] EDUCATIONAL INSTITUTIONS

COLORADO SPRINGS. **The Center at Benet Hill Monastery* Religious/spiritual education & formation, 3190 Benet Ln., 80921-1509. Tel: 719-633-0655; Fax: 719-471-0403. Email: benet@quest.net. Web: www.benethillmonastery.org. Sr. Francine Stallbaumer, O.S.B., Contact Person. Sisters 8; Lay Staff 12; Total Assisted Annually 1,500.

[C] GENERAL HOSPITALS

COLORADO SPRINGS. *St. Francis Health Center* (1968) 825 E. Pikes Peak Ave., 80903. Tel: 719-634-2156; Fax: 303-804-8198. Email: krisordelheide@centura.org. Kris Ordelheide, Contact Person. An operating unit of Catholic Health Initiatives Colorado (an affiliate of Catholic Health Initiatives)
Penrose-St. Francis Health Services, 2222 N. Nevada, P.O. Box 7021, 80907. Tel: 719-776-5007; Fax: 719-776-2770. Email: margaretsabin@centura.org. Web: www.centura.org. Mr. Larry Seidl, Vice Pres. Mission Integration. An operating unit of Catholic Health Initiatives Colorado (an affiliate of Catholic Health Initiatives) Bed Capacity 468; Total Staff 2,800; Patients Assisted Annually 350,528.
Penrose Hospital An operating unit of Catholic Health Initiatives Colorado (an affiliate of Catholic Health Initiatives), 2222 N. Nevada, 80907. Tel: 719-776-5000; Fax: 719-776-2770. Revs. Gerald H. Bruggeman, Sacramental Min. (Retired); Dan Ayers, Sacramental Min.; Rosemary Partridge, Catholic Chap. Sponsored by Catholic Health Initiatives., An operating unit of Catholic Health Initiatives Colorado (an affiliate of Catholic Health Initiatives) Priests 2.
St. Francis Medical Center An operating unit of Catholic Health Initiatives Colorado (an affiliate of Catholic Health Initiatives), 6001 E. Woodmen Rd., 80923. Tel: 719-571-1000. An operating unit of Catholic Health Initiatives Colorado (an affiliate of Catholic Health Initiatives)

[D] NURSING HOMES

COLORADO SPRINGS. **St. Francis Nursing Center*, 7550 Assisi Heights, 80919. Tel: 719-598-1336; Fax: 719-598-6472. Rev. Cyrus Gallagher, O.F.M.Cap., Spiritual Svcs. Dir.; Vivian Booker, Admin. Sisters of St. Francis of Perpetual Adoration. Total Staff 165; Beds 102; Total Assisted Annually 82.

[E] SPECIAL CARE FACILITIES

COLORADO SPRINGS. *Catholic Health Initiatives Colorado Foundation*, 961 E. Colorado Ave., 80903-3776. Tel: 719-634-6725; Fax: 719-630-0873. Email: Jerrybaqq@centura.org. Gerald D. Baqq, Pres. & CEO.
Medalion Foundation An affiliate division of Catholic Health Initiatives Colorado Foundation (an affiliate of Catholic Health Initiatives)
Namaste Alzheimer Foundation An affiliate division of Catholic Health Initiatives Colorado Foundation (an affiliate of Catholic Health Initiatives)
Penrose-St. Francis Health Foundation An affiliate division of Catholic Health Initiatives Colorado Foundation (an affiliate of Catholic Health Initiatives)
Medalion Retirement Community, 1719 E. Bijou St., 80909. Tel: 719-381-1000; Fax: 719-381-4978. Dave Campbell, Chap. An operating unit of Catholic Health Initiatives Colorado. An affiliate of Catholic Health Initiatives. Skilled Nursing Beds 60; Assisted Living Beds 30; Independent Living Apartments 78.
Namaste Alzheimer Center, 2 Penrose Blvd., 80906. Tel: 719-776-6300; Fax: 719-520-9709. JoAnn Harrison, Chap. An operating unit of Catholic Health Initiatives Colorado. An affiliate of Catholic Health Initiatives; Adult Day Programs for seniors with Alzheimer's or dementia. Skilled Nursing/Alzheimer Beds 62.

[F] RESIDENCES FOR MEN RELIGIOUS

COLORADO SPRINGS. *Our Lady of the Angels Friary*, 8095 Walker Rd., 80908. Tel: 719-495-2058. Revs. Frank X. Grinko, O.F.M. Cap., Guardian; John Toepfer, O.F.M.Cap., Vicar; Jeff Ernst, O.F.M.Cap.; Bro. Felix Shinsky, O.F.M.Cap.
Solanus Casey Friary, 15 W. View Place, 80903. Tel: 719-632-7584; Fax: 719-632-7718. Revs. John P. Cousins, O.F.M.Cap., Guardian; Cyrus Gallagher, O.F.M.Cap.; Myron Flax, O.F.M.Cap.; Felix Petrovsky, O.F.M. Cap., Vicar.

CASCADE. *Holy Cross Novitiate*, 7872 W. Hwy. 24, Box 749, 80809. Tel: 719-684-9277. Rev. Thomas F. Lemos, C.S.C., Dir. of Novices & Supr.; Bros. Thomas Moser, C.S.C., Asst. Dir.; Thomas Krieter, C.S.C., Steward & Dir. of Facilities. Congregation of Holy Cross. Priests 2; Brothers 2; Novices 4. In Res. Rev. Donald W. Dilg, C.S.C.

SEDALIA. *Sacred Heart Jesuit Community*, Box 185, 80135-0185. Tel: 303-688-5198; Fax: 303-688-9633. Email: shrinformation@quest.net. Web: www.sacredheartretreat.org. Revs. Vincent E. Hovley, S.J., Supr.; Edward Kinerk, S.J.; Richard W. Dunphy, S.J.; E. Eugene Arthur, S.J.; Bro. Richard P. May, S.J.

[G] RESIDENCES FOR WOMEN RELIGIOUS

COLORADO SPRINGS. **Benet Hill Monastery*, 3190 Benet Ln., 80921-1509. Tel: 719-633-0655; Fax: 719-471-0403. Email: info@benethillmonastery.org. Web: www.benethillmonastery.org. Sisters Anne Stedman, O.S.B., Prioress; Diane Liston, O.S.B., Community Archivist. Motherhouse of the Benedictine Sisters (1963).; Properties owned:

Benet Hill Monastery and Ministry Center. Professed Sisters 33.

Sisters of St. Francis of Perpetual Adoration, 7665 Assisi Hts., 80919-3837. Tel: 719-598-5486; Fax: 719-598-1578. Email: stephanie@stfrancis.org. Web: www.stfrancis.org. Sr. Stephanie McReynolds, O.S.F., Prov. Email: stephanie@stfrancis.org; Rev. Msgr. John F. Slattery, Chap. (Retired). Provincial House. Sisters of St. Francis of Perpetual Adoration, Province of St. Joseph (The Sisters of St. Francis of Colorado Springs). Professed Sisters 61.

[H] RETREAT CENTERS

COLORADO SPRINGS. **Benet Pines*, 15880 Hwy. 83, 80921. Tel: 719-495-2574; Fax: 719-495-4469. Email: bpinescs@hotmail.com. Web: www.benethillmonastery.org. Sr. Josie Sanchez, O.S.B., Center Dir. Total in Residence 2; Total Staff 2.

Franciscan Retreat Center, Inc., 7740 Deer Hill Grove, 80919-3836. Tel: 719-955-7025; Fax: 719-260-8044. Email: frc@stfrancis.org. Web: www.franciscanretreatcenter.org. Sr. Joanne Moeller, F.S.P.A., Dir. Total Guests 11,000; Total Staff 9.

SEDALIA. *Sacred Heart Jesuit Retreat House*, Box 185, 80135-0185. Tel: 303-688-4198; Fax: 303-688-9633. Email: shrinformation@quest.net. Web: www.sacredheartretreat.org. Revs. Edward Kinerk, S.J.; Richard W. Dunphy, S.J.; E. Eugene Arthur, S.J.; Vincent E. Hovley, S.J.; Bro. Richard P. May, S.J.; Sr. Eileen Currie, M.S.C. Total in Residence 5.

[I] MISCELLANEOUS LISTINGS

COLORADO SPRINGS. *All for the Glory of God Ministry*, 5885 Del Paz Dr., 80918. Tel: 719-593-2120; Fax: 719-593-2120.

Ave Maria Catholic School Corporation, 228 N. Cascade Ave., 80903. Tel: 719-636-2345; Fax: 719-636-1216. Michelle Maher, Contact Person.

Catholic Center at the Citadel, 750 Citadel Dr. E., Ste. 3056, 80909. Tel: 719-573-7364. Web: www.catholicchapelmall.org. Revs. Frank X. Grinko, O.F.M. Cap., Dir.; Myron Flax, O.F.M.Cap.; Felix Petrovsky, O.F.M. Cap.; Jeff Ernst, O.F.M.Cap.

Catholic Charities of Colorado Springs, Inc., 228 N. Cascade Ave., 80903. Tel: 719-636-2345; Fax: 719-636-1216. Email: info@ccharitiescs.org. Web: www.ccharitiescs.org. Jason Christensen, Pres. & CEO.

The Catholic Foundation of the Diocese of Colorado Springs, Inc., 228 N. Cascade Ave., 80903. Tel: 719-636-2345; Fax: 719-636-1216. Web: www.diocs.org. Robert G. Doerfler Jr., Pres. & Exec. Dir.

Catholic Housing Corporation of Colorado Springs, 2445 Wimbleton Ct., 80920.

Colorado Springs Cursillo Movement, P.O. Box 25655, 80936.

Douglas County Catholic School Corporation, 228 N. Cascade Ave., 80903.

Fostering Hope Foundation, 3055 Sunnybrook Ln., 80904. Tel: 719-635-6756.

Franciscan Community Counseling, 7665 Assisi Heights, 80919. Tel: 719-955-7008; Fax: 719-598-0346. Email: sharon@stfrancis.org. Web: www.franciscancommunitycounseling.org. Sharon Compono, Exec. Dir.. Email: sharon@stfrancis.org. Total Staff 12; Total Assisted Annually 500.

The Franciscan Foundation of Colorado Springs, 7665 Assisi Hts., 80919-3836. Tel: 719-598-5486; Fax: 719-532-0567. Email: stephanie@stfrancis.org. Sr. Stephanie McReynolds, O.S.F., Pres. & Prov.

**St. Mary's Catholic Education Foundation*, 2501 Yampa St., 80809. LeRoy K. Hoelting, Contact Person.

**Partners in Housing, Inc.*, 455 Gold Pass Heights, 80906. Tel: 719-473-8890; Fax: 719-635-9360. Email: office@partnersinhousing.org. Web: www.partnersinhousing.org. Frank Stampf, Exec. Dir.; Barbara Blumer, Dir. of Support Svcs. Total Staff 21; Total Assisted Annually (Adults 136); (Children 212); (Families 97) 109.

**S.E.T. of Colorado Springs dba S.E.T Family Medical Clinic* 825 E. Pikes Peak Ave., Bldg. 29, 80903. Tel: 719-776-8950; Fax: 719-776-8855. Email: Zelnajoseph@centura.org; info@setofcs.org. Web: www.setofcs.org. Zelna Joseph, Pres. & CEO.

**St. Thomas Aquinas Society*, P.O. Box 62908, 80962-2908. Tel: 719-448-0020. Web: www.StThomasAquinasSociety.org.

**Villa San Jose, Inc.*, 1810 S. Corona Ave., 80905. Tel: 719-632-7444; Fax: 719-520-9345. Web: www.archhousing.com. Total in Residence 50; Total Staff 9.

**Villa Santa Maria, Inc.*, 405 E. St. Elmo Ave., 80906. Tel: 719-520-9344; Fax: 719-520-9345. Web: www.archhousing.com. Total Staff 10; Total in Residence 50.

Women Partnering, 10 S. Institute, 80903. Tel: 719-577-9404; Fax: 719-577-9407. Email: womenpar@comcast.net. Web: stfrancis.org.

NECROLOGY

† Dwyer, Dennis E., (Retired)—Died Jan. 15, 2009

† McHugh, Owen Joseph, (Retired)—Died Feb. 24, 2009

Diocese of Columbus

(Dioecesis Columbensis)

Most Reverend

FREDERICK F. CAMPBELL, PH.D., D.D.

Bishop of Columbus; ordained May 31, 1980; appointed Titular Bishop of Afufenia and Auxiliary Bishop of St. Paul and Minneapolis March 2, 1999; consecrated May 14, 1999; appointed Eleventh Bishop of Columbus October 14, 2004; installed January 13, 2005. *Res.: 198 E. Broad St., Columbus, OH 43215.* Tel: 614-224-2251.

Most Reverend

JAMES A. GRIFFIN, J.D., J.C.L.

Retired Bishop of Columbus; ordained May 28, 1960; consecrated Titular Bishop of Holar and Auxiliary to the Bishop of Cleveland August 1, 1979; appointed Tenth Bishop of Columbus February 7, 1983; installed April 25, 1983; retired October 14, 2004; named Diocesan Administrator October 18, 2004 to January 12, 2005. *Mailing Address: 198 E. Broad St., Columbus, OH 43215.*

(Diocesan Seal)

Chancery Office: 198 E. Broad St., Columbus, OH 43215. Tel: 614-224-2251; Fax: 614-224-6306.

ESTABLISHED 1868.

Square Miles 11,310.

Comprises the following 23 Counties in the State of Ohio: Hardin, Marion, Morrow, Knox, Holmes, Tuscarawas, Union, Delaware, Licking, Coshocton, Madison, Franklin, Muskingum, Fayette, Pickaway, Fairfield, Perry, Ross, Hocking, Pike, Jackson, Vinton and Scioto.

For legal titles of parishes and diocesan institutions, consult the Chancery Office.

STATISTICAL OVERVIEW

Personnel	
Bishop	1
Retired Bishops	1
Priests: Diocesan Active in Diocese	105
Priests: Diocesan Active Outside Diocese	5
Priests: Retired, Sick or Absent	52
Number of Diocesan Priests	162
Religious Priests in Diocese	27
Total Priests in Diocese	189
Extern Priests in Diocese	13
Ordinations:	
Diocesan Priests	1
Transitional Deacons	3
Permanent Deacons in Diocese	102
Total Brothers	1
Total Sisters	267
Parishes	
Parishes	106
With Resident Pastor:	
Resident Diocesan Priests	88
Resident Religious Priests	5
Without Resident Pastor:	
Administered by Priests	10
Administered by Deacons	3
Missions	3
Professional Ministry Personnel:	
Sisters	16
Lay Ministers	32
Welfare	
Catholic Hospitals	6
Total Assisted	803,176
Homes for the Aged	20
Total Assisted	3,125
Special Centers for Social Services	6
Total Assisted	210,428
Educational	
Seminaries, Diocesan	1
Students from This Diocese	18
Students from Other Diocese	102
Diocesan Students in Other Seminaries	7
Total Seminarians	25
Colleges and Universities	2
Total Students	3,849
High Schools, Diocesan and Parish	11
Total Students	4,808
Elementary Schools, Diocesan and Parish	42
Total Students	10,496
Elementary Schools, Private	2
Total Students	82
Catechesis/Religious Education:	
High School Students	876
Elementary Students	14,037
Total Students under Catholic Instruction	34,173
Teachers in the Diocese:	
Priests	15
Sisters	5
Lay Teachers	1,137
Vital Statistics	
Receptions into the Church:	
Infant Baptism Totals	3,536
Minor Baptism Totals	198
Adult Baptism Totals	317
Received into Full Communion	437
First Communions	3,627
Confirmations	3,838
Marriages:	
Catholic	514
Interfaith	539
Total Marriages	1,053
Deaths	1,646
Total Catholic Population	257,374
Total Population	2,511,332

Former Bishops—Rt. Revs. SYLVESTER HORTON ROSECRANS, D.D., ord. June 5, 1852; cons. Titular Bishop of Pompeiopolis and Auxiliary to the Bishop of Cincinnati, March 25, 1862; transferred to Columbus, March 3, 1868; died Oct. 21, 1878; JOHN AMBROSE WATTERSON, D.D., ord. Aug. 9, 1868; cons. Aug. 8, 1880; died April 17, 1899; Most Revs. HENRY MOELLER, D.D., cons. Bishop of Columbus, Aug. 25, 1900; promoted to the Archiepiscopal See of Areopolis and made Coadjutor to the Archbishop of Cincinnati, with the right of succession, April 27, 1903; succeeded to the See of Cincinnati, Oct. 31, 1904; died Jan. 5, 1925; JAMES JOSEPH HARTLEY, D.D., cons. Feb. 25, 1904; died Jan. 12, 1944; MICHAEL JOSEPH READY, D.D., cons. Dec. 14, 1944; died May 2, 1957; CLARENCE GEORGE ISSENMANN, S.T.D., cons. Titular Bishop of Phytea and Auxiliary Bishop of Cincinnati May 25, 1954; appt. Bishop of Columbus Dec. 5, 1957; transferred to Cleveland as Apostolic Administrator. "cum jure successionis," Oct. 7, 1964; died July 27, 1982; His Eminence JOHN CARDINAL CARBERRY, D.D., S.T.D., J.C.D., Ph.D., appt. Titular Bishop of Elis and Coadjutor of Lafayette in Indiana "cum jure successionis," May 3, 1956; cons. July 25, 1956; succeeded to See Nov. 20, 1957; transferred to Columbus Jan. 20, 1965; transferred to the Archdiocese of St. Louis, March 24, 1968; created Cardinal April 28, 1969; Most Revs. CLARENCE E. ELWELL, D.D., cons. Dec. 21, 1962; appt. to Columbus May 29, 1968; died Feb. 16, 1973; EDWARD J. HERRMANN, D.D., appt. Auxiliary Bishop of Washington and Titular Bishop of Lamzella, March 4, 1966; cons. April 26, 1966; appt. Ninth Bishop of Columbus, June 26, 1973; installed Aug. 21, 1973; retired Sept. 18, 1982; named Apostolic Administrator Sept. 1982 to April 1983; died Dec. 22, 1999; JAMES A. GRIFFIN, J.D., J.C.L., ord. May 28, 1960; cons. Titular Bishop of Holar and Auxiliary to the Bishop of Cleveland Aug. 1, 1979; appt. Tenth Bishop of Columbus Feb. 7, 1983; installed April 25, 1983; resigned Oct. 14, 2004.

Vicar General—Rev. Msgr. STEPHAN J. MOLONEY, M.A., M.Div., J.C.L.

Episcopal Moderator for Charities and Social Concerns—MARK H. HUDDY, J.D.

Episcopal Moderator for Education—LUCIA D. MCQUAIDE, M.S.Ed., M.Rel.Ed.

Episcopal Moderator for Spiritual Life and Parish Ministry—Deacon THOMAS M. BERG JR., B.A., M.J., M.P.S., (Acting).

Chancery Office—198 E. Broad St., Columbus, 43215. Tel: 614-224-2251; Fax: 614-224-6306. Office Hours: Mon.-Fri. 8-4:30

Chancellor—Very Rev. SHAWN D. CORCORAN, M.Div., J.C.L.

Vice Chancellor—Deacon THOMAS M. BERG JR., B.A., M.J., M.P.S.

College of Consultors—Most Rev. FREDERICK F. CAMPBELL, D.D., Ph.D.; Rev. Msgr. STEPHAN J. MOLONEY, M.A., M.Div., J.C.L.; Very Rev. SHAWN D. CORCORAN, M.Div., J.C.L.; Rev. KEVIN J. KAVANAGH; Rev. Msgrs. GEORGE J. SCHLEGEL, B.A.; WILLIAM A. DUNN; Revs. JOHN E. STATTMILLER; MATTHEW N. HOOVER; Rev. Msgr. FRANK J. MEAGHER (Retired).

Parochial Examiners—Rev. JAMES A. WALTER; Rev. Msgr. STEPHAN J. MOLONEY, M.A., M.Div., J.C.L.; Revs. CHARLES E. COTTON; JAMES C. CSASZAR; WILLIAM J. FAUSTNER; Very Rev. G. MICHAEL GRIBBLE, M.Div.; Revs. THEODORE F. MACHNIK; JAMES A. KLIMA; F. RICHARD SNOKE; JOHN E. STATTMILLER; JAN C. P. SULLIVAN; PATRICK A. TONER; MICHAEL B. WATSON, M.Div., B.S.; DAVID J. YOUNG.

Deaneries—Deanery 1: Center-South Columbus: Very Rev. G. MICHAEL GRIBBLE, M.Div., St. Joseph Cathedral, 212 E. Broad St., Columbus, 43215-3767. Deanery 2: Northwest: Rev. MICHAEL B. WATSON, M.Div., B.S., St. Andrew Church, 1899 McCoy Rd., Columbus, 43220-4499. Deanery 3: North High: Rev. STANLEY L. (STASH) DAILEY, St. Michael Church, 5750 N. High St., Worthington, 43085-3986. Deanery 4: Northland: Rev. CHARLES E. COTTON, St. Elizabeth Church, 6077 Sharon

Woods Blvd., Columbus, 43229. Deanery 5: West: Rev. PATRICK A. TONER, St. Joseph Church, 640 W. Main St., Plain City, 43064. Deanery 6: East: Rev. JAMES A. KLIMA, Seton Parish, 600 Hill Rd. N., Pickerington, 43147-9201. Deanery 7: Marion: Rev. DAVID J. YOUNG, Our Lady of Lourdes Church, 222 E. Highland Ave., Ada, 45810-1122. Deanery 8: Muskingum-Perry: Rev. JAMES C. CSASZAR, St. Rose Church, 309 N. Main St., New Lexington, 43764-1204. Deanery 9: Knox Licking: Rev. F. RICHARD SNOKE, St. Luke Church, 307 S. Market St., P.O. Box P, Danville, 43014-0616. Deanery 10: Tuscarawas-Holmes-Coshocton: Rev. WILLIAM J. FAUSTNER, St. Francis DeSales Church, 440 River St., Newcomerstown, 43832-1499. Deanery 11: Lancaster: Rev. JAMES A. WALTER, Mailing Address: St. Joseph Church, P.O. Box 209, Sugar Grove, 43155-0209. Deanery 12: Chillicothe: Rev. JAN C. P. SULLIVAN, St. Colman Church, 219 S. North St., Washington Court House, 43160-2250. Deanery 13: Scioto County: Rev. THEODORE F. MACHNIK, St. Mary Church, 524 Sixth St., Portsmouth, 45662-3840.

Presbyteral Council—Most Rev. FREDERICK F. CAMPBELL, D.D., Ph.D., Pres.; Revs. PATRICK A. TONER, Chm.; ANDRE-JOSEPH LACASSE, O.P., Vice Chm.; Very Rev. SHAWN D. CORCORAN, M.Div., J.C.L., Sec.; Revs. CHARLES E. COTTON; F. RICHARD SNOKE; WILLIAM J. FAUSTNER; JAMES C. CSASZAR; JAN C. P. SULLIVAN; STANLEY L. (STASH) DAILEY; THEODORE F. MACHNIK; JAMES A. KLIMA; Very Rev. G. MICHAEL GRIBBLE, M.Div.; Revs. MICHAEL B. WATSON, M.Div., B.S.; DAVID J. YOUNG; Rev. Msgrs. STEPHAN J. MOLONEY, M.A., M.Div., J.C.L.; FRANK J. MEAGHER (Retired).

Diocesan Pastoral Council—Most Rev. FREDERICK F. CAMPBELL, D.D., Ph.D., Pres.; WILLIAM NEUTZLING, Chm.; ELLEN WEILBACHER, Exec. Sec., 197 E. Gay St., Columbus, 43215. Tel: 614-241-2550, Ext. 336.

Bishop's Council—Rev. Msgr. STEPHAN J. MOLONEY, M.A., M.Div., J.C.L., Vicar Gen. & Episcopal Moderator for Admin.; Very Rev. SHAWN D. CORCORAN, M.Div., J.C.L., Chancellor; Deacon THOMAS M. BERG JR., B.A., M.J., M.P.S., Vice Chancellor & Episcopal Moderator for Spiritual Life and Parish Ministry; Ms. LUCIA D. MCQUAIDE, Episcopal Moderator for Educ.; Mr. MARK H. HUDDY, Episcopal Moderator for Catholic Charities & Social Concerns; Mr. RICK H. JERIC, Dir. Devel. & Planning; Mr. WILLIAM S. DAVIS, Dir. Finance; Mr. DOMINIC PRUNTE, Dir. Personnel.

Diocesan Board of Review for the Protection of Children—Rev. Msgr. STEPHAN J. MOLONEY, M.A., M.Div., J.C.L., Victims Asst. Coord.; Dr. LESLIE A. BOSTIC; Mr. MITCHELL J. BROWN; Mrs. MARILYN P. DONO; Dr. MARIAN K. SCHUDA, Chm.; Mr. JOHN J. KULEWICZ; Mrs. MARY GINN RYAN; Rev. PAUL A. NOBLE, M.A., Ph.D.; Mrs. LINDA DAY-MACKESSY; Dr. JUANITA MURAWSKI, 198 E. Broad St., Columbus, 43215. Tel: 614-224-2251.

Diocesan Finance Council—Most Rev. FREDERICK F. CAMPBELL, D.D., Ph.D.; Rev. Msgr. STEPHAN J. MOLONEY, M.A., M.Div., J.C.L.; Very Rev. SHAWN D. CORCORAN, M.Div., J.C.L.; Mr. WILLIAM S. DAVIS; FRANK BETTENDORF, Chm.; THOMAS MCAULIFFE; HUGH DORRIAN; JAMES CSASZAR; TIMOTHY BOTTS; MIKE DEASCENTIS; CHRISTOPHER FIDLER; Rev. MICHAEL B. WATSON, M.Div., B.S.

Tribunal—Ste. 500, 197 E. Gay St., Columbus, 43215-3290. Tel: 614-241-2500; Fax: 614-241-2522.

Judicial Vicar—Rev. Msgr. JAMES L.T. RUEF, M.A., J.C.L., M.Div., J.D.

Adjutant Judicial Vicar—Rev. Msgr. JOHN K. CODY, B.A., M.Div., J.C.L.

Presiding Judges of First Instance—Rev. Msgrs. JOHN K. CODY, B.A., M.Div., J.C.L.; JOHN G. JOHNSON, J.C.D.; Revs. DENNIS E. STEVENSON, J.C.L., M.A., M.Div.; JOSEPH N. BAY, M.A., M.Div., J.C.L.

Presiding Judge in Second Instance—Rev. Msgr. JAMES L.T. RUEF, M.A., J.C.L., M.Div., J.D.

Promoter of Justice—Rev. Msgr. STEPHAN J. MOLONEY, M.A., M.Div., J.C.L.

Defenders of the Bond—Rev. MARK J. HAMMOND, J.C.L., S.T.L.; Sr. WANDA SCHERER, O.S.F., M.A.; Deacon JOHN R. CRERAND, M.A.

Medical Experts—Rev. STEPHEN G. VIRGINIA, Ph.D.; Dr. FRANK J. OROSZ, Ph.D.; Sr. MARIALEIN ANZENBERGER, O.P., M.A.

Diocesan Judges—Rev. WILLIAM ARNOLD, M.E., M.Ed.; Rev. Msgr. ANTHONY BORRELLI, J.C.L.; Rev. LEO L. CONNOLLY, M.Div.; Rev. Msgrs. JOHN J. DREESE (Retired); JAMES A. GEIGER, M.A., Ph.D. (Retired); Very Rev. G. MICHAEL GRIBBLE, M.Div.; Revs. TIMOTHY M. HAYES, S.T.L.; KEVIN J. KAVANAGH; CHARLES F. KLINGER, B.A., M.A., M.Div., Ph.D.; Rev. Msgr. FRANK P. LANE, Ph.D. (Retired); Revs. WILLIAM A. METZGER, B.A.; DANIEL J. MILLISOR, M.Div.; PAUL A. NOBLE, M.A., Ph.D.; CHARLES T. THOMAS, B.A., M.Div., M.A.

Tribunal Staff—Sr. RAYMUNDA BROOKS, O.P., M.A.; Mrs. SUE ULMER; Ms. MARY BETH KRECSMAR; Ms. PATRICIA SMITH.

Advocates—Hon. PEGGY BRYANT, J.D.; Mr. THOMAS LONG, J.D., Esq.; Mrs. BARBARA KEGELMEYER, B.A.

Catholic Conference of Ohio

Catholic Conference of Ohio—CAROLYN JURKOWITZ, Dir., 9 E. Long St., Ste. 201, Columbus, 43215. Tel: 614-224-7147; Fax: 614-224-7150. Email: general@ohiocathconf.org. Web: ohiocathconf.org.

Diocesan Offices and Departments

Department of Administration

Black Catholic Ministries of Columbus—RACHELLE MARTIN, Chm., 244 E. Rich St., Columbus, 43215-5232. Tel: 614-228-0024; Fax: 614-221-1787. Email: blkcathministries@sbcglobal.net.

Building Commission—Deacon JAMES A. ROUSE, A.E., M.S., P.E., Chm.; Mr. PAT DAVIS, Co Chm.

Catholic Center—PATRICK DAVIS, Supt. Bldgs., Diocesan Office Building, 197 E. Gay St., Columbus, 43215. Tel: 614-228-2453.

Catholic Latino Ministry Office—ANGELA JOHNSTON, Dir., 197 E. Gay St., Columbus, 43215. Tel: 614-262-7992. Email: ajohnston@colsdioc.org.

Catholic Record Society—DONALD SCHLEGEL, Vice Chm.; RICK JACKSON, Sec., 197 E. Gay St., Columbus, 43215. Tel: 614-241-2571.

The Catholic Times, Inc.—DAVID A. GARICK, Editor; Deacon STEVEN DEMERS, Business Mgr., 197 E. Gay St., Columbus, 43215. Tel: 614-224-5195.

Cemeteries—RICHARD FINN, Dir., 6440 S. High St., Lockbourne, 43137. Tel: 614-491-2751; Fax: 614-491-4264. Email: ccocrfinn@aol.com.

Censor of Books—Rev. Msgr. JOHN V. WOLF, S.T.D. (Retired); Revs. WILLIAM THOMAS KESSLER; THOMAS J. BUFFER, S.T.D.

Central Purchasing Service—STEVE DEEDRICK, Dir., 197 E. Gay St., Columbus, 43215. Tel: 614-262-0010; 800-842-8319; Fax: 614-262-0013.

Communications Office—Deacon THOMAS M. BERG JR., B.A., M.J., M.P.S., Dir.; CAROL KEENE, Assoc. Dir., 197 E. Gay St., Columbus, 43215. Tel: 614-241-2555; Fax: 614-241-2557.

Deaf Apostolate—Rev. STANLEY BENECKI, St. Mary Magdalene, 473 S. Roys Ave., Columbus, 43204-2598. Tel: 614-274-1121 (Voice); 614-358-7323 (TDD); Fax: 614-274-1122.

Development and Planning Office—Mr. RICK H. JERIC, Exec. Dir., 197 E. Gay St., Columbus, 43215. Tel: 614-241-2550; Fax: 614-241-2567.

Diocesan Charities Membership Corporation—MARK H. HUDDY, J.D., Trustee & Sec., 198 E. Broad St., Columbus, 43215. Tel: 614-224-2251.

Diocesan Finance Office—Mr. WILLIAM S. DAVIS, Dir. Finance, 198 E. Broad St., Columbus, 43215. Tel: 614-224-1221; Fax: 614-241-2573.

Haitian Catholic Coalition of Ohio—NEDY MELIDOR, Founder & Counselor; Rev. FRITZNER VALCIN, Counselor, 1582 Ferris Rd., Columbus, 43224. Tel: 614-778-0459.

Information Technology Office—JAMES RATHBURN, Dir., 197 E. Gay St., Columbus, 43215. Tel: 614-221-1182.

Legion of Mary—Rev. Msgr. CHARLES J. FOELLER, Dir. (Retired), 6555 County Rd. 109, Mount Gilead, 43338-9563. Tel: 419-768-2739. Email: foeller@bright.net.

Personnel Office—Mr. DOMINIC PRUNTE, Dir., 197 E. Gay St., Columbus, 43215. Tel: 614-241-2590.

Real Estate—Diocesan Finance Office, 198 E. Broad St., Columbus, 43215. Tel: 614-224-1221.

Retreats—MARY E. MURPHY, Dir., St. Therese's Retreat Center, 5277 E. Broad St., Columbus, 43213-1389. Tel: 614-866-1611; ROBERT OVERMAN, Dir., Ss. Peter and Paul Retreat Center, 2734 Seminary Rd., S.E., Newark, 43056-9339. Tel: 740-928-6400; Fax: 740-928-1512.

Insurance Office—Mr. DOMINIC PRUNTE, Dir. Insurance Office, 198 E. Broad St., Columbus, 43215. Tel: 614-224-1221.

Victim Assistance Coordinator—Rev. Msgr. STEPHAN J. MOLONEY, M.A., M.Div., J.C.L. Tel: 614-224-2251; 866-448-0217 (Toll Free). Email: helpisavailable@colsdioc.org.

Office of Clergy Personnel

Health Affairs Department (Hospitals)—Rev. MARK J. HAMMOND, J.C.L., S.T.L., Coord., 197 E. Gay St., Columbus, 43215. Tel: 740-392-4711.

Office of the Diaconate—Deacon FRANK A. IANNARINO, Dir., Office, 197 E. Gay St., Columbus, 43215. Tel: 614-241-2545. Email: fiannarino@colsdioc.org; School, 7625 N. High St., Columbus, 43235. Tel: 614-885-5585.

Office of Vocations—Rev. JEFFREY CONING, 197 E. Gay St., Columbus, 43215. Tel: 614-221-5565.

Priests Continuing Education—Very Rev. G. MICHAEL GRIBBLE, M.Div., St. Joseph Cathedral, 212 E. Broad St., Columbus, 43215. Tel: 614-224-1295.

Priests Personnel Board—Rev. LEO L. CONNOLLY, M.Div., Chm., St. Cecilia Church, 434 Norton Rd., Columbus, 43228. Tel: 614-878-5353.

Department for Catholic Charities and Social Concerns

Catholic Charities and Social Concerns—MARK H. HUDDY, J.D., Episcopal Moderator, 197 E. Gay St., Columbus, 43215. Tel: 614-241-2540; Fax: 614-228-7302.

Catholic Campaign for Human Development—ERIN CORDLE, Dir., 197 E. Gay St., Columbus, 43215-3229. Tel: 614-241-2540; Fax: 614-228-7302. Email: ecordle@colsdioc.org.

Catholic Relief Services—ERIN CORDLE, Dir., Office for Social Concerns, 197 E. Gay St., Columbus, 43215. Tel: 614-241-2540; Fax: 614-228-7302. Email: ecordle@colsdioc.org.

J.O.I.N. (Joint Organization for Inner-City Needs)—Mrs. RUTH BECKMAN, Dir., 578 E. Main St., Columbus, 43215. Tel: 614-241-2530.

Office for Social Concerns—MARK H. HUDDY, J.D., Dir., 197 E. Gay St., Columbus, 43215. Tel: 614-241-2540; Fax: 614-228-7302.

Rural Life Apostolate—JERALD FREEWALT, Dir., 197 E. Gay St., Columbus, 43215. Tel: 614-241-2540; Fax: 614-228-7302.

Department for Education

Department for Education—LUCIA D. MCQUAIDE, M.S.Ed., M.Rel.Ed., Episcopal Moderator - Supt., 197 E. Gay St., Columbus, 43215. Tel: 614-221-5829.

Office of Religious Education & Catechesis—BARBARA ROMANELLO-WICHTMAN, Ph.D., Dir., 197 E. Gay St., Columbus, 43215. Tel: 614-221-4633.

Office of Youth and Young Adult Ministry—Mr. MIKE HALL, Dir.; Mr. SEAN ROBINSON, Program Coord., 197 E. Gay St., Columbus, 43215. Tel: 614-241-2565.

Scout Chaplain—Deacon ROBERT KILLOREN. Tel: 614-241-2565.

Council for Religious—198 E. Broad St., Columbus, 43215. Tel: 614-224-2251.

Department for Spiritual Life and Parish Ministry

Marriage and Family Life Office—STEPHANIE JENEMANN, Dir., 197 E. Gay St., Columbus, 43215. Tel: 614-241-2560. Email: flomailbox@colsdioc.org.

Liturgical Commission—Deacon MARTIN H. DAVIES, Dir., 197 E. Gay St., Columbus, 43215. Tel: 614-221-4640.

Office of Liturgy—Deacon MARTIN H. DAVIES, Dir., 197 E. Gay St., Columbus, 43215. Tel: 614-221-4640.

Office of Ministry Formation—SHEILA MURPHY, Ph.D., Dir., 197 E. Gay St., Columbus, 43215. Tel: 614-241-2544.

Pontifical Mission Societies— The Society for the Propagation of the Faith, Holy Childhood Association, The Society of St. Peter Apostle, Missionary Union of Priests & Religious Mr. LEANDRO M. TAPAY, M.A., Dir., 197 E. Gay St., Columbus, 43215. Tel: 614-228-8603. Email: mismailbox@colsdioc.org.

St. Francis Evangelization Center—Sr. LINDA LEWANDOWSKI, O.S.F., Dir., 108 W. Mill St., McArthur, 45651-1229. Tel: 740-596-4316; Fax: 740-596-4316.

Diocesan Sponsored Catholic Social Agencies

Catholic Social Services—DONALD S. WISLER, Pres., 197 E. Gay St., Columbus, 43215. Tel: 614-221-5891.

St. Stephen's Community House—Ms. MICHELLE MILLS, Dir., 1500 E. 17th Ave., Columbus, 43219. Tel: 614-294-6347; Fax: 614-294-0258.

St. Vincent Family Center—MICHELLE WARD, L.S.W., Pres. & CEO; REJEANA HAYNES, L.I.S.W., Prog. Dir., 1490 E. Main St., Columbus, 43205. Tel: 614-252-0731; 614-252-2069 (TDD & TTY); Fax: 614-252-8468.

Affiliates of National Organizations

Diocesan Council of Catholic Women—NANCY MONTGOMERY, Pres., 197 E. Gay St., Columbus, 43215. Tel: 614-228-8601.

CLERGY, PARISHES, MISSIONS AND PAROCHIAL SCHOOLS

CITY OF COLUMBUS

(FRANKLIN COUNTY)

1—ST. JOSEPH CATHEDRAL (1878) Very Rev. G. Michael Gribble, Rector; Deacons Thomas Johnston; James Gorski. In Res., Very Rev. Shawn D. Corcoran.
Res.: 212 E. Broad St., 43215. Tel: 614-224-1295; Fax: 614-224-1176. Email: cathedral@columbus.rr.com. Web: www.saintjosephcathedral.org.
Church: E. Broad St. & N. Fifth St., 43215.
Catechesis/Religious Program—Students 25.

2—ST. AGATHA (Upper Arlington) (1940) Rev. Daniel L. Ochs; Sr. Mary Faith Geelan, O.P., Pastoral Min.
Res.: 1860 Northam Rd., 43221. Tel: 614-488-6149; Fax: 614-488-6596. Email: stagatha@rrohio.com. Web: www.st-agatha.org.
School—1880 Northam Rd., 43221. Tel: 614-488-9000; Fax: 614-488-5783. Web: www.cdeducation.org/schools/ag. Mrs. Joan Mastell, Prin. Lay Teachers 22; Students 283.
Catechesis/Religious Program—Tel: 614-488-4975. Mrs. Jeanne Altiero, D.R.E. Students 262.

3—ST. AGNES (1954) Rev. Homer D. Blubaugh, Priest Moderator; Deacon James Gorski, Parish Admin.
Res.: 2364 W. Mound St., 43204-2903. Tel: 614-276-5413; Fax: 614-276-5413. Email: st-agnes@sbcglobal.net.
Catechesis/Religious Program—4031 Clime Rd., 43228. Tel: 614-274-5589; Fax: 614-272-5200. Students 8.

4—ST. ALOYSIUS (1906) Deacon James Gorski, Parish Admin.; Rev. Homer D. Blubaugh, Priest Moderator. In Res., Rev. Dennis E. Stevenson.
Res.: 32 Clarendon Ave., 43223. Tel: 614-276-6587; Fax: 614-276-1793.
Catechesis/Religious Program—4031 Clime Rd., 43228. Tel: 614-272-5205; Fax: 614-272-5200. Email: stals32@yahoo.com. Students 6.

5—ST. ANDREW (1955) Rev. Michael B. Watson; Deacon Thomas M. Berg Jr. In Res., Rev. Msgr. Kenneth F. Grimes (Retired).
Res.: 1899 McCoy Rd., 43220. Tel: 614-451-4290; Fax: 614-451-8300. Web: www.standrewparish.cc.
School—4081 Reed Rd., 43220. Tel: 614-451-1626; Fax: 614-451-0272. Web: www.standrewschool.com. Joel Wichtman, Prin. Lay Teachers 25; Students 449.
Catechesis/Religious Program—Tel: 614-451-2855; Fax: 614-451-8300. Kris Pellissier, Coord.; Suzanne Emsweller, D.R.E. Students 255.

6—SAINT ANTHONY (1963) Rev. Thomas G. Petry; Deacon Craig Smith; Mrs. Colleen Buzenski, Pastoral Asst.
Rectory—4913 Atwater Dr., 43229. Tel: 614-885-4857. Email: st.anthony@sbcglobal.net. Web: www.stanthonyparishcolumbus.org.
Church: 1300 Urban Dr., 43229.
School—(Grades K-8), 1300 Urban Dr., 43229. Tel: 614-888-4268; Fax: 614-888-4435. Web: stanthony-columbus.org. Chris Iaconis, Prin. Lay Teachers 9; Students 190.
Catechesis/Religious Program—Tel: 614-888-8190. Judy McElwee, D.R.E. Students 60.

7—STS. AUGUSTINE AND GABRIEL (1984) Rev. Joseph N. Bay.
Office: 1567 Loretta Ave., Ste. 111, 43211-1677. Tel: 614-268-3123; Fax: 614-268-8130. Email: stsag@aol.com.
Church: 1550 E. Hudson St., 43211.
Catechesis/Religious Program—Students 11.

8—ST. CATHARINE (1931) Rev. Michael J. Lumpe; Deacon Martin Davies.
Res.: 500 S. Gould Rd., 43209. Tel: 614-231-4509; Fax: 614-231-8366. Email: info@stcatharine.com. Web: www.stcatharine.com.
School—2865 Fair Ave., 43209. Tel: 614-235-1396; Fax: 614-235-9708. Mrs. Janet Weisner, Prin. Lay Teachers 19; Students 272.
Catechesis/Religious Program—Tel: 614-231-4500. Mrs. Chris Schleicher, D.R.E. Students 232.

9—ST. CECILIA (1882) Revs. Leo L. Connolly; Thomas J. Brosmer.
Res.: 434 Norton Rd., 43228. Tel: 614-878-5353; Fax: 614-878-0459. Email: email@saintceciliachurch.org. Web: www.saintceciliachurch.org.
School—440 Norton Rd., 43228. Tel: 614-878-3555; Fax: 614-878-6852. Email: stcecilia@cdeducation.org. Web: www.cdeducation.org/schools/ce. Marge Moretti, Prin. Lay Teachers 21; Students 195.
Catechesis/Religious Program—Tel: 614-878-0133. Kathy Maggied, D.R.E. Students 239.

10—CHRIST THE KING (1946) Rev. Craig R. Eilerman; Deacon Peter C. Labita. In Res., Rev. Joshua J. Wagner.
Res.: 2770 Dover Rd., 43209. Tel: 614-237-0401; Fax: 614-237-4689.
Church: 2777 E. Livingston Ave., 43209.
School—All Saints Academy, (Grades PreSchool-8), 2855 E. Livingston Ave., 43209. Tel: 614-231-3391; Fax: 614-338-2170. Laura Miller, Prin. St. Thomas, St. Phillip & Christ the King. Lay Teachers 15; Students 275.
Catechesis/Religious Program—Students 45.

11—ST. CHRISTOPHER (1947) Rev. Msgr. John K. Cody; Deacon David J. Kruse, Pastoral Admin.
Res.: 1420 Grandview Ave., 43212. Tel: 614-486-0457; Fax: 614-486-0433. Web: www.rc.net/columbus/stchristopher/.
School—Trinity, 1440 Grandview Ave., 43212. Tel: 614-488-7650; Fax: 614-488-4687. Web: www.cdeducation.org/schools/tr/. Jeffrey Grimmett, Prin. Lay Teachers 18; Students 172.
Catechesis/Religious Program—Chris Ross, Catechetical Leader. Students 87.

12—COLUMBUS VIETNAMESE CATHOLIC COMMUNITY (1994) Rev. Joseph N. Bay, Chap.
1567 Loretta Ave., Ste. 111, 43211-1677. Tel: 614-268-3123; Fax: 614-268-8130. Email: josephbay@att.net.

13—COMMUNITY OF HOLY ROSARY AND ST. JOHN (1979), (African American), Deacon William J. Andrews, Parish Admin.; Rev. Joshua J. Wagner, Priest Moderator Pro Tem.
Res.: 648 S. Ohio Ave., 43205. Tel: 614-252-5926; Fax: 614-252-5933. Web: www.hrsj.org.
Catechesis/Religious Program—Tel: 614-252-5926, Ext. 226. Gaye Reissland, D.R.E. Students 37.

14—CORPUS CHRISTI (1925) Rev. John E. Stattmiller; Deacon Jerry J. Butts.
P.O. Box 7825, 43207. Email: pattiejjonesp@prodigy.net.
Res.: 1111 E. Stewart Ave., 43206. Tel: 614-444-9871; Fax: 614-444-1018.
Catechesis/Religious Program—Tel: 614-443-2828; Fax: 614-444-0523. Clustered with St. Ladislas, Columbus. Students 16.

15—ST. DOMINIC (1889), (African American), Rev. James L. Colopy; Deacon Robert A. Neely.
Mailing Address & Res.: 453 N. 20th St., P.O. Box 83572, 43203-0572. Tel: 614-252-4913; Fax: 614-252-1655. Email: stdominic@stdominic-church.org. Web: www.stdominic-church.org.
Catechesis/Religious Program—Students 48.

16—ST. ELIZABETH (1967) Rev. Charles E. Cotton; Deacons Frank X. McDevitt; Dean W. Racine; Rich Krehnovi, Music Min.
Church: 6077 Sharon Woods Blvd., 43229. Tel: 614-891-0150; Fax: 614-891-3243. Email: stelizabethchurch@sbcglobal.net. Web: www.stelizabethchurch.org.
Res.: 1682 Lynnhurst Rd., 43229. Tel: 614-882-1782.
Catechesis/Religious Program—Email: stelizabethreled@sbcglobal.net. Dave Gruber, D.R.E. & RCIA Coord. Students 98.

17—ST. FRANCIS OF ASSISI (1892) Rev. Ronald J. Atwood. In Res., Rev. Fritzner Valcin (Haiti).
Res.: 386 Buttles Ave., 43215. Tel: 614-299-5781; Fax: 614-299-1987. Email: office@sfacolumbus.org. Web: www.sfacolumbus.org.

18—ST. GABRIEL, Merged with St. Augustine. See separate listing.

19—HOLY CROSS (1833), (German), Rev. Jerome D. Stluka.
Res.: 204 S. Fifth St., 43215. Tel: 614-224-3416; Fax: 614-224-9916. Email: admmike@columbus.rr.com. Web: www.holycrosscatholic.com.
Catechesis/Religious Program—Sr. Patricia Pieper, S.N.D.deN., D.R.E.

20—HOLY FAMILY (1877) Rev. Kevin F. Lutz; Deacons W. Earl McCurry; Frank A. Paniccia.
Res.: 584 W. Broad St., 43215-2710. Tel: 614-221-4323; Fax: 614-221-9818. Email: hchurchl@columbus.rr.com. Web: www.holyfamilycolumbus.org.
Catechesis/Religious Program—Students 65.
**The Jubilee Museum*, The Diocesan Museum of Sacred Catholic Art., 57 S. Grubb St., 43215-2747. Tel: 614-461-6204; Fax: 614-461-1737.

21—HOLY NAME OF JESUS (1905) Rev. Antonio Carvalho, Admin. Pro Tem.
Res.: 154 E. Patterson Ave., 43202. Tel: 614-262-0390; Fax: 614-262-0390. Email: holynamechurch@columbus.rr.com. Web: www.holynamercc.com.
Catechesis/Religious Program—

22—HOLY SPIRIT (Whitehall) (1947) Rev. William L. Arnold.
Res.: 4383 E. Broad St., 43213. Tel: 614-861-1521; Fax: 614-861-3746. Web: www.holyspiritcolumbus.org.
School—4382 Duchene Ln., 43213. Tel: 614-861-0475; Fax: 614-861-8608. Web: www.holy-spirit-school.org. Linda Saelzler, Prin. Lay Teachers 14; Students 265.
Catechesis/Religious Program—Kristie Mendes, D.R.E. Students 36.

23—IMMACULATE CONCEPTION (1917) Rev. Msgr. Stephan J. Moloney; Deacon Christopher Campbell.
Res.: 414 E. North Broadway, 43214. Tel: 614-267-9241; Fax: 614-267-7720.
School—366 E. North Broadway, 43214. Tel: 614-267-6579. John Grossman, Prin. Lay Teachers 21; Students 448.
Catechesis/Religious Program—440 E. North Broadway, 43214. Tel: 614-267-0279. John Hoffman, D.R.E. Students 68.

24—ST. JAMES-THE-LESS (1947) Revs. Scott Kramer, C.PP.S.; Patrick Patterson, C.PP.S.; Deacons Joseph P. Checca; Kasuma J. Santos Jr.; Tim Feeney, Business Mgr.
Res.: 1652 Oakland Park Ave., 43224. Tel: 614-262-1179; 614-262-1170; Fax: 614-262-6798. Email: sjamesless@yahoo.com.
School—1628 Oakland Park Ave., 43224. Tel: 614-268-3311; Fax: 614-268-1808. Web: www.saintjames-theless.com. Yvonne Schwab, Prin. Lay Teachers 18; Students 340.
Catechesis/Religious Program—Sr. Pat Dual, O.P., D.R.E. Students 90.

25—ST. JOHN THE BAPTIST (1896), (Italian), Rev. William A. Metzger.
Res.: 720 Hamlet St., 43215-1534. Tel: 614-294-5319; Fax: 614-294-4303. Email: sbaptist@columbus.rr.com.

26—KOREAN CATHOLIC COMMUNITY (1978), (Asian), [CEM] Rev. Peter Kim; Mr. Anthony Kim, Contact Person.
Mailing Address: 221 Hanford St., 43206-3656.
Catechesis/Religious Program—

27—ST. LADISLAS (1908) Rev. John E. Stattmiller.
Mailing Address: 277 Reeb Ave., 43207. Email: pattiejjonesp@prodigy.net.
Catechesis/Religious Program— (Clustered with Corpus Christi.) Students 88.

28—ST. LEO (1903), (German), Closed. For inquiries for parish records please see St. Mary, Columbus.

29—ST. MARGARET OF CORTONA (1921) Rev. Jeffrey J. Rimelspach; Deacon Andrew W. Naporano.
Res.: 1600 Hague Ave., 43204-1606. Tel: 614-279-1690; Fax: 614-279-2386. Email: stmargaretcol@yahoo.com. Web: www.stmargaretcolumbus.org.
Catechesis/Religious Program—Tel: 614-272-1127; 614-274-1922 (Trinity Pre School). Email: stmargaretpsr@yahoo.com. Ruth Ann Wolansky, Dir. Students 168.
Catechesis/Religious Program—Catechesis of the Good Shepherd Lisa LaTorre, Dir. Students 37.

30—ST. MARY CHURCH (1865), (German), Rev. C. Theodore Thomas; Jason Shanks, Pastoral Admin. & Coord., Pastoral Ministries; Deacon Roger Minner.
Office: 672 S. Third St., 43206. Tel: 614-445-9668; Fax: 614-444-1688. Email: info@stmarygv.com. Web: www.stmarygv.com.
School—700 S. Third St., 43206. Tel: 614-444-8994; Fax: 614-445-2853. Web: www.stmaryschoolgv.com. Sr. Regina Snyder, O.S.F., Prin. Lay Teachers 15; Students 233.
Catechesis/Religious Program—(with St. Ladislas, Columbus.) Students 4.

31—ST. MARY MAGDALENE (1928) Rev. Stanley Benecki.
Res.: 473 S. Roys Ave., 43204. Tel: 614-274-1121; Fax: 614-274-1122. Web: www.saintmarymag.org.
School—2940 Parkside Rd., 43204. Tel: 614-279-9935; Fax: 614-279-9575. Rocco Fumi, Prin. Lay Teachers 14; Students 115.
Catechesis/Religious Program—Tel: 614-279-9291. Students 20.

32—ST. MATTHIAS (1956) Rev. James T. Smith; Sr. Marie Shields, S.N.D.deN., Pastoral Assoc.
Res.: 1582 Ferris Rd., 43224. Tel: 614-267-3406. Email: stmatthiascolumbus@sbcglobal.net.
School—1566 Ferris Rd., 43224. Tel: 614-268-3030; Fax: 614-268-4681. Mr. Daniel Kinley, Prin. Sisters 1; Lay Teachers 11; Students 266.
Catechesis/Religious Program—Michelle Mead, D.R.E. Students 70.

33—OUR LADY OF PEACE (1946) Rev. Kevin J. Kavanagh; Deacon Jeffrey D. Fortkamp; Sisters Martha Langstaff, O.P., Pastoral Min.; Barbara Kolesar, O.P., Pastoral Assoc.
Res.: 20 E. Dominion Blvd., 43214. Tel: 614-263-8824; Fax: 614-263-3383. Email: olp@rrohio.com.
School—40 Dominion Blvd., 43214. Tel: 614-267-4535; Fax: 614-267-2333. Email: olp@cdeducation.org. Web: www.olpcolumbus.org. Carol Folian, Prin. Lay Teachers 14; Students 274.
Catechesis/Religious Program—Tel: 614-263-4271. Students 40.
Convent—60 E. Dominion Blvd., 43214. Tel: 614-268-1980.

34—OUR LADY OF THE MIRACULOUS MEDAL (1967) Rev. James Coleman; Deacon Stephen A. Venturini, Pastoral Assoc.

Church & Office: 5225 Refugee Rd., 43232-5398. Tel: 614-861-1242; Fax: 614-861-1499. Email: cool5225@sbcglobal.net. Web: www.home.catholicweb.com/cool5225.
Catechesis/Religious Program—Tel: 614-868-1414. Students 57.

35—OUR LADY OF VICTORY (1922) [CEM] Rev. Msgr. Romano Ciotola; Deacons Richard L. Baumann, (Retired); Rob Joseph.
Res.: 1559 Roxbury Rd., 43212. Tel: 614-488-2428; Fax: 614-488-0507. Email: olvc@sbcglobal.net. Web: www.olvonline.org.
See Trinity, Columbus under St. Christopher, Columbus for details.
Catechesis/Religious Program—Tel: 614-486-7678; Fax: 614-488-0507. Lisa Schechter, D.R.E. (Grades K-5); Amy Frederick, D.R.E. (Grades 6-8). Students 347.

36—ST. PATRICK (1852), (Irish), Revs. Andre-Joseph LaCasse, O.P.; Thomas Blau, O.P. In Res., Revs. J. Jordan Lenaghan, O.P.; John Boll, O.P.
Res.: 280 N. Grant Ave., 43215. Tel: 614-224-9522; Fax: 614-240-5928. Email: stpatrickcolumbus@sbcglobal.net. Web: www.stpatrickcolumbus.catholicweb.net.
Catechesis/Religious Program—Tel: 614-240-5925; Fax: 614-240-5928. Students 254.

37—ST. PETER (1970) Rev. Justin J. Reis; Deacons Joseph E. Schermer; Philip M. Paulucci. In Res., Rev. Stephen G. Virginia.
Res.: 6899 Smoky Row Rd., 43235-1998. Tel: 614-889-2221; Fax: 614-889-6612. Web: www.stpetersnet.org.
Catechesis/Religious Program—Tel: 614-889-1407. Students 481.

38—ST. PHILIP THE APOSTLE (1956) Rev. Patrick W. Rogers; Deacon Joseph W. Farry, Pastoral Assoc.
Res.: 1573 Elaine Rd., 43227. Tel: 614-237-1671; Fax: 614-231-8416. Email: stphilip@rrohio.com. Web: www.stphilipcolumbus.org.
Catechesis/Religious Program—Bradley E. Walters, D.R.E. Students 25.

39—SACRED HEART (1875) Rev. William A. Metzger, Admin.
Res.: 893 Hamlet St., 43201. Tel: 614-299-4191.

40—SANTA CRUZ PARISH (1993), (Spanish), Rev. Jose Perez (Venezuela).
Mailing Address: P.O. Box 82205, 43202.
Church: 143-155 E. Patterson Ave., 43202. Tel: 614-784-9732; Fax: 614-784-9732.
Catechesis/Religious Program—Sr. Celia Palma, D.R.E. Students 69.

41—SHRINE OF BLESSED MARGARET OF CASTELLO (1957) Mailing Address: *c/o St. Patrick*, 280 N. Grant Ave., 43215. Tel: 614-240-5915; Fax: 614-240-5928. Shrine dedicated to promoting the sanctity of life, and the cause of canonization of Blessed Margaret of Castello, O.P.

42—SAINT STEPHEN THE MARTYR (1963) Rev. Thomas J. Buffer.
Res.: 4131 Clime Rd., 43228. Tel: 614-272-5206; Fax: 614-272-5200.
Catechesis/Religious Program—Tel: 614-279-9291. Students 350.

43—ST. THOMAS THE APOSTLE (1900) Rev. Denis S. Kigozi. In Res., Rev. Dean Mathewson, part-time Chap., Riverside Hospital.
Res.: 2692 E. Fifth Ave., 43219. Tel: 614-252-0976; Fax: 614-252-7519.
Catechesis/Religious Program—Students 117.

44—ST. TIMOTHY (1961) Rev. Timothy M. Hayes.
Res.: 1088 Thomas Ln., 43220. Tel: 614-451-2671; Fax: 614-451-4181.
School—1070 Thomas Ln., 43220. Tel: 614-451-0739; Fax: 614-451-3108. George Mosholder, Prin. Lay Teachers 12; Students 274.
Catechesis/Religious Program—Tel: 614-451-3867; Fax: 614-451-3108. Rita Feige, D.R.E. Students 75.

OUTSIDE THE CITY OF COLUMBUS

ADA, HARDIN CO., OUR LADY OF LOURDES (1874) Rev. David J. Young; Deacons John P. Stahl, (Retired); J. Michael Hood; Deb Driscolli, Admin. Asst.
Res.: 222 E. Highland Ave., 45810. Tel: 419-634-2626; Fax: 419-634-6555. Email: oll@wcoil.com. Web: www.oll-ada.com.
Catechesis/Religious Program—Tel: 419-634-2445. Mr. David Savino, D.R.E. Students 85.

BREMEN, FAIRFIELD CO., ST. MARY (1917) [CEM] Rev. William Thomas Kessler.
Res.: 602 Marietta St., 43107. Tel: 740-569-7929. Email: bremenstmary@verizon.net.
Catechesis/Religious Program—Tel: 740-862-8839. Deborah Schmelzer, D.R.E. Students 30.

BUCKEYE LAKE, LICKING CO., OUR LADY OF MT. CARMEL (1929) Rev. William J. Ferguson; Deacon Richard B. Busic, Pastoral Assoc.
Res.: 5133 Walnut Rd., S.E., P.O. Box 45, 43008. Tel: 740-928-3266; Fax: 740-928-3266. Email: olmc@avolve.net. Web: www.olmcparish.org.
Catechesis/Religious Program—Tel: 740-928-3264. Silvia Zaboroski, D.R.E. Students 67.

CANAL WINCHESTER, FAIRFIELD CO., POPE JOHN XXIII (2000) Rev. Msgr. A. Anthony Frecker; Deacons Roger Pry; Charles J. Miller.
Office: 5170 Winchester Southern Rd., N.W., 43110. Tel: 614-920-1563; Fax: 614-920-1564. Email: ppopejoh@insight.rr.com. Web: www.popejohnxxiiiparish.com.
Res.: 7820 White Ash Ct., 43110. Tel: 614-920-1562.
Catechesis/Religious Program—Students 291.

CARDINGTON, MORROW CO., SACRED HEARTS (1868) Rev. John L. Bakle, S.M., Admin.
Res.: 4680 U.S. Rte. 42, 43315. Tel: 419-946-3611. Email: sacredhearts@bright.net.
Catechesis/Religious Program—Kevin Tebbe, D.R.E.; Sharon Tebbe, D.R.E. Students 5.

CHILLICOTHE, ROSS CO.

1—ST. MARY (1837) [CEM] [JC] Rev. Lawrence L. Hummer; Deacon George L. Lovensheimer.
Res.: 61 S. Paint St., 45601. Tel: 740-772-2061; Fax: 740-772-2061. Email: saintmary@roadrunner.com.
School—Bishop Flaget Elementary, (Grades PreSchool-8), 570 Parsons Ave., 45601. Tel: 740-774-2970; Fax: 740-774-2998. Laura Corcoran, Prin. Lay Teachers 15; Students 132.
Catechesis/Religious Program—Email: saintmary@roadrunner.com. Students 47.

2—ST. PETER (1845), (German), [CEM] [JC] Rev. William P. Hahn. In Res., Rev. Charles R. Griffin (Retired).
Office: 126 Church St., 45601. Email: secretary@stpeterchillicothe.com. Web: www.stpeterchillicothe.com.
Res.: 122 Church St., 45601. Tel: 740-774-1407.
School—Bishop Flaget Elementary, (Grades PreK-8), 570 Parsons Ave., 45601. Tel: 740-774-2970; Fax: 740-774-2889. Laura Corcoran, Prin. Lay Teachers 15; Students 132.
Catechesis/Religious Program—Tel: 740-773-3455. Students 45.

CIRCLEVILLE, PICKAWAY CO., ST. JOSEPH (1840) [CEM] Rev. Stephen L. Krile.
Res.: 134 W. Mound St., P.O. Box 40, 43113. Tel: 740-477-2549; Fax: 740-477-1453. Email: church@hocking.net.
Catechesis/Religious Program—Theresa Jenkins, D.R.E. Students 245.

CORNING, PERRY CO., ST. BERNARD (1882) Revs. James C. Csaszar; Victor R. Wesolowski, Parochial Vicar; Sr. Diana Durling, S.C.
Res.: 425 Adams St., 43730. Tel: 740-347-4700.
Catechesis/Religious Program—Students 20.

COSHOCTON, COSHOCTON CO., SACRED HEART (1856) [CEM] Rev. William A. Hritsko; Deacons Frank A. Duda; Douglas Mould.
Res.: 805 Main St., 43812. Tel: 740-622-8817. Email: shrectory@sbcglobal.net.
School—39 Burt Ave., 43812. Tel: 740-622-3728; Fax: 740-622-9151. Mary Stenner, Prin. Lay Teachers 7; Students (K-6) 60; Students (PreK) 25.
Catechesis/Religious Program—Tel: 740-622-8817. Deacon Douglas Mould, D.R.E. Students 54.

CROOKSVILLE, PERRY CO., CHURCH OF THE ATONEMENT (1896) [CEM] Revs. James C. Csaszar; Victor R. Wesolowski, Parochial Vicar.
Mailing Address: 309 N. Main St., New Lexington, 43764-1204. Tel: 740-342-1348; Fax: 740-342-1340.
320 Winter St., 43731.
Catechesis/Religious Program—Tel: 740-982-2386. Mary King, D.R.E. Students 40.

DANVILLE, KNOX CO., ST. LUKE (1820) [CEM] Rev. F. Richard Snoke.
Mailing Address: 307 S. Market St., P.O. Box P, 43014. Email: stluke@ecr.net.
Res.: 305 S. Market St., P.O. Box P, 43014. Tel: 740-599-6362.
Catechesis/Religious Program—St. Luke Community Center, 7 W. Rambo, P.O. Box P, 43014-0616. Tel: 740-599-7367. Thomas Harrmann, D.R.E. Students 157.

DELAWARE, DELAWARE CO., ST. MARY (1835) [CEM] Revs. James P. Black; David A. Schalk; Deacon Felix Azzola.
Res.: 82 E. William St., 43015. Tel: 740-363-4641; 740-369-9644; Fax: 740-363-9915. Email: delawarestmary@rrohio.com. Web: www.delawarestmary.org.
School—66 E. William St., 43015. Tel: 740-362-8961; Fax: 740-362-3733. Web: www.stmarydelaware.org. Becky Piela, Prin. (Grades K-8). Lay Teachers 22; Students 365.
Catechesis/Religious Program—Tel: 740-369-8228. Ann Manning, D.R.E. Students 453.
Convent—59 E. William St., 43015. Tel: 740-363-2998.

DENNISON, TUSCARAWAS CO., IMMACULATE CONCEPTION (1871) [CEM] Rev. Anthony P. Lonzo.
Res.: 206 N. First St., 44621. Tel: 740-922-3533; Fax: 740-922-2486. Email: icdennison@sbcglobal.net.
School—100 Sherman St., 44621. Tel: 740-922-3539; Fax: 740-922-2486. Beth Dennison, Prin. Lay Teachers 10; Students 130.
Catechesis/Religious Program—Kendra Host, D.R.E. Students 24.

DOVER, TUSCARAWAS CO., ST. JOSEPH (1849), (German—Italian), [CEM 2] Rev. Matthew N. Hoover; Deacon Ronald H. Fondriest.
Res.: 613 N. Tuscarawas Ave., 44622. Tel: 330-364-6661; Fax: 330-602-7488. Email: stjosephchurch@roadrunner.com.
School—Tuscarawas Central Catholic Elementary, (Grades PreK-6), 600 N. Tuscarawas Ave., 44622. Tel: 330-343-9134; Fax: 330-364-6509. Theresa Layton, Prin. Lay Teachers 12; Students 220.
Catechesis/Religious Program—Tel: 330-364-8257. Ms. Cindy Teynor, D.R.E. Students 121.

DRESDEN, MUSKINGUM CO., ST. ANN'S (1889) Rev. Jack G. Maynard.
Res.: 405 Chestnut St., Box 107, 43821. Tel: 740-754-2221.
Catechesis/Religious Program—Students 35.
Mission—St. Mary [CEM] 6280 St. Mary's Rd., Nashport, Muskingum Co. 43830.

DUBLIN, FRANKLIN CO., ST. BRIGID OF KILDARE (1987) Rev. Msgr. Joseph M. Hendricks; Deacons Frank A. Iannarino; Donald Poirier; Sisters Patricia McMahon, O.S.F., Pastoral Assoc.; Joan M. Harper, C.D.P., Pastoral Assoc.; Joseph Burger, Business Mgr. In Res., Rev. Jeffrey Coning.
Res.: 7179 Avery Rd., P.O. Box 3130, 43016-0062. Tel: 614-761-3734; Fax: 614-889-6638. Email: kcremeans@midohio.twcbc.com. Web: www.stbrigidofkildare.org.
School—7175 Avery Rd., 43017. Tel: 614-718-5825; Fax: 614-718-5831. Ms. Kathleen O'Reilly, Prin. Lay Teachers 31; Students 550.
Catechesis/Religious Program—Tel: 614-761-1176; Fax: 614-718-5831. Mary Fran Cassidy, D.R.E. Students 1,349.

GAHANNA, FRANKLIN CO., ST. MATTHEW (1959) Revs. Paul A. Noble; Adam A. Streitenberger, Parochial Vicar.
Res.: 807 Havens Corners Rd., 43230. Tel: 614-471-0212; Fax: 614-471-0247. Web: www.stmatthew.net.
School—795 Havens Corners Rd., 43230. Tel: 614-471-4930; Fax: 614-471-1673. Web: www.cdeducation.org/schools/mat. Carole G. Marsh, Prin. Lay Teachers 32; Students 612.
Catechesis/Religious Program—Tel: 614-471-2067; Fax: 614-471-1693. Julie Zarichny, D.R.E. Students 468.

GRANVILLE, LICKING CO., ST. EDWARD THE CONFESSOR (1946) Rev. Msgr. Paul P. Enke, Pastor; Michael Millisor, Pastoral Assoc.
Res.: 785 Newark Rd., 43023-1450. Tel: 740-587-3254; Fax: 740-587-0149. Email: church@saintedwards.org. Web: www.saintedwards.org.
Catechesis/Religious Program—Tel: 740-587-4160. Email: reled@saintedwards.org. Students 458.

GROVE CITY, FRANKLIN CO., OUR LADY OF PERPETUAL HELP (1954) Rev. John L. Swickard.
Church & Mailing Address: 3730 Broadway, 43123. Tel: 614-875-3322; Fax: 614-875-6033. Email: bweber@ourladyofperpetualhelp.net. Web: www.ourladyofperpetualhelp.net.
School—3752 N. Broadway, 43123. Tel: 614-875-6779; Fax: 614-539-5719. Web: www.olphsaints.org. Susan Donovan, Prin. Lay Teachers 23; Students 450.
Catechesis/Religious Program—Tel: 614-875-9345. Mrs. Camille Kopczewski, D.R.E. Students 388.

GROVEPORT, FRANKLIN CO., ST. MARY (1871) Rev. Richard Metzger. In Res., Rev. William J. Metzger (Retired).
Res.: 5684 Groveport Rd., 43125. Tel: 614-497-1324; Fax: 614-497-2706. Email: stmarygroveport@hotmail.com. Web: www.stmarygroveport.org.
Catechesis/Religious Program—Tel: 614-497-1437. Email: stmarypsrgroveport@msn.com. Alice Doran, D.R.E. Students 85.

HEATH, LICKING CO., ST. LEONARD (1962) Rev. Michael J. Reis; Deacon Larry Wilson. In Res., Rev. Ronald Boccali, P.I.M.E. (Retired).
Res.: 57 Dorsey Mill Rd., 43056. Tel: 740-522-5270; Fax: 740-522-5261. Web: www.stleonardchurchheathohiousa.com.
Catechesis/Religious Program—Email: giovannileonardi@roadrunner.com. Students 60.

HILLIARD, FRANKLIN CO., ST. BRENDAN (1957) Rev. Rodric J. DiPietro; Rev. Msgr. John G. Johnson, Parochial Vicar; Deacons Patrick J. Wiggins; Gilbert L. Plummer; James Morris. In Res., Rev. Saulius P. Laurinaitis (Retired).
Res.: 4475 Dublin Rd., 43026. Tel: 614-876-1272; Fax: 614-876-1482. Email: info@stbrendans.net. Web: www.stbrendans.net.
School—(Grades K-8) Tel: 614-876-6132; Fax: 614-529-8929. Mary Lang, Prin. Lay Teachers 22; Students 475.
Catechesis/Religious Program—Tel: 614-876-9533. S. Joanne Fogarty, D.R.E. Students 473.

JACKSON, JACKSON CO., HOLY TRINITY (1875) [CEM] Rev. Joseph J. Trapp II.
Res.: 215 Columbia St., 45640. Tel: 740-286-1428.
Catechesis/Religious Program—Students 38.

JOHNSTOWN, LICKING CO., CHURCH OF THE ASCENSION (1912) [CEM] Rev. J. Lawrence Reichert; Deacon William J. Andrews.
Res.: 501 S. Main St., 43031-1231. Tel: 740-967-7871 (Office); Fax: 740-967-0321 (Office). Email: ascensionparish@embarqmail.com. Web: www.johnstownascension.org.
Catechesis/Religious Program—Tel: 740-967-1338. Jane Laudani, D.R.E. Students 80.

JUNCTION CITY, PERRY CO., ST. PATRICK (1820) [CEM] Revs. James C. Csaszar; Victor R. Wesolowski, Parochial Vicar; Mr. Al Kunkler, Pastoral Assoc.
Mailing Address: c/o 309 N. Main St., New Lexington, 43764-1204. 1170 S.R. 668S, 43748. Tel: 740-342-1348; Fax: 740-342-1340.
Catechesis/Religious Program—Students 25.

KENTON, HARDIN CO., IMMACULATE CONCEPTION (1836) [CEM] Rev. Anthony A. Dinovo Jr.
Res.: 215 E. North St., 43326. Tel: 419-675-1162.
Parish Center—220 E. North St., 44326. Tel: 419-675-9461.
Catechesis/Religious Program—Tel: 419-675-1162. Jean M. Bruner, D.R.E. Students 30.

LA RUE, MARION CO., ST. JOSEPH'S (1864) Closed. For inquiries for parish records contact the Chancery.

LANCASTER, FAIRFIELD CO.

1—ST. BERNADETTE (1963) Rev. William Thomas Kessler; Deacons Paul Deshaies; Mark A. Scarpitti.
Church & Office: 1343 Wheeling Rd., 43130-8701. Tel: 740-654-1893; Fax: 740-687-5926. Email: saintb@stbparish.org. Web: www.stbparish.org.
School—1325 Wheeling Rd., 43130. Tel: 740-654-3137; Fax: 740-654-1602. Email: saintb@greenapple.com. Web: www.stbernadette-school.com. Pam Eltringham, Prin. Lay Teachers 10; Students 175.
Catechesis/Religious Program—Students 44.

2—ST. MARK (1960) [JC] Rev. Peter M. Gideon.
Res.: 324 Gay St., 43130. Tel: 740-653-1229; Fax: 740-653-8329.
Catechesis/Religious Program—331 Gay St., 43130. Tel: 740-654-7154. Kim Kirchgessner, D.R.E. (K-6); Terry Mitchell, D.R.E. (7-12). Students 63.

3—ST. MARY (1818) [CEM] Rev. Donald E. Franks; Sr. Mary Cecil Grandpre, O.P., Pastoral Assoc.; Deacon Frank K. Sullivan, Pastoral Assoc.
Res.: 132 S. High St., 43130. Tel: 740-653-0997; Fax: 740-653-0337. Web: www.stmarylancaster.org.
School—309 E. Chestnut St., 43130. Tel: 740-654-1632; Fax: 740-654-0877. Web: www.greenapple.com/~stmarylab. Carlton B. Rider, Prin. Lay Teachers 23; Students 467.
Catechesis/Religious Program—Tel: 740-653-5054; Fax: 740-653-0337. Sr. Louis Mary Passeri, O.P., D.R.E. Students 167.
Convent—229 E. Chestnut St., 43130. Tel: 740-653-2837.

LOGAN, HOCKING CO., ST. JOHN (1841) [CEM] Rev. Msgr. William A. Dunn; Deacon Donald Robers. In Res., Rev. Msgr. James A. Geiger (Retired).
Res.: 351 N. Market St., 43138. Tel: 740-385-2549; Fax: 740-380-2837. Email: info@stjohnlogan.com. Web: www.stjohnlogan.com.
School—321 N. Market St., 43138. Tel: 740-385-2767; Fax: 740-385-9727. Email: eschorna@cdeducation.org. Web: www.stjohn.cdeducation.org. Erin Schornack, Prin. Lay Teachers 4; Students 74.
Catechesis/Religious Program—Patricia Knoop, D.R.E. Students 57.

LONDON, MADISON CO., ST. PATRICK (1865), (German—Irish), [CEM] Rev. Theodore K. Sill; Deacon Daniel W. Hann.
Res.: 61 S. Union St., 43140. Tel: 740-852-0942; Fax: 740-852-5008. Web: www.stpatricklondon.org.
School—(Grades K-8), 226 Elm St., 43140. Tel: 740-852-0161; Fax: 740-852-0602. Dr. Jacob Froning, Prin. Lay Teachers 11; Students 184.
Catechesis/Religious Program—Bernardine J. Hess, D.R.E. Students 55.

MARION, MARION CO., ST. MARY (1864) [CEM] Rev. Michael Nimocks, Pastor.
Res.: 251 N. Main St., 43302. Tel: 740-382-2118; Fax: 740-382-2110. Email: stmaryinfo@marionstmary.org. Web: www.marionstmary.org.
School—274 N. Prospect St., 44302. Tel: 740-382-1607. Web: www.marioncatholicschools.org. Bob Rush, Prin. Lay Teachers 11; Students 144.
High School—Marion Catholic Jr/Sr High School, (Grades 7-12), 1001 Mt. Vernon Ave., 43302. Tel: 740-389-2381; Fax: 740-389-5243. Web: www.marioncatholicschools.org. Francis C. Voll, Prin. Lay Teachers 17; Students 140.
Catechesis/Religious Program—Tel: 740-382-2262. Students 514.

MARYSVILLE, UNION CO., OUR LADY OF LOURDES (1866) [CEM] Rev. David A. Poliafico; Deacons Gordon T. Kunkler; Charles Knight; Amy Rohyans, Pastoral Assoc.; Paul Cordell, Business Mgr.
Res.: 1033 W. Fifth St., 43040. Tel: 937-644-6020; Fax: 937-644-3297. Email: olol.marysville@rrohio.com.
Catechesis/Religious Program—Tel: 937-644-6030; Fax: 937-644-3297. Alicia Weingates, C.R.E. Students 325.
Mission—Haiti Parish Twinning Program (Saint Thomas d' Aquin) Aquin.

MILLERSBURG, HOLMES CO., ST. PETER (1877) [CEM] [JC] Rev. Ronald J. Aubry.
Res.: 379 S. Crawford St., 44654-1463. Tel: 330-674-1671. Web: www.holmescountycatholic.org.
Catechesis/Religious Program—Fax: 330-674-1673. Email: ron@valkyrie.net. Bonnie Agawa, D.R.E. Students 47.
Mission—SS. Peter and Paul (1857)Tel: 330-674-1671.
Catechesis/Religious Program—Students 9.

MINERAL CITY, TUSCARAWAS CO., SAINT PATRICK, Closed. For sacramental records contact Holy Trinity, Bolivar.

MT. VERNON, KNOX CO., ST. VINCENT DE PAUL (1842) [CEM] Rev. Mark J. Hammond; Greg Henkel, Pastoral Assoc.
Res.: 303 E. High St., 43050. Tel: 740-392-4711; Fax: 740-392-4714. Web: www.stvincentmountvernon.org.
School—206 E. Chestnut St., 43050. Tel: 740-393-3611; Fax: 740-393-0236. Martha Downs, Prin. Lay Teachers 15; Students 145.
Catechesis/Religious Program—Shirley Lower, D.R.E. Students 155.

MURRAY CITY, HOCKING CO., ST. PHILIP NERI, Closed. For inquiries for sacramental records contact St. John, Logan.

NEW ALBANY, FRANKLIN CO., CHURCH OF THE RESURRECTION (1983) Rev. Jerome P. Rodenfels; Deacon Byron Phillips.
Church: 6300 E. Dublin-Granville Rd., 43054. Tel: 614-855-1400; Fax: 614-855-0779. Email: info@churchoftheresurrection.com. Web: www.churchoftheresurrection.com.
Res.: 5575 Morgan Rd., 43054. Tel: 614-855-0476 (Rectory).
Catechesis/Religious Program—Tel: 614-939-1794; Fax: 614-855-0779. Ms. Joan Lucius, D.R.E. Students 480.

NEW BOSTON, SCIOTO CO., ST. MONICA (1915) [CEM] Rev. Joseph T. Yokum; Deacon James M. Sturgeon. In Res., Rev. Joseph C. Klee.
Res.: 4252 Pine St., 45662. Tel: 740-456-5154; Fax: 740-456-5154. Email: stmonica45662@yahoo.com.
Catechesis/Religious Program—Students 39.

NEW LEXINGTON, PERRY CO., ST. ROSE OF LIMA (1867) [JC] Revs. James C. Csaszar; Victor R. Wesolowski; Sr. Diana Durling, S.C., Pastoral Min.
Res.: 309 N. Main St., 43764. Tel: 740-342-1348.
School—119 W. Water St., 43764. Tel: 740-342-3043; Fax: 740-342-1082. Roxanne Demeter, Prin. Lay Teachers 9; Students 144.
Catechesis/Religious Program—Tel: 740-987-2691; 740-342-3043. Students 69.

NEW PHILADELPHIA, TUSCARAWAS CO., SACRED HEART (1895) [CEM 2] Rev. Msgr. George J. Schlegel.
Res.: 139 3rd St., N.E., 44663-3900. Tel: 330-343-6976; Fax: 330-343-1406. Email: shchurch@neohio.twcbc.com. Web: sacreheartnpohio.catholicweb.com.
School—Tuscarawas Central Catholic Elementary, (Grades PreK-6), 600 N. Tuscarawas Ave., Dover, 44622. Tel: 330-343-9134; Fax: 330-364-6509. Theresa Layton, Prin. Lay Teachers 12; Students 220.
Catechesis/Religious Program—Students 85.

NEWARK, LICKING CO.

1—CHURCH OF THE BLESSED SACRAMENT (1904) [JC] Rev. Jonathan F. Wilson; Deacons Charles F. Stevens, (Retired); Robert W. Ghiloni, (Retired); Patrick Wilson.
Mailing Address: 394 E. Main St., 43055. Email: blsac43055@midohio.twcbc.com. Web: www.blsac.net.
Res.: 378 E. Main St., 43055. Tel: 740-345-4290; Fax: 740-345-3890.
School—. Tel: 740-345-4125; Fax: 740-345-6168. Email: svanhorn@cdeducation.org. Mary Packham, Prin. Lay Teachers 10; Students 200.
Catechesis/Religious Program—Tel: 740-763-4304. Debbie Wills, C.R.E. Students 50.

2—ST. FRANCIS DE SALES (1842) [CEM 2] Rev. Robert Penhallurick; Deacons Jack Elam, (Retired); Steven DeMers.
Res.: 66 Granville St., 43055. Tel: 740-345-9874; Fax: 740-345-1585. Web: www.stfrancisparish.net.
School—38 Granville St., 43055. Tel: 740-345-4049; Fax: 740-345-9768. Web: www.cdeducation.org/schools/dse. Cheryl Spain, Prin. Lay Teachers 21; Students 420.
Catechesis/Religious Program—Tel: 740-345-9874, Ext. 222; Fax: 740-345-1585. Lori Mazone, D.R.E. Tel: 740-345-9874, Ext. 222; Theresa DeMers, Pastoral Min. Tel: 740-345-9874, Ext. 224. Students 160.

NEWCOMERSTOWN, TUSCARAWAS CO., ST. FRANCIS DE SALES (1918) [JC] Rev. William J. Faustner.
Res.: 440 River St., 43832. Tel: 740-498-7368. Email: stfran@newsguy.com.
Catechesis/Religious Program—Tel: 740-498-5497; Fax: 740-498-5497 (call first). Students 15.

OTWAY, SCIOTO CO., OUR LADY OF LOURDES (1917) [CEM] Rev. David E. Young.
Res.: 2215 Galena Pike, West Portsmouth, 45663. Tel: 740-858-4600; Fax: 740-858-4600. Email: olosc@zoomnet.net.
Catechesis/Religious Program—Students 19.
Otway Community Service Center—P.O. Box 8, 45657. Tel: 740-372-2202.

PICKERINGTON, FAIRFIELD CO., SETON PARISH (1978) Rev. James A. Klima; Deacon Hector Raymond, Pastoral Min.
Res.: 600 Hill Rd., 43147. Tel: 614-833-0482; Fax: 614-833-4154. Email: bstory@setonparish.com. Web: www.setonparish.com.
Catechesis/Religious Program—Tel: 614-833-0485. Mary Jane Sobczyk, D.R.E.; Barbara Serrano, Youth Min. Students 875.

PLAIN CITY, UNION CO., ST. JOSEPH (1864) Rev. Patrick A. Toner; Deacon Anthony Bonacci; Sarah Reinhard, Admin.; Sue York, Volunteer & Prog. Coord.
Res.: 670 W. Main St., 43064. Tel: 614-873-8850; Fax: 614-873-0735. Email: office@saintjosephplaincity.com. Web: www.saintjosephplaincity.com.
Catechesis/Religious Program—Students 139.
Oratory—Sacred Heart Milford Center, Union Co.

PORTSMOUTH, SCIOTO CO.

1—HOLY REDEEMER (1852), (Irish), [CEM] [JC] Rev. Dwayne A. McNew; Ann Kempf, Pastoral Assoc.
Office, Activities Center & Res.: 1325 Gallia St., 45662. Tel: 740-354-2716; Fax: 740-354-8692. Email: holyredeemer1325@yahoo.com.
School—Notre Dame Elementary, (Grades PreK-6), 1401 Gallia St., 45662. Tel: 740-353-8610; Fax: 740-353-6769. Web: www.nddev.com. Kay Kern, Prin. Serving all 7 parishes in Scioto County. Lay Teachers 15; Students 230.
Catechesis/Religious Program—Students 18.

2—ST. MARY (1841), (German), [CEM] Rev. Theodore F. Machnik; Deacon George E. Horsley.
Res.: 524 Sixth St., 45662. Tel: 740-354-4551; Fax: 740-354-5797. Email: office@stmaryportsmouth.org. Web: www.stmaryportsmouth.org.
Catechesis/Religious Program—Students 15.

POWELL, DELAWARE CO., ST. JOAN OF ARC (1987) Revs. Raymond Larussa; Jeffrey E. Tigyer; Deacons Thomas M. Berg Sr.; James A. Rouse.
Res.: 10700 Liberty Rd. S., 43065-9303. Tel: 614-761-0905; Fax: 614-761-0850. Email: office-staff@rrohio.com. Web: www.stjoanofarcpowell.org.
Catechesis/Religious Program—Tel: 614-761-0903. Email: psr-office@rrohio.com. Emily Winner, D.R.E. Students 1,527.

REYNOLDSBURG, FRANKLIN CO., ST. PIUS X (1958) Rev. Msgr. David R. Funk; Rev. Daniel J. Millisor, Parochial Vicar; Deacons John Vellani; John L. DuPrey; James W. Kelly; Charles Miller, Parish Admin.; Sr. Joan Supel, O.P., Pastoral Assoc.; Leah Kelly, Pastoral Assoc.
Res.: 1051 Waggoner Rd., 43068. Tel: 614-866-2859; Fax: 614-866-1499. Email: st_piusx@ameritech.net. Web: www.spxreynoldsburg.com.
School—1061 Waggoner Rd., 43068. Tel: 614-866-6050; Fax: 614-866-6187. Web: www.coeducation.org/schools/px/index.html. Kathleen DeMatteo, Prin. Lay Teachers 28; Students 534.
Catechesis/Religious Program—Tel: 614-864-3505. Judy Cafmeyer, D.R.E.; Judie Bryant, Dir. Youth Ministry. Students 255.

ROSWELL, TUSCARAWAS CO., ST. ELIZABETH, Closed. For sacramental records contact Sacred Heart Parish, New Philadelphia.

SHAWNEE, PERRY CO., ST. MARY & ST. AUGUSTINE, Closed. For sacramental records contact St. Rose of Lima Parish, New Lexington.

SOMERSET, PERRY CO.

1—HOLY TRINITY (1827) [CEM] Revs. Stephen F. Carmody, O.P.; William Luke Tancrell, O.P., Parochial Vicar; Deacon Eugene C. Dawson, Pastoral Assoc.
Mailing Address: P.O. Box 190, 43783. Tel: 740-743-1317 (Office). Email: stjoe-holytrinity@columbus.rr.com.
Rectory—St. Joseph Rectory, St. Rte. 383, 43783. Tel: 740-743-1399.
School—S. Columbus St., 43783. Tel: 740-743-1324; Fax: 740-743-1324. Joan Miller, Prin. Lay Teachers 8; Students 136.

Catechesis/Religious Program—Tel: 740-743-1855. Students 96.

2—St. Joseph's (1818) [CEM] Revs. Stephen F. Carmody, O.P.; William Luke Tancrell, O.P., Parochial Vicar; Deacon Eugene C. Dawson, Pastoral Assoc.
Rectory—St. Joseph Rectory, State Rte. 383, N.E., P.O. Box 190, 43783. Tel: 740-743-2856; 740-743-1317 (Office). Email: stjoe-holytrinity@columbus.rr.com.
Catechesis/Religious Program—Tel: 740-743-1855. Students 16.

Strasburg, Tuscarawas Co., St. Aloysius (1911) Closed. For sacramental records contact Holy Trinity, Bolivar.

Sugar Grove, Fairfield Co., St. Joseph (1853) [CEM] [JC] Rev. James A. Walter; Barbara A. Uhl, Pastoral Assoc.; Frederick J. Krile, Pastoral Assoc.
Res.: 306 Elm St., P.O. Box 209, 43155-0209. Tel: 740-746-8302; Fax: 740-746-8805.
Catechesis/Religious Program—Tel: 740-746-8302. Rita Dryden, D.R.E. Students 50.

Sunbury, Delaware Co., St. John Neumann (1983) Rev. David W. Sizemore; Deacon Carl A. Calcara Jr.
Res. & Mailing Address: 801 W. Cherry St., Ste. 120, 43074. Tel: 740-965-1358; Fax: 740-965-1377. Email: saintjohnneumann@stjohnsunbury.org. Web: www.saintjohnsunbury.org.
Church: 9633 E. State Rte. 37, 43074-9593. Tel: 740-965-1358.
Social Hall—Tel: 740-965-1358.
Catechesis/Religious Program— Robert M. Steinbauer, D.R.E. Students 377.

Utica, Licking Co., Church of the Nativity (1909) Rev. Stephen A. Metzger.
Res.: 271 Jefferson St., P.O. Box 506, 43080. Tel: 740-892-2321.
Catechesis/Religious Program—Rose Gorius, D.R.E. Students 44.

Wainwright, Tuscarawas Co., Parish Community of St. Therese and St. Paul, Closed. For St. Therese's sacramental records contact Immaculate Conception, Dennison. For St. Paul's sacramental records contact Sacred Heart, New Philadelphia.

Washington Court House, Fayette Co., St. Colman (1885) [CEM] Rev. Jan C. P. Sullivan.
Office: 219 S. North St., 43160. Tel: 740-335-5000; Fax: 740-335-5066.
Res.: 223 E. East St., 43160. Tel: 740-335-3457.
Catechesis/Religious Program—Tel: 740-335-5005. Tracie Rush, D.R.E. (Grades PreK-12). Students 114.

Waverly, Pike Co., St. Mary, Queen of the Missions (1878) [JC] Rev. William P. Hahn.
Res.: 407 S. Market St., 45690. Tel: 740-947-2436. Email: stmary_qm@verizon.net.
Catechesis/Religious Program—Students 23.

Wellston, Jackson Co., SS. Peter and Paul (1881) [CEM] Rev. Donald M. Maroon.
Res.: 227 S. New York Ave., 45692. Tel: 740-384-2359; Fax: 740-384-2945.
School—229 S. New York Ave., 45692. Tel: 740-384-6354. Jeff Plummer, Prin. Lay Teachers 8; Students 80.
Catechesis/Religious Program—Students 90.

West Jefferson, Madison Co., SS. Simon and Jude (1866), (German—Irish), [CEM] Rev. Robert J. Kitsmiller.
9350 High Free Pike, 43162. Web: stsimonjude.org.
Res.: 311 Darbyview Dr., 43162. Tel: 614-879-8562; Fax: 614-879-7373.
Catechesis/Religious Program—Tel: 614-879-8579. Mary Wanner, D.R.E. Students 104.

West Portsmouth, Scioto Co., Our Lady of Sorrows (1944) [CEM] Rev. David E. Young.
Res.: 2215 Galena Pike, 45663. Tel: 740-858-4600; Fax: 740-858-4600. Email: olosc@zoomnet.net.
New To You Service Center—Tel: 740-858-3176. Mary Horn, Dir.
Catechesis/Religious Program—P.O. Box 31, Otway, 45657. Tel: 740-372-7115; Fax: 740-372-7115. Students 10.
Mission—Holy Trinity 2215 Galena Pike, Pond Creek, Scioto Co. 45663.

Westerville, Delaware Co., St. Paul the Apostle (1913) Revs. Charles F. Klinger; David E. Gwinner, Parochial Vicar; Rodney M. Damico, Parochial Vicar; Deacons Thomas Barford; Mickey B. Hawkins; Susan Bellotti, Pastoral Assoc.; Mary Reichley, Pastoral Assoc. In Res., Rev. Mark V. Ghiloni.
Res.: 313 N. State St., 43082. Tel: 614-882-7537. Email: stpaulchurch@stpacc.org. Web: www.stpaulcatholicchurch.org.
School—61 Moss Rd., 43082. Tel: 614-882-2710; Fax: 614-882-5998. Kathleen Norris, Prin.; Sharon Gillivan, Asst. Prin. Lay Teachers 39; Students 866.
Catechesis/Religious Program—Tel: 614-882-5045. Janet Brewer, D.R.E.; Linda Hall, Youth Min. Students 1,005.

Wheelersburg, Scioto Co., St. Peter (1855) [CEM] Rev. Joseph T. Yokum; Deacon James M. Sturgeon.
Res.: 2167 Lick Run Lyra Rd., 45694. Tel: 740-574-5486; Fax: 740-574-6641 (Call before sending). Email: stpeterinchains@verizon.net.
Catechesis/Religious Program—Cindy Gannon, C.R.E. Students 28.

Wills Creek, Coshocton Co., Our Lady of Lourdes, Closed. For sacramental records contact Sacred Heart, Coshocton.

Worthington, Franklin Co., St. Michael (1946) Revs. Richard J. Pendolphi; Stanley L. (Stash) Dailey; Deacons John R. Crerand; Klaus Fricke; William F. Demidovich Jr. In Res., Rev. Carmen J. Arcuri (Retired).
Res.: 5750 N. High St., 43085. Tel: 614-885-7814; Fax: 614-885-3446. Email: saintmichael@ameritech.net. Web: www.saintmichael-cd.org.
School—64 E. Selby Blvd., 43085-3986. Tel: 614-885-3149; Fax: 614-885-1249. Web: www.cdeducation.org/schools/mi. Miss Christine Armbrust, Prin. Lay Teachers 25; Students 585.
Catechesis/Religious Program—Tel: 614-888-5384. James Hahn, D.R.E. Students 286.

Zaleski, Vinton Co., St. Sylvester (1862), (Irish), [CEM] Rev. Joseph J. Trapp II. In Res., Rev. Richard F. Engle (Retired).
Res.: 119 N. Second St., P.O. Box 264, 45698-0264. Tel: 740-596-5474.
Catechesis/Religious Program—Students 11.

Zanesville, Muskingum Co.

1—St. Nicholas (1842), (German), [CEM] Rev. Martin J. Ralko; Deacons Burdette N. (Pete) Peterson Jr., Pastoral Assoc.; Robert E. Staker, Pastoral Assoc.
Res.: 925 E. Main St., 43701. Tel: 740-453-0597; Fax: 740-453-0590. Web: www.stnickparish.org.
School—Bishop Fenwick Middle School, 1030 E. Main St., 43701. Tel: 740-453-2637; Fax: 740-454-0653. Mrs. Mary Walsh, Prin. (Preschool, Kindergarten & 6-8) Lay Teachers 18; Students 283.
Catechesis/Religious Program—Tel: 740-450-7461. Kevin Dooley, D.R.E. Students 98.

2—St. Thomas Aquinas (1820) [CEM 2] Revs. Steven Jordan Turano, O.P.; Joseph Pius Pietrzyk, O.P.; Louis Luke Turon, O.P.; Sr. Maureen Mahon, O.S.F., Pastoral Assoc.
Res.: 130 N. Fifth St., 43701. Tel: 740-453-3301; Fax: 740-453-0333.
School—Bishop Fenwick Elementary School, (Grades 1-5), 139 N. Fifth St., 43701. Tel: 740-454-9731; Fax: 740-454-8775. Mrs. Mary Walsh, Prin. Lay Teachers 12; Students 301.
Catechesis/Religious Program—Tel: 740-453-3301, Ext. 15. Melanie Von Gunten, D.R.E.; Carol A. Luby, Business Mgr. Students 75.

Zoar, Tuscarawas Co., Church of the Holy Trinity (1995) [CEM 4] Rev. Edward Keck. Tel: 330-874-0391; Deacon Lyn Houze.
Mailing Address: 1835 Dover Zoar Rd., N.E., Bolivar, 44612.
Res.: 1841 Dover Zoar Rd., N.E., Bolivar, 44612. Tel: 330-874-4716 (Office & Church).
Catechesis/Religious Program—Kathleen Johnson, D.R.E. Students 72.

Chaplains of Public Institutions

Columbus. *Children's Hospital*. Vacant.
Corrections Medical Center. Mrs. Rose Hamilton.
OSU Hospital East. Rev. James L. Colopy.
OSU Medical Center. Vacant.

Chillicothe. *Chillicothe Correctional Institution*, P.O. Box 5500, 45601. Tel: 740-773-2616, Ext. 248. Rev. Lawrence L. Hummer.
Ross Correctional Institution, P.O. Box 7010, 45601. Tel: 740-774-4182, Ext. 2519. Rev. Charles R. Griffin (Retired).
Res.: 122 Church St., 45601. Tel: 740-773-4391.
Veteran's Affairs Medical Center, 17273 S.R. 104, 45601. Tel: 740-773-1141, Ext. 7203. Rev. Vio O. Joseph, S.A.C.

Lancaster. *Southeastern Correctional Institution*, Tel: 740-653-4324. Deacon Paul DeShaies.

London. *London Correctional Institution*. Rev. Homer D. Blubaugh. Tel: 740-852-2454, Ext. 451.
Madison Correctional Institution. Deacon Gordon T. Kunkler.

Lucasville. *Southern Ohio Correctional Facility*, Tel: 740-259-5544. Rev. Joseph C. Klee.

Marion. *Marion Correctional Institution*. Deacon Robert A. Neely. Tel: 740-382-5781, Ext. 2346.

Marysville. *Ohio Reformatory for Women*. Rev. Patrick A. Toner. Tel: 614-873-8850.

Mount Vernon. *Mount Vernon Developmental Center*, St. Vincent de Paul Parish, 303 E. High St., 43050. Tel: 740-392-4711.

Orient. *Corrections Reception Center*. Rev. Joseph J. Trapp II, Sacramental Min.
Pickaway Correctional Institution, Tel: 614-877-4362. Deacon Donald Robers.

On Duty Outside the Diocese:
Revs.—
Ascencio, Joseph A., Chap., Federal Prison System, Florence, CO 81226.
Everett, Willis E.
Klein, Terrance W., St. Augustine, Brooklyn, NY.
Naughton, Patrick J. (SCR), St. David, Davie, FL.

Military Services:
Rev.—
Subler, Carl A.

Retired:
Rev. Msgrs.—
Bender, Thomas G., The Villas at St. Therese, 5253 E. Broad St., Rm. 309, 43213.
Borrelli, Anthony A., 3140 El Greco Dr., 43204.
Carroll, James J., 12915 Galaxy Dr., Sun City West, AZ.
Clagett, Carl P., 2601 Aspen Rd., Frazeysburg, 43822.
Dreese, John J., P.O. Box 39, New Straitsville, 43766.
Fairchild, Edward, 3306 Beachworth Dr., 43232.
Foeller, Charles J., 6555 County Rd. 109, Mount Gilead, 43338-9563.
Geiger, James A., St. John Church, 351 N. Market St., Logan, 43138-1228.
Grimes, Kevin, St. Andrew, 1899 McCoy Rd., 43220-4499.
Huntzinger, Ralph J., Mohun Health Care Center, 2340 Airport Dr., 43219.
Lane, Frank P., Ph.D., 2025 Lyndon Rd., Franklinville, NY 14737.
McFarland, Edward J., Mother Angelina McCrory Manor, 5199 E. Broad St., 43213-3800.
Meagher, Frank J., The Villas at St. Therese, 5253 E. Broad St., Apt. 207, 43213.
Metzger, Robert E., P.O. Box 227, Junction City, 43748.
Missimi, Anthony N., 1374 Lakeshore Dr., Apt. B, 43204.
Noon, Robert L., The Villas at St. Therese, 5253 E. Broad St. #127, 43213.
Ruef, James L.T., M.A., J.C.L., M.Div., J.D.
Schneider, Robert E., The Villas at St. Therese, 5253 E. Broad St., # 108, 43213.
Schulz, Donald C., Mohun Health Care Center, 2340 Airport Dr., Rm. 322, 43219-2602.
Schweitzer, Francis X., Villas at St. Therese Assisted Living, 25 Noc-Bixby Rd., 43213.
Serraglio, Mario, P.O. Box 703, Canal Winchester, 43110.
Sorohan, David V., M.A., S.T.L., Ph.D., 925 Vernon Rd., Bexley, 43209.
Wolf, John V., S.T.D., 104 N. Mulberry St., Fredericktown, 43019-1051. Tel: 614-694-2505
Revs.—
Arcuri, Carmen J., St. Michael Church, 5750 N. High St., Worthington, 43085.
Arter, Ronald L., 202 Elm St., Box 135, Sugar Grove, 43155.
Bentz, John B., Rte. 1, P.O. Box 604, Sugar Grove, 43155.
Byrne, Patrick J., 4468 Beachwood Lake Dr., Naples, FL 34112.
Carter, Raymond J., Mohun Health Care Center, 2340 Airport Dr., 43219-2602.
Connor, William J., Mohun Health Care Center, 2340 Airport Dr., 43219.
DeVille, William H., 196 S. Grant Ave., Unit 304, 43215-8365.
Ehwald, Joseph A., 1308 Erickson Ave., 43227-2059.
Engle, Richard F., St. Sylvester Church, P.O. Box 264, Zaleski, 45698.
Gately, Robert E., 702 Valley Forge Blvd., Sun City, FL 33573.
Griffin, Charles R., 122 Church St., Chillicothe, 45601.
Laurinaitis, Saulius P., P.O. Box 1417, Hilliard, 43026.
Lavelle, Raymond E., 6415 Pinehurst Pointe, Westerville, 43082.
Losh, Joseph F., Villas at St. Therese, 25 Noe Bixby Rd., 43215.
Loyd, Frederick A., c/o 198 E. Broad St., 43215.
McClory, Bernard J., P.O. Box 3103, Westerville, 43086.
Metzger, John L., P.O. Box 55, New Lexington, 43764.
Metzger, William J., 5684 Groveport Rd., Groveport, 43125.
Schilder, David M., 192 Grand Ave., Chillicothe, 45601.
Schneider, Harold E., 913 Hartney Dr., Gahanna, 43230.
Shonebarger, Thomas, Mohun Health Care Center, 2340 Airport Dr., 43219.
Smith, Paul O., c/o 198 E. Broad St., 43215.

Stanton, Francis M., Villas at St. Therese, Independent Living, 5253 E. Broad St., # 124, 43213-3834.
Stanton, Joseph E., The Villas of St. Therese, 25 Noe Bixby Rd., Rm. 109, 43213.
Totten, Raymond F., 329 Carnegie Pl., Pittsburgh, PA 15208.

Permanent Deacons:
Allison, Mark D., (Leave of Absence)
Andrews, William J., Church of the Ascension, Johnstown; Deacon Parish Administrator: Community of Holy Rosary/St. John the Evangelist
Azzola, Feliz F., St. Mary, Delaware
Ball, Frank X., (Retired)
Barford, Thomas M., St. Paul, Westerville
Baumann, Richard L., (Retired)
Belhorn, Paul C., (Retired)
Berg, Thomas M., Sr., St. Joan of Arc, Powell
Berg, Thomas M., Jr., B.A., M.J., M.P.S., St. Andrew, Columbus; Vice Chancellor, Diocese of Columbus
Bonacci, Anthony C., St. Joseph, Plain City
Busic, Richard B., Our Lady of Mt. Carmel, Buckeye Lake
Butts, Jerome J., Corpus Christi, Columbus
Cain, Albert E., (Retired)
Calcara, Carl A., Jr., St. John Neumann, Sunbury
Campbell, Christopher, Immaculate Conception, Columbus
Checca, Joseph P., St. James the Less, Columbus
Crerand, John R., M.A., St. Michael, Worthington; Defender of the Bond, Diocesan Tribunal
Davies, Martin H., Office of Liturgy, Dir.; St. Catharine of Siena, Columbus
Davis, James R., (Retired)
Davis, William J.F., (Retired)
Dawson, Eugene C., Holy Trinity, Somerset
DeMers, Steven, St. Francis DeSales, Newark; Business Mgr., Catholic Times
Demidovich, William F., Jr., St. Michael, Worthington
Deshaies, Paul, St. Bernadette, Lancaster
Drummer, Kenneth I., (Leave of Absence)
Duda, Frank A., Sacred Heart, Coshocton
DuPrey, John L., St. Pius X, Reynoldsburg
Eiden, Gregory L., Kairos Prison Ministry
Elam, Jack W., (Retired)
Farry, Joseph W., St. Philip, Columbus
Fondriest, Ronald H., St. Joseph, Dover
Fortkamp, Jeffrey D., Our Lady of Peace, Columbus
Fricke, Klaus, St. Michael, Worthington
Ghiloni, Robert W., Blessed Sacrament, Newark
Gorman, William J., (Leave of Absence)
Gorski, James, St. Aloysius & St. Agnes; St. Joseph Cathedral, Columbus; Deacon Parish Admin.
Gundrum, Henry, St. Mark, Lancaster
Hann, Daniel W., St. Patrick, London
Hawkins, Mickey, St. Paul, Westerville
Hood, J. Michael, Our Lady of Lourdes, Ada; Immaculate Conception, Kenton
Horsley, George E., St. Mary, Portsmouth
Houze, Lester, Holy Trinity, Zoar
Iannarino, Francis A., Dir. Diaconate Office, St. Brigid of Kildare, Dublin; Chap., Bishop Watterson High School, Columbus
Johnston, Thomas V., St. Joseph Cathedral, Columbus
Joseph, Robert A., Our Lady of Victory, Columbus
Keating, James, Ph.D., (Excardinated)
Kelly, James W., St. Pius X, Reynoldsburg
Killoren, Robert, (Temporary Leave of Absence)
Knight, Charles, (Retired)
Koebel, Lawrence F., (Retired)
Krick, Richard T., (Retired)
Kruse, David J., St. Christopher, Columbus
Kunkler, Gordon T., Our Lady of Lourdes, Marysville; Chap., Madison Correctional Institution
Labita, Peter C., Christ the King, Columbus
Lampe, Elmer L., (Retired)
Larcomb, Dwight T., (Retired)
Lovensheimer, George L., St. Mary, Chillicothe
McCurry, William E., Chaplain, Marion Youth Services; Holy Family, Columbus
McDevitt, Francis X., St. Elizabeth, Columbus
Miller, Charles J., Pope John XXIII, Canal Winchester
Milne, Maurice N., III, St. Agatha, Columbus
Minner, Roger, St. Mary, Columbus
Morris, James, St. Brendan, Hilliard
Mould, Douglas, Sacred Heart, Coshocton
Mueller, Martin, (Unassigned)
Naporano, Andrew W., St. Margaret of Cortona, Columbus
Neely, Robert A., St. Dominic, Columbus; Chap., Marion Correctional Institute
Paniccia, Frank A., (Retired)
Parsons, Ralph L., (Retired)
Paulucci, Philip M., St. Peter, Columbus
Peterson, Burdette N., St. Nicholas, Zanesville
Phillips, Byron, Church of the Resurrection, New Albany
Plummer, Gil L., Sr., St. Brendan, Hilliard; Business Mgr., St. Joan of Arc, Powell
Poirier, Donald, St. Brigid of Kildare, Dublin
Poland, Joseph D., (Retired)
Pry, Roger F., Pope John XXIII, Canal Winchester
Racine, Dean W., St. Elizabeth, Columbus
Rankin, John, (Retired)
Raymond, Hector, Seton Parish, Pickerington
Robers, Donald, St. John, Logan; Chaplain, Pickaway Correctional
Rouse, James A., A.E., M.S., P.E., St. Joan of Arc, Powell
Rzewnicki, Phil E., (Leave of Absence)
Santos, Kasuma J., Jr., St. James the Less, Columbus; Latino Commission
Scarpitti, Mark A., St. Bernadette, Lancaster
Schermer, Joseph E., St. Peter, Columbus
Smith, Craig, St. Anthony, Columbus
Smithberger, Marion E., St. Timothy, Columbus
Spina, Philip V., Jr., (Leave of Absence)
Stahl, John P., (Retired)
Staker, Eugene R., St. Nicholas, Zanesville
Stevens, Charles F., (Retired)
Sturgeon, James M., St. Peter in Chains, Wheelersburg; St. Monica, New Boston
Sullivan, Frank, St. Mary, Lancaster; Chap., Bishop Hartley High School
Supino, Bart, (Retired)
Turner, Harry, St. Matthew, Gahanna
Varacalli, Christopher, (Temporary Leave of Absence)
Vellani, Albert J., St. Pius X, Reynoldsburg
Venturini, Stephen A., Our Lady of the Miraculous Medal, Columbus
Wiggins, Patrick J., St. Brendan, Hilliard
Wilson, Larry, St. Leonard, Heath
Wilson, Patrick, Blessed Sacrament, Newark
Zimmermann, George A., Holy Spirit, Columbus

INSTITUTIONS LOCATED IN THE DIOCESE

[A] SEMINARIES, PONTIFICAL COLLEGES

COLUMBUS. *Pontifical College Josephinum* (1888) 7625 N. High St., 43235-1498. Tel: 614-885-5585; Fax: 614-885-2307. Web: www.pcj.edu. Faculty 26; Total Enrollment 120.

Chancellor & Vice Chancellor: Most Revs. Pietro Sambi, Apostolic Nuncio to the United States, Chancellor; Frederick F. Campbell, D.D., Ph.D., Vice Chancellor & Bishop of Columbus.

General Administration: Very Rev. James A. Wehner, S.T.D., Rector & Pres.; Rev. Msgr. William Cleves, Ph.D., Vice Rector, School of Theology & Dir. of Formation; Deacon Michael Ross, Ph.D., Academic Dean; David J. DeLeonardis, Ph.D., Asst. Academic Dean; Perry J. Cahall, Ph.D., Dir. of Admissions; Revs. Walter R. Oxley, S.T.D., Dir. Liturgy; Eduardo Nevares, Vice Rector, Dir. Formation, College Liberal Arts; John F. Heisler (ARL), Dean Men, College Liberal Arts; Ervens Mengelle, I.V.E., S.S.L., Dir. Apostolic Works, College Liberal Arts; Michael Ciccone, O.P., S.T.L., Ph.D., Spiritual Dir. - Theology; Paul Hrezo, S.T.L., Spiritual Dir. - College; Rev. Msgr. Christopher Schreck, Ph.D., S.T.D., Vice Pres. Devel., Exec. Dir. Inst. Formation, Min. Perm. Diaconte, Dir.Pastoral Formation & Theolog; John Erwin, M.B.A., C.P.A., Treas.

Administrative Officers: Barbara Couts, Registar; John Heise, Dir. Plant Opers.; Mr. Peter G. Veracka, M.S.L.S., Dir. Library.

School of Theology full-time faculty: Rev. George D. Byers, C.P.M., S.S.L., S.T.D.; Perry J. Cahall, Ph.D.; Rev. Walter R. Oxley, S.T.D.; Rev. Msgrs. William Cleves, Ph.D.; Nevin Klinger, J.C.L.; Revs. Joseph A. Murphy, S.J., S.T.D.; William F. Murphy, S.T.D.; Rev. Msgr. Christopher Schreck, Ph.D., S.T.D.; John J. Clabeaux, Ph.D.; Sr. Elizabeth McDonough, O.P., J.C.D.

Resident Emeritus Professor: Rev. William Dettling, O.P., S.T.D.

Other full-time faculty: Deacon Michael Ross, Ph.D.; Mr. Peter G. Veracka, M.S.L.S.; Julia Parker, M.Mu.Ed.

College of Liberal Arts-full-time faculty: Revs. John Heisler; Eduardo Nevares; Alma Amell, Ph.D.; David J. De Leonardis, Ph.D.; Beverly Lane, M.L.S.; Very Rev. James A. Wehner, S.T.D., Rector & Pres.; Loyann W. Brush, M.A.; Douglas C. Fortner, Ph.D.; Revs. Paul Hrezo, S.T.L.; Ervens Mengelle, I.V.E., S.S.L.; Bradley G. Potter, Ph.D.; Patricia Pintado, Ph.D.; Patricia Polko, M.A.

[B] COLLEGES AND UNIVERSITIES

COLUMBUS. *Ohio Dominican University*, 1216 Sunbury Rd., 43219. Tel: 614-253-2741; Fax: 614-252-0776. Email: admissions@ohiodominican.edu. Web: www.ohiodominican.edu. Ronald J. Seiffert, Interim Pres.; Dr. Linda Schoen, Interim Vice Pres. Academic Affairs; David Archibald, Vice Pres. Enrollment Mgmt. & Mktg.; David Kosanovic, Interim Vice Pres. Fin. & Admin.; Jamie Caridi, Vice Pres. Student Devel.; Sr. Catherine Colby, O.P., Ed.D., Vice Pres., Mission & Identity. Dominican Sisters of the Third Order of St. Dominic of Dominical Sisters of Peace. Sisters 3; Lay Teachers 73; Students 3,051.

[C] HIGH SCHOOLS, DIOCESAN OR INTERPAROCHIAL

COLUMBUS. *Bishop Hartley High School*, 1285 Zettler Rd., 43227. Tel: 614-237-5421; Fax: 614-237-3809. Email: hartley@cdeducation.org. Web: www.bishop-hartley.org. Mike Winters, Prin.; Barbara Recchie, Asst. Prin.; Dave Thompson, Athletic Dir. Lay Teachers 45; Students 649.

Bishop Ready High School (1961) 707 Salisbury Rd., 43204. Tel: 614-276-5263; Fax: 614-276-5116. Email: cseamen@cdeducation.org. Web: www.brhs.org. Celene A. Seamen, Prin.; Jeri Rod, Asst. Prin. Sisters 1; Administrators 2; Lay Teachers 27; Students 450.

Bishop Watterson High School (1954) 99 E. Cooke Rd., 43214. Tel: 614-268-8671; Fax: 614-268-0551. Web: www.cd.education.org/schools/bw. Mrs. Marian Hutson, Prin.; Virginia O'Connor, Asst. Prin.; Bill Weisner, Asst. Prin.; Deacon Frank A. Iannarino, Chap. Deacons 2; Sisters 1; Lay Teachers 88; Students 1,070.

Development Office, 99 E. Cooke Rd., 43214. Tel: 614-268-8671, Ext. 239; Fax: 614-268-4309. Web: www.bishopwatterson.com/.

St. Charles Preparatory School, 2010 E. Broad St., 43209. Tel: 614-252-6714; Fax: 614-251-6800. Email: dcavello@cdeducation.org. Web: www.stcharlesprep.org. Dominic J. Cavello, Prin.; Scott M. Pharion, Asst. Prin.; James Lower, Asst. Prin. Priests 1; Sisters 1; Lay Teachers 27; Students 616.

St. Francis de Sales High School, 4212 Karl Rd., 43224. Tel: 614-267-7808; Fax: 614-265-3375. Email: dgarrick@cdeducation.org. Web: www.cdeducation.org/school/ds. Mr. Dan Garrick, Prin.; Jackie Messerschmitt, Asst. Prin.; Jim Jones, Asst. Prin. Lay Teachers 69; Students 865.

LANCASTER. *William V. Fisher Catholic High School*, 1803 Granville Pike, 43130. Tel: 740-654-1231; Fax: 740-654-1233. Email: jsilcott@cdeducation.org. Web: fishercatholic.org. Mr. Jim Silcott, Pres. & Prin.; Tiffany Wade, Asst. Prin.; Rev. John M. Reade, Chap. Lay Teachers 19; Students 249.

MARION. *Marion Catholic High School*, (Grades 7-12), (Junior/Senior High School), 1001 Mt. Vernon Ave., 43302. Tel: 740-389-2381; Fax: 740-389-5243. Email: fvoll@cdeducatoin.org. Web: www.marioncatholic.org. Francis C. Voll, Pres. & Prin.; Al Seitter, Asst. Prin. Lay Teachers 12; Students 102.

NEW PHILADELPHIA. *Tuscarawas Central Catholic High School*, (Grades 7-12), (Junior/Senior High School), 777 Third St., N.E., 44663. Tel: 330-343-3302; Fax: 330-343-6388. Email: ddidonat@cdeducation.org. Web: www.tccsaints.com. David A. DiDonato, Prin.; Scott Power, Asst. Prin. Lay Teachers 12; Students 131.

NEWARK. *Newark Catholic High School* (1958) 1 Green Wave Dr., 43055. Tel: 740-344-3594; Fax: 740-344-0421. Email: bhill@cdeducation.org. Web: www.newarkcatholic.org/. Beth Hill, Prin.; Rev. Robert Penhallurick, Chap. Lay Teachers 22; Students 269.

PORTSMOUTH. *Notre Dame High School* (1953) (Grades 7-12), (Junior/Senior High School), 2220 Sunrise Ave., 45662. Tel: 740-353-0719; Fax: 740-353-2526. Email: kmilliga@cdeducation.org. Kathleen Milligan, Prin. Lay Teachers 17; Students 158.

ZANESVILLE. *Bishop Rosecrans High School* (1950) 1040 E. Main St., 43701. Tel: 740-452-7504; Fax: 740-455-5080. Email: bzanders@cdeducation.org. Web: www.cdeducation.org/schools/bro. Rev. Martin J. Ralko; F. William Zanders, Prin. Priests 1; Lay Teachers 13; Students 143.

[D] MONTESSORI SCHOOLS

COLUMBUS. *St. Joseph Montessori School* (1968) 933 Hamlet St., 43201-3595. Tel: 614-291-8601; Fax: 614-291-7411. Email: sjmsoffice@cdeducation.org; sjmsdev@cdeducation.org. Web: www.sjms.net. Sr. Carolyn Thomas, S.C.N., Ph.D., Interim Head of School; Ernestine Jackson, Devel. Dir.; Lenn Turner, Transition Coord. Lay Teachers 30; Students 275.

[E] PRIVATE SCHOOLS

COLUMBUS. *Our Lady of Bethlehem School and Childcare*, 4567 Olentangy River Rd., 43214. Tel: 614-459-8285; Fax: 614-451-3706. Email: ldulin@cdeducation.org. Web: www.ourladyofbethlehem.org. Lori Dulin, Dir.; Janelle Obergfell, Librarian. Totally Terrific Twos; Preschool; Pre-Kindergarten; Full & Half Day Kindergarten; Full & Part Time Childcare; Summer Program. Total Staff 10; Children 78.

[F] GENERAL HOSPITALS

COLUMBUS. *Mohun Health Care Center* (1956) 2340 Airport Dr., 43219. Tel: 614-416-6132; Fax: 614-251-0338. Jeffrey Urban, Admin. Total Staff 118; Bed Capacity 72; Patients Assisted Annually 101.

Mount Carmel Health System, 6150 E. Broad St., 43213. Tel: 614-546-4533; Fax: 614-546-4573. Web: mountcarmelhealth.com. Claus von Zychlin, Pres. & CEO. Bed Capacity 1,267; Total Staff 7,990; Patients Assisted Annually 1,213,648.

Legal Holdings:

Mount Carmel Health System Tel: 614-546-4531; Fax: 614-546-4573.

Mount Carmel West (General Hospital) Tel: 614-234-5000; Fax: 614-234-5756.

Mount Carmel East (General Hospital) Tel: 614-234-6000; Fax: 614-234-6408.

Mount Carmel Care Continuum Businesses Tel: 614-234-0224; Fax: 614-234-5756. Web: www.mountcarmelhealth.com.

Mount Carmel College of Nursing Tel: 614-234-5800; Fax: 614-234-2875.

Mount Carmel St. Ann's (General Hospital), Westerville. Tel: 614-898-4000; Fax: 614-898-8668. Web: www.mountcarmelhealth.com.

Mount Carmel New Albany Surgical Hospital, New Albany, 43054. Tel: 614-775-6610.

Mount Carmel Health System Foundation Tel: 614-546-4500; Fax: 614-546-4501. Web: www.mountcarmelfoundation.org.

ZANESVILLE. *Genesis HealthCare System*, 2951 Maple Ave, 43701. Tel: 740-454-4633; Fax: 740-455-4914. Mr. Matthew Perry, CEO & Pres. Franciscan Sisters of Christian Charity 3; Bed Capacity 433; Total Staff 3,539.

[G] HOMES FOR AGED AND HOUSING FOR ELDERLY

COLUMBUS. *Mother Angeline McCrory Manor, Inc.* (2005) 5199 E. Broad St., 43213. Tel: 614-751-5700; Fax: 614-751-8311. Web: www.mangelinemanor.org. Sr. Pauline Ross, O.Carm., Admin.

Nazareth Towers (1967) 300 E. Rich St., 43215. Tel: 614-464-4780; Fax: 614-464-1733. Email: sallyhaban@yahoo.com. Sally Haban, Admin. Total in Residence 152; Total Staff 5.

Seton Coshocton, Inc., 377 Clow Ln., Coshocton, 43812. Tel: 740-622-7664; 740-622-7664 (Coshocton No.); Fax: 740-622-4635. Email: setoncoshocton@midohio.twcbc.com. Roxana Wilson, Property Mgr.; Wayne Patterson, Maintenance; Cindy Smith, Svc. Coord. Apartments 40; Total in Residence 40; Total Staff 3.

Seton South Columbus, Inc. (1995) 155 Highview Blvd., 43207. Tel: 614-492-9944; Fax: 614-492-9955. Suzanne Ambrose, Mgr. Total in Residence 60; Total Staff 2.

Seton Square Dover, II, Inc., 139 Filmore Ave., Dover, 44622. Tel: 330-343-3611; Fax: 330-364-3147. Email: setonsquare@wifi7.com. Bob Campitelli, Mgr.; Mary Campitelli, Asst. Total in Residence 40; Total Staff 3.

Seton Square North, 1776 Drew Ave., 43235. Tel: 614-451-1995; Fax: 614-451-3793. Email: ssnaline@ameritech.net. Aline Taylor, Mgr. Total in Residence 242; Total Staff 5.

Seton Square, West, 3999 Clime Rd., 43228. Tel: 614-274-8550; Fax: 614-308-1550. Dionna Richardson, Mgr. Staff 3; Total in Residence 48.

**The Villas at St. Therese Assisted Living, Inc.*, 25 Noe-Bixby Rd., 43213-1411. Tel: 614-864-3576; Fax: 614-864-3577. Sr. Patricia Michael Sweeney, O.Carm., Admin.; Rev. Msgr. Joseph M. Hendricks, Contact Person.

**The Villas at St. Therese Independent Living, Inc.*, 5253 E. Broad St., 43213. Tel: 614-856-9951; Fax: 614-856-9654. Rev. Msgr. Joseph M. Hendricks, Contact Person.

DOVER. *Seton Development, Inc.*, 501 S. James St., 44622. Tel: 330-343-3611; Fax: 330-364-3147. Email: setonsquare@wifi7.com. Bob Campitelli, Mgr.; Mary Campitelli, Asst. Total in Residence 50; Total Staff 3.

KENTON. *Seton Kenton, Inc.*, 699 Morningside Dr., 43326. Tel: 419-673-7202; Fax: 419-673-7202. Kim Manns, Mgr. Total in Residence 50; In Residence 48; Total Staff 2.

LANCASTER. *Seton Lancaster, Inc.*, 232 Gay St., 43130. Tel: 740-681-1403; Fax: 740-681-9178. Roxanne Bailey, Mgr. Total in Residence 34; Total Staff 2.

LONDON. *Seton London, Inc.*, 350 Cambridge Dr., 43140. Tel: 740-852-4233. Kitty Binion, Mgr. Total in Residence 50; Total Staff 3.

MARION. *Seton Square Marion, Inc.*, 255 Richland Rd., 43302. Tel: 740-389-4746; Fax: 740-389-9780. Email: Seton504@yahoo.com. Debra J. Erwin, Mgr. Total in Residence 110; Total Staff 3.

REYNOLDSBURG. *Seton Square East, Inc.*, 1235 Briarcliff Rd., 43068. Tel: 614-861-4860; Fax: 614-861-8022. Email: dougdecke89r@yahoo.com. Douglas Decker, Mgr. Total in Residence 106; Total Staff 3.

WASHINGTON COURT HOUSE. *Seton Washington Court House*, 400 N. Glenn Ave., 43160. Tel: 740-335-2292; Fax: 740-335-2291. Email: setonwch@sbcglobal.net. Linda Hatmacher, Mgr. Total in Residence 40; Total Staff 2.

WELLSTON. *Seton Square Wellston, Inc.* (1980) 570 W. First St., 45692. Tel: 740-384-6174; Fax: 740-384-1514. Tamra Jolly, Property Mgr. Total in Residence 48; Total Staff 2.

ZANESVILLE. *Seton Housing, Inc.*, 516 Sheridan St., 43701. Tel: 740-453-4422; Fax: 740-453-4950. David Sears, Mgr. Total in Residence 44; Total Staff 1.

[H] MONASTERIES AND RESIDENCES OF PRIESTS AND BROTHERS

COLUMBUS. *Salesian Center* (1967) P.O. Box 2854, 43216. Tel: 614-286-3417. Email: sdb@sbgcc.org. Web: www.sbgcc.org. Bro. Michael Brinkman, S.D.B. Brothers 1; Total Staff 1.

[I] CONVENTS AND RESIDENCES FOR SISTERS

COLUMBUS. *Congregation of the Sisters of the Holy Cross, Mount Carmel East Convent*, 266 McNaughton Rd., 43213-2139. Tel: 614-866-9397.

Sisters of the Holy Cross, Inc. Sisters 2.

Dominican Sisters of Peace, Inc., 2320 Airport Dr., 43219-2098. Tel: 614-416-1900; Fax: 614-252-7435. Email: srpeace@oppeace.org. Web: www.oppeace.org. Sisters 164; Total in Congregation 638.

Leadership Team: Sisters Therese Leckert, O.P., Councilor, Sec.-General; Joan Scanlon, O.P., Vicaress; Margaret Ormond, O.P., Prioress; Gene Poore, O.P., Councilor; Gemma Doll, O.P., Councilor.

Sisters' Residence: Sr. Sheila Marie McIntyre, Mission Group Coord.

Mohun Health Care Center Tel: 614-253-8517; Fax: 614-251-0338. Jeffrey Urban, Admin.; Sr. Mary Patricia Gallagher, O.P., Dir. of Resident Life; Rev. Emmanuel Bertrand, O.P., Chap.

Mother Angeline McCrory Manor Convent, 5199 E. Broad St., 43213. Tel: 614-751-5700. Email: srfcasey@sbcglobal.net. Carmelite Sisters operate the Villas at St. Therese, Assisted Living; Carmelite Sisters for the Aged and Infirm.

Sisters of the Good Shepherd (1865) 2440 Dawnlight Ave., 43211-1934. Tel: 614-416-8747; Fax: 614-428-7995. Email: srrose3@gmail.com. Web: www.handcraftingjustice.org. Handcrafting Justice buys from Good Shepherd Missions in the developing world for resale. Proceeds are sent back to the missions to better the lives of women in the developing world. Sisters of the Good Shepherd 3.

PORTSMOUTH. *St. Joseph Adoration Monastery, Poor Clares of Perpetual Adoration* (Public Chapel), 2311 Stockham Ln., 45662-3049. Tel: 740-353-4713. Email: nuns@stjosephmonastery.com. Web: www.stjosephmonastery.com. Sr. Dolores Marie, P.C.P.A., Abbess; Rev. Joseph C. Klee, Chap. Professed Cloistered Nuns 8; Postulants 1; Novices 1.

[J] NEWMAN CENTERS

COLUMBUS. *Campus Ministry Ohio State University*, 64 W. Lane Ave., 43201. Tel: 614-291-4674; Fax: 614-291-2065. Email: mailbox@thenewmancenter.net. Web: www.thenewmancenter.net. Revs. Vincent W. McKiernan, C.S.P.; Lawrence Rice, C.S.P., Dir.; Charles Cunniff, C.S.P. Priests 4; Members 1,914; Staff 10. In Res. Rev. David W. O'Brien, C.S.P. (Retired).

[K] FOUNDATIONS

COLUMBUS. **The Foundation of the Catholic Diocese of Columbus dba The Catholic Foundation* 1071 S. High St., 43206. Tel: 614-443-8893; Fax: 614-443-8894. Jennifer A. Damiano, Exec. Dir.

Legacy of Catholic Learning Endowment Program, 198 E. Broad St., 43215. Tel: 614-224-1221.

LANCASTER. **William V. Fisher Catholic High School Endowment Fund*, 1803 Granville Pike, 43130. Tel: 740-654-1231; Fax: 740-654-1233. Email: jsilcott@cdeducation.org. Web: fishercatholic.org.

MARION. *Marion Catholic High School Endowment Fund*, 1001 Mount Vernon Ave., 43302. Tel: 740-389-2381; Fax: 740-389-5243. Email: fvoll@cdeducation.org. Web: www.marioncatholic.org.

NEW PHILADELPHIA. *Tuscarawas Central Catholic High School Endowment Fund*, 777 Third St. N.E., 44663. Tel: 330-343-3302; Fax: 330-343-6388. Email: ddidonat@cdeducation.org.

NEWARK. **Newark Catholic High School Foundation*, One Green Wave Dr., 43055. Tel: 740-344-5671; Fax: 740-344-0421. Email: kdellner@laca.org.

ZANESVILLE. *Bishop Rosecrans High School Foundation* (1986) 1040 E. Main St., 43701. Tel: 740-450-7993; Fax: 740-455-5080. Email: jod@brhsfoundation.org. Web: www.rosecrans.cdeducation.

[L] MISCELLANEOUS

COLUMBUS. *Blessed Margaret Guild, Inc. c/o St. Patrick Church*, 262 N. Grant Ave., 43215. Tel: 614-240-5915; Fax: 614-240-5928. Total Staff 1.

Catholic Alumni Club, P.O. Box 695, 43216. Tel: 614-575-0518; Fax: 614-575-0518. Email: peg42@att.net; dwdoell@yahoo.com. Web: www.angelfire.com/oh/CatholicAlumniClub. Peggy Schano, Contact Person. Tel: 614-575-0518; Dan Doell, Contact Person. Tel: 614-846-7489.

Catholic Men's Ministry, 1511 Teeway Dr., 43220. Tel: 614-235-0608. Web: cmmohio.org. Chuck Wilson, Dir.

The Christ Child Society of Columbus, Inc., P.O. Box 340091, 43234-0091. Tel: 614-294-6347, Ext. 305. Email: ccsofcolumbus@yahoo.com. Web: www.rc.net/columbus/christchild. Theresa Lembach, Pres.

Diocesan Charities Membership Corporation, 198 E. Broad St., 43215.

Diocesan Retirement Community Corp., 198 E. Broad St., 43215. Tel: 614-224-2251; Fax: 614-224-6306. Rev. Msgr. Joseph M. Hendricks, Pres. & CEO.

Haitian Catholic Coalition of Ohio, 1582 Ferris Rd., 43224. Tel: 614-778-0459. Nedy Melidor, Founder & Counselor; Rev. Fritzner Valcin (Haiti), Counselor.

St. Stephen's Community House, 1500 E. 17th Ave., 43219. Tel: 614-294-6347; Fax: 614-294-0258. Email: brightenlives@saintstephensch.org. Web: www.saintstephensch.org. Ms. Michelle Mills, Pres. & CEO. Total Assisted 22,000; Total Staff 131.

LANCASTER. **St. Mary of the Assumption Foundation*, 132 S. High St., 43130. Tel: 740-653-0997; Fax: 740-653-0337. Rev. Donald E. Franks, Contact Person.

ZANESVILLE. *St. Nicholas Foundation* (1842) 955 E. Main St., 43701. Tel: 740-453-0597; Fax: 740-453-0590. Web: www.stnickparish.org. Rev. Martin J. Ralko, Pres.

RELIGIOUS INSTITUTES OF MEN REPRESENTED IN THE DIOCESE

For further details refer to the corresponding bracketed number in the Religious Institutes of Men or Women section.

[0350]—*Cistercians Order of the Strict Observance-Trappists*—O.C.S.O.

[0690]—*Jesuit Fathers and Brothers* (Detroit and Maryland Provs.)—S.J.

[0430]—*Order of Preachers-Dominicans* (Prov. of St. Joseph)—O.P.

[1030]—*Paulist Fathers*—C.S.P.

[1050]—*Pontifical Institute for Foreign Missions*—P.I.M.E.

[1190]—*Salesians of St. John Bosco*—S.D.B.

[0760]—*Society of Mary*—S.M.

[0990]—*Society of the Catholic Apostolate*—S.A.C.

[1060]—*Society of the Precious Blood* (Cincinnati Prov.)—C.PP.S.

RELIGIOUS INSTITUTES OF WOMEN REPRESENTED IN THE DIOCESE

[0330]—*Carmelite Sisters for the Aged and Infirm*—O.Carm.

[3710]—*Congregation of the Sisters of St. Agnes*—C.S.A.

[1920]—*Congregation of the Sisters of the Holy Cross*—C.S.C.

[1730]—*Congregation of the Sisters of the Third Order of St. Francis, Oldenburg, IN*—O.S.F.

[1710]—*Congregation of the Third Order of St. Francis of Mary Immaculate, Joliet, IL*—O.S.F.

[1070-13]—*Dominican Sisters* (Adrian, MI)—O.P.

[]—*Dominican Sisters of Our Lady of the Springs of Bridgeport*—O.P.

[1115]—*Dominican Sisters of Peace, Inc.*—O.P.

[1230]—*Franciscan Sisters of Christian Charity* (Manitowoc, WI)—O.S.F.

[3210]—*Poor Clares of Perpetual Adoration*—P.C.P.A.
[0440]—*Sisters of Charity of Cincinnati, Ohio*—S.C.
[0500]—*Sisters of Charity of Nazareth, Kentucky*—S.C.N.
[0990]—*Sisters of Divine Providence*—C.D.P.
[3000]—*Sisters of Notre Dame de Namur*—S.N.D.deN.
[1630]—*Sisters of St. Francis of Penance and Christian Charity* (Stella Niagara, NY)—O.S.F.
[1530]—*Sisters of St. Francis of the Congregation of Our Lady of Lourdes, Sylvania, OH*—O.S.F.
[3830-05]—*Sisters of St. Joseph* (Brentwood, NY)—C.S.J.
[]—*Sisters of the Good Shepherd*—R.G.S.
[3220]—*Sisters of the Poor Child Jesus*—P.C.J.
[3260]—*Sisters of the Precious Blood* (Dayton, OH)—C.PP.S.
[3320]—*Sisters of the Presentation of the B.V.M.*—P.B.V.M.
[1760]—*Sisters of the Third Order of St. Francis of Penance and of Charity* (Tiffin, OH)—O.S.F.
[1720]—*Sisters of the Third Order Regular of St. Francis of the Congregation of Our Lady of Lourdes*—O.S.F.

DIOCESAN CEMETERIES

COLUMBUS. *Mount Calvary*, Mailing Address: 6440 S. High St., Lockbourne, 43137-9208. 518 Mt. Calvary Ave., 43223-2217. Tel: 614-491-2751. Rich Finn, Dir. & Gen. Mgr.

LEWIS CENTER. *Resurrection Cemetery*, 9571 N. High St., 43035-9413. Tel: 614-888-1805; Fax: 614-888-1810. Rich Finn, Dir. & Gen. Mgr.

LOCKBOURNE. *St. Joseph*, 6440 S. High St., 43137-9208. Tel: 614-491-2751; Fax: 614-491-4264. Rich Finn, Dir. & Gen. Mgr.

PATASKALA. *Holy Cross Cemetery*, 11539 National Rd., S.W., 43062-8304. Tel: 740-927-4442; Fax: 740-927-4645. Rich Finn, Dir. & Gen. Mgr.

NECROLOGY

† Corcoran, Rev. Msgr. Lawrence J., (Retired)—Died Aug. 31, 2009
† Dittoe, Rev. Msgr. John T., (Retired)—Died Sept. 14, 2009
† Maroon, Rev. Msgr. William J., (Retired)—Died Jan. 30, 2009
† Nugent, Rev. Msgr. Michael A. (Andy), (Retired)—Died June 30, 2009
† Gamba, John J., (Retired)—Died Nov. 21, 2009
† Schuer, Robert J., (Retired)—Died Jan. 12, 2009

An asterisk (*) denotes an organization that has established tax-exempt status directly with the IRS and is not covered by the USCCB Group Ruling.

Diocese of Corpus Christi

(Dioecesis Corporis Christi)

Most Reverend

WILLIAM M. MULVEY

Eighth Bishop of Corpus Christi; ordained June 29, 1975; appointed Bishop of Corpus Christi January 18, 2010; ordained March 25, 2010. *Mailing Address: P.O. Box 2620, Corpus Christi, TX 78403-2620.* Tel: 361-882-6191; Fax: 361-882-1018.

The Chancery Office: 620 Lipan St., P.O. Box 2620, Corpus Christi, TX 78403-2620. Tel: 361-882-6191; Fax: 361-882-1018; 361-883-8850; 361-654-1270.

Web: www.diocesecc.org

Email: chancery@diocesecc.org

Most Reverend

EDMOND CARMODY, D.D.

Bishop Emeritus of Corpus Christi; ordained June 8, 1957; appointed Auxiliary Bishop of the Archdiocese of San Antonio November 8, 1988; consecrated December 15, 1988; appointed Bishop of the Diocese of Tyler March 24, 1992; installed May 25, 1992; appointed Bishop of the Diocese of Corpus Christi February 3, 2000; installed March 17, 2000; retired Jan. 18, 2010. *Mailing Address: P.O. Box 2620, Corpus Christi, TX 78403-2620.* Tel: 361-882-6191; Fax: 361-654-1270.

Most Reverend

RENE H. GRACIDA, D.D.

Bishop Emeritus of Corpus Christi; ordained May 23, 1959; appointed Titular Bishop of Masuccaba and Auxiliary of Miami December 6, 1971; consecrated January 25, 1972; appointed Bishop of Pensacola-Tallahassee October 1, 1975; transferred to Corpus Christi May 19, 1983; installed July 11, 1983; retired April 1, 1997. *Res.: 4126 Ocean Dr., Corpus Christi, TX 78411-1224. Office: 620 Lipan St., P.O. Box 2620, Corpus Christi, TX 78403-2620.* Tel: 361-882-6191.

Square Miles 10,951.

Erected a Vicariate Apostolic in 1874; elevated to a Diocese March 23, 1912.

The territory embraced by the Diocese of Corpus Christi comprises the Counties of Aransas, Bee, Brooks, Duval, Jim Wells, Kleberg, Kenedy, Live Oak, Nueces, Refugio, San Patricio, and parts of McMullen in the State of Texas.

For legal titles of parishes and diocesan institutions, consult the Chancery Office.

STATISTICAL OVERVIEW

Personnel	
Bishop	1
Retired Bishops	2
Priests: Diocesan Active in Diocese	85
Priests: Diocesan Active Outside Diocese	5
Priests: Retired, Sick or Absent	21
Number of Diocesan Priests	111
Religious Priests in Diocese	35
Total Priests in Diocese	146
Extern Priests in Diocese	22
Ordinations:	
Diocesan Priests	1
Religious Priests	6
Transitional Deacons	1
Permanent Deacons	1
Permanent Deacons in Diocese	85
Total Brothers	7
Total Sisters	145
Parishes	
Parishes	68
With Resident Pastor:	
Resident Diocesan Priests	62
Resident Religious Priests	6
Missions	32
Pastoral Centers	3
Professional Ministry Personnel:	
Brothers	3
Sisters	19
Lay Ministers	212
Welfare	
Catholic Hospitals	6
Total Assisted	516,150
Health Care Centers	6
Total Assisted	75,385
Homes for the Aged	2
Total Assisted	205
Specialized Homes	2
Total Assisted	1,955
Special Centers for Social Services	13
Total Assisted	206,562
Other Institutions	6
Total Assisted	15,445
Educational	
Diocesan Students in Other Seminaries	14
Seminaries, Religious	1
Students Religious	6
Total Seminarians	20
Colleges and Universities	1
Total Students	20
High Schools, Diocesan and Parish	1
Total Students	380
High Schools, Private	1
Total Students	314
Elementary Schools, Diocesan and Parish	14
Total Students	2,416
Elementary Schools, Private	3
Total Students	620
Catechesis/Religious Education:	
High School Students	3,726
Elementary Students	10,160
Total Students under Catholic Instruction	17,656
Teachers in the Diocese:	
Priests	10
Brothers	6
Sisters	37
Lay Teachers	282
Vital Statistics	
Receptions into the Church:	
Infant Baptism Totals	2,517
Minor Baptism Totals	317
Adult Baptism Totals	188
Received into Full Communion	294
First Communions	2,649
Confirmations	1,427
Marriages:	
Catholic	728
Interfaith	119
Total Marriages	847
Deaths	1,737
Total Catholic Population	391,182
Total Population	558,831

Former Bishops—Rt. Revs. DOMINIC MANUCY, ord. Aug. 15, 1850; cons. Dec. 8, 1874; transferred to Mobile March 9, 1884; reappointed to Vicariate Apostolic of Brownsville Feb. 1, 1885; died Dec. 4, 1885, before taking possession; PETER VERDAGUER, ord. Dec. 12, 1862; cons. Nov. 9, 1890; died Oct. 26, 1911; PAUL JOSEPH NUSSBAUM, C.P., D.D., ord. May 30, 1894; cons. May 20, 1913; resigned March 26, 1920; Bishop of Marquette; appt. Nov. 14, 1922; died June 24, 1935; Most Revs. EMMANUEL B. LEDVINA, D.D., LL.D., appt. April 30, 1921; cons. June 14, 1921; Assistant at Pontifical Throne May 30, 1931; resigned March 15, 1949; died Dec. 15, 1952; MARIANO S. GARRIGA, D.D., LL.D., Coadjutor cum jure successionis,; appt. June 20, 1936; cons. Sept. 21, 1936; succeeded to See March 15, 1949; assistant at Pontifical Throne April 14, 1951; died Feb. 21, 1965; THOMAS J. DRURY, D.D., LL.D., Fourth Bishop of Corpus Christi; Bishop of San Angelo; appt. Oct. 16, 1961; cons. Jan. 24, 1962; fourth Bishop of Corpus Christi; appt. July 19, 1965; installed Sept. 1, 1965; retired Bishop of Corpus Christi; appt. May 19, 1983; died July 22, 1992; RENE H. GRACIDA, D.D. (Retired), Bishop Emeritus; Fifth Bishop of Corpus Christi; appt. Titular Bishop of Masuccaba and Auxiliary of Miami Dec. 6, 1971; cons. Jan. 25, 1972; appt. Bishop of Pensacola-Tallahassee Oct. 1, 1975; transferred to Corpus Christi May 19, 1983; installed July 11, 1983; retired April 1, 1997; ROBERTO O. GONZALEZ, O.F.M., Sixth Bishop of Corpus Christi; appt. Titular Bishop of Ursona and Auxiliary Bishop of Boston July 19, 1988; ord. Oct. 3, 1988; appt. Coadjutor Bishop of Corpus Christi May 16, 1995; transferred to Corpus Christi June 26, 1995; succeeded to See April 1, 1997; appt. Apostolic Administrator to Corpus Christi and Archbishop of San Juan, March 26, 1999; installed Archbishop of San Juan, Puerto Rico May 8, 1999; EDMOND CARMODY, D.D., ord. June 8, 1957; appt. Auxiliary Bishop of the Archdiocese of San Antonio Nov. 8, 1988; cons. Dec. 15, 1988; appt. Bishop of the Diocese of Tyler March 24, 1992; installed May 25, 1992; appt. Bishop of the Diocese of Corpus Christi Feb. 3, 2000; installed March 17, 2000; retired Jan. 18, 2010.

Diocesan Curia—620 Lipan St., P.O. Box 2620, Corpus Christi, 78403-2620.

Office of the Bishop—Most Rev. WILLIAM M. MULVEY; Rev. Msgr. RICHARD SHIRLEY, P.A., V.G., Vicar Gen.; Rev. JOSEPH A. LOPEZ, J.C.L., Chancellor; Rev. Msgr. THOMAS P. FEENEY, J.C.L., Judicial Vicar.

Bishop's Office—620 Lipan St., P.O. Box 2620, Corpus Christi, 78403-2620. Tel: 361-882-6191; Fax: 361-693-6726. MARTY WIND, Dir. Communications: Sr. ANNE ELIZABETH CRONIN, D.C.J., Dir. Consecrated Life; Mr. GREG SEAGRAVE, Dir. Human Resources; Deacon MICHAEL MANTZ, Dir. Deacons; Rev. PETER STANLEY; Rev. Msgrs. LEONARD PIVONKA, J.C.D., Health Care; TOM MCGETTRICK, Vicar for Priests; Revs. EDUARDO MONTEMAYOR, S.O.L.T., Dir. Evangelization; JAMES G. STEMBLER, Dir. Seminary Formation & Vocations.

Consultative Bodies—620 Lipan St., P.O. Box 2620, Corpus Christi, 78403-2620.

Council of Religious—Sr. ANNE ELIZABETH CRONIN, D.C.J.

Deans—Rev. Msgr. LEONARD PIVONKA, J.C.D., Alice Deanery; Rev. LUKOSE THIRUNELLIPARAMABIL, Beeville Deanery; Rev. Msgrs. MARK CHAMBERLIN, Corpus Christi Central Deanery; LAWRENCE E. WHITE, Corpus Christi Westside Deanery; MORGAN J. ROWSOME, Fivepoints Deanery; TOM MCGETTRICK, Southside Deanery; Revs. PIOTR A. KOZIEL, S.T.L., Kingsville Deanery; PHILIP PANACKAL, Refugio Deanery.

College of Consultors—Rev. Msgr. MARK CHAMBERLIN; Revs. LUKOSE THIRUNELLIPARAMABIL; JOSEPH A. LOPEZ, J.C.L., Chancellor; Rev. Msgrs. MORGAN J. ROWSOME; TOM MCGETTRICK; Revs. PHILIP PANACKAL; PIOTR A. KOZIEL, S.T.L.; Rev. Msgrs. LEONARD PIVONKA, J.C.D.; RICHARD SHIRLEY, P.A., V.G.; LAWRENCE E. WHITE.

Diaconal Screening Committee—Rev. Msgr. THOMAS P. FEENEY, J.C.L.; NINA JOINER; ELVA MANTZ; DAVID T. GARCIA; Deacons LONI LUGO; ADELFINO PALACIOS JR.; PAUL MOORE, Assoc. Dir. Deacons; ART PROVENCIO, Assoc. Dir. Formation; MICHAEL MANTZ, Dir. Deacons; JOHN R. JOINER, Dir. Formation; LILLIE PROVENCIO.

Finance Council—Most Rev. EDMOND CARMODY, D.D.; Rev. Msgrs. RICHARD SHIRLEY, P.A., V.G.; LOUIS F. KIHNEMAN; MORGAN J. ROWSOME; Sr. AGNES MARIE TENGLER, I.W.B.S.; Rev. JOSEPH A. LOPEZ, J.C.L., Chancellor; Deacon ADELFINO PALACIOS JR.; Mrs. ROBIN PERRONE, CPA; Ms. NELDA MARTINEZ; Mr. MIKE MCLELLAN; Mr. TOM CARLISLE. Consultants: Mr. GREG SEAGRAVE; Mr. GARY A. RAMIREZ; Mr. PAUL A. DAMEROW, CPA.

Building Commission—Most Rev. EDMOND CARMODY, D.D.; Mr. GREG SEAGRAVE, Chm.; Mr. BUD COLWELL, P.E.; Mr. BILL REDFOX, P.E. (Retired); Mr. JAMES ROME, ARCH. (Retired); Mr. JIMMY LAURENCE, P.E.; Mr. MIKE LIPPINCOTT; Mr. TED STEPHENS. Consultants: Mr. JEFF KISEL; JIMMY EARNEST; LEO FARIAS.

Personnel Board - Priests—Rev. Msgrs. RICHARD SHIRLEY, P.A., V.G., Chm.; MORGAN J. ROWSOME; Rev. LUKOSE THIRUNELLIPARAMABIL; Rev. Msgrs. MARK CHAMBERLIN, Vice Chm.; TOM MCGETTRICK; Revs. PHILIP PANACKAL; PIOTR A. KOZIEL, S.T.L.; Rev. Msgrs. LEONARD PIVONKA, J.C.D.; LAWRENCE E. WHITE.

Presbyteral Council—Rev. Msgrs. ROGER R. SMITH, Chm.; MARK CHAMBERLIN, Vice Chm.; Rev. LUKOSE THIRUNELLIPARAMABIL; Rev. Msgr. MICHAEL HOWELL; Revs. JOSEPH A. LOPEZ, J.C.L., Chancellor; PETER STANLEY; JOSE ALMAZAN; PIOTR A. KOZIEL, S.T.L.; Rev. Msgrs. SEAMUS MCGOWAN (Retired); MICHAEL HERAS; Rev. PEDRO T. ELIZARDO; Rev. Msgrs. THOMAS P. FEENEY, J.C.L.; TOM MCGETTRICK; Rev. PHILIP PANACKAL; Rev. Msgrs. LEONARD PIVONKA, J.C.D.; RICHARD SHIRLEY, P.A., V.G.; LAWRENCE E. WHITE; MORGAN J. ROWSOME.

Tribunal—Rev. Msgr. THOMAS P. FEENEY, J.C.L., Judicial Vicar, 620 Lipan St., P.O. Box 2620, Corpus Christi, 78403-2620. Tel: 361-882-6191; Fax: 361-693-6782.

Judges—Rev. Msgrs. THOMAS P. FEENEY, J.C.L.; LEONARD PIVONKA, J.C.D.; Revs. JAMES HAMILTON (Retired); JOSEPH A. LOPEZ, J.C.L.; Rev. Msgrs. MICHAEL HOWELL; ROGER R. SMITH; MARK CHAMBERLIN.

Defenders of the Bond—Rev. Msgr. RICHARD SHIRLEY, P.A., V.G.; Rev. ANGEL MONTANO, J.C.L.

Notaries-Secretaries—BELINDA HARRIS; OLGA RODRIGUEZ.

Instructor—Rev. FLOVER A. OSORIO, J.C.L.

Villa Maria, Inc., Board—3146 Saratoga Blvd., Corpus Christi, 78413. Tel: 361-857-6171; Fax: 361-857-6173. Email: villamaria@stx.rr.com. DAMIEN H. CARVALHO, Pres. Members: Deacon PETER HORSEMAN; Rev. Msgr. ROGER R. SMITH; KENDERA JUSTICE, Sec.; MARTY PENA, Treas.; BARBARA A. MERLIN, Exec. Dir.; TRE MORRIS; ART SALINAS; ELOY CEBALLOS; BILL PORTWOOD, P.E., Vice Pres. Consultors: Most Rev. EDMOND CARMODY, D.D.; Rev. Msgr. RICHARD SHIRLEY, P.A., V.G.; Mr. GREGOR SEAGRAVE.

Administrative Offices

The Chancery Office—620 Lipan St., P.O. Box 2620, Corpus Christi, 78403-2620. Tel: 361-882-6191; Fax: 361-882-1018 (Admin.); 361-693-6753 (Fiscal Office); 361-693-6726 (Bishop's Office). Email: chancery@diocesecc.org. Web: www.goccn.org. Office Hours: Mon.-Fri. 8:30-5. Closed holy days and holidays.

Office of the Bishop—Most Rev. WILLIAM M. MULVEY.

Office of the Bishop Emeritus—Most Rev. RENE H. GRACIDA, D.D. (Retired).

Canonical Affairs—Rev. Msgr. THOMAS P. FEENEY, J.C.L.

Administrative Assistant—MARY SEDBERRY.

Vicar General—Rev. Msgr. RICHARD SHIRLEY, P.A., V.G.

Judicial Vicar—Rev. Msgr. THOMAS P. FEENEY, J.C.L.

Director for Evangelization Department—Rev. EDUARDO MONTEMAYOR, S.O.L.T.

Director Human Resources—Mr. GREG SEAGRAVE.

Director for Diaconate—Deacons MICHAEL MANTZ, 1200 Lantana St., Kolbe Center, Corpus Christi, 78407-2454. Tel: 361-289-2343; Fax: 361-289-2454; PAUL MOORE, Assoc. Dir. Diaconate.

Vicar for Priests—Rev. Msgr. TOM MCGETTRICK.

Chancellor—Rev. JOSEPH A. LOPEZ, J.C.L.

Family Life Office—Rev. JAMES VASQUEZ.

Fiscal Officer—Mr. GREG SEAGRAVE.

Controller—Mr. PAUL A. DAMEROW, CPA.

Bishop's Annual Appeal—

Development & Stewardship Office—Mr. DALE BAIRD, Dir.

Information Technology Services—LEE ALVARADO, MIS Technical Dir.

Web Development Department—MARK HARRIS, Webmaster.

Real Property Office—CY RICHARDS, Mgr.

Alliance for Human Life—Rev. EDUARDO MONTEMAYOR, S.O.L.T.

Operations Manager—SUSAN CAMPBELL.

Personnel Office—Mr. GREG SEAGRAVE.

Propagation of the Faith Office—Rev. RAYNALDO YRLAS JR.

Seminary Formation & Vocations—Rev. JAMES G. STEMBLER, Dir. Vocations.

Archives—CY RICHARDS, Archivist, 1200 Lantana St., Corpus Christi, 78407. Tel: 361-855-2345 Mon.-Thurs. 9-2.

Catholic Schools Office—Mr. RENE GONZALEZ, Supt.

Catholic Cemeteries—Mr. GREG SEAGRAVE.

Office for Child Protection—KRISTI SKROBARCZYK.

Office of Communications—MARTY WIND, Dir. Communications, 1200 Lantana, Corpus Christi, 78407. Tel: 361-289-6437; Fax: 361-289-1420.

Education—Mr. RENE GONZALEZ, Supt.

Natural Family Planning - Understanding Sexuality—JANE GARZA, Dir., 4455 S. Padre Island Dr. #28, Corpus Christi, 78411. Tel: 361-852-0222.

Newspaper "The South Texas Catholic"—Most Rev. EDMOND CARMODY, D.D., Publisher; PAULA GOLDAPP, Editor.

St. Paul School of Catechesis—Rev. PETER STANLEY.

Office for Persons with Disabilities—Mrs. LINDA MCKAMIE, Dir., 1322 Comanche, Corpus Christi, 78401. Tel: 361-814-2181; Fax: 361-654-2020.

Religious Education—Rev. PETER STANLEY.

Office of Youth And Young Adult Ministry—Rev. PETE ELIZARDO, Dir.

Diocese of Corpus Christi Perpetual Benefit Endowment Fund, Inc.—Mailing Address: P.O. Box 2620, Corpus Christi, 78403-2620. Tel: 361-882-6191.

Diocese of Corpus Christi Perpetual Deposit and Loan Fund, Inc.—Mailing Address: P.O. Box 2620, Corpus Christi, 78403-2620. Tel: 361-882-6191.

Office of Worship—Rev. PETE ELIZARDO, Dir.

Juvenile Ministry—Deacon CRISTOBAL E. LUNA JR., Coord., Mailing Address: P.O. Box 2620, Corpus Christi, 78403-2620. Tel: 361-449-8876.

Hispanic Ministry—Rev. EDUARDO MONTEMAYOR, S.O.L.T.

Other Offices and Organizations

Alhambra—MIKE CASPAR, Grand Commander, 5280 CR 3865, Taft, 78390. Tel: 361-854-4638; SHARRON ODLE, Grand Sultana, 309 Palmetto Dr., Corpus Christi, 78412. Tel: 361-991-7656.

Birthright Counseling—MILDRED HOFFER, Pres., 1422 Baldwin, Corpus Christi, 78404. Tel: 361-884-2662.

Blue Army (World Apostolate of Fatima)—Mrs. MARTHA MAJEK, Pres., 12126 Up River Rd., Corpus Christi, 78410. Tel: 361-242-1533.

Campus Ministries—Texas A&M University-Kingsville, St. Thomas Aquinas University Catholic Center, 1119 Santa Gertrudis, Kingsville, 78363. Tel: 361-592-7831; Fax: 362-592-8617. *Del Mar College, St. Thomas More, 2045 18th St., Corpus Christi, 78404*. Tel: 361-883-9308. *The Cardinal John Henry Newman Catholic Student Center, at Texas A&M Univ.-Corpus Christi, 7002 Ocean Dr., Corpus Christi, 78412*. Tel: 361-993-5898.

Catholic Daughters of the Americas—MARY E. GONZALEZ, Dist. 16, Corpus Christi. Tel: 361-854-0688; DIANA GARCIA, Dist. 36, Odem. Tel: 361-368-3521; ALICIA RODRIGUES, Dist. 47, Taft. Tel: 361-528-2683; FRANCES SALAZAR, Dist. 41, Corpus Christi. Tel: 361-993-6654; EVE TREVINO, State Treas., Corpus Christi. Tel: 361-994-8553. Email: evetrevino@yahoo.com; ELVA PENA, Dist. 48, Corpus Christi. Tel: 361-986-9679.

Catholic Charities—Mrs. LINDA MCKAMIE, Dir., 1322 Comanche, Corpus Christi, 78401. Tel: 361-884-0651; Fax: 361-884-3956.

The Catholic Charismatic Renewal Movement—Rev. EDUARDO MONTEMAYOR, S.O.L.T.; RENE PENA, Coord. Tel: 361-643-3449.

Cursillo Movement—IRMA PADILLA, Pres. Secretariat. Tel: 361-688-2064.

English Cursillo—DAN SERRATO, Dir. School. Tel: 361-815-6896.

Spanish Cursillo—OFELIA GARZA, Dir. School. Tel: 361-756-1757.

Diocesan Council of Catholic Women—ROSE HICKEY, Pres., 1205 Palma St., Kingsville, 78364. Tel: 361-595-7663. Email: roseannahickey@yahoo.com; Rev. JAMES G. STEMBLER, Spiritual Dir.

Diocesan Telecommunications Corporation—MARTY WIND, Exec. Vice Pres. & Gen. Mgr., 1200 Lantana, Corpus Christi, 78407. Tel: 361-289-6437; Fax: 361-289-1420.

Disaster Relief—Mrs. LINDA MCKAMIE, Dir., 1322 Comanche St., Corpus Christi, 78401. Tel: 361-884-0651.

Emergency Aid—Mrs. LINDA MCKAMIE, Dir., 1322 Comanche, Corpus Christi, 78401. Tel: 361-884-0651.

Family Counseling—Mrs. LINDA MCKAMIE, Dir., 1322 Comanche St., Corpus Christi, 78401. Tel: 361-884-0651.

Catholic Singles in Christ—Rev. JAMES VASQUEZ, Dir. Tel: 361-882-6191.

Catholic Engaged Encounter—Rev. JAMES VASQUEZ, Dir. Tel: 361-882-6191.

Immigration Services—Mrs. LINDA MCKAMIE, Dir., 1322 Comanche, Corpus Christi, 78401. Tel: 361-884-0651.

Jail Ministries—Deacon MARIO RIVERA, Dir. Tel: 361-664-9724; AMY NOBLE, Chap., Federal Correctional Institute, Three Rivers, 78071. Tel: 361-786-3576, Ext. 321; TOMMY INGLE, Chap., Garza East Unit, Beeville, 78104. Tel: 361-358-9880; ROBERT KIBBE, Chap., McConnel Unit, Beeville, 78104. Tel: 361-362-2300. Chaplains: JOHN ZIMMER; MICHAEL HUBBARD, Garza West Unit, Beeville, 78104. Tel: 361-358-9890.

Knights of Columbus—TOM GARCIA, Diocesan Deputy, 132 Whistlers Cove Dr., Rockport, 78382. Tel: 361-727-9814.

Legion of Mary—VIANN HERMANN, Pres., 610 Wilshire Pl., Corpus Christi, 78411. Tel: 361-855-8321; Deacon SOLOMON WILLIS, Spiritual Dir.

Marriage Encounter—Rev. JAMES VASQUEZ, Dir. Contact Persons: ROLANDO R. GARZA; NELDA GARZA, Corpus Christi, 78407. Tel: 361-851-8306.

Radio Stations - KLUX FM—RUSSEL WAYNE MARTIN, Dir. Broadcast Oper., 1200 Lantana St., Corpus Christi, 78407. Tel: 361-289-2487.

Serra International—Mr. WILBURN H. FISCHER, District Governor, Dist. 126, 4902 Elmhurst, Corpus Christi, 78413. Tel: 361-993-4881; Mr. CLIFF ZARSKY, Pres., 5202 Woolridge, Corpus Christi, 78407. Tel: 361-991-7465.

Theresians—Mrs. HELEN PATREM, Team Leader, 625 Gregory #14, Corpus Christi, 78412. Tel: 361-980-8818.

Victim Assistance Coordinator—KRISTI SKROBARCZYK. Tel: 361-693-6632; Fax: 361-693-6732. Email: ksrobarczyk@diocesecc.org.

Villa Maria, Inc.—BARBARA A. MERLIN, Dir., 3146 Saratoga Blvd., Box 4, Corpus Christi, 78415. Tel: 361-857-6171; Fax: 361-857-6173.

CLERGY, PARISHES, MISSIONS AND PAROCHIAL SCHOOLS

CITY OF CORPUS CHRISTI

(NUECES COUNTY)

1—CORPUS CHRISTI CATHEDRAL (1853) [CEM] Revs. Joseph A. Lopez, Rector; Pedro (Pete) T. Elizardo Jr.; Gustavo Obando; Kuriakose Ouseph; Deacons Michael Mantz; Paul Moore; Adelfino Palacios Jr.

Res.: 505 N. Upper Broadway, 78401. Tel: 361-883-4213; Fax: 361-883-1918. Email: info@cccathedral.com. Web: www.cccathedral.com.

Catechesis/Religious Program—Tel: 361-883-4213. Email: religioused@ccathedral.com. Students 218.

Chapel—Emmanuel

Chapel—Blessed Sacrament

Chapel—Perpetual Eucharistic Adoration

2—SAINT ANDREW BY THE SEA PARISH (1986) Rev. Msgr. Tom McGettrick.

Res.: 14238 Encantada Ave., 78418-6432. Tel: 361-949-7193; Fax: 361-949-0717.

Email: standrewcc@stx.rr.com.
Catechesis/Religious Program—Tel: 361-949-8834. Students 130.

3—ST. ANSELM ANGLICAN USE COMMUNITY (1992) Rev. Jean F. Hart, S.O.L.T.
Church: 1200 Lantana St., 78407-1112. Tel: 361-289-0807; Fax: 361-289-1402. Email: frjeanhart@hotmail.com.

4—CHRIST THE KING (1946) Revs. Glen F. Mullan; Tung Tran; Deacon Israel Blanco.
Res.: 3423 Rojo, 78415. Tel: 361-883-2821; Fax: 361-888-7048.
Catechesis/Religious Program—Tel: 361-883-2821. Natasha Rios, D.R.E. Students 80.
Convent—

5—SS. CYRIL AND METHODIUS (1947), (Hispanic), Rev. Msgr. Lawrence E. White, Pastor; Revs. Peter Martinez, Vicar; P. R. Victor, Vicar; Deacons Ron Dubuque; Raul (Rudy) Ramirez; Kevin Sullivan.
Res.: 3210 S. Padre Island Dr., 78415. Tel: 361-853-7371; Fax: 361-851-1438.
Catechesis/Religious Program—Tel: 361-852-1651. Mona Lucido, D.R.E. Students 470.

6—HOLY CROSS (1914), (African American), Rev. Anthony Muppala, Admin.
Res.: 1109 N. Staples St., 78401. Tel: 361-888-4012; Fax: 361-883-2670. Email: holycrosscorchr@sbcglobal.net.
Catechesis/Religious Program—Students 27.

7—HOLY FAMILY (1946), (Hispanic), Revs. Francisco Xavier Martinez, S.T.L.; Joseph Nirmal Kumar; Jose Naul Ordonez.
Office: 2509 Nogales St., 78416. Tel: 361-882-3245; Fax: 361-882-4968. Email: holyfamilycatholicchurch@bizstx.rr.com. Web: www.holyfamilycc.net.
Priest's Res.: 2530 Presa, 78416.
Catechesis/Religious Program—Tel: 361-882-3245, Ext. 21. Email: Ianes@bizstx.rr.com. Students 287.

8—SAINT JOHN THE BAPTIST (2001) Revs. Paul A. Hesse; John J. Forbus; Deacon Loni G. Lugo.
Mailing Address: 7522 Everhart Rd., 78413. Tel: 361-991-4400; Fax: 361-991-4401. Email: stjohntx@sbcglobal.net. Web: www.stjohnthebaptistcc.org.
Catechesis/Religious Program—Students 232.

9—ST. JOSEPH (1950), (Hispanic), Revs. Thomas L. Goodwin; Joseph Lawless, M.S.F.; Henry Artunduaga; Peter Stanley; Deacon Reynaldo Rojas.
710 S. 19th St., P.O. Box 5196, 78465-5196.
Catechesis/Religious Program—Michelle Padilla, D.R.E. Students 193.

10—MARY, MOTHER OF THE CHURCH MISSION (1965) Rev. Peter Thenan.
Mailing Address: 1755 Frio St., 78417. Tel: 361-852-0249; Fax: 361-852-8463. Email: mmcmission@gmail.com.
Catechesis/Religious Program—Students 61.

11—ST. MICHAEL THE ARCHANGEL LATIN MASS COMMUNITY (1995) Rev. Carlos S. Casavantes, F.S.S.P.
Church, Res. & Mailing Address: 5830 Williams Dr., 78412. Tel: 361-446-1967 (Res.).
Catechesis/Religious Program—

12—MOST PRECIOUS BLOOD (1966) Rev. Bob Dunn; Deacons Ken Bockholt; Garland Frazier; James Gallagher; Sebastian Landagan; Frank N. Newchurch; Erick Simeus.
Res.: 3502 Saratoga Blvd., 78415. Tel: 361-854-3800; Fax: 361-854-9253. Email: mpb@mpbchurch.org. Web: www.mpbchurch.org.
Catechesis/Religious Program—Tel: 361-854-9219. Students 687.

13—OUR LADY OF GUADALUPE (1969), (Hispanic), Revs. Emilio Jimenez; Rodolfo D. Vasquez.
Res.: 540 Hiawatha, 78405. Tel: 361-882-1951; Fax: 361-888-5813.
Catechesis/Religious Program—Emma Botello, D.R.E. Students 236.

14—OUR LADY OF MOUNT CARMEL (1969) Rev. Sebastian Pasupalety.
Church: 1080 S. Clarkwood Rd., 78406. Tel: 361-265-0610; Fax: 361-265-0757. Email: pasupalety@gmail.com.
Catechesis/Religious Program—Students 50.
Mission—St. Vivian 3516 FM 665 W., Robstown, 78380. Tel: 361-767-5557; Fax: 361-767-5557.

15—OUR LADY OF PERPETUAL HELP (1954) Rev. Msgr. Michael Heras; Revs. Carlos Casavates; Stephen Dougherty; M. Susai Gnanapragasm.
Mailing Address: 5830 Williams Dr., 78412. Tel: 361-991-7891; Fax: 361-993-1211. Email: msgrmh@olphcc.net. Web: www.olphcctex.org.
Catechesis/Religious Program—Students 162.

16—OUR LADY OF PILLAR (1964), (Hispanic), Rev. Marcos Martinez; Deacon Armando M. Bolanos.
Res.: 1101 Bloomington St., 78416. Tel: 361-852-6327; Fax: 361-852-6843. Email: pillarchurch@stx.rr.com.
Catechesis/Religious Program—Students 308

17—OUR LADY OF THE ROSARY (1967), (Hispanic), Rev. Varghese Antony.
Res.: 1123 Main Dr., 78409. Tel: 361-241-2004; 361-242-9571; Fax: 361-242-1099. Email: olrosary@awesomenet.net.
Catechesis/Religious Program—Students 16.

18—OUR LADY STAR OF THE SEA (1950) Rev. Eulalio (Yul) P. Ibay, Admin. In Res., Rev. James Vasquez.
Office: 3110 E. Causeway Blvd., P.O. Box 1899, 78403. Tel: 361-883-4507; Fax: 361-888-6411.
Catechesis/Religious Program—Students 56.

19—ST. PATRICK (1944) Rev. Msgr. Roger R. Smith; Revs. Dennis P. Zerr; Joseph Tran (Vietnam).
Res.: 3350 S. Alameda St., 78411. Tel: 361-855-7391; Fax: 361-853-4790. Email: stpatrickschurch@bizstx.rr.com.
Catechesis/Religious Program—Tel: 361-855-7567. Students 597.

20—ST. PAUL THE APOSTLE (1967) Revs. James G. Stembler; Jose Nestor Pocong Lachica; Deacons Edward Nartowicz; Michael T. Noble.
Res.: 2233 Waldron Rd., 78418. Tel: 361-937-3864; Fax: 361-939-7774.
Catechesis/Religious Program—Tel: 361-937-6908. Sr. Ma. Fe Gamotin, O.P., D.R.E. Students 254.

21—ST. PETER PRINCE OF APOSTLES (1967) Rev. Msgr. Morgan J. Rowsome.
Res. & Mailing Address: 3901 Violet Rd., 78410-2924. Tel: 361-241-3249; Fax: 361-241-0533. Email: camolin@swbell.net. Web: www.stpeterprince.net.
Catechesis/Religious Program—Tel: 361-241-3372. Priscilla Chapa, D.R.E. Students 673.
Mission—St. Mary 4849 Cynthia, Nueces Co. 78410. Tel: 361-241-3432.

22—ST. PHILIP THE APOSTLE (1982) Rev. Hanh Van Pham; Deacon Bob Allen.
Res.: 3513 Cimarron Rd., 78414. Tel: 361-815-0505. Web: www.stphilipcc.com.
Church: 3513 Cimarron Rd., 78414. Tel: 361-991-5146; Fax: 361-991-9135.
Catechesis/Religious Program—Tel: 361-993-1710. Sharen Tipton, D.R.E. Students 52.

23—ST. PIUS X (1963) Rev. Msgr. Richard Shirley; Rev. Richard Gonzales; Deacon Salvador Alvarado.
Res.: 5620 Gollihar Rd., 78412. Tel: 361-993-4053; Fax: 361-992-0352. Email: wtoledo@stpiusxcc.org. Web: stpiusxcc.org.
Catechesis/Religious Program—Tel: 361-993-9024. Students 350.

24—SACRED HEART (1916), (Hispanic), [CEM] Rev. Jairo Motta (Colombia).
Res.: 422 N. Alameda St., 78401-2604. Tel: 361-883-6082; Fax: 361-883-6248. Email: sacredheartchurch001@stx.rr.com.
Catechesis/Religious Program—Tel: 361-882-1472. Students 67.
Station—Nueces County Jail, Tel: 361-887-2300.
Station—Navarro Place, Tel: 361-882-4924.

25—SAINT HELENA OF THE TRUE CROSS OF JESUS (2001) Rev. Salvatore James Farfaglia.
Mailing Address: P.O. Box 81210, 78468-1210.
Res. & Office: 7634 Wooldridge Rd., 78414. Tel: 361-994-8783; Fax: 361-994-7918. Email: truecross@sbcglobal.net. Web: www.StHelenacctx.org.
Catechesis/Religious Program—Tel: 361-994-8783, Ext. 21. Email: arsegovia15@gmail.com. Ada Segovia, D.R.E. Students 78.

26—ST. THERESA (1947) Rev. Jose A. Almazan.
Res.: 1302 Lantana St., 78407. Tel: 361-289-2759; Fax: 361-299-2018.
Catechesis/Religious Program—Tel: 361-289-2238. Mrs. Josie Martinez, D.R.E. Students 61.

27—ST. THOMAS MORE PARISH (1990) Rev. Tomasz Kozub.
Church: 2045 18th St., 78404-3862. Tel: 361-888-9308; Fax: 361-888-6119.
Catechesis/Religious Program—Students 120.

OUTSIDE THE CITY OF CORPUS CHRISTI

AGUA DULCE, NUECES CO., ST. FRANCES OF ROME (1934), (Czech—Hispanic), Rev. Jacob John Valayath.
Mailing Address: P.O. Box 598, 78330. Tel: 361-726-4227; Fax: 361-726-4247. 410 Simmons St., 78330.
Catechesis/Religious Program—Students 58.

ALICE, JIM WELLS CO.

1—ST. ELIZABETH OF HUNGARY (1918) Rev. Msgr. Leonard Pivonka; Deacons James A. Carlisle; Alan K. Borse.
Office: 603 E. 5th St., 78332. Tel: 361-664-6481; Fax: 361-664-7243. Email: steliz@stx.rr.com.
Res.: 518 N. Almond St., P.O. Box 1009, 78333.
School—615 E. 5th St., 78332. Tel: 361-664-6271; Fax: 361-668-4250. Email: smgarcia@myctsonline.com. Web: www.stelizabeth-.tx.schoolwebpages.com. Faculty 11; Students 155.
Catechesis/Religious Program—Tel: 361-664-7719. Students 170.

2—ST. JOSEPH (1911), (Hispanic), Revs. Richard A. Libby; Carlos Alberto Bolivar, Parochial Vicar; Deacon Mario Rivera.
Res.: 801 S. Reynolds St., 78332. Tel: 361-664-7551; Fax: 361-664-2388.
School—Students 137.
Catechesis/Religious Program—311 Dewey St. & 801 S. Reynolds, 78332. Students 235.
Convent—801-B S. Reynolds St., 78332. Tel: 361-664-6283. Sisters 3.
Chapel—Perpetual Eucharistic Adoration

3—OUR LADY OF GUADALUPE (1969), (Hispanic), Rev. Raynaldo Yrlas Jr.
Res.: 1318 Guerra St., P.O. Box 411, 78333. Tel: 361-664-2953; Fax: 361-664-4001 (Church Office).
Catechesis/Religious Program—Tel: 361-664-0437. Sr. Claudia X. Ongpin, O.P., D.R.E. Students 545.
Mission—Santo Nino De Atocha PO Box 411, Jim Wells Co. 78333.

ARANSAS PASS, SAN PATRICIO CO., ST. MARY, STAR OF THE SEA (1948) Rev. Roy Jacob Kalayil, Admin.
Res.: 342 S. Rife St., 78336. Tel: 361-758-2662; Fax: 361-758-3964.
Catechesis/Religious Program—Monica Dominguez, D.R.E. Students 100.

BANQUETE, NUECES CO., SAINT MICHAEL THE ARCHANGEL (1857), (Hispanic), [JC] Rev. J. Patrick Serna.
Mailing Address: 4325 Fourth St., P.O. Box 9, 78339. Tel: 361-387-8371; Fax: 361-387-7607. Email: archangelbanquete@yahoo.com. Web: www.stmichaelbanquete.com.
Catechesis/Religious Program—Students 100.

BEEVILLE, BEE CO.

1—ST. JAMES (Alta Vista) (1966), (Hispanic), Rev. Balaswamy Pasala; Deacon Juan Vasquez.
Res.: 605 S. Alta Vista, 78102. Tel: 361-358-4825; Fax: 361-354-5757. Email: st.james2002@sbcglobal.net.
Catechesis/Religious Program—Juanita L. Martinez, D.R.E. Students 80.

2—ST. JOSEPH (1895) [CEM] Rev. Patrick K. Donohoe; Deacons Russell W. Duggins; Paul Matula; Luis Trevino; Rolando R. Salazar. In Res., Rev. Eduardo H. Garcia (Retired).
Res.: 609 E. Gramman St., 78102. Tel: 361-358-3239; Fax: 361-358-4270. Email: staff@stjosephbeeville.org. Web: www.stjosephbeeville.org.
Catechesis/Religious Program—David J. Bayaroo, Dir. Faith Formation. Students 308.

3—OUR LADY OF VICTORY (1908), (Hispanic), [CEM 2] Rev. Lukose Thirunelliparamabil.
Mailing Address: 707 North Ave. E., 78102. Tel: 361-358-0088; Fax: 361-358-2028. Email: churcholv@yahoo.com.
Rectory—403 W. Carter St., 78102. Tel: 361-358-3761; Fax: 361-358-2028.
Catechesis/Religious Program—Email: iantha432@yahoo.com. Iantha Richardson, D.R.E. Students 130.

BENAVIDES, DUVAL CO., SANTA ROSA DE LIMA (1941), (Hispanic), Rev. Johnson J. Machado.
Res.: 203 Santa Rosa de Lima St., P.O. Drawer W, 78341. Tel: 361-256-3427; Fax: 361-256-4780.
Catechesis/Religious Program—Tel: 361-256-3319. Inglantina Y. Casas, D.R.E. Students 123.
Mission—St. Joseph P.O. Box W, San Jose Ranch, Duval Co. 78341.

BEN BOLT, JIM WELLS, CO., ST. PETER MISSION (1927) Rev. Kuriachan Cyriac Valachanath (India).
Mailing Address: 221 Salazar Ave., P.O. Box 678, 78342. Tel: 361-664-1688; Fax: 361-664-1688. Email: benboltparish@yahoo.com. Web: www.stpeterparishofbenbolt.com.
Catechesis/Religious Program—Students 66.

BISHOP, NUECES CO., ST. JAMES (1938) [CEM] Rev. Ryszard Andrzej Koziol, Admin.
Res.: 601 W. 3rd St., P.O. Box 843, 78343. Tel: 361-584-3250; Fax: 361-584-1046. Email: ryszardkoziol@poczta.onet.pl.
Catechesis/Religious Program—Students 175.
Mission—St. James 310 W. Ave. B, Driscoll, Nueces Co. 78351.

EDROY, SAN PATRICIO CO., OUR LADY OF GUADALUPE MISSION (1934) Rev. Varghese Kolencheril.
Mailing Address: P.O. Box 127, 78352. Tel: 361-368-3097; Fax: 361-368-2934.
Catechesis/Religious Program—Students 41.

FALFURRIAS, BROOKS CO., SACRED HEART (1914), (Hispanic), [CEM] Rev. Matthew J. Stephan; Deacon Ricardo E. Costley.
Res.: 304 S. Caldwell St., 78355. Tel: 361-325-3455; Fax: 361-325-2486. Email: shcfal@hotmail.com.
Catechesis/Religious Program— Joan Bostwick, D.R.E. Students 401.
Mission—St. Ann c/o Sacred Heart Parish, Encino, Brooks Co. 78355.

FREER, DUVAL CO., ST. MARY (1968) Rev. Angel Montano; Deacons Eluterio Bitoni; Pete Trevino Jr.; Mary Alice Casas, Sec.; Gracie Uribe-Cano, Bookkeeper.

Res.: 1500 Duval St., PO Drawer B, 78357. Tel: 361-394-6832; Fax: 361-394-6568.
Catechesis/Religious Program—Tel: 361-394-7244. Marleigh Martinez, D.R.E. Students 142.

GEORGE WEST, LIVE OAK CO., ST. GEORGE (1924) Rev. George Johnson (India).
Oratory— [CEM] [JC] 304 Crockett St., P.O. Box 580, Live Oak Co. 78022. Tel: 361-449-1893; Fax: 361-449-1886.
Catechesis/Religious Program— Eleanor (Ellie) Jimerson, D.R.E.; Cris Luna, D.R.E. Students 124.
Mission—St. Joseph [CEM] [JC] Gussetville, Live Oak Co. Fax: 361-449-1886.

GREGORY, SAN PATRICIO CO., IMMACULATE CONCEPTION (1926), (Hispanic), Revs. Raju Thottankara; Jose Ortiz; Deacon Juan Gomez.
Res.: 107 Church St., P.O. Box 108, 78359-0108. Tel: 361-643-8327; Fax: 361-643-1509.
Catechesis/Religious Program—Email: iccgregory@yahoo.com. Web: www.iccgregory.org. Students 320.

INGLESIDE, SAN PATRICIO CO., OUR LADY OF THE ASSUMPTION (1970) Rev. Thomas Wellar; Deacon Art Provenejo.
Res.: 2414 Main, 78362. Tel: 361-776-2446; Fax: 361-776-3963.
Catechesis/Religious Program—Students 237.

KINGSVILLE, KLEBERG CO.
1—ST. GERTRUDE (1908) Rev. Piotr A. Koziel; Deacons John R. Joiner; Edwin N. Rowley.
Res. & Office: 1120 S. 8th St., 78363. Tel: 361-592-7351; Fax: 361-592-0028.
School—Tel: 361-592-6522; Fax: 361-592-0100. Students 122.
Catechesis/Religious Program—Tel: 361-592-2443. Sr. Colette Brehony, I.W.B.S., D.R.E. Students 239.
Mission—St. Thomas Aquinas Catholic Campus Center - Texas A & M P.O. Box 2193, Kleberg Co. 78363. Tel: 361-592-5781.
2—ST. JOSEPH (1973), (Hispanic), Rev. Romeo Salinas.
1400 Brookshire, P.O. Box 1602, 78364-1602.
Catechesis/Religious Program—Fax: 361-516-1397. Robert Arguijo, D.R.E. Students 200.
3—ST. MARTIN (1914), (Hispanic), Revs. Jose Isidoro Garcia, O.M.I.; Jose Torres, O.M.I.; Deacons Tiburcio Garcia; Raul G. Rosales.
Res.: 715 N. Eighth St., 78363. Tel: 361-592-4602; Fax: 361-592-0881. Email: stmartincatholic@sbcglobal.net.
Catechesis/Religious Program—Tel: 361-592-0881. Gloria DeLeon, D.R.E. Students 140.
Convent—919 N. Ninth St., 78363. Tel: 361-595-1087. Sisters 8.
Mission—Christ the King King Ranch, Kleberg Co.
4—OUR LADY OF GOOD COUNSEL (1954) [CEM 3] [JC] Rev. Paul Puthenangady.
Res.: 1102 E. Kleberg, 78363. Tel: 361-592-3489; Fax: 361-592-6370. Email: ourlady78363@sbcglobal.net.
Catechesis/Religious Program—Mary A. Pena, D.R.E. Students 218.
5—ST. THOMAS AQUINAS, UNIVERSITY CATHOLIC CENTER (1990) Rev. Piotr A. Koziel.
Res.: 1120 S. 8th St., 78363. Tel: 361-592-5781. Church: 1119 W. Santa Gertrudis, 78363.

MATHIS, SAN PATRICIO CO.
1—SAINT PATRICK MISSION (1829), (Hispanic), [CEM] Rev. George Thomas.
Res.: 20742 Magnolia, 78368. Tel: 361-547-5748; Fax: 361-547-8004.
Catechesis/Religious Program—Students 34.
2—ST. PIUS X MISSION - SANDIA (1955) Rev. George Thomas.
20742 Magnolia, 78368-4456. Tel: 361-547-5748; Fax: 361-547-8004. Email: stpatrick@awesomenet.net.
Catechesis/Religious Program—Students 50.
3—SACRED HEART (1942) [JC] Revs. James Putenparambil (India); Juan Fernando Gomez.
Res.: 217 W. San Patricio Ave., 78368-2259. Tel: 361-547-9181; Fax: 361-547-6111.
Catechesis/Religious Program—Jean McLerran, D.R.E. Students 414.

ODEM, SAN PATRICIO CO., SACRED HEART (1934), (Hispanic), Rev. Isaias Estepa, O.A.R., Admin.
Res.: 401 W. Willis St., P.O. Box 276, 78370. Tel: 361-368-9156; Fax: 361-368-2746. Email: sacredheartodem@yahoo.com.
Catechesis/Religious Program—Tel: 361-368-2746. Anita Lunoff, D.R.E. Students 316.

ORANGE GROVE, JIM WELLS CO.
1—ST. FRANCIS OF ASSISI MISSION (2005), Independent Mission. Rev. Prince Kuruvila.
Mailing Address: c/o 303 FM534, Sandia, 78383. Tel: 361-384-2795; Fax: 361-547-2442. 303 FM 534 at County Rd. 185, Lagarto, 78371.
Catechesis/Religious Program—Jenny Tobin, D.R.E. Students 7.
2—ST. JOHN OF THE CROSS (1925) [CEM] Rev. Prince Kuruvila.
Mailing Address: 200 S. Metz St., P.O. Box 329, 78372. Tel: 361-384-2795; Fax: 361-384-0056. Email: saintjohn0003@aol.com.
Catechesis/Religious Program—Tel: 361-384-0056. Students 232.
Mission—St. Francis of Assisi Mission 303 FM 534, Sandia, 78383. Tel: 361-547-2510; Fax: 361-547-2442.

PETTUS, BEE CO., SACRED HEART MISSION (1916), (Independent) Rev. Joseph Varghese Vakayil, Admin.; Deacon Manuel G. Carranco.
Mailing Address: 104 N. Bee St., P.O. Box 414, 78146-0414. Tel: 361-375-2512. Email: vakayilachan@yahoo.com.

PORT ARANSAS, NUECES CO., ST. JOSEPH (1860) [JC] Rev. John Xaviour Amepparambil (India).
Mailing Address: 412 Lantana St., 78373. Tel: 512-749-5825; Fax: 512-749-5509. Email: saintjosephchurch@centurytel.net.
Catechesis/Religious Program—Students 26.

PORTLAND, SAN PATRICIO CO., OUR LADY OF MOUNT CARMEL (1961) Rev. Msgr. Mark Chamberlin; Rev. Jerome G. Zurovetz.
Res.: 1008 Austin St., 78374. Tel: 361-643-7533; Fax: 361-643-5544. Email: olmc61@ainternet.biz.
Catechesis/Religious Program—Tel: 361-643-3548. Mrs. Melanee Warner, D.R.E. Students 448.

PREMONT, JIM WELLS CO., ST. THERESA OF THE INFANT JESUS (1958) Rev. John C. Ouellette; Deacon Javier Gonzalez.
Res.: 235 S.W. 4th St., P.O. Box 569, 78375. Tel: 361-348-2202; Fax: 361-348-3533. Email: sttheresas@stx.rr.com. Web: www.st-theresas.com.
Catechesis/Religious Program—Students 97.
Mission—Immaculate Conception Concepcion, Duval Co.
Mission—St. Francis of Assisi Rios, Duval Co.
Mission—Our Lady of Guadalupe Ramirez, Duval Co.

REFUGIO, REFUGIO CO.
1—ST. JAMES THE APOSTLE (1886), (Hispanic), [CEM] [JC] Rev. Zenon Konowalek.
Mailing Address: 202 E. Santiago St., 78377.
Catechesis/Religious Program—Tel: 361-526-4454; Fax: 361-526-2714. Students 109.
Mission—St. Catherine Mission Hwy. 2441.
2—OUR LADY OF REFUGE (1795) [CEM] [JC] Rev. Philip Panackal.
Res.: 1008 S. Alamo St., 78377. Tel: 361-526-2083; Fax: 361-526-5653. Email: olrefuge@yahoo.com.
Catechesis/Religious Program—106 W. Roca, 78377. Tel: 361-526-2053. Students 83.

RIVIERA, KLEBER CO., OUR LADY OF CONSOLATION (1914), (German), [CEM] [JC] Rev. Peter Antony (India).
Res.: 204 Palm Ave., 78379. Tel: 361-297-5255; Fax: 361-297-5155.
Catechesis/Religious Program—Students 34.
Mission—Our Lady of Guadalupe 111 S. Second St., Kleberg Co. 78379.
Mission—Sacred Heart W. County Rd. 2160, Ricardo, Kleberg Co. 78363.

ROBSTOWN, NUECES CO.
1—ST. ANTHONY (1914), (Hispanic), [CEM] Revs. Dennis Walsh, S.O.L.T.; Michael Edward Crump, S.O.L.T., Parochial Vicar; George Nedeff, S.O.L.T., Parochial Vicar; Miguel A. Noyola, S.O.L.T. (Guatemala), Parochial Vicar; Deacon Wayne Lickteig, S.O.L.T.
Res.: 204 Dunne St., P.O. Box 792, 78380-0792. Tel: 361-767-1705; 361-387-2774; Fax: 361-387-5114.
Catechesis/Religious Program—Tel: 361-387-9874. Eva Hernandez, D.R.E. Students 439.
Mission—St. Mary, Nueces Co. Fax: 361-387-5114.
2—ST. JOHN NEPOMUCENE (1924), (Czech), [JC] Revs. Thomas Showalter, S.O.L.T.; John Gaffney, S.O.L.T., Parochial Vicar.
Res.: 603 N. First St., 78380. Tel: 361-387-3705; Fax: 361-387-3681. Email: frtomshowalter@gmail.com.
Catechesis/Religious Program—Felipe Salazar, D.R.E. Students 65.
3—ST. THOMAS THE APOSTLE (1980) Rev. Msgr. Michael Howell; Deacon Bill Cleavelin.
Office: 16602 FM 624, 78380. Tel: 361-387-1312; Fax: 512-387-9311. Web: www.christon624.com.
Catechesis/Religious Program—Michele Hoelscher, D.R.E. Students 260.

ROCKPORT, ARANSAS CO.
1—ST. PETER'S PARISH (1989), (Vietnamese), [JC 2] Rev. Peter Nghi Duc Pham, S.O.L.T.
Mailing Address: P.O. Box 1060, 78382. Tel: 361-729-3008; Fax: 361-727-0191.
Catechesis/Religious Program—2761 FM 1781, 78381-1060. Tel: 361-549-7850. Students 14.
2—SACRED HEART (1838) Rev. Msgr. Louis F. Kihneman; Rev. Encarnacion J. Cabrera, Parochial Vicar; Deacons Jerre H. Ledbetter; George Joe Wiest.
Res.: 704 E. Cornwall St., 78382. Tel: 361-729-2174; Fax: 361-729-1989. Email: shrockport@charter.net. Web: www.sacredheartchurchrockport.org.
Catechesis/Religious Program—Tel: 361-729-8283 (Rel. Educ. Office); 361-727-1333 (Youth Ministry Office); 361-729-9135 (Adult Ed Office); Fax: 361-729-1989. Email: reled@charter.net. Students 356.
Convent—114 N. Church St., 78382. Tel: 361-729-5311.
Mission—Tel: 361-729-9135. Aransas Co.
3—STELLA MARIS CHAPEL (1858) Rev. Ralph O. Jones, S.O.L.T.
P.O. Box 1980, Fulton, 78358.

SAN DIEGO, DUVAL CO., ST. FRANCIS DE PAULA (1866) Revs. Benito Retortillo, O.P.; Epifanio Rodriguez, O.P.; Deacons Abelardo Garza; Carlos Tamayo.
Res.: 401 S. Victoria St., P.O. Box 279, 78384. Tel: 361-279-3596; Fax: 361-279-8288.
Catechesis/Religious Program—411 S. Victoria St., 78384. Tel: 361-279-3586. Students 412.
Mission—St. Joseph Palito Blanco, Jim Wells Co. 78384.

SARITA, KENEDY CO., OUR LADY OF GUADALUPE (1935) Rev. James Foelker, O.M.I.
Mailing Address: P.O. Box 6, 78385. Tel: 361-294-5350; Fax: 361-294-5406.
Catechesis/Religious Program—Students 10.
Mission—Santa Elena Norias Ranch, Kenedy Co.

SINTON, SAN PATRICIO CO.
1—OUR LADY OF GUADALUPE (1954), (Hispanic), [CEM] [JC] Rev. Shaji Varghese, Admin.
Res.: 725 Sodville Ave., 78387. Tel: 361-364-2210; Fax: 361-364-5204.
Catechesis/Religious Program—Tel: 361-364-4007. Students 317.
2—SACRED HEART (1916) Rev. Paul Rajareegam (India).
Res.: 906 E. Sinton St., P.O. Box 266, 78387. Tel: 361-364-1768; Fax: 361-364-5325. Email: shsinton@yahoo.com.
Catechesis/Religious Program—Mary Connors, C.R.E.; Deacon Solomon T. Willis III, C.R.E. Students 176.
Mission—St. Paul P.O. Box 266, St. Paul, San Patricio Co. 78387.

SKIDMORE, BEE CO., IMMACULATE CONCEPTION (1915) [JC] Rev. Sebastian Vettath Thomas, Admin.
Res.: 600 First St., P.O. Box 189, 78389. Tel: 361-287-3256; Fax: 361-287-3696.
Catechesis/Religious Program—Students 43.
Mission—St. Francis Xavier Frio St., Tynan, Bee Co. 78384.

TAFT, SAN PATRICIO CO.
1—HOLY FAMILY (1957) [JC] Rev. Randy N. Cain.
Mailing Address: P.O. Box 173, 78390. Tel: 361-528-3132; Fax: 361-528-3209.
Res.: 701 Fetick, 78390.
Catechesis/Religious Program—Students 145.
2—IMMACULATE CONCEPTION (1928) Rev. Jesus Francisco Lopez.
Res. & Mailing Address: 120 E. Escobedo, P.O. Box 868, 78390. Tel: 361-528-2626; Fax: 361-528-3907.
Catechesis/Religious Program—Students 325.

THREE RIVERS, LIVE OAK CO., SACRED HEART (1948) Rev. Ryszard Zielinski.
303 E. Alexandra, P.O. Box 729, 78071-0729. Tel: 361-786-3398; Fax: 361-786-1010.
Catechesis/Religious Program—Students 65.
Mission—Our Lady of Guadalupe P.O. Box 729, Pawnee, Bee Co. 78071.

TIVOLI, REFUGIO CO., OUR LADY OF GUADALUPE (1936) Rev. Gabriel P. Coelho (India).
Mailing Address: P.O. Drawer I, 77990-0001. Tel: 361-286-3349; Fax: 361-286-3665.
Catechesis/Religious Program—Students 7.
Mission—St. Anthony of Padua Austwell, Refugio Co.
Mission—St. Dennis O'Connor Ranch, Refugio Co.

VIOLET, NUECES CO., ST. ANTHONY (1910) [CEM] Rev. Msgr. William C. Murray; Yvette Cavazos, Sec. & Bookkeeper.
Res.: 3918 Country Rd. 61, Robstown, 78380-5737. Tel: 361-387-4434; Fax: 361-767-3881. Email: stanthonyviolet@yahoo.com.
Catechesis/Religious Program—Jeannie Galufka, D.R.E. Students 20.

WOODSBORO, REFUGIO CO., ST. THERESE, THE LITTLE FLOWER (1915), (Hispanic), [CEM] Rev. Andrew Hejdak (Poland).
Res.: 315 Pugh St., P.O. Box 1076, 78393. Tel: 361-543-4166; Fax: 361-543-5922. Email: sttherese1076@gmail.com.
Catechesis/Religious Program—Students 82.
Mission—St. Mary Bayside, Refugio Co.

Shrines

CORPUS CHRISTI, THE SHRINE OF NUESTRA DE SAN JUAN DE LOS LAGOS Rev. Henry Artunduaga, Dir. 3049 County Rd. 37, 78417-3513. Tel: 361-693-6634.

On Special Assignment:
Revs.—
Downey, Donald, Chap.
Elizardo, Pedro T., Dir. Youth & Young Adult Ministry
Gutirerrez, Jose, Chap.
Martinez, Peter, Chap. & Dir. Institutional Advancement
Nwachukwu, Thomas Kizito, Chap.
Onuoha, Silas, Chap.
Stanley, Peter, Dir. Religious Education
Vasquez, James, Dir. Family Life Office

On Duty Outside the Diocese:
Revs.—
McGerity, Francis X., 2 Rosemere Ct., #3, Roslindale, MA 02131.
Salazar, Jose, St. Mary's Seminary, 9845 Memorial Dr., Houston, 77024-3498.
Taurasi, David, 15 Waldemar Ave., Boston, MA 02128.

Military Chaplains:
Revs.—
Gajda, Piotr J., Green Beret Chap., 5395 Wolfe Dr., Oklahoma City, OK 73145.
Shuley, Keith, C.C., Command Chap., U.S. Merchant Marine Academy, 300 Steamboat Rd., Kings Point, NY 11024.

Retired:
Most Rev.—
Gracida, Rene H., D.D., 4126 Ocean Dr., 78411.
Rev. Msgrs.—
Chilen, Michael D., 1905 CR 648, Hanceville, AL 35077.
McGowan, Seamus, 292 Long Point Rd., Portland, 78374.
Thompson, William P.A., 4809 Fern Forest, 78413.
Revs.—
Ashe, Michael B., Ireland.
Bergin, Paschal, 411 St. Mary St., Kenedy, 78119.
Bradley, Robert, Padus Pl., 80 Peter Baque, San Antonio, 78209. Tel: 361-854-4494
Burke, Michael, Mt Carmel Home, 4130 S. Alameda, 78411.
De Llano, Domingo, 6106 Vance Jackson, #5, San Antonio, 78230.
Dean, Gregory, 15 Charlotte, Rockport, 78382.
Doherty, Charles, 127 Lakeview Rd., Rockport, 78382.
Feminelli, John, Villa Maria, 3146 Saratoga, 78415.
Fidalgo, Federico, 8315 N. Vandiver, #34, San Antonio, 78209.
Garcia, Eduardo H., St. Joseph Parish, 609 E. Gramman St., Beeville, 78102.
Hamilton, James, P.O. Box 1541, Aransas Pass, 78335.
Heese, Henry, 132 E. Front St., Rockport, 78382.
Hernandez, Manuel, Jr., 118 W. Olive, Laredo, 78041.
Killeen, John P., Ireland
Linehan, Michael, P.O. Box 690415, San Antonio, 78261.
Mikolajczyk, Bruno, 120 S. Elizabeth St., Kingsville, 78363.
Ngyen, Joseph Liep Van, Mt. Carmel Home, 4130 S. Alameda, 78411.
O'Donovan, Thomas P., Villa Marie Apts., 3146 Saratoga # 46, 78415.
Walsh, Arthur, 140 Bourne Ave., Rumford, RI 02916.

Permanent Deacons:
Ahlers, Ray, (Retired)
Allen, Bob, Philip the Apostle, Corpus Christi
Alvarado, Salvador, St. Pius X, Corpus Christi
Barbour, Antonio, Our Lady of Good Counsel, Kingsville
Benys, Victor, Our Lady of Perpetual Help, Corpus Christi
Bitoni, Eluterio, St. Mary Parish, Freer
Blanco, Israel, Christ the King, Corpus Christi
Bockholt, Ken, Most Precious Blood, Corpus Christi
Bolanos, Armando M., Our Lady of Pillar, Corpus Christi
Borse, Alan T., St. Elizabeth, Alice
Botello, Armando, St. Joseph, Corpus Christi
Breland, Walter N., (Retired)
Carlisle, James A., St. Elizabeth, Alice
Carranco, Manuel G., Chap., Sacred Heart Mission, Pettus
Carrizales, Alejandro, (Retired)
Cavada, Armando, Our Lady of Guadalupe, Alice
Cicora, Allen, St. Peter Prince of the Apostles, Corpus Christi
Cleavelin, William, St. Thomas the Apostle, Calallen
Costley, Ricardo E., Sacred Heart, Falfurrias
Dubuque, Roland, SS. Cyril & Methodius Parish, Corpus Christi
Duggins, Russell W., St. Joseph, Beeville
Farias, Eluterio, St. Peter Prince of the Apostles, Corpus Christi
Flores, Arturo, (Retired)
Frazier, Garland, Most Precious Blood, Corpus Christi
Garcia, Tiburcio, St. Martin, Kingsville
Garza, Abelardo, St. Francis de Paula, San Diego
Gomez, Juan, Immaculate Conception, Gregory
Gonzalez, Javier, St. Teresa of the Infant Jesus, Premont
Gonzalez, Pilar M., St. Michael the Archangel, Banquete
Gonzalez, Ricardo, St. Joseph, Kingsville
Grassedonio, Roy M., Our Lady, Star of the Sea, Corpus Christi
Hinojosa, Raul, (Retired)
Horseman, M.M. Peter, (Retired)
Joiner, John R., Dir., St. Gertrude, Kingsville
Kaizen, Joseph, (Retired)
Landagan, Sebastian, Most Precious Blood, Corpus Christi
Lara, Antonio S., St. Francis Xavier Mission, Tynan
Ledbetter, Jerre H., Sacred Heart, Rockport
Lewinski, Richard R., St. Peter Prince of the Apostles, Corpus Christi
Lickteig, Wayne, S.O.L.T., Dir., Lay Council of Society, St. Anthony, Robstown
Lugo, Loni, St. John the Baptist, Corpus Christi
Luna, Cristobal E., Jr., Coord. Office of Prison Ministry, St. George, George West
Maldonado, Manuel, Mary, Mother of the Church, Corpus Christi
Mantz, Michael, Dir. Deacons, Corpus Christi Cathedral, Corpus Christi
Martinez, Homer, St. Anthony, Robstown
Martinez, Rodolfo R., Our Lady of Perpetual Help, Corpus Christi
Matula, Paul, St. Joseph, Beeville
Millsap, Stanley, (Retired)
Moore, Paul, Assoc. Dir. Deacons, Cathedral, Corpus Christi
Morin, Richard B., St. Joseph, Kingsville
Nartowicz, Edward, St. Paul the Apostle, Our Lady of Guadalupe Chapel, N.A.S., Corpus Christi
Newchurch, Frank N., Most Precious Blood, Corpus Christi
Noble, Michael T., St. Paul the Apostle & St. Anselm, Corpus Christi
Nolte, Stephen, Holy Family, Corpus Christi
Oliver, Willard F., (Retired)
Ouellette, Roland, (Retired)
Palacios, Adelfino, Jr., Corpus Christi Cathedral, Corpus Christi
Phillips, George, St. Pius X, Corpus Christi
Postert, Anthony K., Sacred Heart, Three Rivers
Provencio, Arthur, Our Lady of the Assumption, Ingleside
Ramirez, Rudy, Ss. Cyril & Methodius, Corpus Christi
Rauen, Mike, Asst., Office for Persons with Disabilities, Corpus Christi
Rivera, Gonzalo, (Retired)
Rivera, Mario, Area Coord. Cursillo Movement, St. Joseph, Alice
Rodriguez, Alonzo, (Retired)
Rodriguez, Eleazar, St. Patrick, Corpus Christi
Rodriguez, Reynaldo, Jr., (Retired)
Rojas, Reynaldo, St. Joseph, Corpus Christi
Rosales, Raul G., St. Martin, Kingsville
Rosenbaum, Rogelio, Our Lady of Victory, Beeville
Rowley, Edwin N., St. Gertrude, Kingsville
Salazar, Rolando R., St. Joseph, Beeville
Simeus, Erick, Most Precious Blood, Corpus Christi
Sullivan, Kevin, Saints Cyril & Methodius, Corpus Christi
Tamayo, Carlos, St. Francis de Paula, San Diego
Trevino, Luis, St. Joseph, Beeville
Trevino, Pedro R., Jr., St. Mary, Freer
Vasquez, Jesus, St. James, Beeville
Vasquez, Lupe, Sacred Heart, Corpus Christi
Wiest, George Joe, Sacred Heart, Rockport; Chap., Prision Ministry
Willis, Solomon T., III, Spiritual Dir. for Legion of Mary, Corpus Christi; Sacred Heart, Sinton
Ybarra, Pedro M., (Retired)

INSTITUTIONS LOCATED IN THE DIOCESE

[A] HIGH SCHOOLS

CORPUS CHRISTI. *Incarnate Word Academy High School* (1871) (Private), 2910 S. Alameda, 78404. Tel: 361-883-0857; Fax: 361-881-8742. Email: lugaresi@iwacc.org. Web: www.iwacc.org. Mr. Gerald Lugaresi, Prin.; Mrs. Susan Edwards, Librarian. Sisters 6; Lay Teachers 26; Staff 7; Students 314.

John Paul II High School (2006) Saratoga Blvd., 78415. Tel: 361-855-5744; Fax: 361-855-1343. Web: www.jpiihighschool.org. Rev. Peter Martinez, Chap.; Perry LeGrange, Prin.; Jane Longoria, Librarian. Priests 4; Lay Teachers 24; Students 317.

[B] JUNIOR HIGH AND ELEMENTARY SCHOOLS

CORPUS CHRISTI. *Bishop Garriga Middle Preparatory School* (1987) (Diocesan), 3114 Saratoga Blvd., 78415. Tel: 361-851-0853; Fax: 361-853-5145. Email: rdavila@bgmps.org. Web: www.bgmps.org. Rosario Davila, Prin.; Jane Longoria, Librarian. Lay Teachers 15; Students 167.

Central Catholic Elementary (1911) (Parochial), 1218 Comanche St., 78401. Tel: 361-883-3873; Fax: 361-883-5879. Email: sisteranne@centralcatholic.us. Web: www.centralcatholic.us. Sr. Anne Brigid Schlegel, I.W.B.S., Prin. Sisters 2; Lay Teachers 6; Students 113.

Christ the King School (Parochial), 1625 Arlington Dr., 78415. Tel: 361-883-5391; Fax: 361-888-9207. Email: schooloffice@ctk-cc.org. Rich Barncord, Prin. Priests 2; Sisters 1; Lay Teachers 8; Students 79.

SS. Cyril and Methodius School (1957) (Parochial), 5002 Kostoryz Rd., 78415. Tel: 361-853-9392; Fax: 361-853-0282. Email: apeter6122@aol.com. Web: www.mahpro.com/sscm.html. Anna Peterson, Prin.; Carol Sanchez, Librarian. Lay Teachers 11; Students 144.

Holy Family Catholic School (1946) (Parochial), 2526 Soledad St., 78416. Tel: 361-884-9142; Fax: 361-884-1750. Sr. Patricia Rodriguez, H.M.S.S., Prin.; Rev. Francisco Xavier Martinez, S.T.L., Pastor; Nancy Davila, Librarian. Sisters 5; Lay Teachers 15; Students 296.

Incarnate Word Academy Elementary Level (1950) (Private), 450 Chamberlain, 78404. Tel: 361-883-0857; Fax: 361-881-9519. Email: sherlihy@iwacc.org. Web: www.iwacc.org. Sr. Camelia Herlihy, Prin.; Mrs. Rhonda Mumme, Librarian. Sisters 4; Lay Teachers 22; Students 298.

Incarnate Word Academy Middle School (Private), 2917 Austin St., 78404. Tel: 361-883-0857, Ext. 113; Fax: 361-882-9193. Email: agarza@iwacc.org. Web: www.iwacc.org. Mr. Adolfo Garza, Prin.; Mrs. Susan Edwards, Librarian. Lay Teachers 31; Students 280.

Most Precious Blood School (Parochial), 3502 Saratoga Blvd., 78415. Tel: 361-852-4800; Fax: 361-855-8707. Web: www.mpbcs.org. Email: principal@mpbcs.org. Nelda Bazan, Prin.; Josie Kaufmann, Librarian. Religious Teachers 1; Lay Teachers 13; Students 192.

Our Lady of Perpetual Help Academy (1955) (Parochial), 5814 Williams Dr., 78412. Tel: 361-991-3305; 361-992-5951; Fax: 361-994-1806. Email: lindaecantu@hotmail.com. Web: www.our.tx.schoolwebpages.com. Ms. Linda Cantu, Prin. Sisters 2; Lay Teachers 16; Students 216.

St. Patrick School (1949-1950) (Parochial), 3340 S. Alameda St., 78411. Tel: 361-852-1211; Fax: 361-852-4855. Email: sps@stpatrickschoolcc.org. Web: www.stpatrickschoolcc.org. Dr. Patricia Stegall, Prin.; Mrs. Constance Burkart, Librarian. Sisters 1; Lay Teachers 22; Students 308.

St. Pius X Catholic School (1965) (Parochial), 737 St. Pius Dr., 78412. Tel: 361-992-1343; Fax: 361-992-0329. Email: spxs@stpiusxschoolcc.org. Web: www.stpiusxschoolcc.org. Kathy Clark, Prin.; Carter Wooster, Librarian. Lay Teachers 15; Students 175.

ALICE. *St. Elizabeth School* (1949) (Parochial), 615 E. Fifth, 78332. Tel: 361-664-6271; Fax: 361-668-4250. Email: smgarcia@myctsonline.com. Selina M. Garcia, Prin.; Lorina Gaytan, Librarian. Lay Teachers 11; Students 155.

St. Joseph School (Parochial), 311 Dewey, 78332. Tel: 361-664-4642; Fax: 361-664-4642. Email: sjsaints@awesomenet.net. Mrs. Mary Sandoval, Prin.; Diana Hughes, Librarian. Sisters 2; Lay Teachers 10; Students 140.

KINGSVILLE. *St. Gertrude School* (Parochial), 400 E. Caesar St., 78363. Tel: 361-592-6522; Fax: 361-592-0100. Email: stgschool@stgertrudeparish.org. Web: www.stgertrudeparish.org. Beverly Lanmon, Prin.; Lisa Tucker, Librarian Mgr. Lay Teachers 9; Students 122.

ROBSTOWN. *St. Anthony School* (1916) (Parochial), 203 Dunne Ave., 78380. Tel: 361-387-3814; Fax: 361-387-3814. Sr. Maria Paz Aribon, O.P., Prin.; Elva Ybarra, Librarian; Norma Hernandez, Sec. Sisters

4; Lay Teachers 12; Students 145.

ROCKPORT. *Sacred Heart School* (Parochial), 111 N. Church St., 78382. Tel: 361-729-2672; Fax: 361-729-9382. Email: shsprin@shsrockport.org. Web: www.shsrockport.org. Katherine K. Barnes, Prin.; Randall E. Barnes, Librarian. Sisters 2; Lay Teachers 8; Students 164.

[C] DAY NURSERY, PRE-KINDER, KINDER

CORPUS CHRISTI. *Our Lady of the Rosary Catholic School* (1992) 2237 Waldron Rd., 78418. Tel: 361-939-9847; Fax: 361-937-0890. Email: rosarylearningcenter@yahoo.com. Sr. Esperanza H. Seguban, O.P., Dir. & Prin. Sisters 7; Lay Staff 2; Students 42.

ROBSTOWN. *St. Joseph's Dream*, 3660 Jack Dr., 78380. Tel: 361-387-9598. Email: paxsolt@aol.com. Sisters 2; Total Assisted 5; Total Staff 2.

[D] GENERAL HOSPITALS

CORPUS CHRISTI. *CHRISTUS Medical Group Dr. Hector P. Garcia Family Medicine Center - Residency Program*, 2606 Hospital Blvd., 5 West, 78405. Tel: 361-902-4470. Mailing Address: 1702 Santa Fe, 78404. Jose R. Hinojosa, Prog. Dir.; William L. Pardue, Corp. Sec. Tel: 281-936-3184; Cynthia G. Zatorski, Asst. Corp. Sec. Tel: 281-936-3176. Total Assisted Annually 14,000; Total Staff 34.

CHRISTUS Spohn Family Health Center - Northside, 1406 Martin Luther King, 78401. Tel: 361-887-8811; Fax: 361-887-8874. Mailing Address: 1702 Sante Fe, 78404. David Foster, M.D., Medical Dir.; William L. Pardue, Corp. Sec. Tel: 281-936-3184; Cynthia G. Zatorski, Asst. Corp. Sec. Tel: 281-936-3176. Total Assisted Annually 10,890; Total Staff 9.

CHRISTUS Spohn Family Health Center - Padre Island, 140202 S. Padre Island Dr., 78418. Tel: 361-949-7660; Fax: 361-949-9372. Mailing Address: 1702 Santa Fe, 78404. David Foster, M.D., Medical Dir.; William L. Pardue, Corp. Sec. Tel: 281-936-3184; Cynthia G. Zatorski, Asst. Corp. Sec. Tel: 281-936-3176. Total Assisted Annually 9,173; Total Staff 8.

CHRISTUS Spohn Family Health Center - Robstown, 403 E. Main St., Robstown, 78380. Tel: 361-767-1200; Fax: 361-767-1208. Mailing Address: 1702 Santa Fe, 78404. David Foster, M.D., Medical Dir.; William L. Pardue, Corp. Sec. Tel: 281-936-3184; Cynthia G. Zatorski, Asst. Corp. Sec. Tel: 281-936-3176. Total Assisted Annually 11,150; Total Staff 11.

CHRISTUS Spohn Family Health Center - Westside, 4617 Greenwood Dr., 78416. Tel: 361-857-2872; Fax: 361-857-2946. Mailing Address: 1702 Santa Fe, 78404. David Foster, M.D., Medical Dir.; William L. Pardue, Corp. Sec. Tel: 281-936-3184; Cynthia G. Zatorski, Asst. Corp. Sec. Tel: 281-936-3176. Total Assisted Annually 14,432; Total Staff 11.

CHRISTUS Spohn Health System, 1702 Santa Fe, 78404. Tel: 361-881-3400; Fax: 361-885-0566. Email: larry.pardue@christushealth.org. Bruce Holstien, Pres. & CEO; Sr. Carol Ann Jokerst, Vice Pres., Mission Integration; William L. Pardue, Corp. Sec. Tel: 281-936-3184; Cynthia G. Zatorski, Asst. Corp. Sec. Tel: 281-936-3176. Email: cindy.zatorski@christushealth.org. Bed Capacity 1,086; Total Staff 4,336; Total Assisted Annually 516,150.

CHRISTUS Spohn Hospital Corpus Christi - Memorial, 1702 Santa Fe, 78404. Tel: 361-881-3400; Fax: 361-885-0566. Email: larry.pardue@christushealth.org. Bed Capacity 199; Total Assisted Annually 185,097; Total Staff 1,256.

2606 Hospital Blvd., 78405. Tel: 361-902-4103; Fax: 361-902-4949. Email: estela.chapa@christushealth.org. Estela Chapa, Vice Pres. & COO; William L. Pardue, Corp. Sec. Tel: 281-936-3184; Cynthia G. Zatorski, Asst. Corp. Sec. Tel: 281-936-3184.

Pastoral Staff: Lynne Blackler, Chap.; Revs. Thomas Kizito Nwachukwu, Chap.; David Saenz, Chap.; Silas Onuoha, Chap.; Cuthbert Machamire, Chap.

CHRISTUS Spohn Hospital Corpus Christi - Shoreline, 1702 Santa Fe, 78404. Tel: 361-881-3141; Fax: 361-885-0566. Email: larry.pardue@christushealth.org.

600 Elizabeth St., 78404. Tel: 361-881-3148; Fax: 361-881-3149. Email: william.mcdonald@christushealth.org. William Mcdonald, Vice Pres. & COO. Tel: 361-881-3610; William L. Pardue, Corp. Sec. Tel: 281-936-3184; Cynthia G. Zatorski, Asst. Corp. Sec. Tel: 281-936-3176. Bed Capacity 422; Total Assisted Annually 121,770; Total Staff 1,565.

Pastoral Staff: Revs. Donald Downey, Chap.; Peter Muroko, Chap.; David Saenz, Chap.; Michael Saxton, System Dir.

CHRISTUS Spohn Hospital Corpus Christi - South, 1702 Santa Fe, 78404. Email: larry.pardue@christushealth.org. Sisters of Charity of the Incarnate Word (San Antonio, TX).

5950 Saratoga Blvd., 78414. Tel: 361-985-5000; Fax: 361-985-5109. Email: steven.daniel@christushealth.org. Steven Daniel, COO & Vice Pres.; Sr. Rose Stewart, Chap.; William L. Pardue, Corp. Sec. Tel: 281-936-3184; Cynthia G. Zatorski, Asst. Corp. Sec. Tel: 281-936-3176. Bed Capacity 153; Patients Assisted Annually 61,665; Total Staff 615.

CHRISTUS Spohn Memorial - Specialty Clinic, 2606 Hospital Blvd., 7 West, 78405. Tel: 361-902-4765. Mailing Address: 1702 Santa Fe, 78404. David Foster, M.D., Medical Dir.; William L. Pardue, Corp. Sec. Tel: 281-936-3184; Cynthia G. Zatorski, Asst. Corp. Sec. Tel: 281-936-3176. Total Assisted Annually 15,740; Total Staff 9.

ALICE. *CHRISTUS Spohn Hospital Alice*, 1702 Santa Fe, 78404. Tel: 361-881-3400; Fax: 361-885-0566. Email: larry.pardue@christushealth.org. Web: www.christusspohn.org. Bed Capacity 148.

2500 E. Main St, 78332. Tel: 361-661-8016; Fax: 361-661-8073. Mark Casanova, COO & Vice Pres.; Sr. Carmen Avila, Chap.; William L. Pardue, Corp. Sec. Tel: 281-936-3184; Cynthia G. Zatorski, Asst. Corp. Sec. Tel: 281-936-3176. Bed Capacity 172; Patients Assisted Annually 64,483; Total Staff 397.

BEEVILLE. *CHRISTUS Spohn Hospital Beeville*, 1702 Santa Fe, 78404. Tel: 361-881-3400; Fax: 361-885-0566. Email: larry.pardue@christushealth.org. Web: www.christusspohn.org. Bed Capacity 69.

1500 E. Houston Hwy., 78102. Tel: 361-354-2125; Fax: 361-358-9322. Email: jerry.rodriguez@christushealth.org. Jerry Rodriguez, COO & Vice Pres.; William L. Pardue, Corp. Sec. Tel: 281-396-3184; Cynthia G. Zatorski, Asst. Corp. Sec. Tel: 281-936-3176. Bed Capacity 68; Patients Assisted Annually 42,825; Total Staff 201.

KINGSVILLE. *CHRISTUS Spohn Hospital Kleberg*, Mailing Address: 1702 Santa Fe, 78404. Tel: 361-881-3400; Fax: 361-885-0566. Email: larry.pardue@christushealth.org. Web: christusspohn.org. Sponsorship: Sisters of Charity of the Incarnate Word (San Antonio, TX). Bed Capacity 100.

1311 General Cavazos Blvd., 78363. Noram McBride, Vice Pres. & COO; Sr. Elizabeth Smith, Chap.; William L. Pardue, Corp. Sec. Tel: 281-936-3184; Cynthia G. Zatorski, Asst. Corp. Sec. Tel: 281-936-3176. Bed Capacity 72; Patients Assisted Annually 40,310; Total Staff 302.

[E] HOMES FOR THE AGED

CORPUS CHRISTI. *Mount Carmel Home* (1954) 4130 S. Alameda St., 78411. Tel: 361-855-6243; Fax: 361-854-8513. Email: mtcarmelhome@yahoo.com. Sr. M. Michelle Carmel, D.C.J., Admin.; Rev. Msgr. Arnold Anders, Chap. Priests 6; Sisters 9; Bed Capacity 60; Total Assisted Annually 25; Total Staff 19.

Villa Maria, Inc., 3146 Saratoga Blvd., 78415. Tel: 361-857-6171; Fax: 361-857-6173. Email: villamaria@stx.rr.com. Apartment complex for senior adults. Total Staff 4; Total in Residence 55.

[F] RETREAT HOUSES

CORPUS CHRISTI. *Queen of Peace Retreat Center*, 1200 Lantana, Bldg. C, 78409. Tel: 361-289-9095, Ext. 13; Fax: 361-289-0087. Rev. Jean F. Hart, S.O.L.T., Dir.

SARITA. *Lebh Shomea House of Prayer* (1973) *Missionary Oblates of Mary Immaculate*, P.O. Box 9, 78385-0009. Tel: 361-294-5369; Fax: 361-294-5791. Email: admin@lebhshomea.org. Web: www.lebhshomea.org. Rev. Francis Kelly Nemeck, O.M.I., Co-Dir. & Treas. Priests 1; Total in Residence 3; Total Staff 10.

[G] MONASTERIES AND RESIDENCES OF PRIESTS AND BROTHERS

HEBBRONVILLE. *Catholic Solitudes* (1994) *Rancho Maria*, 11053 N. Hwy. 16, P.O. Box 748, 78361. Tel: 361-527-4636; Fax: 361-527-4482. Email: cathsol@aol.com. Web: http://catholicsolitudes.org. Rev. Patrick Meaney, Moderator. Special Apostolate: A fraternal community stressing eremitical contemplative prayer, welcoming eremitical vocations and spiritual formational retreats for young people under directives of Diocesan Bishop. Priests 1; Total in Residence 6; Total Assisted Annually 430; Total Staff 3.

ROBSTOWN. *Society of Our Lady of the Most Holy Trinity*, P.O. Box 152, 78380-0152. Tel: 361-387-2754; Fax: 361-387-3818. Email: dahliasolt@hotmail.com. Web: www.solt3.org. 109 W. Ave. F, 78380. Revs. Vincent Albano, S.O.L.T., Vicar Servant; Fred Alexander, S.O.L.T.; Anthony Anderson, S.O.L.T.; Derek Anderson, SO.L.T., Gen. Sec.; John M. Ayang, S.O.L.T.; Alphonsus Bakyil, S.O.L.T.; Anthony Blount, S.O.L.T.; James Blount, S.O.L.T.; Scott Braathan, S.O.L.T., Novice Servant; James Brady, S.O.L.T.; Scott Brossart, S.O.L.T.; Mark Byrne, S.O.L.T.; George Carlin, S.O.L.T.; Robert Chapa, S.O.L.T.; Phillip Chavez, S.O.L.T.; John Corapi, S.O.L.T.; Dale Craig, S.O.L.T., Gen. Lay Servant; Robert J. Cronin, S.O.L.T.; Michael Edward Crump, S.O.L.T.; Jacques Dolbec, S.O.L.T.; Dennis Dolter, S.O.L.T.; Stephen Dougherty; Jerome Drolshagen; Dennis Dugan, S.O.L.T.; Jeff Eppler, S.O.L.T.; Dan Estes, S.O.L.T.; James Flanagan, S.O.L.T.; John Gaffney, S.O.L.T.; Alfredo Gaytan, S.O.L.T.; Scott Giuliani, S.O.L.T.; Paul Grala, S.O.L.T.; Joseph Hadgkiss, S.O.L.T.; Jean F. Hart, S.O.L.T., Gen. Procurator; Michael Hinken, S.O.L.T.; Paul Hu, S.O.L.T.; Paul Johnston, S.O.L.T.; Ralph O. Jones, S.O.L.T.; Michael Jordan, S.O.L.T., Second Asst. to Regl. Priest Servant; James R. Kelleher, S.O.L.T.; Thaddeus Simon Kiwera, S.O.L.T.; Richard Klepac, S.O.L.T.; Brian List, S.O.L.T.; Benjamin Lopez, S.O.L.T.; Mario Lopez Garcia, S.O.L.T., (Leave of Absence); Clement Machado, S.O.L.T.; Eckley Macklin, S.O.L.T.; Guilbert Mariani, (Diocese of S. Tome e Principe); Peter Marsalek, S.O.L.T.; Benjamin Martin, S.O.L.T.; Joseph Mc Manus, S.O.L.T.; John McHugh, S.O.L.T.; Shane McKee, S.O.L.T.; Glenn Meaux, S.O.L.T.; Eduardo Montemayor, S.O.L.T.; James Mulligan, S.O.L.T.; David Mumba, S.O.L.T.; Christopher Myers, S.O.L.T.; George Nedeff, S.O.L.T.; Peter Hung Nguyen, S.O.L.T.; Vincent Nicosia, S.O.L.T.; Miguel A. Noyola, S.O.L.T. (Guatemala); Joseph O'Connell, S.O.L.T.; Morty O'Shea, S.O.L.T.; Frank Papa, S.O.L.T.; John H. Patterson, S.O.L.T.; John Mary Perez, S.O.L.T.; Peter Pham, S.O.L.T.; Santan Pinto; Jack Purtell, S.O.L.T.; John Robinson, S.O.L.T.; Edward Roche, S.O.L.T.; Mark Ropel, S.O.L.T.; Rogel Rosalinas, S.O.L.T., Gen. Priest Servant; James Sanchez, S.O.L.T.; Margarito Sanchez, S.O.L.T.; Ramon Santa Cruz, S.O.L.T.; Robert Shaldone, S.O.L.T.; Zachory Of the Mother of God Shallow, S.O.L.T.; Gerard J. Sheehan, S.O.L.T., Regl. Priest Servant; Thomas Showalter, S.O.L.T., First Asst. to Regl. Priest Servant; James Tambornino, S.O.L.T.; Lawrence E. Tucker, S.O.L.T.; Gabriel Uzondu, S.O.L.T.; Dennis Walsh, S.O.L.T.; Mark Wendling, S.O.L.T.; Mark Wheelan, S.O.L.T.; Glenn Whewell, S.O.L.T., Vocations Dir.; Brady Williams, S.O.L.T., Rector, Theological House of Studies; Dominic Zimmermann, S.O.L.T.; Deacon Wayne Lickteig, S.O.L.T.

SAN DIEGO. *Vicariate of Holy Rosary, St. Francis de Paul Church*, P.O. Box 279, 78384. Tel: 361-279-3596; Fax: 361-279-8288. Email: berem@vsta.com. Revs. Benito Retortillo, O.P., Local Supr.; Epifanio Rodriguez, O.P. Order of Preachers, U.S. Foundation of the Province of Spain.

[H] CONVENTS AND RESIDENCES FOR SISTERS

CORPUS CHRISTI. *Bethany Convent*, 3002 Austin St., 78404-2413. Tel: 361-887-6308. Web: iwbscc.org. Sisters of the Incarnate Word and Blessed Sacrament 2.

Blessed Sacrament Chapel (1970) 4105 Ocean Dr., 78411-1223. Tel: 361-852-6212; Fax: 361-852-8815. Email: bsccc@grandecom.net. Web: www.mountgraceconvent.org. Sr. Mary Margaret Friedl, S.Sp.S. de A.P., Supr. Sister-Servants of the Holy Spirit of Perpetual Adoration (Motherhouse, Steyl, Holland) 9.

Casa de Matel Residence, 2930 S. Alameda St., 78404-2798. Tel: 361-887-5064; Fax: 361-883-2185. Email: smigonzalez@iwbscc.org. Sr. Anna Marie Espinosa, Contact Person. Sisters of the Incarnate Word and Blessed Sacrament. Sisters 4.

Dominicas de Santo Tomas de Aquino (1913) 12217 Hearn Rd., 78410. Tel: 361-242-8829; Fax: 361-242-8829. Sr. Maria P. Vega, Local Supr. Sisters 3.

Incarnate Word Convent (1871) 2930 S. Alameda, 78404. Tel: 361-882-5413; Fax: 361-880-4152. Email: smmkuntscher@iwbscc.org. Web: www.iwbscc.org. Sr. Christina Bradley, Local Sr. in Charge.

Convent Academy of the Incarnate Word. Sisters of the Incarnate Word and Blessed Sacrament. Sisters 34; Total in Residence 35; Total Staff 17.

McKinzie Residence, 2839 McKinzie Rd., #7, 78410-2347. Tel: 361-232-3270. Email: srmortiz@iwbscc.org. Sr. Rosa Ortiz, I.W.B.S., Contact Person. Sisters of the Incarnate Word and Blessed Sacrament 2.

Mercedarian Sisters of the Blessed Sacrament (1910) 1723 Frio St., 78417. Tel: 361-854-2370; 361-854-2257. Sr. Patricia Rodriguez, H.M.S.S., Local Supr. Sisters 8.

Missionaries of the Rosary of Fatima, 2509 Nogales, 78416. Tel: 361-882-3245; Fax: 361-882-4968. Sisters 2.

Mount Carmel Home Convent (1954) 4130 S. Alameda St., 78411. Tel: 361-855-6243; Fax: 361-854-8513. Email: mtcarmelhome@yahoo.com. Priests 6; Carmelite Sisters of the Divine Heart of Jesus 9; Total Staff 25.

Mount Tabor Convent, 12940 Leopard St., 78410. Tel: 361-241-1955; Fax: 361-241-2271. Email: mmbitoni@gmail.com. Sisters Maria Margarita Bitoni, M.J.M.J., Delegation Supr.; Milagros Tormo, M.J.M.J., Local Supr. Central Regional House of the Missionary Sisters of Jesus, Mary, and Joseph. Sisters 6.

The Ark Assessment Center & Emergency Shelter for Youth (1994) 12960 Leopard St., 78410. Tel: 361-241-6566; Fax: 361-241-5279.

Pax Christi Institute (1969) 4601 Calallen Dr., 78410. Tel: 361-241-2833; Fax: 361-241-5479. Email: paxchristiinstitute@stx.rr.com. Sr. Maria Elva Reyes, P.C.I., Supr. Gen. Sisters 9; Total Staff 9; Total Assisted 3,200.

Religious Missionaries of St. Dominic, Inc. (1986) 2237 Waldron Rd., 78418. Tel: 361-937-5978 (Community). Email: crmsdsis@swbell.net.

Our Lady of the Rosary Catholic School (1992) 2237 Waldron Rd., 78418. Tel: 361-939-9847; Fax: 361-937-0890. Sr. Esperanza H. Seguban, O.P., Dir. Sisters 6; Total Staff 9.

Sisters of Adoration of the Blessed Sacrament, 1601 Ocean Dr., Apt. 5, 78404-1223. Tel: 361-884-7136. Email: shprovince@aol.com. Sr. Elizabeth Pathiparambil, Supr. Sisters 3.

KINGSVILLE. *Missionary Daughters of the Most Pure Virgin Mary* (1916) 919 N. Ninth St., 78363. Tel: 361-595-1087; Fax: 361-221-9763. Sr. Consuelo Ramirez, M.D.P.V.M., Supr. Sisters 9.

ROBSTOWN. *Incarnate Word Ranch - Bluntzer*, 5939 FM 666, 78380. Tel: 361-387-7397; Fax: 361-880-4152. Email: socardona@iwbscc.org. Mailing Address: 2930 S. Alameda, 78404. Tel: 361-387-7397. Sisters of the Incarnate Word and Blessed Sacrament 3.

Sisters of the Society of Our Lady of the Most Holy Trinity, Regl. Headquarters - Casa San Jose, P.O. Box 152, 78380. Tel: 361-387-8090; Fax: 361-387-3818. Email: mpt611@earthlink.net. Web: www.soltsisters.org. Sr. Anne M. Walsh, S.O.L.T., Gen. Sister Servant.

Society of Our Lady of the Most Holy Trinity, Holy Family Ecclesial Team Formation Center, 700 W. Ave. D, P.O. Box 152, 78380. Tel: 361-767-9417. Sr. Margaret Mary Loehr, S.O.L.T., Contact Person. Sisters in Residence 4.

ROCKPORT. *Schoenstatt Sisters of Mary* (1926) 130 Front St., 78382-7800. Tel: 361-729-1868; Fax: 361-729-1685. Email: schsisterstx@charter.net. Sr. M. Gabriella Maschita, Prov. Supr. Secular Institute of the Schoenstatt Sisters of Mary. Sisters 34; Total in Residence 17.

SARITA. *Lebh Shomea House of Prayer, Hermits*, P.O. Box 9, 78385-0009. Tel: 361-294-5369; Fax: 361-294-5791. Email: admin@lebhshomea.org. Web: www.lebhshomea.org. Sisters 2; Total Staff 10; Total in Residence 3.

[I] MISCELLANEOUS

CORPUS CHRISTI. *Lifelong Faith Formation Board*, PO Box 2620, 78403-2620. Tel: 361-693-6631; Fax: 361-693-6731. Email: pstanley@diocesecc.org. Rev. Peter Stanley, Dir.

The Cathedral Concert Series (1985) 505 N. Upper Broadway, 78401. Tel: 361-888-6520; 361-888-7444 (Information); Fax: 361-883-1918. Email: lee.gwozdz@cccathedral.com. Web: www.goccn.org/diocese/ccs/. Mr. Lee Gwozdz, Exec. Dir.

The Catholic Campaign for Human Development, P.O. Box 2620, 78403-2620. Tel: 361-882-6191; Fax: 361-882-1018.

Cursillo Movement, P.O. Box 2620, 78403-2620. Tel: 361-882-6191; Fax: 361-852-1018. Irma Padilla, Pres. Tel: 361-855-2621; Ofelia Garza, Spanish Cursillo School Dir. Tel: 361-857-0729; Dan Serrato, English Cursillo School Dir.

Fannie Bluntzer Nason Renewal Center, Inc. (2000) 2930 S. Alameda St., 78404. Tel: 361-882-5413; Fax: 361-880-4152. Email: smmkuntscher@iwbscc.org. Alison Diana Torres, Exec. Dir.

FirePower Retreats, P.O. Box 2620, 78403-2620. Tel: 361-882-6191; Fax: 361-592-0028. Revs. Paul A. Hesse, Spiritual Dir.; Pete Elizardo, Spiritual Dir.; Tim Etzler, Prog. Dir. Total Assisted Annually 2,500.

Hope, Faith & Love, Inc., P.O. Box 2620, 78403. Tel: 361-882-6191; Fax: 361-882-1018. Raymond Reeves, Pres.; Rev. Msgr. Richard Shirley, P.A., V.G., Chm.

Incarnate Word Academy Foundation (1989) 2930 S. Alameda, 78404. Tel: 361-882-5413; Fax: 361-880-4152. Email: smmkuntscher@iwbscc.org. Web: www.iwacc.org. Sr. Michelle Marie Kuntscher, Pres.

Journey to Damascus, Inc., 5620 Gollihar Rd., 78412. Tel: 888-546-7382; Fax: 361-992-0352. Email: j2damascus@yahoo.com. Web: www.journeytodamascus.org. Rev. Msgr. Richard Shirley, P.A., V.G., Spiritual Dir. Assisted 246 men and women in 2009, including approximately 60 on partial or full scholarship.

Mother Teresa Shelter, Inc. (2003) 513 Sam Rankin, 78401. Tel: 361-883-7372. Email: mteresashelter@sbcglobal.net. Web: goccn.org. Sr. Rose Paul Madassery, S.A.B.S., Opers. Supvr. A day shelter used as a homeless gathering facility; providing bath, laundry, limited eating facilities and counseling services. Total Assisted Annually 33,418; Staff 6.

Our Lady of Corpus Christi Catholic Undergraduate Liberal Arts (1998) P.O. Box 9785, 78469. Tel: 361-289-9095; Fax: 361-289-0087. Email: bookkeeper@colcc.com. Web: www.colcc.com. 1200 Lantana, 78407. Revs. James R. Kelleher, S.O.L.T., Pres.; Dan Estes, S.O.L.T., Vice Pres.; Samuel Medley, Chap.; Jean Hart, Librarian & Procurator. Priests 4; Brothers 6; Lay Teachers 6; Total Staff 10; Students 18.

Search Retreats, P.O. Box 2620, 78415. Tel: 361-882-6191; Fax: 361-882-1157. Email: info@searchretreats.org. Web: searchretreats.org. Revs. Pete Elizardo, Prog. Dir.; Richard A. Libby, Spiritual Dir. Students 200.

Secular Institute of the Schoenstatt Fathers aka Schoenstatt Fathers 4343 Gaines St., 78412-2541. Tel: 361-992-9841; Fax: 361-992-9842. Email: schtx@sbcglobal.net. Rev. Hector R. Vega, I.Sch., Supr. & Contact Person.

Small Catholic Community Ministry, P.O. Box 2620, 78403-2620. Tel: 361-882-6191; Fax: 361-882-1157. Peter Rabalais, Diocesan Coord.; Rev. Eduardo Montemayor, S.O.L.T., Dir.

Teens Encounter Christ and Church "TECC", P.O. Box 2620, 78403-2620. Tel: 361-882-6191; Fax: 361-882-1157. Email: pelizardo@diocesecc.org. Rev. Pete Elizardo, Prog. Dir. Total Assisted Annually 5,000.

RELIGIOUS INSTITUTES OF MEN REPRESENTED IN THE DIOCESE

For further details refer to the corresponding bracketed number in the Religious Institutes of Men or Women section.

[]—*Catholic Solitudes (Hermits)*

[]—*Company of St. Paul (Secular Institute)*—C.S.P.

[0630]—*Congregation of the Missionaries of the Holy Family*—M.S.F.

[]—*Congregation of the Rosarians (Society of Apostolic Life)*—C.R.

[0430]—*Dominican, Order of Preachers* (Spain)—O.P.

[]—*Missionary Society of St. Thomas the Apostle (Society of Apostolic Life)* (India)

[0910]—*Oblates of Mary Immaculate*—O.M.I.

[1065]—*Priestly Fraternity of St. Peter, Society of Apostolic Life*—F.S.S.P.

[1190]—*Salesians of St. John Bosco*—S.D.B.

[]—*Schoenstatt Fathers (Secular Institute)*—I.Sch.

[]—*Secular Institute*

[0975]—*Society of Our Lady of the Most Holy Trinity, Society of Apostolic Life*—S.O.L.T.

RELIGIOUS INSTITUTES OF WOMEN REPRESENTED IN THE DIOCESE

[0360]—*Carmelite Sisters of the Divine Heart of Jesus*—Carmel.D.C.

[0470]—*Congregation of Sisters of Charity of the Incarnate Word* (Houston, TX)—C.C.V.I.

[]—*Congregation of Sisters of St. Joseph of 'St. Marc'*—S.J.S.M.

[0460]—*Congregation of the Sisters of Charity of the Incarnate Word* (San Antonio, TX)—C.C.V.I.

[]—*Daughters of Divine Love*—D.D.L.

[1070-19]—*Dominican Sisters* (Houston, TX)—O.P.

[]—*Dominican Sisters of St. Thomas Aquinas*—O.P.

[2590]—*Mercedarian Sisters of the Blessed Sacrament*—H.M.S.S.

[2690]—*Missionary Catechists of Divine Providence* (San Antonio, TX)—M.C.D.P.

[]—*Missionary Daughters of the Most Pure Virgin Mary* (U.S. Foundation-Mexico)—M.D.P.V.M.

[2770]—*Missionary Sisters of Jesus, Mary, and Joseph*—M.J.M.J.

[]—*Missionary Sisters of the Rosary of Fatima*—H.M.R.F.

[]—*Pax Christi Institute*—P.C.I.

[]—*Religious Missionaries of St. Dominic* (Spanish Prov.)—O.P.

[]—*Schoenstatt Sisters of Mary (Secular Institute)*—I.S.S.M.

[3540]—*Sister Servants of the Holy Spirit of Perpetual Adoration*—S.Sp.S.deA.

[]—*Sisters for Christian Community*—S.F.C.C.

[]—*Sisters of Adoration of the Blessed Sacrament* (India)—S.A.B.S.

[3360]—*Sisters of Providence of Saint Mary-of-the-Woods, IN*—S.P.

[3718]—*Sisters of St. Anne*—S.S.A.

[2200]—*Sisters of the Incarnate Word & Blessed Sacrament* (Victoria)—I.W.B.S.

[2205]—*Sisters of the Incarnate Word and Blessed Sacrament* (Corpus Christi)—I.W.B.S.

[]—*Sisters of the Society of Our Lady of the Most Holy Trinity (Society of Apostolic Life)*—S.O.L.T.

NECROLOGY

† Tengler, Rev. Msgr. Alvin, (Retired)—Died July 1, 2009

† Boensch, Gregory A., (Retired)—Died Jan. 31, 2009

† Iglesias, Luis Fernando, (Retired)—Died Nov. 8, 2009

† McNamara, Peter J., (Retired)—Died March 11, 2009

† Noone, Sean, (Retired)—Died Oct. 31, 2009

An asterisk (*) denotes an organization that has established tax-exempt status directly with the IRS and is not covered by the USCCB Group Ruling.

Diocese of Covington

(Dioecesis Covingtonensis)

Most Reverend

ROGER J. FOYS, D.D.

Bishop of Covington; ordained May 16, 1973; appointed Bishop of Covington May 31, 2002; consecrated and installed July 15, 2002. *Mailing Address: P.O. Box 15550, Covington, KY 41015-0550.* Tel: 859-392-1512; Fax: 859-392-1508.

Most Reverend

WILLIAM A. HUGHES

Retired Bishop of Covington; ordained April 6, 1946; appointed Titular Bishop of Inis Cathaig and Auxiliary of Youngstown July 23, 1974; consecrated September 12, 1974; appointed Bishop of Covington April 13, 1979; transferred to Covington May 8, 1979; retired July 4, 1995. *Res.: Carmel Manor, 100 Carmel Manor Rd., Fort Thomas, KY 41075-2395.*

P.O. Box 15550, Covington, KY 41015-0550. Tel: 859-392-1515; Fax: 859-392-1508.

Web: www.covingtondiocese.org

Email: swagner@covingtondiocese.org

ESTABLISHED JULY 29, 1853.

Square Miles 3,359.

Comprises 14 Counties of the Commonwealth of Kentucky in the north and east of the Commonwealth, including Bracken, Boone, Campbell, Carroll, Fleming, Gallatin, Grant, Harrison, Kenton, Lewis, Mason, Owen, Pendleton and Robertson Counties.

For legal titles of parishes and diocesan institutions, consult the Chancery Office.

STATISTICAL OVERVIEW

Personnel	
Bishop	1
Retired Bishops	1
Priests: Diocesan Active in Diocese	47
Priests: Diocesan Active Outside Diocese	2
Priests: Retired, Sick or Absent	37
Number of Diocesan Priests	86
Religious Priests in Diocese	12
Total Priests in Diocese	98
Extern Priests in Diocese	1
Ordinations:	
Diocesan Priests	4
Transitional Deacons	2
Permanent Deacons in Diocese	29
Total Brothers	5
Total Sisters	313
Parishes	
Parishes	47
With Resident Pastor:	
Resident Diocesan Priests	35
Without Resident Pastor:	
Administered by Priests	7
Administered by Deacons	1
Administered by Religious Women	1
Administered by Lay People	1
Completely Vacant	2
Missions	6
Professional Ministry Personnel:	
Sisters	10
Lay Ministers	37
Welfare	
Catholic Hospitals	5
Total Assisted	829,973
Homes for the Aged	3
Total Assisted	833
Residential Care of Children	2
Total Assisted	360
Day Care Centers	1
Total Assisted	86
Special Centers for Social Services	4
Total Assisted	85,859
Other Institutions	1
Total Assisted	2,482
Educational	
Diocesan Students in Other Seminaries	16
Total Seminarians	16
Colleges and Universities	1
Total Students	1,860
High Schools, Diocesan and Parish	7
Total Students	2,546
High Schools, Private	2
Total Students	790
Elementary Schools, Diocesan and Parish	26
Total Students	6,487
Elementary Schools, Private	2
Total Students	479
Catechesis/Religious Education:	
High School Students	310
Elementary Students	4,165
Total Students under Catholic Instruction	16,653
Teachers in the Diocese:	
Brothers	1
Sisters	20
Lay Teachers	709
Vital Statistics	
Receptions into the Church:	
Infant Baptism Totals	1,119
Minor Baptism Totals	207
Adult Baptism Totals	155
Received into Full Communion	106
First Communions	1,568
Confirmations	1,558
Marriages:	
Catholic	328
Interfaith	157
Total Marriages	485
Deaths	784
Total Catholic Population	89,491
Total Population	464,629

Former Bishops—Rt. Revs. GEORGE ALOYSIUS CARRELL, S.J., D.D., ord. Dec. 20, 1827; cons. Nov. 1, 1853; died Sept. 25, 1868; AUGUSTUS MARIA TOEBBE, D.D., ord. Sept. 14, 1854; cons. Jan. 9, 1870; died May 2, 1884; CAMILLUS PAUL MAES, D.D., ord. Dec. 19, 1868; cons. Jan. 25, 1885; died May 11, 1915; FERDINAND BROSSART, D.D., ord. Sept. 1, 1872; cons. Jan. 25, 1916; retired March 14, 1923; died Aug. 6, 1930; Most Revs. FRANCIS WILLIAM HOWARD, D.D., ord. June 16, 1891; cons. July 15, 1923; died Jan. 18, 1944; WILLIAM THEODORE MULLOY, D.D., LL.D., ord. June 7, 1916; cons. Jan. 10, 1945; died June 1, 1959; RICHARD HENRY ACKERMAN, C.S.Sp., D.D., cons. May 22, 1956; transferred to Covington April 6, 1960; retired Nov. 28, 1978; died Nov. 18, 1992; WILLIAM ANTHONY HUGHES, D.D., ord. April 6, 1946; cons. Sept. 12, 1974; appt. April 13, 1979; retired July 4, 1995; ROBERT W. MUENCH, D.D., ord. May 18, 1968; cons. June 29, 1990; appt. Bishop of Covington, Jan. 5, 1996; installed March 19, 1996; transferred to Baton Rouge, Dec. 15, 2001; installed Bishop of Baton Rouge March 14, 2002.

Vicars General—Rev. Msgrs. GILBERT J. RUTZ, J.D., M.A., M.Ed., M.Div.; J. MICHAEL DUE, V.G.

Chancellor—Ms. MARGARET M. SCHACK.

Diocesan Tribunal—Rev. Msgr. DONALD A. ENZWEILER, J.C.L., Judicial Vicar. Adjutant Judicial Vicars: Revs. MICHAEL D. BARTH, J.C.L.; JAMES M. RYAN; Ms. KAREN GUIDUGLI, Case Promoter & Notary; Sr. MARTHA WALTHER, O.S.B., Sec. & Notary.

Judges—Rev. Msgr. JOHN R. SCHULTE, J.C.L.; Rev. BARRY M. WINDHOLTZ; Sr. MARY CATHERINE WENSTRUP, O.S.B., J.C.L.

Defenders of the Bond—Rev. Msgr. DONALD F. HELLMANN, P.A. (Retired); Revs. EDWIN OMOROGBE, J.C.L.; GREGORY E. OSBURG; Mr. CHAD GLENDINNING, J.C.L.; Rev. GERALD E. TWADDELL, V.F.; Rev. Msgr. WILLIAM B. NEUHAUS, V.F., J.C.L., Promoter of Justice.

Diocesan Consultors—Rev. GREGORY J. BACH; Rev. Msgrs. WILLIAM B. NEUHAUS, V.F., J.C.L.; J. MICHAEL DUE, V.G.; GILBERT J. RUTZ, J.D., M.A., M.Ed., M.Div.; DONALD F. HELLMANN, P.A. (Retired); Revs. RICHARD W. WURTH; MICHAEL E. COMER; RYAN L. MAHER; GERALD L. REINERSMAN.

Deans—Rev. Msgr. WILLIAM B. NEUHAUS, V.F., J.C.L., Covington; Very Rev. DANIEL J. VOGELPOHL, V.F., Northern Kenton County; Rev. Msgr. JOHN R. SCHULTE, J.C.L., Southwest; Very Rev. JAMES B. EGBERS, V.F., Campbell County.

Deanery Pastoral Council—Rev. RYAN L. MAHER.

Presbyteral Council—Ms. MARGARET M. SCHACK, Chancery Contact.

Due Process Board of Administrative Review—Mr. STEPHEN KOPLYAY, Sec.

Diocesan Offices and Directors

401 E. 20th St., Third Fl., P.O. Box 15550, Covington, 41015-0550. Tel: 859-392-1510; Fax: 859-392-1508. Email: swagner@covingtondiocese.org. Office Hours: Mon.-Fri. 8:30-4:30.

Archives—Mr. THOMAS S. WARD, Archivist; Rev. Msgr. ALLEN J. MEIER, P.A., Asst. Archivist (Retired).

Board of Total Catholic Education—Mr. MICHAEL T. CLINES; Ms. KIM HALBAUER, Chm.

Campus Ministry-Newman Center—Rev. GREGORY J. BACH, Northern Kentucky Univ., 512 Johns Hill Rd., P.O. Box 76174, Highland Heights, 41076-1449. Tel: 859-781-3775.

Cathedral Foundation, Inc.—Mrs. KRISTI NADER,

Exec. Dir., 1140 Madison Ave., Covington, 41011-3116. Tel: 859-431-2060; Fax: 859-431-8444.

Catholic Charities—Mr. WILLIAM R. JONES, M.S.W., M.Div., B.A.E., Dir., 3629 Church St., Covington, 41015-1499. Tel: 859-581-8974; Fax: 859-581-9595.

Catholic Scouting—Mr. ISAAC ISAAC. Tel: 859-392-1533.

Cemeteries—Mr. JOHN NIENABER, Dir.

Censor Librorum—Rev. JAMES E. QUILL, S.T.D. (Retired).

Charismatic Renewal—Contact Persons: Mr. HARRY HUMPERT; Mr. JOSEPH BESSLER.

Communication—Mr. TIMOTHY L. FITZGERALD, Dir.

Continuing Education of Priests—Rev. GERALD L. REINERSMAN.

Corpus Central Purchasing—Ms. SANDRA NARE, Gen. Mgr. Buyers: MIKE FREUDENBERG; BOB MOELLMAN, 845 Isabella St., Newport, 41071-1338. Tel: 859-491-8100; 800-955-2541; Fax: 859-491-6587. Email: sandien@corpuscentral.com. Web: www.corpuscentral.com.

Cursillo Movement—Mrs. CAROLYN BOSCH, Lay Dir.

Disabilities Committee—Mr. STEPHEN KOPLYAY, Chm.

Ecumenism—Rev. RONALD M. KETTELER, Thomas More College, 333 Thomas More Pkwy., Crestview Hills, 41017-3428. Tel: 859-344-3393.

Initiation—Rev. RYAN L. MAHER. Chancery

Family Ministry—Mr. ISAAC ISAAC. Tel: 859-392-1529.

Finance—Mr. DALE HENSON, Dir.

Hispanic Ministry—Rev. JOHN W. CAHILL, Cristo Rey Parish, P.O. Box 18400, Erlanger, 41018-0400. Tel: 859-538-1175; Fax: 859-538-1181.

Legion of Mary—Rev. MARIO J. TIZZIANI.

Vicar for Retired Priests—Rev. JOHN H. KROGER (Retired).

Ministry Development Program for Lay & Deacons—Rev. Msgr. WILLIAM B. NEUHAUS, V.F., J.C.L.

Mission Services— See Stewardship and Missions.

Missions Among Black and Native Americans—Sr. JANET BUCHER, C.D.P. Tel: 859-491-5872; Fax: 859-431-8444.

Mustard Seed Community—Contact Persons: Mr. JOSEPH BESSLER; Mr. HARRY HUMPERT.

Newspaper "Messenger"—Mr. TIMOTHY L. FITZGERALD, Editor & Gen. Mgr.

Deaf Ministry—Mother of God Parish, 119 W. Sixth St., Covington, 41011-1409. Tel: 859-392-1511; 859-291-2289 (TDD).

Permanent Diaconate Formation—Rev. Msgr. WILLIAM B. NEUHAUS, V.F., J.C.L.

Priest Personnel—Rev. Msgr. DONALD F. HELLMANN, P.A., Dir. (Retired).

Priests' Retirement Committee—Rev. MARK A. KEENE, Chm.

Pro Life—Ms. KATHLEEN KIELY, Dir.

Religious—Rev. Msgr. J. MICHAEL DUE, V.G., Dir.

Religious Education—Mr. ISAAK A. ISAAK, Dir.

Serra Club of Diocese of Covington—Mr. JAMES RASMUSSEN, Pres.; Rev. GREGORY J. BACH, Chap.

St. Vincent de Paul Salvage Bureau—Mr. DANIEL PAZAK, Dir.

St. Vincent de Paul Community Pharmacy, Inc.— aka Faith Community Pharmacy. ROSANA AYDT, Dir.

Stewardship and Missions—Mr. MICHAEL MURRAY, Dir., Includes Pontifical Aid Societies, Campaign for Human Development, Catholic Relief Fund, Holy Childhood Assoc., Inner City Missions.

Catholic Schools—Mr. MICHAEL T. CLINES, Supt.

Vocations Office—Rev. GREGORY J. BACH, Recruiter.

Office of Worship—Rev. RYAN L. MAHER.

Office of Youth and Young Adult Ministry—Mr. ISAAC ISAAC.

Victim Assistance Coordinator—Ms. MARGARET M. SCHACK. Tel: 859-392-1515. Email: mschack@covingtondiocese.org.

CLERGY, PARISHES, MISSIONS AND PAROCHIAL SCHOOLS

CITY OF COVINGTON

(KENTON COUNTY)

1—CATHEDRAL, BASILICA OF THE ASSUMPTION (1837) Rev. Msgr. William B. Neuhaus, Rector; Rev. Raymond N. Enzweiler; Deacon Gerald R. Franzen.
Res.: 1140 Madison Ave., 41011-3116. Tel: 859-431-2060; Fax: 859-431-8444. Web: www.covcathedral.com.
Catechesis/Religious Program—Students 20.

2—ST. AGNES (1930) Revs. Mark A. Keene; Brian K. Wigger; James E. Quill (Retired); Deacons Joseph Cleves; Robert Stoeckle; David Flynn.
Res.: 1680 Dixie Hwy., Fort Wright, 41011-2779. Tel: 859-431-1802; Fax: 859-291-7017.
School—(Grades K-8) Tel: 859-261-0543; Fax: 859-261-9778. Linda Groh, Prin. Lay Teachers 35; Students 446.
Catechesis/Religious Program—Students 69.

3—ST. AUGUSTINE (1870) Rev. Leo C. Schmidt. In Res., Rev. Robert J. Reinke (Retired).
Res.: 1839 Euclid Ave., 41014-1162. Tel: 859-431-3943; Fax: 859-431-4036. Web: www.staugustines.net.
School—(Grades K-8), 1840 Jefferson Ave., 41014-1165. Tel: 859-261-5564; Fax: 859-261-5402. Sr. Maria Therese Schappert, S.N.D., Prin.; Mrs. Toni Ash, Librarian. Sisters of Notre Dame 7; Lay Teachers 10; Students 120.
Catechesis/Religious Program—Students 7.
St. Augustine Outreach Center—Tel: 859-491-4584.

4—ST. BENEDICT (1885) Rev. Ryan L. Maher.
Res.: 338 E. 17th St., 41014-1315. Tel: 859-431-5607; Fax: 859-431-5847.

5—CHURCH OF OUR SAVIOR (1943), (African American), Sr. Janet Marie Bucher, C.D.P., Parish Life Collaborator.
Res.: 246 E. 10th St., 41011-3026. Tel: 859-491-5872; Fax: 859-431-8444. Email: jbucher@fuse.net.
Catechesis/Religious Program—Students 2.

6—HOLY CROSS (1890) Rev. Thomas C. Barnes; Sr. Helen Charles Wilke, O.S.B., Pastoral Assoc.; Mrs. Bernie Whittle, Pastoral Assoc.
Res.: 3612 Church St., 41015-1431. Tel: 859-431-0636; Fax: 859-431-6917.
School—(Grades K-8) Tel: 859-581-6599; Fax: 859-392-3992. Mary Ellen Matts, Prin. Lay Teachers 12; Students 168.
Catechesis/Religious Program—Students 32.

7—ST. JOHN (1854) Rev. G. Michael Greer; Deacon Robert J. Hermann.
Res.: 627 Pike St., 41011-2148. Tel: 859-431-5314; Fax: 859-431-8397.
Catechesis/Religious Program—Students 22.
Mission—St. Ann (1860) 1274 Parkway, Kenton Co. 41011-1060. Tel: 859-261-9548.

8—MOTHER OF GOD (1841) Rev. Raymond S. Hartman; Deacon Steven I. Durkee.
Res.: 119 W. 6th St., 41011-1409. Tel: 859-291-2288; Fax: 859-291-2065. Email: motherofgod@insightbb.com.
Catechesis/Religious Program—Students 14.

OUTSIDE THE CITY OF COVINGTON

ALEXANDRIA, CAMPBELL CO., ST. MARY OF THE ASSUMPTION (1860) [CEM] Very Rev. James B. Egbers; Rev. Johnson L. Thekkudan, C.M.I.
Res.: 8246 E. Main St., 41001. Tel: 859-635-4188; Fax: 859-635-4189. Email: stmaryalex@fuse.net. Web: saintmaryparish.com.
School—(Grades PreSchool-8), 9 S. Jefferson St., 41001-1394. Tel: 859-635-9539; Fax: 859-448-4824. Michele Ulrich, Prin. Sisters of Notre Dame 1; Lay Teachers 30; Students 359.
Catechesis/Religious Program—Students 210.

AUGUSTA, BRACKEN CO., ST. AUGUSTINE (1859) [JC] Deacon Frank Estill.
Res.: 215 E. Fourth St., 41002-1117. Tel: 606-756-2377; Fax: 606-756-2377. Web: www.staugustine-augusta.org.
School—(Grades PreSchool-8) Tel: 606-756-3229; Fax: 606-756-2377. Mr. Michael Ruf, Prin. Sisters of Notre Dame 1; Lay Teachers 5; Students 94.
Catechesis/Religious Program—Students 2.

BELLEVUE, CAMPBELL CO.

1—ST. ANTHONY (1889) Merged with Sacred Heart, Bellevue to form Divine Mercy, Bellevue.

2—DIVINE MERCY (2003) Rev. Phillip W. DeVous; Deacons Charles J. Dietz; David W. Klingenberg. In Res., Rev. John H. Kroger (Retired).
Res.: 320 Poplar St., 41073-1198. Tel: 859-491-4735; Fax: 859-261-0016. Web: divinemercyparish.org.
Catechesis/Religious Program—Students 120.

3—SACRED HEART (1874) Merged with St. Anthony, Bellevue to form Divine Mercy, Bellevue.

BROOKSVILLE, BRACKEN CO., ST. JAMES (1868) [CEM] Deborah Bartlett, Pastoral Assoc.
Res.: 122 Garrett Ave., 41004-0027. Tel: 606-735-2271; Fax: 606-735-2271.
Catechesis/Religious Program—Students 44.
Mission—St. James Kentucky Rd. 435, Minerva, Mason Co. 41062. Tel: 606-735-2271.

BURLINGTON, BOONE CO., IMMACULATE HEART OF MARY (1954) Revs. Michael E. Comer; Andrews Athappilly, C.M.I.; Deacon Gregory L. Meier.
Church: 5876 Veterans Way, 41005-8824. Tel: 859-689-5010; Fax: 859-689-5636.
School—(Grades PreSchool-8) Tel: 859-689-4303; Fax: 859-689-5636. Michael Jacks, Prin. Sisters of Divine Providence of Kentucky 1; Lay Teachers 40; Students 687.
Catechesis/Religious Program—Students 851.

CALIFORNIA, CAMPBELL CO., STS. PETER AND PAUL (1854) [CEM 2] Rev. Martin John Pitstick.
Res.: 2162 California Crossroads, 41007-9713. Tel: 859-635-2924; Fax: 859-635-9184.
School—Tel: 859-635-4382; Fax: 859-635-9184. Harry Luebbers, Prin. Lay Teachers 11; Students 176.
Catechesis/Religious Program—Students 45.
Mission—Immaculate Conception Stepstone, Pendleton Co.

CAMP SPRINGS, CAMPBELL CO., ST. JOSEPH (1845) [CEM] Rev. Gerald E. Twaddell.
Mailing Address: 6833 Four Mile Rd., 41059-9746. Tel: 859-635-2491; Fax: 859-635-7336. Email: stjoschurchcamp@juno.com. Web: www.josephcampsprings.catholicweb.com.
School—Tel: 859-635-5652; Fax: 859-635-7336. Mr. Ronald Christensen, Headmaster. Lay Teachers 4; Students 52.
Catechesis/Religious Program—Students 12.

CARROLLTON, CARROLL CO., ST. JOHN THE EVANGELIST (1853) [CEM] Rev. Kavungal Lonappan Davy, C.M.I.
Res.: 503 Fifth St., 41008-1203. Tel: 502-732-5776; Fax: 502-732-9062. Email: kldavy@stjohntransfig.org. Web: www.home.catholicweb.com/stjohntransfiguration/index.cfm.
Catechesis/Religious Program—Students 96.
Mission—Transfiguration Perry Park, Owen Co.

COLD SPRING, CAMPBELL CO., ST. JOSEPH (1870) [CEM] Revs. Gerald L. Reinersman; Joshua L. Lange, Parochial Vicar. In Res., Deacon Timothy B. Schabell.
Res.: 4011 Alexandria Pk., 41076-1895. Tel: 859-441-1604; Fax: 859-441-7681. Email: stjoseph@stjoeschool.net. Web: www.stjosephcoldspring.com.
School—(Grades K-8) Tel: 859-441-2025; Fax: 859-441-2057. Mrs. Melissa Holzmacher, Prin. Lay Teachers 31; Students 518.
Catechesis/Religious Program—Students 65.

CRESCENT SPRINGS, KENTON CO., ST. JOSEPH (1916) Rev. Edward J. Brodnick; Deacons Marvin B. Holstein; Joseph L. Baker. In Res., Rev. Ronald M. Ketteler.
Res.: 2470 Lorraine Ct., 41017-1406. Tel: 859-341-6609; Fax: 859-578-2741.
School—(Grades K-8) Tel: 859-578-2742; Fax: 859-578-2754. Cathy Stover, Prin.; Susan Barth, Librarian. Lay Teachers 45; Students 475.
Catechesis/Religious Program—Students 113.

CYNTHIANA, HARRISON CO., ST. EDWARD (1864) [CEM] Rev. Douglas J. Lauer.
Res.: 107 N. Walnut St., 41031-1225. Tel: 859-234-5444; Fax: 859-234-9823. Email: churchoffice@stedwardky.org. Web: www.stedwardky.org.
School—(Grades PreSchool-5) Tel: 859-234-2731; Fax: 859-234-9823. Email: schooloffice@stedwardky.org. Sr. M. Ruth Agnes Delaney, S.N.D., Prin. Lay Teachers 5; Students 44.
Catechesis/Religious Program—Students 44.

DAYTON, CAMPBELL CO., ST. BERNARD (1853) Rev. Phillip W. DeVous; Deacons Charles J. Dietz; David W. Klingenberg.
Church: 401 Berry St., 41074-1196. Tel: 859-261-8506; Fax: 859-581-7260. Email: pastor@dmsb.org.
Res.: 318 Division St., Bellevue, 41073-1198. Tel: 859-261-6172.
Catechesis/Religious Program—Students 14.

EDGEWOOD, KENTON CO., ST. PIUS X (1958) [CEM] Revs. Thomas P. Robbins; Baiju Kidaagen, V.C., Parochial Vicar. In Res., Revs. John J. Riesenberg (Retired); Joseph C. Brink (Retired).
Res.: 340 Dudley Rd., 41017-2609. Tel: 859-341-4900, Ext. 2; Fax: 859-578-8597. Web: stpiusx.com.
School—(Grades K-8) Tel: 859-341-4900; Fax: 859-578-8597. Elizabeth Trenkamp, Prin. Lay Teachers 41; Students 593.
Catechesis/Religious Program—Students 153.

ELSMERE, KENTON CO., ST. HENRY (1890) Revs. James M. Ryan; Niby Kannai, C.M.I.; Deacon Jack Alexander, Pastoral Assoc.; Chris Gunkel, Youth Min.; Barbara Barczak, Music Min.
Res.: 3813 Dixie Hwy., 41018-1809. Tel: 859-342-2540; Fax: 859-342-2542. Web: sthenryel.com.
School—(Grades K-8) Tel: 859-342-2551; Fax: 859-342-2554. Phillip Gessner, Prin.; Martha Bohman, Librarian. Religious 1; Lay Teachers 27; Students 343.
Catechesis/Religious Program—Luann Kohl, D.R.E. Students 236.

ERLANGER, BOONE CO.

1—CRISTO REY Rev. John W. Cahill.
947 Donaldson Rd., P.O. Box 18400, 41018. Tel: 859-538-1175; Fax: 859-538-1181. Email: cristorey@nkymail.net.
Centro de Amistad—Email: jmendez@nkymail.net. Sr. Juana Mendez, Dir.

2—MARY, QUEEN OF HEAVEN (1955) Revs. Richard W. Wurth; Matthew A. Cushing, Parochial Vicar; Deacon Thomas Dushney.
Res.: 1150 Donaldson Hwy., 41018-1048. Tel: 859-525-6909; Fax: 859-525-7067. Web: www.mqhparish.com.
School—(Grades PreSchool-8) Tel: 859-371-8100; Fax: 859-371-3362. Ms. Lynn Mowery, Prin. Lay Teachers 12; Students 213.
Catechesis/Religious Program—Students 53.

ERLANGER, KENTON CO., ST. BARBARA (1967) Rev. John J. Sterling; Deacon Bernard J. Kaiser.
Res.: 4042 Turkeyfoot Rd., 41018-2921. Tel: 859-371-3100; Fax: 859-371-0983.
Catechesis/Religious Program—Students 220.

FALMOUTH, PENDLETON CO., ST. FRANCIS XAVIER (1880) [CEM] Rev. Joseph Edakkulathoor, C.M.I.
Res.: 202 W. Second St., 41040-1118. Tel: 859-654-8241; Fax: 859-654-5203. Email: stxoffice@gmail.com. Web: www.fxfalmouth.org.
Catechesis/Religious Program—Students 39.

FLEMINGSBURG, FLEMING CO., ST. CHARLES (1859) Rev. Verne F. Hogan.
Res.: 211 Mt. Carmel Ave., 41041-1315. Tel: 859-845-4601.
Catechesis/Religious Program—Students 13.

FLORENCE, BOONE CO., ST. PAUL (1872) Rev. Msgr. Thomas B. Sacksteder; Rev. David B. Gamm; Deacon Nicholas J. Schwartz. In Res., Rev. Msgr. Donald F. Hellmann (Retired).
Res.: 7301 Dixie Hwy., 41042-2126. Tel: 859-371-8051; Fax: 859-647-4073. Email: stpaul2@saint-paulschool.org. Web: saintpaulflorence.com.
School—(Grades K-8) Tel: 859-647-4070; Fax: 859-647-0644. David Maher, Prin.; Shannon Bosley, Librarian. Lay Teachers 25; Students 446.
Catechesis/Religious Program—Students 302.

FORT MITCHELL, KENTON CO., BLESSED SACRAMENT (1920) Very Rev. Daniel J. Vogelpohl; Rev. Jose Pereppadan, C.M.I.; Deacon James J. Bayne. In Res., Revs. Thomas W. Franxman, S.J.; Paul F. Tenhundfeld (Retired).
Res.: 2415 Dixie Hwy., 41017-2993. Tel: 859-331-4302; Fax: 859-578-4752. Email: parish@bscky.org. Web: www.bscky.org.
School—(Grades K-8) Tel: 859-331-3062; Fax: 859-344-7323. Mrs. Maureen Hannon, Prin.; Virginia Schneider, Librarian. Lay Teachers 35; Students 574; Sisters of Divine Providence 1.
Catechesis/Religious Program—Students 151.

FORT THOMAS, CAMPBELL CO.
1—ST. CATHERINE OF SIENA (1930) Revs. Stef M. Bankemper; Robert A. Rottgers, Parochial Vicar.
Mailing Address: 1803 N. Ft. Thomas Ave., 41075-1170. Tel: 859-441-1352; Fax: 859-572-2686. Email: church@stcatherineofsiena.org. Web: stcatherineofsiena.org.
School—(Grades K-8) Tel: 859-572-2680; Fax: 859-572-2699. Douglas P. Lonneman, Prin.; Sue Perkins, Librarian. Lay Teachers 18; Students 184.
Catechesis/Religious Program—Students 192.
2—ST. THOMAS (1902) Rev. Msgr. Roger P. Cooney; Rev. Lawrence A. Schaeper, Parochial Vicar.
Mailing Address: 26 E. Villa Pl., 41075-2223. Tel: 859-441-1282; Fax: 859-572-4640. Web: www.saint-thoschurch.org. In Res., Rev. Albert E. Ruschman (Retired).
School—(Grades PreSchool-8) Tel: 859-572-4641; Fax: 859-572-4644. Web: sttschool.org. Ms. Sharon Bresler, Prin.; Mrs. Judy Bailey, Librarian. Lay Teachers 20; Students 175.
Catechesis/Religious Program—Students 121.

INDEPENDENCE, KENTON CO., ST. CECILIA (1880) [CEM] Rev. Mario J. Tizziani.
Res.: 5313 Madison Pk., 41051-0186. Tel: 859-363-4311; Fax: 859-363-4312. Email: bweller@stcindependence.org. Web: stcindependence.org.
School—(Grades K-8) Tel: 859-363-4314; Fax: 859-363-4315. Dr. Carole Roberts, Prin. Lay Teachers 17; Students 295.
Catechesis/Religious Program—Students 130.

KENTON, KENTON CO., ST. MATTHEW (1909) [CEM] Rev. Msgr. Donald A. Enzweiler.
Res.: 13782 Decoursey Pk., P.O. Box 82, 41053-0082. Tel: 859-356-6530; Fax: 859-356-6530 *51. Email: denzweiler@covingtondiocese.org.
Catechesis/Religious Program—
Mission—Assumption of the Blessed Virgin 3711 St. Mary Rd., Morning View, Kenton Co. 41063.

LUDLOW, KENTON CO., STS. BONIFACE AND JAMES (1872) Rev. Robert J. Reinke (Retired); Deacon James C. Auton, Parish Life Collaborator.
Res.: 304 Oak St., 41016-1417. Tel: 859-261-5340; Fax: 859-261-0939. Email: stbonjames@fuse.net.
Catechesis/Religious Program—Students 36.

MAY'S LICK, MASON CO., ST. ROSE OF LIMA (1864) Rev. Verne F. Hogan.
Church: 5011 Raymond Rd., P.O. Box 100, 41055-8821. Tel: 606-845-4601.

MAYSVILLE, MASON CO., ST. PATRICK (1847) [CEM] Rev. Ivan Kalamuzi, Parochial Admin.
Res.: 110 E. Third St., P.O. Box 248, 41056-0248. Tel: 606-564-9015; Fax: 606-564-6108. Email: klamzey@yahoo.com.
School—(Grades PreK-12) Tel: 606-564-5949; Fax: 606-564-8795. Web: www.stpatschool.com. Ms. Anne Poe, Prin. Lay Teachers 9; Students 158.
High School—(Grades 1-12) Ms. Anne Poe, Prin. Lay Teachers 8; Students 138.
Catechesis/Religious Program—Students 42.

MELBOURNE, CAMPBELL CO., ST. PHILIP (1910) Rev. Michael D. Barth, Parochial Admin.
Res.: 1402 Mary Ingles Hwy., 41059-9701. Tel: 859-441-8949; Fax: 859-442-0290. Email: mbarth@stphilipky.org. Web: www.stphilipky.org.
School—(Grades K-8) Tel: 859-441-3423; Fax: 859-441-2611. Sr. Dolores Ann Gohs, C.D.P., Prin. Sisters of Divine Providence of Kentucky 3; Lay Teachers 5; Students 82.
Catechesis/Religious Program—Students 28.

NEWPORT, CAMPBELL CO.
1—ST. FRANCIS DE SALES, Closed. For sacramental records contact Holy Spirit, Newport.
2—HOLY SPIRIT (1997) Rev. Gregory E. Osburg.
Res.: 825 Washington Ave., 41071-1999. Tel: 859-431-2533; Fax: 859-431-3247. Email: holyspirit@fuse.net. Web: holyspiritnewport.com.
Catechesis/Religious Program—Students 20.
3—ST. STEPHEN, Closed. For sacramental records contact Holy Spirit, Newport.
4—ST. VINCENT DE PAUL, Closed. For sacramental records contact Holy Spirit, Newport.

SOUTHGATE, CAMPBELL CO., ST. THERESE OF THE INFANT JESUS (1927) Rev. Clarence J. Heitzman. In Res., Rev. Paul L. Berschied.
Res.: 11 Temple Pl., 41071-3133. Tel: 859-441-1654; Fax: 859-441-2395. Web: www.sainttherese.ws.
School—(Grades K-8), 2516 Alexandria Pike, 41071. Tel: 859-441-0449; Fax: 859-441-0449. Dot O'Leary, Prin.; Diana Green, Librarian. Lay Teachers 22; Students 332.
Catechesis/Religious Program—Students 68.

TAYLOR MILL, KENTON CO.
1—ST. ANTHONY (1878) Rev. Joseph A. Gallenstein.
Res.: 485 Grand Ave., 41015-0219. Tel: 859-431-1773; Fax: 859-431-0768. Email: saintanthonychurch@fuse.net. Web: saintanthonytaylormill.org.
School—(Grades K-8) Tel: 859-431-5987; Fax: 859-431-7353. Ms. Joanne Browarsky, Prin. Lay Teachers 10; Students 83.
Catechesis/Religious Program—Students 35.
2—ST. PATRICK (1966) Rev. Jeffrey D. Von Lehmen; Deacon Carl A. Ledbetter.
Mailing Address: 3285 Mills Rd., 41015-2480. Tel: 859-356-5151; Fax: 859-344-7042. Email: parishpastor@fuse.net. Web: www.stpatrickonline.org.
Catechesis/Religious Program—Students 230.

UNION, BOONE CO., ST. TIMOTHY (1989) Revs. Richard G. Bolte; Jacob Varghese, V.C.; Deacons Thomas L. Nolan; Michael J. Keller.
Res.: 10272 Hwy. 42, P.O. Box 120, 41091-0120. Tel: 859-384-1100; Fax: 859-384-1709. Web: www.saint-timothy.org.
Catechesis/Religious Program—Students 650.

VANCEBURG, LEWIS CO., HOLY REDEEMER (1965) Mrs. Michele Bertot, Parish Life Collaborator; Rev. Laurence Goulding, G.H.M.
Mailing Address: P.O. Box 8, 41179-0008. Tel: 606-796-3052; Fax: 606-262-4741.
Catechesis/Religious Program—Students 4.

WALTON, BOONE CO., ALL SAINTS (1951) [CEM 2] Rev. Msgr. John R. Schulte; Deacon Paul V. Yancey.
Res.: 46 Needmore St., 41094-1029. Tel: 859-485-4476; Fax: 859-485-6476.
Catechesis/Religious Program—Students 83.

WARSAW, GALLATIN CO., ST. JOSEPH (1864) [CEM] Rev. B. Gerald Witzemann, Parochial Admin. (Retired).
Mailing Address: P.O. Box 495, 41095-0495.
Res.: 602 Sparta Pike, P.O. Box 495, 41095-0495. Tel: 859-567-2425; Fax: 859-567-2425.
Catechesis/Religious Program—Students 27.
Mission—St. Edward (1958) 1335 Hwy. 22 E., R.R. 4, Owenton, Owen Co. 40359-9003.

WILDER, CAMPBELL CO., ST. JOHN THE BAPTIST (1847) Rev. Paul F. Krebs, Parochial Admin. (Retired).
Res.: 1307 John's Hill Rd., 41076-9762. Tel: 859-781-2117; Fax: 859-781-2117. Email: info@sjtbchurch.com. Web: sjtbchurch.com.

WILLIAMSTOWN, GRANT CO., ST. WILLIAM (1912) [CEM 2] Rev. William H. Hinds; Deacon Michael T. Lyman.
Res.: 6 Church St., 41097-9454. Tel: 859-824-5381; Fax: 859-824-5381 *51. Email: stwilliam@wkybb.net.
Catechesis/Religious Program—Students 102.
Mission—St. John's (1956) Dividing Ridge, Pendleton Co.

Chaplains of Public Institutions

FORT THOMAS. *Veterans Hospital*. Rev. Alexander A. Okoro (Nigeria), Chap., Archdiocese for Military Services.

Leave of Absence:
Rev.—
Witte, Mark G.

Administrative Leave:
Revs.—
Broering, Raymond L. (Retired)
Fortner, Douglas F.
Frazier, Richard W.

Retired:
Most Rev.—
Hughes, William A., Carmel Manor, 100 Carmel Manor Rd., 41075-2395.
Rev. Msgrs.—
Hellmann, Donald F., P.A., St. Paul Rectory, 7301 Dixie Hwy., Florence, 41042-2126.
Meier, Allen J., P.A., St. Joseph Heights, 1601 Dixie Hwy., Park Hills, 41011-2798.
Revs.—
Boschert, Joseph N., St. Charles Lodge, 500 Farrell Dr., Apt. 110, 41011-3798.
Brink, Joseph C., St. Pius X Rectory, 340 Dudley Rd., Edgewood, 41017-2699.
Broering, Raymond L., 2 Cypress Run, Apt. 21 B, Homosassa, FL 34446-4228.
Delange, Maurice, P.O. Box 83, Milford, OH 45150.
Dickmann, Louis H., 6660 Licking Pike, Cold Spring, 41076-8807.
Gerrety, James P., 626 Laurel St., Ludlow, 41016-1341.
Henderson, Robert J., 202 Thornbush Ct., Cold Spring, 41076-1939.
Jasper, Louis H., 1400 Sleepy Hollow, Apt. 2, Park Hills, 41011.
Krebs, Paul F., 14 Orchard St., Southgate, 41071-3126.
Kroger, John H., 320 Poplar St., Bellevue, 41073-1109.
McHugh, James L., 209 E. Second St., Maysville, 41056-1307.
Quill, James E., S.T.D., St. Agnes Rectory, 1680 Dixie Hwy., Park Hills, 41011.
Reinke, Robert J., St. Augustine Rectory, 1839 Euclid Ave., 41014-1162.
Riesenberg, John J., St. Pius X Rectory, 340 Dudley Rd., Edgewood, 41017-2609.
Robotnik, Lawrence R., Passionist Monastery, 1149 Donaldson Rd., Erlanger, 41018-1000.
Rooks, Charles W., St. Charles Lodge, 600 Farrell Dr., Apt. 224, 41011-5165.
Rosing, Robert C., St. Joseph Heights, 1601 Dixie Hwy., Park Hills, 41011-2798.
Rueter, Joseph J., Carmel Manor, 100 Carmel Manor Rd., 41075-2395.
Ruschman, Albert E., St. Thomas Rectory, 26 E. Villa Pl., 41075-2223.
Seiler, John A., 17 Montvale Ct., Apt. 2, 41075-1820.
Smith, R. Leroy, Country Village, 10501 Becoming Dr., Hudson, FL 34667.
Tenhundfeld, Paul F., Blessed Sacrament Rectory, 2415 Dixie Hwy., Fort Mitchell, 4107--936.
Toner, Edward R., Plymouth Harbor, 700 John Ringling Blvd., T-1608, Sarasota, FL 34236-0254.
Urlage, Robert J., 2327 Rolling Hills Dr., Crestview Hills, 41017-5136.
Vater, Robert L., Carmel Manor, 100 Carmel Manor Dr., 41075-2395.
Werner, John P., 500 Farrell Dr., 41011-3798.
Witzemann, B. Gerald, P.O. Box 495, Warsaw, 41095-0495.

Permanent Deacons:
Alexander, John N., St. Henry, Elsmere
Auton, James C., Sts. Boniface & James, Ludlow
Baker, Joseph L., St. Joseph, Crescent Springs
Bayne, James L., Airport Chaplaincy; Blessed Sacrament, Ft. Mitchell
Cleves, Joseph A., St. Agnes, Park Hills
Dietz, Charles J., St. Bernard, Dayton & Divine Mercy, Bellevue
Durkee, Steven I., Mother of God, Covington
Dushney, Thomas M., Mary, Queen of Heaven, Erlanger
Estill, Andrew (Frank), St. Augustine, Augusta
Flynn, David J.
Franzen, Gerald R., Cathedral, Covington
Hermann, Robert J., St. John, Covington
Hillenmeyer, Ernest B., (Retired)
Holstein, Marvin B., St. Joseph, Crescent Springs
Kaiser, Bernard, St. Barbara, Erlanger
Keller, Michael J., St. Timothy, Union
Klingenberg, David W., Divine Mercy, Bellevue and St. Bernard, Dayton
Ledbetter, Carl A., Chaplain, St. Elizabeth Hospice; St. Patrick, Taylor Mill
Lyman, Michael T., St. William, Williamstown

Meier, Gregory L., Immaculate Heart of Mary, Burlington
Nolan, Thomas L., St. Timothy, Union
Norris, Eugene F., (Retired)
O'Donnell, Richard J., (Retired)
Racine, Phillip J., St. Benedict, Covington
Schabell, Timothy B., St. Joseph, Cold Spring
Schwartz, Nicholas J., St. Paul, Florence
Stoeckle, Robert A., St. Agnes, Fort Wright
Sweigart, James H., (Retired)
Yancey, Paul V., Marydale Retreat Center and All Saints, Walton

PILGRIMAGE SHRINES

COVINGTON. *Shrine of St. Ann.* Attached to St. Ann Mission.

SOUTHGATE. *Shrine of the Little Flower.* Attached to St. Therese Church.

INSTITUTIONS LOCATED IN THE DIOCESE

[A] COLLEGES AND UNIVERSITIES

CRESTVIEW HILLS. *Thomas More College* (Coed), 333 Thomas More Pkwy., 41017. Tel: 859-341-5800; Fax: 859-344-3649. Web: www.thomasmore.edu. Sr. Margaret Stallmeyer, C.D.P., J.C.L., Pres.; Ms. Cathy Silvers, Vice Pres. Inst. Advancement; Dr. Bradley A. Bielski, Vice Pres. Academic Affairs; Ms. Peg Bradner Hancock, Vice Pres. Finance & Admin.; Sr. Patricia Dorobek, S.N.D., Dir. Campus Ministry; Mr. James McKellogg, Dir. Library; Ms. Kelly Goyette, Registrar; Ms. Mary Givhan, Dir. Fin. Aid; Dr. Jim Ross, Dir. Student Support Svcs.; Ms. Genie Wambaugh, Dir. Institute Planning & Effectiveness; Mr. Matthew Webster, Vice Pres. Student Svcs.; Ms. Kelly Marsh, Dir. Communications & Media Rels. Priests 3; Lay Teachers 73; Sisters 2; Administration: Lay People 15; Students 1,860.

[B] HIGH SCHOOLS, DIOCESAN

COVINGTON. *Covington Catholic High School*, 1600 Dixie Hwy., 41011-2797. Tel: 859-491-2247; Fax: 859-448-2242. Email: browe@covcath.org. Web: www.covcath.org. Mr. Robert J. Rowe, Prin.; Mr. Michael Guidugli, Asst. Prin.; Mr. Anthony Zechella, Asst. Prin.; Rev. Joseph A. Gallenstein, Chap. Lay Teachers 36; Boys 500.

Covington Latin School (1923) (Grades 8-12), 21 E. 11th St., 41011-3196. Tel: 859-291-7044; Fax: 859-291-1939. Email: headmaster@covingtonlatin.org. Web: www.covingtonlatin.org. Mr. Andrew J. Barczak, Headmaster; Mr. Fred Reuter, Dean; Rev. Raymond N. Enzweiler, Chap.; Mrs. Rhonda Vrabel, Librarian. Lay Teachers 27; Boys 138; Girls 97.

Holy Cross High School, 3617 Church St., 41015-1498. Tel: 859-431-1335; Fax: 859-655-2184. Email: clay.eifert@hchscov.com. Web: hchscov.com. Mr. Clay Eifert, Prin.; Rev. Thomas P. Robbins, Chap. Priests 2; Religious 1; Lay Teachers 37; Students 452.

ALEXANDRIA. *Bishop Brossart High School* (1950) 4 Grove St., 41001-1295. Tel: 859-635-2108; Fax: 859-635-2135. Email: brossart@insightbb.com. Web: www.bishopbrossart.org. Mr. Richard L. Stewart, Prin.; Rev. Joshua L. Lange, Chap.; Susan Rasche, Librarian. Sisters of Notre Dame 1; Lay Teachers 30; Students 368.

ERLANGER. *St. Henry District High School*, 3755 Scheben Dr., 41018-3597. Tel: 859-525-0255; Fax: 859-525-5855. Email: dmotte@SHDHS.org. Web: www.SHDHS.org. Mr. David M. Otte, Prin.; Rev. Matthew A. Cushing, Chap.; Ms. Terri Manning, Librarian. Lay Teachers 39; Students 513.

MAYSVILLE. *St. Patrick High School*, 318 Limestone St., 41056-1248. Tel: 606-564-5949; Fax: 606-564-8795. Email: apoe@stpatschool.com. Rev. Ivan Kalamuzi, Chap.; Ms. Anne Poe, Prin.; Mr. William Hauke, Librarian. Lay Teachers 12; Students 116.

NEWPORT. *Newport Central Catholic High School*, 13 Carothers Rd., 41071-2497. Tel: 859-292-0001; Fax: 859-292-0656. Web: www.ncchs.com. Mr. Robert Noll, Prin.; Revs. Phillip W. DeVous, Chap.; Stephen M. Bankemper, Chap. & Pastoral Admin.; Ms. Joanne Loechel, Admin. Team; Mrs. Jenny Mertle, Admin. Team; Ms. Amy Gurley, Librarian. Sisters 1; Lay Teachers 38; Students 431.

[C] HIGH SCHOOLS, PRIVATE

COVINGTON. *Villa Madonna Academy High School*, 2500 Amsterdam Rd., Villa Hills, 41017-3798. Tel: 859-331-6333; Fax: 859-331-8615. Email: pmcqueen@villamadonna.net. Web: www.villamadonna.net. Mr. Edmond Franchi, Pres.; Ms. Pamela McQueen, Prin.; Rev. Baiju Kidaagen, V.C., Chap.; Ms. Debbie Young, Librarian. Sisters 3; Lay Teachers 21; Students 194.

PARK HILLS. *Notre Dame Academy, Inc.*, 1699 Hilton Dr., 41011-2769. Tel: 859-261-4300; Fax: 859-292-7722. Email: nda@ndapandas.org. Web: www.ndapandas.org. Sr. Elaine Marie Winter, S.N.D., Prin.; Rev. Brian K. Wigger, Chap. Sisters of Notre Dame. Sisters 5; Lay Teachers 41; Girls 600.

[D] ELEMENTARY SCHOOLS, INTERPAROCHIAL

COVINGTON. *Holy Family Catholic School* (1988) (Grades K-8), 338 E. 16th St., 41014-1398. Tel: 859-581-0290; Fax: 859-581-0624. Email: holyfamilyschoolcov@insightbb.com. Ms. Polly Duplace, Prin.; Sylvia Wilson, Librarian. Lay Teachers 5; Students 66.

Prince of Peace School, (Grades K-8), 625 Pike St., 41011-2798. Tel: 859-431-5153; Fax: 859-291-8632. Email: srose@popcov.com. Web: www.popcov.com. Sisters M. Suzanne Rose, S.N.D., Prin.; Ann Marie Pflum, S.N.D., Librarian. Sisters of Notre Dame 3; Lay Teachers 10; Students 120.

BELLEVUE. *Holy Trinity Elementary School*, (Grades K-5), 235 Division St., 41073-1101. Tel: 859-291-6937; Fax: 859-291-6970. Email: jfinke@holytrinity-school.org. Web: holytrinity-school.org. Mr. Jeffrey Finke, Prin.; Ms. Liz Enzweiler, Librarian. Sisters 1; Lay Teachers 5; Students 80.

NEWPORT. *Holy Trinity Junior High School and Child Development Center*, 840 Washington Ave., 41071-2485. Tel: 859-292-0487; Fax: 859-431-8745. Email: jfinke@holytrinity-school.org. Web: holytrinity-school.org. Mr. Jeffrey Finke, Prin. Lay Teachers 5; Students 40.

[E] ELEMENTARY SCHOOLS, DIOCESAN

FORT MITCHELL. *Guardian Angel* (1966) (Grades K-8), Orphanage Rd., P.O. Box 17007, 41017-0007. Tel: 859-331-2040; Fax: 859-344-5022. Email: sommer.alpiger@beechwood.kyschools.us. Ms. Sommer Alpiger, Educ. Prog. Dir. School for the Emotional Behavioral Disabled. Lay Teachers 4; Students 30.

[F] ELEMENTARY SCHOOLS, PRIVATE

COVINGTON. *Villa Madonna Academy*, (Grades K-8), 2500 Amsterdam Rd., Villa Hills, 41017-3798. Tel: 859-331-6333; Fax: 859-331-8615. Web: www.villamadonna.net. Mrs. Soshana Bosley, Prin.; Ms. Wilanne Stangel, Librarian. Lay Teachers 34; Students 331.

WALTON. *St. Joseph Academy* (1976) (Grades PreK-8), 48 Needmore St., 41094-1028. Tel: 859-485-6444; Fax: 859-485-4262. Email: principalsja@insightbb.com. Web: www.saintjosephacademy.net. Sr. Elizabeth Ann Barkett, Prin.; Mrs. Michelle Jones, Librarian. Sisters of St. Joseph the Worker. Sisters 4; Lay Teachers 10; Students 184.

[G] MONTESSORI SCHOOLS (PRESCHOOL)

VILLA HILLS. *Villa Madonna Montessori*, 2402 Amsterdam Rd., 41017-5316. Tel: 859-341-5145; Fax: 859-331-2136. Stacey R. Brosky, Admin. Sisters of Divine Providence 1; Lay Teachers 4; Students 48.

[H] PRESCHOOLS

COVINGTON. *Julie Learning Center, Inc.*, 1601 Dixie Hwy., 41011-2798. Tel: 859-392-8231; Fax: 859-291-1774. Email: smpatrycia@aol.com. Sr. M. Patrycia Sweeney, S.N.D., Dir. Daycare with educational emphasis for ages 4-6. Lay Teachers 6; Students 60.

[I] GENERAL HOSPITALS

EDGEWOOD. *St. Elizabeth Medical Center, Inc.*, 1 Medical Village Dr., 41017-3441. Tel: 859-301-2000; Fax: 859-301-5412. Email: jbozzell@stelizabeth.com. Web: www.stelizabeth.com. Mr. Joseph Gross, Pres. & CEO; Mr. John Dubis, Exec. Vice Pres. & COO; Mr. Joseph Bozzelli, Dir. Pastoral Care; Revs. John H. Kroger (Retired); Joseph C. Brink (Retired); Robert J. Henderson (Retired); James E. Quill, S.T.D. (Retired); Robert C. Rosing (Retired); John A. Seiler (Retired); Paul F. Tenhundfeld (Retired). Bed Capacity 480; Patients Assisted Annually 516,279.

[J] NURSING HOMES

COVINGTON. *St. Charles Care Center, Inc.* (1960) 500 Farrell Dr., 41011-3798. Tel: 859-331-3224; Fax: 859-578-2065. Email: smluann@zoomtown.com. Web: www.stcharlescare.org. Sr. Mary Luann Bender, S.N.D., Admin. Adult Day Health Program; Licensed In and Outpatient Occupational Speech and Physical Therapy Department; and Private Duty Nursing; Independent in home care, skilled nursing facility and Senior Living Accommodations. Sisters of Notre Dame 2; Nursing Bed Capacity 105; Senior Living Apartments 72; Cottages 44; Total Assisted Annually 625; Employees 225.

Madonna Manor (1966) 2344 Amsterdam Rd., Villa Hills, 41017-3712. Tel: 859-341-3981; Fax: 859-578-7475. Email: mariannd@madonnamanor.org. Web: www.madonnamanor.org. Mrs. Susan McConn, Admin. Patients Assisted Annually 60; Bed Capacity 60; Staff 75.

[K] PROTECTIVE INSTITUTIONS

COVINGTON. *Diocesan Catholic Children's Home* (1961) Orphanage Rd., P.O. Box 17007, Fort Mitchell, 41017-2730. Tel: 859-331-2040; Fax: 859-344-5022. Email: jhoffman@dcchome.org. Web: www.dcchome.org. Sisters Jean Marie Hoffman, S.N.D., Exec. Dir.; M. Ann Christine Kathman, S.N.D., Educ. Treatment Dir. Sisters of Notre Dame 2; Lay Staff 67; Children in Residence 34; Students 34.

COLD SPRING. *Campbell Lodge Boys Home*, 5161 Skyline Dr., 41076. Tel: 859-781-1214; Fax: 859-442-3473. Email: bjones@clbh.org. Web: www.clbh.org. Mr. Barry Jones, M.S.W., Interim Exec. Dir. Total Staff 32; Boys 25.

Campbell Lodge Boys' Home Foundation, 5161 Skyline Dr., 41076. Tel: 859-781-1214; Fax: 859-442-3473. Mr. Jim Cutter, Chm.

[L] HOMES FOR AGED

FORT THOMAS. *Carmel Manor*, 100 Carmel Manor Rd., 41075-2395. Tel: 859-781-5111; Fax: 859-781-2337. Email: carmelmanor@fuse.net. Web: carmelmanor.com. Sr. Teresa Kennedy, O.Carm., Admin. Carmelite Sisters for the Aged and Infirm. Total Staff 150; Residents 145; Bed Capacity 145; Total Assisted Annually 125.

Regina Cleri Home for Retired Priests, 100 Carmel Manor Rd., 41075-2395. Tel: 859-781-5111; Fax: 859-781-2337. Sr. Teresa Kennedy, O.Carm., Admin. Carmelite Sisters for the Aged and Infirm.

[M] MONASTERIES AND RESIDENCES OF PRIESTS AND BROTHERS

COVINGTON. *Brothers of the Poor of St. Francis* (International Office), Holy Family Friary, 239 W. Robbins St., 41011-3078. Tel: 859-291-2938. Email: bjcphelan@fuse.net. In Res. Bros. William Anuszkiewicz; Blaise Betley, C.F.P.; Rock Larsen, C.F.P.; James Phelan, C.F.P.; Rev. Eric Lauer, C.F.P.

[N] CONVENTS AND RESIDENCES FOR SISTERS

COVINGTON. *The Franciscan Daughters of Mary (F.D.M.)* (Public Association of the Faithful), St. Benedict Convent, 336 E. 16th St., 41014-1303. P.O. Box 122070, 41012-2070.

St. Walburg Monastery, 2500 Amsterdam Rd., 41017-5316. Tel: 859-331-6324; Fax: 859-331-2136. Web: www.stwalburg.org. Sr. Mary Catherine Wenstrup, O.S.B., Prioress. Benedictine Sisters. Professed Sisters 70.

ERLANGER. *Monastery of the Sacred Passion*, 1151 Donaldson Hwy., 41018-1000. Tel: 859-371-8568; Fax: 859-371-8568. Sr. Margaret Mary, C.P., Supr.; Rev. Lawrence R. Robotnik, Chap. (Retired). Passionist Nuns. Professed 8.

FORT THOMAS. *Sisters of the Good Shepherd*, Pelletier Hall, 930 Highland Ave., 41075-1707. Tel: 859-441-5531; Fax: 859-441-7340. Email: srelise@fuse.net. Web: goodshepherdsisters.org. Sr. Mary Elise Kramer, Admin.; Rev. John A. Seiler, Chap. (Retired). Sisters of the Good Shepherd 18.

MELBOURNE. *St. Anne Convent*, 1000 St. Anne Dr., 41059-9603. Tel: 859-441-0679; Fax: 859-441-1510. Email: cschumacher@cdpkentucky.org. Web: www.cdpkentucky.org. Sr. Frances Moore, C.D.P., Prov. Supr.; Rev. Elmer Nadicksbernd, S.V.D., Chap. (Retired). Provincial House and Novitiate of the Sisters of Divine Providence of Kentucky. Sisters in Community 130; Sisters in Provincial House 11.

Holy Family Home, Rte. 8, 2000 St. Anne Dr., 41059-9604. Tel: 859-781-0712; Fax: 859-781-8854. Email: jack.rudnick@thomasmore.edu. John D. Rudnick Jr., Admin. Sisters in Residence 56.

PARK HILLS. *Provincial House of the Sisters of Notre Dame* Juniorate, Novitiate (1924), 1601 Dixie Hwy., 41011-2701. Tel: 859-291-2040; Fax: 859-291-1774. Email: smcarol@sndky.org. Web: www.sndky.org. Sr. Marla Monahan, S.N.D., Prov. Supr.; Rev. Robert C. Rosing, Chap. (Retired). Sisters in Community 132; Sisters in Prov. House 70.

WALTON. *St. William Convent*, One St. Joseph Ln., 41094-1026. Tel: 859-485-4914; 859-485-4256; Fax: 859-485-4914. Sr. Celeste Marie Downes, S.J.W., Supr. Sisters of St. Joseph the Worker. Sisters in Community 13; Sisters in Motherhouse 6. 13 Mulberry St., 41094-1036. Tel: 859-485-7053.

[O] SECULAR INSTITUTES

ERLANGER. *Society of St. Vincent de Paul* (1923) 2655 Crescent Springs Rd., 41017-1504. Tel: 859-341-3212, Ext. 12; Fax: 859-341-1610. Email: tracy.allen@svdpcovington.org. Web: svdpcovington.org. P.O. Box 17594, 41017. Patti Robinson, Pres. District Council of Northern Kentucky. Executive Offices and Thrift Stores. 27 Parish Conferences in Northern Kentucky Thrift Stores, including Dayton, Newport, Crescent Springs, Falmouth; A Catholic lay organization of over 875,000 members worldwide whose members meet in parish and district groups in order to help in a personal way those in need. Total Stores 4.

[P] SOCIAL SERVICES

COVINGTON. *Catholic Charities*, 3629 Church St., 41015-1499. Tel: 859-581-8974; Fax: 859-581-9595. Email: info@covingtoncharities.org. Web: www.covingtoncharities.org. Mr. William R. Jones, M.S.W., M.Div., B.A.E., Exec. Dir. Total Assisted Annually 11,000; Total Staff 38.

Parish Kitchen (1974) Pike St. & Russell St., P.O. Box 1234, 41012-1234. Tel: 859-581-7745. Email: parishkitchen@fuse.net. Web: parishkitchen.org. Ms. Molly Navin, Dir. Total Assisted Annually 60,000.

[Q] DIOCESAN RETREAT HOUSES

ERLANGER. *Marydale Retreat Center*, 945 Donaldson Hwy., 41018-1093. Tel: 859-371-4224; Fax: 859-371-4604. Email: marydale@marydaleretreat.com. Web: marydaleretreat.com. Deacon Paul V. Yancey, Dir. Total Assisted Annually 3,954; Total Staff 16.

[R] NEWMAN CLUBS

HIGHLAND HEIGHTS. *Catholic Newman Club - Northern Kentucky University* 512 Johns Hill Rd., 41076-1449. Tel: 859-781-3775. Rev. Gregory J. Bach, Chap.

[S] MISCELLANEOUS

COVINGTON. *Notre Dame Urban Education Center, Inc.*, 14 E. 8th St., 41011.

FORT MITCHELL. *Mission Share*, P.O. Box 176356, 41017-6356. Tel: 859-824-5381; 859-341-8405. Rev. William H. Hinds, Pres. Purpose: A mission society whose principle activity is to construct Catholic churches, priest houses, parish centers and other buildings of church work, for the advancement of the Catholic faith among the poorest of the poor, especially focused in Colombia, South America and Mexico.

RELIGIOUS INSTITUTES OF MEN REPRESENTED IN THE DIOCESE

For further details refer to the corresponding bracketed number in the Religious Institutes of Men or Women section.

[0460]—*Brothers of the Poor of St. Francis* (Aachen, Germany)—C.F.P.

[0275]—*Carmelites of Mary Immaculate* (Devamatha, India Province)—C.M.I.

[0570]—*Glenmary Home Missioners*—G.H.M.

[0690]—*Jesuit Fathers and Brothers* (Chicago Prov.)—S.J.

[0730]—*Legionaries of Christ* (Atlanta, Georgia)—L.C.

[]—*Society of the Divine Word* (Chicago Prov.)—S.V.D.

[1335]—*Vincentian Congregation* (Padra, Rewa, India)—V.C.

RELIGIOUS INSTITUTES OF WOMEN REPRESENTED IN THE DIOCESE

[0230]—*Benedictine Sisters of Pontifical Jurisdiction*—O.S.B.

[0330]—*Carmelite Sisters for the Aged and Infirm* (Germantown, NY)—O.Carm.

[3180]—*Congregation of the Passion of Jesus Christ*—C.P.

[0440]—*Sisters of Charity of Cincinnati, Ohio*—S.C.

[1000]—*Sisters of Divine Providence of Kentucky*—C.D.P.

[2990]—*Sisters of Notre Dame*—S.N.D.

[1640]—*Sisters of St. Francis of Perpetual Adoration* (Colorado Springs, CO)—O.S.F.

[3920]—*Sisters of St. Joseph the Worker*—S.J.W.

[1830]—*Sisters of the Good Shepherd*—R.G.S.

DIOCESAN CEMETERIES

COLD SPRING. *St. Joseph*

FORT MITCHELL. *St. John*

St. Mary

FORT THOMAS. *St. Stephen*

WILDER. *St. Joseph*

NECROLOGY

† Brinker, Paul J., (Retired)—Died Dec. 27, 2008

† Mulhern, Raymond F., (Retired)—Died July 22, 2009

† Saner, Daniel J., Brooksville, KY St. James—Died Oct. 20, 2009

† Steidle, Mark A., (Administrative Leave)—Died Aug. 30, 2009

† Weber, Charles E., (Retired)—Died May 24, 2009

An asterisk (*) denotes an organization that has established tax-exempt status directly with the IRS and is not covered by the USCCB Group Ruling.

Diocese of Crookston

(Dioecesis Crookstoniensis)

Most Reverend

MICHAEL J. HOEPPNER, D.D., J.C.L.

Bishop of Crookston; ordained June 29, 1975; appointed seventh Bishop of Crookston September 28, 2007; Episcopal ordination November 30, 2007. *1200 Memorial Dr., Crookston, MN 56716.* Tel: 218-281-4533. Email: mhoeppner@crookston.org.

Most Reverend

VICTOR H. BALKE, D.D., PH.D.

Bishop Emeritus of Crookston; ordained May 24, 1958; appointed July 7, 1976; Episcopal ordination September 2, 1976; retired September 28, 2007. *Res.: 1417 Belsly Blvd., Moorhead, MN 56560.* Tel: 218-287-2828. Email: vhbalke@crookston.org.

Chancery Office: 1200 Memorial Dr., P.O. Box 610, Crookston, MN 56716. Tel: 218-281-4533; Fax: 218-281-3328.

Web: www.crookston.org

Email: dbaumgartner@crookston.org

ESTABLISHED BY HIS HOLINESS PIUS X, DECEMBER 31, 1909.

Square Miles 17,210.

Comprises the Counties of Becker, Beltrami, Clay, Clearwater, Hubbard, Kittson, Lake of the Woods, Marshall, Mahnomen, Norman, Pennington, Polk, Red Lake and Roseau in the State of Minnesota.

Patroness of the Diocese: The Immaculate Conception.

Legal Title: Diocese of Crookston.
For legal titles of parishes and diocesan institutions, consult the Chancery Office.

STATISTICAL OVERVIEW

Personnel	
Bishop	1
Retired Bishops	1
Priests: Diocesan Active in Diocese	30
Priests: Diocesan Active Outside Diocese	3
Priests: Retired, Sick or Absent	12
Number of Diocesan Priests	45
Religious Priests in Diocese	3
Total Priests in Diocese	48
Extern Priests in Diocese	5
Ordinations:	
Transitional Deacons	1
Permanent Deacons in Diocese	16
Total Brothers	1
Total Sisters	84
Parishes	
Parishes	66
With Resident Pastor:	
Resident Diocesan Priests	27
Resident Religious Priests	2
Without Resident Pastor:	
Administered by Priests	36
Administered by Deacons	1
Professional Ministry Personnel:	
Brothers	1
Sisters	8
Lay Ministers	33
Welfare	
Catholic Hospitals	3
Total Assisted	79,723
Homes for the Aged	3
Total Assisted	624
Day Care Centers	1
Total Assisted	49
Educational	
Diocesan Students in Other Seminaries	6
Total Seminarians	6
High Schools, Diocesan and Parish	1
Total Students	94
Elementary Schools, Diocesan and Parish	9
Total Students	1,349
Catechesis/Religious Education:	
High School Students	1,457
Elementary Students	3,083
Total Students under Catholic Instruction	5,989
Teachers in the Diocese:	
Sisters	8
Lay Teachers	120
Vital Statistics	
Receptions into the Church:	
Infant Baptism Totals	498
Adult Baptism Totals	9
Received into Full Communion	57
First Communions	456
Confirmations	421
Marriages:	
Catholic	112
Interfaith	92
Total Marriages	204
Deaths	328
Total Catholic Population	35,285
Total Population	252,944

Former Bishops—Most Revs. TIMOTHY CORBETT, D.D., ord. June 12, 1886; ord. May 19, 1910; resigned See Aug. 6, 1938; appt. Titular Bishop of Vita; died July 20, 1939; JOHN H. PESCHGES, D.D., ord. April 15, 1905; ord. Nov. 9, 1938; died Oct. 30, 1944; FRANCIS J. SCHENK, D.D., ord. June 13, 1926; ord. May 24, 1945; transferred to Duluth Jan. 27, 1960; died Oct. 28, 1969; LAURENCE A. GLENN, D.D., ord. June 11, 1927; ord. Sept. 12, 1956; appt. Bishop of Crookston Feb. 3, 1960; retired July 28, 1970; died Jan. 26, 1985; KENNETH J. POVISH, D.D., ord. June 3, 1950; appt. Bishop of Crookston July 28, 1970; ord. Sept. 29, 1970; transferred to Lansing Oct. 21, 1975; died Sept. 5, 2003; VICTOR H. BALKE, D.D. (Retired), ord. May 24, 1958; appt. July 7, 1976; Episcopal ord. Sept. 2, 1976; retired Sept. 28, 2007.

Vicar General & Moderator of the Curia—Very Rev. Msgr. DAVID BAUMGARTNER, V.G., J.C.L., 1200 Memorial Dr., P.O. Box 610, Crookston, 56716. Tel: 218-281-4533. Email: dbaumgartner@crookston.org.

Chancery Office—1200 Memorial Dr., P.O. Box 610, Crookston, 56716. Tel: 218-281-4533; Fax: 218-281-3328. Web: www.crookston.org. Office Hours Mon.-Fri. 8am-noon & 1-5. All official business should be directed to this office.

Chancellor—Very Rev. ROBERT SCHREINER, 702 Summit Ave., Crookston, 56716. Tel: 218-281-1735.

Information Officer—Very Rev. Msgr. DAVID BAUMGARTNER, V.G., J.C.L. Email: dbaumgartner@crookston.org.

Finance Officer—BRADLEY BREKKEN. Tel: 218-281-4533. Email: bbrekken@crookston.org.

Diocesan Tribunal—Ms. REATHEL GIANNONATTI, 1200 Memorial Dr., P.O. Box 610, Crookston, 56716-0610. Tel: 218-281-4533. Email: tribunal@crookston.com.

Judicial Vicar—Rev. Msgr. ROGER L. GRUNDHAUS, V.G., J.C.L.

Adjutant Judicial Vicar—Rev. Msgr. MICHAEL H. FOLTZ, J.C.L.

Defenders of the Bond—Rev. ROBERT ROLFES, J.C.L.; Very Rev. Msgr. DAVID BAUMGARTNER, V.G., J.C.L.; JOANNE TOLLEFSON; MARY TARVER; MICHELLE FLOOD; Rev. VIRGIL HELMIN, J.C.L.

Promoter of Justice—Very Rev. Msgr. DAVID BAUMGARTNER, V.G., J.C.L.

Notaries—BONNIE SULLIVAN; VICTORIA DATHE; MAUREEN WATELAND.

Psychological Consultant—ELIZABETH BARAGA SUPER, Ph.D.

Diocesan Offices And Directors

Diocesan Consultors—Very Rev. Msgr. DAVID BAUMGARTNER, V.G., J.C.L.; Rev. Msgr. MICHAEL H. FOLTZ, J.C.L.; Very Rev. JERRY ROGERS; Rev. Msgrs. TIMOTHY H. MCGEE; JERRY NOESEN; Very Rev. TODD ARENDS.

Finance Council—Most Rev. MICHAEL J. HOEPPNER, D.D.; Very Rev. Msgr. DAVID BAUMGARTNER, V.G., J.C.L., Vicar Gen.; Rev. Msgrs. MICHAEL H. FOLTZ, J.C.L.; TIMOTHY H. MCGEE; Rev. GARY LAMOINE; Very Rev. ROBERT SCHREINER; KAY MACK; MARGEE KELLER; DAN RUST; GAYLE GUNNERSON; PETER ZAVORAL.

Adoption Referral/Post Adoption Search—Very Rev. Msgr. DAVID BAUMGARTNER, V.G., J.C.L., Mailing Address: P.O. Box 610, Crookston, 56716. Tel: 218-281-4533. Email: dbaumgartner@crookston.org.

Boy Scouts—DON VOTAVA, 32077 State Hwy. #1 N.W., Warren, 56762. Tel: 218-745-5423; Rev. THOMAS FRIEDL.

Catechumenal Commission—Rev. AUGIE GOTHMAN, Dir.; Deacon DENNIS BIVENS; Rev. Msgr. TIMOTHY H. MCGEE; Sisters MARY JEAN GUST, O.S.B.; KATHLEEN MCGEARY, O.S.B.; Deacon OLE "RED" ELTON; CATHY BJORKLUND. Tel: 218-681-3571.

Catholic Campaign for Human Development—Very Rev. Msgr. DAVID BAUMGARTNER, V.G., J.C.L., Mailing Address: P.O. Box 610, Crookston, 56716. Tel: 218-281-4533. Email: dbaumgartner@crookston.org.

Catholic Charities—Very Rev. Msgr. DAVID

BAUMGARTNER, V.G., J.C.L., Dir. Tel: 218-281-4533. Email: dbaumgartner@crookston.org.

Catholic Relief Services—Very Rev. Msgr. DAVID BAUMGARTNER, V.G., J.C.L., Dir., Mailing Address: P.O. Box 610, Crookston, 56716. Tel: 218-281-4533. Email: dbaumgartner@crookston.org.

Commission on Building and Planning—Revs. RICHARD D. LAMBERT; AUGIE GOTHMAN; RICHARD RUDE; ROGER WINTER.

Commission on Hispanic Affairs—Rev. MARIO PRADA, Bishop's Liaison. Tel: 218-935-2503. Email: mprada@crookston.org.

Commission on Liturgy, Sacred Music and Art—Rev. AUGIE GOTHMAN; Sr. MARGUERITE STREIFEL; JULIE MAREK; BONNIE LEE; JULIE HARDMEYER; LINDA WOLF; JIM DOTTENWHY.

Cursillo—ROSE E. WEBER, Lay Dir., Rte. 3, P.O. Box 116, Crookston, 56716. Tel: 218-281-6679.

Deans—Very Revs. LARRY DELANEY, Northwest; TODD ARENDS, Northeast; Rev. JOSEPH DECRANS, Southwest; Rev. Msgr. TIMOTHY H. MCGEE, South-Central; Very Rev. DAVID J. SUPER, Southeast.

Diaconate Office—Rev. Msgr. MICHAEL PATNODE, 601-15th Ave. N., Moorhead, 56560. Tel: 218-233-4780. Email: frmike@stfrancismhd.org.

Diocesan Board of Conciliation and Arbitration—Rev. Msgr. WILLIAM MEHRKENS, Bemidji (Retired); ARTHUR DRENKHAHN, Warren (Attorney); Sr. DOREEN CHAREST, C.S.J., Moorhead.

Director of Schools—ALAN FOLEY. Tel: 218-444-4262.

School Board, Diocesan—Ex Officio Member: Most Rev. MICHAEL J. HOEPPNER, D.D. Members: Rev. Msgr. TIMOTHY H. MCGEE; JIM GRIMM; TIM DUFAULT; RYAN HARLICKER; BILL MOSHER; JIM ABELD; MARK MILLER; SHEILA WELLE; KEVIN MCCULLOUGH; MARY AMUNDSON; ROBERT JUNG; GREG BURD; MIKE LANE; DAN SCHOENBORN; ROGER HEAD; Rev. Msgr. TIMOTHY H. MCGEE.

Hispanic Ministry—Rev. MARIO PRADA, Coord., Mailing Address: 120 W. Jefferson Ave., Mahnomen, 56557. Tel: 218-935-2503. Email: frmprada@gra.midco.net.

Holy Childhood Association—Very Rev. Msgr. DAVID BAUMGARTNER, V.G., J.C.L., Dir., Mailing Address: 1200 Memorial Dr., P.O. Box 610, Crookston, 56716-0610. Tel: 218-281-4533. Email: dbaumgartner@crookston.org.

Native American Indian Commission—Deacon DANIEL HANNIG, Mailing Address: 1200 Memorial Dr., P.O. Box 610, Crookston, 56716-0610. Tel: 218-281-4533. Email: dhannig@crookston.org.

Natural Family Planning—Very Rev. Msgr. DAVID BAUMGARTNER, V.G., J.C.L., Mailing Address: 1200 Memorial Dr., P.O. Box 610, Crookston, 56716-0610. Tel: 218-281-4533. Email: dbaumgartner@crookston.org.

Newspaper, "Our Northland Diocese"—CHARMAINE BARRANCO, Editor, Diocese of Crookston, 1200 Memorial Dr., P.O. Box 610, Crookston, 56716-0610. Tel: 218-281-4533. Email: cbarranco@crookston.org.

Pastoral Office of Administration—VACANT, Dir., 1200 Memorial Dr., P.O. Box 610, Crookston, 56716-0610. Tel: 218-281-4533.

Pastoral Office of Worship/RCIA—Rev. AUGIE GOTHMAN, Dir., 1200 Memorial Dr., P.O. Box 610, Crookston, 56716-0610. Tel: 218-281-4533.

Priests' Council—Most Rev. MICHAEL J. HOEPPNER, D.D., Pres.; Very Rev. Msgr. DAVID BAUMGARTNER, V.G., J.C.L.; Very Rev. TODD ARENDS, Chm.; Rev. Msgrs. TIMOTHY H. MCGEE; JERRY NOESEN; MICHAEL H. FOLTZ, J.C.L., Mailing Address: P.O. Box 610, Crookston, 56716. Tel: 218-281-4533; Very Revs. JERRY ROGERS; ROBERT SCHREINER; Revs. RICK LAMBERT; GARY LAMOINE; XAVIER ILANGO.

Priests' Personnel Board—Most Rev. MICHAEL J. HOEPPNER, D.D.; Very Rev. Msgr. DAVID BAUMGARTNER, V.G., J.C.L., Ex Officio Member; Rev. Msgr. MICHAEL H. FOLTZ, J.C.L.; Revs. RICK LAMBERT; JOHN KLEINWACHTER; AUGUST GOTHMAN.

Priests Retirement Board of Trustees—Revs. JOSEPH DECRANS; GARY LAMOINE; PATRICK A. SULLIVAN.

Propagation of the Faith—Very Rev. Msgr. DAVID BAUMGARTNER, V.G., J.C.L., Dir., Mailing Address: 1200 Memorial Dr., P.O. Box 610, Crookston, 56716-0610. Tel: 218-281-4533. Email: dbaumgartner@crookston.org.

Director of Faith Formation—VACANT, 1200 Memorial Dr., P.O. Box 610, Crookston, 56716-0610. Tel: 218-281-4533. Email: dbaumgartner@crookston.org.

Pastoral Leadership Program Board—Most Rev. MICHAEL J. HOEPPNER, D.D., Ex Officio; BONNIE LEE; GERMAINE RIEGERT; MIGUEL BALDERAS; Rev. THOMAS FRIEDL; MICKY HULST; KRIS JENSEN; LOREE BRUGGEMAN; KATHLEEN SHILSON; Deacon DANIEL HANNIG, Dir.

TEC (Teens Encounter Christ)—RAY HOLLCRAFT, Office of the Word, 1200 Memorial Dr., P.O. Box 610, Crookston, 56716. Tel: 218-281-4533. Email: rhollcraft@crookston.org.

Vocations—Revs. VINCENT MILLER, Dir.; AUGIE GOTHMAN, Assoc. Dir., Mailing Address: P.O. Box 610, Crookston, 56716. Tel: 218-281-4533.

Youth Ministry—RAY HOLLCRAFT, Diocesan Coord., Mailing Address: 1200 Memorial Dr., P.O. Box 610, Crookston, 56716-0610. Tel: 218-281-4533. Email: rhollcraft@crookston.org.

Diocesan Board of Review for the Protection of Children and Young People—Very Rev. Msgr. DAVID BAUMGARTNER, V.G., J.C.L.; JOHN JEFFREY; Very Rev. DAVID J. SUPER; CINDY HULST; BRENDA ANDERSON; PAUL BIERMAIER, Chm.

Victim Assistance Coordinator—LOUANN MCGLYNN, Mailing Address: P.O. Box 610, Crookston, 56716. Tel: 218-281-7895. Email: lmcglynn@crookston.org.

Safe Environment Director—Ms. REATHEL GIANNONATTI, Mailing Address: P.O. Box 610, Crookston, 56716. Tel: 218-281-4533. Email: rgiannonatti@crookston.org.

CLERGY, PARISHES, MISSIONS AND PAROCHIAL SCHOOLS

CITY OF CROOKSTON

(POLK COUNTY)

1—CATHEDRAL OF THE IMMACULATE CONCEPTION Very Rev. Robert Schreiner, Rector; Rev. S. R. AntonySamy; Deacon Dennis Bivens.
Church: 702 Summit Ave., 56716-2736. Tel: 218-281-1735; Fax: 218-281-1747. Email: dpeterson.cathedral@midconetwork.com. Web: www.crookstoncathedral.org.
School—The Cathedral School, (Grades K-6) Tel: 218-281-1835; Fax: 218-281-1747. Email: cathedral@midconetwork.com (Office). Web: www.cathedralschool.org. Adam Hollingsworth, Prin. Lay Teachers 10; Students 88.
Catechesis/Religious Program—Tel: 218-281-1735. Email: cathedral@midconetwork.com. Adam Hollingsworth, D.R.E. (Grades K-6); Mark Hollcraft, D.R.E. (Grades 7-12). Students 262.
Mission—St. Peter Gentilly, Polk Co.

2—ST. ANNE'S, Closed. For inquiries for parish records contact the Cathedral of the Immaculate Conception, Crookston.

OUTSIDE THE CITY OF CROOKSTON

ADA, NORMAN CO., ST. JOSEPH'S (1895) [JC] Rev. Joseph DeCrans.
Res.: 405 E. Thorpe Ave., 56510. Tel: 218-784-4131.
Catechesis/Religious Program—(Grades K-12) Terry Steen, D.R.E. Students 109.
Mission—Holy Family Halstad, Norman Co.
Mission—St. William Twin Valley, Norman Co.

AKELEY, HUBBARD CO., ST. JOHN, Merged with Immaculate Conception, Nevis to form Our Lady of the Pines, Akeley/Nevis Community.

ALMA, MARSHALL CO., ST. JOHN THE BAPTIST, Closed. For inquiries for parish records contact St. Stephen, Stephen. Tel: 218-478-2231.

ARGYLE, MARSHALL CO., ST. ROSE OF LIMA, [CEM], Served by St. Stephen, Stephen. Rev. Bob Stone. P.O. Box 277, 56713. Tel: 218-437-6341. Email: stroser@wiktel.com.
Catechesis/Religious Program—Fax: 218-437-6341. Denise St. Germain, D.R.E. Students 95.

BADGER, ROSEAU CO., ST. MARY'S (1899), Served by Sacred Heart, Roseau. Tel: 218-463-2441, Fax: 218-463-2443., Mailing Address: 504 N. Main St., 56714.
Catechesis/Religious Program—Joni Burkel, D.R.E. Students 22.

BAGLEY, CLEARWATER CO., ST. JOSEPH (1912) Very Rev. David J. Super; Deacon Daniel Hannig.
Mailing Address: P.O. Box 67, 56621. Tel: 218-694-6416; Fax: 218-694-6416. Email: stjoseph@gvtel.com.
Res.: 16 Red Lake Ave., 56621.
Catechesis/Religious Program—Clarissa Dowhower, D.R.E. Students 69.

BARNESVILLE, CLAY CO., ASSUMPTION (1883) [CEM] Rev. Gary LaMoine.
Res.: 307 Front St. N., P.O. Box 339, 56514. Tel: 218-354-7320; Fax: 218-354-7659.
Catechesis/Religious Program—Phyllis Peppel, D.R.E. Students 125.
Mission—St. Cecilia Sabin, Clay Co.

BAUDETTE, LAKE OF THE WOODS CO., SACRED HEART (1908), Served by St. Mary's, Warroad. Deacon James Lukenbill, Pastoral Assoc.
Res.: 104 1st St., S.W., P.O. Box 738, 56623. Tel: 218-634-2689. Email: ourlady@mncable.net.
Catechesis/Religious Program—Students 70.
Mission—St. Joseph [CEM] Williams, Lake of the Woods Co.

BEAULIEU, MAHNOMEN CO., ST. JOSEPH PARISH (1895) [CEM] Unassigned. Served by St. Michael, Mahnomen. Tel: 218-935-2503; Fax. 218-935-2503., Mailing Address: 120 W. Jefferson, Mahnomen, 56557.
Catechesis/Religious Program—Vickie Anderson, D.R.E.

BEJOU, MAHNOMEN CO., IMMACULATE CONCEPTION, Closed. For inquiries for parish records contact St. Michael's, Mahnomen.

BEMIDJI, BELTRAMI CO., ST. PHILIP'S, [CEM] Revs. Vincent Miller; Antony Fernando. In Res., Rev. Msgr. William Mehrkens (Retired).
Res. & Mailing Address: 702 Beltrami Ave., N.W., 56601-3046. Tel: 218-444-4262; Fax: 218-281-1381. Email: rector@stphilipsbemidji.org. Web: stphilipsbemidji.org.
School—(Grades PreK-8) Tel: 218-444-4938; Fax: 218-444-1379. Mrs. Carol Rettinger, Prin. Lay Teachers 21; Students 260.
Catechesis/Religious Program—620 Beltrami Ave., N.W., 56601. Tel: 218-444-5849; Fax: 218-444-1381. Kris Jensen, D.R.E., (Grades PreK-8). Students 329.
Mission—St. Charles Pennington, Beltrami Co.
Mission—Holy Spirit Newman Center, Beltrami Co.

BENWOOD, ROSEAU CO., ST. JOSEPH THE WORKER, Closed. For inquiries for parish records please contact Sacred Heart, Roseau.

BIG ELBOW LAKE, BECKER CO., ST. FRANCES CABRINI, Served by St. Ann, Waubun. Tel: 218-473-2101 Fax: 218-473-2101 Rev. Robert Leising, O.M.I.
Mailing Address: 1112 3rd St., Waubun, 56589.

BLACKDUCK, BELTRAMI CO., ST. ANN'S (1905), Served by St. Patrick's, Kelliher. Tel: 218-647-8392., Mailing Address: P.O. Box 187, Kelliher, 56650.
Catechesis/Religious Program—Rita Rabe, D.R.E. Students 44.

BROOKS, RED LAKE CO., ST. JOSEPH (CHURCH OF BROOKS) (1916) [CEM], Mailing Address: P.O. Box 400, Red Lake Falls, 56750-0400. Email: frchuck@stjosephsrlf.org. Web: www.stjosephsrlf.org. Served by St. Joseph's, Red Lake Falls. Tel: 218-253-2685; Fax. 218-253-2195.
Catechesis/Religious Program—Students 44.

CALLAWAY, BECKER CO., ASSUMPTION (1912) [CEM], Served by Sacred Heart, Frazee Rev. Xavier Ilango.
Res.: 206 Dakota St., P.O. Box 67, 56521. Tel: 218-375-3571.
Catechesis/Religious Program—Students 35.

DETROIT LAKES, BECKER CO., HOLY ROSARY, [CEM] Rev. Msgr. Timothy H. McGee; Deacons James Thomas; Ole "Red" Elton; Gary Hager.
Office: 1043 Lake Ave., 56501-3499. Tel: 218-847-1393; Fax: 218-847-6367. Email: parish@holyrosarycc.org. Web: www.holyrosarycc.org.
School—(Grades PreK-8) Tel: 218-847-5306; Fax: 218-847-6367. Email: kklindt@holyrosarycc.org. Kathleen Klindt, Prin.; Donna Kennedy, Librarian. Lay Teachers 14; Students 157.
Catechesis/Religious Program— Jean Olson, D.R.E. (PreK); JoAnne Knuttila, D.R.E. (Grades 1-6); Patti Spry, D.R.E. (Grade 9); Barbara Schmidt, D.R.E. (Grades 10-11). Students 230.

DILWORTH, CLAY CO., ST. ELIZABETH (1910) Rev. Patrick A. Sullivan.
Mailing Address: P.O. Box 307, 56529-0307. Tel: 218-287-2705. Web: www.stlizdilworth.org.
Catechesis/Religious Program—Karen Owings, D.R.E. Students 200.
Mission—St. Andrew Hawley, Clay Co. 56549. Tel: 218-483-4262.

DOROTHY, RED LAKE CO., ST. DOROTHY, Closed. For inquiries for parish records contact St. Joseph's, Red Lake Falls.

EAST GRAND FORKS, POLK CO., SACRED HEART, [CEM] Very Rev. Larry Delaney; Rev. William DeCrans.
Church: 200 Third St., N.W., 56721-1806. Tel: 218-773-0877; Fax: 218-773-8312. Web: www.sacredheartegf.net.
School—(Grades PreK-6) Tel: 218-773-1579; Fax: 218-773-0318. Mr. David Andrys, Prin. Lay Teachers 15; Students 232.
High School—(Grades 7-12) Tel: 218-773-0230; Fax: 218-773-7042. Mr. Phillip E. Meyer, Prin. Lay Teachers 18; Students 159.
Catechesis/Religious Program—Tel: 218-773-0531; Fax: 218-773-8312. Sarah Effhauser, D.R.E. (Grades PreK-11). Students 258.
Mission—St. Francis Fisher, Polk Co.
Mission—Holy Trinity Tabor, Polk Co.

EUCLID, POLK CO., ST. MARY, Served by Sts. Peter & Paul, Warren. Tel: 218-281-5422. Deacon Dennis Bivens, Admin.
Mailing Address: P.O. Box 213, 56722.
Catechesis/Religious Program—Students 23.

FALUN, ROSEAU CO., ST. PHILIP, Served by Sacred Heart, Roseau., Mailing Address: P.O. Box 118, Roseau, 56751.
Catechesis/Religious Program—Sharon Petrowski, D.R.E. Students 14.

FELTON, CLAY CO., ST. LAWRENCE, Closed. For inquiries for parish records contact St. Joseph's, Ada.

FERTILE, POLK CO., ST. JOSEPH, [CEM] Rev. Msgr. Roger L. Grundhaus; Sr. Mary Jean Gust, O.S.B., Pastoral Assoc.
Mailing Address: 205 S.E. Elm St., 56540. Tel: 218-945-6649.
Res.: 620 Summit Ave., 56716. Tel: 218-281-5951; Fax: 218-281-3328. Web: www.stjosephfertile.com.
Catechesis/Religious Program—Students 59.

FISHER, POLK CO., ST. FRANCIS OF ASSISI (1881) [CEM], (Fisher). Served by Sacred Heart, East Grand Forks. Tel: 218-773-0877., Mailing Address: 302 Park Ave., 56723. Tel: 218-891-2249.
Catechesis/Religious Program—Students 17.

FLORIAN, MARSHALL CO., ASSUMPTION - CHURCH OF FLORIAN, [CEM], Served by St. Stephen, Stephen. Rev. Bob Stone; Deacon Courtney Abel, Pastoral Assoc.
Mailing Address: 26932 390th St. N.W., Strandquist, 56758. Tel: 218-478-3578; Fax: 218-478-3578. Web: www.wiktel.net/assumption.
Catechesis/Religious Program—Beth Budziszewski, D.R.E. Students 23.

FOSSTON, POLK CO., ST. MARY'S (1901) [CEM 2] Very Rev. David J. Super; Sr. Debra Berry, S.M.P., Pastoral Assoc.
Mailing Address: 725 6th St., N.E., 56542. Tel: 218-435-6484.
Catechesis/Religious Program—Email: stmarys@gvtel.com. Students 59.

FRAZEE, BECKER CO., SACRED HEART, [CEM] Rev. Xavier Ilango.
Mailing Address: 202 W. Maple Ave., 56544. Tel: 218-334-4221.
Res.: 306 W. Walnut Ave., 56544. Tel: 218-334-2607.
Catechesis/Religious Program—Students 192.
Mission—Assumption Callaway, Becker Co. 56521.

GENTILLY, POLK CO., ST. PETER'S, [CEM], Mailing Address: 25723-185th Ave., S.W., 56716. Tel: 218-281-1735. Served by Cathedral of the Immaculate Conception, Crookston. Tel: 218-281-1735.
Catechesis/Religious Program—Students 44.

GEORGETOWN, CLAY CO., ST. JOHN (1885), Served by St. Francis de Sales, Moorhead. Tel: 218-233-4780. Rev. Msgr. Michael Patnode.
Mailing Address: P.O. Box 248, 56546.
Catechesis/Religious Program—Students 14.

GOODRIDGE, PENNINGTON CO., ST. ANNE (GOODRIDGE), Served by St. Francis Xavier, Oklee. Tel: 218-435-6484.
Catechesis/Religious Program—Students 16.

GREENBUSH, ROSEAU CO., BLESSED SACRAMENT, [CEM] Very Rev. Todd Arends.
Res.: P.O. Box A, 56726. Tel: 218-782-2467. Email: blessedsacrament@wiktel.com.
Catechesis/Religious Program—Tel: 218-782-2263. Becka Nubson, D.R.E. Students 142.
Mission—St. Joseph Middle River, Marshall Co.
Mission—St. Edward Karlstad, Marshall Co.

GRYGLA, MARSHALL CO., ST. CLEMENT (GRYGLA), Served by St. Francis Xavier, Oklee. Tel: 218-435-6484.
Catechesis/Religious Program—Students 34.

HALLOCK, KITTSON CO., ST. PATRICK'S Rev. Timothy T. Noah.
Res.: 170 S. 5th St., P.O. Box 519, 56728-0519. Tel: 218-843-2323.
Catechesis/Religious Program—Students 70.
Mission—Holy Rosary Lancaster, Kittson Co.

HALSTAD, NORMAN CO., HOLY FAMILY (HALSTAD) (1984), Served by St. Joseph, Ada. Tel: 218-784-4131. [JC], Mailing Address: *Pastoral Administrative Office*, 405 E. Thorpe Ave., Ada, 56510. Email: holyfamily@rrv.net. Web: rrv.net/holyfamily.
Catechesis/Religious Program—Bonnie Lee, D.R.E. Students 19.

HAWLEY, CLAY CO., ST. ANDREW, Served by St. Elizabeth, Dilworth. Tel: 218-287-2705. Rev. Patrick A. Sullivan; Deacon Tom Jirik.
Mailing Address: 1418 Main St., P.O. Box 129, 56549. Tel: 218-483-4264; Fax: 218-483-4158.
Catechesis/Religious Program—Students 111.

KARLSTAD, KITTSON CO., ST. EDWARD THE CONFESSOR, Served by Blessed Sacrament, Greenbush. Tel: 218-782-2467.
Catechesis/Religious Program—Becka Nubson, D.R.E. Students 24.

KELLIHER, BELTRAMI CO., ST. PATRICK (1909) [JC] Rev. Luis Segundo Buitron.
165 5th St. N.E., P.O. Box 187, 56650. Tel: 218-647-8392.
Catechesis/Religious Program—Sissy Neft, D.R.E. Students 32.
Mission—St. Ann Blackduck, Beltrami Co.
Mission—St. John Nebish, Beltrami Co.

LAKE EUNICE TOWNSHIP, BECKER CO., ST. MARY OF THE LAKES, (Lake Eunice Township) Rev. Bob J. LaPlante.
Res.: 20996 County Hwy. #20, Detroit Lakes, 56501. Tel: 218-439-3937. Email: stmaryofthelakes@loretel.net. Web: stmaryofthelakes.cc.
Catechesis/Religious Program—Judy Kostreba, D.R.E. Students 15.
Mission—St. Francis Xavier Lake Park, Becker Co.

LAKE ITASCA, CLEARWATER CO., ST. CATHERINE, Closed. For inquiries for parish records contact St. Peter's, Park Rapids.

LAKE PARK, BECKER CO., ST. FRANCIS XAVIER'S, [CEM], Served by St. Mary of the Lakes, Lake Eunice Township. Rev. Bob J. LaPlante.
Res.: 2066 Second St., 56554-4402. Tel: 218-238-6639; Fax: 218-238-6028. Email: sfxchurch@loretel.net.
Catechesis/Religious Program—Rich Veit, D.R.E. (Grades 7-12); Mary Veit, D.R.E. (Grades 7-12).

LANCASTER, KITTSON CO., HOLY ROSARY, Mailing Address: *St. Patrick's*, P.O. Box 519, Hallock, 56728. Served by St. Patrick, Hallock. Tel: 218-843-2323.
Catechesis/Religious Program—

LAPORTE, HUBBARD CO., ST. THEODORE OF TARSUS - LAPORTE, [CEM 2], Served by Our Lady of the Pines, Nevis Community. Tel: 218-652-4005. Rev. Duane Pribula.
Mailing Address: 205 Main St., W., P.O. Box 378, Nevis, 56467. Fax: 218-652-4022.
Catechesis/Religious Program—Students 16.

LEO, ROSEAU CO., ST. ALOYSIUS, Closed. For inquiries for parish records contact Blessed Sacrament, Greenbush.

MAHNOMEN, MAHNOMEN CO., ST. MICHAEL'S PARISH, [CEM] Rev. Mario Prada.
Res.: 120 W. Jefferson Ave., 56557. Tel: 218-935-2503; Fax: 218-935-2503. Web: stmichaelmahnomen.org.
School—(Grades PreK-6) Tel: 218-935-5222; Fax: 218-935-5222. Email: stmike@arvig.net. Lay Teachers 7; Students 71.
Catechesis/Religious Program—Kathy Haider, D.R.E., (PreK-6); Vickie Anderson, D.R.E., (7-12). Students 162.
Mission—St. Joseph [CEM] Beaulieu, Mahnomen Co.

MENTOR, POLK CO., ST. LAWRENCE (1920) Rev. Msgr. Roger L. Grundhaus.
Church & Mailing Address: P.O. Box 51, 56736. Tel: 218-637-8178. Email: stlawrence@gvtel.com.
Catechesis/Religious Program—Mary Olson, D.R.E. Students 53.

MIDDLE RIVER, MARSHALL CO., ST. JOSEPH, HUSBAND OF MARY, [CEM], Served by Blessed Sacrament, Greenbush., Mailing Address: P.O. Box A, Greenbush, 56726. Tel: 218-782-2467.
Catechesis/Religious Program—Becka Nubson, D.R.E. Students 25.

MOORHEAD, CLAY CO.

1—ST. FRANCIS DE SALES (1948) [JC] Rev. Msgr. Michael Patnode.
601 15th Ave. N., 56560. Tel: 218-233-4780; Fax: 218-233-0270.
Catechesis/Religious Program—Diane Dahlin, D.R.E. (Grades PreK-8); Jim White, D.R.E. (Grades 9-12). Students 137.
Mission—St. John Georgetown, Clay Co. 56546.

2—ST. JOSEPH'S, [JC] Rev. Msgr. Michael H. Foltz; Rev. Raul Perez-Cobo; Sr. Doreen Charest, C.S.J., Pastoral Assoc.; Deacons Tom Cerar; Allen Kukert.
Office: 218 10th St. S., 56560. Tel: 218-236-5066; 218-236-9503 (Res.); Fax: 218-233-0717. Email: stjoes@stjoesmhd.com. Web: www.stjoesmhd.com.
School—(Grades PreK-8) Tel: 218-233-0553. Web: www.stjoesmhdschool.com. Leslie Honebrink, Prin.; Cathy Bjorkland, Librarian. Lay Teachers 26; Students 244.
Catechesis/Religious Program—Tel: 218-236-1979. Email: stjoesmhd@stjoesmhd.com. Joann Koble, D.R.E. Students 509.
Mission—St. Thomas Newman Center 707 11th St. S., Clay Co. 56563. Tel: 218-236-9596.

NAYTAHWAUSH, MAHNOMEN CO., ST. ANNE (1917), (Naytahwaush). Served by St. Ann's, Waubun. Tel: 218-473-2101. Rev. Robert Leising, O.M.I.
Mailing Address: 1112-3rd St., Waubun, 56589. Tel: 218-473-2101; Fax: 218-473-2101. Email: 1112sta@arvig.net.

NEBISH, BELTRAMI CO., ST. JOHN, Served by St. Patrick, Kelliher. Tel: 218-647-8392, Mailing Address: P.O. Box 187, Kelliher, 56650. Tel: 218-647-8392.

NEVIS, HUBBARD CO.

1—IMMACULATE CONCEPTION, Closed. Merged with St. John's, Akeley to form Our Lady of the Pines, Nevis.

2—OUR LADY OF THE PINES (2003) [CEM 2] Rev. Duane Pribula.
Mailing Address: 205 Main St. W., P.O. Box 378, 56467. Tel: 218-652-4005 (Office); 218-652-2785 (Rectory); Fax: 218-652-4022. Email: maryolp@unitelc.com. Web: www.olpparish.org.
Catechesis/Religious Program—Students 65.
Mission—St. Theodore Laporte, Hubbard Co. 56461.

OGEMA, BECKER CO., MOST HOLY REDEEMER, [CEM] Rev. Walter Butor, O.M.I.
Res.: P.O. Box 57, 56569-0057. Tel: 218-983-3261; Fax: 218-983-3808. Email: owep@tvutel.com.
Catechesis/Religious Program—Darlene Ballard, D.R.E. Students 25.
Mission—St. Benedict White Earth, Becker Co. 56591.
Mission—St. Theodore Ponsford, Becker Co. 56575.

OKLEE, RED LAKE CO., ST. FRANCIS XAVIER'S (1881) [CEM] Rev. John Kleinwachter.
301 Governor St., P.O. Box 160, 56742. Tel: 218-796-5844. Email: okstfran@gvtel.com.
Catechesis/Religious Program—Students 18.
Mission—St. Anne Goodridge, Pennington Co.
Mission—St. Clement Grygla, Marshall Co.

OSLO, MARSHALL CO., ST. JOSEPH, [CEM], Served by SS. Peter and Paul, Warren. Tel: 218-745-4511.
Res.: 515 Main St., P.O. Box 97, 56744. Tel: 218-695-2641. Email: stjoseph@wiktel.com.
Catechesis/Religious Program—Susan Heinz, D.R.E.; Terri Reed, D.R.E. Students 21.

PARK RAPIDS, HUBBARD CO., ST. PETER THE APOSTLE (1887) [CEM] Rev. Thomas Friedl.
Res.: 305 W. 5th St., P.O. Box 353, 56470-0353. Tel: 218-732-5142 (Office); 218-237-5881 (Res.); Fax: 218-237-6919.
Catechesis/Religious Program—Email: mrss@unitelc.com. Kathleen Shilson, D.R.E. (PreK-12). Students 134.

PENNINGTON, BELTRAMI CO., ST. CHARLES CATHOLIC CHURCH OF PENNINGTON, Served by St. Philip's, Bemidji. Tel: 218-444-4262, Mailing Address: *St. Philip's*, 702 Beltrami Ave., N.W., Bemidji, 56601-3046.
Catechesis/Religious Program—

PLUMMER, RED LAKE CO., ST. VINCENT DE PAUL, Closed. For inquiries for parish records contact St. Francis Xavier, Oklee.

PONSFORD, BECKER CO., ST. THEODORE OF PONSFORD, Served by Most Holy Redeemer, Ogema. Tel: 218-936-3261., Mailing Address: *Most Holy Redeemer*, P.O. Box 57, Ogema, 56569-0057. Email: owep@tvutel.com.
Catechesis/Religious Program—Students 4.

RED LAKE, BELTRAMI CO., ST. MARY'S MISSION CHURCH, [CEM] Very Rev. Jerry Rogers.
Res.: Hwy. 1, P.O. Box 189, 56671-0189. Tel: 218-679-3614; Fax: 218-679-2212.
School—(Grades K-6) Tel: 218-679-3388. Email: mission@paulbunyan.net. Al Yarnott, Prin. Sisters 3; Lay Teachers 8; Students 61.
Catechesis/Religious Program—
Mission—Sacred Heart Wilton, Beltrami Co.

RED LAKE FALLS, RED LAKE CO., ST. JOSEPH'S (1879) [CEM] Rev. Chuck Huck.
Office & Res.: P.O. Box 400, 56750-0400. Tel: 218-253-2004 (Res.); 218-253-2685 (Office); Fax: 218-253-2195. Email: frchuck@stjosephsrlf.org. Web: www.stjosephsrlf.org.
School—(Grades PreK-6), 112 Edward Ave., N.W., P.O. Box 400, 56750-0400. Tel: 218-253-2188; Fax: 218-253-2195. Geraldine Cyr, Prin. Lay Teachers 6; Students 29.
Catechesis/Religious Program—Students 116.
Mission—St. Joseph [CEM] Brooks, Red Lake Co. 56715.

ROSEAU, ROSEAU CO., SACRED HEART, [CEM] Rev. Manuel Sundaram.
Office: 403 Main Ave. N., 56751. Tel: 218-463-2441; Fax: 218-463-2443.
Catechesis/Religious Program—Michelle Peppel, D.R.E. & Youth Dir. Students 116.
Mission—St. Philip Falun, Roseau Co.
Mission—St. Mary's [CEM] Badger, Roseau Co.

SABIN, CLAY CO., ST. CECILIA (OF SABIN), Served by Assumption, Barnesville. Tel: 218-354-7320., Mailing Address: *Assumption*, P.O. Box 339, Barnesville, 56514-0339.
Catechesis/Religious Program—Students 52.

SHEVLIN, CLEARWATER CO., OUR LADY OF VICTORY, Closed. For inquiries for parish records contact St. Joseph's, Bagley.

STEPHEN, MARSHALL CO., ST. STEPHEN'S, [CEM] Rev. Bob Stone.
Res.: 515 5th St., P.O. Box 507, 56757. Tel: 218-478-2231; Fax: 218-478-2231.
Catechesis/Religious Program—Students 61.
Mission—Assumption Church of Florian Florian, Marshall Co. Tel: 218-478-3578.
Mission—St. Rose of Lima Argyle, Marshall Co. 56713. Tel: 218-437-6341.

TABOR, POLK CO., HOLY TRINITY CATHOLIC (OF TABOR), Served by Sacred Heart, East Grand Forks. Tel: 218-773-0877., Mailing Address: 37639 140th St., N.W., Angus, 56762-8929. Tel: 218-745-5853. Web: www.rc.net/crookston/holytrinity.
Catechesis/Religious Program—Students 20.

TERREBONNE, RED LAKE CO., ST. ANTHONY, Closed. For inquiries for parish records contact St. Joseph's, Red Lake Falls.

THIEF RIVER FALLS, PENNINGTON CO., ST. BERNARDS, [CEM] Rev. Rick Lambert; Deacon John Eisbrenner. Res.: 105 Knight Ave. N., 56701. Tel: 218-681-3571; Fax: 218-681-3560. Web: www.stbernardstrf.org.
School—(Grades PreK-5) Tel: 218-681-1539; Fax: 218-681-2261. Email: srkathy@mncable.net. Sr. Kathy Kuchar, O.S.B., Prin. Lay Teachers 9; Students 129.
Catechesis/Religious Program—Email: margerasmussen@mncable.net; rdplambert@hotmail.com. Web: www.stbernardstrf.org. Margaret Rasmussen, D.R.E.; Jacob Rath, Youth Min. Students 253.

TWIN VALLEY, NORMAN CO., ST. WILLIAM (OF TWIN VALLEY), Served by St. Joseph Pastoral Administrative Office, Ada. Tel: 218-784-4131. Deacon Nick Revier.
Catechesis/Religious Program—Jodi Douville, C.R.E. Students 26.

TWO INLETS, BECKER CO., ST. MARY'S, [CEM] Rev. Jan Klimek; Deacon John Muller.
Mailing Address: 55744 Cty. Hwy. 44, Park Rapids, 56470. Tel: 218-732-4046; Fax: 218-732-4046.
Catechesis/Religious Program—Margaret Sharp, D.R.E. Students 16.

WARREN, MARSHALL CO., SS. PETER AND PAUL, [CEM] Rev. Emmanuel Sylvester.
Res.: 208 N. Seventh St., 56762. Tel: 218-745-4511; Fax: 218-745-5484.
Catechesis/Religious Program—Students 75.
Mission—St. Joseph P.O. Box 97, Oslo, Marshall Co. 56744. Tel: 218-695-2641.
Mission—St. Mary Euclid, Polk Co. 56722. Deacon Dennis Bivens, Admin.

WARROAD, ROSEAU CO., ST. MARY'S, [CEM] Rev. Donald Braukman.
Res.: P.O. Box 33, 56763. Tel: 218-386-1178.
Catechesis/Religious Program—Sue Ripplinger, D.R.E. Students 145.

WAUBUN, MAHNOMEN CO., ST. ANN (1912) [CEM] Revs. Robert Leising, O.M.I.; Jerry Orsino, O.M.I.
Res.: 1112 3rd St., 56589-9402. Tel: 218-473-2101; Fax: 218-473-2101. Email: 1112sta@arvig.net.
Catechesis/Religious Program—Students 38.
Mission—St. Anne 204 County Rd. #4, P.O. Box 157, Naytahwaush, Mahnomen Co. 56566.
Mission—St. Frances Cabrini Big Elbow Lake, Becker Co.

WHITE EARTH, BECKER CO., ST. BENEDICT (OF WHITE EARTH), [CEM], Served by Most Holy Redeemer, Ogema. Tel: 218-936-3261. Bro. William Lundberg, O.M.I., Pastoral Assoc.
Mailing Address: P.O. Box 57, Ogema, 56569-0057. Tel: 218-983-3519; Fax: 218-983-3261. Email: owep@tvutel.com.
Catechesis/Religious Program—Students 21.

WILLIAMS, LAKE OF THE WOODS CO., ST. JOSEPH (OF WILLIAMS), Served by Sacred Heart, Baudette. Tel: 218-634-2689., Mailing Address: P.O. Box 738, Baudette, 56623.

WILTON, BELTRAMI CO., SACRED HEART (WILTON), Served by St. Mary's Mission, Red Lake. Tel: 218-679-3614., Mailing Address: *St. Mary's Mission*, P.O. Box 1897, Bemidji, 56619-1897.
Catechesis/Religious Program—Students 30.

On Duty Outside the Diocese:
Revs.—
Bushy, Timothy F.
Silva, Luis
Wieland, Dennis J.

Retired:
Most Rev.—
Balke, Victor H., D.D., 1417 Belsly Blvd., Moorhead, 56560. Tel: 218-287-2828
Rev. Msgrs.—
Krebs, Donald H., 3344-38th St., S., Moorhead, 56560. Tel: 218-236-6644. Email: dkrebs@gomoorhead.com
Mehrkens, William, 702 Beltrami Ave., N.W., Bemidji, 56601. Tel: 218-444-4262
Noesen, Gerald, 1602 Summerfield Dr., #23, 56716. Tel: 218-281-3060. Email: glnoesen@webtv.net
Revs.—
Bernauer, James, P.O. Box 7, Dent, 56528. Tel: 218-758-3377
Felion, Jerome, 4130 S. Alameda St., Corpus Christi, TX 78411. Tel: 361-225-2165
Kieselbach, Joseph, P.O. Box 161, Barnesville, 56514. Tel: 218-354-7258
Kulhawik, Frank, 705 W. Main St., Apt. 100, Ada, 56510. Tel: 218-784-2247
Noah, Daniel, 24344-265th St., S.W., 56716. Tel: 218-281-7823
Palcisko, Raymond, 2769-28th St., N.W., Baudette, 56623. Tel: 651-276-0205. Email: raypal@ymail.com
Pryor, G. Robert, 286 Grantwood Dr., Henderson, NV 89014. Tel: 702-454-1440. Email: grpryor@embarqmail.com. U.S.A.F
Wesely, Eugene L., Pleasantview Apts., 1111 Washington Ave., #411, Detroit Lakes, 56501. Tel: 218-844-5281
Wieseler, Larry, P.O. Box 262, Rio Grande City, TX 78582.

Permanent Deacons:
Abel, Courtney, Assumption, Florian
Bivens, Dennis, Cathedral of the Immaculate Conception, Crookston; St. Peter's, Gentilly; St. Mary's, Euclid
Bruggeman, John A., St. Lawrence, Mentor
Cerar, Tom, St. Joseph, Moorhead
Eisbrenner, John, (Retired), Trail, MN; St. Bernard, Thief River Falls
Elton, Ole "Red", Holy Rosary, Detroit Lakes
Hager, Gary, Holy Rosary, Detroit Lakes
Hannig, Daniel, St. Joseph Bagley; St. Mary Fosston
Jirik, Tom, St. Andrew, Hawley
Klick, Don, Nevis & Laporte
Kukert, Allen, St. Joseph's, Moorhead
Lukenbill, James, Sacred Heart, Baudette
Muller, John, St. Mary's, Two Inlets
Revier, Nick, St. William, Twin Valley
Thomas, James, Holy Rosary, Detroit Lakes
Thomas, Steve, Sacred Heart, East Grand Forks
Vande Kamp, James, St. Michael, Northome

INSTITUTIONS LOCATED IN THE DIOCESE

[A] GENERAL HOSPITALS

BAUDETTE. *LakeWood Health Center*, 600 Main Ave. S., 56623. Tel: 218-634-2120; Fax: 218-634-3416. Email: lakewood@catholichealth.net. Web: www.lakewoodhealthcenter.org. SharRay Peickert, Pres. & CEO. Affiliate of Catholic Health Initiatives. Bed Capacity: Acute 15; Long Term Care 44; Staff 174; Patients Assisted Annually 18,757.
LakeWood Care Center, 600 Main Ave. S., 56623. Tel: 218-634-3488; Fax: 218-634-3489. Affiliate of Catholic Health Initiatives. Bed Capacity 44; Residents Assisted Annually 42.

DETROIT LAKES. **St. Mary's Regional Health Center*, 1027 Washington Ave., 56501. Tel: 218-847-5611; Fax: 218-847-7674. Web: www.trustedcareforlife.org. Thomas R. Thompson, CEO; Tim Cook, Chap.; Lanny Sweeney, Chap.; Stella Bridgeford, Chap.
St. Mary's EMS, 1240 Washington Ave., P.O. Box 1410, 56501. Tel: 218-847-0817; Fax: 218-847-0842. Thomas R. Thompson, CEO. (Sub. of St. Mary's Regional Health Center) Senior Nursing 88; Staff 600; Beds Acute 87; Long Term Care 96; Patients Assisted Annually 25,000.

PARK RAPIDS. *St. Joseph Area Health Services*, 600 Pleasant Ave., 56470. Tel: 218-732-3311; Fax: 218-732-1368. Email: kathydickinson@catholichealth.net. Mr. Ben Koppelman, Pres. & CEO. Affiliate of Catholic Health Initiatives. Sisters 3; Bed Capacity 50; Patients Assisted Annually 35,966.

[B] HOMES FOR THE AGED

CROOKSTON. *Villa St. Vincent*, 516 Walsh St., 56716. Tel: 218-281-3424; Fax: 218-281-4755. Ms. Judith Hulst, Admin. Co-sponsored by the Benedictine Sisters of Crookston, Mt. St. Benedict Monastery and the Benedictine Health System. Sisters of St. Benedict 2; Assisted Living Apts. 71; Skilled Nursing Beds 80; Alzheimer's Beds 24; Residents 170.

ADA. *Bridges Care Center dba Bridges Care Community* Subs. of Benedictine Health System., 201 9th St. W., Ste. 2, 56510. Tel: 218-784-5500; Fax: 218-784-5574. Email: katie.redig@bhshealth.org. Ms. Katie Redig, Admin. Sponsored by the Benedictine Sisters Benevolent Association, Duluth. Staff 75; Skilled Nursing Beds 49; Residents 44.

DETROIT LAKES. *St. Mary's Nursing Center*, 1027 Washington Ave., 56501. Tel: 218-844-0776; Fax: 218-544-0780. Christy Brinkman, Admin., Sr. Housing. Attended by Staff of St. Mary's Regional Health Center. Assisted Living 30; Independent Living 58; Transitional Care 23; Long Term Care 73.

[C] CONVENTS AND RESIDENCES FOR SISTERS

CROOKSTON. *Mount St. Benedict Monastery*, 620 Summit Ave. E., 56716-2799. Tel: 218-281-3441; Fax: 218-281-6966. Email: sisters@msb.net. Web: www.msb.net. Sisters Lenore Paschke, O.S.B., Prioress; Anne Marie Geray, O.S.B., Subprioress. Motherhouse of the Order of the Sisters of St. Benedict of Pontifical Jurisdiction-The Federation of St. Gertrude. Sisters in Community 84.
Sisters of St. Benedict Initial Formation Tel: 218-281-3441; Fax: 218-281-6966. Sr. Lois Spors, O.S.B., Dir. of Novices.
Sunrise Center for Children and Families Tel: 218-281-6540; Fax: 218-281-6966. Sr. Judith Moen, O.S.B., Dir.

[D] NEWMAN CENTERS

CROOKSTON. *University of Minnesota Cooperative Campus Ministry* 56716. Tel: 218-281-8516; Fax: 218-281-8504. Email: cboike@mail.crk.umn.edu. Web: www.crk.umn.edu. Chris Boike, Dir. Coop. Campus Ministry.

BEMIDJI. *Holy Spirit Newman Center* 1701 Birch Ln., N.E., 56601-2607. Tel: 218-444-4762; Fax: 218-444-7244. Email: ncenter@paulbunyan.net. Web: www.newmancenterbsu.org. Rev. Vincent Miller.

MOORHEAD. *St. Thomas Aquinas Newman Center* 707 11th St. S., 56560. Tel: 218-236-9596. Email: serickson@stjoesmhd.com. Web: www.mnstate.edu/newman. Shawn Erickson, Campus Min.

[E] MISCELLANEOUS

CROOKSTON. **The Diocese of Crookston Catholic Community Foundation*, 1200 Memorial Dr., 56716. Tel: 218-281-4533; Fax: 218-281-3328. Email: ccf@crookston.org. Web: www.crookston.org/ccf.
**Mount Saint Benedict Foundation*, 620 Summit Ave., 56716-2799. Tel: 218-281-3441; Fax: 218-281-6966.

RELIGIOUS INSTITUTES OF MEN REPRESENTED IN THE DIOCESE

For further details refer to the corresponding bracketed number in the Religious Institutes of Men or Women section.

[0910]—*Oblates of Mary Immaculate*—O.M.I.

RELIGIOUS INSTITUTES OF WOMEN REPRESENTED IN THE DIOCESE

[0230]—*Benedictine Sisters of Pontifical Jurisdiction* (Congregation of St. Gertrude)—O.S.B.

[0230]—*Benedictine Sisters of Pontifical Jurisdiction (Federation of St. Benedict)*—O.S.B.

[3832]—*Congregation of the Sisters of St. Joseph*—C.S.J.

[]—*Congregation of the Sisters of the Third Order of St. Francis*—O.S.F.

[]—*Franciscan Sisters*—O.S.F.

[2450]—*Sisters of Mary of the Presentation* (Valley City, ND)—S.M.P.

[]—*Sisters of St. Joseph of Concordia* (KS)—C.S.J.

NECROLOGY

† Nistler, Edward A., (Retired)—Died March 18, 2009

An asterisk (*) denotes an organization that has established tax-exempt status directly with the IRS and is not covered by the USCCB Group Ruling.

Diocese of Dallas

(Dioecesis Dallasensis)

Most Reverend

KEVIN J. FARRELL

Bishop of Dallas; ordained December 24, 1978; appointed Auxiliary Bishop of Washington and Titular Bishop of Rusuccuru December 28, 2001; ordained February 11, 2002; appointed Bishop of Dallas March 6, 2007; installed May 1, 2007.

Most Reverend

CHARLES V. GRAHMANN, D.D.

Retired Bishop of Dallas; ordained March 17, 1956; appointed Titular Bishop of Equilio and Auxiliary of San Antonio June 30, 1981; consecrated August 29, 1981; appointed First Bishop of Victoria April 14, 1982; installed May 29, 1982; appointed Coadjutor of Dallas December 18, 1989; Reception as Coadjutor of Dallas February 21, 1990; appointed Bishop of Dallas July 14, 1990; retired March 6, 2007.

Most Reverend

MARK J. SEITZ

Auxiliary Bishop of Dallas; ordained May 17, 1980; appointed Auxiliary Bishop of Dallas and Titular Bishop of Cozyla March 11, 2010; ordained April 27, 2010.

Diocesan Pastoral Center: 3725 Blackburn, P.O. Box 190507, Dallas, TX 75219. Tel: 214-528-2240; Fax: 214-526-1743.

Web: www.cathdal.org

Email: ccfcdal@cathdal.org

Most Reverend

J. DOUGLAS DESHOTEL

Auxiliary Bishop of Dallas; ordained May 13, 1978; appointed Auxiliary Bishop of Dallas and Titular Bishop of Cova March 11, 2010; ordained April 27, 2010.

ESTABLISHED DIOCESE OF DALLAS ON JULY 15, 1890.

Square Miles 7,523.

Redesignated Diocese of Dallas-Fort Worth on October 20, 1953.

Redesignated Diocese of Dallas on August 27, 1969.

Comprises the following nine Counties in the State of Texas: Collin, Dallas, Ellis, Fannin, Grayson, Hunt, Kaufman, Navarro and Rockwall.

For legal titles of parishes and diocesan institutions, consult the Diocesan Pastoral Center.

STATISTICAL OVERVIEW

Personnel	
Bishop	1
Auxiliary Bishops	2
Retired Bishops	2
Abbots	1
Priests: Diocesan Active in Diocese	61
Priests: Diocesan Active Outside Diocese	6
Priests: Retired, Sick or Absent	32
Number of Diocesan Priests	99
Religious Priests in Diocese	77
Total Priests in Diocese	176
Extern Priests in Diocese	31
Ordinations:	
Diocesan Priests	1
Religious Priests	1
Transitional Deacons	2
Permanent Deacons in Diocese	148
Total Brothers	25
Total Sisters	133
Parishes	
Parishes	67
With Resident Pastor:	
Resident Diocesan Priests	42
Resident Religious Priests	11
Without Resident Pastor:	
Administered by Priests	12
Administered by Deacons	2
Quasi-Parishes	6
Pastoral Centers	3
Professional Ministry Personnel:	
Brothers	3
Sisters	21
Lay Ministers	244
Welfare	
Homes for the Aged	1
Total Assisted	49
Day Care Centers	1
Total Assisted	100
Special Centers for Social Services	7
Total Assisted	57,109
Educational	
Seminaries, Diocesan	2
Students from This Diocese	27
Students from Other Diocese	38
Diocesan Students in Other Seminaries	17
Seminaries, Religious	1
Students Religious	17
Total Seminarians	61
Colleges and Universities	1
Total Students	2,883
High Schools, Diocesan and Parish	3
Total Students	2,349
High Schools, Private	4
Total Students	2,341
Elementary Schools, Diocesan and Parish	28
Total Students	9,704
Elementary Schools, Private	2
Total Students	524
Non-residential Schools for the Disabled	1
Total Students	144
Catechesis/Religious Education:	
High School Students	6,882
Elementary Students	41,360
Total Students under Catholic Instruction	66,248
Teachers in the Diocese:	
Priests	17
Scholastics	3
Brothers	8
Sisters	23
Lay Teachers	1,259
Vital Statistics	
Receptions into the Church:	
Infant Baptism Totals	16,931
Adult Baptism Totals	1,037
Received into Full Communion	762
First Communions	11,271
Confirmations	7,444
Marriages:	
Catholic	1,170
Interfaith	315
Total Marriages	1,485
Deaths	1,363
Total Catholic Population	1,181,980
Total Population	3,785,477

Former Bishops—Rt. Revs. THOMAS F. BRENNAN, D.D., cons. April 5, 1891; resigned Nov. 17, 1892; died March 21, 1916; EDWARD JOSEPH DUNNE, D.D., cons. Nov. 30. 1893; died Aug. 5, 1910; Most Revs. JOSEPH PATRICK LYNCH, D.D., LL.D., appt. June 8, 1911; cons. July 12, 1911; Assistant at Pontifical Throne, May 13, 1936; died Aug. 19, 1954; THOMAS K. GORMAN, D.D., D.Sc.Hist., ord. June 23, 1917; Bishop of Reno; appt. April 24, 1931; cons. July 22, 1931; Assistant at the Pontifical Throne, May 4, 1942; appt. Titular Bishop of Rhasus and Coadjutor to the Bishop of Dallas, Feb. 8, 1952; succeeded to Aug. 19, 1954; resigned and appointed Titular Bishop of Pinhel, Aug. 27, 1969. (Title rescinded); died Aug. 16, 1980; THOMAS TSCHOEPE, D.D., ord. May 30, 1943; appt. Bishop of San Angelo, Jan. 12, 1966; cons. March 9, 1966; appt. Bishop of Dallas, Aug. 27, 1969; installed Oct. 29, 1969; retired July 14, 1990; died Jan. 24, 2009; CHARLES V. GRAHMANN, ord. March 17, 1956; appt. Titular Bishop of Equilio and Auxiliary of San Antonio June 30, 1981; cons. Aug. 29, 1981; appt. First Bishop of Victoria April 14, 1982; installed May 29, 1982; appt. Coadjutor of Dallas Dec. 18, 1989; Reception as Coadjutor of Dallas Feb. 21, 1990; appt. Bishop of Dallas July 14, 1990; retired March 6, 2007.

Vicar General—Most Rev. J. DOUGLAS DESHOTEL, V.G.

Diocesan Pastoral Center—3725 Blackburn, P.O. Box 190507, Dallas, 75219. Tel: 214-528-2240; Fax: 214-526-1743. Office Hours: 9-5.

Episcopal Vicar—Rev. Msgr. MILAM J. JOSEPH.

Vicar for Clergy—Rev. GREGORY KELLY.

Chancellor—MARY EDLUND, J.C.L.

Diocesan Tribunal—Mailing Address: P.O. Box 190507, Dallas, 75219. Tel: 214-379-2840; Fax: 214-523-2437.

Judicial Vicar—Rev. Msgr. JOHN P. BELL, J.C.L.

Director of the Tribunal—WILLIAM C. HARE III, J.C.L.

Assessor—MARGARET GILLETT.

Defensor Vinculi—JOHN P. GARGAN, J.C.D.; Rev. Msgrs. RONNY E. JENKINS, J.C.D.; LEON DUESMAN, J.C.B.; MARY EDLUND, J.C.L.

Adjutant Judicial Vicars—Rev. Msgr. GLENN D. GARDNER, J.C.D.; Very Rev. JOHN LIBONE, J.C.L., V.F.

Promoter of Justice—MARY EDLUND, J.C.L.

Auditors and Notaries—MARIA LONGORIA-CHAVEZ; CAROL PHILLIPS; BRENDA M. SMITH; NORA D. SMITH; ELSA BUENDIA.

Diocesan Judges—WILLIAM C. HARE III, J.C.L.; LYNDA ROBITAILLE, J.C.D.; DIANE L. BARR, J.C.D.; Sr. MARIE BREITENBECK, O.P., J.C.D.; Rev. Msgr. MILAM J. JOSEPH; Rev. PAUL HAI NGUYEN, C.SS.R., J.C.L.; Deacon RAYMOND H. SMITH.

Procurator-Advocates—LARRIE W. ARNOLD, M.D.; DOUGLAS A. BOYD JR.; SUSAN C. BOYD; BEBE CANTU; JUDY CLARK; DIANE DANIELS; Rev. JOHN F. DEEVES, S.J.; ANTHONY R. FLEO; Deacon DON FORBRICH; DEBBIE FOWLER; JEANNE MARIE GIRSCH; SANDRA WARNE GIST; Deacon WALTER GOVE; MARY CATHERINE HARE; LANAY N. HARTMANN; JOAN HEITING; LEO HEITING; MARY L.

IZAK; CECILIA LYNNE JONES; Rev. GREGORY KELLY; Deacon JOHN PAUL KELLY; ANNE C. KEOUGH; CECILIA A. LADDA; BARBARA LANDREGAN; PRISCILLA MAHAFFEY; Rev. JOSEPH A. MEHAN JR.; LINDA MOSES; YOLANDA ORTIZ; DENISE G. PHILLIPS; Deacons KENNETH REISOR; PAUL W. REITTINGER; MARY KAY RITCHIE; MARY ROBINSON; Deacons ROBERT SANCHEZ; WILLIAM J. SCHUSTER; Most Rev. MARK J. SEITZ; MONICA SPARKMAN; Deacons CARL H. THELIN; GARY M. VOGEL.

Consultors of Pastors—Rev. Msgr. ROBERT M. COERVER, V.F.; Very Rev. T. MICHAEL DUGAN, V.F.; Rev. GREGORY KELLY, Vicar for Clergy Ex Officio; Rev. Msgrs. HENRY V. PETTER, V.F.; LAWRENCE PICHARD.

College of Consultors—Rev. GREGORY KELLY; Rev. Msgr. HENRY V. PETTER, V.F.; Most Rev. J. DOUGLAS DESHOTEL, V.G., Ex Officio; Rev. ROBERT WILLIAMS; Rev. Msgr. GLENN D. GARDNER, J.C.D.; Rev. J. EDUARDO GONZALEZ; Most Rev. MARK J. SEITZ; Rev. Msgr. MILAM J. JOSEPH; Very Rev. JOHN LIBONE, J.C.L., V.F.

Presbyteral Council—Appointed Members: Rev. Msgr. MILAM J. JOSEPH; Revs. JOSEPH SON VAN NGUYEN; J. EDUARDO GONZALEZ; Rev. Msgr. GLENN D. GARDNER, J.C.D.

Deans—Very Rev. T. MICHAEL DUGAN, V.F., Southwest; Rev. Msgr. ROBERT M. COERVER, V.F., Eastern; Very Rev. ROBERT R. CRISP, V.F., Northeast; Rev. Msgr. HENRY V. PETTER, V.F., Northern; Very Revs. JOHN LIBONE, J.C.L., V.F., Central; EDMUNDO B. PAREDES, V.F., Southeast; DAVID J. FLORI, V.F., North Central.

At Large Members—Rev. BRUCE BRADLEY; Most Rev. MARK J. SEITZ; Revs. ROBERT WILLIAMS; DONALD ZEILER.

Ex Officio Members—Most Rev. J. DOUGLAS DESHOTEL, V.G.; Rev. GREGORY KELLY, Vicar for Clergy.

Censor Librorum—Rev. Msgrs. GLENN D. GARDNER, J.C.D.; ROBERT M. COERVER, V.F.

Diocesan Pastoral Council—Most Rev. KEVIN J. FARRELL, D.D.; MATTHEW SAVINS; GLORIA ABANAKA; BRIAN CULLEN; KAY YATES; JACK GUILLORY; TERRI DALKE; RENE DE LA FUENTE; BETTY BRUCE; RAUL PAREDES; GAIL HARTIN, Ph.D.; RICHARD KELLY; FELICITAS ALFARO; HUGO PONS; ESTELLA M. CASTILLO; ALEX EDOBOR; MONICA GAYTAN.

Diocesan Boards

Finance Council—Most Rev. KEVIN J. FARRELL, D.D.; EUGENE VILFORDI; MIKE CORBOY; J. OLIVER MCGONIGLE; MICHAEL T. WEIS; Most Rev. J. DOUGLAS DESHOTEL, V.G.; ROGER ENRICO; FRANK HUBACH; HARRY J. LONGWELL; JAMES MORONEY III; KATHY MULDOON; LYDIA NOVAKOV; JACK PRATT; ED SCHAFFLER; DENIS SIMON.

Building Commission—Rev. Msgr. JEROME P. DUESMAN; Deacon BRIAN MITCHELL; JOSEPH SCOLARO; MICHAEL T. WEIS; STEVE MALONE.

Personnel Board—Most Rev. J. DOUGLAS DESHOTEL, V.G.; Revs. GREGORY KELLY; THOMAS CLOHERTY; STEPHEN W. BIERSCHENK; Very Rev. EDMUNDO B. PAREDES, V.F.; Rev. Msgr. HENRY V. PETTER, V.F.; Rev. MICHAEL GUADAGNOLI; Most Rev. KEVIN J. FARRELL, D.D.

Accreditation Board—Revs. BRUCE BRADLEY; GREGORY KELLY; Sr. THERESA KHIRALLAH, S.S.N.D.; Deacon JESSE OLIVAREZ; MARY EDLUND, J.C.L.

Diocesan Offices and Directors

Judicial Vicar—Rev. Msgr. JOHN P. BELL, J.C.L.

Tribunal—

Episcopal Vicar—Rev. Msgr. MILAM J. JOSEPH.

Vicar General—Most Rev. J. DOUGLAS DESHOTEL.

I. Vicar for Clergy—Rev. GREGORY KELLY, Dir.

Priest Personnel—Rev. GREGORY KELLY, Mailing Address: P.O. Box 190507, Dallas, 75219. Tel: 214-379-2848.

Vocations—Revs. RODOLFO GARCÍA, Dir.; ANTHONY F. LACKLAND, Assoc. Dir.

Diaconate—Deacon ARNOLD PICON, Dir., 901 S. Madison Ave., Dallas, 75208. Mailing Address: P.O. Box 190507, Dallas, 75219. Tel: 214-943-6585.

II. Catholic Schools Office—Sr. GLORIA CAIN, S.S.N.D., Supt., Mailing Address: P.O. Box 190507, Dallas, 75219. Tel: 214-379-2831.

III. Director of Ministries—Sr. THERESA KHIRALLAH, S.S.N.D., Mailing Address: P.O. Box 190507, Dallas, 75219. Tel: 214-379-2897.

Catechetical Services—LOURDES MAYER, Mailing Address: P.O. Box 190507, Dallas, 75219. Tel: 214-379-2848.

Youth and Young Adult Ministries—SUSAN DORFMEISTER, Dir., Mailing Address: P.O. Box 190507, Dallas, 75219. Tel: 214-379-2843.

Pastoral Services—Deacon CHARLES STUMP JR., Dir. Tel: 214-379-2882.

Addictions Ministry—PHIL PASCHKE, Coord. Tel: 214-960-2166.

Ministries to People with Disabilities—JOHN AUST, Coord. Tel: 214-379-2866.

Hospital Ministry—Deacon CHARLES STUMP JR. Tel: 214-379-2882.

Prison Ministry—Deacon JOSE TREVINO, Coord. Tel: 214-379-2883.

Liturgy Office—Very Rev. T. MICHAEL DUGAN, V.F., Dir. Tel: 214-379-2860.

Sacramental Ministries—

Sacrament of Marriage—DIANE DANIELS, Dir. Tel: 214-379-2881.

IV. Chief Financial Officer—

Business Office—MICHAEL T. WEIS, Dir. Tel: 214-379-2807.

Retreat/Conference Center— Catholic Conference and Formation Center Deacon JESSE OLIVAREZ, Dir., 901 S. Madison Ave., Dallas, 75208. Mailing Address: P.O. Box 190507, Dallas, 75219. Tel: 214-943-6585.

Catholic Community Appeal—PAUL VITANZA, C.F.R.E., Dir. Tel: 214-379-2862.

V. Director of Construction and Real Estate—STEVE MALONE.

VI. Director of Human Resources—JAY SALEM.

VII. Diocesan Risk Manager—JOHN A. SMITH.

VIII. Director of Parish & School Financial Reporting—FRED VILLELA.

IX. Director of Catholic Charities—Sr. MARY ANNE OWENS, S.S.N.D. Tel: 214-520-6590.

X. Director of Communications—ANNETTE GONZALES TAYLOR, Dir., Mailing Address: P.O. Box 190507, Dallas, 75219. Tel: 214-379-2873.

Texas Catholic and El Catolico— Official Catholic Newspapers of the Diocese of Dallas Web: www.texascatholic.com; www.elcatolico.org. Most Rev. KEVIN JOSEPH FARRELL, D.D., Publisher; DAVID SEDENO, Editor; ANTONIO RAMIREZ JR., Business Mgr. Tel: 214-379-2891; Fax: 214-528-3411.

XI. Director of Development—JIM URBANUS.

Chancellor—MARY EDLUND, J.C.L., Mailing Address: P.O. Box 190507, Dallas, 75219. Tel: 214-379-2819.

Archives—STEVE LANDREGAN, Archivist. Tel: 214-379-2871.

Pastoral Planning and Research—LYNN ROSSOL, Dir. Tel: 214-379-2854.

Networks—LYNN ROSSOL, Mailing Address: P.O. Box 190507, Dallas, 75219. Tel: 214-379-2854.

Family Life Network—BARBARA ERETTO, Chm.

Asian Network—VIVIEN ESCANO, Chm.

Black Network—MILDRED D. POPE, Chm.

Hispanic Network—ALPHONSO MIRABAL, Chm.

Safe Environment Office—BARBARA LANDREGAN, Dir., Mailing Address: P.O. Box 190507, Dallas, 75219. Tel: 214-379-2812.

Victim Assistance Coordinator—MARY EDLUND, J.C.L. Tel: 214-379-2819. Email: medlund@cathdal.org.

CLERGY, PARISHES, MISSIONS AND PAROCHIAL SCHOOLS

CITY OF DALLAS

(DALLAS COUNTY)

1—CATHEDRAL-SANTUARIO DE GUADALUPE (1869) Revs. J. Eduardo Gonzalez; Henry Erazo Herrea; Deacons Benito Garcia; Charles Stump Jr.; Larry Harmon. Mailing Address: 2215 Ross Ave., 75201. Fax: 214-954-1557.
Res.: 2102 Allen, 75204. Tel: 214-871-1362.
Catechesis/Religious Program—Imelda Ramirez, P.C.L. Students 921.

2—ALL SAINTS (1976) Revs. Thomas Cloherty; Stanislau Muthu; Deacons Denis Simon; Vincent Bathea; John R. Costello; Frank M. Milliken.
Res.: 5231 Meadowcreek, 75248. Tel: 972-661-9282; Fax: 972-233-5401.
School—(Grades K-8), 7777 Osage Plaza Pkwy., 75252. Tel: 214-217-3300; Fax: 214-217-3339. Denise Thompson, Prin.; Marian Davis, Vice Prin. Students 336.
Catechesis/Religious Program—Students 492.

3—ST. ANDREW KIM (1977), (Korean), Rev. Tae Sun Kim.
Res.: 2019 Valley View Ln., Farmers Branch, 75234. Tel: 972-620-9150; Fax: 972-484-4628. Email: office@dallaskoreancatholic.org. Web: www.dallaskoreancatholic.org.
Catechesis/Religious Program—Veronica Cho, D.R.E. Sisters 2; Students 151.

4—ST. ANTHONY (1938), (African American), Deacon Denis D. Corbin, Admin.
Res.: 2711 Romine St., 75215. Tel: 214-428-6926.

5—ST. AUGUSTINE CATHOLIC CHURCH (1937) Rev. Anibal Adorno; Deacon Robert Sanchez. In Res., Rev. Solh Saez.
Res.: 1047 N. St. Augustine Dr., 75217. Tel: 214-391-1513; Fax: 214-398-2580. Email: churchoffice@stadallas.com.
School—(Grades K-8), 1064 N. St. Augustine Dr., 75217. Tel: 214-391-1381; Fax: 214-391-8781. Email: office@stadallas.com. Mr. Michael Ronan, Prin. Lay Teachers 17; Students 220.
Catechesis/Religious Program—Maria de Lourdes Marin, C.R.E. Students 800.

6—ST. BERNARD OF CLAIRVAUX (1947), (Hispanic), Rev. Martin Moreno; Deacon John Kelly.
Res.: 1404 Old Gate Ln., 75218. Tel: 214-321-0454; Fax: 214-320-0119. Web: www.stbernards.us.
School—(Grades PreK-8), 1420 Old Gate Ln., 75218. Tel: 214-321-2897; Fax: 214-321-4060. Lay Teachers 17; Students 209.
Catechesis/Religious Program—Sandra Godina, P.C.L. Students 547.

7—BLESSED SACRAMENT (1901) Revs. Francisco J. Orozco-Lopez; Jose I. Figueroa.
Res.: 231 N. Marsalis Ave., 75203. Tel: 214-948-6535; Fax: 214-948-1660. Web: www.bsdallas.org.
Catechesis/Religious Program—Students 797.

8—ST. CECILIA (1933), (Hispanic), Very Rev. Edmundo B. Paredes; Rev. Antonio Salvador Rodriguez, Parochial Vicar; Deacons Gonzalo Gonzales; Onesimo Martinez.
Res.: 1809 W. Davis St., 75208. Tel: 214-941-5821; Fax: 214-946-4466. Email: stceciliachurch@sbcglobal.net.
School—(Grades K-8), 635 Marycliff Rd., 75208. Tel: 214-948-8628. Sisters of St. Mary of Namur 1; Lay Teachers 19; Students 203.
Catechesis/Religious Program—Students 633.

9—CHRIST THE KING (1941) Rev. Msgr. Donald F. Zimmerman; Mary Catherine Hare, Pastoral Assoc.; William C. Hare III, Pastoral Assoc.; Deacon Tim Muldoon. In Res., Rev. Anthony F. Lackland.
Res.: 8017 Preston Rd., 75225. Tel: 214-365-1200; Fax: 214-365-1205.
School—(Grades K-8), 4100 Colgate St., 75225. Tel: 214-365-1234; Fax: 214-365-1236. Lay Teachers 47; Students 423.
Catechesis/Religious Program—Students 489.

10—ST. EDWARD (1903) Revs. Edison Vela; Roberto Merced, O.P.
Res.: 4014 Simpson St., 75246. Tel: 214-823-1291; Fax: 214-823-7535. Web: stedwardparish.org.
Catechesis/Religious Program—Claudio Mora, D.R.E. Students 1,216.

11—ST. ELIZABETH (1956) Very Rev. T. Michael Dugan; Rev. Benjamin Molina; Deacons Denis Simon; Frank Kozarevich; Douglas Boyd. In Res., Rev. Alex Buitrago.
Res.: 4015 S. Hampton Rd., 75224. Tel: 214-331-4328; Fax: 214-331-2464. Web: stelizabethofh.org/parish.htm.
School—(Grades K-8), 4019 S. Hampton Rd., 75224. Tel: 214-331-5139; Fax: 214-467-4346. Web: www.stelizabethofh.org. Monica Connelly, Librarian. Lay Teachers 27; Students 282.
Catechesis/Religious Program—Douglas A. Boyd Jr., P.C.L. Students 254.

12—HOLY CROSS (1956) Rev. Timothy A. Gollob; Deacon Antonio D. Trevino. In Res., Rev. James George McKenna.
Res.: 2926 E. Ledbetter Dr., 75216. Tel: 214-374-7952; Fax: 214-375-7457.
Catechesis/Religious Program—Students 171.

13—HOLY TRINITY (1907) Revs. Juan Antonio Ruiz, C.M.; Richard Rex Hays, C.M., Parochial Vicar; Bro. Thomas Juneman, C.M.; Deacons Don Forbrich; Edward Putonti; Michael Bolesta.
Mailing Address: 3826 Gilbert Ave., 75219. Web: www.htccd.org.
Res.: 3811 Oak Lawn Ave., 75219. Tel: 214-526-8555; Fax: 214-526-3477.
School—(Grades K-8), 3815 Oak Lawn Ave., 75219. Tel: 214-526-5113. Web: www.htcsdallas.org. Brothers 1; Lay Ministers 8; Lay Teachers 16; Students 198.
Catechesis/Religious Program—Students 367.

14—ST. JAMES (1934) Rev. Msgr. Mario Magbanua; Rev. Jimwell Goyo; Deacon Vincent F. Jimenez.
Mailing Address: P.O. Box 763338, 75376.
Res.: 1002 E. Saner Ave., 75216. Tel: 214-371-9209; Fax: 214-371-0226. Email: stjamesdallas@sbcglobal.net.
Catechesis/Religious Program—Students 905.

15—ST. JUDE CHAPEL (Downtown Dallas) (1968) Rev. John Alphonso.
Res.: 3769 Weeburn Dr., 75229. Tel: 214-353-0517. Web: stjudechapel.net.

16—MARY IMMACULATE (1956) Rev. Michael D. Forge; Rev. Msgr. Andrés Sagra; Deacons Patrick Hayes; Philip E. Webb.
Res. & Mailing Address: 2800 Valwood Pkwy.,

75234. Tel: 972-243-7104; Fax: 972-406-1254. Email: anny@maryimmaculatechurch.org. Web: maryimmaculatechurch.org.
School—(Grades K-8) Tel: 972-243-7105; Fax: 972-241-7678. Karen Saldana, Librarian. Lay Teachers 32; Students 526.
Catechesis / Religious Program—Sr. Yolanda Perez, O.C.D., P.C.L. Students 1,271.
17—ST. MARY OF CARMEL (1944) Rev. Jesus Sancho, O.C.D.
Res.: 2900 Vilbig Rd., 75212. Tel: 214-747-1433; Fax: 214-748-7481.
School—(Grades K-8), 1716 Singleton Blvd., 75212. Tel: 214-748-2934; Fax: 214-760-9052. Sisters of the Holy Spirit 2; Lay Teachers 12; Students 169.
Catechesis / Religious Program—Students 186.
18—ST. MONICA (1954) Rev. Stephen W. Bierschenk; Rev. Msgr. John F. Meyers, Pastor Emeritus (Retired); Rev. John Hopka; Deacons Michael Weston; Larry Lucido; Bob Marrinan; Brian Mitchell; Abel Cortes.
Res.: 9933 Midway Rd., 75220. Tel: 214-358-1453; Fax: 214-351-1887. Web: stmonicachurch.org.
School—(Grades PreK-8), 4140 Walnut Hill Ln., 75229. Tel: 214-351-5688; Fax: 214-352-2608. Lay Teachers 60; Students 861.
Catechesis / Religious Program—Marianela Byrne, Dir. Faith Formation. Students 1,572.
19—NUESTRA SENORA DEL PILAR (2001), (Hispanic), Rev. Wilmer de Jesus Daza. In Res., Most Rev. José A. Valbuena.
4455 W. Illinois Ave., 75211. Tel: 214-467-9116; Fax: 214-339-7249. Email: pilar.church@sbcglobal.net.
Catechesis / Religious Program—Students 849.
20—OUR LADY OF LOURDES (1954) Revs. Mario Garcia, O.F.M.Cap. (Spain); Pablo Jaramillo, O.F.M.Cap. (Mexico); Roberto Viveros, O.F.M.Cap. (Mexico); Deacon Pete Rodriguez.
Res.: 5605 Bernal Dr., 75212. Tel: 214-637-6673; Fax: 214-637-2454.
Catechesis / Religious Program—Amy Rodriguez, P.C.L. Students 929.
21—OUR LADY OF PERPETUAL HELP (1942), (Hispanic), Rev. Salvador Gúzman; Deacon Albert Montes.
Res.: 7617 Cortland Ave., 75235. Tel: 214-352-6012; Fax: 214-351-9883. Email: secretary@olphdallas.org. Web: olphdallas.org.
School—(Grades PreK-8), 7625 Cortland Ave., 75235. Tel: 214-351-3396; Fax: 214-351-9889. Web: www.olphdallas.org. Monica Schwarz, Librarian. Lay Teachers 14; Students 178.
Catechesis / Religious Program—Students 454.
Convent—Daughters of the Sacred Heart Sisters 3.
22—ST. PATRICK (1963) Revs. Josef Vollmer-Konig; Paul Nguyen; Deacon John C. Nordick.
Res.: 9643 Ferndale Rd., 75238. Tel: 214-348-7380; Fax: 214-340-5956.
School—(Grades PreK-8), 9635 Ferndale Rd., 75238. Tel: 214-348-8070; Fax: 214-503-7230. Web: www.stpatrickschool.org. Ginger Loshelder, Librarian. Sisters of the Incarnate Word and Blessed Sacrament 2; Lay Teachers 33; Students 520.
Catechesis / Religious Program—Mrs. Martha Noel, P.C.L. Students 326.
23—ST. PETER (1905) Rev. Stanislaw Poszwa, S.Ch.
Res.: 2907 Woodall Rodgers Fwy., 75204. Tel: 214-855-1384; Fax: 214-855-1309. Web: www.stpeterdal.com.
Catechesis / Religious Program—Marcella Savala-Hamilton, P.C.L. Students 67.
24—ST. PETER VIETNAMESE (1996) Rev. Dominic Chinh Pham, I.C.M., Admin.; Deacon Uong Hung.
10123 Garland Rd., 75218. Tel: 214-321-9493; Fax: 214-320-2219. Web: www.giaoxuthanhphero.org.
Catechesis / Religious Program—Students 101.
25—ST. PHILIP (1954) Deacon David T. Obergfell, Admin.; Rev. Juan Carlos Franco.
Res.: 8131 Military Pkwy., 75227. Tel: 214-388-5464; Fax: 214-388-2839. Web: www.stphilipcatholicchurch.org.
School—(Grades K-8), 8151 Military Pkwy., 75227. Tel: 214-381-4973; Fax: 214-381-0466. Linda Garrett, Librarian. Sisters of the Holy Spirit 1; Lay Teachers 12; Students 142.
Catechesis / Religious Program—Ginna Curts, P.C.L. Students 204.
26—ST. PIUS X (1954) Revs. Michael Guadagnoli; Arturo Kannee; Deacons David Leerssen; Michael Shaw; John A. Schell; Paul Powers.
Res.: 3030 Gus Thomasson Rd., 75228. Tel: 972-279-6155; Fax: 972-686-7510.
School—(Grades K-8) Tel: 972-279-2339; Fax: 972-613-2059. Lay Teachers 25; Students 327.
Catechesis / Religious Program—Tel: 972-279-2558. Josie Pacheco, P.C.L. Students 1,142.
27—QUASI-PARISH OF OUR LADY OF SAN JUAN DE LOS LAGOS - ST. THERESA (1928) Deacon Hugo A. Salinas.
Res.: 2601 Singleton Blvd., 75212. Tel: 214-631-9627; Fax: 214-631-9627.
Catechesis / Religious Program—Tel: 214-688-0942. Students 255.
28—ST. RITA (1961) Rev. Msgr. J. Mark Seitz; Revs. John J. Heaney, S.J.; Jacinto Garcia; Deacons William J. Schuster; Charles T. Sylvester; Bill Fobes; Moses Chung.
Office: 12521 Inwood Rd., 75244. Tel: 972-934-8388; Fax: 972-934-8965.
Res.: 12626 Planters Glen, 75244. Tel: 972-239-5205.
School—(Grades K-8), 12525 Inwood Rd., 75244. Tel: 972-239-3203; Fax: 972-934-3657. Dr. Elena Hines, Prin. Lay Teachers 49; Students 670.
Catechesis / Religious Program—Susan Sheetz, Interim P.C.L. Students 503.
Convent—Daughters of the Sacred Heart Sisters 4.
29—SAN JUAN DIEGO (QUASI PARISH) (2006) Rev. Jesus Belmontes, Admin.
10150 Monroe Dr., 75229. Tel: 214-271-4691; Fax: 214-271-4696.
Catechesis / Religious Program—Lupita Frausto, P.C.L. Students 862.
30—SANTA CLARA (1993), (Hispanic), Revs. Michael J. Conway, O.SS.T.; Alberto E. Rodriguez, O.S.S.T.
Res.: 321 Calumet Ave., 75211. Tel: 214-337-3936; Fax: 214-333-9148. Web: www.santaclaracatholicchurch.net.
School—Santa Clara of Assisi Catholic Academy, (Grades PreK-8) Tel: 214-333-9423; Fax: 214-333-2556. Email: smatous@santaclaraacademy.org. Web: santaclaraacademy.org. Stephanie Matous, Prin. Lay Teachers 14; Students 162.
Catechesis / Religious Program—Students 499.
31—ST. THOMAS AQUINAS (1952) Very Rev. John Libone; Rev. Victor Bartolotta; Deacons Kenneth Reisor; Richard Harrington; Edward Leyden.
Res.: 6306 Kenwood Ave., 75214. Tel: 214-821-3360; Fax: 214-821-5395.
School—(Grades 3-8), Upper School, 3741 Abrams Rd., 75214. Tel: 214-826-0566; Fax: 214-826-0251. Lay Teachers 80; Students 872.
School—(Grades K-2), Lower School, 6255 E. Mockingbird, 75214. Tel: 469-341-0911.
Catechesis / Religious Program—Victor Bartolotta, Youth Min. (5-12). Faculty 12; Students 261.

OUTSIDE THE CITY OF DALLAS

ALLEN, COLLIN CO.
1—ST. JUDE (1981) Revs. Timothy A. Church, Admin.; Peter Tuan Le; Deacon Ronald Fejeran.
Res.: 1515 N. Greenville Ave., 75002. Tel: 972-727-1177; Fax: 972-727-1401. Web: www.stjudeparish.com.
Catechesis / Religious Program— Julie Buchanan, P.C.L. Students 2,102.
2—OUR LADY OF ANGELS (2000) Rev. Msgr. John P. Bell; Deacons Mike Picard; John O'Leary.
Church: 1914 Ridgeview Dr., 75013. Tel: 214-495-0473; 469-467-9669; Fax: 469-467-0114. Web: www.ourladyofangels.com.
Catechesis / Religious Program—Elizabeth Adams, C.R.E. (Grade School); Sheila Tullier, C.R.E. (Middle School); Matthew Decker, C.R.E. (High School). Students 683.
BONHAM, FANNIN CO., ST. ELIZABETH Rev. Wilson Blas; Deacon Joseph Culling.
Res.: 916 Maple St., 75418. Tel: 903-583-7734; Fax: 903-583-7359. Email: stebonham@verizon.net. Web: www.se-bonham.com.
Catechesis / Religious Program—Students 68.
CARROLLTON, DALLAS CO., SACRED HEART OF JESUS CHRIST (1999) Rev. Joseph Son Van Nguyen.
2121 N. Denton, 75006. Tel: 972-446-3461; Fax: 972-446-9551.
Catechesis / Religious Program—Nghia Duong, P.C.L. Students 358.
COMMERCE, HUNT CO., ST. JOSEPH (1895) Rev. George P. Monaghan.
Rectory—1508 Cooper St., 75428. Tel: 903-886-7135; Fax: 903-886-8034. Web: www.stjoetx.net. Church: P.O. Box 832, 75429-0832.
Catechesis / Religious Program—Students 45.
COPPELL, DALLAS CO., ST. ANN (1985) Rev. Msgr. Leon Duesman; Deacons Ed Scarbrough; Pete Markwald; Kory Killgo.
Res.: 180 Samuel Blvd., 75019.
Church: Tel: 972-393-5544; Fax: 972-462-1617.
Catechesis / Religious Program—Debbie Matalone, D.R.E. Students 2,564.
CORSICANA, NAVARRO CO., IMMACULATE CONCEPTION (1871) Rev. Danilo Ramos; Deacon Lewis J. Palos.
Res.: 3000 Hwy. 22 W., P.O. Box 798, 75151. Tel: 903-874-4473; Fax: 903-874-2619.
School—James L. Collins Catholic School, (Grades K-8) Tel: 903-872-1751. Lay Teachers 13; Students 183.
Catechesis / Religious Program—Gerardo Alvarado, P.C.L. Students 329.
DENISON, GRAYSON CO., ST. PATRICK (1872) Rev. Stephen J. Mocio.
Res.: 314 N. Rusk Ave., 75020. Tel: 903-463-3275; Fax: 903-463-3447. Web: www.saintpats.net.
Catechesis / Religious Program—Bertha Shock, D.R.E.; Magdalena Nieto, D.R.E. Students 248.
DUNCANVILLE, DALLAS CO., HOLY SPIRIT (1974) Rev. Joseph C. Lee; Deacons Al Evans; Paul Wood.
Res.: 1111 W. Danieldale Rd., 75137-3719. Tel: 972-298-4971; Fax: 972-709-1443. Web: holyspiritcatholic.com.
Catechesis / Religious Program—Anne C. Keough, P.C.L. Students 602.
ENNIS, ELLIS CO., ST. JOHN NEPOMUCENE (1902) [CEM] Revs. John Dick; Antonio Liberman-Ormaza; Deacons Don Griffith; Frutos Vega.
401 E. Lampasas St., 75119. Tel: 972-878-2834; Fax: 972-875-2452. Web: stjohnchurch_ennis.org.
Rectory & Res.: 505 E. Lampasas, 75119. Tel: 972-872-9619.
Catechesis / Religious Program—Students 826.
FERRIS, ELLIS CO., CORPUS CHRISTI (1977), (Hispanic), Deacon Isidro Olvera.
Res.: 117 N. Wood, 75125. Tel: 972-544-2161; Fax: 972-544-2161.
Catechesis / Religious Program—Stephanie Rieter, P.C.L. Students 257.
FORNEY, KAUFMAN CO., ST. MARTIN OF TOURS (1891) Rev. Msgr. Glenn D. Gardner.
Res.: 9470 C.R. 213, 75126. Tel: 972-564-9114; Fax: 972-564-9138. Email: stmchurchoff@aol.com.
Catechesis / Religious Program—Email: stmreleducation@aol.com. Jan Reznicek, P.C.L. Students 173.
FRISCO, COLLIN CO., ST. FRANCIS OF ASSISI (1966) Rev. Msgr. Lawrence Pichard; Rev. Vincent C. Anyama; Deacons Frank Reyna; Carl Macero; Greg Kahrs; Dan Covarrubias.
Res.: 8000 El Dorado Pkwy., 75034. Tel: 972-712-2645; Fax: 972-712-1087. Web: www.stfoafrisco.org. Email: office@stfoafrisco.org.
Catechesis / Religious Program—Students 2,056.
GARLAND, DALLAS CO.
1—GOOD SHEPHERD (1944) Rev. Robert Williams; Deacons Jim Harris; Leopoldo Cortinas III.
Res.: 201 S. 13th St., 75040. Tel: 972-276-8587; Fax: 972-494-3653.
School—(Grades K-8), 214 S. Garland Ave., 75040. Tel: 972-272-6533; Fax: 972-272-0512. Web: www.goodshepherdcatholicschool.org. Gail R. Bassett, Prin. Brothers 1; Sisters 1; Lay Teachers 21; Students 239.
Catechesis / Religious Program—Blanca Alanis, P.C.L. Students 1,763.
2—ST. MARY MALANKARA (1996) Rt. Rev. Geevarghese Mannikarotta.
116 E. Ave. D, 75040. Tel: 972-494-5356.
Res.: *c/o Good Shepherd Church*, 201 S. 13th St., 75040. Tel: 972-276-7069; Fax: 972-494-3653.
Catechesis / Religious Program—
3—ST. MICHAEL THE ARCHANGEL (1980) Rev. Joseph A. Mehan Jr.; Deacon Joe Perez. In Res., Rev. Marcus Chidozie.
Res.: 950 Trails Pkwy., 75043. Tel: 972-279-6581; 972-270-4939 (Rectory); Fax: 972-279-6647. Email: smapgar@sbcglobal.net.
Catechesis / Religious Program—Students 675.
4—MOTHER OF PERPETUAL HELP (1992), (Vietnamese), Revs. Tuan Bui, C.Ss.R.; Paul Nguyen, C.Ss.R.
Res.: 2121 W. Apollo Rd., 75044. Tel: 972-414-7073. Web: www.dmhcg.org.
Catechesis / Religious Program—Students 900.
GRAND PRAIRIE, DALLAS CO.
1—IMMACULATE CONCEPTION (1916) Rev. Manuel Ingelmo-Benavente; Deacon David Maida.
Res.: 610 N.E. 17th St., 75050. Tel: 972-262-5137; Fax: 972-264-7657. Web. www.icgrandprairie.org.
School—(Grades PreK-8), 400 N.E. 17th St., 75050. Tel: 972-264-8777; Fax: 972-264-7742. Web: www.icgrandprairie.org/school. Linda Santos, Prin.; Sr. Catherine Marie Kawa, C.F.S.N., Librarian. Sisters of the Holy Family of Nazareth 4; Lay Teachers 11; Students 126.
Catechesis / Religious Program—Patricia T. Hidalgo, P.C.L. Students 488.
2—ST. JOSEPH VIETNAMESE PARISH (1993) Rev. Ansgar Pham, S.D.D.
Res.: 1902 S. Beltline Rd., 75051. Tel: 972-642-6747; Fax: 972-642-6746.
Catechesis / Religious Program—Students 246.
3—ST. MICHAEL THE ARCHANGEL (1985) Rev. Joseph Hoa Duc Trinh; Deacons Dennis Phillip Bryant; J. Robert Miller.
2910 Corn Valley, 75052. Web: www.stmichaelgptx.org.
Res.: 2925 Lake Park Dr., 75052. Tel: 972-262-0552; Fax: 972-642-5429.
Catechesis / Religious Program—Tel: 972-262-6590. Email: 2910smgptx@sbcglobal.net. Students 445.
GREENVILLE, HUNT CO., ST. WILLIAM (1892) Rev. Paul L. Weinberger; Deacon Lee B. Davis.
Res.: 4300 Stuart St., 75401. Tel: 903-450-1177; Fax: 903-455-7134. Web: www.saintwilliamtheconfessor.com. Email: stwilliam@sbcglobal.net.
Catechesis / Religious Program—Tel: 903-455-8201. Students 230.

IRVING, DALLAS CO.
1—CHURCH OF THE INCARNATION (1973) Rev. Rodolfo García; Denise Phillips, Dir. Campus Ministry; Carol Norris, Dir. Music Ministry.
University of Dallas: 1845 E. Northgate Dr., 75062. Tel: 972-721-5375; Fax: 972-721-5351.
2—HOLY FAMILY OF NAZARETH (1964) Rev. Msgr. Jerome P. Duesman; Deacons Kenneth Hale; Ron Morgan.
Res.: 2330 Cheyenne St., 75062. Tel: 972-252-5521; Fax: 972-252-5523. Web: www.holyfamilychurch.net.
School—(Grades K-8), 2323 Cheyenne St., 75062. Tel: 972-255-0205; Fax: 972-252-4167. Web: www.h-fns.com. Lay Teachers 17; Students 132.
Catechesis/Religious Program—Linda Moses, P.C.L. Students 404.
3—ST. LUKE (1902) Revs. Clair Orso, C.S.; Jorge Bravo, C.S.; Leonardo Rocha, C.S.; Deacons Jose Trevino; Daniel D. Segovia; Roger Gette.
Res.: 1015 Schulze Dr., 75060. Tel: 972-259-3222; Fax: 972-259-3339. Web: www.stlukeirving.org.
School—(Grades K-8), 1023 Schulze Dr., 75060. Tel: 972-253-8285; Fax: 972-253-5535. Lay Teachers 12; Students 133.
Catechesis/Religious Program—Deacon Daniel D. Segovia, P.C.L. Students 1,443.
ITALY, ELLIS CO., EPIPHANY (QUASI PARISH) Rev. John Dick.
434 S. Ward, 76651. Mailing: 401 E Tampasas St., Ennis, 75119.
Catechesis/Religious Program—Paula Guerrero, P.C.L. Students 60.
KAUFMAN, KAUFMAN CO., ST. ANN (1935) Rev. Ely Manondo; Deacons James Burkel; Sergio Morales.
Res.: 806 N. Washington St., 75142. Tel: 972-962-3247; Fax: 972-932-4003.
Catechesis/Religious Program—Email: sguigneaux@mycvc.net. Shelly Guigneaux, P.C.L. Students 348.
LANCASTER, DALLAS CO., ST. FRANCIS OF ASSISI (1973) Rev. Albert B. Becher; Deacon Héctor B. Peña.
Res.: 1537 Rogers Ave., 75134. Tel: 972-227-4124; Fax: 972-227-2882. Email: sfre@subell.net. Web: www.stfrancislancaster.org.
Catechesis/Religious Program—Tel: 972-227-0770. Sherry Granello, P.C.L. Students 407.
MCKINNEY, COLLIN CO.
1—ST. GABRIEL THE ARCHANGEL (1996) Revs. Donald Zeiler; Jose Pazheveettil, M.S.T.; Deacons Ray Smith; Robert Boduch; Victor M. Machiano.
Mailing Address: 110 St. Gabriel Way, 75071. Tel: 972-542-7170; Fax: 972-542-7756. Web: www.stgabriel.org.
Catechesis/Religious Program—Students 1,451.
2—ST. MICHAEL (1892) Revs. Bruce Bradley; Cruz Calderon; Deacon George Polcer.
Res.: 411 Paula Rd., 75069. Tel: 972-542-4667; Fax: 972-542-4641.
Catechesis/Religious Program—Jay Semon, P.C.L. Students 775.
MESQUITE, DALLAS CO., DIVINE MERCY OF OUR LORD (2002) Revs. Ernesto Torres; Manuel Sabando; Deacon Al Lopez.
1585 E. Cartwright Rd., 75149. Tel: 972-591-5294; Fax: 972-289-7445. Email: parish@divinemercytx.org. Web: www.divinemercyofourlord.org.
Rectory—510 Elderwood Loop, 75181. Tel: 972-222-0436.
Catechesis/Religious Program—Tel: 469-828-9163. Email: faithformation@divinemercytx.org. Ana L. Dávila, D.R.E. & P.C.L. Students 582.
PLANO, COLLIN CO.
1—ST. ELIZABETH ANN SETON (1976) Rev. Msgr. Henry V. Petter; Rev. Jason Cargo; Deacons Michael Seibold; Thomas Roche; Bill Flynn; Jack Gulino.
Res.: 2701 W. Piedra Dr., 75023. Tel: 972-596-5505; Fax: 972-985-7573. Web: www.setonparish.org.
Catechesis/Religious Program—3100 W. Spring Creek Pkwy., 75023. Fax: 972-985-0431. Bruce Baumann, P.C.L. Students 1,781.
2—ST. MARK THE EVANGELIST (1966) Revs. Clifford G. Smith; Cirilo Quispe; Deacons Arnold Picon; Sid Little.
Res.: 1100 W. 15th St., 75075. Tel: 972-423-5600; Fax: 972-423-5024. Web: www.stmarkplano.org.
School—(Grades K-8) Tel: 972-578-0610; Fax: 972-423-3299. Web: www.stmarkcatholicschool.com. Ann Hollenbeck, Librarian. Lay Teachers 47; Students 650.
Catechesis/Religious Program—Students 2,135.
3—PRINCE OF PEACE (1991) Rev. Msgr. R. James Balint; Revs. Lawrence A. Beyer (Retired); Roberto Butawan; Deacons Louis L. Munoz; David E. Tompsett.
Res.: 5100 W. Plano Pkwy., 75093. Tel: 972-380-2100; Fax: 972-380-5162. Web: www.popplano.org.
School—(Grades K-8) Tel: 972-380-5505; Fax: 972-380-2570. Kathy Bailey, Librarian. Lay Teachers 38; Students 834.
Catechesis/Religious Program—Students 595.
4—SACRED HEART OF JESUS (1993), (Chinese), Rev. Vincent Lin.
Church: 4201 E. 14th St., 75074. Tel: 972-516-8500. Web: www.chinese-catholic.org.
Catechesis/Religious Program—Lisa Longoria, P.C.L. Students 31.
QUINLAN, HUNT CO., OUR LADY OF FATIMA Rev. Paul L. Weinberger.
1579 E. Quinlan Pkwy., 75474. Mailing Address: 4300 Stuart St., Greenville, 75401.
Catechesis/Religious Program—Students 8.
RICHARDSON, DALLAS CO.
1—ST. JOSEPH (1976) Rev. Msgr. Don L. Fischer; Rev. Louis Chijioke Nwaokeafor, Parochial Vicar; Deacon Randall L. Engel.
Res.: 600 S. Jupiter Rd., 75081. Tel: 972-231-2951; Fax: 972-231-2875. Email: church@stjosephcc.net. Web: www.stjosephcc.net.
School—(Grades K-8) Tel: 972-234-4679; Fax: 972-692-4594. Phil R. Riley, Prin.; Sue Heflin, Librarian. Students 352.
Catechesis/Religious Program—Tel: 972-690-5588; Fax: 972-692-4575. Students 660.
2—ST. PAUL THE APOSTLE (1956) Very Rev. David J. Flori; Deacons Carl H. Thelin; Paul W. Reittinger; Jesse Olivarez.
Church: 720 S. Floyd Rd., 75080.
Res.: 709 James Dr., 75080. Tel: 972-235-6105; Fax: 972-480-8528. Web: www.saintpaulchurch.org.
School—(Grades PreK-8) Tel: 972-235-3263; Fax: 972-690-1542. Web: saintpaulschool.org. Lay Teachers 31; Students 380.
Catechesis/Religious Program—Tel: 972-235-2598; Fax: 972-664-9993. Becky Soto, P.C.L. Students 521.
ROCKWALL, ROCKWALL CO., OUR LADY OF THE LAKE (1978) Rev. Msgr. Robert M. Coerver; Deacons Jesus Cerrato; Warner Washington; Paul Husting; Jim Daniels.
Res.: 1305 Damascus Rd., 75087. Tel: 972-771-6671 (Office); Fax: 972-771-7283. Web: www.ourladyrockwall.org.
Catechesis/Religious Program—Tel: 972-771-6671, Ext. 114. Beth Wright, P.C.L. Students 885.
ROWLETT, DALLAS CO., SACRED HEART (1899) Very Rev. Robert R. Crisp; Deacons Kenneth Melston; Jack Hopkins.
Res.: 3502 Andrea, P.O. Box 1650, 75088. Tel: 972-475-2473. Web: www.sacredheartrowlett.org.
Catechesis/Religious Program—Barbara Eretto, P.C.L. Students 503.
SHERMAN, GRAYSON CO., ST. MARY (1872) Revs. Jeremy Myers; Antonio Aureus; Deacons John Le Blanc; Tomas Avila; Albert Miller.
Res.: 727 S. Travis, 75090. Tel: 903-893-5148; Fax: 903-813-5489. Email: info@stmarych.org. Web: www.stmarych.org.
School—(Grades PreK-8), 713 Travis St., 75090. Tel: 903-893-2127; Fax: 903-892-3233. Karen Martin, Sec. Lay Teachers 15; Students 141.
Catechesis/Religious Program—Annie Kremer, P.C.L. & D.R.E. Students 554.
TERRELL, KAUFMAN CO., ST. JOHN (1876) Rev. James Orosco; Deacon Fermin Rodriquez.
Res.: 702 N. Frances St., 75160. Tel: 972-563-3643; Fax: 972-563-9718. Web: www.stjohnterrell.org.
Catechesis/Religious Program—Susan Warner, D.R.E. Students 514.
VAN ALSTYNE, GRAYSON CO., HOLY FAMILY (1980) Rev. Bruce Bradley.
P.O. Box 482, 75495.
Catechesis/Religious Program—Martha Whitfield, P.C.L. Students 162.
WAXAHACHIE, ELLIS CO., ST. JOSEPH (1875) Rev. Jose Luis Ortega, M.Sp.S.; Deacon Hugo Monsanto.
Office: 512 E. Marvin St., 75165. Fax: 972-923-3501.
Res.: 504 E. Marvin St., 75165. Tel: 972-938-1953.
School—*St. Joseph Catholic School*, (Grades K-8), 506 E. Marvin St., 75165. Tel: 972-937-0956; Fax: 972-937-1742. Mary Kay Volker, Prin. Lay Teachers 14; Students 169.
Catechesis/Religious Program—Cheryl Bain, P.C.L. Students 529.
WHITESBORO, GRAYSON CO., ST. FRANCIS OF ASSISI (QUASI PARISH) Rev. Jeremy Myers.
Mailing Address: 727 Travis St., Sherman, 75090. Church: 807 N. Union, 76273.
Catechesis/Religious Program—Margaret Pack, P.C.L. Students 44.
WYLIE, COLLIN CO., ST. ANTHONY (1858) [CEM] Deacon Walter Gove.
Res.: 404 N. Ballard, 75098. Tel: 972-442-2765; Fax: 972-429-9215. Web: www.saintanthony.com.
Catechesis/Religious Program—Students 630.

Chaplains of Public Institutions

DALLAS. *Baylor University Medical Center*, 3500 Gaston Ave., 75246. Tel: 214-820-2558. Deacon Hugo A. Salinas, Rev. Benito Tamez.
Childrens Medical Center of Dallas, 1935 Motor St., 75235. Tel: 214-456-2822. Mrs. Shannon Burk, Chap.
Dallas/Fort Worth Airport Catholic Chaplain, 180 Samuel Blvd., Coppell, 75019. Tel: 972-393-5544. Deacon Ed Scarbrough.
Doctors Hospital, Tel: 214-321-0454. Rev. Martin Moreno.
Medical City Dallas Hospital, 7777 Forest Ln., 75230. Tel: 972-530-3004. Deacon Carl H. Thelin.
Methodist Charlton Medical Center, 3500 W. Wheatland Rd., 75237. Tel: 214-947-2470. Rev. Daniel Clayton.
Methodist Dallas Medical Center, 1441 N. Beckley Ave., 75265. Tel: 214-947-2470. Rev. Daniel Clayton.
Parkland Health & Hospital System, 5201 Harry Hines Blvd., 75235. Tel: 214-590-8512. Rev. Luis Buitrago, Luz Maria de la Paz Austin, Chap.
Texas Health Presbyterian Hospital - Dallas, 8200 Walnut Hill Ln., 75231. Tel: 214-345-7158. Deacon Paul Husting.
UT Southwestern University Medical Center, 5909 Harry Hines Blvd., 75390. Tel: 214-645-1155. Ryan Campbell, Chap., Merrilee Kralik, Chap.
VA - North Texas Health Care System, 2926 E. Ledbetter Dr., 75216. Tel: 214-374-7952. Rev. Timothy Gollob.
BONHAM. *Sam Rayburn Memorial Veterans Center*, 1201 E. 9th St., 75418. Tel: 214-682-6458. Rev. Wilson Blas.
PLANO. *Children's Medical Center - Legacy*, 7609 Preston Rd., 75024. Tel: 469-303-2822. Mr. Witek Nowosiad, Chap.
SEAGOVILLE. *Federal Correctional Institution*, 2113 N. Hwy. 75, 75159. Tel: 972-287-2911. Rev. Wilmo Candanedo, O.P., Deacon Ismael A. Guerra.
TERRELL. *State Hospital*, 701 N. Frances St., 75160. Tel: 972-563-3643. Rev. Msgr. Glenn D. Gardner, J.C.D.

On Duty Outside the Diocese:
Revs.—
Martin, Sean, Aquinas Institute of Theology, 23 S. Spring Ave., St. Louis, MO 63108.
McKenna, James George, P.O. Box 190507, 75219.
Phan, Cho Dink Peter
Riemeh, Lawrence H., Jaffa Gate, Old City, P.O. Box 14622, Jerusalem, Israel.
Sanchez, Rodolfo, Blessed Sacrament, 4015 Sherman, Houston, 77003-2695.

On Leave of Absence:
Revs.—
Alvarez, Ramon
Austin, Jonathan
Heines, Timothy
Mallinson, Arthur D.
Speiser, Thomas M.

Retired:
Rev. Msgrs.—
Cuschieri, Albert, V.F., 218 Sisters St., Tarxien TNX1046 Malta.
Johnson, Robert, 14 Greccio Ct., Crowley, 76036.
Meyers, John F., 6211 W. Northwest Hwy., Ste. 225, 75225.
Rehkemper, Robert C., 1111 E. Sandy Lake Rd., Coppell, 75019.
Weinzapfel, Thomas, 321 Crooked Creek, Garland, 75043.
Revs.—
Beyer, Lawrence A., 4918 Forest Bend, 75244.
Caldwell, Fred, 1507 Bethlehem Rd., Ennis, 75002.
Chen, Peter, 1135 E. Sandy Lake Rd., Coppell, 75019.
Corcoran, Stanley D., 1115 E. Sandy Lake Rd., Coppell, 75019.
Diez, Oscar
Drozd, Henry J., P.O. Box 42063, Savannah, GA 31409-0001.
Fernandez, Edward P., 1147 E. Sandy Lake Rd., Coppell, 75019.
Fowler, John W., 1444 Rodando, Garland, 75042. Tel: 972-205-9307
Haugh, John, 1139 E. Sandy Lake Rd., Coppell, 75019.
Jayasuriya, Jerome, 305 Blake Ln., Midlothian, 76039.
Ortega, Efren
Pratt, Dean, 906 Lake Paint Cir., Mc Kinney, 75070.
Scott, Raymond, 1147 E. Sandy Lake Rd., Coppell, 75019.
Sharp, James, 5621 Cornerstone Dr., Garland, 75043. Tel: 973-681-8915
Slovacek, Emil C., 1815 Hamlet, 75203.
Villaroya, Ernesto
Weaver, Richard, 15736 Golden Creek Rd., 75248.
White, Gale, 16 St. Louis, Crowley, 76036. Tel: 214-357-4312

Permanent Deacons:
Alt, Les, (Retired)
Argumaniz, Fernando L., (Retired)
Ashley, Frank B., (On Duty Outside the Diocese)
Avila, Tomas
Bathea, Val Vincent
Berens, LeRoy J., (On Duty Outside the Diocese)
Boduch, Robert, (Retired)
Bolesta, Michael
Bourland, Fred, (On Duty Outside the Diocese)
Boyd, Douglas
Bryant, Dennis Phillip
Burkel, James
Carrell, Michael A., (Retired)
Catsoris, John A., (Retired)
Cerrato, Jesus, Jr.
Chung, Hoan Moses
Coffey, Thomas, (On Duty Outside the Diocese)
Corbin, Denis D.
Cortes, Abel
Cortinas, Leopoldo, III
Costello, John R.
Covarrubias, Dan
Crawley, Denver
Culling, Joseph
Daniels, James
Davis, Lee B.
De La Garza, John, (On Duty Outside the Diocese)
Delin, Fred O., (Retired)
Dorsey, Timothy, (On Duty Outside the Diocese)
Ellerbrock, Michael, (On Duty Outside the Diocese)
Elsberg, Alick, (On Duty Outside the Diocese)
Engel, Randall L.
Evans, Al
Fejeran, Ronald
Flynn, Bill
Fobes, Bill
Forbrich, Don
Franklin, Sam, (Retired)
French, Shawn Patrick, (On Duty Outside the Diocese)
Friedman, William L., (On Duty Outside the Diocese)
Garcia, Benito
Gette, Roger
Gonzales, Gonzalo
Gonzalez, Ronald, (On Duty Outside the Diocese)
Gove, Walter
Griffith, Don
Guerra, Ismael A.
Gulino, Jack
Gutting, Justin, (Retired)
Gutting, Paul, (On Duty Outside the Diocese)
Hale, Kenneth
Hancock, John, (On Duty Outside the Diocese)
Harmon, Larry
Harrington, Richard
Harris, Jim
Hatch, Larry G., (On Duty Outside the Diocese)
Havard, Bronson
Hayes, Patrick
Hopkins, Jack
Husting, Paul
Ibarra, Juan, (On Duty Outside the Diocese)
Jimenez, Vincent F.
Jones, Edward S., (On Duty Outside the Diocese)
Kahrs, Greg
Kelly, John Paul
Killgo, Kory
Kozarevich, Frank, (Retired)
LeBlanc, John D.
Leerssen, David
Leicht, Robert R., Jr., (On Duty Outside the Diocese)
Leyden, Edward
Little, Sid
Lopez, Al
Lucido, Larry
Macero, Carl, Sr.
Machiano, Victor M.
Maida, David
Markwald, Pete
Marrinan, Robert, Sr.
Martinez, Onesimo
McAlister, Craig, (On Duty Outside the Diocese)
McAllister, Jerome, (Retired)
Melston, Kenneth
Miller, Albert
Miller, Carl V., (On Duty Outside the Diocese)
Miller, J. Robert
Milliken, Frank M.
Mitchell, Brian
Monsanto, Hugo
Montes, Jesus Alberto
Morales, Sergio
Morgan, Ron
Muldoon, Tim
Munoz, Louis L.
Nordick, John C.
O'Leary, John
Obergfell, David T.
Olivarez, Jesse
Olvera, Isidro
Orozco, Adolph, Jr., (Retired)
Osborne, Charles, (Retired)
Palms, Howard
Palos, Lewis J.
Perez, Joe R.
Peña, Héctor B.
Picard, Michael
Picon, Arnold
Polcer, George
Powers, Paul
Putonti, Edward
Rasins, Michael R., Sr., (On Duty Outside the Diocese)
Reisor, Kenneth
Reittinger, Paul W.
Rener, Bonnie Leo
Reyna, Frank
Roche, Thomas
Rodriguez, Fermin
Rodriguez, Pete
Salinas, Hugo A.
Sanchez, Robert
Scarbrough, Ed
Schell, John A.
Schnurr, Don, (Retired)
Schuster, William J.
Segovia, Daniel D.
Seibold, Michael
Shaw, Michael, (Retired)
Simon, Denis
Smith, Raymond H.
Starr, Jim
Stieber, Lee, (Retired)
Stump, Charles, Jr.
Sykora, Richard, (On Duty Outside the Diocese)
Sylvester, Charles T.
Thelin, Carl H.
Tompsett, David E.
Trevino, Antonio D.
Trevino, Jose
Vega, Frutos
Veyna, Manuel, (Retired)
Vogel, Gary M.
Washington, Warner, (Retired)
Webb, Philip E.
Weston, Michael
Wong, Peter
Wood, Paul
Zacek, George E., (On Duty Outside the Diocese)

INSTITUTIONS LOCATED IN THE DIOCESE

[A] SEMINARIES, DIOCESAN

DALLAS. *The Redemptoris Mater House of Formation*, P.O. Box 211669, 75211. Tel: 214-467-2255; Fax: 214-467-5440. Email: rector@rmdallas.org. Very Rev. Fernando Carranza, Rector & Contact Person; Rev. Eduardo Gonzalez-Martinez, Vice Rector. Students 20.

IRVING. *Holy Trinity Seminary* Diocesan College and Pre-Theology Seminary., P.O. Box 140309, 75014-0309. Tel: 972-438-2212; Fax: 972-438-6530. Email: molson@holytrinityseminary.com. Web: www.holytrinityseminary.com. Very Rev. Michael F. Olson, Rector; Revs. James P. Oberle, S.S., Dir. Spiritual & Liturgical Formation; Ronald Ramson, C.M., Spiritual Dir.; Mr. Henry McDowell, Music Coord.; Juan Rendon, Dir. Pastoral Formation & Field Educ.; Dr. William Brownsberger, Dir. Intellectual Formation. Priests 3; Seminarians 47; Lay Faculty 3; Total Staff 4.

[B] COLLEGES AND UNIVERSITIES

IRVING. *University of Dallas*, President's Office, 1845 E. Northgate, 75062. Tel: 972-721-5203; Fax: 972-721-4040. Students 2,883.

Administrative Officers: Most Rev. Kevin J. Farrell, D.D., Chancellor; Mr. Robert Galecke, Interim Pres.; Mr. Robert Galecke, Exec. Vice Pres.; Geralyn Franklin, Dean, College of Business.

Cistercian Priests: Revs. David Balas, O.Cist., Ph.D., S.T.D.; Ralph March, O.Cist., Ph.D.; Roch Keresz Ty; James Lehrberger, O.Cist., Ph.D.; Robert Maguire, O.Cist., Ph.D.

[C] HIGH SCHOOLS, DIOCESAN

DALLAS. *Bishop Dunne Catholic School, Inc.*, (Grades 6-12), (Coed), 3900 Rugged Dr., 75224. Tel: 214-339-6561; Fax: 214-339-1438. Email: kdailey@bdhs.org. Web: www.bdhs.org. Mr. Patrick O'Sullivan, Prin.; Kate Collins Dailey, Pres.; Lydia Torres, Dir. Devel. & Alumni; Melanie Gibson, Librarian. Sisters (S.S.N.D.) 1; Lay Teachers 51; Administrators 11; Students 614.

Bishop Lynch High School, Inc., 9750 Ferguson Rd., 75228. Tel: 214-324-3607; Fax: 214-324-3600. Email: edleyden@bishoplynch.org. Web: www.bishoplynch.org. Deacon Edward Leyden, Pres.; Evelyn Grubbs, Academic Dean; Rev. Victor Bartolotta, Chap.; Gerry Cantalope, Librarian. Priests 1; Sisters 1; Deacons 2; Lay Teachers 83; Total Staff 116; Students 1,108.

PLANO. *John Paul II High School, Inc.*, 900 Coit Rd., 75075. Tel: 972-867-0005; Fax: 972-867-7555. Web: www.johnpauliihs.org. Mr. Brian McPheeters, Vice Pres. Finance & Admin.

[D] HIGH SCHOOLS, PRIVATE

DALLAS. *Jesuit College Preparatory School* (Boys), 12345 Inwood Rd., 75244. Tel: 972-387-8700; Fax: 972-661-9349. Web: www.jesuitcp.org. Mr. Michael A. Earsing, Prin.; Revs. Philip S. Postell, S.J., Pres.; John F. Deeves, S.J.; Charles A. Leininger, S.J.; Bro. Gerald J. Landry, S.J.; Mr. Kevin Cormier, S.J.; Mr. Robert Murphy, S.J.; Mr. John Nugent, S.J.; Mr. Quan Tran, S.J.; Mark Wester, Librarian. Society of Jesus. Priests 3; Brothers 1; Scholastics 4; Lay Teachers 103; Students 1,040; Total Staff 108.

Ursuline Academy (Girls), 4900 Walnut Hill Ln., 75229. Tel: 469-232-1800; Fax: 469-232-1836. Email: srmoser@ursulinedallas.org. Web: www.ursulinedallas.org. Sr. Margaret Ann Moser, O.S.U., Pres.; Elizabeth C. Bourgeois, Prin.; Christy L. Frazer, Dir. Inst. Advancement. Priests 1; Faculty 86; Students 795.

IRVING. *Cistercian Preparatory School*, (Grades 5-12), 3660 Cistercian Rd., 75039-4500. Tel: 469-499-5400; Fax: 469-499-5440. Email: admissions@cistercian.org. Web: www.cistercian.org. Rev. Peter Verhalen, O.Cist., M.A., M.Th., Headmaster; Saranne Gans, Librarian. Cistercian Fathers of Our Lady of Dallas Abbey., (Boys) Priests 10; Brothers 4; Lay Teachers 36; Students 350.

The Highlands School, 1451 E. Northgate Dr., 75062. Tel: 972-554-1980; Fax: 972-721-1691. Email: highlands@thehighlandsschool.org. Web: www.TheHighlandsSchool.org. John Borley, Exec. Dir.; Dr. Paul Sullivan, Prin.; Revs. Christopher Scroggin, L.C., Supr.; Alfonse Nazzaro, L.C., Dir. Boys School; Michelle Reiff, Dir., Consecrated Women; Rev. Frank Formolo, L.C., Chap.; Catherine Hinkson, Librarian. Consecrated Women 4; Lay Teachers 48; High School 124; Middle 144; Elementary 142; Students 461.

[E] ELEMENTARY SCHOOLS, PRIVATE

DALLAS. **Catholic Charismatic Services of Dallas Texas, Inc. dba Mount St. Michael Catholic School* (Grades PreK-8), 4500 W. Davis St., 75211. Tel: 214-337-0244; Fax: 214-339-1702. Email: gmontgomery@msmcatholic.org. Web: www.msmcatholic.org. Mailing Address: P.O. Box 225159, 75222-5159. Gretchen Montgomery, Prin.; Mary Krieg, M.S., Librarian. Priests 2; Religious Sisters 1; Lay Teachers 20; Students 163; Total Staff 33.

IRVING. *The Highlands School*, (Grades PreK-8), 1451 E. Northgate Dr., 75062. Tel: 972-554-1980; Fax: 972-721-1691. Email: highlands@thehighlandsschool.org. Web: www.thehighlandsschool.org. Dr. Paul Sullivan, Prin.; John Borley, Exec. Dir.; Rev. Alfonse Nazzaro, L.C., Dir.; Michelle Reiff, Dir., Consecrated Women; Revs. Christopher Scroggin, L.C., Supr.; Frank Formolo, L.C., Chap.; Catherine Hinkson, Librarian. Priests 3; Brothers 1; Consecrated Women 4; Lay Teachers 48; Students 461; Total Staff 23.

[F] SPECIAL SCHOOLS, PRIVATE

DALLAS. *Notre Dame of Dallas Schools, Inc.*, 2018 Allen St., 75204. Tel: 214-720-3911; Fax: 214-720-3913. Email: tfrancis@notredameschool.org. Web: www.notredameschool.org. Ms. Theresa Francis, Prin. Day School: Provides instructional education for mentally retarded children, ages 6-15.; Vocational Center: Provides vocational training for young adults, ages 16-21. Sisters 1; Lay Staff 37; Teachers 17; Assistants 13; Students 144.

[G] CATHOLIC CHARITIES

DALLAS. *Catholic Charities of Dallas, Inc.*, 9461 LBJ Fwy., Ste. 100, 75243. Tel: 214-520-6590; Fax: 214-520-6595. Email: mowens@central.catholiccharitiesdallas.org. Web: www.CatholicCharitiesDallas.org. Sr. Mary Anne Owens, S.S.N.D.

Elderly and Family Assistance Services, 4009 Elm St., 75226. Tel: 214-826-8330; Fax: 214-826-8579. Email: mharris@brady.catholiccharitiesdallas.org. Web: www.catholiccharitiesdallas.org. Michelle Harris, Div. Dir. Multiple locations offer bilingual social services. Also includes PAN program.

PAN Program Tel: 214-330-1396, Ext. 121.

Immigration and Legal Services, 5415 Maple Ave., Ste. 400, 75235. Tel: 214-634-7182; Fax: 214-634-2531. Email: vanna@ccicsdallas.org. Web: www.catholiccharitiesdallas.org. Vanna Slaughter, L.C.S.W., Div. Dir.

St. Martin Family Service Center, Inc., 9461 LBJ Freeway, Ste. 100, 75243. Tel: 214-520-6590; Fax: 214-520-6595. Web: www.catholiccharitiesdallas.org. Purpose: To operate facilities in which social services are provided to assist the poor and indigent families of Dallas to become self-reliant.

Professional Counseling and Children's Services, 9461 LBJ Freeway, Ste. 100, 75243. Tel: 214-526-2772; Fax: 214-526-2941. Barbara Tenbroek, Div. Dir.

Maternity and Adoption Program Tel: 214-526-2772; (800) BABY-DUE; Fax: 214-526-2941.

Mary R. Saner Child Development Center, 2827 Lapsley St., 75212. Tel: 214-638-1635; Fax: 214-905-0822. Web: www.catholiccharitiesdallas.org.

Refugee and Empowerment Services, 9850 Walnut Hill Ln., Ste. 228, 75238. Tel: 214-553-9909; Fax: 214-553-8116. Email: mrs@catholiccharitiesdallas.org. Web: www.catholiccharitiesdallas.org. Dionne Davis, Div. Dir.

[H] EDUCATION CENTERS

DALLAS. *Mount Carmel Center*, 4600 W. Davis St., 75211-3498. Tel: 214-331-6224; Fax: 214-330-0844. Web: www.mountcarmelcenter.org. Revs. Stephen Sanchez, O.C.D., Prog. Dir.; Jerome Earley, O.C.D., Supr. Discalced Carmelite Fathers of the Southwestern Province., Adult Center for Catholic Spirituality

Mount St. Michael Spiritual Life Center, 4500 W. Davis St., 75211. Tel: 214-331-1754; Fax: 214-333-1659. Sr. Yolanda Martinez, O.L.C., Supr. Adult Center for Catholic Spirituality Sisters of Our Lady of Charity of Refuge 8.

[I] PERSONAL PRELATURES

IRVING. *Opus Dei* Prelature of the Holy Cross and Opus Dei, 3610 Wingren, 75062. Tel: 972-650-0064; Fax: 972-717-3580. Email: info@opusdei.org. Web: www.opusdei.org. Revs. Derrick Esclanda; John E. Solarski.

[J] MONASTERIES AND RESIDENCES OF PRIESTS

DALLAS. *Capuchin Franciscan Friars, Vice Province of Texas*, 5605 Bernal Dr., 75212. Tel: 214-500-8595; Fax: 214-637-2454. Email: mtellitu@yahoo.com. Revs. Mario Garcia, O.F.M.Cap. (Spain), Vice Prov.; Pablo Jaramillo, O.F.M.Cap. (Mexico); Roberto Viveros, O.F.M.Cap. (Mexico); Bros. Aldo Fabricio Munoz; Cristian Alejandro Barragan. Priests 3; Brothers 2.

Congregation of the Mission, Western Province, 3826 Gilbert Ave., 75219. Tel: 214-526-0234; Fax: 214-526-2421. Email: cmstlouis@vincentian.org. Web: www.vincentian.org. Revs. Juan Antonio Ruiz, C.M.; Dan Paul Borlik, C.M.; Paul Sauerbier, C.M.; Richard Rex Hays, C.M.; F. Patrick Hanser, C.M.; Bro. Thomas Juneman, C.M. Priests 6; Brothers 1.

St. John Neumann Formation House, 3912 S. Ledbetter Dr., 75236. Tel: 972-296-6759; Fax: 972-296-6765. Email: longcssr@yahoo.com. Web: www.chuacunthe.org. Revs. Dominic Long Nguyen, C.Ss.R., Formation Dir. & Contact Person; Joseph Hung Le, C.Ss.R.

Mt. Carmel Center, 4600 W. Davis St., 75211. Tel: 214-331-6224; Fax: 214-330-0844. Web: www.mountcarmelcenter.org. Revs. Stephen Sanchez, O.C.D., Prog. Dir.; Jerome Earley, O.C.D., Contact Person & Supr.

IRVING. *Cistercian Abbey of Our Lady of Dallas*, 3550 Cistercian Rd., 75039. Tel: 972-438-2044; Fax: 972-579-7637. Email: DMFDenis@aol.com. Web: www.cistercian.org. Rt. Rev. Denis M. Farkasfalvy, O.Cist., S.S.L., M.S., S.T.D., Abbot, Vicar of the Abbot Pres. of Zirc; Revs. Peter Verhalen, O.Cist., M.A., M.Th., Prior; Ralph March, O.Cist., Ph.D.; Bernard Marton, O.Cist., S.T.D., Subprior; Benedict Monostori, O.Cist., Ph.D.; Bede Lackner, O.Cist., Ph.D.; Pascal Kis-Horvath, O.Cist.; Aloysius Kimecz, O.Cist., M.A.; David Balas, O.Cist., Ph.D., S.T.D.; Matthew Kovacs, O.Cist., M.A.; Melchior Chladek, O.Cist., M.A.; Rochus Kereszty, O.Cist., S.T.D.; Julius Leloczky, O.Cist., S.T.D.; James Lehrberger, O.Cist., Ph.D.; Robert Maguire, O.Cist., Ph.D.; Gregory Schweers, O.Cist., M.A.; Mark Ripperger, O.Cist., M.A.; Paul McCormick, O.Cist., M.A.; Joseph Van House, O.Cist., S.T.L.; Bros. John Bayer, O.Cist., B.A.; Anthony Bigney, O.Cist., B.A.; Philip Neri Lastimosa, O.Cist., B.A.; Augustine Hoelke, O.Cist., M.T.L.; Thomas Esposito, O.Cist., B.A., S.T.B.; Ignatius Peacher, O.Cist., B.A.; Ambrose Strong, O.Cist., B.A., M.Th.; Stephen Gregg, O.Cist., B.A.; Lawrence Brophy, O.Cist., M.S., B.A.; Nathanael Frei, O.Cist., B.A.; Justin McNamara, O.Cist., B.A. Priests 18; Brothers 11.

Dominican Priory of St. Albert the Great and Novitiate, 3150 Vince Hagan Dr., 75062-4701. Tel: 972-438-1626; Fax: 972-438-6948. Very Rev. Donald Dvorak, O.P., Prior; Revs. Wilmo Candanedo, O.P., Novice Master & Vicar; Roberto Merced, O.P., Subprior; Edward M. Robinson, O.P.; Carl Trutter, O.P.; Bros. Cristobal Torres, Novice; Jose Orozco, Novice; Brian Thomas, Novice; Jeremy Hanzelka, Novice; Mauricio Salazar, O.P. Priests 5; Brothers 6; Deacons 1; Novices 4.

Legionaries of Christ, 3813 Cabeza de Vaca Cir., 75062. Tel: 972-890-3892; Fax: 972-281-5243. Email: dallas@legionaries.org. Web: www.thehighlandsschool.org. Revs. Christopher Scroggin, L.C., Supr., Contact Person; Frank Formolo, L.C.; Alfonse Nazzaro, L.C.; Bros. Lucio Bocacci, L.C.; Michael Sullivan, L.C. Priests 3; Brothers 2.

[K] CONVENTS AND RESIDENCES FOR SISTERS

DALLAS. *Bethany House*, 3017 Mallory, 75216. Tel: 214-371-4867. Email: patricia.ridgley@gmail.com. Web: www.ssmnwestern.com. Sr. Patricia Ann Ridgley, S.S.M.N., Contact Person. Sisters of St. Mary of Namur. Sisters 3.

Daughters of the Sacred Heart, 7621 Cortland Ave., 75235. Tel: 214-351-4338. Sisters 7.

Missionaries of Charity, 2704 Harlandale, 75216. Tel: 214-374-3351. Sr. M. Celian, M.C, Supr. Sisters 4.

Missionary Catechist of the Poor, 950 N. Montclair Ave., 75208. Tel: 214-942-2799; Fax: 214-942-2799. Email: gucadi@yahoo.com. Sr. Guadalupe Carreno Diaz, M.C.P., Supr. Sisters 6.

Monastery of Discalced Carmelites, 600 Flowers Ave., 75211. Tel: 214-330-7440; Fax: 214-623-1885. Sr. Mary Regina, O.C.D., Prioress. Professed Sisters 12.

School Sisters of Notre Dame, P.O. Box 227275, 75222. Tel: 214-330-9152; Fax: 214-330-9197. Web: www.ssnd.org. Sr. Addie L. Walker, S.S.N.D., Provincial. Sisters 19.

Provincial House of the Dallas Province, 4500 W. Davis, 75211. Tel: 214-330-9152; Fax: 214-330-9197. Prov. Sisters 127.

Ursuline Sisters, 9905 Inwood Rd., 75220. Tel: 214-358-3922. Web: www.osucentral.org. Sisters 9.

GRAND PRAIRIE. *Sisters of the Holy Family of Nazareth* (Holy Family Province), 1814 Egyptian Way, 75053. Tel: 972-641-4496; Fax: 972-641-1668. Web: www.nazarethcsfm.org. Sr. Edyta Krawczyk, C.S.F.N., Counselor. Sisters 35.

IRVING. *Congregation of Mary, Queen-American Region (CMR)*, 723 Sunset Dr., 75061. Tel: 469-417-0123. Email: cmrvocation@yahoo.com. Web: www.trinhvuong.org. Sisters Teresita Au, C.M.R., Teacher; Gwen Do, C.M.R., Teacher; Jacinta Tran, C.M.R., D.R.E., Contact Person & P.C.L.; Janine Tran, C.M.R., Vocation Dir. Perpetually Professed Religious 5.

[L] CAMPUS MINISTRY

DALLAS. *Southern Methodist University* Neuhoff Catholic Ctr., 3057 University Blvd., 75205. Tel: 214-987-0044; Fax: 214-987-3731. Anna LeBlanc, Dir. Devel.; John P. Lichon, Campus Min.; Erin Duffy, Campus Min.; Frank Santoni, Dir.

IRVING. *University of Dallas* 1845 E. Northgate Dr., 75062. Tel: 972-721-5375; Fax: 972-721-5351. Rev. Rodolfo García, Chap. & Rector; Denise G. Phillips, Dir. Campus Ministry.

[M] MISCELLANEOUS LISTINGS

DALLAS. *Bishop Dunne Catholic School Building and Endowment Fund*, 3900 Rugged Dr., 75224. Tel: 214-339-6561; Fax: 214-339-1438. Web: www.bdhs.org. Kate Dailey, Pres.

Bishop Grahmann Education Endowment Fund, P.O. Box 190507, 75219. Tel: 214-528-2240; Fax: 214-523-2422. Most Rev. Kevin J. Farrell, D.D., Trustee; Michael T. Weis, Contact Person. Trust Fund for Inner City Diocesan Schools

Bishop Lynch High School Building and Endowment Trust, 9750 Ferguson Rd., 75228. Tel: 214-324-3607; Fax: 214-327-8242. Email: jayniepoff@bishoplynch.org. Deacon Edward Leyden, Pres.

Carmelite Nuns Foundation, 600 Flowers Ave., 75211. Tel: 214-373-2739; Fax: 214-373-2788. Sr. Mary Regina Parrish, Prioress.

Cathedral Restoration and Preservation Fund, Inc., 2215 Ross Ave., 75201. Tel: 214-871-1362; Fax: 214-954-1557. Rev. J. Eduardo Gonzalez, Rector.

**St. Catherine of Siena, Inc.*, 13223 Glad Acres Dr., 75234. Tel: 972-241-1272; Fax: 972-241-1214. Email: usa1@airmail.net. Joseph W. Dingman, Sec. & Treas.

**Catholic Charismatic Services of Dallas Texas, Inc. dba Christian Community of God's Delight* 4500 W. Davis-Clement Hall, P.O. Box 225008, 75211. Tel: 214-333-2337; Fax: 214-333-2595. Email: v.bezner@msmcatholic.org.

Catholic Charities Endowment Trust, 9461 LBJ Fwy., Ste. 100, 75243. Tel: 214-520-6590; Fax: 214-520-6595. Web: www.catholiccharitiesdallas.org. Sr. Mary Anne Owens, S.S.N.D.

Catholic Community Appeal, Inc., 3725 Blackburn St., P.O. Box 190507, 75219. Tel: 214-528-2240; Fax: 214-526-1743. Email: pvitanza@cathdal.org. Web: www.cathdal.org. Paul Vitanza, C.F.R.E., Dir.

Catholic Community Educational Services of Dallas, Inc., P.O. Box 190507, 75219. Tel: 214-379-2873; Fax: 214-520-3247. Email: agtaylor@cathdal.org. Annette G. Taylor, Pres.

The Catholic Pro-Life Committee of North Texas, Inc., P.O. Box 59852, 75229. Tel: 972-267-LIFE; Fax: 972-385-3851. Email: cplc@prolifedallas.org. Web: www.prolifedallas.org. Karen Garnett, Exec. Dir.

Commission on Ecumenism, P.O. Box 190507, 75219. Tel: 214-528-2240; Fax: 214-523-2429. Lynn Rossol, Contact Person; Rev. Robert Williams, Chm.; Margie Medlin, Member; Mildred D. Pope, Member; Sandra Gist, Member.

Dallas Deanery Council of Catholic Women, 2629 Winslow Dr., Grand Prairie, 75052. Tel: 972-660-4257; Fax: 972-660-5871. Liz Mullen, Pres.

Dallas Diocesan Council of Catholic Women, 7306 Heathermore, 75248. Tel: 972-377-9244. Email: roseanddwh@aol.com. Ellen Stelmar, Pres.; Rose Harder, Contact Person.

Dallas Vocation Guild, P.O. Box 12153, 75225. Tel: 214-379-2812. Email: blandregan@cathdal.org. Barbara Landregan.

Dave Fox Inner City Education Fund, P.O. Box 190507, 75219. Tel: 214-528-2240; Fax: 214-523-2422. Most Rev. Kevin J. Farrell, D.D., Trustee; Michael T. Weis, Contact Person. Trust Fund for Inner City Diocesan Schools

Diocesan Seminary Burse Endowment Fund Trust, P.O. Box 190507, 75219. Tel: 214-528-2240; Fax: 214-523-2422. Most Rev. Kevin J. Farrell, D.D., Trustee; Michael T. Weis, Contact Person. Trust Fund for education of seminarians for Diocese of Dallas.

Elementary Principals Association of the Diocese of Dallas, Inc. dba Dallas Parochial League P.O. Box 190507, 75219. Tel: 214-528-2240; Fax: 214-523-2422. Michael T. Weis, Contact Person.

James L. Collins Catholic School Education Trust, P.O. Box 190507, 75219. Tel: 214-528-2240; Fax: 214-523-2422. Michael T. Weis, Contact Person.

St. Joseph Residence, Inc., 330 W. Pembroke, 75208. Tel: 214-948-3597; Fax: 214-948-1209. Email: srab@stjr.org. Sr. Adelaide Bocanegra, Bethl., Admin. For elderly ladies, gentlemen, and couples. Conducted by Daughters of the Sacred Heart of Jesus (Bethlemitas). Sisters 6; Residents 49.

Ladies of Charity of Dallas, P.O. Box 595666, 75359-0666. Tel: 214-821-5713. Email: ladiesofcharitydallas@sbcglobal.net. Web: www.ladiesofcharity.com. Sue Ann Gilman, Pres.

Lieutenancy, Equestrian Order of the Holy Sepulchre of Jerusalem formerly Southwestern Lieutenancy, Equestrian Order of the Holy Sepulchre of Jerusalem 7303 Lane Park Ct., 75225. Tel: 214-369-5705; Fax: 214-239-2202. Email: jkacpa@flash.net. Jim Abney, Dallas Area Representative.

**St. Martin de Porres, Inc.*, 13223 Glad Acres Dr., 75234. Tel: 972-241-1272; Fax: 972-241-1214. Email: usa1@airmail.net. Web: www.wellingtonplaceapts.net. Joseph W. Dingman, Sec. & Treas. Mixed-income housing.

Mary Benavidez Education Fund, P.O. Box 190507, 75219. Tel: 214-528-2240; Fax: 214-523-2422. Most Rev. Kevin J. Farrell, D.D., Trustee; Michael T. Weis, Contact Person. Trust Fund for the education of Hispanics.

St. Mary of Carmel Building Trust, 2900 Vilbig Rd., 75212. Tel: 214-747-1433. Email: smcocd@smcocdschool.org.

Mater Dei Latin Mass Community, 6228 Winton St., 75214.

The National Cursillo Center and Office of the National Secretariat, 4500 W. Davis, 75211. Tel: 214-339-6321; Fax: 214-339-6322. Email: nationalcursillo.center@verizon.net. Web: www.natl-cursillo.org. P.O. Box 210226, 75211.

Tel: 214-339-6321; Fax: 214-339-6322. Victor Lugo, Natl. Exec. Dir.; Joachim Thong Le, Vietnamese Language Coord.; Jorge Barcelo, Hispanic Coord.; Ceferino Aguillon, English Language Coord.

Dallas Cursillo Center, 5605 Bernal Dr., 75212. Tel: 214-631-7775. Rev. Roberto Viveros, O.F.M.Cap. (Mexico), Spiritual Dir.

**New Evangelization of America*, 414 Ridgewood Dr., Richardson, 75080. Tel: 469-867-9650. Email: neamail@msn.com. Web: neawebsite.org. Gracie Stanford, Sec.

Nuestra Senora del Pilar Land & Development Trust, 4455W. Illinois Ave., 75211. Tel: 214-467-9116; Fax: 214-339-7249. Email: pilar.church@sbcglobal.net. Rev. Wilmer de Jesus Daza.

Santa Clara Endowment Fund Trust, P.O. Box 190507, 75219. Tel: 214-528-2240; Fax: 214-523-2422. Most Rev. Kevin J. Farrell, D.D., Trustee; Michael T. Weis, Contact Person. Trust Fund to support Santa Clara School.

School Sisters of Notre Dame of Dallas Charitable Trust, 4500 W. Davis, 75211. Tel: 214-330-9152; Fax: 214-330-9197. Web: www.ssnd.org. P.O. Box 227275, 75222-7275.

**St. Stephen, Inc.*, 13223 Glad Acres Dr., 75234. Tel: 972-241-1272; Fax: 972-241-1214. Email: usa1@airmail.net. Web: westlakevillageapartments.com. Joseph W. Dingman, Sec. & Treas. Mixed-income housing.

The Timon Trust, 3826 Gilbert Ave., 75219.

Ursuline Academy of Dallas Foundation, Inc., 4900 Walnut Hill, 75229. Tel: 469-232-3584; Fax: 469-232-3593. Email: cfrazer@ursulinedallas.org. Web: www.ursulinedallas.org. Sr. Margaret Ann Moser, O.S.U., Pres.; Christy L. Frazer, Dir. Inst. Advancement.

**Villa Santa Maria, Inc.*, 13223 Glad Acres Dr., 75234. Tel: 972-241-1272; Fax: 972-241-1272. Email: usa1@airmail.net. Web: peacerealty.com. Joseph W. Dingman, Sec. & Treas. Affordable senior housing

ALLEN. *St. Jude Parish Building Trust*, 1515 N. Greenville Ave., 75002. Tel: 972-727-1177; Fax: 972-727-1401. Email: shawthorne@stjudeparish.com. Web: www.stjudeparish.com. Sue Hawthorne, Contact Person.

Our Lady of Angels Building Trust, Mailing Address: 1914 Ridgeview Dr., 75013. Tel: 469-467-9669; Fax: 469-467-0114. Email: fsantos@ourladyofangels.com. Web: www.ourladyofangels.com. Fernando Santos, Contact Person.

GRAND PRAIRIE. *One America International, Inc.*, 3702 Iris Dr., 75052. Tel: 972-642-7841. Web: www.oneamericainternational.org. Thomas Matasso, Pres.

IRVING. *CHRISTUS Health*, 6363 N. Hwy. 161, Ste. 450, 75038. Tel: 877-980-0100; Fax: 214-492-8540. Email: john.zipprich@christushealth.org. Web: www.Christushealth.org. Thomas C. Royer, M.D., Pres. & CEO; William Pardue, Contact Person.

CHRISTUS St. Joseph Village, 1201 E. Sandy Lake Rd., Coppell, 75019. Tel: 972-304-0300; Fax: 972-462-1099. Email: kim.bomgardner@christushealth.org. Kim Bomgardner, Exec. Dir.

CHRISTUS Health Foundation, 6363 Hwy. 161 N., Ste. 450, 75038. Tel: 281-936-3184; Fax: 281-936-7802. Email: larry.pardue@christushealth.org.

Holy Trinity Seminary Scholarship Trust, P.O. Box 140309, 75014. Tel: 979-438-2212; Fax: 972-438-6530.

PLANO. *St. Elizabeth Ann Seton Parish Building Trust*, 2701 Piedra Dr., 75023. Tel: 972-596-5505; Fax: 972-985-7573. Email: twooliscroft@eseton.org. Web: www.setonparish.org. Terry Wooliscroft, Dir. Finance & Admin.

John Paul II High School Building and Endowment Fund, 900 Coit Rd., 75075. Tel: 469-229-5112; Fax: 972-867-7555. Email: brianmcpheeters@johnpauliihs.org. Web: www.johnpauliihs.org. Mr. Brian McPheeters, Vice Pres. Finance & Admin.

RICHARDSON. *Pastors Professional Development Endowment Trust*, 923 Creekdale Dr., 75080. Tel: 972-238-9382; Fax: 972-238-9276.

St. Paul Parish Endowment Trust Fund, 709 James Dr., 75080. Tel: 972-235-6105; Fax: 972-480-8528.

RELIGIOUS INSTITUTES OF MEN REPRESENTED IN THE DIOCESE

For further details refer to the corresponding bracketed number in the Religious Institutes of Men or Women section.

[0200]—*Benedictine Monks*—O.S.B.
[0470]—*The Capuchin Friars*—O.F.M.Cap.
[0340]—*Cistercian Fathers*—O.Cist.
[0260]—*Discalced Carmelite Friars* (Oklahoma Prov.)—O.C.D.
[]—*Incarnatio Consecratio Missionaries*
[0690]—*Jesuit Fathers and Brothers* (New Orleans Prov.)—S.J.
[0730]—*Legionaries of Christ*—L.C.
[]—*Misioneros de la Natividad de Maria*—M.N.M.
[1210]—*Missionaries of St. Charles-Scalabrinians*—C.S.
[]—*Missionaries of St. Thomas the Apostle*—M.S.T.
[0430]—*Order of Preachers (Dominicans)* (Southern Dominican Prov.)—O.P.
[1310]—*Order of the Holy Trinity*—O.SS.T.
[1065]—*Priestly Fraternity of St Peter*—F.S.S.P.
[1070]—*Redemptorists, Congregation of Most Holy Redeemer*—C.SS.R.
[1260]—*Society of Christ*—S.Ch.
[]—*Society of Damus Dei*—S.D.D.
[1290]—*Society of the Priests of St. Sulpice*—S.S.
[1330]—*Vincentian Fathers* (Southern Prov.)—C.M.

RELIGIOUS INSTITUTES OF WOMEN REPRESENTED IN THE DIOCESE

[0910]—*Bethlemita, Daughters of the Sacred Heart of Jesus*—Bethl.
[0370]—*Carmelite Sisters of the Sacred Heart*—O.C.D.
[]—*Congregation of Mary Queen*—C.M.R.
[]—*Daughters of the Sacred Heart*—D.S.H.
[0420]—*Discalced Carmelite Nuns*—O.C.D.
[1070-03]—*Dominican Sisters*—O.P.
[2710]—*Missionaries of Charity*—M.C.
[]—*Missionary Catechists of the Poor* (Mexico)—M.C.P.
[2970]—*School Sisters of Notre Dame*—S.S.N.D.
[]—*Sisters of Blessed Korean Martyrs*
[3071]—*Sisters of Our Lady of Charity*—O.L.C.
[3950]—*Sisters of Saint Mary of Namur* (Western Prov.)—S.S.M.N.
[1970]—*Sisters of the Holy Family of Nazareth* (Sacred Heart Vice Prov.)—C.S.F.N.
[2050]—*Sisters of the Holy Spirit and Mary Immaculate*—S.H.Sp.
[2205]—*Sisters of the Incarnate Word and Blessed Sacrament*—I.W.B.S.
[4110]—*Ursuline Nuns (Roman Union)* (Central Prov.)—O.S.U.

DIOCESAN CEMETERIES

DALLAS. *Calvary Hill Cemetery*, Mailing Address: 3235 Lombardy Ln., 75220. Tel: 214-357-5754; Fax: 214-357-1271. Web: www.calvaryhillcemetery.com. A corporation that owns and operates Diocesan cemeteries

Old Cavalry Hill formerly Calvary Hill Cemetery and Old Cavalry Hill 2500 N. Hall St., 75201. Tel: 214-357-5754; Fax: 214-357-1271.

Holy Redeemer Cemetery, Desoto, 75115.

Sacred Heart Cemetery, Rowlett, 75088.

PARISH COLUMBARIA

FARMERS BRANCH. *Mary Immaculate Church*, 2800 Valwood Pkwy., 75234. Tel: 972-243-7104.

PLANO. *Prince of Peace Church*, 5100 Plano Pkwy., 75093.

RICHARDSON. *St. Joseph Church*, 600 S. Jupiter Rd., 75081.

PARISH CEMETERIES

ENNIS. *St. Joseph Cemetery, St. John Nepomucene Parish*, 401 E. Lampasas, 75119. Tel: 972-878-2834; Fax: 972-875-2452.

WYLIE. *St. Paul Cemetery, St. Anthony Parish*, 404 N. Ballard Ave., 75098. Tel: 972-442-2765; Fax: 972-429-9215.

NECROLOGY

† Gray, Paul, Dallas, TX All Saints—Died Oct. 1, 2009

An asterisk (*) denotes an organization that has established tax-exempt status directly with the IRS and is not covered by the USCCB Group Ruling.

Diocese of Davenport

(Dioecesis Davenportensis)

Most Reverend

MARTIN J. AMOS

Bishop of Davenport; ordained May 25, 1968; appointed Titular Bishop of Meta and Auxiliary Bishop of Cleveland April 3, 2001; ordained June 7, 2001; appointed Bishop of Davenport October 12, 2006; installed November 20, 2006. *Office: Diocesan Pastoral Center, 2706 N. Gaines St., Davenport, IA 52804-1998.* Tel: 563-324-1911.

Most Reverend

WILLIAM E. FRANKLIN, D.D.

Bishop Emeritus of Davenport; Retired October 12, 2006. *Res.: 2706 N. Gaines St., Davenport, IA 52804.* Tel: 563-324-4774. *Office: Diocesan Pastoral Center, 2706 N. Gaines St., Davenport, IA 52804-1998.* Tel: 563-324-1911.

Chancery: Diocesan Pastoral Center, 2706 N. Gaines St., Davenport, IA 52804-1998. Tel: 563-324-1911; Fax: 563-324-5842.

Web: www.davenportdiocese.org

ERECTED MAY 8, 1881.

Square Miles 11,438.

Comprises that part of the State of Iowa bounded on the east by the Mississippi River; on the west by the western boundaries of the counties of Jasper, Marion, Monroe and Appanoose; on the south by the State of Missouri; on the north by the northern boundaries of the Counties of Jasper, Poweshiek, Iowa, Johnson, Cedar and Clinton.

For legal titles of parishes and diocesan institutions, consult the Chancery.

STATISTICAL OVERVIEW

Personnel	
Bishop	1
Retired Bishops	1
Priests: Diocesan Active in Diocese	72
Priests: Diocesan Active Outside Diocese	6
Priests: Retired, Sick or Absent	23
Number of Diocesan Priests	101
Religious Priests in Diocese	2
Total Priests in Diocese	103
Permanent Deacons in Diocese	39
Total Brothers	1
Total Sisters	159
Parishes	
Parishes	80
With Resident Pastor:	
Resident Diocesan Priests	52
Resident Religious Priests	2
Without Resident Pastor:	
Administered by Priests	22
Administered by Deacons	2
Administered by Lay People	2
Closed Parishes	1
Welfare	
Catholic Hospitals	3
Total Assisted	347,853
Homes for the Aged	4
Total Assisted	347
Educational	
Diocesan Students in Other Seminaries	12
Total Seminarians	12
Colleges and Universities	1
Total Students	3,729
High Schools, Diocesan and Parish	5
Total Students	1,236
Elementary Schools, Diocesan and Parish	13
Total Students	3,632
Catechesis/Religious Education:	
High School Students	1,645
Elementary Students	6,013
Total Students under Catholic Instruction	16,267
Teachers in the Diocese:	
Lay Teachers	419
Vital Statistics	
Receptions into the Church:	
Infant Baptism Totals	1,405
Minor Baptism Totals	38
Adult Baptism Totals	151
Received into Full Communion	135
First Communions	1,619
Confirmations	1,940
Marriages:	
Catholic	272
Interfaith	246
Total Marriages	518
Deaths	1,122
Total Catholic Population	100,777
Total Population	753,144

Former Bishops—Rt. Revs. JOHN MCMULLEN, D.D., ord. June 20, 1858; cons. July 25, 1881; died July 4, 1883; HENRY COSGROVE, D.D., ord. Aug. 27, 1857; cons. Sept. 14, 1884; died Dec. 22, 1906; JAMES DAVIS, D.D., ord. June 21, 1878; cons. Nov. 30, 1904; died Dec. 2, 1926; Most Revs. HENRY P. ROHLMAN, D.D., ord. Dec. 21, 1901; cons. July 26, 1927; appt. Coadjutor-Archbishop of Dubuque and Titular Archbishop of Macra in Rhodope, June 15, 1944; Archbishop of Dubuque, Nov. 21, 1946; appt. Titular Archbishop of Cotrada, Dec. 2, 1954; died Sept. 13, 1957; RALPH LEO HAYES, D.D., ord. Sept. 18, 1909; appt. Bishop of Helena June 23, 1933; cons. Sept. 21, 1933; appt. Rector of North American College in Rome in Sept. 1935; transferred to Titular See of Hierapolis Oct. 26, 1935; transferred to Davenport Nov. 16, 1944; appt. Assistant at the Pontifical Throne April 30, 1958; transferred to Titular See of Naraggara; retired Oct. 20, 1966; died July 4, 1970; GERALD FRANCIS O'KEEFE, D.D., ord. Jan. 29, 1944; appt. Auxiliary Bishop of St. Paul and Titular Bishop of Candyba May 5, 1961; cons. July 2, 1961; transferred to Davenport Oct. 20, 1966; installed Jan 4, 1967; retired Nov. 12, 1993; died April 12, 2000; WILLIAM E. FRANKLIN, ord. Feb. 4, 1956; appt. Titular Bishop of Surista and Auxiliary Bishop of Dubuque Jan. 29, 1987; ord. April 1, 1987; appt. Bishop of Davenport Nov. 12, 1993; installed Jan. 20, 1994; retired Oct. 12, 2006.

Pastoral Center—2706 N. Gaines St., Davenport, 52804-1998. Tel: 563-324-1911; Fax: 563-324-5842. Email: communication@davenportdiocese.org. Web: www.davenportdiocese.org.

Vicar General and Moderator of the Curia—Rev. Msgr. JOHN M. HYLAND, V.G.

Chancellor—Rev. GEORGE W. MCDANIEL, Ph.D., Send marriage matters to Tribunal.

Vice-Chancellors—CHARLENE MAASKE, CPA, M.B.A.; Rev. JOSEPH M. WOLF, J.C.L.

Executive Secretary to the Bishop—MARY FRICK.

Diocesan Tribunal—Pastoral Center, 2706 N. Gaines St., Davenport, 52804-1998. Tel: 563-324-1911.

Judicial Vicar—Rev. JOSEPH M. WOLF, J.C.L.

Adjutant Judicial Vicar—Rev. Msgr. MICHAEL J. MORRISSEY, M.A., J.C.L. (Retired).

Tribunal Auditor—THERESA M. DORAN.

Promoters of Justice—Rev. Msgrs. FRANCIS C. HENRICKSEN, E.V. (Retired); JAMES F. PARIZEK, J.C.L.

Defenders of the Bond—Rev. JOHN P. GALLAGHER, J.C.L.; Very Rev. WILLIAM E. REYNOLDS, V.F., J.C.L.

Notaries—Rev. GEORGE W. MCDANIEL, Ph.D.; Rev. Msgr. JOHN M. HYLAND, V.G.; Rev. JOSEPH M. WOLF, J.C.L.; CHARLENE MAASKE, CPA, M.B.A.; BETH BLOUGH; THERESA M. DORAN; MARY FRICK.

Judges—Very Rev. ROBERT J. BUSHER; Rev. EDWARD J. FITZPATRICK; Very Rev. RUDOLPH T. JUAREZ, J.C.L., E.V.; Revs. ROBERT T. MCALEER; GEORGE W. MCDANIEL, Ph.D.; Rev. Msgr. MICHAEL J. MORRISSEY, M.A., J.C.L. (Retired); Rev. JOSEPH M. WOLF, J.C.L.

Diocesan Consultors—Rev. Msgr. MICHAEL J. MORRISSEY, M.A., J.C.L. (Retired); Rev. NICHOLAS J. ADAM; Rev. Msgr. JOHN M. HYLAND, V.G.; Revs. PAUL CONNOLLY; KENNETH E. KUNTZ; Very Revs. RUDOLPH T. JUAREZ, J.C.L., E.V.; DAVID G. STEINLE, V.F.

Deans—Very Revs. MICHAEL J. SPIEKERMEIER, V.F., Davenport; ANTHONY J. HEROLD, V.F., Clinton; DAVID F. WILKENING, V.F., Iowa City; DAVID G. STEINLE, V.F., Keokuk; CHARLES J. FLADUNG, V.F., Ottumwa; WILLIAM E. REYNOLDS, V.F., J.C.L., Grinnell.

Diocesan Corporate Board—Most Rev. MARTIN J. AMOS, D.D.; Rev. Msgr. JOHN M. HYLAND, V.G.; Rev. GEORGE W. MCDANIEL, Ph.D.; TIMOTHY L. MCMAHON, J.D.; Ms. ANNE MCATEE, J.D.

Finance Officer—CHARLENE MAASKE, CPA, M.B.A.

Finance Council—Most Rev. MARTIN J. AMOS, D.D.; Rev. Msgr. JOHN M. HYLAND, V.G.; Rev. GEORGE W. MCDANIEL, Ph.D.; Rev. Msgr. MICHAEL J. MORRISSEY, M.A., J.C.L. (Retired); TERRENCE KILBURG, CPA; JOEL DIECKMANN, CPA; RITA BAWDEN; TIMOTHY L. MCMAHON, J.D.; JEFF HYLAND, CPA; Ms. ANNE MCATEE, J.D.

Vicar for Hispanics—Very Rev. RUDOLPH T. JUAREZ, J.C.L., E.V., P.O. Box 2776, Iowa City, 52244-2776.

Diocesan Offices

Pastoral Center—2706 N. Gaines St., Davenport, 52804-1998. Tel: 563-324-1911.

Finance and Administration—CHARLENE MAASKE, CPA, M.B.A.

Accountant—SHERYL LACKEY.

Accounting Coordinator—NANCY KARN.

Receptionist—LAUREN FLORES.

Database Coordinator—LYNNETTE SOWELLS.

Director of Development—Sr. LAURA GOEDKEN, O.P.

Communication Department—

Director of Communication—Deacon DAVID MONTGOMERY.

Director of Technology—ROBERT BUTTERWORTH.

Staff Support—LAURIE HOEFLING.

Archivist—Rev. GEORGE W. MCDANIEL, Ph.D.; ARNOLD WIESER, Archives Asst.

Pastoral Services—Rev. Msgr. JOHN M. HYLAND, V.G.

Director of Faith Formation and Education/ Superintendent of Schools—MARY M. WIESER.

Adult & Family Formation Lay Ministry Coordinator—ILAMAE HANISCH.

Youth Ministry Coordinator—PAT FINAN.

Faith Formation Coordinator—PAT FINAN.

Director of Social Action—KENT E. FERRIS, Pastoral Center, 2706 N. Gaines St., Davenport, 52804-1998. Tel: 563-324-1911.

Immigration Program Counselor—GRICELDA GARNICA.

Director of Vocations—Rev. MARTIN G. GOETZ.

Director of Liturgy—Deacon FRANCIS L. AGNOLI, Pastoral Center, 2706 N. Gaines St., Davenport, 52804-1998. Tel: 563-324-1911.

Scouting—Rev. JEFFRY W. BELGER, 220 E. Jefferson, Iowa City, 52245-2137.

Catholic Relief Services—KENT E. FERRIS, Dir., Pastoral Center, 2706 N. Gaines St., Davenport, 52804-1998. Tel: 563-324-1911.

Cemetery Committee—ROBERT MCCABE, Sec., 614 Main St., Davenport, 52801. Tel: 563-322-4438.

Campaign for Human Development—LOXI HOPKINS, Pastoral Center, 2706 N. Gaines St., Davenport, 52804-1998. Tel: 563-324-1911.

Liturgical Commission—Deacon FRANCIS L. AGNOLI, Pastoral Center, 2706 N. Gaines St., Davenport, 52804-1998. Tel: 563-324-1911.

D.C.C.W.—Mrs. CAROL KAALBERG, Dir., Mailing Address: St. Mary Catholic Church, P.O. Box B, Nichols, 52766-0190. Tel: 319-723-4566.

Holy Childhood, Pontifical Association—Rev. Msgr. W. ROBERT SCHMIDT, Dir., Pastoral Center, 2706 N. Gaines St., Davenport, 52804-1998. Tel: 563-324-1911.

Newspaper— "The Catholic Messenger" BARB ARLAND-FYE, Mng. Editor, P.O. Box 460, Davenport, 52805-0460. Tel: 563-323-9959; Fax: 563-323-6612. Email: messenger@davenportdiocese.org.

Pastoral Council—Most Rev. MARTIN J. AMOS, D.D., Pastoral Center, 2706 N. Gaines St., Davenport, 52804-1998. Tel: 563-324-1911.

Permanent Diaconate—Deacon ROBERT MCCOY, Pastoral Center, 2706 N. Gaines St., Davenport, 52804-1998. Tel: 563-324-1911.

Deacon Formation—Deacon FRANCIS L. AGNOLI, Pastoral Center, 2706 Gaines St., Davenport, 52804-1998. Tel: 563-324-1911.

Personnel Board—Rev. JOSEPH F. ROOST, Chm., 102 E. Penn, Box 119, Williamsburg, 52361.

Presbyteral Council—Rev. JAMES J. VRBA, 701 E. 3rd St., P.O. Box 477, Wilton, 52778-0477. Tel: 563-732-2271.

Priests' Aid Society—Rev. GEORGE W. MCDANIEL, Ph.D., St. Ambrose University, 518 W. Locust St., Davenport, 52803-2898. Tel: 563-333-6299; ANN RATLIFF, Contact, Mailing Address: P.O. Box 1478, Newton, 50208-1478.

Priests Eucharistic League—Rev. MICHAEL T. PHILLIPS, Dir., St. Wenceslaus, 623 Fairchild St., Iowa City, 52245-2829. Tel: 319-337-4975; Fax: 319-337-5822. Email: phillipsm@diodav.org.

Propagation of the Faith—Rev. GEORGE W. MCDANIEL, Ph.D., Dir., Pastoral Center, 2706 N. Gaines St., Davenport, 52804-1998. Tel: 563-324-1911.

Social Action Commission—KENT E. FERRIS, Pastoral Center, 2706 N. Gaines St., Davenport, 52804-1998. Tel: 563-324-1911.

Serra Club—CHARLES MISSEL, 908 Grand Ct., Davenport, 52803. Tel: 563-324-7224.

Sisters Consortium—Sisters LAURA GOEDKEN, O.P., Pastoral Center, 2706 Gaines St., Davenport, 52804-1998. Tel: 563-324-1911; RACHEL BEESON, C.H.M.; MICHELLE SCHIFFGENS, C.H.M.; ANNE MARTIN PHELAN, O.S.F.; MARY PAUL HUMMER, O.S.F.; JUDY HEROLD, S.S.N.D.; JANET KREBER, O.S.F.; JOAN MCCORKELL, O.C.D.

Vicar for Clergy—Rev. Msgr. FRANCIS C. HENRICKSEN, E.V. (Retired), 1113 First St., Tipton, 52772-9289. Tel: 563-886-6285.

Vicar for Religious—Rev. Msgr. FRANCIS C. HENRICKSEN, E.V. (Retired), 1113 First St., Tipton, 52772-9289. Tel: 563-886-6285.

Vicar for Hispanics—Very Rev. RUDOLPH T. JUAREZ, J.C.L., E.V., Mailing Address: P.O. Box 2776, Iowa City, 52244-2776.

Vicar for Vietnamese—Very Rev. HAI D. DINH, E.V., St. Paul the Apostle, 916 E. Rusholme St., Davenport, 52803-7994.

Victim Assistance Coordinator—ALICIA OWENS, Mailing Address: P.O. Box 232, Bettendorf, 52722-0004. Tel: 563-349-5002. Email: vacdav@attglobal.net.

Vocations—Rev. MARTIN G. GOETZ, Pastoral Center, 2706 N. Gaines, Davenport, 52804-1998. Tel: 563-324-1911; Fax: 563-324-5842.

CLERGY, PARISHES, MISSIONS AND PAROCHIAL SCHOOLS

CITY OF DAVENPORT

(SCOTT COUNTY)

1—SACRED HEART CATHEDRAL (1856) [JC] Very Rev. Robert J. Busher; Rev. Hai Duc Dinh; Deacons Robert McCoy; Francis L. Agnoli.
Church: 422 E. 10th St., 52803-5499. Tel: 563-324-3257; Fax: 563-326-6014.
School—Merged with Holy Family, Davenport and St. Alphonsus, Davenport to become All Saints Catholic School, Davenport.
Catechesis/Religious Program—Sr. Mary Schmidt, O.S.B., D.R.E. Students 139.

2—ST. ALPHONSUS (1903) Rev. Thomas L. Parlette.
Res.: 2618 Boies Ave., 52802. Tel: 563-322-0987; Fax: 563-323-1458.
School—(Grades PreSchool) Tel: 563-323-3204. Shelly McIntosh, Dir. Students 75.
Catechesis/Religious Program—Mary Ann Hagemann, D.R.E. Students 47.

3—ST. ANTHONY'S (1837) Rev. John P. Gallagher; Sr. Judy Herold, S.S.N.D., Pastoral Min.; Dennis Flaherty, Business Mgr.
Res.: 417 N. Main St., 52801. Tel: 563-322-3303; Fax: 563-326-5136.
Catechesis/Religious Program—Sr. Roberta Birch, C.H.M., C.R.E. Students 110.

4—HOLY FAMILY (1897) Revs. H. Robert Harness; George W. McDaniel; Deacon Joseph Rosenthal.
Office: 1315 W. Pleasant St., 52804. Tel: 563-322-0901 (Office); 563-322-0902 (Rectory); Fax: 563-884-4965.
School—All Saints Catholic School, (Grades K-8), 1926 N. Marquette St., 52804-2199. Tel: 563-324-3205; Fax: 563-324-9331. Mrs. Tammy Conrad, Prin. Lay Teachers 28; Students 368.
Catechesis/Religious Program—Roberta Pegorick, D.R.E., (Grades K-8); Annie Shortridge, Youth Min. Students 110.

5—ST. JOSEPH'S (1855) Closed. For inquiries for parish records contact Pastoral Center.

6—ST. MARY'S (1867), (Irish), Rev. Edward A. O'Melia; Deacons George D. Strader; Julian Gutierrez.
Res.: 516 Fillmore St., 52802. Tel: 563-322-3383; Fax: 563-322-3383.
Catechesis/Religious Program—Students 160.

7—OUR LADY OF VICTORY (1962) Rev. Msgr. James F. Parizek; Deacons Paul Hittner; Marcel Mosse; Al Boboth. In Res., Rev. William O. Meyer (Retired).
Res.: 4105 N. Division, 52806. Tel: 563-391-4245; Fax: 563-445-1003. Email: olvdav@qwestoffice.net. Web: www.olvjfk.com.
School—John F. Kennedy Catholic, (Grades K-8), 1627 W. 42nd St., 52806. Tel: 563-391-3030; Fax: 563-388-5206. Chad Steimle, Prin.; Janet Thomas, Librarian. Lay Teachers 29; Students 349.
Catechesis/Religious Program—Tel: 563-391-8384. Leigh Boorn, Youth Min.; Patricia Gallagher, D.R.E. Students 202.

8—ST. PAUL THE APOSTLE (1909) Very Rev. Michael J. Spiekermeier; Rev. Hai Duc Dinh; Deacons Robert McCoy; Richard J. Rasmussen.
Res.: 916 E. Rusholme St., 52803. Tel: 563-322-7994; Fax: 563-322-7995.
School—1007 E. Rusholme, 52803. Tel: 563-322-2923; Fax: 563-322-9359. Mrs. Julie Delaney, Prin. Sisters of Charity of the Blessed Virgin Mary 1; Lay Teachers 29; Students 534.
Catechesis/Religious Program—Tel: 319-322-3768. Rosie Megraw, D.R.E. Students 154.

OUTSIDE THE CITY OF DAVENPORT

ALBIA, MONROE CO., ST. MARY'S (1874) [CEM] Rev. Michael Volkmer, C.PP.S.
Res.: 730 Benton Ave., W., P.O. Box 365, 52531. Tel: 641-932-5130; Fax: 641-932-5130.
Catechesis/Religious Program—Tel: 641-932-5589. Jackie Maddy, D.R.E. Students 215.

ARDON, MUSCATINE CO., ST. MALACHY, Closed. For sacramental records, inquiries should be addressed to St. Joseph Parish, Columbus Junction.

AUGUSTA, DES MOINES CO., ST. MARY'S (1881) Closed. For inquiries for parish records contact Pastoral Center.

BAUER, MARION CO., ST. JOSEPH, Closed. For inquiries for parish records contact Pastoral Center.

BETTENDORF, SCOTT CO.

1—ST. JOHN VIANNEY (1967) [JC] Rev. Robert T. McAleer; Deacons William Donnelly, (Retired); Daryl Fortin.
Res.: 4097 18th St., 52722-2120. Tel: 563-332-7910; Fax: 563-332-0833.
School—(Grades PreSchool) Tel: 563-332-5308. Marcia Hamilton, Dir. Students 47.
Catechesis/Religious Program—Tel: 563-332-7564. Nicky Stevenson, D.R.E.; Jan Stevenson, Youth Min. Students 1,077.

2—OUR LADY OF LOURDES (1903) Rev. Timothy J. Sheedy; Deacons Dennis Duff; Charles Metzger; John D. Weber.
Res.: 1506 Brown St., 52722. Tel: 563-359-0345; Fax: 563-344-6017.
School—(Grades PreSchool-8), 1453 Mississippi Blvd., 52722. Tel: 563-359-3466; Fax: 563-823-1595. Mrs. Katie Selden, Prin. Lay Teachers 29; Students 362.
Catechesis/Religious Program—Tel: 563-359-1869. Students 380.

BLOOMFIELD, DAVIS CO., ST. MARY MAGDALEN (1953) Attended by St. Patrick's, Ottumwa.

BLUE GRASS, SCOTT CO., ST. ANDREW (1976) [JC] Revs. John P. Gallagher; Robert L. Grant (DM); Deacon Donald Frericks, Parish Life Admin.
Res.: 333 W. Lotte St., 52726. Tel: 563-381-1363; Fax: 563-381-1363.
Catechesis/Religious Program—Janet Friederichs, D.R.E. Students 142.

BROOKLYN, POWESHIEK CO., ST. PATRICK, [CEM] Rev. Brian J. Shepley.
Mailing Address: P.O. Box 512, 52211-0512. Tel: 641-522-4323. In Res., Rev. Philip V. Ryan (Retired).
Catechesis/Religious Program—Students 102.

BRYANT, CLINTON CO., ST. MARY, Consolidated with St. Joseph, Sugar Creek to form Sts. Mary and Joseph, Sugar Creek.

BUFFALO, SCOTT CO., ST. PETER'S (1912) [CEM] Attended by St. Alphonsus, Davenport. Rev. Thomas L. Parlette; Deacon Larry Dankert.
Mailing Address: 406 Fourth St., P.O. Box 488, 52728. Tel: 563-381-2865; 563-322-0987; Fax: 563-323-1458.
Catechesis/Religious Program—Students 34.

BURLINGTON, DES MOINES CO.

1—SS. JOHN & PAUL (1842) [JC] Revs. Patrick Hilgendorf; Bruce A. DeRammelaere; Sr. Kathy Braun, S.S.N.D., Pastoral Assoc.; Connie Trautner, Pastoral Assoc.
Res.: 700 Division St., 52601-5415. Tel: 319-752-6733; Fax: 319-753-5211.
Catechesis/Religious Program—702 S. Roosevelt Ave., 52601. Tel: 319-753-0277. Mary Edwards, D.R.E. Students 129.

2—ST. JOHN'S (1855) Merged with St. Paul's, Burlington, to form SS. John & Paul, Burlington.

3—ST. PATRICK'S (1870) Merged with St. Mary, West Burlington to form SS. Mary and Patrick, West Burlington.

CAMANCHE, CLINTON CO., CHURCH OF THE VISITATION (1966) Rev. Richard U. Okumu.
1028 Middle Rd., 52730-1032. Tel: 563-259-1188; Fax: 563-259-4462.
Catechesis/Religious Program—Tel: 563-259-8966; 563-522-2654. Pam Drury, D.R.E.; Donna Hines, D.R.E. Students 52.

CENTERVILLE, APPANOOSE CO., ST. MARY'S (1870) Rev. Dennis Schaab, C.PP.S.
Res.: 828 S. 18th St., 52544. Tel: 641-437-1984.
Catechesis/Religious Program—Students 231.

CHARLOTTE, CLINTON CO., ASSUMPTION AND ST. PATRICK'S (1993) [CEM 2] Rev. Scott Lemaster.
Res.: 147 Broadway St., 52731. Tel: 563-677-2758; Fax: 563-677-2739.
Catechesis/Religious Program—Students 71.

CLEAR CREEK, KEOKUK CO., SS. PETER & PAUL, See separate listing. See Holy Trinity, Keota.

CLINTON, CLINTON CO., JESUS CHRIST, PRINCE OF PEACE (1990) [CEM 2] Very Rev. Anthony J. Herold; Rev. Thomas Joseph Hennen; Deacons Jeffrey Schuetzle; Ramon Hilgendorf; Arthur C. Donart; Sr. Jane McCarthy, O.S.F., Pastoral Assoc.; David Schnier, Business Mgr.
Parish Office—1105 LaMetta Wynn Dr., P.O. Box 576, 52733-0578. Tel: 563-242-3311; Fax: 563-242-3323.
St. Mary's—, Closed. See Jesus Christ, Prince of Peace, Clinton.

St. Boniface—, Closed. See Jesus Christ, Prince of Peace, Clinton.
St. Irenaeus—, Closed. See Jesus Christ, Prince of Peace, Clinton.
St. Patrick's—, Closed. See Jesus Christ, Prince of Peace, Clinton.
School—312 S. Fourth St., 52732. Tel: 563-242-1663; Fax: 563-243-8272. Mrs. Nancy Peart, Prin. Students 245.
Catechesis/Religious Program—Tel: 563-243-8269. Brenda Bertram, D.R.E. & Youth Min. Students 184.
Chapel—Sacred Heart

COLFAX, JASPER CO., IMMACULATE CONCEPTION (1898) Rev. Dennis L. Hoffman, Canonical Pastor; Very Rev. William E. Reynolds, Sacramental Min.; Deacon Joe Dvorak, Parish Life Admin.
Mailing Address: 305 E. Howard, 50054-1025. Tel: 515-674-3711.
Catechesis/Religious Program—Students 115.
Oratory—Sacred Heart Valeria, Jasper Co.

COLUMBUS JUNCTION, LOUISA CO., ST. JOSEPH (1853) Revs. Jason Crossen, Admin.; Joseph M. Sia.
Mailing Address: 815 Second St., 52738. Tel: 319-728-8210.
Catechesis/Religious Program—Students 49.

CORALVILLE, JOHNSON CO., ST. THOMAS MORE (1944) [JC] Rev. Walter Helms.
Res.: 3000 12th Ave., 52241. Tel: 319-337-2173; Fax: 319-337-2174.
Catechesis/Religious Program—Tel: 319-337-4231. Deacon Ed Goldsmith, D.R.E. Students 326.

COSGROVE, JOHNSON CO., ST. PETER'S (1878) Attended by St. Mary, Oxford. Rev. Edmond J. Dunn; Deacon David Montgomery.
4022 Cosgrove Rd., S.W., Oxford, 52322. Tel: 319-828-4180; 319-545-2077.
Catechesis/Religious Program—

DEWITT, CLINTON CO., ST. JOSEPH'S (1880) [CEM] Rev. Paul E. Connolly; Sr. Theresa Ann Spitz, R.S.M., Pastoral Assoc.
Res.: 417 Sixth Ave., 52742. Tel: 563-659-3514; Fax: 563-659-2599.
School—Tel: 563-659-3812. Chris Meyer, Prin. Sisters of Mercy 1; Lay Teachers 15; Students 179.
Catechesis/Religious Program—Pat Sheil, D.R.E. Students 149.

DELMAR, CLINTON CO., ST. PATRICK'S (1882) [CEM] Rev. David L. Brownfield.
Res.: P.O. Box 293, 52037-0293. Tel: 563-674-4240.
Catechesis/Religious Program—Students 29.

DODGEVILLE, DES MOINES CO., ST. MARY'S (1850) [CEM] Very Rev. David G. Steinle; Deacon Clifford Beckman.
Mailing Address: P.O. Box 415, West Burlington, 52655-0415. Tel: 319-752-8771. Email: stmdodge@interl.net.
Catechesis/Religious Program—Tel: 319-394-9379. Jennifer Meller, D.R.E. Students 60.

EAST PLEASANT PLAIN, JEFFERSON CO., ST. JOSEPH'S (1902) [CEM] Merged with St. Frances Xavier Cabrini, Richland to form Ss. Joseph and Cabrini, Richland.

EDDYVILLE, MAHASKA CO., ST. MARY'S, Closed. For inquiries for parish records contact the Pastoral Center.

ELDON, WAPELLO CO., ST. ALOYSIUS, Closed. For inquiries for parish records contact the Pastoral Center.

FAIRFIELD, JEFFERSON CO., ST. MARY'S (1864) Rev. Stephen C. Page.
Res.: 402 N. Third, 52556-2466. Tel: 641-472-3179; Fax: 641-472-6137.
Catechesis/Religious Program—Tel: 641-472-5996. Students 109.

FARMINGTON, VAN BUREN CO., ST. BONIFACE (1862) [CEM] Rev. Apo T. Mpanda.
Church: 609 Washington St., P.O. Box 247, 52626. Tel: 319-837-6808; Fax: 319-837-8112.
Res.: 311 Ave. C, P.O. Box 68, West Point, 52656.
Catechesis/Religious Program—Tel: 319-837-8905; Fax: 319-837-6808. Students 29.

FORT MADISON, LEE CO.
1—HOLY FAMILY (2009) [CEM] Revs. Troy A. Richmond; Mark P. Spring; Sr. Peggy Duffy, S.S.N.D., Pastoral Assoc.; Deacons Ronald Stein; Robert Gengengbacher.
Res.: 1013 Ave. E., 52627. Tel: 319-372-2127; Fax: 319-372-2083.
Catechesis/Religious Program—Students 110.
2—ST. JOSEPH'S, Consolidated with St. Mary's to form SS. Mary & Joseph Parish.
3—SS. MARY & JOSEPH (1871) Merged with Sacred Heart, Fort Madison to form Holy Family, Madison.
4—ST. MARY'S, Consolidated with St. Joseph's to form SS. Mary & Joseph Parish.
5—SACRED HEART (1893) Merged with SS. Mary & Joseph, Fort Madison to form Holy Family, Fort Madison.

GEORGETOWN, MONROE CO., ST. PATRICK'S (1851) [CEM] Attended by St. Patrick's, Melrose. Rev. Patrick L. Lumsden; Sharon Crall, Pastoral Assoc.
Mailing Address: P.O. Box 183, Albia, 52531. Tel: 641-726-3529.
Catechesis/Religious Program—Clustered with St. Mary, Albia., Tel: 641-932-5589. Students 18.

GRAND MOUND, CLINTON CO., CHURCH OF ST. PHILIP AND JAMES (1876) [CEM] Rev. David L. Brownfield; Deacon Michael D. Sheil.
Res.: 606 Fulton St., P.O. Box 7, 52751-0007. Tel: 563-847-2271.
Catechesis/Religious Program—Students 65.

GRINNELL, POWESHIEK CO., ST. MARY'S (1924) [CEM] Rev. Nicholas J. Adam; Deacons William D. Olson; Stephen J. Witt.
Res.: 1018 Broad St., P.O. Box 623, 50112. Tel: 641-236-7486 (Church Office); Fax: 641-236-7488.
Catechesis/Religious Program—Tel: 641-236-8838. Students 153.

HARPER, KEOKUK CO., ST. ELIZABETH'S, See separate listing. See Holy Trinity, Keota.

HILLS, JOHNSON CO., ST. JOSEPH'S (1902) Rev. Louis J. Leonhardt.
Res.: 208 Iowa St., 52235. Tel: 319-679-2271.
Catechesis/Religious Program—Students 56.

HOLBROOK, IOWA CO., ST. MICHAEL, Closed. For inquiries for parish records contact the Pastoral Center.

HOUGHTON, LEE CO., ST. JOHN'S (1895) [CEM] Rev. Gary L. Beckman.
Res.: Box 100, 52631. Tel: 319-469-2001; Fax: 319-469-2001.
Catechesis/Religious Program—Tel: 319-837-8905; Fax: 319-837-6808. Dixie Booten, D.R.E. Students 24.

IOWA CITY, JOHNSON CO.
1—ST. MARY (1840) [CEM 2] [JC] Revs. Kenneth E. Kuntz; Jeffry W. Belger; Sr. Mary Agnes Giblin, B.V.M., Pastoral Assoc.
Mailing Address: 302 E. Jefferson, 52245-2137.
Res.: 220 E. Jefferson St., 52245-2137. Tel: 319-337-4314; Fax: 319-337-8551.
Catechesis/Religious Program—Regina Inter-Parish Catholic Education Center, Tel: 319-351-7638; Fax: 319-337-4109. Students 256.
2—ST. PATRICK'S (1872), (Irish), Very Rev. Rudolph T. Juarez.
Res.: P.O. Box 2776, 52244-2776. Tel: 319-337-2856; Fax: 319-354-5590.
Catechesis/Religious Program—2150 Rochester Ave., 52245. Tel: 319-351-7638; Fax: 319-337-4109. Sr. Mary Frances Michalec, D.R.E.
3—ST. WENCESLAUS (1893) [JC] Rev. Michael T. Phillips.
Res.: 623 Fairchild St., 52245. Tel: 319-337-4957; Fax: 319-337-5822.

KEOKUK, LEE CO., ALL SAINTS (1982) Rev. Robert Lathrop; Deacon William Cosgrove.
Res.: 310 S. Ninth St., 52632. Tel: 319-524-8334; Fax: 319-524-8358.
Catechesis/Religious Program—Students 105.

KEOTA, KEOKUK CO.
1—HOLY TRINITY (1992) [CEM 3] Very Rev. Charles J. Fladung.
Res.: 109 N. Lincoln St., 52248-9757. Tel: 641-636-3883; Fax: 641-636-3198.
Catechesis/Religious Program—Tel: 641-636-3731. Becky Becker, D.R.E. Students 113.
2—ST. MARY'S, See separate listing. See Holy Trinity, Keota.

KESWICK, KEOKUK CO., OUR LADY OF LOURDES (1914), (Irish—German), Closed. For inquiries for parish records please see St. Mary's, Sigourney.

KINROSS, KEOKUK CO., SACRED HEART, Closed. For inquiries for parish records contact the Pastoral Center.

KNOXVILLE, MARION CO., ST. ANTHONY'S (1870) [CEM] Rev. Stephen P. Ebel.
Res.: 1202 Woodland St., 50138. Tel: 641-828-7050; Fax: 641-842-2338.
Catechesis/Religious Program—1602 & 1604 N. Lincoln St., 50138. Tel: 641-828-6332. Laura Hollinrake, Dir. Faith Formation. Students 113.

LE CLAIRE, SCOTT CO., OUR LADY OF THE RIVER (1969) Rev. Joseph M. Wolf.
Res.: 28200 226th St. Pl., P.O. Box 32, LeClaire, 52753. Tel: 563-289-5736.
Catechesis/Religious Program—Roberta Pegorick, D.R.E. Students 120.

LONE TREE, JOHNSON CO., ST. MARY'S (1853) [CEM] [JC] Rev. Louis J. Leonhardt; Mrs. Carol Kaalberg, Admin.
Mailing Address: 214 W. Jayne St., Box 416, 52755.
Res.: 214 W. Jayne St., 52755. Tel: 319-629-4225; Fax: 319-629-4944.
Catechesis/Religious Program—Students 56.

LONG GROVE, SCOTT CO., ST. ANN'S (1853) [CEM] Rev. Msgr. Drake R. Shafer.
Res.: 16550 290th St., 52756. Tel: 563-285-4596; Fax: 563-285-4897.
Catechesis/Religious Program—Susan Cleveland, D.R.E.; Julia Jones, D.R.E. & Youth Min. Students 315.

LOST NATION, CLINTON CO., SACRED HEART (1895) [CEM] Rev. Gregory A. Steckel.
Res.: P.O. Box 127, 52254. Tel: 563-678-2200.
Catechesis/Religious Program—Monica Steeper, D.R.E. Students 12.

LOVILIA, MONROE CO., ST. PETER'S (1904) [CEM] Rev. Patrick L. Lumsden.
Mailing Address: P.O. Box 8, 50150. Tel: 641-946-8298.
Res.: 200 Trinity Ave., Melrose, 52569. Tel: 641-326-3457.
Catechesis/Religious Program—Clustered with St. Mary, Albia and St. Patrick, Georgetown., Tel: 641-932-5589. Vicki Nace, D.R.E. Students 11.

MARENGO, IOWA CO., ST. PATRICK'S (1878) [CEM] Rev. Joseph F. Roost.
Mailing Address: P.O. Box 183, 52301. Tel: 319-642-5438; Fax: 319-642-5648.
Catechesis/Religious Program—1526 Howard Ave., 52301. Tel: 319-642-3177. Angie Carney, D.R.E. Students 80.

MECHANICSVILLE, CEDAR CO., ST. MARY'S (1872) Rev. Andrew E. Kelly.
Res.: P.O. Box 457, 52306-0457. Tel: 563-432-6236.
Catechesis/Religious Program—Tel: 563-432-6678. Joan Garner, D.R.E. Students 62.

MELCHER, MARION CO., SACRED HEART (1912) [CEM] [JC] Rev. Stephen P. Ebel.
Res.: 204 S.W. D. St., P.O. Box 277, 50163. Tel: 641-947-4981.
Catechesis/Religious Program—Phyllis Dittmer, D.R.E. Students 45.

MELROSE, MONROE CO., ST. PATRICK'S (1870) [CEM] Rev. Patrick L. Lumsden.
Res.: 200 Trinity St., P.O. Box 154, 52569-0154. Tel: 641-726-3457.
Catechesis/Religious Program—Jane Kamerick, D.R.E. Students 30.

MONTROSE, LEE CO., ST. JOSEPH'S (1860) [JC] Revs. Troy A. Richmond; Mark P. Spring.
Res.: 503 Spruce St., 52639. Tel: 319-463-5443.
Catechesis/Religious Program—Tel: 319-463-5571. Students 8.

MOUNT PLEASANT, HENRY CO., ST. ALPHONSUS (1862) [CEM] Rev. Joseph P. V. Phung.
Res.: 607 S. Jackson St., 52641-2696. Tel: 319-385-8410; Fax: 319-385-0545.
Catechesis/Religious Program—Tel: 319-385-4937. Mary Hassenfritz, D.R.E. (Grades PreK-8); Sr. Ann Marie Dunn, O.S.F., Adult Faith Formation. Students 210.

MUSCATINE, MUSCATINE CO.
1—SS. MARY AND MATHIAS OF MUSCATINE, [CEM] Revs. Jason Crossen; Joseph M. Sia; Deacons James Becker; Juan J. Cadena.
Res.: 215 W. Eighth St., 52761. Tel: 563-263-1878; 563-263-1416 (Parish Office); Fax: 563-263-2782.
Catechesis/Religious Program—Tel: 563-263-3264; 563-363-3848; Fax: 563-263-6700. Sr. Mary Cheryl Demmer, P.B.V.M., D.R.E. Students 558.
2—ST. MARY'S (1876) Merged with St. Mathias to form SS. Mary and Mathias of Muscatine.
3—ST. MATHIAS (1842) Merged with St. Mathias to form SS. Mary and Mathias of Muscatine.
4—OUR LADY OF GUADALUPE CATHOLIC MISSION (1976), (Hispanic), Closed. For inquiries for parish records please see SS. Mary and Mathias of Muscatine, Muscatine.

MYSTIC, APPANOOSE CO., ST. FRANCIS, Closed. For inquiries for parish records contact the Pastoral Center.

NEWPORT, JOHNSON CO., ST. MARY, Closed. For inquiries for parish records contact the Pastoral Center.

NEWTON, JASPER CO., SACRED HEART (1867) [CEM] Very Rev. William E. Reynolds; Tammy Norcross, Pastoral Min.
Mailing Address: P.O. Box 1478, 50208-1478. Tel: 641-792-4625 (Rectory); Fax: 641-792-8639.
McCann Center—1115 S. Eighth Ave. E., P.O. Box 1478, 50208. Tel: 641-792-2050. (Parish Office and Religious Education Center)
Catechesis/Religious Program—Mary Beth Lawson, D.R.E. (Grades K-6). Students 139.

NICHOLS, MUSCATINE CO., ST. MARY'S (1874) [CEM] [JC] Rev. Louis J. Leonhardt, Admin.; Mrs. Carol Kaalberg, Parish Life Admin.
201 Short St., Box B, 52766. Tel: 319-723-4566; Fax: 319-629-4944.
Catechesis/Religious Program—Students 20.

NOLAN SETTLEMENT, JOHNSON CO., ST. BRIDGET'S, Closed. For inquiries for parish records contact the Pastoral Center.

NORTH ENGLISH, IOWA CO., ST. JOSEPH'S (1896) [JC] Rev. Joseph F. Roost.
Res.: 221 N. Knoll Ridge St., 52316. Tel: 319-664-3325.
Catechesis/Religious Program—Tel: 319-639-2550. Students 59.

OSKALOOSA, MAHASKA CO., ST. MARY'S (1871) [CEM] Rev. Thomas J. Spiegel.
Res.: 2021 Edmundson Dr., 52577. Tel: 641-673-6680; Fax: 641-676-1766.
Catechesis/Religious Program—Tel: 641-673-0659. Students 219.
OTTUMWA, WAPELLO CO.
1—ST. MARY OF THE VISITATION (1851) Rev. Bernard E. Weir.
Res.: 216 N. Court St., 52501-2586. Tel: 641-682-4559; Fax: 641-682-4433.
Catechesis/Religious Program—Tel: 641-682-4496. Anna Hanson, D.R.E. Students 186.
2—ST. PATRICK'S (1880) Rev. John D. Spiegel.
Res.: 222 N. Ward St., 52501. Tel: 641-682-4212; Fax: 641-682-7915.
Catechesis/Religious Program—Ottumwa Regional Catholic Religious Education, Tel: 641-682-0320. Anna Hanson, D.R.E.; Gail Bates, D.R.E.; Mary Ryan, D.R.E. Students 88.
3—SACRED HEART, Merged with St. Mary of the Visitation, Ottumwa.
OXFORD, JOHNSON CO., ST. MARY'S (1860) [CEM] Rev. Edmond J. Dunn; Deacon David Montgomery.
Mailing Address: Box 80, 52322-0080. Tel: 319-828-4180; Fax: 319-828-4059.
Catechesis/Religious Program—Tel: 319-828-8190. Students 193.
PARNELL, IOWA CO., ST. JOSEPH'S (1880) [CEM] Closed. For inquiries for parish records, contact the Pastoral Center.
PELLA, MARION CO., ST. MARY'S (1869) [CEM] Rev. Dennis L. Hoffman; Deacon Don Efinger.
726 218th Pl., P.O. Box 144, 50219-0144. Tel: 641-628-3078; Fax: 641-628-3165.
Res.: 1104 Peace St., P.O. Box 144, 50219-0144. Tel: 641-628-4262.
Catechesis/Religious Program—Tel: 641-628-3078. Students 186.
PETERSVILLE, CLINTON CO., IMMACULATE CONCEPTION (1853) [CEM] Rev. Scott Lemaster.
Church: 147 Broadway St., Charlotte, 52731. Tel: 563-677-2758.
Catechesis/Religious Program—Tel: 563-652-6971. Students 8.
RATHBUN, APPANOOSE CO., ST. ANTHONY (1895) Closed. For inquiries for parish records contact the chancery.
RICHLAND, KEOKUK CO.
1—ST. FRANCES XAVIER CABRINI (1946), (German), Merged with St. Joseph's, East Pleasant Plain to form Ss. Joseph and Cabrini, Richland.
2—SS. JOSEPH AND CABRINI (2008) Rev. Robert M. Striegel, Canonical Pastor & Sacramental Min.; Shirley Van Dee, Parish Life Admin.
Res.: 308 W. Main St., P.O. Box 130, 52585-0130. Tel: 319-456-3161; Fax: 319-456-6408.
Catechesis/Religious Program—Students 75.
RICHMOND, WASHINGTON CO., HOLY TRINITY (1854) [CEM] Rev. Richard A. Adam.
Res.: 571 Howard St., Kalona, 52247-9558. Tel: 319-656-2802. Pastor's Res.: 51 St. Mary's St., Riverside, 52327-0482.
Catechesis/Religious Program—Tel: 319-656-5218. Students 108.
RIVERSIDE, WASHINGTON CO., ST. MARY OF THE ASSUMPTION (1877) [CEM] Rev. Richard A. Adam.
Res.: 51 St. Mary's St., P.O. Box C, 52327-0482. Tel: 319-648-2331; Fax: 319-648-5024.
Catechesis/Religious Program—Students 42.
ST. PAUL, LEE CO., ST. JAMES (1838) [CEM] Attended by St. John, Houghton. Rev. Gary L. Beckman.
Mailing Address: P.O. Box 100, Houghton, 52631-0100. Tel: 319-469-2001.
Catechesis/Religious Program—Tel: 319-837-8905; Fax: 319-837-8905. Dixie Booten, D.R.E. Students 25.
SIGOURNEY, KEOKUK CO., ST. MARY'S (1873) [CEM] [JC] Very Rev. Charles J. Fladung; Deacon James Striegel.
Res.: 415 E. Pleasant Valley St., 52591. Tel: 641-622-2316 (Rectory & Business); Fax: 641-622-2389.
Catechesis/Religious Program— Jenny Thompson, D.R.E. Students 63.
SOLON, JOHNSON CO.
1—ST. MARY'S (1858) [CEM] Very Rev. David F. Wilkening.
Res.: 1749 Racine Ave., 52333-0069. Tel: 319-624-2228; Fax: 319-624-3564.
Catechesis/Religious Program—Julie Agne, D.R.E. Students 356.
2—SS. PETER & PAUL, Closed. For inquiries for parish records contact the chancery.
STRING PRAIRIE, LEE CO., ST. MARY, Closed. For inquiries for parish records contact the Parish Center.
SUGAR CREEK, CLINTON CO.
1—ST. JOSEPH'S, Consolidated with St. Mary, Bryant, to form Sts. Mary and Joseph, Sugar Creek.
2—SS. MARY AND JOSEPH (1993) [CEM 2] Rev. Scott Lemaster.
Res.: 147 Broadway St., Charlotte, 52731-9686. Tel: 563-677-2758; Fax: 563-677-2739; 563-689-6422.
Catechesis/Religious Program—Students 14.
TIPTON, CEDAR CO., ST. MARY'S (1856) [CEM] Rev. David Hitch; Deacon Robert Snavely, (Retired).
Res.: 208 Meridian St., P.O. Box 309, 52772-0309. Tel: 563-886-2506; Fax: 563-886-6326.
Catechesis/Religious Program—Tel: 563-886-2545. Mary Barnum, D.R.E. Students 170.
TORONTO, CLINTON CO., ST. JAMES (1855) [CEM] Attended by Sacred Heart, Lost Nation. Rev. Gregory A. Steckel.
Mailing Address: P.O. Box 127, Lost Nation, 52254. Tel: 563-678-2200.
Catechesis/Religious Program—Mary Stevenson, D.R.E. Students 18.
VALERIA, JASPER CO., SACRED HEART (1892) Closed. For inquiries for parish records contact the Pastoral Center.
VICTOR, IOWA CO., ST. BRIDGET (1886) [CEM] [JC] Rev. Brian J. Shepley.
Res.: 104 Third St., 52347. Tel: 319-647-2220; Fax: 319-647-3231.
Catechesis/Religious Program—Tel: 319-647-2221. Students 80.
VILLA NOVA, CLINTON CO., ST. PATRICK, Consolidated with Assumption of the Blessed Virgin Mary, Charlotte, to form Assumption and St. Patrick's, Charlotte.
WAPELLO, LOUISA CO., ST. MARY'S (1867) Closed. For inquiries for parish records contact the Pastoral Center.
WASHINGTON, WASHINGTON CO., ST. JAMES (1860) [JC] Rev. Paul J. Appel.
Res.: 540 W. 3rd St., 52353-1994. Tel: 319-653-5704.
School—Tel: 319-653-3631; Fax: 319-653-3631. Mr. Brad Thiel, Prin. Lay Teachers 12; Students 126.
Catechesis/Religious Program—Tel: 319-653-6318. Janis Vittetoe, C.R.E.; Linda Gent, Youth Min. Coord. Students 330.
WELLER, MONROE CO., ST. MARY, Closed. For inquiries for parish records contact the Pastoral Center.
WELLMAN, WASHINGTON CO., ST. JOSEPH (1969) [CEM] Rev. Richard A. Adam.
Mailing Address: 235 11th St., P.O. Box C, Riverside, 52327-0482. Tel: 319-648-2331; Fax: 319-648-5024.
Catechesis/Religious Program—Tel: 319-646-2933. Cindy Duwa, D.R.E. Students 155.
WELTON, CLINTON CO., ST. ANNE (1910) Attended by St. Patrick, Delmar. Rev. David L. Brownfield.
Mailing Address: P.O. Box 293, Delmar, 52037-0293. Tel: 563-674-4240.
Catechesis/Religious Program—Students 6.
WEST BRANCH, CEDAR CO., ST. BERNADETTE (1960) Attended by St. Joseph, West Liberty. Rev. Dennis C. Martin.
Church & Mailing Address: 507 E. Orange, Box 103, 52358-0103. Tel: 319-643-2095; 319-627-2229 (Pastor Only).
Catechesis/Religious Program—1720 Madison St., Tipton, 52772. Tel: 319-946-2162. Martha Freeman, D.R.E. Students 100.
WEST BURLINGTON, DES MOINES CO., SS. MARY AND PATRICK (1870) [CEM] Very Rev. David G. Steinle.
Res.: 520 W. Mt. Pleasant St., P.O. Box 415, 52655-0415. Tel: 319-752-8771.
Catechesis/Religious Program—700 S. Roosevelt, Burlington, 52601. Tel: 319-754-8431. Mary Edwards, D.R.E. Students 205.
WEST LIBERTY, MUSCATINE CO., ST. JOSEPH'S (1892) [CEM] Rev. Dennis C. Martin.
Res.: 107 W. Sixth St., 52776-1246. Tel: 319-627-2229.
Catechesis/Religious Program—Students 153.
WEST POINT, LEE CO., ASSUMPTION OF THE BLESSED VIRGIN MARY, [CEM] Rev. Apo T. Mpanda.
Res.: 311 Ave. C, P.O. Box 68, 52656. Tel: 319-837-6808; Fax: 319-837-6808.
Catechesis/Religious Program—Students 29.
WHAT CHEER, KEOKUK CO., ST. JOSEPH'S, Closed. For inquiries for parish records contact the Pastoral Center.
WILLIAMSBURG, IOWA CO., ST. MARY'S (1891) [CEM] Rev. Joseph F. Roost.
Res.: 102 E. Penn, Box 119, 52361. Tel: 319-668-1397; Fax: 319-668-2487.
Catechesis/Religious Program—Tel: 319-668-2757. Students 187.
WILTON, MUSCATINE CO., ST. MARY'S (1857) [CEM] Rev. James J. Vrba.
Res.: 701 E. 3rd St., P.O. Box 477, 52778. Tel: 563-732-2271; Fax: 563-732-2269.
Catechesis/Religious Program—Tel: 563-785-6266. Students 70.

Chaplains of Public Institutions

IOWA CITY. *State University of Iowa Hospital*. Revs. Vitolds Valainis, E. William Kaska.
Veteran's Administration Hospital. Rev. Robert M. Striegel.

Special Assignment:
Rev.—
Regan, Timothy J., Genesis Medical Center, 1401 Central Park Ave., 52804.

On Duty Outside the Diocese:
Rev. Msgr.—
Gruss, Robert D., Pontifical North American College 00120 Vatican City State.
Revs.—
Beyer, Richard J., 1315 Chapelwood Dr., Waco, TX 76712.
Burnett, James E., 8505 Hemlock Ln., Darien, IL 60561.
Stecher, John E., 2701 Spring St., Fort Wayne, IN 46808.
Young, Ronald E., 3660 W. San Jose, #218, Fresno, CA 93711.

Military Chaplains:
Rev. Msgr.—
Spiegel, Robert H., CMR 409, Box 616, Apo, AE 09053.
Rev.—
Kneemiller, William C.

Retired:
Rev. Msgrs.—
Henricksen, Francis C., E.V., 1113 First St., Tipton, 52772.
Morrissey, Michael J., M.A., J.C.L., Pastoral Center, 2706 N. Gaines St., 52804.
Mottet, Marvin A., Pastoral Center, 2706 N. Gaines St., 52804-1998.
Schmidt, Robert, 5510 Woodland Ave., 52807.
Walter, Robert J., Pastoral Center, 2706 N. Gaines St., 52804-1998.
Revs.—
Benda, Eugene M., Lantern Park, 2200 Oakdale Rd., Coralville, 52241.
Bevenour, Richard F., 622 W. Escalon St., Fresno, CA 93704.
Borger, Theodore R., 6 Windy Ct., Verona, WI 53593-7904.
Braida, Ernest E., 1009 W. Marion St., Knoxville, 50138-2844.
Brothersen, Maynard J., Pastoral Center, 2706 N. Gaines St., 52804-1998.
Dawson, William F., Ph.D., 518 W. Locust St., 52803.
Doyle, Thomas R., 925 Applewood Ct. #4, Coralville, 52241.
Hoening, Gerald, 1432 Ave. E, Fort Madison, 52627-2629.
Hynes, John F., 3051 Holiday Ct., Bettendorf, 52722-3463.
Khan, Joseph Nguyen, 12772 Louise St., Garden Grove, CA 92841.
Mannhardt, Daniel C., 1360 Kimberly Ridge Rd., Bettendorf, 52722.
Manning, Martin B., 2617 Maplecrest, #102, Bettendorf, 52722.
Meyer, William O., Our Lady of Victory, 4105 N. Division St., 52806.
Mohr, Thomas H., 2122 E. Elm St., 52803.
Reilman, Thomas J., 2301 Agency St., #59, Burlington, 52601.
Rogers, Joseph, Kahl Home, 1101 W. Ninth St., 52804.
Ruppenkamp, Raymond, 4233 180th St., Clinton, 52732-8818.
Ryan, Philip V., St. Patrick Rectory, 215 S. Jackson St., P.O. Box 512, Brooklyn, 52211.
Shortall, Robert, 7100 Chase Oaks, Apt. 2313, Plano, TX 75025.
Stratman, Thomas F., Pastoral Center, 2706 N. Gaines St., 52804-1998.
Whalen, John J., 3001 S. Webster Ave., Apt. 118, Green Bay, WI 54301.
Wiegand, William R., Pastoral Center, 2706 Gaines St., 52804-1998.

Permanent Deacons:
Becker, James L., Muscatine
Beckman, Clifford C., Sperry
Boboth, Albert G., Davenport
Cadena, Juan J., Muscatine
Cosgrove, William T., Keokuk
Dankert, Larry F., Davenport
Donart, Arthur C., Thomson, IL
Donnelly, William G., Bettendorf
Duff, Dennis L., Bettendorf
Dvorak, Joseph F., Colfax
Frericks, Donald E., Blue Grass
Gengenbacher, Robert, Fort Madison
Gutierrez, Julian, Davenport
Hilgendorf, Ramon C., Clinton

Hittner, Paul F., East Moline, IL
Lennon, Patrick, Clinton
McCoy, Robert C., Davenport
Metzger, Charles A., Bettendorf
Miller, Jerome A., Iowa City
Montgomery, David, Oxford
Mosse, Marcel G., Davenport
O'Connor, Arthur, Olatha, KS
Olson, William D., Grinnell
Panther, Adrian, Mechanicsville
Rasmussen, Richard J., Bettendorf
Reha, David, Wellman
Rosenthal, Joseph I., Davenport
Schmitt, John H., Low Moor
Schroeder, William E., Carroll
Schuetzle, Jeffrey C., Clinton
Sheil, Michael D., DeWitt
Snavely, Robert E., Tipton
Stein, Ronald K., Donnellson
Strader, George D., Davenport
Striegel, James L., Delta
Tometich, Anton I., Muscatine
Vonderhaar, James J., West Point
Weber, John R., Bettendorf
Witt, Stephen J., Grinnell

INSTITUTIONS LOCATED IN THE DIOCESE

[A] COLLEGES AND UNIVERSITIES

DAVENPORT. *St. Ambrose University* 52803-2898. Tel: 563-333-6300; Fax: 563-333-6243. Email: admit@sau.edu. Web: www.sau.edu. Dr. Joan Lescinski, C.S.J., Pres.; Dr. Paul Koch, Interim Vice Pres. Academic Affairs; Michael Poster, Vice Pres. Finance; Dr. Edward G. Littig, Vice Pres. Advancement; Dr. James P. Loftus, Vice Pres. Enrollment Mgmt. & Student Svcs.; Rev. Charles A. Adam, Campus Chap.; Sr. Rita Cameron, Dir. Music Ministry & Spirituality; Mackenzie Grondahl, Dir. Service Learning & Justice Ministry; Sheila Deluhery, Assoc. Dir. Campus Min.; Mary Heinzman, Librarian Dir. Priests 8; Total Faculty & Staff 502; Lay Teachers 190; Students 3,729.

Priest Faculty: Revs. Charles A. Adam; William F. Dawson, Ph.D. (Retired); Joseph De Francisco, S.T.D. (BEA); Edmond J. Dunn, Ph.D.; Robert L. Grant, Ph.D. (DM); George W. McDaniel, Ph.D.; Brian Miclot, Ph.D.

[B] HIGH SCHOOLS, INTERPAROCHIAL

DAVENPORT. *Assumption High School*, 1020 W. Central Park Ave., 52804-1899. Tel: 563-326-5313; Fax: 563-326-3510. Email: craiga@mail.assumption.pvt.k12.ia.us. Web: www.assumptionhigh.org. Mr. Chuck Elbert, Prin.; Mr. Andrew Craig, Pres.; Shane Stephens, Dean of Students; Dan Huber, Spiritual Dir. Lay Teachers 29; Students 410.

BURLINGTON. *Notre Dame High School*, 702 S. Roosevelt Ave., 52601-1602. Tel: 319-754-8431; Fax: 319-752-8690. Email: dedwards@nd-burl.pvt.k12.ia.us. Ron Glasgow, Prin. Lay Teachers 16; Students 140.

CLINTON. *Prince of Peace College Preparatory*, 312 S. 4th St., 52732-4499. Tel: 563-242-1663; Fax: 563-243-8272. Email: npeart@prince.pvt.k12.ia.us. Web: www.prince.pvt.k12.ia.us. Mrs. Nancy Peart, Prin.; Sue Bergman, Business Mgr. Lay Teachers 12; Students 86.

[C] EDUCATION CENTERS

CLINTON. *Prince of Peace Preschool and Childcare* (Preschool & PreK), 245 26th Ave., N., 52732. Tel: 563-242-9258. Mrs. Mary Jensen, Dir.; Mrs. Nancy Peart, Prin. Lay Teachers 2; Students 56.

FORT MADISON. *Holy Trinity Schools*, 2600 Ave. A, 52627. Tel: 319-372-2486; Fax: 319-372-6310. Email: doris.turner@gpaea.k12.ia.us. Web: www.holytrinityschools.org. Mrs. Doris Turner, Chief Admin. of Holy Trinity Schools, Inc. Lay Teachers 38; Students 361.

IOWA CITY. *The Regina Inter-Parish Catholic Education Center*, 2140 Rochester Ave., 52245. Tel: 319-337-2580; Fax: 319-337-4109. Web: www.icregina.com.

Regina Junior Senior High School, 2150 Rochester Ave., 52245. Tel: 319-338-5436; Fax: 319-887-3817. Email: dkrummel@regina.pvt.k12.ia.us. David Krummel, Prin. Lay Teachers 31; Students 419.

Regina Elementary School, 2120 Rochester Ave., 52245-3527. Tel: 319-337-5739; Fax: 319-337-4109. Email: cvincent@regina.pvt.k12.ia.us. Ms. Celeste Vincent, Prin. Lay Teachers 31; Students 465.

Regina Religious Education, 2140 Rochester Ave., 52245. Tel: 319-351-7638; Fax: 319-337-4109. Sr. Mary Frances Michalec.

Regina Special Events Office, 2140 Rochester Ave., 52245. Tel: 319-358-2455; Fax: 319-337-4109.

Regina Preschool-Daycare, 2140 Rochester Ave., 52245. Tel: 319-337-6198; Fax: 319-337-4109. Ms. Mary Pechous.

KEOKUK. *Keokuk Catholic Schools, Inc.*, 2981 Plank Rd., 52632-2399. Tel: 319-524-5450; Fax: 319-524-7725. Laurie Mendenhall, Chief Admin. & Prin.

St. Vincent's Extended Day Care Program, 2981 Plank Rd., 52632-5452. Tel: 319-524-6375. Lay Teachers 11; Students 70.

[D] ELEMENTARY SCHOOLS, INTERPAROCHIAL

BURLINGTON. *Burlington Notre Dame Schools, Inc.*, (Grades PreK-6), Notre Dame Elementary School, 700 S. Roosevelt Ave., 52601-1602. Tel: 319-752-3776; 319-754-4417; Fax: 319-752-8690. Robert Carr, Prin.; Connie Siefken, Librarian. Lay Teachers 19; Students 277.

MUSCATINE. *Bishop Hayes Catholic School*, 2407 Cedar St., 52761-2696. Tel: 563-263-3264; Fax: 563-263-6700. Email: ann-gomez@mail.mus-hayes.pvt.k12.ia.us. Web: www.bishophayescatholicschool.com. Ann Gomez, Prin. Lay Teachers 14; Students 191.

OTTUMWA. *Seton Catholic School*, 117 E. Fourth St., 52501-2992. Tel: 641-682-8826; Fax: 641-682-6202. Terri Schofield, Prin.; Garnet Brandt, Librarian. Lay Teachers 11; Students 126.

[E] CATHOLIC STUDENT CENTERS

IOWA CITY. *Newman Catholic Student Center* 104 E. Jefferson St., 52245. Tel: 319-337-3106; Fax: 319-337-6858. Email: newman-center@uiowa.edu. Web: www.newman-ic.org. Revs. Edward J. Fitzpatrick, Dir.; Jeffry W. Belger.

[F] RESIDENTIAL ADOLESCENT CARE CENTERS

CLINTON. *Arch, Inc.*, Box 0278, 52733-0278. Tel: 563-243-9035; Fax: 563-243-7796. Email: larchia@qwest.net. Keith Kalaukoa, Exec. Dir. Total Assisted 19; Total Staff 21.

Arch I, 402 S. Fourth St., 52732. Tel: 563-243-3980.
Arch II, 734 Fifth Ave. S., 52732. Tel: 563-242-5082.
Arch III, 505 7th Ave. S., 52732. Tel: 563-242-8740; Fax: 563-242-8740.

[G] GENERAL HOSPITALS

CENTERVILLE. *Mercy Medical Center - Centerville*, One St. Joseph's Dr., 52544. Tel: 641-437-4111; Fax: 641-437-3304. Web: www.mercycenterville.org. Clint Christianson, Pres. Owned by Mercy Medical Center, Des Moines.; Attended from St. Mary's, Centerville. Bed Capacity 25; Patients Assisted Annually 69,245; Total Staff 235.

Legacies, The Foundation of Mercy Medical Center Tel: 614-437-3434; Fax: 641-437-3304. Ann Young, Pres.

CLINTON. *Mercy Medical Center - Clinton* A subsidiary of Trinity Health., 1410 N. Fourth St., 52732. Tel: 563-244-5555; Fax: 563-244-5592. Web: www.mercyclinton.com. Donna Oliver, Pres. & CEO; Rev. John J. Stack. Bed Capacity 159; Staff 1,014; Total Assisted Annually 187,000.

Mercy Living Center - South, 638 S. Bluff Blvd., 52732. Tel: 563-244-3704; Fax: 563-244-3756. Bed Capacity 97.

Mercy Living Center - North, 600 14th Ave. N., 52732. Tel: 563-244-3884; Fax: 563-244-3882. Bed Capacity 86.

IOWA CITY. *Mercy Hospital*, 500 E. Market St., 52245-2633. Tel: 319-358-2725; Fax: 319-887-2884. Email: mark.mcdermott@mercyic.org. Web: www.mercyiowacity.org. Ronald R. Reed, Pres. & CEO; Mark McDermott, Dir., Pastoral Care; Sr. Theresa Kruml, O.S.U., Chap.; David Oakland, Chap.; Tim Bernemann, Chap. Sisters 2; Bed Capacity 234; Total Staff 1,468; Patients Assisted Annually 91,608.

[H] SOCIAL ACTION DEPARTMENTS

DAVENPORT. *Project Renewal of Davenport, Inc.*, Nazarath House, 906 W. Fifth St., 52802. Tel: 563-324-0800. Email: projectrenewal@revealed.net. Ann Schwickerath, (In Res.); Carl Callaway, (In Res.).

**Thomas Merton House, Inc.*, c/o 2706 N. Gaines St., 52804. Tel: 563-324-1128; Fax: 563-324-5842. Email: marv422@aol.com. Rev. Msgr. Marvin A. Mottet (Retired).

[I] HOMES FOR AGED

DAVENPORT. *Kahl Home for the Aged and Infirm*, 1101 W. Ninth St., 52804. Tel: 563-324-1621; Fax: 563-324-1723. Sr. M. Lois Baniewicz, O.Carm., Asst. Admin. & Prioress; Rev. Joseph Rogers, Chap. (Retired). Carmelite Sisters for the Aged and Infirm. Sisters 5; Bed Capacity 132; Total Assisted 132; Total Staff 195.

CLINTON. *The Alverno Health Care Facility* 52732. Tel: 563-242-1521; Fax: 563-243-3016. Email: lgoodman@thealverno.com. Web: www.alvernohealthcare.com. Libby Goodman, Pres. & CEO. Sisters of St. Francis, Clinton, IA 2; Bed Capacity 132; Total Assisted 243; Total Staff 178.

[J] MONASTERIES AND RESIDENCES FOR PRIESTS AND BROTHERS

DAVENPORT. *St. Vincent Center*, 2706 N. Gaines St., 52804. Tel: 563-324-1911; Fax: 563-324-5842. Email: maaske@davenportdiocese.org. Web: www.davenportdiocese.org. Most Rev. William E. Franklin, D.D., Bishop Emeritus; Rev. Msgrs. John M. Hyland, V.G.; Michael J. Morrissey, M.A., J.C.L. (Retired); Marvin A. Mottet (Retired); Robert J. Walter (Retired); Revs. Maynard J. Brothersen (Retired); Martin G. Goetz; Thomas F. Stratman (Retired); William R. Wiegand (Retired).

IOWA CITY. *O'Keefe Hall*, 104 E. Jefferson St., 52245. Tel: 319-337-3106; Fax: 319-337-6858. Email: newman-center@uiowa.edu. Web: www.newman-ic.org. Rev. Edward J. Fitzpatrick, Dir. In Res. Revs. E. William Kaska; Mansuetus Setonga; Robert M. Striegel; Vitalis Torwel (Nigeria); Vitolds Valainis.

WEVER. *Generalate of the Brothers of the Poor of Saint Francis*, 3405 190th St., 52658. Tel: 319-372-9543; Fax: 319-372-9543. Email: markgast@hughes.net. Web: www.brothersofthepoorofstfrancis.org.

[K] CONVENTS AND RESIDENCES FOR SISTERS

DAVENPORT. *Franciscan Sisters of Christ the Divine Teacher*, 2605 Boies Ave., 52802. Tel: 563-323-1502. Sr. Susan Rueve, O.S.F., Supr. Sisters 3.

Humility of Mary Center - Motherhouse of the Congregation of the Humility of Mary, 820 W. Central Park Ave., 52804. Tel: 563-323-9466; Fax: 563-323-5209. Email: sisters@chmiowa.org. Web: chmiowa.org. Sr. Mary Rehmann, C.H.M., Pres. Total in Residence 43; Total Staff 11.

CLINTON. *The Canticle*, 841 13th Ave. N., 52732-5162. Tel: 563-242-7903; Fax: 563-242-8024. Sr. Janice Cebula, O.S.F., Pres. Residence of the Sisters of St. Francis, Clinton, Iowa. Total in Residence 32.

Sisters of St. Francis, Clinton, Iowa, Administrative Center, 843 13th Ave. N., 52732-5115. Tel: 563-242-7611; Fax: 563-243-0007. Email: sisters@clintonfranciscans.com. Web: www.clintonfranciscans.com. Sr. Janice I. Cebula, O.S.F., Pres. Sisters 70; Novices 1.

ELDRIDGE. *Carmel of the Queen of Heaven Discalced Carmelite Nuns*, 17937 250th St., 52748. Tel: 563-285-8387; Fax: 563-285-7467. Email: solitude@netins.net. Web: www.carmelitesofeldridge.org. Sr. Lynne Elwinger, O.C.D., Prioress. Professed Sisters 10.

IOWA CITY. *Dominican Sisters*, 304 Oberlin St., 52245. Tel: 319-339-0993; Fax: 319-338-7475. Email: dolorescyr@earthlink.net. Web: www.dominicanromanusa.org. Sr. Dolores Cyr, O.P., Local Community Treas. Sisters 2.

[L] RETREAT PROGRAMS-CENTERS

DAVENPORT. *Hope and Healing Ministries*, P.O. Box 2772, 52809-2772. Tel: 563-322-1645; Fax: 563-322-1684. Maria Bain, Dir.

WHEATLAND. *New Horizons of Faith: Our Lady of the Prairie Retreat*, 2664 145th Ave., 52777. Tel: 563-323-9466; Fax: 563-323-5209. Email: mrehmann@chmiowa.org. Mailing Address: 820 W. Central Park Ave., 52804.

[M] MISCELLANEOUS

DAVENPORT. **Assumption Foundation for K-12 Schools*, 1020 W. Central Park Ave., 52804. Tel: 563-326-5313; Fax: 563-326-3510. Email: craiga@mail.assumption.pvt.k12.ia.us. Web: www.assumptionhigh.org.

Catholic Foundation for the Diocese of Davenport, 2706 N. Gaines, 52804. Tel: 563-324-1911; Fax: 563-324-5842. Web: www.davenportdiocese.org. Most Rev. Martin J. Amos, D.D., Contact Person.

Catholic Service Board, 1101 W. 9th St., 52804.

Congregation of the Humility of Mary Charitable Trust, 820 W. Central Park Ave., 52804. Tel: 563-323-9466; Fax: 563-323-5209. Email: sisters@chmiowa.org. Web: www.chmiowa.org. Sr. Mary Rehmann, C.H.M., Contact Person.

Davenport Deanery, St. Paul the Apostle, 916 E. Rusholme St., 52803-2596. Very Rev. Michael J. Spiekermeier, V.F.

Eagles' Wings Incorporated, P.O. Box 4804, 52808.

Humility of Mary Housing, Inc., 1228 E. 12th St.,

52803. Tel: 563-326-1330; Fax: 563-326-0756. Email: hmhiowa@netexpress.net. Web: www.humilityofmaryhousing.com. Sr. M. Johanna Rickl, C.H.M., Chairperson Bd. Directors. Total Assisted 237; Total Staff 15; Total in Residence 138.

**Humility of Mary Shelter, Inc.*, 1016 W. 5th St., 52802-3404. Tel: 563-326-1330; Fax: 563-326-0756. Sr. Mary Ann Vogel, C.H.M., Contact Person.

Kingdom Co., 2706 N. Gaines St., 52804-1998. Tel: 563-324-1911; Fax: 563-324-5842. Email: maaske@davenportdiocese.org. Web: www.davenportdiocese.org. Charlene Maaske, CPA, M.B.A., Contact Person.

St. Paul the Apostle Foundation, 916 E. Rusholme St., 52803. Tel: 563-322-7994. Email: davstpaul@diodav.org. Very Rev. Michael J. Spiekermeier, V.F., Contact Person.

Quad Cities Catholic Deaf Ministry, 4105 N. Division St., 52806-4741. Tel: 563-391-4245; Fax: 563-445-1003. Email: parizekj@diodav.org. Rev. Msgr. James F. Parizek, J.C.L., Contact Person.

Scott County Catholic Education Services, Inc., 1926 Marquette St., 52804. Tel: 563-324-3205; Fax: 530-324-9331. Web: www.saintspvt.k12.ia.us. Mrs. Tammy Conrad, Prin. & Contact Person.

Spirit, Inc., 2214 Harrison St., 52804. Tel: 563-324-1776. Email: spiritinc@netzero.net. Paul Roe, Contact.

Vietnamese Catholic Community of the Quad Cities, 422 E. 10th St., 52803. Tel: 563-326-6279; Fax: 563-326-6014. Rev. Hai Duc Dinh.

St. Vincent Home Corporation, 2706 N. Gaines St., 52804. Tel: 563-324-1911; Fax: 563-324-5842. Email: ferris@davenportdiocese.org. Web: www.davenportdiocese.org. Kent E. Ferris, Contact Person.

BETTENDORF. *Catholic Endowment of Bettendorf, Iowa, Inc.*, 2898 Villa Ct., 52722. Tel: 563-332-4271. Gregory P. Adamson, Vice Pres. & Contact Person.

BROOKLYN. *St. Patrick Parish Foundation*, 215 Jackson St., 52211-0512. Tel: 641-522-7714. Glen J. Kriegel, Pres.

BURLINGTON. *Burlington Notre Dame Foundation*, 702 S. Roosevelt Ave., 52601. Tel: 319-752-8690; Fax: 319-752-8690. Deb Trine, Contact Person.

St. Vincent De Paul Society, St. John the Baptist Church Conference, 700 Division St., 52601. Tel: 319-752-9332. Jim Wade, Contact Person.

Society of St. Vincent de Paul, Council of Waterloo, Iowa

R.E.B.A. (Religious Education Burlington Area) Trust Fund, 700 Division St., 52601. Tel: 319-752-6733; Fax: 319-753-5221.

CENTERVILLE. *St. Mary's Foundation of Centerville*, 828 S. 18th St., 52544. Tel: 641-437-1985.

CLINTON. *Mercy Home Care and Hospice*, 638 S. Bluff, 52732. Tel: 563-244-3766; Fax: 563-244-3719. Email: meistesk@mercyhealth.com. Web: www.mercyclinton.com. Sharon Meister, M.S., Dir.; Donna Oliver, CEO.

Mount St. Clare Speech & Hearing Center, Inc., 562 N. Bluff Blvd., 52732. Tel: 563-242-4070; Fax: 563-242-2426. Email: marcella.narlock@mscspeechandhearingcenter.org. Web: www.clintonfranciscans.com. Sr. Marcella Marie Narlock, O.S.F., Dir. Sisters of St. Francis.

Mount St. Clare Education Foundation, 843 13th Ave. N., 52732-5115. Tel: 563-242-7611; Fax: 563-243-0007. Email: president@clintonfranciscans.com.

Sisters of St. Francis, Clinton, Iowa, Charitable Trust, 843 13th Ave. N., 52732. Tel: 563-242-7611; Fax: 563-243-0007. Email: sisters@clintonfranciscans.com. Web: www.clintonfranciscans.com. Sr. Janice Cebula, O.S.F., Pres.

GRINNELL. *St. Mary's Parish Foundation, Grinnell, Iowa*, 1022 Broad St., P.O. Box 655, 50112. Tel: 641-236-4545; Fax: 641-236-8770. Mr. William D. Olson, Contact Person.

HOUGHTON. *Marquette Foundation*, 309 2nd St., 52631. Gale Thompson, Pres.

IOWA CITY. *Catholic Community Foundation*, 1222 Rochester Ave., P.O. Box 1581, 52244. Tel: 319-354-5866; Fax: 319-354-1911. Email: ccf@mchsi.com. April E. Rouner, Exec. Dir.

Mercy Hospital Foundation, 500 E. Market St., 52245-2689. Tel: 319-339-3657; Fax: 319-358-2624. Julie Johnston, Pres.

Mercy Hospital Guild of Iowa City, Iowa, 500 E. Market St., 52245. Tel: 319-339-3659. Carol Ebinger, Volunteer Coord.

Mercy Outreach Iowa City, Inc., 500 E. Market St., 52245. Tel: 319-339-3540. Ronald Reed, CEO.

Mercy Hospital, Iowa City, Iowa, 500 E. Market St., 52245. Tel: 319-339-3540. Ronald Reed, CEO.

Roman Catholic Ministries of Iowa City, Iowa (2002) 104 E. Jefferson, 52245. Tel: 319-337-3106; Fax: 319-337-6858.

St. Thomas More New Season Charitable Trust, 3000 12th Ave., Coralville, 52241. Tel: 319-337-2173. Web: www.stthomasmoreic.com. Rev. Walter Helms, Contact Person.

KEOKUK. *Ladies of Charity of Keokuk*, 1524 High St., 52632. Tel: 319-524-7517. Lois Waldron, Pres.

OTTUMWA. *The Center for International Resources, Inc. Mexico*, 205 Hill Ave., 52501. Tel: 641-682-4264; Fax: 641-684-4690. Kathryn Bissell, Ph.D., M.A., Chm. & Exec. Dir.

RELIGIOUS INSTITUTES OF MEN REPRESENTED IN THE DIOCESE

For further details refer to the corresponding bracketed number in the Religious Institutes of Men or Women section.

[0460]—*Brothers of the Poor of St. Francis*—C.F.P.

[1060]—*Society of the Precious Blood*—C.PP.S.

RELIGIOUS INSTITUTES OF WOMEN REPRESENTED IN THE DIOCESE

[0230]—*Benedictine Sisters of Pontifical Jurisdiction*—O.S.B.

[0330]—*Carmelite Sisters for the Aged and Infirm*—O.Carm.

[2100]—*Congregation of the Humility of Mary*—C.H.M.

[1780]—*Congregation of the Sisters of the Third Order of St. Francis of Perpetual Adoration*—F.S.P.A.

[0420]—*Discalced Carmelite Nuns*—O.C.D.

[1070-03]—*Dominican Sisters*—O.P.

[1115]—*Dominican Sisters of Peace*—O.P.

[1120]—*Dominican Sisters of the Roman Congregation*—O.P.

[]—*Franciscan Sisters of Christ the Divine Teacher*—O.S.F.

[2575]—*Institute of the Sisters of Mercy of the Americas* (Chicago)—R.S.M.

[2960]—*Institute of the Sisters of Mercy of the Americas* (Cedar Rapids)—R.S.M.

[]—*Notre Dame Sisters*—N.D.

[2970]—*School Sisters of Notre Dame, St. Louis*—S.S.N.D.

[]—*School Sisters of St. Francis of Milwaukee*—S.S.S.F.

[]—*Sisters for Christian Community*

[0430]—*Sisters of Charity of the Blessed Virgin Mary*—B.V.M.

[1540]—*Sisters of Saint Francis, Clinton, Iowa*—O.S.F.

[1570]—*Sisters of St. Francis of the Holy Family*—O.S.F.

[3840]—*Sisters of St. Joseph of Carondelet*—C.S.J.

[3320]—*Sisters of the Presentation of the B.V.M.*—P.B.V.M.

[4120-03]—*Ursuline of Louisville, KY*—O.S.U.

NECROLOGY

† Kelly, Daniel J., (Retired)—Died Jan. 23, 2009

† Kokjohn, Joseph E., (Retired)—Died May 21, 2009

† Linnenbrink, Harry H., (Retired)—Died June 17, 2009

An asterisk (*) denotes an organization that has established tax-exempt status directly with the IRS and is not covered by the USCCB Group Ruling.

Archdiocese of Denver

Archidioecesis Denveriensis

Most Reverend

CHARLES J. CHAPUT, O.F.M.CAP., D.D.

Archbishop of Denver; ordained August 29, 1970; Episcopal ordination July 26, 1988; appointed Bishop of Rapid City April 11, 1988; appointed Archbishop of Denver February 18, 1997.

AS CHRIST LOVED THE CHURCH

Most Reverend

JAMES D. CONLEY, D.D., S.T.L.

Auxiliary Bishop of Denver; ordained May 18, 1985; appointed Auxiliary Bishop of Denver and Titular Bishop of Cissa April 10, 2008; ordained May 30, 2008.

ESTABLISHED A VICARIATE-APOSTOLIC IN 1868.

Square Miles 40,154.

Erected a Diocese August 16, 1887; created an Archdiocese November 15, 1941.

Comprises the northern part of the State of Colorado, including the 25 Counties of Adams, Arapahoe, Boulder, Broomfield, Clear Creek, Denver, Eagle, Garfield, Gilpin, Grand, Jackson, Jefferson, Larimer, Logan, Moffat, Morgan, Phillips, Pitkin, Rio Blanco, Routt, Sedgwick, Summit, Washington, Weld and Yuma.

For legal titles of parishes and archdiocesan institutions, consult the Chancery.

Pastoral Center: 1300 S. Steele St., Denver, CO 80210. Tel: 303-722-4687; Fax: 303-715-2041.

Web: www.archden.org/archden

Email: dcr@archden.org

STATISTICAL OVERVIEW

Personnel	
Archbishops	1
Auxiliary Bishops	1
Abbots	1
Priests: Diocesan Active in Diocese	120
Priests: Diocesan Active Outside Diocese	11
Priests: Diocesan in Foreign Missions	1
Priests: Retired, Sick or Absent	51
Number of Diocesan Priests	183
Religious Priests in Diocese	108
Total Priests in Diocese	291
Extern Priests in Diocese	25
Ordinations:	
Diocesan Priests	4
Transitional Deacons	9
Permanent Deacons	9
Permanent Deacons in Diocese	190
Total Brothers	15
Total Sisters	272
Parishes	
Parishes	119
With Resident Pastor:	
Resident Diocesan Priests	103
Resident Religious Priests	16
Missions	24
New Parishes Created	1
Professional Ministry Personnel:	
Brothers	15
Sisters	272
Welfare	
Catholic Hospitals	4
Total Assisted	296,114
Health Care Centers	6
Total Assisted	26,125
Homes for the Aged	6
Total Assisted	614
Day Care Centers	11
Total Assisted	1,346
Specialized Homes	2
Total Assisted	1,470
Special Centers for Social Services	19
Total Assisted	97,922
Residential Care of Disabled	2
Total Assisted	103
Other Institutions	34
Total Assisted	13,142
Educational	
Seminaries, Diocesan	2
Students from This Diocese	64
Students from Other Diocese	39
Diocesan Students in Other Seminaries	9
Total Seminarians	73
Colleges and Universities	2
Total Students	15,061
High Schools, Diocesan and Parish	2
Total Students	938
High Schools, Private	5
Total Students	3,017
Elementary Schools, Diocesan and Parish	37
Total Students	9,075
Elementary Schools, Private	2
Total Students	578
Non-residential Schools for the Disabled	1
Total Students	85
Catechesis/Religious Education:	
High School Students	4,267
Elementary Students	23,917
Total Students under Catholic Instruction	57,011
Teachers in the Diocese:	
Priests	5
Brothers	3
Sisters	29
Lay Teachers	966
Vital Statistics	
Receptions into the Church:	
Infant Baptism Totals	10,510
Minor Baptism Totals	917
Adult Baptism Totals	424
Received into Full Communion	498
First Communions	7,996
Confirmations	5,450
Marriages:	
Catholic	1,003
Interfaith	311
Total Marriages	1,314
Deaths	2,618
Total Catholic Population	533,809
Total Population	3,248,652

Former Bishops—Most Revs. JOSEPH PROJECTUS MACHEBEUF, D.D., cons. Titular Bishop of Epiphania and Vicar Apostolic of Colorado and Utah, Aug. 16, 1868; first Bishop of Denver in 1887; died July 10, 1889; NICHOLAS CHRYSOSTOM MATZ, D.D., cons. Titular Bishop of Telmessa and Coadjutor of Denver cum jure successionis, Oct. 28, 1887; succeeded to the See of Denver, July 10, 1889; died Aug. 9, 1917; J. HENRY TIHEN, D.D., ord. April 26, 1886; cons. Bishop of Lincoln, July 6, 1911; transferred to the See of Denver, Sept. 21, 1917; resigned Jan. 6, 1931; Apostolic Admin. until July 16, 1931; died Jan. 14, 1940; URBAN J. VEHR, D.D., ord. May 29, 1915; Bishop of Denver; appt. April 17, 1931; cons. June 10, 1931; installed July 16, 1931; elevated to Archiepiscopal dignity, Nov. 15, 1941; appt. Jan. 6, 1942; installed as Archbishop of Denver; resigned Feb. 22, 1967; died Sept. 19, 1973; JAMES V. CASEY, D.D., J.C.D., ord. Dec. 8, 1939; Titular Bishop of Citium and Auxiliary of Lincoln; appt. Auxiliary Bishop April 5, 1957; cons. April 24, 1957; appt. Bishop of Lincoln June 14, 1957; promoted to Archbishop of Denver, Feb. 22, 1967; died March 14, 1986; J. FRANCIS CARDINAL STAFFORD, D.D., ord. Dec. 15, 1957; cons. Auxiliary Bishop of Baltimore, Feb. 29, 1976; installed Bishop of Memphis Jan. 18, 1983; appt. Nov. 16, 1982; installed Archbishop of Denver July 31, 1986; appt. June 3, 1986; appt. President of the Pontifical Council for the Laity in Rome, Aug. 1996; elevated to Cardinal Feb. 21, 1998.

The Pastoral Center—1300 S. Steele St., Denver, 80210-2599. Tel: 303-722-4687; Fax: 303-715-2041.

Executive Assistant to the Archbishop—PATRICIA J. MCDONALD. Tel: 303-715-3129.

Vicars General—Most Rev. JAMES D. CONLEY, D.D., S.T.L.; Rev. Msgr. THOMAS S. FRYAR, V.G.

Moderator of the Curia—Rev. Msgr. THOMAS S. FRYAR, V.G.

Vicar for Clergy—Rev. Msgr. BERNARD A. SCHMITZ. Tel: 303-715-3197. Email: father.schmitz@archden.org.

Vicar for Hispanic Ministry—Rev. Msgr. JORGE DE LOS SANTOS.

Chancellor—FRANCIS X. MAIER.

Vice Chancellor—JAMES DANIEL FLYNN, J.C.L.

Archivist—KARYL KLEIN.

Chief Financial Officer—DAVID A. HOLDEN.

Presbyteral Council—

Archbishop—Most Rev. CHARLES J. CHAPUT, O.F.M.Cap., D.D., Pres.

Auxiliary Bishop—Most Rev. JAMES D. CONLEY, D.D., S.T.L.

Elected Representatives from Deanery to Presbyteral Council—Very Revs. STEPHEN E. ADAMS, V.F.; KEVIN R. AUGUSTYN, V.F.; DANIEL LEONARD, V.F.; JASON M. THUERAUF, V.F.; GREGORY CIOCH, V.F.; JAMES SPAHN, V.F.; GREGORY AMES, V.F.; ANDREW KEMBERLING, V.F.; ROBERT D. FISHER, V.F.; DANIEL J. NORICK, V.F.; JAMES K. GOGGINS, V.F.; DAVID ALLEN, V.F.

Newly Ordained Representative—Rev. STEVEN VOSS.

Religious Order Representative—Rev. THOMAS P. LYNCH, O.P.

Ex Officio Members—Most Rev. JAMES D. CONLEY, D.D., S.T.L.; Rev. NOE CARREON; Rev. Msgrs. JORGE DE LOS SANTOS; THOMAS S. FRYAR, V.G.; MICHAEL G. GLENN, S.T.L.; Very Rev. FLORIAN

MARTIN-CALAMA, S.T.L.; Rev. Msgr. BERNARD A. SCHMITZ; Rev. FRANK MARONEY.

Members At Large—Rev. Msgrs. EDWARD BUELT, J.C.L., Chm.; ROBERT KINKEL.

College of Consultors—Most Revs. CHARLES J. CHAPUT, O.F.M.Cap., D.D.; JAMES D. CONLEY, D.D., S.T.L.; Very Rev. STEPHEN E. ADAMS, V.F.; Rev. Msgrs. EDWARD BUELT, J.C.L.; THOMAS S. FRYAR, V.G.; MICHAEL G. GLENN, S.T.L.; ROBERT J. KINKEL, V.F.; BERNARD A. SCHMITZ; Rev. FRANK MARONEY.

Archdiocesan Finance Council—Most Revs. CHARLES J. CHAPUT, O.F.M.Cap., D.D.; JAMES D. CONLEY, D.D., S.T.L.; Rev. Msgr. THOMAS S. FRYAR, V.G.; MICHAEL L. O'DONNELL, Chm.; DAVID A. HOLDEN; WILLIAM E. KEEFE; REID GODBOLT, Esq.; JAMES S. HARRINGTON; BROOKE LEER; STEVE MARKEL; JENNIFER L. NEPPEL; JOHN A. IKARD; LOWELL A. HARE; MICHAEL J. POLAKOVIC; JEFF SCHMITZ; WILLIAM G. TRAINOR.

Deaneries—Very Revs. DANIEL LEONARD, V.F., East Denver; GREGORY AMES, V.F., North Denver; JAMES K. GOGGINS, V.F., West Denver; ANDREW KEMBERLING, V.F., Southeast Denver; ROBERT D. FISHER, V.F., Southwest Denver; STEPHEN E. ADAMS, V.F., Aurora; KEVIN R. AUGUSTYN, V.F., Boulder; GREGORY CIOCH, V.F., Fort Collins; ROBERT L. WEDOW, Eastern Plains; REINHOLD WEISSBECK, V.F., Greeley; DAVID ALLEN, V.F., Western Slope; DANIEL J. NORICK, V.F., West Central Denver.

Metropolitan Tribunal

Metropolitan Tribunal—1535 Logan St., Denver, 80203. Tel: 303-894-8994.

Judicial Vicar—Very Rev. JAMES S. MORENO, J.C.D.

Executive Director—JAMES DANIEL FLYNN, J.C.L.

Clerk of Due Process—MARK ROHLENA, Esq.

Promoter of Justice—Rev. Msgr. EDWARD BUELT, J.C.L.

Metropolitan Judges—Very Revs. JAMES S. MORENO, J.C.D.; ROBERT P. HUNDT, J.C.L.; JAMES DANIEL FLYNN, J.C.L.; CARLOS VENEGAS, J.C.L.

Defenders of the Bond—Rev. Msgrs. THOMAS S. FRYAR, V.G.; MICHAEL J. CHAMBERLAIN, J.C.L., V.F.; Sr. MARY PIERRE JEAN WILSON, R.S.M.

Judicial Auditors and Assessors—Deacon ANTHONY PIERSON; ANN SANCHEZ.

Advocates— Advocates appointed individually for particular cases.

Ecclesiastical Notaries—RONDA WHITEHURST; ANN SANCHEZ.

Coordinator of Second Instance—RONDA WHITEHURST.

The Archdiocese of Denver, a Colorado Corporation Sole

Archdiocesan Offices and Ministries

Unless otherwise indicated, offices and ministries are located in the Pastoral Center on the campus of The John Paul II Center for the New Evangelization, Inc., 1300 S. Steele St., Denver, Colorado 80210. Tel: 303-722-4687. Web: www.archden.org.

Office of Archbishop—

Archbishop—Most Rev. CHARLES J. CHAPUT, O.F.M.Cap., D.D. Tel: 303-715-3129. Email: shepherd@archden.org.

Executive Assistant—PATRICIA J. MCDONALD. Tel: 303-715-3129. Email: patricia.mcdonald@archden.org.

Archbishop's Secretary—KERRY KOBER. Tel: 303-715-3129. Email: kerry.kober@archden.org.

Secretary—HATTY ARENIVER, Sec. Tel: 303-715-3185. Email: hatty.areniver@archden.org.

Events Coordinator—MERCY GUTTIEREZ. Tel: 303-715-3207. Email: mercy.guttierez@archden.org.

Auxiliary Bishop and Vicar General—Most Rev. JAMES D. CONLEY, D.D., S.T.L. Tel: 303-715-3100. Email: bishop.conley@archden.org.

Executive Assistant—SHARON DOERFLINGER. Tel: 303-715-3100. Email: sharon.doerflinger@archden.org.

Vicar General and Moderator of the Curia—Rev. Msgr. THOMAS S. FRYAR, V.G. Tel: 303-715-3263. Email: msgr.fryar@archden.org.

Administrative Assistant—CARRIE SIGMAN. Tel: 303-715-3263. Email: carrie.sigman@archden.org.

Vicar for Clergy—Rev. Msgr. BERNARD A. SCHMITZ. Tel: 303-715-3197. Email: father.schmitz@archden.org.

Administrative Assistant—MARIE SAILAS. Tel: 303-715-3197. Email: marie.sailas@archden.org.

Vicar for Hispanic Ministry—Rev. Msgr. JORGE DE LOS SANTOS. Tel: 303-715-3169. Email: father.santos@archden.org.

Executive Assistant—URSULA JIMENEZ. Tel: 303-715-3247. Email: ursula.jimenez@archden.org.

Chancellor—FRANCIS X. MAIER. Tel: 303-715-3185. Email: francis.maier@archden.org.

Ecumenical and Interreligious Affairs—PHIL WEB. Tel: 303-715-3160. Email: phil.webb@archden.org.

Master of Ceremonies—Deacon CHARLES W. PARKER JR. Tel: 303-715-3156. Email: deacon.parker@archden.org.

Annual Giving—

Director—TODD J. SMITH. Tel: 303-715-3116. Email: todd.smith@archden.org.

Executive Secretary—BETTY JANE NELSON. Tel: 303-715-3111. Email: bettyjane.nelson@archden.org.

Archives—

Archivist—KARYL KLEIN. Tel: 303-520-9986. Email: archives@archden.org.

Black Catholics—

Director—MARY LEISRING. Tel: 303-715-3165. Email: mary.leisring@archden.org.

Catholic Schools—

Superintendent—RICHARD L. THOMPSON. Tel: 303-715-3132. Email: richard.thompson@archden.org.

Assistant Superintendent—Sr. ELIZABETH YOUNGS, S.C.L. Tel: 303-715-3189. Email: sister.youngs@archden.org.

Special Programs Director and Assistant to the Superintendent—BARBARA ANGLADA. Tel: 303-715-3132. Email: barbara.anglada@archden.org.

Cemeteries and Mortuary—

Director—MICHAEL J. WRIGHT (see also Section S, Archdiocesan Cemeteries) Tel: 303-424-7785. Email: michael.wright@archden.org.

Child and Youth Protection—

Director—CHRISTOPHER POND, O.C.D.S. Tel: 303-715-3226. Email: chris.pond@archden.org.

Safe Environment Coordinator and Assistant to Director—NICKI SCHEURWATER. Tel: 303-715-3241. Email: nicki.scheurwater@archden.org.

Colorado Catholic Conference—1535 Logan St., Denver, 80203. Tel: 303-894-8808. Web: cocatholicconference.org. Email: ccc@cocatholicconference.org.

Executive Director—JENNIFER KRASKA.

Coordinator—DIANE CHAVEZ.

Communications and Periodicals—

Director—JEANETTE DEMELO. Tel: 303-715-3230. Email: info@archden.org.

Denver Catholic Register—ROXANNE KING, Editor. Tel: 303-715-3215. Email: editor@archden.org.

El Pueblo Catolico—ROSSANA GONI, Editor. Tel: 303-715-3219. Email: elpueblo@archden.org.

Diaconate—

Director of Deacon Personnel—Deacon JOSEPH DONOHOE. Tel: 303-715-3198. Email: deacon.donohoe@archden.org.

Diaconate Coordinator—MARY BORDA. Tel: 303-715-3198. Email: mary.borda@archden.org.

Diaconate Formation— (see section A, Seminaries, Religious or Scholasticates: Saint John Vianney Theological Seminary)

Evangelization and Catechesis—

Metro Area Parishes—JAMES CAVANAGH, Dir. Tel: 303-715-3107. Email: james.cavanagh@archden.org.

Northern, Eastern Plains and Western Slope Parishes—DONALD SCHNEIDER, Dir., Mailing Address: P.O. Box 124, Longmont, 80501. Tel: 303-678-0900. Email: archden-northern@msn.com.

Finance, Administration and Planning—

CFO and Executive Director—DAVID A. HOLDEN. Tel: 303-715-3258. Email: david.holden@archden.org.

Executive Assistant—CAROLINE ROSE. Tel: 303-715-3258. Email: caroline.rose@archden.org.

Hispanic Ministry—

Director—LUIS SOTO. Tel: 303-715-3117. Email: luis.soto@archden.org.

Executive Assistant—URSULA JIMENEZ. Tel: 303-715-3247. Email: ursula.jimenez@archden.org.

Centro San Juan Diego—2830 Lawrence St., Denver, 80205. Tel: 303-295-9470. Web: www.centrosanjuandiego.org.

Lay Formation— (see section A, Seminaries, Religious or Scholasticates: Saint John Vianney Theological Seminary)

Legal Department—

Director—REBECCA N. WELBORN, Esq. Email: rebecca.welborn@archden.org.

Liturgy—

Director—Deacon CHARLES PARKER JR. Tel: 303-715-3156. Email: deacon.parker@archden.org.

Associate Director—JOHN MILLER. Tel: 303-715-3156. Email: liturgy.office@archden.org.

Marriage and Family Life—

Director—PHIL WEBB. Tel: 303-715-3160. Email: phil.webb@archden.org.

Coordinator—HEATHER AKERS. Tel: 303-715-3259. Email: heather.akers@archden.org.

Priestly Vocations—

Director—Rev. JAMES H. CRISMAN. Tel: 303-282-3429. Email: vocation@archden.org.

Administrative Assistant—VACANT. Tel: 303-282-3429.

Respect Life—

Director—MIMI ECKSTEIN. Tel: 303-715-3205. Email: respectlife.office@archden.org.

Assistant—MARIE BAUER. Tel: 303-715-3243. Email: respectlife.office@archden.org.

Religious—

Director—Sr. SHARON FORD, R.S.M. Tel: 303-343-2095.

Seminaries— (see section A, Seminaries, Religious or Scholasticates)

St. John Vianney Theological Seminary—Rev. Msgr. MICHAEL G. GLENN, S.T.L., Rector.

The Redemptoris Mater House of Formation—Very Rev. FLORIAN MARTIN-CALAMA, S.T.L., Rector.

Social Ministry—

Director—AL HOOPER. Tel: 303-715-3220. Email: al.hooper@archden.org.

Program Associate—BETSY BUETTGENBACH. Tel: 303-715-3171. Email: betsy.buettgenbach@archden.org.

Youth, Young Adult and Campus Ministry—

Director—CHRIS STEFANICK. Tel: 303-715-3203. Email: chris.stefanick@archden.org.

Associate Director—MICHELLE PETERS. Tel: 303-715-3245. Email: michelle.peters@archden.org.

The Archdiocese of Denver Management Corporation—

President—DAVID A. HOLDEN. Tel: 303-715-3258. Email: david.holden@archden.org.

Executive Assistant—CAROLINE ROSE. Tel: 303-715-3258. Email: caroline.rose@archden.org.

Construction and Planning—PHILLIP J. CRISTE, Dir. Tel: 303-715-3251. Email: deacon.criste@archden.org.

Controller—JOYCE TALBURT, CPA, Dir. Tel: 303-715-3181. Email: joyce.talburt@archden.org.

Human Resources—BARBARA BUCHANAN, Dir. Tel: 303-715-3193. Email: barbara.buchanan@archden.org.

Information Systems—MICHAEL MCKEE, Dir. Tel: 303-715-3299. Email: michael.mckee@archden.org.

Insurance and Risk Management—JAMES KREGER, Dir. Tel: 303-715-3150. Email: james.kreger@archden.org.

Parish Finance—ERNEST W. ARMSTRONG, CPA, Dir. Tel: 303-715-3120. Email: ernie.armstrong@archden.org.

Parish Review and Advisory Services—MAC BRYANT, CPA, Dir. Tel: 303-715-3174. Email: mac.bryant@archden.org.

Real Estate—LINDA BISHOP ESQ., Dir. Tel: 303-715-3194. Email: lou.bishop@archden.org.

CLERGY, PARISHES, MISSIONS AND PAROCHIAL SCHOOLS

CITY OF DENVER

(COUNTY OF DENVER)

1—ALL SAINTS (1950) Rev. James R. Purfield; Deacon Arthur A. Vigil.
Office: 2560 S. Grove St., 80219. Tel: 303-922-3758; Fax: 303-922-3750. Email: churchofallsaint@qwestoffice.net.
2559 S. Federal Blvd., 80219.
Catechesis/Religious Program—Students 193.

2—ANNUNCIATION (1883) Rev. Francisco Ramirez, O.F.M.Cap.; Deacon James W. Blume.
Office: 3621 Humboldt St., 80205. Tel: 303-296-1024; Fax: 303-296-1026. Web: www.lukeone26.org.
School—(Grades K-8), 3536 Lafayette St., 80205. Tel: 303-295-2515; Fax: 303-295-2516. Sr. Jean Anne Panisko, S.C.L., Prin. Sisters of Charity of Leavenworth 1; Lay Teachers 19; Students 194.
Catechesis/Religious Program—Students 278.

3—ST. ANTHONY OF PADUA (1947) Very Rev. Daniel J. Norick.
Office: 3801 W. Ohio Ave., 80219. Tel: 303-935-2431; Fax: 303-935-8969. Email: anthonyofpadua@comcast.net.
Catechesis/Religious Program—Fax: 303-289-2713. Students 107.

4—ASSUMPTION OF THE BLESSED VIRGIN MARY (1912) Rev. Peter Dinh; Deacon Harold Del Real.
Office: 2361 E. 78th Ave., 80229. Tel: 303-288-2442.
School—(Grades K-8), 2341 E. 78th Ave., 80229. Tel: 303-288-2159; Fax: 303-288-4716. Thomas Hamilton, Prin. Lay Teachers 15; Students 118.
Catechesis/Religious Program—Fax: 303-289-2713. Students 107.

5—BLESSED SACRAMENT (1912) Rev. Kenneth J. Liuzzi.
1912 Eudora St., 80207. Tel: 303-355-7361; Fax: 303-355-0894. Email: bsparishoffice@aol.com. Web: www.blessedsacrament.net.

Church: 4900 Montview Blvd., 80207.
School—(Grades PreSchool-8), 1973 Elm St., 80220. Tel: 303-377-8835; Fax: 303-321-7765. Email: parishschool@blessedsacrament.net. Greg Kruthaupt, Prin. Lay Teachers 28; Students 366.
Catechesis/Religious Program—Students 61.

6—St. Cajetan (1922), (Hispanic), Rev. Tomas Fraile, C.R.; Deacons Sid Atencio; Henry Concha.
Mailing Address & Office: 299 S. Stuart St., 80219. Tel: 303-922-6306; 303-922-6307; Fax: 303-936-8285.
Church: 299 S. Raleigh St., 80219. Tel: 303-935-4483.
Catechesis/Religious Program—Students 740.

7—Cathedral Basilica of the Immaculate Conception (1860) Rev. Msgr. Thomas S. Fryar; Rev. Frank Lomica, Parochial Vicar; Deacons Dennis J. Langdon; Robert E. Finan; Robert Rinne. In Res., Rev. Andreas Hock.
Office: 1530 Logan St., 80203. Tel: 303-831-7010; Fax: 303-831-9514. Email: info@denvercathedral.org. Web: www.denvercathedral.org.
Catechesis/Religious Program—Students 78.

8—St. Catherine of Siena (1912) Revs. Gregoire Vidal; John Gregory Cieutat (France), Parochial Vicar; Nathanael Pujos (France), Parochial Vicar.
Office & Church: 4200 Federal Blvd., 80211. Tel: 303-455-9090; Fax: 303-455-6651. Web: saintcatherine.us.
School—(Grades PreSchool-8) Tel: 303-477-8035; Fax: 303-477-0110. Suzanne Scheck, Prin. Lay Teachers 16; Students 117.
Catechesis/Religious Program—Students 120.

9—Christ the King (1947) In Res., Very Rev. Daniel Leonard; Deacon Jack Sutton.
Office: 830 Elm St., 80220-4313. Tel: 303-388-1643; Fax: 303-355-0141. Email: churchoffice@christthekingdenver.com. Web: christthekingdenver.org.
School—(Grades PreSchool-8), 860 Elm St., 80220. Tel: 303-321-2123; Fax: 303-321-2191. James Feldewerth, Prin. Nuns 2; Lay Teachers 17; Students 256.
Catechesis/Religious Program—Students 108.

10—Church of the Ascension (1972) Revs. Gerardo Puga; Mark Kovacik, Parochial Vicar.
Church & Office: 14050 Maxwell Pl., 80239. Tel: 303-373-1840; 303-373-4950 (Church); Fax: 303-373-4954. Web: www.mcpascension.org.
Catechesis/Religious Program—Students 592.

11—Church of the Good Shepherd (1981) Rev. Neal A. Pfister; Deacons Dominic DeProfio; Patrick Whaley.
Church: 2626 E. Seventh Ave. Pkwy., 80206-3809. Tel: 303-322-7706; Fax: 303-399-1382. Email: goodshep@aol.com. Web: goodshepherddenver.org.
Business and D.R.E. Offices—2626 E. Seventh Ave. Pkwy., 80206.
School—(Grades PreSchool-8), 620 Elizabeth St., 80206. Tel: 303-321-6231; Fax: 303-261-1059. Lay Teachers 28; Students 342.
Catechesis/Religious Program—Students 131.

12—Church of the Risen Christ (1967) Rev. Msgr. Kenneth J. Leone; Rev. Lawrence Christenson, C.M., Parochial Vicar; Deacon Joe Babish.
Church: 3060 S. Monaco Pkwy., 80222. Tel: 303-758-8826; Fax: 303-782-9667. Web: risenchristchurch.org.
Catechesis/Religious Program—Students 334.

13—Cure D'Ars (1952) Rev. Simon Kalonga (Congo); Deacon Clarence G. McDavid.
Office: 4701 Martin Luther King Blvd., 80207-1862. Tel: 303-322-1119; Fax: 303-322-9335. Email: curedarsoffice@yahoo.com. Web: curedarschurch.org.
Church: 3201 Dahlia St., 80207.
Catechesis/Religious Program—Students 60.

14—St. Dominic (1889) Rev. Clinton P. Honkomp, O.P.; Deacon Pablo Salas. In Res., Revs. Louis S. Morrone, O.P., Novice Master; Robert F. Staes, O.P.; Bros. Michael T. McGovern, O.P.; Jordan Coonen, O.P.; Very Rev. Gerald L. Stookey, O.P.; Rev. John G. McGreevy, O.P.
Office: 3053 W. 29th Ave., 80211. Tel: 303-455-3613. Web: www.stdominicdenver.org.
Catechesis/Religious Program—Students 69.

15—St. Elizabeth of Hungary (1878) Rev. Chrysostom Frank; Deacon Russell D. Barrows.
Office: 1060 St. Francis Way, 80204. Tel: 303-534-4014; Fax: 303-534-4140.
Catechesis/Religious Program—Students 82.

16—St. Francis de Sales (1892) Rev. Msgr. Frank G. Morfeld.
Office: 301 S. Sherman St., 80209. Tel: 303-744-7211; Fax: 303-777-0305.
Church: 300 S. Sherman St., 80209.
School—235 S. Sherman St., 80209. Tel: 303-744-7231; Fax: 303-744-1028. Sr. Eleanor O'Hearn, C.S.J., Prin. Sisters of St. Joseph 2; Lay Teachers 16; Students 195.
Catechesis/Religious Program—Students 24.

17—Guardian Angels (1954) Rev. Lawrence B. Kaiser; Deacon Henry Sandoval.
Office: 1843 W. 52nd Ave., 80221. Tel: 303-433-8361; Fax: 303-477-2066.
School—Tel: 303-480-9005. Mary Gold, Prin. Lay Teachers 15; Students 161.
Catechesis/Religious Program—Students 90.

18—Holy Family (1889) Very Rev. James S. Moreno. 4377 Utica St., 80212. Tel: 303-455-1664; Fax: 303-455-7732.
Church: 4380 Utica St., 80212.
Catechesis/Religious Program—Students 49.

19—Holy Ghost (1905) Revs. Thomas Carzon, O.M.V.; Jeremy Paulin, O.M.V., Parochial Vicar; Michael Warren, O.M.V., Parochial Vicar; Deacon Vernon L. Rompot.
2161 Tremont Pl., 80205.
Office: 1900 California St., 80202. Tel: 303-292-1556; Fax: 303-292-5378. Email: info@holyghostchurch.info. Web: www.holyghostchurch.info.
Catechesis/Religious Program—Students 72.

20—Holy Rosary (1918) Rev. Joseph A. Meznar (Retired).
Mailing Address: P.O. Box 8685, 80201-8685.
Church: 4695 Pearl St., 80201. Tel: 303-296-3283.
Catechesis/Religious Program—

21—St. Ignatius Loyola (1944) Rev. Eustace Sequiera, S.J.; Deacon Philip Harrington. In Res., Revs. Joseph Tuoc Nguyen, S.J.; Leo F. Weber, S.J.; Stephen T. Yavorsky, S.J.; Bro. Donald R. Schlichter, S.J.
Office: 2309 Gaylord St., 80205. Tel: 303-322-8042; Fax: 303-322-2927. Web: loyoladenver.com.
Church: 2301 York St., 80205.
School—2350 Gaylord, 80205. Tel: 303-355-9900; Fax: 303-355-9911. Email: loyolasc@aol.com. Web: loyolagradeschool.net. Brothers 1; Sisters of Charity of Cincinnati 3; Lay Teachers 10; Students 100.
Catechesis/Religious Program—Students 88.

22—St. James (1904) Rev. Felix P. Medina-Algaba; Deacon Dennis Morales.
Office: 1314 Newport St., 80220. Tel: 303-322-7449; Fax: 303-399-2850. Email: parish.office@stjamesdenver.org. Web: www.stjamesdenver.org.
Church: 1311 Oneida St., 80220.
School—Tel: 303-333-8275; Fax: 303-780-0137. Theresa Loiselle, Prin. Lay Teachers 15; Students 110.
Catechesis/Religious Program—Tel: 303-333-5189. Students 115.

23—St. Joseph (1882) Rev. Mario Ramirez, S.T.B. (Mexico); Deacon Hugo Patino.
623 Fox St., 80204.
Church: 605 W. 6th Ave., 80204. Tel: 303-534-4408; Fax: 303-534-0177. Email: office@stjosephc.com. Web: www.stjosephc.org.
Catechesis/Religious Program—Students 240.

24—St. Joseph Polish (1902) Rev. Jan Mucha.
Office: 517 E. 46th Ave., 80216. Tel: 303-296-3217.
Catechesis/Religious Program—Students 83.

25—St. Mary Magdalene (1907) Rev. Jeffrey Wilborn; Deacons Richard Vieira, Pastoral Admin.; Gary Miller; Wilfred G. Sanchez. In Res., Rev. Luis Ecandon.
Office: 2771 Zenobia St., 80212. Tel: 303-477-4533; Fax: 303-477-2049.
Catechesis/Religious Program—Tel: 303-455-1968. Students 36.

26—Most Precious Blood (1952) Rev. Patrick Dolan.
Res.: 2250 S. Harrison, 80210. Tel: 303-756-3083; Fax: 303-756-5628. Email: parish@mpbdenver.org. Web: www.mpbdenver.org.
Church: 2200 S. Harrison St., 80210.
School—3959 E. Iliff, 80210. Tel: 303-757-1279; Fax: 303-757-1270. Colleen McManamon, Prin. Lay Teachers 26; Students 344.
Catechesis/Religious Program—Students 150.

27—Mother of God (1949) Rev. Msgr. Bernard A. Schmitz; Rev. James H. Crisman.
Office: 475 Logan St., 80203. Tel: 303-744-1715; Fax: 303-744-1716.

28—Notre Dame (1957) Rev. Msgr. Leo R. Horrigan; Rev. Peter Mozdyniewicz, Parochial Vicar; Deacons Charles W. Parker Jr.; Kevin Leiner.
Office: 5100 W. Evans Ave., 80219. Tel: 303-935-3900; Fax: 303-937-6699. Email: info@notredameparishdenver.org. Web: www.notredameparishdenver.org.
Church: 2190 S. Sheridan Blvd., 80219.
School—2165 S. Zenobia St., 80219. Tel: 303-935-3549; Fax: 303-937-4868. Email: cmolis@notredamedenver.org. Web: www.notredamedenver.org. Charlene Molis, Prin. Religious 2; Lay Teachers 22; Students 323.
Catechesis/Religious Program—2160 S. Zenobia St., 80219. Tel: 303-922-9875; Fax: 303-934-9970. Students 283.

29—Our Lady of Grace (1951) Rev. Noe Carreon.
Office: 2645 E. 48th Ave., 80216. Tel: 303-297-3440; Fax: 303-296-3486.
Catechesis/Religious Program—Students 192.

30—Our Lady of Guadalupe (1936), (Hispanic), Revs. Benito A. Hernandez, C.R.; Salvador Cisneros, C.R., Parochial Vicar; Miguel Guzman, C.R., Parochial Vicar; Deacons Manuel Ramirez; Jesus Ramirez.
Office: 1209 W. 36th Ave., 80211. Tel: 303-477-1402; Fax: 303-477-4013.
Catechesis/Religious Program—Students 458.

31—Our Lady of Lourdes (1947) Rev. Msgr. Peter Quang Nguyen; Deacon John Driesbach.
Office: 2200 S. Logan St., 80210. Tel: 303-722-6861; Fax: 303-722-4810. Web: www.ourladyoflourdesparish.org.
Church: 2298 S. Logan St., 80210.
School—2256 S. Logan St., 80210. Tel: 303-722-7525; Fax: 303-765-5305. Robert Sickles, Prin. Lay Teachers 13; Students 110.
Catechesis/Religious Program—Students 23.

32—Our Lady of Mount Carmel (1894), (Italian), Rev. Timothy M. Kremen, O.S.M. In Res., Revs. Gabriel M. Ramacciotti, O.S.M.; Joseph M. Carbone, O.S.M.; Mark Franceschini, O.S.M.; Gabriel M. Weber, O.S.M.
Office: 3549 Navajo St., 80211-3088. Tel: 303-455-0447; Fax: 303-455-5487. Email: omcchurch@qwestoffice.net. Web: www.ourladymountcarmel.com.
Catechesis/Religious Program—Students 30.

33—Presentation of Our Lady (1913), (Hispanic), Rev. Edward J. Poehlmann.
Office: 665 Irving St., 80204. Tel: 303-534-4882; Fax: 303-893-5056.
Church: 695 Julian St., 80204.
School—660 Julian St., 80204. Tel: 303-629-6562. Lay Teachers 14; Students 133.
Catechesis/Religious Program—Students 222.

34—St. Rose of Lima (1924) Rev. Jerome M. Rohr.
Office: 1320 W. Nevada Pl., 80223. Tel: 303-778-7673; Fax: 303-778-6801. Email: strose@qwest.net.
Church: 355 S. Navajo St., 80223.
School—1345 W. Dakota Ave., 80223. Tel: 303-733-5806; Fax: 303-733-0125. Email: stroseschools@netscape.net. Web: www.strosedenver.org. Lay Teachers 12; Students 215.
Catechesis/Religious Program—Tel: 303-778-1397. Students 90.

35—Sacred Heart (1879), (Hispanic), Rev. Gene Emrisek, O.F.M.Cap.
Office: 2760 Larimer St., 80205. Tel: 303-294-9830; Fax: 303-296-0171.
Catechesis/Religious Program—Students 139.

36—St. Vincent De Paul (1926) Rev. Daniel Zimmerschied; Deacon George C. Morin.
Office: 2375 E. Arizona Ave., 80210. Tel: 303-744-6119; Fax: 303-744-6124. Email: svdp2@aol.com. Web: www.svdponline.net.
School—1164 S. Josephine St., 80210. Tel: 303-777-3812; Fax: 303-773-9528. Sr. Mary Gertrude, O.P., Prin. Sisters 3; Lay Teachers 25; Students 453.
Catechesis/Religious Program—Tel: 303-744-6119, Ext. 17. Students 84.

OUTSIDE THE CITY OF DENVER

Akron, Washington Co., St. Joseph (1917) [CEM] Rev. Joseph Blanco.
Office: 551 W. 6th St., 80720. Tel: 970-345-6996; Fax: 970-345-6504.
Catechesis/Religious Program—Students 43.

Arvada, Jefferson Co.

1—St. Joan of Arc (1967) Rev. Joseph T. Cao; Deacons Joseph Gerber; Buddy Fricke; Rex Pilger.
Office: 12735 W. 58th Ave., 80002. Tel: 303-420-1232; Fax: 303-420-0126. Email: office@saintjoancatholic.org. Web: www.saintjoancatholic.org.
Catechesis/Religious Program—Students 415.

2—Shrine of St. Anne (1920) [CEM] Rev. David P. Croak; Deacons Rodger Creel; Ken Hawkins, (Retired).
Office: 7555 Grant Pl., 80002. Tel: 303-420-1280; Fax: 303-420-1341. Web: www.shrineofstanne.org.
School—Tel: 303-422-1800; Fax: 303-422-1011. Email: info@stannescatholic.org. Kathie Kuehl, Prin. Lay Teachers 25; Students 387.
Catechesis/Religious Program—Students 258.

3—Spirit of Christ Catholic Community (1974) Revs. David Bluejacket; Steven Voss, Parochial Vicar; Deacons Richard Baker; Hugh Downey; Earl Webster; Mel Corley; Don St. Louis.
Res.: 7400 W. 80th Ave., 80003. Tel: 303-422-9173; Fax: 303-422-8251. Email: staff@spiritofchrist.org. Web: www.spiritofchrist.org.
Catechesis/Religious Program—Students 977.

Aspen, Pitkin Co., St. Mary (1882) Rev. Michael J. O'Brien.
Office: 533 E. Main St., 81611. Tel: 970-925-7339; Fax: 970-925-1889. Email: stmary@sopris.net. Web: www.stmaryaspen.4lpi.com.
Catechesis/Religious Program—Students 120.
Mission—*Snowmass Chapel* Snowmass Village, Pitkin Co. 81615.

Ault, Weld Co., St. Mary (1953) Mailing Address: P.O. Box 1373, 80610. Tel: 970-834-1609; Fax: 970-686-9169. Administered by Our Lady of the

Valley, Windsor.
Catechesis / Religious Program—
AURORA, ARAPAHOE CO.
1—ST. LAWRENCE KOREAN CATHOLIC CHURCH (1981) Rev. Won-Tae Lee.
Office: 4310 S. Pitkin St., 80015-1974. Tel: 303-617-7400; Fax: 303-617-8265.
Catechesis / Religious Program—
2—ST. MICHAEL THE ARCHANGEL (1978) Rev. James E. Fox; Deacons Willie Liwanag; Anthony Pierson; Craig Fucci. In Res., Rev. Henri Tshibambe.
Parish Center, Office & Mailing Address: 19099 E. Floyd Ave., 80013. Tel: 303-690-6797; Fax: 303-690-6932. Email: stmtac@aol.com. Web: www.st.michael-aurora.com.
Catechesis / Religious Program—Students 846.
3—ST. PIUS X (1954) Very Rev. Stephen E. Adams; Rev. Miguel Enriquez, Parochial Vicar.
Office: 13670 E. 13th Pl., 80011. Tel: 303-364-7435; Fax: 303-340-0122. Web: stpiusxparish.org.
School—13680 E. 14th Pl., 80011. Tel: 303-364-6515; Fax: 303-364-1822. Web: stpiusxschool.net. Mr. Mark Strawbridge. Lay Teachers 23; Students 335.
Catechesis / Religious Program—Students 433.
4—QUEEN OF PEACE (1968) Revs. Martin Lally; Enrique Salazar; Faustinus Anyamele; Deacons John Thunblom; Bill Senger; Ruben Duran.
Office: 13120 E. Kentucky Ave., 80012. Tel: 303-364-1056; Fax: 303-364-3944. Email: info@queenofpeace.net. Web: www.queenofpeace.net.
Catechesis / Religious Program—Students 1,064.
5—ST. THERESE (1926) Revs. Elbert Chilson; Alvaro Panqueva (Colombia); Deacons Geraldo Martinez; Edgar Vale.
Office: 1243 Kingston St., 80010. Tel: 303-344-0132; Fax: 303-344-0133. Web: sttheresechurch.org.
School—Tel: 303-364-7494; Fax: 303-364-1340. Laura Demet, Prin. Sisters 1; Lay Teachers 19; Students 176.
Catechesis / Religious Program—Students 518.
BASALT, EAGLE CO., ST. VINCENT DE PAUL (1970) Rev. José Saenz.
Mailing Address: 397 White Hill Rd., Carbondale, 81623. Tel: 970-704-0820; Fax: 970-704-0830.
Church: 250 Midland Ave., 81621.
Catechesis / Religious Program—
Mission—St. Mary of the Crown Carbondale, Garfield Co. 81623.
BOULDER, BOULDER CO.
1—ST. MARTIN DE PORRES (1968) Rev. Hermanagild Jayachandra; Deacon Karl T. Matz.
Parish Office: 3300 Table Mesa Dr., 80305. Tel: 303-499-7744; Fax: 303-494-8754. Email: parishoffice@stmartindeporreschurch.org. Web: www.stmartindeporreschurch.org.
Catechesis / Religious Program—Students 54.
2—SACRED HEART OF JESUS (1875) [JC] Revs. William E. Breslin; Miljenko Pavkovic, Parochial Vicar; Deacon Walter Sweeney.
Res.: 2312 14th St., 80302. Tel: 303-442-6158; Fax: 303-442-7905. Email: breslinw@shjboulder.org. Web: www.shjboulder.org.
School—(Grades PreK-8) Tel: 303-447-2362; Fax: 303-443-2466. Web: www.shjboulder.org/school. Mary Bartsch, Prin. Lay Teachers 31; Students 320.
Catechesis / Religious Program—Students 499.
Mission—St. Rita Nederland, Boulder Co. 80466.
3—SACRED HEART OF MARY (1873) [CEM] Rev. Marcus Mallick; Deacon David Luksch.
Office: 6739 S. Boulder Rd., 80303. Tel: 303-494-7572; Fax: 303-494-7371. Web: sacredheartofmary.org.
Catechesis / Religious Program—Students 250.
4—ST. THOMAS AQUINAS (1950), (Campus Ministry), University of Colorado. Very Rev. Kevin R. Augustyn; Rev. Peter Mussett, Parochial Vicar.
Pastoral Center—904 14th St., 80302. Tel: 303-443-8383; Fax: 303-443-8399.
Church: 898 14th St., 80302.
Catechesis / Religious Program—Students 154.
BRECKENRIDGE, SUMMIT CO., ST. MARY (1875) Very Rev. David Allen; Revs. Tomasz Wikarski; Dennis K. Ryan (Retired); Deacons Charles Lamar, Admin.; James Doyle.
Mailing Address: P.O. Box 2670, Frisco, 80443.
Church: 109 S. French St., 80424. Tel: 970-668-3141; Fax: 970-668-3213. Web: www.summitcatholic.org.
Catechesis / Religious Program—Students 196.
Mission—Our Lady of Peace Dillon, Summit Co. 80435.
BRIGHTON, ADAMS CO., ST. AUGUSTINE (1887) Revs. Humberto Marquez; Jose Garcia, Parochial Vicar; Deacons Bill Jordan; Modesto Garcia; Gordon Hudec.
Office: 675 E. Egbert St., 80601. Tel: 303-659-1410; Fax: 303-659-6449. Web: www.staugustinebrighton.com.
Catechesis / Religious Program—Students 915.
BROOMFIELD, BOULDER CO., NATIVITY OF OUR LORD (1958) Revs. Michael Carvill, F.S.C.B.; Accursio Ciaccio, F.S.C.B., Parochial Vicar; Deacons Richard Medenwaldt; Leonard "Buz" Onesky; James Gollhofer.
Office & Church: 900 W. Midway Blvd., 80020. Tel: 303-469-5171; Fax: 303-469-5172.
School—Tel: 303-466-4177. Kathy Shadel, Prin. Lay Teachers 28; Students 469.
Catechesis / Religious Program—Tel: 303-469-5171, Ext. 104. Students 710.
BRUSH, MORGAN CO., ST. MARY (1911) Rev. David A. Stahl.
Office: 340 Stanford St., 80723. Tel: 970-842-2216; Fax: 970-842-4461.
Catechesis / Religious Program—Students 120.
BYERS, ARAPAHOE CO., OUR LADY OF THE PLAINS (1972) Rev. Msgr. Michael J. Chamberlain.
Res.: 186 N. McDonnell St., 80103. Tel: 303-822-5880; Fax: 303-822-5780. Web: www.ourladyoftheplains.org.
Catechesis / Religious Program—Students 137.
CENTENNIAL, ARAPAHOE CO., ST. THOMAS MORE (1971) Very Rev. Andrew Kemberling; Revs. Paul Montez, O.S.B.; Melvin F. Thompson; Marlon Rodriguez, O.C.D.; Deacons Gary Rogge; John Neal; Alan Rastrelli; Steven Stemper; Timothy Kenny; Robert Cropp; Dick Rapp, Business Mgr.; Mila Glodava, Dir. Communication & Stewardship.
Office: 8035 S. Quebec St., 80112. Tel: 303-770-1155; Fax: 303-770-1160. Email: stm@stthomasmore.org. Web: www.stthomasmore.org.
School—7071 E. Otero Ave., 80112. Tel: 303-770-0441; Fax: 303-267-1899. Web: www.stmk8.com. Paul Mott, Prin. Lay Teachers 45; Students 650.
Catechesis / Religious Program—Jere Allen, D.R.E.; David Tschumper, Youth Dir. Students 1,179.
CENTRAL CITY, GILPIN CO., ST. MARY OF THE ASSUMPTION (1865), Administered by St. Paul, Idaho Springs., Mailing Address: P.O. Box 848, Idaho Springs, 80452.
Catechesis / Religious Program—Students 6.
COMMERCE CITY, ADAMS CO., OUR LADY MOTHER OF THE CHURCH (1954) Rev. Terrence Kissell.
Office: 6690 E. 72nd Ave., 80022. Tel: 303-289-6489; Fax: 303-289-6480. Email: olmc4@earthlink.net.
Catechesis / Religious Program—Tel: 303-288-2966. Students 450.
CONIFER, JEFFERSON CO., OUR LADY OF THE PINES (1979) Revs. James Baird; Michael J. Flaska; Deacon Gerald F. Kotas.
Mailing Address: 9444 Eagle Cliff Rd., 80433. Tel: 303-838-0338; Fax: 303-838-1663.
Catechesis / Religious Program—Students 190.
Mission—St. Elizabeth Buffalo Creek, Jefferson Co. 80425. Deacon Norman Beabout.
CRAIG, MOFFAT CO., SAINT MICHAEL (1920) Revs. James R. Fox; Randy Dollins, Parochial Vicar.
Office & Mailing Address: 678 School St., 81625. Tel: 970-824-5330; Fax: 970-824-7870. Email: stmichael@nctelecom.net.
Catechesis / Religious Program—Students 96.
CROOK, LOGAN CO., ST. PETER (1924), Administered by St. Anthony of Padua, Julesburg., Mailing Address: 606 W. 3rd St., Julesburg, 80737.
EDWARDS, EAGLE CO., ST. CLARE OF ASSISI (1993) Rev. Msgr. Robert J. Kinkel; Rev. Martin Hernandez.
Mailing Address: 31622 U.S. Hwy. 6, P.O. Box 1390, 81632. Tel: 970-926-2821; Fax: 970-926-5350. Email: stclare@vail.net. Web: www.stclareparish.com.
Catechesis / Religious Program—Tel: 970-328-5457. Students 475.
Mission—St. Mary Church Eagle, Eagle Co. 81631.
Catechesis / Religious Program—Students 250.
ENGLEWOOD, ARAPAHOE CO.
1—ALL SOULS (1954), All Souls Roman Catholic Parish Corporation Very Rev. Robert D. Fisher; Deacons Kevin R. Brath; Martin A. Wager; Alex P. Rohr, Business Mgr.; Kathy Grywusiewicz, Music Min.
Church: 4950 S. Logan St., 80113-6847. Tel: 303-789-0007; Fax: 303-833-2777. Web: allsoulscatholicchurch.org. Email: recept@allsouls55.org.
School—4951 S. Pennsylvania, 80113. Tel: 303-789-2155; Fax: 303-833-2778. Web: allsoulsschool.com. William T. Moore, Prin. Lay Teachers 34; Students 492.
Catechesis / Religious Program—Students 184.
2—HOLY NAME (1894) Rev. Vincent Phung; Deacon Donald Schaefer.
Office: 3290 W. Milan Ave., 80110. Tel: 303-781-6093; Fax: 303-781-6398. Email: holyname32@frii.com.
Catechesis / Religious Program—Students 51.
3—ST. LOUIS (1911) Rev. Robert J. Reycraft.
Office: 3310 S. Sherman St., 80113. Tel: 303-761-3940; Fax: 303-806-5394. Email: stlouischurch@frii.com.
School—3301 S. Sherman St., 80113. Tel: 303-762-8307; Fax: 303-762-0156. Web: www.stlouiscatholicschool.org. Lay Teachers 12; Students 115.
Catechesis / Religious Program—Tel: 303-978-0242. Students 213.
ERIE, WELD CO., ST. SCHOLASTICA (1899), A mission of St. Theresa, Frederick.
ESTES PARK, LARIMER CO., OUR LADY OF THE MOUNTAINS (1915) Rev. Joseph A. Hartmann.
P.O. Box 1706, 80517. Tel: 970-586-8111; Fax: 970-586-8112. Web: www.olmestes.org.
Church: 920 Big Thompson Ave., 80517.
Catechesis / Religious Program—Students 90.
EVERGREEN, JEFFERSON CO., CHRIST THE KING (1932) Rev. Christopher A. Renner; Deacons Brian Kerby; Ronald Roderick. In Res., Rev. Michael J. Flaska.
Office: 4291 Evergreen Pkwy., 80439-7723. Tel: 303-674-3155; Fax: 303-674-3285.
Catechesis / Religious Program—Tel: 303-674-5282. Students 405.
FORT COLLINS, LARIMER CO.
1—BLESSED JOHN XXIII (1967) Revs. Donald C. Willette; Francis Nwaiwu; Deacons Leonard Benzel; William McClellan.
Mailing Address: 1220 University Ave., 80521.
Catechesis / Religious Program—Students 182.
2—ST. ELIZABETH ANN SETON (1981) Very Rev. Gregory Cioch; Rev. Joseph Toledo, Parochial Vicar; Deacons William Trewartha; Donald Weiss.
Church & Mailing Address: 5450 S. Lemay Ave., 80525. Email: seas@frii.com. Web: www.seas-parish.org.
Catechesis / Religious Program—Students 472.
3—HOLY FAMILY (1924), (Hispanic), Rev. Damian De La Cruz, C.R.
Res.: 326 N. Whitcomb St., 80521. Tel: 970-482-6599; Fax: 970-482-8045. Email: holyfamilychurc1@qwest.net.
Catechesis / Religious Program—Students 250.
4—ST. JOSEPH (1879) Rev. Roger L. Lascelle; Deacon Warren G. Lybarger.
Mailing Address: 101 N. Howes St., 80521.
Church: 300 W. Mountain Ave., 80521. Email: sjchurch@stjosephchurchfc.org. Web: www.stjosephchurchfc.org.
School—127 N. Howes St., 80521. Tel: 970-484-1171; Fax: 970-221-0635. Barbara Bullock, Prin. Lay Teachers 30; Students 298.
Catechesis / Religious Program—Email: religioused@stjosephchurchfc.org. Students 198.
Mission—Our Lady of the Lakes Red Feather Lakes, Larimer Co. 80545.
FORT LUPTON, WELD CO., ST. WILLIAM (1909) Rev. Gregorio L. Mirto; Deacon Louis Arambula.
Res.: 1025 Fulton Ave., 80621. Tel: 303-857-6642; Fax: 303-857-6643.
Catechesis / Religious Program—Tel: 303-857-4754. Students 170.
Mission—Our Lady of Grace Wattenburg, Weld Co. 80621.
FORT MORGAN, MORGAN CO., ST. HELENA (1910) Very Rev. Jason M. Thuerauf; Rev. Mauricio Bermudez-Hernandez, Parochial Vicar; Deacons Mario Martha; Richard Wilson.
Office: 917 W. 7th Ave., 80701. Tel: 970-867-2885.
Catechesis / Religious Program—Tel: 970-867-7237. Students 385.
Mission—St. Francis of Assisi Warren St., Weldona, Morgan Co. 80653.
FOXFIELD, ARAPAHOE CO., OUR LADY OF LORETO (1998) Rev. Msgr. Edward Buelt; Rev. John Paul Leyba, Parochial Vicar; Deacons George Brown; Michael Magee; Richard Miller.
Res.: 18000 E. Arapahoe Rd., 80016. Tel: 303-766-3800; Fax: 303-766-3700. Email: mail@ourladyofloreto.org. Web: ourladyofloreto.org.
Catechesis / Religious Program—Shirley McDermott, D.R.E. (Adult); Joan Deeb, D.R.E. (Children); Robert Rickard, D.R.E. (Youth). Students 420.
FREDERICK, WELD CO., ST. THERESA (1923) Rev. Hernan Florez.
Mailing Address: P.O. Box 418, 80530. Tel: 303-833-2966; Fax: 303-833-3000. Email: sttheresafred@earthlink.net. Web: www.sttheresafred.org.
Church: 502 Walnut, 80530.
Catechesis / Religious Program—Students 200.
GILCREST, WELD CO., SACRED HEART (1930) Closed. For inquiries for parish records contact the chancery.
GLENWOOD SPRINGS, GARFIELD CO., ST. STEPHEN (1885) Revs. Cliff J. McMillan; William Smith, Parochial Vicar; Deacons Victor Kimminau; Charles Sprick, (Retired).
515 W. 12th St., 81601.
Office: 1885 Blake Ave., 81601. Fax: 970-945-6677.
School—414 S. Hyland Park Dr., 81601. Tel: 970-945-7746. Dr. Tom Alby, Prin. Lay Teachers 16; Students 184.
Catechesis / Religious Program—Tel: 970-945-6673. Students 322.

GOLDEN, JEFFERSON CO., ST. JOSEPH (1859) Rev. Joseph E. Monahan; Deacons Glenn Allison; Edward Clements.
Res.: 969 Ulysses St., 80401. Tel: 303-279-4464; Fax: 303-273-9811. Email: terrih@stjoegold.org. Web: www.stjoegold.org.
Catechesis/Religious Program—Tel: 303-279-4794. Students 305.

GRAND LAKE, GRAND CO., ST. ANNE (1944) Rev. Michael Freihofer, Admin.; Deacon James R. Moat.
Mailing Address: P.O. Box 2029, Granby, 80446.
Church: 219 Hancock St., 80447. Tel: 970-887-0032; Fax: 970-887-9662. Email: stannes@rkymtnweb.com. Web: www.stanneandmissionchurches.catholicweb.com.
Catechesis/Religious Program—Students 24.
Mission—Our Lady of the Snow Granby, Grand Co. 80446.
Mission—St. Bernard of Montjoux Winter Park, Grand Co. 80482.

GREELEY, WELD CO.

1—ST. MARY (1965) Very Rev. Reinhold Weissbeck; Susan Benke, Business Mgr.; Deacons Joseph H. Meilinger, Liturgy Dir.; Joseph H. Meilinger; Andrew Sanchez; Frederick L. Torrez.
Office: 2222 23rd Ave., 80634. Tel: 970-352-1724; Fax: 970-352-1729.
School—Tel: 970-353-8100; Fax: 970-353-8102. Lay Teachers 17; Students 219.
Catechesis/Religious Program—Tel: 970-352-1722. Mary De Graffenried, D.R.E. Students 219.

2—OUR LADY OF PEACE (1948) Rev. Stephen A. Siebert.
Res.: 1311 3rd St., 80631. Tel: 970-353-1747; Fax: 970-353-4830. Email: ourladyofpeacegreeley@msn.com.
Catechesis/Religious Program—1303 3rd St., 80631. Tel: 970-351-6473; Fax: 970-353-4830. Students 276.

3—ST. PETER (1903) Rev. Rocco Porter.
Office: 915 12th St., 80631. Tel: 970-352-1060; Fax: 970-352-1062. Web: www.stpetergreeley.org.
Catechesis/Religious Program—Tel: 970-352-1060, Ext. 104. Email: kerrigan63@comcast.net. Students 267.

HOLYOKE, PHILLIPS CO., ST. PATRICK (1893) Rev. William Jungmann.
Res.: 519 S. Interocean, 80734. Tel: 970-854-2762; 970-854-2866 (Hall).
Catechesis/Religious Program—Students 89.
Mission—Christ the King Haxtun, Phillips Co. 80731. Tel: 970-774-7640.
Mission—St. Peter the Apostle [CEM] Fleming, Logan Co. 80728. Tel: 970-265-2792.
Catechesis/Religious Program—Students 10.

IDAHO SPRINGS, CLEAR CREEK CO., ST. PAUL (1881) Rev. Michael F. Kerrigan.
Mailing Address: P.O. Box 848, 80452.
Office: 1632 Colorado Blvd., 80452. Tel: 303-567-4662; Fax: 303-567-4662.
Catechesis/Religious Program—Tel: 303-567-4138. Students 10.
Mission—Our Lady of Lourdes [CEM] Georgetown, Clear Creek Co. 80452.

ILIFF, LOGAN CO., ST. CATHERINE OF SIENA (1927), Administered by St. Anthony, Sterling., Mailing Address: 326 S. 3rd St., Sterling, 80751.
Church: 111 S. Fifth St., 80736. Tel: 970-522-6422; Fax: 970-522-6442.
Catechesis/Religious Program—Students 40.

JOHNSTOWN, WELD CO., ST. JOHN THE BAPTIST (1937) Rev. Emilio Franchomme; Mary Raker, Business Mgr.
Office: 809 Charlotte St., 80534. Tel: 970-587-2879; Fax: 970-587-2879. Email: johnstownsjb@netscape.com. Web: www.saintjohns-johnstown.com.
Catechesis/Religious Program—Students 220.

JULESBURG, SEDGWICK CO., ST. ANTHONY (1907) Rev. Joseph Tran.
Res.: 606 W. 3rd St., 80737. Tel: 970-474-2655; Fax: 970-474-2655.
Catechesis/Religious Program—Students 40.

KREMMLING, GRAND CO., ST. PETER (1944), Administered by St. Mary, Breckenridge., Mailing Address: P.O. Box 428, 80459.
Church: 106 S. 5th St., 80459. Tel: 970-724-3428.
Mission—St. Ignatius Walden, Jackson Co. 80459.
Catechesis/Religious Program—Students 12.

LAFAYETTE, BOULDER CO., IMMACULATE CONCEPTION (1907) Rev. Msgr. Robert L. Amundsen.
715 Cabrini Drive, 80026-2676. Tel: 303-665-5103; Fax: 303-604-9077. Email: parishoffice@lafayettecatholic.org. Web: www.lafayettecatholic.org.
Catechesis/Religious Program—Students 325.

LAKEWOOD, JEFFERSON CO.

1—ST. BERNADETTE (1947) Very Rev. James K. Goggins; Deacons Phil Criste; Peter O'Donnell.
Res.: 7240 W. 12th Ave., 80214. Tel: 303-233-1523; Fax: 303-233-7285.
Church: W. 12th Ave. & Teller St., 80214.
School—1100 Upham St., 80214. Tel: 303-237-0401; Fax: 303-237-0608. Mrs. Debra Roberts, Prin. Lay Teachers 14; Students 146.
Catechesis/Religious Program—Students 30.

2—CHRIST ON THE MOUNTAIN PARISH (1975) Rev. John Grabrian; Deacons Mickey Webre; Ken Dreiling.
Church: 13922 W. Utah Ave., 80228-4110. Tel: 303-988-2222; Fax: 303-986-6956. Email: office@christonthemountain.org. Web: www.christonthemountain.org.
Catechesis/Religious Program—Students 218.

3—ST. JUDE (1967) Rev. J. Darrell Schaffer; Deacons Michael L. Bunch; Jay Garland; Alan C. Spears.
Office: 9405 W. Florida Ave., 80232-5111. Tel: 303-988-6435; Fax: 303-988-6438. Web: www.saintjudelakewood.org.
Res.: 1666 S. Jellison St., 80232-6350.
Catechesis/Religious Program—Students 256.

4—OUR LADY OF FATIMA (1958) Revs. Jeffrey Wilborn; Timothy Hjelstrom; Deacons Joseph W. Hawley; Rich Boyd. In Res., Rev. James H. Crisman.
Office: 1985 Miller St., 80215. Tel: 303-233-6236; Fax: 303-237-6097.
School—10530 W. 20th Ave., 80215. Tel: 303-233-2500. Miss Lisa Taylor, Prin. Lay Teachers 24; Students 294.
Catechesis/Religious Program—Students 175.

LITTLETON, ARAPAHOE CO.

1—ST. MARY (1901) [JC] Revs. Alvaro Montero, D.C.J.M. (Spain); Javier O'Connor, D.C.J.M. (Spain), Parochial Vicar; Javier Nieva, D.C.J.M., Parochial Vicar; Jorge Aguera, D.C.J.M., Parochial Vicar; Deacons Timothy M. Kilbarger; Anthony Dudzic; Greg Frank; Joel Paulson.
Office: 6853 S. Prince, 80120. Tel: 303-798-8506; Fax: 303-347-2270. Web: www.stmarylittleton.org.
School—(Grades K-8) Tel: 303-798-2375; Fax: 720-283-4756. Mary Cohen, Prin. Lay Teachers 32; Students 498.
Catechesis/Religious Program—Tel: 720-283-4724; Fax: 303-347-2270. Students 443.

2—OUR LADY OF MOUNT CARMEL (LATIN MASS COMMUNITY) (1997) [CEM] Revs. James Jackson, F.S.S.P., Chap.; Joseph Hearty, F.S.S.P., Asst. Chap.
Mailing Address: 5612 S. Hickory St., 80120.
Res.: 5620 S. Hickory Cir., 80120. Tel: 303-703-8538; Fax: 303-795-5411.
Catechesis/Religious Program—Students 39.

LITTLETON, JEFFERSON CO.

1—ST. FRANCES CABRINI (1972) Revs. Sean J. McGrath; Pawel Zborowski, Parochial Vicar. In Res., Deacons Paul K. Grimm; Chet Ubowski; Witold Engel; Russ Barrows.
Church & Mailing Address: 6673 W. Chatfield Ave., 80128. Tel: 303-979-7688; Fax: 303-972-8566.
Catechesis/Religious Program—Students 1,039.

2—LIGHT OF THE WORLD PARISH (1979) Rev. Michael Pavlakovich; Deacons Eugene Mooneyham; Joseph Donohoe; Rick Montagne.
Church & Mailing Address: 10316 W. Bowles Ave., 80127. Tel: 303-973-3969; Fax: 303-973-2122. Web: lotw.org.
Catechesis/Religious Program—Students 639.

LONGMONT, BOULDER CO.

1—ST. FRANCIS OF ASSISI (1982) [JC] Rev. Frank Maroney.
Church & Office: 2140B Trade Centre Ave., 80503. Tel: 303-772-6322; Fax: 303-772-9415. Email: parish@saintfrancislongmont.org. Web: www.saintfrancislongmont.org.
Catechesis/Religious Program—

2—ST. JOHN THE BAPTIST (1882) [JC] Revs. Brian Morrow; Servando Navarro; Michael J. Flaska; Deacons Bob Howard; Mike Berens.
323 Collyer St., 80501. Tel: 303-776-0737; Fax: 303-772-5636. Web: www.johnthebaptist.org.
School—350 Emery St., 80501. Tel: 303-776-8760. Mrs. Julie Rossi, Prin. Lay Teachers 26; Students 324.
Catechesis/Religious Program—Students 561.

LOUISVILLE, BOULDER CO., ST. LOUIS (1884) Rev. G. Timothy Gaines; Deacons Steven J. Vallero; Ronald Darschewski. In Res., Rev. Daniel J. Flaherty (Retired).
Office: 902 Grant Ave., 80027. Tel: 303-666-6401; Fax: 303-666-0826. Email: stlouis.office@stlouisoflsv.org. Web: www.stlouisoflsv.org.
School—925 Grant Ave., 80027. Tel: 303-666-6220; Fax: 303-666-5244. Web: www.stlouisschool-co.com. Karen Herlihy, Prin. Lay Teachers 28; Students 267.
Early Learning Center—Tel: 303-665-0606.
Catechesis/Religious Program—902 Grant Ave., 80027. Tel: 303-604-6055. Students 230.

LOVELAND, LARIMER CO., ST. JOHN THE EVANGELIST (1902) Revs. Joseph A. Hartmann; Felicien Mbala, Parochial Vicar; Deacons Robert Haigh, (Retired); John McKeown, (Retired); John Kunsemiller, (Retired).
Office & Mailing Address: 1515 Hilltop Dr., 80537. Tel: 970-635-5800; Fax: 970-669-5743. Web: www.saintjohns.net.
Res.: 1523 Hilltop Dr., 80537. Tel: 970-635-5805.
Church: 1730 W. 12th St., 80537.
School—Tel: 970-635-5830; Fax: 970-667-9298. Al Drago, Prin. Lay Teachers 21; Students 238.
Catechesis/Religious Program—Students 270.

MEEKER, RIO BLANCO CO., HOLY FAMILY (1905) Rev. James R. Fox.
Mailing Address: P.O. Box 866, 81641.
Church: 889 Park Ave., 81641.
Catechesis/Religious Program—Students 60.

MINTURN, EAGLE CO., ST. PATRICK (1913) Rev. Hugh M. Guentner, O.S.M.
Administrative Office & Mailing Address: 19 Vail Rd., Vail, 81657. Tel: 970-477-0378; Fax: 970-476-3347. Email: st_patricks@comcast.net. Web: www.stpatricksminturn.com.
Church: 476 Pine St., 81645.
Catechesis/Religious Program—Tel: 970-827-5784; Fax: 970-827-5784. Students 95.
Mission—Vail Interfaith Chapel
Mission—Our Lady of Mt. Carmel Red Cliff, Eagle Co. 81649.

NORTHGLENN, ADAMS CO., IMMACULATE HEART OF MARY (1967) Very Rev. Gregory Ames; Rev. Matthew Hartley; Deacons Leo Oehrle, (Retired); Taylor Elder; Jerome Durnford.
Offices & Mailing Address: 11385 Grant Dr., 80233. Tel: 303-452-2041; Fax: 303-452-7546. Email: admin@ihmco.org. Web: ihmco.org.
Res.: 335 E. 112th Dr., 80233.
Catechesis/Religious Program—Students 725.
Mission—Guardian Angels Mead, Weld Co. 80542.
Mission—St. Scholastica Erie, Weld Co. 80516.

OAK CREEK, ROUTT CO., ST. MARTIN OF TOURS, Mission of Holy Name, Steamboat Springs.

PEETZ, LOGAN CO., SACRED HEART (1914) [CEM], Administered by St. Anthony, Sterling., Mailing Address: P.O. Box 99, 80747.
Church: 621 Logan, 80747. Tel: 970-334-2227; Fax: 970-334-2227.
Catechesis/Religious Program—

PLATTEVILLE, WELD CO., ST. NICHOLAS (1889), Administered by St. John the Baptist, Johnston. Mary Raker, Business Mgr.
Mailing Address: P.O. Box 546, 80651.
Church: 514 Marion Ave., 80651. Tel: 970-785-2143. Email: stnickschurch@gwestoffice.net.
Catechesis/Religious Program—Students 157.

RANGELY, RIO BLANCO CO., ST. IGNATIUS OF ANTIOCH (1931), Administered by St. Michael, Craig.
Church: 109 S. Stanolind Ave., 81648. Tel: 970-675-8935; Fax: 970-675-8935. Email: stmich@nctelecom.net.
Catechesis/Religious Program—Students 27.

RIFLE, GARFIELD CO., ST. MARY (1910) Rev. Robert E. Hehn.
Mailing Address: P.O. Box 191, 81650. In Res., Rev. Jude Geilen Kirchen.
Church: 761 Birch Ave., 81650. Tel: 970-625-2547; Fax: 970-625-9025.
Catechesis/Religious Program—Students 339.
Mission—St. Brendan Parachute, Garfield Co. 81650.

ROGGEN, WELD CO., SACRED HEART (1924) Rev. Hector Chiapa-Villarreal, Admin.
Res.: 38044 Weld County Rd. 16, 80652. Tel: 303-849-5313; Fax: 303-849-5674.
Catechesis/Religious Program—Students 140.
Mission—Holy Family
Mission—Our Lady of Lourdes

STEAMBOAT SPRINGS, ROUTT CO., HOLY NAME (1907) Rev. Ernest Bayer; Deacon John Franklin. In Res., Rev. Msgr. Thomas Dentici (Retired).
Office: 504 Oak St., P.O. Box 774198, 80477-4198. Tel: 970-879-0671; Fax: 970-879-7406. Email: holyname@holynamecc.org. Web: www.holynamecc.org.
Catechesis/Religious Program—Tel: 970-879-1225. Students 162.
Mission—St. Martin of Tours Oak Creek, Routt Co. 80467.

STERLING, LOGAN CO., ST. ANTHONY (1888) Very Rev. Robert L. Wedow.
Mailing Address: 326 S. 3rd St., 80751. Tel: 970-522-6422; Fax: 970-522-6442.
Church: 331 S. 3rd St., 80751.
School—324 S. 3rd St., 80751. Tel: 970-522-7567. Lay Teachers 16; Students 120.
Catechesis/Religious Program—Students 155.

STONEHAM, WELD CO., ST. JOHN (1916), Administered by St. Mary, Brush, Mailing Address: 340 Stanford St., Brush, 80723.
Church: 41629 Granite, 80754.
Catechesis/Religious Program—Students 12.

THORNTON, ADAMS CO., HOLY CROSS (Thornton) (1957) Rev. Thomas Coyte; Deacons Russell Halpine; Joe Benedetto; Nehemias Ruiz.
Office: 9371 Wigham St., 80229. Tel: 303-289-2258

(Voice TDD); Fax: 303-289-2259. Email: holy.cross@comcast.net. Web: www.holycrossthornton.com.
Catechesis/Religious Program—Students 442.

WESTMINSTER, ADAMS CO.

1—HOLY TRINITY (1956) Very Rev. John L. Hilton; Revs. Lorenzo Ricci; Carlos Bello, Parochial Vicar; Deacon Lloyd Quintana.
Res.: 7595 N. Federal, 80030. Tel: 303-428-3594; Fax: 303-427-4125. Web: www.htcatholic.org.
School—3050 W. 76th Ave., 80030. Tel: 303-427-5632. Mr. Dave Baker, Prin. Lay Teachers 15; Students 209.
Catechesis/Religious Program—Tel: 303-427-3594, Ext. 32. Students 614.
Mission—Our Lady of Visitation

2—ST. MARK (1973) Rev. Kenneth Koehler; Deacon Gordon D. Hudec.
Office: 3141 W. 96th Ave., 80031. Tel: 303-466-8720; Fax: 303-466-0998.
Catechesis/Religious Program—Students 200.

WHEAT RIDGE, JEFFERSON CO.

1—SS. PETER AND PAUL (1949) Revs. Reuben Payo; Walter Watson, S.J., Parochial Vicar; Deacons John Pontillo; James R. Wall.
Office: 3900 Pierce St., 80033. Tel: 303-424-3706; Fax: 303-424-0819. Email: dianam@peterandpaulcatholic.org. Web: peterandpaulcatholic.org.
School—3920 Pierce St., 80033. Tel: 303-420-0402; Fax: 303-456-1888. Email: pglassmeyer@sppscatholic.com. Kathy Byrnes, Prin. Religious 3; Lay Teachers 20; Students 291.
Catechesis/Religious Program—Students 33.
Convent—4040 Pierce St., 80033. Tel: 303-422-6419.

2—QUEEN OF VIETNAMESE MARTYRS (1976), (Asian), Revs. Joseph M. Vu Kim Ngan, C.M.C.; Leo Dinh Huyen Vu, C.M.C.; Deacons Joseph Le Van Tam; Peter Hung Phi Dang; Lawrence Tong Ngo.
Res.: 4655 Harlan St., 80033. Tel: 303-431-0382; Fax: 303-431-1876. Email: queenvietnam@gmail.com. Web: www.giaoxudenver-.org.

WINDSOR, WELD CO., OUR LADY OF THE VALLEY (1969) Very Rev. James Spahn; Deacon Harold Kimble.
Office: 1250 7th St., 80550. Tel: 970-686-5084; Fax: 970-686-9169. Email: ella@ourladyofthevalley.net. Web: www.ourladyofthevalley.net.
Catechesis/Religious Program—Students 257.

WRAY, YUMA CO., ST. ANDREW (1888) Rev. Jonathan Dellinger.
Office: 412 Dexter St., 80758. Tel: 970-332-5858; Fax: 970-332-4604. Email: standrewapostle@centurytel.net.
Catechesis/Religious Program—Students 124.

YUMA, YUMA CO., ST. JOHN THE EVANGELIST (1888) Rev. Jonathan Dellinger.
Office: 508 S. Ash St., 80759. Tel: 970-848-5973; Fax: 970-848-2817.
Catechesis/Religious Program—Students 119.

On Duty Outside the Archdiocese:
Rev. Msgr.—
McDaid, J. Anthony, Congregation for the Clergy, 00120, Vatican City State.
Revs.—
Denig, Philip P., Chap. (Capt.), 9 B Ardsley Ave., Whiting, NJ 08759.
Gass, Michael W., 3321 7th St., Urbandale, IA 50322.
Kelly, Thomas D., 2315 Alma Ave., Manhattan Beach, CA 90266.
Murphy, John J., St. Gabriel the Archangel, 203 E. Arnold Ave., Port Allegany, PA 16743.
Romero, Donald, PSC2 Box 8352, Apo, AE 09012.
Simko, James, Sts. Peter & Paul the Apostles, 2850 75th St. W., Bradenton, FL 34209.

Graduate Studies:
Revs.—
Capucci, Giovanni
Perez, Angel

Retired:
Rev. Msgrs.—
Dentici, Thomas, St. Mary of the Crown, 397 White Hill Rd., Carbondale, 81623.
Jones, Raymond N., V.G., P.A., 700 S. Yarrow St., Lakewood, 80226.
Jones, William H., Mullen Home, 3629 W. 29th Ave., 80211.
Madden, Edward T., 565 Mohawk Dr., #B1, Boulder, 80303.
Rasby, James W., 460 S. Marion Pkwy., #1206-C, 80209.
Schroeder, George, St. Patrick Parish, 10815 N. 84th St., Scottsdale, AZ 85260.
Revs.—
Banigan, Herbert, 606 Sundance Dr., Loveland, 80538.
Blach, Leo M., Gardens St. Elizabeth, 2835 W. 32nd Ave., #12, 80211.
Bradtke, Thomas, 142 Country Rd. 156, Glenwood Springs, 81601.
Canjar, John A., 6780 E. Cedar Ave., Apt. 706A, Denver 80224.
Cuneo, James J., 6991 Nile Ct., Arvada, 80007.
DeLazzer, Dorino, St. Mary, 2222 23rd Ave., Greeley, 80634.
Deml, Francis S., 625 S. Alton Way, #7C, 80231.
Flaherty, Daniel J., 902 Grant St., Louisville, 80027.
Gabel, Emanuel, 8983 W. Jewell, Apt. #304, Lakewood, 80232.
Gibbons, John M., Mullen Home, 3629 W. 29th Ave., 80211.
Kane, James E., 2397 S. Xanadu Way, Bldg. 9, #402, Aurora, 80014.
Kennedy, Patrick J., 9360 E. Center Ave., #3D, 80247.
Kleiner, James, P.O. Box 300545, 80203-0545.
McCormick, Thomas, V.F., c/o St. Therese, 1243 Kingston St., Aurora, 80010.
Medrano, Marcus, 2576 104th Cir., Westminster, 80234.
Meznar, Joseph A., P.O. Box 211067, 80221.
Meznar, Robert P., 4330 Thompson Ct., 80216.
O'Malley, Joseph M., 1542 E. Nicholas Dr., Centennial, 80122-2945.
Ossino, Angelo, 13800 E. Marina Dr., #312, Aurora, 80014.
Ryan, Dennis K., P.O. Box 131, Frisco, 80443.
Smith, Vincent Leo, P.O. Box 82, Fairplay, 80440.
Sobieszczyk, David, 7074 S. Clermont Dr., Centennial, 80122-1180.
Urban, Peter, 110 W. Simpson St., Lafayette, 80026.
Walsh, Michael, 1893 E. Lake Dr., Centennial, 80121.
Woerth, Thomas, 700 Washington St., #40, 80203.

Permanent Deacons:
Allison, Glenn, St. Joseph, Golden
Anderson, Ernest J., (Retired)
Ansay, Ronald J., (Retired)
Arambula, Louis, St. Williams, Fort Lupton
Armijo, Edward, St. John the Evangelist, Loveland
Atencio, Sidney, St. Cajetan, Denver
Babish, Joseph, Risen Christ, Denver
Baez, David, Queen of Peace, Aurora
Baker, Richard L., Spirit of Christ Catholic Community, Arvada
Barrows, Russell D., St. Frances Cabrini, Littleton
Beabout, Norman, St. Elizabeth, Buffalo Creek
Benedetto, Joseph, Holy Cross, Thornton
Benjamin, Joseph G., St. Joseph, Akron
Benzel, Leonard, (Retired)
Berens, Michael, St. John the Baptist, Longmont
Blake, Stephen M., (Retired)
Blume, James W., Annunciation, Denver
Borda, Richard S., Buckley Air Force Base Chapel
Boselli, Francis "Bud", (Retired)
Boyd, Richard M., Our Lady of Fatima, Lakewood
Brath, Kelvin All Souls Englewood
Brown, George, Our Lady of Loreto
Bunch, Michael L., St. Jude, Lakewood
Clements, Edward R., St. Joseph, Golden
Concha, Henry, St. Cajetan, Denver
Corley, Melvin G., Spirit of Christ, Arvada
Cosados, Ross, Spirit of Christ, Arvada
Coursey, Nathan D., (Retired)
Creel, Rodger L., Shrine of St. Anne, Arvada
Criste, Philip, St. Bernadette, Lakewood
Cropp, Robert, St. Thomas More, Centennial
Dang, Peter Hung Phi, Queen of Vietnamese Martyrs, Wheatridge
Darschewski, Ronald, St. Louis, Louisville
Del Real, Harold, Assumption Parish, Welby
DelVillar, Oscar, Immaculate Conception, Lafayette
DeProfio, Dominic, Good Shepherd, Denver
Devlin, James "Jim", St. Theresa, Frederick; St. Scholastica, Erie
DiPentino, John L., Our Lady of Mount Carmel
Donohoe, Joseph H., Archdiocese of Denver, Dir. & Deacon Personnel
Dorwart, Jason, (Retired)
Downey, Hugh, Missionary in Africa, Spirit of Christ
Doyle, James, Our Lady of Peace, Dillon
Dreiling, L. Kenneth, (Retired)
Driesbach, John, Our Lady of Lourdes, Denver
Dudzic, Anthony, St. Mary's, Littleton
Dunn, Darryl, (Retired)
Duran, Ruben, Queen of Peace, Aurora
Durnford, Jerome, Immaculate Heart of Mary, Northglenn
Elder, R. Taylor, Immaculate Heart of Mary, Northallen
Engel, Witold, (Retired)
Ertmer, William, Holy Family Parish, Meeker
Estrada, Ruben, Sacred Heart, Denver
Finan, Robert E., Cathedral Basilica of the Immaculate Conception
Fitterer, George, (Retired)
Fortunato, George R., St. Ignatius of Antioch, Rangely
Frank, Gregory L., St. Mary, Littleton
Franklin, John, Holy Name Parish, Steamboat Springs
Fricke, Franklin, III, St. Joan of Arc Arvada
Frisinger, Howard, (Retired)
Fucci, Craig, St. Michael the Archangel, Aurora
Gallagher, Michael, St. Patrick, Minturn
Garcia, Modesto, St. Augustine, Brighton
Garland, Jay, St. Jude, Lakewood
Gerber, Joseph, St. Joan of Arc, Arvada
Gollhofer, James D., Nativity of Our Lord Parish, Broomfield
Gregorius, Robert, St. Thomas More, Centennial
Grimler, Richard, (Retired)
Grimm, R. Paul, St. Frances Cabrini, Littleton
Haigh, Robert, (Retired)
Halpine, Russell, Holy Cross, Thornton
Harrington, Philip, St. Ignatius of Loyola, Denver
Hastings, William O., St. Peter, Greeley
Hawkins, Kenneth I., Jr., (Retired)
Hawley, Joseph W., (Retired)
Hegarty, Marvin A., (Retired)
Hetzel, Martin, St. Thomas Acquinas, Boulder
Howard, Michael J., (Retired)
Howard, Robert J., St. John the Baptist, Longmont
Hronek, Dennis R., (Retired)
Hudec, Gordon D., St. Mark, Westminster
Jordan, Bill, St. Augustine, Brighton
Kenny, Timothy M., St. Thomas More, Centennial
Kerby, Brian J., Christ the King, Evergreen
Kilbarger, Timothy M., St. Mary, Littleton
Kimble, Harold, Our Lady of the Valley, Windsor
Kimminau, Victor H., St. Stephen Parish, Glenwood Springs
Kotas, Gerald F., Our Lady of the Pines, Conifer
Kulinski, Jerome N., (Retired)
Kunsemiller, John, (Retired)
Lamar, Charles, St. Mary, Breckenridge
Langdon, Dennis J., Cathedral Basilica of the Immaculate Conception, Denver
Le, Joseph Tam Van, (Retired)
Lee, William S., (Retired)
Leiner, Kevin, Notre Dame, Denver
Liwanag, Wilfred B., St. Michael the Archangel, Aurora
Lopez, Samuel, Church of the Ascension, Denver
Loushin, Albert J., St. Vincent, Basalt
Luksch, David, Sacred Heart of Jesus, Boulder
Lybarger, Warren G., (Retired)
Magee, Michael, Our Lady of Loreto, Foxfield
Martha, Mario, St. Helena, Ft. Morgan
Marthe, Daniel M., (Retired)
Martin, Gregory "Dusty", St. Pius X, Aurora
Martinez, Gerardo, St. Therese, Aurora
Martinez, William, Our Lady of Guadalupe, Denver
Matz, Karl T., (Retired)
McClellan, William, St. John XXIII, Ft. Collins
McDavid, Clarence G., Cure D'Ars
McKeown, John, (Retired)
Medenwaldt, Richard A., Nativity of Our Lord, Broomfield
Meilinger, Joseph H., St. Mary, Greeley
Menogan, Guffie E., (Retired)
Michieli, Ronald, St. Anthony, Sterling
Miller, Gary E., St. Mary Magdalene, Denver
Miller, Richard, Our Lady of Loreto, Foxfield
Moat, James, St. Anne, Grand Lake
Montagne, Eric, Light of the World, Littleton
Mooneyham, E. Gene, Light of the World, Littleton
Morales, Dennis, St. James Parish, Denver
Morin, George C., St. Vincent de Paul, Denver
Neal, John R., St. Thomas More, Centennial
Ngo, Lawrence Tong, Queen of Vietnamese Marytrs, Wheatridge
Oehrle, Leo A., (Retired)
Onesky, Leonard "Buz", Nativity of Our Lord, Broomfield
Padilla, Carlos L., (Retired)
Parker, Charles W., Jr., Notre Dame Parish, Denver
Patino, Hugo, St. Joseph, Denver
Paulson, Joel, St. Mary, Littleton
Pelis, Richard F., (Retired)
Perez, Cesar, Our Lady of Peace, Greeley
Pierson, Anthony, St. Michael the Archangel, Aurora
Pilger, Rex H., Jr., St. Joan of Arc
Polak, Leonard E., (Retired)
Pontillo, John E., Sts. Peter & Paul, Wheatridge
Quinlan, Thomas, (Retired)
Quintana, Lloyd, (Retired)

Ramirez, Mamuel de Jesus, Our Lady of Guadalupe, Denver
Rastrelli, Alan, M.D., St. Thomas More, Centennial
Reinert, George J., (Retired)
Rinne, Robert, Cathedral Basilica of Immaculate Conception
Ritz, Michael P., (Retired)
Roderick, Ronald, II, Christ the King, Evergreen
Rogge, Gary, St. Thomas More, Centennial
Rompot, Vernon L., K.H.S., Holy Ghost, Denver
Rouco, Anthony F., (Retired)
Ruiz, Nehemias, Holy Cross Parish, Thornton
Salas, Pablo, St. Dominic, Denver
Salvato, Mark, Cathedral Basilica of the Immaculate Conception
Sanchez, Alfredo, (Retired)
Sanchez, Andrew, St. Mary's, Greeley
Sanchez, Maclovio, (Retired)
Sanchez, Wilfred G., (Retired)
Sandoval, Alfonso M., St. Pius X, Aurora
Sandoval, Antonio A., Our Lady Mother of the Church, Commerce City
Sandoval, Henry, Guardian Angels, Denver
Schaefer, Donald, Holy Name, Englewood
Senger, William, Jr., Queen of Peace, Aurora
Smith, John L., Ph.D., Dir. Formation
Sorber, William M., (Retired)
Spears, Alan C., St. Jude Parish, Lakewood
Spellman, William, (Retired)
Sprick, Charles B., (Retired)
St. Louis, Donald, Spirit of Christ, Arvada
Stemper, Steven, St. Thomas More Parish, Centennial
Stephenson, Billy C., (Retired)
Stow, William J., Kateri Catholic Comm., Lakewood
Sutton, Jack, Christ the King, Denver
Sweeney, Walter, St. Elizabeth of Hungary, Denver
Thunblom, John, Queen of Peace Parish, Aurora
Torrez, Eugeno, Presentation of Our Lady, Denver
Torrez, Frederick L., St. Mary, Greeley
Trewartha, William, St. Elizabeth Ann Seton, Fort Collins
Trujillo, Samuel R., (Retired)
Ubowski, Chester W., St. Frances Cabrini, Littleton
Valle, Edgar, St. Therese, Aurora
Vallero, Steven J., St. Louis, Louisville
Vieria, Richard, St. Mary Magdalene Parish, Denver
Vigil, Arthur A., (Retired)
Volk, John, St. John the Baptist; St. Nichlas of Antioch, Platteville
Wager, Martin A., All Souls, Englewood
Wall, James R., SS. Peter and Paul, Wheatridge
Ward, William, (Retired)
Webre, Milton G., Christ on the Mountain, Lakewood
Webster, Earl, Spirit of Christ, Arvada
Wehrman, John J., St. Peter, Greeley
Weiss, Donald, St. Elizabeth Ann Seton, Fort Collins
Whaley, Patrick, Church of the Good Shepherd, Denver
Wilhelm, Martin A., (Retired)
Wilson, Richard, Archdiocese of Denver, Formation
Wolfe, James, Immaculate Conception, Lafayette
Young, John Joseph, (Retired)
Zajac, Paul M., St. Anthony of Padua, Denver

INSTITUTIONS LOCATED IN THE ARCHDIOCESE

[A] SEMINARIES, RELIGIOUS OR SCHOLASTICATES

DENVER. *Saint John Vianney Theological Seminary*, 1300 S. Steele St., 80210. Tel: 303-282-3427; Fax: 303-282-3453. Rev. Msgr. Michael G. Glenn, S.T.L., Rector; Rev. Jorge Rodriguez, Vice Rector. Students 104.

Redemptoris Mater House of Formation, 3434 E. Arizona Ave., 80210. Tel: 303-733-2220; Fax: 303-733-2223. Email: redemptoris.mater@archden.org. Very Rev. Florian Martin-Calama, S.T.L., Rector for Redemptoris Mater Archdiocesan Missionary Seminary; Revs. Federico Colautti, S.T.D., Vice Rector; Jose Maria Fuenmayor, Spiritual Dir. Priests 3; Diocesan Seminarians 28; Total Staff 5.

[B] COLLEGES AND UNIVERSITIES

DENVER. **Augustine Institute, Inc.*, 3001 S. Federal Blvd., Box 1126, 80236. Tel: 303-937-4420; Fax: 303-468-2933. Email: info@augustineinstitute.org. Web: www.augustineinstitute.org. Dr. Tim Gray, Pres. Faculty 4; Adjunct 4; Students 220.

Regis University (1877) 3333 Regis Blvd., 80221-1099. Tel: 303-458-4100; Fax: 303-458-4921. Web: www.regis.edu. John P. Box, Chm. Bd. of Trustees; Revs. Michael J. Sheeran, S.J., Pres.; David M. Clarke, S.J., Chancellor; Diane M. Cooper, Dean of Students; Dr. Patricia A. Ladewig, Acting Provost & Vice Pres. Academic Affairs; Ms. Karen Webber, Vice Pres. Admin.; Dr. Thomas E. Reynolds, Vice Pres. Mission & Student Devel.; Ms. Julie Crockett, Vice Pres. Univ. Rels.; Dr. Paul Ewald, Dean Regis College; Dr. William J. Husson, Vice Pres. Professional Studies & Strategic Alliances; Dr. Janet Houser, Acting Academic Dean, Rueckert-Hartman College for Health Professions; Mr. Ivan Gaetz, Dean Libraries; Peter Rogers, Dir. University Min.; Marcel Dumestre, Academic Dean, CPS & Ignatian Mission & Values Faculty; Mr. Lawrence Heller, Vice Provost Fin. & Budget; Sandra Mitchell, Asst. Provost for Diversity; Mr. D. Paul Brocker, Exec. Asst. to the Pres. A university conducted under the auspices of the Society of Jesus. Jesuits 9; Sisters 1; (full time) 205; (part time) 741; Students 14,841.

[C] INTER-PAROCHIAL HIGH SCHOOLS

DENVER. *Bishop Machebeuf High School, Inc.*, 458 Uinta Way, 80230-6934. Tel: 303-344-0082; Fax: 303-344-1582. Web: www.machebeuf.org. Jessie Skipwith, Prin.; Stephanie Chaney, Librarian. Brothers 1; Sisters 1; Lay Teachers 31; Students 365.

BROOMFIELD. *Holy Family High School, Inc.*, 5195 W. 144th Ave., 80023. Tel: 303-440-1411; Fax: 303-466-1935. Web: www.holyfamilyhs.com. Email: patty.gabriel@holyfamilyhs.com. Mr. Michael G. Gabriel, Interim Prin.; Stephanie Brown, Librarian. Sisters 3; Lay Teachers 46; Students 575.

[D] HIGH SCHOOLS, PRIVATE

DENVER. *Arrupe Jesuit High School* (2003) 4343 Utica St., 80212. Tel: 303-455-7449; Fax: 303-455-7453. Email: planningsj@arrupejesuit.com. Web: www.arrupejesuit.com. Rev. Stephen W. Planning, S.J., Pres.; Mr. Michael O'Hagan, Prin.; Rev. Gerard E. Menard, S.J., Asst. Prin. Priests 4; Religious 3; Lay Teachers 12; Volunteers 5; Administrators 20; Students 302.

J K Mullen High School (1931) 3601 S. Lowell Blvd., 80236. Tel: 303-761-1764; Fax: 303-761-0502. Web: www.mullenhigh.com. Greg Gotchey, Prin.

The Christian Brothers of J.K. Mullen High School Brothers of the Christian Schools, Coed High School Brothers 1; Lay Teachers 98; Students 942.

AURORA. *Regis Jesuit High School Corporation* (1877) Co-Institutional, *Boys Div.*, 6300 S. Lewiston Way, 80016. Tel: 303-269-8000 (Boys Div.); Fax: 303-766-2240 (Boys Div.). Web: www.regisjesuit.com. *Girls Div. & Central Admin.*, 6300 S. Lewiston Way, 80016. Tel: 303-269-8100 (Girls Div.); Fax: 303-221-4772 (Girls Div.). Revs. Philip G. Steele, S.J., Pres. Boys & Girls Division; David A. Wayne, S.J., Facilities Mgr. Emeritus; Robert L. Sullivan, S.J., Faculty Chap.; Christopher P. Pinne, S.J., Supr. of Community & Theology Teacher; Mr. James M. Gmelich, Prin., Boys Div.; Ms. Gretchen Kessler, Prin. Girls Div.; Bruce Raymond, Librarian Boys Division; Carol Ann Sass, Librarian Girls Division. Day School for Boys.; Day School for Girls. Priests 4; Seminarians 1; Sisters 1; Lay Staff 190; Students - Boys Division 872; Students - Girls Division 642.

ENGLEWOOD. *St. Mary's Academy High School* (1864) 4545 S. University Blvd., 80113. Tel: 303-762-8300; Fax: 303-783-6201. Web: www.smanet.org. Deirdre V. Cryor, Pres.; Kathryn McNamee, Prin.; Kristen Ferguson, Librarian. Sisters of Loretto at the Foot of the Cross. Lay Teachers 30; Students 256.

[E] ELEMENTARY SCHOOLS, PRIVATE

DENVER. *Escuela De Guadalupe Elementary School*, (Grades K-5), 3401 Pecos St., 80211. Tel: 303-964-8456; Fax: 303-964-0755. Email: david_card@escuelaguadalupe.org. Web: www.escuelaguadalupe.org. Dr. Vernita M. Vallez, Prin.; David A. Card, Pres. Lay Teachers 20; Students 107.

ENGLEWOOD. *St. Mary's Academy Lower School* (1864) (Grades K-5), 4545 S. University Blvd., 80113. Tel: 303-762-8300; Fax: 303-783-6201. Web: www.smanet.org. Deirdre V. Cryor, Pres.; Mary Jane Frederick, Prin.; Margaret Gross, Librarian. Sisters of Loretto at the Foot of the Cross. Lay Teachers 23; Students 245.

St. Mary's Academy Middle School (1864) (Grades 6-8), 4545 S. University Blvd., 80113. Tel: 303-762-8300; Fax: 303-783-6201. Web: www.smanet.org. Martha Ashley, Prin.; Deirdre V. Cryor, Pres.; Kristen Ferguson, Librarian. Lay Teachers 30; Students 230.

[F] SPECIAL EDUCATION

DENVER. *Mount St. Vincent Home, Inc.* (1883) (Grades PreSchool-8), (Special Education), 4159 Lowell Blvd., 80211. Tel: 303-458-7220; Fax: 303-477-7559. Web: www.msvhome.org. Sr. Amy Willcott, S.C.L., Exec. Dir.; Lori McClurg, Admin. Therapeutic Residential Child Care Facility. Mount Saint Vincent Sisters 3; Special Education Teachers 8; Mental Health Workers 8; Crisis Team 6; Students 95.

LITTLETON. **Havern Center, Inc.* (1966) (Grades K-8), 4000 S. Wadsworth Blvd., 80123. Tel: 303-986-4587; Fax: 303-986-0590. Email: cathyp@haverncenter.org. Web: www.haverncenter.org. Cathleen M. Pasquariello, Head of School & Contact Person. Sisters 2; Faculty & Staff 32; Students 85.

[G] MINISTRY TO THE HANDICAPPED

DENVER. *The Bridge Community, Inc.*, 3101 W. Hillside Pl., 80219. Tel: 303-935-4740; Fax: 303-935-7795. Email: rishabridge@comcast.net. Risha Dimas, Contact Person & Dir. Sisters 1; Priests 1; Lay Staff 6; Bed Group Home 8.

Special Religious Education-Pastoral Care of Developmentally Disabled Persons (1976) (An office of the Archdiocese of Denver), 3101 W. Hillside Pl., 80219. Tel: 303-934-1999; Fax: 303-935-7795. Rev. Roland P. Freeman, Dir. Special Educ. & Chap.; Sr. Mary Catherine Widger, S.L., Assoc. Dir. Spec. Educ., Founder & staff of group home. Religious education of mentally retarded children and adults. Priests 1; Total Assisted Annually 394.

[H] GENERAL HOSPITALS

DENVER. *Saint Joseph Hospital*, 1835 Franklin St., 80218. Tel: 303-837-7111; Fax: 303-837-7123. Robert Minkin, CEO; Revs. John J. Waters, S.J., Chap.; Gabriel Okafor, Chap.; Deacon Dominic DeProfio, Chap.; Bro. Donald R. Schlichter, S.J., Chap. Bed Capacity 565; Inpatients Assisted Annually 19,939; Outpatients Assisted Annually 185,242.

St. Anthony Central Hospital, Mailing Address: 188 Inverness Dr., W., Ste. 500, Englewood, 80112. 4231 W. 16th Ave., 80204. Tel: 303-629-4224; Fax: 303-595-6909. Email: krisordelheide@centura.org. Peter Makowski, CEO; Kris Ordelheide, Contact & Gen Counsel. An operating unit of Catholic Health Initiatives Colorado (an affiliate of Catholic Health Initiatives). Bed Capacity 593; Total Assisted Annually 69,060; Total Staff 1,108.

FRISCO. *St. Anthony Summit Medical Center* (1968)Mailing Address: 188 Inverness Dr., W., Ste. 500, Englewood, 80112. 340 Peak One Dr., P.O. Box 738, 80443. Tel: 303-804-8103; Fax: 303-804-8198. Email: krisordelheide@centura.org. Kris Ordelheide, Contact Person. An operating unit of Catholic Health Initiatives Colorado (an affiliate of Catholic Health Initiatives). Bed Capacity 35; Total Assisted Annually 21,873; Total Staff 253.

WESTMINSTER. *St. Anthony North Hospital*, Mailing Address: 188 Inverness Dr., W., Ste. 500, Englewood, 80112. 2551 W. 84th Ave., 80030. Tel: 303-804-8103; Fax: 303-804-8198. Email: krisordleheide@centura.org. Kris Ordelheide, Contact Person. An operating unit of Catholic Health Initiatives Colorado (an affiliate of Catholic Health Initiatives). Bed Capacity 196; Total Assisted Annually 70,548; Total Staff 769.

[I] HOSPICE AND HOMEBOUND SERVICE

DENVER. *St. Anthony Hospice* (1968) Mailing Address: 188 Inverness Dr., W., Ste. 500, Englewood, 80112. 1391 Speer Blvd., Ste. 600, 80204. Tel: 303-804-8103; Fax: 303-804-8198. Email: krisordelheide@centura.org. Kris Ordelheide, Gen. Counsel & Contact. An operating unit of Catholic Health Initiatives Colorado (an Affiliate of Catholic Health Initiatives). Total Assisted Annually 198; Total Staff 16.

**Health S.E.T.* (1988)Mailing Address: 188 Inverness Dr., W., Ste. 500, Englewood, 80112. Raleigh Bldg., 4200 N. Conejos, #436, 80204-1312. Tel: 303-595-6633; Fax: 303-595-6645. Email: jannastieg@centura.org. Web: www.healthset.org. An Operating Unit of Catholic Health Initiatives Colorado (an affiliate of Catholic Health Initiatives); Services for Home-Bound Seniors. Total Staff 11; Total Volunteers 173; Total Assisted 750.

The Villas at Sunny Acres (1968) Mailing Address: 188 Inverness Dr., W., Ste. 500, Englewood, 80112. 2501 E. 104th Ave., Thornton, 80233. Tel: 303-452-4181; Fax: 303-457-9885. Web: www.centura.org. An operating unit of Catholic Health Initiatives Colorado (an affiliate of

Catholic Health Initiatives).; Independent, Assisted & Nursing Home. Total Apartments 283; Bed Capacity 160; Assisted Living 35; Independent Living 283; Total Assisted 478.

[J] INDEPENDENT AND ASSISTED LIVING

DENVER. *Gardens at St. Elizabeth* (1968) Mailing Address: 188 Inverness Dr., W., Ste. 500, Englewood, 80112. 2835 W. 32nd Ave., 80211. Tel: 303-804-8103; Fax: 303-804-8198. Email: krisordelheide@centura.org. Web: www.centura.org. Beth Breen, Admin.; Sr. Jacqueline Leech, Chap.; Kris Ordelheide, Contact Person. Sisters of St. Francis of Colorado Springs (O.S.F.).Catholic Health Care Federation, (Men and Women); An operating unit of Catholic Health Initiatives Colorado (an affiliate of Catholic Health Initiatives). Sisters 6; Independent Living 144; Assisted Living 145; Total Staff 100.

Little Sisters of the Poor (1918) 3629 W. 29th Ave., 80211. Tel: 303-433-7221; Fax: 303-455-9184. Email: msdenver@littlesistersofthepoor.org. Sr. Mary Paul Magyar, L.S.P., Admin.; Rev. Ralph Talkin, S.J. Little Sisters of the Poor 10; Total Staff 90; Assisted Living Rooms 7; Bed Capacity 70; Long-Term Care Beds 44; Independent Apartments 18; Total Assisted 70.

Marycrest Assisted Living, 2850 Columbine Rd., 80221. Tel: 303-433-0906; Fax: 303-433-1254. Email: ppmarycrest@comcast.net. Web: www.marycrest.org. Paula Padilla, Exec. Admin. & Contact. Residents 138.

AURORA. *St. Anna's Home (Congregation of Sisters of Charity of St. Vincent de Paul, Colorado Chapter Inc.)*, 3147 S. Pagosa St., 80013. Tel: 303-627-2986; Fax: 303-627-2986. Email: st.annashome@hotmail.com. Sisters Elizabeth Kim, Dir.; Caecilia Yi, Dir. Total Assisted Annually 3; Total Staff 2.

WESTMINSTER. *Clare of Assisi Homes - Westminster, Inc.* (1995) 2451 W. 82 Pl., 80003. Tel: 303-427-4406; 303-462-9271 (Corporate). Housing and services for elderly and disabled. Total Apartments 62; Total Staff 5.

Villa Maria, Inc. (1996) 2461 W. 82nd Pl., 80031-4065. Tel: 303-427-4406; Fax: 303-412-5771. Housing and services for elderly and disabled. Total Assisted 40; Total Staff 5.

[K] SPECIAL TRANSITIONAL HOUSING

DENVER. *Decatur Place*, Mailing Address: 1999 Broadway, #1000, 80202. 1155 Decatur St., 80204. Tel: 303-830-3300; Fax: 303-830-3301. Web: www.mercyhousing.org. Brian Shuman, Pres.; Patricia O'Roark, Contact. Two year single parent transitional housing program. Residents 196.

Sacred Heart House of Denver (1980) 2844 Lawrence St., 80205. Tel: 303-296-6686; Fax: 303-296-2903. Web: sacredhearthouse.org. Ms. Janet L. Morris, Exec. Dir. Housing and services for homeless mothers and children and for single women. Homeless Women and Children served annually 1,150; Staff 8.

[L] AFFORDABLE HOUSING AND SERVICES FOR SENIORS, FAMILIES, AND THE DISABLED

DENVER. *Archdiocesan Housing, Inc.* (1968) 4045 Pecos St., Ste. A, 80211. Tel: 303-830-0215; Fax: 303-830-2885. Email: jrussell@archdiocesanhousing.org. Web: www.archdiocesanhousing.com. Total Assisted Annually 1,083.

Archdiocesan Family Housing, Inc. (1968) 4045 Pecos St., Ste. A, 80211. Tel: 303-830-0215; Fax: 303-830-2885. Housing for Low-Income Families.

Cathedral Plaza Inc. (1980) 4045 Pecos St., Ste. A, 80211. Tel: 303-830-0215; Fax: 303-830-2885. Web: www.archdiocesanhousing.org.

Holy Family Plaza, Inc. (1981) 4045 Pecos St., Ste. A, 80211. Tel: 303-830-0215; Fax: 303-830-2885. Web: www.archdiocesanhousing.org.

Marian Plaza, Inc. (1983) 4045 Pecos St., Ste. A, 80211. Tel: 303-830-0215; Fax: 303-830-2885. Web: www.archdiocesanhousing.org.

Higgins Plaza, Inc. (1990) 4045 Pecos St., Ste. A, 80211. Tel: 303-830-0215; Fax: 303-830-2885. Web: www.archdiocesanhousing.org.

Madonna Plaza, Inc. (1989) 4045 Pecos St., Ste. A, 80211. Tel: 303-830-0215; Fax: 303-830-2885. Web: www.archdiocesanhousing.org.

St. Martin Plaza, Inc. (1988) 4045 Pecos St., Ste. A, 80211. Tel: 303-830-0215; Fax: 303-830-2885. Web: www.archdiocesanhousing.org.

Colorado Affordable Catholic Housing Corp. (1991) 4045 Pecos St., Ste. A, 80211. Tel: 303-830-0215; Fax: 303-830-2885. Web: www.archdiocesanhousing.org.

Housing Management Services, Inc. (1986) 4045 Pecos St., Ste. A, 80211. Tel: 303-830-0215; Fax: 303-830-2885. Web: www.archdiocesanhousing.org.

Clare Gardens, Inc. (1972) 2626 Osceola St., 80212. Tel: 303-433-6268; Fax: 303-455-5359. Web: www.nfhealthcare.org. Franciscan Sisters, Daughters of the Sacred Hearts of Jesus and Mary (Wheaton, IL)., Housing Ministry, low-income family units. Housing Units 128; Residents 448; Total Staff 14.

Dayspring Villa, Inc. (1993) 3777 W. 26th Ave., 80211. Tel: 303-455-5066; Fax: 303-455-8966. Susan M. Dillberg, Chairperson. Total Assisted 45; Total Staff 34.

Francis Heights, Inc. (1970) 2626 Osceola St., 80212. Tel: 303-433-6268; Fax: 303-455-5359. Web: www.wfhealthcare.org. Franciscan Sisters, Daughters of the Sacred Hearts of Jesus and Mary, (Wheaton, IL)., Housing Ministry and Senior Citizens. Housing Units 383; Total Staff 14; Residents 422.

Machebeuf Apartments, Inc., 4045 Pecos St., Ste. A, 80211. Tel: 303-830-0215. Email: jrussell@archdiocesanhousing.org. Web: www.archdiocesanhousing.org. Josh Russell, Exec. Dir. Low income housing for families located in Glenwood Springs, CO. Total Assisted 55.

Mercy Holly Park East (1996) 1999 Broadway, Ste. 1000, 80202. Tel: 303-830-3300; Fax: 303-830-3301. Patricia O'Roark, Contact. Affordable housing for singles and families. Units 72; Residents 145; Total Staff 3; Total Assisted Annually 200.

Mercy Holly Park West (1996) 1999 Broadway, Ste. 1000, 80202. Tel: 303-830-3300; Fax: 303-830-3301. Affordable housing for singles and families. Units 15; Residents 45; Total Staff 1; Total Assisted Annually 55.

Prairie Rose Plaza, 4045 Pecos St., Ste. A, 80211.

The Sacred Heart of Jesus Housing Foundation (1999) 1300 S. Steele St., 80210. Tel: 303-715-3194; Fax: 303-715-2041. Independent Living 16.

Willow Street Apartments (1996) 1999 Broadway, Ste. 1000, 80202. Tel: 303-830-3300; Fax: 303-830-3301. Affordable housing for persons with chronic mental illness. Units 12; Residents 13.

CARBONDALE. *Villas de Santa Lucia, Inc.*, Mailing Address: 4045 Pecos St., Ste. A, 80211. 302 Meadowood Dr. #K, 81623. Low income housing for families.

[M] CATHOLIC CHARITIES & COMMUNITY SERVICES

DENVER. *Catholic Charities and Community Services of the Archdiocese of Denver, Inc.*, 4045 Pecos St., 80211. Tel: 303-742-0828; Fax: 303-742-0774. Email: info@ccdenver.org. Web: www.ccdenver.org. Jonathan Reyes, Pres., CEO & Admin. Shelters for the Homeless, Emergency Assistance Services, Individual & Family Counseling Services, Adoption Services, Pregnancy Counseling, Youth & Senior Services, Child Care, Foster Care, Immigration Services Day Care Centers 8; Total Assisted 1,012; Special Centers for Social Services 32; Total Assisted 98,466.

Catholic Charities Samaritan House, 2301 Lawrence St., 80205. Tel: 303-294-0241; Fax: 303-294-9523. Homeless Shelter

Catholic Charities Fr. Ed Judy House, 4024 S. Newton St., 80236. Tel: 303-866-7641; Fax: 303-866-7643. Homeless Shelter

Catholic Charities Transitional Housing and Homeless Prevention, 4045 Pecos St., 80211. Tel: 303-742-0828; Fax: 303-455-3176.

Catholic Charities The Carron Center Serving People with Disabilities, 4045 Pecos St., 80211. Tel: 303-742-0828; Fax: 303-742-4373. Services for developmentally disabled adults and ministry to deaf persons.

Catholic Charities Margery Reed Mayo Day Nursery, 1128 28th St., 80205. Tel: 303-308-1420; Fax: 303-308-1421. Child Care, Colorado Preschool & Kindergarten Program, Head Start & Early Head Start.

Catholic Charities Child Development Center, 1155 Decatur St., 80204. Tel: 303-629-5466; Fax: 303-629-6710. Child Care, Colorado Preschool & Kindergarten Program, Head Start & Early Head Start.

Catholic Charities Head Start Services, 4045 Pecos St., 80211. Tel: 303-742-0828; Fax: 303-742-4410.

Catholic Charities Family Services, 4045 Pecos St., 80211. Tel: 303-742-0828; Fax: 303-742-4373. Counseling, Adoption, Foster Care, Youth & Senior Services.

Catholic Charities Immigration Services, 4045 Pecos St., 80211. Tel: 303-742-0828; Fax: 303-742-4410.

Catholic Charities Homeless Prevention Services, 4045 Pecos St., 80211. Tel: 303-742-0828; Fax: 303-742-0774.

Catholic Charities Larimer Regional Office, 460 Linden Center Dr., Fort Collins, 80524. Tel: 970-484-5010; Fax: 970-484-0259. The Mission Shelter for Homeless, Job Bank, Emergency Assistance, Senior Services, Immigration Services & Farm Labor Housing Corp.

Catholic Charities The Mission Shelter for Homeless, Hostel of Hospitality, 460 Linden Center Dr., Fort Collins, 80524. Tel: 970-484-5010; Fax: 970-484-0259. Homeless Shelter

Catholic Charities Weld Regional Office, 2500 1st Ave., Bldg. CB, Greeley, 80631. Tel: 970-353-6433; Fax: 970-353-3861. Emergency Assistance, Senior Services, Case Management, Immigration Services.

Catholic Charities Guadalupe Shelter, 1518 N. 25th Ave., Greeley, 80631. Tel: 970-353-3720. Homeless Shelter

Catholic Charities Western Slope Office, 1004 Grand Ave., Glenwood Springs, 81601. Tel: 970-384-2060; Fax: 970-945-2089. Immigration Services, Emergency Assistance, Transitional Housing.

Catholic Charities Aurora Family Assistance Center, 1300 Potomac St., Ste. 156, Aurora, 80012. Tel: 303-597-0464; Fax: 303-337-2431. Serving Adams & Arapahoe Counties.

Catholic Charities Byers Place Emergency Assistance Center, 1205 W. Byers Pl., Ste. A, 80223. Tel: 303-922-5205; Fax: 303-922-5045. Serving Denver & Jefferson Counties.

Catholic Charities Mulroy Senior Center, 3550 W. 13th Ave., 80204. Tel: 303-892-1540.

Catholic Charities St. Joseph's Group Home, 4626 Pennsylvania St., 80216. Tel: 303-292-2591; Fax: 303-292-1860.

Catholic Charities Farm Labor Housing Corporation, 460 Linden Center Dr., Fort Collins, 80524. Tel: 970-484-5010. Email: info@ccdenver.org. Web: www.ccdenver.org.

Catholic Charities Plaza Del Milagro, 2501 1st Ave., #CC, Greeley, 80631. Tel: 970-346-2888. Migrant & Seasonal Housing.

Catholic Charities Plaza Del Sol, 2501 Ash St., #36, Greeley, 80631. Tel: 970-378-1171; Fax: 970-378-1176. Migrant & Seasonal Housing.

[N] MONASTERIES AND RESIDENCES OF PRIESTS AND BROTHERS

DENVER. *Capuchin Province of Mid-America, Inc.* (1977) 3613 Wyandot St., 80211-2950. Tel: 303-477-5436; Fax: 303-477-6925. Web: www.midamcaps.org. Revs. Charles Polifka, O.F.M.Cap., Provincial Min.; John Lager, O.F.M.Cap., Vocation Dir.; Blaine Burkey, O.F.M.Cap., Communications Dir. & Archivist. *St. Francis of Assisi Friary*, 3553 Wyandot St., 80211-2948. Tel: 303-477-5542; Fax: 303-477-6925. (Order of Friars Minor Capuchin) Total in Residence 8; Total Staff 3. In Res. Revs. Charles Polifka, O.F.M.Cap., Provincial Min. & Guardian; Blaine Burkey, O.F.M.Cap.; John Lager, O.F.M.Cap.; Matthew Gross, O.F.M.Cap.; David Gottschalk, O.F.M.Cap.; Michael Suchnicki, O.F.M.Cap.; Simeon Gallagher, O.F.M.Cap. *San Antonio Friary*, 3554 Humboldt St., 80205-3940. Tel: 303-292-5110; Fax: 303-292-5148. Postulants 5. In Res. Revs. Gene Emrisek, O.F.M.Cap., Guardian; Francisco Ramirez, O.F.M.Cap., Vicar; William Kraus, O.F.M.Cap., Guardian, Dir. of Postulants; Benignus Scarry, O.F.M.Cap., Vicar. *San Damiano Friary*, 605 W. 6th St., 80204. Tel: 303-893-6770. In Res. Revs. Christopher Popravak, O.F.M.Cap., Guardian; Regis Scanlon, O.F.M.Cap.; Bros. Larry Browers, O.F.M.Cap.; Barnabus Eichor, O.F.M.Cap.; Joseph Mary Elder, O.F.M.Cap.; Augustine Rhode, O.F.M.Cap.; Ryan Tidball, O.F.M.Cap.

Catholic Foreign Mission Society of America, Inc. (Maryknoll Fathers and Brothers, M.M.), 3053 W. 29th Ave., 80211. Tel: 303-455-5669; 303-854-7326; Fax: 303-455-2069. Email: ddarling@maryknoll.org. Web: www.maryknoll.org. David A. Darling, Dir.

Congregation of the Mission Western Province: De Paul House, 2340 S. University Blvd., 80210. Tel: 303-715-9123. Revs. Prudencio Rodriguez de Yurre, C.M., Supr.; Paul L. Golden, C.M.; Richard R. Ryan, C.M.; Thomas J. Nelson, C.M.; Bro. F. Joseph Hess, C.M.

Dominican Friars, 3005 W. 29th Ave., 80211-3701. Tel: 303-455-3614; Fax: 303-455-3087. Very Rev. Gerald L. Stookey, O.P., Prior; Bro. Jordan Coonen, O.P.; Revs. Robert F. Staes, O.P.; Louis S. Morrone, O.P., Novice Master; Clinton P. Honkomp, O.P.; Thomas P. Lynch, O.P.; Patrick Roarden, O.P.; John G. McGreevy, O.P. Novitiate & Priory; Province of St. Albert the Great Priests 7; Brothers 1; Novices 7.

The Redemptorists/Denver Province (1996) 1230 S. Parker Rd., 80231. Tel: 303-370-0035; 303-565-5405 (Mission Advancement Ministry); 303-370-9013 (Office of Financial Services); Fax: 303-370-0036. Email: info@redemptorists-denver.org; development@redemptorists-denver.org. Web: www.redemptorists-denver.org. Very Rev. Thomas D. Picton, C.Ss.R., Prov. Supr.; Revs. Richard Mevissen, C.Ss.R., Prov. Vicar; Robert Halter, C.Ss.R., Prov. Consultor; Allan

Weinert, C.Ss.R., Office Fin. Svcs., Treas. Priests 178; Deacons 3; Brothers 25.

Serving abroad: Most Rev. Alfred Novak, C.Ss.R. (Retired), Residencia do Bispro C.P.531 83203-970, PR, Brazil. Tel: 55-41-422-7717; Fax: 55-41-422-7717; Very Rev. Joseph W. Tobin, C.Ss.R., Supr. Gen., Casa Sant'Alfonso, C.P. 2458, 00100 Rome, Italy. Tel: 39-06-49490-1; Fax: 39-06-44660-12; Rev. William Fitzgerald, C.Ss.R., C.P. 400, 48900 Juazeiro, Bahia, Brazil.

Serving elsewhere, not listed: Revs. John Steingraeber, C.Ss.R., Assoc. Dir. CMSM; George Rassley, C.Ss.R., Loyalton #39, 205 E. Anton, Coeur d'Alene, ID 83815. Tel: 208-659-8511; Ricardo Elford, C.Ss.R., 3662 S. 7th Ave., Tucson, AZ 85713-6115. Tel: 520-206-9772; Dr. William Green, C.Ss.R., P.O. Box 1209, Coeur D Alene, ID 83816. Tel: 208-765-1894; Fax: 208-666-1598; Rev. Timothy Watson, C.Ss.R., Chap. *The Redemptorists of Denver, Colorado* (1981) 1230 S. Parker Rd., 80231. Tel: 303-370-0035; Fax: 303-370-0036. *Regis High Jesuit Community*, 16810 E. Caley Ave., Centennial, 80016-1005. Tel: 303-690-4782; Fax: 303-680-7662. Revs. John Apel, S.J., Supr.; David A. Wayne, S.J.; Chris Pinne, S.J.; Philip G. Steele, S.J., Pres. Regis Jesuit High School In Res. Joe Laramie, S.J., Seminarian.

Regis Jesuit Community (The Jesuits at Regis University), Jesuit House M12, 3333 Regis Blvd., 80221-1099. Tel: 303-458-4100; Fax: 303-964-5525. Revs. J. Daniel Daly, S.J., Rector & Contact Person for Regis Univ.; David M. Clarke, S.J.; Marco Tulio Gomez, S.J.; James B. Guyer, S.J.; Donald E. Highberger, S.J.; Gerard E. Menard, S.J.; Stephen W. Planning, S.J.; Michael J. Sheeran, S.J.; Charles M. Shelton, S.J.

Society of Jesus - St. Ignatius Loyola Jesuit Community (1944) 2309 Gaylord St., 80205-5627. Tel: 303-322-8042; Fax: 303-322-2927. Email: loyoladenver@eschelon.com. Web: www.loyoladenver.com. Revs. C. Thomas Jost, S.J., Supr.; Leo F. Weber, S.J.; Joseph Tuoc Nguyen, S.J.; Stephen T. Yavorsky, S.J.; Bro. Donald R. Schlichter, S.J.

The Theatine Fathers (1923) 1050 S. Birch St., 80246. Tel: 303-756-5522; Fax: 303-691-2969. Very Rev. Jospeh Larry Gallegos, C.R., Prov. Supr. Theatine Fathers. Priests 1.

Xavier Jesuit Center (1993) 3450 W. 53rd, 80221-6568. Tel: 303-480-3900; Fax: 303-480-3913. Revs. John J. Waters, S.J., Supr. & Contact for Xavier Center; Richard S. Anthonysamy, S.J.; David E. Barry, S.J.; Joseph F. Bona, S.J.; John R. Daly, S.J.; Robert R. DeRouen, S.J.; Edward F. Flaherty, S.J.; Harry E. Hoewischer, S.J.; William T. Miller, S.J.; Donald W. Reck, S.J.; Curtis E. Van Del, S.J.; John J. Waters, S.J.; Walter Watson, S.J.; Martin J. Whealen, S.J.; William W. Williams, S.J., Min.; Bro. Alors H. Dorsey, S.J. (Society of Jesus)

SNOWMASS. *St. Benedict's Monastery* (1956) 1012 Monastery Rd., 81654. Tel: 970-927-3311; Fax: 970-927-3399. Email: retreat@rof.net. Web: www.snowmass.org. Rt. Rev. Joseph Boyle, O.C.S.O.; Revs. Thomas Keating, O.C.S.O.; William Meninger, O.C.S.O.; Charles Albanese, O.C.S.O.; Micah Schonberger, O.C.S.O. The Order of Cistercians of the Strict Observance (Trappists). Professed Monks 13.

[O] CONVENTS AND RESIDENCES FOR SISTERS

DENVER. *Missionaries of Charity*, 633 Fox St., 80204. Tel: 303-860-8040. Sr. M. Sharon, M.C., Supr. & Contact. Shelter for Homeless Women (8 Beds) Total Assisted 320.

Monastery of Our Lady of Light (Capuchin Poor Clares), 3325 Pecos, 80211. Tel: 303-458-6339; Fax: 303-477-6925. Web: www.capuchinpoorclares.org/denver/index.html. Sr. Maria de Cristo Palafox, O.S.C.Cap., Abbess. *Capuchin Poor Clares of Denver, Inc.* Sisters 9.

Our Lady of Mercy Convent, 1300 S. Steele St., 80210. Tel: 303-765-4592; Fax: 303-765-4595. Email: denver@rsmofalma.org. Web: rsmofalma.org. Sr. Mary Prudence Allen, R.S.M., Local Supr. Religious Sisters of Mercy (Alma, Michigan). Sisters 6.

Sisters of St. Francis of Penance and Christian Charity (1939) 2851 W. 52nd Ave., 80221. Tel: 303-458-6270; Fax: 303-433-5865. Web: www.marycrest.org. Sisters Karen Crouse, Prov. Min.; Macrina Scott, O.S.F., First Asst.

Sisters of St. Francis, Denver, CO Sisters in Province 50; Total Assisted 41; Total Staff 2.

Queen of Peace Convent (1968) Additional Residence: 5360 Columbine Rd., 80221-1277. Tel: 303-433-4104. Web: www.marycrest.org. Sisters of St. Francis of Penance and Christian Charity. Sisters 7.

GOLDEN. *Mother Cabrini Shrine*, 20189 Cabrini Blvd., 80401. Tel: 303-526-0758; Fax: 303-526-9795. Email: mcs@mothercabrinishrine.org. Web: www.mothercabrinishrine.org. Sr. Bernadette Casciano, M.S.C., Admin. Missionary Sisters of the Sacred Heart of Jesus (M.S.C.) 3.

LITTLETON. *Carmel of Holy Spirit* (1947) 6138 S. Gallup St., 80120-2702. Tel: 303-798-4176. Sr. Gemma Marie of the Passion Hughes, O.C.D., Prioress. Discalced Carmelites (O.C.D.). Sisters 11.

Loretto Center (1964) 4000 S. Wadsworth, 80123-1309. Tel: 303-986-1541; Fax: 303-986-8453. Sr. Marlene Spero, S.L., Co-Coord. (Sisters of Loretto) Sisters 13.

Sisters of Benedict of Colorado, Inc., 4264 W. Ponds View Dr., 80123. Tel: 303-795-2378. Email: judiosb@aol.com. Sr. Judith Elms, O.S.B., Supr.

VIRGINIA DALE. *Abbey of St. Walburga* (1935) 32109 N. U.S. Hwy. 287, 80536-8942. Tel: 970-472-0612; Fax: 970-484-4342. Email: abbey@walburga.org. Web: www.walburga.org. Sr. Maria-Michael Newe, O.S.B., Abbess. Benedictine Nuns 19; Novices 2; Claustral Oblate 1.

WHEAT RIDGE. *Carmelite Sisters of the Most Sacred Heart of Los Angeles, Sts. Peter & Paul Convent*, 4040 Pierce St., 80033. Tel: 303-422-6419.

[P] RETREAT CENTERS

DENVER. *St. Joseph Retreat Center*, 3060 S. Monaco Pkwy., 80222. Tel: 303-758-8826. Rev. Msgr. Kenneth J. Leone, Dir.

ALLENSPARK. *Catholic Retreat, Conference and Spiritual Center - Camp St. Malo*, 10758 Hwy. 7, 80510. Tel: 303-747-0201; Fax: 303-747-2892. Web: www.saintmalo.org. Mailing Address: 1300 S. Steele St., 80210. Jose Ambrozic, Dir.; Theresa B. Donohoe, Dir.

LITTLETON. *Jesus Our Hope Hermitage*, 10519 S. Deer Creek Rd., 80127. Tel: 303-697-7539; Fax: 303-697-7539. Web: www.jesus-our-hope.org. Deacon Joseph H. Donohoe, Dir.

[Q] CAMPUS MINISTRY

DENVER. *Youth, Young Adult and Campus Ministry Office* 1300 S. Steele St., 80210. Tel: 303-715-3203; Fax: 303-715-2042. Email: chris.stefanick@archden.org. Web: www.archden.org. Chris Stefanick, Dir.; Deacon Don Schaefer. Please contact this office directly for a complete listing of campus ministry offices in Northern Colorado.

NORTHGLENN. **Fellowship of Catholic University Students (FOCUS)* (1999) 11990 Grant St., 80233. Tel: 303-962-5750; Fax: 303-565-5738. Email: info@focusonline.org. Web: www.focusonline.org. Mailing Address: P.O. Box 33656, 80233. Katherine LeBlane, CFO.

[R] ASSOCIATIONS OF CONSECRATED LIFE

DENVER. *The Catholic Community of the Beatitudes*, 2924 W. 43rd Ave., 80211. Tel: 720-855-9412; Fax: 303-455-6651. Email: beatitudes.denver@gmail.com. Web: www.beatitudes.us. Rev. Nathanael Pujos (France), Shepherd.

Companions of Christ, 1050 Pennsylvania St., 80203. Email: denver.companions@gmail.com. Web: www.denvercompanionsofchrist.org. Matthew Book, Moderator.

ALLENSPARK. *Sodalitium Christianae Vitae*, 10758 Hwy. 7, 80510. Tel: 303-747-0201, Ext. 321; Fax: 303-747-2892. Email: contact@sodalitium.com. Web: www.sodalitium.com.

WHEAT RIDGE. *Denver - Marian Community of Reconciliation* (1991) 1060 St. Francis Way, 80204. Tel: 303-629-0500; Fax: 303-629-5100. Email: rgoni@fraternas.org. Web: www.fraternasusa.org/colorado. Rossana Goni, Supr.

[S] MISCELLANEOUS LISTINGS

DENVER. *St. Anthony Health Foundation*, Mailing Address: 188 Inverness Dr., W., Ste. 500, Englewood, 80112. 4231 W. 16th Ave., 80204. Tel: 303-629-4446; Fax: 303-629-4241. Kris Ordelheide, Gen. Counsel. An operating unit of Catholic Health Initiatives Colorado Foundation.

Archbishops Guild, 2191 E. 97th Ave., 80229. Rev. Patrick Dolan, Spiritual Advisor.

The Archdiocese of Denver Cemeteries Perpetual Care Trust, 1300 S. Steele St., 80210.

The Archdiocese of Denver Irrevocable Revolving Trust, 1300 S. Steele St., 80210. Tel: 303-715-3258; Fax: 303-715-2046.

The Archdiocese of Denver Management Corporation, 1300 S. Steele St., 80210. Tel: 303-715-3258.

The Archdiocese of Denver Risk Management Property/Casualty Insurance Trust, 1300 S. Steele St., 80210.

The Archdiocese of Denver Welfare Benefits Trust, 1300 S. Steele St., 80210.

Arrupe Corporate Work-Study Program (2003) 4343 Utica, 80212. Tel: 303-455-7449, Ext. 237; Fax: 303-455-7453. Email: tmallary@arrupejesuit.com. Web: www.arrupejesuit.com. Thomas C. Mallary, Pres.

Blessed Sacrament Catholic Educational Foundation (1989) 4930 Montview Blvd., 80207. Tel: 303-355-7361. Rev. Kenneth J. Liuzzi, V.F., Exec. Officer & Contact Person.

Catholic Alumni Club of Colorado, P.O. Box 503, Wheat Ridge, 80034. Tel: 303-477-3572; 303-237-2185. Email: cacofco@hotmail.com. Web: www.caci.org/cac/colorado.html.

**The Catholic Foundation for the Roman Catholic Church in Northern Colorado*, 3801 E. Florida Ave., Ste. 725, 80210. Tel: 303-468-9885; Fax: 303-468-9889. Email: info@thecatholicfoundation.com. Web: www.thecatholicfoundation.com. Total Staff 5.

Catholic Health Initiatives (2004) 1999 Broadway, Ste. 4000, 80202. Tel: 303-298-9100; Fax: 303-298-9690. Email: peggymartin@catholichealth.net. Web: www.catholichealthinit.org. Kevin Lofton, Pres. & CEO; Sr. Peggy Ann Martin, O.P., J.C.L., Contact.

Christian Life Movement, Inc. (1985) 1060 11th St., 80204. Tel: 303-629-5100; Fax: 303-629-5100. Email: denverclm@clmusa.org. Web: www.clmusa.org.

**Colorado Vincentian Volunteers* (1994) 1732 Pearl St., 80203. Tel: 303-863-8141; Fax: 303-863-8141 (Call office first). Email: cvv@covivo.org. Web: www.covivo.org. Bill Jaster, Co-Dir.

ENDOW, 1300 S. Steele St., 80210. Tel: 303-715-3224; Fax: 303-715-2040. Email: terry.polakovic@archden.org. Web: www.endowonline.com. Mrs. Therese A. Polakovic, Exec. Dir.; Kate E. Sweeney, Assoc. Dir.

Franciscan Sisters Charitable Fund of Colorado, Inc., 2626 Osceola St., 80212. Tel: 303-433-6268; Fax: 303-455-5359. Email: theresalan@aol.com. Sr. Theresa Langfield, O.S.F., Pres. & Admin. Franciscan Sisters, Daughters of the Sacred Heart of Jesus and Mary, (Wheaton, IL).

**Saint Joseph Hospital Foundation* (1977) 1835 Franklin St., 80218. Tel: 303-837-7043; Fax: 303-837-7115. Email: unreinc@exempla.org. Web: www.sjhfdenver.org. Carl Unrein, Pres. & CEO.

Marycrest Franciscan Ministries (1983)Mailing Address: 2851 W. 52nd Ave., 80221-7636. Tel: 303-458-6270; Fax: 303-433-5865. Sr. Cecilia Linenbrink, O.S.F., Pres.

Mercy Housing Colorado, 1999 Broadway, Ste. 1000, 80202. Tel: 303-830-3300; Fax: 303-830-3301. Web: www.mercyhousing.org. Jennifer Erixon, Pres.

**Mercy Housing, Inc.* (1981) 1999 Broadway, Ste. 1000, 80202. Tel: 303-830-3300; Fax: 303-830-3301. Email: mail@mercyhousing.org. Web: www.mercyhousing.org. Sr. Lillian Murphy, CEO. Affordable Housing Properties. Units 835; Total Served 2,040; Day Care Centers 3; Total Served 334.

Mercy Portfolio Services, 1999 Broadway, Ste. 1000, 80202.

Mercy Services Corp. (1983) 1999 Broadway, Ste. 1000, 80202. Tel: 303-830-3300; Fax: 303-830-3301. Cheryll O'Bryan, Pres.

Mercy Commercial Finance Properties (1990) Richard Banks, Pres.

Mercy Housing Properties (1994) Richard Banks, Pres.

**Mercy Properties, Inc.* (1991) Richard Banks, Pres.

**Queen of Apostles Mission Association, Inc.* (1992) c/o St. Hungary of Elizabeth Church, 1060 St. Francis Way, 80204. Tel: 720-234-7223. Email: qama@aol.com. Web: www.qama.org. Matt Werner, Pres. Supporting Catholic missionary priests and religious in the former Soviet Union with spiritual and financial support. More than $1.5 Million given since 1994.

Redemptorist Fathers (1914) (Inactive), c/o The Redemptorists/Denver Province, 1230 S. Parker Rd., 80231. Tel: 303-370-0035.

The Redemptorist of Greeley, Colorado, Inc. (1983) (Inactive), c/o The Redemptorist/Denver Province, 1230 S. Parker Rd., 80231. Tel: 303-370-0035.

Redemptorist Society of Alaska (1964) (Inactive), c/o The Redemptorist/Denver Province, 1230 S. Parker Rd., 80231. Tel: 303-370-0035.

Redemptorist Society of Iowa (1908) (Inactive), c/o The Redemptorist/Denver Province, 1230 S. Parker Rd., 80231. Tel: 303-370-0035.

Redemptorist Society of Oregon (1906) (Inactive), c/o The Redemptorist/Denver Province, 1230 S. Parker Rd., 80231. Tel: 303-370-0035.

Seeds of Hope Charitable Trust (1996) 1300 S. Steele St., 80210. Tel: 303-715-3127; Fax: 303-715-2042. Email: info@seedsofhopetrust.org. Web: www.seedsofhopetrust.org. Betsy Boudreau, Exec. Dir.

St. Vincent de Paul Stores, Inc., Store Location: 6260 E. Colfax Ave., 80205. Tel: 303-388-3315.

ARVADA. **Buena Vista, Inc.*, P.O. Box 745475, 80006-5475. Tel: 303-477-0180. Email: info@sccconnect.org. Web: www.sccconnect.org. William Breay, Admin. Asst. to the Bd.

BOULDER. *Sacred Heart School Foundation*, Mailing Address: 2525 Arapahoe Ave., Ste. E4-205, 80302. 2312 14th St., 80304. Tel: 303-444-3478. Mr. James Mullen, Contact.

CENTENNIAL. *LC Pastoral Services Inc.*, 8077 S. Quince Cir., 80112. Tel: 303-689-9932; Fax: 303-721-9492. Rev. Jon Budke, L.C., Dir.

ENGLEWOOD. *Association for Catholic Information* (2003) 3392 S. Broadway, 80113. Tel: 303-747-2684; Fax: 303-484-2824. Email: jluna@catholicna.com. Web: www.catholicnewsagency.com. Bro. Jorge S. Luna Diaz del Olmo.

Catholic Health Initiatives Colorado (1968) 188 Inverness Dr. W, Ste. 500, 80112. Tel: 303-290-6500; Fax: 303-804-8198. Mr. Gary S. Campbell, Pres. & CEO; Kris Ordelheide, Contact. An affiliate of Catholic Health Initiatives.

**Centura Health* (1996) 188 Inverness Dr. W, Ste. 500, 80112. Tel: 303-804-8103; Fax: 303-804-8198. Email: krisordelheide@centura.org. Web: www.centura.org. Kris Ordelheide, Contact Person; Mr. Gary S. Campbell, Pres. & CEO. An operating unit of Colorado Health Initiatives Colorado. (An affiliate of Catholic Health Initiatives.)

Family of Nazareth, Inc., 3151 S. Bannock St., 80110. Tel: 303-758-1280; Fax: 303-758-1380. Email: steve.waymel@acs-inc.com. Donald McLeod, Pres.

ESTES PARK. **Our Lady of Tenderness, Poustinia* (1983) Box 4311, 80517. Tel: 970-577-1383. Web: www.ourladyoftenderness.org. Lucille Dupuis, Dir.

FORT COLLINS. *West African Development Support Organization*, 3124 Appaloosa Ct., 80526. Tel: 970-226-2817. Email: steveh291@comcast.net. Web: www.wadso.org. Rev. Donald C. Willette; John Nystom, Pres.; Steve Henry, Contact Person.

GREELEY. *St. Mary's Catholic Education Foundation Greeley*, 2222 23rd Ave., 80634. Tel: 970-352-1724; Fax: 970-352-1729. Email: benke99714@yahoo.com. Susan Benke, Contact.

LAKEWOOD. *Vines of Our Faith Inc.*, 9405 W. Florida Ave., 80232.

LITTLETON. *Sisters of Loretto: Administrative Offices*, 4000 S. Wadsworth Blvd., 80123. Tel: 303-783-0450; Fax: 303-783-0611. Web: www.lorettocommunity.org. Sr. Catherine Mueller, S.L., Pres.

LONGMONT. **From Mission To Mission*, 303 Atwood St., 80501. Tel: 720-494-7211; Fax: 720-494-7211. Email: missiontomission@hotmail.com. Web: www.missiontomission.org. Julie Lupien, Exec. Dir.

LOVELAND. *St. John the Evangelist Education Foundation*, 1515 Hilltop Dr., 80537. Tel: 970-635-5819; Fax: 970-669-5743. Rev. Joseph A. Hartmann.

RELIGIOUS INSTITUTES OF MEN REPRESENTED IN THE ARCHDIOCESE

For further details refer to the corresponding bracketed number in the Religious Institutes of Men or Women section.

[0330]—*Brothers of the Christian Schools*—F.S.C.
[0460]—*Brothers of the Poor of St. Francis*—C.F.P.
[0470]—*The Capuchin Friars* (Denver, CO); (St. Francis of Assisi Friary)—O.F.M.Cap.
[0350]—*Cistercians of the Strict Observance-Trappists* (St. Benedict Monastery)—O.C.S.O.
[]—*Congregation of Mother Coredemptrix* (Carthage, MO); (Queen of Vietnamese Martyrs)—C.M.C.
[1330]—*Congregation of the Mission Western Province* (Vincentians)—C.M.
[]—*Cor Jesu (Societas Cordis Jesu, Fontis Vitae et Sanctitatis)*
[]—*Disciples of the Hearts of Jesus and Mary*
[0690]—*Jesuit Fathers and Brothers* (Missouri, Milwaukee, Oregon, Maryland Provs.)—S.J.
[0730]—*Legionaires of Christ*—L.C.
[0800]—*Maryknoll Fathers & Brothers* (Denver)—M.M.
[0940]—*Oblates of the Virgin Mary* (Holy Ghost Parish)—O.M.V.
[0430]—*Order of Preachers-Dominicans* (Prov. of St. Albert the Great)—O.P.
[1030]—*Paulist Fathers* (Sacred Heart of Jesus)—C.S.P.
[1065]—*Priestly Fraternity of St. Peter*—F.S.S.P.
[1070]—*Redemptorist Fathers* (St. Louis Prov.)—C.SS.R.
[1240]—*Servites* (Western Prov.); (Our Lady of Mt. Carmel)—O.S.M.
[1300]—*Theatine Fathers* (Rome, Italy); (St. Andrew Seminary)—C.R.

RELIGIOUS INSTITUTES OF WOMEN REPRESENTED IN THE ARCHDIOCESE

[0190]—*Benedictine Nuns*—O.S.B.
[0230]—*Benedictine Sisters of Pontifical Jurisdiction* (Colorado Springs, CO; Boulder, CO; Denver, CO; Oklahoma City, OK)—O.S.B.
[3765]—*Capuchin Poor Clares*—O.S.F.Cap.
[0370]—*Carmelite Sisters of the Most Sacred Heart of Los Angeles*—O.C.D.
[3110]—*Congregation of Our Lady of the Retreat in the Cenacle*—R.C.
[2100]—*Congregation of the Humility of Mary* (Davenport, IA)—C.H.M.
[1920]—*Congregation of the Sisters of the Holy Cross*—C.S.C.
[1780]—*Congregation of the Sisters of the Third Order of St. Francis of Perpetual Adoration* (La Crosse, WI)—F.S.P.A.
[0420]—*Discalced Carmelite Nuns*—O.C.D.
[1070-14]—*Dominican Sisters*—O.P.
[1070-03]—*Dominican Sisters* (Sinsinawa)—O.P.
[1105]—*Dominican Sisters of Hope*—O.P.
[1115]—*Dominican Sisters of Peace*—O.P.
[1070-07]—*Dominican Sisters of the Congregation of St. Cecilia* (Nashville)—O.P.
[1240]—*Franciscan Sisters, Daughters of the Sacred Hearts of Jesus and Mary* (Wheaton, IL)—O.S.F.
[1845]—*Guadalupan Missionaries of the Holy Spirit*—M.G.Sp.S.
[2575]—*Institute of the Sisters of Mercy of the Americas*—R.S.M.
[2340]—*Little Sisters of the Poor*—L.S.P.
[2710]—*Missionaries of Charity*—M.C.
[]—*Missionaries of Charity of Mary Immaculate*—M.C.M.I.
[2860]—*Missionary Sisters of the Sacred Heart*—M.S.C.
[2960]—*Notre Dame Sisters*—N.D.
[3130]—*Our Lady of Victory Missionary Sisters*—O.L.V.M.
[2519]—*Religious Sisters of Mercy of Alma, Michigan*—R.S.M.
[2970]—*School Sisters of Notre Dame*—S.S.N.D.
[1680]—*School Sisters of St. Francis* (Milwaukee, WI)—O.S.F.
[0440]—*Sisters of Charity of Cincinnati, Ohio*—S.C.
[0480]—*Sisters of Charity of Leavenworth, Kansas*—S.C.L.
[0655]—*The Sisters of Charity of St. Vincent De Paul of Suwon* (Suwon, Korea)—S.C.V.
[0430]—*Sisters of Charity of the Blessed Virgin Mary*—B.V.M.
[2360]—*Sisters of Loretto at the Foot of the Cross* (Nerinx, KY)—S.L.
[1705]—*Sisters of St. Francis of Assisi* (Milwaukee, WI)—O.S.F.
[1630]—*Sisters of St. Francis of Penance and Christian Charity*—O.S.F.
[1640]—*Sisters of St. Francis of Perpetual Adoration* (Colorado Springs, CO)—O.S.F.
[1530]—*Sisters of St. Francis of the Congregation of Our Lady of Lourdes*—O.S.F.
[3830-15]—*Sisters of St. Joseph*—C.S.J.
[3840]—*Sisters of St. Joseph of Carondelet*—C.S.J.
[3260]—*Sisters of the Precious Blood* (Dayton, OH)—C.PP.S.
[1720]—*Sisters of the Third Order Regular of St. Francis of the Congregation of Our Lady of Lourdes* (Rochester, MN)—O.S.F.

ARCHDIOCESAN CEMETERIES

AURORA. *St. Simeon Cemetery Association* (2003) 22001 E. State Hwy. 30, 80018. Tel: 720-859-9785; Fax: 720-859-9788. Email: lloyd.swint@archden.org. Web: www.stsimeondenver.org.

WHEAT RIDGE. *Archdiocese of Denver Mortuary at Mount Olivet, Inc.* (1981) 12801 W. 44th Ave., 80033. Tel: 303-425-9511; Fax: 303-425-0242.

The Mount Olivet Cemetery Association, 12801 W. 44th Ave., 80033. Tel: 303-424-7785; Fax: 303-424-5263.

NECROLOGY

† Breunig, Robert L., (Retired)—Died Oct. 15, 2009
† DeGante, Adalberto, (Retired)—Died Oct. 31, 2009
† McInerney, Maurice, (Retired)—Died Jan. 4, 2009

An asterisk (*) denotes an organization that has established tax-exempt status directly with the IRS and is not covered by the USCCB Group Ruling.

Diocese of Des Moines

(Dioecesis Desmoinensis)

Most Reverend

RICHARD E. PATES

Bishop of Des Moines; ordained December 20, 1968; appointed Titular Bishop of Suacia and Auxiliary Bishop of Saint Paul and Minneapolis December 22, 2000; ordained March 26, 2001; appointed Bishop of Des Moines April 10, 2008; installed May 29, 2008. *Office: 601 Grand Ave., Des Moines, IA 50309.*

Most Reverend

JOSEPH L. CHARRON, C.PP.S., S.T.D.

Retired Bishop of Des Moines; ordained June 3, 1967; appointed Titular Bishop of Bencenna and Auxiliary Bishop of Saint Paul and Minneapolis November 6, 1989; consecrated January 25, 1990; appointed Bishop of Des Moines November 12, 1993; installed January 21, 1994; retired April 10, 2007.

Chancery: 601 Grand Ave., Des Moines, IA 50309. Tel: 515-243-7653; Fax: 515-237-5070.

Web: www.dmdiocese.org

Email: bishop@dmdiocese.org

ERECTED BY POPE ST. PIUS X, AUGUST 12, 1911.

Square Miles 12,446.

Comprises that part of the State of Iowa which is bounded on the east by the eastern boundaries of the Counties of Polk, Warren, Lucas and Wayne; on the south by the State of Missouri; on the west by the Missouri River; and on the north by the northern boundaries of the Counties of Harrison, Shelby, Audubon, Guthrie, Dallas and Polk.

Patrons of the Diocese: I. Blessed Virgin Mary Queen; II. Pope Saint Pius X. Diocese solemnly consecrated to the Immaculate Heart of Mary on May 16, 1948.

Legal Title: "The Roman Catholic Diocese of Des Moines."
For legal titles of parishes and diocesan institutions, consult the Chancery Office.

STATISTICAL OVERVIEW

Personnel	
Bishop	1
Retired Bishops	1
Priests: Diocesan Active in Diocese	54
Priests: Diocesan Active Outside Diocese	2
Priests: Retired, Sick or Absent	30
Number of Diocesan Priests	86
Religious Priests in Diocese	8
Total Priests in Diocese	94
Extern Priests in Diocese	4
Ordinations:	
Diocesan Priests	2
Transitional Deacons	1
Permanent Deacons in Diocese	77
Total Sisters	65
Parishes	
Parishes	82
With Resident Pastor:	
Resident Diocesan Priests	49
Resident Religious Priests	4
Without Resident Pastor:	
Administered by Priests	29
New Parishes Created	1
Closed Parishes	1
Professional Ministry Personnel:	
Sisters	12
Lay Ministers	50
Welfare	
Catholic Hospitals	3
Total Assisted	1,693,252
Homes for the Aged	1
Total Assisted	423
Specialized Homes	1
Total Assisted	364
Special Centers for Social Services	5
Total Assisted	43,690
Educational	
Diocesan Students in Other Seminaries	10
Total Seminarians	10
Colleges and Universities	1
Total Students	778
High Schools, Diocesan and Parish	2
Total Students	1,497
Elementary Schools, Diocesan and Parish	15
Total Students	4,817
Catechesis/Religious Education:	
High School Students	2,067
Elementary Students	10,610
Total Students under Catholic Instruction	19,779
Teachers in the Diocese:	
Priests	2
Scholastics	4
Sisters	4
Lay Teachers	449
Vital Statistics	
Receptions into the Church:	
Infant Baptism Totals	1,842
Minor Baptism Totals	87
Adult Baptism Totals	113
Received into Full Communion	253
First Communions	1,927
Confirmations	1,994
Marriages:	
Catholic	248
Interfaith	238
Total Marriages	486
Deaths	747
Total Catholic Population	100,943
Total Population	742,190

Former Bishops—Most Revs. AUSTIN DOWLING, D.D., first Bishop of Des Moines; ord. June 24, 1891; appt. Bishop Jan. 31, 1912; cons. April 25, 1912; promoted to the See of St. Paul, Jan. 1919; THOMAS W. DRUMM, D.D., Bishop of Des Moines; ord. Dec. 21, 1901; cons. May 21, 1919; died Oct. 24, 1933; GERALD T. BERGAN, D.D., ord. Oct. 28, 1915; appt. March 24, 1934; cons. June 13, 1934; Enthroned June 21, 1934; elevated to Archiepiscopal dignity and promoted to Omaha Feb. 9, 1948; EDWARD C. DALY, O.P., S.T.M., Bishop of Des Moines; ord. June 12, 1921; appt. March 13, 1948; cons. May 13, 1948; named Asst. at Papal Throne, May 23, 1958; died Nov. 23, 1964; GEORGE J. BISKUP, D.D., ord. March 19, 1937; appt. Auxiliary Bishop of Dubuque, March 9, 1957; cons. April 24, 1957; appt. Bishop of Des Moines, Feb. 3, 1965; appt. Coadjutor Archbishop of Indianapolis, July 26, 1967; succeeded to See Jan. 14, 1970; MAURICE J. DINGMAN, D.D., Bishop of Des Moines; ord. Dec. 8, 1939; appt. Bishop of Des Moines April 2, 1968; cons. June 19, 1968; installed July 7, 1968; retired Oct. 14, 1986; died Feb. 1, 1992; WILLIAM H. BULLOCK, ord. June 7, 1952; appt. Auxiliary Bishop of St. Paul and Minneapolis and Titular Bishop of Natchez June 3, 1980; cons. Aug. 12, 1980; appt. Bishop of Des Moines Feb. 10, 1987; installed April 2, 1987; appt. to Diocese of Madison April 13, 1993; JOSEPH L. CHARRON, C.PP.S. (Retired), ord. June 3, 1967; appt. Titular Bishop of Bencenna and Auxiliary Bishop of Saint Paul and Minneapolis Nov. 6, 1989; cons. Jan. 25, 1990; appt. Bishop of Des Moines Nov. 12, 1993; installed Jan. 21, 1994; retired April 10, 2007.

Vicar General—Rev. CHRISTOPHER HARTSHORN.

Chancery—601 Grand Ave., Des Moines, 50309. Tel: 515-243-7653; Fax: 515-237-5070. Office Hours: Mon.-Fri. 8:30-4:30.

Chancellor—Sr. JUDE FITZPATRICK, C.H.M., Chm., All Matrimonial Correspondence to Tribunal.

Secretary to the Bishop—ANGIE HEMMINGSEN, 601 Grand Ave., Des Moines, 50309. Tel: 515-237-5039; Fax: 515-237-5071.

Finance Officer—TAMERA MASON, 601 Grand Ave., Des Moines, 50309. Tel: 515-237-5012.

Vicar for Finance—Rev. Msgr. EDWARD HURLEY. Tel: 515-223-4577.

Judicial Vicar—Rev. CHRISTOPHER PISUT.

Director of Tribunal—Deacon MICHAEL E. RILEY, J.C.L.

Defenders of the Bond—Revs. MICHAEL AMADEO; LAWRENCE R. HOFFMANN; DAVID J. POLICH; Deacon ROBERT L. HOWE.

Judges—Rev. Msgr. LAWRENCE A. BEESON, J.C.D. (Retired); Revs. CHRISTOPHER PISUT; DANIEL F. KRETTEK; Deacon MICHAEL E. RILEY, J.C.L.; Rev. Msgrs. STEPHEN L. ORR; EDWARD B. PFEFFER, J.C.L. (Retired).

Notary—DORIS KLANG.

Advocates—Revs. EUGENE R. KOCH (Retired); JOHN P. LUDWIG; JOHN DORTON; HOWARD E. FITZGERALD; Mrs. PHYLLIS CACCIATORE; Mrs. SARAH LUFT; Mrs. JOYCE RILEY; Deacon DENNIS LUFT.

Diocesan Consultors—Revs. JOHN M. FROST; CHRISTOPHER HARTSHORN; LAWRENCE R. HOFFMANN; PAUL MONAHAN (Retired); DEAN NIMERICHTER; Rev. Msgr. STEPHEN ORR.

Diocesan Corporation Board—Most Rev. RICHARD PATES; Rev. CHRISTOPHER HARTSHORN; Sr. JUDE FITZPATRICK, C.H.M.; SARA EIDE; MATT MADSEN; TAMMY MASON.

Diocesan Offices and Directors

Campus Ministry—Rev. JOEL MCNEIL, Dir.

Catholic Charities—NANCY GALEAZZI, Exec. Dir., 601

Grand Ave., Des Moines, 50309. Tel: 515-237-5055.

Social Service Division—Des Moines Office, 601 Grand Ave., Des Moines, 50309. Tel: 515-237-5055.

Council Bluffs Office—300 W. Broadway, Ste. 223, Council Bluffs, 51503-4117. Tel: 712-328-3086; Fax: 712-328-1348.

Charismatic Renewal Liaison—Rev. DANIEL F. KRETTEK, 1521 Center St., Des Moines, 50314. Tel: 515-282-4839.

Communications, Office of—ANNE MARIE COX, Dir., 601 Grand Ave., Des Moines, 50309. Tel: 515-237-5057; Fax: 515-237-5070.

Continuing Education for Clergy—Rev. RAYMOND MCHENRY.

Deaf-Handicapped, Office of—PEGGY CHICOINE, Coord. Tel: 515-289-1311. Email: dpchicoine@msn.com.

Development Office—JOAN BINDEL, Dir. Devel. Tel: 515-237-5079. 601 Grand Ave., Des Moines, 50309.

Diocesan Council of Catholic Women—SHIRLEY CHAMBERLAIN, Pres., 3898 194th St., Panama, 51562. Tel: 712-489-2442.

Diaconate (Permanent)—Deacon MICHAEL E. RILEY, J.C.L., Dir., 601 Grand Ave., Des Moines, 50309.

Diaconate Formation—Directors: Deacon RON MYERS; TAMMY MYERS, 601 Grand Ave., Des Moines, 50309. Tel: 515-237-5037.

Evangelization, Office of—VACANT.

Holy Childhood, Pontifical Association—Dr. LUVERN GUBBELS, 601 Grand Ave., Des Moines, 50309. Tel: 515-237-5013.

Legislative Activities, Office of—VACANT.

Newspaper— "The Catholic Mirror" ANNE MARIE COX, Editor, 601 Grand Ave., Des Moines, 50309. Tel: 515-237-5057.

Priests' Pension Fund Society—Rev. GREGORY LEACH; Rev. Msgr. EDWARD HURLEY; Revs. CHRISTOPHER HARTSHORN; ROBERT L. SCHOEMANN; Rev. Msgr. LAWRENCE A. BEESON, J.C.D. (Retired).

Propagation of the Faith—Sr. JUDE FITZPATRICK, C.H.M.

Office of Catechetical Services—JOANNE DALHOFF, Dir., 601 Grand Ave., Des Moines, 50309. Tel: 515-237-5052.

St. Vincent de Paul Society—Deacon TROY THOMPSON, Spiritual Dir., 3210 74th St., Urbandale, 50322. Tel: 515-278-2957.

Schools—Dr. LUVERN GUBBELS, Supt. & Dir. Educ.; STEPHANIE WILSON, Dir. Teaching & Learning. Tel: 515-237-5035; TONYA EATON, Dir. Educational Svcs., 601 Grand Ave., Des Moines, 50309. Tel: 515-237-5015.

Seminarians—Rev. DANIEL KIRBY, Dir.

Office of Social Justice—VACANT, 601 Grand Ave., Des Moines, 50309. Tel: 515-237-5047.

Vocations—Rev. DAVID MUENCHRATH, Dir., 601 Grand Ave., Des Moines, 50309. Tel: 515-237-5014; Mr. JASON KURTH, Vocations Specialist. Tel: 515-237-5061.

Office of Worship (Liturgy, Music, Art and Architecture)—Mr. KYLE LECHTENBERG, Dir., 601 Grand Ave., Des Moines, 50309. Tel: 515-237-5046.

Youth Ministry, Office of—BOB PERRON, Dir., St. Thomas More Center, 6177 Panorama Rd., Panora, 50216. Tel: 515-755-3164.

Office of Adult Faith Formation—CHERYL FOURNIER, Dir., 601 Grand Ave., Des Moines, 50309. Tel: 515-237-5006.

Office of Lay Ministry—Rev. P. TIMOTHY FITZGERALD, 601 Grand Ave., Des Moines, 50309. Tel: 515-237-5026.

Office of Marriage Ministry—Deacon DENNIS LUFT; Mrs. SARAH LUFT, 601 Grand Ave., Des Moines, 50309. Tel: 515-237-5056.

Victim Assistance Coordinator—MARY MCCOY. Tel: 515-286-2024. Email: advocate@dmdiocese.org.

CLERGY, PARISHES, MISSIONS AND PAROCHIAL SCHOOLS

CITY OF DES MOINES

(POLK COUNTY)

1—ST. AMBROSE CATHEDRAL (1856) [JC] Rev. John Bertogli, Rector; Sr. Patricia Scherer, Pastoral Min.; Deacons Michael E. Riley; Lee Pao Yang; Michael McCarthy; Debbie S. Rohrer, Liturgy Coord.; Brenda McDonald, Business Mgr.
Res.: 607 High St., 50309. Tel: 515-288-7411; Fax: 515-288-3969. Web: www.saintambrosecathedral.org.
Catechesis/Religious Program—Dorothy Miller, D.R.E. Students 149.

2—ALL SAINTS (1914) [JC] Rev. Robert Harris; William Connet, Music Min.; Sue A. Christensen, Sec.
Mailing Address: 650 N.E. 52nd Ave., 50313. Tel: 515-265-5001; Fax: 515-265-5636. Web: www.dmallsaints.org.
Catechesis/Religious Program—Students 146.

3—ST. ANTHONY'S (1905) Rev. Msgr. Frank Chiodo; Rev. Thomas V. Dooley, Parochial Vicar; Deacons William Smith; Thomas Starbuck.
Res.: 15 Indianola Rd., 50315. Tel: 515-244-4709; Fax: 515-280-6959. Email: comphelp@ecity.net. Web: www.stanthonydsm.org/church/main.a+.
School—(Grades PreK-8), 16 Columbus Ave., 50315. Tel: 515-243-1874; Fax: 515-243-4467. Dr. Joseph F. Cordaro, Prin. Sisters 1; Lay Teachers 17; Students 340.
Catechesis/Religious Program—Tel: 515-244-1119. Susan Ort, D.R.E. (K-6). Students 285.

4—ST. AUGUSTIN'S (1920) Revs. James C. Polich; Emmanuel S. Agwuoke, C.S.Sp., Parochial Vicar; Deacon Kevin Heim; Mrs. Patricia Neal, Music Min.; C. Andy Ball, Business Finance Officer.
Church: 545 42nd St., 50312. Tel: 515-255-1175; Fax: 515-255-7969. Email: info@staugustin.org. Web: www.staugustin.org.
School—(Grades PreK-8), 4320 Grand Ave., 50312. Tel: 515-279-5947; Fax: 515-279-8049. Dr. Nancy Dowdle, Prin. Lay Teachers 20; Students 289.
Catechesis/Religious Program—Cassie Sheik, D.R.E. Students 361.

5—BASILICA OF SAINT JOHN (1905) Rev. Aquinas Nichols, O.S.B., Admin.; Deacon Frank Lopez.
Church: 1915 University Ave., 50314. Tel: 515-244-3101; Fax: 515-244-3165. Email: basilicadm@msn.com. Web: www.basilicaofstjohn.org.
Catechesis/Religious Program—William Brandle, D.R.E. Students 130.

6—ST. CATHERINE OF SIENA CATHOLIC STUDENT CENTER (1969), (Non-Territorial University Parish) Rev. Joel McNeil (AUS).
Church: 1150-128th St., 50311-4142. Tel: 515-271-4747; Fax: 515-271-1918. Web: www.stcatherinedrake.org.
Catechesis/Religious Program—Margaret Cavanah, D.R.E. Students 80.

7—CHRIST THE KING (1939) Rev. Msgr. Frank E. Bognanno; Deacons Larry Kehoe; Charles Putbrese; Mary Jane Harper, Pastoral Assoc.; Christopher Aldinger, Business Mgr.
Res. & Office: 5711 S.W. 9th St., 50315. Tel: 515-285-2888; Fax: 515-285-8182. Email: msgr@dmchristtheking.com. Web: www.christthekingparish.org.
School—(Grades PreK-8), 701 Wall St., 50315. Tel: 515-285-3349; Fax: 515-285-0381. Becky Johnson, Prin. Sisters 1; Lay Teachers 14; Students 234.
Catechesis/Religious Program—Barbara Graham, D.R.E. Students 483.

8—CHURCH OF ST. PETER VIETNAMESE CATHOLIC COMMUNITY, Mailing Address: 1746 Des Moines St., 50316.
Church: 612 E. 18th St., 50316.

9—HOLY TRINITY (1920) Rev. Michael Amadeo; Deacon Thomas Bradley; Helen Roberts, Pastoral Assoc.; Steve Tatz, Youth Min.
Res.: 2926 Beaver Ave., 50310-4040. Tel: 515-255-3162; Fax: 515-255-1381. Email: dianet@holytrinitydm.org; parishoffice@holytrinitydm.org. Web: www.holytrinitydm.org.
School—(Grades PreK-8) Audra Meyer, Prin. Lay Teachers 21; Students 504.
Catechesis/Religious Program—Paulette Chapman, D.R.E. Students 76.

10—ST. JOSEPH'S (1924) Rev. Msgr. Robert J. Chamberlain; Deacon Marvin Brewer; Dan Gehler, Liturgy Coord.; Bill Konnath, Business Mgr.
Res.: 3300 Easton Blvd., 50317. Tel: 515-266-2226; Fax: 515-266-8348. Email: stjoseph@stjosephdsm.org. Web: www.dmdiocese.org/mass.htm.
School—(Grades PreK-8), 2107 E. 33rd St., 50317. Tel: 515-266-3433; Fax: 515-266-2860. Phyllis Konchar, Prin. Lay Teachers 17; Students 188.
Catechesis/Religious Program—Tel: 515-266-2449. Amy Thompson, D.R.E. Students 118.

11—ST. MARY OF NAZARETH (1964) Rev. Gregory Leach; Deacon George Catanzano Jr.; John Robert Hanna, Youth Min.
Res.: 4600 Meredith Dr., P.O. Box 13170, 50310. Tel: 515-276-4042; Fax: 515-252-1995. Email: stmarydsm@aol.com. Web: www.dmdiocese.org/mass.htm.
Catechesis/Religious Program— JoAnn Kimmel, D.R.E. Students 497.

12—OUR LADY OF THE AMERICAS (1882) Rev. Christopher Reising, Parochial Vicar; Deacon Gene Jager.
Mailing Address: 1271 E. 9th St., 50316. Tel: 515-266-6695; Fax: 515-266-9803. Email: oloa@dwx.com.
Catechesis/Religious Program—Irma Jaime-Cruz, D.R.E. Students 446.
Worship Center—
Visitation: 1271 E. 9th St., 50316. Tel: 515-266-6695; Fax: 515-266-9803.

13—ST. PETER'S (1915) Merged with Visitation, Des Moines to form Our Lady of the Americas, Des Moines.

14—ST. THERESA OF THE CHILD JESUS (1951) [JC] Rev. Lawrence R. Hoffmann; Sr. Barbara Marshall, Pastoral Assoc.; Deacons Joe Cortese II; Earl Weisenhorn; John Gaffney, Youth Min.; Bob Wrobel, Business Mgr.
Res.: 1230 Merle Hay Rd., 50311-2098. Tel: 515-279-4654; Fax: 515-277-0838. Email: parishoffice@yahoo.com. Web: www.sainttheresaiowa.org.
School—54810 Cara Carpenter, 50311. Tel: 515-277-0178; Fax: 515-255-2415. Ellen Stemler, Prin. Lay Teachers 26; Students 329.
Catechesis/Religious Program—Kathy Wipf, D.R.E.; Barbara Woods, D.R.E. Students 334.

15—VISITATION (1882) Merged with St. Peter's, Des Moines to form Our Lady of the Americas, Des Moines.

OUTSIDE THE CITY OF DES MOINES

ADAIR, ADAIR CO., ST. JOHN (1879) Attended by All Saints, Stuart Rev. Raymond Higgins.
Mailing Address: *c/o All Saints*, 216 All Saints Dr., P.O. Box 605, Stuart, 50250. Tel: 515-523-1943; Fax: 515-523-1954.
Church: 501 Adair St., 50002. Tel: 712-762-3773 (Office); Fax: 712-762-3484.
Catechesis/Religious Program—Included with All Saints Parish in Stuart, Tel: 712-762-3484. Students 18.

ADEL, DALLAS CO., ST. JOHN (1917) Rev. Albert Sherbo; Tonia Pals, Youth Min.
Mailing Address: 24043 302nd Pl., P.O. Box 185, 50003-0185. Tel: 515-993-4482; Fax: 515-993-3973. Email: saintjc3@aol.com. Web: www.dmdiocese.org/mass.htm.
Catechesis/Religious Program—Tel: 515-993-4590; Fax: 515-993-3973. Majorie Livermore, D.R.E. Students 210.

AFTON, UNION CO., ST. EDWARD (1878) Attended by Paul VI Pastoral Ministry from Creston. Rev. Joseph Pins; Sheila Brown, Liturgy Coord.
Mailing Address: 406 W. Clark, Creston, 50801. Tel: 641-782-5278; Fax: 515-782-7628. Email: holyspiritst.edward@iowatelecom.net. Web: www.geocities.com/spirit_edwards/.
Church: 104 W. Union, 50830. Tel: 641-347-8452.
Catechesis/Religious Program—Kathy Simmerman, D.R.E./Youth Min. Students 12.

ALTOONA, POLK CO., SS. JOHN AND PAUL (1983) Rev. Timothy Fitzgerald; Deacon Dennis Luft; Joan Ammons, Youth Min.; David Ortega, Business Mgr.
Mailing Address: 1401 1st Ave. S., 50009. Tel: 515-967-3796; Fax: 515-967-7197. Email: ssjohnpaul@ssjohnpaul.org. Web: www.ssjohnpaul.org.
Catechesis/Religious Program—Tel: 515-967-8047. Sr. Virginia Jennings, Dir. Faith Formation; Shirley Koeppel, D.R.E.; Janet Elwer, Asst. D.R.E. Students 177.

ANITA, CASS CO., ST. MARY (1924) Attended by parishioners from SS. Peter & Paul, Atlantic. Rev. Daniel Siepker.
Church: 302 Chestnut St., P.O. Box 277, 50020. Tel: 712-762-3773. Web: www.dmdiocese.org/mass.htm.
Catechesis/Religious Program—Brenda Wedemeyer, D.R.E. Students 14.

ANKENY, POLK CO., OUR LADY'S IMMACULATE HEART (1961) Rev. Msgr. Stephen L. Orr; Deacon Jeffrey Boehlert; Mike Coonan, Youth Min.; Becky J. Robovsky, Business Mgr.
Res.: 510 E. First St., 50021. Tel: 515-964-3038; Fax: 515-964-5997. Email: elaine@olih.org. Web: www.olih.org.
Catechesis/Religious Program—Tel: 515-964-3545. Joyce Clawson, D.R.E. (Grades Pre-K-3); Patsy Carlson, D.R.E. (Grades 4-7); Susan Roupe, D.R.E. (Grades 8-12). Students 1,295.

ATLANTIC, CASS CO., SS. PETER AND PAUL (1871) Rev. Daniel Siepker; Manda Thomas, Youth Min.
Res.: 106 W. 6th St., 50022. Tel: 712-243-4721; Fax: 712-243-2064. Email: petepaul@metc.net. Web: www.metc.net/petepaul/index.htm.
Catechesis/Religious Program—Tel: 712-243-2144. Julie Williamson, D.R.E. Students 115.

AUDUBON, AUDUBON CO., ST. PATRICK (1918) [CEM] Rev. Wayne Gubbels.
Res.: 116 E. Division St., 50025. Tel: 712-563-2283; Fax: 712-563-3238. Email: sph@iowatelecom.net. Web: www.dmdiocese.org/mass.htm.
Catechesis/Religious Program—Candy Chambers, D.R.E. Students 110.

AVOCA, POTTAWATTAMIE CO., ST. MARY, MEDIATRIX OF ALL GRACES (1882) Rev. John M. Frost; Pamela Paulson, Liturgy Coord.; Charlotte Wise, Liturgy Coord.
Res.: 109 N. Maple St., P.O. Box 38, 51521-0038. Tel: 712-343-6948. Email: smpavoca@walnutel.net. Web: stmaryavoca.tripod.com.
Catechesis/Religious Program—Christie Martin, D.R.E.; Julie Gilland, D.R.E. Students 83.

BAYARD, GUTHRIE CO., ST. PATRICK (1882) Rev. Michael G. Peters.
Mailing Address: *St. Mary*, 603 Main St., Guthrie Center, 50115. Email: stmstc@netins.net. Web: showcase.netins.net/web/pgcatholic.
Res.: 214 Prairie St., 50029. Tel: 641-747-2569.
Catechesis/Religious Program—Students 30.

BEDFORD, TAYLOR CO., SACRED HEART, Attended by St. Clare, Clarinda. Rev. Joy Vincent Thaiparambil.
Mailing Address: 300 E. Lincoln Blvd., Clarinda, 51632. Tel: 712-542-2030. Email: stclare@clarinda.heartland.net. Web: www.dmdiocese.org/mass.htm.
Church: 700 Main St., 50833.
Catechesis/Religious Program—Dee Rankin, D.R.E.

CARLISLE, WARREN CO., ST. ELIZABETH SETON (1979) Rev. Jim Kirby.
Mailing Address: 2566 Scotch Ridge Rd., P.O. Box 35, 50047. Tel: 515-989-0659; Fax: 515-989-4525. Email: steliz256@aol.com.
Catechesis/Religious Program—Christine Stickley, D.R.E.; Stacie Henkelman, D.R.E. Students 84.

CARTER LAKE, POTTAWATTAMIE CO., OUR LADY OF CARTER LAKE (1970), Attended by Our Lady, Queen of Apostles, Council Bluffs. Revs. Daniel J. Kirby; George Komo, Parochial Vicar; Deacons Darwin Kruse; Monty Montagne; Jean Plourde.
Church: 3501 N. 9th St., 51510. Tel: 712-347-6631; Fax: 712-325-2411. Web: www.ourladyofcarterlake.org.
Catechesis/Religious Program—Sharon Allen, D.R.E. Students 17.

CASEY, GUTHRIE CO., ST. JOSEPH (1898) Closed. For inquiries for parish records contact the chancery.

CHARITON, LUCAS CO., SACRED HEART (1869) Rev. Christopher Pisut; Kristy Schultz, Youth Min.
Res.: 407 N. Main, 50049. Tel: 641-774-4978; Fax: 641-774-4978. Web: www.dmdiocese.org.
Catechesis/Religious Program—Sheila Adams, D.R.E. Students 109.

CHURCHVILLE, WARREN CO., ASSUMPTION (1855) Rev. Christopher Fontanini, Admin.; Karen Spick, Liturgy Coord.
Mailing Address: P.O. Box 88, St. Mary's, 50241. Tel: 515-297-2267. Email: assumptionc@hotmail.com. Web: www.dmdiocese.org.
Res.: 897 South St., Norwalk, 50211.
Catechesis/Religious Program—Lola Hill, D.R.E.; Josh Hart, Youth Min.; Jessica Hart, Youth Min. Students 23.

CLARINDA, PAGE CO., ST. CLARE (1942) Rev. Joy Vincent Thaiparambil.
Res.: 300 E. Lincoln Blvd., 51632. Tel: 712-542-2030. Email: stclare@clarinda.heartland.net.
Catechesis/Religious Program—Mark Baldwin, D.R.E. Students 60.

CORNING, ADAMS CO., ST. PATRICK'S (1869) [CEM] Rev. Tan Van Tran.
Res.: 504 Grove Ave., 50841. Tel: 515-322-3363. Email: pat_corning@yahoo.com. Web: www.dmdiocese.org/mass.htm.
Catechesis/Religious Program—Jane Rychnoysky, D.R.E. Students 35.

CORYDON, WAYNE CO., ST. FRANCIS (1969) Attended by Chariton of the South Central Catholic Ministry Team. Rev. Christopher Pisut; Mary Rita Van Valkenburg, Business Mgr.
Mailing Address: 407 N. Main St., Chariton, 50049. Web: www.dmdiocese.org/mass.htm.
Church: *c/o United Methodist Church of Corydon*, 213 W. Jackson St., 50060. Tel: 641-774-4978; Fax: 641-774-4978.
Catechesis/Religious Program—Tel: 712-328-7272. Shelly Morgan, D.R.E.; Leanne Downs, D.R.E. Classes held at Methodist Church. Students 7.

COUNCIL BLUFFS, POTTAWATTAMIE CO.

1—HOLY FAMILY (1908) Revs. Daniel J. Kirby; George Komo, Parochial Vicar; Deacons Darwin Kruse; Monty Montagne; Jean Plourde.
Res.: 2217 Ave. B, 51501. Tel: 712-328-3869; Fax: 712-322-1819. Email: holyfamilycb@aol.com. Web: www.holyfamilycb.org/.
Catechesis/Religious Program—Jill Faust, D.R.E. Students 35.

2—OUR LADY, QUEEN OF APOSTLES (1957) Revs. Daniel J. Kirby; George Komo, Parochial Vicar; Deacons Darwin Kruse; Monty Montagne; Jean Plourde.
Res.: 3304 4th Ave., 51501. Tel: 712-323-2916; Fax: 712-323-4716. Email: queen3304@juno.com. Web: www.gapostles.org/.
Catechesis/Religious Program—Catherine Jayjack, D.R.E. Students 85.

3—ST. PATRICK (1924) Rev. David Fleming; Deacons Charles Hannan; James Mason; Emmet Tinley.
Res.: 223 Harmony St., 51503. Tel: 712-323-1484; Fax: 712-328-7595. Web: www.saintpatschurch.org.
Catechesis/Religious Program—LuAnn Baumker, D.R.E. Students 176.

4—ST. PETER (1887), (German), Rev. Charles Kottas; Deacons Stephen Rallis; Dennis Kirlin.
Res.: One Bluff St., 51503. Tel: 712-322-8889; Fax: 712-323-8267. Email: ckottas@aol.com. Web: www.dmdiocese.org/mass.htm.
Catechesis/Religious Program—Jennifer Hundtofte, D.R.E. Students 295.
St. Francis Worship Center—238 6th St., 51501. Tel: 712-328-7272.

CRESTON, UNION CO., HOLY SPIRIT (1975) Rev. Joseph Pins.
Res.: 107 W. Howard St., 50801. Tel: 641-782-5278; Fax: 641-782-7628. Email: holyspiritst.edward@iowatelecom.net.
Church: 104 W. Union St., Afton, 50801. Also serving the parish of St. Edward, Afton.
School—St. Malachy, (Grades PreK-8), 403 W. Clark, 50801. Fax: 641-782-7125; 641-782-5924. John Walsh, Prin. Lay Teachers 14; Students 185.
Catechesis/Religious Program—Barb Hudson, D.R.E.; Deb Peterson, Liturgy Coord. Students 67.

CUMBERLAND, CASS CO., ST. TIMOTHY (Reno) (1883) Rev. Dean Nimerichter.
Mailing Address: 69488 Wichita Rd., 50843. Tel: 712-778-4540. Email: pacm@netins.net. Web: www.dmdiocese.org/mass.htm.
Catechesis/Religious Program—

DEFIANCE, SHELBY CO., ST. PETER (1882), Served from Earling. Nancy Schaben, Business Mgr.
Res.: 501 Fifth St., P.O. Box 127, 51527. Tel: 712-748-3501; Fax: 712-748-3500. Email: stpeters@netins.net. Web: www.dmdiocese.org.
Catechesis/Religious Program—Tel: 712-748-3602. Brenda Kloewer, D.R.E.; Diane Mulligan, Liturgy Coord. Students 47.

DUNLAP, HARRISON CO., ST. PATRICK Rev. Paul J. Strittmatter, S.J.; Deacons Marvin Klein; Gail Stressman.
Res.: 509 S. 3rd St., 51529. Tel: 712-643-5808. Email: dwchurch@iowatelecom.net. Web: www.dmdiocese.org.
Catechesis/Religious Program—2005 Beech Rd., 51529. Tel: 712-643-2222. Elizabeth Mahlberg, D.R.E.; Susan Cogdill, D.R.E. Students 121.

EARLING, SHELBY CO., ST. JOSEPH (1882), (German), Elaine Kramer, Business Mgr.
Res.: 212 2nd St., P.O. Box 225, 51530-0225. Tel: 712-747-2091; Fax: 712-747-9501. Email: stjoseph@fmctc.com. Web: www.dmdiocese.org/mass.htm.
See Shelby County Board of Catholic Education, Panama under Education Centers located in the Institution section.
Catechesis/Religious Program—Joanie Erlbacher, D.R.E. Students 32.

ELKHART, POLK CO., ST. MARY/HOLY CROSS (1885) Rev. Daniel F. Krettek; Deacon Jerry Barnwell.
Res.: 214 N. Washington Ave., P.O. Box 110, 50073. Tel: 515-367-2685; Fax: 515-367-2685.
Church: 12704 N.E. 98th St., Maxwell, 50161.
Catechesis/Religious Program—Michelle Wirth, D.R.E. Students 217.

EXIRA, AUDUBON CO., HOLY TRINITY, Attended by St. Patrick. Rev. Wayne Gubbels.
Mailing Address: 116 E. Division St., Audubon, 50025.
Church & Res.: 208 Kilworth St. N., 50076. Tel: 712-563-2283; Fax: 712-268-3238. Email: spht@metc.net. Web: www.holytrinityexira.parishesonline.com.
Catechesis/Religious Program—Judy Bintner, D.R.E. Students 14.

GLENWOOD, MILLS CO., OUR LADY OF THE HOLY ROSARY (1955) Rev. Donald Bruck; Deacon Ronald Kohn.
Res.: 24116 Marian Ave., 51534-5291. Tel: 712-527-5211; Fax: 712-527-3829. Email: holyrosary@aol.com. Web: www.ourladyoftheholyrosaryglenwood.parishesonline.com.
Catechesis/Religious Program—Fax: 712-527-3829. Theresa Romens, D.R.E. Students 268.

GRAND RIVER, DECATUR CO., ST. PATRICK, Served from St. Bernard, Osceola Rev. Glen Wilwerding.
Mailing Address: 222 E. Pearl St., Osceola, 50213. Tel: 641-342-2850. Web: www.dmdiocese.org.
Res.: 460 Wabonsy St., 50108. Tel: 641-342-2850. Web: www.dmdiocese.org.
Catechesis/Religious Program— Twinned with St. Bernard, Osceola. Students 5.

GRANGER, DALLAS CO., ASSUMPTION OF THE BLESSED VIRGIN MARY (1871) Rev. Remigius C. Okere, C.S.Sp.; Deacons Daniel McGuire, Admin.; Gregg Erickson.
1906 Sycamore, P.O. Box 159, 50109. Tel: 515-999-2239; Fax: 515-999-2208. Email: assumptionp@mchsi.com. Web: www.parishesonline.com/assumption.
School—(Grades PreK-8), 1904 Sycamore, P.O. Box 100, 50109. Tel: 515-999-2211. Dr. Marvin Dick, Prin. Lay Teachers 11; Students 85.
Catechesis/Religious Program—Cathy Davidson, D.R.E. Students 255.

GREENFIELD, ADAIR CO., ST. JOHN (1907) Rev. Michael McLaughlin.
Res.: 303 N.E. Elm St., 50849. Tel: 515-343-7065. Web: www.dmdiocese.org.
Catechesis/Religious Program—Tel: 515-343-7065. Renee Schwartz, D.R.E. Students 73.

GRISWOLD, CASS CO., OUR LADY OF GRACE (1911) Rev. Dean Nimerichter.
Mailing Address: 16493 Contrail Ave., 51535. Tel: 712-778-4540. Email: frdean@netins.net. Web: www.dmdiocese.org/mass.htm.
Res.: 203 Adair, 51535.
Catechesis/Religious Program—Kristine Keiser, D.R.E. Students 24.

GUTHRIE CENTER, GUTHRIE CO., ST. MARY (1906) [JC] Rev. Michael G. Peters; Deacons Richard Ziller; Hans Seeman.
Res.: 603 Main St., 50115. Tel: 515-747-2569; Fax: 641-747-3843. Email: stmstc@netins.net. Web: www.showcase.netins.net/web/pgcatholic.
Catechesis/Religious Program—Cynthia Ahrens, D.R.E. Students 39.

HAMBURG, FREMONT CO., ST. MARY (1874) Attended by St. Mary, Shenandoah. Rev. Vernon Smith, Admin.
1306 Washington St., 51640. Tel: 712-382-2871. Web: www.stmaryparishhamburg.pa. Mailing Address: P.O. Box 67, 51640.
Catechesis/Religious Program—Monica Whitehead, D.R.E. Students 37.

HARLAN, SHELBY CO., ST. MICHAEL (1888) Rev. Robert A. Hoefler; Deacon Patrick Davitt.
Mailing Address: 1912 18th St., 51537.
Church & Res.: 2001 College Pl., 51537. Tel: 712-755-5244. Web: www.stmichaelparish.com/.
School—(Grades PreK-8), 2005 College Pl., 51537. Tel: 712-755-5634. Mrs. Ann Anderson, Prin. Lay Teachers 14; Students 144.
See Shelby County Board of Catholic Education, Panama under Education Centers located in the Institution section.
Catechesis/Religious Program—Tel: 712-755-5366. Charlotte Willenborg, D.R.E. Students 251.

IMOGENE, FREMONT CO., ST. PATRICK (1880), (Irish), Rev. Kenneth Gross.
Res. & Mailing Address: 304 Third St., 51645. Tel: 712-386-2277. Web: www.rc.net/desmoines/stpatrick.
Catechesis/Religious Program—Tel: 712-386-2239. Vicki Kelly, D.R.E.; Janet Shough, Youth Min. Students 76.

INDIANOLA, WARREN CO., ST. THOMAS AQUINAS (1958) Rev. Raymond McHenry; Ellen Miller, Youth Min.
Res.: 1202 W. Iowa Ave., 50125. Tel: 515-961-3026; Fax: 515-961-3458. Web: www.stthomasindianola.com.
Catechesis/Religious Program—Tel: 515-961-3458. Heidi Klodd, D.R.E. Students 305.

IRISH SETTLEMENT, MADISON CO., ST. PATRICK (1852) Rev. Christopher Fontanini, Admin.
Mailing Address: P.O. Box 88, St. Marys, 50241. Tel: 641-297-2267. Web: www.dmdiocese.org.
Church: 3396 155th St., Cumming, 50061.
Catechesis/Religious Program—3183 155th St., Cumming, 50061. Tel: 515-981-4686. Jennifer Lynch, D.R.E.; Drew Dinsmore, Youth Min. Students 35.

JAMAICA, GUTHRIE CO., ST. JOSEPH (1903) Closed. For inquiries for parish records contact the chancery.

LACONA, WARREN CO., HOLY TRINITY CHURCH OF SOUTHEAST WARREN COUNTY (1978) Rev. Felix A. Onuora, C.S.Sp.
Res.: 304 N. Washington Ave., P.O. Box 145, 50139-0145. Tel: 641-534-4691; Fax: 641-534-4691. Email: ofxval@direcway.com. Web: www.dmdiocese.org/mass.htm.
Worship Centers—
St. Mary of the Assumption Church: 50139. Tel: 641-534-4691.
St. Augustine Church: Milo, 50166.
Catechesis/Religious Program—Amy Welch, D.R.E. Students 21.

LENOX, TAYLOR CO., ST. PATRICK (1872) Attended by St. Patrick, Corning. Rev. Tan Van Tran.
Church: 600 W. Michigan, 50851. Tel: 641-336-2893. Web: www.dmdiocese.org/mass.htm.
Catechesis/Religious Program—1041 130th St., Diagonal, 50845. Tel: 641-336-2893. Kathy Ecklin, D.R.E. Students 35.

LEON, DECATUR CO., ST. BRENDAN (1856), (Irish), Rev. Christopher Pisut; Deacon Reinhold Kunze.
Res.: 1001 N.W. Church St., 50144. Tel: 515-446-4789; Fax: 641-446-8110. Email: southch3@grm.net. Web: www.dmdiocese.org.
Catechesis/Religious Program—Linda Buckingham,

D.R.E. Students 61.

LOGAN, HARRISON CO., ST. ANNE (1920) Rev. Michael Berner; Deacons Dennis Lovell; Mike Woltanski.
Res.: 112 W. 3rd St., 51546. Tel: 712-644-2535; Fax: 712-644-2535. Email: pesser@iowatelecom.net. Web: www.dmdiocese.org.
Catechesis/Religious Program—Joe Esser, D.R.E. Students 90.

MALOY, RINGGOLD CO., IMMACULATE CONCEPTION (1874) [CEM] Closed. For inquiries for parish records contact the chancery.

MASSENA, CASS CO., ST. PATRICK (1888), Served from Greenfield. Rev. Michael McLaughlin; Julie Symonds, Liturgy Coord.
Res.: 503 Main St., 50853. Tel: 712-779-3397; Fax: 712-779-3397. Email: stjohns@iowatele.com.net.
Catechesis/Religious Program—Students 39.

MISSOURI VALLEY, HARRISON CO., ST. PATRICK (1877) Rev. Michael Berner; Deacons Mike Woltanski; Charles Wolford.
Res.: 215 N. Seventh St., 51555. Tel: 712-642-2611; Fax: 712-642-2518. Email: stpatsch@loganet.net. Web: www.dmdiocese.org.
Catechesis/Religious Program—Regina Lubash, D.R.E. Students 72.

MONDAMIN, HARRISON CO., HOLY FAMILY (1970) Attended by St. Patrick. Rev. Paul J. Strittmatter, S.J.; Deacon James Herman.
Mailing Address: 509 S. 3rd St., Dunlap, 51529.
Church: 307 Mulberry, 51557. Tel: 712-644-2535. Email: pesser@iowatelecom.net. Web: www.dmdiocese.org/mass.htm.
Catechesis/Religious Program—St. Anne, 104 W. 3rd St., Logan, 51546. Tel: 712-644-2520. Christine Hussing, D.R.E.

MT. AYR, RINGGOLD CO., ST. JOSEPH (1913) Attended by St. Bernard, Osceola Rev. Glen Wilwerding.
Mailing Address: 222 E. Pearl St., Osceola, 50213.
Church: 100 N. Polk, 50854. Tel: 515-446-4789; Fax: 641-446-8110. Web: www.dmdiocese.org.
Catechesis/Religious Program—Students 16.

NEOLA, POTTAWATTAMIE CO., ST. PATRICK (1882) Rev. Raphael Masabakhwa; Deacon James Mason; Sr. Rosie Restelli, C.H.M, Pastoral Min.
Res.: 308 4th St., P.O. Box 127, 51559. Tel: 712-485-2124; Fax: 712-485-2124. Email: stpats@novia.net. Web: www.dmdiocese.org/mass.htm.
Catechesis/Religious Program—Students 203.

NORWALK, WARREN CO., ST. JOHN THE APOSTLE CHURCH (1892) Rev. John P. Ludwig; Deacon David Miller.
Res.: 720 Orchard St., 50211. Tel: 515-981-4855; Fax: 515-981-9475. Email: stjohns@stjohnsnorwalk.org. Web: www.stjohnsnorwalk.org.
Catechesis/Religious Program—Sharon Ewell, D.R.E. Students 252.

ORIENT, ADAIR CO., ST. MARK, Closed. For inquiries for parish records contact the chancery.

OSCEOLA, CLARKE CO., ST. BERNARD (1885) Rev. Glen Wilwerding.
Res.: 222 E. Pearl, 50213. Tel: 641-342-2850; Fax: 641-342-2850. Email: stbernar@pionet.net. Web: www.dmdiocese.org.
Catechesis/Religious Program—530 N. Fillmore, 50213. Marsha Glenn, D.R.E. Students 50.

PANAMA, SHELBY CO., ST. MARY OF THE ASSUMPTION (1899) Rev. John Dorton.
Res.: 104 N. 2nd St., 51562.
See Shelby County Board of Catholic Education, Panama under Education Centers located in the Institution section.
Catechesis/Religious Program—P.O. Box 209, 51562. Tel: 712-489-2504. Marilyn Keane, Youth Min. Students 58.

PANORA, GUTHRIE CO., ST. CECILIA (1907) [JC] Attended by St. Mary, Guthrie Center Tel: 515-747-2569. Rev. Michael G. Peters; Deacons Richard Ziller; Hans Seeman.
Mailing Address: 603 Main St., Guthrie Center, 50115. Tel: 641-747-2569; Fax: 641-747-3843. Email: stmstc@netins.net. Web: www.showcase.netins.net/web/pages.
Church: 221 N. First St., 50216.
Catechesis/Religious Program—Students 72.

PERRY, DALLAS CO., ST. PATRICK (1881) Rev. David J. Polich; Robin Smith, Business Mgr.
Res.: 1312 3rd St., 50220. Tel: 515-465-4387; Fax: 515-465-4387. Email: stpatsperry@iowatelecom.net. Web: www.dmdiocese.org.
School—(Grades PreSchool-8), 1302 5th St., 50220. Tel: 515-465-4186; Fax: 515-465-9808. Corey Wentke, Prin. Lay Teachers 11; Students 92.
Catechesis/Religious Program—Barbara Wolter, D.R.E. Students 259.

PORTSMOUTH, SHELBY CO., ST. MARY (1885) Rev. John Dorton.
Res.: 412 Fourth St., P.O. Box 98, 51565. Tel: 712-743-2625; Fax: 712-743-2625. Email: hankhu@iowatelecom.net. Web: www.dmdiocese.org.
Catechesis/Religious Program—Henrietta (Hank) Hughes, D.R.E. Students 81.

RED OAK, MONTGOMERY CO., ST. MARY (1902) Rev. Kenneth Gross.
Res.: 1510 Highland Ave., 51566. Tel: 712-623-2744. Email: stmarysredoak@msn.com. Web: www.stmaryredoak.parishesonline.com.
Catechesis/Religious Program—Cindee Hays, D.R.E. Students 121.

ST. MARYS, WARREN CO., IMMACULATE CONCEPTION (1871) Rev. Christopher Fontanini, Admin.; Carol Kubik, Liturgy Coord.
Res.: 101 St. James, P.O. Box 88, 50241. Tel: 641-297-2267. Email: immacula@netins.net. Web: www.diocese.org.
Catechesis/Religious Program—220 Iowa St., P.O. Box 113, Saint Marys, 50241. Michelle Fick, D.R.E.; Jolene Gehringer, Youth Min. Students 97.

SHENANDOAH, PAGE CO., ST. MARY Rev. Vernon Smith, Admin.
Mailing Address: 512 W. Thomas Ave., 51601. Tel: 712-246-1718; Fax: 712-246-1776. Email: stmarys@heartland.net. Web: www.dmdiocese.org.
Catechesis/Religious Program—Steve Sauvain, D.R.E. & Youth Min.; Patti Sauvain, D.R.E. & Youth Min. Students 66.

STUART, GUTHRIE CO., ALL SAINTS (1876) Rev. Raymond Higgins; Barb Marnin, Business Mgr.
Res.: 216 All Saints Dr., P.O. Box 605, 50250. Tel: 515-523-1943; Fax: 515-523-1954. Email: stuartsaints@netins.net.
Catechesis/Religious Program—Tel: 515-523-1943. Ginger Peterson, D.R.E. Students 119.

URBANDALE, POLK CO., ST. PIUS X (1955) Rev. Msgr. Joseph McDonnell; Rev. John Harmon, Parochial Vicar; Deacons Dave Bartemes; Rick Condon.
Mailing Address: 3663 66th St., 50322. Tel: 515-276-2059; Fax: 515-276-8351. Email: skatch@dowling.pvt.k12.ia.us. Web: www.stpiusx-urbandale.e-paluch.com.
School—(Grades PreK-8), 3601 66th St., 50322. Tel: 515-276-1061; Fax: 515-276-0350. Lawrence Zahm, Prin. Lay Teachers 30; Students 382.
Catechesis/Religious Program—Tel: 515-278-5684. Mary Heinrich, D.R.E.; William Brandle, D.R.E.; Barb Mease, Youth Min. Students 385.

VILLISCA, MONTGOMERY CO., ST. JOSEPH (1947) Attended by St. Clare, Clarinda. Rev. Joy Vincent Thaiparambil.
Mailing Address: 300 E. Lincoln Blvd., Clarinda, 51632. Tel: 712-542-2030. Web: www.dmdiocese.org/mass.htm.
Church: 131 W. High St., 50864.
Catechesis/Religious Program—Donna Williams, D.R.E.

WALNUT, POTTAWATTAMIE CO., ST. PATRICK (1882) Attended by St. Mary, Mediatrix of All Graces, Avoca. Rev. John M. Frost; Donna Muell, Liturgy Coord.; Ellen Holtz, Liturgy Coord.
Mailing Address: c/o 109 N. Maple St., P.O. Box 38, Avoca, 51521-0038. Tel: 712-343-6948. Email: smpavoca@walnutel.net. Web: www.stmaryavoca.tripod.com.
Church & Res.: 718 Antique City Dr., 51577.
Catechesis/Religious Program—Gwen Blum, D.R.E. Students 8.

WAUKEE, DALLAS CO., ST. BONIFACE (1880) Rev. Vince G. Rosonke; Steve Dressel, Pastoral Min.
Res.: 1200 Warrior Ln., 50263-9587. Tel: 515-987-4597; Fax: 515-987-5272. Email: office@saintbonifacechurch.org. Web: www.dmdiocese.org.
Catechesis/Religious Program—Sue Peterson, D.R.E. Students 892.

WEST DES MOINES, POLK CO.

1—ST. FRANCIS OF ASSISI (1991) Rev. Msgr. Edward Hurley; Rev. Kenneth Halbur, Parochial Vicar; Deacon David O'Brien.
Mailing Address: 7075 Ashworth Rd., 50266. Tel: 515-223-4577; Fax: 515-223-4768. Email: info@saintfrancischurch.org. Web: www.saintfrancischurch.org.
School—Tel: 515-457-7167. Mrs. Misty Hade, Prin. Lay Teachers 44; Students 680.
Catechesis/Religious Program—Mary Green, D.R.E.; Deb Ryan, D.R.E.; Jade Wadding, D.R.E.; Jeanne Mullenbach, Youth Min. Students 840.

2—SACRED HEART (1892) Revs. Michael N. Hess; Lazarus Kirigia, Parochial Vicar; Deacon Ron Myers.
Mailing Address: 1627 Grand Ave., 50265. Tel: 515-225-6414; Fax: 515-225-0286. Email: pbaliff@dowling.pvt.k12.ia.us. Web: www.sacredheartwdm.org/.
School—(Grades PreK-8), 1601 Grand Ave., 50265. Tel: 515-223-1284; Fax: 515-223-9413. Frank Vito, Prin. Lay Teachers 27; Students 499.
Catechesis/Religious Program—Tel: 515-225-1641. Kayla Richer, D.R.E.; Deb Chalik, D.R.E., Coord.; Marcia Schaul, D.R.E. Students 570.

WESTON, POTTAWATTAMIE CO., ST. COLUMBANUS (1883) Attended by St. Patrick, Neola. Rev. Raphael Masabakhwa.
Mailing Address: P.O. Box 127, Neola, 51559. Tel: 712-485-2124. Web: www.dmdiocese.org.
Church: 22720 Weston Ave., Underwood, 51576.
Catechesis/Religious Program—23232 Magnolia Rd., Underwood, 51576. Tel: 712-566-2603. Denise Stuhr, D.R.E. Students 45.

WESTPHALIA, SHELBY CO., ST. BONIFACE (1873) Rev. John Dorton; Joan Schneider, Liturgy Coord.
Church & Res.: 207 Duren Strasse, 51578. Tel: 712-627-4151; Fax: 712-627-4151. Email: stboniface@fmctc.com. Web: www.dmdiocese.org.
Catechesis/Religious Program—Sandi Schwery, D.R.E. Students 28.

WINTERSET, MADISON CO., ST. JOSEPH (1893) Rev. Christopher Hartshorn.
Res.: 607 W. Green St., 50273. Tel: 515-462-1083; Fax: 515-462-2378. Email: office@saintjosephchurch.net. Web: www.saintjosephchurch.net.
Catechesis/Religious Program—Teresa Hoffelmeyer, D.R.E.; Gerene Farrell, Youth Min. Students 150.

WOODBINE, HARRISON CO., SACRED HEART (1902) Attended by St. Patrick's, Dunlap. Rev. Paul J. Strittmatter, S.J.
Mailing Address: 509 S. 3rd St., Dunlap, 51529. Tel: 712-643-5115. Email: dwchurch@iowatelecom.net. Web: www.dmdiocese.org.
Church: 33 - 7th St., 51579.
Catechesis/Religious Program—710 Weare St., 51579. Tel: 712-647-3057. Andrea Reisz, D.R.E. Students 66.

WOODWARD, DALLAS CO., ST. ANN (1934) Closed. For inquiries for parish records contact Assumption Church, Granger.

Chaplains of Public Institutions

DES MOINES. *Des Moines City Chaplaincy Program*, c/o P.O. Box 371, Dexter, 50070. Rev. Robert J. Aubrey.
United States Veterans Hospital, 3600 30th St., 50310.

CLARINDA. *State Hospital*. Served from St. Clare Church, Clarinda.

COUNCIL BLUFFS. *Iowa School for the Deaf*, 411 E. Broadway, 51503. Tel: 712-322-2449. Vacant.

GLENWOOD. *Glenwood State School*. Vacant.

MITCHELLVILLE. *Iowa Correctional Institution for Women*. Kay Kopatich, Chap. & Coord., Svcs. to Catholic Residents.

On Special Assignment:
Revs.—
Fitzgerald, P. Timothy, Offices of Lay Ministry and Worship
Kirby, Daniel, Diocesan Dir. Seminarians
McNeil, Joel (AUS), Diocesan Dir. Campus Ministry
Muenchrath, David, Vocations

On Duty Outside the Diocese:
Revs.—
Chevalier, Martin, St. Joseph Medical Center, Kansas City, MO
Grant, Robert, St. Ambrose University, Davenport, 52803.

On Sabbatical:
Revs.—
Coenen, Thomas
Fitzgerald, Howard E.

Leave of Absence:
Rev.—
Peters, Lyle

Retired:
Rev. Msgrs.—
Beeson, Lawrence A., J.C.D.
Pfeffer, Edward B., J.C.L., 1390 Buffalo Rd., West Des Moines, 50265.
Ryan, Gerald E.
Stessman, Gerald, 1390 Buffalo Rd., West Des Moines, 50265.
Revs.—
Acrea, John, 2115 Summit Ave., Saint Paul, MN 55105.
Aiello, Anthony
Bergman, Richard, 1390 Buffalo Rd., West Des Moines, 50265.
Culver, Garry, 1050 Capri Isle Blvd., #H 106, Venice, FL 34292.
Cunningham, John E., 1390 Buffalo Rd., West Des Moines, 50265.

Fenelon, David, 934 Lincoln St., Waterloo, 50703.
Freeman, James, 2500 N. Desert Links Rd., Apt. # 6205, Tucson, AZ 85715.
Kenkel, Benedict J., St. Francis Rectory, 238 S. 6th St., #3, Council Bluffs, 51501.
Kenkel, Leonard A., 1390 Buffalo Rd, West Des Moines, 50265.
Kiernan, James W., 1390 Buffalo Rd., West Des Moines, 50265.
Kleffman, James, 4624 Navajo St., #17, Council Bluffs, 51501.
Koch, Eugene R., 1390 Buffalo Rd., West Des Moines, 50265.
Koch, Paul M., 238 S. 6th St., Council Bluffs, 51501.
Laurenzo, James, 1205 Lewis, 50315.
Leto, Nelo A., 710 Davis, 50315.
Lorenz, John F., 1390 Buffalo Rd., West Des Moines, 50265.
Maier, John, 507 Spencer Pl., Leavenworth, KS 66048.
McCann, Arthur L., 1610 60th St., 50322.
Monahan, Paul, 238 S. 6th St., Council Bluffs, 51501.
Palmer, Frank S., 4960 - 88th St., Urbandale, 50322.
Reischl, Fred P., St. Francis Rectory, 238 S. 6th St., Council Bluffs, 51503.
Schoemann, Robert

Permanent Deacons:
Ayers, John
Barnwell, Jerry
Bartemes, David
Blankenship, Joseph, (Retired)
Boehlert, Jeffrey
Bradley, Thomas
Bray, Robert, (Retired)
Brewer, Marvin
Catanzano, George, Jr.
Coan, Joseph II, (Retired)
Condon, Rick
Cornwell, Fred
Cortese, Joseph
Davitt, Patrick
Doyle, James, (Retired)
Erickson, Gregg
Garza, David, (Retired)
Gaul, Leo, (Retired)
Hannan, Charles
Heim, Kevin
Herman, James
Horn, Randy
Howe, Robert, (Retired)
Huynh, Joseph, (Retired)
Inman, Jack, (Retired)
Jacobi, Donald, (Retired)
Jager, Gene
Kehoe, Laurence
Kirkman, Patrick, (Retired)
Kirlin, Dennis, (Retired)
Klein, Marvin
Knotek, Lawrence, (Retired)
Kohn, Ronald
Krawczyk, Gene, (Retired)
Kruse, Darwin
Kunze, Reinhold
Leininger, Jerry, (Retired)
Lopez, Frank
Lovell, David, (Retired)
Lovell, Dennis
Luft, Dennis M.
Maiers, Richard, (Retired)
Maly, Thomas, (Retired)
Mason, James
McCarthy, Michael
McGuire, Dan
Miller, Dave
Montagne, Monty
Myers, Ron
O'Brien, David
Pantaloni, Ed, (Retired)
Pins, Fred
Plourde, Jean
Putbrese, Charles
Rallis, Stephen
Richardson, Alan, (Retired)
Richer, William
Riley, Mike
Rohwer, Chris, (Retired)
Romeo, Tony, (Retired)
Schroeder, William, (Retired)
Scurlock, Joseph, (Retired)
Seeman, Hans
Smith, William
Starbuck, Tom
Stessman, Gail
Stessman, John, (Retired)
Sullivan, Robert, (Retired)
Sullivan, Sam
Thompson, Troy
Tinley, Emmet
Tong, Quan
Webering, James, (Retired)
Weisenhorn, Earl
Wolford, Charles
Woltanski, Mike
Yang, LyPao
Ziller, Richard

INSTITUTIONS LOCATED IN THE DIOCESE

[A] EDUCATION CENTERS

DES MOINES. *Holy Family School*, 1265 E. 9th St., 50316. Tel: 515-262-8025; Fax: 515-262-9665. Email: sgood@dowling.pvt.k12.ia.us. Web: hfsdm.org. Martin P. Flaherty, Prin.; Janet Holmes, Asst. Prin.; Rebecca Nichols, Librarian. Participating parishes: Our Lady of the Americas, Des Moines; Basilica of St. John, Des Moines; St. Ambrose Cathedral, Des Moines; All Saints, Des Moines; St. Peter, Des Moines. Lay Teachers 16; Students 237.

COUNCIL BLUFFS. *St. Albert High School*, 400 Gleason Ave., 51503. Tel: 712-328-2316; Fax: 712-328-8316. Web: www.saintalbertschools.org. Jonna Andersen, Prin.; Rev. Mark Neal, Faculty; Donella Pauli, Librarian. Priests 1; Lay Teachers 32; Students 206.

Council Bluffs Area Catholic Education Systems, Inc., 400 Gleason Ave., 51503. Tel: 712-329-9000; Fax: 712-328-0228. Web: www.saintalbertschools.org. Jonna Andersen, Prin. Priests 1; Lay Teachers 50; Total Staff 126; Total Enrollment (K-12) 726.

St. Albert High School, 400 Gleason Ave., 51503. Tel: 712-328-2316; Fax: 712-328-8316. Jonna Andersen, Prin.; Donella Pauli, Librarian. Priests 1; Lay Teachers 29; Total Staff 46; Students 206.

St. Albert Junior High School (Grades 7-8), 400 Gleason Ave., 51503. Tel: 712-328-2316; Fax: 712-328-8316. Lay Teachers 10; Students 126.

St. Albert Intermediate School (Grades 4-6), 400 Gleason Ave., 51503. Tel: 712-322-7004; Fax: 712-322-0399. Lay Teachers 13; Students 185.

St. Albert Primary School (Grades PreK-3), 2912 9th Ave., 51501. Tel: 712-323-3703; Fax: 712-323-6132. Anne Jensen, Prin.; Donella Pauli, Librarian. Lay Teachers 15; Students 278.

HARLAN. *Elementary School: Shelby County Catholic School*, (Grades PreK-8), 2005 College Pl., 51537. Tel: 712-755-5634; Fax: 712-755-3332. Email: sassman@shelcocath.pvt.k12.ia.us. Web: www.shelcocath.pvt.k12.ia.us. Ann Andersen, Prin.; Brenda Blum, Librarian. Lay Teachers 14; Total Staff 22; Students 144.

WEST DES MOINES. *St. Joseph Educational Center*, 1400 Buffalo Rd., 50265. Tel: 515-225-3000; Fax: 515-222-1056. Web: stjosepheducationalcenter.org. Dr. Jerry Deegan, Pres.

Religious Education Tel: 515-225-3000; Fax: 515-222-1056.

[B] COLLEGES AND UNIVERSITIES

DES MOINES. *Mercy College of Health Sciences* (1995) 928-6th Ave., 50309-1239. Tel: 515-643-3180; Fax: 515-643-6698. Email: admissions@mchs.edu. Web: www.mchs.edu. Barbara Q. Decker, Pres.; Brian Tingleff, B.A., Vice Pres. Institute Advancement; Eileen Hansen, M.A., Dir., Librarian & Media Svcs.; Shirley Beaver, Dean of Nursing; Jeannine Matz, Assoc. Dean of Liberal Arts & Sciences; Theresa Smith, Assoc. Dean of Allied Health; Joan McCleish, Dean of Research, Assessment & Distance Education. Member of Mercy Health Network; Sponsored by Catholic Health Initiatives. Lay Teachers 43; Students 778.

[C] HIGH SCHOOLS, INTERPAROCHIAL

COUNCIL BLUFFS. *Saint Albert Catholic Schools*, 400 Gleason Ave., 51503. Tel: 712-329-9000; Fax: 712-328-0228. Email: vansoelen@stalbert.pv.k12.ia.us; kochj@stalbert.pvt.k12.ia.us. Web: www.saintalbertschools.org. Jonna Andersen, Prin.; James W. Rouse, Pres.; Rev. Mark Neal. Serving all parishes in Council Bluffs; St. Patrick, Missouri Valley; St. Patrick, Neola; Holy Rosary, Glenwood; St. Columbanus, Weston. Priests 1; Lay Teachers 50; Total Staff 126; Students 726.

WEST DES MOINES. *Dowling Catholic High School*, 1400 Buffalo Rd., 50265. Tel: 515-225-3000; Fax: 515-222-1056. Email: Jdeegan@dowlingcatholic.org. Web: www.dowlingcatholic.org. Dr. Jerry Deegan, Pres.; Dr. James Dowdle, Prin.; Carol McConnell, Registrar; Rev. Christopher Fontanini, Chap. Serving all parishes in Des Moines; Sacred Heart, West Des Moines; St. Francis of Assisi, West Des Moines; St. Boniface, Waukee; Assumption, Granger; St. John, Cumming; St. Mary, Elkhart; Holy Cross, Elkhart; SS. John and Paul, Altoona; Immaculate Heart, Ankeny. Priests 1; Lay Teachers 85; Students 1,292.

[D] GENERAL HOSPITALS

DES MOINES. *Mercy Medical Center*, 1111 Sixth Ave., 50314-2611. Tel: 515-247-3121; Fax: 515-247-4259. Web: www.mercydesmoines.org. Dave Vellinga, Pres. & CEO; Rev. Anthony Adibe, C.S.Sp. Catholic Health Initiatives Denver, CO. Patients Assisted Annually 1,461,951; Bed Capacity 917; Total Staff 7,000.

Mercy Clinics, Inc.
Mercy Court
Mercy College of Health Sciences
Mercy Foundation
Mercy Foundation of Des Moines dba Mercy Foundation, Bishop Drumm Retirement Center, Mercy Hospice-Johnston
Mercy Hospice and Home Care
Mercy Park Apartments
Mercy Professional Practice Associates
Clark Street House of Mercy
Graduate Medical Education

CORNING. *Alegent Health Mercy Hospital*, 603 Rosary Dr., P.O. Box 368, 50841. Tel: 641-322-3212; Fax: 651-322-4872. James C. Ruppert, Admin.; Rev. Tan Van Tran, Chap. Inpatients 421; Outpatients 48,560.

COUNCIL BLUFFS. *Alegent Health: Mercy Hospital*, 800 Mercy Dr., 51503. Tel: 712-328-5000; Fax: 712-325-2432. Web: www.alegent.org. Sheila Burke, Chap. Bed Capacity 284; Patients Assisted Annually 59,919.

[E] HOMES FOR AGED

JOHNSTON. *Bishop Drumm Retirement Center* (1939) 5837 Winwood Dr., 50131-1651. Tel: 515-270-1100; Fax: 515-276-1714. Mr. Brian E. Farrell, Pres. & CEO; Mrs. Heather Rehmer, Admin. (Affiliate of Catholic Health Initiatives, Mercy Health Network & Mercy Medical Center-Des Moines). Sisters of Mercy of the Americas (Omaha Province) 5; Congregation of the Humility of Mary Sisters 22; Care Center Residents 150; Bed Capacity 293; Total Staff 244; Total Assisted Annually 423. In Res. Rev. Thomas M. DeCarlo, Resident Chap.

McAuley Terrace Apts. (1981) 5921 Winwood Dr., 50131-1670. Tel: 515-270-6640; Fax: 515-331-8875. Sandra Dzankovic, Mgr. Apartment Residents 79.

Martina Place Assisted Living Residence (1997) 5815 Winwood Dr., 50131-1666. Tel: 515-251-7999; Fax: 515-331-8860. Mrs. Sharon Brown, Mgr. Assisted Living Residents 64.

[F] SPECIAL CARE FACILITIES

DES MOINES. *House of Mercy*, 1409 Clark St., 50314-1964. Tel: 515-643-6500; Fax: 515-643-6598. Email: tbeveridge@mercydesmoines.org. Web: houseofmercydesmoines.org. Mr. Todd Beveridge, Dir.

[G] SECULAR INSTITUTES

DES MOINES. *Institute of the Heart of Jesus* (1791) P.O. Box 4634, 50305-4634. Tel: 515-222-1089; Fax: 515-222-1056. Email: fatherjfl1@aol.com. Web: www.secularinstitutes.org. Rev. John F. Lorenz (Retired). Secular Priests and Lay People.

[H] SPIRITUAL MINISTRY TO THE DIOCESE

DES MOINES. *Emmaus House*, 1521 Center St., 50314. Tel: 515-282-4839. Email: emmaus_house@yahoo.com. Rev. Daniel F. Krettek, Co-Dir.; Sr. Joyanne Mueller, O.S.F., Co-Dir.

[I] NEWMAN CENTERS

DES MOINES. *St. Catherine of Siena Catholic Student Center* , (Drake Newman Community), 1150-28th St., 50311-4142. Tel: 515-271-4747; Fax: 515-271-1918. Email: saint.catherine@drake.edu. Rev. Joel McNeil (AUS). Students 190; Non-Students 500.

[J] MISCELLANEOUS LISTINGS

DES MOINES. *Bishop's Endowment Fund Foundation*, 601 Grand Ave., 50309.

Catholic Tuition Organization, Diocese of Des Moines, 601 Grand Ave., 50309. Tel: 515-237-5010; Fax: 515-237-5070. Email: jwells@dmdiocese.org. Jeanne Wells, Exec. Dir.

City Hospital Chaplaincy Service, 3429 Belmar Dr., 50317-5840. Tel: 515-681-0404. Email: baubrey@infionline.net. Rev. Robert J. Aubrey. Serving all non-Catholic hospitals in Des Moines.

Dowling-St. Joseph Alumni Association Investment Co. L.L.C., 1400 Buffalo Rd., West Des Moines, 50265. Tel: 515-225-3000; Fax: 515-222-1056. Email: jdeegan@dowling.pvt.k12.ia.us. Web: www.dowlingcatholic.org. Dr. Jerry Deegan, Mgr.

Dowling-St. Joseph Alumni Foundation, 1400 Buffalo Rd., West Des Moines, 50265. Tel: 515-225-3000; Fax: 515-222-1056. Email: jdeegan@dowling.pvt.k12.ia.us. Web: www.dowlingcatholic.org. Jim Willer, Pres.; Dr. Jerry Deegan, Sec.

Endowment for Educational Excellence, 601 Grand Ave., 50309. Most Rev. Richard Pates; Rev. Christopher Hartshorn, Dir.; Sr. Jude Fitzpatrick, C.H.M., Dir.

Holy Family School Inner-City Youth Foundation, P.O. Box 8437, 50301. Tel: 515-262-7466; Fax: 515-263-8172. Email: hfsfoundation@qwest.net. Web: www.hfsdm.org. Pat Floersch, Foundation Admin.

Iowa Catholic Conference, 530-42nd St., 50312-2707. Tel: 515-243-6256; Fax: 515-243-6257. Email: info@iowacatholicconference.org. Thomas Chapman, Exec. Dir.

St. Joseph Emergency Shelter, 1535 11th St., 50314. Tel: 515-282-1235. Email: jshelter@dmdiocese.org. Sol Varisco, Outreach Coord., 601 Grand Ave., 50309.

Larry Breheny Endowment Fund, 601 Grand Ave., 50309. Most Rev. Richard Pates; Sr. Jude Fitzpatrick, C.H.M., Chancellor; Nancy Galeazzi, Dir.

Life in the Spirit Community, Inc., 5419 S.E. 32nd St., 50320. Tel: 515-287-4480. Eric Zingler, Contact Person.

St. Mary Family Center, 1815 Hubbell Ave., 50316. Tel: 515-262-7290; Fax: 515-262-4036. Email: stmarys@dmdiocese.org. Nancy Galeazzi, Exec. Dir.; Sol Varisco, Outreach Coord., 601 Grand Ave., 50309.

Mercy Child Development Center, 6th & University, 50314. Tel: 515-243-6232. Diane Engelking, Dir.

Mercy Foundation of Des Moines - Affiliate of Catholic Health Initiatives, 1111 6th Ave., 50314. Tel: 515-247-3248. Bob Ravenscroft, Pres.

National Catholic Rural Life Conference (1923) 4625 Beaver Ave., 50310-2145. Tel: 515-270-2634; Fax: 515-270-9447. Email: ncrlc@mchsi.com. Web: www.ncrlc.com. Most Rev. Frank J. Dewane (VEN), Pres., (Bishop of Venice, FL); James F. Ennis, Dir.

Roman Catholic Pastoral Center Foundation, 601 Grand Ave., 50309. Tel: 515-237-5044; Fax: 515-237-5070. Email: finance@dmdiocese.org. Web: www.dmdiocese.org. Most Rev. Richard Pates; Rev. Christopher Hartshorn, Vicar Gen.

Roman Catholic Priests' Medical Fund Foundation, 601 Grand Ave., 50309.

Roman Catholic Seminary Fund Foundation, 601 Grand Ave., 50309. Email: tmason@dmdiocese.org. Tamera Mason, Contact Person.

Society of Saint Vincent de Paul, 1426 6th Ave., 50314. Tel: 515-282-8327. Tom Varilek, Pres.

COUNCIL BLUFFS. *St. Albert Educational Foundation*, 400 Gleason Ave., 51503. Tel: 712-329-9000; Fax: 712-328-0228. Email: vansoelenj@stalbert.pvt.k12.ia.us. Web: www.saintalbertschools.org.

St. Joseph Catholic Cemetery Association, 17510 Sunnydale Rd., 51503. Tel: 712-322-7963. John E. O'Connor, Mgr.

Mercy Hospital Foundation, Council Bluffs, 800 Mercy Dr., P.O. Box 1C, 51502. Tel: 712-328-5372; Fax: 712-325-2425. Emmet Tinky, Pres.

GRISWOLD. *Creighton University Retreat Center* (1967) 16493 Contrail Ave., 51535. Tel: 712-778-2466; Fax: 712-778-2467. Email: curc@netins.net. Web: www.creighton.edu/CURC/. Revs. David L. Smith, S.J., Dir. & Contact Person; William F. Gerut, S.J., Retreat/Pastoral Ministry.

HARLAN. *Shelby County Catholic Education Foundation*, 2005 College Pl., 51537. Tel: 712-755-5634; Fax: 712-755-3332. Email: sassmann@shelcocath.pvt.k12.ia.us. Web: shelcocath.pvt.k12.ia.us. Sue Assmann, Admin.

JOHNSTON. *Bishop Drumm Development Office*, 5921 Winwood Dr., Ste. 1, 50131. Tel: 515-331-8890; Fax: 515-331-8875. Email: afletcher@mercydesmoines.org. Amanda Fletcher. A division of Mercy Foundation - Affiliate of Catholic Health Initiatives and Mercy Health Network.

PANORA. *St. Thomas More Center*, 6177 Panorama Rd., 50216. Tel: 515-309-1936; Fax: 515-309-1885. Email: office@stmcenter.com. Web: www.stmcenter.com. Robert Perron, Dir.; Rev. David Muenchrath.

WEST DES MOINES. *St. Francis of Assisi Roman Catholic School Foundation*, 7075 Ashworth Rd., 50266. Tel: 515-223-4577; Fax: 515-223-4768. Email: info@saintfrancischurch.org. Web: www.saintfrancischurch.org. Rev. Msgr. Edward Hurley, Sec.

RELIGIOUS INSTITUTES OF MEN REPRESENTED IN THE DIOCESE

For further details refer to the corresponding bracketed number in the Religious Institutes of Men or Women section.

[0600]—*Brothers of the Congregation of the Holy Cross*—C.S.C.

[]—*Congregation of the Holy Ghost* (Nigeria)

[0690]—*Jesuit Fathers and Brothers* (Wisconsin Prov.)—S.J.

[0430]—*Order of Preachers-Dominicans*—O.P.

[0200]—*Order of St. Benedict* (Conception, MO)—O.S.B.

RELIGIOUS INSTITUTES OF WOMEN REPRESENTED IN THE DIOCESE

[0230]—*Benedictine Sisters of Pontifical Jurisdiction*—O.S.B.

[2100]—*Congregation of the Holy Humility of Mary*—C.H.M.

[1920]—*Congregation of the Sisters of the Holy Cross*—C.S.C.

[1070-14]—*Dominican Sisters*—O.P.

[1070-03]—*Dominican Sisters*—O.P.

[1070-13]—*Dominican Sisters*—O.P.

[1120]—*Dominican Sisters of the Roman Congregation*—O.P.

[1310]—*The Franciscan Sisters of Little Falls, MN*—F.S.M.

[2575]—*Institute of the Sisters of Mercy of the Americas* (Cedar Rapids, IA; Omaha, NE; Chicago, IL)—R.S.M.

[2960]—*Notre Dame Sisters* (Omaha, NE)—N.D.

[1680]—*School Sisters of St. Francis*—O.S.F.

[3580]—*Servants of Mary*—O.S.M.

[0480]—*Sisters of Charity of Leavenworth, Kansas*—S.C.L.

[0430]—*Sisters of Charity of the Blessed Virgin Mary*—B.V.M.

[2630]—*Sisters of Mercy of the Holy Cross*—S.C.S.C.

[3000]—*Sisters of Notre Dame de Namur*—S.N.D.de.N

[3320]—*Sisters of Presentation of the Blessed Virgin Mary*—P.B.V.M.

[1540]—*Sisters of Saint Francis, Clinton, Iowa*—O.S.F.

[1705]—*The Sisters of St. Francis of Assisi*—O.S.F.

[1570]—*Sisters of St. Francis of the Holy Family*—O.S.F.

[1930]—*Sisters of the Holy Cross*—F.D.N.S.C.

NECROLOGY

† Conley, Rev. Msgr. Raymond J., (Retired)—Died Feb. 9, 2009

† Clarke, John, (Retired)—Died Oct. 23, 2009

An asterisk (*) denotes an organization that has established tax-exempt status directly with the IRS and is not covered by the USCCB Group Ruling.

Archdiocese of Detroit

(Archidioecesis Detroitensis)

His Eminence

EDMUND CARDINAL SZOKA, J.C.L., D.D.

Archbishop Emeritus of Detroit; ordained June 5, 1954; appointed Bishop of Gaylord June 15, 1971; consecrated and installed July 20, 1971; promoted to See of Detroit March 28, 1981; installed May 17, 1981; created Cardinal June 28, 1988; appointed President, Prefacture for Economic Affairs of the Holy See June 25, 1990; President, Pontifical Commission for Vatican City State October 14, 1997; President emeritus of the Pontifical Commission for Vatican City State; President of the government of Vatican City State February 22, 2001; resigned September 15, 2006.

His Eminence

ADAM CARDINAL MAIDA, J.C.L., J.D., S.T.L.

Archbishop Emeritus of Detroit; ordained May 26, 1956; appointed to Green Bay November 8, 1983; consecrated January 25, 1984; installed as Archbishop of Detroit June 12, 1990; created Cardinal on November 26, 1994; retired January 5, 2009.

Most Reverend

THOMAS J. GUMBLETON, D.D.

Retired Auxiliary Bishop of Detroit; ordained June 2, 1956; appointed Auxiliary Bishop of Detroit and Titular Bishop of Ululi March 8, 1968; consecrated May 1, 1968; retired February 2, 2006. *Office: 1234 Washington Blvd., Detroit, MI 48226.*

Most Reverend

ALLEN H. VIGNERON, D.D.

Archbishop of Detroit; ordained July 27, 1975; appointed Auxiliary Bishop of Detroit and Titular Bishop of Sault Ste. Marie June 12, 1996; consecrated July 9, 1996; appointed Coadjutor Bishop of Oakland January 10, 2003; installed February 26, 2003; succeeded to See October 1, 2003; appointed Archbishop of Detroit January 5, 2009; installed January 28, 2009.

Archbishop's Office: 1234 Washington Blvd., Detroit, MI 48226. Tel: 313-237-5816; Fax: 313-237-4642.

Most Reverend

MOSES B. ANDERSON, S.S.E., D.D.

Retired Auxiliary Bishop of Detroit; ordained May 30, 1958; appointed Auxiliary Bishop of Detroit and Titular Bishop of Vatarba December 3, 1982; consecrated January 27, 1983; retired October 24, 2003. *Office: 1234 Washington Blvd., Detroit, MI 48226.*

Most Reverend

FRANCIS R. REISS, D.D.

Auxiliary Bishop of Detroit; ordained June 4, 1966; appointed Auxiliary Bishop of Detroit and Titular Bishop of Remesiana July 7, 2003; consecrated August 12, 2003. *Office: 1234 Washington Blvd., Detroit, MI 48226.*

Square Miles 3,901.

Established March 8, 1833; Created An Archbishopric August 3, 1937.

Comprises the Counties of Lapeer, Macomb, Monroe, Oakland, St. Clair and Wayne.

For legal titles of parishes and archdiocesan institutions, consult the Cardinal's Office.

STATISTICAL OVERVIEW

Personnel	
Retired Cardinals	2
Archbishops	1
Auxiliary Bishops	1
Retired Bishops	2
Priests: Diocesan Active in Diocese	252
Priests: Diocesan Active Outside Diocese	8
Priests: Diocesan in Foreign Missions	1
Priests: Retired, Sick or Absent	135
Number of Diocesan Priests	396
Religious Priests in Diocese	199
Total Priests in Diocese	595
Extern Priests in Diocese	50
Ordinations:	
Diocesan Priests	5
Transitional Deacons	7
Permanent Deacons	11
Permanent Deacons in Diocese	205
Total Brothers	75
Total Sisters	1,245
Parishes	
Parishes	271
With Resident Pastor:	
Resident Diocesan Priests	241
Resident Religious Priests	30
Without Resident Pastor:	
Administered by Priests	32
Missions	1
Closed Parishes	6
Professional Ministry Personnel:	
Brothers	3
Sisters	57
Lay Ministers	499
Welfare	
Catholic Hospitals	10
Total Assisted	1,096,535
Health Care Centers	4
Total Assisted	4,987
Homes for the Aged	20
Total Assisted	18,968
Specialized Homes	14
Total Assisted	2,498
Special Centers for Social Services	45
Total Assisted	35,843
Residential Care of Disabled	1
Total Assisted	38
Educational	
Seminaries, Diocesan	2
Students from This Diocese	50
Students from Other Diocese	51
Seminaries, Religious	2
Students Religious	21
Total Seminarians	71
Colleges and Universities	3
Total Students	13,004
High Schools, Diocesan and Parish	9
Total Students	3,597
High Schools, Private	12
Total Students	6,535
Elementary Schools, Diocesan and Parish	76
Total Students	22,852
Elementary Schools, Private	1
Total Students	354
Catechesis/Religious Education:	
High School Students	5,751
Elementary Students	55,644
Total Students under Catholic Instruction	107,808
Teachers in the Diocese:	
Priests	19
Brothers	5
Sisters	88
Lay Teachers	2,586
Vital Statistics	
Receptions into the Church:	
Infant Baptism Totals	9,544
Minor Baptism Totals	542
Adult Baptism Totals	704
Received into Full Communion	960
First Communions	11,768
Confirmations	10,481
Marriages:	
Catholic	1,992
Interfaith	783
Total Marriages	2,775
Deaths	9,496
Total Catholic Population	1,434,622
Total Population	4,438,006

Former Bishops—Rt. Revs. FREDERIC RESE, D.D., cons. Oct. 6, 1833; resigned Aug. 19, 1840; died Dec. 30, 1871; PETER PAUL LEFEVERE, D.D., cons. Nov. 22, 1841; Bishop of Zela, coadjutor and admin. of Detroit; died March 4, 1869; CASPAR HENRY BORGESS, D.D., cons. April 24, 1870; Bishop of Calydon, coadjutor and admin. of Detroit; became Bishop of Detroit Dec. 30, 1871; resigned April 16, 1887; died May 3, 1890; JOHN SAMUEL FOLEY, D.D., cons. Nov. 4, 1888; died Jan. 5, 1918; Most Rev. MICHAEL JAMES GALLAGHER, D.D., cons. Sept. 8, 1915; Bishop of Tipasa, coadjutor of Grand Rapids; became Bishop of Grand Rapids Dec. 26, 1916; transferred to Detroit July 18, 1918; died Jan. 20, 1937; His Eminence EDWARD CARDINAL MOONEY, D.D., appt. Apostolic Delegate in India Jan. 8, 1926; appt. Titular Archbishop of Irenopolis Jan. 18, 1926; cons. Jan. 31, 1926; appt. Apostolic Delegate in Japan Feb. 25, 1931; transferred to the Diocese of Rochester Aug. 28, 1933; transferred to the Archdiocese of Detroit Aug. 3, 1937; created Cardinal Priest of the title of S. Susanna Feb. 18, 1946; died Oct. 25, 1958; JOHN CARDINAL DEARDEN, D.D., S.T.D., ord. Dec. 8, 1932; cons. Titular Bishop of Sarepta and Coadjutor Bishop of Pittsburgh Dec. 22, 1950; installed Archbishop of Detroit Jan. 29, 1959; created Cardinal April 28, 1969; resigned as Archbishop July 15, 1980; died Aug. 1, 1988; EDMUND CARDINAL SZOKA, J.C.L., D.D., Archbishop Emeritus of Detroit; ord. June 5, 1954; appt. Bishop of Gaylord June 15, 1971; cons. July 20, 1971; installed July 20, 1971; promoted to See of Detroit March 28, 1981; installed May 17, 1981; created Cardinal June 28, 1988; appt. Pres., Prefacture for Economic Affairs of the Holy See June 25, 1990; Pres., Pontifical Commission for Vatican City State Oct. 14, 1997; Pres. emeritus of the Pontifical Commission for Vatican City State; Pres. of the government of Vatican City State Feb. 22, 2001; resigned Sept. 15, 2006; ADAM CARDINAL MAIDA, J.C.L., J.D., S.T.L., ord. May 26, 1956; appt. to Green Bay Nov. 8, 1983; cons. Jan. 25, 1984; installed as Archbishop of Detroit June 12, 1990; created Cardinal on Nov. 26, 1994; retired Jan. 5, 2009.

College of Consultors—Rev. Msgr. RICARDO E. BASS; Revs. THOMAS JOHNSON; GERALD A. MCENHILL; Rev. Msgr. JAMES A. MOLONEY, P.A.; Revs. THEODORE K. PARKER; WILLIAM TINDALL; Rev. Msgr. ANTHONY M. TOCCO; Rev. STANLEY A. ULMAN; Rev. Msgr. JOHN P. ZENZ.

Presbyteral Council—Revs. DONALD ARCHAMBAULT; RICHARD BARTOSZEK; RALPH BESTERWITCH, S.A.C.; DAVID J. BLAZEK; DAVID A. BUERSMEYER; Rev. Msgr. G. MICHAEL BUGARIN; Revs. PATRICK CASEY; MICHAEL N. COONEY; JEFFREY DAY; Rev. Msgr. WILLIAM H. EASTON; Rev. MARK GAWRONSKI; Rev. Msgr. DONALD F. HANCHON; Revs. JAIME HINOJOS; TIMOTHY D. HOGAN; JOSEPH R. HORN; DANIEL J. JONES; ALEXANDER KRATZ, O.F.M.; RONALD KURZAWA (Retired); DON A. LACUESTA; JOSEPH MALLIA; CLINT W. MCDONELL; SAMA F. MUMA; MICHAEL C. NKACHUKWU; ROMAN PASIECZNY; TIMOTHY R. PELC; ROBERT J. SCULLIN, S.J.; WILLIAM D. SINATRA (Retired); RICHARD L. TREML; STANLEY A. ULMAN.

Archdiocesan Vicars—Revs. DONALD ARCHAMBAULT, Trinity; DAVID J. BLAZEK, Lakes; DAVID A. BUERSMEYER, North Macomb; Rev. Msgr. G. MICHAEL BUGARIN, SERF; Revs. PATRICK CASEY, Northwest Wayne; MICHAEL N. COONEY, Central Macomb; JEFFREY DAY, West Wayne; Rev. Msgr. WILLIAM H. EASTON; Revs. MARC A. GAWRONSKI,

Monroe; MARIE-ELIE HABY, Southwest; JOSEPH R. HORN, Blue Water; Rev. Msgr. MICHAEL C. LEFEVRE, J.C.L., Genesis; Revs. JOSEPH MALLIA, Downriver; MICHAEL C. NKACHUKWU, Renaissance; RICHARD L. TREML, Thumb; STANLEY A. ULMAN, Pontiac Area.

Archdiocesan Pastoral Council—Contact: Ms. CATHERINE WAGNER. Tel: 313-237-5934.

Archdiocesan Departments and Offices

General Information and Reference—Tel: 313-237-5800.

Office of the Archbishop— All official mail should be directed to this office. *1234 Washington Blvd., Detroit, 48226*. Tel: 313-237-5816; Fax: 313-237-4642. Rev. CHARLES D. FOX, Personal Sec. to Archbishop.

Moderator of the Curia—Rev. Msgr. ROBERT J. MCCLORY. Tel: 313-237-5783; Fax: 313-237-4642; Mrs. KRISTA BAJOKA, Special Projects Coord. Tel: 313-596-7147; Fax: 313-237-4642.

Office of the Chancellor—Mr. MICHAEL R. TRUEMAN, J.C.L., Chancellor. Tel: 313-237-5847; Fax: 313-237-4643; 313-237-4642.

Archives—Ms. HEIDI CHRISTEIN, Archivist. Tel: 313-237-5864; Fax: 313-596-7199.

Marriage Permissions/Dispensations—Rev. CHARLES D. FOX, Delegate of the Archbishop. Tel: 313-237-5816; Fax: 313-237-4642.

The Metropolitan Tribunal—305 Michigan Ave., Detroit, 48226. Tel: 313-237-5865; Fax: 313-237-5872. Office Hours: Mon.-Fri. 8:30-4:30.

Judicial Vicar—Most Rev. FRANCIS R. REISS, J.C.L.

Adjutant Judicial Vicars—Revs. JEROME SLOWINSKI, J.C.L.; ROBERT HAYES WILLIAMS, J.C.L.

Administrative Director—Mr. TIMOTHY FERGUSON, J.C.L.

Judges—Revs. TIMOTHY F. BABCOCK; JAMES L. BJORUM, J.C.L.; Mr. TIMOTHY FERGUSON, J.C.L.; Revs. JOHN GAGALA, J.C.L. (Retired); RONALD J. JOZWIAK, J.C.L.; KENNETH R. KAUCHECK, J.C.D.; Rev. Msgrs. MICHAEL C. LEFEVRE, J.C.L.; ROBERT J. MCCLORY; GEORGE P. MILLER, J.C.L.; Revs. JOVITA OKOLI, J.C.L.; GARY M. TIERNEY, J.C.L. (Retired); GEORGE W. WILLIAMS, J.C.L.

Defenders of Bond—Rev. Msgr. RICARDO E. BASS; Revs. RICHARD CAVELLIER, J.C.L.; MICHAEL LOYSON; Ms. PATRICIA MKTRUMIAN; Rev. NORMAN D. NAWROCKI, J.C.L.; Mr. FRANCIS SYLVESTER; Mr. MICHAEL R. TRUEMAN, J.C.L.

Advocates—Mr. ROBERT CADOTTE, All priests, deacons, and certified lay advocates (ad actum).

Notaries—Mr. ADAM DWORNICK; Ms. MARIA JEROME; Ms. JACQUELINE L. LOVE; Ms. LINDSAY MARTINEZ; Ms. DOLORES PAULL.

Coordinator of Administrative Support Staff—Ms. JACQUELINE L. LOVE.

Office for Clergy and Consecrated Life—Rev. Msgr. PATRICK F. HALFPENNY, Dir., 1234 Washington Blvd., Detroit, 48226. Tel: 313-596-7155; Fax: 313-237-4643.

Pastoral Care for Priests—Rev. Msgr. MICHAEL C. LEFEVRE, J.C.L., Assoc. Dir. Tel: 313-596-7152; Fax: 313-237-4643.

Pastoral Care for Senior Priests—Rev. Msgr. GEORGE T. BROWNE, Coord. (Retired). Tel: 313-237-5840; Fax: 313-237-4643.

Permanent Diaconate Program—Deacon MICHAEL J. MCKALE, Assoc. Dir. Tel: 313-596-7142; Fax: 313-237-4643.

Delegate for Consecrated Life—Contact: Rev. Msgr. PATRICK F. HALFPENNY. Tel: 313-596-7155.

Immigration Legal Services for Clergy, Consecrated Life and Schools—Ms. VIVIANA LANDE, Esq., Immigration Lawyer. Tel: 313-596-7148.

Office of Priestly Vocations—Rev. TIMOTHY P. BIRNEY, Dir., 2701 Chicago Blvd., Detroit, 48206. Tel: 313-237-5875; Fax: 313-883-6070; Mrs. JAN DEFOUR, Coord. Fax: 313-237-5839.

Department of Communications—Mr. NED MCGRATH, Dir., 305 Michigan Ave., Detroit, 48226. Tel: 313-237-5943; Fax: 313-237-4644.

Office of Public Relations—Mr. JOSEPH KOHN, Dir. Tel: 313-237-5802; Fax: 313-237-4644.

Office of Digital Media— For Associate Director and CTND inquiries contact Mr. Joseph Kohn. Tel: 313-237-5802 Rev. Msgr. THOMAS G. RICE, The Michigan Catholic Newspaper, Editor & Assoc. Publisher. Tel: 313-224-8000; Mrs. CASSANDRA ZAKENS, Web Mgr. Tel: 313-237-5973.

Office of Printing and Publications—Mr. DENNIS MILLIGAN, Dir. Tel: 313-237-5967; Fax: 313-965-8471.

Department of Development and Stewardship—Mr. DAVID KELLEY, Dir., 2701 Chicago Blvd., Detroit, 48206. Tel: 313-883-8657; 800-986-3925; Fax: 313-883-8681.

Planned Giving—Mr. THOMAS P. SCHOLLER, Assoc. Dir. Tel: 313-883-8657; Ms. DIANA MENDIOLA, Scholarship Prog. Coord. Tel: 313-883-8532.

Special Services—Mr. DAVID P. CASNOVSKY, Assoc. Dir. Tel: 313-883-8684.

Marketing—Ms. KATHRYN BUA, Dir. Mktg. Tel: 313-883-8533; Mr. DANIEL GALLIO, Editor. Tel: 313-883-8773.

Charitable Gift Planning—Mr. DARREN HOGAN, Assoc. Dir. Tel: 313-883-8748.

Major Gifts—Contact: Mr. DAVID KELLEY, Dir. Tel: 313-883-8657; 800-986-3925.

Annual Giving—Ms. JAN STUART, Assoc. Dir. Tel: 313-883-8567.

Catholic Services Appeal—Ms. THERESA J. KACH, Assoc. Dir. Tel: 313-883-8656.

Development Services—Ms. JESSICA I. ORZECHOWSKI, Coord. Tel: 313-883-8629.

Department of Evangelization, Catechesis and Schools—Dr. MARGIE CROOKS, Dir., 305 Michigan Ave., Detroit, 48226. Tel: 313-596-7305; Fax: 313-237-5867.

Office of Catholic Schools—Regional Associate Superintendents: Ms. BERNADETTE SUGRUE. Tel: 313-237-5763; Ms. SUSAN LESLIE. Tel: 313-237-5772; Mrs. GEORGENE WOJCIECHOWSKI. Tel: 313-237-4654; Ms. MARY SWINKEY. Tel: 313-237-4658.

Health, Athletics and Physical Safety—Mr. VICTOR MICHAELS, Admin. Tel: 313-237-5960; Mr. MICHAEL EVOY, Assoc. Admin. Tel: 313-237-5960.

Office of Evangelization and Catechesis—Rev. JOHN RICCARDO, Dir. Tel: 313-237-4664; Fax: 313-237-5867. Coordinators, Catechetical Programming & Formation: Sisters RUTH PLATTE, S.L.W. Tel: 313-237-5758; KATHLEEN MATZ, C.D.P. Tel: 313-237-4667; Mr. DANIEL BARRIBALL, Coord. RCIA. Tel: 313-237-5956. Adult Evangelization Coordinators: Mr. PACO GAVRILIDES. Tel: 313-237-4689; Ms. JUDITH MATEN. Tel: 313-237-5832.

Marriage and Family Life—Mr. DAVID P. GROBBEL, Assoc. Dir. Tel: 313-237-5894; Ms. SOCORRO TRUCHAN, Coord. Tel: 313-237-4691; Mrs. DOROTHY STAPEL, Natural Family Planning. Tel: 313-237-4679.

Cultural Ministries—Mr. JOHN THORNE, Coord. Black Catholic Ministries. Tel: 313-596-7103; Mr. FERNANDO PERALES-HERNANDEZ, Coord. Hispanic Ministries. Tel: 313-570-1975.

Ministerial Certification—Ms. SALLY MCCUEN, Assoc. Dir. Tel: 313-596-7312.

Youth, Young Adults and Campus Ministries—Mrs. RAKHI MCCORMICK, Assoc. Dir. Tel: 313-237-4687.

Department of Finance and Administration—Mr. DANIEL OLIVER, Dir., 1234 Washington Blvd., Detroit, 48226. Tel: 313-237-5834; Fax: 313-237-5868.

Office of Financial Services—Mrs. FRANCES ASHE, Dir. Tel: 313-237-5903.

Accounting Services—Mr. DAVID SMITH, Assoc. Dir. Tel: 313-237-5825.

Parish Support Services—Ms. PATRICIA HOJNACKI, Assoc. Dir. Tel: 313-237-5860.

Audit—Mrs. LORI RAFFERTY, Assoc. Dir. Tel: 313-237-5841.

Office of Facilities Services—Mr. JOHN DUNCAN, Dir. Tel: 313-883-8599; Fax: 313-883-8699.

Sacred Heart Major Seminary/Cathedral Campus Building Administration—Deacon LAZARUS DER-GHAZARIAN, Assoc. Dir. Tel: 313-883-8506.

Archdiocesan Properties—Mr. MICHAEL MORAN, Dir. Tel: 313-237-5830; Fax: 313-237-5791.

Buildings—Mr. FRANK MACDONELL, Contractor, PMNet. Tel: 313-237-5829; Fax: 313-596-7187.

Office of Computing and Network Services—Mr. CHRISTOPHER SNYDER, Dir. Tel: 313-237-5797; Fax: 313-237-5979.

Department of Human Resources—Ms. PAMELA BEECH, Dir., 1234 Washington Blvd., Detroit, 48226. Tel: 313-237-5947; Fax: 313-237-5791.

Benefits and School Personnel—Ms. ERIN TAFT, Coord. Tel: 313-237-1574.

Safe Environments—Ms. SHARON GORMAN, Coord. Tel: 313-237-5886.

Department of Parish Life—Ms. CATHERINE WAGNER, Dir., 305 Michigan Ave., Detroit, 48226. Tel: 313-237-5934; Fax: 313-237-5869.

Office of Pastoral Planning and Leadership Services—Mrs. LORY MCGLINNEN, Dir. & Regl. Coord. Tel: 313-237-5798; Fax: 313-237-5869; Mr. MICHAEL MCCALLION, Regl. Coord. - Research. Tel: 313-237-5760. Regl. Coord. - Pastoral Staffs, Contact: Mrs. LORY MCGLINNEN. Tel: 313-237-5798; Mr. ANTHONY LATARSKI, Regl. Coord. - Leadership Svcs. Tel: 313-237-5765; Ms. JANET SHAY, Statistics Coord. Tel: 313-237-5785; Ms. MEGAN LAMONT, Mapping and Surveys Coord. Tel: 313-237-8011.

Office of Christian Worship—Mr. DANIEL MCAFEE, Dir. Tel: 313-237-4697; Fax: 313-237-5869; Sr. GEORGETTE ZALESKA, Coord. Tel: 313-237-6064; Mr. LOUIS CANTER, Coord. Music Ministries - AOD. Tel: 313-237-5782; Ms. STACEY MASON, Coord. Music Ministries - St. John Ctr. Tel: 734-414-1161; Fax: 734-414-1150.

Office of Catholic Charities—Mr. MICHAEL HARNING, Dir. Tel: 313-237-5978; Fax: 313-237-5869.

Christian Service and Health Care Ministries—Ms. JOYCE HYTTINEN, Assoc. Dir. Tel: 313-237-5905; Fax: 313-237-5869.

Ecumenical/Interfaith Relations—Rev. Msgr. PATRICK F. HALFPENNY, Archbishop's Ecumenical/Interfaith Advisor, 1234 Washington Blvd., Detroit, 48226. Tel: 313-596-7155; Fax: 313-237-4643; Mr. MICHAEL HOVEY, Coord. Tel: 313-237-4678; Fax: 313-237-5869.

Victim Assistance Coordinator—Ms. MARGARET A. HUGGARD, M.S.W. Tel: 866-343-8055.

Promoter of Ministerial Standards—Ms. INA GRANT. Tel: 313-237-4813; Fax: 313-237-5844.

Propagation of the Faith (Missions)—Rev. Msgr. JAMES A. MOLONEY, P.A., 1230 Washington Blvd., Detroit, 48226. Tel: 313-237-5807.

Association of the Holy Childhood—1230 Washington Blvd., Detroit, 48226. Tel: 313-237-5807.

Catholic Youth Organization—Ms. SUZANNE HEATH, Dir., 305 Michigan Ave., Detroit, 48226. Tel: 313-963-7172; Fax: 313-963-7179.

Archdiocesan Theological Commission—Rev. Msgr. ROBERT J. MCCLORY. Tel: 313-237-5783.

Priests Conference for Polish Affairs of the Archdiocese of Detroit—Rev. Msgr. STANLEY E. MILEWSKI, Pres. (Retired).

CLERGY, PARISHES, MISSIONS AND PAROCHIAL SCHOOLS

CITY OF DETROIT

(WAYNE COUNTY)

1—CATHEDRAL, CHURCH OF THE MOST BLESSED SACRAMENT Rev. Msgrs. Michael C. LeFevre, Rector; James P. Robinson, S.S.E., Rector Emeritus.
Res.: 9844 Woodward Ave., 48202. Tel: 313-865-6300; Fax: 313-867-4613.
Catechesis/Religious Program—Students 19.

2—ALL SAINTS Rev. Guy Christopher Snyder, P.I.M.E.; Deacon Norbert Motowski.
Res.: 7824 W. Fort St., 48209. Tel: 313-841-1428; Fax: 313-841-3009.
All Saints Soup Kitchen and Food Pantry—Denise Balogh, Outreach Dir.
Catechesis/Religious Program—Students 171.

3—ST. ALOYSIUS Rev. Tod Laverty, O.F.M.; Bros. Al Mascia, O.F.M., Pastoral Assoc.; Michael Radomski, O.F.M. In Res., Rev. Alexander Kratz, O.F.M.
Chancery Bldg.—1234 Washington Blvd., 48226. Tel: 313-237-5810; Fax: 313-963-9076.
Catechesis/Religious Program—Sr. Grace Keane, O.S.F., D.R.E. Students 35.

4—ST. ANDREW, (Polish), Merged into Our Lady Queen of Angels, Detroit.

5—SS. ANDREW AND BENEDICT Rev. Edward F. Zaorski.
Res.: 2430 S. Beatrice St., 48217. Tel: 313-381-1184; Fax: 313-381-0416.
Catechesis/Religious Program—Mary Ann Wallace, D.R.E. Students 11.

6—ST. ANTHONY, Merged with Our Lady of Sorrows, Detroit to form Good Shepherd, Detroit.

7—ST. ANTHONY, (Lithuanian), Rev. Gintaras Jonikas.
Res.: 1750 25th St., 48216. Tel: 313-554-1284.

8—ASSUMPTION GROTTO, [CEM] Revs. Eduard Perrone; John Christopher Bustamante; Paul T. Ward.
Res.: 13770 Gratiot Ave., 48205. Tel: 313-372-0762; Fax: 313-372-2064.
Catechesis/Religious Program—Students 25.

9—ST. AUGUSTINE AND ST. MONICA Rev. Daniel J. Trapp.
Res.: 4151 Seminole St., 48214. Tel: 313-921-4107; Fax: 313-921-1115.
Catechesis/Religious Program—Students 10.

10—ST. BARTHOLOMEW, Merged with St. Rita, Detroit to form St. Bartholomew/St. Rita, Detroit.

11—ST. BARTHOLOMEW/ST. RITA Rev. Ronald Borg, C.S.B.
Res.: 2291 E. Outer Dr., 48234. Tel: 313-892-1446; Fax: 313-892-1149.
School—20001 Wexford, 48234. Tel: 313-366-3640; Fax: 313-366-0257. Ms. Sharon Perko, Prin. Lay Teachers 9; Students 90.
Convent—2251 E. Outer Dr., 48234. Tel: 313-366-0525. Sisters 2.

12—ST. BRENDAN, Closed. For inquiries for parish records contact the chancery.

13—ST. CATHERINE OF SIENA, Closed. For inquiries for parish records contact the chancery.

14—ST. CECILIA Rev. Theodore K. Parker.
Res.: 10400 Stoepel Ave., 48204. Tel: 313-933-6788;

Fax: 313-933-1439.
Church: Livernois at Stearns, 48204.
School—6327 Burlingame, 48204. Tel: 313-933-2400 (PreK-8); Fax: 313-933-9332. Ms. Darlisa Rickman, Prin. Lay Teachers 5; Students 84.
Catechesis/Religious Program—Students 61.

15—ST. CHARLES BORROMEO Rev. Raymond Stadmeyer, O.F.M.Cap.
Res.: 1491 Baldwin Ave., 48214. Tel: 313-331-0253; Fax: 313-331-4834.
Catechesis/Religious Program—Students 20.

16—CHRIST THE KING Rev. Victor Clore; Sr. Fiorentina D'Amore, H.V.M., Pastoral Assoc. & D.R.E.
Res.: 16805 Pierson, 48219. Tel: 313-532-1211; Fax: 313-532-1216.
Church: 20800 Grand River & Burt Rd., 48219.
School—16800 Trinity, 48219. Tel: 313-532-1213; Fax: 313-532-1050. Mrs. Rosanne Jodway, Prin. Lay Teachers 15; Students 149.
St. Christine Christian Services—22261 Fenkell, 48223. Office: 15317 Dacosta, 48223. Tel: 313-535-7272.
Catechesis/Religious Program—Students 70.

17—ST. CHRISTINE, Closed. For inquiries for parish records contact the chancery.

18—ST. CHRISTOPHER Rev. James Smalarz.
Res.: 7800 Woodmont Ave., 48228. Tel: 313-584-7460; Fax: 313-584-6361.
Convent—7800 Woodmont Ave., 48228. Tel: 313-584-7579.
Catechesis/Religious Program—Theresa Zaleski, D.R.E. Students 5.

19—CORPUS CHRISTI (2006) Rev. Donald Archambault; Sr. Stephanie Holub, R.S.M., Pastoral Assoc.; Deacon Paul Mueller; Beryl Harriott, Pastoral Assoc.
Res.: 19800 Pembroke Ave., 48219-2145. Tel: 313-537-5770; Fax: 313-537-5773.
Catechesis/Religious Program—Sheri Dargin, D.R.E. Students 40.

20—ST. CUNEGUNDA Rev. Zbigniew Grankowski.
Res.: 5900 St. Lawrence Ave., 48210. Tel: 313-843-4717; Fax: 313-841-4255.
Catechesis/Religious Program—Michael Peck, D.R.E. Students 45.

21—ST. ELIZABETH Rev. Norman P. Thomas, Admin.
Res.: 3138 E. Canfield Ave., 48207. Tel: 313-921-9225; Fax: 313-921-9475.
Catechesis/Religious Program—Velma Coleman, D.R.E. Students 55.

22—ST. FRANCIS D'ASSISI Rev. Robert J. Wojciechowski.
Res.: 4500 Wesson St., 48210. Tel: 313-897-7229; Fax: 313-897-7485.
Catechesis/Religious Program—Leonard Meir, D.R.E.

23—ST. FRANCIS DE SALES, Merged with Precious Blood, Detroit to form St. Peter Claver, Detroit.

24—ST. GABRIEL Rev. Jaime Hinojos.
Res.: 8118 W. Vernor Hwy., 48209-1524. Tel: 313-841-0753; Fax: 313-841-0916.
Catechesis/Religious Program—Tel: 313-841-0419. Students 400.

25—ST. GEMMA GALGANI, Closed. For inquiries for parish records contact the chancery.

26—ST. GERARD, Merged with Immaculate Heart of Mary, Detroit to form Corpus Christi, Detroit.

27—GESU Rev. Robert J. Scullin, S.J.
Office: 17180 Oak Dr., 48221. Tel: 313-862-4400; Fax: 313-862-1083.
School—17139 Oak Dr., 48221. Tel: 313-863-4677; Fax: 313-862-4395. Mr. John Champion, Prin. Lay Teachers 10; Students 218.
Catechesis/Religious Program—Laura Silveri, D.R.E. Students 40.

28—GOOD SHEPHERD (2006) Rev. Michael C. Nkachukwu; Alton M. James, Pastoral Assoc.
Res.: 1265 Parkview Ave., 48214. Tel: 313-822-1262; Fax: 313-822-8988.
Catechesis/Religious Program—Ms. Gayle Koyton, D.R.E. Students 16.

29—ST. GREGORY THE GREAT Rev. Msgr. Michael C. LeFevre, Admin.; Rev. Timothy J. Kane.
Res.: 9844 Woodward Ave., 48202. Tel: 313-865-6300; Fax: 313-867-4613.
Catechesis/Religious Program—Students 29.

30—GUARDIAN ANGELS, Closed. For inquiries for parish records contact the chancery.

31—ST. HEDWIG Revs. Robert J. Wojciechowski; Noel Cornelio, P.I.M.E.; Deacon Rafael Jimenez.
Res.: 3245 Junction Ave., 48210. Tel: 313-894-5409; Fax: 313-894-4730.

32—HOLY CROSS, (Hungarian), Revs. Barnabas G. Kiss, O.F.M.; Angelus Ligeti, O.F.M.
Res.: 8423 South St., 48209. Tel: 313-842-1133; Fax: 313-842-2773. Email: sztkereszt@comcast.net.
Catechesis/Religious Program—Emma T. Mahar, D.R.E. Students 25.

33—HOLY FAMILY, (Italian), Rev. Edward J. Vilkauskas, C.S.Sp., Admin.
Res.: 641 Walter P. Chrysler Expwy., 48226. Tel: 313-963-2046; Fax: 313-963-0646.

34—HOLY REDEEMER Rev. Msgr. Donald F. Hanchon; Rev. Charles K. Altermatt; Deacon Ronald L. McIntyre.
Res.: 1721 Junction Ave., 48209. Tel: 313-842-3450; Fax: 313-849-0539.
School—Tel: 313-841-5230; Fax: 313-841-3640. Sr. Elizabeth Fleckenstein, I.H.M., Prin. Sisters Servants of the Immaculate Heart of Mary 2; Sisters of St. Joseph 1; Sisters of Mercy 1; Lay Teachers 9; Students 153.
Catechesis/Religious Program—Marcela Solis, D.R.E. Students 550.

35—ST. HYACINTH, (Polish), Rev. Janusz Iwan.
Res.: 3151 Farnsworth Ave., 48211. Tel: 313-922-1507; Fax: 313-922-2459.

36—IMMACULATE HEART OF MARY, Merged with St. Gerard, Detroit to form Corpus Christi, Detroit.

37—ST. JOHN CANTIUS, (Polish), Closed. For inquiries for parish records contact the chancery.

38—ST. JOSAPHAT, (Polish), Rev. Mark Borkowski, Admin.; Deacon Bill Stimpson.
Office: 4440 Russell St., 48202.
Church: 691 E. Canfield Ave., 48201. Tel: 313-831-6659; Fax: 313-831-8522.

39—ST. JOSEPH Rev. Mark Borkowski, Admin.; Deacon Bill Stimpson.
Office: c/o 4440 Russell St., 48202.
Church: 1828 Jay St., 48207. Tel: 313-831-6659; Fax: 313-891-8522.

40—ST. JUDE Rev. Robert S. Liberty; Rev. Msgr. George P. Miller.
Res.: 15889 E. Seven Mile Rd., 48205. Tel: 313-527-0380; Fax: 313-527-3511.
Catechesis/Religious Program—Students 18.

41—ST. LEO Rev. Theodore K. Parker; Angela Thomas-Weldon, Pastoral Assoc.
Church & Res.: 4860 15th St., 48208. Tel: 313-894-1176; Fax: 313-894-1176 (call first).
Catechesis/Religious Program—Sandra Hill, D.R.E. Students 10.

42—ST. LOUIS THE KING Rev. Boleslaus Krol.
Res.: 18891 St. Louis Ave., 48234. Tel: 313-891-1766; Fax: 313-891-7959.

43—ST. LUKE Rev. Tyrone Robinson, Admin.; Sr. Marie Roy, S.S.J., Pastoral Assoc.
Res.: 8017 Ohio Ave., 48204. Tel: 313-935-6161; Fax: 313-935-0788.
Catechesis/Religious Program—Students 10.

44—MADONNA Rev. Msgr. Michael C. LeFevre, Admin.; Rev. Timothy J. Kane.
Res.: 9844 Woodward, 48202. Tel: 313-868-4308; Fax: 313-868-9771.
Catechesis/Religious Program—Students 69.

45—MARTYRS OF UGANDA, Closed. For inquiries for parish records contact the chancery.

46—ST. MARY Revs. Edward J. Vilkauskas, C.S.Sp.; John Owusu-Achiaw.
Res.: 646 Monroe Ave., 48226. Tel: 313-961-8711; Fax: 313-961-4994.
Catechesis/Religious Program—Students 8.

47—ST. MARY'S OF REDFORD Rev. Tyrone Robinson, Admin.
Mailing Address: 14750 St. Mary's, 48227. Tel: 313-273-1100; Fax: 313-273-2002. In Res., Rev. William Lunnon.
Catechesis/Religious Program—Ada Taylor, D.R.E. Students 36.

48—ST. MATTHEW Rev. Duane R. Novelly.
Res.: 6021 Whittier Ave., 48224. Tel: 313-884-4470; Fax: 313-884-4276.
Catechesis/Religious Program—Students 13.

49—MOST HOLY TRINITY Rev. Russell E. Kohler.
Res.: 1050 Porter St., 48226. Tel: 313-965-4450; Fax: 313-965-4453.
School—1229 Labrosse, 48226. Tel: 313-961-8855; Fax: 313-961-5797. Ms. Kathleen McBride, Prin. Lay Teachers 8; Students (K-7) 113; Preschool 20.
Catechesis/Religious Program—Students 113.

50—NATIVITY OF OUR LORD Rev. Jerome C. Singer.
Res.: 5900 McClellan Ave., 48213. Tel: 313-922-0033; Fax: 313-922-8553.
Catechesis/Religious Program—Sr. Jolene Van Handel, O.P., D.R.E. Students 54.

51—OUR LADY GATE OF HEAVEN, Closed. For inquiries for parish records please see St. Suzanne/Our Lady Gate of Heaven, Detroit.

52—OUR LADY HELP OF CHRISTIANS, (Polish), Merged with Transfiguration, Detroit to form Transfiguration-Our Lady Help of Christians, Detroit.

53—OUR LADY OF GOOD COUNSEL Rev. Robert J. Kotlarz.
20103 Joann, 48205.
Church: 17142 Rowe Ave., 48205. Tel: 313-372-1698; Fax: 313-372-1211.
Catechesis/Religious Program—Mrs. My Xiong, C.R.E. Students 21.

54—OUR LADY OF MT. CARMEL, Closed. For inquiries for parish records contact the chancery.

55—OUR LADY OF THE ROSARY Rev. Robert Morand.
Res.: 5930 Woodward Ave., 48202. Tel: 313-875-6011; Fax: 313-872-0758.
Catechesis/Religious Program—Students 46.

56—OUR LADY QUEEN OF ANGELS Rev. Albert C. Sescon.
Res.: 4200 Martin Ave., 48210. Tel: 313-897-8160; Fax: 313-897-8126.
Catechesis/Religious Program—Students 153.

57—OUR LADY QUEEN OF HEAVEN Rev. Donald A. Sopiak.
Res.: 8200 Rolyat Ave., 48234. Tel: 313-891-4553; Fax: 313-891-5782.
Catechesis/Religious Program—Mary Beth Lewinski, D.R.E.

58—ST. PATRICK Rev. Tod Laverty, O.F.M.; Floria Ellison, Pastoral Assoc.
Church: 58 Parsons, 48201. Tel: 313-833-0857; Fax: 313-831-1619.
St. Patrick Senior Center, Inc.—Tel: 313-833-7080; Fax: 313-833-0128.

59—SS. PETER AND PAUL (West Side) Rev. Stan Tokarski. In Res., Rev. Mitchell Szarek.
Res.: 7685 Grandville Ave., 48228. Tel: 313-846-2222; Fax: 313-584-1484.
Catechesis/Religious Program—Lawrence Kowalski, D.R.E. Students 25.

60—SS. PETER AND PAUL JESUIT Revs. Mark George, S.J.; Ben Jimenez, S.J., Dir. Warming Center.
Res.: 438 St. Antoine St., 48226. Tel: 313-961-8077; Fax: 313-963-5134.

61—ST. PETER CLAVER Rev. James E. O'Reilly, S.J.
13305 Grove Ave., 48235. Tel: 313-342-5292; Fax: 313-342-3513.
Catechesis/Religious Program—Mary Caroline Jonah, D.R.E. Students 25.

62—ST. PHILOMENA Rev. Peter S. Lentine.
Res.: 4281 Marseilles Ave., 48224. Tel: 313-882-4300; Fax: 313-882-1661.
Catechesis/Religious Program—4500 Marseilles, 48224. Kelly Woolums, D.R.E. Tel: 313-884-2422. Students 129.

63—PRECIOUS BLOOD, Merged with St. Francis de Sales, Detroit to form St. Peter Claver, Detroit.

64—PRESENTATION/OUR LADY OF VICTORY Rev. Michael J. Byrnes; Deacon Hubert Sanders, Pastoral Admin.
Res.: 19760 Meyers Rd., 48235. Tel: 313-342-1333; Fax: 313-342-4182.
Catechesis/Religious Program—Students 12.

65—ST. RAYMOND Rev. Robert J. Kotlarz.
Res.: 20103 Joann Ave., 48205. Tel: 313-527-0525; Fax: 313-527-9776.
Community Center—20055 Joann Ave., 48205. Tel: 313-372-0437.
Catechesis/Religious Program—Sr. Rosemarie Abate, H.V.M., D.R.E. & Evangelization Coord. Students 28.

66—ST. RITA, Merged with St. Bartholomew, Detroit to form St. Bartholomew/St. Rita, Detroit.

67—SACRED HEART OF JESUS Rev. Norman P. Thomas, Admin.
Res.: 1000 Eliot St., 48207. Tel: 313-831-1356; Fax: 313-831-8603.
Catechesis/Religious Program—Barbara Hunt, D.R.E. Students 165.

68—ST. SCHOLASTICA Rev. Michael R. Green, O.S.B.
Res.: 17320 Rosemont Rd., 48219. Tel: 313-531-0140; Fax: 313-531-0739.
Church: Southfield Rd. & W. Outer Dr., 48219.
School—Tel: 313-532-1916; Fax: 313-532-0140. Faye Vaughn, Elementary Prin. Lay Teachers 11; Students 153.
Convent—17305 Ashton, 48219. Tel: 313-541-4368.
Catechesis/Religious Program—Bro. Gregory David Jones, O.S.B., D.R.E. Students 13.

69—STE. ANNE DE DETROIT Rev. Thomas W. Sepulveda, C.S.B. In Res., Revs. José Jaime DelToro, C.S.B.; A. Leo Reilly, C.S.B.; Manuel J. Chircop, C.S.B.
Res.: 1000 Ste. Anne St., 48216-2027. Tel: 313-496-1701; Fax: 313-496-0429.
Catechesis/Religious Program—Students 260.

70—ST. STEPHEN-MARY MOTHER OF THE CHURCH Revs. Edward F. Zaorski, Admin.; Marie-Elie Haby.
Res.: 4311 Central Ave., 48210. Tel: 313-841-0783; Fax: 313-841-4868.
Catechesis/Religious Program—Armando Bravo, D.R.E. Students 150.

71—ST. SUZANNE/OUR LADY GATE OF HEAVEN Rev. Richard Lewnau; Deacon Alex Jones Jr.
Res.: 9357 Westwood Ave., 48228. Tel: 313-838-6780; Fax: 313-838-1063.
Catechesis/Religious Program—Students 21.

72—SWEETEST HEART OF MARY, (Polish), [CEM] Rev. Mark Borkowski; Deacon Bill Stimpson.
Res.: 4440 Russell St., 48207. Tel: 313-831-6659; Fax: 313-831-8522.

73—ST. THOMAS AQUINAS Rev. Richard Lewnau; Deacon Alex Jones Jr.; Micheleen Troutman, Pastoral Min.; Catherine Odom Prowse, Music Min.
Parish Center—5780 Evergreen Rd., 48228. Tel: 313-271-3266; Fax: 313-271-8773.
Catechesis/Religious Program—Tel: 313-271-0813. Penny Vanderkerckhove, D.R.E. Students 10.

74—TRANSFIGURATION-OUR LADY HELP OF CHRISTIANS Rev. Andrew Wesley.
Res.: 5830 Simon K. St., 48212. Tel: 313-892-1310; Fax: 313-893-2478.
Convent—5821 Rupert, 48212. Tel: 313-891-9273.
Catechesis/Religious Program—Sr. Angelica Zajkowski, D.R.E.

OUTSIDE THE CITY OF DETROIT

ALGONAC, ST. CLAIR CO., ST. CATHERINE OF ALEXANDRIA, [CEM] Merged with Holy Cross, Marine City & St. Mark, Harsens Island to form Our Lady on the River, Marine City.

ALLEN PARK, WAYNE CO., ST. FRANCES CABRINI Rev. Joseph Mallia.
Res.: 9000 Laurence Ave., 48101. Tel: 313-381-5601; Fax: 313-381-7837.
School—St. Frances Cabrini Elementary, 13500 Wick Rd., 48101. Tel: 313-928-6610; Fax: 313-928-8502. Patricia Pollick, Prin. Lay Teachers 31; Students 498.
High School—Cabrini High School, Tel: 313-388-0110; Fax: 313-388-1876. James J. Wasukanis, Pres.; Cheryl Szczodroski, Prin. Lay Teachers 35; Students 461.
Catechesis/Religious Program—Peggy Durocher, D.R.E. Students 297.

ALLENTON, ST. CLAIR CO., ST. JOHN THE EVANGELIST Revs. Wayne G. Ureel; Rajaian Suresh, S.A.C.
Res.: 872 Capac Rd., 48002. Tel: 810-395-7074; Fax: 810-395-7718.
Catechesis/Religious Program—883A Capac Rd., 48002. Tel: 810-395-2301. Students 192.

ARMADA, MACOMB CO., ST. MARY MYSTICAL ROSE Rev. Siaosi E. Patau.
Res.: 24040 Armada Ridge, 48005. Tel: 586-784-5966; Fax: 586-784-9330.
Catechesis/Religious Program—Tel: 586-784-4157. Students 214.

AUBURN HILLS, OAKLAND CO.

1—ST. JOHN FISHER CHAPEL UNIVERSITY PARISH Rev. Jerome A. Brzezinski; Sr. Mary Van Gilder, Pastoral Assoc.; Mrs. Lisa Brown, Pastoral Assoc.; Mr. Paul Borucki, Pastoral Assoc.; Mrs. Susan Buratto, Pastoral Assoc.; Mrs. Nancy Mason Bordley, Pastoral Assoc.
Res.: 3665 Walton Blvd., 48326. Tel: 248-373-6457; Fax: 248-373-5479. Web: www.stfisherparish.org.
Catechesis/Religious Program—Tel: 248-373-3130. Michelle Pittel, D.R.E. Students 333.

2—SACRED HEART Rev. Richard Cavellier.
Res.: 3400 Adams Rd., 48326. Tel: 248-852-4170; Fax: 248-852-5745.
Catechesis/Religious Program—Tel: 248-852-3620. Students 235.

BELLEVILLE, WAYNE CO., ST. ANTHONY Rev. Thomas H. Cusick; Edward Haggerty, Parish Admin.; Deacon Peter Cornell.
Res.: 409 W. Columbia Ave., 48111. Tel: 734-697-1211; Fax: 734-697-6217.
Catechesis/Religious Program—Tel: 734-699-3373. Students 225.
Convent—371 W. Columbia Ave., 48111. Tel: 734-697-6661.

BERKLEY, OAKLAND CO., OUR LADY OF LA SALETTE Rev. Patrick J. Connell; Deacons Daniel M. Darga, Pastoral Assoc.; Brian Carroll, Pastoral Assoc.
Res.: 2600 Harvard Rd., 48072. Tel: 248-541-3762; Fax: 248-541-4250.
School—(Grades PreK-8), 2219 Coolidge Hwy., 48072. Tel: 248-542-3757; Fax: 248-541-6559. Mr. William J. Dogan, Prin.; Ms. Meg Bowker, Librarian. Lay Teachers 10; Students 149.
Catechesis/Religious Program—Students 152.

BEVERLY HILLS, OAKLAND CO., OUR LADY QUEEN OF MARTYRS Rev. Scott A. Thibodeau; Sr. Michael Clare Mauntel, S.C., Pastoral Min.
32340 Pierce Ave., 48025. Tel: 248-644-8620; Fax: 248-644-8623.
School—(Grades PreK-8), 32460 Pierce Ave., 48025. Tel: 248-642-2616; Fax: 248-642-3671. Peter J. Ferguson, Prin. Lay Teachers 32; Students 285.
Catechesis/Religious Program—Tel: 248-647-6068. Sarah Hogan, D.R.E. Students 300.

BIRMINGHAM, OAKLAND CO.

1—ST. COLUMBAN Rev. Donald L. Demmer; Deacon John Parent; Robert Mervak, Music Min.
Church: 1775 Melton, 48009. Tel: 248-646-5224; Fax: 248-642-7889. Email: stcbhm@aol.com. Web: www.saintcolumbanchurch.com.
Catechesis/Religious Program—Tel: 248-646-5225. Betty Sheehan, D.R.E.

2—HOLY NAME Rev. Msgr. John P. Zenz; Sr. Shirlee Hoski, S.S.J.-T.O.S.F., Pastoral Assoc.; Mary A. Pineau, Pastoral Assoc.; Deacon Michael J. McKale.
Parish Office—630 Harmon St., 48009. Tel: 248-646-2244; Fax: 248-646-2286.
School—(Grades PreK-8) Tel: 248-644-2722; Fax: 248-644-1191. Mary Ann Grady, Prin.; Sue Lambert, Librarian. Lay Teachers 27; Students 374.
Catechesis/Religious Program—Tel: 248-642-4130. Mary Morian, D.R.E. Students 440.

BLOOMFIELD HILLS

1—ST. HUGO OF THE HILLS Rev. Msgr. Anthony M. Tocco; Rev. Michael Wilkes; Sr. Barbara Rund, O.P., Pastoral Assoc.; Deacon Michael T. Smith.
Res.: 2215 Opdyke Rd., 48304. Tel: 248-644-5460; Fax: 248-644-1758. Web: www.sthugo.org.
School—380 E. Hickory Grove, 48304. Tel: 248-642-6131; Fax: 248-642-4457. Sr. Margaret Van Velzen, I.H.M., Prin. Sisters, Servants of the Immaculate Heart of Mary 3; Lay Teachers 41; Students 721.
Catechesis/Religious Program—Tel: 248-642-6062. Margaret Bucchi, C.R.E. Students 328.

2—ST. OWEN Rev. James F. Cronk; Sisters Carolyn Nelson, Pastoral Min.; Susanne Hofweber, O.P., Pastoral Min.; Mary Mills, Youth Min.; Sharon Dreisig, Youth Min.
Res.: 6869 Franklin Rd., 48301. Tel: 248-626-0840; Fax: 248-626-0345. Web: www.stowen.org.
Catechesis/Religious Program—6855 Franklin Rd., 48301. Tel: 248-626-3200; Fax: 248-626-1415. Sue Fredenberg, D.R.E.; Karen Heuer, D.R.E.; Patricia Watanabe, Music Min. Students 439.

3—ST. REGIS Rev. Norman D. Nawrocki.
Res.: 3695 Lincoln Rd., 48301. Tel: 248-646-2686; Fax: 248-646-4643.
School—3691 Lincoln Rd., 48301-4055. Tel: 248-646-2686, Ext. 300; Fax: 248-644-0944. Chris Ciagne, Prin. Lay Teachers 33; Students 501.
Catechesis/Religious Program—Students 225.

CANTON, WAYNE CO.

1—SAINT JOHN NEUMANN Revs. George W. Williams; Theodore D'Cunha, S.A.C.; Eugene Kijek, Pastoral Assoc.
Res.: 44800 Warren Rd., 48187. Tel: 734-455-5910; Fax: 734-455-6779.
Catechesis/Religious Program—Donna Franke, D.R.E. Students 839.

2—RESURRECTION Rev. Richard A. Perfetto.
48755 Warren Rd., 48187-1216. Tel: 734-451-0444; Fax: 734-451-0454.
Catechesis/Religious Program—Students 550.

3—ST. THOMAS A BECKET Revs. Patrick Casey; Mathew C. George.
Res.: 555 S. Lilley Rd., 48188. Tel: 734-981-1333; Fax: 734-981-1481.
Catechesis/Religious Program—Tel: 734-981-6680. Students 1,157.

CAPAC, ST. CLAIR CO., ST. NICHOLAS Revs. Wayne G. Ureel; Rajaian Suresh, S.A.C.
Church: 4331 Capac Rd., Box 129, 48014. Tel: 810-395-7572; Fax: 810-395-7830.
Catechesis/Religious Program—Julie Laeder, D.R.E. Students 105.

CARLETON, MONROE CO., ST. PATRICK, [CEM 3] Rev. Robert A. Bauer.
Res.: 2996 W. Labo Rd., 48117. Tel: 734-654-2500; Fax: 734-654-6594.
School—Tel: 734-654-2522; Fax: 734-654-8120. Ms. Ruth Meiring, Prin. Lay Teachers 11; Students 133.
Catechesis/Religious Program—Tel: 734-654-6444. Jan Doederlien, D.R.E. Students 154.

CENTER LINE, MACOMB CO., ST. CLEMENT, [CEM] Revs. Michael R. Gawlowski; Thomas Puzio; Deacon Eric Sorensen.
Res.: 8155 Ritter Ave., 48015-1499. Tel: 586-757-3306; Fax: 586-757-5390.
School—Tel: 586-757-7500; Fax: 586-757-4724. Michelle Sheppard, Prin. Lay Teachers 12; Students 152.
Catechesis/Religious Program—Tel: 586-427-2761. Alice Baron, D.R.E.; Donna VanGheluwe, D.R.E. Students 234.
Mission—St. Joseph Malankara

CLARKSTON, OAKLAND CO., ST. DANIEL Rev. Christopher P. Maus; Deacon Stephen Marks.
Res.: 7010 Valley Park Dr., 48346. Tel: 248-625-4580; Fax: 248-620-9839.
Catechesis/Religious Program—Betty Haran, D.R.E. Students 680.

CLAWSON, OAKLAND CO., GUARDIAN ANGELS Revs. Gerard LeBoeuf; Hoang Chi Lam; Deacon Eugene Tombler.
Res.: 581 E. 14 Mile Rd., 48017. Tel: 248-588-1222; Fax: 248-588-8767.
School—Tel: 248-588-5545; Fax: 248-589-7356. Ms. Sharon Hammerschmidt, Prin. Lay Teachers 20; Students 291.
Catechesis/Religious Program—Denise Ficorelli, D.R.E. Students 202.

CLINTON TWP., MACOMB CO.

1—ST. CLAUDE, Merged with St. Thecla, Clinton Twp.

2—ST. LOUIS Rev. Lawrence A. Pettke; Deacon Donald C. Junak, Pastoral Assoc.
Res.: 24415 Crocker Blvd., 48036. Tel: 586-468-8734; Fax: 586-468-9647.
Catechesis/Religious Program—39140 Ormsby St., Clinton Township, 48036. Tel: 586-468-8734, Ext. 104. Sr. Kathy Onderbeke, I.H.M., D.R.E. Students 153.

3—ST. PAUL OF TARSUS Rev. Ronald Essman; Deacon Thomas Carter.
Res.: 41300 Romeo Plank Rd., 48038. Tel: 586-228-1210; Fax: 586-228-8935. Email: parishoffice@stpauloftarsus.com. Web: www.stpauloftarsus.com.
Catechesis/Religious Program—Claudia Dombrowski, D.R.E. Students 733.

4—ST. RONALD Rev. James Andres, O.F.M.Cap.; Diane McDonald, Pastoral Assoc.
Res.: 17701 15 Mile Rd., 48035-2401. Tel: 586-792-1190; Fax: 586-792-0765.
Catechesis/Religious Program—Tel: 586-792-1276. Students 290.

5—SAN FRANCESCO COMMUNITY Rev. Giulio Schiavi, P.I.M.E.
Res.: 22870 S. Nunneley Rd., 48035. Tel: 586-792-5346; Fax: 586-792-5119.
Catechesis/Religious Program—Students 150.

6—ST. THECLA, Merged with St. Claude, Clinton Twp. Rev. Charles Ratnasamy, S.D.B., Admin.
Res.: 20740 S. Nunneley Rd., 48035-1628. Tel: 586-791-3930; Fax: 586-791-3890. Email: baronol@stthecla.com.
School—Tel: 586-791-2170; Fax: 586-791-2356. Sr. Mary Kathleen White, C.S.S.F., Prin. Felician Sisters 1; Lay Teachers 26; Students 454.
Catechesis/Religious Program—Tel: 586-792-0550. Students 288.

7—ST. VALERIE OF RAVENNA, Merged into St. Louis, Clinton Township.

COLUMBUS, ST. CLAIR CO., ST. PHILIP NERI, [CEM] Merged with All Saints, Memphis & Holy Rosary Mission, Smiths Creek to form Holy Family, Memphis.

DAVISBURG, OAKLAND CO., DIVINE MERCY Rev. Msgr. John G. Budde.
4055 Parker, 48350-2321. Tel: 248-634-7015; Fax: 248-634-7029.
Catechesis/Religious Program—Students 84.

DEARBORN, WAYNE CO.

1—ST. ALPHONSUS Rev. David Lesniak.
Res.: 7455 Calhoun Ave., 48126. Tel: 313-581-5218; Fax: 313-584-9560.
Catechesis/Religious Program—Tel: 313-581-5218. Students 4.
Convent—13541 Gould Ave., 48126. Tel: 313-584-4350.

2—ST. BARBARA Rev. Zbigniew Grankowski.
Res.: 13534 Colson Ave., 48126. Tel: 313-582-8383; Fax: 313-582-1581.
Catechesis/Religious Program—Michael Peck, D.R.E. Students 45.

3—ST. CLEMENT Rev. Charles S. Fontana; Sr. Mary Downey, I.H.M., Pastoral Assoc.; Deacon Robert Rowland.
Res.: 5275 Kenilworth St., 48126. Tel: 313-581-7495; Fax: 313-581-4233.
Catechesis/Religious Program—Tel: 313-846-2443. Maurine Dailey, D.R.E. Students 42.

4—DIVINE CHILD Revs. James D. Bilot; Clint W. McDonell; Deacon Roger O'Donnell.
Res.: 25001 Hollander, 48128. Tel: 313-277-3110; Fax: 313-277-3211.
School—Tel: 313-562-1090; Fax: 313-562-9306. Sr. Cecilia Bondy, Elementary Prin. Bernardine Sisters 3; Lay Teachers 32; Students 671.
High School—1001 N. Silvery Ln., 48128. Tel: 313-562-1990; Fax: 313-562-9361. Margaret Knuth, High School Prin. Bernardine Sisters 2; Lay Teachers 54; Students 837.
Catechesis/Religious Program—Karen Mitchell, D.R.E. Students 166.
Convent—1045 N. Silvery Ln., 48128. Tel: 313-561-5455.

5—ST. JOSEPH, Clustered with St. Martha, Dearborn. Rev. Terrence D. Kerner.
Res.: 16101 Rotunda Dr., 48120. Tel: 313-336-3227; Fax: 313-441-6769.

6—ST. MARTHA, Clustered with St. Joseph, Dearborn. Rev. Terrence D. Kerner.
Mailing Address: 18200 Oakwood Blvd., 48124. Tel: 313-336-4090; Fax: 313-336-3318.
Res.: 16101 Rotunda, 48120. Tel: 313-336-3227; Fax: 313-441-6769.
Catechesis/Religious Program—Kathleen Kelly, D.R.E.; Gloria Koss, D.R.E. Students 61.

7—SACRED HEART, [CEM] Rev. Peter Petroske; Fran Helner, Pastoral Assoc. In Res., Rev. John F. Child (Retired).
Res.: 22430 W. Michigan Ave., 48124. Tel: 313-278-5555; Fax: 313-278-8582.
School—22513 Garrison, 48124. Tel: 313-561-9192; Fax: 313-561-1598. Lisa Powaser, Prin. Lay Teachers 20; Students 283.
Catechesis/Religious Program—Julie Wieleba-Milkie, Youth Min. Students 238.

DEARBORN HEIGHTS, WAYNE CO.

1—ST. ALBERT THE GREAT Rev. Daniel Zaleski; Sr. Barbara Ennis, S.S.J.-T.O.S.F., Pastoral Assoc.; Deacons Henry J. Kibit; Ray Gabel.

Res.: 4855 Parker, 48125. Tel: 313-292-0430; Fax: 313-292-8565.
Catechesis/Religious Program—Tel: 313-292-9370. Students 70.

2—ST. ANSELM Rev. Msgr. James A. Moloney, Pastor & Dir., Society for The Propagation of The Faith.
Res.: 17650 W. Outer Dr., 48127. Tel: 313-565-4808; Fax: 313-565-7514.
School—Tel: 313-563-3430. Mrs. Stephanie Tozer, Prin. Sisters 1; Lay Teachers 10; Students 160.
Catechesis/Religious Program—Tel: 313-561-0512. Maryanne Walkuski, D.R.E. Students 80.

3—ST. JOHN THE BAPTIST Rev. Edwin W. Balazy.
Res.: 26123 McDonald Ave., 48125. Tel: 313-292-9693; Fax: 313-292-1755.

4—ST. LINUS Rev. Robert A. LaCroix; Deacon Jerry Schiffer.
Parish Office—6466 Evangeline, 48127-2086. Tel: 313-274-4500; Fax: 313-562-2821.
School—Tel: 313-274-5320. Dena Jayson, Prin. Lay Teachers 11; Students 252.
Catechesis/Religious Program—Tel: 313-274-5778. Students 90.
Convent—25450 Hass, 48127.

5—ST. MEL Rev. Thomas J. Kramer.
Church: 7506 Inkster Rd., 48127. Tel: 313-274-0684; Fax: 313-274-4248.
Catechesis/Religious Program—Tel: 313-274-3977. Donna Trudell, D.R.E. Students 60.

6—OUR LADY OF GRACE Rev. Donald L. Walker, Admin. (Retired); Deacon Robert DeWitt, Pastoral Min.
Res.: 8679 Riverview, 48127. Tel: 313-561-6373; Fax: 313-359-2727.
Church: 23700 Joy Rd., 48127.

7—ST. SABINA Rev. Raymond H. Bucon.
Res.: 25605 Ann Arbor Tr., 48127. Tel: 313-561-1977; Fax: 313-561-1315.
Catechesis/Religious Program—Tel: 313-274-5635. Students 115.

8—ST. SEBASTIAN Rev. Jeffrey Day; Deacons Lawrence Girard; Stephen Bussa; James Thibodeau.
Res.: 20710 Colgate, 48125. Tel: 313-562-5356; Fax: 313-562-0058.
School—Tel: 313-563-6640; Fax: 313-563-6641. Sr. Geraldine Kaczynski, F.S.S.J., Prin. Franciscan Sisters of St. Joseph 2; Lay Teachers 12; Students 200.
Catechesis/Religious Program—Tel: 313-563-0960; Fax: 313-562-0058. Susan Campbell, D.R.E. Students 211.
Convent—20700 Colgate Ave., 48125. Tel: 313-562-7733.

DRYDEN, LAPEER CO., ST. CORNELIUS Revs. Wayne G. Ureel; Rajaian Suresh, S.A.C.
Res.: 3834 Mill St., P.O. Box 208, 48428. Tel: 810-796-2926; Fax: 810-796-9713.
Catechesis/Religious Program—Donna Sandoffsky, D.R.E. Students 268.

DUNDEE, MONROE CO., ST. IRENE Rev. Michael A. Woroniewicz.
Res.: 576 Main St., 48131. Tel: 734-529-2160; Fax: 734-529-3463.
Catechesis/Religious Program—Mary Mead, D.R.E. Students 63.

EASTPOINTE, MACOMB CO.

1—ST. BARNABAS, Merged with Holy Innocents, Roseville to form Holy Innocents-St. Barnabas, Roseville.

2—ST. BASIL Rev. Anthony P. Sulkowski.
Parish Center—22851 Lexington Ave., 48021. Tel: 586-777-5610; Fax: 586-779-3341.
Catechesis/Religious Program—Tel: 586-772-5434. Students 60.

3—OUR LADY OF GRACE VIETNAMESE PARISH (1999) Rev. Vincent Nguyen An Ninh.
19300 Stephens Dr., 48021. Tel: 586-447-0504.
Res.: 19341 Stephens Dr., 48021. Tel: 586-322-0047; Fax: 586-447-8082.
Catechesis/Religious Program—Phil Long Nguyen, D.R.E. Students 106.

4—ST. VERONICA Revs. Stanley L. Pachla Jr.; Kulan-Daisamy Arokiasamy (India).
Res.: 21440 Universal Dr., 48021-2998. Tel: 586-777-0331; Fax: 586-777-0615.
Catechesis/Religious Program—Tel: 586-777-5810. Mary Fortunate, D.R.E. Students 85.
Convent—21357 Redmond, 48021. Tel: 586-777-0321.

ECORSE, WAYNE CO., ST. FRANCIS XAVIER, [CEM] Rev. Victor Roman.
Res.: 4250 W. Jefferson Ave., 48229. Tel: 313-383-8514; Fax: 313-383-7508.
Catechesis/Religious Program—Jason Lubaway, D.R.E. Students 50.

EMMETT, ST. CLAIR CO., OUR LADY OF MOUNT CARMEL Rev. Paul Czarnota; Deacon William Kolarik.
Rectory—10828 Brandon Rd., 48022. Tel: 810-384-1338; Fax: 810-384-8708.
Catechesis/Religious Program—10817 Brandon Rd., 48022. Students 186.

ERIE, MONROE CO., ST. JOSEPH, [CEM] Rev. Frederik Kalaj.
Res.: 2214 Manhattan Ave., 48133. Tel: 734-848-6125; Fax: 734-848-2784.
School—2238 Manhattan St., 48133. Tel: 734-848-6985. Sr. Jean Walczak, S.N.D., Prin. Sisters 2; Lay Teachers 10; Students 111.
Catechesis/Religious Program—Students 70.
Convent—2238 Manhattan Ave., 48133.

FARMINGTON, OAKLAND CO.

1—ST. COLMAN Rev. Norbert V. Kendzierski.
Res.: 32500 Middlebelt Rd., Farmington Hills, 48334. Tel: 248-626-0285; Fax: 248-626-5420. Email: colmancloyne@att.net.
Catechesis/Religious Program—Tel: 248-626-0287. Students 77.

2—ST. GERALD Rev. Festus N. Ejimadu.
Res.: 21300 Farmington Rd., 48336. Tel: 248-477-7470; Fax: 248-477-3878.
Catechesis/Religious Program—Tel: 248-476-7677. Mary Taylor, D.R.E. Students 249.

3—OUR LADY OF SORROWS Revs. Mark S. Brauer; David Cybulski; Deacon Clement Stankiewicz; Sr. Christine Mihelcic, S.J., Dir. Pastoral Svcs.; Mrs. Patricia Ernst, Pastoral Assoc.
Res.: 23815 Power Rd., 48336. Tel: 248-474-5720; Fax: 248-474-1340.
School—(Grades PreK-8), 24040 Raphael, 48336-2465. Tel: 248-476-0977; Fax: 248-615-5567. Mariann Lupinacci, Prin.; Andrea Lencione, Librarian. Lay Teachers 39; Students 787.
Catechesis/Religious Program—Tel: 248-474-6480. Students 263.

FARMINGTON HILLS, OAKLAND CO.

1—ST. ALEXANDER Rev. Robert McGrath; Deacon Mark Springer.
Res.: 27835 Shiawassee, 48336. Tel: 248-474-5748; Fax: 248-427-0883.
Catechesis/Religious Program—Tel: 248-474-8126. Students 123.

2—ST. CLARE OF ASSISI Rev. Gregory Tokarski.
Res.: 29200 W. Ten Mile, 48336. Tel: 248-477-9870; Fax: 248-477-4785.
Catechesis/Religious Program—Lawrence Kowalski, D.R.E. Students 15.

3—ST. FABIAN Rev. Brian J. Chabala; Celia St. Charles, Pastoral Assoc.; Deacon Jene Baughman.
Church & Office: 32200 W. 12 Mile Rd., 48334. Tel: 248-553-4610; Fax: 248-553-6296.
School—Tel: 248-553-2750; Fax: 248-848-3035. John Gilboe, Prin. Lay Teachers 22; Students 457.
Catechesis/Religious Program—Tel: 248-553-4860; Fax: 248-553-2041. Nancy Pawlukiewicz, D.R.E.; Andy Karl, Youth Min.; Lara Druffner, Middle School Coord. Students 433.

FERNDALE, OAKLAND CO., ST. JAMES Rev. Steven A. Wertanen.
Res.: 241 W. Pearson St., 48220-1824. Tel: 248-542-8835; Fax: 248-542-0267.
Catechesis/Religious Program—Beth LeAnnais, D.R.E. Students 86.

FLAT ROCK, WAYNE CO., ST. ROCH Rev. Richard A. Hartmann.
Res.: 25022 Gibraltar Rd., 48134. Tel: 734-782-4471; Fax: 734-782-5450.
Catechesis/Religious Program—Timothy Stokes, D.R.E. Students 292.

FRASER, MACOMB CO., OUR LADY QUEEN OF ALL SAINTS Rev. Ronald J. Babich; Sr. Nancy Zajac, O.P., Pastoral Assoc.
Res.: 31740 Cyril Ave., 48026. Tel: 586-293-4050; Fax: 586-293-1041.
Catechesis/Religious Program—Tel: 586-293-4050, Ext. 5. Sr. Nancy Zajac, O.P., D.R.E. Students 163.

GARDEN CITY, WAYNE CO.

1—ST. DUNSTAN Revs. Ronald Richards; Manuel J. Chircop, C.S.B.; Deacon Ziggy Kucharek.
Church: 1526 Belton Ave., 48135. Tel: 734-425-6720; Fax: 734-425-8411.
Res.: 1646 Belton Ave., 48135.
Catechesis/Religious Program—Sabrina S. Queen, C.R.E./Youth Ministry Coord.; Priscilla Steenburg, C.R.E. & Adult Faith Formation. Students 112.

2—ST. RAPHAEL THE ARCHANGEL Rev. Raymond H. Lewandowski; Deacon Frederick Burrell; Sr. Ritamary Pyzick, O.S.F., Pastoral Min.
Parish Center—31530 Beechwood, 48135. Tel: 734-427-1533; Fax: 734-744-2148.
School—(Grades K-8) Tel: 734-427-9771; Fax: 734-427-8895. DeAnn Brzezinski, Prin. Lay Teachers 10; Students 207.
Catechesis/Religious Program—Tel: 734-425-5550; Fax: 734-744-2148. Carol Bregand, D.R.E. Students 245.

GIBRALTAR, WAYNE CO., ST. VICTOR Revs. Roger A. Knapp; Robert J. Shafer.
Res.: 14100 Navarre, 48173. Tel: 734-675-0100; Fax: 734-675-6952. Email: stvictor@comcast.net.
Catechesis/Religious Program—Students 22.

GROSSE ILE, WAYNE CO., SACRED HEART, [CEM] Rev. Michael Molnar; Deacon Robert Tremmel.
Parish Center—21599 Parke Ln., 48138. Tel: 734-676-1378; Fax: 734-676-3623.
Catechesis/Religious Program—Students 351.

GROSSE POINTE, WAYNE CO., OUR LADY STAR OF THE SEA Revs. Gary T. Smetanka; Jovita Okoli; Deacon William E. Jamieson.
Church: 467 Fairford, 48236. Tel: 313-884-5554; Fax: 313-885-5591.
School—Tel: 313-884-1070; Fax: 313-884-0406. Michael Reece, Prin. Religious 1; Lay Teachers 30; Students 377.
Catechesis/Religious Program—Tel: 313-884-7407. John Lajiness, D.R.E. Students 361.
Convent—19950 Morningside Dr., 48236. Tel: 313-884-4074.

GROSSE POINTE FARMS, WAYNE CO., ST. PAUL CATHOLIC CHURCH, [CEM] Rev. Msgr. Patrick F. Halfpenny; Revs. John Wynnycky; Sama F. Muma; Deacon Richard Shubik, Pastoral Assoc.
Res.: 157 Lake Shore Rd., 48236. Tel: 313-885-8855; Fax: 313-886-6467.
School—170 Grosse Pointe Blvd., 48236. Tel: 313-885-3430; Fax: 313-885-9357. Mary Miller, Prin. Lay Teachers 37; Students 524.
Catechesis/Religious Program—Tel: 313-885-7022; Fax: 313-885-9316. Mrs. Judith Jones, D.R.E. Students 500.

GROSSE POINTE PARK, WAYNE CO.

1—ST. AMBROSE Rev. Timothy R. Pelc; Deacon Michael H. Cummins; Mr. Charles J. Dropiewski, Pastoral Assoc.
Res.: 15020 Hampton, 48230. Tel: 313-822-2814; Fax: 313-822-9838.
Catechesis/Religious Program—Elizabeth Haley, D.R.E. Students 304.

2—ST. CLARE OF MONTEFALCO Rev. James J. Sheridan, O.S.A.; Janet Guensche, Pastoral Assoc.
Res.: 1401 Whittier Rd., 48230. Tel: 313-647-5000; Fax: 313-647-5005.
School—16231 Charlevoix, 48230. Tel: 313-647-5100; Fax: 313-647-5105. Sr. Kathleen Jo Avery, O.S.M., Prin. Sisters 2; Lay Teachers 15; Students 212.
Catechesis/Religious Program—Tel: 313-647-5050; Fax: 313-647-5055. Paula Miller, D.R.E.; David Troiano, Music Min. Students 330.

HAMTRAMCK, WAYNE CO.

1—ST. FLORIAN Revs. Miroslaw Frankowski, S.Ch.; Jan Michalski, S.Ch.
Res. & Church: 2626 Poland Ave., 48212. Tel: 313-871-2778; Fax: 313-871-5947.
Catechesis/Religious Program—Students 90.

2—ST. LADISLAUS, (Polish), Rev. Andrew Wesley, Admin.
Res.: 2730 Caniff Ave., 48212. Tel: 313-872-0709; Fax: 313-872-5906.

3—OUR LADY QUEEN OF APOSTLES, (Polish), Rev. Bogdan Milosz.
Res.: 3851 Prescott Ave., 48212-3115. Tel: 313-891-1520; 313-891-1521; Fax: 313-891-3552.
Catechesis/Religious Program—Debbie Warren, D.R.E. Students 54.

HARPER WOODS, WAYNE CO.

1—OUR LADY QUEEN OF PEACE Rev. William J. Herman. In Res., Rev. John M. Fee, SS.CC.
Res.: 20955 Bournemouth Ave., 48225. Tel: 313-881-5212; Fax: 313-881-7813.
Catechesis/Religious Program—Tel: 313-884-8744.

2—ST. PETER THE APOSTLE Rev. Robert J. Keller.
Res.: 19851 Anita St., 48225. Tel: 313-886-1770; Fax: 313-886-1489.
Catechesis/Religious Program—Michaline Chmielewski, D.R.E. Students 50.

HARRISON TWP., MACOMB CO., ST. HUBERT Rev. Robert H. Blondell.
Res.: 38775 Prentiss, Harrison Township, 48045. Tel: 586-463-5877; Fax: 586-463-1734.
Catechesis/Religious Program—Tel: 586-463-5875; Fax: 586-463-4520. Mrs. Sandra Tapp, C.R.E. Students 512.

HARSENS ISLAND, ST. CLAIR CO., ST. MARK, Merged with Holy Cross, Marine City & St. Catherine of Alexandria, Algonac to form Our Lady on the River, Marine City.

HAZEL PARK, OAKLAND CO.

1—ST. JUSTIN Rev. Robert Hayes Williams.
Res.: 1631 E. Elza St., 48030. Tel: 248-542-2129; Fax: 248-542-2715.
Catechesis/Religious Program—Connie M. Giden, D.R.E. Students 25.

2—ST. MARY MAGDALEN Rev. Bede Louzon, O.F.M.Cap.
Res.: 50 E. Annabelle, 48030. Tel: 248-542-8060; Fax: 248-542-4563.
Catechesis/Religious Program—Tel: 248-547-0323. David Troiano, D.R.E. Students 65.

HIGHLAND, OAKLAND CO., CHURCH OF THE HOLY SPIRIT Rev. Leo T. Lulko; Deacon Arthur Van Brook.
Church: 3700 Harvey Lake Rd., 48356. Tel: 248-887-5364; Fax: 248-889-1374.
Catechesis/Religious Program—Tel: 248-887-1634. Jillian Peck, D.R.E. Students 378.

HIGHLAND PARK, WAYNE CO., ST. BENEDICT Rev. Msgr. Michael C. LeFevre; Rev. Timothy J. Kane.
Res. & Mailing Address: 9844 Woodward Ave., 48202. Tel: 313-865-6300; Fax: 313-867-4613.
Church: 60 Church Ave., 48203. Tel: 313-868-3876; Fax: 313-868-0110.
Catechesis/Religious Program—Students 7.

HOLLY, OAKLAND CO., ST. RITA Rev. David J. Blazek.
Res.: 309 E. Maple, 48442. Tel: 248-634-4841; Fax: 248-634-4858.
Catechesis/Religious Program—Tel: 248-634-1658; Fax: 248-634-4863. Email: stritasym@sbcglobal.net. Shelly Rau, D.R.E. Students 180.

IDA, MONROE CO., ST. JOSEPH, [CEM] Rev. Michael A. Woroniewicz.
Res.: 8295 Van Akin St., 48140. Tel: 734-269-3895.
Catechesis/Religious Program—Tel: 734-269-3414; Fax: 734-269-2153. Linda Wilson, D.R.E. Students 175.

IMLAY CITY, LAPEER CO., SACRED HEART, [CEM] Rev. Ezequiel Mondragon; Deacon Joseph A. Hulway.
Res.: 700 Maple Vista, 48444. Tel: 810-724-1135; Fax: 810-724-0870.
Catechesis/Religious Program—Tel: 810-724-1145. Students 145.

INKSTER, WAYNE CO., HOLY FAMILY PARISH Revs. David G. Burgard, Admin.; Gary Morelli.
Res.: 27800 Annapolis Rd., 48141. Tel: 313-563-8242; Fax: 313-563-0696.
Catechesis/Religious Program—Ruth Burney, D.R.E. Students 14.

IRA TOWNSHIP, ST. CLAIR CO., IMMACULATE CONCEPTION, [CEM] Rev. Tomek Maka; Deacon Kenneth Nowicki.
Mailing Address: 7043 Church Rd., 48023. Tel: 586-725-3051; Fax: 586-725-2474.
School—7043 Church Rd., 48023. Tel: 586-725-0078; Fax: 586-725-8240. Kathleen Steele, Prin. Lay Teachers 12; Students 212.
Catechesis/Religious Program—Jane Petitpren, D.R.E. Tel: 586-725-1762. Students 348.

LAKE ORION, OAKLAND CO., ST. JOSEPH Revs. C. Michael Verschaeve; Anthony E. Camilleri; Deacon Steven Mitchell; Mary Martin, Pastoral Assoc.; Kathy Hasty, Pastoral Assoc.; Leszek Bartkiewicz, Music Min.
Res.: 715 N. Lapeer Rd., 48362. Tel: 248-693-0440; Fax: 248-693-3724.
School—Tel: 248-693-6215; Fax: 248-693-0958. Sr. Theresa Darga, O.S.F., Prin. Lay Teachers 23; Students 425.
Catechesis/Religious Program—Kim Myers, D.R.E. Students 975.

LAKEPORT, ST. CLAIR CO., ST. EDWARD'S ON THE LAKE, [CEM] Rev. Joseph M. Esper.
Res.: 6945 Lakeshore Rd., 48059. Tel: 810-385-4340; Fax: 810-385-6972.
School—(Grades K-5) Tel: 810-385-4461; Fax: 810-385-6070. Ms. Rachael Becker, Prin. For grades 6-8 please refer to St. Mary/McCormick Catholic Academy, Port Huron, under Elementary Schools, Inter-Parochial in the Institutions Located in the Archdiocese section. Sisters 1; Lay Teachers 6; Students 95.
Catechesis/Religious Program—Students 95.
Convent—6995 Lakeshore Rd., 48059.

LAPEER, LAPEER CO., IMMACULATE CONCEPTION OF THE BLESSED VIRGIN MARY, [CEM] Revs. Douglas J. Terrien; Aaron J. DePeyster; Deacon Gerald DeShaw.
Res.: 814 W. Nepessing, 48446. Tel: 810-664-8594; Fax: 810-664-4564. Email: office@lapeercatholic.org. Web: www.lapeercatholic.org.
School—Bishop Kelley School, 926 W. Nepessing St., 48446. Tel: 810-664-5011; Fax: 810-664-5606. Lay Teachers 14; Students 233.
Catechesis/Religious Program—Mrs. Kenlin Botello, D.R.E. Students 267.

LINCOLN PARK, WAYNE CO.
1—CHRIST THE GOOD SHEPHERD Rev. Anthony Charles Richter; Deacon John Szwarc.
Res.: 1540 Riverbank Ave., 48146. Tel: 313-928-1324; Fax: 313-928-1326.
School—Tel: 313-386-0633. Thomas Caruso, Prin. Lay Teachers 12; Students 150.
Catechesis/Religious Program—Students 160.
2—ST. HENRY Rev. Gerard J. Cupple.
Res.: 1358 Council Ave., 48146. Tel: 313-381-0711; 313-381-0712; Fax: 313-381-6746.
Catechesis/Religious Program—Christine Brennan, D.R.E. Students 60.

LIVONIA, WAYNE CO.
1—ST. AIDAN Rev. Kevin Thomas.
Res.: 17500 Farmington Rd., 48152. Tel: 734-425-5950; Fax: 734-425-3687.
Catechesis/Religious Program—Tel: 734-425-9333. David Conrad, D.R.E. Students 380.
2—ST. COLETTE Rev. Henry W. Roodbeen; Deacons Alfred J. Morad; Gary Pardo.
Res.: 17600 Newburgh, 48152-2699. Tel: 734-464-4433; Fax: 734-464-1694.
Catechesis/Religious Program—Tel: 734-464-4435. Elizabeth Haley, D.R.E. Students 480.
3—ST. EDITH Rev. Michael Kazer; Deacon Richard Misiak.
Res.: 15089 Newburgh, 48154. Tel: 734-464-1222; Fax: 734-464-7582.
School—Tel: 734-464-1250; Fax: 734-464-6765. Sr. Margaret Kijek, C.S.S.F., Prin. Felician Sisters 1; Lay Teachers 9; Students 238.
Catechesis/Religious Program—Tel: 734-464-2020. Diana Seim, D.R.E. Students 415.
4—ST. GENEVIEVE Rev. Howard L. Vogan; Deacon Kevin Breen, Pastoral Assoc.
Res.: 29015 Jamison St., 48154-4021. Tel: 734-427-5220; Fax: 734-422-1763.
School—28933 Jamison St., 48154-4019. Tel: 734-425-4420; Fax: 734-458-3915. Marie E. Flack, Prin. Lay Teachers 10; Students 241.
Catechesis/Religious Program—Tel: 734-261-5920. Sheryl Nordstrom, D.R.E.; Diane Montes, Dir. Youth Ministry. Students 195.
5—ST. MAURICE Rev. Howard L. Vogan; Mr. David A. Carignan, Pastoral Assoc.
Church: 32765 Lyndon Ave., 48154. Tel: 734-522-1616; Fax: 734-522-5092.
Res.: 29015 Jamison, 48154-4021. Tel: 734-427-5220; Fax: 734-427-1763.
Catechesis/Religious Program—Tel: 734-421-5240. Sr. Deborah Ciolek, F.S.S.J., D.R.E. Students 90.
6—ST. MICHAEL Revs. William Tindall; Raymond Arwady.
Res.: 11441 Hubbard Ave., 48150. Tel: 734-261-1455; Fax: 734-522-1123.
School—11311 Hubbard, 48150. Tel: 734-421-7360; Fax: 734-466-9713. Sr. M. Carolyn Ratkowski, C.S.S.F., Prin. Lay Teachers 28; Students 785.
Catechesis/Religious Program—Tel: 734-261-1790. Students 204.
Convent—11400 Fairfield, 48154. Tel: 734-421-7522.
7—ST. PRISCILLA Rev. James McNulty; Deacon Robert C. Fitzgerald.
19120 Purling Brook Rd., 48152. Tel: 248-476-4700; Fax: 248-476-7831. Web: www.saintpriscilla.org.
Catechesis/Religious Program—Tel: 248-476-4702. Students 150.

MACOMB, MACOMB CO.
1—ST. ISIDORE Revs. Michael Hrydziuszko; John Britto Chinnapa, M.S.F.S.; Deacon Anthony Kendzierski.
Res.: 18201 Twenty-Three Mile Rd., 48042. Tel: 586-286-1700; Fax: 586-286-8753.
Catechesis/Religious Program—Tel: 586-286-4433. Diane Bucko, D.R.E. Students 1,300.
2—ST. MAXIMILIAN KOLBE, Merged with St. Francis of Assisi, Ray Township to form St. Francis of Assisi-St. Maximilian Kolbe, Ray Township.

MADISON HEIGHTS, OAKLAND CO., ST. VINCENT FERRER Rev. John C. Esper; Deacon Andrew Fairbanks.
Res.: 1087 E. Gardenia Ave., 48071. Tel: 248-542-8720; Fax: 248-542-8721.
Catechesis/Religious Program—Mrs. Sue Gordon, D.R.E. Students 106.

MARINE CITY, ST. CLAIR CO.
1—HOLY CROSS, [CEM] Merged with St. Catherine of Alexandria, Algonac & St. Mark, Harsens Island to form Our Lady on the River, Marine City.
2—OUR LADY ON THE RIVER Revs. James F. Lopez; Matthew Ellis; Sr. Mary Ann Ankoyiak, C.S.J., Pastoral Assoc.
610 S. Water St., 48039-1557. Tel: 810-765-3568; Fax: 810-765-2974. Web: www.ourladyontheriver.net.
School—(Grades PreK-8), 618 S. Water St., 48039. Tel: 810-765-3591; Fax: 810-765-9074. Amanda Lund, Prin. Lay Teachers 8; Students 87.
Catechesis/Religious Program—Mrs. Margie Smith, D.R.E. Students 310.

MARYSVILLE, ST. CLAIR CO., ST. CHRISTOPHER Rev. Arthur R. Baranowski.
Res.: 1000 Michigan Ave., 48040. Tel: 810-364-4100; Fax: 810-364-5947.
Catechesis/Religious Program—Tel: 810-364-7080. Theresa Doyle, D.R.E. Students 221.

MAYBEE, MONROE CO., ST. JOSEPH, [CEM] Revs. Robert A. Bauer, Admin.; Richard Luberti, C.Ss.R.
Res.: 9207 Joseph St., Box 125, 48159. Tel: 734-587-8835; Fax: 734-587-3490.
Convent—9147 Joseph St., Box 118, 48159. Tel: 734-587-8785.
Catechesis/Religious Program—Patricia Eisenhauer, D.R.E. Students 90.

MELVINDALE, WAYNE CO.
1—ST. CONRAD, Merged into St. Mary Magdalen, Melvindale.
2—ST. MARY MAGDALEN Rev. Jeffrey J. Anifer.
Res.: 19624 Wood St., 48122. Tel: 313-381-8566; Fax: 313-381-1319.
Catechesis/Religious Program—Tel: 313-381-8566, Ext. 104. Cheryl Reynolds, D.R.E. Students 99.

MEMPHIS, MACOMB CO.
1—ALL SAINTS, Merged with St. Philip Neri, Columbus & Holy Rosary Mission, Smiths Creek to form Holy Family, Memphis.
2—HOLY FAMILY Rev. Joseph R. Horn. In Res., Rev. Erwin J. Bauer (Retired).
Church: 79780 Main St., 48041. Tel: 810-392-2056; Fax: 810-392-2043.
Catechesis/Religious Program—Susan Finley, D.R.E. Students 323.

MILFORD, OAKLAND CO., ST. MARY, OUR LADY OF THE SNOWS, [CEM] Rev. Ronald Anderson; Valerie Thompson, Pastoral Assoc.
Res.: 1955 E. Commerce, 48381. Tel: 248-685-1482; Fax: 248-684-5642.
Catechesis/Religious Program—Tel: 248-685-2702. Anita Daroczy, D.R.E. Students 1,041.

MONROE, MONROE CO.
1—ST. ANNE Revs. William F. Fisher, O.S.F.S.; Robert C. Mossett, O.S.F.S.
Res.: 2420 N. Dixie Hwy., 48162. Tel: 734-289-2910; Fax: 734-289-1098.
Catechesis/Religious Program—Barbara Rumschlag, D.R.E.
2—ST. JOHN THE BAPTIST Rev. Jack Quinlan.
Res.: 511 S. Monroe St. S., 48161. Tel: 734-241-8910; Fax: 734-241-1943.
School—Tel: 734-241-1670; Fax: 734-241-8782. Cheryl Tibai, Prin. Lay Teachers 10; Students 225.
Catechesis/Religious Program—Monica Pope, D.R.E. Students 15.
3—ST. JOSEPH, [JC] Rev. William F. Fisher, O.S.F.S.
Res.: 924 E. Second St., 48161. Tel: 734-241-9590; Fax: 734-241-5296.
Catechesis/Religious Program—Mrs. Joan Allor, D.R.E. Students 125.
4—ST. MARY, [JC] Rev. Marc A. Gawronski. In Res., Rev. Robert K. Singelyn (Retired).
Res.: 127 N. Monroe St., 48162. Tel: 734-241-1644; Fax: 734-241-3077.
School—151 N. Monroe St., 48162. Tel: 734-241-3377; Fax: 734-241-0497. Mrs. Melody M. Curtis, Prin. Lay Teachers 11; Students 195.
Catechesis/Religious Program—Tel: 734-241-6097. Lorie Bronson, D.R.E. Students 163.
5—ST. MICHAEL, [JC] Rev. Stephen L. Vileo; Sr. Dorothy Jayne Krupp, Pastoral Assoc.
Res.: 502 W. Front St., 48161. Tel: 734-241-8645; Fax: 734-241-6132.
School—510 W. Front St., 48161. Tel: 734-241-3923; Fax: 734-241-7314. Karen Pilon, Prin. Lay Teachers 10; Students 169.
Catechesis/Religious Program—Tel: 734-241-8663. Mrs. Kathleen Dubay, D.R.E. Students 117.

MOUNT CLEMENS, MACOMB CO., ST. PETER, [CEM] Rev. Michael N. Cooney; Sheila Roy, Pastoral Min.; Moira Shaum, Admin.
Admin. Bldg.—110 New St., 48043. Tel: 586-468-4578; Fax: 586-468-3199. Web: www.saintpeterchurch.us.
School—St. Mary, 105 Market St., 48043. Tel: 586-468-4570; Fax: 586-468-6454. Tina Forsythe, Prin. Lay Teachers 26; Students 511.
Catechesis/Religious Program—Judy Coll, D.R.E. Students 590.

NEW BALTIMORE, MACOMB CO., ST. MARY QUEEN OF CREATION, [CEM] Rev. Nicholas Zukowski; Sue Ann Lugo, Parish Nurse Coord.; Deacon Anthony Lewandoski, (Retired).
Res.: 51041 Maria St., 48047. Tel: 586-725-2441; Fax: 586-725-3647.
Catechesis/Religious Program—36254 Main, 48047. Tel: 586-725-7579. Carolyn Bissett, D.R.E. Students 959.

NEW BOSTON, WAYNE CO., ST. STEPHEN, [CEM] Rev. John P. Hedges; Deacon Kenneth Trabbic.
Res.: 18858 Huron River Dr., 48164-9272. Tel: 734-753-5268; Fax: 734-753-5828.
School—Tel: 734-753-4175. Sr. M. Thaddea, C.S.S.F., Prin. Felician Sisters 2; Lay Teachers 9; Students 169.
Convent—Tel: 734-753-9937.
Catechesis/Religious Program—Sr. M. Josepha, D.R.E. Students 140.

NEWPORT, MONROE CO., ST. CHARLES BORROMEO, [CEM] Rev. Frederick Misiolek.
Res.: 8109 Swan Creek Rd., 48166. Tel: 734-586-2531; Fax: 734-586-3900.
School—Tel: 734-586-2531, Ext. 3. Lay Teachers 9; Students 177.
Catechesis/Religious Program—Tel: 734-586-2531, Ext. 4. Gina Baker, D.R.E.; Mrs. Karen Johnson, D.R.E. Students 339.

NORTH BRANCH, LAPEER CO.
1—ST. MARY'S BURNSIDE, [CEM] Rev. Richard L. Treml.
Res.: 5622 Summers Rd., P.O. Box 268, 48461. Tel: 810-688-3648; Fax: 810-688-9068.
Catechesis/Religious Program—Lisa Verellen, D.R.E. Twinned with SS. Peter and Paul, North Branch.

2—SS. PETER AND PAUL, [CEM] Rev. Richard L. Treml.
Res.: 6645 Washington, Box 208, 48461. Tel: 810-688-3797; Fax: 810-688-2969.
Catechesis/Religious Program—Tel: 810-688-8343. Lisa Verellen, D.R.E. Twinned with St. Mary's Burnside, North Branch. Students 181.
Chapel—St. Patrick's Clifford, Lapeer Co.

NORTHVILLE, WAYNE CO.

1—ST. ANDREW KIM KOREAN CATHOLIC CHURCH Rev. Dong Hyuk Jeon.
Res.: 21155 Halsted Rd., 48167. Tel: 248-442-9026; Fax: 248-442-9020.

2—OUR LADY OF VICTORY Rev. Denis B. Theroux; Deacons Donald Quigley; Kenneth Fry; Kathryn Ling, Pastoral Assoc.
Church & Res.: 133 Orchard Dr., 48167. Tel: 248-349-2621; Fax: 248-349-7329.
School—132 Orchard Dr., 48167. Tel: 248-349-3610; Fax: 248-380-7247. Paula Nemeth, Prin. Lay Teachers 26; Students 438.
Catechesis/Religious Program—Tel: 248-349-2559. Mary Ellen Skene, Dir. Faith Formation. Students 469.

NOVI, OAKLAND CO.

1—HOLY FAMILY Revs. Timothy D. Hogan; Peter Mendes, S.A.C.; Deacons William L. Waldmann; Timothy Pilon; Robert Ervin.
Res.: 41445 Fawn Tr., 48375. Tel: 248-349-8847; Fax: 248-349-3711.
Catechesis/Religious Program—Tel: 248-349-8837. Maria Koncius, Pastoral Min. Students 902.

2—ST. JAMES Rev. George Charnley.
Church: 46325 Ten Mile Road, 48374-3007. Tel: 248-347-7778; Fax: 248-347-9625.
Catechesis/Religious Program—Sylvia Shorter, D.R.E. Students 875.

OAK PARK, OAKLAND CO., OUR LADY OF FATIMA Rev. Paul F. Chateau. In Res., Rev. John T. Nowlan (Retired).
Res.: 13500 Oak Park Blvd., 48237. Tel: 248-545-2310; Fax: 248-545-2312.
Catechesis/Religious Program—Natalie LaCroix, D.R.E. Students 60.

ORCHARD LAKE, OAKLAND CO., OUR LADY OF REFUGE Rev. Gerald A. McEnhill.
Parish Office: 3725 Erie Dr., 48324.
Res.: 3663 Erie Dr., 48324. Tel: 248-682-0933.
School—3750 Commerce Rd., 48324. Tel: 248-682-3422; Fax: 248-683-2265. Sally Chaney, Prin. Lay Teachers 32; Students 250.
Catechesis/Religious Program—Tel: 248-682-6381. Marianne Gdowski, C.R.E. Students 280.

ORION TOWNSHIP, OAKLAND CO., CHRIST THE REDEEMER Rev. Joseph E. Dailey.
Res.: 2700 Waldon Rd., Lake Orion, 48360. Tel: 248-391-1621; Fax: 248-391-3412.
Catechesis/Religious Program—Tel: 248-391-4074. Nancy Clancy, D.R.E. Students 953.

ORTONVILLE, OAKLAND CO., ST. ANNE Rev. Gerard Frawley, S.A.C.
Res.: 825 S. Ortonville Rd., 48462. Tel: 248-627-3965; Fax: 248-627-5153.
Catechesis/Religious Program—Gloria Boesch, D.R.E. Students 287.

PLYMOUTH, WAYNE CO.

1—ST. KENNETH Rev. Thomas A. Belczak.
Res.: 14951 N. Haggerty Rd., 48170. Tel: 734-420-0288; Fax: 734-420-2921. Web: www.stkenneth.org.
Catechesis/Religious Program—Tel: 734-420-3031. Mrs. Gretchen Hennen, D.R.E. Students 604.

2—OUR LADY OF GOOD COUNSEL Revs. John Riccardo; Lee E. Acervo; Charles White IV; Deacons Timothy Sullivan; Donald Leach, Pastoral Assoc.; Vincent Small. In Res., Rev. Stanislaw Obloj.
Office: 1062 Penniman Ave., 48170.
Res.: 1160 Penniman Ave., 48170. Tel: 734-453-0326; Fax: 734-416-9257.
School—1151 William St., 48170. Tel: 734-453-3053; Fax: 734-357-5331. Kay Reilly, Prin. Lay Teachers 30; Students 626.
Catechesis/Religious Program—Mary DelPup, D.R.E. Students 870.

PONTIAC, OAKLAND CO.

1—ST. DAMIEN OF MOLOKAI PARISH (2009) [CEM] Revs. James F. Kean; John J. O'Keefe; Deacon Brian S. White.
Rectory—46408 Woodward Ave., 48342. Tel: 248-332-0283; Fax: 248-332-7041.
Catechesis/Religious Program—Ms. Maria Charria, D.R.E. Students 599.

2—ST. JOSEPH, Merged with St. Vincent de Paul, Pontiac & St. Michael, Pontiac, to form St. Damien of Molokai, Pontiac.

3—ST. MICHAEL, Merged with St. Vincent de Paul, Pontiac & St. Joseph, Pontiac to form St. Damien of Molokai, Pontiac.

4—ST. VINCENT DE PAUL, Merged with St. Michael, Pontiac & St. Joseph, Pontiac to form St. Damien of Molokai, Pontiac.

PORT HURON, ST. CLAIR CO.

1—HOLY TRINITY, [CEM] Rev. Brian K. Cokonougher. 325 32nd St., 48060. Tel: 810-984-2689; Fax: 810-984-8559.
Catechesis/Religious Program—Karen Clor, D.R.E. Students 190.
Mission—Our Lady of Guadalupe Mission 3110 Goulden St., St. Clair Co. 48060. Tel: 810-985-5212; Fax: 810-985-5314.

2—ST. JOSEPH, [JC] Merged with St. Stephen, Port Huron & Our Lady of Guadalupe Mission, Port Huron to form Holy Trinity, Port Huron.

3—ST. MARY Rev. Zbigniew Zomerfeld, Admin.
Res.: 1505 Ballentine St., 48060. Tel: 810-982-7906; Fax: 810-987-8255.
School—Mrs. Deborah A. Krueger, Prin. Lay Teachers 10; Students 174.
Catechesis/Religious Program—Patricia Isaacson, D.R.E. Students 219.

4—OUR LADY OF GUADALUPE MISSION, Merged with St. Joseph, Port Huron & St. Stephen, Port Huron to form Holy Trinity, Port Huron.

5—ST. STEPHEN, Merged with St. Joseph, Port Huron & Our Lady of Guadalupe Mission, Port Huron to form Holy Trinity, Port Huron.

RAY TOWNSHIP, MACOMB CO.

1—ST. FRANCIS OF ASSISI, Merged with St. Maximilian Kolbe, Macomb Township to form St. Francis of Assisi-St. Maximilian Kolbe, Ray Township.

2—ST. FRANCIS OF ASSISI-ST. MAXIMILIAN KOLBE Rev. Christopher Talbot.
Res.: 23965 23 Mile Rd., Macomb, 48042. Tel: 586-598-3314; Fax: 586-598-3346.
Church: 62811 New Haven Rd., Ray Twp., 48096. Tel: 586-749-9584; Fax: 586-749-6021.
Catechesis/Religious Program—Jane Van Belle, D.R.E. Students 330.

REDFORD, WAYNE CO.

1—ST. AGATHA, Closed. For inquiries for parish records contact the chancery.

2—ST. HILARY Rev. Donald L. Walker, Admin. (Retired); Sr. Marie Miller, I.H.M.
Res.: 23901 Elmira, 48239. Tel: 313-533-1560; Fax: 313-533-1735.
Catechesis/Religious Program—Christin Laing, D.R.E. Students 10.

3—ST. JOHN BOSCO Rev. Richard A. Osebold.
Res.: 12100 Beech-Daly Rd., 48239. Tel: 313-937-9690; Fax: 313-937-2927.
Catechesis/Religious Program—Sr. Helen Gazarek, D.R.E. Students 25.

4—OUR LADY OF LORETTO Rev. Ralph Besterwitch, S.A.C.; Sr. Margretta Wojcik, O.S.F., Pastoral Assoc.
Res.: 17116 Olympia Ave., 48240. Tel: 313-534-9000; Fax: 313-534-6744.
Catechesis/Religious Program—Tel: 313-532-3707. Donna Kohn, D.R.E. Students 65.

5—ST. ROBERT BELLARMINE Rev. Richard M. Leliaert; Liela Abass, Pastoral Assoc.
Res.: 27101 W. Chicago, 48239. Tel: 313-937-1500; Fax: 313-937-1185. Web: www.strobertbellarmine.com.
School—27201 W. Chicago, 48239. Tel: 313-937-1655; Fax: 313-937-9795. Nancy Kuszczak, Prin. Lay Teachers 10; Students 174; Preschool 27.
Catechesis/Religious Program—Tel: 313-937-1531. Mrs. Dawn Dwyer, Faith Formation Coord. Students 90.

6—ST. VALENTINE Rev. Paul Coutinha, S.A.C.; Deacon Lawrence Toth.
Res.: 25881 Dow, 48239. Tel: 313-532-4394; Fax: 313-537-2237.
School—(Grades PreK-8), 25875 Hope St., 48239. Tel: 313-533-7149; Fax: 313-533-3060. Rachel Damuth, Prin. Lay Teachers 15; Students 193.
Catechesis/Religious Program—Tel: 313-538-9161. Stephanie Toth, D.R.E. Students 120.

RICHMOND, MACOMB CO., ST. AUGUSTINE, [CEM] Revs. Joseph A. Plawecki; John Nedumcheril.
Church: 68035 Main St., 48062. Tel: 586-727-5215; Fax: 586-727-3760. Email: stjosepherie@yahoo.com.
Res.: 36341 Franklin St., 48062. Tel: 586-727-6469.
School—67901 Howard, 48062. Tel: 586-727-9365. Mr. Gerald Bagierek, Prin. Lay Teachers 18; Students 183.
Catechesis/Religious Program—Tel: 586-727-9290. Students 161.

RIVER ROUGE, WAYNE CO., OUR LADY OF LOURDES Rev. James F. Wieging; Dr. Paul D. Bodrie, Pastoral Assoc.
Res.: 1440 Coolidge Highway, 48218. Tel: 313-842-3320; 313-842-3321; Fax: 313-842-4507.
Catechesis/Religious Program—Pamela Gori, D.R.E. Students 40.

RIVERVIEW, WAYNE CO., ST. CYPRIAN Rev. William J. Promesso.
Res.: 13249 Pennsylvania, 48193. Tel: 734-283-1366; Fax: 734-283-2809.
Catechesis/Religious Program—Tel: 734-283-2239. Mrs. Stacey Sutowski-Shurtz, D.R.E. Students 230.

ROCHESTER, OAKLAND CO., ST. ANDREW Rev. Thomas F. Slowinski; Sr. Rebecca Hodge, O.P., Pastoral Assoc.
Res.: 1400 Inglewood, 48307. Tel: 248-651-7486; Fax: 248-651-3950.
Catechesis/Religious Program—Tel: 248-651-6401; Fax: 248-651-2844. Students 1,574.

ROCHESTER HILLS, OAKLAND CO.

1—ST. IRENAEUS Rev. A. Frank Pollie.
Res.: 771 Old Perch Rd., 48309. Tel: 248-651-9595; Fax: 248-651-1504.
Catechesis/Religious Program—Tel: 248-651-2443; Fax: 248-651-8767. Patricia Egan-Myers, D.R.E. Students 408.

2—ST. MARY OF THE HILLS Rev. Stanley A. Ulman.
Res.: 971 Briston Dr., 48307. Tel: 248-853-5390; Fax: 248-853-7989.
2675 John R., 48307-4652.
Catechesis/Religious Program—Tel: 248-844-8662. Peggy Casing, D.R.E. Students 493.

3—ST. PAUL ALBANIAN CATHOLIC COMMUNITY Rev. Anton Kcira, Admin.
Office: 525 Auburn Rd., 48307. Tel: 248-844-8201; Fax: 248-844-8092.
Catechesis/Religious Program—Franz Grishaj, D.R.E.

ROCKWOOD, WAYNE CO., ST. MARY, [CEM] Rev. James R. Rafferty.
Res.: 32477 Church, 48173. Tel: 734-379-9248; Fax: 734-379-6548.
School—Tel: 734-379-9285; Fax: 734-379-9088. Kevin DuFresne, Prin. Lay Teachers 10; Students 168.
Catechesis/Religious Program—Laurel Nadeau, Catechism Coord.

ROMEO, MACOMB CO., ST. CLEMENT OF ROME Revs. Stephen C. Reckker; John Ortman.
Res.: 343 S. Main St., 48065. Tel: 586-752-9611; Fax: 586-752-1601.
Catechesis/Religious Program—Tel: 586-752-6951; Fax: 586-752-7093. Deborah Knoblock, D.R.E. Students 783.

ROMULUS, WAYNE CO., ST. ALOYSIUS Rev. John M. Currin.
Res.: 37200 Neville St., 48174. Tel: 734-941-5056; Fax: 734-941-6018.
Catechesis/Religious Program—Roseann Farnstrom, D.R.E. Students 50.

ROSEVILLE, MACOMB CO.

1—ST. ANGELA Rev. Andrew Czarnecki. In Res., Rev. Dennis J. Nowinski; Deacon Lee Smith.
Res.: 25001 Chippendale, 48066.
Church: Ten Mile Rd. and Chippendale, 48066. Tel: 586-445-6360; Fax: 586-445-6366.
Catechesis/Religious Program—Tel: 586-775-4650. Angela Laesch, D.R.E.; Alyssa Ouellette, Youth Min. Students 14.

2—ST. ATHANASIUS Rev. Ronald J. Victor; Deacon Michael O'Keefe.
Res.: 18720 Thirteen Mile Rd., 48066. Tel: 586-772-1170; Fax: 586-776-2945.
Catechesis/Religious Program—Carol Buboi, D.R.E. Students 187.

3—ST. DONALD Rev. Michael A. Donovan.
Res.: 16330 Twelve Mile Rd., 48066. Tel: 586-773-3440; Fax: 586-773-1235.
Catechesis/Religious Program—

4—HOLY INNOCENTS-ST. BARNABAS Rev. Robert Schuster.
Res. & Mailing Address: 26100 Ridgemont, 48066. Tel: 586-777-7543; Fax: 586-777-1536.
Catechesis/Religious Program—24800 Phlox, Eastpointe, 48021. Tel: 586-775-4650; Fax: 586-775-6933. Angela Laesch, D.R.E. Students 213.

5—HOLY INNOCENTS, Merged with St. Barnabas, Eastpointe to form Holy Innocents-St. Barnabas, Roseville.

6—SACRED HEART Rev. Eugene Katcher; Deacons Lawrence Sullivan; Paul Lippard.
Res.: 18430 Utica Rd., 48066. Tel: 586-777-9116; Fax: 586-777-7958.
Catechesis/Religious Program—Tel: 810-777-8150; Fax: 586-777-3288. Paula Davis, D.R.E. Students 78.

ROYAL OAK, OAKLAND CO.

1—ST. DENNIS Rev. John P. Christ, O.S.C.; Deacon Francis X. Chau Ngoc Doan.
Res.: 2200 E. 12 Mile Rd., 48067-1504. Tel: 248-544-2181; Fax: 248-544-9443.
School—1415 N. Stephenson, 48067-1504. Tel: 248-398-6555; Fax: 248-398-2878. Gregory Pilarski, Prin. Lay Teachers 15; Students 112.
Catechesis/Religious Program—Tel: 248-545-1926. Christine Wagberg, D.R.E. Students 128.

2—ST. MARY, [CEM] Rev. Steven A. Wertanen.
Res.: 730 Lafayette Ave. S., 48067. Tel: 248-547-1818; Fax: 248-547-4577.
School—628 Lafayette Ave. S., 48067. Tel: 248-545-2140; Fax: 248-545-2303. Greg Carnacchi, Prin. Lay Teachers 10; Part-Time Teachers 7; Students 147.
Catechesis/Religious Program—Tel: 248-547-1810.

Ms. Bridget Nemzek, D.R.E. Students 110.
3—NATIONAL SHRINE OF THE LITTLE FLOWER Rev. Msgr. William H. Easton; Revs. Pawel Kaczmarczyk; Krzysztof Nowak; Joseph Lang; Deacon Thomas Avery.
Res. & Church: 2100 W. 12 Mile Rd., 48073-3973. Tel: 248-541-4122 (Office); Fax: 248-541-2838.
School—1621 Linwood, 48067. Tel: 248-541-4622; Fax: 248-541-6969. Sharon Dixon, Prin.; Kelly Neighbors, Asst. Prin. Lay Teachers 30; Students 556.
School—Academy, 3500 W. Thirteen Mile Rd., 48073. Tel: 248-549-2928; Fax: 248-546-2953. Ms. Gabrielle Erken, Prin. Lay Teachers 10; Students 151.
High School—Tel: 248-549-2925. Lay Teachers 26; Students 276.
Catechesis/Religious Program—Tel: 248-541-5133. Students 451.
ST. CLAIR, ST. CLAIR CO., ST. MARY, [CEM] Rev. Gregory J. Deters.
Res.: 415 N. 6th St., 48079. Tel: 810-329-2255; Fax: 810-329-5997.
School—Tel: 810-329-4150; Fax: 810-329-5705. Mr. Gary Tomlin, Prin. Lay Teachers 10; Students 157.
Catechesis/Religious Program—Tel: 810-329-7801. Mrs. Mary Beth Blum, D.R.E. Students 382.
Community Center—811 Orchard St., 48079. Tel: 810-329-2400.
ST. CLAIR SHORES, MACOMB CO.
1—ST. GERMAINE, Merged with St. Gertrude, St. Clair Shores to form Our Lady of Hope, St. Clair Shores.
2—ST. GERTRUDE, [CEM] Merged with St. Germaine, St. Clair Shores to form Our Lady of Hope, St. Clair Shores.
3—ST. ISAAC JOGUES Rev. Timothy P. Mazur.
Parish Center—21120 Benjamin Dr., 48081. Tel: 586-778-5100; Fax: 586-778-4458.
School—Tel: 586-771-3525; Fax: 586-778-8183. Patricia Domagala, Prin. Lay Teachers 23; Students 340.
Catechesis/Religious Program—Jean Hartman, Faith Formation. Students 276.
4—ST. JOAN OF ARC Rev. Msgr. G. Michael Bugarin; Sr. Carol Juhasz, I.H.M., Pastoral Min. & Coord.
Parish Center—22412 Overlake, 48080. Tel: 586-777-3670; Fax: 586-774-5528.
School—22415 Overlake, 48080. Tel: 586-777-8370; Fax: 586-447-3574. Mr. Don Ancypa, Prin. Lay Teachers 32; Students 525.
Catechesis/Religious Program—Tel: 586-772-1282. Suzanne Cornelius, D.R.E. Students 450.
5—ST. LUCY Rev. James E. Commyn; Deacon Robert Herta. In Res., Rev. Michael Loyson.
Res.: 23401 Jefferson, 48080. Tel: 586-771-8300; Fax: 586-447-4220.
Catechesis/Religious Program—Tel: 586-447-4223. Mrs. Maureen Ortwein, D.R.E. Students 72.
6—ST. MARGARET OF SCOTLAND Rev. Ronald DeHondt; Deacon Ronald Channell.
Church: 21201 Thirteen Mile Rd., 48082. Tel: 586-293-2240; Fax: 586-293-0116.
Res.: 21101 Thirteen Mile Rd., Saint Clair Shores, 48082. Tel: 586-296-3190.
Catechesis/Religious Program—Tel: 586-293-3280. Students 336.
7—OUR LADY OF HOPE Rev. James L. Bjorum, Admin.; Deacon Terrance E. Downey, Pastoral Assoc.
Office: 28301 Little Mack, 48081. Tel: 586-771-1750; Fax: 586-771-7634.
School—Tel: 586-771-0890. Mrs. Julie DeGrez, Prin. Lay Teachers 13; Students 257.
Catechesis/Religious Program—28839 Jefferson, Saint Clair Shores, 48081. Kathleen Thompson, D.R.E. Students 285.
SHELBY TWP.
1—ST. JOHN VIANNEY CHURCH Rev. Jerome J. Machlik; Fritzi Bohlmann, Pastoral Assoc.; Barbara Bakotich, Youth Min.
Res.: 54045 Schoenherr Rd., 48315. Tel: 586-781-6525; Fax: 586-781-6527.
Catechesis/Religious Program—Tel: 586-781-2627. Mary Lundgaard, D.R.E. Students 1,901.
2—ST. KIERAN Rev. H. Thomas Johnson; Patricia Radacsy, Pastoral Assoc.
Res.: 53600 Mound Rd., 48316. Tel: 586-781-4901; Fax: 586-781-6516.
Catechesis/Religious Program—Tel: 586-781-6515. Students 1,110.
3—ST. THERESE OF LISIEUX Revs. Andrew J. Tomasko; Jaroslaw Pilus; Deacon Donald Sandstrom.
Church: 48115 Schoenherr Rd., 48315-4225. Tel: 586-254-4433; Fax: 586-254-5463.
Catechesis/Religious Program—Students 1,075.
SOUTH LYON, OAKLAND CO., ST. JOSEPH Rev. Kenneth M. Chase; Deacon Chris Booms.
Church: 830 S. Lafayette, 48178. Tel: 248-446-8700; Fax: 248-446-8746. Email: office@saintjosephsouthlyon.com. Web: www.saintjosephsouthlyon.com.
Res.: 810 S. Lafayette St., 48178.
Catechesis/Religious Program—Tel: 248-446-8728. Laura Quinn Rector, D.R.E. Students 1,164.
SOUTHFIELD, OAKLAND CO.
1—ST. BEATRICE, Merged with St. Bede, Southfield, St. Ives, Southfield & St. Michael, Southfield to form Church of the Transfiguration, Southfield.
2—ST. BEDE, Merged with St. Beatrice, Southfield, St. Ives, Southfield & St. Michael, Southfield to form Church of the Transfiguration, Southfield.
3—CHURCH OF THE TRANSFIGURATION Rev. William Ollendick, O.F.M.; Deacon John Liddle.
25225 Code Rd., 48034-5807. Tel: 248-356-8787; Fax: 248-356-1240.
Catechesis/Religious Program—Laurie Spano-Rinehart, D.R.E. Students 58.
4—DIVINE PROVIDENCE, (Lithuanian), Rev. Gintaras Jonikas.
Res.: 25335 W. 9 Mile Rd., 48033-3933. Tel: 248-354-3429; Fax: 248-354-1773.
5—ST. IVES, Merged with St. Beatrice, Southfield, St. Bede, Southfield & St. Michael, Southfield to form Church of the Transfiguration, Southfield.
6—ST. MICHAEL, Merged with St. Beatrice, Southfield, St. Bede, Southfield & St. Ives, Southfield to form Church of the Transfiguration, Southfield.
7—OUR LADY OF ALBANIANS Rev. Nue Gjergji, Admin. 29350 Lahser Rd., 48034. Tel: 248-353-3410; Fax: 248-353-5412.
Catechesis/Religious Program—Dr. Gjecka Gjelaj, D.R.E. Students 125.
SOUTHGATE, WAYNE CO.
1—ST. HUGH, Merged into St. Francis Cabrini Parish, Allen Park.
2—ST. PIUS X Rev. Robert J. McCabe.
Office: 14101 Superior Ave., 48195. Tel: 734-285-1100; Fax: 734-285-5310.
Res.: 14160 Longtin Ave., 48195.
School—14141 Pearl St., 48195. Tel: 734-284-6500; Fax: 734-285-6525. Michelle E. Seward, Elementary Prin. Lay Teachers 11; Students 262.
Catechesis/Religious Program—Philippa Monteleon, D.R.E. Students 150.
STERLING HEIGHTS, MACOMB CO.
1—ST. BLASE Rev. Randall Phillips; Dr. Mary Dumm, Pastoral Assoc.
Res.: 12151 E. 15 Mile Rd., 48312-5120. Tel: 586-268-2244; Fax: 586-268-1174.
Catechesis/Religious Program—Students 409.
2—SS. CYRIL AND METHODIUS Revs. Benjamin Kosnac (Slovakia), Admin.; Libor Marek; Deacons Gerald Smigell; James Gennette.
Res.: 41233 Ryan Rd., 48314. Tel: 586-726-6911; Fax: 586-685-1070.
Catechesis/Religious Program—Paul Schuller, D.R.E.; Carroll Schuller, D.R.E. Students 310.
3—ST. EPHREM Rev. Ronald Milligan; Deacon Edwin McLeod.
Res.: 38900 Dodge Rd., 48312. Tel: 586-264-1230; Fax: 586-264-2757.
Catechesis/Religious Program—Tel: 586-264-2777; Fax: 586-264-2783. Students 126.
4—ST. JANE FRANCES DE CHANTAL Rev. Jerome Slowinski.
Res.: 38750 Ryan Rd., 48310. Tel: 586-977-8080; Fax: 586-977-9305.
Catechesis/Religious Program—Tel: 586-977-0310. Students 227.
5—ST. MALACHY Rev. Joseph J. Gembala.
Res.: 14115 14 Mile Rd., 48312-6506. Tel: 586-264-1220; Fax: 586-264-1656.
Catechesis/Religious Program—Tel: 586-268-4430. Ms. Patricia Whelan, D.R.E. Students 368.
6—ST. MATTHIAS Rev. Francisco Restrepo.
Res.: 12509 Nineteen Mile Rd., 48313. Tel: 586-731-1300; Fax: 586-731-2576.
Catechesis/Religious Program—Tel: 586-731-0650. Donna Latimer, D.R.E. Students 252.
7—ST. MICHAEL Revs. Michael W. Quaine; Artemio Galos; Deacon Lawrence Healy.
Church: 40501 Hayes Rd., 48313. Tel: 586-247-0020; Fax: 586-247-4081.
Res.: 39443 Heatherheath, Clinton Twp., 48038. Tel: 313-268-6379.
Catechesis/Religious Program—Tel: 586-247-0098. Cathy McInerney, D.R.E. Students 534.
8—OUR LADY OF CZESTOCHOWA Revs. Slawomir Murawka, S.Ch.; Robert Bedzinski, S.Ch.; Witalij Guz, S.Ch. In Res., Revs. Konrad Urbanowski, S.Ch.; Stanislaw Drzal, S.Ch.
Res.: 3100 18 Mile Rd., 48314-3810. Tel: 586-977-7267; Fax: 586-977-2074. Web: www.olcsh.org.
Catechesis/Religious Program—Sr. Jadwiga Kokolus, D.R.E. Students 355.
9—ST. RENE GOUPIL Rev. Steven C. Koehler; Deacon David Fleming.
Res.: 35955 Ryan Rd., 48310. Tel: 586-939-7500; Fax: 586-939-7839. Email: mmay@strene.org.
Catechesis/Religious Program—Tel: 586-939-7688. Michael Novak, D.R.E. Students 190.
TAYLOR, WAYNE CO.
1—ST. ALFRED Rev. Maurice Henry Sands; Deacon Gerard McGowan. In Res., Rev. Godfrey Nana Andoh.
Res.: 9500 Banner, 48180. Tel: 313-291-6464; Fax: 313-291-2733.
School—9540 Telegraph Rd., 48180. Tel: 313-291-0247. Ann Tonissen, Prin. Lay Teachers 12; Students 165.
Catechesis/Religious Program—Tel: 313-291-3210; Fax: 313-291-2162. Karen Kerr, D.R.E.; Stephen Siemion, Music Min. Students 223.
2—ST. CONSTANCE Rev. Leo F. Sabourin; Deacon Joseph Mouro.
Res.: 21555 Kinyon Rd., 48180. Tel: 313-291-4050; Fax: 313-291-5655.
Catechesis/Religious Program—Bernadine Shook, D.R.E. Students 176.
3—ST. CYRIL OF JERUSALEM, Merged with St. Paschal, Taylor to form Our Lady of the Angels, Taylor.
4—OUR LADY OF THE ANGELS Rev. Dariusz Strzalkowski; Deacons Daniel J. Hurley; William A. Thome.
Church: 6442 Pelham Rd., 48180. Tel: 313-381-3000; Fax: 313-381-5528.
Catechesis/Religious Program—Michael Grube, D.R.E. Students 160.
5—ST. PASCHAL, Merged with St. Cyril of Jerusalem, Taylor to form Our Lady of the Angels, Taylor.
TEMPERANCE, MONROE CO.
1—ST. ANTHONY, [CEM] Rev. Brian K. Hurley.
Res.: 4605 St. Anthony Rd., 48182. Tel: 734-854-1143; Fax: 734-854-4622.
School—4609 St. Anthony Rd., 48182. Tel: 734-854-1160. Fran Sweet, Prin. Sisters of St. Francis 1; Lay Teachers 4; Students 34.
Catechesis/Religious Program—Students 103.
Convent—4607 St. Anthony Rd., 48182. Tel: 734-854-2779.
2—OUR LADY OF MT. CARMEL Rev. Stephen Rooney; Christine Zaums, Pastoral Assoc.
Res.: 8330 Lewis Ave., 48182. Tel: 734-847-2805; Fax: 734-847-8970.
Catechesis/Religious Program—Tel: 734-847-1725. Students 459.
TRENTON, WAYNE CO.
1—ST. JOSEPH, [JC] Rev. Bradley Forintos; Donald Scott Anastasia, Pastoral Assoc.
Parish Center—2565 Third St., 48183. Tel: 734-676-9082; Fax: 734-676-6255.
School—2675 Third St., 48183. Tel: 734-676-2565; Fax: 734-676-9744. Wanda Rovenskie, Prin. Lay Teachers 10; Students 213.
Catechesis/Religious Program—Tel: 734-676-7115; Fax: 734-676-9082. Thomas J. Clark, D.R.E. Students 319.
2—ST. TIMOTHY Rev. Robert J. Shafer.
Parish Office—2901 Manning Dr., 48183. Tel: 734-676-5115; Fax: 734-676-6863.
Catechesis/Religious Program—Tel: 734-676-5616. Dennae Petrlich, D.R.E.; Theresa Kramer, D.R.E. Students 75.
TROY, OAKLAND CO.
1—ST. ALAN Rev. Donald L. Demmer, Admin.; Sr. Mary Choiniere, S.S.J., Pastoral Assoc.
Church: 3077 Glouchester, 48084. Tel: 248-649-5510; Fax: 248-649-6729.
Res.: 2345 Coolidge Rd., 48084. Tel: 248-649-5511.
Catechesis/Religious Program—Betty Sheehan, D.R.E. Students 78.
2—ST. ANASTASIA Revs. John J. Mech; Mark P. Prill; Deacon Ronald W. Cook, Pastoral Assoc.
Res.: 4571 John R. Rd., 48085. Tel: 248-689-8380; Fax: 248-689-7489.
Catechesis/Religious Program—Patty Chase, D.R.E. Students 885.
3—ST. ELIZABETH ANN SETON Rev. Ronald J. Jozwiak.
Church: 280 E. Square Lake Rd., 48085. Tel: 248-879-1310; Fax: 248-879-2886.
Res.: 301 Tara, 48085.
Catechesis/Religious Program—Tel: 248-879-1314. Students 204.
4—ST. LUCY, (Croatian), Rev. Jozo Cuic, O.F.M.
Res.: 200 E. Wattles Rd., 48085. Tel: 248-619-9910; Fax: 248-619-9912. Email: stlucy@sbcglobal.net.
5—ST. THOMAS MORE Rev. Edward A. Belczak; Deacon John Vanneste.
Res.: 4580 Adams Rd., 48098. Tel: 248-647-2222; Fax: 248-647-8192.
Catechesis/Religious Program—Tel: 248-647-4680. Students 734.
UTICA, MACOMB CO., ST. LAWRENCE Revs. Robert J. Fisher; Philip Ching; Sr. Janet Sullivan, I.H.M., Pastoral Assoc.
Church: 44633 Utica Rd., 48317. Tel: 586-731-7347; Fax: 586-731-5393.
Res.: 44657 Utica Rd., 48317. Tel: 586-731-5347; Fax: 586-731-5393.
School—44429 Utica Rd., 48317. Tel: 586-731-0135. Christine Lee, Prin. Lay Teachers 33; Students

692.
Catechesis / Religious Program—Tel: 586-731-5072. Mary Paonessa, D.R.E. Students 731.

WALLED LAKE, OAKLAND CO., ST. WILLIAM Rev. Michael G. Savickas; Deacon Michael Somervell.
Res.: 531 Common St., 48390-3417. Tel: 248-624-1421; Fax: 248-624-5273.
School—135 O'Flaherty, 48390. Tel: 248-669-4440; Fax: 248-669-2245. Linda Jackson, Prin. Lay Teachers 17; Students 192.
Catechesis / Religious Program—Tel: 248-624-1371. Jeanne Martin, D.R.E. Students 407.

WARREN, MACOMB CO.
1—ST. ANNE Revs. Alberto P. Bondy; Koshy Chirakkarottu.
Res.: 32000 Mound Rd., 48092. Tel: 586-264-0713; Fax: 586-264-0718.
School—Tel: 586-264-2911; Fax: 586-264-4533. Anthony Sahadi, Prin. Lay Teachers 23; Students 525.
Catechesis / Religious Program—Students 180.
2—ASCENSION, Merged into St. Clement, Center Line.
3—ST. CLETUS Rev. Sidney J. Eckert, Admin.
Office: 26256 Ryan Rd., 48091. Tel: 586-755-1313; Fax: 586-393-6623.
Res.: 26262 Ryan Rd., 48091.
Catechesis / Religious Program—Peggy DeClercq, D.R.E. Students 80.
4—ST. DOROTHY, Merged with St. Leonard of Port Maurice, Warren to form St. Teresa of Avila, Warren.
5—ST. EDMUND Rev. Robert J. Witkowski.
Res.: 14025 Twelve Mile Rd., 48088. Tel: 586-772-2720; Fax: 586-772-5576.
Catechesis / Religious Program—Tel: 586-773-9220; Fax: 586-772-5021. Students 204.
6—ST. LEONARD OF PORT MAURICE, [CEM] Merged with St. Dorothy, Warren to form St. Teresa of Avila, Warren.
7—ST. LOUISE Rev. Msgr. Thomas G. Rice; Deacons Wilhelm Kessler; Art Majewski.
Res.: 2500 Twelve Mile Rd., 48092. Tel: 586-751-3340; Fax: 586-751-0603.
Catechesis / Religious Program—Tel: 586-751-3486. Peggy DeClercq, D.R.E. Students 169.
8—ST. MARK Rev. Robert A. Ruedisueli; Deacon George R. Posavetz.
Res.: 4401 Bart, 48091. Tel: 586-759-3020; Fax: 586-759-3024.
Catechesis / Religious Program—Students 100.
9—ST. MARTIN DE PORRES Rev. Roman Pasieczny.
Res.: 31555 Hoover Rd., 48093. Tel: 586-264-7515; Fax: 586-264-4013.
Catechesis / Religious Program—Tel: 586-264-7970. Mrs. Christine Cabe, D.R.E. Students 369.
10—ST. SYLVESTER Rev. Gary Schulte; Deacon John L. Skladanowski, Pastoral Assoc.
Res.: 11200 Twelve Mile Rd., 48093. Tel: 586-751-3636; Fax: 586-751-1766.
Catechesis / Religious Program—Tel: 586-751-3510; Fax: 586-751-3512. Students 178.
11—ST. TERESA OF AVILA Revs. Michael R. Gawlowski; Thomas Puzio.
12255 Frazho Rd., 48089-1200. Tel: 586-757-3306; Fax: 586-754-3152.
Catechesis / Religious Program—Alice Baron, D.R.E. Students 62.

WASHINGTON, MACOMB CO., SS. JOHN AND PAUL Rev. David A. Buersmeyer; Deacon John Wright.
Church: 7777 W. 28 Mile Rd., 48094. Tel: 586-781-9010; Fax: 586-781-7061.
Res.: 61847 Glenwood Trail, 48094.
Catechesis / Religious Program—Tel: 586-781-9488. Students 290.

WATERFORD, OAKLAND CO.
1—ST. BENEDICT Rev. H. Thomas Kuehnemund.
Parish Office—80 S. Lynn, 48328. Tel: 248-681-1534; Fax: 248-681-4501.
Catechesis / Religious Program—Students 140.
2—OUR LADY OF THE LAKES Revs. Lawrence Delonnay; Don A. LaCuesta.
Mailing Address: 5481 Dixie Hwy., 48329. Tel: 248-623-0274; Fax: 248-623-2723.
School—5501 Dixie Hwy., 48329. Tel: 248-623-0250; Fax: 248-623-2274. Lauri Hoffman, Elementary Prin. Lay Teachers 22; Students 356.
High School—5495 Dixie Hwy., 48329. Tel: 248-623-0340; Fax: 248-623-7536. Carl Uberti, Pres. Sisters 1; Lay Teachers 14; Students 174.
Catechesis / Religious Program—Tel: 248-623-0291; Fax: 248-623-1280. Patricia Bell, D.R.E. Students 325.
3—ST. PERPETUA Rev. Jack H. Baker.
Res.: 134 Airport Rd., 48327. Tel: 248-682-6431; Fax: 248-682-7088.
Catechesis / Religious Program—Pauline Zorza, D.R.E. Students 235.

WAYNE, WAYNE CO., ST. MARY, [CEM] Rev. David G. Burgard.
34530 W. Michigan Ave., 48184-1748. Tel: 734-721-8745; Fax: 734-721-0260. Email: parishoffice@waynestmarys.org. Web: www.waynestmarys.org.
School—34516 Michigan Ave., 48184-1748. Tel: 734-721-1240; Fax: 734-467-7381. Mr. Donald Lipinski, Prin. Lay Teachers 11; Students 244.
Catechesis / Religious Program—Tel: 734-721-8745, Ext. 42. Students 154.

WEST BLOOMFIELD, OAKLAND CO., PRINCE OF PEACE Rev. Msgr. Ricardo E. Bass.
Res.: 4300 Walnut Lake Rd., 48323. Tel: 248-681-9424; Fax: 248-681-5543.
Catechesis / Religious Program—Tel: 248-681-5070. Carol Kania, D.R.E. Students 195.

WESTLAND, WAYNE CO.
1—ST. BERNARDINE Rev. Salvino Briffa.
Res.: 31463 Ann Arbor Tr., 48185. Tel: 734-427-5150; Fax: 734-427-3319.
Catechesis / Religious Program—Tel: 313-261-3050. Judith A. Bedard, D.R.E. (part time). Students 52.
2—CHURCH OF THE DIVINE SAVIOR Rev. Alexander A. Kuras; Deacon Paul F. Pelchat.
Church: 39375 Joy Rd., 48185. Tel: 734-455-3620; Fax: 734-455-7998.
Res.: 9249 Caprice, Plymouth, 48170. Tel: 734-664-1592.
Catechesis / Religious Program—Sr. Gemma Legel, O.S.F., D.R.E. Students 76.
3—ST. DAMIAN Rev. Lawrence Zurawski.
Res.: 30055 Joy Rd., 48185-1728. Tel: 734-421-6130; Fax: 734-513-4916.
School—29891 Joy Rd., 48185. Tel: 734-427-1680; Fax: 734-427-1272. Mary Stempin, Prin. Lay Teachers 10; Students 171.
Catechesis / Religious Program—Tel: 734-522-5383. Students 135.
4—ST. RICHARD Rev. Terence Treppa.
Res.: 35637 Cherry Hill, 48186. Tel: 734-729-2240; Fax: 734-729-3132.
Church Office: 35637 Cherry Hill Rd., 48186. Tel: 734-729-4420.
Catechesis / Religious Program—Tel: 734-729-4411. Judy Gorman, D.R.E. Students 75.
5—SS. SIMON AND JUDE Rev. Gerard V. Bechard.
Office: 32500 Palmer Rd., 48186. Tel: 734-722-1343; Fax: 734-326-5466.
Catechesis / Religious Program—Mary Ann Kocsis, D.R.E.; Margaret Reyez, D.R.E. Students 81.
6—ST. THEODORE OF CANTERBURY Rev. Gary Michalik; Theresa Lisiecki, Dir. Educational Ministry; Kathleen Galoch, Parish Admin.
Res.: 8200 Wayne Rd., 48185. Tel: 734-425-4421; Fax: 734-425-0650.
Catechesis / Religious Program—Tel: 734-425-7310. Students 130.

WHITE LAKE, OAKLAND CO., ST. PATRICK Revs. Thomas L. Meagher; John Peter Arulanandam, M.S.F.S.; Deacon Michael Chesley.
Res.: 9086 Hutchins Rd., 48386. Tel: 248-698-3100; Fax: 248-698-2350.
School—9040 Hutchins Rd., 48386. Tel: 248-698-3240; Fax: 248-698-4339. Carol Budchuk, Prin. Lay Teachers 25; Students 425.
Catechesis / Religious Program—Students 778.

WOODHAVEN, WAYNE CO., OUR LADY OF THE WOODS Rev. Richard Macey.
Res.: 21892 Gudith Rd., 48183. Tel: 734-671-5101; Fax: 734-671-2901.
Catechesis / Religious Program—Tel: 734-671-0525. Jeanette Russell, D.R.E. Students 898.

WYANDOTTE, WAYNE CO.
1—ST. ELIZABETH, [JC] Rev. Charles M. Morris.
Res.: 138 Goodell St., 48192. Tel: 734-284-7727; Fax: 734-284-7891.
Catechesis / Religious Program—Julie Dzanbazoff, D.R.E. Students 33.
2—ST. HELENA, Closed. For inquiries for parish records contact the chancery.
3—ST. JOSEPH Rev. Michael Cremin, S.A.C.
Res.: 353 Elm St., 48192. Tel: 734-285-9840; Fax: 734-285-9745.
School—Wyandotte Catholic Consolidated Elementary, Tel: 734-285-2030; Fax: 734-285-0327. David McCarney, Prin. Lay Teachers 12; Students 114.
Catechesis / Religious Program—Tel: 734-285-6453. Jason Lubaway, D.R.E. Students 180.
4—OUR LADY OF MT. CARMEL, (Polish), [CEM] Rev. Walter J. Ptak; Deacon Richard Bloomfield.
Res.: 976 Pope John Paul II Ave., 48192. Tel: 734-284-9135; Fax: 734-284-1367.
School—2609 Tenth St., 48192. Tel: 734-285-5520; Fax: 734-285-9245. Mr. Timothy Scanlon, Elementary Prin. Felician Sisters 2; Lay Teachers 9; Students 105.
High School—Tel: 734-284-7311; Fax: 734-284-6235. Timothy Scanlan, High School Prin. Lay Teachers 10; Students 70.
Catechesis / Religious Program—Tel: 734-284-6145. Mrs. Karen Cameron, D.R.E. Students 4.
Convent—2609 Tenth St., 48192. Tel: 734-284-7253.
5—ST. PATRICK, [JC] Rev. Charles M. Morris, Admin.
Office: 135 Superior Blvd., 48192. Tel: 734-285-9470; Fax: 734-285-1623. Email: stpatrick1857@gmail.com.
Res.: 105 Superior Blvd., 48192. Tel: 734-285-9472.
School—Wyandotte Catholic Consolidated School, Tel: 734-285-2030; Fax: 734-285-0327. David McCarney, Elementary Prin. Lay Teachers 12; Students 114.
Catechesis / Religious Program—Darlene Fritz, D.R.E. Students 90.
6—ST. STANISLAUS KOSTKA, (Polish), Rev. Walter J. Ptak.
Church & Mailing Address: 266 Antoine St., 48192-3496.
Res.: 976 Pope John Paul Ave., 48192. Tel: 734-285-9509; Fax: 734-285-0124.
Catechesis / Religious Program—Debbie Lesko, C.R.E.; Rod Lesko, C.R.E. Students 56.

YALE, ST. CLAIR CO., SACRED HEART, [CEM] Rev. Paul Czarnota; Deacon William Kolarik.
Res.: 310 N. Main St., P.O. Box 155, 48097-2845. Tel: 810-387-9800; Fax: 810-387-0538.
Catechesis / Religious Program—Melissa Francis, D.R.E. Students 87.
Mission— P.O. Box 479, Brown City, Sanilac Co. 48416. Tel: 810-346-3036; Fax: 810-346-3036. Email: sacredheart@greatlakes.net.

Chaplains of Public Institutions

DETROIT. *Children's Hospital*, Tel: 313-745-5917. Sr. Beverly Hindson, I.H.M.
Cottage Hospital, Tel: 810-785-8855. Vacant. Attended from St. Paul on the Lake Parish, Grosse Pointe Farms, MI
Detroit Osteopathic Hospital, Tel: 313-865-6300. Attended from Cathedral of the Most Blessed Sacrament, Detroit.
Detroit Receiving Hospital 48226. Tel: 313-745-3000. Vacant.
DMC Sinai-Grace Hospital, Tel: 313-966-3300. Vacant.
Harper University Hospital, Tel: 313-745-6000. Vacant.
Henry Ford Hospital, Tel: 800-436-7936. Sr. Ellen Burke, O.S.F.
Hutzel Hospital, Tel: 313-831-3139. Vacant.
John D. Dingell Veterans Administration Medical Center, Tel: 313-576-1000. Rev. Joseph Duc Vu.
St. John Hospital, 22101 Moross Rd., 48236. Tel: 313-343-7850. Rev. Janusz Marzynski, Sr. Jane Dutkiewicz.
Karmanos Cancer Institute, Tel: 800-527-6266. Vacant.
Mound Correctional Facility, 17601 Mound Rd., 48212. Mr. Anthony Latarski.
Ryan Correctional Facility, 17600 Ryan Rd., 48212. Mr. Anthony Latarski.
Wayne County Jail, 1231 St. Antoine, 48226. Mr. Anthony Latarski.
Wayne County Juvenile Detention Facility, 1326 St. Antoine, 48226. Ida Johns. Tel: 313-237-6056.

DEARBORN. *Oakwood Hospital*, Tel: 313-593-7000. Rev. Luke Iwuji.

FARMINGTON HILLS. *Botsford Hospital*, Tel: 248-471-8000. Rev. Paschal Igwe.

GARDEN CITY. *Garden City Hospital*, Tel: 734-421-3300. Rev. Bernard Pilarski.

GROSSE POINTE. *Beaumont Hospital*, Tel: 313-343-1000. Rev. Richard Bartoszek.

LAPEER. *Lapeer County Jail*, 3231 John Conley Dr., 48446. Mr. Anthony Latarski.
Thumb Correctional Facility, 3225 John Conley Dr., 48446. Mr. Anthony Latarski.

MONROE. *Monroe County (juveniles), HCCS, Moreau Center*, 3500 Comboni Way, 48162. Ida Johns. Tel: 313-237-6056. (fka Boysville)
Monroe County Jail, 100 E. Second St., 48161. Mr. Anthony Latarski.

MOUNT CLEMENS. *Macomb County Jail*, 43565 Elizabeth Rd., 48043. Tel: 586-307-9326. Jo Kudela.
Macomb County Juvenile Justice Center, 400 N. Rose Rd., 48043. Ida Johns. Tel: 313-237-6056. Attended from St. Peter's, Mount Clemens.
Mount Clemens General Hospital, Tel: 586-493-8500. Vacant.

NEW HAVEN. *Macomb Correctional Facility*, 26 Mile Rd, 48048. Mr. Anthony Latarski.

PONTIAC. *St. Clair County Jail*, 1170 Michigan Rd., Port Huron, 48060. Mr. Anthony Latarski.
Doctors' Hospital of Michigan, 461 W. Huron, 48341. Tel: 248-857-7200. Vacant.
Oakland County Children's Village, 1200 N. Telegraph Rd., 48341. Tel: 313-237-6056. Ida Johns, Coord. of Min. to Youth in Detention, Carleen Ward, Chap. Tel: 248-858-1183.
Oakland County Jail, 1201 N. Telegraph, 48341. Tel: 248-338-9310; Fax: 248-338-2695. Sr. Margaret Devaney.

Pontiac Osteopathic Hospital, Tel: 248-338-5000. Vacant.

PORT HURON. *St. Clair County Juvenile Intervention Center*, 1170 Michigan, 48060. Tel: 313-237-6056. Ida Johns, Coord. of Min to Youth in Detention, Kevin Totty, Chap. Tel: 810-966-4106.

Port Huron Hospital, Tel: 810-985-7750. Attended from Holy Trinity Parish, Port Huron.

PLYMOUTH. *Robert Scott Correctional Facility*, 47500 Five Mile Rd., 48170. Mr. Anthony Latarski.

ROCHESTER. *Crittendon Hospital*, Tel: 248-652-5000. Rev. Joy Chakian.

ROYAL OAK. *Beaumont Hospital*, Tel: 248-898-5000. Rev. Christopher Welsh.

TRENTON. *Oakwood Southshore Medical Center*, Tel: 734-671-7779. Beverly Beltramo.

TROY. *Beaumont Hospital*, Tel: 248-964-5000. Rev. Joy Chakian.

WARREN. *Henry Ford Macomb Hospital*, Tel: 586-759-7300. Rev. Luke Krotkiewicz.

WAYNE. *Oakwood Annapolis Hospital*, Tel: 734-467-4000. Rev. Bernard Pilarski.

WHITE LAKE. *Camp White Lake*, 8110 E. White Lake, 48386. Mr. Anthony Latarski.

WYANDOTTE. *Henry Ford Wyandotte Hospital*, Tel: 734-246-6000. Rev. Gary Morelli, Karen Gorski.

YALE. *Yale Community Hospital*, Tel: 810-387-2998. Attended from Sacred Heart Parish, Yale, MI.

Special Assignment:
Rev. Msgr.—
Bugarin, G. Michael, Archbishop's Delegate to the Archdiocesan Review Board
Revs.—
Babcock, Timothy F., Coord. Acculturation Services & Coord. Mentors
Banazak, Gregory, Faculty SS. Cyril and Methodius Seminary
Cassidy, Richard, Faculty, S.H.M.S.
Fabian, John V., Companions of Christ the Lamb, Paradise
Jones, Daniel J., Faculty, S.H.M.S.
Kiselica, John J., Faculty St. Mary's Preparatory
Lumpkin, Thomas
Lunnon, William
Ventline, Lawrence M.

Graduate Studies:
Revs.—
Battersby, Gerard, Pontifical University of St. Thomas Aquinas, Rome
Laboe, Timothy A., Pontifical North American College, Rome
Urban, Thomas E., Pontifical North American College, Rome

On Duty Outside the Archdiocese:
Rev. Msgr.—
Sable, Robert M., Prelate Auditor of the Roman Rota, Vatican
Revs.—
Ballien, Paul K., St. Ignatius Parish, Cayman Islands
Blanchette, Melvin, S.S., Rector, Theological College at CUA
Browne, Ronald T., J.C.L., Moderator of the Curia, Diocese of Marquette.
Walsh, Jerome, Faculty Univ. of Dallas, TX

Military Chaplains:
Rev.—
Kaul, John L., U.S. Naval Reserves

Absent on Leave:
Revs.—
Bloomfield, Andrew
Brady, Reginald
Brewczynski, Jacek M.
Fraser, Bernard
Hogan, Richard
Kaucheck, Kenneth R., J.C.D.
Knapp, Roger A.
Mistor, Todd C.
Prince, Michael J.
Stochmal, Marek
Sylvester, Sean

Absent on Sick Leave:
Revs.—
Nowinski, Dennis J.
Obloj, Stanislaw
Redwanski, Dale H., O.S.C.
Siroskey, Paul Larry

Retired:
Rev. Msgrs.—
Baldwin, Edward J., Sacred Heart Major Seminary, 2701 Chicago Blvd., 48206.
Browne, George T., 165 S. Water St., Apt. 204, Marine City, 48039.
DeCneudt, Ferdinand, American House East II, 18750 Thirteen Mile Rd., Apt. C108, Roseville, 48066-1378.
Edyk, Eugene, 45000 Geddes Rd., Canton, 48188.
Flanigan, Gerald A., 14469 Levan Rd., Apt. B, Livonia, 48154-5094.
Harrity, Dennis, 1401 S. 33rd Ave., Hollywood, FL 33021.
Humitz, Robert S., 6160 Brockway, Commerce Township, 48382.
Milewski, Stanley E., SS. Cyril & Methodius Seminary, 3535 Indian Trail, Orchard Lake, 48324.
Monticello, Robert V., 14469 Levan Rd., Apt. C, Livonia, 48154-5094.
Schweder, John F., 900 N. 70th Ave., Hollywood, FL 33024.
Villerot, Thomas H., 14453 Levan Rd., Apt. A, Livonia, 48154-5090.
Ziemba, Walter J., SS. Cyril & Methodius Seminary, 3535 Indian Trail, Orchard Lake, 48324.
Revs.—
Alder, Ronald J., St. Francis Cabrini Parish, 9000 Laurence, Allen Park, 48101-1598.
Babonas, Alphonse, 22525 Fairway Dr., Southfield, 48033.
Bauer, Erwin J., St. Philip Neri Rectory, 9735 Dolan Rd., Columbus, 48063-1105.
Blaska, John A., 875 W. Avon Rd., Apt. 128 C., Rochester Hills, 48307-2757.
Bodde, Frederick A., 6116 River Rd., East China, 48054-4731.
Bonnici, William C., 2189 Cat Lake Hills, Mayville, 48744.
Brock, David F., 41464 White Tail Ln., Canton, 48188-2073.
Broderick, Leo P., 407 S. Parkway, Algonac, 48001.
Byrne, Thomas R., St. Constance Parish, 21555 Kinyon, Taylor, 48180-3798.
Canavan, John D., 11395 Oakwood Dr., Jerome, 49249-9516.
Child, John F., Sacred Heart Parish, 22430 Michigan Ave., Dearborn, 48124.
Chmura, Julian, 41842 Lindsay Dr., Plymouth, 48170.
Complo, Daniel C., 38 E. Willow, Apt. C, Monroe, 48162-2644.
Cusmano, John C., Deerwood Manor, 1095 W. Hummer Lake Rd., Oxford, 48371.
Cyr, Richard E., 5971 Fordham Dr., Shelby Twp, 48316-2528.
D'Achille, Arnold V., 7518 Hazleton, Dearborn Heights, 48127-1544.
Dacey, Donald, Fairlane Meadows, 5148 Heather Dr., #116, Dearborn, 48126-2884.
Dunn, John F., Lourdes Nursing Home, 2300 Watkins Lake Rd., Waterford, 48328-1439.
Esper, Thomas, 164 Shoreline Dr. E., Port Sanilac, 48469.
Fares, Lawrence T., 31980 Mark Adam Lange, Warren, 48093.
Flynn, Thomas P., 22034 Sunnyside, St. Clair Shores, 48080.
Forish, Andrew J., Marywood Nursing Care Center, 36975 W. Five Mile Rd., Livonia, 48154.
Gagala, John, J.C.L., 22750 Ten Mile Rd., Southfield, 48033.
Gagnon, Joseph A., 1000 St. Joseph Ln., Marysville, 48040-1596.
Gattari, Valentine A., 15894 Nineteen Mile Rd., Clinton Twp, 48038.
Grandpre, Louis, 555 Brush St. #3108, 48226.
Hall, John F., Sacred Heart Major Seminary, 2701 Chicago Blvd., 48206.
Hayes, James L., Marywood Nursing Care Center, 36975 W. Five Mile Rd., Livonia, 48154-1871.
Higdon, C. Paul, 4170 24th Ave., Apt. 127, Fort Gratiot, 48059.
Hoffmaster, Harry E., 2500 River Rd., Apt. 41, Marysville, 48040-1949.
Jackson, Lawrence J., 24348 Eastwood Village Ct., Apt. 106, Clinton Twp., 48035.
Jacobi, Arthur, 49726 Alpine Dr., Apt. 147, Macomb, 48044-6125.
Jagielski, James J.
Janiga, Joseph, 873 W. Avon Rd., Rochester Hills, 48307-2705.
Kaiser, Lawrence H., 14465 Levan Rd., Apt. B., Livonia, 48154-5092.
Kirwan, Thomas P., 2450 Watkins Lake Rd., Waterford, 48328.
Klettner, Frederick J., 2208 Bowman Rd., Franklin, TN 37064.
Konopka, Edward F., 7950 N. McNab, Bldg. 10, Apt. 210, Tamarac, FL 33321-8436.
Kosicki, Bohdan W., 5630 Klettner, St. Clair, 48079-1918.
Kowalczyk, Sigismund C., 879 N. Channel Dr., Harsens Island, 48028.
Kowalski, George, 12765 Walnut St., Southgate, 48195.
Kuntz, Donald B., 9245 North River Rd., Algonac, 48001-4007.
Kurzawa, Ronald, 38694 L'Anse Creuse, Harrison Township, 48045.
LaCasse, John P., IHM Motherhouse, 610 W. Elm Ave., Monroe, 48162-7909.
Lombardi, Albert U., Marywood Nursing Care Center, 36975 W. Five Mile Rd., Livonia, 48154.
Maciejewski, Norbert F.
MacLennan, Donald B., 30105 Avenida Alvera, Cathedral City, CA 92234-2869.
Mayworm, James A., 48726 Alpine Dr., Macomb, 48044-6125.
McGoldrick, William J., St. John's Senior Community, 18300 E. Warren, #211, Gross Pointe, 48224.
Meyer, James, 4600 Woodward Ave., Ste. 308, 48201-1894.
Mikus, Elemir, 90863 Oreske 5, Skalica, Slovakia.
Mitchell, Edward J., 14467 Levan Rd., Apt. C, Livonia, 48154-5093.
Muir, Edmund D., 14465 Levan Rd., Apt. C, Livonia, 48154.
Murphy, Daniel J., 14455 Levan Rd., Apt A, Livonia, 48154-5091.
Murphy, William J., 14455 Levan Rd., Apt. D, Livonia, 48154-5091.
Nitoski, Gerald A., St. Benedict Parish, 60 Church St., Highland Park, 48203-2893.
Nowlan, John T., Our Lady of Fatima Parish, 13500 Oak Park Blvd., Oak Park, 48237-2099.
O'Brien, Kevin P., 14465 Levan Rd., Apt. D, Livonia, 48154-5092.
O'Dea, Loren F., Our Lady of Sorrows Parish, 23815 Power, Farmington, 48336-2461.
O'Hagan, James P., 2450 Watkins Lake Rd., #317, Waterford, 48328.
O'Leary, James J., American House East I, 17255 Common Rd., Apt. 126C, Roseville, 48066.
O'Sullivan, Daniel, 3941 Crooks Rd., Troy, 48084.
Page, Leon J., 12109 Avondale, Warren, 48089-3922.
Partensky, Leonard J., 6737 N. Wayne Rd., Apt. 105B, Westland, 48185-7055.
Petron, William G., 15745 Charleston Dr., Clinton Township, 48038-1016.
Phalen, John L., 9314 Top Flight Dr., Lakeland, FL 33810.
Profota, James H., 34594 Maple Ln., Sterling Heights, 48312-5213.
Prus, Edward J., St. James Parish, 241 Pearson, Ferndale, 48220-1896.
Rakoczy, Richard S., 999 Stratton Dr., Waterford, 48328.
Reckinger, Robert A., 14455 Levan Rd., Apt. C, Livonia, 48154-5091.
Reyesmedina, Carlos, Our Lady of Mt. Thabor Monastery, 1295 Bald Eagle Lake, Ortonville, 48462-9096.
Ritter, Edward, 5325 Pointe Dr., East China, 48054.
Romano, Joseph L., 14453 Levan Rd., Apt. B, Livonia, 48154-5090.
Ruskowski, Clifford F., 8200 E. Jefferson, Apt. 409, 48214.
Russell, Robert, S.S., Casa de Nuestra Senora Dolorosa/Chuburna de Hidalgo, Calle 31 No. 78, Chuburna de Hidalgo, Merida 97200 Mexico.
Rutkowski, George A., 15171 Granada Plaza, Warren, 48088.
Ryder, Joseph F., 3015 Moon Lake Dr., West Bloomfield, 48323-1844.
Samonie, Jacob, 36975 W. Five Mile Rd., Livonia, 48154.
Sayers, Raymond J., 408 Fox Hills Dr., Apt. 2, Bloomfield Hills, 48304-1346.
Sayes, Ronald E., Andover Heights, 8401 Eighteen Mile Rd., #217, Sterling Heights, 48313-3064.
Scheick, James C., 14469 Levan Rd., Apt. D, Livonia, 48154-5094.
Scheuerman, Edward L., 14453 Levan Rd., Apt. D, Livonia, 48154-5090.
Schmidberger, Richard, 4171 Fourth St., P.O. Box 535, Brown City, 48416.
Siebert, William P., 16041 Vergi Ct., Clinton Township, 48038.
Sinatra, William D., 43225 Polo Cir., Apt. 3, Sterling Heights, 48313-2064.
Singelyn, Robert K., St. Mary Parish, 127 N. Monroe St., Monroe, 48162-2686.
Skalski, Francis S., Sunrise of Northville, 16100 N. Haggerty, Plymouth, 48170.
Slominski, Fabian B., 5405 Christi Dr., Warren, 48091-4196.
Stanievich, J. Walter, Marquette House, 36000 Campus Dr., #423, Westland, 48185.
Strain, Eugene R., 320 Elm, Rochester, 48307.
Sullivan, John J., St. Frances Cabrini Parish, 9000 Laurence, Allen Park, 48101-1598.
Sutherland, Thomas J., 49230 Arlington Ct., Shelby Township, 48315-3903.

Szarek, Mitchell, SS. Peter & Paul Parish (Westside), 7685 Grandville Ave., 48228.
Taube, Sylvester, 9008A Bissonette, Oscoda, 48750.
Tierney, Gary M., J.C.L., 5568 N. Adams Way, Bloomfield Hills, 48302-4000.
Trent, James F., 2487 Bluejay Bluff Ln., Green Valley, AZ 85614.
Villerot, Henry E., American House East I, 17255 Common Rd., Apt. B-200, Roseville, 48066-1954.
Walker, Donald L., 26900 Van Buren, Dearborn Heights, 48127.
Weingartz, Francis A., 19737 Colman, Clinton Township, 48035.
Welsh, Richard C., 26560 Burg Rd., Bldg. B, Apt. 324, Warren, 48089-3503.
Wojcicki, Wojciech, 14453 Levan Rd., Apt. C, Livonia, 48154-5090.
Wojtewicz, Eugene E., 14467 Levan Rd., Apt. D, Livonia, 48154-5093.
Worthy, Donald L., St. Philomena Parish, 4281 Marseilles, 48224.
Wurm, Robert L., 66 Lakeshore Ln., Grosse Pointe Shores, 48236.
Wytrwal, Alexander J., Henry Ford Village, 15101 Ford Rd., #208, Dearborn, 48126.
Xuereb, Paul D., 17825 Fifteen Mile Rd., Clinton Twp., 48035.
Zielinski, Francis A., 2477 Yordy Rd., Mio, 48647.

Permanent Deacons:
Abler, Donald, Senior Status
Avery, Stanley, St. Theresa of Avila, Warren
Avery, Thomas, National Shrine of the Little Flower, Royal Oak
Ball, John H., Senior Status
Barbera, John, St. Louis, Clinton Twp.
Barthel, Michael, St. Joan of Arc; St. Clair Shores
Baughman, Jene, St. Fabian, Farmington Hills
Berch, James, St. Isaac Jogues, St. Clair Shores
Bloomfield, Richard, Our Lady of Mt. Carmel, Wyandotte
Booms, Chris, St. Joseph, South Lyon
Bousamra, Thomas, (Unassigned)
Bovitz, Robert, Senior Status
Breen, Kevin, St. Genevieve, Livonia
Brown, Oscar, St. Hugo of the Hills, Bloomfield Hills
Bruen, Patrick T., Senior Status
Burke, John, St. Theodore of Canterbury, Westland
Burrell, Frederick, St. Raphael, Garden City
Busch, Robert F., Senior Status
Bussa, Stephen, Senior Status
Buyle, Valere, St. Hubert, Harrison Twp.
Campernel, Jerome, St. John Vianney, Shelby Twp.
Carroll, Brian, Our Lady of La Salette, Berkley
Carter, Thomas, St. Paul of Tarsus, Clinton Twp.
Channell, Ronald, St. Margaret of Scotland, St. Clair Shores
Chesley, Michael, St. Patrick, White Lake
Conlen, Patrick, St. John Neumann, Canton; St. Paul of the Cross Retreat House, Detroit
Conlin, Richard R., Senior Status
Connors, John J., Holy Trinity, Port Huron
Cook, Ronald W., St. Anastasia, Troy
Cornell, Peter, St. Anthony, Belleville; St. Paul of the Cross Retreat Center, Detroit
Cousino, George, St. Joseph, Maybee; St. Patrick, Carleton
Cousino, Wesley, Senior Status
Cox, Donald J., St. Cornelius, Dryden
Cummins, Michael H., St. Ambrose, Grosse Pointe Park
D'Argis, Leo, Senior Status
Damaske, Richard, Senior Status
Darga, Daniel M., Our Lady of La Salette, Berkley
Delbeke, Robert G., Senior Status
DeShaw, Gerald, Senior Status
Desjarlais, Eugene B., Senior Status
DeWitt, Robert, Our Lady of Grace, Dearborn Heights
Doan, Francis X. Chau Ngoc, St. Dennis, Royal Oak
Donnelly, Thomas, (Unassigned)
Downey, Terrance E., Our Lady of Hope, St. Clair Shores
Dreyer, Charles R., St. William, Walled Lake
Ervin, Robert, Holy Family, Novi
Fairbanks, Andrew, St. Vincent Ferrer, Madison Heights
Feliciano, Raul, Senior Status
Fitzgerald, Robert C., St. Priscilla, Livonia
Fleming, David, St. Rene Goupil, Sterling Hts.
Fleming, Michael J., St. Damian of Molokai, Pontiac
Flores, Luis A., St. Frances Cabrini, Allen Park
Formanczyk, Gregory, St. Elizabeth Ann Seton, Troy
Fosmire, Charles, Senior Status
Friend, Harry, (On Duty in Diocese of Gaylord, MI)
Fry, Kenneth, Our Lady of Victory, Northville
Gabel, Raymond, St. Albert the Great, Dearborn Heights
Gajda, Robert, St. Perpetua, Waterford
Gardner, Jack Jr., St. Robert Bellarmine, Redford
Gemellaro, Marc, St. Andrew, Rochester
Gennette, James, SS. Cyril & Methodius, Sterling Heights
Gergosian, Edward, (Unassigned)
Girard, Lawrence, Senior Status
Godfryd, Kurt, St. Clement of Rome, Romeo
Goetz, Robert, (Unassigned)
Gonos, Daniel, St. Regis, Bloomfield Hills
Goodhue, Harold, (Unassigned)
Grenda, Ronald, St. Gerald, Farmington
Gwozdz, Alan, Holy Family, Memphis
Healy, Lawrence, St. Michael, Sterling Heights
Hensel, James L., Senior Status
Herta, Robert, St. Lucy, St. Clair Shores
Hoffer, Franz, St. Ronald, Clinton Twp.
Hogrebe, Alfons, Senior Status
Hulan, Richard, Senior Status
Hulway, Joseph A., Sacred Heart, Imlay City
Hurley, Daniel J., Our Lady of the Angels, Taylor
Igoe, James, St. Richard, Westland
Ingels, Michael M., St. Mary, Monroe
Iskra, Joseph, SS. Augustine & Monica, Detroit
Jablonowski, Alexander, St. John Fisher University Chapel, Auburn Hills
Jackson, Douglas, St. Cecilia, Detroit
Jamieson, William E., Our Lady Star of the Sea, Grosse Pointe Woods
Jimenez, Rafael, St. Hedwig, Detroit
Johnson, Charles, Senior Status
Jones, Alex, Jr., St. Mary of Redford, Detroit; St. Suzanne/Our Lady Gate of Heaven, Detroit; St. Thomas Aquinas, Detroit
Junak, Donald C., St. Louis, Clinton Twp.
Jurewicz, Marion, St. Martin de Porres, Warren
Karle, Joseph, III, Sacred Heart, Auburn Hills
Kendzierski, Anthony, St. Isidore, Macomb
Kessler, Wilhelm, St. Louise, Warren
Kibit, Henry J., St. Albert the Great, Dearborn Hills
Kolarik, William, Our Lady of Mt. Carmel, Emmett
Kowalski, Eugene, St. Mary of the Hills, Rochester Hills
Krueger, Gary R., Senior Status
Krzeminski, Eugene, (On Duty at Diocese of Las Vegas, NV)
Kucharek, Zigment, St. Dunstan, Garden City
Kunik, Raymond L., (On Duty at Diocese of Lansing, MI)
LaForest, Scott, St. Joseph, Dearborn; St. Martha, Dearborn
Lalone, Norman, Senior Status
Lang, Michael, Sr., Holy Innocents & St. Barnabas, Roseville
Leach, Donald, Resurrection, Canton
Lennon, Joseph, St. Clare of Assisi, Farmington Hills
Lewandoski, Anthony, Senior Status
Liddle, John, Church of the Transfiguration, Southfield
Lippard, Paul, Sacred Heart, Roseville
Loffreda, Dennis, St. Francis of Assisi-St. Maximilian Kolbe, Ray
Majkowski, Arthur, St. Louise, Warren
Malloy, John, Jr., St. Roch, Flat Rock
Marks, Stephen, St. Daniel, Clarkston
Marku, John, Senior Status
McGowan, Gerard, St. Alfred, Taylor
McIntyre, Ronald L., Senior Status
McKale, Michael J., Holy Name, Birmingham; Assoc. Dir. for Deacons
McLeod, Edwin, St. Ephrem, Sterling Heights
McLeod, Robert E., Senior Status
Meahan, William, (Unassigned)
Meerschaert, Gary, (Unassigned)
Melenyk, Glenn, St. James, Novi
Misiak, Richard, St. Edith, Livonia
Mitchell, Steven, St. Joseph, Lake Orion
Modes, Robert, St. John Bosco, Redford
Morad, Alfred J., Senior Status
Morello, Steven, (Unassigned)
Morici, Anthony, St. Lawrence, Utica
Motowski, Norbert, All Saints, Detroit; SS. Andrew & Benedict, Detroit
Mouro, Joseph, Senior Status
Mueller, Paul, Corpus Christi, Detroit
Murphy, Thomas P., Our Lady of the Woods, Woodhaven
Nelson, Joseph, (Unassigned)
Noon, Archie J., Senior Status
Nowicki, Kenneth, Immaculate Conception, Ira Twp.
O'Donnell, C. Roger, Divine Child, Dearborn
O'Keefe, Michael, St. Athanasius, Roseville
Otto, William, St. Joseph, South Lyon
Ovies, Robert, Senior Status
Pardo, Gary, St. Colette, Livonia
Parent, John, St. Columban, Birmingham
Pelchat, Paul F., Senior Status
Pilon, Timothy, Holy Family, Novi
Piro, Rudolph P., Senior Status
Posavetz, George R., Senior Status
Quigley, Donald, Our Lady of Victory, Northville
Redwine, Mark, Our Lady of the Woods, Woodhaven
Riopelle, Ernest, Senior Status
Rivera, Rafael, Senior Status
Rodriguez, Brigido, Senior Status
Rohlman, Ronald E., St. Joseph Mercy Hospital, Pontiac; Our Lady Queen of Martyrs, Beverly Hills
Root, Joseph, (Retired)
Rowland, Robert, St. Clement, Dearborn
Ruehlen, Lawrence, St. Isaac Jogues; St. Clair Shores
Sanders, Hubert, Presentation/Our Lady of Victory, Detroit
Sandstrom, Donald, St. Therese of Lisieux, Shelby Twp.
Santeramo, John, St. Joseph, Lake Orion
Schiffer, Gerald, St. Linus, Dearborn Hts.
Schlesser, Peter, (Unassigned)
Schmitz, William, St. Mary Queen of Creation, New Baltimore
Schulte, John, Our Lady of the Lakes, Waterford
Schwartz, Robert, St. Jane Frances de Chantal, Sterling Heights
Shubik, Richard, St. Paul, Grosse Pointe Farms
Skladanowski, John L., St. Sylvester, Warren
Skubick, Charles G., Senior Status
Small, Vincent, Our Lady of Good Counsel, Plymouth
Smigell, Gerald, SS. Cyril & Methodius, Sterling Heights
Smith, Lee, St. Angela, Roseville
Smith, Michael T., St. Hugo of the Hills, Bloomfield Hills
Smith, Richard T., (On Duty at Diocese of Phoenix, AZ)
Sobolewski, Don, (On Duty in Diocese of Lansing, MI)
Somervell, Michael, St. William, Walled Lake
Sorensen, Eric, St. Clement, Center Line
Springer, Mark, St. Alexander, Farmington Hills
Stankiewicz, Clement, Our Lady of Sorrows, Farmington; St. Paul of the Cross Retreat Center, Detroit
Stevens, Paul, St. Ladislaus, Hamtramck; Transfiguration/Our Lady Help of Christians, Detroit
Stewart, Michael, St. John the Baptist, Monroe
Stimpson, Bill, Sweetest Heart of Mary, Detroit
Strzyzewski, Marvin, Senior Status
Sullivan, Lawrence, Sacred Heart, Roseville
Sullivan, Timothy, Our Lady of Good Counsel, Plymouth
Swartz, Edward, St. Teresa of Avila, Warren
Szwarc, John, Christ the Good Shepherd, Lincoln Park
Talbot, Stephen, St. Matthias, Sterling Hts.
Thibodeau, James, St. Sebastian, Dearborn Hts.
Thomas, Thomas, St. Clement, Center Line; St. Teresa of Avila, Warren
Thome, William A., Our Lady of the Angels, Taylor
Thompson, John, St. Basil, Eastpointe
Tombler, Eugene, Guardian Angels, Clawson
Toth, Lawrence, St. Valentine, Redford
Trabbic, Kenneth, St. Stephen, New Boston
Tremmel, Robert, Sacred Heart, Grosse Ile
Urbiel, Joseph, Christ the King, Detroit
Vader, Ronald, Our Lady of Loretto, Redford
Valade, Ronald, St. Irenaeus, Rochester Hills
Van Brook, Arthur, Holy Spirit, Highland
Vanneste, John, St. Thomas More, Troy
Vasquez, Jesus, Senior Status
Von Ende, Michael, Prince of Peace, West Bloomfield
Waldmann, William L., Senior Status
Wallace, John, (Unassigned)
Ward, James, St. Thomas A'Becket, Canton
Weiss, Kenneth, St. Mary Mystical Rose, Armada
White, Brian S., St. Damian of Molokai, Pontiac
Wilder, James, Assumption Grotto, Detroit
Wilson, Edward C., Jr., St. Paul of Tarsus, Clinton Township
Wright, John, SS. John & Paul, Washington Twp.
Yezak, Thomas, Senior Status

INSTITUTIONS LOCATED IN THE DIOCESE

[A] SEMINARIES, ARCHDIOCESAN

DETROIT. *Sacred Heart Major Seminary, Inc.*, 2701 Chicago Blvd., 48206. Tel: 313-883-8500; Fax: 313-868-8685. Email: information@shms.org. Web: www.shms.edu. Rev. Msgr. Jeffrey M. Monforton, Rector & Pres.; Revs. Michael J. Byrnes, Vice

Rector & Dean of Formation; Todd Lajiness, Dean of Studies; Ms. Jane Jeffrey, Asst. Dean; Ms. Astrid Caicedo, Asst. Dean; Ms. Ann Marie Connolly, Dir. Finance & Treas.; Mr. John D. Meldrum, Registrar; Mr. David Kelley, Vice Pres. Devel & External Affairs.

The College of Liberal Arts Revs. Stephen Burr, Dir. Undergraduate Seminarians; Robert Spezia, Spiritual Dir. Undergraduate Seminarians; Sr. Mary Finn, H.V.M., Dir. The Apostolic Experience Prog., Pastoral Formation Dir.; Mr. Christopher Spilker, Dir. Libraries; Dr. Ronald Prowse, Dir. Music.

The School of Theology Revs. Daniel J. Trapp, Spiritual Dir. Grads.; Douglas Bignall, Dir. Graduate Pastoral Formation.

The Institute for Pastoral Ministry Mrs. Janet Diaz, Dean Institute for Ministry. Priests 17; Sisters 2; Lay Faculty 16; Students 424.

ORCHARD LAKE. *SS. Cyril and Methodius Seminary*, 3535 Indian Tr., 48324. Tel: 248-683-0311; Fax: 248-738-6735. Web: www.sscms.edu. Very Rev. Msgr. Charles Kosanke, Rector/Pres.; Sr. Karen Shirilla, S.J., Dir. Lay Ministry Programs; Rev. Msgr. Francis Koper, Dean Pastoral Formation; Rev. Robert Marczewski, Dean of Spiritual Formation; Timothy Bailey, Comptroller; Rev. Miroslaw Krol, Dean of Students; Rev. Msgr. John C. Kasza, Dean of Studies; Ms. Caryn Noel, Librarian; Rev. Timothy Whalen, Chancellor of Orchard Lake Schools. Students 95.

[B] SEMINARIES, RELIGIOUS OR SCHOLASTICATES

BERKLEY. *Loyola House* (Novitiate of the Chicago-Detroit-Wisconsin Provinces of the Society of Jesus), 2599 Harvard Rd., 48072. Tel: 248-399-8132; Fax: 248-399-0910. Revs. Christopher J. Manahan, S.J., Supr.; William L. Verbryke, S.J., Dir. Novices; David G. DeMarco, S.J., Asst. Dir. Novices. Priests 3; Sisters 1; Novices 21.

OXFORD. *St. Benedict Monastery*, 2711 E. Drahner Rd., 48370. Tel: 248-628-2249; Fax: 248-628-0014. Web: www.benedictinemonks.com. Revs. Daniel J. Homan, O.S.B., Conventual Prior & Retreat Dir.; Michael R. Green, O.S.B., Subprior; Damien Gjonaj, O.S.B.; John Martin Shimkus, O.S.B. Headquarters Novitiate House of Sylvestrine Benedictine Monks in the United States. Priests 3; Brothers 7; Chapels 2.

[C] COLLEGES AND UNIVERSITIES

DETROIT. *Marygrove College* (Coed); Incorporated, 8425 W. McNichols Rd., 48221. Tel: 313-927-1200; Fax: 313-927-1345. Email: info@marygrove.edu. Web: www.marygrove.edu. Dr. David J. Fike, Pres.; Ms. Jane Hammang-Buhl, Vice Pres. Academic Affairs; Mr. William Johnson, Vice Pres. Finance & Admin.; Mr. Kenneth Malecke, Vice Pres. Institutional Advancemnet; Ms. JoAnn Cusmano, Vice Pres. Strategic Initiatives; Dr. Darrin Q. Rankin, Vice Pres. Student Affairs & Enrollment Mgmt.; Ms. Gladys Smith, Registrar; Ms. Linnea M. Dudley, Librarian, Head of Reference. Sisters, Servants of the Immaculate Heart of Mary. I.H.M. 5; Lay Staff 165; Students 2,869.

University of Detroit Mercy, McNichols Campus, 4001 W. McNichols Rd. at Livernois, 48221-3038. Tel: 313-993-1000; Fax: 313-993-3317. Web: www.udmercy.edu. Priests 11; Sisters 6; Lay Staff 525; Faculty 290; Total Enrollment 5,725.

Law School, 851 E. Jefferson, 48226. Tel: 313-596-0210; Fax: 313-596-0280. Web: www.law.udmercy.edu.

Dental School, 2700 Martin Luther King Blvd., 48208-2576. Tel: 313-494-6621; Fax: 313-494-6627. Web: www.dental.udmercy.edu. Rev. Gerard L. Stockhausen, S.J., Ph.D., Pres.; Ms. Pamela Zarkowski, Vice Pres. Academic Affairs; Mr. Michael Joseph, Exec. Vice Pres.; Mr. Vincent Abatemarco, Vice Pres. Business & Finance; Mr. Gregory Cascione, Vice Pres. Univ. Advancement; Ms. Denise Williams Mallett, Vice Pres. Enrollment Mgmt. & Student Affairs; Rev. John M. Staudenmaier, S.J., Asst. to the Pres. for Mission & Identity; Ms. Monica Barbour, Sr. Attorney & Sec. to the University.

LIVONIA. *Madonna University*, 36600 Schoolcraft Rd., 48150. Tel: 734-432-5300; 800-852-4951; Fax: 734-432-5393. Web: www.madonna.edu. Sr. Rose Marie Kujawa, C.S.S.F., Pres.; Ms. Andrea R. Nodge, Vice Pres. Univ. Advancement; Dr. Ernest Nolan, Vice Pres. Academic Affairs; Dr. Connie Tingson-Gatuz, Vice Pres. Student Svcs.; Ms. Dina Dubuis, Registrar; Mr. Leonard Wilhelm, Vice Pres. Finance; Mr. Michael Kenney, Vice Pres. Planning & Enrollment Mgmt.; Sr. Serafina Dixon, C.S.S.F., Dir. Information Systems; Mr. Chris Ziegler, Dir. Fin. Aid; Sr. Anita M. Taddonio, C.S.S.F., Interim Dir. Campus Ministry; Ms. Joanne Lumetta, Librarian. Coeducational, resident & non-resident.; Conducted by the Felician Sisters. Priests 6; Sisters 12; Lay Staff 620; Students 4,100.

Madonna Outreach Centers:

Madonna University Orchard Lake Center, 3535 Indian Tr., Orchard Lake, 48324. Tel: 248-683-1757; Fax: 248-683-1756. Email: lmcintyre@madonna.edu. James Novak, Ph.D., Dean, Outreach & Distance Learning. Lay Staff 12; Students 250.

SWEEP Center, 2051 Rosa Parks Blvd., 48216. Tel: 734-432-5733. Lay Staff 2; Students 60.

Macomb University Center, 44575 Garfield Rd., Clinton Township, 48038-1139. Tel: 586-263-6330. Email: lmcintyre@madonna.edu. Linda McIntyre, Coord. Lay Staff 1.

[D] HIGH SCHOOLS, INTER-PAROCHIAL

MADISON HEIGHTS. *Bishop Foley Catholic High School*, 32000 Campbell Rd., 48071. Tel: 248-585-1210; Fax: 248-585-3667. Email: molnar@bishopfoley.org. Web: www.bishopfoley.org. Rev. Gerard LeBoeuf, Pres.; Ms. Joanne Molnar, Prin.; Mr. Gary Rushton, Pres., Bd. of Ed.; Mr. Eric Haley, Dean, Academic Affairs; Ms. Elizabeth Luzenski, Librarian. Priests 1; Lay Teachers 24; Students 360.

Bishop Foley Venture Fund, 32000 Campbell Rd., 48071. Tel: 248-585-1210; Fax: 248-585-3667. Email: fry@bishopfoley.org.

MARINE CITY. *Cardinal Mooney Catholic School*, 660 S. Water St., 48039. Tel: 810-765-8825; Fax: 810-765-7164. Web: www.cardinalmooneycatholic.com. Sr. Karen Lietz, O.P., Prin.; Ms. Mary Patrick, Librarian. Sisters 1; Lay Teachers 16; Students 189.

MONROE. *St. Mary Catholic Central High School* (Coed), 108 W. Elm Ave., 48162. Tel: 734-241-7622; Fax: 734-241-9042. Web: www.smccmonroe.com. Mrs. Jenny Biler, Prin.; Mr. Sean Jorgensen, Pres.; Mr. Jack Giarmo, COO; Mary Steinhauser, Librarian. Lay Teachers 28; Students 423.

PONTIAC. *Notre Dame Preparatory School and Marist Academy* (Consists of three schools), 1300 Giddings Rd., 48340-2108. Tel: 248-373-5300; Fax: 248-373-8024. Email: ndp@ndpma.org. Web: www.ndpma.org. Revs. Leon M. Olszamowski, S.M., Pres.; Joseph C. Hindelang, S.M., Upper School Prin.; James Strasz, S.M.; Brian J. Cidlevich, S.M.; Deacon Anthony Morici; Ms. Sandra J. Favrow, Middle School Prin.; Ms. Diana C. Atkins, Lower School Prin.; Ms. Marna Nemon, Upper & Middle School Librarian; Ms. Suzanne Braverman, Lower School Librarian. Priests 4; Brothers 1; Deacons 1; Sisters 2; Lay Teachers 87; Students 985.

RIVERVIEW. *Gabriel Richard High School*, 15325 Pennsylvania Rd., 48193. Tel: 734-284-1875; Fax: 734-284-9304. Email: admin@grriverview.org. Web: www.grriverview.org. Bro. James Rottenbucher, C.S.C., Prin.; Mrs. Joan Fitzgerald, Asst. Prin. Brothers 1; Lay Teachers 28; Students 410.

ROYAL OAK. *Shrine Catholic High School*, 3500 W. 13 Mile Rd., 48073. Tel: 248-549-2925; Fax: 248-549-2953. Email: erken@shrineschools.com. Web: www.shrineschools.com. Rev. Msgr. William H. Easton, Pres.; Ms. Gabrielle Erken, Prin.; Ms. Barbara Myler, Librarian. Sisters 1; Lay Teachers 30; Students 471.

[E] HIGH SCHOOLS, PRIVATE

DETROIT. *Detroit Cristo Rey High School, Inc.*, 5679 Vernor Highway, 48209. Tel: 313-843-2747; Fax: 313-843-2750. Email: info@detroitcristorey.org. Web: www.detroitcristorey.org. Michael J. Khoury, Pres.; Ms. Susan A. Rowe, Prin.; Mr. Robert S. Quinn, Dir. Devel.; Mr. Bruce A. Brinson, Dir. Admin.; Ms. Pamela A. Kelly Ford, Dir. Admissions; Mr. David K. McIntyre, Dir. CWSP; Mr. Leon Dixon, Dean Students. Priests 1; Sisters 1; Lay Teachers 5; Students 137.

Detroit Cristo Rey High School Corporate Work Study Program, Inc., 5679 W. Vernor Hwy., 48209. Mr. David K. McIntyre, CWSP Dir.; Richard Stacy, CWSP Coord.

Loyola High School, 15325 Pinehurst, 48238-1633. Tel: 313-861-2407; Fax: 313-861-4718. Email: dmastrangelo@loyolahsdetroit.org. Web: www.loyolahsdetroit.org. Revs. David F. Mastrangelo, S.J., Pres.; James E. O'Reilly, S.J., Chap.; Mrs. DeLisa Jones, Prin.; Ms. Carla Barrett, Librarian. Priests 2; Lay Teachers 14; Students 170. In Res. Rev. Justin J. Kelly, S.J.

Loyola Work Experience Program, Inc., 15325 Pinehurst, 48238. Tel: 313-861-3407; Fax: 313-861-4718. Web: www.loyolahsdetroit.org. Rev. David F. Mastrangelo, S.J., Pres.; Mrs. DeLisa Jones, Prin.; Ms. Carla Barrett, Librarian.

University of Detroit Jesuit High School and Academy, (Grades 7-12), 8400 S. Cambridge, 48221. Tel: 313-862-5400; Fax: 313-862-3299. Web: www.uofdjesuit.org. Revs. Karl Kiser, S.J., Pres.; Mark George, S.J.; Patrick F. Peppard, S.J.; Ben Jimenez, S.J.; Brian J. Lehane, S.J., Supr.; James F. Riley, S.J.; Bro. John Moriconi, S.J.; Mr. Ryan Duns, S.J., Jesuit Regent, Seminarian & Theology Teacher; Mr. Gary Marando, Prin.; Mrs. Vondra Abbott, Librarian. Priests 3; Lay Teachers 61; Students 792; Chapels 1.

BLOOMFIELD HILLS. *Academy of the Sacred Heart*, 1250 Kensington Rd., 48304-3029. Tel: 248-646-8900; Fax: 248-646-4143. Web: www.ashmi.org. Sr. Bridget Bearss, R.S.C.J., Headmistress; Ms. Sandra Jeffries, Media Center Coord. Religious of the Sacred Heart. Lay Teachers 25; Students 133.

Brother Rice Endowment Fund (The "Foundation"), 7101 Lahser Rd., 48301-4045. Tel: 248-647-2526; Fax: 248-647-2532. Web: www.brrice.edu. Mr. John Birney, Pres.; Mr. Edward Shaffer, Dir. Advancement & Contact Person; Mr. Mike Tyranski, Bd. Pres.; Mr. Neal Kuehn, Dir. Fin.

Brother Rice High School, 7101 Lahser Rd., 48301-4045. Tel: 248-647-2526; Fax: 248-647-8170. Mr. John Birney, Pres.; Mr. David Kozlowski, Prin.; Ms. Cathy Treboldi, Librarian. Congregation of Christian Brothers. Brothers 3; Sisters 2; Lay Teachers 46; Students 715.

Marian High School for Young Women, 7225 Lahser Rd., 48301. Tel: 248-644-1750; Fax: 248-644-6107. Web: www.marian-hs.org. Sr. Lenore Pochelski, I.H.M., Pres. & Prin.; Mr. Richard Copland, Asst. Prin. & Dean; Mrs. Stefanie Hughes, Librarian. Sisters 2; Lay Teachers 38; Students 586.

FARMINGTON HILLS. *Mercy High School for Girls*, 29300 Eleven Mile Rd., 48336. Tel: 248-476-8020; Fax: 248-476-3691. Email: mhs@mhsmi.org. Web: www.mhsmi.org. Mrs. Carolyn R. Witte, Prin.; Mr. Lawrence B. Davenport, Librarian. Sisters of Mercy. Sisters 1; Lay Teachers 44; Faculty 45; Students 743.

LIVONIA. *Ladywood High School*, 14680 Newburgh Rd., 48154. Tel: 734-591-1544; Fax: 734-591-4214. Web: www.ladywood.org. Sr. Mary Ann Smith, C.S.S.F., Prin.; Mrs. Molly Stewart, Librarian. (Private School for Girls) Priests 1; Sisters 3; Lay Teachers 33; Students 386.

MACOMB TOWNSHIP. *Austin Catholic Academy*, 18201 Twenty-Three Mile Rd., 48042. Tel: 586-306-9611; Fax: 586-286-8753. Mr. Leonard J. Brillati, Pres.; Rev. David L. Brecht, O.S.A., Headmaster.

ORCHARD LAKE. *St. Mary's Preparatory*, 3535 Indian Tr., 48324. Tel: 248-683-0530; Fax: 248-683-1740. Email: lkosco@stmarysprep.com. Web: www.stmarysprep.com. Mr. James Glowacki, Headmaster; Rev. Timothy Whalen, Chancellor; Mr. Leonard Karschnia, Dir. Admissions & Vice Headmaster. Priests 2; Sisters 1; Lay Teachers 33; Students 477.

NOVI. *Catholic Central High School*, 27225 Wixom Rd., 48374. Tel: 248-596-3810; Fax: 248-596-3811. Email: rarcsb@catholiccentral.net. Web: www.catholiccentral.net. Revs. Richard J. Elmer, C.S.B., Pres.; John J. Ward, C.S.B.; Raymond Paramo, C.S.B.; Christopher Valka, C.S.B.; Edwin J. Kline, C.S.B.; Robert W. Moslosky, C.S.B.; James M. O'Neill, C.S.B.; Jefferson M. Thompson, C.S.B.; Dennis Kauffman, C.S.B.; Richard A. Ranalletti, C.S.B., Prin.; Roy Kronsbein, Librarian. Basilian Fathers. Priests 10; Lay Teachers 65; Students 1,062.

WARREN. *De La Salle Collegiate*, 14600 Common Rd., 48088-3387. Tel: 586-778-2207; Fax: 586-778-5118. Web: www.delasallehs.com. Bro. Robert Carnaghi, F.S.C., Pres.; Mr. Patrick Adams, Prin.; Mrs. Nanette Maltz, Librarian. High School Brothers of the Christian Schools. Brothers 1; Sisters 2; Lay Teachers 45; Students 834.

Regina High School for Girls, 13900 Masonic Blvd., 48088. Tel: 586-585-0500; Fax: 586-585-0507. Web: www.reginahs.com. Sisters Mary Leanne, S.S.J.-T.O.S.F., Prin.; Mary Hyacinth, S.S.J.-T.O.S.F., Asst. Prin.; Mrs. Karen Forys, Asst. Prin.; Donald Kalpin, Business Mgr.; Ms. Julie Bedard, Librarian. Sisters of St. Joseph of the Third Order of St. Francis 2; Dominican Sisters 1; I.H.M. Sisters 1; Lay Teachers 32; Students 500.

[F] ELEMENTARY SCHOOLS, INTER-PAROCHIAL

CANTON. *All Saints Catholic School*, (Grades PreSchool-8), 48735 Warren Rd., 48187-1233. Tel: 734-459-2490; Fax: 734-459-0981. Email: ascs9@hotmail.com. Web: www.allsaintscs.com. Ms. Kristen Strausbaugh, Prin. Lay Teachers 31; Total Enrollment 535.

CLARKSTON. *Everest Academy*, 5935 Clarkston Rd., 48348. Tel: 248-620-3390; Fax: 248-620-3942. Email: mnalepa@everestacademy.org. Web:

www.everestacademy.org. Rev. Scott Reilly, L.C., Pres.; Ms. Susan Ender, Academic Coord.; Ms. Christine Cataldi, Academic Coord. Priests 3; Consecrated Women 3; Lay Teachers 34; Students 440.

PORT HURON. *St. Mary/McCormick Catholic Academy*, (Grades PreK-8), 1429 Ballentine St., 48060. Tel: 810-982-7906; Fax: 810-987-8255. Email: stmaryacademy@hotmail.com. Web: www.stmarypthuron.org. Mrs. Deborah A. Krueger, Prin.; Ms. Candice Mendoza, Librarian. (2 schools merged) Lay Teachers 10; Students 174.

ROCHESTER. *Holy Family Regional School - North Campus*, (Grades K-3), 1240 Inglewood, 48307. Mailing Address: 2633 John R. Rd., Rochester Hills, 48307. Tel: 248-656-1234; Fax: 248-656-3494. Sr. Karen Hawver, S.C., Prin.; Mrs. Adelia Parent, Librarian.

Holy Family Regional School - South Campus (Grades 4-8), 2633 John R. Rd., Rochester Hills, 48307. Tel: 248-299-3798; Fax: 248-299-3843. Sr. Karen Hawver, S.C., Prin.; Mrs. Mary Coppola, Librarian. Sisters 2; Lay Teachers 60; Students 1,130.

[G] ELEMENTARY, PRIVATE

BLOOMFIELD HILLS. *Academy of the Sacred Heart*, (Grades PreK-8), 1250 Kensington Rd., 48304-3029. Tel: 248-646-8900; Fax: 248-646-4143. Web: www.ashmi.org. Sr. Bridget Bearss, R.S.C.J., Headmistress; Ms. Sandra Jeffries, Media Center Coord. Religious of the Sacred Heart. Lay Teachers 53; Students 354.

[H] GENERAL HOSPITALS

DETROIT. *St. John Hospital and Medical Center* (a unit of St. John Health System), 22101 Moross Rd., 48236. Tel: 313-343-4000; Fax: 313-343-7533. Ms. Diane Radloff, Pres. Sisters of Saint Joseph (Nazareth, Michigan) 12; Bed Capacity 804; Total Staff 4,500; Patients Assisted Annually 181,595; Outpatients 91,819.

BRIGHTON. *Brighton Hospital Chemical Dependency and Dual Diagnosis Residential Treatment* (a unit of St. John Health), 12851 E. Grand River Rd., 48116. Tel: 888-215-2700. Web: www.brightonhospital.org. Denise Bertin-Epp, Pres. & Chief Nursing Officer. Bed Capacity 92; Total Staff 247; Patients Assisted Annually 6,118.

EAST CHINA. *St. John River District Hospital* (a unit of St. John Health), 4100 River Rd., 48054. Tel: 810-329-7111; Fax: 810-329-8920. Web: www.stjohn.org/riverdistrict. Frank Poma, Pres. Bed Capacity 68; Total Staff 506; Inpatient 2,233; ER Patients 9,957.

LIVONIA. *St. Mary Mercy Hospital*, 36475 W. Five Mile Rd., 48154. Tel: 734-655-4800; Fax: 734-655-1620. Web: www.stmarymercy.org. Mr. David Spivey, Pres. & CEO; Revs. Luke Okecukwu Iwuji; Peter Ben Opara. (A Division of Trinity Health-Michigan) Sisters 5; Bed Capacity 304; Patients Assisted Annually 206,606; RN's 495; LPN's 10; Total Inpatient Days 78,220; Total Staff 1,400.

MADISON HEIGHTS. *St. John Macomb-Oakland Hospital, Oakland Center* (a unit of St. John Health), 27351 Dequindre, 48071. Tel: 248-967-7000. Web: www.stjohn.org/macomb-oakland. Mr. Michael Beaubien, COO; Mr. Joseph Tasse, Pres. Bed Capacity 180; Total Staff 1,077; Patients Assisted Annually 88,804.

NOVI. *Providence Park Hospital* (a unit of St. John Health), 47601 Grand River Ave., 48374. Tel: 248-465-4100; Fax: 248-465-4501. Jean Meyer, Pres.; Michael Wiemann, M.D., Exec. V.P. Bed Capacity 200; Staff 1,300.

PONTIAC. *St. Joseph Mercy Oakland* (Div. of Trinity Health-Michigan), 44405 Woodward Ave., 48341-2985. Tel: 248-858-3000; Fax: 248-858-3299. Web: www.stjoesoakland.com. Mr. Jack Weiner, Pres. & CEO; Ms. Ann Suziedelis, Vice Pres. Mission & Ethics; Ms. Linda Thompson, Chap.; Ms. Alice Murphy, Chap.; Deacon Ronald E. Rohlman, Chap. Bed Capacity 428; Total Staff 2,500; Total Assisted Annually 20,070.

PORT HURON. *St. Joseph Mercy Port Huron* (Div. of Trinity Health-Michigan), 2601 Electric, 48060-6518. Tel: 810-985-1510; Fax: 810-985-1579. Mr. Peter Karadjoff, Pres. & CEO; Rev. C. Paul Higdon, Chap. (Retired); Sisters LuAnn Hannasch, R.S.M., Dir. Mission Svcs.; Mary Mercita Logan, R.S.M., Chap.; Susan Stockwell, S.S.J., Chap. Bed Capacity 119; Patients Assisted Annually 154,019; Total Staff 775.

SOUTHFIELD. *Providence Hospital* (A unit of St. John Health), 16001 W. Nine Mile Rd., 48037. Tel: 248-849-3000; Fax: 248-849-3035. Michael Wiemann, M.D., Pres.; Ms. Susan Prokop, Dir. Mission Integration; Rev. Felix S. Alsola (Philippines), Chap. Daughters of Charity of St. Vincent de Paul 6; Bed Capacity 459; Bassinets 65; Lay Staff 3,160; Patients Assisted Annually 651,616; Total Staff 7,836.

WARREN. *St. John Macomb-Oakland Hospital, Macomb Center* (a unit of St. John Health), 11800 E. 12 Mile Rd., 48093. Tel: 586-573-5000. Web: www.stjohn.org/macombFax: 586-573-5541. Mr. Joseph Tasse, Pres.; Mr. Michael Beaubien, Vice Pres., East Region; Sr. Diane Rondeau, R.S.M., Chap.; Deacon Kenneth Weiss, Chap. Bed Capacity 376; Total Staff 1,375; Patients Assisted Annually 21,065.

[I] SPECIAL HOSPITALS AND SANATORIA FOR INVALIDS

FRASER. *Sanctuary at Fraser Villa* (a unit of Trinity Senior Living Communities), 33300 Utica Rd., 48026. Tel: 586-293-3300. Email: sliwinsg@trinity-health.org. Web: www.trinityseniorsanctuary.org. Ms. Gail Sliwinski, Admin.

LAKE ORION. *Guest House, Inc.*, 1601 Joslyn Rd., P.O. Box 420, 48361. Tel: 248-391-4445; Fax: 248-391-0210. Web: www.guesthouse.org. Mr. Daniel A. Kidd, Pres. & CEO; Mr. Michael P. Morgan, M.A., Exec. Dir. Management Services Offices; State licensed, CARF-accredited residential treatment centers and women information for priests, brothers, deacons, sisters and seminarians. Bed Capacity 39.

Guest House for Women Religious, 1720 W. Scripps Rd., Box 68, 48360. Tel: 248-391-3100; Fax: 248-393-0186. Web: www.guesthouse.org. Sr. Lee Anne Farrell, S.S.N.D., V.P. Women's Svcs. A state-licensed and CARF accredited endorsed residential treatment center for Catholic sisters and women in formation.; Central Admissions Office, from U.S. & Canada call: 800-626-6910. Bed Capacity 16.

Guest House Recovery Residence, 444 Nakomis Rd., 48362. Tel: 248-693-8973. Bro. Richard D. Hittle, S.J., Residential Mgr.

Guest House Institute, 1601 Joslyn Rd., 48360. Tel: 248-391-4445; Fax: 248-391-0210. Web: www.guest-houseinstitute.org. The Insitute promotes health and wellness of Catholics by providing educational services regarding alcoholism and other addictions and by promoting and providing research in alcoholism and other addictions affecting the Catholic Church.

LIVONIA. *Marycrest Manor*, 15475 Middlebelt Rd., 48154. Tel: 734-427-9175; Fax: 734-427-5044. Mr. James Butler, Admin. Served by Marianhill Fathers., Ownership: Franciscan Sisters of St. Joseph. Sisters 3; Residents 55; Bed Capacity 55; Total Staff 72; Total Assisted Annually 240.

Marywood Nursing Care Center, 36975 W. Five Mile Rd., 48154. Tel: 734-464-0600; Fax: 734-464-4846. Mr. John Mimnaugh, N.H.A., Admin. Skilled Nursing Facility. Sisters 4; Capacity 103; Total Staff 180.

MEMPHIS. *Sacred Heart Rehabilitation Center, Inc.*, 400 Stoddard Rd., Box 41038, 48041-1038. Tel: 810-392-2167; Fax: 810-392-3385. Mr. John Sass Jr., Pres. Treatment for alcoholism and drug dependency to adult men and women. Detox and residential services. Bed Capacity 112.

ROCHESTER HILLS. *Sanctuary at Bellbrook* (A unit of Trinity Senior Living Communities), 873 W. Avon Rd., 48307. Tel: 248-656-3239. Email: moulism@trinity-health.org. Web: www.trinityseniorsanctuary.org. Ms. Carrie Beaulieu, Admin. Bed Capacity 116; Total Staff 175.

ROYAL OAK. *Sanctuary at Alexander* (A unit of Trinity Senior Living Communities), 718 W. Fourth St., 48067. Tel: 248-545-0571. Email: larsonjo@trinity-health.org. Web: www.trinityseniorsanctuary.org. Ms. Judy Thayer, Admin.

WARREN. *Sanctuary at the Abbey* (a unit of Trinity Senior Living Communities), 12250 E. Twelve Mile Rd., 48093. Tel: 586-751-6200. Email: loriusl@trinity-health.org. Web: www.trinityseniorsanctuary.org. Lisa Lorius, Admin.

WATERFORD. *Lourdes Alzheimers Special Care Center*, 2400 Watkins Lake Rd., 48328. Tel: 248-674-4732; Fax: 248-618-6376. Web: www.lourdescampus.com. Sr. Maureen Comer, O.P., CEO. Bed Capacity 20; Total Assisted Annually 27; Total Staff 25.

Lourdes Nursing Home, 2300 Watkins Lake Rd., 48328. Tel: 248-674-2241; Fax: 248-674-1211. Web: www.lourdes-sc.org. Sr. Maureen Comer, O.P., CEO. Skilled & basic nursing facility for men and women rehabilitation and 24 hour nursing care. Residents 106; Bed Capacity 108; Total Assisted Annually 184; Total Staff 182.

[J] HOUSING AND/OR COMMUNITY FACILITIES FOR THE AGING

BLOOMFIELD HILLS. *St. Elizabeth Briarbank Home for the Aged*, 39315 Woodward Ave., 48304. Tel: 248-644-1011; Fax: 248-644-1596. Daughters of Divine Charity. Sisters 8; Aged Residents 38; Bed Capacity 38; Total Assisted Annually 25; Total Staff 16.

CLINTON TOWNSHIP. *A Friend's House Adult Day Services*, 15945 Canal, Clinton Twp., 48038. Tel: 586-412-8494; Fax: 586-412-8084. Email: csmseniors@csmacomb.org. Web: www.csmacomb.org. 26238 Ryan, Warren, 48091. Tel: 586-759-8700; Fax: 586-759-8789. Adrianna Chamberlain, Dir. Adult Day Services. Daytime care for older adults. Support services for caregiving families. A service of Catholic Services of Macomb. Total Staff 10; Total Assisted Annually 200.

Sanctuary at Clinton Villa, 17825 Fifteen Mile Rd., 48035. Tel: 586-792-0358; Fax: 586-792-4409. Email: nelsonsh@trinity-health.org. Web: www.trinityseniorsactuary.org. Ms. Dianne Wettergren, Admin. A unit of Trinity Senior Living Communities. Total Staff 15; Units 78; Total Assisted Annually 1,032.

FARMINGTON HILLS. *Sanctuary at Marian Oakland*, 29250 W. Ten Mile Rd., 48336. Tel: 248-474-7204; Fax: 248-474-8662. Web: www.sanctuaryatmarianoakland.org. Mr. Joseph Theisen, Dir. Hospitality. A unit of Trinity Senior Living Communities. Total Staff 12; Units 81; Total Assisted Annually 1,080.

FORT GRATIOT. *Sanctuary at Mercy Village* (A unit of Trinity Senior Living Communities), 4170 24th Ave., 48059. Tel: 810-989-7440. Email: cooperd@trinity-health.org. Web: www.villagemercy.org. Christine Jones, Admin.

IMLAY CITY. *Sanctuary at Maple Vista*, 600 Maple Vista, 48444. Tel: 810-724-6300. Email: campagnc@trinity-health.org. Web: www.trinityseniorsanctuary.org. Ms. Crystal Campagne, Admin. A unit of Senior Living Communities. Total Staff 15; Units 69; Total Assisted Annually 1,080.

LIVONIA. *Sanctuary at Villa Marie*, 15131 Newburgh, 48154. Tel: 734-464-9494; Fax: 734-464-4010. Web: www.trinityseniorsanctuary.org. Ms. Sharon Powell, Dir. A unit of Trinity Senior Living Communities. Total Staff 10; Units 70; Total Assisted Annually 1,080.

Trinity Continuing Care Services dba Trinity Senior Living Communities 17410 College Pkwy., Ste. 200, 48152-2363. Tel: 734-542-8349; Fax: 248-488-9169. Email: harrisj@trinity-health.org. Web: www.trinityccs.org. Ms. Jaclyn Harris, Pres. & CEO. Bed Capacity 3,075; Total Assisted Annually 6,000; Total Staff 2,400.

MONROE. *Sanctuary at Marian Place*, 408 W. Front St., 48161. Tel: 734-241-2414. Email: austinde@trinity-health.org. Web: www.mercymarianplace.org. Ms. Karen Morrin, Admin. A unit of Trinity Senior Living Communities. Total Staff 11; Units 53; Total Assisted Annually 636.

PORT HURON. *Sanctuary at Marydale*, 3147 Tenth Ave., 48060. Tel: 810-985-9683. Email: hungerr@trinity-health.org. Web: www.trinityseniorsanctuary.org. Ms. Maura Koppel, Admin. A unit of Trinity Senior Living Communities. Total Staff 13; Units 51; Total Assisted Annually 612.

SOUTHGATE. *Sanctuary at Maryhaven*, 11350 Reeck Rd., 48195. Tel: 734-287-2111; Fax: 734-287-6905. Web: www.trinityseniorsanctuary.org. Shanita Bradley, Regional Admin. A unit of Trinity Senior Living Communities. Total Staff 12; Units 85; Total Assisted Annually 700.

WATERFORD. *Fox Manor, Inc.*, 2350 Watkins Lake Rd., 48328. Tel: 248-674-9590; Fax: 248-674-3463. Web: www.lourdes-sc.org. Sr. Maureen Comer, O.P., CEO. Dominican Sisters., Residential facility for independent senior citizens of moderate or limited means. Bed Capacity 57; Total Staff 21; Total Assisted Annually 64.

Lourdes Assisted Living Corporation, 2450 Watkins Lake Rd., 48328. Tel: 248-618-6362; Fax: 248-618-6361. Web: www.lourdes-sc.org. Sr. Maureen Comer, O.P., CEO; Ms. Cori Sharrard, Dir. Bed Capacity 80; Total Assisted Annually 113; Total Staff 55.

[K] MONASTERIES AND RESIDENCES OF PRIESTS AND BROTHERS

DETROIT. *St. Bonaventure Friary*, 1740 Mt. Elliott Ave., 48207-3496. Tel: 313-579-2100; Fax: 313-579-5388.

Province of St. Joseph of the Capuchin Order, Inc. Provincialate, 1820 Mt. Elliott Ave., 48207. Tel: 313-579-2100; Fax: 313-579-2275. Very Rev. John Celichowski, O.F.M.Cap., Prov. Min.; Bro. Robert Smith, O.F.M.Cap., Prov. Vicar; Revs. William Cieslak, O.F.M.Cap., Public Rels. & Devel. Tel: 313-579-2100, Ext. 151; Patrick McSherry, O.F.M.Cap., Archivist.

Priests of the Province Assigned Outside the U.S.: Revs. Carmel Flora, O.F.M.Cap., St. Lawrence Community, 545 Tingal Rd., Wynnum, Qld. 4178, Australia. Fax: 011-61-73348-5141; Glenn Gessner, O.F.M.Cap.; Thomas Schmeid, O.F.M.Cap.; Walter Kasuboski, O.F.M.Cap.; Paul Koenig, O.F.M.Cap.; Benjamin Markwell, O.F.M.Cap.; Andre Weller, O.F.M.Cap.; Paul Craig, O.F.M.Cap.; Kevin Heagerty, O.F.M.Cap.; Bro. Jozef Timmers, O.F.M.Cap.

Assigned to St. Bonaventure Friary: Very Rev. John Celichowski, O.F.M.Cap.; Bro. Larry LaCross, O.F.M.Cap., Local Min.; Revs. Philip Naessens, O.F.M.Cap.; Joseph Maloney, O.F.M.Cap.; Albert Sandor, O.F.M.Cap.; Lloyd Thiel, O.F.M.Cap.; Patrick McSherry, O.F.M.Cap.; Malcolm Maloney, O.F.M-.Cap.; Bros. Michael Drobnicki, O.F.M.Cap.; Paul Hanisko, O.F.M.Cap.; David Heffron, O.F.M.Cap.; Thomas Kroll, O.F.M.Cap.; Richard Merling, O.F.M.Cap., Vicar; Leo Wollenweber, O.F.M.Cap.

Jesuit Community at the University of Detroit Mercy, Lansing-Reilly Hall, 4001 W. McNichols Rd., 48221-3038. Tel: 313-993-1000; Fax: 313-993-1653. Revs. R. Gerard Albright, S.J.; Frederick J. Benda, S.J.; Gerald F. Cavanagh, S.J.; Simon J. Hendry, S.J.; Richard M. Mackowski, S.J.; Oswald A. Mascarenhas, S.J. (India); John D. O'Neill, S.J.; John A. Saliba, S.J.; Robert J. Scullin, S.J.; James K. Serrick, S.J.; Raphael Shen, S.J. (China); John M. Staudenmaier, S.J.; Gerard L. Stockhausen, S.J., Ph.D.; Gilbert Sunghera, S.J.; David E. Watson, S.J.; Gary R. Wright, S.J.; Bro. Richard D. Hittle, S.J. (Corporate Title: The Jesuit Community Corporation at the University of Detroit).

Jesuit Provincial Office-Detroit Province of the Society of Jesus, 2050 N. Clark St., Chicago, IL 60614-4788. Tel: 773-975-6888; Fax: 733-975-0230. Email: provincial@jesuits-chgdet.org. Web: www.jesuitdet.org. Very Rev. Timothy P. Kesicki, S.J., Prov. Superior; Revs. Walter C. Deye, S.J., Exec. Asst. Prov.; Theodore G. Munz, S.J., Treas.; Richard H. Twohig, S.J., Asst., Health Care; James S. Prehn, S.J., Asst. Secondary Educ.; Ms. Jenene Francis, Asst. Pastoral Ministry; Rev. Raymond P. Guiao, S.J., Asst. for Formation; Mr. Timothy J. Freeman, Asst. Devel. & Communications. Priests 111; Brothers 16; Scholastics 23.

Treasurer, Social & International Ministries, & Devel./Mission Offices: 7303 W. Seven Mile Rd., 48221-2121. Tel: 313-861-7500; Fax: 313-861-4230.

Priests assigned outside the U.S.: Revs. Michael A. Evans, S.J., Loyola House, Ngong Rd., P.O. Box 21399, Nairobi 00505 Kenya. Tel: 254-20-3869-494; Fax: 254-20-3866-873; Theodore W. Walters, S.J., St. Augustine University of Tanzania, P.O. Box 307, Mwanza, Tanzania. Tel: 255-0744-617396; Fax: 255-28-2550167; Kevin L. Flannery, S.J., Pontifica Universita Gregoriana, Piazza Della Pilotta 4, Rome 00187 Italy. Tel: 39-6-6701-5213; Fax: 39-6-6701-5413; Joseph E. Mulligan, S.J., Colegio Centroamericano, Apdo. 2419, Managua, Nicaragua. Tel: 505-278-6965; Joseph P. Daoust, S.J., Borgo S. Spirito, 4, Rome 00193 Italy; Timothy J. Meier, S.J., Chap., A CO, STB, 41D, Unit 43119, APO, AE 09344-3119.

Members in the U.S. not listed elsewhere: Revs. Thomas S. Acker, S.J., 200 Main St., Beckley, WV 25801; Martin T. Connell, S.J., P.O. Box 1079, Dodoma, Tanzania; Edward J. Mattimoe, S.J., St. Patrick Church, 400 Main St., Huntington, NY 11743. Tel: 631-385-3311; James F. Riley, S.J., 7303 W. Mile Rd., 48221.

St. Mary's Friary, 1057 Parker, 48214-2612. Tel: 313-821-5883; Fax: 313-922-0404; 313-579-5365. Email: jhast@thecapuchins.org. Web: www.thecapuchins.org. Revs. Lawrence E. Webber, O.F.M.Cap.; James C. Hast, O.F.M.Cap.; Bros. Michael Gaffney, O.F.M.Cap.; Joseph Monachino, O.F.M.Cap.

P.I.M.E. Missionaries (Pontifical Institute for Foreign Missions), 17330 Quincy, 48221. Tel: 313-342-4066; Fax: 313-342-6816. Email: info@pimeusa.org. Web: www.pimeusa.org. Very Rev. Kenneth Mazur, P.I.M.E., North American Regional Supr.; Revs. Sergio Fossati, P.I.M.E., Mission Center Dir.; Dino Vanin, P.I.M.E., Treas.; George Berendt, P.I.M.E.; Noel Cornelio, P.I.M.E.; Guy Christopher Snyder, P.I.M.E.

St. Paul of the Cross Community, Congregation of the Passion, 23335 Schoolcraft, 48223. Tel: 313-531-0562; Fax: 313-535-8468. Revs. Robert Weiss, C.P., Supr.; Rene Champagne, C.P.; John Devany, C.P.; James Thoman, C.P., Dir. Retreat Center; Randal Joyce, C.P.; Blaise Czaja, C.P.; Ronald Corl, C.P.; Bro. William Baalman, C.P. A center for the Passionist Fathers & Brothers in mid-western & north central United States. Members of this community conduct parish missions, renewals & retreats for laity, clergy & religious, Forty Hours Devotion & other ministries. Priests 6; Brothers 1.

St. Sylvester Monastery, 17320 Rosemont Rd., 48219. Tel: 313-532-6064; Fax: 313-531-0739. Rev. Michael R. Green, O.S.B., Prior; Bro. Gregory David Jones, O.S.B., Rel. Dir. St. Scholastica School.

BLOOMFIELD HILLS. *Congregation of Christian Brothers, Mater Dei Community*, 7350 Parkstone Ln., 48301. Tel: 248-258-1186; Fax: 248-647-8170. Email: macintyre@brrice.edu. Bros. David A. MacIntyre, C.F.C., Supr.; Arthur M. Arndt, C.F.C.; Benjamin L. Favero, C.F.C. Brothers 3.

CLARKSTON. *Colombiere Center*, 9075 Big Lake Rd., 48346-1015. Tel: 248-625-5611; Fax: 248-625-3526. Revs. Richard H. Twohig, S.J., Supr. & Dir.; R. James Kurtz, S.J., Asst. Supr.; Thomas F. Ankenbrandt, S.J.; Thomas J. Bain, S.J.; Robert E. Beckman, S.J.; Joseph H. Boel, S.J.; R. Michael Brophy, S.J.; Francis X. Budovic, S.J.; Paul F. Conen, S.J.; Matthew E. Creighton, S.J.; Cornelius L. Curtin, S.J.; J. Peter Deane, S.J.; Joseph F. Downey, S.J.; Robert C. Dressman, S.J.; Raymond A. Dunne, S.J.; Eugene F. Dwyer, S.J.; Edward A. Flint, S.J.; Thomas M. Gannon, S.J.; Vincent A. Hagarman, S.J.; John H. Kleinhenz, S.J.; John A. Knapek, S.J.; Daniel P. Liderbach, S.J.; Stephen A. Meder, S.J.; Harold R. Meirose, S.J.; Benjamin R. Morin, S.J.; Robert J. Murphy, S.J.; Edward M. Nemeth, S.J.; Lothar Nurnberger, S.J.; Frank M. Oppenheim, S.J.; Donald J. O'Shaughnessy, S.J.; John F. Pennington, S.J.; John J. Powell, S.J.; Herbert J. Raterman, S.J.; John E. Reilly, S.J.; L. Harold Sanford, S.J.; Francis J. Smith, S.J.; Jerome F. Treacy, S.J.; Gerald C. Walling, S.J.; Earl A. Weiss, S.J.; Glenn Williams, S.J.; Bros. Robert G. Cardosi, S.J.; Richard C. Conroy, S.J.; Herman F. Elsaesser, S.J.; James F. Gates, S.J.; William R. Haas, S.J.; David L. Henderson, S.J.; Henry C. Kuhn, S.J.; Daniel J. McCullough, S.J.; John J. Petrus, S.J.; Bernard L. Polinak, S.J.; Jerome Pryor, S.J.; John J. Sebian, S.J. Jesuit Health Care Community for the Detroit Province and Chicago Province.

DEARBORN. *Society of St. Paul*, 7050 Pinehurst, 48126. Tel: 313-582-2033; Fax: 313-582-2970. Email: sspdearborn@comcast.net. Rev. Arthur Palisada, S.S.P.; Bro. Aloysius Milella, S.S.P. Priests 1; Brothers 1.

DEARBORN HEIGHTS. *All Saints Friary*, 23755 Military Rd., 48127. Tel: 313-278-5129; Fax: 313-278-5828. Email: jupy46@aol.com. Web: www.franciscancommunity.com. Very Rev. Patrick Greenough, O.F.M.Conv., Provincial; Revs. John Joseph Mikula, O.F.M.Conv.; Justin Kusibab, O.F.M.Conv.; Bros. Juniper Kriss, O.F.M.Conv., Guardian; Thomas Hercegovics, O.F.M.Conv. (This is a subsidiary of St. Bonaventure, Chicago, IL.) Priests 3; Brothers 2.

Our Lady of Grace Monastery, Mariannhill Mission Society, 23715 Ann Arbor Tr., 48127. Tel: 313-561-7140; 313-561-8888; Fax: 313-561-9486. Email: cmm-usa@juno.com. Web: www.rc.net/detroit/mariannhill/leaves.htm. *Vocation Office* Tel: 313-561-7140, Ext. 25; Fax: 313-561-9486. Email: vheier@juno.com. Web: www.mariannhill.org. Revs. Raymond Lucasinsky, C.M.M.; Timothy Mock, C.M.M., Asst. Prov. Treas.; Thomas Szura, C.M.M., Prov. Treas.; Thomas Heier, C.M.M., Editor of LEAVES & American Regional; Vergil Heier, C.M.M., Vocation Dir. & Supr. of House; Michael Sheehy, C.M.M., Mission Procurator. Priests 6; Brothers 3. In Res. Bros. Francis Berridge, C.M.M.; Jamie Miller, C.M.M.; Otto Waldmueller, C.M.M.

GROSSE POINTE. *Order of Canons Regular of the Holy Cross*, 576 Neff Rd., 48230. Tel: 313-884-1121; Fax: 313-882-1763. Email: frwolfgang@opusangelorum.org. Web: www.cruzios.org. Revs. Wolfgang Seitz, O.R.C.; Michael Hincks, O.R.C.

LIVONIA. *Marist Fathers & Brothers Community*, 32509 Scone, 48154-4165. Tel: 734-266-1475; Fax: 734-266-0197. Revs. Ronald G. DesRosiers, S.M., Local Supr. & Madonna Univ.; Frank Grispino, S.M., Madonna Univ.; John Sajdak, S.M., Chm., Rel. Studies Dept., Madonna University.

NORTHVILLE. *Miles Christi*, P.O. Box 701200, Plymouth, 48170. Tel: 248-596-9677; Fax: 248-596-9678. Email: infousa@mileschristi.org. Web: www.mileschristi.org. Revs. Caesar Bertolacci, M.C., Supr.; Patrick Wainwright, Apostolate Dir.

REDFORD. *Society of the Catholic Apostolate-Indian Province of the State of Michigan*, 17116 Olympia, 48240. Tel: 313-534-9000; Fax: 313-534-6744. Rev. Ralph Besterwitch, S.A.C., Prov. Delegate; Deacon Robert Bovitz, Contact Person.

WYANDOTTE. *Society of the Catholic Apostolate (Pallottine Fathers)* (Irish Province), 3352 Fourth St., 48192. Tel: 734-285-2966; Fax: 734-285-1059. Rev. Hubert Flanagan, S.C.A., Pres., Rector & Mission Promotion Dir.; Bro. Faustino Paez, S.C.A., Mission Promotion Associate. *Pallottine Missionary Center (Irish Province)*, 424 Orange St., 48192. Tel: 734-282-3019; Fax: 734-285-1059. Revs. Eamonn Monson, S.C.A., Prov.; John Kelly, S.C.A., Prov. Bursar, Treas.; Hubert Flanagan, S.C.A., Pres. *Pallottine Peer Ministry*, P.O. Box 66, 48192. Tel: 734-770-8262; Fax: 734-752-6545. Rev. Brendan Walsh, S.C.A., Chap.

[L] CONVENTS AND RESIDENCES FOR SISTERS

DETROIT. *Missionaries of Charity*, 1917 Cabot St., 48209. Tel: 313-841-1394. Sr. M. Davis, M.C., Supr.

Sisters of Jesus the Savior (1985) (Founded in Elele, Nigeria), St. Bartholomew Convent, 2291 E. Outer Dr., 48234-1897. Tel: 313-363-7774. Sr. Maria Goretti Ojiobianu, Supr. Ministry in Education and Social Assistance. Sisters 4.

Sisters, Home Visitors of Mary Convent, 121 E. Boston, 48202. Tel: 313-869-2160. Email: homevisitors@att.net. Sr. Rosemarie Abate, H.V.M., Admin. Sisters 21.

ALLEN PARK. *Little Sisters of the Poor*, P.O. Box 610, 48101-0610. Tel: 419-698-4331; Fax: 419-698-1109. Email: msoregon@littlesistersofthepoor.org. Web: www.littlesistersofthepoor.org. Sr. Anne Joseph, L.S.P., Pres. & Contact Person.

BLOOMFIELD HILLS. *Daughters of Divine Charity - Holy Trinity Province* (1972) Holy Trinity Provincialate, 39315 N. Woodward Ave., 48304. Tel: 248-644-1011; Fax: 248-644-1596. Sr. Hyacinth Vamos, F.D.C., Prov. Supr. Sisters in Community 26.

CLINTON TWP. *Monastery of St. Therese of the Child Jesus*, 35750 Moravian Dr., 48035-2138. Tel: 586-790-7255; Fax: 586-790-7271. Email: carmelctwp@sbcglobal.net. Web: www.rc.net/detroit/carmelite. Sr. Mary Elizabeth, O.C.D., Prioress. Discalced Carmelite Nuns. Professed Nuns 6; Extern Sisters 1; Novices 1.

DEARBORN HEIGHTS. *Sisters of the Good Shepherd (RGS)*, 20651 W. Warren Ave., 48127-2698. Tel: 313-271-3050, Ext. 270; Fax: 313-271-6250.

EASTPOINTE. *Marist Sisters, Inc.*, 16057 Hauss, 48021. Tel: 586-772-2577; Fax: 586-772-8302. Email: maristsep@yahoo.com. Sisters Linda Sevcik, S.M., Sector Leader; Constance Dodd, S.M., Sec. & Treas.

FARMINGTON HILLS. *Bernardine Franciscan Sisters of Michigan*, Our Lady of the Rosary Convent, 27405 W. 10 Mile Rd., 48336-2201. Tel: 248-476-4111; Fax: 248-476-6950. Web: www.bfranciscan.org. Sr. Madonna Marie Harvath, O.S.F., Congregational Min. Bernardine Sisters of the Third Order of St. Francis. Sisters in Area 28.

Monastery of the Blessed Sacrament, 29575 Middlebelt Rd., 48334-2311. Tel: 248-626-8253; Fax: 248-626-8724. Email: opnunsfh@sbcglobal.net. Web: www.opnuns-fh.org. Sr. Mary Thomas, O.P., Prioress; Rev. David J. Santoro, O.P, Chap. Nuns of the Order of Preachers (Cloistered Dominican Nuns, Perpetual Adoration). Cloistered Sisters 33; Extern Sisters 3.

Sisters of Mercy of the Americas West Midwest Community, Inc. (As of July 1, 2008, the Sisters of Mercy of the Americas Regional Communities of Auburn, CA; Burlingame, CA; Cedar Rapids, IA; Chicago, IL; Detroit, MI; and Omaha, NE, merged to create Sisters of Mercy of the Americas West Midwest Community, Inc.), 29000 Eleven Mile Rd., 48336. Tel: 248-476-8000; Fax: 248-476-4222. Email: info@mercywmw.org. Web: www.mercywestmidwest.org. Sisters Norita Cooney, R.S.M., Pres.; Judith Frikker, R.S.M., Substitute for Pres.; Sheila Megley, R.S.M., Treas.; Judith Cannon, R.S.M., Sec.; Kathy Thornton, R.S.M., Leadership Team; Michelle Gorman, R.S.M., Leadership Team; Kim Kinsel, Community Oper. Officer; Carol Kelley, Community Fin. Officer; Sandy Goetzinger-Comer, Dir. Communications. Sisters 810; Associates 565.

West Midwest FIDES, Inc., 29000 Eleven Mile Rd., 48336. Tel: 248-476-8000; Fax: 248-476-4222. Email: info@mercywmw.org. Web: www.mercywestmid-west.org. Sisters Sheila Megley, R.S.M., Pres.; Sheila Browne, R.S.M., Vice Pres.; Judith Frikker, R.S.M., Sec. & Treas.; Helen Amos, R.S.M., Governing Bd. Member; Katherine Graber, R.S.M., Governing Bd. Member.

Sisters of Mercy of the Americas, 29000 Eleven Mile Rd., 48336. Tel: 248-476-8000; Fax: 248-476-4222. Regional Community of Detroit, Charitable Trusts 1 & 2.

LIVONIA. *Provincial House and Novitiate of the Sisters of St. Felix*, 36800 Schoolcraft Rd., 48150. Tel: 734-591-1730; Fax: 734-591-1710. Email: cssf@feliciansilvonia.org. Web: www.feliciansisters.org. Sr. Mary Renetta Rumpz, C.S.S.F., Prov. Min.

Provincial House and Novitiate of the

Congregation of the Sisters of St. Felix, C.S.S.F., Felician Sisters Professed Sisters 156; Novices 1.

MONROE. *Sisters, Servants of the Immaculate Heart of Mary, Leadership Council*, 610 W. Elm Ave., 48162-7909. Tel: 734-240-9700; Fax: 734-240-9784. Web: www.ihmsisters.org. Sisters Mary Frances Gilleran, I.H.M., Pres.; Joan Mumaw, I.H.M., Vice Pres. & Mission Councilor; Helen Ingles, I.H.M., CFO; Carol Quigley, I.H.M., Leadership Council & Mission Councilor; Margaret Sweeney, I.H.M., Leadership Council & Mission Councilor; Janet Ryan, I.H.M., Leadership Council & Mission Councilor.

Intercultural Consultation Services, 8531 W. McNichols Rd., 48221-2500. Tel: 313-341-4841; Fax: 313-342-7421. Sr. Kathryn Pierce, I.H.M., Pres. & Exec. Dir.

ORTONVILLE. *Our Lady of Mt. Thabor Monastery*, 1295 Bald Eagle Lake Rd., 48462. Tel: 248-627-4355. Email: mtthabor@aol.com. Web: www.mtthabornunsop.com. Sr. Anne Mary, O.P., Prioress. Dominican Nuns of Mt. Thabor.

RIVERVIEW. *Sisters of Mary Reparatrix*, 17320 Grange Rd., 48193. Tel: 734-285-4510; Fax: 734-285-8147. Sisters 13.

Mary Reparatrix Retreat House, 17380 Grange Rd., 48193. Tel: 734-324-0901; Fax: 734-324-0903. Email: mrretreats@comcast.net. Web: www.mrretreats.org. Ms. Denise LaPorte, Dir.

[M] HOMES FOR MEN AND WOMEN

DETROIT. *St. Mary's Residence Adult Foster Care*, 2120 Orleans St., 48207. Tel: 313-259-6874; 313-259-0459; Fax: 313-259-2001. Sr. M. Hyacinthe, F.D.C., Admin. Daughters of Divine Charity., A residence for women desiring home-like surroundings. Sisters 3; Residents 32.

[N] CATHOLIC SOCIAL SERVICE AGENCIES

DETROIT. *Catholic Social Services of Wayne County*, 9851 Hamilton Ave., 48202. Tel: 313-883-2339; Fax: 313-883-3957. Email: csswc@csswayne.org. Web: www.csswayne.org. Mr. Patrick J. Heron, Pres. & CEO. Educational programs; Adoption services; Services to unwed mothers; Substance abuse counseling and prevention; foster family care and services to youth and older persons including Foster Grandparent, Senior Companion and Retired Senior Volunteer Programs; Domestic Violence counseling and services to parolees and probationers; literacy project; residential program for homeless teen moms and children.

Branches:

20382 Van Born Rd., Dearborn Heights, 48125. Tel: 313-792-9286; Fax: 313-792-0444. Email: csswc@csswayne.org. Web: www.csswayne.org.

15200 E. Jefferson, Ste. 105, Grosse Pointe Park, 48230. Tel: 313-821-2590; Fax: 313-821-1046. Email: csswc@csswayne.org. Web: www.csswayne.org.

Teen, Infant, Parent Services (TIPS), 9851 Hamilton, 48202. Tel: 313-873-0117; Fax: 313-873-0136.

CLINTON TOWNSHIP. *Catholic Services of Macomb*, 15945 Canal Rd., 48038. Tel: 586-416-2300; Fax: 586-416-2311. Web: www.csmacomb.org. Mr. Thomas Reed, Pres. & CEO.

Branch Offices:

18720 Thirteen Mile Rd., Roseville, 48066. Tel: 586-416-2300; Fax: 586-416-2311.

347 S. Main, Romeo, 48065. Tel: 586-336-6844; Fax: 586-336-6843.

26238 Ryan Rd., Warren, 48091. Tel: 586-759-8700; Fax: 586-759-8789.

Christian Family Services of Lapeer County, Inc., 15945 Canal Rd., 48038. Tel: 586-416-2300; Fax: 586-416-2311.

MONROE. *Catholic Charities of Monroe County*, 14930 LaPlaisance Rd., Ste. 123, 48161. Tel: 734-240-3850; Fax: 734-240-3863. Web: www.ccmonroe.org. Greg Schafer, Dir. Bd.

Carleton Head Start Program, 1735 Ash St., Carleton, 48117. Tel: 734-654-2866; Fax: 734-654-2886.

Dundee Head Start Program, 130 Viking Dr., Dundee, 48131. Tel: 734-529-7008, Ext. 3101.

Harwood 1 and 2 Head Start, 14930 LaPlaisance Rd., Ste. 121 & 122, 48161. Tel: 734-242-0165; 734-242-0190 (Family Advocates).

Harwood Head Start 3, 14930 LaPlaisance Rd., 48161. Tel: 734-240-2606.

Monroe Townsite 1, 2, 3, 4, & 5 Head Start, 15488 Eastwood St., 48161. Tel: 734-265-5000; Fax: 734-265-5001.

Temperance Head Start Program, 9144 Lewis Ave., Temperance, 48182. Tel: 734-847-3460; Fax: 734-847-3460.

PORT HURON. *Catholic Social Services of St. Clair County, Inc.*, 2601 Thirteenth St., 48060. Tel: 810-987-9100; Fax: 810-987-9105. Patrick L. Cogley, M.A., Pres.

ROYAL OAK. *Catholic Social Services of Oakland County*, 1424 E. Eleven Mile Rd., 48067. Tel: 248-548-4044; Fax: 248-548-9239. Web: www.cssoc.org. Ms. Margaret A. Huggard, M.S.W., Pres.

Branches:

53 Franklin Blvd., Pontiac, 48341. Tel: 248-334-3595; Fax: 248-334-3781.

6637 Highland Rd., Waterford, 48327. Tel: 248-666-8870; Fax: 248-666-5023.

1424 E. Eleven Mile Rd., 48067. Tel: 248-548-4044; Fax: 248-548-9239.

3300 S. Adams Rd., Auburn Hills, 48326. Tel: 248-537-3300; Fax: 248-537-3306.

715 N. Lapeer Rd., Lake Orion, 48362. Tel: 248-693-7526; Fax: 248-693-2426.

St. Francis Family Services, 17500 W. Eight Mile Rd., Southfield, 48075. Tel: 248-552-0750; Fax: 248-552-9019.

Older Adult Services, 18310 W. 12 Mile Rd., Southfield, 48076. Tel: 248-557-7373; Fax: 248-559-1140.

Hispanic Outreach, Pontiac. Tel: 248-338-4250; Fax: 248-335-8130.

[O] SPECIALIZED CHILD CARE FACILITIES AND SCHOOLS

DETROIT. *Christ Child House*, 15751 Joy Rd., 48228. Tel: 313-584-6077; Fax: 313-584-1148. Email: jyablonky@christchildhouse.org. Web: www.christchildhouse.org. Mr. John Yablonky, A.C.S.W, M.S.W., L.M.S.W., Exec. Dir. Educational Specialist 1; Educational Coordinator 1; Volunteer Tutors 12.

Don Bosco Hall, Inc., 2340 Calvert, 48206. Tel: 313-869-2200; Fax: 313-869-8220. Email: csmall@donboscohall.org. Web: www.donboscohall.org. Mr. Charles Small, Pres. & CEO. Residential treatment center for boys, ages 12-17, in need of care, guidance and therapy. Lay Staff 125; Residents 140; Transitional Services 180; Mentoring Program 155.

Holy Cross Children's Services, 5555 Conner, 48213. Tel: 888-377-5060, Ext. 7558; Fax: 313-267-1185. Email: fboylan@hccsnet.org. Web: www.hccsnet.org. Bro. Francis Boylan, C.S.C., Pres.; Mr. Gary Tester, Vice Pres. Advocacy & Govt. Relations; Loren Brown, Exec. Dir. Residential and community based treatment programs for troubled youth and families with facilities located throughout the state of Michigan under the auspices of the Brothers of Holy Cross at Notre Dame.

Bowman House/Holy Cross Children's Services, 17200 Rowe St., 48205. Tel: 313-372-7320; Fax: 313-372-8623. Email: fboylan@hccsnet.org. Web: www.hccsnet.org.

Holy Cross Family & Community Support Program, 5690 Cecil Ave., 48210. Tel: 313-895-2200; Fax: 313-895-4010. Email: fboylan@hccsnet.org. Web: www.hccsnet.org. Bro. Francis Boylan, C.S.C., Pres.; Loren Brown, Exec. Dir.; William Geddes, Regl. Dir. Includes specialized foster care, supervised independent living, in-home family treatment.

Hitchcock Center/Holy Cross Children's Services, 5675 Larkins, 48210. Tel: 313-895-5135; Fax: 313-895-5133. Email: fboylan@hccsnet.org. Web: www.hccsnet.org.

Holy Cross Center/Holy Cross Children's Services, 5690 Cecil, 48210. Tel: 313-895-2200; Fax: 313-895-4010. Email: fboylan@hccsnet.org. Web: www.hccsnet.org. Day treatment, education, recreation program for Detroit region.

King House/Holy Cross Children's Services, 24455 Crocker Blvd., Clinton Twp, 48036. Tel: 810-463-7130; Fax: 810-463-7131. Email: fboylan@hccsnet.org. Web: www.hccsnet.org.

Moreau Center/Holy Cross Children's Services, 3500 Comboni Way, Monroe, 48162. Tel: 734-242-5898; Fax: 734-242-6828. Email: fboylan@hccsnet.org. Web: www.hccsnet.org. Loren Brown, Exec. Dir.; William Geddes, Regl. Dir.

Kennedy House/Holy Cross Children's Services, 7001 Burlingame St., 48204. Tel: 313-935-7500; Fax: 313-935-0605. Email: fboylan@hccsnet.org. Web: www.hccsnet.org.

St. Thomas Center, 8333 Townsend, 48213. Tel: 313-924-9515; Fax: 313-924-9547. Email: fboylan@hccsnet.org. Web: www.hccsnet.org.

St. Vincent and Sarah Fisher Center, 16800 Trinity, 48219. Tel: 313-535-9200; Fax: 313-535-7804. Email: nanci.swain@svsfcenter.org. Nanci Swain, CEO. (Educational) Staff 9.

DEARBORN HEIGHTS. *Vista Maria*, 20651 W. Warren Ave., 48127. Tel: 313-271-3050; Fax: 313-271-6250. Web: www.vistamaria.org. Mr. Cameron Hosner, Pres. & CEO. Residential treatment programs for adolescent girls, and community-based programs, e.g. foster care for boys and girls all involved in The Juvenile Justice & Child Welfare Systems. Sponsored by the Sisters of the Good Shepherd. Sisters 1; Girls Residential 163; Lay Staff 300; Foster Care 100; Youth Assistance Program 30.

[P] RETREAT HOUSES

DETROIT. *St. Paul of the Cross Passionist Retreat and Conference Center, Inc.* Conducted by the Passionist Community., 23333 Schoolcraft Rd., 48223-2499. Tel: 313-535-9563; Fax: 313-535-9207. Email: stpauls@passionist.org. Web: www.passionist.org/stpauls. Revs. James Thoman, C.P., Retreat Dir.; Ronald Corl, O.P., Staff Member; Sr. Rosemarie Kieffer, O.P., Team Member; Deacons Patrick Conlen, Team Member; Peter Cornell, Team Member; Clement Stankiewicz, Team Member; Mrs. Cathy Anthony, Team Member; Ms. Bernadette Beach, Admin.; Ms. Joyce Hansen, Dir. Youth Svcs.

BLOOMFIELD HILLS. *Manresa Jesuit Retreat House*, 1390 Quarton Rd., 48304-3554. Tel: 248-644-4933; Fax: 248-644-8291. Email: office@manresa-sj.org. Web: www.manresa-sj.org. Revs. Gregory J. Hyde, S.J., Exec. Dir.; Walter L. Farrell, S.J., Retreat Dir. & Spiritual Dir.; Leo P. Cachat, S.J., Retreat Dir. & Spiritual Dir.; Peter J. Fennessy, S.J., Retreat Dir., Community Supr.; Bernard J. Owens, S.J., Dir. Internship in Ignatian Spirituality. Priests 5.

MONROE. *River House - IHM Spirituality Center*, 805 W. Elm Ave., 48162. Tel: 734-240-5494; Fax: 734-240-5495. Email: riverhouse@ihmsisters.org. Web: www.ihmsisters.org. Sponsorship of I.H.M. Congregation. Sisters 3.

Visitation North Spirituality Center, 7227 Lahser Rd., Bloomfield Hills, 48301. Tel: 248-433-0950; Fax: 248-433-0952. Email: visitationnorth@ihmsisters.org. Web: www.visitationnorth.org. Sisters 4.

OXFORD. *Queen of the Family Retreat Center*, 751 W. Drahner Rd., 48371. Tel: 248-625-5560; Fax: 248-628-4898. Email: ccarter@arcol.org. Web: www.qfrc.org. Rev. Lorenzo Gomez, L.C., Dir.

PLYMOUTH. *The Retreat Center at St. John's*, 44011 Five Mile Rd., 48170-2555. Tel: 313-237-5800; Fax: 313-237-5868.

WASHINGTON. *Capuchin Retreat*, 62460 Mt. Vernon Rd., P.O. Box 396, 48094. Tel: 248-651-4826; Fax: 248-650-4910. Revs. Kenneth Reinhart, O.F.M.Cap., Dir.; Gerald Kessel, O.F.M.Cap.; John Guimond, O.F.M. Cap.; Bros. Patrick Forton, O.F.M.Cap.; Joseph Howe, O.F.M.Cap.; Sr. Joanne Peters, O.P.

[Q] SPECIAL SERVICES

DETROIT. *Capuchin Soup Kitchen*, 1820 Mt. Elliott, 48207. Tel: 313-579-2100; Fax: 313-571-1822. Jerry Smith, O.F.M.Cap., Exec. Dir.; Bob Malloy, O.F.M.Cap., Pastoral Dir.; Ray Stadmeyer, O.F.M.Cap., Site Dir.

On the Rise Bakery, 6110 McClellan, 48213. Tel: 313-922-8510.

Conner Kitchen Mike Breen, Site Dir.; Nancyann Turner, O.P., Mgr. Children & Youth Program. Tel: 313-822-8606, Ext. 21.

Capuchin Services, 6333 Medbury, 48211. Tel: 313-925-1730, Ext. 100. George Gaerig, Opers. Mgr.

Meldrum Kitchen, 1264 Meldrum, 48207. Tel: 313-579-2100. Alison Costello, Site Dir.; Ed Conlin, S.W., Chap.

Jefferson House, 8311 E. Jefferson, 48214. Tel: 313-331-8900; Fax: 313-331-2322. Joe Monachino, O.F.M.Cap., Site Dir. Transitional alcohol-drug residence.

Catholic Community Services of the Archdiocese of Detroit, Inc., 1234 Washington Blvd., 48226. Tel: 313-237-5885; Fax: 313-237-4642. Most Rev. Allen J. Vigneron, D.D., Pres.; Rev. Msgr. Robert J. McClory, Sec.; Mr. Daniel Oliver, Treas.

Manna Community Meal (Soup Kitchen), 1950 Trumbull, 48226. Tel: 313-963-8708.

St. Patrick Senior Center, Inc., 58 Parsons, 48201. Tel: 313-833-7080; Fax: 313-833-0128. Web: www.stpatseniorcenter.com. Mrs. Satrice Coleman-Betts, Exec. Dir. Lay Staff 10; Patients Assisted Annually 1,600.

Pope John XXIII Hospitality House, 3977 2nd Ave., 48201. Tel: 313-965-4450; Fax: 313-965-4453. Rev. Russell E. Kohler. Cancer outpatient-residents, Transportation for Area Pediatric Cancer Patients.

Society of St. Vincent de Paul, 3000 Gratiot Ave., 48207. Tel: 313-393-2925; Fax: 313-393-2934. Email: bbrazier@svdpdet.org. Web: www.svdpdet.org. Mr. William D. Brazier, Exec. Dir.

HARRISVILLE. *The Oratory*, 407 N. Lake St., 48740. Tel: 313-965-4450; Fax: 313-965-4453. Email: corktown99@sbcglobal.net. Rev. Russell E. Kohler, Dir.

ONSTED. *St. Patrick's Retreat*, 11528 Killarney Hwy., 49265. Tel: 313-965-4450; Fax: 313-965-4453. Email: corktown99@sbcglobal.net. Rev. Russell E. Kohler, Dir. Tel: 313-832-4357. Retreats for Family with cancer outpatient; small groups of handicapped-developmentally disabled; small parish team meetings; hospice & chaplain's meetings and offers assistance for patient visits to world shrines.

St. Patrick's Chapel, Tipton, Michigan 4345 US12, Tipton, 49287. Tel: 313-965-4450; Fax: 313-965-4453. Email: corktown99@sbcglobal.net. 14-acre site for children's chapel and nature sanctuary to memorialize victims of childhood cancer and programs of aftercare for bereaved family members.

TROY. *Gabriel Richard Institute*, 3641 Estates Dr., 48084. Tel: 248-643-8887; 248-229-6877; Fax: 248-643-8887. Ms. Dolores Ammar, Exec. Dir. Adult and youth Christopher Leadership training for Catholic laymen, women, clergy & religious.

WARREN. *St. John's Deaf Center*, 14057 E. Nine Mile Rd., 48089. Tel: 586-758-0710 (TDD); 866-281-7108 (VP); 586-774-8476 (Voice); Fax: 586-774-8476. Rev. Richard J. Yost, O.S.F.S., Dir.

[R] CAMPS AND COMMUNITY CENTERS

DETROIT. *C.Y.O. Boys Camp*, 305 Michigan Ave., 48226. Tel: 313-963-7172; Fax: 313-963-7179. Email: ckrucker@cyodetroit.org. Web: www.cyocamps.org.

C.Y.O. Girls Camp, 305 Michigan Ave., 48226. Tel: 313-963-7172; Fax: 313-963-7179. Email: ckrucker@cyodetroit.org. Web: www.cyocamps.org.

Camp Ozanam, 3000 Gratiot Ave., 48207. Tel: 313-393-2930; 877-788-4623; Fax: 313-393-2934. Web: www.svdpdet.org/camp.cfm. Mr. William D. Brazier, Exec. Dir. A free week-long Christian camping experience for boys 8-12. Recruitment through Parish Conferences of the Society of St. Vincent de Paul.

Camp Stapleton, 3000 Gratiot Ave., 48207. Tel: 313-393-2930; 877-788-4623; Fax: 313-393-2934. Web: www.svdpdet.org/camp.cfm. Mr. William D. Brazier, Exec. Dir. A free week long Christian camping experience for girls 8-12. Recruitment through Parish Conferences of the Society of St. Vincent de Paul.

[S] CAMPUS MINISTRIES

DETROIT. *Center for Creative Studies Campus Ministry* 5221 Gullen Mall, #761, 48202. Tel: 313-577-3462. Ms. Aundrea Klesko, Campus Min.

Marygrove College Campus Ministry 8425 W. McNichols Rd., 48221. Tel: 313-927-1404; Fax: 313-927-1345. Sr. Barbara Beesley, Campus Ministry & Svc. Learning Coord.

University of Detroit Mercy University Ministry University Ministry UC106, 4001 W. McNichols Rd., 48221-3038. Web: www.udmercy.edu/ministry.

McNichols Campus Tel: 313-993-1560. Rev. Gary R. Wright, S.J., Dir.; Sisters Beth Ann Finster, S.S.J., Asst. Dir.; Katherine Hill, R.S.M., Campus Min.; Drew Peters, Campus Min.

Wayne County Community College 305 Michigan Ave., 48226. Tel: 313-237-4687.

Wayne State Medical School 5221 Gullen Mall #761, 48202. Tel: 313-577-3462. Ms. Aundrea Klesko, Campus Min.

Wayne State University, Newman Center 5221 Gullen Mall, #761, 48202. Tel: 313-577-3462. Ms. Aundrea Klesko, Campus Min.

DEARBORN. *Archdiocesan Catholic Campus Ministry Association, Gabriel Richard Campus Ministry, University of Michigan-Dearborn*, 5001 Evergreen, 48128. Tel: 313-271-6000. Email: grcministry@yahoo.com. Ms. Jennifer Horn, Campus Min.; Rev. Brendan Walsh, S.C.A., Campus Min.

Univ. of Michigan, Dearborn, Henry Ford Community College Newman Center 5001 Evergreen Rd., 48128. Tel: 313-271-6000. Ms. Jennifer Horn, Campus Min.; Rev. Brendan Walsh, S.C.A., Campus Min. Gabriel Richard Campus Ministry Center.

FARMINGTON HILLS. *Oakland Community College* 305 Michigan Ave., 48226. Tel: 313-237-4687.

LIVONIA. *Madonna University Campus Ministry* 36600 Schoolcraft, 48150. Tel: 734-432-5419; Fax: 734-432-5393. Sr. Anita M. Taddonio, C.S.S.F., Interim Dir. & Campus Min.

Schoolcraft Community College 305 Michigan Ave., 48226. Tel: 313-237-4687.

MONROE. *Monroe Community College* 305 Michigan Ave., 48226. Tel: 313-237-4687.

PORT HURON. *Blue Water/Thumb Regional Campus Ministry* 305 Michigan Ave., 48226. Tel: 313-237-4687. (Baker College and St. Clair Community College)

ROCHESTER. *St. John Fisher Campus Ministry-Oakland University, Rochester* 3665 Walton Blvd., Auburn Hills, 48326. Tel: 248-370-2189. Web: www.oucampusministry.com. Mrs. Lisa Brown, Campus Min.

SOUTHFIELD. *Lawrence Technological University* Mailing Address: 305 Michigan Ave., 48226. Tel: 313-237-4687.

WARREN. *Macomb Community College Campus Ministry* 305 Michigan Ave, 48226. Tel: 313-237-4687.

[T] MISCELLANEOUS LISTINGS

DETROIT. *Annunciation Institute*, 2701 Chicago Blvd., 48206. Tel: 313-980-0622.

St. Catherine of Siena Academy Foundation, 500 Woodward Ave., Ste. 3500, 48226-3435. Tel: 313-965-8293; Fax: 313-965-8252.

Christ Child Society, 15751 Joy Rd., 48228. Tel: 313-584-6077. Rev. Msgr. John P. Zenz, Spiritual Dir.; Jill Barker, Pres.

Clergy Health Plan, Chancery Building, 1234 Washington Blvd., 48226.

Dominican Center for Religious Development, 23333 Schoolcraft, 48228. Tel: 313-387-9574; Fax: 313-535-9207. Email: info@dominicancenter.org. Web: www.dominicancenter.org. Sisters Joanne Podlucky, O.P., Dir.; Rosemarie Kieffer, O.P., Staff/Spiritual Dir.; Rev. Victor Clore; Sr. Teresa Disch, O.P., Staff/Spiritual Dir.

Dominican Literacy Center, 11148 Harper, 48213. Tel: 313-267-1000. Sr. Janice Brown, O.P., Exec. Dir.

Gabriel Richard Historical Society, 1000 Ste. Anne St., 48216. Tel: 313-963-1888; Fax: 313-496-0429. Rev. Thomas W. Sepulveda, C.S.B., Contact Person.

Institute for Communal Contemplation and Dialogue, 8531 W. McNichols, 48221. Tel: 313-971-3668; Fax: 313-342-7421. Email: circles@engagingimpasse.org. Web: www.engagingimpasse.org. Sr. Nancy Sylvester, I.H.M., Exec. Dir.

Jesuit Seminary Association, 7303 W. Seven Mile Rd., 48221. Tel: 313-861-7500; Fax: 313-861-4230. Email: sjdetroit@aol.com. Web: www.jesuitdet.org. Rev. James E. Von Tobel, S.J., Dir. of Devel. & Communications.

Jesuit International Missions Tel: 248-625-5611; Fax: 248-625-3526. Email: dictwo@aol.com. Web: wwww.colombiere.com. Rev. Richard H. Twohig, S.J.

Jesuit Volunteer Corps. Midwest, Inc., 7333 W. Seven Mile Rd., 48221. Tel: 313-345-3480; Fax: 313-345-5410. Email: jvcmw@jesuitvolunteers.org. Web: www.jesuitvolunteers.org. P.O. Box 21936, 48221-0936. Angela Moloney, Exec. Dir.

Latino Cultural Pastoral Center, 4329 Central, 48210. Tel: 248-398-4565.

**Mercy Education Project*, 1450 Howard St., 48216. Tel: 313-963-5881; Fax: 313-963-0209. Email: mep@mercyed.net. Web: www.mercyed.net. Sr. Maureen Mulcrone, R.S.M., Dir. Devel. & Mktg.

Missionary Medical Relief, 17330 Quincy St., 48221. Tel: 313-342-4066; Fax: 313-342-6816. Email: mmr@pimeusa.org. Web: www.pimeusa.org. Ms. Barbara J. Rubaie, Dir. An agency of the P.I.M.E. Missionaries.

PIME Foster Parents, 17330 Quincy Ave., 48221. Tel: 313-342-4066; Fax: 313-342-6816. Rev. Sergio Fossati, P.I.M.E., Mission Center Dir.; Ms. Maria Biernacki, Dir. An agency of the PIME Missionaries.

Pontiac Vision 2000 Schools, Inc., 1234 Washington Blvd., 48226. Tel: 313-237-5803. Mr. Daniel Oliver, Sec. & Treas.

Pope John Paul II Cultural Foundation, Inc. His Eminence Adam Cardinal Maida, J.C.L., J.D., S.T.L., Contact Person (Retired).

Foundation Office, 1234 Washington Blvd., 48226. Tel: 313-237-5816; Fax: 313-237-4642. Web: www.jp2cc.org.

Operations Office, Pope John Paul II Cultural Center, 3900 Harewood Rd., N.E., Washington, DC 20017-1555. Tel: 202-635-5400; Fax: 202-635-5411. His Eminence Adam Cardinal Maida, J.C.L., J.D., S.T.L., Pres.; Most Revs. John J. Myers, D.D., J.C.D., First Vice Pres.; Donald W. Wuerl, S.T.D., Vice Pres.; Bernard J. Harrington, D.D., Sec.; Mr. Daniel Oliver, Treas.; Rev. Steven C. Boguslawski, O.P., M.A., M.Div., S.T.M., S.T.L., Ph.D., Acting Exec. Dir.; Dr. Hugh Dempsey, K.M.O.B., Deputy Dir. & Dir. Devel.

Siena Literacy Center, 16161 Winston St., 48219. Tel: 313-532-8404; Fax: 313-532-8409. Email: info@sienaliteracy.org. Web: www.sienaliteracy.org. Donna J. Nesbitt, Dir.

Solanus Casey Center, 1780 Mt. Elliott, 48207-3596. Tel: 313-579-2100, Ext. 130; Fax: 313-579-5365. Web: www.solanuscaseycenter.org. Revs. Lawrence E. Webber, O.F.M.Cap., Dir.; James C. Hast, O.F.M.Cap., Asst. Dir., Pastoral Care.

BLOOMFIELD HILLS. *Detroit Catholic Charismatic Renewal Center*, 1390 Quarton Rd., 48304. Tel: 248-593-4888; Fax: 248-593-4889. Email: dccrcenter@aol.com. Web: www.bobandmaryann.com. Rev. John C. Esper, Liaison; Arlene Apone, Assoc. Liaison.

Logos, Inc. (Michigan), 2460 Opdyke Rd., 48304. Tel: 248-644-2954; Fax: 248-642-4668. Revs. Lorenzo Gomez, L.C., Rector; Daniel Pajerski, L.C.; Bro. Gerardo Gonzalez, L.C., Vice Rector.

Mercy Homecare - Oakland, 281 Enterprise Dr., Ste. 200, 48302. Tel: 248-858-7735; Fax: 248-858-8323. Web: www.trinity-health.org. Ms. Mary Ann Rayrat, Exec. Dir.

**Mercy Hospice*, 281 Enterprise Ct., Ste. 200, 48302. Tel: 800-832-1155; Fax: 248-858-8323. Ms. Mary Ann Rayrat, Exec. Dir.

Opdyke, Inc., 2460 Opdyke Rd., 48304. Tel: 248-644-2954; Fax: 248-642-4668. Rev. Jose Felix Ortega, L.C., Contact.

Voluntas Dei Institute, 2104 Eagle Pointe, 48304. Tel: 248-499-9576; Fax: 248-644-1758. Web: www.voluntasdeiusa.org. Rev. George F. Hazler, District Dir.

WCVA, Inc. - Michigan Catholic Radio, 38710 Woodward Ave., Ste. 220, 48304-2964. Tel: 248-642-6226; Fax: 248-642-6027. Web: www.catholicradio.org. Mr. John F.X. Browne, Pres.

CLARKSTON. *Clarkston Pastoral Center, Inc.*, 5935 Clarkson Rd., 48348. Tel: 248-241-9043; Fax: 248-922-2084. Revs. Lorenzo Gomez, L.C.; Jose Antonio Rivas, L.C., Everest Academy Chap.; Daniel Pajerski, L.C., Everest Academy Boys School Dir.

DEARBORN. *Council of Catholic Women*, P.O. Box 5097, 48128. Tel: 313-563-1734. Lorraine McFee, Pres.

Leo XIII Society, 1840 N. Melborn, 48128. Tel: 313-359-1499; Fax: 313-359-1767. P.O. Box 666, Elmore, OH 43416. Ernie Scarano, Pres.

EASTPOINTE. *Servants of Jesus of The Divine Mercy*, 16103 Chesterfield, 48021-1106. Tel: 586-777-8591; Fax: 586-777-7989. Email: sdivine2013@wowway.com. Web: www.sjdivinemercy.org. Ms. Catherine M. Lanni, Spiritual Moderator/Pres.

FARMINGTON HILLS. *Trinity Health International*, 34605 Twelve Mile Rd., 48331. Tel: 248-489-6100; Fax: 248-488-9220. Mr. Joseph Swedish, Bd. Chm.; Mr. Jim Cotelingam, Pres.

GROSSE POINTE. *John Paul II Foundation of Michigan, Inc.*, 1 Elmsleigh Ln., 48230. Tel: 313-882-2140; Fax: 313-882-1292. Conducts religious, cultural, educational, humanitarian and fund raising activities in Michigan in liaison with the John Paul Foundation in Rome. Regular, supporting and life memberships.

LIVONIA. **Angela Hospice Home Care, Inc.*, 14100 Newburgh Rd., 48154-5010. Tel: 734-464-7810; Fax: 734-779-4601. Email: ahospice@aol.com. Web: www.angelahospice.org. Bed Capacity 16; Total Assisted Annually (with home care) 1,600; Total Staff 135.

Felician Sisters of Livonia Foundation, 36800 Schoolcraft, 48150. Tel: 734-591-1730; Fax: 734-591-1710. Email: cssf@felicianslivonia.org. Web: www.felicianslivonia.org. Sr. Mary Renetta Rumpz, C.S.S.F., Pres.

Marian Village Corporation aka Marywood Nursing Care Center 36800 Schoolcraft, 48150. Tel: 734-591-1730; Fax: 734-591-1710. Email: cssf@felicianslivonia.org. Web: www.feliciansisters.org. Sr. Mary Renetta Rumpz, C.S.S.F., Pres. & CEO.

Mercy Services for Aging, Non-profit Housing Corporation Wholly owned subsidiary of Trinity Continuing Care Services, 17410 College Pkwy., Ste. 200, 48152-2363. Tel: 734-542-8349; Fax: 248-488-9169. Email: harrisj@trinity-health.org. Web: www.trinityccs.org. Jaclyn Harris, Pres. & CEO.

Trinity Continuing Care Services - Indiana, Inc., 17410 College Pkwy., Ste. 200, 48152-2363. Tel: 734-542-8349; Fax: 248-488-9169. Email: harrisj@trinity-health.org. Web: www.trinityccs.org. Ms. Jaclyn Harris, Pres. & CEO.

MARYSVILLE. *National Alliance of Parishes Restructuring into Communities (NAPRC)*, 1000 Michigan Ave., 48040. Tel: 810-364-3228; Fax: 810-364-5947. Email: naprcoffice@ameritech.net. Rev. Arthur R. Baranowski, Dir.

MONROE. *SSIHM Charitable Trust (Retired and Infirm Sisters)*, 610 W. Elm Ave., 48162-7909. Tel: 734-240-9700; Fax: 734-240-9784. Sr. Helen Ingles, I.H.M., Trustee.

NOVI. *Trinity Health Corporation*, 27870 Cabot Dr., 48377-2920. Tel: 248-489-6000; Fax: 248-489-6775. Email: HaleD@Trinity-Health.org. Web: www.trinity-health.org. Mr. Joseph Swedish, Pres. & CEO.

Trinity Health-Michigan, 27870 Cabot Dr., 48377-2920. Tel: 248-489-6000; Fax: 248-489-6775. Web: www.trinity-health.org. Mr. Joseph Swedish, Pres. Organization owns & operates 7 hospital divisions in Michigan. In addition to acute care facilities, Trinity Health - Michigan operates other related health care programs and facilities. Trinity Health - Michigan is part of Trinity Health, a multi-state health care organization.

**Trinity Home Health Services, Inc.*, 39500 Orchard Hills Pl., Ste. 400, 48375. Tel: 248-305-7920; Fax: 248-305-7632. Email: kingslel@trinity-health.org. Web: www.trinityhomehealth.com. Ms. Grace C. McCauley, CEO.

ORCHARD LAKE. *American Friends of the Vatican Library*, 3535 Indian Tr., 48324. Tel: 248-683-0311; Fax: 248-738-6735. Rev. Msgr. Charles G. Kosanke, Pres.

PONTIAC. *Mt. Hope Catholic Cemetery Association*, 46408 Woodward Ave., 48342. Tel: 248-332-1079. Rev. James F. Kean; Joseph E. Alessi, Supt.

PORT HURON. *Port Huron Mercy Family Care*, 2601 Electric Ave., P.O. Box 610669, 48061-0669. Tel: 810-985-1868. Ms. Nancy Mason, Dir. (A unit of Trinity Health).

REDFORD. *Catholic Biblical School of Michigan, Ltd.*, 26234 Graham Rd., 48239. Tel: 313-570-8105; Fax: 586-774-4040.

ROMEO. **BVM Foundation*, 11070 W. Gates, 48065. Tel: 586-752-6744; Fax: 888-950-3329. Email: info@bvmfoundation.com. Mr. Brian Palmer, Pres.

SHELBY TWP. *Holy Trinity Apostolate*, 53565 Sherwood Ln., 48315. Tel: 586-781-6051; Fax: 568-781-6051. Barbara Middleton, Pres.

ST. CLAIR SHORES. *Catholic Kolping Society of America, Detroit Branch, Inc.*, 24409 Jefferson, 48080. Tel: 586-775-9159. Mrs. Rosalinda Seubert, Pres.; Ms. Thekla Abels, Contact Person. Tel: 313-885-1189; Very Rev. Daniel J. Fox, O.F.M.Cap.

**Celebrate Life Ministries*, P.O. Box 537, Roseville, 48066. Tel: 586-778-4446. Sr. Loretta Mellon, O.P., Exec. Dir.

WARREN. *St. John Health System* Holding Company sponsored by Sisters of St. Joseph, the Daughters of Charity of St. Vincent de Paul and Sisters of St. Joseph of Carondelet which operates: St. John Hospital & Medical Center; Medical Resources Group; Affiliated Health Services, Inc.; St. John Senior Community; Eastwood Community Clinics; St. John River District Hospital; St. John Macomb-Oakland Hospital; Father Murray Nursing Center; St. John Home Care; St. John Health Foundation; Providence Hospital and Medical Centers, Inc.; Seton Health Corporation of Southeast Michigan; St. John Community Health Investment Corporation; St. John Hospital Foundation; St. John Macomb Foundation., 28000 Dequindre Rd., 48092. Tel: 586-753-0911; Fax: 586-753-0491. Mr. Elliot Joseph, Pres. & CEO.

WATERFORD. *Dominican Health Care Corporation*, 2300 Walkins Lake Rd., 48328. Tel: 248-674-2241; Fax: 248-674-1211. Web: www.lourdes-sc.org. Sr. Maureen Comer, O.P., CEO.

Lourdes Campus Fund, 2300 Watkins Lake Rd., 48328. Tel: 248-674-2241; Fax: 248-674-1211. Web: www.lourdes-sc.org. Sr. Maureen Comer, O.P., CEO.

WESTLAND. *Chinese Catholic Society of Michigan, Inc.*, 39375 Joy Rd., 48185. Tel: 248-855-4517; Fax: 248-647-7736. Mr. Francis G. King, Pres.; Mr. Thomas McGuire, Spiritual Dir.

[U] CLOSED INSTITUTIONS

DETROIT. *Archdiocesan Archives* The following institutional sacramental records can be found at the following address unless otherwise indicated., 1234 Washington Blvd., 48226. Tel: 313-237-5846; Fax: 313-237-4643.

St. Agnes
St. Albertus
Anawim Community
St. Andrew Records at Our Lady Queen of Angels, Detroit.
Annunciation Records at Good Shepherd, Detroit.
Annunciation/Our Lady of Sorrows Records at Good Shepherd, Detroit.
St. Anthony Records at Good Shepherd, Detroit.
Assumption of the Blessed Virgin Mary
St. Augustine
St. Bartholomew Records at St. Bartholomew-St. Rita, Detroit.
St. Benedict the Moor
St. Bernadette Chapel
St. Bernard
St. Boniface
St. Brendan
St. Brigid
St. Camillus
Cardinal Leger Community
St. Casimir
St. Catherine
St. Catherine of Siena
St. Christine
Corpus Christi
St. David
St. Dominic
St. Edward
Emmaus Community
Epiphany
St. Eugene
St. Francis de Sales Records at St. Peter Claver, Detroit.
St. Francis Hospital
St. Gemma
St. George (Lithuanian)
St. Gerard Records at Corpus Christi, Detroit.
Guardian Angels
Holy Ghost
Holy Name of Jesus
St. Ignatius of Antioch
Immaculate Conception
Immaculate Heart of Mary Records at Corpus Christi, Detroit.
St. Jerome Records at St. Lucy Croatian, Troy
St. Joachim
St. John Berchmans
St. John Berchmans/St. Juliana
St. John Cantius
St. John the Evangelist
St. John Nepomucene
St. Joseph Mercy Hospital
St. Juliana
St. Lawrence
St. Margaret Mary
St. Martin of Tours
Martyrs of Uganda
St. Mary Hospital - Detroit Memorial Hospital
St. Monica
Mother of Consolation
Mother of Our Savior
Mount Carmel Mercy Hospital
Our Lady Gate of Heaven Records at St. Suzanne/Our Lady Gate of Heaven, Detroit
Our Lady of Guadalupe
Our Lady of Help
Our Lady Help of Christians Records at Transfiguration-Our Lady Help of Christians, Detroit.
Our Lady of Mt. Carmel
Our Lady Queen of Hope
Our Lady of Sorrows Records at Good Shepherd, Detroit.
St. Paul Maltese
Patronage of St. Joseph
St. Peter Claver Records at Sacred Heart, Detroit
St. Peter (Lithuanian)
St. Philip Neri
Precious Blood Records at St. Peter Claver, Detroit.
Resurrection
St. Rita Records at St. Bartholomew-St. Rita, Detroit.
St. Rose of Lima
St. Stanislaus Bishop and Martyr
St. Suzanne Records at St. Suzanne/Our Lady Gate of Heaven, Detroit
St. Theresa
St. Thomas the Apostle
Transfiguration Records at Transfiguration-Our Lady Help of Christians, Detroit.
St. Vincent de Paul
Santa Maria
Visitation
St. Wenceslaus

ALGONAC. *St. Catherine of Alexandria* Records at Our Lady on the River, Marine City.

CLINTON TOWNSHIP. *St. Claude* Records at St. Thecla, Clinton Twp.

St. Valerie of Ravenna Records at St. Louis, Clinton Twp.

COLUMBUS. *Holy Rosary Mission* Records at Holy Family Parish - All Saints Church, Memphis.

St. Philip Neri Records at Holy Family Parish - All Saints Church, Memphis.

DEARBORN. *St. Bernadette*

EASTPOINTE. *St. Barnabas* Records at Holy Innocents-St. Barnabas, Roseville.

HARSENS ISLAND. *St. Mark* Records at Our Lady of the River, Marine City.

HIGHLAND PARK. *St. John Vianney*

INKSTER. *St. Kevin*
SS. Kevin & Norbert
St. Norbert

MACOMB. *St. Maximilian Kolbe* Records at St. Francis of Assisi-St. Maximilian Kolbe, Ray.

MARINE CITY. *Holy Cross* Records at Our Lady on the River, Marine City.

MELVINDALE. *St. Conrad* Records at St. Mary Magdalen, Melvindale.

MEMPHIS. *All Saints* Records at Holy Family, Memphis.

NORTH BRANCH. *St. Patrick Mission* Records at SS. Peter & Paul, North Branch.

PONTIAC. *St. Joseph* Records at St. Damien of Molokai, Pontiac.

St. Michael Records at St. Damien of Molokai, Pontiac.

St. Vincent de Paul Records at St. Damien of Molokai, Pontiac.

PORT HURON. *St. Joseph* Records at Holy Trinity, Port Huron.

Our Lady of Guadalupe Mission Records at Holy Trinity, Port Huron.

St. Stephen Records at Holy Trinity, Port Huron.

RAY. *St. Francis of Assisi* Records at St. Francis of Assisi-St. Maximilian Kolbe, Ray.

REDFORD. *St. Agatha*

ROSEVILLE. *Holy Innocents* Records at Holy Innocents-St. Barnabas, Roseville.

ST. CLAIR SHORES. *St. Germaine* Records at Our Lady of Hope, St. Clair Shores.

St. Gertrude Records at Our Lady of Hope, St. Clair Shores.

SOUTHFIELD. *St. Beatrice* Records at Church of the Transfiguration, Southfield.

St. Bede Records at Church of the Transfiguration, Southfield.

St. Ives Records at Church of the Transfiguration, Southfield.

St. Michael Records at Church of the Transfiguration, Southfield.

SOUTHGATE. *St. Hugh* Records at St. Frances Cabrini, Allen Park.

TAYLOR. *St. Cyril of Jerusalem* Records at Our Lady of the Angels, Taylor.

St. Paschal Baylon Records at Our Lady of the Angels, Taylor.

TROY. *Our Lady of the Hills*

UTICA. *Vida Nueva Community*

WARREN. *Ascension* Records at St. Clement, Center Line.

St. Dorothy Records at St. Teresa of Avila, Warren.

St. Leonard of Port Maurice Records at St. Teresa of Avila Parish.

WYANDOTTE. *St. Helena*

RELIGIOUS INSTITUTES OF MEN REPRESENTED IN THE ARCHDIOCESE

For further details refer to the corresponding bracketed number in the Religious Institutes of Men or Women section.

[0140]—*The Augustinians* (Chicago)—O.S.A.
[0170]—*Basilian Fathers* (Toronto, Ont.)—C.S.B.
[0200]—*Benedictine Monks* (Detroit Prov.)—O.S.B.
[0330]—*Brothers of the Christian Schools* (District of Eastern North America)—F.S.C.
[0600]—*Brothers of the Congregation of Holy Cross* (Midwest Prov.)—C.S.C.
[]—*Canons Regular of the Holy Cross*—O.R.C.
[0470]—*The Capuchin Friars* (St. Joseph Prov.)—O.F.M.Cap.
[0310]—*Congregation of Christian Brothers* (American Prov.)—C.F.C.
[0750]—*Congregation of Marianhill Missionaries*—C.M.M.
[]—*Congregation of the Holy Spirit*—C.S.Sp.
[1000]—*Congregation of the Passion* (Western Prov.)—C.P.
[1140]—*Congregation of the Sacred Hearts of Jesus and Mary*—SS.CC.
[0480]—*Conventual Franciscans*—O.F.M.Conv
[0520]—*Franciscan Friars (Custody of the Holy Family/Croatian)* (Prov. of St. John the Baptist; Prov. of St. Stephen, King of Hungary)—O.F.M.
[0690]—*Jesuit Fathers and Brothers* (Detroit, Chicago, New Orleans, New York, Maryland Provinces)—S.J.
[0730]—*Legionaries of Christ*—L.C.
[]—*Little Brothers of Jesus*
[0780]—*Marist Fathers* (Northeastern Prov.)—S.M.
[]—*Miles Christi Institute*—M.C.
[]—*Missionaries of St. Francis de Sales* Visakhapatnam Province, India—M.S.F.S.
[]—*Missionary Society of St. Paul*—M.S.S.P.
[0920]—*Oblates of St. Francis De Sales*—O.S.F.S.
[0430]—*Order of Preachers-Dominicans* (Prov. of St. Albert the Great)—O.P.
[1020]—*Pious Society of St. Paul*—S.S.P.
[1050]—*Pontifical Institute for Foreign Missions*—P.I.M.E.
[1070]—*Redemptorist Fathers* (Denver Prov.)—C.SS.R.
[]—*Salesians of Don Bosco*—S.D.B.
[1260]—*Society of Christ* (American-Canadian Prov.)—S.Ch.
[0440]—*Society of Saint Edmund*—S.S.E.
[]—*Society of St. Paul*—S.S.P.
[0990]—*Society of the Catholic Apostolate*—S.A.C.
[]—*Voluntas Dei Institute, I.V. Dei*

RELIGIOUS INSTITUTES OF WOMEN REPRESENTED IN THE ARCHDIOCESE

[1810]—*Bernardine Sisters of the Third Order of St. Francis*—O.S.F.
[3810]—*Catholic Mission Sisters of St. Francis Xavier*—X.S.
[]—*Congregation of Sisters of Bon Secours*—C.B.S.

[]—*Congregation of the Sisters of Divine Providence*—C.D.P.
[3832]—*Congregation of the Sisters of St. Joseph*—C.S.J.
[0760]—*Daughters of Charity of St. Vincent de Paul*—D.C.
[0790]—*Daughters of Divine Charity*—F.D.C.
[]—*Daughters of Mary* (India)—D.M.
[]—*Daughters of Mary Immaculate (Chaldean)*—D.M.I.
[]—*Daughters of Mary, Mother of Mercy*—D.M.M.M.
[]—*Daughters of the Heart of Mary*—D.H.M.
[0420]—*Discalced Carmelite Nuns*—O.C.D.
[1050]—*Dominican Contemplative Nuns*—O.P.
[1070-13]—*Dominican Sisters (Adrian, MI)*—O.P.
[1070-14]—*Dominican Sisters (Grand Rapids, MI)*—O.P.
[]—*Dominican Sisters of Mt. Thabor*—O.P.
[1115]—*Dominican Sisters of Peace*—O.P.
[1170]—*Felician Sisters*—C.S.S.F.
[]—*Franciscan Missionaries of Jesus Crucified*—F.M.J.C.
[]—*Franciscan Sisters of St. Joseph*—F.S.S.J.
[]—*Franciscan Sisters of the Atonement*—S.A.
[1440]—*Franciscan Sisters of the Poor*—S.F.P.
[]—*Holy Name of Jesus and Mary*—S.N.J.M.
[2430]—*Marist Sisters Congregation of Mary*—S.M.
[]—*Mission Helpers of the Sacred Heart*—M.H.S.H.
[2710]—*Missionaries of Charity*—M.C.
[]—*Missionaries of the Kingship of Christ*—S.I.M.
[M.Chr.]—*Missionary Sisters of Christ the King for Polonia*
[]—*Order of St. Basil the Great*—O.S.B.M.
[2970]—*School Sisters of Notre Dame*—S.S.N.D.
[3560]—*Servants of Jesus*—S.J.
[3590]—*Servants of Mary (Servite Sisters)*—O.S.M.
[0440]—*Sisters of Charity of Cincinnati, Ohio*—S.C.
[0520]—*Sisters of Charity of Our Lady, Mother of Mercy*—S.C.M.M.
[2245]—*Sisters of Jesus the Savior*—S.J.S.
[2575]—*Sisters of Mercy of the Americas* (Mid-Atlantic Community; West Midwest Community)—R.S.M
[2990]—*Sisters of Notre Dame*—S.N.D.
[]—*Sisters of St. Francis* Oldenburg
[1530]—*Sisters of St. Francis of the Congregation of Our Lady of Lourdes* (Sylvania, OH & Tiffin, OH)—O.S.F.
[3930]—*Sisters of St. Joseph of the Third Order of St. Francis*—S.S.J.-T.O.S.F.
[1830]—*Sisters of the Good Shepherd*—R.G.S.
[]—*Sisters of the Holy Cross*
[1970]—*Sisters of the Holy Family of Nazareth*—C.S.F.N.
[]—*Sisters of the Imitation of Christ* (India)—S.I.C.
[2350]—*Sisters of the Living Word*—S.L.W.
[]—*Sisters of the Precious Blood*—C.P.P.S.
[2090]—*Sisters, Home Visitors of Mary*—H.V.M.
[2150]—*Sisters, Servants of the Immaculate Heart of Mary*—I.H.M.
[2460]—*Society of Mary Reparatrix*—S.M.R.
[4070]—*Society of the Sacred Heart*—R.S.C.J.
[]—*Vestiarski Sisters of Jesus*—V.S.

ARCHDIOCESAN CEMETERIES

DETROIT. *Holy Cross*, 8850 Dix Ave., 48209. Tel: 313-841-0545. (owned & operated by the Archdiocese of Detroit)
Mt. Elliott, 1701 Mt. Elliott Ave., 48207. Tel: 313-567-0048. (owned & operated by the Mt. Elliott Cemetery Assoc.)
Mt. Olivet, 17100 Van Dyke, 48234. Tel: 313-365-5650. (owned & operated by the Mt. Elliott Cemetery Assoc.)

CLINTON TOWNSHIP. *Resurrection*, 18201 Clinton River Rd., 48038. Tel: 586-286-9020. (owned & operated by the Mt. Elliott Cemetery Assoc.)

DEARBORN HEIGHTS. *St. Hedwig*, 23755 Military, 48127. Tel: 313-562-1900. (owned & operated by the Conventual Franciscan Friars)

MONROE. *St. Joseph Cemetery*, 909 N. Monroe St., 48162. Tel: 734-241-1411. James Duboy, Gen. Mgr.

ROCHESTER. *Guardian Angel*, 4701 Rochester Rd., 48306. Tel: 800-275-9574. (owned & operated by the Mt. Elliott Cemetery Assoc.)

SOUTHFIELD. *Holy Sepulchre*, 25800 W. Ten Mile Rd., P.O. Box 68, 48037. Tel: 248-350-1900. Sr. Mary V. Korb, R.S.M., Dir. Archdiocesan Cemeteries. (owned & operated by the Archdiocese of Detroit)

SOUTHGATE. *Our Lady of Hope*, 18303 Allen Rd., P.O. Box 1125, 48195. Tel: 734-285-2155. (owned & operated by the Archdiocese of Detroit)

WATERFORD. *All Saints*, 4401 Nelsey Rd., 48329. Tel: 248-623-9633. (owned & operated by the Mt. Elliott Cemetery Assoc.)

NECROLOGY

† Kucyk, Rev. Msgr. Herman W., Dearborn, MI Divine Child—Died May 15, 2009
† Berg, Paul C., (Retired)—Died Jan. 26, 2009
† Burke, Walter E., (Retired)—Died Nov. 25, 2009
† Decker, Maurice C., (Retired)—Died June 23, 2009
† Fauser, Arthur W., (Retired)—Died April 1, 2009
† Ferens, Joseph F., (Retired)—Died Nov. 30, 2009
† Heidelberger, Ronald L., (Retired)—Died Jan. 29, 2009
† Herman, Jerome A., (Retired)—Died Oct. 18, 2009
† Immel, A. William, (Retired)—Died June 16, 2009
† Kowalski, Ralph E., (Retired)—Died Jan. 6, 2009
† Kreft, Henry S., (Retired)—Died Aug. 15, 2009
† Porcari, Ernest, (Retired)—Died June 21, 2009
† Repsys, Ricardas, Southfield, MI Divine Providence—Died 2010
† Ugolik, Richard A., (Retired)—Died July 16, 2009
† Wolber, Ferdinand A., (Retired)—Died Jan. 4, 2009
† Zeeb, Charles M., (Retired)—Died Sept. 9, 2009

An asterisk (*) denotes an organization that has established tax-exempt status directly with the IRS and is not covered by the USCCB Group Ruling.

Diocese of Dodge City

(Dioecesis Dodgepolis)

Most Reverend

RONALD M. GILMORE, S.T.L., D.D.

Bishop of Dodge City; ordained June 7, 1969; appointed Bishop of Dodge City May 12, 1998; installed July 16, 1998. *Office: 910 Central Ave., P.O. Box 137, Dodge City, KS 67801.*

Most Reverend

STANLEY G. SCHLARMAN, D.D.

Bishop Emeritus of Dodge City; ordained July 13, 1958; appointed to the Titular See of Capri and Auxiliary Bishop of Belleville, March 13, 1979; consecrated May 14, 1979; appointed Bishop of Dodge City March 1, 1983; installed May 4, 1983; retired May 12, 1998. *Res.: 2620 Lebanon Ave., Belleville, IL 62221.*

Catholic Church Offices: 910 Central Ave., P.O. Box 137, Dodge City, KS 67801-0137. Tel: 620-227-1500; Fax: 620-227-1570.

Web: www.dcdiocese.org

Email: dcdiocese@dcdiocese.org

ESTABLISHED MAY 19, 1951.

Square Miles 23,000.

Comprises the following Counties in the State of Kansas: Barton, Stafford, Pratt, Barber, Rush, Ness, Lane, Scott, Wichita, Greeley, Hamilton, Kearny, Finney, Hodgeman, Pawnee, Edwards, Ford, Gray, Haskell, Grant, Stanton, Morton, Stevens, Seward, Meade, Clark, Kiowa and Comanche.

Principal Patron: Our Lady of Guadalupe.

Secondary Patron: St. John the Baptist.

For legal titles of parishes and diocesan institutions, consult the Chancery Office.

STATISTICAL OVERVIEW

Personnel	
Bishop	1
Retired Bishops	1
Priests: Diocesan Active in Diocese	18
Priests: Diocesan Active Outside Diocese	2
Priests: Retired, Sick or Absent	10
Number of Diocesan Priests	30
Religious Priests in Diocese	5
Total Priests in Diocese	35
Extern Priests in Diocese	7
Permanent Deacons in Diocese	8
Total Sisters	68
Parishes	
Parishes	48
With Resident Pastor:	
Resident Diocesan Priests	14
Resident Religious Priests	3
Without Resident Pastor:	
Administered by Priests	23
Administered by Religious Women	2
Administered by Lay People	2
Completely Vacant	4
Quasi-Parishes	1
Professional Ministry Personnel:	
Sisters	15
Lay Ministers	16
Welfare	
Catholic Hospitals	2
Total Assisted	178,847
Special Centers for Social Services	4
Total Assisted	6,220
Educational	
Diocesan Students in Other Seminaries	4
Total Seminarians	4
Elementary Schools, Diocesan and Parish	7
Total Students	1,050
Catechesis/Religious Education:	
High School Students	1,387
Elementary Students	3,547
Total Students under Catholic Instruction	5,988
Teachers in the Diocese:	
Sisters	1
Lay Teachers	87
Vital Statistics	
Receptions into the Church:	
Infant Baptism Totals	1,081
Minor Baptism Totals	83
Adult Baptism Totals	48
Received into Full Communion	67
First Communions	1,109
Confirmations	1,072
Marriages:	
Catholic	173
Interfaith	67
Total Marriages	240
Deaths	358
Total Catholic Population	44,182
Total Population	215,585

Former Bishops—Most Revs. JOHN BAPTIST FRANZ, D.D., cons. Aug. 29, 1951; transferred to the See of Peoria Aug. 8, 1959; retired June 1, 1971; died July 3, 1992.; MARION F. FORST, D.D., cons. March 24, 1960; transferred to See of Kansas City, KS as Auxiliary Oct. 16, 1976; retired as Auxiliary Bishop Dec. 23, 1986; died June 2, 2007; EUGENE J. GERBER, D.D., cons. Dec. 14, 1976; transferred to See of Wichita, KS Nov. 23, 1982; STANLEY G. SCHLARMAN, D.D. (Retired), cons. May 14, 1979; appt. Bishop of Dodge City March 1, 1983; installed May 4, 1983; retired May 12, 1998.

Chancery Office and Administration— Unless otherwise noted, the mailing address is: *P.O. Box 137, Dodge City, 67801-0137.* Tel: 620-227-1500; Fax: 620-227-1545. Office Hours: Mon.-Fri. 9-4:30.

Vicar General and Moderator of the Curia—Rev. ROBERT A. SCHREMMER, V.G. Tel: 620-227-1555. Email: rschremmer@dcdiocese.org.

Chancellor—Sr. JANICE GROCHOWSKY, C.S.J., J.C.L. Tel: 620-227-1527. Email: jgrochowsky@dcdiocese.org.

Diocesan Archivist—Mr. TIMOTHY F. WENZL. Tel: 620-227-1556. Email: twenzl@dcdiocese.org.

Finance Officer—Mr. DANIEL M. STREMEL, CPA. Tel: 620-227-1517. Email: dmstremel@dcdiocese.org.

Safe Environment—

Coordinator—Sr. JANICE GROCHOWSKY, C.S.J., J.C.L. Tel: 620-227-1527. Email: jgrochowsky@dcdiocese.org.

Diocesan Fitness Review Administrator—Mr. DAVID H. SNAPP. Tel: 620-225-5051 (office); 620-225-2412 (home).

Assistance Minister—Mrs. DONNA STAAB, M.S.N., R.N., B.C. Tel: 620-792-2098; 620-786-5785. Email: donna@cpcis.net.

Office of Stewardship—Mr. ERIC HASELHORST, Dir. Tel: 620-227-1537. Email: ehaselhorst@dcdiocese.org.

Office of Finance—Mr. DANIEL M. STREMEL, CPA, Dir. Tel: 620-227-1517. Email: dmstremel@dcdiocese.org.

Development and Accounting Services—Mr. JOHN ACKERMAN. Tel: 620-227-1534; Fax: 620-227-1545. Email: jackerman@dcdiocese.org.

Receptionist/Accounts Payable—Mrs. AMY SEACHRIS. Tel: 620-227-1500. Email: aseachris@dcdiocese.org.

Matrimonial Tribunal—

Judicial Vicar—Rev. JOHN V. HOTZE (WCH).

Defender of the Bond—Rev. DAVID H. KRAUS, J.C.L. (Retired).

Judge—Rev. JAMES E. BAKER, J.C.L. (Retired).

Advocates—Revs. TED A. SKALSKY, V.F.; ROBERT A. SCHREMMER, V.G.; Sr. CATHERINE THERESE PAULIE, C.S.J.; Rev. WESLEY W. SCHAWE.

Notary—Sr. JANICE GROCHOWSKY, C.S.J., J.C.L.

Promoter of Justice—Rev. DAVID H. KRAUS, J.C.L. (Retired).

All matrimonial correspondence may be sent to the attention of Sr. Janice Grochowsky, C.S.J., J.C.L. Tel: 620-227-1527; Fax: 620-227-1570. Email: jgrochowsky@dcdiocese.org.

Catholic Education and Formation—

Catholic Elementary Schools—Mr. BILL BIERMANN, Supt. Tel: 620-227-1513; Fax: 620-227-1570. Email: bbiermann@dcdiocese.org.

Diocesan School Council—Mr. BILL BIERMANN, Supt. Schools, 910 Central Ave., Dodge City, 67801. Tel: 620-227-1514; COURTNEY RANKIN, Sacred Heart School, 905 Central, Dodge City, 67801. Tel: 620-225-6532; LORIN HAAS, Sacred Heart School, 330 N. Oak, Pratt, 67124. Tel: 620-672-3687; LORI BILLINGER, St. Joseph School, 111 W. Third, Ellinwood, 67526. Tel: 620-564-2721; ANITA GARCIA, St. Mary School, 503 St. John St., Garden City, 67846. Tel: 620-275-2241; ELOISE DORAN, Holy Family School, 4200 Broadway, Great Bend, 67530. Tel: 620-793-3265; ALAN ROTHS, Sacred Heart School, 510 S. School St., Ness City, 67560. Tel: 785-798-3530; LYNN DUNFORD, St. Dominic School, 617 JC St., Garden City, 67846. Tel: 620-276-8981.

Pastoral Ministry Formation—Rev. Msgr. BRIAN R. MOORE, Dir. Tel: 620-227-1533; Fax: 620-227-1545. Email: bmoore@dcdiocese.org; Mrs. COLEEN STEIN, Coord. Tel: 620-227-1538; Fax: 620-227-1570. Email: cstein@dcdiocese.org.

Youth/Family Ministry and Religious Formation—Mr. STEVEN D. POLLEY, Dir. Tel: 620-227-1540; Fax: 620-227-1570. Email: spolley@dcdiocese.org; Rev. TED D. STOECKLEIN, Assoc. Dir. Young Adult Ministry, P.O. Box 187,

Spearville, 67876-0187. Tel: 620-385-2212; Fax: 620-385-2396. Email: frstoecklein@hotmail.com.

Catechist Formation—VACANT, Coord., Spanish; Mrs. COLEEN STEIN, Coord., English. Tel: 620-227-1538; Fax: 620-227-1570. Email: cstein@dcdiocese.org.

Catholic Social Service: Catholic Charities for Southwest Kansas—Web: www.catholicsocialservice.org. DEBBIE SNAPP, Exec. Dir., 906 Central, Dodge City, 67801. Tel: 620-227-1588; Fax: 620-227-1572. Email: dsnapp@catholicsocialservice.org; Mailing Address: P.O. Box 137, Dodge City, 67801-0137.

Satellite Offices—Garden City: 708 N. Main, Garden City, 67846. Great Bend: 2201 16th St., Great Bend, 67530. Family Crisis Center, 2008 11th St., P.O. Box 1543, Great Bend, 67530. Tel: 620-793-1965; 620-793-1966; 620-792-1885 (Crisis Line); Fax: 620-293-1964. *Sommerset Place, 5830 16th Ter., Great Bend, 67530.* Tel: 620-793-8075; Fax: 620-793-7417.

Pro-Life Activities—VACANT.

Hispanic Ministry—Sr. ANGELA EREVIA, M.C.D.P., Dir. Tel: 620-227-1542. Email: aerivia@dcdiocese.org.

Vietnamese Ministry—Rev. TRONG TRAN, Chap., Mailing Address: 804 N. Colorado, Ulysses, 67880-1734. Tel: 620-356-1532; Fax: 620-424-1065.

Mission Outreach and Propagation of the Faith—Mr. JOHN ACKERMAN, Coord. Tel: 620-227-1534; Fax: 620-227-1545. Email: jackerman@dcdiocese.org.

Migration and Refugee Services—Mrs. LEVITA RUPP, Exec. Dir., 1510 Taylor Plaza E., Garden City, 67846. Tel: 620-276-7610; Fax: 620-276-9228.

Clergy Formation—

Deacon Personnel—Rev. TED A. SKALSKY, V.F., Dir., Mailing Address: P.O. Box 670, Dodge City, 67801-0670. Tel: 620-227-3442; Fax: 620-338-8268.

Priest Continuing Formation—Rev. Msgr. BRIAN R. MOORE, Dir. Tel: 620-227-1533; Fax: 620-227-1545. Email: bmoore@dcdiocese.org.

Vocation and Seminarian—

Director of Seminarians—Rev. Msgr. BRIAN R. MOORE. Tel: 620-227-1533; Fax: 620-227-1545. Email: bmoore@dcdiocese.org.

Diocesan Vocation Coordinator—Mrs. BECKY HESSMAN. Tel: 620-227-1530; Fax: 620-227-1570. Email: bhessman@dcdiocese.org.

Liturgy—VACANT, Diocesan Liturgist.

Media and Communications—

Diocesan Newspaper— bimonthly, "Southwest Kansas Register" Mr. DAVID MYERS, Editor. Tel: 620-227-1519; Fax: 620-227-1545. Email: skregister@dcdiocese.org.

Interactive Television Network—Mrs. COLEEN STEIN, Coord. Tel: 620-227-1538; Fax: 620-227-1570. Email: cstein@dcdiocese.org.

Media/Press Liaison—Mr. TIMOTHY F. WENZL. Tel: 620-227-1556; Fax: 620-227-1570. Email: twenzl@dcdiocese.org.

Scouting—

Catholic Committee on Scouting—Mr. DAVE GEIST. Tel: 620-225-8230; 620-225-0161. Email: daveg@starrtech.net.

Legal Services—

Diocesan Attorney—Foulston & Siefkin, L.L.P., 9 Corporate Woods, 9200 Indian Creek Pkwy., Ste. 450, Overland Park, 66210. Tel: 913-498-2100; Fax: 913-498-2101. TAMARA L. DAVIS, P.A., 100 Military Plaza, Ste. 214, Dodge City, 67801. Tel: 620-225-1674; Fax: 620-227-2770.

Consultative Bodies—

Presbyteral Council—Most Rev. RONALD M. GILMORE, S.T.L., D.D.; Revs. ROBERT A. SCHREMMER, V.G.; HENRY F. HILDEBRANDT; CHARLES MAZOUCH, V.F., Chm.; REGINALD A. URBAN; BERNARD H. FELIX; Rev. Msgr. BRIAN R. MOORE; Rev. DAVID H. KRAUS, J.C.L. (Retired).

College of Consultors—Rev. Msgr. BRIAN R. MOORE; Revs. TED A. SKALSKY, V.F.; ROBERT A. SCHREMMER, V.G.; TED D. STOECKLEIN; JOHN R. STRASSER; JOHN J. MAES (Retired).

Diocesan Finance Council—Most Rev. RONALD M. GILMORE, S.T.L., D.D., Ex Officio; Mr. DANIEL M. STREMEL, CPA, Ex Officio, Sec. & Treas.; Mr. JOHN ACKERMAN, Ex Officio; CLARINE HEIMAN; EUGENE HEIMAN; Revs. JOHN R. STRASSER; JOHN J. MAES (Retired); Sr. JUDITH LINDELL, O.P.; STEVE RICE, CPA; MATILDA SCHEURER; RICHARD GLEASON; JOHN ALIG.

Diocesan Review Board—Mr. DAVID H. SNAPP, Chm.; Mrs. DEBBIE SCHARTZ-ROBINSON; Dr. PATRICK STANG, M.D.; Mrs. HATTIE STEIN; Rev. JOHN R. STRASSER; Mr. MIKE MARTINEZ.

Deans—Revs. CHARLES MAZOUCH, V.F., Great Bend; TED A. SKALSKY, V.F., Dodge City; JAMES P. DIEKER, V.F., Garden City.

CLERGY, PARISHES, MISSIONS AND PAROCHIAL SCHOOLS

CITY OF DODGE CITY

(FORD COUNTY)

1—CATHEDRAL OF OUR LADY OF GUADALUPE CATHOLIC CHURCH OF DODGE CITY, KANSAS (2001) [JC] Rev. Ted A. Skalsky; Rev. Msgr. Brian R. Moore; Rev. Ted D. Stoecklein, Parochial Vicar; Sisters Rose Mary Stein, O.P., Pastoral Min./Coord.; Maria Rea, C.F.P., Hispanic Pastoral Min.; Enedina Lulo, Hispanic Pastoral Min.; Jodi D. Lix, Dir. Administration & Stewardship.

Mailing Address: 3231 N. 14th St., P.O. Box 670, 67801. Tel: 620-225-4802; 620-227-3442; Fax: 620-338-8268. Email: colg@starrtech.net. Web: www.dodgecitycathedral.com.

Church: 3231 N. 14th St., 67801.

School—905 Central Ave., 67801. Tel: 620-227-6532; Fax: 620-227-3221. Email: schutte.shcs@gmail.com. Bonnie Schuette, Prin. Lay Teachers 18; Students 242.

Catechesis/Religious Program—Email: norma@starrtech.net. Mr. Dave Geist, D.R.E., (High School); Norma Alvarez, D.R.E.; Anne Shaughnessy, D.R.E. Students 433.

2—CHURCH OF THE SACRED HEART, Closed. For inquiries for sacramental records, please contact The Cathedral of Our Lady of Guadalupe, Dodge City.

OUTSIDE THE CITY OF DODGE CITY

ASHLAND, CLARK CO., ST. JOSEPH CATHOLIC CHURCH OF ASHLAND, KANSAS (1886) [JC] Rev. Maurice H. Cummings, O.Carm.

512 Cedar St., P.O. Box 577, 67831-0577.

Res.: 514 Main St., P.O. Box 577, 67831-0577. Tel: 620-635-2338; 620-635-2240 (office).

Catechesis/Religious Program—Tel: 620-635-2679. Becky Luerman, D.R.E. Students 26.

BEAVER, BARTON CO., ST. JOSEPH, Closed. Sacramental records can be found at St. John, Hoisington.

BELPRE, EDWARDS CO., ST. BERNARD CATHOLIC CHURCH OF BELPRE, KANSAS (1901) Rev. Bernard H. Felix; Sr. Catherine Therese Paulie, C.S.J., Pastoral Min. Res.: 203 Hudson St., P.O. Box 188, 67519-0188. Tel: 620-995-4305.

Catechesis/Religious Program—Tel: 620-324-5472. Denise Wheaton, D.R.E. Students 35.

BUCKLIN, FORD CO., ST. GEORGE, Closed. Sacramental records can be found at Our Lady of Guadalupe, Dodge City.

BURDETT, PAWNEE CO., HOLY ROSARY, Closed. Sacramental records can be found at Sacred Heart, Larned.

CLAFLIN, BARTON CO., IMMACULATE CONCEPTION CATHOLIC CHURCH OF CLAFLIN, KANSAS (1904) [JC] Rev. Charles Mazouch.

Mailing Address: P.O. Box 197, 67525. Tel: 620-587-3628; Fax: 620-588-3628.

Catechesis/Religious Program—Sr. Andre Kravec, O.P., D.R.E. Students 89.

COLDWATER, COMANCHE CO., HOLY SPIRIT, Quasi-parish. Sacramental records can be found at St. Joseph, Ashland.

DEERFIELD, KEARNEY CO., CHRIST THE KING CATHOLIC CHURCH OF DEERFIELD, KANSAS (1937) Rev. Michael L. Helms.

Mailing Address: P.O. Box 455, 67838. Tel: 620-355-6405.

Catechesis/Religious Program—Tel: 620-277-0309. Twinned with St. Anthony, Lakin.

DIGHTON, LANE CO., ST. THERESA CATHOLIC CHURCH OF DIGHTON, KANSAS (1927) [JC] Rev. Warren L. Stecklein.

Res.: 322 S. First St., P.O. Box 787, 67839. Tel: 620-397-5357.

Catechesis/Religious Program—Rene Roberts, D.R.E. Students 57.

DUBUQUE, BARTON CO., ST. CATHERINE, Closed. Sacramental records can be found at St. John the Evangelist, Hoisington.

ELKHART, MORTON CO., ST. JOAN OF ARC CATHOLIC CHURCH OF ELKHART, KANSAS (1921) [JC] Rev. Pascal L. Klein, Parochial Admin.

Res.: 723 S. Baca Ave., P.O. Box 570, 67950-0570. Tel: 620-697-4622. Email: stjoan@elkhart.com.

Catechesis/Religious Program—Tel: 620-697-4587. Traci O'Hanlon, D.R.E. Students 60.

ELLINWOOD, BARTON CO., ST. JOSEPH CATHOLIC CHURCH OF ELLINWOOD, KANSAS (1876) [JC] Rev. Charles Mazouch.

Res.: 214 N. Main St., 67526. Tel: 620-564-2534; Fax: 620-564-2613.

School—111 W. Third, 67526. Tel: 620-564-2721; Fax: 620-564-2714. Lay Teachers 7; Students 63.

Catechesis/Religious Program—Raechel Manley, D.R.E. Students 44.

FOWLER, MEADE CO., ST. ANTHONY CATHOLIC CHURCH OF FOWLER, KANSAS (1910) [JC] Rev. Angel Dy; Judy Dewell, Pastoral Assoc.; Steve Dewell, Pastoral Assoc.

Res.: 411 Fourth St., P.O. Box 80, 67844. Tel: 620-646-5297; Fax: 620-646-5207.

Catechesis/Religious Program—Sarah Weber, D.R.E. Students 55.

GARDEN CITY, FINNEY CO.

1—ST. DOMINIC CATHOLIC CHURCH OF GARDEN CITY, KANSAS (1965) Rev. Wesley W. Schawe; Jennifer Mai, Dir. Adult Formation; Alissa Bell, Dir. Admin. & Stewardship; Veronica Aguiniga, Sec.

Office: 615 J. C. St., 67846. Tel: 620-276-2024; Fax: 620-276-2086. Email: stdomoffice@st-dominic.org. Web: www.st-dominic.org.

School—617 J. C. St., 67846. Tel: 620-276-8981. Email: jneuman@st-dominic.org. Web: www.st-dominic.org/school/. Trina Delgado, Prin. Lay Teachers 13; Students (Preschool to 6th) 192.

Catechesis/Religious Program—Tel: 620-276-3500. Email: rformation@st-dominic.org. Sr. Myra Arney, O.P., D.R.E. & Dir. Youth Formation. Students 224.

2—ST. MARY CATHOLIC CHURCH OF GARDEN CITY, KANSAS (1898) [CEM 2] [JC 2] Revs. Francis Khoi Nguyen; Efiri Matthias Selemobri, M.S.P.; Sr. Marie Elena Martinez-SiFuentes, M.C.M.I., Pastoral Min./Coord. Tel: 620-275-4204.

Res.: 509 St. John St., 67846. Fax: 620-272-9971.

School—503 W. St. John St., 67846. Tel: 620-276-2241; Fax: 620-276-7067. Trina Delgado, Prin. Lay Teachers 10; Students 138.

Catechesis/Religious Program—Tel: 620-276-2716. Patricia Nieman, D.R.E. Students 670.

GREAT BEND, BARTON CO.

1—ST. PATRICK (1960) [JC] Merged with St. Rose to form Prince of Peace, Great Bend.

2—PRINCE OF PEACE CATHOLIC CHURCH OF GREAT BEND, KANSAS (2006) Revs. Reginald A. Urban; Pedro de la Cruz Fernandez Jr.

4100 Broadway, P.O. Box 87, 67530-0087.

Res. & Mailing Address: 1423 Holland, P.O. Box 87, 67530-0087. Tel: 620-792-1396; Fax: 620-792-3642.

Church: 4100 Broadway, 67530-0087. Email: bookkeeper@gbpeace.kscoxmail.com.

School—Holy Family School, (Grades PreK-6), 4200 Broadway, 67530. Tel: 620-793-3265; Fax: 620-792-2798. Email: office@gbholyfamily.org. Mrs. Karen Moeder, Prin. Total Staff 24; Students 242.

Catechesis/Religious Program—Email: mmoshier@gbpeace.kscoxmail.com. Michelle Moshier, D.R.E.; Pam Vainer, D.R.E. Merged with St. Rose of Lima, Great Bend. Students 403.

3—ST. ROSE OF LIMA (1878) [JC] Merged with St. Patrick, Great Bend to form Prince of Peace, Great Bend.

GREENSBURG, KIOWA CO., ST. JOSEPH CATHOLIC CHURCH OF GREENSBURG, KANSAS (1952) Ellen Peters, Parish Life Coord.; Rev. Robert A. Schremmer, Priest Supvr.

820 Walnut, 67054. Cell: 620-255-3636. Email: kdvigness67@hotmail.com.

Catechesis/Religious Program—Tel: 620-723-2534; Fax: 620-723-2534. Students 14.

HANSTON, HODGEMAN CO., ST. ANTHONY CATHOLIC CHURCH OF HANSTON, KANSAS (1908) [CEM] Rev. Benjamin Dande, M.S.F.S., Parochial Admin.

Mailing Address: *c/o St. Lawrence Church*, P.O. Box 278, Jetmore, 67854. Tel: 620-357-8791.

Catechesis/Religious Program—Students 26.

HOISINGTON, BARTON CO., ST. JOHN THE EVANGELIST CATHOLIC CHURCH OF HOISINGTON, KANSAS (1892) [CEM] Rev. Dwight J. Birket (WCH).

Office: 122 E. 5th St., 67544. Tel: 620-653-2963; Fax: 620-653-2934. Email: stjohnevangel@dc.kscoxmail.com.

Rectory—108 E. 5th St., 67544. Tel: 620-653-2695.

Catechesis/Religious Program— Pam Willis, D.R.E. Students 142.

HUGOTON, STEVENS CO., ST. HELEN CATHOLIC CHURCH OF HUGOTON, KANSAS (1948) Rev. Pascal L. Klein, Parochial Admin.

Parish Office—1011 S. Jefferson St., 67951-2823. Tel: 620-544-2551. Email: sthelenc@pld.com.

Catechesis/Religious Program—Tel: 316-544-7544. Amanda Mangels, D.R.E. Students 98.

INGALLS, GRAY CO., ST. STANISLAUS CATHOLIC CHURCH OF INGALLS, KANSAS (1909) [JC] Marlene Miller, Parish Life Coord.; Revs. Wesley W. Schawe, Priest Supvr.; Francis G. Jordan (Retired).

Mailing Address: 200 N. Rush, P.O. Box 175, 67853. Tel: 620-335-5202; Fax: 620-335-5865.

Church Address: 200 N. Rush St., 67853. Tel: 620-335-5753.

Catechesis/Religious Program—Kathy Hornung, D.R.E. Students 83.

JETMORE, HODGEMAN CO., ST. LAWRENCE CATHOLIC CHURCH OF JETMORE, KANSAS (1923) Rev. Benjamin Dande, M.S.F.S., Parochial Admin.

Mailing Address: P.O. Box 278, 67854. Tel: 620-357-8791.
Catechesis/Religious Program—P.O. Box 278, 67854. Cheryl Shuler, D.R.E. Students 42.

JOHNSON, STANTON CO., ST. BERNADETTE CATHOLIC CHURCH OF JOHNSON, KANSAS (1949) Rev. Trong Binh Tran.
Mailing Address: *c/o Mary, Queen of Peace Church*, 804 Colorado, Ulysses, 67880. Tel: 620-356-1532; Fax: 620-424-1065.
Catechesis/Religious Program—Tel: 620-492-1554. Students 90.

KINSLEY, EDWARDS CO., ST. NICHOLAS CATHOLIC CHURCH OF KINSLEY, KANSAS (1883) [CEM] Rev. John R. Strasser.
Res.: 706 E. Sixth St., 67547. Tel: 620-659-2692; Fax: 620-659-2049.
Catechesis/Religious Program— Twinned with St. Joseph, Offerle. Students 83.

KIOWA, BARBER CO., ST. JOHN THE APOSTLE CATHOLIC CHURCH OF KIOWA, KANSAS (1885) Rev. Cosmas Okey Nwosuh, M.S.P., Admin.
Res.: 300 Curry Ln., Medicine Lodge, 67104. Tel: 620-886-3596. Email: ccbc@sctelcom.net.
Church: 920 E. Main St., 67070. Tel: 620-825-4361.
Catechesis/Religious Program—Tel: 620-825-4836. Lori Schrock, D.R.E. Students 38.

LACROSSE, RUSH CO., ST. MICHAEL CATHOLIC CHURCH OF LACROSSE, KANSAS (1911) [JC] Rev. Rene Labrador.
Res.: 918 Lincoln St., P.O. Box 309, 67548. Tel: 785-222-2561; Fax: 785-222-3292. Email: church@gbta.net.
Catechesis/Religious Program—Tel: 913-222-2869. Email: rbbaalmann@gbta.net. Ruth Baalmann, D.R.E. Students 60.

LAKIN, KEARNY CO., ST. ANTHONY OF PADUA CATHOLIC CHURCH OF LAKIN, KANSAS (1909) [JC] Rev. Michael L. Helms.
Res.: 600 Soderberg St., P.O. Box 983, 67860. Tel: 620-355-6405; Fax: 620-355-6406.
Catechesis/Religious Program—Tel: 620-355-8050; 620-355-6663. Joyce Frederiksen, D.R.E.; Julie Rains, D.R.E. Students 138.

LARNED, PAWNEE CO., SACRED HEART OF JESUS CATHOLIC CHURCH OF LARNED, KANSAS (1912) [CEM] [JC] Rev. Bernard H. Felix.
Res.: 1111 State St., 67550. Tel: 620-285-2035; Fax: 620-285-3025.
Catechesis/Religious Program— Brenda Johnson, D.R.E. Students 123.

LEOTI, WICHITA CO., ST. ANTHONY OF PADUA CATHOLIC CHURCH OF LEOTI, KANSAS (1887) [JC] Rev. Benjamin Martin.
Res.: P.O. Box D, 67861. Tel: 620-379-4431; Fax: 620-379-4428.
Catechesis/Religious Program—Tel: 620-379-4427. Students 29.

LIBERAL, SEWARD CO., ST. ANTHONY OF PADUA CATHOLIC CHURCH OF LIBERAL, KANSAS (1916) Revs. James P. Dieker; Enrique Estrada; Deacons Victor Mencos; Ruben Sigala; Oscar Rodriguez; Hector Rios; Araceli LaPoint, Office Mgr.; Jana Widener, Bookkeeper.
Office: 1510 N. Calhoun, 67901. Tel: 620-624-4135; Fax: 620-624-3553.
Rectory—1230 N. Pershing, 67901. Tel: 620-624-7846.
Catechesis/Religious Program—Tel: 620-624-1552. Matilda Scheurer, D.R.E. Students 415.

LIEBENTHAL, RUSH CO., ST. JOSEPH CATHOLIC CHURCH OF LIEBENTHAL, KANSAS (1876) [CEM] Rev. Rene Labrador.
Mailing Address: P.O. Box 98, 67553. Tel: 785-222-3160.
Catechesis/Religious Program—Tel: 785-222-2561. (attending St. Michael's Program at LaCrosse, KS) Students 4.

LORETTO, ST. MARY, HELP OF CHRISTIANS, Closed. Sacramental records can be found at St. Joseph, Liebenthal.

MARIENTHAL, WICHITA CO., ST. MARY CATHOLIC CHURCH OF MARIENTHAL, KANSAS (1886) [CEM] Rev. Benjamin Martin.
Mailing Address: P.O. Box 7, 67863. Tel: 620-379-4427; Fax: 620-379-4428.
Catechesis/Religious Program— Jenni Winter, D.R.E. Students 39.

MCCRACKEN, RUSH CO., ST. MARY (1886) Closed. For inquiries for sacramental records please contact St. Michael, La Crosse.

MEADE, MEADE CO., ST. JOHN THE BAPTIST CATHOLIC CHURCH OF MEADE, KANSAS (1889) [JC] Rev. Angel Dy.
Res.: 408 W. Carthage St., P.O. Box 1207, 67864. Tel: 620-873-2003.
Catechesis/Religious Program—Tel: 620-873-2654. Audrey Flowers, D.R.E. Students 46.

MEDICINE LODGE, BARBER CO., HOLY ROSARY CATHOLIC CHURCH OF MEDICINE LODGE, KANSAS (1952) Rev. Cosmas Okey Nwosuh, M.S.P., Admin.
Mailing Address: 300 Curry Ln., 67104. Tel: 620-886-3596; 887-886-1255. Email: ccbc@sctelcom.net.
Catechesis/Religious Program—Students 72.

NESS CITY, NESS CO., SACRED HEART CATHOLIC CHURCH OF NESS CITY, KANSAS (1912) [CEM] Rev. Henry F. Hildebrandt.
Res.: 510 S. School St., 67560. Tel: 785-798-3195. Email: sacredheart@gbta.net.
School—(Grades PreK-8), 510 S. School St., 67560. Tel: 785-798-3530; Fax: 785-798-3004. Don Ruda, Prin. Lay Teachers 7; Students 78.
Catechesis/Religious Program—Students 41.

NORTH ELLINWOOD, BARTON CO., STS. PETER & PAUL, Closed. Sacramental records can be found at St. Joseph, Ellinwood.

NORTH KINSLEY, EDWARDS CO., SS. PETER AND PAUL, Closed. Sacramental records can be found at St. Nicholas, Kinsley.

ODIN, BARTON CO., HOLY FAMILY CATHOLIC CHURCH OF ODIN, KANSAS (1879) [CEM] Rev. Dwight J. Birket (WCH).
Mailing Address: *c/o St. John the Evangelist Parish*, 122 E. 5th St., Hoisington, 67544. Tel: 620-653-2963; Fax: 620-653-2934.
Catechesis/Religious Program— Teresa Hickel, D.R.E. Students 32.

OFFERLE, EDWARDS CO., ST. JOSEPH CATHOLIC CHURCH OF OFFERLE, KANSAS (1876) [CEM 2] Rev. John R. Strasser.
Res.: c/o 706 E. Sixth St., Kinsley, 67547. Tel: 620-659-2692.
Catechesis/Religious Program—Twinned with St. Nicholas, Kinsley.

OLMITZ, BARTON CO., ST. ANN CATHOLIC CHURCH OF OLMITZ, KANSAS (1889) [CEM] Rev. Ultan P. Murphy, Admin.
Res.: 115 Cleveland St., P.O. Box 8, 67564. Tel: 620-586-3306; Cell: 620-923-5766. Email: lisabahr15@hotmail.com.
Catechesis/Religious Program—Tel: 620-923-4225; Cell: 620-923-3228. Lisa Starr, D.R.E. Students 52.

PLAINS, MEADE CO., ST. PATRICK CATHOLIC CHURCH OF PLAINS, KANSAS (1916) [JC] Rev. Angel Dy.
Mailing Address: P.O. Box 247, 67869.
Res.: 601 Superior, 67869. Tel: 620-873-2003.
Catechesis/Religious Program—P.O. Box 247, 67869. Tel: 620-563-6162 (Home). Traci Eakes, D.R.E.; Martha Saucedo, D.R.E. Students 94.

PRATT, PRATT CO., SACRED HEART CATHOLIC CHURCH OF PRATT, KANSAS (1887) Rev. Floyd E. McKinney (WCH); Glenna Borho, Parish Administrative Mgr.
Res.: 332 N. Oak St., 67124. Tel: 620-672-6352; Fax: 620-672-3748.
School—(Grades PreK-5), 330 N. Oak St., 67124. Tel: 620-672-3687. Email: csacredheartre1@cox.net. Web: home.catholicweb.com/sacredheartholychild/index.cfm?reinit=y. Linda Conkle, Prin. Lay Teachers 9; Students 95.
Catechesis/Religious Program— Erin Crouch, D.R.E. Students 157.

RANSOM, NESS CO., ST. ALOYSIUS CATHOLIC CHURCH OF RANSOM, KANSAS (1903) [CEM] Rev. Henry F. Hildebrandt.
Mailing Address: *c/o Sacred Heart*, 510 S. School St., Ness City, 67560. Tel: 785-731-2497.
Catechesis/Religious Program—Students 12.

ST. JOHN, STAFFORD CO., ST. JOHN THE APOSTLE CATHOLIC CHURCH OF ST. JOHN, KANSAS (1949) Sr. Catherine Therese Paulie, C.S.J., Parish Life Coord.; Rev. Charles Mazouch, Priest Supvr.
Res., Church & Office: 609 E. Fourth St., Box 475, 67576. Fax: 620-549-3538.
Catechesis/Religious Program—Tel: 620-549-3428; 620-549-3847; Fax: 620-549-6188. Johnna Stanford, D.R.E. Students 65.

ST. MARY, HODGEMAN CO., ST. MARY, Closed. Sacramental records can be found at St. John the Baptist, Spearville.

SATANTA, HASKELL CO., ST. ALPHONSUS CATHOLIC CHURCH OF SATANTA, KANSAS (1946) Sr. Matilde Monterrosso, M.C.M.I., Parish Life Coord.; Rev. James P. Dieker, Priest Supvr.
Res.: 603 Tecumseh, Box 65, 67870. Tel: 620-649-2692; Fax: 620-649-2550. Email: catholic@pld.com.
Church: 601 Tecumseh, 67870.
Catechesis/Religious Program—P.O. Box 452, 67870. Tel: 620-649-2200, Ext. 508; Fax: 620-649-2776. Email: cfolk@satantahospital.org. Cherie Folk, D.R.E. Students 99.

SCOTT CITY, SCOTT CO., ST. JOSEPH CATHOLIC CHURCH OF SCOTT CITY, KANSAS (1911) [JC] Rev. Warren L. Stecklein.
Res.: 606 W. 10th, P.O. Box 228, 67871-0228. Tel: 620-872-7388; 620-872-3644 (Sec.); Fax: 620-872-3644. Email: stjosephsc@att.net.
Catechesis/Religious Program—Tel: 620-872-5630. Denise Strecker, D.R.E. Students 159.

SEWARD, STAFFORD CO., ST. FRANCIS XAVIER CATHOLIC CHURCH OF SEWARD, KANSAS (1886) Rev. Rene Guesnier, O.S.B.
Mailing Address: 504 Main St., 67576. Tel: 620-458-5691. Email: ccsc@ruraltel.net.
Catechesis/Religious Program— Attended at St. John Students 6.

SHARON, BARBER CO., ST. BONIFACE CATHOLIC CHURCH OF SHARON, KANSAS (1904) [CEM] Rev. Cosmas Okey Nwosuh, M.S.P., Admin.; Sr. Nancy Jane Kuntz, O.P., Pastoral Min.
Res.: 300 Curry Ln., Medicine Lodge, 67104. Tel: 620-886-3596. Email: ccbc@sctelcom.net.
Church: 410 N. Main St., P.O. Box 118, 67138. Tel: 620-294-5526.
Catechesis/Religious Program—Tel: 620-294-5258. Margonie Eck, D.R.E. Students 57.

SPEARVILLE, FORD CO., ST. JOHN THE BAPTIST CATHOLIC CHURCH OF SPEARVILLE, KANSAS (1904) [CEM] [JC 2] Rev. Ted D. Stoecklein.
Res.: 100 S. Main St., P.O. Box 187, 67876. Tel: 620-385-2212.
Catechesis/Religious Program—Tel: 620-385-2881. Judy Gleason, D.R.E. Students 156.

SYRACUSE, HAMILTON CO., ST. RAPHAEL CATHOLIC CHURCH OF SYRACUSE, KANSAS (1906) [CEM] [JC] Rev. Michael L. Helms.
Mailing Address: P.O. Box 731, 67878. Tel: 620-384-7357; Fax: 620-384-5946. Email: st.raphael2007@gmail.com.
Catechesis/Religious Program—Tel: 620-384-5582. Email: gama@wbsnet.org. Mary Ann Fair, D.R.E. Students 65.

TIMKEN, RUSH CO., HOLY TRINITY CATHOLIC CHURCH OF TIMKEN, KANSAS (1904) [CEM] [JC] Rev. Rene Labrador.
Mailing Address: *c/o St. Michael Church*, P.O. Box 309, LaCrosse, 67548. Tel: 785-222-2561.
Catechesis/Religious Program—Tel: 785-623-1917. Don Erb, D.R.E.; Brian Stejskal, D.R.E.; JoAnn Tomecek, D.R.E. Students 25.

TRIBUNE, GREELEY CO., ST. JOSEPH THE WORKER CATHOLIC CHURCH OF TRIBUNE, KANSAS (1950) [JC] Rev. Benjamin Martin.
Mailing Address: Box 67, 67879. Tel: 620-376-2292.
Catechesis/Religious Program—Tel: 620-376-2490. Teressa Ricke, D.R.E. Students 35.

ULYSSES, GRANT CO., MARY, QUEEN OF PEACE CATHOLIC CHURCH OF ULYSSES, KANSAS (1948) Rev. Trong Binh Tran; Deacon Apolonio Rodriguez.
Res.: 804 N. Colorado, 67880. Tel: 620-356-1532; 620-356-3994 (Parish Hall); Fax: 620-424-1065. Email: mqop@pld.com. Web: www.mqopp.org.
Catechesis/Religious Program—Tel: 620-356-1532; Fax: 620-424-1065. Email: mqopdre@pld.com. Dana Gaspar, D.R.E. Students 215.

WINDTHORST, FORD CO., IMMACULATE HEART OF MARY, Closed. Sacramental records can be found at St. John the Baptist, Spearville.

WRIGHT, FORD CO., ST. ANDREW CATHOLIC CHURCH OF WRIGHT, KANSAS (1909) [CEM] Rev. Robert A. Schremmer.
Mailing Address: 10893 St. Andrew Rd., P.O. Box 125, 67882. Tel: 620-227-3363; Fax: 620-227-9979.
Parish Center—11792 Jewel Rd., 67882. Tel: 620-225-7345.
Catechesis/Religious Program—Tel: 620-225-1299. Regina Lix, D.R.E. Students 35.

On Special Diocesan Assignment:
Rev.—
Tran, Trong Binh, Diocesan Chap. Vietnamese Community

On Duty Outside the Diocese:
Rev.—
Trung Dinh Hoang, Louis, Diocese of Honolulu

Retired:
Revs.—
Baker, James E., J.C.L., 1707 Belmont, Garden City, 67846.
Fiedler, Donald J.
Herrmann, Gilbert P., 808 Fitz St., Garden City, 67846.
Jordan, Francis G., P.O. Box 175, Ingalls, 67853.
Kelly, James, 6900 E. 45th St. N., Apt. D-4, Wichita, 67226.
Kenny, Eugene, 6900 E. 45th St. N., Apt. E-4, Wichita, 67226.
Kraus, David H., J.C.L., P.O. Box 18, Ransom, 67572.
Maes, John J., 6900 E. 45th St. N., Apt. F2, Bel Aire, 67226.
Pottorff, Lisle J., 6900 E. 45th St. N., Apt. D2, Bel Aire, 67226.
Suellentrop, Anthony J., 226 W. San Jacinto Ave., Ulysses, 67880.
Tighe, Dermot F., 1420 Wilson, Great Bend, 67530.

Permanent Deacons:
Hermocillo, Martin, Diaconate Convenor
Lampe, Dwaine, (Retired)

Mencos, Victor A., St. Anthony, Liberal
Rael, Gilbert E., Larned State Hospital/Larned Mental Health Correctional Facility, Larned
Rios, Hector, St. Anthony, Liberal
Rodriguez, Apolonio, Mary Queen of Peace, Ulysses
Rodriguez, Erasmo, (Retired)
Rodriguez, Oscar, St. Anthony, Liberal
Rondeau, Richard, (Retired)
Sigala, Ruben, St. Anthony, Liberal

INSTITUTIONS LOCATED IN THE DIOCESE

[A] GENERAL HOSPITALS

GARDEN CITY. *St. Catherine Hospital*, 401 E. Spruce, 67846-5679. Tel: 620-272-2222; Fax: 620-272-2566. Web: www.stcath-hosp.org. Scott J. Taylor, Pres. & CEO; John E. Yox, Senior Vice Pres.; Bonnie Peters, Vice Pres. Patient Svcs.; Amanda Vaughan, CFO; Victor Hawkins, Exec. Dir. & Mktg.; Kathy Morrison, Exec. Dir. Human Resources; Doug Williams, Chap.; Remigius Ekweariri, Chap. Affiliated with Catholic Health Initiatives. Bed Capacity 132; Patients Assisted Annually 126,114; Total Staff 574.

GREAT BEND. *Central Kansas Medical Center* (1902) 3515 Broadway, 67530. Tel: 620-792-2511; Fax: 620-786-6298. Email: ckmc@greatbend.com. Web: www.ckmc.org. Sharon Lind, Pres. & CEO; Matthew Heyn, CFO; Sr. Mary Klinge, Dir. Mission. Sisters of the Third Order of St. Dominic., Member-Catholic Health Initiatives. Sisters 2; Bed Capacity 62; Total Staff 383; Patients Assisted Annually 50,912.

St. Rose Campus, 3515 Broadway, 67530. Tel: 620-792-2511; Fax: 620-792-1605.

LARNED. *St. Joseph Memorial Hospital, Inc.*, 923 Carroll St., 67550. Tel: 620-285-3161; Fax: 620-285-8883. Sharon Lind, Pres./CEO; Matthew Heyn, C.F.O. Bed Capacity 55; Total Staff 73; Total Assisted Annually 8,446.

St. Joseph Campus, 923 Carroll St., 67550.

[B] RETREAT CENTERS

GREAT BEND. *Heartland Center for Spirituality* (1985) 3600 Broadway, 67530-3692. Tel: 620-792-1232; Fax: 620-792-1746. Email: office@heartlandspirituality.org. Web: www.heartlandspirituality.org. Sisters Louise Hageman, O.P., Co-Dir.; Renee Dreiling, O.P., Co-Dir. Retreat Center. Total Staff 6.

PAWNEE ROCK. *Heartland Farm* (1988) 1049 County Rd. 390, 67567-7002. Tel: 620-923-4585. Email: hfarm@gbta.net. Sr. Mary Terence Wasinger, O.P., Contact Person. A Ministry of the Dominican Sisters of Great Bend, KS., Organic sustainable agriculture, body massage, retreat opportunities in rural setting. Total Membership 9.

[C] EDUCATIONAL ENDOWMENT FUNDS

DODGE CITY. *Sacred Heart Cathedral School Endowment Fund*, 3231 N. 14th St., P.O. Box 670, 67801. Tel: 620-225-4802; Fax: 620-338-8268. Email: colg@starrtech.net.

ELLINWOOD. *St. Joseph School Education Endowment Fund*, 109 W. 3rd, 67526. Tel: 620-564-2534; Fax: 620-564-2613. Rev. Charles Mazouch, V.F., 109 W. 3rd, 67526. Tel: 620-564-2290.

GARDEN CITY. *St. Dominic Grade School Endowment Fund*, 615 J.C. St., 67846. Tel: 620-276-2024; Fax: 620-276-2086.

St. Mary Catholic Education Endowment Fund, 509 St. John St., 67846. Tel: 620-275-4204; Fax: 620-272-9971.

GREAT BEND. *The Holy Family Grade School Education Endowment Fund*, 4200 Broadway, 67530. Tel: 620-792-1396; Fax: 620-792-3642. Email: bookkeeper@gbpeace.kscoxmail.com.

KINSLEY. *St. Nicholas School Endowment*, 401 E. 9th, P.O. Box 285, 67547. Tel: 620-659-2692; Fax: 620-659-2049.

LARNED. *The Sacred Heart Grade School of Larned Educational Endowment Fund*, 1111 State St., 67550. Tel: 620-285-2035; Fax: 620-285-3025.

LIBERAL. *St. Anthony School Endowment Fund*, 1510 N. Calhoun St., 67901. Tel: 620-624-4135; Fax: 620-624-3553.

NESS CITY. *The Sacred Heart School Endowment Fund*, 510 S. School St., 67560. Tel: 785-798-3530; Fax: 785-798-3004.

PRATT. *The Sacred Heart School Education Endowment, Inc.*, 332 N. Oak St., 67124. Tel: 620-672-6352; Fax: 620-672-3748.

[D] CONVENTS AND RESIDENCES FOR SISTERS

GREAT BEND. *Dominican Sisters of Peace*, 3600 Broadway, 67530-3692. Tel: 620-792-1232; Fax: 620-792-1746. Email: srpeace@oppeace.org. Web: www.oppeace.org. Sr. Ann Metzen, O.P., Mission Group Coord.

Dominican Sisters of Peace, Inc. Dominican Sisters of Peace. Final Professed Sisters in Diocese 58; Lay Associates in Diocese 31; Partners in Mission in Diocese 2; Total Sisters in Congregation 638.

[E] SERVICES FOR THE ELDERLY

GREAT BEND. *Cedar Park Place, Inc.*, 3910 Cedar Park Pl., 67530-3692. Tel: 620-793-8115; Fax: 620-793-6702. Email: jmurray@mercyhousing.org. Low and Middle Income Housing for Elderly and Handicapped.

[F] MISCELLANEOUS

DODGE CITY. *Catholic Social Service Endowment Fund* (1989) 906 Central Ave., 67801. Tel: 620-227-1562; Fax: 620-227-1572. Email: mlegleiter@dcdiocese.org.

Dechant Foundation, 910 Central, P.O. Box 137, 67801.

The Diocese of Dodge City Priest Retirement Fund, Inc., 2210 1st Ave., 67801. Rev. Msgr. Brian R. Moore; Revs. Ted D. Stoecklein; Charles Mazouch, V.F., Sec./Treas,; John R. Strasser, Chairperson; Dermot F. Tighe (Retired); Warren L. Stecklein.

Manna House, 1012 First, 67801. Tel: 620-227-6707. Laura Koehn, Exec. Dir.; Maria Musick, Pres.; David Oreelion, Pres.; Louise Jambor, Contact Person, 1707 Ave. A, 67801. Tel: 620-227-6767; Marsha Morrison, Treas. & Contact Person, 925 Club View, 67801. Tel: 620-227-6767; Ronald Schneweis, Treas. & Contact Person. Short-term housing and food distrubution need. Total Staff 3; Total Assisted 3,583.

Newman University, 236 San Jose #39, 67801. Tel: 620-227-9616; Fax: 620-227-9688. Email: heydmant@newmanu.edu. Tom Heydman, Dir.

GARDEN CITY. *St. Catherine Hospital Development Foundation*, 401 E. Spruce, 67846. Tel: 620-272-2567; Fax: 620-272-2180. Email: victorhawkins@catholichealth.net. Web: www.schdf.org. Victor Hawkins, Exec. Dir. & Contact Person.

GREAT BEND. *Heartland Center for Wholistic Health* (1988) 1005 Williams, 67530. Tel: 620-793-9067; Fax: 620-793-5817. Email: anita@hcwh.net. Web: www.hcwh.net. Sr. Anita Schugart, O.P., Dir., Contact Person. A Ministry of the Dominican Sisters of Great Bend, KS., Body massage, herbals, chiropractic, natural remedies. Total Staff 6.

St. Rose - Dominican Nurses Alumnae Association, 3600 Broadway, 67530. Tel: 620-792-1232; Fax: 620-792-1746. Email: sisters@ksdom.org. Sr. Mary Terence Wasinger, O.P., Sec. & Contact Person.

RELIGIOUS INSTITUTES OF MEN REPRESENTED IN THE DIOCESE

For further details refer to the corresponding bracketed number in the Religious Institutes of Men or Women section.

[0200]—*Benedictine Monks*—O.S.B.

[]—*Missionaries of St. Francis de Sales*—M.S.F.S.

[]—*Missionaries of St. Paul*—M.S.P.

[0270]—*Order of Carmelites*—O.Carm.

RELIGIOUS INSTITUTES OF WOMEN REPRESENTED IN THE DIOCESE

[3832]—*Congregation of St. Joseph*—C.S.J.

[1115]—*Dominican Sisters of Peace*—O.P.

[]—*Mexican Passionist Sisters*—C.F.P.

[]—*Missionaries of the Charity of Mary Immaculate*—M.C.M.I.

NECROLOGY

† Leahy, Rev. Msgr. Patrick Joseph, (Retired)—Died April 30, 2009

An asterisk (*) denotes an organization that has established tax-exempt status directly with the IRS and is not covered by the USCCB Group Ruling.

Archdiocese of Dubuque

(Archidioecesis Dubuquensis)

Most Reverend

JEROME HANUS, O.S.B., D.D.

Archbishop of Dubuque; ordained July 30, 1966; appointed Bishop of St. Cloud July 6, 1987; ordained and installed August 24, 1987; appointed Coadjutor Archbishop of Dubuque August 23, 1994; welcomed October 27, 1994; succeeded to the See October 16, 1995.

PRODESSE MAGIS QUAM PRÆESSE

Chancery-Archdiocesan Center: P.O. Box 479, Dubuque, IA 52004-0479. Tel: 563-556-2580; Fax: 563-556-5464.

Web: www.arch.pvt.k12.ia.us

Email: dbqcco@arch.pvt.k12.ia.us

Most Reverend

DANIEL W. KUCERA, O.S.B., PH.D., D.D.

Retired Archbishop of Dubuque; ordained May 26, 1949; appointed Titular Bishop of Natchez and Auxiliary Bishop of Joliet June 6, 1977; ordained Bishop July 21, 1977; appointed Bishop of Salina March 11, 1980; installed May 7, 1980; appointed Archbishop of Dubuque December 20, 1983; installed February 23, 1984; retired October 16, 1995. *Villa Raphael, 1155 Mt. Loretta Ave., Dubuque, IA 52003.*

Square Miles 17,403.

Established July 28, 1837; Created an Archdiocese June 15, 1893.

Patrons of the Archdiocese: Primary: St. Raphael, the Archangel; Secondary: St. John Mary Vianney, Cure of Ars.

Corporate Title: The Archdiocese of Dubuque.

Comprises 30 Counties, that part of the State of Iowa north of the Counties of Polk, Jasper, Poweshiek, Iowa, Johnson, Cedar and Clinton and east of the Counties of Kossuth, Humboldt, Webster and Boone.

For legal titles of parishes and archdiocesan institutions, consult the Chancery.

STATISTICAL OVERVIEW

Personnel	
Archbishops	1
Retired Archbishops	1
Abbots	1
Retired Abbots	2
Priests: Diocesan Active in Diocese	109
Priests: Diocesan Active Outside Diocese	3
Priests: Retired, Sick or Absent	87
Number of Diocesan Priests	199
Religious Priests in Diocese	30
Total Priests in Diocese	229
Extern Priests in Diocese	2
Ordinations:	
Diocesan Priests	2
Permanent Deacons	14
Permanent Deacons in Diocese	97
Total Brothers	24
Total Sisters	737
Parishes	
Parishes	176
With Resident Pastor:	
Resident Diocesan Priests	79
Resident Religious Priests	1
Without Resident Pastor:	
Administered by Priests	86
Administered by Deacons	3
Administered by Religious Women	5
Administered by Lay People	2
Pastoral Centers	1
Professional Ministry Personnel:	
Brothers	1
Sisters	30
Lay Ministers	380
Welfare	
Catholic Hospitals	7
Total Assisted	1,235,282
Health Care Centers	2
Total Assisted	181
Homes for the Aged	4
Total Assisted	657
Special Centers for Social Services	3
Total Assisted	570
Other Institutions	1
Total Assisted	15
Educational	
Seminaries, Diocesan	1
Students from This Diocese	9
Students from Other Diocese	2
Diocesan Students in Other Seminaries	5
Seminaries, Religious	1
Students Religious	90
Total Seminarians	104
Colleges and Universities	3
Total Students	4,436
High Schools, Diocesan and Parish	7
Total Students	2,570
Elementary Schools, Diocesan and Parish	44
Total Students	9,731
Catechesis/Religious Education:	
High School Students	5,187
Elementary Students	13,460
Total Students under Catholic Instruction	35,488
Teachers in the Diocese:	
Sisters	14
Lay Teachers	900
Vital Statistics	
Receptions into the Church:	
Infant Baptism Totals	2,621
Minor Baptism Totals	81
Adult Baptism Totals	101
Received into Full Communion	225
First Communions	2,931
Confirmations	2,330
Marriages:	
Catholic	642
Interfaith	376
Total Marriages	1,018
Deaths	2,031
Total Catholic Population	205,252
Total Population	980,903

Former Bishops—Most Revs. MATHIAS LORAS, D.D., cons. Dec. 10, 1837; died Feb. 19, 1858; CLEMENT SMYTH, O.C.S.O., D.D., named Coadjutor Bishop of Dubuque Jan. 9, 1857; cons. May 3, 1857; Succeeded Feb. 19, 1858; died Sept. 22, 1865; JOHN HENNESSY, D.D., First Archbishop; named Bishop of Dubuque April 24, 1866; cons. Sept. 30, 1866; raised to the Archiepiscopal Dignity, June 16, 1893; died March 4, 1900; JOHN J. KEANE, D.D., cons. Bishop of Richmond, Aug. 25, 1878; transferred to the Titular See of Jasso, Aug. 12, 1888; elevated to the Archiepiscopal Dignity with the title of Archbishop of Damascus, Jan. 29, 1897; transferred to the See of Dubuque, July 24, 1900; resigned April 3, 1911; appt. Titular Archbishop of Cios, April 28, 1911; died June 22, 1918; JAMES JOHN KEANE, D.D., ord. Dec. 23, 1882; cons. Bishop of Cheyenne, Oct. 28, 1902; elevated to the Archiepiscopal Dignity and transferred to Dubuque, Aug. 11, 1911; died Aug. 2, 1929; FRANCIS J. L. BECKMAN, S.T.D., Titular Archbishop of Phulli; ord. June 20, 1902; appt. Bishop of Lincoln, Dec. 23, 1923; cons. Bishop of Lincoln, May 1, 1924; Apostolic Administrator of Omaha, June 1, 1926 to July 4, 1928; elevated to Archiepiscopal Dignity and transferred to Dubuque, Jan. 17, 1930; appt. Assistant at the Pontifical Throne, April 21, 1928; resigned Nov. 11, 1946; died Oct. 17, 1948; HENRY P. ROHLMAN, D.D., appt. Bishop of Davenport, May 20, 1927; cons. July 25, 1927; appt. Coadjutor Archbishop of Dubuque "cum jure successionis" and Apostolic Administrator, June 15, 1944; installed Sept. 12, 1944; succeeded Nov. 11, 1946; named Assistant at Pontifical Throne, Sept. 2, 1950; resigned and named Titular Archbishop of Cotrada, Dec. 2, 1954; died Sept. 13, 1957; LEO BINZ, D.D. (Retired), ord. March 15, 1924; appt. Titular Bishop of Pinara, Coadjutor Bishop and Apostolic Administrator of Winona, Nov. 21, 1942; cons. Dec. 21, 1942; named Titular Archbishop of Silyum and Coadjutor to the Archbishop of Dubuque "cum jure successionis," Oct. 15, 1949; named Assistant at the Pontifical Throne, June 11, 1954; Archbishop of Dubuque, Dec. 2, 1954; Pallium conferred, June 12, 1958; appt. Archbishop of St. Paul, Dec. 16, 1961; retired July, 1975; died Oct. 9, 1979; JAMES J. BYRNE, S.T.D., appt. Titular Bishop of Etenna and Auxiliary Bishop of St. Paul, May 10, 1947; ord. Bishop, July 2, 1947; transferred to Boise, ID, June 16, 1956; appt. Archbishop of Dubuque, March 19, 1962; retired Aug. 23, 1983; named Apostolic Administrator; died Aug. 2, 1996; DANIEL W. KUCERA, O.S.B., Ph.D., D.D. (Retired), ord. May 26, 1949; appt. Titular Bishop of Natchez and Auxiliary Bishop of Joliet, June 6, 1977; ord. Bishop, July 21, 1977; appt. Bishop of Salina, KS, March 11, 1980; installed May 7, 1980; named Archbishop of Dubuque, Dec. 20, 1983; installed Feb. 23, 1984; retired Oct. 16, 1995.

Archbishop—Most Rev. JEROME HANUS, O.S.B., D.D., Archdiocesan Center, 1229 Mt. Loretta Ave., P.O. Box 479, Dubuque, 52004-0479. Tel: 563-556-2580.

Vicar General and Episcopal Vicar for Dubuque Region—Rev. Msgr. THOMAS E. TOALE, Ph.D., Archdiocesan Center, 1229 Mt. Loretta Ave., P.O. Box 479, Dubuque, 52004-0479. Tel: 563-556-2580; Fax: 563-556-5464.

Episcopal Vicar for Cedar Rapids Region—Rev. Msgr. RUSSELL M. BLEICH, S.T.L., 6300 42nd St., N.E.,

Cedar Rapids, 52411. Tel: 319-366-1647; Fax: 319-366-0426.

Episcopal Vicar for Waterloo Region—Rev. Msgr. LYLE L. WILGENBUSCH, 320 Mulberry St., Waterloo, 50703. Tel: 319-236-0241; Fax: 319-232-1118.

Vicar for Hispanic Ministry—Rev. Msgr. LEON L. CONNOLLY (Retired), Stonehill Care Center, 3485 Windsor Ave., Dubuque, 52001.

Judicial Vicar—Rev. THOMAS R. ZINKULA, J.D., J.C.L., Archdiocesan Center, 1229 Mt. Loretta Ave., P.O. Box 479, Dubuque, 52004-0479. Tel: 563-556-2580.

Chancellor—BETTY SCHUELLER, Archdiocesan Center, 1229 Mt. Loretta Ave., P.O. Box 479, Dubuque, 52004-0479. Tel: 563-556-2580.

Director of the Pastoral Center—LYNN OSTERHAUS, Archdiocesan Center, 1229 Mt. Loretta Ave., P.O. Box 479, Dubuque, 52004-0479. Tel: 563-556-2580.

Finance Officer—RICHARD L. RUNDE, Archdiocesan Center, 1229 Mt. Loretta Ave., P.O. Box 479, Dubuque, 52004-0479. Tel: 563-556-2580.

Archbishop's Cabinet—Most Rev. JEROME HANUS, O.S.B., D.D.; Rev. Msgr. RUSSELL M. BLEICH, S.T.L.; LYNN OSTERHAUS; DAN ROHNER; RICHARD L. RUNDE; BETTY SCHUELLER; Rev. Msgrs. THOMAS E. TOALE, Ph.D.; LYLE L. WILGENBUSCH.

College of Consultors—Most Rev. JEROME HANUS, O.S.B.; Rev. Msgrs. RUSSELL M. BLEICH, S.T.L.; JAMES O. BARTA, Ph.D. (Retired); LYLE L. WILGENBUSCH; THOMAS E. TOALE, Ph.D.; CARL L. SCHMITT; Revs. DANIEL J. KNEPPER; WALTER J. KLEINFEHN (Retired); DANIEL A. KRAPFL (Retired).

Deans—Very Revs. JOHN A. GOSSMAN, Cedar Rapids; MARVIN C. SALZ, Decorah; DWAYNE J. THOMAN, Dubuque; PHILLIP F. KRUSE, Dyersville; RICHARD G. GAUL, Elkader; JOHN R. KREMER, Independence; MICHAEL J. MESCHER, Marshalltown; KENNETH B. GEHLING, Mason City; Rev. Msgr. CARL L. SCHMITT, New Hampton; Very Revs. JERRY F. KOPACEK, Waterloo; BERNARD C. GRADY, Webster City.

Archdiocesan Central Offices

Archdiocesan Pastoral Center—1229 Mt. Loretta Ave., Dubuque, 52003-7826. Tel: 563-556-2580; Fax: 563-556-5464. *Mailing Address: P.O. Box 479, Dubuque, 52004-0479.* Most Rev. JEROME HANUS, O.S.B., D.D.; Rev. Msgrs. THOMAS E. TOALE, Ph.D., Vicar Gen.; RUSSELL M. BLEICH, S.T.L., Episcopal Vicar - Cedar Rapids Region; LYLE L. WILGENBUSCH, Episcopal Vicar - Waterloo Region; BETTY SCHUELLER, Chancellor. Office Hours: Mon.-Fri. 8:30-4:30. Secretaries: SARAH OTTING; JULIE KAPSCH, Cedar Rapids Region.

Adult Faith—Sr. MARCI BLUM, O.S.F., Dir.; JUDY ARLEN, Sec., Archdiocesan Center, 1229 Mt. Loretta Ave., Dubuque, 52003-7286. Tel: 563-556-2580.

Archives—Revs. LORAS C. OTTING, Dir. (Retired); MARK J. MCGOVERN, Asst. to Archivist.

Campaign for Human Development—TRACY MORRISON, M.S., L.M.H.C., N.C.C., Dir., 1229 Mt. Loretta Ave., P.O. Box 1309, Dubuque, 52004-1309. Tel: 563-556-2580.

Campus Ministry—Rev. JOHN S. HAUGEN, Dir., Mailing Address: Loras College, P.O. Box 178, Dubuque, 52004-0178. Tel: 563-588-7108.

Catholic Cemeteries of the Archdiocese of Dubuque—RICHARD L. RUNDE, Dir., Finance Office, 1229 Mt. Loretta Ave., Dubuque, 52003-7826. Tel: 563-556-2580.

Catholic Charities—

Administrative Offices—Business Office: 1229 Mt. Loretta Ave., P.O. Box 1309, Dubuque, 52004-1309. Tel: 563-588-0558. TRACY MORRISON, M.S., L.M.H.C., N.C.C., Exec. Dir.; JOSEPH FEATHERSTON, Assoc. Dir.; DEBRA JASPER, Exec. Asst.; ED HABERKORN, Admin. Asst.; Sr. JANICE HANCOCK, P.B.V.M., Admin. Asst.; CHERYL WOOD, Office Mgr.; CAROL CALLAHAN, Business Mgr.

Branch Offices—

Ames—MARY JO PFEIFER-WULF, 2210 Lincoln Way, Ames, 50014. Tel: 515-296-2759.

Cedar Rapids—GARY STEJSKAL, Clinical Dir.; CARLA HUGHES.

Decorah—LORI EASTWOOD, Mailing Address: P.O. Box 1309, Dubuque, 52004-1309. Tel: 800-772-2758.

Dubuque—Mailing Address: P.O. Box 1309, Dubuque, 52004-1309. Tel: 563-556-2580; Fax: 563-588-0558. JOSEPH FEATHERSTON, Supvr.; AMY MAHONEY; ANGELLA LINK; JOANN WEITZ; Deacon WILLIAM HICKSON, Jail & Prison Min. Coord.

Mason City—THOMAS FLAHERTY, Regl. Mgr., Will F. Muse Center, 600 First St. N.W., Ste. 105, Mason City, 50401. Tel: 641-424-9683.

Waterloo—KELLEY DICKEY-CUDDY, Regl. Mgr. & Counselor; ORLYN WATHIER; Rev. KENNETH C. STECHER; MICHELLE SPRIO, Office Mgr., Kimball Ridge Center, 2101 Kimball Ave., LL 11, Waterloo, 50702. Tel: 319-272-2080.

Special Programs—

Adoption—JOANN WEITZ, Dubuque Office; CHERYL WOOD, Adoption Asst.

Barnabas Uplift—TRACY MORRISON, M.S., L.M.H.C., N.C.C.

Disaster Services Coordinator—KATHY HARMON.

Case Advocate Volunteer & Office Coordinator—TERINA HEIDELBERG.

Hispanic Counselor—BILL DEUTSCH.

Jail and Prison Ministry—Deacon WILLIAM HICKSON, Coord.

Pregnancy Services—JOANN WEITZ, Dubuque Office.

Refugee Resettlement and Immigration—JOSEPH FEATHERSTON.

Immigration Outreach Services—TERRI REYNOLDS.

Social Concerns/Iowa Catholic Conference—TRACY MORRISON, M.S., L.M.H.C., N.C.C.

St. Mary's Home—TRACY MORRISON, M.S., L.M.H.C., N.C.C., Dir., Mailing Address: P.O. Box 1309, Dubuque, 52004. Tel: 563-556-2580; STEVE JACOBS, Housing Admin. Tel: 563-556-5125.

Catholic Committee on Scouting—G. J. (JERRY) HOLBACH, Chm., Mailing Address: P.O. Box 1977, Waterloo, 50704-1977. Tel: 319-236-1672; Deacon MICHAEL KLAPPHOLZ, Chap., Mailing Address: All Saints Parish, 720 29th St., S.E., Cedar Rapids, 52403. Tel: 319-363-6130.

Continuing Formation of Priests—Rev. Msgrs. JAMES O. BARTA, Ph.D., Dir., Sabbaticals & Priests' Graduate Studies (Retired); LYLE L. WILGENBUSCH, Dir. Continuing Educ. & Priests' Convocation; BEV RECH, Sec., Mailing Address: Archdiocesan Center, 1229 Mt. Loretta Ave., Dubuque, 52003-7826. Tel: 563-556-2580.

Council of Catholic Women—Rev. Msgr. W. DEAN WALZ, J.C.D., Moderator (Retired); ANN DIETRICH, Pres., Mailing Address: P.O. Box 101, Earlville, 52041. Tel: 563-923-5415.

Faith Formation and Educational System—

Office of Faith Formation & Education—JAMES OSTERBERGER, Dir.; ITZA HEIM, Office Mgr.

Catholic Schools—JEFF HENDERSON, Supt. Schools; DEB FLECKENSTEIN, Special Projects Coord.; ALICE CONLON, Dir. Pre K-12 Prog.; JULIE KAPSCH, Sec. Cedar Rapids Office.

Office of Youth Catechesis—MARGE KRAWCZUK, Dir.; JULIE SANDERS, Sec.

Office of Youth Evangelization—KEVIN FEYEN, Dir.; JUDY ARLEN, Sec.

Associate Directors of Youth Catechesis & Evangelization—JULIE JOHNSON, Cedar Rapids; JOANNE POHLAND, Dubuque.

Family Life Office—Ms. LINDA MANTERNACH, Dir.; DIANE KONSHAK, Sec., Archdiocesan Center, 1229 Mt. Loretta Ave., Dubuque, 52003-7826. Tel: 563-556-2580.

Befriender Ministry— Contact Family Life Office

Beginning Experience—SARA JOHNSON, Contact. Tel: 563-556-6501.

Christian Family Movement—Contact: Deacon GARY AITCHISON; KAY AITCHISON, 3312 Ross Rd., Ames, 50014. Tel: 515-296-2966.

Courage—Very Rev. JERRY F. KOPACEK, Contact, St. Edward Parish, 1423 Kimball Ave., Waterloo, 50702. Tel: 319-233-8060.

Engaged Encounter—Rev. PHILLIP E. SCHMITT, Spiritual Advisor (Retired), 212 1/2 7th St., S.E., Mt. Vernon, 52314-1518. Tel: 319-895-0404.

For Registration—Family Life Office, 1229 Mt. Loretta Ave., Dubuque, 52003-7826. Tel: 563-556-2580.

Marriage Retorno—Rev. MELVIN D. HEMANN, Dir. (Retired). Tel: 319-266-3889.

Marrying & Trusting Together (M.A.T.T.) Remarriage Preparation Program—Contact: Family Life Office, 1229 Mt. Loretta Ave., Dubuque, 52003-7826. Tel: 563-556-2580.

Ministry of Mothers Sharing (M.O.M.S.)—Contact: Family Life Office, 1229 Mt. Loretta Ave., Dubuque, 52003-7826. Tel: 563-556-2580.

Natural Family Planning and Fertility Care—Archdiocesan Coordinators: Deacon SEAN SMITH; SARA SMITH, 2620 2nd Ave., Marion, 52302. Tel: 319-373-1385.

Parish Nurses and Healthcare Ministry— Contact: Family Life Office

Pre-Cana—Family Life Office, 1229 Mt. Loretta Ave., Dubuque, 52003-7826. Tel: 563-556-2580. Dubuque Area: SANDY ERNSDORFF, Contact, 2085 Hale St., Dubuque, 52001. Tel: 563-556-2859; TOM DANNER, Co Dir.; MARY JO DANNER, Co Dir., 16247 Country Club Dr., Peosta, 52068. Tel: 563-588-4069. Dyersville Area Contacts: MARK FALLON; LAURIE FALLON, 1029 1st St., S.W., Dyersville, 52040. Tel: 563-875-2276. Independence & Waterloo Areas: LISA GEISLER, St. Stephen the Witness Student Center, 1019 W. 23rd St., Cedar Falls, 50613. Tel: 319-266-9863. Cedar Rapids Area: PAT MURPHY, Co Dir.; SANDY MURPHY, Co Dir., 1130 33rd St. S.E., Cedar Rapids, 52403. Tel: 319-365-9839. Ames, Marshalltown & Webster City Areas: BRENDA NEPPLE, Contact, St. Thomas Aquinas, 2210 Lincoln Way, Ames, 50010. Tel: 515-292-8696. Mason City Area, Directors: Deacon DENNIS POPOWSKI; CHAR POPOWSKI, 560 Center Ave., Garner, 50438. Tel: 641-923-6045. North/Northeast Iowa Area: JOHN O'NEILL, Lansing; MARY O'NEILL, Lansing. Tel: 563-586-2380; Deacon VICTOR J. DESLOOVER, New Hampton; NANCY DESLOOVER, New Hampton. Tel: 563-429-2773; JOE KREINER, Ossian; KRISTIN KREINER, Ossian. Tel: 563-532-7065.

Sponsor Couple— Contact local parish for more information

Finance Office—RICHARD L. RUNDE, Finance Officer; PENNY MINNIHAN, Auditor; PAULA MONTAG, Controller; KEN RAHE, Business Mgr.; JANICE TUEGEL, Accounting Clerk; ELAINE HILDEBRAND, Bookkeeper/Sec., Mailing Address: P.O. Box 479, Dubuque, 52004-0479. Tel: 563-556-2580.

Health Care Ethics & Life Issues—JANINE MARIE IDZIAK, Ph.D., Consultant, Mailing Address: P.O. Box 479, Dubuque, 52004-0479. Tel: 563-556-2580; NANCY EISBACH, Sec.

Hispanic Offices and Personnel—

Vicar for Hispanic Ministry—Rev. Msgr. LEON L. CONNOLLY (Retired).

Director—Sr. JUDY CALLAHAN, B.V.M.

Secretary—PATRICIA NEISES.

Immigration Services—TERRI REYNOLDS. Tel: 563-556-5372; TERESA RUBIO, Sec.

Human Resources—LYNN OSTERHAUS, Dir.; BARB GLEASON, Sec., 1229 Mt. Loretta Ave., Dubuque, 52003-7826. Tel: 563-556-2580.

Information Technology—JOHN NIGG, Dir.; ROB AESCHLIMAN, Email Admin.; DENISE AIRD, Sec.

Print Shop Manager—ROBERT GOLDTHORPE.

Insurance: Property and Liability (Dubuque Archdiocesan Protection Program)—RICH EARLES, Claims Risk Mgr., Archdiocesan Center, 1229 Mt. Loretta Ave., Dubuque, 52003-8787. Tel: 563-556-2580; PATRICIA NEISES, Sec.

Lay Formation—Sr. MARCI BLUM, O.S.F., Dir.; DIANE KONSHAK, Sec., Archdiocesan Center, 1229 Mt. Loretta Ave., P.O. Box 479, Dubuque, 52004-0479. Tel: 563-556-2580.

Leadership Development and Pastoral Planning—DAN ROHNER, Dir., Mailing Address: P.O. Box 479, Dubuque, 52004-0479. Tel: 563-556-2580.

Media Services—KIM FELDMAN, Dir.; Sr. CAROL HOVERMAN, O.S.F., Dir. Communications; LARRY GAUL, Media Technician, 1229 Mt. Loretta Ave., Dubuque, 52003-7826. Tel: 563-556-2580; TRICIA TRANEL, Resource Center Specialist.

Metropolitan Tribunal—Mailing Address: P.O. Box 479, Dubuque, 52004-0479. Tel: 563-556-2580. (Please send all dispensation requests to the Tribunal.)

Director—Sr. MAUREEN MCPARTLAND, O.P., J.C.L.

Judicial Vicar—Rev. THOMAS R. ZINKULA, J.D., J.C.L.

Defenders of the Bond—Rev. Msgr. RICHARD P. FUNKE, J.C.L. (Retired); Sr. MARY LIANA GLYNN, O.P., J.C.L.; Rev. DONALD J. PLAMONDON, J.C.L.

Judges—Revs. SCOTT E. BULLOCK, J.C.L.; JOSEPH L. HAUER, J.C.D.; Deacon GERALD T. JORGENSEN, Ph.D., J.C.L.; Revs. DOUGLAS J. LOECKE, J.C.L.; MARK R. NEMMERS (Retired); Sr. FRANCINE QUILLIN, P.B.V.M., J.C.L.; Rev. Msgr. W. DEAN WALZ, J.C.D. (Retired); Rev. THOMAS R. ZINKULA, J.D., J.C.L.

Promoter of Justice—Deacon GERALD T. JORGENSEN, Ph.D., J.C.L.

Office Secretaries—MADONNA WHITAKER, Notary; BARB GLEASON.

Newly Ordained Program—Rev. SCOTT E. BULLOCK, J.C.L., Dir.; BEV RECH, Sec., 1229 Mt. Loretta Ave., Dubuque, 52003-7826. Tel: 563-556-2580.

Newspaper "The Witness"—Sr. CAROL HOVERMAN, O.S.F., Editor, Archdiocesan Center, 1229 Mt. Loretta Ave., P.O. Box 917, Dubuque, 52004-0917. Tel: 563-588-0556; Fax: 563-588-0557. Staff: BRET FEAR, Production & Design; CATHY WHITE, Circulation & Sec.; STEVE MCMAHON, Staff Writer & Copy Editor; AMBER MORRISSEY, Reporter.

Permanent Diaconate Program—Deacon TOM LANG, Dir., 1229 Mt. Loretta Ave., P.O. Box 479, Dubuque, 52004-0479. Tel: 563-556-2580. Assistant Directors: Deacons RICHARD WALLACE; GERALD T. JORGENSEN, Ph.D., J.C.L.; RAYMOND LARSEN.

Persons With Disabilities—Sr. MARCI BLUM, O.S.F., Dir.; JUDY ARLEN, Sec.; MARY KOETZ, Coord. Retreats/Renewal Days.

Pontifical Missions/Mission Awareness—Rev. Msgr. JOHN R. MCCLEAN, Dir. (Retired), Archdiocesan Center, 1229 Mt. Loretta Ave., Dubuque, 52003-7826. Tel: 563-556-2580; NANCY EISBACH, Sec.

Protection of Children and Young People—JOANNE POHLAND, Dir.; BARB GLEASON, Sec.

Respect Life—JANINE MARIE IDZIAK, Ph.D., Dir.; ED HABERKORN, Sec.

School Tuition Organization (STO)—JAMIE HENLEY, Dir.; LOIS THILMANY, Sec., 1229 Mt. Loretta Ave., P.O. Box 479, Dubuque, 52004-0479. Tel: 563-556-2580.

Seminarians—Rev. SCOTT E. BULLOCK, J.C.L., Dir.; BEV RECH, Sec., 1229 Mt. Loretta Ave., Dubuque, 52003-7826. Tel: 563-556-2580.

Stewardship & Development—JAMIE HENLEY, Dir.; PAUL J. FROMMELT, Dir. Educational Devel. Emeritus. Secretaries: LOIS THILMANY. Tel: 563-556-2580; DENISE AIRD.

Vocation Awareness—Rev. DAVID A. SCHATZ, M.A., Dir. Associate Directors: Revs. KENNETH J. GLASER; DENNIS W. MILLER; BEV RECH, Sec., Archdiocesan Center, 1229 Mt. Loretta Ave., Dubuque, 52003-7826. Tel: 563-556-2580.

Worship Office—THERESA HARVEY, Dir.; GINNY NEUWOHNER, Sec., 1229 Mt. Loretta Ave., P.O. Box 479, Dubuque, 52004-0479. Tel: 563-556-2580.

Young Adult Ministry—KATIE PFIFFNER, Dir., Archdiocesan Center, 1229 Mt. Loretta Ave., Dubuque, 52003-7826. Tel: 563-556-2580.

Archdiocesan Boards, Commissions and Councils

The Archdiocese of Dubuque Corporate Board—Most Rev. JEROME HANUS, O.S.B.; Rev. Msgr. THOMAS E. TOALE, Ph.D.; RICHARD L. RUNDE, Treas. (non-voting); BETTY SCHUELLER; Sr. DOLORES MARIE MCHUGH, B.V.M.; MARK MOLO.

Archdiocese of Dubuque Deposit & Loan Fund Board—Most Rev. JEROME HANUS, O.S.B., D.D.; Rev. Msgr. THOMAS E. TOALE, Ph.D.; Sr. DOLORES MARIE MCHUGH, B.V.M.; MARK MOLO; BETTY SCHUELLER; RICHARD L. RUNDE, Treas. (non-voting).

Archdiocese of Dubuque Education Fund Board—Most Rev. JEROME HANUS, O.S.B., D.D., Pres.; PAUL J. FROMMELT, Vice Pres.; JAMIE HENLEY, Sec., Ex-Officio; RICHARD L. RUNDE, Treas., Ex-Officio; MATTHEW BRANDES; EDWARD J. GALLAGHER JR.; C. RICHARD STARK; Rev. Msgr. THOMAS E. TOALE, Ph.D.

Archdiocese of Dubuque Perpetual Care Fund Board—Most Rev. JEROME HANUS, O.S.B., D.D.; Rev. Msgr. THOMAS E. TOALE, Ph.D.; ARNOLD HONKAMP; Sr. HELEN HUEWE, O.S.F.; BETTY SCHUELLER; RICHARD L. RUNDE, Treas. (non-voting).

Archdiocese of Dubuque Seminarian Education Fund Board—Most Rev. JEROME HANUS, O.S.B., D.D.; Rev. Msgr. THOMAS E. TOALE, Ph.D.; Sr. DOLORES MARIE MCHUGH, B.V.M.; MARK MOLO; BETTY SCHUELLER; RICHARD L. RUNDE, Treas. (non-voting).

Advisory Committee in Partnership with Persons with Disabilities—Sr. MARCI BLUM, O.S.F.; MARTHA HANLEY; ANDY HASLEY; D. J. JAEGER; NORMA LEIBOLD; Deacons STEPHEN MACDONALD; MICHAEL MOETSCH; RUTH PALMER; ANNA STAMAT; Rev. JAMES STARBUCK; JEAN TRAINOR.

American Martyrs Retreat House Advisory Board—Sr. M. JEANINE KUHN, P.B.V.M, Dir.; JANINE WHIPPS, Chm.; BRIAN A'HEARN; EDWARD J. GALLAGHER JR.; Sr. MARY MICHELLE GALLAGHER, P.B.V.M.; Rev. LOUIS M. JAEGER; ROGER KUETER; RON LEIBOLD; Rev. Msgr. LYLE L. WILGENBUSCH, Ex Officio.

Audit Committee—KAREN STURM, Chm.; DENISE DOLAN; STEPHEN J. SCHMALL; RICHARD L. RUNDE, Staff (non-voting).

Archdiocesan Faith Formation Commission—Ex-Officio: Most Rev. JEROME HANUS, O.S.B.; LEANN BELKEN; DAVE CUSHING; SHIRLEY FORD; MARILYN GORUN; KIM HERMSEN; Deacon MICHAEL KLAPPHOLZ; LEON KEUHNER; SUSAN KEUNE; Rev. NICHOLAS B. MARCH; KATHY OBERREUTER; MATT O'LAUGHLIN; RUTH PALMER; JOSEPH SCHMALL; ERIC STROMBERG; SUE VERNON.

Archdiocesan Catholic School Board—Ex-Officio: JAMES OSTERBERGER; MILISSA BAILEY; CORRINE HEIMER BREITSPRECKER; TIM KNEELAND; WILLIAM MCCARTAN; MARY NICHOLS; Deacon JIM PATERA; MARTHA REAL; Sr. CATHERINE STEWART, O.P.; Rev. PHILIP E. THOMPSON.

Building Commission—Rev. Msgr. RUSSELL M. BLEICH, S.T.L., Chair; RALPH EMERSON; Deacon LAVERNE FLAGEL; THERESA HARVEY; Rev. Msgr. STANLEY J. HAYEK (Retired); JAMES HYNES; Deacon RAY LARSEN; Rev. NEIL J. MANTERNACH; JAMES OSTERBERGER; KEN RAHE, Recording Sec.; RICHARD L. RUNDE, Exec. Sec.; Rev. Msgr. CARL L. SCHMITT; ED WINEINGER.

Catholic Charities Board of Directors—Most Rev. JEROME HANUS, O.S.B., Pres.; Rev. Msgr. THOMAS E. TOALE, Ph.D., Vice Pres.; TRACY MORRISON, M.S., L.M.H.C., N.C.C., (Staff Non-Voting); MARY COAN; Sr. MARGARET MARY COSGROVE, B.V.M.; NANCY ZACHAR FETT; JUSTIN GULLEKSON; JAMES JACKSON; MARY JO RATER; STEPHANIE SAVAGE; RICHARD SCHRAD; PAUL SIGWARTH; JEFFREY FITZPATRICK; Deacon TOM SINK, Diaconate Representative.

CEW Advisory Board—ROGER BERNING; BARBARA BRUMM; MIKE DUDLEY; DAVE FANGMAN; DENISE HAGER; Rev. GEORGE W. KARNIK (Retired); DEBBIE LANDUYT; BOB RAHE; CATHY ROBERTSON; STEVE SCHMIT; BECKY SEYMOUR; MYRNA UDELHOFEN; PAM WASHINGTON; LORAS WEBER; CAROLYN WEBER; LUANN YANECEK.

Christian Initiation Advisory Committee—Sr. MARY L. LECHTENBERG, O.S.F.; KAREN BYRNE; Rev. KENNETH J. GLASER, Chm.; THERESA HARVEY; JAMES HAWKINS; JOHN HAYES; Deacon WILLIAM HICKSON; Sr. CONNIE HOWE, R.S.M.; JO ANN KRAMER; JO MEISTER, Vice Chm.; Sr. FRANCINE QUILLIN, P.B.V.M., J.C.L.; Deacon TOM SINK; Sr. JEANNE TRANEL, O.P.

Church Design/Renovation Commission—Rev. DAVID G. KUCERA; THERESA HARVEY, Exec. Sec.; PAM JOHNSTON, Vice Chm.; Rev. NEIL J. MANTERNACH, Chm.; Sr. RUTH JACKSON, S.V.M.; Revs. DENNIS D. JUHL; PHILIP E. THOMPSON.

Diaconal Community Council—Most Rev. JEROME HANUS, O.S.B., Pres.; Deacon TOM LANG, Exec. Sec.

Ames Region—Deacons JEFF HARRIS; RON SMITH.

Cedar Rapids Region—Deacons MICHAEL KLAPPHOLZ; SEAN SMITH.

Dubuque Region—JOAN STEGER; Deacon JAMES THILL.

Northeast Region—Deacons JAMES PFAFFLY; PATRICK J. MALANAPHY.

Mason City Region—Deacon MICHAEL G. BYRNE; JENNIFER COOPER.

Waterloo Region—Deacon MICHAEL MOETSCH; KAREN SINK.

Appointed By The Archbishop—PAM WHITTERS; Deacons JOHN MCCULLY; SEAN SMITH, APC Liaison.

Catholic Charities/St. Mary's Home— Board of Directors Social Concern Committee Liaison Deacon TOM SINK.

Due Process Board—Sr. MARY MCCAULEY, B.V.M., Chm.; Rev. GABRIEL C. ANDERSON; DAVID HEIAR; JULIE NIEMEYER; Deacon STEVEN W. STRANG; KAREN A. VOLZ; JOHN WALDMEIR; Rev. Msgr. THOMAS E. TOALE, Ph.D., Staff (non-voting).

Family Life & Marriage Advisory Committee—Sr. LINDA BECHEN, R.S.M.; KAREN BONFIG; MIKE ERIKSON; JEAN LEUTE; JANICE LOECKE, L.P.N., B.S.; Ms. LINDA MANTERNACH; Rev. PHILLIP E. SCHMITT (Retired); Deacon SEAN SMITH; SARAH SMITH; ERIK STROMBERG; MARY BETH WAGNER.

Finance Council—Most Rev. JEROME HANUS, O.S.B., Chm.; RICHARD L. RUNDE, Exec. Sec.; PAULA MONTAG, Recording Sec.; Rev. Msgr. JAMES O. BARTA, Ph.D. (Retired); DONALD BERGAN; Deacon MATTHEW F. BERRY; Sr. MARGARET MARY COSGROVE, B.V.M.; THOMAS W. HANLEY; Revs. JOSEPH L. HAUER, J.C.D.; DONALD L. KLEIN; MAGGIE JACKSON; ROBERT KUCHARSKI; JASON MCDERMOTT; KAREN STURM; Rev. Msgr. THOMAS E. TOALE, Ph.D.; STEVE WEISS.

Human Resources Advisory Committee—LYNN OSTERHAUS, Chm.; Sr. JEAN GORDON, B.V.M.; KATHY KRUSIE; JULIE NEIMEYER.

Investment Committee—ROBERT KUCHARSKI, Chm.; Rev. Msgr. JAMES O. BARTA, Ph.D. (Retired); DON FLYNN; PAUL J. FROMMELT; EDWARD J. GALLAGHER JR.; GREG GRECO; Rev. DOUGLAS J. LOECKE, J.C.L.; RICHARD L. RUNDE.

Lay Formation Advisory Board—Rev. Msgr. JAMES O. BARTA, Ph.D. (Retired); Sr. MARCI BLUM, O.S.F.; PATRICIA BRUSH; DAVE CUSHING; Rev. LOUIS M. JAEGER; DEAN MANTERNACH; JERRY MANTERNACH; KATHY OBERREUTER; SUSAN M. SCHLETTER; MAUREEN UTTER.

Medical-Moral Commission—JANINE MARIE IDZIAK, Ph.D., Chm.; Sr. JAMES MARIE DONAHUE, R.S.M., Ph.D.; KEVIN HEALY, M.D.; Rev. WILLIAM M. JOENSEN, Ph.D.; JANICE LOECKE, L.P.N., B.S.; Rev. STEPHEN A. LUNDGREN; CAROL SCHMIDT, R.N.C., M.S.H.; RICHARD WHITTY, J.D.

PAMAD (Pastoral Associates/Ministers of the Archdiocese of Dubuque)—ANN PETZELKA, Pres.; Sr. LINDA BECHEN, R.S.M., Vice Pres.; SHARON BAINBRIDGE, Sec.; ANN WERTZ, Treas.

Pastoral Council—Most Rev. JEROME HANUS, O.S.B., Pres.; Sr. LINDA BECHEN, R.S.M., Chm.; BOB CELICHOWSKI, Vice Chm.; FLORINE SWANSON, Sec.; DAN ROHNER, Exec. Sec.; Rev. Msgrs. THOMAS E. TOALE, Ph.D.; RUSSELL M. BLEICH, S.T.L.; JIM BAILEY; PATRICK BYRNE; JOE DAVIS; PETER GONZALEZ; DANIEL HAYES; NORMA LEIBOLD; DAVID MITCHELL; Sr. SUSAN O'CONNOR, R.S.M., Sec.; BILL OFFERMAN; NANCY RIGEL; BETSY SCHMITZ; RICHARD SCHRAD; CLAIRA SIEVERDING; Sisters DOROTHY SCHWENDINGER, O.S.F.; JEANNE TRANEL, O.P.; Deacon SEAN SMITH; JOSEPH SUAREZ; Rev. Msgr. LYLE L. WILGENBUSCH; BERNICE TOEPFER; ROSE YADDOF.

Permanent Diaconate Formation Board—Deacon TOM LANG, Chm.; JOAN M. HEAD; Deacons DANIEL HOEGER; GERALD T. JORGENSEN, Ph.D., J.C.L.; JOANN KOOPMANN; Deacon RAY LARSEN; Revs. JAMES L. MILLER; DAVID H. O'CONNOR; Deacon MICHAEL WHITTERS.

Personnel Advisory Board—Very Rev. BERNARD C. GRADY, Age Group II; Revs. NEIL J. MANTERNACH, At Large; DONALD L. KLEIN, Age Group I; THOMAS R. ZINKULA, J.D., J.C.L., Sec., Age Group III; DENNIS J. QUINT, Age Group IV.

Priests' Council—Most Rev. JEROME HANUS, O.S.B., Pres.; Revs. PHILIP E. THOMPSON, Chm.; DAVID M. BECKMAN, Vice Chm.; Very Rev. DWAYNE J. THOMAN, Sec. Ex Officio Members: Rev. Msgrs. RUSSELL M. BLEICH, S.T.L.; LYLE L. WILGENBUSCH; THOMAS E. TOALE, Ph.D.

Retired Priests' Representatives—Rev. Msgr. RALPH P. SIMINGTON (Retired); Rev. DANIEL A. KRAPFL (Retired).

Religious Priests Representative—Rev. ROBERT MERTES, S.V.D.

Deanery Representatives—Revs. PHILIP E. THOMPSON, Cedar Rapids Deanery; MARK J. REASONER, Cedar Rapids Deanery; DAVID M. BECKMAN, Decorah Deanery; DANIEL J. KNEPPER, Dubuque Deanery; Very Rev. DWAYNE J. THOMAN, Dubuque Deanery; Rev. G. ROBERT GROSS, Dyersville Deanery; Very Rev. RICHARD G. GAUL, Elkader Deanery; Revs. DAVID J. AMBROSY, Independence Deanery; DENNIS W. MILLER, Marshalltown Deanery; HENRY P. HUBER, Mason City Deanery; Rev. Msgr. WALTER L. BRUNKAN, New Hampton Deanery; Revs. KENNETH C. STECHER, Waterloo Deanery; SCOTT F. BOONE, Webster City Deanery.

Priestly Life and Ministry Committee— (Standing Committee of the Priests' Council) Rev. SCOTT E. BULLOCK, J.C.L.; Very Rev. JERRY F. KOPACEK; Revs. LOUIS M. JAEGER; DAVID H. O'CONNOR; DENNIS J. QUINT; Rev. Msgr. LYLE L. WILGENBUSCH.

Review Board for Sexual Abuse of Minors by Clergy and Other Church Personnel—JAMES ANASTASI, Mason City; JOHN E. BECKMAN, Waterloo; CHERIE CASEY, Dyersville; ELIZABETH CORKEN DEEGAN, Cedar Rapids; Rev. DARREL GERRIETTS, Waverly; Sr. CORITA HEID, R.S.M., Mason City; Very Rev. JERRY F. KOPACEK, Waterloo; Judge RANDAL NIGG, Dubuque; PAM WHITTERS; Deacon GERALD T. JORGENSEN, Ph.D., J.C.L., Promoter of Justice; Dr. BARBARA SULLIVAN WOODWARD, Chm., Dubuque.

St. Mary's Home Board of Directors—Most Rev. JEROME HANUS, O.S.B., D.D., Pres.; Rev. Msgr. THOMAS E. TOALE, Ph.D., Vice Pres.; GREG BURBACH; Sr. MARGARET MARY COSGROVE, B.V.M.; MICHAEL COYLE; STEPHANIE SAVAGE; NICHOLAS SCHRUP III; TRACY MORRISON, M.S., L.M.H.C., N.C.C., (Staff Non-Voting).

Saint Raphael Priest Fund Society—

Board of Directors/Priest Pension Plan Board of Trustees—Most Rev. JEROME HANUS, O.S.B., Pres.; Rev. Msgr. THOMAS E. TOALE, Ph.D., Vice Pres.; Rev. DANIEL A. KRAPFL, Sec. & Treas. (Retired); RICHARD L. RUNDE, Plan Admin. Directors: Rev. Msgrs. JAMES O. BARTA, Ph.D. (Retired); WALTER L. BRUNKAN; STANLEY J. HAYEK (Retired); Revs. DOUGLAS J. LOECKE, J.C.L.; DANIEL A. KRAPFL (Retired); Rev. Msgr. JOHN R. MCCLEAN (Retired); Rev. THOMAS J. MCDERMOTT; Very Rev. MICHAEL J. MESCHER; Rev. MARK J. REASONER; Rev. Msgrs. CARL L. SCHMITT; RALPH P. SIMINGTON (Retired); Rev. THOMAS R. ZINKULA, J.D., J.C.L.

Seminary Admissions and Advisory Board—Revs. SCOTT E. BULLOCK, J.C.L., Chm.; THOMAS J. MCDERMOTT; MARY JO PFEIFER-WULF; Revs. NEIL J. MANTERNACH; DUSTIN L. VU.

School Tuition Organization Board of Directors—Rev. Msgr. THOMAS E. TOALE, Ph.D., Pres.; JAMES OSTERBERGER, Vice Pres.; JEFF HENDERSON, Sec.; MAE BECKER; JEFF ENGEL; JULIE HERMANN; JUDY RUDMAN; JOSEPH SCHMALL.

Stewardship Committee—SUE BAHLS, (Elkader Deanery); JIM BERGKAMP, (Webster City Deanery); ROBERT BREITFELDER, (Dyersville Deanery); SHIRLEY FORD, (Marshalltown Deanery); Deacon JIM FREET, (Waterloo Deanery); Very Rev. BERNARD C. GRADY; Sr. MARY HARGRAFEN, O.S.F., Pastoral Admin.; JAMES HAWKINS, (Decorah Deanery); JOANNE KOOPMAN, (Dyersville Deanery); Deacon TIMOTHY LOBIANCO, (Dubuque Deanery); SUSAN MARTINEK, (Cedar Rapids Deanery); JODY DOYLE, (Independence Deanery); MAUREEN UTTER, (Mason City Deanery); CONNIE WAGNER, (New Hampton Deanery); Rev. Msgr. LYLE L. WILGENBUSCH, Regl. Vicar; JAMIE HENLEY, Staff.

Victim Assistance Coordinators—Dr. THOMAS ANDEREGG. Tel: 563-556-1225; JOAN HOFFMANN. Tel: 866-319-4636.

Vocation Awareness Advisory Committee—Very Rev. JOHN A. GOSSMAN; Rev. JOHN S. HAUGEN; Very Rev. PHILLIP F. KRUSE.

Witness Advisory Committee—Sr. CAROL HOVERMAN, O.S.F., Chm.; BRIAN COOPER; MARILYN GORUN; AL GRIVETTI; DALE KUETER; PAULA MONTAG; Sr. MIRA MOSLE, B.V.M.; Deacon SEAN SMITH; Rev. DENNIS J. QUINT.

Worship Commission—CHRISTINE CARRIER, Chm.; THERESA HARVEY, Exec. Sec.; RICHARD BEAVES, Vice Chm.; Revs. GREG E. BAHL; SCOTT E. BULLOCK, J.C.L.; Sisters SHEILA DOUGHERTY, P.B.V.M.; LINDA BECHEN, R.S.M.; KATHLEEN GRACE, O.S.F.; Rev. DANIEL J. KNEPPER; JOANN KOOPMANN; Rev. DENNIS J. QUINT; ANASTASIA NICKLAUS SCHMELZER; Deacon ROBERT STIRM.

Youth Commission—KEVIN FEYEN, Exec. Dir. Adult Members: Rev. GREG E. BAHL; ANGELA BULMAN; THERESA DEUTSCH; BOB GARDNER; VONIS HARTIGAN; ANNA STEELE. Youth Members: HALEY BRIMMER, Youth Chm.; CORY RUDE, Vice Chm.; CLAIRA SIEVERDING, APC 11th Grade Representative; EMILY FOEGEN; KRISTI HARTIGAN; EMILY HOGAN; ALEX HOLBACH; ASHLEY LABARGE; JOCELYN MULDER; KELSEY PIEPER, Sec.; MOLLY MURPHY; CAITLIN O'LOUGHLIN; BETSY SCHMITZ, APC 12th Grade Representative; SARAH SCHWENDINGER; KAY PAUL; CHELSEA REICKS; NICOLE SCHROEDER; NICOLE SCHULTE; BETHANY SCHWAN.

CLERGY, PARISHES, MISSIONS AND PAROCHIAL SCHOOLS

CITY OF DUBUQUE

(DUBUQUE COUNTY)

1—ST. RAPHAEL CATHEDRAL (1833) [JC] Rev. Msgr. Wayne A. Ressler, Rector; Deacon Paul Peckosh; Barbara Gatch, Pastoral Assoc.; James Mandralla, Music Dir. & Liturgist. In Res., Rev. Ardel H. Barta (Retired).
Church, Res. & Office: 231 Bluff St., 52001-6918. Tel: 563-582-7646; Fax: 563-556-6796.
See Holy Family Catholic Schools under Consolidated K-12 Systems located in the Institution section
Catechesis/Religious Program—Jean Leute, D.R.E. Students 125.

2—ST. ANTHONY (1867) [JC] Rev. Daniel J. Knepper; Deacons William Mauss; William Hickson; Sr. Margaret Anne Kramer, P.B.V.M., Pastoral Assoc.
Res. & Office: 1870 St. Ambrose St., 52001-4196. Tel: 563-588-0571; Fax: 563-588-0572.
Church: 1880 St. Ambrose St., 52001.
See Holy Family Catholic Schools under Consolidated K-12 Systems located in the Institution Section.
Catechesis/Religious Program—Carol A. Witry, D.R.E. Students 215.

3—CHURCH OF THE NATIVITY (1923) [JC] Very Rev. Dwayne J. Thoman; Deacon David McGhee, Pastoral Assoc.
Church & Office: 1225 Alta Vista St., 52001. Tel: 563-582-1839; Fax: 563-582-1830.
Res.: 1075 University, 52001. Tel: 563-582-0703.
See Holy Family Catholic Schools under Consolidated K-12 Systems located in the Institution section
Catechesis/Religious Program—Judith Calcari, D.R.E. Students 89.

4—CHURCH OF THE RESURRECTION (1857) [CEM] Revs. Joseph L. Hauer; Steven M. Garner; Deacons Michael Blouin; Gerald T. Jorgensen; Timothy LoBianco, Pastoral Assoc.; Sr. Francine Quillin, P.B.V.M., Pastoral Assoc.
Church & Office: 4300 Asbury Rd., 52002. Tel: 563-556-7511; Fax: 563-556-7419.
Res.: 2525 St. Anne Dr., 52001. Tel: 563-582-5634.
See Holy Family Catholic Schools under Consolidated K-12 Systems located in the Institution Section.
Catechesis/Religious Program—Joseph Hancock, D.R.E. Students 468.

5—ST. COLUMBKILLE (1887) [JC] Rev. Gabriel C. Anderson; Deacon William Biver; Alice Noethe, Pastoral Assoc.
Church, Res. & Office: 1240 Rush St., 52003-7598. Tel: 563-583-9117; Fax: 563-583-5909.
See Holy Family Catholic Schools under Consolidated K-12 Systems located in the Institution Section.
Catechesis/Religious Program—Alice Noethe, D.R.E. Students 80.

6—HOLY GHOST (1896) [JC] Revs. Thomas R. Zinkula; Gary A. Mayer; Deacons James J. Thill; Dave Brinkmoeller; John Stierman.
Res.: 2917 Central Ave., 52001-1999. Tel: 563-582-5443.
Church: 2921 Central Ave., 52001.
Office: 2215 Windsor Ave., 52001-0698. Tel: 563-583-1709; Fax: 563-583-1700.
See Holy Family Catholic Schools under Consolidated K-12 Systems located in the Institution Section
Catechesis/Religious Program—Victoria Wadle, D.R.E. Students 122.

7—HOLY TRINITY (1910) [JC] Revs. Thomas R. Zinkula; Gary A. Mayer; Deacons James J. Thill; Dave Brinkmoeller; John Stierman.
Office: 2215 Windsor Ave., 52001-0698. Tel: 563-583-1709; Fax: 563-583-1700.
Church: 1701 Rhomberg, 52001.
Rectory—2917 Central Ave., 52001. Tel: 563-582-5443.
See Holy Family Catholic Schools under Consolidated K-12 Systems located in the Institution Section
Catechesis/Religious Program—Victoria Wadle, D.R.E. Students 41.

8—ST. JOSEPH THE WORKER (1949) [JC] Rev. Mark A. Ressler; Deacon Stephen MacDonald.
Res.: 90 S. Algona St., 52001-5605. Tel: 563-588-2934.
Office: 60 S. Algona, 52001-5605. Tel: 563-588-1433; Fax: 563-588-4108.
Church: 2001 St. Joseph St., 52001.
See Holy Family Catholic Schools under Consolidated K-12 Systems located in the Institution Section.
Catechesis/Religious Program—Sr. Marilyn Breen, P.B.V.M., D.R.E. Students 158.

9—ST. MARY (1850) [JC] Rev. Steven J. Rosonke; Deacon Horacio Quiles; Ann Wertz, Pastoral Assoc.
Church, Res., & Office: 1584 White St., 52001-4905. Tel: 563-582-5469; Fax: 563-582-5460.
See Holy Family Catholic Schools under Consolidated K-12 Systems located in the Institution Section
Catechesis/Religious Program—Linked with St. Patrick, Dubuque. Susan Dazey, D.R.E. Students 46.

10—ST. PATRICK (1862) [JC] Rev. Steven J. Rosonke; Deacon Horacio Quiles; Ann Wertz, Pastoral Assoc.; Sr. Jeanette McCarthy, P.B.V.M., Hispanic Min. Coord.
Parish Office—1425 Iowa St., 52001-4890. Tel: 563-583-9749.
Church: 15th & Iowa St., 52001.
See Holy Family Catholic Schools under Consolidated K-12 Systems located in the Institution Section
Catechesis/Religious Program—Susan Dazey, D.R.E. Linked with St. Mary, Dubuque. Students 20.

11—SACRED HEART (1879) [JC] Revs. Thomas R. Zinkula; Gary A. Mayer; Deacons James Thill; Dave Brinkmoeller; John Stierman. In Res., Rev. Harold J. Drexler (Retired).
Church & Office: 2215 Windsor Ave., 52001-0698. Tel: 563-583-1709.
Res.: 2917 Central Ave., 52001. Tel: 563-582-5443.
See Holy Family Catholic Schools under Consolidated K-12 Systems located in the Institution Section
Catechesis/Religious Program—Linked with Holy Trinity Victoria Wadle, D.R.E. Students 147.

OUTSIDE THE CITY OF DUBUQUE

ACKLEY, FRANKLIN CO., ST. MARY (1891) [CEM] Very Rev. Bernard C. Grady; Deacon David Jones.
Mailing Address: 1405 N. Federal, Hampton, 50441-1005.
Office & Church: 611 Sherman Ave., P.O. Box 2, 50601. Tel: 641-847-2329.
Res.: 2 19th Ave., N.E., Hampton, 50441. Tel: 641-456-3406.
Catechesis/Religious Program—Jolene Harms, D.R.E. Students 80.

ALLISON, BUTLER CO., IMMACULATE CONCEPTION, Closed. For sacramental records, contact St. Mary, Greene.

ALTA VISTA, CHICKASAW CO., ST. BERNARD (1897) [CEM] Rev. Ray E. Atwood.
Office: 203 Seventh St., P.O. Box 38, Elma, 50628-0038. Tel: 641-393-2520; Fax: 641-393-2069.
Church: 116 E. Washington, 50603.
Catechesis/Religious Program—Sheila Kobliska, D.R.E. Students 28.

AMES, STORY CO.

1—ST. CECILIA (1899) Rev. James L. Secora; Deacons Gary Aitchison; John McCully, Hispanic Min. Coord.; Richard Tondra; Ron Smith; Alan Christy.
Res.: 1642 Reagan Dr., 50010. Tel: 515-233-9477.
Church & Office: 2900 Hoover Ave., 50010-4498. Tel: 515-233-3092; Fax: 515-233-6423.
School—(Grades PreSchool-5) Tel: 515-232-5290. Tom Budnik, Prin. Lay Teachers 13; Students 252.
Catechesis/Religious Program—Tel: 515-232-3514. John Hayes, D.R.E. Students 373.

2—ST. THOMAS AQUINAS CHURCH (AND CATHOLIC STUDENT CENTER) (1947) Revs. Jon M. Seda; Dennis W. Miller. Tel: 515-292-3097; Sr. Lorraine Schmaltz, P.B.V.M., Pastoral Assoc.; Bobby LeBlanc, Business Mgr.; Shari Reilly, Dir. Campus Ministry; Misty Heinen, Campus Ministry.
Church & Office: 2210 Lincoln Ave., 50014-7184. Tel: 515-292-3810; Fax: 515-292-3841.
Pastor's Res.: 2801 Bristol Dr., 50010.
Assoc. Pastor's Res.: 3007 Wessex Dr., #162, 50014.
Catechesis/Religious Program—Kathy White, D.R.E. Students 237.

ANAMOSA, JONES CO., ST. PATRICK (1861) [CEM] Sr. Susan Dunnwald, R.S.M., Pastoral Admin.; Very Rev. John A. Gossman, Priest Supvr.; Rev. Wayne J. Droessler, Sacramental Priest.
Res. & Office: 215 N. Garnavillo St., 52205-1121. Tel: 319-462-2141.
Church: 217 N. Garnavillo St., 52205.
School—(Grades PreSchool-6), 216 N. Garnavillo St., 52205-1122. Tel: 319-462-2688; Fax: 319-462-3239. Charlotte Scheckel, Prin. Lay Teachers 8; Students 74.
Catechesis/Religious Program—Charlotte Scheckel, D.R.E. Students 64.

ANDREW, JACKSON CO., ST. JOHN (1914) [CEM] Revs. James T. Chappell; Paul E. Lippstock, Sacramental Priest; Deacon Robert Head.
Res. and Mailing Address: 200 S. Vermont, Maquoketa, 52060. Tel: 563-652-6931.
Church: 107 S. Main St., 52030.
Catechesis/Religious Program—Sr. Helen Stejskal, S.S.N.D., D.R.E. Students 37.

BALDWIN, JACKSON CO., HOLY TRINITY, [CEM] Closed. Sacramental Records are located at Sacred Heart, Maquoketa.

BALLTOWN, DUBUQUE CO., ST. FRANCIS OF ASSISI (1891) [CEM] Rev. Raymond A. Burkle; Bro. Stephen W. Markham, F.S.C., Pastoral Assoc.
Parish Office & Mailing Address: 875 Church St., P.O. Box 398, Holy Cross, 52053. Tel: 563-870-4041.
Pastor's Res.: 103 S. Andres St., P.O. Box 140, Luxemburg, 52056. Tel: 563-853-3369.
Church: 468 Balltown Rd., Sherrill, 52073.
See LaSalle Elementary Schools, Holy Cross under Elementary School Systems located in the Institution section.
Catechesis/Religious Program—Students 22.

BANKSTON, DUBUQUE CO., ST. CLEMENT (1859) [CEM] Rev. Dennis R. Cain; Deacons James Kean; Gerald Koopmann; Betty Pins, Pastoral Assoc.
Office: 104 First St., S.E., P.O. Box 286, Epworth, 52045-0286. Tel: 563-876-5540.
Res.: 22511 E. Pleasant Grove Rd., Epworth, 52045. Tel: 563-876-5501.
Church: 24287 New Vienna Rd., Epworth, 52045-9732.
See Seton Catholic Schools, Farley under Elementary School Systems located in the Institution section.
Catechesis/Religious Program—Betty Pins, C.R.E. Students 60.

BARCLAY, BLACKHAWK CO., ST. FRANCIS (1862) [CEM] Rev. Kenneth C. Stecher.
Office: 7837 E. Airline Hwy., Dunkerton, 50626. Tel: 319-822-7477.
Res.: 634 Stevens St., P.O. Box 316, Jesup, 50648. Tel: 319-827-3003.
Church: 7830 E. Airline Hwy., Dunkerton, 50626.
Catechesis/Religious Program—Arlene Widdel, C.R.E. Students 46.

BELLE PLAINE, BENTON CO., ST. MICHAEL (1885) Very Rev. Michael J. Mescher; Deacon Joseph Behounek, Pastoral Assoc.; Bette Kratoska, Pastoral Min.
Church & Mailing Address: 1304 Ninth Ave., 52208-1614. Tel: 319-444-3106; Fax: 319-444-3737.
Catechesis/Religious Program—Jeffrey Lumpa, D.R.E. Students 73.

BELLEVUE, JACKSON CO., ST. JOSEPH (1841) [CEM] Revs. Stephen L. Meyer; Scott E. Bullock; Mary Jane Keppler, Pastoral Assoc.
Church, Res., & Office: 405 Franklin St., 52031-1596. Tel: 563-872-3234.
See Bellevue, Marquette High School under Consolidated K-12 Systems located in the Institution section.
Catechesis/Religious Program—Students 111.

BELMOND, WRIGHT CO., ST. FRANCIS XAVIER (1870) [CEM] Rev. Nils Hernandez; Deacons Michael Whitters; Pedro Garcia; Jerry Temeyer; Phyllis Koschmeder, Pastoral Assoc.
Church, Parish Office & Mailing Address: 1207 Third St. N.E., 50421-1608. Tel: 641-444-3249; Fax: 641-444-4499.
Catechesis/Religious Program—Tamra Frakes, C.R.E. Students 83.

BLAIRSTOWN, BENTON CO., ST. JOHN (1948) Rev. Jack H. McClure, C.PP.S.

Rectory, Office & Mailing Address: 405 4th Ave., P.O. Box 250, Van Horne, 52346-0250. Tel: 319-228-8131; Fax: 319-228-8800.
Church: 105 West St. N.W., 52209-0170.
Catechesis/Religious Program—Students 37.

BLESSING, BLACKHAWK CO., IMMACULATE CONCEPTION (1875) [CEM] Closed. For inquiries for parish records contact St. Mary of Mt. Carmel, Eagle Center.

BLUFFTON, WINNESHIEK CO., ST. BRIDGET ORATORY (1858) [CEM] Closed. For sacramental records, contact Notre Dame, Cresco.
Church: 3094 253rd Ave., Ridgeway, 52165.

BRITT, HANCOCK CO., ST. PATRICK (1880) [CEM] Revs. Henry P. Huber; Brian M. Dellaert; Deacon Dennis Popowski.
Office & Mailing Address: 139 Third St. S.E., 50423-1726. Tel: 641-843-3215; Fax: 641-843-3557.
Pastor's Res.: 906 W. O St., Forest City, 50436. Tel: 641-585-4856.
Assoc. Pastor's Res.: 660 Bush Ave., Garner, 50438. Tel: 641-923-2329.
Church: 335 First Ave. S.E., 50423.
Catechesis/Religious Program—Sheryl Chiezek, D.R.E. Students 124.

BUFFALO CENTER, WINNEBAGO CO., ST. PATRICK (1899) Revs. Henry P. Huber. Tel: 641-585-4856; Brian M. Dellaert. Tel: 641-923-2329; Deacon Dennis Popowski.
Office, Pastor's Res. & Mailing Address: 906 W. O St., Forest City, 50436. Tel: 641-585-4856.
Church: 115 5th Ave. N.W., 50424.
Catechesis/Religious Program—Jody Smith, D.R.E. Students 25.

CALMAR, WINNESHIEK CO., ST. ALOYSIUS (1875) [CEM] Rev. Donald J. Hawes.
Church, Res. & Mailing Address: 304 S. Maryville, P.O. Box 819, 52132-0819. Tel: 563-562-3603; Fax: 563-562-3292.
See Calmar-Festina-Spillville Catholic School, Calmar under Elementary School Systems located in the Institution section.
Catechesis/Religious Program—Patty Frana, C.R.E. Students 84.

CARROLL TOWNSHIP, CARROLL CO., ST. WENCESLAUS ORATORY, Parish closed. Sacramental Records are located at St. Paul, Traer.

CARTERSVILLE, CERRO GORDO CO., ST. JOHN, Closed. Sacramental Records located at Sacred Heart, Rockwell.

CASCADE, DUBUQUE CO.

1—ST. MARTIN (1848) Closed. Merged with St. Mary, Cascade to form St. Matthias, Cascade. Sacramental records located at St. Matthias, Cascade.

2—ST. MARY (1857) Closed. Merged with St. Martin, Cascade to form St. Matthias, Cascade. Sacramental records located at St. Matthias, Cascade.

3—ST. MATTHIAS (1995) [CEM] Rev. Douglas J. Loecke; Deacons Steven W. Strang; Marvin Recker; Ray Noonan; Jean Conrad, Pastoral Assoc.
Mailing & Parish Office Address: 408 Third Ave., N.W., P.O. Box 699, 52033. Tel: 563-852-3524.
Church: 410 3rd Ave., NW, 52033.
See Aquin Educational System, Cascade under Consolidated K-12 Systems located in the Institution section.
Catechesis/Religious Program—Rebecca Smith, D.R.E. Students 169.

CASTLE GROVE, JONES CO., IMMACULATE CONCEPTION ORATORY (1877) [CEM] Closed. For sacramental records contact Sacred Heart, Monticello.

CEDAR FALLS, BLACKHAWK CO., ST. PATRICK (1855) Rev. Everett Hemann; Deacons Tom Sink, Pastoral Assoc.; Michael Moetsch.
Mailing & Parish Office Address: 705 Main St., 50613-2950. Tel: 319-266-3523; Fax: 319-266-2179.
Church: 8th & Washington St., 50613.
School—(Grades Day Care-8), 615 Washington St., 50613. Tel: 319-277-6781; Fax: 319-266-5806. Sr. Marilou Irons, P.B.V.M., Prin. Sisters 1; Lay Teachers 20; Students 253.
Catechesis/Religious Program—Amy Hoyer, C.R.E.; Katie Wilson, C.R.E. Students 409.

CEDAR RAPIDS, LINN CO.

1—ALL SAINTS (1947) [JC] Rev. David H. O'Connor; Deacon Michael Klappholz; Linda Stavropoulos, Pastoral Assoc.; Joanne Meister, Pastoral Assoc. In Res., Rev. Nicholas B. March.
Church, Parish Office & Mailing Address: 720 29th St., S.E., 52403-3099. Tel: 319-363-6130; Fax: 319-861-2240.
Res.: 830 Beaver Ridge Ct. S.E., 52403. Tel: 319-362-1691.
School—(Grades Day Care-5), 720 29th St., SE, 52403. Tel: 319-363-4110; Fax: 319-363-9547. Marlene Bartlett, Prin. Lay Teachers 16; Students 239.
Catechesis/Religious Program—Deanna Gerber, D.R.E.; Dan Thraen, C.R.E. Students 111.

2—IMMACULATE CONCEPTION (1858) [JC] Rev. Christopher R. Podhajsky; Deacons William J. Cisler; Diego Ramirez; Naida Garza, Pastoral Assoc. & Hispanic Min. Coord.; Sr. Brian Kelly, R.S.M., Pastoral Min.
Mailing Address: P.O. Box 1247, 52406-1247.
Church, Office & Res.: 857 Third Ave. S.E., 52403. Tel: 319-362-7181; Fax: 319-369-9528.
Catechesis/Religious Program—Mary Ann McEniry, D.R.E. Students 182.

3—JOHN XXIII (2000) [JC] Rev. Dustin L. Vu; Ann Petrzelka, Pastoral Assoc.
Pastor's Res.: 3108 80th St., S.W., 52404. Tel: 319-846-3142.
Church & Mailing Address: 8100 Roncalli Dr., S.W., 52404. Tel: 319-846-3139; Fax: 319-846-3159.
Catechesis/Religious Program—Students 132.

4—ST. JUDE (1962) [JC] Revs. Mark J. Reasoner; Donald A. Hertges.
Res.: 3601 First Ave. S.W., 52404. Tel: 319-396-8827.
Church & Office: 50 Edgewood Rd., N.W., 52405. Tel: 319-390-3520; Fax: 319-390-3457.
See Holy Family School, Cedar Rapids under Elementary School Systems located in the Institution section.
Catechesis/Religious Program—June Speltz, C.R.E.; Jesse Sheedy, D.R.E. Students 224.

5—ST. LUDMILA (1922) [JC] Rev. Thomas J. McDermott; Deacons Richard Manning; Paul "Jim" Berger; Sr. Mary L. Lechtenberg, O.S.F., Pastoral Assoc.
Office & Res.: 2107 J St., S.W., 52404-3615. Tel: 319-362-7282; Fax: 319-398-0352.
Church: 211 21st Ave., S.W., 52404.
See Holy Family School, Cedar Rapids under Elementary School Systems located in the Institution section.
Catechesis/Religious Program—Sue Berger, D.R.E. Students 323.

6—ST. MATTHEW (1922) [JC] Rev. Mark Osterhaus; Deacons Phil Saunders; Richard Wallace; Becky Shaffer, Pastoral Min. In Res., Rev. David J. Ambrosy.
Church, Res. & Office: 2310 First Ave. N.E., 52402-4999. Tel: 319-363-8269; Fax: 319-363-8260.
School—(Grades Day Care-5), 125 24th St., NE, 52402. Tel: 319-362-3021; Fax: 319-362-7946. Joe Wolf, Prin. Sisters 1; Lay Teachers 20; Students 292.
Catechesis/Religious Program—Betsy Schmuck, D.R.E.; Sarah White, C.R.E. Students 239.

7—ST. PATRICK (1886) [JC] Rev. Philip E. Thompson; Deacon Daniel Hoeger; Sr. Linda Bechen, R.S.M., Pastoral Assoc.
Parish Office & Mailing Address: 3100 E Ave., N.W., Ste. 102, 52405. Tel: 319-362-7966; Fax: 319-366-7260.
Church: 500 First Ave. N.W., 52405.
Catechesis/Religious Program—Penny Ackerman, C.R.E. Students 122.

8—ST. PIUS X (1959) [JC] Revs. Donald L. Klein; Dennis H. Cahill, Sacramental Priest; Deacons Paul Zimmerman; Lanny Peterson; Anne Johnson, Pastoral Assoc.; Sr. Joellen Price, P.B.V.M., Pastoral Assoc.
Church and Office: 4949 Council St. N.E., 52402-2492. Tel: 319-393-4445; Fax: 319-393-9424.
Pastor's Res.: 1500 48th St. N.E., 52402. Tel: 319-395-0452.
See St. Pius and St. Elizabeth Ann Seton Schools under Elementary School Systems located in the Institution section.
Catechesis/Religious Program—Linda Van Etten, D.R.E. Students 323.

9—ST. WENCESLAUS (1874) [JC] Rev. Christopher R. Podhajsky; Deacons William J. Cisler; Diego Ramirez.
Parish Office & Mailing Address: 510 16th Ave. S.E., 52401.
Pastor's Res.: 857 Third Ave., S.E., P.O. Box 1247, 52406-1247. Tel: 319-362-7181; Fax: 319-369-9528.
Church: 1224 Fifth St. S.E., 52401.
Catechesis/Religious Program—Mary McEniry, D.R.E. Students 18.

CENTRAL CITY, LINN CO., ST. STEPHEN (1932) Rev. Wayne J. Droessler; Sr. Anne Kisting, O.S.F., Pastoral Min.
Res. & Mailing Address: 410 Terrace Dr., P.O. Box 496, 52214-0496. Tel: 319-438-6625.
Parish Office Address—211 3rd St. N., P.O. Box 47, Coggon, 52218-0047. Tel: 319-435-2236.
Church: 4700 Valley Farm Rd., 52214.
Catechesis/Religious Program—Marci Luedeman, C.R.E. Students 67.

CHARLES CITY, FLOYD CO., IMMACULATE CONCEPTION (1857) [CEM] Rev. Carl A. Ries; Sr. M. Diana Blong, P.B.V.M., Pastoral Assoc.
Church, Res. & Office: 106 Chapel Ln., 50616-2810. Tel: 641-228-1071; Fax: 641-228-1072.
School—(Grades PreSchool-6), 1203 Clark St., 50616. Tel: 641-228-1225; Fax: 641-228-7692. Mindy Hart, Prin. Lay Teachers 14; Students 194.
Catechesis/Religious Program—Wendy Wandro, D.R.E. Students 152.

CHELSEA, TAMA CO., ST. JOSEPH (1867) [CEM] Very Rev. Michael J. Mescher; Deacon Joseph Behounek, Pastoral Assoc.; Bette Kratoska, Pastoral Min.
Mailing Address: 900 Park St., Tama, 52339. Tel: 641-484-3039; Fax: 641-484-8039.
Church: 307 Station St., 52215.
Catechesis/Religious Program—Jeffrey Lumpa, D.R.E. Students 26.

CHERRY MOUND, ALLAMAKEE CO., ST. PIUS (1863) [CEM] Rev. Louis J. Trzil.
Mailing Address: 1416 Great River Rd., Lansing, 52151. Tel: 563-586-2150.
Church: 699 State Forest Rd., Harpers Ferry, 52146.
Catechesis/Religious Program—Shari Curran, D.R.E. Students 16.

CHESTER, HOWARD CO., ST. STEPHEN ORATORY (1916), Parish closed. For sacramental records, contact Immaculate Conception, Elma.

CLARION, WRIGHT CO., ST. JOHN (1883) [CEM] Rev. Nils Hernandez; Deacons Michael Whitters; Pedro Garcia; Jerry Temeyer; Jo Ann Kramer, Pastoral Assoc.
Church and Mailing Address: 608 Second Ave., N.E., 50525. Tel: 515-532-3586; Fax: 515-532-2478.
Catechesis/Religious Program—Gloria Kisor, C.R.E. Students 161.

CLEAR LAKE, CERRO GORDO CO., ST. PATRICK (1901) Rev. John R. Tilp.
Church, Res. & Office: 1001 Ninth Ave. S., 50428-2615. Tel: 641-357-3214; Fax: 641-357-3210.
Catechesis/Religious Program—Ann Kunst, C.R.E. Students 170.

CLERMONT, FAYETTE CO., ST. PETER (1855) [CEM] Rev. Dale J. Rausch.
Parish Office—128 N. Walnut, West Union, 52175. Tel: 563-422-3184.
Church and Mailing Address: 608 Larrabee, P.O. Box 25, 52135-0025.
Catechesis/Religious Program—Mary Olson, D.R.E. Students 72.

CLUTIER, TAMA CO.
ORATORY—IMMACULATE CONCEPTION ORATORY (1900), For sacramental records, contact St. Paul, Traer. Parish closed.

COGGON, LINN CO., ST. JOHN THE EVANGELIST (1912) [CEM] Rev. Wayne J. Droessler; Sr. Anne Kisting, O.S.F., Pastoral Assoc.
Mailing Address: 211 Third St. N., P.O. Box 47, 52218-0047. Tel: 319-435-2236; Fax: 319-435-2236.
Church: 211 Third St. N., 52218.
Catechesis/Religious Program—Pamela Klima, C.R.E. Students 59.

COLESBURG, DELAWARE CO., ST. PATRICK (1862) [CEM] Rev. Stephen A. Lundgren.
Mailing Address: 203 S. Locust, P.O. Box 365, Edgewood, 52042-0365. Tel: 563-928-7200.
Pastor's Res.: 207 S. Locust, P.O. Box 365, Edgewood, 52042-0365. Tel: 563-928-6938.
Church: Delaware St., 52035.
Catechesis/Religious Program—Deanne Wulfekuhle, D.R.E.; Mary Fischer, C.R.E. Students 46.

COLO, STORY CO., ST. MARY, [CEM] Rev. Rick D. Dagit; Deacon Steven Van Kerckvoorde.
Pastor's Res. & Mailing Address: 410 Bailey, P.O. Box 236, 50056-0236. Tel: 641-377-2710.
Church: 422 Fourth St., 50056.
Catechesis/Religious Program—Tracy Birchmier, C.R.E. Students 17.

CORWITH, HANCOCK CO., ST. MARY (1912) [CEM] Closed. For sacramental records, please contact St. Patrick, Britt.

CRESCO, HOWARD CO.

1—ASSUMPTION OF THE BLESSED VIRGIN MARY (1858) Closed. Merged with St. Joseph's, Cresco to form Notre Dame, Cresco. Sacramental records are located at Notre Dame, Cresco.

2—ST. JOSEPH (1870) Closed. Merged with Assumption of the Blessed Virgin Mary, Cresco to form Notre Dame, Cresco. Sacramental records are located at Notre Dame, Cresco.

3—NOTRE DAME (1999) [JC] Rev. Richard J. Ament; LeRoy Webb, Pastoral Min.
Mailing Address & Parish Office: 116 Third St. E., 52136. Tel: 563-547-3565; Fax: 563-547-3835.
Pastor's Res.: 1019 N. Elm St., #4, 52136. Tel: 563-547-5826.
Church: 223 2nd Ave. E., 52136.
School—(Grades PreSchool-6), 221 Second Ave. E., 52136. Tel: 563-547-4513. Wendy Schatz, Prin. Teachers 12; Students 151.
Catechesis/Religious Program—Tel: 563-547-3760. Pam Daley, D.R.E. Students 178.

DECORAH, WINNESHIEK CO., ST. BENEDICT (1864) [CEM] Rev. Phillip G. Gibbs; Deacon Nick Francois; Luke Jansen, Pastoral Min.
Church, Res. & Office: 307 W. Main St., 52101-1778. Tel: 563-382-9631; Fax: 563-382-6436.
School—(Grades PreSchool-8), 402 Rural Ave., 52101. Tel: 563-382-4668; Fax: 563-382-3193. Ruth Palmer, Prin. Lay Teachers 14; Students 142.

Catechesis/Religious Program—June Francois, Dir. Faith Formation. Students 258.

DELHI, DELAWARE CO., ST. JOHN (1872) [CEM] Very Rev. John R. Kremer.
Office, Pastor's Res. & Mailing Address: 307 South St., P.O. Box 187, 52223-0187. Tel: 563-922-2251.
Church: 303 South St., 52223.
Catechesis/Religious Program—JoLynn Heims, D.R.E.; Linda Jay, D.R.E. Students 130.

DIKE, GRUNDY CO., ST. MARY (1880) [CEM] Closed. Merged with Sacred Heart, Grundy Center; St. Patrick, Parkersburg; Queen of Heaven, Reinbeck to form Holy Family, Reinbeck. For parish records contact Holy Family, Reinbeck.

DORCHESTER, ALLAMAKEE CO., ST. MARY (1865) [CEM] Rev. Joseph M. Schneider; Deacon Michael Ward, Pastoral Assoc.
Mailing Address: 109 2nd St., S.W., P.O. Box 146, Waukon, 52172. Tel: 563-568-3671; Fax: 563-568-4432.
Church: 590 Waterloo Creek Rd., 52140.
Catechesis/Religious Program—Peggy Teff, C.R.E. Students 28.

DOUGHERTY, CERRO GORDO CO., ST. PATRICK (1870) [CEM] Rev. James W. Dubert, Parochial Admin.
Res.: 305 Elm St., P.O. Box 30, Rockwell, 50469-0030. Tel: 641-822-4957.
Church, Parish Office & Mailing Address: 410 E. Patrick St., 50433. Tel: 641-794-3416.
Catechesis/Religious Program—Kim Staudt, C.R.E. Students 10.

DUMONT, BUTLER CO., ST. FRANCIS (1890) Closed. For sacramental records please contact St. Patrick, Hampton.

DUNCAN, HANCOCK CO., ST. WENCESLAUS (1900) [CEM] Revs. Henry P. Huber; Brian M. Dellaert; Deacon Dennis Popowski.
Res. & Mailing Address: 660 Bush Ave., Garner, 50438-1513. Tel: 641-923-2329; Fax: 641-923-2480.
Church: 2343 Navy Ave., Britt, 50423.
Catechesis/Religious Program—Rebecca Rolling, D.R.E. Students 34.

DYERSVILLE, DUBUQUE CO., BASILICA OF ST. FRANCIS XAVIER (1859) [CEM] Very Rev. Phillip F. Kruse; Rev. G. Robert Gross; Deacons Fredrick J. Pins; James Steger; Jerry Miller; Cookie Scherrman, Pastoral Min.
Res. & Mailing Address: 104 Third St. S.W., 52040-1696. Tel: 563-875-7325; Fax: 563-875-8716.
Church: Second St. S.W., 52040.
Catechesis/Religious Program—Students 141.

DYSART, TAMA CO., ST. JOSEPH (1878) [CEM] Closed. For inquiries for sacramental records please contact St. Paul, Traer.

EAGLE CENTER, BLACKHAWK CO., ST. MARY OF MT. CARMEL (1859) [CEM] Rev. Jerry W. Blake.
Church & Mailing Address: 1435 E. Eagle Rd., Waterloo, 50701-9545. Tel: 319-342-3491; Fax: 319-342-3491.
Catechesis/Religious Program—Jessica Ollinger, D.R.E. Students 101.

EAGLE GROVE, WRIGHT CO., SACRED HEART (1882) [CEM] Rev. Nils Hernandez; Deacons Michael Whitters; Pedro Garcia; Jerry Temeyer; Carla Kem, Pastoral Assoc.
Parish Office & Mailing Address: 221 S. Jackson Ave., 50533-2311. Tel: 515-603-4765; Fax: 515-603-6131.
Pastor's Res.: 608 2nd Ave., N.E., Clarion, 50525.
Church: 201 S. Jackson Ave., 50533.
Catechesis/Religious Program—Michele Choquette, C.R.E. Students 89.

EARLVILLE, DELAWARE CO., ST. JOSEPH (1887) [CEM] Rev. Herbert L. Tegeler; Deacons James Steger; Fredrick J. Pins; Jerry Miller.
Res. & Mailing Address: 307 Mary St., P.O. Box 187, 52041-0187. Tel: 563-923-3135; Fax: 563-923-2895.
Church: 303 Mary St., 52041.
Catechesis/Religious Program—Joan Steger, D.R.E. Students 82.

EDGEWOOD, DELAWARE CO., ST. MARK (1916) [CEM] Rev. Stephen A. Lundgren.
Church & Office: 203 S. Locust St., P.O. Box 365, 52042. Tel: 563-928-7200.
Pastor's Res.: 207 S. Locust, P.O. Box 365, 52042. Tel: 563-928-6938.
Catechesis/Religious Program—Jody Kerns, D.R.E. Students 152.

ELDORA, HARDIN CO., ST. MARY (1868) [CEM] Rev. Paul C. Baldwin; Sr. Connie Howe, R.S.M., Pastoral Assoc.
Church & Parish Office: 614 Washington, 50627-1257. Tel: 641-939-5545.
Pastor's Res.: 415 Main St., P.O. Box 368, Iowa Falls, 50126-0368. Tel: 641-648-9547; Fax: 641-648-9562.
Catechesis/Religious Program—LeAnn Belken, D.R.E. Students 58.

ELKADER, CLAYTON CO., ST. JOSEPH (1844) [CEM] Rev. Paul R. Peters.
Church & Office: 330 First St., S.W., P.O. Box 626, 52043-0626. Tel: 563-245-2548; Fax: 563-245-2937.
Pastor's Res.: Tel: 563-245-1325.
Catechesis/Religious Program—Deborah Deitchler, C.R.E. Students 106.

ELMA, HOWARD CO., IMMACULATE CONCEPTION (1887) [CEM] Rev. Ray E. Atwood.
Parish Office, Pastor's Res. & Mailing Address: 203 Seventh St., P.O. Box 38, 50628-0038. Tel: 641-393-2520; Fax: 641-393-2069.
Church: 207 Seventh St., 50628.
Catechesis/Religious Program—Sheila Kobliska, D.R.E. Students 38.

EPWORTH, DUBUQUE CO., ST. PATRICK (1879) [CEM] Rev. Dennis R. Cain; Deacons James Kean; Gerald Koopmann; Joann Koopmann, Pastoral Assoc.
Parish Office & Mailing Address: 104 First St., S.E., P.O. Box 286, 52045-0286. Tel: 563-876-5540; Fax: 563-876-9062.
Pastor's Res.: 22511 E. Pleasant Grove Rd., 52045. Tel: 563-876-5501.
Church: 102 1st St. S.E., 52045.
See Seton Catholic Schools, Farley under Elementary School Systems located in the Institution section.
Catechesis/Religious Program—Marilyn Connor Ryan, C.R.E. Students 152.

EVANSDALE, BLACKHAWK CO., ST. NICHOLAS (1951) Closed. Merged with St. Mary, St. John & St. Joseph, Waterloo to form Queen of Peace, Waterloo. Sacramental records are located at Queen of Peace, Waterloo.

FAIRBANK, BUCHANAN CO., IMMACULATE CONCEPTION (1858) [CEM] Rev. Harry H. Koelker; Deacon Jim Patera.
Church, Office and Mailing Address: 302 W. Main St., P.O. Box 505, 50629. Tel: 319-635-2211.
Pastor's Res.: 628 S. Frederick Ave., Oelwein, 50662. Tel: 319-283-3743.
Catechesis/Religious Program—Dan Cutsforth, D.R.E. Students 136.

FAIRFAX, LINN CO., ST. PATRICK (1875) [CEM] Rev. Dustin L. Vu, Parochial Admin.
Parish Office & Mailing Address: 8100 Roncalli Dr., S.W., Cedar Rapids, 52404. Tel: 319-846-3139; Fax: 319-846-3159.
Res.: 3108 80th St., S.W., Cedar Rapids, 52404. Tel: 319-846-3142.
Church: 324 Church St., 52228.
Catechesis/Religious Program—Geralyn Ward, C.R.E. Students 142.

FARLEY, DUBUQUE CO., ST. JOSEPH (1914) [CEM] Rev. Dennis R. Cain; Deacons James Kean; Gerald Koopmann; Sr. Sharon Kelchen, P.V.B.M., Pastoral Assoc.
Office & Mailing Address: 104 First St., S.E., P.O. Box 286, Epworth, 52045. Tel: 563-876-5540; Fax: 563-876-9062.
Pastor's Res.: 22511 E. Pleasant Grove Rd., Epworth, 52045. Tel: 563-876-5501.
Church: 202 2nd Ave., S.E., 52046.
See Seton Catholic Schools, Farley under Elementary School Systems located in the Institution section.
Catechesis/Religious Program—Betty Pins, C.R.E.; Marian Bourek, C.R.E. Students 135.

FAYETTE, FAYETTE CO., ST. FRANCIS OF ASSISI (1879) [CEM] Rev. James P. Brokman.
Mailing Address: P.O. Box 276, 52142-0276.
Office & Pastor's Res.: 413 W. First St., Sumner, 50674. Tel: 563-578-5366; Fax: 563-578-3286.
Church: 205 Lovers Ln., 52142.
Catechesis/Religious Program—Holly Streeter, D.R.E. Students 53.

FESTINA, WINNESHIEK CO., OUR LADY OF SEVEN DOLORS (1843) [CEM] Rev. Msgr. Cletus J. Hawes.
Mailing Address: 418 E. Main St., Ossian, 52161. Tel: 563-532-9366; Fax: 563-532-9353.
Church: 2348 County Rd. B 32, 52144-7701.
See Calmar-Festina-Spillville Catholic School, Calmar under Elementary School Systems located in the Institution section.
Catechesis/Religious Program—Patty Frana, C.R.E. Students 27.

FILLMORE, DUBUQUE CO., SACRED HEART (1890) [CEM] Rev. Douglas J. Loecke; Deacons Marvin Recker; Steven W. Strang; Ray Noonan.
Mailing Address: 19589 Sacred Heart Ln., Bernard, 52032.
Pastor's Res.: 401 3rd Ave., N.W., P.O. Box 699, Cascade, 52033-0699. Tel: 563-852-7805.
Church: 19661 Sacred Heart Ln., Bernard, 52032.
See Aquin Educational System, Cascade under Consolidated K-12 Systems located in the Institution section.
Catechesis/Religious Program—Rebecca Smith, D.R.E. Students 20.

FOREST CITY, WINNEBAGO CO., ST. JAMES (1870) [CEM] Revs. Henry P. Huber; Brian M. Dellaert; Deacon Dennis Popowski.
Church, Mailing & Parish Office Address: 906 W. O St., 50436. Tel: 641-585-4856; Fax: 641-585-3336.
Catechesis/Religious Program—Rita Kleemeier, D.R.E. Students 92.

FORT ATKINSON, WINNESHIEK CO., ST. JOHN NEPOMUCENE (1875) [CEM] Rev. David M. Beckman; Very Rev. Marvin C. Salz, Sacramental Priest; Tyler Wheeler, Pastoral Min.; Lynette Wheeler, Pastoral Min.
Office & Mailing Address: 110 Commercial Ave., P.O. Box 205, Protivin, 52163. Tel: 563-569-8259.
Church: 201 Oak St., 52144.
See Trinity Catholic School, Protovin under Elementary School Systems located in the Institution section.
Catechesis/Religious Program—Martin Ahrndt, D.R.E. Students 83.

GARBER, CLAYTON CO., ST. MICHAEL (1917) [CEM] Closed. For parish records, please contact St. Joseph, Garnavillo.

GARNAVILLO, CLAYTON CO., ST. JOSEPH (1846) [CEM] Rev. Marvin J. Bries; Deacon James Pfaffly.
Mailing Address, Parish Office & Res.: 520 2nd St., P.O. Box 847, Guttenberg, 52052. Tel: 563-252-1247.
Church: 204 W. Oak St., 52049.
Catechesis/Religious Program—Lisa Robinson, D.R.E. Students 56.

GARNER, HANCOCK CO., ST. BONIFACE (1883) [CEM] Revs. Henry P. Huber; Brian M. Dellaert; Deacon Dennis Popowski.
Office & Res.: 660 Bush Ave., 50438-1513. Tel: 641-923-2329; Fax: 641-923-2480.
Church: 600 Bush Ave., 50438.
Catechesis/Religious Program—Rebecca Rolling, D.R.E. Students 130.

GARRYOWEN, JACKSON CO., ST. PATRICK (1840) [CEM] Rev. Douglas J. Loecke; Deacons Steven W. Strang; Marvin Recker; Ray Noonan; Jean Conrad, Pastoral Assoc.
Parish Office & Mailing Address: 408 3rd Ave., N.W., P.O. Box 699, Cascade, 52033-0699. Tel: 563-852-3524.
Church: 28914 46th Ave., Bernard, 52032-9289. Tel: 563-879-3303.
Pastor's Res.: 401 3rd Ave., N.W., P.O. Box 699, Cascade, 52033-0699. Tel: 563-852-7805.
See Aquin Educational System, Cascade under Consolidated K-12 Systems located in the Institution section.
Catechesis/Religious Program—Rebecca Smith, D.R.E. Students 38.

GARWIN, TAMA CO., ST. BONIFACE (1884) Very Rev. Michael J. Mescher; Deacon Joe Behounek, Pastoral Assoc.; Bette Kratoska, Pastoral Min.
Office, Res. & Mailing Address: 900 Park St., Tama, 52339-1238. Tel: 641-484-3039; Fax: 641-484-8039.
Church: 306 4th St., 50632.
Catechesis/Religious Program—Christopher DiTomo, D.R.E. Students 20.

GENEVA, FRANKLIN CO., ST. PAUL, [CEM] Closed. Sacramental records are located at St. Mary, Ackley.

GILBERT, STORY CO., SS. PETER AND PAUL (1882) [CEM] Revs. Jon M. Seda; Dennis W. Miller.
Mailing Address: P.O. Box 327, 50105. Tel: 515-292-3810.
Pastor's Res.: 2821 Bristol Dr., Ames, 50010. Tel: 515-292-1192.
Assoc. Pastor's Res.: 3007 Wessex Dr., #162, Ames, 50014. Tel: 515-292-3097.
Church: 14238 500th Ave., 50105.
Catechesis/Religious Program—Tony Gustafson, D.R.E.; Erin Wilgenbusch, D.R.E. Students 92.

GILBERTVILLE, BLACKHAWK CO., IMMACULATE CONCEPTION (1875) [CEM] Rev. Dennis J. Colter.
Office & Res.: 311 15th Ave., P.O. Box 136, 50634. Tel: 319-296-1092; Fax: 319-296-2087.
Church: 325 15th Ave., 50634-0136.
See Gilbertville-Raymond, Don Bosco High School, Gilbertville-Raymond Elementary under Consolidated K-12 Systems located in the Institution section.
Catechesis/Religious Program—Students 13.

GREELEY, DELAWARE CO., ST. JOSEPH (1870) [CEM] Closed. For parish records, contact St. Mary, Manchester.

GREEN ISLAND, JACKSON CO., SACRED HEART, Closed. For sacramental records, please contact St. Peter, Sabula.

GREENE, BUTLER CO., ST. MARY (1872) [CEM] Rev. Msgr. Walter L. Brunkan.
Church & Res.: 105 N. Main, P.O. Box 480, 50636-0480. Tel: 641-823-4146.
Catechesis/Religious Program—Sherilyn Backer, D.R.E. Students 117.

GRUNDY CENTER, GRUNDY CO., SACRED HEART (1885) Closed. Merged with St. Mary, Dike, St. Patrick, Parkersburg & Queen of Heaven, Reinbeck to form Holy Family, Reinbeck. Sacramental records located at Holy Family, Reinbeck.

GUTTENBERG, CLAYTON CO., ST. MARY (1851) [CEM] Rev. Marvin J. Bries; Deacon James Pfaffly.

Res. & Office: 520 S. Second St., P.O. Box 847, 52052-0847. Tel: 563-252-1247; Fax: 563-252-1363.
Church: 520 S. 2nd St., 52052.
See St. Mary and Immaculate Conception School System, Guttenberg under Elementary School Systems located in the Institution section.
Catechesis/Religious Program—Becky Pfaffly, D.R.E. Students 99.

HAMPTON, FRANKLIN CO., ST. PATRICK (1870) Very Rev. Bernard C. Grady; Deacon David Jones.
Res.: 2 19th Ave. N.E., 50441. Tel: 641-456-3406.
Church & Parish Office: 1405 N. Federal, 50441-1005. Tel: 641-456-4857.
Catechesis/Religious Program—Judy Nelson, D.R.E. Students 175.

HANOVER, ALLAMAKEE CO., ST. MARY (1875) [CEM] Rev. Joseph M. Schneider; Deacon Michael Ward.
Mailing Address: *c/o St. Patrick Parish*, 109 Second St. S.W., Waukon, 52172-0146. Tel: 563-568-3671; Fax: 563-568-4432.
Church: 2096 Hwy. 76, Waukon, 52172.
Catechesis/Religious Program—Jackie Johnson, D.R.E. Students 14.

HARPERS FERRY, ALLAMAKEE CO., ST. ANN-ST. JOSEPH (1855) [CEM] Rev. Louis J. Trzil.
Res. & Mailing Address: Immaculate Conception (Wexford), 1416 Great River Rd., Lansing, 52151-7519. Tel: 563-586-2150.
Church: 307 W. Orange, Harper's Ferry, 52146.
Catechesis/Religious Program—Brigid Cota, D.R.E. Students 41.

HAVERHILL, MARSHALL CO.
ORATORY—IMMACULATE CONCEPTION ORATORY (1877), For sacramental records, contact St. Henry, Marshalltown.

HAWKEYE, FAYETTE CO., ST. FRANCIS XAVIER (1891) Closed. For sacramental records, contact Immaculate Conception, Sumner.

HAZLETON, BUCHANAN CO., ST. MARY (1881) [CEM] Closed. For sacramental records, contact Sacred Heart, Oelwein.

HIAWATHA, LINN CO., ST. ELIZABETH ANN SETON PARISH (1989) [JC] Revs. Neil J. Manternach; Dennis H. Cahill; Deacon Dennis Mulherin; Sr. Annette Kestel, P.B.V.M., Pastoral Assoc. In Res., Rev. Philip E. Thompson.
Church & Office: 1350 Lyndhurst Dr., 52233. Tel: 319-393-3778; Fax: 319-393-7165.
Res.: 1385 Lyndhurst Dr., 52233. Tel: 319-393-2646.
See St. Pius and St. Elizabeth Ann Seton Schools under Elementary School Systems located in the Institution section.
Catechesis/Religious Program—Tricia Lokmer, D.R.E. Students 465.

HOLY CROSS, DUBUQUE CO., HOLY CROSS (1845) [CEM] Rev. Raymond A. Burkle; Bro. Stephen W. Markham, F.S.C., Pastoral Assoc.
Church & Office: 875 Church St., P.O. Box 398, 52053. Tel: 563-870-4041.
Pastor's Res.: 103 S. Andres St., P.O. Box 140, Luxemburg, 52056. Tel: 563-853-3369.
See LaSalle Elementary Schools, Holy Cross under Elementary School Systems located in the Institution section.
Catechesis/Religious Program—Students 20.

HOPKINTON, DELAWARE CO., ST. LUKE (1922) Very Rev. John R. Kremer.
Office & Mailing Address: 206 First St., S.E., P.O. Box 159, 52237-0159. Tel: 563-926-2613.
Pastor's Res.: 307 South St., P.O. Box 187, Delhi, 52223. Tel: 563-922-2251.
Church: 206 First St. S.E., 52237.
Catechesis/Religious Program—Patricia Hucker, D.R.E. Students 70.

INDEPENDENCE, BUCHANAN CO., ST. JOHN THE EVANGELIST (1856) [CEM] Rev. Donald J. Plamondon; Deacon Tim Post; Sharon Bainbridge, Pastoral Assoc.
Church, Res. & Office: 209 Fifth Ave. N.E., 50644-1998. Tel: 319-334-7191; Fax: 319-334-7192.
School—(Grades PreSchool-8), 314 Third St., NE, 50644. Tel: 319-334-7173; Fax: 319-334-9088. Peter Bellaver, Prin. Lay Teachers 12; Students 175.
Catechesis/Religious Program—Sharon Bainbridge, C.R.E. Students 177.

IONIA, CHICKASHAW CO., ST. BONIFACE (1899) [CEM] Rev. Msgr. Carl L. Schmitt; Deacon Victor J. DeSloover; Sr. Jeanne Tranel, O.P., Pastoral Assoc.; Christine Carrier, Pastoral Assoc.
Parish Office & Mailing Address: 202 N. Broadway, New Hampton, 50659. Tel: 641-394-2105.
Pastor's Res.: 619 Rural St., New Hampton, 50659. Tel: 641-394-2744.
Church: 204 E. Prairie, 50645.
Catechesis/Religious Program—Christine Carrier, D.R.E.; Karen Bonfig, C.R.E. Students 22.

IOWA FALLS, HARDIN CO., ST. MARK (1855) [CEM] Rev. Paul C. Baldwin; Sr. Connie Howe, R.S.M., Pastoral Assoc.
Church, Res. & Office: 415 Main St., P.O. Box 368, 50126-0368. Tel: 641-648-9547; Fax: 641-648-9562.
Catechesis/Religious Program—LeAnn Belken, D.R.E. Students 61.

JESUP, BUCHANAN CO., ST. ATHANASIUS (1880) [CEM] Rev. Kenneth C. Stecher; Sr. Donna Burke, O.S.F., Pastoral Assoc.
Res. & Mailing Address: 634 Stevens St., P.O. Box 316, 50648-0316. Tel: 319-827-3003; Fax: 319-827-1124.
Church: 623 Stevens St., 50648.
School—(Grades K-8), 641 Stevens St., P.O. Box 288, 50648-0288. Tel: 319-827-1314. Julie Niemeyer, Prin. Lay Teachers 8; Students 68.
Catechesis/Religious Program—Carla Even, C.R.E. Students 77.

JEWELL, HAMILTON CO., GOOD SHEPHERD (1915) Closed. For sacramental records, contact St. Cecelia, Ames.

KEY WEST, DUBUQUE CO., ST. JOSEPH (1872) Rev. Donald V. Bakewell; Deacon Tom Lang.
Office & Res.: 10204 Key West Dr., 52003-8936. Tel: 563-582-7392; Fax: 563-582-7392.
Church: 10270 Key West Dr., 52003.
See Holy Family Catholic Schools under Consolidated K-12 Systems located in the Institution Section.
Catechesis/Religious Program—Linda Frommelt, C.R.E. Students 167.

LA MOTTE, JACKSON CO., HOLY ROSARY (1893) [CEM] Closed. For sacramental records please contact Sacred Heart, Maquoketa.

LA PORTE CITY, BLACKHAWK CO., SACRED HEART (1887) Rev. Jerry W. Blake.
Mailing Address, Church & Parish Office: 1021 Poplar St., 50651. Tel: 319-342-2991.
Pastor's Res.: 1102 Walnut St., Traer, 50675. Tel: 319-478-2222.
Catechesis/Religious Program—Jessica Ollinger, C.R.E. Students 117.

LAKE MILLS, WINNEBAGO CO., ST. PATRICK (1870) [CEM] Revs. Henry P. Huber; Brian M. Dellaert; Deacon Dennis Popowski.
Mailing Address: 906 W. O St., Forest City, 50436-1131. Tel: 641-585-4856; Fax: 641-585-3336.
Church: 406 S. Grant St., 50450.
Catechesis/Religious Program—Carla Langfald, D.R.E. Students 28.

LAMONT, BUCHANAN CO., ST. MARY (1894) [CEM] Closed. For sacramental records, contact St. Mary, Strawberry Point.

LANSING, ALLAMAKEE CO., IMMACULATE CONCEPTION (1855) [CEM] Rev. Daniel J. Knipper.
Church, Res. & Office: 648 Main St., 52151. Tel: 563-538-4171.
Catechesis/Religious Program—Karen Weber, D.R.E. Students 62.

LATTNERVILLE, DUBUQUE CO., ANNUNCIATION ORATORY, Parish closed. For sacramental records, contact St. John the Baptist, Peosta.

LAWLER, CHICKASAW CO., OUR LADY OF MT. CARMEL (1869) [CEM] Rev. David M. Beckman; Very Rev. Marvin C. Salz, Sacramental Priest; Tyler Wheeler, Pastoral Min.; Lynette Wheeler, Pastoral Min.
Church, Mailing Address & Parish Office: 3040 Iowa Hwy. 24, P.O. Box 119, 52154. Tel: 563-238-3444.
Pastor's Res.: 110 Commercial Ave., P.O. Box 205, Protivin, 52163-0205. Tel: 563-569-8259.
Catechesis/Religious Program—Martin Ahrndt, D.R.E. Students 60.

LITTLE TURKEY, CHICKASAW CO., ASSUMPTION OF THE B.V.M. (1902) [CEM] Rev. David M. Beckman; Very Rev. Marvin C. Salz, Sacramental Priest; Tyler Wheeler, Pastoral Min.; Lynette Wheeler, Pastoral Min.
Office, Res. & Mailing Address: 110 Commercial Ave., P.O. Box 205, Protivin, 52163. Tel: 563-569-8259.
Church: 3303 160th St., Lawler, 52154.
Catechesis/Religious Program—Martin Ahrndt, D.R.E. Students 54.

LITTLEPORT, CLAYTON CO., SACRED HEART, [CEM] Closed. For sacramental records, please contact St. Joseph, Garnavillo.

LOURDES, HOWARD CO., OUR LADY OF LOURDES (1875) [CEM] Rev. Ray E. Atwood.
Office, Res. & Mailing Address: 203 7th St., P.O. Box 38, Elma, 50628-0038. Tel: 641-393-2520; Fax: 641-393-2069.
Church: 14068 175th St., Elma, 50628.
Catechesis/Religious Program—Sheila Kobliska, D.R.E. Students 40.

LUXEMBURG, DUBUQUE CO., HOLY TRINITY (1865) [CEM] Rev. Raymond A. Burkle; Bro. Stephen W. Markham, F.S.C., Pastoral Assoc.
Office & Mailing Address: 875 Church St., P.O. Box 398, Holy Cross, 52053. Tel: 563-870-4041.
Church & Rectory: 103 S. Andres St., 52056. Tel: 563-853-3369.
See LaSalle Elementary Schools, Holy Cross under Elementary School Systems located in the Institution section.
Catechesis/Religious Program—Students 22.

LYCURGUS, ALLAMAKEE CO.
ORATORY—ST. MARY ORATORY (1859), For sacramental records please contact St. Patrick, Waukon.

MANCHESTER, DELAWARE CO., ST. MARY (1872) [CEM] Revs. John R. Flaherty; Greg E. Bahl; Deacon Dave Loecke.
Church, Res. & Office: 119 W. Fayette St., 52057-1596. Tel: 563-927-4710; Fax: 563-927-9949.
School—(Grades K-6), 132 W. Butler, 52057-1502. Tel: 563-927-3689; Fax: 563-927-1437. Justin Nosbisch, Prin. Sisters 1; Lay Teachers 13; Students 159.
Catechesis/Religious Program—Kathy Oberrueter, C.R.E. Students 352.

MANLY, WORTH CO., SACRED HEART (1883) [CEM] Rev. David G. Kucera.
Res. & Office: 120 E. North, P.O. Box 160, 50456-0160. Tel: 641-454-2586.
Church: 412 N. Broadway, 50456.
Catechesis/Religious Program—Kelley O'Keefe, D.R.E. Students 53.

MAQUOKETA, JACKSON CO., SACRED HEART (1873) [CEM] Rev. James T. Chappell; Deacon Robert Head.
Church, Res. & Office: 200 S. Vermont St., 52060-0635. Tel: 563-652-6931; Fax: 563-652-6931.
School—(Grades PreK-6), 806 Eddy St., 52060. Tel: 563-652-3743; Fax: 563-652-2698. Sr. Shirley Steines, S.S.N.D., Prin. Sisters 1; Lay Teachers 8; Students 102.
Catechesis/Religious Program—Sr. Helen Stejskal, S.S.N.D., D.R.E. Students 98.

MARION, LINN CO., ST. JOSEPH (1890) [JC] Very Rev. John A. Gossman; Rev. Rodney M. Allers; Deacon Sean Smith; Rodney Bluml, Pastoral Assoc.; Mary Hauschildt, Pastoral Min.
Res.: 1483 14th St., 52302. Tel: 319-377-2605.
Church & Office: 1790 14th St., 52302-2267. Tel: 319-377-4869; Fax: 319-377-9043.
School—(Grades PreSchool-8), 1430 14th St., 52302-2499. Tel: 319-377-6348; Fax: 319-377-9358. Tony Voss, Prin. Lay Teachers 20; Students 248.
Catechesis/Religious Program—Ruth Ard, D.R.E.; Elizabeth Lockhart, C.R.E. Students 521.

MARSHALLTOWN, MARSHALL CO.
1—ST. HENRY (1959) Rev. Donald J. Czapla; Deacons Roger Polt; Gary Pusillo; Karen Mroz, Pastoral Min.
Church & Parish Office: 221 W. Olive St., 50158-4248. Tel: 641-753-7374; Fax: 641-753-1499.
Pastor's Res.: 1610 Crestview Dr., 50158. Tel: 641-752-2043.
See Marshalltown Area Catholic Schools, Marshalltown under Elementary School Systems located in the Institution section.
Catechesis/Religious Program—Patty Mayer, D.R.E. Students 153.

2—ST. MARY (1869) Rev. James L. Miller; Deacons Jeff Harris; Felix Hernandez; Sr. Christine Feagan, O.P., Coord. Hispanic Ministry.
Office & Res.: 9 W. Linn St., 50158. Tel: 641-753-6278; Fax: 641-753-1279.
Church: 11 W. Linn St., 50158.
See Marshalltown Area Catholic Schools, Marshalltown under Elementary School Systems located in the Institution section.
Catechesis/Religious Program—Jeannine Grady, C.R.E. Students 193.

MASON CITY, CERRO GORDO CO.
1—HOLY FAMILY (1908) Rev. Michael G. Schueller; Deacons Matthew F. Berry; Charles Cooper; Lisa Paloma, Pastoral Assoc.
Church: 716 N. Adams St., 50401.
Res. & Office: 714 N. Adams St., 50401-2199. Tel: 641-423-7301; Fax: 641-423-7663.
See Newman Catholic School System, Mason City under Consolidated K-12 Systems located in the Institution section.
Catechesis/Religious Program—Jennifer Clancy, D.R.E. Students 75.

2—ST. JOSEPH (1873) Rev. Craig E. Steimel; Deacon Michael G. Byrne; Karen Byrne, Pastoral Assoc.
Pastor's Res.: 507 4th St., S.E., 50401. Tel: 641-424-3940.
Church & Parish Office: 302 Fifth St. S.E., 50401-4005. Tel: 641-423-5001; Fax: 641-423-8553.
See Newman Catholic School System, Mason City under Consolidated K-12 Systems located in the Institution section.
Catechesis/Religious Program—Jennifer Clancy, D.R.E. Students 205.

MASONVILLE, DELAWARE CO., IMMACULATE CONCEPTION (1883) [CEM] Revs. John R. Flaherty; Greg E. Bahl; Deacon Dave Loecke.
Mailing Address & Office: 119 W. Fayette St., Manchester, 52057. Tel: 563-927-4710; Fax: 563-927-9949.
Church: 606 Bernhart St., 50654.
Catechesis/Religious Program—Kathy Oberrueter,

C.R.E. Students 38.

MCGREGOR, CLAYTON CO., ST. MARY (1873) [CEM] Deacon Patrick J. Malanaphy, Pastoral Admin.; Rev. Msgr. Thomas E. Toale, Priest Supvr.; Very Rev. Richard G. Gaul, Sacramental Priest.
Office: 405 S. East St., P.O. Box U, Monona, 52159. Tel: 563-539-4442; Fax: 563-539-4383.
Church: 311 Seventh St., 52157.
Catechesis/Religious Program—Meagan Bee, C.R.E. Students 65.

MCINTIRE, MITCHELL CO., ST. MEL, Closed. For sacramental records, please contact Sacred Heart, Osage.

MEYER, MITCHELL CO., SACRED HEART ORATORY (1900) [CEM], Parish closed. For sacramental records, please contact, Sacred Heart, Osage.

MONONA, CLAYTON CO., ST. PATRICK (1856) [CEM] Deacon Patrick J. Malanaphy, Pastoral Admin.; Rev. Msgr. Thomas E. Toale, Priest Supvr.; Very Rev. Richard G. Gaul, Sacramental Priest.
Office & Mailing Address: 405 East St. S., P.O. Box U, 52159-0557. Tel: 563-539-4442; Fax: 563-539-4383.
Church: 407 S. East St., 52159.
Catechesis/Religious Program—Carla Pester, D.R.E. Students 115.

MONTI, BUCHANAN CO., ST. PATRICK ORATORY (1855) [CEM], Parish closed. For sacramental records, contact, St. John the Evangelist, Independence.

MONTICELLO, JONES CO., SACRED HEART (1868) [CEM] Rev. Keith L. Birch; Sr. Sheila Geraghty, R.S.M., Pastoral Assoc.
Office: 210 E. Third St., 52310-1535. Tel: 319-465-5944; Fax: 319-465-7065.
Pastor's Res.: 410 N. Maple St., Unit #301, 52310. Tel: 319-465-3034.
Church: 302 N. Sycamore, 52310.
School—(Grades PreSchool-6), 234 N. Sycamore, 52310-1515. Tel: 319-465-4605; Fax: 319-465-6183. Jim Zimmerman, Prin. Lay Teachers 10; Students 168.
Catechesis/Religious Program—Leanna Manternach, C.R.E. Students 189.

MOUNT VERNON, LINN CO., ST. JOHN THE BAPTIST (1843) [CEM] Susan M. Schettler, Pastoral Admin.; Very Rev. John A. Gossman, Priest Supvr. In Res., Rev. Philip E. Schmitt.
Church & Office: 212 7th St. S.E., P.O. Box 169, 52314-0169. Tel: 319-895-6246; Fax: 319-895-0973.
Catechesis/Religious Program—Linda Hamsmeier, D.R.E. Students 297.

NASHUA, CHICKASAW CO., ST. MICHAEL (1870) [CEM] Rev. Carl A. Ries.
Mailing Address & Parish Office: 612 Cedar St., P.O. Box 308, 50658-0308. Tel: 641-435-2070.
Pastor's Res.: 106 Chapel Ln., Charles City, 50616. Tel: 641-228-1071.
Church: 602 Cedar St., 50658.
Catechesis/Religious Program—Ann Demro, D.R.E. Students 74.

NEVADA, STORY CO., ST. PATRICK (1870) [CEM] Rev. Rick D. Dagit; Deacon Steven Van Kerckvoorde.
Parish Office: 1110 11th St., 50201. Tel: 515-382-2974.
Res. and Mailing Address: 410 Bailey St., P.O. Box 236, Colo, 50056-0236. Tel: 641-377-2710.
Church: 1127 Tenth St., 50201.
Catechesis/Religious Program—Barb Kuebler, D.R.E. Students 168.

NEW ALBIN, ALLAMAKEE CO., ST. JOSEPH (1910) [CEM] Rev. Daniel J. Knipper.
Parish Office: 114 3rd St., N.E., P.O. Box 404, 52160-0404. Tel: 563-544-4855.
Pastor's Res. & Mailing Address: 648 Main St., Lansing, 52151. Tel: 563-538-4171.
Church: 154 Third St. N.E., Lansing, 52151.
Catechesis/Religious Program—Karen Weber, D.R.E. Students 32.

NEW HAMPTON, CHICKASAW CO.

1—HOLY FAMILY (2002) [CEM] Rev. Msgr. Carl L. Schmitt; Deacon Victor J. DeSloover; Christine Carrier, Pastoral Assoc.; Sr. Jeanne Tranel, O.P., Pastoral Assoc. & Hispanic Min. Coord.
Parish Office & Mailing Address: 202 N. Broadway, 50659. Tel: 641-394-2105; Fax: 641-394-5154.
Pastor's Res.: 619 Rural St., 50659. Tel: 641-394-2744.
Churches:—St. Joseph, 202 N. Broadway, 50659.
St. Mary, 239 S. Walnut Ave., 50659.
School—(Grades PreSchool-8), 216 N. Broadway, 50659. Tel: 641-394-2865. Beth Wright, Prin. Sisters 1; Lay Teachers 12; Students 181.
Catechesis/Religious Program—Karen Bonfig, C.R.E. Students 246.

2—ST. JOSEPH (1870) Closed. Merged with St. Mary, New Hampton to form Holy Family, New Hampton. Sacramental records are located at Holy Family, New Hampton.

3—ST. MARY (1894) Closed. Merged with St. Joseph, New Hampton to form Holy Family, New Hampton.; Sacramental records are located at Holy Family, New Hampton.

NEW HARTFORD, BUTLER CO., ST. JOSEPH, Closed. For sacramental records contact Holy Family, Grundy Center.

NEW HAVEN, MITCHELL CO., ST. PETER (1876) [CEM] Rev. Ray E. Atwood.
Mailing Address, Res. & Office: 203 7th St., P.O. Box 38, Elma, 50628-0038. Tel: 641-393-2520; Fax: 641-393-2069.
Church: 2985 360th St., Osage, 50461.
Catechesis/Religious Program—Meg Schutjer, D.R.E. Students 58.

NEW MELLERAY, DUBUQUE CO., HOLY FAMILY (1850) [CEM] Rev. Richard W. Kuhn.
Office & Mailing Address: 241 Peosta Rd., Peosta, 52068-9507. Tel: 563-582-4217; Fax: 563-582-4217.
Pastor's Res.: 476 Lezlie Dr., Apt. 1, Peosta, 52068. Tel: 563-582-2821.
Church: 16500 Holy Family Ln., Peosta, 52068.
Catechesis/Religious Program—Kay Goedken, D.R.E. Students 105.

NEW VIENNA, DUBUQUE CO., ST. BONIFACE (1845) [CEM] Rev. John J. O'Connor; Deacons Jerry Miller; Fredrick J. Pins; James Steger.
Church, Res. & Mailing Address: 7401 Columbus St., P.O. Box 215, 52065. Tel: 563-921-2465.
Parish Office: 7420 Columbus St., P.O. Box 170, 52065. Tel: 563-921-2635; Fax: 563-921-3003.
See Archbishop Hennessy Catholic School, New Vienna under Elementary School Systems located in the Institution section.
Catechesis/Religious Program—Students 13.

NEWHALL, BENTON CO., ST. PAUL (1914) Rev. Jack H. McClure, C.PP.S.
Office, Pastor's Res. & Mailing Address: 405 Fourth Ave., P.O. Box 250, Van Horne, 52346-0250. Tel: 319-228-8131; Fax: 319-228-8800.
Church: 303 Third St. E., 52315.
Catechesis/Religious Program—Students 81.

NORTH BUENA VISTA, CLAYTON CO., IMMACULATE CONCEPTION (1898) [CEM] Rev. Marvin J. Bries; Deacon James Pfaffly.
Mailing Address & Office: 520 S. 2nd St., P.O. Box 847, Guttenberg, 52052-0847. Tel: 563-252-1247.
Church: 218 Main St., 52066.
See St. Mary & Immaculate Conception School System, Guttenberg under Elementary School Systems located in the Institution Section
Catechesis/Religious Program—Students 6.

NORTH WASHINGTON, CHICKASAW CO., IMMACULATE CONCEPTION (1868) [CEM] Rev. Msgr. Carl L. Schmitt; Deacon Victor J. DeSloover; Sr. Jeanne Tranel, O.P., Pastoral Assoc.; Christine Carrier, Pastoral Assoc.
Mailing & Office Address: 202 N. Broadway, New Hampton, 50659. Tel: 641-394-2105; Fax: 641-394-5154.
Pastor's Res.: 619 Rural St., New Hampton, 50659. Tel: 641-394-2744.
Church: 114 N. Wapsie St., 50661.
Catechesis/Religious Program—Karen Bonfig, C.R.E. Students 46.

NORWAY, BENTON CO., ST. MICHAEL (1867) [CEM] Rev. Jack H. McClure, C.PP.S.
Office, Pastor's Res. & Mailing Address: 405 Fourth Ave., P.O. Box 250, Van Horne, 52346-0250. Tel: 319-228-8131; Fax: 319-228-8800.
Church: 512 Evergreen, 52318.
Catechesis/Religious Program—Students 106.

OELWEIN, FAYETTE CO., SACRED HEART (1876) [CEM] Rev. Harry H. Koelker; Deacon Jim Patera; Carol Hamilton, Pastoral Assoc.
Church, Office & Res.: 628 S. Frederick Ave., 50662. Tel: 319-283-3743.
School—(Grades PreSchool-6), 601 First Ave., S.W., 50662. Tel: 319-283-1366; Fax: 319-283-5279. Nick Trenkamp, Prin. Lay Teachers 11; Students 126.
Catechesis/Religious Program—Michael Meyer, D.R.E. Students 117.

OSAGE, MITCHELL CO., SACRED HEART (1878) [CEM] Rev. John A. Moser; Sr. Millie Leuenberger, O.S.F., Pastoral Assoc.
Office: 1209 State St., 50461. Tel: 641-732-4342; Fax: 641-832-2447.
Pastor's Res.: 1203 State St., 50461. Tel: 641-732-4509.
Church: 1204 State St., 50461.
School—(Grades PreSchool-6), 218 S. 12th St., 50461-1725. Tel: 641-732-5221; Fax: 641-732-3248. Kim Weigle, Prin. Lay Teachers 7; Students 83.
Catechesis/Religious Program—Lisa Krones, C.R.E.; Beth Hoppel, C.R.E. Students 166.

OSSIAN, WINNESHIEK CO., ST. FRANCIS DE SALES (1876) [CEM] Rev. Msgr. Cletus J. Hawes.
Res. & Office: 418 E. Main St., 52161-9998. Tel: 563-532-9366.
Church: 420 E. Main St., 52161.
School—(Grades Day Care-8), 414 E. Main St., 52161. Tel: 563-532-9352; Fax: 563-532-9353. Mae Becker, Prin. Lay Teachers 8; Students 107.
Catechesis/Religious Program—Patricia Frana, C.R.E. Students 65.

OTTER CREEK, JACKSON CO., ST. LAWRENCE (1854) [CEM] Rev. James T. Chappell; Deacon Robert Head.
Parish Office, Res. & Mailing Address: 200 S. Vermont, Maquoketa, 52060. Tel: 563-652-6931.
Church: 17434 Bellevue-Cascade Rd., Zwingle, 52079.
Catechesis/Religious Program—Sr. Helen Stejskal, S.S.N.D., C.R.E. Students 14.

OXFORD JUNCTION, JONES CO., SACRED HEART (1890) Rev. Gregory A. Steckel (DAV), Parochial Admin.
Parish Office, Pastor's Res. & Mailing Address: 903 Main St., P.O. Box 127, Lost Nation, 52254-0127. Tel: 563-678-2200.
Church: 301 Church St., 52323.
Catechesis/Religious Program—Dena Jensen, D.R.E.; Stacy Agnitsch, D.R.E. Students 75.

PARKERSBURG, BUTLER CO., ST. PATRICK, [CEM] Closed. Merged with St. Mary, Dike, Sacred Heart, Grundy Center & Queen of Heaven, Reinbeck to form Holy Family, Reinbeck. For inquiries for sacramental records contact Holy Family, Reinbeck.

PEOSTA, DUBUQUE CO., ST. JOHN THE BAPTIST CHURCH OF PEOSTA, IOWA (1874) [CEM] Rev. Richard W. Kuhn; Sr. Mary Kent Pearson, O.P., Pastoral Assoc.
Mailing Address & Office: 241 Peosta St., 52068-9507. Tel: 563-582-4217; Fax: 563-582-4217.
Pastor's Res.: 476 Lezlie Dr., Apt. 1, 52068. Tel: 563-582-2821.
Church: 235 Peosta St., 52068.
See Seton Catholic Schools, Farley under Elementary School Systems located in the Institution section.
Catechesis/Religious Program—Marybeth Wagner, D.R.E. Students 191.

PETERSBURG, SS. PETER AND PAUL (1867) [CEM] Rev. John J. O'Connor.
Pastor's Res.: 7401 Columbus St., P.O. Box 215, New Vienna, 52065. Tel: 563-921-2465.
Church & Mailing Address: 1625 300th Ave., Dyersville, 52040. Tel: 563-875-7992.
See Archbishop Hennessy Catholic School, New Vienna under Elementary School Systems located in the Institution section.
Catechesis/Religious Program—Students 1.

PINHOOK, ST. BRIDGET ORATORY, [CEM] Closed. Sacramental Records located at Immaculate Conception, Sumner.

PLACID, DUBUQUE CO., ST. JOHN (1874) [CEM] Rev. Dennis R. Cain; Deacons Gerald Koopmann; James Kean; Joann Koopmann, Pastoral Assoc.
Office: 104 First St., S.E., P.O. Box 286, Epworth, 52045. Tel: 563-876-5540; Fax: 563-876-9062.
Church & Res.: 22511 E. Pleasant Grove Rd., Epworth, 52045. Tel: 563-876-5501.
See Seton Catholic Schools, Farley under Elementary School Systems located in the Institution section.
Catechesis/Religious Program—Marilyn Connor Ryan, D.R.E. Students 25.

PLYMOUTH ROCK, WINNESHIEK CO., ST. AGNES ORATORY (1857) [CEM], Parish closed. Sacramental records are located at Notre Dame, Cresco.

PLYMOUTH, CERRO GORDO CO., ST. MICHAEL, Closed. For sacramental records, contact Sacred Heart, Manly.

POSTVILLE, ALLAMAKEE CO., ST. BRIDGET (1872) Deacon Patrick J. Malanaphy, Pastoral Admin.; Rev. Msgr. Thomas E. Toale, Priest Supvr.; Very Rev. Richard G. Gaul, Sacramental Priest; Paul Rael, Hispanic Min. Coord.
405 S. East St., P.O. Box U, Monona, 52159-0557.
Parish Office: 135 W. Williams St., P.O. Box 369, 52162-0369. Tel: 563-864-3138; Fax: 563-864-7000.
Church: 141 W. Williams St., 52162.
Catechesis/Religious Program—Jennifer Benda, C.R.E. Students 48.

PRAIRIE, DUBUQUE CO., ST. JOSEPH, [CEM] Closed. For parish records, contact St. John the Baptist, Peosta.

PRAIRIEBURG, LINN CO., ST. JOSEPH (1874) [CEM] Rev. Wayne J. Droessler; Sr. Anne Kisting, O.S.F., Pastoral Min.
Parish Office & Mailing Address: 211 3rd St. N., P.O. Box 47, Coggon, 52218-0047. Tel: 319-435-2236; Fax: 319-435-2236.
Pastor's Res.: 410 Terrace Dr., P.O. Box 496, Central City, 52214-0496. Tel: 319-438-6625.
Church: 300 West Ave., 52219.
Catechesis/Religious Program—Marci Luedeman, C.R.E. Students 23.

PRESTON, JACKSON CO., ST. JOSEPH (1881) [CEM] Rev. Paul E. Lippstock.
Church, Res. & Mailing Address: 250 S. Faith St., P.O. Box 309, 52069-0309. Tel: 563-689-5161.
Catechesis/Religious Program—Irene Entsminger, D.R.E.; Rosemary Sievers, D.R.E. Students 244.

PROTIVIN, HOWARD CO., HOLY TRINITY (1878) [CEM] Rev. David M. Beckman; Very Rev. Marvin C. Salz, Sacramental Priest; Tyler Wheeler, Pastoral Min.; Lynette Wheeler, Pastoral Min.
Res. & Mailing Address: 110 Commercial Ave., P.O. Box 205, 52163-0205. Tel: 563-569-8259.
Church: 124 N. Main St., 52163.
See Trinity Catholic School, Protovin under Elementary School Systems located in the Institution Section.
Catechesis/Religious Program—Martin Ahrndt, D.R.E. Students 36.

RAYMOND, BLACKHAWK CO., ST. JOSEPH (1905) [CEM] Rev. Dennis J. Colter.
Res., Office & Mailing Address: 311 15th Ave., P.O. Box 136, Gilbertville, 50634. Tel: 319-296-1092; Fax: 319-296-2087.
Church: 313 E. Central St., 50667.
See Gilbertville-Raymond, Don Bosco High School, Gilbertville-Raymond Elementary under Consolidated K-12 Systems located in the Institution section.
Catechesis/Religious Program—Students 3.

REILLY SETTLEMENT, CHICKASAW CO., SACRED HEART, [CEM] Closed. For sacramental records, please contact Holy Trinity, Protivin.

REINBECK, GRUNDY CO.
1—HOLY FAMILY CHURCH, REINBECK, IOWA (2004) [CEM] Rev. Dennis J. Quint.
Office, St. Gabriel Church & Mailing Address: 21275 U Ave., 50669. Tel: 319-345-2006; Fax: 319-345-2006.
Pastor's Res.: 702 Grant St., Parkersburg, 50665.
St. Patrick Church: 304 Second St., Parkersburg, 50665.
Catechesis/Religious Program—Lyndsay Petersen, D.R.E. Students 194.
2—QUEEN OF HEAVEN (1958) [CEM] Closed. Merged with St. Mary, Dike, Sacred Heart, Grundy Center & St. Patrick, Parkersburg to form Holy Family, Reinbeck. Sacramental records are located at Holy Family, Reinbeck.

RHODES, MARSHALL CO., ST. JOSEPH, [CEM] Closed. For sacramental records, please contact St. Joseph, State Center.

RICEVILLE, HOWARD CO., IMMACULATE CONCEPTION (1879) [CEM] Rev. Ray E. Atwood.
Res. and Mailing Address: 203 7th St., Elma, 50628-0038. Tel: 641-393-2520; Fax: 641-393-2069.
Church: 211 Main St., 50466.
Catechesis/Religious Program—Deborah Oulman, C.R.E. Students 79.

RICKARDSVILLE, DUBUQUE CO., ST. JOSEPH (1840) [CEM] Rev. Raymond A. Burkle; Bro. Stephen W. Markham, F.S.C., Pastoral Assoc.
Office: 875 Church St., P.O. Box 398, Holy Cross, 52053. Tel: 563-870-4041.
Pastor's Res.: 103 S. Andres St., Luxemburg, 52056. Tel: 563-853-3369.
Church: 20249 St. Joseph Dr., 52039-9757.
See LaSalle Elementary Schools, Holy Cross under Elementary School Systems located in the Institution section.
Catechesis/Religious Program—Students 22.

ROCKFORD, FLOYD CO., HOLY NAME (1910) Rev. James W. Dubert, Parochial Admin.
Church & Parish Office: 507 First Ave. N.W., 50468. Tel: 641-756-3569.
Rectory—305 Elm St. E., Rockwell, 50469. Tel: 641-822-4957.
Catechesis/Religious Program—Mabel Zeran, D.R.E. Students 68.

ROCKWELL, CERRO GORDO CO., SACRED HEART (1878) [CEM] Rev. James W. Dubert, Parochial Admin.
Church, Res. & Mailing Address: 305 Elm St. E., P.O. Box 30, 50469. Tel: 641-822-4957.
Catechesis/Religious Program—Thomas Novotney, D.R.E. Students 55.

ROSEVILLE, FLOYD CO., ST. MARY (1867) [CEM] Rev. Msgr. Walter L. Brunkan.
Office & Mailing Address: 105 N. Main, P.O. Box 480, Greene, 50636-0480. Tel: 641-823-4146.
Church: 2397 Hwy. 14, Marble Rock, 50653.
Catechesis/Religious Program—Janet Willert, D.R.E. Students 68.

ROWLEY, BUCHANAN CO., ALL SAINTS (1896) Closed. For sacramental records, contact St. John the Evangelist, Independence.

RYAN, DELAWARE CO., ST. PATRICK (1882) [CEM] Revs. John R. Flaherty; Greg E. Bahl; Deacon Dave Loecke.
Office & Mailing Address: 615 Howard St., P.O. Box 219, 52330-0219. Tel: 563-932-2151.
Res.: 119 W. Fayette St., Manchester, 52057. Tel: 563-927-4710.
Church: 606 Franklin St., 52330.
Catechesis/Religious Program—Kathy Oberrueter, D.R.E. Students 81.

ST. ANSGAR, MITCHELL CO., ST. ANSGAR (1951) Closed. For sacramental records, contact Sacred Heart, Osage.

ST. ANTHONY, MARSHALL CO., SACRED HEART (1878) [CEM] Closed. For sacramental records contact St. Mary, Colo.

ST. CATHERINE, DUBUQUE CO., ST. CATHERINE (1887) [CEM] Revs. Stephen L. Meyer; Scott E. Bullock; Mary Jane Keppler, Pastoral Assoc.
Office & Mailing Address: 405 Franklin St., Bellevue, 52031. Tel: 563-872-3234.
Church: 5189 St. Catherine Rd., 52003.
See Marquette High School Bellevue under Consolidated K-12 Systems located in the Institution section.
Catechesis/Religious Program—Students 31.

ST. CECILIA, HOWARD CO., ST. PATRICK, [CEM] Closed. Sacramental records are located at Immaculate Conception, Elma.

ST. DONATUS, JACKSON CO., ST. DONATUS (1853) [CEM] Revs. Stephen L. Meyer; Scott E. Bullock; Mary Jane Keppler, Pastoral Assoc.
Office & Mailing Address: 405 Franklin St., Bellevue, 52031. Tel: 563-872-3234.
Church: 97 E. First St., 52071.
See Marquette High School, Bellevue under Consolidated K-12 Systems located in the Institution section.
Catechesis/Religious Program—Students 22.

ST. LUCAS, FAYETTE CO., ST. LUKE (1855) [CEM] Rev. David M. Beckman; Very Rev. Marvin C. Salz, Sacramental Priest; Tyler Wheeler, Pastoral Min.; Lynette Wheeler, Pastoral Min.
Pastor's Res. & Mailing Address: 110 Commercial Ave., P.O. Box 205, Protivin, 52163-0205.
Church: 207 E. Main St., 52166.
See Trinity Catholic School, Protovin under Elementary School Systems located in the Institution section.
Catechesis/Religious Program—Martin Ahrndt, D.R.E. Students 72.

ST. THERESA, JACKSON CO., ST. THERESA (1853) [CEM] Closed. Sacramental records are located at Sacred Heart, Maquoketa.

SABULA, JACKSON CO., ST. PETER (1840) [CEM] Sr. Lou Ann Kilburg, O.S.F., Pastoral Admin.; Rev. Paul E. Lippstock, Priest Supr. & Sacramental Priest.
Church & Parish Office: 504 Elk St., P.O. Box 429, 52070. Tel: 563-687-2525.
Catechesis/Religious Program—Sr. Lou Ann Kilburg, O.S.F., D.R.E. Students 11.

SAND SPRINGS, DELAWARE CO., IMMACULATE CONCEPTION, Closed. For sacramental records, please contact St. Luke, Hopkinton.

SCHLEY, HOWARD CO., HOLY CROSS ORATORY, [CEM] Closed. For sacramental records, contact Holy Trinity, Protivin.

SHELL ROCK, BUTLER CO., HOLY NAME, Closed. Sacramental records are located at St. Mary, Waverly.

SHERRILL, DUBUQUE CO., SS. PETER AND PAUL (1852) [CEM] Rev. Raymond A. Burkle; Bro. Stephen W. Markham, F.S.C., Pastoral Assoc.
Office & Mailing Address: 875 Church St., P.O. Box 398, Holy Cross, 52053. Tel: 563-870-4041.
Pastor's Res.: 103 S. Andres St., Luxemburg, 52056. Tel: 563-853-3369.
Church: 5131 Sherrill Rd., 52073-9612.
See LaSalle Elementary Schools, Holy Cross under Elementary School Systems located in the Institution section.
Catechesis/Religious Program—Students 80.

SOUTH GARRYOWEN, JACKSON CO., ST. ALOYSIUS, [CEM] Closed. For sacramental records, contact St. Patrick, Garryowen.

SPILLVILLE, WINNESHIEK CO., ST. WENCESLAUS (1860) [CEM] Rev. Donald J. Hawes.
Church & Parish Office: 207 Church St., P.O. Box 128, 52168-0128. Tel: 563-562-3637.
Pastor's Res.: 304 S. Maryville, P.O. Box 819, Calmar, 52132. Tel: 563-562-3603.
See Calmar-Festina-Spillville Catholic School, Calmar under Elementary School Systems located in the Institution section.
Catechesis/Religious Program—Helen Pinter, C.R.E. Students 15.

SPRINGBROOK, JACKSON CO., SS. PETER AND PAUL (1864) [CEM] Rev. Paul E. Lippstock.
Mailing Address: 105 E. Main St., P.O. Box 97, 52075. Tel: 563-872-3875.
Pastor's Res.: 250 S. Faith St., Preston, 52069. Tel: 563-689-5161.
Church: 107 E. Main St., 52075.
See Marquette High School, Bellevue under Consolidated K-12 Systems located in the Institution section.
Catechesis/Religious Program—Mary Jane Keppler, D.R.E. Students 36.

SPRINGVILLE, LINN CO., ST. ISIDORE (1961) Susan M. Schettler, Pastoral Admin.; Very Rev. John A. Gossman, Priest Supvr.
Office & Mailing Address: 603 6th St., P.O. Box 318, 52336. Tel: 319-854-6141; Fax: 319-854-7161.
Church: 603 6th St. S., 52336.
Catechesis/Religious Program—Michele Loehr, D.R.E. Students 77.

STACYVILLE, MITCHELL CO., CHURCH OF THE VISITATION (1894) [CEM] Rev. John A. Moser; Sr. Millie Leuenberger, O.S.F., Pastoral Assoc.
Parish Office & Mailing Address: 1209 State St., Osage, 50461. Tel: 641-732-4342; Fax: 641-832-2447.
Pastor's Res.: 1203 State St., Osage, 50461. Tel: 641-732-4509.
Church: 604 N. Broad St., 50476.
Catechesis/Religious Program—Barb Brumm, C.R.E. Students 104.

STATE CENTER, MARSHALL CO., ST. JOSEPH (1870) [CEM] Rev. Rick D. Dagit; Deacon Steven Van Kerckvoorde.
Office: 1110 11th St., Nevada, 50201. Tel: 515-382-2974; Fax: 515-382-2974.
Pastor's Res. & Mailing Address: 410 Bailey St., P.O. Box 236, Colo, 50056. Tel: 641-377-2710.
Church: 610 Third St. S.W., 50247.
Catechesis/Religious Program—Sr. Mary Ann Aman, C.H.M., D.R.E. Students 67.

STONE CITY, JONES CO., ST. JOSEPH ORATORY, Parish closed. Sacramental records are located at St. Patrick, Anamosa.

STRAWBERRY POINT, CLAYTON CO., ST. MARY (1876) [CEM] Rev. Paul R. Peters.
Mailing Address: 314 W. Mission St., 52076-9432. Tel: 563-933-6166.
Pastor's Res.: 330 1st St. S.W., P.O. Box 626, Elkader, 52043. Tel: 563-245-2548.
Church: 320 W. Mission St., 52076.
Catechesis/Religious Program—Patty Hilton, C.R.E.; Jennifer Palmersheim, C.R.E. Students 139.

SUMNER, BREMER CO., IMMACULATE CONCEPTION (1894) [CEM] Rev. James P. Brokman.
Church, Res. & Office: 413 W. First St., 50674-1313. Tel: 563-578-5366.
Catechesis/Religious Program—Sarah Kass, D.R.E. Students 100.

SWALEDALE, CERRO GORDO CO., ST. LAWRENCE, Closed. For sacramental records, contact Sacred Heart, Rockwell.

SYLVIA, DUBUQUE CO., ASSUMPTION (1896) [CEM] Closed. For sacramental records, please contact Sacred Heart, Maquoketa.

TAMA, TAMA CO., ST. PATRICK (1864) [CEM] Very Rev. Michael J. Mescher; Deacon Joe Behounek, Pastoral Assoc.; Bette Kratoska, Pastoral Assoc.; Laura Galvez, Hispanic Min. Coord.
Church, Pastor's Res. & Parish Office: 900 Park St., 52339. Tel: 641-484-3039; 641-484-4242; Fax: 641-484-8039.
Catechesis/Religious Program—Jeffrey Lumpa, D.R.E. Students 176.

TEMPLE HILL, JONES CO., ST. PETER (1852) [CEM] Rev. Douglas J. Loecke; Deacons Marvin Recker; Steven W. Strang; Ray Noonan.
Res. & Office: 20121 Temple Hill Rd., Cascade, 52033. Tel: 563-852-3448.
Church: 20123 Temple Hill Rd., Cascade, 52033.
See Aquin Educational System, Cascade under Consolidated K-12 Systems located in the Institution section.
Catechesis/Religious Program—Rebecca Smith, C.R.E. Students 28.

TRAER, TAMA CO., ST. PAUL (1912) [CEM] Rev. Jerry W. Blake.
Church, Res. & Office: 1102 Walnut St., 50675-1440. Tel: 319-478-2222; Fax: 319-478-2222.
Catechesis/Religious Program—Jessica Ollinger, D.R.E. Students 111.

URBANA, BENTON CO., ST. MARY (1872) [JC] Sr. Mary Hargrafen, O.S.F., Pastoral Admin.; Rev. Msgr. Russell M. Bleich, Priest Supvr.; Rev. Ardel H. Barta, Sacramental Priest (Retired).
Mailing Address: 516 Rowley St., P.O. Box 116, Walker, 52352-0116. Tel: 319-448-4241; Fax: 319-448-4241.
Church: 402 Ash Ave., 52345.
Catechesis/Religious Program—Diane Walston, D.R.E.; Melissa Holthaus, C.R.E. Students 177.

VAN HORNE, BENTON CO., IMMACULATE CONCEPTION (1869) [CEM] Rev. Jack H. McClure, C.PP.S.
Pastor's Res., Church & Parish Office: 405 Fourth Ave., P.O. Box 250, 52346-0250. Tel: 319-228-8131; Fax: 319-228-8800.
Catechesis/Religious Program—Students 74.

VINING, TAMA CO., ST. MARY ORATORY (1874) [CEM] Closed. Parish. For sacramental records, contact St. Paul, Traer.

VINTON, BENTON CO., ST. MARY (1878) [CEM] Sr. Mary Hargrafen, O.S.F., Pastoral Admin.; Rev. Msgr. Russell M. Bleich, Priest Supvr.; Rev. Ardel H. Barta, Sacramental Priest (Retired).
Church, Res. & Office: 2200 Second Ave., 52349. Tel: 319-472-3368; Fax: 319-472-3042.
Catechesis/Religious Program—Diane Walston, D.R.E. Students 161.

VOLGA, CLAYTON CO., SACRED HEART (1889) [CEM] Rev. Paul R. Peters.
Mailing Address: P.O. Box 135, 52077-0135.
Parish Office & Rectory: 330 1st St., S.W., P.O. Box 626, Elkader, 52043-0626. Tel: 563-245-2548.
Church: 306 White St., 52077.
Catechesis/Religious Program—Elise Bergan, D.R.E. Students 49.

WADENA, FAYETTE CO., ST. JOSEPH, [CEM], Parish closed. Sacramental records located at St. Joseph, Elkader.

WALFORD, LINN CO., HOLY TRINITY (1890) Closed. For sacramental records, contact John XXIII, Cedar Rapids.

WALKER, LINN CO., SACRED HEART (1885) [CEM] Sr. Mary Hargrafen, O.S.F., Pastoral Admin.; Rev. Msgr. Russell M. Bleich, Priest Supvr.; Rev. Ardel H. Barta, Sacramental Priest (Retired).
Mailing & Parish Office: 516 Rowley St., P.O. Box 116, 52352-0116. Tel: 319-448-4241; Fax: 319-448-4241.
Church: 518 Rowley St., 52352.
Catechesis/Religious Program—Diane Walston, D.R.E.; Melissa Holthaus, C.R.E. Students 138.

WATERLOO, BLACKHAWK CO.

1—BLESSED SACRAMENT (1947) [JC] Rev. Dennis D. Juhl; Deacons John Herman; James Freet; Norman Schauls; Robert Stirm; Sr. Madonna M. Friedman, O.S.F., Pastoral Min.
Church, Res. & Office: 650 Stephan Ave., 50701. Tel: 319-233-6179; Fax: 319-233-6051.
See Cedar Valley Catholic Schools under Consolidated K-12 Systems located in the Institution Section.
Catechesis/Religious Program—Barbara Duggan, D.R.E.; Lori Zabler, C.R.E. Students 126.

2—ST. EDWARD (1945) [JC] Very Rev. Jerry F. Kopacek; Deacons John Baker; Raymond Larsen; Richard Lynch; Karol Rae Hoth, Pastoral Assoc.
Church, Res. & Office: 1423 Kimball Ave., 50702. Tel: 319-233-8060; Fax: 319-233-3808.
See Cedar Valley Catholic Schools under Consolidated K-12 Systems located in the Institution Section.
Catechesis/Religious Program—Hazel Martin, D.R.E. Students 111.

3—ST. JOHN (1923) Closed. Merged with St. Mary & St. Joseph, Waterloo and St. Nicholas, Evansdale to form Queen of Peace, Waterloo. Sacramental records located at Queen of Peace, Waterloo.

4—ST. JOSEPH, Closed. Merged with St. Mary & St. John, Waterloo and St. Nicholas, Evansdale to form Queen of Peace, Waterloo. Sacramental records located at Queen of Peace, Waterloo.

5—ST. MARY (1898) Closed. Merged with St. John & St. Joseph, Waterloo and St. Nicholas, Evansdale to form Queen of Peace, Waterloo. Sacramental records located at Queen of Peace, Waterloo.

6—QUEEN OF PEACE (2002) [JC] Rev. Jose Luis Comparan; Deacons Larry Gram II; Ed Weber; Rigoberto Real.
Mailing, Parish Office & Church Address: 320 Mulberry St., 50703. Tel: 319-226-3655; Fax: 319-232-1118.
Pastor's Res.: 327 Alta Vista Ave., 50703.
See Cedar Valley Catholic Schools under Consolidated K-12 Systems located in the Institution Section
Catechesis/Religious Program—Bev Byford, D.R.E. Students 60.

7—SACRED HEART (1909) [JC] Rev. Louis M. Jaeger; Deacon Alan Weber; Nancy Rigel, Pastoral Assoc.
Office: 627 W. Fourth St., 50702. Tel: 319-234-4996; Fax: 319-233-0531.
Pastor's Res.: 3711 Loralin Dr., 50701. Tel: 319-236-6530.
Church: 623 W. Fourth St., 50702.
See Cedar Valley Catholic Schools under Consolidated K-12 Systems located in the Institution Section.
Catechesis/Religious Program—Pam Johnston, D.R.E.; Cathy Mills, C.R.E. Students 113.

WATKINS, BENTON CO., ST. PATRICK (1880) [CEM] Rev. Jack H. McClure, C.PP.S.
Parish Office, Pastor's Res. & Mailing Address: 405 Fourth Ave., P.O. Box 250, Van Horne, 52346. Tel: 319-228-8131; Fax: 319-228-8800.
Church: 109 2nd St., 52354.
Catechesis/Religious Program—Students 13.

WAUCOMA, FAYETTE CO., ST. MARY (1898) [CEM] Rev. David M. Beckman; Very Rev. Marvin C. Salz, Sacramental Priest; Tyler Wheeler, Pastoral Min.; Lynette Wheeler, Pastoral Min.
Mailing Address & Church: 218 3rd St., N.W., P.O. Box 215, 52171. Tel: 563-776-6364.
Pastor's Res.: 110 Commercial Ave., P.O. Box 205, Protivin, 52163-0205. Tel: 563-569-8259.
Catechesis/Religious Program—Martin Ahrndt, D.R.E. Students 47.

WAUKON, ALLAMAKEE CO., ST. PATRICK (1851) [CEM] Rev. Joseph M. Schneider; Deacon Michael Ward, Pastoral Assoc.
Res., Office & Mailing Address: 109 Second St., S.W., Box 146, 52172. Tel: 563-568-3671; Fax: 563-568-4432.
Church: 101 2nd St., S.W., 52172.
School—(Grades PreSchool-6), 200 Second St., S.W., 52172. Tel: 563-568-2415; Fax: 563-568-2170. Richard Wede, Prin. Lay Teachers 11; Students 130.
Catechesis/Religious Program—Michael Erickson, D.R.E. Students 257.

WAVERLY, BREMER CO., ST. MARY (1856) [CEM] Rev. Michael L. Tauke; Theresa Buss, Pastoral Min.
Parish Office, Church & Mailing Address: 2700 Horton Rd., 50677. Tel: 319-352-2493; Fax: 319-352-3122.
Pastor's Res.: 313 Third Ave., N.E., 50677. Tel: 319-483-9009.
Catechesis/Religious Program—Eric Stromberg, D.R.E. Students 343.

WEBSTER CITY, HAMILTON CO., ST. THOMAS AQUINAS (1870) [CEM] Rev. Scott F. Boone; Amy Shannon, Pastoral Assoc.
Mailing & Office: 1000 Des Moines St., 50595-2147. Tel: 515-832-1190; Fax: 515-832-3757.
Church: 1008 Des Moines St., 50595.
Pastor's Res.: 2209 Summit Dr., 50595. Tel: 515-832-1977.
School—(Grades PreSchool-6), 624 Dubuque St., 50595-2245. Tel: 515-832-1346; Fax: 515-832-1212. Michael Pavik, Prin. Lay Teachers 10; Students 115.
Catechesis/Religious Program—Lynn Houdeshell, C.R.E. Students 149.

WEST RIDGE, ALLAMAKEE CO., ST. JOHN THE BAPTIST, [CEM], Parish closed. Sacramental records are located at St. Patrick, Waukon.

WEST UNION, FAYETTE CO., HOLY NAME (1870) [CEM] Rev. Dale J. Rausch.
Office, Pastor's Res. & Church: 128 N. Walnut St., 52175. Tel: 563-422-3184.
Catechesis/Religious Program—Marion Broghammer, C.R.E.; Sue McDonough, C.R.E. Students 152.

WEXFORD, ALLAMAKEE CO., IMMACULATE CONCEPTION (1851) [CEM] Rev. Louis J. Trzil.
Res., Church & Mailing Address: 1416 Great River Rd., Lansing, 52151. Tel: 563-586-2150.
Catechesis/Religious Program—Shari Curran, D.R.E. Students 28.

WILLIAMS, HAMILTON CO., ST. MARY (1875) [CEM] Rev. Scott F. Boone.
Parish Office & Mailing Address: 1000 Des Moines St., Webster City, 50595. Tel: 515-832-1190; Fax: 515-832-3757.
Pastor's Res.: 2209 Summit Dr., Webster City, 50595. Tel: 515-832-1977.
Church: 404 Fourth St., 50271.
Catechesis/Religious Program—Lynn Houdeshell, C.R.E. Students 15.

WINTHROP, BUCHANAN CO., ST. PATRICK (1894) [CEM] Rev. Donald J. Plamondon; Deacon Tim Post; Sharon Bainbridge, Pastoral Assoc.
Office, Res. & Mailing Address: 209 5th Ave. N.E., Independence, 50644-1998. Tel: 319-334-7191; Fax: 319-334-7192.
Church: 555 First St. S., 50682.
Catechesis/Religious Program—Deb Steffen, C.R.E. Students 153.

WODEN, HANCOCK CO., SACRED HEART (1900) Closed. For sacramental records, please contact St. Patrick, Britt.

WORTHINGTON, DUBUQUE CO., ST. PAUL (1875) [CEM] Very Rev. Phillip F. Kruse; Rev. G. Robert Gross; Deacons Fredrick J. Pins; Jerry Miller; James Steger.
Parish Office & Mailing Address: 309 Third Ave., S.W., P.O. Box 38, 52078.
Church: 301 S. 2nd Ave. S.W., 52078.
School—(Grades PreSchool-6), 309 Third Ave., S.W., P.O. Box 68, 52078-0068. Tel: 563-855-2125; Fax: 563-855-2022. Jayne Intlekofer, Prin. Lay Teachers 5; Students 43.
Catechesis/Religious Program—Students 24.

ZEARING, STORY CO., ST. GABRIEL (1904) Rev. Rick D. Dagit; Deacon Steven Van Kerckvoorde.
Mailing Address: 410 Bailey St., P.O. Box 236, Colo, 50056-0236.
Office: 1110 11th St., Nevada, 50201. Tel: 515-382-2974; Fax: 515-382-5966.
Church: 302 N. Center, 50278.
Catechesis/Religious Program—Rex Gogerty, D.R.E. Students 9.

On Special or Other Archdiocesan Assignment:
Rev. Msgrs.—
Bleich, Russell M., S.T.L., Episcopal Vicar, Cedar Rapids Region
Connolly, Leon L. (Retired), Vicar for Hispanic Min.
Toale, Thomas E., Ph.D., Vicar General & Dubuque Region Episcopal Vicar
Wilgenbusch, Lyle L., Episcopal Vicar, Waterloo Region
Revs.—
Bullock, Scott E., J.C.L., Dir. Seminarians, Vianney House, 1235 Mt. Loretta Ave., 52003.
Glaser, Kenneth J., Dir. Campus Ministry, St. Stephen the Witness Student Center, 1019 W. 23rd, Cedar Falls, 50613. Tel: 319-266-9863
Haugen, John S., 1450 Alta Vista St., 52001. Dean, Campus Spirtual Life at Loras College, Dubuque
Krapfl, Gary F., P.O. Box 479, 52004-0479.
McGovern, Mark J., 971 Mt. Loretta Ave., 52003. Tel: 563-543-5178
Nienhaus, Ivan R., P.O. Box 479, 52004-0479.
Podhajsky, Michael J., (Advanced Studies), St. Philip the Apostle Parish, 5416 Henderson Way, Camp Springs, MD 20746. Tel: 301-423-4244
Schatz, David A., M.A., Dir. Vocation Awareness, Vianney House, 1235 Mt. Loretta Ave., 52003. Tel: 563-556-2580
Wild, Alexander, P. O. Box 479, 52004-0479.

Military Chaplains:
Revs.—
Lawrence, Andrew Ch. (Cpt.) 8235 Forrester Blvd., Springfield, VA 22152.
Remy, David P., CDR, CHC, USN, 3101 Marcus Pointe Blvd., Pensacola, FL 32505. Tel: 850-473-9426

On Leave of Absence (Not Authorized for Priestly Ministry):
Revs.—
Landherr, Clayton
McDermott, John J.
O'Brien, Steven G.
Rastrelli, Thomas P.

Retired:
Rev. Msgrs.—
Barta, James O., Ph.D., Villa Raphael, 1155 Mt. Loretta Ave., 52003. Tel: 563-583-2321
Connolly, Leon L., Stonehill Care Center, 3485 Windsor Ave., 52001.
Dalton, John W., 1301 Rhodes, Naperville, IL 60540. Tel: 630-355-2664
Friedl, Francis P., Villa Raphael, 1155 Mt. Loretta Ave., 52003. Tel: 563-588-8018
Funke, Richard P., J.C.L., 7974 Sailboat Key Blvd., Box 602, South Pasadena, FL 33707. Tel: 727-363-1754
Glovik, Karl L., 150 Thompson Dr., S.E., #102, Cedar Rapids, 52403. Tel: 319-364-4652
Hayek, Stanley J., 307 Meadow Ln., Charles City, 50616. Tel: 641-228-1664
Heineman, Donald P., 108 3rd St., S.E., P.O. Box 187, Fort Atkinson, 52144-0187. Tel: 563-534-3052
Hemann, John W., 481 N. Shore Dr., Apt. #301, Clear Lake, 50428-1368. Tel: 641-357-4539
Heuring, Alvan P., 3458 Edison St., San Mateo, CA 94403-3401. Tel: 650-341-1645
Lang, Charles E., Ph.D., 8727 W. Bryn Mawr, #409, Chicago, IL 60631. Tel: 773-391-2888
Laughlin, Martin T., 119 Broad St., P.O. Box 818, Charleston, SC 29402.
Lechtenberg, Edward W., 321 Diagonal St., Lansing, 52151. Tel: 563-538-4773
Manternach, Albert V., Villa Raphael, 1155 Mt. Loretta Ave., 52003. Tel: 563-582-2189
McClean, John R., 1539 Bies Dr., 52002. Tel: 563-556-1922
O'Brien, Joseph, Villa Raphael, 1155 Mt. Loretta Ave., 52003. Tel: 563-556-4326
Ralph, Thomas J., 400 Woodland Ridge, 52003. Tel: 563-587-1977
Simington, Ralph P., 931 E. Ridgeway Ave., Waterloo, 50702. Tel: 319-236-6638
Slepicka, Joseph J., 313 N. 13th St., Clear Lake, 50428. Tel: 641-357-2448
Steimel, Paul T., 3709 W. 9th St., Apt. 8, Waterloo, 50702. Tel: 319-233-5287
Vogl, Robert R., Villa Raphael, 1155 Mt. Loretta Ave, 52003. Tel: 563-556-4997
Walz, W. Dean, J.C.D., 24701 207th Ave., P.O. Box 182, Delhi, 52223-0182. Tel: 563-927-6672
Revs.—
Ament, Robert J., 67 Brandon, Glen Ellyn, IL 60137. Tel: 630-858-0043
Auer, Robert F., CH (COL), 1027 N. Third St., P.O. Box 674, Guttenberg, 52052. Tel: 563-252-2109
Barnes, John G., 114 S. Sheakley #8, New Hampton, 50659. Tel: 641-394-2394
Barta, Ardel H. Tel: 563-581-2760
Blocklinger, James L., 1331 Oak Park Pl., Unit 361, 52002.
Bodensteiner, Peter C., 108 W. Spring St., Apt. A-1, Lawler, 52154. Tel: 563-238-8751
Braak, Thomas E., 205 W. Ingledue St.,

Marshalltown, 50158. Tel: 641-752-3846
Bruggeman, Donald R., 411 Burdette Dr., S.W., Apt. 1022, Cedar Rapids, 52404. Tel: 319-396-0504
Burke, Clement J., 1510 11th Ave. S., Apt. 1108, Minneapolis, MN 55404. Tel: 612-238-5189
Carpender, John W., 720 Duggan Dr., #1, 52003-0250. Tel: 563-582-6993
Carpender, Thomas J., Aberdeen Heights Assisted Living, 7220 S. Yale Ave., Tulsa, OK 74136. Tel: 918-879-8223
Charipar, Henry W., Stonehill Care Center, 3485 Windsor Ave., 52001. Tel: 563-588-8620
Condon, Gerald A., 130 Thompson Dr., S.E., #120, Cedar Rapids, 52403. Tel: 319-366-1287
Devine, William P., 2302 Rick Collins Way, Apt. 6, Eldora, 50627-8357. Tel: 641-858-2222
Drexler, Harold J., Sacred Heart Rectory, 2215 Windsor Ave., 52001-1698. Tel: 563-583-1709
Engler, Ernest J., 14300 W. Bell Rd., #210, Surprise, AZ 85374. Tel: 623-975-1965
Fangmann, Frederick C., Villa Raphael, 1155 Mount Loretta Ave., 52003. Tel: 563-557-3717
Flanagan, James W., 1723 Vickers Cir., Decatur, GA 30030-1033. Tel: 404-378-0366
Friedell, John C., 1920 Cox St., Apt. #3, 52001. Tel: 563-556-9176
Geary, Patrick G., 518 Crawford Ave., Ames, 50010. Tel: 515-233-4191
Heimerman, Francis D., 151 Main St., P.O. Box 623, Nashua, 50658. Tel: 641-435-2261
Hemann, Melvin D., 127 Kaspend Pl., Cedar Falls, 50613-1683. Tel: 319-266-3889
Herzog, John M., 1004 Mesa Verde Pl., Ames, 50014. Tel: 515-292-0558
Hussmann, John R., Stonehill Care Center, 3485 Windsor Ave., 52001.
Karnik, George W., 750 River Forest Rd., #35, Evansdale, 50707. Tel: 319-226-5412
Katz, Roger L., 400 17th St. W., Clear Lake, 50428. Tel: 641-357-2003
Keppler, Daniel J., 505 Cherry Dr., P.O. Box 0445, Monona, 52159. Tel: 563-539-4186
Kissling, John M., 419 3rd St., P.O. Box 356, Chetek, WI 54728-0356. Tel: 715-924-3514
Kleinfehn, Walter J., 4850 16th Ave., S.W., Apt. 103, Cedar Rapids, 52404. Tel: 319-390-0643
Krapfl, Daniel A., 786 Stone Ridge Pl., 52001. Tel: 563-582-1039
Kurt, Allan J., P.O. Box 479, 52004-0479.
Kutsch, Eugene C., 2622 New Haven St., 52001. Tel: 563-583-1638
Levenhagen, Robert J., 6158 Forest Hills Dr., Asbury, 52002. Tel: 563-582-5041
Maichen, Richard F., 1009 New St., Manchester, 52057. Tel: 563-927-8137
Manternach, Carl J., 420 N. Maple, Monticello, 52310. Tel: 319-465-6348
McAndrew, Thomas F., 14258 Sagewood Dr., 52002. Tel: 563-588-3389
McDonald, Paul F., Villa Raphael, 1155 Mt. Loretta Ave., 52003. Tel: 563-583-5105 U.S.A.F.
McGuire, Joseph E., Mercy Medical Center-Hallmar, 701 Tenth St., S.E., Cedar Rapids, 52403.
McManus, Paul C., 419 3rd St., N.W., Independence, 50644. Tel: 319-332-0411
Nemmers, Mark R., 801 Davis St., #212, 52001. Tel: 563-557-5094
O'Brien, William D., Villa Raphael, 1155 Mt. Loretta Ave., 52003. Tel: 563-582-9933
Otting, Loras C., Villa Raphael, 1155 Mt. Loretta Ave., 52003. Tel: 563-583-3866
Otting, Paul J., Villa Raphael, 1155 Mt. Loretta Ave., 52003. Tel: 563-582-2709
Ouderkirk, Lloyd Paul, 24876 Mississippi Rd., Garnavillo, 52409. Tel: 563-252-1248
Paisley, John C., 816 Euclid St., 52001-8123. Tel: 563-583-9242
Pepper, J. David, 102 W. Spring, Box 120, Lawler, 52154. Tel: 563-238-2701
Perry, Francis J., Stonehill Care Center, 3485 Windsor Ave., 52001.
Ptacek, John P., 206 7th St. S.E., Farley, 52046. Tel: 563-744-9105
Purtell, John J., 105 Union St., Apt. 10, Sumner, 50674. Tel: 563-578-3234
Purtell, Thomas W., Hillcrest Home, 915 W. 1st St., Sumner, 50674. Tel: 563-578-8593
Rasing, Linus E., 615 W. Prospect St., New Hampton, 50659. Tel: 641-394-4504
Recker, Philip F., 1849 Doral Park Rd., S.E., Rio Rancho, NM 87124-7118. Tel: 505-896-9449
Reuter, Lloyd E., 1905 5th St., P.O. Box 114, Gilbertville, 50634. Tel: 319-296-0848
Rhomberg, Thomas W., Villa Raphael, 1155 Mt. Loretta Ave., 52003. Tel: 563-582-3545
Rogers, Daniel J., 7678 Moonlight Ln., Bellevue, 52031. Tel: 563-582-6605
Schmidt, Florian J., 2130 Woodland #6, 52002. Tel: 563-582-4066
Schmitt, Phillip E., 212-1/2 7th St., S.E., Mt. Vernon, 52314-1518. Tel: 319-895-0404
Schueller, La Verne L., CH (COL), 622 Cottage Grove Ave., P.O. Box 1983, Cedar Rapids, 52406. Tel: 319-365-0500
Vorwald, Aloysius J., 203 3rd St., S.W. #2, Dyersville, 52040. Tel: 563-875-2627
Walsh, John J., Villa Raphael, 1155 Mt. Loretta Ave., 52003. Tel: 563-556-4897
Wilkie, William E., Ph.D., 1920 Cox St., #4, 52001. Tel: 563-588-7100
Zee, Louis C., Ascension Catholic Church, 4605 Jetty Lane, Houston, TX 77072. Tel: 281-575-8855

Permanent Deacons:
Aitchison, Gary, St. Cecilia, Ames
Baker, John, St. Edward, Waterloo
Baltes, Robert, (Retired), New Hampton
Behounek, Joseph, St. Joseph, Chelsea; St. Michael, Belle Plaine; St. Boniface, Garwin; St. Patrick, Tama
Berger, Paul "Jim", St. Ludmila, Cedar Rapids
Berry, Matthew F., Holy Family, Mason City
Biver, William, St. Columbkille, Dubuque
Blouin, Michael, Church of the Resurrection, Dubuque
Brinkmoeller, Dave, Holy Ghost, Holy Trinity and Sacred Heart, Dubuque
Brustkern, Leo J., (Retired), La Porte City
Byrne, Michael G., St. Joseph, Mason City
Cashatt, Wayne, (Retired), Eldora
Christy, Alan, St. Cecilia, Ames
Cisler, William J., St. Wenceslaus and Immaculate Conception, Cedar Rapids
Cooper, Charles, Holy Family, Mason City
DeSloover, Vic, Holy Family, New Hampton; St. Boniface, Ionia; Immaculate Conception, North Washington
Dunn, Frank, (Retired), Dubuque
Flagel, LaVerne, (Retired), Marion
Francois, Nick, St. Benedict, Decorah
Freet, James, Blessed Sacrament, Waterloo
Froyen, Leonard, Ph.D., (Retired)
Garcia, Pedro, St. Francis Xavier, Belmond; St. John, Clarion; Sacred Heart, Eagle Grove
Gehrke, Richard, (Retired), Oelwein
Gram, Clarence, Queen of Peace, Waterloo
Harris, Jeff, St. Mary, Marshalltown
Hayes, Joseph, (Retired), Cascade
Head, Robert, Sacred Heart, Maquoketa; St. John, Andrew; St. Lawrence, Otter Creek
Herman, John, Blessed Sacrament, Waterloo
Hernandez, Felix, St. Mary, Marshalltown
Hickson, William, St. Anthony, Dubuque
Hoeger, Daniel, St. Patrick, Cedar Rapids
Hurych, Robert F., (Leave of Absence)
Jones, David, St. Mary, Ackley; St. Patrick, Hampton
Jorgensen, Gerald T., Ph.D., J.C.L., Resurrection, Dubuque
Kean, James, St. Patrick, Epworth; St. John, Placid; St. Clement, Bankston; St. Joseph, Farley
Klappholz, Mike, All Saints, Cedar Rapids
Koopmann, Gerald, St. John, Placid; St. Patrick, Epworth; St. Clement, Bankston; St. Joseph, Farley
Lang, Tom, St. Joseph, Key West
Larsen, Raymond, St. Edward, Waterloo
LoBianco, Timothy, Resurrection, Dubuque
Loecke, Dave, St. Mary, Manchester; Immaculate Conception, Masonville; St. Patrick, Ryan
Lynch, Richard, St. Edward, Waterloo
MacDonald, Stephen, St. Joseph the Worker, Dubuque
Malanaphy, Patrick J., St. Mary, McGregor; St. Patrick, Monona & St. Bridget, Postville
Malone, John, (Retired), Cedar Rapids
Manning, Richard, St. Ludmila, Cedar Rapids
Mauss, William, St. Anthony, Dubuque
McCully, John, St. Cecilia, Ames
McGhee, David, Nativity, Dubuque
Mead, Edward J., (Retired), Marshalltown
Miller, Jerry, St. Francis Xavier, Dyersville; St. Joseph, Earlsville; St. Boniface, New Vienna; SS. Peter & Paul, Petersburg; St. Paul, Worthington
Moetsch, Michael, St. Patrick, Cedar Falls
Mulherin, Dennis, St. Elizabeth Ann Seton, Hiawatha
Noonan, Ray, St. Matthias, Cascade; Sacred Heart, Fillmore; St. Patrick, Garryowen; St. Peter, Temple Hill
Pantaloni, Ed, (Retired Outside the Archdiocese) Grimes
Patera, Jim, Sacred Heart, Oelwein; Immaculate Conception, Fairbank
Peckosh, Paul, St. Raphael Cathedral, Dubuque
Peterson, Lanny, St. Pius X, Cedar Rapids
Pfaffly, James, St. Mary, Guttenberg; Immaculate Conception, North Buena Vista; St. Joseph, Garnavillo
Pins, Fredrick J., St. Francis Xavier, Dyersville; St. Paul, Worthington; St. Joseph, Earlville; St. Boniface, New Vienna; SS. Peter & Paul, Petersburg
Polt, Roger, St. Henry, Marshalltown
Popowski, Dennis, St. Patrick, Britt; St. Patrick, Buffalo Center; St. Wenceslaus, Duncan; St. James, Forest City, St. Boniface, Garner; St. Patrick, Lake Mills
Post, Tim, St. John the Evangelist, Independence; St. Patrick, Winthrop
Pusillo, Gary, St. Henry, Marshalltown
Quiles, Horacio, St. Mary, Dubuque; St. Patrick, Dubuque
Ramirez, Diego, Immaculate Conception, Cedar Rapids; St. Wenceslaus, Cedar Rapids
Real, Rigoberto, Queen of Peace, Waterloo
Recker, Marvin, St. Matthias, Cascade; Sacred Heart, Fillmore; St. Patrick, Garryowen; St. Peter, Temple Hill
Saunders, Phil, St. Matthew, Cedar Rapids
Scharosch, Albert, (Retired), Cedar Rapids
Schauls, Norman, Blessed Sacrament, Waterloo
Schmit, Nick, (Retired), Belmond
Sink, Tom, St. Patrick, Cedar Falls
Smith, Ron, St. Cecilia, Ames
Smith, Sean, St. Joseph, Marion
Steger, James, St. Joseph, Earlville; St. Francis Xavier, Dyersville; St. Boniface, New Vienna; SS. Peter & Paul, Petersburg; St. Paul, Worthington
Stierman, John, Holy Ghost, Dubuque; Holy Trinity, Dubuque; Sacred Heart, Dubuque
Stirm, Bob, Blessed Sacrament, Waterloo
Strang, Steven W., St. Matthias, Cascade; Sacred Heart, Fillmore & St. Patrick, Garryowen; St. Peter, Temple Hill
Temeyer, Jerry, St. Francis Xavier, Belmond; St. John, Clarion; Sacred Heart, Eagle Grove
Thill, James J., Holy Ghost & Holy Trinity & Sacred Heart, Dubuque
Tondra, Richard, St. Cecilia, Ames
Van Kerckvoorde, Steven, St. Mary, Colo; St. Patrick, Nevada; St. Joseph, State Center; St. Gabriel, Zearing
Vaske, Irvin, (Retired), Marshalltown
Wallace, Richard, St. Matthew, Cedar Rapids
Walsh, Tom, (Retired), Cedar Rapids
Ward, Mike, St. Patrick, Waukon; St. Mary, Dorchester; St. Mary, Hanover
Weber, Alan, Sacred Heart, Waterloo
Weber, Ed, Queen of Peace, Waterloo
Whitters, Michael, St. Francis Xavier, Belmond; St. John, Clarion; Sacred Heart, Eagle Grove
Wilson, James, (Retired), Waterloo
Zimmerman, Paul, St. Pius X, Cedar Rapids

Deacons Active Outside the Archdiocese:
Deacons—
Brock, Cary, Irrigon, OR
Brown, Paul, Auburn, AL
DiPietre, Dennis, Columbia, MO
Fortin, Daryl, LeClaire
Jenney, William, Brooklyn, MN

INSTITUTIONS LOCATED IN THE DIOCESE

[A] SEMINARIES, ARCHDIOCESAN

DUBUQUE. *Seminary of St. Pius X, Loras College*, 1450 Alta Vista St., P.O. Box 178, 52004-0178. Tel: 563-588-7662. Revs. Scott E. Bullock, J.C.L., Rector; David A. Schatz, M.A., Vice Rector; William M. Joensen, Ph.D., Spiritual Dir. Students for Archdiocese of Dubuque 8; Other Diocesan Students 2.

[B] SEMINARIES, RELIGIOUS OR SCHOLASTICATES

EPWORTH. *Divine Word College*, 102 Jacoby Dr., S.W., P.O. Box 380, 52045-0380. Tel: 563-876-3353; Fax: 563-876-3407. Email: hutchins@dwci.edu. Web: www.dwci.edu. Revs. William Shea, S.V.D.; Michael Hutchins, S.V.D., Pres.; Kenneth Anich, S.V.D.; Khien Luu, S.V.D., Vice Pres. Formation & Dean of Students; Joseph McDermott, S.V.D.; James Bergin, S.V.D., Rector SVD Community; Walter Bunofsky, S.V.D.; Paul LaForge, S.V.D.; Joseph Chau Nguyen, S.V.D.; Stephen Kha Nguyen, S.V.D.; Thang Hoang, S.V.D.; Trung Thanh Mai, S.V.D.; Robert Mertes, S.V.D.; Quy Ngoc Dang, S.V.D.; Linh Pham, S.V.D.; Nahn Van Tran, S.V.D.; Bros. Kevin Diederich, S.V.D.; Tony

Kreinus, S.V.D.; Wayne Till, S.V.D. Society of the Divine Word (S.V.D.). Priests 16; Brothers 3; Sisters 1; Lay Teachers 19; Students 90.

[C] COLLEGES AND UNIVERSITIES

DUBUQUE. *Clarke College*, 1550 Clarke Dr., 52001. Tel: 563-588-6300; Fax: 563-588-6789. Email: clarke-info@clarke.edu. Web: www.clarke.edu. Sr. Joanne M. Burrows, S.C., Ph.D., Pres.; Kristi Droessler, Registrar; Sr. Joan Lingen, B.V.M., Vice Pres. Academic Affairs & Provost; Graciela Canerio-Livingston, Academic Dean & Provost; Kate Zanger, Vice Pres. Student Life & Enrollment Mgmt.; Deanna McCormick, Vice Pres. Business & Finance; Kristi Gimmel Becker, Dir. Career Svcs. Liberal Arts College. (Coed); Conducted by Sisters of Charity, B.V.M. Sisters 6; Lay Teachers 132; Students 1,202.

Loras College, 1450 Alta Vista St., P.O. Box 178, 52004-0178. Tel: 563-588-7100; Fax: 563-588-7964. Email: jim.collins@loras.edu. Web: www.loras.edu. Mr. Jim Collins, Pres.; Lisa L. Bunders, Vice Pres. Enrollment Mgmt. Tel: 563-588-7103; Fax: 563-588-7824; Stephen J. Schmall, C.P.A., Vice Pres. Finance & Admin. Svcs.; Rev. John S. Haugen, Dean, Campus Spiritual Life; Cheryl Jacobsen, Ph.D., Provost/Academic Dean; Arthur Sunleaf, Asst. Vice Pres. Student Devel./Dean of Students; Joyce A. Meldrem, Dir. Academic Resource Ctr.; Rev. Msgr. Charles E. Lang, Ph.D. (Retired). (Accredited by the North Central Assoc. of Colleges and Secondary Schools) Priests 3; Students 1,568.

College Faculty: Revs. Robert R. Beck; Douglas O. Wathier, S.T.D.; William M. Joensen, Ph.D. In Res. Revs. John C. Friedell (Retired); William E. Wilkie, Ph.D. (Retired).

CEDAR RAPIDS. *Mount Mercy College*, 1330 Elmhurst Dr., N.E., 52402-4797. Tel: 319-363-8213; Fax: 319-368-5270. Email: admission@mtmercy.edu. Web: www.mtmercy.edu. Christopher R. L. Blake, Ph.D., Pres.; Dr. Sue Oatey, Ph.D., Vice Pres. for Enrollment; Barb Pooley, C.P.A., C.M.A., Vice Pres. Finance & Business Operations; John P. Marsden, Ph.D., Provost & Vice Pres. Academic Affairs; Lori Heying, Dir. Inst. Research. Priests 1; 76 full-time; 85 part-time 161; Students 1,666.

[D] HIGH SCHOOLS, INTERPAROCHIAL

CEDAR RAPIDS. *Metropolitan Office of Catholic Education, Cedar Rapids Metro Office*, 6300 42nd St., N.E., 52411. Tel: 319-366-2517; Fax: 319-366-0426. Email: dbqasup@arch.pvt.k12.ia.us. Web: www.cr-cath.pvt.k12.ia.us. Jeff Henderson, Supt. Schools. Priests 1; Sisters 1; Lay Teachers 210.

Xavier High School (Coed), 6300 42nd St., N.E., 52411. Tel: 319-294-6635; Fax: 319-294-6712. Email: DBQH02@arch-pvt.k12.ia.us. Rev. Philip E. Thompson, Pastoral Coord.; Tom Keating, Prin. & Contact Person; Elizabeth Globokar, Asst. Prin. Serving St. Patrick, Fairfax; John XXIII; St. Jude, St. Ludmila, St. Patrick, Immaculate Conception, St. Wenceslaus, St. Matthew, All Saints, St. Pius X, Cedar Rapids; St. Joseph, Marion; St. Elizabeth Ann Seton, Hiawatha. Lay Teachers 51; Students 792.

Xavier High School Foundation, 6300 42nd St., N.E., P.O. Box 10956, 52410-0956. Tel: 319-378-4571; Fax: 319-378-2953. Email: jruff@xavierfoundation.org. Jody Ruff, Dir. & Contact Person; Rev. Philip E. Thompson, Pastoral Coord.

DYERSVILLE. *Beckman High School*, (Grades 7-12), (Coed), 1325 Ninth St. S.E., 52040. Tel: 563-875-7188; Fax: 563-875-7242. Email: dbqh05@arch.pvt.k12.ia.us. Pat Meade, Prin.; Pat Lehmann, Asst. Prin.; Very Rev. Phillip F. Kruse, Pastoral Coord.; Emmy Brehm, Librarian; Melissa Kenkel, Librarian. Serving the following parishes: St. Francis Xavier, Dyersville; St. Joseph, Earlville; St. Boniface, New Vienna; Ss. Peter and Paul, Petersburg; St. Paul, Worthington. Lay Teachers 35; Students 481.

[E] SCHOOLS OF RELIGION

CALMAR. *Christian Family School of Religion* Serving: St. Aloysius, Calmar; Our Lady of Seven Dolors, Festina; St. Francis de Sales, Ossian; St. Wenceslaus, Spillville, 107 E. South St., P.O. Box 821, 52312. Tel: 563-562-3045; Fax: 563-562-3292. Email: cfsrstaff@mchsi.com. Rev. Msgr. Cletus J. Hawes, Pastoral Coord.; Patty Frana, D.R.E. Priests 1; Lay Teachers 1; Students 158.

MANCHESTER. *St. Paul School of Religion*, (Grades 7-12), Serving: St. Mary, Manchester; Immaculate Conception, Masonville; St. Patrick, Ryan, 408 Clara Ave., 52057. Tel: 563-927-2900; Fax: 563-927-6506. Email: stpaulsor@iowatelecom.net. Rev. John R. Flaherty, Pastoral Coord.; Kathy Oberrueter, Dir. of Catechetical Programming. Priests 1; Lay Teachers 3; Students 295.

NEW HAMPTON. *St. John School of Religion* Serving: St. Bernard, Alta Vista; St. Boniface, Ionia; Our Lady of Lourdes, Lourdes; Holy Family, New Hampton; Immaculate Conception, North Washington, 823 W. Main St., Box 108, 50659. Tel: 641-394-3171. Email: dbqrt4@arch.pvt.k12.ia.us. Rev. Msgr. Carl L. Schmitt, Pastoral Coord.; Marjorie Zipse, Dir. Priests 1; Lay Teachers 3; Students 149.

[F] ELEMENTARY SCHOOL SYSTEMS

CALMAR. *Calmar-Festina-Spillville Catholic School*, (Grades PreSchool-8), 302 S. Maryville, Box 815, 52132. Tel: 563-562-3291; Fax: 563-562-3292. Email: dbqe05@arch.pvt.k12.ia.us. Katie Schmitt, Prin.; Rev. Donald J. Hawes, Pastoral Coord. Consolidation of the following parishes: Our Lady of Seven Dolors (St. Mary), Festina; St. Wenceslaus, Spillville; St. Aloysius, Calmar; St. Wenceslaus (Grades K-3); St. Aloysius (Grades 4-8). Lay Teachers 12; Students 121.

CEDAR RAPIDS. *Holy Family Consolidated School*, (Grades Day Care-8) Rick Louk, Prin.; Rev. Philip E. Thompson, Pastoral Coord. Parishes Served: John XXIII, St. Jude, St. Ludmila and St. Patrick, Cedar Rapids; St. Patrick, Fairfax. Lay Teachers 42; Students 545.

LaSalle Middle School (Grades 5-8), 3700 First Ave. N.W., 52405. Tel: 319-396-7792; Fax: 319-390-6527. Email: dbqe12@arch.pvt.k12.ia.us. Rick Louk, Prin.; Rev. Philip E. Thompson, Pastoral Coord.

St. Ludmila Center (Grades Day Care-4), 215 21st Ave. S.W., 52404. Tel: 319-362-1943; Fax: 319-364-4149. Email: dbqe10@arch.pvt.k12.ia.us. Janet Whitney, Assoc. Admin.

St. Jude Elementary (Grades Day Care-2), 3700 First Ave. N.W., 52405. Tel: 319-396-7818; Fax: 319-390-0952. Email: dbqe09@arch.pvt.k12.ia.us. Ronda Krystofiak, Assoc. Admin.

St. Pius and St. Elizabeth Ann Seton Schools, (Grades PreSchool-5), 4901 Council St. N.E., 52402-2402. Tel: 319-393-4507; Fax: 319-393-0216. Email: dbqe13@arch.pvt.k12.ia.us. Candace Hurley, Prin.; Marilyn Olson, Librarian. Lay Teachers 25; Students 492.

Regis Middle School, (Grades 6-8), Parishes Served: All Saints, Immaculate Conception, St. Matthew, St. Pius X, Cedar Rapids; St. Elizabeth Ann Seton, Hiawatha, 735 Prairie Dr. N.E., 52402. Tel: 319-363-1968; Fax: 319-247-6099. Email: dbqmM02@arch.pvt.k12.ia.us. Rev. Donald L. Klein, Pastoral Coord.; Rick Blackwell, Prin.; Cindy Glynn, Asst. Prin. Lay Teachers 26; Students 426.

DYERSVILLE. *St. Francis Xavier School, Dyersville, Iowa*, (Grades PreSchool-6), 203 Second St., S.W., 52040. Tel: 563-875-7376; Fax: 563-875-7037. Peter Smith, Prin. Lay Teachers 28; Students 425.

FARLEY. *Seton Catholic Schools*, (Grades PreK-8), St. Joseph Center: 210 Second St. S.E., 52046. Tel: 563-744-3290; Fax: 563-744-3450. Email: dbqe28@arch.pvt.k12.ia.us. St. Patrick Center: 106 First St., S.E., Epworth, 52045. Tel: 563-876-5586; Fax: 563-876-3055. St. John Center: 10801 Sundown Rd., Peosta, 52068. Tel: 563-556-5967; Fax: 563-556-7579. Mary Smock, Prin.; Melissa O'Brien, Asst. Prin.; Rev. Richard W. Kuhn, Pastoral Coord. Consolidation of the following parishes: St. Patrick, Epworth; St. John, Peosta; St. John, Placid; St. Joseph, Farley; St. Clement, Bankston. Lay Teachers 27; Students 383.

GUTTENBERG. *St. Mary and Immaculate Conception School System*, (Grades K-8), 510 S. Second St., P.O. Box 100, 52052. Tel: 563-252-1577; Fax: 563-252-1363. Email: dbqe32@arch.pvt.k12.ia.us. Sr. Suzanne Gallagher, P.B.V.M., Prin.; Rev. Marvin J. Bries, Pastoral Coord. Consolidation of the following parishes: St. Mary, Guttenberg; Immaculate Conception, North Buena Vista. Sisters 1; Lay Teachers 8; Students 106.

HOLY CROSS. *LaSalle Elementary Schools*, (Grades PreSchool-8), Holy Cross Center: 835 Church St., P.O. Box 368, 52053-0368. Tel: 563-870-2405; Fax: 563-870-4101. Email: dbqe34@arch.pvt.k12.ia.us. Holy Trinity Center: 100 W. Main St., P.O. Box 139, Luxemburg, 52056. Tel: 563-853-2325. John Pesetski, Prin.; Rev. Raymond A. Burkle, Pastoral Coord. Consolidation of the following parishes: St. Joseph, Rickardsville; Holy Cross, Holy Cross; Holy Trinity, Luxemburg (Grades K-3); SS. Peter and Paul, Sherrill; St. Francis of Assisi, Balltown. Lay Teachers 13; Students 130.

MARSHALLTOWN. *Marshalltown Area Catholic Schools*, (Grades Day Care-6), St. Mary Center: 10 W. Linn St., 50158. Tel: 641-753-7977; Fax: 641-753-0337. Email: dbqe40@arch.pvt.k12.ia.us. St. Henry Center: 310 Columbus Dr., 50158. Tel: 641-753-8744. James Wessling, Prin.; Rev. James L. Miller, Pastoral Coord.; Carol Johnson, Librarian. Serving the following parishes: St. Mary, Marshalltown (Grades 3-6); St. Henry, Marshalltown (Grades K-2). Lay Teachers 16; Students 216.

NEW VIENNA. *Archbishop Hennessy Catholic School*, (Grades PreK-6), St. Boniface Center: 7420 Columbus, P.O. Box 170, 52065. Tel: 563-921-2635; Fax: 563-921-3003. Email: dbqe33@arch.pvt.k12.ia.us. SS. Peter & Paul Center: 1623 300th Ave., Dyersville, 52040. Tel: 563-875-7572. Vicki Palmer, Prin.; Rev. John J. O'Connor, Pastoral Coord. Consolidation of the following parishes: St. Boniface Center (Grades K-3), New Vienna; SS. Peter & Paul Center (Grades PreK, 4-6), Petersburg. Sisters 2; Lay Teachers 8; Students 66.

PROTIVIN. *Trinity Catholic School*, (Grades K-6), 116 N. Main St., 52163-0246. Tel: 563-569-8556; Fax: 563-569-8477. Email: dbqe47@arch.pvt.k12.ia.us. Dana Spry, Prin.; Rev. David M. Beckman, Pastoral Coord. Consolidation of the following parishes: Holy Trinity, Protivin; St. Luke, St. Lucas; St. John, Fort Atkinson. Lay Teachers 8; Students 52.

[G] CONSOLIDATED K-12 SYSTEMS

DUBUQUE. *Holy Family Catholic Schools*, (Grades Day Care-12), 2005 Kane St., 52001. Tel: 563-582-5456; Fax: 563-583-3885. Steven Cornelius, Chief Admin.; Todd Wessels, Curriculum Dir.; Rev. Msgr. Wayne A. Ressler, Pastoral Coord. Serving the parishes of Dubuque and Key West. Sisters 3; Lay Teachers 140; K-12 2,186.

St. Joseph the Worker Early Childcare Center, 2105 Saint Joseph St., 52001. Tel: 563-582-1246; Fax: 563-588-3960.

St. Mary Childcare Center, 1600 White St., 52001. Tel: 563-583-5153; Fax: 563-585-1818.

Trinity Square Childcare Center, 1703 Rhomberg Ave., 52001. Tel: 563-582-2578; Fax: 563-582-1048.

Holy Ghost School (Grades PreSchool-5), 2981 Central Ave., 52001. Tel: 563-556-1511; Fax: 563-556-4768. Email: dbqe17@arch.pvt.k12.ia.us. Denise Grant, Prin.

Resurrection School (Grades Day Care-5), 4300 Asbury Rd., 52002. Tel: 563-583-9488; Fax: 563-557-7995. Email: dbqe20@arch.pvt.k12.ia.us. Dave Gross, Prin.

St. Anthony School (Grades Day Care-5), 2175 Rosedale, 52001. Tel: 563-556-2820; Fax: 563-556-2131. Email: dbqe17@arch.pvt.k12.ia.us. Denise Grant, Prin.

St. Columbkille School (Grades Day Care-5), 1198 Rush St., 52003. Tel: 563-582-3532; Fax: 563-583-4884. Email: dbqe22@arch.pvt.k12.ia.us. Barb Roling, Prin.

Mazzuchelli Catholic Middle School (Grades 6-8), 2005 Kane St., 52001. Tel: 563-582-1198; Fax: 563-582-5428. Email: dbqm03@arch.pvt.k12.ia.us. Kim Hermsen, Prin.; Doug Varley, Asst. Prin.

Wahlert High School, 2005 Kane St., 52001. Tel: 563-583-9771; Fax: 563-583-9775. Email: dbqh04@arch.pvt.k12.ia.us. Donald Sisler, Prin.; Cyndi Wagner, Asst. Admin. Parishes Served: The Parishes in Dubuque; Holy Family, New Melleray; St. Joseph's, Key West.

BELLEVUE. *Marquette High School*, 502 Franklin St., 52031. Tel: 563-872-3356; Fax: 563-872-3285. Email: dbqe04@arch.pvt.k12.ia.us. Jim Squiers, Prin.; Randy Rubel, Curriculum Dir. & Business Mgr.; Rev. Stephen L. Meyer, Pastoral Coord. Parishes Served: St. John, Andrew; St. Joseph, Bellevue; St. Peter, Sabula; St. Catherine, St. Catherine; St. Donatus, St. Donatus; SS. Peter and Paul, Springbrook. Sisters 1; Lay Teachers 19; Students 271.

Bellevue Area Elementary School (Grades Day Care-8), 403 Park St., 52031. Tel: 563-872-3284; Fax: 563-872-3285. Jim Squiers, Prin.; Randy Rubel, Curriculum Dir. & Business Mgr.; Rev. Stephen L. Meyer, Pastoral Coord. Parishes Served: St. Joseph, Bellevue; SS. Peter & Paul, Springbrook; St. Donatus, St. Donatus.

CASCADE. *Aquin Educational System*, (Grades Day Care-12), Serving: St. Matthais, Cascade; Sacred Heart, Fillmore; St. Patrick, Garryowen; St. Peter, Temple Hill, 608 Third Ave., N.W., P.O. Box 460, 52033-0460. Tel: 563-852-7875; Fax: 563-852-5269. Email: dbqcdir@arch.pvt.k12.ia.us. Bro. Stephen W. Markham, F.S.C., Pastoral Coord.; Rebecca Smith, D.R.E. Brothers 1; Lay Teachers 20; K-8 248.

Little Angels (Grades Day Care), 608 Third Ave., N.W., P.O. Box 460, 52033-0460. Tel: 563-852-7020.

Aquin Elementary School (Grades PreSchool-8), 608 Third Ave., N.W., P.O. Box 460, 52033-0460. Tel: 563-852-3331; Fax: 563-852-5269. Email: dbqe06@arch.pvt.k12.ia.us. Mary Yamoah, Prin.

Aquin School of Religion (Grades 9-12), 608 Third Ave., N.W., P.O. Box 460, 52033-0460. Tel: 563-852-7875; Fax: 563-852-5269. Email: dbq023re@arch.pvt.k12.ia.us. Rebecca Smith, D.R.E.

GILBERTVILLE. *Don Bosco High School*, (Grades K-12), 405 16th Ave., 50634. Tel: 319-296-1692; Fax: 319-296-1693. Email: dbqH06@arch.pvt.k12.ia.us. Eric Eckerman, Prin.; Rev. Dennis J. Colter, Spiritual Dir. Parishes Served: St. Francis, Barclay; St. Mary of Mt. Carmel, Eagle Center; Immaculate Conception, Gilbertville; St. Athanasius, Jesup; Sacred Heart, LaPorte City; St. Joseph, Raymond. Lay Teachers 37; Students 413.

Gilbertville-Raymond Consolidation (Grades K-8), *Immaculate Conception Center*, 311 16th Ave., 50634. Tel: 319-296-1089; Fax: 319-296-3847. *St. Joseph Center*, 6916 Layafette Rd., P.O. Box 158, Raymond, 50667. Tel: 319-233-5980. Email: dbqe31@arch.pvt.k12.ia.us. Julie Niemeyer, Prin.; Rev. Kenneth C. Stecher, Pastoral Coord. Parishes served: Immaculate Conception, Gilbertville & St. Joseph, Raymond

MASON CITY. *Newman School System* formerly Newman Catholic School System , (Grades Day Care-12), 2000 S. McKinley Ave., 50401. Tel: 641-423-3101; Fax: 641-422-1181. Parishes served: Holy Family, St. Joseph, Mason City. Sisters 1; Lay Teachers 42; K-12 592.

Newman Child Care formerly Newman Catholic Child Care 2050 S. McKinley Ave., 50401. Tel: 641-423-0168; Fax: 641-423-3521. Kathy Lloyd, Early Childhood Dir.

Newman Elementary School (Grades K-8), 2000 S. McKinley Ave., 50401. Tel: 641-423-3101; Fax: 641-422-1181. Email: dbqe41@arch.pvt.k12.ia.us. Jan Avery, Admin.; Rev. Michael G. Schueller, Pastoral Coord.

Newman High School, 2445 19th St. S.W., 50401. Tel: 641-423-6939; Fax: 641-423-6653. Email: dbqh07@arch.pvt.k12.ia.us. Tony Adams, Prin.; Rev. Michael G. Schueller, Pastoral Coord. Parishes Served: St. Patrick, Clear Lake; Sacred Heart, Manly; Holy Family, St. Joseph, Mason City; Sacred Heart, Rockwell.

WATERLOO. *Cedar Valley Catholic Schools*, (Grades Day Care-12), 3231 W. 9th St., 50702. Tel: 319-232-1422; Fax: 319-232-3977. Cathy Walz, Dir. Educ.; Rev. Louis M. Jaeger, Pastoral Coord. Lay Teachers 78; Students (K-12) 1,054.

Blessed Sacrament School (Grades Day Care-8), 600 Stephan Ave., 50701. Tel: 319-233-7863; Fax: 319-233-8237. Email: dbqe49@arch.pvt.k12.ia.us. Nancy Stirm, Prin.

Sacred Heart School (Grades Day Care-8), 620 W. 5th St., 50702. Tel: 319-234-6593; Fax: 319-235-7987. Email: dbqe50@arch.pvt.k12.ia.us. Amy Sandvold, Prin.

St. Edward School (Grades Day Care-8), 139 E. Mitchell, 50702. Tel: 319-233-6202; Fax: 319-235-2898. Email: dbqe51@arch.pvt.k12.ia.us. Pam Schowalter, Prin.

Columbus High School, 3231 W. 9th St., 50702. Tel: 319-233-3358; Fax: 319-235-0733. Email: dbqh08@arch.pvt.k12.ia.us. Mr. Tom Ulses, Prin.; Rev. Louis M. Jaeger, Pastoral Coord. Parishes Served: St. Patrick's, Cedar Falls; Blessed Sacrament, Queen of Peace, Sacred Heart and St. Edward, Waterloo.

[H] GENERAL HOSPITALS

DUBUQUE. *Mercy Medical Center-Dubuque* (A Division of Mercy Health Services-Iowa), 250 Mercy Dr., 52001. Tel: 563-589-8000; Fax: 563-589-8073. Web: www.mercydubuque.com. Russell Knight, Pres.; Patrick Conlon, Dir. Pastoral Care Dept.; Sisters Maureen Fury, B.V.M., Chap.; Rosalyn Ulfers, P.B.V.M., Chap.; Gabrielle Hoefer, R.S.M., Chap.; Maryann Dunn, Chap.; Rev. Richard L. Schaefer, Chap.; Deacon William Biver, Chap. Bed Capacity 263; Total Staff 1,265; Patients Assisted Annually 47,376.

CEDAR FALLS. **Sartori Health Care Foundation, Inc.*, 515 College St., 50613. Tel: 319-268-3161; Fax: 319-268-3270. Heather Bremer-Miller, Devel. Dir.

Sartori Memorial Hospital, Inc. (Formerly known as S.F.H., Inc.), 515 College St., 50613. Tel: 319-268-3000; Fax: 319-268-3270. Email: jack.dusenbery@wfhc.org. Jack Dusenbery, Contact Person. Bed Capacity 101; Patients Assisted Annually 42,138; Total Staff 217.

CEDAR RAPIDS. *Mercy Medical Center, Endowment Foundation, Inc., Cedar Rapids, IA*, 701 Tenth St. S.E., 52403. Tel: 319-398-6206. Sue Hawn, Pres.; Sr. James Marie Donahue, R.S.M., Ph.D., Chairwoman of the Bd.

Mercy Medical Center-Cedar Rapids (Sisters of Mercy-Regional Community of Cedar Rapids), 701 Tenth St. S.E., 52403. Tel: 319-398-6011. Email: kcrist@mercycare.org. Web: www.mercycare.org. Tim Charles, Pres. & CEO; Revs. David J. Ambrosy, Resident Chap.; Ken Glandorf, Chap.; Susan Sweeney, Dir. Pastoral Care Office; Mark Eccles, Chap.; Deacon Daniel Hoeger, Chap.; Sr. Margaret Murphy, R.S.M., Chap. Sponsored by the Sisters of Mercy, West Midwest Community. Total Staff 2,184; Bed Capacity Acute 369; Skilled Nursing 21; Patients Assisted Annually 300,000.

Mercycare Service Corporation (Parent Corp.), 701 10th St. S.E., 52403. Tel: 319-398-6011. Tim Charles, CEO & Pres. Sponsored by the Sisters of Mercy, West Midwest Community.

DYERSVILLE. *Mercy Medical Center-Dubuque (Dyersville)* (A Division of Mercy Health Services Iowa), 1111 Third St. S.W., 52040. Tel: 563-875-7101; Fax: 563-875-2957. Web: www.mercydubuque.com. Russell Knight, Pres. Bed Capacity 25; Total Staff 44; Patients Assisted Annually 4,915.

MASON CITY. *Mercy Medical Center-North Iowa* (Member of Mercy Health Network), 1000 4th St. S.W., 50401. Tel: 641-422-7000; Fax: 641-422-7827. James G. Fitzpatrick, Pres. & CEO; Very Rev. Kenneth B. Gehling, Chap.; Rev. Barbara McCaulley, Chap. (Episcopal); Sisters Joyce Kolbert, S.S.N.D., Chap.; Carmen Hernandez, P.B.V.M., Spec. Populations Outreach Coord.; Susan Kennedy, Chap. (Evangelical). Bed Capacity 346; Total Staff 2,625; Patients Assisted Annually 542,595.

NEW HAMPTON. *Mercy Medical Center-New Hampton* (Member of Mercy Health Network), 308 N. Maple Ave., 50659. Tel: 641-394-4121; Fax: 641-394-1669. Web: www.mercynewhampton.com. Bruce Roesler, Pres. & CEO; Richard Kriener, Bd. Chm., Member Organization Board; Rev. John Harpel, S.V.D., Chap. Bed Capacity 18; Patients Assisted Annually 33,047; Total Staff 127.

OELWEIN. *Mercy Hospital of Franciscan Sisters, Inc.* formerly Mercy Hospital of Franciscan Sisters , 201 8th Ave. S.E., 50662. Tel: 319-283-6000; Fax: 319-283-6004. Jack Dusenbery, Contact Person, Pres. & CEO. Franciscan Sisters. Daughters of the Sacred Hearts of Jesus and Mary, Wheaton, IL. Bed Capacity 64; Patients Assisted Annually 26,908; Total Staff 142.

WATERLOO. *Covenant Foundation, Inc.*, 3421 W. Ninth St., 50702. Tel: 319-272-7676; Fax: 319-272-5093. Email: heather.bremermiller@wfhc.org. Heather Bremer-Miller, Exec. Dir.

Covenant Medical Center, Inc., 3421 W. Ninth St., 50702. Tel: 319-272-8000; Fax: 319-272-7313. Email: jack.dusenbery@wfhc.org. Web: www.covhealth.com. Jack Dusenbery, Pres. & Contact Person. Franciscan Sisters. Daughters of the Sacred Hearts of Jesus and Mary, Wheaton, IL. Total Staff 1,297; Bed Capacity 346; Patients Assisted Annually 238,303.

Wheaton Franciscan Healthcare-Iowa, Inc., 3421 W. Ninth St., 50702. Tel: 319-272-8000; Fax: 319-272-7313. Jack Dusenbery, Pres. & Contact Person.

[I] SPECIAL HEALTH CENTERS

DUBUQUE. *Holy Family Hall Infirmary*, 3340 Windsor Ave., 52001-1300. Tel: 563-583-9786; Fax: 563-583-6080. Email: info@osfdbq.org. Web: www.osfdbq.org. Rev. Ronald G. Friedell, Chap.; Sisters Helen Nelson, O.S.F., Dir. Sister Support Svcs.; Nancy Schreck, O.S.F., Pres. Sisters of St. Francis, Dubuque. Bed Capacity 94; Professed Sisters 75; Total Staff 100; Patients Assisted Annually 100.

Marian Hall Infirmary, 1050 Carmel Dr., 52003. Tel: 563-556-5474; Fax: 563-588-1975. Email: bvmcenter@bvmcong.org. Web: www.bvmcong.org. Rev. Msgr. Robert R. Vogl, Chap. (Retired); Joyce Cravens, Admin. Professed Sisters 87; Bed Capacity 106; Total Staff 107.

Caritas Center, 1130 Carmel Dr., 52003-7911. Tel: 563-556-3240. Email: bvmcenter@bvmcong.org. Web: www.bvmcong.org. Joyce Cravens, Admin. Professed Sisters 46; Bed Capacity 53; Total Staff 98.

[J] HOMES FOR AGED

DUBUQUE. *Stonehill Franciscan Services, Inc.*, 3485 Windsor Ave., 52001-1312. Tel: 563-557-7180; Fax: 563-584-9282. Email: ethomas@stonehilldbq.com. Web: www.stonehilldbq.com. Terry Friedman, Svcs. Bd. Pres.; Eric L. Thomas, Pres. & CEO. Bed Capacity 290; Total Staff 305; Total Assisted Annually 490; Residents-Retirement Units 51.

Stonehill Benevolent Foundation Tel: 563-557-7180; Fax: 563-584-9282. Stephen J. Schmall, Chair, Stonehill Benevolent Foundation Board. Sponsored by Sisters of St. Francis of the Holy Family.

Villa Raphael, 1155 Mt. Loretta Ave., 52003. Tel: 563-588-2049. Email: dbqvilla@arch.pvt.k12.ia.us. Patricia Flores, Dir. Administered by the Archdiocese of Dubuque.; Accommodations for 16 priests. Total in Residence 15; Total Staff 5.

CEDAR RAPIDS. *Hallmar-Mercy Medical Center*, 701 Tenth St. S.E., 52403. Tel: 319-398-6241. Tim Charles, CEO/Pres. Sisters of Mercy, West Midwest Community., Cedar Rapids Regional, owned and operated by Mercy Medical Center. Home for Aged. Total Assisted 50; Residents 55; Total Staff 50.

DYERSVILLE. *Ellen Kennedy Living Center*, 1177 7th St., S.W., 52040. Tel: 563-875-6323; Fax: 563-875-6268. Jeanette C. Digmann, Vice Pres. & Contact Person. Sponsor: Mercy Medical Center.; Purpose: to provide funds to assure person of limited resources will be able to access programs and services at the Ellen Kennedy Living Center. Assisted Living 32; Independent Living 26; Total Staff 29.

Mercy Medical Center-Dubuque-Dyersville-Oakcrest Manor (A Division of Mercy Health Services - Iowa), 1111 Third St. S.W., 52040. Tel: 563-875-7101; Fax: 563-875-2957. Web: www.mercydubuque.com. Russell Knight, Pres. Bed Capacity 40; Patients Assisted Annually 60; Total Staff 42.

[K] MONASTERIES AND RESIDENCES OF PRIESTS AND BROTHERS

PEOSTA. *New Melleray Abbey, Order of Cistercians of the Strict Observance*, 6632 Melleray Cir., 52068. Tel: 563-588-2319; Fax: 563-588-4117. Email: monks@newmelleray.org. Web: www.newmelleray.org. Rt. Rev. David R. Bock, O.C.S.O., Retired Abbot (Retired); Revs. Bernard J. Cullen, O.C.S.O.; Xavier L. Dieter, O.C.S.O.; Alberic R. Farbolin, O.C.S.O.; Rt. Rev. Brendan J. Freeman, O.C.S.O., Abbot; Revs. James B. Henderson, O.C.S.O.; Thaddeus J. Kennedy, O.C.S.O.; Rt. Rev. James J. Kerndt, O.C.S.O., Retired Abbot; Revs. Daniel F. Lenihan, O.C.S.O.; Thomas A. MacMaster, O.C.S.O.; James E. O'Connor, O.C.S.O.; Neil Paquette, O.C.S.O., Prior; Kenneth F. Tietjen, O.C.S.O.; Stephen Verbest, O.C.S.O., Novice, Sub-Prior & Vocation Dir.; Jonah Wharff, O.C.S.O.; Bros. Albert Bracket, O.C.S.O.; Gilbert B. Cardillo, O.C.S.O.; Juan Diego, O.C.S.O., Novice; Michael Gajarski, O.C.S.O., Novice; Cyprian Griffith, O.C.S.O.; Paul Halaburt, O.C.S.O.; Kevin Knox, O.C.S.O.; Nicholas Koenig, O.C.S.O.; Joseph Kronebusch, O.C.S.O.; Felix Leja, O.C.S.O.; John O'Driscoll, O.C.S.O.; Ephrem Poppish, O.C.S.O.; Walter Schoenberg, O.C.S.O.; Tobias Shanahan, O.C.S.O.; Robert Simon, O.C.S.O.; Paul Andrew Tanner, O.C.S.O.; Dennis Vavra, O.C.S.O.; Placid Zilka, O.C.S.O.; Rt. Rev. David Wechter, O.C.S.O., Retired Abbot (Retired).

Corporation of New Melleray Total in Residence 33; Priests 15; Brothers 19; Absent on Medical Leave 3; Chaplains 1.

[L] CONVENTS AND RESIDENCES FOR SISTERS

DUBUQUE. *St. Joseph's Convent, Mount Carmel*, 1150 Carmel Dr., 52003. Tel: 563-556-3240. Email: bvmcenter@bvmcong.org. Web: www.bvmcong.org. Joyce Cravens, Admin.; Rev. Msgr. Thomas E. Toale, Ph.D., Chap.; Sr. Thea O'Meara, B.V.M., Contact Person. Motherhouse of the Sisters of Charity of the Blessed Virgin Mary. Professed Sisters 71; Total Staff 37; Bed Capacity 81.

Mt. Loretto Convent, 2360 Carter Rd., 52001-2997. Tel: 563-588-2008; Fax: 563-588-4463. Email: jennifer@dubuquepresentations.org. Web: www.dubuquepresentations.org. Sisters Jennifer Rausch, P.B.V.M., Pres.; Ruth Ann Takes, P.B.V.M., Dir.; Rev. Douglas O. Wathier, S.T.D., Chap. Motherhouse and Novitiate of the Sisters of the Presentation of the B.V.M. Professed Sisters 68.

International Presentation Association Tel: 212-370-0075; Fax: 212-370-0075. Email: ipanetworker@pbvm.org.au. Web: ipa.ozehosting.com.

Mt. St. Francis, 3390 Windsor Ave., 52001-1311. Tel: 563-583-9786; Fax: 563-583-3250. Email: info@osfdbq.org. Web: www.osfdbq.org. Sisters Marie Cigrand, O.S.F., Contact Person; Nancy Schreck, O.S.F., Pres.; Pat R. Farrell, O.S.F., Vice Pres.; Rev. Robert R. Beck, Chap. Sisters of St. Francis of the Holy Family Charitable Trust., Motherhouse and Novitiate of the Sisters of St. Francis of the Holy Family. Professed Sisters 100.

Our Lady of the Mississippi Abbey, 8400 Abbey Hill Ln., 52003. Tel: 563-582-2595; Fax: 563-582-5511. Email: sisters@olmabbey.org. Web: www.mississippiabbey.org. Sr. Nettie Gamble, O.C.S.O., Abbess; Rev. Xavier L. Dieter, O.C.S.O., Chap. The Cistercian Nuns of the Strict Observance., (Monastery of Trappistine Nuns). Professed Nuns 21; Novices 1.

Sisters of Charity of the Blessed Virgin Mary, BVM Center, Mount Carmel, 1100 Carmel Dr., 52003-7991. Tel: 563-588-2351; Fax: 563-588-4832. Email: bvmcenter@bvmcong.org. Web: www.bvmcong.org. Sisters Mary Ann Zollmann, B.V.M., Pres. Congregation; Mira Mosle, B.V.M., 1st Vice Pres.; Teri Hadro, B.V.M., 2nd Vice Pres.; Deanna Marie Carr, B.V.M., Archivist. Total Staff 31.

Sisters of the Visitation, 2950 Kaufmann Ave., 52001-1631. Tel: 563-556-2440. Email: dbqsvm@arch.pvt.k12.ia.us. Sr. Patricia Clark, S.V.M., Pres. & Contact Person. Sisters of the Visitation of the Congregation of the Immaculate Heart of Mary. Professed Sisters 5.

CEDAR RAPIDS. *Sisters of Mercy of the Americas West Midwest Community, Inc. Sacred Heart Convent*, 1125 Prairie Dr., N.E., 52402-4737. Tel: 319-364-5196; Fax: 319-364-7383. Email: info@mercywmw.org. Web: www.mercywestmidwest.org. Theresa Baldus-Kokontis, Admin.; Sisters Norita Cooney, R.S.M., Pres.; Judith Frikker, R.S.M., Substitute for Pres.; Sheila Megley, R.S.M., Treas.; Judith Cannon, R.S.M., Sec.; Kathy Thornton, R.S.M., Leadership Team; Michelle Gorman, R.S.M., Leadership Team; Kim Kinsel, Community Oper. Officer; Carol Kelley, Community Fin. Officer; Sandy Goetzinger-Comer, Dir. Communications. Motherhouse of the Sisters of Mercy of the Americas - West Midwest Community.; (As of July 1, 2008 the Sisters of Mercy of the Americas Regional Communities of Auburn, CA; Burlingame, CA; Cedar Rapids, IA; Chicago, IL; Detroit, MI; and Omaha, NE merged to create Sisters of Mercy of the Americas West Midwest Community, Inc.) Sisters 810; Associates 565.

Sisters of Mercy Charitable Trust Tel: 319-364-5196; Fax: 319-364-7383.

Catherine McAuley Center, Cedar Rapids Tel: 319-363-4993; Fax: 319-363-8332.

Mount Mercy College, Cedar Rapids Tel: 319-363-8213; Fax: 319-363-5270. Web: www.mtmercy.edu.

Mercy Medical Center, Cedar Rapids Tel: 319-398-6011; Fax: 319-398-6912.

[M] RETREAT HOUSES

DUBUQUE. *New Melleray Guest House*, 6632 Melleray Cir., Peosta, 52068. Tel: 563-588-2319; Fax: 563-588-4117. Email: monks@newmelleray.org. Web: www.newmelleray.org.

Shalom Retreat Center, 1001 Davis St., 52001-1398. Tel: 563-582-3592; Fax: 563-582-5872. Email: info@shalomretreats.org. Web: www.shalomretreats.org. Sr. Margaret Jungers, O.S.F., Dir. Retreatants 7,500; Total Staff 8.

CEDAR FALLS. *American Martyrs Retreat House*, 2209 North Union Rd., 50613-0028. Tel: 319-266-3543; Fax: 319-266-3543. Email: dbqamrh@arch.pvt.k12.ia.us. Web: americanmartyrs.tripod.com. Sr. Jeanine Kuhn, P.B.V.M., Dir. Total Staff 18.

HIAWATHA. *Prairiewoods Franciscan Spirituality Center*, 120 E. Boyson Rd., 52233-1277. Tel: 319-395-6700; Fax: 319-395-6703. Email: ecospirit@prairiewoods.org. Web: www.prairiewoods.org. Sr. Helen Elsbernd, F.S.P.A., Dir. & Contact Person.

[N] NEWMAN CENTERS

AMES. *St. Thomas Aquinas Church and Catholic Student Center (Iowa State University)* 2210 Lincoln Way, 50014-7184. Tel: 515-292-3810; Fax: 515-292-3841. Email: dbq004@arch.pvt.k12.ia.us. Web: www.staparish.net. Revs. Jon M. Seda; Dennis W. Miller, Campus Min. & Assoc. Pastor; Shari Reilly, Dir. Campus Ministry & Charity, Justice & Peace Coord.; Todd Flowerday, Dir. Liturgy & Music; Robert LeBlanc, Church Business Mgr. & Contact Person; Misty Heinen, Campus Min.; Kathy White, D.R.E.

CEDAR FALLS. *St. Stephen the Witness Catholic Student Center, University of Northern Iowa* 1019 W. 23rd St., 50613-3550. Tel: 319-266-9863; Fax: 319-266-3706. Email: kjglaser@ststephenuni.org. Web: www.ststephenuni.org. Rev. Kenneth J. Glaser, Dir. Campus Ministry; Deacon Leonard Froyen, Ph.D.; Erin Kass, Campus Min.; Anastasia Nicklaus Schmelzer, Dir. of Liturgy & Music; Kelly McCormick, Devel. Coord. & Business Mgr.; Lisa Geisler, Office Mgr. Total Staff 6.

FAYETTE. *Upper Iowa University* 605 Washington St., P.O. Box 1857, 52142. Tel: 563-425-5200; Fax: 563-425-5323.

[O] MISCELLANEOUS

DUBUQUE. *Archdiocese of Dubuque Deposit and Loan Fund*, 1229 Mt. Loretta, 52003-8787. Tel: 563-556-2580; Fax: 563-556-5464. Email: DBQCFO@arch.pvt.k12.ia.us. Richard L. Runde, Finance Officer.

Archdiocese of Dubuque Education Fund, 1229 Mt. Loretta, 52003-8787. Tel: 563-556-2580; Fax: 563-556-5464. Email: DBQCFO@arch.pvt.12.ia.us. Richard L. Runde, Finance Officer.

Archdiocese of Dubuque Perpetual Care Fund, 1229 Mt. Loretta, 52003-8787. Tel: 563-556-2580; Fax: 563-556-5464. Email: DBQCFO@arch.pvt.k12.ia.us. Richard L. Runde, Finance Officer.

Archdiocese of Dubuque Seminarian Education Fund, 1229 Mt. Loretta, 52003-8787. Tel: 563-556-2580; Fax: 563-556-5464. Email: DBQCFO@arch.pvt.k12.ia.us. Richard L. Runde, Finance Officer.

Cistercian Studies Quarterly, Inc., Mississippi Abbey, 8400 Abbey Hill, 52003. Tel: 563-582-2595; Fax: 563-582-5511. Email: csq@mississippiabbey.org. Web: www.cistercian-studies-quarterly.org. Carrie Stolmeier, Admin. & Contact Person. Sponsor: Cistercian Order of the Strict Observance of the USA Region.

Declaration of Trust of the Paul & Janet Auterman Charitable Educational Trust, 4300 Asbury Rd., 52002. Tel: 563-556-7511; Fax: 563-556-7419. Mr. Virgil Blocker, Co-Trustee & Contact Person. Archdiocese of Dubuque, Resurrection Parish, Purpose: To establish a fund to assist students in attending Catholic schools, Pre-K through grade 12, and for such related purposes as allowed by Internal Revenue code Section 501(c)(3) of the 1986 Internal Revenue Code, as amended, or any successor section.

Heartland Housing Initiative, 90 Main St., 52001. Tel: 563-583-9653; Fax: 563-583-6490. Email: jschmidt@mercyhousing.org. Julie Schmidt, Contact Person & Property Mgr., Sponsored by the Wheaton Franciscan Sisters, Wheaton, IL and a corporation of Wheaton Franciscan System. (A member of the Mercy Housing System, Mercy Housing Corp.) Total Staff 3; Total Assisted 282.

Hennessy Charitable Trust, 2360 Carter Rd., 52001-2997. Tel: 563-588-2008; Fax: 563-588-4463. Email: lynn@dubuquepresentations.org. Web: www.dubuquepresentations.org. Sisters Jennifer Rausch, P.B.V.M., Pres.; Lynn Fangman, P.B.V.M., Contact Person. Sponsored by the Sisters of the Presentation.

Opening Doors, 1561 Jackson St., 52001. Tel: 563-582-7480; Fax: 563-582-7467. Email: mbrown@openingdoorsdbq.org. Web: www.openingdoorsdbq.org. Art Roche, Bd. Pres.; Michelle Brown, Exec. Dir. & Contact Person. Sponsors: Sinsinawa Dominicans, Sisters of the Presentation, Sisters of Charity, B.V.M, Sisters of the Visitation and Dubuque Franciscan Sisters., Purpose: Maria House provides transitional housing and related support services for women and children at 1561 Jackson Street. Teresa Shelter provides emergency shelter for women and children at 1111 Bluff Street. Total Assisted Annually 320.

Maria House, 1561 Jackson St., 52001.

Teresa Shelter, 1111 Bluff St., 52001. Tel: 563-690-0086.

Our Faith, Our Children, Our Future, School Tuition Organization formerly Our Faith, Our Children, Our Future School Tuition Organization, Inc. 1229 Mt. Loretta Ave., 52003-7800. Tel: 563-556-2580. Richard L. Runde, Contact Person. Purpose: to provide tuition assistance to students enrolled in accredited non-public schools located within the Archdiocese of Dubuque in conformance with the Iowa law.

Presentation Lantern, 1501 Jackson St., Ste. B, 52001. Tel: 563-557-7134; Fax: 563-557-7466. Email: corinemurray@aol.com. Sr. Corine Murray, P.B.V.M., Exec. Dir. & Contact Person.

Second Chances, 2600 Dodge St., 52003. Tel: 563-583-5474. Lynn Siegert, Contact Person. Sponsored by the Archdiocese of Dubuque., Purpose: providing financial assistance for the operation of Wahlert High School and Holy Family Catholic Schools of Dubuque.

Society of St. Vincent de Paul Particular Council of the City of Dubuque, Iowa Gary Anglin, National Trustee & Contact Person.

Dubuque Council, 4990 Radford Rd., 52002. Tel: 563-584-2226; Fax: 563-690-1581. Gary Anglin, Natl. Trustee & Contact Person.

CEDAR RAPIDS. *Sisters of Mercy of the Americas. Regional Community of Cedar Rapids, Iowa Charitable Trust*, 1125 Prairie Dr., N.E., 52402-4737. Tel: 319-364-5196; Fax: 319-364-7383. Sr. Laura Reicks, R.S.M., Chm.; Theresa Baldus-Kokontis, Admin. Sisters of Mercy of the Americas, West Midwest Community.

St. Vincent de Paul Particular Counsel of Cedar Rapids, Iowa, 928 7th St., S.E., 52401. Tel: 319-365-5091. Robert Crawford, Pres.

WATERLOO. *Ridgeway Place, Inc.*, 155 E. Ridgeway Ave., 50702. Tel: 319-272-2622; Fax: 319-272-2633. Susan Dillberg, Chm. & Contact Person. Assisted Living Housing Units 96; Residents 91; Total Staff 32.

Society of St. Vincent de Paul District Council of Waterloo, Iowa, 320 Broadway St., 50703. Tel: 319-232-3366; Fax: 319-232-5114. Patrick A. Russo, Exec. Dir.; William McGrane, Pres.

WEBSTER CITY. *St. Thomas Aquinas Foundation*, 1000 Des Moines St., 50595-2147. Tel: 515-832-1190; Fax: 515-832-3757. Web: www.stthomaswc.org. Rev. Scott F. Boone, Contact Person. St. Thomas Aquinas Parish.

RELIGIOUS INSTITUTES OF MEN REPRESENTED IN THE ARCHDIOCESE

For further details refer to the corresponding bracketed number in the Religious Institutes of Men or Women section.

[1180]—*Brothers of Saint Pius X*—C.S.P.X.

[0330]—*Brothers of the Christian Schools* (Midwest Prov.)—F.S.C.

[0350]—*Order of Cistercians of the Strict Observance-Trappists* (Our Lady of New Melleray)—O.C.S.O.

[0420]—*Society of the Divine Word* (Northern Prov.)—S.V.D.

[1060]—*Society of the Precious Blood* (Kansas City Province)—C.PP.S.

RELIGIOUS INSTITUTES OF WOMEN REPRESENTED IN THE ARCHDIOCESE

[0670]—*Cistercian Nuns of the Strict Observance*—O.C.S.O.

[2100]—*Congregation of the Humility of Mary* (Davenport, IA)—C.H.M.

[1780]—*Congregation of the Sisters of the Third Order of St. Francis of Perpetual Adoration*—F.S.P.A.

[1070-03]—*Dominican Sisters Congregation of the Most Holy Rosary* (Sinsinawa, WI)—O.P.

[3530]—*Missionary Sisters Servants of the Holy Spirit*—S.Sp.S.

[2960]—*Notre Dame Sisters* (Omaha, NE)—N.D.

[3130]—*Our Lady of Victory Missionary Sisters*—O.L.V.M.

[2970]—*School Sisters of Notre Dame* (Mankato, MN)—S.S.N.D.

[1680]—*School Sisters of St. Francis* (Milwaukee, WI)—O.S.F.

[0430]—*Sisters of Charity of the Blessed Virgin Mary*—B.V.M.

[2575]—*Sisters of Mercy of the Americas* (West Midwest Community)—R.S.M.

[1540]—*Sisters of St. Francis* (Clinton, IA)—O.S.F.

[1570]—*Sisters of St. Francis of the Holy Family*—O.S.F.

[3320]—*Sisters of the Presentation of the B.V.M.* (Dubuque, IA; Fargo, SD)—P.B.V.M.

[4200]—*Sisters of the Visitation of the Congregation of the Immaculate Heart of Mary* (Dubuque, IA)—S.V.M.

CEMETERIES

DUBUQUE. *Catholic Cemeteries of Dubuque, Inc.*, P.O. Box 479, 52004-0479. Tel: 563-556-2580; Fax: 563-556-5464. Email: dbqcfo@arch.pvt.k12.ia.us.

Mount Calvary

Mount Olivet

CEDAR RAPIDS. *St. John*

St. Joseph

Mount Calvary

MCINTIRE. *St. Patrick*

WATERLOO. *Catholic Cemeteries, Inc.*

NECROLOGY

† Leonard, Rev. Msgr. William P., (Retired)—Died Dec. 10, 2008

† Tobin, Rev. Msgr. Neil W., (Retired)—Died Feb. 10, 2009

† Wheeler, Rev. Msgr. David A., (Retired)—Died March 26, 2009

† Hess, Richard J., (Retired)—Died Sept. 1, 2009

† Hirsch, Robert M., (Retired)—Died March 21, 2009

† Schwinn, Thomas J., (Retired)—Died July 19, 2009

An asterisk (*) denotes an organization that has established tax-exempt status directly with the IRS and is not covered by the USCCB Group Ruling.

Diocese of Duluth

(Dioecesis Duluthensis)

Most Reverend

PAUL D. SIRBA

Bishop of Duluth; ordained May 31, 1986; appointed Bishop of Duluth October 15, 2009; ordained December 14, 2009. *Pastoral Center: 2830 E. Fourth St., Duluth, MN 55812.*

Pastoral Center: 2830 E. Fourth St., Duluth, MN 55812. Tel: 218-724-9111; Fax: 218-724-1056.

Web: www.dioceseduluth.org

Email: duluth@dioceseduluth.org

ESTABLISHED OCTOBER 3, 1889.

Square Miles 22,354.

Corporate Title: Diocese of Duluth.

Comprises the counties of Aitkin, Carlton, Cass, Cook, Crow Wing, Itasca, Koochiching, Lake, Pine and St. Louis in the State of Minnesota.

For legal titles of parishes and diocesan institutions, consult the Chancery Office.

STATISTICAL OVERVIEW

Personnel	
Bishop	1
Priests: Diocesan Active in Diocese	47
Priests: Diocesan Active Outside Diocese	3
Priests: Retired, Sick or Absent	28
Number of Diocesan Priests	78
Religious Priests in Diocese	9
Total Priests in Diocese	87
Extern Priests in Diocese	5
Ordinations:	
Diocesan Priests	2
Transitional Deacons	1
Permanent Deacons in Diocese	42
Total Sisters	115
Parishes	
Parishes	94
With Resident Pastor:	
Resident Diocesan Priests	41
Resident Religious Priests	5
Without Resident Pastor:	
Administered by Priests	47
Administered by Deacons	1
Professional Ministry Personnel:	
Lay Ministers	29
Welfare	
Catholic Hospitals	2
Total Assisted	456,954
Homes for the Aged	5
Total Assisted	697
Day Care Centers	1
Total Assisted	95
Educational	
Diocesan Students in Other Seminaries	20
Total Seminarians	20
Colleges and Universities	1
Total Students	3,746
Elementary Schools, Diocesan and Parish	12
Total Students	1,623
Catechesis/Religious Education:	
High School Students	2,949
Elementary Students	3,455
Total Students under Catholic Instruction	11,793
Teachers in the Diocese:	
Priests	1
Sisters	5
Lay Teachers	305
Vital Statistics	
Receptions into the Church:	
Infant Baptism Totals	679
Minor Baptism Totals	27
Adult Baptism Totals	29
Received into Full Communion	123
First Communions	702
Confirmations	717
Marriages:	
Catholic	138
Interfaith	116
Total Marriages	254
Deaths	831
Total Catholic Population	63,423
Total Population	439,543

Former Bishops—Rt. Revs. JAMES MCGOLRICK, D.D., ord. June 11, 1867; cons. Dec. 27, 1889; died Jan. 23, 1918; JOHN T. MCNICHOLAS, O.P., S.T.D., cons. Sept. 8, 1918; appt. Archbishop of Cincinnati July 8, 1925; died April 22, 1950; Most Revs. THOMAS A. WELCH, D.D., cons. Feb. 3, 1926; died Sept. 9, 1959; FRANCIS J. SCHENK, D.D., cons. May 24, 1945; appt. to Duluth Jan. 19, 1960; resigned April 30, 1969; died Oct. 28, 1969; PAUL F. ANDERSON, D.D., appt. Titular Bishop of Polignando and Coadjutor Bishop with right of succession July 19, 1968; cons. Oct. 17, 1968; succeeded to See April 10, 1969; resigned Aug. 7, 1982; appt. Apostolic Administrator Aug. 7, 1982; appt. Auxiliary Bishop of Sioux Falls, SD March 25, 1983; died Jan. 4, 1987; ROBERT H. BROM, D.D., cons. May 23, 1983; appt. Coadjutor Bishop of San Diego, CA, May 9, 1989; ROGER SCHWIETZ, O.M.I., D.D., ord. Dec. 20, 1967; appt. Bishop of Duluth Dec. 12, 1989; cons. Feb. 2, 1990; appt. Coadjutor Archbishop of Anchorage, Jan. 18, 2000; installed March 24, 2000; succeeded to See March 3, 2001; DENNIS M. SCHNURR, ord. July 20, 1974; appt. Bishop of Duluth Jan. 18, 2001; ord. April 2, 2001; appt. Coadjutor Archbishop of Cincinnati Oct. 17, 2008.

Pastoral Center—2830 E. Fourth St., Duluth, 55812. Tel: 218-724-9111; Fax: 218-724-1056. Office Hours: Mon.-Fri. 8:30-12 & 12:30-4:30.

Vicar General—VACANT.

Finance Officer—Rev. PETER MUHICH, Interim.

Moderator of the Curia—Rev. PETER MUHICH, Interim.

Safe Environment—Rev. DALE NAU.

Chancellor—Rev. JAMES B. BISSONETTE.

Vice Chancellor—Rev. ERIC F. HASTINGS.

Diocesan Tribunal—2830 E. Fourth St., Duluth, 55812. Tel: 218-724-9111.

Judicial Vicar—Rev. JAMES B. BISSONETTE.

Adjutant Judicial Vicar—Rev. ERIC F. HASTINGS.

Vicar for Canonical Affairs—Rev. JAMES B. BISSONETTE.

Defender of the Bond—Rev. DALE NAU.

Promoter of Justice—Rev. DALE NAU.

Advocate—Ms. ELIZABETH DAMBERG.

Auditor—Rev. RICHARD KUNST.

Notary—Mrs. ROSE MARIE EICHMUELLER.

College of Consultors—Revs. FREDRICK METHOD; JOHN O'DONNELL; MICHAEL PATULLO; JEROME WEISS; ANTHONY WROBLEWSKI.

Diocesan Deans—VACANT.

Diocesan Corporate Board—Rev. JAMES B. BISSONETTE; Mr. DARRYL LISOWSKI; Mrs. MARILYN GRATTO.

Diocesan Finance Council—Rev. PETER MUHICH, Interim.

Diocesan Offices and Departments

Archivist (Historical)—Mrs. CHRISTINE SKALKO, 2830 E. Fourth St., Duluth, 55812. Tel: 218-724-9111.

Boy Scouts—Rev. LLOYD MUDRAK, Mailing Address: P.O. Box 290, Coleraine, 55722. Tel: 218-245-1684.

Campus Ministry—Rev. MICHAEL SCHMITZ, 421 St. Marie St., Duluth, 55811. Tel: 218-728-3757.

Cemeteries—Rev. JAMES B. BISSONETTE, 2830 E. Fourth St., Duluth, 55812. Tel: 218-724-9111.

Censor of Books—Rev. ERIC F. HASTINGS.

Council of Catholic Women—Rev. PAUL FRUTH, Moderator, 299 Red Oak Dr., Aitkin, 56431. Tel: 218-927-6581.

Cursillo Movement—Rev. WILLIAM SKARICH, Spiritual Advisor, Mailing Address: 231 E. Camp St., Ely, 55731-1495. Tel: 218-365-4017; WILLIAM SPEISS, Lay Dir., Mailing Address: P.O. Box 402, Emily, 56447.

Department of Catechesis, RCIA, and Lay Apostolate—Mr. BRIAN PIZZALATO, 2830 E. Fourth St., Duluth, 55812. Tel: 218-724-9111.

Department of Catholic Schools—Ms. CYNTHIA ZOOK, 2830 E. Fourth St., Duluth, 55812. Tel: 218-724-9111.

Department of Communications—Mr. KYLE ELLER, 2830 E. Fourth St., Duluth, 55812. Tel: 218-724-9111.

Department of Continuing Formation of Clergy—Rev. DALE NAU, 2830 E. Fourth St., Duluth, 55812. Tel: 218-724-9111.

Department of Development—Mr. MIKE BILDEN, 2830 E. Fourth St., Duluth, 55812. Tel: 218-724-9111.

Department of Indian Ministry—Sr. MARIE ROSE MESSINGSCHLAGER, C.D.P., 2830 E. Fourth St., Duluth, 55812. Tel: 218-724-9111.

Department of Liturgy—Rev. JOEL HASTINGS, 2830 E. Fourth St., Duluth, 55812. Tel: 218-724-9111.

Department of Marriage and Family Life—Ms. GRACE ROMANEK, Contact Person, 2830 E. Fourth St., Duluth, 55812. Tel: 218-724-9111.

Department of Ministry Formation—

Department of Vocations and Priestly Formation—Rev. RICHARD KUNST; Deacon MICHAEL KNUTH, 2830 E. Fourth St., Duluth, 55812. Tel: 218-724-9111.

Department of Permanent Diaconate—Deacon DAVID CRAIG, 2830 E. Fourth St., Duluth, 55812. Tel: 218-724-9111.

Department of Protection of Children & Young People—Mr. ERNIE STAUFFENECKER, 2830 E. Fourth St., Duluth, 55812. Tel: 218-724-9111.

Victim Assistance Coordinators—Mrs. ESTHER REAGAN. Tel: 218-820-9220; Mr. TAB BAUMGARTNER. Tel: 218-249-5495; Mrs. DAYLE PETERSON. Tel: 218-724-5310.

Department of Social Apostolate and CHD—Ms. PATRICE CRITCHLEY-MENOR, 2830 E. Fourth St., Duluth, 55812. Tel: 218-724-9111.

Department of Youth and Young Adult Ministry—Rev. MICHAEL SCHMITZ, 2830 E. Fourth St., Duluth, 55812. Tel: 218-724-9111.

Mission Outreach and Propagation of the Faith—Rev. PETER MUHICH, 2830 E. Fourth St., Duluth, 55812. Tel: 218-724-9111.

Diocesan Newspaper "The Northern Cross"—Mr. KYLE ELLER, Editor, 2830 E. Fourth St., Duluth, 55812. Tel: 218-724-9111.

CLERGY, PARISHES, MISSIONS AND PAROCHIAL SCHOOLS

CITY OF DULUTH

(ST. LOUIS COUNTY)

1—CATHEDRAL OF OUR LADY OF THE ROSARY Revs. Peter Muhich; Joseph T. Sobolik; Deacon Rodger Brannan.
Office: 2801 E. 4th St., 55812. Tel: 218-728-3646; Fax: 218-728-3647. Email: cathdulth@aol.com.
School—Holy Rosary, (Grades K-8) Tel: 218-724-8565. Jesse Murray, Prin. Lay Teachers 24; Students 301.
Catechesis / Religious Program—Tel: 218-728-6985. Tisha Frost, D.R.E.; Ben Frost, D.R.E. Students 180.

2—ST. ANTHONY, Closed. For inquiries for parish records contact St. Benedict Church, Duluth.

3—ST. BENEDICT (1950) Rev. Eric F. Hastings; Deacons Dennis Anderson; John Weiske; Scott Peters.
Parish Office—1419 St. Benedict St., 55811. Tel: 218-724-4828; Fax: 218-728-2683. Web: www.stbensduluth.org.
Res.: 1419 Arrowhead Rd., 55811. Tel: 218-724-8926.
Catechesis / Religious Program—Colleen McDonald, D.R.E.; Nic Davidson, Youth Min. Students 162.

4—SS. CLEMENT AND JEAN, Closed. For inquiries for parish records contact Holy Family Church, Duluth.

5—ST. ELIZABETH Rev. Jon Anthony Wild.
Office: 610 99th Ave. W., 55808. Tel: 218-626-2283.
Catechesis / Religious Program—Mrs. Ann Menart, D.R.E. Students 31.

6—GOOD SHEPHERD, Closed. For inquiries for parish records contact St. James Church, Duluth.

7—HOLY FAMILY Rev. Terence Figel, O.M.I.; Deacon Timothy Kittelson. In Res., Rev. James Datko, O.M.I.
Parish Office—2430 W. 3rd St., 55806-1801. Tel: 218-722-4445; Fax: 218-722-8979. Email: info@holyfamilyduluth.org. Web: www.holyfamilyduluth.org.
Res.: 202 N. 25th Ave W., 55806. Tel: 218-722-0730.
Catechesis / Religious Program—Desiree Taylor, D.R.E. Students 55.

8—ST. JAMES (1888) Rev. James B. Bissonette.
Office: 721 N. 57th Ave. W., 55807. Tel: 218-624-0125; Fax: 218-624-3435.
School—St. James, (Grades PreSchool-8) Tel: 218-624-1511. Web: www.stjamesduluth.org. Mr. William VanLoh, Prin. Lay Teachers 20; Students 134.
Catechesis / Religious Program—Mary Ann Rotondi, D.R.E. Students 77.

9—ST. JOHN (Woodland) (1915) Rev. Richard Kunst; Deacon Walt Beier.
Office: 4230 St. John's Ave., 55803. Tel: 218-724-6332; Fax: 218-724-4605.
Church: 3 W. Chisholm St., 55803.
School—St. John, (Grades PreSchool-6), 1 W. Chisholm St., 55803. Tel: 218-724-9392; Fax: 218-724-9368. Peggy Frederickson, Prin. Lay Teachers 11; Students 130.
Catechesis / Religious Program—Students 131.

10—ST. JOSEPH (1921) Rev. William Fider; Deacon Chico Anderson.
Office: 2410 Morris Thomas Rd., 55811. Tel: 218-722-2259; Fax: 218-733-0414. Email: stlawrencechurch@msn.com. Web: www.stjosephchurchduluth.org.
Catechesis / Religious Program—Coordinated with St. Lawrence, Duluth. Karen Ball, D.R.E. Students 10.

11—ST. LAWRENCE (1959) Rev. William Fider; Deacon Chico Anderson.
Office: 2410 Morris Thomas Rd., 55811. Tel: 218-722-1900; 218-722-2259; Fax: 218-733-0414. Email: stlawrencechurch@msn.com.
Catechesis / Religious Program—Tel: 218-722-6965. Karen Ball, D.R.E. Students 290.

12—ST. MARGARET MARY (1917), (Morgan Park) Rev. John C. Petrich.
Office: 1467 88th Ave. W., 55808. Tel: 218-626-2379; 218-626-4724.
Catechesis / Religious Program—Students 28.

13—ST. MARY STAR OF THE SEA (1883) Rev. Kuriakose Nediakala, M.C.B.S.
Office: 325 E. Third St., 55805. Tel: 218-722-3078; Fax: 218-279-5070. Email: stmarys@cpinternet.com.
Catechesis / Religious Program—Tel: 218-722-3078. Shirley Baker, D.R.E. Students 45.

14—ST. MICHAEL (1914) Rev. Thomas Radaich; Deacon Richard Laumeyer.
Office: 4901 E. Superior St., 55804. Tel: 218-525-1902; Fax: 218-525-1904.
School—St. Michael Lakeside School, (Grades PreSchool-5), 4628 Pitt St., 55804. Tel: 218-525-1931; Fax: 218-525-0296. Web: www.smlsduluth.org. Amy Flaig, Prin. Teachers 6; Students 97.
Catechesis / Religious Program—Students 146.

15—OUR LADY OF MERCY Rev. Kuriakose Nediakala, M.C.B.S.
Mailing Address: 325 E. Third St., 55805. Tel: 218-722-3078; Fax: 218-279-5070.
Church: 2002 Minnesota Ave., 55802.

16—ST. PETER Rev. Kuriakose Nediakala, M.C.B.S. Mailing Address: 325 E. Third St., 55805. Tel: 218-722-3078; Fax: 218-279-5070.
Church: 810 W. 3rd St., 55805.

17—SS. PETER AND PAUL, Closed. For inquiries for parish records contact Holy Family Church, Duluth.

18—ST. RAPHAEL (1959) Rev. Dale Nau.
Parish Office—5779 Seville Rd., 55811. Tel: 218-729-7537 (Office); 218-729-5546 (Rectory); Fax: 218-729-8122. Email: raphaelchurch@yahoo.com.
Catechesis / Religious Program—Tel: 218-729-7537. Rebecca Kroll, D.R.E. Students 190.

OUTSIDE THE CITY OF DULUTH

AITKIN, AITKIN CO., ST. JAMES (1881) [CEM] Rev. Justin Fish; Deacons William Stein; Luverne Anderson.
Office: 299 Red Oak Dr., 56431. Tel: 218-927-6581. Email: mary.stiago@embarqmail.com.
Catechesis / Religious Program—Deb Mueller, D.R.E. Students 121.

AURORA, ST. LOUIS CO., HOLY ROSARY (1908) Rev. Keith Bertram.
Office: 16 W. Fifth Ave. N., 55705. Tel: 218-229-3210; Fax: 218-229-3434. Email: holy.rosary@hotmail.com.
Catechesis / Religious Program—Tel: 218-229-3434. Students 33.

BABBITT, ST. LOUIS CO., ST. PIUS X (1957) Rev. William Skarich; Deacon Gregory Hutar, Parish Coord.
Parish Office—15 Ash Blvd., 55706. Tel: 218-827-2291.
Res.: 231 E. Camp St., Ely, 55731. Tel: 218-365-4017.
Catechesis / Religious Program—Students 26.

BALL CLUB, ITASCA CO., ST. JOSEPH, [CEM] Rev. Stephen Solors.
Office: 51061 Wolf Dr., Deer River, 56636. Tel: 218-246-8105.
Catechesis / Religious Program—Students 23.

BAXTER, CROW WING CO., ALL SAINTS (2007) Rev. Kristoffer McKusky; Deacon Michael Knuth.
Parish Office—P.O. Box 464, Brainerd, 56401-0464. Tel: 218-828-7738.
Catechesis / Religious Program—Students 92.

BENA, CASS CO., ST. ANNE, [CEM] Closed. For inquiries for parish records contact St. Joseph, Ball Club.

BEROUN, PINE CO., ST. JOSEPH (1896) [CEM] Rev. Cornelius Kelleher.
Parish Office: P.O. Box 490, Hinckley, 55037. Tel: 320-384-6313; 320-384-6313 (Office); Fax: 320-384-6357. Email: frcon@live.com.
Church: 19390 Praha Ave., 55063.

BIGFORK, ITASCA CO., OUR LADY OF THE SNOWS (1960) Rev. Thomas Galarneault.
Parish Office—P.O. Box 11, 56628. Tel: 218-743-3255; Fax: 218-743-3257. Email: olschurch@bigfork.net. Web: www.olschurch.net.
Catechesis / Religious Program—Students 36.

BIWABIK, ST. LOUIS CO., ST. JOHN Rev. Keith Bertram.
Parish Office—Box 569, 55708. Tel: 218-865-6774.
Res.: 16 W. 5th Ave. N., Aurora, 55705. Tel: 218-229-3210.
Catechesis / Religious Program—Students 19.

BRAINERD, CROW WING CO.

1—ST. ANDREW Revs. Anthony Wroblewski; Steven L. La Flamme; Deacons Roger Marks; Mike Koecheler; David Brown.
1108 Willow St., 56401. Tel: 218-822-4040; Fax: 218-829-1340. Email: baccoffice@lakescatholic.org. Web: www.lakescatholic.org.
Catechesis / Religious Program—Martha Ray, D.R.E.; Celeste Badger, D.R.E. Students 194.

2—ST. FRANCIS, [CEM] Revs. Anthony Wroblewski; Steven L. La Flamme; Deacons Roger Marks; Michael Koecheler; David Brown.
Office: 1108 Willow St., 56401.
Res.: 1205 S. Ninth St., 56401. Tel: 218-828-1192.
Church: 404 9th St., N., 56401. Tel: 218-822-4040; Fax: 218-829-1340. Email: baccoffice@lakescatholic.org. Web: www.lakescatholic.org.
School—St. Francis of the Lakes, (Grades PreK-8) Tel: 218-829-2344; Fax: 218-828-4157. Email: info@stfranciscatholicschool.org. Web: www.stfranciscatholicschool.org. Debra Euteneuer, Prin. Lay Teachers 17; Students 236.
Catechesis / Religious Program—Celeste Badger, D.R.E. Students 425.

BRUNO, PINE CO., SACRED HEART, [CEM] Rev. Lourdusamy Kanagarajan.
Office: Box 644, Sandstone, 55072. Tel: 320-245-5175.

BUHL, ST. LOUIS CO., OUR LADY OF THE SACRED HEART (1905) Rev. Fredrick Method.
Parish Office—P.O. Box 27, 55713-0027. Tel: 218-254-5703; Fax: 218-254-3636. Email: stjoes@cpinternet.com.
Pastor Res.: 113 4th St. S.W., Chisholm, 55719-2017. Tel: 218-254-5703; Fax: 218-254-3636.
Catechesis / Religious Program—Deanne Hildenbrand, D.R.E. Students 3.

CARLTON, CARLTON CO., ST. FRANCIS (1928) [CEM] Rev. David Tushar.
Parish Office: 509 Sunrise Dr., 55718. Tel: 218-384-4563.
Catechesis / Religious Program—Students 92.

CASS LAKE, CASS CO., ST. CHARLES Rev. Anselm Thevarkunnel.
Office: 308 Central Ave., P.O. Box 368, 56633. Tel: 218-335-2359; Fax: 218-335-2618.
Catechesis / Religious Program—Students 11.

CHISHOLM, ST. LOUIS CO., ST. JOSEPH (1905) [CEM] Rev. Fredrick Method.
Office: 113 Fourth St. S.W., 55719. Tel: 218-254-5703; Fax: 218-254-3636. Email: stjoes@cpinternet.com.
Catechesis / Religious Program—Students 143.

CLOQUET, CARLTON CO.

1—HOLY FAMILY (1889) [CEM] Rev. Rick Banker; Deacon Terry Twomey.
Office: 102 4th St., 55720. Tel: 218-879-6793.
Church: 280 Reservation Rd., 55720. Tel: 218-879-9047.
Catechesis / Religious Program—Students 14.

2—QUEEN OF PEACE (1881) [CEM 2] Rev. Rick Banker; Deacon Terry Twomey.
Office: 102 4th St., 55720. Tel: 218-879-6793. Email: qop@familink.com.
Church: 102 4th St., 55720. Tel: 218-879-6793; Fax: 218-879-8930.
School—Queen of Peace, (Grades K-6) Tel: 218-879-8516. Sr. Therese Gutting, Prin. Lay Teachers 6; Students 49.
Catechesis / Religious Program—Irene McKay, D.R.E. Students 282.

COHASSET, ITASCA CO., ST. AUGUSTINE (1908) Rev. Paul Larson.
Office: P.O. Box 98, Deer River, 56636. Tel: 218-246-8582; Fax: 218-246-4017. Email: stmary@paulbunyan.net.
Catechesis / Religious Program—Lisa Neurerer, D.R.E. Students 35.

COLERAINE, ITASCA CO., MARY IMMACULATE (1964) Rev. Lloyd Mudrak.
Office: Box 290, 55722. Tel: 218-245-1684.
Catechesis / Religious Program—Students 102.

COOK, ST. LOUIS CO., ST. MARY (1906) [CEM] Rev. Joseph M. Thomas, M.C.B.S. (India).
Office: Box 609, 55723. Tel: 218-666-5334.
Catechesis / Religious Program—Students 12.

CROMWELL, CARLTON CO., IMMACULATE CONCEPTION, [CEM] Rev. Msgr. Aleksander Suchan.
Office: Box 378, Floodwood, 55736. Tel: 218-476-1617. Email: churchstlouis@gmail.com.
Church: Tel: 218-476-2367.
Catechesis / Religious Program—Tanya Davis, D.R.E. Students 10.

CROSBY, CROW WING CO., ST. JOSEPH Rev. Timothy Deutsch; Deacons Philip Mayer; John Reed.
Office: P.O. Box 69, 56441. Tel: 218-546-6559; Fax: 218-545-1548.
Catechesis / Religious Program—Students 80.

CROSSLAKE, CROW WING CO., IMMACULATE HEART (1955) Rev. Michael Patullo; Deacons James Baskfield; James Kirzeder; Barry Olson.
Mailing Address: P.O. Box 155, 56442. Tel: 218-692-3731 (Office); Fax: 218-692-3732.
Res.: 35162 County Rd. 37, 56442. Tel: 218-692-2233. Email: ihc@crosslake.net. Web: ihccrosslake.org.
Catechesis / Religious Program—Students 111.
Chapel—Our Lady of Snows

DEER RIVER, ITASCA CO., ST. MARY (1908) Rev. Paul Larson.
Office: P.O. Box 98, 56636. Tel: 218-246-8582; Fax: 218-246-4017. Email: stmarys@paulbunyan.net.
Catechesis / Religious Program—Lisa Neurerer, D.R.E. Students 70.

DEERWOOD, CROW WING CO., ST. JOSEPH Rev. Timothy Deutsch; Deacons Philip Mayer; John Reed.

Office: P.O. Box 69, Crosby, 56441. Tel: 218-546-6559; 218-534-3182 (Church).
Catechesis/Religious Program—Students 23.

ELY, ST. LOUIS CO., ST. ANTHONY (1888) Rev. William Skarich; Deacon Gregory Hutar.
Office: 231 E. Camp St., 55731. Tel: 218-365-4017; Fax: 218-365-3296. Email: stefaniessaintant@frontiernet.net.
Catechesis/Religious Program—Barbara Condor, D.R.E. Students 96.

EMILY, CROW WING CO., ST. EMILY Rev. Michael Patullo; Deacons Barry Olson; Jim Baskfield; Jim Kirzeder.
Office: Box 25, 56447. Tel: 218-763-2101; 218-763-2301 Res.
Catechesis/Religious Program—Students 8.

EVELETH, ST. LOUIS CO., RESURRECTION Rev. Charles P. Flynn; Deacon Herb Riley.
Office: Box 586, 55734. Tel: 218-744-3277; Fax: 218-744-1723. Email: reschurch@msn.com.
Catechesis/Religious Program—Tel: 218-744-3305. Pam Rapacz, D.R.E., (Grades K-11). Students 187.

FEDERAL DAM, CASS CO., SACRED HEART Rev. Stephen Solors.
Office: 51061 Wolf Dr., Deer River, 56636. Tel: 218-246-8105. Email: joemiss@paulbunyan.net.
Catechesis/Religious Program—

FINLAYSON, PINE CO., ST. JOSEPH, [CEM] Rev. Lourdusamy Kanagarajan.
Office: Box 644, Sandstone, 55702. Tel: 320-245-5175.
Catechesis/Religious Program—James Mostek, D.R.E.; Nancy Mostek, D.R.E. Students 2.

FLOODWOOD, ST. LOUIS CO., ST. LOUIS, [CEM] Rev. Msgr. Aleksander Suchan.
Office: Box 378, 55736. Tel: 218-476-2367; 218-476-1617; Fax: 218-476-2376. Email: churchstlouis@gmail.com.
Catechesis/Religious Program—Students 51.

FORT RIPLEY, CROW WING CO., ST. MATHIAS, [CEM] Revs. Anthony Wroblewski; Steven L. La Flamme. In Res., Rev. Richard G. Oberstar, M.S.F. (Retired).
Office: 1108 Willow St., S.E., Brainerd, 56401. Tel: 218-822-4040.
Church: 4529 County Rd. 121, 56449. Tel: 218-822-4041. Web: www.lakescatholic.org.
Catechesis/Religious Program—Students 105.
Station—Crow Wing State Park St. Mathias.

GARRISON, CROW WING CO., OUR LADY OF FATIMA (1954) Rev. Justin Fish.
Office: c/o 299 Red Oak Dr., Aitkin, 56431. Tel: 218-927-6581.
Church: 27332 Central St., 56450. Tel: 320-692-4466.

GILBERT, ST. LOUIS CO., ST. JOSEPH Revs. Charles P. Flynn; Joseph Valliyamthadathil, M.C.B.S.
Office: Box 788, 55741. Tel: 218-741-9551. Email: stjosephs@mchsi.com.
Res.: 515 Summit St., S., 55741.
Catechesis/Religious Program—Students 42.

GNESEN, ST. LOUIS CO., ST. JOSEPH (1896) [CEM] Rev. Richard Kunst; Deacon Walt Beier.
Office: 4230 St. John's Ave., 55803. Tel: 218-724-6332.
Catechesis/Religious Program—Students 18.

GRAND MARAIS, COOK CO., ST. JOHN (1933) [CEM] Rev. Seamus Walsh; Deacon Peter Mueller.
Office: 10 E. 5th St., Box 549, 55604. Tel: 218-387-1409. Email: stjohns@boreal.org. Web: www.northshorecatholic.org.
Catechesis/Religious Program—Students 43.

GRAND PORTAGE, COOK CO., HOLY ROSARY, [CEM] Rev. Seamus Walsh; Deacon Peter Mueller.
P.O. Box 549, Grand Marais, 55604.
Office: 10 E. St., P.O. Box 549, Grand Marais, 55604. Tel: 218-387-1409.

GRAND RAPIDS, ITASCA CO., ST. JOSEPH Revs. Jerome P. Weiss; Francis Kabiru; Deacon Jerome Sura.
Parish Office—P.O. Box 110, 55744. Tel: 218-326-2843; 218-326-3959; Fax: 218-326-1663.
School—(Grades PreSchool-6) Tel: 218-326-6232; Fax: 218-326-6034. Teresa Matetich, Prin. Lay Teachers 13; Students 188.
Catechesis/Religious Program—Tel: 218-326-3720. Lori Dowling, D.R.E., (Grades 6-12); Holli Busching, D.R.E., (Grades K-5). Students 420.

HACKENSACK, CASS CO., SACRED HEART, Unassigned.
Office: Box 874, Walker, 56484. Tel: 218-547-1054. Email: stagnes@arvig.net. Web: www.hackensack-catholic.org.

HIBBING, ST. LOUIS CO.
1—BLESSED SACRAMENT Revs. Gabriel Waweru; Ryan John Moravitz; Deacons James Griffiths; Ray Sampson.
Office: 2310 7th Ave. E., 55746. Tel: 218-262-5541; Fax: 218-263-3682. Email: parish@blsachibbing.org. Web: www.blsachibbing.org.
Res.: 2328 Seventh Ave. E., 55746. Tel: 218-263-3681.
School—(Grades PreSchool-6) Tel: 218-263-3054; Fax: 218-263-5058. Email: assump@mchsi.com. Susan Scipioni, Prin.; Glenda Larkin, Librarian. Lay Teachers 15; Students 165.
Catechesis/Religious Program—Ann Stocco, D.R.E. Students 323.
Chapel—Side Lake, Blessed Sacrament Chapel
2—IMMACULATE CONCEPTION, Consolidated with Blessed Sacrament, Hibbing.
3—ST. LEO, Consolidated with Blessed Sacrament, Hibbing.

HILL CITY, AITKIN CO., ST. JOHN Rev. Jerome P. Weiss.
Office: c/o St. Joseph's Church, P.O. Box 110, Grand Rapids, 55744. Tel: 218-326-2843.
Church: 55748. Tel: 218-697-2465.

HILLMAN, CROW WING CO., HOLY FAMILY (1925) [CEM] Rev. Justin Fish.
Office: 299 Red Oak Dr., Aitkin, 56431. Tel: 218-927-6581.
Church: 1182 County Rd. 8, 56338. Tel: 320-277-3386.
Catechesis/Religious Program—Deb Mueller, D.R.E. Students 18.

HINCKLEY, PINE CO., ST. PATRICK (1875) [CEM] Rev. Cornelius Kelleher.
Office: 203 Lawler Ave. S., Box 490, 55037-0490. Tel: 320-384-6313; Fax: 320-384-6357.
Church: 203 Lawler Ave. S., 55037.
Catechesis/Religious Program—Students 92.

HOYT LAKES, ST. LOUIS CO., QUEEN OF PEACE Rev. Keith Bertram.
Office: P.O. Box 211, 55750. Tel: 218-225-2867.
Catechesis/Religious Program—Tel: 218-229-3434. Students 25.

INTERNATIONAL FALLS, KOOCHICHING CO., ST. THOMAS AQUINAS, [CEM] Rev. Mitch Byeck, O.M.I.; Deacon Francis Zaren.
Office: 810 Fifth St., 56649. Tel: 218-283-3293; Fax: 218-283-3553.
School—St. Thomas Aquinas, (Grades PreSchool-8) Tel: 218-283-3430. Mike Gerard, Prin. Lay Teachers 7; Students 61.
Catechesis/Religious Program—Mary Morrisseau, D.R.E. Students 152.

KEEWATIN, ITASCA CO., ST. MARY Rev. Dennis H. Hoffman.
Office: 326 2nd St., Nashwauk, 55769. Tel: 218-885-1126. Email: stcekema@uslink.net.
Church: Box 219, 55753. Tel: 218-778-6379.

LITTLEFORK, KOOCHICHING CO., ST. COLUMBAN Rev. Mitch Byeck, O.M.I.
Office: 810 5th St., International Falls, 56649. Tel: 218-283-3293; Fax: 218-283-3553.
Church: Box 44, 56653. Tel: 218-278-6638.
Catechesis/Religious Program—Students 29.

LONGVILLE, CASS CO., ST. EDWARD (1917) Rev. Joseph A. Sirba.
Office: P.O. Box 38, 56655-0038. Tel: 218-363-2799.
Catechesis/Religious Program—Students 18.

MARBLE, ITASCA CO., ST. MARY (1937) Rev. Lloyd Mudrak.
Office & Church: Box 411, 55764. Tel: 218-245-1684.

MCGRATH, AITKIN CO., OUR LADY OF FATIMA, [CEM] Rev. Paul Fruth; Deacon Michael Barta.
Office: Box 156, McGregor, 55760. Tel: 218-768-2702.

MCGREGOR, AITKIN CO., HOLY FAMILY Rev. Paul Fruth; Deacon Michael Barta.
Office: Box 156, 55760. Tel: 218-768-2702; Fax: 218-768-2131.
Catechesis/Religious Program—Students 32.

MEADOWLANDS, ST. LOUIS CO., ST. MARY, [CEM] Rev. Msgr. Aleksander Suchan.
Office: Box 378, Floodwood, 55736. Tel: 218-476-1617.
Church: Box 184, 55765. Tel: 218-427-2626.
Catechesis/Religious Program—Students 12.

MOOSE LAKE, CARLTON CO., HOLY ANGELS (1926) [CEM] Rev. Eamonn Boland.
Office: P.O. Box 487, 55767. Tel: 218-485-4909. Email: holyangelschurch@hotmail.com.
Church: 60 Hartman Dr., 55767.
Catechesis/Religious Program—Tel: 218-485-8214. Kari Janz, D.R.E.; Kathy Burke, D.R.E. Students 114.

MOUNTAIN IRON, ST. LOUIS CO., SACRED HEART (1925) Revs. John O'Donnell; John Doyle (Retired); Deacon Daniel Schultz.
Church: 8861 Main St., 55768. Tel: 218-735-8248.
Catechesis/Religious Program—Students 26.

NASHWAUK, ITASCA CO., ST. CECILIA'S (1905) Rev. Dennis H. Hoffman; Deacon Richard Johnston.
Office: 326 Second St., 55769. Tel: 218-885-1126; Fax: 218-885-1145. Email: stcekema@uslink.net.
Catechesis/Religious Program—Julie Dasovich, D.R.E.; Deanne Faulkner, D.R.E. Students 76.

NISSWA, CROW WING CO., ST. CHRISTOPHER (1949) Rev. George Zeck.
Office: P.O. Box 759, Pequot Lakes, 56472.
Church: 25574 Church St., P.O. Box 12, 56468. Tel: 218-963-2766; 218-963-1119 (Liturgy Office); Fax: 218-568-6707. Email: stchris_judy@msn.com. Web: www.lakecountryparishes.4lpi.com.
Catechesis/Religious Program—Students 105.

NORTHOME, KOOCHICHING CO., ST. MICHAEL (1906) Rev. Thomas Galarneault; Deacon James VandeKamp.
Office: c/o Our Lady of the Snows, P.O. Box 11, Bigfork, 56628. Tel: 218-743-3255; Fax: 218-743-3257.
Church: P.O. Box 52, 56661. Tel: 218-897-5628.
Catechesis/Religious Program—Students 25.

ORR, ST. LOUIS CO., HOLY CROSS (1958) Rev. Joseph M. Thomas, M.C.B.S. (India).
Office: P.O. Box 218, 55771. Tel: 218-757-3273.
Church: 10696 Shady Grove Ln. S., Box 218, 55771. Tel: 218-757-3273.
Catechesis/Religious Program—Students 25.
Chapel—Buyck, St. Joseph's

PENGILLY, ITASCA CO., ST. KEVIN (1947) Rev. Dennis H. Hoffman; Deacon Richard Johnston.
Office: 326 2nd St., Nashwauk, 55769. Tel: 218-885-1126.

PEQUOT LAKES, CROW WING CO., ST. ALICE Rev. George Zeck; Deacons David Craig; Richard Paine.
Office: Box 759, 56472. Tel: 218-568-4760; Fax: 218-568-6707. Email: stalice@uslink.net. Web: www.lakecountryparishes.4lpi.com.
Catechesis/Religious Program—Students 175.

PINE BEACH, CROW WING CO., ST. THOMAS, [CEM] Rev. Anthony Wroblewski.
Parish Office: 1108 Willow St., Brainerd, 56401. Tel: 218-822-4040.

PINE CITY, PINE CO., IMMACULATE CONCEPTION, [CEM] Rev. David Forsman; Deacons Eugene Biever; Mark Pulkrabek.
Office: 535 8th St. S.W., 55063. Tel: 320-629-2935; Fax: 320-629-1438.
School—St. Mary, (Grades PreK-6), 815 Sixth Ave., S.W., 55063. Tel: 320-629-3953. Rev. David Forsman, Prin. Lay Teachers 8; Students 79.
Catechesis/Religious Program—Tel: 320-629-3911. Students 133.

PINE RIVER, CASS CO., OUR LADY OF LOURDES (1917) Rev. George Zeck. In Res., Rev. Bruce Engen (Retired).
Office: Box 44, 56474. Tel: 218-587-4163; Fax: 218-568-6707. Email: stalice@uslink.net. Web: www.lakecountryparishes.4lpi.com.
Catechesis/Religious Program—Tel: 218-587-4203. Students 46.

PROCTOR, ST. LOUIS CO., ST. ROSE Rev. Joel Hastings.
Office: 3 Sixth Ave., 55810. Tel: 218-624-0007; Fax: 218-628-1462. Email: saintroseproctor@qwestoffice.net. Web: www.stroseproctor.org.
School—(Grades PreK-6) Tel: 218-624-0818; Fax: 218-624-0984. Nicole M. Paulson, Prin. Lay Teachers 6; Students 79.
Catechesis/Religious Program—Tel: 218-624-9580. Becky Kubat, D.R.E. Students 70.

REMER, CASS CO., ST. PAUL Rev. Joseph A. Sirba.
Office: P.O. Box 38, Longville, 56655. Tel: 218-363-2799.
Catechesis/Religious Program—Students 30.

SAGINAW, ST. LOUIS CO., ST. PHILIP NERI Rev. Joel Hastings.
Office: c/o 3 Sixth Ave., Proctor, 55810. Tel: 218-624-0007; Fax: 218-628-1462.
Church: 4904 Independence Rd., 55779.
Catechesis/Religious Program—Students 14.

SANDSTONE, PINE CO., ST. LUKE, [CEM] Rev. Lourdusamy Kanagarajan.
Office: 122 Commercial Ave. N., Box 644, 55072. Tel: 320-245-5175. Email: saintlukes@scicable.com.
Catechesis/Religious Program—Tel: 320-245-5367. James Mostek, D.R.E.; Nancy Mostek, D.R.E. Students 51.

SAWYER, CARLTON CO., SS. MARY & JOSEPH (1859) Rev. David Tushar.
Office: 509 Sunrise Dr., Carlton, 55718. Tel: 218-879-4563.
Church: 1225 Mission Rd., 55780. Tel: 218-384-4563.
Catechesis/Religious Program—Students 29.

SILVER BAY, LAKE CO., ST. MARY (1955) Revs. Michael J. Lyons; Francis Paquette (Retired); Deacons Fred Wright; Jack Ferris.
Office: 57 Horn Blvd., 55614. Tel: 218-226-3100; Fax: 218-226-3116. Email: stmary@mchsi.com. Web: www.northshorecatholic.org.
Catechesis/Religious Program—Students 32.

SQUAW LAKE, ITASCA CO., ST. CATHERINE (1942) Rev. Thomas Galarneault.
Office: P.O. Box 11, Bigfork, 56628-0011. Tel: 218-743-3255; Fax: 218-743-3257.
Church: 52265 State Hwy 46, 56681. Tel: 218-659-4353.
Catechesis/Religious Program—

STURGEON LAKE, PINE CO., ST. ISIDORE (1887) [CEM] Rev. Steven Daigle.
Office: c/o St. Mary Church, 8118 Lake St., Willow River, 55795. Tel: 218-372-3284.
Church: 9010 Main St., 55783. Tel: 218-372-3208.
Catechesis/Religious Program—Michelle Malone, D.R.E. Students 27.

TACONITE, ITASCA CO., ST. JOSEPH (1965) Rev. Lloyd Mudrak.

Office: Box 290, Coleraine, 55722. Tel: 218-245-1684.

TOWER, ST. LOUIS CO., ST. MARTIN (1884) Rev. Joseph M. Thomas, M.C.B.S. (India).
Office: Box 757, 55790. Tel: 218-753-4310.
Catechesis/Religious Program—Students 41.

TWO HARBORS, LAKE CO., HOLY SPIRIT, [CEM] Rev. Michael J. Lyons.
Office: 227 Third St., 55616. Tel: 218-834-4313; Fax: 218-834-7082. Email: hspirit@mchsi.com. Web: www.northshorecatholic.org.
Catechesis/Religious Program—Students 149.

VIRGINIA, ST. LOUIS CO.
1—HOLY SPIRIT Revs. John O'Donnell; John Doyle (Retired); Deacon Daniel Schultz.
Office: 306 S. Second St., 55792. Tel: 218-741-6344; Fax: 218-741-6345. Email: holyspirit@2z.net. Web: www.catholic-parishes.org.
See Marquette Catholic School under Elementary Schools, Interparochial located in the Institution section
Catechesis/Religious Program—Tel: 218-741-6345. Nick Strle, D.R.E. Students 215.
2—SACRED HEART (1950) Revs. John O'Donnell; John Doyle (Retired); Deacon Daniel Schultz.
Office: 306 S. Second St., 55792.
Church: 603 12th St. N., 55792. Tel: 218-741-2322.

WALKER, CASS CO., ST. AGNES, Unassigned.
Office: Box 874, 56484. Tel: 218-547-1054. Email: stagnes@arvig.net. Web: www.walkercatholic.org.
Catechesis/Religious Program—Students 99.

WARBA, ITASCA CO., ST. PAUL Rev. Jerome P. Weiss.
Office: c/o St. Joseph Church, P.O. Box 110, Grand Rapids, 55744. Tel: 218-326-2843.
Church: Hwy. 2, 55793. Tel: 218-697-2465.

WILLOW RIVER, PINE CO., ST. MARY (1907) [CEM] Rev. Steven Daigle.
Office: 8118 Lake St., 55795. Tel: 218-372-3446. Email: st.mary.church@frontiernet.net.
Catechesis/Religious Program—Students 16.

INDIAN MISSIONS

DULUTH, ST. LOUIS CO., INDIAN MISSIONS Sr. Marie Rose Messingschlager, C.D.P.
c/o Chancery Office, 2830 E. Fourth St., 55812. Tel: 218-724-9111; Fax: 218-724-1056.

Chaplains of Public Institutions
Hospitals

DULUTH. *St. Luke's Hospital*, Tel: 218-726-5555. Rev. John C. Petrich, Chap., 1467 88th. Ave. W., 55808. Tel: 218-626-4724.
Miller Dwan Hospital. Mrs. Jan Rohweder, Dir. of Chaplains. Tel: 218-727-1089.

MOOSE LAKE. *Moose Lake State Hospital*. Rev. Eamonn Boland, Chap., 60 Hartman Dr., 55767. Tel: 218-485-4909.

Correctional Institutions

DULUTH. *Duluth Federal Prison*. Rev. Noel Stretton (Retired), 610 99th Ave. W., 55808. Tel: 218-626-2283.

SAGINAW. *Northeast Regional Correctional Institution*. Rev. John C. Petrich, Chap. Tel: 218-626-4724.

WILLOW RIVER. *Youth Conservation Camp*. Rev. Timothy Deutsch, Chap. Tel: 218-372-3446.

On Duty Outside the Diocese:
Revs.—
Fournier, William, Sacred Heart Church, 1201 Bogard Rd., Wasilla, AK 99654.
Hauver, James, Church of St. Patrick, 137 Moseman Rd., Yorktown Heights, NY 10598.
Johnson, Lawrence P., 1820 Froude St., San Diego, CA 92107.
Kaster, Alfred D., 6716 Woodland Dr., Paradise, CA 95969.

Retired:
Rev. Msgrs.—
O'Shea, Lawrence, Westwood, 925 Kenwood Ave., Apt. 3132, 55811.
Popesh, Bernard, 1181 Ring Rock Rd., Ely, 55731. Tel: 218-365-6085
Revs.—
Antus, Roland, 221 Boulder Dr., Cloquet, 55720. Tel: 218-393-7900
Arimond, Vincent
Bouchard, Thomas, 20 6th St., S.W., Chisholm, 55712. Tel: 218-254-4529
Cossette, Raymond, 12788 County Rd. 8, S.E., Brainerd, 56401. Tel: 218-764-2941
Crossman, James, 330 E. Third St., # 219, 55805. Tel: 218-740-5076
Doyle, John, P.O. Box 475, Mountain Iron, 55768. Tel: 218-735-8248
Engen, Bruce, P.O. Box 44, Pine River, 56474. Tel: 218-587-4163
Foster, Edward, 3 Cliftonville, Crosshaven, Co. Cork Ireland.
Gagne, Ronald, 6894 Paulson Rd., Cotton, 55724. Tel: 218-482-3415
Golden, James, 204 4th Ave., Keewatin, 55753. Tel: 218-778-6949
Golobich, John, 330 E. Third St., 55805. Tel: 218-723-1566
Kosciesza, Bogumil, 2301 Douglas Ct., Silver Spring, MD 20902. Tel: 301-933-1896
La Patka, Gerald, 4202 E. Broadway Rd., #75, Mesa, AZ 85206. Tel: 480-325-5103
Lyttle, Eugene, 1115 S. Lake Ave., 55802. Tel: 218-726-0602
Moran, Patrick, Strokestown Rd., Ballyleague, Lanesboro, Co. Longford Ireland.
Paquette, Francis, 57 Horn Blvd., Silver Bay, 55614. Tel: 218-220-0122
Partika, Richard, 925 Kenwood Ave., #1157, 55811. Tel: 218-728-3498
Perkovich, Frank, 12 1/2 S.W. 2nd. St., Chisholm, 55719. Tel: 218-254-5444
Scheuer, James, 151 W. Linden, 55811. Tel: 218-722-2356
Schultz, Brian, 1346 W. Arrowhead Rd. #188, 55811. Tel: 218-786-0458
Spors, Roman, 35 N. 1st Ave. #210, Waite Park, 56387. Tel: 480-459-9374
Stretton, Noel, 4926 Pitt St., 55804. Tel: 218-464-1292
Sustarsic, John, 330 E. 3rd St., #519, 55805. Tel: 218-279-4001
White, Stephen, 122 Ridge Rd, New London, 56273. Tel: 320-354-3397

Permanent Deacons:
Anderson, Dennis, St. Benedict, Duluth
Anderson, H. L., St. Lawrence, Duluth
Anderson, Luverne, St. James, Aitkin
Barta, Michael, Holy Family, McGregor
Baskfield, Jim, Immaculate Heart, Crosslake
Beier, Walter, St. John, Duluth
Biever, Eugene, Immaculate Conception, Pine City
Birkland, Roger, St. Mary Star of the Sea, Duluth
Brannan, Rodger, Cathedral of Our Lady of the Rosary, Duluth
Brown, David, Brainerd Area Catholic Churches
Craig, David, St. Alice, Pequot Lakes
Ferris, Jack, (Retired)
Griffiths, James, Blessed Sacrament, Hibbing
Hutar, Gregory, St. Anthony, Ely
Johnston, Richard, Nashwauk, Keewatin, Pengilly
Kirzeder, James, Immaculate Heart, Crosslake
Kittelson, Timothy, Holy Family, Duluth
Knuth, Michael, All Saints, Baxter
Koecheler, Michael, Brainerd Area Catholic Churches
Kubat, Thomas, St. Rose, Proctor
Laumeyer, Richard, St. Michael's, Duluth
Marks, Roger, Holy Family, Hillman
Mayer, Philip, St. Joseph, Crosby
Moravitz, Richard, St. Anthony, Ely
Mueller, Peter, St. John, Grand Marais
Olson, Barry, St. Emily, Emily
Paine, Richard, St. Alice, Pequot Lakes
Peters, Scott, St. Benedicts, Duluth
Pulkrabek, Mark, Immaculate Conception, Pine City
Ramsey, Herbert, St. Agnes, Walker
Reed, John, St. Joseph, Crosby
Riley, Herbert, (Retired)
Sampson, Ray, Blessed Sacrament, Hibbing
Schultz, Daniel, Holy Spirit, Virginia
Skala, Mark, (On Duty Outside the Diocese)
Stein, William, St. James, Aitkin
Sura, Jerome, St. Joseph, Grand Rapids
Twomey, Terence, Queen of Peace, Cloquet
Vande Kamp, James, St. Michael's, Northome
Weiske, John, St. Benedict, Duluth
Windus, Theodore, Sr., St. Mary of the Sea, Duluth
Wright, Fred, St. Mary, Silver Bay
Zaren, Francis, St. Thomas, International Falls

INSTITUTIONS LOCATED IN THE DIOCESE

[A] COLLEGES AND UNIVERSITIES

DULUTH. *College of St. Scholastica*, 1200 Kenwood Ave., 55811. Tel: 218-723-6000; Fax: 218-723-6290. Web: www.css.edu. Dr. Larry Goodwin, Pres.; Steve Lyons, Vice Pres. for Student Affairs & Dean of Students; Kevin McGrew, Dir., Library. A coed Benedictine college for resident, day and evening students. Priests 1; Sisters 4; Lay Faculty 162; Students 3,746.

[B] ELEMENTARY SCHOOLS, INTERPAROCHIAL

DULUTH. *Duluth Area Catholic Schools System*, (Grades PreK-8), 2830 E. Fourth St., 55812-1501. Ms. Cynthia Zook, Area Coord. Tel: 218-724-9111; Fax: 218-724-1056. Holy Rosary School, Duluth, Tel: 218-724-8565; St. James Catholic School, Duluth, Tel: 218-624-1511; St. John the Evangelist School, Duluth, Tel: 218-724-9392; St. Michael's Lakeside School, Duluth, Tel: 218-525-1931; St. Rose School, Proctor, Tel: 218-624-0818. Priests 1; Lay Teachers 48.

VIRGINIA. *Marquette Catholic School*, (Grades PreSchool-6), 311 Third St. S., 55792. Tel: 218-741-6811; Fax: 218-741-2158. Email: mcs@cpinternet.com. Georgia Brown Epp, Prin.; Janet Schultze, Librarian. Serving the parishes of Holy Spirit & Sacred Heart. Lay Teachers 10; Students 104.

[C] GENERAL HOSPITALS

DULUTH. *St. Mary's Medical Center*, 407 E. Third St., 55805. Tel: 218-786-4000; Fax: 218-786-4383. Email: shofer@smdc.org. Web: www.smdc.org. Sr. Kathleen Hofer, O.S.B., Pres.; John Gibbs, M.Div., Dir. of Chap. Svcs.; Rev. Thomas J. Foster, Chap. Sisters 4; Nurses 859; Patients Assisted Annually 304,067; Bed Capacity 313; Bassinets 43; Total Staff 2,460.

BRAINERD. *St. Joseph's Medical Center*, 523 N. Third St., 56401. Tel: 218-829-2861; Fax: 218-828-3103. Email: sjmc@brainerdlakeshealth.org. Web: www.brainerdlakeshealth.org. Jani M. Wiebolt, Admin.; Karen DuBord, Dir. Spiritual Care. Nurses 386; Patients Assisted Annually 152,887; Bed Capacity 162; Total Staff 1,070.

[D] HOMES FOR AGED

DULUTH. *St. Ann's Senior Residence*, 330 E. Third St., 55805. Tel: 218-727-8831; Fax: 218-727-8833. Web: www.stanns.com. Sisters of St. Benedict 1; Residents 176.
Benedictine Health Center (Sub. of Benedictine Health System), 935 Kenwood Ave., 55811. Tel: 218-723-6408; Fax: 218-723-6449. Mark Broman, Admin. & CEO. Senior Housing Apartments 45; Assisted Living Apartments 35; Skilled Nursing Beds 120; Day Care (Adults) 25; Children 70; Westwood Terrace Memory Care 21.
St. Eligius Health Center (Sub. of Benedictine Health System); A Benedictine Care Center, 7700 Grand Ave., 55807. Tel: 218-628-2341; Fax: 218-628-0395. Steve Baukner, Admin. Skilled Nursing Beds 112.

EVELETH. *Arrowhead Senior Living Community dba St. Raphael's Health and Rehab Center* 601 Grant Ave., 55734. Tel: 218-744-9800; Fax: 218-744-9829. Dawn Chiabotti, Admin. Assisted Units 14; Skilled Beds 86.

VIRGINIA. *Arrowhead Senior Living Community dba St. Michael's Health and Rehabilitation Center* 1201 8th St., S., 55792. Tel: 218-748-7800; Fax: 218-748-7890. Cheri High, Admin. Skilled Beds 102.

[E] CONVENTS AND RESIDENCES FOR SISTERS

DULUTH. *Motherhouse and Novitiate of the Sisters of Saint Benedict*, St. Scholastica Monastery, 1001 Kenwood Ave., 55811. Tel: 218-723-6555; Fax: 218-723-5902. Email: lois@duluthosb.org. Web: www.duluthbenedictines.org. Sr. Margaret Clarke, O.S.B., Archivist. Professed Sisters 103.

[F] NEWMAN CENTERS

DULUTH. *Newman Catholic Campus Ministry* 421 W. Marie St., 55811. Tel: 218-728-3757. Heather Serena, Coord.; Rev. Michael Schmitz, Dir.

[G] MISCELLANEOUS LISTINGS

DULUTH. *Benedictine Sisters Benevolent Association* (Parent Co.), 1001 Kenwood Ave., 55811-2300. Tel: 218-728-1817; Fax: 218-723-5902. Email: lois@duluthosb.org. Web: www.duluthbenedictines.org. Sr. Lois Eckes, O.S.B., Pres.
Benedictine Health System, 503 E. Third St., Ste. 400, 55805. Tel: 218-786-2370; Fax: 218-786-2373. Web: www.bhshealth.org. Dale M. Thompson, Pres. & CEO. Sponsored by Benedictine Sisters Benevolent Association, (Affiliated with Essentia Health) Entities not located in the Diocese: St. Francis Regional Medical Center, Shakopee, MN; St. Mary's Hospital, Cottonwood, ID; St. Mary's Regional Health Center, Detroit Lakes, MN; St. Benedict's Family Medical Center, Jerome, ID., Sponsored by Benedictine Sisters Benevolent Association, Benedictine Health System Subsidiaries and Sponsored Entities Not Located In The Diocese: Benedictine

Care Centers; (St. Brigid's at Hi-Park & The Villa at Hi-Park, Red Wing, MN; St. Isidore Health Center of Greenwood Prairie & Green Prairie Place, Plainview, MN; Benedictine Health Center at Innsbruck, New Brighton, MN; St. Eligius Health Center, Duluth, MN; Benedictine Health Dimensions, Inc. Benedictine Living Communities, Inc. (Benedictine Living Center of Garrison, Garrison, ND; Benedictine Living Communities Bismarck, Inc; Prince of Peace Care Center and Evergreen Place, Ellendale, ND; St. Benedict's Health Center and Benedict's Court, Dickenson, ND; St. Catherine's Living Center, Wahpeton, ND; St. Rose Care Center and Rosewood Court, LaMoure, ND; Benedictine Living Communities Foundation, Bismarck, ND); Benedictine Living Community of St. Peter, St. Peter, MN; Bridges Care Community, Ada, MN; Madonna Towers of Rochester, Inc., Rochester, MN; Saint Anne of Winona, Winona, MN; St. Gertrude's Health and Rehabilitation Center, Shakopee, MN; Tekakwitha Living Center, Inc., Sisseton, SD; Villa St. Benedict, Lisle, IL; Villa St. Vincent, Crookston, MN; Benedictine Health Center of Minneapolis, MN; Madonna Meadows of Rochester, Rochester, MN; Living Community of St. Joseph, St. Joseph, MO; Benedictine Senior Living at Steeple Pointe, Osseo, MN. 502 E. Second St., 55805. Tel: 218-786-8376. Web: www.essentiahealth.org. Peter Person, M.D., CEO.

St. Mary's Medical Center, 407 E. Third St., 55805. Tel: 218-786-4000; Fax: 218-786-4383. Sr. Kathleen Hofer, O.S.B., Pres. & Chm. Bd.; Thomas Patnoe, M.N., Pres.; Mari Beth Olson, COO; Rev. Thomas J. Foster, Chap. Affiliate: St. Mary's Hospital of Superior, WI

St. Joseph's Medical Center, Brainerd Affiliated with Essentia Health, 523 N. Third St., Brainerd, 56401. Tel: 218-829-2861; Fax: 218-828-3103. Jani M. Weibolt, Pres. & CEO.

Benedictine Health System Foundation, Inc., 503 E. Third St., Ste. 400, 55805. Tel: 218-786-2370; Fax: 218-786-2373. Lowell Larson, Pres. (Sub. of Benedictine Health System) Comprised of the following Associated Foundations: Benedictine Health Center Foundation, Duluth, MN; Benedictine Health Center of Minneapolis Foundation, Minneapolis, MN; Benedictine Living Communities Foundation, Bismarck, ND (serving Benedictine Living Center of Garrison, Prince of Peace Care Center, St. Benedict's Health Center, St. Catherine's Living Center and St. Rose Care Center); Benedictine Living Community of St. Peter Foundation, St. Peter, MN; Bridges Care Community Foundation, Ada, MN; Cerenity Foundation, St. Paul, MN (serving Cerenity Care Center-Bethesda of South St. Paul, Cerenity Care Center on Humboldt, Cerenity Care Center on Dellwood Place, Cerenity Care Center-Marian of St. Paul and Cerenity Care Center-White Bear Lake); Hi-Park Foundation, Red Wing, MN; Innsbruck Foundation, New Brighton, MN; Living Community of St. Joseph Foundation, St. Joseph, MO; Madonna Living Community Foundation of Rochester, Rochester, MN; Saint Anne Foundation, Winona, MN; Saints Healthcare Foundation, Shakopee, MN; St. Eligius Foundation, Duluth MN; St. Isidore Health Center of Greenwood Prairie Foundation, Plainview, MN; St. Michael's Foundation, Virginia, MN; St. Raphael's Foundation, Eveleth, MN; Tekakwitha Living Center Foundation, Sisseton, SD; Villa St. Benedict Foundation, Lisle, IL; Villa St. Vincent/The Summit Foundation, Crookston, MN.

Benedictine Health Center (Sub. of Benedictine Health System), 935 Kenwood Ave., 55811. Tel: 218-723-6408; Fax: 218-723-6449. Mark Broman, Admin. & CEO.

Polinsky Medical Rehabilitation Center, 530 E. Second St., 55805. Tel: 218-786-5360; Fax: 218-786-5340. Barb Westberg, Dir. (Sub. of St. Mary's Medical Center)

Benedictine Living Communities Inc., 503 E. Third St., Ste. 400, 55805. Tel: 218-786-2370; Fax: 218-786-2373. Kevin Greff, Pres. & CEO. (Sub. of Benedictine Health System)

The Blessed Nuno Society, P.O. Box 3484, 55803. Tel: 218-310-5110. Email: director@blessednuno.org. Web: www.blessednuno.org. Tim Heinan, Dir.

Holy Rosary Parish Endowment Fund, 2801 E. Fourth St., 55812. Tel: 218-728-3646. Email: cathdulth@aol.com.

The Human Life and Development Fund of the Diocese of Duluth, 2830 E. Fourth St., 55812. Tel: 218-724-9111; Fax: 218-724-1056.

The Seminary Endowment Fund of the Diocese of Duluth, 2830 E. 4th St., 55812. Tel: 218-724-9111; Fax: 218-724-1056. Mr. Mike Bilden, Devel. Dir.

The Catholic Religious Education Endowment Fund of the Diocese of Duluth, 2830 E. 4th St., 55812. Tel: 218-724-9111; Fax: 218-724-1056. Mr. Mike Bilden, Devel. Dir.

St. Vincent de Paul Society, 630 S. 66th Ave. W., 55807-2129. Tel: 218-723-8751. Email: svdpdul@aol.com. Joseph Jodouin, Pres.

CLOQUET. *Educational Endowment Trust, Queen of Peace Church*, 102 4th St., 55720. Tel: 218-879-6793. Rev. Rick Banker.

HACKENSACK. *S.W. Deanery Chapter of Magnificat of the Diocese of Duluth*, 3989 Bayview Dr., N.W., 56452. Tel: 218-675-6180. Email: garoutte@tds.net.

HIBBING. *Hibbing Catholic Schools Endowment Fund*, 2310 7th Ave., E., 55746. Tel: 218-262-5541; Fax: 218-263-3682. Rev. Gabriel Waweru, Contact Person.

**Sister Thea Bowman Black Catholic Educational Foundation*, 627 E. 39 St., 55746. Tel: 216-263-4865. Email: maryloujll@aol.com. Mrs. Mary Lou Jennings, Exec. Dir.

RELIGIOUS INSTITUTES OF MEN REPRESENTED IN THE DIOCESE

For further details refer to the corresponding bracketed number in the Religious Institutes of Men or Women section.

[]—*Missionary Congregation of the Blessed Sacrament*—M.C.B.S.

[0910]—*Oblates of Mary Immaculate*—O.M.I.

RELIGIOUS INSTITUTES OF WOMEN REPRESENTED IN THE DIOCESE

[0230]—*Benedictine Sisters of Pontifical Jurisdiction* (St. Joseph, MN; Watertown, SD; St. Paul, MN; Duluth, MN)—O.S.B.

[1000]—*Congregation of Divine Providence of Kentucky*—C.D.P.

[1250]—*The Institute of the Franciscan Sisters of the Eucharist* (Meriden, CT)—F.S.E.

[3840]—*Sisters of St. Joseph of Carondelet*—C.S.J.

[2150]—*Sisters Servants of the Immaculate Heart of Mary*—I.H.M.

DIOCESAN CEMETERIES

DULUTH. *Calvary Cemetery*, 4820 Howard Gnesen Rd., 55803. Tel: 218-724-3376; Fax: 218-724-9700. Rev. Peter Muhich, Dir.; Mr. Tim Stresow, Supt.

NECROLOGY

† McDowell, Rev. Msgr. Patrick, (Retired)—Died May 19, 2009

† Dolsina, Stanley, (Retired)—Died July 27, 2009

An asterisk (*) denotes an organization that has established tax-exempt status directly with the IRS and is not covered by the USCCB Group Ruling.

Diocese of El Paso

(Dioecesis Elpasensis)

Most Reverend

ARMANDO X. OCHOA, D.D.

Bishop of El Paso; ordained May 23, 1970; appointed Titular Bishop of Sitifi and Auxiliary of the Archdiocese of Los Angeles December 29, 1986; ordained Bishop February 23, 1987; appointed Bishop of El Paso April 1, 1996; installed June 26, 1996.

Chancery Office: 499 St. Matthews St., El Paso, TX 79907. Tel: 915-872-8407; Fax: 915-872-8413.

Web: www.elpasodiocese.org

ERECTED MARCH 3, 1914.

Square Miles 26,686.

Comprises in Texas, the Counties of El Paso, Brewster, Culberson, Hudspeth, Jeff Davis, Loving, Presidio, Reeves, Ward and Winkler.

For legal titles of parishes and diocesan institutions, consult the Chancery Office.

STATISTICAL OVERVIEW

Personnel	
Bishop	1
Priests: Diocesan Active in Diocese	45
Priests: Diocesan Active Outside Diocese	4
Priests: Retired, Sick or Absent	28
Number of Diocesan Priests	77
Religious Priests in Diocese	41
Total Priests in Diocese	118
Extern Priests in Diocese	9
Ordinations:	
Transitional Deacons	3
Permanent Deacons in Diocese	25
Total Brothers	10
Total Sisters	127
Parishes	
Parishes	57
With Resident Pastor:	
Resident Diocesan Priests	37
Resident Religious Priests	7
Without Resident Pastor:	
Administered by Priests	10
Administered by Deacons	2
Administered by Religious Women	1
Missions	19
Professional Ministry Personnel:	
Sisters	1
Welfare	
Health Care Centers	2
Total Assisted	62,885
Homes for the Aged	1
Total Assisted	330
Special Centers for Social Services	3
Total Assisted	40,878
Educational	
Seminaries, Diocesan	1
Students from This Diocese	13
Diocesan Students in Other Seminaries	7
Seminaries, Religious	1
Students Religious	12
Total Seminarians	32
High Schools, Private	3
Total Students	1,130
Elementary Schools, Diocesan and Parish	8
Total Students	2,444
Elementary Schools, Private	2
Total Students	460
Catechesis/Religious Education:	
High School Students	6,974
Elementary Students	11,762
Total Students under Catholic Instruction	22,802
Teachers in the Diocese:	
Brothers	6
Sisters	13
Lay Teachers	290
Vital Statistics	
Receptions into the Church:	
Infant Baptism Totals	4,662
Minor Baptism Totals	374
Adult Baptism Totals	165
Received into Full Communion	215
First Communions	4,721
Confirmations	3,697
Marriages:	
Catholic	696
Interfaith	53
Total Marriages	749
Deaths	2,108
Total Catholic Population	649,648
Total Population	826,611

Former Bishops—Most Revs. JOHN J. BROWN, S.J., preconized Bishop of El Paso, Jan. 22, 1915; resigned June 16, 1915; ANTHONY J. SCHULER, S.J., D.D., cons. Oct. 28, 1915; died June 3, 1944; SIDNEY M. METZGER, S.T.D., J.C.D., cons. April 10, 1940; succeeded to See, Nov. 29, 1942; retired May 29, 1978; died April 12, 1986; PATRICK F. FLORES, D.D., cons. May 5, 1970; installed Bishop of El Paso, May 29, 1978; appt. Archbishop of San Antonio, Aug. 28, 1979; RAYMUNDO J. PENA, D.D., cons. Dec. 13, 1976; appt. Bishop of El Paso, April 29, 1980; appt. Bishop of Brownsville, May 23, 1995.

Vicars General—Rev. Msgr. FRANCIS J. SMITH, P.A., V.G.; Rev. JOHN STOWE, O.F.M.Conv., V.G.

Vicar for Clergy—Rev. Msgr. DAVID G. FIERRO.

Moderator of the Curia—Rev. JOHN STOWE, O.F.M.Conv., V.G.

Chancellor—Rev. JOHN STOWE, O.F.M.Conv., V.G.

Diocesan Pastoral Staff—Rev. JOHN STOWE, O.F.M.Conv., V.G., Moderator of the Curia; Rev. Msgr. DAVID G. FIERRO.

Liaison for Women Religious—Sr. ISABEL FIERRO, D.C., 499 St. Matthews St., El Paso, 79907. Tel: 915-872-8407.

Diocesan Pastoral Center—499 St. Matthews St., El Paso, 79907. Tel: 915-872-8400; Fax: 915-872-8423. Refer all official business to this address.

Presbyteral Council—Revs. FRANCISCO HERRERA (Retired); PABLO MATTA; EDWARD C. CARPENTER; EMANUEL ALCAZAR; LEONIDES RIVERO, Council Pres.; ROLANDO FONSECA; ANTHONY C. CELINO, J.C.L. Ex Officio Members: Rev. Msgr. FRANCIS J. SMITH, P.A., V.G.; Rev. JOHN STOWE, O.F.M.Conv., V.G.; Rev. Msgr. DAVID G. FIERRO.

Diocesan Tribunal—499 St. Matthews St., El Paso, 79907. Tel: 915-872-8402. Rev. ANTHONY C. CELINO, J.C.L., Judicial Vicar. Adjutant Vicars: Revs. STEPHEN PETERS; ROBERT S. KOBE.

Judges—Revs. ANTHONY C. CELINO, J.C.L.; STEPHEN PETERS; ROBERT S. KOBE; Bro. JAMES WORCHUCK, O.F.M.Conv., J.C.L.; Revs. JAMES W. HALL; GILES CARIE, O.F.M.Conv.

Defenders of the Bond—Rev. Msgr. DAVID G. FIERRO; Revs. TRINIDAD FUENTEZ; VIDAL ROBLES JR., J.D., J.C.L.; Sr. DIANE MASSON, C.S.S.F., J.C.L.

Advocates—Rev. Msgr. FRANCIS J. SMITH, P.A., V.G.; Revs. ROLANDO FONSECA; EDWARD C. CARPENTER; Deacon JOSE LUIS SANCHEZ, J.D.

Lay Advocates—Ms. CARMEN RODRIGUEZ; Judge SUE KURITA, J.D.; Ms. LORETTA BUCHANAN; Ms. CARMEN HAGEMANN, J.D.

Tribunal Ecclesiastical Notary—Ms. YOLANDA RUIZ.

Peritus—VACANT.

Vicar for Clergy—Rev. Msgr. DAVID G. FIERRO.

Promoter of Justice—Rev. VIDAL ROBLES JR., J.D., J.C.L.

Vicars-Vicariates—St. Peter: Rev. RICHARD A. MATTY, St. Patrick Cathedral, 1118 N. Mesa, El Paso, 79902. Tel: 915-533-4451. St. Paul: Rev. ANTONIO LASHERAS, O.A.R., Little Flower Parish, 171 Polo Inn Rd., El Paso, 79915. Tel: 915-772-1285. St. John: VACANT. St. Mark and St. Luke: Rev. JOHN LUCIDO, St. John the Apostle Parish, 5th & S. Ike St., Monahans, 79756. Tel: 432-943-5114. St. Matthew: Rev. RAUL TRIGUEROS, Cristo Rey Parish, 8011 Williamette, El Paso, 79907. Tel: 915-591-0688. Our Lady of Guadalupe: Rev. FRANK LOPEZ, St. Frances Xavier Cabrini Parish, 12200 Vista del Sol, El Paso, 79936. Tel: 915-857-1263.

Diocesan Master of Ceremonies—Rev. MARCUS MCFADIN.

Peace & Justice Office—Mr. MARCO RAPOSO, Dir., 499 St. Matthews, El Paso, 79907. Tel: 915-872-8422.

Finance Council—Most Rev. ARMANDO X. OCHOA, D.D.; Rev. Msgr. FRANCIS J. SMITH, P.A., V.G.; Rev. JOHN STOWE, O.F.M.Conv., V.G.; Rev. Msgr. DAVID G. FIERRO; Mr. E. H. BAEZA; Mr. FRANK GORMAN; Ms. MARIA ELENA FLOOD; Mr. PHILLIP MULLIN; Mr. JOSE VILLA, CPA.

Diocesan Building Committee—Most Rev. ARMANDO X. OCHOA, D.D.; Mr. CRUZ GARCIA; Mr. JORGE VERGEN; Mr. RICARDO BACA; Revs. MARCUS MCFADIN; FRANK LOPEZ; Mr. PETE HERRERA; Ms. IRENE RAMIREZ; Ms. VERONICA ROSALES-SOTO.

Priests' Personnel Advisory Committee—Rev. Msgr. FRANCIS J. SMITH, P.A., V.G.; Revs. RICHARD A. MATTY; ANTONIO LASHERAS, O.A.R.; FRANK LOPEZ; JOHN LUCIDO; RAUL TRIGUEROS; ANTHONY C. CELINO, J.C.L.; Rev. Msgr. DAVID G. FIERRO; Rev. JOHN STOWE, O.F.M.Conv., V.G.

Diocesan Review Board—Ms. JULIETA CASTANEDA, R.N.; MAUREEN DE LA ROSA, M.S.; Mr. ENRIQUE MORENO, J.D.; Rev. RICHARD A. MATTY; Sr. ELIZABETH ANNE SWARTZ, S.S.N.D.; Mr. JOSE CASTRELLON; Mr. WALTER DEINES, L.C.S.W.; Mrs. YOLANDA DEINES, L.C.S.W.; Mrs. SUSAN MARTINEZ, L.C.S.W.; Dr. ROBERT RANKIN, Ph.D.

Youth and Young Adult Ministry—NORMA VALDEZ, Dir.; Sr. JANET GILDEA, S.C., M.D., Dir. Young Adult; Mrs. GRACIE CONCHA, Asst., 499 St. Matthews, El Paso, 79907. Tel: 915-872-8438.

Catholic Communications Ministry—Rev. RAUL TRIGUEROS, 499 St. Matthews St., El Paso, 79907. Tel: 915-872-8414.

Diocesan Newspaper— "Rio Grande Catholic" ANDY SPARKE, Editor, 499 St. Matthews St., El Paso, 79907. Tel: 915-872-8414.

Campaign for Human Development—Mr. MARCO RAPOSO, 499 St. Matthews St., El Paso, 79907. Tel: 915-872-8422.

Office of Marriage and Family Life—Mrs. DIANA BULKO, 499 St. Matthews St., El Paso, 79907. Tel: 915-872-8401.

Permanent Diaconate Office—Rev. ROBERT DUEWEKE, O.S.A., 499 St. Matthews, El Paso, 79907. Tel: 915-872-8420.

Priests' Retirement and Disability Plan—Most Rev. ARMANDO X. OCHOA, D.D.; Rev. Msgrs. JOHN PETERS; FRANCIS J. SMITH, P.A., V.G., Pres.; Revs. JOHN STOWE, O.F.M.Conv., V.G.; EDILBERTO LOPEZ; LEONIDES RIVERO; Mr. YAZBIK DAW; Ms. CAROLYN MORA, CPA.

Missions Office/Propagation of the Faith/Catholic Relief Services—Rev. JOHN STOWE, O.F.M.Conv., V.G., 499 St. Matthews St., El Paso, 79907. Tel: 915-872-8407.

Office of Education—Sr. ELIZABETH ANNE SWARTZ, S.S.N.D., Supt., 499 St. Matthews St., El Paso, 79907. Tel: 915-872-8426.

Tepeyac Institute—Rev. ROBERT DUEWEKE, O.S.A., Dir.; Dr. VERONICA RAYAS, Assoc. Dir., 499 St. Matthews St., El Paso, 79907. Tel: 915-872-8420.

Reverence for Life Ministry—Ms. MARIA ACOSTA, 499 St. Matthews St., El Paso, 79907. Tel: 915-872-8401.

Vocations & Seminarians—Revs. MIGUEL ANGEL SANCHEZ, Dir., 499 St. Matthews, El Paso, 79907. Tel: 915-872-8403; JOHN TELLES, Rector, 8330 Park Haven, El Paso, 79907. Tel: 915-872-8460; Sr. RACHEL VALLARTA, M.J.M.J., Asst., 499 St. Matthews St., El Paso, 79907. Tel: 915-872-8403.

Religious Formation—Sr. GLORIA RODRIGUEZ, M.J.M.J., 499 St. Matthews, El Paso, 79907. Tel: 915-872-8432.

Native American (Tigua) Ministry—MIKE LARA, 131 S. Zaragosa, El Paso, 79907. Tel: 915-859-9848.

Victim Assistance Coordinator—Mrs. SUSAN MARTINEZ, L.C.S.W. Tel: 915-872-8465. Email: smartinez@elpasodiocese.org.

Catholic Campus Ministry—2230 N. Oregon, El Paso, 79902. Tel: 915-838-0300. Rev. HENRY BECK, O.F.M., Dir.

Finance Office—Mr. CHARLES CASIANO, CPA, Dir. Tel: 915-872-8404.

Human Resources—Ms. PATRICIA FIERRO, Dir. Tel: 915-872-8421.

Office of Worship—Revs. MARCUS MCFADIN; FRANK LOPEZ.

Office of Safe Environment—Ms. ELENA BEJARANO, Coord. Tel: 915-872-8427.

CLERGY, PARISHES, MISSIONS AND PAROCHIAL SCHOOLS

CITY OF EL PASO

(EL PASO COUNTY)

1—ST. PATRICK CATHEDRAL Rev. Richard A. Matty, Rector; Deacons Jose Luis Sanchez; Ernesto Rodriguez.
Res.: 1118 N. Mesa St., 79902. Tel: 915-533-4451; Fax: 915-532-8761.
School—(Grades K-8), 1111 N. Stanton St., 79902. Tel: 915-532-4142. Email: stpat1111@netzero.net. Liliana Esparza, Prin. Lay Teachers 20; Students 362.
Catechesis/Religious Program—Rosa M. Thorpe, P.C.L. Students 478.

2—ALL SAINTS (1967) Rev. Kennon Y. Ducre.
Res.: 1415 Dakota St., 79930. Tel: 915-566-9711; Fax: 915-566-9737.
Catechesis/Religious Program—Students 55.

3—BLESSED SACRAMENT Rev. Stephen Peters.
Res.: 9025 Diana Dr., 79904. Tel: 915-755-7658.
Catechesis/Religious Program—Tel: 915-755-7658, Ext. 15. Teri Valdez, P.C.L. Students 412.

4—CHRIST THE SAVIOR (1982) Rev. Robert S. Kobe; Deacon Tom Wauson.
Res.: 5301 Wadsworth Ave., 79924. Tel: 915-821-3766.
Catechesis/Religious Program—Mrs. Irma Mejia, P.C.L. Students 412.

5—CORPUS CHRISTI Rev. Wilson Cuevas.
Res.: 9205 N. Loop Dr., 79907. Tel: 915-858-0488; Fax: 915-858-0812. Email: corpuschristi@netzero.com.
Catechesis/Religious Program—Lorena Enriquez, P.C.L. Students 606.

6—CRISTO REY CHURCH Rev. Raul Trigueros; Deacon Ignacio M. Bustillos.
Res.: 8011 Williamette, 79907. Tel: 915-591-0688; Fax: 915-593-0470.
Catechesis/Religious Program—Gloria Ibarra, P.C.L. Students 369.

7—EL BUEN PASTOR MISSION Rev. Roberto Alvarado.
Church: 311 Peyton, 79928. Tel: 915-852-4010.
Mission—La Resurreccion Mission 1140 Timothy, El Paso Co. 79928.
Catechesis/Religious Program—Students 201.

8—ST. FRANCES XAVIER CABRINI PARISH (1993) Rev. Frank Lopez.
Church: 12200 Vista del Sol, 79936. Tel: 915-857-1263; Fax: 915-921-1709. Email: mothercabrini@sbcglobal.net. Web: www.stfrancesxcabrini.com.
Catechesis/Religious Program—Ms. Rosie Torres, P.C.L. Students 464.

9—ST. FRANCIS OF ASSISI MISSION Rev. J. Alejandro Juarez, O.F.M.
Mailing Address: P.O. Box 220034, 79932. Tel: 915-584-7130.
Church & Res.: 5750 Doniphan, 79932.
Catechesis/Religious Program—Students 207.

10—ST. FRANCIS XAVIER (1932) Rev. Esteban Sescon.
Res.: 519 S. Latta St., 79905. Tel: 915-532-2761; Fax: 915-544-5103.
Catechesis/Religious Program—Gloria Serna, P.C.L. Students 215.

11—GUARDIAN ANGEL (1908) Revs. Jesus Maria Mena, O.A.R.; Jose Luis Duenas, O.A.R.
Res.: 3021 Frutas Ave., 79905. Tel: 915-533-2077; Fax: 915-533-3649.
Catechesis/Religious Program—Salvador Vargas, P.C.L. Students 175.

12—HOLY FAMILY (1916), (Hispanic), Rev. Msgr. Victor Kayrouz.
Rectory & Mailing Address: 104 Fewel St., 79902. Tel: 915-532-8462; Fax: 915-577-0236.
Catechesis/Religious Program—Angie Escarciga, P.C.L. Students 47.

13—ST. IGNATIUS OF LOYOLA Revs. Angel M. Maldonado, O.S.M.; Jorge M. Palacio, O.S.M.; Deacon Aurelio MeLucci.
Res.: 408 Park St., 79901. Tel: 915-532-9534; Fax: 915-532-9534.
Catechesis/Religious Program—Robert Hernandez, P.C.L. Students 119.

14—IMMACULATE CONCEPTION Rev. Msgr. William H. Ryan, Pastor Emeritus (Retired).
Res.: 118 N. Campbell St., 79901-2404. Tel: 915-533-3427; Fax: 915-533-3228.

15—ST. JOSEPH'S Revs. Joseph Hermoso; Benjamin Mones.
Res.: 1315 Travis St., 79903. Tel: 915-566-9396; Fax: 915-566-5606.
School—(Grades K-8), 1300 Lamar, 79903. Tel: 915-566-1661; Fax: 915-566-2006. Email: stjosephs@aol.com. Bro. Edwin Gallagher, Prin. Brothers 3; Lay Teachers 27; Students 518.
Catechesis/Religious Program— Rose Lowe, P.C.L. Students 88.

16—LA PURISIMA (1863) Deacon William Reyes, Parish Life Coord.
Res.: 328 S. Nevarez St., 79927. Tel: 915-859-7718; Fax: 915-859-9452. Email: lapurisima@earthlink.net.
Catechesis/Religious Program—Eloy Carmona, P.C.L. Students 164.

17—ST. LUKE (1992) Rev. Msgr. John Peters; Rev. Edilberto Lopez; Deacon Frederick C. Rotchford.
Res.: 930 E. Redd Rd., 79912. Tel: 915-585-0255; Fax: 915-585-6355.
Catechesis/Religious Program—Mary L. Hernandez, P.C.L. Students 1,044.

18—ST. MARK (1992) Rev. Leonides Rivero; Deacons Jesus A. Cardenas; Francisco Segura.
Church: 11700 Pebble Hills, 79936. Tel: 915-857-2955; Fax: 915-857-7133. Email: stmarkcatholic@sbcglobal.net. Web: home.catholicweb.com/StMarkCatholic/.
Catechesis/Religious Program—Yolanda Valdez, P.C.L. Students 1,583.

19—ST. MATTHEW Rev. Msgr. David G. Fierro.
Res.: 400 W. Sunset Rd., 79922. Tel: 915-584-3461; Fax: 915-584-2107.
School—(Grades K-6) Tel: 915-581-8801; Fax: 915-581-8816. Email: cmontoya@stmatthewcatholicschool.org. Carol Montoya, Prin.; Estela Loy, Librarian. Lay Teachers 9; Students 142.
Catechesis/Religious Program—Tel: 915-587-1524. Mrs. Jane Fuller, P.C.L. Students 450.

20—MOST HOLY TRINITY (1967) Rev. Msgr. Robert S. Calles; Deacon Paul Andrade Jr.
Res.: 10000 Pheasant Rd., 79924. Tel: 915-751-6416; Fax: 915-751-5440.
School—(Grades K-8) Tel: 915-751-2566; Fax: 915-751-2596. Email: holytrinityschoolep@yahoo.com. Rosa Gandara, Prin. Lay Teachers 10; Students 88.
Catechesis/Religious Program—Bernie Collins, P.C.L. Students 444.

21—OUR LADY OF ASSUMPTION Revs. Joe Molina; John Canu.
Res.: 4800 Byron St., 79930. Tel: 915-566-4040; Fax: 915-566-1104.
School—(Grades PreK-8) Tel: 915-565-3411; Fax: 915-565-3411. Email: olacs@elp.rr.com. Karen Biddle, Prin.; Nikki Duran, Librarian. Lay Teachers 11; Students 105.
Catechesis/Religious Program—Daniel Hernandez, P.C.L. Students 272.

22—OUR LADY OF GUADALUPE (1929) Revs. Luis Rodolfo Bernal, O.F.M.; Erasmo Rodriguez Vega, Vicar; Gerardo Francisco Salgado.
Res.: 2709 Alabama St., 79930. Tel: 915-562-4304; Fax: 915-562-3509.
Catechesis/Religious Program—Fax: 915-566-3307. Students 250.

23—OUR LADY OF MT. CARMEL Rev. Charles McCarthy, O.F.M.Conv. In Res., Revs. John Stowe, O.F.M-.Conv.; Maurice C. Hayes, O.F.M.Conv.; Bro. James Worchuck, O.F.M.Conv.
Res.: 131 S. Zaragoza, 79907. Tel: 915-859-9848; Fax: 915-860-9340. Email: olmcsecretary@sbcglobal.net. Web: www.ysletamission.org.
Catechesis/Religious Program—Leonor Armstrong, P.C.L. Students 405.

24—OUR LADY OF SORROWS Revs. Enrique M. Camps, O.S.M.; Tomas M. Xotta, O.S.M.; Aldo M. Quelin, O.S.M.
Res.: 7712 Rosedale St., 79915. Tel: 915-772-4834; Fax: 915-772-9078.
Catechesis/Religious Program—Gloria Moreno, P.C.L. Students 237.

25—OUR LADY OF THE LIGHT Deacon Roberto E. Saucedo, Parish Life Coord.
Res.: 4700 Delta Dr., 79905. Tel: 915-532-1757; Fax: 915-532-1757.
Catechesis/Religious Program—Cookie Valdiviez, P.C.L. Students 400.

26—OUR LADY OF THE VALLEY (1945) Rev. Maurice C. Hayes, O.F.M.Conv., Admin.; Deacon Carlos E. Rubio.
Res.: 8600 Winchester, 79907. Tel: 915-859-7939; Fax: 915-859-7576. Email: olvchurch@elp.rr.com.
School—(Grades PreK-8) Tel: 915-859-6448; Fax: 915-859-3908. Email: olvschool@msn.com. Sr. Caroline Vasquez, O.S.F., Prin.; Janice Cook, Librarian. Lay Teachers 14; Students 240.
Catechesis/Religious Program—David Perez, P.C.L. Students 218.

27—ST. PAUL THE APOSTLE (1963) Rev. Emanuel Alcazar; Deacon Vicente Aguirre.
Res.: 7424 Mimosa Ave., 79915. Tel: 915-778-5304; Fax: 915-778-5398. Email: stplap@netzero.net.
Catechesis/Religious Program—Concepcion Pantoja, P.C.L. Students 137.

28—STS. PETER AND PAUL Rev. Saul de Jesus Uribe.
Res.: 673 Old Hueco Tanks Rd., 79927. Tel: 915-859-3758; Fax: 915-858-1501. Email: stspeterandpaulelp@yahoo.com.
Catechesis/Religious Program—Hector Manuel Decanini, P.C.L. Students 607.

29—ST. PIUS X Rev. Msgr. Arturo Banuelas; Deacons Jim Szostek; Juan M. Alvarez; Rolando Lujan.
Res.: 1050 N. Clark Rd., 79905. Tel: 915-772-3226; Fax: 915-771-6665. Email: stpiusxparish@sbcglobal.net. Web: groups.yahoo.com/group/stpiusxchurch_elpaso.
School—(Grades PreK-8) Tel: 915-772-6598; Fax: 915-225-0010. Email: gomezstpius@sbcglobal.net. Web: www.stpiusxschelpaso.org. Mr. Carlos Gomez, Interim Prin.; Lucy Loveridge, Librarian. Sisters 3; Lay Teachers 23; Students 462.
Catechesis/Religious Program—Tel: 915-772-0224. Email: formation.stpiusx@sbcglobal.net. Eva Rodriguez, P.C.L. Students 757.

30—QUEEN OF PEACE Rev. Trinidad Fuentez.
Res.: 1551 Belvidere, 79912. Tel: 915-584-5817; Fax: 915-584-7761.
Catechesis/Religious Program—Elizabeth Mata, P.C.L. Students 667.

31—ST. RAPHAEL (1967) Rev. Msgr. Francis J. Smith; Revs. Vicente Calderon Jr.; Wallace Blake Fry.
Res.: 2301 Zanzibar Rd., 79925. Tel: 915-598-3431; 915-598-3432; Fax: 915-598-0944.
School—(Grades PreK-8), 2310 Woodside, 79925. Tel: 915-598-2241; Fax: 915-598-3002. Email: st_raphael_principal@hotmail.com. Elizabeth Wiehe, Prin. Lay Teachers 27; Students 575.
Catechesis/Religious Program—Eva Morales-Casas, P.C.L. Students 940.

32—SACRED HEART Revs. Edwin L. Gros, S.J.; Louis Lambert, S.J.; Frank Renfroe, S.J.; Bro. Peter Zagone, S.J., Scholastic. In Res., Revs. Antonio Concha, S.J.; Samuel Rosales, S.J.; John L. Vessels, S.J.
Res.: 602 S. Oregon St., 79901. Tel: 915-532-5447; Fax: 915-533-0013. Web: www.sacredheartelpaso.org.
Catechesis/Religious Program—Sr. Maria de la Luz Oseguera, O.P., P.C.L. Students 91.

33—SAN ANTONIO (1917), (Mexican—American), Rev. Benjamin Flores.
Res.: 503 Hunter Dr., 79915. Tel: 915-598-1457; Fax: 915-590-1312. Web: www.paduaofelpaso.org.
Catechesis/Religious Program—Zulema Frausto, P.C.L. Students 458.
34—SAN JOSE Rev. Jose Alcocer.
Res.: 8100 San Jose Rd., 79907. Tel: 915-598-6285.
Catechesis/Religious Program—Rosa Aguon, P.C.L. Students 91.
35—SAN JUAN BAUTISTA Rev. Michael Rodriguez, Admin.
Res.: 5649 Dailey Ave., 79905. Tel: 915-779-1583; Fax: 915-778-7127.
Catechesis/Religious Program—Mrs. Martha Drake, P.C.L. Students 32.
36—SAN JUAN DIEGO PARISH (1992) Rev. Edward Paul Roden-Lucero.
Res.: 14520 E. Montana, 79938. Tel: 915-855-2217; Fax: 915-855-7716. Email: jubileejuan@aol.com.
Catechesis/Religious Program—Mr. Christopher Romero, P.C.L. Students 265.
37—SAN JUDAS TADEO (1982) Revs. Pablo Matta; Eddy Mendoza.
Res.: 4006 Hidden Way, 79922. Tel: 915-584-1095. Email: pmatta@elp.rr.com. Web: www.santuariosanjudastadeo.com.
Catechesis/Religious Program—Rudy Gonzales, P.C.L. Students 676.
Mission—Santa Teresita 3400 Zapal St., El Paso Co. 79922.
38—SANTA LUCIA Rev. Anthony C. Celino, Admin.
Res.: 518 Gallagher St., 79915. Tel: 915-592-5245; Fax: 915-592-5336. Email: santaluciachurch@sbcglobal.net.
Catechesis/Religious Program—Students 146.
39—SANTO NINO DE ATOCHA Rev. Ikechi Korie, O.P., Admin.
Res.: 210 S. Clark, 79905. Tel: 915-779-3164; Fax: 915-779-1811. Email: secretarysantonino@sbcglobal.net.
Catechesis/Religious Program—Laura Lopez, P.C.L.; Lucy Herrera, Confirmation Coord. Students 175.
40—ST. STEPHEN, DEACON AND MARTYR Rev. Marcus McFadin; Deacons Gus J. Rodriguez Sr.; Hector E. Grijalva.
Church: 1700 George Dieter, 79936. Tel: 915-855-1661; Fax: 915-857-5800.
Catechesis/Religious Program—Gus Rodriguez Jr., P.C.L. Students 532.
41—SAINT THERESE OF THE LITTLE FLOWER PARISH Rev. Antonio Lasheras, O.A.R.
Church: 171 Polo Inn, 79915. Tel: 915-772-1285. Email: littleflower@elp.rr.com.
Catechesis/Religious Program—Steve Serna, P.C.L. Students 133.
42—ST. THOMAS AQUINAS (1981) Rev. James W. Hall; Deacons Jose E. Soto; Ignacio J. Torres.
Church: 10970 Bywood, 79936. Tel: 915-592-1313; Fax: 915-592-9733. Email: saintthomasa@aol.com.
Catechesis/Religious Program—Betty Vigil, P.C.L. Students 486.

OUTSIDE THE CITY OF EL PASO

ALPINE, BREWSTER CO., OUR LADY OF PEACE, [CEM] Rev. Miguel Alcuino, Admin.; Deacon Paul A. Lister.
Mailing Address: 406 S. Sixth, 79830. Tel: 432-837-3304; Fax: 432-837-1752.
Mission—St. Mary P.O. Box 268, Marathon, Brewster Co. 79842.
Catechesis/Religious Program—Claudia Saucedo, P.C.L. Students 197.
BALMORHEA, REEVES CO., CHRIST THE KING, Under pastoral care of Santa Rosa, Pecos.
Res.: Rte. 1, Box 3, 79718. Tel: 432-375-2347.
Catechesis/Religious Program—Prescilla Garcia, P.C.L.; Caro Garcia, P.C.L. Students 25.
Mission—Our Lady of Guadalupe Saragosa, Reeves Co. Tel: 432-375-2636.
CANUTILLO, EL PASO CO., ST. PATRICK (1912) [CEM] Rev. Pablo Matta, Admin.
Mailing Address: P.O. Box 10, 79835.
Res.: 7065 Second St., 79835. Tel: 915-877-3997.
Catechesis/Religious Program— Maria Teresa C. Rivera, P.C.L. Students 231.
Mission—Immaculate Heart of Mary 8701 Joplin Rd., Westway, El Paso Co. 79835. Tel: 915-886-3539.
Catechesis/Religious Program—Students 146.
CLINT, EL PASO CO., SAN LORENZO (1914) Rev. Edward C. Carpenter.
Mailing Address: P.O. Box 215, 79836.
Res.: 13021 Center Way, 79836. Tel: 915-851-2255; Fax: 915-851-5251. Email: sanlorenzo1914@sbcglobal.net.
Catechesis/Religious Program—Sr. Angeles Berrozpe, P.C.L. Students 198.
FABENS, EL PASO CO., OUR LADY OF GUADALUPE, [CEM] Rev. Antonio Mena.
Mailing Address: P.O. Box 356, 79838.
Res.: 127 W. Main St., 79838. Tel: 915-764-3942.
Catechesis/Religious Program—Terry Avila, P.C.L. Students 187.
Mission—San Jose Cuadrilla, El Paso Co.
Mission—Santa Rita Tornillo, El Paso Co.
Mission—San Luis La Isla, El Paso Co.
FORT DAVIS, JEFF DAVIS CO., ST. JOSEPH, [CEM] Rev. Miguel Alcuino, Admin.
Res.: P.O. Box 787, 79734. Tel: 432-426-3284.
FORT HANCOCK, HUDSPETH CO., SANTA TERESA (1920) Sr. Silvia Chacon, A.S.C., Pastoral Life Coord.
Res.: P.O. Box 215, 79839. Tel: 915-769-3771; Fax: 915-769-3771. Email: santa_teresa215@netscape.com.
Catechesis/Religious Program—Students 40.
HORIZON CITY, EL PASO CO., HOLY SPIRIT, (Independent Mission) Rev. Ralph Solis Jr., Admin.
Res.: 14132 McMahon, 79928. Tel: 915-852-3582; Fax: 915-852-0585.
Church: 14100 Horizon Blvd., 79928.
Catechesis/Religious Program—Students 387.
KERMIT, WINKLER CO.
1—ST. JOSEPH THE WORKER, Consolidated with St. Thomas in 1990.
2—ST. THOMAS & ST. JOSEPH Revs. John Lucido; Richard Waiwood (Retired).
Res.: 838 Bellaire Rd., 79745. Tel: 432-586-3922.
Catechesis/Religious Program—Lorina Lujan, P.C.L. Students 237.
MARFA, PRESIDIO CO., ST. MARY'S, [CEM] Rev. Rolando Fonseca, Admin.
Mailing Address: Box 356, 79843. Tel: 432-729-4694. Email: churchmarfa@gmail.com.
Catechesis/Religious Program—Students 55.
MONAHANS, WARD CO., ST. JOHN THE APOSTLE AND EVANGELIST, [JC] Revs. John Lucido; Richard Waiwood (Retired).
Res.: 5th & S. Ike St., 79756. Tel: 432-943-5114.
Catechesis/Religious Program—Renee French, P.C.L.; Eloiza Collazo, P.C.L. Students 155.
Mission—St. Gertrude P.O. Box 181, Grandfalls, Ward Co. 79742. Tel: 432-547-2484.
PECOS, REEVES CO.
1—ST. CATHERINE Rev. Fabian Marquez; Deacon George Vasquez.
Mailing Address: P.O. Box 686, 79772.
Res.: 1201 S. Plum, 79772. Tel: 432-447-9231.
Mission—St. Emily Toyah, Reeves Co.
2—SANTA ROSA DE LIMA, [CEM] Rev. Fabian Marquez; Deacon George Vasquez.
Mailing Address: P.O. Box 686, 79772.
Res.: 620 E. 4th St., 79772. Tel: 432-445-2309; Fax: 432-445-2977.
Catechesis/Religious Program—Sam Anchondo, P.C.L. Students 335.
Mission—Our Lady of Refuge Barstow, Ward Co.
PRESIDIO, PRESIDIO CO., SANTA TERESA DE JESUS, [CEM] Rev. Jose Alfredo Hinojosa, Admin.
Mailing Address: P.O. Box 2049, 79845.
Res.: 1101 W. O'Reilly, 79845. Tel: 432-229-3235; Fax: 432-229-3953.
Catechesis/Religious Program—Patricia Venegas, P.C.L.; Leticia Juarez, P.C.L. Students 190.
Mission—Sgdo. Corazon de Jesus Shafter, Presidio Co. Tel: 432-229-4679.
Mission—San Jose Redford, Presidio Co.
Mission—Our Lady of Peace Candelaria, Presidio Co.
Mission—Lajitas Mission Lajitas, Brewster Co.
SAN ELIZARIO, EL PASO CO.
1—SAN ELCEARIO, [JC] Rev. Edward C. Carpenter; Deacon Pilar Grijalva Jr.
Res.: P.O. Box 910, 79849. Tel: 915-851-2333.
Catechesis/Religious Program—Students 208.
2—SAN FELIPE DE JESUS Rev. Celimo Osorio.
Mailing Address: P.O. Box 1070, 79849.
Res.: 401 Passmore, 79849. Tel: 915-851-3039.
Catechesis/Religious Program—Romualda Miranda, P.C.L. Students 340.
VAN HORN, CULBERSON CO., OUR LADY OF FATIMA Rev. Rodolfo Lacerna, Admin.
Mailing Address: P.O. Box 398, 79855.
Res.: 308 Almond St., 79855. Tel: 432-283-2042.
Catechesis/Religious Program—Corina Flores, P.C.L. Students 131.
Mission—Our Lady of Miracles P.O. Box 144, Sierra Blanca, Hudspeth Co. 79851.
Mission—San Isidro P.O. Box 65, Dell City, Hudspeth Co. Tel: 915-964-2601. Rev. Wallace Blake Fry, Admin.
Mission—Sacred Heart General Delivery, Valentine, Jeff Davis Co. 79854.

Chaplains of Public Institutions

EL PASO. *El Paso County Jail*. Vacant.
El Paso Juvenile Detention Center. Vacant.
ANTHONY. *La Tuna Federal*. Rev. Vidal Robles Jr., J.D., J.C.L.
7045 Second St., P.O. Box 10, Canutillo, 79835.

On Duty Outside of Diocese:
Revs.—
Aguilera, Salvador, U.S. Naval Academy, Annapolis, MD 21402. U.S. Navy
Kim, Nam Joseph (Society of St. Sulpice)
Rowland, Thomas, Madonna House, Combermere ON K0J 1L0 Canada.
Zamorano, Richard (Diocese of Tucson)

Absent on Leave:
Revs.—
Bengert, Tony
Knopp, John
Lopez, Richard
Maraya, Felipe
Marin, Miguel
Munoz, Manuel
Narez, Juan
Olivas, J. Alfredo
Ponce, Demetrio
Ramirez, Jose Nieves
Ruiz, Rick

Retired:
Rev. Msgrs.—
Frias, Carlos
Ryan, William H.
Revs.—
Acevedo, Luis H.
Burkus, John
Cervantes, Fidel
Herrera, Francisco
Lafrenz, James
Lucero, Lorenzo
Meneses, Miguel
Rini, John
Rizzo, Mark
Stegman, Leonard F.
Weiss, Richard

Permanent Deacons:
Aguirre, Vicente G., St. Paul, El Paso
Alvarez, Juan M., St. Pius X, El Paso
Andrade, Paul, Jr., Most Holy Trinity, El Paso
Bustillos, Ignacio M., Cristo Rey, El Paso
Cardenas, Jesus A., St. Mark, El Paso
Grijalva, Hector E., St. Stephen, El Paso
Grijalva, Pilar, Jr., San Elizario, El Paso
Lister, Paul A., Our Lady of Peace, Alpine
Lujan, Rolando, St. Pius X, El Paso
MeLucci, Aurelio, St. Ignatius, El Paso
Reyes, William, Our Lady of Guadalupe, El Paso
Rodriguez, Ernesto, St. Patrick Cathedral, El Paso
Rodriguez, Gus J., Sr., St. Stephen, El Paso
Rotchford, Frederick C., St. Luke, El Paso
Rubio, Carlos E., Our Lady of the Valley, El Paso
Sanchez, Jose L., St. Patrick Cathedral, El Paso
Saucedo, Roberto E., Santo Nino, El Paso
Segura, Francisco R., St. Mark, El Paso
Solis, Ralph, (Retired)
Soto, Jose E., St. Thomas Aquinas, El Paso
Szostek, James T., St. Pius X, El Paso
Torres, Ignacio J., St. Thomas Aquinas, El Paso
Vasquez, George, (Retired)
Wauson, Thomas J., (Retired), Christ the Savior, El Paso

INSTITUTIONS LOCATED IN THE DIOCESE

[A] SEMINARIES, DIOCESAN

EL PASO. *St. Charles Seminary* (1961) 8330 Park Haven, 79907. Tel: 915-872-8460; Fax: 915-872-8468. Rev. John Telles, Rector; Sr. Darlene Stoecklein, A.S.C., Librarian/Formation Staff; Rev. Stephen Peters, Spiritual Dir. Seminarians 12.

[B] SEMINARIES, RELIGIOUS OR SCHOLASTICATES

EL PASO. *St. Anthony's School of Theology* (1935) 4601 Hastings Dr., 79903. Tel: 915-566-2261; Fax: 915-566-8851. Email: sas1936@hotmail.com. Revs. Maximino J. Rangel, O.F.M., Rector & Prof.; Mauro Munoz, Guardian & Prof.; J. Alejandro Juarez, O.F.M., Fin. Off. & Prof.; Jaime Yanez, O.F.M.; Jose Alfredo Ramirez, O.F.M., Students Master & Prof.; Bro. Hermenegildo Resendiz. Franciscan Fathers of St. Peter and St. Paul Province, Michoacan, Mexico. Priests 5;

Scholastics 16; Brothers 1; Sisters 3.

Roger Bacon College (1940) 2400 Marr St., 79903. Tel: 915-565-2921; Fax: 915-562-4756. Email: rogerbaconcollege@juno.com. Revs. Juan Pedro Murrillo, O.F.M., Rector; Romauldo Rangel, O.F.M.; Jose Vera-Perez, O.F.M. Minor Seminary of the Franciscan Fathers, Province of the Holy Gospel. Priests 3; Brothers 1.

[C] HIGH SCHOOLS, PRIVATE

EL PASO. *Cathedral High School, Inc.* (Boys), 1309 N. Stanton St., 79902. Tel: 915-532-3238; Fax: 915-533-8248. Email: sgovea80@cathedral-elpaso.org. Web: cathedral-elpaso.org. Mr. Sam Govea, Prin.; Peter Solis, Librarian. Brothers 3; Lay Teachers 34; Students 490.

Father Yermo Schools, (Grades PreK-12), High School/Elementary/Learning Center., 220 Washington St., 79905. Tel: 915-532-6875; Fax: 915-532-2827. Email: srmariafys@hotmail.com. Web: fatheryermoschools.com. Sisters Maria Jesus Munguia, S.S.H.J.P., High School Prin.; Angelica Omana, S.S.H.J.P., Elem. Prin.; Grace Galvan, S.S.H.J.P., Librarian. Servants of the Sacred Heart of Jesus and of the Poor. Sisters 7; Lay Teachers 43; Students 509.

Loretto Academy, (Grades PreK-12), 1300 Hardaway, 79903. Tel: 915-566-8400; Fax: 915-566-0636. Email: bboesen@loretto.org. Web: www.loretto.org. Sr. Mary E. Boesen, S.L., Pres.; Mr. Abe Ramirez, Middle/High School Prin.; Ms. Jane German, Elementary Prin.; Ms. Margie Niemira, Librarian; Ms. Connie Hartley, Librarian. Sisters of Loretto at the Foot of the Cross. Sisters 2; Lay Teachers 47; Students 655.

[D] CLINICS

EL PASO. *Centro San Vicente* (1988) 8061 Alameda, 79915. Tel: 915-859-7545; Fax: 915-859-9862. Email: csv@csv.tachc.org. Web: www.sanvicente.org. Donald M. Tufts, CEO.

Centro San Vicente Total Assisted 51,586; Total Staff 160.

La Clinica Guadalupana, Inc. (1995) 901 Ascencion, 79928. Tel: 915-852-3328; Fax: 915-852-4246. Email: dbenedict@umcelpaso.org. Deborah Benedict, Exec. Dir. Total Assisted Annually 1,540.

[E] DAY CARE CENTERS

EL PASO. *St. Joseph of the Valley* (Multi-purpose Center), 7681 Barton, 79915. Tel: 915-778-3407; Fax: 915-778-3407. Sisters 1; Total Assisted Annually 50.

[F] HOMES FOR AGED

EL PASO. *Nazareth Hall Nursing Center*, 4614 Trowbridge, 79903. Tel: 915-565-4677; Fax: 915-565-5118. Email: bcarpenter@nazarethhall.org. Web: nazarethhallnursing.com.

[G] MONASTERIES & RESIDENCES FOR PRIESTS & BROTHERS

EL PASO. *Christian Brothers*, 1204 N. Mesa, 79902-4012. Tel: 915-532-9314.

[H] CONVENTS AND RESIDENCES FOR WOMEN

EL PASO. *Adorers of the Blood of Christ (A.S.C.)* (1834) 199 Pendale Rd., 79907. Tel: 915-566-5855. Email: micasa2chante@msn.com. Sr. Darlene Stoecklein, A.S.C., Contact Person. Sisters 2.

Daughters of Charity of St. Vincent De Paul (D.C.), 3014 Taylor St., 79930. Tel: 915-564-5921; Fax: 915-859-9862. Email: dctaylorelpaso@gmail.com. Sisters 4.

11540 Montana, D1, 79936. Tel: 915-855-6451. Email: dcredsails@aol.com. Sisters 3.

Hermanas Contemplativas del Buen Pastor (H.C.B.P.) (1835) (Cloistered), *Good Shepherd Convent*, 8824 Old County Rd., P.O. Box 17254, 79917. Tel: 915-859-3683; Fax: 915-872-0698. Sr. Ernestina Estrada, Supr. Sisters 5.

Hermanas del Servicio Social (1945) 6372 Saint Lo Dr., 79925-1807. Tel: 915-771-0780. Email: hsscarmena@yahoo.com.

Hermanas Dominicas de la Doctrinia Cristiana (O.P.) (1948) *San Alberto Provincial Magno Convent*, 634 Hampton Rd., 79907. Tel: 915-590-3107; Fax: 915-590-6169. Email: provincia_norte_stacatalina@yahoo.com.mx; provincianorte@gmail.com. Sisters Maria Refugio Vazquez, O.P., Prov. Supr.; Maria de la Luz Oseguera, O.P., Local Supr.; Teresa Aguayo, O.P., Provincial Vicar. Sisters 55.

Missionary Sisters of Jesus, Mary & Joseph (M.J.M.J.), 7681 Barton Dr., 79915. Tel: 915-778-3407. Email: menobye@hotmail.com. Sr. Julia Donez, Supr. Sisters 5.

Servants of the Sacred Heart of Jesus and of the Poor (S.S.H.J.P.), Father Yermo Convent, 237 Tobin Pl., 79905. Tel: 915-533-3338; Fax: 915-532-7511. Sr. Elia Lucia Hernandez, S.S.H.J.P., Supr. Sisters 10.

Queen of Peace Convent, 3119 Pera Ave., 79905. Tel: 915-533-0590; Fax: 915-838-9640. Sr. Martha Sagrario Santamaria, Supr. Sisters 7.

Sisters of Loretto at the Foot of the Cross (S.L.), 1300 Hardaway St., 79903. Tel: 915-566-8400; Fax: 915-566-0636. Web: www.lorettocommunity.org. Sisters 10.

Sisters of Our Lady of Charity (1931) 415 N. Glenwood Dr., 79905. Tel: 915-772-0737; Fax: 915-779-2664. Email: mescobar1125@hotmail.com. Web: nauolc.org. Sr. Martha Escobar, Supr. Sisters 11.

Sisters of Our Lady of Charity of the Good Shepherd (R.G.S.) (1835) *Good Shepherd Convent*, 8824 Old County Rd., P.O. Box 17635, 79917. Tel: 915-858-0692. Sr. Maria del Rocio Hernandez, Supr. Sisters 4.

Sisters of Perpetual Adoration (A.P.) (1937) Corpus Christi Monastery, 451 Mockingbird Ln., 79907. Tel: 915-591-5662; Fax: 915-598-6203. Email: ccmonast@aol.com. Sr. Maria Sagrario Perez, A.P., Supr. (Cloistered) Sisters 8.

Sisters of Perpetual Adoration (A.P.) (1979) *Cristo Rey Monastery*, 145 Cotton St., 79901. Tel: 915-533-5323. Sr. Maria Isabel De La Trinidad, Supr. Sisters 13.

Sisters of St. Joseph of Carondelet (C.S.J.), 335 Valle Sereno, 79907. Tel: 915-629-8297.

MARFA. *Missionary Sisters of Jesus, Mary & Joseph*, P.O. Box 1118, 79843. Tel: 432-729-3385. Sisters 2.

[I] NEWMAN CENTERS

EL PASO. *Catholic Campus Ministry at University of Texas at El Paso* 2230 N. Oregon, 79902. Tel: 915-838-0300. Email: campusministry@elpasodiocese.org. Rev. Henry Beck, O.F.M., Campus Minister.

ALPINE. *Sul Ross State University Newman Center* P.O. Box C 78, 79832. Tel: 432-837-8790; Fax: 915-837-8714. Email: joecal3ramirez@sbcglobal.net.

[J] MISCELLANEOUS LISTINGS

EL PASO. *Adoracion Nocturna (Nocturnal Adoration)*, c/o 499 St. Matthews St., 79907.

Annunciation House (1978) 1003 E. San Antonio, 79901. Tel: 915-533-4675; Fax: 915-351-1343. Email: rubengarcia@annunciationhouse.org. Web: www.annunciationhouse.org. Mr. Ruben Garcia, Dir.

Apostolado de la Cruz (Apostolate of the Cross), c/o 499 St. Matthews St., 79907.

Blue Army, c/o 499 St. Matthews St., 79907. Rev. Ikechi Korie, O.P.

Casa Vides (Shelter for displaced families), 325 Leon St., 79901. Mr. Ruben Garcia, Dir.

Catholic Counseling Services, Inc., 499 St. Matthews St., 79907. Tel: 915-872-8424; Fax: 915-872-8425. Email: jcastrellon@elpasodiocese.org. Mr. Jose Castrellon, Exec. Dir.

Catholic Daughters of America, c/o 499 St. Matthews St., 79907.

Catholic Knights of America, c/o 499 St. Matthews St., 79907.

Catholic Legal Immigration Network, Inc. (CLINIC) Subsidiary of the USCCB Southwest Regional Office., 2400-A E. Yandell, 79903. Tel: 915-532-3975; Fax: 915-532-4071. Email: clinictx@aol.com. Services: National immigration support network to the Catholic Dioceses throughout the U.S. Southwest regional CLINIC office provides technical assistance, basic organizational program services, management assessments, and immigration law training for its diocesan affiliates. CLINIC assists dioceses in applying for agency recognition and staff accreditation before the Immigration Board of Appeals. CLINIC assists dioceses and religious congregations in obtaining legal status for foreign clergy as non-immigrant and legal permanent residents.

Catholic Properties of El Paso, Inc., 499 St. Matthews St., 79907. Tel: 915-872-8406. Mr. Jorge Vergen, Exec. Dir.

Christ Child Society, 10560 Lakewood, 79925. Tel: 915-241-5440.

Cursillos de Cristianidad, c/o 499 St. Matthews St., 79907. Rev. Pablo Matta, Diocesan Dir.

Diocesan Migrant and Refugee Services, Inc. (1987) 2400-A E. Yandell, 79903. Tel: 915-532-3975; Fax: 915-532-4071. Web: www.dmrs-ep.org. Mrs. Iliana Holguin, J.D., Exec. Dir.

Diocese of El Paso Charity Trust, 499 St. Matthews St., 79907. Tel: 915-872-8400.

Diocese of El Paso Clergy Continuing Education Trust, 499 St. Matthews St., 79907.

Diocese of El Paso Education Assistance Fund, Inc., c/o 499 St. Matthews, 79907. Tel: 915-872-8426; Fax: 915-872-8464. Email: elpasocs@elpasodiocese.org.

Diocese of El Paso Historic Missions Restoration Trust, 499 St. Matthews St., 79907.

Diocese of El Paso Insurance Trust, 499 St. Matthews St., 79907.

Diocese of El Paso Investment Trust, 499 St. Matthews St., 79907.

Diocese of El Paso Seminarian Education Trust, 499 St. Matthews St., 79907.

El Paso Villa Maria, 920 S. Oregon, 79901. Tel: 915-544-5500; Fax: 915-544-5502. Email: villamaria_elp@sbcglobal.net. Sisters Helen Santamaria, S.L., Exec. Dir.; Mary Margaret Murphy, S.L., Case Mgr.

Foundation for the Diocese of El Paso (2001) 499 St. Matthews, 79907. Tel: 915-872-8412; Fax: 915-872-8411. Email: tyellen@elpasodiocese.org. Web: www.elpasodiocesefoundation.org. Ms. Tracy Yellen, COO. Tel: 915-872-8412, Ext. 170; Fax: 915-872-8411.

Franciscans, Secular Order of Franciscans, c/o 499 St. Matthews St., 79907. Rev. John Stowe, O.F.M.Conv., V.G., Spiritual Asst.

Historic Missions Restoration, Inc., 499 St. Matthews St., 79907.

Knights of Columbus, c/o 499 St. Matthews St., 79907. Rev. Msgr. Francis J. Smith, P.A., V.G.

Knights of St. Gregory, c/o 499 St. Matthews St., 79907.

Knights of the Holy Sepulchre, c/o 499 St. Matthews St., 79907. Rev. Msgr. Francis J. Smith, P.A., V.G.

La Posada Home (1986) 1020 N. Campbell, 79902. Tel: 915-544-4595; Fax: 915-544-2373. Email: monyalmuina@hotmail.com. Shelter for displaced families.

Ladies of the Holy Sepulchre, c/o 499 St. Matthews St., 79907. Rev. Msgr. Francis J. Smith, P.A., V.G.

Legion of Mary, c/o 499 St. Matthews St., 79907.

Mount Carmel Cemetery Perpetual Care Trust, 499 St. Matthews St., 79907. Tel: 915-872-8400.

Open Arms Community, Centro Santa Fe (1972) 8210 N. Loop Dr., 79907. Tel: 915-595-0589; Fax: 915-851-2251. Email: openarms@openarmscommunity.org. Web: openarmscommunity.org. Joanne D. Ivey, Dir.

Our Lady's Youth Center (1953) 501 E. Paisano, P.O. Box 1422, 79948. Tel: 915-533-5260; 915-533-9122; Fax: 575-233-3829. Email: olyc77@gmail.com. Rev. John L. Vessels, S.J., Dir. The Lord's Ranch & The Lord's Food Bank.

Serra Club, c/o 499 St. Matthews St., 79907. Elizabeth Rios Carl, Contact Person.

St. Vincent de Paul Society, c/o 499 St. Matthews St., 79907. Rebecca Montelongo, Contact Person.

Zaragosa, Texas Catholic Relief Trust, 499 St. Matthews St., 79907. Tel: 915-872-8407.

RELIGIOUS INSTITUTES OF MEN REPRESENTED IN THE DIOCESE

For further details refer to the corresponding bracketed number in the Religious Institutes of Men or Women section.

[0330]—*Brothers of the Christian Schools* (New Orleans and Santa Fe Provs.)—F.S.C.

[0460]—*Brothers of the Poor of St. Francis*—C.F.P.

[]—*Catholic Foreign Mission Society of American, Inc*—M.M.

[0480]—*Conventual Franciscan Friars* (Province of Our Lady of Consolation)—O.F.M.Conv

[0520]—*Franciscan Friars* (Holy Gospel Prov. and St. Peter & Paul Prov.)—O.F.M.

[0520]—*Franciscan Friars* (Prov. of Saint John the Baptist.)—O.F.M.

[0690]—*Jesuit Fathers and Brothers* (Prov. of New Orleans)—S.J.

[0370]—*Missionary Society of Saint Columban*—S.S.C.

[]—*Order of Augustinian* (Province of Our Mother of Good Counsel)—O.S.A.

[]—*Order of Preachers* (Province of St. Joseph the Worker Nigeria & Ghana)—O.P.

[0150]—*Order of the Augustinian Recollects* (Prov. of San Nicolas of Tolentino, Italy)—O.A.R.

[1240]—*Servites* (Province of Mexico)—O.S.M.

RELIGIOUS INSTITUTES OF WOMEN REPRESENTED IN THE DIOCESE

[3190]—*Adoratrices del Santisimo Sacramento*—A.P.

[0100]—*Adorers of the Blood of Christ*—A.S.C.

[]—*Adrian Dominican Sisters*—O.P.

[]—*Congregation of St. Joseph*—C.S.J.

[3832]—*Congregation of the Sisters of St. Joseph*—C.S.J.

[0760]—*Daughters of Charity of St. Vincent de Paul*—D.C.

[1370]—*Franciscan Missionaries of Mary*—F.M.M.

[1430]—*Franciscan Sisters of Our Lady of Perpetual Help*—O.S.F.

[]—*Franciscan Sisters of Perpetual Adoration*—F.S.P.A.

[]—*Hermanas Contemplativas del Buen Pastor*—H.C.B.P.

[]—*Hermanas de San Jose de Lyon* (Prov. Mex.)

[]—*Hermanas del Servico Social*—H.S.S.

[]—*Hermanas Dominicas de la Doctrina Cristiana*—O.P.

[]—*Hermanas Franciscanas de San Jose*—H.F.S.J.

[2470]—*Maryknoll Sisters of St. Dominic*—M.M.

[2770]—*Missionary Sisters of Jesus, Mary and Joseph*—M.J.M.J.

[2970]—*School Sisters of Notre Dame*—S.S.N.D.

[1680]—*School Sisters of St. Francis*—S.S.S.F.

[3660]—*Servants of the Sacred Heart of Jesus and of the Poor*—S.S.H.J.P.

[]—*Sisters of Charity of Cincinnati*—S.C.

[]—*Sisters of Charity of New Jersey*—S.C.

[0460]—*Sisters of Charity of the Incarnate Word*—C.C.V.I.

[2360]—*Sisters of Loretto at the Foot of the Cross*—S.L.

[]—*Sisters of Mercy*—R.S.M.

[]—*Sisters of Our Lady of Charity*—O.L.C.

[]—*Sisters of Our Lady of Charity of the Good Shepherd*—R.G.S.

[1630]—*Sisters of St. Francis of Penance and Christian Charity*—O.S.F.

[3840]—*Sisters of St. Joseph of Carondelet* (Province of St. Louis)—C.S.J.

[3840]—*Sisters of St. Joseph of Carondelet* (Prov. of St. Paul)—C.S.J.

[]—*Sisters of St. Joseph of Concordia, Kansas*—C.S.J.

[]—*Sisters of the Living Word*—S.L.W.

DIOCESAN CEMETERY

EL PASO. *Mount Carmel*, Box 17655, 79917. Tel: 915-860-0606.

NECROLOGY

† Saez, Jose Vincente, (Retired)—Died Oct. 24, 2008

An asterisk (*) denotes an organization that has established tax-exempt status directly with the IRS and is not covered by the USCCB Group Ruling.

Diocese of Erie

(Dioecesis Eriensis)

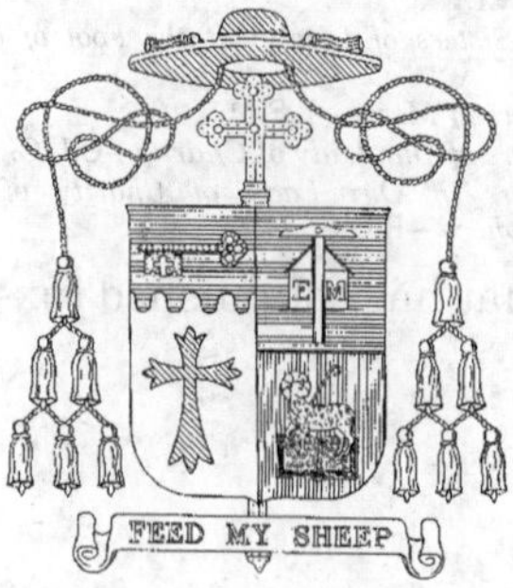

Most Reverend

DONALD W. TRAUTMAN, S.T.D., S.S.L.

Bishop of Erie; ordained April 7, 1962; appointed Titular Bishop of Sassura and Auxiliary Bishop of Buffalo February 27, 1985; consecrated April 16, 1985; appointed to Erie June 12, 1990; installed July 16, 1990. *Res.: 205 West 9th St., Erie, PA 16501.* Tel: 814-824-1120; Fax: 814-824-1124.

Chancery: St. Mark Catholic Center, P.O. Box 10397, Erie, PA 16514. Tel: 814-824-1111; Fax: 814-824-1128.

Web: www.eriercd.org

ESTABLISHED 1853.

Square Miles 9,936.

Comprises the following Counties in Northwestern Pennsylvania: Erie, Crawford, Mercer, Venango, Forest, Clarion, Jefferson, Clearfield, Cameron, Elk, McKean, Potter and Warren.

For legal titles of parishes and diocesan institutions, consult the Chancery.

STATISTICAL OVERVIEW

Personnel	
Bishop	1
Priests: Diocesan Active in Diocese	138
Priests: Diocesan Active Outside Diocese	7
Priests: Retired, Sick or Absent	48
Number of Diocesan Priests	193
Religious Priests in Diocese	6
Total Priests in Diocese	199
Extern Priests in Diocese	5
Ordinations:	
Diocesan Priests	2
Transitional Deacons	5
Permanent Deacons	4
Permanent Deacons in Diocese	56
Total Sisters	350
Parishes	
Parishes	120
With Resident Pastor:	
Resident Diocesan Priests	95
Resident Religious Priests	2
Without Resident Pastor:	
Administered by Priests	23
Missions	18
New Parishes Created	2
Closed Parishes	4
Professional Ministry Personnel:	
Lay Ministers	11
Welfare	
Catholic Hospitals	1
Total Assisted	480,800
Homes for the Aged	4
Total Assisted	1,612
Day Care Centers	1
Total Assisted	110
Specialized Homes	3
Total Assisted	110
Special Centers for Social Services	24
Total Assisted	49,900
Other Institutions	1
Total Assisted	200
Educational	
Seminaries, Diocesan	1
Students from This Diocese	11
Students from Other Diocese	8
Diocesan Students in Other Seminaries	9
Total Seminarians	20
Colleges and Universities	2
Total Students	7,454
High Schools, Diocesan and Parish	6
Total Students	1,648
High Schools, Private	1
Total Students	595
Elementary Schools, Diocesan and Parish	32
Total Students	5,326
Elementary Schools, Private	1
Total Students	236
Catechesis/Religious Education:	
High School Students	5,658
Elementary Students	8,130
Total Students under Catholic Instruction	29,067
Teachers in the Diocese:	
Priests	9
Sisters	10
Lay Teachers	534
Vital Statistics	
Receptions into the Church:	
Infant Baptism Totals	1,543
Minor Baptism Totals	63
Adult Baptism Totals	119
Received into Full Communion	90
First Communions	2,021
Confirmations	1,962
Marriages:	
Catholic	365
Interfaith	252
Total Marriages	617
Deaths	2,542
Total Catholic Population	221,958
Total Population	860,340

Former Bishops—Most Revs. MICHAEL O'CONNOR, cons. Bishop of Pittsburgh, Aug. 15, 1843; transferred from Pittsburgh as first Bishop of Erie in 1853; transferred back to Pittsburgh in 1854; died Oct. 18, 1872; JOSUE M. YOUNG, cons. April 23, 1854; died Sept. 18, 1866; TOBIAS MULLEN, D.D., cons. Aug. 2, 1868, Bishop of Erie; resigned Aug. 10, 1899, and appt. to Titular See of Germanicopolis; died April 22, 1900; JOHN E. FITZMAURICE, D.D., cons. Feb. 24, 1898; died June 18, 1920; EDWARD P. MCMANAMAN, S.T.D., Titular Bishop of Floriana and Auxiliary Bishop of Erie; cons. Oct. 28, 1948; died July 18, 1964; JOHN MARK GANNON, D.D., Archbishop-Bishop of Erie; ord. Dec. 21, 1901; appt. Titular Bishop of Nilopolis, Nov. 13, 1917; cons. Feb. 6, 1918; transferred to Erie, Aug. 26, 1920; installed Dec. 16, 1920; appt. Assistant at the Pontifical Throne Nov. 4, 1944; appt. Archbishop "ad personam" Nov. 25, 1953; resigned Sept. 21, 1966 and transferred to Titular See of Tacarata, Dec. 14, 1966; died Sept. 5, 1968; JOHN F. WHEALON, D.D., appt. Titular Bishop of Andrapa and Auxiliary Bishop of Cleveland, June 2, 1961; cons. July 6, 1961; transferred to the See of Erie, Dec. 14, 1966; transferred to the Archdiocese of Hartford; died Aug. 2, 1991; ALFRED M. WATSON, D.D., Bishop of Erie; ord. May 10, 1934; Titular Bishop of Nationa and Auxiliary Bishop of Erie; appt. May 17, 1965; cons. June 29, 1965; succeeded to See, March 19, 1969; retired July 16, 1982; died Jan. 4, 1990 Cleveland; MICHAEL J. MURPHY, D.D., S.T.L., Titular Bishop of Arindela and Auxiliary Bishop of Cleveland; appt. April 20, 1976; cons. June 11, 1976; Coadjutor Bishop of Erie; appt. Nov. 28, 1978; succeeded to See, July 16, 1982; retired July 16, 1990; died April 3, 2007.

Vicar General—Rev. Msgr. ROBERT J. SMITH, J.C.L., V.G., Mailing Address: St. Mark Catholic Center, P.O. Box 10397, Erie, 16514-0397. Tel: 814-824-1130; Fax: 814-824-1124.

Office of the Bishop—ROBERTA PALMISANO, Sec. to the Bishop, Mailing Address: St. Mark Catholic Center, P.O. Box 10397, Erie, 16514. Tel: 814-824-1120; Fax: 814-824-1124.

Chancery—Mailing Address: St. Mark Catholic Center, P.O. Box 10397, Erie, 16514. Tel: 814-824-1135; Fax: 814-824-1124.

Chancellor—Rev. EDWARD M. LOHSE, J.C.L.

Vice Chancellor—Sr. CATHERINE MANNING, S.S.J.

Diocesan Archivist— Contact the Chancellor

Episcopal Vicars—

Northern Vicariate—Rev. Msgr. ROBERT J. SMITH, J.C.L., V.G., Mailing Address: St. Mark Catholic Center, P.O. Box 10397, Erie, 16514. Tel: 814-824-1130.

Eastern Vicariate—Rev. Msgr. CHARLES A. KAZA, E.V., 1135 Hewett St., Brockway, 15824. Tel: 814-265-1374.

Western Vicariate—Rev. Msgr. JOHN W. SWOGER, E.V., 35 Pearl Ave., Oil City, 16301. Tel: 814-677-4004.

Vicar for Religious—Sr. MARY RITA KUHN, S.S.J., Mailing Address: St. Mark Catholic Center, P.O. Box 10397, Erie, 16514-0397. Tel: 814-824-1125.

Office for the Protection of Children and Youth—KAREN STREETT, Coord., Mailing Address: St. Mark Catholic Center, P.O. Box 10397, Erie, 16514-0397. Tel: 814-824-1222.

Advisory To Bishop

Administrative Cabinet—Rev. Msgrs. ROBERT J. SMITH, J.C.L., V.G.; CHARLES A. KAZA, E.V.; Sr. MARY RITA KUHN, S.S.J.; Rev. NICHOLAS J. ROUCH, S.T.D.; MARY C. MAXWELL, M.A.; DAVID MURPHY; Rev. EDWARD M. LOHSE, J.C.L.; Rev. Msgr. JOHN W. SWOGER, E.V.; Dr. EMMA LEE MCCLOSKEY, C.F.R.E., Consultant.

College of Consultors—Rev. EDWARD M. LOHSE, J.C.L.; Rev. Msgrs. CHARLES A. KAZA, E.V.; ROBERT J. SMITH, J.C.L., V.G.; JOHN W. SWOGER, E.V.; DANIEL E. MAGRAW; ROBERT M. MALENE; H. DESMOND MCGEE, V.F.; Very Rev. GREGORY A. KIRSCH, V.F.

Finance Council—Most Rev. DONALD W. TRAUTMAN, S.T.D., S.S.L.; Rev. Msgr. JOHN W. SWOGER, E.V.; THOMAS C. GUELCHER; JOSEPH M. HILBERT; Ms. MAUREEN BARBER-CAREY, Ed.D.; JAMES E. MARTIN; Ms. C. ANGELA BONTEMPO, F.A.C.H.E.; AL LANDER, Esq.; Rev. Msgrs. ROBERT L. BRUGGER; CHARLES A. KAZA, E.V. Ex Officios: Rev. Msgr. ROBERT J. SMITH, J.C.L., V.G.; DAVID J. MURPHY.

Deans—Rev. Msgr. BERNARD J. URBANIAK, Erie East; Very Revs. JOHN J. DETISCH, V.F., Erie West; JOSEPH C. GREGOREK, V.F., Ph.D., Gannon University; JEFFERY J. NOBLE, V.F., Sharon; Rev. Msgr. JOHN J. HERBEIN, V.F., Oil City; Very Revs. PHILLIP A. PINCZEWSKI, V.F., Bradford; GREGORY A. KIRSCH, V.F., Clearfield; Rev. Msgrs. LAWRENCE T.

SPEICE, V.F., Meadville; JOSEPH J. RICCARDO, V.F., DuBois; Rev. THOMAS L. TYLER, V.F., St. Marys; Rev. Msgr. JOHN J. LUCAS, V.F., Warren.

Presbyteral Council—Most Rev. DONALD W. TRAUTMAN, S.T.D., S.S.L., Pres.; Very Rev. GREGORY A. KIRSCH, V.F., Chm.; Rev. Msgr. DANIEL E. MAGRAW, Sec.

Priest Personnel Board—Rev. Msgrs. ROBERT J. SMITH, J.C.L., V.G., Chm.; H. DESMOND MCGEE, V.F.; WILLIAM C. KARG; Revs. GEORGE E. STROHMEYER, M.A., Sec.; PHILIP PINCZEWSKI; GLENN R. WHITMAN; JOHN P. MALTHANER; MARC J. SOLOMON.

Priest Retirement Board—Most Rev. DONALD W. TRAUTMAN, S.T.D., S.S.L., Chm. Members: THOMAS C. GUELCHER; Rev. Msgrs. ERNEST J. DALEY (Retired); JOHN B. HAGERTY (Retired); ROBERT J. SMITH, J.C.L., V.G.; Rev. EDWARD M. LOHSE, J.C.L.; Deacon WILLIAM SABORSKY; SAMUEL ZAFFUTO. Staff: DAVID J. MURPHY.

Episcopal Delegate for Retired Priests—Rev. Msgrs. ERNEST J. DALEY (Retired); JOHN B. HAGERTY (Retired).

Pennsylvania Catholic Conference—Rev. Msgr. MARK L. BARTCHAK, J.C.D., Personal Rep. of the Bishop, Mailing Address: St. Mark Catholic Center, P.O. Box 10397, Erie, 16514. Tel: 814-824-1140.

The Bishop's Theological Advisory Committee—Rev. Msgr. GERALD L. ORBANEK, M.A., Chm.; Revs. EDWARD KRAUSE, C.S.C., Ph.D.; CASIMIR WOZNIAK, Ph.D.; Very Rev. MICHAEL T. KESICKI, S.S.L.; Mr. PATRICK O'CONNELL, Ph.D.; Sr. MICHELLE HEALY, S.S.J., M.A.; Rev. SCOTT P. DETISCH, Ph.D.

Matrimonial Concerns

All requests for marriage dispensations, permissions, and rogatory commissions should be sent to this office.

Diocesan Tribunal—Mailing Address: St. Mark Catholic Center, P.O. Box 10397, Erie, 16514. Tel: 814-824-1140; Fax: 814-824-1149.

Judicial Vicar—Rev. Msgr. MARK L. BARTCHAK, J.C.D.

Promoter of Justice—Rev. EDWARD M. LOHSE, J.C.L.

Defender of the Bond—Very Rev. GREGORY A. KIRSCH, V.F.

Matrimonial Judges—Rev. Msgrs. ROBERT J. SMITH, J.C.L., V.G.; RICHARD J. STACK, J.C.L. (Retired); MARK L. BARTCHAK, J.C.D.; Rev. JOHN P. BEAL, J.C.D.; Deacon RICHARD D. SHEWMAN, J.C.L.; BARBARA A. BETTWY, J.C.L.

Auditors—Sisters JEAN BAPTISTE DILUZIO, S.S.J.; SYLVIA BURNETT, O.S.B.M.

Secretaries/Notaries—PATRICIA WIERBINSKI; CINDY MANGIARACINA.

Office of Conciliation & Arbitration—Mailing Address: St. Mark Catholic Center, P.O. Box 10397, Erie, 16514. Tel: 814-824-1140; Fax: 814-824-1149. Rev. Msgr. MARK L. BARTCHAK, J.C.D., Dir.

Catholic Education

Unless otherwise indicated, all correspondence for Catholic Education should be directed to St. Mark Catholic Center, P.O. Box 10397, Erie, PA 16514-0397.

Vicar for Catholic Education—Rev. NICHOLAS J. ROUCH, S.T.D. Tel: 814-824-1220.

Special Assistant to the Vicar—Mr. RONALD FRONZAGLIA. Tel: 814-824-1220.

Elementary Curriculum and Teacher Personnel—KIMBERLY LYTLE, Dir. Tel: 814-824-1248.

Government Programs—ROBERTA BUCCI, Dir. Govt. Programs. Tel: 814-824-1238.

Director of Catholic Schools and Principal Personnel—Ms. PATRICIA MCLAUGHLIN. Tel: 814-824-1247.

Elementary Athletic Programs—DOUGLAS CHUZIE, Dir. Athletics. Tel: 814-824-1245.

Diocesan Director of Athletics—DOUGLAS CHUZIE. Tel: 814-824-1245.

Religious Education—Mr. JOSEPH STREETT, D.R.E. Tel: 814-824-1210; Sr. NANCY FISCHER, S.S.J., Dir. Community Formation & Lay Ministry Training. Tel: 814-824-1210; Rev. STEPHEN J. SCHREIBER, Dir. Office of Youth & Young Adults. Tel: 814-824-1210; BARBARA BURKETT, B.S., Dir. NFP & Coord. Chastity Educ. Tel: 814-824-1259; KAREN STREETT, Coord. Media Resources & Office for the Protection of Children and Youth. Tel: 814-824-1222; Sr. NANCY FISCHER, S.S.J., Dir. RCIA.

Campus Ministry—Deacon STEPHEN J. WASHEK, Diocesan Dir. Campus Min., Gannon University, 109 University Sq., Erie, 16541. Tel: 814-871-7435 See Separate listing in the Institution Section for details on Campus Ministry and Newman Centers.

Catholic Charities

Affiliated Offices, Agencies and Institutions

Central Administration

All communication for the Catholic Charities Central Administration should be directed to St. Mark Catholic Center, P.O. Box 10397, Erie, PA 16514-0397. Tel: 814-824-1251.

Office of Catholic Charities—MARY C. MAXWELL, M.A., Exec. Dir.

Catholic Charities of the Diocese of Erie, Inc.—MARY C. MAXWELL, M.A., Charities program and fiscal development corporation.

Director of Development—Dr. EMMA LEE MCCLOSKEY, C.F.R.E., Dir.

Pastoral Social Services

Unless otherwise indicated, all communication for Catholic Charities Pastoral Social Services should be directed to St. Mark Catholic Center, P.O. Box 10397, Erie, PA 16514-0397. Tel: 814-824-1251.

Family Life—ANN BADACH, B.S., Dir., Office includes Marriage Preparation and Enrichment Programs, Family Ministry, Retrouvaille.

Parish Social Ministry/Respect Life—ERIN LANDINI-GROGAN, M.S., Dir., Consultant for Parish Care and Concern and Social Justice & Respect Life Programs.

Refugee Ministry—JOSEPH J. HAAS, L.P.C., Dir. Tel: 800-673-2535. Email: jhaas@cccas.org.

Catholic Rural Ministry - Bradford Deanery—Co Directors: Sisters PHYLLIS SCHLEICHER, O.S.B.; MARY WILLIAM HOFFMAN, O.S.B., 472 Sartwell Creek Rd., Port Allegany, 16743. Tel: 814-544-8017.

Catholic Rural Ministry - Oil City Deanery—Co Directors: Sisters CLARE MARIE BEICHNER, S.S.J., L.S.W.; MARIAN WEHLER, O.S.B., Mailing Address: 7 Pulaski St., Oil City, 16301. Tel: 814-677-2032.

Rainbows—Sr. ANN BANNON, O.S.B., Dir.

Office of Diocesan and International Mission Activities—PAT MARSHALL, Supvr.

Office of Disabilites/Deaf Ministry/Healing Ministries—JACKLYN JOHNSON, R.N., Dir.

Victim Assistance Coordinator—Dr. ROBERT NELSEN. Tel: 814-871-7723. Email: nelsen001@gannon.edu.

Community Counseling Services

Catholic Charities Counseling and Adoption Services—JOSEPH J. HAAS, L.P.C., Agency Dir. Tel: 814-456-2091.

Northern Vicariate - Erie Office—JEFFREY ROSE, Area Supvr., 329 W. Tenth St., Erie, 16502. Tel: 814-456-2091.

Western Vicariate - Sharon Office—CONNIE MASIAN, L.S.W., Area Supvr., 995 Linden St., Sharon, 16146. Tel: 412-346-4142.

Eastern Vicariate - DuBois Office—NANCI MATTISON, M.A., Area Supvr., 90 Beaver Dr., Ste. 119 D, Box 2, DuBois, 15801. Tel: 814-371-4717.

Residential Services for Older Persons

John XXIII Home—KIRK HAWTHORNE, Admin., 2250 Shenango Fwy., Hermitage, 16148. Tel: 814-981-3200.

Christ the King Manor—SAMUEL ZAFFUTO, Admin., 1100 W. Long Ave., Du Bois, 15801. Tel: 814-371-3180.

Community Social Services

**St. Martin Center*CHERYL KOBEL, M.A., Dir., 1701 Parade St., Erie, 16503. Tel: 814-452-6113.

Harborcreek Youth Services—Mr. JOHN D. PETULLA, A.C.S.W., M.S.W., 5712 Iroquois Ave., Harborcreek, 16421. Tel: 814-899-7664.

Prince of Peace Center—JOSEPH FLECHER, Dir., 502 Darr Ave., Box 89, Farrell, 16121. Tel: 412-346-5777.

Better Housing for Erie—KAREN MCLELLAN, Site Mgr., 515 State St., Erie, 16501. Tel: 814-456-0510.

Good Samaritan Center—Deacon ANTHONY INDELICATO, Dir., 1 E. Locust St., Clearfield, 16830. Tel: 814-768-7229.

St. Elizabeth Center—Deacon JOHN WREN, 311 Emerald St., Oil City, 16301. Tel: 814-677-0203.

Parish Services

Unless otherwise noted, all communication for Parish Services should be directed to St. Mark Catholic Center, P.O. Box 10397, Erie, PA 16514-0397. Tel: 814-824-1274.

Office of Evangelization for Worship—MATTHEW CLARK, Admin.

Office of Communications—ANNE-MARIE WELSH, Dir.

Faith Magazine— The Magazine of the Catholic Diocese of Erie ANNE-MARIE WELSH, Exec. Editor, 429 E. Grandview Blvd., Erie, 16504. Tel: 814-824-1167; Fax: 814-824-1128. Email: faith@eriercd.org.

Financial Services

Unless otherwise noted, all communication for Financial Services should be directed to St. Mark Catholic Center, P.O. Box 10397, Erie, PA 16514-0397. Tel: 814-824-1180.

Chief Financial Officer—DAVID J. MURPHY.

Financial Services Office—DAVID J. MURPHY, Dir.; JAMES L. BOGNIAK, Dir. Accounting; THOMAS E. BURIK, CPA, Dir. Parish Financial Svcs.; Deacon WILLIAM SABORSKY, Consultant, Human Resources; CHARLES BANDUCCI, Dir. School Financial Svcs.

Stewardship and Annual Appeals Office—JOSEPH W. HOAG, Dir.

Diocesan Attorney—FRANK L. KROTO JR., Esq., Quinn, Buseck, Leemhuis, Toohey & Kroto, Inc., 2222 W. Grandview Blvd., Erie, 16506. Tel: 814-833-2222.

Erie Diocesan Cemeteries—Board of Members: Most Rev. DONALD W. TRAUTMAN, S.T.D., S.S.L.; Rev. Msgr. ROBERT J. SMITH, J.C.L., V.G.; Revs. EDWARD M. LOHSE, J.C.L.; THOMAS M. FIALKOWSKI, Bishop's Liaison; DAVID J. MURPHY; JOHN HROMYAK, Dir., 3325 West Lake Rd., Erie, 16505. Tel: 814-838-7724.

Clergy Formation

Clergy Personnel—Rev. Msgr. ROBERT J. SMITH, J.C.L., V.G., Dir., Mailing Address: St. Mark Catholic Center, P.O. Box 10397, Erie, 16514-0397. Tel: 814-824-1130; Fax: 814-824-1124.

Clergy Continuing Education and Formation—Rev. Msgr. RICHARD R. SIEFER, Coord., St. Catherine Parish, 116 S. State St., DuBois, 15801. Tel: 814-371-8556. Mailing Address: St. Mark Catholic Center, P.O. Box 10397, Erie, 16514-0397. Tel: 814-824-1195.

Vocation Office—Revs. EDWARD M. LOHSE, J.C.L., Dir.; STEPHEN J. SCHREIBER, Assoc. Dir., Mailing Address: St. Mark Catholic Center, P.O. Box 10397, Erie, 16514-0397. Tel: 814-824-1200.

St. Mark Seminary—Very Rev. MICHAEL T. KESICKI, S.S.L., Rector & Dir. Seminarians; Revs. NICHOLAS J. ROUCH, S.T.D., Vice Rector & Assoc. Dir. Seminarians; STEPHEN J. SCHREIBER, Resident Spiritual Dir.; Sr. MARY ANDREW HIMES, R.S.M., Dir. Liturgical Music, Mailing Address: St. Mark Catholic Center, P.O. Box 10397, Erie, 16514-0397. Tel: 814-824-1200.

Special Apostolates

Hispanic Apostolate—Rev. JORGE C. VILLEGAS, Dir., 1237 W. 21st St., Erie, 16502. Tel: 814-459-0543.

Apostleship of the Sea and Chaplain to the Port of Erie—Rev. Msgr. L. THOMAS SNYDERWINE, Dir., c/o St. Luke Church, 421 E. 38th St., Erie, 16504-1699. Tel: 814-825-6920.

World Apostolate of Fatima (Blue Army)—Rev. DAVID L. POULSON, Dir., 502 Peach St., Erie, 16501-1104. Tel: 814-454-6494.

Cursillo Movement—Co Directors: Rev. JOHN B. JACQUEL; Rev. Msgr. WILLIAM E. SUTHERLAND, Mailing Address: St. Mark Catholic Center, P.O. Box 10397, Erie, 16514. Tel: 814-824-1111.

Legion of Mary—Rev. JAMES T. O'HARA, Spiritual Dir., 913 Fulton St., Erie, 16503. Tel: 814-452-4832.

Charismatic Movement—MICHAEL VEHEC, Diocesan Liaison, Mailing Address: St. Mark Catholic Center, P.O. Box 10397, Erie, 16514-0397.

Bread of Life Community—Rev. LAWRENCE R. RICHARDS, Moderator, St. Joseph Parish, 147 W. 24th St., Erie, 16502-2897. Tel: 814-452-2982.

Word of Life Charismatic Renewal—St. Mark Catholic Center, 429 E. Grandview Blvd., P.O. Box 10397, Erie, 16514-0397. Tel: 814-824-1286.

Inner-City Outreach—Rev. JAMES G. GUTTING, St. Mary of the Immaculate Conception Parish, 315 E. 9th St., Erie, 16503. Tel: 814-452-2410; Sr. ROSEMARY O'BRIEN, S.S.J.; Deacon ROBERT WALKER.

Ecumenism

Pennsylvania Conference on Inter-Church Cooperation—Rev. Msgr. MARK L. BARTCHAK, J.C.D., Diocesan Rep.

Ecumenical Officers—

Eastern Vicariate—Very Rev. PHILLIP A. PINCZEWSKI, V.F., St. Callistus Church, 342 Chase St., Kane, 16735. Tel: 814-837-6694.

Western Vicariate—Rev. STEPHEN A. ANDERSON, Mailing Address: Our Lady Queen of the Americas, P.O. Box 110, Conneaut Lake, 16316. Tel: 814-382-7252.

Northern Vicariate—Rev. Msgr. WILLIAM E. BIEBEL, V.F., St. Peter Cathedral, 230 W. 10th St., Erie, 16501. Tel: 814-453-6677.

CLERGY, PARISHES, MISSIONS AND PAROCHIAL SCHOOLS

CITY OF ERIE

(ERIE COUNTY)

1—ST. PETER CATHEDRAL (1893) Rev. Msgr. William E. Biebel, Rector; Rev. John L. Miller, Parochial Vicar. In Res., Rev. Msgr. Robert G. Barcio, Archivist (Retired).
Res.: 230 W. 10th St., 16501. Tel: 814-453-6677; Fax: 814-456-1351.
Church: 10th St. & Sassafras St., 16501.
School—(Grades K-8), 160 W. 11th St., 16501. Tel: 814-452-4276; Fax: 814-452-0479. Kathleen Lane, Prin.; Miss Helen McQuown, Librarian. Lay Teachers 23; Students 258; Preschool 27.
Catechesis/Religious Program—Karen Hund, D.R.E. Students 53.

2—ST. ANDREW (1871) Rev. Msgr. Richard J. Sullivan; Deacon Ralph DeCecco. In Res., Rev. Michael G. DeMartinis.
Res.: 1116 W. Seventh St., 16502. Tel: 814-454-2486; Fax: 814-456-4443.
Catechesis/Religious Program—Carol Hoffman, D.R.E. Students 68.

3—ST. ANN (1887) Merged with St. Casimir and Holy Family to create Our Mother of Sorrows.

4—BLESSED SACRAMENT (1938) Rev. Msgr. Daniel E. Magraw; Deacon Kevin Kunik. In Res., Rev. Msgrs. John B. Hagerty (Retired); Richard J. Stack (Retired); Richard G. Mayer.
Res.: 1626 W. 26th St., 16508. Tel: 814-454-0171; Fax: 814-459-6832.
School—(Grades K-8) Tel: 814-455-1387; Fax: 814-461-0247. Sheri Kurczewski, Prin.; Alice Kelley, Librarian. Lay Teachers 24; Students 331; Religious 1; Clergy 1; Preschool 94.
Catechesis/Religious Program—Tracey Kunik, D.R.E. Students 181.

5—ST. BONIFACE (1857) [CEM] Rev. John M. Schultz; Deacon Timothy Good.
Res.: 7615 Wattsburg Rd., 16509. Tel: 814-825-4439; Fax: 814-825-2819.
School—(Grades K-8) Tel: 814-825-4238; Fax: 814-825-4274. Barbara Portenier, Prin. Lay Teachers 9; Students 88; Preschool 22; Religious 2.
Catechesis/Religious Program—Tel: 814-825-4439, Ext. 230. Sr. Rose Kuzma, O.S.F., D.R.E.

6—ST. CASIMIR (1914), (Polish), Merged with St. Ann and Holy Family to create Our Mother of Sorrows.

7—ST. GEORGE (1922) Rev. Msgr. Robert L. Brugger; Rev. Timothy R. Balliett, Parochial Vicar; Sr. Josephine Vuodi, F.S.O., Pastoral Min.; Deacons Robert Ball; Norbert Smith; Stephen Washek.
Res.: 5145 Peach St., 16509. Tel: 814-864-0622; Fax: 814-866-7532.
School—(Grades K-8) Tel: 814-864-4821; Fax: 814-866-7532. Lawrence Neubauer, Prin. Lay Teachers 35; Students 475; Preschool 90.
Catechesis/Religious Program—Tel: 814-864-0622, Ext. 277. Mary Lou Pacoe, D.R.E.; Kris Rudy, D.R.E. Students 411.

8—ST. HEDWIG (1910) Rev. Msgr. Henry A. Kriegel; Deacon Jerome Peterson.
Res.: 521 E. 3rd St., 16507. Tel: 814-454-8096.
Catechesis/Religious Program—Tel: 814-454-8085. Sr. Marie Stephen Kebort, S.S.J., D.R.E.

9—HOLY FAMILY/ST. ANN/ST. CASIMIR (1902), (Slovak), Merged with St. Ann and St. Casimir to create Our Mother of Sorrows.

10—HOLY ROSARY (1927) Rev. Joseph R. Czarkowski.
Res.: 2701 East Ave., 16504. Tel: 814-456-4254; Fax: 814-459-8082.
Catechesis/Religious Program—Tel: 814-454-6322. Kathleen Kutz, D.R.E., Eastside Faith Formation.

11—HOLY TRINITY (1903), (Polish), Rev. Msgr. Thomas J. McSweeney.
Res.: 2220 Reed St., 16503. Tel: 814-456-0671; Fax: 814-461-1150.

12—IMMACULATE CONCEPTION (1946), (African American), Closed. For inquiries for parish records contact the chancery.

13—ST. JAMES (1921) Revs. James McCormick; Scott W. Jabo; Deacon Charles Adamczyk. In Res., Sisters Susan Freitag, O.S.B., Sec.; Collette Hilow, C.D.S.
Res.: 2635 Buffalo Rd., 16510. Tel: 814-899-6178; Fax: 814-899-7681.
School—(Grades K-8) Tel: 814-899-3429; Fax: 814-898-8285. Sr. Collette Hilow, C.D.S., Prin.; Mrs. Kathy Sebunia, Librarian. Sisters of the Congregation of the Divine Spirit 4; Lay Teachers 12; Students 241; Preschool 26.
Catechesis/Religious Program—Sr. Collette Hilow, C.D.S., D.R.E. Students 102.

14—ST. JOHN THE BAPTIST (1870) Rev. John B. Jacquel; Deacon Denis Coan.
Res.: 509 E. 26th St., 16504. Tel: 814-454-2873; Fax: 814-456-7073.
School—St. John-Holy Rosary Eastside Catholic School, (Grades K-8), St. John merged with Holy Rosary to form St. John-Holy Rosary Eastside Catholic School., Tel: 814-452-6874; Fax: 814-455-0358. Mary Hoffman, Prin. Religious 1; Lay Teachers 12; Students 148; Preschool 17.

15—ST. JOSEPH (1867) Rev. Lawrence R. Richards. In Res., Rev. Gerald Wright, O.M.V.; Deacon Andrew Froberg.
Res.: 147 W. 24th St., 16502. Tel: 814-452-2982; Fax: 814-452-4400.
Catechesis/Religious Program—Alex Francani, D.R.E.

16—ST. JUDE THE APOSTLE (1955) Revs. Thomas M. Brooks; Johnathan P. Schmolt, Parochial Vicar. In Res., Rev. Msgr. Ernest J. Daley (Retired); Deacons David Pratt; James B. McGuinness.
Res.: 2801 W. 6th St., 16505. Tel: 814-833-0927; Fax: 814-833-9692.
School—Our Lady's Christian, (Grades K-8) Tel: 814-838-7676; Fax: 814-838-6860. Patty Landenberger, Prin. Lay Teachers 26; Students 350; Preschool 76.
Catechesis/Religious Program—Anne Osborn, D.R.E. Students 328.

17—ST. JULIA (1938) Rev. Msgr. Bruce R. Allison.
Res.: 638 Roslyn Ave., 16505. Tel: 814-833-4347; Fax: 814-833-4596.
See Our Lady's Christian, Erie under St. Jude the Apostle, Erie for details.
Catechesis/Religious Program—Cheryl Ann Morrison, D.R.E. Students 151.

18—ST. LUKE (1954) Rev. Msgr. L. Thomas Snyderwine; Very Rev. Thomas M. Aleksa; Deacons Richard Shewman; Glenn Kuzma; Jerome Sobrowski.
Res.: 421 E. 38th St., 16504. Tel: 814-825-6920; Fax: 814-825-6905.
School—(Grades K-8) Tel: 814-825-7105; Fax: 814-825-7169. Marietta Stalsky, Prin.; Paula Mielnik, Librarian. Lay Teachers 24; Students 320; Preschool 44.
Catechesis/Religious Program—Mary Tirak, C.R.E. Students 164.

19—ST. MARK THE EVANGELIST (Lawrence Park) (1938) Rev. Michael P. Allison; Deacons Frederick Weaver; James Kaschalk.
Res.: 4306 Morse St., 16511. Tel: 814-899-3000; Fax: 814-899-5212.
Catechesis/Religious Program—Pat Marshall, D.R.E. (6-12); Geri Hadlock, D.R.E. (K-5) & Youth Min. Students 187.

20—ST. MARY OF THE IMMACULATE CONCEPTION (2009) Rev. James G. Gutting; Sr. Rosemary O'Brien, S.S.J., Pastoral Assoc.
Res.: 315 E. 9th St., 16503. Tel: 814-452-2410; Fax: 814-455-7992.
Catechesis/Religious Program—Kathleen Kutz, D.R.E. Eastside Faith Formation, Twinned with Holy Rosary.

21—ST. MATTHEW IN THE WOODS (1966) Merged to become All Saints, Waterford.

22—MOUNT CALVARY (1951) Rev. Christopher M. Hamlett, Admin.
Res.: 2022 E. Lake Rd., 16511. Tel: 814-454-0061; Fax: 814-454-7177.
Catechesis/Religious Program—Don McClallen, D.R.E. Students 1.

23—OUR LADY OF MERCY (1946) Rev. Gerald T. Ritchie; Sr. Mary Rose Romeo, S.J., Liturgical Min.; Deacon John Brophy.
Res.: 837 Bartlett Rd., Harborcreek, 16421. Tel: 814-899-5342; Fax: 814-898-3306.
Catechesis/Religious Program—Irene Lucas, D.R.E.; Donna Clark, D.R.E. Students 245.

24—OUR LADY OF MT. CARMEL (1960) Rev. Raymond W. Hahn; Deacon Frank Pregler.
Res.: 1553 E. Grandview Blvd., 16510. Tel: 814-825-7313; Fax: 814-825-4190.
School—(Grades K-8) Tel: 814-825-2822; Fax: 814-824-7437. Veronica Antoske, Prin.; Patty Drabina, Librarian. Lay Teachers 15; Students 161; Preschool 29.
Catechesis/Religious Program—Melissa Hanley, D.R.E. Students 117.

25—OUR LADY OF PEACE (1955) Very Rev. Theodore B. Marconi; Rev. William R. Barron, Parochial Vicar; Deacon Anthony Alleruzzo.
Res.: 2401 W. 38th St., 16506. Tel: 814-833-7701; Fax: 814-833-7702.
School—(Grades K-8) Tel: 814-838-3548; Fax: 814-838-9133. Jeffrey Lipiec, Prin. Lay Teachers 27; Students 388; Preschool 72.
Catechesis/Religious Program—Laura Drapcho, D.R.E. Students 54.

26—OUR MOTHER OF SORROWS (2009) Rev. James T. O'Hara.
913 Fulton St., 16503. Tel: 814-452-4832; Fax: 814-453-2275. In Res., Rev. Msgr. Gerald J. Koos; Revs. Ronald E. Gmerek; Jerry S. Priscaro.
St. Ann Church—921 East Ave., 16503.
St. Casimir Church—629 Hess Ave., 16503.
Holy Family Church—913 Fulton St., 16503.
School—Holy Family, (Grades PreSchool-8) Tel: 814-452-4720. Sr. M. Kevin Berdis, O.S.F., Prin.; Mrs. Charlotte Newcamp, Librarian. Religious 1; Lay Teachers 8; Students 106; Preschool students 2.
Catechesis/Religious Program—Patricia Devore, D.R.E. Students 20.

27—ST. PATRICK (1834) Rev. Msgr. Henry A. Kriegel; Deacon Jerome Peterson. In Res., Rev. Msgr. Joseph V. Wardanski; Revs. Daniel J. Prez; John E. Santor.
Res.: 130 E. 4th St., 16507. Tel: 814-454-8085; Fax: 814-459-8685.
Catechesis/Religious Program—Eastside Faith Formation, 2701 East Ave., 16504. Sr. Marie Stephen Kebort, S.S.J., D.R.E. Students 17.

28—ST. PAUL (1891), (Italian), Rev. Alexander D. Amico.
Res.: 1617 Walnut St., 16502. Tel: 814-459-3173; Fax: 814-459-3173.

29—SACRED HEART (1894) Very Rev. John J. Detisch. In Res., Rev. Jerome S. Simmons.
Res.: 816 W. 26th St., 16508. Tel: 814-456-6256; Fax: 814-459-9533.
Catechesis/Religious Program—Tony Del Rio, D.R.E. Students 130.

30—ST. STANISLAUS (1885), (Polish), [CEM] Rev. Msgrs. Bernard J. Urbaniak; Mark L. Bartchak.
Res.: 516 E. 13th St., 16503. Tel: 814-452-6606; Fax: 814-452-6606.
Catechesis/Religious Program—Michelle Inter, D.R.E. Students 21.

31—ST. STEPHEN (1917), (Hungarian—Hispanic), Rev. Jorge C. Villegas; Deacon Miguel Alvarez.
Res.: 1237 W. 21 St., 16502. Tel: 814-459-0543.

OUTSIDE THE CITY OF ERIE

ALBION, ERIE CO., ST. LAWRENCE (1914) Rev. Philip M. Oriole.
Res.: 180 E. State St., 16401. Tel: 814-756-3623; Fax: 814-756-5918.
St. Lawrence Catechetical Center—129 E. Pearl St., 16401. Tel: 814-756-4840.
Catechesis/Religious Program—Kathleen Peterson, D.R.E. Students 132.

ANITA, JEFFERSON CO., ST. JOSEPH, HUBAND OF MARY Rev. Msgr. Joseph J. Riccardo.
Res.: 616 Mahoning St., Punxsutawney, 15767. Tel: 814-938-6540; Fax: 814-938-7439.

BRADFORD, MCKEAN CO.

1—ST. BERNARD (1880) [CEM] Rev. Leo J. Gallina; Deacon Gerald Beeman.
Res.: 95 E. Corydon St., 16701-5394. Tel: 814-362-6825; Fax: 814-362-1479.
School—(Grades K-8) Tel: 814-368-5302; Fax: 814-368-1464. Kimberly Mooney, Prin.; Lisa Webster, Librarian. Lay Teachers 14; Students 157; Preschool 27.
Catechesis/Religious Program—Students 137.

2—ST. FRANCIS OF ASSISI (1846) [JC] Rev. Samuel B. Slocum.
Res.: 574 E. Main St., 16701. Tel: 814-368-6959; Fax: 814-368-6959.
Catechesis/Religious Program—Students 49.

BRANDY CAMP, ELK CO., HOLY CROSS (1908), (Italian), [CEM] Rev. Msgr. Charles A. Kaza, Admin.
Mailing Address: 1135 Hewett St., Brockway, 15824. Tel: 814-268-3655; Fax: 814-268-1147.

BROCKWAY, JEFFERSON CO., ST. TOBIAS (1898) [CEM] Rev. Msgr. Charles A. Kaza; Deacon Robert P DeNoon.
Res.: 1135 Hewett St., 15824. Tel: 814-268-3655; Fax: 814-268-1147.
Catechesis/Religious Program—Joanne Bruno, C.R.E.; Tara Starr, D.R.E. Students 186.

BROOKVILLE, JEFFERSON CO., IMMACULATE CONCEPTION (1852) [CEM] Rev. William M. Laska.
Res.: 129 Graham Ave., 15825. Tel: 814-849-8697; Fax: 814-849-5265.
Catechesis/Religious Program—Penny Rakovan, D.R.E.
Mission—St. Dominic [CEM] Sigel, Jefferson Co.

CAMBRIDGE SPRINGS, CRAWFORD CO., ST. ANTHONY (1899) Rev. Msgr. Lawrence T. Speice.
Res.: 165 Beach Ave., P.O. Box 214, 16403. Tel: 814-398-4234; Fax: 814-398-1531.
Catechesis/Religious Program—Sue Parkin, D.R.E. Students 98.

CLARION, CLARION CO., IMMACULATE CONCEPTION (1855) [CEM] Rev. Monty Sayers.
Res.: 720 Liberty St., 16214. Tel: 814-226-8433; Fax: 814-226-1092.
School—(Grades K-8) Tel: 814-226-9690; Fax: 814-226-4998. Donna Gaydash, Prin. Lay Teachers 13; Students 94; Preschool 22.
Catechesis/Religious Program—Dawn Kidney, D.R.E.; Ann Enderle Liska, D.R.E. Students 280.

CLEARFIELD, CLEARFIELD CO., ST. FRANCIS (1830) [CEM] Rev. Msgr. H. Desmond McGee; Rev. John G. Chaplin. In Res., Rev. Msgr. Henry L. Krebs;

Deacon Eugene Miller Jr.
Res.: 212 S. Front St., 16830. Tel: 814-765-9671; Fax: 814-765-9489.
School—(Grades K-8) Tel: 814-765-2618; Fax: 814-765-6704. Dr. Michael Spencer, Prin.; Sheila Clancy, Librarian. Lay Teachers 15; Students 156; Preschool 34.
Catechesis/Religious Program—Rita McConnell, D.R.E. Students 135.

COALPORT, CLEARFIELD CO., ST. BASIL THE GREAT (1887) [CEM] Rev. Zab Amar.
Res.: 183 Locust St., 16627. Tel: 814-672-5561; Fax: 814-672-5954.
Catechesis/Religious Program—Kathleen Pino, D.R.E. Students 110.

CONNEAUT LAKE, CRAWFORD CO., OUR LADY QUEEN OF THE AMERICAS (1958) [CEM] Rev. Stephen A. Anderson.
Res.: 9th & Water Sts., Box 110, 16316. Tel: 814-382-7252; Fax: 814-382-9575.
Catechesis/Religious Program—Tel: 814-382-7256. Pam Davis, D.R.E. Students 141.

CONNEAUTVILLE, CRAWFORD CO., ST. PETER (1853), (Irish), [CEM] In Res., Rev. John A. Walsh.
Res.: 501 Washington St., P.O. Box F, 16406. Tel: 814-587-3435; Fax: 814-587-6436.
Catechesis/Religious Program—Debbie Monnie, D.R.E. Students 44.

CORRY, ERIE CO.
1—ST. ELIZABETH (1876) [CEM] Rev. Thomas E. Brown; Deacons William Saborsky; William Sproveri.
Res.: 26 W. Pleasant St., 16407. Tel: 814-664-7105; Fax: 814-663-0505.
Catechesis/Religious Program—Vickie Stull, D.R.E.
2—ST. THOMAS THE APOSTLE (1856) [CEM] Rev. Thomas E. Brown; Deacons William Saborsky; William Sproveri.
Res.: 26 W. Pleasant St., 16407. Tel: 814-663-3041; Fax: 814-663-0505.
School—(Grades PreK-7) Tel: 814-665-7375; Fax: 814-664-4025. Karen Beer, Prin. Lay Teachers 7; Students 62.
Catechesis/Religious Program—Sue Vinca, D.R.E. Students 51.

COUDERSPORT, POTTER CO., ST. EULALIA (1891) [CEM] Rev. James C. Campbell.
Res.: 6 E. Maple St., 16915. Tel: 814-274-8646; Fax: 814-274-8586.
Catechesis/Religious Program—Tel: 814-274-8552. Andrea Streich, D.R.E.

CROSSINGSVILLE, CRAWFORD CO., ST. PHILIP (1840) [CEM] Rev. Thaddeus T. Kondzielski.
Res.: 25797 State Hwy. 98, Crossingville, R.D. 2, Edinboro, 16412. Tel: 814-734-7395.
Catechesis/Religious Program—25797 State Hwy. 98, Edinboro, 16412. Kris Gajdowski, D.R.E. Students 32.

CROWN, CLARION CO., ST. MARY (1848) [CEM 2] Rev. Gregory P. Passauer.
Res.: 117 Lancer Dr., P.O. Box 41, 16220. Tel: 814-744-9919; Fax: 814-744-8624.
Catechesis/Religious Program—Lynn Tarr, C.R.E. Students 75.
Mission—St. Anne Marienville, Forest Co.

CURWENSVILLE, CLEARFIELD CO., ST. TIMOTHY (1915) [CEM] Rev. Mark J. Mastrian.
Res.: 306 Walnut St., 16833. Tel: 814-236-1845; Fax: 814-236-1196.
Catechesis/Religious Program—Terri A. Clarkson, D.R.E. Students 76.

DAGUSCAHONDA, ELK CO., ST. BENEDICT, Closed. Effective April 30, 1995, St. Benedict in Daguscahonda became a Public Oratory (Cannon 1223).

DU BOIS, CLEARFIELD CO.
1—ST. CATHERINE (1877) [CEM] Rev. Msgr. Richard R. Siefer; Rev. Thomas S. Hoderny; Deacon William Wright.
Res.: 116 S. State St., 15801. Tel: 814-371-8556; Fax: 814-371-0592.
School—(Grades K-5) Tel: 814-371-2570; Fax: 814-371-1551. Mary Mike Sayers, Prin. Lay Teachers 18; Students 197; Preschool 51.
Catechesis/Religious Program—Pat McAllister, D.R.E.
2—ST. JOSEPH (1893), (Lithuanian), [CEM] Rev. V. David Foradori.
Res.: 25 Robinson St., 15801. Tel: 814-371-5773; Fax: 814-371-5028.
Catechesis/Religious Program—Students 63.
3—ST. MICHAEL (1912), (Polish), [CEM] Rev. V. David Foradori.
Res.: 25 Robinson St., 15801. Tel: 814-371-5773; Fax: 814-371-5028.
Catechesis/Religious Program—Kathleen Clement, C.R.E. Students 149.

EAST BRADY, CLARION CO., ST. EUSEBIUS (1877) [CEM] Rev. William M. Kuba.
Res.: 301 E. 2nd St., 16028. Tel: 724-526-3366; Fax: 724-526-3294.
Catechesis/Religious Program—
Mission—St. Richard Rimersburg, Clarion Co.

EDINBORO, ERIE CO., OUR LADY OF THE LAKE (1950) Rev. William E. Sutherland.
Res.: 128 Sunset Dr., Box 838, 16412. Tel: 814-734-3113; Fax: 814-734-3085.
Catechesis/Religious Program—Mary Rose Shinsky, D.R.E.

ELDRED, MCKEAN CO., ST. RAPHAEL (1847) [CEM 2] Rev. John J. Murphy.
Res.: 16 First St., Box 252, 16731. Tel: 814-225-4231; Fax: 814-225-4298.
Catechesis/Religious Program—Students 37.
Mission—St. Mary [CEM] Sartwell, McKean Co.

EMLENTON, VENANGO CO., ST. MICHAEL (1867) [CEM] Rev. Msgr. Jan C. Olowin.
Res.: Chestnut St., P.O. Box 177, 16373. Tel: 724-867-2422; Fax: 724-867-6815.
Catechesis/Religious Program—Pam Gent, D.R.E. Students 28.

EMPORIUM, CAMERON CO., ST. MARK (1888) [CEM] Rev. Paul S. Siebert.
Res.: 235 E. 4th St., 15834. Tel: 814-486-0569; Fax: 814-486-3298.
Catechesis/Religious Program—Jennifer Guisto, C.R.E. Students 130.
Mission—St. James Driftwood, Cameron Co.

FAIRVIEW, ERIE CO., HOLY CROSS (1963) Rev. Scott P. Detisch.
7100 W. Ridge Rd., P.O. Box 10, 16415.
Res.: 7125 W. Ridge Rd., P.O. Box 10, 16415. Tel: 814-474-2605; Fax: 814-474-1256.
Catechesis/Religious Program—Sylvia Smith, D.R.E. Students 296.

FALLS CREEK, JEFFERSON CO., ST. BERNARD (1952) Rev. Marc Stockton, Admin.
Res.: 205 Taylor Ave., 15840. Tel: 814-371-7419.
Catechesis/Religious Program—Tel: 814-449-3624.

FARRELL, MERCER CO.
1—ST. ADALBERT (1913) [CEM] Rev. Daniel J. Kresinski.
1035 Fruit Ave., 16121.
Res.: 804 Idaho St., Sharon, 16146. Tel: 724-342-7391; Fax: 724-342-3349.
Catechesis/Religious Program—Mary Lou Nogay, D.R.E.; Cyndi Serafin, D.R.E. Students 30.
2—ST. ANN (1904), (Slovak), [CEM] Closed. For inquiries for parish records contact the chancery.
3—HOLY TRINITY (1915), (Hungarian), [CEM] Closed. For inquiries for parish records contact the chancery.
4—OUR LADY OF FATIMA-ST. ANN (1952) [CEM 3] Rev. Donald E. Berdis.
Res.: 601 Roemer Blvd., 16121. Tel: 724-346-3359; Fax: 724-346-2326.
School—Monsignor Geno Monti School, (Grades K-8), 1225 Union St., 16121. Tel: 724-347-1440; Fax: 724-347-1440. Alice Connelly, Prin. Lay Teachers 9; Students 69; Clergy 1.
Catechesis/Religious Program—Deacon Joseph Messina, D.R.E.

FORCE, ELK CO., ST. JOSEPH (1906) [CEM] Rev. Thomas L. Tyler.
Res.: 17735 Bennetts Valley Hwy., P.O. Box 124, 15841. Tel: 814-787-4151; Fax: 814-787-4478.
Catechesis/Religious Program—Mary Stoker, Coord. Faith Formation. Students 88.

FRANKLIN, VENANGO CO., ST. PATRICK (1867) [CEM] Rev. Msgr. John J. Herbein; Deacons Walter Jones; Richard Reed.
Res.: 949 Liberty St., 16323. Tel: 814-437-5763; Fax: 814-437-6326.
School—(Grades K-8) Tel: 814-432-8689; Fax: 814-437-6538. Carol Long, Prin. Lay Teachers 12; Students 97; Preschool 20.
Catechesis/Religious Program—Therese Marshall, D.R.E.

FRENCHTOWN, CRAWFORD CO., ST. HIPPOLYTE (1838) [CEM] Rev. Dennis J. Veltri.
Res.: 25997 Hwy. 27, Guys Mills, 16327. Tel: 814-789-2022; Fax: 814-789-2025.
Catechesis/Religious Program—Joyce Tarr, D.R.E.
Mission—Our Lady of Lourdes Cochranton, Crawford Co.
Chapel— Sts. Peter & Paul, Pettis. (Devotional Chapel)

FRENCHVILLE, CLEARFIELD CO., ST. MARY OF THE ASSUMPTION (1840) [CEM] Rev. David A. Perry; Deacons Joseph Lyncha; Robert Hoover.
Res.: P.O. Box 159, 16836. Tel: 814-263-4354; Fax: 814-263-4219.
Catechesis/Religious Program—Ann Butler, D.R.E. (Elementary); Tina Hicks, D.R.E. (High School); Shelly Cowder, D.R.E. (Elementary & High School). Students 33.
Mission—SS. Peter & Paul [CEM] Grassflat, Clearfield Co. 16839.
Mission—St. Severin [CEM] Drifting, Clearfield Co.
Catechesis/Religious Program— Twinned with Mission - SS. Peter & Paul. Students 43.

FRYBURG, CLARION CO., ST. MICHAEL (1846) [CEM] Rev. David L. Poulson.
Res.: 18765 Rt. 208, P.O. Box 27, 16326. Tel: 814-354-2467; Fax: 814-354-6375.
Catechesis/Religious Program—Bernice Strauser, D.R.E. Students 148.

GALETON, POTTER CO., ST. BIBIANA (1888), (Italian), [CEM] Rev. Joseph V. Dougherty.
Res.: 111 Germania, 16922. Tel: 814-435-2303.
Catechesis/Religious Program—David Pope, D.R.E. Students 20.
Mission—St. Augustine [CEM] Austin, Potter Co.
Mission—Sacred Heart Genesee, Potter Co.
Chapel— St. Germain, Germania. (Devotional Chapel)

GIRARD, ERIE CO., ST. JOHN THE EVANGELIST (1853) [CEM] Rev. William J. O'Brien; Sr. Geraldine Kasper, O.S.F., D.R.E.
Res.: 32 Penn Ave., Box 336, 16417. Tel: 814-774-4108; Fax: 814-774-2097.
Catechesis/Religious Program—Tel: 814-774-4061. Sr. Geraldine Kasper, O.S.F., D.R.E. Students 153.

GRAMPIAN, CLEARFIELD CO., ST. BONAVENTURE (1833) [CEM] Rev. Mark J. Mastrian; Deacon Anthony Indelicato Sr.
Res.: 461 Main St., P.O. Box F, 16838. Tel: 814-236-0364; Fax: 814-236-0733.
Catechesis/Religious Program—Terri A. Clarkson, D.R.E. Students 65.

GREENVILLE, MERCER CO., ST. MICHAEL (1850) [CEM] Rev. Msgr. Andrew H. Karg; Rev. Daniel R. Hoffman, Parochial Vicar; Sr. Mary Gertrude McElhinny, S.C., Pastoral Min.; Deacon William Brown. In Res., Rev. Paul A. Schill (Retired).
Office: Tel: 412-588-9800; Fax: 412-588-7053.
Res.: 81 N. 2nd St., 16125.
School—(Grades K-8), 80 N. High St., 16125. Tel: 724-588-7050; Fax: 724-588-7056. Mary Jo Lipani, Prin. Lay Teachers 12; Students 137; Preschool 29.
Catechesis/Religious Program—Elaine Shearer, D.R.E. Students 255.
Mission—St. Margaret 701 Denver St., Jamestown, Mercer Co. Tel: 724-932-5959.

GROVE CITY, MERCER CO., BELOVED DISCIPLE (1925) [CEM] Rev. Mark A. Hoffman.
1310 S. Center St. Ext., 16127.
Res.: 321 N. Broad St., 16127. Tel: 724-748-6700.
Catechesis/Religious Program—Fax: 724-458-9166. Emily Zgonc, D.R.E. Students 242.

HERMITAGE, MERCER CO., CHURCH OF NOTRE DAME (1960) Very Rev. Jeffery J. Noble; Rev. Msgr. Edward J. Zeitler (Retired); Deacons W. Jack Tupper; Owen Wagner.
Res.: 2325 Highland Rd., 16148. Tel: 724-981-5566; Fax: 724-981-3215.
School—(Grades K-8) Tel: 724-342-2205; Fax: 724-704-7397. Victoria Wagner, Prin. Lay Teachers 17; Students 153; Preschool 58.
Catechesis/Religious Program—Pat Polesnak, D.R.E.; Kathy Higgins, D.R.E. Students 274.

HOUTZDALE, CLEARFIELD CO., CHRIST THE KING (1970) [CEM] Very Rev. Gregory A. Kirsch.
Res.: 123 Good St., 16651. Tel: 814-378-7653; Fax: 814-378-8333.
Catechesis/Religious Program—Tel: 814-378-6125. Nancy Yarger, D.R.E. Students 149.
Mission—Immaculate Conception Madera, Clearfield Co.

JOHNSONBURG, ELK CO., HOLY ROSARY (1896) [CEM] Rev. David J. Wilson.
Res.: 606 Penn St., 15845. Tel: 814-965-2819; Fax: 814-965-3482.
Catechesis/Religious Program—Tel: 814-965-2812. Margaret Griffin, D.R.E. Students 241.

KANE, MCKEAN CO., ST. CALLISTUS (1866) [CEM] Very Rev. Phillip A. Pinczewski.
Res.: 342 Chase St., 16735. Tel: 814-837-6694; Fax: 814-837-4304.
Catechesis/Religious Program—Sr. Francis Therese Matia, S.S.J., D.R.E.
Convent—116 Haines St., 16735.
Chapel— Sts. John & Stephen, James City, 16734. (Devotional Chapel)

KERSEY, ELK CO., ST. BONIFACE (1832) [CEM] Rev. John A. Kuzilla.
Res.: 355 Main St., 15846. Tel: 814-885-8941.
School—(Grades K-5) Tel: 814-885-8093; Fax: 814-885-8931. Marie Giazzoni, Prin. Lay Teachers 10; Students 69; Preschool 48.
Catechesis/Religious Program—Tel: 814-885-6195. Paula Micale, D.R.E. Students 210.

LEWIS RUN, MCKEAN CO., OUR MOTHER OF PERPETUAL HELP (1946) Rev. Samuel B. Slocum.
Res.: 31 Lafayette, 16738. Tel: 814-368-6355.
Catechesis/Religious Program—Students 27.

LINESVILLE, CRAWFORD CO., ST. PHILIP (1957) [CEM] Rev. John A. Walsh.
Res.: 401 S. Mercer St., 16424. Tel: 814-683-5313; Fax: 814-683-5824.
Catechesis/Religious Program—Maria Pilarcik, C.R.E.

LUCINDA, CLARION CO., ST. JOSEPH (1840) [CEM] Rev. William C. Miller.
Rectory—112 Rectory Ln., P.O. Box 9, 16235. Tel: 814-226-7288; Fax: 814-226-5538.
School—(Grades K-6), 72 Rectory Ln., 16235. Tel: 814-226-8018; Fax: 814-223-9620. Sr. Monica Steiner, O.S.B., Prin.; Susie Beary, Librarian. Sisters 1; Lay Teachers 11; Students 78; Preschool 29.
Catechesis/Religious Program—Mr. Norm Wolbert, D.R.E.; Mrs. Judy Wolbert, D.R.E. Students 68.
MCKEAN, ERIE CO., ST. FRANCIS XAVIER (1838) [CEM] Rev. Mark A. Nowak.
Res.: 8880 W. Main St., P.O. Box 317, 16426. Tel: 814-476-7657; Fax: 814-476-0160.
Catechesis/Religious Program—Cynthia Zemcik, D.R.E.
MEADVILLE, CRAWFORD CO.
1—ST. AGATHA (1849) [CEM] Rev. Raymond Gramata; Deacon Harvey McQueen.
Res.: 353 Pine St., 16335. Tel: 814-336-1112; Fax: 814-724-4051.
School—Seton School, (Grades K-8) Tel: 814-336-2320; Fax: 814-336-2328. Regina Merritt, Prin.; Amanda Foulk, Librarian. Lay Teachers 15; Students 148; Preschool 30.
Catechesis/Religious Program—Tel: 814-336-1112. Eileen O'Day, D.R.E. Students 100.
Mission—St. Bernadette 222 Renner Ln., Saegertown, Crawford Co. 16433. Tel: 814-763-2831.
2—ST. BRIGID (1865), (Irish), [CEM] Revs. Mark O'Hern; Rocco A. Tito.
Res.: 967 Chancery Ln., 16335. Tel: 814-336-4459; Fax: 814-724-2996.
Catechesis/Religious Program—Shari Bronson, D.R.E. Students 97.
3—ST. MARY OF GRACE (1909), (Italian), Rev. Richard Toohey.
Res.: 1085 Water St., 16335. Tel: 814-333-6161; Fax: 814-336-3145.
Catechesis/Religious Program—Tel: 814-333-6161, Ext. 5. Kathleen Allen, D.R.E. Students 46.
MERCER, MERCER CO., IMMACULATE HEART (1838) [CEM] Rev. James J. Kennelley; Rev. Msgr. Charles S. Murcko (Retired).
Res.: 16137. Tel: 724-662-2999; Fax: 724-662-5094.
Catechesis/Religious Program—Barb Kehlbeck, D.R.E.
Chapel— St. Hermenegild, Pardoe. (Devotional Chapel)
MORRISDALE, CLEARFIELD CO., ST. AGNES (1891) [CEM] Rev. Robert Horgas.
Res.: 16858. Tel: 814-342-2583; Fax: 814-342-6377.
Catechesis/Religious Program—Tel: 814-342-2583. Dennis Socash, D.R.E. Students 72.
Mission—SS. Peter & Paul [CEM] Hawk Run, Clearfield Co.
MOUNT JEWETT, MCKEAN CO., ST. JOSEPH (1898) Rev. Vincent P. Cieslewicz.
Res.: 22 Division St., P.O. Box 520, 16740. Tel: 814-778-5520; Fax: 814-887-5271.
Catechesis/Religious Program—Carol Walker, D.R.E. Students 17.
NEW BETHLEHEM, CLARION CO., ST. CHARLES (1872) [CEM] Rev. Samuel Bungo.
Res.: 201 Washington St., 16242. Tel: 814-275-3446; Fax: 814-275-7550.
Catechesis/Religious Program—Amy Toth, D.R.E.
Mission—St. Nicholas [CEM] Crates, Clarion Co.
NORTH EAST, ERIE CO., ST. GREGORY THAUMATURGUS (1875) [CEM] Rev. David E. Prenatt.
Res.: 136 W. Main St., 16428. Tel: 814-725-9691; Fax: 814-725-1225.
School—(Grades PreSchool-8), 140 W. Main St., 16428. Tel: 814-725-4571; Fax: 814-725-4572. Nancy Pierce, Prin. Lay Teachers 7; Students 62; Preschool 27.
Catechesis/Religious Program—Loraine Fetzer, D.R.E. Students 240.
OIL CITY, VENANGO CO.
1—ASSUMPTION OF THE BLESSED VIRGIN MARY (1899), (Polish), Rev. Msgr. John W. Swoger, Admin.
Rectory—35 Pearl St., 16301. Tel: 814-677-4004; Fax: 814-677-5977.
2—ST. JOSEPH (1865) [CEM 2] Rev. Msgr. John W. Swoger.
Res.: 35 Pearl Ave., 16301. Tel: 814-677-4004; Fax: 814-677-5977.
Catechesis/Religious Program—Dianne Phillips, C.R.E. Students 62.
3—OUR LADY HELP OF CHRISTIANS (1914) Rev. John P. Mathaner, Admin.
Res.: 69 Willow St., 16301. Tel: 814-677-3078; Fax: 814-676-9216.
Catechesis/Religious Program— Twinned with St. Stephen.
4—ST. STEPHEN (1898) Rev. Matthew J. Ruyechan; Rev. Msgr. William C. Karg; Deacon Terry Schmader.
Res.: 210 Reed St., 16301. Tel: 814-677-3020; Fax: 814-678-8841.
School—(Grades K-8) Tel: 814-677-3035; Fax: 814-677-2053. Marge Hajduk, Prin. Lay Teachers 14; Students 157; Preschool 15.
Catechesis/Religious Program—Dianne Phillips, D.R.E. Students 99.
PORT ALLEGANY, MCKEAN CO., ST. GABRIEL THE ARCHANGEL (1876) [CEM] Rev. James C. Campbell.
Res.: 203 E. Arnold Ave., 16743. Tel: 814-642-2847; Fax: 814-642-7990.
Catechesis/Religious Program—Theresa Gigliotti, D.R.E.
Mission—St. Mary Roulette, Potter Co.
PUNXSUTAWNEY, JEFFERSON CO., SS. COSMAS AND DAMIAN (1885) [CEM] Rev. Msgr. Joseph J. Riccardo; Rev. Justin P. Pino, Parochial Vicar.
Res.: 616 W. Mahoning St., 15767. Tel: 814-938-6540; Fax: 814-938-7439.
School—(Grades PreSchool-8), 205 N. Chestnut St., 15767. Tel: 814-938-4224; Fax: 814-939-3759. Dawn Bressler, Prin. Lay Teachers 10; Students 89; Preschool 31.
Catechesis/Religious Program—Sue Dahrouge, D.R.E. Students 163.
RAMEY, CLEARFIELD CO., HOLY TRINITY (1937) [CEM] Rev. Zab Amar.
Mailing Address: Box 196, 16671. Tel: 814-378-7193; Fax: 814-378-4855.
Res.: 183 Locust St., Coalport, 16627. Tel: 814-672-3561; Fax: 814-672-5954.
REYNOLDSVILLE, JEFFERSON CO., ST. MARY (1872) [CEM] Rev. Marc J. Solomon.
Res.: 607 E. Main St., 15851. Tel: 814-653-8586; Fax: 814-653-8586.
Catechesis/Religious Program—Barb Murray, D.R.E. Students 71.
RIDGWAY, ELK CO., ST. LEO THE GREAT (1874) [CEM] Revs. Brian E. Vossler; Joseph C. Campbell.
Res.: 111 Depot St., 15853. Tel: 814-772-3135; Fax: 814-772-6627.
School—(Grades K-8) Tel: 814-772-9775; Fax: 814-772-9295. Mary Detwiler, Prin. Lay Teachers 12; Students 104; Preschool 33.
Catechesis/Religious Program—Erin Ciccone, D.R.E. Students 250.
ROUSEVILLE, VENANGO CO., ST. VENANTIUS (1872) Rev. Matthew J. Ruyechan, Admin.
Res.: 210 Reed St., Oil City, 16301. Tel: 814-677-3020; Fax: 814-678-8841.
Church: 401 Main St., 16344.
Catechesis/Religious Program—Students 5.
ST. MARYS, ELK CO.
1—ST. MARY (1842), (German), [CEM] Revs. Meinrad Lawson, O.S.B.; Daniel C. Wolfel, O.S.B.
139 Church St., 15857.
Res.: 325 Church St., 15857. Tel: 814-781-1019; Fax: 814-834-6795.
School—St. Mary's Catholic Elementary School System, (Grades PreSchool-5) Tel: 814-834-4169; Fax: 814-834-7830. Mary Beth Schaut, Prin.; Mrs. Patty Cotter, Librarian. Lay Teachers 20; Students 263; Preschool 138.
School—St. Mary's Catholic Middle School, (Grades 6-8), 303 Church St., 15857. Tel: 814-834-2665; Fax: 814-834-5339. Ms. Mary Agnes Marshall, Prin. Lay Teachers 15; Students 175.
Catechesis/Religious Program—Georgia Wagner, D.R.E. Students 549.
2—QUEEN OF THE WORLD (1954) Revs. Daniel C. Wolfel, O.S.B.; Michael P. Ferrick.
Res.: 134 Queens Rd., 15857. Tel: 814-834-4701; Fax: 814-834-3422.
Catechesis/Religious Program—Tel: 814-834-9077. Georgia Wagner, D.R.E. Students 157.
3—SACRED HEART OF JESUS (1876) [JC] Revs. Eric Vogt, O.S.B.; Jeremy Bolha, O.S.B.; Deacon William Gibson.
325 Center St., 15857.
Res.: 144 Church St., 15857. Tel: 814-834-7861; Fax: 814-834-1376.
Catechesis/Religious Program—Georgia Wagner, D.R.E. Teachers 549.
SHARON, MERCER CO.
1—ST. ANTHONY (1924), (Croatian), [CEM] Rev. Daniel J. Kresinski.
Res.: 804 Idaho St., 16146. Tel: 724-342-7391; Fax: 724-342-3349.
Catechesis/Religious Program—Mary Lou Nogay, C.R.E.; Cyndi Serafin, C.R.E. Students 21.
2—ST. JOSEPH (1860) [CEM] [JC] Revs. Glenn R. Whitman; J. Thomas Dugan.
Res.: 79 Case Ave., 16146. Tel: 724-981-3232; Fax: 724-981-4174.
School—(1892), (Grades K-8) Tel: 724-983-8382; Fax: 724-983-8383. Marian Smith, Prin.; Renee Azalos, Librarian. Lay Teachers 17; Students 149; Preschool 21.
Catechesis/Religious Program—Sr. Sandy Pedone, H.M., D.R.E.; Mary Beth Jones, Asst. High School Dir.
3—SACRED HEART (1864) [CEM] Rev. Henry C. Andrae.
Res.: 40 S. Irvine Ave., 16146. Tel: 724-346-3567; Fax: 724-346-4464.
Catechesis/Religious Program—
4—ST. STANISLAUS KOSTKA-HOLY TRINITY (1931), (Polish—Hungarian), [CEM 2] Rev. Stanley J. Swacha.
Res.: 370 Spruce Ave., 16146. Tel: 724-347-7526; Fax: 724-347-1760.
Catechesis/Religious Program—Nancy Radachy, C.R.E. Students 31.
SHARPSVILLE, MERCER CO., ST. BARTHOLOMEW (1874) Rev. Matthew J. Kujawinski.
Res.: 311 W. Ridge Ave., 16150. Tel: 724-962-7130; Fax: 724-962-1771.
Catechesis/Religious Program—
SHEFFIELD, WARREN CO., ST. ANTHONY (1878) Rev. James G. Faluszczak.
Res.: Four Mile Rd., P.O. Box 518, 16347. Tel: 814-968-5915; Fax: 814-968-4214.
Catechesis/Religious Program—Mona Champion, C.R.E.; Sara Korchak, C.R.E. Students 31.
SHINGLEHOUSE, POTTER CO., ST. THERESA (1901) [CEM] Rev. John J. Murphy.
Mailing Address: P.O. Box 277, 16748. Tel: 814-225-4231; Fax: 814-225-4298.
Res.: P.O. Box 252, Eldred, 16731.
Catechesis/Religious Program—Gail McGee, D.R.E. Students 17.
SMETHPORT, MCKEAN CO., ST. ELIZABETH (1875) [CEM] Rev. Vincent P. Cieslewicz.
Res.: 307 Franklin St., 16749. Tel: 814-887-9254; Fax: 814-887-5271.
Catechesis/Religious Program—Amy Sage, D.R.E.
STONEBORO, MERCER CO., ST. COLUMBKILLE (1874) [CEM] Rev. Robert A. Manning, Admin.
Res.: 70 Franklin St., P.O. Box 206, 16153. Tel: 724-376-3393; Fax: 724-376-3396.
Catechesis/Religious Program—Students 18.
SYKESVILLE, JEFFERSON CO., ASSUMPTION OF BLESSED VIRGIN MARY (1923) [CEM] Rev. Marc J. Solomon.
Res.: 20 Shaffer St., 15865. Tel: 814-894-2772; Fax: 814-894-2445.
Catechesis/Religious Program—Elaine Fike, D.R.E. Students 34.
TIDIOUTE, WARREN CO., ST. JOHN (1866) [CEM] Rev. James A. Reardon.
Res.: 25 First St., 16351. Tel: 814-484-7747; Fax: 814-484-0275.
Catechesis/Religious Program—Jane Downey, D.R.E. Students 42.
Mission—St. Anthony Tionesta, Forest Co.
TITUSVILLE, CRAWFORD CO.
1—ST. TITUS (1962) [CEM] [JC] Rev. D.G. "Skip" Davis.
Res.: 513 W. Main St., 16354. Tel: 814-827-4636; Fax: 814-827-3958.
Catechesis/Religious Program—Tel: 814-827-7250. Frances Schneider, D.R.E.
Mission—Immaculate Conception Mageetown, Crawford Co. Tel: 814-827-2075.
2—ST. WALBURGA (1872), (German), [CEM] Rev. D.G. "Skip" Davis.
Mailing Address: 513 W. Main St., 16354. Tel: 814-827-4636; Fax: 814-827-3958.
Res.: 120 Brook St., 16354.
Catechesis/Religious Program—Frances Schneider, D.R.E.
UNION CITY, ERIE CO., ST. TERESA OF AVILA (1906) [CEM] Rev. F. Thomas Suppa.
Res.: 9 Third Ave., 16438. Tel: 814-438-2000; Fax: 814-438-2073.
Catechesis/Religious Program—Tel: 814-438-3408. Cheryl Godak-Nothum, D.R.E. Students 150.
Mission—Our Lady of Fatima Canadohta Lake, Crawford Co.
WALSTON, JEFFERSON CO., ST. ANTHONY OF PADUA (1898) Rev. Msgr. Joseph J. Riccardo; Rev. Justin P. Pino, Parochial Vicar.
Res.: *SS Cosmas & Damian*, 616 W. Mahoning St., Punxsutawney, 15767. Tel: 814-938-9687; Fax: 814-938-1257.
Catechesis/Religious Program—Mary Butler, D.R.E.
Mission—St. Adrian Delancey.
WARREN, WARREN CO.
1—HOLY REDEEMER (1912) Rev. Msgr. John J. Lucas; Deacons Joseph Lucia Jr.; Raymond Wiehagen.
Res.: 11 Russell St., 16365. Tel: 814-726-3360; Fax: 814-726-3361.
Catechesis/Religious Program—Diana Lillard, D.R.E. Students 199.
2—ST. JOSEPH (1858) [CEM] [JC] Rev. Walter E. Packard.
Res.: 600 Penna Ave., W., 16365. Tel: 814-723-2090; Fax: 814-723-6042.
School—(Grades K-3) Tel: 814-723-2030; Fax: 814-723-6042. Dr. Howard Ferguson, Prin. Lay Teachers 6; Students 56.
Catechesis/Religious Program—Jennifer Wortman, D.R.E. Students 164.
WATERFORD, ERIE CO.
1—ALL SAINTS Rev. Thomas J. Whitman; Deacon William C. Spinks.

11264 Rte. 97, 16441. Tel: 814-796-3023; Fax: 814-796-3025.

2—ST. CYPRIAN (1878) Closed. For inquiries for parish records contact the chancery.

WEST MIDDLESEX, MERCER CO., GOOD SHEPHERD (1955) [JC] Rev. Msgr. Robert M. Malene. In Res., Rev. Jeffery J. Lucas.
Res.: P.O. Box 226, 16159. Tel: 724-528-3539; Fax: 814-528-2928.
Catechesis / Religious Program—Judy Miller, D.R.E. Students 126.

WILCOX, ELK CO., ST. ANNE (1890) [JC] Rev. David Willson.
Mailing Address: *c/o Holy Rosary*, 606 Penn St., Johnsonburg, 15845. In Res., Rev. John G. Barwin (Retired).
Res.: Clarion St., P.O. Box 65, 15870. Tel: 814-965-2819; Fax: 814-965-3482.

WINBURNE, CLEARFIELD CO., SS. CYRIL AND METHODIUS (1904), (Slovak—Hungarian), Closed. For inquiries for parish records contact the chancery. Listed as a chapel under St. Agnes parish, Morrisdale.

YOUNGSVILLE, WARREN CO., ST. LUKE (1957) Rev. John Neff; Deacon Philip Skerda.
Res.: 420 N. Main St., 16371. Tel: 814-563-4432; Fax: 814-563-9686.
Catechesis / Religious Program—Dolores Stec, D.R.E. Students 28.

Chaplains of Public Institutions

ERIE. *Erie County Prison* (1961). Rev. Philip M. Oriole.
Hamot Medical Center, 201 State St., 16550. Rev. Msgr. Gerald J. Koos.
Pleasant Ridge Manor East. Rev. Msgr. Gerald L. Orbanek, M.A.
Pleasant Ridge Manor West. Rev. Daniel J. Prez.
Shriners Hospital for Crippled Children, 1116 W. 7th St., 16550. Vacant.
Soldiers and Sailors Home. Deacon James B. McGuinness.
Veterans Administration Hospital. Rev. Gerald Wright, O.M.V., Chap.
St. Vincent's Health Center, 232 W. 25th St., 16544. Rev. Dennis A. Martin, Chap.

ALBION. *Albion State Correctional Facility*. Deacon Ralph DeCecco.

BRADFORD. *Federal Correction Institution*, P.O. Box 5000, 16701-0950. Rev. Vincent P. Cieslewicz.

CAMBRIDGE SPRINGS. *Cambridge Springs Correction Institution*. Rev. Daniel J. Prez.

DU BOIS. *Du Bois Regional Hospital*, 100 Hospital Ave., 15801. Deacon Robert P DeNoon, Chap.

MEADVILLE. *Crawford County Care Center*, 967 Chancery Ln., 16335. Rev. Rocco A. Tito.

MERCER. *State Correctional Facility*, Box 530, 16137. Rev. Msgr. Charles S. Murcko, Chap. (Retired).

POLK. *Polk Center*, Box 94, 16342. Sr. Claire Hudert, O.S.B., M.A.

WARREN. *Warren State Hospital*. Rev. James G. Faluszczak.

On Duty Outside Diocese:
Revs.—
Allen, Richard J.
Beal, John P., J.C.D., Washington, DC
Gula, Richard, S.S.
Jeselnick, Stephen E., AFB
Kalinowski, Joseph J., CHC
Singer, Christopher J.
Witherup, Ronald, S.S.

On Leave of Absence:
Rev.—
Hadberg, Dennis C.

Retired:
Rev. Msgrs.—
Adams, George
Barcio, Robert G., Ph.D.
Bobal, Joseph K., V.F.
Bogniak, Casimir
Carter, John T.
Daniszewski, John D.
DeWalt, Homer C.
Dollinger, John M.
Hagerty, John B.
Heberlein, Louis J.
McGuire, Richard J.
Mitchell, Salvatore P.
Murcko, Charles S.
Peterson, James W.
Reilly, Robert J.
Sanner, James E.
Schauerman, Henry J.
Snyder, John R.
Stack, Richard J., J.C.L.
Zeitler, Edward J., V.F.
Revs.—
Andersen, Emil
Barwin, John G.
Bauer, John F.
Burke, John R.
Buzga, John P.
Collins, Stephen L.
Cooper, Donald J.
Dipre, Gilio L., Ph.D.
Dymski, J. Daniel
Fedor, Robert P.
Fischer, John M.
Levis, Robert J., Ph.D.
Lynch, John S.
Maloney, William J.
Maryland, Joseph A.
Matuszak, Edward S.
Powers, Richard E.
Rice, William A.
Schill, Paul A.
Schmitt, Charles R.
Skinner, Charles D.
Somers, Eldon K.
Susa, Robert P., M.A.
Wolf, Norbert G.

INSTITUTIONS LOCATED IN THE DIOCESE

[A] SEMINARIES, DIOCESAN

ERIE. *St. Mark's Seminary*, 429 E. Grandview Blvd., P.O. Box 10397, 16514. Tel: 814-824-1200. Very Rev. Michael T. Kesicki, S.S.L., Rector; Revs. Nicholas J. Rouch, S.T.D., Vice Rector; Stephen J. Schreiber, Res. Spiritual Dir.

[B] COLLEGES AND UNIVERSITIES

ERIE. *Gannon University*, University Square, 16541. Tel: 814-871-7000; Fax: 814-871-5372. Web: www.gannon.edu. Dr. Antoine M. Garibaldi, Ph.D., Pres.; Very Rev. Joseph C. Gregorek, V.F., Ph.D.; Revs. Gilio L. Dipre, Ph.D. (Retired); Edward Krause, C.S.C., Ph.D.; Robert J. Levis, Ph.D. (Retired); Casimir Wozniak, Ph.D.; Very Rev. Michael T. Kesicki, S.S.L.; Revs. George E. Strohmeyer, M.A.; Jason A. Glover, S.T.L. Priests 8; Sisters 3; Lay Teachers 193; Students 4,238.
Mercyhurst College, 501 E. 38th St., 16546. Tel: 814-824-2000; Fax: 814-824-3333. Web: www.mercyhurst.edu. Thomas J. Gamble, Ph.D., Pres.; Rev. James Piszker, Chap.; Sue Johnson, Asst. to the Pres.; Darcy Jones, Librarian. Priests 1; Sisters 3; Lay Teachers 147; Students 3,216.

[C] HIGH SCHOOLS, DIOCESAN

ERIE. *Cathedral Preparatory School*, 225 W. Ninth St., 16501. Tel: 814-453-7737; Fax: 814-459-6188. Rev. Scott W. Jabo, Pres.; Sr. Claudia Dombrowski, S.S.J., Prin.; Gail Dragich, Librarian. Priests 6; Sisters 2; Laymen 26; Laywomen 14; Students 555.
Faculty: Rev. Msgr. Bruce R. Allison; Revs. Michael G. DeMartinis; T. Shane Mathew; James McCormick; John L. Miller; Sr. James Francis Mulligan.

DU BOIS. *DuBois Area Catholic School*, (Grades PreK-12), P.O. Box 567, 15801. Tel: 814-371-3060; Fax: 814-371-3215. Email: rtomasone@duboiscatholic.com. Very Rev. Richard C. Tomasone, V.F., Pres.; Revs. Marc Stockton, Prin., High & Middle School.; Edward J. Walk, Asst. Headmaster. Priests 3; Lay Teachers 47; Students 520.
Du Bois Area Catholic School dba Central Catholic High School Tel: 814-371-3060; Fax: 814-371-3215.
Du Bois Area Catholic School dba Central Catholic Middle School (Grades 6-8) Tel: 814-371-3060; Fax: 814-371-3215. Rev. Marc Stockton, Prin.

HERMITAGE. *Kennedy Catholic High School*, 2120 Fwy., 16148. Tel: 724-346-5531; Fax: 724-346-3011. Email: kchs@kennedy-catholic.org. Mr. Peter Iacino, Pres.; Mr. Joseph Kenneally, Prin. Priests 1; Sisters 1; Lay Teachers 20; Students 250.

OIL CITY. *Venango Catholic High School*, 1505 W. 1st St., 16301-3298. Tel: 814-677-3098; Fax: 814-676-4453. Email: jpsm5.vchs@choiceonemail.com. Rev. John P. Malthaner, Headmaster; Barbara Reszkowski, Librarian. Priests 2; Lay Teachers 14; Students 89.

SAINT MARYS. *Elk County Catholic High School*, 600 Maurus St., St. Marys, 15857. Tel: 814-834-7800; Fax: 814-781-3441. Email: ecchs@ncentral.com. Mr. John W. Kowach, Headmaster; Jen Meyer, Campus Ministry Coord. Priests 1; Lay Teachers 25; Students 289.

[D] HIGH SCHOOLS, PRIVATE

ERIE. *Mercyhurst Preparatory School*, 538 E. Grandview Blvd., 16504. Tel: 814-824-2210; Fax: 814-824-2116. Email: maste@mpslakers.com. Sr. Mary Ann Bader, R.S.M., Pres.; Margaret Aste, Prin.; Marcia DiTullio, Contact Person; Ms. Deborah Servey, Librarian. Priests 1; Sisters 3; Lay Teachers 44; Students 595.
Villa Maria Academy, 2403 W. 8th St., 16505. Tel: 814-838-2061; Fax: 814-836-0881. Email: villa@villamaria.com. Web: www.villamaria.com. Rev. Scott W. Jabo, Pres.; Sr. Mary Drexler, S.S.J., Prin.; Mrs. Kathleen DiNicola, Asst. Prin.; Sue Dobson, Librarian. Sisters 5; Lay Teachers 23; Students 298.

[E] ELEMENTARY SCHOOLS, PRIVATE

ERIE. *Villa Maria Elementary School*, (Grades PreK-8), 2551 W. 8th St., 16505. Tel: 814-838-5451; Fax: 814-833-6132. Mr. Damon Finazzo, Prin. Sisters of St. Joseph 2; Lay Teachers 26; Students 322.

[F] SPECIAL MINISTRIES

ERIE. *St. Benedict Child Development Center*, 345 E. 9th St., 16503. Tel: 814-454-4514; Fax: 814-452-1905. Email: admin@stbenedictctr.com. Sr. Diane Rabe, O.S.B., Admin. Students 50.
St. Benedict Education Center, 330 E. 10th St., 16503. Tel: 814-452-4072, Ext. 234; Fax: 814-454-2686. Email: mmashank@stben.org. Sr. Miriam Mashank, O.S.B., Exec. Dir. Students 2,800; Personnel 60.
Erie East Coast Migrant Programs, 345 E. 9th St., 16503. Tel: 814-454-4514; Fax: 814-452-1905. Email: admin@stbenedictctr.com. Sr. Diane Rabe, O.S.B., Dir. Benedictine Sisters of Erie. Students 55.
Inner-City Neighborhood Art House, 210 East Ave., 16503. Tel: 814-455-5508; Fax: 814-480-8942. Sr. Anne Wambach, O.S.B., Exec. Dir.
L'Arche Erie, 3745 W. 12th St., 16505. Tel: 814-452-2065; Fax: 814-452-4188. Email: office@larcheerie.org.
Mercy Center of the Arts, 444 E. Grandview Blvd., 16504. Tel: 814-824-2519; Fax: 814-824-2127. Email: catherine_ed@yahoo.com.
Word of Life Catholic Charismatic Renewal, St. Mark Catholic Center, 429 E. Grandview Blvd., P.O. Box 10397, 16514-0397. Tel: 814-824-1286; Fax: 814-824-1128. Email: wolccrc@aol.com. Web: www.wordoflifeccrc.org.

FAIRVIEW. *Camp Notre Dame*, 400 Eaton Rd., P.O. Box 74, 16415. Tel: 814-474-5001; Fax: 814-474-4818. Email: cnd3@earthlink.net. Web: www.campnotredame.com. William Hilbert Jr., Pres.; Kathleen Bastow, Vice Pres.; John Yonko, Exec. Dir.

OIL CITY. *Catholic Rural Ministry - Oil City Deanery*, 7 Pulaski St., 16301. Tel: 814-677-2032. Sisters Clare Marie Beichner, S.S.J., L.S.W., Co-Dir.; Marian Wehler, O.S.B., Co-Dir.

PORT ALLEGANY. *Catholic Rural Ministry - Bradford Deanery*, 472 Sartwell Creek Rd., 16743. Tel: 814-544-8017; Fax: 814-544-8017. Email: crm@zitomedia.net. Sr. Phyllis Schleicher, O.S.B., Dir.

[G] GENERAL HOSPITALS

ERIE. **Saint Vincent Health Center*, 232 W. 25th St., 16544. Tel: 814-452-5000; Fax: 814-452-7611. Web: www.saintvincenthealth.com. Ms. Angela Bontempo, Pres. & CEO; Rev. Dennis A. Martin, Chap.; Julie M. DeMarco, Dir. Tel: 814-452-7611.
Saint Vincent Health System Ms. Angela Bontempo, Pres. & CEO, Saint Vincent Health System.

[H] PROTECTIVE INSTITUTIONS

ERIE. *Gannondale, Inc.*, 4635 E. Lake Rd., 16511. Tel: 814-899-7659; Fax: 814-898-4266. Email: gdale@gannondale.org. Web: www.gannondale.org. Sr. Carol Pregno, O.L.C., Pres.; Nancy Sabol, Exec. Dir. North American Union of Sisters of Our Lady of Charity-Erie. Residents 47.

HARBORCREEK. *Harborcreek Youth Services*, 5712 Iroquois Ave., 16421. Tel: 814-899-7664; Fax: 814-899-3075. Email: jpetulla@hys-erie.org. Mr. John D. Petulla, A.C.S.W., M.S.W., C.E.O. Children 70.

[I] APARTMENTS FOR SENIOR CITIZENS

ERIE. *Mercy Terrace Apartments*, 430 E. Grandview Blvd., 16504. Tel: 814-825-6791; Fax: 814-824-2127. Email: mta430@verizon.net. Sr. M. Felice Duska, R.S.M., Mgr. Sponsored by Sisters of Mercy of the Americas - New York, Pennsylvania, Pacific West Community.

HARBORCREEK. **Benetwood Apartments for Persons Elderly and Disabled*, 641 Troupe Rd., 16421-1048. Tel: 814-899-0088; Fax: 814-898-2513.

Email: benetwood@neohio.twcbc.com. Sr. Patricia Hause, O.S.B., Admin. Benedictine Sisters of Erie. Residents 80.

[J] RESIDENCES FOR RETIRED PRIESTS

ERIE. *Bishop Michael J. Murphy Residence for Retired Priests*, 400 E. Gore Rd., 16509. Tel: 814-825-0680; Fax: 814-825-9761. Rev. Msgr. Robert J. Smith, J.C.L., V.G., Dir.

[K] NURSING HOMES

ERIE. *Saint Mary's Home of Erie*, Mailing Address: 607 E. 26th St., 16504. Tel: 814-459-0621; Fax: 814-454-0909. Email: pmccracken@stmaryshome.org. Web: www.stmaryshome.org. Sr. Phyllis McCracken, S.S.J., M.S., R.N., N.H.A., Pres., CEO & Contact Person.

Saint Mary's Home of Erie dba Saint Mary's East 607 E. 26th St., 16504. Tel: 814-459-0621; Fax: 814-454-0909. Sisters Phyllis McCracken, S.S.J., M.S., R.N., N.H.A., Pres., CEO & Contact Person; Mary Fromknecht, S.S.J., Admin.; Rev. Msgr. Joseph V. Wardanski, Chap. Sisters 9; Residents 131; Adult Day Services 49; Patients in Nursing Home 139.

Saint Mary's Home of Erie dba Saint Mary's at Asbury Ridge 4855 W. Ridge Rd., 16506. Tel: 814-836-5300; Fax: 814-836-5326. Sr. Phyllis McCracken, S.S.J., M.S., R.N., N.H.A., Pres., CEO & Contact Person; Audrey Urban, Admin.; Rev. G. William Fischer, O.S.F.S., Chap. Sisters 3; Residents 164; Patients in Nursing Home 80; Carriage Homes Independent Living 26.

Saint Mary's Home of Erie dba Carleton Court 2710 Carleton Ct., 16506. Tel: 814-833-2787. Apartments (Independent Living) 60; Total Assisted Annually 82.

DU BOIS. *Christ the King Manor, Inc.*, 1100 W. Long Ave., 15801. Tel: 814-371-3180; Fax: 814-371-4101. Email: ctkm@penn.com. Web: www.christthekingmanor.org. Very Rev. Richard C. Tomasone, V.F. Residents 220.

HERMITAGE. *John XXIII Home*, 2250 Shenango Fwy., 16148. Tel: 724-981-3200; Fax: 724-981-1677. Email: klhawthorne@johnxxIIIhome.org. Web: www.johnXXIIIhome.org. Rev. Regis Meenihan, Chap.; Kirk L. Hawthorne, Admin. Residents 198.

[L] SHELTERS FOR MEN AND WOMEN

ERIE. *Maria House Project*, P.O. Box 10682, 16514. Tel: 814-454-0891. Rev. Msgr. James W. Peterson, Dir. (Retired).

St. Patrick Haven, Inc., 147 E. 12th St., 16501. Tel: 814-454-7219; 814-836-5301; Fax: 814-454-7219. Sr. Marie Eileen Moyer, S.S.J., Admin.

[M] CONVENTS AND RESIDENCES FOR SISTERS

ERIE. *Benet Priory*, 330 E. 10th St., 16503. Tel: 814-459-5103. Benedictine Sisters of Erie 2.

Congregation of the Divine Spirit, 409 W. 6th St., 16507. Tel: 814-455-3590; Fax: 814-454-8899. Email: AdSum409@aol.com. Sr. Michele Beauseigneur, C.D.S., Supr. Gen.; Revs. Casimir Wozniak, Ph.D., Chap.; Edward Krause, C.S.C., Ph.D., Chap. Members 40.

Holy Family Monastery, 510 E. Gore Rd., 16509-3799. Tel: 814-825-0846; Fax: 814-825-0865. Sr. Emmanuel of the Mother of God, O.C.D., Prioress; Very Rev. Michael T. Kesicki, S.S.L., Chap.; Rev. Nicholas J. Rouch, S.T.D., Chap. Discalced Carmelites 5.

Julia House, 608 Walnut St., 16502. Tel: 814-871-5756. Sr. Kathleen Dietz, F.S.O., Supr. The Spiritual Family the Work Members 2.

Kraus House Priory, 436 E. 9th St., 16503. Tel: 814-454-4846. Benedictine Sisters of Erie. Sisters 2.

Mount Saint Benedict Monastery, 6101 E. Lake Rd., 16511. Tel: 814-899-0614; Fax: 814-898-4004. Email: prioress@mtstbenedict.org. Web: www.eriebenedictines.org. Sisters Christine Vladimiroff, O.S.B., Prioress; Patricia McGreevy, O.S.B., Admin. Assoc. to the Prioress. Benedictine Sisters of Erie. Professed Sisters in Community 105.

Om Shanti, 1239 W. 7th St., 16502. Tel: 814-459-3215. Email: mdcookosb@yahoo.com. Web: www.eriebenedictines.org.

Sophia House, 1245 W. 10th St., 16502. Tel: 814-454-1212. Email: sbenedictine002@neo.rr.com. Benedictine Sisters of Erie 3.

Bethany House, 218 E. 11th St., 16503. Tel: 814-455-4574. Email: bethany2@peoplepc.com. Benedictine Sisters of Erie 3.

Peace House, 103 E. 35th St., 16504. Tel: 814-455-6066. Email: mmashank@stben.org. Benedictine Sisters of Erie 2.

Benedicta Riepp Priory, 3904 Tuttle Ave., 16504. Tel: 814-825-2767. Email: mjaneosb@peoplepc.org. Benedictine Sisters of Erie 2.

Pax Priory, 345 E. Ninth St., 16503. Tel: 814-452-6318; Fax: 814-459-8066. Email: PAXPRIORY@peoplepc.com. Web: www.eriebenedictines.org. Benedictine Sisters of Erie 5.

St. Scholastica Priory, 355 E. 9th St., 16503. Tel: 814-454-4052; Fax: 814-459-8066. Email: scholpriory@benetvision.org. Web: eriebenedictines.org. Benedictine Sisters of Erie 3.

Sisters of Mercy of the Americas - New York, Pennsylvania, Pacific West Community, 444 E. Grandview Blvd., 16504. Tel: 814-824-2516; Fax: 814-824-2127. Web: www.sistersofmercy.org. Sr. Nancy Hoff, R.S.M., Pres. (Erie Diocese) 47; Total in Community 490.

Sisters of Saint Joseph of Northwestern Pennsylvania, 5031 W. Ridge Rd., 16506-1249. Tel: 814-836-4100; Fax: 814-836-4278. Email: smedwyer@ssjerie.org. Web: www.ssjerie.org. Sr. Mary Ellen Dwyer, S.S.J., Pres.; Rev. Jerome S. Simmons, Chap. The Sisters of St. Joseph of Northwestern PA. Professed Sisters in Community 120.

Union of Our Lady of Charity/United States Province, 4635 E. Lake Rd., 16511. Tel: 814-899-1052; Fax: 814-899-1573. Email: srcgentile@hotmail.com. Sisters Catherine Gentile, Local Supr.; Carol Pregno, O.L.C., Provincial. Sisters 4.

St. Walburga Priory, 302 E. 10th St., 16503. Tel: 814-454-3706. Email: walburga@peoplepc.com. Web: www.eriebenedictines.org. Benedictine Sisters of Erie 2.

ST. MARYS. *Benedictine Sisters of Elk County St. Joseph Monastery*, 303 Church St., 15857. Tel: 814-834-2267; Fax: 814-834-3270. Email: srjacintaconklin@yahoo.com. Sr. Jacinta Conklin, O.S.B., Prioress. Professed Sisters 18.

[N] SOCIOLOGICAL

ERIE. *Saint Benedict Community Center*, 320 E. 10th St., 16503. Tel: 814-459-2406. Email: iluv2kayak@hotmail.com. Sr. Dianne Sabol, O.S.B., Dir.

Emmaus Ministries, Inc., 345 E. 9th St., 16503. Tel: 814-459-8349; Fax: 814-459-8066. Sr. Mary Miller, O.S.B., Dir.

ERIE DAWN, 2549 W. 8th St., 16505-4430. Tel: 814-453-5921; Fax: 814-453-5831. Email: maureen@eriedawn.org. Web: www.eriedawn.org. Maureen Dunn, Admin.

Mercy Center for Women, 1039 E. 27th St., 16504. Tel: 814-455-4577; Fax: 814-459-7012. Email: ctombaugh@mcwerie.org. Web: www.mcwerie.org. Christine Tombaugh, Exec. Dir.

Mercy Center on Aging, Inc., 444 E. Grandview Blvd., 16504-2604. Tel: 814-824-2214; Fax: 814-824-2127. Web: mercycenteronaging.com. Sr. Mary Dolores Jablonski, R.S.M., Exec. Dir.

Partnership of Women Religious, 6101 E. Lake Rd., 16511. Tel: 814-899-0614.

Sisters of St. Joseph Neighborhood Network, Inc., 425 W. 18th St., 16502. Tel: 814-454-7814; Fax: 814-454-7915. Email: mherrmann@ssjnn.org. Web: ssjnn.org. Sr. Mary Herrmann, S.S.J., Exec. Dir.

[O] RETREAT & RENEWAL CENTERS

ERIE. *Ecclesia Ministry*, 1626 W. 26th St., 16508. Tel: 814-454-0810. Email: ecclesia@adelphia.net. Web: www.ecclesiacenter.org. Rev. Jerome S. Simmons; Sr. Marilyn Zimmerman, S.S.J., Contact Person.

Glinodo Center, 6270 E. Lake Rd., 16511. Tel: 814-899-0614; Fax: 814-898-4004. Email: physical@mstbenedict.org. Web: www.eriebenedictines.org. Sr. Charles Marie Holze, O.S.B., Dir. Benedictine Sisters of Erie.

FRENCHVILLE. *Young People Who Care Inc.*, 1031 Germania Rd., P.O. Box 129, 16836. Tel: 814-263-4855; Fax: 814-263-7106. Email: bethanyyouth@pennswoods.net. Web: www.ypwcministries.org. Sr. Therese Dush, C.A., Dir.

UNION CITY. *Avila Retreat Center*, 61 E. High St., 16438. Tel: 814-438-7020. Richard Raid, Contact Person.

[P] CAMPUS MINISTRY

ERIE. *Newman Centers and Campus Ministry* Gannon Univ., 109 University Sq., 16541. Tel: 814-871-7435. Deacon Stephen J. Washek.

Allegheny College 520 N. Main St., P.O. Box 101, Meadville, 16335. Tel: 814-332-2800; Fax: 814-332-2340. Rev. Richard Toohey.

University of Pittsburgh - Bradford Campus St. Bernard Parish, P.O. Box 2394, Bradford, 16701. Tel: 814-362-6825; Fax: 814-362-1497. Deacon Gerald Beeman.

Clarion University of Pennsylvania P.O. Box 177, Emlenton, 16373. Tel: 724-867-2422; Fax: 724-867-6815. Rev. Msgr. Jan C. Olowin.

Lockhaven University - Clearfield Campus 212 S. Front St., Clearfield, 16830. Tel: 814-765-9671; Fax: 814-226-1090.

Penn State University - Du Bois Campus 116 State St., DuBois, 15801. Tel: 814-371-8556.

Edinboro University of PA Newman Center, 128 Sunset Dr., P.O. Box 820, Edinboro, 16412. Tel: 814-734-1651; Fax: 814-734-3085. Rev. William E. Sutherland.

Gannon University University Sq., 16541. Tel: 814-871-7435. Deacon Stephen J. Washek, Campus Min.; Rev. George E. Strohmeyer, M.A., Chap.

Grove City College Beloved Disciple Parish, 321 N. Broad St., Grove City, 16127. Tel: 412-458-7145.

Mercyhurst College 501 E. 38th St., 16546. Tel: 814-456-6189. Greg Baker, Campus Min.; Rev. James Piszker, Chap. & Dir. Tel: 814-824-2467; Paul Mocosko, Campus Min. Tel: 814-456-6189.

Mercyhurst College, North East 204 W. 6th St., 16507. Tel: 814-456-6189.

Clarion State University of PA - Venango Campus St. Stephen Parish, 210 Reed St., Oil City, 16301. Tel: 814-677-3020.

Penn State Erie, The Behrend College 5091 Station Rd., 16563-0901. Tel: 814-898-6245; Fax: 814-898-6608.

Indiana University of PA - Punxsutawney Campus Ss. Cosmas & Damian Parish, 616 W. Mahoning St., Punxsutawney, 15767. Tel: 814-938-6540.

Penn State University - Shenango Valley Campus St. Joseph Parish, 74 Case Ave., Sharon, 16146. Tel: 412-981-3232.

Thiel College, St. Michael Parish, 85 N. High St., Greenville, 16125. Tel: 724-588-9800.

University of Pittsburgh - Titusville Campus St. Titus Parish, 513 W. Main St., Titusville, 16354. Tel: 814-827-4636.

[Q] MISCELLANEOUS

ERIE. *Alliance for International Monasticism (AIM)-USA Secretariat (AIM-USA)*, 345 E. 9th St., 16503-1107. Tel: 814-453-4724; Fax: 814-459-8066. Email: aim@aim-usa.org. Web: www.aim-usa.org. Sr. Susan Doubet, O.S.B., Exec. Dir. AIM is an organization founded to assist Benedictine and Cistercian monasteries in Africa, Asia and Latin America.

Star Foundation, c/o St. Mark Catholic Center, 429 E. Grandview Blvd., P.O. Box 10397, 16514-0397. Tel: 814-824-1188; Fax: 814-824-1181. Email: cbanducci@eriercd.org. Charles Banducci, Coord.

The Catholic Foundation of the Roman Catholic Diocese of Erie, Inc., Mailing Address: *St. Mark Catholic Center*, P.O. Box 10397, 16514-0397. Tel: 814-824-1236; Fax: 814-824-1264. Email: thecatholicfoundation@eriercd.org. 429 E. Grandview Blvd., 16504.

St. Thomas More Society, P.O. Box 10397, 16514-0397. Tel: 814-824-1140; Fax: 814-824-1149.

FRENCHVILLE. *Anawim Community of Frenchville*, 1031 Germania Rd., P.O. Box 129, 16836. Tel: 814-263-4855; Fax: 814-263-7106. Email: anawimco@pennswoods.net. Web: www.anawimcommunity.org. Sr. Therese Dush, C.A., Dir.

ST. MARYS. *Opportunity for Parochial Education Network (OPEN)*, 575 Charles St., 15857. Tel: 814-834-6181. Richard J. Reuscher, Trustee.

RELIGIOUS INSTITUTES OF MEN REPRESENTED IN THE DIOCESE

For further details refer to the corresponding bracketed number in the Religious Institutes of Men or Women section.

[0200]—*Benedictine Monks* (St. Vincent's Archabbey)—O.S.B.

[0290]—*Oblates of St. Francis de Sales*—O.S.F.S.

[0940]—*Oblates of the Virgin Mary*—O.M.V.

[0610]—*Priests of the Congregation of Holy Cross*—C.S.C.

RELIGIOUS INSTITUTES OF WOMEN REPRESENTED IN THE DIOCESE

[0230]—*Benedictine Sisters of Elk Co.*—O.S.B.

[0160]—*Benedictine Sisters of Erie*—O.S.B.

[]—*Congregation of Divine Providence* (Pittsburgh)—C.D.P.

[]—*Congregation of the Divine Spirit*—C.D.S.

[]—*Congregation of the Sisters of St. Joseph* Pittsburgh—C.S.J.

[0420]—*Discalced Carmelite Nuns*—O.C.D.

[2720]—*Mission Helpers of the Sacred Heart*—M.H.S.H.

[2820]—*Missionary Sisters of Our Lady of Africa*—M.S.O.L.A.

[3070]—*North American Union of Sisters of Our Lady of Charity*—N.A.U.-O.L.C.

[1690]—*School Sisters of the Third Order of St. Francis*—O.S.F.

[0507]—*Sisters of Charity of Seton Hill, Greenburg, PA*—S.C.

[2570]—*Sisters of Mercy of the Americas* (New York, PA, Pacific West Community)—R.S.M.

[]—*Sisters of St. Basil the Great*—O.S.B.M.

[3830]—*Sisters of St. Joseph*—S.S.J.
[2110]—*Sisters of the Humility of Mary*—H.M.
[]—*Spiritual Family the Work*—F.S.O.

DIOCESAN CEMETERIES

ERIE. *Queen of Peace*
Trinity, Calvary & Gate of Heaven

NECROLOGY

† Kraus, Rev. Msgr. Conrad, (Retired)—Died May 13, 2009
† Mignot, Rev. Msgr. John W., Reynoldsville, PA St. Mary—Died Feb. 19, 2009
† Sperry, Rev. Msgr. James E., (Retired)—Died May 17, 2009

An asterisk (*) denotes an organization that has established tax-exempt status directly with the IRS and is not covered by the USCCB Group Ruling.

Diocese of Evansville

(Dioecesis Evansvicensis)

Most Reverend

GERALD ANDREW GETTELFINGER

Bishop of Evansville; ordained May 7, 1961; appointed Fourth Bishop of Evansville March 11, 1989; ordained and installed April 11, 1989. *Res.: 3980 Woodcastle, Evansville, IN 47711. Mailing Address: Catholic Center, 4200 N. Kentucky Ave., P.O. Box 4169, Evansville, IN 47724-0169.* Fax: 812-436-7450.

Catholic Center: 4200 N. Kentucky Ave., P.O. Box 4169, Evansville, IN 47724-0169. Tel: 812-424-5536; Fax: 812-421-1334.

Web: www.evansville-diocese.org

ESTABLISHED NOVEMBER 11, 1944.

Square Miles 5,010.

Comprises twelve Counties in the Southwestern part of Indiana: Daviess, Dubois, Gibson, Greene, Knox, Martin, Pike, Posey, Spencer (except township of Harrison), Sullivan, Vanderburgh, Warrick.

The Diocese of Evansville was established by decree of Pope Pius XII, November 11, 1944, and the See was fixed at Evansville.

For legal titles of parishes and diocesan institutions, consult the Chancery.

STATISTICAL OVERVIEW

Personnel	
Bishop	1
Priests: Diocesan Active in Diocese	47
Priests: Diocesan Active Outside Diocese	1
Priests: Retired, Sick or Absent	28
Number of Diocesan Priests	76
Religious Priests in Diocese	5
Total Priests in Diocese	81
Extern Priests in Diocese	1
Ordinations:	
Diocesan Priests	1
Permanent Deacons	12
Permanent Deacons in Diocese	52
Total Sisters	250
Parishes	
Parishes	69
With Resident Pastor:	
Resident Diocesan Priests	39
Resident Religious Priests	3
Without Resident Pastor:	
Administered by Priests	20
Administered by Deacons	6
Administered by Religious Women	1
Pastoral Centers	7
Professional Ministry Personnel:	
Sisters	13
Lay Ministers	75
Welfare	
Catholic Hospitals	2
Total Assisted	922,897
Health Care Centers	1
Total Assisted	60
Homes for the Aged	4
Total Assisted	187
Day Care Centers	1
Total Assisted	156
Special Centers for Social Services	10
Total Assisted	159,075
Educational	
Diocesan Students in Other Seminaries	8
Total Seminarians	8
High Schools, Diocesan and Parish	4
Total Students	1,518
High Schools, Private	1
Total Students	6
Elementary Schools, Diocesan and Parish	24
Total Students	5,802
Catechesis/Religious Education:	
High School Students	2,036
Elementary Students	4,587
Total Students under Catholic Instruction	13,957
Teachers in the Diocese:	
Sisters	8
Lay Teachers	477
Vital Statistics	
Receptions into the Church:	
Infant Baptism Totals	1,180
Adult Baptism Totals	92
Received into Full Communion	142
First Communions	1,281
Confirmations	1,047
Marriages:	
Catholic	272
Interfaith	164
Total Marriages	436
Deaths	800
Total Catholic Population	85,079
Total Population	496,795

Former Bishops—Most Revs. HENRY JOSEPH GRIMMELSMAN, D.D., appt. Nov. 11, 1944; cons. Dec. 21, 1944; retired and named Titular Bishop of Tabla Oct. 20, 1965; died June 26, 1972; PAUL F. LEIBOLD, D.D., J.C.D., appt. Titular Bishop of Trebenna and Auxiliary of Cincinnati April 10, 1958; cons. June 17, 1958; appt. to Evansville April 6, 1966; translated to Archbishop of Cincinnati July 23, 1969; died June 1, 1972; FRANCIS R. SHEA, appt. Dec. 10, 1969; retired April 11, 1989; died Aug. 18, 1994.

Catholic Center—4200 N. Kentucky Ave., P.O. Box 4169, Evansville, 47724-0169. Tel: 812-424-5536; Fax: 812-421-1334. Office Hours: Mon.-Thurs. 8-5, Fri. 8-4:30.

Vicar General—Rev. Msgr. KENNETH R. KNAPP, A.C.S.W., M.S.

Chief Operating Officer—TIMOTHY J. MCGUIRE.

Chancellor—JUDITH A. NEFF.

Secretary to the Bishop—DEANNA RUSTON.

Treasurer—ROBERT J. COX, CPA.

Associate Treasurer—SCOTT BRITT.

Assistant Treasurer—PHYLLIS HIGGINS.

Diocesan Tribunal—Mailing Address: P.O. Box 4169, Evansville, 47724-0169.

Judicial Vicar—Rev. J. KENNETH WALKER, B.A., M.Div., M.C.L., J.C.L.; MARY GEN BLITTSCHAU, M.A., M.C.L., J.C.L., Asst. to Judicial Vicar & Judge.

Defender of the Bond—Rev. JOSEPH ERBACHER.

Judges—Rev. Msgr. CLINTON F. HIRSCH, J.C.L. (Retired); Revs. RAYMOND L. KUPER (Retired); DAVID G. FLECK; STEPHEN P. LINTZENICH.

Advocates—Revs. JOHN H. SCHIPP; MICHAEL MADDEN.

Secretaries and Notaries—CHARLEEN KAELIN; GAYLE SPALDING.

Archivist—JUDITH A. NEFF.

Diocesan Consultors—Rev. Msgr. KENNETH R. KNAPP, A.C.S.W., M.S.; Revs. J. KENNETH WALKER, B.A., M.Div., M.C.L., J.C.L.; BERNARD ETIENNE; GARY EDWARD KAISER; JAMES KORESSEL; STEPHEN P. LINTZENICH; BERNARD A. LUTZ (Retired); MICHAEL MADDEN; DAVID G. FLECK.

Diocesan Council of Priests—Rev. Msgr. KENNETH R. KNAPP, A.C.S.W., M.S.; Revs. J. KENNETH WALKER, B.A., M.Div., M.C.L., J.C.L.; JACK J. DURCHHOLZ; DAVID A. MARTIN; GREGORY CHAMBERLIN, O.S.B.; DAVID G. FLECK; JOHN BROSMER; STEPHEN P. LINTZENICH; JAMES KORESSEL; MICHAEL MADDEN; GARY EDWARD KAISER; BERNARD ETIENNE; BERNARD A. LUTZ (Retired); EUGENE SCHMITT.

Clergy Personnel Board—Rev. STEPHEN P. LINTZENICH, Dir.; Deacon DAVID RICE, Asst. Dir.; Revs. RONALD S. ZGUNDA; DONALD K. ACKERMAN (Retired); KENNETH H. HERR; JACK DURCHHOLZ; EUGENE SCHMITT; JAMES BLESSINGER.

Deans—Revs. BERNARD ETIENNE, Evansville, East; DAVID H. NUNNING, Evansville, West; RAYMOND BRENNER, Jasper; JOSEPH ZILIAK, S.T.L., Newburgh; RONALD S. ZGUNDA, Princeton; DAVID G. FLECK, Vincennes; JAMES KORESSEL, Washington.

Censors of Books—Revs. J. KENNETH WALKER, B.A., M.Div., M.C.L., J.C.L.; JOSEPH ZILIAK, S.T.L.

Diocesan Offices And Directors

Boy Scouts—Deacon CHARLES KORESSEL, Chap.

Campus Ministry—CHRISTINE HOEHN, Coord.

Catholic Charities—JAMES F. COLLINS, Exec. Dir., Court Bldg., Ste. 603, 123 N.W. Fourth St., Evansville, 47708. Tel: 812-423-5456.

Catholic Diocese of Evansville, Inc.—Most Rev. GERALD A. GETTELFINGER.

Catholic Education Endowment, Inc. (Washington)—JAMES WERNE, Pres.

Catholic Education Foundation, Inc. (Evansville)—MARGARET ANGERMEIER, Exec. Dir.

The Catholic Foundation of Southwestern Indiana, Inc.—LINDA COX, Exec. Dir., Mailing Address: P.O. Box 4169, Evansville, 47724-0169.

Holy Family Catholic School Foundation, Inc.—WILFRED WEINZAPFEL, Pres., 950 Church Ave., Jasper, 47546.

Catholic Education, Office of—DONNA HALVERSON, Interim Dir. Schools; RHONDA SCHROEDER, Sec.; STEVE BAGBEY, Safety & Security Coord.

Catholic Communication Office—PAUL LEINGANG, Dir., Mailing Address: P.O. Box 4169, Evansville, 47724-0169.

Catholic Hospitals, Diocesan Representative—Deacon MICHAEL BURNS, 1490 Holler Rd., Mount Vernon, 47620.

Catholic Relief Services—JAMES F. COLLINS, Court Building, Ste. 603, 123 N.W. Fourth St., Evansville, 47708. Tel: 812-423-5456.

Cemeteries—Rev. EUGENE A. SCHROEDER, Dir., 6202 W. St. Joseph Rd., Evansville, 47720. Tel: 812-963-3273.

Christian Educational Foundation of Vincennes, Inc.—MIKE RUSCH, Pres.

Continuing Education of Clergy—Rev. BERNARD A. LUTZ, Dir. (Retired), Mailing Address: 4200 N. Kentucky Ave., Evansville, 47711.

Cursillos in Christianity—BRUCE BONENBERGER, Lay Dir.

Deaf Ministry—Rev. HENRY KUYKENDALL, 3635 Pollack, Evansville, 47714. Tel: 812-491-3173.

Diocesan Finance Council—Ex Officio: Most Rev. GERALD A. GETTELFINGER; Rev. Msgr. KENNETH R. KNAPP, A.C.S.W., M.S.; TIMOTHY J. MCGUIRE; ROBERT COX; GARY BECKMAN; ALAN HOFFMAN;

JAMES MUEHLBAUER; STEVE WITTING; JAMES ROACH; DEAN HAPPE; WILLIAM KAISER; MARGARET CONWAY.

Diocese of Evansville Retirement Trust Agreement and Plan for Priests—Office of the Bishop: 4200 N. Kentucky Ave., P.O. Box 4169, Evansville, 47724-0169. Tel: 812-424-5536.

Ecumenism—4200 N. Kentucky Ave., P.O. Box 4169, Evansville, 47724-0169. Tel: 812-424-5536.

Evangelization, Office of—4200 N. Kentucky Ave., P.O. Box 4169, Evansville, 47724-0169. Tel: 812-424-5536.

Girl Scouts—Deacon CHARLES KORESSEL, Chap.

Spanish Speaking Ministry—Sr. KAREN DURLIAT, O.S.B., Dir.; Rev. EUGENE HEERDINK, Sacramental Min. (Retired), Guadalupe Center, 511 E. 4th St., Ste. 1, Huntingburg, 47542. Tel: 812-683-5212.

Propagation of the Faith and Holy Childhood Association—CATHY CROWDUS, 4200 N. Kentucky Ave., P.O. Box 4169, Evansville, 47724-0169. Tel: 812-424-5536.

Justice and Peace— (Please refer to Catholic Charities for further information).

Legion of Mary—VACANT, Evansville; Deacon DONALD HAAG, Washington.

Message, The— Catholic Press of Evansville; Publisher, Most Rev. GERALD A. GETTELFINGER; PAUL LEINGANG, Editor.

Permanent Diaconate Program—Rev. JEAN VOGLER, Dir., 219 N.W. Third St., Evansville, 47708; Deacon DAVID SEIBERT, Assoc. Dir.

Adult Formation/RCIA—Sr. GERALDINE HEDINGER, O.S.B., Dir.; DONNA GISH, Asst. Dir.

Rural Life Conference—Rev. JOHN BOEGLIN, Dir., Holy Family Church, 950 E. Church Ave., Jasper, 47546-3797.

Sarto Retreat House—JULIE YOUNG, Coord.; GEORGE FLEMING, Dir. Maintenance.

Secretariat for Charismatic Renewal—VACANT.

Stewardship/Development, Office of—VACANT, Mailing Address: P.O. Box 4169, Evansville, 47724-0169. Tel: 812-424-5536.

Victim Assistance Coordinator—REBECCA LUZIO, Ph.D. Tel: 812-490-9565 (local); 866-200-3004 (long distance). Email: rluzio@luzioassociates.com.

Vocation Office—Rev. BERNARD ETIENNE, Vocation Dir. Associate Directors: Revs. ALEX ZENTHOEFER; JASON GRIES; Sr. AGNES MARIE DAUBY, O.S.B., Mailing Address: P.O. Box 4169, Evansville, 47724-0169. Tel: 812-424-5536.

Worship—MATT J. MILLER, 4200 N. Kentucky, P.O. Box 4169, Evansville, 47724-0169. Tel: 812-424-5536.

Youth and Young Adult Ministry—STEVEN DABROWSKI JR., Dir., 4200 N. Kentucky, P.O. Box 4169, Evansville, 47724-0169. Tel: 812-424-5536.

CLERGY, PARISHES, MISSIONS AND PAROCHIAL SCHOOLS

CITY OF EVANSVILLE

(VANDERBURGH COUNTY)

1—ST. BENEDICT CATHEDRAL Rev. Gregory D. Chamberlin, O.S.B.; Sr. Patricia McGuire, O.S.B., Pastoral Assoc.; Deacons David Cook; James Flynn; Kevin Bach.
Parish Center—1328 Lincoln Ave., 47714-1598. Tel: 812-425-3369; Fax: 812-425-3378.
Res.: 1312 Lincoln Ave., 47714.
School—(Grades PreK-8), 530 S. Harlan Ave., 47714-1598. Tel: 812-425-4596. Sr. Karlene Sensmeier, O.S.B., Prin.; Jeanne McGinnis, Librarian. Sisters of St. Benedict 2; Lay Teachers 24; Students 452.
Catechesis/Religious Program—Marty Horning, D.R.E. Students 74.

2—ST. AGNES, [CEM] Rev. David H. Nunning; Deacons William Heberling; Thomas Kempf.
Res.: 1600 Glendale Ave., 47712. Tel: 812-425-9140; Fax: 812-423-4240.
School—Westside Catholic Consolidated, (Grades K-4) Cynthia Schneider, Prin.; Doriene Markin, Librarian. Lay Teachers 8; Students 94.
Catechesis/Religious Program—Jenny Mayer, D.R.E. Students 15.

3—ST. ANTHONY Rev. John Davidson; Sr. Jackie Kissel, O.S.B., Pastoral Assoc.; Lisa Covington, Pastoral Assoc.
Res.: 704 First Ave., 47710. Tel: 812-423-5209; Fax: 812-424-5498.
Catechesis/Religious Program—Sr. Jackie Kissel, O.S.B., D.R.E. Students 43.

4—ASSUMPTION CATHEDRAL, Closed. For inquiries for parish records contact Holy Trinity.

5—ST. BONIFACE Rev. Kenneth H. Herr; Deacons Richard Preske; David Franklin.
Res.: 418 N. Wabash Ave., 47712. Tel: 812-425-8375; Fax: 812-401-7690.
School—(Grades 5-8) Cynthia Schneider, Prin.; Doriene Markin, Librarian. Lay Teachers 11; Students 87.
Catechesis/Religious Program—Jenny Mayer, D.R.E. Students 6.

6—CHRIST THE KING Rev. Msgr. Kenneth R. Knapp, A.C.S.W.; Deacons Francis Hillenbrand; Vincent Bernardin, Pastoral Assoc.
Office: 3010 E. Chandler Ave., 47714-2602. Tel: 812-476-3061; Fax: 812-476-3062.
School—(Grades PreK-8) Sr. Mary Karen Bahlmann, C.D.P., Prin. Lay Teachers 17; Students 205.
Catechesis/Religious Program—

7—CORPUS CHRISTI Rev. James Blessinger; Deacon Tom Goebel.
Res.: 5528 Hogue Rd., 47712-3218. Tel: 812-422-2027; Fax: 812-421-8316.
School—(Grades PreK-8) Martha Craig, Prin.; Donna Martin, Librarian. Lay Teachers 17; Students 273.
Catechesis/Religious Program—Kathryn Curtis, D.R.E. Students 23.

8—GOOD SHEPHERD Deacon Edward Wilkerson, Pastoral Life Coord.; Rev. Attila Frohlich, Sacramental Min.; Deacon Cyril Will.
Res.: 2301 N. Stockwell, 47715. Tel: 812-477-5405; Fax: 812-469-2907.
School—(Grades K-8) Judy Van Hoosier, Prin.; Lucy Ashley, Librarian. Lay Teachers 25; Students 327.
Catechesis/Religious Program—Sue Kroupa, D.R.E. Students 58.

9—HOLY REDEEMER Revs. Paul Anthony Ferguson; Christopher A. Forler; Deacons Robert Hayden; David Mayer.
Office: 918-A W. Mill Rd., 47710. Tel: 812-424-8344; Fax: 812-424-7166.
School—(Grades PreK-8) Marianne Webster, Prin.; Jennifer Gossman, Librarian. Lay Teachers 17; Students 237.
Catechesis/Religious Program—Doug Rasler, D.R.E. Students 120.

10—HOLY ROSARY Revs. Bernard Etienne; Alex Zenthoefer; Sr. Mary Mundy, S.P., Pastoral Assoc.; Ruth Girten, Pastoral Assoc.; Deacon Christian Borowiecki.
Office: 1301 S. Green River Rd., 47715. Tel: 812-477-8923; Fax: 812-471-7226.
School—(Grades PreK-8) Joan Fredrich, Prin.; Robin Gilliam, Librarian. Lay Teachers 22; Students 420.
Catechesis/Religious Program—Carol Ann Gaddis, D.R.E. Students 69.

11—HOLY SPIRIT Rev. Claude Thomas Burns; Deacon Anthony Schapker.
Church: 1800 S. Lodge Ave., 47714. Tel: 812-477-1738; Fax: 812-469-6633.
School—(Grades PreK-8) Nancy Mills, Prin. Lay Teachers 17; Students 162.

12—HOLY TRINITY Revs. Jean Vogler; Gregory D. Chamberlin, O.S.B., Admin.; Deacon Charles Koressel.
219 N.W. Third St., 47708-1233. Tel: 812-422-5150.
Catechesis/Religious Program—Gail Shetler, D.R.E. Students 33.

13—ST. JOHN THE APOSTLE Sr. Jane Nesmith, S.B.S., Pastoral Life Coord.; Rev. Stephen P. Lintzenich, Pastoral Moderator.
Church: 617 Bellemeade Ave., 47713-1707. Tel: 812-424-9261; Fax: 812-424-5933.
Catechesis/Religious Program—Sr. Jane Nesmith, S.B.S., D.R.E. Students 28.

14—ST. JOHN THE EVANGELIST, [CEM] Rev. John Silva.
Church: 5301 Daylight Dr., 47725-7636. Tel: 812-867-3718.
Catechesis/Religious Program—Leah Haley, D.R.E. Students 131.

15—ST. JOSEPH Rev. Stephen P. Lintzenich, Moderator; Deacons Richard Grannan, Parish Life Coord.; Emil Altmeyer.
Office: 607 E. Iowa, 47711. Tel: 812-422-5668; Fax: 812-425-2730.
Catechesis/Religious Program—Lisa Foster, D.R.E. Students 7.

16—ST. JOSEPH, [CEM] Rev. Eugene A. Schroeder.
Res.: 6202 W. St. Joseph Rd., 47720. Tel: 812-963-3273; Fax: 812-963-6254.
School—(Grades PreK-8) Melba Wilderman, Prin.; Donna Hiestand, Librarian. Sisters 1; Lay Teachers 13; Students 202.
Catechesis/Religious Program—Sharon Vogler, D.R.E. Students 41.
Convent—Sisters of St. Benedict Sisters 2.

17—ST. MARY Rev. Stephen P. Lintzenich; Deacons Joseph Stofleth, Pastoral Assoc.; Dennis Russell.
Parish Office—613 Cherry St., 47713.
Res.: 609 Cherry St., 47713. Tel: 812-425-1577; Fax: 812-426-1416.
Catechesis/Religious Program—Students 48.

18—NATIVITY Rev. Henry Kuykendall; Sr. Sharon Haskins, D.C., Pastoral Assoc.; Deacon John McMullen.
Res.: 3635 Pollack, 47714. Tel: 812-476-7186; Fax: 812-476-7956.
Catholic Ministry of the Deaf Office—Tel: 812-491-3173.
Catechesis/Religious Program—Abraham Brown, D.R.E. Students 41.

19—RESURRECTION Rev. Philip Kreilein.
Res.: 5301 New Harmony Rd., 47720-1774. Tel: 812-963-3121; Fax: 812-963-1141.
School—(Grades PreK-8) Angie Johnson, Prin.; Sue Gretler, Librarian. Sisters of St. Benedict 1; Lay Teachers 25; Students 359.
Catechesis/Religious Program—Karen Muensterman, D.R.E. Students 80.
Convent—Sisters of St. Benedict Sisters 2.

20—SACRED HEART Rev. David H. Nunning; Deacon Tom Lehman.
Office: 2701 W. Franklin St., 47712. Tel: 812-425-5505; Fax: 812-425-8443.
School—Westside Catholic Consolidated, (Grades PreK) Cynthia Schneider, Prin. Lay Teachers 5; Students 43.
Catechesis/Religious Program—Jenny Mayer, D.R.E. Students 7.

21—ST. THERESA Rev. Msgr. Kenneth R. Knapp, A.C.S.W., Moderator; Deacons David Seibert, Pastoral Life Coord.; Donald Yochum.
Mailing Address: 600 Herndon Dr., 47711-3830.
Res.: Tel: 812-422-8211; Fax: 812-422-5345.
School—(Grades PreK-8) Theresa Berendes, Prin.; Peggy Epley, Librarian. Lay Teachers 12; Students 88.
Catechesis/Religious Program—Deacon David Seibert, D.R.E. Students 21.
Convent—Sisters of St. Benedict Sisters 3.

22—ST. WENDEL, [CEM] Rev. Edward Schnur; Deacon Mark McDonald.
Parish Office—10542 W. Boonville-New Harmony Rd., 47720-7901. Tel: 812-963-3733; Fax: 812-963-3835.
School—(Grades PreK-8) Ron Pittman, Prin. Lay Teachers 15; Students 162.
Catechesis/Religious Program—Twinned with St. Francis, Poseyville Sr. Leta Zeller, O.S.B., D.R.E. Students 189.

OUTSIDE CITY OF EVANSVILLE

BICKNELL, KNOX CO., ST. PHILIP NERI Rev. Jason Gries.
Res.: 605 W. Fourth St., 47512. Tel: 812-735-4069.
Catechesis/Religious Program—Carol Wampler, D.R.E. Students 41.

BLOOMFIELD, GREENE CO., HOLY NAME, [CEM] Rev. Michael Madden.
Res.: 700 Lincoln Dr., 47424-0124. Tel: 812-384-8415.
Catechesis/Religious Program—Lora Burris, D.R.E. Students 6.

BOONVILLE, WARRICK CO., ST. CLEMENT Rev. Lowell Will; Deacon Tom Lambert.
Res.: 422 E. Sycamore, 47601. Tel: 812-897-4653; Fax: 812-897-4653.
Catechesis/Religious Program—Jaynie Gayhart, D.R.E. Students 60.

CANNELBURG, DAVIESS CO., ALL SAINTS, Attended by St. Peter, Montgomery. Revs. James Koressel; Ryan Paul Hilderbrand; Deacon Michael Jones.
Tel: 812-486-3149.
Catechesis/Religious Program—Twinned with St. Peter Montgomery Donna Bradley, D.R.E.; Karen Kane, D.R.E. Students 100.

CELESTINE, DUBOIS CO., ST. PETER CELESTINE, [CEM] Rev. Ronald Kreilein; Deacon Michael Seibert.
Res.: 6864 E. State Rd. 164, P.O. Box 1, 47521-0001. Tel: 812-634-1875; Fax: 812-634-1875.
Catechesis/Religious Program—Glenda Prechtel, D.R.E. Students 257.

CHRISNEY, SPENCER CO., ST. MARTIN, [CEM] Rev. Eugene Schmitt; Deacon Michael Waninger.
Office:—58 S. Church St., 47611-0147. Tel: 812-362-7313; Fax: 812-362-7390.
Catechesis/Religious Program—Deacon Michael Waninger, D.R.E. Students 36.

DALE, SPENCER CO., ST. JOSEPH, [CEM] Rev. John Brosmer; Deacon James Woebkenberg.
Res.: 8 E. Maple St., R.R. 1, Box 684, 47523. Tel: 812-937-2200; Fax: 812-937-4349.
Catechesis/Religious Program—Kristel Riffert, D.R.E. Students 90.

DUBOIS, DUBOIS CO., ST. RAPHAEL, [CEM] Rev. Ronald Kreilein; Deacon Michael Seibert.
Res.: 5564 E. St. Raphael St., 47527. Tel: 812-678-2011; Fax: 812-678-5096.
Catechesis/Religious Program—Lavone Magin, D.R.E. Students 209.

FERDINAND, DUBOIS CO.
1—ST. FERDINAND, [CEM] Rev. Jack Durchholz; Deacon James King; Sr. Jayn Lein, O.S.B., Pastoral Assoc.; Deanna Youngs, Pastoral Assoc.
Res.: 840 Maryland, P.O. Box 156, 47532. Tel: 812-367-1212; Fax: 812-367-1066.
Spiritual Life Center—Tel: 812-367-1092.
Catechesis/Religious Program—Sheila Hurst, D.R.E. Students 449.
2—ST. HENRY, [CEM] Rev. Damian Schmelz, O.S.B.
Res.: 1311 W. 1100 S., 47532-9710. Tel: 812-367-2731.
Catechesis/Religious Program—Laura McAninch, D.R.E. Students 103.
FORT BRANCH, GIBSON CO.
1—ST. BERNARD, [CEM] Revs. Anthony Ernst; John Sasse; Deacon Steve Hall.
Res.: 5342 E. State Rd., 47648-9632. Tel: 812-753-4568.
Catechesis/Religious Program—Rose Obert, D.R.E.; Jeanne Vieke, D.R.E. Students 54.
2—HOLY CROSS, [CEM] Revs. Anthony Ernst; John Sasse; Deacon Steve Hall.
Office: 305 E. Walnut St., 47648. Tel: 812-753-3548.
School—(Grades PreK-5) Tracey Unfried, Prin.; Mary Jane Buehner, Librarian. Lay Teachers 11; Students 142.
Catechesis/Religious Program—Liz Hirsch, C.R.E. Students 95.
HAUBSTADT, GIBSON CO.
1—ST. JAMES, [CEM] Rev. Kenneth Betz.
Res.: 12300 S. 50 W., 47639-9752. Tel: 812-867-5175; Fax: 812-867-5589.
School—(Grades PreK-8) Michelle Priar, Prin. Sisters 1; Lay Teachers 13; Students 157.
Catechesis/Religious Program—Connie Baehl, D.R.E. Students 52.
2—SS. PETER AND PAUL, [CEM] Revs. Anthony Ernst; John Sasse; Deacon William Brandle.
Res.: 211 N. Vine St., 47639. Tel: 812-768-6457; Fax: 812-768-6521.
School—(Grades PreK-5) Kalyn Herrmann, Prin. Lay Teachers 12; Students 169.
Catechesis/Religious Program—Stephanie Stoll, C.R.E. Students 177.
HUNTINGBURG, DUBOIS CO., VISITATION OF THE BLESSED VIRGIN MARY, [CEM] Rev. Mark O'Keefe, O.S.B.
Res.: 313 Washington St., 47542. Tel: 812-683-4903; Fax: 812-683-2747.
Catechesis/Religious Program—Michelle Fischer, D.R.E. Students 353.
IRELAND, DUBOIS CO., ANNUNCIATION OF THE BLESSED VIRGIN MARY, [CEM], (St. Mary's) Rev. Zachary J. Etienne.
Res.: P.O. Box 67, 47545. Tel: 812-482-7041; Fax: 812-482-3699.
Catechesis/Religious Program—Mickie Paulin, D.R.E. Students 516.
JASONVILLE, GREENE CO., ST. JOAN OF ARC, Attended by St. Mary, Sullivan, Tel: 812-268-4088. Rev. Frank G. Renner.
JASPER, DUBOIS CO.
1—HOLY FAMILY, [JC] Rev. John Boeglin; Deacons Michael Helfter; David McDaniel.
Res.: 950 E. Church Ave., 47546-3797. Tel: 812-482-3076; Fax: 812-634-6998.
School—(Grades PreK-8) Jeanne Heltzel, Prin.; Sr. Mary Jane Kinghorn, Librarian. Lay Teachers 18; Students 264.
Catechesis/Religious Program—Mary Altman, D.R.E. Students 58.
2—ST. JOSEPH, [JC] Revs. Raymond Brenner; James Sauer; Deacon Levi Schnellenberger.
Res.: 1020 Kundek St., 47546. Tel: 812-482-1805; Fax: 812-482-1814.
Catechesis/Religious Program—Pam Freyberger, D.R.E. Students 493.
3—PRECIOUS BLOOD, [JC] Rev. Gary Edward Kaiser; Sisters Betty Koressel, S.P., Pastoral Assoc.; Gloria Memmering, S.P., Pastoral Assoc.; Deacon Gerald Gagne.
Res.: 1517 Gregory Ln., 47546.
Church: 1385 W. Sixth St., 47546. Tel: 812-482-3589; Fax: 812-482-3589.
School—(Grades PreK-5) Joseph Brake, Prin.; Judy Buechlein, Librarian. Lay Teachers 17; Students 254.
Catechesis/Religious Program—Bernadette Heeke, D.R.E. Students 190.
Convent—Sisters of Providence Sisters 2.
LINTON, GREENE CO., ST. PETER, [CEM] Rev. Michael Madden.
Res.: 489 E St. N.E., 47441. Tel: 812-847-7821; Fax: 812-847-8892.
Catechesis/Religious Program—Marcia Waters, D.R.E. Students 50.
LOOGOOTEE, MARTIN CO.
1—ST. JOHN, [CEM] Rev. Joseph Erbacher.
Office: 408 Church St., 47553. Tel: 812-295-2225; Fax: 812-295-2031.
Catechesis/Religious Program—Julie Sutton, C.R.E. Students 265.
2—ST. MARTIN, [CEM] Rev. Joseph Erbacher.
Mailing Address: 408 Church St., 47553. Tel: 812-295-2225; Fax: 812-295-3445.
Catechesis/Religious Program—Roberta Burch, C.R.E.; Denise Craney, C.R.E. Students 39.
MARIAH HILL, SPENCER CO., MARY, HELP OF CHRISTIANS, [CEM] Deacon James Woebkenberg, Parish Life Coord.
Church: P.O. Box 170, 47556. Tel: 812-937-4326.
Catechesis/Religious Program—Twinned with St. John Chrysostom. Marilyn Satkamp, D.R.E. Students 91.
MONTGOMERY, DAVIESS CO., ST. PETER, [CEM] Revs. James Koressel; Ryan Paul Hilderbrand; Deacon Michael Jones.
Res.: P.O. Box 10, 47558. Tel: 812-486-3149; Fax: 812-486-2571.
Catechesis/Religious Program—Twinned with All Saints Cannelburg Donna Bradley, D.R.E.; Karen Kane, D.R.E. Students 100.
Chapel—Corning, St. Patrick's
MOUNT VERNON, POSEY CO.
1—ST. MATTHEW, [CEM] Rev. Kenneth Steckler; Deacon Thomas Evans.
Res.: 421 Mulberry St., 47620. Tel: 812-838-2535; Fax: 812-838-0237.
School—(Grades PreK-5) Vickie Wannemuehler, Prin. Lay Teachers 9; Students 90.
Catechesis/Religious Program—Irene Evans, D.R.E. Students 78.
2—ST. PHILIP, [CEM] Rev. Thomas Kessler.
Res.: 3500 St. Philip Rd. S., Mt. Vernon, 47620. Tel: 812-985-2275; Fax: 812-985-2590.
School—(Grades PreK-8) Andrea Lodato Dickel, Prin.; Joan Frazer, Librarian. Lay Teachers 18; Students 216.
Catechesis/Religious Program—Students 29.
NEW BOSTON, SPENCER CO., ST. JOHN CHRYSOSTOM, [CEM] Deacon Michael Waninger, Temporary Parish Life Coord.
Mailing Address: c/o P.O. Box 178, Chrisney, 47611.
NEW HARMONY, POSEY CO., HOLY ANGELS Rev. Kenneth Steckler; Deacon Thomas Evans.
Mailing Address: 423 South St., P.O. Box 795, 47631. Tel: 812-682-4224.
Catechesis/Religious Program—Irene Evans, D.R.E. Students 15.
NEWBURGH, WARRICK CO., ST. JOHN THE BAPTIST, [CEM] Revs. Joseph Ziliak; David A. Martin; Sr. Jeanne Voges, O.S.B., Pastoral Assoc.; Lynda Provence, Pastoral Assoc.; Marty Brown, Pastoral Assoc.; Deacons Joseph Seibert; David Rice.
Res.: 625 Frame Rd., 47630. Tel: 812-490-1000; Fax: 812-490-1010.
School—(Grades PreK-8) Dr. Charlotte Bennett, Prin.; Colleen Walsh, Librarian. Lay Teachers 26; Students 425.
Catechesis/Religious Program—Connie Schnapf, D.R.E.; Cindy Shoulders, D.R.E. Students 447.
OAKLAND CITY, GIBSON CO., BLESSED SACRAMENT Rev. Ronald S. Zgunda; Deacon Mark Wade; Sr. Kim Mandelkow, Pastoral Assoc.
Res.: 11092 E. Lincoln Hts. Rd., 47660. Tel: 812-749-4474.
Catechesis/Religious Program—Susan Williams, D.R.E. Students 31.
PETERSBURG, PIKE CO., SS. PETER AND PAUL Revs. James Koressel; Ryan Paul Hilderbrand; Deacon Donald Haag.
Res.: 711 Walnut St., 47567. Tel: 812-354-6942.
Catechesis/Religious Program—Stacy Mosby, D.R.E. Students 28.
POSEYVILLE, POSEY CO., ST. FRANCIS XAVIER, [CEM] Rev. Edward Schnur; Sr. Leta Zeller, O.S.B., Pastoral Assoc.
Res.: 10 N. St. Francis Ave., 47633. Tel: 812-874-2258; Fax: 812-874-2639.
Catechesis/Religious Program—Twinned with St. Wendel Sr. Leta Zeller, O.S.B., D.R.E. Students 189.
PRINCETON, GIBSON CO., ST. JOSEPH, [CEM] Rev. Ronald S. Zgunda; Deacon Mark Wade; Sr. Kim Mandelkow, Pastoral Assoc.
Res.: 410 S. Race St., 47670. Tel: 812-385-2617; Fax: 812-385-2603.
School—(Grades PreK-8) Dan Gilbert, Prin.; Tamrun Sokeland, Librarian. Lay Teachers 11; Students 161.
Catechesis/Religious Program—Susan Williams, D.R.E. Students 79.
RED BRUSH, WARRICK CO., ST. RUPERT, [CEM] Rev. Lowell Will.
Church: 1244 Red Brush Rd., Newburgh, 47630. Tel: 812-853-3040.
Catechesis/Religious Program—Denice Martin, D.R.E. Students 13.
ROCKPORT, SPENCER CO., ST. BERNARD, [CEM] Rev. Eugene Schmitt; Deacon Michael Waninger.
Res.: 547 Elm St., 47635. Tel: 812-649-4811; Fax: 812-649-4176.
School—(Grades PreK-8) Sara Guth, Prin. Lay Teachers 10; Students 155.
Catechesis/Religious Program—Carolyn Thorpe, D.R.E. Students 74.
ST. ANTHONY, DUBOIS CO., ST. ANTHONY, [CEM] Rev. Timothy Tenbarge; Deacon Ken Johanning.
Res.: 4444 S. Ohio St., P.O. Box 98, 47575-0098. Tel: 812-326-2777; Fax: 812-326-9028.
Catechesis/Religious Program—Janie Kempf, D.R.E. Students 209.
ST. JOSEPH, MARTIN CO., ST. JOSEPH, [CEM] Rev. Joseph Erbacher.
Mailing Address: 408 Church St., Loogootee, 47553. Tel: 812-295-2225.
Catechesis/Religious Program—Karen Wittmer, C.R.E.; Darin Holder, C.R.E. Students 31.
Chapel—Barr Township, St. Mary
SANTA CLAUS, SPENCER CO., ST. NICHOLAS Rev. John Brosmer; Deacon James Woebkenberg.
Res.: 181 Balthazar, P.O. Box 351, 47579. Tel: 812-937-2380; Fax: 812-937-2385.
Catechesis/Religious Program—Kristel Riffert, D.R.E. Students 197.
SCHNELLVILLE, DUBOIS CO., SACRED HEART, [CEM] Rev. Timothy Tenbarge; Deacon Ken Johanning.
Res.: 2504 Walnut St., 47580. Tel: 812-389-2535.
Catechesis/Religious Program—Diane Verkamp, D.R.E. Students 117.
SHOALS, MARTIN CO., ST. MARY'S, [CEM] Attended by St. John, Loogootee, Tel: 812-295-2225. Rev. Joseph Erbacher.
Catechesis/Religious Program—Alice Boyd, C.R.E. Students 19.
SULLIVAN, SULLIVAN CO., ST. MARY Rev. Frank G. Renner.
Res.: 105 E. Jackson St., P.O. Box 506, 47882. Tel: 812-268-4088.
Catechesis/Religious Program—Nannette Stone, D.R.E. Students 41.
VINCENNES, KNOX CO.
1—BASILICA OF ST. FRANCIS XAVIER, [JC] Rev. John H. Schipp.
Res.: 205 Church St., 47591. Tel: 812-882-5638; Fax: 812-882-4042.
See Vincennes Schools Consolidated, Vincennes under St. John the Baptist, Vincennes for details.
Catechesis/Religious Program—Patricia Earley, D.R.E. Students 37.
2—ST. JOHN THE BAPTIST, [JC] Rev. David G. Fleck; Ron Shafer, Pastoral Assoc.
Res.: 803 Main St., 47591. Tel: 812-882-1762; Fax: 812-886-9151.
Parish Center—828 Vigo St., 47591.
School—Vincennes Schools Consolidated, (Grades PreK-5) Anne Pratt, Prin.; Mary Nowaskie, Librarian. Lay Teachers 15; Students 225.
Catechesis/Religious Program—Sr. Regina Baker, D.R.E. Students 67.
3—SACRED HEART, [JC] Rev. Jason Gries; Deacon Philip Pierpont.
Res.: 2004 N. Second St., 47591. Tel: 812-882-8382; Fax: 812-886-4676.
See Vincennes Schools Consolidated, Vincennes under St. John the Baptist, Vincennes for details.
Catechesis/Religious Program—Lucille Pierpont, D.R.E. Students 87.
4—ST. THOMAS THE APOSTLE, [CEM] Rev. John H. Schipp, Mod.; Deacon Earl Ruppel, Parish Life Coord.
Office: 6268 S. St. Thomas Rd., 47591. Tel: 812-882-2478.
Catechesis/Religious Program—Students 41.
5—ST. VINCENT DE PAUL, [CEM] Rev. David G. Fleck.
Office: 1837 S. Hart St. Rd., 47591. Tel: 812-882-8968.
Catechesis/Religious Program—Pat West, D.R.E. Students 18.
WASHINGTON, DAVIESS CO.
1—IMMACULATE CONCEPTION, [JC] Closed. For inquiries for parish records contact the chancery.
2—OUR LADY OF HOPE, [JC] Rev. Gordon Mann; Deacon Dennis Hilderbrand; Yvonne Evans, Pastoral Assoc.
Office: 315 N.E. Third St., 47501. Tel: 812-254-2883; Fax: 812-254-2884.
School—(Grades PreK-5), 310 N.E. Second St., 47501. David Memmer, Prin. Washington Catholic Interparochial Schools Elementary. Lay Teachers 14; Students 280.
School—Washington Catholic Interparochial Schools Middle, (Grades 6-8), 200 W. Main St., 47501. David Memmer, Prin.; Roberta Collison, Librarian. Lay Teachers 13; Students 59.
High School—(Grades 6-8) David Memmer, Prin.; Roberta Collison, Librarian. See High Schools, Diocesan under Institutions Located in the Diocese for details.
Catechesis/Religious Program—Gayle Ostby, D.R.E. Students 106.

Special Assignment:
Rev. Msgr.—
Knapp, Kenneth R., A.C.S.W., M.S., Vicar Gen., 3010 E. Chandler, 47714.
Revs.—
Etienne, Bernard, 1301 S. Green River Rd., 47715-5617.
Gries, Jason, 918 W. Mill Rd., 47710-3956.
Lintzenich, Stephen P., 613 Cherry St., 47713.
Lutz, Bernard A. (Retired), 5044 E. 750 St., Fort Branch, 47648.
Nemergut, Robert S., P.O. Box 432, Carlisle, 47838.
Walker, J. Kenneth, B.A., M.Div., M.C.L., J.C.L., Judicial Vicar, P.O. Box 4169, 47724-0169.
Zenthoefer, Alex, 1301 S. Green River Rd., 47715.

On Duty Outside the Diocese:
Rev.—
Kissel, Anthony, 14235 21st St., Dade City, FL 33523.

On Leave:
Rev.—
Traylor, William

Absent on Medical Leave:
Rev.—
Breidenbach, John

Retired:
Rev. Msgrs.—
Hirsch, Clinton F., J.C.L., Heritage Center Nursing Care, 1201 W. Buena Vista Dr., 47710.
Koch, Charles J., S.T.L., J.C.L., 1655 Sweetgum Dr., Greenwood, 46143.
Revs.—
Ackerman, Donald K., 310 W. 4th, Jasper, 47546.
Busch, August, 5221 New Harmony Rd., 47720.
Deig, Robert A., St. John's Home, 1236 Lincoln Ave., 47714.
Dick, Firmus, 3203 E. 1160S, Ferdinand, 47532.
Dietsch, William, 2562 E. County Rd. 8505, Fort Branch, 47648.
Dilger, Donald, 6621 Smith Diamond Rd., 47712.
Egloff, Adolph, 2017 N. Second St., Vincennes, 47591.
Endress, James, S.T.L., M.S., M.A., 600 Cullen Ave., Apt. 510.
Graehler, Kenneth, 104 Southside Ave., 47501.
Heerdink, Eugene, 212 W. 13th St., Jasper, 47546.
Hut, Clemens, Friendship Village, 2525 E. Southern Ave., Tempe, AZ 85282.
Kane, Joseph, 8427 Gannon, Saint Louis, MO 63132-4906.
Kiesel, Leo C., 315 Doyle Ave., Loogootee, 47553.
Kuper, Raymond L., 1404 Timberlake Ln., 47710.
Lefler, John, Woodmont Health Campus, 1325 N. Rockport Rd., Boonville, 47601.
Loehrlein, Sylvester, c/o 3316 W. Maryland, 47720.
Lutz, Bernard A., 5044 E. 750 S., Fort Branch, 47648-9607.
Rogers, James, 801 N. Shortridge Rd., Apt. F4, Indianapolis, 46219.
Rohleder, Earl, 2540 Calle Rincon Bonito, Santa Fe, NM 87505.
Schipp, Ralph, 278 S. Tinsel Cir. E., Santa Claus, 47579.
Spaulding, Donald E., 112 W. Third St., Cannelburg, 47519.
Tempel, Theodore, 1236 Lincoln Ave., 47714.
Wannemuehler, Robert, 1611 S. Bosse, 47712.
Wargel, William, 3130 N. Chigger Ridge Rd., Birdseye, 47513.

Permanent Deacons:
Altmeyer, Emil, St. Joseph Church, Evansville
Bach, Kevin, St. Benedict Cathedral; Catholic Center
Bernardin, Vincent, St. John the Baptist, Newburgh; Christ the King, Evansville
Borowiecki, Christian, Holy Rosary, Evansville
Brandle, William, Sts. Peter & Paul, Haubstadt
Burns, Michael, Chaplain, Evansville Hospitals; Chaplain, Westside Nursing Homes
Cook, David, St. Benedict Cathedral, Evansville
Dow, Lancaster, Jr., (Unassigned)
Evans, Thomas, St. Matthew, Mt. Vernon; Holy Angels, New Harmony
Flynn, James, St. Benedict Cathedral, Evansville
Franklin, David, St. Boniface
Gagne, Gerald, Precious Blood, Jasper
Goebel, Thomas, Corpus Christi, Evansville
Grannan, Richard, St. Joseph Parish, Evansville
Haag, Donald, SS. Peter & Paul Parish, Petersburg
Hall, Steve, St. Bernard Parish & Holy Cross, Fort Branch
Hayden, Robert, Holy Redeemer, Evansville
Heberling, William, St. Agnes, Evansville
Helfter, Michael, Holy Family Parish, Jasper
Hilderbrand, Dennis, Our Lady of Hope, Washington
Hillenbrand, Francis, Christ the King, Evansville
Holsworth, Thomas, Master of Ceremony
Johanning, Kenneth, St. Anthony, Indiana; Sacred Heart, Schnellville
Jones, Michael R., St. Peter, Montgomery; All Saints, Cannelburg
Kempf, Thomas, St. Agnes, Evansville
King, James, St. Ferdinand, Ferdinand
Koressel, Charles, Holy Trinity, Evansville
Lambert, Thomas, St. Clement, Boonville
Lehman, Thomas, Sacred Heart, Evansville
Mayer, David, Holy Redeemer, Evansville
McDaniel, David, Holy Family, Jasper
McDonald, Mark, St. Wendel, St. Wendel; St. Francis Xavier, Poseyville
McMullen, John, Nativity, Evansville; Chap., Evansville State Hospital
Morris, Michael, Prison Ministry
Pierpont, Philip, Sacred Heart, Vincennes
Preske, Richard, (Retired)
Rice, David, Assoc. Clergy Personnel Dir., St. John the Baptist, Newburgh
Ruppel, Earl, St. Thomas, Vincennes
Russell, Dennis, St. Mary, Evansville
Schapker, Anthony, Holy Spirit, Evansville
Schnellenberger, Levi, St. Joseph, Jasper
Seibert, David, Asst. Deacon Dir., St. Theresa, Evansville
Seibert, Joseph S., St. John, Newburgh
Seibert, Michael, St. Peter, Celestine; St. Raphael, Dubois
Stofleth, Joseph, St. Mary, Evansville
Sturgis, Joseph V., (Retired)
Wade, Mark, St. Joseph, Princeton; Blessed Sacrament, Oakland City
Waninger, Michael, St. Martin, Chrisney, St. Bernard, Rockport & St. John Chrysostom, New Boston
Wilkerson, Edward, Good Shepherd, Evansville
Will, Cyril, Good Shephard, Evansville
Woebkenberg, James, Mary, Help of Christians, Mariah Hall, St. Joseph, Dale & St. Nicholas, Santa Claus
Yochum, Donald, St. Theresa, Evansville

INSTITUTIONS LOCATED IN THE DIOCESE

[A] HIGH SCHOOLS, DIOCESAN

EVANSVILLE. *Mater Dei High School*, 1300 Harmony Way, 47712. Tel: 812-426-2258; Fax: 812-421-5717. Web: www.materdeiwildcats.com. Timothy Dickel, Prin.; Rev. Alex Zenthoefer, Chap. Priests 1; Sisters 1; Lay Teachers 38; Students 538.

Reitz Memorial High School, 1500 Lincoln Ave., 47714. Tel: 812-476-4973; Fax: 812-474-2942. Web: www.memorial.evansville.net. Mrs. Gwen Godsey, M.Ed., Prin.; Mr. Rick Wilgus, Asst. Prin., Student Svcs.; Rev. Alex Zenthoefer, Chap.; Mrs. Lisa Popham, Asst. Prin., Curriculum & Instruction. Clergy 1; Lay Teachers 52; Students 791.

VINCENNES. *Jean Francois Rivet High School*, (Grades 6-12), (Vincennes Area), 210 Barnett St., 47591. Tel: 812-882-6215; Fax: 812-886-1939. Web: www.vincennescatholicschools.org. Janice Jones, Prin. Lay Teachers 13; Students 198.

WASHINGTON. *Washington Catholic Interparochial Schools*, (Grades 6-12), 201 N.E. Second St., 47501. Tel: 812-254-2050; Fax: 812-254-2050. David Memmer, Prin.; Roberta Collison, Librarian. Sisters 1; Lay Teachers 13; Students 85.

[B] DAY CARE CENTERS

EVANSVILLE. *St. Vincent Day Care Center*, 730 W. Delaware, 47710. Tel: 812-424-4780; Fax: 812-425-2502. Sr. Brenda Fritz, Exec. Dir. Daughters of Charity of St. Vincent de Paul 7; Children 156.

[C] GENERAL HOSPITALS

EVANSVILLE. *St. Mary's Medical Center of Evansville, Inc.*, 3700 Washington Ave., 47750. Tel: 812-485-4000; Fax: 812-485-4927. Web: www.stmarys.org. Tim Flesch, Pres. & CEO St. Mary's Health System; Sr. Jane Burger, D.C., Sr. Vice Pres., Mission Integration. Daughters of Charity of St. Vincent de Paul 7; Bed Capacity 509; Patients Assisted Annually 663,647.

JASPER. *Memorial Hospital and Health Care Center, Little Company of Mary Hospital of Indiana, Inc.*, 800 W. Ninth St., 47546. Tel: 812-482-2345; Fax: 812-482-0302. Ray Snowden, Pres. & CEO; Sr. M. Adrian Davis, L.C.M., Bd. Chairperson; Deacon Michael Jones, Chap. Sisters of the Little Company of Mary 2; Bed Capacity 144; Patients Assisted Annually 233,000; Palliative Care Patients 60.

Memorial Hospital Foundation, Inc., 800 W. 9th St., 47546. Tel: 812-481-8426; Fax: 812-481-8427. William A. Rubino, Chair Person; Michael A. Jones, Exec. Dir.

[D] HOMES FOR AGED

EVANSVILLE. *St. John's Home for the Aged*, 1236 Lincoln Ave., 47714. Tel: 812-464-3607; Fax: 812-464-2141. Sr. Rose Marie Mayock, L.S.P., Pres.; Rev. Theodore Tempel, Chap. (Retired). Little Sisters of the Poor 11; Residents 47; Apartments 22.

Seton Residence, 9200 New Harmony Rd., 47720-8918. Tel: 812-963-7600; Fax: 812-963-7654. Marvin Kemper, Admin.; Sr. Judy Flowers, D.C., Supr. Home for the Senior Sisters of the Daughters of Charity of St. Vincent de Paul. Senior Sisters 63; Sisters on Staff 8.

FERDINAND. *Hildegard Health Center, Inc.*, 802 E. 10th St., 47532-9239. Tel: 812-367-2022; Fax: 812-367-1309. Web: www.thedome.org. Sr. Kristine Harpenau, O.S.B., Chm. Sisters on Staff 5; Sisters in Residence 17.

JASPER. *Providence Home, Nursing Home for the Needy*, 520 W. Ninth St., 47546. Tel: 812-482-6603; Fax: 812-481-1778. Deacon David McDaniel, Admin.; Rev. Angelo Quadrini, Supr. Conducted by the Sons of Divine Providence. Residents 60; Staff 72.

[E] RETREAT HOUSES

EVANSVILLE. *Sarto Retreat House*, 4200 N. Kentucky Ave., P.O. Box 4169, 47724-0169. Tel: 812-424-5536; Fax: 812-421-1334. Julie Young, Coord.

FERDINAND. *Kordes Center*, 841 E. 14th St., 47532-9216. Tel: 812-367-1411; Fax: 812-367-2313. Email: kordes@thedome.org. Web: www.thedome.org/kordes. Sr. Marilyn Schroering, O.S.B., Dir.

[F] CONVENTS AND RESIDENCES FOR SISTERS

EVANSVILLE. *Daughters of Charity of St. Vincent de Paul of Indiana, Inc.*, 9400 New Harmony Rd., 47720. Tel: 812-963-3341; Fax: 812-963-7589. Sr. Honora Remes, D.C., Visitatrix; Rev. William Hartenbach, C.M., Prov. Dir.

Daughters of Charity of St. Vincent de Paul of Indiana, Inc., Mater Dei Provincialate, Inc. Sisters in Residence 18.

Monastery of St. Clare, 6825 Nurrenbern Rd., 47712. Tel: 812-425-4396; Fax: 812-425-0089. Sisters Jeanne Maffet, O.S.C., Abbess; Catherine K. Janeway, O.S.C., Vicaress. Franciscan Poor Clare Nuns. Solemnly Professed Cloistered Nuns 9.

FERDINAND. *Sisters of St. Benedict of Ferdinand, IN, Inc., Monastery Immaculate Conception*, 802 E. Tenth St., 47532. Tel: 812-367-1411; Fax: 812-367-2313. Web: www.thedome.org. Sr. Kristine Harpenau, O.S.B., Prioress; Rev. Tobias Colgan, O.S.B., Chap., St. Meinrad Chaplain Team Coord. Sisters of St. Benedict. Professed Sisters in Community 160; Temporary Commitment 6; Postulants 1.

[G] NEWMAN CENTERS & CAMPUS MINISTRY

EVANSVILLE. *Newman Center for the University of Evansville* 1901 Lincoln Ave., 47714. Tel: 812-477-6446.

University of Southern Indiana Newman Center 8113-A O'Daniel Ln., 47712. Tel: 812-465-7095. Christine Hoehn, Dir.

OAKLAND CITY. *Oakland City College Newman Center* R.R. 1, Box 72-A, 47660. Tel: 812-749-4474.

VINCENNES. *Vincennes University-Newman Center c/o St. John Parish*, 803 Main St., 47591. Tel: 812-882-1762.

[H] MISCELLANEOUS

EVANSVILLE. *Catholic Education Foundation, Inc.*, 520 S. Bennighof, 47714. Tel: 812-402-6700, Ext. 302. Margaret Angermeier, Dir.

Evansville Catholic Interparochial High Schools, 520 S. Benninghof, 47714. Tel: 812-474-2943, Ext. 308.

Marian Educational Outreach, 520 S. Benninghof, 47714. Tel: 812-402-6700, Ext. 312; Fax: 812-474-2949. Bev Williamson, Dir.

Mission and Ministry, Inc., 9404 New Harmony Rd., 47720. Tel: 812-963-7584; Fax: 812-963-7526. Mary Wildeman, Exec. Dir.

Seton Health Corporation of Southern Indiana, 3700 Washington Ave., 47750. Tel: 812-485-1502; Fax: 812-485-7800. Gwen Sandefur, Senior Vice Pres., Strategic Devel. & Regl. Opers.

HUNTINGBURG. *Guadalupe Center*, 511 E. 4th St., Ste. 1, 47542.

JASPER. **Regional Catholic School Corporation*, P.O. Box 247, 47547-0247.

LOOGOOTEE. *American-Innsbruck Alumni Association*, 315 Doyle Ave., 47553. Tel: 812-295-3214. Rev. Leo C. Kiesel, Contact Person (Retired).

VINCENNES. *Old Cathedral Library & Museum, Inc.*, 205 Church St., 47591. Tel: 812-882-7016. Web: www.evansville-diocese.org/chancellor/oldcath.htm. Rev. John H. Schipp, Registered Agent.

RELIGIOUS INSTITUTES OF MEN REPRESENTED IN THE DIOCESE

For further details refer to the corresponding bracketed number in the Religious Institutes of Men or Women section.

[0200]—*Benedictine Monks*—O.S.B.

[1330]—*Congregation of the Mission Western Province*—C.M.

RELIGIOUS INSTITUTES OF WOMEN REPRESENTED IN THE DIOCESE

[0230]—*Benedictine Sisters of Pontifical Jurisdiction*—O.S.B.

[1000]—*Congregation of Divine Providence*

[1730]—*Congregation of the Third Order of St. Francis*—O.S.F.

[0760]—*Daughters of Charity of St. Vincent de Paul*—D.C.

[2340]—*Little Sisters of the Poor*—L.S.P.

[3760]—*Order of St. Clare*—O.S.C.

[]—*Sisters for Christian Community*—S.F.C.C.

[3360]—*Sisters of Providence of Saint Mary-of-the-Woods, Indiana*—S.P.

[0260]—*Sisters of the Blessed Sacrament*—S.B.S.

[2270]—*Sisters of the Little Company of Mary*—L.C.M.

JOINT CEMETERIES

EVANSVILLE. *St. Joseph*, 2500 Mesker Park Dr., 47712.

JASPER. *Fairview*, 1215 Newton St., 47546.

VINCENNES. *Calvary*, P.O. Box 4, 47591.

WASHINGTON. *St. John*, 101 N. Meridian St., 47501-2931.

NECROLOGY

† Foster, Patrick, (Retired)—Died April 10, 2009

† Reising, Raymond, (Retired)—Died July 14, 2009

† Schneider, Edward, Petersburg, IN Sts. Peter and Paul—Died Dec. 28, 2008

† Schroering, Raymond A., (Retired)—Died July 19, 2009

† Vieck, Hilary F., Linton, IN St. Peter—Died Nov. 27, 2008

An asterisk (*) denotes an organization that has established tax-exempt status directly with the IRS and is not covered by the USCCB Group Ruling.

Diocese of Fairbanks

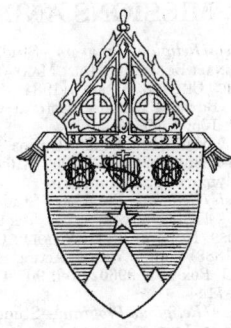

Most Reverend

DONALD J. KETTLER

Bishop of Fairbanks; ordained May 29, 1970; appointed Bishop of Fairbanks June 7, 2002; installed August 22, 2002. *Office: 1316 Peger Rd., Fairbanks, AK 99709.*

Chancery Office: 1316 Peger Rd., Fairbanks, AK 99709. Tel: 907-374-9500; Fax: 907-374-9580.

Web: www.cbna.info

Email: info@cbna.org

Square Miles 409,849.

Corporate Title: "Catholic Bishop of Northern Alaska."

Established as the Prefecture Apostolic of Alaska, July 27, 1894.

Erected into the Vicariate of Alaska, Dec. 22, 1916; elevated to a Diocese, Aug. 8, 1962.

Comprises all of the State of Alaska, north of the old Territorial Third Judicial Division whose boundary extended in a northwesterly direction from the Canadian Border along the crest of the Alaska range to Mount McKinley, thence southwesterly to Cape Newenham and west along the 58 parallel north of the Pribilof Islands.

For legal titles of parishes and diocesan institutions, consult the Chancery Office.

STATISTICAL OVERVIEW

Personnel	
Bishop	1
Priests: Diocesan Active in Diocese	11
Priests: Diocesan Active Outside Diocese	1
Priests: Retired, Sick or Absent	1
Number of Diocesan Priests	13
Religious Priests in Diocese	7
Total Priests in Diocese	20
Extern Priests in Diocese	4
Ordinations:	
Diocesan Priests	1
Permanent Deacons	1
Permanent Deacons in Diocese	30
Total Brothers	2
Total Sisters	12
Parishes	
Parishes	46
With Resident Pastor:	
Resident Diocesan Priests	10
Resident Religious Priests	2
Without Resident Pastor:	
Administered by Deacons	2
Administered by Religious Women	1
Administered by Lay People	15
Administered by Pastoral Teams, etc.	16
Pastoral Centers	2
Professional Ministry Personnel:	
Brothers	2
Sisters	11
Welfare	
Special Centers for Social Services	1
Total Assisted	2,000
Educational	
Diocesan Students in Other Seminaries	1
Total Seminarians	1
High Schools, Diocesan and Parish	1
Total Students	210
Elementary Schools, Diocesan and Parish	1
Total Students	266
Catechesis/Religious Education:	
High School Students	312
Elementary Students	848
Total Students under Catholic Instruction	1,637
Teachers in the Diocese:	
Lay Teachers	54
Vital Statistics	
Receptions into the Church:	
Infant Baptism Totals	309
Minor Baptism Totals	30
Adult Baptism Totals	17
Received into Full Communion	23
First Communions	223
Confirmations	104
Marriages:	
Catholic	32
Interfaith	22
Total Marriages	54
Deaths	119
Total Catholic Population	15,071
Total Population	167,000

Former Bishops—Most Revs. JOSEPH RAPHAEL CRIMONT, S.J., D.D., Vicar-Apostolic of Alaska; ord. Aug. 26, 1888; appt. Prefect-Apostolic March 28, 1904; appt. Vicar-Apostolic of Alaska Feb. 15, 1917; preconized Titular Bishop of Ammaedera, March 22, 1917; cons. July 25, 1917; died May 20, 1945; WALTER J. FITZGERALD, S.J., D.D., Vicar-Apostolic of Alaska; ord. May 16, 1918; appt. Coadjutor Vicar-Apostolic of Alaska cum jure successionis, Dec. 14, 1938; cons. Titular Bishop of Tymbrias, Feb. 24, 1939; succeeded to as Vicar-Apostolic of Alaska, May 20, 1945; died July 19, 1947; GEORGE T. BOILEAU, S.J., D.D., appt. Coadjutor Bishop cum jure successionis, April 21, 1964; cons. Titular Bishop of Ausuccura, July 31, 1964; died Feb. 25, 1965; FRANCIS D. GLEESON, S.J., D.D., ord. July 29, 1926; appt. Titular Bishop of Cotenna and Vicar-Apostolic of Alaska Jan. 8, 1948; cons. April 5, 1948; appt. First Bishop of Fairbanks Aug. 8, 1962; retired Nov. 30, 1968; transferred to Titular See of Cuicul in Numidia and Assistant at the Pontifical Throne by Pope Paul VI, Feb. 3, 1969; died April 30, 1983; ROBERT LOUIS WHELAN, S.J., D.D., retired Bishop of Fairbanks; ord. June 17, 1944; appt. Titular Bishop of Sicilibba and Coadjutor Bishop of Fairbanks, cum jure successionis Dec. 6, 1967; cons. Feb. 22, 1968; succeeded to Nov. 30, 1968; retired July 28, 1985; died Sept. 15, 2001; MICHAEL J. KANIECKI, S.J., D.D., ord. June 5, 1965; appt. Coadjutor Bishop cumjure successionis, March 8, 1984; cons. May 1, 1984; succeeded to July 28, 1985; died Aug. 6, 2000.

Vicar General—Rev. PATRICK D. BERGQUIST, V.G.

Superior Regular—Rev. GREGG D. WOOD, S.J., Pastoral Ministry, Mailing Address: Bro. Joe Prince House, P.O. Box 49, Saint Marys, 99658.

Chancery Office—1316 Peger Rd., Fairbanks, 99709. Tel: 907-374-9500; Fax: 907-374-9580.

Chancellor and Special Assistant—ROBERT HANNON, 1316 Peger Rd., Fairbanks, 99709. Tel: 907-374-9510.

Secretary to Bishop—GERALDINE JAUHOLA.

Treasurer—Deacon GEORGE W. BOWDER.

Diocesan Tribunal—

Tribunal Administrator—BARBARA THIEME TOLLIVER.

Judicial Vicar—Rev. PATRICK TRAVERS, J.C.L., J.D.

Defenders of the Bond—Revs. SCOTT GARRETT, J.C.L.; TOM BRUNDAGE, J.C.L.

Promoter of Justice—Sr. CAROLYN A. ROEBER, O.P.

Auditor—BARBARA THIEME TOLLIVER.

Notaries—Tribunal: BARBARA THIEME TOLLIVER; GERALDINE JAUHOLA.

Presbyteral Council—Revs. GREGG D. WOOD, S.J.; GERALD ORNOWSKI, M.I.C.; PATRICK D. BERGQUIST, V.G.; JACK DE VERTEUIL; JOSEPH HEMMER, O.F.M.; ROBERT FATH; ROSS TOZZI; STANISLAW JASZEK; CHARLES J. PETERSON, S.J.

Consultors—Revs. CHARLES J. PETERSON, S.J.; GREGG D. WOOD, S.J.; JACK DE VERTEUIL; JOSEPH HEMMER, O.F.M.; ROSS TOZZI; GERALD ORNOWSKI, M.I.C.; STANISLAW JASZEK.

Diocesan Archivist—VACANT, Archivist; DAVID SCHIENLE, Archives Clerk.

Diocesan Offices and Directors

Alaskan Shepherd Office—Mrs. PATTY WALTER, Editor & Dir. Direct Mail Fundraising. Tel: 907-374-9536; LIN CRAIG, Office Mgr., 1312 Peger Rd., Fairbanks, 99709. Tel: 907-374-9532.

Beginning Experience—Rev. TIMOTHY SANDER, O.S.B., Dir., Mailing Address: P.O. Box 74401, Fairbanks, 99707. Tel: 907-457-1858; SHANNA KARELLA, Facilitator.

Catholic Campaign for Human Development—Mr. THOMAS BUZEK.

Campus Ministry—Sr. DOROTHY GILOLEY, S.S.J., 514 Copper Ln. - UAF, P.O. Box 750166, Fairbanks, 99775. Tel: 907-474-6776.

Communications, Radio and TV—NORMAN "RIC" E. SCHMIDT, Gen. Mgr.; KELLY BRABEC, Prog. Dir., Mailing Address: P.O. Box 988, Nome, 99762. Tel: 907-443-5221.

The Children and Family Life Center—VACANT.

Construction Committee—JAMES WALTER; Deacons PAUL PERREAULT, Chm.; GEORGE W. BOWDER.

Engaged Encounter—Deacon ROBERT P. BARNARD.

Fairbanks Counseling and Adoption—CAMILLE CONNELLY-TERHUNE, Exec. Dir., 912 Barnette, P.O. Box 71544, Fairbanks, 99707. Tel: 907-456-4729.

Finance Advisory Board—CYNTHIA KLEPASKI; SUSAN MURPHY; Rev. PATRICK D. BERGQUIST, V.G.; JEFF JOHNSON; HAROLD ESMAILKA; JOSEPH PASKVAN; Sr. KATHLEEN RADICH, O.S.F.; BOB FROEHLE; NICK TUCKER; CLAIRE WINGFIELD.

Hispanic Ministry—Rev. NORMAND A. PEPIN, S.J.

Human Resources—RONNIE ROSENBERG, Dir.

Native Alaskan Ministries Coordinators—Sr. KATHLEEN RADICH, O.S.F., Mailing Address: St. Mary's Conf. Ctr., P.O. Box 29, St. Marys, 99658; Bro. ROBERT J. RUZICKA, O.F.M., Mailing Address: Our Lady of the Snows, P.O. Box 89, Nulato, 99765.

Ministry of Sick, Aged and Imprisoned—SHANNA KARELLA, Dir. Stephen Ministry. Tel: 907-374-9553.

Office of Child Protection—BARBARA THIEME TOLLIVER, Dir. Tel: 907-374-9516.

Office of Religious Education—Sr. DOROTHY GILOLEY, S.S.J., Dir. Tel: 907-374-0752.

Office of Native Permanent Diaconate—Rev. THEODORE E. KESTLER, S.J., Mailing Address: P.O. Box 29, St. Marys, 99658. Tel: 907-438-2336; Fax: 907-438-2536.

Office of Urban Permanent Diaconate—VACANT.

Office of Worship—VACANT.

Pontifical Association of the Holy Childhood—Chancery Office.

Pontifical Society for Propagation of the Faith—Deacon GEORGE W. BOWDER, Chancery Office.

Schools—NANCY HANSON, Acting Exec. Dir., 615 Monroe St., Fairbanks, 99701. Tel: 907-456-7970.

Victim Assistance Coordinator—BARBARA THIEME TOLLIVER.

Vocation Director—Rev. ROSS TOZZI, Mailing Address: P.O. Box 1010, Nome, 99762. Tel: 907-443-5527.

Urban Native Ministry Liaison—Sr. MARITA SOUCY, C.S.J. Tel: 907-374-9563.

Retrouvaille—Deacon GEORGE W. BOWDER; WANDA BOWDER.

Youth Ministry—VACANT.

Catholic Relief Services—Mr. THOMAS BUZEK.

Catholic Trust of Northern Alaska—Deacon GEORGE BOWDER, Exec. Officer.

CLERGY, PARISHES, MISSIONS AND PAROCHIAL SCHOOLS

CITY OF FAIRBANKS

NORTH STAR BOROUGH

1—SACRED HEART CATHEDRAL CATHOLIC CHURCH FAIRBANKS (1966) Most Rev. Donald J. Kettler; Rev. Frederick C. Bayler, Parochial Vicar; Dr. Charles Geist, Parish Admin.
Res.: 2890 N. Kobuk Ave., 99709. Tel: 907-374-9938.
Church: 2501 Airport Way, 99709. Tel: 907-474-9032; Fax: 907-479-3327. Email: shc@mosquitonet.com. Web: www.sacredheartak.org.
Catechesis/Religious Program—Gigi Martinez, D.R.E. Students 116.

2—IMMACULATE CONCEPTION CATHOLIC CHURCH FAIRBANKS (1904) [JC] Rev. Miroslaw Woznica, Parochial Admin.; Deacons Robert Mantei; Sean Stack.
Res.: 115 N. Cushman St., 99701. Tel: 907-452-3533; Fax: 907-456-3336.
Catechesis/Religious Program—Deacon Robert P. Barnard, D.R.E. Students 50.

3—ST. MARK UNIVERSITY CATHOLIC PARISH FAIRBANKS (1977) Rev. Kasparaj Mallavarapu, Parochial Admin.
Res.: 1265 Deborah Ave., 99709. Tel: 907-456-4853.

4—ST. RAPHAEL CATHOLIC CHURCH FAIRBANKS (1991) Rev. Patrick D. Bergquist; Nancy Hanson, Pastoral Co-coord. & Admin.; Gloria Slagle, Pastoral Co-coord. & Admin.
Res.: P.O. Box 10508, 99710. Tel: 907-457-4115; Fax: 907-457-4461. Web: www.alaska.net~raphael.
Catechesis/Religious Program—Students 75.

OUTSIDE CITY OF FAIRBANKS

ALAKANUK, ST. IGNATIUS CATHOLIC CHURCH ALAKANUK (1954), (Yup'ik), [CEM] [JC] Mary Ayunerak, Parish Admin.; Deacons Denis Shelden, Pastoral Co-ord.; Joseph Phillip, (Retired); Emmanuel Stanislaus; John Ayunerak.
Res.: P.O. Box 53, 99554. Tel: 907-238-3914.
Mission—St. Peter Catholic Church Nunam Iqua P.O. Box 45, Nunam Iqua, 99666. Tel: 907-498-4246.

ANIAK, ST. THERESA CATHOLIC CHURCH ANIAK (1935), (Yup'ik), [CEM] Sr. Marian Leaf, O.S.F., Ministerial Residence; Elizabeth Murphy, Acting Parish Admin.
Res.: P.O. Box 308, 99557. Tel: 907-675-4448.
Catechesis/Religious Program—Angela Morgan, D.R.E.

BARROW, NORTH SLOPE BOROUGH, ST. PATRICK CATHOLIC CHURCH BARROW (1954) [JC], (Served out of Fairbanks) Sue Bowen, Parish Admin.
Mailing Address: P.O. Box 389, 99723. Tel: 907-852-3515. Email: stpatrickschurch@barrow.com.
Catechesis/Religious Program—Students 3.

BETHEL, IMMACULATE CONCEPTION CATHOLIC CHURCH BETHEL (1942) Rev. Charles J. Peterson, S.J.; Susan Murphy, Parish Admin.; Deacons Peter Aluska; Louie Andrew; Brian McCaffery; Joe Asuluk.
Res.: 775 2nd Ave., P.O. Box 429, 99559. Tel: 907-543-2464; Fax: 907-543-3142.
Catechesis/Religious Program—Students 107.

CHEFORNAK, ST. CATHERINE OF SIENA CATHOLIC CHURCH CHEFORNAK (1937), (Yup'ik), [CEM] Agnes Kairaiuak, Acting Parish Admin.; Cecelia Kanigak, Acting Parish Admin.; Deacons David Panruk; Joe Avugiak.
Res.: P.O. Box 90, 99561. Tel: 907-867-8702.
Catechesis/Religious Program—Students 156.

CHEVAK, SACRED HEART CATHOLIC CHURCH CHEVAK (1952), (Cup'ik), [CEM] Deacons Stephan F. Smart Sr.; David Boyscout, (Retired); Peter Boyscout.
Res.: P.O. Box 249, 99563. Tel: 907-858-7826.
Catechesis/Religious Program—Charlene Tuluk, D.R.E. Students 35.

DELTA JUNCTION, OUR LADY OF SORROWS CATHOLIC CHURCH DELTA JUNCTION (1959) Rev. John Martinek.
Res.: 2565 Deborah St., Box 446, 99737. Tel: 907-895-5232. Email: olsdelta@wildak.net.
Catechesis/Religious Program—Students 31.
Mission— Eagle.

EMMONAK, SACRED HEART CATHOLIC CHURCH EMMONAK (1953), (Yup'ik), [JC] Larry Yupanik, Acting Parish Admin.; Rev. Roman Caly; Deacons Bart Agathluk; Raymond Waska.
P.O. Box 69, 99581.
Res.: P.O. Box 190, 99581. Tel: 907-949-1012.
Catechesis/Religious Program—Matrona Kozevenikoff, D.R.E.; Patrick Tam, Dir. Adult Faith Formation. Students 40.

GALENA, ST. JOHN BERCHMANS CATHOLIC CHURCH GALENA (1923), (Athabascan), Agnes Sweetsir, Admin.; Bro. R. Justin Huber, O.F.M., Pastoral Min.
Res.: P.O. Box 131, 99741. Tel: 907-656-1240.
Catechesis/Religious Program—Students 10.

HEALY, DENALI BOROUGH, HOLY MARY OF GUADALUPE CATHOLIC CHURCH HEALY (1984) Rev. Jack de Verteuil; Barbara Walters, Pastoral Min.
P.O. Box 10508, 99743.
Church & Mailing Address: P.O. Box 32, 99743. Tel: 907-683-2535; 907-683-1007 (Rectory). Web: www.holymaryofguadalupe.org.
Catechesis/Religious Program—Students 33.
Mission— [JC] Cantwell, 99729. Tel: 907-768-2768.

HOLY CROSS, HOLY FAMILY CATHOLIC CHURCH HOLY CROSS (1888) Connie Werba, Acting Parish Admin.
Res.: P.O. Box 101, 99602. Tel: 907-476-7144; Fax: 907-476-7144.
Catechesis/Religious Program—Students 9.

HOOPER BAY, LITTLE FLOWER OF JESUS CATHOLIC CHURCH HOOPER BAY (1928), (Yup'ik), [JC] Unassigned.
Res.: P.O. Box 9, 99604. Tel: 907-758-4620.
Catechesis/Religious Program—Students 11.

HUSLIA, ST. FRANCIS REGIS CATHOLIC CHURCH HUSLIA Bro. R. Justin Huber, O.F.M., Parish Admin.
P.O. Box 89, 99746-0089. Tel: 907-656-1240.

KALSKAG, IMMACULATE CONCEPTION CATHOLIC CHURCH KALSKAG, Unassigned.P.O. Box 11, Bethel Census Area 99607. Tel: 907-471-2298.
Catechesis/Religious Program—Julia Durous, D.R.E.; Marous Dammeyer, D.R.E.

KALTAG, ST. TERESA CATHOLIC CHURCH, (Athabascan), [JC] Rev. Joseph Hemmer, O.F.M.
P.O. Box 69, 99748.
Res.: P.O. Box 69, 99748. Tel: 907-534-2218.
Catechesis/Religious Program—Students 10.

KOTLIK, ST. JOSEPH CATHOLIC CHURCH KOTLIK (1949), (Yup'ik), Pius Akran, Parish Admin.; Delle Hunt, Acting Pastoral Coord.; Deacon Raymond Teluk.
Church: P.O. Box 20228, 99620. Tel: 907-899-4715.
Catechesis/Religious Program—Students 15.

KOTZEBUE, NORTHWEST ARCTIC BOROUGH, ST. FRANCIS XAVIER CATHOLIC CHURCH KOTZEBUE (1929) [CEM] [JC], (Served out of Nome) Rev. Ross Tozzi.
342 Second St., 99752.
Res.: Box 358, 99752. Tel: 907-442-3239.
Catechesis/Religious Program—Students 26.

KOYUKUK, ST. PATRICK CATHOLIC CHURCH GALENA, (Athabascan), (Served out of Galena) Eliza Jones, Acting Parish Admin.
Res.: P.O. Box 10, 99754. Tel: 907-927-2240.
Catechesis/Religious Program—Elizabeth Jones, D.R.E. Students 3.

MARSHALL, IMMACULATE HEART OF MARY CATHOLIC CHURCH MARSHALL (1930) Ms. Clara Shorty, Parish Admin.
Mailing Address: P.O. Box 69, 99585. Tel: 907-679-6639; Fax: 907-679-6639.
Catechesis/Religious Program—Students 14.
Mission—Our Lady of Guadalupe Catholic Church Russian Mission P.O. Box 56, Russian Mission, Wade Hampton Co. 99657. Tel: 907-584-5173.

McGRATH, ST. MICHAEL CATHOLIC CHURCH McGRATH (1960) Sharon Strick, Parish Admin.; Roger Seavoy, Co-Parish Admin.; Izabelle Harrinton, Co-Parish Admin.
Res.: P.O. Box 141, 99627. Tel: 907-524-3928.

MOUNTAIN VILLAGE, ST. LAWRENCE CATHOLIC CHURCH MOUNTAIN VILLAGE Margaret Waskey, Parish Admin.; Kate Thompson, Pastoral Coord.; Deacon Elmer Beans.
Res. & Mailing Address: P.O. Box 32205, 99632. Tel: 907-591-2348; Fax: 907-591-2348 (Prior Arrangement).
Catechesis/Religious Program—Students 22.

NENANA, ST. THERESA CATHOLIC CHURCH NENANA (1922) [JC 2], Served out of Healy, AK. Penelope A. Forness, Acting Admin.
Mailing Address: P.O. Box 312, 99760. Tel: 907-832-5617.
Catechesis/Religious Program—Students 9.

NEWTOK, HOLY FAMILY CATHOLIC CHURCH NEWTOK (1950), (Yup'ik), [CEM] Ignatius Tommy, Acting Parish Admin.; Deacons Mark Tom, (Retired); John F. Andy.
Res.: P.O. Box 5569, 99559. Tel: 907-237-2427.
Catechesis/Religious Program—Freida Carl, D.R.E. Students 19.

NIGHTMUTE, OUR LADY OF PERPETUAL HELP CATHOLIC CHURCH NIGHTMUTE (1950), (Yup'ik), [CEM] Jane Tulik, Acting Parish Admin.; Anne Tom, Acting Parish Admin.; Deacons Thomas Jumbo, (Retired); Camillus Tulik, (Retired); Ignatius Matthias; Christopher Tulik.
Res.: 99690. Tel: 907-647-6428.
Catechesis/Religious Program—Students 73.

NOME, ST. JOSEPH CATHOLIC CHURCH NOME (1901) [CEM] Rev. Ross Tozzi; Maureen Koezuna, Parish Admin.
Rectory—100 W. King Pl., P.O. Box 1010, 99762. Tel: 907-443-5527.
Church: 409 Steadman, 99762.
Catechesis/Religious Program—Students 45.
Mission—St. Jude Catholic Church Little Diomede P.O. Box 7999, Little Diomede, Nome Census Area 99762-7999.

NORTH POLE, FAIRBANKS, NORTH STAR BOROUGH, ST. NICHOLAS CATHOLIC CHURCH NORTH POLE (1975) Rev. Robert Fath; Anne Armour, Pastoral Coord.; Deacon Walt Gelinas.
Res.: 707 St. Nicholas Dr., 99705. Tel: 907-488-2595; Fax: 907-488-9625. Email: stnicks@acsalaska.net. Web: www.saintnicholasnorthpole.parishesonline.com.
Catechesis/Religious Program—Eileen Wehner, C.R.E.; Lisa Sagers, Youth Min. Students 157.

NULATO, OUR LADY OF SNOWS CATHOLIC CHURCH NULATO (1877), (Served out of Galena) Bro. Robert J. Ruzicka, O.F.M., Pastoral Admin.
Res.: P.O. Box 89, 99765. Tel: 907-898-2242.
Catechesis/Religious Program—

PILOT STATION, ST. CHARLES SPINOLA CATHOLIC CHURCH PILOT STATION (1914), (Yup'ik), [JC] Rev. Stanislaw Jaszek, Ministerial Residence; Abraham Kelly, Acting Parish Admin.; Annie Greene, Acting Pastoral Coord.
Mailing Address: P.O. Box 5120, 99650. Tel: 907-549-3231; Fax: 907-549-3231.
Catechesis/Religious Program—Students 11.

RUBY, ST. PETER-IN-CHAINS CATHOLIC CHURCH GALENA (1912) [JC] Unassigned. (Served out of Kaltag)
Res.: P.O. Box 207, 99768. Tel: 907-468-4413.
Catechesis/Religious Program—Students 6.

ST. MARYS, CHURCH OF THE NATIVITY CATHOLIC CHURCH ST. MARYS (1970) Rev. Theodore E. Kestler, S.J.
Mailing Address: P.O. Box 109, 99658.
Res.: P.O. Box 49, 99658. Tel: 907-438-2536.
Catechesis/Religious Program—

ST. MICHAEL, ST. MICHAEL CATHOLIC CHURCH ST. MICHAEL (1895) [JC] Rita Oyoumick, Acting Parish Admin.
Res.: P.O. Box 29, 99659. Tel: 907-923-3151.
Catechesis/Religious Program—

SCAMMON BAY, BLESSED SACRAMENT CATHOLIC CHURCH SCAMMON BAY (1968) [JC] Unassigned.
Res.: P.O. Box 170, 99662. Tel: 907-558-5229.
Catechesis/Religious Program—Elizabeth Kasayuli, D.R.E.

STEBBINS, ST. BERNARD CATHOLIC CHURCH STEBBINS (1908) [JC] Margaret Marlin, Acting Parish Admin.
Res.: P.O. Box 71102, 99671. Tel: 907-934-3151.

TANANA, ST. ALOYSIUS CATHOLIC CHURCH GALENA (1887) [JC], (Served out of Fairbanks) Lois Huntington, Admin.
Res.: P.O. Box 6, 99777. Tel: 907-366-7238.

TELLER, ST. ANN CATHOLIC CHURCH TELLER (1909) Unassigned. (Served out of Nome), General Delivery, 99778.
Res.: 100 W. King Pl., Nome, 99762. Tel: 907-443-5527.

TOK, HOLY ROSARY CATHOLIC CHURCH TOK (1949), (Served out of Delta Junction) Sr. Margaret Butler, S.S.J., Parish Admin.
Res.: P.O. Box 369, 99780. Tel: 907-883-4111. Email: hrtok@aptalaska.net.
Catechesis/Religious Program—Students 22.

TOKSOOK BAY, ST. PETER THE FISHERMAN CATHOLIC CHURCH TOKSOOK BAY (1964) [CEM] Maggie John, Parish Admin./Pastoral Coord.; Deacons James Charlie; Nick Therchik Sr.
Mailing Address: P.O. Box 37046, 99637. Tel: 907-427-7813; Fax: 907-427-7813. Email: stpeter@gci.net.
Catechesis/Religious Program—Tel: 907-427-7826; Fax: 907-427-7820. Students 215.

TUNUNAK, ST. JOSEPH CATHOLIC CHURCH TUNUNAK (1889), (Yup'ik), [CEM] Josephine M. Link, Acting Parish Admin.; Sophie Oscar, Acting Pastoral Coord.; Deacon Dick Lincoln, (Retired).
Res.: P.O. Box 9, 99681. Tel: 907-652-6214.
Catechesis/Religious Program—Students 12.

UNALAKLEET, CHURCH OF THE HOLY ANGELS CATHOLIC CHURCH UNALAKLEET (1952) Anne Ivanoff, Parish Admin.

Res.: P.O. Box 152, 99684. Tel: 907-624-3711. *Catechesis/Religious Program*—Students 4.

Leave of Absence:
Rev.—
Wallner, Gerhard

Retired:
Rev.—
Hinsvark, John (Retired), 200 W. 34th Ave., #545, Anchorage, 99503.

Permanent Deacons:
Agathluk, Bart, Sacred Heart, Emmonak
Andrew, Louie, Immaculate Conception, Bethel
Andy, John F., Holy Family, Newtok
Asuluk, Joe, St. Peter Fisherman, Toksook Bay
Avugiak, Joe, St. Catherine, Chefornak
Ayunerak, John, St. Ignatius, Alakanuk
Barnard, Robert P., Immaculate Conception, Fairbanks
Beans, Elmer, Mountain Village
Bowder, George, St. Raphael, Fairbanks
Boyscout, David, (Retired), Sacred Heart Church, Chevak
Boyscout, Peter, Sacred Heart, Chevak
Charlie, James, St. Peter the Fisherman, Toksook Bay
Gelinas, Walt, St. Nicholas, North Pole
Jumbo, Thomas, (Retired), Our Lady of Perpetual Help, Nightmute
Lincoln, Dick, (Retired), St. Joseph's, Tununak
Mantei, Robert, Immaculate Conception, Fairbanks
Matthias, Ignatius, St. Bernard, Stebbins
McCaffrey, Brian, Immaculate Conception, Bethel
Panruk, David, St. Catherine, Chefornak
Perreault, Paul, Fairbanks
Phillip, Joseph, (Retired), St. Ignatius, Alakanuk
Shelden, Denis, St. Ignatius, Alakanuk
Smart, Stephan F., Sr., Sacred Heart Church, Chevak
Stack, Sean, Immaculate Conception, Fairbanks
Stanislaus, Emmanuel, St. Ignatius, Alakanuk
Therchik, Nick, St. Peter the Fisherman, Toksook Bay
Tom, Mark, (Retired), Holy Family, Newtok
Tulik, Christopher, Our Lady of Perpetual Help, Nightmute
Waska, Ray, Sacred Heart, Emmonak
Wasuli, Aloysius, Immaculate Conception, Bethel

INSTITUTIONS LOCATED IN THE DIOCESE

[A] HIGH SCHOOLS, DIOCESAN

FAIRBANKS. *Monroe Catholic Junior-Senior High School*, (Grades 7-12), 615 Monroe St., 99701. Tel: 907-452-2044; Fax: 907-452-5978. Email: monroeprincipal@catholic-schools.org. Web: www.catholic-schools.org. Vincent Fantazzi, Prin.; Rev. Normand A. Pepin, S.J. Priests 1; Lay Teachers 27; Students 210.

[B] GRADE SCHOOLS, DIOCESAN

FAIRBANKS. *Immaculate Conception Grade School*, (Grades K-6), 615 Monroe St., 99701. Tel: 907-456-4574; Fax: 907-452-5978. Email: icsprincipal@catholic-schools.org. Web: www.catholic-schools.org. Amanda Angaiak, Prin.; Rev. Normand A. Pepin, S.J. Lay Teachers 27; Students 266.

[C] RESIDENCES FOR PRIESTS AND BROTHERS

FAIRBANKS. *Kobuk Center*, 2890 Kobuk Ave., 99709. Revs. Miroslaw Woznica; Kasparaj Mallavarapu; Frederick C. Bayler; Sean P. Thomson; Clint Landry, Seminarian.

[D] CONVENTS AND RESIDENCES OF SISTERS

NOME. *Little Sisters of Jesus*, Box 845, 99762. Tel: 907-443-2094. Sisters 3.

[E] MISCELLANEOUS LISTINGS

FAIRBANKS. *Catholic Trust of Northern Alaska*, 1320 Peger Rd., 99709. Tel: 907-374-9530. Deacon George Bowder, Exec. Officer.

House of Prayer, 1310 Peger Rd., 99709. Tel: 907-474-9379. Rev. Normand A. Pepin, S.J., Dir.

**Monroe Foundation, Inc.*, 718 Betty St., 99707. Tel: 907-456-7970; Fax: 907-456-7481. Email: director@catholic-schools.org. Web: www.catholic-schools.org. Nancy Hanson, Acting Exec. Dir.

Voice in the Wilderness Prayer Community, 4028 Birch Ln., 99709. Tel: 907-479-8512. Email: spiritfilled@gci.net. Gail Riedman, Dir.

GALENA. *Kateri Tekakwitha Center*, 1316 Peger Rd., 99709. Robert Hannon.

NOME. *Alaska Radio Mission, KNOM*, 107 W. Third Ave., Box 988, 99762. Tel: 907-443-5221; Fax: 907-443-5757. Email: knomgeneralmanager@gmail.com. Web: www.knom.org. Norman "Ric" E. Schmidt, Gen. Mgr.; Kelly Brabec, Prog. Dir. Total Staff 12; Total in Residence 4.

ST. MARYS. *Brother Joe Prince Jesuit Community*, P.O. Box 49, 99658. Tel: 907-438-2536. Email: jprincesj@juno.com. Revs. Gregg D. Wood, S.J., Supr., Pastoral Ministry, Nelson Island, Hooper Bay, Scammon Bay, Chevak, AK & SW Coast; Theodore E. Kestler, S.J., Asst. in Native Ministry Training Prog. & Deacon Prog., Pastoral Ministry, St. Mary's; Thomas G. Provinsal, S.J., Pastoral Ministry, Villages of Nelson Island & SW Coast; Charles J. Peterson, S.J. Pastoral Ministry, Bethel, AK; Normand A. Pepin, S.J.; Vincent J. Beuzer, S.J. Priests 6; Total Assisted 6,000.

Native Ministry Training Program, P.O. Box 29, 99658-0029. Tel: 907-438-2832; Fax: 907-438-2823. Email: nmtp@juno.com. Sr. Ellen Callaghan, O.S.F., Dir.; Rev. Theodore E. Kestler, S.J., Scripture/Theology Resource Person; Sr. Kathleen Radich, O.S.F. Staff 2; Total in Residence 2.

RELIGIOUS INSTITUTES OF MEN REPRESENTED IN THE DIOCESE

For further details refer to the corresponding bracketed number in the Religious Institutes of Men or Women section.

[0200]—*Benedictine Monks*—O.S.B.
[0520]—*Franciscan Friars and Brothers*—O.F.M.
[0690]—*Jesuit Fathers and Brothers*—S.J.
[0740]—*Marian Fathers*—M.I.C.

RELIGIOUS INSTITUTES OF WOMEN REPRESENTED IN THE DIOCESE

[2330]—*Little Sisters of Jesus*—L.S.J.
[0590]—*Sisters of Charity of Saint Elizabeth, Convent Station* (Northern Prov.)—S.C.
[1650]—*The Sisters of St. Francis of Philadelphia*—O.S.F.
[3830-12]—*Sisters of St. Joseph* Philadelphia, PA—S.S.J.
[3850]—*Sisters of St. Joseph of Chambery*—C.S.J.
[4110]—*Ursuline Nuns*—O.S.U.

NECROLOGY

(No Deaths)

An asterisk (*) denotes an organization that has established tax-exempt status directly with the IRS and is not covered by the USCCB Group Ruling.

Diocese of Fall River

(Dioecesis Riverormensis)

Most Reverend

GEORGE W. COLEMAN

Bishop of Fall River; ordained December 16, 1964; appointed Bishop of Fall River April 30, 2003; consecrated July 22, 2003. *Office: P.O. Box 2577, Fall River, MA 02722.*

ESTABLISHED MARCH 12, 1904.

Square Miles 1,194.

Comprises Bristol, Barnstable, Dukes and Nantucket Counties, and the Towns of Marion, Mattapoisett and Wareham in Plymouth County, Massachusetts.

For legal titles of parishes and diocesan institutions, consult the Chancery Office.

The Chancery: P.O. Box 2577, Fall River, MA 02722. Tel: 508-675-1311; Fax: 508-730-2447.

Email: chancery@dioc-fr.org

STATISTICAL OVERVIEW

Personnel	
Bishop	1
Priests: Diocesan Active in Diocese	99
Priests: Diocesan Active Outside Diocese	9
Priests: Diocesan in Foreign Missions	1
Priests: Retired, Sick or Absent	46
Number of Diocesan Priests	155
Religious Priests in Diocese	103
Total Priests in Diocese	258
Extern Priests in Diocese	6
Ordinations:	
Diocesan Priests	2
Transitional Deacons	1
Permanent Deacons in Diocese	88
Total Brothers	17
Total Sisters	182
Parishes	
Parishes	91
With Resident Pastor:	
Resident Diocesan Priests	77
Resident Religious Priests	10
Without Resident Pastor:	
Administered by Priests	4
Missions	12
Professional Ministry Personnel:	
Sisters	7
Lay Ministers	68
Welfare	
Catholic Hospitals	1
Total Assisted	204,595
Homes for the Aged	5
Total Assisted	1,193
Residential Care of Children	1
Total Assisted	100
Day Care Centers	1
Total Assisted	45
Specialized Homes	2
Total Assisted	39
Special Centers for Social Services	4
Total Assisted	43,727
Residential Care of Disabled	2
Total Assisted	223
Other Institutions	103
Total Assisted	666
Educational	
Diocesan Students in Other Seminaries	7
Total Seminarians	7
Colleges and Universities	1
Total Students	2,430
High Schools, Diocesan and Parish	5
Total Students	2,871
Elementary Schools, Diocesan and Parish	22
Total Students	4,824
Catechesis/Religious Education:	
High School Students	4,077
Elementary Students	23,961
Total Students under Catholic Instruction	38,170
Teachers in the Diocese:	
Priests	9
Brothers	3
Sisters	12
Lay Teachers	730
Vital Statistics	
Receptions into the Church:	
Infant Baptism Totals	3,109
Minor Baptism Totals	197
Adult Baptism Totals	58
Received into Full Communion	186
First Communions	3,702
Confirmations	3,546
Marriages:	
Catholic	762
Interfaith	181
Total Marriages	943
Deaths	3,613
Total Catholic Population	319,853
Total Population	826,616

Former Bishops—Most Revs. WILLIAM STANG, D.D., ord. June 15, 1878; appt. March 12, 1904; cons. May 1, 1904; died Feb. 2, 1907; DANIEL F. FEEHAN, D.D., ord. Dec. 20, 1879; appt. July 2, 1907; cons. Sept. 19, 1907; died July 19, 1934; JAMES E. CASSIDY, D.D., ord. Sept. 8, 1898; appt. Titular Bishop of Ibora and Auxiliary, March 21, 1930; cons. May 27, 1930; succeeded to the See, July 28, 1934; died May 17, 1951; JAMES L. CONNOLLY, D.D., D.Sc.H., ord. Dec. 21, 1923; appt. Titular Bishop of Mylasa and Coadjutor "cum jure successionis," April 18, 1945; cons. May 24, 1945; succeeded to See, May 17, 1951; retired Oct. 30, 1970; died Sept. 12, 1986; DANIEL A. CRONIN, D.D., S.T.D., ord. Dec. 20, 1952; appt. Titular Bishop of Egnatia and Auxiliary Bishop of Boston, June 10, 1968; cons. Sept. 12, 1968; transferred to Fall River, Oct. 30, 1970; installed Dec. 16, 1970; transferred to Hartford, Dec. 9, 1991; His Eminence SEAN CARDINAL O'MALLEY, O.F.M.Cap., Ph.D., ord. Aug. 29, 1970; appt. Coadjutor Bishop of St. Thomas, Virgin Islands May 30, 1984; ord. Aug. 2, 1984; succeeded to See Oct. 16, 1985; appt. Bishop of Fall River June 16, 1992; installed Aug. 11, 1992; transferred to Palm Beach Sept. 3, 2002; installed Oct. 19, 2002; transferred to Boston July 1, 2003; installed July 30, 2003; Named Cardinal Priest with the title of Santa Maria della Vittoria, in the consistory of March 24, 2006; installed October 1, 2006.

Vicar General—Rev. Msgr. JOHN A. PERRY, V.G., Mailing Address: P.O. Box 2577, Fall River, 02722.

The Chancery—450 Highland Ave., Fall River, 02720. Mailing Address: P.O. Box 2577, Fall River, 02722-2577. Tel: 508-675-1311; Fax: 508-730-2447.

Chancellor—Rev. MICHAEL K. MCMANUS.

Secretary to the Bishop—Rev. KARL C. BISSINGER, 47 Underwood St., Fall River, 02720.

Diocesan Tribunal—887 Highland Ave., Fall River, 02720. Tel: 508-675-7150; Fax: 508-675-7295.

Judicial Vicar—Rev. PAUL F. ROBINSON, O.Carm., J.C.D.

Promotor Justitiae—Rev. Msgr. DANIEL F. HOYE, J.C.L.

Judges—Revs. PAUL F. ROBINSON, O.Carm., J.C.D.; THOMAS L. RITA; RODNEY E. THIBAULT, J.C.L.; Very Rev. JAY T. MADDOCK, J.C.L., V.F.

Defenders of the Bond—Rev. Msgrs. THOMAS J. HARRINGTON, J.C.L. (Retired); DANIEL F. HOYE, J.C.L.; Revs. GERARD A. HEBERT, J.C.L.; THOMAS E. MCGLYNN, J.C.L.

Procurator-Advocates—Revs. MARC H. BERGERON; BRUCE M. NEYLON.

Auditors—Revs. DANIEL W. LACROIX; JOHN J. PERRY; HENRY J. DAHL; MARK R. HESSION, J.C.L.; THOMAS E. MCGLYNN, J.C.L.; Deacon ROBERT L. SURPRENANT.

Office Manager—Mrs. DENISE D. BERUBE.

Notaries—Mrs. DENISE D. BERUBE; Mrs. HELENE P. BEAUDOIN.

Diocesan Consultors—Rev. HENRY J. DAHL; Rev. Msgr. EDMUND J. FITZGERALD, V.F.; Revs. THOMAS C. LOPES (Retired); MICHAEL K. MCMANUS; Very Rev. JOHN J. OLIVEIRA, V.F.; Rev. Msgr. JOHN A. PERRY, V.G.; Rev. DAVID M. STOPYRA, O.F.M.Conv.

Deans—Fall River Deanery: Rev. Msgr. EDMUND J. FITZGERALD, V.F., St. Thomas More Rectory, 386 Luther Ave., Somerset, 02726. Taunton Deanery: Very Rev. JAY T. MADDOCK, J.C.L., V.F., 370 Middleboro Ave., P.O. Box 619, East Taunton, 02718. Attleboro Deanery: Rev. Msgr. STEPHEN J. AVILA, V.F., St. Mary's Rectory, 330 Pratt St., Mansfield, 02048. Cape Cod Deanery: Very Rev. GEORGE C. BELLENOIT, V.F., St. Pius Tenth Rectory, 5 Barbara St., South Yarmouth, 02664. New Bedford Deanery: Very Rev. JOHN J. OLIVEIRA, V.F., Our Lady of Mount Carmel Rectory, 230 Bonney St., New Bedford, 02744.

Diocesan Offices and Directors

Apostolate for Persons with Disabilities—MATTHEW DANSEREAU, Coord., 1600 Bay St., Fall River, 02724. Tel: 508-997-7337; 508-679-8373.

Campus Ministry—

Director—Rev. MICHAEL A. CIRYAK.

Bristol Community College—Rev. MICHAEL A. CIRYAK, Interim, 777 Elsbree St., Fall River, 02720. Tel: 508-678-2811, Ext. 301.

University of Massachusetts Dartmouth—Rev. MICHAEL JOSEPH FITZPATRICK; Sr. MADELEINE TACY, O.P., 285 Old Westport Rd., North Dartmouth, 02747. Tel: 508-999-8872.

Wheaton College—Rev. JAMES R. LACKENMIER, C.S.C., Norton.

Massachusetts Maritime Academy—VACANT.

Cape Cod Campus Ministry—Rev. DAVID C. FREDERICI, 230 S. Main St., Centerville, 02632. Tel: 508-362-8122; Fax: 508-771-0170.

Catholic Youth Organization—Very Rev. JAY T. MADDOCK, J.C.L., V.F., Dir., 403 Anawan St., Fall River, 02720.

Catholic Charities Appeal—VACANT.

Diocesan Apostolate to Hispanics—Rev. RICHARD D. WILSON, J.C.L., Diocesan Dir., Mailing Address: 233 County St., New Bedford, 02740. Tel: 508-996-5862; Fax: 508-990-0575. Area Offices: Fall River: Rev. GERMAN CORREA AGUDELO, Dir., Saint Mary's Cathedral, 327 Second St., Fall River, 02721. Tel:

508-672-9303. Attleboro: Rev. JOHN M. MURRAY, Dir., Saint Joseph's Church, 208 S. Main St., Attleboro, 02702. Tel: 508-222-1730. Taunton: Revs. WILLIAM H. KELLEY, C.S.C., Dir. Tel: 508-822-7116; Fax: 508-822-7117; MARC F. FALLON, C.S.C., St. Mary's Church, 14 St. Mary's Square, Taunton, 02780. Tel: 508-880-0410. New Bedford: Revs. RICHARD D. WILSON, J.C.L., Dir., Our Lady of Guadalupe Parish, 233 County St., New Bedford, 02740. Tel: 508-996-5862; Fax: 508-990-0575; HUGO G. CARDENAS, I.V.E., Dir., Mailing Address: St. Kilian's Church, 306 Ashley Blvd., New Bedford, 02746. Tel: 508-992-7587; Fax: 508-994-0281. Nantucket: Revs. PAUL E. CANUEL, Pastor; CARLOS ALBERTO PATINO VILLA, Dir., Mailing Address: St. Mary/Our Lady of the Isle, P.O. Box 1168, Nantucket, 02554-1168; NOE PINEDA, Contact Person, Mailing Address: P.O. Box 2067, Nantucket, 02584. Tel: 508-843-5873; Fax: 508-325-7991. Cape Cod: Rev. CARLOS ALBERTO PATINO VILLA, Dir., 246 Main St., P.O. Box 428, West Harwich, 02671. Tel: 774-238-0714; Fax: 508-771-5940.

Director of Portuguese Ministry—Very Rev. JOHN J. OLIVEIRA, V.F., 230 Bonney St., New Bedford, 02744.

Diocesan Archives—Rev. BARRY W. WALL (Retired), Mailing Address: P.O. Box 2577, Fall River, 02722.

Diocesan Office of Communications—JOHN E. KEARNS JR., Dir., 887 Highland Ave., Fall River, 02720. Tel: 508-675-0211; Fax: 508-675-5204. Mailing Address: P.O. Box 7, Fall River, 02722.

Diocesan Director of Cemeteries—Rev. JOHN J. PERRY, 249 Whittenton St., Taunton, 02780.

Diocesan Education Center—Dr. GEORGE A. MILOT, Supt. Schools; Dr. DONNA BOYLE, Asst. Supt. Curriculum; KATHLEEN A. SIMPSON, Asst. Supt. Personnel; CLAIRE M. MCMANUS, S.T.L., Dir. Faith Formation; Deacons BRUCE J. BONNEAU, Asst. Dir. Faith Formation; ROBERT D. LEMAY, Dir., Rite of Christian Initiation for Adults (RCIA); CRYSTAL-LYNN MEDEIROS, Asst. Dir. Youth & Young Adult Ministries, Catholic Education Center, 423 Highland Ave., Fall River, 02720. Tel: 508-678-2828; Fax: 508-674-4218.

Diocesan Department of Pastoral Care for the Sick—Rev. MAREK S. TUPTYNSKI, Dir., Office: 306 South St., Somerset, 02726. Tel: 508-672-1523; Fax: 508-675-5787.

St. Anne's Hospital—795 Middle St., Fall River, 02721. Rev. PAUL C. FEDAK; Sr. CAROLE V.M. MELLO, O.P.; Deacon DAVID B. PEPIN; Sisters MARIE THERESE DYER, F.C.J.; GLORINA JUGO, O.P.; Mr. CHARLES FOLEY; Mr. DANIEL SULLIVAN; Mrs. MEREKA HULL.

Charlton Memorial Hospital—Highland Ave. at New Boston Rd., Fall River, 02720. Rev. ANDREW JOHNSON, O.S.C.O.; Sisters ROBERTA O'CONNELL, F.C.J.; LUCILLE SOCCIARELLI, R.S.M.; Mrs. JANICE M. HART.

Sturdy Memorial Hospital—211 Park St., P.O. Box 649, Attleboro, 02703. Rev. MICHEL G. CORRIVEAU, C.P.M.; Deacon PAUL M. FOURNIER; Sr. ANNETTE LANGLOIS, S.A.S.V.

Cape Cod Hospital—27 Park St., Hyannis, 02601. Revs. DAVID C. FREDERICI; PETER J. FOURNIER; Deacon GREGORY J. BECKEL; Mrs. KATHERINE SULLIVAN.

St. Luke's Hospital—101 Page St., New Bedford, 02741. Revs. RODNEY E. THIBAULT, J.C.L.; MICHAEL JOSEPH FITZPATRICK; Deacon ROBERT G. LORENZO; Sr. JUDITH COSTA, S.S.D., M.Div.; DENISE BENJAMIN.

Morton Hospital—Taunton, 02780. Revs. EDWARD A. MURPHY; KEVIN A. COOK; Deacon PHILIP E. BEDARD.

Tobey Hospital and Rehabilitation Hospital of the Cape and Islands—Toby Hospital, 43 High St., Wareham, 02571. Rehabilitation Hospital of the Cape and Islands, 311 Service Rd., East Sandwich, 02537. Ms. LEONA LEONARD, Tobey Hospital, 43 High St., Wareham, 02571. Rehabilitation Hospital of the Cape and Islands, 311 Service Rd., East Sandwich, 02537.

Falmouth Hospital—100 Ter Heun Dr., Falmouth, 02540. Rev. JOSEPH H. MAURITZEN.

Diocesan Department of Catholic Social Services—ARLENE A. MCNAMEE, L.C.S.W., Exec. Dir., Office, 1600 Bay St., Box M, S. Station, Fall River, 02724. Tel: 508-674-4681; Fax: 508-675-2224.

Diocesan Finance Council—Members: Rev. Msgr. JOHN A. PERRY, V.G.; Mr. PAUL KAWA; FREDERIC J. TORPHY, Esq.; Mr. WILLIAM N. WHELAN; Rev. MICHAEL K. MCMANUS, Finance Officer, Mailing Address: P.O. Box 2577, Fall River, 02722. Tel: 508-675-1311.

Diocesan Guild for the Blind—Rev. BRUCE M. NEYLON, 36 Rockland St., P.O. Box 111, Fall River, 02724. Tel: 508-672-0423.

Diocesan Health Facilities—Rev. Msgr. EDMUND J. FITZGERALD, V.F., Dir., Office, 368 N. Main St., Fall River, 02720. Tel: 508-679-8154; Fax: 508-679-1422.

Diocesan Insurance Department—JOSEPH A. FIGLOCK, Benefits Mgr. & Insurance Coord.; SHAUN P. KERRIGAN, Asst. Benefits Mgr., Mailing Address: P.O. Box 2577, Fall River, 02722. Tel: 508-675-1311; Fax: 508-672-3802.

Diocesan Newspaper— "The Anchor" Rev. ROGER J. LANDRY, Exec. Editor; Mr. DAVID B. JOLIVET, Editor, Office, 887 Highland Ave., Fall River, 02722. Tel: 508-675-7151. Mailing Address: P.O. Box 7, Fall River, 02722.

Ecumenical Officer—Rev. MARC H. BERGERON, 818 Middle St., Fall River, 02721. Tel: 508-674-5651.

Episcopal Representative for Religious—Sr. CATHERINE DONOVAN, R.S.M., 500 Slocum Rd., North Dartmouth, 02747. Tel: 508-992-9921.

Family Ministry—Rev. GREGORY A. MATHIAS, Dir., Family Life Center, 500 Slocum Rd., North Dartmouth, 02747. Tel: 508-999-6420.

Holy Childhood Association, The—Rev. Msgr. JOHN J. OLIVEIRA, P.A., Dir., 106 Illinois St., New Bedford, 02745. Tel: 508-995-3593.

Missionary Cooperative Plan—Rev. Msgr. JOHN J. OLIVEIRA, P.A., Dir., 106 Illinois St., New Bedford, 02745. Tel: 508-995-3593.

Office for Divine Worship—Rev. Msgr. STEPHEN J. AVILA, V.F., St. Mary's Rectory, 330 Pratt St., Mansfield, 02048. Tel: 508-339-2981; Fax: 508-339-0612.

Office of AIDS Ministry, Inc.—KRYSTEN WINTER-GREEN, Ph.D., Exec. Dir., 243 Forest St., Clemence Hall, Rm. 225, Fall River, 02721. Tel: 508-674-5600, Ext. 2295.

Office of Pastoral Planning—DOUGLAS RODRIGUES, Dir.; DIANE RINKACS, Assoc. Dir., Mailing Address: P.O. Box 2577, Fall River, 02722. Tel: 508-675-1311; Fax: 866-515-2933.

Permanent Diaconate Program—Rev. Msgr. JOHN J. OLIVEIRA, P.A., Dir.

Pro-Life Apostolate—Mrs. MARIAN DESROSIERS, Dir., 500 Slocum Rd., North Dartmouth, 02747. Tel: 508-997-2290; Fax: 508-997-2923.

Propagation of the Faith—Rev. Msgr. JOHN J. OLIVEIRA, P.A., Dir., Office, 106 Illinois St., New Bedford, 02745. Tel: 508-995-3593; Fax: 508-995-2453.

St. Vincent De Paul Society—VACANT.

Television Apostolate—Rev. Msgr. STEPHEN J. AVILA, V.F., Coord., St. Mary's Rectory, 330 Pratt St., Mansfield, 02048. Tel: 508-339-2981; Fax: 508-339-0612.

Victim Assistance Coordinator—ARLENE A. MCNAMEE, L.C.S.W. Tel: 508-674-4681. Email: aam@cssdioc.org.

Vocations—Revs. KARL C. BISSINGER, Dir.; KEVIN A. COOK, Assoc. Dir. Recruitment, 47 Underwood St., Fall River, 02720. Tel: 508-675-1311; Fax: 508-679-9220.

Commissions and Councils

Campaign for Human Development—ARLENE A. MCNAMEE, L.C.S.W., Mailing Address: S. Station, P.O. Box M, Fall River, 02724. Tel: 508-674-4681; Fax: 508-675-2224.

Catholic Scouting Program—Rev. DAVID C. FREDERICI, Dir., 230 S. Main St., Centerville, 02632. Tel: 508-362-8122; Fax: 508-771-0170.

Continuing Education of the Clergy—Rev. MARK R. HESSION, J.C.L., Dir., 230 S. Main St., Centerville, 02632. Tel: 508-775-5744; Fax: 508-771-0170.

Mentoring Program for Priests—Very Rev. JOHN J. OLIVEIRA, V.F., Dir., 230 Bonney St., New Bedford, 02744. Tel: 508-993-4704; Fax: 508-991-5536.

Diocesan Council of Catholic Nurses—Rev. MARK R. HESSION, J.C.L., Moderator, 230 S. Main St., Centerville, 02632. Tel: 508-775-5744; Fax: 508-771-0170.

Diocesan Council of Catholic Women—Sr. EUGENIA BRADY, S.J.C., Moderator, Cluny Convent, 90 Brenton Rd., Newport, RI 02840. Tel: 401-924-0953.

Diocesan Liaison with Charismatic Groups—Rev. EDWARD A. MURPHY, Dir., 249 Whittenton St., Taunton, 02780. Tel: 508-824-7794; Fax: 508-880-3865.

Diocesan Liaison with Portuguese Charismatic Groups—Rev. HENRY S. ARRUDA, St. Anthony's Rectory, 126 School St., Taunton, 02780. Tel: 508-822-0714.

Diocesan Pastoral Council—Rev. Msgr. JOHN A. PERRY, V.G., Mailing Address: P.O. Box 2577, Fall River, 02722.

Legion of Mary—Rev. BARRY W. WALL (Retired), 120 Beattie St., Fall River, 02723. Tel: 508-672-7232.

CLERGY, PARISHES, MISSIONS AND PAROCHIAL SCHOOLS

CITY OF FALL RIVER

(BRISTOL COUNTY)

1—CATHEDRAL OF ST. MARY OF THE ASSUMPTION (1838) Rev. Paul Bernier, Rector; Deacon Peter R. Cote. In Res., Revs. Thomas E. McGlynn; Paulo Barbosa, Dir. Brazilian Apostolate; German Correa Agudelo, Spanish Apostolate.
Res.: 327 Second St., 02721. Tel: 508-673-2833; Fax: 508-672-0667.
Catechesis/Religious Program—467 Spring St., 02721. Tel: 508-672-5531. Alizabeth Camara, D.R.E. Students 77.

2—ST. ANNE'S (1869), (French), Revs. Marc H. Bergeron; Krzysztof Stanibula. In Res., Rev. Roger J. Levesque (Retired).
Res.: 818 Middle St., 02721. Tel: 508-674-5651; 508-678-5322; Fax: 508-672-0939. Web: www.stanneshrine.com.
420 Bradford Ave., 02721. Fax: 508-300-0242.
Catechesis/Religious Program—Tel: 508-678-1510. Susan Chapdelaine, D.R.E. Students 320.

3—ST. ANTHONY OF PADUA (1911), (Portuguese), Rev. Brian E. Albino.
Res.: 48 Sixteenth St., 02723. Tel: 508-673-2402; Fax: 508-730-2519.
Catechesis/Religious Program—Tel: 508-674-1986. Deborah Polselli, C.R.E. (1st & 2nd grades); John Janeiro, C.R.E. (3rd - 9th grades). Students 183.

4—BLESSED SACRAMENT (1902), (French), Merged with Our Lady of the Angels and St. Patrick's, Fall River to form the Parish of the Good Shepherd, Fall River.

5—ST. ELIZABETH'S (1915) Merged with St. Jean Baptiste and St. William to form Holy Trinity.

6—ESPIRITO SANTO (1904), (Portuguese), Rev. James Ferry; Deacon Thomas Souza.
Res.: 311 Alden St., 02723. Tel: 508-672-3352; Fax: 508-646-1787.
School—(Grades PreK-8), 143 Everett St., 02723. Tel: 508-672-2229; Fax: 508-672-7724. Louise Kane, Prin. Lay Teachers 25; Students 257.
Catechesis/Religious Program—Students 384.

7—HOLY CROSS (1916), (Polish), Merged with SS. Peter & Paul, Fall River.

8—HOLY NAME (1923) Rev. George E. Harrison. In Res., Revs. Paul C. Fedak; John A. Raposo.
Res.: 709 Hanover St., 02720. Tel: 508-679-6732; Fax: 508-675-4755. Email: office@holynamefr.com. Web: www.holynamefr.com.
School—850 Pearce St., 02720. Tel: 508-674-9131; Fax: 508-679-0571. Web: www.holynamefr-school.com. Dr. Patricia M. Wardell, Prin. Religious Sisters of Mercy 1; Lay Teachers 18; Students 243.
Catechesis/Religious Program—Tel: 508-678-7532. Email: faithformation@holynamefr.com. Diane Baron, D.R.E. Students 174.

9—HOLY TRINITY (2000) Rev. David M. Andrade; Deacon John F. Branco.
Res.: 951 Stafford Rd., 02721. Tel: 508-672-3200; Fax: 508-673-5518. Email: holytrinityparish@comcast.net. Web: www.holytrinityfallriver.com.
School—64 Lamphor St., 02721. Tel: 508-673-6772; Fax: 508-730-1864. Brenda Gagnon, Prin. Lay Teachers 15; Students 221.
Catechesis/Religious Program—Tel: 508-673-1284; Fax: 508-730-1864. Patricia Pasternak, Faith Formation Coord. Students 147.

10—ST. JEAN BAPTISTE (1901) Merged with St. Elizabeth and St. William to form Holy Trinity Parish.

11—ST. JOSEPH'S (1873) Rev. Hugh J. McCullough.
Res.: 1335 N. Main St., 02720. Tel: 508-673-1123; Fax: 508-673-7230.
Catechesis/Religious Program—Students 184.

12—ST. LOUIS (1885) Closed. Sacramental records can be found at St. Mary's Cathedral.

13—ST. MICHAEL (1902), (Portuguese), Rev. Edward E. Correia; Deacon Jose Medeiros. In Res., Rev. Andrew Johnson, O.S.C.O.
Res.: 189 Essex St., 02720. Tel: 508-672-6713; Fax: 508-679-1841. Email: smfr929@comcast.net. Web: www.smpfr.org.
School—(Grades PreK-8), 209 Essex St., 02720. Tel: 508-678-0266; Fax: 508-324-4433. Email: stmfr@comcast.net. Web: www.smfr.org. Sr. Marie Baldi, S.U.S.C., Prin. Religious of the Holy Union of the Sacred Hearts 1; Lay Teachers 17; Students 192.
Catechesis/Religious Program—Tel: 508-678-0266. Students 202.

14—NOTRE DAME DE LOURDES (1874), (French), Revs. Richard L. Chretien; Kenneth R. Gumbert, O.P.
Res.: 529 Eastern Ave., 02723. Tel: 508-679-1991; Fax: 508-676-5276. Email: chreechie@aol.com.
Catechesis/Religious Program—Tel: 508-679-1991;

Fax: 508-676-5276. Ms. Colleen Laliberte, D.R.E. Students 90.

15—OUR LADY OF HEALTH (1924), (Portuguese), Closed. For inquiries for parish records, please see Espirito Santo Parish, Fall River.

16—OUR LADY OF THE ANGELS (1915), (Portuguese), Merged with Blessed Sacrament and St. Patrick's, Fall River to form the Parish of the Good Shepherd, Fall River.

17—OUR LADY OF THE HOLY ROSARY (1904), (Italian), Closed. For inquiries for parish records contact Cathedral of St. Mary of the Assumption, Fall River.

18—OUR LADY OF THE IMMACULATE CONCEPTION (1882) Rev. Richard L. Chretien.
Res.: 15 Thomas St., 02723. Tel: 508-673-2122; Fax: 508-730-1694.
Catechesis/Religious Program—Tel: 508-679-1991. Ms. Colleen Laliberte, D.R.E. Students 70.

19—PARISH OF THE GOOD SHEPHERD (2002) Rev. Fred Babiczuk; Deacon John F. Branco.
Res.: 1598 S. Main St., 02724-2586. Tel: 508-678-7412; Fax: 508-673-1280. Email: goodshepherdfallriver@yahoo.com.
Catechesis/Religious Program—Tel: 508-677-4702. Marion Carrier, D.R.E. Students 228.

20—ST. PATRICK'S (1873) Merged with Blessed Sacrament and Our Lady of the Angels, Fall River to form the Parish of the Good Shepherd, Fall River.

21—SS. PETER AND PAUL (1882) Rev. Stephen B. Salvador.
Res.: 250 Snell St., 02721. Tel: 508-676-8463; Fax: 508-678-8070. Email: ssppchurch@aol.com. Web: www.saintspeterandpaulparish.org.
Worship Site—Holy Cross Church, 47 Pulaski St., 02721.
School—(Grades PreK-8), 240 Dover St., 02721. Tel: 508-672-7258; Fax: 508-674-6042. Ms. Kathleen A. Burt, Prin. Lay Teachers 17; Students 248.
Catechesis/Religious Program—Tel: 508-672-3720. Gayle Riley, D.R.E. Students 83.

22—SACRED HEART (1872) Rev. Raymond Cambra.
Res.: 160 Seabury St., 02720. Tel: 508-673-0852; Fax: 508-678-0873. Email: sacred_heart_church@comcast.net.
Catechesis/Religious Program—Tel: 508-730-1481; Fax: 508-730-1481. Students 93.

23—SANTO CHRISTO (1892), (Portuguese), Revs. Gastao A. Oliveira; Thomas M. Kocik.
Res.: 185 Canal St., 02721. Tel: 508-676-1184; Fax: 508-676-9701. Email: scp1892@yahoo.com.
Catechesis/Religious Program—Tel: 508-675-3007. Mr. Osvaldo Pacheco, D.R.E. Students 330.

24—ST. STANISLAUS (1898), (Polish), Rev. Bruce M. Neylon.
Res.: 36 Rockland St., P.O. Box 300, 02724. Tel: 508-672-0423; Fax: 508-677-1378. Email: saintstanislaus@cox.net. Web: www.saintstanislaus.com.
School—(Grades PreK-8), 37 Rockland St., 02724. Tel: 508-674-6771; Fax: 508-677-1622. Miss Jean Willis, Prin. Lay Teachers 17; Students 198.
Catechesis/Religious Program—Eileen Hadfield, D.R.E. Students 33.

25—ST. WILLIAM'S (1905) Merged with St. Elizabeth and St. Jean Baptiste to form Holy Trinity Parish.

OUTSIDE THE CITY OF FALL RIVER

ACUSHNET, BRISTOL CO., ST. FRANCIS XAVIER'S (1915) Rev. Msgr. Gerard P. O'Conner; Deacon David B. Pepin.
Res.: 125 Main St., 02743. Tel: 508-995-7600; Fax: 508-995-1794. Email: stfrancisx@comcast.net. Web: www.sfxacushnet.org/churchhome.htm.
School—223 Main St., 02743. Tel: 508-995-4313; Fax: 508-995-0456. Donald A. Pelletier, Prin. Religious 1; Lay Teachers 11; Students 226.
Catechesis/Religious Program—Tel: 508-998-7445. Email: stfrancisxreled@aol.com. Janine Hammarquist, D.R.E. Students 266.

ASSONET, BRISTOL CO., ST. BERNARD'S (1938) Rev. Michael S. Racine.
Res.: 32 S. Main St., P.O. Box 370 (Freetown), 02702. Tel: 508-644-5585; Fax: 508-644-2136. Email: stbernardassonet@aol.com. Web: www.stbernardassonet.org.
Catechesis/Religious Program—Tel: 508-644-2032; Fax: 508-644-2032. Email: stbernardreled@verizon.net. Brian Correia, D.R.E.; Dr. Marlene Correia, D.R.E. Students 400.

ATTLEBORO, BRISTOL CO.

1—HOLY GHOST (1921) Rev. John M. Murray; Deacon Paul M. Fournier.
Res.: 71 Linden St., 02703. Tel: 508-222-3266; Fax: 508-222-3292. Email: hgchurch@verizon.net.
Catechesis/Religious Program—Tel: 508-222-6756. Students 52.

2—ST. JOHN THE EVANGELIST (1883) [CEM] Rev. Richard M. Roy; Deacon Adelbert F. Malloy.
Res.: One St. John Pl., 02703-2249. Tel: 508-222-1206; Fax: 508-226-6461. Email: sjparish@naiimail.net. Web: www.stjohns-attleboro.org.
School—13 Hodges St., 02703. Tel: 508-222-5062; Fax: 508-223-1737. Email: sje-school@naiimail.net. Web: www.sje-school.com. Sr. Mary Holden, C.P., Prin. Sisters 3; Lay Teachers 14; Students 258.
Catechesis/Religious Program—Tel: 508-222-0707; Fax: 508-222-0701. Email: mkennan@sje-scvhool.com. Margaret Keenan, D.R.E. Students 716.

3—ST. JOSEPH'S (1905) Rev. John M. Murray; Deacon Paul M. Fournier.
Res.: 208 S. Main St., 02703. Tel: 508-226-1115; Fax: 888-239-9322. Email: stjosephattleboro@gmail.com.
Catechesis/Religious Program—10 Maple St. Tel: 508-222-1730. Students 62.

4—ST. STEPHEN'S (1875) [CEM] Rev. James H. Morse.
Res.: 683 S. Main St., 02703-6397. Tel: 508-222-0641; Fax: 508-222-1855. Web: www.ststephensattleboro.org.
Catechesis/Religious Program—Chris Adams; Patty Adams. Students 154.

5—ST. THERESA OF THE CHILD JESUS (1925) Rev. Jon-Paul Gallant.
Res.: 18 Baltic St., South Attleboro, 02703. Tel: 508-761-8111; Fax: 508-761-5475. Email: sttcj@aol.com.
Catechesis/Religious Program—Tel: 508-761-5367. Mrs. Theresa Paquette, D.R.E. Students 460.

ATTLEBORO FALLS, BRISTOL CO., ST. MARK'S (1967) Rev. Thomas A. Frechette; Deacon Richard J. Gundlach.
Res.: 105 Stanley St., P.O. Box 1240, 02763-0240. Tel: 508-699-7566; Fax: 508-643-0103. Email: stmarkoffice@comcast.net. Web: www.stmarks-attleborofalls.org.
Catechesis/Religious Program—Tel: 508-695-7773. Mrs. Elaine Corvese, D.R.E. Students 830.

BREWSTER, BARNSTABLE CO., OUR LADY OF THE CAPE (1961) Revs. Bernard Baris, M.S.; John R. Dolan, M.S., Parochial Vicar; Robert J. Campbell, M.S., Parochial Vicar; Deacons R. Donald Biron; James P. Leavitt.
Res.: 468 Stony Brook Rd., P.O. Box 1799, 02631-7799. Tel: 508-385-3252; Fax: 508-385-6864. Email: ourladyofthecape@yahoo.com. Web: www.ourladyofthecape.org.
Catechesis/Religious Program—Tel: 508-385-2115. Mrs. Priscilla Silva, D.R.E. Students 295.
Mission—*Immaculate Conception* 2580 Main St., Rte. 6A, Barnstable Co. 02631. P.O. Box 1799, 02631.

BUZZARDS BAY, BARNSTABLE CO., ST. MARGARET (1915) [JC] Revs. Francis de Sales Paolo, O.F.M.; Giles Barreda, O.F.M.; Deacon Ernest J. Gendron.
Res.: 141 Main St., 02532. Tel: 508-759-7777; Fax: 508-759-3920. Email: stmargarets.rectory@verizon.net. Web: www.saintmargaretsparish.com.
School—143 Main St., 02532. Tel: 508-759-2213; Fax: 508-759-8776. Paul Hudson, Prin. Lay Teachers 13; Students 204.
Catechesis/Religious Program—Tel: 508-743-4604. Manuel Subda, D.R.E. Students 271.
Mission—*St. Mary Star of the Sea* Onset, Plymouth Co.

CENTERVILLE, BARNSTABLE CO., OUR LADY OF VICTORY (1957) Revs. Mark R. Hession; John P. Kelleher, O.S.B.; Deacons James M. Barrett; Theodore Lukac; Ralph A. Babusci Jr., Pastoral Assoc.; Patricia Clock, Pastoral Assoc.
In Res—Rev. David C. Frederici.
Res.: 230 S. Main St., 02632. Tel: 508-775-5744; Fax: 508-771-0170. Email: office@olvparish.org. Web: www.olvparish.org.
Catechesis/Religious Program—Tel: 508-771-1614. Karen Perella, D.R.E.; Helen L. Curran, D.R.E. Students 850.
Mission—*Our Lady of Hope* Rte. 6A, West Barnstable, Barnstable Co. 02668.

CHATHAM, BARNSTABLE CO., HOLY REDEEMER (1955) [JC] Rev. George Scales.
Res.: 57 Highland Ave., Box 687, 02633. Tel: 508-945-0677; Fax: 508-945-3186. Email: parish@holyredeemerchatham.org.
Catechesis/Religious Program—Students 94.
Chapel—*Our Lady of Grace Chapel* 60 Meetinghouse Rd. (Rte. 137), South Chatham, 02659.

DIGHTON, BRISTOL CO., ST. PETER'S (1904) Closed. For inquiries for parish records contact St. Nicholas of Myra Parish, North Dighton.

EAST FALMOUTH, BARNSTABLE CO., ST. ANTHONY'S (1923) [CEM] Rev. William M. Costello.
Res.: 167 E. Falmouth Hwy., 02536. Tel: 508-548-0108; Fax: 508-457-1723. Email: stanthonyschurch@yahoo.com. Web: www.stanthonyscapecod.org.
Catechesis/Religious Program—Tel: 508-548-3515; Fax: 508-548-3515. Email: stanthonyfaithformation@comcast.net. Patricia Friel, D.R.E. Students 419.

EAST FREETOWN, BRISTOL CO., ST. JOHN NEUMANN (1984) Rev. Richard E. Degagne; Deacon Robert L. Surprenant.
Res.: 157 Middleboro Rd., Box 718, 02717. Tel: 508-763-2240; Fax: 508-763-3040. Email: contact@sjnfreetown.org. Web: www.sjn.freetown.org.
Catechesis/Religious Program—Tel: 508-763-8122. Dr. Doris Thibault, D.R.E.; Ms. Jane Ayer, D.R.E.; Mrs. Suzanne Medeiros, D.R.E. Students 552.

EAST SANDWICH, BARNSTABLE CO., CORPUS CHRISTI (1830) [CEM] Revs. Marcel H. Bouchard; Rodney E. Thibault; Deacons David Boucher; Robert Alence; Arthur LaChance; Dennis O'Connell.
Res. & Parish Center: 324 Quaker Meetinghouse Rd., 02537-1327. Tel: 508-888-0209; Fax: 508-888-8961. Email: pastor@corpuschristiparish.org. Web: www.corpuschristiparish.org.
Catechesis/Religious Program—Email: dmboucher@corpuschristiparish.org. Deborah M. Boucher, D.R.E. Students 1,015.
Mission—*St. Theresa* Sagamore, Barnstable Co.

EAST TAUNTON, BRISTOL CO., HOLY FAMILY (1900) Very Rev. Jay T. Maddock; Deacon John J. Fitzpatrick.
Res.: 370 Middleboro, P.O. Box 619, 02718. Tel: 508-824-5707; Fax: 508-822-2915. Email: secretary@holyfamilytaunton.org. Web: hfparish.net.
Catechesis/Religious Program—Karen Coughlin, D.R.E. Students 445.

EDGARTOWN, DUKES CO., ST. ELIZABETH (1925) Closed. For inquiries for parish records contact Good Shepherd Parish, Oak Bluffs.

FAIRHAVEN, BRISTOL CO.

1—ST. JOSEPH'S (1905) Rev. Thomas McElroy, SS.CC.; Deacons Robert Lorenzo; Douglas Medeiros.
41 Walnut St., 02719.
Res.: 74 Spring St., 02719. Tel: 508-994-9714; Fax: 508-979-4659. Email: stjosephparish@comcast.net.
School—(Grades PreK-8), Spring St. and Homestead Ave., 02719. Tel: 508-996-1983; Fax: 508-996-1998. Ms. Julie Vareika, Prin. Lay Teachers 11; Students 234.
Catechesis/Religious Program—Tel: 508-994-8679. Mary Lorenzo, D.R.E. Students 150.

2—ST. MARY'S (1933) Rev. Patrick Killilea, SS.CC.; Deacon Bruce Bonneau.
Res.: 41 Harding Rd., 02719. Tel: 508-992-7300; Fax: 508-992-0685. Email: stmarysfairhaven@comcast.com. Web: www.sscc.org/stmaryfhvn.
Catechesis/Religious Program—Tel: 508-992-8721. Sr. Eleanor Cyr, SS.CC., D.R.E. Students 238.

FALMOUTH, BARNSTABLE CO., ST. PATRICK'S (1928) [CEM] Rev. Msgr. John A. Perry; Rev. James Doherty, C.S.C; Deacons Patrick J. Mahoney; John E. Simonis. In Res., Rev. Messias Alburquerque.
Res.: 511 Main St., P.O. Box 569, 02541. Tel: 508-548-1065; Fax: 508-495-0875. Web: www.stpatricksonline.org.
Res.: 30 Deacons Ave., 02540.
Catechesis/Religious Program—Tel: 508-548-2306. Cynthia O'Connor, D.R.E. Students 189.
Chapel—*St. Thomas* Falmouth Heights Rd., 02540.

HYANNIS, BARNSTABLE CO., ST. FRANCIS XAVIER'S (1904) [CEM 2] Revs. Daniel W. Lacroix; Peter J. Fournier, Parochial Vicar; Deacons Richard M. Dresser; Richard J. Murphy.
Res.: 21 Cross St., 02601. Tel: 508-775-0818; Fax: 508-771-5940. Email: stfrancis@stfrancishyannis.org. Web: stfrancishyannis.org.
School—(Grades 5-8), 33 Cross St., 02601. Tel: 508-771-7200; Fax: 508-771-7233. Robert H. Deburro, Headmaster. Lay Teachers 21; Students 253.
Catechesis/Religious Program—Tel: 508-775-6200; Fax: 508-771-7233. Mrs. Mary Offiler, D.R.E. Students 88.
Mission—*Sacred Heart Chapel* 32 Summer St., Yarmouth Port, Barnstable Co. 02675.

MANSFIELD, BRISTOL CO., ST. MARY'S (1894) [CEM] Rev. Msgr. Stephen J. Avila; Rev. William M. Sylvia, Parochial Vicar; Sr. Ann William Publicover, M.S.B.T., Pastoral Min.; Deacon Thomas P. Palanza.
Res.: 330 Pratt St., 02048-1581. Tel: 508-339-2981; Fax: 508-339-0612. Email: office@stmarymans.org. Web: www.stmarymans.org.
School—Tel: 508-339-4800; Fax: 508-337-2063. Email: info@stmarymansschool.org. Web: www.stmarymansschool.org. Gayle N. Riley, Prin. Religious 2; Lay Teachers 10; Students 219.
Catechesis/Religious Program—Tel: 508-339-4621; 508-339-2064 Confirmation. Mrs. Ellen Westlund, D.R.E.; Jeffrey Cahill, Dir. Youth Min. Students 1,713.

MARION, PLYMOUTH CO., ST. RITA'S (1972) Rev. Paul A. Caron.
Res.: 113 Front St., Box 902, 02738. Tel: 508-748-1497; Fax: 508-748-0604. Email: stritamarion@comcast.net.

Catechesis/Religious Program—Tel: 508-748-2072. Email: stritamarion@comcast.net. Theresa Fitzpatrick, D.R.E. Students 164.

MASHPEE, BARNSTABLE CO., CHRIST THE KING (1984) Rev. Msgr. Daniel F. Hoye; Sr. Dympna Smith, R.S.M., Pastoral Assoc.; Deacons Robert D. Lemay, Pastoral Assoc.; Gregory J. Beckel; Frank D. Fantasia.
The Commons: P.O. Box 1800, 02649. Tel: 508-477-7700; Fax: 508-477-8158. Email: ctk@cape.com. Web: www.christthekingparish.com.
Catechesis/Religious Program—Tel: 508-477-7700, Ext. 21. Sisters Claire Sinotte, O.P., D.R.E.; Annette Roach, O.P., Faith Formation Coord.; Shirley Agnew, R.S.M., Faith Formation. Students 412.

MATTAPOISETT, PLYMOUTH CO., ST. ANTHONY'S (1908) [CEM] Rev. Paul A. Caron.
Mailing Address: P.O. Box 501, 02739-0501.
Res.: 22 Barstow St., 02739. Tel: 508-758-3719; Fax: 508-758-3735. Email: st.anthony@verizon.net. Web: www.mystanthonys.org.
Catechesis/Religious Program—Tel: 508-758-3735. Email: stanthony.ed@verizon.net. Ms. Mary Chaplain, D.R.E. Students 300.

NANTUCKET, NANTUCKET CO., ST. MARY'S, OUR LADY OF THE ISLE (1903) [CEM] Rev. Paul E. Canuel; Deacon Donald L. Battiston.
Res.: 6 Orange St., P.O. Box 1168, 02554. Tel: 508-228-0100; Fax: 508-325-7991. Email: stmarys@nantucket.net. Web: www.stmarysnantucket.org.
Catechesis/Religious Program—Tel: 508-228-4852. Ms. Elaine Boehm, D.R.E. Students 240.

NEW BEDFORD, BRISTOL CO.

1—ST. ANNE (1908), (French), Closed. For inquiries for parish records contact Our Lady of Guadalupe Parish, New Bedford.

2—ST. ANTHONY OF PADUA'S (1895), (French), Rev. Roger J. Landry.
Res.: 1359 Acushnet Ave., 02746. Tel: 508-993-1691; Fax: 508-999-4775. Email: fatherlandry@saintanthonynewbedford.com. Web: www.saintanthonynewbedford.com.
Catechesis/Religious Program—Marijanna Lokitis, Youth Min.; Philip Martin, D.R.E. Students 53.
Convent—106 Bullard St., 02746.

3—ST. CASIMIR (1927), (Polish), Closed. For inquiries for parish records, please see Our Lady of Perpetual Help, New Bedford.

4—ST. FRANCIS OF ASSISI (1928), (Italian), Rev. Kevin Harrington.
Res.: 247 North St., 02740. Tel: 508-997-7732; Fax: 508-991-6630. Email: jbelli72@comcast.net.
Catechesis/Religious Program—Students 34.

5—ST. HEDWIG, Closed. For inquiries for Parish records, please contact Our Lady of Guadalupe, New Bedford.

6—HOLY NAME, Merged with Sacred Heart, New Bedford to form Holy Name of the Sacred Heart of Jesus, New Bedford.

7—HOLY NAME OF THE SACRED HEART OF JESUS (1999) Rev. Robert A. Oliveira; Deacon Eugene H. Sasseville.
Res.: 121 Mt. Pleasant St., 02740. Tel: 508-992-3184; Fax: 508-984-3406. Email: holynamesacredheartparish@comcast.net.
School—(Grades PreK-8) Tel: 508-993-3547; Fax: 508-993-8277. Ms. Cecilia Felix, Prin. Sisters 1; Lay Teachers 17; Students 290.
Catechesis/Religious Program—Tel: 508-996-8654. Theodore Machado, D.R.E. Students 180.

8—ST. JAMES (1888) Closed. For inquiries for parish records contact Our Lady of Guadalupe Parish, New Bedford.

9—ST. JOHN THE BAPTIST (1871), (Portuguese), [CEM] Very Rev. John J. Oliveira; Deacon Paul J. Macedo.
Res.: 344 County St., 02740. Tel: 508-992-7727; Fax: 508-997-1462.
Catechesis/Religious Program—Tel: 508-996-3087. Ms. Marge Ferreira, D.R.E. Students 123.

10—ST. JOSEPH (1910) Merged with St. Theresa, New Bedford to form St. Joseph-St. Therese, New Bedford.

11—ST. JOSEPH-ST. THERESE (1999) Rev. Philip N. Hamel.
Res.: 51 Duncan St., 02745-6108. Tel: 508-995-5235; Fax: 508-995-7266. Email: stjosstherese@aol.com.
School—(Grades PreK-8), 35 Kearsarge St., 02745-6117. Tel: 508-995-2264; Fax: 508-995-0038. Sherri Swainamer, Prin. Religious 1; Lay Teachers 13; Students 153.
Catechesis/Religious Program—Fax: 508-995-7266. Students 143.

12—ST. KILIAN (1896) Rev. Hugo G. Cardenas, I.V.E.
Res.: 306 Ashley Blvd., 02746. Tel: 508-992-7587; Fax: 508-994-0281.
Catechesis/Religious Program—Fax: 508-994-0281. Ana Aldarondo, D.R.E. Students 78.

13—ST. LAWRENCE MARTYR (1821) Rev. Marek Chmurski; Deacon Maurice A. Ouellette. In Res., Rev. Marc F. Fallon, C.S.C.
Res.: 110 Summer St., 02740. Tel: 508-992-4251; Fax: 508-984-4136. Email: stloffice@saintlawrencemartyr.com. Web: saintlawrencemartyr.com.
School—Holy Family-Holy Name, 91 Summer St., 02740. Tel: 508-993-3547; Fax: 508-993-8277. Web: www.hfhn.org. Ms. Cecilia Felix, Prin. Sisters 1; Lay Teachers 18; Students 302.
Catechesis/Religious Program—Tel: 508-993-3547. Mrs. Teresa Ouellette, D.R.E. Students 71.

14—ST. MARY'S (1927) Rev. Msgr. John J. Oliveira, P.A.
Res.: 106 Illinois St., 02745. Tel: 508-995-3593. Email: stmarysnb@gmail.com. Web: www.stmarysnb.com.
School—(Grades PreK-8), 115 Illinois St., 02745. Tel: 508-995-3696; Fax: 508-995-0840. Email: smselemnb@aol.com. Cathy Lacroix, Prin. Lay Teachers 11; Students 200.
Catechesis/Religious Program—Tel: 508-995-3693. Sue Richard, D.R.E. Students 186.

15—NUESTRA SENORA DE GUADALUPE (1993), (Hispanic), Closed. For inquiries for parish records contact Our Lady of Guadalupe Parish, New Bedford.

16—OUR LADY OF FATIMA (1966) Rev. John C. Ozug.
Res.: 4256 Acushnet Ave., 02745. Tel: 508-995-7351; Fax: 508-995-4401. Email: olofnb@comcast.net. Web: www.fatimanewbedford.org.
Parish Center—980 Tobey St., 02745.
Catechesis/Religious Program—Tel: 508-995-6685. Students 168.

17—OUR LADY OF GUADALUPE (2004) Rev. Richard D. Wilson; Deacon Lawrence A. St. Onge. In Res., Rev. Michael Joseph Fitzpatrick.
Res.: 233 County St., 02740. Tel: 508-992-9408; Fax: 508-990-0575. Email: rdwilson1@comcast.net. Web: www.saintjames-nb.org.
School—St. James-St. John, (Grades PreK-8), 180 Orchard St., 02740. Tel: 508-996-0534. Mrs. Cristina Raposo, Prin. Lay Teachers 11; Students 258.
Catechesis/Religious Program—Timothy Mitchell, D.R.E. Students 154.

18—OUR LADY OF MT. CARMEL (1902), (Portuguese), Very Rev. John J. Oliveira; Rev. Michael M. Camara, Parochial Vicar; Deacon Abilio Pires; Rev. William Rodrigues.
Res.: 230 Bonney St., 02744. Tel: 508-993-4704; Fax: 508-991-5536. Email: olmcnb@comcast.net.
Catechesis/Religious Program—Tel: 508-984-7097. Nancy Morin, D.R.E. Students 436.

19—OUR LADY OF PERPETUAL HELP (1905), (Polish), Rev. Roman Chwaliszewski, O.F.M.Conv.
Res.: 235 N. Front St., 02746. Tel: 508-992-9378; Fax: 508-993-4881. Email: olphrectory@comcast.net. Web: www.olphchurchnb.org.
Catechesis/Religious Program—Students 26.

20—OUR LADY OF THE ASSUMPTION (1905), (Cape Verdean), Rev. Christopher Santangelo, SS.CC.; Deacon Eduardo M. Pacheco.
47 S. 6th St., 02740. Tel: 508-994-7602 Parish Center; Fax: 508-994-9461.
Res. & Parish Center: 54 S. 6th St., 02740. Tel: 508-994-0106. Email: oloaoffice@verizon.net.

21—OUR LADY OF THE IMMACULATE CONCEPTION (1909), (Portuguese), Rev. Daniel O. Reis; Deacon Albertino F. Pires.
Res.: 136 Earle St., 02746. Tel: 508-992-9892; Fax: 508-992-9907. Email: i.conception@comcast.net.
Catechesis/Religious Program—Tel: 508-990-0249. Students 331.

22—SACRED HEART (1874), (French), Merged With Holy Name, New Bedford to form Holy Name of the Sacred Heart of Jesus, New Bedford.

23—ST. THERESA (1926), (French), Merged with St. Joseph's, New Bedford to form St. Joseph-St. Therese, New Bedford.

NORTH ATTLEBORO, BRISTOL CO.

1—ST. MARY'S (1890) [CEM] Rev. David A. Costa; Deacon James J. Meloni Jr.; Sr. Kathleen Corrigan, S.U.S.C., Pastoral Assoc.
Res.: 14 Park St., 02760. Tel: 508-695-6161; Fax: 508-695-5248. Email: stmary@noozi.com. Web: www.saintmaryna.com.
See St. Mary's-Sacred Heart Consolidated School, North Attleboro under Sacred Heart, North Attleboro details.
Catechesis/Religious Program—Tel: 508-695-3823. Email: michelecre@comcast.net. Michele Dillon, C.R.E. Students 338.

2—SACRED HEART (1904) Rev. David A. Costa; Deacon Joseph E. Regali; Sr. Kathleen Corrigan, S.U.S.C., Pastoral Assoc.
Res.: 58 Church St., 02760. Tel: 508-699-8383; Fax: 508-699-7016. Email: shna@comcast.net. Web: www.shna.org.
School—St. Mary-Sacred Heart School, 57 Richards Ave., 02760. Tel: 508-695-3072; Fax: 508-695-9074. Email: smsh@comcast.net. Web: www.smsh-na.com. Mrs. Denise M. Peixoto, Prin. Religious 1; Lay Teachers 21; Students 218.
Catechesis/Religious Program—Tel: 508-643-9009. Mrs. Bernadette Marland, C.R.E. Students 364.

NORTH DARTMOUTH, BRISTOL CO., ST. JULIE BILLIART (1969) Revs. Gregory A. Mathias; Jay Mello, Parochial Vicar; Deacon Claude A. LeBlanc.
Res.: 494 Slocum Rd., 02747. Tel: 508-993-2351; Fax: 508-993-2437. Email: stjuliebilliart@gmail.com. Web: www.saintjulies.org.
Catechesis/Religious Program—Tel: 508-990-0287. Peter Healy, D.R.E.; Paula Raposo, Adult Education; David Dearden, Youth Min. Students 665.

NORTH DIGHTON, BRISTOL CO.

1—ST. JOSEPH'S (1913) [JC 2] Closed. For inquiries for parish records contact St. Nicholas of Myra Parish, North Dighton.

2—ST. NICHOLAS OF MYRA PARISH (2008) Rev. Timothy J. Goldrick.
499 Spring St., P.O. Box 564, 02764. Tel: 508-822-1425; Fax: 508-822-3886. Email: st.nicholasofmyra@comcast.net. Web: saintnicholasofmyra.org.
Res.: 2039 County St., Dighton, 02715. Tel: 508-669-6743.
Catechesis/Religious Program—Gregory Bettencourt, D.R.E. Students 465.

NORTH EASTON, BRISTOL CO., IMMACULATE CONCEPTION (1871) [CEM] Rev. James W. Fahey.
Res.: 193 Main St., 02356. Tel: 508-238-3232; Fax: 508-238-7849. Email: rectory@icceaston.org. Web: www.icceaston.org.
Catechesis/Religious Program—Tel: 508-238-3230; Fax: 508-238-7849. Email: religioused@icceaston.org. Students 540.

NORTH FALMOUTH, BARNSTABLE CO., ST. ELIZABETH SETON (1977) Rev. Arnold R. Medeiros; Deacons William A. Martin; Vincent J. Coates Jr.; Peter M. Guresh.
Res.: 481 Quaker Rd., Box 861, 02556. Tel: 508-563-7770; Fax: 508-563-7794. Email: saintelizabethseton@comcast.net. Web: www.stelizabethseton.net.
Catechesis/Religious Program—Tel: 508-563-7774. Margaret Bushy, D.R.E. Students 251.

NORTON, BRISTOL CO., ST. MARY'S (1925) Rev. Marc P. Tremblay; Deacons Michael T. Zonghetti; John Conner.
Res.: 133 S. Worcester St., 02766-0430. Tel: 508-285-4462; Fax: 508-285-5589. Email: stmarysnorton@comcast.net. Web: www.stmarysnorton.com.
Catechesis/Religious Program—1 Powers St., 02766. Tel: 508-285-3237. Web: www.saintmaryccd.org. Laura Vergow, Faith Formation Coord. Students 855.

OAK BLUFFS, DUKES CO.

1—GOOD SHEPHERD (2004) [CEM] Revs. Michael R. Nagle; Messias Alburquerque; Deacons Fred Lapiana; Karl G. Buder.
Mailing Address: P.O. Box 1058, Vineyard Haven, 02568. Tel: 508-693-0342. Email: mnagle@vineyard.net. Web: mvcatholic.net.
Res.: 56 Franklin St., Vineyard Haven, 02568. Fax: 508-693-8517. Email: frnagle@goodshepherdmv.com. Web: www.goodshepherdmv.com.
Res.: 86 Main St., P.O. Box 156, Edgartown, 02539.
Church: 22 Massasoit Ave., 02557.
Catechesis/Religious Program—55 School St., 02557. Martha Rheaume, D.R.E. Students 172.

2—SACRED HEART (1880) [CEM] Closed. For inquiries for parish records contact Good Shepherd Parish, Oak Bluffs.

ORLEANS, BARNSTABLE CO., ST. JOAN OF ARC (1947) Rev. Robert J. Powell; Deacons Donald Joslin; Norman McEnaney; John Twerago.
Res.: 61 Canal Rd., 02653. Tel: 508-255-0170; Fax: 508-240-6741. Email: joanarc@c4.net. Web: joanarc.org.
Catechesis/Religious Program—Tel: 508-255-1257. Email: religed@c4.net. Judith Burt-Walker, D.R.E. Students 160.

OSTERVILLE, BARNSTABLE CO., OUR LADY OF THE ASSUMPTION (1928) Rev. Philip A. Davignon; Deacon Paul K. Roma.
Res.: 76 Wianno Ave., P.O. Box E., 02655. Tel: 508-428-2011; Fax: 508-428-2891. Web: www.assumption-capecod.org.
Church: 86 Wianno Ave., P.O. Box E, 02655.
Catechesis/Religious Program—Students 138.

POCASSET, BARNSTABLE CO., ST. JOHN THE EVANGELIST (1969) Rev. Robert C. Donovan; Deacons Leonard C. Dexter Jr.; David E. Pierce.
Res.: 15 Virginia Rd., P.O. Box 1558, 02559. Tel: 508-563-3121; 508-563-5887; Fax: 508-563-3102. Email: stjohnpocasset@aol.com; stjohn.rectory@verizon.net. Web: stjohnspocasset.org.
Catechesis/Religious Program—Liz Henry, D.R.E. Students 234.

PROVINCETOWN, BARNSTABLE CO., ST. PETER THE APOSTLE (1874) [CEM] Rev. Henry J. Dahl; Deacons

Joseph K. Kane; Steven M. Minninger.
Res.: 11 Prince St., 02657. Tel: 508-487-0095; Fax: 508-487-2564. Email: stpetersptown@aol.com. Web: www.stpeters-provincetown.4lpi.com.
Catechesis/Religious Program—Students 59.

RAYNHAM CENTER, BRISTOL CO., ST. ANN (1960) Rev. Michael K. McManus; Deacon Joseph A. McGinley.
Res.: 660 N. Main St., P.O. Box 247, 02768. Tel: 508-823-9833; 508-823-9834; Fax: 508-823-8935. Email: office@stannsraynham.org. Web: www.stannsraynham.org.
Catechesis/Religious Program—725 N. Main St., Box 247, 02768. Tel: 508-824-9021; Fax: 508-824-1090. Kristin Kreckler, D.R.E.; Patricia Desrochers, D.R.E. Students 965.

SEEKONK, BRISTOL CO.

1—ST. MARY'S (1906) Rev. Thomas L. Rita. In Res., Rev. Michel G. Corriveau, C.P.M.
Res.: 385 Central Ave., 02771. Tel: 508-399-8440; Fax: 508-399-7398. Email: stmaryseekonk@comcast.net.
Catechesis/Religious Program—Tel: 508-399-7534. James Souza, D.R.E. Students 468.

2—OUR LADY OF MT. CARMEL (1922) Revs. Brian J. Harrington; Thomas E. Costa, Parochial Vicar; Deacon Richard G. Lemay; Barbara A. Wenc, Business Mgr.
Res.: 984 Taunton Ave., P.O. Box 519, 02771. Tel: 508-336-5549; Fax: 508-336-9010. Email: mountcarmel1@verizon.net. Web: www.mountcarmel1.com.
Catechesis/Religious Program—1040 Taunton Ave., 02771. Tel: 508-336-8608 (Grades 1-6); 508-336-9015 (Grades 7-8). Christine Gregorek, Faith Formation Coord.; Sr. Irene Rivard, F.C.S.C.J., D.R.E. Students 563.

SOMERSET, BRISTOL CO.

1—ST. JOHN OF GOD (1928), (Portuguese), [CEM] Rev. Raul M. Lagoa; Deacon Robert A. Faria. In Res., Rev. Luciano J. de M. Pereira (Retired).
Res.: 996 Brayton Ave., Box 113, 02726. Tel: 508-678-5513; Fax: 508-678-6458. Web: stjohnofgodsomerset.org.
Catechesis/Religious Program—1036 Brayton Ave., 02726. Tel: 508-678-5139. Students 379.

2—ST. PATRICK'S (1883) [CEM] Rev. Marek S. Tuptynski; Deacon Edward Hussey; Anne Bouchard, Pastoral Assoc.
Res.: 306 South St., 02726-5617. Tel: 508-672-1523; Fax: 508-675-5787. Email: stpatparish@comcast.net. Web: www.stpatricksomerset.com.
Catechesis/Religious Program—Tel: 508-675-1073. Janet Rausch, D.R.E.; Gregory J. Wholean, D.R.E. Students 267.

3—ST. THOMAS MORE (1949) Rev. Msgr. Edmund J. Fitzgerald; Deacon Victor Haddad.
Res.: 386 Luther Ave., 02726. Tel: 508-673-7831; Fax: 508-730-1396. Email: stmsomerset@comcast.net. Web: home.comcast.net/~stmsomerset.
Catechesis/Religious Program—Tel: 508-679-1236. Janis Johnson, D.R.E. Students 215.

SOUTH DARTMOUTH, BRISTOL CO., ST. MARY'S (1930) Revs. John A. Gomes; Francis J. Moy, S.J.
Res.: 783 Dartmouth St., 02748. Tel: 508-992-7163; Fax: 508-992-5209. Email: info@stmarysdartmouth.org. Web: www.stmarysdartmouth.org.
Catechesis/Religious Program—789 Dartmouth St., 02748. Tel: 508-992-7505. Ken Sylvia, D.R.E. (Grades 7-9); Beni Costa-Reedy, Faith Formation Coord.; David Dearden, Youth Min. Students 504.

SOUTH EASTON, BRISTOL CO., HOLY CROSS (1967) Revs. James Fenstermaker, C.S.C.; Lawrence A. Jerge, C.S.C.; Deacon George Zarella.
Res.: 225 Purchase St., 02375. Tel: 508-238-2235; Fax: 508-238-0500. Web: www.holycrosseaston.org. Email: info@holycrosseaston.org.
Catechesis/Religious Program—Anne Tarallo, D.R.E. Students 1,125.

SOUTH YARMOUTH, BARNSTABLE CO., ST. PIUS TENTH (1954) Very Rev. George C. Bellenoit; Revs. David C. Deston Jr.; John M. Murray; Deacons David Akin; Thomas Bailey; William Gallerizzo; Michael C. Hickey; Richard C. Zeich, (Retired).
Res.: 5 Barbara St., 02664. Tel: 508-398-2248; Fax: 508-398-7233. Email: stpiusxoffice@comcast.net. Web: www.stpiusxsy.com.
School—(Grades PreK-8), 321 Wood Rd., 02664. Tel: 508-398-6112; Fax: 508-398-6113. Email: info@spxschool.org. Web: www.spxschool.org. Mr. John Regan, Prin. Lay Teachers 16; Students 208.
Catechesis/Religious Program—Station Ave., 02664. Tel: 508-394-0709; 508-394-0708. Email: stpiusxreled@comcast.net. Mrs. Jean Kelly, D.R.E. Students 427.
Chapel—Bass River, Our Lady of the Highway Rte. 28, 02664. Tel: 508-760-3332.

SWANSEA, BRISTOL CO.

1—ST. DOMINIC'S (1911) Rev. Joseph F. Viveiros.
Res.: 1277 Grand Army Hwy., 02777. Tel: 508-675-7206; Fax: 508-675-4626.
Catechesis/Religious Program—Tel: 508-675-7002. Students 280.

2—SAINT FRANCIS OF ASSISI (1922) Rev. Michael A. Ciryak.
Church: 530 Gardner's Neck Rd., 02777.
Res.: 270 Ocean Grove Ave., 02777. Tel: 508-673-2808; Fax: 508-672-6241. Email: stfrancisswansea@comcast.net. Web: www.stfrancisswansea.com.
Catechesis/Religious Program—Tel: 508-674-0024. Students 285.

3—ST. LOUIS DE FRANCE (1928), (French), Rev. Richard R. Gendreau; Deacon Robert G.L. Normandin.
Res.: 56 Buffington St., 02777. Tel: 508-674-1103; Fax: 508-672-8889. Email: sldfc@comcast.net. Web: stlouisdefrance.net.
Catechesis/Religious Program—Tel: 508-672-0615. Mrs. Paulette J. Normandin, D.R.E. Students 612.

4—ST. MICHAEL'S, Closed. For inquiries for parish records please see Saint Francis of Assisi, Swansea

5—OUR LADY OF FATIMA (1958) Closed. For inquiries for parish records, please see Saint Francis of Assisi, Swansea.

TAUNTON, BRISTOL CO.

1—SAINT ANDREW THE APOSTLE PARISH (2008) Rev. Timothy P. Reis; Deacon Alan J. Thadeu.
Res.: 19 Kilmer Ave., 02780. Tel: 508-824-5577; Fax: 508-822-1401. Email: standrewtaunton@comcast.net. Web: www.standrewtaunton.org.
Catechesis/Religious Program—Tel: 508-822-9672. Students 486.

2—ANNUNCIATION OF THE LORD (2001) Rev. Timothy Paul Driscoll. In Res., Rev. Kevin A. Cook.
Res.: 311 Somerset Ave., 02780. Tel: 508-823-2521; Fax: 508-823-2522. Web: www.annunciationtaunton.com.
School—Our Lady of Lourdes, (Grades K-5), 52 First St., 02780. Tel: 508-822-3746; Fax: 508-822-1450. Lincoln De Moura, Prin. Sisters 3; Lay Teachers 5; Students 121.
Catechesis/Religious Program—Tel: 508-824-6791. Susan Finney, D.R.E. Students 230.
Convent—49 First St., 02780. Tel: 508-822-0357.

3—ST. ANTHONY'S (1903), (Portuguese), Rev. Henry S. Arruda; Deacon Jose H. Medina.
Res.: 126 School St., 02780. Tel: 508-822-0714; Fax: 508-828-5844. Email: hsarruda@comcast.net. Web: www.stanthonytaunton.com.
Catechesis/Religious Program—Tel: 508-824-6241. Jane R. Santos, D.R.E.; Annalee Nystrom, D.R.E. Students 237.

4—ST. JAMES (1904), (French), Closed. For inquiries for parish records contact St. Jude the Apostle Parish, Taunton.

5—ST. JOSEPH'S (1896) Closed. For inquiries for parish records contact St. Andrew the Apostle Parish.

6—ST. JUDE THE APOSTLE (2007) Rev. John J. Perry; Deacon Philip E. Bedard.
Mailing Address: 249 Whittenton St., 02780. Tel: 508-824-3330; Fax: 508-880-3865. Email: whittenton@verizon.net. In Res., Rev. Edward A. Murphy.
Res.: 438 Bay St, 02780. Tel: 508-824-4545.
Catechesis/Religious Program—Tel: 508-824-3535. Students 240.
Convent—279 Whittenton St., 02780. Tel: 508-824-8946.

7—ST. MARY'S (1828) Rev. William H. Kelley, C.S.C. In Res., Revs. John P. Phalen, C.S.C.; David S. Marcham.
Res.: 14 St. Mary's Square, 02780. Tel: 508-822-7116; Fax: 508-822-7117. Email: saintmarystaunton@verizon.net.
School—(Grades PreK-5), 106 Washington St., 02780. Tel: 508-822-9480; Fax: 508-822-7164. Web: www.saintmarystaunton.com. Mr. Brian Cote, Prin.; Mrs. Sandra Parker, Asst. Prin. Lay Teachers 17; Students 276.
Catechesis/Religious Program—Tel: 508-822-7116; Fax: 508-822-7117. Judith Silvia, D.R.E. Students 165.
Dolan Parish Center—

8—OUR LADY OF LOURDES (1905), (Portuguese), Merged with Sacred Heart, Taunton to form Annunciation of the Lord, Taunton.

9—OUR LADY OF THE HOLY ROSARY (1909), (Polish), [JC] Rev. David M. Stopyra, O.F.M.Conv.
Res.: 80 Bay St., 02780. Tel: 508-823-3046; Fax: 508-823-0585. Email: myholyrosary@comcast.net. Web: holyrosarytaunton.org.
Catechesis/Religious Program—Tel: 508-824-3910. Students 62.

10—OUR LADY OF THE IMMACULATE CONCEPTION (1883) Closed. For inquiries for parish records contact St. Jude the Apostle Parish, Taunton.

11—ST. PAUL'S (1904) Closed. For inquiries for parish records contact St. Andrew the Apostle Parish.

12—SACRED HEART (1873) Merged with Our Lady of Lourdes, Taunton to form Annunciation of the Lord, Taunton.

VINEYARD HAVEN, DUKES CO., ST. AUGUSTINE (1962) Closed. For inquiries for parish records contact Good Shepherd Parish, Oak Bluffs.

WAREHAM, PLYMOUTH CO., ST. PATRICK'S (1911) [CEM] Revs. John M. Sullivan; Ronnie Paul Floyd, Parochial Vicar; Deacons Daniel M. Donovan; Henry A. Gardyna.
Res.: 82 High St., P.O. Box 271, 02571-0271. Tel: 508-295-2411; Fax: 508-295-2417. Email: stpatrickwareham@verizon.net. Web: stpatricks.netfirms.com.
Catechesis/Religious Program—Tel: 508-295-0780; Fax: 508-295-2417. Email: stpatricksre@yahoo.com. Paula Wilk, D.R.E. Students 388.
Mission—St. Anthony Gault Rd., Plymouth Co. 02571.

WELLFLEET, BARNSTABLE CO., OUR LADY OF LOURDES (1911) [CEM 2] Rev. John F. Andrews; Deacons Joseph K. Kane; Steven M. Minninger.
Res.: 137 Fresh Brook Ln., P.O. Box 1414, 02667-1414. Tel: 508-349-2222; Fax: 508-349-9612. Email: webmaster@ololwellfleet.org. Web: www.ololwellfleet.org.
Catechesis/Religious Program—Students 32.
Mission—Visitation Church 930 Massasoit Rd., North Eastham, Barnstable Co. 02651. Fax: 508-349-9612.

WEST HARWICH, BARNSTABLE CO., HOLY TRINITY (1918) [CEM] Revs. Edward J. Healey; Maurice O. Gauvin, Parochial Vicar; Deacons John W. Foley; Vincent P. Walsh; Ralph F. Cox. In Res., Rev. Carlos Patino Villa.
Res.: 246 Rte. 28, 02671. Tel: 508-432-4000; Fax: 508-432-3494. Email: htchurch@comcast.net. Web: www.htchurch.4lpi.com.
School—(Grades PreK-5), 245 Main St., 02671. Tel: 508-432-8216; Fax: 508-432-9349. Linda Mattson, Prin. Lay Teachers 12; Students 92.
Catechesis/Religious Program—Tel: 508-432-2898. Catherine Kane, D.R.E. Students 199.
Mission—Our Lady of the Annunciation [CEM] P.O. Box 428, Dennis Port, Barnstable Co. 02671. Upper County Rd., Dennis Port, 02639.

WESTPORT, BRISTOL CO.

1—ST. GEORGE'S (1914) Rev. Gerard A. Hebert. In Res., Rev. Msgr. Edmond R. Levesque (Retired).
Res.: 12 Highland Ave., 02790. Tel: 508-636-4965; Fax: 508-636-4188.
Catechesis/Religious Program—Students 240.

2—ST. JOHN THE BAPTIST (1930) Rev. Leonard P. Hindsley.
Res.: 945 Main Rd., Box 3328, 02790. Tel: 508-636-2251; Fax: 508-636-8306. Email: stjb@sprintout.net. Web: stjohnthebaptistwestport.org.
Catechesis/Religious Program—924 Main Rd., P.O. Box 3328, 02790. Tel: 508-636-5506. Email: stjohnccd@sprintout.net. Susan Orzeck, D.R.E. Students 357.

3—OUR LADY OF GRACE (1954) Rev. Horace J. Travassos.
Res.: 569 Sanford Rd., 02790. Tel: 508-674-6271; Fax: 508-675-4128. Email: ologwestportma@aol.com.
Catechesis/Religious Program—Tel: 508-675-5857. Students 172.

WOODS HOLE, BARNSTABLE CO., ST. JOSEPH'S (1882) Rev. Joseph H. Mauritzen.
Church: 33 Millfield St., P.O. Box 3, 02543. Tel: 508-548-0990; Fax: 508-457-7849. Email: stjosephchurch@verizon.net.
Catechesis/Religious Program—Tel: 508-540-3723. Students 10.

Chaplains of Public Institutions

BARNSTABLE. *Barnstable County House of Correction.* 82 High St., P.O. Box 271, Wareham, 02571. Deacon Daniel M. Donovan, Coord.

NEW BEDFORD. *Bristol Co. House of Correction & Eastern Massachusetts Correctional Alcohol Center.*
824 Tucker Rd., North Dartmouth, 02747. Tel: 508-996-2413. Vacant.

Awaiting Assignment:
Revs.—
Blyskosz, Joseph J.
Harrington, John P.
Kozanko, Andrzej J.
Swiercz, Pawel A.

Special Assignment:
Rev.—
Pregana, Craig A., St. Rose of Lima & St. Francis of Assisi, Casa Cural, Guaimaca, Honduras.

Graduate Studies:
Revs.—
Cabral, Jeffrey, Little Flower Rectory, 5607 Massachusetts Ave., Bethesda, MD 20816-1930.
Kalinowski, Dariusz, 3015 4th St. N.E., Washington, DC 20017.
Pignato, David A., S.T.L., Pontifical North American College, Casa Santa Maria Via del'Umilta 30, Rome 00187 Italy.

On Duty Outside the Diocese:
Revs.—
Dominguez, Ramon, McLean, VA
Engo, Michael, Padre Pio Friary, 345 N. 63rd St., Philadelphia, PA 19139.
Kuhn, Michael F., McLean, VA
Magee, Patrick, St. Theresa Parish, 80 13th Ave., Paterson, NJ 07544.
Pacholczyk, Tadeusz, The National Catholic Bioethics Center, 6399 Drexel Rd., Philadelphia, PA 19151.
Sharland, David, McLean, VA

Absent on Sick Leave:
Rev.—
Fitzpatrick, James M.

Retired:
Rev. Msgrs.—
Harrington, Thomas J., J.C.L., 375 Elsbree St., 02720.
Levesque, Edmond R., 12 Highland Ave., Westport, 02790.
Moore, John F., P.O. Box 2114, Cotuit, 02635.
Munroe, Henry T., P.A., 375 Elsbree St., 02720.
Regan, John J., P.O. Box 1094, North Falmouth, 02556.
Smith, John J., 375 Elsbree St., 02720.
Tosti, Ronald A., P.O. Box 814, Cotuit, 02635-0814.
Revs.—
Almeida, George F., 375 Elsbree St., 02720.
Barnwell, Gerald P., 430 Eastern Ave., 02723.
Blottman, William P., 375 Elsbree St., 02720.
Boivin, Louis R., 2446-2474 Highland Ave., 02720.
Bousquet, Roland, 53 California St., 02723-3905.
Buckley, James F., 209 Union St., Yarmouthport, 02675.
Buote, Martin L., 54 Salisbury St., 02744.
Burns, Edward J., 4234 N. Main St., Apt. 301, 02720.
Byington, Edward J., P.O. Box 571, Taunton, 02780.
Campbell, William G., 16 White Pine Ave., W., West Wareham, 02576.
Cardoso, Luis A., 375 Elsbree St., 02720.
Delano, Kenneth J., 22 Ingell St., Taunton, 02780.
Dos Santos, Jose A.F., 375 Elsbree St., 02720.
Driscoll, John P., 375 Elsbree St., 02720.
Ferreira, Manuel P., 375 Elsbree St., 02720.
Freitas, Daniel L., P.O. Box 411154, Melbourne, FL 32941-1154.
Graziano, Peter N., S.T.L., M.A., M.S.W., 185 Woodside Ave., Winthrop, 02152.
Keenan, Terence, 375 Elsbree St., 02720.
Kirby, Robert F., 50 Otis Trailer Village, Buzzards Bay, 02542-1302.
Kropiwnicki, Henry, 19 Rutland St., 02745-5830.
Lamb, Paul T., 15 Toby Cir., Hyannis, 02601.
LeDuc, Roger D., P.O. Box 2538, Tehachapi, CA 93581-2538.
Levesque, Roger J., 818 Middle St., 02721-1734.
Lopes, Thomas C., P.O. Box 4321, Vineyard Haven, 02568.
McLellan, James R., 375 Elsbree St., 02720.
Mullaney, Leonard M., 523 River Rd., Westport, 02790.
Murphy, Clarence, 375 Elsbree St., 02720.
Pereira, Luciano J., P.O. Box 113, Somerset, 02726.
Ryan, Albert J., 375 Elsbree St., 02720.
Shovelton, Gerald T., 419 Chula Vista Ave., Lady Lake, FL 32159.
Shovelton, William J., 419 Chula Vista Ave., Lady Lake, FL 32159.
Wall, Barry W., 375 Elsbree St., 02720.
Wallace, Francis X., P.O. Box 3737, Pocasset, 02559.
Wingate, Arthur K., 375 Elsbree St., 02720.

Permanent Deacons:
Akin, David P., St. Pius X, South Yarmouth
Alence, Robert, (Retired), Corpus Christi, East Sandwich
Bailey, Thomas C., (Retired), St. Pius Tenth, South Yarmouth
Barrett, James M., Our Lady of Victory, Centerville
Battiston, Donald L., St. Mary, Our Lady of the Isle, Nantucket
Beckel, Gregory J., Christ the King, Mashpee
Bedard, Philip E., St. Jude the Apostle, Taunton
Biron, Donald R., Our Lady of the Cape, Brewster
Bonneau, Bruce J., St. Mary, Fairhaven
Boucher, David R., Corpus Christi, Sandwich
Bousquet, Louis A., (Unassigned)
Branco, John F., Good Shepherd & Holy Trinity, Fall River
Buder, Karl G., Good Shepherd, Martha's Vineyard
Camacho, Francis, Florida
Cipriano, A. Anthony, Fall River
Coates, Vincent, Jr., (Retired), St. Elizabeth Seton, North Falmouth
Connor, John, St. Mary, Norton; Boston, MA
Cook, Chester O., (Retired), St. Peter the Apostle, Provincetown
Cote, Peter R., St. Mary's Cathedral, Fall River
Cox, Ralph F., (Retired), Holy Trinity, West Harwich
Dexter, Leonard C., Jr., St. John the Evangelist, Pocasset
Donovan, Daniel M., St. Patrick, Wareham
Dresser, Richard M., (Retired), St. Francis Xavier, Hyannis
Drinkwater, Oscar T., (Retired), South Carolina
Emmert, John J., (Unassigned)
Fantasia, Frank D., Christ the King, Mashpee
Faria, Robert A., St. John of God, Somerset
Fitzpatrick, John J., Holy Family, East Taunton
Foley, John W., Holy Trinity, West Harwich
Fournier, Paul M., St. Joseph & Holy Ghost, Attleboro
Gallerizzo, William, St. Pius X, South Yarmouth; Washington
Gardyna, Henry A., (Retired), St. Patrick, Wareham; Boston, MA
Gendron, Ernest J., St. Margaret, Buzzards Bay
Grant, John D., (Unassigned)
Gundlach, Richard J., St. Mark, Attleboro Falls
Guresh, Peter M., St. Elizabeth Seton, North Falmouth
Guy, Michael P., New Hampshire
Haddad, Victor, (Retired), St. Thomas More, Somerset
Hickey, Michael C., St. Pius X, South Yarmouth; Boston, MA
Hill, Robert J., (Retired)
Hussey, Edward J., St. Patrick, Somerset
Joslin, Donald, St. Joan of Arc, Orleans; Syracuse, NY
Kane, Joseph K., Our Lady of Lourdes, Wellfleet; St. Peter the Apostle, Provincetown
LaChance, Arthur L., Jr., Corpus Christi, Sandwich
LaPiana, Fred G., III, Good Shepherd, Martha's Vineyard
Leavitt, James P., (Retired), Our Lady of the Cape, Brewster
LeBlanc, Claude A., St. Julie Billiart, North Dartmouth
Lemay, Richard G., Our Lady of Mt. Carmel, Seekonk
Lemay, Robert D., Christ the King, Mashpee
Liegey, Gabriel J., (Retired), Vermont
Lorenzo, Robert G., Camden, NJ; St. Joseph, Fairhaven
Lukac, Theodore E., Our Lady of Victory, Centerville
Macedo, Paul J., St. John the Baptist & Our Lady of Mt. Carmel, New Bedford
Mador, Joseph F., Holy Redeemer, Chatham
Mahoney, Patrick J., (Retired), St. Patrick, Falmouth
Malloy, Adelbert F., St. John the Evangelist, Attleboro
Martin, William A., St. Elizabeth Seton, North Falmouth
Massoud, Donald P., St. Anthony of the Desert, Fall River
Mattar, Jean E., Our Lady of Purgatory, New Bedford
McCarthy, Dana G., Florida
McEnaney, Norman F., St. Joan of Arc, Orleans
McGinley, Joseph A., St. Ann, Raynham
Medeiros, Douglas R., St. Joseph, Fairhaven
Medeiros, Joseph P., St. Michael, Fall River
Medina, Jose H., St. Anthony, Taunton
Meloni, James J., Jr., (Retired), St. Mary's, North Attleboro
Metilly, Paul, Florida
Minninger, Steven M., Our Lady of Lourdes, Wellfleet; St. Peter the Apostle, Provincetown
Mis, Franciszek W., (Retired), St. Stanislaus Church, Fall River
Moniz, John de A., Florida
Morency, Marcel G., (Retired), Our Lady of Fatima, New Bedford
Murphy, Richard J., St. Francis Xavier, Hyannis
Nogueira, Benjamin, Diocese of Worcester
Normandin, Robert G.L., St. Louis de France, Swansea
Norton, Victor K., Texas
O'Connell, Dennis G., Corpus Christi, Sandwich
Ouellette, Maurice A., St. Lawrence, New Bedford
Pacheco, Eduardo M., (Retired), Our Lady of the Assumption, New Bedford
Palanza, Thomas P., St. Mary, Mansfield
Pelland, Robert W., (Retired), Rhode Island
Pepin, David B., St. Francis Xavier, Acushnet
Pierce, David E., St. John the Evangelist, Pocasset
Pires, Abilio dos A., Our Lady of Mt. Carmel & St. John the Baptist, New Bedford
Pires, Albertino F., Our Lady of the Immaculate Conception, New Bedford
Racine, Leo W., (Retired), St. Joseph-St. Therese, New Bedford
Reardon, Jeremiah J., (Unassigned)
Regali, Joseph E., Sacred Heart, North Attleboro
Roma, Paul K., Our Lady of the Assumption, Osterville
Sasseville, Eugene H., Holy Name of the Sacred Heart of Jesus, New Bedford
Simonis, John E., St. Patrick, Falmouth
Souza, Thomas J., Espirito Santo, Fall River
St. Onge, Lawrence A., Our Lady of Guadalupe at St. James Church, New Bedford
Stenberg, Richard S., Holy Redeemer, Chatham; Bridgeport CT
Surprenant, Robert L., St. John Neumann, East Freetown
Thadeu, Alan J., St. Andrew the Apostle, Taunton
Thomas, Walter D., Florida
Twerago, John P., St. Joan of Arc, Orleans
Wallace, Forrest, Cincinnati, Ohio
Walsh, Vincent, (Retired), Holy Trinity, West Harwich
Welch, John, (Retired), St. Ann, Raynham
Zarella, George H., Holy Cross, South Easton
Zeich, Richard C., St. Pius X, South Yarmouth
Zonghetti, Michael T., St. Mary, Norton
Nasser, Andre P., (Retired), St. Anthony of the Desert, Fall River

INSTITUTIONS LOCATED IN THE DIOCESE

[A] COLLEGES AND UNIVERSITIES

NORTH EASTON. *Holy Cross Fathers Religious*, 480 Washington St., 02356. Tel: 508-238-5942; Fax: 508-238-1297. Email: jlack@hcep.com. Web: www.holycrosscsc.org. Revs. James R. Lackenmier, C.S.C., Supr.; Richard E. Gribble, C.S.C.; David J. Arthur, C.S.C.; Joseph F. Callahan, C.S.C.; Thomas L. Campbell; Rudolph V. Carchidi, C.S.C., Asst. Supr.; James W. Chichetto, C.S.C.; Mark T. Cregan, C.S.C.; John F. Denning, C.S.C.; Marc F. Fallon, C.S.C.; Thomas P. Gariepy, C.S.C.; Thomas M. Halkovic, C.S.C.; Bro. Harold Hathaway, C.S.C.; Revs. Francis J. Hurley, C.S.C.; Robert J. Kruse, C.S.C.; Bro. Patrick L. Lynch, C.S.C., Asst. Supr.; Revs. Bartley MacPhaidin, C.S.C.; Robert Malone, C.S.C.; James H. Phalan, C.S.C.; George Piggford, C.S.C.; Leo Polselli, C.S.C.; Richard J. Segreve, C.S.C.; Patrick J. Sullivan, C.S.C.; Francis M. Walsh, C.S.C.; Stephen S. Wilbricht, C.S.C.

Stonehill College (1948) 320 Washington St., 02357. Tel: 508-565-1301; Fax: 508-565-1432. Email: mcregan@stonehill.edu. Web: www.stonehill.edu. Revs. Mark T. Cregan, C.S.C., Pres.; Rudolph V. Carchidi, C.S.C.; James W. Chichetto, C.S.C.; John F. Denning, C.S.C.; Thomas P. Gariepy, C.S.C.; Richard E. Gribble, C.S.C.; Thomas M. Halkovic, C.S.C.; Francis J. Hurley, C.S.C.; Walter E. Jenkins, C.S.C., Dir. Campus Min.; Robert J. Kruse, C.S.C.; George Piggford, C.S.C.; Kevin P. Spicer, C.S.C.; Francis M. Walsh, C.S.C.; Stephen S. Wilbricht, C.S.C., Campus Min. Priests 6; Lay Teachers 148; Students 2,430.

[B] HIGH SCHOOLS, DIOCESAN

FALL RIVER. *Bishop Connolly High School*, 373 Elsbree St., 02720. Tel: 508-676-1071; Fax: 508-676-8594. Email: bchs@bishopconnolly.com. Web: www.bishopconnolly.com. Michael Scanlan, Prin.; Deacon Anthony A. Cipriano. Brothers 3; Lay Teachers 19; Students 277.

ATTLEBORO. *Bishop Feehan High School*, 70 Holcott Dr., 02703. Tel: 508-226-6223; Fax: 508-226-7696. Email: webmaster@bishopfeehan.com. Web: www.bishopfeehan.com. Mr. Christopher E. Servant, Pres.; William Runey, Prin.; Rev. Thomas E. Costa, Chap. Priests 1; Sisters 1; Lay Teachers 108; Students 1,099.

HYANNIS. *Pope John Paul II High School*, 120 High School Rd., 02601. Tel: 508-862-6336; Fax: 508-862-6339. Email: ckeavy@pjp2hs.org. Web: www.pjp2hs.org. Christopher W. Keavy, Prin. Lay Teachers 20; Students 100.

NORTH DARTMOUTH. *Bishop Stang High School*, 500 Slocum Rd., 02747-2999. Tel: 508-996-5602; Fax: 508-994-6756. Email: office@bishopstang.com. Web: www.bishopstang.com. Theresa E. Dougall, Pres.; Mary Ann Miskel, Academic Prin.; Michael P. O'Brien, Prin. of Students; Rev. Jay Mello, Chap.; Kathleen Ruginis, Dir. Guidance; Jennifer Thomas, Librarian. Priests 1; Lay Teachers 59; Support Staff 21; Students 785.

TAUNTON. *Coyle and Cassidy High School* (1971) 2 Hamilton St., 02780. Tel: 508-823-6164; Fax: 508-823-2530. Email: gchaves@coylecassidy.com. Web: www.coylecassidy.com. Dr. Mary Patricia Tranter, Ph.D., Pres.; Paul Cartier, Prin.; Rev. Kevin A. Cook, Chap.; Carolyn Hoye, Librarian. Priests 1; Lay Teachers 45; Students 660.

[C] ELEMENTARY SCHOOLS, DIOCESAN

TAUNTON. *Taunton Catholic Middle School* (1971) (Grades 5-8), 61 Summer St., 02780. Tel: 508-822-0491; Fax: 508-824-0469. Email: tcms@catholicmiddle.com. Web: www.catholicmiddle.com. Margaret S. Menear, Prin.; Linda St. Laurent, Librarian. Lay Teachers 19; Students 237.

[D] RESIDENTIAL CHILD CARE FACILITIES

FALL RIVER. *St. Vincent's Home Corp.*, Main Campus: 2425 Highland Ave., 02720. Tel: 508-679-8511; Fax: 508-672-2558. Web: www.stvincentshome.org. Mr. John T. Weldon, Exec. Dir.; Sheila Wilkins, M.Ed., Prin. Sisters 5; Lay Teachers 7; Total Staff 285; Children Residents 100.

[E] GENERAL HOSPITALS

FALL RIVER. *Saint Anne's Health Care Management Services, Inc.* (1985) 795 Middle St., 02721-1798. Tel: 508-674-5741; Fax: 508-675-5647. Web: www.saintanneshospital.com. Joseph E. Ciccolo Jr., Pres.

Saint Anne's Health Care System, Inc., 795 Middle St., 02721-1798. Tel: 508-674-5741; Fax: 508-675-5647. Web: www.saintanneshospital.com. Joseph E. Ciccolo Jr., Pres.

Saint Anne's Hospital Corporation (1906) 795 Middle St., 02721-1798. Tel: 508-674-5741; Fax: 508-675-5647. Web: www.saintanneshospital.org. Joseph E. Ciccolo Jr., Pres. Dominican Sisters of Charity of the Presentation of the Blessed Virgin Mary. Sisters 6; Total Staff 1,293; Bed Capacity 144; Patients Assisted Annually 175,752.

[F] HOMES FOR AGED

FALL RIVER. *Catholic Memorial Home Inc.*, 2446 Highland Ave., 02720-4599. Tel: 508-679-0011; Fax: 508-672-5858. Email: thealy@dhfo.org. Thomas F. Healy, Supr. & Admin.; Rev. John A. Raposo. Total Assisted Annually 489; Total Staff 421; Bed Capacity 294.

FAIRHAVEN. *Our Lady's Haven of Fairhaven Inc.*, 71 Center St., 02719. Tel: 508-999-4561; Fax: 508-997-0254. Email: mmedeiros@dhfo.org. Web: www.dhfo.org. Michael Medeiros, Admin.; Rev. Ambrose Forgit, SS.CC., Chap. Bed Capacity 117; Residents 117; Total Staff 160; Total Assisted Annually 183.

NEW BEDFORD. *Sacred Heart Home*, 359 Summer St., 02740. Tel: 508-996-6751; Fax: 508-992-3145. Web: www.dhfo.org. Manuel Benevides, M.S., Admin. Sisters of Charity of Quebec 2; Total Staff 275; Residents 197; Bed Capacity 217; Total Assisted Annually 217.

NORTH ATTLEBORO. *Madonna Manor Inc.* (1966) 85 N. Washington St., 02760. Tel: 508-699-2740; Fax: 508-699-0481. Email: mmurpy@dhfo.org. Web: www.dhfo.org. Mary-Ellen Murphy, R.N., B.S.N., M.S., Admin.; Rev. Robert Malone, C.S.C.; Sr. Mary Duffy, S.S.J., Dir. of Pastoral Care. Bed Capacity 129; Total Assisted Annually 188; Total Staff 208.

TAUNTON. *Bethany House Adult Day Care*, 72 Church Green, 02780. Tel: 508-822-9200. Raymond A. McAndrews, Admin. Bed Capacity 30; Total Assisted 45; Total Staff 6.

Marian Manor Inc., 33 Summer St., 02780. Tel: 508-822-4885; Fax: 508-880-3386. Email: rmcandrews@dhfo.org. Raymond A. McAndrews, Admin.; Rev. Bernard Vanasse, Chap.; Sr. Paulina Cardenas, O.P., Dir. Pastoral Care. Dominican Sisters of Charity of the Presentation of the Blessed Virgin Mary 1; Total Staff 160; Bed Capacity 116; Patients Assisted Annually 116.

[G] MONASTERIES AND RESIDENCES OF PRIESTS AND BROTHERS

FALL RIVER. *Brothers of Christian Instruction*, 555 Eastern Ave., 02723. Tel: 508-672-5763; Fax: 508-676-8594. Email: fallriverfic@comcast.net. Web: ficbrothers.org. Bros. Daniel Caron, F.I.C., Local Supr.; Roger Millette, F.I.C.; Norman Simoneau, F.I.C., (Retired); Walter Zwierchowski, F.I.C. Brothers 4; Faculty of Bishop Connolly High 3.

Cardinal Medeiros Residence-Retirement Facility for Priests, 375 Elsbree St., 02720-7211. Tel: 508-675-1050; Fax: 508-675-2181.

Priests' Hostel, 2402 Highland Ave., 02720. Tel: 508-672-1632; Fax: 508-679-1422. In Res. Revs. Joseph J. Blyskosz; Andrzej J. Kozanko; Michael J. O'Hearn; Pawel A. Swiercz; Bernard Vanasse.

ATTLEBORO. *La Salette Missionary Association*, 947 Park St., 02703. Tel: 508-222-0027; Fax: 508-222-2504. Email: lsmajp@aol.com. Web: www.lasalettemissionary.org. Very Rev. Joseph G. Bachand, M.S., Provincial; Rev. Bernard Baris, M.S., Dir.

Missionaries of La Salette (MA), Inc.

La Salette Shrine, 947 Park St., 02703. Tel: 508-222-5410; Fax: 508-222-6770. Email: programsoffice@lasalette-shrine.org. Web: www.lasalette-shrine.org. Rev. Ronald A. Beauchemin, M.S., Supr.; Bro. Robert W. Russell, M.S., Dir. Shrine. Priests 12; Brothers 7. In Res. Revs. Henry C. Brodeur, M.S.; Fernand Cassista, M.S.; Victor Chaupetta, M.S.; Pedro Chingandu, M.S.; Ronald G. Gagne, M.S., Prov. Communications Dir.; Gilles M. Genest, M.S. (Retired); Roger Leroux, M.S. (Retired); Cyriac Mattathilanickal, M.S., Dir. Retreat House; Donald Paradis, M.S. (Retired); John P. Sullivan, M.S.; John A. Welch, M.S., Vocation Dir.; Bros. Paul Boucher, M.S.; Lucien Brodeur, M.S.; Roger Moreau, M.S.; Roger St. Germain, M.S., (Retired); Ronald Taylor, M.S.; Raymond Tetreault, M.S., (Retired).

FAIRHAVEN. *Sacred Hearts Provincial House*, 77 Adams St., P.O. Box 111, 02719-0111. Tel: 508-993-2442; Fax: 508-996-5499. Web: www.sscc.org. Revs. Thomas McElroy, SS.CC., Vicar Provincial; William F. Petrie, SS.CC., Prov.; Bro. Paul R. Alves, SS.CC., Treas., Prov. Councilor. Congregation of the Sacred Hearts of Jesus and Mary. Fathers 1. *National Center of the Enthronement*, P.O. Box 111, 02719-0111. Tel: 508-999-2680; Fax: 508-993-8233. Email: necenter@juno.com. Web: www.sscc.org. Congregation of the Sacred Hearts of Jesus and Mary. Total Staff 2.

Damien Residence, 73 Adams St., P.O. Box 111, 02719-0111. Tel: 508-999-0500; Fax: 508-990-7173. Revs. Matthias Shanley, SS.CC., Dir.; Michael Annunziato, SS.CC., Asst. Dir. (Retired); William Heffron, SS.CC., Mission Procurator; Richard Lifrak, SS.CC., Vocation Dir.; Albert Dagnoli, SS.CC.; John Fee, SS.CC.; Benedict Folger, SS.CC.; Ambrose Forgit, SS.CC.; Owen F. Goodwin, SS.CC. (Retired); Gabriel Healy, SS.CC. (Retired); Leo King, SS.CC. (Retired); David Lupo, SS.CC.; Brian Marggraf, SS.CC. (Retired); Austin Nagle, SS.CC.; Michael Shanahan, SS.CC.; Roy Yurco, SS.CC. (Retired). Fathers 12; Brothers 1.

Priests of the Province Serving Abroad - In Reynosa, Mexico: Rev. Gerry Shanley, SS.CC.

In Nassau, Bahamas: Revs. Martin Gomes, SS.CC.; Michael Kelly, SS.CC.; Patrick F. Fanning, SS.CC.

In India: Revs. David P. Reid, SS.CC.; Alexis Nayak, SS.CC.; Subal Nayak, SS.CC.; Sudhir Nayak, SS.CC.; Sudhir Cristo Das Nayak, SS.CC.; Roche Iruthayaraj Thiruchiluvai, SS.CC.; Joseph Anthony Raja, SS.CC.; Stephen Joseph Sarto, SS.CC.; Ajith Kumar Dass, SS.CC.; Tony Biswas, SS.CC.

In Rome, Italy: Rev. Richard McNally, SS.CC., Vicar Gen.

NEW BEDFORD. *Marian Friary of Our Lady, Queen of the Seraphic Order*, 600 Pleasant St., 02740-6299. Tel: 508-996-8274; Fax: 508-996-8296. Email: ffi@marymediatrix.com. Web: www.marymediatrix.com. P.O. Box 3003, 02741-3003. Revs. Raphael M. Magee, F.I., Vicar; Dominic Sario M. Murphy, F.I., Father Guardian; Alphonsus M. Sutton, F.I.; Maximilian M. Warnisher, F.I. Priests 5; Brothers 2.

NORTH DARTMOUTH. *Holy Cross Residence* (1934) 824 Tucker Rd., 02747. Tel: 508-993-2238; Fax: 508-984-4339. Revs. Fred Serraino, C.S.C., Supr.; Douglas W. Hawkins, C.S.C. (Retired); William G. Condon, C.S.C. (Retired); Albert A. Croce, C.S.C. (Retired); John F. Dias, C.S.C. (Retired); Donald W. Whipple, C.S.C. (Retired); J. Robert Rioux, C.S.C. (Retired); Joseph Tate, C.S.C. (Retired); Charles L. Wallen, C.S.C. (Retired); James F. Boyle, C.S.C. (Retired); Bro. Robert Vozzo, C.S.C.

St. Joseph's Hall, 800 Tucker Rd., 02747-3599. Tel: 508-996-2413; Fax: 508-984-4339. Email: cscda@aol.com. Revs. J. Robert Rioux, C.S.C., Dir. (Retired); John F. Dias, C.S.C. (Retired); William G. Condon, C.S.C. (Retired); Bro. Robert Vozzo, C.S.C., (Retired).

ONSET. *St. Joseph Friary-Franciscan Friars*, 46 Robinwood Rd., P.O. Box 63, 02558. Tel: 508-759-7280; Fax: 508-743-9551. Email: gjsilverio17@hotmail.com. Revs. Gilbert J. Silverio, O.F.M., M.E.D., Guard.; Brennan Egan, O.F.M., Ph.D. Total Staff 2; Total in Residence 2.

[H] CONVENTS AND RESIDENCES FOR SISTERS

FALL RIVER. *Bishop's Residence Convent*, 394 Highland Ave., 02720. Tel: 508-675-1311. Sisters of St. Jeanne d'Arc.

DIGHTON. *Dominican Sisters of Charity of the Presentation of the Blessed Virgin*, 3012 Elm St., 02715. Tel: 508-669-5425; 508-669-5023 (Novitiate); Fax: 508-669-6521. Email: domsis@dominicansistersofthepresentation.org. Web: www.dominicansistersofthepresentation.org. Sr. Vimala Vadakumpadan, O.P., Major Supr. Provincial House-Residence, Residence for Aged Sisters, Novitiate. Sisters 37.

FAIRHAVEN. *Sisters of the Sacred Hearts, Community Headquarters*, 35 Huttleston Ave., 02719-3154. Tel: 508-994-9341. Email: srmuriellebeau@cs.com. Sr. Helen Wood, SS.CC., Prov. Supr.

Sisters of the Sacred Hearts of Jesus and Mary and of Perpetual Adoration, SS.CC. Sisters in Community 3.

HARWICHPORT. *Contemplative Sisters of the Good Shepherd* (1831) 88 Bank St., 02646. Tel: 508-432-5582; Fax: 508-432-6293. Email: aureenb@aol.com.

NEW BEDFORD. *Franciscan Sisters of the Immaculate*, 106 Bullard St., 02746. Tel: 508-990-0335. Email: fsiusa@verizon.net. Web: www.marymediatrix.com; www.franciscansoftheimmaculate.com. Sr. Maria Consolatrice, F.I., Dir. Vocation. Professed Sisters 5.

NORTH DARTMOUTH. *Diocesan Family Life Center*, 500 Slocum Rd., 02747. Tel: 508-993-4930; Fax: 508-999-6430. Email: flcdartmouth@aol.com. Total Staff 3.

Dominican Sisters of Hope (1995) 856 Tucker Rd., 02747. Tel: 508-996-1305. Web: www.ophope.org. Sisters 4.

TAUNTON. *Villa Fatima* (1934) 90 County St., 02780. Tel: 508-822-6282; Fax: 508-823-0825. Email: sr.dot@att.net; srdot@fctuplus.net. Web: www.ssdmission.org; www.sistersofsaintdorothy.org. Sr. Rosalie Patrello, S.S.D., Local Coord. Sisters of St. Dorothy. Professed Sisters 6.

WAREHAM. *St. Patrick's Missionary Cenacle*, 86 High St., 02571. Tel: 508-295-0799. Email: srcathl@verizon.net. Outreach to the homebound.

[I] RETREAT HOUSES

ATTLEBORO. *La Salette Retreat Center*, 947 Park St., 02703-0965. Tel: 508-222-8530; Fax: 508-236-9089. Email: lasaletteretreats@hotmail.com. Web: www.lasalette-shrine.org. Revs. Cyriac Mattathilanickal, M.S., Dir.; Fernand Cassista, M.S.; John A. Welch, M.S., Retreat Facilitator; Bro. Roger A. Moreau, M.S.; Claire Lamoureux, Ph.D., Retreat Leader, Counseling; Dorothy J. Levesque, Retreat Leader; Mrs. Karen Laroche, M.A., Youth Leader; Margaret Ormond, Steubenville Coord. Priests 3; Total Staff 11; Total Assisted 4,200.

EAST FREETOWN. *Cathedral Camp and Retreat Center* (1919) 167 Middleboro Rd., P.O. Box 428, 02717-0428. Tel: 508-763-8874; Fax: 508-763-2230. Email: rena@cathedralcamp.net. Web: www.cathedralcamp.net. Rena Lemieux, Asst. Dir. Total Staff 60.

Cathedral Camp Retreat Center, 167 Middleboro Rd., P.O. Box 428, 02717-0428. Tel: 508-763-3994; Fax: 508-763-2230. Email: rena@cathedralcamp.net. Web: www.cathedralcamp.org. Total Staff 6.

NORTH EASTON. *Holy Cross Retreat House*, 490 Washington St., 02356-1294. Tel: 508-238-2051; Fax: 508-238-0164. Email: jfcal44@hotmail.com. Web: www.retreathouse.org. Rev. Joseph F. Callahan, C.S.C., Spiritual Dir. Priests 1.

WAREHAM. *Sacred Hearts Retreat Center*, 226 Great Neck Rd., 02571. Tel: 508-295-0100; Fax: 508-291-2624. Email: retreats@sscc.org. Web: www.sscc.org/wareham. Rev. Stanley Kolasa, SS.CC., Dir.; Sr. Claire Bouchard, SS.CC., Admin. Congregation of the Sacred Hearts of Jesus and Mary and of the Perpetual Adoration of the Most Blessed Sacrament. Priests 1; Sisters 1; Total Staff 5.

[J] DEPARTMENT OF CATHOLIC SOCIAL SERVICES AND SPECIAL APOSTOLATES

FALL RIVER. *Campaign For Human Development Apostolate*, 1600 Bay St., P.O. Box M, South Station, 02724. Tel: 508-674-4681; Fax: 508-675-2224. Email: aam@cssdioc.org. Arlene A. McNamee, L.C.S.W., Coord.

Office for Persons with Disabilities Tel: 508-679-8373; 508-997-7337 (Voice); 508-679-4277 (TTY);

508-674-4681; Fax: 508-984-1667; 508-675-2224. Mathew Dansereau, Coord.; Dennis Canuela.

Spanish Apostolate P.O. Box 2577, 02722. Tel: 508-675-1311; Fax: 508-679-9220. Rev. Richard D. Wilson, J.C.L., Dir.

P.O. Box 40605, New Bedford, 02744-0006. Tel: 508-675-1311; Fax: 508-679-9220.

Catholic Social Services of Fall River, 1600 Bay St., P.O. Box M, S. Station, 02724. Tel: 508-674-4681; Fax: 508-675-2224. Email: aam@cssdioc.org. Arlene A. McNamee, L.C.S.W., Exec. Dir.

Program Directors: Debora Jones, Office Child Protecticy; Elaine Abdow, Pregnancy & Adoption Svcs.; Patricia McGann, L.I.C.S.W., Residential Prog.; Maria A. Pereira, L.I.S.C.W., Counseling Svcs.; Matt Dausereau, Office for Persons with Disabilities; Carol Hernandez, Coord. Basic Needs & Housing Counseling; Aaron McNamee, Coord. Supportive Housing Programs.

Catholic Social Services of New Bedford, 238 Bonney St., New Bedford, 02744. Tel: 508-997-7337; Fax: 508-984-1667.

Catholic Social Services of Cape Cod, 261 South St., Hyannis, 02601. Tel: 508-771-6771; Fax: 508-771-4711.

Catholic Social Services of Taunton, 78 Broadway, Taunton, 02780. Tel: 508-824-3264; Fax: 508-880-1903.

Adoption By Choice, 311 Hooper St., Tiverton, RI 02878. Tel: 401-624-9270; Fax: 508-675-2224.

HYANNIS. *St. Clare's Residence for Women* 02601. Bed Capacity 5; Total Staff 2; Total Assisted Annually 19.

[K] CAMPS AND COMMUNITY CENTERS

EAST TAUNTON. *Diocesan Catholic Youth Organization*, P.O. Box 619, 02718. Tel: 508-824-5707; Fax: 508-824-5665. Very Rev. Jay T. Maddock, J.C.L., V.F., Diocesan Dir.

Fall River Area Catholic Youth Organization, Sullivan-McCarrick CYO Center, 403 Anawan St., 02720. Tel: 508-672-9644; Fax: 508-824-5665.

New Bedford Area Catholic Youth Organization, Kennedy Youth Center, 377 County St., New Bedford, 02740. Tel: 508-996-0536; Fax: 508-824-5665. Mr. George Viveiros, Area Dir.

Taunton Area Catholic Youth Organization, 61 Summer St., Taunton, 02780. Tel: 508-822-5218; Fax: 508-824-5665. Mr. Donald Morrison, Area Dir.; Mr. Ronald Benoit, Area Dir.

[L] NEWMAN CENTERS AND CAMPUS MINISTRY

FALL RIVER. *Bristol Community College Newman Center* 777 Elsbree St., 02720-7395. Tel: 508-678-2811, Ext. 2247; Fax: 508-730-3286. Email: sistercynthia.bauer@bristolcc.edu. Web: www.bristol.mass.edu/students/counseling/min_cath.html. Rev. Michael A. Ciryak, Campus Minister. Total Staff 1.

Diocesan Education Center 423 Highland Ave., 02720. Tel: 508-678-2828; Fax: 508-674-4218. Email: gmilot@dfrcec.com. Web: www.dfrcec.com. Dr. George A. Milot, Supt. of Schools; Dr. Donna Boyle, Asst. Supt. Curriculum; Kathleen A. Simpson, Asst. Supt. Personnel; Claire M. McManus, S.T.L., Dir. Faith Formation.

HYANNIS. *Cape Cod Campus Ministry* 21 Cross St., 02601. Tel: 508-775-0818, Ext. 16; Fax: 508-771-5940. Email: youngadultfaith@gmail.com. Rev. David C. Frederici, Chap.

NORTH DARTMOUTH. *Catholic Campus Ministry University of Massachusetts Dartmouth* 285 Old Westport Rd., 02747-2300. Tel: 508-999-8872. Email: mfitzpatrick@umassd.edu. Rev. Michael Joseph Fitzpatrick, Chap.; Sr. Madeleine Tacy, O.P., Campus Min. Total Staff 2.

NORTH EASTON. *Wheaton College Newman Center* 480 Washington St., 02356. Tel: 508-238-5942. Web: catholiccampusministry.com. Rev. James R. Lackenmier, C.S.C.

[M] MISCELLANEOUS LISTINGS

FALL RIVER. *Carmelite Convent of Dartmouth, Inc.*, P.O. Box 2577, 02722.

Community Action for Better Housing, Inc., 1600 Bay St., P.O. Box M, S. Station, 02724. Tel: 508-674-4681; Fax: 508-675-2224. Email: AAM@cssdioc.org. Ed Allard, Prog. Coord.

Diocesan Facilities Self-Insurance Group, Inc., P.O. Box 1110, 02722.

Saint Mary's Education Fund, Inc., P.O. Box 2577, 02722. Tel: 508-675-1311.

St. Dominic's Apartments, Inc., 1600 Bay St., 02724. Tel: 508-674-4681; Fax: 508-675-2224. Arlene A. McNamee, L.C.S.W., Dir.

NEW BEDFORD. *The Institute of the Incarnate Word, Inc.*, 306 Ashley Blvd., 02746. Tel: 508-992-7587; Fax: 508-994-0281. Rev. Hugo G. Cardenas, I.V.E. Priests 1; Total Staff 4; Total Assisted 150.

St. Mary's Home of New Bedford, Inc., P.O. Box 2577, 02722. Tel: 508-675-1311.

Missionaries of Charity, 556 County St., 02740. Tel: 508-997-7347. Shelter for homeless women. Total in Residence 4; Total Assisted 203.

NORTH EASTON. *Holy Cross Family Ministries* (1942) 518 Washington St., 02356-1200. Tel: 508-238-4095; Fax: 508-238-3953. Email: mission@HCFM.org. Web: www.hcfm.org. Robert Alzapiedi, Chief Admin. Officer; Revs. John P. Phalen, C.S.C., Pres.; James H. Phalan, C.S.C., Intl. Dir. Family Rosary; Wilfred Raymond, C.S.C., Natl. Dir. of Family Theater Productions; Beth Mahoney, Mission Dir. Corporate Name: The Family Rosary, Inc.; Sponsored by Congregation of Holy Cross (Eastern Province).

RELIGIOUS INSTITUTES OF MEN REPRESENTED IN THE DIOCESE

For further details refer to the corresponding bracketed number in the Religious Institutes of Men or Women section.

[0320]—*Brothers of Christian Instruction*—F.I.C.
[0600]—*Brothers of the Congregation of Holy Cross*—C.S.C.
[]—*Brothers of the Congregation of the Sacred Hearts*—SS.CC.
[]—*Carmelite Fathers*—O.Carm.
[1140]—*Congregation of the Sacred Hearts of Jesus and Mary*—SS.CC.
[0480]—*Conventual Franciscans* (Buffalo, NY)—O.F.M.Conv.
[0520]—*Franciscan Friars* (Immaculate Conception Prov.)—O.F.M.
[0533]—*Franciscan Friars of the Immaculate*—F.I.
[]—*The Institute of the Incarnate Word*—I.V.E.
[0690]—*Jesuit Fathers and Brothers*—S.J.
[0720]—*Missionaries of Our Lady of La Salette*—M.S.
[]—*Order of Cistercians of Strict Observance*—O.C.S.O.
[0430]—*Order of Preachers (Dominicans)*—O.P.
[]—*Order of St. Benedict*—O.S.B.
[0610]—*Priests of the Congregation of the Holy Cross* (Eastern Prov.)—C.S.C.

RELIGIOUS INSTITUTES OF WOMEN REPRESENTED IN THE DIOCESE

[]—*Bernadine Franciscan Sisters*—O.S.F.
[3815]—*Congregation of the Sisters of St. Joan of Arc*—S.J.A.
[1830]—*Contemplative Sisters of the Good Shepherd*—C.G.S.
[0750]—*Daughters of the Charity of the Sacred Heart of Jesus* (Sacred Heart Prov.)—F.C.S.C.J.
[1100]—*Dominican Sisters of Charity of the Presentation of the Blessed Virgin*—O.P.
[]—*Dominican Sisters of Hope*—O.P.
[]—*Franciscan Sisters of the Immaculate*—F.I.
[2580]—*Institute of the Sisters of Mercy of the Americas* (Northeast NY, CA)—R.S.M.
[3790]—*Institute of the Sisters of St. Dorothy*—S.S.D.
[2790]—*Missionary Servants of the Most Blessed Trinity*—M.S.B.T.
[]—*Missionary Sisters of Charity*—M.C.
[2070]—*Religious of the Holy Union of the Sacred Hearts* (Immaculate Heart and Sacred Heart Provs.)—S.U.S.C.
[0560]—*Sisters of Charity of Quebec (Grey Nuns)*—S.C.Q.
[0640]—*Sisters of Charity of St. Vincent de Paul (Halifax)*—S.C.
[]—*Sisters of Our Lady of LaSalette*—S.N.D.S.
[3720]—*Sisters of Saint Anne*—S.S.A.
[3830-16]—*Sisters of St. Joseph* (Springfield, MA)—S.S.J.
[]—*Sisters of the Cross and Passion*—C.P.
[1830]—*Sisters of the Good Shepherd*—R.G.S.
[]—*Sisters of the Presentation of the Blessed Virgin Mary*—P.B.V.M.
[3690]—*Sisters of the Sacred Hearts of Perpetual Adoration*—SS.CC.
[4048]—*Society of the Sisters, Faithful Companions of Jesus*—F.C.J.

DIOCESAN CEMETERIES

FALL RIVER. *St. John*
St. Mary
Notre Dame
St. Patrick
ATTLEBORO. *St. John*
St. Stephen
EAST FALMOUTH. *St. Anthony*
HYANNIS. *St. Francis*
MANSFIELD. *St. Mary*
MATTAPOISETT. *St. Anthony*
NANTUCKET. *St. Mary*
NEW BEDFORD. *St. John*
St. Mary
Sacred Heart
NORTH ATTLEBORO. *St. Mary*
NORTH EASTON. *Immaculate Conception*
OAK BLUFFS. *Sacred Heart*
PROVINCETOWN. *St. Peter*
SANDWICH. *St. Peter*
SOMERSET. *St. Patrick*
TAUNTON. *St. Francis*
St. James
St. Joseph
St. Mary
TRURO. *Sacred Heart*
WAREHAM. *St. Patrick*
WELLFLEET. *Our Lady of Lourdes*
WEST HARWICH. *Holy Trinity*

NECROLOGY

† Dufour, Clement E., (Retired)—Died Sept. 26, 2009

An asterisk (*) denotes an organization that has established tax-exempt status directly with the IRS and is not covered by the USCCB Group Ruling.

Diocese of Fargo

(Dioecesis Fargensis)

Most Reverend

SAMUEL J. AQUILA, D.D.

Bishop of Fargo; ordained June 5, 1976; appointed Coadjutor Bishop of Fargo June 12, 2001; ordained August 24, 2001; appointed Bishop of Fargo March 18, 2002. *Mailing Address: 5201 Bishops Blvd., Ste. A, Fargo, ND 58104-7605.*

Chancery Office: 5201 Bishops Blvd., Ste. A, Fargo, ND 58104-7605. Tel: 701-356-7900; Fax: 701-356-7999.

Web: www.fargodiocese.org

Email: webadmin2007@fargodiocese.org

Square Miles 35,786.

Corporate Title: The Diocese of Fargo.

Formerly Diocese of Jamestown.

Established November 12, 1889; Transferred to Fargo, April 6, 1897.

Comprises the Counties of Barnes, Benson, Bottineau, Cass, Cavalier, Dickey, Eddy, Foster, Grand Forks, Griggs, Kidder, LaMoure, Logan, McHenry, McIntosh, Nelson, Pembina, Pierce, Ramsey, Ransom, Richland, Rolette, Sargent, Sheridan, Steele, Stutsman, Towner, Traill, Walsh and Wells in the State of North Dakota.

For legal titles of parishes and diocesan institutions, consult the Chancery Office.

STATISTICAL OVERVIEW

Personnel	
Bishop	1
Priests: Diocesan Active in Diocese	80
Priests: Diocesan Active Outside Diocese	11
Priests: Retired, Sick or Absent	45
Number of Diocesan Priests	136
Religious Priests in Diocese	9
Total Priests in Diocese	145
Extern Priests in Diocese	7
Ordinations:	
Diocesan Priests	1
Permanent Deacons	3
Permanent Deacons in Diocese	45
Total Sisters	124
Parishes	
Parishes	132
With Resident Pastor:	
Resident Diocesan Priests	64
Resident Religious Priests	5
Without Resident Pastor:	
Administered by Priests	63
Closed Parishes	1
Professional Ministry Personnel:	
Sisters	6
Lay Ministers	50
Welfare	
Catholic Hospitals	8
Total Assisted	160,090
Homes for the Aged	13
Total Assisted	126,038
Specialized Homes	1
Total Assisted	37
Special Centers for Social Services	5
Total Assisted	10,348
Educational	
Seminaries, Diocesan	1
Students from This Diocese	6
Students from Other Diocese	4
Diocesan Students in Other Seminaries	11
Total Seminarians	17
Colleges and Universities	1
Total Students	480
High Schools, Diocesan and Parish	1
Total Students	337
Elementary Schools, Diocesan and Parish	12
Total Students	1,685
Catechesis/Religious Education:	
High School Students	1,949
Elementary Students	5,957
Total Students under Catholic Instruction	10,425
Teachers in the Diocese:	
Priests	1
Sisters	1
Lay Teachers	158
Vital Statistics	
Receptions into the Church:	
Infant Baptism Totals	1,262
Minor Baptism Totals	47
Adult Baptism Totals	36
Received into Full Communion	146
First Communions	1,028
Confirmations	1,120
Marriages:	
Catholic	223
Interfaith	163
Total Marriages	386
Deaths	874
Total Catholic Population	85,229
Total Population	377,979

Former Bishops—Rt. Rev. JOHN SHANLEY, D.D., ord. 1874; cons. Dec. 27, 1889; died July 16, 1909; Most Rev. JAMES O'REILLY, D.D., ord. June 24, 1880; cons. May 19, 1910; installed June 1, 1910; died Dec. 19, 1934; His Eminence ALOISIUS CARDINAL MUENCH, ord. June 8, 1913; appt. Bishop of Fargo, Aug. 10, 1935; cons. Oct. 15, 1935; installed Nov. 6, 1935; appt. Apostolic Visitator for Germany, July 8, 1946; granted personal title of Archbishop, Nov. 1, 1950; appt. Papal Nuncio to Germany, March 10, 1951; created Cardinal Priest and elevated to the Roman Curia, Dec. 14, 1959; died Feb. 15, 1962; Most Revs. LEO F. DWORSCHAK, D.D., ord. May 29, 1926; appt. Coadjutor Bishop of Rapid City, June 23, 1946; cons. Aug. 22, 1946; appt. Auxiliary Bishop of Fargo, April 10, 1947; succeeded to See, May 10, 1960; retired Sept. 8, 1970; died Nov. 5, 1976; JUSTIN A. DRISCOLL, D.D., ord. July 28, 1945; appt. Bishop of Fargo, Sept. 8, 1970; cons. and installed Oct. 28, 1970; died Nov. 19, 1984; JAMES S. SULLIVAN, ord. June 4, 1955; cons. Auxiliary Bishop of Lansing Sept. 21, 1972; appt. Bishop of Fargo April 2, 1985; installed May 30, 1985; retired March 18, 2002; died June 12, 2006.

Chancery Office—5201 Bishops Blvd., Fargo, 58104. Tel: 701-356-7900; Fax: 701-356-7999.

Moderator of the Curia—Rev. Msgr. JOSEPH P. GOERING, V.G.

Vicar General—Rev. Msgr. JOSEPH P. GOERING, V.G.

Chancellor and Secretary to the Bishop—Very Rev. LUKE D. MEYER.

Vicar for Clergy—Rev. Msgr. JOSEPH P. GOERING, V.G.

Vice Chancellor—Rev. Msgr. JEFFREY WALD.

Archivist—Very Rev. LUKE D. MEYER.

Chief Financial Officer—Mr. SCOTT A. HOSELTON, CPA.

Diocesan Tribunal—5201 Bishops Blvd., Fargo, 58104. Tel: 701-356-7940.

Judicial Vicar—Very Rev. K. S. KOPACZ, J.C.L.

Promotor Justitiae—VACANT.

Defensor Vinculi—Rev. Msgr. DANIEL J. PILON, J.C.L.

Presiding Judge—Very Rev. K. S. KOPACZ, J.C.L.

Judges—Rev. Msgr. WENDELYN VETTER, V.F. (Retired); Revs. JARED KADLEC, J.C.L.; JAMES GOODWIN, J.C.L.

Advocates—JONI TOLLEFSON; Ms. ELLEN O'CONNOR; Ms. JOAN HOUDEK.

Auditor—Ms. MARILYN BITTNER.

Notaries—Very Rev. LUKE D. MEYER, Chancellor; Rev. Msgr. GREGORY J. SCHLESSELMANN; Mr. SCOTT A. HOSELTON, CPA; Ms. JENNIFER LAGEIN; Ms. JOLETTE KRABBENHOFT.

Diocesan College of Consultors—Revs. RICHARD FINEO; ANDREW JASINSKI; Rev. Msgr. DENNIS A. SKONSENG; Very Rev. ROSS LAFRAMBOISE; Revs. GARY LUITEN; JAMES A. MEYER.

Deans—Deanery 1: Very Rev. DALE LAGODINSKI, Wahpeton. Deanery 2: Very Rev. JAMES MEYER, Fargo. Deanery 3: Very Rev. PHILLIP ACKERMAN, Grand Forks. Deanery 4: Very Rev. SAMUEL EZEIBEKWE, Pisek. Deanery 5: Very Rev. DALE H. KINZLER, Devils Lake. Deanery 6: Very Rev. JAMES GROSS, Velva. Deanery 7: Very Rev. AL M. BITZ, Jamestown. Deanery 8: Very Rev. ROSS LAFRAMBOISE, Napoleon.

Diocesan Offices and Directors

Corporate Board—Most Rev. SAMUEL J. AQUILA, D.D.; Rev. Msgr. JOSEPH P. GOERING, V.G.; Very Rev. LUKE D. MEYER; Mr. BOB WILMOT; Mr. SCOTT A. HOSELTON, CPA; Mr. TERRY W. KNOEPFLE ESQ.

Apostleship of Prayer—Very Rev. CHAD F. WILHELM, Dir.

Diocesan Finance Council—Most Rev. SAMUEL J. AQUILA, D.D.; Rev. Msgr. JOSEPH P. GOERING, V.G.; Very Rev. LUKE D. MEYER; Mr. GRANT SHAFT; Ms. SHARON FROLEK; Mr. FRANCIS KRITZBERGER; Ms. KAREN LESTER; Mr. PAUL LEIER; Mr. SCOTT A. HOSELTON, CPA; Ms. TERRI CLARK; Mr. LARRY EXNER; Ms. JULIE FLATEN; Mr. BRIAN SCHANILEC; Mr. BOB WILMOT; Mr. RICK SIMONSON.

Catholic Church Deposit & Loan Fund of Eastern North Dakota— Same as corporate board.

Pension Plan—Mr. SCOTT A. HOSELTON, CPA.

Censor Librorum—Rev. Msgr. ROBERT LALIBERTE, Ph.D.

Office of Worship and Sacraments—Very Rev. LUKE D. MEYER.

Continuing Education of Priests—Rev. ANDREW JASINSKI.

Arbitration & Conciliation Board—JENNIFER HASELBERGER; Sr. MARLYSS DIONNE, S.M.P.; MICHAEL MOE; PAUL RICHARD; Rev. Msgr. JOSEPH P. GOERING, V.G.; BARB AUGDAHL.

Ecumenical Commission—VACANT.

Director of Stewardship and Development—Mr. PAUL LEIER.

Holy Childhood Association—Very Rev. LUKE D. MEYER.

Communications—Ms. TANYA WATTERUD.

The "New Earth" (Diocesan Newspaper)—Ms. TANYA WATTERUD, Editor.

North Dakota Catholic Conference—Mr. CHRISTOPHER

DODSON, 103 S. 3rd St., Ste. 10, Bismarck, 58501-3800.

Permanent Diaconate—Rev. PAUL C. DUCHSCHERE, Sec. Diaconate; Deacons DAVID EBLEN, Dir. Formation; MATTHIAS PROM, Dir. Life & Ministries; STUART LONGTIN, Asst. Dir. Life & Ministries.

Presbyteral Council—Rev. JAMES GOODWIN, J.C.L., Chm.

Propagation of the Faith—Very Rev. LUKE D. MEYER.

Rural Life—Rev. THOMAS GRANER, Dir., Mailing Address: 218 3rd St., S.E., Rugby, 58368. Tel: 701-776-6388.

Technology/Computer Office—Ms. JOCELYN SLOAN.

Catholic Education and Formation—Mr. TOM FREI, Dir.

Evangelization/Catechesis—Ms. KATIE DUBAS.

Healthcare Director—Very Rev. DALE H. KINZLER.

Youth/Young Adults—Ms. KATHY LONEY.

Catholic Schools—Mr. THOMAS A. FREI.

Education in Parish Service (EPS)—Deacon DAVID EBLEN.

Engaged Encounter—VACANT. Tel: 701-356-7900.

Respect Life Office—Ms. RACHELLE L. SAUVAGEAU.

Vocation Director—Rev. PAUL C. DUCHSCHERE, Cardinal Muench Seminary, 100-35th Ave., N.E., Fargo, 58102. Tel: 701-271-1212.

Catholic Cemeteries—Mr. SCOTT A. HOSELTON, CPA.

Hispanic Ministry—Rev. TIMOTHY SCHROEDER, Mailing Address: St. John the Evangelist, P.O. Box 636, Grafton, 58237-0636.

Native American Ministries—Rev. EDWARD SHERMAN, Chap. at Large (Retired).

Apostolate for Native Americans—Rev. GERALD A. MCCARTHY (Retired), 304 3rd Ave. W., Box 155, Bisbee, 58317.

Prison Apostolate—Rev. PAUL R. SCHUSTER; Deacon STUART LONGTIN.

Liaison with Charismatic Movement—Rev. DONALD A. LEIPHON (Retired).

CLERGY, PARISHES, MISSIONS AND PAROCHIAL SCHOOLS

CITY OF FARGO

(CASS COUNTY)

1—ST. MARY'S CATHEDRAL OF FARGO (1880) [JC] Very Rev. Chad F. Wilhelm, Rector; Rev. Joseph Christensen; Deacon George Loegering. In Res., Rev. Charles Fischer.
Office: 619 7th St. N., 58102. Tel: 701-235-4289; 701-235-4280; Fax: 701-235-2986. Email: cathedral@cathedralofstmary.com. Web: www.cathedralofstmary.com.
Res.: 679 6th Ave. N., 58102. Tel: 701-235-4280.
Catechesis/Religious Program—Students 112.

2—STS. ANNE & JOACHIM CHURCH OF FARGO (1995) [JC] Revs. Jude Okafor; Kurtis Gunwall, Temp. Admin.; Deacon David Eblen.
5202 25th St. S., 58104. Tel: 701-235-5757; Fax: 701-235-0764. Email: stsaaj@stsaaj.org. Web: www.stsaaj.org. In Res., Revs. Duaine Cote (Retired); Charles LaCroix.
Res.: 5202 25th St. S., 58104. Tel: 701-235-1514.
Catechesis/Religious Program—Students 391.

3—ST. ANTHONY OF PADUA'S CHURCH OF FARGO (1917) [JC] Rev. Raymond P. Courtright; Rev. Msgr. Robert Laliberte; Deacons Stuart Longtin; Mathias Prom; Donald Bunce.
Church: 710 S. 10th St., 58103. Tel: 701-237-6063; Fax: 701-237-6064.
Catechesis/Religious Program—Tel: 701-232-3995. Students 112.

4—HOLY SPIRIT CHURCH OF FARGO (1951) [JC] Rev. Msgr. Jeffrey Wald; Rev. Jason Asselin. In Res., Rev. Msgr. Val Gross (Retired); Rev. Jose Mundadan.
Church: 1420 N. 7th St., 58102. Tel: 701-232-5900; Fax: 701-232-5902. Web: holyspirit-church.org.
School—(Grades PreSchool-5), 1441 8th St. N., 58102. Tel: 701-232-4087; Fax: 701-232-8240. Jason Kotrba, Prin. Lay Teachers 17; Students 167.
Catechesis/Religious Program—Students 240.

5—NATIVITY CHURCH OF FARGO (1960) [JC] Revs. Kevin Boucher; Gary Luiten; Duane Koble, Admin.
Church: 1825 11th St. S., 58103. Tel: 701-232-2414; Fax: 701-232-4491. Email: duanek@nativitycatholicchurch.net. Web: www.nativitycatholicchurch.net.
School—(Grades K-5) Tel: 701-232-7461; Fax: 701-298-8981. Web: www.fcsn.k12nd.us/index2ntm. Cindy Hutchins, Prin.; Jan Nowatzki, Librarian. Lay Teachers 27; Students 350.
Catechesis/Religious Program—Students 256.

6—ST. PAUL'S NEWMAN CHURCH OF FARGO (1957) [JC] Rev. James Cheney.
Church: 1141 N. University Dr., 58102. Tel: 701-235-0142; Fax: 701-298-6431. Email: ndsunewmanctr@yahoo.com. Web: www.ndsunewman.org.
Catechesis/Religious Program—Students 26.

OUTSIDE THE CITY OF FARGO

ALICE, CASS CO., ST. HENRY (1902) Closed. For inquiries for parish records contact the Chancellor's Office. Sacramental records are at St. Patrick in Enderlin.

ANAMOOSE, MCHENRY CO., ST. FRANCIS XAVIER CHURCH OF ANAMOOSE (1899) [CEM], Also serving Drake. Rev. Robert Wapenski.
Mailing Address: P.O. Box 49, 58710-0049.
Church: 605 1st St. W., 58710. Tel: 701-465-3780; Fax: 773-496-3780. Email: stfx@gondtc.com.

ANETA, NELSON CO., SACRED HEART CHURCH OF ANETA (1907), Served from Cooperstown. Rev. Richard Fineo.
Mailing Address: *c/o St. George*, P.O. Box 217, Cooperstown, 58425. Tel: 701-797-2624.
Catechesis/Religious Program—Students 9.

ARDOCH, WALSH CO., ST. JOHN THE BAPTIST (1883) [CEM] Closed. For inquiries for parish records contact the chancery. Sacramental records are at Sacred Heart, Minto.

ARGUSVILLE, CASS CO., ST. WILLIAM (1942) [JC], Served from Hillsboro. Rev. Leo Kinney.
Mailing Address: P.O. Box 1, Harwood, 58042-0001.
Church: 107 Drake Ave., 58005.
Catechesis/Religious Program—Tel: 701-484-5211. Students 54.

ASHLEY, MCINTOSH CO., ST. DAVID (1920), Served from Wishek. Rev. Thomas Feltman.
Mailing Address: *c/o St. Patrick*, P.O. Box 293, Wishek, 58495. Tel: 701-423-5494.
Catechesis/Religious Program—Students 15.

BALFOUR, MCHENRY CO., ST. JOSEPH (1906) Closed. For inquiries for parish records please contact the Chancellor's office. Sacramental records are at St. Margaret Mary, Drake.

BALTA, PIERCE CO., OUR LADY OF MT. CARMEL CHURCH OF BALTA (1902) [CEM], Served from Esmond. Rev. Julian Kupisz.
Mailing Address: *c/o St. Boniface*, P.O. Box 37, Esmond, 58332-0037.
Church: 301 Main St. N., 58313.

BATHGATE, PEMBINA CO., ST. ANTHONY (1883) Closed. For inquiries for parish records contact the Chancellor's Office. Sacramental records are at St. Brigid, Cavalier.

BECHYNE, STS. PETER & PAUL CHURCH OF BECHYNE (1886) [CEM], Served from Pisek. Very Rev. Samuel Ezeibekwe.
Mailing Address: P.O. Box 27, Pisek, 58273. Tel: 701-284-6060.
Catechesis/Religious Program—Students 9.

BELCOURT, ROLETTE CO.

1—ST. ANN (1885) [CEM], Also serving St. Anthony. Revs. Mark Ropel, S.O.L.T.; Robert J. Cronin, S.O.L.T.; Scott Brossart, S.O.L.T.; Shane Mckee, S.O.L.T.; Deacon Francis Davis.
Church: Box 2000, 58316. Tel: 701-477-5601; Fax: 701-477-0602.
School—St. Ann, (Grades K-6), P.O. Box 2020, 58316-2020. Tel: 701-477-2667. Angela Zaccardelli, Prin. Sisters 3; Lay Teachers 6; Students 38.
Catechesis/Religious Program—Students 150.

2—ST. ANTHONY (1885) [CEM], Served from Belcourt. Rev. Mark Ropel, S.O.L.T.
Mailing Address: *c/o St. Ann*, P.O. Box 2000, 58316. Tel: 701-477-5601.
Catechesis/Religious Program—Students 10.

3—ST. BENEDICT'S CHURCH OF BELCOURT (1940), Served from St. John. Rev. Mark Wheelan, S.O.L.T., Admin.
Mailing Address: P.O. Box 170, St. John, 58369-0170. Tel: 701-477-3081; Fax: 701-477-0256.

BISBEE, TOWNER CO., HOLY ROSARY (1889) [CEM], Served from Rolette. Rev. Philip Chacko.
Mailing Address: P.O. Box 155, 58317. In Res., Rev. Gerald A. McCarthy (Retired).
Church: 304 3rd Ave. W., 58317. Tel: 701-656-3307; Fax: 701-246-3449.

BOTTINEAU, BOTTINEAU CO., ST. MARK'S CHURCH OF BOTTINEAU (1901) [CEM], Also serving Westhope. Rev. Paul R. Schuster.
322 Sinclair St., 58318-1024. Tel: 701-228-3164.
Catechesis/Religious Program—Students 108.

BREMEN, WELLS CO., ST. JOSEPH (1896) [CEM] Closed. For inquiries for parish records contact the chancery. Sacramental records located at St. John, New Rockford.

BROCKET, RAMSEY CO., ST. JOSEPH (1910) Closed. For inquiries for parish records contact the Chancellor's Office. Sacramental records are at St. Mary, Lakota.

BUCHANAN, STUTSMAN CO., ST. MARGARET ALACOQUE (1924) [CEM], Served from Jamestown. Very Rev. Al M. Bitz.
Mailing Address: *c/o Basilica of St. James*, 622 1st Ave. S., Jamestown, 58401-4648. Tel: 701-252-0119; Fax: 701-952-6992. Email: parish@csicable.net.
Catechesis/Religious Program—Twinned with St. Michael in Pingree. Students 6.

BUFFALO, CASS CO., ST. THOMAS (1900) [JC], Served from Casselton. Rev. James Ermer.
Mailing Address: *c/o St. Leo*, P.O. Box 340, Casselton, 58012. Tel: 701-347-4609.
Church: 401 3rd St. N. Buffalo, 58011. Tel: 701-633-5150.
Catechesis/Religious Program—Students 14.

BURNSTAD, LOGAN CO., ST. CLARE OF ASSISI (1915) Closed. For inquiries for parish records contact the chancery. Sacramental records are at St. Philip Meri, Napoleon.

CANDO, TOWNER CO., SACRED HEART CHURCH OF CANDO (1893) [CEM], Also serving Leeds. Rev. Joseph D'Aco; Deacon James Eggl.
Mailing Address: P.O. Box 399, 58324.
Church: 310 3rd Ave., 58324. Email: shparish@dvl.midco.net.
Catechesis/Religious Program—Tel: 701-968-3830. Students 47.

CARRINGTON, FOSTER CO., SACRED HEART CHURCH OF CARRINGTON (1887) [CEM], Also serving Sykeston. Rev. David Syverson.
Mailing Address: P.O. Box 420, 58421. Tel: 701-652-2519.
Church: 663 1st St. S., 58421. Fax: 701-652-2518.
Catechesis/Religious Program—Tel: 701-652-2072. Students 155.

CASSELTON, CASS CO., ST. LEO'S CHURCH OF CASSELTON (1880) [CEM], Also serving Buffalo. Rev. James Ermer.
Mailing Address: P.O. Box 340, 58012.
Church: 211 Langer Ave., 58012. Tel: 701-347-4609; Fax: 701-347-4611. Email: stleo@casselton.net.
Catechesis/Religious Program—Students 188.

CAVALIER, PEMBINA CO., ST. BRIGID OF IRELAND CHURCH OF CAVALIER (1883) [CEM], Also serving Crystal. Rev. Robert Pecotte.
Mailing Address: P.O. Box 280, 58220-0280. Tel: 701-265-8877; Fax: 701-265-8848.
Church: 201 W. 1st Ave. S., 58220.
Catechesis/Religious Program—Students 35.

CAYUGA, SARGENT CO., STS. PETER & PAUL CHURCH OF CAYUGA (1916), Served from Lidgerwood. Rev. Robert Smith.
Mailing Address: *c/o St. Boniface*, P.O. Box 449, Lidgerwood, 58053-0449. Tel: 701-538-4604; Fax: 701-538-4600.
Church: 229 Franklin Ave. W., 58032.
Catechesis/Religious Program—Students 3.

COGSWELL, SARGENT CO., OUR LADY OF MERCY (1903) [CEM] Closed. For inquiries for parish records contact the chancery. Sacramental records are at St. Mary, Forman.

CONWAY, WALSH CO., ST. MARK (1884) Closed. For inquiries for parish records contact the Chancellor's Office. Sacramental records are at St. John, Pisek.

COOPERSTOWN, GRIGGS CO., ST. GEORGE (1939) [CEM], Also serving Aneta, Jessie, Finley. Rev. Richard Fineo.
Mailing Address: P.O. Box 217, 58425.
Church: 804 Foster Ave. N.W., 58425. Tel: 701-797-2624; Fax: 701-797-2632.
Catechesis/Religious Program—Students 20.

COURTENAY, STUTSMAN CO., ST. MARY, [CEM] Closed. For inquiries for parish records contact the chancery. Sacramental records are at St. Boniface, Wimbledon.

CRARY, RAMSEY CO., ST. BENEDICT (1910) [CEM] Closed. For inquiries for parish records contact the chancery. Sacramental records are at St. Joseph, Devil Lake.

CROW HILL, BENSON CO., ST. JEROME'S CHURCH OF CROW HILL (1892), (Native American), [CEM], Served from Fort Totten. Rev. Charles J. Leute, O.P.
Mailing Address: Box 299, Fort Totten, 58335. Tel: 701-766-4314.
Catechesis/Religious Program—Students 12.

CRYSTAL, PEMBINA CO., ST. PATRICK'S CHURCH OF CRYSTAL (1892) [CEM], Served from Cavalier. Rev. Robert Pecotte.
Mailing Address: P.O. Box 280, Cavalier, 58220. Tel: 701-265-8877; Fax: 701-265-8848.
Catechesis/Religious Program—Students 20.

DAZEY, BARNES CO., ST. MARY'S CHURCH OF DAZEY (1899) [CEM], Served from Wimbledon. Rev. Steven J. Meyer.
Mailing Address: P.O. Box 9, Wimbledon, 58492.
Church: 1606 16th St., S.E., 58429. Tel: 701-435-2310.
Catechesis/Religious Program—Students 13.

DEVILS LAKE, RAMSEY CO., ST. JOSEPH'S CHURCH OF DEVILS LAKE (1884) Very Rev. Dale H. Kinzler; Rev. Peter Sharpe.

Mailing Address & Church: 501 4th St., N.E., Box 898, 58301. Tel: 701-662-7558; Fax: 701-662-7559. Email: stjosephschurch@dvl.midco.net.
School—(Grades PreK-6), 824 10th Ave., N.E., 58301. Tel: 701-662-5016; Fax: 701-662-5017. Tom Burckhard, Prin. Lay Teachers 15; Students 141.
Catechesis / Religious Program—Students 215.

DICKEY, LAMOURE CO., ASSUMPTION OF MARY (1909) [CEM], Served from LaMoure. Rev. William Callery.
Mailing Address: *c/o Holy Rosary*, P.O. Box 217, Lamoure, 58458. Tel: 701-883-5987; Fax: 701-883-4359.
Church: 106 Main St., 58431.

DRAKE, MCHENRY CO., ST. MARGARET MARY (1910) [CEM], Served by Anamoose. Rev. Robert Wapenski.
Res.: 605 Main St., P.O. Box 197, 58736. Tel: 701-465-3284; Fax: 773-496-3780.
Catechesis / Religious Program—Students 38.

DRAYTON, PEMBINA CO., ST. EDWARD'S CHURCH OF DRAYTON (1889) [CEM], Also serving Pembina. Rev. Joseph Okogba.
Mailing Address: P.O. Box 215, 58225. Tel: 701-454-6171; Fax: 701-454-6171. Email: stedward@polarcomm.com.
Church: 211 N. Main St., 58225.
Catechesis / Religious Program—Students 16.

DUNSEITH, ROLETTE CO.
1—IMMACULATE HEART OF MARY (1948) [CEM] Closed. For inquiries for parish records please see St. Michael's Church, Dunseith.
2—ST. LOUIS KING OF FRANCE (1882) [CEM] Closed. For inquiries for parish records please St. Michael's Church, Dunseith.
3—ST. MICHAEL THE ARCHANGEL DUNSEITH (2007) Rev. Jeff Eppler, S.O.L.T., Admin.
Mailing Address: P.O. Box 160, 58329. Tel: 701-244-5738.
Res.: 112 First St., N.W., 58329.
Catechesis / Religious Program—Students 44.

EDGELEY, LAMOURE CO., TRANSFIGURATION CHURCH OF EDGELEY (1889) [CEM], Also serving Nortonville. Rev. Thaines Arulandu.
Mailing Address: 205 Second St., P.O. Box 347, 58433. Tel: 701-493-2387; Fax: 701-493-2387.
Catechesis / Religious Program—Students 82.

ELLENDALE, DICKEY CO., ST. HELENA'S CHURCH OF ELLENDALE (1888) [CEM], Also serving Fullerton. Rev. John Fisher Kizito.
Mailing Address: P.O. Box 796, 58436. Tel: 701-349-3297; Fax: 701-349-3297.
Church: 421 N. 2nd St., 58436.
Catechesis / Religious Program—Tel: 701-349-4128. Students 80.

ENDERLIN, RANSOM CO., ST. PATRICK'S CHURCH OF ENDERLIN (1901) [CEM], Also serving Sheldon and Fingal. Rev. Msgr. Daniel J. Pilon.
Mailing Address: 302 Bluff St., 58027. Tel: 701-437-2791; Fax: 262-437-2791. Email: stpatrick@mlgc.com. Web: www.fargodiocese.org/parish/enderlin.
Catechesis / Religious Program—Students 23.

ESMOND, BENSON CO., ST. BONIFACE (1909) [CEM], Also serving Maddock and Balta. Rev. Julian Kupisz.
Mailing Address: P.O. Box 37, 58332-0037. Tel: 701-249-8360; Fax: 701-249-3459.
Church: 108 Alta Ave. N., 58332.
Catechesis / Religious Program—Students 6.

FAIRMOUNT, RICHLAND CO., ST. ANTHONY'S CHURCH OF FAIRMOUNT (1909) [CEM], Served from Hankinson. Rev. Scott Sautner.
Mailing Address: Box 292, 58030. Tel: 701-474-5518.
Church: 204 2nd St. N., 58030.
Catechesis / Religious Program—Students 29.

FESSENDEN, WELLS CO., ST. AUGUSTINE'S CHURCH OF FESSENDEN (1896), Also serving Hurdsville and McClusky. Rev. Jerome Okafor.
105 7th Ave. S., 58438-7404. Tel: 701-547-3430.
Catechesis / Religious Program—Students 11.

FINGAL, BARNES CO., HOLY TRINITY CHURCH OF FINGAL (1889) [CEM 2], Served by Enderlin. Rev. Msgr. Daniel J. Pilon.
Mailing Address: 302 Bluff St., Enderlin, 58027. Tel: 701-437-2791; Fax: 701-437-2791. Web: www.fargodiocese.org/parish/fingal.
Catechesis / Religious Program—Students 13.

FINLEY, STEELE CO., ST. OLAF (1948) [JC], Served from Cooperstown. Rev. Richard Fineo.
Mailing Address: P.O. Box 217, Cooperstown, 58425. Tel: 701-797-2624.
Church: 100 Taft St., 58230.
Catechesis / Religious Program—Tel: 701-524-1101. Students 13.

FORMAN, SARGENT CO., ST. MARY (1913) [CEM], Served from Oakes. Rev. Kevin Willis, Admin.
Mailing Address: 480 4th St. S.W., 58032. Tel: 701-724-3319; Fax: 701-724-3310. Email: 4steeples@drtel.net.
Catechesis / Religious Program—Tel: 701-724-3440. Students 22.

FORT TOTTEN, BENSON CO., SEVEN DOLORS (1875), (Native American), [CEM], Also serving Crow Hill, Tokio. Rev. Charles J. Leute, O.P.; Deacon Anthony McDonald.
Mailing Address: P.O. Box 299, 58335. Tel: 701-766-4314; Fax: 701-766-1842.
Catechesis / Religious Program—Tel: 701-766-4314. Students 12.

FRIED, STUTSMAN CO., SACRED HEART (1888) Closed. For inquiries for parish records contact the Chancellor's Office. Sacramental records are at Basilica St. James, Jamestown.

FULDA, MCHENRY CO., ST. ANSELM (1901) [CEM] Closed. For inquiries for parish records contact the chancery. Sacramental records are at St. Therese, Rugby.

FULLERTON, DICKEY CO., ST. PATRICK (1921) [CEM], Served from Ellendale. Rev. John Fisher Kizito.
Mailing Address: *c/o St. Helena*, P.O. Box 796, Ellendale, 58436. Tel: 701-349-3297.
Church: 207 Monroe St. N., 58441.
Catechesis / Religious Program—Students 8.

GACKLE, LOGAN CO., ST. ANNE (1951) Closed. For inquiries for parish records contact the chancery. Sacramental records are at St. Philip Neri, Napoleon.

GENESEO, SARGENT CO., ST. MARTIN'S CHURCH OF GENESEO (1907) [CEM], Served from Lidgerwood. Rev. Robert Smith.
413 Main St., 58053. Tel: 701-538-4604.
Catechesis / Religious Program—Students 10.

GRAFTON, WALSH CO., ST. JOHN THE EVANGELIST'S CHURCH OF GRAFTON (1881) [CEM] Rev. Timothy Schroeder; Deacon Michael Grzadzielewski.
Church: 344 15th St. W., 58237. Tel: 701-352-1648; Fax: 701-352-1608.
St. John's Catechetical Center— 58237. Brent Hermans, D.R.E.; Rose Marie Kerner, D.R.E.; Brian Herding, Pastoral Assoc. Students 252.
Catechesis / Religious Program—Students 250.

GRAND FORKS, GRAND FORKS CO.
1—HOLY FAMILY CHURCH OF GRAND FORKS (1960) [JC] Very Rev. Phillip Ackerman; Rev. Richard LaCorte (Retired).
1018 18th Ave. S., 58201-6828. Tel: 701-746-1454; Fax: 701-746-1456. Web: holyfamilygrandforks.parishesonline.com.
School—(Grades K-5) Tel: 701-775-9886; Fax: 701-775-0221. Mr. Charles Scherr, Prin.; Loria Novak, Librarian. Lay Teachers 6; Students 70.
Catechesis / Religious Program—Fax: 701-746-1456. Students 115.
2—ST. MARY (1915) [JC] Rev. Daniel Mrnarevic; Deacon Don Litzinger.
216 Belmont Rd., 58201. Tel: 701-775-9318; Fax: 701-775-7568. Email: stmarysgfnd@yahoo.com.
Catechesis / Religious Program—Tel: 701-775-2842. Students 83.
3—ST. MICHAEL'S CHURCH OF GRAND FORKS (1872) [JC] Revs. H. Gerard Braun; William Peter Gerlach.
520 N. Sixth St., 58203. Tel: 701-772-2624. Email: gfstmichaels@yahoo.com. Web: www.stmichaelsgf.com.
School—(Grades PreK-6), 504 5th Ave. N., 58203. Tel: 701-772-1822; Fax: 701-772-0211. Stephanie Schuster, Prin. Lay Teachers 13; Students 101.
Catechesis / Religious Program—Tel: 701-772-2282; Fax: 701-772-2282. Students 214.
4—ST. THOMAS AQUINAS NEWMAN CHURCH OF GRAND FORKS (1951) [JC] Rev. Jason Lefor; Deacon Samuel Pupino.
410 Cambridge St., 58203. Tel: 701-777-6850; Fax: 701-777-6851. Web: www.und.nodak.edu/dept/newman.
Catechesis / Religious Program—Students 55.

GRANVILLE, MCHENRY CO., OUR LADY OF PERPETUAL HELP (1933) Closed. For inquiries for parish records contact the chancery. Sacramental records are at St. Cecilia, Towner.

GWINNER, SARGENT CO., ST. VINCENT'S CHURCH OF GWINNER (1984) [CEM], Served from Lisbon. Rev. Jerald L.C. Finnestad.
Mailing Address: *c/o St. Aloysius*, 701 Oak St., Lisbon, 58054. Tel: 701-683-4620; Fax: 701-683-5703.
Church: 302 Hwy. 13 E., 58040. Tel: 701-683-4620.
Catechesis / Religious Program—Tel: 701-678-2364. Students 30.

HANKINSON, RICHLAND CO., ST. PHILIP'S CHURCH OF HANKINSON (1889) [CEM] Rev. Scott Sautner.
612 S. Main, P.O. Box 419, 58041. Tel: 701-242-7327; Fax: 701-242-7773.
Catechesis / Religious Program—Students 109.

HANSBORO, TOWNER CO., SACRED HEART, Closed. For inquiries for parish records please contact the Chancellor's Office. Sacramental records are at St. Joachim, Rolla.

HARVEY, WELLS CO., ST. CECILIA'S CHURCH OF HARVEY (1895) [CEM], Also serving Selz. Rev. Franklin Miller; Deacon Jeffrey M. Faul.
413 E. Brewster St., 58341. Tel: 701-324-2144; Fax: 701-324-2637.
Catechesis / Religious Program—Tel: 701-324-2637. Students 84.

HILLSBORO, TRAILL CO., ST. ROSE OF LIMA'S CHURCH OF HILLSBORO (1892) [CEM], Also serves Argusville. Rev. Leo Kinney.
Mailing Address: P.O. Box 459, 58045-0459. Tel: 701-636-4541.
Church: 503 3rd St. S.E., 58045.
Catechesis / Religious Program—Students 103.

HOPE, STEELE CO., ST. AGATHA'S CHURCH OF HOPE (1907), Served from Oriska. Rev. Timothy Johnson.
Mailing Address: *c/o St. Bernard's Church of Oriska*, 606 5th St., Oriska, 58063. Tel: 701-845-3713; Fax: 701-845-0172. Email: oriska_tri_parish@yahoo.com.
Church: 819 Steele Ave., 58046.
Catechesis / Religious Program—Students 24.

HUNTER, CASS CO., ST. AGNES (1898), Served by Mayville. Rev. Matthew Attansey.
Mailing Address: c/o Our Lady of Peace, 846 5th St. S.E., Mayville, 58257. Tel: 701-788-3234.
Church: 102 1st St. E., 58048.
Catechesis / Religious Program—Tel: 701-967-8970. Students 26.

HURDSFIELD, WELLS CO., ST. PATRICK'S CHURCH OF HURDSFIELD (1907), Served from Fessenden. Rev. Jerome Okafor.
Mailing Address: *c/o St. Augustine*, 105 7th Ave S., Fessenden, 58438. Tel: 701-547-3430; Fax: 701-547-3766.
Church: 12 3rd St. W., 58451.
Catechesis / Religious Program—Students 18.

JAMESTOWN, STUTSMAN CO., ST. JAMES BASILICA OF JAMESTOWN (1881) [CEM], Also Serving Buchanan, Windsor and Pingree. Very Rev. Al M. Bitz; Revs. John Arthur McGinnis; Joseph Barrett; Sr. Michaeleen Jantzer, O.S.B., Pastoral Min.; Deacons Thomas Geffre; Geary McCleery.
Mailing Address: 622 1st Ave. S., 58401-4648. Tel: 701-252-0119; Fax: 701-952-6992. Email: basilica@stjamesbasilica.org. Web: www.stjamesbasilica.org.
Church: 622 1st Ave. S., 58401.
School—St. John Academy, (Grades PreK-6), 215 5th St., S.E., 58401. Tel: 701-252-3397; Fax: 701-252-2434. Email: charles.stastny@sendit.nodak.edu. Web: www.stjamesbasilica.org/stjohn. Charles Stastney, Prin. Lay Teachers 14; Students 232.
St. James Faith Formation—214 4th St., S.E., 58401. Tel: 701-252-0478; Fax: 701-252-0478. Email: faithformation@csicable.net. Shirley Wallace, D.R.E. Lay Teachers 43.
Catechesis / Religious Program—Students 126.

JESSIE, GRIGGS CO., ST. LAWRENCE (1888) [CEM], Served from Cooperstown. Rev. Richard Fineo.
Mailing Address: *c/o St. George*, P.O. Box 217, Cooperstown, 58425. Tel: 701-797-2624.
Church: 105 Dewey St., 58452.
Catechesis / Religious Program—Students 10.

KARLSRUHE, MCHENRY CO., STS. PETER & PAUL CHURCH OF KARLSRUHE (1905) [CEM], Served from Velva. Very Rev. James Gross.
Mailing Address: *c/o St. Cecilia*, P.O. Box K, Velva, 58790-0496. Tel: 701-338-2663; Fax: 701-338-2883.
Church: 401 N. Main, 58744.
Catechesis / Religious Program—Students 11.

KENSAL, STUTSMAN CO., ST. JOHN'S CHURCH OF KENSAL (1917) [CEM], Served from Wimbledon. Rev. Steven J. Meyer.
Mailing Address: *c/o St. Boniface*, P.O. Box 9, Wimbledon, 58492. Tel: 701-435-2310.
Church: 407 Pleasant Ave., 58455.

KINDRED, CASS CO., ST. MAURICE (1965), Served from Wild Rice. Rev. Jared Kadlec; Deacon Clarence Vetter.
Mailing Address & Church: 5313 165th Ave., S.E., P.O. Box 272, 58051. Tel: 701-428-3094; Fax: 701-428-3094. Web: www.fargodiocese.org/parish/kindred.
Catechesis / Religious Program—Tel: 701-428-3094. Students 76.

KINTYRE, LOGAN CO., ST. BONIFACE (1905) [CEM] Closed. For inquiries for parish records contact the chancery. Sacramental records are at St. Philip Neri, Napleon.

KNOX, BENSON CO., ST. MARY'S CHURCH OF KNOX (1936) [CEM], Served from Rugby. Rev. Thomas Graner.
c/o St. Therese, 218 3rd St., S.E., Rugby, 58368-1814. Tel: 701-776-5327.
Church: 129 Morgan, 58343.
Catechesis / Religious Program—Students 7.

LA MOURE, LA MOURE CO., HOLY ROSARY CHURCH OF LA MOURE (1890) [CEM], Also serving Dickey and Verona. Rev. William Callery.
Mailing Address: P.O. Box 217, 58458.
Church: 209 1 St., S.E., 58458. Tel: 701-883-5987; Fax: 701-883-4359.
Catechesis / Religious Program—Students 74.

LAKE WILLIAMS, KIDDER CO., OUR LADY OF THE LAKE (1946) Closed. For inquiries for parish records contact the Chancellor's Office. Sacramental records are at St. Francis de Sales, Steele.

LAKOTA, NELSON CO., ST. MARY'S CHURCH OF LAKOTA (1902), Also serving Tolna and Michigan. Rev. John F. Aerts.
Mailing Address: P.O. Box 509, 58344. Tel: 701-247-2594. Email: smcc@polarcomm.com.
Church: 109 East Ave. E., 58344.
Catechesis/Religious Program—Tel: 701-247-2584. Students 41.

LANGDON, CAVALIER CO., ST. ALPHONSUS CHURCH OF LANGDON (1888) [CEM], Also serving Nekoma and Wales. Rev. William McDermott.
Mailing Address: 1010 3rd St., 58249. Tel: 701-256-5966; Fax: 701-256-2358.
School—(Grades K-8), 209 10th Ave., 58249. Tel: 701-256-2354. Sr. Anne Frawley, P.B.V.M., Prin. Sisters 1; Lay Teachers 11; Students 82.
Catechesis/Religious Program—Students 40.

LANKIN, WALSH CO., ST. JOSEPH'S CHURCH OF LANKIN (1906) [CEM], Served by Pisek. Very Rev. Samuel Ezeibekwe.
Mailing Address: *c/o St. John Nepomucene*, P.O. Box 27, Pisek, 58273.
Church: 506 4th St., 58250. Tel: 701-284-6060.
Catechesis/Religious Program—Students 10.

LANSFORD, BOTTINEAU CO., ST. JOHN'S CHURCH OF LANSFORD (1903) Rev. Chris B. Walter, Admin.
303 E. Main St., 58750. Tel: 701-756-6601; Fax: 701-756-6901.

LARIMORE, GRAND FORKS CO., ST. STEPHEN'S CHURCH OF LARIMORE (1882) Rev. James Goodwin.
Mailing Address: P.O. Box 778, 58251. Tel: 701-343-2377; Fax: 701-343-2316. Email: ststlarimore@msn.com.
Church: 311 W. Front St., 58251.
Catechesis/Religious Program—Tel: 701-343-2747. Students 138.

LEEDS, BENSON CO., ST. VINCENT DE PAUL CHURCH OF LEEDS (1897) [CEM], Served from Cando. Rev. Joseph D'Aco.
Mailing Address: P.O. Box 399, Cando, 58324. Tel: 701-968-3462; Fax: 701-968-3830.
Church: 315 Central Ave., Cando, 58324.
Catechesis/Religious Program—Students 38.

LEROY, PEMBINA CO., ST. JOSEPH (1873) [CEM] Closed. For inquiries for parish records contact the chancery. Sacramental records are at St. Boniface, Walhalla.

LIDGERWOOD, RICHLAND CO., ST. BONIFACE CHURCH OF LIDGERWOOD (1887) [CEM], Also serving Geneseo and Cayuga. Rev. Robert Smith.
Mailing Address: P.O. Box 449, 58053.
Church: 230 1st St., N.W., 58053. Tel: 701-538-4600.
Catechesis/Religious Program—Tel: 701-538-4604. Students 75.

LISBON, RANSOM CO., ST. ALOYSIUS CHURCH OF LISBON (1884) [CEM], Also serving Gwinner. Rev. Jerald L.C. Finnestad.
Church & Mailing Address: 701 Oak St., 58054-4256. Tel: 701-683-4620; Fax: 701-683-5703.
Catechesis/Religious Program—Students 97.

LOMICE, WALSH CO., ST. CATHERINE (1936) [CEM] Closed. For inquiries for parish records contact the chancery. Sacramental records are at St. Mary, Lakota.

MADDOCK, BENSON CO., ST. WILLIAM (1954), Served from Esmond. Rev. Julian Kupisz.
Mailing Address: *c/o St. Boniface*, P.O. Box 37, Esmond, 58332. Tel: 701-249-8360.
Catechesis/Religious Program—Students 12.

MANTADOR, RICHLAND CO., STS. PETER & PAUL CHURCH OF MANTADOR (1881) [CEM], Served from Mooreton. Rev. Peter J. Anderl.
Mailing Address: P.O. Box 39, 58058. Tel: 701-274-8259.
Church: 609 County Rd. 25, 58058.
Catechesis/Religious Program—Students 9.

MANVEL, GRAND FORKS CO., ST. TIMOTHY'S CHURCH OF MANVEL (1882) [CEM] Rev. Bernard Schneider.
Church: 1207 Oldham Ave., 58256-4335. Tel: 701-696-2219.
Catechesis/Religious Program—Students 69.

MARION, LA MOURE CO., ST. FRANCIS (1910) [CEM] Closed. For inquiries for parish records contact the chancery. Sacramental records are at Holy Rosary, La Moure.

MAYVILLE, TRAILL CO., OUR LADY OF PEACE CHURCH OF MAYVILLE (1945), Also serving Hunter. Rev. Matthew Attansey.
Church: 846 5th St., S.E., 58257. Tel: 701-788-3234; Fax: 701-788-3234.
Catechesis/Religious Program—Students 67.

MCCLUSKY, SHERIDAN CO., HOLY FAMILY (1905), Served from Fessenden. Rev. Jerome Okafor.
Mailing Address: *c/o St. Augustine*, 105 7th Ave S., Fessenden, 58438. Tel: 701-547-3430; Fax: 701-547-3766.
Church: 409 Ave. B E., 58463.
Catechesis/Religious Program—Students 2.

MCHENRY, FOSTER CO., STS. PETER & PAUL CHURCH OF MCHENRY (1912) [CEM], Served from New Rockford. Rev. Bernard Pfau.
Mailing Address: *c/o St. John*, P.O. Box 389, New Rockford, 58356. Tel: 701-947-5325; Fax: 701-947-5325. Web: www.newrockford.com.
Church: 391 Conn St., 58464.
Catechesis/Religious Program—Students 7.

MEDINA, STUTSMAN CO., ST. MARY'S CHURCH OF MEDINA (1905) [CEM], Served from Steele. Rev. Jerome Hunkler.
Mailing Address: P.O Box 87, Steele, 58482-0087. Tel: 701-475-2333.
Church: 105 3rd Ave. S.E., 58467.
Catechesis/Religious Program—Students 20.

MICHIGAN, NELSON CO., ST. LAWRENCE O'TOOLE'S CHURCH OF MICHIGAN (1883), Served from Lakota. Rev. John F. Aerts.
Mailing Address: P.O. Box 509, Lakota, 58344. Tel: 701-247-2594.
Church: 214 Broadway St., 58259.
Catechesis/Religious Program—Students 8.

MILNOR, SARGENT CO., ST. ARNOLD'S CHURCH OF MILNOR (1905) [CEM], Served from Wyndmere. Rev. Leonard Loegering.
Mailing Address: P.O. Box 295, 58060.
Church: 107 3rd St., 58060. Tel: 701-427-9288.
Catechesis/Religious Program—Tel: 701-427-5327. Students 57.

MILTON, CAVALIER CO., ST. CLOTILDE (1893) Closed. For inquiries for parish records contact the Chancellor's Office. Sacramental records are at St. Alphonsus, Langdon.

MINNEWAUKAN, BENSON CO., ST. JAMES (1899) Closed. For inquiries for parish records, contact the Chancellor's Office. Sacramental records are at St. Joseph, Devil's Lake.

MINTO, WALSH CO., SACRED HEART CHURCH OF MINTO (1905) [CEM], Also serving Warsaw. Rev. John Kleinschmidt.
Mailing Address: P.O. Box 316, 58261. Tel: 701-248-3589; Fax: 701-248-3139. Email: shpastor@invisimax.com.
Church: 621 3rd St., 58261.
Catechesis/Religious Program—Students 55.

MOORETON, RICHLAND CO., ST. ANTHONY'S (1884) [CEM], Also serving Mantador. Rev. Peter J. Anderl.
204 Mooreton Ave. N., 58061. Tel: 701-274-8259.
Catechesis/Religious Program—Students 58.

MOUNT CARMEL, CAVALIER CO., OUR LADY OF MOUNT CARMEL (1888) [CEM] Closed. For inquiries for parish records contact the chancery. Sacramental records located at St. Alphonsus, Langdon.

MUNICH, CAVALIER CO., ST. MARY (1916) [CEM 3], Also serving Starkweather. Rev. Anthony Hession.
Mailing Address: P.O. Box 159, 58352-0159. Tel: 701-682-5178; Fax: 701-682-5124.
Church: 607 Main, 58352.
Catechesis/Religious Program—Tel: 701-682-5124. Students 26.

NAPOLEON, LOGAN CO., ST. PHILIP'S CHURCH OF NAPOLEON (1906) [CEM] Very Rev. Ross Laframboise; Deacons Allen Baumgartner; Gary Schumacher.
401 Broadway, 58561-7013. Tel: 701-754-2860.
Catechesis/Religious Program—Students 145.

NECHE, PEMBINA CO., STS. NEREUS & ACHILLEUS CHURCH OF NECHE (1887) [CEM], Served from Walhalla. Rev. Thomas Krupich.
Mailing Address: *c/o St. Boniface*, P.O. Box 228, Walhalla, 58282-0228. Tel: 701-549-2729; Fax: 701-549-3256.
Church: 6th St., 58265.
Catechesis/Religious Program—Students 15.

NEKOMA, CAVALIER CO., ST. EDWARD (1907) [CEM], Served from Langdon. Rev. William McDermott.
Mailing Address: *c/o St. Alphonsus*, 1010 3rd St., Langdon, 58249. Tel: 701-256-5966; Fax: 701-256-2358.
Church: 323 Main.
Catechesis/Religious Program—Students 3.

NEW ROCKFORD, EDDY CO., ST. JOHN'S CHURCH OF NEW ROCKFORD (1904) [CEM], Also serving McHenry. Rev. Bernard Pfau.
Mailing Address: P.O. Box 389, 58356. Tel: 701-947-5325.
Church: 116 1st Ave. N., 58356.
Catechesis/Religious Program—Students 96.

NORTONVILLE, LAMOURE CO., HOLY SPIRIT CHURCH OF NORTONVILLE (1912) [JC], Served from Edgeley. Rev. Thaines Arulandu.
Mailing Address: *c/o Transfiguration*, P.O. Box 347, Edgeley, 58433. Tel: 701-493-2387; Fax: 701-493-2387.
Church: 705 1st St., 58454.
Catechesis/Religious Program—Students 21.

OAKES, DICKEY CO., ST. CHARLES CHURCH OF OAKES (1905) [CEM], Also serving Forman. Rev. Kevin Willis, Admin.
410 Seventh St. N., 58474. Tel: 701-742-2418; Fax: 701-742-2418.
Catechesis/Religious Program—Tel: 701-742-2911. Students 113.

OAKWOOD, WALSH CO., SACRED HEART CHURCH OF OAKWOOD (1881) [CEM], Also serving St. Thomas. Rev. James P. Lauerman.
7010 County Rd. 4, Grafton, 58237-8860. Tel: 701-352-1392.
Catechesis/Religious Program—Students 29.

OLGA, CAVALIER CO., OUR LADY OF THE SACRED HEART (1882) [CEM 2] Closed. For inquiries for parish records contact the chancery. Sacramental records are at St. Boniface, Walhalla.

ORISKA, BARNES CO., ST. BERNARD'S CHURCH OF ORISKA (1881) [CEM], Also serving Hope and Sanborn. Rev. Timothy Johnson; Deacon Jim McAllister.
606 Fifth St., 58063. Tel: 701-845-3713; Fax: 701-845-0172. Email: oriska_tri_parish@yahoo.com.
Catechesis/Religious Program—Students 14.

ORRIN, PIERCE CO., SACRED HEART (1903) [CEM] Closed. For inquiries for parish records contact the chancery. Sacramental records located at St. Therese, Rugby.

OSNABROCK, CAVALIER CO., ST. JOSEPH (1909) Closed. For inquiries for parish records contact the Chancellor's Office. Sacramental records are at St. Alphonsus, Langdon.

PAGE, CASS CO., ST. JAMES (1909) [CEM] Closed. For inquiries for parish records contact the chancery. Sacramental records are at St. Bernard, Oriska.

PARK RIVER, WALSH CO., ST. MARY (1888) [CEM], Also serving Veseleyville. Rev. Robert P. Unger; Deacon Gerald F. Sobolik.
Mailing Address: P.O. Box 110, 58270-0110. Tel: 701-284-6165; Fax: 701-284-7789.
Church: 505 Park St. E., 58270.
Catechesis/Religious Program—Tel: 701-284-7789. Students 87.

PEMBINA, PEMBINA CO., ASSUMPTION CHURCH OF PEMBINA (1818) [CEM], Served from Drayton. Rev. Joseph Okogba.
Church: 143 Hayden St., 58271. Tel: 701-825-6266; Fax: 701-825-6266.
Catechesis/Religious Program—Students 26.

PENN, RAMSEY CO., IMMACULATE CONCEPTION (1986) Closed. For inquiries for parish records contact the Chancellor's Office. Sacramental records are at St. Vincent de Paul, Leeds.

PINGREE, STUTSMAN CO., ST. MICHAEL (1905) [CEM], Served from Jamestown. Very Rev. Al M. Bitz.
Mailing Address: *c/o Basilica of St. James*, 622 1st. Ave. S., Jamestown, 58401-4648. Tel: 701-252-0119; Fax: 701-952-6992.
Catechesis/Religious Program—Students 2.

PISEK, WALSH CO., ST. JOHN NEPOMUCENE'S CHURCH OF PISEK (1886) [CEM], Also serving Lankin and Bechyne. Very Rev. Samuel Ezeibekwe.
Mailing Address: P.O. Box 27, 58273. Tel: 701-284-6060; Fax: 701-284-6692.
Church: 167 Newton Ave., 58273.
Catechesis/Religious Program—Students 4.

REYNOLDS, GRAND FORKS CO., OUR LADY OF PERPETUAL HELP CHURCH OF REYNOLDS (1895) [CEM], Serves Thompson. Rev. John Cavanaugh.
Mailing Address: Box 68, 58275. Tel: 701-847-3096.
Church: 424 5th St., 58275.
Catechesis/Religious Program—Students 51.

ROCK LAKE, TOWNER CO., IMMACULATE HEART OF MARY CHURCH OF ROCK LAKE (1949), Served from Rolla. Rev. Jake Miller.
Mailing Address: *c/o St. Joachim*, P.O. Box 788, Rolla, 58367. Tel: 701-477-3568.
Catechesis/Religious Program—Students 7.

ROLETTE, ROLETTE CO., SACRED HEART (1918) [CEM 3], Also serving Willow City and Bisbee. Rev. Philip Chacko.
Mailing Address: P.O. Box 127, 58366. Tel: 701-246-3449; Fax: 701-246-3449. Email: shrolette@fargodiocese.org.
Church: 505 Main, 58366.
Catechesis/Religious Program—Students 39.

ROLLA, ROLETTE CO., ST. JOACHIM'S CHURCH OF ROLLA (1894) [CEM], Also serving Rock Lake. Rev. Jake Miller.
Mailing Address: P.O. Box 788, 58367-0788. Tel: 701-477-3568. Email: stjhm@utma.com.
Church: 210 2nd St., 58367.
Catechesis/Religious Program—Students 62.

RUGBY, PIERCE CO., ST. THERESA, LITTLE FLOWER CHURCH OF RUGBY (1910) [CEM], Also serves Knox. Revs. Thomas Graner; John Ejike; Deacon Arlen Blessum.
218 Third St., S.E., 58368-1814. Tel: 701-776-6388; Fax: 701-776-5327. Email: lfparish@gondtc.com. Web: www.littleflowerrugby.org.
School—(Grades PreSchool-6), 306 Third Ave., S.E., 58368. Tel: 701-776-6258. Bruce Gannarelli, Prin.; Sr. Jean Louise Schafer, O.S.F., Librarian. Sisters of St. Francis of the Immaculate Heart of

Mary (Hankinson, ND) 2; Lay Teachers 9; Students 80.
Catechesis/Religious Program—Tel: 701-776-5327. Students 184.

ST. JOHN, ROLETTE CO., ST. JOHN'S CHURCH OF ST. JOHN (1882) [CEM], Also serves St. Benedict, Belcourt. Rev. Mark Wheelan, S.O.L.T., Admin.
Mailing Address: P.O. Box 170, 58369. Tel: 701-477-3081.
Church: 107 St. Ann St., S.E., 58369.

ST. MICHAEL, BENSON CO., ST. MICHAEL'S CHURCH OF ST. MICHAEL (1874), (Native American), [CEM] Rev. Brian Moen.
Mailing Address: P.O. Box 42, 58370. Tel: 701-766-4151; Fax: 701-766-1085.
Catechesis/Religious Program—Students 29.

ST. THOMAS, PEMBINA CO., ST. THOMAS CHURCH OF ST. THOMAS (1882) [CEM], Served from Oakwood. Rev. James P. Lauerman.
Mailing Address: *c/o Sacred Heart*, 7010 Country Rd. 4, Grafton, 58237. Tel: 701-352-1392.
Church: 640 Main St., 58276.
Catechesis/Religious Program—Students 18.

SANBORN, BARNES CO., SACRED HEART CHURCH OF SANBORN (1904) [CEM], Served from Oriska. Rev. Timothy Johnson.
Mailing Address: *c/o St. Bernard's Church of Oriska*, 606 5th St., Oriska, 58063. Tel: 701-845-3713.
Church: 711-4th St., 58480.

SELZ, PIERCE CO., ST. ANTHONY (1916) [CEM], Served from Harvey. Rev. Franklin Miller.
Mailing Address: 29 Girard St., 58341. Tel: 701-324-4059.
Catechesis/Religious Program— Twinned with St. Cecilia, Harvey. Students 4.

SHELDON, RANSOM CO., OUR LADY OF THE SCAPULAR CHURCH OF SHELDON (1883) [CEM], Served from Enderlin. Rev. Msgr. Daniel J. Pilon.
Mailing Address: *c/o St. Patrick*, 302 Bluff St., Enderlin, 58027. Tel: 701-437-2791. Web: www.fargodiocese.org/parish/sheldon.
Church: 14025 55th St., S.E., 58068.
Catechesis/Religious Program—Students 30.

STARKWEATHER, RAMSEY CO., ASSUMPTION CHURCH OF STARKWEATHER (1905) [CEM], Served from Munich. Rev. Anthony Hession.
Mailing Address: *c/o St. Mary*, P.O. Box 159, Munich, 58352-0159. Tel: 701-682-5178; Fax: 701-682-5124.
Church: 502 Main St., 58377.
Catechesis/Religious Program—Students 15.

STEELE, KIDDER CO., ST. FRANCIS DE SALES (1958) [CEM], Also serves Tappen and Medina. Rev. Jerome Hunkler.
Mailing Address: P.O. Box 87, 58482-0087. Tel: 701-475-2333; Fax: 701-475-2335.
Church: 318 2nd St., S.W., 58482-0087.
Catechesis/Religious Program—Students 57.

STIRUM, SARGENT CO., ST. VINCENT (1986) Closed. For inquiries for parish records contact the Chancellor's Office. Sacramental records are at St. Aloysius, Lisbon.

SYKESTON, WELLS CO., ST. ELIZABETH'S CHURCH OF SKYESTON (1906), (German), [CEM], Served from Carrington. Rev. David Syverson.
Mailing Address: P.O. Box 397, 58486. Tel: 701-984-2266.
Church: 130 Anson Ave., S.E., 58486.
Catechesis/Religious Program—Students 8.

TAPPEN, KIDDER CO., ST. PAUL (1924), Served from Steele. Rev. Jerome Hunkler.
Mailing Address: *c/o St. Francis*, P.O. Box 87, Steele, 58482-0087. Tel: 701-475-2333; Fax: 701-475-2335.
Church: 218 1st St. , N.E., 58487.
Catechesis/Religious Program—Students 5.

THOMPSON, GRAND FORKS CO., ST. JUDE'S CHURCH OF THOMPSON (1895) [CEM], Served from Reynolds. Rev. John Cavanaugh; Deacon Jim West.
Mailing Address: P.O. Box 305, 58278. Tel: 701-599-2574.
Res.: 421 Sanborn St., Reynolds, 58275. Tel: 701-847-3096.
329 Broadway St., 58278.
Catechesis/Religious Program—Students 62.

TOKIO, BENSON CO., CHRIST THE KING CHURCH OF TOKIO (1938), (Native American), Served from Fort Totten. Rev. Charles J. Leute, O.P.
Mailing Address: *c/o Seven Dolors*, P.O. Box 299, Fort Totten, 58335. Tel: 701-766-4314; Fax: 701-766-1842.
Church: 134 2nd St., 58379.

TOLNA, NELSON CO., ST. JOSEPH (1911) [CEM], Served from Lakota. Rev. John F. Aerts.
Mailing Address: *c/o St. Mary*, P.O. Box 509, Lakota, 58344.
Church: 220 Main St., 58380.
Catechesis/Religious Program—Students 9.

TOWNER, MCHENRY CO., ST. CECILIA'S CHURCH OF TOWNER (1903) [CEM] Rev. Wenceslaus Katanga.
Mailing Address: Box 267, 58788-0267. Tel: 701-537-5133. Email: stcs@srt.com.
Church: 503 1st St., S.W., 58788.
Catechesis/Religious Program—Students 40.

VALLEY CITY, BARNES CO., ST. CATHERINE'S CHURCH OF VALLEY CITY (1882) [CEM] Rev. Michael Schommer; Deacons Arlie Braunberger; Raphael Grim; Edward Didier; Carl M. Orthman.
540 Third Ave., N.E., 58072-2628. Tel: 701-845-0354; Fax: 701-845-0556.
School—(Grades K-6) Tel: 701-845-1453; Fax: 701-845-0556. Mr. Ralph Dyrness, Prin. Lay Teachers 6; Students 69.
St. Catherine's Parish Education Center—540 Third Ave., N.E., 58072. Mr. Ralph Dyrness, Parish Education Dir. Lay Teachers 20.
Catechesis/Religious Program—Students 141.

VELVA, MCHENRY CO., ST. CECILIA'S CHURCH OF VELVA (1905) [CEM], Also serving Karlsruhe. Very Rev. James Gross.
Mailing Address: P.O. Box K, 58790-0496. Tel: 701-338-2663; Fax: 701-338-2883. Email: velvakarls@srt.com.
Church: 201 2nd Ave. W., 58790.
Catechesis/Religious Program—Students 106.

VERONA, LAMOURE CO., ST. RAPHAEL'S CHURCH OF VERONA (1898) [CEM], Served from Lamoure. Rev. William Callery.
Mailing Address: *c/o Holy Rosary*, P.O. Box 217, Lamoure, 58458. Tel: 701-883-5987.
Church: 205 1st St., 58490.
Catechesis/Religious Program—Students 7.

VESELEYVILLE, WALSH CO., ST. LUKE'S CHURCH OF VESELEYVILLE (1880) [CEM], Served from Park River. Rev. Robert P. Unger.
Mailing Address: 14207 63rd St., N.E., Grafton, 58237.

WAHPETON, RICHLAND CO., ST. JOHN'S CHURCH OF WAHPETON (1876) [CEM] Very Rev. Dale Lagodinski; Rev. Terry Dodge; Deacons Douglas Campbell; James Anderson.
Office: 115 Second St. N., 58075. Tel: 701-642-6982; Fax: 701-642-2601. Web: www.stjohns-wahpeton.org.
Res.: 222 Dakota Ave., 58075. Tel: 701-642-4985.
School—(Grades PreK-6), 122 Second St. N., 58075. Tel: 701-642-6116; Fax: 701-642-9134. Renee Langenwalter, Prin. Lay Teachers 11; Students 126.
St. John Day Care Center—Tel: 701-642-4922. Joyce Holkup, Dir. Total Staff 23; Students 88.
Catechesis/Religious Program—Students 282.

WALES, CAVALIER CO., ST. MICHAEL'S (1889) [CEM], Served from Langdon. Rev. William McDermott.
Mailing Address: *c/o St. Alphonsus*, 1010 3rd St., Langdon, 58249-2415. Tel: 701-256-5966.
Church: 221 2nd Ave., 58281.

WALHALLA, PEMBINA CO., ST. BONIFACE CHURCH OF WALHALLA (1848) [CEM], Also serving Neche. Rev. Thomas Krupich; Deacon Stanley (Jim) Carpenter.
Mailing Address: P.O. Box 228, 58282. Tel: 701-549-2729; Fax: 701-549-3256. Email: boniface@utma.com.
Church: 801 Central Ave., 58282.
Catechesis/Religious Program—Tel: 701-549-2750. Students 87.

WARSAW, WALSH CO., ST. STANISLAUS CHURCH OF WARSAW (1882) [CEM], Served from Minto. Rev. John Kleinschmidt.
P.O. Box 316, Minto, 58261. Tel: 701-248-3589; Fax: 701-248-3139. Email: shpastor@invisimax.com.
Catechesis/Religious Program—Students 62.

WEST FARGO, CASS CO.
1—BLESSED SACRAMENT CHURCH OF WEST FARGO (1945) [CEM] Rev. Bert Miller; Deacon James Hunt.
210 Fifth Ave. W., 58078-1747. Tel: 701-282-3321; Fax: 701-282-6503. Web: www.blessedsacramentwestfargo.org.
Catechesis/Religious Program—Tel: 701-282-4554. Students 144.
2—HOLY CROSS CHURCH OF WEST FARGO (1981) [CEM] Very Rev. James Meyer; Rev. Mathew V. Pamplaniyil; Deacons John Lane; James Eggl.
1420 16th St. E., 58078-3411. Tel: 701-282-7217; Fax: 701-282-2753. Email: holycrosscc@ideaone.net. Web: www.holycrosscatholicchurch.com.
Catechesis/Religious Program—Students 433.

WESTHOPE, BOTTINEAU CO., ST. ANDREW'S CHURCH OF WESTHOPE (1904) [CEM], Served from Bottineau. Rev. Paul R. Schuster.
Mailing Address: P.O. Box 365, 58793. Tel: 701-245-6171.
Church: 260 1st Ave. E., 58793.
Catechesis/Religious Program—Students 35.

WILD RICE, CASS CO., ST. BENEDICT'S CHURCH OF WILD RICE (1870) [CEM], Also serving Kindred. Rev. Jared Kadlec.
Mailing Address: 11743 38th St. S., Horace, 58047-9512. Tel: 701-588-4288; Fax: 701-588-9290. Email: office@stbensnd.org. Web: www.stbensnd.org.
Catechesis/Religious Program—Michelle Herrington, D.R.E. Students 89.

WILLOW CITY, BOTTINEAU CO., NOTRE DAME DE LA VICTOIRE CHURCH OF WILLOW CITY (1895) [CEM 2], Served by Rolette. Rev. Philip Chacko.
Mailing Address: P.O. Box 115, 58384. Tel: 701-246-3449; Fax: 701-246-3449.
Church: 215 1st St., 58384.
Catechesis/Religious Program—Students 15.

WIMBLEDON, BARNES CO., ST. BONIFACE CHURCH OF WIMBLEDON (1886) [CEM], Also serving Kensal and Dazey. Rev. Steven J. Meyer.
Mailing Address: P.O. Box 9, 58492. Tel: 701-435-2310.
Church: 301 1st Ave., 58492.
Catechesis/Religious Program—Students 34.

WINDSOR, STUTSMAN CO., ST. MATHIAS CHURCH OF WINDSOR (1910) [CEM], Served from Jamestown. Very Rev. Al M. Bitz.
c/o Basilica of St. James, 622 1st Ave. S., Jamestown, 58401-4648. Tel: 701-252-0119; Fax: 701-952-6992. Email: parish@csicable.net.
Church: 207 Washington Ave., 58424.
Catechesis/Religious Program—Students 6.

WISHEK, MCINTOSH CO., ST. PATRICK (1925) [CEM], Also serving Zeeland and Ashley. Rev. Thomas Feltman.
Mailing Address: P.O. Box 293, 58495-0293.
Church: 322 Centennial St. S., 58495. Tel: 701-452-2970.
Catechesis/Religious Program—Students 42.

WYNDMERE, RICHLAND CO., ST. JOHN THE BAPTIST (1912) [CEM], Also serving Milnor. Rev. Leonard Loegering.
630 Sixth St., 58081. Tel: 701-439-2200.
Catechesis/Religious Program—Students 79.

ZEELAND, MCINTOSH CO., ST. ANDREW'S CHURCH OF ZEELAND (1906) [CEM 2], Served from Wishek. Rev. Thomas Feltman.
Mailing Address: *c/o St. Patrick*, P.O. Box 293, Wishek, 58495. Tel: 701-423-5494.
Church: 301 1st Ave., S.E., 58581.
Catechesis/Religious Program—Students 33.

INDIAN MISSIONS

FORT TOTTEN RESERVATION
MISSION—CHRIST THE KING - TOKIO (1938) *c/o Seven Dolors*, Box 299, Benson Co. 58335-0299. Tel: 701-766-4314. Rev. Charles J. Leute, O.P.
Mission—St. Jerome - Crow Hill (1892) *c/o Seven Dolors*, Box 299, Benson Co. 58334-0299. Tel: 701-766-4314.
Mission—Seven Dolors Indian Mission [CEM] Seven Sorrows Dr., Box 299, Benson Co. 58335. Tel: 701-766-4314. Rev. Charles J. Leute, O.P.; Deacon Anthony McDonald. Also serving Crow Hill, Tokio.

ST. MICHAEL
MISSION—ST. MICHAEL'S CHURCH OF ST. MICHAEL (1874) P.O. Box 42, 58370-0042. Tel: 701-766-4151; Fax: 701-766-1085. Rev. Brian Moen.

TURTLE MOUNTAIN RESERVATION
MISSION—ST. ANN Belcourt, Rolette Co. Revs. Mark Ropel, S.O.L.T.; Robert J. Cronin, S.O.L.T.; Shane Mckee, S.O.L.T.; Scott Brossart, S.O.L.T.; Deacon Francis Davis.
Mission—St. Anthony St. Anthony, Rolette Co. Served from Belcourt.
Mission—St. Benedict Belcourt, Rolette Co. Rev. Mark Wheelan, S.O.L.T. Served from Saint John.

Chaplains of Public Institutions

GRAND FORKS. *Altru Hospital*. Rev. Bernard Schneider, Chap., P.O. Box 6002, 58206-6002.
Grand Forks Air Force Base. Jane Hutzol, Contact Person. Tel: 701-747-3073.
Our Lady of the Snows, 319 ARW/HC Blvd., 58205-6335.

Special Assignment:
Rev. Msgrs.—
Schlesselmann, Gregory J., Rector of Cardinal Muench Seminary, 100 35th Ave., N.E., 58102.
Skonseng, Dennis A., Vicar Gen. & Spiritual Dir., Cardinal Muench Seminary
Very Revs.—
Kopacz, K. S., J.C.L., Judicial Vicar, 5201 Bishops Blvd., 58104.
Meyer, Luke D., Chancellor & Priest Sec. to the Bishop, 5201 Bishops Blvd., Ste. A, 58104-7605.
Revs.—
Brooks, Armand L., Chaplain Sisters of St. Francis, Hankinson, 58041.
Duchschere, Paul C., 100 35th Ave., N.E., 58102.
Hughes, Peter, C.S.Sp., Chap., 100 35th Ave., N.E., 58102.
Jasinski, Andrew, Dir., Cardinal Muench, 100 35th Ave., N.E., 58102.
LaCroix, Charles, Chap., Shanley High School, 5600 25th St. S., 58104.
Mundadan, Joe, Chap., Prairie St. John's, 510 4th St. S., 58103.
Seeberger, Claude, O.S.B., Chap., 11550 River Rd., Valley City, 58072.

On Duty Outside the Diocese:
Revs.—
Alilonu, Augustine, Cape Girardeau, MO
Evans, John, II, Chap., Mayo Clinic, Rochester, MN
Hickin, Michael, North American College
Irwin, Robert (SD), San Diego, CA
Mikes, Pavel, Zahradni 32/2 41002 Czech Republic.
Mudd, Joachim, F.I., Marian Friary, Bloomington, IN
Schill, Damien, Chap., VA, St. Paul, MN
Smith, Vernon, Shenandoah, IA
Tiu, Jimmy Lim, Montrose, CA
Yee Mon, Ronald, Schreiver, LA

Military Chaplains:
Rev. Msgr.—
Donahue, Brian G., Chap. (MAJ)
Revs.—
Herron, Jack B., Chap. CMR, El Paso, TX
Kawczynski, Ronald, Chap., CDR, USN, Washington State

Absent on Leave:
Revs.—
Bachmeier, Brian
Fallon, John P.
Fitzpatrick, J. Vincent
Okonmah, Emmanuel, J.C.L., M.C.L.
Vos, Jude

Retired:
Rev. Msgrs.—
Anderson, John D., Hankinson, ND
Gross, Val, Fargo, ND
Huebsch, Joseph R., Hankinson, ND
Nilles, Allan F., Fargo, ND
Senger, Joseph, Minot, ND
Vetter, Wendelyn, V.F., Grand Forks, ND
Revs.—
Bachmeier, A. Bernard, San Diego, CA
Billman, George, Lehigh, FL
Campbell, Joseph, Bella Vista, AR
Cosentino, Jack, Venice, FL
Cote, Duaine
Davis, John E., Peru
Fish, Eugene J., Swartz Creek, MI
Flisk, Louden-Hans W.
Goellen, Richard M.
Grady, Peter W., Fargo, ND
Gross, Richard J., Grand Forks, ND
Haas, Lawrence W., Carrington, ND
Hasey, Adam, Oakes, ND
Jeffrey, C. James, Belleville, IL; Boqueron, PR
Lanz, Matt, Corvallis, OR
Leiphon, Donald A.
Lewandowski, John, Mountain View, AR
McCarthy, Gerald A., Bisbee, ND
Myers, Gerald, Tucson, AZ
Ovsak, William, Chap., Wahpeton, ND
Parrotta, Michael, North Palm Beach, FL
Potter, Gerald, Grand Forks, ND
Roehrich, Andrew, Hankinson, ND
Ruge, Paul, Washington, NJ
Sherman, Edward, Grand Forks, ND
Sherman, William C., Hillsboro, ND
Snell, Roger K., Edgeley, ND
Stelten, Leo F., Frazee, MN
Tuchscherer, Vincent, Fargo, ND

Permanent Deacons:
Anderson, James, St. John's, Wahpeton
Baumgartner, Allen, St. Phillip Neri, Napoleon
Biss, Richard, St. Arnold, Milnor
Blessum, Arlen, St. Therese Little Flower, Rugby
Braunberger, Arlie, St. Catherine, Valley City
Bunce, Donald A., St. Anthonys, Fargo; Shanley High School
Buresh, Leonard, (Retired)
Carpenter, Stanley (Jim), St. Boniface, Walhalla
Davis, Francis R., St. Ann, Belcourt
Desjarlais, Raymond, St. Joachim, Rolla
Didier, Edward, St. Catherine, Valley City
Didier, Harry, Jr., (Retired)
Eberle, Edward, (Retired)
Eblen, David, Sts. Anne, Joachim, Fargo
Eggl, James, Sacred Heart, Cando
Ethier, George, (Retired)
Faul, Jeffrey, St. Cecilia, Harvey
Geffre, Thomas, St. James Basilica, Jamestown
Grim, Raphael, St. Catherine, Valley City
Grzadzielewski, Michael, St John the Evangelist, Grafton
Ham, Thurston, (Retired)
Haney, David, Holy Cross, West Fargo
Hoefs, Gene, (Retired)
Hunt, James, Blessed Sacrament, West Fargo
Johnson, Edward J.
Klein, Eugene, (Retired)
Lane, John, Holy Cross, West Fargo
Leitner, Joseph, St. Catherine, Valley City
Litzinger, Donald, St. Mary, Grand Forks
Loegering, George, St. Mary Cathedral, Fargo
Longtin, Stuart, St. Anthony, Fargo
Marcy, Timothy, Missions
McAllister, James, St. Bernard, Oriska
McCleery, Geary, Basilica St. James, Jamestown
McDonald, Anthony, Seven Dolors, Fort Totten
Mears, Emery, St. Joachim, Rolla
Mrozla, Julian, (Retired)
Orthman, Carl M., St. Catherine, Valley City
Perius, James, (Retired)
Prom, Mathias, St. Anthony, Fargo
Pupino, Samuel, St. Thomas Aquinas Newman Center, Grand Forks
Schumacher, Gary, St. Philip Neri, Napoleon
Schuster, Conrad, (Retired)
Sobolick, Gerald, St. Mary, Park River
Tinguely, Donald, (Retired)
Uline, James, (Retired)
Vetter, Clarence, St. Maurice, Kindred
West, James, St. Jude, Thompson

INSTITUTIONS LOCATED IN THE DIOCESE

[A] SEMINARIES, DIOCESAN

FARGO. *Cardinal Muench Seminary*, 100 35th Ave., N.E., 58102. Tel: 701-232-8969; Fax: 701-271-1250. Email: cms2@cardinalmuench.org. Web: www.cardinalmuench.org. Rev. Msgr. Gregory J. Schlesselmann, Rector; Rev. Andrew Jasinski, Dir. Formation; Rev. Msgr. Dennis A. Skonseng, Spiritual Dir. Corporate Title: The Cardinal Muench Seminary. Priests 3; Lay Teachers 5; 4-Year College Students 12.

[B] HIGH SCHOOLS, DIOCESAN

FARGO. *Fargo Catholic Schools Network*, (Grades K-12), 5600 25th St. S.W., 58104. Tel: 701-893-3200; Fax: 701-893-3277. Email: kyle.edgerton@sendit.nodak.edu. Web: www.fcsn.k12.nd.us. Most Rev. Samuel J. Aquila, D.D., Pres.; Rev. Msgr. Gregory J. Schlesselmann, Chm.; Kyle Edgerton, Supt. Priests 1; Lay Teachers 77; Total Enrollment 1,112.

Shanley High School and Sullivan Middle School, (Grades 6-12), 5600 25th St. S.W., 58104. Tel: 701-893-3227; Fax: 701-893-3277. Email: sean.safranski@sendit.nodak.edu; darrin.roach@sendit.nodak.edu. Web: www.fcsn.k12.nd.us. Mr. Sean Safranski, Prin., Shanley Middle School; Mr. Darrin Roach, Prin. Sullivan Middle School; Deacon Don Bunce, Student Asst. Coord.; Rev. Charles LaCroix, Chap.; Pam Brusegaard, Librarian. Priests 1; Lay Teachers 35; Students 583.

[C] PROTECTIVE INSTITUTIONS

FARGO. *Villa Nazareth dba Friendship, Inc.* 801 Page Dr., 58103. Tel: 701-235-8217; Fax: 701-235-7538. Email: jeffpederson@catholichealth.net. Jeff Pederson, CEO. Presentation Sisters (P.B.V.M.). Catholic Health Initiatives., A community-based facility providing an array of residential, vocational, educational, social and clinical services for children and adults with mental retardation and other developmental disabilities. Total Assisted 250; Total Staff 350.

[D] GENERAL HOSPITALS

BOTTINEAU. *St. Andrew's Health Center*, 316 Ohmer St., 58318. Tel: 701-228-9300; Fax: 701-228-9384. Email: sahc@utma.com. Web: www.standrewshealth.com. Jodi Atkinson, C.E.O. Sisters of Mary of the Presentation 2; Bed Capacity 25; Total Staff 102; Patients Assisted Annually 10,950.

CARRINGTON. *Carrington Health Center* Catholic Health Initiatives., P.O. Box 461, 58421. Tel: 701-652-3141; Fax: 701-652-2884. Web: www.carringtonhealthcenter.org. Bed Capacity 25; Staff 180; Patients Assisted Annually 21,511.

DEVILS LAKE. *Mercy Hospital*, 1031 7th St., N.E., 58301-2798. Tel: 701-662-2131; Fax: 701-662-9651. Email: jamesmarshall@catholichealth.net. Web: www.mercyhospitaldl.com. James Marshall, Admin. Total Staff 182; Bed Capacity 25; Bassinets 7; Patients Assisted Annually 23,318.

HARVEY. *St. Aloisius Medical Center* (1938) 325 E. Brewster St., 58341. Tel: 701-324-4651; Fax: 701-324-4687. Email: rockyz@staloisius.com. Web: www.staloisius.com. Rockford Zastoupil, Admin. Sisters of Mary of the Presentation. Total Staff 320; Bed Capacity 25; Long Term Care 106; Patients Assisted Annually 53,000.

LISBON. *Lisbon Area Health Services, Catholic Health Initiatives*, 905 Main St., Box 353, 58054. Tel: 701-683-5241; Fax: 701-683-4345. Email: peggylarson@catholichealth.net. Bed Capacity 25; Total Assisted Annually 12,500; Total Staff 115; Home Health Care Agency 1.

OAKES. *Oakes Community Hospital*, 1200 N. 7th St., 58474-2502. Tel: 701-742-3291; Fax: 701-742-3639. Email: leeboyles@catholichealth.net. Sr. M. Dianna Hell, O.S.F., Supr.; Lee Boyles, Inst. Admin. Sisters of St. Francis of the Immaculate Heart of Mary (Hankinson, ND) 2; Total Staff 95; Bed Capacity 20; Bassinets 2; Patients Assisted Annually 6,365.

ROLLA. *Presentation Medical Center*, 213 Second Ave., N.E., P.O. Box 759, 58367-0759. Tel: 701-477-3161; Fax: 701-477-5564. Email: pmc@utma.com. Web: www.pmc-rolla.com. Kimber L. Wraalstad, CEO. Sisters of Mary of the Presentation 3; Total Staff 110; Acute Beds 25; Patients Assisted Annually 12,500.

VALLEY CITY. *Mercy Hospital* (1928) Catholic Health Initiatives., 570 Chautauqua Blvd., 58072. Tel: 701-845-6400; Fax: 701-845-6413. Email: johnosse@catholichealth.net. Bed Capacity 25; Bassinets 4; Patients Assisted 21,064; Total Staff 150.

[E] HOMES FOR AGED

FARGO. *Riverview Place* (1987) 5300 12th St. S., 58104. Tel: 701-237-4700; Fax: 701-235-5738. Email: jeffpederson@catholichealth.net. Web: www.riverviewplace.org. Jeff Pederson, Admin. Residents 180; Total Staff 90; Total Assisted Annually 180.

Rosewood on Broadway, SMP Health System, 1351 Broadway, 58102. Tel: 701-277-7999; Fax: 701-277-7989. Email: meldinetang@smphs.org. Web: rosewoodonbroadway.com. Meldine Tang, Admin. Bed Capacity 111; Total Staff 185; Resident Days 40,004.

Villa Maria, SMP Health System, 3102 University Dr. S., 58103. Tel: 701-293-7750; Fax: 701-293-5845. Email: michael.pfeifer@smphs.org. Michael Pfeifer, CEO & Pres. Bed Capacity 140; Total Staff 200; Resident Days 48,800.

EDGELEY. *Manor St. Joseph*, 404 Fourth Ave., P.O. Box 305, 58433. Tel: 701-493-2477; Fax: 701-493-2477. Email: stjoseph@drtel.net. Tammy Jangula, Admin. Sister Servants of Christ the King 2; Total Assisted Annually 28; Bed Capacity 40; Staff 33.

ELLENDALE. *Prince of Peace Care Center*, 201 8th St. N., 58436. Tel: 701-349-3312; Fax: 701-349-3944. Mr. Tony Hanson, Admin. Operated by Benedictine Living Communities, Inc. Bed Capacity 55; Total Staff 75; Total Assisted Annually 84.

ENDERLIN. *Maryhill Manor, SMP Health System*, 110 Hillcrest Dr., 58027. Tel: 701-437-3544; Fax: 701-437-3816. Email: nancy.farnham@smphs.org. Web: www.maryhillmanor.net. Nancy Farnham, Admin. Bed Capacity 54; Total Staff 86; Resident Days 18,866; Total Assisted Annually 91.

GRAND FORKS. *St. Anne's Guest Home*, 524 N. 17th St., 58203. Tel: 701-746-9401; Fax: 701-795-7825. Email: stannes@midconetwork.com. Sr. Rebecca Metzger, O.S.F., Admin. Sisters of St. Francis of the Immaculate Heart of Mary (Hankinson, ND) 4; Total Staff 36; Guests 84; Total Assisted Annually 152; Beds 84.

HANKINSON. *St. Gerard Community Nursing Home*, P.O. Box 448, 58041. Tel: 701-242-7891; Fax: 701-242-7896. Email: stgerard@prairietech.net. Karen Gabbert, Admin.; Sr. Mary Louise, O.S.F., Asst. Admin. Sisters of St. Francis of the Immaculate Heart of Mary (Hankinson, ND) 3; Bed Capacity 67; Patients Assisted Annually 76; Independent Living Unit Beds 11; Children in Daycare 18; Total Staff 70.

JAMESTOWN. *Ave Maria Village, SMP Health System*, 501 19th St., N.E., 58401. Tel: 701-252-5660; Fax: 701-251-2643. Email: tim.burchill@smphs.org. Timothy N. Burchill, Admin. Bed Capacity 100; Total Staff 180; Resident Days 36,192; Total Assisted Annually 225.

LA MOURE. *St. Rose Care Center*, P.O. Box 627, 58458. Tel: 701-883-5363; Fax: 701-883-5711. Email: tony.hanson@bhshealth.org. Mr. Tony Hanson, Admin. Operated by Benedictine Living Communities, Inc. Bed Capacity 40; Total Staff 65.

VALLEY CITY. *Sheyenne Care Center, SMP Health System*, 979 N. Central Ave., 58072. Tel: 701-845-8222; Fax: 701-845-8270. Email: craig.christianson@smphs.org. Craig Christianson, CEO. Bed Capacity 170; Total Staff 290; Resident Days 60,041; Total Assisted Annually 239.

WAHPETON. *St. Catherine's Living Center*, 1307 N. Seventh St., 58075. Tel: 701-642-6667; Fax: 701-642-2485. Emmy Tretter, Admin. Operated by Benedictine Living Communities, Inc. Long Term Care Beds 104; Basic Care Beds 16; Total Staff 150.

[F] CATHOLIC CHARITIES

FARGO. *Catholic Charities North Dakota - Fargo* (1923) 5201 Bishops Blvd., Ste. B, 58104. Tel: 701-235-4457; Fax: 701-356-7993. Email: fargo@catholiccharitiesnd.org. Web: www.catholiccharitiesnd.org. Briston Fernandes, Exec. Dir. Statewide social service agency providing adoption services, child welfare, guardianship services, pregnancy services, and Adults Adopting Special Kids (AASK). Total Staff 48.

St. Vincent de Paul Society (1967) 1425 First Ave. S., 58103. Tel: 701-235-5944; Fax: 701-232-6576. George Lacher, Treas. Total Assisted Annually 974.

GRAND FORKS. *Catholic Charities North Dakota - Grand Forks*, c/o 5201 Bishops Blvd., Ste. B, 58104. Tel: 701-775-4196; Fax: 701-775-0129. Email: fargo@catholiccharitiesnd.org. Web: www.catholiccharities.org.

St. Vincent de Paul, 620 8th Ave. S., 58201. Tel: 701-795-8614; Fax: 701-746-6648. Email: jbrundin@msn.com. Jo Ann Brundin, Dir. Total Assisted Annually 8,000.

MINTO. *Saint Gianna's Home Inc.* Residence for pregnant women and their children., 15605 Country Rd. 15, 58261. Tel: 701-248-3077; Fax: 701-248-2068. Email: saintgiannahome@hotmail.com. Web: www.saintgiannahome.com. Mary Pat Jahner, Dir.; Rev. Joseph Christensen, Spiritual Dir. Priests 1; Staff 5.

[G] CONVENTS AND RESIDENCES FOR SISTERS

FARGO. *Presentation Center-Sacred Heart Convent*, 1101 32nd Ave. S., 58103. Tel: 701-237-4857; Fax: 701-237-9822. Web: www.presentationsistersfargo.com. Sr. Mary Margaret Mooney, P.B.V.M., Pres. Sisters 48.

HANKINSON. *Sisters of St. Francis of the Immaculate Heart of Mary*, P.O. Box 447, 58041-0447. Tel: 701-242-7195; Fax: 701-242-7198. Email: osfhank2009@rrt.net. Web: www.fargodiocese.org/sfc/index.html. 102 6th St., S.E., 58041. Sr. Donna Welder, O.S.F., Prov. Supr. Sisters 34.

VALLEY CITY. *Sisters of Mary of the Presentation*, 11550 River Rd., 58072. Tel: 701-845-2864; Fax: 701-845-0805. Email: carol.kuntz@fargodiocese.org. Sr. Carol Jean Kuntz, S.M.P., Prov. Supr.; Rev. Claude Seeberger, O.S.B., Chap. Sisters 33.

WAHPETON. *Carmel of Mary* (1954) 17765 78th St., S.E., 58075. Tel: 701-642-2360. Sr. Joseph-Marie of the Child of Jesus, O.Carm., Prioress; Rev. William Ovsak, Chap. (Retired). Carmelite Nuns of the Ancient Observance. Solemn Professed Nuns 9.

[H] RETREAT HOUSES

FARGO. *St. Joseph's House of Retreat*, P.O. Box 1323, 58107.

Presentation Prayer Center (1981) 3001 11th St. S., 58103. Tel: 701-235-8246; Fax: 701-237-9822. Email: presprayerctr@cableone.net. Web: www.presentationsistersfargo.com. Sr. Andrea Arendt, P.B.V.M., Dir. Sisters 2.

[I] NEWMAN FOUNDATIONS

FARGO. *St. Paul's Newman Church of Fargo* (1928) 1141 N. University Dr., 58102. Tel: 701-235-0142; Fax: 701-298-6431. Email: ndsunewmanctr@yahoo.com. Web: www.ndsunewman.org. Rev. James Cheney, Dir. Campus Ministry. Total Staff 15; Catholic Students 400.

GRAND FORKS. *St. Thomas Aquinas Newman Church of Grand Forks* (1951) 410 Cambridge St., 58203. Tel: 701-777-6850; Fax: 701-777-6851. Email: father.courtright@und.nodak.edu. Web: www.und.nodak.edu/dept/newman. Rev. Jason Lefor. Total Staff 13; Catholic Students 2,500.

WAHPETON. *State College of Science Newman Student Parish* 701 N. Seventh St., 58075. Tel: 701-642-6982; Fax: 701-642-2601. Very Rev. Dale Lagodinski.

[J] MISCELLANEOUS LISTINGS

FARGO. *Catholic Chaplains Association, Diocese of Fargo*, Pastoral Center, 5201 Bishops Blvd., 58104. Tel: 701-356-7950. Email: luke.meyer@fargodiocese.org. Very Rev. Luke D. Meyer.

Catholic Development Foundation (1989) *Diocese of Fargo*, Pastoral Center, 5201 Bishops Blvd., 58104-7605. Tel: 701-356-7900; Fax: 701-356-7998. Email: scott.hoselton@fargodiocese.org. Web: www.fargodiocese.org. A nonprofit foundation for religious charitable and educational purposes.

Cursillo Movement, 5202 25th St. S., 58104. Tel: 701-493-2387. Web: www.natl-cursillo.org. Rev. Duaine Cote, Spiritual Advisor (Retired).

Fargo Catholic Schools Network Foundation, c/o Todd Mickelson, 5600 25th St. S., 58104. Tel: 701-893-3200; Fax: 701-893-3277. Email: todd.mickelson@sendit.nodak.edu. Web: www.fcsn.k12.nd.us. A nonprofit foundation for religious charitable and educational purposes. The Foundation is organized to financially support, assist, promote, expand and strengthen religious educational institutions affiliated with and under the governance of the Fargo Catholic Schools Network.

Hughes, Inc., 1101 32nd Ave. S., 58103. Tel: 701-237-4857; Fax: 701-237-9822. Email: foundation@presentationsistersfargo.com. Web: www.presentationsistersfargo.com. Sr. Mary Margaret Mooney, P.B.V.M., Pres. Assisting, providing and expanding low-cost housing (in part for senior citizens along with other groups).

Marriage Encounter, P.O. Box 898, Devils Lake, 58301. Tel: 701-662-7558; Fax: 701-662-7559. Very Rev. Dale H. Kinzler.

Prairieland Home Care, 1102 Page Dr., S.W., 58103. Tel: 701-232-1245; Fax: 701-232-0813. Email: lynn.elliot@smphs.org. Web: www.prairielandhomecare.org.

The Presentation Foundation, Sacred Heart Convent, 1101 32nd Ave. S., 58103. Tel: 701-237-4857; Fax: 701-237-9822. Email: foundation@presentationsistersfargo.com. Web: www.presentationsistersfargo.com. Sr. Stella Olson, P.B.V.M., Dir.

Presentation Partners in Housing, 1101 32nd Ave S., 58103. Tel: 701-235-6861; Fax: 701-237-9822. Email: skk1978@hotmail.com. Web: www.presentationsistersfargo.com.

BATHGATE. *Bethlehem Community*, 10194 Garfield St., S., 58216. Tel: 701-265-3717; Fax: 701-265-3716. Email: contact@bethlehembooks.com. Web: www.vmcenter.org. Lydia Reynolds, Contact Person.

GRAND FORKS. *Grand Forks Catholic Schools Association*, 216 Belmont Rd., 58201. Tel: 701-775-4818; Fax: 701-775-7568. Mr. Charles Scherr, Contact Person. A nonprofit organization developing curriculum study, scholarship, transportation, personnel and fund raising.

JAMESTOWN. *Jamestown College*, 214 4th St. S.E., 58401. Tel: 701-252-0478; Fax: 701-252-0478. Email: swallace@jc.edu. Very Rev. Al M. Bitz; Shirley Wallace, Pastoral Min. & Campus Min. Catholic Students 214.

LANGDON. *St. Alphonsus School Foundation*, 1211 10th St., 58249. Tel: 701-256-3717; Fax: 701-256-3720. Gerald Mikkelsen, Pres.

MANVEL. *Beginning Experience Apostolate, c/o St. Timothy's Catholic Church*, 1207 Oldham Ave., 58256-4335. Tel: 701-696-2219. Email: bernard.schneider@fargodiocese.org. Rev. Bernard Schneider.

VALLEY CITY. *Valley City State University*, c/o St. Catherine, 540 3rd Ave., N.E., 58072. Tel: 701-845-0354; Fax: 701-845-0556. Catholic Students 150.

RELIGIOUS INSTITUTES OF MEN REPRESENTED IN THE DIOCESE

For further details refer to the corresponding bracketed number in the Religious Institutes of Men or Women section.

[0200]—*Benedictine Monks* (Assumption Abbey, Richardton, ND)—O.S.B.

[0650]—*Holy Ghost Fathers*—C.S.Sp.

[0430]—*Order of Preachers-Dominicans*—O.P.

[0975]—*Society of Our Lady of the Most Holy Trinity*—S.O.L.T.

RELIGIOUS INSTITUTES OF WOMEN REPRESENTED IN THE DIOCESE

[0300]—*Calced Carmelites*—O.Carm.

[3832]—*Congregation of the Sisters of St. Joseph*—C.S.J.

[1310]—*Franciscan Sisters of Little Falls, MN*—O.S.F.

[2575]—*Institute of the Sisters of Mercy of the Americas* (Omaha, NE)—R.S.M.

[3510]—*Sister Servants of Christ the King*—S.S.C.K.

[2450]—*Sisters of Mary of the Presentation* (Valley City, ND)—S.M.P.

[1590]—*Sisters of St. Francis of the Immaculate Heart of Mary* (Hankinson, ND)—O.S.F.

[3320]—*Sisters of the Presentation of the B.V.M.* (Fargo, ND)—P.B.V.M.

[]—*Sisters of the Society of Our Lady of the Most Holy Trinity*—S.O.L.T.

NECROLOGY

† Graven, John P., (Retired)—Died Aug. 29, 2009
† Knoke, Kenneth, (Retired)—Died June 8, 2009
† Lommel, George D., (Retired)—Died Dec. 30, 2008

An asterisk (*) denotes an organization that has established tax-exempt status directly with the IRS and is not covered by the USCCB Group Ruling.

Diocese of Fort Wayne - South Bend

(Dioecesis Wayne Castrensis-South Bendensis)

Most Reverend

JOHN M. D'ARCY, D.D., M.D., S.T.D.

Retired Bishop of Fort Wayne-South Bend; ordained February 2, 1957; appointed Auxiliary Bishop of Boston and Titular Bishop of Mediana December 31, 1974; consecrated February 11, 1975; appointed Bishop of Fort Wayne-South Bend February 26, 1985; installed May 1, 1985; retired November 14, 2009. *Mailing Address: P.O. Box 390, Fort Wayne, IN 46801.*

Most Reverend

KEVIN C. RHOADES

Bishop of Fort Wayne-South Bend; ordained July 9, 1983; appointed Bishop of Harrisburg October 14, 2004; consecrated December 9, 2004; appointed Bishop of Fort Wayne-South Bend November 14, 2009; installed Bishop of Fort Wayne-South Bend January 13, 2010. *Mailing Address: P.O. 390, Fort Wayne, IN 46801.*

Archbishop Noll Catholic Center: 915 S. Clinton St., P.O. Box 390, Fort Wayne, IN 46801. Tel: 260-422-4611; Fax: 260-969-9145.

Web: www.diocesefwsb.org

Email: dlewandowski@fw.diocesefwsb.org

ESTABLISHED SEPTEMBER 22, 1857.

Square Miles 5,792.

Redesignated Diocese of Fort Wayne-South Bend on July 22, 1960.

Comprises the Counties of Adams, Allen, Dekalb, Elkhart, Huntington, Kosciusko, La Grange, Marshall, Noble, St. Joseph, Steuben, Wabash, Wells, Whitley in the State of Indiana.

For legal titles of parishes and diocesan institutions, consult the Chancery Office.

STATISTICAL OVERVIEW

Personnel	
Bishop	1
Retired Bishops	1
Priests: Diocesan Active in Diocese	59
Priests: Retired, Sick or Absent	19
Number of Diocesan Priests	78
Religious Priests in Diocese	137
Total Priests in Diocese	215
Extern Priests in Diocese	21
Ordinations:	
Diocesan Priests	2
Religious Priests	3
Transitional Deacons	2
Permanent Deacons in Diocese	11
Total Brothers	142
Total Sisters	489
Parishes	
Parishes	80
With Resident Pastor:	
Resident Diocesan Priests	55
Resident Religious Priests	14
Without Resident Pastor:	
Administered by Priests	11
Missions	1
Pastoral Centers	3
Closed Parishes	1
Professional Ministry Personnel:	
Sisters	9
Lay Ministers	100
Welfare	
Catholic Hospitals	2
Total Assisted	216,965
Health Care Centers	4
Total Assisted	56,731
Homes for the Aged	7
Total Assisted	2,291
Day Care Centers	1
Total Assisted	119
Special Centers for Social Services	11
Total Assisted	216,883
Other Institutions	4
Total Assisted	10,042
Educational	
Diocesan Students in Other Seminaries	16
Seminaries, Religious	1
Students Religious	18
Total Seminarians	34
Colleges and Universities	5
Total Students	16,557
High Schools, Diocesan and Parish	4
Total Students	3,180
Elementary Schools, Diocesan and Parish	39
Total Students	9,701
Catechesis/Religious Education:	
High School Students	1,309
Elementary Students	9,054
Total Students under Catholic Instruction	39,835
Teachers in the Diocese:	
Sisters	5
Lay Teachers	745
Vital Statistics	
Receptions into the Church:	
Infant Baptism Totals	2,596
Minor Baptism Totals	235
Adult Baptism Totals	163
Received into Full Communion	474
First Communions	2,964
Confirmations	2,770
Marriages:	
Catholic	524
Interfaith	265
Total Marriages	789
Deaths	1,370
Total Catholic Population	171,499
Total Population	1,262,788

Former Bishops—Rt. Revs. JOHN HENRY LUERS, D.D., ord. Nov. 11, 1846; cons. Jan. 10, 1858; died June 29, 1871; JOSEPH DWENGER, C.PP.S., D.D., ord. Sept. 4, 1859; cons. April 14, 1872; died Jan. 27, 1893; JOSEPH RADEMACHER, D.D., ord. Aug. 2, 1863; cons. Bishop of Nashville, June 24, 1883; transferred to Fort Wayne, July 14, 1893; died Jan. 12, 1900; HERMAN JOSEPH ALERDING, D.D., cons. Nov. 30, 1900; died Dec. 6, 1924; Most Revs. JOHN FRANCIS NOLL, D.D., ord. June 4, 1898; cons. June 30, 1925; promoted to rank of Archbishop "ad personam," Sept. 2, 1953; died July 31, 1956; LEO A. PURSLEY, D.D., ord. June 11, 1927; cons. Sept. 19, 1950; retired Oct. 19, 1976; died Nov. 15, 1998; WILLIAM E. MCMANUS, D.D., ord. April 15, 1939; appt. Auxiliary Bishop of Chicago, June 21, 1967; appt. Bishop of Fort Wayne, Aug. 31, 1976; installed as 7th Bishop of Fort Wayne, Oct. 19, 1976; retired Feb. 25, 1985; died March 3, 1997; JOHN M. D'ARCY, M.D., S.T.D. (Retired), ord. Feb. 2, 1957; appt. Auxiliary Bishop of Boston and Titular Bishop of Mediana Dec. 31, 1974; cons. Feb. 11, 1975; appt. Bishop of Fort Wayne-South Bend Feb. 26, 1985; installed May 1, 1985; retired Nov. 14, 2009.

Diocese of Fort Wayne-South Bend, Inc.—(Incorporated Aug. 29, 1955). Board of Directors: Most Rev. KEVIN C. RHOADES, Pres.; Rev. Msgr. ROBERT C. SCHULTE, Vice Pres.; Mr. JOSEPH RYAN, Sec. & Treas. Finance Council: Most Rev. KEVIN C. RHOADES; Rev. Msgr. ROBERT C. SCHULTE; THOMAS BLEE; JOSEPH DAHM; ARTHUR DECIO; RICHARD DOERMER; JAMES FITZPATRICK; Mr. JERRY HAMMES; MICHAEL HAMMES; JEROME KEARNS; Sr. JANE MARIE KLEIN, O.S.F.; ALICE KOPFER; SCOTT MALPASS; Mr. JOSEPH RYAN, Sec. & Treas.; THOMAS SKIBA; VINCENT TIPPMANN.

Chancery Office—Archbishop Noll Catholic Center, 915 S. Clinton St., P.O. Box 390, Fort Wayne, 46801. Tel: 260-422-4611; Fax: 260-969-9145. Office Hours: Mon.-Fri. 8:30-4:30. Other times by appointment.

Vicar General-Chancellor—Rev. Msgr. ROBERT C. SCHULTE.

Vicar for Retired Clergy—Rev. Msgr. J. WILLIAM LESTER, P.A. (Retired).

Episcopal Vicar for Education—Rev. Msgr. ROBERT C. SCHULTE, Archbishop Noll Catholic Center, 915 S. Clinton St., P.O. Box 390, Fort Wayne, 46801. Tel: 260-422-4611; Fax: 260-969-9145.

South Bend Chancery—114 W. Wayne St., South Bend, 46601. Tel: 574-234-0687; Fax: 574-232-8483.

Diocesan Tribunal—Archbishop Noll Catholic Center, 915 S. Clinton St., Fort Wayne, 46802. Tel: 260-422-4611; Fax: 260-969-9140. *Mailing Address: P.O. Box 390, Fort Wayne, 46801. South Bend Office, 114 W. Wayne St, P.O. Box 1432, South Bend, 46624.* Tel: 574-287-6531; Fax: 574-287-9391.

Judicial Vicar—Rev. Msgr. BRUCE PIECHOCKI, J.C.L.; Rev. FRANCIS CHUKWUMA, J.C.L., Judge.

Defender of the Bond—MONICA KLUESNER.

Pro-Synodal Judges—Revs. PHILIP DEVOLDER; MARK GURTNER, J.C.L.; LAWRENCE A. KRAMER; Rev. Msgr. BRUCE PIECHOCKI, J.C.L.

Court Consultant—Dr. SUSAN FEATHERGILL.

Fort Wayne Office—JANICE BRELL, Tribunal Administrative Asst. Advocates: VICKI FERRIER; ELLEN BECKER. Auditors: DEBORAH PAINTER;

PAULA SHOAF.
Notary—JANICE BRELL.
South Bend Office Manager—DIANA HEIDT. Office Auditor: DEBRA HANSEN.
Advocate—SUZANNE DALY.
Consultors—Rev. Msgrs. ROBERT C. SCHULTE; J. WILLIAM LESTER, P.A. (Retired); Rev. MARK GURTNER, J.C.L.; Rev. Msgr. BRUCE PIECHOCKI, J.C.L.; Revs. DANIEL D. SCHEIDT; THOMAS SHOEMAKER; Rev. Msgr. MICHAEL W. HEINTZ, Ph.D.; Revs. DERRICK SNEYD; DAVID W. VOORS.

Diocesan Offices and Directors

Business Administration Office—Archbishop Noll Catholic Center, 915 S. Clinton St., Fort Wayne, 46802. Tel: 260-422-4611; Fax: 260-423-3382. *Mailing Address: P.O. Box 390, Fort Wayne, 46801.* Mr. JOSEPH RYAN, CFO.
Buildings and Improvements—Advisory Board: Rev. Msgr. ROBERT C. SCHULTE; Rev. DALE A. BAUMAN; JOHN BERGHOFF; Revs. DOMINIQUE A. CARBONEAU; JOHN DELANEY; MICHAEL KINDER; Rev. JOHN OVERMYER; Mr. JOSEPH RYAN; Revs. DERRICK SNEYD; WILLIAM SULLIVAN.
Budget Committee—Rev. Msgrs. ROBERT C. SCHULTE; BERNARD J. GALIC; Rev. JOHN F. PFISTER; Mr. JOSEPH RYAN; Rev. Msgr. JOHN N. SUELZER.
Diocesan Services Agency—JOHN KLEIN; MARY LOU O'KEEFFE, Purchasing, Archbishop Noll Catholic Center, 915 S. Clinton St., Fort Wayne, 46802. Tel: 260-422-4611; 800-856-4611; Fax: 260-420-6306. Mailing Address: P.O. Box 390, Fort Wayne, 46801.
Diocesan Office of Development—HARRY W. VERHILEY, Dir., 1328 W. Dragoon Trail, Mishawaka, 46544. Tel: 574-258-6571; Fax: 574-256-2709.
Campus and Young Adult Ministry—MARY L. GLOWASKI, Dir., Archbishop Noll Catholic Center, 915 S. Clinton St., Fort Wayne, 46802. Tel: 260-422-4611; 260-483-3661; Fax: 260-483-1881. Mailing Address: P.O. Box 390, Fort Wayne, 46801.
Diocesan Archives—JANICE CANTRELL, Archivist, Archbishop Noll Catholic Center, 915 S. Clinton St., Fort Wayne, 46802. Tel: 260-422-4611, Ext. 3386; Fax: 260-420-6306. Mailing Address: P.O. Box 390, Fort Wayne, 46801.
Catholic Campaign for Human Development—ANN HELMKE, Dir., 2827 Holton Ave., Fort Wayne, 46806. Tel: 260-456-4172; Fax: 260-456-4075.
Catholic Charities—DEBRA SCHMIDT, Dir., 315 E. Washington, Fort Wayne, 46802. Tel: 260-422-5625; 800-686-7459; Fax: 260-422-5657.
Censor Librorum—Rev. Msgr. MICHAEL W. HEINTZ, Ph.D., 1701 Miami St., South Bend, 46613. Tel: 574-289-5539; Fax: 574-289-0227.
Cemeteries—THOMAS E. ALTER, Dir., Catholic Cemetery Assoc., 3500 Lake Ave., Fort Wayne, 46805. Tel: 260-426-2044; Fax: 260-426-7418.
Communications—VINCE LABARBERA, Dir., Archbishop Noll Catholic Center, 915 S. Clinton St., Fort Wayne, 46802. Tel: 260-422-4611; 260-744-0012; Fax: 260-744-1473. Mailing Address: P.O. Box 390, Fort Wayne, 46801.
Continuing Education of the Clergy—Rev. Msgr. ROBERT C. SCHULTE, Mailing Address: P.O. Box 390, Fort Wayne, 46801. Tel: 260-422-4611; Fax: 260-399-1419.
Presbyteral Council—Revs. DOMINIC CARBONEAU; TERRY FISHER; JASON FREIBURGER; JOSEPH GAUGHAN; MARK GURTNER, J.C.L.; Rev. Msgr. MICHAEL W. HEINTZ, Ph.D.; Rev. WILLIAM KUMMER; Rev. Msgr. JOHN M. KUZMICH; Rev. JOHN PFISTER; Rev. Msgr. BRUCE PIECHOCKI, J.C.L.; Rev. DAVID RUPPERT; Rev. Msgr. ROBERT C. SCHULTE; Revs. JAMES F. SECULOFF; THOMAS SHOEMAKER; WILLIAM SULLIVAN; NEIL WACK, C.S.C.
Cursillo—Rev. PAUL BUETER. Tel: 574-267-5842 (Spanish); Fax: 574-268-1030; DON NAPOLI. Tel: 574-234-9177 (English).
Hispanic Ministry Services—ENID ROMAN-DEJESUS, Dir., 1328 W. Dragoon Trail, Mishawaka, 46544. Tel: 574-259-9994, Ext. 211; Fax: 574-258-6569.
Angola—St. Anthony of Padua, 700 W. Maumee St., Angola, 46703. Tel: 260-665-2259. Rev. MARK WEAVER, O.F.M.Conv.
Bremen—St. Dominic, 803 W. Bike St., Bremen, 46506. Tel: 574-546-3601.
Elkhart—St. Vincent de Paul, 1108 S. Main St., Elkhart, 46516. Tel: 574-389-9634. Revs. GLENN KOHRMAN; KEVIN M. BAUMAN.
Fort Wayne—St. Patrick, 2120 Harrison St., Fort Wayne, 46802. Tel: 260-744-1450. Rev. THOMAS ASCHEMAN, S.V.D.
Fort Wayne—St. Joseph, 2213 Brooklyn, Fort Wayne, 46802. Tel: 260-432-5113. Rev. TIMOTHY A. WROZEK.
Goshen—St. John the Evangelist, 109 W. Monroe St., Goshen, 46526-3957. Tel: 574-534-7554. Rev. CONSTANTINO ROCHA.
LaGrange—St. Joseph, P.O. Box 69, LaGrange, 46761. Tel: 260-463-3472. Rev. MARK WEAVER, O.F.M.Conv.
Ligonier—St. Patrick, 300 Ravine Park Dr., Ligonier, 46767-1301. Tel: 260-894-4946. Rev. WILSON O. CORZO.
Plymouth—St. Michael, 612 N. Walnut St., Plymouth, 46563. Tel: 574-936-4935. Rev. ELOY JIMENEZ.
South Bend—St. Adalbert, 2420 W. Huron, South Bend, 46619-3395. St. Casimir, 1308 W. Dunham St., South Bend, 46619. Rev. CHRISTOPHER COX, C.S.C.
Warsaw—Our Lady of Guadalupe, 225 Gillian Dr., Warsaw, 46580. Tel: 574-658-9384. *Sacred Heart, 125 N. Harrison St., Warsaw, 46580.* Sr. JOAN HASTREITER, S.S.J.
Encuentro Matrimonial - (Marriage Encounters)—South Bend: GREG GERMANN; NORMA GERMANN. Tel: 574-281-6432. Fort Wayne: RON LEE; LEANNE LEE. Tel: 260-637-5124.
Diocesan Council of Catholic Women—Rev. RICHARD HIRE, Priest Moderator; GEORGETTA GUNTHORP, Pres., 0240 N. 850 E., LaGrange, 46761. Tel: 260-367-2359.
Diocesan Family Life—FRED EVERETT; LISA EVERETT, 114 W. Wayne St., South Bend, 46601. Tel: 574-234-0687; Fax: 574-232-8483. Email: fredeverett@sbglobal.net; lisaanneverett@sbglobal.net.
Ecumenical Affairs—Rev. Msgr. ROBERT C. SCHULTE, Dir., East, Mailing Address: P.O. Box 390, Fort Wayne, 46801. Tel: 260-422-4611; Fax: 260-969-1383. Email: rschulte@fw.diocesefwsb.org.
Liturgical Commission—Rev. Msgr. MICHAEL W. HEINTZ, Ph.D.; Rev. PETER D. ROCCA, C.S.C.; ENID ROMAN-DEJESUS; Rev. Msgr. WILLIAM C. SCHOOLER, Chm.; JAMES FITZPATRICK; Rev. MICHAEL DRISCOLL, Ph.D.; CINDY BLACK; JEREMY HOY; DAVID FAGERBERG, Ph.D.; Rev. MARK GURTNER, J.C.L.
Environment and Art—CHRISTOPHER SCHENKEL; BILL COLEMAN, AIA; Revs. DANIEL D. SCHEIDT; MARK GURTNER, J.C.L.; SAM JONES, A.I.A.; Bro. DENNIS MEYERS, C.S.C.
Diocesan Music Committee—JEREMY HOY, Chm.; KEVIN DEMETROFF; MEGAN HARTZ; MICHAEL DULAC; THERESA SLOTT; MICHAEL BECHTOL; ANN BECHTOL; BEN WEDLER.
Office of Worship—BRIAN MACMICHAEL, Dir., Archbishop Noll Catholic Center, 915 S. Clinton St., Fort Wayne, 46802. Tel: 260-422-4611; Fax: 260-423-3382. Mailing Address: P.O. Box 390, Fort Wayne, 46801.
Official Publication "Today's Catholic"—TIMOTHY JOHNSON, Editor, Archbishop Noll Catholic Center, 915 S. Clinton St., Fort Wayne, 46802. Tel: 260-422-4611; 260-456-2824; Fax: 260-744-1473. Mailing Address: P.O. Box 390, Fort Wayne, 46801.
Permanent Diaconate—MARY SZYMCZAK, Dir., 114 W. Wayne St., South Bend, 46601. Tel: 574-234-0687; Fax: 574-232-8483.
Pro-Life—FRED EVERETT; LISA EVERETT, 114 W. Wayne St., South Bend, 46601. Tel: 574-234-0687.
Propagation of the Faith and Holy Childhood Association—Dr. KATHLEEN SCHNEIDER, Mailing Address: P.O. Box 390, Fort Wayne, 46801.
Office of Catechesis—JAMES TIGHE, Dir.; Sr. M. JANE CAREW, O.V., Consultant, Archbishop Noll Catholic Center, 915 S. Clinton St., Fort Wayne, 46802. Tel: 260-422-4611; Fax: 260-969-1475. Mailing Address: P.O. Box 390, Fort Wayne, 46801.
Catechetical Consultant—Sr. M. JANE CAREW, O.V., Cathedral Bookstore, 915 S. Clinton St., Fort Wayne, 46802.
South Bend-Mishawaka Office of Catechesis—MEGGAN YOUNG, Assoc. Dir., 1328 W. Dragoon Trail, Mishawaka, 46554. Tel: 574-259-9994; Fax: 574-258-6569.
Refugee Resettlement Program—DEBRA SCHMIDT, Dir., 315 E. Washington, Fort Wayne, 46802. Tel: 260-422-5625; 800-686-7459; Fax: 260-422-5657.
Retired Clergy Committee—Rev. WILLIAM KUMMER; Rev. Msgrs. J. WILLIAM LESTER, P.A. (Retired); ROBERT C. SCHULTE; Rev. JAMES F. SECULOFF; Rev. Msgr. JOHN N. SUELZER; Rev. PHILLIP A. WIDMANN; Rev. Msgr. JAMES J. WOLF.
RSVP St. Joseph County & Elkhart County—JENNIFER TINDELL, Prog. Coord., Auburn: 120 S. Taylor St., South Bend, 46601. Tel: 574-287-0500; Fax: 574-287-3320.
Serra International—Fort Wayne: DEB ANDREWS, Pres., 9829 Tamar Trail, Fort Wayne, 46825. Tel: 260-490-2170; Rev. GLENN KOHRMAN, Chap., 124 College Ave., Culver, 46511. Tel: 574-842-2522. South Bend Office: RICHARD WASOSKI, Pres., 21943 Auten Rd., South Bend, 46637. Tel: 574-272-9043; Rev. PAUL MCCARTHY, Chap., 55756 Tulip Rd., New Carlisle, 46552-9734. Tel: 574-654-3781.
Schools—MARK MYERS, Ph.D., Supt., 915 S. Clinton St., P.O. Box 390, Fort Wayne, 46801. Tel: 260-422-4611; Fax: 260-426-3077; JOHN GAUGHAN, Asst. Dir. High Schools, Fort Wayne Office: Archbishop Noll Catholic Center, 915 S. Clinton St., Fort Wayne, 46802. Tel: 260-422-4611; Fax: 260-426-3077. Mailing Address: P.O. Box 390, Fort Wayne, 46801. South Bend Office: 1328 W. Dragoon Trail, Mishawaka, 46544. Tel: 574-255-1387; Fax: 574-256-2709.
School Board, Diocesan—MARK MYERS, Ph.D., Supt.; BURT BRUNNER; Rev. TERRY FISHER; JOHN GAUGHAN; JACQUELINE GILL; JUAN GIRON; JIM HOCH; JOHN LESZCZYNSKI; ROBERTA POLOVIK; ANDY SCHNEIDER; LISA SOWERS; JOHN STAUD.
Ex Officio Member—Most Rev. JOHN M. D'ARCY, D.D., M.A., S.T.D.
Scouting—Fort Wayne: Rev. ANTHONY STEINACKER, Chap. Tel: 260-482-2186; VACANT, Chm. South Bend: VACANT, Chap.; LAURA RAY, Vice Chm. Tel: 574-273-2081.
Spiritual Development—Fort Wayne: VACANT, Dir., Archbishop Noll Catholic Center, 915 S. Clinton St., Fort Wayne, 46802. Tel: 260-422-4611; Fax: 260-426-3077. Mailing Address: P.O. Box 390, Fort Wayne, 46801. South Bend: VACANT.
Office of Youth Ministry and Spiritual Formation—CINDY BLACK, Dir., Archbishop Noll Catholic Center, 915 S. Clinton St., Fort Wayne, 46802. Tel: 260-422-4611; Fax: 260-483-1881. Mailing Address: P.O. Box 390, Fort Wayne, 46801.
Vocations—Rev. Msgr. BERNARD J. GALIC, Dir., 114 W. Wayne St., South Bend, 46601. Tel: 574-234-0687; Fax: 574-232-8483.
Youth Organizations—Mailing Address: P.O. Box 445, Monroeville, 46773. Tel: 260-623-6007.
CYO Office—AVA MEYER, Business Mgr., Mailing Address: P.O. Box 445, Monroeville, 46773. Tel: 260-623-6007; Fax: 260-623-6007; VACANT, Moderator; Ms. MARY SCHREIBER, Pres., 2021 Reckeweg Rd., Fort Wayne, 46804. Tel: 260-432-1921.
Inter City Catholic League—Rev. Msgr. MICHAEL W. HEINTZ, Ph.D., Moderator, St. Matthew Cathedral, 1701 Miami St., South Bend, 46613. Tel: 574-289-5539; TONY VIOLI, Pres., 225 Omer Ave., Mishawaka, 46545. Tel: 574-259-1638; 574-255-9776; Fax: 574-259-0995.
Victim Assistance Coordinator—MARY L. GLOWASKI, 4525 Arlington Ave., Fort Wayne, 46807. Tel: 260-744-3682. Email: mglowaski@diocesefwsb.org.
Safe Environment Program—CATHIE CICCHIELLO, Coord. Tel: 260-672-1510.

CLERGY, PARISHES, MISSIONS AND PAROCHIAL SCHOOLS

CITY OF FORT WAYNE

(ALLEN COUNTY)

1—CATHEDRAL OF THE IMMACULATE CONCEPTION (1836), (Calhoun, between Lewis and Jefferson Sts.). Rev. Msgr. Robert C. Schulte, Rector; Revs. Dale A. Bauman; Fernando Jimenez; James Stoyle.
Mailing Address: P.O. Box 10898, 46854. Web: cathedralfw.catholicweb.com.
Tel: 260-424-1485; Fax: 260-424-7625.
Catechesis/Religious Program—Fax: 260-424-7625. Sr. Marilyn Ellert, O.S.F., D.R.E./Pastoral Min. Students 65.
Chapel—MacDougal Memorial Chapel 1139 S. Calhoun St., 46802.

2—ST. ANDREW (1910) Closed. Parish closed June 28, 2003. Sacramental records are located in the Diocesan Archives Office, P.O. Box 390, Fort Wayne, IN. Tel: 260-422-4611.

3—ST. CHARLES BORROMEO (1957) [CEM] Rev. Msgr. John N. Suelzer; Revs. Anthony Steinacker; James Kumbakkeel, O.S.B. (India); Casey Ryan, Dir. Adult Formation; Margaret Sorg, Business Admin.
Res.: 4916 Trier Rd., 46815. Tel: 260-482-2186; Fax: 260-471-2144. Web: stcfw.org.
School—(Grades K-8), 4910 Trier Rd., 46815. Tel: 260-484-3392; Fax: 260-482-2006. Robert Sordelet, Prin. Franciscan Sisters of the Sacred Heart 1; Lay Teachers 44; Students 736.
Catechesis/Religious Program—Tel: 260-484-7322. Amy Johns, D.R.E. Students 121.

4—ST. ELIZABETH ANN SETON (1988) Revs. James A. Shafer; Andrew Curry.
Office: 10700 Aboite Center Rd., 46804. Tel: 260-432-0268; Fax: 260-436-5851.
Catechesis/Religious Program—Students 1,310.

5—ST. HENRY (1956) Rev. Daniel Durkin.
Parish Office: 4643 Gaywood Dr., 46806. Tel: 260-744-2519; Fax: 260-387-5044. Email: sainthenry@verizon.net.

Res.: 2929 E. Paulding Rd., 46816. Tel: 260-447-4100; Fax: 260-447-4100.
Catechesis/Religious Program—Students 2.

6—ST. HYACINTH (1910) Closed. Parish closed November 4, 1995. Sacramental records are located in the Diocesan Archives Office, P.O. Box 390, Fort Wayne, IN. Tel: 260-422-4611.

7—ST. JOHN THE BAPTIST (1929) Rev. Cyril Fernandes; Mary L. Glowaski, Pastoral Assoc.
Res.: 4525 Arlington Ave., 46807. Tel: 260-744-4393; Fax: 260-456-3072. Web: www.stjohnsfw.org.
School—(Grades PreK-8), 4500 Fairfield Ave., 46807. Tel: 260-456-3321. Jane Sandor, Prin. Lay Teachers 20; Students 315.
Catechesis/Religious Program—Tel: 260-744-3578. David Fleischacker, D.R.E.; Amy Woodfill, Youth Min. Students 65.

8—ST. JOSEPH (1914), (Italian), Rev. Timothy A. Wrozek; Ken Jehle, Music Dir. In Res., Rev. Adam Schmitt (Retired).
Office: 2213 Brooklyn Ave., 46802.
Res.: 1910 Hale Ave., 46802. Tel: 260-432-5113; Fax: 260-432-4711.
School—(Grades PreK-8), 2211 Brooklyn Ave., 46802. Tel: 260-432-4000; Fax: 260-432-8642. Ms. Lois Widner, Prin. Lay Teachers 33; Students 526.
Catechesis/Religious Program—Students 130.

9—ST. JOSEPH (1851) [CEM] Rev. Thomas Lombardi.
Res.: 11337 Old U.S. 27 S., 46816. Tel: 260-639-3748; Fax: 260-639-3331.
School—(Grades PreK-8), 11521 Old U.S. 27 S., 46816. Tel: 260-639-3580; Fax: 260-639-3675. Louise Schultheis, Prin. Lay Teachers 13; Students 134.
Catechesis/Religious Program—Students 28.

10—ST. JUDE (1929) Revs. Thomas Shoemaker; Robert D'Souza; Mary Pohlman, Pastoral Assoc.
Res.: 2130 Pemberton Dr., 46805. Tel: 260-484-6609; Fax: 260-969-1607. Web: www.stjudefw.org.
School—(Grades PreK-8), 2110 Pemberton Dr., 46805. Tel: 260-484-4611; Fax: 260-969-1607. Web: www.stjudefw.org/school. Sr. Kathleen Marie Knueven, Prin. Sisters of Notre Dame 3; Lay Teachers 36; Students 507.
Catechesis/Religious Program—Sue Sherburne, D.R.E. Students 176.

11—ST. MARY (1848), (German), [CEM] Rev. Phillip A. Widmann.
Mailing Address: P.O. Box 11383, 46857-1383. Tel: 260-424-8231; Fax: 260-426-2029. Email: stmarysfw@verizon.net.
Res.: 518 E. Dewald, 46803.
Catechesis/Religious Program—Students 15.

12—MOST PRECIOUS BLOOD (1897) Rev. Joseph Gaughan.
Res.: 1515 Barthold St., 46808. Tel: 260-424-5535; Fax: 260-426-7765.
School—(Grades PreK-8), 1529 Barthold St., 46808. Tel: 260-424-4832. Mrs. Alexandria Bergman, Prin. Lay Teachers 12; Students 182.
Catechesis/Religious Program—Students 30.

13—OUR LADY OF GOOD HOPE (1969) Rev. Msgr. Bruce Piechocki; David Zehr, Pastoral Assoc.; Ben Wedler, Liturgy & Music Dir.; Herman Riecke, Business Mgr.
Res.: 7215 St. Joe Rd., 46835. Tel: 260-485-9615; Fax: 260-485-4463.
Catechesis/Religious Program—Tel: 260-485-9615, Ext. 107. Natalie Kohrman, D.R.E.; Jackie Oberhausen, Youth Dir. (K-8). Students 161.

14—ST. PATRICK (1889), (Vietnamese), Revs. Chau Pham, S.V.D. (Vietnam); Thomas Ascheman, S.V.D.
Res.: 2120 S. Harrison St., 46802. Tel: 260-744-1450; Fax: 260-745-3643. Email: stpartrick063@verizon.net.
Catechesis/Religious Program—Students 281.

15—ST. PAUL (1865) Closed. Parish closed June 28, 2003. Sacramental records are located at St. Patrick Catholic Church, 2120 Harrison St., Fort Wayne, IN 46802. Tel: 260-744-1450.

16—ST. PETER (1872), (German), Rev. Phillip A. Widmann.
Res.: 518 E. De Wald St., 46803. Tel: 260-744-2765; Fax: 260-744-1972. Web: www.stpeterscatholicfw.org.
Catechesis/Religious Program—

17—QUEEN OF ANGELS (1947) [CEM] Rev. Gary L. Sigler.
Res.: 1500 W. State Blvd., 46808. Tel: 260-482-9411; Fax: 260-471-0005.
School—1600 W. State Blvd., 46808. Tel: 260-483-8214; Fax: 260-482-9412. Mrs. Marsha Jordan, Prin. Lay Teachers 17; Students 251.
Catechesis/Religious Program—Students 60.

18—SACRED HEART (1947) Revs. Daniel Durkin; George Gabet, F.S.S.P.
Church & Office: 4643 Gaywood Dr., 46806. Tel: 260-744-2519. Email: sacredheartcc@verizon.net.
Res.: 2929 E. Paulding Rd., 46816. Tel: 260-447-4100; Fax: 260-387-5044.
Catechesis/Religious Program—Students 25.

19—ST. THERESE (1947) Rev. David Ruppert.
Res.: 2304 Lower Huntington Rd., 46819. Tel: 260-747-9139; Fax: 260-747-1494. Email: sttheresefw@fw.diocesefwsb.org. Web: www.sttheresefw.org.
School—2222 Lower Huntington Rd., 46819. Tel: 260-747-2343; Fax: 260-747-4767. Charles Grimm, Prin. Lay Teachers 14; Students 170.
Catechesis/Religious Program—Students 51.

20—ST. VINCENT DE PAUL (1846) [CEM] Rev. Msgr. John M. Kuzmich; Rev. Jason Eugene Freiburger; Dorothy Schuerman, Pastoral Assoc.; Mrs. Sherry Miller, Admin.; Judy Mockenhaupt, Pastoral Assoc.
Res.: 1502 E. Wallen Rd., 46825. Tel: 260-489-3537; Fax: 260-497-9405. Email: stvincentchurch@hotmail.com. Web: www.saintv.org.
School—1720 E. Wallen Rd., 46825. Tel: 260-489-3537, Ext. 213; Fax: 260-489-5318. Mrs. Sandra Guffey, Prin. Lay Teachers 43; Students 752.
Catechesis/Religious Program—Tel: 260-489-3537, Ext. 235. Beth Amick, D.R.E. Students 555.

CITY OF SOUTH BEND

(ST. JOSEPH COUNTY)

1—ST. ADALBERT (1910), (Polish), Revs. Christopher Cox, C.S.C.; David Scheidler, C.S.C.
Mailing Address: 2505 W. Grace St., 46619. In Res., Revs. Leonard J. Collins, C.S.C.; Thomas W. Smith, C.S.C.
Res.: 2420 W. Huron St., 46619. Tel: 574-288-5708; Fax: 574-251-2786.
School—519 S. Olive St., 46619. Tel: 574-288-6645; Fax: 574-251-2788. Mary Ann Bachman, Prin. Lay Teachers 10; Students 190.
Catechesis/Religious Program—Students 300.

2—ST. ANTHONY DE PADUA (1949) Rev. Mark Gurtner; Deacon Brian L. Miller.
Res.: 2120 E. Jefferson Blvd., 46617. Tel: 574-282-2308; Fax: 574-288-8877.
School—2310 E. Jefferson Blvd., 46615. Tel: 574-233-7169; Fax: 574-233-7290. Chad Barwick, Prin. Lay Teachers 22; Students 299.
Catechesis/Religious Program—Students 17.

3—ST. AUGUSTINE (1928), (African American), Rev. Leonard J. Collins, C.S.C.
Mailing Address: P.O. Box 3198, 46619-0198. Tel: 574-234-7082; Fax: 574-251-2786.
Res.: 2505 Grace St., 46619. Tel: 574-251-2789.
Catechesis/Religious Program—Students 10.

4—ST. CASIMIR (1899), (Polish), Revs. Christopher Cox, C.S.C.; David Scheidler, C.S.C.
Mailing Address: 2505 W. Grace St., 46619. 1308 W. Dunham St., 46619. Tel: 574-287-9551; Fax: 574-251-2786. Email: stcas145@aol.com. Web: stcasimirparish.org.
Res.: 2420 W. Huron, 46619. Tel: 574-288-5708.
Catechesis/Religious Program—

5—ST. CATHERINE OF SIENA PARISH AT ST. JUDE (1948) Revs. John Delaney; Paul Choorathottiyil, V.C.
Res.: 19704 Johnson Rd., 46614. Tel: 574-291-0570; Fax: 574-299-3051. Email: stjudesb@juno.com. Web: www.stjudeparish.net.
School—19657 Hildebrand St., 46614. Tel: 574-291-3820; Fax: 574-299-3053. Email: principal@stjudeschool.net. Mr. Steve Donndelinger, Prin. Lay Teachers 18; Students 165.
Catechesis/Religious Program—Tel: 574-291-2797. Students 9.

6—CHRIST THE KING (1933) Revs. Neil F. Wack, C.S.C.; Ronald Tripi, C.S.C.; Stephen A. Lacroix, C.S.C.
Res.: 52473 Indiana State Rte. 933, 46637. Tel: 574-272-3113; Fax: 574-273-6702. Email: xtherex@aol.com. Web: christthekingonline.org.
School—Tel: 574-272-3922; Fax: 574-273-6707. Stephen Hoffmann, Prin. Lay Teachers 36; Students 498.
Catechesis/Religious Program—Students 60.

7—CORPUS CHRISTI (1961) Rev. Daryl Rybicki.
Res.: 2822 Corpus Christi Dr., 46628. Tel: 574-272-9982; Fax: 574-272-2545. Email: corpuschristi2005@sbcglobal.net. Web: www.corpuschristisb.org.
School—2817 Corpus Christi Dr., 46628. Tel: 574-272-9868; Fax: 574-272-9894. Web: www.corpuschristischool-southbend.org. Maggie Mackowiak, Prin. Daughters of Divine Charity 1; Lay Teachers 23; Students 300.
Catechesis/Religious Program—Students 20.

8—FAITH & HOPE & CHARITY CHAPEL (1975) Revs. William H. Donahue, C.S.C. (Retired); James F. Blaes, C.S.C. (Retired); Leonard F. Chrobot; John Klimczyk; Joseph P. Browne, C.S.C. (Retired).
Res.: 114 W. Wayne St., 46601. Tel: 574-289-4263.

9—ST. HEDWIG (1877), (Polish), Revs. Leonard F. Chrobot; John Klimczyk.
Res.: 331 S. Scott St., 46601. Tel: 574-287-8932; Fax: 574-232-9787.
Catechesis/Religious Program— Twinned with St. Patrick.

10—HOLY CROSS (1929) Revs. Michael C. Mathews, C.S.C.; Bradley Metz, C.S.C. In Res., Rev. Thomas E. Seidel, C.S.C.
Res.: 1520 Vassar Ave., 46628. Tel: 574-233-2179; Fax: 574-237-6736. Web: www.hcssparish.org.
School—(Grades PreSchool-8), 1020 Wilber St., 46628. Tel: 574-234-3422; Fax: 574-237-6725. Web: www.holycrosscrusaders.org. Mrs. Angela Budzinski, Prin. Lay Teachers 23; Students 329.
Catechesis/Religious Program—Students 35.

11—HOLY FAMILY (1945) [JC] Rev. Msgr. Bernard J. Galic. In Res., Rev. Camillo Tirabassi (Retired).
Res.: 56405 Mayflower Rd., 46619. Tel: 574-282-2317; Fax: 574-282-2318. Web: www.holyfamilysouthbend.org.
School—56407 Mayflower Rd., 46619. Tel: 574-289-7375; Fax: 574-289-7386. Sr. Joan Marie Shillinger, C.S.S.F., Prin. Felician Sisters (Livonia, MI) 3; Lay Teachers 24; Students 355.
Catechesis/Religious Program—Linda Lagodney, D.R.E. Students 75.

12—ST. JOHN THE BAPTIST (1956) Rev. Charles A. Herman.
Res.: 3526 St. Johns Way, 46628. Tel: 574-233-5414; Fax: 574-233-5414. Email: johnthebaptistcc@aol.com.
School—3616 St. John Way, 46628. Tel: 574-232-9849; Fax: 574-232-9849. Janet Wroblewski, Prin. Lay Teachers 9; Students 126.
Catechesis/Religious Program—Students 25.

13—ST. JOSEPH (1853) Revs. John M. DeRiso, C.S.C.; John P. Riley, C.S.C.; Kevin Grove, C.S.C.
Res.: 226 N. Hill St., 46617. Tel: 574-234-3135.
Parish Office—211 N. St. Louis Blvd., 46617. Tel: 574-234-3134; Fax: 574-234-2822. Web: www.stjoeparish.com.
School—216 N. Hill St., 46617. Tel: 574-234-0451; Fax: 574-234-0524. Web: www.stjosephgradeschool-.com. Mrs. Suzanne Wiwi, Prin. Lay Teachers 25; Students 445.
Catechesis/Religious Program—Students 35.

14—ST. MARY OF THE ASSUMPTION (1882), (German), Closed. For inquiries for parish records see St. Jude, South Bend.

15—ST. MATTHEW CATHEDRAL (1921) Rev. Msgr. Michael W. Heintz, Rector; Rev. Jacob Runyon; Deacon Emilio Gizzi; David Laux, Business Mgr.
Res.: 1701 Miami St., 46613. Tel: 574-289-5539; Fax: 574-289-0227. Email: info@stmatthewcathedral.org. Web: stmatthewcathedral.org.
School—(Grades K-8), 1015 E. Dayton, 46613. Tel: 574-289-4535; Fax: 574-289-5439. Ms. Mary Ann Retseck, Prin. Lay Teachers 23; Students 365.
Catechesis/Religious Program—1721 Miami St., 46613. Tel: 574-289-0940; Fax: 574-289-0940. Richard Becker, D.R.E.; Nancy Becker, D.R.E. Students 85.

16—OUR LADY OF HUNGARY (1921) [CEM] Rev. Lawrence Teteh, C.S.Sp. (Nigeria); Deacon Ervin Kuspa.
Res.: 829 W. Calvert St., 46613. Tel: 574-287-1700; Fax: 574-289-6704. Email: olhp@sbcglobal.net. Web: www.ourladyofhungary.com.
School—(Grades PreK-8), 735 W. Calvert St., 46613. Tel: 574-289-3272; Fax: 574-289-3272. Mr. Clem Wroblewski, Prin. Lay Teachers 9; Students 122.
Catechesis/Religious Program—Tel: 574-289-8314. Students 10.

17—ST. PATRICK (1858) Revs. Leonard F. Chrobot; John Klimczyk.
Office: 309 S. Taylor St., 46601. Tel: 574-232-5839; Fax: 574-232-5830. Web: www.sspatrickhedwig.org.
Res.: 331 S. Scott St., 46601. Tel: 574-239-5839; Fax: 574-232-9787.
Catechesis/Religious Program—Tel: 574-239-5839. Students 30.

18—ST. STANISLAUS (1899), (Polish), Revs. Michael C. Matthews, C.S.C.; Bradley Metz, C.S.C. In Res., Rev. Thomas E. Seidel, C.S.C.
Res.: 920 Wilber St., 46628. Tel: 574-233-2179; Fax: 574-237-6736. Web: www.hcssparish.org.

19—ST. STEPHEN (1909), (Hispanic—Hungarian), Closed. Parish closed May 31, 2003. Sacramental records are located at St. Adalbert Catholic Church, 2420 W. Huron St., South Bend, IN 46619. Tel: 574-288-5708.

20—ST. THERESE, LITTLE FLOWER (1937) Rev. Cornelius Ryan, C.S.C.
54191 N. Ironwood Dr., 46635. Tel: 574-272-7070; Fax: 574-243-3434. Email: littleflowerchurch@sbcglobal.net. Web: www.littleflowerchurch.org.
Catechesis/Religious Program—Tel: 574-243-3439. Students 179.

OUTSIDE THE CITIES OF FORT WAYNE AND SOUTH BEND

ALBION, NOBLE CO., BLESSED SACRAMENT (1875) [JC] Rev. Lourdino Fernandes.
Res.: 807 Rolling River Run, 46701. Tel: 260-239-4017.

Church: State Rd. 9 S., 46701-0102. Tel: 260-636-2072.
Catechesis/Religious Program—Students 61.

ANGOLA, STEUBEN CO., ST. ANTHONY (1926) Revs. Fred Pasche, O.F.M.Conv.; Mark Weaver, O.F.M.Conv., Hispanic Ministry; Andrew Martinez, O.F.M.Conv. In Res., Rev. Philip Schneider, O.F.M.Conv.
Res.: 700 W. Maumee St., 46703. Tel: 260-665-2259; Fax: 260-665-2268.
Catechesis/Religious Program—Cathy Bryan, D.R.E.; Lisa Lysaght, Youth Min. Students 230.

ARCOLA, ALLEN CO., ST. PATRICK (1846) [CEM] Rev. Alexius Dodrai (India).
Res.: 12305 Arcola Rd., 46818. Tel: 260-625-4151; Fax: 260-625-3095. Email: stpatarcola@earthlink.net.
Catechesis/Religious Program—Tel: 260-625-4104. Students 127.

AUBURN, DE KALB CO., IMMACULATE CONCEPTION (1872) [CEM] Rev. Derrick Sneyd.
Res.: 500 E. 7th St., 46706. Tel: 260-925-3930; Fax: 260-925-3186.
Catechesis/Religious Program—Tel: 260-925-1621, Ext. 5. Phyllis Gurtner, D.R.E.; Melanie Rolston, D.R.E. Students 140.

AVILLA, NOBLE CO., ST. MARY OF THE ASSUMPTION (1853) [CEM] Rev. Edward Erpelding.
Res.: 228 N. Main St., Box 700, 46710-0700. Tel: 260-897-3261; Fax: 260-897-2284.
School—232 N. Main St., 46710. Tel: 260-897-3481; Fax: 260-897-3706. Mrs. Kathy Garlitz, Prin. Lay Teachers 10; Students 143.
Catechesis/Religious Program—Students 70.

BESANCON, ALLEN CO., ST. LOUIS (1846), (French), [CEM 2] Rev. Stephen E. Colchin.
Res.: 15535 Lincoln Hwy. E., New Haven, 46774. Tel: 260-749-4525.
School—15529 Lincoln Hwy. E., New Haven, 46774. Tel: 260-749-5815; Fax: 260-748-2072. Ms. Cheryl Layton, Prin. Lay Teachers 5; Students 63.
Catechesis/Religious Program—Students 35.

BIG LONG LAKE, LAGRANGE CO., ST. MARY OF THE ANGELS (1937) Closed. Parish closed February 25, 2006. Sacramental records are located at St. Michael Catholic Church, 1098 County Rd. 39, Waterloo, IN. Tel: 260-837-7115.

BLUFFTON, WELLS CO., ST. JOSEPH (1875) Rev. Francis Chukwuma.
Res.: 1300 N. Main St., 46714-1127. Tel: 260-824-1380; Fax: 260-824-2792. Email: stjosephchurch@adamswell.com.
Catechesis/Religious Program—Students 109.

BREMEN, MARSHALL CO., ST. DOMINIC (1947) [JC] Rev. Polycarp Fernando.
803 W. Bike St., 46506.
Church: 212 N. Maryland St., 46506. Tel: 574-546-3601; Fax: 574-546-3659.
Catechesis/Religious Program—803 W. Bike St., 46506. Students 251.

BRISTOL, ELKHART CO., ST. MARY OF THE ANNUNCIATION (1942) [JC] Rev. Robert Van Kempen.
Res.: 411 W. Vistula St., Box 245, 46507. Tel: 574-848-4305; Fax: 574-848-4305.
Catechesis/Religious Program—Students 338.

CHURUBUSCO, WHITLEY CO., ST. JOHN BOSCO (1971) Rev. Danny Pinto (Sri Lanka), Admin.
Res.: 216 N. Main St., 46723. Tel: 260-693-9578; Fax: 260-693-1608.
Catechesis/Religious Program—Tel: 260-693-3332. Students 70.

CLEAR LAKE, STEUBEN CO., ST. PAUL CHAPEL (1941) Rev. Philip Schneider, O.F.M.Conv., Admin.
Rectory—St. Anthony Rectory, 700 W. Maumee, Angola, 46703. Tel: 260-665-2259; Fax: 260-665-2268.
Church: 8780 E. 700 N., Fremont, 46737. Tel: 260-495-9913.
Catechesis/Religious Program—Tel: 260-238-2047. Margaret Carlson, D.R.E. Students 29.

COLUMBIA CITY, WHITLEY CO., ST. PAUL OF THE CROSS (1860) [CEM] [JC] Rev. Lawrence A. Kramer.
Mailing Address: 315 S. Line St., 46725. Email: saintpaulchurch@earthlink.net. Web: www.saintpaulofthecross.org.
Res.: 308 S. Chauncey St., 46725. Tel: 260-244-5723; Fax: 260-244-2833.
Catechesis/Religious Program—Tel: 260-244-2926. Students 203.

CULVER, MARSHALL CO., ST. MARY OF THE LAKE, [JC] Rev. Thadeus Balinda (Uganda).
Office: 605 N. Plymouth St., 46511-1015. Email: stmarys@culcom.net. Web: www.culcom.net/~stmarys.
Res.: 124 College Ave., 46511. Tel: 574-842-2522; Fax: 574-842-5009.
Catechesis/Religious Program—Tel: 574-842-3667; Fax: 574-842-2549. Students 108.

DECATUR, ADAMS CO., ST. MARY OF THE ASSUMPTION (1840), (German), [CEM] Revs. David W. Voors; Benedict Kakwezi (Uganda); Sr. Margaret Rose Donnelly, S.S.N.D., Pastoral Assoc.; Ron Gage, Music Dir.
Res.: 414 W. Madison St., 46733. Tel: 260-724-9159; Fax: 260-724-8948. Email: tdebolt@stmarysdecatur.org. Web: www.stmarysdecatur.org.
School—St. Joseph, (Grades PreK-8), 127 N. Fourth St., 46733. Tel: 260-724-2765; Fax: 260-724-4953. Web: www.stjosephdecatur.org. Karla Hormann, Prin. Lay Teachers 23; Students 344.
Catechesis/Religious Program—Teresa Schurger, D.R.E.; Amber Heimann, Youth Min. Students 81.

EGE, NOBLE CO., IMMACULATE CONCEPTION (1876) [CEM] Rev. Danny Pinto (Sri Lanka), Admin.
216 N. Main St., Churubusco, 46723. Tel: 260-693-9578; Fax: 260-693-1608.
Catechesis/Religious Program—Students 70.

ELKHART, ELKHART CO.

1—ST. THOMAS THE APOSTLE (1949) [JC] Rev. William Sullivan.
Res.: 1405 N. Main St., 46514. Tel: 574-262-1505; Fax: 574-264-4186.
School—(Grades K-8), 1331 N. Main St., 46514. Tel: 574-264-4855; Fax: 574-262-8477. Lay Teachers 25; Students 395.
Catechesis/Religious Program—Tel: 574-264-0491. Students 149.

2—ST. VINCENT DE PAUL (1868) [CEM] Revs. Glenn Kohrman; Kevin M. Bauman.
Res.: 1108 S. Main St., 46516. Tel: 574-293-8231; Fax: 574-293-1105.
School—(Grades PreK-6), 1114 S. Main St., 46516. Tel: 574-293-8451; Fax: 574-295-9702. Ms. Donna Quinn, Prin. Lay Teachers 7; Students 120.
Catechesis/Religious Program—Tel: 574-293-8071. Students 515.

GARRETT, DE KALB CO., ST. JOSEPH (1876) [CEM] Rev. Andrew L. Nazareth (India); Deacon Harris Hoeffel.
Office: 300 W. Houston, 46738-1424. Tel: 260-357-3122.
Res.: 307 S. Ijams St., 46738. Tel: 260-357-0381.
School—(Grades PreK-6), 301 W. Houston, 46738. Tel: 260-357-5137; Fax: 260-357-5138. Kristine Call, Prin. Lay Teachers 7; Students 120.
Catechesis/Religious Program—Students 15.

GENEVA, ADAMS CO., ST. MARY OF THE PRESENTATION (1883) [CEM] Rev. J. Bosco Perera (Sri Lanka).
Res.: 5790 E. 1100 S., 46740-9132. Tel: 260-997-6558.
Catechesis/Religious Program—Students 11.

GOSHEN, ELKHART CO., ST. JOHN THE EVANGELIST (1840) [CEM] Revs. Christopher L. Smith; Constantino Rocha.
Res.: 109 W. Monroe St., 46526. Tel: 574-533-3385; Fax: 574-533-1814. Email: parishoffice@stjohncatholic.com. Web: stjohncatholic.com.
School—(Grades PreSchool-6), 117 W. Monroe, 46526. Tel: 574-533-9480. Amy Weidner, Prin.; Angela Hein, Librarian. Sisters 1; Lay Teachers 8; Students 144.
Catechesis/Religious Program—Darlene Leitz, D.R.E. Students 340.

GRANGER, ST. JOSEPH CO., ST. PIUS X (1955) Rev. Msgr. William C. Schooler; Rev. Bob J. Lengerich.
Res.: 52553 Fir Rd., 46530. Tel: 574-272-8462; Fax: 574-272-8493. Web: www.stpius.net.
School—(Grades PreK-8) Tel: 574-272-4935; Fax: 574-533-1814. Elaine Holmes, Prin. Students 540.
Catechesis/Religious Program—Tel: 574-277-5760. Students 780.

HUNTINGTON, HUNTINGTON CO.

1—ST. MARY (1896) [JC] Rev. John F. Pfister.
Office & Res.: 903 N. Jefferson St., 46750. Tel: 260-356-4398; Fax: 260-356-3529. Email: stmary083@comcast.net.
School—Middle Building, 960 Warren St., 46750. Tel: 260-356-1926; Fax: 260-356-8419. Jason Woolard, Prin. Faculty 16; Students 217.
Catechesis/Religious Program—Students 115.

2—SS. PETER AND PAUL (1843) [JC] Revs. Ronald Rieder, O.F.M.Cap.; Augustine Rochuparathanathu, V.C. (India).
Res.: 860 Cherry St., 46750. Tel: 260-356-4798; Fax: 260-356-7154.
See Huntington Catholic School, Huntington under St. Mary, Huntington for details.
Catechesis/Religious Program—Sr. Miriam Gill, S.S.N.D., D.R.E. Students 282.

KENDALLVILLE, NOBLE CO., IMMACULATE CONCEPTION (1867) [CEM] Rev. James Stoyle.
Res. & Mailing Address: 319 E. Diamond St., 46755. Tel: 260-347-2522; Fax: 260-347-4045.
Church: 301 E. Diamond St., 46755.
Catechesis/Religious Program—Students 43.

LAGRANGE, LAGRANGE CO., ST. JOSEPH (1930) [JC] Rev. Mark Weaver, O.F.M.Conv.
Res.: 050 N. 100 E., 46761. Tel: 260-463-3472; Fax: 260-456-3472. Email: stjosephlagrange@embarq.com.
Catechesis/Religious Program—Students 200.

LAGRO, WABASH CO., ST. PATRICK (1838) Closed. Parish closed February 1, 1997. Sacramental records are located at St. Bernard Catholic Church, 207 North Cass St., Wabash, IN 46992-2441. Tel: 260-563-4750.

LAKEVILLE, ST. JOSEPH CO., ST. CATHERINE OF SIENA PARISH AT SACRED HEART OF JESUS (1932) [JC] Revs. John Delaney; Paul Choorathottiyil, V.C.
Res.: 63568 U.S. 31 S., 46614-9409. Tel: 574-291-2826; Fax: 574-291-3775. Email: sacredheart11@juno.com.
Catechesis/Religious Program—Twinned with St. Jude., Tel: 574-291-2826.

LIGONIER, NOBLE CO., ST. PATRICK (1860) [JC] Rev. Wilson O. Corzo (Colombia).
Res.: 300 Ravine Park Dr., 46767-1301. Tel: 260-894-4946; 260-894-4911.
Catechesis/Religious Program—Students 220.

MISHAWAKA, ST. JOSEPH CO.

1—ST. BAVO (1903) Rev. Barry C. England; Deacon Kevin M. Ranaghan.
Res.: 511 W. 7th St., 46544. Tel: 574-255-1437; Fax: 574-255-0404. Web: www.stbavochurch.com.
School—524 W. 8th St., 46544. Tel: 574-259-4214; Fax: 574-258-0403. Linda Hixon, Prin. Lay Teachers 13; Students 200.
Catechesis/Religious Program—Students 70.

2—ST. JOSEPH (1848) [CEM] Rev. Terry Fisher; Deacon Ronald Moser.
Res.: 225 S. Mill St., 46544. Tel: 574-255-6134; Fax: 574-255-6387.
School—(Grades PreK-8), 230 S. Spring St., 46544. Tel: 574-255-5554; Fax: 574-255-6381. Mrs. Mary Geist, Prin. Lay Teachers 13; Students 199.
Catechesis/Religious Program—Students 86.

3—ST. MICHAEL UKRAINIAN CATHOLIC CHURCH (1916), (Ukrainian), [CEM] [JC] Rev. Thomas R. Dobrowolski.
Res.: 712 E. Lawrence St., 46545-6835. Tel: 574-259-7173.
Catechesis/Religious Program—Students 12.

4—ST. MONICA (1915) Rev. Jeffery A. Largent.
Res.: 222 W. Mishawaka Ave., 46545. Tel: 574-255-2247; Fax: 574-255-8375.
School—(Grades PreK-8), 223 W. Grove St., 46545. Tel: 574-255-0709; Fax: 574-255-0311. Email: schooloffice@stmonicamish.org. Web: www.stmonicamish.org. Sr. Pat Gavin, S.S.N.D., Prin. Sisters 1; Lay Teachers 15; Students 161.
Catechesis/Religious Program—Students 60.

5—QUEEN OF PEACE (1957) Rev. Daniel D. Scheidt.
Res.: 4508 Vistula Rd., 46544. Tel: 574-255-9674; Fax: 574-255-9675. Web: www.queenofpeace.cc.
School—(Grades PreSchool-8) Tel: 574-255-0392; Fax: 574-255-1029. Email: schoolinfo@queenofpeace.cc. Web: www.queenofpeace.cc/school. Chad Berndt, Prin.; Lynette Delahanty, Librarian. Lay Teachers 11; Students 240.
Catechesis/Religious Program—Carol Cone, D.R.E. Students 175.

MONROEVILLE, ALLEN CO., ST. ROSE OF LIMA (1868) [CEM] Rev. Stephen E. Colchin.
Res.: 206 Summit St., P.O. Box 406, 46773. Tel: 260-623-6437. Web: www.saintrosechurch.com.
School—St. Joseph, (Grades K-8), 209 Mulberry St., 46773. Tel: 260-623-3447; Fax: 260-623-3447. Mrs. Carolyn Kirkendall, Prin. Lay Teachers 5; Students 69.
Catechesis/Religious Program—Catrina O'Shaughnessey, D.R.E.

NAPANEE, ELKHART CO., ST. ISIDORE, Closed. Parish closed August 1, 1995. Sacramental records are located at St. Dominic, 803 W. Bike St., Bremen, IN. Tel: 574-546-3601.

NEW CARLISLE, ST. JOSEPH CO., ST. STANISLAUS KOSTKA (1884), (Polish), Rev. Paul McCarthy.
Res.: 55756 Tulip Rd., 46552. Tel: 574-654-3781; Fax: 574-654-3781.
Catechesis/Religious Program—Tel: 574-654-8132. Jacqueline Sheedy, D.R.E. Students 65.

NEW HAVEN, ALLEN CO., ST. JOHN THE BAPTIST (1859) [CEM] Rev. James F. Seculoff.
Res.: 943 Powers St., 46774. Tel: 260-493-4553; Fax: 260-749-6164.
School—(Grades PreK-8), 204 Rufus St., 46774. Tel: 260-749-9903; Fax: 260-749-6047. Janice Comito, Prin. Lay Teachers 16; Students 318.
Catechesis/Religious Program—Students 140.

NIX SETTLEMENT, WHITLEY CO., ST. CATHARINE (1850) [CEM] Rev. Kenneth J. Sarrazine.
Rectory—St. Joseph, 641 N. Main St., P.O. Box 250, Roanoke, 46783-0250. Tel: 260-672-2838; Fax: 260-672-3069.
Church: Ind. Hwy. 9 & Whitley Co. Rd., 1,000 S., Columbia City, 46725.
Catechesis/Religious Program—Dr. Kathleen Schneider, D.R.E. Students 29.

NORTH MANCHESTER, WABASH CO., ST. ROBERT BELLARMINE (1963) [JC] Rev. Thomas Kodakassery, O.S.B. (India).
Res.: 1203 State Rd., 114 E., 46962. Tel: 260-982-4404; Fax: 260-982-6979.

Catechesis / Religious Program—Students 28.
NOTRE DAME, ST. JOSEPH CO., SACRED HEART (1842) [CEM] [JC] Revs. Thomas J. Jones, C.S.C.; Timothy O'Connor, C.S.C.
Res.: 104 The Presbytery, 46556-5658. Tel: 574-631-7511; Fax: 574-631-8080.
Catechesis / Religious Program—Tel: 574-631-9436; Fax: 574-631-9687. Students 45.
PIERCETON, KOSCIUSKO CO., ST. FRANCIS XAVIER (1841) [CEM] Rev. Dale A. Bauman.
Mailing Address: P.O. Box 376, 46562.
Church: 408 W. Catholic St., 46562. Tel: 574-594-5750; Fax: 574-594-2347.
Catechesis / Religious Program—Tel: 574-594-5750, Ext. 12. Students 43.
PLYMOUTH, MARSHALL CO., ST. MICHAEL (1862) [CEM] Revs. William Kummer; Eloy Jimenez.
Res., Office & Mailing Address: 612 N. Walnut St., 46563. Tel: 574-936-4935; Fax: 574-936-9293. Web: www.stmichaelchurchplymouth.com.
School—(Grades PreK-8), 612 N. Center St., 46563. Tel: 574-936-4329; Fax: 574-936-1151. Web: www.saintmichaelschool.org. Miss Gertrude Nawara, Prin.; Mrs. Barbara Blad, Librarian. Lay Teachers 12; Students 202.
Catechesis / Religious Program—Gregory Lenburg, D.R.E. Students 168.
ROANOKE, HUNTINGTON CO., ST. JOSEPH (1867) [CEM] Rev. Kenneth J. Sarrazine.
Res.: 641 N. Main St., P.O. Box 250, 46783-0250. Tel: 260-672-2838; Fax: 260-672-3069.
Catechesis / Religious Program—Dr. Kathleen Schneider, D.R.E. Students 46.
ROME CITY, NOBLE CO., ST. GASPAR DEL BUFALO (1957) [CEM] Rev. Bernard Ramenaden, O.S.B. (Sri Lanka).
Res.: 10871 N. State Rd. 9, 46784. Tel: 260-854-3100; Fax: 260-854-4083. Email: stgaspar@kuntrynet.com.
Catechesis / Religious Program—Students 44.
SYRACUSE, KOSCIUSKO CO., ST. MARTIN DE PORRES (1966) Rev. Richard Hire.
Res.: 6941 E. Waco Dr., 46567-9496. Tel: 574-457-8176; Fax: 574-457-3542.
Catechesis / Religious Program—Students 79.
WABASH, WABASH CO., ST. BERNARD (1864) Rev. Sextus Don (Sri Lanka); Deacon Ted Krizman.
Res.: 207 N. Cass St., 46992. Tel: 260-563-4750; Fax: 260-563-0313.
School—(Grades PreK-5), 191 N. Cass St., 46992. Tel: 260-563-5746; Fax: 260-563-4898. Theresa Carroll, Prin. Lay Teachers 6; Students 78.
Catechesis / Religious Program—Students 86.
WALKERTON, ST. JOSEPH CO., ST. PATRICK (1856) Rev. Pius N. Illechukwu (Nigeria); Mrs. Sue Steininger, Music Min.
7807 Tyler St., 46574.
Office: 807 Tyler St., 46574. Fax: 574-586-7152.
Res.: 801 Tyler St., 46574. Tel: 574-586-7404.
Letko Hall—811 Tyler St., 46574.
Catechesis / Religious Program—Wendy Bocian, D.R.E. Students 70.
WARSAW, KOSCIUSKO CO.
1—OUR LADY OF GUADALUPE (1972), (Hispanic), [CEM] Rev. Philip DeVolder.
Mailing Address: P.O. Box 1136, 46581-1136.
Res.: 125 N. Harrison, 46580. Tel: 574-267-5842, Ext. 115; Fax: 574-268-1030.
Church: 225 Gilliam Dr., 46581. Tel: 574-267-5324.
Catechesis / Religious Program—Students 170.
2—SACRED HEART (1852) [JC] Rev. Msgr. James J. Wolf.
Res.: 125 N. Harrison St., 46580. Tel: 574-267-5842; Fax: 574-268-1030.
School—(Grades K-6), 135 N. Harrison, 46590. Tel: 574-267-5874; Fax: 574-267-5136. Mr. James L. Faroh Sr., Prin. Lay Teachers 13; Students 210.
Catechesis / Religious Program—Students 198.
WATERLOO, DEKALB CO., ST. MICHAEL THE ARCHANGEL (1880) [CEM] Rev. David Carkenord.
Res.: 1098 County Rd. 39, 46793-9779. Tel: 260-837-7115; Fax: 260-837-7727.
Catechesis / Religious Program—Students 175.
Mission—St. Mary of the Angels 5725 S. 1025 E., Hudson, Steuben Co. 46747-9605. Tel: 260-837-5401.
YODER, ALLEN CO., ST. ALOYSIUS (1859) Rev. Dominique A. Carboneau.
Res.: 14623 Bluffton Rd., 46798-9741. Tel: 260-622-4491. Email: office@staloysiusyoder.org. Web: staloysiusyoder.org.
School—14607 Bluffton Rd., 46798-9741. Tel: 260-622-7151; Fax: 260-622-7961. Charles Grimm, Prin. Lay Teachers 6; Students 92.
Catechesis / Religious Program—Students 37.

Chaplains of Public Institutions

FORT WAYNE. *St. Joseph Medical Center*, 700 Broadway, 46802-1402. Tel: 260-425-3000. Rev. Daniel Chukwuleta, Chap.
Lutheran Hospital, Tel: 260-435-7001. Roseann Bloomfield. Tel: 260-435-7722.
Parkview Memorial Hospital, Tel: 260-484-6636, Ext. 26311. Rev. Robert D'Souza, Chap.
Veterans Administration Hospital. Rev. Daniel R. Leeuw, Chap. (Retired).

On Special Assignment:
Rev. Msgr.—
Piechocki, Bruce, J.C.L., Officialis of Diocese, Chancery

Retired:
Rev. Msgr.—
Lester, J. William, P.A., Saint Anne Home, 1900 Randallia Dr. #1012, 46805.
Revs.—
Balzer, Raymond, c/o Rev. Robert Schulle, P.O. Box 390, 46801.
Bly, Walter J., Castle Point Apts., 2701 Royal Huntsmen, 46637.
Doriot, Thomas E., 2724 Elvyra Way, Apt. 2, Sacramento, CA 95821. Tel: 916-484-6145
Gall, Jacob M., 51958 Fawn Meadow Dr., Elkhart, 46514. Tel: 574-264-1119
Hammond, Robert, P.O. Box 390, 46801.
Leeuw, Daniel R., 1608 Tyler Ave., 46808. Tel: 260-424-0645
McNulty, Patrick J., 2888 Dafoe Rd., RR 2, Combermere ON KOJILO Canada.
Miller, Paul D., St. Anne Home, 1900 Randallia Dr., 46805. Tel: 260-748-4042
Peil, William, St. Anne Home, 1900 Randallia Dr., #1023, 46805. Tel: 260-339-3066
Rose, James, 536 Fallen Oaks Dr., Coldwater, MI 49036. Tel: 517-238-5522
Ruetz, Edward J., 621 Portage, 46616. Tel: 574-234-5652
Schmitt, Adam, St. Joseph Church, 1910 Hale Ave., 46802. Tel: 260-432-5113
Sienkiewicz, Matthew, 19080 Three Oaks Rd., Three Oaks, MI 49128. Tel: 269-756-6316
Tippmann, Laurence, 1608 Reckeweg Rd., 46804. Tel: 260-432-3197
Tirabassi, Camillo, Holy Family Church, 56405 Mayflower Rd., 46619.
Traub, Robert, Saint Anne Home, 1900 Randallia Dr. #1020, 46805. Tel: 260-399-3305
Yast, Robert A., St. Joseph Church, 4631 Lake Ave., 46815. Tel: 260-755-1499

Permanent Deacons:
Baumgartner, Paul E., (Retired), 417 Howard St., 46617.
Dits, Paul, (Retired), 17433 Battles Rd., 46614.
Folds, Milton, (Retired), 3700 S. Westport Ave. #3651, Sioux Falls, SD 57106-6360.
Gizzi, Emilio, 1136 E. Fairview Ave., 46614.
Hoeffel, Harris H., (Retired), 1245 Rohm, Auburn, 46707.
Krizman, Ted, 134 W. Sinclair, Wabash, 46992.
Kuspa, Ervin, 434 S. Liberty, 46619.
Lyczak, Edward, 4645 Mariner Blvd., Spring Hill, FL 34609.
Miller, Brian L., 2120 E. Jefferson, 46617.
Moser, Ronald J., 51812 Whitestable, 46627.
Ranaghan, Kevin, 1003 St. Vincent, 46617.
Tugman, John, 15932 Preswick Ln., Granger, 46530.
Walsh, James M., (Retired), 2212 Broadmoor Dr., Elkhart, 46514.

INSTITUTIONS LOCATED IN THE DIOCESE

[A] SEMINARIES, RELIGIOUS, OR SCHOLASTICATES

NOTRE DAME. *Moreau Seminary*, P.O. Box 668, 46556. Tel: 574-631-7735; Fax: 574-631-9233. This is a college level and Theological Seminary run by the Indiana Province of the Congregation of Holy Cross for Religious Priesthood and Brotherhood candidates. Priests 20; Brothers 3; Seminarians 45; Total Staff 8.
Formation Staff: Revs. Patrick M. Neary, C.S.C., Rector & Supr.; Frank Cafarelli, C.S.C.; Peter D. Rocca, C.S.C.; Kevin M. Russeau, C.S.C.; Charles Kohlerman, C.S.C.; Stephen Kempinger, C.S.C.; Sr. Susan Dunn, O.P., Ph.D.; Bro. Edward C. Luther, C.S.C In Res. Revs. Frank Cafarelli, C.S.C.; Andrew Hofer, O.P.; Stephen Kempinger, C.S.C.; Jerome E. Knoll, C.S.C.; Stephen M. Koeth, C.S.C.; Charles Kohlerman, C.S.C.; Emery Longanga; Wilson D. Miscamble, C.S.C.; Austin Murphy, O.S.B.; Patrick M. Neary, C.S.C.; Emeka Ngowke; Charles Oyo, C.S.C.; Peter D. Rocca, C.S.C.; Douglas Smith, C.S.C.; John H. Pearson, C.S.C., Asst. Supr. Moreau Seminary; Neil Roy; Bros. John Britto, C.S.C.; John Platte, C.S.C.
Vocations Office: Revs. Peter M. McCormick, C.S.C.; James T. Gallagher, C.S.C.; Ralph L. Haag, C.S.C.; Tom Cashore, Librarian.
Old College, Box 638, 46556-0638. Tel: 574-631-0778; Fax: 574-631-0111. Email: kevin.m.russeau.3@nd.edu. Web: oldcollege.nd.edu. Rev. Kevin M. Russeau, C.S.C., Dir.; Bro. Edward Luther, C.S.C. College candidates study here for up to three years before entering Moreau Seminary. Priests 2; Brothers 1; Candidates for the Priesthood in the First Three Years of Undergraduate Formation 22; Total Staff 3.

[B] COLLEGES AND UNIVERSITIES

FORT WAYNE. *University of Saint Francis* (1890) 2701 Spring St., 46808-3994. Tel: 260-399-7700. Email: ekriss@sf.edu. Web: www.sf.edu. Sr. M. Elise Kriss, O.S.F., B.Ed., M.S., Ph.D., Pres.; Ms. Karla Alexander, Librarian. Conducted by Sisters of St. Francis of Perpetual Adoration. Priests 1; Sisters 9; Students 2,166; Lay Teachers 124; Total Staff 206.
DONALDSON. *Ancilla Domini College*, P.O. Box 1, 46513. Tel: 574-936-8898; Fax: 574-935-1773. Email: admissions@ancilla.edu. Web: www.ancilla.edu. Ronald L. May, Pres.; Sr. Carleen Wrasman, P.H.J.C., Coord. Pastoral Min. & Mission Integration Coord.; Michael Brown, Exec. Dir. Finance & Admin.; Joanna Blount, Dean, Academic & Student Svcs.; Todd Zeltwanger, Exec. Dir. Inst. Advancement; Glenda Bockman, Head Librarian. Poor Handmaids of Jesus Christ (Ancilla Domini Sisters). Sisters 1; Lay Teachers 48; Students 553.
NOTRE DAME. *Holy Cross College, Holy Cross College, Inc.* (1966) 54515 State Rd., 933 N., 46556-0308. Tel: 574-239-8400; Fax: 574-239-8323. Email: rgilman@hcc-nd.edu. Web: www.hcc-nd.edu. Bro. Richard Gilman, C.S.C., Pres.; Robert Benjamin, Dir. Fin. Aid; Mark P. Mullaney, B.B.A., Vice Pres. Admin.; Mary Ellen Hegedus, Librarian; Richard J. Sullivan, B.B.A., M.B.A., Registrar; Marie E. Bensman, Dean Admissions & Enrollment Mngt.; Robert Kloska, M.A., Vice Pres. Mission Advancement; Tina Holland, Ph.D., Sr. Vice Pres.; Daniel Cochran, B.S., M.S., Dean Students; Andrew Polaniecki, Dir. Campus Ministry; Bro. Chris Dreyer, C.S.C., B.A., M.S., B.S.W., Dir. Student Counseling Svcs.
Holy Cross College, Inc. Priests 2; Brothers 6; Lay Professors 44; Students 444; Total Staff 52.
Saint Mary's College (1844) 46556. Tel: 574-284-4556; Fax: 574-284-4707. Email: jhersche@saintmarys.edu. Web: www.saintmarys.edu. Carol A. Mooney, J.D., Pres.; Janet Fore, Librarian. Sisters of the Holy Cross., An institution of higher education for women. Lay Professors 134; Total Enrollment 1,664.
**University of Notre Dame Du Lac* (1842) Provost Office, 300 Main Bldg., 46556. Tel: 574-631-5000; 574-631-6631 (Provost); Fax: 574-631-6897. Email: cleichty@nd.edu. Web: www.nd.edu. The Graduate School (29 departments). The Law School. The Undergraduate School (four colleges, 36 departments). Institutes and Radiation Laboratory, Center for Study of Man, Institute for Urban Studies and Institute for International Studies. Priests 63; Sisters 8; Total Staff 1,013; Total Enrollment 11,731.
Officers Group: Rev. John I. Jenkins, C.S.C., Pres.; Thomas G. Burish, Ph.D., Provost; John Affleck-Graves, Ph.D., Exec. Vice Pres.; Christine Maziar, Ph.D., Vice Pres. & Senior Assoc. Provost; Don Pope-Davis, Ph.D., Vice Pres. & Assoc. Provost; Dennis Jacobs, Ph.D., Vice Pres. & Assoc. Provost; Revs. James E. McDonald, C.S.C., Assoc. Vice Pres. & Counselor to the Pres.; Mark L. Poorman, C.S.C., Vice Pres. Student Affairs; Peter A. Jarret, C.S.C., Holy Cross Supr.; Frances Shavers, Ph.D., Chief of Staff & Spec. Asst. to Pres.; Robert Bernhard, Ph.D., Vice Pres. Research; Janet Botz, Vice Pres. for Public Affairs & Communications; Marianne Corr, J.D., Vice Pres. & General Counsel; Gregory E. Sterling, Ph.D., Dean, Graduate School; James J. Lyphout, Vice Pres. for Business Opers.; Scott C. Malpass, M.B.A., Vice Pres. & Chief Investment Officer; Louis M. Nanni, Vice Pres. Univ. Rels.; John A. Sejdinaj, Vice Pres. for Finance.
Administrative Group: Sr. Susan Dunn, O.P., Ph.D., Asst. Vice Pres. Student Affairs; Ann Firth, Assoc. Vice Pres. Student Affairs; Jannifer Crittendon, Dir. of Inst. Equity; Gilberto Cardenas, Dir. Institute for Latino Studies; Roger P. Mahoney, Chief Audit Exec.; William W. Kirk, Assoc. Vice Pres. for Residence Life; Jennifer Monahan, Exec. Asst. to the Vice Pres. Student Affairs; Robert K. McQuade,

Assoc. Vice Pres. for Human Resources; David Moss, Asst. Vice Pres. Student Affairs; Iris Outlaw, Dir. Multicultural Student Programs & Svcs.; Daniel J. Saracino, Asst. Provost, Enrollment; Jack Swarbrick, Dir. Athletics; Jennifer Younger, Dir. Univ. Libraries.

Assistant Vice Presidents & Counsels: Lisa Anderson, Assoc. Dir., Career Svcs., Graduate School Career Prog.; Dolly Duffy, Assoc. Exec. Dir. Alumni Assoc.; Drew Buscareno, Asst. Vice Pres. Univ. Rels.; Maureen Collins, Mgr. Data & Report, Graduate School; Micki Kidder, Asst. Vice Pres. Devel.; Susan Vissage, Business Mgr., Graduate School; Timothy J. Flanagan, Assoc. Vice Pres. & Counsel; David Harr, Assoc. Vice Pres. Auxiliary Svcs.; Lois C. Jackson, Asst. Vice Pres. & Counsel; Charles F. Lennon Jr., Assoc. Vice Pres. Univ. Rels. & Exec. Dir., Alumni Association; Jean Gorman, Asst. Vice Pres. for Devel.; David Morrissey, Asst. Vice Pres. Univ. Rels.; Harold L. Pace, Registrar; Andrew M. Paluf, Asst. Vice Pres. Finance & Controller; Brandon Roach, Exec. Asst. to the Provost; Daniel G. Reagan, Assoc. Vice Pres. for Univ. Rels.; Joseph A. Russo, Dir. Student Finance Strategies, Fin. Aid; Dennis Brown, Asst. Vice Pres News & Information; Barbara Turpin, Assoc. Dean Academic Policies & Programs, Graduate School; Gordon D. Wishon, Assoc. Provost, Assoc. Vice Pres. & Chief Information Officer.

C.S.C. Faculty & Personnel: Revs. Robert J. Austgen, C.S.C., Emeritus Faculty; Nicholas Ayo, C.S.C.; Leonard N. Banas, C.S.C.; Ernest J. Bartell, C.S.C.; Thomas E. Blantz, C.S.C.; James Bracke, C.S.C.; Richard S. Bullene, C.S.C.; Joseph H. Carey, C.S.C., Campus Min.; Austin I. Collins, C.S.C.; John E. Conley, C.S.C.; Michael Connors, C.S.C.; Joseph Corpora, C.S.C.; Louis A. Delfra, C.S.C.; Robert A. Dowd, C.S.C.; Paul F. Doyle, C.S.C.; John S. Dunne, C.S.C.; Carl F. Ebey, C.S.C.; Tom Eckert, C.S.C.; James F. Flanigan, C.S.C.; James K. Foster, C.S.C.; Patrick D. Gaffney, C.S.C.; James T. Gallagher, C.S.C.; Thomas E. Gaughan, C.S.C.; Eugene F. Gorski, C.S.C.; Gregory A. Green, C.S.C.; Daniel G. Groody, C.S.C.; Ralph L. Haag, C.S.C.; Peter A. Jarret, C.S.C., Prof. Theology & Supr. Corby Hall; John I. Jenkins, C.S.C., Pres.; Thomas J. Jones, C.S.C.; James King, C.S.C.; Paul V. Kollman, C.S.C.; William M. Lies, C.S.C.; Edward A. Malloy, C.S.C., Prof. Theology; Patrick H. Maloney, C.S.C.; Peter M. McCormick, C.S.C.; James E. McDonald, C.S.C., Senior Exec. Asst. & Counselor to the Pres.; Sean D. McGraw, C.S.C.; Donald McNeill, C.S.C.; Leon J. Mertensotto, C.S.C.; Wilson D. Miscamble, C.S.C.; Robert H. Moss, C.S.C.; Martin Lam Nguyen, C.S.C.; Edwin H. Obermiller, C.S.C.; Edward D. O'Connor, C.S.C.; Robert S. Pelton, C.S.C.; Mark L. Poorman, C.S.C., Vice Pres. Student Affairs; Randall C. Rentner, C.S.C.; Peter D. Rocca, C.S.C.; George A. Rozum, C.S.C.; Kevin M. Russeau, C.S.C.; Timothy R. Scully, C.S.C.; William B. Simmons, C.S.C.; S. Douglas Smith, C.S.C.; Thomas G. Streit, C.S.C.; Michael Bruce Sullivan, C.S.C. (Eastern Prov.); Thomas C. Tallarida, C.S.C.; Mark B. Thesing, C.S.C.; Merwyn J. Thomas, C.S.C.; Joseph L. Walter, C.S.C.; Richard V. Warner, C.S.C.; Oliver F. Williams, C.S.C.; Bros. Francis Gorch, C.S.C.; Louis Hurcik, C.S.C.; Edward Luther, C.S.C.; Jerome Meyer, C.S.C. (Midwestern Prov.); Thomas Tucker, C.S.C.

Non-C.S.C. Religious Faculty: Revs. Joseph P. Amar (SAM); James J. Bacik; Paul F. Bradshaw; William Buggert, O.Carm.; Francis Cafarelli; Richard Clifford; John J. Coughlin, O.F.M.; Brian Daley, S.J.; Michael Driscoll, Ph.D.; Bro. William Dygert, C.S.C.; Revs. Virgilio P. Elizondo; Michael D. Findikyan; Thomas Florek, S.J.; Rev. Msgr. Michael W. Heintz, Ph.D.; Rev. Maxwell E. Johnson; Daniel P. Kroger; Revs. Donald LaSaile, S.M.M.; James B. Lewis; Richard P. McBrien; Michael B. McGarry; John P. Meier; James Murphy-O'Connor; Ronald J. Nuzzi; Paulinus I. Odozor, C.S.Sp.; Hugh R. Page; Keith Pecklers; Robert B. Peiffer; Frederick W. Pfotenhauer; Revs. Robert E. Sullivan; Robert F. Taft; Sisters Kathleen Cannon, O.P.; Kathleen J. Dolphin, P.B.V.M.; Mary Jane Herb, I.H.M.; Mary Catherine Hilkert, O.P.; Irene Martineau; Gail Mayotte; LaReine-Marie Veronica Mosely; Mary Shaughnessy, S.C.N.; Margaret Oravez, S.S.J.

[C] HIGH SCHOOLS, DIOCESAN

FORT WAYNE. *Bishop Dwenger High School* (1963) 1300 E. Washington Center Rd., 46825. Tel: 260-496-4700; Fax: 260-496-4702. Email: bdhs@bishopdwenger.com. Web: www.bishopdwenger.com. Mr. J. Fred Tone, Prin.; Mr. Jason Schiffli, Asst. Prin.; Mr. Chris Svarczkopf, Asst. Prin.; Mr. Dennis Fech, Devel. Dir.; Diane Stein, Librarian. Priests 2; Lay Teachers 67; Students 1,070; Total Staff 110.

Bishop Luers High School (1959) 333 E. Paulding Rd., 46816. Tel: 260-456-1261; Fax: 260-456-1262. Email: mkeefer@bishopluers.org. Web: www.bishopluers.org. Mary Keefer, Prin.; Tiffany Albertson, Asst. Prin.; Rev. David Ruppert, Chap.; Jane Anderson, Librarian. Priests 3; Lay Teachers 33; Students 536.

SOUTH BEND. *Saint Joseph's High School* (1953) 1441 N. Michigan St., 46617. Tel: 574-233-6137; Fax: 574-232-3482. Email: sbdstjoehs@saintjoehigh.com. Web: www.saintjoehigh.com. Mrs. Susan Richter, Prin.; Mr. Marty Harshman, Asst. Prin.; Mrs. Marilyn Gibbs, Asst. Prin.; Revs. Walter J. Bly, Chap. (Retired); Camillo Tirabassi, Chap. (Retired); Neil F. Wack, C.S.C., Chap.; Bob J. Lengerich, Chap.; Jane Goldsberry, Librarian. Priests 4; Sisters of the Holy Cross 1; Lay Teachers 59; Students 809.

MISHAWAKA. *Marian High School* (1964) 1311 S. Logan St., 46544. Tel: 574-259-5257; Fax: 574-258-7668. Email: cmoretti@marianhs.org. Web: www.marianhs.org. Mr. Carl Loesch, B.A., M.A., Prin.; Carol Miller, Pastoral Min.; Debbie Conn, Librarian. Priests 1; Sisters 1; Lay Teachers 48; Students 707.

[D] GENERAL HOSPITALS

MISHAWAKA. *Saint Joseph Regional Medical Center*, 5215 Holy Cross Pkwy., 46545. Tel: 574-335-5000; Fax: 574-335-1002. Email: paintelm@sjrmc.com. Web: www.sjmed.com. Nancy R. Hellyer, C.E.O.; Lori Price, COO; Sr. Laureen M. Painter, O.S.F., Vice Pres., Mission Integration. Bed Capacity 254; Patients Assisted Annually 145,571; Total Staff 1,680.

PLYMOUTH. *Saint Joseph Regional Medical Center - Plymouth*, 1915 Lake Ave., P.O. Box 670, 46563. Tel: 574-936-3181; Fax: 574-935-2235. Email: jaegerl@sjrmc.com. Web: www.sjmed.com. Nancy R. Hellyer, C.E.O.; Lori Price, Chief Operating Officer; Sr. Laureen M. Painter, O.S.F., Vice Pres. Mission Integration; Lee Jaeger, Exec. Vice Pres. Total Staff 343; Bed Capacity 58; Patients Assisted Annually 71,394.

[E] SPECIAL HOSPITALS

NOTRE DAME. *University Health Services* 46556. Tel: 574-239-8013; Fax: 574-631-6047. Email: Ann.E.Kleva.4@nd.edu. Web: www.nd.edu/~uhs. Rev. Robert J. Austgen, C.S.C., Health Center Chap. Bed Capacity 8; Total Staff 36; Patients Assisted Annually 18,000.

[F] HOMES FOR THE AGED

FORT WAYNE. *Saint Anne Home & Retirement Community*, 1900 Randallia Dr., 46805. Tel: 260-484-5555; Fax: 260-482-8929. Email: skendrick@sah1900.com. Web: www.saintannehome.com. Mary E. Haverstick, Admin. A Service of the Fort Wayne-South Bend Diocese, Inc. Residents 262; Bed Capacity 334; Total Apartments 168; Total Assisted Annually 509; Total Staff 308. In Res. Rev. Msgr. J. William Lester, P.A. (Retired); Rev. Robert Traub (Retired).

AVILLA. *Provena LaVerna Terrace*, 517 N. Main St., 46710. Tel: 260-897-2093; Fax: 260-897-2086. Email: laverna@dominiorgroup.org. Thomas F. Nehring, Vice Pres. & Mission Leadership Devel.; Rev. Daniel R. Leeuw (Retired); Betty Bower, Property Mgr.

LaVerna Terrace Housing Corp., Conducted by Franciscan Sisters Health Care Corp. whose sole member is Provena Health. Total Staff 2; Apartments 51; Total Assisted 55.

Provena Sacred Heart Home, 515 N. Main St., 46710-9602. Tel: 260-897-2841; Fax: 260-897-3724. Email: craig.prokupek@provena.org. Web: www.provena.org/sacredheart. Craig Prokupek, Admin.; Sr. Theresa Renninger, O.S.F., Religious Leader; Rev. Babasino Fernandes (India), Chap. & Dir. Pastoral Care.

Provena Senior Services Bed Capacity 163; Residents 155; Total Assisted Annually 250; Total Staff 190.

[G] PERSONAL PRELATURES

SOUTH BEND. *Prelature of the Holy Cross and Opus Dei*, Windmoor Center, 1121 N. Notre Dame Ave., 46617. Tel: 574-232-0550; Fax: 574-287-4798. Web: www.opusdei.org. Rev. Mark S. Mannion. Total Staff 4; Total in Residence 14.

[H] MONASTERIES AND RESIDENCES OF PRIESTS AND BROTHERS

NOTRE DAME. *Congregation of Holy Cross, Indiana Province, Provincial House* (1841) *Provincial Administrative Offices*, 54515 State Rd. 933 N., P.O. Box 1064, 46556-1064. Tel: 574-631-6196; Fax: 574-631-5655. Email: david.t.tyson.4@nd.edu. Revs. David T. Tyson, C.S.C., Prov. Supr.; Kenneth M. Molinaro, C.S.C., First Asst. Prov. & Vicar; Anthony V. Szakaly, C.S.C., Second Asst. Prov.; Edwin H. Obermiller, C.S.C., Third Asst. Prov.; E. William Beauchamp, C.S.C., Councilor; Thomas E. Blantz, C.S.C., Councilor; Charles W. Kohlerman, C.S.C., Councilor; William M. Lies, C.S.C., Councilor; Peter A. Jarret, C.S.C., Councilor; Patrick M. Neary, C.S.C., Councilor; Bro. Edward C. Luther, C.S.C; Revs. Francis J. Murphy, C.S.C., Councilor; Neil F. Wack, C.S.C., Councilor; James E. Kelly, C.S.C.; H. Thomas McDermott, C.S.C.; Jeffrey L. Allison, C.S.C.; Robert A. Dowd, C.S.C.; Michael C. Mathews, C.S.C., Councilor; James E. McDonald, C.S.C., Councilor; Thomas E. Chambers, C.S.C., Ph.D. Willwoods Community, Metarie, LA; Thomas P. Doyle, C.S.C. University of Portland.

Priests of Holy Cross, Indiana Province, Inc.

Holy Cross Priests Serving in Foreign Countries:

Chile: Revs. Jose E. Ahumanda, C.S.C., Communidad Egana, Congregacion de Santa Cruz, Casilla 1271, Santiago 1, Chile. Tel: 56-2-673-3278; Fax: 56-2-206-9339; Gerald R. Barmasse, C.S.C., Parroquia Nuestra Senora de la Merced, Congregacion de Santa Cruz, Casilla 1271, Santiago 1, Chile. Tel: 56-2-673-3278; Fax: 56-2-206-9339; Jorge A. Canepa, C.S.C., Congregacion de Santa Cruz, Casilla 1271, Santiago 1, Chile. Tel: 56-2-673-3278; Fax: 56-2-206-9339 St. George's College, Chile; Charles A. Delaney, C.S.C., Congregacion de Santa Cruz, Casilla 1271, Santiago 1, Chile. Tel: 56-2-673-3278; Fax: 56-2-206-9339; Fermin J. Donoso, C.S.C., Parroquia Nuestra Senora de Andacollo, Congregacion de Santa Cruz, Casilla 1271, Santiago 1, Chile. Tel: 56-2-673-3278; Fax: 56-2-206-9339; Joseph A. Dorsey, C.S.C., Congregacion de Santa Cruz, Casilla 1271, Santiago 1, Chile. Tel: 56-2-673-3278; Fax: 56-2-206-9339 St. George's College, Chile; Erwin A. Fonseca, C.S.C., Communidad Egana, Congregacion de Santa Cruz, Casilla 1271, Santiago 1, Chile. Tel: 56-2-673-3278; Fax: 56-2-206-9339; Roberto M. Gilbo, C.S.C., Parroquia Nuestra Senora de la Merced, Congregacion de Santa Cruz, Casilla 1271, Santiago 1, Chile. Tel: 56-2-673-3278; Fax: 56-2-206-9339; Gerald T. Papen, C.S.C., Parroquia Nuestra Senora de Andacollo, Casilla 1271, Santiago 21, Chile. Tel: 56-2-673-3278; Fax: 56-2-206-9339; Pedro Parra, C.S.C., Congregacion de Santa Cruz, Casilla 1271, Santiago 1, Chile. Tel: 56-2-673-3278; Fax: 56-2-206-9339 Casa Andes, Chile; Bro. Joaquin R. Parada, C.S.C., Congregacion de Santa Cruz, Casilla 1271, Santiago 1, Chile. Tel: 56-2-673-3278; Fax: 56-2-206-9339; Rev. Robert G. Simon, C.S.C., Congregacion de Santa Cruz, Casilla 1271, Santiago 1, Chile. Tel: 56-2-673-3278; Fax: 56-2-206-9339 St. George College; Bro. Marcelo Solar, C.S.C.; Rev. Romulo E. Vera, C.S.C., Parroquia Nuestra Senora de Andacolla, Congregacion de Santa Cruz, Casilla 1271, Santiago 1, Chile. Tel: 56-2-673-3278; Fax: 56-2-206-9339.

Peru: *Instituto de Estudios Aymaras*, Apartado 295, Puno, Peru. Fax: 011-51-54-351574. Rev. Philip T. Devlin, C.S.C., Apartado 313, Lima, Peru.

District of East Africa (Uganda): Revs. David Kashangaki, C.S.C., Fort Portal, Uganda; Russell K. McDougall, C.S.C., Holy Cross Bugembe, P.O. Box 1037, Jinja, Uganda. Tel: 011-256-43-120013; Fax: 011-256-43-121322; Prosper Tesha, C.S.C., Holy Cross Bugembe, P.O. Box 1037, Jinja, Uganda. Tel: 011-256-43-120013; Fax: 011-256-43-121322; Leopold Temba, C.S.C.; Serapio Wamara, C.S.C., Holy Cross Bugembe, P.O. Box 1037, Jinja, Uganda. Tel: 011-256-43-120013; Fax: 011-256-43-121322; Lucius Atwine, C.S.C., Kyarusozi Parish Community, P.O. Box 46, Fort Portal, Uganda. Tel: 011-256-077-548-307 King's College; Andrew Massawe, C.S.C., Holy Cross Novitiate, Lake Saaka, P.O. Box 176, Fort Portal, Uganda. Tel: 011-256-77-609469; Pascal Mugabe, C.S.C.; Francis J. Murphy, C.S.C., Holy Cross Novitiate, Lake Saaka, P.O. Box 176, Fort Portal, Uganda. Tel: 011-256-77-609469; Richard L. Potthast, C.S.C., Holy Cross Novitiate, Lake Saaka, P.O. Box 176, Fort Portal, Uganda. Tel: 011-256-77-609469; Richard E. Stout, C.S.C., Holy Cross Novitiate, Lake Saaka, P.O. Box 176, Fort Portal, Uganda. Tel: 011-256-77-609469; James Burasa, C.S.C., District Supr., Bishop McCauley House, P.O. Box 25827, Kampala, Uganda. Tel: 001-256-41-510662; Fulgentius Katende, C.S.C., Bishop McCauley House, P.O. Box 25827, Kampala, Uganda. Tel: 001-256-41-510662; George Muganyizi, C.S.C., Bishop McCauley House, P.O. Box 25827, Kampala, Uganda. Tel: 001-256-41-510662; Leonard Olobo, C.S.C., Bishop McCauley House, P.O. Box 25827, Kampala, Uganda. Tel: 001-256-41-510662; Fred Jenga, C.S.C.

District of East Africa (Kenya): Revs. Bernard Amani (KCK); Richard Kyazze, C.S.C., P.O. Box 58078-00200, Nairobi, Kenya. Tel: 011-254-20-791157; Fax: 001-254-20-780506; Silvester Makwali, C.S.C., P.O. Box 58078-00200, Nairobi, Kenya. Tel:

011-254-20-791157; Fax: 001-254-20-780506; Simon Mwangi, C.S.C.; Willy Frank Lukati, C.S.C., McCauley House of Formation, Box 355-00517, Uhuru Gardens, Nairobi, Kenya. Tel: 011-254-2-601014.

Tanzania: Revs. Aristides Massawe, C.S.C., St. Brendan, P.O. Box 39, Karatu, Arusha, Tanzania; Comfort Agele, C.S.C., St. Brendan, P.O. Box 39, Karatu, Arusha, Tanzania.

On Leave for Higher Studies: Revs. Gary S. Chamberland, C.S.C., 1201 Perry St., Washington, DC 20017-2525. Tel: 202-635-8515; Terrence P. Ehrman, C.S.C., 1201 Perry St., Washington, DC 20017. Tel: 202-635-8515; Brent A. Kruger, C.S.C., 1201 Perry St., Washington, DC 20017. Tel: 202-635-8515; Stephen S. Wilbricht, C.S.C., 1201 Perry St., Washington, DC 20017. Tel: 202-635-8515; William R. Dailey, C.S.C., Holy Trinity Parish, 213 W. 82nd St., New York, NY 10024. Tel: 212-787-0634; John P. Donato, C.S.C., Holy Trinity Parish, 213 W. 82nd St., New York, NY 10024. Tel: 212-787-0634. Our Lady Help of Christians Parish, 573 Washington St., Newton, MA 02458. Tel: 617-527-7560, Ext. 25 Univ. of Portland; Sean D. McGraw, C.S.C., Our Lady Help of Christians Parish, 573 Washington St., Newton, MA 02458. Tel: 617-527-7560, Ext. 25; James E. McDonald, C.S.C., Corby Hall, P.O. Box 514, 46556. Tel: 574-631-7325; Fax: 574-631-6715; James M. Lies, C.S.C., 325 Prior Ave. S., Saint Paul, MN 55105. Tel: 651-696-5426; Randall C. Rentner, C.S.C., 85 Overlook Cir., New Rochelle, NY 10804-4501.

Military Chaplains: Revs. S. Douglas Smith, C.S.C., LTCDR, CHC, USNR Commander, Marine Corp. Air Station Yuma, P.O. Box 99130, Yuma, AZ 85369-9130. Tel: 928-269-2371; Robert E. Roetzel, C.S.C., 411th BSB Chaplain's Office, CMR 419, Box 1811, APO AE09102. Tel: 011-49-06221-57-1570.

Priests of the Province in Residences Not Listed Elsewhere: Revs. Milton Adamson, C.S.C.; Robert Antonelli, C.S.C.; Duane Balcerski, C.S.C.; Richard Berg, C.S.C.; George Bernard, C.S.C.; Thomas Bill, C.S.C.; James T. Banas, C.S.C., Mathis House, P.O. Box 5, Motijhell, Dhaka 1000, Bangladesh. Tel: 011-88-02-710324; Michael T. Belinsky, C.S.C., 3320 Toledo Pl., Apt. G, Hyattsville, MD 20782. Tel: 240-893-7273; Harold L. Bride, C.S.C., Servants of the Paraclete, Vianney Renewal Center, 6476 Eime Rd., P.O. Box 130, Dittmer, MO 63023. Tel: 636-274-5226; William Brinker, C.S.C.; James Burtchaell, C.S.C.; Joseph H. Carey, C.S.C.; Bruce Cecil, C.S.C.; Thomas E. Chambers, C.S.C., Ph.D., Sacred Heart of Jesus, 139 S. Lopez, New Orleans, LA 70119-5109. Tel: 504-827-1481; James Connelly, C.S.C.; John Connor, C.S.C.; Richard Conyers, C.S.C.; Jeffrey Cooper, C.S.C.; Joseph Corpora, C.S.C.; Michael D. Couhig, C.S.C.; Christopher Cox, C.S.C.; Maurice E. Amen, C.S.C., Columba Hall, P.O. Box 47, 46556. Tel: 574-631-8440; Michael DeLaney, C.S.C.; Donald W. Dilg, C.S.C., Our Lady of the Woods Parish, P.O. Box 416, Woodland Park, CO 80866. Tel: 719-687-9345; John M. DeRiso, C.S.C.; Lawrence E. Calhoun, C.S.C., 13645 Riverside Dr., Sherman Oaks, CA 91423. Tel: 818-386-1931; John Dougherty, C.S.C.; Bro. Thomas Dziekan, C.S.C.; Revs. Harry B. Eichorn, C.S.C., Stonehill College, 480 Washington St., North Easton, MA 02356. Tel: 508-238-4515; James T. Gallagher, C.S.C., University of Portland; Stephen C. Gibson, C.S.C.; Charles Gordon, C.S.C.; Richard E. Gribble, C.S.C., Province-Eastern, Stonehill College, 480 Washington St., North Easton, MA 02356. Tel: 508-238-4515; Donald F. Guertin, C.S.C.; David L. Guffey, C.S.C.; Andrew Guljas, C.S.C.; LeRoy E. Clementich, C.S.C., Archdiocese of Anchorage, 225 Cordova St., Anchorage, AK 99501. Tel: 907-297-7734; Fax: 907-279-3885; Lawrence J. Henry, C.S.C., 1406 Buffalo, Michigan City, 46360. Tel: 219-873-2410; Charles W. Corso, C.S.C., 43326 Mission Blvd., Fremont, CA 94539-5829. Tel: 510-659-9717; Edward J. Kaminski, C.S.C., 3220 W. Greenway Rd., Phoenix, AZ 85053. Tel: 602-993-1213; Harry C. Cronin, C.S.C., Holy Cross Center, 2597 Virginia St., Berkeley, CA 94709. Tel: 510-548-8515; Fax: 510-548-7903; William W. Faiella, C.S.C., Holy Cross Center, 2597 Virginia St., Berkeley, CA 94709. Tel: 510-548-8515; Fax: 510-548-7903; James J. Denn, C.S.C., Holy Cross House, P.O. Box 1048, 46556; Thomas F. Elliott, C.S.C., School Sisters of Notre Dame, 345 Belden Hill Rd., Wilton, CT 06897. Tel: 203-762-3318; William G. Blum, C.S.C., Holy Cross House, P.O. Box 1048, 46556-1064. Tel: 574-631-6196; William D. Dorwart, C.S.C., University of Portland, 5000 Willamette Blvd., Portland, OR 97203-5798; John T. Ford, C.S.C., M.A., S.T.D., Catholic University, Cardinal Station, 125.12 Caldwell Hall, Box 236, Washington, DC 20064. Tel: 202-319-6501; Fax: 202-319-5875; 202-319-4967 Hyattsville, MD; James W. Irwin, C.S.C., Calle Esmeralda, Holy Cross Center, 2597 Virginia St., Berkeley, CA 94709. Tel: 510-548-8515; Michael W. Glockner, C.S.C., St. Paul's Retirement Community, 3602 S. Ironwood Dr., 46614. Tel: 574-231-8647; Fax: 574-291-0858; Mark R. Ghyselinck, C.S.C., Holy Cross College, P.O. Box 308, 46556. Tel: 574-631-9484; Fax: 219-631-9233 University of Portland; Kenneth E. Grabner, C.S.C., Holy Cross Village; W. Hannon, C.S.C.; John Herman, C.S.C.; Gregory P. Haake, C.S.C., Holy Cross & St. Stanislaus Parish, South Bend, IN; Thomas Hosinski, C.S.C.; William Hund, C.S.C.; Thomas J. Jones, C.S.C.; John Keefe, C.S.C.; Thomas King, C.S.C.; Jerome E. Knoll, C.S.C.; Stephen M. Koeth, C.S.C., Holy Redeemer Parish, Portland, OR; Edward C. Krause, C.S.C., Gannon University, Erie, PA 16541. Tel: 814-871-7702; Christopher Kuhn, C.S.C.; Howard Kuhns, C.S.C.; John Kurtzke, C.S.C.; Richard Laurick, C.S.C.; Vincent A. Kuna, C.S.C.; Aaron J. Michka, C.S.C.; Charles F. McCoy, C.S.C.; Charles J. Lavely, C.S.C.; Thomas Lemos, C.S.C.; Robert Loughery, C.S.C.; Stephen P. Newton, C.S.C., St. Cletus, 101 N. Horner Ln., Mount Prospect, IL 60056. Tel: 847-824-5049; David E. Schlaver, C.S.C., Holy Cross Mission Center, P.O. Box 543, 46556. Tel: 219-631-8884; 574-631-5477; Fax: 574-631-6813; Thomas W. Smith, C.S.C., Holy Cross Mission Center, P.O. Box 543, 46556. Tel: 219-631-6814; 574-631-5477; Fax: 574-631-6813; Bro. J. Rodney Struble, C.S.C., Mathis House, Norte Dame College, G.P.O. Box 5, Motijhell, Dhaka 1000, Bangladesh; Revs. Patrick H. Maloney, C.S.C.; Jose M. Martelli, C.S.C., Valley Missionary Program, 52-565 Oasis Palms St., Coachella, CA 92236. Tel: 760-398-9277; Fax: 760-398-9281; Michael C. Mathews, C.S.C.; Peter M. McCormick, C.S.C., Notre Dame, IN; Thomas McNally, C.S.C.; Donald McNeill, C.S.C.; Bradley Metz, C.S.C.; Bros. Dennis Meyers, C.S.C.; Thomas Moser, C.S.C.; Revs. John M. Mulcahy, C.S.C., Morris Camp, Box 550, Atikokan ON Canada. Tel: 807-929-2341; Fax: 807-929-7181; William Neidhart, C.S.C.; Joseph O'Donnell, C.S.C.; Peter Pacini, C.S.C.; Claude Pomerleau, C.S.C.; Chester Prusynski, C.S.C.; Ronald Raab, C.S.C.; James Rigert, C.S.C.; H. Rutherford, C.S.C.; Cornelius Ryan, C.S.C.; Kevin Sandberg, C.S.C.; David Scheidler, C.S.C.; Eric Schimmel, C.S.C.; Arthur Schoenfeldt, C.S.C.; Most Rev. Charles A. Schleck, C.S.C., Congregazione di Santa Croce, Via Framura, 85, Rome 00168 Italy. Tel: 011-39-06-612-962-10; Fax: 011-39-06-614-7547; Revs. Stephen J. Sedlock, C.S.C.; Charles Sherrer, C.S.C.; Norbert J. Sinski, C.S.C., 319 Ave. C, Apt. 2B, New York, NY 10009. Tel: 212-673-1101; John A. Struzzo, C.S.C., St. Louise De Marillac, 1720 E. Covina Blvd., Covina, CA 91724-1640. Tel: 626-915-7873; James Thornton, C.S.C.; Ronald Tripi, C.S.C.; John V. VandenBossche, C.S.C., St. Francis High School, 1885 Miramonte Ave., Mountain View, CA 94040. Tel: 650-961-4276; Fax: 650-698-3241; David H. Verhalen, C.S.C., Holy Cross Mission House, P.O. Box 929, 46556. Tel: 574-631-4757; Neil F. Wack, C.S.C.; William Wack, C.S.C.; Ronald Wasowski, C.S.C.; James N. Watzke, C.S.C., 400 E. Randolph St., Apt. 3230, Chicago, IL 60601. Tel: 312-861-0651; Ambrose Wheeler, C.S.C.; Arthur Wheeler, C.S.C.; Bro. Ronald Whelan, C.S.C.; Revs. William Wickham, C.S.C.; Nathan D. Wills, C.S.C.; John Wironen, C.S.C.; Michael Wurtz, C.S.C.; Herbert C. Yost, C.S.C., Holy Cross Association, P.O. Box K, 46556. Tel: 574-631-6022; Fax: 574-631-7291; Richard P. Zang, C.S.C., Holy Cross Mission House, P.O. Box 929, 46556-0929. Tel: 574-631-5492; Francis D. Zagorc, C.S.C., Holy Cross Mission House, P.O. Box 929, 46556-0929. Tel: 574-631-5492; Thomas Zurcher, C.S.C. *Holy Cross House, Casa de Formacion*, 5 de Febeno 124, Guadalupe, NL 6701 Mexico. Tel: 574-631-6337; Fax: 574-631-5172. Revs. Charles W. Kohlerman, C.S.C.; David J. Porterfield, C.S.C., Supr. (Retired); James F. Blaes, C.S.C. (Retired); William G. Blum, C.S.C.; Eugene A. Burke, C.S.C.; Joseph H. Fey, C.S.C. (Retired); James B. Gillis, C.S.C. (Retired); Theodore M. Hesburgh, C.S.C.; Robert M. Hoffman, C.S.C. (Retired); George G. Kahle, C.S.C.; Bro. James Lakofka, C.S.C.; Revs. James McGrath, C.S.C.; William P. Melody, C.S.C.; Timothy O'Connor, C.S.C.; William O'Connor, C.S.C.; Louis W. Rink, C.S.C. (Retired); Robert C. Steigmeyer, C.S.C. (Retired); Richard Teall, C.S.C. (Retired), (Southern Prov.); James R. Trepanier, C.S.C. (Retired); Paul G. Wendel, C.S.C.; Bros. Clarence J. Breitenbach, C.S.C.; Thomas J. Combs, C.S.C.; Revs. James R. Blantz, C.S.C., Holy Cross Sisters, 1931 Poli St., Ventura, CA 93001. Tel: 805-648-7651; John J. Blazek, C.S.C., Gilmour Academy, 34001 Cedar Rd., Gates Mills, OH 44040-9356. Tel: 440-473-3560; Fax: 440-473-8010; Joseph P. Browne, C.S.C. (Retired), St. Birgitta Parish, 11820 N.W. St. Helens Rd., Portland, OR 97231-2319. Tel: 503-286-3929; Michael J. Heppen, C.S.C., National Shrine of the Little Flower, 2123 Roseland Ave., Royal Oak, MI 48073. Tel: 248-541-4122; Joseph W. Koma, C.S.C., St. Mark Parish, 3 N. 19th St., Niles, MI 49120-2117. Tel: 269-683-8650; Fax: 269-683-9314; Robert J. Nogosek, C.S.C., Our Lady of the Rosary Cathedral, 265 W. 25th St., San Bernardino, CA 92405. Tel: 909-648-1562; Thomas E. Seidel, C.S.C., Sacred Heart, 201 S. Walnut St., Bangor, MI 49013. Tel: 269-427-7514; Fax: 269-427-5558.

Congregation of Holy Cross, Midwest Province, Provincial Admin., 54515 State Rd. 933 N., P.O. Box 460, 46556-0460. Tel: 574-631-4000; Fax: 574-631-2999. Email: cfreel@brothersofholycross.com. Web: www.brothersofholycross.com. Bros. Chester Freel, C.S.C., Prov. Supr.; Raymond Papenfuss, C.S.C., Asst. Prov. & Vicar; Kenneth Haders, C.S.C., Prov. Steward; Richard Gilman, C.S.C., Prov. Councilor; Thomas Minta, C.S.C., Prov. Sec.; Robert Lavelle, C.S.C., Prov. Councilor; Lewis Brazil, C.S.C., Prov. Councilor.

Brothers of Holy Cross, Inc. Holy Cross Village, P.O. Box 839, 46556. Tel: 574-251-2214; Fax: 574-631-2999. Rev. Kenneth E. Grabner, C.S.C., Chap.; Bro. Joseph Fox, C.S.C., Dir. of Religious. Religious 50; Laity 180. *Dujarie House, Infirmary*, P.O. Box 706, 46556-0706. Tel: 574-287-1838; Fax: 574-289-7277. Jack Mueller, Admin. Total in Residence 36; Laity 18. *Helen D. Schubert Villa, Assisted Living*, P.O. Box 706, 46556-1020. Tel: 574-287-1986; Fax: 574-289-7277. Jack Mueller, Admin. Total in Residence 24.

Columba Hall, P.O. Box 776, 46556. Tel: 574-631-6284; Fax: 574-631-9882. Bro. Walter Gluhm, C.S.C., Supr.; Rev. William G. Blum, C.S.C., Chap. Total in Residence 35.

Holy Cross Community, Corby Hall, University of Notre Dame 46556. Tel: 574-631-7325; Fax: 574-631-6715. Revs. Robert J. Austgen, C.S.C., Emeritus Faulty; Nicholas Ayo, C.S.C.; Leonard N. Banas, C.S.C.; Ernest J. Bartell, C.S.C.; Thomas E. Blantz, C.S.C.; James Bracke, C.S.C.; Richard S. Bullene, C.S.C.; Joseph H. Carey, C.S.C., Campus Min.; Austin I. Collins, C.S.C.; John E. Conley, C.S.C.; Michael E. Connors, C.S.C.; Joseph Corpora, C.S.C.; Louis A. Delfra, C.S.C.; Robert A. Dowd, C.S.C.; Paul F. Doyle, C.S.C.; John S. Dunne, C.S.C.; Carl F. Ebey, C.S.C.; Thomas J. Eckert, C.S.C.; James F. Flanigan, C.S.C.; James K. Foster, C.S.C.; Patrick D. Gaffney, C.S.C.; James T. Gallagher, C.S.C.; Thomas E. Gaughan, C.S.C.; Bro. Francis J. Gorch, C.S.C.; Revs. Eugene F. Gorski, C.S.C.; Gregory A. Green, C.S.C.; Daniel G. Groody, C.S.C.; Ralph L. Haag, C.S.C.; Bro. Louis F. Hurcik, C.S.C.; Revs. Peter A. Jarret, C.S.C., Rel. Supr. Corby Hall; John I. Jenkins, C.S.C., Pres. of Univ. Notre Dame; Thomas J. Jones, C.S.C.; James B. King, C.S.C.; Paul V. Kollman, C.S.C., Asst. Prof. Theology; Andre E. Leveille, C.S.C.; William M. Lies, C.S.C.; Bro. Edward C. Luther, C.S.C; Revs. Edward A. Malloy, C.S.C., Prof. Theology; Patrick H. Maloney, C.S.C.; Peter M. McCormick, C.S.C.; James E. McDonald, C.S.C., Senior Exec. & Counselor to Pres.; Sean D. McGraw, C.S.C.; Donald McNeill, C.S.C.; Leon J. Mertensotto, C.S.C.; Bro. Jerome Meyer, C.S.C., (Midwest Prov.); Revs. Robert H. Moss, C.S.C.; Edwin H. Obermiller, C.S.C., Vocation Dir.; Edward D. O'Connor, C.S.C.; Robert S. Pelton, C.S.C.; Mark L. Poorman, C.S.C.; Randall C. Rentner, C.S.C.; George A. Rozum, C.S.C.; Kevin M. Russeau, C.S.C.; Timothy R. Scully, C.S.C.; William B. Simmons, C.S.C.; Thomas G. Streit, C.S.C.; Michael Bruce Sullivan, C.S.C., (Eastern Prov.); Thomas C. Tallarida, C.S.C.; Mark B. Thesing, C.S.C.; Merwyn J. Thomas, C.S.C.; Bro. Thomas P. Tucker, C.S.C.; Revs. Joseph L. Walter, C.S.C.; Richard V. Warner, C.S.C.; Oliver F. Williams, C.S.C.

[I] CONVENTS AND RESIDENCES OF SISTERS

FORT WAYNE. *Marian Convent* (St. Joseph Hospital), 4138 S. Harrison, 46807. Tel: 260-745-4041. Web: www.poorhandmaids.org. Poor Handmaids of Jesus Christ 2.

Sisters of St. Joseph of the Third Order of St. Francis Residences S.S.J.-T.O.S.F., 5123 Truemper Way, 46835. Tel: 260-492-6520. Email: trueway@msn.com.

Other Location:

Sisters of St. Joseph of the Third Order of St. Francis Residences S.S.J.-T.O.S.F., 2222 Abbey Dr., 46835. Tel: 260-485-4616.

SOUTH BEND. *Handmaids of the Most Holy Trinity Monastery-Hermitage* (1968) 23089 Adams Rd., 46628-9674. Tel: 574-272-9425. Sr. Mary Emmanuel Baggoo, H.T., Representative. Contemplative Community; Prayer Ministry; Prayer Witness which includes Retreats and Spiritual Direction.

Sarah House (1996) 1213 E. Bronson, 46615. Tel: 574-287-8342; Fax: 574-287-8342. Email: connie.ss@att.net. Owned by the Poor Handmaids of Jesus Christ. Sisters 2.

The Sisters of St. Joseph of the Third Order of St. Francis, S.S.J.-T.O.S.F. (1901) 1425 Clayton Dr., 46614. Tel: 574-287-5435; Fax: 574-291-1555. Email: Chiarahome@att.net. Sisters Rose Margaret Firkus, Novice Min.; Gretchen Clark, S.S.J.-T.O.S.F., Contact Person. Sisters 2.

DONALDSON. *Convent Ancilla Domini* (1922) 9601 Union Rd., P.O. Box 1, 46513. Tel: 574-936-9936; Fax: 574-935-1785. Email: nhahn@poorhandmaids.org. Web: www.poorhandmaids.org. Sr. Nora Hahn, P.H.J.C., Prov. Provincialate, Poor Handmaids of Jesus Christ (The Ancilla Domini Sisters) Professed Sisters 30.

Catherine's Cottage, 9601 Union Rd., P.O. Box 1, 46513. Tel: 574-935-1703; Fax: 574-935-1785. Email: nhahn@poorhandmaids.org. Web: www.poorhandmaids.org. Professed Sisters 10.

Catherine Kasper Home, 46513. Tel: 574-935-1742. Nursing home for retired sisters & laity. Rooms 81.

Catherine Kasper Life Center, Inc. (1970) Tel: 574-935-1742; Fax: 574-935-1755. Retired Sisters 29.

Maria Center 46513. Tel: 574-935-1784; Fax: 574-935-1790. Senior Apartments (Efficiency and Singles) Apartments 27.

Poor Handmaids of Jesus Christ Community Support Trust Tel: 574-936-9936; Fax: 574-935-1785.

Ancilla College Tel: 574-936-8898; Fax: 574-935-1779. Email: admissions@ancilla.edu. Web: www.ancilla.edu.

Lindenwood, Retreat & Conference Center Tel: 574-935-1780; Fax: 574-935-1728. Email: lw@lindenwood.org. Web: www.lindenwood.org.

St. Joseph Community Health Foundation Tel: 260-969-2001; Fax: 260-969-2004. Email: mdistler@stjosephhealthfdn.org. Web: www.stjosephhealthfdn.org.

Earthworks, Inc., 9815 Union Rd., Plymouth, 46563. Tel: 574-935-4164. Email: earthworks@fourway.net. Web: www.earthworksonline.org.

HUNTINGTON. *Victory Noll--Motherhouse of Our Lady of Victory Missionary Sisters* (1922) 1900 W. Park Dr., P.O. Box 109, 46750-0109. Tel: 260-356-0628; Fax: 260-358-1504. Email: victorynoll@olvm.org. Web: www.olvm.org. Rev. Thomas C. Fahey, O.F.M., Chap. (Retired). Legal Holding: Victory Noll Sisters Community Support Trust. Professed Sisters 121.

MISHAWAKA. *St. Francis Provincialate*, 1515 Dragoon Tr., P.O. Box 766, 46546-0766. Tel: 574-259-5427; Fax: 574-256-0822. Web: www.ssfpa.org. Sr. M. Angela Mellady, O.S.F., Prov. Supr.; Rev. Francis Affelt, O.F.M., Chap. Sisters of St. Francis of Perpetual Adoration, Inc., St. Francis Convent and Novitiate of Immaculate Heart of Mary Province. Sisters 117; Novices 4; Postulants 2.

Our Lady of the Angels Convent, 1515 Dragoon Tr., P.O. Box 766, 46546-0766. Tel: 574-259-5427; Fax: 574-256-0822. Web: www.ssfpa.org. Sr. M. Blanche Rausch, O.S.F., Supr.; Rev. James Kendzierski, O.F.M., Chap. Convent for retired and infirm sisters. Sisters 39.

NOTRE DAME. *Congregation of the Sisters of the Holy Cross*, Saint Mary's of the Immaculate Conception, 309 Bertrand Hall, 46556-5000. Tel: 574-284-5550; Fax: 574-284-5779. Web: www.cscsisters.org. Sisters Joan Marie Steadman, C.S.C., B.S., M.A., Pres.; Mary Louise Full, C.S.C., B.A., M.A., First Councilor; Geraldine Hoyler, C.S.C., B.A., B.S., M.S., C.P.A., General Treas.; Philomena Quiah, C.S.C., B.A., B.Ed., M.Sc., M.Phil., Councilor; Sharlet Ann Wagner, C.S.C., B.J., J.D., General Sec.

Sisters of the Holy Cross, Inc.; Sisters of the Holy Cross, Inc. dba CSC Consultation Services., Generalate, Candidate Program, Associate Program. Professed Sisters in Congregation 441; Temporarily Incorporated 32; Novices 8.

Sisters of the Holy Cross Other Residences and Programs: *Rainbow House*, 2710 Trader Ct. W., 46628. Tel: 574-247-2512. Sisters 2. 52700 Shellbark Ave., 46628-4082. Tel: 574-273-9598. Sisters 5. 727 Forest Ave., 46616-1310. Tel: 574-246-0673; Fax: 574-246-0674. Sisters 2. 1023 Portage Ave., 46616. Tel: 574-234-3208. Sisters 2. 2121 W. Madison St., 46617. Tel: 574-287-6071. *Immaculata Convent*, 200 Augusta Hall- Saint Mary's, 46556-5002. Tel: 574-284-5707. Sisters 2. *Moreau Convent*, 100 Lourdes Hall St. Mary's, 46556-5030. Tel: 574-284-5663. *Rosary Convent*, 100 Rosary Convent, Saint Mary's, 46556-5013. Tel: 574-284-5841. Sisters 32. *House of Shalem*, 100 House of Shalem, Saint Mary's, 46556-5025. Tel: 574-284-5740. Sisters 2. *St. Bridget's Convent*, 100 Saint Bridget's Convent, Saint Mary's, 46556-5024. Tel: 574-284-5752. Sisters 2. *St. John's Convent*, 100 Saint John's Convent, Saint Mary's, 46556-5022. Tel: 574-284-5695. Sisters 4. *Bethany Convent*, 100 Bethany Convent, Saint Mary's, 46556-5038. Tel: 574-284-5674. Sisters 4. *Saint Mary's Convent*, 100 Saint Mary's Convent, 46556-5007. Tel: 574-284-5688; Fax: 574-284-5801. Sisters 69. *Loretto Convent*, 100 Loretto Convent, Saint Mary's, 46556-5039. Tel: 574-284-5667. Sisters 8. *Holy Spirit Convent*, 300 Augusta Hall Saint Mary's, 46556-5002. Tel: 574-284-5715. Sisters 3. *Kateri Convent*, 400 Augusta Hall Saint Mary's, 46556-5002. Tel: 574-284-5993. Sisters 3. *Madonna Convent*, 400 Augusta Hall St. Mary's, 46556-5002. Tel: 574-284-5890. Sisters 5. *Nazareth Convent*, 200 Augusta Hall St. Mary's, 46556-5002. Tel: 574-284-5822. Sisters 2. *Saint Ann's Convent*, 300 Augusta Hall St. Mary's, 46556-5002. Tel: 574-284-5713. Sisters 2. *Saint Claire Convent*, 400 Augusta Hall St. Mary's, 46556-5002. Tel: 574-284-5892. Sisters 2. *Visitation Convent*, 200 Augusta Hall St. Mary's, 46556-5002. Tel: 574-284-5820. Sisters 2. *Guadalupe Convent*, 300 Augusta Hall St. Mary's, 46556-5002. Tel: 574-284-5717. Sisters 2. *Andre House - East*, 100 Andre House-E., Saint Mary's, 46556-5015. Tel: 574-284-5644. Sisters 4. *Andre House - West*, 100 Andre House-W., Saint Mary's, 46556-5016. Tel: 574-284-5645. Sisters 3. *Marian Convent*, 300 Augusta Hall St. Mary's, 46556-5002. Tel: 574-284-5710. Sisters 5. *Novitiate at the Solitude, Saint Mary's*, 100 Saint Mary's Solitude, 46556-5002. Tel: 574-284-5120. Sisters 3; Novices 6. *Saint Theresa Convent*, 400 Augusta Hall - Saint Mary's, 46556-5002. Tel: 574-284-5995. Sisters 2. *Queen of Peace Convent*, 100 Lourdes Hall - St. Mary's, 46556-5014. Tel: 574-284-5579. Sisters 11.

All Saints Convent, 100 Lourdes Hall-St. Mary's, 46556-5014. Tel: 574-284-5660. Sisters 7.

Sisters of the Holy Cross, 5016-2 Belleville Cir., 46619. Tel: 574-233-6978. Sisters 2.

Sisters of the Holy Cross, 701 Marquette Ave., 46617. Tel: 574-520-1447. Sisters 2.

Sisters of the Holy Cross

The Corporation of Saint Mary's College Sponsored Ministry.

[J] RETREAT HOUSES & EDUCATIONAL CENTERS

SOUTH BEND. *Forever Learning Institute, Inc.* (1974) 54191 Ironwood Rd., 46635. Tel: 574-282-1901; Fax: 574-282-1901. Email: jmloranger@comcast.net. Web: www.foreverlearninginstitute.org. Christopher Bowman, Pres. & Bd. Member; William Darden, Vice Pres. & Bd. Member; Joan Loranger, Exec. Dir. To promote and support the quality and dignity of older adults and to assist older adults in finding enrichment, joy and fellowship through educational and recreational activities.

DONALDSON. *Lindenwood Retreat & Conference Center* (1986) PHJC Ministry Center, P.O. Box 1, 46513-0001. Tel: 574-935-1706; Fax: 574-935-1728. Email: lw@lindenwood.org. Web: www.lindenwood.org. Loretta Peters, Dir. Overnight facilities for 100, Conference rooms for 250, Handicapped accessibility. Total Staff 8; Total in Residence 2.

[K] MISCELLANEOUS

FORT WAYNE. *Cathedral Museum* (1980) P.O. Box 390, 46801. Tel: 260-744-2765; Fax: 260-744-1972. 915 S. Clinton St., 46802. Tel: 260-422-4611, Ext. 3307. Rev. Phillip A. Widmann, Dir.

Catholic Charities of the Diocese of Ft. Wayne-South Bend, Inc. (1922) Tel: 260-422-5625; Fax: 260-422-5657. Email: fwoffice@ccfwsb.org. Web: www.ccfwsb.org.

Fort Wayne Community Service Center, 315 E. Washington Blvd., 46802. Tel: 260-422-5625; Fax: 260-422-5657. Debbie Schmidt, Exec. Dir. Total Staff 64; Total Assisted 17,678.

South Bend Community Service Center, 1817 Miami St., 46613. Tel: 574-234-3111; Fax: 574-289-1034. Email: sboffice@ccfwsb.org. Total Staff 6.

Villa of the Woods-Catholic Charities Residential Living, 5610 Noll Ave., 48606. Tel: 260-745-7039; Fax: 260-744-4887. Cheryl Smith, Admin. Residential facilities for the elderly including housing, meals, laundry services and planned activities. Total Staff 11; Residents 19.

Children's Cottage, 2820 Reed St., 46803. Tel: 260-745-4929; Fax: 260-456-6100. Day care center serving children 6 weeks- 12 years old, year round. Total Staff 20; Students 98.

RSVP St. Joseph County & Elkhart County, 120 S. Taylor St., 46601. Tel: 574-287-0500; Fax: 574-287-3320. Total Staff 2; Volunteers Placed 481.

RSVP (Retired Senior Volunteer Program), 107 W. 5th St., Auburn, 46706. Tel: 260-925-0917; Fax: 260-925-1732. Total Staff 3; Volunteers Placed 602.

Catholic Charities Children's Services, 2220 Reed St., 46808. Tel: 260-745-4929; Fax: 260-456-6100. Rhonda Lewis, Dir. Lay Teachers 9; Aides 9; Enrollment 90.

Catholic Community Foundation of Northeast Indiana, Inc., 915 S. Clinton St., P.O. Box 390, 46801. Tel: 260-422-4611; Fax: 260-423-3382. Email: rschulte@fw.diocesefwsb.org. Web: www.diocesefwsb.org. Most Rev. John M. D'Arcy, D.D., M.A., S.T.D., Contact Person.

**The Christ Child Society of Fort Wayne, Inc.* (1997) P.O. Box 12708, 46864. Web: www.christchildsocietyfw.org. Sherri Miller, Pres. Total Assisted Annually 5,000.

Crosier Fathers of Fort Wayne, 1721 Magnavox Way, 46802. Tel: 320-532-5225; Fax: 320-532-5222. Email: ABecker@Crosiers.org. William G. Niezer, Registered Agent. Total Staff 1.

Diocese of Fort Wayne-South Bend Investment Trust, Inc., 915 S. Clinton St., P.O. Box 390, 46801. Tel: 260-422-4611; Fax: 260-423-3382. Most Rev. John M. D'Arcy, D.D., M.A., S.T.D., Admin.; Joseph Ryan, Contact Person & Chief Fin. Officer. To invest money received from qualified 501(c)(3) organizations that buy shares offered by the organization. All investments of share purchase proceeds shall be directed and conducted consistent with the investment policies and objectives established by the organization that are applicable to the type of share(s) sold to the participating 501 (c)(3) entities. All gains and any losses on investments, after administrative and money management fees, shall be reflected in share values.

**Fort Wayne Catholic Radio Group, Inc.* (Redeemer Radio, Catholic Radio AM 1450), 4705 Illinois Rd., Ste. 104, 46804. Tel: 260-436-9598; Fax: 260-432-6179. Web: www.redeemerradio.com. Mike Kelly, Chm.

The St. Joseph Community Health Foundation, Inc. (1998) 2826 S. Calhoun St., 46807. Tel: 260-969-2001; Fax: 260-969-2004. Email: mdistler@sjchf.org; ckronstain@sjchf.org. Web: www.sjchf.org. Meg Distler, Exec. Dir.; Connie Kronstain, Office Program Asst.; Loaine Hagerty, Community Initiatives; Aye Ma, Community Health Educator. Total Staff 6.

Scholarship Granting Organization of Northeast Indiana, Inc., 915 S. Clinton St., P.O. Box 390, 46801. Tel: 260-422-4611; Fax: 260-426-3077. Email: mmyers@fw.diocesefwsb.org. Mark Myers, Ph.D., Supt.

SOUTH BEND. *Chiara Home, Inc.* (1993) 1425 Clayton Dr., 46614. Tel: 574-287-5435; Fax: 574-291-1555. Email: chiarahome@att.net. Web: www.chiarahomerespite.org. Sr. Gretchen Clark, S.S.J.-T.O.S.F., Pres. & Admin. Respite Care for people with special needs. Total Staff 3; Families Served 400.

Christ Child Society of South Bend, P.O. Box 1286, 46624. Tel: 574-288-6028; Fax: 574-288-4282. Web: www.christchildsb.org. Total Assisted 4,400.

The Foundation of Saint Joseph Regional Medical Center, 837 E. Cedar St., Ste. 350, 46617. Tel: 574-237-7377; Fax: 574-472-6800. Email: thefoundation@sjrmc.com. Web: www.sjmed.com. Andrew J. Snyder, Vice Pres. Community Devel. & Mktg.

The Foundation of Saint Joseph Regional Medical Center, Inc. Total Staff 5.

Jesuit Community, 1713 Burdette St., 46637. Tel: 574-243-0601. Revs. Brian Daley, S.J.; Thomas Florek, S.J.; John S. Thiede, S.J.; Andrew N. Downing, S.J.; Edoth Mukasa, S.J.; Jean Ngoy Nyembo, S.J. Priests 6.

HUNTINGTON. *Our Sunday Visitor, Inc.* (1912) 200 Noll Plaza, 46750. Tel: 260-356-8400; Fax: 260-359-0029. Email: osvinc@osv.com. Web: www.osv.com. Most Rev. John M. D'Arcy, D.D., M.A., S.T.D., Bd. Chm. Publishers of Catholic Periodicals, Books, Religious Education Materials, Offering Envelopes and Curriculum.

MISHAWAKA. **Hills Insurance Company, Inc.*, P.O. Box 1290, 46544-4797. Sr. Jane Marie Klein, O.S.F., Admin.

Saint Joseph Regional Medical Center, Inc., 5215 Holy Cross Pkwy., 46545. Tel: 574-335-5000; Fax: 574-335-1002. Email: hellyern@sjrmc.com. Web: www.sjmed.com. Nancy R. Hellyer, C.E.O.; Sr. Laureen M. Painter, O.S.F., Vice Pres. Mission Integration. Merged with St. Joseph's Visiting Nurse Association, Inc. Total Staff 513; Total Assisted 187,460.

Sisters of St. Francis Health Services, Inc. (1974) P.O. Box 1290, 46546-1290. Tel: 574-256-3935; Fax: 574-257-8669. Web: www.ssfhs.org.

Sisters of St. Francis of Perpetual Adoration, Inc., P.O. Box 766, 46546-0766. Tel: 574-259-5427; Fax: 574-256-0822. Web: www.ssfpa.org.

Sisters of St. Francis of Perpetual Adoration, Inc., Medical Benefits Trust Tel: 574-259-5427; Fax: 574-256-0822.

Sisters of St. Francis of Perpetual Adoration, Inc. Capital Improvements Trust, 1515 Dragoon Tr., P.O. Box 766, 46546-0766. Tel: 574-259-5427; Fax: 574-256-0822. Web: www.ssfpa.org.

Sisters of St. Francis Charitable Mission Trust Tel: 574-259-5427; Fax: 574-256-0822.

Sisters of St. Francis Retirement Fund Tel: 574-259-5427; Fax: 574-256-0822.

SSFPA Ministry Corporation, 1515 Dragoon Tr., P.O. Box 766, 46546. Tel: 574-259-5427; Fax: 574-256-0822. Web: www.ssfpa.org. Sr. M. Angela Mellady, O.S.F., Prov. Supr.

Yves R. Simon Institute (1988) 3921 Glenview Dr., 46628. Tel: 574-271-1187. Email: aos1936@comcast.net. Mr. Anthony O. Simon, Dir. & Contact Person. Catholic academic institute. Total Staff 2.

NOTRE DAME. *American Maritain Association, Jacques Maritain Center,* 714 Hesburgh Library, 46556. Tel: 574-631-5825. Email: osberger.l@nd.edu. Web: www.jacquesmaritain.org. Alice Osberger, Admin.; John Tripani, Pres. & Dir. Purpose: For the purpose of perpetuating the wisdom, influence and inspiration of Jacques Maritain as a Catholic intellectual, saintly Christian and classical creative exponent of the philosophia perennis. To promote research, study and critical interpretations of the life and work of Jacques Maritain especially as that work continues and expands into a broader area of the tradition of the thought of Saint Thomas, to develop social and formative cultural movement based on the results of this research and study, cooperation with the Institute International "Jacques Maritain and its national and regional branches, and the promotion of publications, lecturers, study groups and similar activities."

Ave Maria Press, Inc. (1865) P.O. Box 428, 46556. Tel: 574-287-2831; Fax: 574-239-2904. Email: avemariapress.1@nd.edu. Web: www.avemariapress.com. Thomas Grady, Pres. & Publisher. Owned and operated by the Congregation of Holy Cross, Indiana Province, Inc.

Brothers of Holy Cross Life Development Trust, P.O. Box 460, 46556. Tel: 574-631-4000; Fax: 574-631-2999. Bro. Peter Graham, C.S.C., Trustee; J. Lynne Pawlick, Trustee; Fred G. Botek, Trustee; Bros. William Dygert, C.S.C., Trustee & Chairperson; Paul Kelly, C.S.C., Trustees; Robert Lavelle, C.S.C., Trustees; Lawrence Skitzki, C.S.C., Trustees.

Holy Cross Village at Notre Dame, Inc. dba Dujarie House 54515 State Rd. 933 N., P.O. Box 303, 46556-0303. Tel: 574-251-3252; Fax: 574-232-7933. Email: skastner@holycrossvillage.com. Web: www.holycrossvillage.com. Bros. Thomas Shaughnessy, C.S.C., Chm. Bd.; Joseph Fox, C.S.C., Dir. of Religious.

PLYMOUTH. *Catherine Kasper Life Center, Inc.,* 9601 Union Rd., P.O. Box 1, Donaldson, 46513. Tel: 574-935-1742; Fax: 574-936-9366. Email: nhahn@poorhandmaids.org. Sisters Nora Hahn, P.H.J.C., Prov.; Judith Diltz, P.H.J.C., Vice Pres. & Sec.; Margaret Anne Henss, P.H.J.C., Treas. Sponsored by the Poor Handmaids of Jesus Christ. (The Ancilla Domini Sisters), Purpose: To provide quality care and address the spiritual, emotional, and physical needs of the aged, sick and disabled. Total Assisted 170.

Earthworks, Inc., 9815 Union Rd., 46563. Tel: 574-935-4164. Email: earthworks@fourway.net. Web: www.earthworksonline.org. Sr. Suzanne Rogers, Dir. An environmental education center; a sponsored entity of the Poor Handmaids of Jesus Christ (P.H.J.C.) affiliated with Convent Ancilla Domini, Donaldson, IN.

RELIGIOUS INSTITUTES OF MEN REPRESENTED IN THE DIOCESE

For further details refer to the corresponding bracketed number in the Religious Institutes of Men or Women section.

[0600]—*Brothers of the Congregation of Holy Cross* (Midwest Province)—C.S.C.

[0470]—*The Capuchin Friars* (Prov. of St. Joseph)—O.F.M.Cap.

[0480]—*Conventual Franciscans* (Prov. of Our Lady of Consolation)—O.F.M.Conv

[0520]—*Franciscan Friars* (Prov. of St. John the Baptist)—O.F.M.

[0690]—*Jesuit Fathers and Brothers*—S.J.

[]—*Missionaries of the Holy Spirit*—M.Sp.S.

[]—*Priestly Fraternity of Saint Peter*—F.S.S.P.

[0610]—*Priests of the Congregation of Holy Cross* (Indiana Province)—C.S.C.

[]—*Society of the Divine Word*—S.V.D.

[1060]—*Society of the Precious Blood* (Cincinnati Province)—C.PP.S.

RELIGIOUS INSTITUTES OF WOMEN REPRESENTED IN THE DIOCESE

[3710]—*Congregation of the Sisters of Saint Agnes*—C.S.A.

[3832]—*Congregation of the Sisters of St. Joseph*—C.S.J.

[1920]—*Congregation of the Sisters of the Holy Cross*—C.S.C.

[1710]—*Congregation of the Third Order of St. Francis of Mary Immaculate* (Joliet, IL)—O.S.F.

[0790]—*Daughters of Divine Charity* (Holy Trinity Province)—F.D.C.

[]—*Daughters of Mary Mother of Mercy*—D.M.M.M.

[1070-03]—*Dominican Sisters* (Adrian Dominican Sisters)—O.P.

[1170]—*Felician Sisters* (Presentation of the B.V.M. Province)—C.S.S.F.

[1450]—*Franciscan Sisters of the Sacred Heart*—O.S.F.

[]—*Handmaids of the Most Holy Trinity*—H.T.

[3130]—*Our Lady of Victory Missionary Sisters*—O.L.V.M.

[3230]—*Poor Handmaids of Jesus Christ*—P.H.J.C.

[2970]—*School Sisters of Notre Dame*—S.S.N.D.

[]—*Sisters of Divine Providence*—C.D.P.

[2990]—*Sisters of Notre Dame* (Province of Toledo)—S.N.D.

[3360]—*Sisters of Providence of Saint Mary-of-the-Woods, Indiana*—S.P.

[]—*Sisters of Saint Agnes*—C.S.A.

[1640]—*Sisters of St. Francis of Perpetual Adoration* (Province of the Immaculate Heart of Mary)—O.S.F.

[3930]—*Sisters of St. Joseph of the Third Order of St. Francis*—S.S.J.-T.O.S.F.

DIOCESAN CEMETERY

FORT WAYNE. *Catholic Cemetery Association of Fort Wayne, Inc.,* 3500 Lake Ave., 46805-5572. Tel: 260-426-2044; Fax: 260-422-7418. Web: www.catholic-cemetery.org. Thomas E. Alter, Diocesan Dir. Cemeteries/Supt. Catholic Cemetery.

NECROLOGY

† Dombrowski, Robert J., (Retired)—Died April 22, 2009

† Ramenaden, Ronald, North Manchester, IN St. Robert Bellarmine—Died Sept. 9, 2009

An asterisk (*) denotes an organization that has established tax-exempt status directly with the IRS and is not covered by the USCCB Group Ruling.

Diocese of Fort Worth

(Dioecesis Arcis-Vorthensis)

Most Reverend

KEVIN W. VANN

Bishop of Fort Worth; ordained May 30, 1981; appointed Coadjutor Bishop of Fort Worth May 17, 2005; succeeded July 12, 2005; ordained July 13, 2005. *Office: 800 West Loop 820 S., Fort Worth, TX 76108.*

The Catholic Center: 800 West Loop 820 S., Fort Worth, TX 76108. Tel: 817-560-3300; Fax: 817-244-8839.

Web: www.fwdioc.org

ESTABLISHED AUGUST 09, 1969.

Square Miles 23,950.

Comprises the following twenty-eight Counties in the State of Texas: Archer, Baylor, Bosque, Clay, Comanche, Cooke, Denton, Eastland, Erath, Foard, Hardeman, Hill, Hood, Jack, Johnson, Knox, Montague, Palo Pinto, Parker, Shackleford, Stephens, Somervell, Tarrant, Throckmorton, Wichita, Wilbarger, Wise and Young.

For legal titles of parishes and diocesan institutions, consult the Chancery Office.

STATISTICAL OVERVIEW

Personnel	
Bishop	1
Priests: Diocesan Active in Diocese	45
Priests: Diocesan Active Outside Diocese	1
Priests: Diocesan in Foreign Missions	1
Priests: Retired, Sick or Absent	23
Number of Diocesan Priests	70
Religious Priests in Diocese	52
Total Priests in Diocese	122
Extern Priests in Diocese	8
Ordinations:	
Diocesan Priests	2
Transitional Deacons	3
Permanent Deacons in Diocese	143
Total Brothers	9
Total Sisters	65
Parishes	
Parishes	89
With Resident Pastor:	
Resident Diocesan Priests	38
Resident Religious Priests	21
Without Resident Pastor:	
Administered by Priests	21
Administered by Deacons	8
Administered by Professed Religious Men	1
Missions	2
Professional Ministry Personnel:	
Brothers	1
Sisters	16
Lay Ministers	300
Welfare	
Homes for the Aged	4
Total Assisted	342
Special Centers for Social Services	18
Total Assisted	82,939
Educational	
Diocesan Students in Other Seminaries	27
Total Seminarians	27
Colleges and Universities	1
Total Students	50
High Schools, Diocesan and Parish	5
Total Students	1,479
Elementary Schools, Diocesan and Parish	16
Total Students	4,753
Elementary Schools, Private	1
Total Students	180
Catechesis/Religious Education:	
High School Students	10,135
Elementary Students	21,320
Total Students under Catholic Instruction	37,944
Teachers in the Diocese:	
Sisters	15
Lay Teachers	525
Vital Statistics	
Receptions into the Church:	
Infant Baptism Totals	5,658
Minor Baptism Totals	432
Adult Baptism Totals	257
Received into Full Communion	753
First Communions	5,941
Confirmations	3,767
Marriages:	
Catholic	858
Interfaith	292
Total Marriages	1,150
Deaths	1,077
Total Catholic Population	573,529
Total Population	3,189,134

Former Bishops—Most Revs. JOHN J. CASSATA, D.D., ord. Dec. 8, 1932; Titular Bishop of Bida and Auxiliary of Dallas-Fort Worth; appt. March 20, 1968; cons. June 5, 1968; first Bishop, Fort Worth; appt. Aug. 22, 1969; retired Sept. 16, 1980; died Sept. 8, 1989; JOSEPH P. DELANEY, ord. Dec. 18, 1960; appt. Bishop of Fort Worth July 10, 1981; ord. Bishop Sept. 13, 1981; died July 12, 2005.

Vicar General—Very Rev. STEPHEN BERG.

Chancellor and Moderator of the Curia—Very Rev. E. JAMES HART.

Vicar for Priests—Rev. JUAN RIVERO.

Deans—Rev. Msgr. JOSEPH S. SCANTLIN, Arlington Area Deanery; Revs. ANH TRAN, Northeast Deanery; JOSEPH PEMBERTON, West Central Deanery; DAVID BRISTOW, East Central Deanery; JOHN SWISTOVICH, Northwest Deanery; RAYMUND A. MULLAN, Southwest Deanery; Rev. Msgr. CHARLES KING, P.A., North Deanery; VACANT, South Deanery.

Diocesan Pastoral Council—Ms. BECKY LUCAS; Deacon POPO GONZALEZ; Mr. JOE FRANCIS; Dr. LOUIS GASPER; Mr. CHARLIE MARTINEZ; Mr. JOHN PATRICK HORN; Mr. LAWRENCE JORDAN; Mr. VINCENT KEIS; Ms. LISA KUPPER; Ms. DOLORA LEDER; Ms. KATHERINE LUBKE; Mr. JIM MCSORLEY; Mr. HECTOR SALDUA; Ms. ANDREA SCANLAND; Mr. MARK SHADOWENS; Mr. RONALD SUMCIZK; Ms. CHRISTINA TOMCZAK; Sr. MARY LOUISE SWIFT, C.S.F.N.; Rev. RICHARD ELDREDGE, T.O.R.; Very Revs. STEPHEN BERG; E. JAMES HART, Ex Officio; Most Rev. KEVIN W. VANN; Mr. JOE RODRIGUEZ, Staff.

Presbyteral Council and Consultors—Revs. MEL BESSELLIEU; RICHARD ELDREDGE, T.O.R.; HECTOR MEDINA; Very Rev. STEPHEN BERG; Rev. D. TIMOTHY THOMPSON; Very Rev. E. JAMES HART; Revs. DANIEL KELLEY; HOA NGUYEN; THOMAS CRAIG.

Diocesan Finance Council—Mr. CHUCK BARTUSH JR.; Mr. JOHN HERNANDEZ; Rev. Msgr. PHILIP L. JOHNSON; Ms. BARBARA MAY; Mr. DAVID MORITZ; Ms. ELAINE PETRUS; Mr. ROBERT SCHUMACHER; Mr. EARLE SHIELDS JR.; Mr. PETER FLYNN, Staff; Very Revs. E. JAMES HART, Ex Officio; STEPHEN BERG, Ex Officio.

Catholic Foundation of North Texas—Mr. PETER FLYNN, Exec. Dir.; Mr. CHUCK BARTUSH JR.; Mr. JOHN HERNANDEZ; Rev. Msgr. PHILIP L. JOHNSON; Ms. BARBARA MAY; Mr. DAVID MORITZ; Ms. ELAINE PETRUS; Mr. ROBERT SCHUMACHER; Mr. EARLE SHIELDS JR.; Very Revs. E. JAMES HART; STEPHEN BERG.

Catholic Schools' Trust—Mr. EARLE SHIELDS JR., Chm.; Ms. LYNN ALPAR; Ms. GILDA JACKSON; Mr. RICHARD MARX; Ms. LAURA RICHARDS; Dr. JOAN MORAN; Mr. DONALD MILLER, Supt. Schools; Mr. PETER FLYNN, Exec. Officer.

Catholic Cemeteries Trust—Mr. JOHN ECKELKAMP; Mr. JOSEPH BEZNER; Mr. DAN SHINE; Mr. BENNY LINDEMANN.

St. Joseph's Health Care Trust—Very Rev. E. JAMES HART.

North Texas San Benito, Inc.—Mr. PETER FLYNN.

Boards and Associations

Building Commission—Rev. Msgr. HUBERT NEU (Retired); Very Rev. E. JAMES HART, Chm.; Mr. W. J. DICKENS III; Mr. JACK DREWETT; Mr. GARY JONES; Mr. BRAD RUPAY; Mr. RICHARD FLORES; Mr. ROBERT BARHAM; Mr. GARY FRAGOSSO, Staff.

Diocesan Pastoral Finance Committee—Very Rev. E. JAMES HART, Chm.

Diocesan School Advisory Council—Mr. JASON BATESON; Ms. ANNE BLOESSER; Mr. JEFF MARTINEZ; Dr. RICHARD URSO; Mr. JAMES LEITO III; Rev. STEPHEN JASSO, T.O.R. Ex Officio: Mr. DONALD MILLER; Ms. TESSY ROSS.

Mission Council—Mr. DARYL CLEMENTS; Ms. JUANITA CLEMENTS; Mr. PETER FLYNN; Mr. MARTIN PENA; Ms. LETTY ZATARAIN; Ms. AMY ZEDER; Mr. STEVE ZEDER; Rev. THOMAS CRAIG; Deacon LEN SANCHEZ, Chm.; Ms. HILDA FLORES, Staff; Ms. COLLEEN CARGILE; Mr. JULIO CARRILLO; Rev. RICHARD ELDREDGE, T.O.R.; Sr. MILDRED GORDON; Rev. JOHN MCKONE; Mr. THANH NGUYEN; Ms. FELICIA GEHRIG; Mr. AL MIRABAL.

Priests' Personnel Board—VACANT, Chm.

Priests' Pension Plan Trustees—Rev. JUAN RIVERO, Chm.; Ms. BARBARA MAY; Mr. FRANKLIN MOORE; Revs. THOMAS CRAIG; D. TIMOTHY THOMPSON; Mr. PETER FLYNN, Staff; Mr. EARLE SHIELDS; Mr. MARK SIMEROTH, Staff.

Diocesan Programs

Vocations and Seminarians—Revs. KYLE WALTERSCHEID; JAMES PEMBERTON; RICHARD FLORES. Tel: 817-451-9395. Email: flores84rita@yahoo.com.

Deacons—Deacon DON WARNER.

Permanent Deacon Formation Program—Dr. ANN HEALEY; Ms. JUDY LOCKE.

Conduct Review Board—Very Rev. E. JAMES HART.

Victims' Assistance—Ms. JUDY LOCKE.

Tribunal—Rev. D. TIMOTHY THOMPSON, Judicial Vicar. Tel: 940-387-6223. Email: fr.tim@stmarkdenton.org; Ms. MEG HOGAN, Dir. Case Coordinators: Ms. JOLEEN DUBOIS; Ms. ANNA MARIE CHAMBLEE.

Finance & Administrative Services—Mr. PETER FLYNN.

Financial Services—Mr. PETER FLYNN; Ms. CAROLYN

JONES; Mr. KEVIN O'BRIEN; Mr. JORGE MONTENEGRO.
Construction—Mr. GARY FRAGOSSO.
Claims and Risk Management - Catholic Mutual—Mr. MICHAEL SHANNON.
Stewardship and Development—Ms. PATRICIA MILLER.
Cemeteries—Mr. KEVIN O'BRIEN.
Catechetical Department—Mr. LUCAS POLLICE.
Adult Catechesis—Mr. LUCAS POLLICE.
Respect Life—Ms. CHANACEE RUTH-KILLGORE Catholics for Life.
Family Life—Ms. SUZANNA ORDONEZ; Ms. DIANE SCHWIND.
Children's Catechesis—Sr. YOLANDA CRUZ, S.S.M.N.
Cursillo Center—Rev. FRANCIS X. FERNANDEZ, O.F.M.Cap. Tel: 817-624-9411; 817-624-8526. Email: cursillocntr@aol.com.
Pope John Paul II Institute for Lay Ministry—Rev. CARMEN MELE, O.P.
Respect Life—Mr. LUCAS POLLICE.
Youth & Young Adult Ministry and Campus Ministry—Mr. KEVIN PREVOU; ELVIRA MATA; Rev. CHARLES CALABRESE, TCU Catholic Campus Ministry, P.O. Box 297310, Fort Worth, 76129. Tel: 817-257-7830; Ms. DEBRA NEELY, Catholic Campus Center, 3410 W. Louis Rodriguez Dr., Wichita Falls, 76308. Tel: 940-692-9778. Email: neelydeb@yahoo.com; Ms. JANET WOLF, University of North Texas/Texas Woman's University, 1303 Eagle Dr., Denton, 76201. Tel: 940-566-0004; Ms. STEPHANIE MILLIGAN, UTA, 303 Lampe St., Arlington, 76010. Tel: 817-460-1155.
Catholic Schools Department—Mr. DONALD MILLER.
Catholic Schools—Mr. DONALD MILLER, Supt. Schools; CHARLENE HYMEL, Assoc. Supt.
Marketing—Ms. TESSY ROSS.
School Nurses—Ms. NANCY EDER.
School Athletics—Ms. MICHELLE GUNTER.
Communications Department—Mr. PAT SVACINA.
Communications—Mr. PAT SVACINA.
Internet Services—Mr. CHRIS KASTNER.
Newspaper— "North Texas Catholic" Mr. JEFF HENSLEY; Mr. TONY GUTIERREZ, Assoc. Editor; Ms. NICKI PREVOU.
Human Resources and Personnel Department—Mr. MARK SIMEROTH.
Personnel—Mr. MARK SIMEROTH.
Benefits—Ms. SHARON FIELDER.
Office of Child & Youth Protection—Ms. RUTH SMITH.
Liturgy Department—Deacon DON WARNER.
Community and Pastoral Services—Deacon LEONARD SANCHEZ.
Peace and Justice—Deacon LEONARD SANCHEZ.
Multicultural Ministries—ELVIRA MATA.
Deaf Ministry—Ms. MARY CINATL.
Hospital Chaplaincy—Rev. GEORGE THENNATTIL, T.O.R.
Jail Ministry—Deacon LEONARD SANCHEZ.
Mission Outreach—Ms. HILDA FLORES.
Miscellaneous—
Coordinator of Council Development—Mr. JOE RODRIGUEZ.
Delegate for Hispanic Ministry—Mr. ANDRES ARANDA.
Society for the Propagation of the Faith—Rev. THOMAS CRAIG, Dir.
Scouting—Rev. ANH TRAN, The Catholic Center, 800 W. Loop 820 S., Fort Worth, 76108. Tel: 817-560-3300.
Clergy and Religious Personnel Services—Very Rev. STEPHEN BERG.
Priests' Care Fund—Very Rev. STEPHEN BERG.
Continuing Pastoral Formation—Rev. JOSEPH PEMBERTON.
Catholic Women, Council of—Rev. IVOR KOCH, Sacred Heart Parish, 1504 10th St., Wichita Falls, 76301. Tel: 817-723-5288.
Campaign for Human Development—Deacon LEONARD SANCHEZ.
Ecumenism, Office of—Rev. Msgr. CHARLES KING, P.A., Immaculate Conception Church, 1215 N. Elm, Denton, 76201. Tel: 940-565-1770.
St. Vincent de Paul Society—Mr. RALPH E. HASSEL, 3005 Phoenix Dr., Fort Worth, 76116. Tel: 817-244-4624.
Holy Childhood Association—Mr. DONALD MILLER, Supt. Schools.

CLERGY, PARISHES, MISSIONS AND PAROCHIAL SCHOOLS

CITY OF FORT WORTH

(TARRANT COUNTY)

1—ST. PATRICK CATHEDRAL (1870) Revs. Richard Flores, Rector; Joy Joseph, T.O.R.
1206 Throckmorton St., 76102. Tel: 817-332-4915; Fax: 817-338-1988. Email: stpatricktx@sbcglobal.net.
Catechesis/Religious Program—Tel: 817-338-4441. Students 303.

2—ALL SAINTS (1902) Revs. Stephen Jasso, T.O.R.; Angel Infante, T.O.R.
214 N.W. 20th St., 76104. Tel: 817-626-3055; Fax: 817-626-3050.
School—2006 N. Houston St., 76164. Tel: 817-624-2670; Fax: 817-624-1221. Christina Mendez, Prin. Lay Teachers 8; Students 85.
Catechesis/Religious Program—Tel: 817-740-9176. Students 828.

3—ST. ANDREW (1953) Revs. Thomas Stabile, T.O.R.; Gerald Gordon, T.O.R. In Res., Revs. Gerald Gordon, T.O.R.; Robert Hilz, T.O.R.; Warren L. Murphy, T.O.R.; Luke Robertson, T.O.R.
Res.: 46 Chelsea Dr., 76134. Tel: 817-927-5383; Fax: 817-927-8507. Web: www.standrewcc.org.
Church: 3717 Stadium Dr., 76109.
School—St. Andrew Catholic School, 3304 Dryden Rd., 76109. Tel: 817-924-8917. Clarice Peninger, Prin. Lay Teachers 42; Students 701.
Catechesis/Religious Program—Students 426.

4—ST. BARTHOLOMEW (1969) Bro. Paul McMullen, T.O.R., Pastoral Admin.; Deacons Gary Brooks; Manuel Pereda. In Res., Rev. Raphael Eagle, T.O.R.
Res.: 3601 Altamesa Blvd., 76133. Tel: 817-292-7703; Fax: 817-292-2568. Email: stbarts@stbartsfw.org. Web: www.stbartsfw.org.
Catechesis/Religious Program—Students 632.

5—CHRIST THE KING Rev. Louis Pham Ha, C.M.C.
1112 Eagle Dr., 76111. Tel: 817-831-7200; Fax: 817-881-7200.

6—ST. GEORGE (1941) Rev. Thu Nguyen.
825 Karnes, 76111. Tel: 817-831-4404; Fax: 817-834-0121.
School—824 Hudgins Ave., 76111. Tel: 817-222-1221; Fax: 817-838-0424. Email: principalsg@charter.net. Olga Ferris, Prin. Lay Teachers 13; Students 213.
Catechesis/Religious Program—Tel: 817-831-4404. Students 477.

7—HOLY FAMILY (1942) Revs. Joseph Pemberton; Balaji Boyalla, S.A.C.; Deacons Joseph L. Milligan Jr.; Michael Mocek.
6150 Pershing Ave., 76107. Tel: 817-737-6768; Fax: 817-737-6876. Email: pastoraloffice@holyfamilyfw.org. Web: www.holyfamilyfw.org.
School—Tel: 817-737-4201. Dr. John Shreve, Prin. Lay Teachers 20; Students 242.
Catechesis/Religious Program—Students 252.

8—HOLY NAME OF JESUS (1952) Rev. Rodrigo Serrano.
2637 Avenue L., 76105. Tel: 817-536-9604.
Catechesis/Religious Program—Tel: 817-535-8495. Students 780.

9—IMMACULATE HEART OF MARY (1961) Revs. Antonio Bandres, O.F.M.Cap.; Jesse Torre, O.F.M.Cap.; Greg Goicoechea, O.F.M.Cap.
Mailing Address: 100 E. Pafford St., 76110. Tel: 817-923-6323; Fax: 817-923-6523.
Catechesis/Religious Program—Tel: 817-923-8582. Students 1,898.

10—ST. JOHN THE APOSTLE (North Richland Hills) (1964) Revs. Karl Schilken; James Flynn.
7341 Glenview Dr., 76180. Tel: 817-284-4811; Fax: 817-284-1729.
School—7421 Glenview Dr., 76180. Tel: 817-284-2228; Fax: 817-284-1800. Cynthia Cummins, Prin. Lay Teachers 25; Students 288.
Catechesis/Religious Program—Students 760.

11—ST. MARY OF THE ASSUMPTION (1909) Rev. David Bristow.
509 W. Magnolia Ave., 76104. Tel: 917-923-1911; Fax: 817-923-0769. Email: stmarysfw@catholicweb.com. Web: stmarysftw-.catholic.com. In Res., Revs. George Thennattil, T.O.R.; Philip Brembah; Robert Strittmatter.
Catechesis/Religious Program—Students 785.

12—OUR LADY OF FATIMA Rev. Mark Huynh Thanh Nguyen, C.M.C.
Mailing Address: 5109 E. Lancaster Ave., 76112. Tel: 817-446-4196. Email: ourladyoffatima@sbcglobal.net. Web: nhathofatima-.com.

13—OUR LADY OF GUADALUPE (1977), (Hispanic), Revs. Domingo Romero, O.F.M.Cap.; Francis Garces, O.F.M.Cap.; Sabino Erro, O.F.M.Cap.
4100 Blue Mound Rd., 76106. Tel: 817-626-7421; Fax: 817-626-4461. Email: doromero@yahoo.com. In Res., Rev. Francis X. Fernandez, O.F.M.Cap.
Catechesis/Religious Program—Tel: 817-624-3240. Students 1,600.

14—OUR MOTHER OF MERCY (1929), (African American), Rev. Jerome LeDoux, S.V.D.
1007 E. Terrell Ave., 76104-3788. Tel: 817-335-1695.
School—(Grades K-12), 1003 E. Terrell Ave., 76104-3799. Tel: 817-336-2880; Fax: 817-338-4227. Dr. Carolyn Yusuf, Prin. Lay Teachers 8; Students 85.

15—ST. PAUL THE APOSTLE (1952) Rev. Ellsworth T. Wigginton; Deacon Ron Aziere.
5508 Black Oak Ln., 76114. Tel: 817-738-9925; Fax: 817-735-8579.
Church: 5508-B Black Oak Ln., 76114.
Catechesis/Religious Program—Students 340.

16—ST. PETER THE APOSTLE (1952) Very Rev. Stephen Berg; Deacon Patrick Bresler.
Office: 1201 S. Cherry Ln., 76108. Tel: 817-246-3622.
School—Tel: 817-246-2032; Fax: 817-246-3686. Ms. Erin Vader, Prin. Lay Teachers 10; Students 124.
Catechesis/Religious Program—Students 320.

17—ST. RITA (1910) Rev. Paul Kahan, S.V.D.
5550 E. Lancaster, 76112. Tel: 817-451-9395; Fax: 817-451-9421.
School—712 Weiler Blvd., 76112. Tel: 817-451-9383. Kathleen Krick, Prin. Lay Teachers 15; Students 211.
Catechesis/Religious Program—Students 324.

18—SAN MATEO (1939) Rev. Robert Strittmatter.
Mailing Address: c/o 1206 Throckmorton St., 76102.
Office: 2909 Photo Ave., 76107. Tel: 817-737-5470.
Catechesis/Religious Program—Students 174.

19—ST. THOMAS (1937) Rev. Antony Matthew, T.O.R.
2920 Azle Ave., 76106. Tel: 817-624-2184; Fax: 817-624-9688.
Catechesis/Religious Program—Students 470.
Mission—Holy Trinity 800 High Crest Dr., Azle, Tarrant Co. 76020. Tel: 817-444-3063; Fax: 817-444-2217. Email: holytrinity1@prodigy.net.

20—ST. THOMAS MORE, Closed. For inquiries for parish records contact the chancery.

OUTSIDE THE CITY OF FORT WORTH

ABBOTT, HILL CO., IMMACULATE HEART OF MARY (1946) [CEM] Rev. Baby George Pullambryayil.
601 W. Houston St., 76621. Tel: 254-582-3092; Fax: 254-582-0613.
Catechesis/Religious Program—Students 85.

ALBANY, SHACKELFORD CO., JESUS OF NAZARETH (1970) Rev. Jerome Jayasuriya.
Catechesis/Religious Program—Students 8.

ALEDO, PARKER CO., HOLY REDEEMER PARISH Rev. Publius Xuereb; Deacon Scott France; Ms. Judie Woodall, Pastoral Assoc.
Mailing Address: P.O. Box 550, 76008. Tel: 817-441-3500. Email: parishoffice@holyredeemerEPC.org. Web: www.holyredeemeraledo.org.
Catechesis/Religious Program—Students 223.

ARLINGTON, TARRANT CO.

1—CHURCH OF ST. MARY THE VIRGIN (1994) Rev. Allan R.G. Hawkins.
1408 N. Davis Dr., 76012. Tel: 817-460-2278; Fax: 817-277-9927. Email: stmaryarl@sbcglobal.net.
Catechesis/Religious Program—Students 60.

2—CHURCH OF THE VIETNAMESE MARTYRS (2000) Revs. Polycarp Nguyen, C.M.C.; John Nghia Hoang, C.M.C.
801 E. Mayfield Rd., 76014. Tel: 817-466-0800. Email: vpgxtd@yahoo.com. Web: www.cttdvn.com.

3—ST. JOSEPH'S (1988) Revs. Daniel Kelley; Cyprian J. Mercieca, T.O.R.
Office: 1927 S.W. Green Oaks Blvd., 76017-2734. Tel: 817-472-5181; Fax: 817-467-9319. Email: frdkelley@stjoe88.org. Web: www.stjoe.org.
Catechesis/Religious Program—Students 953.

4—ST. MARIA GORETTI (1941) Revs. James Gigliotti, T.O.R.; Michael Ciski, T.O.R.
Res.: 306 Cecile Ct., 76013. Tel: 817-274-0643; Fax: 817-277-4193.
School—Tel: 817-275-5081. Mary Ellen Doskocil, Prin. Lay Teachers 35; Students 451.
Catechesis/Religious Program—Tel: 817-274-0643, Ext. 226. Students 301.

5—ST. MATTHEW (1964) Revs. Hector Medina; John Pacheco; Jonathan Wallis; Deacons Eduardo Garcia; Benito Serenil.
2021 New York Ave., 76010-6097. Tel: 817-860-0130; Fax: 817-277-7159.
Catechesis/Religious Program—Students 2,143.

6—MOST BLESSED SACRAMENT (1978) Rev. Msgr. Joseph S. Scantlin; Deacon Mike Krempp.
2100 N. Davis Dr., 76012. Tel: 817-460-2751; Fax: 817-460-2761. Web: mostblessedsacrament.org.
Catechesis/Religious Program—Students 505.

7—ST. VINCENT DE PAUL (1976) Rev. Thomas Craig; Deacon Charles Castleberry.
5819 W. Pleasant Ridge Rd., 76016. Tel: 817-478-8206; Fax: 817-478-8513. Email: svdpcc@svdpcc.org.
Catechesis/Religious Program—Fax: 817-478-8513. Students 860.

BEDFORD, TARRANT CO., ST. MICHAEL (1977) Rev. Msgr. Philip Johnson; Rev. Thomas Kennedy; Deacon Harold Heinz.
3713 Harwood, 76021-4097. Tel: 817-283-8746; Fax: 817-283-1908. Web: www.smcchurch.org.

Catechesis/Religious Program—Students 818.

BOWIE, MONTAGUE CO., ST. JEROME (1986) Attended by St. Mary, Henrietta. Rev. Richard Collins.
Mailing Address: 105 S. Barrett, Henrietta, 76365. Tel: 940-538-4214. Email: stmaryhenrietta@yahoo.com.
Catechesis/Religious Program—Students 60.

BRECKENRIDGE, STEPHENS CO., SACRED HEART (1920) Rev. Jerome Jayasuriya, Sacramental Min.
208 S. Miller St., 76424. Tel: 254-559-2860; Fax: 254-559-5289. Email: galilee@pgrb.com.
Catechesis/Religious Program—Students 182.

BRIDGEPORT, WISE CO., ST. JOHN THE BAPTIZER (1889) Rev. Sojan George, H.G.N.
1801 Irvin, 76426. Tel: 940-683-2743; Fax: 940-683-5958. Email: stjohns76426@embarqmail.com. Web: jackandwisecatholics.org.
Catechesis/Religious Program—Students 120.

BURKBURNETT, WICHITA CO., ST. JUDE THADDEUS (1965) Rev. Joseph Meledom.
600 Davey Dr., 76354. Tel: 940-569-1222; Fax: 940-569-2714. Email: stjudeth@yahoo.com.
Catechesis/Religious Program—Students 70.

BURLESON, TARRANT CO., ST. ANN (1971) Rev. Mel Bessellieu.
100 S.W. Alsbury Blvd., 76028. Tel: 817-295-5621; Fax: 817-295-5482. Email: stannoffice@sbcglobal.net.
Catechesis/Religious Program—Tel: 817-426-1101; Fax: 817-426-1106. Email: stannccd@sbcglobal.net. Web: www.stanninburleson.com. Students 579.

CARROLLTON, DENTON CO., ST. CATHERINE OF SIENA (1981) Rev. Mathew Kavipurayidam, T.O.R.
Mailing Address: 1705 Peters Colony, 75007-3704. Tel: 972-492-3237; Fax: 972-394-0676. Email: churchinfo@stcatherine.org. Web: www.stcatherine.org.
Catechesis/Religious Program—Students 512.

CISCO, EASTLAND CO., HOLY ROSARY (1920) Attended by St. Rita, Ranger. Rev. Kyle Walterscheid, Sacramental Min.; Deacon Ruben Castaneda, Pastoral Admin.
1109 Blackwell St., Ranger, 76470. Tel: 254-647-3167.
Catechesis/Religious Program—Students 8.

CLEBURNE, JOHNSON CO., ST. JOSEPH (1888) Rev. Sergio Rizo.
Mailing Address: 807 N. Anglin St., 76031. Tel: 817-645-4478; Fax: 817-558-9938. Email: stjolv123@sbcglobal.net.
Catechesis/Religious Program—Tel: 817-645-8079. Students 529.

CLIFTON, BOSQUE CO., HOLY ANGELS (1954) Deacon James Poole.
1915 W. Fifth St., 76634. Tel: 254-675-8877. Email: holyangels@embarqmail.com.
Catechesis/Religious Program—Tel: 254-675-3165. Students 108.

COLLEYVILLE, TARRANT CO., GOOD SHEPHERD (1992) Rev. Richard Eldredge, T.O.R.
1000 Tinker Rd., 76034. Tel: 817-421-1387; Fax: 817-421-4709.
Catechesis/Religious Program—Students 1,319.
See Holy Trinity Catholic School, Grapevine under Elementary and Secondary Schools, Parochial located in the Institution section.

COMANCHE, COMANCHE CO., SACRED HEART (1964) Attended by St. Brendan, Stephenville. Rev. Philip McNamara, S.A.C.; Deacon Tomie Diza.
Mailing Address: 1444 W. Washington Ave., Stephenville, 76401. Tel: 254-965-5693.
Catechesis/Religious Program—Tel: 325-356-2040. Students 90.

CROWELL, FOARD CO., ST. JOSEPH (1910) Attended by Holy Family, Vernon. Rev. John McKone.
Res. & Mailing Address: 2200 Roberts, Vernon, 76384. Tel: 940-552-2895; 940-552-9870 (Rel. Ed.); Fax: 940-552-6084.

DE LEON, COMANCHE CO., OUR LADY OF GUADALUPE (1975) Attended by St. Brendan, Stephenville. Rev. Philip McNamara, S.A.C.
1444 W. Washington, Stephenville, 76401. Tel: 254-965-5693.
Catechesis/Religious Program—Students 31.

DECATUR, WISE CO., ASSUMPTION OF THE BLESSED VIRGIN MARY (1938) Attended by St. John the Baptizer, Bridgeport. Rev. Sojan George, H.G.N.
1305 Deer Park Rd., 76234-9701. Tel: 940-627-3307; Fax: 940-683-5958. Email: stjohns76426@embarqmail.com. Web: jackandwisecatholics.org.
Church Rectory: 1801 Irvin, Bridgeport, 76426.
Catechesis/Religious Program—Tel: 940-683-2743. Students 286.

DENTON, DENTON CO.

1—IMMACULATE CONCEPTION (1894) Rev. Msgr. Charles King; Rev. Alfredo Barba; Deacon Popo Gonzalez.
Res.: 2237 Northway Dr., 76207. Tel: 940-565-1770; Fax: 940-382-7939.
Catechesis/Religious Program—Martha Tona, Dir. Faith Formation. Students 876.

2—ST. MARK (1995) Rev. D. Timothy Thompson.
2800 Pennsylvania, 76205. Tel: 940-387-6223; Fax: 940-382-1641. Email: cwalker@stmarkdenton.org. Web: www.stmarkdenton.org.
Catechesis/Religious Program—Students 455.

DODSON PRAIRIE, PALO PINTO CO., ST. BONIFACE (1913) Closed. For inquiries for parish records contact the chancery.

DUBLIN, ERATH CO., ST. MARY (1916) Attended by St. Brendan, Stephenville., 1444 W. Washington Ave., Stephenville, 76401. Tel: 254-965-5693.
Catechesis/Religious Program—Tel: 254-445-0237. Students 127.

EASTLAND, EASTLAND CO., ST. FRANCIS XAVIER (1920) Attended by St. Rita, Ranger. Rev. Kyle Walterscheid, Sacramental Min.; Deacon Ruben Castaneda, Pastoral Admin.
1109 Blackwell St., Ranger, 76470. Tel: 254-647-3167; Fax: 254-647-3167.

ELECTRA, WICHITA CO., ST. PAUL (1966) [JC] Attended by Christ the King, Iowa Park. Deacon Patrick Burke, Admin.
Mailing Address: 3422 Stirling St., Wichita Falls, 76310.
Office: 1008 First St., Iowa Park, 76367. Tel: 940-592-2802; Fax: 940-592-2802.
Res.: 4807 Heisman Dr., Wichita Falls, 76310. Tel: 940-691-7893.
Church: 500 N. Bailey, 76360. Tel: 940-495-3464; 940-592-2802.

GAINESVILLE, COOKE CO., ST. MARY (1879) Rev. James Pemberton.
Res.: 805 N. Weaver St., 76240. Tel: 940-665-5395, Ext. 2; Fax: 940-665-0957. Web: stmaryscatholic.com.
School—931 N. Weaver St., 76240. Tel: 940-665-5395; Fax: 940-668-1881. Carol Hermes, Prin. Lay Teachers 15; Students 190.
Catechesis/Religious Program—Students 305.
Convent—825 N. Weaver St., 76240.

GLEN ROSE, SOMERVELL CO., ST. ROSE OF LIMA (1969) [JC] Attended by St. Frances Cabrini. Rev. Juan Rivero; Deacon Franklin Eschbach.
P.O. Box 7324, 76048.
Catechesis/Religious Program—Students 40.

GRAFORD, PALO PINTO CO., ST. FRANCIS OF ASSISI (1949) Attended by Our Lady of Lourdes.
Res.: P.O. Box 404, 76449. Tel: 254-779-2023.

GRAHAM, YOUNG CO., ST. MARY (1922) [JC] Rev. Raymund A. Mullan.
Res.: 1218 S. Rodgers Dr., Box 547, 76450. Tel: 940-549-4314; Fax: 940-549-2690. Email: stmarygm@sbcglobal.net. Web: www.stmarygraham.org.
Catechesis/Religious Program—Tel: 940-549-1058. Students 205.

GRANBURY, HOOD CO., ST. FRANCES CABRINI (1976) [JC] Revs. Juan Rivero; Gonzalo Morales; Deacons Jim Bell; Richard Stojak; Jim Fuller; Craig McAlister.
2301 Acton Hwy., 76049. Tel: 817-326-2131; Fax: 817-326-3211.
Catechesis/Religious Program— 76048. Tel: 817-326-2131. Students 484.

GRAPEVINE, TARRANT CO., ST. FRANCIS OF ASSISI (1949) Revs. Anh Tran; Jacob Alvares, S.A.C.; Deacons Joseph Salvo; M. C. Marquez.
Res.: 861 Wildwood, 76051-3398. Tel: 817-481-2685; Fax: 817-488-3169. Web: www.sfatx.org.
See Holy Trinity Catholic School, Grapevine under Elementary and Secondary Schools, Parochial located in the Institution section.
Catechesis/Religious Program—Students 1,291.

HENRIETTA, CLAY CO., ST. MARY (1879) [CEM] Rev. Richard Collins.
105 S. Barrett St., 76365. Tel: 940-538-4214; Fax: 940-538-6638. Email: stmaryhenrietta@yahoo.com.
Catechesis/Religious Program—Students 25.

HILLSBORO, HILL CO., OUR LADY OF MERCY (1887) Rev. Baby George Pullambryayil; Deacon James Poole.
Interstate 35, P.O. Box 567, 76645. Tel: 254-582-5640; Fax: 254-582-0347. Email: olm@hillsboro.net.
Catechesis/Religious Program—Students 226.

HURST, TARRANT CO., KOREAN MARTYRS, Unassigned.415 Brown Tr., 76053. Tel: 817-788-5530; Fax: 817-485-2460. Email: chrysantpaul@yahoo.com. Web: www.koreancatholic.us.

IOWA PARK, WICHITA CO., CHRIST THE KING (1980) Deacon Patrick Burke, Pastoral Admin.
Mailing Address: P.O. Box 239, 76367.
Office: 1008 First St., 76367. Tel: 940-592-2802; Fax: 940-592-2802. Email: ctkip@sbcglobal.net.
Res.: 3422 Stirling St., Wichita Falls, 76310. Tel: 940-691-7893.
Catechesis/Religious Program—Students 20.

JACKSBORO, JACK CO., ST. MARY (1911) Attended by St. John the Baptizer, 1801 Irvin St., Bridgeport, TX 76426. Tel: 940-683-2743; Fax: 940-683-5958; 940-683-2743 (Rel. Ed.). Rev. Sojan George, H.G.N.

KELLER, TARRANT CO., ST. ELIZABETH ANN SETON (1985) Revs. Dennis Smith; Isaac Orozco; Deacons Klaus Gutbier; Myles Miller; Robert Montini; Donald E. Warner.
Office: 2016 Willis Ln., 76248. Tel: 817-431-3857; Fax: 817-431-9568. Web: www.seascc.org.
School—(Grades PreK-8) Tel: 817-431-4845; Fax: 817-431-1865. Web: www.seascc.org. Kay Burrell, Prin.; Ms. Nancy Stone, Librarian. Students 739.
Catechesis/Religious Program—Tel: 817-431-6023; Fax: 817-431-3871. Students 1,656.

KNOX CITY, KNOX CO., SANTA ROSA (1948) [JC] Attended by St. Joseph, Rhineland Rev. Charles Gorantla, H.G.N., Sacramental Min.; Deacons Jim Novak, Pastoral Admin.; Ben Vasquez.
Mailing Address: P.O. Box 428, 79529. Tel: 940-658-5062.
Church: N. 3rd and Ave. G, 79529. Tel: 940-658-5062.

LEWISVILLE, DENTON CO., ST. PHILIP THE APOSTLE (1976) Rev. John Stasiowski; Deacons Raymond G. Lamarre; John Kerrigan; Ramiro Rodriguez.
Office: 1897 W. Main St., 75067. Tel: 972-436-9581; Fax: 972-436-5302. Email: connieg@stphilipcc.org. Web: www.stphilipcc.org.
Catechesis/Religious Program—Tel: 972-219-7448. Students 838.

LINDSAY, COOKE CO., ST. PETER (1892) [CEM] Unassigned. Rev. Raymond McDaniel.
Res.: 424 Main St., P.O. Box 148, 76250. Tel: 940-668-7609; Fax: 940-668-7723. Email: stpeterschurch@ntin.net.
Catechesis/Religious Program—Tel: 940-665-6763. Students 313.

MANSFIELD, TARRANT CO., ST. JUDE (1898) [CEM] Rev. George Foley; Deacons Rubén Curiel; Edward Bowden.
500 E. Dallas St., 76063. Tel: 817-473-6709; Fax: 817-477-2088. Web: www.stjudecc.org.
Catechesis/Religious Program—Tel: 817-473-0768. Students 934.

MEGARGEL, ARCHER CO., ST. MARY (1909) [CEM] Attended by Sacred Heart, Seymour. Rev. Charles Gorantla, H.G.N., Sacramental Min.; Deacon Jim Novak.
13th St. & St. Mary St., 76370. Tel: 940-889-5252; Fax: 940-889-2136. Email: shseymour@srcaccess.net.

MINERAL WELLS, PALO PINTO CO., OUR LADY OF LOURDES (1960) Rev. Jeff Poirot.
Res.: 108 N.W. 4th Ave., 76067. Tel: 940-325-4789; Fax: 940-327-8170.
Catechesis/Religious Program—Students 292.

MONTAGUE, MONTAGUE CO., ST. WILLIAM (1899) [CEM] Attended by St. Mary Rev. Richard Collins.
105 S. Barrett, Henrietta, 76365. Tel: 940-538-4214; Fax: 940-538-6638. Email: stmaryhenrietta@yahoo.com.
Catechesis/Religious Program—Students 100.

MORGAN, BOSQUE CO., OUR LADY OF GUADALUPE (1987) Attended by Our Lady of Mercy, Hillsboro. Deacon James Poole.

MUENSTER, COOKE CO., SACRED HEART (1889) [CEM] Rev. Ken Robinson.
714 N. Main St., 76252. Tel: 940-759-2511; Fax: 940-759-4422. Email: sacredheart@ntin.net. Web: ntin.net/sacredheart.
Preschool—Lay Teachers 3; Students 23.
School—Dr. Rafael Rondon, Prin. Lay Teachers 11; Students 129.
High School—Lay Teachers 14; Students 81.
Catechesis/Religious Program—Tel: 940-759-2511, Ext. 16. Students 240.

NOCONA, MONTAGUE CO., ST. JOSEPH (1948) Attended by St. Mary. Rev. Richard Collins.
105 S. Barrett, Henrietta, 76365. Tel: 940-538-4214; Fax: 940-538-6638. Email: stmaryhenrietta@yahoo.com.
Catechesis/Religious Program—Students 40.

OLNEY, YOUNG CO., ST. THERESA OF THE INFANT JESUS (1935) [JC] Attended by St. Mary, Graham. Rev. Raymund A. Mullan.
P.O. Box 547, Graham, 76450. Tel: 940-549-4314. Email: stmarygm@sbcglobal.net.
Church: Oak & Ave. E, 76374.

PENELOPE, HILL CO., NATIVITY OF THE BLESSED VIRGIN MARY (1909) [CEM 2] Attended by Immaculate Heart of Mary, Abbot. Rev. Baby George Pullambryayil.
Mailing Address: P.O. Box 98, 76676. Tel: 254-582-3092; Fax: 254-582-3092.
Catechesis/Religious Program—Tel: 254-533-2486. Students 44.

PILOT POINT, DENTON CO., ST. THOMAS AQUINAS (1891) [CEM] Rev. Aloysius Muthaya, S.A.C.
Res.: 400 St. Aquinas Ave., 76258. Tel: 940-686-2088; Fax: 360-925-2952. Email: office@stthomaspilotpoint.org. Web: www.stthomaspilotpoint.org.
Catechesis/Religious Program—400 E. Gibbons, 76258. Tel: 940-686-2360. Students 291.

QUANAH, HARDEMAN CO., ST. MARY (1914) [JC] Attended by Holy Family, Vernon. Rev. John McKone.

2200 Roberts, Vernon, 76384. Tel: 940-552-2895; Fax: 940-552-6084.

RANGER, EASTLAND CO., ST. RITA (1919) Rev. Kyle Walterscheid; Deacon Ruben Castaneda, Pastoral Admin.
Res.: 1109 Blackwell St., 76470. Tel: 254-647-3167; Fax: 254-647-3167. Email: ruben1@classicnet.net.

RHINELAND, KNOX CO., ST. JOSEPH (1895) [CEM] Rev. Charles Gorantla, H.G.N., Sacramental Min.; Deacons Jim Novak, Pastoral Admin.; Ben Vasquez.
Res.: 10180 CR 6010, Munday, 76371. Tel: 940-422-4994; Fax: 940-422-4994.
Catechesis/Religious Program—Students 132.

SCOTLAND, ARCHER CO., ST. BONIFACE (1911) [CEM] Attended by St. Mary, Windthorst. Rev. David Kraeger, T.O.R.
Tel: 940-423-6687; Fax: 940-423-6657. Email: windscot@comcell.net. Web: www.st-boniface.org.

SEYMOUR, BAYLOR CO., SACRED HEART (1910) [CEM] Rev. Charles Gorantla, H.G.N., Sacramental Min.; Deacon Jim Novak.
Sacred Heart Pastoral Center—206 N. Cedar St., 76380. Tel: 940-889-5252; Fax: 940-889-2136. Email: shseymour@srcaccess.net.
Catechesis/Religious Program—Students 76.

STEPHENVILLE, ERATH CO., ST. BRENDAN (1958) Rev. Philip McNamara, S.A.C.; Deacons William Bolf; Joe Stanridge.
Res.: 1444 W. Washington Ave., 76401. Tel: 254-965-5693.
Catechesis/Religious Program—Students 247.

STRAWN, PALO PINTO CO., ST. JOHN (1912) Attended by St. Rita. Rev. Kyle Walterscheid; Deacon Ruben Castaneda, Pastoral Admin.
Res.: 1109 Blackwell Rd., Ranger, 76470. Tel: 254-647-3167.

THE COLONY, DENTON CO., HOLY CROSS (1981) Rev. J. Michael Holmberg; Deacons Tomas Baca; Simon Torrez.
Church: 7000 Morning Star, P.O. Box 560156, 75056. Tel: 972-625-5252; Fax: 972-370-5524.
Catechesis/Religious Program—Students 363.

THROCKMORTON, THROCKMORTON CO., SAN PATRICIO (1964) Closed. For inquiries for parish records contact the chancery.

VALLEY VIEW, COOKE CO., ST. JOHN (1946) [JC] Unassigned.709 Lee St., 76272. Tel: 940-726-3524.

VERNON, WILBARGER CO., HOLY FAMILY (1891) Rev. John McKone.
2200 Roberts, 76384. Tel: 940-552-2895; Fax: 940-552-6084.
Catechesis/Religious Program—Tel: 940-553-1580. Students 100.

WEATHERFORD, PARKER CO., ST. STEPHEN (1882) Rev. John Casey, S.A.C.; Deacon Carlos Frias.
Office: 1802 Bethel Rd., 76086. Tel: 817-596-9585; Fax: 817-613-0808. Web: www.ss-cc.org.
Res.: 1904 Bethel Rd., 76086. Tel: 817-596-9586.
Catechesis/Religious Program—Students 623.

WICHITA FALLS, WICHITA CO.

1—IMMACULATE CONCEPTION OF MARY, [CEM] [JC] Rev. Louis Pham Ha, C.M.C.
2901 Barnett Rd., 76310. Tel: 940-692-1825.

2—OUR LADY OF GUADALUPE (1927) [JC] Rev. John Robert Skeldon; Deacon Anastasio Perez.
421 Marconi, 76301. Tel: 940-766-2735; Fax: 940-766-4052. Email: guadalupewf@sbcglobal.net. Web: www.guadalupewf.org.
Catechesis/Religious Program—Students 179.

3—OUR LADY QUEEN OF PEACE (1956) [JC] Rev. John Swistovich; Deacon Larry W. Bills.
4040 York Ave., 76309. Tel: 940-696-1253; Fax: 940-696-1216. Email: olqp@wf.net. Web: olqpwf.org.
Catechesis/Religious Program—Fax: 940-696-1253. Students 196.

4—SACRED HEART (1891) [JC] Revs. Hoa Nguyen; Charles Gorantla, H.G.N.
Mailing Address: 1504 Tenth St., 76301. Tel: 940-723-5288; Fax: 940-767-0160.
Catechesis/Religious Program—Students 281.

WINDTHORST, ARCHER CO., ST. MARY (1892) [CEM] Rev. David Kraeger, T.O.R.
Res.: P.O. Box 230, 76389. Tel: 940-423-6687; Fax: 940-423-6657. Email: windscot@comcell.net. Web: www.st-boniface.com.
Catechesis/Religious Program—Students 327.

Chaplains of Public Institutions

FORT WORTH. *Federal Medical Center* 76199.

DENTON. *State School*, 1215 E. Elm St., 76201. Tel: 817-387-1755. Deacon Emilio (Popo) Gonzalez.

GAINESVILLE. *Texas Youth Council Youth Facility*, 805 N. Weaver, 76240. Tel: 817-665-2413.

WICHITA FALLS. *State Hospital*, Tel: 817-723-4111.

On Duty Outside the Diocese:
Very Rev.—
Olson, Michael F., Dallas, TX.
Revs.—
Spong, William, Ogdensburg, NY.
Thames, Robert, Residencia de Arzobispado, Casilla 25, Santa Cruz, Bolivia.

On Leave of Absence:
Revs.—
Gremmels, John
Hennessy, John

Retired:
Rev. Msgrs.—
Neu, Hubert, 174 Rieti Dr., Crowley, 76036.
Schumacher, Joseph A.
Revs.—
Beaumont, Richard, 6240 Horton Circle, Apt. D, 76133.
Blank, Severius, 1022 Sheridan St., Burkburnett, 76354.
Cooney, Gerald, c/o 1824 Clark Rd., Crowley, 76036-9714.
Curtsinger, George, P.O. Box 101148, 76185.
Edwards, Dale
Miller, James, St. Francis Village, 134 St. Anthony Dr., Crowley, 76036.
Miranda, Luke, 3240 Daniels, Apt. 101, Dallas, 75205.
O'Toole, James, c/o The Catholic Center, 800 W. Loop 820 S., 76108.
Perez, Salvador, Calle 22 #678, N. con Avenida Guerrero, Torreon, Coah 27000 Mexico.

Permanent Deacons:
Aguirre, Ruben
Amos, Clarence
Aragon, Jose
Archer, William
Baca, Tomas
Bates, Thomas
Beaton, William
Bell, James
Benoit, Roland
Berens, LeRoy
Bills, Larry
Bindel, James
Blake, Vincent
Bolf, William
Bowden, Edgar
Bressler, Patrick
Brooks, Gary
Burke, Patrick
Camargo, Moisés
Cardenas, Jesus Esteban
Carranza, Marcelino
Casias, Arturo
Castaneda, Ruben
Castellon, Damaso
Castleberry, Charles
Clark, John
Corbett, Bruce
Crites, James
Curiel, Ruben
Detwiler, Russell
Diaz, Tommy
Escamilla, Juan
Eschbach, Franklin
France, Scott
Frias, Carlos
Fuller, Jim
Galbraith, James
Garcia, Eduardo
Garcia, Gelasio
Garcia, Martin
Garcia, Pedro
Garza, Dave
Geiger, Wendell
Germann, Joe
Giovannitti, Thomas
Gonzalez, Adolfo
Gonzalez, Emilio
Gray, Glen Eldon
Greene, Clifford
Griego, Richard
Gutbier, Klaus
Guzman, N. John
Harvey, James
Heinz, Harold
Hernandez, Mauricio
Hoang, Dominic T.
Hoang, Michael
Howard, Terrance
Huerta, Lauro
Jasso, Juan
Johnson, William
Kerrigan, John
Krempp, Michael
Kunath, Wolfgang
Lagunas, Matias
Lamarre, Raymond
Lavery, Patrick
Leyva, Rigoberto
Marquez, Mario
Maskow, Kurt
McAlister, Craig
McDermott, John
Miller, Myles
Milligan, Joseph
Mocek, Michael
Montini, Robert
Nguyen, John Ban
Norton, Victor
Novak, Jim
Onofre, Jose
Pereda, Manuel
Perez, Anastasio
Perez, Julio
Poole, James
Poth, Louis J.
Ramirez, Alfonso
Reyes, Juan
Rodriguez, Jose
Rustand, Gerald
Salva, Hector
Salvo, Joseph
Sanchez, Jose
Sanchez, Leonard
Sandoval, Larry
Serenil, Benito
Sowers, Lynn
Standridge, Joe
Stojak, Richard
Stone, Walter
Stuart, Robert
Sweeden, Barry
Tello, Reyes, Jr.
Torrez, Simon
Ulupano, Sangote
Vasquez, Ben
Warner, Don
Weaver, Lonnie, Jr.
Wolf, George
Wuenchel, Douglas

INSTITUTIONS LOCATED IN THE DIOCESE

[A] COLLEGES & UNIVERSITIES

FORT WORTH. *The College of St. Thomas More*, 3020 Lubbock St., 76109. Tel: 817-923-8459; Fax: 817-924-3206. Email: skirk@sctm.edu. Web: www.cstm.edu. Priests 1; Fellows 4; Lay Teachers 7; Students 50.

[B] HIGH SCHOOLS, DIOCESAN

FORT WORTH. *Cassata High School* (Coed Secondary)., 1400 Hemphill St., 76104-4796. Tel: 817-926-1745; Fax: 817-926-3132. Email: nmartin@cassatahs.org. Web: www.cassata.us. Nancy F. Martin, Prin. Teachers 7; Students 273.

Nolan Catholic High School (Coed), 4501 Bridge St., 76103. Tel: 817-457-2920; Fax: 817-496-9775. Email: cbuckingham@nolancatholichs.org. Web: www.nolancatholichs.org. Rev. Richard Villa, S.M., Pres.; Stephen Hiner, Prin. Society of Mary. Priests 2; Sisters 2; Brothers 5; Lay Teachers 83; Students 1,035.
Nolan School Trust

ROANOKE. *Our Lady of Grace High School*, 13517 Alta Vista Dr., 76262. Tel: 817-933-6516; Fax: 817-491-4399. Email: olghsdonohue@gmail.com. Web: www.olghs.com. Ms. Denise Donohue, Prin.; Ms. Debra Austin, Librarian.

WICHITA FALLS. *Notre Dame Middle-High School*, 2821 Lansing Blvd., 76309. Tel: 940-692-6041; Fax: 940-692-2811. Web: www.notredamecatholic.org. Mrs. Cindy Huckabee, Prin. Lay Teachers 17; Students 103.

[C] HIGH SCHOOLS, PAROCHIAL

MUENSTER. *Sacred Heart School*, (Grades PreK-12), 153 E. Sixth, Box 588, 76252. Tel: 940-759-2511; Fax: 940-759-4422. Email: principalshs@ntin.net. Web: www.sacredheartschoolmuenster.com. Dr. Rafael Rondon, Prin.; Ms. Dolores Hofbauer, Librarian. Sisters 2; Lay Teachers 30; Students 258.
**Sacred Heart Teachers Trust Fund*

[D] ELEMENTARY AND SECONDARY SCHOOLS, PAROCHIAL

ARLINGTON. *Holy Rosary Catholic School*, (Grades PreK-8), 2015 S.W. Green Oaks Blvd., 76017. Tel: 817-419-6800; Fax: 817-419-7080. Email: holy_rosary@hotmail.com. Web: www.hrcstx.com. Mr. Chad Riley, Prin. Total Staff 38; Students 465.

DENTON. *Immaculate Conception Catholic School*, (Grades PreK-8), 2301 N. Bonnie Brae, 76207. Tel: 940-381-1155; Fax: 940-381-1837. Email:

eschad@runbox.com. Web: www.catholicschooldenton.org. Mrs. Elaine Schad, Prin.; Mrs. Rebecca Bevilacqua, Library Mgr. Lay Teachers 26; Students 258.

GRAPEVINE. *Holy Trinity Catholic School*, (Grades PreK-8), 3750 William D. Tate Ave., 76051. Tel: 817-421-8000; Fax: 817-421-4468. Web: www.holytcs.org. Dr. Valerie Johnson, Prin.; Mrs. Andrea Volding, Asst. Prin.; Ms. Marianne Lippert, Librarian. Lay Teachers 29; Students 441.

WICHITA FALLS. *Notre Dame Elementary School*, 4060 York Ave., 76309. Tel: 940-696-1011; Fax: 940-691-6913. Web: www.notredamecatholic.org. Mrs. Cindy Huckabee, Prin.; Suzanne Prosser, Librarian. Sisters 1; Lay Teachers 12; Students 129.

[E] ELEMENTARY SCHOOLS, PRIVATE

FORT WORTH. *Our Lady of Victory Catholic School*, 3320 S. Hemphill St., 76110. Tel: 817-924-5123; Fax: 817-923-9621. Email: tmiller@olvfw.com. Web: www.olvfw.com. Ms. Trudy Miller, Prin.; Ann Edmonds, Librarian. Sisters 1; Lay Teachers 16; Students 180.

[F] SOCIAL AGENCIES, CATHOLIC CHARITIES

FORT WORTH. *Catholic Charities, Diocese of Fort Worth, Inc.*, 2701 Burchill Rd. N., 76105-3012. Tel: 817-534-0814; Fax: 817-536-1556. Email: infoccdofw@ccdofw.org. Web: www.ccdofw.org. Heather Reynolds, Pres., CEO. An Independent Corporation Founded by the Diocese of Fort Worth.

Office Sites:

Senior Disabled Housing, 2701 Burchill Rd. N., 76105-3012. Tel: 817-534-0814; Fax: 817-535-8779. Administers residential programs for the elderly, and disabled.

Program Sites:

Nuestro Hogar, Inc., 709 Magnolia St., Arlington, 76012. Tel: 817-216-0608; Fax: 817-861-6178.

CASA, Inc., 3201 Sondra Dr., 76107. Tel: 817-332-7276; Fax: 817-877-0487.

CASA Brendan & CASA II, Inc., 1300 Hyman St., Stephenville, 76401. Tel: 817-965-6964; Fax: 817-968-3072.

Program Sites: Immigration Counseling, Refugee Resource Center and Refugee Resettlement. Assistance in migration matters: family reunification, adjustment of status, naturalization, ESL, and employment services.; Coordinates the Emergency Assistance Association of Tarrant County, Social Concerns, Holiday Network, Disaster Relief, Public Relations.

Healthy Start, 2701 Burchill Rd. N., 76105. Tel: 817-534-0814; Fax: 817-536-4671.

Assessment Center of Tarrant, 2701 Burchill Rd. N., 76105. Tel: 817-534-0814; Fax: 817-531-2996. (Children's Shelter)

School Based Services, 2701 Burchill Rd., 76105. Tel: 817-534-0814; Fax: 817-536-1556.

Therapeutic Foster and Respite Care, 2701 Burchill Rd. N., 76105. Tel: 817-534-0814; Fax: 817-535-8779.

Clinical Counseling Department, 2701 Burchill Rd., 76104. Tel: 817-534-0814; Fax: 817-536-1556.

Immigration & Refugee Services, La Gran Plaza, 4200 South Fwy., Ste. 200, 76115. Tel: 817-920-7733; Fax: 817-923-3415.

Lady Hogan Project, 2701 Burchill Rd. N., 76105. Tel: 817-534-0814; Fax: 817-536-4671.

Enrollment Solutions, La Gran Plaza, 4200 South Fwy., Ste. 200, 76115. Tel: 817-920-7733; Fax: 817-923-3415.

CARE, 2701 Burchill Rd. N., 76105. Tel: 817-534-0814; Fax: 817-536-1556.

Pathways, 2701 Burchill Rd. N., 76105. Tel: 817-534-0814; Fax: 817-536-1556.

Pharmaceutical Services, La Gran Plaza, 4200 South Fwy., Ste. 200, 76115. Tel: 817-920-7733; Fax: 817-923-3415.

Family P.A.C.T., 2701 Burchill Rd. N., 76105. Tel: 817-534-0814; Fax: 817-536-1556.

Compassion Resource Network (CRN), 1404 Hemphill, 76104. Tel: 817-922-0384; Fax: 817-923-6818.

Financial Stability, 1404 Hemphill, 76104. Tel: 817-922-0384; Fax: 817-923-6818.

School Based Services, 2701 Burchill Rd. N., 76105. Tel: 817-534-0814; Fax: 817-536-1556.

St. Joseph's Health Care Trust, La Gran Plaza, 4200 South Fwy., Ste. 200, 76115. Tel: 817-920-7733; Fax: 817-923-3415.

Disaster Response Service, 2701 Burchill Rd., N., 76105. Tel: 817-534-0834; Fax: 817-535-6280.

Translation and Interpreter Network (TIN), La Gran Plaza, 4200 S. Fwy., Ste. 200, 76115. Tel: 817-920-7733; Fax: 817-923-3415.

Unaccompanied Refugee Minor (URM), 2701 Burchill Rd. N., 76105. Tel: 817-534-0815; Fax: 817-536-1556.

Central Intake, 2701 Burchill Rd. N., 76105. Tel: 817-534-0815; Fax: 817-536-1556.

Housing Opportunity Model for Empowerment and Stability (HOMES), 2701 Burchill Rd. N., 76105. Tel: 817-534-0815; Fax: 817-536-1556.

Alliance for Infant Survival (AIS), 2701 Burchill Rd. N., 76105. Tel: 817-534-0815; Fax: 817-536-1556.

[G] RETIREMENT & DISABILITY HOUSING

FORT WORTH. *Casa, Inc. Housing for the Elderly and Handicapped*, 3201 Sondra Dr., 76107. Tel: 817-332-7276; Fax: 817-877-0487. Email: infoccdofw@ccdofw.org. Web: www.ccdofw.org. Units 200; Total in Residence 189; Total Staff 10.

ARLINGTON. *Nuestro Hogar, Inc. Catholic Charities*, 709 Magnolia St., 76012. Tel: 817-261-0608. Email: infoccdofw@ccdofw.org. Web: www.ccdofw.org. 65 unit apartment complex for the elderly and disabled. Total in Residence 65; Total Staff 6.

CROWLEY. *St. Francis Village, Inc.*, 4070 St. Francis Village Rd., 76036. Tel: 817-292-5786; Fax: 817-294-2989. Email: deanah@saintfrancisvillage.com. Web: www.saintfrancisvillage.com. Deana Harris, Executive Dir.; Rev. John Abts, O.F.M. Active Retirement village, on shores of Lake Benbrook near Fort Worth, for retirees and the elderly sponsored by Franciscan Tertiary Provinces Foundation & SFV, Inc. (Illinois). Residents 550. In Res. Rev. Msgr. W. Robert Johnson (Retired); Rev. James Miller (Retired).

Franciscan Tertiary Provinces Foundation, 4070 St. Francis Village Rd., 76036. Tel: 817-292-5786. Sponsor corporation of St. Francis Village (retirement village) in Crowley, TX. Total Staff 17.

San Damiano, Inc., 4070 St. Francis Village Rd., 76036. Tel: 817-292-5786; Fax: 817-294-2989. Email: deanah@saintfrancisvillage.com. Web: saintfrancisvillage.com.

STEPHENVILLE. *CASA Brendan & CASA II, Inc. Catholic Charities*, 1300 Hyman, 76401. Tel: 254-965-6964; Fax: 254-968-3072. Email: infoccdofw@ccdofw.org. Web: www.ccdofw.org. 86 unit apartment complex for the elderly and handicapped. Total in Residence 88; Total Staff 9.

[H] MONASTERIES AND RESIDENCES OF PRIESTS AND BROTHERS

FORT WORTH. *Sacred Heart Friars of the Renewal*, 1003 E. Terrell, 76104. Tel: 817-332-2435; Fax: 817-334-7930. Revs. Michael Kmiotek, C.F.R; Joseph Mary Deane, C.F.R.; Bros. Peter Marie Westhall, C.F.R.; Patrick Crowley, C.F.R.; Mariano Joseph Demma, C.F.R.

CARROLLTON. **Third Order Regular of St. Francis, Province of St. Thomas*, 1705 E. Peter's Rd., 75007.

CROWLEY. *St. Maximilian Kolbe Friary* (Fort Worth), One Marquard Cir., St. Francis Village, 76036. Tel: 817-370-9747; Fax: 817-361-9522. Revs. John J. Abts, O.F.M.; Richard Baranski, O.F.M.; Vincent Elsen, O.F.M.; Cal Giesen; Robert Leonhardt, O.F.M.; Lambert Leykam, O.F.M.; Luis Runde, O.F.M.; Bro. Lester Kocklin.

[I] CONVENTS AND RESIDENCES FOR SISTERS

FORT WORTH. *Hermanas Catequistas Guadalupanas*, 1001 Altamont Dr., 76106. Tel: 817-386-4161. Sisters 3.

Provincialate, Our Lady of Victory Center, 909 W. Shaw St., 76110. Tel: 817-923-8393; Fax: 817-921-5064. Email: mercycom@sbcglobal.net. Web: web2.airmail.net/ssmn. Sr. Patricia Ste. Marie, S.S.M.N., Prov. Supr. Provincial House of the Western Province, Sisters of St. Mary of Namur.

Sisters of St. Mary Namur, 909 W. Shaw, 76110. Tel: 817-923-8393; Fax: 817-921-5064. Email: mercycom@sbcglobal.net. Web: web2.airmail.net/ssmn/. Sr. Patricia Ste. Marie, S.S.M.N. Sisters of St. Mary of Namur.

ARLINGTON. *Monastery of the Most Holy Trinity, Discalced Carmelites*, 5801 Mt. Carmel Dr., 76017. Tel: 817-468-1781; Fax: 817-468-1782. Email: supcarmel@aol.com. Web: www.carmelnuns.com. Sr. Maria Brinkley, O.C.D., Prioress. Solemn Professed Nuns 11; Novices 1.

WICHITA FALLS. *Mercy Convent*, 3000 Lansing Blvd., 76309. Tel: 940-692-9770; Fax: 940-689-0139. Email: mercycom@sbcglobal.net. Web: www.ssmnwestern.com. Sisters 4.

Notre Dame House of Prayer and Hospitality, 2820 Lansing Blvd., 76309. Tel: 940-692-2043. Email: sjstewart99@gmail.com. Sisters 2.

[J] RETREAT HOUSES

LAKE DALLAS. *Montserrat Jesuit Retreat House*, 600 N. Shady Shores Rd., P.O. Box 1390, 75065. Tel: 940-321-6020; 940-321-6030; Fax: 940-321-6040. Email: montserratquestions@gmail.com. Web: www.montserratretreat.org. Revs. Joseph Tetlow, S.J., Dir.; Ronald J. Boudreaux, S.J., Assoc.Dir.; Edmundo Rodriguez, Assoc. Dir.; Jose Fetzer, S.J.

Montserrat Foundation, Inc. Tel: 940-321-6010; Fax: 940-321-6040.

Board Members & Directors: Mr. Adam Auten; Mr. Archy Roper.

[K] SOCIETY OF ST. VINCENT DE PAUL

FORT WORTH. *St. Vincent de Paul Diocesan Council of Fort Worth*, 1901 Layton, Haltom City, 76117. Tel: 817-975-3255. Email: fwcouncilPresident@gmail.com. Web: www.svdpfw.org. Mr. Ralph E. Hassel, Pres.

WICHITA FALLS. *Particular Council of Wichita Falls, St. Vincent de Paul Society*, 4516 Lake Park Dr., 76302. Tel: 817-322-2920. Mr. Walter Brady.

[L] COLLEGE CAMPUS MINISTRIES

FORT WORTH. *Texas Christian University Catholic Community* TCU Box 297310, 76129-0001. Tel: 817-257-7830; Fax: 817-257-7304. Email: c.calabrese@tcu.edu. Web: www.catholic.tcu.edu. Rev. Charles L. Calabrese (STU).

ARLINGTON. *UTA Catholic Campus Center* 1010 Benge Dr., 76013-2643. Tel: 817-460-1155. Email: smilligan@fwdioc.org. Web: utacatholics.org. Ms. Stephanie Milligan, Dir.

University of Texas at Arlington University Catholic Community

DENTON. *University of North Texas* 1303 Eagle Dr., 76201. Tel: 940-566-0004. Email: jwolf@fwdioc.org. Ms. Janet Wolf, Campus Min.

HILLSBORO. *Hill College (United Christian Fellowship)* 2006 Brandon Rd., Box 1628, 76645. Tel: 254-580-0022. Email: director@UCCFHill.org. Web: UCFHill.org. Deacon Jim Poole, Campus Min.

WICHITA FALLS. *Catholic Campus Ministry* Midwestern State University, 3410 Louis Rodriguez Dr., 76308. Tel: 940-692-9778. Email: msuccc@yahoo.com. Ms. Debra Neely.

[M] MISCELLANEOUS

FORT WORTH. *Catholic Diocese of Fort Worth Advancement Corporation*, 800 W. Loop 820 S., 76108. Tel: 817-560-3300; Fax: 817-244-8839. Email: pflynn@fwdioc.org. Mr. Peter Flynn, Pres.

The Catholic Renewal Center of North Texas, Inc., 4503 Bridge St., 76103. Tel: 817-429-2920 (Metro); Fax: 817-492-8668. Email: crcwomen@sbcglobal.net. Ms. Gail Schatzman, Dir.

Beginning Experience

Special Days for Special People

National Marriage Encounter of North Texas

Engaged Encounter of North Texas

CRC Ministries Outreach Tel: 940-382-3594. Sisters Pat Miller, S.S.N.D., Contact Person; Kay Kolb, S.S.N.D., Contact Person.

Rachel's Vineyard Post Abortion Ministry, 800 W. Loop 820 S., 76108. Tel: 817-457-4757.

Franciscan Renewal Ministries of Texas, Inc., 1003 E. Terrell Ave., 76104. Tel: 817-332-2435; Fax: 817-334-7930. Bro. Peter Marie, C.F.R., Apostolate Dir.

Magnificat, Grapevine Chapter, Catholic Center, 800 West Loop 820 South, 76108-2919. Gloria Salerno, Coord. Tel: 214-587-3487.

RELIGIOUS INSTITUTES OF MEN REPRESENTED IN THE DIOCESE

For further details refer to the corresponding bracketed number in the Religious Institutes of Men or Women section.

[0470]—*The Capuchin Friars*—O.F.M.Cap.

[]—*Dominicans*—O.P.

[0520]—*Franciscan Friars*—O.F.M.

[]—*Franciscan Friars of the Renewal*—C.F.R.

[0585]—*Heralds of Good News*—H.G.N.

[0690]—*Jesuit Fathers and Brothers*—S.J.

[]—*Priests and Brothers of the Congregation of Mother Coredemptrix*—C.M.C.

[0420]—*Saviors of the Divine Word*—S.V.D.

[0760]—*Society of Mary (Marianists)*—S.M.

[0990]—*Society of the Catholic Apostolate*—S.A.C.

[0560]—*Third Order Regular of Saint Francis*—T.O.R.

RELIGIOUS INSTITUTES OF WOMEN REPRESENTED IN THE DIOCESE

[0100]—*Adorers of the Blood of Christ*—A.S.C.

[0420]—*Discalced Carmelite Nuns*—O.C.D.

[1115]—*Dominican Sisters of Peace*—O.P.

[1900]—*Hermanas Catequistas Guadalupanas*—H.C.G.

[]—*Hermanas Franciscanas de la Inmaculada Concepcion*—H.F.I.C.

[]—*Olivetan Benedictine Sisters*—O.S.B.

[3950]—*Sisters of Saint Mary of Namur*—S.S.M.N.

[1970]—*Sisters of the Holy Family of Nazareth*—C.S.F.N.

NECROLOGY

(No Deaths)

An asterisk (*) denotes an organization that has established tax-exempt status directly with the IRS and is not covered by the USCCB Group Ruling.

Diocese of Fresno

(Dioecesis Fresnensis)

Most Reverend

JOHN T. STEINBOCK, D.D.

Bishop of Fresno; ordained May 1, 1963; appointed Titular Bishop of Midila and Auxiliary Bishop of Orange May 29, 1984; consecrated July 14, 1984; appointed Bishop of Santa Rosa January 27, 1987; appointed Bishop of Fresno October 15, 1991. *Office: 1550 N. Fresno St., Fresno, CA 93703-3788.* Tel: 559-488-7400; Fax: 559-488-7464.

Chancery Office: 1550 N. Fresno St., Fresno, CA 93703-3788. Tel: 559-488-7400; Fax: 559-488-7464.

ESTABLISHED DECEMBER 15, 1967.

Square Miles 36,072.

Formerly Diocese of Monterey-Fresno.

Comprises the Counties of Fresno, Inyo, Kern, Kings, Madera, Mariposa, Merced and Tulare in the State of California.

Diocesan Patroness: St. Therese of the Child Jesus.

Legal titles of parishes and institutions, the Roman Catholic Bishop of Fresno, a Corporation Sole, Diocese of Fresno Education Corporation (for schools).

STATISTICAL OVERVIEW

Personnel	
Bishop	1
Priests: Diocesan Active in Diocese	83
Priests: Diocesan Active Outside Diocese	3
Priests: Retired, Sick or Absent	38
Number of Diocesan Priests	124
Religious Priests in Diocese	40
Total Priests in Diocese	164
Extern Priests in Diocese	22
Ordinations:	
Diocesan Priests	3
Religious Priests	2
Transitional Deacons	3
Permanent Deacons in Diocese	45
Total Brothers	1
Total Sisters	110
Parishes	
Parishes	88
With Resident Pastor:	
Resident Diocesan Priests	55
Resident Religious Priests	9
Without Resident Pastor:	
Administered by Priests	17
Administered by Deacons	1
Missions	43
Professional Ministry Personnel:	
Brothers	1
Sisters	23
Lay Ministers	75
Welfare	
Catholic Hospitals	3
Total Assisted	703,694
Homes for the Aged	2
Total Assisted	220
Special Centers for Social Services	6
Total Assisted	200,000
Educational	
Diocesan Students in Other Seminaries	21
Total Seminarians	21
High Schools, Diocesan and Parish	2
Total Students	1,245
Elementary Schools, Diocesan and Parish	20
Total Students	4,708
Catechesis/Religious Education:	
High School Students	8,974
Elementary Students	28,457
Total Students under Catholic Instruction	43,405
Teachers in the Diocese:	
Priests	1
Sisters	24
Lay Teachers	368
Vital Statistics	
Receptions into the Church:	
Infant Baptism Totals	21,212
Minor Baptism Totals	716
Adult Baptism Totals	455
Received into Full Communion	752
First Communions	12,263
Confirmations	5,778
Marriages:	
Catholic	1,695
Interfaith	256
Total Marriages	1,951
Deaths	3,334
Total Catholic Population	1,074,941
Total Population	2,756,266

Former Prelates of Diocese of Monterey-Fresno—Most Revs. JOHN B. MACGINLEY, D.D., ord. June 8, 1895; cons. May 10, 1910; First Bishop of Monterey-Fresno, July 31, 1924; resigned Sept. 30, 1932; died Oct. 18, 1969; PHILIP G. SCHER, ord. June 6, 1903; appt. April 28, 1933; cons. June 29, 1933; died Jan. 3, 1953; ALOYSIUS J. WILLINGER, C.Ss.R., ord. July 2, 1911; cons. Bishop of Ponce, Puerto Rico, Oct. 28, 1929; Coadjutor Bishop of Monterey/Fresno "cum jure successionis," Dec. 12, 1946; succeeded to the See, Jan. 3, 1953; resigned Oct. 25, 1967; died July 25, 1973; HARRY ANSELM CLINCH, D.D., ord. June 6, 1936; cons. Feb. 27, 1957; appt. Auxiliary to the Bishop of Monterey-Fresno, Dec. 5, 1956; transferred to the See of Monterey, Dec. 14, 1967; retired Jan. 19, 1982; died March 8, 2003.

Former Bishops of the Diocese of Fresno—His Eminence TIMOTHY CARDINAL MANNING, D.D., J.C.D., ord. June 16, 1934; appt. Titular Bishop of Lesvi and Auxiliary of Los Angeles, Aug. 3, 1946; consecrated Oct. 15, 1946; installed as First Bishop of Fresno, Dec. 15, 1967; elevated to Coadjutor Archbishop of Los Angeles "cum jure successionis," May 26, 1969; succeeded to the See, Jan. 21, 1970; created Cardinal, March 5, 1973; died June 23, 1989; Most Rev. HUGH A. DONOHOE, D.D., Ph.D., ord. June 14, 1930; appt. Auxiliary in San Francisco, Aug. 2, 1947; consecrated Oct. 7, 1947; appt. Bishop of Stockton, Feb. 21, 1962; appt. Second Bishop of Fresno, Aug. 28, 1969; resigned July 1, 1980; died Oct. 26, 1987; His Eminence ROGER CARDINAL MAHONY, D.D., ord. May 1, 1962; appt. Auxiliary Bishop of Fresno, Jan. 7, 1975; ord. Bishop, March 19, 1975; transferred to Diocese of Stockton, Feb. 26, 1980; installed April 17, 1980; appt. Archbishop of Los Angeles, July 16, 1985; installed Sept. 5, 1985; created Cardinal, June 28, 1991; Most Rev. JOSEPH J. MADERA, M.Sp.S., D.D., ord. June 15, 1957; consecrated March 4, 1980; succeeded to the See on July 1, 1980; transferred to Archdiocese for the Military Services, Washington, DC May 28, 1991; retired 2004.

Vicar General and Moderator of the Curia—Rev. Msgr. MYRON J. COTTA, V.G.

Chancellor—Deacon JESSE J. AVILA. Email: javila@dioceseoffresno.org.

Chancery Office—1550 N. Fresno St., Fresno, 93703-3788. Tel: 559-488-7400; Fax: 559-488-7464. Web: www.dioceseoffresno.org.

Diocesan Tribunal—1550 N. Fresno St., Fresno, 93703-3788. Tel: 559-488-7490; Fax: 559-488-7498. Email: tribunal@dioceseoffresno.org.

Judicial Vicar—Rev. MICHAEL A. BURCHFIELD, J.C.L.

Adjutant Judicial Vicar—VACANT.

Tribunal Director—NANCY S. STEVENS, J.C.L. Email: nstevens@dioceseoffresno.org.

Tribunal Judges—Rev. MICHAEL A. BURCHFIELD, J.C.L.; NANCY S. STEVENS, J.C.L.

Assessor & Tribunal Bilingual Auditor—PATRICIA RUIZ. Tel: 559-488-7425. Email: pruiz@dioceseoffresno.org.

Tribunal Secretaries—ESTELA MANZANO. Email: estela@dioceseoffresno.org; HORTENSIA RUBIO. Email: hrubio@dioceseoffresno.org; ADELINA GAMEZ. Email: lina@dioceseoffresno.org.

Ecclesiastical Notaries—ADELINA GAMEZ; ESTELA MANZANO; HORTENSIA RUBIO; Rev. THOMAS TIMMINGS; Rev. Msgr. PERRY KAVOOKJIAN; MARIA ALANIS FLORES.

Defenders of the Bond—Rev. Msgrs. MICHAEL BRAUN; PATRICK JOSEPH MCCORMICK.

Advocates—Rev. Msgrs. JOHN ESQUIVEL, V.F.; JOHN GRIESBACH; RICHARD URIZALQUI.

Promoter of Justice—NANCY S. STEVENS, J.C.L.

Diocesan Consultors—Rev. Msgrs. JOHN ESQUIVEL, V.F.; RAYMOND C. DREILING, V.F.; RAUL SANCHEZ, V.U.; CRAIG F. HARRISON, V.F.; HARVEY FONSECA, V.F.; MYRON J. COTTA, V.G.; E. JAMES PETERSEN (Retired).

Vicar Urbanis—Rev. Msgr. RAUL SANCHEZ, V.U.

Vicars Forane—Rev. Msgrs. CRAIG F. HARRISON, V.F.; RAYMOND C. DREILING, V.F.; HARVEY FONSECA, V.F.; JOHN ESQUIVEL, V.F.

Diocesan Offices and Directors

Catechetical Ministries—MADELINE LOIACONO, Coord.

Catholic Charities—CATHERINE MANFREDO, Exec. Dir., 149 N. Fulton, Fresno, 93701. Tel: 559-237-0851; Fax: 559-237-7050.

Channel 49 (KNXT)—COLIN DOUGHERTY, Gen. Mgr., 1550 N. Fresno St., Fresno, 93703-3788. Tel: 559-488-7400; Fax: 559-488-7444.

Cursillo Movement—

English—Deacon LEONARD RODRIGUEZ, Mailing Address: 1742 N. 10th Ave., Hanford, 93230. Tel: 559-582-6471.

Spanish—Deacon JIM NUNEZ, 1650 18th Ave., Kingsburg, 93631. Tel: 559-897-8130.

Development Director—GILBERT J. HARO.

Diocese of Fresno Education Corporation—1550 N. Fresno St., Fresno, 93703-3788. Tel: 559-488-7414.

Diocesan Newspaper— "Central California Catholic Life" Deacon JESSE J. AVILA, Exec. Editor. Email: javila@dioceseoffresno.org; PHILIP G. TORREZ, Mng. Editor, 1550 N. Fresno St., Fresno, 93703-3788. Tel: 559-488-7400; Fax: 559-493-2880. Email: cccl@dioceseoffresno.org.

Finance Committee—Rev. Msgrs. MYRON J. COTTA, V.G., 1550 N. Fresno St., Fresno, 93703-3788. Tel: 559-488-7400; MICHAEL BRAUN; LEROY GILSDORF; GARY BETHKE, CPA; LARRY STEFANI; GARY RENNER; GARY MARSELLA.

Deposit and Loan Fund—Rev. Msgr. MICHAEL BRAUN; JOSEPH ZIEMANN; JAMES F. SWEENEY; ROSEMARY MCCAVE; GARY BETHKE, CPA.

Detention Ministry—CLAUDE A. MUNCEY, 1550 N. Fresno St., Fresno, 93703-3788. Tel: 559-488-7474; Fax: 559-493-2847.

Holy Childhood Association—Rev. Msgr. MYRON J. COTTA, V.G., Dir., 1550 N. Fresno St., Fresno, 93703-3788. Tel: 559-488-7400; Fax: 559-488-7464.

Italian Catholic Federation—NETTIE DESCALSO, Pres. Tel: 209-383-4819.

Legion of Mary—Sr. LAURENCE MARIE DIAZ, O.P., Spiritual Dir.; CYNTHIA LAGRAFF, Pres. Tel: 559-673-2336.

Federacion Mariana de Guadalupe—Rev. Msgr. DANIEL LOPEZ, Diocesan Chap., 2441 Dockery Ave., Selma, 93662. Tel: 559-896-1052.

Newman Apostolate—Deacon JOHN SUPINO, Parish Life Coord., St. Paul Newman Center, 1572 E. Barstow Ave., Fresno, 93710. Tel: 559-436-3434.

Office of Catholic Education—RICHARD SEXTON, Supt., 1510 N. Fresno St., Fresno, 93703-3711. Tel: 559-488-7420; Fax: 559-488-7422; Sr. MARY JEAN WILLIAMS, O.P., Asst. Supt.

Diocesan Advisory Board of Education—DEBORAH LEARY, Pres., 1510 N. Fresno St., Fresno, 93703-3711. Tel: 559-488-7420; Fax: 559-488-7422.

Property/Construction Management—DOUGLAS DURIVAGE, 1550 N. Fresno St., Fresno, 93703-3788. Tel: 559-493-2872.

Office of Finances—GARY BETHKE, CPA, Fiscal Mgr., 1550 N. Fresno St., Fresno, 93703-3788. Tel: 559-488-7426; Fax: 559-488-7461.

Office of Human Resources—KATHLEEN ANDREWS, Dir. Human Resources, 1550 N. Fresno St., Fresno, 93703-3788. Tel: 559-488-7488.

Office of Ministries—PATRICIA JIMENEZ, Dir.; PAUL MENTLEWSKI, Admin. Asst., 1550 N. Fresno St., Fresno, 93703-3788. Tel: 559-488-7474.

Multicultural and Campesino Ministry (Spanish)—Rev. MICHAEL MCANDREW, C.SS.R.

Family Life Ministry—Sr. JOANNE BAUER, C.S.C., Coord.

School of Ministry—Rev. DAVID J. NORRIS, D.Min., Dir., 1550 N. Fresno St., Fresno, 93703-3788. Tel: 559-493-2871.

Youth Ministry—ALEJANDRO BARRAZA, Coord.

Worship and Evangelization—Rev. JEAN-MICHAEL LASTIRI, Dir., 1550 N. Fresno St., Fresno, 93703-3788. Tel: 559-642-3452; Fax: 559-642-4655.

Ecumenical Affairs—Rev. GREGORY J. BEAUMONT, Mailing Address: P.O. Box 798, Kingsburg, 93631. Tel: 559-897-5953.

Master of Ceremonies—Rev. Msgr. PATRICK JOSEPH MCCORMICK, Mailing Address: 671 E. Yosemite, Merced, 95340. Tel: 209-383-9261; Fax: 209-383-6796.

St. Anthony Retreat Center—Co Directors: Rev. Msgr. JOHN GRIESBACH; Sr. DANIELLE WITT, S.S.N.D., Mailing Address: P.O. Box 249, Three Rivers, 93271. Tel: 559-561-4595. Web: www.stanthonyretreat.org.

Permanent Diaconate Office—Deacons EDWARD HARMON, Dir.; CHARLES REYBURN, 1550 N. Fresno St., Fresno, 93703-3788. Tel: 559-493-2840.

Personnel Board—Rev. Msgrs. PERRY KAVOOKJIAN; ROBERT D. WENZINGER; JOHN ESQUIVEL, V.F.; E. JAMES PETERSEN (Retired); MYRON J. COTTA, V.G.; RAUL SANCHEZ, V.U.; RAYMOND C. DREILING, V.F.; CRAIG F. HARRISON, V.F.; PATRICK MCCORMICK, V.F.

Priests' Council—Rev. Msgrs. MYRON J. COTTA, V.G.; RAUL SANCHEZ, V.U.; CRAIG F. HARRISON, V.F.; HARVEY FONSECA, V.F.; RICHARD URIZALQUI; Rev. SALVADOR GONZALEZ JR.; Rev. Msgrs. RAYMOND C. DREILING, V.F.; JAMES T. LOGAN (Retired); Revs. JOHN SCHMOLL; EFRAIN MARTINEZ; JEAN-MICHAEL LASTIRI; Deacon JESSE J. AVILA; Rev. Msgr. JOHN ESQUIVEL, V.F.; Rev. GABRIEL RUIZ, C.M.F.

The Society for the Propagation of the Faith/The Society of St. Peter Apostle—Rev. Msgr. MYRON J. COTTA, V.G., 1550 N. Fresno St., Fresno, 93703-3788. Tel: 559-488-7400.

Scouting—Rev. GERALD NORTHRUP, S.F.O., Chap., Sequoia Council (Retired), P.O. Box 410, Bass Lake, 93604.

Vicar for Priests—Rev. Msgr. MYRON J. COTTA, V.G., 1550 N. Fresno St., Fresno, 93703-3788. Tel: 559-488-7400; Fax: 559-488-7464.

Continuing Formation of Priests—Rev. Msgr. MYRON J. COTTA, V.G., 1550 N. Fresno St., Fresno, 93703-3788. Tel: 559-488-7400; Fax: 559-488-7464.

Vicar for Religious—Sr. CLARA ANN BUDENZ, O.P., 1550 N. Fresno St., Fresno, 93703-3788. Tel: 559-493-2882; Fax: 559-488-7464.

Safe Environment/Victim Assistance—TERESA DOMINGUEZ, Mgr., 1550 N. Fresno St., Fresno, 93703-3788. Tel: 559-584-4349; Fax: 559-584-2592. Email: tadominguez@sbcglobal.net; Mailing Address: P.O. Box 1306, Hanford, 93232-1306.

Vocations—Rev. SALVADOR GONZALEZ JR., Dir., 1550 N. Fresno St., Fresno, 93703-3788. Tel: 559-488-7478; Fax: 559-488-7475.

CLERGY, PARISHES, MISSIONS AND PAROCHIAL SCHOOLS

CITY OF FRESNO

(FRESNO COUNTY)

1—ST. JOHN CATHEDRAL (1882) Rev. Msgr. Raul Sanchez, Rector; Rev. Guillermo Preciado; Deacon Salvador de la Torre.
Res.: 2814 Mariposa St., 93721. Tel: 559-485-6210; Fax: 559-485-8409.
Catechesis/Religious Program—Tel: 559-485-0161. Students 911.
Mission—St. Francis 1046 S. 9th St., Fresno Co. 93702. Tel: 559-485-9467; Fax: 559-485-8548. Rev. Joseph Nguyen, (Vietnamese Ministry).

2—ST. ALPHONSUS (1908) Revs. Dominic Savio Rajappa; Jim Torrens, S.J.
351 E. Kearney Blvd., 93706. Tel: 559-233-8275; Fax: 559-233-9379. Email: stalphonsus_church@yahoo.com.
Catechesis/Religious Program—Email: stalphonsus_church@yahoo.com. Students 85.

3—ST. ANTHONY CLARET (Calwa Area) (1952) Revs. Gabriel Ruiz, C.M.F.; Albert Vazquez, C.M.F., Parochial Vicar; Ralph Berg, C.M.F., Parochial Vicar.
Res.: 2494 S. Chestnut Ave., 93725. Tel: 559-255-4260; Fax: 559-255-6329.
Catechesis/Religious Program—Tel: 559-255-0223.
Mission—Christ the King 3565 Calvin St., Malaga, Fresno Co. 93725. Fax: 559-255-6329.

4—ST. ANTHONY OF PADUA (1953) Rev. Msgr. Robert D. Wenzinger; Revs. Loren Blessing; Ricardo Magdaleno, Parochial Vicar, Chap., Fresno Heart Hospital & Children's Hospital; Rev. Msgr. Laserian Byrne (Retired); Deacon Edward C. Valdez.
Office: 5770 N. Maroa Ave., 93704-2038. Tel: 559-439-0124; Fax: 559-439-3050. Web: www.stanthonyfresno.org.
School—(Grades K-8), 5680 N. Maroa Ave., 93704-2038. Tel: 559-435-0700; Fax: 559-435-6749. Web: www.sasfresno.com. Mr. Tim McConnico, Prin.; Thomas Neumeier, Vice Prin.; Mrs. Maryclaire Polacek, Librarian. Lay Teachers 24; Students 615.
Catechesis/Religious Program—5770 N. Maroa St., 93704. Tel: 559-439-0124. Students 1,000.
Mission—St. Agnes 111 W. Birch, Pinedale, Fresno Co. 93650. Tel: 559-439-2100; Fax: 559-439-0248.

5—ST. GENEVIEVE (1941) [CEM] Rev. Victor T. Dinh.
Church: 1127 Tulare St., 93706. Tel: 559-486-2988; Fax: 559-442-4318.
Catechesis/Religious Program—Email: stgenevieve@yahoo.com. Students 40.

6—ST. HELEN (1955) Revs. Salvador Gonzalez Jr.; John Nelliparambil, Parochial Vicar; Deacon Jesse J. Avila.
Office: 4870 E. Belmont, 93727. Tel: 559-255-3871; Fax: 559-255-7625. Email: office.sthelens@sbcglobal.net.
School—(Grades K-8), 4888 E. Belmont, 93727. Tel: 559-251-5855; Fax: 559-251-5948. Dr. Toni Amodio, Prin. Lay Teachers 13; Students 295.
Junior Kindergarten—Monica Kay, Dir.
Catechesis/Religious Program—4875 E. Grant, 93727. Students 271.

7—HOLY SPIRIT (1981) Rev. Eric Swearingen; Sharon Tellifson, Business Mgr.
355 E. Champlain Dr., 93720-1273. Tel: 559-434-7701; Fax: 559-434-7734. Email: holyspiritchurchfresno@yahoo.com. Web: www.holyspiritfresno.catholicweb.com.
Catechesis/Religious Program—Tel: 559-434-3522. Email: tafolla4@hotmail.com. Tomas Tafolla, D.R.E. Students 610.
Life Teen—Tel: 559-434-7708. Email: holyspirityouthminister@yahoo.com. Web: www.holyspiritlifeteen.catholicweb.com. Martha Perry, Youth Min. Tel: 559-434-7708.
Mission—Infant Jesus of Prague 32054 Whispering Spring Rd., Tollhouse, Fresno Co. 93667. Tel: 559-855-4659; Fax: 559-855-4659. Mailing Address: P.O. Box 357, Prather, 93651.
Station—Shaver Lake Comm. Chapel 41340 Tollhouse Rd., Shaver Lake, 93634.

8—ST. MARY QUEEN OF APOSTLES CATHOLIC CHURCH (1967) [CEM] Rev. Timothy N. Cardoza.
Res.: 4636 W. Dakota, 93722. Tel: 559-275-2022; Fax: 559-275-2040. Email: stmarysfresno@sbcglobal.net.
Catechesis/Religious Program—Tel: 559-271-1459. Students 480.

9—OUR LADY OF MT. CARMEL (1955) Rev. Joaquin S. Arriaga.
Office: 816 Pottle Ave., 93706. Tel: 559-264-2587; Fax: 559-264-2539. Email: olmcfresno@gmail.com.
Catechesis/Religious Program—Students 209.

10—OUR LADY OF VICTORY (1950) Rev. Msgr. John Moreton; Deacon Nai Her.
Parish Center & Rectory: 2850 N. Crystal Ave., 93705. Tel: 559-226-1163; Fax: 559-226-2093. Email: olvchurch@gmail.com.
Church: 2838 N. West Ave., 93705.
School—(Grades PreSchool-8), 1626 W. Princeton Ave., 93705. Tel: 559-229-0205; Fax: 559-229-3230. Email: olvoffice@fresnoolv.org. Web: www.fresnoolv.org. Mrs. Deborah Nettell, Prin. Lay Teachers 11; Students 178.
Catechesis/Religious Program—Students 300.

11—ST. PAUL NEWMAN CENTER (1964) Rev. David J. Norris; Deacon John Supino, Parish Life Coord.
California State University: 1572 E. Barstow Ave., 93710. Tel: 559-436-3434; Fax: 559-436-3430. Web: www.csufnewman.com.
Catechesis/Religious Program—Students 188.

12—SACRED HEART (1947) Rev. Alejandro Ignacio.
Res.: 2140 N. Cedar Ave., 93703. Tel: 559-237-4121; Fax: 559-237-0122. Email: sacredheartfresno@att.net. Web: shfresno.org.
School—(Grades K-8), 4460 E. Yale, 93703. Tel: 559-251-3171; Fax: 559-251-7778. Web: www.shsfresno.net. Sr. Kathleen Drilling, S.S.N.D., Prin. Lay Teachers 11; Students 135.
Catechesis/Religious Program—Fax: 559-237-4121. Students 190.

13—SHRINE OF ST. THERESE (1925) Revs. Michael Burchfield; Flordito Redulla, S.V.D.
Mailing & Res.: 855 E. Floradora Ave., 93728. Tel: 559-268-6388; Fax: 559-268-0852.
Catechesis/Religious Program—Email: religioused@shrineofsttherese.com. Students 288.

OUTSIDE THE CITY OF FRESNO

ARVIN, KERN CO., ST. THOMAS THE APOSTLE (1941) Rev. Jorge de la Torre.
Res.: 350 E. Bear Mountain Blvd., 93203. Tel: 661-854-6150; Fax: 661-854-2564.
Catechesis/Religious Program—Students 300.

ATWATER, MERCED CO., ST. ANTHONY (1909) Rev. Thomas Timmings; Deacon Albert Montejano.
Office: 1799 Winton Way, 95301. Tel: 209-358-5743; Fax: 209-358-2423.
Res.: 1999 Juniper Ave., 95301.
School—(Grades PreK-8), 1801 Winton Way, 95301. Tel: 209-358-3341. Dianne Silva, Prin.; Susie Henriques, Librarian. Lay Teachers 8; Students 170.
Preschool—Tel: 209-358-3341. Debbie Flores, Dir.
Catechesis/Religious Program—Tel: 209-357-3259. Susie Ramirez, D.R.E. Students 869.
Mission—Immaculate Conception 1799 Winton Way, Buhach, Merced Co. 95301.

AVENAL, KINGS CO., ST. JOSEPH (1941) Revs. Raul Silva; Juan Pineda Lira, M.S.C.
Res.: 428 E. Kern St., 93204. Tel: 559-386-9523; Fax: 559-386-1068. Email: st.josephsparish@yahoo.com.
Catechesis/Religious Program—Students 382.
Mission—St. Cecilia Milham & 8th St., Kettleman City, Kings Co. 93239.

BAKERSFIELD, KERN CO.

1—CHRIST THE KING (1952) Rev. Msgr. Stephen A. Frost; Deacon David Rodriguez.
Res.: 1800 Bedford Way, 93308. Tel: 661-391-4640; Fax: 661-391-4649.
Catechesis/Religious Program—Tel: 661-399-1956. Students 331.

2—ST. ELIZABETH ANN SETON Rev. Msgr. Perry Kavookjian; Deacons David Rodriguez; Nicholas Amicone.
Church: 12803 Montbatten Pl., 93312-6799. Tel: 661-587-3626; Fax: 661-587-3844. Email: pkavookjian@setoncatholicchurch.org. Web: www.setoncatholicchurch.org.
Catechesis/Religious Program—Students 203.

3—ST. FRANCIS OF ASSISI (1881) Rev. Msgr. Craig F. Harrison.
Res.: 900 H St., 93304. Tel: 661-327-4734; Fax: 661-327-4930. Email: jjacobs@stfran.org. Web: stfran.org.
School—(Grades PreK-8), 2516 Palm St., 93304. Tel: 661-326-7955; Fax: 661-327-0395. Email: stfran@inreach.com. Cynthia Meek, Prin. Lay Teachers 33; Students 499.
Day Care/Preschool—Tel: 661-326-7958. Mary Johnson, Dir. Students 92.
Catechesis/Religious Program—Tel: 661-323-8800. Alice Fry, D.R.E. Students 1,194.

4—ST. JOSEPH (1907) Revs. Miguel Flores; Anthony Iromenu, Parochial Vicar.
Mailing Address: 1515 Baker St, 93305.
Res.: 2701 Panorama Dr., 93306. Tel: 661-327-2744; Fax: 661-327-0133.
Catechesis/Religious Program—Tel: 661-325-2581. Students 1,490.

5—OUR LADY OF GUADALUPE (1925) Revs. Larry Toschi, O.S.J.; Chummar Chirayath, O.S.J.; Steve Peterson, O.S.J.; Matthew Spencer, O.S.J., Parochial Vicar.
Res.: 601 E. California Ave., 93307. Tel: 661-323-3148; Fax: 661-323-6016.
School—(Grades PreK-8), 609 E. California Ave.,

93307. Tel: 661-323-6059. Sr. Eva Lujano, S.J.S., Prin. Sisters 4; Lay Teachers 8; Students 153.
Catechesis/Religious Program—Tel: 661-323-7642. Sofia Mendez, D.R.E. Students 628.
Mission—Holy Spirit 720 E. Belle Terrace, Kern Co. 93307. Tel: 661-834-7095.
Mission—St. Jude 825 Chapman, Kern Co. 93307. Tel: 661-323-2347.

6—OUR LADY OF PERPETUAL HELP (1948) Rev. Msgr. Michael Braun.
Res.: 124 Columbus St., 93305. Tel: 661-323-3108; Fax: 661-325-7067. Email: olphbaker@aol.com. Web: olphbakersfield.org.
School—(Grades PreSchool-8) Tel: 661-327-7741. Email: dsmith@olph1.com. Web: olph1.com. Donna Smith, Prin. Lay Teachers 20; Students 340.
Catechesis/Religious Program—Tel: 661-322-7200. Students 223.

7—ST. PHILIP THE APOSTLE (1968) Rev. Msgr. Ronald J. Swett; Rev. Ivan Hernandez, Parochial Vicar; Deacons John Monsma; Michael Richard.
Mailing Address: 7100 Stockdale Hwy., 93309-1399. Tel: 661-834-7483; Fax: 661-834-2214. Web: stphilipchurch.org.
Preschool—Mrs. Karen Cerri, Dir.
Catechesis/Religious Program—Diana Akroush, D.R.E. Students 1,190.

8—SACRED HEART (1952) Rev. Dan Coyle.
Res.: 9915 Ramos St., 93307. Tel: 661-831-8905; Fax: 661-837-8075. Web: sacredheartbfl.org.
Catechesis/Religious Program—Tel: 661-831-6223; Fax: 661-837-8073. Students 253.

9—SAN CLEMENTE MISSION PARISH Rev. Joachim Cheon.
1305 Water St., Kern Co. 93305. Tel: 661-871-9190; Fax: 661-873-7286.
Catechesis/Religious Program—Students 1,189.

BISHOP, INYO CO., OUR LADY OF PERPETUAL HELP (1947) Rev. John Gracey.
Res.: 849 N. Home St., 93514. Tel: 760-872-7231; Fax: 760-873-8862. Email: olph2@verizon.net. Web: olphbishop.com.
Catechesis/Religious Program—Tel: 760-873-8862. Email: davidbruce.olph@verizon.net. Students 169.
Mission—St. Stephen 461 S. Main St., Big Pine, Inyo Co. 93513. Tel: 760-872-7231.

BUTTONWILLOW, KERN CO., ST. MARY (1941) Rev. Gilbert Chacon, S.J.
Res.: 420 N. Main St., Box 875, 93206. Tel: 661-764-5486.
Catechesis/Religious Program—Students 55.

CALIFORNIA CITY, KERN CO., OUR LADY OF LOURDES (1982) Rev. Kris Sorenson.
Catechesis/Religious Program—Students 36.
Mission—St. Joseph (1969) P.O. Box 2060, Kern Co. 93504.

CHOWCHILLA, MADERA CO., ST. COLUMBA (1921) [JC] Rev. Angel Sotelo.
Res.: 213 Orange Ave., 93610. Tel: 559-665-3376.
Catechesis/Religious Program—Tel: 559-665-5104. Students 340.
Mission—St. George El Nido, 95317.

CLOVIS, FRESNO CO., OUR LADY OF PERPETUAL HELP (1929) Revs. Robert Borges; Adrian Kim, C.P., Parochial Vicar; Craig Plunkett, Parochial Vicar; Deacon Gary Stevens.
Res.: 929 Harvard Ave., 93612. Tel: 559-299-4270; Fax: 559-299-7126. Web: olphclovis.org.
Church: Ninth & DeWitt, 93612.
School—(Grades K-8), 886 DeWitt, 93612. Tel: 559-299-7504; Fax: 559-299-4627. Web: olphschool.net. Kimberly Cochran, Prin. Immaculate Conception Sisters 3; Lay Teachers 7; Students 206.
Catechesis/Religious Program—(Grades K-8) Students 881.

COALINGA, FRESNO CO., ST. PAUL THE APOSTLE (1907) [JC] Rev. Viktor Perez, O.F.M.Conv.; Bro. Andres Amador, O.F.M.Conv.
Res.: 637 Sunset St., P.O. Box 812, 93210. Tel: 559-935-1872; Fax: 559-935-3763.
Catechesis/Religious Program—Students 136.

CORCORAN, KINGS CO., OUR LADY OF LOURDES (1939) Rev. Alfredo Arias.
Res.: 1404 Hanna, 93212. Tel: 559-992-4414; Fax: 559-992-2512. Email: ourladyoflourdescorcoran@comcast.net.
Catechesis/Religious Program—Tel: 559-992-4698. Students 525.
Mission—Sacred Heart 3860 Ave. 54, Alpaugh, Tulare Co. 93201. Tel: 559-949-8352.

CUTLER, TULARE CO., ST. MARY (1953) Rev. Israel Avila.
Res.: 12588 Avenue 407, 93615. Tel: 559-528-3566.
Catechesis/Religious Program—Tel: 559-528-3077; Fax: 559-528-3535. Students 370.

DEL REY, FRESNO CO., ST. KATHERINE (1956), (Quasi-parish included with St. Mary, Sanger). Revs. Jupeter Quinto, R.C.J.; Philip Puntrello, R.C.J., Parochial Vicar; Renato Panlasigui, R.C.J.; Deacon John Biedermann.
Res.: 828 "O" St., P.O. Box 335, Sanger, 93657. Tel: 559-888-2889; 559-875-2025; Fax: 559-875-2618. Email: stmarysanger@msn.com.
Catechesis/Religious Program—Students 41.

DELANO, KERN CO.

1—ST. MARY OF THE MIRACULOUS MEDAL (1920) Rev. Rick Fierros.
Res.: 916 Lexington St., 93215. Tel: 661-725-8456; Fax: 661-725-8485.
Catechesis/Religious Program—Tel: 661-725-9041. Students 641.
Mission—St. Vincent 1732 11th Ave., Richgrove, Tulare Co. 93215.

2—OUR LADY OF GUADALUPE (1954) Revs. Javier Alvarez, O.F.M.; Ervan Beers, O.F.M.
Res.: 1015 Clinton St., 93215. Tel: 661-725-9087; 661-725-9115; Fax: 661-725-7129.
Catechesis/Religious Program—Tel: 661-725-2777. Students 560.

DINUBA, TULARE CO., ST. CATHERINE OF SIENA (1948) Rev. Raul Diaz.
Res.: 356 N. Villa Ave., 93618. Tel: 559-591-0931; Fax: 559-591-2965.
Catechesis/Religious Program—Tel: 559-591-2988. Tomi Castilleja, D.R.E. Students 669.

DOS PALOS, MERCED CO., SACRED HEART (1924) Rev. Robert R. Vanoncini; Deacon David Mumby.
Res.: 1650 Lucerne, 93620-2623. Tel: 209-392-2724; Fax: 209-392-1037. Email: sacredheartchurch1655@comcast.net.
Catechesis/Religious Program—Students 500.

EARLIMART, TULARE CO., ST. JUDE THADDEUS (1968) Rev. Pastor Hermosillo Lomeli, M.S.C.
Mailing Address: 1270 E. Washington Ave., P.O. Box 12187, 93219. Tel: 661-849-3170; Fax: 661-849-0704.
Res.: 964 Dove St., 93219. Tel: 661-849-2858.
Catechesis/Religious Program—Students 195.

EASTON , FRESNO CO., ST. JUDE (1967) Rev. Jerry Amerando.
208 W. Jefferson, 93706. Tel: 559-485-3870; Fax: 559-485-3880. Email: stjudechurch@attitude.com.
Catechesis/Religious Program—Students 268.
Mission—Our Lady of the Assumption 13540 S. Henderson Ave., Caruthers, Fresno Co. 93609. Tel: 559-864-8224; Fax: 559-864-3656. P.O. Box 388, Caruthers, 93609-0388.

EXETER, TULARE CO., SACRED HEART (1950) Rev. Juan Manuel Flores.
Res.: 417 North E St., 93221. Tel: 559-592-2465; Fax: 559-592-6075.
Catechesis/Religious Program—Tel: 559-592-1020. Students 667.
Mission—St. Anthony of Egypt 521 W. Visalia Rd., Farmersville, Tulare Co. 93223. Tel: 559-747-0234 (Religious Educ. Office).

FIREBAUGH, FRESNO CO., ST. JOSEPH (1950) Rev. Efrain Martinez.
Res.: 1900 Saipan, 93622. Tel: 559-659-2225; Fax: 559-659-0408.
Church: 1558 12th St., 93622.
Catechesis/Religious Program—Tel: 559-659-2943. Students 292.

FOWLER, FRESNO CO., ST. LUCY 1st Church (1943); 2nd Church (1965) Rev. William Paiz, C.M.F.
Res.: 512 S. 5th, 93625. Tel: 559-834-2624; Fax: 559-834-6814. Email: stlucyparish@hotmail.com.
Catechesis/Religious Program—Students 126.

FRAZIER PARK, KERN CO., OUR LADY OF THE SNOWS MISSION (1968), (Quasi-parish) Rev. Thomas O'Neill. 7115 Lakewood Dr. Lake of the Woods, 93225. Tel: 661-245-3741; Fax: 661-245-1680.
Catechesis/Religious Program—Students 33.

GOSHEN, TULARE CO., ST. THOMAS THE APOSTLE (1963) [CEM] Rev. Msgr. Raymond C. Dreiling; Revs. Rod L. Craig; David Bustamante; Daniel C. Avila; John Bosco Prasit Kruesuwan; Deacons Julian Ponce; Paul Hernandez; James Rooney.
Mailing Address: P.O. Box 287, Visalia, 93279.
Res.: 6735 Ave. 308, 93227. P.O. Box 287, Visalia, 93279. Tel: 559-734-9522; Fax: 559-734-3435.
Catechesis/Religious Program—Students 130.

GUSTINE, MERCED CO., SHRINE OF OUR LADY OF MIRACLES (1919) Rev. Leonard J. Trindade.
Res.: 370 Linden Ave., 95322. Tel: 209-854-6692; Fax: 209-854-1344.
School—(Grades PreK-8) Tel: 209-854-3180; Fax: 209-854-3961. Adrienne Lopes, Co-Admin.; Barbara Dompe, Co-Admin. Lay Teachers 8; Students 120.
Preschool—Tel: 209-854-3180. Terri Amarante, Dir. Students 45.
Catechesis/Religious Program—Tel: 209-854-2834. Karen Souza, D.R.E. Students 300.

HANFORD, KINGS CO.

1—ST. BRIGID (1886) [CEM] Revs. Michael Moore; Julian Policetti (India); Deacon Anthony Silveira.
Office & Mailing Address: 200 E. Florinda, 93230. Tel: 559-582-2533; Fax: 559-582-9193. Email: stbrigid@sierratel.com.
School—St. Rose-McCarthy Memorial School, (Grades K-8), 1000 N. Harris St., 93230. Tel: 559-584-5218; Fax: 559-584-0899. Web: www-.strosemccarthy.org. Jim Carpenter, Prin. Religious Teachers 2; Lay Teachers 8; Students 149.
Catechesis/Religious Program—Tel: 559-583-6563; Fax: 559-582-9193. Students 410.

2—IMMACULATE HEART OF MARY (1948) Rev. Stephen M. Devine.
Res.: 10355 Hanford Armona Rd., 93230. Tel: 559-584-8576; Fax: 559-584-0436.
Catechesis/Religious Program—Tel: 559-582-5688. Students 364.

HILMAR, MERCED CO., HOLY ROSARY (1948) Rev. Hilary Silva.
Res.: 8471 Cypress, P.O. Box 429, 95324. Tel: 209-667-8961; Fax: 209-667-5239.
Catechesis/Religious Program—Tel: 209-632-7163. Students 300.
Mission—St. Mary 2809 Railroad, Stevinson, Merced Co. 95374.

HURON, FRESNO CO., ST. FRANCES CABRINI (1961) Revs. Juan Pineda Lira, M.S.C.; Raul Silva Arredondo.
Res.: 36986 Los Angeles St., P.O. Box 939, 93234. Tel: 559-945-2507; Fax: 559-945-2630. Email: s.cabrini@att.net.
Catechesis/Religious Program—Students 163.

KERMAN, FRESNO CO., ST. PATRICK (1953) Revs. David Reed; Marcelinus Okenedo, S.M.M.M.
Mailing Address: 567 S. 6th St., P.O. Box 375, 93630. Tel: 559-846-8190; Fax: 559-846-7705.
Res.: 567 S. Sixth St., 93630.
Catechesis/Religious Program—Students 420.

KINGSBURG, FRESNO CO., HOLY FAMILY (1950) [JC] Rev. Gregory J. Beaumont.
Res.: 1301 Smith St., P.O. Box 798, 93631-0798. Tel: 559-897-5953; Fax: 559-897-8599.
Church: 1700 Lewis St., 93631.
Catechesis/Religious Program—Students 271.
Mission—Santa Cruz 5626 Ave. 378, London, Tulare Co. 93631.
Mission—St. John the Baptist Educational Center 4204 Merritt Dr., Traver, Tulare Co. 93673.

LAMONT, KERN CO., ST. AUGUSTINE (1962) Rev. John Schmoll, O.S.B. oblate.
Res.: 10601 Myrtle Ave., 93241-2111. Tel: 661-845-0003; Fax: 661-845-0259.
Catechesis/Religious Program—Tel: 661-845-3622. Students 1,090.

LATON, FRESNO CO., SHRINE OF OUR LADY OF FATIMA (1953) Rev. Richard Smith; Deacon Jesus Hernandez.
Res.: P.O. Box 119, 93242. Tel: 559-923-4935; Fax: 559-923-2284.
Catechesis/Religious Program—Tel: 559-923-3715. Students 205.

LEMOORE, KINGS CO., ST. PETER PRINCE OF APOSTLES (1912) Rev. Msgr. John Coelho-Harguindeguy; Rev. Jojappa (Joseph) Bandanadam; Deacon Joseph Biangone.
19 Follett St., 93245. Tel: 559-924-2562; Fax: 559-924-5727. Email: stpeters@lemoorenet.net.
Res.: 951 Murphy Dr., 93245.
School—(Grades K-8), 884 N. Lemoore Ave., 93245. Tel: 559-924-3424; Fax: 559-924-7848. Email: miqprince@lemoorenet.com. Web: miqschool.com. Sr. Tessy Pius, C.S.S.T., Prin. Carmelite Sisters of St. Teresa 5; Lay Teachers 6; Students 237.
Catechesis/Religious Program—Tel: 559-924-2826. Shirley Roberts, D.R.E. Students 500.
Mission—St. Joseph, Kings Co. 93245.
Mission—Santa Rosa [CEM] 16111 Alkaki, Tache Indian Reservation, Kings Co. 93245.

LINDSAY, TULARE CO., SACRED HEART (1925) Rev. Kenneth Bozzo.
Res.: 217 Lindero Ave., 93247-2623. Tel: 559-562-4008; Fax: 559-562-5511. Email: sacredheartlindsay@verizon.net.
Catechesis/Religious Program—Tel: 559-562-2295. Students 510.
Mission—St. Anthony Church 21631 Brooks Ave., Tonyville, Tulare Co. 93247.
Mission—St. James Catholic Church 19752 Guthrie Rd., P.O. Box 4010, Strathmore, Tulare Co. 93267. Tel: 559-568-0435.
Station—Plainview, Santa Cruz Plainview.

LIVINGSTON, MERCED CO., ST. JUDE THADDEUS (1937) Rev. Msgr. Harvey Fonseca.
Office: 330 Franci St., 95334. Tel: 209-394-7512; Fax: 209-394-3089.
Catechesis/Religious Program—Tel: 209-394-7516. Rosa Maria Alejandre, D.R.E. Students 648.
Mission—Blessed Teresa of Calcutta P.O. Box 86, Delhi, Merced Co. 95315.

LONE PINE, INYO CO., SANTA ROSA (1919) Rev. Douglas Walker.
Res.: P.O. Box 246, 93545. Tel: 760-876-4350.
Catechesis/Religious Program—Students 13.
Mission—St. John the Baptist Shoshone-Tecopa, CA.
Mission—St. Vivian Independence, Inyo Co.
Station— Death Valley.
Station— Olancha, CA.

LOS BANOS, MERCED CO., ST. JOSEPH (1905) Revs. Robert E. Gamel; Guadalupe Rios, Parochial Vicar; Deacon Leon Miller.
Res.: 1516 Center Ave., 93635. Tel: 209-826-4246; Fax: 209-827-3457. Email: stjosephlb@sbcglobal.net.
School—Our Lady of Fatima, (Grades PreK-8), 1625 Center Ave., 93635. Tel: 209-826-2709; Fax: 209-826-7320. Email: cmcghee@olfdof.org. Web: olfdof.org. Connie McGhee, Prin. Lay Teachers 11; Students 219.
Catechesis/Religious Program—Tel: 209-826-1512. Students 652.

MADERA, MADERA CO., ST. JOACHIM (1881) Revs. Carlos Esquivel, O.S.J.; Gustavo Lopez, O.S.J.; Rafael Lavilla, O.S.J.
Res.: 401 W. Fifth St., 93637. Tel: 559-673-3290; Fax: 559-673-6471. Email: church@sjoachim.org. Web: sjoachim.org.
School—(Grades K-8) Tel: 559-674-7628; Fax: 559-674-8770. Email: school@sjoachim.org. Thomas Spencer, Prin. Immaculate Conception Sisters 1; Lay Teachers 11; Students 262.
Catechesis/Religious Program—Tel: 559-674-5871. Students 1,500.
Convent—310 N. "J" St., 93637. Tel: 559-674-4085. Sisters of the Immaculate Conception (RCM)
Mission—St. Agnes 7308 Hwy. 145, Madera Co. 93637.
Mission—St. Anne Raymond-Knowles, Raymond, Madera Co. 93653.

MARIPOSA, MARIPOSA CO., ST. JOSEPH (1863) [CEM 3] Rev. Stephen C. Bulfer.
Mailing Address: P.O. Box 215, 95338-0215. Tel: 209-966-2522; Fax: 209-966-2522. Email: sjccoff@yahoo.com.
Res.: 4985 Bullion St., 95338.
Catechesis/Religious Program—Students 22.
Mission—St. Catherine of Siena Hornitos, Mariposa Co.

MCFARLAND, KERN CO., ST. ELIZABETH (1966) Rev. Antero Sanchez, M.S.C.
Res.: 835 E. Perkins, 93250. Tel: 661-792-3225; Fax: 661-792-5645.
Catechesis/Religious Program—Tel: 661-792-3429. Esperanza Melendez, D.R.E. Students 407.

MENDOTA, FRESNO CO., OUR LADY OF GUADALUPE (1953) Rev. Gaspar Bautista.
Res.: P.O. Box 248, 93640. Tel: 559-655-3631; 559-655-4237; Fax: 559-655-3785. Email: padregaspar@yahoo.com.
Catechesis/Religious Program—Students 165.
Mission—Our Lady of Lourdes 161015 S. Derrick, Three Rocks, Fresno Co. 93608. Tel: 559-829-3358.

MERCED, MERCED CO.
1—OUR LADY OF MERCY/ST. PATRICK'S (1868) [JC] Rev. Msgr. Patrick Joseph McCormick; Revs. John Okeke Agwu, S.M.M.M., Parochial Vicar; David Greskowiak, Parochial Vicar; Deacons Joseph Smith; Charles Reyburn; Jose Morales.
Mailing Address: 671 E. Yosemite, 95340.
(1968) St. Patrick Church & Mailing Address: 671 E. Yosemite, 95340. Tel: 209-383-3924; 209-383-3930 (Mass recording); Fax: 209-723-6510. Email: info@olmstpatrick.org. Web: olmstpatrick.org.
(1867) Our Lady of Mercy: 459 W. 21st St., 95340.
Res.: 334 & 338 Snowhaven Ct., 95348.
School—Our Lady of Mercy Elementary, (Grades PreSchool-8), 1400 E. 27th St., 95340. Tel: 209-722-7496; Fax: 209-722-7532. Email: olmsch@elite.net. Web: www.olmlancers.com. Mrs. Judy Blackburn, Prin. Lay Teachers 15; K-8 289; Pre-School 107.
Preschool—Tel: 209-722-6657. Jill Serpa, Vice Prin.
Catechesis/Religious Program—Tel: 209-723-8888; Fax: 209-723-8888. Brenda Feehan, D.R.E. Students 449.

2—SACRED HEART (1945) Rev. Jose de Jesus Reynaga.
Res.: 519 W. 12th St., 95340. Tel: 209-383-6604; Fax: 209-383-6608. Email: sacredheart1merced@sbcglobal.net. Web: jeaf.com/shc.
Catechesis/Religious Program—Tel: 209-383-1528; Fax: 209-383-0187. Sr. Gloria Torres, D.R.E. Students 860.

OAKHURST, MADERA CO., OUR LADY OF THE SIERRA (1999) Rev. Jean-Michael Lastiri, Admin.; Deacon Ernie Molloy.
P.O. Box 2499, 93644.
Res.: 49552 Pierce Dr., 93644. Tel: 559-642-3452; Fax: 559-642-4655. Email: olsparish@sti.net. Web: olscatholic.org.
Catechesis/Religious Program—Students 84.
Mission—St. Joseph the Worker 56522 Rd. 200, North Fork, Madera Co. 93643.
Mission—St. Dominic Savio (1961) 40077 Rd. 222, Bass Lake, Madera Co. 93604.

ORANGE COVE, FRESNO CO., ST. ISIDORE THE FARMER (1978) Rev. David Enriquez.
Mailing & Res. Address: 480 Adams Ave., 93646. Tel: 559-626-4943; Fax: 559-626-4648. Email: stisidore3802@sbcglobal.net.
Catechesis/Religious Program—Tel: 559-626-2420. Students 84.
Mission—St. Rita 30673 George Smith Rd., Squaw Valley, Fresno Co. 93675.

PARLIER, FRESNO CO., OUR LADY OF SORROWS (1965) Rev. Jose Luis Rico.
Res.: 830 Tulare St., 93648. Tel: 559-646-2161; Fax: 559-646-9511.
Catechesis/Religious Program—Students 220.

PLANADA, MERCED CO., SACRED HEART (1966) [JC] Rev. Msgr. Patrick Joseph McCormick, Admin.; Revs. John Okeke Agwu, S.M.M.M., Parochial Vicar; David Greskowiak, Parochial Vicar; Deacons Javier Higareda; Higinio Yanez.
Res.: 9360 E. Amistad St., P.O. Box 278, 95365. Tel: 209-382-0459; Fax: 209-382-0814. Email: sacredheartplanada@sbcglobal.net.
Catechesis/Religious Program—9317 Amistad St., P.O. Box 278, 95365. Students 131.
Mission—Our Lady of Lourdes 13145 Le Grand Rd., LeGrand, Merced Co. 95333.

PORTERVILLE, TULARE CO., ST. ANNE (1896) Rev. Scott Daugherty; Rev. Msgr. Ronald Royer (Retired); Revs. Juan Garcia; Samuel Borbon; Deacon James Dieterle.
Res.: 378 N. F St., 93257. Tel: 559-784-2800; Fax: 559-784-4338. Email: stannes@ocsnet.net. Web: stannesparish.com.
School—(Grades PreK-8), 385 N. F St., 93257. Tel: 559-784-4096. Sr. Carmen Fernandez, R.A.D., Prin. Sisters of the Love of God 3; Lay Teachers 7; Students 215.
Preschool—331 F St., 93257. Tel: 559-781-8614. Rhonda Dotters, Dir.
Catechesis/Religious Program—Students 1,061.
Mission—Mater Dolorosa Tule Indian Reservation, Tulare Co. Tel: 559-784-2800.
Mission—Blessed Miguel Agustin Pro 9120 Rd. 236, Terra Bella, Tulare Co. 93270.
Station—Springville, Community Church 35725 Hwy. 190, Springville, 93265.

REEDLEY, FRESNO CO., ST. ANTHONY OF PADUA (1906) Rev. Msgr. John Esquivel; Rev. Juan Madera, Parochial Vicar.
Res.: P.O. Box 188, 93654. Tel: 559-638-2012; Fax: 559-638-8211. Email: stanthonychurch_reedley@comcast.net.
LaSalle Preschool/Child Care Center—Tel: 559-638-2621; Fax: 559-638-5542. Email: hannibalmarylucy@yahoo.com. Web: www.stlasalle-.com. Sr. Lucy Cassarino, F.D.Z., Prin., Preschool & School.
School—St. La Salle Grammar School, (Grades PreK-8), 404 E. Manning Ave., 93654. Tel: 559-638-2621; Fax: 559-638-5542. Sisters 3; Lay Teachers 8; Students 261.
Catechesis/Religious Program—Tel: 559-638-5608. Students 520.

RIDGECREST, KERN CO., ST. ANN (1965) [JC] Rev. Paul Kado.
Res.: 446 W. Church St., P.O. Box 127, 93556. Tel: 760-375-2110; Fax: 760-375-8899. Web: parishofsaintann.org.
School—(Grades K-8) Tel: 760-375-4713. Email: school@parishofsaintann.org. Mary Little, Prin. Lay Teachers 12; Students 128.
Catechesis/Religious Program—Students 285.
Mission—Santa Barbara 72 Lexington Ave., Randsburg, Kern Co. 93554.

RIVERDALE, FRESNO CO., ST. ANN (1928) [JC] Rev. Victor Piansay.
Res.: 3047 W. Mt. Whitney, P.O. Box 335, 93656. Tel: 559-867-3035.
Catechesis/Religious Program—Tel: 559-867-4996. Students 209.
Mission—Holy Family Chapel c/o St. Ann, Riverdale Ca. 93656, Diener Ranch At Five Points, Fresno Co.

ROSAMOND, KERN CO., ST. MARY OF THE DESERT (1999) Rev. Patrick Geo, Admin.
Mailing Address: 3100 Fifteenth St. W., 93560. Tel: 661-256-4505; Fax: 661-256-7127. Email: st.mary3100@att.net.
Catechesis/Religious Program—Students 278.
Mission—St. Francis of Assisi Church 15382 Meyer Rd., Mojave, 93501.

SANGER, FRESNO CO., ST. MARY (1922) [JC] Revs. Jupeter Quinto, R.C.J.; Philip Puntrello, R.C.J.; Deacon John Biedermann. In Res., Revs. Salvatore Ciranni, R.C.J. (Retired); Renato Panlasigui, R.C.J.
Res.: 828 O St., P.O. Box 335, 93657. Tel: 559-875-2025; Fax: 559-875-1281. Email: stmarysanger@verizon.net.
Catechesis/Religious Program—2590 North Ave., 93657. Tel: 559-875-6340; Fax: 559-875-6340. Students 640.

SELMA, FRESNO CO., ST. JOSEPH (1913) Rev. Msgr. Daniel Lopez; Deacon Ed Harmon III.
Res.: 2441 Dockery Ave., 93662. Tel: 559-896-1052; Fax: 559-896-3975.
Catechesis/Religious Program—Tel: 559-896-2620. Students 510.

SHAFTER, KERN CO., ST. THERESE (1952) Rev. Pedro Umana, O.F.M.
Res.: 300 W. Lerdo, P.O. Box 1448, 93263. Tel: 661-746-4471; Fax: 661-746-0945.
Catechesis/Religious Program—Students 345.

TAFT, KERN CO., ST. MARY (1918) Rev. Genaro C. Demecias.
Res.: 110 E. Woodrow St., 93268. Tel: 661-765-4292.
Catechesis/Religious Program—Students 95.

TEHACHAPI, KERN CO., ST. MALACHY (1887) Rev. Joel Davadilla.
Res.: 407 W. "E" St., 93561-1642. Tel: 661-822-3060; Fax: 661-822-3159.
Catechesis/Religious Program—Tel: 661-822-6327. Students 268.

TIPTON, TULARE CO., ST. JOHN THE EVANGELIST (1945) Rev. Miguel Campos.
Res.: 232 S. Adam Rd., 93272. Tel: 559-752-4544; Fax: 559-752-4313. Email: st.johnchurch93272@sbcglobal.net.
Catechesis/Religious Program—Tel: 559-752-4313. Students 505.
Mission—St. Francis of Assisi 16410 Ave. 168, Woodville, Tulare Co. 93258. Tel: 559-688-8412.
Station—Our Lady of the Assumption Pixley.

TRANQUILLITY, FRESNO CO., ST. PAUL (1924) Revs. David Reed; Marcelinus Okenedo, S.M.M.M., Parochial Vicar.
Res.: 25592 Doughty St., 93668. Tel: 559-698-7429; Fax: 559-698-1059.
Catechesis/Religious Program—Tel: 559-693-4320. Students 80.
Mission—St. Vincent de Paul San Joaquin, Fresno Co.

TULARE, TULARE CO.
1—ST. ALOYSIUS (1905) Rev. Msgrs. Richard Urizalqui; Raul Marta.
Res.: 125 E. Pleasant Ave., 93274. Tel: 559-688-1796; 559-688-1797; Fax: 559-688-0948.
School—(Grades K-8) Tel: 559-686-6250; Fax: 559-686-0479. Joel Nunes, Prin. Lay Teachers 14; Students 209.
Catechesis/Religious Program—Tel: 559-688-8644. Students 400.

2—ST. RITA (1967) Revs. Ignacio Villafan; Reynaldo Hernandez.
Res.: 954 S. O St., 93274. Tel: 559-686-3847; Fax: 559-686-9672.
Catechesis/Religious Program—Tel: 559-686-0802. Students 700.

VISALIA, TULARE CO.
1—HOLY FAMILY (1950) Rev. Msgr. Raymond C. Dreiling; Revs. Rod L. Craig; David Bustamante; Daniel C. Avila; John Bosco Prasit Kruesuwan; Deacons Paul Hernandez; Julian Ponce; James Rooney.
Mailing Address: P.O. Box 287, 93279. Res.: 1908 N. Court St., 93291. Tel: 559-734-9522; Fax: 559-734-3435. Email: rparlier@ccov.org.
Catechesis/Religious Program—Tel: 559-732-9651. Irma Gaitan, C.R.E. Students 900.
Mission—San Felipe de Jesus 32809 Rd. 159, Ivanhoe, Tulare Co. 93235.
Catechesis/Religious Program—Tel: 559-798-2172. Susana Gomez, D.R.E.

2—ST. MARY (1861) Rev. Msgr. Raymond C. Dreiling; Revs. Rod L. Craig; David Bustamante; Daniel C. Avila; John Bosco Prasit Kruesuwan; Deacons Ken Ramage; Rick Miller; Doug Pingel; Charles Culbreth, Dir., Music.
Res.: 608 N. Church St., P.O. Box 287, 93279. Tel: 559-734-9522; Fax: 559-734-3435. Web: tccov.org.
School—George McCann Memorial School, (Grades PreK-8), 200 E. Race St., 93291. Tel: 559-732-5831; Fax: 559-741-1562. Web: gmccatholicschool.org. Sheila Rast, Prin. Lay Teachers 11; Students 238.
Catechesis/Religious Program—Tel: 559-733-3929; Fax: 559-733-1255. Mrs. Joan Bell, D.R.E.; Ruben Cabatic, Youth Min. Students 925.

WASCO, KERN CO., ST. JOHN THE EVANGELIST (1913) Rev. John P. Fluetsch.
Res.: 1300 Ninth Pl., 93280. Tel: 661-758-6688; Fax: 661-758-7751.
Preschool—Tel: 661-758-6829.
Mission—Nuestra Senora de la Paz Lost Hills. 14846 Hwy. 33, Blackwell's Corner, Kern Co. 93249.

WOFFORD HEIGHTS, KERN CO., ST. JUDE (1969) Rev. Patrick Persinger.
Mailing Address: P.O. Box 1190, 93285.
Res.: 86 Nellie Dent Dr., 93285. Tel: 760-376-2416; Fax: 760-376-2253.
Catechesis/Religious Program—Students 35.
Station—

WOODLAKE, TULARE CO., ST. FRANCES CABRINI (1963) Rev. Jesse C. Venzor.
Res.: 599 N. Valencia Blvd., P.O. Box 459, 93286. Tel: 559-564-2647; Fax: 559-564-2647.
Catechesis/Religious Program—Students 280.
Mission—St. Clair Alta Acres Dr., Three Rivers, Tulare Co. 93271.

YOSEMITE NATIONAL PARK, MARIPOSA CO., OUR LADY OF THE SNOWS (1963) Rev. Msgr. Anthony Janelli (Retired).
Res.: P.O. Box 457, 95389. Tel: 209-372-4729; Fax: 209-372-4767.
Catechesis/Religious Program—

Chaplains of Public Institutions

FRESNO. *Children's Hospital Central California*, Tel: 559-353-5250. Rev. Ricardo Magdaleno, Chap.
Community Medical Center, Clovis, Tel: 559-324-4000. Rev. Adrian Kim, C.P., Chap.
Community Regional Medical Center & University Medical Center, Tel: 559-459-6461; 559-459-4000 University Medical Center. Rev. Dominic Savio Rajappa, Chap.
Kaiser Permanente Medical Center. Tel: 559-448-4500. Rev. Ricardo Magdaleno, Chap.
Veterans Administration Medical Center, 3636 N. First St., 93726. Tel: 559-487-5660. Revs. Dominic Savio Rajappa, Chap., Victor T. Dinh, Chap.
AVENAL. *Avenal State Prison*, Tel: 559-386-0587, Ext. 6384. Rodney Ornellas, Chap.
BAKERSFIELD. *Bakersfield Memorial Hospital & San Joaquin Community Hospital*, Tel: 661-237-4734. Rev. Msgr. Ralph Belluomini.
CHOWCHILLA. *Department of Corrections, Central California Women's Facility*, P.O. Box 1501, 93610-1501. Tel: 559-665-5531, Ext. 7232. Sr. Mary Anne DiVicenzo, C.S.J., Chap.
Valley State Prison for Women, P.O. Box 92, 93610-0092. Tel: 559-665-6100, Ext. 6060. Danilo Grajales, Chap.
COALINGA. *Coalinga State Hospital*, Tel: 559-935-4300. Bro. Andres Amador, O.F.M.Conv.
Pleasant Valley State Prison, P.O. Box 8500, 93210-8500. Tel: 559-935-4900, Ext. 6777. Brian Phillips, Chap.
CORCORAN. *California State Prison*, P.O. Box 8800, 93212. Tel: 559-992-8800, Ext. 6412.
California Substance Abuse Treatment Facility & State Prison - Corcoran, P.O. Box 7100, 93212-7100. Tel: 559-992-7100, Ext. 7037. Sr. Rosa Maria Guembe, R.C.M., Chap., Jose Ojeda, Chap.
DELANO. *Kern Valley State Prison*, P.O. Box 6000, 93216-6000. Tel: 661-721-6300. Rev. Francisco Diaz, Chap.
North Kern State Prison, P.O. Box 567, 93216-0567. Tel: 661-721-2345, Ext. 6861. John Messina, Chap.
PORTERVILLE. *Developmental Center*, P.O. Box 2000, 93258-2000. Tel: 559-782-2402, Ext. 2401. Sr. Marion Morua, M.C.D.P. Tel: 559-782-2401.
TEHACHAPI. *California Correctional Institution*, P.O. Box 1031, 93581-1031. Tel: 661-822-4402, Ext. 4387. Deacon Clyde Davis, Chap.
WASCO. *State Prison*, P.O. Box 8800, 93280-8800. Tel: 661-758-8400, Ext. 5649. Rev. Daniel Bringas, Chap.

On Special Assignment:
Rev. Msgrs.—
Cotta, Myron J., V.G., 1550 N. Fresno St., 93703-3788.
Griesbach, John, St. Anthony Retreat Center, Dir.
Revs.—
Burchfield, Michael A., J.C.L., Asst. Tribunal Dir. & Adjutant Vicar
Norris, David J., D.Min., Dean - School of Ministry

On Duty Outside the Diocese:
Revs.—
Congdon, John, Military Chap.
Okorie, Onyema

Absent on Sick Leave:
Revs.—
Baca, Joseph
Bray, Kevin
Chavez, Gerald F.

Sabbatical:
Rev.—
del Angel, Jesus

Retired:
Rev. Msgrs.—
Barnes, Joseph C.
Bezunartea, Herman O.
Byrne, Laserian
Cleary, Kevin
Herrero, Nicolas
Janelli, Anthony
Logan, James T.
Marth, Loydell J.
Meyer, Gilbert, 328 del Mar Ln., Ridgecrest, 93555.
Minhoto, Walter F., 2814 Mariposa, 93721.
O'Friel, John
Petersen, E. James
Pointek, Francis J.
Poschen, Ed
Riccomini, Dino
Revs.—
Alabart, Francis X.
Alvernaz, Dennis
Azpericueta, Lucas
Burns, John P.
Casale, Charles B.
Duffy, Raymond
Flickinger, Don D.
Gonzalez, Angel
Gonzalez, Antonio
Heffernan, Joseph A.
Kudilil, James
Montiel, Jose
Northrup, Gerald, S.F.O.
Pascual, Manuel
Raffel, Godfrey
Shenoy, Leslie
Simeone, Francis
Varo, Jose Luis
Vega, Jose Luis

INSTITUTIONS LOCATED IN THE DIOCESE

[A] HIGH SCHOOLS, DIOCESAN

FRESNO. *San Joaquin Memorial High School* (1945) 1406 N. Fresno St., 93703-3789. Tel: 559-268-9251; Fax: 559-268-1351. Web: www.sjmhs.org. Edward R. Borges, Prin.; Rev. David J. Norris, D.Min., Rector; James Sherman, Librarian. Lay Teachers 41; Students 556.
BAKERSFIELD. *Garces Memorial High School* (1947) 2800 Loma Linda Dr., 93305. Tel: 661-327-2578; Fax: 661-327-5427. Email: kbears@garces.org. Web: www.garces.org. Kathleen Bears, Prin.; Susan Rizo, Dir. Campus Ministry; Rev. James LaCasse, S.J., Chap.; Rev. Msgr. Michael Braun, Rector; Darla Brown, Librarian. Lay Teachers 42; Students 689.

[B] GENERAL HOSPITALS

FRESNO. *Saint Agnes Medical Center* (1929) 1303 E. Herndon, 93720. Tel: 559-450-3000; Fax: 559-450-2143. Email: Thomas.Anderson@samc.com. Web: www.samc.com. Thomas Anderson, CEO; Craig Saladino, Chm., Bd. of Trustees; Rev. Gregori Neri, Chap. Trinity Health. Sisters 8; Nurses 918; Bed Capacity 436; Patients Assisted Annually 38,324; Total Staff 2,820.
Professional Office Corporation, Saint Agnes Medical Center, 1303 E. Herndon Ave., 93720. Tel: 559-449-3000; Fax: 559-449-2143. Thomas Anderson, CEO; Craig Saladino, Chm. P.O.C. Bd.
BAKERSFIELD. *Mercy Hospital dba Catholic Healthcare West* (1910) Mercy Southwest is a campus of Mercy Hospital., 2215 Truxtun Ave., 93301. Tel: 661-632-5000; Fax: 661-327-2592. Web: www.mercybakersfield.org. Russell V. Judd, Pres. Sponsored by Sisters of Mercy of the Americas West Midwest Community Patients Assisted Annually 150,544; Bed Capacity 269; Sisters 2; Total Staff 1,458.
Mercy Southwest Hospital dba Catholic Healthcare West 400 Old River Rd., 93311. Tel: 661-663-6000; Fax: 661-663-6570. Web: mercybakersfield.org.
Mercy Foundation, Bakersfield dba Friends of Mercy Foundation 2215 Truxtun Ave., 93302. Tel: 661-632-5683; Fax: 661-322-8543. Web: mercybakersfield.org. Stephanie Weber, Vice Pres., Fund Devel.
MERCED. *Mercy Medical Center Merced - Dominican Campus dba Catholic Healthcare West* (1923) 2740 M St., 95340. Tel: 209-384-6444; Fax: 209-722-2902. Web: mercymercedcares.org. David Dunham, Pres. Sponsored by the Dominican Sisters of St. Catherine of Siena of Kenosha, Wisconsin. Bed Capacity 287; Staff 1,145; Patients Assisted Annually 169,826.

[C] HOMES FOR INVALID AND AGED

FRESNO. *Nazareth House*, 2121 N. First St., 93703. Tel: 559-237-2257; Fax: 559-237-1958. Email: sr.marie@nazarethfresno.org. Sr. Margaret Brody, S.N., Admin. Sisters of Nazareth of Fresno Inc. 3; Residential Care/Assisted Living 110; Total Staff 80.
LOS BANOS. *New Bethany Residential Care and Skilled Nursing Community*, 1441 Berkeley Dr., 93635. Tel: 209-827-8933; Fax: 209-827-8989. Email: jdf2003@yahoo.com. Web: www.newbethanyfhic.org. Sisters Helen Petrovich, F.H.I.C., Dir. Nurses; Julia Fonseca, F.H.I.C., Pres.; Lucinda Fonseca, F.H.I.C., Skilled Nursing Admin.; Rev. Richard F. O'Halloran (MRY), Chap. Franciscan Hospitaller Sisters of the Immaculate Conception 10; Residential Care 75; Skilled Nursing 35; Total Staff 70; Capacity 110.

[D] CATHOLIC CHARITIES

FRESNO. *Catholic Charities of the Diocese of Fresno*, 149 N. Fulton St., 93701. Tel: 559-237-0851; Fax: 559-237-7050. Email: cmanfredo@ccdof.org. Catherine Manfredo, Exec. Dir. Total Staff 78; Total Assisted in all 6 Locations 200,000.
Catholic Charities Thrift Store, 149 N. Fulton St., 93701-1607. Tel: 559-237-0851; Fax: 559-237-7050. Email: jhudson@ccdof.org. Jody Hudson, Retail & Food Distribution Center. Total Staff 2.
Immigration Services, 149 N. Fulton St., 93701. Tel: 559-264-6400; Fax: 559-237-7050. Email: arodriguez@ccdof.org. Web: www.ccdof.org. Anna Rodriguez, Immigration Counselor. Total Staff 1; Total Assisted 102,500.
Senior Companion Program, 149 N. Fulton St., 93701. Tel: 559-498-6377. Email: kcox@ccdof.org. Alan Lopes, Sr. Companion Prog. Total Staff 6; Total Assisted 324.
BAKERSFIELD. *Catholic Charities, Diocese of Fresno, Kern and Inyo County Resource Center*, 825 Chester Ave., 93301. Tel: 661-281-2130; Fax: 661-281-2139. Email: acastaneda@ccdof.org. Andy Castaneda, Site Dir. Total Staff 7; Total Assisted Annually 38,000.
MERCED. *Catholic Charities*, 366 W. Main #1, 95340. Tel: 209-383-2494; 209-383-5220; Fax: 209-383-3975. Total Staff 4.
Catholic Charities Social Services, Office Mgr., 366 W. Main, #1, 95340. Tel: 209-383-2494; Fax: 209-383-3975.
Immigration Program, 336 W. Main, #1, 95340. Tel: 209-383-2494; 209-383-5220; Fax: 209-383-3975.
PORTERVILLE. *Catholic Charities, Family Resource Center (FRC)*, 271 S. Wallace, 93257. Tel: 559-781-5555; Fax: 559-781-5301. Leonor Alvarado, Site Dir. Total Staff 2.
VISALIA. *The Good News Center* (1968) 1724 N. Dinuba Blvd., 93291. Tel: 559-734-1572; Fax: 559-734-4921. Email: lmoheno@ccdof.org. Web: ccdof.org. Total Staff 3.
Catholic Charities, Diocese of Fresno, Visalia Family Resource Center (1985) 1724 N. Dinuba Blvd., 93291. Tel: 559-734-1572; Fax: 559-734-4921.

[E] CONVENTS AND RESIDENCES FOR SISTERS

FRESNO. *St. Agnes Medical Center Convent* (1975) 1261 E. Los Altos Ave., 93710. Tel: 559-431-3376. Congregation of the Sisters of the Holy Cross. Sisters of the Holy Cross, Inc. 6.
Congregation of the Sisters of Nazareth, 2121 N. First St., 93703. Tel: 559-237-2257; Fax: 559-237-2323. Email: nazfresno@aol.com. Sr. Margaret Brody, S.N., Supr. Sisters 4.
Pious Disciples of the Divine Master, 3700 N. Cornelia Ave., 93722. Tel: 559-275-1656; Fax: 559-275-2725. Sr. M. Peter Mendes, P.D.D.M., Supr. Sisters 10.
BAKERSFIELD. *Sister Servants of the Blessed Sacrament (SJS)*, 1100 S. Kern St., 93307. Tel: 661-631-1061 (Convent); 661-323-6059 (School); Fax: 661-323-6058. Email: lbakersfielsjs@yahoo.com. Sisters 4.
CLOVIS. *Sisters of the Immaculate Conception (RCM)* (1892) 859 Harvard Ave., 93612. Tel: 559-299-8407; Fax: 559-299-4627. Email: rcmclovis@cvip.net. Web: www.rc.net/conception. Sisters 4.
LEMOORE. *Carmelite Sisters of St. Teresa (CSST)*, 884 N. Lemoore Ave., 93245. Tel: 559-924-2347; Fax: 559-924-7848. Email: tessypius@hotmail.com. Sisters 5.
LOS BANOS. *Franciscan Hospitallers of the Immaculate Conception (FHIC)*, 1441 Berkeley Dr., 93635-9599. Tel: 209-826-0770; Fax: 209-827-8989. Email: confhic@sbcglobal.net. Web: www.fhiccalp.org. Sisters 10.
REEDLEY. *Daughters of Divine Zeal (FDZ)* (1897) 379 E. Manning Ave., 93654. Tel: 559-638-1916; Fax: 559-638-5542. Email: hannibalmarylucy@yahoo.com. Web: www.figliedivinozelo.it. Sisters 3.

[F] RETREAT HOUSES

THREE RIVERS. *St. Anthony's Retreat Center*, P.O. Box 249, 93271. Tel: 559-561-4595; Fax: 559-561-4493. Email: thomas@stanthonyretreat.org. Web: stanthonyretreat.org. Rev. Msgr. John Griesbach, Dir.; Sr. Danielle Witt, S.S.N.D., Co-Dir. Priests 1; Religious 1.

[G] NEWMAN CENTERS

FRESNO. *St. Paul Newman Center* (1964) 1572 E. Barstow Ave., 93710. Tel: 559-436-3434; Fax: 559-436-3430. Web: csufnewman.com. Deacon John Supino, Parish Life Coord.
California State University at Fresno & Fresno City

College 93740. Tel: 559-436-3434; Fax: 559-436-3430. Web: csufnewman.com. Karey Spach, Campus Min.

[H] MISCELLANEOUS & AGENCIES

FRESNO. *Catholic Professional and Business Club of Fresno*, P.O. Box 9454, 93792-9454. Tel: 559-434-2722. Email: president@cpbcfresno.org. Patrick Ogle, Pres.

Our Faith, Our Family, Our Future Foundation, Inc., 1550 N. Fresno St., 93703. Tel: 559-488-7426; Fax: 559-488-7461.

The Sisters of Nazareth of Fresno Real Estate Holdings, Inc., 2121 N. First St., 93703. Tel: 559-237-2257. Sr. Margaret Brody, S.N., Pres.

MERCED. **Apostoles de la Palabra of California*, 168 Cone Ave., 95341.

Catholic Professional & Business Club of the Fresno Diocese, 260 W. 21st St., 95340. 1550 N. Fresno St., 93703-3788. Robert Tomasetti, Pres.

SANGER. *Fr. Hannibal House Social Service Center*, 1401 14th St., P.O. Box 37, 93657. Tel: 559-875-0564; Fax: 559-875-1281. Email: hannibalhouse@aol.com. Teresa Ramirez, Exec. Dir. Total Assisted: Food Distribution 6,500.

TEHACHAPI. *Norbertine Association of St. Joseph*, 17831-A Water Canyon Rd., 93561.

RELIGIOUS INSTITUTES OF MEN REPRESENTED IN THE DIOCESE

For further details refer to the corresponding bracketed number in the Religious Institutes of Men or Women section.

[0360]—*Claretian Missionaries* (Western Prov.)—C.M.F.
[0480]—*Conventual Franciscans* (St. Joseph Cupertino Prov.)—O.F.M.Conv.
[0520]—*Franciscan Friars* (St. Barbara Prov.)—O.F.M.
[0690]—*Jesuit Fathers* (Los Gatos, CA)—S.J.
[]—*Missionaries of St. Paul*—M.S.P.
[]—*Missioneros del Sagrado Corazon y Santa Maria de Guadalupe*—M.S.C.
[0930]—*Oblates of St. Joseph* (Asti, Italy)—O.S.J.
[]—*Redemptorists*—C.Ss.R.
[1090]—*Rogationist Fathers*—R.C.J.
[0420]—*Society of the Divine Word* (Philippines)—S.V.D.
[]—*Sons of Mary Mother of Mercy* (Umvahia, Nigeria)—S.M.M.M.

RELIGIOUS INSTITUTES OF WOMEN REPRESENTED IN THE DIOCESE

[]—*Carmelite Sisters of St. Teresa* (Gidellahalli, Bangalore-India)—C.S.S.T.
[3830-13]—*Congregation of Sisters of St. Joseph* Baden, PA)—C.S.J.
[3242]—*Congregation of the Sisters of Nazareth* (Los Angeles, CA)—C.S.N.
[1920]—*Congregation of the Sisters of the Holy Cross* (Notre Dame, IN)—C.S.C.
[0795]—*Daughters of Divine Zeal* (Rome, Italy)—F.D.Z.
[1070-20]—*Dominican Sisters* (Congregation of St. Thomas Aquinas, Marymount, Tacoma, WA)—O.P.
[1070-13]—*Dominican Sisters* (Congregation of the Most Holy Rosary, Adrian, MI)—O.P.
[107012]—*Dominican Sisters* (Congregation of the Most Holy Rosary Mission, San Jose, CA)—O.P.
[1070-25]—*Dominican Sisters* (Congregation of of St. Catherine of Siena of Kenosha)—O.P.
[1270]—*Franciscan Hospitaller Sisters of the Immaculate Conception* (San Jose, CA)—F.H.I.C.
[1190]—*Franciscan Sisters of the Atonement* (Garrison, NY)—S.A.
[]—*Hijas del Sagrado Corazon de Jesus y Santa Maria* (Mexico)—H.S.C.M.G.
[2180]—*Immaculate Heart Community* (Los Angeles, CA)—I.H.M.
[]—*Instituto Misionero Apostoles de la Palabra*—I.M.A.P.
[]—*Misioneras Carmelitas de Santa Teresa del Nino Jesus* (Puebla, Puebla Mexico)—M.C.S.T.N.J.
[]—*Misioneras Eucaristicas de Maria Inmaculada* (Colima, Mexico)—M.E.M.I.
[]—*Missionary Catechists of Divine Providence*—M.C.D.P.
[]—*Norbertine Sisters of the Bethlehem Priory of St. Joseph*
[4120-06]—*Order of St. Ursula, Toledo OH*—O.S.U.
[3130]—*Our Lady of Victory Missionary Sisters* (Huntington, IN)—O.L.V.M.
[0980]—*Pious Disciples of the Divine Master* (Staten Island, NY)—P.D.D.M.
[2970]—*School Sisters of Notre Dame* (St. Louis, MO)—S.S.N.D.
[3499]—*Servants of the Blessed Sacrament* (El Segundo, CA)—S.J.S.
[0430]—*Sisters of Charity of Blessed Virgin Mary* (Dubuque, IA)—B.V.M.
[2570]—*Sisters of Mercy of the Americas* (Silver Spring, MD)—R.S.M.
[]—*Sisters of Our Lady of Nazareth* (Fiji)—S.O.L.N.
[3840]—*Sisters of St. Joseph of Carondelet* (Los Angeles, CA)—C.S.J.
[1960]—*Sisters of the Holy Family* (Mission San Jose, CA)—S.H.F.
[2130]—*Sisters of the Immaculate Conception* (San Francisco, CA & Spain)—R.C.M.
[]—*Sisters of the Love of God* (La Puente, CA & Spain)—R.A.D.
[3320]—*Sisters of the Presentation of the Blessed Virgin Mary* (San Francisco, CA)—P.B.V.M.

DIOCESAN CEMETERIES

FRESNO. *Fresno Catholic Cemeteries*, 264 N. Blythe, 93706. Tel: 559-488-7449; Fax: 559-488-7485.

NECROLOGY

† Balker, Rev. Msgr. Joseph W., (Retired)—Died April 1, 2009
† Doherty, Rev. Msgr. Patrick G., (Retired)—Died Sept. 7, 2009
† Flood, Rev. Msgr. Patrick, (Retired)—Died July 12, 2009
† Herdegen, Rev. Msgr. Anthony, (Retired)—Died March 17, 2009

An asterisk (*) denotes an organization that has established tax-exempt status directly with the IRS and is not covered by the USCCB Group Ruling.

Diocese of Gallup

(Dioecesis Gallupiensis)

Most Reverend

JAMES S. WALL

Bishop of Gallup; ordained June 6, 1998; appointed Bishop of Gallup February 5, 2009; ordained and installed April 23, 2009. *Office: 711 S. Puerco Dr., P.O. Box 1338, Gallup, NM 87305.*

Chancery: 711 S. Puerco Dr., P.O. Box 1338, Gallup, NM 87305. Tel: 505-863-4406; Fax: 505-722-9131.

ESTABLISHED DECEMBER 16, 1939.

Square Miles 55,468.

Comprises Apache, Navajo and those parts of the Navajo and Hopi Reservations in Coconino Counties in the State of Arizona; San Juan, McKinley, Catron, Cibola and those parts of Rio Arriba, Sandoval, Bernalillo and Valencia Counties lying west of 106, 52', 41" meridian in the State of New Mexico.

Legal Title: New Mexico: Roman Catholic Church of the Diocese of Gallup. Arizona: Bishop of the Roman Catholic Church of the Diocese of Gallup.
For legal titles of parishes and diocesan institutions, consult the Chancery Office.

STATISTICAL OVERVIEW

Personnel	
Bishop	1
Retired Bishops	1
Priests: Diocesan Active in Diocese	23
Priests: Diocesan Active Outside Diocese	4
Priests: Retired, Sick or Absent	13
Number of Diocesan Priests	40
Religious Priests in Diocese	17
Total Priests in Diocese	57
Extern Priests in Diocese	6
Ordinations:	
Permanent Deacons	2
Permanent Deacons in Diocese	28
Total Brothers	8
Total Sisters	100
Parishes	
Parishes	52
With Resident Pastor:	
Resident Diocesan Priests	22
Resident Religious Priests	10
Without Resident Pastor:	
Administered by Priests	14
Administered by Religious Women	3
Completely Vacant	3
Missions	22
Professional Ministry Personnel:	
Brothers	6
Sisters	54
Lay Ministers	51
Welfare	
Homes for the Aged	1
Total Assisted	50
Specialized Homes	1
Total Assisted	24
Special Centers for Social Services	12
Total Assisted	75,000
Educational	
Diocesan Students in Other Seminaries	2
Total Seminarians	2
High Schools, Diocesan and Parish	1
Total Students	95
High Schools, Private	1
Total Students	42
Elementary Schools, Diocesan and Parish	10
Total Students	1,060
Elementary Schools, Private	1
Total Students	120
Catechesis/Religious Education:	
High School Students	782
Elementary Students	2,702
Total Students under Catholic Instruction	4,803
Teachers in the Diocese:	
Sisters	18
Lay Teachers	138
Vital Statistics	
Receptions into the Church:	
Infant Baptism Totals	550
Minor Baptism Totals	133
Adult Baptism Totals	89
Received into Full Communion	58
First Communions	743
Confirmations	475
Marriages:	
Catholic	116
Interfaith	39
Total Marriages	155
Deaths	523
Total Catholic Population	61,990
Total Population	495,000

Former Bishop—Most Revs. BERNARD T. ESPELAGE, O.F.M., D.D., ord. May 16, 1918; appt. Bishop of Gallup, July 20, 1940; cons. Oct. 9, 1940; resigned Sept. 3, 1969; died Feb. 19, 1971; JEROME J. HASTRICH, D.D., ord. Feb. 9, 1941; cons. Auxiliary Bishop of Madison and Titular Bishop of Gurza, July 31, 1963; transferred to the See of Gallup, Sept. 3, 1969; installed Dec. 3, 1969; retired March 20, 1990; died May 12, 1995; DONALD E. PELOTTE, S.S.S., D.D., Ph.D., ord. Sept. 2, 1972; appt. Coadjutor Bishop of Gallup Feb. 24, 1986; cons. May 6, 1986; succeeded to See, March 20, 1990; retired April 30, 2008; died Jan. 7, 2010.

Vicar General—Very Rev. JAMES E. WALKER, Ph.D., V.G.

Judicial Vicar—Very Rev. MICHAEL A. VIGIL, J.C.L., J.V.

Office of the Bishop—711 S. Puerco Dr., P.O. Box 1338, Gallup, 87305. Tel: 505-863-4406.

Chancery—711 S. Puerco Dr., P.O. Box 1338, Gallup, 87305. Tel: 505-863-4406; Fax: 505-722-9131. Office Hours: Mon.-Fri. 8:30-12 & 1-4:30.

Chancellor—Rev. MATTHEW A. KELLER, Chancellor Pro tem; Mrs. VERA PLACENCIO, Exec. Sec. to the Bishop.

Financial Secretary—Mrs. ANNA J. DIGREGORIO.

Diocesan Tribunal (First Instance)—711 S. Puerco Dr., P.O. Box 1338, Gallup, 87305. Tel: 505-863-4406; Fax: 505-722-9324.

Adjutant Judicial Vicar—Very Rev. LAWRENCE J. O'KEEFE, J.C.D.

Judges—Very Revs. LAWRENCE J. O'KEEFE, J.C.D.; MICHAEL A. VIGIL, J.C.L., J.V.; Deacon JIM HOY.

Defenders of the Bond—Rev. THOMAS R. MAIKOWSKI, Ph.D., Ed.D.; Very Rev. KEVIN H. FINNEGAN, J.C.L.; Rev. JEROME R. HERFF, C.M.

Notary—MARGIE MARES.

Promoter of Justice—Very Rev. KEVIN H. FINNEGAN, J.C.L.

Vicars Forane—Very Revs. KEVIN H. FINNEGAN, J.C.L., McKinley Vicariate; GILBERT SCHNEIDER, O.F.M., Apache Vicariate; CLAY KILBURN, C.M., Navajo Vicariate; JOHN SAUTER, Lower Arizona Vicariate; DANIEL F. KASSIS, San Juan Vicariate; ALBERTO AVELLA, Cibola Vicariate.

Bishop's Delegate for Religious—VACANT.

Presbyteral Council—Most Rev. JAMES S. WALL; Very Revs. JAMES E. WALKER, Ph.D., V.G.; FRANK CHACON; KEVIN H. FINNEGAN, J.C.L.; JOACHIM BLONSKI, Moderator; ALBERTO AVELLA, Vice Moderator; EDUARDO ESPINOSA, O.F.M.; LAWRENCE J. O'KEEFE, J.C.D.; CLAY KILBURN, C.M.; JOHN SAUTER; GILBERT SCHNEIDER, O.F.M.; MICHAEL A. VIGIL, J.C.L., J.V.; DANIEL F. KASSIS; Mrs. VERA PLACENCIO, Sec., Mailing Address: P.O. Box 1338, Gallup, 87305.

Diocesan Consultors—Very Revs. JAMES E. WALKER, Ph.D., V.G.; LAWRENCE J. O'KEEFE, J.C.D.; JOACHIM BLONSKI; EDUARDO ESPINOSA, O.F.M.; GILBERT SCHNEIDER, O.F.M.; FRANK CHACON.

Diocesan Offices and Directors

Archivist—VACANT.

Catholic Committee on Scouting—Rev. JEFFREY KING, Mailing Address: P.O. Box 489, Reserve, 87830-0489. Tel: 575-533-6719.

Budget and Finance—Deacon JAMES P. HOY, Dir.

Catholic Charities—Sr. KATHLEEN DRISCOLL, D.C., Dir., Main Office, Gallup: P.O. Box 3146, Gallup, 87305. Tel: 505-722-4407. Chinle: P.O. Box 417, Chinle, AZ 86053. Tel: 928-674-3238. Grants-Milan: 2595 W. Hwy. 66, Grants, 87020. Tel: 505-285-5451. Farmington: 119 W. Broadway, Farmington, 87401. Tel: 505-325-3734. Holbrook: P.O. Box 41, Holbrook, AZ 86025. Tel: 928-524-9720. White Mountain: P.O. Box 552, McNary, AZ 85930. Tel: 928-334-2244.

Cursillos—ROBERT KRAKOW, Dir., No. 10 Rd. 5280, Bloomfield, 87413. Tel: 505-632-7322; Rev. ROBERT E. MATHIEU, Spiritual Dir., 307 N. Church St., Bloomfield, 87413. Tel: 505-632-2014.

Diocesan Superintendent of Catholic Schools—VACANT.

Ecumenical Affairs in Arizona, Arizona Ecumenical Council—VACANT.

Ecumenical Affairs in New Mexico—Rev. RAYMOND MAHLMANN, Mailing Address: P.O. Box 668, Grants, 87020.

Newspaper— "Voice of the Southwest" CHARLES L. LAMB, Editor in Chief, Mailing Address: P.O. Box 1338, Gallup, 87305. Tel: 505-863-4406.

Diocesan Director of Religious Education—Sr. EVE MARIE KORZYM, O.S.F., Mailing Address: P.O. Box 1338, Gallup, 87305. Tel: 505-863-4406, Ext. 32.

Priests' Retirement Board—Revs. JOACHIM BLONSKI; WILLIAM F. DAY (Retired); MATTHEW A. KELLER; TIMOTHY W. FARRELL.

Propagation of the Faith—Deacon JOSEPH F. KRIKAWA, Dir., Mailing Address: P.O. Box 1338, Gallup, 87305.

Radio—LEE LAMB; Rev. CORMAC ANTRAM, O.F.M., Mailing Address: P.O. Box 668, Saint Michaels, AZ 86511.

Search—TED GOMEZ, Dir., Mailing Address: P.O. Box 5243, Farmington, 87499-5243.

Life, Peace, Justice and Creation Stewardship—Sr. ROSE MARIE CECCHINI, M.M., Mailing Address: P.O. Box 3146, Gallup, 87305. Tel: 505-722-4407, Ext. 103.

Vocations— For Priesthood: Rev. MATTHEW A. KELLER, Mailing Address: P.O. Box 1338, Gallup, 87305. Tel: 505-863-4406, Ext. 14. Deacon Vocations: Deacon FRANK T. CHAVEZ, Mailing Address: 3023 E. 22nd St., Farmington, 87401. Tel: 505-793-5735. Bishop's Delegate for Religious: VACANT.

Gallup. Cure of Ars House of Discernment— (2009) *300 Mount Carmel Ave., Gallup, 87301.* Tel: 505-863-4406; Fax: 505-722-9131. Email: gallupvocationsoffice@gmail.com. Web:

dioceseofgallup.org. Rev. MATTHEW A. KELLER, Dir. Vocations.

Youth Ministry—CHRISTINE RAYNER, Coord., Mailing Address: P.O. Box 972, Saint Michaels, AZ 86511. Tel: 928-871-3567.

Ministry Formation Program—Mailing Address: P.O. Box 1338, Gallup, 87305. Tel: 505-863-4406, Ext. 24. Rev. BLANE GREIN, O.F.M., Builders of the New Earth & Native American Formation; Deacon FRANK T. CHAVEZ, Dir. Diaconate Life & Ministry. Email: ftchavez@mac.com; bookie@frontier.netTel: 505-793-5735; 480-620-7063; Sisters ROSE MARIE CECCHINI, M.M., Lay Spirituality; RENE BACKE, C.S.A., Academics, Diaconate Candidates: 2; Lay Ministry Candidates: 16.

Diocesan Review Board for Sexual Abuse & Misconduct by Clergy, Religious and Other Church Personnel—Rev. JEROME R. HERFF, C.M., Mailing Address: P.O. Box 3932, Gallup, 87305; KATHLEEN BOWMAN; MARJORIE TRUJILLO, Ph.D.; FLOYD J. KEZELE, J.D., Chm.; Sr. DONNA STEVENS, F.S.P.A.; Det. ROBERT PEREZ.

Victim Assistance Coordinator Team—Sr. MARY THURLOUGH, D.C. Tel: 505-722-4407; HELEN GALLAGHER. Tel: 505-862-7465.

CLERGY, PARISHES, MISSIONS AND PAROCHIAL SCHOOLS

CITY OF GALLUP

(MCKINLEY COUNTY)

1—CATHEDRAL OF THE SACRED HEART (1939), (Dedicated June 19, 1955) Very Rev. Lawrence J. O'Keefe, Rector; Rev. Ravi Kiran; Deacons Randolf Copeland; James P. Hoy; Michael Sullivan.
Res. & Mailing Address: 415 E. Green Ave., 87301. Tel: 505-722-6644; Fax: 505-722-6645.
Catechesis/Religious Program—Tel: 505-722-5485. Debbie Trujillo, D.R.E. Students 226.

2—ST. FRANCIS OF ASSISI (1943), (Hispanic), Revs. Eduardo Espinoza, O.F.M.; Patrick Schaffer, O.F.M.; Deacon Paul Endter.
Res.: 411 N. Second, 87301. Tel: 505-863-3033; Fax: 505-863-6887.
Catechesis/Religious Program—Tel: 505-863-5291. Cynthia Rangel, D.R.E. Students 375.

3—ST. JEROME, Closed. For inquiries for parish records contact Sacred Heart Cathedral.

4—ST. JOHN VIANNEY (1973) Very Rev. James E. Walker.
Res.: 3408 Zia Dr., 87301. Tel: 505-722-3361.
Catechesis/Religious Program—Tel: 505-722-5085. Ethel Kayate, D.R.E. Students 19.

OUTSIDE THE CITY OF GALLUP, NEW MEXICO

ACOMA, CIBOLA CO., SAN ESTEBAN, ACOMA CATHOLIC INDIAN MISSION (1629), (Native American), [CEM 3] Revs. Larry Bernard, O.F.M.; Don Billiard, O.F.M.; Deacon Larry Valdo.
Res.: P.O. Box 448, Pueblo of Acoma, 87034-0448. Tel: 505-552-6403; Fax: 505-522-6221.
Catechesis/Religious Program—Melody Simpson, D.R.E. Students 22.
Mission—St. Anne Pueblo of Acoma, P.O. Box 448, Acomita, Cibola Co. 87034.
Mission—Santa Maria de Acoma McCartys, Cibola Co. 87034.

ARAGON, CATRON CO., SANTO NINO (1910), (Hispanic), Rev. Jeffrey King; Deacon Juan Aragon.
Res.: P.O. Box 489, Reserve, 87830-0489. Tel: 575-533-6240 (Parish); 575-533-6719 (Office).
Catechesis/Religious Program—Students 6.
Mission—Nativity of the Blessed Virgin Mary Datil, Catron Co.
Mission—San Isidro Lower San Francisco, Catron Co.
Mission—St. Francis Reserve, Catron Co.
Mission—St. Anne Horse Springs, Catron Co.
Station— Apache Creek.

AZTEC, SAN JUAN CO., ST. JOSEPH (1946), (Hispanic), Revs. Robert E. Mathieu, Canonical Pastor; Thomas Pudota; Deacon Steve Moffett.
Res.: 500 N. Mesa Verde St., 87410. Tel: 505-334-6535; Fax: 505-334-5902.
Catechesis/Religious Program—Tel: 505-334-3542. Sr. Sara Marie Gomez, O.S.U., D.R.E. Students 158.

BLANCO, SAN JUAN CO., ST. ROSE OF LIMA (1900) [CEM] Rev. Robert E. Mathieu; Deacons Roger Garcia; Patrick R. Valdez.
Res.: 307 N. Church St., Bloomfield, 87413. Tel: 505-632-2014; Fax: 505-634-0312.
Catechesis/Religious Program—Abby Florez, D.R.E. Students 51.
Mission—Our Lady of Guadalupe Los Martinez, San Juan Co.

BLOOMFIELD, SAN JUAN CO., ST. MARY (1960) [CEM] Rev. Robert E. Mathieu; Deacons Roger Garcia; Patrick R. Valdez.
Res.: 307 N. Church St., 87413. Tel: 505-632-2014.
Catechesis/Religious Program—Roselie Valdez, D.R.E. Students 174.

CHICHILTAH, MCKINLEY CO., ST. PATRICK (1965), (Native American), Rev. Eugene Bowski. (Navajo Mission)
Res.: P.O. Box 267, Vanderwagen, 87326. Tel: 505-778-5410.
Catechesis/Religious Program—Sr. M. Cristena, M.C., D.R.E. Students 36.
Mission—Good Shepherd Catholic Mission
Catechesis/Religious Program—Students 12.

CHURCH ROCK, MCKINLEY CO., ST. PHILIP BENIZI, Closed. For inquiries for parish records please see Sacred Heart Cathedral, Gallup.
Station— Pindale.

CROWNPOINT, MCKINLEY CO., ST. PAUL (1961), (Native American), [JC] Very Revs. Lawrence J. O'Keefe, Canonical Pastor; Kevin H. Finnegan, Sacramental Min.; Sr. Maureen Farrar, A.S.C., Pastoral Admin.; Deacon Sherman Manuelito, Pastoral Admin.
Res.: P.O. Box 268, 87313. Tel: 505-786-5376; Fax: 505-786-5376.
Catechesis/Religious Program—Christine Smith, D.R.E.
Mission—Risen Savior Thoreau. H.C. 62, Box 5095, Bluewater, McKinley Co. 87323-9517.
Station— Lake Valley.
Station—St. Bonaventure Thoreau.

CUBA, SANDOVAL CO., IMMACULATE CONCEPTION (Nacimiento) (1914) [CEM 4] Rev. Timothy Cervantes, Pastoral Admin.
Res.: P.O. Box 40, 87013. Tel: 505-289-3803.
Catechesis/Religious Program—Students 73.
Mission—Santo Nino La Jara, Sandoval Co.
Mission—Saint Aloysius Gonzaga San Luis, Sandoval Co.
Mission—San Jose Cabezon, Sandoval Co.

FARMINGTON, SAN JUAN CO.

1—ST. MARY'S (1976), (Hispanic), Very Rev. Michael A. Vigil; Rev. Mohana R. Bathineni, Parochial Vicar; Deacon Frank T. Chavez, Pastoral Assoc.
Res.: 2100 E. 20th, 87401. Tel: 505-325-0287; Fax: 505-564-8515.
Catechesis/Religious Program—Tel: 505-325-0287, Ext. 115; 505-325-0287, Ext. 122. Teresa Garcia, D.R.E. Students 345.

2—SACRED HEART (1929) Rev. Timothy W. Farrell. In Res., Rev. Gil Mangampo.
Res.: 414 N. Allen Ave., 87401. Tel: 505-325-9743; Fax: 505-325-8860.
Catechesis/Religious Program—Tel: 505-564-8164. Sr. Ana Maria Lopez, O.S.F., D.R.E. Students 463.

FLORA VISTA, SAN JUAN CO., HOLY TRINITY (1986), (Hispanic), Revs. Robert E. Mathieu, Canonical Pastor; Thomas Pudota.
Res.: 500 N. Mesa Verde Ave., Aztec, 87410. Tel: 505-334-6535; Fax: 505-334-5902.
Catechesis/Religious Program—Sr. Sara Marie Gomez, O.S.U., D.R.E. Students 16.

FORT WINGATE, MCKINLEY CO., ST. ELEANOR, Closed. For inquiries for parish records contact Sacred Heart Cathedral.
Station— Iyanbito.

GRANTS, CIBOLA CO., ST. TERESA OF AVILA (1942) Very Rev. Alberto Avella; Revs. Edwin Bryan Diesen; Raymond Mahlmann; Deacons Timoteo Lujan; Rogelio Fernandez-Rojo; Larry Chavez.
Res.: 213 Smith St., P.O. Box 668, 87020. Tel: 505-285-6645; Fax: 505-285-6646.
Catechesis/Religious Program—Tel: 505-287-3549. Barbara Rawdon, D.R.E. Students 420.

LAGUNA, CIBOLA CO., ST. JOSEPH (Laguna Indian Pueblo) (1699) Revs. Larry Bernard, O.F.M.; Don Billiard, O.F.M.; Deacon Larry Valdo, Pastoral Assoc.
Res.: P.O. Box 1000, 87026. Tel: 505-552-9330.
Catechesis/Religious Program—Tel: 505-552-7464; Fax: 505-552-9330. Florence Chino, D.R.E.; Virginia Siow, D.R.E. Students 31.
Mission—Nativity of the Blessed Virgin Mary Encinal, Valencia Co.
Mission—Sacred Heart Mesita, Valencia Co.
Mission—St. Elizabeth of Hungary Paguate, Valencia Co.
Mission—St. Margaret Mary Paraje, Valencia Co.
Mission—St. Anne Seama, Valencia Co.

LUMBERTON, RIO ARRIBA CO., ST. FRANCIS OF ASSISI (1910), (Hispanic—Native American), Rev. Peter Morello (Retired).
Res.: P.O. Box 1147, Dulce, 87528. Tel: 505-759-1307.
Catechesis/Religious Program—Valerie Gomez, D.R.E. Students 13.
Mission—St. Anthony 3760 Sandhill, Dulce, Rio Arriba Co. 87528.

MILAN, CIBOLA CO., ST. VIVIAN (1969) Very Rev. Alberto Avella; Revs. Edwin Bryan Diesen; Raymond Mahlmann; Deacons Larry Chavez; Timoteo Lujan; Rogelio Fernandez-Rojo.
Res.: P.O. Box 2938, 87201-2938. Tel: 505-287-9327.
Catechesis/Religious Program—Combined with St. Teresa, Grants, NM.

NAVAJO, MCKINLEY CO., ST. BERARD (1963), (Native American), [JC] Very Rev. Gilbert Schneider, O.F.M.; Sr. Magdalena Studer, S.C., Pastoral Assoc.; Deacon Wilson Gorman.
Res.: P.O. Box 1284, 87328. Tel: 505-777-2251.
Catechesis/Religious Program—Tel: 505-777-2490. Students 22.
Mission—St. Francis Mission P.O. Box 41, Sawmill, Apache Co., AZ 86549. Tel: 602-729-5224.
Station— Crystal.

PINEHAVEN, MCKINLEY CO., GOOD SHEPHERD CATHOLIC MISSION (1972), (Native American), [CEM] Unassigned.
Res.: P.O. Box 2170, 87305. Tel: 505-778-5658.
Catechesis/Religious Program—Combined with St. Patrick, Chichiltah. Students 16.
Convent—Missionaries of Charity, Box 267, Vanderwagen, 87326. Tel: 505-778-5740. Sisters 4.

QUEMADO, CATRON CO., SACRED HEART (1881), (Hispanic), [CEM] Revs. Daniel P. Daley, Canonical Pastor; Kingsley George-Obilonu, Pastoral Admin.
Res.: P.O. Box 339, 87829. Tel: 575-773-4631.
Catechesis/Religious Program—

SAN FIDEL, CIBOLA CO., ST. JOSEPH MISSION (1920), (Hispanic), [CEM] Attended by Acoma, NM. Sr. Ellen Corcoran, S.C.S.J.A., Admin.
Res.: P.O. Box 370, 87049. Tel: 505-552-6257.

SAN MATEO, CIBOLA AND MCKINLEY COS., SAN MATEO Very Rev. Alberto Avella; Revs. Edwin Bryan Diesen; Raymond Mahlmann; Deacons Larry Chavez; Timoteo Lujan; Rogelio Fernandez-Rojo.
Mailing Address: P.O. Box 2938, Milan, 87021. Tel: 505-287-9327.
Catechesis/Religious Program—Combined with St. Teresa, Grants, NM.

SAN RAFAEL, CIBOLA CO., SAN RAFAEL Very Rev. Alberto Avella; Revs. Edwin Bryan Diesen; Raymond Mahlmann; Deacons Larry Chavez; Timoteo Lujan; Rogelio Fernandez-Rojo.
Mailing Address: P.O. Box 2938, Milan, 87201.
Catechesis/Religious Program—Combined with St. Teresa, Grants, NM.

SEBOYETA, CIBOLA CO., OUR LADY OF SORROWS (1774), (Hispanic), [CEM] Very Rev. Alberto Avella, Canonical Pastor; Rev. Raymond Mahlmann, Sacramental Min.; Sr. Ellen Corcoran, S.C.S.J.A., Admin.
Res.: H.C. 77, P.O. Box 13, 87014. Tel: 505-552-6301.
Catechesis/Religious Program—Students 15.
Mission—Our Lady of Light Cubero, Cibola Co. 87014.
Mission—Our Lady of Loretto Bibo, Cibola Co.
Mission—Santa Rosalia Moquino, Valencia Co.
Station— Marquez.

SHIPROCK, SAN JUAN CO., CHRIST THE KING (1924), (Native American), [JC] Very Rev. Daniel F. Kassis; Rev. Benjamin Onwumelu.
Res.: P.O. Box 610, 87420. Tel: 505-368-4532.
Catechesis/Religious Program—Tel: 505-368-5845. Jerome Herbert, D.R.E. Students 7.

THOREAU, MCKINLEY CO., ST. BONAVENTURE, Unassigned.Mailing Address: P.O. Box 268, Crownpoint, 87313. Tel: 505-786-7110.

TINAJA, CIBOLA CO., SAN LORENZO (1981), (Hispanic—Native American), Attended by St. Teresa, Grants, NM.
Res.: State Rte. 2, Box 47, Ramah, 87321. Tel: 505-783-4301.
Catechesis/Religious Program—
Mission—El Morro Fence Lake, Valencia Co.

TOHATCHI, MCKINLEY CO., ST. MARY CHURCH (1920), (Native American), [CEM] Revs. John Mittelstadt, O.F.M.; Bob Ross, S.J., Sacramental Min.; Bro. Maynard Shurley, O.F.M.; Deacon Marcellino Morris Jr. In Res., Rev. Terance Rhoades, O.F.M.
Res.: Box 39, 87325. Tel: 505-733-2243; Fax: 505-733-2243.
Catechesis/Religious Program—Tel: 505-733-2382. Sisters Marlene Kochert, O.S.F., D.R.E.; Pat Bietsch, O.S.F., D.R.E.; Carole Ann Hoppe, O.S.F., D.R.E. Students 27.
Mission—St. Anthony Naschitti, San Juan Co. Tel: 505-733-2468.
Station— Mexican Springs.
Station— Twin Lakes.
Station— Sheep Springs.
Station— Chuska.

WATERFLOW, SAN JUAN CO., SACRED HEART (1917) [CEM] Very Rev. Daniel F. Kassis; Deacon Joseph Didde.
Res.: 9 Rd. 6820, 87421. Tel: 505-598-5454.
Catechesis/Religious Program—Tel: 505-598-9856. Deacon Joseph Didde. Students 33.
Mission—San Juan Catholic Center P.O. Box 857, Kirtland, San Juan Co. 87417. Tel: 505-598-6799.

Mission—Sacred Heart Missionary Cenacle Fruitland. P.O. Box 1037, Ojo Armarillo, San Juan Co. 87416. Tel: 505-598-9856. Sr. Ann Regis Barrett, M.S.B.T., Dir.

ZUNI, MCKINLEY CO., ST. ANTHONY, OUR LADY OF GUADALUPE (Zuni Indian Pueblo) (1923) Rev. Sean Murnan, O.F.M. In Res., Bro. Michael Haag, O.F.M.
Res.: P.O. Box 486, 87327. Tel: 505-782-2888; Fax: 505-782-2888.
Catechesis/Religious Program—Tel: 505-782-2527. Sr. Jean Glach, O.P., D.R.E. Students 3.

ARIZONA

ALPINE, APACHE CO., ST. HELENA (1971) Very Rev. John Sauter.
Res.: P.O. Box 229, AZ 85920. Tel: 928-339-4363.
Catechesis/Religious Program—
Mission—Santo Nino Glenwood, Catron Co. Rev. Msgr. Arthur F. MacDonald (Retired).

CHINLE, APACHE CO., OUR LADY OF FATIMA (1905), (Native American), Rev. Blane Grein, O.F.M. In Res., Bro. Gordon Boykin, O.F.M.
Res.: P.O. Box 2119, AZ 86503. Tel: 928-674-5413; Fax: 928-674-5813.
Mission—St. Anthony P.O. Box 578, Many Farms, Apache Co., AZ 86538. Tel: 928-781-6350.
Catechesis/Religious Program—Sr. Christa McGill, S.B.S., D.R.E.
Mission—St. Mary of the Rosary P.O. Box 432, Pinon, Navajo Co., AZ 86510. Tel: 928-725-3365.
Catechesis/Religious Program—Tel: 928-674-5029. Sr. Nancy Auster, S.B.S., D.R.E. Students 23.

CIBECUE, NAVAJO CO., ST. CATHERINE (1929), (Native American), Rev. Edward Fronske, O.F.M.
Res.: P.O. Box 80156, AZ 85911. Tel: 928-338-4432; Fax: 928-338-1568.
Mission—St. Anthony Cedar Creek, Gila Co., AZ. (TUC)

CONCHO, APACHE CO., SAN RAFAEL (1977) Rev. Yeruva Lourdu Marreddy; Deacon Filomeno Ulibarri.
Church: P.O. Box 309, St. Johns, AZ 85936-0309. Tel: 928-337-4390.
Catechesis/Religious Program—Combined with St. John the Baptist, St. Johns, AZ. Andrea Borg, D.R.E. Students 17.

FORT DEFIANCE, APACHE CO., OUR LADY OF BLESSED SACRAMENT (1915), (Native American), [JC] Very Rev. Gilbert Schneider, O.F.M.; Revs. Ignacio Candelas, O.F.M.; Robert Sprott, O.F.M., Sacramental Min.
Res.: P.O. Box 70, AZ 86504-0070. Tel: 928-729-5068; Fax: 928-729-5069.
Catechesis/Religious Program—Sr. Mary Hottenroth, S.B.S., D.R.E. Students 66.

GANADO, APACHE CO., ALL SAINTS (1968), (Native American), Rev. Flann O'Neil, O.F.M.
Res.: P.O. Box 119, AZ 86505. Tel: 928-755-3401.
Catechesis/Religious Program—Tel: 928-652-3236; Fax: 928-652-3236. Sr. Monica Dubois, O.P., D.R.E. Students 10.
Mission—St. Anne Klagetoh, AZ. #50, HC 58, P.O. Box 90, Apache Co., AZ 86505. Tel: 928-652-3264. Sr. Monica Dubois, O.P.
Mission—Our Lady of the Rosary #161, HC 58, Box 70, Greasewood, Navajo Co., AZ 86505. Tel: 928-654-3236. Bro. Paul O'Brien, O.F.M.
Station— Cornfields, AZ.
Station— Wide Ruins, AZ.

HOLBROOK, NAVAJO CO., OUR LADY OF GUADALUPE (1923) Rev. Anthony O. Dike, Pastoral Admin.
Res.: 212 E. Arizona St., P.O. Box 849, AZ 86025. Tel: 928-524-3261; Fax: 928-524-1507.
Catechesis/Religious Program—Tel: 928-288-3565. Michael Ashenfelder, D.R.E. Students 50.

HOUCK, APACHE CO., ST. JOHN THE EVANGELIST (Tekakwitha Mission) (1927), (Native American), Rev. Robert Sprott, O.F.M.
Res.: P.O. Box 48, AZ 86506. Tel: 928-688-2921; Fax: 928-688-2921.
Catechesis/Religious Program—Students 20.
Mission—St. Rose Pine Springs, Apache Co., AZ.

KAYENTA, NAVAJO CO., OUR LADY OF GUADALUPE (1967) Rev. Jerome R. Herff, C.M.
Res.: P.O. Box 517, AZ 86033. Tel: 928-697-3429; Fax: 928-697-3429.
Catechesis/Religious Program—

KEAMS CANYON, NAVAJO CO., ST. JOSEPH'S INDIAN MISSION (1920), (Hopi-Navajo), Very Rev. Clay Kilburn, C.M.
Res.: P.O. Box 128, AZ 86034. Tel: 928-738-2325; Fax: 928-738-2325.
Catechesis/Religious Program—Students 15.
Station— Toyei, AZ.

LUKACHUKAI, APACHE CO., ST. ISABEL (1910), (Native American), Rev. Blane Grein, O.F.M.
P.O. Box 128, AZ 86507. Tel: 928-787-2322.
Catechesis/Religious Program—Anna Sandoval, D.R.E. Students 6.
Mission—Our Lady of Guadalupe Round Rock, Apache Co., AZ.
Mission—St. Ann Tsaile, Apache Co., AZ.
Mission—Our Lady of the Lake Wheatfields, Apache Co., AZ.

MCNARY, APACHE CO., ST. ANTHONY (1922) Rev. Robert Hyman.
Res.: SAC 628, AZ 85930-0628. Tel: 928-334-2394.
Catechesis/Religious Program—

OVERGAARD, NAVAJO CO., OUR LADY OF ASSUMPTION (1982) Very Rev. John Sauter; Deacon Ronald Wilson.
P.O. Box 628, AZ 85933. Tel: 928-535-5329; Fax: 928-535-6602.
Res.: 455 S. Lake Powell Blvd., Page, AZ 86040.
Catechesis/Religious Program—Jo McKernan, D.R.E. Students 16.

PAGE, COCONINO CO., IMMACULATE HEART OF MARY (1958) Rev. Thomas Maikowski, Admin.; Deacons Jerry Lindsay; Gerald Kocjan.
Res.: 455 S. Lake Powell Blvd., P.O. Box 1387, AZ 86040. Tel: 928-645-2301; Fax: 928-645-1261.
Catechesis/Religious Program—Tel: 928-645-3124. Carla Corn, C.R.E. Students 61.

PINETOP, NAVAJO CO., ST. MARY OF THE ANGELS (1974) Rev. Daniel P. Daley.
Res.: 1915 S. Penrod Ln., Box 819, AZ 85935. Tel: 928-367-2080; Fax: 928-367-2085. Web: www.stmaryoftheangels.us.
Catechesis/Religious Program—Fax: 928-367-2085. Beverly Cloud, D.R.E. Students 158.

PINON, NAVAJO CO., ST. MARY OF THE ROSARY (1937), (Native American), Attended by Chinle, AZ.
Res.: P.O. Box 432, AZ 86510. Tel: 928-725-3365.
Catechesis/Religious Program—Students 6.
Station— Tachee, AZ.
Station— Blue Gap, AZ.
Station— Forest Lake, AZ.
Station— Whippoorwill Spring, AZ.
Station— Hardrock, AZ.
Station— Kits'iiLi, AZ.

ST. JOHNS, APACHE CO., ST. JOHN THE BAPTIST (1890) Very Rev. Joachim Blonski, Canonical Pastor; Rev. Yeruva Lourdu Marreddy, Admin.; Deacon Filomeno Ulibarri.
Res.: P.O. Box 309, AZ 85936. Tel: 928-337-4390.
Catechesis/Religious Program—Tel: 928-337-4461. Sr. Angelina Chavez, O.S.F., D.R.E. Students 106.

ST. MICHAELS, APACHE CO., ST. MICHAEL (1898), (Native American), [JC] Very Rev. Gilbert Schneider, O.F.M.; Revs. Robert Sprott, O.F.M., Sacramental Min.; Ignacio Candelas, O.F.M., Sacramental Min. In Res., Revs. Cormac Antram, O.F.M.; Flann O'Neil, O.F.M.
Res.: P.O. Box 680, AZ 86511-0680. Tel: 928-871-4171; Fax: 928-871-4186.
Catechesis/Religious Program—Tel: 928-871-4173. Christine Rayner, Youth Min.; Sr. Josephine Goebel, C.S.A., D.R.E. Students 40.
Mission—St. Michael's Mission for Navajo Indians, Apache Co., AZ.

SHOW LOW, NAVAJO CO., ST. RITA (1962) Very Rev. Joachim Blonski; Deacon John Heal.
Res.: 1400 E. Owens St., P.O. Box 1449, AZ 85901. Tel: 928-537-2543; Fax: 928-532-8441.
Catechesis/Religious Program—Rebecca Quintana, D.R.E. Students 128.

SNOWFLAKE, NAVAJO CO., OUR LADY OF THE SNOWS (1963) Rev. William J. Welch; Deacon Raymond Melcher.
Res.: 1655 S. Main St., AZ 85937. Tel: 928-536-4559; Fax: 928-536-5852.
Catechesis/Religious Program—Tel: 928-243-1562. Judith Carrillo, D.R.E. Students 64.

SPRINGERVILLE, APACHE CO., ST. PETER (1880), (Hispanic), Revs. Daniel P. Daley, Canonical Pastor; Kingsley George-Obilonu, Admin.; Deacon Jorge Campos, Pastoral Admin.
Res.: P.O. Box 1566, AZ 85938. Tel: 928-333-4423.
Catechesis/Religious Program—Tel: 928-333-5328. Lora Harrison, D.R.E. Students 94.

TUBA CITY, COCONINO CO., ST. JUDE (1956) Rev. J. Godden Menard, C.M., Sacramental Min.; Sr. Mary Rogers, D.C., Admin.
Res.: P.O. Box 248, AZ 86045. Tel: 928-283-5391.
Catechesis/Religious Program—Mary Jo Parys, D.R.E. Students 72.

WHITERIVER, NAVAJO CO., ST. FRANCIS (1921), (Native American), Rev. Edward Fronske, O.F.M.
Res.: 9 W. Elm St., P.O. Box 679, AZ 85941. Tel: 928-338-4432.
Catechesis/Religious Program—Fax: 928-338-1568. Phyllis Esquibel, D.R.E. Students 27.

WINSLOW, NAVAJO CO.
1—ST. JOSEPH'S (1896) Very Rev. Frank Chacon.
Res.: 300 W. Hillview St., AZ 86047. Tel: 928-289-2350; Fax: 928-289-9226.
Catechesis/Religious Program—Laura Osuna, D.R.E.; David Sanchez, D.R.E. Students 202.
2—MADRE DE DIOS (1950), (Hispanic), Very Rev. Frank Chacon.
Res.: 300 W. Hillview St., AZ 86047. Tel: 928-289-2350; Fax: 928-289-9226.
Catechesis/Religious Program—Laura Osuna, D.R.E.; David Sanchez, D.R.E. Twinned with St. Joseph's, Winslow. Students 202.

Chaplains of Public Institutions

GALLUP. *Gallup Area Hospitals & Nursing Homes*, Tel: 505-722-0999. Vacant.

FARMINGTON. *Farmington Area Hospitals*, 414 N. Allen Ave., 87401. Tel: 505-325-9743. Rev. Gil Mangampo.

On Duty Outside of Diocese:
Revs.—
Curran, Oliver, 850 W. Fourth St., Fallon, NV 89406.
Hussey, Daniel C., Chap. (Maj.), St. Joseph Church, 1035 C St., Elko, NV 89801.
Juric, Jakov, Gospinica 18, 21000 Split, Croatia.
Kugler, Michael, 5852 N. Sherman Blvd., Milwaukee, WI 53208.

On Leave of Absence:
Revs.—
Boland, John
McConvey, Michael
Obersteiner, Ernest
Sanchez, Raul N., Ch. Lt. Col.

Retired:
Rev. Msgrs.—
Gomez, Leo, V.G., 100098 Bridgepointe N.E., Albuquerque, 87111.
MacDonald, Arthur F., P.O. Box 222, Glenwood, AZ 88039.
Revs.—
Day, William F., 2828 Park Cir., Unit 3, Pinetop, AZ 85935.
Downie, Arley T., #15 Rd. 6015, 87401.
Franz, Lou, C.M., P.O. Box 1208, Flagstaff, AZ 86002.
Levy, Cyril
Mesley, Jerome T., P.O. Box 1947, 87305.
Morello, Peter, P.O. Box 1147, Dulce, 87528.
O'Neill, Hugh, 1900 Mark Ave., 87301.
Richardson, Donald
Smith, Norman, Mullen Home, 3629 W. 29th Ave., Denver, CO 80211.
Stanfield, Francis E., The Pines, No. 38-9544 Mission Rd., Overland Park, KS 66206.
Tachias, Alfred A., J.C.L., 1900 Mark Ave., 87301.
Universal, Patrick J., 24 Clark St., Boston, MA 02109.

Permanent Deacons:
Aragon, Juan, HC62, Box 637, Aragon, 87820.
Beaton, William P., (Retired), 1815 Wrsteria St., Denton, TX 76205.
Berhost, Paul, (Retired), 1717 E. 23rd St., 87020.
Campos, Jorge, 639 South Ave., Springerville, AZ 85938.
Chavez, Frank T., 3023 E. 22nd St., 87401.
Chavez, Larry, P.O. Box 1883, Grants, 87020.
Copeland, Randolf, M.D., 1609 Red Rock Dr., 87301.
Didde, Joseph, 12 CR 6427, Kirtland, 87417.
Endter, Paul, 3071 Red Bluff Ct., 87301.
Fernandez-Rojo, Rogelio, 80011 Lobo Canyon Rd., Grants, 87020.
Garcia, Roger, 14 CR 4989, Bloomfield, 87413.
Gorman, Wilson C., P.O. Box 218, Fort Defiance, AZ 86504-0218.
Guoladdle, Bobby, Rte. 2, Box 493, Carnegie, OK 73015.
Heal, John, P.O. Box 2845, Snowflake, AZ 85937.
Hoy, James, 411 East Logan, 87301.
Kelley, Timothy, 416 Valentine Dr., 87301. (On Leave of Absence)
Kocjan, Gerald, P.O. Box 3748, Page, AZ 86040.
Krikawa, Joseph, 2410 W. Calle Retana, Tucson, AZ 85745.
Lente, Michael, 133 Camino del Pueblo, Bernalillo, 87004.
Lindsay, Jerry, P.O. Box 3607, Page, AZ 86040-3607.
Lujan, Timoteo, P.O. Box 2612, Milan, 87021-2612.
Majesky, Russel, 212 S. Nichols, San Manuel, AZ 85631.
Manuelito, Sherman, P.O. Box 538, Crownpoint, 87313.
Martin, Daniel Nez, P.O. Box 724, Window Rock, AZ 86515.
Melcher, Raymond, P.O. Box 1266, Snowflake, AZ 85937-1226.
Moffett, Stephen, P.O. Box 1892, Aztec, 87410.
Morris, Marcelino, P.O. Box 768, Fort Defiance, AZ 86505.
Peterson, Charles, 30 Rd. 3011, Aztec, 87410.
Racicot, Robert, P.O. Box 697, Ruidoso, 88355.
Richtsmeier, Thomas, M.D., 2901 8th St., S.E., East Wenatchee, WA 98802.
Rogers, Earl, 7915 Springfield-Jamestown Rd., Springfield, OH 45502.

Rogers, William, P.O. Box 217, Taylor, AZ 85939-0217.
Stando, Matthew, 2446 Harlem Rd., Cheektowaga, NY 14225.
Stringfellow, Roy, 379 W. Strawberry Dr., Pueblo West, CO 81007.
Sullivan, Michael, P.O. Box 3327, 87305.
Ulibarri, Fiomeno, P.O. Box 453, Concho, AZ 85924.
Valdez, Patrick R., P.O. Box 526, Blanco, 87412.
Valdo, Larry, P.O. Box 352, Pueblo Of Acoma, 87034.
Valencia, Ernest, P.O. Box 461, Blanco, 87412. (On Leave of Absence)
Wilson, Ronald, P.O. Box 574, Overgaard, AZ 85933.

INSTITUTIONS LOCATED IN THE DIOCESE

[A] HIGH SCHOOLS

GALLUP. *Gallup Catholic High School*, 515 Park Ave., 87301. Tel: 505-722-6089; Fax: 505-726-8142. Email: gcschool@cnetco.com. Web: www.gcschool.pvt.k12.nm.us. David Boyd, Prin. Lay Teachers 11; Students 118.

ST. MICHAELS, AZ. *St. Michael High School*, P.O. Box 650, AZ 86511. Tel: 928-871-4443; Fax: 928-871-3191. Email: principal@smis1902.org. Thomas Sorci, Prin. Brothers 1; Sisters 4; Lay Teachers 13; Students 156.

[B] ELEMENTARY SCHOOLS

GALLUP. *St. Francis of Assisi School*, (Grades PreK-5), 215 W. Wilson, 87305. Tel: 505-863-3145; Fax: 505-863-3145. Don Joseph Frank, Prin. Sisters 3; Lay Teachers 10; Students 86.

Gallup Catholic School, (Grades PreK-8), 515 Park Ave., 87301. Tel: 505-863-6652; Fax: 505-726-8142. Email: gcshool@cnetco.com. Web: www.gcschool.pvt.k12.nm.us. David Boyd, Prin. Lay Teachers 10; Students 189.

FARMINGTON. *Sacred Heart School*, (Grades PreK-5), 404 N. Allen Ave., 87401. Tel: 505-325-7152; Fax: 505-325-6157. Email: olybrook@shcsfarmington.com. Web: www.shcsfarmington.org. Orla Lybrook, Prin. Lay Teachers 12; Students 100.

GRANTS. *St. Teresa of Avila School*, (Grades PreK-8), 402 E. High St., 87020. Tel: 505-287-2261; Fax: 505-285-4350. Email: stteresaschool@hotmail.com. Maria Mirabal, Prin. Lay Teachers 8; Students 70.

LUMBERTON. *St. Francis School*, (Grades K-8), HC 71, Box 26, 87528. Tel: 505-759-3252; Fax: 505-759-3844. Email: lumbertonschool@yahoo.com. Leonard Meyer, Prin.; Jerome Smith, Librarian. Lay Teachers 8; Students 73.

ST. MICHAELS, AZ. *St. Michael Elementary School*, (Grades K-8), P.O. Box 650, AZ 86511. Tel: 928-871-4636; Fax: 928-871-3027. Email: smis1902@aol.com. Web: www.rc.net/gallup/stmichael. Tracie Lee, Prin.; Mary Roanhorse, Librarian. Brothers 1; Sisters 2; Lay Teachers 12; Students 218.

SAN FIDEL. *St. Joseph School*, (Grades K-3), P.O. Box 370, 87049. Tel: 505-552-6362; Fax: 505-552-0168. Sr. Consolata Beecher, S.B.S., Prin. Lay Teachers 3; Students 14.

SHOW LOW. *Our Lady of Perpetual Help dba St. Anthony Catholic School* (Grades PreK-4), P.O. Box 696, Lakeside, AZ 85929-0696. Robert Higgins, Prin. Lay Teachers 8; Students 87.

THOREAU. *St. Bonaventure School*, (Grades PreK-8), 25 Navarre Blvd. W., P.O. Box 909, 87323. Tel: 505-862-7465; Fax: 505-862-7790. Web: www.sbms.k12.nm.us. Sr. Natalie Bussiere, S.N.D.deN., Prin. Sisters 5; Lay Teachers 13; Students 205.

ZUNI. *St. Anthony Indian School*, (Grades PreK-8), P.O. Box 486, 87327. Tel: 505-782-4596; Fax: 505-782-2013. Deborah Goering, Prin. Sisters 3; Lay Teachers 17; Students 100.

[C] CONVENTS AND RESIDENCES FOR SISTERS

GALLUP. *Casa Reina*, 217 E. Wilson, 87301. Tel: 505-722-5511; Fax: 505-863-0075. Email: casareina@questoffice.net. Sr. Magda Garcia, H.N.S.G., Supr. Sisters of Guadalupe and St. Joseph., Perpetual Adoration Chapel. Immigration and Naturalization Services, Hispanic Ministry. Sisters 9.

Catholic Charities of Gallup, Inc., 506 W. Hwy. 66, P.O. Box 3146, 87301. Tel: 505-722-4407; Fax: 505-722-7512. Email: director@catholiccharitiesgallup.com. Web: www.catholiccharitiesgallup.com. Sr. Kathleen Driscoll, D.C., Exec. Dir.

[D] HOMES FOR THE AGED

GALLUP. *Villa Guadalupe Home for the Aged*, 1900 Mark Ave., 87301. Tel: 505-863-6894; Fax: 505-722-4121. Email: msgallup@littlesistersofthepoor.org. Sr. Andrea Munarriz, L.S.P.; Rev. Alfred A. Tachias, J.C.L., Chap. (Retired). Little Sisters of the Poor 9; Total Assisted 50; Total Staff 50.

[E] MISCELLANEOUS LISTINGS

GALLUP. *Blue Army* (Fatima Apostolate), 217 E. Wilson Ave., 87301. Tel: 505-722-5511; Fax: 505-863-0075. Email: casareina@questoffice.net. Sisters Magda Leticia Garcia, H.N.S.G., Spiritual Dir.; Rosa M. Zuniga, H.N.S.G., Contact Person.

Casa San Martin, Mailing Address: 207 E. Wilson St., 87301. Tel: 505-722-5261. 411 W. Wilson Ave., 87301. Tel: 505-722-5156. Sr. M. Mirjana, M.C., Supr. & Contact Person. Missionaries of Charity., Soup Kitchen & Shelter for Native American Clients. Missionaries of Charity 6; Total Assisted 49,800.

Catholic Peoples' Foundation, Inc., P.O. Box 369, 87305. Tel: 505-726-8295; Fax: 505-726-8295. Email: dot@catholicpeoplesfoundation.com. Web: www.catholicpeoplesfoundation.com. Dot Teso, Exec. Dir.

Gallup Catholic School Foundation, Inc., 515 Park Ave., 87301. Tel: 505-722-6966; Fax: 505-726-8142. Email: gc.school@hotmail.com. Web: www.edline.net/pages/Gallup_Catholic_School. Amy Collar, Exec. Dir.

Sacred Heart Retreat, P.O. Box 1338, 87305. Tel: 505-722-6755. Email: rbcsa@cnetco.com. Web: www.dioceseofgallup.org. Sr. Rene Backe, C.S.A., Program Dir.

Southwest Indian Foundation, 100 W. Coal Ave., P.O. Box 307, 87305. Tel: 505-863-2837; Fax: 505-863-2760. Email: swif@cia-g.com. Web: www.southwestindian.com. Mr. William McCarthy, CEO.

Board of Directors: Most Rev. James S. Wall; Mr. James Mason, Pres.; Mr. John Dowling, Vice Pres.; Mrs. Mary Constant, Sec.; Very Rev. Gilbert Schneider, O.F.M.; Hon. Judge Marie Nezwood; Phillip G. Garcia; Victoria Taliman; Angelo Di Paolo.

CHINLE, AZ. *Talbot House-Catholic Charities*, P.O. Box 417, AZ 86503. Tel: 928-674-3238; Fax: 928-674-5813. Web: www.catholiccharitiesgallup.com. Sr. Kathleen Driscoll, D.C., Interim Dir. Total Assisted 2,600; Total Staff 3.

GRANTS-MILAN. *Casa San Jose*, 2595 W. Hwy. 66, 87020-9626. Tel: 505-285-5451; Fax: 505-285-6436. Email: casa@7cities.net. Web: www.cnetco/~Catholiccharities.com. Sr. Francine Schuster, A.S.C., Admin. Residence of pregnant & parenting teenagers. Operated by Catholic Charities. Sisters Adorers of the Blood of Christ 1; Sinsinawa Dominicans of the Most Holy Rosary 1; Total Staff 10; Total Assisted 24.

PINETOP, AZ. *St. Vincent DePaul Society* (1990) P.O. Box 376, AZ 85935. Tel: 928-367-2029 (Thrift Shop); 928-367-3057 (Emergency Aid Office). Email: Lucysvdp@wmonline.com. Mary Alcon Young, Pres.; Lucy Wallace, Asst. Officer. Thrift Shop & Emergency Aid Office. Total Assisted 1,080; Total Staff 3.

THOREAU. *St. Bonaventure Indian Mission & School*, 25 Navarre Blvd. W., P.O. Box 610, 87323. Tel: 505-862-7847; Fax: 505-862-7029. Email: chaltar@stbonaventuremission.org. Web: www.stbonaventuremission.org.

TUBA CITY, AZ. *Life Sharing Center, Inc., St. Jude Food Bank*, P.O. Box 1277, AZ 86045. Tel: 928-283-6886; Fax: 928-283-6614. Email: stjudefoodbank@frontiernet.net. Sr. Maureen Houlihan, D.C., Exec. Dir.

WINSLOW, AZ. *La Casa de Nuestra Senora (Madonna House)* (1957) 213 Jefferson St., AZ 86047. Tel: 928-289-9284. Web: www.madonnahouse.org. Email: madonnahouse@cableone.net. Kathy McVady, Dir. Mission of Madonna House Apostolate Combermere, Ontario, Canada; Prayer and Community Service Center; Catechesis of the Good Shepherd Program for 3 - 5 yr. olds. Total in Residence 6.

RELIGIOUS INSTITUTES OF MEN REPRESENTED IN THE DIOCESE

For further details refer to the corresponding bracketed number in the Religious Institutes of Men or Women section.

[1100]—*Brothers of the Sacred Heart*—S.C.
[1330]—*Congregation of the Mission* (Western Prov.)—C.M.
[0490]—*Franciscan Brothers of Brooklyn, NY*—O.S.F.
[0520]—*Franciscan Friars* (Provs. of Our Lady of Guadalupe; St. John the Baptist & Santa Barbara)—O.F.M.

RELIGIOUS INSTITUTES OF WOMEN REPRESENTED IN THE DIOCESE

[0100]—*Adorers of the Blood of Christ*—A.S.C.
[3710]—*Congregation of the Sisters of Saint Agnes*—C.S.A.
[1780]—*Congregation of the Sisters of the Third Order of St. Francis of Perpetual Adoration*—F.S.P.A.
[0760]—*Daughters of Charity of St. Vincent de Paul*—D.C.
[1070-13]—*Dominican Sisters (Adrian, MI)*—O.P.
[1115]—*Dominican Sisters of Peace*—O.P.
[1070-09]—*Dominican Sisters (Racine, WI)*—O.P.
[1390]—*Franciscan Missionary Sisters of Our Lady of Sorrow*—O.S.F.
[1350]—*Franciscan Missionary Sisters of the Immaculate Conception*—O.S.F.
[1180]—*Franciscan Sisters of Allegany* (New York)—O.S.F.
[1415]—*Franciscan Sisters of Mercy*—F.S.M.
[1425]—*Franciscan Sisters of Peace*—F.S.P.
[2340]—*Little Sisters of the Poor*—L.S.P.
[2470]—*Maryknoll Sisters of St. Dominic*—M.M.
[2490]—*Medical Mission Sisters*—M.M.S.
[2710]—*Missionaries of Charity*—M.C.
[2790]—*Missionary Servants of the Most Blessed Trinity*—M.S.B.T.
[2760]—*Missionary Sisters of the Immaculate Conception of the Mother of God*—S.M.I.C.
[3640]—*Poor Servants of the Mother of God*—S.M.G.
[0480]—*Sisters of Charity Levenworth*—S.C.L.
[0600]—*Sisters of Charity of St. Joan Antide*—S.C.S.J.A.
[2360]—*Sisters of Loretto*—S.L.
[2990]—*Sisters of Notre Dame*—S.N.D.
[3000]—*Sisters of Notre Dame de Namur*—S.N.D.deN.
[0590]—*Sisters of St. Elizabeth* (Convent Station)—S.C.
[1510]—*Sisters of St. Francis*—O.S.F.
[1705]—*Sisters of St. Francis of Assisi*—O.S.F.
[1730]—*Sisters of St. Francis of Oldenburg*—O.S.F.
[1650]—*The Sisters of St. Francis of Philadelphia*—O.S.F.
[3830-13]—*Sisters of St. Joseph of Boden, PA*—C.S.J.
[0260]—*Sisters of the Blessed Sacrament for Indians and Colored People*—S.B.S.
[1830]—*The Sisters of the Good Shepherd*—R.G.S.
[1990]—*Sisters of the Holy Name of Jesus and Mary*—S.N.J.M.
[]—*Sisters of the Immaculate Heart of Mary* Nigeria
[1440]—*Sisters of the Poor of St. Francis*—S.F.P.
[4120-05]—*Ursuline Nuns of the Congregation of Paris*—O.S.U.

NECROLOGY

✠ Pelotte, Most Rev. Donald E., Retired Bishop of Gallup—Died Jan. 7, 2010

An asterisk (*) denotes an organization that has established tax-exempt status directly with the IRS and is not covered by the USCCB Group Ruling.

Archdiocese of Galveston-Houston

(Archidioecesis Galvestoniensis Houstoniensis)

His Eminence

DANIEL CARDINAL DiNARDO

Archbishop of Galveston-Houston; ordained July 16, 1977; appointed Coadjutor Bishop of Sioux City August 19, 1997; consecrated October 7, 1997; appointed Bishop of Sioux City November 28, 1998; appointed Coadjutor Bishop of Galveston-Houston January 16, 2004; installed March 26, 2004; appointed Coadjutor Archbishop December 29, 2004; succeeded to the See February 28, 2006; elevated to Cardinal November 24, 2007. *Mailing Address: P.O. Box 907, Houston, TX 77001-0907.* Tel: 713-659-5461.

Most Reverend

JOSEPH A. FIORENZA, D.D.

Retired Archbishop of Galveston-Houston; ordained May 29, 1954; appointed Bishop of San Angelo September 4, 1979; consecrated and installed October 25, 1979; appointed Bishop of Galveston-Houston December 18, 1984; installed February 18, 1985; appointed Archbishop December 29, 2004; retired February 28, 2006. *Mailing Address: P.O. Box 907, Houston, TX 77001-0907.* Tel: 713-659-5461.

Chancery Office: P.O. Box 907, Houston, TX 77001-0907. Tel: 713-659-5461; Fax: 713-759-9151.

Most Reverend

VINCENT M. RIZZOTTO, J.C.L.

Retired Auxiliary Bishop of Galveston-Houston; ordained May 26, 1956; appointed Auxiliary Bishop of Galveston-Houston June 22, 2001; ordained July 31, 2001; retired November 6, 2006.

ESTABLISHED IN 1847.

Square Miles 8,880.

Redesignated Diocese of Galveston-Houston on July 25, 1959; created Archdiocese December 29, 2004.

Comprises the Counties of Austin, Brazoria, Fort Bend, Galveston, Grimes, Harris, Montgomery, San Jacinto, Walker and Waller in the State of Texas.

For legal titles of parishes and archdiocesan institutions, consult the Chancery Office.

STATISTICAL OVERVIEW

Personnel	
Cardinals	1
Retired Archbishops	1
Retired Bishops	1
Priests: Diocesan Active in Diocese	138
Priests: Diocesan Active Outside Diocese	3
Priests: Diocesan in Foreign Missions	2
Priests: Retired, Sick or Absent	57
Number of Diocesan Priests	200
Religious Priests in Diocese	199
Total Priests in Diocese	399
Extern Priests in Diocese	38
Ordinations:	
Diocesan Priests	4
Permanent Deacons in Diocese	386
Total Brothers	15
Total Sisters	456
Parishes	
Parishes	146
With Resident Pastor:	
Resident Diocesan Priests	102
Resident Religious Priests	39
Without Resident Pastor:	
Administered by Priests	4
Missions	6
Pastoral Centers	19
New Parishes Created	1
Closed Parishes	7
Welfare	
Catholic Hospitals	2
Total Assisted	226,461
Health Care Centers	9
Total Assisted	133,462
Homes for the Aged	4
Total Assisted	437
Residential Care of Children	4
Total Assisted	661
Day Care Centers	37
Total Assisted	3,675
Specialized Homes	5
Total Assisted	5,420
Special Centers for Social Services	11
Total Assisted	737,241
Educational	
Seminaries, Diocesan	1
Students from This Diocese	18
Students from Other Diocese	71
Diocesan Students in Other Seminaries	26
Seminaries, Religious	5
Students Religious	10
Total Seminarians	54
Colleges and Universities	1
Total Students	3,246
High Schools, Private	9
Total Students	4,201
Elementary Schools, Diocesan and Parish	44
Total Students	11,849
Elementary Schools, Private	7
Total Students	2,060
Catechesis/Religious Education:	
High School Students	20,125
Elementary Students	67,747
Total Students under Catholic Instruction	109,282
Teachers in the Diocese:	
Sisters	21
Lay Teachers	1,428
Vital Statistics	
Receptions into the Church:	
Infant Baptism Totals	11,534
Minor Baptism Totals	10,576
Adult Baptism Totals	1,782
Received into Full Communion	775
First Communions	19,588
Confirmations	9,857
Marriages:	
Catholic	2,744
Interfaith	728
Total Marriages	3,472
Deaths	3,720
Total Catholic Population	1,146,908
Total Population	5,811,010

Former Bishops—Rt. Revs. J. M. ODIN, C.M., D.D., ordained May 4, 1823; cons. Bishop of Claudiopolis and Vicar-Apostolic of Texas, March 6, 1842; transferred to Galveston 1847; promoted to New Orleans in 1861; died in Ambierle, France, May 25, 1870; C. M. DUBUIS, D.D., ordained June 1, 1844; cons. Nov. 23, 1862; resigned 1881; remained Titular Bishop of Galveston till 1892, when he was promoted to an Archbishopric i.p.i.; died May 21, 1895; at Vernaison, France; P. DUFAL, C.S.C., D.D., ordained Sept. 29, 1852; cons. Nov. 25, 1860; Bishop of Delcon, and Vicar-Apostolic of Eastern Bengal; transferred to Galveston; as Coadjutor of Rt. Rev. C. M. Dubuis, cum jure successionis, May 14, 1878; resigned 1880; died in Paris 1898; NICHOLAS A. GALLAGHER, D.D., ordained Dec. 25, 1868; consecrated Titular Bishop of Canopus, April 30, 1882; succeeded to Galveston, Dec. 16, 1892; died Jan. 21, 1918; Most Revs. CHRISTOPHER E. BYRNE, D.D., appt. July 18, 1918; cons. Nov. 10, 1918; made Assistant at the Pontifical Throne, May 8, 1941; died April 1, 1950; WENDELIN J. NOLD, S.T.D., appt. Nov. 29, 1947; consecrated Feb. 25, 1948; died Oct. 1, 1981; JOHN L. MORKOVSKY, S.T.D., ord. Dec. 5, 1933; Titular Bishop of Hieron and Auxiliary Bishop of Amarillo; appt. Dec. 22, 1955; cons. Feb. 22, 1956; succeeded to See Aug. 18, 1958; transferred to Galveston-Houston as Titular Bishop of Tigava and Coadjutor and Apostolic Administrator "cum jure successionis"April 1963; installed June 11, 1963; succeeded to the See of Galveston-Houston, April 22, 1975; retired Aug. 16, 1984; died March 24, 1990; JOSEPH A. FIORENZA, ord. May 29, 1954; appt. Bishop of San Angelo Sept. 4, 1979; cons. and installed Oct. 25, 1979; appt. Bishop of Galveston-Houston Dec. 18, 1984; installed Feb. 18, 1985; appt. Archbishop Dec. 29, 2004; retired Feb. 28, 2006.

Chancery Office—1700 San Jacinto St., Houston, 77002-8291. Mailing Address: P.O. Box 907, Houston, 77001-0907. Tel: 713-659-5461; Fax: 713-759-9151. Office Hours: Mon.-Fri. 8:30-4:30.

Chancellor and Moderator of the Curia—VACANT, 1700 San Jacinto St., Houston, 77002-8291. Tel: 713-659-5461.

Vice Chancellor and Associate General Counsel—Ms. CHRISTINA DEAJON, 1700 San Jacinto St., Houston, 77002-8291. Tel: 713-659-5461.

Vicars General—Most Rev. VINCENT M. RIZZOTTO, D.D., J.C.L.; Rev. Msgr. FRANK H. ROSSI, S.T.L.

Ethnic Vicars—Deacon ANDREW B. MALVEAUX SR., Vicar of African American Catholics; VACANT, Vicar of Hispanic Catholics; Rev. JOSEPH THANH VA, Vicar of Vietnamese Catholics; Rev. Msgr. SETH F. HERMOSO, Vicar of Filipino Catholics.

Vicar for Religious—Sr. HELOISE CRUZAT, O.P., 2403 Holcombe, Houston, 77021. Tel: 713-741-8733.

Deans and Vicariates—

Central Vicariate—Revs. WENCIL C. PAVLOVSKY, V.F. Tel: 713-946-8968; SALVATORE DEGEORGE, O.M.I., Central Dean. Tel: 713-695-0631; ALBERT ZANATTA, C.R.S., Northeast Dean. Tel: 281-447-6381; OSCAR M. CASTRO, Southeast Dean. Tel: 713-645-6614.

Northern Vicariate—Revs. JOSEPH A. GIETL, Episcopal Vicar. Tel: 713-942-3447; HUBERT J. KEALY, Northern Dean. Tel: 936-756-8186; JOHN

A. ZABELSKAS, V.F., Eastern Dean. Tel: 281-843-2422; FRED W. VALONE, San Jacinto Dean. Tel: 281-351-8106.
Southern Vicariate—Rev. Msgr. LEO WLECZYK. Tel: 979-297-3041; Revs. PAUL G. FELIX, V.F.; DOMINIC PISTONE, V.F., Bay Area Dean. Tel: 281-485-2421; ROBERT J. DUGGAN, C.S.B. Tel: 979-849-2421.
Western Vicariate—Rev. Msgr. DANIEL L. SCHEEL, Episcopal Vicar. Tel: 713-468-9555; Rev. STEPHEN B. REYNOLDS, Western Dean. Tel: 979-793-4477; Rev. Msgr. BILL YOUNG, V.F., Southwest Dean. Tel: 713-729-0221; Revs. JOHN E. CAHOON, J.C.L., Northwest Dean. Tel: 713-692-9123; ERIC J. PITRE, M.Div. Tel: 979-885-3868.

Secretariat Directors—
Secretariat For Administration—VACANT, 1700 San Jacinto St., Houston, 77002-8291. Tel: 713-659-5461.
Secretariat For Clergy Formation and Chaplaincy Services—Rev. Msgr. GEORGE A. SHELTZ, E.V., Dir., 1700 San Jacinto St., Houston, 77002-8291. Tel: 713-659-5461.
Secretariat For Communication—Mrs. JENNY FABER, 1700 San Jacinto St., Houston, 77002-8291. Tel: 713-659-5461.
Secretariat For Finance—Mr. DAVID HESSELL, 1700 San Jacinto St., Houston, 77002-8291. Tel: 713-659-5461.
Secretariat For Pastoral and Educational Ministries—Mr. JIM BARRETTE, Dir., 2403 Holcombe, Houston, 77021-2099. Tel: 713-741-8786.
Secretariat for Catholic Schools—Sr. KEVINA KEATING, C.C.V.I., 2403 Holcombe Blvd., Houston, 77021.
Secretariat for Social Concerns—VACANT, Dir., 2403 Holcombe, Houston, 77021-2099. Tel: 713-741-8769.

Tribunal Judicial—
Metropolitan Tribunal—Very Rev. LAWRENCE W. JOZWIAK, J.C.L., Judicial Vicar, Mailing Address: P.O. Box 907, Houston, 77001-0907. Tel: 713-807-9286; Fax: 713-807-9296. Email: tribunal@archgh.org.
Adjutant Judicial Vicar—Rev. RICHARD A. WAHL, C.S.B., J.C.L., Mailing Address: P.O. Box 907, Houston, 77001-0907. Tel: 713-807-9286; Fax: 713-807-9296. Email: tribunal@archgh.org.
Director of the Tribunal—Ms. ANNE BRYANT, J.C.L.
Archdiocesan Judges—Rev. Msgr. PHILIPPE LE-XUAN THUONG, J.C.D.; Revs. TRUNG V. NGUYEN, J.C.L.; ERIC J. PITRE, M.Div.; THU NGOC NGUYEN.
Promoter of Justice—Rev. JOHN E. CAHOON, J.C.L.
Defenders of the Bond—Rev. Msgrs. DAVID KENNEDY, J.C.L.; WILLIAM M. PICKARD, J.C.D. (Retired); Rev. EDWIN A. COREAS, J.C.L.; Ms. ANNE BRYANT, J.C.L.
Censor Librorum—Rev. TERENCE BRINKMAN, S.T.D., 915 Runneburg Rd., Crosby, 77532. Tel: 281-328-4871.

Archdiocesan Councils, Commissions and Committees
Archdiocesan Presbyteral Council—1700 San Jacinto St., Houston, 77002-8291.
Presbyteral Council—His Eminence DANIEL CARDINAL DINARDO, Pres. Ex Officio Members: Most Rev. VINCENT M. RIZZOTTO, D.D., J.C.L., Vicar Gen.; Rev. Msgrs. FRANK H. ROSSI, S.T.L., Vicar Gen.; GEORGE A. SHELTZ, E.V. Appointees: Rev. Msgr. LEO WLECZYK; Rev. WENCIL C. PAVLOVSKY, V.F.; Rev. Msgrs. DANIEL L. SCHEEL; CHESTER L. BORSKI; Rev. JOSEPH A. GIETL. Elected Members: Revs. RONALD F. CLOUTIER, Chap.; DANIEL K. LAHART, S.J., Educational; VACANT, Spiritual and Admin. Area Representatives: VACANT, Northern, Western and Bluebonnet; VACANT, Galveston-Mainland and Southern; Revs. RIVERS PATOUT, Bay Area and Southeast; SEAN HORRIGAN, Southwest and Northwest; DAVID CANIZARES, Eastern and San Jacinto.
College of Consultors—Most Rev. VINCENT M. RIZZOTTO, D.D., J.C.L.; Rev. Msgrs. DANIEL L. SCHEEL; LEO WLECZYK; FRANK H. ROSSI, S.T.L.; GEORGE A. SHELTZ, E.V.; CHESTER L. BORSKI; Revs. JOSEPH A. GIETL; WENCIL C. PAVLOVSKY, V.F.
Priests Personnel Committee—His Eminence DANIEL CARDINAL DINARDO; Rev. Msgr. GEORGE A. SHELTZ, E.V., Chm., 1700 San Jacinto, Houston, 77002. Tel: 713-659-5461, Ext. 8241; Revs. HUBERT J. KEALY; THU NGOC NGUYEN; Rev. Msgr. FRANK H. ROSSI, S.T.L. (16-24 yrs.); Rev. CLINT C. RESSLER; Rev. Msgr. CHESTER L. BORSKI; Rev. ITALO DELL'ORO, C.R.S.
Building and Planning Commission—Rev. NORBERT J. MADUZIA JR., D.Min.; Rev. Msgr. GEORGE A. SHELTZ, E.V.; Ms. CHRISTINA DEAJON; Deacon GERALD W. DUPONT; Mr. DON SENGER; Mr. STEVE FAUGHT, Chm., 1700 San Jacinto, Houston, 77002. Tel: 713-659-5461.
Archdiocesan School Council—ERNEST A. FORZANO. Tel: 713-241-1424.
Ecumenism and Interreligious Affairs Commission—Rev. JOHN ROONEY, 1700 San Jacinto, Houston, 77002. Tel: 713-659-5461.
Liturgical Commission—Rev. JAMES M. BURKART, Chm., 11011 Hall Rd., Houston, 77089. Tel: 281-481-6816.

Secretariat for Administration—VACANT, 1700 San Jacinto St., Houston, 77002-8291. Tel: 713-659-5461.
Administrative Service Department—Deacon CHARLES DUCK, 1700 San Jacinto, Houston, 77002. Tel: 713-659-5461, Ext. 4484.
Archives and Current Records—Ms. LISA MAY, Dir., 1700 San Jacinto St., Houston, 77002-8291. Tel: 713-659-5461.
Catholic Cemeteries—Mr. GUS HOLLIS, Dir., Gulf Fwy. at Hughes Rd., P.O. Box 965, Dickinson, 77539. Tel: 281-337-1641; 409-948-1455.
Construction/Preventative Maintenance—Mr. STEVE FAUGHT, Dir.; Mr. DON SENGER, Preventive Maintenance, 1700 San Jacinto St., Houston, 77002-8291. Tel: 713-659-5461.
Information Services—Mr. ED HERRERA, 1700 San Jacinto St., Houston, 77002-8921. Tel: 713-659-5461.
Internal Auditor—Mr. WILLIAM PRIME, 1700 San Jacinto St., Houston, 77002-8291. Tel: 713-659-5461.
Legal Services—Mr. JOHN SIEGER, Dir. Gen. Counsel, 1700 San Jacinto St., Houston, 77002-8291. Tel: 713-659-5461.
Real Estate—Mr. KEN SYKES, 1700 San Jacinto St., Houston, 77002-8291. Tel: 713-659-5461.
Human Resources—DIANE BLANKENSHIP, Dir., 1700 San Jacinto St., Houston, 77002. Tel: 713-659-5461.

Secretariat for Clergy Formation and Chaplaincy Services—Rev. Msgr. GEORGE A. SHELTZ, E.V., Dir., 1700 San Jacinto St., Houston, 77002-8291. Mailing Address: P.O. Box 907, Houston, 77001-0907. Tel: 713-659-5461.
Apostleship of the Sea (Port Ministry)—Rev. RIVERS PATOUT, Houston Dir. Tel: 713-923-5843. Mailing Address: Houston International Seaman's Center, P.O. Box 9506, Houston, 77261. Tel: 713-672-0511; Mrs. KAREN PARSONS, Galveston, P.O. Box 2742, League City, 77574. Tel: 409-762-0021; Fax: 409-762-1436.
Catholic Chaplain Corps (Hospital Chaplains)—Rev. PAGE E. POLK, O.F.M., 4206 MacGregor Way S., Houston, 77021-1598. Tel: 713-526-6438.
Catholic Relief Services—Mrs. HILDA HERNANDEZ, Dir., 1700 San Jacinto St., Houston, 77002-8921. Tel: 713-659-5461.
Correctional Ministries (Jail Chaplains)—Rev. RONALD F. CLOUTIER, Dir. (Chaplain Office at Harris County Jail), Office and Mailing Address, 2403 E. Holcombe, Houston, 77021-2098. Tel: 713-741-8745; 713-755-5326 (Jail).
Director of Ministry to Priests—Rev. ITALO DELL'ORO, C.R.S., Somascan Formation House, 610 W. Melwood, Houston, 77009. Tel: 713-880-8243.
Diaconal Formation/Diaconal Ministry—Deacon GERALD W. DUPONT, Dir., 1700 San Jacinto St., Houston, 77002-8291. Tel: 713-659-5461.
Permanent Deacons—Deacon GERALD W. DUPONT, Dir., 1700 San Jacinto St., Houston, 77002-8291. Tel: 713-659-5461.
Mission Office—Mrs. HILDA HERNANDEZ, Dir., 1700 San Jacinto St., Houston, 77002-8291. Tel: 713-659-5461 Holy Childhood, Propagation of the Faith.
Seminarian Support—Rev. DAT HOANG, Dir., 1700 San Jacinto St., Houston, 77002-8291. Tel: 713-659-5461.
Vocations Office—Rev. DAT HOANG, Dir., 1700 San Jacinto St., Houston, 77002-8291. Tel: 713-659-5461.

Secretariat for Communication—Mrs. JENNY FABER, Dir., 1700 San Jacinto St., Houston, 77002-8291. Tel: 713-659-5461.
Radio—Mrs. MADELINE JOHNSON, 1700 San Jacinto St., Houston, 77002-8291. Tel: 713-659-5461.
Texas Catholic Herald—Ms. MELANIE SPENCER, Editor, 1700 San Jacinto St., Houston, 77002-8291. Tel: 713-659-5461; Fax: 713-659-3444.

Secretariat for Finance—Mr. DAVID HESSELL, Dir., 1700 San Jacinto St., Houston, 77002-8291. Tel: 713-659-5461.
Accounting Department—HEIDI HENRICHS, Controller, 1700 San Jacinto St., Houston, 77002-8291. Tel: 713-659-5461.
Development Office—Mrs. ROZ HILL, Dir., 1700 San Jacinto St., Houston, 77002-8291. Tel: 713-659-5461.
Insurance & Risk Manager—Ms. MEREDITH B. SMITH, CPCU, ARM Dir., 1700 San Jacinto St., Houston, 77002-8291. Tel: 713-659-5461.
Claims Risk Manager—Mrs. CHRISTINA SANDOVAL, Dir., 2403 Holcombe, Houston, 77021-2099. Tel: 713-741-8758; 800-856-4040; Fax: 713-748-3205.
Parish Accounting Services (PAS)—Mrs. JANIE MORALES, Dir., 1700 San Jacinto St., Houston, 77002-8291. Tel: 713-659-5461.

Secretariat for Pastoral and Educational Ministries—Mr. JIM BARRETTE, Dir., 2403 Holcombe, Houston, 77021-2099. Tel: 713-741-8786.
Aging Ministry—Mrs. KATHY BINGHAM, Dir., 2403 Holcombe, Houston, 77021-2098. Tel: 713-741-8712.
Boy and Girl Scouts—Rev. Msgr. WILLIAM L. YOUNG, Dir., 10330 Hillcroft, Houston, 77096. Tel: 713-729-0221.
Campus Ministry and Young Adults—ROBERTO NAVARRO, Dir., 2403 Holcombe, Houston, 77021-2098. Tel: 713-741-8786.
Continuing Christian Education—Mrs. ANNE COMEAUX, Dir., 2403 Holcombe, Houston, 77021-2099. Tel: 713-741-8730.
Circle Lake Retreat Center—GLORIA BUSTILLO, Dir., Mailing Address: P.O. Box 1410, Pinehurst, 77362-1410. Tel: 281-356-6764, Ext. 11; Fax: 281-356-6678. Email: circlelake@sbcglobal.net.
Deaf Apostolate—Rev. LEONARD BRONIAK, C.Ss.R., Dir., 2403 Holcombe Blvd., Houston, 77021-2099. Tel: 713-741-8721.
Family Life Ministry—Deacon ARTURO MONTERRUBIO, Dir., 2403 Holcombe, Houston, 77021-2099. Tel: 713-741-8710.
Resource Center—Mrs. DIANE O'CONNOR, 2403 E. Holcombe, Houston, 77021-2099. Tel: 713-741-8781.
Respect Life Office—Dr. MARCELLA COLBERT, Dir., 2403 Holcombe, Houston, 77021-2098. Tel: 713-741-8730 (Main Tel.).
Worship—Mr. DAVID WOOD, Dir., 2403 Holcombe, Houston, 77021-2099. Tel: 713-741-8760.
Youth Ministry—Mr. BRIAN JOHNSON, Dir., 2403 Holcombe, Houston, 77021-2099. Tel: 713-741-8723.
Special Youth Services (Juvenile Detention Ministry)—Ms. MARILU BALLOW, Dir., 2403 Holcombe, Houston, 77021-2099. Tel: 713-527-1894; 832-541-4718.

Secretariat for Catholic Schools—Sr. KEVINA KEATING, C.C.V.I., 2403 Holcombe Blvd., Houston, 77021. Tel: 713-741-8704.
Catholic School Office—Sr. KEVINA KEATING, C.C.V.I., Supt., 2403 Holcombe, Houston, 77021-2099. Tel: 713-741-8704.
School of Environmental Education - Camp Kappe—Sr. THOMAS ANN LA COUR, O.P., Prin., 7738 Camp Kappe Rd., Navasota, 77363. Tel: 936-894-2141.

Secretariat for Social Concerns—VACANT, Dir., 2403 Holcombe, Houston, 77021-2099. Tel: 713-741-8769.
Campaign for Human Development—Deacon SAM DUNNING, Dir., 2403 Holcombe, Houston, 77021-2098. Tel: 713-741-8731.
Catholic Charities—BONNA KOL, Pres. & CEO, 2900 Louisiana St., Houston, 77006. Tel: 713-526-4611; Fax: 713-526-1546. Mailing Address: P.O. Box 66508, Houston, 77266; MICHAEL J. PIERI, CPA, Exec. Vice Pres. Tel: 713-874-6740.
Program Services—JIM GAJEWSKI, Vice Pres. Tel: 713-874-6739.
Finance and Human Resources—KATHY FOUNTAIN, CPA. Tel: 713-874-6741.
Fund Development/Marketing—Tel: 713-526-4611. VACANT, Vice Pres. Tel: 713-874-6659.
Community Relations and Advocacy—Deacon JOE RUBIO, Vice Pres. Tel: 713-874-6657.
Technology and Facilities—MICHAEL GILLESPIE, Vice Pres. Tel: 713-874-6729.
Human Resources—GLENDA BATES. Tel: 713-874-6748.
Children & Family Services—VALERIE PERALES, L.M.S.W.-A.C.P., Admin. Tel: 713-874-6589.
Children Placement Services Adoption and Foster Care—SHARON JORGESON, L.M.S.W., Supvr. Tel: 713-874-6594.
Services to Pregnant and Parenting Adolescents—CAROL SHULSE, C.C.A. Supvr. Tel: 713-874-6593.
Post Adoption Services—LILLIAN SALINAS, L.M.S.W. Tel: 713-874-6575.
St. Jerome Emiliani's Home for Children—MICHELLE MITCHELL, M.S., N.C.C., S.W.A., Supvr. Tel: 713-874-6587.
Community Outreach Services—VACANT.
AIDS Ministry—VACANT, Supvr., 2900 Louisiana St., Houston, 77006. Tel: 713-874-6699.
Guadalupe Center—ANA RAUSH, Dir. Housing, 326 S. Jensen, Houston, 77003-1599. Family Assistance Program, Villa Guadalupe-Transitional Housing for Women.

Parish Social Ministry—VACANT. Tel: 713-526-4611.

Services to the Alone and Frail Elderly—VACANT, Supvr. Tel: 713-874-6670.

Family Counseling—VALERIE PERALES, L.M.S.W.-A.C.P., Dir. Admin.; Sr. CARMEN SANCHEZ. Tel: 713-874-6590 (Appointments); 713-874-6608 (Direct).

Immigration and Refugee Services—VACANT, Admin.

St. Frances Cabrini Center for Immigrant Legal Assistance—WAFA ABDIN, J.D., Supvr. Tel: 713-874-6570.

Refugee Resettlement Services—DANIELLE BOLKS, Supvr. Tel: 713-874-6527.

St. Michael's Home for Children—LETICIA HARMON, Supvr. Tel: 713-526-4611.

Serenity House—CONNIE HIDALGO. Tel: 713-874-6668.

Galveston County Center—ELIZABETH KINARD, Supvr., 4418 Ave. M, Galveston, 77550-3726. Tel: 409-762-2143; 409-949-9884 (Texas City Office); Fax: 409-762-2088.

Justice and Peace—Deacon SAM DUNNING, Dir., 2403 E. Holcombe, Houston, 77021-2099. Tel: 713-741-8730.

St. Vincent de Paul Society—WENDY GARAGHTY, Exec. Dir., 2403 Holcombe, Houston, 77021-2099. Tel: 713-741-8783.

Council of Catholic Women—Rev. Msgr. DANIEL L. SCHEEL, Archdiocesan Moderator, 8825 Kempwood Dr., Houston, 77080. Tel: 713-468-9555.

Cursillos in Christianity—Deacon HECTOR MORALES, Admin.; Rev. EUGENE CANAS, O.M.I., Spiritual Dir., St. Paul Cursillo Center, 4000 Belk St., Houston, 77087. Tel: 713-643-7682.

Disaster Relief—VACANT, 1700 San Jacinto, Houston, 77002. Tel: 713-659-5461.

Oremus Pro Invicem—Rev. Msgr. FRANCIS G. WEARDEN, Dir. (Retired), John XXIII.

Rural Life Bureau—VACANT, 1700 San Jacinto St., Houston, 77002-8291. Tel: 713-659-5461.

Victim Assistance Coordinator—Sr. MAUREEN O'CONNELL, O.P. Tel: 713-659-5461, Ext. 499; 713-654-5799. Email: moconnell@archgh.org.

CLERGY, PARISHES, MISSIONS AND PAROCHIAL SCHOOLS

CITY OF GALVESTON

(GALVESTON COUNTY)

1—ST. MARY'S CATHEDRAL BASILICA (1840), (Unattended)
Res., Church & Mailing Address: 2011 Church St., 77550-2091. Email: cathedralstmary@sbcglobal.net. Web: www.marycath.org.

2—HOLY FAMILY Revs. John P. Bok, O.F.M.; John Paul Flajole, O.F.M., Parochial Vicar; E. J. Stein, O.F.M., Parochial Vicar; Deacons Louis (Sam) Dell'Olio; Henry Herrera; Douglas W. Matthews; Robert Standridge; Henry Becker, (Retired); John S. Pistone, (Retired).
1010 35th St., 77550. In Res., Rev. Nils Thompson, O.F.M.

3—HOLY ROSARY (1888) Closed. For parish records contact the Archives of Galveston-Houston.

4—OUR LADY OF GUADALUPE, Closed. August 1992. Contact St Patrick, Galveston for further information.

5—ST. PATRICK (1870) Closed. For parish records contact the Archives of Galveston-Houston.

6—ST. PETER THE APOSTLE (1965) Closed. For parish records contact the Archives of Galveston-Houston.

7—SACRED HEART (1884) Closed. For parish records contact the Archives of Galveston-Houston.

CITY OF HOUSTON

(HARRIS COUNTY)

1—ST. ALBERT OF TRAPANI (1970) Rev. Philip A. Wilhite; Deacons Carlito Buhay; Alvaro Casas Jr.; Larry T. Longley.
Church & Mailing Address: 11027 S. Gessner Dr., 77071-3599. Tel: 713-771-3596; Fax: 713-270-0441. Email: secretary@stalbertoftrapani.org. Web: www.stalbertoftrapani.org.
Catechesis/Religious Program— Peggy Popkey, D.R.E. Students 340.

2—ALL SAINTS (1908) Rev. Msgr. Adam S. McClosky; Deacons Gary Hilbig; Rodolfo Cerda. In Res., Rev. Ronald F. Cloutier.
Res., Church & Mailing Address: 215 E. 10th St., 77008-7025. Tel: 713-864-2653; Fax: 713-864-0761. Email: information@allsaints.ws. Web: www.allsaints.us.
Catechesis/Religious Program— Daniel Schwieterman, D.R.E. Students 412.

3—ST. ALPHONSUS (1966) Rev. Rivers Patout, Admin.
Res., Church & Mailing Address: 9217 E. Ave. L, 77012-2727. Tel: 713-923-5843; Fax: 713-923-5866. Email: stalphonsusch@aol.com.
Catechesis/Religious Program—Mrs. Mary Elizondo, D.R.E. Students 507.

4—ST. AMBROSE (1958) Revs. Benjamin Smaistrla; Jeffrey Allen Reed, Parochial Vicar; Franklin Simmons (Retired); Deacon Miguel Vazquez.
Res., Church & Mailing Address: 4213 Mangum Rd., 77092-5599. Tel: 713-686-3497; Fax: 713-686-6604. Web: www.stambrosehouston.org.
School—Tel: 713-686-6990; Fax: 713-686-6902. Email: info@sashornets.org. Web: www.sashornets.org. Judy A. Fritsch, Prin. Lay Teachers 33; Students 460.
Catechesis/Religious Program—Tel: 713-686-3857. Miguel Vences, D.R.E. Students 510.

5—ST. ANDREW KIM (1977), (Korean), Rev. Yong Huyk Lee.
Church & Mailing Address: 1706 Bingle Rd., 77055-2336. Tel: 713-465-2682; Fax: 713-932-7401. Email: standrewkimhouston@yahoo.com. Web: www.stakim.org.
Rectory—8557 Hiridge St., 77055. Tel: 713-465-2926.
Convent—Handmaids of the Sacred Heart of Jesus (H.S.H.), Tel: 713-465-1196; Fax: 713-465-2682. Email: sea4628@hotmail.com. Sisters 2.
Catechesis/Religious Program—Tel: 281-489-9952. Students 176.

6—ST. ANNE (1925) Revs. John F. Robbins, C.S.B.; Jay Francis Walsh, C.S.B.; William J. Frankenberger, C.S.B.; Alvin A. Sinasac, C.S.B.; Deacons William Garrett; Jean-Paul Budinger; Joan O'Leary, Pastoral Assoc.
Res., Church & Mailing Address: 2140 Westheimer, 77098-1419. Tel: 713-526-3276; Fax: 713-526-3079. Email: church@saintanne.org. Web: www.stanne.org.
School—2120 Westheimer, 77098. Tel: 713-526-3279. Kathy Barnosky, Prin. Sisters 1; Lay Teachers 33; Students 452.
Catechesis/Religious Program—Tel: 713-526-2936. Jeff Crandall, D.R.E. Students 499.

7—ST. ANNE DE BEAUPRE (1948) Rev. Oliver O. Obele, M.S.P.
Res., Church & Mailing Address: 2810 Link Rd., 77009-1196. Tel: 713-869-1319; Fax: 713-869-4527. Email: stanne@prodigy.net.
Catechesis/Religious Program—Tel: 281-537-6825. Pam McCarthy, D.R.E. Students 30.

8—ANNUNCIATION (1869) Rev. Msgr. James L. Golasinski; Deacons Bart Hock; Robert George Alexander.
Mailing Address: P.O. Box 214, 77001-0214. Tel: 713-222-2289; Fax: 713-222-2280. Email: info@annunciationcc.org.
Church: 1618 Texas Ave., 77001-0214. Email: info@annunciationcc.org.
Catechesis/Religious Program—Herman Jadloski, S.T.L., D.R.E. Students 93.

9—ASCENSION CHINESE MISSION (1988), (Chinese), Rev. Louis C. Zee; Deacon Paul Kiang.
Office Mailing Address: P.O. Box 749, Alief, 77411-0749.
Church: 4605 Jetty Ln., 77411-0749. Tel: 281-575-8855; Fax: 281-575-6940. Email: ascensioncc@sbcglobal.net. Web: www.ascensionchinesemission.org.
Catechesis/Religious Program—Tel: 281-495-9257. Gladys Shen, D.R.E. Students 63.

10—ASSUMPTION (1948) Revs. Albert Zanatta, C.R.S.; Julian Gerosa, C.R.S.; Deacons Dan Addis; Mario Ortega. In Res., Rev. Tiziano Marconato, C.R.S.
Res., Church & Mailing Address: 901 Rose Ln., 77037-4699. Tel: 281-447-6381; Fax: 281-447-6382. Email: acchurch@houston.rr.com.
Catechesis/Religious Program—Tel: 281-931-1460. Mario Ortega, D.R.E. Students 857.

11—ST. AUGUSTINE (1955) Rev. Wencil C. Pavlovsky; Deacon Benito Meza.
Mailing Address: 5438 Laurel Creek Way, 77017-6746.
Church & Res.: 5560 Laurel Creek Way, 77017-6729. Tel: 713-946-8968; Fax: 713-946-0080. Email: sacc@staugustinecc.com. Web: www.staugustinecc.com.
School—5500 Laurel Creek Way, 77017. Tel: 713-946-9050; Fax: 713-943-3444. Mrs. Carol Bruns, Prin. Lay Teachers 17; Students 197.
Catechesis/Religious Program—Alicia Perez, D.R.E. Students 559.

12—ST. BENEDICT THE ABBOT (1963) Rev. Benoit K. Mukamba, C.S.Sp.
Church & Mailing Address: 4025 Grapevine, 77045-6320. Tel: 713-433-9836; Fax: 713-433-3949. Email: stbenedictabbotcc@sbcglobal.net. Web: www.stbenedictchurchhouston.org.
Rectory—3931 Grapevine, 77045.
Catechesis/Religious Program—Tel: 713-433-2436. Adela Tijerina, Interim D.R.E. Students 293.

13—ST. BERNADETTE SOUBIROUS (1977) Revs. Robert Barras; Matthew Thottiyil, M.S.F.S.; Ruben C. Nwankwor, Chap.; Deacon Joe Rubio.
Church & Mailing Address: 15500 El Camino Real, 77062-5793. Tel: 281-486-0337; Fax: 281-218-9440. Email: office@stbchurch.org. Web: www.stbchurch.org.
Rectory—959 El Dorado Blvd., 77062.
School— Pam Calandra, Prin. Lay Teachers 13; Students 268.
Catechesis/Religious Program—Tel: 281-486-0337, Ext. 112. Barbara Aubuchon, D.R.E. (K-5); Marianne Bartos, D.R.E. (6-8). Students 1,238.

14—BLESSED SACRAMENT (1910) Rev. Rudolfo Sanchez, Admin.
Res., Church & Mailing Address: 4015 Sherman, 77003-2695. Tel: 713-224-5291; Fax: 713-224-5292.
Catechesis/Religious Program—Students 298.

15—ST. CATHERINE OF SIENA (1975) Rev. Michael J. Carmody; Deacons Louis Horr; Lee Tollett.
Church & Mailing Address: 10688 Shadow Wood Dr., 77043-2826. Tel: 713-467-8170; Fax: 713-467-7149. Email: stcat7433@sbcglobal.net. Web: www.stcat.net.
Rectory—1902 Stebbins Dr., 77043-2417.
Catechesis/Religious Program— Ruth Yanez, D.R.E. Students 62.

16—ST. CECILIA (1956) Revs. John E. Cahoon; Vincente Agila; Jaimon Kurian Pathiyil, O.S.H.; Deacons Donald E. Bradley; Gregory Evans; Carlos Porras; Roberto Chavez. In Res., Rev. Jacques Weber, S.J. (Retired).
Church & Mailing Address: 11720 Joan of Arc Dr., 77024-2602. Tel: 713-465-3414; Fax: 713-465-1305. Email: frcahoon@saintcecilia.org. Web: www.saintcecilia.org.
Rectory—11701 Joan of Arc Dr., 77024.
School—11740 Joan of Arc Dr., 77024. Tel: 713-468-9515; Fax: 713-468-4698. Ms. Bridget Collins, Prin. Lay Teachers 48; Students 547.
Catechesis/Religious Program— Rosemary Munoz, D.R.E. Students 1,203.

17—ST. CHARLES BORROMEO (1962) Revs. Miguel A. Solorzano; Eduardo Lopez, C.M.; Deacons Charles R. Conant; Rodrigo Lozano.
Res., Church & Mailing Address: 501 Tidwell, 77022-2121. Tel: 713-692-6303; Fax: 713-692-6314. Email: miguel@solorzano.com.
Rectory—601 Cravens, 77076.
School—Tel: 713-692-4898; Fax: 713-692-1376. Tray Stogsdill, Prin. Sisters 1; Lay Teachers 12; Students 185.
Catechesis/Religious Program—Sr. Marcella I. Perez, D.J., D.R.E. Students 1,283.

18—CHRIST THE KING (1928) Revs. Giulio Veronesi, C.R.S.; Romualdo Lopez, C.R.S., Parochial Vicar; Deacon Gerardo J. Garcia. In Res., Rev. Italo Dell'Oro, C.R.S.
Res., Church & Mailing Address: 4419 N. Main St., 77009-5199. Tel: 713-869-1449; Fax: 713-869-1491. Email: secretary@ctkcc.org. Web: www.ctkcc.org.
Catechesis/Religious Program—Tel: 713-869-3140. Deacon Gerry Garcia, D.R.E. Students 1,042.

19—CHRIST THE REDEEMER (1980) Revs. Sean P. Horrigan; Arthur P. Alban; Deacons James H. Osterhaus; Ralph R. Gregory Jr.; Phillip Jackson; Robert Henkel Sr.
Church & Mailing Address: 11507 Huffmeister Rd., 77065-1051. Tel: 281-469-5533; Fax: 281-469-8441. Email: office@ctrcc.com. Web: www.ctrcc.com.
Catechesis/Religious Program—Tel: 281-469-5533. Mary Phillips, D.R.E. Students 1,841.

20—CHRIST, THE INCARNATE WORD (1997), (Vietnamese), Rev. Msgr. Philippe Le-Xuan Thuong; Rev. Joseph T.P. Bui; Deacons Dinh Van Nguyen; Joseph Si Nguyen Bach.
Res., Church & Mailing Address: 8503 S. Kirkwood Rd., 77099-4056. Tel: 281-495-8133; Fax: 281-495-4220.
Catechesis/Religious Program—Tel: 281-495-3741. Anthony Phan, D.R.E. Students 660.

21—ST. CHRISTOPHER (1924) Rev. Msgr. Ralph C. Salazar; Rev. Joseph Thu Le; Deacons Allan Fredericksen; Merce C. Leal Jr.; Benito Tristan Jr.
Res., Church & Mailing Address: 8150 Park Place Blvd., 77017-3033. Tel: 713-645-6614; Fax: 713-640-1640. Email: stchris1924@netzero.net. Web: www.stchristopherhouston.org.
School—8134 Park Place Blvd., 77017. Tel: 713-649-0009; Fax: 713-649-1104. Jo Ann Prater, Prin. Sisters 3; Lay Teachers 16; Students 242.
Catechesis/Religious Program—Tel: 713-645-6142. Maria Fernandez, D.R.E. Students 536.

22—ST. CLARE OF ASSISI (1990) Rev. Dominic J. Pistone Jr.; Deacons Thomas Berna; John H. Dean; Jim Wright. In Res., Rev. Robert J. Matzinger, C.S.B.

Res., Church & Mailing Address: 3131 El Dorado Blvd., 77059-5100. Tel: 281-286-7729; Fax: 281-286-1256. Email: officemgr@stclarehouston.ort. Web: www.stclarehouston.org.
Rectory—15906 Laurelfield, 77059.
School—Tel: 281-286-3395. Al Varisco, Prin. Lay Teachers 20; Students 146.
Catechesis/Religious Program—Tel: 281-486-0874. Sandra Trevino, D.R.E. Students 741.

23—CO-CATHEDRAL OF THE SACRED HEART (1896) Revs. Lawrence W. Jozwaik; Thu Ngoc Nguyen; David W. Garnier; Deacons Marvin R. Fikac; John Salinas; Leonard P. Lockett.
Res.: 1111 St. Joseph Pkwy., 77002-8127. Tel: 713-659-1561; Fax: 713-739-1185. Email: office@sacredhearthouston.org. Web: www.sacredhearthouston.org.
Catechesis/Religious Program— Debbie Elizondo, D.R.E. Students 352.

24—CORPUS CHRISTI (1956) Revs. Dana Pelotte, S.S.S.; Robert A. Chabot, S.S.S. In Res., Rev. Arul Tharcius, S.S.S.; Bro. Anthony Ornelas.
Res., Church & Mailing Address: 9900 Stella Link Rd., 77025-4718. Tel: 713-667-0497; Fax: 713-668-4742. Email: danagsss@blessedsacrament.com. Web: www.blessedsacrament.com/usa/corpus.
School—4005 Cheena St., 77025. Tel: 713-664-3351; Fax: 713-664-6095. Email: cmueller@corpuschristihouston.org. Web: www.corpuschristihouston.org. Ms. Claire Mueller, Prin. Lay Teachers 17; Students 160.
Catechesis/Religious Program—Tel: 713-667-0497. Susie Way, D.R.E.; Leonor Castillo, D.R.E. Students 374.

25—ST. CYRIL OF ALEXANDRIA (1963) Rev. Mario J. Arroyo; Deacon Eduardo M. Dolpher.
Res., Church & Mailing Address: 10503 Westheimer Rd., 77042-3502. Tel: 713-789-1250; Fax: 713-780-0967. Email: fmja@stcyrilhouston.org. Web: www.stcyrilhouston.org.
Catechesis/Religious Program—Tel: 713-789-1250. Rebecca Giles, D.R.E. Students 656.

26—ST. DOMINIC (1965) Rev. Roger O. Estorgue, O.P.; Deacon Philip Arlen Wiles.
Res., Church & Mailing Address: 8215 Reservoir St., 77049-1728. Tel: 281-458-2910; Fax: 281-458-7114. Email: stdominic@houston.rr.com. Web: stdominicchurch.home.att.net.
Catechesis/Religious Program—Tel: 832-465-8851. Sr. Olga Rivera, D.R.E. Students 165.

27—ST. ELIZABETH ANN SETON (1977) Revs. Paul E. Lockey, Admin.; Bernadine Tan Minh Dang; Deacons German Godoy; Tuu Hoang; Charles G. Pennell; Gilbert R. Johnson; Alfonse Sosa; William A. Weaver.
Church & Mailing Address: 6646 Addicks-Satsuma Rd., 77084-1599. Tel: 281-463-7878; Fax: 281-463-4822. Email: seasoffice@sbcglobal.com. Web: www.seascatholic.org.
School—Tel: 281-463-1444; Fax: 281-463-8707. Jan Krametbauer, Prin. Lay Teachers 33; Students 422.
Catechesis/Religious Program—Tel: 281-463-7356. Mrs. Selma DeMarco, D.R.E. Students 2,645.

28—ST. FRANCES CABRINI (1962) Rev. Frank T. Fabj; Sr. Maria Loretta Caeti, M.S.C., Pastoral Assoc.; Deacons Fernandez Ramirez; Robert Gregory Stevens; Charles F. Roessler Jr.
Church & Mailing Address: 10727 Hartsook St., 77034-3523. Tel: 713-946-5768; Fax: 713-946-3282. Email: cabrini@sfchoutx.org. Web: www.sfchoutx.org.
Rectory—10726 Bessemer St., 77034.
Catechesis/Religious Program— Mrs. Nancy Patyrak, D.R.E. Students 1,003.

29—ST. FRANCIS DE SALES (1962) Rev. Wayne W. Wilkerson; Deacon Antonio Flores Jr.
Church & Mailing Address: 8200 Roos Rd., 77036-6399. Tel: 713-774-7475; Fax: 713-774-6591. Email: lalvarado_sfds@sbcglobal.net. Web: www.sfds-hou.org.
Res.: 8018 Roos Rd., 77036. Tel: 713-774-7475; Fax: 713-774-6591.
School—8100 Roos Rd., 77036. Tel: 713-774-4447; Fax: 713-271-6744. Sandra Mendez, Prin. Lay Teachers 45; Students 491.
Catechesis/Religious Program—Tel: 713-774-9631. Mrs. Ann Cashiola, D.R.E. Students 750.

30—ST. FRANCIS OF ASSISI (1950) Rev. Edmund C. Nnadozie, M.S.P.; Deacons Ignatius Joseph; Michael St. Julian.
Res., Church & Mailing Address: 5102 Dabney St., 77026-3015. Tel: 713-672-7773; Fax: 713-673-1913. Email: stfrancisofhouston@yahoo.com. Web: www.sfahouston.org.
School—5100 Dabney St., 77026. Tel: 832-325-0480; Fax: 713-674-9901. Clarice Campbell, Prin. Sisters 2; Lay Teachers 11; Students 167.
Catechesis/Religious Program—Tel: 713-672-7773, Ext. 106. Mrs. Delores Melvin, D.R.E.

31—ST. FRANCIS XAVIER (1952) Rev. Kenneth J. Howard, S.S.J.; Deacons Albert Henry; Michael V. Jenkins; Frank Laugerman.
Res., Church & Mailing Address: 4600 Reed Rd., 77051-2857. Tel: 713-738-2311; Fax: 713-738-3337. Email: stfrancisxavier@sbcglobal.net. Web: www.josephite.com/parish/tx/sfx.
Catechesis/Religious Program—Tel: 281-431-7666. Leesha Miller, D.R.E.; Kimberly Chandler, D.R.E. Students 133.

32—ST. GREGORY THE GREAT (1962) Rev. Francis Huan Ton Ngo; Deacons Julio M. Ramirez; Abner Brown Sr. In Res., Rev. Frank Guenter.
Res., Church & Mailing Address: 10500 Nold Dr., 77016-2921. Tel: 713-631-3681; Fax: 713-631-6114.
Catechesis/Religious Program—Tel: 713-631-0058. Sr. Ann Theresa Nguyen, D.R.E. Students 365.

33—HOLY CROSS CHAPEL (Downtown) (1982) Rev. Michael J. Barrett, S.T.D.
Chapel— 905 Main St., 77002-6408. Tel: 713-650-1323; Fax: 713-650-8836. Email: info@holycrosschapel.org. Web: www.holycrosschapel.org.

34—HOLY GHOST (1946) Revs. Gregory May, C.Ss.R.; Anh Tuan Pham, C.Ss.R.; Peter H. Voelker, C.Ss.R.; Scott Katzenberger, C.Ss.R. In Res., Revs. Leonard Broniak, C.Ss.R.; Luong Uong, C.Ss.R.; Bro. John (Patrick) F. Concidine, C.Ss.R.; Deacon Robert T. Brueggerhoff.
Res., Church & Mailing Address: 6921 Chetwood Dr., 77081-5697. Tel: 713-668-0463; Fax: 713-661-4645. Email: hgc@holyghostchurch.net. Web: www.holyghostchurch.net.
School—6920 Chimney Rock Rd., 77081. Tel: 713-668-5327; Fax: 713-667-4410. Sr. Judy Scheffler, S.S.N.D., Prin. Lay Teachers 13; Students 128.
Catechesis/Religious Program—Tel: 713-668-8001. Ms. Marilynn Wilson, D.R.E. Students 849.

35—HOLY NAME (1920) Revs. Michael G. Earthman; Mark Czarnecki; Deacon Juan Francisco Pareja; Minnie Martinez, Pastoral Assoc. In Res., Rev. Jan Kubisa.
Church: 1920 Marion St., 77009. Email: holynameparish@sbcglobal.net. Web: holynamecatholic.org.
Res.: 1917 Cochran St., 77009-8497. Tel: 713-222-1255; Fax: 713-222-1260.
School—1912 Marion St., 77009-8649. Tel: 713-227-9529; Fax: 713-227-0224. Tina Lewis, Prin. Sisters 1; Lay Teachers 13; Students 138.
Catechesis/Religious Program—Tel: 713-223-4059. Rosario Munoz, D.R.E. Students 477.

36—HOLY ROSARY (1913) Revs. Ian G. Bordenave, O.P.; Joseph D. Konkel, O.P.; Isidore V. Vicente, O.P.; Juan M. Torres, O.P.; James Burke, O.P., Parochial Vicar; Art Kerwin, O.P., Parochial Vicar; Deacon Douglas W. Matthews. In Res., Revs. Austin Greer, O.P.; Ronald H. Henry, O.P.
Res. & Mailing Address: 3600 Travis St., 77002-9591. Tel: 713-529-4854; Fax: 713-522-3967. Email: office@holyrosaryparish.org. Web: www.holyrosaryparish.org.
Church: 3600 Milan St., 77002.
Catechesis/Religious Program—Tel: 713-529-4854. Marisa Mendoza, D.R.E. Students 99.

37—IMMACULATE CONCEPTION (1911) Revs. Kevin A. Collins, O.M.I.; Marco A. Ortiz, O.M.I.
Res., Church & Mailing Address: 7250 Harrisburg Blvd., 77011-4791. Tel: 713-921-1261; Fax: 713-921-2304. Email: iccsec@comcast.net.
Catechesis/Religious Program— Teresa Martinez, D.R.E. Students 526.

38—IMMACULATE HEART OF MARY (1926) Revs. Ramiro Cortez, O.M.I.; Edward M. Ward, O.M.I. In Res., Rev. Eugene Canas, O.M.I.
Res., Church & Mailing Address: 7539 Ave. K, 77012-1033. Tel: 713-923-2394; Fax: 713-923-6497. Email: ihmhouston@hotmail.com.
Catechesis/Religious Program—Tel: 713-921-5431. Becky Arcizo, D.R.E. Students 507.

39—ST. JEROME (1960) Rev. Msgr. Daniel L. Scheel; Revs. Michael S. Van Cleve; Vincent Tran; Deacons Pedro Salas; Antonio Moya.
Church & Mailing Address: 8825 Kempwood, 77080-4199. Tel: 713-468-9555; Fax: 713-464-0325. Email: stjeromehou@msn.com. Web: www.stjeromechurch.org.
Rectory—9011 Friendship, 77080.
School—Tel: 713-468-7946. Sharon Makulski, Prin. Sisters 1; Lay Teachers 22; Students 327.
Catechesis/Religious Program—Tel: 713-464-5029. Ms. Gabriela DePavia, D.R.E. Students 1,380.

40—ST. JOHN NEUMANN (1977) Rev. Msgr. Seth F. Hermoso.
Church & Mailing Address: 2730 Nelwood Dr., 77038-1025. Tel: 281-931-0684; Fax: 281-931-5363. Email: stjneumannparish@hotmail.com.
Rectory—2715 Nelwood Dr., 77038-1025.
Catechesis/Religious Program—Tel: 281-580-5415. Gina Pasket, D.R.E. Students 294.

41—ST. JOHN VIANNEY (1966) Revs. R. Troy Gately; Gregorio Filipe Can-Vasquez; Charles J. Talar; Deacons Dale W. Steffes; Albert E. Vacek Jr.; Frederick Kossegi; Robert J. Hesse; Marcelino Villarreal; Hector J. Romeu.
Res., Church & Mailing Address: 625 Nottingham Oaks Tr., 77079-6234. Tel: 281-497-1500; Fax: 281-584-2024. Email: sjv@stjohnvianney.org. Web: www.stjohnvianney.org.
Catechesis/Religious Program—Tel: 281-497-6665. Daniel Marcantel, D.R.E. Students 1,075.

42—ST. JOSEPH (1880) Rev. Jan Kubisa; Deacon Reynaldo S. Gil.
Res., Church & Mailing Address: 1505 Kane St., 77007-7711. Tel: 713-222-6193; Fax: 713-222-1729. Email: stjosephcch@yahoo.com. Web: www.stjosephparish.cc.
Catechesis/Religious Program—Tel: 713-222-6579. Marina Ramirez, D.R.E. Students 138.

43—ST. JUSTIN MARTYR (1982) Revs. Paul R. Chovanec; Greg Viet Nguyen, I.C.M.; Deacons Gene Festa; Cornelius C. Llorens; Louis Provenzano; Nhat Tran.
Church & Mailing Address: 13350 Ashford Point Dr., 77082-5100. Tel: 281-556-5116; Fax: 281-556-6932. Email: sjm@sjmtx.com. Web: www.sjmtx.org.
Rectory—3142 W. Hampton, 77082.
Catechesis/Religious Program— Debbie Lazarou, D.R.E. Students 808.

44—ST. LEO THE GREAT (1973) Revs. Rafael Becerra, C.S.; J. Humberto Chacon, C.S., Parochial Vicar.
Res., Church & Mailing Address: 2131 Lauder Rd., 77039-3199. Tel: 281-449-2344; Fax: 281-442-3156. Email: stleohou@sbcglobal.net.
Catechesis/Religious Program— Nohemi Lara, D.R.E. Students 394.

45—ST. LUKE THE EVANGELIST (1975) Revs. James M. Burkart; Thomas Joseph Puthusseril, O.S.H.; Deacons John E. Devine Jr.; James Sharpless; Jesse Tollett; Alvin Birsinger; Rainaldo J. Egusquiza.
Church & Mailing Address: 11011 Hall Rd., 77089-2999. Tel: 281-481-6816; Fax: 281-481-8780. Email: parishsecretary@stlukecatholic.com. Web: www.stlukecatholic.com.
Rectory: 8402 Kirkville, 77089.
Catechesis/Religious Program—Marilyn Kiel, D.R.E. Students 1,112.

46—ST. MARK THE EVANGELIST (1974) Deacon John Benoit.
Church and Mailing Address: 5430 W. Ridgecreek Dr., 77053-3211. Email: stmarkhouston@aol.com.
Rectory—5302 Castlecreek Ln., 77053. Tel: 281-437-9114; 281-437-4828; Fax: 281-835-6303.
Catechesis/Religious Program—Tel: 281-416-0186. Zulema Perez, D.R.E. Students 387.

47—ST. MARY OF THE PURIFICATION (1929) Rev. Francis Borgia Aubespin, S.V.D.; Deacons Leonard P. Lockett; Andrew B. Malveaux Sr. In Res., Revs. Tan Viet Nguyen, S.V.D.; Roben C. Vwankor.
Res., Church & Mailing Address: 3006 Rosedale, 77004-6128. Tel: 713-528-0571; Fax: 713-528-0572. Email: baubespin@stmaryshouston.org. Web: www.stmaryshouston.org.
School—3002 Rosedale, 77004. Tel: 713-522-9276; Fax: 713-522-1879. Mrs. Mazie McCoy, Prin. Sisters 1; Lay Teachers 13; Students 185.
Catechesis/Religious Program—Tel: 281-437-4110. Dr. Evelyn Hunter, D.R.E. Students 221.

48—ST. MATTHEW THE EVANGELIST (1974) Revs. Luis Evardoni; Joven S. Saavedra, D.S.; Deacon John W. Adams.
Res., Church & Mailing Address: 9915 Hollister Dr., 77040-1702. Tel: 713-466-4030; Fax: 713-896-7235. Email: admin@stmatthewhou.org. Web: www.stmatthewhou.org.
Catechesis/Religious Program—Tel: 713-466-0510. Anna Brent, D.R.E. Students 368.

49—ST. MAXIMILIAN KOLBE (1983) Rev. John F. Ulm; Deacons Dennis Hayes; Stacy Millsap; Denver Crawley. In Res., Rev. Msgr. Milam Kleas (Retired).
Church and Mailing Address: 10135 West Rd., 77064-5361. Tel: 281-955-7324; Fax: 281-955-7328. Email: stmaximilian@stmaximilian.org. Web: www.stmaximilian.org.
Rectory—10218 Great Plains, 77064.
Catechesis/Religious Program— Stephanie Slattery, D.R.E. Students 991.

50—ST. MICHAEL (1925) Rev. Msgr. Frank H. Rossi; Revs. Michael T. Grey, C.S.Sp, Parochial Vicar; J. Christopher C. Nguyen; Deacons Thomas C. Newhouse; Henry Woods Martin; Jack Alexander; James Nicholas Caruso. In Res., Rev. Leon Strieder.
Res., Church & Mailing Address: 1801 Sage Rd., 77056-3502. Tel: 713-621-4370; Fax: 713-850-8341. Email: parishoffice@stmichaelchurch.net. Web: www.stmichaelchurch.net.
School—1833 Sage Rd., 77056-3502. Tel: 713-621-6847; Fax: 713-877-8812. Stephen P. Parsons, Prin. Sisters 1; Lay Teachers 27; Students 499.
Catechesis/Religious Program—Tel: 713-840-8213. Mrs. Mary Jo Wilt, D.R.E. Students 422.

51—ST. MONICA (1960) Rev. John M. Ayangl, S.O.L.T.; Deacon John Lane.

Res., Church & Mailing Address: 8421 W. Montgomery Rd., 77088-7116. Tel: 281-447-5837; Fax: 281-447-8410. Email: stmonica@sbcglobal.net. Web: www.stmonicahouston.com.
Catechesis/Religious Program—Tel: 281-445-0334. Jennifer Sims, D.R.E. Students 164.

52—ST. NICHOLAS (1887) Rev. Desmond C. Ohankwere, M.S.P.
Res., Church & Mailing Address: 2508 Clay St., 77003-4406. Tel: 713-223-5210; Fax: 713-222-0424.
Catechesis/Religious Program— Anita Garvey, D.R.E. Students 25.

53—NOTRE DAME (1969) Rev. Msgr. Rolando V. Diokno; Rev. Francis Z. Kizhakkethazhe, M.S.F.S.; Deacons F.L. Ostrowski; Ernesto Abadejos; Elie P. Calonge.
Rectory—11226 Pompano Ln., 77072-3595.
Church & Mailing Address: 7720 Boone Rd., 77072-3595. Tel: 281-498-4653; Fax: 281-879-1527. Email: pastor@notredamechurch.org. Web: notredamechurch.org.
Catechesis/Religious Program—Tel: 281-498-1256. Farah Najjar, D.R.E.; Josephine Lowell, D.R.E. Students 778.

54—OUR LADY OF CZESTOCHOWA (1982), (Polish), Rev. Jacek Nowak, S.Ch.; Deacon Anthony Rudnicki.
Mailing Address: 1712 Oak Tree, 77080-7240. Tel: 713-973-1081; Fax: 713-984-9501.
Church: 1731 Blalock Rd., 77080. Tel: 713-973-1081; Fax: 713-984-9501. Email: parish@parafiahouston.com. Web: www.parafiahouston.com.
Catechesis/Religious Program—Students 40.

55—OUR LADY OF GUADALUPE (1912) [JC] Revs. Edward Kilianski, S.C.J.; Richard Dileo, S.C.J.; Peter Mastrobuono, S.C.J.; Deacons Manuel A. Laurel; Gabriel Z. Quiroga.
Res., Church & Mailing Address: 2405 Navigation Blvd., 77003-1599. Tel: 713-222-0203; Fax: 713-225-2235. Email: parish@olghouston.org. Web: www.olghouston.org.
School—Tel: 713-224-6904; Fax: 713-225-2122. Christina Skowronek, Prin. Sisters 1; Lay Teachers 18; Students 219.
Catechesis/Religious Program— Sr. Anne Garcia, M.C.D.P., D.R.E. Students 846.

56—OUR LADY OF LAVANG CHURCH (1985), (Vietnamese), Revs. Dominic Huy The Trinh, O.P.; Joseph Chung Van Do, O.P.; John Baptist Minh Doan, O.P., Parochial Vicar; Deacon Michael Nguyen.
Mailing Address: 12320 Old Foltin Rd., 77086-3514. Tel: 281-999-1672; Fax: 281-820-7095. Email: info@lavangchurch.org. Web: www.lavangchurch.org.
Church: 12311 Old Foltin Rd., 77086-3513. Email: lavangchurch@yahoo.com.
Catechesis/Religious Program—Tel: 281-955-9395. Deacon Michael Nguyen, D.R.E. Students 611.

57—OUR LADY OF LOURDES (1994) Rev. Peter Thien Van Hoang, O.P.; Deacon Joseph Chuong Nguyen Do.
Church & Mailing Address: 6550 Fairbanks N. Houston, 77040-4307. Tel: 713-939-1906; Fax: 713-939-0771. Email: lourdes@loduc.org. Web: www.loduc.org.
Catechesis/Religious Program— Rev. Peter Thien Van Hoang, O.P.; Tina Cao, D.R.E. Students 615.

58—OUR LADY OF MT. CARMEL (1952) Revs. Sean A. Wenger, C.C.; Ben St. Croix, Parochial Vicar; Deacons Federico Guajardo; Juan Aguilar.
Church: 6723 Whitefriars Dr., 77087. Tel: 713-645-6673; Fax: 713-645-6674. Email: olmcparish@olmchou.org. Web: www.olmchou.org.
School—6703 Whitefriars Dr., 77087. Tel: 713-643-0676; Fax: 713-649-1835. Mrs. Abigail Doheny, Prin. Lay Teachers 14; Students 180.
Catechesis/Religious Program— Diana Zamora, C.R.E. Students 146.

59—OUR LADY OF SORROWS (1936) Rev. Norberto Conde.
Church & Mailing Address: 3006 Kashmere St., 77026-5999. Tel: 713-673-5600; Fax: 713-673-5667. Email: olosch@sbcglobal.net.
Catechesis/Religious Program—Tel: 713-695-3928. Mrs. Rose Mary Cadena, Prin. Students 114.

60—OUR LADY OF ST. JOHN (1947) Rev. Edwin A. Coreas.
Church & Mailing Address: 7500 Hirsch Rd., 77016-6215. Tel: 713-631-0810; Fax: 713-631-0781. Email: sanjuan@comcast.com. Web: www.ourladyofstjohn.org.
Catechesis/Religious Program— Jessica Romero, D.R.E. Students 218.

61—OUR LADY OF WALSINGHAM (1984) Rev. James Ramsey; Deacon James Barnett. In Res., Rev. Michael G. Earthman.
Church & Mailing Address: 7809 Shady Villa Ln., 77055-5011. Tel: 713-683-9407; Fax: 713-683-1518. Email: office@walsingham-church.org. Web: www.walsingham-church.org.
Rectory—1502 Shadyvilla Fern, 77055.
Catechesis/Religious Program—Mark Baker, D.R.E. Students 36.

62—OUR LADY STAR OF THE SEA (1950) Rev. Lowell D. Case, S.S.J.; Deacons Charles J. Allen Sr.; Irvin Johnson Jr.; Rick L. Simon. In Res., Rev. Rawlin B. Enette, S.S.J.
Church & Mailing Address: 1401 Fidelity St., 77029-4624. Tel: 713-674-9206; Fax: 713-675-7842. Email: ourlady2@comcast.com.
Catechesis/Religious Program— Daisy Fields, D.R.E. Students 91.

63—OUR MOTHER OF MERCY (1930) Rev. Lowell D. Case, S.S.J.; Deacons Irvin Johnson Jr.; Rick L. Simon; Charles J. Allen Sr.
Res., Church & Mailing Address: 4000 Sumpter St., 77020-2497. Tel: 713-672-0026; Fax: 713-672-2031. Email: pastor@ourmotherofmercy.net. Web: www.ourmotherofmercy.net.
School—2010 Benson St., 77020. Tel: 713-673-1862; Fax: 713-673-1041. Linda Mabrie, Prin. Sisters 3; Lay Teachers 11; Students 117.
Catechesis/Religious Program—Tel: 713-672-2037. Sr. Theresa Healy, D.R.E. Students 259.

64—ST. PATRICK (1880) Revs. Salvatore DeGeorge, O.M.I.; Osvaldo F. Velazquez, O.M.I.; Deacon Reynaldo Torres.
Church & Mailing Address: 4918 Cochran St., 77009-2117. Tel: 713-695-0631; Fax: 713-695-6255. Email: stpatric4918@sbcglobal.net. Web: www.stpatrickhouston.us.
Catechesis/Religious Program—Tel: 713-697-4325. Ms. Rita Ann Martinez, D.R.E. Students 740.

65—ST. PAUL (1964) Revs. Alberto A. Maullon Jr.; Cyriacus N. Onyejegbu; Deacon Luis Lopez.
Church & Mailing Address: 18223 Point Lookout Dr., 77058-3594. Tel: 281-333-3891; Fax: 281-333-3815. Email: parishadministrator@stpaulcatholic.org. Web: www.stpaulcatholic.org.
Rectory—18326 Point Lookout Dr., 77058.
Catechesis/Religious Program—Tel: 281-335-5701. Priscilla Munoz, D.R.E. Students 680.

66—ST. PETER CLAVER (1964) Revs. Romanus O. Muoneke; Rawlin B. Enette, S.S.J.; Deacon Raymond L. Despania Sr.
Church & Mailing Address: 6005 N. Wayside Dr., 77028-4494. Tel: 713-674-3338; Fax: 713-674-6524. Email: spclaver1@aol.com. In Res., Rev. Damian Odunze, C.S.Sp.
Catechesis/Religious Program— Helen H. Wilson, D.R.E. Students 105.

67—ST. PETER THE APOSTLE (1941) Revs. Emmanuel Esukpa, M.S.P.; Anthony O. Anike, M.S.P.; Alphonsus Enelichi, M.S.P., Parochial Vicar; Deacons Dan Gilbert; Clarence B. Johnson.
Res., Church & Mailing Address: 6220 La Salette Dr., 77021-1323. Tel: 713-747-7800; Fax: 713-747-9671. Email: stpetercc@sbcglobal.net.
School—Tel: 713-747-9484; Fax: 713-747-2621. Sr. Maria Babatunde, Prin. Sisters 2; Lay Teachers 8; Students 53.
Catechesis/Religious Program—Tel: 713-842-1226. Stephanie Jackson, D.R.E. Students 60.

68—ST. PHILIP NERI (1961) Revs. Robert T. Kajoh, M.S.P.; Clement N. Kanu, M.S.P.; Deacons Ronald Simon; James Brooks; Orrin D. Burroughs.
Mailing Address: P.O. Box 330190, 77233-0190. Tel: 713-734-0320; Fax: 713-734-0331. Email: stphlpnr@houston.rr.com. Web: www.spnchurch.org.
Church: 10960 Martin Luther King Jr. Blvd., 77048.
School—10950 Martin Luther King Jr. Blvd., 77048. Tel: 713-733-2343. Mrs. Melina Harris, Prin. Priests 2; Sisters 1; Lay Teachers 8; Students 64.
Catechesis/Religious Program—Tel: 713-734-0320. Mary E. Freeman, D.R.E. Students 129.

69—ST. PHILIP OF JESUS (1958) Rev. Jesus E. Suarez; Deacon Roy Breaux.
Church & Mailing Address: 9700 Villita St., 77013-3851. Tel: 713-672-6141; Fax: 713-672-8675. Email: stphilipofjesus@gmail.com.
Catechesis/Religious Program— Ana Maria DiAnastacio, D.R.E. Students 1,242.

70—PRINCE OF PEACE (1971) Revs. John T. Keller; Theo Lam; Alfonso Delgado, SS.CC.; Deacons Allen W. Prescott; Fred Dinges; Charles Butler; C. J. Mangano; Jeronimo R. Bazan; George Trosclair.
Church & Mailing Address: 19222 Tomball Pkwy., 77070-3510. Tel: 281-469-2686; Fax: 281-469-8418. Email: info@houstonpopcc.org. Web: www.houstonpopcc.org.
Catechesis/Religious Program— Jill McAboy, D.R.E. Students 2,900.

71—QUEEN OF PEACE (1942) Revs. John P. Vandenkker, C.C.; Michael J. Minifie, C.C.; John A. Bolger, C.C., Parochial Vicar; Deacons Jose L. Liendo; Jose M. Galvan. In Res., Rev. Ed Wade, C.C.
Res., Church & Mailing Address: 3011 Telephone Rd., 77023-5312. Tel: 713-921-6127; Fax: 713-921-6128. Email: queenofpeace@sbcglobal.net. Web: www.queenofpeacecatholicparish.net.
School—2320 Oakcliff St., 77023. Tel: 713-921-1558; Fax: 713-921-0855. Deena Wolf, Prin. Sisters 1; Lay Teachers 10; Students 205.
Catechesis/Religious Program—Tel: 713-921-1917; Fax: 713-921-6127. Mrs. Tammy Juarez, D.R.E. Students 701.

72—ST. RAPHAEL THE ARCHANGEL (1961) Rev. Jaime C. Arrambide, C.Ss.R.; Deacons Antonio Marquez; Juan De Dios Perez.
Mailing Address: P.O. Box 630787, 77263-0787. Tel: 713-781-9511; Fax: 713-278-9705.
Res. & Church Address: 3915 Ocee, 77063-5417. Email: straphaelcc@houston.rr.com.
Catechesis/Religious Program—Araceli Perez, D.R.E. Students 605.

73—RESURRECTION (1920) Revs. Jose A. Cobos, Admin.; Blas P. Herrador.
Res., Church & Mailing Address: 915 Zoe St., 77020-6898. Tel: 713-675-5333; Fax: 713-673-3605. Email: resurrectiondc@sbcglobal.net. Web: www.resurrectioncc.org.
School—916 Majestic St., 77019. Tel: 713-674-5545; Fax: 713-678-4036. Dora Tillman, Prin. Priests 2; Sisters 1; Lay Teachers 12; Students 105.
Catechesis/Religious Program—Tel: 713-673-1443. Gloria Hewitt, D.R.E. Students 550.
Station—La Divina Providencia Port Houston.

74—ST. ROSE OF LIMA (1946) Rev. Clint C. Ressler, Admin.; Deacons Brick Hodge; John T. Murrell; Connie Swenceski, Pastoral Assoc.
Church & Mailing Address: 3600 Brinkman St., 77018-6329. Tel: 713-692-9123; Fax: 713-692-5638. Email: parishmail@stroselima.org. Web: www.stroselima.org.
Rectory—802 Judiway, 77018-6329.
School—Tel: 713-691-0104; Fax: 713-692-8073. Mrs. Maria Luisa Rodriquez, Prin. Lay Teachers 17; Students 133.
Catechesis/Religious Program— Deacon John T. Murrell, D.R.E. Students 501.

75—ST. STEPHEN (1941) Revs. Gabriel Camilo, M.J.; Eduardo Roque, M.J.; Ramon J. Arechua, M.J.
Rectory—Rectory & Mailing Address: 2019 Center St., 77007-6106.
Church: 1910 Center St., 77007. Tel: 713-864-4075; Fax: 713-880-8611. Email: gc.ststephen@sbcglobal.net.
Catechesis/Religious Program—Tel: 281-827-4484. Ms. Maria Torres, D.R.E. Students 231.

76—ST. THERESA (1946) Rev. Philip P. Lloyd; Deacons Larry A. Vaclavik; John Froning. In Res., Rev. Donald S. Nesti, C.S.Sp.
Church & Mailing Address: 6622 Haskell St., 77007-2097. Tel: 713-869-3783; Fax: 713-869-3784. Email: britishbulldog@sttheresa.cc. Web: www.sttheresa.cc.
School—Tel: 713-864-4536; Fax: 713-869-5184. Ms. Frances Ramsey, Prin. Lay Teachers 15; Students 194.
Catechesis/Religious Program—Tel: 713-869-9725. Ginger Tamborello, D.R.E. Students 252.

77—ST. THOMAS MORE (1962) Revs. William A. Oliver; Hugh G. Cullen; Deacons Edwin F. Gosline; Edward T. Stoessel; Anthony V. Alessi. In Res., Revs. Don A. Neumann; Job Kalluvilayil.
Church & Mailing Address: 10330 Hillcroft, 77096-4795. Tel: 713-729-0221; Fax: 713-729-3294. Web: www.stmhouston.org.
School—5927 Wigton, 77096. Tel: 713-729-3434. Mrs. Nadine Mouser, Prin. Lay Teachers 38; Students 574.
Catechesis/Religious Program—Tel: 713-729-3435. Marianne Strzelecki, D.R.E. Students 775.

78—VIETNAMESE MARTYRS (1986), (Vietnamese), Revs. Joseph Thanh Vu; Loc D. Phan; Deacon Joseph Pham Nguyen.
Mailing Address: 10612 Kingspoint Rd., 77075-4114.
Rectory—10614 Kingspoint Rd., 77075-4114. Tel: 713-941-0521.
Church: 10610 Kingspoint Rd., 77075-4114. Fax: 713-941-2464. Email: vnmartyrs@hotmail.com.
Catechesis/Religious Program— Pham Nguyen, D.R.E. Students 420.

79—ST. VINCENT DE PAUL (1939) Rev. Msgr. William L. Young; Rev. Jonathan K. Kathenge; Deacons Joseph E. Lorino; Daniel Pagnano. In Res., Revs. Anthony Tam H. Pham; Antony Paulose, C.M.I.
Church & Mailing Address: 6800 Buffalo Speedway, 77025-1499. Tel: 713-667-9111; Fax: 713-667-3453. Web: www.stvincentcatholicchurch.org.
School—6802 Buffalo Speedway, 77025. Tel: 713-666-2345; Fax: 713-663-3562. Dr. Thomas W. O'Neill, Prin. Lay Teachers 46; Students 502.
Catechesis/Religious Program—Tel: 713-663-3524. Sr. Jean Marie Goukas, C.V.I., D.R.E. Students 1,010.

OUTSIDE THE CITIES OF GALVESTON AND HOUSTON

ALVIN, BRAZORIA CO., ST. JOHN THE BAPTIST (1952) Revs. Charles J. Borski, O.M.I.; John Franko, O.M.I.; Deacons Robert Kacz; David Bowman; B.

Edward Stoughton; Dale Hayden. In Res., Rev. Henry A. Laenen, O.M.I.
Res., Church & Mailing Address: 110 E. South St., 77511-3570. Tel: 281-331-3751; Fax: 281-331-5430. Email: stjohns110@att.net.
Catechesis/Religious Program—Tel: 281-824-0877. Mrs. Mary Voight, D.R.E. Students 598.

ANDERSON, GRIMES CO., ST. STANISLAUS (1866) [CEM] Rev. Raul A. Marterior.
Mailing Address: P.O. Box 210, 77830-0210.
Church: 1511 Hwy. 90 S., 77830. Tel: 936-873-2291; Fax: 936-873-3304. Email: stananders@mscc.net.
Catechesis/Religious Program— Dana Wagner, D.R.E. Students 54.

ANGLETON, BRAZORIA CO., MOST HOLY TRINITY (1960) Revs. Robert J. Duggan, C.S.B.; Jamie M. Abercrombie, C.S.B.; Deacons Andrew Shefts; Robert Ward; Cheryl Scott, Pastoral Assoc.
Church & Mailing Address: 1713 N. Tinsley St., 77515-3551. Tel: 979-849-2421; Fax: 979-849-2425. Email: ccang@mostholytrinitychurch.org. Web: www.mostholytrinitychurch.org.
Catechesis/Religious Program— Cheryl Scott, D.R.E. Students 476.

BARRETT STATION, HARRIS CO., ST. MARTIN DE PORRES (1944) [JC] Rev. Alphonsus Enelichi, M.S.P.
Church & Mailing Address: 12606 Crosby-Lynchburg Rd., 77532-8628. Tel: 281-328-4451; Fax: 281-328-7306. Email: smdpbarret@aol.com.
Catechesis/Religious Program—Tel: 281-328-1972. Mrs. Louise Salandy, D.R.E. Students 245.

BAYTOWN, HARRIS CO.

1—ST. JOHN THE EVANGELIST (1974) Rev. Terence P. Brinkman; Deacons Justin J. Wewer; Robert Hennessy; John Singer; Dan Foley; Robert Corbett, Pastoral Assoc.
Church & Mailing Address: 800 W. Baker Rd., 77521-2311. Tel: 281-837-8180; Fax: 281-837-8181. Email: noreenpro@verizon.net.
Catechesis/Religious Program—Tel: 281-837-0532. Mrs. Cynthia Hill, D.R.E. Students 786.

2—ST. JOSEPH (1924) Rev. Dwight M. Canizares; Deacon John Singer.
Res., Church & Mailing Address: 1907 Carolina St., 77520-6098. Tel: 281-420-3588; Fax: 281-422-3044. Email: st_josephbaytown@yahoo.com. Web: home-houston.rr.com/stjoseph.
School—1811 Carolina St., 77520-6099. Tel: 281-422-9749. Ms. Ann Mullins, Prin. Sisters 1; Lay Teachers 9; Students 127.
Catechesis/Religious Program—Tel: 281-427-5720. Mrs. Jude Arceneaux, D.R.E. Students 224.

3—OUR LADY OF GUADALUPE (1958) Rev. J. Jesus Guerrero, O.S.A.; Deacons Fernando Gonzalez Bangs; Rudy Venegas; George Rincon.
Church & Mailing Address: 1124 Beech St., 77520-4198. Tel: 281-428-1507; Fax: 281-422-4554. Email: olguadalupe@galvestonbay.net.
Catechesis/Religious Program—Tel: 281-427-5836. Deacon George Rincon, D.R.E. Students 786.

BEASLEY, FT. BEND CO., ST. WENCESLAUS MISSION (1923) [CEM], (Independent Mission) Rev. Henry C. Rachunek.
Mailing Address: P.O. Box 121, Hungerford, 77448-0121. Tel: 979-532-4747; Fax: 979-532-8713.
Church: 407 S. 3rd St., 77448-0121.
Catechesis/Religious Program—Angie Reid, D.R.E. Students 156.

BELLVILLE, AUSTIN CO., STS. PETER & PAUL (1860) Rev. Timothy P. Bucek; Deacon Gerald W. DuPont.
Mailing Address: P.O. Box 808, 77418-0808. Tel: 979-865-2368; Fax: 979-865-9929.
Church: 936 S. Front St., 77418-0176. Email: stspandp@sbcglobal.net.
Catechesis/Religious Program—Tel: 979-865-8601. Whitney Malhmann, D.R.E. Students 166.
Mission—Immaculate Conception (1875) Industry, Austin Co.

BRAZORIA, BRAZORIA CO., ST. JOSEPH ON THE BRAZOS (1840) Rev. Tin Cosmas Kim Pham; Deacons Raul A. Castillo; Jimmy Smith.
Church & Mailing Address: 219 Country Rd. 762, 77422-7621. Tel: 979-798-2288; Fax: 979-798-2271. Email: stjoseph@brazoriainet.com.
Catechesis/Religious Program—Tel: 979-798-4702. Deacon Jimmy T. Smith, D.R.E. Students 164.

CHANNELVIEW, HARRIS CO., ST. ANDREW (1970) Rev. Christopher Shackelford; Deacons John Santos; Javier Gomez; Carlos Vences.
Res., Church & Mailing Address: 827 Sheldon Rd., 77530-3511. Tel: 281-452-9865; Fax: 281-452-2157. Email: standrew7067@sbcglobal.net. Web: standrewcatholicchurch.com.
Catechesis/Religious Program—Ms. Rosa Guerrero, D.R.E. Students 823.

CLUTE, BRAZORIA CO., ST. JEROME (1969) Rev. James F. Lynes; Deacon Julio Garcia; Dina A. Tonche, Pastoral Assoc.
Mailing Address: 201 N. Lazy Ln., 77531-4000. Tel: 979-265-5179; Fax: 979-265-4601. Email: jerome-clute@earthlink.net.
Rectory—100 Oak Dr. S., Lake Jackson, 77566-5630.
Church: 107 N. Lazy Ln., 77531-4001.
Catechesis/Religious Program—Tel: 979-266-8634. Dina A. Tonche, D.R.E. Students 431.

CONROE, MONTGOMERY CO., SACRED HEART (1916) Revs. Hubert J. Kealy; Christopher M. Plant; Thomas W. Hopper, Parochial Vicar; Deacons Ricardo Garcia; John W. Ehrman Jr.; Steve Miller.
Church & Mailing Address: 109 N. Frazier St., 77301-2889. Tel: 936-756-8186; Fax: 936-756-8105. Email: parishoffice@shconroe.org. Web: www.shconroe.org.
School—615 McDade St., 77301-2758. Tel: 936-756-3848. Gerard Kubelka, Prin. Sisters 2; Lay Teachers 21; Students 275.
Catechesis/Religious Program—Tel: 936-756-8186. Becki Lipari, D.R.E. Students 974.

CROSBY, HARRIS CO., SACRED HEART (1935) Rev. Arnel B. Barrameda; Deacon Archie Benham.
Res., Church & Mailing Address: 915 Runneburg Rd., 77532-5826. Tel: 281-328-4871; Fax: 281-328-1075. Email: sacredheartchurch@comcast.net. Web: www.sacredheartcrosby.org.
School—907 Runneberg Rd., 77532. Tel: 281-328-6561; Fax: 281-462-0072. Cathy Stephen, Prin. Sisters 3; Lay Teachers 11; Students 127.
Catechesis/Religious Program—Tel: 281-328-4871, Ext. 16. Mrs. Margaret Benham, D.R.E. Students 222.

DAMON, BRAZORIA CO., STS. CYRIL AND METHODIUS (1925) [CEM] Rev. Joseph Son Thanh Phan.
Mailing Address: P.O. Box 309, 77430-0309.
Rectory—P.O. Box 95, Needville, 77461.
Church: 603 Parrott Ave., 77430-0309. Tel: 979-742-3383; Fax: 979-742-3395. Email: patsystcyril@consolidated.net.
Catechesis/Religious Program—Tel: 979-553-3755. Mrs. Jolia Mueck, D.R.E. Students 62.

DANBURY, BRAZORIA CO., ST. ANTHONY DE PADUA (1911) [CEM] Rev. David G. Harris; Deacon Gerald Peltier; Camilla Cheolester, Pastoral Assoc.
Mailing Address: P.O. Box 299, 77534-0299.
Rectory—1603 Main St., 77534. Tel: 979-922-1253.
Church: 1523 Main St., 77534-0299. Tel: 979-922-1240; Fax: 979-922-8643. Email: st1523@sbcglobal.net.
Catechesis/Religious Program—Tel: 409-922-1241. Monica Sebesta, C.R.E. Students 147.

DEER PARK, HARRIS CO., ST. HYACINTH (1965) Rev. Antonio Castro; Deacons Dennis M. Hickey; Richard F. Camunez; Tom C. Mesa Jr.
Church & Mailing Address: 2921 Center St., 77536-4997. Tel: 281-479-4298; Fax: 281-478-6123. Email: info@sthyacinthchurch.org. Web: www.sthyacinthchurch.org.
Catechesis/Religious Program—Tel: 281-479-8832. Mr. Joseph F. Maire, D.R.E. Students 747.

DICKINSON, GALVESTON CO., SHRINE OF THE TRUE CROSS (1909) Revs. Paul G. Felix; Lawrence Clifton Wilson; Deacons Sam Ausmus III; Jose Duplan Jr.; Alberto Ospina; Neil Lewis.
Mailing Address: P.O. Box 687, 77539-0687.
Res.: 3720 Spruce, 77539. Tel: 281-337-4112; Fax: 281-337-5779. Email: info@truecrosschurch.org. Web: www.truecrosschurch.org.
Church: 300 FM 517 E., 77539.
School—400 FM 517 E., 77539. Tel: 281-337-5212. Marc Martinez, Prin. Lay Teachers 16; Students 255.
Catechesis/Religious Program—Tel: 281-337-3130. Raquel Hinojosa, D.R.E. Students 635.

FREEPORT, BRAZORIA CO.

1—ST. HENRY (1932) Closed. For inquiries for parish records contact the chancery.

2—ST. MARY: STAR OF THE SEA (1926) Rev. Edmund P. Eduarte; Deacon Wallace Shaw.
Church, Rectory & Mailing Address: 1019 W. 6th St., 77541-5423. Tel: 979-233-5271; Fax: 979-233-4418. Email: stmarysos@sbcglobal.net. Web: www.stmarystarofthesea.org.
Catechesis/Religious Program—Tel: 979-233-2771. Barbara Flores, D.R.E. Students 482.

FRIENDSWOOD, GALVESTON CO., MARY, QUEEN (1965) Revs. Phil "Skip" M. Negley, M.S.; Benny Joseph Thadathilkunnel, M.S.; Deacons James A. Lockwood; Paul Robinson; Bro. Robert Belliveau, M.S.
Church & Mailing: 606 Cedarwood Dr., 77546. Tel: 281-482-1391; Fax: 281-482-4886. Email: baezrm@maryqueenchurch.org. Web: www.maryqueenchurch.org.
Catechesis/Religious Program—Cynthia Newman, D.R.E. Students 1,027.

FRYDEK, AUSTIN CO., ST. MARY (1908) [CEM] Rev. Thuy Quang Nguyen, Admin.; Deacon Jerome D. Losack Sr.
Mailing Address: 10471 Grotto Rd., Sealy, 77474-9801. Tel: 979-885-3131; Fax: 979-885-4555.
Catechesis/Religious Program—Tel: 979-885-3178. Gloria Howard, D.R.E. Students 91.

GALENA PARK, HARRIS CO., OUR LADY OF FATIMA (1946) Rev. Josefino P. Templado; Deacons Jerry Peter Kulhanek Sr.; Hector Hernando Morales.
Mailing Address: P.O. Box 644, 77547-0644.
Res. & Church Address: 1705 Eighth St., 77547-0644. Tel: 713-675-0981; Fax: 713-675-0982. Email: ourladyoffatimacc@houston.rr.com.
School—1702 Ninth St., 77547. Tel: 713-674-5832; Fax: 713-674-3877. David Guite, Prin. Lay Teachers 9; Students 101.
Catechesis/Religious Program—Tel: 713-671-0717. Margarita Alaniz, D.R.E. Students 415.

HEMPSTEAD, WALLER CO.

1—ST. KATHERINE DREXEL (2001) Rev. Joseph Phiet The Nguyen. In Res., Deacon John Pelletier.
Church & Rectory: 800 F.M. 1488 Rd., 77445-1700. Tel: 979-826-2275; Fax: 979-826-8057. Email: pastorskd@sbcglobal.net. Web: www.stkdrexel.org.
Catechesis/Religious Program— Lucille Pavlock, D.R.E. Students 435.

2—MARY, MOTHER OF GOD (1879) Merged with St. Martin de Porres, Prairie View to form St. Katherine Drexel, Hempstead.

HIGHLANDS, HARRIS CO., ST. JUDE THADDEUS (1946) Rev. John A. Zabelskas.
Church & Mailing Address: 800 S. Main St., 77562-4236. Tel: 281-843-2422; Fax: 281-426-3671. Email: frwho@houston.rr.com.
Catechesis/Religious Program—Tel: 281-426-6800. Mrs. Claudine Lewis, D.R.E. Students 114.

HITCHCOCK, GALVESTON CO., OUR LADY OF LOURDES (1953) Rev. John H. Kappe; Deacon Joseph R. Kelly Sr.
Church & Mailing Address: 10114 Hwy. 6, 77563-4515. Tel: 409-925-3579; Fax: 409-925-5094. Email: jgrassmuch@dolchurch.org.
School—Tel: 409-925-3224. Mrs. Lisa Burnam, Prin. Sisters 2; Lay Teachers 6; Students 124.
Catechesis/Religious Program— Yvonne Routh, D.R.E. Students 190.

HUFFMAN, HARRIS CO., ST. PHILIP THE APOSTLE (1977) Rev. Richard E. Barker.
Mailing Address: P.O. Box 2363, 77336-2363.
Church: 2308 Third St., 77336. Tel: 281-324-1478; Fax: 281-324-2775. Email: stphiliphuffmantx@verizon.net.
Catechesis/Religious Program— Lisa Griffin, D.R.E. Students 160.

HUMBLE, HARRIS CO., ST. MARY MAGDALENE (1911) Revs. Edmund P. Eduarte; Daniel S. Baguio; Fernando Anaya-Maida; Deacons David W. Illingworth; James Meshell.
Church & Mailing Address: 527 S. Houston Ave., 77338-4763. Tel: 281-446-8211; Fax: 281-446-8213. Email: jlemoine@st-mm.com. Web: www.st-mm.com.
Rectory—525 S. Houston Ave., 77338-4763.
School—530 Ferguson, 77338. Tel: 281-446-8535; Fax: 281-446-8527. Jean Johnson, Prin. Lay Teachers 17; Students 190.
Catechesis/Religious Program—Tel: 281-446-2933. Waldemar Karaszewski, D.R.E. Students 1,161.

HUNTSVILLE, WALKER CO., ST. THOMAS THE APOSTLE (1963) Rev. Stephen J. Payne; Deacons Frank P. Ortego; Ivy C. Floyd; Richard Lopez.
Church & Mailing Address: 1323 16th St., 77340-4431. Tel: 936-295-8159; Fax: 936-295-3543. Email: stthomashuntsville@sbcglobal.net.
Rectory—1608 Ave. M, 77340-4431.
Catechesis/Religious Program— Sharyn Pezant, D.R.E.; Kathy Boscarino, D.R.E. Students 438.

KATY, HARRIS CO.

1—ST. BARTHOLOMEW THE APOSTLE (1965) Revs. John Kha Tran; Humberto Sanchez; Deacons Leroy Hamilton; William C. Wagner; Michael J. McGuire; Arthur Chin-Fatt; Rolando J. Garcia.
Church & Mailing Address: 5356 11th St., 77493-1748. Tel: 281-391-4758; Fax: 281-391-3978. Email: contact@st-bart.org. Web: www.st-bart.org.
Rectory—5356-B 11th St., 77493-1748.
Catechesis/Religious Program—Tel: 281-391-0839. Mrs. Isabel Chandler, D.R.E. Students 1,017.

2—ST. EDITH STEIN (1999) Rev. Ryszard Kulma; Deacons Leonard J. Broussard; Timothy Borbas; Lawrence Biediger Jr.; Samuel Hull III; Gary Walsh PP; Chris Tuadowski, Pastoral Assoc.
Church & Mailing Address: 3311 N. Fry Rd., 77449-6235. Tel: 281-492-7500; Fax: 281-492-0266. Email: pm@stedithstein.org. Web: www.stedithstein.org.
Rectory—2903 Sinton Ct., 77449.
Catechesis/Religious Program— Amy Auzenne, D.R.E. Students 496.

3—EPIPHANY OF THE LORD (1981) Rev. Msgr. Jack M. Dinkins; Deacons Don Kish; Jim Hite.
Church & Mailing Address: 1530 Norwalk Dr., 77450-4918. Tel: 281-578-0707; Fax: 281-578-9161. Email: epiphany@epiphanycatholic.org. Web: www.epiphanycatholic.org.
Catechesis/Religious Program—Tel: 281-578-8271. Students 2,606.

KINGWOOD, HARRIS CO., ST. MARTHA (1979) Rev. Msgr. Chester L. Borski; Revs. Linh N. Nguyen; Thomas Joseph T.J. Dulce; Deacons Alfred J.

O'Brien; Gerard Ostrand; Robert MacFarlane; Ed. Kleinguetl; John Schuster; Alfredo Soto.
Mailing Address: 2302 Oak Shores Dr., 77339-1801. Tel: 281-358-6637; Fax: 281-358-7973. Email: franp@stmartha.com. Web: www.stmartha.com.
Church: 3702 Woodland Hills Dr., 77339-1801.
School—2411 Oakshores Dr., 77339. Tel: 281-358-5523; Fax: 281-358-5526. Leslie Flickenger, Prin. Lay Teachers 20; Students 308.
Catechesis/Religious Program—Tel: 281-358-1959, Ext. 212. Linda Cussen, D.R.E. Students 1,782.

LA MARQUE, GALVESTON CO., QUEEN OF PEACE (1951) Rev. Chacko Puthumayil; Deacon Harold B. Eskew Jr.
Mailing Address: 1224 Cedar Dr., 77568-3932.
Church: 1200 Cedar Dr., 77568. Tel: 409-938-7000; Fax: 409-935-9791. Email: queenofpeaclm@sbcglobal.net.
Rectory—626 Laurel, 77568.
Catechesis/Religious Program—Tel: 409-935-3535. Martha Cantu, D.R.E. Students 149.

LA PORTE, HARRIS CO., ST. MARY (1954) Rev. Gary A. Rickles; Deacons Hector Cantu; Edward Thomas Lewis; Julio C. Matallana.
Church & Mailing Address: 816 Park Dr., 77571-5811. Tel: 281-471-2000; Fax: 281-471-9365. Email: stmaryslaportecc@sbcglobal.net. Web: www.stmaryslaporte.com.
Catechesis/Religious Program— Gloria Leal, D.R.E. Students 502.

LAKE JACKSON, BRAZORIA CO., ST. MICHAEL (1966) Rev. Msgr. Leo Wleczyk; Rev. Marty Pham; Deacon David Mitchell.
Church & Mailing Address: 100 Oak Dr. S., 77566-5630. Tel: 979-297-3041; Fax: 979-297-7895. Email: winnie@smlj.org. Web: www.smlj.org.
Catechesis/Religious Program—Tel: 979-297-3043. Marsha Jacklitsch, D.R.E. Students 526.

LEAGUE CITY, GALVESTON CO., ST. MARY (1910) Rev. Msgr. Eugene Cargill; Deacon George Blanford Jr.
Church & Mailing Address: 1612 E. Walker St., 77573-4137. Tel: 281-332-3031; 281-332-7211 (Rectory); Fax: 281-332-8328. Web: www.stmarylc.org.
School—Tel: 281-332-4014. Ruth Ann Winsor, Prin. Lay Teachers 21; Students 290.
Catechesis/Religious Program—Tel: 281-332-7459. Lisa Sabatier, D.R.E. Students 889.

MAGNOLIA, MONTGOMERY CO., ST. MATTHIAS THE APOSTLE (1978) Rev. Nicolas O. Pasadilla.
Church & Mailing Address: 302 S. Magnolia Blvd., 77355-8535. Tel: 281-356-2000; Fax: 832-446-0080. Email: stmatthias@st-matthias.net. Web: www.st-matthias.net.
Catechesis/Religious Program— Marlene Grauvogl, D.R.E. Students 580.

MANVEL, BRAZORIA CO., SACRED HEART OF JESUS (1945) Revs. David J. Zapalac, C.S.B.; Charles E. Lynch, C.S.B., Parochial Vicar; John S. Broussard, C.S.B.; Deacons Robert Reed Leicht Jr.; Brian Lambert; Hector J. Ibarra; Arturo Monterrubio.
Church & Mailing Address: 6502 County Rd. 48, 77578-4146. Tel: 281-489-8720; Fax: 281-489-8727. Email: admin@sacredheartofjesuschurch.org. Web: www.sacredheartofjesuschurch.org.
Catechesis/Religious Program—Tel: 281-489-7603. Connie Bowers, D.R.E. Students 809.

MCNAIR, HARRIS CO., HOLY FAMILY (1945) [JC] Rev. Rodney J. Armstrong, S.S.J.; Deacon Steve Arceneaux Jr.
Church & Mailing Address: 7122 Whiting Rock St., Baytown, 77521-1124. Tel: 281-426-8448; Fax: 281-426-8449. Email: hfrcc7122@houston.rr.com.
Catechesis/Religious Program—Tel: 281-421-7042. Charlotte Allen, D.R.E. Students 50.

MISSOURI CITY, FT. BEND CO.
1—ST. ANGELA MERICI (2007) Rev. John Rooney; Deacon Kevin McCarthy.
Mailing Address: PMB 99, 6140 Hwy. 6, 77549-3802. Tel: 281-778-0096. Email: frjrmerici@entouch.net.
Catechesis/Religious Program—Anne Sanford, D.R.E.
2—HOLY FAMILY (1915) Revs. Sunny Joseph Plammoottil, O.S.H.; Kurian Stephen Chooshukunnel, O.S.H., Parochial Vicar; Jose Mathai Mampuzhakkal, O.S.H., Parochial Vicar; Deacons Alfred Abram Sr.; William E. Seifert Jr.; Jose Melendez.
Church & Mailing Address: 1510 Fifth St., 77489-1298. Tel: 281-499-9688; Fax: 281-499-9680. Email: h1050@houston.rr.com. Web: www.holyfamilychurch.us.
Catechesis/Religious Program—Tel: 281-499-4612. Yolanda Pena, D.R.E. Students 863.

NAVASOTA, GRIMES CO., CHRIST OUR LIGHT (1869) Rev. Raul A. Marterior, Admin.; Deacons Grant E. Holt; Gregory N. Jelinek.
Res. & Mailing Address: 510 Manley St., 77868-3926. Tel: 936-825-3920; Fax: 936-825-7612. Email: info@christourlight.org. Web: www.christourlight.org.
Church: 9677 Hwy. 6, 77868.
Rectory—9685 Hwy. 6, 77868-3905.
Catechesis/Religious Program—Tel: 936-825-1869. Eva Rico, D.R.E. Students 260.

NEEDVILLE, FORT BEND CO., ST. MICHAEL (1913) [CEM] Rev. Joseph Son Thanh Phan.
Mailing Address: P.O. Box 95, 77461-0095.
Church: 9202 Main St., 77461. Tel: 979-793-4477; Fax: 979-793-7456.
Catechesis/Religious Program—Tel: 281-232-5290. Jacki Mikel, D.R.E. Students 650.

NEW CANEY, MONTGOMERY CO., ST. JOHN OF THE CROSS (1989) Rev. Hai Duc Dang; Deacons Winfield S. Matz; Robert Keller.
Church & Mailing Address: 20000 Loop 494, 77357-8213. Tel: 281-399-9008; 281-399-5541 (Rectory); Fax: 281-399-1500. Email: stjohn@argolink.net. Web: www.stjohnofthecross.com.
Catechesis/Religious Program— Debbie Davis, D.R.E. Students 415.

NEW WAVERLY, WALKER CO., ST. JOSEPH (1869) [CEM 2] Rev. Daokim Nguyen; Deacon Klaus Petereit.
Church & Mailing Address: 101 Elmore, 77358-4105. Tel: 936-344-6104; Fax: 936-344-2818. Email: stjonw@consolidated.net. Web: www.stjosephnewwaverlytx.net.
Catechesis/Religious Program—Tel: 936-856-3713. Deacon Klaus Petereit, D.R.E. Students 158.
Mission—St. Stephen the Martyr 101 Stagecoach, Pointblank, San Jacinto Co. 77364. Deacon Melvin Mouton.

PASADENA, HARRIS CO.
1—ST. JUAN DIEGO (1954), (Hispanic), (Formerly Guardian Angel) Revs. Jose Romero, O.S.A.; David Klotz, O.S.A.; Deacons Valeriano Leija; Jose Jimenez; Adolfo Mejia-Parada; Servando J. Rojas.
Church & Mailing Address: 3301 Pasadena Blvd., 77503-3201. Tel: 713-477-6693; Fax: 713-477-0523. Email: sjdchurch@sjdchurch.org. Web: www.sjdchurch.org.
Catechesis/Religious Program—Tel: 832-661-3404. Diego Monroy, D.R.E. Students 907.
2—ST. PIUS THE FIFTH (1941) Revs. Oscar M. Castro; Julian Michael A. Barrosa, D.S.; Deacons Celestino M. Perez Jr.; James L. Bart.
Church & Mailing Address: 824 S. Main St., 77506-3532. Tel: 713-473-9484; Fax: 713-473-2731. Web: www.stpiusv.com.
School—812 S. Main St., Pasaena, 77506. Tel: 713-472-5172. Sr. Krysia A. Pilon, M.C.D.P., Prin. Sisters 1; Lay Teachers 17; Students 214.
Catechesis/Religious Program— Alicia Alvarado, D.R.E. Students 1,400.

PATTISON/BROOKSHIRE, WALLER CO., SACRED HEART (1914) Rev. David J. DuBois.
Mailing Address: P.O. Box 300, 77466-0300.
Church: 4445 F.M. 359 N., 77466. Tel: 281-375-6799; Fax: 281-375-5799. Email: shpoffice@consolidated.net.
Catechesis/Religious Program—Tel: 281-375-6638. Mrs. Marie Pattison, D.R.E. Students 201.

PEARLAND, BRAZORIA CO., ST. HELEN (1952) Rev. Msgr. Reginald R. Nesvadba; Rev. Rodolfo L. Cal-Ortiz Jr.; Deacons Darvin A. Bordelon; Pete Calvillo; J. Cruz Trujillo; Dale Almonario.
Res., Church & Mailing Address: 2209 Old Alvin Rd., 77581-4499. Tel: 281-485-2421; Fax: 281-485-6789. Email: sthelen@sthelenchurch.org. Web: www.sthelenchurch.org.
School—2213 Old Alvin Rd., 77581. Tel: 281-485-2845; Fax: 281-485-7607. Mary Margaret Hitt, Prin. Lay Teachers 21; Students 222.
Catechesis/Religious Program—Tel: 281-485-5457. Julie Martinez, D.R.E. Students 1,640.

PLANTERSVILLE, GRIMES CO., ST. MARY (1894) [CEM] Rev. Edward C. Kucera Jr.; Deacon David Garvis.
Mailing Address: P.O. Box 388, 77363-0388. In Res., Rev. William T. Kelly (Retired).
Church: 8227 County Rd. 205, 77363. Tel: 936-894-2223; Fax: 936-894-3613. Email: info@smsj.org. Web: www.smsj.org.
Catechesis/Religious Program—Tel: 936-894-2223. Cheryl Schratwieser, D.R.E. Students 225.
Mission—St. Joseph Stoneham, Grimes Co11323 County Rd. 304, 77363-0388.

PORT BOLIVAR, GALVESTON CO., OUR MOTHER OF MERCY (1968) Closed. For parish records contact the Archives of Galveston-Houston.

PRAIRIE VIEW, WALLER CO., ST. MARTIN DE PORRES (1962) Merged with Mary, Mother of God, Hempstead to form St. Katherine Drexel, Hempstead.

RICHMOND, FORT BEND CO.
1—ST. JOHN FISHER (1952) Rev. Manuel LaRosa-Lopez; Deacons Ruben Torres; Hector L. Rodriguez.
Church & Mailing Address: 410 Clay St., 77469-1708. Tel: 281-342-5092; Fax: 281-633-9465. Email: info@st-john-fisher-church.org. Web: www.stjfisher.com.
Rectory—610 N. Fourth St., 77469.
Catechesis/Religious Program—Mrs. Helen Mata, D.R.E. Students 403.
2—SACRED HEART (1935) Rev. Howard E. Drabek. In Res., Deacons Donald G. Ries; Billy Guerrero Jr.; Don Murrile.
Church & Mailing Address: 507 S. Fourth St., 77469-3599. Tel: 281-342-3609; Fax: 281-342-9833. Email: info@sacredheartrichmond.com. Web: www.sacredheartrichmond.com.
Rectory—303 Houston, 77469.
Catechesis/Religious Program—Tel: 281-342-8371. Betty Holub, D.R.E.; Emily Kucherka, D.R.E. Students 1,457.

ROSENBERG, FORT BEND CO.
1—HOLY ROSARY (1911) Rev. William D. Bartniski.
Church & Mailing Address: 1416 George St., 77471-3198. Tel: 281-342-3089; Fax: 281-342-7688. Email: office@hrccr.com. Web: www.hrccr.com.
School—1408 James St., 77471. Tel: 281-342-5813; Fax: 281-344-1107. Mrs. Nancy Moore, Prin. Lay Teachers 23; Students 195.
Catechesis/Religious Program— Tina Hollopeter, D.R.E. Students 253.
2—OUR LADY OF GUADALUPE (1936) [CEM] Rev. Lee A. Flores; Deacons D. Naranjo; Enrique G. Avila; Albert Yanez.
Mailing Address: 1600 Avenue D, 77471-1814.
Church: 514 Carlisle St., 77471-1822. Tel: 281-232-5113; Fax: 281-342-4008. Email: olgc1936@yahoo.com.
Catechesis/Religious Program—Tel: 281-232-4322. Pauline Cano, D.R.E. Students 608.

SEALY, AUSTIN CO., IMMACULATE CONCEPTION (1889) [CEM] Rev. Eric J. Pitre; Rev. Msgr. Boleslaus Zientek (Retired); Deacons Frank Laredo; Robert Kent; Ben Munguia.
Mailing Address: P.O. Box 337, 77474-0337.
Rectory—525 5th St., 77474. Tel: 979-885-3868; Fax: 979-885-2246. Email: iccsealy@aol.com. Web: www.iccsealy.com.
Church: 600 4th St., 77474-2607.
Catechesis/Religious Program— Carol Thormaehlin, D.R.E. Students 265.

SOUTH HOUSTON, HARRIS CO., OUR LADY OF GRACE (1971) Rev. Jesus M. Martinez-Irigoyen, Admin.
Mailing Address: P.O. Box 164, 77587-0164.
Church: 1211 Michigan St., 77587. Tel: 713-946-6461; Fax: 713-946-0647. Email: ourladyofgracecc@sbcglobal.net.
Res.: 1204 Michigan St., 77587.
Catechesis/Religious Program—Tel: 281-461-9417. Rosa Elly Garcia, D.R.E. Students 169.

SPRING, HARRIS CO.
1—CHRIST THE GOOD SHEPHERD (1978) Revs. John Upton; Joseph Hoang Huy Bui; Deacons Pat W. Camerino; Alberto J. Patetta; Pat Hancock.
Church & Mailing Address: 18511 Klein Church Rd., 77379-4998. Tel: 281-376-6831; Fax: 281-376-8945. Email: center@cgsccdogh.org. Web: www.cgsccdogh.org.
Catechesis/Religious Program— Camilla Chedester, D.R.E. Students 835.
2—ST. EDWARD (1969) Revs. Joseph A. Gietl; Mark Czarnecki, Parochial Vicar; Patrick Stuart Garrett, Parochial Vicar; Deacons Nicholas Thompson; Dominic Romaguera; Kenneth Martin.
Church & Mailing Address: 2601 Spring Stuebner Rd., 77389-4824. Tel: 281-353-9774; Fax: 281-353-9786. Email: cklos@saintedward.com. Web: www.saintedward.com.
School—Tel: 281-353-4570; Fax: 281-353-8255. Mr. Gregory J. Sawka, Prin. Lay Teachers 27; Students 352.
Catechesis/Religious Program—Tel: 281-353-4930. Students 593.
3—ST. IGNATIUS OF LOYOLA (1985) Revs. Norbert J. Maduzia Jr.; Wilfred A. Legal, O.S.B.; Deacons John Baker; William Sheffield; Glen H. Cupier; Michael E. Higgins; Larry Vines.
Church & Mailing Address: 7810 Cypresswood Dr., 77379-7101. Tel: 281-370-3401; Fax: 281-370-9306. Email: ignatiusloyola@silcc.org. Web: www.ignatiusloyola.org.
Rectory—7802 King Arthur Ct., 77379.
Catechesis/Religious Program— Mary Wright, D.R.E. Students 1,393.
4—ST. JAMES THE APOSTLE (1976) Revs. Charles J. Samperi; Joseph Manappuram; Deacons Ray Oden; Arthur Zepeda.
Church & Mailing Address: 22800 Aldine Westfield Rd., 77373-6565. Tel: 281-353-5053; Fax: 281-355-8847. Email: saintjta@wbell.net. Web: www.stjamestheapostle.org.
Catechesis/Religious Program— Peggy Hay, D.R.E. Students 675.

SUGAR LAND, FORT BEND CO.
1—ST. LAURENCE (1985) Revs. William Andrew Wood; Santy M. Kurian, M.S.F.S.; Reginald Wayne Samuels; Deacons Don Burns; Charles Plant; Albert G. Bothe; Renato Arellano.
Church & Mailing Address: 3100 Sweetwater Blvd., 77479-2630. Tel: 281-980-9812; Fax: 281-980-0686. Email: contact@stlaurenceparish.com. Web:

www.stlaurenceparish.com.
School—2630 Austin Pkwy., 77479. Tel: 281-980-0500; Fax: 281-980-0026. Debra Haney, Prin. Lay Teachers 54; Students 744.
Catechesis/Religious Program—Tel: 281-265-5774. Ms. Pat Kerlin, D.R.E. Students 1,572.

2—ST. THERESA (1924) Revs. Stephen B. Reynolds; Miguel A. Alvizures; Jose J. Tharayil; Deacons Glenn F. Haller; Frank P. Cromer; Joaquin Garcia.
Mailing Address: P.O. Box 968, 77487-0968.
Res. & Church Address: 115 Seventh St., 77478. Tel: 281-494-1156; Fax: 281-242-1393. Email: fcromer@sttheresasugarland.org. Web: www.sttheresasugarland.org.
School—St. Theresa Academy, Tel: 281-494-1157. Jonathan M. Beeson, Headmaster.
Catechesis/Religious Program—Rosa Michel, D.R.E. Students 1,249.

3—ST. THOMAS AQUINAS (1978) Rev. Joseph K. Kalladan; Verna Patout, Pastoral Assoc.; Deacons Sam Dunning; Bob Dunham; Robert Kirkpatrick. In Res., Rev. James A.C. Cheruvil (SYM).
Church & Mailing Address: 12627 W. Bellfort Ave., 77478-1844. Tel: 281-240-6721; Fax: 281-240-6733. Email: contact@stthomasaquinas.info. Web: www.stthomasaquinas.info.
Rectory—10415 Huntington Wood Dr., 77099-3721.
Catechesis/Religious Program— Rebecca Gotting, D.R.E. Students 429.

SWEENY, BRAZORIA CO., OUR LADY OF PERPETUAL HELP (1954) Rev. Ralph O. Roberts.
Church & Mailing Address: 310 N. McKinney St., 77480-2899. Tel: 979-548-2020; Fax: 979-548-4253. Web: www.olphsja.org.
Catechesis/Religious Program—Tel: 979-798-8129. Students 117.
Mission—St. John the Apostle 807 Loggins, West Columbia, Brazoria Co. 77486-3843.

TEXAS CITY, GALVESTON CO., ST. MARY (1911) Rev. Thomas V. Ponzini; Deacons Joseph A. Hensley; Miguel Hernandez; Stephen A. Mistretta; Sue Mistretta, Pastoral Assoc.
Mailing Address: 1604 Ninth Ave. N., 77590-5468.
Church: 722 Third Ave. N., 77590. Tel: 409-948-8448; Fax: 409-945-8662. Email: st_marys@swbell.net. Web: www.stmarycctc.org.
School—Our Lady of Fatima, 1600 Ninth Ave. N., 77590. Tel: 409-945-3326; Fax: 409-945-3389. Susan Flanagan, Prin. Sisters 2; Lay Teachers 10; Students 155.
Catechesis/Religious Program—Tel: 409-948-1383. Deacon Joseph A. Hensley, D.R.E. Students 514.

THE WOODLANDS, MONTGOMERY CO.

1—ST. ANTHONY OF PADUA (1997) Revs. Thomas F. Rafferty; George Vattapara Devasia, M.S.F.S.; Deacons Joe Mignogna; Michael Mims; Tom Vicknair; Charles Duck.
Church & Mailing Address: 7801 Bay Branch Dr., 77382-5359. Tel: 281-296-2800; Fax: 281-296-7238. Email: trafferty@staoptw.org. Web: www.staoptw.org.
Rectory—7979 Bay Branch Dr., 77382-5312.
School—7901 Bay Branch Dr., 77382. Tel: 281-296-0300. Renee Nunez, Prin. Lay Teachers 22; Students 383.
Catechesis/Religious Program— Mike Quigley, D.R.E. Students 2,244.

2—STS. SIMON AND JUDE (1979) Rev. Msgr. Charles C. Domec; Rev. Vincent Vuong-Quoc Nguyen; Deacons John E. Charnisky Jr.; Robert E. Flynn Sr.; Sid Sandiford; Glendon Michael Schmidt; Anthony G. Cantania.
Res., Church & Mailing Address: 26777 Glen Loch Dr., 77381-2921. Tel: 281-367-9885; Fax: 281-367-9888. Email: webmaster@ssjwoodlands.com. Web: www.ssjwoodlands.com.
Catechesis/Religious Program—Sonya Thibert, D.R.E. Students 716.

TOMBALL, HARRIS CO., ST. ANNE (1964) Rev. Fred W. Valone; Deacons Ted F. Heap; Thomas Davis; Garry Janota.
Church & Mailing Address: 1111 S. Cherry St., 77375-6675. Tel: 281-351-8106; Fax: 281-351-8142. Email: fvalone@stanne-tomball.org. Web: www.stanne-tomball.org.
School—Tel: 281-351-0093. Margaret Morgan, Prin. Lay Teachers 20; Students 269.
Catechesis/Religious Program— Laura Hinton, D.R.E. Students 714.

WALLIS, AUSTIN CO., GUARDIAN ANGEL (1892) [CEM] Rev. Thuy Quang Nguyen, Admin.; Deacon Jerome D. Losack Sr.
Mailing Address: P.O. Box 487, 77485-0487. Tel: 979-478-6532; Fax: 979-478-7275.
Church & Res.: 5610 Demel St., 77485.
Catechesis/Religious Program—Tel: 979-478-6717. Barbara Litzmann, D.R.E. Students 164.

Chaplains of Public Institutions

GALVESTON. *Galveston County Jail*, 715 19th St., 77550. Tel: 409-766-2315. Deacon Javier Gomez.
John Sealy Hospital, 809 Harborside Dr, 77555. Tel: 409-762-1810. Deacon Javier Gomez. Prison Unit

HOUSTON. *Federal Correctional Center*, 1200 Texas Ave., 77002. Tel: 713-229-4172. Rev. Frank Guenter.
George Bush Intercontinental Airport. Rev. Edmund P. Eduarte, Chap. (Retired).
Harris County Jail. Rev. Ronald F. Cloutier. Tel: 713-755-5326, Deacon Eddie Stoughton. Tel: 713-741-8745.
Res.: 1200 Baker St., 77002. Tel: 713-755-5326.
701 San JacintoBldg., 77002. Tel: 713-755-8562.
INS Houston Process Center, 15850 Export Plaza Dr., 77032. Tel: 281-449-1481. Vacant.
Juvenile Detention Center. Ms. Marilu Ballow. Tel: 713-741-8779. Special Youth Svcs.
Kegan State Jail, 707 Top St., 77002. Tel: 713-224-6584.
William P. Hobby Airport. Rev. Wencil C. Pavlovsky, V.F., Chap.

ANGLETON. *Brazoria County Jail*, 3602 Co. Rd. 45, 77515. Tel: 979-849-2441. Vacant.
Pam Lychner State Jail.
2350 Atoscocita Rd., Humble, 77396. Tel: 281-454-5036, Ext. 358. Deacon Al O'Brien.
Scott Unit. Vacant.
6999 Retrieve County Rd. 290, 77515. Tel: 979-849-9306.

CONROE. *Montgomery County Jail*, #1 Criminal Justice Dr., 77301. Tel: 936-760-5870. Vacant.

BRAZORIA. *Clemens Unit*. Vacant.
11034 Hwy. 36, 77422. Tel: 979-798-2188.

DICKINSON. *Young Unit/Young Medical Facility*, 5509 Attwater Ave., 77539. Tel: 409-948-0001. Deacon Ron Simon, Chap.

HUNTSVILLE. *Byrd Unit*. Vacant.
21 FM 247, 77320. Tel: 936-295-5786.
Diagnostic Unit.
P.O. Box 100, 77340. Tel: 936-295-8459. Anthony Velasquez.
Ellis I Unit, 1697 FM 980, 77343. Tel: 936-295-5756, Ext. 217. Vacant.
Estelle Unit, 264 FM 3478, 77320. Tel: 936-291-4200, Ext. 2274. Vacant.
Goree Unit. Vacant.
7504 Hwy. 75 S., 77344. Tel: 936-295-6331.
Holliday Unit, 295 IH-45N, 77320. Tel: 936-437-1975. Vacant.
Huntsville Walls Unit, 815 12th St., 77340. Tel: 936-295-8159; 409-291-4200. Vacant.
Texas Department of Criminal Justice, 1060 State Hwy. 190 E, 77340. Tel: 936-294-6548 (Regl. Program Admin.). Deacon Richard Lopez.
Wynne Unit.
FM 2821, 77349. Tel: 936-295-9126. Linda Hill.

NAVASOTA. *Luther Unit*, 1800 Luther Dr., 77868. Tel: 936-825-7547.
Pack Unit, 2400 Wallispack Rd., 77869. Tel: 409-825-3728. Vacant.

RICHMOND. *Central Unit*.
One Circle Dr., 77478. Tel: 281-491-2146. Deacon Brent Larsen.
Jester I, III, IV Unit/Vance Unit/Central Unit. Deacon Brent Larsen, Chap.
Rte. 2, 77469. Tel: 281-277-3700.

ROSHARON. *Darrington Unit*.
59 Darrington Rd., 77583. Tel: 281-595-3465, Ext. 275. Vacant.
Ramsey I Unit. Deacon Bob Leicht.
1100 FM 655, 77583. Tel: 281-595-3491.
Stringfellow Unit.
1200 FM 655, 77583. Tel: 281-595-3413. Vacant.
Terrell Unit. Vacant.
1300 FM 655, 77583. Tel: 281-595-3481.

On Duty Outside the Archdiocese:
Revs.—
McGinnis, Jack P., Chap., P.O. Box 2456, Idyllwild, CA 92549-2456.
Perez, Joseph, The Chancery, P.O. Box 907, 77001.

Retired:
Rev. Msgrs.—
Beck, Albert J., Pope John XXIII Residence, 2407 Holcombe Blvd., #B1, 77021-2023. Tel: 713-748-0644
Crosthwait, Joseph H., Maloney Hall Nursing Home, 2409 Holcombe Blvd., #307, 77021-2023. Tel: 713-440-0030
Francis, Eugene, 6651 Camptown Cir., 77069-1214. Tel: 281-440-1303
Fruge, Donald J., 5000 Montrose Apt. 7F, 77006-6560. Tel: 713-521-3267
Kennedy, David W., V.F., 12121 Maverick Dr., Willis, 77378-4814. Tel: 936-228-5209
Kleas, Milam, St. Maximilan Kolbe, 10135 West Rd., 77064-5361.
Lee, Lawrence F., Maloney Hall Nursing Home, 2409 Holcombe Blvd., #308, 77021-2023. Tel: 713-741-7267
O'Connor, Fred P., St. John the Evangelist Church, 800 W. Baker Rd., Baytown, 77521-2311. Tel: 281-837-8180
Pickard, William M., J.C.D., Pope John XXIII Residence, 2407 Holcombe Blvd., Apt. A-4, 77021-2023. Tel: 713-842-7770
Procella, Paul, 1101 Parthenon Pl., New Caney, 77357-3276. Tel: 281-785-0017
Randall, Edward, P.O. Box 444, Coldspring, 77331-0444. Tel: 936-767-8313
Wearden, Francis G., Pope John XXIII Residence, 2407 Holcombe Blvd., #B9, 77021-2023. Tel: 713-747-1928
Wells, Patrick R., Land Fall Towers, 6403 Padre Blvd., Unit #85, South Padre Island, 78597-7708. Tel: 956-761-3953
Zientek, Boleslaus, Immaculate Conception Church Rectory, P.O. Box 788, Sealy, 77474-0788. Tel: 281-797-5916

Revs.—
Abell, Edward, Cenacle Retreat House, 420 North Kirkwood, 77079-6807. Tel: 713-417-6272
Antle, Nicholas C., Pope John XXIII Residence, 2407 Holcombe Blvd., #A8, 77021-2023. Tel: 713-748-1553
Anton, Ronald J., S.J., Pope John XXIII Residence, 2407 Holcombe Blvd., 77021-2023. Tel: 713-748-1553
Asenjo, Jose Maria, P.O. Box 464, South Houston, 77587-0464. Tel: 832-428-8832
Carlson, Robert D., Maloney Hall Nursing Home, 2409 Holcombe Blvd., #304, 77021-2033. Tel: 713-741-8701
Cejudo, Serafin, 6618 Limestone St., 77092-5794. Tel: 713-703-8074
Chia, Luis P., St. Dominic Village-Maloney Hall Room 305, 2409 Holcombe Blvd., 77021-2023. Tel: 713-741-8700
Chu, Peter Ngoc Thanh, Pope John XXIII Residence, 2407 Holcombe Blvd., #B6, 77021-2023. Tel: 713-747-8774
Connelly, Laurence D., 7 Tourney Cove, Austin, 78738-1119. Tel: 512-261-8063
Corrigan, Michael T., Pope John XXIII Residence, 2407 Holcombe Blvd., #B4, 77021-2023. Tel: 832-578-6860
Doroin, Elias E., 2432 Sheridan St., 77030-1922. Tel: 713-922-1230
Ferguson, Peter A., P.O. Box 552, Ellenton, FL 34222-0552. Tel: 813-671-6967
Guenter, Frank, 2008 Southgate, #2, 77030.
Heberlein, Kenneth, 7811 Rolling Brook Dr., 77071-1707. Tel: 713-988-2468
Hoang, John Minh Toan, Pope John XXIII Residence, 2407 Holcombe Blvd., #A1, 77021-2023. Tel: 713-747-7707
Jones, Frank W., Pope John XXIII Residence, 2407 Holcombe Blvd., #B7, 77021-2023. Tel: 713-842-1977
Kellick, John W., 6517 Burdock Dr., Santa Fe, 77510-9340. Tel: 409-925-6817
Kelly, William T., St. Mary Church, P.O. Box 388, Plantersville, 77363-0388. Tel: 936-894-2016
Lee, Lawrence, Pope John XXIII Residence, 2407 Holcombe Blvd., 77021-2023. Tel: 713-741-7267
Linan, Jesse S., P.O. Box 250, Anderson, 77830-0250. Tel: 409-873-2945
Mandry, Stephen, Pope John XXIII Residence, 2407 Holcombe Blvd., #B2, 77021-2023. Tel: 713-747-2593
Martin, Roosevelt, Jr., 3560 Dixie Dr., Apt. 723, 77021-1263. Tel: 713-962-8652
McGinnis, John P., 11734 Wilshire Blvd., #C 1103, Los Angeles, CA 90025-6450. Tel: 760-902-6925
Mikulik, Kenneth E., St. Dominic Village Assisted Living, 2401 Holcombe Blvd., Tower Rm. 507, 77021-2099. Tel: 713-741-3522
Moore, James T., 5478 County Rd. 113A, Iola, 77861-5378. Tel: 936-394-1940
Morfin, John N., 8429 Sands Point Dr., Bldg. #18, 77036-2769. Tel: 281-650-7629
Olsovsky, George J., P.O. Box 292, Huffman, 77336-0292. Tel: 281-324-2873
Rodriguez, Armando J., Pope John XXIII Residence, 2407 Holcombe Blvd., #A6, 77021-2023. Tel: 713-842-2053
Sanchez, Jose M., Pope John XXIII Residence, 2407 Holcombe Blvd., A3, 77021-2023. Tel: 713-440-6329
Schwarting, J. Donald, 679 Ashmore St., New Braunfels, 78130-4601. Tel: 830-214-7177
Sikorski, Louis S., Pope John XXIII Residence, 2407 Holcombe Blvd., #B8, 77021-2023. Tel: 936-870-5133
Simmons, Franklin, 2000 Westborough Dr., #1104, Katy, 77449-3291. Tel: 713-397-3057
Snock, Bernard C., 4044 Chew Rd., Sealy, 77474. Tel: 979-885-3930
Tenhundfeld, Carl Anthony, 11002 Hammerly #167, 77043. Tel: 713-932-8977
Walker, Anselm, 1815 Parker, 77093. Tel: 713-697-7109

Warden, Daniel L., V.F., 1815 Parker Rd., 77093-5221. Tel: 713-697-7109

Permanent Deacons:
Abadejos, Ernesto, Notre Dame, Houston
Abram, Alfred, Sr., (Unassigned)
Adame, David, St. Matthew, Houston
Adams, John W., St. Matthew the Evangelist, Houston
Addis, Daniel, Assumption, Houston
Aguilar, Juan, Our Lady of Mount Carmel, Houston
Alessi, Anthony V., St. Thomas More, Houston
Alexander, Jack, St. Michael, Houston
Alexander, Robert George, Annunciation and St. Paul, Houston
Allen, Charles J., Sr., Our Mother of Mercy, Houston
Almenario, Adelfo, St. Helen, Pearland
Arceneaux, Leon, St. Anthony, The Woodlands
Arceneaux, Steve, Jr., Holy Family, McNair
Arellano, Jose, Immaculate Heart of Mary, Houston
Arellano, Renato, St. Laurence, Sugar Land
Ausmus, Sam, III, Shrine of the True Cross, Dickinson
Avila, Enrique G., Our Lady of Guadalupe, Rosenberg
Baker, J. M., St. Ignatius, Spring
Barnett, James, Our Lady of Walsingham, Houston
Bart, James L., St. Pius V, Pasadena
Bazan, Jeronimo, Prince of Peace, Houston
Becker, Henry, Holy Family, Galveston
Benham, Archie, Sacred Heart, Crosby
Benoit, John, St. Mark the Evangelist, Houston
Berna, Thomas, St. Clare of Assisi, Houston
Biediger, Lawrence, Jr., Sr. Edith Stein, Katy
Birsinger, Alvin, St. Luke the Evangelist, Houston
Blanford, George, Jr., St. Mary, League City
Bobb, William J., (Retired), St. George Villa, Rosewell
Borbas, Timothy, St. Edith Stein, Katy
Bordelon, Darvin A., St. Helen, Pearland
Bothe, Albert G., St. Lawrence, Sugar Land
Bottjer, Albert, Assumption, Houston; Ben Taub Hospital; Jail Chap.
Bowman, David, St. John the Baptist, Alvin
Bradley, Donald V., Jr., St. Cecilia, Houston
Breaux, Roy, St. Phillip of Jesus, Houston
Brinkman, Fred H., TDC-Ramsey Units I, II, III/Drug Trustee Camp
Brooks, James, St. Philip Neri, Houston
Broussard, Leonard J., St. Edith Stein
Brown, Abner, Sr., St. Gregory the Great, Houston
Brueggerhoff, Robert T., Holy Ghost, Houston
Budinger, Jean-Paul, St. Anne, Houston
Buhay, Carlito, St. Albert, Houston
Burns, Don, St. Laurence, Sugar Land
Burroughs, Orrin D., St. Philip Neri, Houston
Butler, Charles, Prince of Peace, Houston
Cabler, Paul Stephen, Unassigned
Calonge, Elie P., Notre Dame, Houston
Calvillo, Pedro, St. Helen, Pearland
Calvo, Clement S., Hispanic Ministry Office, Houston
Camerino, Pat W., Christ the Good Shepherd, Spring
Camunez, Richard F., St. Hyacinth, Deer Park
Cantu, Hector, St. Mary, La Porte
Carranza, Joe, On Duty Outside the Archdiocese
Caruso, James, St. Michael, Houston
Casas, Alvaro, Jr., St. Albert, Houston
Castaneda, Guillermo F., Jr., Diocese of Brownsville
Castillo, Raul A., St. Joseph, Brazoria
Catania, Anthony, SS. Simon & Jude, The Woodlands
Cerda, Rodolfo, All Saints, Houston
Charnisky, John E., Jr., St. Simon & St. Jude, The Woodlands
Chavez, Roberto, St. Cecilia, Houston
Chin-Fatt, Arthur, St. Bartholomew
Coenen, Jerry, On Duty Outside the Archdiocese
Conant, Charles, St. Charles Borromeo, Houston
Contla, Juan M., St. John Neumann, Houston
Cooper, Leslie F., (Unassigned)
Coussirat, John F., (Retired)
Cox, Ralph, Holy Trinity
Crawford, J. R., Diocese of Little Rock
Crawley, Denver, St. Maximilian Kolbe, Houston
Cromer, Frank P., St. Theresa, Sugarland
Cuiper, Glen H., St. Ignatius of Loyola, Spring
D'Agnolo, Louis, On Duty Outside the Archdiocese
Dalecki, Robert, St. Leo the Great, Centerville
Davies, Martin, On Duty of the Archdiocese
Davis, Thomas, St. Anne, Tomball
Dean, John H., St. Clare of Assisi, Houston
Dell-Olio, L. S., Holy Family, Galveston
Despania, Raymond L., Sr., St. Peter Claver, Houston
Devine, John E., Jr., St. Luke the Evangelist, Houston
Dinges, Adrian F., Jr., Prince of Peace, Houston
Do, Joseph Chuong Nguyen, Our Lady of Lourdes, Houston
Dolpher, Eduardo M., St. Cyril of Alexandria, Houston
Duck, Charles, St. Anthony, The Woodlands
Dunham, Bob, Unassigned
Dunning, Sam, St. Thomas Aquinas, Sugar Land
Duplan, Jose, Jr., Shrine of the True Cross, Dickenson
Dupont, Gerald W., SS. Peter & Paul, Bellville
Durden, Jonathon, On Duty Outside of Archdiocese
Egusquiza, Reinaldo, St. Luke the Evangelist, Houston
Ehrman, John W., Jr., Sacred Heart, Conroe
Eskew, Harold B., Jr., Queen of Peace, La Marque
Evans, Gregory, St. Cecilia, Houston
Festa, Gene, St. Justin Martyr, Houston
Fikac, Marvin R., Sacred Heart Co-Cathedral, Houston
Flores, Antonio, Jr., St. Francis de Sales, Houston
Floyd, Ivy C., St. Thomas the Apostle, Huntsville
Flynn, Robert E., Sr., Sts. Simon & Jude, The Woodlands
Foley, Dan, St. John the Evangelist, Baytown
Frederiksen, Allan, St. Christopher, Houston
Froning, John, St. Theresa, Houston
Fuentes, Jose, St. Augustine, Houston
Gallagher, James, Christ the Good Sheperd, Spring
Galvan, Jose M., Queen of Peace, Houston
Garcia, Gerardo J., Christ the King, Houston
Garcia, Joaquin, St. Theresa, Sugar Land
Garcia, Jorge, Catholic Charismatic Center, Houston
Garcia, Julio, St. Jerome, Clute
Garcia, Ricardo, Sacred Heart, Conroe
Garcia, Rolando J., St. Bartholomew, Katy
Garrett, William, St. Anne, Houston
Garvis, David, St. Mary, Plantersville
Germann, Joseph, On Duty Outside of the Archdiocese
Gil, Reynaldo S., St. Joseph, Houston
Gilbert, Daniel W., St. Peter the Apostle, Houston
Glor, Richard J.L., Unassigned
Godinez-Galvan, Jorge, On Duty Outside the Archdiocese
Godoy, German, St. Elizabeth Ann Seton, Houston
Gomez, Javier, St. Andrew, Channelview
Gonzales, Emiliano, On Duty Outside of Archdiocese
Gonzalez, Enrique, St. Charles Borromeo, Houston
Gonzalez, Guadalupe, St. Charles, Houston
Gonzalez, Miguel A., St. Mary Magdalene, Humble
Gonzalez Bangs, Fernando, Our Lady of Guadalupe, Baytown
Gosline, Edwin F., St. Thomas More, Houston
Graham, Michael G., Unassigned
Granado, Alfred E., Jr., Leave of Absence
Gregory, Ralph R., Jr., Christ the Redeemer, Houston
Griesmyer, Steven, Sr., Catholic Charismatic Center, Houston
Guajardo, Fredrico, Our Lady of Mt. Carmel, Houston
Guerra, Daniel, Sr., St. Cecilia, Houston
Guerrero, Billy, Jr., Sacred Heart, Richmond
Hall, Raymond J., Unassigned
Haller, Glenn F., St. Theresa, Sugar Land
Hamilton, L. William, St. Bartholomew, Katy
Hancock, James, Christ the Good Sheperd, Spring
Harper, Stephen Edwin, On Duty Outside of Archdiocese
Hayden, Dale, St. John the Baptist, Alvin
Hayes, Dennis, St. Maximilian Kolbe, Houston
Heap, Theodore, Jr., St. Anne, Tomball
Henkel, Robert, Sr., Christ the Redeemer, Houston
Hennessy, Robert, St. John the Evangelist, Baytown
Henry, Albert, St. Francis Xavier, Houston
Hensley, Joseph, Jr., St. Mary of the Miraculous Medal, Texas City
Hernandez, Miguel, St. Mary of the Miraculous Medal, Texas City
Herrera, Enrique, Holy Family, Galveston
Herrera, Rolando, Archdiocese of San Antonio
Hesse, Robert J., St. John Vianney, Houston
Hickey, Dennis, St. Hyacinth, Deer Park
Higgins, Michael E., St. Ignatius, Spring
Hilbig, Gerard, All Saints, Houston
Hill, Russell, On Duty Outside of the Archdiocese
Hite, James, Epiphany of the Lord, Katy
Hoang, Tuu, St. Elizabeth Ann Seton, Houston
Hock, Leslie Bart, Annunciation, Houston
Hodge, Brick, St. Rose, Houston
Holt, Grant E., Christ Our Light, Navasota
Horbowy, Thaddeus J., Chap. Fed. Bureau of Prisons and Medical Center, Lexington, KY
Horr, Louis, St. Catherine of Siena, Houston
Hull III, Samuel, St. Edith Stein, Katy
Hunsucker, Paul, St. Thomas the Apostle, Canyon Lake
Ibarra, Hector J., Sacred Heart of Jesus, Manvel
Illingworth, David W., St. Mary Magdalene, Humble
Jackson, Clifford X., Unassigned
Jackson, Phillip, Christ the Redeemer, Houston
Janota, Garry, St. Anne, Tomball
Jelinek, Gregory N., M.D., Christ Our Light-Navasota; O.C. Luther TDC
Jenkins, Michael V., St. Francis Xavier, Houston
Jimenez, Jose, St. Juan Diego, Pasadena
Johnson, Gilbert R., St. Elizabeth Ann Seton, Houston
Johnson, Irvin, Jr., Our Mother of Mercy, Houston
Joseph, Ignatius, St. Francis of Assisi, Houston
Kacz, Robert, St. John the Baptist, Alvin
Keller, Robert C., St. John of the Cross, Houston
Kelly, Joseph R., Sr., Our Lady of Lourdes, Hitchcock
Kent, Robert, Immaculate Conception, Sealy
Kiang, Paul, Ascension Chinese Mission, Houston
Kirkpatrick, Robert, St. Thomas Aquinas, Sugar Land
Kish, Don, Epiphany of the Lord, Katy
Kleinguetl, Edward, St. Martha, Kingwood
Koch, William E., Sr., Deaf Ministry Center
Kossegi, Frederick, St. John Vianney, Houston
Kulhanek, Jerry Peter, Sr., Our Lady of Fatima, Galena Park
LaBonte, Stephen L., Catholic Chaplain Corps.
Labrecque, Richard, On Duty Outside of Archdiocese
Lambert, Bernard, Sacred Heart of Jesus, Manvel
Landry, Burke J., Unassigned
Lane, John, St. Monica, Houston
Lansch, John, St. Justin Martyr, Houston
Laredo, Frank, Immaculate Conception, Sealy
Laugermann, Frank J., Jr., St. Francis Xavier, Houston
Laurel, Manuel A., Our Lady of Guadalupe, Houston
Leach, Bruce, On Duty Outside of the Archdiocese
Leal, Merce C., Jr., St. Christopher, Houston
Leicht, Robert Reed, Jr., Sacred Heart, Manvel
Leija, Valeriano, Blessed Juan Diego, Pasadena
Lerma, Pedro, Sr., Blessed Sacrament, Houston
Lewis, Edward Thomas, St. Mary, La Porte
Lewis, George, Shrine of the True Cross, Dickinson
Liendo, Jose L., Queen of Peace, Houston
Llorens, Cornelius C., St. Justin Martyr, Houston
Lockett, Leonard P., Sacred Heart Co-Cathedral, Houston
Lockwood, James A., Mary, Queen, Friendswood
Longley, Larry T., St. Albert of Trapani, Houston
Lopez, Luis, St. Paul, Houston
Lopez, Richard, St. Thomas the Apostle, Huntsville
Lorino, Joseph E., St. Vincent de Paul, Houston
Losack, Jerome D., Sr., Guardian Angel, Wallis
Loving, Peter, On Duty Outside of the Archdiocese
Lozano, Rodrigo, St. Charles Borromeo, Houston
Lugo, Loni G., Unassigned
MacFarlane, Robert, St. Martha, Kingwood
Malveaux, Andrew B., Sr., St. Mary of the Purification, Houston
Mancuso, Salvatore, St. Cecilia, Houston
Mangano, Collie J., Jr., Prince of Peace, Houston
Marquez, Antonio, St. Raphael, Houston
Martin, Henry Woods, St. Michael, Houston
Martin, Kenneth, St. Edward, Spring
Matallana, Julio C., St. Mary, La Porte
Matthews, Douglas W., Holy Rosary, Galveston
Matula, Francis L., All Saints, Houston
Matz, Winfield S., St. John of the Cross, New Caney
McAllister, Jerome, On Duty Outside the Archdiocese
McCarthy, Kevin, St. Angela Merici, Missouri City
McGuire, Michael J., St. Bartholomew the Apostle, Katy
Mejia Parada, Adolfo, St. Juan Diego, Pasadena
Melendez, Jose, Holy Family, Missouri City
Meshell, James, St. Mary, Humble
Meza, Benito, St. Augustine, Houston
Michalec, Jerry J., St. Michael, Needville
Middleton, Carl L., On Duty Outside of the Archdiocese
Mignogna, Joe, St. Anthony of Padua, The Woodlands
Miller, Arthur, Unassigned
Miller, Steve, Sacred Heart, Conroe
Millsap, Stacy, St. Maximillian Kolbe, Houston
Mims, Michael, St. Anthony of Padua, The Woodlands
Mistretta, Stephen A., St. Mary of the Miraculous Medal, Texas City
Mitchell, David D., St. Michael, Lake Jackson
Monterrubio, Arturo, Sacred Heart of Jesus, Manvel
Morales, Hector Hernando, Our Lady of Fatima, Galena Park
Moreno, Aurelio Frank, Jr., St. Frances Cabrini, Houston

Moreno, Leopold R., Catholic Charismatic Center, Houston
Motley, John M., Unassigned
Moulton, Darrell, Covenant House, Houston
Mouton, Melvin, St. Stephen the Martyr Mission, Point Blank
Moya, Antonio, St. Jerome, Houston
Mulcare, Terrance D., On Duty Outside the Archdiocese
Munguia, Ben, Immaculate Conception, Sealy
Murrell, John T., St. Rose of Lima, Houston
Murrile, Donald, Sacred Heart, Richmond
Naranjo, Danilo, Our Lady of Guadalupe, Rosenberg
Nelms, D. Cade, St. Cecilia, Houston
Newhouse, Thomas C., St. Michael, Houston
Nguyen Kim Khanh, Michael, Our Lady of Lavang, Houston
Nguyen Pham, Joseph, Vietnamese Martyrs, Houston
Nguyen Si Bach, Joseph, Christ the Incarnate Word, Houston
O'Brien, Alfred J., St. Martha, Kingwood
Oden, Edgar, St. James the Apostle, Spring
Ortego, Frank P., St. Thomas the Apostle, Huntsville
Ortego, Mario, Assumption, Houston
Ospina, Alberto, Shrine of the True Cross, Dickinson
Osterhaus, James H., Christ the Redeemer, Houston
Ostrand, Gerard, St. Martha, Kingwood
Ostrowski, F. L., Notre Dame, Houston
Pagnano, Daniel, St. Vincent de Paul, Houston
Pareja, Juan Francisco, Holy Name, Houston
Parr, Kenneth, Catholic Charismatic Center, Houston
Patetta, Alberto J., Christ the Good Sheperd, Spring
Pelletier, John, St. Katherine Drexel, Hempstead
Peltier, Gerald, St. Anthony, Danbury
Pennell, Charles G., St. Elizabeth Ann Seton, Houston
Perez, Celestino M., Jr., St. Pius V, Pasadena
Perez, Juan de Dios, St. Raphael the Archangel, Houston
Petereit, Klaus, St. Joseph, New Waverly
Pistone, John Salvadore, Holy Family, Galveston
Plant, Charles, St. Laurence, Sugar Land
Porras, Carlos, St. Cecilia, Houston
Poth, Louis, On Duty Outside the Archdiocese
Prescott, Allen W., Prince of Peace, Houston
Provenzano, Luis, St. Justin Martyr, Houston
Quiroga, Gabriel Z., Our Lady of Guadalupe, Houston
Ramirez, Fernando, St. Frances Cabrini, Houston
Ramirez, Julio M., St. Gregory the Great, Houston
Rangel, Francisco M., St. Joseph, Houston
Rapp, Donald, St. Albert of Trapini, Houston
Ries, Donald G., Sacred Heart, Richmond
Rincon, George, Our Lady of Guadalupe, Baytown
Risk, Ralph F., On Duty Outside the Archdiocese
Robison, Paul L., Jr., Mary Queen, Friendwood
Rodriguez, Hector L., St. John Fisher, Richmond
Rodriguez, Luis, St. Albert of Trapani, Houston
Roessler, Charles F., Jr., St. Frances Cabrini, Houston
Rojas, Servando J., St. Juan Diego, Pasadena
Romaguera, Dominic, St. Edward, Spring
Romeu, Hector J., St. John Vianney, Houston
Rowan, Vincent A., (Retired)
Rubio, Jesus J., St. Bernadette, Houston
Rudnicki, Anthony, Our Lady of Czestochowa, Houston
Rumford, Robert, St. Bernadette
Salas, Pedro, St. Jerome, Houston
Salinas, Johnny, Sacred Heart Co-Cathedral, Houston
Saltzmann, Peter, Catholic Charismatic Center, Houston
Sanchez, Martin G., St. Joseph, Houston
Sandiford, Sid, Sts. Simon & Jude, The Woodlands
Santos, John, St. Andrew, Channelview
Satterwhite, Michael, (Unassigned)
Schmidt, Glendon Michael, SS. Simon & Jude, The Woodlands
Schuster, John, St. Martha, Kingwood
Seifert, William E., Jr., Holy Family, Missouri City
Sharpless, James, St. Luke the Evangelist, Houston
Shaw, Wallace, St. Mary Star of the Sea, Freeport
Sheffield, William L., St. Ignatius, Spring
Shefts, Andrew, Most Holy Trinity, Angleton
Simon, Rick L., Our Mother of Mercy, Houston
Simon, Ronald, St. Philip Neri, Houston
Singer, John, St. Joseph, Baytown
Smaistrla, Denis J., St. Mary's Seminary, Houston
Smith, Jimmy, St. Joseph, Brazoria
Sosa, Alfonso, St. Elizabeth Ann Seton, Houston
Soto, Alfredo, St. Martha, Kingwood
St. Aubin, Leo F., St. Anthony of Padua, The Woodlands
St. Julian, Michael, St. Francis of Assisi
Standridge, Robert, Holy Family, Galveston
Stasiulis, Stan, (Retired)
Steffes, Dale W., St. John Vianney, Houston
Stevens, Robert Gregory, St. Francis Cabrini, Houston
Stoessel, Edward T., St. Thomas More, Houston
Stoughton, Bruce, St. John the Baptist, Alvin
Sullivan, John, On Duty Outside of Archdiocese
Suriano, Julio S., Sacred Heart Co-Cathedral
Thompson, Edward, (Retired)
Thomson, Nicholas, St. Edwards, Spring
Tollett, Jesse, St. Luke, Houston
Tollett, Lee, St. Catherine of Siena, Houston
Torres, Reynaldo, St. Patrick, Houston
Torres, Ruben, St. John Fisher, Richmond
Tran, Nhat, St. Justin Martyr, Houston
Trevino, Jose, Christ the Redeemer, Houston
Tripp, Edwin, St. Edith Stein, Katy
Tristan, Benito, Jr., St. Christopher, Houston
Trosclair, George, Prince of Peace, Houston; St. Mary, Plantersville
Trujillo, J. Cruz, St. Helen, Pearland
Vacek, Albert E., Jr., St. John Vianney, Houston
Vaclavik, Larry A., St. Theresa, Houston
Vasquez, Miguel, St. Ambrose, Houston
Vences, Carlos, St. Andrew, Channelview
Venegas, Rudy, Our Lady of Guadalupe, Baytown
Vicknair, Tom Jude, St. Anthony of Padua, The Woodlands
Vigil, Benjamin, On Duty Outside of the Archdiocese
Villarreal, Marcelino, St. John Vianney, Houston
Vines, Larry, St. Ignatius, Spring
Vocelka, Frank Jay, Jr., Duty Outside of Archdiocese
Wagner, William C., St. Bartholomew, Katy
Walsh, Gary, PP, St. Edith Stein, Katy
Ward, Robert, Most Holy Trinity, Angleton
Waterman, John H., On Duty Outside of Archdiocese
Weaver, William A., St. Elizabeth Ann Seton, Houston
Wewer, Justin J., St. John the Evangelist, Baytown
Wiles, Philip Arlen, St. Dominic, Houston
Wright, Jim, St. Clare of Assisi
Yanez, Albert, Our Lady of Guadalupe, Rosenberg
Zamora, Joe, St. Elizabeth Ann Seton, Houston
Zbylut, Robert, On Duty Outside of the Archdiocese
Zepeda, Arthur, St. James the Apostle, Spring

INSTITUTIONS LOCATED IN THE ARCHDIOCESE

[A] SEMINARIES, ARCHDIOCESAN

HOUSTON. *St. Mary's Seminary* (1901) 9845 Memorial Dr., 77024-3498. Tel: 713-686-4345; Fax: 713-681-7550. Email: seminary@stthom.edu. Rev. Trung V. Nguyen, J.C.L., Vice Rector; Rev. Msgr. Charles Elmer (AUS); Very Rev. Brendan J. Cahill, Rector; Revs. Jose Salazar (CC), Formation Dir.; Rafael R. Davila, M.M.; Damon Geiger, O.SS.T., Spiritual Dir.; James Mueller, O.Carm.; Sisters Barbara Tovar, M.C.D.P., Dir. Cultural Formation; Patricia Regan, C.D.P., Business Mgr.; Sandra Magie, S.T.D., Dean School of Theology; Mrs. Laura Olejnik, Librarian; Rev. Msgr. James B. Anderson, Prof. Priests 9; Sisters 1; Lay Teachers 5; Diocesan Seminarians 81; Religious Seminarians 7; Total Enrollment 88.

[B] SEMINARIES, RELIGIOUS OR SCHOLASTICATES

HOUSTON. *Holy Ghost Fathers and Brothers, Spiritan Hall*, 4410 Yoakum Blvd., 77006-5820. Tel: 713-529-0405; Fax: 713-529-4236. Web: www.spiritans.org. Rev. J.M. Huy Quang Dinh, C.S.Sp., Dir. Priests 1; Brothers 1; Consecrated Religious 2.

SUGAR LAND. *Basilian Fathers of Sugarland* (2004) 106 Fifth St., 77498. Tel: 281-491-1565; Fax: 281-491-1178. Email: vdulock@earthlink.net. Revs. Vincent Dulock, C.S.B., V.F., Rector & Supr.; Roy J. Oggero, C.S.B. (Retired); Paul F. English, C.S.B., Gen. Counsellor; Jamie M. Abercrombie, C.S.B. Priests 4.

[C] COLLEGES AND UNIVERSITIES

HOUSTON. **University of St. Thomas* (1947) 3800 Montrose Blvd., 77006-4696. Tel: 713-522-7911; Fax: 713-525-2125. Email: president@stthom.edu. Web: www.stthom.edu. Dr. Robert Ivany, Pres.; Dr. Dominic A. Aquila, Vice Pres. Academic Affairs; Mr. James Piccininni, Dir., Doherty Library; Dr. Sandra C. Magie, Dean School of Theology; Dr. Bahman Mirshab, Dean Cameron School of Business; Dr. Robert LeBlanc, Dean, School Educ.; Ms. Lynda McKendree, Dean Scholarships & Fin. Aid; Ms. Kia Wissmiller, Dir. Major Constituents; Ms. Joanna Palasoda, Dir. Admin. Computing & Institutional Research; Mr. James Booth, Vice Pres. Finance; Dr. John Palasoda, Assoc. Vice Pres.; Dr. Ravi Srinivas, Dir., Master in Liberal Arts Prog. & Dean, Extended Programs; Dr. Rose Signorello, Exec. Dir. Counseling, Wellness, & Disability Svcs.; Dr. Mary Catherine Sommers, Dir. Center for Thomistic Studies; Mr. Gary McCormack, Vice Pres. Information Technology & Special Assistant to Pres.; Mr. H. Ken DeDominicis, Vice Pres. Inst. Advancement; Mr. Matthew Prasifka, Dir. Campus Life; Mr. Daryl Bissett, Dir. Security; Mr. Howard Rose, Asst. Vice Pres. Facilities Opers.; Ms. Karen Burns, Controller; Ms. Susan Rose, Treas.; Rev. Donald S. Nesti, C.S.Sp., Dir. Center for Faith and Culture; Dr. Daryl Koehn, Dir. Center for Business Ethics & Cullen Trust for Higher Educ.; Ms. Patricia McKinley, Dean of Students, Dir. Career Svcs. & Testing, & Interim Vice Pres. Student Affairs; Ms. Vickie Alleman, Vice Pres. Mktg., Communications & Enrollment Mgmt.; Ms. Marionette Mitchell, Dir. Publications; Ms. Laura Dozier, Dir. Special Events; Ms. Susan Bradford, Advancement Exec. Dir.; Mr. Tony Reyna, Dir. Network & Campus Computing; Ms. Christine Barry, Dir. Central Computing Svcs.; Mr. Mark Henderson, Dir., Technology Support Svcs.; Sr. Paula Jean Miller, FSE, Dir. Catholic Studies Prog.; Ms. Laura P. Olejnik, Dir. Cardinal Beran Library; Dr. Terry Hall, Dir. Honors Prog.; Dr. Sophia Esquiff, Dir. Learning and Writing Center; Ms. Deborah Crofoot-Morley, Dir. Major Constituents; Ms. Roya Esfandi, Dir. Information Resources; Ms. Yolanda Norman, Dir. Residence Life; Ms. Diane Thornton, Dir. Planned Giving; Mr. John Meuser, Dir. Human Resources; Ms. Sara Laidlaw, Dir., Advising; Dr. Linda Pett-Conklin, Dir. Center for Intl. Studies; Rev. Joseph E. Pilsner, C.S.B., Dean Arts & Sciences; Mr. Hank Emery, Dir. Alumni Rels. & Annual Giving; Ms. Lori Gallagher, Dir., Center for Irish Studies; Mr. Todd Smith, Dir. Athletics; Ms. Monica Clem, Dir. Devel. & External Rels.; Ms. Elsie Biron, Advisor to Pres., Catholic Outreach Efforts; Rev. Michael Buentello, C.S.B., Univ. Chap.; Ms. Poldi Tschirsch, Dir., Nursing Programs Devel.; Ms. Shannon Wilson, Dir. Veteran Svcs. & Graduate Programs; Mr. Lee Holm, Dir. Admissions; Dr. John Burke, Dir. Catholic Social Justice Learning; Dr. Jean-Philippe Faletta, Dir. Svc. Learning. Founded in 1947, Graduate Division (Four Schools). Undergraduate Division (21 Departments). Center for Thomistic Studies. Center for International Studies. Center for Business Ethics.; Liberal Arts University. Priests 14; Sisters 5; Lay Professors 135; Total Enrollment 3,246; Total Staff 205.

[D] JUNIOR HIGH SCHOOLS, ARCHDIOCESAN

HOUSTON. *Assumption Catholic School*, 801 Roselane St., 77037-4696. Tel: 281-447-2132; Fax: 281-447-1825. Email: PWClark@houstonassumption.org. Web: www.houstonassumption.org. Mr. Patrick W. Clark, Prin.; Sr. Francis Marie Bordages, Librarian. Sisters 3; Lay Teachers 16; Students 263; Total Staff 32.

[E] HIGH SCHOOLS, PRIVATE

GALVESTON. *O'Connell College Preparatory School*, 1320 Tremont St., 77550-4513. Tel: 409-765-5534; Fax: 409-765-5536. Email: pdanesi@ochsgalv.org. Web: www.ochsgalv.org. Mr. Patrick Danesi, Prin.; Janice Vinson, Librarian. Priests 1; Lay Teachers 15; Total Staff 20; Students 114.

HOUSTON. *St. Agnes Academy* (1906) 9000 Bellaire Blvd., 77036-4683. Tel: 713-219-5400; Fax: 713-219-5499. Email: sjmeyer@st-agnes.org. Web: www.st-agnes.org. Sr. Jane Meyer, O.P., Head of School. Tel: 713-219-5400; Fax: 713-219-5499; Herman Sutter, Librarian. Dominican Sisters 1; Lay Teachers 54; Full time faculty 75; Girls 874.

Duchesne Academy of the Sacred Heart (1960) (Girls), 10202 Memorial Dr., 77024-3299. Tel: 713-468-8211; Fax: 713-465-9809. Email: administration@duchesne.org. Web: www.duchesne.org. Sr. Jan Dunn, R.S.C.J., Headmistress; Dr. Rae Flory, Prin. (Upper School); Ms. Julie Meyer, Prin. (Middle School); Ms. Debra Johnson, Prin. (Lower School); Barbara Weathers, Librarian (Upper School); Aria Tatelman, Librarian (Middle School); Jean Pfluger, Librarian (Lower School). Religious of the Sacred Heart. Sisters 1; Lay Teachers 89; Students (9-12) 263; Total Enrollment (PreK-12) 700.

Incarnate Word Academy (1873) 609 Crawford St., 77002-3668. Tel: 713-227-3637; Fax: 713-227-1014.

Email: mgetschow@incarnateword.org. Web: www.incarnateword.org. Sr. Lauren Beck, C.V.I., Pres.; Mary Getschow, Prin.; Rebecca Shields, Librarian. Sisters of the Incarnate Word and Blessed Sacrament. Sisters 4; Lay Teachers 19; Girls 262.

St. Pius X High School, Inc. (1956) 811 W. Donovan, 77091-5699. Tel: 713-692-3581; Fax: 713-692-5725. Email: pollardd@stpiusx.org. Web: www.stpiusx.org. Sr. Donna M. Pollard, O.P., B.S., M.A., M.Ed., Head of School; Diane Larsen, Academic Dean; Jeff Donaruma, Dean of Students; Susie Kramer, Dir. of Admissions; Marilyn McEvoy, Librarian. Dominican Sisters 2; Lay Teachers 60; Students 694; Total Staff 85.

Strake Jesuit College Preparatory Inc., 8900 Bellaire Blvd., 77036-4699. Tel: 713-774-7651; Fax: 713-774-6427. Email: sjcom@strakejesuit.org. Web: www.strakejesuit.org. Mr. Richard Nevle, Prin.; Revs. Christopher A. Billac, S.J., Faculty; Flavio Bravo, S.J., Pastoral Ministry; John N. Folzenlogen, S.J., Faculty; Daniel K. Lahart, S.J., Pres.; Bro. Castenzio A. Ferlita, S.J., Prefect of Discipline; Ms. Susan Penny, Librarian. Priests 4; Brothers 1; Scholastics 2; Lay Teachers 80; Boys 900.

St. Thomas High School (1900) 4500 Memorial Dr., 77007-7332. Tel: 713-864-6348 (School); 713-868-9209 (Residence); Fax: 713-864-5750. Web: www.sths.org. Revs. Jack H. Hanna, C.S.B., Treas.; John Huber, C.S.B., Prin.; Ronald G. Schwenzer, C.S.B., Pres.; Albert R. Gaelens, C.S.B.; Richard A. Wahl, C.S.B., J.C.L.; Kevin J. Storey, Supr.; Robert H. Glass, C.S.B.; Les F. Schaefer, C.S.B.; James F. Blocher, C.S.B. Basilian Residence, Basilian Fathers. Priests 7; Lay Teachers 65; Total Staff 100; Total Enrollment 709.

KATY. *Pope John XXIII High School, Inc.* (2004) 1800 W. Grand Pkwy., 77449. Tel: 281-693-1000; Fax: 281-693-1001. Email: tpetersen@pj23.org. Web: www.pj23.org. Tim Petersen, Prin.; Michelle Ponder, Admissions; Lauren Gavulic, Advancement; Ms. Theresa Bramanti, Bd. Pres.; Jenelle Drymalla, Librarian. Teachers 27; Total Staff 41; Total Enrollment 268.

[F] ELEMENTARY SCHOOLS, PRIVATE

HOUSTON. *St. Catherine's Montessori* (1966) 9821 Timberside, 77025. Tel: 713-665-2195; Fax: 713-665-1478. Email: jmccullough@stcathmont.org. Judy McCullough, Prin.; Sarah Case, Librarian. Lay Teachers 17; Students 240; Total Staff 42.

John Paul II Catholic School (1988) 1400 Parkway Plaza Dr., 77077-1503. Tel: 281-496-1500; Fax: 281-496-2943. Email: principal@jp2.org. Web: www.jp2.org. Janie Hengst, Prin.; Kristen Thome, Asst. Prin.; Don Courtney, Asst. Prin.; Sherry Lamb, Librarian. Lay Teachers 50; Students 719; Total Staff 73.

The Regis School, 7330 Westview Dr., 77055-5122. Tel: 713-682-8383; Fax: 713-682-8388. Email: ntaylor@theregisschool.org. Web: www.theREGISschool.org. Dr. Nancy O. Taylor, Headmistress; Laura Luong, Librarian; Mrs. Kay Pickett, Prin. Catholic School for Boys. Lay Teachers 32; Students 224; Total Staff 51.

[G] ELEMENTARY SCHOOLS, CONSOLIDATED

GALVESTON. *Galveston Catholic School* (1986) (Consolidation) 2601 Ursuline Ave., 77550-4398. Tel: 409-765-6607; Fax: 409-765-5154. Email: mnix@galvestoncatholicschool.org. Web: www.galvestoncatholicschool.org. Madeleine P. Nix, Prin.; Dawn Cromie, Librarian & Mgr. Sisters 1; Lay Teachers 13; Students 102; Total Staff 20.

GALVESTON/HOUSTON. *School of Environmental Education - Camp Kappe* (1982) (Grades 5), 7738 Camp Kappe Rd., Plantersville, 77363. Tel: 936-894-2141; Fax: 936-894-2198. Email: stalsee@aol.com. Sr. Thomas Ann LaCour, O.P., Prin. Sisters 1; Lay Teachers 3; Total Staff 4; Total Enrollment 1,400.

RICHWOOD. *Our Lady Queen of Peace*, 1600 Hwy. 2004, 77531. Tel: 979-265-3909; Fax: 979-265-9780. Email: devdir@olqpschool.org. Web: www.olqpschool.org. Mrs. Debra Kyle, Prin. Serving the parishes of Holy Trinity, Angleton; St. Jerome, Clute; St. Anthony, Danbury; St. Mary Star of the Sea, Freeport; Lady of Perpetual Help, Sweeny; St. John the Apostle Mission, West Columbia; St. Joseph's, Brazoria, TX; St. Michaels, Lake Jackson. Lay Teachers 20; Students 237.

[H] SOCIAL AGENCIES CATHOLIC CHARITIES

HOUSTON. *Catholic Charities of the Archdiocese of Galveston-Houston* (1943) P.O. Box 66508, 77266. 2900 Louisiana St., P.O. Box 66508, 77006. Tel: 713-526-4611; Fax: 713-526-1546. Email: info@catholiccharities.org. Web: www.catholiccharities.org. Bonna Kol, Pres.

AIDS Ministry Tel: 713-526-4611; Fax: 713-526-1546.

Beacon of Hope, Beacon of Hope Center. Tel: 409-739-2318; Fax: 409-762-2088.

Guadalupe Center Tel: 713-227-9981; Fax: 713-225-1242. (Family Assistance)

Children's and Family Services Tel: 713-526-4611; Fax: 713-526-1546. (Adoption and Foster Care)

Disaster Recovery Tel: 713-526-4611; Fax: 713-526-1546.

Services to Pregnant and Parenting Adolescents Tel: 713-526-4611; Fax: 713-526-1546.

Post Adoption Services Tel: 713-526-4611; Fax: 713-526-1546.

Family Counseling Tel: 713-526-4611; Fax: 713-526-1546.

St. Frances Cabrini Center for Immigrant Legal Assistance Tel: 713-874-6553; Fax: 713-874-6792.

St. Jerome Emiliani's Home for Children Tel: 713-526-4611; Fax: 713-526-1546.

Refugee Resettlement Program Tel: 713-526-4611; Fax: 713-526-1546.

St. Michael's Home for Children Tel: 713-526-4611; Fax: 713-526-1546.

Services to the Alone and Frail Elderly Tel: 713-526-4611; Fax: 713-526-1546.

Serenity House Tel: 713-526-4611; Fax: 713-526-1546.

Parish Social Ministry Tel: 713-526-4611; Fax: 713-526-1546.

Villa Guadalupe Tel: 713-227-9981; Fax: 713-225-1242. Transitional Housing

[I] HEALTH AND HOSPITALS

HOUSTON. *CHRISTUS Health Gulf Coast*, 1700 W. Loop S., #1200, 77027. Tel: 713-277-2772; Fax: 713-277-2778. Email: rae.korczynski@christushealth.org. Web: www.christushealth.org. Patrick B. Carrier, Pres. & CEO. Total Staff 1,153; Total Assisted Annually 200,254; Bed Capacity 232.

Christus Literacy Center, 2420 Winnie, 77550. Tel: 409-621-1337. Personnel 2.

CHRISTUS Our Daily Bread (1985) Tel: 409-765-6971; Fax: 409-765-8547. Staff 7.

KATY. *CHRISTUS St. Catherine Hospital*, 701 S. Fry Rd., 77450. Tel: 281-599-5700; Fax: 281-398-2265. Bed Capacity 102; Patients Assisted Annually 97,819; Total Staff 705.

NASSAU BAY. *CHRISTUS St. John Hospital*, 18300 St. John Dr., 77058. Tel: 281-333-5503 (Hospital); Fax: 281-333-8891. Email: tom.permetti@christushealth.org. Web: www.christusstjohn.org. Tom Permetti, Admin. Tel: 281-333-8898. Bed Capacity 178; Patients Assisted Annually 128,642; Total Staff 850.

[J] CLINICS

HOUSTON. *San Jose Clinic* (1922) 2615 Fannin, 77002. Tel: 713-228-9411; Fax: 713-228-6371. Email: staciecokinos@sanjoseclinic.org. Web: www.sanjoseclinic.org. Stacie Cokinos, Exec. Dir. Patients Assisted Annually 5,000; Lay Staff 50.

[K] PROTECTIVE INSTITUTIONS

HOUSTON. *Casa de Esperanza De Los Ninos, Inc.* (1982) P.O. Box 66581, 77266-6581. Tel: 713-529-0639; Fax: 713-529-9179. Email: casa@casahope.org. Web: www.casahope.org. Kathleen Foster, Dir.; Mr. William Jones, Assoc. Dir. Homes for children in crisis situations, foster care, adoption. Sisters 4; Served 3,000; Total Assisted 400; Total Staff 42; Bed Capacity 50.

Casa Juan Diego (1980) P.O. Box 70113, 77270. Tel: 713-869-7376; Fax: 713-864-7295. Email: info@cjd.org. Web: www.cjd.org. 4818 Rose, 77007. Mr. Mark Zwick, Dir.; Mrs. Louise Zwick, Dir. Houses 10; People Served Annually 71,420; Personnel 16.

Casa Maria de Guadalupe Medical Clinic and Social Service Center, 6101 Edgemoor, 77081. Tel: 713-869-7376; Fax: 713-864-7295. Email: info@cjd.org. Web: www.cjd.org. (Catholic Worker) Patients Assisted Annually 21,450; Total Staff 4.

Covenant House Texas, 1111 Lovett Blvd., 77006. Tel: 713-523-2231; Fax: 713-523-6904. Email: Rgrobinson@covenanthouse.org. Web: www.covenanthousetx.org. Kevin M. Ryan, Pres.; Ronda G. Robinson, Exec. Dir. & CEO; Martin Galicia, Pastoral Min. Bed Capacity 128; Total Assisted Annually 4,539; Total Staff 90.

Magnificat Houses Inc. (1968) P.O. Box 25415, 77265. Tel: 713-520-0461; Fax: 713-520-0461. Email: magnificathousesion@sbcglobal.net. Web: www.mhihouston.org. Rose Mary Badami, Founder, Pres. & Exec. Dir. Bed Capacity 187; Staff 12; Resident Staff 4; Contract Staff 4; Total Assisted Annually (Houses) 2,602; Meals Served Annually (Houses) 1,947; Meals Served Annually (Soup Kitchen) 96,649.

Santa Maria Hostel, 2605 Parker Rd., 77093. Tel: 713-691-0900; 713-957-2413; Fax: 713-691-0910; 713-400-1119. Email: kaustin@santamariahostel.org. Web: www.santamariahostel.org. 807 Paschall, 77009. Tel: 713-222-0699; Fax: 713-222-6245. Kay Austin, CEO. Intensive and supportive residential treatment; housing, shelter and outpatient services (substance abuse) for women ages 18 and above and women with their children. Treatment for co-occurring disorders is also provided. Residents 136; Patients Assisted Annually 1,662; Total Staff 130; Bed Capacity 225.

[L] HOMES FOR THE AGED

HOUSTON. *St. Dominic Village* (1998) 2409 Holcombe Blvd., 77021. Tel: 713-741-8701; Fax: 713-741-9811. Email: rstanley@stdominicvillage.org. Web: www.stdominicvillage.org. Ruth Stanley, Admin. & COO. Bed Capacity 349; Total Assisted Annually 401; Total Staff 185.

Pope John Paul XXIII Priests' Residence (1981) 2407 Holcombe Blvd., 77021-2023. Tel: 713-748-4608; Fax: 713-748-4608. Revs. Gabre-Tinsaye Adhana (Retired). Tel: 713-748-4425; Nicholas Neal Antle (Retired); Peter Ngoc Thanh Chu (Retired). Tel: 713-747-8774; Lawrence Lee (Retired). Tel: 713-741-7267; Armando J. Rodriguez (Retired). Tel: 713-842-2053; Charles K. Schoppe (Retired). Tel: 713-748-4596; Hoang Toan (Retired); Jose M. Sanchez (Retired); Joseph Crossthwait (Retired). Total in Residence 17; Total Staff 2.

St. Dominic Nursing Home (1981) 2409 Holcombe Blvd., 77021. Tel: 713-741-8701; Fax: 713-741-9811. Web: www.stdominicvillage.org. Email: rstanley@stdominicvillage.org. Ruth Stanley, Admin. & COO. Aged Residents 304; Total Staff 140.

St. Dominic Residence Hall (1975) 2401A Holcombe Blvd., 77021. Tel: 713-741-8700; Fax: 713-748-8305. Ruth Stanley, Admin. & COO. Total in Residence 177; Total Staff 20.

[M] RESIDENTIAL TREATMENT AND RENEWAL CENTERS

SPLENDORA. *Shalom Center, Inc.* (1980) 13516 Morgan Dr., 77372-3121. Tel: 281-399-0520; Fax: 281-399-3366. Email: info@shalomcenterinc.org. Web: www.shalomcenterinc.org. Rev. Andre Estephan, M.L.M., Exec. Dir. A residential treatment center for priests, brothers and sisters. Bed Capacity 16; Total Assisted Annually 376; Total Staff 14.

[N] PERSONAL PRELATURES

HOUSTON. *Opus Dei*, 5505 Chaucer Dr., 77005-2631. Tel: 713-528-4081; Fax: 713-523-6829. Web: www.opusdei.org. Very Rev. Paul D. Kais, B.A., M.A., Ph.D., Vicar Opus Dei in Texas; Rev. Msgr. William H. Stetson; Revs. Michael Barrett; Michael J. Manz. Prelature of the Holy Cross and Opus Dei.

[O] MONASTERIES AND RESIDENCES OF PRIESTS AND BROTHERS

HOUSTON. *Companions of the Cross (Texas), Companions of the Cross (Texas)*, 6725 Reed Rd., 77087-6830. Tel: 713-644-8400. Email: companionstx@gmail.com. Web: www.companionscross.org. Rev. Francis Donnelly, Local Supr.

Congregation of the Holy Spirit, Province of the United States (1964) 1700 W. Alabama St., 77098-2808. Tel: 713-522-2882; Fax: 713-522-8063. Email: spiritans@aol.com. Web: www.spiritans.org. Revs. Daniel L. Walsh, C.S.Sp., Supr.; Thomas J. Byrne, C.S.Sp.; Joseph A. Seiter, C.S.Sp.; Bro. Michael Suazo, C.S.Sp. Total in Residence 4.

Congregation of the Passion, Holy Name Passionist Community and Retreat Center, 430 Bunker Hill Rd., 77024. Tel: 713-464-4932; Fax: 713-932-7303. Email: arthurcp@passionist.org. Web: www.passionist.org. Very Rev. Arthur Carrillo, C.P., Local Supr.; Revs. Joseph Moons, C.P., Retreat Center Dir.; Peter Berendt, C.P.; Simon Herbers, C.P.; Cedric Pisegna, C.P.; Robert Bovenzi, C.P.; Bro. Carl Hund, C.P., Retreat Center Team.

Dillon House, 1302 Kipling, 77006-4297. Tel: 713-529-3994; Fax: 713-942-7623. Revs. Philip Anthony Acquaro, C.S.B., Supr. (Retired); Wilfred S. Canning, C.S.B. (Retired); Gerald F. Dillon, C.S.B. (Retired); Donald E. Kuder, C.S.B. (Retired); Thomas J. McReavy, C.S.B. (Retired); Robert G. Ritz, C.S.B. (Retired); John M. Wilson, C.S.B. (Retired); Joseph Charles Mitrano, C.S.B. (Retired); Carl L. Belisch, C.S.B. (Retired); Thomas Bernard Mailldoux, C.S.B. (Retired). Basilian Fathers.

Disciples of Hope (Texas) (1995) 15403 Palmway St., 77071. Tel: 713-721-2894; 713-721-2879; Fax:

713-721-2894. Web: www.disciplesofhope.org. Rev. Enrique V. Salen, D.S., Procurator. *St. Matthew the Evangelist*, 9915 Hollister Dr., 77040-1702. Tel: 713-466-4030; Fax: 713-896-7235. Email: minorstar0817@yahoo.com. Web: www.disciplispei.org. Revs. Luis Paolo Agostino V. Evardoni, D.S.; Joven Vincent Romuald Saavedra, D.S.; Deacon Julian Venida Jr.

Dominican Friars, St. Mark Priory, Inc., 10430 Hunington Point Dr., 77099. Tel: 713-667-1101; Fax: 713-667-1807. Revs. Richard Martin Patrick, O.P., Subprior; Anthony Hung N. Tran, O.P., Prior.

Maryknoll Fathers and Brothers, 2360 Rice Blvd., 77005-2652. Tel: 713-529-1912; Fax: 713-529-0372. Email: mklhouston@maryknoll.org. Web: www.maryknoll.org. Revs. Gerald E. Kelly, M.M., Dir.; Edward R. Schoellmann, M.M., (African Mission).

Priests Residing Elsewhere: Revs. Rafael R. Davila, M.M., St. Mary Seminary, 9845 Memorial Dr., 77024-3498. Tel: 713-686-4345; Fax: 713-681-7550; Richard E. Paulissen, M.M., P.O. Box 9592, 77261. Tel: 713-921-2736.

Residence of the Basilian Fathers of the University of St. Thomas (1947) 4019 Yoakum Blvd., 77006-4833. Tel: 713-525-3515; Fax: 713-529-0844. Revs. Robert W. Crooker, C.S.B.; Edward J. Baenziger, C.S.B.; Robert J. Barringer, C.S.B., Supr.; Patrick O. Braden, C.S.B.; Michael A. Buentello, C.S.B.; John C. Gallagher, C.S.B.; Anthony E. Giampietro, C.S.B.; George H. Hosko, C.S.B.; Janusz Ihnatowicz (Poland); James J. Keon, C.S.B.; Harold V. O'Leary, C.S.B.; Joseph E. Pilsner, C.S.B.; T. Patrick Warden, C.S.B.; John R. Whitley, C.S.B.

MISSOURI CITY. *The Society of the Oblates of Sacred Heart*, 1510 Fifth St., 77489-1298. Tel: 281-630-0688; Fax: 281-499-9680. Email: kurian.stephen@holyfamilychurch.us. Web: www.askcongregation.org. Revs. Kurian Steephen Choozhukunnel, O.S.H., Supr.; Sunny Joseph Plammoottil, O.S.H.; Thomas Joseph Puthusseril, O.S.H.; Jaimon Kurian Pathiyil, O.S.H.

NEW CANEY. *Congregation of the Mother Coredemptrix* (1985) 23404 Oak Shadows Pl., 77357-8516. Tel: 281-354-4764. Rev. Joseph Doan Huy Chuong, Admin. (Retired). Total in Residence 1.

SUGAR LAND. *Basilian Mission Center* (1936) 414 Main St., P.O. Box 708, 77487-0708. Tel: 281-242-3148; Fax: 281-242-3149. Email: basmissions@earthlink.net. Web: www.basilianfathersmissions.org. Revs. John L. Boscoe, C.S.B., Mission Procurator, Treas.; Robert J. Klem, C.S.B. Associates 3; Scholastics 5.

Priests Serving in Foreign Missions: Revs. Francis A. Amico, C.S.B.; Jose D. Delgado, C.S.B.; Thomas P. Dugan, C.S.B.; Alberto A. Ferrara, C.S.B.; Rafael I. Lopera, C.S.B., (Supr. of Colombia); Pedro M. Mora, C.S.B.; Bernard C. Owens, C.S.B.; Philip Wallace Platt, C.S.B.; Juan Carlos Rojas, C.S.B.; Roberto P. Rojas, C.S.B.; Alejandro Romero, C.S.B., (Supr. of Mexico); Robert J. Seguin, C.S.B.; Charles Daniel Porter, C.S.B.

Franciscan Missionary Brothers, St. Francis Friary, 11710 Cobblestone Point Dr., 77498. Tel: 281-495-1558; Fax: 281-561-8659. Email: brothersfriary@yahoo.com. Web: www.cmsf-brothers.org. Bro. Rogi Ignatius, C.M.S.F.

[P] CONVENTS AND RESIDENCES FOR SISTERS

HOUSTON. *Carmelite Sisters of the Sacred Heart (C.S.H.)* (1904) 22 Farrell, 77022-2609. Tel: 713-697-6020; Fax: 713-697-6020. Email: Carmelitas200@hotmail.com. Sr. Mary Esther Alonso, Supr. Total Staff 3.

Casa Providencia, 3907 Rotman, 77003. Tel: 713-227-2555; Fax: 713-923-5866.

Congregation of Divine Providence (1762) (France) *Providence House*, 1339 Friarcreek Ln., 77055. Tel: 713-984-8041; Fax: 713-339-9559. Email: pjregancdp@att.net. Sisters 3.

Congregation of Our Lady of the Retreat in the Cenacle (R.C.), Cenacle Retreat House, 420 N. Kirkwood, 77079. Tel: 281-497-3131; Fax: 281-497-7632. Email: ministry@cenacleretreathouse.org. Web: www.cenacleretreathouse.org. Sisters 6.

Congregation of the Incarnate Word & Blessed Sacrament (C.V.I.) (Houston) (1873) Incarnate Word Convent, 3400 Bradford Pl., 77025-1398. Tel: 713-668-0423; Fax: 713-668-1857. Email: rpurcell@incarnateword.org. Web: www.incarnateword.org. Sisters 29. *Casa Pacis Convent*, 3428 Bradford Pl., 77025. Tel: 713-661-3785. Sisters 2. *Incarnate Word Academy Convent*, 609 Crawford St., 77002-3668. Tel: 713-223-4143. Sisters 5. *St. Christopher Convent*, 8711 Glen Loch, 77061. Tel: 713-649-4700. *Visitation Convent*, 3418A Bradford Pl., 77025-1328. Tel: 713-664-8370. Sisters 3. *St. Michael Convent*, 3810 Costa Rica, 77092-6653. Tel: 713-682-2242. Sisters 1.

Marian Convent, Marian Convent, 3719 Glen Haven, 77025-1204. Tel: 713-667-2238. Sisters 2.

Congregation of the Sisters of Charity of the Incarnate Word, Houston, Texas (CCVI) (1866) 6510 Lawndale, P.O. Box 230969, 77223-0969. Tel: 713-928-6053; Fax: 713-928-8148. Email: lhealy@ccvi-vdm.org. Web: www.sistersofcharity.org. Sr. M. Rose Scanlan, Contact Person. Total Sisters in Congregation (Professed) 166. *St. Anne Community* Tel: 713-928-6053; Fax: 713-921-1070. Sisters 6. *Annunciation Community* Tel: 713-928-6053; Fax: 713-928-9962. Sisters 7.

Bernice Place Community Tel: 713-928-6053; Fax: 713-928-9962.

Casa de la Paz Community, 6641 Wildwood Way, 77023. Tel: 713-928-6053; Fax: 713-928-8148. Sisters 4. *De Matel Community* Tel: 713-928-6053; Fax: 713-928-8148. Sisters 5. *Edith Stein Community*, 6405 Pinehurst, 77023-3329. Tel: 713-926-6024; Fax: 713-926-6024.

Incarnate Word Charitable Trust Tel: 713-928-6053; Fax: 713-926-3085. Sr. Elizabeth Ann Hayes, CCVI, Chairperson. *St. Jeanne Community* Tel: 713-928-6053. Sisters 2. *Marian Community* Tel: 713-928-6053; Fax: 713-928-8148. Sisters 17.

Dubuis Community Tel: 713-928-6053; Fax: 713-218-7339. Sisters 2.

Placidus Place Community Tel: 713-928-6053. Sisters 5. *St. Placidus Community* Tel: 713-928-6053; Fax: 713-928-8148. Sisters 27.

Shalom Community Tel: 713-921-5305.

St. Veronica Community Tel: 713-928-6053. Sisters 4. *St. John Community*, 1623 Antigua Ln., Nassau Bay, 77058-4126. Tel: 281-333-9363.

Mater Christi Convent, 6123 Valley Forge Dr., 77057. Tel: 713-278-9262; Fax: 713-782-1480. Sisters 3.

Discipulas de Jesus, 9601 McGallion Rd., 77076. Tel: 713-691-3960; Fax: 713-691-3960. Email: discipulasdejesushouston@yahoo.com. Web: www.discipulasdejesus.org. Sr. Maria Rosalinda Navarro, D.J., Local Supr.

Dominican Sisters of Houston (1882) Motherhouse Complex & Administrative Offices: 6501 Almeda Rd., 77021-2095. Tel: 713-747-3310; Fax: 713-747-4707. Email: houstonop@domhou.org. Web: www.houstonop.org. Sr. Adrian Dover, O.P., Prioress.

Dominican Sisters of Houston, Texas Inc. (O.P.), The Sacred Heart Convent Retirement Trust.; St. Agnes Academy, Inc.; St. Agnes Academy Foundation, Inc.; St. Pius X High School, Inc.; St. Pius X High School Foundation, Inc.; The Sacred Heart Convent Retirement Trust.

Dominican Sisters-Vietnamese (O.P.), Inc. (1978) Provincial House, 5250 Gasmer Dr., 77035. Tel: 713-723-8250; Fax: 713-723-8229. Web: www.nutudaminh.org. Professed in Province 93. *Vietnamese Dominican Sisters Provincial House (St. Catherine Convent)*, 5250 Gasmer Dr., 77035. Tel: 713-723-4815; 713-723-8250; Fax: 713-723-8229. Sisters 44. *Mary Immaculate Convent*, 5900 Chippewa Blvd., 77086. Tel: 281-445-9574; Fax: 281-445-6716. Sisters 16. *Our Lady of the Rosary Convent (Novitiate)*, 1602 Adams St., Missouri City, 77489. Tel: 281-403-9300; Fax: 281-403-9300. Sisters 16.

Sacred Heart Convent, 911 Runneburg, Crosby, 77532. Tel: 281-328-4073; Fax: 281-328-4073. Sisters 4.

Marian Convent, 3719 Glenhaven Blvd., 77025-1204. Tel: 713-667-2238. Sisters Lauren Beck, C.V.I., Pres., Incarnate Word Academy; Carmel O'Malley, C.V.I., Teacher, Incarnate Word Academy.

Maryknoll Sisters of St. Dominic (M.M.), 7490 Brompton, No. 265, 77025. Tel: 713-666-5245; Fax: 713-666-5245. Email: joyagnes000@sbcglobal.net.

Missionary Carmelites of St. Teresa (C.M.S.T.) (1903) Holy Family Provincial House, 9548 Deer Trail Dr., 77038. Tel: 281-445-5520; Fax: 281-445-5748. Email: hfamprovcmst@yahoo.com. Sisters 5. *Divine Providence Convent*, 9600 Deer Trail Dr., 77038. Tel: 281-847-3328. Sisters 6.

Infant Jesus of Prague Convent, 9600 Deer Trail Dr., 77038. Tel: 281-445-8830. Sisters 11.

St. Joseph Convent, 9815 Marek Rd., 77038. Tel: 281-820-8961. Sisters 5. *St. Therese Novitiate*, 9819 Marek Rd., 77038. Tel: 281-820-3732. Sisters 4.

St. Teresa Postulancy, 9608 Deer Trail Dr., 77038. Tel: 281-999-4435. Sisters 6.

Missionary Sisters of the Eucharist, P.O. Box 88147, 77288-0147. 3301 San Jacinto St., 77004. Tel: 713-523-8831. Sr. Leocadia Otzoy, M.S.E., Contact Person. Sisters 3.

Missionary Sisters of the Immaculate Conception (S.M.I.C.), 10680 Westbrae Pkwy, Apt. 156, 77031-2450. Tel: 713-484-5620.

Religious of the Sacred Heart (R.S.C.J.) (1960) Duchesne Community, 10204 Memorial Dr., 77024. Tel: 713-467-5312; Fax: 713-465-9809. Email: acaire@rscj.org. Web: www.rscj.org. Sisters 4. 2020 Harvard St., 77008. Tel: 713-868-9607. Sisters 2.

Sisters for Christian Community (S.F.C.C.) Tel: 936-756-8288; Fax: 936-756-8105. *SFCC Community*, 109 N. Frazier, Conroe, 77301. Tel: 409-756-3051; Fax: 409-756-8105. *Sacred Heart Convent*, 105 N. Frazier St., Conroe, 77301. Tel: 936-756-8288; Fax: 936-756-8105.

Sisters of the Holy Spirit and Mary Immaculate (S.H.Sp.), St. Charles Borromeo Convent, 9601 McGallion, 77076-5122. Tel: 713-694-4264 (Convent); 281-447-2132 (School); Fax: 713-692-1376. Sr. Miriam Mitchell, S.H.Sp., Gen. Supr. Tel: 210-533-5149; 210-533-5522; Fax: 210-533-3434.

Sisters of the Incarnate Word and Blessed Sacrament (C.V.I.), Marian Convent, 3719 Glen Haven, 77025-1204.

Sisters of the Sacred Heart (S.S.C.J.) (1816) Sacred Heart Convent, 1707 Chapman St., 77009-8715. Tel: 713-236-9294; Fax: 713-227-0224. Email: maryssscj@hotmail.com. Sisters 4.

MISSOURI CITY. *Schoenstatt Sisters of Mary (I.S.S.M.)*, Holy Family Church, 1510 Fifth St., 77489. Tel: 281-499-6246, Ext. 339; Fax: 281-499-9680. Sr. M. Carmen Rodriguez, Coord., Social Min.

NEW CANEY. *Discalced Carmelite Nuns of New Caney, Texas* (1958) 1100 Parthenon Pl., 77357-3276. Tel: 281-399-0270, Ext. 4; Fax: 281-689-3615. Email: newcaneycarmel@icansurf.net. Web: www.icansurf.com/ocdnewcaney. Sisters 9.

PEARLAND. *Handmaids of the Holy Child Jesus* (1931) 3614 Englewood Dr., 77584. Tel: 281-692-0098; Fax: 281-692-0049; 713-995-6706. Email: handmaidsusa@handmaidsisters.org. Web: www.hhcjsisters.org. P.O. Box 740099, 77274. Sisters Felicia Agibi, H.H.C.J., Dir. Devel.; Leonie-Martha Okaraga, H.H.C.J., Supr.Gen., Generalate H.H.C.J., P.O. Box 155, Ifuho-Ikot Ekpene, Akwa Ibom Nigeria. Sisters 774.

Mission Development Office, Office: P.O. Box 740099, 77274. Tel: 281-914-4664; Fax: 281-500-1948. Email: missiondev@hhcjsisters.org. Web: www.hhcjsisters.org. Sr. Caroline Onyeoziri, Supr.

ROSENBURG. *Missionary Catechists of the Sacred Hearts of Jesus and Mary (M.C.S.H.)* (1918) Our Lady of Guadalupe Convent: 504 Carlisle St., Rosenberg, 77471. Tel: 281-232-9881; Fax: 281-342-4008. Sisters Antonieta Salazar, Coord.; Enriqueta Salgado. Sisters 3.

STAFFORD. *Missionary Sisters of Mary Immaculate*, 630 Easy Jet Dr., 77477-6358. Tel: 281-499-0030; Fax: 281-499-0030. Email: msmisisters@hotmail.com. Sisters Betsy Ulahannan; Agnes Maria, M.S.M.I., Supr. & Contact Person.

[Q] RETREAT HOUSES

HOUSTON. *Cenacle Retreat House*, 420 N. Kirkwood Rd., 77079. Tel: 281-497-3131; Fax: 281-497-7632. Email: ministry@cenacleretreathouse.org. Web: www.cenacleretreathouse.org. Sisters Dorothy Briscoe, r.c.; Pat Burke, r.c., Treas.; Lois Dideon, r.c.; Mary Dennison, r.c., Sabbatical (Houston Area); Rosell Haas, r.c.; Ann Goggin, r.c.; Mary Guido, r.c., Local Leader; Sue Ellen Ruggles, Exec. Dir. Congregation of Our Lady of the Retreat in the Cenacle. Sisters 6.

Holy Name Retreat Center, 430 Bunker Hill Rd., 77024-6399. Tel: 713-464-0211; Fax: 713-464-0671. Email: holyname@passionist.org. Web: passionist.org/holyname. Bro. Carl Hund, C.P., Assoc. Dir.; Revs. Joseph Moons, C.P., Dir.; Peter Berendt, C.P. Total in Residence 1; Total Staff 2.

DICKINSON. *Christian Renewal Center*, 1515 Hughes Rd., P.O. Box 699, 77539-0699. Tel: 281-337-1312 (Center); Fax: 281-337-2615. Email: crc1515@retreatcentercrc.org. Web: www.retreatcentercrc.org. Total in Residence 1; Total Staff 13.

[R] NEWMAN CENTERS

GALVESTON. *Galveston Newman Center* 602 Seawolf Pkwy., Ste. B, Pelican Island #5, 77550. Tel: 409-740-3797; Fax: 409-740-3798. Email: gal.newmancenterum@gmail.com. Carl Erickson, Dir. Texas A & M University at Galveston; University of Texas Medical Branch; Galveston College; College of the Mainland.

HOUSTON. *Catholic Newman Association at the University of Houston Central Campus* (1968) Catholic Center, 4805 Calhoun Rd., 77004. Tel: 713-748-2529; Fax: 713-748-8412. Email: catholic@uh.edu. Web: www.uh.edu/catholic. Rev. Daniel L. Walsh, C.S.Sp., Dir. Priests 2; Total Assisted 10,000; Total Staff 4.

Satellite Office (1964) 203 AD Bruce Religion Center, 77204-3050. Tel: 713-748-2529; Fax: 713-748-8412. Rev. Daniel L. Walsh, C.S.Sp., Campus Min. & Dir.; Dolores Perez, Sec.; Giovan Cuchapin, Campus Min.

Rice University/Texas Medical Center Schools; Catholic Student Center 1703 Bolsover Rd., 77005. Tel: 713-526-3809; Fax: 713-526-6010. Email: cathcen@rice.edu. Web: www.rice.edu/catholic. Sr. Antoinette "Kitty" Carter, O.P., Dir.; Rev. Binh T. Ta, C.Ss.R., Chap.; Rita M. Seng, Sec. & Ministry Asst. Total Staff 3.

Texas Southern University Catholic Newman Hall 3535 Wheeler Ave., 77004. Tel: 713-747-9595; Fax: 713-747-3198. Email: tsunewmanhall@sbcglobal.net. Vivian Gathright, Campus Min. Asst.; Rev. Daniel Walsh, C.S.Sp., Dir. Total Assisted 300; Total Staff 2.

University of St. Thomas Campus Ministry 3800 Montrose Blvd., 77006. Tel: 713-525-3589; Fax: 713-525-3524. Email: campusministry@stthom.edu. Web: www.stthom.edu. Sr. Maura Behrenfeld, F.S.E., Dir. Campus Ministry; Rev. Michael A. Buentello, C.S.B., Chap.

HUNTSVILLE. *Catholic Student Center, S.H.S.U.* 1310 17th St., 77340-4415. Tel: 936-291-2620; Fax: 936-291-2620. Email: org_cath@shsu.edu. Web: www.shsu-catholic.org. Joseph Magee, Ph.D., Dir. Total Assisted 350; Total Staff 3.

PRAIRIE VIEW. *Prairie View A & M University Catholic Center* P.O. Box 1688, 77446. Tel: 832-372-8056. Deacon Irvin Johnson Jr., Campus Min. Total Staff 1.

[S] MISCELLANEOUS

GALVESTON. *The Bishop's Palace* (1886) 1402 Broadway, 77550. Tel: 409-762-2475; Fax: 409-762-1801. Rev. William D. Bartniski, Exec. Dir.

HOUSTON. *Angela House*, 425 Shane, #18, 77037. Tel: 281-445-9696. Email: moconnell@angelahouse.org. Web: www.angelahouse.orgFax: 281-445-8891. Sr. Maureen O'Connell, O.P., Exec. Dir./Contact Person.

The Catholic Chaplain Corps (1967) 4206 S. MacGregor Way, 77021-1598. Tel: 713-747-8445; Fax: 713-747-3642. Revs. Joseph Bang-Doan; Patrick J. Cummings; Arul Dhairiam, S.S.S.; Don A. Neumann; David H. Noble; Page E. Polk, O.F.M.; Teodoro Tim Y. Prado; Enrique V. Salen, D.S. Cell: 713-922-0700; Michael S. Van Cleve; Yohanes K. Taosan; Bruce H. Noble; Sr. Beatrice Cruz, I.W.B.S. Houston Hospitals: St. Luke's Episcopal, Texas Children's Hospital, Methodist, M. D. Anderson Cancer Center, The Institute of Rehabilitation and Research, Ben Taub General Hospital, Kindred Hospital, LBJ General Hospital, Memorial Hermann Medical Center, Memorial Hermann Southwest, Spring Branch Medical Center, Univ. of Texas Medical Branch, Galveston.

Catholic Charismatic Center (1972) 1949 Cullen, P.O. Box 230287, 77023-0287. Tel: 713-236-9977; Fax: 713-236-0073. Email: ccc@catholiccharismaticcenter.org. Web: www.catholiccharismaticcenter.org. Revs. Michael G. Scherrey, Dir.; Francis A. Frankovich, C.C., Assoc. Dir.; Ed Wade, C.C., Assoc. Dir.; Carlos Martins, Assoc. Dir.

Catholic Clerical Student Fund (1933) 2531 Rosefield, 77080. Tel: 713-939-1430. His Eminence Daniel Cardinal DiNardo, Chm.; Mrs. Marie Walsh, Pres. Higher learning for the priesthood.

The Catholic Endowment Foundation of Galveston-Houston, P.O. Box 907, 77001-0907. Tel: 713-654-1133; Fax: 713-654-1188. Boone Schwartzel, Sec.

Charity Guild of Catholic Women (1922) 1203 Lovett Blvd., 77006-3857. Tel: 713-529-0995; Fax: 713-529-9263. Web: www.charityguild.com.

Charity Guild of St. Joseph (1988) P. O. Box 570728-319, 77257-0728. Tel: 713-965-0965.

CHRISTUS Health (1999) 2707 N. Loop W., 77008. Tel: 281-936-3184; Fax: 281-936-7802. Email: larry.pardue@christushealth.org. Web: www.christushealth.org. Thomas C. Royer, M.D., Pres. & CEO; William L. Pardue, Corp. Sec.; Cynthia G. Zatorski, M.B.A., Asst. Corp. Sec.

CHRISTUS Health Liability Retention Trust Tel: 281-936-3184; Fax: 281-936-7802.

CHRISTUS Health Cash Balance Plan Trust Tel: 281-936-3184; Fax: 281-936-7802.

CHRISTUS Health Matched Savings Plan Tel: 281-936-3184; Fax: 281-936-7802.

CHRISTUS Tax-Deferred Annuity Plans

CHRISTUS Health Rabbi Trust

St. Dominic Center, Inc., 2401 E. Holcombe, 77021. Tel: 713-741-8743; Fax: 713-741-8705. Email: wknight@archgh.org. Wayne Knight, Diocesan Facility Admin.

Equestrian Order of the Holy Sepulchre of Jerusalem, 2001 Kirby Dr., Ste. 902, 77019.

Equestrian Order of the Holy Sepulchre of Jerusalem, Congregation of the Passion, Holy Name Passionist Community and Retreat Center, 2001 Kirby Dr., Ste. 902, 77019-1402. Tel: 713-522-5444; Fax: 713-522-5333. Email: Lieutenant@EOHSsouthwest.com; lieutenant@EOHSsouthwest.com. Mr. Dennis M. Malloy, Knight Grand Cross.

St. Francis de Sales School Foundation, 8100 Roos, 77036. Tel: 713-774-4447; Fax: 713-271-6744. Email: webmaster@st-francis-de-sales.org. Web: www.st-francis-de-sales.org. Tom Overbeck, Pres.; Bill St. Cyr, Treas.; Thomas Norman, Advisor & Finance Council.

Martha's Kitchen Food Services (1992) 322 S. Jensen Dr., 77003. Tel: 713-224-2522; Fax: 713-224-7814. 2302 Oak Shores Dr., Kingwood, 77339. Rev. Msgr. Chester L. Borski. Sisters 2.

St. Mary's Children's Relief Fund, Chancery Bldg., 1700 San Jacinto, P.O. Box 907, 77001-0907. Tel: 713-659-5461; Fax: 713-759-9151. His Eminence Daniel Cardinal DiNardo, Pres.

St. Pius X High School Foundation, Inc., 811 W. Donovan, 77091-5699. Tel: 713-692-3581; Fax: 713-692-5725. Email: pollardd@stpiusx.org. Web: www.stpiusx.org. Edgar Hancock, Pres.; Sisters Donna M. Pollard, O.P., B.S., M.A., M.Ed., Head of School; Lavergne Schwender, O.P., Sec.; Patrick Svrcek, Treas.

Sociedad San Martin de Porres, 931 Euclid, 77009. Tel: 713-869-0999; 713-860-6631. Email: ccampbell@abhr.com.

The Society of the Holy Spirit, 1700 W. Alabama, 77098-2808. Tel: 713-522-2882; Fax: 713-522-8064. Email: nesti@stthom.edu. Web: www.spiritans.org. Rev. Donald S. Nesti, C.S.Sp., Contact Person.

UST Chapelle, 3034 Quenby Ave., 77005. Tel: 713-349-0921; Fax: 832-201-7556. Alain Maury, Contact Person.

RELIGIOUS INSTITUTES OF MEN REPRESENTED IN THE ARCHDIOCESE

For further details refer to the corresponding bracketed number in the Religious Institutes of Men or Women section.

[0140]—*The Augustinians*—O.S.A.
[0170]—*Basilian Fathers* (Toronto, Canada)—C.S.B.
[]—*Benedictine Monks*—O.S.B.
[0275]—*Carmelites of Mary Immaculate*—C.M.I.
[]—*Companions of the Cross* (Ottowa, Canada)—C.C.
[0220]—*Congregation of the Blessed Sacrament*—S.S.S.
[]—*Congregation of the Holy Spirit (Spiritans)*—C.S.Sp.
[]—*Congregation of the Mother Coredemptrix*—C.M.C.
[1130]—*Congregation of the Priests of the Sacred Heart*—S.C.J.
[]—*Disciples of Hope* Careres, Philippines—D.S.
[]—*Divine Word Fathers*—S.V.D.
[0520]—*Franciscan Friars*—O.F.M.
[]—*Franciscan Missionary Brothers*—C.M.S.F.
[0650]—*Holy Ghost Fathers* (Western Prov.)—C.S.Sp.
[0690]—*Jesuit Fathers and Brothers* (New Orleans Prov.)—S.J.
[]—*Legionaries of Christ*—L.C.
[0800]—*Maryknoll*—M.M.
[0720]—*The Missionaries of Our Lady of La Salette* (Prov. of Mary Queen)—M.S.
[]—*Missionaries of St. Joseph* (Mexico)—M.J.
[]—*Missionaries of St. Paul*—M.S.P.
[1110]—*Missionaries of the Sacred Heart*—M.S.C.
[0910]—*Oblates of Mary Immaculate*—O.M.I.
[0920]—*Oblates of St. Francis de Sales*—O.S.F.S.
[0430]—*Order of Preachers-Dominicans* (Prov. of St. Albert the Great)—O.P.
[1070]—*Redemptorist Fathers* (New Orleans Vice Prov.)—C.SS.R.
[]—*Scalabrinians*—C.S.
[1260]—*Society of Christ*—S.Ch.
[0975]—*Society of Our Lady of the Most Holy Trinity*—S.O.L.T.
[0420]—*Society of the Divine Word*—S.V.D.
[]—*Society of the Precious Blood Sanguinist Fathers*—C.PP.S.
[1250]—*Somascan Fathers*—C.R.S.

RELIGIOUS INSTITUTES OF WOMEN REPRESENTED IN THE ARCHDIOCESE

[0230]—*Benedictine Sisters of the Sacred Heart*—O.S.B.
[0390]—*Carmelite Missionaries of St. Teresa*—C.M.S.T.
[]—*Carmelite Sisters of the Sacred Heart*—C.S.C.
[]—*Communidad Apostolica de Maria Siempre Virgen*—C.A.M.S.V.
[]—*Community of the Holy Spirit (A Private Association of the Faithful)*—C.H.S.
[1010]—*Congregation of Divine Providence*—C.D.P.
[3110]—*Congregation of Our Lady of the Retreat in the Cenacle*—R.C.
[3830-01]—*Congregation of St. Joseph* (Boston, MA)—C.S.J.
[]—*Congregation of the Lovers of the Cross* (N. Vietnam)—H.C.L.
[0470]—*Congregation of the Sisters of Charity of the Incarnate Word* (Houston)—CCVI
[]—*Daughters of Divine Love* (Nigeria)—D.D.L.
[]—*Daughters of Mary Mother of Mercy*—D.M.M.M.
[0420]—*Discalced Carmelite Nuns of New Caney, Texas*—O.C.D.
[]—*Discipulas de Jesus*—D.J.
[1070-13]—*Dominican Sisters* (Adrian, MI)—O.P.
[1070-19]—*Dominican Sisters, Congregation of the Sacred Heart* (Houston)—O.P.
[]—*Eucharistic Missionaries of St. Theresa* (Mexico)—M.E.S.T.
[]—*Family of the Visitation of Mary*—F.M.V.
[]—*Franciscan Sisters of the Eucharist*—F.S.E.
[]—*Handmaids of the Holy Child Jesus* (Nigeria)—H.H.C.J.
[]—*La Salle Sisters*—L.S.S.
[2470]—*Maryknoll Sisters of St. Dominic*—M.M.
[]—*Missionaries of Charity*—M.C.
[2690]—*Missionary Catechists of Divine Providence*—M.C.D.P.
[2700]—*Missionary Catechists of the Sacred Hearts of Jesus and Mary*—M.C.S.H.
[]—*Missionary Sisters of Mary Immaculate*—M.S.M.I.
[2725]—*Missionary Sisters of the Eucharist*—M.S.E.
[2760]—*Missionary Sisters of the Immaculate Conception*—S.M.I.C.
[4070]—*Religious of the Sacred Heart*—R.S.C.J.
[4110]—*Roman Union of the Order of St. Ursula*—O.S.U.
[]—*Schoenstatt Sisters of Mary*—I.S.S.M.
[2970]—*School Sisters of Notre Dame*—S.S.N.D.
[]—*Sisters for Christian Community*—S.F.C.C.
[]—*Sisters of Loretto*—S.L.
[]—*Sisters of St. Michael the Archangel*—S.S.M.A.
[2050]—*Sisters of the Holy Spirit and Mary Immaculate*—S.H.Sp.
[2150]—*Sisters of the Immaculate Heart of Mary*—I.H.M.
[2190]—*Sisters of the Incarnate Word and Blessed Sacrament* (Houston)—C.V.I.
[2200]—*Sisters of the Incarnate Word and Blessed Sacrament* (Corpus Christi)—I.W.B.S.
[3310]—*Sisters of the Presentation of Mary*—P.M.
[3670]—*Sisters of the Sacred Heart of Jesus*—S.S.C.J.
[]—*Vietnamese Dominican Sisters*—O.P.

ARCHDIOCESAN CEMETERIES

GALVESTON. *Old Catholic, Calvary*
HOUSTON. *Holy Cross*
St. Vincent
DICKINSON. *Mount Olivet*

NECROLOGY

† Braden, Rev. Msgr. Leroy H., (Retired)—Died July 23, 2009
† Culver, Rev. Msgr. T. Joseph, (Retired)—Died April 7, 2009
† Madden, Rev. Msgr. James J., (Retired)—Died Sept. 6, 2009
† Chanh, John Chan Tran, (Retired)—Died Oct. 25, 2009
† Fernandez, Jose Maria, (Retired)—Died Oct. 15, 2009
† Hughes, Royce, (Retired)—Died May 2, 2009
† Tran, John Chinh Chan—Died Oct. 25, 2009

An asterisk (*) denotes an organization that has established tax-exempt status directly with the IRS and is not covered by the USCCB Group Ruling.

Diocese of Gary

(Dioecesis Gariensis)

Most Reverend

DALE J. MELCZEK, D.D.

Bishop of Gary; ordained June 6, 1964; appointed Auxiliary Bishop of Detroit and Titular Bishop of Trau December 3, 1982; consecrated January 27, 1983; appointed Apostolic Administrator of Gary August 19, 1992; appointed Coadjutor Bishop of Gary October 20, 1995; succeeded to the See of Gary June 1, 1996. *Office: 9292 Broadway, Merrillville, IN 46410.* Tel: 219-769-9292; Fax: 219-769-2066.

Chancery: 9292 Broadway, Merrillville, IN 46410. Tel: 219-769-9292; Fax: 219-738-9034.

Web: www.dcgary.org

ESTABLISHED DECEMBER 17, 1956.

Square Miles 1,807.

Comprises the Counties of Lake, LaPorte, Porter and Starke in the State of Indiana.

For legal titles of parishes and diocesan institutions, consult the Chancery.

STATISTICAL OVERVIEW

Personnel	
Bishop	1
Priests: Diocesan Active in Diocese	62
Priests: Diocesan Active Outside Diocese	6
Priests: Diocesan in Foreign Missions	1
Priests: Retired, Sick or Absent	33
Number of Diocesan Priests	102
Religious Priests in Diocese	46
Total Priests in Diocese	148
Extern Priests in Diocese	9
Ordinations:	
Transitional Deacons	1
Permanent Deacons	8
Permanent Deacons in Diocese	58
Total Brothers	13
Total Sisters	75
Parishes	
Parishes	69
With Resident Pastor:	
Resident Diocesan Priests	54
Resident Religious Priests	5
Without Resident Pastor:	
Administered by Priests	10
Missions	4
Pastoral Centers	6
Closed Parishes	3
Professional Ministry Personnel:	
Brothers	4
Sisters	6
Lay Ministers	67
Welfare	
Catholic Hospitals	6
Total Assisted	1,167,973
Homes for the Aged	2
Total Assisted	226
Residential Care of Children	2
Total Assisted	200
Day Care Centers	2
Total Assisted	500
Specialized Homes	2
Total Assisted	700
Special Centers for Social Services	7
Total Assisted	10,000
Educational	
Diocesan Students in Other Seminaries	11
Seminaries, Religious	1
Students Religious	6
Total Seminarians	17
Colleges and Universities	1
Total Students	1,275
High Schools, Diocesan and Parish	3
Total Students	1,225
High Schools, Private	1
Total Students	36
Elementary Schools, Diocesan and Parish	21
Total Students	4,947
Catechesis/Religious Education:	
High School Students	808
Elementary Students	8,982
Total Students under Catholic Instruction	17,290
Teachers in the Diocese:	
Sisters	4
Lay Teachers	400
Vital Statistics	
Receptions into the Church:	
Infant Baptism Totals	1,650
Minor Baptism Totals	119
Adult Baptism Totals	64
Received into Full Communion	238
First Communions	2,040
Confirmations	1,972
Marriages:	
Catholic	328
Interfaith	158
Total Marriages	486
Deaths	1,603
Total Catholic Population	184,750
Total Population	790,527

Former Bishops—Most Revs. ANDREW GREGORY GRUTKA, D.D., ord. Dec. 5, 1933; appt. Bishop of Gary Dec. 29, 1956; cons. Feb. 25, 1957; retired July 9, 1984; died Nov. 11, 1993; NORBERT F. GAUGHAN, D.D., Ph.D., ord. Nov. 4, 1945; appt. Auxiliary Bishop of Greensburg April 2, 1975; cons. June 26, 1975; appt. Bishop of Gary July 9, 1984; retired June 1, 1996; died Oct. 1, 1999.

Vicar General—Rev. Msgr. JOHN J. SIEKIERSKI, J.C.L.

Deans—Rev. JON J. PLAVCAN, Gary-Hobart Deanery; Rev. Msgr. JOHN J. SIEKIERSKI, J.C.L., North Lake County Deanery; Revs. MICHAEL J. YADRON, South Lake County Deanery; GERALD H. SCHWEITZER, Porter-Starke County Deanery; DAVID W. KIME, LaPorte County Deanery.

Chancery—9292 Broadway, Merrillville, 46410. Tel: 219-769-9292; Fax: 219-738-9034.

Administrative Assistant to the Bishop—Rev. JON J. PLAVCAN.

Bishop's Delegate for Sexual Misconduct Matters—KELLY VENEGAS, SPHR.

Director of Finance and Administration—KARL P. DYTRYCH.

Executive Secretary to the Bishop—VALERIE D. MCMANUS. Tel: 219-769-9181; Fax: 219-769-2066.

Diocesan Tribunal—9292 Broadway, Merrillville, 46410. Tel: 219-769-9292.

Judicial Vicar—Rev. BRIAN D. CHADWICK, J.C.L.

Director of the Tribunal—Sr. EVELYN OVALLES, S.P., J.C.L.

Judges—Rev. BRIAN D. CHADWICK, J.C.L.; Sr. EVELYN OVALLES, S.P., J.C.L.

Defender of the Bond—Rev. LOURDU PASALA, J.C.L.

Second Instance—Judges: Rev. Msgrs. EDWARD F. LITOT (Retired); VINCENT L. LENGERICH (Retired); Rev. LOURDU PASALA, J.C.L. Defender of the Bond: Sr. EVELYN OVALLES, S.P., J.C.L.

Adjutant Defenders of the Bond—Revs. MICHAEL J. KOPIL; RICHARD C. HOLY.

Auditors—Deacon SHERMAN BROWN; DONNA V. CALLAWAY.

Notaries—VALERIE MCMANUS; MARY ANN O'CONNELL; JEAN DAVID.

Bishop's Council of Priests—Revs. DAVID W. KIME; JON J. PLAVCAN; GERALD H. SCHWEITZER; KEVIN R. HUBER, D.Min.; LAWRENCE M. HEEG (Retired); JOSEPH E. VAMOS (Retired); MICHAEL J. YADRON; JAMES E. WOZNIAK; WILLIAM F. O'TOOLE; RICHARD A. ORLINSKI; TERRENCE R. CHASE; Rev. Msgrs. JOHN J. SIEKIERSKI, J.C.L.; JOSEPH F. SEMANCIK; Revs. DERRICK F. DUDASH; EDUARDO MALAGON; KEITH J. MCCLELLAN.

Consultors—Revs. GERALD H. SCHWEITZER; MICHAEL J. YADRON; DAVID W. KIME; JON J. PLAVCAN; Rev. Msgr. JOHN J. SIEKIERSKI, J.C.L.

Priests' Personnel Board—Revs. GERALD H. SCHWEITZER; KEVIN P. MCCARTHY; JON J. PLAVCAN; JOHN V. SCOTT; MICHAEL J. YADRON; DAVID W. KIME; Rev. Msgr. JOHN J. SIEKIERSKI, J.C.L.; Revs. BRIAN D. CHADWICK, J.C.L.; EDWARD J. MOSZUR.

Diocesan Offices and Directors

African American Catholic Ministry—PEARLETTE SPRINGER, Dir., 9292 Broadway, Merrillville, 46410. Tel: 219-769-9292; Fax: 219-738-9034.

Blue Army—Rev. WALTER M. CIESLA, Chap., Mailing Address: P.O. Box 3036, Munster, 46321. Tel: 219-836-8779.

Boy Scouts Liaison—Rev. IAN J. WILLIAMS, Chap.; SANDRA PYLE, Chm., 1830 Govert, Schererville, 46375. Tel: 219-322-8446.

Catholic Campaign for Human Development—Rev. JAMES M. DIXON, S.J., 6819 Indianapolis Blvd., Hammond, 46324. Tel: 219-844-7515; Fax: 219-844-7566.

Campus Ministry— St. Teresa of Avila Catholic Student Center (Valparaiso University) Rev. KEVIN P. MCCARTHY, Chap., 1511 LaPorte St., Valparaiso, 46383. Tel: 219-464-4042; Fax: 219-462-2711.

Catholic Relief Services— Operation Rice Bowl, annual Lenten collection, and disaster relief collections. Sr. JEAN AUGUSTINE, S.C., M.S.W., M.B.A., Exec. Dir. Catholic Charities, 176 S. West St., Crown Point, 46307. Tel: 219-663-8417, Ext. 329; Fax: 219-663-8421.

Global Solidarity Partnership Program—Rev. JAMES M. DIXON, S.J., 6819 Indianapolis Blvd., Hammond, 46324. Tel: 219-844-7515; Fax: 219-844-7566.

Catholic Foundation for the Diocese of Gary—DIANA MURRAY, Dir., 9292 Broadway, Merrillville, 46410. Tel: 219-769-9292; Fax: 219-738-9034.

Catholic Services Appeal—JOYCE ILLYES, 9292 Broadway, Merrillville, 46410. Tel: 219-769-9292; Fax: 219-738-9034.

Catholic Youth Organization (CYO) Office—PAUL WENGEL, 7725 Broadway, Ste. C, Merrillville, 46410. Tel: 219-736-8931; Fax: 219-736-9457.

Cemeteries—Rev. ROY T. BEECHING, Dir., 5885 Harrison St., Merrillville, 46410. Tel: 219-980-2693; MICHAEL P. WELSH, 1547 167th St., Hammond, 46324. Tel: 219-844-9475.

Charismatic Apostolate—Rev. BRIAN D. CHADWICK, J.C.L., Dir., 801 W. 73rd Ave., Merrillville, 46410. Tel: 219-769-8534; BRITTA NEINAST, 204 Appletree Ln., Valparaiso, 46383. Tel: 219-531-4194.

Charities—Sr. JEAN AUGUSTINE, S.C., M.S.W., M.B.A., Exec. Dir., 176 S. West St., Crown Point, 46307. Tel: 219-663-8417, Ext. 329; Fax: 219-663-8421.

Communications Office—4137 W. Andrea, La Porte, 46350. Tel: 219-324-6026. Deacon MARK PLAISS, Dir.

Council of Catholic Women—Rev. ROY T. BEECHING, Diocesan Moderator, 5885 Harrison St., Merrillville, 46410. Tel: 219-980-2693.

Cursillos in Christianity—Rev. EDUARDO MALAGON, Chap. (Spanish), 2447 Putnam St., Lake Station, 46405. Tel: 219-962-8626; Deacon JOSEPH CODESPOTI, (English), 10503 Woodmar Lane, Saint John, 46373. Tel: 219-365-4048.

Diaconate—Deacons MARK PLAISS, Deacon Formation Dir., 4137 W. Andrea, La Porte, 46350. Tel: 219-324-6026; DALE WALSH, Diaconate Dir. - Post Ordination, 82 Gingerwood Ct., Valparaiso, 46385. Tel: 219-464-0557.

Ecumenical Officer—JOAN CRIST, 7 Detroit St., Hammond, 46320. Tel: 219-932-2706.

Employee Benefits—KAREN WALSH, Coord., 9292 Broadway, Merrillville, 46410. Tel: 219-769-9292; Fax: 219-738-9034.

Family Life Ministry—176 S. West St., Crown Point, 46307. Tel: 219-663-8417.

Finance Council—DENNIS BIELFELDT; CALVIN E. BELLAMY; MITCH GAFFIGAN; KARL DYTRYCH; JOHN J. DIEDERICH; DONNA SMITH; Rev. JOSEPH M. PAWLOWSKI; DOUGLAS S. ROBSON; ANA GRANDFIELD.

Girl Scout Liaison—Rev. THEODORE A. NORDQUIST; JACKIE KRILICH, Chm., 10621 State Line Rd., Dyer, 46311. Tel: 219-365-5217.

Heartland Center—Rev. JAMES DIXON, S.J., 6819 Indianapolis Blvd., Hammond, 46324. Tel: 219-844-7515; Fax: 219-844-7566.

Holy Childhood Association— cf. Mission Office

Hispanic Diocesan Ministries—ADELINE TORRES, Mailing Address: P.O. Box 3027, East Chicago, 46312. Tel: 219-397-2125; Fax: 219-397-2168.

Human Resources—KELLY VENEGAS, SPHR, Mgr., 9292 Broadway, Merrillville, 46410. Tel: 219-769-9292; Fax: 219-769-7567.

Indiana Catholic Conference—Rev. JAMES DIXON, S.J., Diocesan Coord., 6819 Indianapolis Blvd., Hammond, 46324. Tel: 219-844-7515; Fax: 219-844-7566.

Lay Ministry Formation Office—Mrs. ANNE VERBEKE, Dir., 9292 Broadway, Merrillville, 46410. Tel: 219-769-9292; Fax: 219-738-9034.

Legal Counsel—ROBERT M. SCHWERD, 2637 45th St., Highland, 46322. Tel: 219-924-2427.

Marriage Dispensations—Rev. GERALD H. SCHWEITZER, Mailing Address: P.O. Box 386, Wanatah, 46390. Tel: 219-733-2955.

Marriage Encounter—MARK WYSOCK; MARY WYSOCK, 9618 Crestwood Ave., Munster, 46321. Tel: 219-838-3962.

Ministry to Deaf—Rev. JOHN J. ZEMELKO, 356 W. Seven Mile Rd., Valparaiso, 46385. Tel: 219-759-2400.

Mission Office—Rev. JOHN J. ZEMELKO, Dir., 356 W. Seven Mile Rd., Valparaiso, 46385. Tel: 219-759-2400.

Newspaper— "Northwest Indiana Catholic" STEVE EUVINO, Editor; CAROL MACINGA, Circulation Mgr., 9292 Broadway, Merrillville, 46410. Tel: 219-769-9292; Fax: 219-738-9034.

Parish Pastoral Councils—Mrs. ANNE VERBEKE, Dir., 9292 Broadway, Merrillville, 46410. Tel: 219-769-9292; Fax: 219-738-9034.

Peace and Social Justice, Office of—Rev. JAMES M. DIXON, S.J., 6819 Indianapolis Blvd., Hammond, 46324. Tel: 219-844-7515; Fax: 219-844-7566.

Priestly Life—Rev. KEVIN R. HUBER, D.Min., Dir., 9292 Broadway, Merrillville, 46410. Tel: 219-769-9292; Fax: 219-738-9034.

Pro-Life Activities—Rev. THEODORE J. MENS, Dir., 525 N. Broad St., Griffith, 46319. Tel: 219-924-4163.

Propagation of the Faith and Holy Childhood Association— cf. Mission Office

Religious Education Office—FRANK J. ZOLVINSKI, Dir., 9292 Broadway, Merrillville, 46410. Tel: 219-769-9292; Fax: 219-738-9034.

Religious, Liaison for Women—Sr. M. CAROL ANN TERLICHER, S.S.C.M., 5959 Broadway, Merrillville, 46410. Tel: 219-887-5287.

Retirement Plan of the Diocese of Gary, Indiana—KELLY VENEGAS, SPHR, Plan Admin., 9292 Broadway, Merrillville, 46410. Tel: 219-769-9292; Fax: 219-769-7567.

Rural Life Conference—Rev. JAMES M. DIXON, S.J., Dir., 6819 Indianapolis Blvd., Hammond, 46324. Tel: 219-844-7515.

Safe Environment Program—KELLY VENEGAS, SPHR, Bishop's Delegate for Sexual Misconduct Cases, 9292 Broadway, Merrillville, 46410. Tel: 219-769-9292; Fax: 219-769-7567.

Victim Assistance Coordinator—STEVEN J. BUTERA, M.S., 12490 Marshall St., Crown Point, 46307. Tel: 219-662-7066, Ext. 25; Fax: 219-662-3478.

St. Vincent de Paul Society—DIANE MCKERN, Pres., 7132 Arizona Ave., Hammond, 46324. Tel: 219-845-7531.

Schools Office—BARBARA O'BLOCK, Ed.D., Supt. Schools, 9292 Broadway, Merrillville, 46410. Tel: 219-769-9292; Fax: 219-738-9034.

Spiritual Life/Seimetz Center—1441 Hoffman St., Hammond, 46327. Tel: 219-932-8321.

Stewardship—Mrs. ANNE VERBEKE, Dir., 9292 Broadway, Merrillville, 46410. Tel: 219-769-9292; Fax: 219-738-9034.

Vocations—Rev. KEVIN R. HUBER, D.Min., Dir., 9292 Broadway, Merrillville, 46410. Tel: 219-769-9292; Fax: 219-738-9034.

Worship and Spirituality, Office of—Rev. MARTIN J. DOBRZYNSKI, Dir.; KRISTOPHER SEAMAN, Assoc. Dir., 9292 Broadway, Merrillville, 46410. Tel: 219-769-9292; Fax: 219-738-9034.

Youth and Young Adult Ministry—KEVIN DRISCOLL, Dir., 9292 Broadway, Merrillville, 46410. Tel: 219-769-9292; Fax: 219-738-9034.

CLERGY, PARISHES, MISSIONS AND PAROCHIAL SCHOOLS

CITY OF GARY

(LAKE COUNTY)

1—CATHEDRAL OF HOLY ANGELS (1906) Rev. Jon J. Plavcan, Rector; Deacon Robert Angelich.
Res.: 640 Tyler St., Gary, 46402-2299. Tel: 219-882-6079; Fax: 219-882-0133. Web: www.garycluster.org.
Catechesis/Religious Program—Students 3.

2—ST. ANN (1942) Rev. Theodore J. Mens, Admin.
Res.: 525 N. Broad St., Griffith, 46319. Tel: 219-924-4163; Fax: 219-922-2291.
Catechesis/Religious Program—Sr. Paula Hammersley, D.R.E. Students 25.

3—ST. ANTHONY (1918) Closed. For inquiries for parish records contact Cathedral of Holy Angels, Gary.

4—BLESSED SACRAMENT (1947) Closed. For inquiries for parish records, contact Ss. Peter and Paul, Merrillville.

5—ST. CASIMIR (1916), (Lithuanian), Closed. For inquiries for parish records contact Holy Angels Cathedral.

6—ST. EMERIC (1911) Closed. For inquiries for parish records contact Holy Trinity (Hungarian), East Chicago.

7—ST. HEDWIG MISSION (1908), (Polish), [JC] Attended by Salvatorian Fathers., 1746 Pennsylvania St., Gary, 46407. Tel: 219-882-2584; Fax: 219-981-9224.

8—HOLY FAMILY (1926), (Polish), Closed. For inquiries for parish records, contact St. Bridget, Hobart.

9—HOLY ROSARY (1931) Rev. Thomas E. Mischler; Deacon Martin Gomez.
Res.: 6060 Miller Ave., Gary, 46403. Tel: 219-938-1373. Email: hrosaryp@yahoo.com. Web: www.garycluster.org.
Catechesis/Religious Program—

10—HOLY TRINITY (1911), (African American), Closed. For inquiries for parish records contact Cathedral of Holy Angels, Gary.

11—ST. JOSEPH THE WORKER (1912), (Croatian), Rev. Stephen Loncar, O.F.M.Conv.
Res.: 330 E. 45th Ave., Gary, 46409. Tel: 219-980-1846.

12—ST. LUKE (1917) See separate listing. See Sts. Monica-Luke, Gary.

13—ST. MARK (1921) Rev. J. Patrick Gaza.
Mailing Address: P.O. Box 2100, Gary, 46409-0100. Tel: 219-887-0514. Email: stmarkch@yahoo.com.
Res.: 6060 Miller Ave., Gary, 46403.
Church: 505 W. Ridge Rd., Gary, 46408. Tel: 219-887-0514.
Catechesis/Religious Program—Generations of Faith, Tel: 219-801-5722. Mrs. Ester Serrano, D.R.E. Students 200.
Convent—Missionaries of Charity (1999) 509 W. Ridge Rd., Gary, 46408. Tel: 219-884-2140. Missionaries of Charity 4.

14—ST. MARY OF THE LAKE (1929) Rev. Thomas E. Mischler.
Res.: 6060 Miller Ave., Gary, 46403. Tel: 219-938-1373; Fax: 219-938-1316. Email: smlake1929@sbcglobal.net. Web: www.garycluster.org.
Catechesis/Religious Program—Tel: 219-938-9115. Debra Lightsey, D.R.E. Students 2.

15—SS. MONICA-ST. LUKE (1927; 1917) Rev. J. Patrick Gaza.
Mailing Address: 645 Rhode Island, Gary, 46402.
Res.: 6060 Miller Ave., Gary, 46403. Tel: 219-883-1861.
Catechesis/Religious Program—Generations of Faith Mrs. Tyra Serrano, D.R.E. Students 80.

16—SACRED HEART (1918), (Polish), Closed. For inquiries for parish records contact Cathedral of Holy Angels, Gary.

OUTSIDE THE CITY OF GARY

BEVERLY SHORES, PORTER CO., ST. ANN (1950), (Lithuanian), Rev. John B. Barasinski.
Res.: P.O. Box 727, 46301. Tel: 219-879-7565; Fax: 219-879-8893. Email: stannesdunnes@comcast.net. Web: www.st-ann-of-the-dunes.org.
Catechesis/Religious Program—Students 48.

CEDAR LAKE, LAKE CO., HOLY NAME (1859) [CEM] Rev. Edward G. Tlucek, O.F.M.
Res.: 11000 W. 133rd Ave., 46303. Tel: 219-374-7160; Fax: 219-374-7165. Email: holyname4884@att.net.
Parish Center—13209 Schneider St., 46303. Tel: 219-374-8798.
Catechesis/Religious Program—Generations of Faith, Tel: 219-374-8798. Students 130.

CHESTERTON, PORTER CO., ST. PATRICK (1858) [CEM] Rev. James W. Meade; Deacons Nicholas Juracevich; William Jones. In Res., Rev. James P. McGrogan (Retired).
Res.: 638 N. Calumet Rd., 46304. Tel: 219-926-1282; Fax: 219-395-1560. Email: churchoffice@stpatsparish.org. Web: www.stpatsparish.org.
Rectory—642 N. Calumet Rd., 46304. Tel: 219-926-9633.
School—640 N. Calumet Rd., 46304. Tel: 219-926-1707; Fax: 219-921-1922. Email: schooloffice@stpatsparish.org. Lee Ann Cosh, Prin. Lay Teachers 17; Students 356.
Catechesis/Religious Program—Tel: 219-926-1265. Students 295.

CROWN POINT, LAKE CO.

1—ST. MARY (1865), (German), [CEM] Rev. Patrick J. Kalich.
Res.: 321 E. Joliet St., 46307. Tel: 219-663-0044; Fax: 219-663-1027. Email: stmarycp2004@yahoo.com. Web: www.stmarycrownpoint.org.
School—405 E. Joliet St., 46307. Tel: 219-663-0676; Fax: 219-663-1347. L. Thomas Ruiz, Prin. Lay Teachers 25; Students 545.
Catechesis/Religious Program—Marian Weeks, D.R.E. Students 1,116.

2—ST. MATTHIAS (1967) Rev. James E. Wozniak; Deacon Gregory Fabian.
Res.: 101 W. Burrell Dr., 46307. Tel: 219-663-2201; Fax: 219-663-2567. Email: office@stmatthiasparish.net. Web: www.stmatthiasparish.net.
Catechesis/Religious Program—Tel: 219-663-4281. Email: faith.formation@stmatthiasparish.net. Maura Carpenter, D.R.E. Students 230.

DYER, LAKE CO.

1—ST. JOSEPH (1867) [CEM] Rev. Terrence J. Steffens.
Res.: 440 Joliet St., 46311. Tel: 219-865-2271; Fax: 219-865-2350. Email: dyerstjoe@sbcglobal.net.
School—Tel: 219-865-2750; Fax: 219-865-3740. Email: stjoseph22@comcast.net. Web: www.saint-joseph-school.org. Jane Smith, Prin. Lay Teachers 10; Students 125.
Catechesis/Religious Program—430 Joliet St., 46311. Tel: 219-865-2355. Students 160.

2—ST. MARIA GORETTI (1977) Rev. Charles W. Niblick.
Res.: 500 Northgate Dr., 46311. Tel: 219-865-8956; Fax: 219-322-1670. Email: goretti@stmariagoretticchurch.org. Web: www.stmariagoretticchurch.org.
Catechesis/Religious Program—Tel: 219-322-6124; Fax: 219-865-4677. Email: smg.religed@yahoo.com. Web: www.stmariagoretticchurch.org. Bernadine Smierciak, D.R.E.; Kimberly Hoogeveen, D.R.E. Students 289.

EAST CHICAGO, LAKE CO.

1—ASSUMPTION (1915), (Slovak), Closed. For inquiries for parish records contact St. Patrick, East Chicago.

2—ST. FRANCIS (1913), (Lithuanian), Closed. For inquiries for parish records contact St. John Cantius, East Chicago.

3—HOLY TRINITY (1916), (Croatian), Rev. Msgr. John J. Siekierski, Admin.; Deacon James Haugh.
Res.: 4754 Carey St., 46312. Tel: 219-398-3061. Email: holytrinitycroatia@sbcglobal.net.
Catechesis/Religious Program—Mrs. Rose Dado, D.R.E.; Mrs. Pauline Dergo, D.R.E. Students 20.

4—HOLY TRINITY (1906), (Hungarian), Rev. Alphonse Skerl.
Res.: 4759 McCook Ave., 46312. Tel: 219-397-1907; Fax: 219-397-1907.
5—IMMACULATE CONCEPTION (1933), (Italian), Closed. For inquiries for parish records contact St. Stanislaus, East Chicago.
6—ST. JOHN CANTIUS (1905), (Polish), Closed. For inquiries for parish records, contact St. Stanislaus, East Chicago
7—ST. JOSEPH (1916), (Polish), Closed. For inquiries for parish records contact St. John Cantius, East Chicago.
8—ST. JUDE (1933) Closed. For inquiries for parish records contact Our Lady of Guadalupe, East Chicago.
9—ST. MARY (1890) Rev. Stephen G. Gibson.
822 W. 144th St., 46312. Tel: 219-398-2409; Fax: 219-391-8999. Email: stephengibson@aol.com.
School—816 W. 144th St., 46312. Tel: 219-397-4404; Fax: 219-397-0924. Lay Teachers 4; Students 56.
Catechesis/Religious Program—Students 472.
10—OUR LADY OF GUADALUPE (1927), (Hispanic), Rev. Juan Gonzalez, C.PP.S.
Res.: 3510 Deodar St., P.O. Box 3400, 46312. Tel: 219-398-0253; Fax: 219-398-0257. Email: olguadalupe@hotmail.com.
Catechesis/Religious Program—Marilyn A. Baron, D.R.E. Students 111.
11—ST. PATRICK (1902), (Hispanic), Revs. William F. O'Toole; Fernando de Cristobal (Retired); Deacon Raymond E. Helfen.
Res.: 3810 Grand Blvd., 46312. Tel: 219-398-1036; Fax: 219-397-6901. Email: churchoffice@st-pat-ec-in.org. Web: www.st-pat-ec-in.org.
School—
Catechesis/Religious Program—3802 Grand Blvd., 46312. Students 35.
12—SACRED HEART (1926), (Slovak), Rev. Msgr. Joseph F. Semancik.
Res.: 4423 Olcott Ave., 46312. Tel: 219-397-5857.
Catechesis/Religious Program—Students 11.
13—ST. STANISLAUS (1900), (Polish), Rev. Msgr. John J. Siekierski.
Res.: 808 W. 150th St., 46312. Tel: 219-398-2341; Fax: 219-398-2388.
School—4930 Indianapolis Blvd., 46312. Tel: 219-398-1316; Fax: 219-398-9080. Web: myschoolonline. Kathleen A. Lowry, Prin. Lay Teachers 13; Students 212.
Catechesis/Religious Program—Tel: 219-397-7059. Students 20.
Convent—4914 Magoun Ave., 46312. Tel: 219-397-7059.
FISH LAKE, LA PORTE CO., ST. ANTHONY OF PADUA (1948) Rev. Michael G. Heimer.
Res.: 7732 E. State Rd. 4, Walkerton, 46574. Tel: 219-369-1210; Fax: 219-369-9500. (Fish Lake)
Catechesis/Religious Program—Students 4.
GRIFFITH, LAKE CO., ST. MARY (1928) Rev. Theodore J. Mens.
Res.: 525 N. Broad St., 46319-2225. Tel: 219-924-4163; Fax: 219-922-2291.
School—(Grades PreK-8) Tel: 219-924-8633; Fax: 219-922-2279. Mrs. Rebecca Maskovich, Prin. Sisters of St. Francis of Perpetual Adoration 1; Lay Teachers 12; Students 237.
Catechesis/Religious Program—Tel: 219-922-2277. Students 212.
Convent—508 N. Lafayette St., 46319. Tel: 219-922-2278.
HAMLET, STARKE CO., HOLY CROSS (1888) [CEM] Rev. Anthony L. Spanley.
Res.: 6 W. Pearl St., P.O. Box 230, 46532. Tel: 574-867-2461.
Catechesis/Religious Program—Students 5.
Mission—St. Dominic (1981)Tel: 574-867-2461.
HAMMOND, LAKE CO.
1—ALL SAINTS (1896) Rev. Stephen D. Kosinski.
Res.: 570 Sibley St., P.O. Box 836, 46325-0836. Tel: 219-932-0204; Fax: 219-932-4507. Email: allsaint@comcast.net.
Catechesis/Religious Program—Josephine Perez, D.R.E. Students 97.
2—ST. CASIMIR (1890), (Polish), [JC] Revs. William F. O'Toole; Kevin R. Huber; Frank D. Torres; Vladimir Janeczek, Senior Priest (Retired); Deacon Martin J. Brown.
Res.: 4340 Johnson St., 46327. Tel: 219-931-2589; Fax: 219-932-0467. Email: saintcasimirchurch@comcast.net. Web: www.saintcasimirchurch.org.
School—4329 Cameron St., 46327. Tel: 219-932-2686; Fax: 219-932-2686. Mr. Daniel McCabe, Prin. Lay Teachers 11; Students 267.
Catechesis/Religious Program—Tel: 219-931-2589, Ext. 16. Email: an-jo-lu@sbcglobal.net. Maria Marsh, D.R.E. Tel: 219-931-8130. Students 97.
3—ST. CATHERINE OF SIENA (1956) Rev. Larry J. Kew.
Res.: 6605 Kentucky Ave., 46323. Tel: 219-845-1939; Fax: 219-845-4772. Web: www.scos.catholicweb.com.
Catechesis/Religious Program—Mrs. Shirley Brown, D.R.E. Students 50.
4—ST. JOHN BOSCO (1934) Rev. Richard A. Orlinski.
Res.: 7113 Columbia Ave., 46324. Tel: 219-844-9027, Ext. 319; Fax: 219-844-6986. Email: sjboffice@comcast.net. Web: www.sjbhammond.org.
Pastoral Center—1247 171st Pl., 46324. Fax: 219-989-7947.
School—(Grades PreK-8), 1231 171st Pl., 46324. Tel: 219-845-6226; Fax: 219-989-7946. Email: sjbprincipalmk@gmail.com. Mark Kielbania, Prin.; Yvette Markovic, Librarian. Lay Teachers 13; Students 253.
Catechesis/Religious Program—Tel: 219-844-9027, Ext. 310. Mrs. Vickie Blackwood, D.R.E. Students 160.
5—ST. JOSEPH (1879) Rev. Richard A. Orlinski.
Res.: 5304 Hohman Ave., 46320-1808. Tel: 219-932-0702; Fax: 219-932-0059. Email: SaintJoe5304@SBCglobal.net.
Catechesis/Religious Program—Tel: 219-932-7294. Patricia A. Malinowski, D.R.E. Students 72.
6—ST. MARGARET MARY (1947) [CEM] Rev. James W. Schulz, S.J.
Res.: 1445 Hoffman St., 46327. Tel: 219-931-5229; Fax: 219-937-4357. Email: stmargaretmary@sbcglobal.net.
Catechesis/Religious Program—Students 215.
7—ST. MARY (1912) Closed. For inquiries for parish records, contact St. John Bosco, Hammond.
8—OUR LADY OF PERPETUAL HELP (1937) Rev. Charles A. Mosley.
Res.: 7132 Arizona St., 46323. Tel: 219-844-3438; Fax: 219-844-3580. Web: olphparish.net.
Catechesis/Religious Program—7128 Arizona St., 46323. Robert Meaney, D.R.E. Students 207.
HEBRON, PORTER CO., ST. HELEN (1946) Rev. Derrick F. Dudash.
Res.: 302 N. Madison St., 46341. Tel: 219-996-4611.
Catechesis/Religious Program—Tel: 219-996-4612. Karen Yankauskas, D.R.E. Students 92.
HIGHLAND, LAKE CO.
1—ST. JAMES THE LESS (1967) Rev. Keith M. Virus; Deacons Martin Denkhoff; Raymond Dec; Michael W. Halas; Michael L. Hogan.
Mailing Address: 9640 Kennedy Ave., 46322.
Res.: 2703 45th St., 46322. Tel: 219-924-4220; Fax: 219-924-4295.
Catechesis/Religious Program—Tel: 219-924-4222. Email: dre@stjameshighland.org. Emily Watroba, D.R.E. Students 392.
2—OUR LADY OF GRACE (1949) Rev. Edward J. Moszur; Deacon Edward J. Shultz.
Office: 3005 Condit St., 46322. Tel: 219-838-0395; Fax: 219-972-6372. Email: ourladygrace@sbcglobal.net.
School—3025 Highway Ave., 46322. Tel: 219-838-2901; Fax: 219-972-6389. Email: garyolg@yahoo.com. Web: www.olgraceschool.org. Marilyn Tomko, Prin. Lay Teachers 14; Students 165.
Catechesis/Religious Program—Tel: 219-838-6790. Patricia Franz, D.R.E. Students 135.
HOBART, LAKE CO., ST. BRIDGET (1873) Rev. Dominic V. Bertino; Deacon Jamie D. Lewis.
Res.: 568 E. Second St., 46342. Tel: 219-942-6441; Fax: 219-942-4573. Email: stbride@verizon.net. Web: www.stbridgethobart.org.
School—(Grades PreK-8), 107 Main St., 46342. Tel: 219-942-1894; Fax: 219-942-0939. Mr. Douglas A. Pearson, Prin.; Debbie Replin, Librarian. Lay Teachers 14; Students 180.
Catechesis/Religious Program—Tel: 219-955-0186. Students 158.
KINGSFORD HEIGHTS, LA PORTE CO., IMMACULATE HEART OF MARY (1953) Closed. For inquiries for parish records contact St. Anthony, Fish Lake.
KNOX, STARKE CO., ST. THOMAS AQUINAS (1923) Rev. John V. Scott.
Res.: 406 E. Washington St., 46534. Tel: 574-772-4134.
Catechesis/Religious Program—Tel: 574-772-3237. Mrs. Linda Kelly, D.R.E. Students 61.
KOUTS, PORTER CO., ST. MARY (1884) [CEM] Rev. Thomas T. Tibbs.
Res.: P.O. Box 663, 46347. Tel: 219-766-3680. Email: stmarykouts@verizon.net.
Catechesis/Religious Program—Lynn Wichlinski, D.R.E.; Debra Magiera, D.R.E. Students 92.
LA PORTE, LA PORTE CO.
1—ST. JOSEPH (1858) [CEM] Rev. David W. Kime; Deacon Robert Bucheit.
Res.: 109 C St., 46350. Tel: 219-362-9595; Fax: 219-325-9021. Email: stjosephch@verizon.net.
School—101 C St., 46350. Tel: 219-362-6472; Fax: 219-362-2707. Web: st-joe.net. Fonda Mauch, Prin. Sisters of St. Francis of Perpetual Adoration 2; Lay Teachers 7; Students 109.
Catechesis/Religious Program—Students 300.
Convent—102 B St., 46350. Tel: 219-362-2587.
2—ST. PETER (1853) Rev. Joseph A. Angotti.
Res.: 1104 Monroe St., 46350. Tel: 219-362-6186; Fax: 219-324-9277. Email: stpeterlaport@csinet.net. Web: members.csinet.net/stpeterschurch.
Catechesis/Religious Program—Tel: 219-362-2509; Fax: 219-362-2748. Sandra Ransom, D.R.E. & Pastoral Assoc. Students 92.
3—SACRED HEART (1912), (Polish), [JC] Rev. Ian J. Williams.
Res.: 130 Bach St., 46350. Tel: 219-362-2815; Fax: 219-362-4822. Email: office@sacredheartlp.org. Web: www.sacredheartlp.org.
Catechesis/Religious Program—Tel: 219-362-4822. Karen Vidler, D.R.E. Students 125.
LAKE STATION, LAKE CO., ST. FRANCIS XAVIER (1930) [CEM] Rev. Eduardo Malagon; Deacon Leonard Holland.
Res.: 2447 Putnam St., 46405. Tel: 219-962-8626; Fax: 219-962-8627. Email: st.francis@verizon.net.
Catechesis/Religious Program—Tel: 219-962-4507. LaVerne Papich, D.R.E. Students 163.
LOWELL, LAKE CO., ST. EDWARD (1870) [CEM] Rev. Theodore A. Nordquist; Deacon William Hathaway.
Res.: 216 S. Nichols St., 46356. Tel: 219-696-7307; Fax: 219-696-3525. Email: stedwardchurch@sbcglobal.net. Web: home.catholicweb.com/stedwardlowell.
School—(Grades PreSchool-8), 210 S. Nichols St., 46356. Tel: 219-696-9876; Fax: 219-696-2524. Lay Teachers 7; Students 90.
Catechesis/Religious Program—Tel: 219-696-4282; Fax: 219-696-3525. Students 222.
MERRILLVILLE, LAKE CO.
1—ST. ANDREW (1965) Rev. Brian D. Chadwick; Deacon Thomas Gryzbek.
Res.: 801 W. 73rd Ave., 46410. Tel: 219-769-8534; Fax: 219-769-8543. Email: standrew73rd@sbcglobal.net.
School—Tel: 219-769-2049. Bruce Schooler, Prin. Lay Teachers 10; Students 125.
Catechesis/Religious Program—Tel: 219-769-2049. Students 53.
2—ST. JOAN OF ARC (1968) Rev. Roy T. Beeching.
Res.: 5885 Harrison, 46410. Tel: 219-980-2693.
Catechesis/Religious Program— Candice Hanusin, D.R.E. Students 33.
St. Joan of Arc Center—Fax: 219-769-9056.
3—OUR LADY OF CONSOLATION (1947) Rev. Peter J. Muha; Deacon Robert E. Gill.
Res.: 8303 Taft St., 46410. Tel: 219-769-2785; Fax: 219-769-2177. Email: olcsec@sbcglobal.net. Web: www.olcweb.org.
Catechesis/Religious Program—Tel: 219-769-2295. Email: olcffp@live.com. Carole Sluce, D.R.E. Students 256.
4—SS. PETER AND PAUL (1841) [CEM] Rev. Roy T. Beeching.
Res.: 5885 Harrison St., 46410. Tel: 219-980-2693; Fax: 219-980-2851.
Catechesis/Religious Program—Tel: 219-887-2940. Dawn Wojkovich, D.R.E. Students 120.
5—ST. STEPHEN, MARTYR (1968) Rev. Michael L. Maginot.
Res.: 5920 Waite St., 46410. Tel: 219-980-9348; Fax: 219-980-9354.
Catechesis/Religious Program—5885 Harrison, 46410. Tel: 219-887-2940.
MICHIGAN CITY, LA PORTE CO.
1—ST. MARY OF THE IMMACULATE CONCEPTION (1867) Rev. Walter J. Rakoczy.
Res.: 411 W. 11th St., 46360. Tel: 219-874-7231. Email: saintmary.school@comcast.net.
Catechesis/Religious Program—Students 15.
Mission—Sacred Heart 1001 W. Eighth St., 46360.
2—NOTRE DAME (1953) Rev. Keith J. McClellan.
Res.: 1010 Moore Rd., 46360. Tel: 219-872-4844; Fax: 219-872-2510. Email: fatherkeith@notredameparish.net. Web: notredameparish.net.
School—(Grades PreK-8) Tel: 219-872-6216; Fax: 219-872-6273. Mrs. Karen Breen, Prin. Lay Teachers 18; Students 211.
3—QUEEN OF ALL SAINTS (1950) Revs. Terrence R. Chase; Selvaraj Selladurai; Deacon Mark Plaiss.
Res.: 606 S. Woodland Ave., 46360. Tel: 219-872-9196; Fax: 219-872-9176.
School—1715 E. Barker Ave., 46360. Tel: 219-872-4420; Fax: 219-872-1943. Anita Peters, Prin. Lay Teachers 15; Students 204.
Catechesis/Religious Program—Tel: 219-878-9348. Kathy Moskovich, D.R.E. Students 130.
Convent—
4—SACRED HEART MISSION (1915), (Lebanese), Rev. Walter J. Rakoczy, Admin.
Res.: 411 W. 11th St., 46360. Tel: 219-874-7231; Fax: 219-873-1322.
Catechesis/Religious Program—
5—ST. STANISLAUS KOSTKA (1891), (Polish), Rev. Walter M. Ciesla; Deacon Daniel Bowmar.
Mailing Address: 1506 Washington St., 46360.
Res.: 109 Ann St., 46360. Tel: 219-879-9281; Fax:

219-872-2295. Email: ststanskostka@yahoo.com.
School—1506 Washington St., 46360. Tel: 219-872-2258; Fax: 219-872-2295. Lay Teachers 16; Students 167.
Catechesis/Religious Program—203 Benton St., 46360. Tel: 219-872-1257. Antoinette Sajewski, D.R.E. Students 144.

MUNSTER, LAKE CO., ST. THOMAS MORE (1945) Revs. Michael J. Yadron; Richard C. Holy; Deacons Joseph Stodola; Napoleon Tabion; Daniel W. Zurawski.
Res.: 8501 Calumet Ave., 46321. Tel: 219-836-8610; Fax: 219-836-9185. Email: parish.office@stm-church.com. Web: www.stm-church.com.
School—8435 Calumet Ave., 46321. Tel: 219-836-9151; Fax: 219-836-0982. Web: www.stm-school.com. Chet A. Nordyke, Prin. Lay Teachers 30; Students 641.
Catechesis/Religious Program—Tel: 219-836-9152. Mrs. Sandi Morgan, D.R.E. Students 545.

NEW CHICAGO, LAKE CO., ASSUMPTION OF THE BLESSED VIRGIN MARY (P.O. Hobart) (1917), (Polish), Rev. Lourdu Pasala.
Res.: 3530 Illinois St., Hobart, 46342. Tel: 219-962-1073; Fax: 219-962-1073.
Catechesis/Religious Program—Tel: 219-962-6678. Students 40.

NORTH JUDSON, STARKE CO., SS. CYRIL AND METHODIUS (1881) [CEM] Rev. Terrence W. Bennis, Admin.; Peggy Okeley, Pastoral Assoc.
Res.: 303 Keller Ave., 46366. Tel: 574-896-2195; Fax: 574-896-5131.
Catechesis/Religious Program—Email: smallvillejz@yahoo.com. Students 62.

OTIS, LA PORTE CO., ST. MARY (1873), (Polish), [CEM] Rev. Gerald H. Schweitzer; Deacon Dale Walsh.
P.O. Box 386, Wanatah, 46390.
Church: 199 W. Snyder Rd., Westville, 46391-9551.
Res.: 202 N. Ohio, Wanatah, 46390. Tel: 219-733-2955; Fax: 219-733-0001. Web: stmaryotis.org.
Catechesis/Religious Program—Students 75.

PORTAGE, PORTER CO., NATIVITY OF OUR SAVIOR (1964) Rev. Andrew J. Corona; Deacons Robert J. Bonta; Richard Huber; Dennis M. Guernsey.
Res.: 2949 Willowcreek Rd., 46368. Tel: 219-762-4858; Fax: 219-762-6678. Email: staff@crown.net.
School—2929 Willowcreek Rd., 46368. Tel: 219-763-2400. Kemberly Markham, Prin. Lay Teachers 12; Students 169.
Catechesis/Religious Program—Tel: 219-764-3143. Jackie Gentry, D.R.E. Students 400.

ROLLING PRAIRIE, LAPORTE CO., ST. JOHN KANTY (1888), (Polish), [CEM] Rev. Michael G. Heimer, Admin.
Res.: 7732 E. State Rd. 4, Walkerton, 46574. Tel: 219-369-1210; Fax: 219-369-9500.
Catechesis/Religious Program— Sharon DeGroote, D.R.E. Students 60.

ST. JOHN, LAKE CO., ST. JOHN THE EVANGELIST (1839) [CEM] Rev. Sammie L. Maletta.
Res. & Office: 11301 W. 93rd Ave., 46373. Tel: 219-365-5678; Fax: 219-365-2703. Web: www.stjohnparish.org.
School—9400 Wicker Ave., 46373. Tel: 219-365-5451; Fax: 219-365-6173. Web: www.stjohnparish.org/sjeschool. Candace Scheidt, Prin. Lay Teachers 22; Students 341.
Catechesis/Religious Program—Tel: 219-365-3709. Joan Backe, D.R.E. Students 373.

SAN PIERRE, STARKE CO., ALL SAINTS (1858) [CEM] Rev. William J. Spranger.
Res.: 201 W. Eliza St., P.O. Box 56, 46374. Tel: 219-828-4281.
Catechesis/Religious Program—Tel: 219-828-4111. Students 4.

SCHERERVILLE, LAKE CO., ST. MICHAEL (1874) [CEM] Revs. Martin J. Dobrzynski; Michael J. Kopil; Deacons Edwin Gatons; Jack Krol.
Res.: One Wilhelm St., 46375. Tel: 219-322-4505; Fax: 219-322-4508. Web: stmichaels-parish.org.
Preschool—Tel: 219-322-3077. (Good Shepherd Program) Students 35.
School—16 W. Wilhelm St., 46375. Tel: 219-322-4531; Fax: 219-322-1710. Web: saintmichaelscher-.org. Franciscan Sisters of the Sacred Heart 1; Lay Teachers 27; Students 302.
Catechesis/Religious Program—Tel: 219-322-3077. Students 696.

SHELBY, LAKE CO., ST. THERESA (1939) Closed. Records kept at St. Edward, Lowell.

VALPARAISO, PORTER CO.
1—ST. ELIZABETH SETON (1978) Rev. Douglas J. Mayer; Deacons James J. Keough; Michael Prendergast; Brian Nosbusch.
Res.: 509 W. Division Rd., 46385. Tel: 219-464-1624; Fax: 219-465-7673. Email: ffseseton@comcast.net. Web: www.seton.com.
Catechesis/Religious Program—Tel: 219-462-2202. Students 302.
2—OUR LADY OF SORROWS (South Haven) (1967) Rev. John J. Zemelko; Deacon Sherman Brown.
Res.: 356 W. 700 N., 46385. Tel: 219-759-2400; Fax: 219-759-0054. Email: ourladyofsorrows@verizon.net.
Catechesis/Religious Program—Tel: 219-759-2286. Students 84.
3—ST. PAUL (1858) [CEM] Revs. Joseph M. Pawlowski; Michael J. Hoffman; Deacons John Roscoe; Michael Foster; James Caristi; David A. Bergstedt.
Mailing Address: P.O. Box 1475, 46384-1475.
Res.: 452 W. Chicago St., 46383. Tel: 219-465-3723.
Church: P.O. Box 1475, 46384-1475. Tel: 219-464-4831; Fax: 219-464-4833. Email: stpaulcathvalpo@netnitco.net.
School—1755 W. Harrison Blvd., 46385. Tel: 219-462-3374; Fax: 219-477-1763. Email: principal@stpaulvalpo.org. Web: www.stpaulvalpo.org. Jane Scupham, Prin. Lay Teachers 25; Students 373.
Catechesis/Religious Program—Tel: 219-464-8502; Fax: 219-531-6854. Joanne White, D.R.E.; Meghan Conley, Youth Min. Students 560.
Tiny Tim's Child Development Center—1857 Harrison Blvd., 46385. Tel: 219-465-0882; Fax: 219-531-2047. Email: sptinytim@aol.com. Janet McCorkle, Dir.
St. Agnes Adult Day Service Center—1859 Harrison Blvd., 46385. Tel: 219-477-5433; Fax: 219-462-9553. Barbara Kubiszak, Dir.

WANATAH, LA PORTE CO., SACRED HEART (1887) [CEM] Rev. Gerald H. Schweitzer; Deacon Dale Walsh.
Res.: 202 N. Ohio St, P.O. Box 386, 46390. Tel: 219-733-2955; Fax: 219-733-0001. Web: sacredheartwanatah.org.
Catechesis/Religious Program—Tel: 219-733-2315. Email: shreligioused@thecatholiccommunities.org. Students 117.
Mission—St. Martin (1860) Lowell & Dominic Sts., LaCrosse, LaPorte Co. 46348.

WHITING, LAKE CO.
1—ST. ADALBERT (1902), (Polish), Revs. John E. Kalicky, C.PP.S.; Stanley J. Dominik, Admin. (Retired).
1340 121st St., 46394.
Res.: 1849 Lincoln Ave., 46394. Tel: 219-659-0733; Fax: 219-659-0195. Email: sheartwhiting@sbcglobal.net.
Catechesis/Religious Program—Sacred Heart Parish, 1723 LaPorte Ave., 46394. Tel: 219-473-7557; Fax: 219-473-7553.
2—IMMACULATE CONCEPTION (1922), (Slovak), Revs. John E. Kalicky, C.PP.S.; Stanley J. Dominik, Admin. (Retired).
Res.: 1717 LaPorte Ave., 46394. Tel: 219-659-0733; Fax: 219-659-0195. Email: sheartwhiting@sbcglobal.net.
Catechesis/Religious Program—1723 LaPorte Ave., 46394. Tel: 219-473-7557. Students 4.
3—ST. JOHN THE BAPTIST (1897), (Slovak), [JC] Revs. John E. Kalicky, C.PP.S.; Gary Scherer, C.PP.S.; Stanley J. Dominik, Senior Priest (Retired); Leon Flaherty, C.PP.S.; Deacon Joseph Manchak. In Res., Bro. Terrence Nufer, C.PP.S.
Res.: 1849 Lincoln Ave., P.O. Box 711, 46394. Tel: 219-659-0023; Fax: 219-473-7551. Email: churchparishoffice@yahoo.com. Web: sjbcatholicparish.org.
School—1844 Lincoln Ave., 46394. Tel: 219-659-3042; Fax: 219-473-7553. Mark Topp, Prin. Lay Teachers 21; Students 363.
Catechesis/Religious Program—Tel: 219-473-7557; Fax: 219-473-7553. Students 151.
4—STS. PETER AND PAUL (1910) Closed. For inquiries of parish records, contact Sacred Heart, Whiting.
5—SACRED HEART (1889) Revs. John E. Kalicky, C.PP.S.; Stanley Dominik, Admin.
Res.: 1731 Laporte Ave., 46394. Tel: 219-659-0733; Fax: 219-659-0195. Email: sheartwhiting@sbcglobal.net.
Catechesis/Religious Program—1723 LaPorte Ave., 46394. Tel: 219-473-7557; Fax: 219-473-7551. Students 29.

WINFIELD TOWNSHIP, LAKE CO., HOLY SPIRIT (1998) Rev. Joseph V. Murphy.
Res.: 7667 E. 109th Ave., Crown Point, 46307. Tel: 219-661-0644; Fax: 219-662-2611. Email: information@holy-spiritchurch.org. Web: www.holy-spiritchurch.org.
Catechesis/Religious Program—Students 280.

Chaplains of Public Institutions

MICHIGAN CITY. *Indiana State Prison*. Rev. David T. Link, 306 Outlook Cove Dr., La Porte, 46350. Tel: 574-807-2631, Deacon Michael Prendergast.
123 Shorewood Dr., Valparaiso, 46385.

ROLLING PRAIRIE. *Sharing Meadows*. Rev. Dennis J. Blaney (Retired).
P.O. Box 400, 46371. Tel: 219-778-9130.

WESTVILLE. *Westville Correctional Center*. Deacon James Etter.
P.O. Box 473, 46391. Tel: 219-785-2511.

On Duty Outside the Diocese:
Revs.—
Coriden, James A., 6896 Laurel St., N.W., Washington, DC 20012.
Gajardo, Leonardo J., 2665 Woodley Rd. N.W., Washington, DC 20008.
Hand, Dennis M., Pje. 6, Poligno E-Casa #101, Col. San Luis, San Martin, Depto. de San Salvador, El Salvador.
Hendricks, Clare, 1428 Lyon St., Columbia, TN 38401.
Mazza, Mark G. (SF), Archdiocese of San Francisco

Military Chaplains:
Rev.—
Nondorf, Aloysius J., 1962 Bay City Pl., El Paso, TX 79936.

Retired:
Rev. Msgrs.—
Charlebois, Robert L., 161 E. Chicago Ave., Chicago, IL 60611.
Lengerich, Vincent L., 2860 U.S. Rte. 127, Carthagena, OH 45822.
Litot, Edward F., 317 Waverly Rd., La Porte, 46350.
Melevage, F. J., 3214 Milestone Creek Ct., Valparaiso, 46383.
Morales, John F., 333 N. Palm Dr., #305, Beverly Hills, CA 90210.
Tomaszewski, Michael J., 2605 Hermoine Dr., Michigan City, 46360.
Urbonas, Ignatius L., 14911 127th St., Lemont, IL 60439.
Zollinger, Richard, 301 S. Main St., Knox, 46534.
Revs.—
Blaney, Dennis J., P.O. Box 400, Rolling Prairie, 46371.
Daniels, John W., 425 Birch St., N.W., DeMotte, 46310.
de Cristobal, Fernando, 3810 Grand Blvd., East Chicago, 46312.
Dettmer, Alfred J., 1134 Bluebird Ln., Munster, 46321.
Dominik, Stanley J., 1731 LaPorte Ave., Whiting, 46394.
Doyle, Charles E., 105 Autumn Tr., Michigan City, 46360.
Evers, Robert B., P.O. Box 3546, Munster, 46321.
Gehring, Robert P., 419 Autumn Tr. S., Michigan City, 46360.
Gosnell, David H., 917 Beechnut Blvd., 46391.
Heeg, Lawrence M., 1159 N. 325 E, Chesterton, 46304.
Hogan, John A., 318 Garden Tr., Michigan City, 46360.
Janeczek, Vladimir, 211 Autumn Tr., Michigan City, 46360.
Kashmer, George B., P.O. Box 53643, Albuquerque, NM 87153.
Kish, Matthew J., 1501 Hoffman St., Hammond, 46327.
Kronkowski, Leonard J., 2440 Polish Lane Rd., Cheboygan, MI 49721.
McGrogan, James P., 638 N. Calumet Rd., Chesterton, 46304.
Minnich, John F., P.O. Box 537, Georgetown, 47122.
Peil, William L., 1841 N. Anthony Blvd., Fort Wayne, 46805.
Sroka, Gerald A., 209 Autumn Tr., Michigan City, 46360.
Strebig, John J., 135 Kingsbury Ave., La Porte, 46350.
Teles, Dennis J., 230 Lilac Dr., Walkerton, 46574.
Vamos, Joseph E., 10789 Pike St., Crown Point, 46307.
Winterlin, John R., 8724 Manor Ave., Munster, 46321.

Permanent Deacons:
Angelich, Robert
Bacon, John
Bergstedt, David A.
Bonta, Robert J., Senior Deacon
Bowmar, Daniel L., Senior Deacon
Brown, Martin J.
Brown, Sherman, Senior Deacon
Bucheit, Robert J.
Caristi, James
Cichoracki, Eugene, Senior Deacon
Codespoti, Joseph
Dec, Raymond, Senior Deacon
Denkhoff, Martin J., Senior Deacon
Etter, James
Fabian, Gregory G.
Foster, Michael
Gatons, Edwin
Gill, Robert E.
Gomez, Martin, Senior Deacon
Gryzbek, Thomas
Guernsey, Dennis M.

Halas, Michael W.
Hathaway, William R.
Haugh, James
Hawkins, Christopher
Hawkins, Dennis, Senior Deacon
Helfen, Raymond E.
Hogan, Michael L.
Holland, Leonard D.
Huber, Richard
Janowski, Victor
Jones, William E., Jr.
Jurasevich, Nicholas J.
Keough, James J., Senior Deacon
Kozub, Edward
Kreidler, Thomas, Senior Deacon
Krilich, Paul M.
Krol, Jack
Lewis, Jamie D.
Litavecz, Robert J.
Lunsford, Malcolm
Maldonado, Felipe
Manchak, Joseph C.
Mendoza, Roberto
Muvich, Phillip L.
Neher, Norman
Nosbusch, Brian
Plaiss, Mark
Prendergast, Michael
Roscoe, John, Senior Deacon
Shultz, Edward J.
Stodola, Joseph
Tabion, Napoleon
Viviano, Robert L.
Walsh, Dale
Webdell, Dale P.
Zubel, Steven
Zurawski, Daniel W.

INSTITUTIONS LOCATED IN THE DIOCESE

[A] COLLEGES AND UNIVERSITIES

WHITING. *Calumet College of St. Joseph*, 2400 New York Ave., 46394. Tel: 219-473-7770; Fax: 219-473-4259. Web: www.ccsj.edu. Dr. Dennis Rittenmeyer, Pres.; Revs. Alphonse Spilly, C.PP.S., Chap. & Faculty; Jerome Stack, C.PP.S., Faculty; Bros. James Ballmann, C.PP.S., Computer Svcs.; Jerry Schwieterman, C.PP.S., Campus Ministry; Basile Benjamin, C.PP.S., Faculty. Priests 2; Brothers 3; Lay Teachers 126; Total Staff 140; Total Enrollment 1,275.

[B] HIGH SCHOOLS, DIOCESAN

HAMMOND. *Bishop Noll Institute* (1921) 1519 Hoffman St., 46327. Tel: 219-932-9058; Fax: 219-853-1736. Email: cmmccoycejka@bishopnoll.org. Web: www.bishopnoll.org. Colleen McCoy-Cejka, Prin.; Mary Lou Cowperthwaite, Librarian. Students 520; Lay Teachers 40; Total Staff 70; Total Enrollment 630.

MERRILLVILLE. *Andrean High School*, 5959 Broadway, 46410. Tel: 219-887-5281; Fax: 219-981-5072. Web: www.andreanhs.com. Rev. Paul E. Quanz, C.S.B., Prin.; Mrs. Tracy Hadt, Asst. Prin. Basilian Fathers 1; Sisters of Sts. Cyril and Methodius 2; Lay Teachers 45; Total Staff 50; Students 620.

MICHIGAN CITY. *Marquette Catholic High School*, 306 W. Tenth St., 46360. Tel: 219-873-1325; Fax: 219-873-1327. Web: www.marquette-hs.org. James G. White, Prin. Email: jwhite1117@att.net. Lay Teachers 15; Total Staff 22; Students 162.

[C] ELEMENTARY SCHOOLS, INTERPAROCHIAL

ROLLING PRAIRIE. *Sacred Heart Apostolic School, Inc.*, 5901 N. 500 E., 46371. Tel: 219-778-4596; Fax: 219-778-9018. P.O. Box 7, 46371. Rev. Daren Weisbrod, L.C., Vice Pres., Rector & Prin. Priests 2; Brothers 4; Lay Teachers 5; Students 36.

[D] GENERAL HOSPITALS

CROWN POINT. *Saint Anthony Medical Center* (1974) 1201 S. Main St., 46307-8483. Tel: 219-738-2100; Fax: 219-757-6242. Email: david.ruskowski@ssfhs.org. Web: www.stanthonymedicalcenter.com. David Ruskowski, Pres.; Revs. Anthony F. Janik, O.F.M., Chap.; Patrick Okoroh, Chap. Sisters of St. Francis Health Services, Inc. Sisters of St. Francis of Perpetual Adoration 1; Franciscan Sisters of Chicago 3; Bed Capacity (Includes 30 bassinets) 268; Total Staff 1,653; Patients Assisted Annually 310,766.

DYER. *St. Margaret Mercy Healthcare Centers, South Campus*, 24 Joliet, 46311. Tel: 219-865-2141; Fax: 219-933-2585. Email: tom.gryzbek@ssfhs.org. Web: www.smmhc.com. Thomas Gryzbek, Pres.; Rev. Ignatius Ijere, Chap. Sisters of St. Francis Health Services, Inc. Sisters 2; Bed Capacity 297; Total Staff 945; Patients Assisted Annually 202,257.

EAST CHICAGO. *St. Catherine Hospital* (1928) 4321 Fir St., 46312. Tel: 219-392-1700; Fax: 219-392-7002. Web: www.comhs.org. JoAnn Birdzell, Admin. & CEO; Joe Winterhaler, Vice Pres., Finance & CFO; Sr. Mary Ellen Goeller, P.H.J.C., Regl. Dir. Mission Integration. Sisters 1; Bed Capacity 181; Bassinets 9; Total Staff 1,242; Patients Assisted Annually 125,997.

HAMMOND. *St. Margaret Mercy Healthcare Centers - North Campus*, 5454 Hohman Ave., 46320. Tel: 219-932-2300; Fax: 219-933-2585. Email: Tom.Gryzbek@ssfhs.org. Web: www.smmhc.com. Thomas Gryzbek, Pres.; Rev. Gregory Holicky. Sisters of St. Francis Health Services, Inc. Sisters 5; Bed Capacity 485; Bassinets 46; Total Staff 1,250; Patients Assisted Annually 126,506.

HOBART. *St. Mary Medical Center*, 1500 S. Lake Park Ave., 46342. Tel: 219-942-0551; Fax: 219-947-6037. Web: www.stmary-hobart.com. Janice Ryba, Admin. & CEO; Sr. Mary Ellen Goeller, P.H.J.C., Regl. Dir., Mission Integration; Art Vasquez, Controller. Sisters 2; Bed Capacity 190; Bassinets 18; Total Staff 1,173; Patients Assisted Annually 157,484.

MICHIGAN CITY. *Saint Anthony Memorial Health Centers* (1904) 301 W. Homer St., 46360. Tel: 219-879-8511; Fax: 219-877-1409. Email: darla.ream@ssfhs.org. Web: www.saintanthonymemorial.org. James T. Callaghan III, M.D., M.B.A., Pres.; Revs. Jose Pottokaran, C.M.I., Chap.; Lawrence Henry, C.S.C., Chap. Sisters of St. Francis Health Services, Inc. Sisters 3; Staffed Beds (plus 26 research beds) 198; Bassinets 20; Total Staff 1,036; Patients Assisted Annually 244,963.

[E] PROTECTIVE INSTITUTIONS

EAST CHICAGO. *Carmelite Home for Girls/Holy Innocents Shelter* (1913) 4840 Grasselli Ave., 46312. Tel: 219-397-1085; Fax: 219-392-3574. Email: carmeliteec@aol.com. Web: www.carmelitedcjnorth.org. Sr. Maria Giuseppe Moxley, Supr. & Admin. Carmelite Sisters of the Divine Heart of Jesus 10; Total Staff 110; Tauscher Center 32; Holy Innocents Children 30; Residential Girls 34; Total Assisted Annually 190.

[F] HOMES FOR THE AGED

CROWN POINT. *Franciscan Communities at St. Anthony Campus*, 203 Franciscan Dr., 46307-4824. Tel: 219-661-5100; Fax: 219-661-5102. Web: www.stanthonyhome.com. Linda O'Neill, Exec. Dir.; Rev. Myron Lowisz, O.F.M., Pastoral Care. Priests 1; Franciscan Sisters of Chicago 4; Deacons 2; Total Staff 476.

St. Anthony Home Tel: 219-661-5100; Fax: 219-661-5102. Web: www.stanthonyhome.com. Capacity 190.

St. Anthony Assisted Living Apartments Tel: 219-661-5150. Web: www.stanthonyhome.com. Capacity 60.

St. Anthony Hospice Tel: 219-661-5306; Fax: 219-661-5305. Web: www.stanthonyhome.com.

Franciscan Community Services Adult Day Care Tel: 219-661-5200. Web: www.stanthonyhome.com. Capacity 25.

Holy Family Child Care Tel: 219-661-5250. Children 175.

HAMMOND. *Albertine Home*, 1501 Hoffman St., 46327. Tel: 219-937-0575; Fax: 219-937-0575. Email: albertineusa@att.net. Sr. Loretta Soja, Dir. Albertine Sisters 9; Guests 36.

[G] PERSONAL PRELATURES

VALPARAISO. *Opus Dei*, 359 West 200 North, 46385. Tel: 219-462-6594; 219-462-0931; Fax: 219-465-6241. Email: shellbourne2@aol.com. Web: www.shellbourne.org. Prelature of the Holy Cross and Opus Dei, Shellbourne Conference Center.

[H] MONASTERIES AND RESIDENCES OF PRIESTS AND BROTHERS

CEDAR LAKE. *Our Lady of Lourdes Friary*, 12915 Parrish St., P.O. Box 156, 46303. Tel: 219-374-5931. Revs. Anthony F. Janik, O.F.M., Guardian; Francis Affelt; Bronislaus Jaskulski, O.F.M.; James Kendzierski; Myron Lowisz, O.F.M.; Bert Pepowski; Edward G. Tlucek, O.F.M.; Bro. DeSales Wisniewski; Rev. Sergius Worbleski, O.F.M. Franciscan Friars of the Assumption of the B.V.M. Province (Order of Friars Minor). Priests 7; Brothers 2.

San Damiano Friary, 12921 Parrish St., P.O. Box 500, 46303. Tel: 219-374-5741; Fax: 219-374-9650. Web: www.ofmnovitiate.org. Revs. Dennet Jung, O.F.M., Supr.; Joachim Studwell, O.F.M., Member Formation Team; Ralph Parthie, O.F.M., Novice Dir.; Bro. Norbert Bertram, O.F.M., Member Formation Team. Cedar Lake Franciscan Friars (Order of Friars Minor). Interprovinicial Novitiate. Priests 3; Novices 6.

EAST CHICAGO. *Roque Gonzalez Residence-Jesuit Fathers*, 3905 Fir St., 46312. Tel: 219-397-1885; 219-397-3906; Fax: 219-844-7566. Email: jdixon@heartlandctr.org. Web: www.heartlandctr.com. Rev. James M. Dixon, S.J.

MERRILLVILLE. *Basilian Fathers Residence* (1959) 5959 Broadway, 46410. Tel: 219-887-5284; Fax: 219-981-5072. Email: pquanz@andreanhs.com. Revs. John J. Fiore, C.S.B. (Retired); Paul E. Quanz, C.S.B., Rector. Priests 2.

Salvatorian Fathers (Society of the Divine Savior) (1954) 5755 Pennsylvania St., 46410. Tel: 219-884-0714; Fax: 219-981-9224. Email: mail@salvatorianfathers.us. Web: www.salvatorianfathers.us. Revs. Tadeusz Majcher, S.D.S., Supr.; Joseph R. Zuziak, S.D.S.; Edward Kawa, S.D.S.; Walter M. Pawlik, S.D.S.; Stanislaw Pieczara, S.D.S., US Air Force Chap.; Bro. Marek Miazga. Mission House for Polish Priests and Brothers. Priests 5; Brothers 1.

MUNSTER. *Discalced Carmelite Fathers Monastery*, 1628 Ridge Rd., 46321. Tel: 219-838-7111; Fax: 219-838-7214. Email: carmelmunster@yahoo.com. Revs. Jacek Palica, O.C.D., Prior; Casimir Adalbert Borcz, O.C.D.; Joseph Ivans, O.C.D.; Edward C. Spyrka, O.C.D.; Waclaw L. Lech, O.C.D.; Bronislaw F. Socha, O.C.D.; Bartlomiej Stanowski, O.C.D.; Michael G. Veneklase, O.C.D.; Jacek Chodzynski, O.C.D.; Franciszek Czaicki, O.C.D.; Pawel Furdzik, O.C.D.; Lurasz Nowak, O.C.D.; Bros. Marian Leszewicz, O.C.D.; Tomasz S. Paczek, O.C.D. Priests 12; Brothers 2.

[I] CONVENTS AND RESIDENCES OF SISTERS

GARY. *Missionaries of Charity* (1999) 509 W. Ridge Rd., 46408. Tel: 219-884-2140. Sr. Maria Agnes, M.C., Supr. Sisters 4.

EAST CHICAGO. *St. Catherine Convent*, 4325 Elm St., 46312. Tel: 219-398-0403. Email: magdalenhellmann@yahoo.com. Web: www.poorhandmaids.org. Sisters Annemarie Kampwerth, P.H.J.C.; Pamela Thelkes, P.H.J.C. Poor Handmaids of Jesus Christ 5.

HAMMOND. *Albertine Sisters (Prov. of Krakow, Poland)*, 1501 Hoffman St., 46327. Tel: 219-937-0575; Fax: 219-937-0575. Email: albertineusa@att.net. Sr. Danuta Karwacka, Supr. Sisters 9.

MERRILLVILLE. *Andrean H.S. Sisters' Residence*, 5959 Broadway, 46410. Tel: 219-887-5287. Email: barbarasable@hotmail.com. Web: www.sscm.org. Sr. Joanne Marie Schutz, SS.C.M., Pastoral Assoc., St. Mary, Crown Point, IN. Sisters of SS. Cyril and Methodius Sisters 3.

[J] RETREAT HOUSES

EAST CHICAGO. *Bethany Retreat House* (1992) 2202 Lituanica Ave., 46312. Tel: 219-398-5047; Fax: 219-398-9329. Email: bethanyrh@sbcglobal.net. Web: www.bethanyretreathouse.org. Sr. Joyce Diltz, P.H.J.C., D.Min., M.Chr.Sp., Spiritual Dir. & Dir. Retreat House. Total Staff 2; Guests 400.

MICHIGAN CITY. *Angela House* (1994) Congregation of the Sisters of the Holy Cross, 412 W. 10th St., 46360. Tel: 219-873-1324. Email: prayercentermc@sbcglobal.net. Sisters Rita Bray, C.S.C., Co-Dir.; Julia Marie Jacomet, C.S.C., Co-Dir.

Sisters of the Holy Cross, Inc. Total Staff 2; Total in Residence 2.

[K] DIOCESAN CHARITIES

CROWN POINT. *Catholic Charities* (1937) 176 S. West St., 46307. Tel: 219-663-8417; Fax: 219-663-8421. Email: jaugustine@catholic-charities.org. Web: www.catholic-charities.org. Sr. Jean Augustine, S.C., M.S.W., M.B.A., Exec. Dir.

Catholic Family Service, 176 S. West St., 46307. Tel: 219-663-8417; Fax: 219-663-8421.

176 S. West St., 46307. Tel: 219-663-8417; Fax: 219-663-8421.

3901 Fir St., East Chicago, 46312. Tel: 219-397-5803; Fax: 219-397-5804.

6919 Indianapolis Blvd., Hammond, 46324. Tel: 219-844-4883; Fax: 219-844-4885.

6350 Central Ave., Portage, 46368. Tel: 219-762-1177; Fax: 219-762-1827.

321 W. 11th St., Michigan City, 46360. Tel: 219-879-9312; Fax: 219-879-9073.

166 S. West St., 46307. Tel: 219-662-7677; Fax: 219-662-7678.

Family Life Ministry, Gary. Tel: 219-663-8417; Fax: 219-663-8421.

Family Life Ministry, Marriage Preparation & Anniversary Mass.

176 S. West St., 46307. Tel: 219-663-8417; Fax: 219-663-8421.

Services to the Aging, Retired & Senior Volunteer Program

LaPorte & Starke Co., 321 W. 11th St., Michigan City, 46360. Tel: 219-874-8195; Fax: 219-879-9073.

Lake Co., 6919 Indianapolis Blvd., Hammond, 46324. Tel: 219-844-5174; Fax: 219-844-4885.

Senior Companion Program, 6919 Indianapolis Blvd., Hammond, 46324. Tel: 219-844-4883; Fax: 219-844-4885.

Lake Co., 6919 Indianapolis Blvd., Hammond, 46324. Tel: 219-844-4883; Fax: 219-844-4885.

Foster Grandparent Program, 6919 Indianapolis Blvd., Hammond, 46324. Tel: 219-844-4883; Fax: 219-844-4885.

[L] NEWMAN APOSTOLATES

VALPARAISO. *Newman Apostolate-Valparaiso University* (1974) 1511 La Porte Ave., 46383-5818. Tel: 219-464-4042; Fax: 219-462-2711. Email: kevin.mccarthy@valpo.edu. Rev. Kevin P. McCarthy, Chap. St. Teresa of Avila Catholic Student Center; Chapel and Center for Students attending Valparaiso University. Students 836.

[M] MISCELLANEOUS

CROWN POINT. *Franciscan Home Care Services, Inc.*, 203 Franciscan Dr., 46307. Tel: 219-661-5321; Fax: 219-661-5305. Email: cgrantner@franciscancommunities.com. Catherine Grantner-Coltun, Exec. Dir.

EAST CHICAGO. *Office of Hispanic Ministry* (1983) 1709 E. 138th St., P.O. Box 3027, 46312. Tel: 219-397-2125; Fax: 219-397-2168. Email: atorres@dcgary.org. Web: www.dcgary.org. Adeline Torres, Coord. Total Staff 3.

HAMMOND. **Alverno Provena Hospital Laboratories, Inc.*, 2434 Interstate Plaza Dr., 46324. Tel: 219-989-3714; Fax: 219-989-3900. Email: cheryl.vance@ssfhs.org. Cheryl Vance, Pres.

HealthVisions Midwest, 3700 179th St., 46323. Tel: 219-397-4335; Fax: 219-397-4651. Email: akampwerth@hvusa.org. Web: www.hvusa.org. Mr. Donald G. Barnes, Pres. & CEO.

Heartland Center, 6819 Indianapolis Blvd., 46324. Tel: 219-844-7515; Fax: 219-844-7566. Email: mail@heartlandctr.org. Web: www.heartlandctr.org. Rev. James M. Dixon, S.J. Office of Peace and Social Justice of the Diocese of Gary. Total Staff 3.

Spiritual Life/Seimetz Center, 1441 Hoffman St., 46327. Tel: 219-932-8321; Fax: 219-932-8321. Email: xctb29c@prodigy.com. Bed Capacity 64; Total Assisted Annually 1,000; Total Staff 3.

HOBART. *Ancilla Systems Incorporated* (1967) 1419 S. Lake Park Ave., 46342. Tel: 219-947-8570; Fax: 219-947-3708. Email: tmola@ancilla.org. Web: www.ancilla.org. Sr. Nora Hahn, P.H.J.C., Chairperson; Toni Mola, Admin.

Ancilla Domini Hospitals Self Insurance Trust Tel: 219-947-8570; Fax: 219-947-3708.

St. Joseph Medical Center of Fort Wayne, Inc. Tel: 219-947-8665; Fax: 219-947-3708.

Nazareth Home, East Chicago, 46312. Tel: 219-947-8570; Fax: 219-947-3708. Web: www.nazarethhome-.com. Toni Mola, Admin.

VALPARAISO. *Camp Lawrence* Diocesan Spiritual Center and Youth Camp., 68 E. 700 N., 46383. Tel: 219-462-8243; 219-462-5261. Email: camplawrence@verizon.net.

Catholic Youth Organization, 77725 Broadway, Ste. C, 46410. Tel: 219-736-8931; Fax: 219-736-9457.

RELIGIOUS INSTITUTES OF MEN REPRESENTED IN THE DIOCESE

For further details refer to the corresponding bracketed number in the Religious Institutes of Men or Women section.

[]—*Association of the Immaculate Conception*
[0170]—*Basilian Fathers* (Toronto)—C.S.B.
[0200]—*Benedictine Monks*—O.S.B.
[0600]—*Brothers of the Congregation of Holy Cross*—C.S.C.
[0275]—*Carmelites of Mary Immaculate*—C.M.I.
[1130]—*Congregation of the Priests of the Sacred Heart*—S.C.J.
[0480]—*Conventual Franciscans* (Croatia)—O.F.M.Conv.
[0260]—*Discalced Carmelite Friars* (Holy Ghost Prov., Poland)—O.C.D.
[0520]—*Franciscan Friars* (Prov. of Assumption of B.V.M.; Prov. of St. John the Baptist; Prov. of the Sacred Heart)—O.F.M.
[0690]—*Jesuit Fathers*—S.J.
[0610]—*Priests of the Congregation of Holy Cross*—C.S.C.
[1200]—*Society of the Divine Savior*—S.D.S.
[1060]—*Society of the Precious Blood*—C.PP.S.

RELIGIOUS INSTITUTES OF WOMEN REPRESENTED IN THE DIOCESE

[]—*Albertine Sisters* (Prov. of Krakow, Poland)—C.S.A.
[0230]—*Benedictine Sisters of the Pontifical Jurisdiction*—O.S.B.
[0360]—*Carmelite Sisters of the Divine Heart of Jesus*—Carmel D.C.
[3710]—*Congregation of the Sisters of Saint Agnes*—C.S.A.
[1920]—*Congregation of the Sisters of the Holy Cross*—C.S.C.
[1070-03]—*Dominican Sisters*—O.P.
[1070-13]—*Dominican Sisters*—O.P.
[1115]—*Dominican Sisters of Peace*—O.P.
[1210]—*Franciscan Sisters of Chicago*—O.S.F.
[1450]—*Franciscan Sisters of the Sacred Heart*—O.S.F.
[2710]—*Missionaries of Charity*—M.C.
[3130]—*Our Lady of Victory Missionary Sisters*—O.L.V.M.
[3230]—*Poor Handmaids of Jesus Christ*—P.H.J.C.
[2970]—*School Sisters of Notre Dame*—S.S.N.D.
[3340]—*Sisters of Providence*—S.P.
[3780]—*Sisters of Saints Cyril and Methodius*—SS.C.M.
[]—*Sisters of St. Anne of Bangalore*—S.A.B.
[1640]—*Sisters of St. Francis of Perpetual Adoration*—O.S.F.
[3930]—*Sisters of St. Joseph of the Third Order of St. Francis* (Immaculate Conception Prov.)—S.S.J.-T.O.S.F.

DIOCESAN CEMETERIES

HAMMOND. *Saint John-Saint Joseph*, 1547 167th St., 46320. Tel: 219-844-9475; Fax: 219-844-3770. Email: garycathcems@sbcglobal.net. Rev. Roy T. Beeching, Dir. of Cemeteries; Michael P. Welsh, Cemetery Mgr. Employees 10.

MICHIGAN CITY. *Saint Stanislaus*, 1015 Greenwood Ave., P.O. Box 642, 46360. Tel: 219-874-4310.

NECROLOGY

† Charlebois, Rev. Msgr. John J.—Died Sept. 22, 2009
† Murzyn, John A., (Retired)—Died April 20, 2009

An asterisk (*) denotes an organization that has established tax-exempt status directly with the IRS and is not covered by the USCCB Group Ruling.

Diocese of Gaylord

(Dioecesis Gaylordensis)

Most Reverend

BERNARD A. HEBDA, J.C.L., J.D.

Bishop of Gaylord; ordained July 1, 1989; appointed Bishop of Gaylord October 7, 2009; ordained December 1, 2009. *Diocesan Pastoral Center: 611 W. North St., Gaylord, MI 49735-8349.*

Diocesan Pastoral Center: 611 W. North St., Gaylord, MI 49735-8349. Tel: 989-732-5147; Fax: 989-705-3589.

Web: www.dioceseofgaylord.org

Email: msteffel@dioceseofgaylord.org

ESTABLISHED JULY 20, 1971.

Square Miles 11,171.

Comprises the following 21 Counties in the State of Michigan: Alcona, Alpena, Antrim, Benzie, Charlevoix, Cheboygan, Crawford, Emmet, Grand Traverse, Iosco, Kalkaska, Leelanau, Manistee, Missaukee, Montmorency, Ogemaw, Oscoda, Otsego, Presque Isle, Roscommon and Wexford.

For legal titles of parishes and diocesan institutions, consult the Chancery Office.

STATISTICAL OVERVIEW

Personnel	
Bishop	1
Retired Bishops	1
Priests: Diocesan Active in Diocese	35
Priests: Diocesan Active Outside Diocese	2
Priests: Retired, Sick or Absent	25
Number of Diocesan Priests	62
Religious Priests in Diocese	6
Total Priests in Diocese	68
Extern Priests in Diocese	16
Ordinations:	
Diocesan Priests	1
Transitional Deacons	1
Permanent Deacons in Diocese	22
Total Sisters	32
Parishes	
Parishes	80
With Resident Pastor:	
Resident Diocesan Priests	30
Resident Religious Priests	3
Without Resident Pastor:	
Administered by Priests	40
Administered by Religious Women	3
Administered by Lay People	1
Closed Parishes	1
Professional Ministry Personnel:	
Sisters	6
Lay Ministers	47
Welfare	
Catholic Hospitals	3
Total Assisted	375,000
Residential Care of Children	4
Total Assisted	295
Day Care Centers	11
Total Assisted	342
Specialized Homes	1
Total Assisted	250
Special Centers for Social Services	23
Total Assisted	28,972
Educational	
Diocesan Students in Other Seminaries	7
Total Seminarians	7
High Schools, Diocesan and Parish	4
Total Students	501
Elementary Schools, Diocesan and Parish	16
Total Students	1,882
Catechesis/Religious Education:	
High School Students	745
Elementary Students	2,660
Total Students under Catholic Instruction	5,795
Teachers in the Diocese:	
Sisters	1
Lay Teachers	186
Vital Statistics	
Receptions into the Church:	
Infant Baptism Totals	577
Minor Baptism Totals	48
Adult Baptism Totals	64
Received into Full Communion	124
First Communions	815
Confirmations	845
Marriages:	
Catholic	169
Interfaith	102
Total Marriages	271
Deaths	853
Total Catholic Population	60,837
Total Population	507,722

Former Bishops—Most Revs. EDMUND C. SZOKA, J.C.L., D.D., First Bishop of Gaylord; ord. June 5, 1954; cons. July 20, 1971; installed July 20, 1971; appt. Archbishop of Detroit March 28, 1981; installed May 17, 1981; named Cardinal Priest May 29, 1988; elevated June 28, 1988; Assigned to the Vatican, 1990; ROBERT J. ROSE, S.T.L., D.D., ord. Dec. 21, 1955; appt. Bishop of Gaylord Oct. 13, 1981; installed Dec. 6, 1981; transferred to Diocese of Grand Rapids July 11, 1989; installed Aug. 30, 1989; PATRICK R. COONEY, S.T.B., S.T.L., ord. Dec. 20, 1959; appt. Titular Bishop of Hodelm and Auxiliary Bishop of Detroit Dec. 3, 1982; cons. Jan. 27, 1983; appt. Bishop of Gaylord Nov. 21, 1989; installed Jan. 28, 1990; retired Oct. 7, 2009.

Vicar General—Rev. FRANCIS J. MURPHY, St. Ann Parish, 800 W. 13th, Cadillac, 49601. Tel: 231-775-2471.

Diocesan Offices and Departments

Diocesan Pastoral Center—611 W. North St., Gaylord, 49735-8349. Tel: 989-732-5147; Fax: 989-705-3589. Office Hours: Mon.-Fri. 8-4:30; All business should be directed to this office.

Members of the College of Consultors—Revs. CHARLES G. DONAJKOWSKI; MICHAEL S. JANOWSKI; WILLIAM W. LIPSCOMB; DONALD L. LIBBY; T. PATRICK MAHER; JOHN E. MCCRACKEN, Ex Officio.

Administrative Services, Secretariat for—MICHAEL E. STEFFEL, Dir., 611 W. North St., Gaylord, 49735. Tel: 989-732-5147.

Audiovisual Resource Center—CANDACE NEFF, 611 W. North St., Gaylord, 49735. Tel: 989-732-5147.

Archivist—Rev. GERALD F. MICKETTI, 611 W. North St., Gaylord, 49735. Tel: 989-732-5147.

Communications, Secretariat for—CANDACE NEFF, Dir., 611 W. North St., Gaylord, 49735. Tel: 989-732-5147.

Council of Catholic Women, Diocesan—DIANE BLEVINS, Pres., 3210 Putnam Rd., Hale, 48739-9250.

Cursillo—Rev. LAWRENCE J. SERGOTT, Mailing Address: P.O. Box 150, Onekama, 49675. Tel: 231-889-4254.

Ecumenical and Interreligious Affairs, Delegate for—Rev. JOSEPH P. GRAFF, 150 W. Main St., Harbor Springs, 49740.

Faith Development, Secretariat for—DANORA BRZEZINSKI, Dir., 611 W. North St., Gaylord, 49735-8349. Tel: 989-732-5147.

Finance Council, Diocesan—Most Rev. PATRICK R. COONEY, S.T.B., S.T.L., D.D.; Rev. FRANCIS J. MURPHY; JAMES S. BERISH JR.; STAN DOMBROWSKI; LORI A. REICHARD; ROSEMARY SMITH; TODD STACHNIK.

Holy Childhood Pontifical Association—Rev. ROBERT H. BISSOT, 2188 Nicholson Hill Rd., Ossineke, 49766.

Native American Apostolate—Rev. ANDREW G. BUVALA, O.F.M., Coord., Blessed Kateri Tekakwitha Parish, P.O. Box 369, Suttons Bay, 49682. Tel: 231-271-6651.

Knights of Columbus—MICHAEL J. STANCHINA, Eastern Diocesan Prog. Dir., 937 Joyce Court, Mio, 48647. Tel: 989-848-5322; RUSSELL SCHOLTENS, Western Diocesan Prog. Dir., Mailing Address: P.O. Box 37, Suttons Bay, 49682. Tel: 231-271-6865.

Worship and Liturgical Formation, Secretariat for—Rev. DUANE A. WACHOWIAK JR., Dir., 611 W. North St., Gaylord, 49735. Tel: 989-732-5147.

Marriage Enrichment, Secretariat for—DANORA BRZEZINSKI, Dir., 611 W. North St., Gaylord, 49735. Tel: 517-732-5147.

Hispanic Apostolate—SILVIA CORTES-LOPEZ, 1026 Hannah, Ste. A, Traverse City, 49686. Tel: 231-929-4738.

Justice and Peace—Rev. WAYNE H. DZIEKAN, 611 W. North St., Gaylord, 49735. Tel: 989-732-5147.

Continuing Spiritual Formation of Clergy, Pastoral Administrators and Women Religious—Rev. JOHN E. MCCRACKEN, Delegate, 611 W. North St., Gaylord, 49735. Tel: 989-732-5147.

Priests' Retirement Fund—Most Rev. BERNARD A. HEBDA, J.C.L., J.D. Elected Members: Revs. ROBERT W. NALLEY; CHARLES G. DONAJKOWSKI; JAMES P. HAYDEN (Retired); JOHN E. MCCRACKEN. Appointed Member: DON BARTOSH, Chm.

Vocations and Pastoral Care of Seminarians, Delegate for—Rev. DONALD R. GEYMAN, Diocese of Gaylord, 611 W. North St., Gaylord, 49735. Tel: 989-732-5147.

Propagation of the Faith—Rev. ROBERT H. BISSOT, Dir., 2188 Nicholson Hill Rd., Ossineke, 49766. Tel: 989-471-5121.

St. Vincent De Paul, Society of—District Councils: Council of Tawas, 115 First St., Tawas City, 49763. Roscommon County, 117 Woodcrest Dr., Roscommon, 48653. Grand Traverse County: Traverse Bay Conference, 715 Beitner St., Traverse City, 49686. Alpena, 805 W. Chisholm, Alpena, 49707. Also particular councils in Cheboygan, Hillman, Hale, Prescott, and Mikado.

Spiritual Formation—MICHAEL FONSECA, Dir., 611 W. North St., Gaylord, 49735. Tel: 989-732-5147.

Tribunal Diocesan—Rev. ROBERT W. NALLEY, Judicial Vicar. Judge: Rev. PETER O. EKE. Defender of the Bond: PETE VERE, J.C.L. Procurator-Advocate: MARY DICKERSON, Notary Inquiries may be made through the local pastors or directed to this office: 611 W. North St., Gaylord, 49735. Tel: 989-732-5147.

Victim Assistance Coordinator—THOMAS TENEROVICZ. Tel: 800-727-5147, Ext. 3525 (Toll Free); 989-705-3525. Email: ttenerovicz@dioceseofgaylord.org.

CLERGY, PARISHES, MISSIONS AND PAROCHIAL SCHOOLS

CITY OF GAYLORD

(OTSEGO COUNTY), ST. MARY CATHEDRAL, [CEM] Revs. James M. Bearss, Rector; Peter O. Eke; Sr. Cecilia Faber, O.P., Pastoral Min.
Res.: 606 N. Ohio Ave., 49735-1999. Tel: 989-732-5448; Fax: 989-705-3585.
Catechesis / Religious Program—Students 412.

OUTSIDE THE CITY OF GAYLORD

ACME, GRAND TRAVERSE CO., CHRIST THE KING Rev. Gerald F. Micketti.
Res. & Mailing: P.O. Box 95, 49610. Tel: 231-938-9214; Fax: 231-938-3266.
Church: 3801 Shore Rd., Williamsburg, 49690.
See Grand Traverse Area Catholic School, Traverse City, under Interparochial Parish Schools located in the Institution section.
Catechesis / Religious Program—Denise Elsenheimer, D.R.E. Students 146.

AFTON, CHEBOYGAN CO., ST. MONICA, [CEM] Rev. Arthur F. Duchnowicz.
Res.: 585 S. Third St., Rogers City, 49779. Tel: 989-734-2753; Fax: 989-734-2753.
Church: M-68, 49705.

ALPENA, ALPENA CO.
1—ST. ANNE, [JC] Revs. Gregory P. McCallum; Rolando Silva.
Res.: 817 Sable St., 49707. Tel: 989-356-0622; Fax: 989-354-3918.
Church: 201 S. Ninth Ave., 49707.
Catechesis / Religious Program—Jacqueline Benson, D.R.E. All 4 Alpena parishes combined Students 257.
2—ST. BERNARD, [JC] Revs. Gregory P. McCallum; Rolando Silva.
Mailing Address: 322 W. Chisholm St., 49707. Tel: 989-354-2676; Fax: 989-354-5142. Email: sbc@charterinternet.com.
Catechesis / Religious Program—Tel: 989-354-8655. Anne Kelley, D.R.E.
3—ST. JOHN THE BAPTIST Revs. Gregory P. McCallum; Rolando Silva.
Res.: 2550 S. First Ave., 49707. Tel: 989-354-3019; Fax: 989-358-9079.
Catechesis / Religious Program—William Morford, D.R.E.
4—ST. MARY, [JC] Revs. Gregory P. McCallum; Rolando Silva.
Res.: 120 E. Miller St., 49707. Tel: 989-354-2322; Fax: 989-354-2030.
Catechesis / Religious Program—Tel: 989-354-8655. Anne Kelley, D.R.E. Combined with other Alpena parishes.

ALVERNO, CHEBOYGAN CO., ST. FRANCIS OF ASSISI, Closed. For sacramental records contact St. Mary-St. Charles Parish, Cheboygan.

ATLANTA, MONTMORENCY CO., JESUS THE GOOD SHEPHERD Rev. Raymond C. Cotter.
Res. & Mailing: P.O. Box 216, Hillman, 49746. Tel: 989-742-4542; Fax: 989-742-8090.
Church: 4521 County Rd. 491, 49709. Email: staug.jtgs@src-milp.com.
Catechesis / Religious Program—Debra Banks, D.R.E.

BAY SHORE, EMMET CO., ST. FRANCIS SOLANUS, Closed. For inquiries for parish records contact the chancery.

BEAVER ISLAND, CHARLEVOIX CO., HOLY CROSS, [CEM] Revs. Gerard A. Hunko; Patrick T. Cawley, Admin.
Res.: P.O. Box 145, 49782.
Office: Kings Hwy., 49782. Tel: 231-448-2230; Fax: 231-448-2230.
Catechesis / Religious Program—Students 9.

BELLAIRE, ANTRIM CO., ST. LUKE Rev. James K. Gardiner.
Res.: 3088 S. M-88, P.O. Box 799, 49615-0799. Tel: 231-533-8121; Fax: 231-533-9254. Email: stluke@torchlake.com. Web: www.stlukebellaire.com.
Catechesis / Religious Program—Debbie Balon, D.R.E. Students 60.

BLACK RIVER, ALCONA CO., ST. GABRIEL, [CEM] Rev. Robert H. Bissot.
Res.: 2188 W. Nicholson Hill Rd., Ossineke, 49766-9736. Tel: 989-471-2556; Fax: 989-471-2697.
Church: 5570 N. Lake Shore Dr., 48721. Tel: 989-471-5121.
Catechesis / Religious Program—Cathy MacFalda, D.R.E.

BOYNE CITY, CHARLEVOIX CO., ST. MATTHEW, [JC] Rev. Duane A. Wachowiak Jr.
Res.: 1303 Boyne Ave., 49712. Tel: 231-582-7718; Fax: 231-582-7490. Email: parishoffice@jamcc.org.
Catechesis / Religious Program—Patty Furtaw, D.R.E. & Pastoral Assoc. Students 100.

BOYNE FALLS, CHARLEVOIX CO., ST. AUGUSTINE, [CEM] Rev. Duane A. Wachowiak Jr.
Res.: 1303 Boyne Ave., Boyne City, 49712. Tel: 231-582-7718; Fax: 231-582-7490. Email: parishoffice@jamcc.org.
Church: Grove St., 49713. Tel: 231-549-2350.
Catechesis / Religious Program—Patty Furtaw, D.R.E. & Pastoral Assoc. Students 20.

BURT LAKE, CHEBOYGAN CO., ASSUMPTION OF ST. MARY
Res.: P.O. Box 122, Pellston, 49769. Tel: 231-539-8805; Fax: 231-539-8572.

CADILLAC, WEXFORD CO., ST. ANN, [CEM] Revs. Francis J. Murphy; Santiago Hoyumpa; Deacons James Barton, Pastoral Min.; James Siler, Pastoral Min.
Res.: 800 W. 13th St., 49601-9281. Tel: 231-775-2471; Fax: 231-775-0161. Email: ellenhovey@yahoo.com.
Catechesis / Religious Program—Therese Abee, D.R.E.; Geralyn Kohler, D.R.E. Students 62.

CEDAR, LEELANAU CO., HOLY ROSARY, [CEM] Rev. Donald L. Libby.
Res.: 3919 E. Gatzke Rd., 49621. Tel: 231-228-5429; Fax: 231-228-5529.
Church: 6982 S. Schomberg Rd., 49621.
Catechesis / Religious Program—Students 76.

CHARLEVOIX, CHARLEVOIX CO., ST. MARY Rev. Gerard A. Hunko.
Res.: 1003 Bridge St., 49720. Tel: 231-547-6652.
Catechesis / Religious Program—Students 23.

CHEBOYGAN, CHEBOYGAN CO., ST. MARY-ST. CHARLES, [JC] Rev. Paul Megge; Mrs. Patricia Watson, Pastoral Assoc.
Mailing Address: P.O. Box 40, 49721. Tel: 231-627-2105; Fax: 231-627-5362. Email: chebcathcom@nmo.net.
Church: 120 N. D St., 49721.
Catechesis / Religious Program—Students 51.

COPEMISH, MANISTEE CO., ST. RAPHAEL, [CEM] Rev. Lawrence J. Sergott.
P.O. Box 56, 49625.
Res.: P.O. Box 150, Onekama, 49675. Tel: 231-378-2984; Fax: 231-378-4953.
Church: M-115, 49625. Tel: 231-889-4254; Fax: 231-889-3706.
Catechesis / Religious Program—Carlina Breitner, D.R.E. Students 12.

CROSS VILLAGE, EMMET CO., HOLY CROSS, [CEM] Rev. Joseph P. Graff.
Mailing Address & Res.: 150 W. Main, Harbor Springs, 49740.
Church: 6624 N. Lake Shore Dr., 49740. Tel: 231-526-2017; Fax: 231-526-9299.

EAST JORDAN, CHARLEVOIX CO., ST. JOSEPH, [CEM] Rev. James K. Gardiner.
Res.: P.O. Box 379, 49727. Tel: 231-536-2934; Fax: 231-536-2988.
Catechesis / Religious Program—Barbara Kowal, D.R.E. Students 50.

EAST TAWAS, IOSCO CO.
1—HOLY FAMILY Rev. Charles G. Donajkowski.
Res.: P.O. Box 472, 48730. Tel: 989-362-9020.
Church: 516 W. Lincoln, 48730. Tel: 989-362-3162; Fax: 989-362-9077. Email: holyfamily3@hotmail.com.
Catechesis / Religious Program—Pattie Rioux, D.R.E. Students 101.
2—ST. JOSEPH, Merged with Immaculate Heart of Mary, Tawas City to form Holy Family, East Tawas.

ELK RAPIDS, ANTRIM CO., SACRED HEART, [CEM] Rev. Robert J. Zuchowski.
Res.: 143 Charles St., 49629. Tel: 231-264-8087; Fax: 231-264-6350. Email: sacredheart@sacredheartelkrapids.org.
Catechesis / Religious Program—Denise Elsenheimer, D.R.E. Students 84.

ELMIRA, ANTRIM CO., ST. THOMAS AQUINAS, [CEM] Revs. James M. Bearss; Peter O. Eke.
Res.: P.O. Box 128, 49730. Tel: 231-546-3326.
Church: 2567 Buell Rd., 49730.
Catechesis / Religious Program—Students 3.

EMPIRE, LEELANAU CO., ST. PHILIP NERI, [CEM] Rev. Michael S. Janowski.
Res.: P.O. Box 257, 49630. Tel: 231-326-5255; Fax: 231-326-5839. Email: stphilipneri@charter.net.
Church: 11411 La Core Ave., 49630.
Catechesis / Religious Program—Mary Boissoneau, D.R.E. Students 51.

FIFE LAKE, GRAND TRAVERSE CO., ST. ALOYSIUS, [CEM] Rev. Norman Dickson, S.J., Admin.
Res.: 0438 County Rd. 612, Kalkaska, 49646. Tel: 231-258-5021; Fax: 231-258-2842.
Church: 403 E. Merritt St., 49633. Tel: 231-258-2752.
Catechesis / Religious Program—Robert Bowersox, D.R.E. Students 7.

FRANKFORT, BENZIE CO., ST. ANN Rev. John F. Porter, Sacramental Min. (Retired).
Res.: 508 Crystal Ave., P.O. Box 1168, 49635. Tel: 231-352-4421; Fax: 231-352-9940.
Catechesis / Religious Program—

GILLS PIER, LEELANAU CO., ST. WENCESLAUS, [CEM] Rev. Andrew G. Buvala, O.F.M., Sacramental Min.; Martin Korson, Lay Admin.
Church & Res.: 8500 E. Kolarik Rd., Suttons Bay, 49682. Tel: 231-271-3574.

GLENNIE, ALCONA CO., ST. FRANCIS OF ASSISI, Closed. For inquiries for parish records contact the chancery.

GOOD HART, EMMET CO., ST. IGNATIUS, [CEM] Rev. Joseph P. Graff.
Mailing Address & Res.: 150 W. Main St., Harbor Springs, 49740. Tel: 231-526-2017; Fax: 231-526-9299.
Church: 101 Lamkin Rd., Good Heart.

GRAYLING, CRAWFORD CO., ST. MARY Revs. James M. Bearss; Peter O. Eke.
Res.: 707 Spruce St., 49738-1259. Tel: 989-348-7657 (Office); Fax: 989-348-7658.
Catechesis / Religious Program—Students 79.

HALE, IOSCO CO., ST. PIUS X Rev. J. August Franczek.
Res.: P.O. Box 428, 48739. Tel: 989-728-2278; Fax: 989-728-7487.
Church: 3900 M-65, 48739. Email: spxhale@centurytel.net.
Catechesis / Religious Program—Tel: 989-728-2278; Fax: 989-728-7487. Karol Shellenbarger, D.R.E. Students 9.

HANNAH, GRAND TRAVERSE CO., ST. MARY, [CEM] Rev. Michael P. Conner.
Res.: 6955 Hannah Rd., Kingsley, 49649. Tel: 231-263-2430; Fax: 231-263-7489. Email: pstmaryhannah@inbox.com.
Catechesis / Religious Program—2912 W. M-113, Kingsley, 49649. Norm Schichtel, D.R.E. Students 50.

HARBOR SPRINGS, EMMET CO., HOLY CHILDHOOD OF JESUS, [CEM] Rev. Joseph P. Graff.
Res.: 150 W. Main St., 49740. Tel: 231-526-2017; Fax: 231-526-9299. Email: office@holychildhoodchurch.org. Web: www.holychildhoodchurch.org.
Catechesis / Religious Program—Tel: 231-526-9299; Fax: 231-526-7181. Students 92.

HARRIETTA, WEXFORD CO., ST. EDWARD Rev. Francis J. Murphy.
Res.: 800 W. 13th St., Cadillac, 49601-9281. Tel: 231-775-2471; Fax: 231-775-0161.
Church: 207 W. Gaston, 49638.

HARRISVILLE, ALCONA CO., ST. ANNE, [CEM] Rev. William T. Livinus.
Res.: P.O. Box 345, 48740. Tel: 989-724-6713; Fax: 989-724-5210.
Church: 110 State St., 48740. Email: stanne@charter.net.
Catechesis / Religious Program—Students 19.

HERRON, ALPENA CO., ST. ROSE OF LIMA Rev. Gregory P. McCallum; Theresa M. Zbytowski, Office Mgr.
Church: 3439 Herron Rd., 49744. Tel: 989-379-4316; Fax: 989-379-3796. Email: strose@i2k.com.
Catechesis / Religious Program—Dianne Blissland, D.R.E. Students 42.

HIGGINS LAKE, ROSCOMMON CO., ST. HUBERT Revs. Joseph A. Blasko; Bernard L. Tyler, Admin. (Retired).
Res.: P.O. Box 75, 48627. Tel: 989-821-5591; Fax: 989-821-5895. Email: jambert@charter.net.
Church: 7612 W. Higgins Lake Dr., 48627.
Catechesis / Religious Program—

HILLMAN, MONTMORENCY CO., ST. AUGUSTINE, [CEM] Rev. Raymond C. Cotter.
Res.: P.O. Box 216, 49746. Tel: 989-742-4542; Fax: 989-742-8090.
Church: 24140 Veterans Memorial Hwy., 49746. Email: staug.jtgs@src-milp.com.
Catechesis / Religious Program—Debra Banks, D.R.E. Students 30.

HOUGHTON LAKE, ROSCOMMON CO., ST. JAMES Revs. Joseph A. Blasko; Bernard L. Tyler, Admin. (Retired); Anthony J. Cureton.
Res.: P.O. Box 75, Higgins Lake, 48627. Tel: 989-821-5591; Fax: 989-821-5895.
Church: 7878 E. Houghton Lake Dr., 48629. Tel: 989-422-3925.

INDIAN RIVER, CHEBOYGAN CO., CROSS IN THE WOODS CATHOLIC SHRINE, [CEM] Revs. Michael Fowler, O.F.M.; Harry Speckman, O.F.M.; Albert Langheim, O.F.M.; Thomas Vos, O.F.M.; Miro Wiese, O.F.M.
Res.: 7078 M-68, 49749. Tel: 231-238-8973; Fax: 231-238-7012.

Catechesis/Religious Program— 49749. Tel: 231-238-8542; Fax: 231-238-7012. Shirley Ronk, D.R.E. Students 80.

KALKASKA, KALKASKA CO., ST. MARY OF THE WOODS, [CEM] Rev. Norman Dickson, S.J., Admin.
Res.: 0438 County Rd. 612, 49646. Tel: 231-258-5021; Fax: 231-258-2842.
Catechesis/Religious Program—Robert Bowersox, D.R.E. Students 27.

KLACKING CREEK, HOLY FAMILY, [CEM] Rev. T. Patrick Maher.
Res.: 402 W. Peters Rd., West Branch, 48661. Tel: 989-345-3422.
Catechesis/Religious Program—Glen Painter, D.R.E. Students 17.

LAKE CITY, MISSAUKEE CO., ST. STEPHEN Revs. Francis J. Murphy; Santiago Hoyumpa.
Res.: P.O. Box 379, 49651. Tel: 231-839-2121; Fax: 231-839-3755.
Church: 506 Union St., 49651.
Catechesis/Religious Program—Patricia Crane, Dir. Adult Ed.; Geralyn Kohler, D.R.E. Students 35.

LAKE LEELANAU, LEELANAU CO., ST. MARY, [CEM] Rev. Michael S. Janowski.
Mailing Address: P.O. Box 340, 49653. Tel: 231-256-9676; Fax: 231-256-7812.
Res.: 307 S. St. Mary St., 49653.
Church: 403 S. St. Mary St., 49653.
Catechesis/Religious Program—Michael Collins, D.R.E. Students 25.

LARKS LAKE, EMMET CO., ST. NICHOLAS, [CEM] Rev. Joseph P. Graff.
Mailing Address: P.O. Box 120, Cross Village, 49723.
Res.: 150 W. Main St., Harbor Springs, 49740. Tel: 231-526-9299.
Catechesis/Religious Program—Students 16.

LEWISTON, MONTMORENCY CO., ST. FRANCIS OF ASSISI, [CEM] Rev. Raymond C. Cotter.
Res.: P.O. Box 182, 49756. Tel: 989-786-2235; Fax: 989-786-7685.
Church: 4086 Salling Ave., 49756. Email: stfrancisassisi@i2k.net.
Catechesis/Religious Program—Students 15.

MACKINAW CITY, EMMET CO., ST. ANTHONY OF PADUA, [CEM] Sr. Chris Herald, O.P., Pastoral Admin.
Res.: P.O. Box 460, 49701. Tel: 231-436-5561; 231-436-5601; Fax: 231-436-5699.
Church: 600 W. Central Ave., 49701.
Catechesis/Religious Program—Students 22.

MANCELONA, ANTRIM CO., ST. ANTHONY OF PADUA, [CEM] Rev. R. Dale Magoon.
Mailing Address: P.O. Box 677, 49659-0677.
Church: 209 Jefferson St., 49659. Tel: 231-587-8401; Fax: 231-587-5643. Email: st.anthony@torchlake.com.

MANISTEE, MANISTEE CO.
1—GUARDIAN ANGELS, [JC] Revs. John E. McCracken; Joseph Muszkiewicz.
Res.: 254 Sixth St., 49660. Tel: 231-723-2619.
Convent—501 Michael St., 49660. Tel: 231-723-6332.
Catechesis/Religious Program— Combined for all three Manistee parishes. Students 175.
2—ST. JOSEPH, [JC] Revs. John E. McCracken; Joseph Muszkiewicz.
Res.: 254 Sixth St., 49660. Tel: 231-723-2619; Fax: 231-723-6827.
Catechesis/Religious Program—Tel: 231-723-3732. Liz Hainstock, D.R.E. Combined for all three Manistee parishes. Students 175.
3—ST. MARY OF MT. CARMEL SHRINE, [JC] Revs. John E. McCracken; Joseph Muszkiewicz.
Res.: 254 Sixth St., 49660. Tel: 231-723-2619; Fax: 231-723-2157.
Catechesis/Religious Program—Liz Hainstock, D.R.E. Combined for all three Manistee parishes. Students 175.

MANTON, WEXFORD CO., ST. THERESA Revs. Francis J. Murphy; Santiago Hoyumpa.
Res.: P.O. Box 379, Lake City, 49651. Tel: 231-839-2121.
Church: 9475 14th & 1/4 Rd., 49663.

MAPLE CITY, LEELANAU CO., ST. RITA-ST. JOSEPH Rev. Donald L. Libby.
Mailing Address: P.O. Box 75, 49664-0075. Tel: 231-228-5823; Fax: 231-228-5823.
Church: 8707 Hill St., 49664. Tel: 231-228-5823.
Catechesis/Religious Program—

MAPLETON, GRAND TRAVERSE CO., ST. JOSEPH, [CEM] Rev. Edwin A. Thome, Sacramental Min. (Retired).
Mailing Address: 13400 Center Rd., Traverse City, 49686. Tel: 231-223-7211. Email: stjoeofc@pentel.net.
Catechesis/Religious Program—Kerry Marsh, D.R.E. Students 165.

MCBAIN, MISSAUKEE CO., ST. RITA, Closed. For inquiries for parish records contact the chancery.

METZ, PRESQUE ISLE CO., ST. DOMINIC, [CEM] Sr. Rita Epple, R.S.M., Pastoral Admin.
Res.: 9269 County Rd. 441, Posen, 49776. Tel: 989-766-2694; Fax: 989-766-8654.
Catechesis/Religious Program—Carolyn Haske, D.R.E. Students 22.

MIKADO, ALOCONA CO., ST. RAPHAEL, [CEM] Rev. William T. Livinus, Temporary Admin.
Res.: P.O. Box 345, Harrisville, 48740. Tel: 989-724-6713; Fax: 989-724-5210.
Church: 2531 E. Mikado Rd., 48745. Tel: 989-736-6071. Email: stanne@charter.net.
Catechesis/Religious Program—Ruth Johnson, D.R.E. Students 17.

MIO, OSCODA CO., ST. MARY Rev. Raymond C. Cotter.
Res.: P.O. Box 189, 48647. Tel: 989-826-5509; Fax: 989-826-1333. Email: stmarymio@m33access.com.
Church: 100 Deyarmond St., 48647.
Ministry Office—
Catechesis/Religious Program—Students 21.

NORTHPORT, LEELANAU CO., ST. GERTRUDE Rev. James Doherty, Admin.
Res.: P.O. Box 9, Suttons Bay, 49682. Tel: 231-271-3744; Fax: 231-271-3733.
Church: 701 Warren, 49670. Tel: 231-386-5221.
Catechesis/Religious Program—315 Broadway, Suttons Bay, 49682. Mary Mills, D.R.E.

ONAWAY, PRESQUE ISLE CO., ST. PAUL, [CEM] Rev. Arthur F. Duchnowicz, Admin.
Res.: 585 S. Third St., Rogers City, 49779. Tel: 989-734-2753.
Church & Office: 3856 Oak St., P.O. Box 130, 49765. Tel: 989-733-4043; Fax: 989-733-6053.
Catechesis/Religious Program—

ONEKAMA, MANISTEE CO., ST. JOSEPH, [CEM] Rev. Lawrence J. Sergott.
Res.: P.O. Box 150, 49675. Tel: 231-889-4254; Fax: 231-889-3706.
Church: 8380 Fifth St., 49675. Email: stjosephch3706@esagelink.com.
Catechesis/Religious Program—Students 20.

OSCODA, IOSCO CO., SACRED HEART, [CEM] Rev. Charles G. Donajkowski; Sr. Linda Schoenborn, O.P., Pastoral Assoc.
Res.: 5300 N. U.S.-23, 48750. Tel: 989-739-9511; Fax: 989-739-3010. Email: sacredheartoscoda@charterinternet.com.
Catechesis/Religious Program—Tel: 989-739-9062. Mrs. Jackie Welles, D.R.E. Students 30.

OSSINEKE, ALPENA CO., ST. CATHERINE, [CEM] Rev. Robert H. Bissot.
Res.: 2188 W. Nicholson Hill Rd., 49766-9736. Tel: 989-471-2556; Fax: 989-471-2697.
Catechesis/Religious Program—Tel: 989-471-5121. Cathy MacFalda, D.R.E. Students 59.

PELLSTON, EMMET CO., ST. CLEMENT, [CEM] Revs. Paul Megge; Robbie Deka.
Res.: 118 N. D St., Cheboygan, 49721. Tel: 231-627-5795.
Church: 202 Maple, 49769. Tel: 231-539-8805; Fax: 231-539-8572.
Catechesis/Religious Program—Larry Cassidy, Dir. Faith Formation. Students 20.

PESHABESTOWN, LEELANAU CO., BLESSED KATERI TEKAKWITHA Rev. Andrew G. Buvala, O.F.M.
Res.: P.O. Box 369, Suttons Bay, 49682. Tel: 231-271-6651. Email: kateri369@aol.com.

PETOSKEY, EMMET CO., ST. FRANCIS XAVIER, [CEM] Rev. Dennis R. Stilwell.
Res.: 513 Howard St., 49770. Tel: 231-347-4133; Fax: 231-347-4134. Email: sfxpetoskey@hotmail.com. Web: www.petoskeystfrancis.org.
School—(Grades K-8), 414 Michigan St., 49770. Tel: 231-347-3651; Fax: 231-348-6475. Phyllis Daily, Prin. Students 215.
Catechesis/Religious Program—Tel: 231-347-2681. Students 98.

POSEN, PRESQUE ISLE CO., ST. CASIMIR, [CEM] Revs. Arthur F. Duchnowicz; Clarence D. Smolinski, Sacramental Min. (Retired).
Res.: 10075 M-65 N., P.O. Box 217, 49776. Tel: 989-766-2660.
Church: 10075 M-65 N., 49776-0217. Web: stcasimirposen.catholicweb.com.
Catechesis/Religious Program—Joan Chappa, D.R.E. Students 95.

PRAGA, ANTRIM CO., ST. JOHN NEPOMUCENE, [CEM] Rev. Duane A. Wachowiak Jr.
Res.: 1303 Boyne Ave., Boyne City, 49712. Tel: 231-582-7718; Fax: 231-582-7490.
Catechesis/Religious Program—Students 5.

PRUDENVILLE, ROSCOMMON CO., OUR LADY OF THE LAKE, Unassigned. Revs. Joseph A. Blasko; Anthony J. Cureton.
Res.: 1037 W. Houghton Lake Dr., P.O. Box 800, 48651. Tel: 989-366-5533; Fax: 989-366-5988. Email: olotlparish@gmail.com.
Catechesis/Religious Program—Students 30.

RIGGSVILLE, CHEBOYGAN CO., SACRED HEART Revs. Paul Megge; Robbie Deka.
Mailing Address: P.O. Box 122, Pellston, 49769.
Church: 4989 Polish Line Rd., Cheboygan, 49721. Tel: 231-539-8805 (Parish); Fax: 231-539-8572.
Catechesis/Religious Program—Kim Socolovitch, D.R.E. Students 56.

ROGERS CITY, PRESQUE ISLE CO., ST. IGNATIUS, [CEM] Rev. Arthur F. Duchnowicz.
Business Office & Mailing Address: 585 S. Third St., 49779. Tel: 989-734-2753; Fax: 989-734-7671. Email: stignatius@i2k.net.
Catechesis/Religious Program—Tel: 989-734-3443. Students 119.

ROSCOMMON, ROSCOMMON CO., ST. MICHAEL Rev. Joseph A. Blasko.
Res.: 104 N. 6th St., P.O. Box 248, 48653. Tel: 989-275-5212; Fax: 989-275-9020.
Catechesis/Religious Program—Tel: 989-275-5212. Tim Harris, D.R.E. Students 95.

ST. HELEN, ROSCOMMON CO., ST. HELEN Sr. Barbara Matievich, O.P., Parish Life Coord.
Mailing Address: P.O. Box 318, Saint Helen, 48656.
Res.: 737 N. St. Helen Rd., Saint Helen, 48656. Tel: 989-389-4959; Fax: 989-389-4959. Email: st.helen@sbcglobal.net.
Catechesis/Religious Program—

SKIDWAY LAKE, OGEMAW CO., ST. STEPHEN OF HUNGARY Rev. T. Patrick Maher.
Res.: 2811 E. Greenwood Rd., Prescott, 48756. Tel: 989-873-3340; Fax: 989-873-5209. Email: ststephenofhungary@verizon.net.
Catechesis/Religious Program—Wayne Winter, D.R.E. Students 10.

SUTTONS BAY, LEELANAU CO., ST. MICHAEL THE ARCHANGEL, [CEM] Rev. James Doherty.
Res.: 315 Broadway, P.O. Box 9, 49682. Tel: 231-271-3744.
Church: 104 Elm St., 49682.
Catechesis/Religious Program—Mary Mills, D.R.E. Students 43.

TAWAS CITY, IOSCO CO., IMMACULATE HEART OF MARY, Merged with St. Joseph, East Tawas to form Holy Family, East Tawas.

TRAVERSE CITY, GRAND TRAVERSE CO.
1—ST. FRANCIS OF ASSISI Rev. Kenneth R. Stachnik.
Res.: 1025 S. Union St., 49684. Tel: 231-947-4620; Fax: 231-947-4693. Email: ann@sfparish.org. Web: www.sfparish.org.
Catechesis/Religious Program—Beth Hicks, D.R.E. Students 943.
2—IMMACULATE CONCEPTION Revs. Anthony M. Citro; Ruben Munoz.
Res.: 720 W. Second, 49684. Tel: 231-946-4211; Fax: 231-946-0567. Email: imc@gbctc.net.
Catechesis/Religious Program—Tel: 231-946-2782. Fred Robb, D.R.E. Students 130.
3—ST. PATRICK Rev. Robert W. Nalley.
Res.: 630 W. Silver Lake Rd. S., 49684-8526. Tel: 231-943-4633; Fax: 231-943-8886. Email: stpattc@chartermi.net. Web: www.stpatricktc.org.
Catechesis/Religious Program—Students 116.

VANDERBILT, OTSEGO CO., HOLY REDEEMER Revs. James M. Bearss; Peter O. Eke.
Res. & Mailing: 606 N. Ohio Ave., 49735-1999. Tel: 989-732-5448.
Church: 8075 Lincoln St., 49795.
Catechesis/Religious Program—Students 5.

WEST BRANCH, OGEMAW CO., ST. JOSEPH, [CEM] Rev. T. Patrick Maher.
Mailing Address: 961 W. Houghton Ave., 48661. Tel: 989-345-0064; Fax: 989-345-8757. Email: stjoseph@m33access.com. Web: www.stjosephwestbranch.org.
Res.: 907 W. Houghton Ave., 48661.
School—(Grades K-8), 935 W. Houghton Ave., 48661. Tel: 989-345-0220; Fax: 989-345-3030. Lorrene Spaulding, Prin. Students 151.
Catechesis/Religious Program—Tel: 989-345-0670. Students 17.

WHITTEMORE, IOSCO CO., ST. JAMES, [CEM] Rev. J. August Franczek.
Res.: P.O. Box 206, 48770. Tel: 989-756-2591; Fax: 989-756-3255.
Church: 202 E. Sherman, 48770.

Special Assignment:
Revs.—
Gallagher, Daniel B., Secretariat of State Office, Rome
Greene, John C.
Zielinski, Chad W., Military Service

Retired:
Revs.—
Bereda, Stanislaw J., 1180 Barepoint Rd., Alpena, 49707.
Boks, Lawrence E., 5853 Nancy Ct., Tawas City, 48763.
Brucksch, James L., 10208 Tennesse St., Oscoda, 48750.
Dominiak, Thomas M., 7150 Tuscarora Cir., Indian River, 49749.
Fox, Gabriel, 5020 Park Lake Dr., Pinellas Park, FL 33782.
Gietzen, Albin J., P.O. Box 311, Buckley, 49620.

Hannon, Richard T., 61 Augur Rd. Ext., Northford, CT 06472.
Hayden, James P., 13071 Beechwood Dr., Charlevoix, 49720.
Kelleher, Lawrence A., Senior Clergy Village, 14469-A Levan Rd., Livonia, 48154-5094.
Kosterman, Richard A., P.O. Box 613, Antigo, WI 54409.
Ladd, John O., 3069 E. Snover Rd., Mayville, 48744.
Marek, Walter, P.O. Box 203, Whitehall, 49461.
Mulka, Arthur C., 2388 Emmett, Alpena, 49707.
Mulka, Raymond C., 300 Washington, Alpena, 49707.
Partridge, Francis C., P.O. Box 84, Conway, 49722.
Reitz, Joseph A., 52 Marble Rd., Lowell, 49331.
Seifferly, Richard R., P.O. Box 422, West Branch, 48661-0422.
Sitar, Richard T., 12039 Leer Rd., Posen, 49776.
Smolinski, Clarence D., 14692 Lakeside Dr., Presque Isle, 49777.
Suchocki, James A., 7525 N.W. Second Ave., Miami, FL 33150.
Tamulis, John J., 1189 S. 35 Mile Rd., Cadillac, 49601.
Thome, Edwin A., 6844 Deepwater Point Rd., Acme, 49610.

Permanent Deacons:
Ashmore, John
Barton, James, St. Ann, Cadillac
Bousamra, Thomas, (Retired)
Duggan, Dennis, St. Francis, Petoskey
Falicki, John, Christ the King, Acme
Fifer, Paul, St. Francis Xavier, Petoskey
Friend, Harry, St. Philip, Empire
Goetz, Robert, (Unassigned)
Goodhue, Harold
Hoenscheid, Rene, St. Patrick, Traverse City
Krupka, James, St. Joseph of Mapleton, Traverse City
LoVetere, Arthur, Jesus the Good Shepherd, Atlanta
Lyberg, Matthew, Christ the King, Acme
Moeggenberg, John, (Retired), (Outside of Diocese)
Nelson, Joseph B., (Retired)
Painter, Glen, Holy Family, Klacking Creek
Riley, Charles, St. Francis of Assisi, Traverse City
Trapp, Richard, (Retired)
Wallace, John, (Retired)
Wendell, Max, (Unassigned)
Wigton, Douglas, Holy Rosary, Cedar

INSTITUTIONS LOCATED IN THE DIOCESE

[A] INTERPAROCHIAL SCHOOLS

MANISTEE. *Manistee Catholic Central Schools*, (Grades PreK-12), 1200 U.S. 31 S., 49660. Tel: 231-723-2529; Fax: 231-723-0669. Web: www.manisteecatholiccentral.org. Jan Bigalke, Prin.; Ed Kolanowski, Dean of Students. Lay Teachers 15; Students 258.

TRAVERSE CITY. *St. Elizabeth Ann Seton Middle School*, (Grades 6-8), 1601 Three Mile Rd. N., 49686. Tel: 231-932-4810; Fax: 231-932-4814. Web: www.gtacs.org. Lori Phillips, Prin.; Donna Grayson, Librarian. Lay Teachers 9; Students 216.

St. Francis High School, 123 E. 11th St., 49684. Tel: 231-946-8038; Fax: 231-946-1878. Email: echitt@gtacs.org. Web: www.gtacs.org. Erick Chittle, Prin.; Carol Niemi, Librarian. Lay Teachers 25; Students 299.

Grand Traverse Area Catholic Schools, (Grades PreK-12), 123 E. 11th St., 49684. Tel: 231-946-8100; Fax: 231-946-1878. Web: www.gtacs.org. Michael R. Buell, Supt.; Erick Chittle, Prin.; Carol Niemi, Librarian. Lay Teachers 62; Students 995.

Holy Angels Elementary, (Grades PreK-2), 130 E. 10th, 49684. Tel: 231-946-5961; Fax: 231-946-1878. Web: www.gtacs.org. Janet M. Troppman, Prin.; Margaret Wilson, Librarian; Donna Grayson, Librarian. Lay Teachers 13; Students 236.

Immaculate Conception Elementary School, (Grades 3-5), 218 Vine St., 49684. Tel: 231-947-1252; Fax: 231-947-2508. Web: www.gtacs.org. Matt Bauman, Prin.; Margaret Wilson, Librarian. Lay Teachers 12; Students 241.

[B] PAROCHIAL SCHOOLS

GAYLORD. *St. Mary Cathedral School*, (Grades PreK-12), 321 N. Otsego Ave., 49735. Tel: 989-732-5801; Fax: 989-732-2085. Cynthia Pineda, Prin. Lay Teachers 25; Students 322.

ALPENA. *All Saints Catholic School*, (Grades PreK-6), (Consolidation of St. Anne Elementary, Alpena and St. Mary Elementary, Alpena), 500 N. Second Ave., 49707. Tel: 989-354-4911; Fax: 989-354-3752. Email: allsaints@speednetllc.com. Web: alpenaallsaints.org. Mary Lightner, Prin.; Eileen Clase, Librarian. Lay Teachers 6; Students 60; PreK Students 18.

CADILLAC. *St. Ann Elementary*, (Grades PreK-7), 800 W. 13th, 49601. Tel: 231-775-1301; Fax: 231-775-5433. Email: saintannschool@yahoo.com. Craig King, Prin. Lay Teachers 9; Students 170; PreK Students 42.

CHARLEVOIX. *St. Mary Elementary*, (Grades PreK-6), 1005 Bridge St., 49720. Tel: 231-547-9441; Fax: 231-547-6658. Email: stmaryschool@chartermi.net. Web: www.stmaryschoolcharlevoix.com. Keisha Veryser, Prin.; Monica Mailloux, Librarian. Lay Teachers 7; Students 81; PreK Students 17.

CHEBOYGAN. *Bishop Baraga Catholic School*, (Grades PreK-6), 623 W. Lincoln Ave., 49721. Tel: 231-627-5608; Fax: 231-627-6048. Email: principal@nmo.net. Web: www.bishopbaraga.com. Kitty LaBlance, Prin.; Maryann Schoch, Librarian. Lay Teachers 8; Students 152.

EAST TAWAS. *Holy Family Elementary School*, (Grades K-6), 411 N. Wilkinson, 48730. Tel: 989-362-5651; Fax: 989-362-6916. Email: howel@charterinternet.com. Linda Howe, Prin. Lay Teachers 8; Students 77.

KINGSLEY. *St. Mary's Hannah School*, (Grades PreK-6), 2912 M-113, 49649. Tel: 231-263-5288; Fax: 231-263-5288. Email: smh.school@inbox.com. Lisa Medina, Prin. Lay Teachers 4; Students 69.

LAKE LEELANAU. *St. Mary School*, (Grades PreK-12), 303 S. St. Mary St., 49653. Tel: 231-256-9636; Fax: 231-256-7239. Web: www.stmarysll.org. P.O. Box 340, 49653. Mark Gaubatz, Prin.; Donna Allington, Librarian. Lay Teachers 19; Students 205; PreK Students 18.

PETOSKEY. *St. Francis Xavier*, (Grades K-8), 414 Michigan, 49770. Tel: 231-347-3651; Fax: 231-348-6475. Web: www.petoskeystfrancis.com. Phyllis Daily, Prin.; Mary Daniels, Librarian. Lay Teachers 16; Students 186.

PRUDENVILLE. *Our Lady of the Lake*, (Grades PreK-8), 1039 W. Houghton Lake Dr., 48651. Tel: 989-366-5592; Fax: 989-366-1348. Email: olotlschool@gmail.com. Michalina Wargo, Prin.; April Silva, Librarian. Lay Teachers 5; Students 54; PreK Students 39.

ROGERS CITY. *St. Ignatius*, (Grades 1-7), 545 S. Third, 49779. Tel: 989-734-3443; Fax: 989-734-3443. Web: home.catholicweb.com/stignatiasparishschool. Amy Rabeau, Prin.; Donna Dubbs, Librarian. Sisters 1; Lay Teachers 6; Students 92.

WEST BRANCH. *St. Joseph*, (Grades K-8), 935 W. Houghton Ave., 48661. Tel: 989-345-0220; Fax: 989-345-3030. Web: www.stjosephwestbranch.org. Lorrene Spaulding, Prin. Lay Teachers 9; Students 151.

[C] GENERAL HOSPITALS

CADILLAC. *Mercy Hospital* Mercy Health Services North, Ministry Organization of Trinity Health, Novi, MI, 400 Hobart St., 49601. Tel: 231-876-7200; Fax: 231-876-7439. Email: mercycadillac@trinity-health.org. Web: www.mercycadillac.com. Mr. John L. MacLeod, CEO. Bed Capacity 97; Total Staff 594; Patients Assisted Annually 75,000.

GRAYLING. *Mercy Hospital*, 1100 E. Michigan Ave., 49738. Tel: 989-348-5461; Fax: 989-348-0477. Email: bwoods@trinity-health.org. Stephanie J. Riemer-Matuzak, CEO. Member Organization of Trinity Health. Acute Care 90; Continued Care Nursing Unit 40; Patients Assisted Annually 100,000.

TAWAS CITY. *St. Joseph Health System*, 200 Hemlock, P.O. Box 659, 48764-0659. Tel: 989-362-3411; 989-362-4611; Fax: 989-362-7277. Email: csmedley@sjhsys.org. Web: www.sjhsys.org. Mr. Patrick J. Murtha, Pres. & CEO; Michael Sullivan, Chap. & Mgr. Spiritual Care. Associated with Ascension Health, St. Louis, MO. Congregation of St. Joseph (Nazareth, MI) 2; Bed Capacity 49; Total Staff 489; Patients Assisted Annually 200,000.

[D] CONVENTS AND RESIDENCES FOR SISTERS

CONWAY. *Sacramentine Monastery of Perpetual Adoration*, P.O. Box 86, 49722. Tel: 231-347-0447. Sr. Mary Rosalie, O.S.S., Prioress. Sacamentine Sisters 2.

TRAVERSE CITY. *Infant Jesus of Prague Monastery*, 3501 Silver Lake Rd., 49684-8949. Tel: 231-946-4960; Fax: 231-947-7729. Web: carmelitenunsstjoseph.org. Sr. Mary of Jesus Markey, O.C.D. Carmelite Nuns 4; In Formation 2.

[E] CHILD CARE FACILITIES

ALPENA. *Huron House/Holy Cross Children's Services*, 4761 U.S. 23 N., 49707. Tel: 989-356-3573; Fax: 989-356-4910. *Holy Cross Children's Services*, 8759 Clinton-Macon Rd., Clinton, 49236. Bro. Francis Boylan, C.S.C., Pres. Residential and community-based treatment programs for troubled youth and families, with facilities located throughout the state of Michigan. Boys 30; Total Staff 17.

Kenquest House/Holy Cross Children's Services, 3951 Jones Lake Rd., P.O. Box 683, Grayling, 49738. Tel: 989-348-5922; Fax: 989-348-6583.

ONAWAY. *Russell House/Holy Cross Children's Services*, P.O. Box 599, 49765. Tel: 989-733-5201; Fax: 989-733-8678. Boys 15; Total Staff 17.

TRAVERSE CITY. *Holy Cross Children's Services*, 207 W. Grandview Pkwy., Ste. 200, 49684. Tel: 231-922-9664; 800-235-9664; Fax: 231-922-9675. Web: www.hccsnet.org. Bro. Francis Boylan, C.S.C., Pres.; Sharon Berkobien, Regl. Dir.; Loren Brown, Exec. Dir. Youths 250.

[F] RETREAT CENTERS AND CAMPS

GAYLORD. *Camp Sancta Maria*, P.O. Box 338, 49734. Tel: 231-546-3878; Fax: 866-875-1933. Email: office@campsanctamaria.org. Web: www.campsanctamaria.org. Michael Hickey, Exec. Dir.; Andrew Dawson, Contact Person. Total Staff 50; Campers 555.

CONWAY. *Augustine Center*, P.O. Box 84, 49722-0084. Tel: 231-347-3657; Fax: 231-347-9502. Email: augustinecenter@gmail.com. Sr. Barbara Hubeny, O.P., Dir.

[G] CATHOLIC SOCIAL SERVICE AGENCIES

GAYLORD. *Catholic Human Services*, 611 W. North St., 49735. Tel: 989-732-5147; Fax: 989-705-3589. Email: chstraverse@catholichumanservices.org. Web: www.catholichumanservices.org. Mr. David Martin, Pres. & CEO.

Area Offices:

154 S. Ripley Blvd., Alpena, 49707. Tel: 989-356-6385; Fax: 989-356-4909. Email: chsalpena@catholichumanservices.org. Web: www-.catholichumanservices.org. Joseph Garant, Admin.

421 S. Mitchell, Cadillac, 49601. Tel: 231-775-6581; Fax: 231-775-5421. Email: chscadillac@catholichumanservices.org. Web: www-.catholichumanservices.org. Mr. David Martin, Admin.

2090 W. M-32, 49735. Tel: 989-732-6761; Fax: 989-732-6763. Email: chsgaylord@catholichumanservices.org. Web: www-.catholichumanservices.org. Nancy Morgridge, Admin.

1000 Hastings St., Traverse City, 49686. Tel: 231-947-8110; Fax: 231-947-3522. Email: chstraverse@catholichumanservices.org. Web: www.catholichumanservices.org. Mr. David Martin, Admin.

[H] MISCELLANEOUS

GAYLORD. *Northern Michigan Catholic Foundation, Inc.*, 611 W. North St., 49735. Tel: 989-732-5147; Fax: 989-705-3589. Email: dparish@dioceseofgaylord.org. Joel Myler, Pres.; Brian Bartosh, Vice Pres.; Jean Stevenson, Sec.; Philip Potvin, Treas.; Most Rev. Bernard A. Hebda, J.C.L., J.D.

ALPENA. *Madonna House Apostolate*, 309 Lockwood, 49707-2543. Tel: 989-354-4073. Rosemary Horan, Dir.

HARBOR SPRINGS. *Christ Child Society of Northern Michigan, Inc.*, P.O. Box 132, 49740-0132. Tel: 231-526-7271. Laura Kors, Pres.

INDIAN RIVER. **Baraga Broadcasting, Inc.*, 7119 W. M-68, P.O. Box 1109, 49749. Tel: 231-238-0811; Fax: 231-238-0803.

JOHANNESBURG. *Stella Maris Hermitage*, 19920 Black River Rd., 49751-9645. Tel: 989-732-9580. Email: rwkropf@stellamar.net. Web: www.stellamar.net. Rev. Richard Kropf.

TAWAS CITY. *House of the Holy Shroud*, 2922 W. M-55, 48763. Tel: 989-305-6236. Bro. Michael W. Whitman, Dir.

WEST BRANCH. *St. Vincent de Paul Conference of West Branch Division*, P.O. Box 53, 48661. Tel: 989-345-0779.

RELIGIOUS INSTITUTES OF MEN REPRESENTED IN THE DIOCESE

For further details refer to the corresponding bracketed number in the Religious Institutes of Men or Women section.

[0520]—*Franciscan Friars* (Assumption, Sacred Heart Provs.)—O.F.M.

RELIGIOUS INSTITUTES OF WOMEN REPRESENTED IN THE DIOCESE

[3832]—*Congregation of the Sisters of St. Joseph*—C.S.J.

[0420]—*Discalced Carmelite Nuns*—O.C.D.

[1070]—*Dominican Sisters*—O.P.

[2580]—*Institute of the Sisters of Mercy of the Americas*—R.S.M.

[3490]—*Sacramentine Nuns*—O.S.S.

[3560]—*Servants of Jesus*—S.J.

[3590]—*Servants of Mary*—O.S.M.

[3830]—*Sisters of St. Joseph*—S.S.J.

NECROLOGY

† Mausolf, James H., (Retired)—Died Aug. 6, 2009

† Mikulski, Isidore J., (Retired)—Died Oct. 6, 2009

† Wiekierak, Joseph F., (Retired)—Died Dec. 3, 2008

An asterisk (*) denotes an organization that has established tax-exempt status directly with the IRS and is not covered by the USCCB Group Ruling.

Diocese of Grand Island

(Dioecesis Insulae Grandis)

Most Reverend

WILLIAM J. DENDINGER, D.D., M.A.

Bishop of Grand Island; ordained May 29, 1965; appointed Bishop of Grand Island October 14, 2004; ordained December 13, 2004. *Mailing Address: P.O. Box 1531, Grand Island, NE 68802.* Tel: 308-382-6565; Fax: 308-382-6569.

Square Miles 40,000.

Erected at Kearney, March 8, 1912; See Transferred to Grand Island, April 11, 1917.

Comprises the Counties of Arthur, Banner, Blaine, Box Butte, Brown, Buffalo, Cherry, Cheyenne, Custer, Dawes, Deuel, Garden, Garfield, Grant, Greeley, Hooker, Howard Keyapaha, Kimball, Logan, Loup, McPherson, Morrill, Rock, Scotts Bluff, Sheridan, Sherman, Wheeler, Sioux, Thomas, Valley, and those portions of Dawson, Hall, Lincoln and Keith lying north of the South Platte River in the State of Nebraska.

For legal titles of parishes and diocesan institutions, consult the Chancery Office.

Chancery Office: 2708 Old Fair Rd., P.O. Box 996, Grand Island, NE 68802. Tel: 308-382-6565; Fax: 308-382-6569.

STATISTICAL OVERVIEW

Personnel	
Bishop	1
Priests: Diocesan Active in Diocese	35
Priests: Diocesan Active Outside Diocese	1
Priests: Retired, Sick or Absent	32
Number of Diocesan Priests	68
Total Priests in Diocese	68
Extern Priests in Diocese	4
Ordinations:	
Diocesan Priests	3
Transitional Deacons	1
Permanent Deacons in Diocese	3
Total Sisters	61
Parishes	
Parishes	36
With Resident Pastor:	
Resident Diocesan Priests	31
Resident Religious Priests	4
Without Resident Pastor:	
Administered by Priests	1
Completely Vacant	8
Missions	33
Closed Parishes	1
Welfare	
Health Care Centers	2
Total Assisted	178,000
Homes for the Aged	1
Total Assisted	75
Educational	
Diocesan Students in Other Seminaries	8
Total Seminarians	8
High Schools, Diocesan and Parish	4
Total Students	495
Elementary Schools, Diocesan and Parish	6
Total Students	932
Catechesis/Religious Education:	
High School Students	2,177
Elementary Students	3,961
Total Students under Catholic Instruction	7,573
Teachers in the Diocese:	
Sisters	2
Lay Teachers	106
Vital Statistics	
Receptions into the Church:	
Infant Baptism Totals	916
Minor Baptism Totals	76
Adult Baptism Totals	61
Received into Full Communion	161
First Communions	869
Confirmations	670
Marriages:	
Catholic	159
Interfaith	133
Total Marriages	292
Deaths	478
Total Catholic Population	54,644
Total Population	301,328

Former Bishops—Most Revs. JAMES ALBERT DUFFY, D.D., cons. April 16, 1913; resigned See, May 7, 1931; appt. Titular Bishop of Silando; died Feb. 12, 1968; STANISLAUS V. BONA, D.D., appt. Bishop of Grand Island, Dec. 18, 1931; cons. Feb. 25, 1932; appt. Coadjutor Bishop of Green Bay and Titular Bishop of Mela, Dec. 2, 1944; succeeded to See, March 3, 1945; died Dec. 1, 1967; EDWARD J. HUNKELER, D.D., ord. June 14, 1919; appt. March 10, 1945; cons. May 1, 1945; transferred to Kansas City in Kansas, March 31, 1951; died Oct. 1, 1970; JOHN L. PASCHANG, D.D., Ph.D., J.C.D., ord. June 12, 1921; appt. July 28, 1951; cons. Oct. 9, 1951; resigned July 25, 1972; died March 21, 1999; JOHN J. SULLIVAN, D.D., ord. Sept. 23, 1944; appt. July 25, 1972; cons. Sept. 19, 1972; transferred to Kansas City-St. Joseph in Missouri, Aug. 17, 1977; died Feb. 11, 2001; LAWRENCE J. MCNAMARA, D.D., S.T.L., ord. May 30, 1953; appt. Jan. 10, 1978; cons. March 28, 1978; retired Oct. 14, 2004; died Dec. 17, 2004.

Vicar General—Very Rev. CHARLES L. TORPEY, S.T.L., J.C.L., St. Leo, 2410 S. Blaine, Grand Island, 68801. Tel: 308-382-4753.

Chancery Office—2708 Old Fair Rd., P.O. Box 996, Grand Island, 68802. Tel: 308-382-6565; Fax: 308-382-6569. Office Hours: 9-5.

Chancellor—KATHLEEN M. HAHN, J.C.L.

Vice Chancellor—Sr. MARGARET A. PROSKOVEC, N.D.

Diocesan Tribunal—Mailing Address: P.O. Box 5405, Grand Island, 68802. Tel: 308-382-6364.

Vicar-Judicial—Rev. MICHAEL F. MCDERMOTT, J.C.L.

Adjutant Vicars-Judicial—Rev. RICHARD L. PIONTKOWSKI JR., S.T.L., J.C.L.; Very Rev. CHARLES L. TORPEY, S.T.L., J.C.L.

Defender of the Bond—Rev. THOMAS A. RYAN.

Promoter Justitiae—Very Rev. CHARLES L. TORPEY, S.T.L., J.C.L.

Judges—Very Rev. CHARLES L. TORPEY, S.T.L., J.C.L.; Revs. RICHARD L. PIONTKOWSKI JR., S.T.L., J.C.L.; MICHAEL F. MCDERMOTT, J.C.L.

Procurator—Rev. JAMES M. HUNT.

Advocates—Rev. JAMES M. HUNT; CONNIE RUHLMAN; KATHLEEN M. HAHN, J.C.L.

Associate Director-Notary—MARIE RYAN.

Diocesan Consultors—Revs. DONALD A. BUHRMAN; LOUIS A. NOLLETTE; PAUL J. COLLING; JOSEPH A. HANNAPPEL; JAMES E. NOVAKOWSKI; RICHARD L. PIONTKOWSKI JR., S.T.L., J.C.L.; MICHAEL F. MCDERMOTT, J.C.L.; Very Rev. CHARLES L. TORPEY, S.T.L., J.C.L.; Rev. MARTIN L. EGGING.

Vicar for Religious Communities of Women—VACANT.

Diocesan Offices and Directors

Charismatic Renewal—Rev. HAROLD R. KURTENBACH, Dir. (Retired), 2647 Brennen Lane, Grand Island, 68803.

Charities—Rev. CHRISTOPHER KUBAT, Dir., Catholic Social Svcs., 515 W. 3rd St., Hastings, 68901. Tel: 402-463-2112.

Communications—Most Rev. WILLIAM J. DENDINGER, D.D., M.A., Dir.

Ongoing Formation for Clergy and Liturgy—Revs. JAMES R. GOLKA, Mailing Address: P.O. Box 399, North Platte, 69103. Tel: 308-532-0942; LOUIS A. NOLLETTE, Mailing Address: P.O. Box 7, Ainsworth, 69210. Tel: 402-387-1275.

Council of Catholic Women, Diocesan—Rev. STEPHEN F. DEAVER, Diocesan Moderator (Retired).

Hispanic Ministry—Rev. PAUL J. COLLING, Vicar, Mailing Address: P.O. Box 578, Lexington, 68850. Tel: 308-324-4647; Sr. M. VERONICA RIVAS, M.C.D.P., Dir., 1225 S. Poplar, North Platte, 69101. Tel: 308-532-2707.

Newspaper— "The West Nebraska Register" MARY PARLIN, Editor; COLLEEN GALLION, Assoc. Editor, Address all correspondence to: P.O. Box 608, Grand Island, 68802. Tel: 308-382-4660; Fax: 308-382-6569.

Personnel Board—Revs. MATTHEW J. KOPERSKI; MICHAEL D. MCDONALD; JOSEPH A. HANNAPPEL; JAMES R. GOLKA; JAMES E. HEITHOFF; JAMES E. NOVAKOWSKI; BRYAN D. ERNEST.

Priests' Advisory Board (Presbyteral Council)—Revs. MICHAEL F. MCDERMOTT, J.C.L.; NEAL P. NOLLETTE; BRYAN D. ERNEST; LOUIS A. NOLLETTE; JAMES E. NOVAKOWSKI; PAUL J. COLLING; VINCENT L. PARSONS; Very Rev. CHARLES L. TORPEY, S.T.L., J.C.L.

Catholic Relief Services—Most Rev. WILLIAM J. DENDINGER, D.D., M.A., Dir.

Priests' Pension and Welfare Board— Address all mail to: Rev. LAWRENCE W. COULTER (Retired), Mailing Address: 1301 S. "D" St., Broken Bow, 68822.

Propagation of the Faith—Rev. MICHAEL D. MCDONALD, Dir., 1210 E. 11th, Kearney, 68847. Tel: 308-236-9171.

Religious Education—DONALD KURRE, Dir., 1225 S. Poplar, North Platte, 69101. Tel: 308-532-2707.

Rural Life Conference—Rev. NEAL P. NOLLETTE, Dir., Mailing Address: P.O. Box 586, Chappell, 69129.

Schools—Rev. THOMAS A. RYAN, Diocesan Supt. of Schools, 2708 Old Fair Rd., P.O. Box 996, Grand Island, 68802. Tel: 308-682-6565; Fax: 308-382-6569.

Vocations—Rev. MATTHEW J. KOPERSKI, Dir., P.O. Box 1024, Kearney, 68848. Tel: 308-234-1539.

Youth & Young Adult—KEVIN FULLER, Dir., 1225 S. Poplar, North Platte, 69101. Tel: 308-532-2707.

CEC (Catholics Encounter Christ)—Rev. PAUL J. COLLING, Spiritual Dir., Mailing Address: P.O. Box 578, Lexington, 68850.

Community Mental Health—MICHAEL F. MCDERMOTT, L.M.H.P., Mailing Address: P.O. Box 996, Grand Island, 68802.

Victim Assistance Coordinators—Grand Island: ELIZABETH HEIDT, Ph.D. Tel: 308-379-1949. Email: cpo@gidiocese.org; AILEEN D. GRUENDEL, Ph.D. Tel: 308-381-2233. Email: gruendel@hamilton.net. Ravenna: CHERYL ALBRIGHT, M.S. Tel: 308-440-7644. Email: calbright@gidiocese.org. Scottsbluff: MATTHEW HUTT, Ph.D. Tel: 308-632-8080; ANNE TALBOT, Ph.D. Tel: 308-632-8547; OLIVIA GONZALEZ, DAC. Tel: 308-635-3171.

Office of Child Protection—ELIZABETH HEIDT, Ph.D., Dir.; CHERYL ALBRIGHT, M.S., Outreach Coord., Mailing Address: P.O. Box 1531, Grand Island, 68802. Tel: 308-382-6565; Fax: 308-382-6569. Email: cpo@gidiocese.org.

Office of Planning and Lay Ministry—MICHAEL S. DAVIS, Dir., 1225 S. Poplar #100, North Platte, 69101.

CLERGY, PARISHES, MISSIONS AND PAROCHIAL SCHOOLS

CITY OF GRAND ISLAND

(HALL COUNTY)

1—CATHEDRAL OF THE NATIVITY OF THE BLESSED VIRGIN MARY (1864) Revs. Richard L. Piontkowski Jr.; Jonathan D. Sorensen.
Res.: 207 S. Elm St., 68801. Tel: 308-384-2523; Fax: 308-384-2527. Email: office@stmarysgi.com.
Catechesis/Religious Program—112 S. Cedar, 68801. Tel: 308-382-1198. Students 278.

2—BLESSED SACRAMENT (1949) Revs. Todd K. Philipsen; Mark Maresh; Sr. Nadine Heimann, O.S.F., Pastoral Min.
Res.: 1724 N. Walnut, 68801. Tel: 308-381-1361.
Church: 518 W. State St., 68801. Tel: 308-384-0532; Fax: 308-384-0424. Email: bscc_1@msn.com. Web: blsachurch.net.
Catechesis/Religious Program—518 W. State St., 68801. Tel: 308-395-8521. Ms. Debra Wetzel, D.R.E. Students 338.

3—ST. LEO (1972) Very Rev. Charles L. Torpey; Sr. Mary Margaret McGowen, Pastoral Min.
Church: 2410 S. Blaine, 68801. Tel: 308-382-4753.
Catechesis/Religious Program—Jodi Stauffer, D.R.E. Students 252.

4—RESURRECTION (1973) Rev. Michael F. McDermott.
Res.: 4110 Cannon Rd., 68803. Tel: 308-382-8644; Fax: 308-382-1845.
Catechesis/Religious Program—Tel: 308-382-0976. Therese Stump, D.R.E.; Michalene Iverson, Youth Dir. Students 245.

OUTSIDE THE CITY OF GRAND ISLAND

AINSWORTH, BROWN CO., ST. PIUS X (1955) Rev. Louis A. Nollette.
Res.: P.O. Box 7, 69210. Tel: 402-387-1275. Email: stpiusxne@msn.com.
Catechesis/Religious Program—Tel: 402-387-2260. Wanda Raymond, D.R.E. Students 105.
Mission—Holy Cross Bassett, Rock Co. Tel: 402-684-3640.

ALLIANCE, BOX BUTTE CO., HOLY ROSARY (1894) [CEM] Rev. James H. Heithoff.
Parish Offices—1104 Cheyenne Ave., 69301. Tel: 308-762-2009; Fax: 308-762-7474.
Res.: 916 Cheyenne Ave., 69301. Tel: 308-762-1418.
School—St. Agnes Academy, (Grades PreSchool-8) Tel: 308-762-2315. Email: saasecretary@stagnesacademy.com. Web: www.stagnesacademy.com. Doyle Christensen, Prin. Lay Teachers 12; Students 160; Preschool 21.
Catechesis/Religious Program—Tel: 308-762-2830. Email: faithformation@bbc.net. Web: www.2bcatholic.org. Noreen Placek, D.R.E.; Ralph Yeager, Youth Min. Students 113.
Mission—St. Bridget (1888) 801 Niobrara Ave., P.O. Box 67, Hemingford, Box Butte Co. 69348. Tel: 308-487-3617; Fax: 308-487-3608. Email: stbridget@bbc.net. Sr. Sarah Manchester, O.S.F., Pastoral Min.
Catechesis/Religious Program—Students 43.

BRIDGEPORT, MORRILL CO., ALL SOULS (1919) [CEM] Rev. David L. Rykwalder.
Res.: P.O. Box 250, 69336-0250. Tel: 308-262-1332; Fax: 308-262-0709.
Catechesis/Religious Program— Colleen Cruise, D.R.E.; Beth Freeze, D.R.E.; Paula Contraras, D.R.E. Students 101.
Mission—St. Mary P.O. Box 346, Dalton, Cheyenne Co. 69131-0346. Tel: 308-377-2440.
Mission—Sacred Heart P.O. Box 190, Bayard, Morrill Co. 69334-0190. Tel: 308-586-1160.

BROADWATER, CHEYENNE CO., ST. DOMINIC, Closed. For inquiries for parish records contact the chancery.

BROKEN BOW, CUSTER CO., ST. JOSEPH'S (1888) [CEM] Rev. James M. Hunt.
Mailing Address: P.O. Box 405, 68822. Tel: 308-872-5809 (Office); Fax: 308-872-5809.
Res.: 1407 S. E St., 68822. Tel: 308-872-5716; Fax: 308-872-5809.
Catechesis/Religious Program— Rashelle Ryan, D.R.E. Students 125.
Mission—St. Anselm's [CEM 2] Anselmo, Custer Co.
Catechesis/Religious Program— Connie Chandler, D.R.E. (Grades P-12). Students 61.
Mission—Assumption of the Blessed Virgin Mary Sargent, Cluster Co.
Catechesis/Religious Program—Students 52.

CHADRON, DAWES CO., ST. PATRICK'S (1886) [CEM] Rev. Timothy L. Stoner.
Office: 340 Cedar St., P.O. Box 231, 69337. Tel: 308-432-2626; Fax: 308-432-4969. Email: stpats@chadronstpatricks.org.
Catechesis/Religious Program—Tel: 308-432-2161. Linda Yeradi, D.R.E.; Terri Connealy, Youth Min. Students 100.

CHAPPELL, DEUEL CO., ST. JOSEPH'S (1909) [CEM] Rev. Neal P. Nollette.
Res.: 1049 2nd St., P.O. Box 586, 69129. Tel: 308-874-3221. Email: joelizgal@embarqmail.com.
Catechesis/Religious Program—Students 28.
Mission—St. Elizabeth 300 W. 4th, P.O. Box 586, Oshkosh, Garden Co. 69154. Tel: 308-772-3221; Fax: 308-772-3221.
Catechesis/Religious Program—Tel: 308-722-3445. Students 14.
Mission—St. Gall 307 1st St., Lisco, Garden Co. 69148.

COZAD, DAWSON CO., CHRIST THE KING (1951), (Irish), Rev. Donald J. O'Brien.
Res.: 1220 Ave. M, 69130. Tel: 308-784-3959.
Catechesis/Religious Program—512 E. 19th. Tel: 308-784-2696. Donna Kolbo, D.R.E. Students 176.
Mission—Our Lady of Good Counsel 1915 Ave. J, Gothenburg, Dawson Co. 69138.

CRAWFORD, DAWES CO., ST. JOHN THE BAPTIST (1896), (German—Irish), [CEM 2] Rev. Bernard M. Berger.
Res.: 808 4th St., 69339. Tel: 308-665-1584. Email: stjohnscrawford@bbc.net.
Catechesis/Religious Program—Tel: 308-665-2240. Email: lindam@kdsi.net. Linda Moloney, D.R.E. Students 25.
Mission—Church of the Nativity of the Blessed Virgin Mary 426 Kate St., Harrison, Sioux Co. 69339. Tel: 308-668-2181.
Catechesis/Religious Program—Students 13.

ELM CREEK, BUFFALO CO., IMMACULATE CONCEPTION (1879) [CEM] Rev. Jose M. Chavez.
Res.: 314 N. Church, 68836. Tel: 308-856-4375; Fax: 308-856-4017.
Church: P.O. Box 530, 68836.
Catechesis/Religious Program—Students 120.
Mission—Holy Rosary 503 D St., Overton, Dawson Co. 68863.
Mission—St. John Capistran 118 N. Ash, Amherst, Buffalo Co. 68812.

GERING, SCOTTS BLUFF CO., CHRIST THE KING (1958) Rev. Gerald J. Harr.
Res.: 1730 'N' St., P.O. Box 33, 69341. Tel: 308-436-4000; Fax: 308-436-2923.
Catechesis/Religious Program—P.O. Box 33, 69341. Tel: 308-436-2290. Micki Walker, D.R.E. & Dir. Youth Ministry. Students 236.

GORDON, SHERIDAN CO., ST. LEO'S (1887) [JC] Rev. James Joseph, S.D.B.
Res.: 228 N. Maverick, 69343. Tel: 308-282-0427.
Catechesis/Religious Program—Students 89.
Mission—Immaculate Conception 606 Church St., P.O. Box 279, Rushville, Sheridan Co. 69360. Tel: 308-327-2430.
Mission—St. Columbkille 545 N. Main, Hay Springs, Sheridan Co. 69347.

KEARNEY, BUFFALO CO.

1—ST. JAMES (1881) Revs. Joseph A. Hannappel; Matthew J. Koperski; Mary Bowman, Adult Faith Formation.
Church Office: 3801 Ave. A, 68847. Tel: 308-234-5536.
Res.: 7 Sioux Ln., 68847. Tel: 308-233-5051.
High School—Kearney Catholic, (Grades 6-12), 110 E. 35th St. Tel: 308-234-2610; Fax: 308-234-4986. Mr. Terrence Torson, Admin. Lay Teachers 23; Students 300.
Catechesis/Religious Program—Tel: 308-234-9695. Deb Kratochvil, D.R.E.; Ann Sucha, Youth Min. Students 270.

2—PRINCE OF PEACE (1986) Rev. Michael D. McDonald; Sisters Mary Chamberlain, O.S.M., Pastoral Min.; Doris Durant, O.S.M., Pastoral Min.
Church: 1210 E. 11th St., 68847. Tel: 308-236-9171. Email: popchurch@charterinternet.com.
Catechesis/Religious Program— Ms. Jane Bettles, D.R.E. Students 235.

KIMBALL, KIMBALL CO., ST. JOSEPH'S (1921) Rev. Robert Karnish.
Mailing Address: P.O. Box 576, 69145.
Res.: 511 S. Howard, 69145. Tel: 308-235-2162.
Catechesis/Religious Program—Students 97.

LEXINGTON, DAWSON CO., ST. ANN'S (1883) [CEM] Revs. Paul J. Colling. Tel: 308-324-4648; Jorge Canela; Sr. Mary Ann Flax, C.S.J., Pastoral Min. Tel: 308-324-2450.
Res.: 303 E. 6th St., P.O. Box 578, 68850. Tel: 308-324-4648. Email: stanns@cozadtel.net.
Catechesis/Religious Program—St. Ann's Parish Center, 10th & Taft St., 68850. Tel: 308-324-4647; Fax: 308-324-5320. Linda Saiz, D.R.E. (Grades K-5); DeLinda Glaze, D.R.E. (Grades 6-12); Frances Peterson, Youth Dir. Students 400.

LOUP CITY, SHERMAN CO., ST. JOSAPHAT'S (1882), (Polish), Rev. Martin L. Egging.
Res.: 704 N. 9th St., P.O. Box 626, 68853. Tel: 308-745-0315. Email: josaphatsaint@yahoo.com.
Catechesis/Religious Program—Tel: 308-745-1235. Students 152.
Mission—St. Francis [CEM] Ashton, Sherman Co. 68817.
Catechesis/Religious Program—Loretta Halinsky, D.R.E. Students 39.
Mission—St. Gabriel Hazard, Sherman Co. 68844.
Catechesis/Religious Program—Annette Siegel, D.R.E. Students 35.

MITCHELL, SCOTTS BLUFF CO., ST. THERESA'S (1930) Rev. Anthony Madhichetti.
Res.: 1715 17th St., 69357. Tel: 308-623-1745. Email: frsttheresa@embarqmail.com.
Catechesis/Religious Program—Tel: 308-623-2245. Students 75.
Mission—St. Ann Hwy. 26 & Walsh, Morrill, Scotts Bluff Co. 69358.
Mission—Sacred Heart 203 E. "O" St., Lyman, Scotts Bluff Co. 69352.

MULLEN, HOOKER CO., ST. MARY'S (1910) Rev. Loren G. Pohlmeier.
Res.: 302 S. Blaine, P.O. Box 191, 69152. Tel: 308-546-2250.
Catechesis/Religious Program—Students 74.
Mission—All Saint's Hyannis, Grant Co. 69152.
Mission—St. Thomas of Canterbury Thedford, Thomas Co. 69152.

NORTH PLATTE, LINCOLN CO.

1—HOLY SPIRIT (1973) Rev. James E. Novakowski.
Res.: 2120 West C, P.O. Box 427, 69103. Tel: 308-534-4334; 308-534-6623 (Church).
Church: Tel: 308-534-6623.
Catechesis/Religious Program—Tel: 308-534-7906; Fax: 308-534-6525. Kathy Schroeder, D.R.E. Students 213.
Mission—Sacred Heart P.O. Box 398, Sutherland, Lincoln Co. 69165. Tel: 308-386-4300.

2—ST. PATRICK (1875) [CEM] Rev. James R. Golka.
Res.: 415 N. Chestnut, P.O. Box 399, 69103. Tel: 308-532-0942; Fax: 308-532-0944. Email: office@st-pats-online.org. Web: www.st-pats-online.org.
School—McDaid Elementary, (Grades K-6), 1000 East E St., P.O. Box 970, 69101. Tel: 308-532-1874; Fax: 308-532-8015. Web: athena.esu16.org/~npcs/1npcsHome.html. Mr. Rick Carpenter, Prin. Lay Teachers 20; Students 319.
High School—(Grades 7-12), 500 S. Silber, 69101. Tel: 308-532-1874. *c/o North Platt Catholic Schools*, P.O. Box 970, 69103. Mark Skillstad, Prin.; Mr. William McGahan Jr., Supt. Lay Teachers 18; Students 116.
Catechesis/Religious Program—Tel: 308-532-6388, Ext. 203. Email: formation@st-pats-online.org; religioused@st-pats-online.org. Web: www.st.pats-online.org. Mary Wyatt, Dir. Faith Formation; Teresa Smith, C.R.E. Students 120.

OGALLALA, KEITH CO., ST. LUKE'S (1887) [JC] Rev. Bryan D. Ernest; Sr. Shirley Simmons, O.S.U., Pastoral Min.
Res.: 417 E. Third, 69153. Tel: 308-284-3196; Fax: 308-284-3599. Email: stlukerectory@charter.net.
School—(Grades PreSchool-5), 406 E. 3rd St., 69153. Tel: 308-284-4841; Fax: 308-284-9839. Email: stlukesschool@charterinternet.com. Sr. Loretta Krajewski, O.S.U., Prin. Lay Teachers 5; Students 58.
St. Luke Catholic School Endowment—Office: 417 E. 3rd., 69153. Fax: 308-284-3599.
Catechesis/Religious Program—Tel: 308-520-4094. Lori Beckins, Faith Formation. Students 112.
Mission—St. Patrick's Church Paxton, Keith Co. 69155.

ORD, VALLEY CO., OUR LADY OF PERPETUAL HELP (1908) [CEM] Rev. Thomas A. Ryan.
Res.: 527 N. 19th St., P.O. Box 123, 68862. Tel: 308-728-3351; Fax: 308-728-3360.
School—(Grades K-8) Tel: 308-728-5389. Sisters 1; Lay Teachers 7; Students 50.
Catechesis/Religious Program—Students 142.
Mission—Sacred Heart Burwell, Garfield Co. 68823. Tel: 308-346-4190.
Catechesis/Religious Program—Betty Kovarik, D.R.E. Students 74.

RAVENNA, BUFFALO CO., OUR LADY OF LOURDES (1887), (German), Rev. Martin L. Egging; Sr. Paulette Kuta, Pastoral Min.
Res.: 515 Sicily Ave., Box 90, 68869. Tel: 308-452-3314; Fax: 308-452-9102. Email: ourladyoflourdes@nctc.net. Web: oll-Ravenna.com.
Catechesis/Religious Program—Joan Clifton, D.R.E. & Youth Min. Students 118.
Mission—St. Mary's [CEM] 406 Fair St., Rockville, Sherman Co. 68871.
Mission—St. Mary's (1909) [CEM] [JC] 504 N. Syracuse St., Box 134, Pleasanton, Buffalo Co. 68866. Tel: 308-388-2181.

ST. LIBORY, HOWARD CO., ST. LIBORY'S (1884) [CEM] Revs. Donald A. Buhrman; Sidney B. Bruggeman.
Res.: P.O. Box 7, 68872. Tel: 308-687-6276; Fax: 308-687-6093.
Catechesis/Religious Program—Tel: 308-687-6273. Rachel Duoiak, D.R.E. Students 80.

ST. PAUL, HOWARD CO., SS. PETER AND PAUL (1878) [JC] Rev. Raymond Kosmicki.
Res.: 405 7th St., 68873. Tel: 308-754-4649; Fax: 308-754-4002.
Catechesis/Religious Program—713 Elm St., 68873. Tel: 308-754-4002. Sandi Mudloff, Youth Min. Students 245.
Mission—St. Joseph 1803 Hwy. 11, Elba, Howard Co. 68838. Tel: 308-336-3323.
Catechesis/Religious Program—Students 50.
Mission—St. Anthony of Padua (1877) [CEM 3] 103 Kearns Ave., Box 156, Farwell, Howard Co. 68838. Tel: 308-336-3323.
Catechesis/Religious Program—Tel: 308-754-3351. Kathy Gorecki, D.R.E. Tel: 308-336-3351; Shelly Wolinski, D.R.E. Tel: 308-863-2232. Students 45.

SCOTTSBLUFF, SCOTTS BLUFF CO.
1—ST. AGNES (1912) Rev. Vincent L. Parsons; Sr. Vera Meis, C.S.J., Pastoral Min.
Office: 2314 3rd Ave., 69361. Tel: 308-632-2541; Fax: 308-632-2146. Email: office@st-agnes-church.com. Web: www.stagnesscottsbluff.com.
Res.: 2201 2nd Ave., 69363.
School—(Grades K-5) Tel: 308-632-6918; Fax: 308-632-6918. Sue Gerdau, Prin. Lay Teachers 9; Students 73.
Catechesis/Religious Program—Email: dre@st-agnes-church.com. Terri Calvert, D.R.E. Students 180.
2—OUR LADY OF GUADALUPE (1955), (Hispanic), Rev. Phil Flott.
Res.: 1103 12th Ave., P.O. Box 2485, 69361. Tel: 308-632-2845; Fax: 308-632-7356. Email: frph.l@embarqmail.com.
Catechesis/Religious Program— Monica Longoria, D.R.E. (High School); Laura Lopez, D.R.E., Elementary; Paul Vostades, Asst. D.R.E. Students 211.

SIDNEY, CHEYENNE CO., ST. PATRICK'S (1878) [JC] Rev. Arthur A. Faesser; Sr. Marietta Spenner, O.S.F., Pastoral Assoc.
Res.: 1039 14th Ave., P.O. Box 99, 69162. Tel: 308-254-2828; Fax: 308-254-2830.
Catechesis/Religious Program— Sr. Marietta Spenner, O.S.F., D.R.E.; Pat Mertz, Youth Min. Students 202.

SPALDING, GREELEY CO., ST. MICHAEL'S (1887) [CEM 2] Rev. Donald A. Buhrman; Maggie Smith, Youth Coord.
Res.: 150 E. Marguerite, P.O. Box 310, 68665. Tel: 308-497-2662.
School—Spalding Academy, (Grades K-12) Tel: 308-497-2103; Fax: 308-497-2105. Amy McKay, Prin. Lay Teachers 17; Students 107.
Catechesis/Religious Program—Students 79.
Mission—St. Theresa of the Child Jesus Ericson, 68637.
Catechesis/Religious Program—Students 20.
Mission—Sacred Heart P.O. Box 99, Greeley, Greeley Co. 68842. Tel: 308-428-2855.
Catechesis/Religious Program—Students 73.

STAPLETON, LOGAN CO., ST. JOHN THE EVANGELIST (1913), (German), [CEM] Rev. Antony Thekkekara.
Res.: 304 H St., P.O. Box 309, 69163. Tel: 308-636-2421. Email: stjohnscatholic@hotmail.com.
Catechesis/Religious Program—Students 39.
Mission—St. Agnes 503 N. Carroll, Arnold, Custer Co. 69163. Tel: 308-848-2442.
Catechesis/Religious Program—Students 15.
Mission—St. Boniface 204 S. Morgan Ave., Callaway, Logan Co. 68825. Tel: 308-836-2606.
Catechesis/Religious Program—Students 20.

VALENTINE, CHERRY CO., ST. NICHOLAS (1893) [JC] Rev. John Kakkuzhiyil, S.D.B.
Res.: P.O. Box 510, 69201. Tel: 402-376-1672; Fax: 402-376-1672. Email: stnicholas@shwisp.net.
Catechesis/Religious Program—Wanda Nielson, D.R.E.; Jessica McGinley, D.R.E. Students 112.
Mission—St. Mary [CEM] Nenzel, Cherry Co. 69201.

WOOD RIVER, HALL CO., ST. MARY'S (1884) [CEM] Rev. James J. Janovec.
Res.: P.O. Box 37, 68883. Tel: 308-583-2464. Email: stmary-sheart@hotmail.com.
Catechesis/Religious Program—Students 103.
Mission—Sacred Heart P.O. Box 190, Shelton, Buffalo Co. 68876. Tel: 308-647-5123.
Catechesis/Religious Program—Students 68.

Chaplains of Public Institutions

GRAND ISLAND. *Nebraska Veterans Home*. Vacant.
U.S. Veterans' Hospital. Rev. Harold Kurtenbach (Retired).

KEARNEY. *Youth Development Center*, W. Hwy. 30, 68847. Tel: 308-237-3181. Vacant.

Military Chaplains:
Rev.—
Borzych, Alexander J.

Retired:
Rev. Msgr.—
Hayden, Carl T., Heritage Estates, 2325 Lodge Dr., Gering, 69341.
Revs.—
Augustyn, Andrew M., 404 Woodland Dr., #71, 68801.
Bauer, Jacob F., 404 Woodland Dr., #208, 68801.
Carlson, Gerald J., 3720 State St., Apt J3, 68803.
Chamberlain, Robert F., 1220 Estates Dr., Gering, 69341.
Cortney, Edward P., 781 Parry Dr., Chadron, 69337.
Coulter, Lawrence W., 1301 S. D St., Broken Bow, 68822.
Curran, Francis T., 4000 S. 56th St., Unit 105A, Lincoln, 68506.
Deaver, Stephen F., 615 W. 42nd St., Scottsbluff, 69361.
Dillon, Thomas J., 901 S. Bryan St., #A-8, North Platte, 69101.
Dowd, Thomas M., 6340 W. 38th Ave., #1002, Wheat Ridge, CO 80033.
Fenton, Lawrence E., 10351 Sprague St., Omaha, 68134.
Ferris, Carl A., 716 N. Main, Valentine, 69201.
Guevara, Miguel H., 1010 W. 8th St., North Platte, 69103.
Koprowski, Mitchell J., P.O. Box 521, Mullen, 69152.
Krystosek, Robert H., Box 425, Clara City, MN 56222.
Kurtenbach, Harold R., 2647 Brennen Ln., 68803.
Larmore, Donald E., J.C.D., 4358 N. Rio Cancion #312, Tucson, AZ 85718.
Mullowney, Thomas E., 3915 Ave. H, 68847.
Murphy, James E., 82167 509th Ave., Spalding, 68665.
Nekoliczak, Ted A., 1516 E. 43rd St., 68848.
O'Kane, James D., 105 S. 9th St., #702, Omaha, 68102.
Phelan, Walter M., 515 N. Cluster, 68803.
Phillips, Walter W., 512 Community Dr., Seneca, KS 66538.
Pruss, Rodney Lee A., 15723 W. Amelia Dr., Goodyear, AZ 85338.
Rademacher, John R., 2497 Marston Hts., Colorado Springs, CO 80920.
Rooney, Robert B., 4419 Ave. P, 68847.
Schlaf, John E., 708 W. 7th St., Concordia, KS 66901.
Schmitt, James C., 23 Chantilly, 68803.
Snyder, Frederick, St. Mary's Convent, 2649-US20, Swanton, OH 43558.
Spanel, Hubert J., 745 N. 5th Ave., Broken Bow, 68822.
Warner, James P., 726 E. Carrol, Harlingen, TX 78552.

INSTITUTIONS LOCATED IN THE DIOCESE

[A] HIGH SCHOOLS, DIOCESAN

GRAND ISLAND. *Central Catholic Schools*, (Grades 6-12), 1200 Ruby Ave., 68803. Tel: 308-384-2440; Fax: 308-389-3274. Email: glogsdon@gicentralcatholic.org. Web: www.gicentralcatholic.org. John Golka, Prin.; Howard Schumann, Asst. Prin.; Greg Logsdon, Supt. Lay Teachers 29; Students 318.

[B] GENERAL HOSPITALS

GRAND ISLAND. *Saint Francis Medical Center, Affiliate of Catholic Health Initiatives*, 2620 W. Faidley Ave., P.O. Box 9804, 68802. Tel: 308-398-4600; Fax: 308-389-5589. Email: dsanders@sfmc-gi.org. Web: www.saintfrancisgi.org. Mr. Dan McElligott, Pres. & CEO. Catholic Health Initiatives. Bed Capacity 163; Bassinets 17; Patients Assisted Annually 124,350; Total Staff 1,100.

KEARNEY. *Good Samaritan Hospital, Affiliate of Catholic Health Initiatives*, 10 E. 31st St., P.O. Box 1990, 68848-1990. Tel: 308-865-7100. Email: robertsmoot@catholichealth.net. Web: www.gshs.org. John W. Allen, Pres. & CEO. Sisters 4; Total Staff 1,472; Bed Capacity 210.
Richard H. Young Hospital, 4600 17th Ave., 68847. Tel: 308-865-2000. Bed Capacity 80.

[C] HOMES FOR THE AGED

KEARNEY. *Mount Carmel Home-Keens' Memorial*, 412 W. 18th St., 68847. Tel: 308-338-1263; Fax: 308-236-9380. Email: brownun@yahoo.com. Web: www.corpuschristicarmelites.org. Sr. Dorothy Cavaness, O.Carm., Supr. Sisters (Carmelites) 9; Residents 75; Total Staff 114.

[D] NEWMAN CENTERS

CHADRON. *Chadron State College-Newman House* 907 Main St., 69337. Tel: 308-432-4286. Email: newmanhousecsc@yahoo.com. Total in Residence 1; Total Staff 1.

KEARNEY. *University of Nebraska at Kearney Newman Apostolate* 821 W. 27th St., 68845. Tel: 308-234-1539; Fax: 308-233-5718. Email: cathnewman@unk.edu. Web: http://newmancenter.unk.edu. Rev. Matthew J. Koperski, Chap.; Sr. Rosemarie Maly, O.S.B., Dir.; Dianne Keiter, Dir. Music Ministry; Pam Cinfel, Admin. Asst. Total in Residence 7; Total Staff 4.

[E] MISCELLANEOUS

KEARNEY. *Magnificat-Mary Full of Grace, Inc.*, 1516 First Ave., 68847.

RELIGIOUS INSTITUTES OF WOMEN REPRESENTED IN THE DIOCESE
For further details refer to the corresponding bracketed number in the Religious Institutes of Men or Women section.
[0230]—*Benedictine Convent of the Sacred Heart*
[0350]—*Carmelite Sisters (Corpus Christi)*—O.Carm.
[3832]—*Congregation of the Sisters of St. Joseph*—C.S.J.
[1115]—*Dominican Sisters of Peace*—O.P.
[2690]—*Missionary Catechists of Divine Providence*
[2960]—*Notre Dame Sisters*—N.D.
[]—*School Sisters of St. Francis, WI*
[3580]—*Servants of Mary* (Omaha, NE)—O.S.M.
[]—*Sinsinawa Sisters, WI*
[1630]—*Sisters of St. Francis of Penance and Christian Charity*—O.S.F.
[1640]—*Sisters of St. Francis of Perpetual Adoration*—O.S.F.
[3830-18]—*Sisters of St. Joseph*—C.S.J.
[3930]—*Sisters of St. Joseph of the Third Order of St. Francis P*—S.S.J.-T.O.S.F.
[2110]—*Sisters of the Humility of Mary*—H.M.
[4120-03]—*Ursuline Nuns of the Congregation of Paris* (Louisville, KY)—O.S.U.

NECROLOGY
† Cook, John N., (Retired)—Died July 4, 2009

An asterisk (*) denotes an organization that has established tax-exempt status directly with the IRS and is not covered by the USCCB Group Ruling.

Diocese of Grand Rapids

(Dioecesis Grandormensis)

Most Reverend

WALTER A. HURLEY

Bishop of Grand Rapids; ordained June 5, 1965; appointed Titular Bishop of Chunavia and Auxiliary Bishop of Detroit July 7, 2003; consecrated August 12, 2003; appointed Bishop of Grand Rapids June 21, 2005; installed August 4, 2005. *Office: Cathedral Square Center, 360 Division Ave., S., Grand Rapids, MI 49503-4539*. Tel: 616-243-0491.

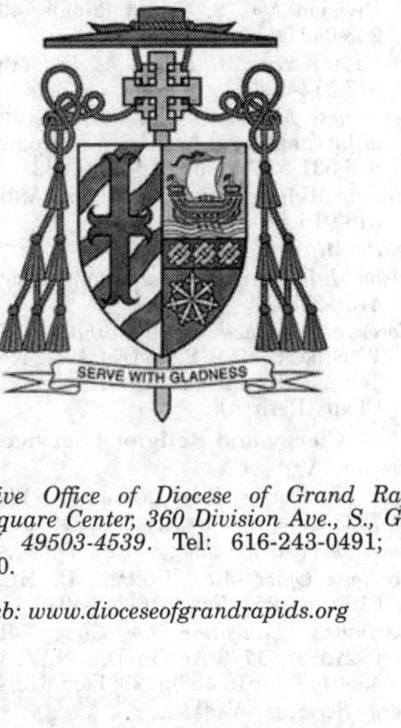

Most Reverend

ROBERT J. ROSE, S.T.L., D.D.

Retired Bishop of Grand Rapids; ordained December 21, 1955; appointed Bishop of Gaylord October 13, 1981; consecrated December 6, 1981; appointed Bishop of Grand Rapids July 11, 1989; installed August 30, 1989; retired October 13, 2003. *Res.: 1200 104th, Apt. A, Byron Center, MI 49315*. Tel: 616-583-1260.

Most Reverend

JOSEPH C. MCKINNEY, D.D.

Retired Auxiliary Bishop of Grand Rapids; ordained December 20, 1953; appointed Titular Bishop of Lentini and Auxiliary of Grand Rapids July 24, 1968; consecrated September 26, 1968; retired October 3, 2001. *Res.: St. Ann's Home, 2161 Leonard N.W., Grand Rapids, MI 49504*. Tel: 616-735-1046.

Administrative Office of Diocese of Grand Rapids: Cathedral Square Center, 360 Division Ave., S., Grand Rapids, MI 49503-4539. Tel: 616-243-0491; Fax: 616-243-4910.

Web: www.dioceseofgrandrapids.org

ESTABLISHED MAY 19, 1882.

Square Miles 6,795.

Comprises the following Counties of the Lower Peninsula of the State of Michigan: Ionia, Kent, Lake, Mason, Mecosta, Montcalm, Muskegon, Newaygo, Oceana, Osceola, Ottawa.

For legal titles of parishes and diocesan institutions, consult the Chancery Office.

STATISTICAL OVERVIEW

Personnel	
Bishop	1
Retired Bishops	2
Priests: Diocesan Active in Diocese	66
Priests: Retired, Sick or Absent	41
Number of Diocesan Priests	107
Religious Priests in Diocese	17
Total Priests in Diocese	124
Extern Priests in Diocese	15
Ordinations:	
Diocesan Priests	2
Transitional Deacons	1
Permanent Deacons in Diocese	41
Total Brothers	1
Total Sisters	326
Parishes	
Parishes	91
With Resident Pastor:	
Resident Diocesan Priests	77
Resident Religious Priests	7
Without Resident Pastor:	
Administered by Priests	5
Administered by Lay People	2
Missions	12
Pastoral Centers	1
Welfare	
Catholic Hospitals	2
Total Assisted	1,737,952
Homes for the Aged	3
Total Assisted	906
Specialized Homes	15
Total Assisted	3,500
Special Centers for Social Services	4
Total Assisted	212,080
Educational	
Diocesan Students in Other Seminaries	12
Total Seminarians	12
Colleges and Universities	1
Total Students	2,312
High Schools, Diocesan and Parish	3
Total Students	1,456
High Schools, Private	1
Total Students	203
Elementary Schools, Diocesan and Parish	27
Total Students	4,433
Elementary Schools, Private	1
Total Students	286
Catechesis/Religious Education:	
High School Students	2,168
Elementary Students	10,818
Total Students under Catholic Instruction	21,688
Teachers in the Diocese:	
Sisters	3
Lay Teachers	397
Vital Statistics	
Receptions into the Church:	
Infant Baptism Totals	2,829
Adult Baptism Totals	338
Received into Full Communion	544
First Communions	3,234
Confirmations	2,132
Marriages:	
Catholic	420
Interfaith	1,519
Total Marriages	1,939
Deaths	1,188
Total Catholic Population	178,000
Total Population	1,283,717

Former Bishops—Most Revs. HENRY JOSEPH RICHTER, D.D., cons. April 22, 1883; died Dec. 26, 1916; MICHAEL JAMES GALLAGHER, D.D., ord. March 19, 1893; appt. titular Bishop of Tipasa and Coadjutor Bishop of Grand Rapids July 5, 1915; cons. Sept. 8, 1915; succeeded to the Diocese of Grand Rapids, Dec. 26, 1916; transferred to the See of Detroit, July 18, 1918; died Jan. 20, 1937; EDWARD D. KELLY, ord. June 16, 1886; cons. Auxiliary Bishop of Detroit, Jan. 26, 1911; transferred to the See of Grand Rapids, Jan. 16, 1919; died March 26, 1926; JOSEPH G. PINTEN, D.D., ord. Nov. 1, 1890; cons. Bishop of Superior May 3, 1922; transferred to See of Grand Rapids June 25, 1926; resigned and appt. Titular Bishop of Sela Nov. 1, 1940; died Nov. 6, 1945; JOSEPH CASIMIR PLAGENS, ord. July 5, 1903; cons. Sept. 30, 1924, Auxiliary Bishop of Detroit and Titular Bishop of Rhodiopolls; transferred to See of Marquette Nov. 16, 1935; transferred to See of Grand Rapids Dec. 16, 1940; installed as Bishop of Grand Rapids Feb. 18, 1941; died March 31, 1943; FRANCIS J. HAAS, D.D., ord. June 11, 1913; appt. Sept. 26, 1943; cons. and installed as Bishop of Grand Rapids, Nov. 18, 1943; died Aug. 29, 1953; ALLEN J. BABCOCK, D.D., ord. March 7, 1925; appt. Titular Bishop of Irenopolis and Auxiliary of Detroit Feb. 15, 1947; cons. March 25, 1947; appt. to Grand Rapids March 23, 1954; died June 27, 1969; JOSEPH M. BREITENBECK, D.D., ord. May 30, 1942; appt. Titular Bishop of Tepelta and Auxiliary of Detroit Oct. 18, 1965; cons. Dec. 20, 1965; appt. Bishop of Grand Rapids Oct. 15, 1969; installed Dec. 2, 1969; retired Aug. 3, 1989; died March 12, 2005; ROBERT J. ROSE, D.D., S.T.L. (Retired), ord. Dec. 21, 1955; appt. Bishop of Gaylord Oct. 13, 1981; cons. Dec. 6, 1981; appt. Bishop of Grand Rapids July 11, 1989; installed Aug. 30, 1989; retired Oct. 13, 2003; KEVIN M. BRITT, ord. June 28, 1970; appt. Auxiliary Bishop of Detroit, Titular Bishop of Esco Nov. 23, 1993; cons. Jan. 6, 1994; appt. Coadjutor Bishop of Grand Rapids Dec. 10, 2002; Succeeded to See Oct. 13, 2003; died May 15, 2004.

Office of the Bishop

Office of the Bishop—Most Rev. WALTER ALLISON HURLEY, Cathedral Square Center, 360 Division Ave., S., Grand Rapids, 49503-4539. Tel: 616-243-0491.

Administrative Assistant—SR. SARAH DOSER, F.S.E.

Vicar General/Moderator of the Curia—Rev. Msgr. WILLIAM H. DUNCAN, Cathedral Square Center, 360 Division Ave., S., Grand Rapids, 49503-4539. Tel: 616-243-9508.

Chancellor—VACANT.

Vice Chancellor—Mr. T. EDWARD CAREY JR. Tel: 616-475-1247.

Director of Finance and Administration—Mr. T. EDWARD CAREY JR. Tel: 616-475-1247; Mr. JOHN S. CZACHORSKI, Comptroller. Tel: 616-475-1253; Sr. MARIA SERRA GARCIA, F.S.E., Dir. Parish Accounting Svcs. Tel: 616-243-1463; Mr. MARK MORROW, Dir. Stewardship & Devel., Cathedral Square Center, 360 Division Ave., S., Grand Rapids, 49503-4539. Tel: 616-475-1251.

Tribunal Office—Rev. EDWARD A. HANKIEWICZ, J.C.L., Officialis, Diocese of Grand Rapids: Cathedral Square Center, 360 Division Ave., S., Grand Rapids, 49503-4539. Tel: 616-551-5672.

Director of Planning—VACANT.

Director of Communications—MARY HAARMAN, Cathedral Square Center, 360 Division Ave., S., Grand Rapids, 49503-4539. Tel: 616-475-1240.

Victim Assistance Coordinator—MARYANNE L KOWALSKI. Tel: 231-730-1060.

Clergy Fund—Rev. GEORGE E. DARLING. Tel: 616 7339.

Deans—Revs. JOSEPH J. FIX, Big Rapids

Address: P.O. Box 778, Evart, 49631. Tel: 231-734-3171; JOSEPH W. KENSHOL, Grand Rapids North, 1 Maple St., P.O. Box 140, Sand Lake, 49343. Tel: 616-636-5671; THEODORE KOZLOWSKI, Grand Rapids South, 101 Hall, S.E., Grand Rapids, 49507. Tel: 616-243-0222; Rev. Msgr. ERNEST SCHNEIDER, Grand Rapids East, 2750 Burton St., S.E., Grand Rapids, 49546. Tel: 616-949-4170; Revs. EDWARD J. HANKIEWICZ, Grand Rapids West, 156 Valley, S.W., Grand Rapids, 49504. Tel: 616-459-7390; LARRY KING, Ionia, 140 Church St., Portland, 48875-1095. Tel: 517-647-6505; RONALD F. SCHNEIDER, Northwest Lake Shore Deanery, Mailing Address: St. Ann Parish, P.O. Box 729, Baldwin, 49304. Tel: 231-745-7997; WILLIAM F. ZINK, Grand Haven Deanery, 15164 Juniper Dr., Marne, 49435. Tel: 616-677-3934; THOMAS J. BROWN, Muskegon Deanery, 150 E. Summit Ave., Muskegon, 49444. Tel: 231-733-2440.

Presbyteral Council—Revs. RONALD F. SCHNEIDER, Exec. Coord.; JOSEPH KENSHOL, Asst. Exec. Coord.; MICHAEL CILIBRAISE; JOACHIM LALLY, C.S.P.; GODFREY C. ONYEKWERE, and the Deans of the Diocese.

College of Consultors—Rev. Msgrs. ERNEST SCHNEIDER; WILLIAM H. DUNCAN; Revs. THEODORE KOZLOWSKI; GODFREY C. ONYEKWERE; LARRY KING; WILLIAM F. ZINK.

Diocesan Finance Council Membership—Mr. THOMAS CZERNEY; Mr. JOHN NOWAK; Mr. WILLIAM J. MCCALL; Mrs. NANCY KENNEDY; MARY LEHMAN PANEK; Rev. LEONARD SUDLIK; Mr. GEORGE SHARPE JR.; Mr. RICHARD WENDT; Sr. AQUINAS WEBER, O.P.; Rev. Msgr. WILLIAM H. DUNCAN, Vicar Gen.; Mr. T. EDWARD CAREY JR., Dir. Finance & Admin.; Mr. JOHN S. CZACHORSKI, Comptroller.

Finance Council—Most Rev. WALTER ALLISON HURLEY, Cathedral Square Center, 360 Division Ave., S., Grand Rapids, 49503-4539. Tel: 616-243-0491.

Finance—

Parish Review Services—Mr. THOMAS CZERNEY, Dir. Tel: 616-551-5670.

Delegate for Religious—Sr. SARAH DOSER, F.S.E.

Catholic Services Appeal—Cathedral Square Center, 360 Division Ave., S., Grand Rapids, 49503-4539. Tel: 616-243-0491. LISA DAVIS.

Vicar For Priests—Rev. DONALD E. WEBER (Retired), 7523 Pinegrove Dr., Jenison, 49428.

Associate Vicar for Priests—Rev. THOMAS P. PAGE.

Moderator of the Curia—Rev. Msgr. WILLIAM H. DUNCAN, Cathedral Square Center, 360 Division Ave., S., Grand Rapids, 49503-4539. Tel: 616-475-1250.

Pro-Life Ministry—Sr. COLLEEN ANN NAGLE, F.S.E., Dir., Cathedral Square Center, 360 Division Ave. S., Grand Rapids, 49503. Tel: 616-551-5633.

Inclusion/Diversity Initiatives—Rev. GODFREY C. ONYEKWERE, Office for Black Catholic Ministry; Mr. LUIS BETETA, Office for Hispanic Ministry.

Worship—Rev. CHRIS W. ROUECH, Dir., Cathedral Square Center, 360 Division Ave. S., Grand Rapids, 49503. Tel: 616-475-1241.

Catechesis—Sr. BARBARA CLINE, F.S.E. Tel: 616-551-4742.

Music—Mr. DENNIS RYBICKI. Tel: 616-243-5590.

Faith Formation—Sr. BARBARA CLINE, F.S.E. Tel: 616-551-4743.

Family and Youth—Mr. MARK MANN. Tel: 616-475-1243.

Evangelization—Catholic Information Center, 360 Division Ave., S. 2A, Grand Rapids, 49503. Tel: 616-459-7267. Revs. MARK-DAVID JANUS, C.S.P.; JOHN J. KENNY, C.S.P.; THOMAS TAVELLA, C.S.P.

Hispanic Ministry—Mr. LUIS BETETA. Tel: 616-246-0598.

Black Catholic Ministry—Rev. GODFREY C. ONYEKWERE, Dir., Cathedral Square Center, 360 Division Ave. S, Grand Rapids, 49503. Tel: 616-243-0491.

Native American Ministry—Ms. DEBRA GUTOWSKI. Tel: 616-514-6065.

Vietnamese Ministry—Rev. PETER NGHIEM, Our Lady of LaVang, 2420 Avon, S.W., Wyoming, 49519. Tel: 616-531-5213; Fax: 616-261-0232.

Campus Ministry—Rev. DONALD A. ANDRIE, C.S.P. Tel: 616-916-4290.

Health Ministry—VACANT.

Prison/Jail Ministry—Ms. JUDE GRANSTROM. Tel: 616-475-1255.

Diocesan Council of Catholic Women—HELEN WEISNECK, 4979 S. Ferris Ave., Newaygo, 49337. Tel: 231-924-4709; Rev. ANTHONY C. VAINAVICZ, Chap. (Retired).

Clergy and Religious Services Division

Director—VACANT.

Vicar for Clergy—Rev. DONALD E. WEBER (Retired), 7523 Pinegrove Dr., Jenison, 49428.

Associate Vicar for Clergy—Rev. THOMAS P. PAGE.

Vocations Office—Rev. RONALD D. HUTCHINSON. Tel: 616-475-1254; Fax: 616-243-4910.

Continuing Education for Clergy—Rev. MARK C. PRZYBYSZ, 1776 Acacia Dr., N.W., Grand Rapids, 49504. Tel: 616-453-8229; Fax: 616-453-8053.

Clergy Services—VACANT.

Permanent Diaconate—VACANT, Cathedral Square Center, 360 Division Ave., S., Grand Rapids, 49503-4539. Tel: 616-243-0491, Ext. 1551; Fax: 616-243-1442.

Ecumenical Affairs—Rev. MARK-DAVID JANUS, C.S.P., 50 Bellevue St., S.W., Wyoming, 49548-3144. Tel: 616-531-1480.

Pastoral Council Membership— (In formation)

Education Division

Superintendent of Elementary Schools—Dr. BERNARD STANKO, Cathedral Square Ctr., 360 Division Ave., S., Grand Rapids, 49503-4539. Tel: 616-475-1257.

Associate Superintendent—VACANT.

Catholic Secondary Schools Pastor and President—Rev. R. LOUIS STASKER, Cathedral Square Center, 360 Division Ave., S., Grand Rapids, 49503-4539. Tel: 616-233-5979.

Catholic Charities of West Michigan

Catholic Charities of West Mighigan—Cathedral Square Center, 360 Division Ave., S., Grand Rapids, 49503-4539. DEBORAH NYKAMP, Pres. Tel: 616-243-9122; Mr. ROBERT ENDERS, CFO. Tel: 616-475-1252.

Bishops Overseas Appeal—

Catholic Relief Services—

Catholic Charities West Michigan, Grand Rapids—40 Jefferson Ave., S.E., Grand Rapids, 49506. Tel: 616-456-1443. *212 1/2 Maple St., Big Rapids, 49307.* Tel: 231-796-1583. *601 E. Washington St., Ste. A, Ionia, 48846.* Tel: 616-522-0836. *212 W. Main, Ste. B, Stanton, 48888.* Tel: 989-831-8306. *303 Division Ave., S., Grand Rapids, 49503.* Tel: 616-454-4110. *1935 Plainfield Ave., N.E., Grand Rapids, 49505.* Tel: 616-364-0845. *1195 E. Wilcox, White Cloud, 49349.* Tel: 231-689-6701.

Catholic Charities West Michigan, Lakeshore—1095 Third St., Ste. 125, Muskegon, 49441. Tel: 231-726-4735. *11 Washington, Hart, 49420.* Tel: 231-726-4735. *5816 W. US 10, Ludington, 49431.* Tel: 231-843-4899. *6660 Blair Ln., Holland, 49424.* Tel: 616-796-9595. *540 E. Hackley Ave., Muskegon Heights, 49444.* Tel: 231-725-7579.

Administration Division

Director of Finance and Administration—Mr. T. EDWARD CAREY JR., Cathedral Square Center, 360 Division Ave., S., Grand Rapids, 49503-4539. Tel: 616-475-1247; Fax: 616-475-1247.

Catholic Services Appeal—Mr. MARK MORROW; JANE CAMPEAU.

Accounting—Mr. JOHN S. CZACHORSKI, Comptroller.

Parish Audits—Mr. THOMAS CZERNEY. Tel: 616-551-5670.

Human Resources Management—LAURA PLOOF. Tel: 616-475-1242.

Facilities/Real Estate—Mr. T. EDWARD CAREY JR. Tel: 616-475-1247.

Technology—Ms. SUE SWANSON.

Cemeteries—Mr. ROBERT MENZEL, 4100 Clyde Park, S.W., Wyoming, 49509-0063. Tel: 616-531-9320; Fax: 616-531-9780 Resurrection Cemetery; Mt. Calvary Cemetery; St. Andrew Cemetery; Holy Cross Cemetery.

Deposit and Loan Program—Mr. JOHN S. CZACHORSKI, Comptroller.

Catholic Foundation of West Michigan—Mr. MARK MORROW, Dir. Tel: 616-475-1251.

Self-Insurance Program—Mr. T. EDWARD CAREY JR.

Building and Planning Committee—Mr. T. EDWARD CAREY JR., Cathedral Square Center, 360 Division Ave., S., Grand Rapids, 49503-4539. Tel: 616-475-1247.

Archivist—Rev. DENNIS W. MORROW, Cathedral Square Center, 360 Division Ave., S., Grand Rapids, 49503-4539. Tel: 616-246-0580.

CLERGY, PARISHES, MISSIONS AND PAROCHIAL SCHOOLS

CITY OF GRAND RAPIDS

(KENT COUNTY)

1—CATHEDRAL OF ST. ANDREW (1833) [CEM] Revs. Mark-David Janus, C.S.P.; Joachim Lally, C.S.P., Parochial Vicar; Thomas Tavella, C.S.P., Parochial Vicar; Deacons Stanley Lechtanski; Carlos Gutierrez.
Res.: 265 Sheldon S.E., 49503. Tel: 616-456-1454; Fax: 616-456-5110. Email: standrewcathedral@sbcglobal.net. Web: cathedralofsaintandrew.org.
School—(Grades K-8), 302 Sheldon Blvd., S.E., 49503. Tel: 616-451-8463; Fax: 616-451-2354. Web: www.saintandrewsschool.org. Sisters 1; Lay Teachers 12; Students 113.
Catechesis/Religious Program—Students 128.

2—ST. ALPHONSUS (1888) [JC] Revs. Denis J. Ryan, C.Ss.R.; Andrew J. Thompson, C.Ss.R.; Bernard Carlin, C.Ss.R.; Edward P. Vella, C.Ss.R. In Res., Revs. Rudy Papes, C.Ss.R.; Robert Balser, C.Ss.R.
Res.: 224 Carrier St., N.E., 49505. Tel: 616-451-3043; Fax: 616-458-5667. Email: stalphonsusgr@catholicweb.com. Web: www.stalphonsusre.org.
See All Saints Academy under Diocesan Elementary Schools, located in the Institution section
Catechesis/Religious Program—Tel: 616-459-5472. Students 115.

3—ST. ANTHONY OF PADUA (1906) Rev. Mark C. Przybysz; Deacon Leo Ferguson.
Res.: 2510 Richmond St., N.W., 49504. Tel: 616-453-8229; Fax: 616-453-8053. Email: parishoffice@saparish.com. Web: www.saparish.com.
School—(Grades K-8) Julie Whalen, Prin. Lay Teachers 20; Students 411.
Catechesis/Religious Program— Lynne Haley, D.R.E. Students 350.

4—BASILICA OF ST. ADALBERT (1881), (Polish), [JC] Rev. R. Louis Stasker; Deacon Stanley Lechtanski, Homebound Ministry.
Parish Office:—701 4th St., N.W., 49504-5199. Tel: 616-458-3065; Fax: 616-458-0563. Email: aoatley@basilicagr.org. Web: basilicagr.org.
Church: 4th and Davis, N.W., 49504.
Catechesis/Religious Program—Margaret Downer, C.R.E. Students 12.

5—BLESSED SACRAMENT (1946) [JC] Rev. George E. Darling.
Res.: 2275 Diamond Ave., N.E., 49505-4313. Tel: 616-361-7339; Fax: 616-361-1327. Email: church@bsacrament.net. Web: bsacrament.net.
See All Saints Academy under Diocesan Elementary Schools, located in the Institution section
Catechesis/Religious Program—Tel: 616-361-7738; Fax: 616-361-1327. Jody DeGraw, D.R.E. Students 90.

6—ST. DOMINIC (1974) Rev. Charles R. Dautremont.
Office: 50 Bellevue, S.W., 49548-3144. Tel: 616-531-1480; Fax: 616-531-0759. Email: ccastano@iserv.net.

7—HOLY NAME OF JESUS (1908) [JC] Rev. Stephen S. Dudek; Deacons Jeffrey Burns; Carlos Gutierrez.
Res.: 1630 Godfrey Ave., S.W., 49509. Tel: 616-241-6489; Fax: 616-241-6480. Email: holynameofjesus@comcast.net.
School—(Grades K-8), 1650 Godfrey Ave., S.W., 49509. Tel: 616-243-1126; Fax: 616-243-0862. Email: rlfraga@yahoo.com. Web: hnjschool.com. Lay Teachers 6; Students 109.
Catechesis/Religious Program—Tel: 616-245-3359. Students 133.

8—HOLY SPIRIT Rev. John F. Vallier; Daryl E. Nowicki, Business Mgr.
Res.: 2230 Lake Michigan Dr., N.W., 49504. Tel: 616-453-6369; Fax: 616-453-0244. Email: office@hsparish.com. Web: www.hsparish.com.
School—(Grades PreK-8), 2222 Lake Michigan Dr., N.W., 49504. Tel: 616-453-2772; Fax: 616-453-0018. Email: sgrant@hsparish.com. Web: www.holyspiritschoolgr.com. Sharon Grant, Prin. Lay Teachers 20; Students 360.
Catechesis/Religious Program—Tel: 616-453-1591. Students 141.

9—IMMACULATE HEART OF MARY Rev. Troy Nevins.
Res.: 1935 Plymouth Rd., S.E., 49506. Tel: 616-241-4477; Fax: 616-241-2832. Email: parish@ihmparish.com. Web: ihmparish.com.
School—(Grades K-8), 1915 Plymouth, S.E., 49506. Tel: 616-241-4633; Fax: 616-241-4418. Kathleen Vafadari, Prin.; Beth McDermott, Librarian. Sisters 1; Lay Teachers 27; Students 372.
Catechesis/Religious Program—Tel: 616-241-4477, Ext. 107. Mark Postma, D.R.E. Students 153.

10—ST. ISIDORE (1897), (Polish), [JC] Rev. Donald E. Lomasiewicz; Deacon Daniel Schneider.
Res.: 628 Diamond Ave., N.E., 49503. Tel: 616-459-4731; Fax: 616-454-5832. Email: casajo359@aol.com.
See All Saints Academy under Diocesan Elementary Schools, located in the Institution section
Catechesis/Religious Program—Polly Sare, C.R.E. Students 110.

11—ST. JAMES (1870) Rev. Dennis W. Morrow; Deacons Thomas Jurek; Robert McClintick.
Res.: 733 Bridge St., N.W., 49504. Tel: 616-458-3213; Fax: 616-458-9002. Email: stjamesgr@catholicweb.com. Web: stjamesparish.catholicweb.com.
Catechesis/Religious Program—Students 9.

12—ST. JOHN VIANNEY, [JC] Rev. Michael Alber; Jim Kulfan, Parish Admin.
Res.: 4101 Clyde Park, S.W., 49509. Tel: 616-534-5449; Fax: 616-530-8224. Email:

parish@stjohnvianney.net. Web: www.stjohnvianney.net.
School—(Grades K-8) Tel: 616-532-7001; Fax: 616-532-1884. Mr. Tom Priest, Prin. Lay Teachers 25; Students 288.
Catechesis/Religious Program—Tel: 616-532-2397. Students 99.

13—St. Joseph The Worker Rev. Steven D. Cron; Deacons Martin Zapata, Pastoral Assoc.; Carlos Gutierrez, Pastoral Assoc.
Office: 3138 Birchwood, S.W., 49548. Tel: 616-456-7982; Fax: 616-301-1759.
Church: 225 32nd St., S.W., Wyoming, 49548.
Catechesis/Religious Program—Students 265.

14—St. Jude (1946) Rev. Thomas P. Page; Deacon Larry Hoogeboom.
Office: 1120 Four Mile, N.E., 49525. Tel: 616-363-6885; Fax: 616-363-1470. Web: www.stjudes.net.
See All Saints Academy under Diocesan Elementary Schools, located in the Institution section
Catechesis/Religious Program—1120 Four Mile, N.E., 49525. Tel: 616-363-6897; Fax: 616-363-1470. Students 154.

15—St. Mary Magdalen (1956) Rev. Godfrey C. Onyekwere; Deacons Michael Dordan; Michael L. Wood.
Res.: 1213 52nd St., S.E., 49508. Tel: 616-455-9310; Fax: 616-455-4139. Email: witness@stmmagdalen.org. Web: stmmagdalen.org.
Catechesis/Religious Program—Students 246.

16—St. Mary's (1857) Rev. Dick Host; Deacon Edward Harwood.
Res.: 423 First St., N.W., 49504. Tel: 616-459-7390; Fax: 616-459-9630. Email: parish@stmarygr.org. Web: www.stmarygr.org.
Catechesis/Religious Program—David Bulkowski, D.R.E. Students 117.

17—Our Lady of Sorrows (1908), (Italian), Rev. Theodore Kozlowski.
Office: 116 Green St., S.E., 49525.
Res.: 101 Hall St., S.E., 49507. Tel: 616-243-0222; Fax: 616-243-6612; 616-247-0545 (Rectory). Web: ourladyofsorrows-gr.org.
Catechesis/Religious Program—Students 49.

18—St. Paul the Apostle (1965) Rev. Msgr. Ernest Schneider; Deacon Richard Radecki; Sr. Rosanne Szocinski, O.P., Pastoral Assoc.
Mailing Address: 2750 Burton St., S.E., 49546. Tel: 616-949-4170; Fax: 616-949-5295. Web: www.stpaulapostle.com.
School—Tel: 616-949-1690; Fax: 616-949-0836. Web: www.stpaul-school.org. Lori Salva, Prin. Lay Teachers 11; Students 214.
Catechesis/Religious Program— Beth Kolenda, D.R.E. Students 251.

19—SS. Peter and Paul (1904), (Lithuanian), [CEM] Rev. Dennis W. Morrow; Deacon Manuel E. Herrera.
Res.: 520 Myrtle St., N.W., 49504-3277. Tel: 616-454-6000; Fax: 616-454-4532.
Catechesis/Religious Program—1433 Hamilton Ave. N.W., 49504. Tel: 616-454-5611. Students 57.

20—Sacred Heart of Jesus (1904) [JC] Rev. Edward A. Hankiewicz.
Res.: 156 Valley Ave., S.W., 49504. Tel: 616-459-8362; Fax: 616-458-0602. Email: mayss052459@aol.com.
School—(Grades K-8), 1200 Dayton S.W., 49504. Tel: 616-459-0948; Fax: 616-459-0899. Web: www.sacredheartgr.org. Christine Peplinski, Prin. Lay Teachers 10; Students 175.
Catechesis/Religious Program—Jacqueline Kozal, D.R.E. Students 25.

21—Shrine of St. Francis Xavier and Our Lady of Guadalupe (1914) [JC] Rev. Jose Quintana; Deacon Ken Baldwin.
Res.: 250 Brown St., S.E., 49507. Tel: 616-241-2485; Fax: 616-241-2079. Email: sfxgr@sfxgr.org. Web: www.sfxgr.org.
Catechesis/Religious Program—Ignacio Vidal, D.R.E. (Spanish).

22—St. Stephen Catholic Church (1925) [JC] Rev. Paul Milanowski; Deacon Dale Hollern.
Res.: 760 Gladstone Ave., S.E., East Grand Rapids, 49506. Tel: 616-243-8998; Fax: 616-245-7360. Email: parishofbce@ststephenparish.com. Web: www.ststephenparish.com.
School—(Grades K-8), 740 Gladstone Dr., S.E., East Grand Rapids, 49506. Tel: 616-243-8998, Ext. 206; Fax: 616-243-0451. Web: ststephenschoolgr-.com. Cindy Thomas, Prin.; J. Klein, Librarian; N. Mulvihill, Librarian. Lay Teachers 22; Students 259.
Catechesis/Religious Program—Donna Francisco, D.R.E. Students 325.

23—St. Thomas the Apostle (1924) [JC] Rev. James A. Chelich; Deacons James Thorndill; Dennis Williams.
Res.: 1449 Wilcox Park Dr., S.E., 49506. Tel: 616-459-4662; Fax: 616-458-4047. Web: www.stthomasgr.org.
School—(Grades K-8) Tel: 616-458-4228; Fax: 616-458-4583. Web: www.stthomasapostle.catholicweb.com. David A. Faber, Prin. Lay Teachers 16; Students 315.
Catechesis/Religious Program—Students 146.

OUTSIDE THE CITY OF GRAND RAPIDS

Ada, Kent Co., St. Robert (1951) Sr. Ann Michael Farnsworth, O.P., Pastoral Assoc.
Res.: 6477 Ada Dr., S.E., 49301. Tel: 616-676-9111; Fax: 616-676-0950. Email: parishmail@strobertchurch.org. Web: www.strobertchurch.org.
Catechesis/Religious Program—Tel: 616-676-1488. Mary Ann Snyder, D.R.E.; Anne Gruscinski. Students 989.

Allendale, Ottowa Co., St. Luke University Parish (2007) Revs. Bradford C. Schoeberle, C.S.P.; Donald A. Andrie, C.S.P., Parochial Vicar.
6261-A Lake Michigan Dr., 49401-8456. Tel: 616-895-2247; Fax: 616-895-2249. Web: www.lukespot.com.
Mission—Grand Valley State University - Catholic Campus Ministry

Alpine, Kent Co., Holy Trinity, [CEM] Rev. Thomas G. Simons; Deacon Gerald Roersma.
Res.: 1200 Alpine Church Rd., N.W., 49321. Tel: 616-784-0677; Fax: 616-784-0678. Email: holytrinityalpine@gmail.com.
School—(Grades K-8), Comstock Park, 49321. Tel: 616-784-0696; Fax: 616-988-9415. Web: holytrinity-catholic.net. Kathy Rand, Prin.; Linda Fuller, Librarian. Lay Teachers 9; Students 220.
Catechesis/Religious Program—Tel: 616-784-3242. Rebecca Dunneback, D.R.E. Students 222.

Baldwin, Lake Co., St. Ann's (1912) Rev. Ronald F. Schneider.
Res.: 740 Ninth St., P.O. Box 729, 49304. Tel: 231-745-7997; Fax: 231-745-9844. Email: annigna@triton.net.
Catechesis/Religious Program—Students 16.
Mission—St. Ignatius Luther, Lake Co.

Belding, Ionia Co., St. Joseph's (1894) [CEM] Rev. G. Fredrick Brucker; Deacon Howard Scheid.
Office: 409 S. Bridge St., 48809. Tel: 616-794-2145; Fax: 616-794-2145. Email: sjsmoffice@charterinternet.com. Web: joseph-mary.catholicweb.com.
Catechesis/Religious Program—Students 86.

Belmont, Kent Co., Assumption of the Blessed Virgin Mary (1913) [CEM] Rev. Peter G. Vu; Deacon Peter P. Conigliaro.
Res.: 6369 Belmont Ave., 49306. Tel: 616-361-5126; Fax: 616-361-5503. Email: officesecretary@assumptionbvm.com. Web: www.assumptionbvm.com.
School—(Grades K-8), 6393 Belmont Ave., 49306. Tel: 616-361-5483; Fax: 616-361-2553. Michael Micele, Prin.; Noreen Eshleman, Librarian. Lay Teachers 10; Students 173.
Catechesis/Religious Program—6391 Belmont Ave., 49306. Tel: 616-361-5126, Ext. 257. Email: religiouseddirector@assumption.com. Students 359.

Big Rapids, Mecosta Co.

1—St. Mary's (1873) [CEM] Rev. Lam T. Le.
1009 Marion Ave., 49307. Tel: 231-796-5202; Fax: 231-796-9231.
School—(Grades K-8), 927 Marion Ave., 49307. Tel: 231-796-6731; Fax: 231-976-9293. Email: bnostram@stmarybr.org. Web: www.stmarybr.org. Barbara J. Borth, Prin. Lay Teachers 6; Students 78.
Catechesis/Religious Program—Students 38.

2—St. Paul's Campus Parish (1958) Rev. Lam T. Le.
Res.: One Damascus Rd., 49307. Tel: 231-796-7393; Fax: 231-796-3990. Email: stpauls1@charterinternet.com.
Catechesis/Religious Program—Students 47.

Brunswick, Newaygo Co., St. Michael (1886) [CEM] Rev. Roc Majalla, S.A.C.
Res.: 6382 S. Maple Island Rd., Fremont, 49412. Tel: 231-924-3389; Fax: 231-924-0402. Email: stmctk@wmis.net.
Catechesis/Religious Program—Students 25.
Mission—Christ the King Hesperia, Oceana Co.

Byron Center, Kent Co., St. Sebastian's (1852) [CEM] Rev. Msgr. William H. Duncan.
Res.: 9408 Wilson Ave., S.W., 49315. Tel: 616-878-1893. Web: www.sebastianmi.org.
Catechesis/Religious Program—Tel: 616-878-1619; Fax: 616-878-0715. Debbie Mayer, D.R.E.; Patrick Rossi, Youth Min. Students 180.

Caledonia, Kent Co., Holy Family (1970) [CEM 3] Rev. Mark Bauer.
Res.: 9669 Kraft Ave., S.E., 49316. Tel: 616-891-1160 (Rectory); 616-891-9259 (Office); Fax: 616-891-1346. Web: www.holyfamilycaledonia.org.
Catechesis/Religious Program—Tel: 616-891-8867. Christine Shafer, D.R.E. Students 588.

Carson City, Montcalm Co., St. Mary's (1896) [CEM] Nancy Woodcock, Pastoral Dir.
Office: 404 N. Division St., 48811. Tel: 989-584-6044; 989-762-5320; Fax: 989-584-6044. Email: smsjchurch@cmsinter.net.
Catechesis/Religious Program— Nancy Woodcock, D.R.E. Students 94.

Conklin, Ottawa Co., St. Francis Xavier (1892) [CEM] Revs. William F. Zink, Admin.; Philip A. Silwinski, Sacramental Asst.
Res.: 2044 Gooding Rd., 49403. Tel: 616-899-2471; Fax: 231-853-2191. Email: stfrancisconklin@aol.com.
Catechesis/Religious Program—Students 21.

Coopersville, Ottawa Co., St. Michael's (1950) [CEM] [JC] Rev. Norman P. Droski, Admin. (Retired).
Res.: 17151 88th Ave., 49404. Tel: 616-837-8792; 616-837-8158 (Parish Office); Fax: 616-837-7893. Email: secretary@stmichaels.us. Web: www.saintmichaels.us.
School—(Grades K-6), 17150 88th Ave., 49404. Tel: 616-837-6346. Web: www.saintmichaels.us. Peter Emmerson, Prin. Lay Teachers 5; Students 55.
Catechesis/Religious Program—Students 147.

Custer, Mason Co., St. Mary's (1933) [CEM] [JC] Rev. Michael Cilibraise, Admin.
85 S. Madison, P.O. Box 68, 49405.
Res.: 80 S. Monroe St., P.O. Box 68, 49405. Tel: 231-757-3709.
Catechesis/Religious Program—Combined with St. Jerome, Scottville., Tel: 231-757-9711. Kathy Papes, D.R.E. Students 11.

Edmore, Montcalm Co., St. Margaret Mary (1963) Rev. Antony Britto, S.A.C.
Res.: 1051 E. Howard City Rd., 48829. Tel: 989-427-5645; Fax: 989-427-3268. Email: smmchurch@charter.com.
Catechesis/Religious Program—Students 30.

Evart, Osceola Co., Sacred Heart (1874) Rev. Joseph J. Fix.
Res.: 9878 E. US 10, P.O. Box 778, 49631. Tel: 231-734-3171; Fax: 231-734-6880. Email: sacred@netonecom.net.
Catechesis/Religious Program—Tel: 231-734-3165. Ann Johnson, D.R.E. Students 37.

Free Soil, Mason Co., St. John Cantius (1906) [CEM] Rev. Dennis O'Donnell.
Res.: 2845 E. Michigan, 49411-9691. Tel: 231-464-5672; Fax: 231-464-5859.
Catechesis/Religious Program—Tel: 231-464-5698. Students 11.

Fremont, Newaygo Co., All Saints, [CEM] Rev. Peter M. Chukwu, Admin.
Res.: 500 Iroquois Dr., 49412. Tel: 231-924-7705; Fax: 231-924-7708. Email: allsaintspriest@sbcglobal.net. Web: www.rc.net/grandrapids/allsaints.
Catechesis/Religious Program—Tel: 231-924-7571. Students 74.

Grand Haven, Ottawa Co., St. Patrick's (1857) Rev. William A. Langlois; Deacons Richard Fett; Joseph Finnigan.
Res.: 920 Fulton St., 49417. Tel: 616-842-0001; Fax: 616-842-1174. Web: stpatsgh.org.
Catechesis/Religious Program—Tel: 616-842-8230. Jeff Andrini, D.R.E.
Mission—St. Anthony 13421 Green St., Robinson Township, Ottawa Co. 49417. Tel: 616-846-3548; Fax: 616-846-1085.
Catechesis/Religious Program—Jose Astua, D.R.E. Students 20.

Grandville, Kent Co., St. Pius X (1953) Rev. Chris W. Rouech.
Res.: 3937 Wilson Ave., S.W., 49418. Tel: 616-532-9344; Fax: 616-538-6340. Email: parishofsce@spxcatholic.org. Web: www.spxcatholic.org.
Catechesis/Religious Program—Tel: 616-538-2600. Students 510.

Greenville, Montcalm Co., St. Charles Borromeo (1849) [CEM] Rev. Philip P. Salmonowicz.
Res.: 109 W. Oak St., 48838. Tel: 616-754-3512; Fax: 616-754-2357. Web: home.catholicweb.com/stcharles.
School—(Grades K-8), 502 S. Franklin St., 48838. Tel: 616-754-3416; Fax: 616-754-9262. Margaret Karpus, Prin.; Sr. David Therese Korson, O.P., Librarian. Lay Teachers 9; Students 134.
Catechesis/Religious Program—Tel: 616-754-3196. Dave Mendrea, Youth Min. Students 116.
Mission—St. Margaret [CEM] Cedar Springs. 10195 16 Mile Rd., Harvard, Kent Co. 49319. Tel: 616-696-3904. Web: www.vritsworks.com/church.

Hart, Oceana Co., St. Gregory's (1908) Rev. M. Thomas Bolster.
Res.: 316 Peach St., 49420. Tel: 231-873-2660; Fax: 616-551-5623.
Catechesis/Religious Program—Tel: 231-873-2578. Andrea Bosse, D.R.E. Students 112.
Mission—Kateri Tekawitha Native American Center & St. Joseph Center Elbridge, Oceana Co.

Holland, Ottawa Co.

1—St. Francis de Sales (1903) Rev. Charles D. Brown; Deacon Juan Garcia.
Office: 195 W. 13th St., 49423. Tel: 616-396-7641; Fax: 616-392-2474. Email:

cbrown@stfrancisholland.org. Web: www.stfrancisholland.org.
School—(Grades K-8), 12100 Quincy St., 49424. Tel: 616-994-9864; Fax: 616-994-9870. Judi Koepnick, Prin. Corpus Christi Catholic School Lay Teachers 15; Students 130.
Catechesis/Religious Program—195 W. 13th St., 49423. Tel: 616-392-6700. Marilyn Torborg, D.R.E. (Including Adults) 407.

2—OUR LADY OF THE LAKE (1979) Rev. Charles D. Hall; Sr. Brigid Clingman, Pastoral Assoc.
Office: 480 152nd Ave., 49424. Tel: 616-399-1062; Fax: 616-399-5766. Email: cdhall@oll.org. Web: www.oll.org.
School—(Grades K-8), 12100 Quincy St., 49424. Tel: 616-994-9864; Fax: 616-994-9870. Joanne Swan-Jones, Prin. Corpus Christi Catholic School Lay Teachers 18; Students 129.
Catechesis/Religious Program—Students 553.

HOWARD CITY, MONTCALM CO., CHRIST THE KING (1975) [CEM] Rev. James B. Wyse; Deacon Richard Dubridge.
Res.: 9596 N. Reed Rd., 49329. Tel: 231-937-5757; Fax: 231-937-8211. Email: ctknsf@charternet.com. Web: king-francis.catholicweb.com.
Catechesis/Religious Program— Sandy Weiks, D.R.E. Students 61.
Mission—St. Frances de Sales 829 E. Richardson, Lakeview, Montcalm Co. 48850. Tel: 989-352-7293.

HUBBARDSTON, IONIA CO., ST. JOHN THE BAPTIST (1853) [CEM] Nancy Woodcock, Pastoral Dir.
Res.: c/o 404 N. Division St., Carson City, 48811. Tel: 989-584-6044; Fax: 989-584-6044. Email: nwoodcock@cmsinter.net.
Catechesis/Religious Program—Tel: 989-981-6668. Nancy Woodcock, D.R.E. Students 73.

IONIA, IONIA CO., SS. PETER AND PAUL (1861) [CEM] Rev. Thomas F. Boufford; Deacon Zenon Cardenas Sr.
Parish Office—434 High St., 48846. Tel: 616-527-3610; Fax: 616-527-3697. Web: www.ssppcatholic.com.
School—(Grades K-8), 317 Baldie St., 48846. Tel: 616-527-3561; Fax: 616-527-3562. Julie Palmer, Prin.; Patricia Zander, Librarian. Lay Teachers 8; Students 103.
Catechesis/Religious Program—Tel: 616-527-3575. Students 118.

IRONS, LAKE CO., ST. BERNARD'S Rev. Dennis O'Donnell.
Res.: One Oak St., P.O. Box 155, 49644. Tel: 231-266-5155; Fax: 231-266-8948.
Catechesis/Religious Program—

JENISON, OTTAWA CO., HOLY REDEEMER (1975) Rev. Ronald D. Hutchinson; Deacon Richard Pitt.
Res.: 2700 Baldwin Dr., 49428. Tel: 616-669-9220; Fax: 616-669-9360. Web: www.holyredeemerparish.org.
Catechesis/Religious Program—Tel: 616-669-0820. Bobby DeVries, D.R.E. Students 410.

LAKE ODESSA, IONIA CO., ST. EDWARD'S (1945) Rev. Victor Kynam.
Res.: 531 Jordan Lake St., 48849-6200. Tel: 616-374-7253; Fax: 616-374-1559. Email: frvictor@cablespeed.com.
Catechesis/Religious Program—Tel: 616-374-8809. Gary Coates, D.R.E. Students 55.

LAKEVIEW, MONTCALM CO., ST. FRANCIS DE SALES (1943) Rev. James B. Wyse; Deacon Richard Dubridge.
Res.: 9596 N. Reed Rd., Howard City, 49329. Tel: 231-937-5757; Fax: 231-937-8211. Email: ctknsf@charterinternet.com. Web: king-francis.catholicweb.com.
Church: 829 E. Richardson, 48850.
Catechesis/Religious Program— Patricia Berry, D.R.E. Students 33.

LAKEWOOD CLUB, MUSKEGON CO., ST. MARY OF THE WOODS (1916) Rev. Donn Tufts; Sr. Donna Brown, O.P., Pastoral Assoc.
Church: 150 Church St., Twin Lake, 49457. Tel: 231-894-5887; Fax: 231-894-9397.
Catechesis/Religious Program—Students 20.

LOWELL, KENT CO., ST. MARY'S (1879) [CEM] Rev. Eugene Okoli.
Res.: 402 Amity St., 49331-1308. Tel: 616-897-9820; Fax: 616-897-9683. Email: stmarylowell@att.net. Web: stmarylowell.com.
Catechesis/Religious Program—300 Amity St., 49331. Tel: 616-897-7915; Fax: 616-897-7915. Preston (Pete) Wiggins, D.R.E. & Youth Min. Students 73.

LUDINGTON, MASON CO.

1—ST. SIMON'S, [CEM] Rev. Wayne B. Wheeler Jr.
Res.: 702 E. Bryant Rd., 49431. Tel: 231-843-8606; Fax: 231-843-2052. Email: stsimon@stsimonchurch.com. Web: www.stsimonchurch.com.
School—(Grades K-6) Tel: 231-843-3188. Collin Thompson, Prin. & Librarian. Lay Teachers 10; Students 167.
Catechesis/Religious Program—Tel: 231-843-3497. Students 142.

2—ST. STANISLAUS, [JC] Rev. Wayne B. Wheeler Jr.
Res.: 702 E. Bryant Rd., 49431. Tel: 231-843-8606; Fax: 231-843-2052.
Mission—Sacred Heart-Victory

MARION, OSCEOLA CO., ST. AGNES (1888) Rev. Joseph J. Fix.
Res.: P.O. Box 778, Evart, 49631. Tel: 231-734-3171. Church: Tel: 231-743-6401; Fax: 231-734-6880.
Catechesis/Religious Program—Tel: 231-825-2971; Fax: 231-825-0230. Lynne Nolan, D.R.E. Students 35.

MARNE, OTTAWA CO., ST. MARY'S, [CEM] Rev. William F. Zink.
Res.: 15164 Juniper Dr., 49435. Tel: 616-677-3934; Fax: 616-677-5866.
Catechesis/Religious Program—Tel: 616-677-3753. Students 150.

MIRIAM, IONIA CO., ST. MARY'S (1871) [CEM] Rev. G. Fredrick Brucker.
Office: 409 S. Bridge St., Belding, 48809. Tel: 616-794-2145; Fax: 616-794-2145. Email: sjsmofnce@charterinternet.com. Web: www.joseph-mary.catholicweb.com.
See St. Joseph-St. Mary under St. Joseph, Belding for details.
Catechesis/Religious Program—Twinned with St. Joseph, Belding. Students 33.

MONTAGUE, MUSKEGON CO., ST. JAMES (1876) [CEM] Rev. Donn Tufts; Deacon Gregory Anderson.
Res.: 5149 Dowling St., 49437. Tel: 231-893-3085; Fax: 231-894-9929. Email: parishoffice@stjamescatholicparish.org. Web: www.stjamescatholicparish.org.
Catechesis/Religious Program—Email: faithformation@stjamescatholicparish.org. Pat Jackson, Faith Formation Coord. Students 174.

MUSKEGON, MUSKEGON CO.

1—ST. FRANCIS DE SALES (1948) [JC] Revs. Dung Anton Tran; Julian Reginato (Retired); Deacon William McCabe.
Res.: 2929 McCracken St., 49441. Tel: 231-755-1953; Fax: 231-759-7074. Email: sfnorton@iserv.net. Web: www.sfnortonshores.com.
Catechesis/Religious Program—Tel: 231-755-1307. Students 145.

2—ST. JEAN BAPTISTE (1883) [JC] Rev. Matthew J. Barnum; Deacon William Cook.
Res.: 1292 Jefferson St., 49441. Tel: 231-722-2793; Fax: 231-726-5976. Email: stjeanbaptiste@verizon.net. Web: stjeanbaptiste.catholicweb.com.
Catechesis/Religious Program—Mary Yack, D.R.E. Students 58.

3—ST. JOSEPH'S, Closed. For inquiries for parish records contact the chancery.

4—ST. MARY'S (1856) [JC] Rev. Matthew J. Barnum.
Res.: 239 W. Clay Ave., 49440-1213. Tel: 231-722-2844; Fax: 231-722-0733. Email: stmaryschurch@verizon.net. Web: www.stmaryschurchmuskegon.org.
Catechesis/Religious Program—Students 60.

5—ST. MICHAEL'S (1909) [JC] Rev. Thomas J. Brown.
Res.: 1716 Sixth St., 49441. Tel: 231-722-3071; Fax: 231-722-3243. Email: stmichaelmusk@aol.com.
Catechesis/Religious Program— Sr. Agnes Mary Wojtkowiak, O.P., D.R.E. Students 66.

6—OUR LADY OF GRACE (1923) [JC] Revs. Michael P. Olson; Aaron R. Ferris; Deacon David Kasprzyk.
Res.: 451 S. Getty St., 49442. Tel: 231-722-2803; Fax: 231-722-3622. Email: ourladyofgracechurch@comcast.net.
Catechesis/Religious Program—Students 50.

7—ST. THOMAS THE APOSTLE (1948) Revs. Michael P. Olson; Aaron R. Ferris; Deacon David Kasprzyk.
Office: 3252 Apple Ave., 49442. Tel: 231-773-3160; Fax: 231-777-7866. Email: saint_thomas@verizon.net. Web: www.stthomasmuskegon.catholicweb.com.
Catechesis/Religious Program—451 S. Getty, 49442. Students 75.

MUSKEGON HEIGHTS, MUSKEGON CO., SACRED HEART (1919) [JC] Rev. Thomas J. Brown.
Res.: 150 E. Summit Ave., 49444. Tel: 231-733-2440; Fax: 231-733-5128.
Catechesis/Religious Program—Tel: 231-733-2440. Students 37.

NEWAYGO, NEWAYGO CO., ST. BARTHOLOMEW'S (1885) [CEM] Rev. Peter Schafer; Sr. Jean Marie Wojtas, Pastoral Assoc.
Res.: 599 W. Brooks St., 49337. Tel: 231-652-1286; Fax: 231-652-6669. Email: stbarts1@sbcglobal.net. Web: www.catholicweb.com/stbartourlady.
Catechesis/Religious Program—Lorae Sokolowski, D.R.E. Students 150.
Mission—Our Lady of Guadalupe Church Grant, Newaygo Co. 49327.

NORTH MUSKEGON, MUSKEGON CO., PRINCE OF PEACE (1975) Rev. Anthony M. Pelak; Deacon James J. Schlitz.
Res.: 1110 Dykstra, 49445. Tel: 231-744-3321; Fax: 231-744-4859. Email: pofpeace.church@verizon.net. Web: www.princeofpeacemusk.org.
Catechesis/Religious Program—Tel: 231-744-5445. Walter Elliott, Youth Min.; Joann McQuone, D.R.E. Students 184.

PARNELL, KENT CO., ST. PATRICK'S (1844) [CEM] Rev. Mark E. Peacock.
Res.: 4351 Parnell, Ada, 49301. Tel: 616-691-8541; Fax: 616-691-6309. Email: secrepat@wmis.net. Web: stpatrickparnell.org.
School—(Grades K-3), 4333 Parnell Ave., N.E., Ada, 49301. Tel: 616-691-8833. Web: www.stpatrickparnell.org/school. Sean Donovan, Prin.; Kathy Leeuwenburg, Librarian. Lay Teachers 5; Students 83.
Catechesis/Religious Program—Email: rciaham@wmis.net. Students 190.

PEWAMO, IONIA CO., ST. JOSEPH'S (1903) [CEM] Rev. Charlon O. Mason.
Res.: 106 East St., 48873. Tel: 989-593-2913; Fax: 989-593-3184. Email: stjoseph@cablespeed.com. Web: www.stjosephpewamo.org.
School—(Grades 2-8), 160 East St., P.O. Box 38, 48873. Tel: 989-593-3400; Fax: 989-593-3400. Patricia O'Mara, Prin. Lay Teachers 6; Students 90.
Catechesis/Religious Program—126 East St., P.O. Box 37, 48873. Tel: 989-593-3384. Email: religioused@cablespeed.com. Aaron Epkey. Students 84.

PORTLAND, IONIA CO., ST. PATRICK'S (1878) Rev. Larry King; Deacon Don F. Sobolewski, Pastoral Assoc.
Res.: 140 Church St., 48875. Tel: 517-647-6505; Fax: 517-647-7807. Email: stpats@cablespeed.com. Web: www.stpatrickportland.com.
School—(Grades K-8), 122 West St., 48875. Tel: 517-647-7551; Fax: 517-647-4545. Email: office@portlandstpats.org. Anne Bennett, Librarian. Lay Teachers 15; Students 215.
High School—Randy Hodge, Prin. Lay Teachers 7; Students 92.
Catechesis/Religious Program— Thomas Jandernoa, D.R.E. Students 284.

RAVENNA, MUSKEGON CO., ST. CATHERINE (1908) [CEM] Revs. William F. Zink, Admin.; Philip A. Silwinski, Sacramental Asst.
Res.: 12285 Hts. Ravenna Rd., P.O. Box 216, 49451. Tel: 231-853-6222; Fax: 231-853-2191. Email: stcatherinealex@aol.com.
School—(Grades K-6), 3375 Thomas St., 49451. Tel: 231-853-6743; Fax: 231-853-8673. Sr. Peter Mary Korson, O.P., Prin. Sisters 1; Lay Teachers 4; Students 42.
Catechesis/Religious Program—Tel: 231-853-2191. Students 21.

REED CITY, OSCEOLA CO., ST. PHILIP NERI, [CEM] Rev. Loc Trinh.
Res.: 831 S. Chestnut, 49677. Tel: 231-832-5544; Fax: 231-832-5545.
Catechesis/Religious Program—Pat Schoenherr, D.R.E. Students 56.
Mission—St. Anne 23949 22 Mile Rd., Paris, Mecosta Co. 49338.

REMUS, MECOSTA CO., ST. MICHAEL'S (1888) [CEM] Revs. Michael E. Burt, Admin.; James B. Wyse, Canonical Pastor; Deacon Robert Cathcart.
Res.: 8929 50th Ave., 49340. Tel: 989-967-3520; Fax: 989-967-8246. Email: stmichael@winntel.net. Web: stmichaelsremus.net.
School—(Grades K-6), 8944 50th Ave., 49340. Tel: 989-967-3681; Fax: 989-967-3061. Web: www.stmike-s.us. Mrs. Mary Schoner, Prin. Lay Teachers 5; Students 79.
Catechesis/Religious Program—Students 51.

ROCKFORD, KENT CO., OUR LADY OF CONSOLATION (1972) Revs. Anthony S. Russo; Dominic Tirkey, Parochial Vicar; Deacon James Hessler, Business Mgr.
Office: 4865 Eleven Mile Rd., 49341. Tel: 616-866-0931; Fax: 616-866-3668. Email: olcparish@olcparish.net. Web: www.olcparish.net.
School—(Grades K-8) Tel: 616-866-2427; Fax: 616-866-5475. Email: olcschool@olcparish.net. Kevin Varner, Prin.; Mandy McGregor, Librarian. Lay Teachers 12; Students 268.
Catechesis/Religious Program—Tel: 616-866-2577. Students 855.

ROTHBURY, OCEANA CO., OUR LADY OF THE ASSUMPTION (1923) [CEM], Twinned with Our Lady of Fatima, Rothbury Rev. Phillip J. Witkowski.
Res.: 1372 S. Oceana Dr., Shelby, 49455. Tel: 231-861-2620; Fax: 231-861-6878.
Church: 3000 Winston Rd., P.O. Box 8, 49452. Tel: 231-893-0905.

SAND LAKE, KENT CO., MARY QUEEN OF APOSTLES, [CEM 2] Rev. Joseph W. Kenshol.
Res.: 1 Maple St., P.O. Box 140, 49343-0140. Tel: 616-636-5671; Fax: 616-636-4570. Email: mqapostles@sbcglobal.net.
Catechesis/Religious Program—Tel: 616-636-5923. Students 100.

Mission—St. Clara 4584 N. Bailey Rd., Coral, Montcalm Co. 49322.

SARANAC, IONIA CO., ST. ANTHONY (1951) Rev. Victor Kynam.
Res.: 3927 Jackson Rd., 48881. Tel: 616-642-6119; Fax: 616-642-0390. Email: frvictor@cablespeed.com.
Catechesis/Religious Program—Janice Diaz, D.R.E.; Michele Westbrook, D.R.E. Students 50.

SCOTTVILLE, MASON CO., ST. JEROME (1912) [CEM] Rev. Michael Cilibraise, Admin.
Office: 203 W. State St., 49454. Tel: 231-757-2855; Fax: 231-757-2855. Email: fathermike@hotmail.com. 85 Madison Ave., Custer, 49405. Tel: 231-757-4709; Fax: 231-757-4709.
Catechesis/Religious Program—Barbara Burwell, D.R.E.

SHELBY, OCEANA CO., OUR LADY OF FATIMA Rev. Phillip J. Witkowski.
Res.: 1372 S. Oceana Dr., 49455. Tel: 231-861-2620; Fax: 231-861-6878.
Catechesis/Religious Program—Students 81.
Mission—St John 5179 Dowling St., Montague, Muskegon Co. 49437.

SPARTA, KENT CO., HOLY FAMILY (1947) Rev. Msgr. Terrence L. Stewart.
Res.: 425 S. State St., 49345. Tel: 616-887-8222; Fax: 616-887-0681.
Catechesis/Religious Program—Tel: 616-887-8857. Students 121.

SPRING LAKE, OTTAWA CO., ST. MARY'S (1863) Rev. Daniel R. DePew; Deacon William Charron.
Res.: 406 E. Savidge, 49456. Tel: 616-842-1702; Fax: 616-842-3392.
School—(Grades K-8), 421 E. Exchange, 49456. Tel: 616-842-1282; Fax: 616-842-8048. Web: www-.stmaryschoolspringlake.com. Mike Devitt, Prin. Lay Teachers 13; Students 165.
Catechesis/Religious Program—Tel: 616-842-2840. Jim Penrice, D.R.E. Students 205.
Convent—421 E. Exchange St., 49456. Tel: 616-842-1615.

STANTON, MONTCALM CO., ST. BERNADETTE OF LOURDES (1963) Rev. Antony Britto, S.A.C.
Res.: 1051 E. Howard City, Edmore, 48829. Tel: 989-427-5645; Fax: 989-427-3268. Email: smmchurch@charter.net.
Catechesis/Religious Program—Students 33.

WEARE TWP., OCEANA CO., ST. JOSEPH'S (1884) [CEM] Rev. Philip Shangraw.
Office: 2380 W. Jackson Rd., Hart, 49420. Tel: 231-873-2683; Fax: 231-873-5327. Email: st.joseph@lakeshore.net.
Catechesis/Religious Program—Renee Dennert, D.R.E. Students 50.
Mission—St. Vincent 637 E. Sixth, Pentwater, Oceana Co. 49449. Tel: 231-869-2601.

WHITE CLOUD, NEWAYGO CO., ST. JOSEPH'S, [CEM] Rev. Peter M. Chukwu, Admin.
Office: 500 Iroquois, Fremont, 49412.
Church: 965 Newell St., 49349. Tel: 231-924-7705; Fax: 231-924-7708. Email: allsinsfremont2@sbcglobal.net.
Catechesis/Religious Program—Students 45.

WRIGHT TOWNSHIP, OTTAWA CO., ST. JOSEPH'S (1853) [CEM] Rev. Msgr. Leo S. Rosloniec.
Res.: 18876 Eighth Ave., Conklin, 49403. Tel: 616-899-2286; Fax: 616-899-2212. Email: stjoseph@rfbii.com.
School—(Grades K-8), 18784 Eighth Ave., Conklin, 49403. Tel: 616-899-5300; Fax: 616-899-5491. Web: www.stjoseph-school.org. Shannon Saxton-Murphy, Prin. Lay Teachers 6; Students 64.
Catechesis/Religious Program—Tel: 616-899-2384. Students 132.

WYOMING, CHISAGO CO., OUR LADY OF LAVANG (1999) [JC] Rev. Peter Nghiem; Deacon Thanh Van Nguyen. 2420 Avon S.W., 49519. Tel: 616-261-9422; Fax: 616-531-1948.
Catechesis/Religious Program—Students 230.

CHAPELS

GRAND RAPIDS
CHAPEL OF OUR LADY OF AGLONA, LATVIAN APOSTOLATE—Cathedral Square Center, 360 Division Ave., S., 49503-4539. Tel: 616-243-0491.
Michigan Veterans' Facility Catholic Chapel—3000 Monroe Ave., N.E., 49505. Tel: 616-364-5323.

On Special Assignment:
Rev. Msgr.—
Duncan, William H., Vicar Gen. & Moderator of the Curia, 660 Burton, S.E., 49507. Tel: 616-243-0491
Revs.—
Brucker, G. Fredrick, Adjutant Judicial Vicar for the Tribunal. Tel: 616-794-2145
Dudek, Stephen S., Dir., Missions Office and the Society for the Propagation of Faith, Cathedral Square Center, 360 Division Ave., S., 49503. Tel: 616-459-4516; Fax: 616-243-4910
Hankiewicz, Edward A., J.C.L., Judicial Vicar, Tribunal Office. Tel: 616-551-5672
Hutchinson, Ronald D., Dir., Priestly Vocations. Tel: 616-475-1274
Janus, Mark-David, C.S.P., Diocesan Ecumenical Officer. Tel: 616-456-1454
Morrow, Dennis W., Adjutant Judicial Vicar for the Tribunal; Diocesan Archivist; Chap. Grand Rapids Fire Dept. & Grand Rapids Police Dept.
Nghiem, Peter, Dir. Vietnamese Apostolate, 2420 Avon S.W., 49509. Tel: 616-531-5213 National service to community of Vietnamese Clergy and Religious; Serving Vietnamese Catholic Federation of USA.
Onyekwere, Godfrey C., Dir., Office of Black Catholic Ministry, Cathedral Square Center, 360 Division Ave., S., 49503. Tel: 616-243-0491
Page, Thomas P., Assoc. Vicar for Priests. Tel: 616-363-1093
Przybysz, Mark C., Dir. of Continuing Formation of Priests. Tel: 616-453-8229
Quintana, Jose, Liaison & Delegate, Cursillo Movement, 250 Brown St., S.E., 49507. Tel: 616-241-2485
Rouech, Chris W., Dir., Office of Worship, Cathedral Center, 360 Division Ave., S., 49503. Tel: 616-475-1241
Shangraw, Philip, Projects as assigned by Bishop
Sliwinski, Philip, Projects as assigned by Bishop
Stasker, R. Louis, Pastor & Pres., Catholic Secondary Schools. Tel: 616-233-5979
Vainavicz, Anthony C., Chap. (Retired), Diocesan Council of Catholic Women
Weber, Donald E., Vicar for Priests (Retired). Tel: 616-457-1378

Personal Leave:
Revs.—
Badgerow, Rock J.
Nguyen, Phillip D.

Faculties Suspended:
Revs.—
Cook, Daniel
Harpe, David L.
Kurylowicz, Martin

Retired:
Rev. Msgrs.—
Ancona, Gaspar F., 5920 W. Lyn Haven Dr., Kentwood, 49512.
Giammona, John J., 3803 Old Elm Dr., S.E., Kentwood, 49512.
Porter, John F., 7332 Chippewa Hwy., Kaleva, 49645.
Zerfas, Herman H., 2161 Leonard N.W., #225, 49504.
Revs.—
Anderson, Louis, 4753 Rock Valley Dr., N.E., 49525.
Antekeier, Charles R.
Bernott, Ernest J., 1409 Quarry Ave., N.W., 49504.
Bozung, James M., 601 Spring Ave., N.E., 49503.
Bruck, Raymond E., 1200 104th, S.W., Byron Center, 49315.
Cawley, Patrick, c/o General Delivery, Vanderbilt, 49795.
Danner, Michael A.
DeYoung, Thomas J., 3543 Brook Tr., S.E., 49508.
Droski, Norman P., 2858 Oak Ct., Spring Lake, 49456. Tel: 231-865-6171
Fekete, George J., 628 Diamond, N.E., 49503.
Fox, Melvin E.
Garcia, Pedro, 13685 New Holland St., Holland, 49424.
Gargantiel, Isidro T., 436 Maple St., Custer, 49405.
Gillespie, Robert B., St. Ann's Home, 2161 Leonard, N.W., 49504.
Golas, Eugene S., 601 Spring Ave., N.E., 49503.
Hack, Thomas, 601 Spring Ave., N.E., 49503.
La Goe, John P., 3119 Scenic Dr., North Muskegon, 49445.
Leyrita, Norbert, 6253 E. Woodrow Rd., Hesperia, 49421.
Lowie, Richard J., 4223 Valleyside Dr., N.E., 49525.
McKinney, Thomas A., St. Ann's Home, 2161 Leonard, N.W., 49504.
Mitchell, Mark E., 601 Spring Ave., N.E., 49503.
Pettit, Joseph, 950 4 Mile Rd. N.W., #1D, 49544.
Reginato, Julian, 17468 Dunewood Ct., D, Spring Lake, 49456.
Reitz, William J., 52 Marble Rd., Lowell, 49331.
Schichtel, Kenneth H., 17502 Meadow Wood, Spring Lake, 49456.
Schiller, Thomas A., 3816 Fountain R., Ludington, 49431.
Toolis, Martin, 317 N. Lavina St., Ludington, 49431.
Vainavicz, Anthony C., 11968 Reyburn Dr., Sparta, 49345.
Vesbit, Thomas, 2608 Inverness Rd., S.E., 49546.
Weber, Donald E., 7523 Pinegrove Dr., Jenison, 49428.
Wing, Kenneth A., St. Ann's Home, 2161 Leonard N.W., 49504.
Wisneski, John J., 2066 Ter Van Dr., 49505.

Permanent Deacons:
Anderson, Gregory, St. James, Montague
Baldwin, Kenneth, Shrine of St. Francis Xavier, Grand Rapids
Burns, Jeffrey, Holy Name of Jesus, Wyoming
Cardenas, Zenon, Sr., SS. Peter and Paul, Ionia; St. Patrick, Grand Haven
Cathcart, Robert, St. Michael, Remus
Charron, William, St. Mary, Spring Lake
Conigliaro, Pietro, Assumption of the Blessed Virgin Mary, Belmont; Jail Ministry
Cook, William, St. Jean Baptiste, Muskegon
Dordan, Michael, St. Mary Magdalen, Kentwood
Dubridge, Richard, Christ the King, Howard City
Ferguson, Leo, St. Anthony of Padua, Grand Rapids
Fett, Richard, Jail Ministry, Ottawa Co.
Finnigan, Joseph, St. Patrick, Grand Haven
Garcia, Juan, St. Francis de Sales, Holland
Gutierrez, Carlos, Cathedral of St. Andrew, Holy Name of Jesus, St. Joseph the Worker, Grand Rapids
Harwood, Edward, St. Mary, Grand Rapids
Herrera, Manuel E., SS. Peter and Paul, Grand Rapids
Hessler, James, Our Lady of Consolation, Rockford
Hollern, Dale, St. Stephen, E. Grand Rapids, MI
Hoogeboom, Larry, St. Jude, Grand Rapids
Jankowski, Leon, (Retired)
Jurek, Thomas, St. James, Grand Rapids
Kasprzyk, David, St. Thomas the Apostle & Our Lady of Grace, Muskegon
Lechtanski, Stanley, Basilica of St. Adalbert, Grand Rapids
Mauer, Michael J., Catholic Information Center, Grand Rapids
McCabe, William, St. Francis de Sales, Muskegon
McClintic, Robert, St. James, Grand Rapids; Prison & Jail Ministry
Nguyen, Thanh Van, Our Lady of LaVang, Wyoming
Pitt, Richard, Holy Redeemer, Jenison
Radecki, Richard, (Retired), St. Paul the Apostle, Grand Rapids
Riksen, Norman, (Retired)
Roersma, Gerald, Holy Trinity, Comstock Park
Scheid, Howard, (Retired)
Schlitz, James, Prince of Peace, North Muskegon
Schneider, Daniel, St. Isidore, Grand Rapids
Sobolewski, Donald F., St. Patrick, Portland
Thorndill, James, St. Thomas, Grand Rapids
VandeVoren, Lawrence
Williams, Dennis, St. Thomas, Grand Rapids
Wood, Michael, St. Mary Magdalen, Grand Rapids
Zapata, Martin, St. Joseph the Worker, Grand Rapids

INSTITUTIONS LOCATED IN THE DIOCESE

[A] COLLEGES AND UNIVERSITIES

GRAND RAPIDS. *Aquinas College*, 1607 Robinson Rd., S.E., 49506. Tel: 616-632-8900; Fax: 616-732-4589. Web: www.aquinas.edu. C. Edward Balog, Ph.D., Pres.; Charles Gunnoe, Ph.D., Provost; Michael C. Keller, M.S.A., Vice Pres. Planning & Research; Greg McAleenan, B.A., J.D., Vice Pres. Advancement; Paula Meehan, Vice Pres.; Nanette Clatterbuck, M.Ed., Assoc. Provost; Thomas Mikowski, B.S., Dean of Admissions; Marty Fahey, APR, Dir. College Rels.; Cecilia Mesler, B.A., Registrar; David J. Steffee, Dir. Financial Aid; Mary Clark-Kaiser, Dir. Campus Ministry; Terry Marshall, Liturgist; Eric Bridge, Service Learning Coord.; Brandon Spence, Pastoral Musician; Francine Paolini, Co-Dir. Library; Shellie Jeffries, Co-Dir. Library; Patricia Chase, Ed.D., Dean Students; Terrence Bocian, M.A., Dir. Athletics. Sisters 5; Lay Teachers 89; Students 2,312.

[B] HIGH SCHOOLS, DIOCESAN

GRAND RAPIDS. *Catholic Central High School*, 319 Sheldon Ave., S.E., 49503. Tel: 616-233-5899; Fax: 616-459-0257. Web: www.grcatholiccentral.com. Mr. Steve Passinault, Prin.; Ann Wheeler, Librarian. Sisters of St. Dominic 1; Lay Teachers 44; Students 775.

West Catholic High School, 1801 Bristol, N.W., 49504. Tel: 616-233-5900; Fax: 616-453-4320. Web: grwestcatholic.org. Mr. Tom Maj, Prin.; Mr. Chuck Pitsch, Librarian. Lay Teachers 36; Students 582.

[C] HIGH SCHOOLS, PRIVATE

MUSKEGON. *Greater Muskegon Catholic Schools*, 1145 W. Laketon Ave., 49441. Tel: 231-755-2201; Fax: 231-755-2415. Robert Bridges, Supt.; Patrick O'Neill, Prin.; Margaret Alexander, Librarian. Lay Teachers 35; Students 490.

[D] INTERPAROCHIAL ELEMENTARY SCHOOLS

HOLLAND. *Corpus Christi School*, (Grades K-8), 12100 Quincy St., 49424. Tel: 616-994-9864; Fax: 616-994-9870. Web: www.corpuschristischool.us. Joanne Swan Jones, Prin. Lay Teachers 14; Students 131.

[E] DIOCESAN ELEMENTARY SCHOOLS

GRAND RAPIDS. *All Saints Academy*, (Grades PreSchool-8), PS-4 Campus: 2233 Diamond Ave., N.E., 49505. Tel: 616-364-9453; Fax: 616-361-6991. 5-8 Campus: 1120 Four Mile N.E., 49525. Tel: 616-363-7725; Fax: 616-363-3086. Christine Burns, Prin.; Anne Harpold, Asst. Prin.

[F] GRADE SCHOOLS, PRIVATE

MUSKEGON. *Muskegon Catholic Central Elementary School*, (Grades PreSchool-4), 2947 McCracken St., 49441. Tel: 231-755-1045; Fax: 231-759-7009. Web: www.gmcs.org. Penny Johnson, Prin. Lay Teachers 10; Students 191.

[G] GENERAL HOSPITALS

GRAND RAPIDS. *Saint Mary's Health Care*, 200 Jefferson, S.E., 49503. Tel: 616-685-6090; Fax: 616-685-6151. Web: www.smhc.org. Philip McCorkle, Pres. & CEO; Rev. Ayub Nasar, Chap.; Sr. Myra Bergman, R.S.M., Vice Pres. Mission Svcs. Sponsored by Catholic Health Ministries. Bed Capacity 336; Patients Assisted Annually 860,000; Total Staff 2,495.

MUSKEGON. *Mercy Health Partners*Roger Spoelman, Pres. & CEO; Rev. Bartholomew Okagbue, Chap. Sponsored by Trinity Health. Bed Capacity 457; Total Assisted Annually 20,811; Total Staff 3,836.

Mercy Health Partners, Mercy Campus, 1500 E. Sherman Blvd., 49444. Tel: 231-672-2000; Fax: 231-672-3074.

Mercy Health Partners, General Campus, 1700 Oak Ave., 49242. Priests 1; Sisters 1.

Mercy Health Partners, Hackley Campus, 1700 Clinton Ave., 49442.

Mercy Health Partners, Lakeshore Campus, 72 S. State St., Shelby, 49455.

[H] HOMES FOR THE AGED

GRAND RAPIDS. *St. Ann's Home* (1951) 2161 Leonard St., N.W., 49504. Tel: 616-453-7715; Fax: 616-453-7359. Email: sisterg@stannshome.com. Carmelite Sisters of the Divine Heart of Jesus. Priests 7; Sisters 8; Residents 150; Total Assisted 150; Total Staff 200.

[I] CONVENTS AND RESIDENCES FOR SISTERS

GRAND RAPIDS. *Dominican Center at Marywood*, 2025 E. Fulton St., 49503-3895. Tel: 616-454-1241; Fax: 616-454-2861. Web: www.dominicancenter.com. Sr. Diane Zerfas, O.P., Interim Prog. Dir.

Marywood Health Center, 111 Lakeside Dr., N.E., 49503-3811. Tel: 616-643-0272; Fax: 616-454-6105. Sisters 48; Bed Capacity 50.

Motherhouse of the Dominican Sisters, Marywood, 2025 E. Fulton St., 49503-3895. Tel: 616-459-2910; Fax: 616-454-6105. Web: www.grdominicans.org. Sisters Nathalie Meyer, O.P., Prioress; Janet Brown, O.P., Dir. Pastoral Life; Maureen Geary, O.P., Treas.

Sisters of St. Dominic of the Congregation of Our Lady of the Sacred Heart (The Religious Institute) Sisters of the Order of St. Dominic of Grand Rapids, Michigan (The Corporation)., Motherhouse and Novitiate for the Sisters of the Order of St. Dominic of the Congregation of Our Lady of the Sacred Heart. Sisters 261.

ADA. *Discalced Carmelite Nuns, Monastery of Our Lady of Guadalupe* (1916) (Parnell), 4300 Mount Carmel Dr., N.E., 49301-9784. Tel: 616-691-7625; Fax: 616-691-8538. Sr. Elizabeth Ann, O.C.D., Prioress. Professed Carmelite Nuns 12; Extern Sisters 1.

BELMONT. *Motherhouse of the Consolata Missionary Sisters* (1954) 6801 Belmont Rd., P.O. Box 371, 49306. Tel: 616-361-2072; Fax: 616-361-2049. Email: mcregus@consolatasisters.org. Web: www.consolatasisters.org. Sr. Zelita M. Bragagnolo, M.C., Supr. Consolata Sisters 10.

LOWELL. *Franciscan Sisters of the Eucharist*, 11600 Downes St., 49331-9489. Tel: 616-897-5590; Fax: 616-897-5088. Email: smaschmitz@fsecommunity.org. Sr. Rita Brunner, F.S.E., Supr. Sisters 14.

[J] RETREAT HOUSES

SPRING LAKE. *St. Lazare Retreat House*, 18600 W. Spring Lake Rd., 49456. Tel: 616-842-3370; Fax: 616-842-6815. Email: secretaryst@triton.net. Web: www.stlazareretreat.org. Revs. Michael J. Shea, C.M.; Thomas M. Finley, C.M.

[K] NEWMAN CENTERS

ALLENDALE. *St. Luke University Parish and Catholic Campus Ministry* Cook-Dewitt Center, GVSU, Rm. 120, 49401-9403. Tel: 616-331-3131. Email: frbrad@gvsucatholic.org. Revs. Bradford C. Schoeberle, C.S.P., Campus Min.; Donald A. Andrie, C.S.P., Campus Min.

BIG RAPIDS

St. Paul Campus Parish listed under Parishes Outside the City of Grand Rapids

[L] MISCELLANEOUS LISTINGS

GRAND RAPIDS. *Basilica of St. Adalbert Education Foundation* (1985) 701 4th St., N.W., 49504. Tel: 616-458-3065; Fax: 616-458-0563. Email: stasker@basilicagr.org. Web: basilicagr.org.

Bishops' Housing Corporation, Cathedral Square Center, 360 Division Ave., S., 49503-4539. Tel: 616-475-1247; Fax: 616-551-5635.

Cathedral Square, Inc., Cathedral Square Center, 360 Division Ave., S., 49503-4539. Tel: 616-475-1247; Fax: 616-551-5635.

Catholic Charities West Michigan, Cathedral Square Center, 360 Division Ave., S., 49503-4539. Tel: 616-551-4747; Fax: 616-243-1442. Web: www.ccwestmi.org. Deborah Nykamp, Pres. & CEO.

The Catholic Foundation of West Michigan, 360 Division Ave. S., 49503. Tel: 616-243-0491; Fax: 616-243-4910. T. Edward Carey Jr.

Catholic Information Center, Cathedral Square Center, 360 Division Ave. S., Ste. 2A, 49503-4539. Tel: 616-459-7267; Fax: 616-459-4645. Rev. Mark-David Janus, C.S.P., Dir.

Christopher House, Cathedral Square Center, 360 Division Ave., S., 49503-4539. Tel: 616-475-1247; Fax: 616-551-5635.

The Foundation for Catholic Secondary Education of Greater Grand Rapids, Inc., Cathedral Square Center, 360 Division Ave., S., 49503-4539. Tel: 616-233-5977; Fax: 616-514-6055. Email: cindysielawa@grcss.org.

Marywood Academy, 2025 E. Fulton St., 49503-3895. Tel: 616-454-2910; Fax: 616-454-6105.

Ministry Ventures, 2025 E. Fulton St., 49503-3895. Tel: 616-643-0133; Fax: 616-454-6105. Email: mgeary@grdominicans.org. Sr. Maureen Geary, O.P., Treas.; Jack Peltier, Dir. Finance.

SS. Peter and Paul Parish Education Endowment Fund, 520 Myrtle St., N.W., 49504. Tel: 616-454-6000; Fax: 616-454-4532.

Sisters of St. Dominic Charitable Trust, 2025 E. Fulton St., 49503-3895. Tel: 616-459-2910; Fax: 616-454-6105. Sr. Nathalie Meyer, O.P.

Sisters of St. Dominic of the Congregation of Our Lady of the Sacred Heart Charitable Trust (The Trust).

The Society of the Redemptorists of the City of Grand Rapids, 224 Carrier St., N.E., 49505. Tel: 616-451-3043; Fax: 616-458-5667. Email: stalphonsusgr@catholicweb.com. Web: stalphonsusgr.com. Revs. Denis J. Ryan, C.Ss.R.; Andrew J. Thompson, C.Ss.R.; Rudy Papes, C.Ss.R.; Robert Balser, C.Ss.R.; Edward P. Vella, C.Ss.R.; Bernard Carlin, C.Ss.R.; Bro. Andrew Patin, C.Ss.R. Represented in the Diocese.

Steepletown Neighborhood Services, Inc. (1994) 671 Davis, N.W., Steepletown Center, 49504. Tel: 616-451-4215; Fax: 616-451-0557. Email: dick@steepletowncenter.org. Neighborhood Center for Social Service and Assistance.

The Society For The Propagation Of The Faith, Cathedral Square Center, 360 Division Ave., S., 49503-4539. Tel: 616-459-4516; Fax: 616-243-4910. Revs. Stephen S. Dudek, Dir.; Stephen S. Dudek, Dir.

BELMONT. *Grand Rapids Catholic Committee on Scouting*, 6550 Belmont Ave., 49306. Tel: 616-780-9088; 616-364-9093. Email: scottharvey@prodigy.net. Web: www.grccscouting.org. Scott Harvey, Treas.

LOWELL. *Franciscan Life Process Center* (1999) 11650 Downes St., 49331-9489. Tel: 616-897-7842; Fax: 616-897-7054. Email: scanagle@lifeprocesscenter.org. Sr. Colleen Ann Nagle, F.S.E., Dir.

PORTLAND. *The Father Flohe Foundation*, 140 Church St., 48875. Tel: 517-647-6505; Fax: 517-647-7807.

VESTABURG. *Emmaus Monastery*, 10154 N. Pine Grove Rd., 48891. Tel: 989-268-5494. Email: emmaus.monastery@gmail.com. Web: www.emmausmonastery.org. Sr. Diane Stier, E.C., Prioress.

WYOMING. *Catholic Cemeteries Extended Care Fund*, 4100 Clyde Park, S.W., 49509-0063. Tel: 616-531-9320; Fax: 616-531-9780. Mr. Robert Menzel, Dir. & Mgr.

RELIGIOUS INSTITUTES OF MEN REPRESENTED IN THE DIOCESE

For further details refer to the corresponding bracketed number in the Religious Institutes of Men or Women section.

[1330]—*Congregation of the Mission*—C.M.
[1030]—*Paulist Fathers*—C.S.P.
[1070]—*Redemptorist Fathers* (Denver Prov.)—C.SS.R.
[0990]—*Society of the Catholic Apostolate*—S.A.C.

RELIGIOUS INSTITUTES OF WOMEN REPRESENTED IN THE DIOCESE

[0360]—*Carmelite Sisters of the Divine Heart of Jesus Carmel*—C.D.C.J.
[3832]—*Congregation of the Sisters of St. Joseph*—C.S.J.
[0720]—*Consolata Missionary Sisters*—M.C.
[0420]—*Discalced Carmelite Nuns*—O.C.D.
[1070-14]—*Dominican Sisters*—O.P.
[]—*Emmaus Community*—E.C.
[1430]—*Franciscan Sisters of Our Lady of Perpetual Help*—O.S.F.
[2575]—*Institute of the Sisters of Mercy of the Americas*—R.S.M.
[]—*Mexican Passionist Sisters*—C.F.P.
[2970]—*School Sisters of Notre Dame*—S.S.N.D.
[3560]—*Servants of Jesus*—S.J.
[0470]—*Sisters of Charity of the Incarnate Word*—C.C.V.I.
[2990]—*Sisters of Notre Dame*—S.N.D.
[]—*Sisters of St. Paul De Chartres*—S.D.C.
[1250]—*The Institute for the Franciscan Sisters of the Eucharist*—F.S.E.

NECROLOGY

† Jude, Rev. Msgr. Walter F., (Retired)—Died May 5, 2009

† Bielskas, Edward J., (Retired)—Died Dec. 31, 2008

An asterisk (*) denotes an organization that has established tax-exempt status directly with the IRS and is not covered by the USCCB Group Ruling.

Diocese of Great Falls - Billings

(Dioecesis Magnocataractensis-Billingensis)

Most Reverend

MICHAEL W. WARFEL

Bishop of Great Falls-Billings; ordained April 26, 1980; appointed Bishop of Juneau November 19, 1996; ordained December 17, 1996; appointed Apostolic Administrator of Fairbanks October 23, 2001; resigned June 7, 2002; appointed Bishop of Great Falls-Billings November 20, 2007; installed January 16, 2008. *Office: 121 23rd St. S., Great Falls, MT 59401-3939.* Tel: 406-727-6683.

ALWAYS TO WALK IN CHRIST

Most Reverend

ANTHONY M. MILONE, D.D.

Bishop Emeritus of Great Falls-Billings; ordained December 15, 1957; appointed Titular Bishop Plestia and Auxiliary of Omaha November 10, 1981; Episcopal ordination January 6, 1982; appointed Bishop of Great Falls-Billings December 14, 1987; installed February 23, 1988; resigned July 12, 2006. *Res.: St. Bernadette, 7600 S. 42nd St., Bellevue, NE 68147-1702.* Tel: 402-933-8707. Email: bishopmilone@cox.net.

ERECTED MAY 18, 1904.

Square Miles 94,158.

Corporation Title: "Roman Catholic Bishop of Great Falls, Montana, a corporation sole."

Comprises the eastern part of the State of Montana and is made up of the following Counties: Big Horn, Blaine, Carbon, Carter, Cascade, Chouteau, Custer, Daniels, Dawson, Fallon, Fergus, Garfield, Golden Valley, Hill, Judith Basin, Liberty, McCone, Musselshell, Park, Petroleum, Phillips, Powder River, Prairie, Richland, Roosevelt, Rosebud, Sheridan, Stillwater, Sweet Grass, Treasure, Valley, Wibaux, Yellowstone and parts of Toole.

For legal titles of parishes and diocesan institutions, consult the Pastoral Office.

Pastoral Office: 121 23rd St. S., Great Falls, MT 59401-3939. Mailing Address: P.O. Box 1399, Great Falls, MT 59403-1399. Tel: 406-727-6683; 800-332-9998 (Toll Free Montana only); Fax: 406-454-3480.

Web: www.dioceseofgfb.org

Email: chancery@dioceseofgfb.org

STATISTICAL OVERVIEW

Personnel	
Bishop	1
Retired Bishops	1
Priests: Diocesan Active in Diocese	31
Priests: Diocesan Active Outside Diocese	4
Priests: Retired, Sick or Absent	29
Number of Diocesan Priests	64
Religious Priests in Diocese	14
Total Priests in Diocese	78
Extern Priests in Diocese	6
Ordinations:	
Diocesan Priests	1
Permanent Deacons in Diocese	5
Total Brothers	1
Total Sisters	56
Parishes	
Parishes	55
With Resident Pastor:	
Resident Diocesan Priests	29
Resident Religious Priests	10
Without Resident Pastor:	
Administered by Priests	8
Administered by Deacons	4
Administered by Religious Women	1
Missions	52
Professional Ministry Personnel:	
Brothers	1
Sisters	9
Lay Ministers	39
Welfare	
Catholic Hospitals	2
Total Assisted	463,532
Homes for the Aged	1
Total Assisted	84
Day Care Centers	7
Total Assisted	347
Educational	
Diocesan Students in Other Seminaries	5
Total Seminarians	5
Colleges and Universities	1
Total Students	858
High Schools, Diocesan and Parish	2
Total Students	421
High Schools, Private	1
Total Students	121
Elementary Schools, Diocesan and Parish	9
Total Students	1,463
Elementary Schools, Private	4
Total Students	478
Catechesis/Religious Education:	
High School Students	922
Elementary Students	2,620
Total Students under Catholic Instruction	6,888
Teachers in the Diocese:	
Priests	2
Brothers	1
Sisters	4
Lay Teachers	294
Vital Statistics	
Receptions into the Church:	
Infant Baptism Totals	654
Minor Baptism Totals	100
Adult Baptism Totals	58
Received into Full Communion	51
First Communions	673
Confirmations	799
Marriages:	
Catholic	88
Interfaith	68
Total Marriages	156
Deaths	698
Total Catholic Population	47,773
Total Population	434,299

Former Bishops—Most Revs. MATHIAS C. LENIHAN, D.D., ord. Dec. 20, 1879; cons. First Bishop of Great Falls, Sept. 21, 1904; resigned Jan. 18, 1930; created Titular Archbishop of Preslavo, Feb. 14, 1930; died Aug. 19, 1943; EDWIN V. O'HARA, D.D., ord. June 10, 1905; appt. Aug. 1, 1930; cons. Oct. 28, 1930; appt. Bishop of Kansas City April 15, 1939; made asst. at the Pontifical Throne Jan. 5, 1949; appt. Archbishop "Ad Personam" June 29, 1954; died Sept. 11, 1956, Milan, Italy; WILLIAM J. CONDON, D.D., ord. Oct. 14, 1917; appt. Aug. 5, 1939; cons. Oct. 18, 1939; asst. at the Pontifical Throne Dec. 9, 1964; died Aug. 17, 1967; ELDON BERNARD SCHUSTER, D.D., ord. May 27, 1937; appt. Titular Bishop of Amblada; cons. Dec. 21, 1961; appt. Bishop of Great Falls Dec. 2, 1967; resigned Dec. 27, 1977; died Sept. 4, 1998; THOMAS JOSEPH MURPHY, D.D., S.T.D., ord. April 12, 1958; appt. Bishop of Great Falls July 5, 1978; Episcopal ordination and installation Aug. 21, 1978; appt. Coadjutor Archbishop of Seattle May 26, 1987; died June 26, 1997; ANTHONY M. MILONE, D.D., ord. Dec. 15, 1957; appt. Titular Bishop Plestia and Auxiliary of Omaha Nov. 10, 1981; Episcopal ord. Jan. 6, 1982; appt. Bishop of Great Falls-Billings Dec. 14, 1987; installed Feb. 23, 1988; resigned July 12, 2006.

Vicar General—Very Rev. JAY H. PETERSON, V.G. Email: vicargeneral@dioceseofgfb.org.

Pastoral Office—121 23rd St. S., P.O. Box 1399, Great Falls, 59403. Tel: 406-727-6683; 800-332-9998 (Montana Toll Free Number Only); Fax: 406-454-3480. All applications for dispensations and official communications should be addressed to this office.

Chancellor—Sr. LYNN CASEY, S.C.L. Email: chancellor@dioceseofgfb.org. Send all Marriage Correspondence to the Director of the Tribunal.

Moderator of the Curia—Very Rev. JAY H. PETERSON, V.G.

Business Manager/Fiscal Officer—JOSEPH LONCKI. Email: business@dioceseofgfb.org.

Diocesan Tribunal—121 23rd St. S., P.O. Box 1399, Great Falls, 59403. Tel: 406-727-6683; 800-332-9998 (Montana Toll Free Number Only). Email: tribunal@dioceseofgfb.org.

Judicial Vicar—Rev. ROBERT D. GROSCH, J.C.L.

Promoter of Justice—Rev. JOHN W. ROBERTSON, J.C.L.

Defender of the Bond—Rev. MICHAEL SCHNEIDER, J.C.L. (Cand.).

Director of the Tribunal—TERRYAL ANN REAVLEY.

Notary—TERRYAL ANN REAVLEY.

Diocesan Consultors—Revs. JAMES O'NEILL; DAVID REICHLING, O.F.M.Cap.; DALE E. YURKOVIC; ROBERT SEWVELLO; TED F. SZUDERA; WILLIAM D'SOUZA; DANIEL WATHEN; ROBERT OSWALD; PATRICK ZABROCKI.

Personnel Board—Revs. STEPHEN L. TOKARSKI; PETER E. GUTHNECK; DANIEL O'ROURKE; JOSEPH PONESSA; GREGORY STAUDINGER.

Vicars Forane—Revs. STEPHEN J. ZABROCKI, Billings; RICHARD SCHLOSSER, Great Falls; PETER E. GUTHNECK, Havre; ROBERT OSWALD, Miles City;

FRANCIS SCHREIBER, Wolf Point.

Cemetery Board—Mount Olivet Cemetery (Great Falls): Most Rev. MICHAEL W. WARFEL; JOSEPH LONCKI. Holy Cross Cemetery (Billings): Rev. ROBERT GROSCH; JOHN GLEN, Chm.

Vicar for Clergy—VACANT.

Cum Christo/Cursillo—VACANT.

Vicar for Ministry to Native Americans—VACANT.

Diocesan Offices and Directors

Boy Scouts—EDWARD LAWLER, Chm. Catholic Committee on Scouting; Rev. LEO G. MCDOWELL, Chap., Mailing Address: P.O. Box 849, Fort Benton, 59442. Tel: 406-622-3726. Email: frleo@frleo.org.

Catholic Campaign for Human Development—Sr. LYNN CASEY, S.C.L., Diocesan Dir., 121 23rd St. S., Great Falls, 59401. Mailing Address: P.O. Box 1399, Great Falls, 59403. Tel: 406-727-6683; Fax: 406-454-3480.

Office of Stewardship—VACANT, Dir.; STELLA ZIEGLER, Committee Chm. Email: business@dioceseofgfb.org.

Catechesis—ANTHONY ALLEN, Dir. Youth Ministry & Catechesis, Mailing Address: Pastoral Center, P.O. Box 1399, Great Falls, 59403. Tel: 406-727-6683. Email: 7treasures@dioceseofgfb.org.

Catholic Relief Services—Sr. LYNN CASEY, S.C.L.

Clerical Benefit Association—Most Rev. MICHAEL W. WARFEL; Revs. PATRICK ZABROCKI, Pres.; DANIEL WATHEN, Sec. & Treas.; JAMES BIRKMAIER, Retired Priest Rep.; TERRY REGAN; ROBERT D. GROSCH, J.C.L.; JAMES R. SIKORA; RICHARD SCHLOSSER; JOSEPH LONCKI, Consultant.

Continuing Formation of Clergy—Most Rev. MICHAEL W. WARFEL.

Diocesan Pastoral Council—Sisters LYNN CASEY, S.C.L., Exec. Coord.; BERNADETTE HELFERT, S.C.L., Chm., Mailing Address: 121 23rd St. S., P.O. Box 1399, Great Falls, 59403-1399. Tel: 406-727-6683; Fax: 406-454-3480.

Membership—JARED HARRIS, Billings; RICHARD HALL, Billings; ROGER SEILSTAD, Great Falls; JOAN BENNETT, Great Falls; KIM BRIESE, Havre; JEROME MAIN, Havre; TERRIE MCDONALD, Miles City; JOHN LANE, Miles City; MIKE FISHER, Wolf Point; ANNE O'BRIEN, Wolf Point; JOSEPH LONCKI, Finance Council Liaison; Rev. FRANCIS SCHREIBER, Priest Council; Sr. CATHERINE KINSELLA, O.P., Sister Council.

Diocesan School Board—HARRY PLUMMER, Supt. Email: hplummer@dioceseofgfb.org; CHRIS READ, Chm., Mailing Address: P.O. Box 31158, Billings, 59107-1158. Tel: 406-252-9595; Fax: 406-252-9875.

D.C.C.W.—JOBY PARKER, Pres.; Rev. ROBERT OSWALD, Moderator.

Ecumenical Officer—VACANT.

Education—HARRY PLUMMER, Diocesan School Supt., Mailing Address: P.O. Box 1399, Great Falls, 59403-1399. Tel: 406-727-6683; 800-332-9998; Fax: 406-454-3480. Email: hplummer@dioceseofgfb.org.

Finance Council—Most Rev. MICHAEL W. WARFEL; BILL BELINSKI; JERE MANNING; Rev. THOMAS TOBIN; Very Rev. JAY H. PETERSON, V.G., Vicar Gen. Ex Officio; FRANK FRENCH; STELLA ZIEGLER; Rev. STEPHEN J. ZABROCKI; Sisters JEAN DAWSON, S.C.L.; LYNN CASEY, S.C.L., Chancellor; JOSEPH LONCKI, Consultant; MARILYN HARMON; JOHN NELSON; ALBERT MARTENS; MARILYN ROSE; ELLEN SOLEM; Rev. LEO G. MCDOWELL.

Lay Ministry Programs—Sr. EILEEN HURLEY, S.C.L. Email: layministry@dioceseofgfb.org.

Liturgical Commission—Sr. MARILYN WINTER, O.P., Chm.; LARRY GUILBAULT; ROSALIE FOSTER; JOBY PARKER; Sr. MARGARET MARY O'DOHERTY, O.P.; Most Rev. MICHAEL W. WARFEL; ANTHONY ALLEN; COLLEEN EISENMAN; Rev. STEPHEN J. ZABROCKI; TIMOTHY MARONEY.

Office of Worship—Sr. MARILYN WINTER, O.P., Dir. Email: worship@dioceseofgfb.org.

Newspaper— "The Harvest" Very Rev. JAY H. PETERSON, V.G., Editor.

RCIA—Sr. MARILYN WINTER, O.P., Dir.

Pastoral Outreach—Very Rev. JAY H. PETERSON, V.G., Coord.; ANTHONY ALLEN; Sisters EILEEN HURLEY, S.C.L.; LYNN CASEY, S.C.L.; MARILYN WINTER, O.P.; HARRY PLUMMER; TERRYAL ANN REAVLEY; DEB WAGNER; JOSEPH LONCKI.

Priests' Council—Most Rev. MICHAEL W. WARFEL; Revs. DALE E. YURKOVIC; ROBERT SEWVELLO; TED F. SZUDERA; ROBERT OSWALD; WILLIAM D'SOUZA; DANIEL WATHEN; PATRICK ZABROCKI; DAVID REICHLING, O.F.M.Cap.; JAMES O'NEILL; Very Rev. JAY H. PETERSON, V.G., Ex Officio.

Sister's Council—Liaisons: Sisters LYNN CASEY, S.C.L.; EILEEN HURLEY, S.C.L.

Director of Vocations—Rev. LEO G. MCDOWELL, Mailing Address: Immaculate Conception Church, P.O. Box 849, Fort Benton, 59442. Tel: 406-622-3726. Email: frleo@frleo.org.

Inter-Diocesan Organizations

Montana Catholic Conference—MOE WOSEPKA, Exec. Dir., Mailing Address: P.O. Box 1708, Helena, 59624. Tel: 406-442-5761; Fax: 406-442-9047. Email: mccadmin@bresnan.net. Web: www.montanacc.org.

Catholic Social Services of Montana—ROSEMARY MILLER, Dir., 1301 11th Ave., Helena, 59601. Mailing Address: P.O. Box 907, Helena, 59624-0907. Tel: 406-442-4130; 800-222-9383; Fax: 406-442-4192. Web: www.cssmt.org. Email: rosemary@catholicsocialservicesofmontana.org. Provides adoption and counseling services for families, children and infants.

Billings Office—BECKY HUBBERT, 1048 N. 30th St., Billings, 59101. Tel: 406-252-3399; Fax: 406-252-9173. Email: billings@cssmt.org.

Columbus Office—SAM HUBBERT, P.O. Box 707, Columbus, 59019-0707. Tel: 406-322-4264. Email: cssm@cablemt.net.

Great Falls Office—KYLA WRIGHT; DELJEAN WADSWORTH, Mailing Address: 410 Central Ave., #601, Great Falls, 59401. Tel: 406-771-7805. Email: greatfalls@cssmt.org.

Helena Office—HELEN BEAUSOLEI, Mailing Address: P.O. Box 907, Helena, 59601. Tel: 406-442-4130; Fax: 406-442-4192.

Missoula Office—BETSY ROBEL, 420 W. Pine St., Missoula, 59802. Tel: 406-728-5429; Fax: 406-327-8537. Email: missoula@cssmt.org.

Montana Association of Churches—Rev. DAN KREBILL, Yellowstone Presbytery, P.O. Box 1150, Bozeman, 59771; PAM SHELDON, Exec. Sec., 25 S. Ewing St., Ste. 408, Helena, 59601-6072. Tel: 406-449-6010; Fax: 406-449-6657. Web: www.montana-churches.org.

Victim Assistance Coordinator—Sr. KATHLEEN KANE, O.P. Tel: 406-378-2250. Email: asstcoord@dioceseofgfb.org.

CLERGY, PARISHES, MISSIONS AND PAROCHIAL SCHOOLS

CITY OF GREAT FALLS

(CASCADE COUNTY)

1—ST. ANN'S CATHEDRAL Rev. Oliver Doyle, Admin. Res.: 715 Third Ave. N., P.O. Box 1708, 59403. Tel: 406-761-5456; Fax: 406-761-5457. Email: stannscathedral@mt.net. Web: www.stannscathedral.org.

Catechesis/Religious Program—Georgia Miller, Youth Min.; Patty Jo Sheldon, D.R.E. Students 28.

2—ST. GERARD MAJELLA, Closed. For inquiries for parish records contact the chancery.

3—HOLY FAMILY, Closed. See Holy Spirit.

4—HOLY SPIRIT (1998) Rev. Richard Schlosser; Sr. Catherine Kinsella, O.P., Pastoral Assoc.; Mark Meyer, Parish Admin.

Parish Office—201 44th St. S., 59405. Tel: 406-452-6491; Fax: 406-452-6495. Email: hsparish@holyspiritgf.org. Web: www.holyspiritgf.org.

Sts. Peter & Paul Education Center—200 44th St. S., 59405. Tel: 406-761-4805.

School—(Grades PreK-8), 2820 Central Ave., 59401. Tel: 406-761-5775; Fax: 406-761-5887. Email: rorohscs@hotmail.com. Web: www.holyspiritschool-.net. Roger Robbins, Prin. Lay Teachers 20; Students 235.

Catechesis/Religious Program—Students 260.

Chapel—*Holy Family* 2800 Central Ave., 59401.

5—ST. JOSEPH (1912) Very Rev. Jay H. Peterson, Canonical Pastor; Rev. Wm. Paul McKane, O.S.B., Parochial Vicar; Jean Sobolik, Pastoral Assoc. Church: 420-2nd. Ave., S.W., 59404. Tel: 406-453-9331.

Parish Center: 500-2nd Ave. S.W., 59404.

Catechesis/Religious Program—Tel: 406-453-9331. Carmen Thorsen, D.R.E. Students 32.

6—ST. LUKE THE EVANGELIST (1967) Very Rev. Jay H. Peterson, Canonical Pastor; Rev. Wm. Paul McKane, O.S.B., Parochial Vicar; Mary Lynn Wojtowick, Pastoral Assoc.

Res.: 410 22nd Ave., N.E., 59404. Tel: 406-453-6546. Email: stlukes@bresnan.net.

Catechesis/Religious Program—Jeanne Tonkovich, D.R.E. (K-5); Laura Toeckes, D.R.E. (Youth). Students 219.

7—OUR LADY OF LOURDES Rev. Lothar Krauth; Barbara Brown, Pastoral Assoc.

Res.: 409 13th St. S., 59405. Tel: 406-452-6464; Fax: 406-452-6464. Email: lourdes@bresnan.net. Web: www.angelfire.com/mt/ollgf.

School—(Grades PreK-8), 1305 Fifth Ave. S., 59405. Tel: 406-452-0551; Fax: 406-761-7180. Web: www.ollschool.info. Mrs. Sherri Schmitz, Prin. Lay Teachers 14; Students 245.

Catechesis/Religious Program—Roslyn Gallagher, D.R.E.; Mary Jo Bailly, Youth Min. Students 70.

8—STS. PETER & PAUL, Closed. See Holy Spirit.

CITY OF BILLINGS

(YELLOWSTONE COUNTY)

1—ST. BERNARD Rev. David Reichling, O.F.M.Cap. Office: 226 Wicks Ln., 59105. Tel: 406-259-4350; Fax: 406-259-0433. Email: davidr@stbernardblgs.org. Web: www.stbernardblgs.org.

Catechesis/Religious Program—Brian Shea, D.R.E. (Youth Group); Ann Salisburg, D.R.E. (Elementary). Students 254.

Mission—*Sts. Cyril & Methodius* c/o St. Bernard's Church, 226 Wicks Ln., Yellowstone Co. 59105. Tel: 406-259-4350. Church: 16 S. Corner Rd., Ballantine, 59006.

2—HOLY ROSARY Deacon Melvin A. Melius, Pastoral Admin.; Lynne Gillig, Pastoral Assoc.

501 Custer Ave., 59101. Mailing Address: P.O. Box 20938, 59104.

Office: 521 Custer Ave., 59101. Tel: 406-259-7611; Fax: 406-248-8921. Email: holyrosary1@qwestoffice.net.

Catechesis/Religious Program—Students 79.

3—LITTLE FLOWER (1931) Deacon Melvin A. Melius, Pastoral Admin.; Rev. Paul Reichling, O.F.M.Cap., Sacramental Min.

Mailing Address: P.O. Box 20938, 59104.

Res.: 209 S. 35th St., 59101. Tel: 406-245-6711; Fax: 406-245-0494.

Catechesis/Religious Program—Amy Aguirre, D.R.E. Tel: 406-256-6333. Students 34.

4—OUR LADY OF GUADALUPE (1953) Deacon Melvin A. Melius, Pastoral Admin.; Rev. Paul Reichling, O.F.M.Cap., Sacramental Min.

Mailing Address: P.O. Box 20938, 59104.

Res.: 209 S. 35th St., 59101. Tel: 406-259-7611; Fax: 406-245-0494.

Church: 523 S. 29th St., 59101. Tel: 406-245-4717.

Catechesis/Religious Program—Tel: 406-256-6333. Students 65.

5—ST. PATRICK CO-CATHEDRAL Rev. Robert Grosch. Res.: 215 N. 31st St., 59101. Tel: 406-259-3389; Fax: 406-248-1185. Email: stpatrickblgs@yahoo.com. Web: www.catholic-church.org/stpatricksbillings.

Catechesis/Religious Program— Brenda Estill, D.R.E. Students 120.

6—ST. PIUS X (1958) Rev. Stephen L. Tokarski; Deacon Robert W. Daem; Bob Bender, Admin. & Business Mgr.; Mary Ronan, Campus Ministry Dir.

Parish Center—717 18th St. W., 59102. Tel: 406-656-2522; Fax: 406-656-2584.

Catechesis/Religious Program— Barbara Burleson, D.R.E. Students 193.

Billings Catholic Campus Ministry Program—Tel: 406-850-4488. Email: billingsccm@gmail.com.

7—ST. THOMAS THE APOSTLE Rev. Stephen Zabrocki; Deacon Tim Birkle; Kathy Lombardozzi, Outreach Coord.

Res.: 2101-24th St. W., 59102. Tel: 406-656-5578.

Church: 2055 Woody Dr., 59102. Tel: 406-656-5800; Fax: 406-656-8260. Email: st_thomas@qwestoffice.net.

Catechesis/Religious Program—Joyce Hollowell, D.R.E.; Cathy Day, Youth Min. Students 111.

OUTSIDE THE CITIES OF GREAT FALLS AND BILLINGS

ASHLAND, ROSEBUD CO., ST. LABRE (1884) Rev. Paschal Siler, O.F.M.Cap.

Res.: P.O. Box 228, 59003. Tel: 406-784-4536. Email: psiler@stlabre.org.

Catechesis/Religious Program—Pam Kania, D.R.E. Students 25.

BAKER, FALLON CO., ST. JOHN THE EVANGELIST Rev. Thomas Tobin.

Res.: P.O. Box 1519, 59313. Tel: 406-778-2297.

Church: 210 W. Center Ave., 59313.

Catechesis/Religious Program—Joan Grammond, D.R.E.; Gail Brence, D.R.E. Students 50.

Mission—*St. Joan of Arc* Ekalaka, Carter CoChurch: 100 Church Ave., Ekalaka, 59324.

Mission—*St. Anthony* [CEM] Plevna, Fallon CoChurch: 201 W. Conser Ave., Plevna, 59344.

BELT, CASCADE CO., ST. MARK THE EVANGELIST Rev. Ted F. Szudera.

Res.: P.O. Box 213, 59412. Tel: 406-277-3537.

Church: 132 Castner St., 59412.

Catechesis/Religious Program—Tel: 406-277-3366. Bob Williams, D.R.E. Students 49.

Mission—*St. Clement* Monarch, Cascade CoChurch: 62 Cascade Ave., Monarch, 59463.

Mission—*St. Mary* Raynesford, Judith Basin CoChurch: 100 Main St., Raynesford, 59469.

Mission—*Holy Trinity* Centerville, Cascade CoChurch: 692 Stockett Rd., Centerville.

BIG SANDY, CHOUTEAU CO., ST. MARGARET MARY (1910) Rev. Peter E. Guthneck; Sisters Margaret Mary O'Doherty, O.P., Pastoral Assoc. & D.R.E.; Kathleen Kane, O.P., Pastoral Assoc.
Res.: P.O. Box 3009, Box Elder, 59521. Tel: 406-395-4380.
Church: 400 Johannes, 59520.
St. Mary's Rocky Boy Indian Reservation: P.O. Box 3009, Box Elder, 59521. Tel: 406-395-4380.
Catechesis/Religious Program—Tel: 409-395-4870. Students 104.
Mission—St. Anthony Box Elder, Hill CoChurch: 235 E. Main, Box Elder, 59521.
Mission—St. Mary Rocky Boys Indian Reservation, Hill CoChurch: 99 Church Hill Rd., Box Elder, 59521.

BIG TIMBER, SWEET GRASS CO., ST. JOSEPH Rev. Wayne M. Pittard.
Res.: P.O. Box 871, 59011. Tel: 406-932-4728.
Church: 910 McLeod, 59011.
Catechesis/Religious Program—MaryAnn Finnan, D.R.E. Students 27.

BLACK EAGLE, CASCADE CO., MOST BLESSED SACRAMENT Very Rev. Jay H. Peterson, Canonical Pastor; Rev. Domenico Pizzonia, Parochial Vicar.
Res.: 1325 Smelter Ave., 59414. Tel: 406-453-8425; Fax: 406-453-8425. Email: frdom@live.com.
Catechesis/Religious Program—Sandy Wedel, D.R.E. Students 10.

BRIDGER, CARBON CO., SACRED HEART Sr. Nancy Malburg, O.P., Pastoral Admin.
Mailing Address: P.O. Box 309, 59014-0309.
Res.: 209 S. 4th St., 59014-0309. Tel: 406-662-3550; Fax: 406-662-3550. Email: trinity@brmt.net.
Catechesis/Religious Program—Students 55.
Mission—St. Joseph Fromberg, Carbon CoChurch: 202 N. Montana St., Fromberg, 59029.
Mission—St. John Joliet, Carbon CoChurch: 404 W. Central, Joliet, 59041.

BROADUS, POWDER RIVER CO., ST. DAVID (1931) Rev. Chester Poppa, O.F.M.Cap.
Mailing Address: P.O. Box 52, 59317. Tel: 406-436-2348. 217 N. Wilbur, 59317.
Catechesis/Religious Program—Students 20.

CHESTER, LIBERTY CO., ST. MARY Rev. Joseph Diekhans; Natalie Ghekiere, Parish Coord.
Res.: 504 Main, P.O. Box 647, 59522. Tel: 406-759-5377; Fax: 406-759-5568.
Catechesis/Religious Program—Tel: 406-759-5389. Natalie Ghekiere, D.R.E. Students 64.

CHINOOK, BLAINE CO., ST. GABRIEL (1896) Rev. Jose Valliparambil.
Res.: 404 Eighth St., P.O. Box 1089, 59523. Tel: 406-357-2073; Fax: 406-357-2173.
Catechesis/Religious Program—Mrs. Ellen Pyette, D.R.E., (Elementary); Mrs. Carol Elliot, D.R.E., (High School). Students 47.
Mission—St. Thomas the Apostle 210 1st Ave., S.E., Harlem, Blaine Co. 59526. P.O. Box 1125, Harlem, 59526. Tel: 406-353-4643.
Mission—St. Thomas Aquinas 10610 Wing Rd., Hogeland, Blaine Co. 59529. *c/o Mary Ann Olszewski*, 1570 Poland Rd., Hogeland, Blaine Co. 59529. Tel: 406-379-2582; Fax: 406-379-2582.

CIRCLE, MCCONE CO., ST. FRANCIS XAVIER Revs. Robert Oswald; Cory D. Sticha, Parochial Vicar.
Res.: 1102 C Ave., P.O. Box 160, 59215-0160. Tel: 406-485-3520; Fax: 406-485-3520. Email: stx@midrivers.com.
Church: 1100 C Ave., 59215.
Catechesis/Religious Program—Janna Munson, D.R.E. Students 10.
Mission—St. John the Baptist Jordan, Garfield Co. Tel: 406-557-6135. Email: stjohn@midrivers.com. Church: 412 Leavitt Ave., Jordan, 59337.
Catechesis/Religious Program—Students 21.
Mission—St. Francis de Sales Richey, Dawson CoChurch: 301 S. Main St., Richey, 59259.

COLSTRIP, ROSEBUD CO., ST. MARGARET MARY (1924) Deacon William Medved, Pastoral Admin.; Rev. William D'Souza, Sacramental Min.; Terri McDonald, Pastoral Assoc.
Res.: P.O. Box 305, 59323. Tel: 406-748-2214; Fax: 406-748-2214. Email: stmm@bhwi.net. Web: bhwi.net/stmm.
Church: 320 Water Ave., 59323. Tel: 406-748-2234.
Catechesis/Religious Program—Students 57.

COLUMBUS, STILLWATER CO., ST. MARY (1916) Rev. Michael Schneider.
Mailing Address: P.O. Box 956, 59019. Tel: 406-322-5541. Email: secretary@stmarycolumbus.org. Web: stmarycolumbus.org.
Church: 240 N. 4th St., 59019.
Catechesis/Religious Program—Students 25.
Mission—St. Michael Absarokee, Stillwater CoChurch: 307 S. Woodard St., Absorokee.

CROW AGENCY, BIG HORN CO., ST. DENNIS (1892) Rev. Charles Robinson, O.F.M.Cap.; Sr. Loretta Sedlmayer, R.S.M., Pastoral Assoc.
Res.: P.O. Box 57, 59022. Tel: 406-638-2641.
Church: 8750 Magic Carpet Rd., 59022.
Catechesis/Religious Program—Students 36.
Mission—St. Francis Xavier P.O. Box 138, St. Xavier, Big Horn Co. 59075. Tel: 406-666-2380. Church: 5936 W. 18300 S., St. Xavier, 59075. Leah Big Hair, Pastoral Assoc.

CULBERTSON, ROOSEVELT CO., ST. ANTHONY, Now a mission of Our Lady of Lourdes, Poplar.

FORSYTH, ROSEBUD CO., IMMACULATE CONCEPTION Rev. William D'Souza.
Res.: 591 N. 12th Ave. N., P.O. Box 166, 59327. Tel: 406-346-2101 (Rectory); 406-346-9239 (Parish Center). Email: wilphilet@yahoo.com.
Catechesis/Religious Program—Students 15.
Mission—St. Joseph Hysham, Treasure CoChurch: 206 Orchard Ave., Hysham.

FORT BENTON, CHOUTEAU CO., IMMACULATE CONCEPTION (1846) Rev. Leo G. McDowell.
Res.: P.O. Box 849, 59442. Tel: 406-622-3726.
Church: 1223-16th St., 59442. Email: icc@itstriangle.com.
Catechesis/Religious Program—Tel: 406-622-5288. Students 12.
Mission—St. Margaret P.O. Box 50, Geraldine, Chouteau Co. 59446-0050. Tel: 406-737-4573. Church: 700 Brewster St., Geraldine, 59446.

FORT SHAW, CASCADE CO., ST. ANN Rev. J. D. Dobbin (Retired).
Res.: 13327 MT. Hwy 200, 59443. Tel: 406-264-5554.
Catechesis/Religious Program—Carla Blanchard, D.R.E., (St. Ann). Tel: 406-264-5495; David Konecny, D.R.E., (Sacred Heart). Tel: 406-468-2368. Students 90.
Mission—Sacred Heart Cascade, Cascade Co.

GLASGOW, VALLEY CO., ST. RAPHAEL Rev. Robert Sewvello.
Office: 412 Third Ave. N., P.O. Box 1047, 59230. Tel: 406-228-9800; Fax: 406-228-9717. Email: straphael@nemontel.net.
Church: 402 Third Ave. N., 59230.
Catechesis/Religious Program—Tel: 406-228-4651. Amanda Bell, D.R.E.; Sheila Malone, Sec. Students 146.
Mission—Holy Family Glentana, Valley CoChurch: 102 1st Ave., N., Glentana, 59240.
Mission—St. Albert Hinsdale, Valley CoChurch: 304 Minnesota, Hinsdale, 59241.
Mission—Queen of the Angels Nashua, Valley CoChurch: 206 Hobart, Nashua, 59248.
Chapel—Our Lady of the Lake Fort Peck, Valley CoChurch: 150 Missouri, Fort Peck, 59223.

GLENDIVE, DAWSON CO., SACRED HEART (1907) Rev. Joseph Ponessa.
Res.: 316 W. Benham St., P.O. Box 36, 59330. Tel: 406-377-2585. Email: sacred@midrivers.com.
Catechesis/Religious Program—Tel: 406-377-4569. Monica Christianson, D.R.E. (Sacred Heart); Patti Goroski, D.R.E. (St. Philip's); Judy Bushman, D.R.E. (St. Peter's). Students 196.
Mission—St. Peter P.O. Box 217, Wibaux, Wibaux Co. 59353. Tel: 406-796-2215. Church: 312 W. 1st Ave., S., Wibaux, 59353. Rev. Jolly Pathiyamoola Ouseph, Parochial Vicar.
Mission—St. Philip P.O. Box 217, Wibaux, Wibaux Co. 59353. Tel: 406-796-8188. Church: 61 Lanesteer Rd., Wibaux, 59353.

HARDIN, BIG HORN CO., ST. JOSEPH Rev. Fabian Fehring, O.F.M.Cap.
Res.: 710 N. Custer, P.O. Box 510, 59034. Tel: 406-665-1432; Fax: 406-665-1432.
Catechesis/Religious Program—Students 45.
Mission—St. Mary Custer, Yellowstone Co.

HAVRE, HILL CO., ST. JUDE THADDEUS (1904) Rev. Dale E. Yurkovic; Timothy Maroney, Pastoral Assoc.
Res.: 440 7th Ave., P.O. Box 407, 59501. Tel: 406-265-4261; Fax: 406-265-4408. Email: stjude@ttc-cmc.net. Web: www.stjudehavre.catholicweb.com.
School—(Grades PreK-8), 430 7th Ave., 59501. Tel: 406-265-4613; Fax: 406-265-1315. Email: stjude2@ttc-cmc.net. Web: stjudeschoolmt.org. Mrs. Carol Ortman, Prin. Lay Teachers 11; Students 163.
Catechesis/Religious Program—Students 92.
Chapel—St. John the Baptist Cottonwood.

HAYS, BLAINE CO., ST. PAUL'S INDIAN MISSION (1886) Revs. Joseph R. Retzel, S.J.; Robert L. Erickson, S.J.; Sr. Laura Fucito, O.P., Pastoral Assoc.
Res.: Mission Dr. #1, P.O. Box 40, 59527. Tel: 406-673-3300; Fax: 406-673-3403. Email: josephrr@mtintouch.net.
School—(Grades K-6) Tel: 406-673-3123. Sr. Helen Durso, O.P., Prin. Sisters 3; Lay Teachers 7; Students 99.
Catechesis/Religious Program—Students 60.
Mission—St. Joseph Zortman, Phillips CoChurch: 300 Azure Ave., Zortman, 59546.
Mission—St. Thomas HC63, Box 5240, Lodgepole, Blaine Co. 59524. Tel: 406-673-3677; Fax: 406-673-3454. Sr. Laura Fucito, O.P., Pastoral Assoc.
Mission—Sacred Heart, Fort Belknap 303 Chipewa Ln., P.O. Box 429, Harlem, Blaine Co. 59526. Tel: 406-353-2257; Fax: 406-353-2927. Linda Azure, Pastoral Admin.

HINGHAM, HILL CO., OUR LADY OF RANSOM (1910) Rev. Joseph Diekhans.
Mailing Address: P.O. Box 647, Chester, 59522-0647.
Church: 201-2nd. St., 59528. Tel: 406-759-5377; Fax: 406-759-5568.
Catechesis/Religious Program—Dianne Folk, D.R.E. Students 26.
Mission—Sacred Heart 630 Main, Inverness, Hill Co.
Church: 630 Main, Inverness, 59530.

LAME DEER, ROSEBUD CO., BLESSED SACRAMENT Deacon Joseph Kristufek, Pastoral Admin.; Rev. Paschal Siler, O.F.M.Cap., Sacramental Min.; Sr. LeAnn Probst, O.P., Pastoral Assoc.
Res.: P.O. Box 100, 59043. Tel: 406-477-6384; Fax: 406-477-6224.
Church: 630 Cheyenne Ave., 59043.
Catechesis/Religious Program—Students 20.
Mission—Christ the King P.O. Box 315, Busby, Big Horn Co. 59016. Tel: 406-592-3568. Church: 13268 S. 5th St., Busby, 59016.

LAUREL, YELLOWSTONE CO., ST. ANTHONY (1907) [CEM] Rev. Thomas C. Harney.
Res.: 317 W. 7th St., P.O. Box 955, 59044. Tel: 406-628-7182.
Church: 700 3rd Ave., 59044.
Catechesis/Religious Program—Tel: 406-628-7484. Barb Hoppel, D.R.E. Students 139.

LEWISTOWN, FERGUS CO., ST. LEO (1888) [CEM] Rev. Daniel O'Rourke.
Res.: P.O. Box 421, 59457. Tel: 406-538-9306; Fax: 406-538-7624. Email: stleos@midrivers.com.
Church: 102 W. Broadway, 59457.
Catechesis/Religious Program— Pam Zerr, D.R.E., (Grades K-6). Students 120.
Mission—Holy Family Winifred, Fergus CoP.O. Box 421, 59457. Church: 530 Main St., Winifred, 59489. Jody DeMars, Coord.
Chapel—Danvers, St. Wenceslaus 7724 Danvers Rd., Danvers, 59430.

LIVINGSTON, PARK CO., ST. MARY, [CEM] Rev. Wayne M. Pittard; Joannie Lee, Pastoral Min.
Res.: 511 S. F St., P.O. Box 646, 59047-0646. Tel: 406-222-1393; Fax: 406-222-1405.
School—(Grades PreK-8) Tel: 406-222-3303. Judy Jagodzinski, Prin. Lay Teachers 13; Students 62.
Catechesis/Religious Program—Students 26.
Mission—St. Margaret 206 1st. Ave. N., Clyde Park, Park Co. 59018.
Mission—St. William 705 Scott St., W., Gardiner, Park Co. 59030.

LODGE GRASS, BIG HORN CO., OUR LADY OF LORETTO (1910) Rev. James Antoine, O.F.M.Cap.
Res.: P.O. Box 509, 59050. Tel: 406-639-2254; Fax: 406-639-2688. Email: jimanto@nemont.net.
Church: 219 S. Helen St., 59050.
Catechesis/Religious Program—Rosaline Old Bear, D.R.E. Students 15.
Mission—Blessed Kateri Tekakwitha Wyola, Big Horn CoChurch: 309 S. Mondel Ave., Wyola, 59089.

MALTA, PHILLIPS CO., ST. MARY Rev. Jim O'Neil.
Res.: 27 S. Seventh St. W., P.O. Box 70, 59538. Tel: 406-654-1446; Fax: 406-654-1467. Email: smp1435@hotmail.com. Web: saintmarysmalta.org.
Catechesis/Religious Program—Tel: 406-654-1311. Carly Bishop, D.R.E. Students 147.
Mission—Sacred Heart Dodson, Phillips CoChurch: 225 2nd St., E., Dodson, 59524.
Mission—St. Francis of Assisi Saco, Phillips CoChurch: 500 Wilson Ave., Saco, 59261.
Chapel—St. John 230 1st Ave. E., Whitewater.

MILES CITY, CUSTER CO., SACRED HEART Revs. Robert Oswald; Alex Pulickaparambil, Parochial Vicar; Michael Darsey, Pastoral Assoc.
Mailing Address: P.O. Box 1016, 59301. Tel: 406-234-1691; Fax: 406-234-9233.
Res.: 110 N. Montana, 59301. Tel: 406-234-7585.
Church: 120 N. Montana Ave., 59301.
Parish Center—520 N. Montana Ave., 59301.
School—(Grades PreSchool-8), 519 N. Center Ave., 59301. Tel: 406-234-3850. Web: www.midrivers.com/~shschool. Bart Freese, Prin. Lay Teachers 5; Students 65.
Catechesis/Religious Program—Students 150.
Mission—Sacred Heart P.O. Box 526, Terry, Prairie Co. 59349. Tel: 406-635-5569.

PLENTYWOOD, SHERIDAN CO., ST. JOSEPH Rev. Patrick Zabrocki.
Res.: P.O. Box 167, 59254. Tel: 406-765-2250; Fax: 406-765-2345.
Church: 301 N. Main St., 59254.
Catechesis/Religious Program—Students 28.
Mission—St. Patrick Medicine Lake, Sheridan CoChurch: 401 Main St., Medicine Lake, 59247.

POPLAR, ROOSEVELT CO., OUR LADY OF LOURDES Rev. Francis Anton Schreiber.
Res.: 105 D St. W., P.O. Box 187, 59255. Cell: 406-768-7488; Tel: 406-768-3305 (Office); Fax: 406-768-3305.

Catechesis / Religious Program—Students 12.
Mission—St. Anthony Culbertson, Roosevelt Co. 59218. Tel: 406-787-6666. Church: 413 3rd St., W., Culbertson, 59218.
Mission—St. Thomas Brockton, Roosevelt Co. 59213. Church: 3022 BIA Rd. 173, Brockton, 59213.
Mission—Sacred Heart Bainville, Roosevelt Co. 59212. Church: 314 Clinton St., Bainville, 59212.
Chapel—Fort Kipp, St. Anthony

PRYOR, BIG HORN CO., ST. CHARLES BORROMEO CHURCH Rev. Randolph Graczyk, O.F.M.Cap.
Res.: P.O. Box 29, 59066. Tel: 406-259-9747; Fax: 406-259-7092.
Church: 21228 S. Pryor Gap Rd., 59066.
Catechesis / Religious Program—Students 35.

RED LODGE, CARBON CO., ST. AGNES Rev. Denis J. Keane.
Res.: P.O. Box 1067, 59068. Tel: 406-446-1237; Fax: 406-446-1237. Email: sachurch1003@qwestoffice.net.
Church: 1 N. Word Ave., 59068.
Catechesis / Religious Program—Students 37.

ROUNDUP, MUSSELSHELL CO., ST. BENEDICT (1908) Rev. Daniel Wathen.
Res.: 503 Main St., 59072. Tel: 406-323-1019; Fax: 406-323-1054. Email: stbenedict@midrivers.com.
Catechesis / Religious Program—Students 30.
Mission—Our Lady of Mercy Melstone, Musselshell CoChurch: 121 6th Ave., Melstone, 59054.
Mission—St. Aloysius Winnett, Petroleum CoChurch: 112 W. Main St., Winnett.
Mission—St. Theresa the Little Flower Broadview, Yellowstone Co.
Mission—St Mathias Ryegate, Golden Valley CoChurch: 305 Kemp St., Ryegate, 59074.
Chapel—St. Honorata Musselshell, . Church: 22 3rd Ave., Musselshell, 59059.
Chapel—Our Lady of the Assumption Broadview, 59015.

SCOBEY, DANIELS CO., ST. PHILIP BONITUS Rev. Patrick Zabrocki.
Res.: P.O. Box 827, 59263. Tel: 406-487-5525; Fax: 406-487-5566.
Church: 404 Timmons St., 59263.
Catechesis / Religious Program—Matt Goettle, D.R.E. Students 40.

SIDNEY, RICHLAND CO., ST. MATTHEW Rev. Gregory Staudinger; Linda Latka, Parish Admin.
Res.: 219 Seventh St., S.E., 59270. Tel: 406-433-1068; Fax: 406-433-4373. Email: wst@midrivers.com.
Catechesis / Religious Program—Tel: 406-433-2510. Robyn Heck, D.R.E. Students 120.
Mission—St. Catherine P.O. Box 494, Fairview, Richland Co. 59221. Tel: 406-742-5293. Church: 317 7th St., W., Fairview, 59221.
Mission—St. Theresa P.O. Box 153, Lambert, Richland Co. 59243. Tel: 406-774-3360. Church: 212 N. Main St., Lambert, 59243.
Mission—St. Bernard Charley Creek, Richland Co. Tel: 406-774-3401. Church: 301 Rd. 148, Charley Creek. Mailing Address: 31789 CR148, Box 409, Brockton, 59213. Regina Murray, Pastoral Assoc.; Rita Rauschendorfer, Pastoral Assoc.
Mission—St. Michael P.O. Box 95, Savage, Richland Co. 59262. Church: 120 2nd Ave., Savage, 59262.

STANFORD, JUDITH BASIN CO., ST. ROSE OF LIMA (1908) Rev. Terrence P. Regan.
Mailing Address: P.O. Box 250, 59479. Tel: 406-566-2531.
Res.: 305 S. 2nd, 59479.
Church: 101 Fourth St. W., 59479.
Catechesis / Religious Program—Students 25.
Mission—St. Anthony P.O. Box 333, Denton, Fergus Co. 59430. Tel: 406-567-2438.
Church: 1100 Main Ave., Denton, 59430.
Mission—St. Cyril R.R. 1, Box 50A, Geyser, Judith Basin Co. 59447. Tel: 406-735-4388.
Church: 100 Hill Ave., Geyser, 59447.
Mission—St. Mathias P.O. Box 104, Moore, Fergus Co. 59464.
Church: 310-2nd St., N.E., Moore, 59464.
Mission—Sacred Heart P.O. Box 225, Hobson, Judith Basin Co. 59452.
Church: 100-2nd Ave. E., Hobson, 59452.

WOLF POINT, ROOSEVELT CO., IMMACULATE CONCEPTION, [CEM] Revs. Francis Anton Schreiber; Anselm Ofodum, Parochial Vicar.
Res.: 500 Fifth Ave. S., P.O. Box 789, 59201. Tel: 406-653-2610.
Church: 513 Dawson St., 59201.
Catechesis / Religious Program—Ann Wienke, D.R.E. Students 84.
Mission—St. Joseph Frazer, Valley CoChurch: 331 Moccasin, Frazer, 59225.
Mission—St. Ann Vida, McCone CoChurch: 102 Shell St., Vida, 59274. Tel: 406-525-3378.
Chapel—Sacred Heart 1022 Hwy. 201, Riverside, .

Special Assignment:
Revs.—
Doyle, Oliver, St. Ann's Cathedral, P.O. Box 1708, 59403-1708.
Erlenbush, Ryan, Pontifical American College 00120 Vatican City State.
Ofodum, Anselm, Immaculate Conception Church, P.O. Box 789, 59201. Tel: 406-653-2610
Pathiyamoola Ouseph, Jolly, St. Peter Church/St. Philip Church, Wibaux, MT
Pittapilly, Thomas, Ursuline Center Chaplin, 2300 Central Ave., 59401.
Pulickaparambil, Alex, Sacred Heart Church, P.O. Box 1016, Miles City, 59301.
Sikora, James, University of Great Falls, 1301 20th St., S., 59405.
Valliparambil, Jose, St. Gabriel Church, P.O. Box 1089, Chinook, 59523.
Vogel, Marcel, 2810 Central Ave., 59405.

On Duty Outside of the Diocese:
Revs.—
Cawley, William M., St. Patrick Rectory, 231 S. Beaver St., York, PA 17403-5499.
Kirkness, Michael D., 3243 Lemon Ave., Signal Hill, CA 90755-5124.
Krier, John P., P.O. Box 125, Medical Lake, WA 99022-0125.

Leave of Absence:
Rev.—
Munsell, Richard F.

Retired:
Revs.—
Arbanas, Harold P., 3475 16th St., #6, San Francisco, CA 94114-1751.
Beggin, Thomas M., 1631-41st St. W., 59106-1742.
Birkmaier, James E., 1701 26th St. S., #1, 59405-5173.
Bourke, Nathaniel J., 2003 Woody Dr., #2, 59102-2891.
Coady, John, P.O. Box 57128, Tucson, AZ 85732-7128.
Connolly, Jerry, P.O. Box 456, Joliet, 59041.
Dobbin, J. D., St. Ann Church, 13327 MT Hwy. 200, Fort Shaw, 59443-9409.
Fisher, Martin, 507 Parkhill Dr., 59102-3619.
Fox, Robert J., 1000-6th St. N., Apt. 16, 59201-1867.
Gedvila, Izidorius, 1718 Haverhill Cir., Chipley, FL 32428-3179.
Gorman, Charles, Moate, Ballinakill, Portlaois, County Laois Ireland.
Gregori, Anthony F., 1711 Smelter Ave., 59414-1222.
Guinan, Michael, 1701 26th St. S., #4, 59405-5173.
Hoffman, Emmett G., 745 Indian Tr., 59105-2750.
Hogan, William A., Ballyneety, Pallasgreen, County Limerick, Ireland.
Hopkins, Richard J., Mother of Confidence Church, 3131 Governor Dr., San Diego, CA 92122-2229.
Houlihan, John J., 2003 Woody Dr., Apt. 4, 59102.
Hruska, Eugene P., 1701 26th St. S., Apt. 2, 59405.
Kelly, Frank F., 2115 Central Ave., 59102.
Kozikowski, Thad, P.O. Box 421, Lewistown, 59457-0421.
Lobo, Benjamin, Ben's Ark, Alake, Mangalore 575 003 India.
McInnis, Francis L., 1701-26th St. S. #3, 59404-5173.
Nyquist, Raymond J., 2003 Woody Dr., Apt. 1, 59102.
O'Hanlon, Michael A., Danesfort, Dromahane Mallow, County Cork 022-50140 Ireland.
Osterman, Richard, P.O. Box 1093, Red Lodge, 59068-1093.
Schuster, Anthony J., 3842 Ave., E., 59102.
Shinnick, Edward P., 11499 Hwy. 2, Savage, 59262-9420.
Tarrant, Patrick J., P.O. Box 275, Yarmouth Port, MA 02675-0275.

Permanent Deacons:
Birkle, Timothy J., 3820 Towhee Ln., 59102-7723.
Daem, Robert W., 220 34th St. W., 59102-4473.
Kristufek, Joseph M., P.O. Box 100, Lame Deer, 59043-0100.
Medved, William, P.O. Box 305, Colstrip, 59323-0305.
Melius, Melvin A., 1437 Ave. D, 59102-3124.

INSTITUTIONS LOCATED IN THE DIOCESE

[A] COLLEGES AND UNIVERSITIES

GREAT FALLS. *University of Great Falls* (1932) 1301 20th St. S., 59405. Tel: 406-791-5300; Fax: 406-791-5391. Email: rsanne01@ugf.edu. Web: www.ugf.edu. Richard McDowell, Provost; Eugene J. McAllister, Pres.; Sr. Karen Hawkins, S.P., Campus Min.; Rev. James R. Sikora, Academic Dean; David Bibb, Library Dir.; Peggy Boord, Vice Pres. Admin. & Finance. Sponsored by the Sisters of Providence, Mother Joseph Province Priests 2; Brothers 1; Sisters 2; Lay Teachers 39; Students 858.
Associate Professors of Theology & Ministry: Revs. James R. Sikora, Academic Dean; Jon Taylor; Bro. Jeremy D. Bryja, S.C.S., Adjunct Prof. Theology; Dan McGuire, Asst. Prof. Theology & Ministry; Sr. Mary Kaye Nealen, S.P., Prof. Theology & Ministry & Dir. Mission Intergration.

[B] HIGH SCHOOLS, DIOCESAN

GREAT FALLS. *Great Falls Central Catholic High School*, 2800-18th Ave. S., 59405. Tel: 406-216-3344; Fax: 406-216-3343. Email: hsmith@greatfallscentral.org. Web: greatfallscentral.org. Hugh Smith, Prin.; Sarah Zook, Asst. Prin.; Rev. Francis McInnis, Chap.; Luella Kinzler, Librarian. Lay Teachers 13; Students 82.

BILLINGS. *Central Catholic High School*, 3 Broadwater Ave., 59101. Tel: 406-245-6651; Fax: 406-259-3124. Email: shelhanser@billingscatholicschools.org; jhawbaker@billingscatholicschools.org. Web: www.billingscatholicschools.org. Sheldon Hanser, Prin.; Jim Hawbaker, Assoc. Prin.; Kathy Harris, Librarian. Sisters 1; Lay Teachers 32; Students 341.

[C] HIGH SCHOOLS, PRIVATE

ASHLAND. *St. Labre Indian Catholic High School*, P.O. Box 216, 59003. Tel: 406-784-4500; Fax: 406-784-4565. Email: bbailey@stlabre.org. Web: www.stlabre.org. Ivan Small, Dir. Schools; Bart Bailey, Prin. Lay Teachers 21; Students 120.

[D] ELEMENTARY SCHOOLS, DIOCESAN

BILLINGS. *St. Francis Intermediate School*, (Grades 3-5), 1734 Yellowstone Ave., 59102. Tel: 406-656-2300; Fax: 406-656-2301. Email: cread@billingscatholicschools.org. Web: billingscatholicschools.org. Chris Read, Prin.; Jennifer Nieva, Librarian. Lay Teachers 15; Students 171.
St. Francis Primary School, (Grades PreK-2), 511 Custer Ave., 59101. Tel: 406-259-6421; Fax: 406-245-0176. Email: kpetermann@billingscatholicschools.org. Web: www.billingscatholicschools.org. Karen Petermann, Prin.; Amy Brown, Librarian. Lay Teachers 14; Students 219.
St. Francis Upper School, (Grades 6-8), 205 N. 32nd St., 59101. Tel: 406-259-5037; Fax: 406-259-7981. Email: jstanton@billingscatholicschools.org. Jim Stanton, Prin.; Donna Petriccione, Librarian. Lay Teachers 18; Students 191.

[E] ELEMENTARY SCHOOLS, PRIVATE

ASHLAND. *St. Labre Indian Catholic Elementary School*, (Grades PreK-4), P.O. Box 216, 59003. Tel: 406-784-4500; Fax: 406-784-4565. Email: twendt@stlabre.org. Ivan Small, Dir. of Schools; Toni Wendt, Prin. Lay Teachers 15; Students 153.
St. Labre Academy (Grades 5-8) Tel: 406-784-4500; Fax: 406-784-4565. Email: linda@stlabre.org. Linda Pease-Brien, Prin. Lay Teachers 11; Students 85.

PRYOR. *St. Charles Mission School*, (Grades PreK-8), P.O. Box 29, 59066. Tel: 406-259-9976; Fax: 406-259-7092. Email: dfritzler@stlabre.org. Web: www.stlabre.org. Dell Fritzler, Prin.; Barb Garritson, Librarian. Priests 1; Lay Teachers 14; Students 124.

ST. XAVIER. *Pretty Eagle Catholic Academy*, (Grades K-8), P.O. Box 310, 59075. Tel: 406-666-2215; Fax: 406-666-2245. Email: gwilliamson@stlabre.org. Web: www.stlabre.org. Garla Williamson, Prin.; Anne Smith, Librarian. Lay Teachers 16; Students 116.

[F] CHILD CARE & YOUTH SERVICES

GREAT FALLS. *St. Thomas Child and Family Center*, 1710 Benefis Ct., 59405. Tel: 406-761-6538; Fax: 406-727-0670. Email: carrie@stthomaskids.org. Web: stthomaskids.org. Carrie Doty, Exec. Dir. Sisters of Providence, Mother Joseph Province. Lay Staff 30; Child Care & Pre-School Children 106.

BILLINGS. *Little Flower Day Care*, 120 S. 34th St., P.O. Box 31158, 59107. Tel: 406-252-5697; Fax: 406-252-5697. Email: kseibel@billingscatholicschools.org. Web: www.billingscatholicschools.org. Katie Seibel, Dir.
St. Francis Primary Early Childcare Center, 511 Custer Ave., 59101. Tel: 406-254-7548; Fax: 406-252-5697. Katie Seibel, Dir.
Wm. R. Lowe Childcare, 2630 Normal Ave., 59102. Tel: 406-896-5820; Fax: 406-252-5697. Katie Seibel, Dir.
Saint Francis Day West Childcare, 2821 Augusta Ln., 59102. Tel: 406-256-3562; Fax: 406-252-5697.

Katie Seibel, Dir.

[G] GENERAL HOSPITALS

BILLINGS. *St. Vincent Healthcare*, 1233 N. 30th St., P.O. Box 35200, 59107-5200. Tel: 406-237-7000; Fax: 406-237-3078. Web: svhhc.org. James Paquette, Pres. & CEO; Sr. Catrina Bones, S.C.L., Vice Pres. Mission Integration; Rev. William Burke, S.J., Chap. Sisters of Charity of Leavenworth, Kansas. Sisters 4; Bed Capacity 314; Patients Assisted Annually 423,532; Total Staff 2,174.

MILES CITY. *Holy Rosary Healthcare*, 2600 Wilson St., 59301. Tel: 406-233-2600; 800-843-3820; Fax: 406-233-2611. Web: www.holyrosaryhealthcare.org. Ron Webb, CEO. Sponsored by Sisters of Charity of Leavenworth. Beds: Acute Care 49; Extended Care 84; Patients Assisted Annually 11,226; Total Staff 400.

[H] CONVENTS AND RESIDENCES FOR SISTERS

GREAT FALLS. *Poor Clares of Montana, Inc.*, 3020-18th Ave. S., 59405. Tel: 406-453-7891; Fax: 406-453-8689. Email: sisters@poorclaresmt.org. Web: www.poorclaresmt.org. Sisters 4.

Ursuline Convent, 2300 Central Ave., 59401. Tel: 406-452-8585; Fax: 406-452-8586. Email: ursuline@in-tch.com. Sr. Francis Xavier Porter, O.S.U., Supr. Ursuline Sisters 3.

BILLINGS. *Mercy Convent*, 2420 Elm St., 59101. Tel: 406-259-2550; Fax: 406-259-2550. Email: valmcge@yahoo.com. Web: www.sistersofmercy.ie.

Sisters of Charity of Leavenworth, 2703 Gregory Dr. S., 59102. Tel: 406-252-2508. Sisters 3.

[I] RETREAT HOUSES

GREAT FALLS. *Ursuline Retreat & Conference Centre*, 2300 Central Ave., 59401. Tel: 406-452-8585; Fax: 406-452-8586. Email: ursuline@in-tch.com. Web: www.ursulinecentre.com. Harry J. Tholen, Dir.

[J] MISCELLANEOUS LISTINGS

GREAT FALLS. *Big Sky Cum Christo/Cursillo*, P.O. Box 1399, 59403-1399. Web: www.bigskycumchristo.org. Rev. Gregory Staudinger. Tel: 406-433-4372; Neil Baquet. Tel: 406-535-2187 (Lewistown, MT); Bob Meyers. Tel: 406-453-5304 (Great Falls, MT); Carolyn Miller. Tel: 406-248-6617 (Billings/Laurel, MT); Mary Miller. Tel: 406-377-7973 (Glendive, MT); Dan Williams, (Landusky, MT).

Big Sky Marriage Encounter, c/o P.O. Box 1399, 59403-1399. Web: www.wwmemontana.org. Wade Kynette. Tel: 406-423-5564; Mary Kynette.

**Cascade County Council of the St. Vincent de Paul Society*, 426 Central Ave. W., P.O. Box 1562, 59403. Tel: 406-761-0870. Email: svdp@in-tch.com. Dione Leidholt, Opers. Dir.

Catholic Foundation of Eastern Montana, Inc., P.O. Box 1399, 59403-1399. Tel: 406-727-6683; Fax: 406-454-3480. Web: www.dioceseofgfb.org.

Committee for a Great Falls Catholic High School, P.O. Box 1399, 59403-1399. Tel: 406-727-6683; Fax: 406-454-3480. Email: business@dioceseofgfb.org. Web: www.dioceseofgfb.org. Joseph Loncki, Diocesan Finance Officer.

Engaged Encounter, c/o P.O. Box 1399, 59403-1399. Web: www.engagedencounter.org. Bob Williamson; Vickie Williamson. Tel: 406-727-5507.

Frank & Isabell Stites Memorial Center (Retired Priests & Lay People Living), *Pastoral Center*, P.O. Box 1399, 59403. Tel: 406-727-6683; Fax: 406-454-3480. Email: business@dioceseofgfb.org. Web: www.dioceseofgfb.org. 1701 26th St. S., 59403. Joseph Loncki, Contact Person.

Heisey Memorial Trust Fund, 313 Seventh St. N., 59401. Tel: 406-453-1211; Fax: 406-453-0607. Sandra Fermo, Exec. Dir.

Heisey Memorial Youth Center, 313 Seventh St. N., 59401. Tel: 406-453-1211; Fax: 406-453-0607. Email: heiseyyc@hotmail.com. Web: heiseyyouthcenter.com. Sandra Fermo, Exec. Dir. Recreation center serving the adults and youth of the community.

Holy Spirit Catholic School Endowment Trust, 2820 Central Ave., 59401-3412. Tel: 406-761-5775; Fax: 406-761-5887. Email: wingerter@holyspiritschool.net. Marge Sitzman, Contact Person.

St. Joseph's Education Trust, 500 2nd Ave., S.W., 59404. Tel: 406-453-9331. Very Rev. Jay H. Peterson, V.G.

**St. Martin De Porres Mission of Great Falls*, P.O. Box 141, 59403-0141. Tel: 406-868-0528.

Retrouvaille of Montana, P.O. Box 4, 59403-0004. Tel: 800-470-2330; 406-761-4830. Email: MT1Retrouvaille@aol.com. Rev. Robert Noonan. Tel: 406-258-6815 (Bonner, MT); Bill Wademan, Co-Coord.; Rose Wademan, Co-Coord.

Tekakwitha Conference National Center, P.O. Box 6768, 59406-6768. Tel: 406-727-0147; 800-842-9635; Fax: 406-452-9845. Email: tekconf@gmail.com. Web: www.tekconf.org. Sr. Kateri Mitchell, S.S.A., Exec. Dir.

BILLINGS. *Billings Area Catholic Education Trust* (BACET), P.O. Box 31158, 59107-1158. Tel: 406-252-0252; Fax: 406-252-5731. Janyce Haider, Exec. Dir.; Cori Cook, Chair.

Mayfair Auction, Billings Catholic Schools, P.O. Box 31158, 59107. Janyce Haider, Exec. Dir.

Regina Cleri, Pastoral Center: P.O. Box 1399, 59403. Tel: 406-727-6683; Fax: 406-454-3480. Email: business@dioceseofgfb.org. Web: www.dioceseofgfb.org. 2003 Woody Dr., 59102. Joseph Loncki, Contact Person. (Retired Priests Living).

St. Vincent Healthcare Foundation, 1106 N. 30th St., 59101. Tel: 406-237-3600; Fax: 406-237-3619. Email: david.irion@svh-mt.org. Web: www.svfoundation.org. David Irion, Exec. Dir.; Bill Underriner, Chm.

ASHLAND. *St. Labre Indian School Educational Association*, P.O. Box 77, 59003. Tel: 406-784-4500; Fax: 406-784-4512. Email: executivedirector@atlabre.org. Web: www.stlabre.org. Curtis Yarlott, Pres. & Exec. Dir. A Nonprofit Corporation.; Four Catholic schools for Native Americans: St. Labre Indian School at Ashland (PreK-8 Students 240); (High School Students 123); Pretty Eagle Catholic Academy, St. Xavier (Students 115); St. Charles Mission School, Pryor (Students 116).

St. Labre Youth & Family Services, P.O. Box 458, 59003. Tel: 406-784-4521; 877-785-4457; Fax: 406-784-4527. Email: vanderson@stlabre.org. Web: www.stlabre.org. Vicki Anderson, Dir. Residential Group Homes:; Shilo Home for Native American Children; Licensed for 8 children.; Other Services: St. Labre Clothes Room Thrift Store; St. Labre Daycare Center

HAVRE. *St. Jude's Education Trust*, P.O. Box 407, 59501. Tel: 406-265-4261; Fax: 406-265-4408. Email: stjude@ttc.cmc.net. Web: stjudehavre.catholicweb.com. Rev. Dale E. Yurkovic.

LEWISTOWN. *St. Leo's Catholic Education Trust*, P.O. Box 421, 59457. Tel: 406-538-9306; Fax: 406-538-7624. Email: stleos@midrivers.com. Rev. Daniel O'Rourke, Chm.

MALTA. *St. Mary's Catholic Education Trust*, P.O. Box 70, 59538. Tel: 406-654-1446; Fax: 406-654-1467. Web: www.saintmarysmalta.org. Rev. James O'Neil.

MILES CITY. **Custer County Conference of the Society of Saint Vincent de Paul and Thrift Store*, 407 Main St., 59301. Tel: 406-234-3011. Linda Life, Exec. Dir.

Holy Rosary Healthcare Foundation, 2600 Wilson St., 59301. Tel: 406-233-4043; Fax: 406-233-4214. Web: www.hrhfoundation.com. Jackie Muri, Dir.

MONARCH. *Thieltges-St. Thomas Camp*, P.O. Box 46, 59463. Tel: 406-236-5385. Email: jimhoxter@3rivers.net.

RELIGIOUS INSTITUTES OF MEN REPRESENTED IN THE DIOCESE

For further details refer to the corresponding bracketed number in the Religious Institutes of Men or Women section.

[0200]—*Benedictine Monks* (Assumption Abbey, Richardton, ND; Cleveland, OH)—O.S.B.

[0470]—*The Capuchin Friars* (Prov. of St. Joseph, Detroit)—O.F.M.Cap.

[0690]—*Jesuit Fathers and Brothers* (Oregon Prov.)—S.J.

RELIGIOUS INSTITUTES OF WOMEN REPRESENTED IN THE DIOCESE

[0230]—*Benedictine Sisters of Pontifical Jurisdiction* (St. Paul, MN)—O.S.B.

[2100]—*Congregation of the Humility of Mary* (Davenport, IA)—C.H.M.

[1730]—*Congregation of the Sisters of the Third Order of St. Francis* (Oldenburg, IN)—O.S.F.

[1070-14]—*Dominican Congregation of Our Lady of the Sacred Heart* (Grand Rapids, MI)—O.P.

[1070-13]—*Dominican Congregation of the Most Holy Rosary* (Adrian, MI)—O.P.

[1115]—*Dominican Sisters of Peace*—O.P.

[1070-11]—*Dominican Sisters, Congregation of Our Lady of the Rosary* (Sparkill, NY)—O.P.

[1070-03]—*Dominican Sisters, Sinsinawa Dominican Congregation of the Most Holy Rosary* (Sinsinawa, WI)—O.P.

[3760]—*Order of St. Clares, Holy Name Federation* (Great Falls, MT)—O.S.C.

[3720]—*Sister of Saint Anne* (Marborough, MA)—S.S.A.

[0480]—*Sisters of Charity of Leavenworth, Kansas*—S.C.L.

[2560]—*Sisters of Mercy - US Prov.* (Redlands, CA)—R.S.M.

[2575]—*Sisters of Mercy of the Americas* (Omaha, NE)—R.S.M.

[3350]—*Sisters of Providence* (Spokane, WA)—S.P.

[]—*Sisters of Sainte Anne* (Victoria, BC, Canada)—S.S.A.

[1720]—*Sisters of the Third Order Regular of St. Francis of the Congregation of Our Lady of Lourdes* (Rochester, MN)—O.S.F.

[4110]—*Ursuline Nuns* (Santa Rosa, CA)—O.S.U.

DIOCESAN CEMETERIES

BILLINGS. *Holy Cross*

GREAT FALLS. *Calvary*

Mount Olivet

NECROLOGY

† Bofto, Robert C., (Retired)—Died Dec. 2, 2008

An asterisk (*) denotes an organization that has established tax-exempt status directly with the IRS and is not covered by the USCCB Group Ruling.

Diocese of Green Bay

(Dioecesis Sinus Viridis)

Most Reverend

DAVID LAURIN RICKEN, D.D., J.C.L.

Bishop of Green Bay; ordained September 12, 1980; appointed Coadjutor Bishop of Cheyenne December 14, 1999; Episcopal Ordination January 6, 2000; succeeded to See September 26, 2001; appointed Bishop of Green Bay July 9, 2008; installed August 28, 2008. *Office: 1825 Riverside Dr., Green Bay, WI 54301. Mailing Address: P.O. Box 23825, Green Bay, WI 54305-3825.*

Chancery: 1825 Riverside Dr., Green Bay, WI 54301. Tel: 920-437-7531; Fax: 920-435-1330. *Mailing Address: P.O. Box 23825, Green Bay, WI 54305-3825*

Web: www.gbdioc.org

Most Reverend

ROBERT J. BANKS, D.D.

Retired Bishop of Green Bay; ordained December 20, 1952; consecrated September 19, 1985; appointed Auxiliary Bishop to the Archbishop of Boston and Titular Bishop of Taraqua on June 26, 1985; appointed to Green Bay October 16, 1990; installed December 5, 1990; retired December 12, 2003. *Office: 1825 Riverside Dr., Green Bay, WI 54301. Mailing Address: P.O. Box 23825, Green Bay, WI 54305-3825.*

Most Reverend

ROBERT F. MORNEAU, D.D.

Auxiliary Bishop of Green Bay; ordained May 28, 1966; appointed Auxiliary Bishop of Green Bay and Titular Bishop of Massa Lubrense December 19, 1978; consecrated February 22, 1979. *Res.: 333 Hilltop Dr., Green Bay, WI 54301-2713. Office: 1825 Riverside Dr., Green Bay, WI 54301.* Tel: 920-437-7531. *Mailing Address: P.O. Box 23825, Green Bay, WI 54305-3825.*

ESTABLISHED MARCH 3, 1868.

Square Miles 10,728.

Incorporated January 16, 1907.

Comprises these 16 Counties: Brown, Calumet, Door, Florence, Forest, Kewaunee, Langlade, Manitowoc, Marinette, Menominee, Oconto, Outagamie, Shawano, Waupaca, Waushara and Winnebago in the State of Wisconsin.

Legal Title: Catholic Diocese of Green Bay, Inc.
For legal titles of parishes and diocesan institutions, consult the Chancery Office.

STATISTICAL OVERVIEW

Personnel	
Bishop	1
Auxiliary Bishops	1
Retired Bishops	1
Abbots	1
Retired Abbots	1
Priests: Diocesan Active in Diocese	91
Priests: Diocesan Active Outside Diocese	6
Priests: Diocesan in Foreign Missions	2
Priests: Retired, Sick or Absent	88
Number of Diocesan Priests	187
Religious Priests in Diocese	97
Total Priests in Diocese	284
Extern Priests in Diocese	10
Ordinations:	
Diocesan Priests	2
Transitional Deacons	1
Permanent Deacons	4
Permanent Deacons in Diocese	133
Total Brothers	36
Total Sisters	489
Parishes	
Parishes	157
With Resident Pastor:	
Resident Diocesan Priests	66
Resident Religious Priests	21
Without Resident Pastor:	
Administered by Priests	46
Administered by Deacons	7
Administered by Religious Women	10
Administered by Lay People	7
Missions	2
Pastoral Centers	17
Closed Parishes	3
Professional Ministry Personnel:	
Sisters	43
Lay Ministers	152
Welfare	
Catholic Hospitals	8
Total Assisted	1,050,383
Homes for the Aged	15
Total Assisted	974
Day Care Centers	2
Total Assisted	110
Specialized Homes	4
Total Assisted	8,108
Special Centers for Social Services	8
Total Assisted	214,584
Residential Care of Disabled	1
Total Assisted	4
Educational	
Diocesan Students in Other Seminaries	22
Seminaries, Religious	1
Students Religious	3
Total Seminarians	25
Colleges and Universities	2
Total Students	3,677
High Schools, Diocesan and Parish	5
Total Students	1,329
High Schools, Private	1
Total Students	720
Elementary Schools, Diocesan and Parish	55
Total Students	9,132
Catechesis/Religious Education:	
High School Students	9,075
Elementary Students	20,320
Total Students under Catholic Instruction	44,278
Teachers in the Diocese:	
Priests	3
Sisters	14
Lay Teachers	740
Vital Statistics	
Receptions into the Church:	
Infant Baptism Totals	3,729
Adult Baptism Totals	102
Received into Full Communion	190
First Communions	3,725
Confirmations	3,143
Marriages:	
Catholic	887
Interfaith	329
Total Marriages	1,216
Deaths	2,954
Total Catholic Population	304,614
Total Population	989,997

Former Bishops—Rt. Revs. JOSEPH MELCHER, D.D., ord. March 27, 1830; cons. July 12, 1868; died Dec. 20, 1873; FRANCIS XAVIER KRAUTBAUER, D.D., ord. July 16, 1850; cons. June 29, 1875; died Dec. 17, 1885; FREDERICK XAVIER KATZER, D.D., ord. Dec. 21, 1866; appt. July 13, 1886; cons. Sept. 21, 1886; appt. Archbishop of Milwaukee, Jan. 30, 1891; died July 20, 1903; SEBASTIAN GEBHARD MESSMER, D.D., ord. July 23, 1871; cons. Bishop of Green Bay, March 27, 1892; appt. Archbishop of Milwaukee, Nov. 28, 1903; died Aug. 4, 1930; JOSEPH J. FOX, D.D., ord. June 7, 1879; cons. Bishop of Green Bay, July 25, 1904; resigned Dec. 4, 1914; appt. Titular Bishop of Ionopolis; died March 14, 1915; Most Revs. PAUL P. RHODE, D.D., ord. June 17, 1894; cons. Titular Bishop of Barca and Auxiliary to the Archbishop of Chicago, July 29, 1908; transferred to the See of Green Bay, July 5, 1915; died March 3, 1945; STANISLAUS V. BONA, D.D., ord. Nov. 1, 1912; appt. Bishop of Grand Island, NE Dec. 18, 1931; cons. Feb. 25, 1932; appt. Coadjutor Bishop of Green Bay, Dec. 2, 1944; succeeded to See, March 3, 1945; died Dec. 1, 1967; ALOYSIUS J. WYCISLO, D.D., ord. April 7, 1934; appt. Titular Bishop of Stadia and Auxiliary Bishop of Chicago Oct. 17, 1960; cons. Dec. 21, 1960; appt. to Green Bay, March 8, 1968; retired May 10, 1983; died Oct. 11, 2005; ADAM J. MAIDA, J.C.L., J.D., S.T.L., ord. May 26, 1956; appt. to Green Bay, Nov. 8, 1983; cons. Jan. 25, 1984; installed as Archbishop of Detroit, June 12, 1990; created Cardinal on Nov. 26, 1994; ROBERT J. BANKS, D.D., J.C.D. (Retired), ord. Dec. 20, 1952; cons. Sept. 19, 1985; appt. Auxiliary Bishop to the Archbishop of Boston and Titular Bishop of Taraqua on June 26, 1985; appt. to Green Bay Oct. 16, 1990; installed Dec. 5, 1990; retired Dec. 12, 2003; DAVID A. ZUBIK, ord. May 3, 1975; appt. Auxiliary Bishop of Pittsburgh and Titular Bishop of Jamestown Feb. 18, 1997; cons. April 6, 1997; appt. Bishop of Green Bay Oct. 10, 2003; installed Dec. 12, 2003; appt. Bishop of Pittsburgh July 18, 2007.

Vicars General—Most Rev. ROBERT F. MORNEAU, D.D.; Very Rev. JOHN F. DOERFLER, S.T.D., J.C.L.

Chancery—1825 Riverside Dr., Green Bay, 54301. Tel: 920-437-7531; Fax: 920-435-1330. *Mailing Address: P.O. Box 23825, Green Bay, 54305-3825.* Office Hours: Mon.-Fri. 8-4:30; other times by appointment only.

Director of Administration—Deacon TIMOTHY G. REILLY. Tel: 920-272-8171.

Associate Director of Administration—DORIS V. VINCENT. Tel: 920-272-8175.

Chancellor—Very Rev. JOHN F. DOERFLER, S.T.D., J.C.L. Tel: 920-272-8180.

Vice-Chancellor—Rev. Msgr. BRIAN P. COLEMAN, J.C.L. (Retired).

Archivist—Mr. JOHN LEDOUX. Tel: 920-272-8186.

Secretaries to Bishop—NANCY LUCAS. Tel: 920-272-8194; GLADYS POWELL. Tel: 920-272-8167.

Secretary to Director of Administration—TERRI WICKMAN. Tel: 920-272-8189.

Chancery Secretary—MARY JO KRUEGER. Tel: 920-272-8188.

Diocesan Tribunal—1825 Riverside Dr., Green Bay, 54301. Tel: 920-437-7531. *Mailing Address: P.O. Box 23825, Green Bay, 54305-3825.*

Judicial Vicar—Very Rev. ROBERT J. KABAT, J.C.L. Tel: 920-272-8172.

Adjutant Judicial Vicars—Rev. Msgr. BRIAN P. COLEMAN, J.C.L. (Retired); Rev. RICHARD GETCHEL, J.C.L.

Judges—Most Rev. ROBERT J. BANKS, D.D., J.C.D. (Retired); Rev. Msgr. BRIAN P. COLEMAN, J.C.L. (Retired); Very Rev. ROBERT J. KABAT, J.C.L.; Rt. Rev. GARY J. NEVILLE, O.Praem., J.C.D.; Revs. WILLIAM L. VAN DE KREEKE, J.C.L. (Retired); RICHARD GETCHEL, J.C.L.

Promoter of Justice—Sr. ANN F. REHRAUER, J.C.L., M.A.

Defenders of the Bond—Rev. LEE J. KAHRS, B.A. (Retired); Sr. ANN F. REHRAUER, J.C.L., M.A.; Rev. BENJAMIN SEMBER, J.C.L.

Notaries—JOANN VANDER LOOP; GLADYS POWELL.

College of Consultors—Most Revs. DAVID L. RICKEN, D.D., J.C.L.; ROBERT F. MORNEAU, D.D.; Rev. JOHN J. BECKER; Rev. Msgr. BRIAN P. COLEMAN, J.C.L. (Retired); Very Revs. JOHN F. DOERFLER, S.T.D., J.C.L.; JOHN W. GIROTTI; Revs. ROBERT J. KARUHN; PAUL J. PAIDER; THOMAS J. REYNEBEAU; JEREMIAH F. WORMAN (Retired); DAVID M. ZIMMERMAN.

Regional Vicars—Very Revs. JOSEPH E. DORNER, Vicariate I - North; CELESTINE BYEKWASO, Asst. Vicar, Vicariate I - North; Very Rev. Msgr. JAMES E. DILLENBURG, Vicariate II - Mid-North; Very Revs. DOUGLAS E. LECAPTAIN, Vicariate III - Southwest; DONALD M. ZULEGER, Vicariate IV - Mid-South; RICHARD H. KLINGEISEN, Vicariate V - Southeast; LARRY J. SEIDL, Vicariate VI - Mid-East; ANTHONY J. BIRDSALL, Vicariate VII - Peninsula.

Diocesan Pastoral Council—Most Rev. DAVID L. RICKEN, D.D., J.C.L., Chm.

Ecumenical Liaison—Rev. JAMES P. MASSART.

Presbyteral Council Membership—

President—Most Rev. DAVID L. RICKEN, D.D., J.C.L.

Appointed Members—Revs. JOHN J. BECKER; GERALD J. FOLEY (Retired); THOMAS WOJCIECHOWSKI, O.F.M.; Very Rev. DONALD M. ZULEGER.

Elected Members—Vicariate: Revs. MICHAEL E. BETLEY, I - North; RICHARD GETCHEL, J.C.L., II - Mid-North; JAMES R. JUGENHEIMER, III - Southwest; JAMES A. HABLEWITZ, IV - Mid-South; MATHEW J. SIMONAR, V - Southeast; RONALD C. BELITZ, VI - Mid-East; CARL E. SCHMITT, VII - Peninsula.

Ex Officio—Most Rev. ROBERT F. MORNEAU, D.D.; Very Revs. JOHN F. DOERFLER, S.T.D., J.C.L.; PAUL E. DEMUTH.

Resource—Deacon TIMOTHY G. REILLY.

Bishop's Finance Council—Most Rev. DAVID L. RICKEN, D.D., J.C.L.; Rev. ROBERT K. FINNEGAN, O.Praem.; Mrs. JOANN COTTER; Mr. W. PAUL JONES; Mr. MICHAEL ARIENS; Mr. RON JOHNSON; Mr. ROBERT C. GALLAGHER; Mr. PAUL GEHL; Mr. THOMAS VORPAHL; Mr. JOSEPH VARKOLY; Deacon TIMOTHY G. REILLY; Most Rev. ROBERT F. MORNEAU, D.D.; JASON HAEN, Resource.

Censores Librorum—Revs. GORDON J. GILSDORF; MILTON M. SUESS.

Ministry Formation

Vicar for Ministers—Very Rev. PAUL E. DEMUTH, Mailing Address: P.O. Box 23825, Green Bay, 54305-3825. Tel: 920-272-8165.

Vocations and Ongoing Formation of Priests and Parish Directors—Revs. W. THOMAS LONG, Dir. Tel: 920-272-8293; QUENTIN A. MANN, Assoc. Vocations Dir.

Representative for Religious—Sr. FLORENCE YOUNGWIRTH, A.N.G.

Department of the Permanent Diaconate—Deacon PAUL K. GRIMM, Dir., Prog. Coord. & Vicar for Deacons, Mailing Address: P.O. Box 23825, Green Bay, 54305-3825. Tel: 920-272-8290.

Lay Ministry Formation—Mr. TONY PICHLER, Dir., Mailing Address: P.O. Box 23825, Green Bay, 54305-3825. Tel: 920-272-8268.

Safe Environment—Ms. ANN FOX, Assistance Coord. Tel: 920-272-8174; Ms. KAREN R. BASS, Asst. Tel: 920-272-8198.

Diocesan Department of Education

Director—Dr. JOSEPH BOUND. Tel: 920-272-8266.

Administrative Services Supervisor—DEBBIE LINNANE. Tel: 920-272-8266.

Catholic Schools—HOLLY ROTTIER, Dir. Tel: 920-272-8273; DIANE WALTERS, Dir. Curriculum & Instruction. Tel: 920-272-8212; Deacon RAYMOND L. DUBOIS, Dir. Promotional Svcs. Tel: 920-272-8272; JACALYN VANKAUWENBERG, Administrative Asst. Tel: 920-272-8279.

Religious Education and Youth Ministry—ROSEMARY G. BARTEL, Dir. Tel: 920-272-8288; CAROL FOUNTAIN, Administrative Asst. Tel: 920-272-8270.

Adult Faith Formation and Young Adult Ministry—JULIANNE STRANZ, Dir. Tel: 920-272-8270; SHEILA SCHAUT, Administrative Asst. Tel: 920-437-7531, Ext. 8276.

Liaisons-Office of Education—

The Diocesan Charismatic Renewal Center—

Serra Clubs—Rev. W. THOMAS LONG, Mailing Address: P.O. Box 23825, Green Bay, 54305-3825. Tel: 920-437-7531.

World Apostolate of Fatima—Deacon ROBERT ELLIS, 1372 Nienhaus Dr., De Pere, 54115-8600. Tel: 920-337-6263.

Cursillo—Rev. DAVID J. PLEIER, 2040 Hillside Ln., Green Bay, 54302-4098. Tel: 920-468-4811.

Xavier Guild—Rev. DENNIS M. RYAN, Chap., St. Bernard Parish, 1617 W. Pine St., Appleton, 54914-5118. Tel: 920-739-0331.

Diocesan Council of Catholic Women—TERRY OLIVAS, Pres., Mailing Address: P.O. Box 384, Plainfield, 54966; Rev. CHARLES W. MOCCO, Chap. (Retired).

Evangelization and Worship

Evangelization and Worship—Sr. ANN REHRAUER, Dir. Tel: 920-272-8292; NANCY MOOREN, Administrative Asst. Tel: 920-272-8310.

Campus Ministry—SAM WOOD, Dir., Newman Center of Oshkosh, Inc., 514 Scott Ave., Oshkosh, 54901-3741. Tel: 920-233-5555.

Family & Married Life—HELEN SCIESZKA, Dir. Tel: 920-272-8315.

Respect Life—CHRISTINA PALLINI, Volunteer Consultant. Tel: 920-272-8286.

Retreat & Shrine Operations—

Camp Tekawitha Retreat and Conference Center, Inc.—Tel: 715-526-2316.

Holy Name Retreat House, Inc.—CHARLOTTE DURAN, Admin.

The Shrine of Our Lady of Good Help, Inc.—Very Rev. JOHN F. DOERFLER, S.T.D., J.C.L., Rector. Tel: 920-272-8180; STEVE TIPPS, Facility Mgr. Tel: 920-866-2571.

Spirituality and Evangelization—Dr. KRISTINA DENEVE. Tel: 920-272-8304.

Worship and Sacraments—CLARE STURM, Dir. Tel: 920-272-8311.

Stewardship and Pastoral Services

Stewardship and Pastoral Services—1825 Riverside Dr., Green Bay, 54301. Tel: 920-437-7531; Fax: 920-437-0694. Email: pastserv@gbdioc.org. *Mailing Address: P.O. Box 23825, Green Bay, 54305-3825.* MARK MOGILKA, Dir. Tel: 920-272-8297. Email: mmogilka@gbdioc.org; PATTY YOUNG, Administrative Svcs. Supvr. Tel: 920-272-8295.

Coordinators—

Hispanic Ministry—CARLOS HERNANDEZ. Tel: 920-272-8308.

Pastoral Care—Rev. PETER J. RENARD, O. Praem. Tel: 920-272-8307; MARY SHERMAN. Tel: 920-272-8300.

Parish Planning & Collaboration—DEBORAH WEGNER-HOHENSEE. Tel: 920-272-8286.

Prison Ministry—MARY SHERMAN. Tel: 920-272-8300; Deacon ROBERT VINCENT. Tel: 920-731-0356.

Rural Life—Bro. STEVEN J. HERRO, O.Praem. Tel: 920-272-8299.

Social Concerns—Bro. STEVEN J. HERRO, O.Praem. Tel: 920-272-8299.

Stewardship—MARY ANN OTTO. Tel: 920-272-8301.

Community Services

Catholic Charities—KAREN JOHNSTON, Dir., 1825 Riverside Dr., Green Bay, 54301. Tel: 920-272-8234; Fax: 920-437-0694. Mailing Address: P.O. Box 23825, Green Bay, 54305-3825.

Apostleship of the Sea—Deacon GLENN TESKE, Port Chap., 2839 S. Broadway, Green Bay, 54304-5309. Tel: 920-499-0035.

Diocesan Health Services—Very Rev. RICHARD H. KLINGEISEN, Coord., 601 N. 8th St., Manitowoc, 54220-3919. Tel: 920-684-3718.

McCormick Memorial Home for the Aged—212 Iroquois St., Green Bay, 54301-1995. Tel: 920-437-0883. JAMES GENRICH, Admin.; Rev. MICHAEL R. KOCH, Chap. (Retired).

Liaisons - Community Services—

Society of St. Vincent de Paul—VINCENT NICHOLAS, Pres., Mailing Address: 1437 Grignon St., Green Bay, 54301; EVERETT JOHNSON, Exec. Sec.

Knights of Columbus—Rev. PETER J. RENARD, O. Praem., Diocesan Chap.

Our Lady of Charity Center, Inc.—Sr. DONNA TRACKEY, O.L.C., Dir., 2560 Shawano Ave., P.O. Box 10357, Green Bay, 54307-0357. Tel: 920-434-8208.

Catholic Veterans of War—RAYMOND WOZNICK, Commander, 418 Forrest Ave., Fond du Lac, 54935.

Menominee Pastoral Program—Rev. DAVID S. BARRETT (Retired), N6772 Black Oak Circle, Shawano, 54166. Tel: 715-853-1285.

Administrative Services

Administrative Services—Mailing Address: P.O. Box 23825, Green Bay, 54305-3825. Tel: 920-437-7531; Fax: 920-435-1330. Deacon TIMOTHY G. REILLY, Dir. Admin. Tel: 920-272-8171.

Department of World Mission Services—CINDI BRAWNER, Dir. Tel: 920-272-8173; MARGIE SUMNICHT, Coord. Mission Svcs., Mailing Address: P.O. Box 23825, Green Bay, 54305-3825. Tel: 920-272-8192; Fax: 920-435-1330.

Agencies— Propagation of the Faith, St. Peter the Apostle, Holy Childhood Association, Catholic Relief Services

Annual Bishop's Appeal—JOSH DIEDRICH, Dir. Tel: 920-272-8197.

Bishop's Charities Game—JAMES HOGAN, Dir., Mailing Address: P.O. Box 23825, Green Bay, 54305-3825. Tel: 920-272-8219.

Communications—Mailing Address: P.O. Box 23825, Green Bay, 54305-3825. Tel: 920-272-8213. RENAE BAUER, Dir. Tel: 920-272-8213.

Diocesan Newspaper— "The Compass" *Mailing Address: P.O. Box 23825, Green Bay, 54305-3825.* Tel: 920-437-7531. *Appleton Area.* Tel: 920-233-5555. RENAE BAUER, Gen. Mgr. Tel: 920-272-8214; SAM LUCERO, Editor. Tel: 920-272-8210.

Computer Services—RENAE BAUER, Mailing Address: Box 23825, Green Bay, 54305-3825. Tel: 920-272-8214; ROY VERSTEGEN, Database Mgr. Tel: 920-272-8255; DAN LEE, Systems Admin. Tel: 920-272-8253; NICK GRIFFIE, Intranet Coord.

Financial Services—JASON HAEN, Dir., Mailing Address: P.O. Box 23825, Green Bay, 54305-3825. Tel: 920-272-8206. Accounting Managers: MIKE SPEEL. Tel: 920-272-8259; CATHERINE HOEFT. Tel: 920-272-8267.

Facilities, Properties and Cemeteries—Ms. TAMMY BASTEN, Dir. Diocesan Properties, Mailing Address: P.O. Box 23825, Green Bay, 54305-3825. Tel: 920-272-8260.

Human Resources—CATHY LARSON, Dir., Mailing Address: P.O. Box 23825, Green Bay, 54305-3825. Tel: 920-272-8216.

Medical Insurance and Benefits—MARY VANKAUWENBERG, Mailing Address: Box 23825, Green Bay, 54305-3825. Tel: 920-272-8201.

Sacred Heart Seminary, Corp.—Mailing Address: P.O. Box 23825, Green Bay, 54305-3825. Tel: 920-437-7531.

Sacrificial Giving Program—CINDI BRAWNER, Dir., Mailing Address: P.O. Box 23825, Green Bay, 54305-3825. Tel: 920-272-8173.

St. Joseph Corporation and Central Services—Ms. TAMMY BASTEN, Mailing Address: P.O. Box 23825, Green Bay, 54305-3825. Tel: 920-272-8260.

The Catholic Foundation for the Diocese of Green Bay, Inc.—CINDI BRAWNER, Mailing Address: P.O. Box 23825, Green Bay, 54305-3825. Tel: 920-272-8173.

Priests' Personnel Board—Mailing Address: P.O. Box 23825, Green Bay, 54305-3825. Tel: 920-437-7531. Most Revs. DAVID L. RICKEN, D.D., J.C.L.; ROBERT F. MORNEAU, D.D., Resource Person; Very Rev. PAUL E. DEMUTH, Chm.; Revs. JOHN J. BECKER; BRIAN S. BELONGIA; Very Rev. JOHN F. DOERFLER, S.T.D., J.C.L.; Rev. Msgr. JAMES B. FEELY (Retired); Rev. DAVID R. SCHMIDT; Rev. Msgr. JOHN H. SCHUH (Retired).

Conciliation and Arbitration Board—Very Revs. JOHN F. DOERFLER, S.T.D., J.C.L., Pres.; ROBERT J. KABAT, J.C.L., Clerk, Mailing Address: P.O. Box 23825, Green Bay, 54305-3825. Tel: 920-437-7531.

Liaisons--Personnel—

Association of Pastoral Associates—HELEN SCIESZKA, Mailing Address: P.O. Box 23825, Green Bay, 54305-3825.

Leo Benevolent Association—Rev. Msgr. MARK J. SCHOMMER, Chm. (Retired), N2614 Bughs Lake Rd., Wautoma, 54982-7130. Tel: 920-787-1666.

Clergy Credit Union—Rev. CHARLES W. MOCCO, Treas. (Retired), 401 Gray St., Green Bay, 54303. Tel: 920-680-4045.

Community of Our Lady—Very Rev. REGIS N. BARWIG, Prior, 2804 Oakwood Ln., Oshkosh, 54904-8406. Tel: 920-233-5633.

A New Genesis—Sr. DIANE BAUMAN, Moderator, Mailing Address: P.O. Box 8642, Green Bay, 54308. Tel: 715-752-3374.

Victim Assistance Coordinator—Ms. ANN FOX. Tel: 920-272-8174. Email: afox@gbdioc.org.

CLERGY, PARISHES, MISSIONS AND PAROCHIAL SCHOOLS

CITY OF GREEN BAY

(BROWN COUNTY)

1—ST. FRANCIS XAVIER CATHEDRAL, Also serves SS. Peter and Paul, Green Bay. Rev. John W. Girotti; Deacon Thomas Mahoney. In Res., Rev. Richard L. Thomas (Retired).
Res.: 139 S. Madison St., 54301-4501. Tel: 920-432-4348; Fax: 920-435-5068. Email: sfxavier@sbcglobal.net.
School—St. Thomas More, 650 S. Irwin Ave., 54301-3398. Tel: 920-432-8242; Fax: 920-432-1562. Email: stmore@stmoregb.org. Eric Weydt, Prin. Consolidated with SS. Peter & Paul and St. Mary of the Angels.
Catechesis/Religious Program—1420 Harvey St., 54302-1918. Tel: 920-437-0651. Deacon Michael C. Vincent, D.R.E. Associated with Ss Peter & Paul, Green Bay.

2—ST. AGNES Rev. Richard Getchel; Deacon James R. Gauthier.
Res.: 1484 9th St., 54304-3061. Tel: 920-494-2534; Fax: 920-617-3118. Email: rgtchl@aol.com.
School—Holy Family, 1204 S. Fisk St., 54304-2299. Tel: 920-494-1931; Fax: 920-494-4942. Email: potto@gbhfs.org. Pamela S. Otto, Prin.
Catechesis/Religious Program—Email: religioused@stagnesgreenbay.org. Mrs. Carrie A. Aimers, D.R.E.; Peter J. Leitermann, D.R.E. Students 377.

3—ANNUNCIATION OF THE BLESSED VIRGIN MARY, Served from St. Joseph, Green Bay. Revs. Donald E. Everts; Timothy Brandt, Parochial Vicar; Deacons Michael J. Mervilde; Daniel Wagnitz.
Mailing Address: 1420 Division St., 54303-3122. Tel: 920-496-2160; Fax: 920-496-2167. Email: deverts@allofuswestgb.org.
Catechesis/Religious Program—Faith Formation Center-St. Joseph Site, Combined with St. Joseph, Green Bay, St. Joseph, Green Bay and St. Patrick, Green Bay., 936 - 9th St., 54304-3439. Tel: 920-497-7042. Email: tmeyer@allofuswestgb.org. Maxine Geiger, D.R.E.; Tina Meyer, D.R.E.

4—ST. BERNARD, Also serves St. Philip the Apostle, Green Bay. Revs. David J. Pleier; Anthony Cirignani, O.F.M.; Deacons Keith P. Holschbach; John H. Laurant; Larry V. Mastalish.
Res.: 2040 Hillside Ln., 54302-4098. Tel: 920-468-4811; Fax: 920-468-1396. Email: dave@stbernardcong.org.
School—2020 Hillside Ln., 54302-4099. Tel: 920-468-5026; Fax: 920-468-3478. Email: kfranz@stbernardcong.org. Kay L. Franz, Prin.
Catechesis/Religious Program—Tel: 920-468-4390. Email: amy@stbernardcong.org. Amy M. Matz, D.R.E.; Holly Meyer, D.R.E.; Becky Pieters, Contact Person.

5—ST. ELIZABETH ANN SETON Very Rev. Msgr. James E. Dillenburg; Deacon Steven J. Meyer.
Res.: 2771 Oakwood Dr., 54304-1618. Tel: 920-499-1546; Fax: 920-499-2207. Email: seas@seasgb.org.
School: See Holy Family, Green Bay under St. Agnes, Green Bay for details.
Catechesis/Religious Program—Email: asabor@seasgb.org. Andrea Sabor, D.R.E.

6—HOLY MARTYRS OF GORCUM, [CEM] Merged with Holy Trinity, Pine Grove to form Prince of Peace, Green Bay.

7—ST. JOHN Rev. Guy Blair, S.C.J.
Res.: 413 St. John St., 54301-4116. Tel: 920-436-6380; Fax: 920-436-6382. Email: stjevan@sbcglobal.net.
Catechesis/Religious Program—Tel: 920-432-4348. Email: susan.perrault@gmail.com. Susan K. Perrault, D.R.E.

8—ST. JOSEPH, Also serves Annunciation, Green Bay, St. Jude, Green Bay and St. Patrick, Green Bay. Revs. Donald E. Everts; Timothy Brandt, Parochial Vicar; Deacons Michael J. Mervilde; Daniel Wagnitz.
Res.: 1420 Division St., 54303-3122. Tel: 920-496-2160; Fax: 920-496-2167. Email: deverts@allofuswestgb.org.
Catechesis/Religious Program—Combined with Annunciation of the Blessed Virgin Mary, Green Bay, St. Joseph, Green Bay and St. Patrick, Green Bay., Tel: 920-497-7042. Email: tmeyer@allofuswestgb.org.

9—ST. JUDE, Served from St. Joseph, Green Bay. Revs. Donald E. Everts; Timothy Brandt, Parochial Vicar; Deacons Michael J. Mervilde; Daniel Wagnitz.
Res.: 1420 Division St., 54303-3122. Tel: 920-496-2160; Fax: 920-496-2167. Email: deverts@allofuswestgb.org.
Catechesis/Religious Program—Combined with Annunciation of the Blessed Virgin Mary, Green Bay, St. Joseph, Green Bay and St. Patrick, Green Bay., Tel: 920-497-7042. Email: tmeyer@allofuswestgb.org.

10—ST. MARY OF THE ANGELS Rev. Thomas Wojciechowski, O.F.M.; Deacon Paul P. Umentum.
Res.: 645 S. Irwin Ave., 54301-3303. Tel: 920-437-1979; Fax: 920-965-9127. Email: stmary12@juno.com.
School: See St. Thomas More, Green Bay under St. Francis Xavier Cathedral, Green Bay for details.
Catechesis/Religious Program—Tel: 920-432-2747. Email: stmaryangel@att.net. Mary S. Sedlacek, D.R.E.

11—ST. MATTHEW Very Rev. Larry J. Seidl; Deacon Paul J. Cibula.
Res.: 130 St. Matthews St., 54301-2999. Tel: 920-435-6811; Fax: 920-435-0065. Email: parishoffice@stmattsgb.org.
School—2575 S. Webster Ave., 54301-2998. Tel: 920-432-5223; Fax: 920-432-5139. Email: stmatthews1@new.rr.com. Renee Engels, Prin.
Catechesis/Religious Program—Email: mwestenberg@stmattsgb.org. Michael Westenberg, D.R.E.

12—NATIVITY OF OUR LORD Revs. John J. Becker; Benjamin Sember; Deacon Michael E. Schmidt.
Res.: 2270 S. Oneida St., 54304-4712. Tel: 920-499-5156; Fax: 920-490-9285. Email: natscene@nativityparish.com.
Catechesis/Religious Program—Tel: 920-499-6012. Email: natjw@nativityparish.com. James R. Whalen, D.R.E.

13—ST. PATRICK, Served from St. Joseph, Green Bay. Revs. Donald E. Everts; Timothy Brandt, Parochial Vicar; Deacons Michael J. Mervilde; Daniel Wagnitz.
1420 Division St., 54303-3122.
Res.: 211 N. Maple Ave., 54303-2749. Tel: 920-496-2160; Fax: 920-437-3274. Email: deverts@allofuswestgb.org.
Catechesis/Religious Program—Combined with Annunciation of the Blessed Virgin Mary, Green Bay, St. Joseph, Green Bay and St. Jude, Green Bay., Tel: 920-497-7042. Email: tmeyer@allofuswestgb.org.

14—SS. PETER AND PAUL, Served from St. Francis Xavier Cathedral, Green Bay. Very Rev. Larry J. Seidl, Temporary Admin.; Rev. Harry G. Hafeman; Deacons Michael C. Vincent; Thomas Mahoney.
Res.: 710 N. Baird St., 54302-1997. Tel: 920-435-7548; Fax: 920-432-1321. Email: cfssp@hotmail.com.
School: See St. Thomas More, Green Bay under St. Francis Xavier Cathedral, Green Bay for details.
Catechesis/Religious Program—1420 Harvey St., 54302-1999. Tel: 920-437-0651. Email: mdkvincent@sbcglobal.net. Michael F. Lee, D.R.E.

15—ST. PHILIP THE APOSTLE, Served from St. Bernard, Green Bay. Revs. David J. Pleier, Admin.; Anthony Cirignani, O.F.M.
Res.: 312 Victoria St., 54302-2818. Tel: 920-468-7848; Fax: 920-468-1025. Email: edymond@stphilipcong.org.
Catechesis/Religious Program—Mary A. Peters, D.R.E.

16—PRINCE OF PEACE, Merger of Holy Trinity, Pine Grove and Holy Martyrs of Gorcum, Green Bay. Rev. Ronald C. Belitz; Deacon William J. Burkel.
Mailing Address: 3425 Willow Rd., 54311-8232. Tel: 920-468-5718; Fax: 920-468-5713. Email: pop-parish-office@new.rr.com.
School—3542 Finger Rd., 54311-7733. Tel: 920-468-7262. Email: holymartyrs@itol.com. Theresa M. Williams, Prin.
Catechesis/Religious Program—Email: cwhitcomb@princeofpeaceparish.com. JoAnne Adrians, D.R.E.; Carolyn Whitcomb, D.R.E.

17—RESURRECTION Most Rev. Robert F. Morneau; Very Rev. Paul E. Demuth, Sacramental Min.; Deacons Michael G. Grzeca; Donald J. Ropson; Timothy G. Reilly.
Res.: 333 Hilltop Dr., 54301-2799. Tel: 920-336-7768; Fax: 920-336-1949. Email: resurrectionparish@gbres.org.
School—Tel: 920-336-3230. Email: jschueller@bgres.org. Jane Schueller, Prin.
Catechesis/Religious Program—Email: rvanzeeland@gbres.org. Rachel R. Van Zeeland, D.R.E.

18—ST. WILLEBRORD Rev. Kenneth J. De Groot, O.Praem.; Deacon Luis Sanchez.
Res.: 209 S. Adams St., 54301-4584. Tel: 920-435-2016; Fax: 920-435-2039. Email: frken@stwillys.org.
Catechesis/Religious Program—Email: rita@stwillys.org. Rita M. Bauldry, D.R.E.; Alma Vazquez, D.R.E.

OUTSIDE THE CITY OF GREEN BAY

ABRAMS, OCONTO CO., ST. LOUIS, [JC] Merged with St. Joseph, Chase and St. John Cantius, Sobieski to form St. Maximilian Kolbe, Sobieski.

ALGOMA, KEWAUNEE CO., ST. MARY (1860) [CEM], Also serves Holy Rosary, Kewaunee. Rev. William D. Swichtenberg.
Res.: 118 Church St., 54201-1098. Tel: 920-487-5005; Fax: 920-487-5002.
School—214 Church St., 54201-1035. Tel: 920-487-5004. Email: lkrzysiak@yahoo.com. Mrs. Laura L. Krzysiak, Prin. & D.R.E.
Catechesis/Religious Program—214 Church St., 54201-1035. Email: lkrzysiak@yahoo.com.

ALVERNO, MANITOWOC CO., ST. JOSEPH, Merged with St. Casimir, Northeim; St. Isidore, Osman; and St. Wendel, Cleveland to form St. Thomas the Apostle, Northeim.

AMBERG, MARINETTE CO., ST. AGNES, Served from St. Augustine, Wausaukee. Revs. Ronald C. Belitz, Priest Moderator; John J. Hephner, Sacramental Min. (Retired); Deacon Patrick J. Whitcomb, Pastoral Coord.
Mailing Address: 507 Church St., Wausaukee, 54177-9749. Tel: 715-856-5276; Fax: 715-856-5276. Email: staugustine@centurytel.net.
Catechesis/Religious Program—Ms. Linda Suzawith, D.R.E.

ANIWA, SHAWANO CO., ST. BONIFACE, [CEM], Served from St. Philomena, Birnamwood. Rev. Everard Scesney, O.F.M.
Res.: P.O. Box K, Birnamwood, 54414-0911. Tel: 715-449-2104; Fax: 715-449-9828. Email: eversces@charter.net.
Catechesis/Religious Program—

ANTIGO, LANGLADE CO.

1—ST. HYACINTH, Merged with St. Mary, Antigo to form SS. Mary & Hyacinth, Antigo.

2—ST. JOHN, [JC] Rev. Charles G. Hoffmann.
Res.: 415 6th Ave., 54409-2104. Tel: 715-623-2024; Fax: 715-627-0234. Email: carolyn@stjohnantigo.com.
School: See All Saints Catholic Schools, Inc., Antigo located under Consolidated Schools Antigo located in the Institution Section for details.
Catechesis/Religious Program—Email: religioused@stjohnantigo.com. Dawn Kratzke, Contact Person.

3—ST. MARY, Merged with St. Hyacinth, Antigo to form SS. Mary & Hyacinth, Antigo.

4—SS. MARY & HYACINTH, [JC], Also serves St. Wenceslaus, Neva. Has records for St. Mary and St. Hyacinth, Antigo. Rev. Michael E. Betley; Deacon Thomas J. Hanley.
Res.: 819 3rd Ave., 54409-1930. Tel: 715-623-4938; Fax: 715-623-5255. Email: ssmhy@dwave.net.
School: See All Saints Catholic Schools, Inc., Antigo located under Consolidated Schools in the Institution Section for details.
Catechesis/Religious Program—Tel: 715-623-5255. Susan Brettingen, D.R.E.; Thomas Hanley, D.R.E.

APPLETON, OUTAGAMIE CO.

1—ST. BERNADETTE Very Rev. Donald M. Zuleger; Deacon Michael A. Madden.
Church: 2331 E. Lourdes Dr., 54915-3615. Tel: 920-739-4157; Fax: 920-739-2795. Email: peichhorst@saint-bernadette.org.
School—ACES/Xavier Education System, Inc. (St. Bernadette Campus), Tel: 920-739-5391; Fax: 920-739-0061. Web: www.acesys.org/st_bernadette/index.htm. Elizabeth A. Watson, Prin.
Catechesis/Religious Program—Tel: 920-734-7502. Email: sriley@saint-bernadette.org. Shirley Riley, D.R.E.; Peter J. Gagnon, D.R.E.

2—ST. BERNARD Rev. Dennis M. Ryan; Deacons Maurice F. Reed; Robert Vincent.
1617 W. Pine St., 54914-5118. Tel: 920-739-0331; Fax: 920-749-9771. Email: stbernard@stbernardappleton.org.
School—ACES/Xavier Educational System Inc., 101 E. Northland Ave., 54911-2104. Tel: 920-735-9380; Fax: 920-735-1787. Email: tabts@acesys.org. Anthony J. Abts, Pres.
Catechesis/Religious Program—Tel: 920-739-8912. Jane Angha, D.R.E.; Lisa M. Hecht, D.R.E.

3—ST. JOSEPH Rev. Lawrence E. Abler, O.F.M.Cap.; Deacons Mark J. Farrell; Roy J. Baumruk.
Res.: 404 W. Lawrence St., 54911-5855. Tel: 920-734-7195; Fax: 920-734-0227. Email: labler@saintjosephparish.org.
School—ACES/Xavier Educational System, Inc. (St. Joseph Middle School Campus), 2626 Oneida St., 54911-2099. Tel: 920-730-8849; Fax: 920-703-4147. Email: jlinsmeier@acesys.org. Bradley Norcross, Prin.
Catechesis/Religious Program—Tel: 920-738-7413. Email: iprf@athenet.net. Andrew J. Russell, D.R.E. Associated with St. Mary's, Appleton.

4—ST. MARY, [CEM] Rev. Michael K. O'Rourke; Deacons Gerard J. Schraufnagel; William J. Burke.
Church: 312 S. State St., 54911-5926. Tel: 920-739-5119; Fax: 920-739-5111. Email: stmary@stmaryparish.org.
School—ACES/Xavier Educational System, Inc. (Catholic Central Campus), 313 S. State St., 54911-5929. Tel: 920-733-3709; Fax: 920-733-8142. Email: jstaddler@acesxavier.k12.wi.us. Jeffrey Staddler, Prin.
Catechesis/Religious Program—404 W. Lawrence St., 54911-5817. Tel: 920-738-7413. Email:

iprf@athenet.net. Andrew J. Russell, D.R.E. Associated with St. Joseph-St. Mary Interparish.

5—ST. PIUS X Revs. Thomas J. Farrell; Andrew T. Kysely, Parochial Vicar; Deacon Richard S. Simon.
Office:—500 W. Marquette St., 54911-1996. Tel: 920-733-0575; Fax: 920-749-8056. Email: stpius@stpiusxappleton.com.
School—ACES/Xavier Educational System, Inc. (St. Pius X Campus), Tel: 920-733-4918; Fax: 920-733-7269. Email: scjpeterson@acesxavier.k12.wi.us. Sr. Carol Jean Peterson, C.S.J., Prin.
Catechesis/Religious Program—Tel: 920-733-4919. Email: kathleenschommer@stpiusxappleton.com. Kathy Schommer, D.R.E.

6—SACRED HEART Rev. Robert J. Karuhn; Deacons Daniel T. Koszalinski; Gilbert Schmidt.
Res.: 222 E. Fremont St., 54915-1890. Tel: 920-739-3196; Fax: 920-739-4062. Email: shchurch@athenet.net.
Catechesis/Religious Program—Email: shgeorgia@athenet.net. Maurine Overesch, D.R.E.; Kelly Koszalinski, D.R.E.

7—ST. THERESE Rev. William A. Hoffman; Deacon Patrick J. Whitcomb.
Office:—213 E. Wisconsin Ave., 54911-4875. Tel: 920-733-8568; Fax: 920-954-5727. Email: william.hoffman@st-therese.com.
School—ACES/Xavier Educational System, Inc., 101 E. Northland Ave., 54911-2104. Tel: 920-735-9380; Fax: 920-735-1787. Email: tabts@acesys.org. Anthony J. Abts, Pres.
Catechesis/Religious Program—Email: patrick.whitcomb@st-therese.com. Sr. Gemma T. Harvey, S.S.N.D., D.R.E.

8—ST. THOMAS MORE Rev. Gerald R. Falk; Deacons Donald J. Wetzel; Craig W. Merrick; Paul J. Klein; Timothy Downey.
Res.: 1810 N. McDonald St. B, 54911-3498. Tel: 920-739-7758; Fax: 920-749-3743. Email: stmparish@stmcath.org.
School—ACES/Xavier Educational System, Inc. (St. Thomas More Campus), Tel: 920-739-7826; Fax: 920-739-2376. Email: stm@acesxavier.k12.wi.us. Mr. David L. Callan, Prin. Sisters 2; Lay Teachers 19; Students 229.
Catechesis/Religious Program—Tel: 920-739-8172. Email: irene@stmcath.org. Irene Skarban, D.R.E.; Carolyn M. Coutu, D.R.E.; Anna M. Donnermeyer, D.R.E.

ARGONNE, FOREST CO., ST. MARY, Merged with St. Joseph, Crandon.

ARMSTRONG CREEK, FOREST CO., ST. STANISLAUS KOSTKA, Served from St. Mary of the Lake, Lakewood. Rev. David R. Schmidt, Admin.; Rev. Msgr. Paul P. Koszarek, Sacramental Min. (Retired); Deacon Gerald H. Cross, Parish Dir.
Mailing Address: P.O. Box 39, 54103-0039. Tel: 715-336-2334. Email: ststanislausarmstrong@gmail.com.
Catechesis/Religious Program—Mrs. Vinnie Duda, D.R.E. Associated with St. Joan of Arc, Goodman.

AURORA, FLORENCE CO., SACRED HEART, Served from St. Anthony, Niagara. Rev. Matthew W. Settle.
Mailing Address: 1432 River St., Niagara, 54151-1544. Tel: 715-251-3879; Fax: 715-528-3052.

BAILEYS HARBOR, DOOR CO., ST. MARY OF THE LAKE, Merged with St. John the Baptist, Egg Harbor; St. Paul, Fish Creek; St. Michael, Jacksonport and St. Rosalia, Sister Bay to form Stella Maris, Egg Harbor.

BAY SETTLEMENT, BROWN CO., HOLY CROSS, [CEM] Rev. Thomas A. Hagendorf, O.Praem.; Deacon James P. Heider.
Res.: 3009 Bay Settlement Rd., 54311-7301. Tel: 920-468-0595; Fax: 920-468-4764. Email: thagen@netnet.net.
School—3002 Bay Settlement Rd., 54311-7302. Tel: 920-468-0625; Fax: 920-468-0625. Email: rjensen@holycrossfamily.org. Robin J. Jensen, Prin.
Catechesis/Religious Program—Tel: 920-468-6554. Martha Burkard, D.R.E.

BEAR CREEK, OUTAGAMIE CO., ST. MARY, [CEM], Served from St. Rose, Clintonville. Mr. Lincoln Wood, Parish Dir.; Revs. John W. Girotti, Priest Mod.; John T. Mullarkey, Sacramental Min. (Retired); Deacons Thomas V. Jozwiak; Joseph M. Lehman.
Mailing Address: P.O. Box 27, 54922-0027. Tel: 715-752-4177; Fax: 715-752-3249. Email: ssrmbs@frontiernet.net.
Catechesis/Religious Program—140 Auto St., Clintonville, 54929-1712. Tel: 715-823-4360. Mary Rose Morse, D.R.E. Associated with St. Rose, Clintonville.

BIRNAMWOOD, SHAWANO CO., ST. PHILOMENA, [CEM], Also serves St. Boniface, Aniwa. Rev. Everard Scesney, O.F.M.
Res.: P.O. Box K, 54414-0911. Tel: 715-449-2104; Fax: 715-449-9828. Email: eversces@charter.net.
Catechesis/Religious Program—

BLACK CREEK, OUTAGAMIE CO., ST. MARY, [CEM] Rev. Theodore J. Hendricks.
Res.: P.O. Box 217, 54106-0217. Tel: 920-984-3319.
Catechesis/Religious Program—Rita Theobald, D.R.E.

BRILLION, CALUMET CO.

1—HOLY FAMILY, [JC], Merger of St. Mary, Brillion and St. Mary-St. Patrick, Reedsville/Maple Grove. (Has records for St. Mary, Brillion and St. Mary-St. Patrick.) Rev. Mathew J. Simonar; Deacon Stephen T. Letourneaux.
Res.: 1100 W. Ryan St., 54110-1074. Tel: 920-756-2535; Fax: 920-756-9802. Email: parishoffice@holyfamily-parish.org.
School—209 N. Custer St., 54110-1236. Tel: 920-756-2502; Fax: 920-756-9702. Email: HolyFamilyBrillon@charter.net. Scott Smith, Prin.
Catechesis/Religious Program—Email: bobbie@holyfamily-parish.org. Roberta Whittaker, D.R.E.; Theresa Lambrecht, D.R.E.; Nick Vogel, Contact Person.

2—ST. MARY, Merged with St. Mary-St. Patrick, Reedsville to form Holy Family, Brillion.

BRUSSELS, DOOR CO.

1—ST. FRANCIS XAVIER, Merged with St. Mary, Namur to form St. Francis-St. Mary, Brussels.

2—ST. FRANCIS-ST. MARY PARISH, [CEM 3], Merger of St. Francis Xavier, Brussels and St. Mary, Namur. (Has records for St. Francis Xavier, Brussels and St. Mary, Namur.) Rev. Pius Cotter, O.F.M.Cap., Admin.
Res.: 9716 Cemetery Rd., 54204-9749. Tel: 920-825-7555; Fax: 920-825-1492. Email: stfrancis@centurytel.net.
Catechesis/Religious Program—Tel: 920-825-7713. Susan M. Johnson, D.R.E.; Tinamarie L. DeJardin, D.R.E.

CASCO/SLOVAN, KEWAUNEE CO., HOLY TRINITY, [CEM] Rev. Milton M. Suess; Deacon Robert J. Miller. Merger of Holy Trinity, Casco and Mission of St. Adalbert, Slovan. (Has records for Holy Trinity, Casco and St. Adalbert, Slovan)
Res.: 510 Church Ave., 54205-9712. Tel: 920-837-7531; Fax: 920-837-2361.
School—510 Church Ave., 54205-9712. Email: holytrinitycasco@hotmail.com.
Catechesis/Religious Program—

CECIL, SHAWANO CO., ST. MARTIN, [CEM] Deacon Thomas M. Craig, Parish Dir.; Rev. Leonard M. Evers, Priest Moderator; Very Rev. John F. Doerfler, Sacramental Min.; Deacon Kenneth Banker.
Church: 418 S. Warrington St., P.O. Box 144, 54111-0144. Tel: 715-745-6681; Fax: 715-745-4289. Email: stmartin_cecil@frontiernet.net.
Catechesis/Religious Program—Deacon Thomas M. Craig, D.R.E.

CHAMPION, BROWN CO., ST. JOSEPH, [CEM] Rev. Dean W. Dombroski.
Mailing Address: 5996 County Rd. K, New Franken, 54229-9456. Tel: 920-866-9961. Email: stjosephchampion@centurytel.net. Served from St. Thomas the Apostle, Humboldt.
Catechesis/Religious Program—Lisa Laurent, D.R.E.; Patricia Ratajczak, D.R.E.; Mary E. Murphy, Contact Person.

CHARLESBURG, CALUMET CO., ST. CHARLES BORROMEO, Merged with St. Augustine, Chilton; St. Mary, Chilton; St. Martin, Charlestown; Holy Trinity, Jericho and St. Elizabeth, Kloten to form Good Shepherd, Chilton.

CHARLESTOWN, CALUMET CO., ST. MARTIN, Merged with St. Augustine, Chilton; St. Mary, Chilton; St. Charles Borromeo, Charlesburg; Holy Trinity, Jericho and St. Elizabeth, Kloten to form Good Shepherd, Chilton.

CHASE, OCONTO CO., ST. JOSEPH, [CEM] Merged with St. Louis, Abrams and St. John Cantius, Sobieski to form St. Maximilian Kolbe, Sobieski.

CHILTON, CALUMET CO.

1—ST. AUGUSTINE, Merged with St. Mary, Chilton; St. Charles Borromeo, Charlesburg; St. Martin, Charlestown; Holy Trinity, Jericho and St. Elizabeth, Kloten to form Good Shepherd, Chilton.

2—GOOD SHEPHERD, [CEM] Rev. Robert Kollath; Deacon Dennis G. Bennin. Merger of St. Augustine, Chilton; St. Mary, Chilton; St. Charles Borromeo, Charlesburg; St. Martin, Charlestown; Holy Trinity, Jericho and St. Elizabeth, Kloten
Res.: 62 E. Main St., 53014-1428. Tel: 920-849-9363; Fax: 920-849-7270.

3—ST. MARY, Merged with St. Augustine, Chilton; St. Charles Borromeo, Charlesburg; St. Martin, Charlestown; Holy Trinity, Jericho and St. Elizabeth, Kloten to form Good Shepherd, Chilton.

CLARKS MILLS, MANITOWOC CO., IMMACULATE CONCEPTION, [CEM], Also serves St. Michael, Whitelaw. Rev. David M. Zimmerman; Deacon Thomas J. Koch.
Res.: 15 S. County Rd. J, Cato, 54230-8329. Tel: 920-775-4365; Fax: 920-775-4365. Email: stmarycm@tds.net.
School: See St. Mary/St. Michael School, Cato under Consolidated Schools located in the Institution section.
Catechesis/Religious Program—Tel: 920-775-4876. Teresa Pederson, D.R.E.

CLEVELAND, MANITOWOC CO., ST. WENDEL, Merged with St. Isidore, Osman; St. Joseph, Alverno; and St. Casimir, Northeim to form St. Thomas the Apostle, Northeim.

CLINTONVILLE, WAUPACA CO., ST. ROSE, [CEM], Also serves St. Mary, Bear Creek. Mr. Lincoln Wood, Parish Dir.; Revs. John W. Girotti, Priest Mod.; John T. Mullarkey, Sacramental Min. (Retired); Deacons Joseph M. Lehman; Thomas V. Jozwiak.
Mailing Address: P.O. Box 27, Bear Creek, 54922-0027.
Res.: 24 7th St., 54929-1733. Tel: 715-823-3416; Fax: 715-752-3249. Email: ssrmbs@frontiernet.net.
School—140 Auto St., 54929-1758. Tel: 715-823-4360; Fax: 715-823-3402. Email: stroseschool@charter.net. Mary Rose Morse, Prin. Lay Teachers 9; Students 77.
Catechesis/Religious Program—Tel: 715-823-5266. Jennifer Wood, D.R.E.

COLEMAN, MARINETTE CO.

1—ST. ANNE PARISH CORP., (Merger of SS. Francis-Wenceslaus, Coleman & Holy Cross, Lena/Spruce) Very Rev. Celestine Byekwaso, Admin.
228 E. Main St., 54112-9407. Tel: 920-897-3226; Fax: 920-897-4677. Email: stanne1@centurytel.net.
Catechesis/Religious Program—Tel: 920-897-4677. Email: ssfranreled@ex-net.com. Theresa M. Alberts, D.R.E.; Kathryn Lieburn, D.R.E.

2—ST. FRANCIS OF ASSISI, Merged with St. Wenceslaus, Klondike to form SS. Francis-Wenceslaus, Coleman.

COMBINED LOCKS, OUTAGAMIE CO., ST. PAUL, [CEM] Very Rev. James W. Lucas; Deacon George J. Schraufnagel.
Res.: 410 Wallace St., 54113-1128. Tel: 920-788-4553; Fax: 920-788-6822. Email: stpaulcl@newbc.rr.com.
Catechesis/Religious Program—Tel: 920-788-5711. Email: stpaulff@newbc.rr.com.

COOPERSTOWN, MANITOWOC CO., ST. JAMES, [CEM], Served from All Saints, Denmark. Revs. Ronald A. Colombo; David J. Koch, Sacramental Min.
Res.: 18228 County Rd. R, Denmark, 54208-9554. Tel: 920-863-2585; Fax: 920-863-5445. Email: stjamescoop@tm.net.
Catechesis/Religious Program—Ann M. Habeck, D.R.E.; Katherine A. Styer, D.R.E.

CRANDON, FOREST CO., ST. JOSEPH, (Has records for St. Mary, Argonne and St. Michael Station, Hiles.) Rev. Ralph J. Gillis.
Res.: 208 N. Park Ave., 54520-1351. Tel: 715-478-3396.
Catechesis/Religious Program—

CRIVITZ, MARINETTE CO., ST. MARY, [CEM], Also serves Station at Caldron Falls. Rev. Walter P. Stumpf; Deacon Patrick Whitcomb, Contact Person.
Mailing Address: P.O. Box 159, 54114-0159. Tel: 715-854-2501.
Catechesis/Religious Program—

DARBOY, OUTAGAMIE CO. (APPLETON P.O.), HOLY ANGELS, [CEM] Merged with Holy Name of Jesus, Kimberly to form Holy Spirit, Kimberly/Darboy.

DE PERE, BROWN CO.

1—ST. BONIFACE, Merged with St. Joseph, De Pere to form Our Lady of Lourdes, De Pere.

2—ST. FRANCIS XAVIER, [JC], Served from St. Mary, De Pere. Very Rev. John H. Harper; Rev. Joel A. Sember, Parochial Vicar; Deacon Kevin DeCleene.
Res.: 220 S. Michigan St., 54115-2730. Tel: 920-336-1813; Fax: 920-336-1814.
School—Notre Dame School, 221 S Wisconsin St., 54115-2797. Tel: 920-337-1115; Fax: 920-337-1117. Email: ndprin@itol.com. Mrs. Mary A. VandenBusch, Prin.

3—ST. JOSEPH, Merged with St. Boniface, De Pere to form Our Lady of Lourdes, De Pere.

4—ST. MARY, [JC], Also serves St. Francis Xavier, De Pere. Very Rev. John H. Harper; Rev. Joel A. Sember, Parochial Vicar; Deacon Kevin DeCleene.
Mailing Address: P.O. Box 70, 54115-0070. Tel: 920-337-2330; Fax: 920-337-2332. Email: office@stmarydepere.org.
School—Notre Dame School, 221 S. Wisconsin St., 54115-2797. Tel: 920-337-1115; Fax: 920-337-1117. Email: vandenbuschm@notredameofdepere.com. Mrs. Mary A. VandenBusch, Prin.
Catechesis/Religious Program—Sr. Charlene Hockers, O.S.F., D.R.E.; Michael Lotto, D.R.E.

5—ST. NORBERT COLLEGE Revs. James T. Baraniak, O.Praem.; Salvatore H. Cuccia, O.Praem.
Mailing Address: 100 Grant St., 54115-2099. Tel: 920-403-3010; Fax: 920-403-4432. Email: parish@snc.edu.
Catechesis/Religious Program—Tel: 920-403-3559. Margaret VandeHey, D.R.E.

6—Our Lady of Lourdes (1996) [CEM], (Has records for St. Joseph, De Pere and St. Boniface, De Pere.) Rev. Timothy D. Shillcox, O.Praem.; Deacons Michael D. Vander Bloomen; Harvey J. Quinette.
Res.: 1307 Lourdes Ave., 54115-1018. Tel: 920-336-4033; Fax: 920-336-3910. Email: parish@lourdesdepere.org.
School—1305 Lourdes Ave., 54115-1018. Tel: 920-336-3091; Fax: 920-337-6806. Email: school@lourdesdepere.org. Mrs. Susan Sands, Prin.
Catechesis/Religious Program—Tel: 920-337-0443. Email: knienhaus@lourdesdepere.org. Mrs. Karen Nienhaus, D.R.E.; Angela Bieda, Contact Person.

Denmark, Brown Co., All Saints, [CEM], Also serves St. James, Cooperstown and Holy Trinity Mission, New Denmark. Revs. Ronald A. Colombo; David J. Koch, Sacramental Min.
P.O. Box 787, 54208-0787. Email: asden_parish@charter.net.
School—Tel: 920-863-2449; Fax: 920-863-5425. Email: lmeles@allsaintsschool.net. LeRoy Meles, Prin.
Catechesis/Religious Program—Tel: 920-863-5256. Email: lwagner@allsaintsschool.net. Lori Wagner, D.R.E. Associated with Holy Trinity, New Denmark.

Dyckesville, Kewaunee Co., St. Louis, [CEM 2] Sr. Marlene M. Dimmerling, O.P., Parish Dir.; Rev. John H. Van Deuren, Priest Mod. & Sacramental Min. (Retired).
Res.: N8726 County Line Rd., Luxemburg, 54217-8629. Tel: 920-866-2410; Fax: 920-866-9531. Email: mardim@greenbaynet.com.
Catechesis/Religious Program—Tel: 920-866-2842; Fax: 920-866-2611. Mrs. Kathleen Cornette, D.R.E.

Eaton, Brown Co., SS. Cyril and Methodius, Merged with Our Lady Queen of Peace, Humboldt to form St. Thomas the Apostle, Humboldt

Egg Harbor, Door Co.

1—St. John the Baptist, Merged with St. Mary of the Lake, Baileys Harbor; St. Paul, Fish Creek; St. Michael, Jacksonport and St. Rosalia to form Stella Maris, Egg Harbor.

2—Stella Maris, Merger of St. John the Baptist, Egg Harbor; St. Mary of the Lake, Baileys Harbor; St. Paul, Fish Creek; St. Michael, Jacksonport; St. Rosalia, Sister Bay and the Station at Washington Island. Rev. David C. Ruby; Deacon David J. Kowalski.
Mailing Address: P.O. Box 49, 54209-0049. Tel: 920-868-3241. Email: churchoffice@dcwis.comFax: 920-868-1481.

Eland, Shawano Co., St. William, Merged with Holy Family, Wittenberg to form Holy Family-St. William, Wittenberg.

Elcho, Langlade Co., Holy Family, [CEM], Also serves St. Mary Parish, Pickerel. Rev. Roger W. Strebel, Admin.
Mailing Address: P.O. Box 128, 54428-0128. Tel: 715-275-3750. Email: holyfamilyelcho@frontiernet.net.
Catechesis/Religious Program—Tel: 715-275-3114. Roger LeBouton, Contact Person.

Fish Creek, Door Co., St. Paul, Merged with St. John the Baptist, Egg Harbor; St. Mary of the Lake, Baileys Harbor; St. Michael, Jacksonport and St. Rosalia, Sister Bay to form Stella Maris, Egg Harbor.

Flintville, Brown Co., SS. Edward and Isidore, [CEM] Rev. David D. Kasperek; Deacon Earl L. Kunzer.
Mailing Address: 3667 Flintville Rd., 54313-8330. Tel: 920-865-7844; Fax: 920-865-4375. Email: clom@stedwardisidore.org.
Office:—3752 Elm Tree Rd., 54313.
Catechesis/Religious Program—Tel: 920-865-7677. June L. Ingold, D.R.E.

Florence, Florence Co., Immaculate Conception, [CEM] Mrs. Christine Gall, Parish Dir.; Revs. David R. Schmidt, Priest Mod; Jeremiah F. Worman, Sacramental Min. (Retired); Matthew W. Settle, Sacramental Min.
Res.: P.O. Box 166, 54121-0166. Tel: 715-528-3310; Fax: 715-528-3052. Email: stmary@borderlandnet.net.
Catechesis/Religious Program—Tel: 715-582-4992. Sr. Marla J. Clercx, A.N.G., D.R.E.

Francis Creek, Manitowoc Co., St. Anne, [CEM], Served from Holy Cross, Mishicot. Rev. Paul J. Paider.
Res.: P.O. Box 218, 54214-0218. Tel: 920-682-6640. Email: stannefc@lsol.net.
Catechesis/Religious Program—Sara Tuma, D.R.E.

Freedom, Outagamie Co., St. Nicholas, [CEM] Very Rev. David J. Hoffman; Deacon Donald W. Newhouse.
Res.: W2037 County Rd. S., 54131. Tel: 920-788-1492; Fax: 920-788-1492. Email: parish@stnicholasfreedom.org.
School—W2035 County Rd. S., Kaukauna, 54130-7565. Tel: 920-788-9371. Rosemary F. Perrino, Prin.
Catechesis/Religious Program—Tel: 920-788-1451. Email: bschwandt@stnicholasfreedom.org. Betty Schwandt, Contact Person; Angela Kempen, D.R.E.; Rebecca S. Tappen, D.R.E.

Gillett, Oconto Co., St. John, [CEM], Also serves St. Michael, Suring and Chute Lake Station. Sr. Marla J. Clercx, A.N.G., Parish Dir.; Revs. John J. Becker, Priest Mod.; David S. Barrett, Sacramental Min. (Retired); Deacon William V. Doran.
Res.: 127 Garden St., 54124-9413. Tel: 920-855-2542; Fax: 920-855-1449. Email: jcoopmans@centurytel.net.
Catechesis/Religious Program—Haley Baraniak, D.R.E.; Danelle Schuh-Philippi, Contact Person.
Station—Chute Lake, Chute Lake Station P.O. Box 248, Suring, 54174-248.

Glenmore, Brown Co., Immaculate Conception, Merged with St. Mary, Stark to form St. Mary, Glenmore/Stark.

Glenmore/Stark, Brown Co., St. Mary, [CEM 2], Merger of Immaculate Conception, Glenmore and St. Mary, Stark. (Has records for St. Mary, Stark) ; Served from All Saints, Denmark. Rev. Ronald A. Colombo; Deacon Clarence Naidl.
Mailing Address: 5840 Big Apple Rd., De Pere, 54115-9766. Tel: 920-864-7641.
Catechesis/Religious Program—Denis Lotto, D.R.E.

Goodman, Marinette Co., St. Joan of Arc, Served from St. Mary of the Lake, Lakewood. Revs. David R. Schmidt, Admin.; Matthew W. Settle; Rev. Msgr. Paul P. Koszarek, Sacramental Min. (Retired).
Church: P.O. Box 218, 54125. Tel: 715-336-2334. Email: stjoanofarc@gmx.com.
Catechesis/Religious Program—P.O. Box 39, Armstrong Creek, 54103-0039. Deborah Thompson, D.R.E. Associated with St. Stanislaus Kosta, Armstrong Creek.

Greenleaf, Brown Co., St. Clare Corp., (Merger of St. Mary, Greenleaf; St. Patrick, Askeaton & St. Paul, Wrightstown) Rev. Dennis L. Bergsbaken; Deacon Kenneth J. Kabat.
2218 Day St., 54126-9200. Tel: 920-864-2550; Fax: 920-864-2979. Email: office@stclareagw.org.
School—St. Clare School, 425 Main St., Wrightstown, 54180-057. Tel: 920-532-4833.
Catechesis/Religious Program—Tel: 920-864-2586. Email: stclarere@gmail.org. Gloria Kennedy, D.R.E.

Greenville, Outagamie Co., St. Mary, [CEM], Also serves St. Edward, Mackville. Rev. Mark P. Vander Steeg; Deacon David L. DeYoung.
Res.: N2385 Municipal Dr., 54942-9713. Tel: 920-757-6555; Fax: 920-757-6560. Email: parish@stmarygreenville.org.
School—(Grades PreK-8), N2387 Municipal Dr., 54942-9713. Tel: 920-757-5516. Email: dfuller@stmarygreenville.org. Debra Fuller, Prin.

Gresham, Shawano Co., St. Francis Solanus, [CEM], Served from St. Michael, Keshena. Deacon Thomas M. Craig, Pastoral Coord.; Rev. Leonard M. Evers, Priest Mod.
Mailing Address: P.O. Box 177, 54128-0177. Tel: 715-787-3250. Email: sfrancis@frontiernet.net.
Catechesis/Religious Program—Sr. Mary S. Brunner, O.S.F., D.R.E.

Hilbert, Calumet Co., St. Mary, [CEM], Served from St. John-Sacred Heart, Sherwood/Saint John. Very Rev. Philip Dinh-Van-Thiep.
Res.: P.O. Box 386, 54129-0386. Tel: 920-853-3252.
School—P.O. Box 249, 54129-0249. Tel: 920-853-3216; Fax: 920-853-3216. Email: stmary@new.rr.com. Chandra L. Stomek, Prin.
Catechesis/Religious Program—N369 Military Rd., Sherwood, 54169-9661. Tel: 920-989-2400. Michael F. Brummond, D.R.E.

Hofa Park, Shawano Co., St. Stanislaus, [CEM], Served from Assumption BVM, Pulaski. Very Rev. Patrick M. Gawrylewski, O.F.M., Admin.
Res.: W1888 Hofa Park Dr., Seymour, 54165-9510. Tel: 920-822-5512; Fax: 920-822-8030.
Catechesis/Religious Program—Deanne Wilinski, Contact Person.

Hollandtown, Brown Co., St. Francis, [CEM] Merged with St. Mary of the Annunciation, Kaukauna and St. Aloysius, Kaukauna to form St. Katharine Drexel, Kaukauna.

Hortonville, Outagamie Co., SS. Peter and Paul, [CEM] Greg Layton, Parish Dir.; Rev. David J. Lewis, Priest Moderator; Rev. Msgr. James B. Feely, Sacramental Min. (Retired); Deacon Kenneth D. Bilgrien.
Res.: P.O. Box 238, 54944-0238. Tel: 920-779-6133; Fax: 920-779-6164. Email: peterandpaul@juno.com. See St. Mary School under St. Mary Parish, Greenville.
Catechesis/Religious Program—105 N. Olk St., 54944-9434. Tel: 920-779-0551. Email: ssevegney@execpc.com. Kim A. Schroeder, D.R.E.

Howard, Brown Co., St. John the Baptist, [CEM] Rev. John P. Bergstadt; Deacons Manuel Torres; Nicholas J. Williams.
Res.: 2597 Glendale Ave., 54313-6899. Tel: 920-434-2145; Fax: 920-434-5015. Email: jbergstadt@sjbh.org.
School—2561 Glendale Ave., 54313-6898. Tel: 920-434-3822; Fax: 920-434-5016. Email: vmarotz@sjbh.org. Vicki Marotz, Prin.
Catechesis/Religious Program—880 Cardinal Ln., 54313-6816. Email: tschelter@sjbn.org. Mrs. Therese M. Schelter, D.R.E.; Marie Francis, D.R.E.; Amy E. Koehler, Contact Person; Rebecca S. Tappen, Contact Person.

Humboldt, Brown Co.

1—Our Lady Queen of Peace, Merged with SS. Cyril & Methodius, Eaton to form St. Thomas the Apostle, Humbolt.

2—St. Thomas the Apostle, [JC 4], Also serves St. Kilian, New Franken and St. Joseph, Champion. Rev. Dean W. Dombroski.
Res.: 5930 Humboldt Rd., Luxemburg, 54217-9325. Tel: 920-863-6113; Fax: 920-845-5180. Email: sttomhum@baycomwi.com.
Catechesis/Religious Program—Email: stthomastheapostlecre@yahoo.com. Nancy Metzler, D.R.E.

Institute, Door Co., SS. Peter and Paul, [CEM], Served from St. Joseph, Sturgeon Bay. Rev. Dominic Peluse, S.C.J.; Deacon Kenneth D. Kopydlowski.
Res.: 4767 Dunn Rd., Sturgeon Bay, 54235-8822. Tel: 920-743-4842; Fax: 920-743-3885. Email: ssppchurch@charter.net.
See St. John Bosco Catholic School, Inc., Sturgeon Bay under Elementary Schools, Diocesan in the Institution Section.
Catechesis/Religious Program—Penny Biwer, D.R.E.

Isaar, Outagamie Co., St. Sebastian, [CEM], Served from St. John, Seymour. Very Rev. Robert J. Kabat, Admin.; Deacon Donald F. Coenen.
Res.: N9269 Isaar Rd., Seymour, 54165-9428. Tel: 920-833-2558. Email: stsebastian@gbonline.com.
Catechesis/Religious Program—Jodi M. Soltvedt, D.R.E.; Pat Posbrig, Contact Person.

Jacksonport, Door Co., St. Michael, Merged with St. John the Baptist, Egg Harbor; St. Mary of the Lake, Baileys Harbor; St. Paul, Fish Creek and St. Rosalia, Sister Bay to form Stella Maris, Egg Harbor.

Jericho, Calumet Co., Holy Trinity, Merged with St. Augustine, Chilton; St. Mary, Chilton; St. Charles Borromeo, Charlesburg; St. Martin, Charlestown and St. Elizabeth, Kloten to form Good Shepherd, Chilton.

Kaukauna, Outagamie Co.

1—St. Aloysius, Merged with St. Mary of the Annunciation, Kaukauna and St. Francis, Hollandtown to form St. Katharine Drexel, Kaukauna.

2—Holy Cross, [CEM] Rev. Thomas Pomeroy.
Res.: 309 Desnoyer St., 54130-2187. Tel: 920-766-3773; Fax: 920-766-3774. Email: tschmahl@holycrosskaukauna.org. Web: www.holycrosskaukauna.org.
School—Kaukauna Catholic Schools System, 220 Doty St., 54130-2188. Tel: 920-766-0186; Fax: 920-759-2428. Email: jleege@kcssonline.org. Jeanine Leege-Jankowski, Prin.
Catechesis/Religious Program—212 Doty St., 54130-2108. Tel: 920-766-3510. Email: jwallace@holycrosskaukauna.org. Jacqueline Wallace, Contact Person.

3—St. Katharine Drexel Rev. Jerome P. Pastors; Deacons Randall A. Haak; Gerald G. Kuborn.
119 W. 7th St., 54130-2356. Tel: 920-766-1445; Fax: 920-766-1476. Email: stkatharineparish@new.rr.com.
School—Kaukauna Catholic Schools System, Tel: 920-766-5199. Email: jleege@kessonline.org. Jeanine Leege-Jankowski, Prin.
Catechesis/Religious Program—Jean Olson, D.R.E.

4—St. Mary of the Annunciation, [JC] Merged with St. Aloysius, Kaukauna, and St. Francis, Hollandtown to form St. Katharine Drexel, Kaukauna.

Kellnersville, Manitowoc Co., St. Joseph, [CEM 2] Revs. Ronald A. Colombo, Admin.; David J. Koch, Sacramental Min.
Res.: P.O. Box 27, 54215-0027. Tel: 920-732-3770; Fax: 920-732-4612. Email: stjoseph@tm.net.
Catechesis/Religious Program—Jane Y. Kalies, D.R.E.

Keshena, Menominee Co., St. Michael, (Native American), [CEM], Also serves St. Francis Solanus, Gresham. Deacon Thomas M. Craig, Pastoral Coord.; Rev. Leonard M. Evers, Priest Mod.
Mailing Address: P.O. Box 610, 54135-0610. Tel: 715-799-3811; Fax: 715-799-5092. Email: saintmichaels@frontiernet.net.
Catechesis/Religious Program—Tel: 715-799-3234. Sandra Gawryleski, D.R.E.

Kewaunee, Kewaunee Co., Holy Rosary, [CEM], Served from St. Mary, Algoma. Rev. William D. Swichtenberg.

Res.: 521 Juneau St., 54216-1397. Tel: 920-388-2285; Fax: 920-388-3822. Email: mrsvan2001@yahoo.com.
School—519 Kilbourn St., 54216-1343. Tel: 920-388-2431. Email: raebly1264@yahoo.com. Richard C. Aebly, Prin.
Catechesis/Religious Program—Email: kzeman-hr-smp-@sbcglobal.net. Kathleen E. Zeman, D.R.E.

KIEL, MANITOWOC CO., SS. PETER AND PAUL, [CEM] Joe Zenk, Parish Dir.; Revs. Robert Kollath, Priest Mod.; Loren Nys, S.D.S., Sacramental Min.; Deacon Bernard (Pat) P. Knier.
Res.: 413 Fremont St., 53042-1398. Tel: 920-894-3553; Fax: 920-894-4462. Email: secretary@sspeternpaul.org.
School—Divine Savior Catholic School, 423 Fremont St., 53042-1316. Tel: 920-894-3533; Fax: 920-894-4959. Email: principal@spps.pvt.k12.wi.us. Lawrence Konetzke, Prin.
Catechesis/Religious Program—409 Fremont St., 53042-1316. Email: rel.ed@sspeternpaul.org. Mary Jo Meyer, D.R.E.

KIMBERLY, OUTAGAMIE CO., HOLY NAME OF JESUS, [CEM] Merged with Holy Angels, Darboy to form Holy Spirit, Kimberly/Darboy.

KIMBERLY/DARBOY, OUTAGAMIE CO., HOLY SPIRIT, [CEM], Merger of Holy Name of Jesus, Kimberly and Holy Angels, Darboy. Rev. David B. Beaudry; Deacon Cyril J. Klister.
Res.: 620 E. Kimberly Ave., 54136-1513. Tel: 920-788-7640; Fax: 920-788-7658. Email: hspkim@holyspirit-parish.org.
School—Holy Spirit School, W2796 County Rd. KK, Appleton, 54915. Tel: 920-733-2651; Fax: 920-733-5440. Sue Simonsen, Prin.
Catechesis/Religious Program—Sr. Elise Cholewinski, O.S.F., D.R.E.

KING, WAUPACA CO., ST. GEORGE, Closed. For inquiries for parish records, please see St. Mary Magdalene, Waupaca.

KLONDIKE, OCONTO CO., ST. WENCESLAUS, Merged with St. Francis of Assisi, Coleman, to form SS. Francis-Wenceslaus, Coleman.

KLOTEN, CALUMET CO., ST. ELIZABETH, Merged with St. Augustine, Chilton; St. Mary, Chilton; St. Charles Borromeo, Charlesburg; St. Martin, Charlestown and Holy Trinity, Jericho to form Good Shepherd, Chilton.

KOSSUTH, MANITOWOC CO., ST. AUGUSTINE, [CEM], Served from Holy Cross, Mishicot. Rev. Paul J. Paider.
Mailing Address: P.O. Box 218, Francis Creek, 54214-0218. Tel: 920-682-6640.
Catechesis/Religious Program—Sara Tuma, D.R.E. Associated with St. Anne, Francis Creek.

KRAKOW, SHAWANO CO., ST. CASIMIR, [CEM] Rev. James Esser, O.F.M.
Mailing Address: P.O. Box 66, 54137-0066. Tel: 920-899-3621. Email: stcasimir@netnet.net.
Catechesis/Religious Program—William Mihalski, D.R.E.

KROK, KEWAUNEE CO., ST. JOHN, Merged with St. Joseph, Montpelier to form St. Joseph-St. John, Montpelier.

LAKEWOOD, OCONTO CO., ST. MARY OF THE LAKE, [CEM], Also serves St. Ambrose, Wabeno; St. Stanislaus, Armstrong Creek; St. Joan of Arc, Goodman and stations at Crooked Lake and Silver Cliff. Revs. David R. Schmidt; Matthew W. Settle.
Res.: P.O. Box 219, 54138-0219. Tel: 715-276-7364. Email: stmary01@centurytel.net.
Catechesis/Religious Program—Kendra Yingling, D.R.E.
Station—Crooked Lake, Crooked Lake Station
Station—Silver Cliff, Silver Cliff Station

LANGLADE, LANGLADE CO., ST. STANISLAUS KOSTKA, Merged with St. James, White Lake to form SS. James-Stanislaus, White Lake.

LAONA, FOREST CO., ST. LEONARD, [JC], Also serves St. Norbert, Long Lake and St. Hubert Mission, Newald. Rev. John W. Cerkas.
Res.: 5330 Beech St., 54541-9340. Tel: 715-674-3241. Email: tunbles@ez-net.com.
Catechesis/Religious Program—Tel: 715-674-3306. Cynthia Beairl, D.R.E.

LEBANON, DODGE CO., ST. PATRICK, [CEM] Rev. Msgr. Dennis M. Lally, Admin.
Res.: N5705 County Rd. T, New London, 54961-8464. Tel: 920-982-5475.
Catechesis/Religious Program—Barbara Tate, D.R.E.

LENA, OCONTO CO., ST. CHARLES BORROMEO, Merged with Sacred Heart, Spruce to form Holy Cross, Lena.

LEOPOLIS, SHAWANO CO., ST. MARY, [CEM], Served from St. Anthony, Tigerton. Deacons Patrick G. Berg; Kenneth F. Sambs; Clay Wildenberg.
Mailing Address: P.O. Box 106, Tigerton, 54486-0106. Tel: 715-535-2571; Fax: 715-535-2953. Email: sacctig@frontiernet.net.
Church: W11842 3rd St., 54948.
Catechesis/Religious Program—Sally Korbisch, D.R.E.

LINCOLN, KEWAUNEE CO., ST. PETER, Merged with St. Hubert, Rosiere to form St. Peter-St. Hubert, Rosiere.

LITTLE CHUTE, OUTAGAMIE CO., ST. JOHN NEPOMUCENE, [CEM] Revs. James A. Hablewitz; David J. Funk, O.F.M.Cap.; Deacon Bruce H. Corey.
Res.: 323 Pine St., 54140-1854. Tel: 920-788-9061; Fax: 920-687-0851. Email: parish@stjn.org.
School—328 Grand Ave., 54140-1797. Tel: 920-788-9082; Fax: 920-788-7046. Email: mawelch@stjn.org. Mary Terrien, Interim Prin.
Catechesis/Religious Program—325 Pine St., 54140-1854. Tel: 920-788-9033. Email: reledu@stjn.org. Nancy Schmoll, D.R.E.; Charlene A. Kilsdonk, D.R.E.

LITTLE SUAMICO, OCONTO CO., ST. PIUS, Served from St. Benedict, Suamico. Rev. Gary J. Dantinne.
Mailing Address: P.O. Box 66, Suamico, 54173-0066. Tel: 920-434-2024.
Catechesis/Religious Program—Tammi LaLuzerne, D.R.E.

LONG LAKE, FLORENCE CO., ST. NORBERT, Served from St. Leonard, Laona (Laona also serves St. Hubert Mission, Newald). Rev. John W. Cerkas.
Res.: 5330 Beech St., Laona, 54541-9340. Tel: 715-674-3241.
Catechesis/Religious Program—Cynthia Beairl, D.R.E.; Sr. Marla J. Clercx, A.N.G., D.R.E. Associated with St. Leonard, Laona.

LUXEMBURG, KEWAUNEE CO., IMMACULATE CONCEPTION, [CEM], Also serves Holy Trinity, Casco/Slovan. Rev. Milton M. Suess; Deacon Robert J. Miller.
Res.: 1412 Main St., 54217-1308. Tel: 920-845-2056. Email: stmaryoffice@itol.com.
School—Immaculate Conception, 1406 Main St., 54217-1308. Tel: 920-845-2224; Fax: 920-845-5581. Email: bmatchefts@itol.com. William Matchefts, Prin.
Catechesis/Religious Program—Email: stmaryoffice@itol.com. Lee Treml, D.R.E.

MACKVILLE, OUTAGAMIE CO., ST. EDWARD, [CEM], Served from St. Mary, Greenville. Rev. Mark P. Vander Steeg, Admin.; Deacons Jeffrey J. Hofacker; Raymond G. Ambrosius Jr.
Res.: N2921 State Rd. 47, Appleton, 54913-9564. Tel: 920-733-9266; Fax: 920-733-7964. Email: stedwardparish@new.rr.com.
School—N2944 State Rd. 47, Appleton, 54913-9564. Tel: 920-733-6276; Fax: 920-733-1005. Email: saintedward@catholicweb.com. Becky Morrin, Prin.
Catechesis/Religious Program—Tel: 920-733-6070. Email: stedwardre@new.rr.com. Patricia Coonen, D.R.E.

MANAWA, WAUPACA CO., SACRED HEART, [JC], Served from SS. Peter & Paul, Weyauwega. Rev. Bertin L. Samsa, O.F.M.Cap., Admin.
Res.: P.O. Box 10, 54949-0010. Tel: 920-596-3323; Fax: 920-596-3323.
Catechesis/Religious Program—Email: nickizip@hotmail.com; shmanawa@wolfnet.net.

MANITOWOC, MANITOWOC CO.

1—ST. ANDREW, Merged with St. Boniface, Manitowoc; Holy Innocents, Manitowoc; St. Mary, Manitowoc; St. Paul, Manitowoc and Sacred Heart, Manitowoc to form St. Francis of Assisi, Manitowoc.

2—ST. BONIFACE, Merged with St. Andrew, Manitowoc; Holy Innocents, Manitowoc; St. Mary, Manitowoc; St. Paul, Manitowoc and Sacred Heart, Manitowoc to form St. Francis of Assisi, Manitowoc.

3—ST. FRANCIS OF ASSISI, [CEM], Merger of St. Andrew, Manitowoc; St. Boniface, Manitowoc; Holy Innocents, Manitowoc; Sacred Heart, Manitowoc; St. Mary, Manitowoc; and St. Paul, Manitowoc. Revs. Daniel J. Felton; John W. Schuetze; Very Rev. Richard H. Klingeisen, Sacramental Min.; Rev. Daniel J. Schuster; Deacons Robert L. Beehner; Richard D. Bahnaman; Alan L. Boeldt; Robert F. Drobka; Paul A. Kieffer; Kenneth R. Nelesen; Michael Dolezal.
Mailing Address: 601 N. 8th St., 54220-3919. Tel: 920-684-3718; Fax: 920-682-1096. Email: dan.felton@sfamanitowoc.com.
School—St. Francis Catholic School
Catechesis/Religious Program—Roxanne Dyzak, D.R.E.; Barbara K. Kratz, D.R.E.

4—HOLY INNOCENTS, Merged with St. Andrew, Manitowoc; St. Boniface, Manitowoc; St. Mary, Manitowoc; St. Paul, Manitowoc and Sacred Heart, Manitowoc to form St. Francis of Assisi, Manitowoc.

5—ST. MARY, Merged with St. Andrew, Manitowoc; St. Boniface, Manitowoc; Holy Innocents, Manitowoc; St. Paul, Manitowoc and Sacred Heart, Manitowoc to form St. Francis of Assisi, Manitowoc.

6—ST. PAUL, Merged with St. Andrew, Manitowoc; St. Boniface, Manitowoc; Holy Innocents, Manitowoc; St. Mary, Manitowoc and Sacred Heart, Manitowoc to form, St. Francis of Assisi, Manitowoc.

7—SACRED HEART, Merged with St. Andrew, Manitowoc; St. Boniface, Manitowoc; Holy Innocents, Manitowoc; St. Mary, Manitowoc and St. Paul, Manitowoc to form St. Francis of Assisi, Manitowoc.

MAPLE GROVE, MANITOWOC CO., ST. PATRICK, Merged with St. Mary, Reedsville to form St. Mary-St. Patrick, Reedsville.

MAPLEWOOD, DOOR CO., ST. MARY, [CEM 2] Rev. Robert Konkol, O.F.M., Admin.
Mailing Address: P.O. Box 308, 54226-0308. Tel: 920-856-6440. Email: holynameofmary@doorpi.net.
Catechesis/Religious Program—Janet Babler, D.R.E.; Dawn Lardinois, D.R.E.

MARCHAND, DOOR CO., ST. FRANCIS DE PAUL (Duvall) Closed. For inquiries for parish records contact St. Louis, Dyckesville.

MARINETTE, MARINETTE CO.

1—ST. ANTHONY, Merged with St. Joseph, Sacred Heart, and Our Lady of Lourdes, Marinette to form Holy Family, Marinette.

2—HOLY FAMILY, [CEM 2], Has records for St. Anthony, St. Joseph, Our Lady of Lourdes and Sacred Heart, Marinette. Very Rev. Joseph E. Dorner; Deacon Jerome E. Thetreau.
Office:—2715 Taylor St., 54143-1537. Tel: 715-735-9100; Fax: 715-735-9650. Email: holyfamily@holyfamparish.com.
School—St. Thomas Aquinas Academy, 1045 Water St., 54143-2524. Tel: 715-735-7481; Fax: 715-735-7146. Email: mcchs@hotmail.com. Mrs. Jennifer Elfering, Prin.
Catechesis/Religious Program—Kim M. Duffrin, D.R.E.

3—ST. JOSEPH, Closed. For inquiries for parish records please see Holy Family, Marinette.

4—OUR LADY OF LOURDES, Closed. For inquiries for parish records please see Holy Family, Marinette.

5—SACRED HEART CONGREGATION, Merged with St. Anthony, St. Joseph, and Our Lady of Lourdes, Marinette to form Holy Family, Marinette.

MARION, WAUPACA CO., ST. MARY, [CEM], Served from St. Anthony, Tigerton. Deacons Patrick G. Berg; Clay Wildenberg; Kenneth F. Sambs.
Mailing Address: P.O. Box 106, Tigerton, 54486-0106. Tel: 715-535-2571; Fax: 715-535-2953. Email: sacctig@frontiernet.net.
Catechesis/Religious Program—Sally Korbisch, D.R.E. Tel: 715-235-2571. Associated with St. Anthony, Tigerton.

MATTOON, SHAWANO CO., HOLY FAMILY, [CEM] Merged with St. Joseph, Phlox, to form St. Joseph-Holy Family Parish, Phlox. Served from St. Anthony, Neopit.

MENASHA, WINNEBAGO CO.

1—ST. JOHN, [CEM], Served from St. Mary, Menasha. Revs. Paul J. Radetski; Lawrence J. Canavera; Deacon Gerald H. Cross.
Res.: 516 Depere St., 54952-2847. Tel: 920-722-8922; Fax: 920-729-9248. Email: jjulius@tcces.k12.wi.us.
See Twin Catholic Education System, Neenah/Mensha under Consolidated Schools, Neenah/Mensha located in the Institution Section for details.
Catechesis/Religious Program—Email: despielbauer@tcces.k12.wi.us. Deborah A. Spielbauer, D.R.E.; Sally Michalkiewicz, D.R.E.

2—ST. MARY, [CEM], Also serves St. John and St. Patrick, Menasha. Revs. Paul J. Radetski; Lawrence J. Canavera; Deacons Richard B. Dvorak; Gerald H. Cross.
Res.: 528 2nd St., 54952-3112. Tel: 920-725-7714; Fax: 920-725-7612. Email: mgyrion@tcces.k12.wi.us.
See Twin Catholic Education System, Neenah/Mensha under Consolidated Schools, Neenah/Mensha located in the Institution Section for details.
Catechesis/Religious Program—Tel: 920-722-4830. Email: despielbauer@tcces.k12.wi.us. Sally Michalkiewicz, D.R.E.; Deborah A. Spielbauer, D.R.E.

3—ST. PATRICK, [JC], Served from St. Mary, Menasha. Revs. Paul J. Radetski; Lawrence J. Canavera.
Res.: 324 Nicolet Blvd., 54952-3334. Tel: 920-725-8381; Fax: 920-725-5544. Email: stpatmen@gmail.com.
School—Seton Catholic Middle School, 312 Nicolet Blvd., 54952. Tel: 920-727-0279. Monica Bausom, Prin.
See Twin Catholic Education System, Neenah/Mensha under Consolidated Schools, Neenah/Mensha located in the Institution Section for details.
Catechesis/Religious Program—Email: bmauthe@tcees.k12.wi.us. Barbara A. Mauthe, D.R.E.

MISHICOT, MANITOWOC CO., HOLY CROSS, [JC], Also serves St. Anne, Francis Creek & St. Augustine,

Kossuth. Rev. Paul J. Paider.
Res.: 423 S. Main St., 54228-9777. Tel: 920-755-2550. Email: holycrossparish@charterinternet.net.
Catechesis/Religious Program—Email: hcsoffice@charter.net. Marie T. Steeber, D.R.E.

MONTPELIER, KEWAUNEE CO.
1—ST. JOSEPH, Merged with St. John, Krok to form St. Joseph-St. John, Montpelier.
2—ST. JOSEPH-ST. JOHN, Merged with St. Lawrence, Stangelville and St. Hedwig, West Kewaunee to form St. Therese de Lisieux, Stangelville.

NAMUR, DOOR CO., ST. MARY, Merged with St. Francis Xavier, Brussels to form St. Francis-St. Mary, Brussels.

NAVARINO, SHAWANO CO., ST. LAWRENCE, [CEM] Deacon Donald F. Coenen, Pastoral Coord.; Very Rev. Robert J. Kabat, Priest Moderator; Rev. Theodore J. Hendricks, Sacramental Min.
Res.: W5125 State Hwy. 156, Bonduel, 54107-8614. Tel: 715-758-8161; Fax: 715-758-7562. Email: stlawrence@granitewave.com.
Catechesis/Religious Program—Karlyn Pennings, D.R.E.

NEENAH, WINNEBAGO CO.
1—ST. GABRIEL THE ARCHANGEL, [JC] Rev. Richard L. Allen; Deacon Raymond L. DuBois.
Res.: 900 Geiger St., 54956-2302. Tel: 920-722-4914; Fax: 920-722-2566. Email: reverendallen@tcces.k12.wi.us.
See Twin Catholic Education System, Neenah/Mensha under Consolidated Schools, Neenah/Mensha located in the Institution Section for details.
Catechesis/Religious Program—Tel: 920-725-0660. Email: spable@tcces.k12.wi.us. Stephen C. Pable, D.R.E.; Jennifer L. Schneider, D.R.E.
2—ST. MARGARET MARY, [JC] Rev. Michael L. Ingold.
Mailing Address: 439 Washington Ave., 54956-3398. Tel: 920-729-4560; Fax: 920-729-4572. Email: sbellile@tcces.k12.wi.us.
Church: 666 Division St., 54956-3398.
See Twin Catholic Education System, Neenah/Mensha under Consolidated Schools, Neenah/Mensha located in the Institution Section for details.
Catechesis/Religious Program—Tel: 920-729-4562. Sr. Diane Baumann, A.N.G., D.R.E.; Cindy M. Kyles-Werth, D.R.E.

NEOPIT, MENOMINEE CO., ST. ANTHONY, [CEM], Also serves St. Joseph, Phlox; Holy Family, Mattoon and Ss. James & Stanislaus, White Lake/Langlade. Rev. R. David Kiefer; Deacon Thomas W. Hartman.
Mailing Address: P.O. Box 241, 54150-0241. Tel: 715-756-2361; Fax: 715-756-2756. Email: stanthonyneopit@Frontiernet.net.
Catechesis/Religious Program—Email: mccn@frontiernet.net. Charlotte Ann Wagner, D.R.E.; Sandra Gawryleski, D.R.E.

NEVA, LANGLADE CO., ST. WENCESLAUS, [CEM], Served from SS. Mary & Hyacinth, Antigo. Rev. Jeremiah F. Worman (Retired); Deacon Thomas J. Hanley.
Mailing Address: P.O. Box 50, Deerbrook, 54424-0050. Tel: 715-627-2126.
Res.: N5340 Church Rd., Deerbrook, 54424-9413. Tel: 715-623-7019.
See All Saints Catholic School, Antigo under SS. Mary & Hyacinth, Antigo for details.
Catechesis/Religious Program—Susan Brettingen, D.R.E.; Lisa Ourada, D.R.E.

NEW DENMARK, BROWN CO., HOLY TRINITY MISSION, [CEM], Served from All Saints, Denmark. Revs. Ronald A. Colombo; David J. Koch, Sacramental Min.
Res.: P.O. Box 787, Denmark, 54208-0787. Tel: 920-863-2357; Fax: 920-863-5425.

NEW FRANKEN, BROWN CO., ST. KILIAN, [CEM], Served from St. Thomas the Apostle, Humboldt. Rev. Dean W. Dombroski.
Res.: P.O. Box 83, 54229-0083. Tel: 920-866-3541; Fax: 920-866-3541. Email: stkiliandre@hotmail.com.
Catechesis/Religious Program—Tel: 920-863-5297. Nancy Meltzer, D.R.E. Students 122.

NEW HOLSTEIN, CALUMET CO., HOLY ROSARY, [CEM], Also serves St. Ann, Saint Anna. Rev. Harold L. Berryman, Admin.
Res.: 1724 Madison St., 53061-1389. Tel: 920-898-4884; Fax: 920-898-4884. Email: hrparish_1@charter.net.
School—Divine Savior Catholic School, 423 Fremont St., Kiel, 53042-1316. Tel: 920-894-3533; Fax: 920-894-4959. Lawrence Konetzke, Prin.
Catechesis/Religious Program—1814 Madison St., 53061-1347. Tel: 920-898-9248. Jean M. Vogel, D.R.E.

NEW LONDON, WAUPACA CO., MOST PRECIOUS BLOOD, [CEM] Rev. David J. Lewis.
Res.: 712 S. Pearl St., 54961-1861. Tel: 920-982-2346; Fax: 920-982-8381. Email: pglocke@mpbnewlondon.org.
School—120 E. Washington St., 54961-1891. Tel: 414-982-2134; Fax: 920-982-1572. Email: jquinn@mpbnewlondon.org. James Quinn, Prin.
Catechesis/Religious Program—Tel: 920-982-9025. Email: eclarke@mpbnewlondon.org. Ellen E. Clarke, D.R.E.; Tina L. Noel, Contact Person.

NEWALD, ARGONNE CO., ST. HUBERT MISSION, Served from St. Leonard, Laona. Rev. John W. Cerkas.
Res.: 5330 Beech St., Laona, 54541-9340. Tel: 715-674-3241. Email: tumbles@ez-net.com.
Catechesis/Religious Program—Tel: 715-674-2654. Cynthia Beairl, D.R.E.

NEWTON, MANITOWO CO., ST. THOMAS THE APOSTLE (2000) [CEM], Has records for St. Joseph, Alverno; St. Wendel, Cleveland; St. Isidore, Osman & St. Casimir, Northeim. Sr. Marlita Henseler, Parish Dir.; Revs. Daniel J. Felton, Priest Moderator; Thomas Long, Sacramental Min.
Res.: 8100 Brunner Rd., 53063-9607. Tel: 920-726-4228; Fax: 920-726-4229. Email: churchlady@lakefield.net.
Catechesis/Religious Program—Pamela Fischer, D.R.E.

NIAGARA, MARINETTE CO., ST. ANTHONY, Also serves St. Margaret, Pembine and Sacred Heart, Aurora. Revs. Matthew W. Settle; Michael E. Betley; Deacon Gerald A. Nardi.
Res.: 1432 River St., 54151-1544. Tel: 715-251-3879. Email: stanthony@borderlandnet.net.
Catechesis/Religious Program—Rebecca S. Adedrman, D.R.E.; Debra Maszka, D.R.E.

NORMAN, KEWAUNEE CO., ST. JOSEPH, Merged with Nativity of the Blessed Virgin Mary, Tisch Mills to form St. Isidore the Farmer, Tisch Mills.

NORTHEIM, MANITOWOC CO., ST. CASIMIR, Merged with St. Joseph, Alverno; St. Wendel, Cleveland; and St. Isidore, Osman to form St. Thomas the Apostle, Northeim.

OCONTO, OCONTO CO.
1—HOLY TRINITY (1996) [CEM], (Has records for St. Joseph, Oconto and St. Peter, Oconto). Rev. Patrick C. Beno Jr., Admin.; Deacon Walter P. Kaszynski.
Res.: 716 Madison St., 54153-1668. Tel: 920-835-5900; Fax: 920-835-5907. Email: htcommun@bayland.net.
Catechesis/Religious Program—Gail Eichhorn, D.R.E.
2—ST. JOSEPH, Merged with St. Peter, Oconto to form Holy Trinity, Oconto.
3—ST. PETER, Merged with St. Joseph, Oconto to form Holy Trinity, Oconto.

OCONTO FALLS, OCONTO CO., ST. ANTHONY, [CEM], Served from Holy Trinity, Oconto. Rev. Patrick C. Beno Jr., Admin.
Church: 253 N. Franklin St., 54154-1042. Tel: 920-846-2276; Fax: 920-846-2180. Email: admsec@plbb.us.
School—Email: stant84@plbb.us. Ms. Rosemary Marifke, Prin.
Catechesis/Religious Program—Lynn Beaumier, D.R.E. Associated with St. Patrick, Stiles.

OMRO, WINNEBAGO CO., ST. MARY, Served from St. Mary, Winneconne. Sr. Pamela A. Biehl, O.S.F., Parish Dir.; Very Rev. Douglas E. LeCaptain, Priest Mod.; Revs. William Kuhr, Sacramental Min.; David J. Funk, O.F.M.Cap., Sacramental Min.; Jason J. Blahnik, Sacramental Min.
Res.: 730 Madison St., 54963-1630. Tel: 920-685-2258; Fax: 920-685-7343. Email: stmaryomro@charter.net.
Catechesis/Religious Program—Janet Abalan, D.R.E.

ONEIDA, BROWN CO., ST. JOSEPH, [CEM], Also serves Immaculate Conception, Oneida. Rev. David A. Duffeck; Deacon Everett L. Doxtator.
Res.: 145 Saint Joseph Dr., 54155-8914. Tel: 920-869-2244; Fax: 920-869-2219. Email: ruthboyea@aol.com.
Catechesis/Religious Program—Ann Van Schyndel, D.R.E.; Mary Van Schyndel, D.R.E.

ONEIDA TOWNSHIP, OUTAGAMIE CO., IMMACULATE CONCEPTION, [CEM], Served from St. Joseph, Oneida. Rev. David A. Duffeck; Deacon Donald F. Coenen.
Res.: N5589 County Rd. E., De Pere, 54115-8529. Tel: 920-869-2281. Email: cnndnld@yahoo.com.
Catechesis/Religious Program—Tel: 920-869-2950. Rochelle Bastien, D.R.E.

OSHKOSH, WINNEBAGO CO.
1—ST. JOHN, [JC] Merged with Sacred Heart, Oshkosh and St. Vincent de Paul, Oshkosh to form St. Jude the Apostle, Oshkosh.
2—ST. JOSAPHAT, Merged with St. Mary, Oshkosh and St. Peter, Oshkosh to form Most Blessed Sacrament, Oshkosh.
3—ST. JUDE THE APOSTLE Revs. Thomas J. Reynebeau; Joel A. Sember; Deacons Frederick C. Fischer; G. Patrick Gelhar; Kurt L. Grube; Robert Penzenstadler.
1025 W. 5th Ave., 54902-5725. Tel: 920-235-7412. Email: office@stjudeoshkosh.org.
See Unified Catholic Schools of Oshkosh, Oshkosh under Consolidated Schools located in the Institution section.
4—ST. MARY, Merged with St. Josaphat, Oshkosh and St. Peter, Oshkosh to form Most Blessed Sacrament, Oshkosh.
5—MOST BLESSED SACRAMENT Very Rev. James R. Jugenheimer; Deacons Joseph F. Gates; Kurt L. Grube; Richard A. Hocking.
449 High Ave., 54901-4708. Tel: 920-231-9782; Fax: 920-231-9808. Email: aflanagan@mbsoshkosh.org.
See Unified Catholic Schools of Oshkosh, Oshkosh under Consolidated Schools located in the Institution section.
6—ST. PETER, [JC] Merged with St. Josaphat, Oshkosh and St. Mary, Oshkosh to form Most Blessed Sacrament, Oshkosh.
7—ST. RAPHAEL THE ARCHANGEL, [JC] Very Rev. Douglas E. LeCaptain; Rev. Jason J. Blahnik; Deacons Gregory A. Grey; Peter A. Cheskie; John Ingala.
Church & Mailing Address: 830 S. Westhaven Dr., 54904-7977. Tel: 920-233-8044; Fax: 920-233-2360. Email: parishoffice@raphael.org.
See Unified Catholic Schools of Oshkosh, Oshkosh under Consolidated Schools located in the Institution section.
Catechesis/Religious Program—Mr. Rich F. Curran, Contact Person.
8—SACRED HEART, [CEM] Merged with St. John, Oshkosh and St. Vincent de Paul, Oshkosh to form St. Jude the Apostle, Oshkosh.
9—ST. VINCENT DE PAUL, [JC] Merged with St. John, Oshkosh and Sacred Heart, Oshkosh to form St. Jude the Apostle, Oshkosh.

OSMAN, MANITOWOC CO., ST. ISIDORE, Merged with St. Wendel, Cleveland; St. Joseph, Alverno; and St. Casimir, Northeim to form St. Thomas the Apostle, Northeim.

PEMBINE, MARINETTE CO., ST. MARGARET, Served from St. Anthony, Niagara. Revs. Matthew W. Settle; Jeremiah F. Worman, Temporary Admin. (Retired).
Mailing Address: P.O. Box 235, 54156-0235. Tel: 715-324-5849; Fax: 715-324-6571.

PESHTIGO, MARINETTE CO., ST. MARY, Also serves SS. Joseph & Edward, Walsh. Sr. Helen M. Plum, S.S.N.D., Parish Dir.; Revs. Dean W. Dombroski, Priest Moderator; Michael J. Clifford, Sacramental Min. (Retired); Deacon Charles R. Schumacher.
Res.: 171 S. Wood Ave., 54157-1426. Tel: 715-582-3876; Fax: 715-582-0970. Email: cte47017@centurytel.net.
School—141 S. Wood Ave., 54157-1426. Tel: 715-582-4041; Fax: 715-582-1165. Email: cte46995@centurytel.net. Linda Bjorkman, Prin.
Catechesis/Religious Program—Tel: 715-582-4897. Email: maryarmbrus@hotmail.com. Mary Armbrust, Contact Person.

PHLOX, LANGLADE CO.
1—ST. JOSEPH, [CEM] Merged with Holy Family, Mattoon to form St. Joseph-Holy Family Parish, Phlox. Served from St. Anthony, Neopit.
2—ST. JOSEPH-HOLY FAMILY PARISH, Served from St. Anthony, Neopit, Has records from St. Joseph, Phlox and Holy Family Mattoon. Rev. R. David Kiefer; Deacon Thomas W. Hartman.
Mailing Address: P.O. Box 73, 54464-0073. Tel: 715-489-3330. Email: sjhfphlox@granitewave.com.

PICKEREL, LANGLADE CO., ST. MARY, [CEM], Served from Holy Family, Elcho. Rev. Roger W. Strebel, Admin.
Mailing Address: P.O. Box 77, 54465-0077. Tel: 715-484-4300; Fax: 715-484-8949. Email: stmarysp@newnorth.net.
Catechesis/Religious Program—Sue Koleczek, D.R.E.

PINE GROVE, BROWN CO., HOLY TRINITY, [CEM] Merged with Holy Martyrs of Gorcum, Green Bay to form Prince of Peace, Green Bay.

PLAINFIELD, WAUSHARA CO., ST. PAUL (1898) [CEM] Deacon Robert L. Precourt, Parish Dir.; Very Rev. Robert Stegmann, Priest Mod.
Res.: 622 S. Beach St., 54966-9637. Tel: 715-335-4314; Fax: 715-335-6016. Email: stpaul@uniontel.net.
Catechesis/Religious Program—Heather Burns, D.R.E.; Cheryl Pionke, D.R.E.

POY SIPPI, WAUSHARA CO., SACRED HEART OF JESUS (1920), Served from St. Mark, Redgranite. Karen J. Nesbit, Parish Dir.; Very Rev. Robert Stegmann, Priest Mod.; Rev. Joseph A. Mattern, Sacramental Min. (Retired).
Mailing Address: P.O. Box 273, Redgranite, 54970-0273. Tel: 920-566-4442; Fax: 920-566-4559. Email: sacredheartps@centurytel.net.
Catechesis/Religious Program—Barbara M. Breest, Contact Person.

PULASKI, BROWN CO., ASSUMPTION OF THE BLESSED VIRGIN MARY (1887) [CEM], Also serves St. Stanislaus, Hofa Park. Very Rev. Patrick M. Gawrylewski, O.F.M., Admin.; Deacon Dennis G. Majewski.

Res.: P.O. Box 379, 54162-0379. Tel: 920-822-3279; Fax: 920-822-8030. Email: parishoffice@abvm.org.
School—109 E. Pulaski St., 54162-9287. Tel: 920-822-5650; Fax: 920-822-8003. Email: dwilinski@hotmail.com. Deanne Wilinski, Prin.
Catechesis/Religious Program—Email: dwilinski@hotmail.com. Deanne Wilinski, D.R.E.

REDGRANITE, WAUSHARA CO., ST. MARK (1906) [CEM], Also serves Sacred Heart of Jesus, Poy Sippi. Karen J. Nesbit, Parish Dir.; Very Rev. Robert Stegmann, Priest Mod.; Rev. Joseph A. Mattern, Sacramental Min. (Retired).
Mailing Address: P.O. Box 273, 54970-0273. Tel: 920-566-4442; Fax: 920-566-4559. Email: stmarkredgranite@centurytel.net.
Catechesis/Religious Program—Barbara M. Breest, D.R.E.

REEDSVILLE, MANITOWOC CO.
1—ST. MARY, Merged with St. Patrick's, Maple Grove to form St. Mary-St. Patrick, Reedsville.
2—ST. MARY-ST. PATRICK, Merged with St. Mary, Brillion to form Holy Family, Brillion.

ROSIERE, KEWAUNEE CO., ST. HUBERT, Merged with St. Peter, Lincoln to form St. Peter-St. Hubert, Rosiere.

ROSIERE/LINCOLN, KEWAUNEE CO., ST. PETER-ST. HUBERT (1994) [JC 4], Merger of St. Peter, Lincoln and St. Hubert, Rosiere. (Has records for St. Peter, Lincoln) Rev. Robert Konkol, O.F.M., Admin.
Res.: E3085 County Rd. X, Casco, 54205-9787. Tel: 920-837-2852.
Catechesis/Religious Program—Donna L. Bredael, D.R.E.; Tammy Barta, Contact Person.

SAINT ANNA, CALUMET CO., ST. ANN (1851) [CEM], Served from Holy Rosary, New Holstein. Rev. Harold L. Berryman, Admin.
Res.: N188 School St., New Holstein, 53061-9776. Tel: 920-894-3147; Fax: 920-894-3147.
Catechesis/Religious Program—June Winkel, D.R.E.; Susan Mintner, D.R.E.

SAINT JOHN, CALUMET CO., ST. JOHN THE BAPTIST, Merged with Sacred Heart, Sherwood, to form St. John-Sacred Heart, Sherwood.

SAINT NAZIANZ, MANITOWOC CO., ST. GREGORY (1854) [CEM], Also serves Holy Trinity, School Hill. Rev. Michael Bigley, S.D.S.; Deacon James E. Steffen.
Mailing Address: P.O. Box 199, St. Nazianz, 54232-0199. Tel: 920-773-2511; Fax: 920-773-3086. Email: stgregory100@hotmail.com.
School—Tel: 920-773-2530. Email: stgregs100@hotmail.com. Rita A. Steffen, Prin.
Catechesis/Religious Program—Rosemary G. Bartel, D.R.E.

SCHOOL HILL, MANITOWOC CO., HOLY TRINITY (1869) [CEM], Served from St. Gregory, St. Nazianz. Rev. Michael Bigley, S.D.S.; Deacon James E. Steffen.
Res.: 11928 Marken Rd., Kiel, 53042-9750. Tel: 920-773-2380. Email: holytrinitysh@excel.net.
Catechesis/Religious Program—Rosemary G. Bartel, D.R.E.

SEYMOUR, OUTAGAMIE CO., ST. JOHN (1873) [CEM] Very Rev. Robert J. Kabat; Deacons Paul K. Grimm; Orvell A. DeBruin.
Res. & Mailing Address: 915 Ivory St., 54165-1629. Tel: 920-833-6140; Fax: 920-833-7098. Email: office@stjohnseymour.com.
Catechesis/Religious Program—Tel: 920-833-2122. Mary P. Carter, D.R.E.

SHAWANO, SHAWANO CO., SACRED HEART (1867) [CEM 2] Rev. Leonard M. Evers.
Office & Mailing Address: 321 S. Sawyer St., 54166-2437. Tel: 715-526-2023; Fax: 715-526-4105. Email: shinto@sacredheartofshawano.org.
School—124 E. Center St., 54166-2499. Tel: 715-526-5328; Fax: 715-526-4107. Email: principal@shcscardinals.org. Lois R. Maczuzak, Prin.
Catechesis/Religious Program—Tel: 715-526-4104. Email: shdre@sacredheartofshawano.org. Linda Patzke, D.R.E.

SHERWOOD, CALUMET CO.
1—ST. JOHN-SACRED HEART (1995), Also serves St. Mary, Stockbridge & St. Mary, Hilbert (Has records for St. John the Baptist, Saint John). Very Rev. Philip Dinh-Van-Thiep.
Res.: N369 Military Rd., 54169-9661. Tel: 920-989-1515; Fax: 920-989-8585. Email: triparish@tds.net.
School—N361 Military Rd., 54169-9661. Tel: 920-989-1373; Fax: 920-989-1689. Email: heart@tds.net. Kerry Sievert, Prin.
Catechesis/Religious Program—Tel: 920-989-2400. Michael F. Brummond, D.R.E.
2—SACRED HEART, Merged with St. John the Baptist, St. John to form St. John-Sacred Heart, Sherwood.

SHIOCTON, OUTAGAMIE CO., ST. DENIS (1898) [CEM], Served from St. Patrick, Stephensville. Sr. Pauline Feiner, S.D.S., Parish Dir.; Very Rev. Patrick M. Gawrylewski, O.F.M., Priest Moderator; Rev. John P. Kastenholz, O.Praem., Sacramental Min.
Mailing Address: N3686 State Rd. 76, Hortonville, 54944-8320. Tel: 920-757-5090; Fax: 920-757-5010. Email: stpatdenis@new.rr.com.
Catechesis/Religious Program—Email: dcherry@new.rr.com. Mrs. Donna Cherry, D.R.E.

SISTER BAY, DOOR CO., ST. ROSALIA, Merged with St. John the Baptist, Egg Harbor; St. Mary of the Lake, Baileys Harbor; St. Paul, Fish Creek and St. Michael, Jacksonport to form Stella Maris, Egg Harbor.

SLOVAN, KEWAUNEE CO., ST. ADALBERT, Merged with Holy Trinity, Casco.

SOBIESKI, OCONTO CO.
1—ST. JOHN CANTIUS, [CEM] Merged with St. Louis, Abrams and St. Joseph, Chase to form St. Maximilian Kolbe, Sobieski.
2—ST. MAXIMILIAN KOLBE Rev. Gerald A. Prusakowski, O.F.M.
6051 Noble St., 54171-9724. Tel: 920-822-5255; Fax: 920-822-1859. Email: frg33ofm6051@netnet.net. Has records for St. John Cantius, Sobieski, St. Louis, Abrams and St. Joseph, Chase.
Catechesis/Religious Program—Donna Rae VanKauwenbergh, D.R.E.

SOUTH BRANCH, MENOMINEE RESERVATION, ST. JOSEPH OF THE LAKE, Closed. For inquiries for parish records contact the chancery.

SPRUCE, OCONTO CO., SACRED HEART OF JESUS, Merged with St. Charles Borromeo, Lena to form Holy Cross, Lena.

STANGELVILLE, KEWAUNEE CO.
1—ST. LAWRENCE, Merged with St. Joseph-St. John, Montpelier and St. Hedwig, West Kewaunee to form St. Therese de Lisieux, Stangelville.
2—ST. THERESE DE LISIEUX (2000) [JC], Also serves St. Isidore the Farmer Parish, Tisch Mills. (Has records for St. Joseph-St. John, Montpelier/Krok; St. Lawrence, Strangelville and St. Hedwig, West Kewaunee). Rev. Dennis G. Drury; Deacon Robert J. Pribek.
Mailing Address: N2085 County Rd. AB, Denmark, 54208-7705. Tel: 920-863-8747; Fax: 920-863-5768. Email: parish@stthereseonline.com.
Catechesis/Religious Program—Sandy Salentine, D.R.E.

STEPHENSVILLE, OUTAGAMIE CO., ST. PATRICK (1867) [CEM], Also serves St. Denis, Shiocton. Sr. Pauline Feiner, S.D.S., Parish Dir.; Very Rev. Patrick M. Gawrylewski, O.F.M., Priest Moderator; Rev. John P. Kastenholz, O.Praem., Sacramental Min.
Res.: N3686 State Rd. 76, Hortonville, 54944-8320. Tel: 920-757-5090; Fax: 920-757-5010. Email: stpatdenis@new.rr.com.
Catechesis/Religious Program—Email: dcherry@newrr.com. Mrs. Donna Cherry, D.R.E.

STILES, OCONTO CO., ST. PATRICK (1870) [JC], Served from Holy Trinity, Oconto. Rev. Patrick C. Beno Jr., Admin.
Mailing Address: 253 N. Franklin St., Oconto Falls, 54154-1042.
Res.: 5246 St. Patrick's Rd., Lena, 54139-9105. Tel: 920-846-2276; Fax: 920-846-2180. Email: admsec@plbb.us.
Catechesis/Religious Program—Email: relcoor@plbb.us. Lynn Beaumier, D.R.E. Associated with St. Anthony, Oconto Falls.

STOCKBRIDGE, CALUMET CO., ST. MARY (1882) [CEM], Served from St. John-Sacred Heart, Sherwood/Saint John. Very Rev. Philip Dinh-Van-Thiep.
Res.: P.O. Box 8, 53088-0008. Tel: 920-439-1515. Email: stmarystockbridge@tds.net.
Catechesis/Religious Program—N369 Military Rd., Sherwood, 54169-9661. Tel: 920-898-2400. Michael F. Brummond, D.R.E.

STURGEON BAY, DOOR CO.
1—CORPUS CHRISTI (1904) [JC] Rev. Carl E. Schmitt; Deacon Paul T. Zenefski.
Mailing Address: 25 N. Elgin Ave., 54235-2963.
Oratory— [JC] Mailing Address & Oratory: 25 N. Elgin Ave., 54235-2963. Tel: 920-743-4716; Fax: 920-743-3711. Email: christiparish@hotmail.com.
Res.: 722 W. Maple St., 54235.
See St. John Bosco Catholic School, Inc., Sturgeon in the Institution Section under Elementary Schools, Diocesan.
Catechesis/Religious Program—Email: jdalberts@charter.net. Amy Alberts, D.R.E.
2—ST. JOSEPH (1865), Also serves SS. Peter & Paul, Institute. Rev. Dominic Peluse, S.C.J.; Deacon Kenneth D. Kopydlowski.
Church & Office Address: 526 Louisiana St., 54235-1796. Tel: 920-743-2062; Fax: 920-743-6786. Email: mvandertie@hotmail.com.
See St. John Bosco Catholic School, Inc., Sturgeon Bay in the Institution Section under Elementary Schools, Diocesan.
Catechesis/Religious Program—Penny Biwer, D.R.E.

SUAMICO, BROWN CO., ST. BENEDICT (1917) [CEM], Also serves St. Pius, Little Suamico. Rev. Gary J. Dantinne.
Mailing Address: P.O. Box 66, 54173-0066. Tel: 920-434-2024; Fax: 920-662-2301.
Catechesis/Religious Program—Betty Nier, D.R.E.

SURING, OCONTO CO., ST. MICHAEL (1906) [CEM], Served from St. John, Gillett, with Station at Chute Pond. Sr. Marla J. Clercx, A.N.G., Parish Dir.; Revs. John J. Becker, Priest Mod.; David S. Barrett, Sacramental Min. (Retired); Deacon William V. Doran.
Mailing Address: P.O. Box 248, 54174-0248. Tel: 920-842-2580; Fax: 920-842-9825. Email: patsystmsuring@centurytel.net.
Catechesis/Religious Program—Haley Baraniak, D.R.E.

THIRY DAEMS, KEWAUNEE CO., ST. ODILE, Closed. For inquiries for parish records, please see St. Joseph, Champion.

TIGERTON, SHAWANO CO., ST. ANTHONY (1881), Also serves St. Mary, Marion St. Mary, Leoplis and Holy Family-St. William, Wittenberg. Deacons Patrick G. Berg; Howard Bricco; Kenneth F. Sambs; Clay Wildenberg.
Mailing Address: P.O. Box 106, 54486-0106. Tel: 715-535-2571; Fax: 715-535-2953. Email: sacctig@frontiernet.net.
Catechesis/Religious Program—Sally Korbisch, D.R.E.

TISCH MILLS, MANITOWOC CO.
1—ST. ISIDORE THE FARMER (2002), Served from St. Therese Parish, Stangelville. (Has records for St. Joseph, Norman and Nativity of the BVM, Tisch Mills.) Rev. Dennis G. Drury; Deacon Robert J. Pribek.
Mailing Address: 18424 Tisch Mills Rd., Denmark, 54208-9508. Tel: 920-776-1555; Fax: 920-776-1814. Email: st.isidore@tm.net.
Catechesis/Religious Program—Linda French, D.R.E.; Christal Wavrunek, D.R.E.
2—NATIVITY OF THE BLESSED VIRGIN MARY, Merged with St. Joseph, Norman to form St. Isidore the Farmer, Tisch Mills.

TONET, KEWAUNEE CO., ST. MARTIN, Closed. For inquiries for parish records, please see St. Joseph, Champion.

TWO RIVERS, MANITOWOC CO.
1—HOLY REDEEMER - SACRED HEART (2000) Merged with St. Luke and St. Mark, Two Rivers to form St. Peter the Fisherman, Two Rivers.
2—ST. LUKE, Merged with St. Mark and Holy Redeemer-Sacred Heart, Two Rivers to form St. Peter the Fisherman, Two Rivers.
3—ST. MARK, Merged with St. Luke and Holy Redeemer-Sacred Heart, Two Rivers to form St. Peter the Fisherman, Two Rivers.
4—MOST HOLY REDEEMER, Merged with Sacred Heart, Two Rivers to form Holy Redeemer-Sacred Heart, Two Rivers.
5—ST. PETER THE FISHERMAN (2002) [CEM], Merger of St. Luke, St. Mark and Holy Redeemer-Sacred Heart, Two Rivers. (Has records for St. Luke, St. Mark, Most Holy Redeemer.) Rev. William O'Brien.
Mailing Address: 3218 Tannery Rd., 54241-1648. Tel: 920-793-4531; Fax: 920-793-8067. Email: parish@stpeterthefisherman.org.
School—1322 33rd St., 54241-1747. Tel: 920-794-7622; Fax: 920-553-7625. Email: spfcs@stpeterthefisherman.org. Sr. Mary Lee Schommer, O.S.F., Prin.
Catechesis/Religious Program—Sr. Jacqueline Spaniola, O.S.F., D.R.E.; Jacinda J. Thiele, D.R.E.
6—SACRED HEART, Merged with Most Holy Redeemer, Two Rivers to form Holy Redeemer-Sacred Heart, Two Rivers.

WABENO, FOREST CO., ST. AMBROSE (1905) [CEM], Served from St. Mary of the Lake, Lakewood. Revs. David R. Schmidt, Admin.; Matthew W. Settle; Deacon Harold R. Orlowski.
Mailing Address: P.O. Box 280, 54566-0280. Tel: 715-473-2511.
Catechesis/Religious Program—Email: ljmcewen@ez-net.com. Linda McEwen, D.R.E.

WAGNER, MARINETTE CO., ST. EDWARD, [CEM] Merged with St. Joseph, Walsh to form SS. Joseph & Edward, Walsh. For inquiries for parish records contact St. Joseph & Edward, Walsh.

WALHAIN, KEWAUNEE CO., ST. AMAND, Closed. For inquiries for parish records, please see St. Joseph, Champion.

WALSH, MARINETTE CO.
1—ST. JOSEPH, Merged with St. Edward, Wagner to form SS. Joseph & Edward, Walsh. For inquiries for parish records contact St. Joseph & Edward, Walsh.
2—SS. JOSEPH & EDWARD (1894), Served from St. Mary, Peshtigo. (Has records for St. Edward, Wagner & St. Joseph, Walsh.) Sr. Helen M. Plum, S.S.N.D., Parish Dir.; Revs. Dean W. Dombroski, Priest Moderator; William J. Stengel, Sacramental Min. (Retired); Deacon Charles R. Schumacher.
Mailing Address: W3308 County Road G, Porterfield, 54159-9736. Tel: 715-789-2254; Fax: 715-789-2293. Email: stsjosed@centurytel.net.
Catechesis/Religious Program—Tel: 715-582-4897.

Mary Armbrust, D.R.E.

WAUPACA, WAUPACA CO., ST. MARY MAGDALENE (1890) [CEM], (Has records for St. George, King.) Rev. Brian S. Belongia.

Office & Mailing Address: P.O. Box 409, 54981-0409. Tel: 715-258-2088; Fax: 715-258-5708. Email: melissa@smm-waupaca.org.

Catechesis/Religious Program—Email: bettymanion@yahoo.com. Elizabeth Manion, D.R.E.; Catherine Miller, D.R.E.

WAUSAUKEE, MARINETTE CO., ST. AUGUSTINE (1890), Also serves St. Agnes, Amberg. Revs. Matthew W. Settle, Admin.; Ronald C. Belitz, Priest Moderator; John J. Hephner, Sacramental Min. (Retired); Deacon Patrick J. Whitcomb, Pastoral Coord.

Mailing Address: 507 Church St., 54177-9749. Tel: 715-856-5276; Fax: 715-856-5276. Email: staugustine@centurytel.net.

Catechesis/Religious Program—Ms. Linda Suzawith, D.R.E.

WAUTOMA, WAUSHARA CO., ST. JOSEPH (1885) [CEM] Very Rev. Robert Stegmann.

Res.: 364 S. Cambridge St., 54982-8101. Tel: 920-787-3848; Fax: 920-787-4781. Email: sjcc@centurytel.net.

Catechesis/Religious Program—Nancy Reilly, D.R.E.

WEST KEWAUNEE, KEWAUNEE CO., ST. HEDWIG, Merged with St. Joseph-St. John, Montpelier and St. Lawrence, Stangelville to form St. Therese de Lisieux, Stangelville.

WEYAUWEGA, WAUPACA CO., SS. PETER AND PAUL (1890) [CEM], Also serves Sacred Heart, Manawa. Rev. Bertin L. Samsa, O.F.M.Cap.

Res.: P.O. Box 548, 54983-0548. Tel: 920-867-2179; Fax: 920-867-2074. Email: sspeterpaul@charter.net.

Catechesis/Religious Program—Tel: 920-867-2170. Cheryl Rothrock, D.R.E.

WHITE LAKE, LANGLADE CO.

1—ST. JAMES, Merged with St. Stanislaus Kostka, Langlade to form SS. James-Stanislaus, White Lake/Langlade.

2—SS. JAMES-STANISLAUS (1992) [CEM 2] Revs. R. David Kiefer, Admin.; Jeremiah F. Worman, Sacramental Min.

Mailing Address: P.O. Box 36, 54491-0036. Tel: 715-882-2551. Served from St. Anthony, Neopit. Has records for St. James, White Lake and Stanislaus Kotska, Langlade.

Res.: 252 Bissell St., 54491.

Catechesis/Religious Program—Sr. Marie A. Miszewski, S.S.N.D., D.R.E.

WHITELAW, MANITOWOC CO., ST. MICHAEL (1872) [CEM], Served from Immaculate Conception, Clarks Mills. Rev. David M. Zimmerman; Deacon Thomas J. Koch.

Mailing Address: P.O. Box 206, 54247-0206. Tel: 920-732-3901. Email: stmichaelwzipperer@yahoo.com.

See St Mary/St. Michael School, Cato under Consolidated Schools located in the Institution Section.

Catechesis/Religious Program—

WINNECONNE, WINNEBAGO CO., ST. MARY (1884) [JC], Also serves St. Mary Omro. Sr. Pamela A. Biehl, O.S.F., Parish Dir.; Very Rev. Douglas E. LeCaptain, Priest Mod. & Sacramental Min.; Rev. Jason J. Blahnik, Sacramental Min.

Res.: P.O. Box 487, 54986-0487. Tel: 920-582-7712; Fax: 920-582-0181. Email: stmarywinneconne@sbcglobal.net.

Catechesis/Religious Program—Tel: 920-582-4601. Email: sharonstmary@sbcglobal.net. Sharon M. Baker, D.R.E.; Andrea Krueger, Contact Person.

WITTENBERG, SHAWANO CO., HOLY FAMILY, Merged with St. William, Eland to form Holy Family-St. William, Wittenberg/Eland.

WITTENBERG/ELAND, SHAWANO CO., HOLY FAMILY-ST. WILLIAM (2000) [CEM], Served from St. Anthony, Tigerton. (Has records for St. William, Eland.) Deacons Patrick G. Berg; Clay Wildenberg; Kenneth F. Sambs.

Mailing Address: P.O. Box 106, Tigerton, 54486-0106. Tel: 715-535-2571; Fax: 715-535-2953. Email: sacctig@frontiernet.net.

Res.: 106 N. Ellms St., 54499-9099.

Catechesis/Religious Program—Sally Korbisch, D.R.E.

Special Assignment:

Very Revs.—

Demuth, Paul E., P.O. Box 23825, 54305-3825.
Doerfler, John F., S.T.D., J.C.L., P.O. Box 23825, 54305-3825.
Klingeisen, Richard H., Chap., 1114 S. 21st St., Manitowoc, 54220.

Revs.—

Gilsdorf, Gordon J., 3788 Cottage Row, Suamico, 54173-8254.
Groher, Robert C., 5082 Lucas Rd., Oconto, 54153.
Koch, David J., Chap., 145 St. Joseph Dr., Oneida, 54155.
Long, W. Thomas, P.O. Box 23825, 54305-3825.
Mann, Quentin A., Assoc. Vocs. Dir., 500 W. Marquette St., Appleton, 54911.
Massart, James P., P.O. Box 23825, 54305-3825.
Weber, Frank N., Chap., St. Paul Villa, 312 E. 14th St., Apt. 214, Kaukauna, 54130.

On Duty Outside the Diocese:

Revs.—

Ashbeck, David K., (Diocese of Phoenix, AZ)
Reuter, John F., Apartado 46, Tlaxiaco, Oaxaca 69800 Mexico.
Schiavone, Robert W., Sacred Heart School of Theology, P.O. Box 429, Hales Corners, 53130-0429. Tel: 414-425-0630
Seis, Michael, BM # 7047, 3508 N.W. 114th Ave., Doral, FL 33178-1841.
Vander Heyden, William F., Chap., V.A. Medical Center, 3001 Green Bay Rd., North Chicago, IL 60064-3049.

Military Chaplains:

Revs.—

Dory, Michael, Lt. Cmdr., 3811 Marquette Pl., Apt. 2A, San Diego, CA 92106-1033.
LaCombe, Terrence, 3811 Marquette Pl., #3C, San Diego, CA 92106.
Schuetze, John W., Chap. U.S.A.F.

Absent on Leave, Sick or Disabled:

Revs.—

Carroll, Michael
Geiser, Allen A.
Hoffmann, Philip
Mastalir, Peter
Schneider, Ronald
Shebuski, Charles J.
Somers, Michael

Retired:

Most Revs.—

Banks, Robert J., D.D., J.C.D., P.O. Box 23825, 54305-3825.
Schmitt, Mark (MAR), 224 Iroquois Ave., #12, 54101.

Rev. Msgrs.—

Coleman, Brian P., J.C.L., 224 Iroquois Ave., #14, 54101.
Dewane, John B., M.A., S.T.L., D.Min., P.O. Box 442, Two Rivers, 54241-0442.
Feely, James B., 2785 Taurus Rd., 54311.
Klauck, Peter N., 224 Iroquois Ave., #2, 54301-1994.
Koszarek, Paul P., 2788 W. Shore Ln., Crandon, 54520.
Rose, Donald, 865 Mill Rd., Sturgeon Bay, 54235-9267.
Schommer, Mark J., N2614 Bughs Lake Rd., Wautoma, 54982.
Schuh, John H., 226 S. Walnut St., Kimberly, 54136.
Vanden Hogen, James, 925 Wilson St., Little Chute, 54140.

Very Rev.—

Birdsall, Anthony J., 2105 Shiloh Rd., Sturgeon Bay, 54235.

Revs.—

Baeten, David, 224 Nicolet Pl., De Pere, 54115-1922.
Barrett, David S., N6772 Black Oak Cir., Shawano, 54166.
Bauschka, Joseph, 3001 Riverside Dr., 54301.
Beerntsen, Harold, 5151 Van Laenen Rd., Lena, 54139-9127.
Bernardy, Patrick, 1341 Wilson St., Niagara, 54151.
Bestler, Joseph, 5319B Sunset Bluff Dr., Unit B, 54311-9133.
Brooks, Charles R., 4721 Everbreeze Cir., Unit C, Appleton, 54913.
Browne, Stanley, 224 Iroquois Ave., #11, 54301.
Buhl, Wilbert L., 224 Iroquois Ave., #1, 54301.
Burkardt, Donald, N7374 Birchwood Rd., Crivitz, 54114.
Clifford, Michael J., 4775 Pine Ridge Trail, Abrams, 54101.
Conard, Ray J., McCormick Memorial Home, 212 Iroquois Ave. Rm. 407, 54301. Tel: 920-438-1673
Conrad, John F., 1039 Covington Dr., Sheboygan Falls, 53085.
Dewane, Daniel, 1828 S. 18th St., Manitowoc, 54220.
Dolski, V. Anthony, 340 W. St. Joseph St., #8, 54301.
Dowling, Raymond, 11300 W. Parmer Ln., #1114, Cedar Park, TX 78613.
DuCharme, Paul, 224 Iroquois Ave., #8, 54301-1998.
Foley, Gerald J., 1700 S. 18th St., #214, Manitowoc, 54220.
Fox, Martin F., 224 Iroquois Ave., #16, 54301.
Frozena, Kenneth R., W5045 Golf Course Rd., Sherwood, 54169.
Gallagher, John M., 985 N. Broad, Apt. 71, De Pere, 54115.
Geigel, Francis, 2937 Trump Lake Rd., Wabeno, 54566-9273.
Gerend, Lawrence, 216 Catherine St., Kaukauna, 54130-2136.
Gilsdorf, Daniel C., N518 Robinhood Way, Sherwood, 54169-9660.
Golden, Thomas, 1110 S. Baird St., 54301.
Hephner, John J., N15211 Beazley Rd., Amberg, 54102-9177.
Heymen, Richard, 3400 Yorkshire Ln., Apt. 318, Manitowoc, 54220.
Jacobs, James T., 2792 W. Shore Ln., Crandon, 54520.
Kahrs, Lee J., B.A., 1751 Eldorado Dr., #13, 54302.
Kelley, Omer C., 918 Elm St., Antigo, 54409-1525.
Kerscher, Francis, 2005 Division St., Rm. 2066, Manitowoc, 54220.
Koch, Michael R., 224 Iroquois Ave, #7, 54301-1994.
Krutzik, Norman, 622 Pershing St., Appleton, 54911-2870.
Kutiuk, Casimir, 1246 W. 20th Ave., Oshkosh, 54902-6620.
Lenzner, George, 1157 Packerland Dr., 54304-1376.
Lessard, Leo, 17725 Munger Lake Ln., Lakewood, 54138-9615.
Lexa, Robert, 232 S. Pleasant Dr., Appleton, 54914-4205.
Marquardt, Donald, 224 Iroquois Ave., #3, 54301-1994.
Mattern, Joseph A., 320 N. Webster Ave., Omro, 54963.
Mauthe, Richard, Old Orchard Apts., 3001 S. Webster Ave., #216, 54301.
Mayefske, Thomas J., 1017 Florida St. S.E., Albuquerqe, NM 87108-4823.
Melchior, Frank, E2783 Rockledge Rd., Casco, 54205.
Merkatoris, Ralph, 2808 Taurus Rd., 54311-4600.
Mocco, Charles W., 401 Gray St., 54303.
Mullarkey, John T., 1409 Alcan Dr., Menasha, 54952.
Neuser, John, 1700 S. 18th St., Apt. 118, Manitowoc, 54220-6047.
Nickel, Leander, 224 Iroquois Ave., # 6, 54301-1998.
Nowakowski, Edward S., 224 Iroquois Ave., #10, 54301.
O'Brien, John, 502 N. Front St., Apt. 4, De Pere, 54115-2546.
Reinke, Francis P., 1820 Ridgeway Dr., Apt. 12B, De Pere, 54115.
Rhyner, Robert E., 340 W. St. Joseph St., 54301.
Rickert, William, 224 Iroquois Ave., #5, 54301-1998.
Sammut, Tito, P.O. Box 23825, 54305-3825.
Samter, James W., 1600 Rustic Oaks Ct., #11, 54301-2465.
Schumacher, Paul, 2427 County Rd. J, Abrams, 54101.
Smet, Leroy R., N3640 Rocky Mountain Dr., New London, 54961.
Stencil, Rallen, 224 Iroquois Ave., #16, 54301.
Stengel, William J., W8445 Germantown Rd., Crivitz, 54114.
Stingle, Lawrence A., 2777 He Nis Ra Ln., 54304-1357.
Taddy, Jerome J., 6106 Hwy. O, Two Rivers, 54241.
Taylor, Peter, 224 Iroquois Ave., #15, 54301-1969.
Thomas, Richard L., 139 S. Madison St., 54301.
Van De Kreeke, William L., J.C.L., 376-A Wyldewood Dr., Oshkosh, 54904.
Van De Loo, Willard J., 825 E. River Dr., #4, De Pere, 54115.
Van Deuren, John H., 1490 Capitol Dr., #12, 54303.
Vanden Hogen, Paul, 1030 County Rd. QQ, Apt. 6, Waupaca, 54981.
Vandenberg, Robert H., 705 Kramer Lane, Keshena, 54135.
Vennix, James J., E1277 Cleghorn Rd., Waupaca, 54981-9552.
Werner, Justin, N1682 Ridgeway Dr., Greenville, 54942.
Worman, Jeremiah F., N9065 Waterpower Rd., Deerbrook, 54424.
Worzalla, Dennis A., 224 Iroquois Ave., #13, 54301.

Permanent Deacons:

Ambrosius, Raymond G., Jr., St. Edward Church, Mackville
Asmuth, James, (Retired), Neenah
Bahnaman, Richard D., St. Francis of Assisi Church, Manitowoc
Banker, Kenneth, St. Martin Church, Cecil
Baumruk, Roy J., St. Joseph Church, Appleton
Beehner, Robert, St. Francis of Assisi Church, Manitowoc
Bennin, Dennis G., Good Shepherd Church, Chilton
Berg, Patrick G., St. Anthony, Tigerton; St. Mary, Marion; Holy Family-St. William, Wittenberg; St. Mary, Leopolis

Bilgrien, Kenneth, SS. Peter & Paul Church, Hortonville
Boeldt, Alan L., St. Francis of Assisi Church, Manitowoc
Boucher, Paul, (Retired), Gresham
Brandenstein, Raymond L., (Retired), Oshkosh
Bricco, Howard, St. Anthony, Tigerton; St. Mary, Marion; Holy Family-St. William, Wittenberg; St. Mary, Leopolis
Burke, William, St. Mary Church, Appleton
Burkel, William J., Prince of Peace Church, Green Bay
Charlier, Earl, (Retired), Green Bay
Cheskie, Peter A., St. Raphael the Archangel Church, Oshkosh
Cibula, Paul J., St. Matthew Church, Green Bay
Clark, Kenneth, Green Bay
Coenen, Donald F., Par. Dir., St. Lawrence Church, Navarino, and Diac. Service; St. Sebastian, Isaar
Corey, Bruce H., St. John Nepomucene Church, Little Chute
Craig, Thomas M., Parish Dir., St. Martin, Cecil
Cross, Gerald H., Par. Dir., St. Stanislaus Kostka, Armstrong Creek & St. Joan of Arc, Goodman
Dahlen, Joseph, Hortonville
De Bruin, Orvell, St. John Church, Seymour
De Groot, Vincent M., (Retired)
DeCleene, Kevin, St. Mary Church, St. Francis Xavier, DePere
DeYoung, David L., St. Mary Church, Greenville
Dolezal, Michael, St. Francis of Assisi, Manitowoc
Doran, William V., St. John Church, Gillet; St. Michael Church, Suring
Downey, Timothy, St. Thomas More, Appleton
Doxtator, Everett L., St. Joseph Church, Oneida; Immaculate Conception, Oneida
Drobka, Robert F., St. Francis of Assisi Church, Manitowoc
DuBois, Raymond L., St. Gabriel the Archangel Church, Neenah
Dvorak, Richard B., St. Mary Church, Menasha
Ellis, Robert, De Pere
Farrell, Mark J., St. Joseph Church, Appleton
Fischer, Frederick, St. Jude the Apostle, Oshkosh
Garcia, Benjamin, (Retired), Shawano
Gauthier, James R., St. Agnes Church, Green Bay
Gelhar, G. Patrick, St. Jude the Apostle, Oshkosh
Gigure, Donald J., Sacred Heart Church, Appleton
Gleichner, Paul J., Silver Lake College, Manitowoc
Grey, Gregory A., St. Raphael the Archangel, Oshkosh
Gribowski, Mark A., 4106 106th Dr., Phoenix, AZ 85037. (Diocese of Phoenix, AZ)
Grimm, Paul K., Dir. Office of Permanent Diaconate, St. John Church, Seymour
Grube, Kurt L., Most Blessed Sacrament, St. Jude the Apostle, Oshkosh
Grzeca, Michael G., Resurrection Church, Green Bay
Haak, Randall A., St. Katharine Drexel Church, Kaukauna
Hanley, Thomas J., SS. Mary & Hyacinth Church, Antigo; St. Wenceslaus Church, Neva
Hartman, Thomas W., St. Anthony Church, Neopit; St. Joseph-Holy Family Church, Plox
Hayek, Hilary W., (Retired), Tigerton
Heider, James P., Holy Cross, Bay Settlement
Hocking, Richard A., Most Blessed Sacrament, Oshkosh
Hofacker, Jeffrey J., St. Edward Church, Mackville
Holschbach, Keith, St. Bernard Church, Green Bay
Humpal, Gregory J., St. Nicholas Church, Freedom
Ingala, John, St. Raphael the Archagel, Oshkosh
Jacqmin, Robert, (Retired), Green Bay
Jozwiak, Thomas V., St. Rose Church, Clintonville; St. Mary Church, Bear Creek
Kabat, Kenneth, St. Clare Church, Greenleaf
Kaszynski, Walter, Holy Trinity Church, Oconto
Kieffer, Paul A., St. Francis of Assisi Church, Manitowoc
Klein, Paul, St. Thomas More Church, Appleton
Klein, William, (Retired), Manitowoc
Klister, Cyril, Holy Spirit Church, Kimberly/Darboy
Knier, Bernard (Pat) P., SS. Peter & Paul Church, Kiel
Koch, Thomas J., Immaculate Conception Church, Clarks Mills; St. Michael, Whitelaw
Kopydlowski, Kenneth D., St. Joseph, Sturgeon Bay; SS. Peter & Paul, Institute
Koszalinski, Daniel T., Sacred Heart Church, Appleton
Kowalski, David J., Stella Maris, Egg Harbor (Door County)
Kuborn, Gerald G., St. Katharine Drexel Church, Kaukauna
Kunzer, Earl L., SS. Edward/Isidore Church, Flintville
Laurant, John H., St. Bernard Church, Green Bay
Le Mere, David, Gresham
Lehman, Joseph M., St. Mary Church, Bear Creek; St. Rose Church, Clintonville
Letourneaux, Stephen T., Holy Family, Brillion
Lowe, Russ, (Retired), Waupaca
Madden, Michael, St. Bernadette Church, Appleton
Madsen, Roger, Sturgeon Bay
Mahoney, Thomas, St. Francis Xavier Cathedral & SS. Peter & Paul, Green Bay
Majewski, Dennis, Assumption of the BVM Church, Pulaski
Maloney, John R., (Retired), Suamico
Mastalish, Larry V., St. Bernard Church, Green Bay
Meidl, Richard, Peoria, AZ
Merrick, Craig, St. Thomas More Church, Appleton
Mervilde, Michael J., St. Joseph, St. Jude, Annunciation & St. Patrick, Green Bay
Meyer, Steven J., St. Elizabeth Ann Seton, Green Bay
Miech, Richard M., (Richmond, VA)
Miller, Robert J., Immaculate Conception, Luxemburg; Holy Trinity, Casco
Naidl, Clarence, All Saints, Denmark; Holy Trinity, New Denmark; St. James, Cooperstown; St. Joseph, Kellnersville; St. Mary, Glenmore/Stark
Nardi, Gerald A., St. Anthony, Niagara
Nass, Donald, (Retired), Redgranite
Nelesen, Ken, St. Francis of Assisi Church, Manitowoc
Newhouse, Don, St. Nicholas Church, Freedom
Nooker, Robert L., Green Bay
Nowak, Richard, (Retired), Green Bay
Orlowski, Harold R., St. Ambrose Church, Wabeno
Otradovec, Byron A., (Retired), Florida
Penzenstadler, Robert, St. Jude the Apostle, Oshkosh
Plantico, Paul, (Retired), Woodstock, GA
Precourt, Robert L., St. Paul Church, Plainfield
Pribek, Robert J., St. Therese de Lisieux, Stangelville; St. Isidore the Farmer, Tisch Mills
Quinette, Harvey J., Our Lady of Lourdes Church, De Pere
Reed, Maurice F., St. Bernard Church, Appleton
Reilly, Timothy G., Dir. of Admin.; Resurrection Church, Green Bay
Reinl, Peter M., Appleton
Rocchi, Steven, (Retired), Wild Rose
Ropson, Donald J., Resurrection Church, Green Bay
Sambs, Kenneth F., St. Anthony Church, Tigerton; St. Mary Church, Marion; Holy Family-St. William, Wittenberg; St. Mary, Leopolis
Sanchez, Luis, St. Willebrord Church, Green Bay
Schmidt, Gilbert, Sacred Heart Church, Appleton
Schmidt, Michael, Nativity of Our Lord Church, Green Bay
Schraufnagel, George J., St. Paul Church, Combined Locks
Schraufnagel, Gerard J., St. Mary, Appleton
Schumacher, Charles R., St. Mary Church, Peshtigo; SS. Joseph & Edward, Walsh
Simon, Richard S., St. Pius X, Appleton
Spielbauer, Norman, Neenah
Steffen, James E., Holy Trinity Church, School Hill; St. Gregory Church, St. Nazianz
Sustman, James, Mishicot
Swinford, Norval, (Retired), New London
Teske, Glenn, Port Chap., Apostleship of the Sea, Green Bay
Thetreau, Jerome E., Holy Family Church, Marinette
Torres, Manuel, St. John the Baptist, Howard; Asst. Episcopal/Diocesan Master of Ceremonies
Umentum, Paul, St. Mary of the Angels Church, Green Bay; Asst. Episcopal & Diocesan Master of Ceremonies
Vande Hey, Steven, St. John - Sacred Heart, Sherwood; St. Mary, Hilbert; St. Mary, Stockbridge
Vanden Heuvel, Lee P., Appleton
Vander Bloomen, Michael D., Our Lady of Lourdes Church, DePere
Vincent, John, Manitowoc
Vincent, Michael C., SS. Peter & Paul Church, Green Bay; Episcopal & Diocesan Master of Ceremonies
Vincent, Robert, St. Bernard Church, Appleton
Wagnite, Daniel, Annunciation of the BUM, St. Joseph, St. Jude & St. Patrick, Green Bay
Wetzel, Donald J., St. Thomas More Church, Appleton
Whitcomb, Patrick, Past. Coord.; St. Augustine, Wausankee & St. Agnes, Amberg
Wildenberg, Clay, St. Anthony, Tigerton; St. Mary, Marion; Holy Family-St. William, Wittenberg; St. Mary, Leopolis
Williams, Nicholas J., St. John the Baptist Church, Howard
Zenefski, Paul T., Corpus Christi Church, Sturgeon Bay; St. Mary, Maplewood; St. Peter & St. Hubert, Rosiere/Lincoln

INSTITUTIONS LOCATED IN THE DIOCESE

[A] SEMINARIES, RELIGIOUS OR SCHOLASTICATES

GREEN BAY. *St. Mary of the Angels Friary*, 645 S. Irwin Ave., 54301-3303. Tel: 920-437-7411; Fax: 920-437-7411. Rev. Richard Tulko, O.F.M., Guardian & Librarian. Priests 4; Lay Teachers 7.

DE PERE. *St. Norbert Abbey*, 1016 N. Broadway, 54115-2697. Tel: 920-337-4300; Fax: 920-337-4328. Email: john.kastenholz@snc.edu. Web: www.norbertines.org. Rt. Revs. Gary J. Neville, O.Praem., J.C.D., Abbot; John P. Kastenholz, O.Praem., Sec. & Treas.; E. Thomas De Wane, O.Praem., Abbot Emeritus; Jerome G. Tremel, O.Praem., Abbot Emeritus; Very Rev. James B. Herring, O.Praem., J.C.D., Prior; Revs. John M. Tourangeau, O.Praem., Vocation Coord.; Conrad J. Kratz, O.Praem., Dir. Norbertine Center for Spirituality. Priests 65; Brothers 2; Novices 3; Total Staff 70.

[B] COLLEGES AND UNIVERSITIES

DE PERE. *St. Norbert College* (1898) 54115-2099. Tel: 920-403-3165; Fax: 920-403-4063. Email: amy.sorenson@snc.edu. Web: www.snc.edu. Mr. Thomas Kunkel, Pres.; Dr. Michael Marsden, Vice Pres. Academic Affairs & Dean of College; Ms. Eileen Jahnke, C.P.A., Vice Pres. Business & Finance; Dr. Mary Oling-Sisay, Vice Pres. Student Life; Revs. Jay J. Fostner, O.Praem., Ph.D., Vice Pres. Mission & Heritage; James T. Baraniak, O.Praem., Pastor, St. Norbert College Parish; Salvatore H. Cuccia, O.Praem., Assoc. Pastor, St. Norbert College.

St. Norbert College, Inc. Priests 7; Sisters 1; Lay Teachers 174; Lay Staff 458; Students 2,137.

Faculty: Revs. John Bostwick, O.Praem.; Jay J. Fostner, O.Praem., Ph.D.; David R. McElroy, O.Praem.; James P. Neilson, O.Praem.; Brian J. Prunty, O.Praem.; Sr. Sally Ann Brickner, Ph.D., Assoc. Prof.

St. Norbert College Tel: 920-403-3005; Fax: 920-403-4096. Email: admit@snc.edu. Web: www.snc.edu. Felice E. Maciejewski, Dir., Library.

MANITOWOC. *Silver Lake College of the Holy Family* (1935) 2406 S. Alverno Rd., 54220-9319. Tel: 920-684-6691; Fax: 920-684-7082. Email: garnold@silver.sl.edu. Web: www.sl.edu. George Arnold, Pres.; Sr. Ritarose Stahl, Librarian. Sponsored by the Franciscan Sisters of Christian Charity. Priests 1; Sisters 19; Lay Faculty 27; Students 1,540.

[C] HIGH SCHOOLS, DIOCESAN

APPLETON. *Xavier High School* (1959) Coed, 1600 W. Prospect Ave., 54914. Tel: 920-733-6632; Fax: 920-733-5513. Email: mreynebeau@acesxavier.k12.wi.us. Web: www.acesxavier.k12.wi.us. Mr. Matt Reynebeau, Prin.; Mrs. Donna Fahrenkrug, Assoc. Prin.; Andrew Mahoney, Dir. Guidance Dept.; Ms. Sarah Simon, Campus Min.; Mrs. Mary Micke, Librarian. (Part of ACES Xavier Educational System, Inc.) Lay Teachers 33; Students 522.

MANITOWOC. *Roncalli High School* (1965) 2000 Mirro Dr., 54220-6799. Tel: 920-682-8801; Fax: 920-686-8110. Mr. John Stelzer, Pres.; Mr. Tim Olson, Prin.; Mr. Frank Birr, Campus Min.; Mrs. Sue Rohrer, Librarian. Christian Brothers and Franciscan Sisters of Christian Charity. Brothers 1; Sisters 2; Lay Teachers 28; Students 352.

MARINETTE. *St. Thomas Aquinas Academy (Secondary Campus)*, 1200 Main St., 54143-2594. Tel: 715-735-7481; Fax: 715-735-3375. Email: mcchs@hotmail.com. Mrs. Jennifer Elfering, Pres.; Mr. James Aldrich, Lead; Anita Folgert, Librarian. Lay Teachers 17; Students 97.

NEENAH/MENASHA. *St. Mary Central High School*, 1050 Zephyr Dr., 54956-1389. Tel: 920-722-7796; Fax: 920-722-5940. Email: pbatey@tcces.k12.wi.us. Web: www.smc.k12.wi.us. Mr. Patrick Batey, Prin.; Jane Sturn, Contact Person; Anne Shelley, Librarian. (part of Twin City Catholic Education System) Lay Teachers 24; Students 192.

OSHKOSH. *Lourdes High School* (1959) (Coed.), 110 N. Sawyer St., 54902. Tel: 920-235-5670; Fax: 920-235-7453. Web: www.lourdes.k12.wi.us. Mr. Jim LaDue, Prin.; Mary Mueller, Librarian. (Part of Unified Catholic Schools of Oshkosh) Lay Teachers 22; Students 229.

[D] HIGH SCHOOLS, PRIVATE

GREEN BAY. *Notre Dame de la Baie Academy*, 610 Maryhill Dr., 54303-2092. Tel: 920-429-6100;

Fax: 920-429-6168. Email: dradecki@notredameacademy.com. Web: www.notredameacademy.com. Rev. Dane J. Radecki, O.Praem., Pres.; Mr. John Ravizza, Prin.; Mr. Greg Masarik, Assoc. Prin.; Mr. Ken Flaten, Business Mgr.; Mary Schmidt, Librarian. Priests 2; Sisters 1; Lay Teachers 45; Students 720.

[E] ELEMENTARY SCHOOLS, DIOCESAN

GREEN BAY. *Green Bay Area Catholic Education, Inc., (GRACE)*, 1087 Kellogg St., P.O. Box 33084, 54303-3058. Tel: 920-499-7330. Email: cconwaygerhardt@gbdioc.org. Dr. Carol Conway-Gerhardt, System Pres.

NEW HOLSTEIN/KIEL. *Divine Savior Catholic Elementary School, Inc.*, 1814 Madison St., 53061. Tel: 920-898-4210; Fax: 920-898-4220. Email: info@divinesaviorschool.org. Rev. Harold L. Berryman, Admin.; Lawrence Konetzke, Prin.

STURGEON BAY. *St. John Bosco Catholic School, Inc.*, (Grades PreK-8), 15 N. Elgin Ave., 54235. Tel: 920-743-4144; Fax: 920-743-3711. James A. Tabaska, Prin.; Marcia Egeland, Librarian. Priests 2; Lay Teachers 13.

[F] CONSOLIDATED SCHOOLS

ANTIGO. *All Saints Catholic Schools, Inc.* (1998) 419 6th Ave., 54409. Tel: 715-623-4835; 715-623-2211; Fax: 715-623-3202. Email: cfleischman@ascscrusaders.org. Web: www.ascscrusaders.org. John Reetz, Admin. & Prin.; Michele Nagel, Librarian. Lay Teachers 16; Total Enrollment 214.

APPLETON. *ACES Xavier Educational System, Inc.*, 101 E. Northland Ave., 54911. Tel: 920-735-9380; Fax: 920-735-1787. Email: aces@acesxavier.k12.wi.us. Web: acesxavier.k12.wi.us. Anthony J. Abts, Pres. Sisters 3; Lay Teachers 124; Total Enrollment 1,717.

CATO. *St. Mary/St. Michael School*, (Grades PreSchool-8), 19 S. County Rd. J, 54230-8329. Tel: 920-775-4366; Fax: 920-775-4365. Email: 1stmarysschoo2@new.rr.com. Lori Scheffler, Admin.; Ronald Nesper, Prin.; Carol Wetenkamp, Librarian. Priests 1; Sisters 1; Lay Staff 8.

MANITOWOC. *St. Francis Catholic School*, 601 N. 8th St., 54220. Tel: 920-683-6880; Fax: 920-683-6881. Email: bob.beehner@sfamanitowoc.com. Deacon Bob Beehner, Dir. of Admin. Sisters 3; Lay Teachers 35; Total Enrollment 475.

St. Francis de Sales School (Grades K-5), 1408 Waldo Blvd., 54220-2610. Tel: 920-683-6892; Fax: 920-683-6889. Mrs. Linda Bender, Prin.

St. Francis Xavier School (Grades PreK-5), 1418 Grand Ave., 54220-6197. Tel: 920-683-6888; Fax: 920-683-6897. Mrs. Linda Bender, Prin.

St. Frances Cabrini Middle School (Grades 6-8), 2109 Marshall St., 54220-4959. Tel: 920-683-6884; Fax: 920-683-6882. Mr. James Clark, Prin.

NEENAH/MENASHA. *Twin Cities Catholic Educational System (TCCES)*, 1050 Zephyr Dr., 54956. Tel: 920-967-0021; Fax: 920-722-5940. Email: msullivan@tcces.k12.wi.us. Michael Sullivan, System Dir.; Shelley Wautlet, Contact Person. (Consolidation of St. Gabriel, St. Margaret Mary, Neenah and St. Mary, St. John, St. Patrick, Menasha.) Lay Teachers 88; Total Enrollment 942.

OSHKOSH. *Unified Catholic Schools of Oshkosh*, 110 N. Sawyer St., 54902. Tel: 920-426-3626; Fax: 920-303-6682. Mr. Tony Blando, Pres. Sisters 3; Lay Teachers 51; Total Enrollment 800.

TWO RIVERS. *St. Peter the Fisherman Catholic School*, (Grades PreSchool-8), 1322 33rd St., 54241. Tel: 920-794-7622; Fax: 920-553-7625. Email: spfcs@stpeterthefisherman.org. Sr. Mary Lee Schommer, O.S.F., Prin. (Consolidation of St. Luke and St. Mark. Holy Redeemer Schools.) Sisters 3; Lay Teachers 18; Students 182.

[G] GENERAL HOSPITALS

GREEN BAY. *St. Mary's Hospital-Medical Center*, 1726 Shawano Ave., 54303-3282. Tel: 920-498-4200; Fax: 920-497-3707. Email: cbecker@stmgb.org. Web: www.stmgb.org. Mr. Larry Connors, COO; Ms. Cynthia L. Becker, Dir. Pastoral Care; Deacon Nick Williams, Pastoral Care Assoc.; Rev. David J. Koch, Chap. Hospital Sisters of Third Order of St. Francis. Bed Capacity 158; Total Staff 740; Patients Assisted Annually 90,432.

St. Vincent Hospital (1888) P.O. Box 13508, 54307-3508. Tel: 920-433-0111; 920-433-8155; Fax: 920-431-3215. Email: cbecker@smg.hshs.org. Web: www.stvgb.org. Thomas R. Bayer, COO; Ms. Cynthia L. Becker, Dir. Pastoral Care; Sisters Paulette Hupfauf, O.S.F., Chap.; Monica Bongert, O.S.F., Chap.; Marilyn Herr, O.S.F., Chap. Hospital Sisters of the Third Order of St. Francis. Bassinets 24; Bed Capacity 547; Patients Assisted Annually 122,022; Total Staff 2,030.

ANTIGO. *Langlade Hospital - Hotel Dieu of St. Joseph of Antigo Wisconsin*, 112 E. 5th Ave., 54409. Tel: 715-623-2331; Fax: 715-623-9359. Email: jbricco@langhosp.org; rhsj@antigopro.net. Web: www.langladehospital.org. Sr. Dolores Demulling, Mission & Philosophy Advocate & Trustee, Dir. of LeRoyer Hospice; Mr. David Schneider, Exec. Dir.; Sisters Jean Bricco, Dir. Pastoral Care, Trustee & Contact Person; Adele Demulling, R.H.S.J., Supr., Coord. LeRoyer Hospice; Rev. Omer C. Kelley, Part-time Chap. (Retired). Religious Hospitallers of St. Joseph. Bed Capacity 25; Total Assisted Annually 75,000; Total Staff 525.

Religious Hospitalliers of St. Joseph (1636) Sisters Res.: 644 Longlade Rd., 55409. Tel: 715-623-4615; Fax: 715-623-4615. Email: rhsj@antigopro.net. Web: www.rhsj.org/. Sisters 3; Priests 1; Staff 525; Bed Capacity 25; Patients Assisted Annually 75,000.

APPLETON. *St. Elizabeth Hospital, Inc.*, 1506 S. Oneida St., 54915-1305. Tel: 920-831-8913; Fax: 920-831-8916. Email: dschoono@affinityhealth.org. Web: www.affinityhealth.org. Travis Andersen, Pres.; Revs. Karin Derenne, Chap. & Spiritual Svcs. Dir.; Roy Rogers, Chap.; Calvin Reyburn, Chap.; Sisters Gerri Krautkramer, Chap.; Anne Arthur Klinker, Chap.; Annette Johnson, Chap.; Linda Stipe, Chap.; Debra Langacker, Contact Person.

St. Elizabeth Hospital, Inc., Corporate Sponsors: Wheaton Franciscan Services, Inc. (Wheaton, IL) and Affinity Health System (Menasha, WI) Franciscan Sisters, Daughters of the Sacred Hearts of Jesus and Mary (Wheaton, IL) 1; Bed Capacity 203; Total Staff 1,137; Patients Assisted Annually 158,247.

CHILTON. *Calumet Medical Center*, 614 Memorial Dr., 53014-1568. Tel: 920-849-2386. Timothy Richman, Pres.& CEO. Email: timothy.richman@affinity.org. Affinity Health System, Spiritual Services Dept: Chaplain support from St. Elizabeth Hospital, Appleton. Bed Capacity 25; Total Staff 181; Patients Served 34,764.

MANITOWOC. *Holy Family Memorial, Inc.* (1898) 2300 Western Ave., P.O. Box 1450, 54221-1450. Tel: 920-320-2011; Fax: 920-320-3500. Email: services@hfmhealth.org. Web: www.hfmhealth.org. Mr. Mark Herzog, Pres.; Rev. Joel Szydlowski, O.F.M., Dir. Pastoral Care & Chap.; John Vincent, Chap.; Rahlf Proulx, Chap.; Molly La Fond, Chap. Franciscan Sisters of Christian Charity 9; Licensed Beds 62; Maternity Rooms 7; Patients Assisted Annually 287,879; Total Staff 1,295.

OSHKOSH. *Mercy Medical Center of Oshkosh, Inc.*, 500 S. Oakwood Rd., P.O. Box 3370, 54903-3370. Tel: 920-223-0504; Fax: 920-223-0508. Email: wcalhoun@affinityhealth.org. Web: www.affinityhealth.org. Daniel Neufelder, CEO; Bill Calhoun, COO; Sr. Johnette Marek, S.S.M., Chap.; Revs. Karin Derenne, Dir., Spiritual Svcs. & Clinical Ethics; Phil Dewitt, Chap.; Donna Greischar, Chap.; Ronald Michels, Chap.; Julianna Hirsch, Chap.

Mercy Medical Center of Oshkosh, Inc. Corporate Sponsors: Ministry Health Care, Inc. (Milwaukee, WI) and Affinity Health System (Menasha, WI). Sisters of the Sorrowful Mother 1; Bed Capacity 172; Total Staff 835; Bassinets 25; Patients Assisted Annually 91,295.

STURGEON BAY. **Door County Memorial Hospital* (1943) 323 S. 18th Ave., 54235-1495. Tel: 920-743-5566; Fax: 920-743-8165. Email: Gerald.Worrick@ministryhealth.org. Web: www.ministryhealth.org. Gerald M. Worrick, Pres.& CEO; Susan Johnson, Contact Person & Spiritual Svcs. Dir. Corporate Sponsor: Ministry Health Care, Inc. (Milwaukee, WI); Sponsored by Sisters of the Sorrowful Mother. Bed Capacity, Critical Access Hospital 25; Patients Assisted Annually 190,744; Total Staff 630.

[H] PROTECTIVE INSTITUTIONS

GREEN BAY. *Libertas Treatment Center for Chemically Dependent*, 1701 Dousman St., 54303-3282. Tel: 920-498-8600; Fax: 920-496-2027. David B. Fish, Pres.; Patrick W. Ryan, Prog. Dir. Hospital Sisters of the Third Order of St. Francis., Hospital Sisters Health System. Bed Capacity 24; Patients Assisted Annually 8,041; Total Staff 31.

McClosky Program, Inc., 2560 Shawano Ave., P.O. Box 10357, 54313. Tel: 920-434-8208; Fax: 920-662-0047. Sr. Barbara Jean Arnsmeyer, O.L.C., Dir. A Community based residential facility for women 18 years old and over who are pregnant or in a crisis situation and in need of transitional supervision and guidance. Needs addressed are personal and family problems. Also, shelter offered during crisis or unemployment. Bed Capacity 4; Total Staff 2; Total Assisted 6.

Our Lady of Charity Center, Inc., 2560 Shawano Ave., P.O. Box 10357, 54313. Tel: 920-434-8208; Fax: 920-662-0047. Sr. Donna Truckey, Admin. Total Staff 2; Total Assisted 10.

OSHKOSH. *The Convent Project, Inc.*, 449 High Ave., 54901. Tel: 920-233-1894. Email: baker8983@sbcglobal.net. Barbara Baker, Treas. For victims of domestic abuse. Bed Capacity 32; Total Assisted 51; Total Staff 1.

TWO RIVERS. *Sisters Treatment Home*, 3904 Martin Ln., 54241. Tel: 920-553-1524; Fax: 920-553-2442. Sisters Irmina Bula, S.S.J.-T.O.S.F., Co-Dir.; Edmund Antoniewicz, S.S.J.-T.O.S.F., Co-Dir. For physically and mentally handicapped children. Children 1; Adults 2; Bed Capacity 4; Total Staff 5; Total Assisted 4.

[I] HOMES FOR AGED

GREEN BAY. *The McCormick Memorial Home for the Aged* (1921) 212 Iroquois Ave., 54301-1918. Tel: 920-437-0883; Fax: 920-437-2696. Email: jim@mmhgb.com. James Genrich, Admin.; Rev. Michael R. Koch, Chap. (Retired). Bed Capacity 56; Total Staff 27; Nursing Staff 6; Residents 50.

KAUKAUNA. *St. Paul Elder Services, Inc.*, 316 E. Fourteenth St., 54130. Tel: 920-766-6020; Fax: 920-766-7945. Email: jimf@stpaulelders.org. Web: stpaulelders.org. James J. Fett, Pres.; Todd Greenway, COO & Admin. Bed Capacity 254; Total Assisted Annually 250; Total Staff 345.

St. Paul Home, 316 E. 14th St., 54130. Tel: 920-766-6020; Fax: 920-766-9161. Rev. Frank N. Weber, Asst. Chap. Bed Capacity 129.

St. Paul Villa, 312 E. Fourteenth St., 54130. Tel: 920-766-6020; Fax: 920-766-7945. Total Apartments 89.

St. Paul Manor, 509 W. Wisconsin Ave., 54130. Tel: 920-766-6027; Fax: 920-766-6035. Rooms 27.

MANITOWOC. *Felician Village* Tel: 920-684-7171; Fax: 920-684-0240. Web: www.felicianvillage.org.

Felician Village Inc. dba The Gardens at Felician Village 1635 S. 21st St., 54220-5652. Tel: 920-684-7171; Fax: 920-684-0240. Email: pkaldor@felicianvillage.org. Web: felicianvillage.org. Patricia Kaldor, CEO. Apartments 122.

St. Mary's Home for the Aged, Inc. dba St. Mary's at Felician Village 1635 S. 21st St., 54220-5652. Tel: 920-684-7171; Fax: 920-684-0240. Email: pkaldor@felicianvillage.org. Web: felicianvillage.org. Patricia Kaldor, CEO. Sisters 6; Aged Residents 121.

St. Mary's Home for the Aged, Inc. dba The Court at Felician Village 2005 Division St., 54220-5652. Tel: 920-684-7171; Fax: 920-684-0240. Email: pkaldor@felicianvillage.org. Web: felicianvillage.org. Patricia Kaldor, CEO. Total Apartments 32.

St. Mary's Home for the Aged, Inc. dba The Villas at Felician Village 1635 S. 21st St., 54220-5652. Tel: 920-684-7171; Fax: 920-684-0240. Email: pkaldor@felicianvillage.org. Web: felicianvillage.org. Beds 32.

NEENAH. *Assisi Homes of Neenah, Inc.* (1989) 210 Byrd Ave., 54956. Tel: 920-729-1771; Fax: 920-729-1797. Web: www.wfhealthcare.org. *Assisi Homes of Neenah, Inc.*, 26W171 Roosevelt Rd., Wheaton, IL 60187. Susan M. Dillberg, Chm. & Contact. (An independent living community for Seniors.) Total Staff 3; Total in Residence 39; Housing Units 38.

Villa St. Clare, Inc. (1993) 130 Byrd Ave., 54946. Tel: 920-722-5100; Fax: 920-722-5171. Web: www.wfs-inc.org. 26W71 Roosevelt Rd., Wheaton, IL 60189. Susan M. Dillberg, Chm. & Contact. Special care facility, affordable housing with supportive accommodations in an independent setting for seniors 55+. Bed Capacity 45; Total in Residence 45; Total Assisted 45; Total Staff 30; Housing Units 45.

NEW LONDON. *St. Joseph Residence, Inc., New London*, 107 E. Beckert Rd., 54961. Tel: 920-982-5354; Fax: 920-982-5420. Robert Fietsch, CEO. Residents 107.

Trinity Terrace, 107 E. Beckert Rd., 54961. Tel: 920-982-9354. Total in Residence 32.

Marion Heights Apartments, 101 E. Beckert Rd., 54961. Tel: 920-982-5354. Residents 26.

St. Joseph Residence - The Washington Center, Inc., 500 Washington St., 54961. Tel: 920-982-9200. Robert Fietsch, CEO. Apartments 33.

NIAGARA. *Maryhill Manor (SNF)*, 501 Madison Ave., 54151. Tel: 715-251-3172; Fax: 715-251-1200. Email: maryhill@borderlandnet.net. Web: www.maryhillmanor.org. Jana Clement, Admin., Pres. & CEO. Sponsored by School Sisters of St. Francis, Milwaukee. Bed Capacity 75; Nursing Care Residents 75; Total Staff 105; Total Assisted Annually 155.

[J] MONASTERIES AND RESIDENCES OF PRIESTS AND BROTHERS

GREEN BAY. *St. Mary of the Angels Friary*, 645 S. Irwin Ave., 54301-3303. Tel: 920-437-7411; 920-437-1979 (Res.); Fax: 920-437-7411. Email: RJTOFM@aol.com. Rev. Joachim Swarick, O.F.M.,

Guardian. Franciscan Friars, Assumption of the Blessed Virgin Mary Province (Order of Friars Minor). Priests 4; Brothers 1. In Res. Revs. Thomas Wojciechowski, O.F.M.; Bede Hepnar; Joachim Swarick, O.F.M.; Bro. Joseph Molinari, O.F.M. *St. Thomas More*, 650 S. Irwin Ave., 54301. Fax: 920-432-1562. Administrators 1; Lay Teachers 15; Students 161.

APPLETON. *St. Fidelis Friary*, 1100 N. Ballard Rd., 54911-5100. Tel: 920-954-8954; Fax: 920-954-1095. Web: www.thecapuchins.org. Revs. William Alcuin, O.F.M.Cap. (Retired); Silas Baumann, O.F.M.Cap. (Retired); David Belongea, O.F.M.Cap.; Donald Brody, O.F.M.Cap. (Retired); Ralph Fellenz, O.F.M.Cap. (Retired); Leopold Gleissner, O.F.M.Cap. (Retired); Gilbert Hemauer, O.F.M.Cap. (Retired); Kieran Hickey, O.F.M. (Retired); John Francis Samsa, O.F.M.Cap. (Retired); Giles Soyka, O.F.M.Cap. (Retired); Ambrose Simon, O.F.M.Cap. (Retired); Robert Udulutsch, O.F.M.Cap. (Retired); Ellis Zimmer, O.F.M.Cap. (Retired); Bros. John Gau, O.F.M.Cap., (Retired); Conrad Heinen, O.F.M.Cap., (Retired); Rob Roemer, O.F.M.Cap., Local Minister; Kenneth Stewart, O.F.M.Cap., (Retired); Cyrus Toschik, O.F.M.Cap., (Retired). Order of Friars Minor Capuchin. Priests 13; Brothers 5; Total Staff 5.

St. Joseph Friary, 404 W. Lawrence St., 54911-5855. Tel: 920-734-7195; Fax: 920-734-0227. Web: www.saintjosephparish.org. Rev. Lawrence E. Abler, O.F.M.Cap. Order of Friars Minor Capuchin.

DE PERE. *St. Joseph Priory*, 103 Grant St., 54115-2001. Tel: 920-403-3572 (Office); Fax: 920-403-4430. Revs. James T. Baraniak, O.Praem.; John Bostwick, O.Praem.; Rowland C. De Peaux, O.Praem.; Conrad J. Kratz, O.Praem.; Alfred A. McBride, O.Praem., House Supr.; Brendan J. McKeough, O.Praem.; Gery G. Meehan, O.Praem.; Brian J. Prunty, O.Praem.; Joseph S. Rekasi, O.Praem.; Peter J. Renard, O. Praem.; Timothy D. Shillcox, O.Praem. Residence for Norbertine Community. Priests 11.

St. Norbert Abbey (1898) 1016 N. Broadway, 54115-2697. Tel: 920-337-4300; Fax: 920-337-4328. Email: john.kastenholz@snc.edu. Web: www.norbertines.org. Rt. Revs. Gary J. Neville, O.Praem., J.C.D., Abbot; Jerome G. Tremel, O.Praem., Abbot Emeritus; Revs. Bartholomew A. Agar, O.Praem.; Robert E. Carson, O.Praem.; Xavier G. Colavechio, O.Praem.; Joseph R. Coopmans, O.Praem.; Andrew G. Cribben, O.Praem.; Salvatore H. Cuccia, O.Praem.; Mark D. Falcone, O.Praem; Robert M. Feller, O.Praem.; Robert K. Finnegan, O.Praem.; Michael F. Frisch, O.Praem.; Very Rev. James B. Herring, O.Praem., J.C.D., Prior; Revs. Gilbert H. Jacobs, O.Praem.; John P. Kastenholz, O.Praem., Treas.; Gerald B. Kempen, O.Praem.; David R. McElroy, O.Praem.; Gilbert Mihayli, O.Praem.; Conan P. Mulrooney, O.Praem.; James P. Neilson, O.Praem.; Christian T. O'Brien, O.Praem. (Retired); Dane J. Radecki, O.Praem.; Robert B. Reppen, O.Praem.; William H. Ribbens, O.Praem.; Stephen J. Rossey, O.Praem.; John M. Tourangeau, O.Praem.; Roman R. Vanasse, O.Praem.; Steven J. Vanden Boogard, O.Praem., Chap., (United States Navy, VA); Albin V. Veszelovszky, O.Praem., (Godollo, Hungary); Michael J. Weber, O.Praem., Chap., (United States Air Force, Witchita Falls, TX); Bros. Robert J. Craanen, O.Praem.; Steven J. Herro, O.Praem.
The Premonstratensian Fathers
NORBERT & CO., a nominee of The Premonstratensian Fathers, Norbertine Fathers
St. Norbert Abbey, Inc.
Augustine Stewardship Fund Trust
Norbertine Retirement Fund Trust
St. Norbert Abbey Seminary and Education Fund Trust
The Walnut Markets, Inc.
Los Amigos del Peru, Inc. Canons Regular of Premontre. Brothers 2; Priests 65; Priests 27; Novices 3.
Priests serving in foreign countries: Rev. John P. MacCarthy, O.Praem., Archdiocese of Iquitos, Peru, Santa Clotilde, Rio Napo, Apartado 216, Iquitos, Peru. Tel: 011-51-94-25-1932; Fax: 011-51-94-25-1922.

NEW HOLSTEIN. *Salvatorian Center*, 2021 Mason St., 53061-1141. Tel: 920-898-5605. Email: sds@salvatoriancenter.com. Web: www.salvatoriancenter.org. Brothers 4.
Salvatorian Public Relations, Salvatorian Center, 53062. Tel: 920-898-5605; Fax: 920-898-4736. Rev. Gregory Coulthard, S.D.S. *Salvatorian Mission Warehouse*, 53061. Tel: 920-898-5898; Fax: 920-898-4736. Bro. Regis Fust, S.D.S., Dir. Mission Supply Prog.

OSHKOSH. *Community of Our Lady* (1968) (Diocesan Pious Union), 2804 Oakwood Ln., 54904-8406. Tel: 920-233-5633; Fax: 920-233-5604. Very Rev. Regis N. Barwig, Prior; Revs. Eugene E. Kalinski; Augustine Serafini; Bro. Joseph G. Le Sanche. Priests 3; Brothers 1.

PULASKI. *Assumption of B.V.M. Friary* (1887) 143 E. Pulaski St., P.O. Box 100, 54162-0100. Tel: 920-822-8125; Fax: 920-822-5423. Email: blwofm@aol.com. Web: www.ofm.abvm.org. (Order of Friars Minor). *Friary*, 54162. Tel: 920-822-8125; Fax: 920-822-5423. Revs. Anthony Chojnacki, O.F.M., Vice-Guardian; Sebastian Kus, O.F.M.; Joachim Swarick, O.F.M.; Melvin Wierzbicki, O.F.M.; Brendan Wroblewski, O.F.M., Guardian; Bros. James Buda, O.F.M.; Anthony Gancarz, O.F.M.; Andrew Giba, O.F.M.; Henry Kolbok, O.F.M.; Jude Lustyk, O.F.M.; Austin Mysliwiec, O.F.M.; Gerald Tokarz, O.F.M.; Peter Rydza, O.F.M.; Robert Sembrat, O.F.M.; Gregory Stasinski, O.F.M.; David Typek, O.F.M.; Didacus Weber. *Villa Alverna*, N. 11450 Rademaker Rd., Wausaukee, 54177. Tel: 715-732-6612.
Outside of Diocese: Revs. James Esser, O.F.M.; Adam Szufel, O.F.M.; Very Rev. Patrick M. Gawrylewski, O.F.M.; Revs. Gerald A. Prusakowski, O.F.M.; Everard Scesney, O.F.M.

[K] CONVENTS AND RESIDENCES FOR SISTERS

GREEN BAY. *The Sisters of St. Francis of the Holy Cross* (1881) 3110 Nicolet Dr., 54311-7212. Tel: 920-468-1828; Fax: 920-468-1207. Email: CommSecretary@gbfranciscans.org. Web: www.gbfranciscans.org. Sr. Donna Koch, Pres. Sisters 69; In Diocese 67.
Union of Our Lady of Charity United States Province (1882) 2560 Shawano Ave., P.O. Box 10357, 54307-0357. Tel: 920-434-8208; Fax: 920-662-0047. Web: www.nauolc.org. Sr. Donna Truckey, Supr. Sisters 8.

DENMARK. *Monastery of the Holy Name of Jesus, Ltd.* (1992) Discalced Carmelite Nuns, *Monastery of the Holy Name of Jesus, Ltd.*, 6100 Pepper Rd., 54208. Tel: 920-863-5055. Email: holynamecarmel@catholic.org. Sr. Mary Elizabeth, O.C.D., Prioress. Total 9.

MANITOWOC. *St. Clare Convent*, 3 Riverview Dr., 54220. Tel: 920-682-5145. Sr. Michael Majeskie, Dir. Franciscan Sisters of Christian Charity. Sisters 7.
St. Francis Convent (1869) 6835 Calumet Ave., 54220. Tel: 920-684-7884; Fax: 920-682-4195. Web: www.sl.edu/FSCC. Sr. June Smith, Sec. Franciscan Sisters of Christian Charity. Sisters 43.
Holy Family Convent of Franciscan Sisters of Christian Charity (1869) Motherhouse and Novitiate dedicated to the Holy Family, 2409 S. Alverno Rd., 54220-9320. Tel: 920-682-7728; Fax: 920-682-4195. Email: slouise@fscc-calledtobe.org. Web: www.fscc-calledtobe.org. Revs. Finian Andrew Zaucha, O.F.M., Chap.; Samuel D. Jadin, O.Praem., Chap.; Sr. Louise Hembrecht, Community Dir. Sisters 339; In Diocese 281; Total in Residence 166.

OSHKOSH. *SSM Franciscan Courts*, 815 S. Westhaven Dr., 54904-7978. Tel: 920-426-2440; Fax: 920-426-3196. Email: jbelongie@ssm-courts.org. Jane Belongie, Facility Mgr.; Sr. Raphael Narcisi, S.S.M., Community Dir.; Rev. William Kuhr, Chap. Sisters of the Sorrowful Mother. Sisters 35.

[L] SHRINES

CHILTON. *St. Peregrine Shrine* 62 E. Main St., 53014. Tel: 920-849-9363; Fax: 920-849-7270. Rev. Robert Kollath, Pastor Good Shepherd, Chilton.

NEW FRANKEN. *The Chapel of Our Lady of Good Help (Diocesan Shrine)-Robinsonville* 4047 Chapel Dr., 54229-9768. Tel: 920-866-2571. Very Rev. John F. Doerfler, J.C.L., S.T.L., Rector.

[M] RETREAT HOUSES

APPLETON. *Monte Alverno Retreat & Spirituality Center*, 1000 N. Ballard Rd., 54911-5198. Tel: 920-733-8526; Fax: 920-733-7562. Email: montealverno@juno.com. Web: www.montealverno.org. Revs. Keith Clark, O.F.M.Cap., Dir.; Adrian Staehler, O.F.M.Cap.; Bro. John Kocian, O.F.M.Cap.; Sr. Marlene Weber, F.S.P.A. The Province of St. Joseph of the Capuchin Order, Inc. Priests 2; Brothers 1; Retreatants Annually 3,000; Total in Residence 3; Total Staff 17.

CHAMBERS ISLAND. *Holy Name Retreat House* (1951) 1825 Riverside Dr., 54301. Mailing Address: P.O. Box 23825, 54305-3825. Tel: 920-437-7531; Fax: 920-437-0694. Doris V. Vincent, Assoc. Dir. Admin. Conducted by Diocese of Green Bay.

DENMARK. *The Bridge-Between Retreat Center, Inc.*, 4471 Flaherty Ln., 54208. Tel: 920-864-7230; Fax: 920-864-7044. Email: bbrci@theglobalnet.net. Web: www.bridge-between.org. Mary Failey, Business Mgr. & Contact Person; Sr. Caroline Sullivan, O.P., Dir.

DE PERE. *Norbertine Center for Spirituality* (1979) (An Apostolate of the Norbertine Fathers), St. Norbert Abbey, 1016 N. Broadway, 54115-2697. Tel: 920-337-4315; Fax: 920-337-4385. Email: norbertinecenter@yahoo.com. Web: www.norbertines.org. Rev. Conrad J. Kratz, O.Praem., Dir. Total in Residence 1; Total Staff 6.

MENASHA. *Mount Tabor Center* (1983) 522 2nd St., 54952-3112. Tel: 920-722-8918; Fax: 920-722-8918. Email: mttabor1@sbcglobal.net. Web: mttabor.net. Eden Foord, Dir.; Katherine Foord, Asst. Dir. Total Staff 4.

OSHKOSH. *Jesuit Retreat House* (1961) 4800 Fahrnwald Rd., 54902-7598. Tel: 920-231-9060; Fax: 920-231-9094. Email: office@jesuitretreathouse.org. Web: www.jesuitretreathouse.org. Revs. John Schwantes, S.J., Dir.; Eugene Donahue, S.J., Retreat Dir.; Sr. Kerry Larkin, O.S.M., Assoc. Dir. Society of Jesus.

SHAWANO. *Camp Tekawitha Retreat and Conference Center, Inc.*, W5248 Lake Dr., 54166. Tel: 920-272-8162. Email: eblumreich@gbdioc.org. Web: www.gbdioc.org. P.O. Box 23825, 54305-3825. Eric Blumereich, Dir. & Contact Person; Doris V. Vincent, Assoc. Dir. Admin.

[N] NEWMAN CENTERS

GREEN BAY. *Ecumenical Center-UWGB* P.O. Box 23825, 54305-3825. Tel: 920-366-3661; Fax: 920-465-0128. Email: info@ecumenical-center.org. Web: www.ccm-uwgb.blogspot.com. Rev. W. Thomas Long, Chap.
Lawrence University Newman Center , (Appleton)
University of Wisconsin Marinette Campus Newman Center , (Marinette)
University of Wisconsin Fox Valley Campus Newman Center , (Menasha)
University of Wisconsin Oshkosh, Newman Center 514 Scott Ave., Oshkosh, 54901. Tel: 920-233-5555; Fax: 920-233-5556. Rev. Quentin A. Mann, Chap.

[O] MISCELLANEOUS LISTINGS

GREEN BAY. *The Catholic Foundation for the Diocese of Green Bay, Inc.* (1998) 1825 Riverside Dr., 54301. Mailing Address: P.O. Box 22128, 54305-2835. Tel: 920-272-8173; Fax: 920-272-8435. Email: catholicfoundation@gbdioc.org. Web: www.gbdioc.org. Cindi Brawner, Exec. Dir.
The Diocesan Charismatic Renewal Center, 1227 13th Ave., 54304. Tel: 920-405-1960. Email: dcrc@att.net. Rev. Arthur Cooney, O.F.M.Cap., Liaison; Judy Goolsbey, Office Mgr.
St. Francis Xavier Investment Corp. (1998) 1825 Riverside Dr., 54301. Mailing Address: P.O. Box 23825, 54305-3825. Tel: 920-437-7531, Ext. 8206; Fax: 920-437-0694. Email: jhaen@gbdioc.org. Web: gbdioc.org. Jason Haen, Diocesan Finance Officer.
Green Bay Area Catholic High School Foundation, L.T.D., P.O. Box 23825, 54305-3825. Tel: 920-272-8166. Mr. Thomas Olejniczak, Pres.
Green Bay Diocese Cemetery Corporation, 2121 Riverside Dr., P.O. Box 23825, 54305-3825. Tel: 920-432-7585; Fax: 920-432-0425. Email: dvanpay@gbdioc.org. Web: www.gbdioc.org. Ms. Tammy Basten, Dir., Facilities & Properties.
St. John the Evangelist Homeless Shelter, Inc., 1825 Riverside Dr., 54301. Mailing Address: P.O. Box 23825, 54305-3825. Tel: 920-272-8171. Email: treilly@gbdioc.org. Mary Kelly, Exec. Dir.
St. Joseph Real Estate Services Corporation, Diocesan Central Offices, P.O. Box 23825, 54305-3825. Tel: 920-272-8260; Fax: 920-437-0694. Email: dvanpay@gbdioc.org. Web: www.gbdioc.org. Ms. Tammy Basten, Dir., Facilities & Properties.
A New Genesis (ANG) An Association of the Faithful, P.O. Box 8642, 54308. Tel: 920-729-4562; 715-752-3374; Fax: 920-729-4572. Email: dbaumann@tcces.k12.wi.us. Web: www.anewgenesis.org. Sr. Diane Baumann, A.N.G., Coord. Total Members 25; In Diocese 22; Vowed in Diocese 17.
Notre Dame de la Baie Foundation, Inc., 610 Maryhill Dr., 54303. Tel: 920-429-6100; Fax: 920-429-6140. Rev. Dane J. Radecki, O.Praem., Pres.
Oratory of St. Joseph Institute of Christ the King, 211 N. Maple Ave., 54303. Tel: 920-437-9660; Fax: 920-437-5154. Email: stjoseph@institute-christ-king.org. Web: institute-christ-king.org/greenbay/. Rev. Andreas Hellmann, Rector.
Sacred Heart Seminary Corporation, P.O. Box 23825, 54305-3825. Tel: 920-437-7531; Fax: 920-435-1330. Deacon Timothy G. Reilly, Admin.; Rev. John F. Doefler, Chancellor.
Society for Faith and Children's Education, Inc., 423 Woodfield Dr., 54313. Tel: 920-434-2420; Fax: 920-434-1884. Email: sfacegreenbay@yahoo.com.

Web: www.sfacemission.org. June L. Ingold, Pres. & Contact Person; Rev. Savio J. Samala, Sec. & Treas.

St. Luke Benefit & Insurance Services Corp., 1910 S. Webster Ave., P.O. Box 23825, 54305-3825. Tel: 920-437-7531, Ext. 8216; Fax: 920-437-9296. Email: clarson@gbdioc.org. Web: www.gbdioc.org. Catherine Larson, Contact Person.

**Starboard Media Foundation, Inc. dba Relevant Radio* 1496 Bellevue St., Ste. 202, 54311. Tel: 800-342-0306; Fax: 920-465-9986. Web: www.relevantradio.com. Margaret Kleinschmidt, O.C.D.S., Exec. Asst. to CEO. Email: mmarino@relevantradio.com. Total Staff 80.

Teens Encounter Christ (TEC), Green Bay Chapter, P.O. Box 23825, 54305-3825. Tel: 920-437-7531; Fax: 920-272-8430. Email: vocations@gbdioc.org. Rev. Tom Long, Spiritual Dir.

St. Therese of the Little Flower, Inc., 1825 Riverside Dr., 54305-3825. Tel: 920-272-8206; Fax: 920-437-0694. Email: jhaen@gbdioc.org. Web: gbdioc.com.

ANTIGO. *Religious Hospitallers of St. Joseph Health Corporation "RHSJ Health Corporation"*, 112 E. Fifth Ave., 54409. Tel: 715-623-2331.

APPLETON. *Catholic Youth Expeditions, Inc.*, P.O. Box 272, 54912-0272. Tel: 920-312-0070. Email: fatherquinnmann@gmail.com. Web: www.cyexpeditions.org. Rev. Quentin A. Mann, Chm. & Treas.

St. Elizabeth Hospital Community Foundation, Inc., 1506 S. Oneida St., 54915-1397. Tel: 920-738-2859; Fax: 920-738-2061. Daniel Neufelder, CEO Affinity Health System; Tonya L. Dedering, Exec. Dir. Franciscan Sisters, Daughters of the Sacred Heart of Jesus and Mary (Wheaton, IL) & Ministry Health Care (Sisters of the Sorrowful Mother).

Global Outreach, Inc. (1994) 4815 Whitetail Way, 54914. Tel: 920-734-5967. Email: boryczkabb@sbcglobal.net. Web: www.globaloutreachprogram.com. Barbara Tota-Boryczka, Exec. Dir.; Jackie Martin, Pres.; Tom Kropidlowski, Vice Pres.; Gary Elmer, Treas.; Jerry Greany, Co-Treas.; David Raupp, Sec.

**ISECP, Inc.* (1975) 418 E. Grant St., 54911. Tel: 920-733-3210. Email: jroemer1@msn.com. Web: www.isecp.org. Sr. Judith A. Roemer, Pres.

DE PERE. *Augustine Stewardship Fund Trust* (1986) 1016 N. Broadway, 54115-2697. Tel: 920-337-4300; Fax: 920-337-4328. Email: john.kastenholz@snc.edu. Web: www.norbertines.org.

Canons Regular of Magnovarad, Ltd. (1981) 1016 N. Broadway, 54115-2697. Tel: 920-337-4300; Fax: 920-337-4328. Email: rkfinn@netnet.net. Web: www.norbertines.org. Rev. Albin V. Veszelovszky, O.Praem., Pres.; Rt. Rev. Jerome G. Tremel, O.Praem., Vice Pres.; Revs. Joseph S. Rekasi, O.Praem.; Robert K. Finnegan, O.Praem., Sec. & Treas.

Los Amigos del Peru, Inc. (1991) 1016 N. Broadway St., 54115-2697. Tel: 920-337-4300; Fax: 920-337-4328. Email: john.kastenholz@snc.edu. Web: www.norbertines.org.

NORBERT & CO. (1978) A nominee of The Premonstratensian Fathers, 1016 N. Broadway, 54115-2697. Tel: 920-337-4300; Fax: 920-337-4328. Email: john.kastenholz@snc.edu. Web: www.norbertines.org. Rt. Rev. Gary J. Neville, O.Praem., J.C.D., Abbot; Very Rev. James B. Herring, O.Praem., J.C.D., Prior; Rev. John P. Kastenholz, O.Praem., Sec.& Treas.

St. Norbert Abbey Seminary and Education Fund Trust (1989) 1016 N. Broadway, 54115-2697. Tel: 920-337-4300; Fax: 920-337-4328. Email: john.kastenholz@snc.edu. Web: www.norbertines.org.

Norbertine Generalate, Inc. (1989) 1016 N. Broadway, 54115-2697. Tel: 920-337-4300; Fax: 920-337-4328. Email: rkfinn@netnet.net. Web: www.premontre.org. Rt. Revs. Thomas A. Handgratinger, O.Praem., Pres., Rome, Italy; Gary J. Neville, O.Praem., J.C.D., Vice Pres.; Rev. Robert K. Finnegan, O.Praem., Sec. & Treas.

Norbertine Retirement Fund Trust (1986) 1016 N. Broadway, 54115-2697. Tel: 920-337-4300; Fax: 920-337-4328. Email: john.kastenholz@snc.edu. Web: www.norbertines.org.

Thea Bowman Spirituality Center, Inc. (2001) 1016 N. Broadway, 54115. Tel: 920-337-4300; Fax: 920-337-4328. Email: gjn@netnet.net. Rt. Rev. Gary J. Neville, O.Praem., J.C.D., Abbot.

DEERBROOK. **Living Waters International, Inc.* (1996) N7544 County Rd. S., 54424. Tel: 715-627-4782; Fax: 715-627-4782. Email: livingh2o@livingwatersinternational.org. Web: www.livingwatersinternational.org. Dr. Stephen L. Zimmerman, Ph.D., Pres.

MANITOWOC. *Franciscan Sisters of Christian Charity HealthCare Ministry, Inc.* (1985) 1415 S. Rapids Rd., 54220-9302. Tel: 920-684-7071; Fax: 920-684-6417. Email: lwolf@fhcm.org. Web: www.fhcm.org. Sr. Laura J. Wolf, O.S.F., Pres.

MENASHA. **Affinity Health System*, 1570 Midway Pl., 54952. Tel: 920-720-1713; Fax: 920-720-1720. Email: svandenh@affinityhealth.org. Web: affinityhealth.org. Daniel Neufelder, Pres. & CEO. Sponsored by Wheaton Franciscan Services, Inc. (Wheaton, IL) and Ministry Health Care, Inc. (Milwaukee, WI).

**Network Health System, Inc.*, 1570 Midway Pl., 54952-8005. Tel: 920-720-1734. Web: www.affinityhealth.org. Daniel Neufelder, CEO. Total Staff 1,084; Total Assisted 394,116.

NEENAH. *St. Mary High School Foundation, Inc.*, 1050 Zephyr Dr., 54956-1389. Tel: 920-722-7796; Fax: 920-722-5940. Web: www.smc.k12.wi.us.

Twin Cities Catholic Perpetual Eucharistic Adoration Chapel, Inc., 1615 Nicolet Blvd., 54956-2984. Tel: 920-722-8574. James Asmuth, Contact Person, (Retired).

NEW FRANKEN. *The Chapel of Our Lady of Good Help, Inc.*, 4047 Chapel Dr., 54229. Tel: 920-866-2571. Email: chapel000@centurytel.net. Web: www.shrineofourladyofgoodhelp.com. P.O. Box 23825, 54305-3825. Very Rev. John F. Doerfler, J.C.L., S.T.L., Rector.

OSHKOSH. *Christ Child Society, Oshkosh Chapter, c/o St. Raphael the Archangel*, 830 Westhaven Rd., 54904. Tel: 920-232-9453. Marie Combs, Contact Person.

STURGEON BAY. *Christ Child Society of Door County* (1996) P.O. Box 572, 54235. Tel: 920-823-2200. Diane Stracka, Pres.

[P] CLOSED AND MERGED PARISHES

GREEN BAY. *Green Bay Diocesan Archives*, 1910 S. Webster Ave., P.O. Box 23825, 54305-3825. Tel: 920-437-7531, Ext. 8186; Fax: 920-435-1330. Email: jledoux@gbdioc.org. Web: www.gbdioc.org. Parish sacramental records for parishes that have closed or merged can be found at the locations listed below. As the location of sacramental records can change periodically, inquiries for records of parishes on this list should be directed to the above address.

St. Louis, Abrams Please see St. Maximilian Kolbe, Sobieski.

St. Joseph, Alverno Tel: 920-726-4228; Fax: 920-726-4229. Please see St. Thomas the Apostle, Newton.

St. Hyacinth, Antigo Please see SS. Mary & Hyacinth, Antigo.

St. Mary, Antigo Please see SS. Mary & Hyacinth, Antigo.

St. Mary, Argonne Tel: 715-478-3396. Please see St. Joseph, Crandon.

St. Patrick, Askeaton Please see St. Clare Corp., Greenleaf.

St. Mary of the Lake, Baileys Harbor Please see Stella Maris, Egg Harbor.

St. Mary, Brillion Tel: 920-753-2535; Fax: 920-753-9802. Please see Holy Family, Brillion.

St. Charles Borromeo, Charlesburg Please see Good Shepherd, Chilton.

St. Martin, Charlestown Please see Good Shepherd, Chilton.

St. Joseph, Chase Please see St. Maximilian Kolbe, Sobieski.

St. Augustine, Chilton Please see Good Shepherd, Chilton.

St. Mary, Chilton Please see Good Shepherd, Chilton.

St Wendel, Cleveland Tel: 920-726-4228; Fax: 920-726-4229. Please see St. Thomas the Apostle, Newton.

St. John the Baptist, Coleman Tel: 920-897-3226; Fax: 920-897-4677. Please see St. Anne Parish, Corp., Coleman.

St. Francis of Assisi, Coleman Tel: 920-897-3226; Fax: 920-897-4677. Please see St. Anne Parish, Corp., Coleman.

SS. Francis-Wenceslaus, Coleman Please see St. Anne Parish Corp., Coleman.

Holy Angels, Darboy Tel: 920-788-7640; Fax: 920-788-7658. Please see Holy Spirit, Kimberly.

St. Boniface, De Pere Tel: 920-336-4033; Fax: 920-336-3910. Please see Our Lady of Lourdes, De Pere.

St. Joseph, De Pere Tel: 920-336-4033; Fax: 920-336-3910. Please see Our Lady of Lourdes, De Pere.

SS. Cyril and Methodius, Eaton Tel: 920-863-2593; Fax: 920-845-5180. Please see St. Thomas the Apostle, Humboldt.

St. John the Baptist, Egg Harbor Please see Stella Maris, Egg Harbor.

St. William, Eland Tel: 715-253-2050; Fax: 715-253-3020. Please see Holy Family-St. William, Wittenberg.

St. Paul, Fish Creek Please see Stella Maris, Egg Harbor.

Holy Marytrs of Gorcum, Green Bay See Prince of Peace, Green Bay.

St. Mary, Greenleaf Please see St. Clare Corp., Greenleaf.

St. Michael, Hiles Tel: 715-478-3396. Please see St Joseph, Crandon.

St. Francis, Hollandtown Please see St. Katharine Drexel, Kaukauna.

Our Lady Queen of Peace, Humboldt Tel: 920-863-2593; Fax: 920-845-5180. Please see St. Thomas the Apostle, Humboldt.

St. Michael, Jacksonport Please see Stella Maris, Egg Harbor.

Holy Trinity, Jericho Please see Good Shepherd, Chilton.

Holy Trinity, Kasson Please see Holy Family, Brillion.

St. Aloysius, Kaukauna Please see St. Katharine Drexel, Kaukauna.

St. Mary of the Annunciation, Kaukauna Please see St. Katharine Drexel, Kaukauna.

Holy Name of Jesus, Kimberly Please see Holy Spirit, Kimberly.

St. George, King Tel: 715-258-3000; Fax: 715-258-5708. Please see St. Mary Magdalene, Waupaca.

St. Wenceslaus, Klondike Tel: 920-897-3226; Fax: 920-897-4677. Please see St. Anne Parish, Corp., Coleman.

St. Elizabeth, Kloten Please see Good Shepherd, Chilton.

St. John, Krok Tel: 920-863-8747; Fax: 920-863-5768. Please see St. Therese de Lisieux, Stangelville.

St. Stanislaus Kostka, Langlade Tel: 715-882-2551. Please see SS. James and Stanislaus, White Lake.

St. Charles Borromeo, Lena Tel: 920-829-5222. Please see Holy Cross, Lena.

Holy Cross, Lena Please see St. Anne Parish Corp., Coleman.

St. Peter, Lincoln Tel: 920-837-2852. Please see St. Peter and St. Hubert, Rosiere.

St. Andrew, Manitowoc Please see St. Francis of Assisi, Manitowoc.

St. Boniface, Manitowoc Please see St. Francis of Assisi, Manitowoc.

Holy Innocents, Manitowoc Please see St. Francis of Assisi, Manitowoc.

St. Mary, Manitowoc Please see St. Francis of Assisi, Manitowoc.

St. Paul, Manitowoc Please see St. Francis of Assisi, Manitowoc.

Sacred Heart, Manitowoc Please see St. Francis of Assisi, Manitowoc.

St. Patrick, Maple Grove Tel: 920-756-2535; Fax: 920-756-9802. Please see Holy Family, Brillion/Reedsville.

St. Francis De Paul, Marchand (Duvall) Tel: 920-866-2410; Fax: 920-866-3591. Please see St. Louis, Dyckesville.

Our Lady of Lourdes, Marinette Tel: 715-735-9100; Fax: 715-735-9650. Please see Holy Family, Marinette.

Sacred Heart of Jesus, Marinette Tel: 715-735-9100; Fax: 715-735-9650. Please see Holy Family, Marinette.

St. Anthony, Marinette Tel: 715-735-9100; Fax: 715-735-9650. Please see Holy Family, Marinette.

St. Joseph, Marinette Tel: 715-735-9100; Fax: 715-735-9650. Please see Holy Family, Marinette.

Holy Family Church, Mattoon Please see St. Joseph-Holy Family, Phlox.

St. Joseph, Montpelier Tel: 920-863-8747; Fax: 920-863-5768. Please see St. Therese de Lisieux, Stangelville.

St. Joseph-St. John, Montpelier Tel: 920-863-8747; Fax: 920-863-5768. Please see St. Therese de Lisieux, Stangelville.

St. Mary, Namur Tel: 920-825-7555; Fax: 920-825-1492. Please see St. Francis and St. Mary, Brussels.

St, Joseph, Norman Tel: 920-776-1555; Fax: 920-776-1555. Please see St. Isidore the Farmer, Tisch Mills

St. Casimir, Northeim Tel: 920-726-4228; Fax: 920-726-4229. Please see St. Thomas the Apostle, Newton.

St. Joseph, Oconto Tel: 920-835-5900; Fax: 920-835-5907. Please see Holy Trinity, Oconto.

St. Peter, Oconto Tel: 920-835-5900; Fax: 920-835-5907. Please see Holy Trinity, Oconto.

St. John, Oshkosh Please see St. Jude the Apostle, Oshkosh.

St. Josaphat, Oshkosh Please see Most Blessed Sacrament, Oshkosh.

St. Mary, Oshkosh Please see Most Blessed Sacrament, Oshkosh.

St. Peter, Oshkosh Please see Most Blessed Sacrament, Oshkosh.

Sacred Heart, Oshkosh Please see St. Jude the Apostle, Oshkosh.

St. Vincent De Paul, Oshkosh Please see St. Jude the Apostle, Oshkosh.

St. Isidore, Osman Tel: 920-726-4228; Fax: 920-726-4229. Please see St. Thomas the Apostle, Newton.

Holy Trinity, Pine Grove See Prince of Peace, Green Bay.

St. Leo, Pound Tel: 920-897-3226; Fax: 920-897-4677. Please see St. Anne Parish, Corp., Coleman.

St. Mary, Reedsville Tel: 920-756-2535; Fax: 920-756-9802. Please see Holy Family, Brillion.

St. Mary-St. Patrick, Reedsville/ Maple Grove Tel: 920-756-2535; Fax: 920-756-9802. Please see Holy Family, Brillion.

St. Rosalia, Sister Bay Please see Stella Maris, Egg Harbor.

St. Adalbert, Slovan Tel: 920-837-7234; Fax: 920-837-2361. Please see Holy Trinity, Casco.

St. John Cantius, Sobieski Please see St. Maximilian Kolbe, Sobieski.

St. Joseph of the Lake, South Branch Tel: 715-799-3811; Fax: 715-799-5092. Please see St. Michael, Keshena.

Sacred Heart, Spruce Tel: 920-829-5222. Please see Holy Cross, Lena.

St. John the Baptist, St. John Tel: 920-989-1515; Fax: 920-989-8585. Please see St. John-Sacred Heart, Sherwood.

St. Lawrence, Stangelville Tel: 920-863-8747; Fax: 920-863-5768. Please see St. Therese de Lisieux, Stangelville.

St. Mary, Stark Tel: 920-864-7641. Please see St. Mary, Glenmore.

St. Odile, Thiry Daems Tel: 920-866-9961. Please see St. Joseph, Champion.

Nativity of the BVM, Tisch Mills Tel: 920-776-1555; Fax: 920-776-1555. Please see St. Isidore the Farmer, Tisch Mills.

St. Martin, Tonet Tel: 920-866-9961. Please see St. Joseph, Champion.

Holy Redeemer-Sacred Heart, Two Rivers Tel: 920-793-4531; Fax: 920-793-8067. Please see St. Peter the Fisherman, Two Rivers.

Sacred Heart, Two Rivers Tel: 920-793-4531; Fax: 920-793-8067. Please see St. Peter the Fisherman, Two Rivers.

St. Luke, Two Rivers Tel: 920-793-4531; Fax: 920-793-8067. Please see St. Peter the Fisherman, Two Rivers.

St. Mark, Two Rivers Tel: 920-793-4531; Fax: 920-793-8067. Please see St. Peter the Fisherman, Two Rivers.

St. Edward, Wagner See St. Joseph & Edwards, Walsh.

St. Amand, Walhain Tel: 920-866-9961. Please see St. Joseph, Champion.

St. Joseph, Walsh Please see SS. Joseph & Edward, Walsh.

St. Hedwig, West Kewaunee Tel: 920-863-8747; Fax: 920-863-5768. Please see St. Therese de Lisieux, Stangelville.

St. James, White Lake Please see SS. James & Stanislaus, White Lake/Langlade.

St. Paul, Wrightstown Please see St. Clare Corp., Greenleaf.

RELIGIOUS INSTITUTES OF MEN REPRESENTED IN THE DIOCESE

For further details refer to the corresponding bracketed number in the Religious Institutes of Men or Women section.

[0330]—*Brothers of the Christian Schools* (Midwest Province), Burr Ridge, IL—F.S.C.

[0900]—*Canons Regular of Premontre*—O.Praem.

[0470]—*The Capuchin Friars* (Province of St. Joseph)—O.F.M.Cap.

[1130]—*Congregation of the Priests of the Sacred Heart*—S.C.J.

[0690]—*Franciscan Friars*—O.F.M.

[0305]—*Institute of Christ the King*—I.C.

[0690]—*Jesuit Fathers and Brothers* (Wisconsin Province)—S.J.

[0910]—*Oblates of Mary Immaculate*—O.M.I.

[1200]—*Society of the Divine Savior*—S.D.S.

RELIGIOUS INSTITUTES OF WOMEN REPRESENTED IN THE DIOCESE

[3710]—*Congregation of the Sisters of St. Agnes*—C.S.A.

[0420]—*Discalced Carmelite Nuns*—O.C.D.

[1070-03]—*Dominican Sisters* Adrian, MI—O.P.

[1070-09]—*Dominican Sisters* Racine, WI—O.P.

[1070-14]—*Dominican Sisters* Sinsinawa, WI—O.P.

[1115]—*Dominican Sisters of Peace*—O.P.

[1170]—*Felician Sisters*—C.S.S.F.

[]—*Felician Sisters (Congregation of the Sisters of St. Felix)*—C.S.S.F.

[1230]—*Franciscan Sisters of Christian Charity*—O.S.F.

[]—*Franciscan Sisters of Perpetual Adoration*—F.S.P.A.

[1240]—*Franciscan Sisters, Daughters of the Sacred Hearts of Jesus and Mary*—O.S.F.

[]—*Handmaids of the Divine Redeemer*—H.D.R.

[1820]—*Hospital Sisters of the Third Order of St. Francis*—O.S.F.

[3070]—*North American Union Sisters of Our Lady of Charity*—N.A.U.-O.L.C.

[3440]—*Religious Hospitallers of Saint Joseph*—R.H.S.J.

[2970]—*School Sisters of Notre Dame*—S.S.N.D.

[1680]—*School Sisters of St. Francis*—S.S.S.F.

[]—*Servants of Mary*—O.S.M.

[]—*Sisters of St. Elizabeth*—S.S.E.

[1705]—*The Sisters of St. Francis of Assisi*—O.S.F.

[1550]—*Sisters of St. Francis of the Holy Cross*—O.S.F.

[3840]—*Sisters of St. Joseph of Carondelet* (Prov. of St. Louis)—C.S.J.

[3930]—*Sisters of St. Joseph of the Third Order of St. Francis*—S.S.J.-T.O.S.F.

[1030]—*Sisters of the Divine Savior*—S.D.S.

[4100]—*Sisters of the Sorrowful Mother (Third Order of St. Francis)*—S.S.M.

[]—*Society of Sisters for the Church*—S.S.C.

DIOCESAN CEMETERIES

GREEN BAY. *Diocesan Cemeteries*, P.O. Box 23825, 54305-3825. Tel: 920-437-7531, Ext. 8229. Ms. Tammy Basten, Diocesan Dir.

Allouez Catholic Cemetery and Mausoleum, 2121 Riverside Dr., 54301.

Queen of Peace Cemetery & Mausoleum, 101 6th St., P.O. Box 535, Antigo, 54409.

Calvary Cemetery & Calvary Chapel Mausoleum, 2601 S. 14th St., Manitowoc, 54220-6467.

Oshkosh Catholic Cemeteries, 1905 Roosevelt Ave., Oshkosh, 54901.

NECROLOGY

† Schneider, Rev. Msgr. Alfred, (Retired)—Died April 25, 2009

† Bedessem, Henry W., (Retired)—Died Feb. 11, 2009

† Van Der Horst, John, (Retired)—Died Sept. 11, 2009

An asterisk (*) denotes an organization that has established tax-exempt status directly with the IRS and is not covered by the USCCB Group Ruling.

Diocese of Greensburg

(Dioecesis Greensburgensis)

Most Reverend

LAWRENCE E. BRANDT, J.C.D., PH.D.

Bishop of Greensburg; ordained December 19, 1969; appointed Bishop of Greensburg January 2, 2004; installed March 4, 2004. *Office: 723 E. Pittsburgh St., Greensburg, PA 15601.*

Most Reverend

ANTHONY G. BOSCO, D.D., J.C.L.

Retired Bishop of Greensburg; ordained June 7, 1952; appointed Auxiliary Bishop of Pittsburgh and Titular Bishop of Labico May 14, 1970; consecrated June 30, 1970; appointed Bishop of Greensburg April 14, 1987; installed June 30, 1987; retired January 2, 2004.

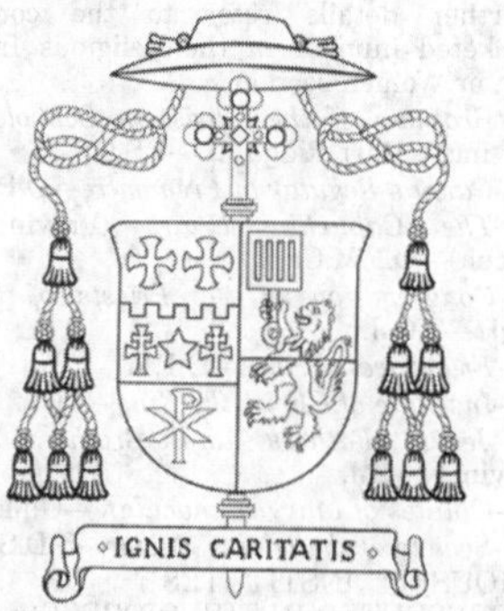

Pastoral Center: 723 E. Pittsburgh St., Greensburg, PA 15601. Tel: 724-837-0901; Fax: 724-837-0857.

Web: www.catholicgbg.org

ESTABLISHED MARCH 10, 1951.

Square Miles 3,334.

Comprises the Counties of Armstrong, Fayette, Indiana and Westmoreland in the State of Pennsylvania.

For legal titles of parishes and diocesan institutions, consult the Chancery Office.

STATISTICAL OVERVIEW

Personnel	
Bishop	1
Retired Bishops	1
Abbots	1
Priests: Diocesan Active in Diocese	77
Priests: Diocesan Active Outside Diocese	3
Priests: Retired, Sick or Absent	34
Number of Diocesan Priests	114
Religious Priests in Diocese	69
Total Priests in Diocese	183
Ordinations:	
Religious Priests	2
Permanent Deacons	2
Permanent Deacons in Diocese	2
Total Brothers	47
Total Sisters	198
Parishes	
Parishes	85
With Resident Pastor:	
Resident Diocesan Priests	58
Resident Religious Priests	12
Without Resident Pastor:	
Administered by Priests	15
Professional Ministry Personnel:	
Sisters	13
Lay Ministers	78
Welfare	
Homes for the Aged	2
Total Assisted	264
Special Centers for Social Services	6
Total Assisted	15,916
Residential Care of Disabled	1
Total Assisted	89
Educational	
Diocesan Students in Other Seminaries	8
Seminaries, Religious	1
Students Religious	24
Total Seminarians	32
Colleges and Universities	2
Total Students	3,930
High Schools, Diocesan and Parish	2
Total Students	655
Elementary Schools, Diocesan and Parish	15
Total Students	2,915
Elementary Schools, Private	3
Total Students	238
Catechesis/Religious Education:	
High School Students	1,794
Elementary Students	7,330
Total Students under Catholic Instruction	16,894
Teachers in the Diocese:	
Priests	10
Brothers	4
Sisters	11
Lay Teachers	299
Vital Statistics	
Receptions into the Church:	
Infant Baptism Totals	1,329
Minor Baptism Totals	42
Adult Baptism Totals	65
Received into Full Communion	302
First Communions	1,625
Confirmations	1,737
Marriages:	
Catholic	413
Interfaith	267
Total Marriages	680
Deaths	2,419
Total Catholic Population	161,959
Total Population	673,477

Former Bishops—Most Revs. HUGH L. LAMB, S.T.D., First Bishop of Greensburg; ord. May 29, 1915; appt. Titular Bishop of Helos and Auxiliary of Philadelphia Dec. 19, 1935; cons. March 19, 1936; promoted to Greensburg May 28, 1951; installed Jan. 16, 1952; died Dec. 8, 1959; WILLIAM G. CONNARE, D.D., ord. June 14, 1936; appt. Feb. 23, 1960; cons. May 4, 1960; retired Jan. 20, 1987; died June 12, 1995; ANTHONY G. BOSCO, D.D., J.C.L., ord. June 7, 1952; appt. Auxiliary Bishop of Pittsburgh and Titular Bishop of Labico May 14, 1970; cons. June 30, 1970; appt. Bishop of Greensburg April 14, 1987; installed June 30, 1987; retired Jan. 2, 2004.

Pastoral Center—723 E. Pittsburgh St., Greensburg, 15601-2697. Tel: 724-837-0901; Fax: 724-837-0857. Office Hours: Mon.-Fri. 8:45-5.

Vicar General/Chancellor—Rev. Msgr. LAWRENCE T. PERSICO, J.C.L., V.G. Tel: 724-837-0901.

Chief Financial Officer—Mr. MICHAEL J. MCGEE.

Deaneries—Rev. Msgr. JAMES T. GASTON, V.F., Deanery 1; Very Revs. PAUL A. LISIK, V.F., Deanery 2; KENNETH G. ZACCAGNINI, V.F., Deanery 3; DANIEL C. MAHONEY, V.F., Deanery 4; Rev. Msgr. MICHAEL W. MATUSAK, V.F., Deanery 5.

Director for Religious—VACANT, Office, 723 E. Pittsburgh St., Greensburg, 15601-2697. Tel: 724-837-0901.

Tribunal— Address all correspondence to *723 E. Pittsburgh St., Greensburg, 15601-2697.* Tel: 724-837-0901.

Judicial Vicar—Rev. Msgr. WILLIAM R. RATHGEB, J.C.L.

Defender of Bond—Rev. Msgr. LAWRENCE T. PERSICO, J.C.L., V.G.

Judges—Rev. RICHARD J. KOSISKO, J.C.L.; Rev. Msgr. WILLIAM G. CHARNOKI, P.A., J.C.L.; Rev. ANTHONY J. CARBONE, J.C.L.

Advocate—VACANT.

Notaries—Mrs. CINDY J. OZZELLO; Ms. KATHLEEN POLOSKY.

Tribunal Coordinator—Ms. KATHLEEN POLOSKY.

Advisory Bodies

College of Consultors—Most Rev. LAWRENCE E. BRANDT, J.C.D., Ph.D.; Rev. Msgr. LAWRENCE T. PERSICO, J.C.L., V.G.; Very Rev. KENNETH G. ZACCAGNINI, V.F.; Rev. Msgr. MICHAEL W. MATUSAK, V.F.; Rev. JOHN A. MOINEAU; Very Rev. PAUL A. LISIK, V.F.; Rev. LAWRENCE L. MANCHAS, V.F.

Diocesan Pastoral Council— (none at this time)

Bishop's Priests Council—Rev. Msgr. LAWRENCE T. PERSICO, J.C.L., V.G.; Very Rev. PAUL A. LISIK, V.F.; Rev. Msgr. JAMES T. GASTON, V.F.; Very Revs. DANIEL C. MAHONEY, V.F.; KENNETH G. ZACCAGNINI, V.F.; Revs. JOHN A. MOINEAU; JOHN M. FORISKA; ALEXANDER L. PLEBAN, S.T.L.; JAMES D. TRINGHESE; MICHAEL J. CROOKSTON; Rev. Msgr. MICHAEL W. MATUSAK, V.F.; Rev. RICHARD J. KOSISKO, J.C.L.

Finance Council—Most Rev. LAWRENCE E. BRANDT, J.C.D., Ph.D.; Rev. Msgr. LAWRENCE T. PERSICO, J.C.L., V.G.; Mr. JOSEPH G. KLOCEK; Mr. JOHN A. ROBERTSHAW JR.; Mrs. NORMA F. SCHERER; Rev. THADDEUS J. KACZMAREK; Mr. CHARLES A. FAGAN III; Mr. B. PATRICK COSTELLO; Mr. WILLIAM MCCABE; Ms. MARIE HUSS; Mrs. RUTH GRANT.

Diocesan Offices, Commissions and Special Programs

The Catholic Foundation for the Diocese of Greensburg— The Catholic Foundation for the Diocese of Greensburg (the Foundation) is a not-for-profit, tax-exempt corporation established by the Diocese of Greensburg (diocese) in 1986. Effective July 1, 2009, Bishop Lawrence E. Brandt announced the restructuring of The Catholic Foundation and new by-laws were adopted for the Foundation. These by-laws provide for a three-tier management structure designed to enhance monitoring of policies and procedures, and ensure effective accomplishment of the Foundation's mission. As the philanthropic arm of the Diocese, the Foundation exists to support the pastoral, educational, and social service ministries of the Diocese of Greensburg. This includes, but is not exclusive to parishes, Catholic schools, Catholic Charities, Catholic Cemeteries, and other Diocesan ministries. *723 E. Pittsburgh St., Greensburg, 15601.*

Members of the Corporation—Most Rev. LAWRENCE E. BRANDT, J.C.D., Ph.D., Chm.; Rev. Msgr. LAWRENCE T. PERSICO, J.C.L., V.G., Vice Chm.; VACANT, Assoc. Vice Chm.

Board of Trustees—Mr. LAWRENCE S. BUSCH, Pres.; VACANT, Vice Pres.; Mr. MARC B. ROBERTSHAW, Sec.; Mr. DANIEL L. CHESS, CPA, C.V.A., Treas.; Mr. LEO N. HITT; Mr. RAYMOND J. HANLEY.

Ex-Officio Trustees—

College of Deans—Rev. Msgr. JAMES T. GASTON, V.F., Deanery I; Very Revs. PAUL A. LISIK, V.F., Deanery II; KENNETH G. ZACCAGNINI, V.F., Deanery III; DANIEL C. MAHONEY, V.F., Deanery IV; Rev. Msgr. MICHAEL W. MATUSAK, V.F., Deanery V.

Diocese of Greensburg - Managing Directors—Mr. TRENT D. BOCAN, Supt. Catholic Schools; Mr. MICHAEL J. MCGEE, CFO; Rev. Msgr. RAYMOND E. RIFFLE, M.S.W., M.P.A., Catholic Charities; Mr. ROBERT A. SHERWIN, Evangelization & Faith Formation; Mr. MATTHEW J. STOESSEL, The Catholic Foundation; Mr. JEROME ZUFELT, Communications.

Diocese of Greensburg - Development Personnel—Mrs. JUDY M. MODECKI, Catholic Charities; Mr. JOSEPH G. KLOCEK, Catholic Schools.

The Catholic Institute of Greensburg— A Corporation, not-for-profit, incorporated under the law of the Commonwealth of Pennsylvania on the 4th day of June, 1954 having as its purpose the support of any Roman Catholic benevolent, charitable, educational or missionary undertaking.

Board of Members of the Corporation—Most Rev. LAWRENCE E. BRANDT, J.C.D., Ph.D., Pres.; Rev. Msgr. LAWRENCE T. PERSICO, J.C.L., V.G., Sec.

Board of Trustees—Mr. PAUL D. PULEO, Pres.; Mr. MICHAEL J. MCGEE, Sec.; Mr. MARK E. LOPUSHINSKY; Mr. JOHN N. STEVENS; Rev. Msgr. J. EDWARD MCCULLOUGH. Staff: Mrs. SHEILA R. MURRY, Financial Officer; Mrs. CARLA C. PELLIS, Accountant.

Greensburg Catholic Accent and Communications, Inc.— A corporation, not-for-profit, under the laws of the Commonwealth of Pennsylvania having as its purpose the support of any Roman Catholic benevolent, charitable, educational or missionary undertaking. Most Rev. LAWRENCE E. BRANDT, J.C.D., Ph.D.; Rev. Msgr. LAWRENCE T. PERSICO, J.C.L., V.G.; Mr. MICHAEL J. MCGEE, Treas., 723 E. Pittsburgh St., Greensburg, 15601-2697. Tel: 724-837-0901; Fax: 724-837-0857.

Catholic Charities of the Diocese of Greensburg, PA, Inc.— A corporation not-for-profit incorporated under the law of the Commonwealth of Pennsylvania on the 27th day of August, 1954, having as its purpose, the support of any Roman Catholic benevolent, charitable, educational or missionary undertaking. Most Rev. LAWRENCE E. BRANDT, J.C.D., Ph.D., Chm. Bd. Members of the Corp.; CHARLES DELUZIO, Pres. Bd. of Trustees; Rev. Msgr. RAYMOND E. RIFFLE, M.S.W., M.P.A., Mng. Dir., 711 E. Pittsburgh St., Greensburg, 15601-2636. Tel: 724-837-1840; Fax: 724-837-4077.

Archives—723 E. Pittsburgh St., Greensburg, 15601. Tel: 724-837-0901.

Catholic Charities—Rev. Msgr. RAYMOND E. RIFFLE, M.S.W., M.P.A., Mng. Dir.; Mr. ROBERT MCHENRY, Dir. Oper. & Finance; Mrs. JUDY M. MODECKI, Dir., Coordinated Svcs. & Devel., 711 E. Pittsburgh St., Greensburg, 15601-2636. Tel: 724-837-1840; Fax: 724-837-4077.

Catholic Relief Services Representative—Rev. Msgr. J. EDWARD MCCULLOUGH, 723 E. Pittsburgh St., Greensburg, 15601-2697. Tel: 724-837-0901.

The Catholic Accent & Media Relations—Mr. JERRY ZUFELT, Mng. Dir. Communications & Editor, Catholic Accent; Mrs. ELIZABETH FAZZINI, Asst. Dir., 725 E. Pittsburgh St., P.O. Box 850, Greensburg, 15601-2697. Tel: 724-834-4010; Fax: 724-836-5650.

Diocesan Ecumenical Office—Rev. THOMAS A. FEDERLINE, 820 Carbon Rd., Greensburg, 15601. Email: tfederline@dioceseofgreensburg.org.

Office of Information Technology—Ms. KAREN CORNELL, Dir.; Mr. BRIAN LOOSZ, Network Analyst; Mr. TONY KRANCE, Internet/Lotus Notes System Admin.; Mr. GREGG WHITFIELD, Client Technology Analyst & Telecommunication Specialist; Mr. DARREN DORN, Client Technology Specialist; JORDAN GOVI, Database & System Admin.; KATHERINE FINFROCK, Instructional Technology Analyst; Mrs. CINDY STICKLE, IT Asset Management & Contract Admin.

Office for Planning—Rev. WILLIAM J. LECHNAR, Dir., 723 E. Pittsburgh St., Greensburg, 15601-2697. Tel: 724-837-0901; Fax: 724-837-0857.

Office of Catholic Schools—Mr. TRENT D. BOCAN, Supt. Schools; Mrs. KAREN MCCLAMON, Dir. Catholic School Svcs. Email: kmcclamon@dioceseofgreensburg.org; Mr. JOSEPH G. KLOCEK, Dir. Advancement for Catholic Schools & Scholarship Partners Foundation.

Office for Worship—Rev. MICHAEL P. SIKON, Dir.

Office for Faith Formation—Mr. ROBERT A. SHERWIN, Mng. Dir. Email: rsherwin@dioceseofgreensburg.org.

Youth & Young Adult Ministry and Adult Initiation—CHRISTINA M. SMITH.

Marriage Formation—Coordinators: RICHARD RYBA; LEEANNA RYBA.

Consultant for Catechesis of the Good Shepherd—BONNIE MILAN.

Athletics—Mr. MICHAEL COLLETT, Athletic Dir. Email: mcollett@dioceseofgreensburg.org.

Diocesan Catholic Scoutmaster—Rev. E. GEORGE SALETRIK, 723 E. Pittsburgh St., Greensburg, 15601-2697. Tel: 724-837-0901; Fax: 724-837-0857.

Office for Lay Ecclesial Ministry—Ms. MARSHA KABLE, Dir., 723 E. Pittsburgh St., Greensburg, 15601-2697. Tel: 724-837-0901; Fax: 724-837-0857.

Office for Clergy Vocations—Revs. LARRY J. KULICK, Dir.; TIMOTHY J. KRUTHAUPT, Asst. Dir. Email: tkruthaupt@dioceseofgreensburg.org.

Office for the Permanent Diaconate—Rev. Msgr. ROGER A. STATNICK, S.T.L., Ph.D., Dir.; Ms. MARSHA KABLE, 723 E. Pittsburgh St., Greensburg, 15601. Tel: 724-837-0901; Fax: 724-837-0857.

Missions— Society for the Propagation of the Faith and Holy Childhood, Rev. Msgr. J. EDWARD MCCULLOUGH, 723 E. Pittsburgh St., Greensburg, 15601-2697. Tel: 724-837-0901; Fax: 724-837-0857.

Newspaper— "The Catholic Accent" Mailing Address: 725 E. Pittsburgh St., P.O. Box 850, Greensburg, 15601-2697. Tel: 724-834-4010; Fax: 724-836-5650.

Mr. JEROME ZUFELT, Editor; Mrs. ELIZABETH FAZZINI, Asst. Dir.

Engineering and Facility Management Office—Mr. EDGAR R. TURNER, Dir., 723 E. Pittsburgh St., Greensburg, 15601-2697. Tel: 724-837-0901; 724-552-2570; Fax: 724-836-5592.

SPECIAL PROGRAMS

Apostleship of Prayer—Rev. Msgr. J. EDWARD MCCULLOUGH, Dir., 459 Ranch Rd., Dunbar, 15431. Tel: 724-277-4236; Fax: 724-277-0192.

Apostolate for the Deaf—VACANT, Diocese of Greensburg, 723 E. Pittsburgh St., Greensburg, 15601. Tel: 724-837-0901.

Catholic Business and Professional Women's Association—Rev. LARRY J. KULICK, Spiritual Moderator, 723 E. Pittsburgh St., Greensburg, 15601-2697. Tel: 724-837-0901; Fax: 724-837-0857.

Catholic Daughters of America—Rev. Msgr. J. EDWARD MCCULLOUGH, Dir., 459 Ranch Rd., Dunbar, 15431. Tel: 724-277-4236; Fax: 724-277-0192.

Cemeteries—723 E. Pittsburgh St., Greensburg, 15601-2697. Tel: 724-837-0901.

Charismatic—Sr. ANN INFANGER, S.C., Moderator, Seton Hill College, Greensburg, 15601. Tel: 724-834-2200, Ext. 374.

Cursillo—c/o Diocese of Greensburg, 723 E. Pittsburgh St., Greensburg, 15601. Tel: 724-837-0901; Fax: 724-837-0857.

Diocesan Council of Catholic Women—Rev. Msgr. DONALD J. MONDELLO, Dir., Newmann House, 2900 Seminary Dr., Greensburg, 15601. Tel: 724-834-2409.

Holy Childhood Association—Rev. Msgr. J. EDWARD MCCULLOUGH, Dir., 723 E. Pittsburgh St., Greensburg, 15601-2697. Tel: 724-837-0901; Fax: 724-837-0857.

Holy Name Society—Rev. RICHARD P. KARENBAUER, Dir., St. Joseph Church, 1125 Leishman Ave., New Kensington, 15068. Tel: 724-337-6412; Fax: 724-337-4022.

Legion of Mary—Rev. ALAN W. GROTE, 857 Kenneth Ave., New Kensington, 15068. Tel: 724-335-8212. Email: agrote@dioceseofgreensburg.org.

Pilgrimages—Rev. Msgr. J. EDWARD MCCULLOUGH, Dir., 459 Ranch Rd., Dunbar, 15431. Tel: 724-277-4236.

Priests' Eucharistic League—Rev. Msgr. J. EDWARD MCCULLOUGH, 459 Ranch Rd., Dunbar, 15431. Tel: 724-277-4236.

St. Luke Society for Health Care Professionals—Rev. Msgr. LAWRENCE T. PERSICO, J.C.L., V.G., Chap., 723 E. Pittsburgh St., Greensburg, 15601. Tel: 724-837-0901.

St. Thomas More Society for Lawyers—Rev. TIMOTHY J. KRUTHAUPT, Chap., 723 E. Pittsburgh St., Greensburg, 15601-2697. Tel: 724-837-0901.

St. Vincent de Paul Society—Rev. JOHN A. SEDLAK, Spiritual Dir., Mailing Address: St. Joseph Church, P.O. Box 3, Everson, 15631. Tel: 724-887-6714.

Bishop's Delegate—Rev. Msgr. LAWRENCE T. PERSICO, J.C.L., V.G Tel: 724-837-0901, Ext. 221. Email: lpersico@dioceseofgreensburg.org.

Victim Assistance Coordinators—Rev. Msgr. RAYMOND E. RIFFLE, M.S.W., M.P.A.; Dr. PAUL NIEMIEC. Tel: 724-837-1840.

CLERGY, PARISHES, MISSIONS AND PAROCHIAL SCHOOLS

CITY OF GREENSBURG

(WESTMORELAND COUNTY)

1—BLESSED SACRAMENT CATHEDRAL, [CEM] Rev. Msgr. Roger A. Statnick; Rev. William G. Berkey; Sandi Kocian, Coord. Social & Care Ministries; Susan Gimigliano, Dir. Business Svcs.; John Sittard, Dir. Liturgy & Music.
Res.: 300 N. Main St., 15601. Tel: 724-834-3710; Fax: 724-834-1518.
See Aquinas Academy, Greensburg under Elementary Schools, Inter-Parochial located in the Institution section.
Catechesis/Religious Program—Sara Thomas, C.R.E.; Kathi Probo, Dir. Faith Formation. Students 317.

2—ST. BRUNO Revs. Martin R. Bartel, O.S.B.; Alan N. Polczynski, Parochial Vicar.
Res.: 1715 Poplar St., 15601. Tel: 724-836-0690; Fax: 724-834-9980.
See Aquinas Academy, Greensburg under Elementary Schools, Inter-Parochial located in the Institution section.
Catechesis/Religious Program—Tel: 724-836-0690, Ext. 11; Fax: 724-834-9980. Christine Gannon, D.R.E. Students 113.

3—OUR LADY OF GRACE Rev. Msgr. Raymond E. Riffle; Hollie Uccellini, Pastoral Min.; Greg Petrucci, Dir. Faith Formation; Marisa Cazden, Music Min. In Res., Rev. Larry J. Kulick.
Res.: 1011 Mount Pleasant Rd., 15601. Tel: 724-838-9480; Fax: 724-838-1842.
See Aquinas Academy, Greensburg under Elementary Schools, Inter-Parochial located in the Institution section.
Catechesis/Religious Program—Tel: 724-832-6730. Students 377.

4—ST. PAUL Rev. Thomas A. Federline. In Res., Rev. Msgr. William R. Rathgeb.
Res.: 820 Carbon Rd., 15601. Tel: 724-834-6880; Fax: 724-834-1492.
See Aquinas Academy, Greensburg under Elementary Schools, Inter-Parochial located in the Institution section.
Catechesis/Religious Program—Students 166.

OUTSIDE THE CITY OF GREENSBURG

APOLLO, ARMSTRONG CO., ST. JAMES THE GREATER Rev. John T. Euker.
Res.: 109 Owens View Rd., 15613. Tel: 724-478-4958.
Catechesis/Religious Program—Megan Krachanko, Rel. Educ. Coord. Students 53.

ARNOLD, WESTMORELAND CO., ALL SAINTS, (Slovak), Closed. For inquiries for parish records, see St. Joseph, New Kensington.

AVONMORE, WESTMORELAND CO., ST. AMBROSE Rev. Salvatore R. Lamendola.
Res.: 505 Cambria Ave., P.O. Box 617, 15618. Tel: 724-697-4129; Fax: 724-697-4484.
Catechesis/Religious Program—Grace Sikora, D.R.E. Students 46.

BELLE VERNON, WESTMORELAND CO., ST. SEBASTIAN Rev. Lawrence L. Manchas.
801 Broad Ave., 15012.
Res.: 712 Henry St., 15012. Tel: 724-929-9300; Fax: 724-930-7611.
School—815 Broad Ave., 15012. Tel: 724-929-5143; Fax: 724-929-3038. Mr. Steven J. Dorko, Prin. Lay Teachers 21; Students 242.
Catechesis/Religious Program—Mr. Scott J. Martin, D.R.E. Students 133.

BLAIRSVILLE, INDIANA CO., SS. SIMON AND JUDE Rev. Chester J. Raimer.
Res.: 155 N. Brady St., 15717. Tel: 724-459-7103; Fax: 724-459-5314.
Catechesis/Religious Program—Becky Feldbusch, D.R.E. Students 69.

BOVARD, WESTMORELAND CO., ST. BEDE, Closed. For inquiries for parish records, see Blessed Sacrament Cathedral, Greensburg.

BRADY'S BEND, ARMSTRONG CO., ST. PATRICK, [CEM 2] Rev. Ronald L. Cyktor Jr.
Res.: 915 State Rte. 68, 16028. Tel: 724-526-5079; Fax: 724-526-3028.
Catechesis/Religious Program—Mrs. Margaret Craig, C.R.E. (PreK-6th); Mrs. Mary Anne Seybert, C.R.E. (Grades 7-12). Students 83.
Chapel—Sugar Creek, Chapel of St. Patrick, Brady's Bend [CEM]

BROWNSVILLE, FAYETTE CO.
1—ST. MARY, (Slovak), [CEM] Closed. For inquiries for parish records please see St. Peter Parish.
2—ST. PETER, [CEM 2] Rev. Vincent J. Gigliotti.
Office: 118 Church St., 15417.
Church: 300 Shaffner Ave., 15417.
Res.: 304 Shaffner Ave., 15417. Tel: 724-785-7781; Fax: 724-785-0844.
Catechesis/Religious Program—Anita Lamendola, D.R.E. Students 77.

CADOGAN, ARMSTRONG CO., ST. LAWRENCE, [CEM] Rev. Bryan F. Summers, C.O., Admin.; Deacon F. William Frescura.
Res.: 736 Fifth Ave., Ford City, 16226. Tel: 724-763-1196.
Church: 114 Main St., P.O. Box 114, 16212.
Catechesis/Religious Program—Tel: 724-763-7973. Patricia Shevchuk, D.R.E. Students 81.
Chapel—Nicholson Run, Guardian Angel Cemetery and Chapel

CALUMET, WESTMORELAND CO., ST. STANISLAUS, (Polish), [CEM] Closed. For inquiries for parish records, see Saint Florian, United.

CARDALE, FAYETTE CO., MADONNA OF CZESTOCHOWA, (Polish), [CEM] Rev. Stephen R. Bugay, Admin.
Res.: 1043 Main St., Republic, 15475. Tel: 724-246-9639; Fax: 724-246-8081. In Res., Rev. James W. Clark.
Catechesis/Religious Program—Kathleen Dunlevy, D.R.E. Students 20.

CLYMER, INDIANA CO., CHURCH OF THE RESURRECTION, [CEM] Very Rev. Paul A. Lisik; Revs. Timothy J. Kruthaupt; Rudolph J. Koser.
Administration Center—349 Morris St., 15728-1266. Tel: 724-254-3041; Fax: 724-254-3045.
Catechesis/Religious Program—Students 113.
Chapel—Camerons Bottom, Chapel of Church of the Resurrection, Clymer, Suppressed June 21, 1995.

CONNELLSVILLE, FAYETTE CO.
1—HOLY TRINITY, (Polish), [CEM] Closed. For inquiries for parish records, see Immaculate Conception, Connellsville.
2—IMMACULATE CONCEPTION, [CEM 5] Rev. Joseph E. Bonafed; Deacon William J. Hisker.
Res.: 148 E. Crawford Ave., 15425. Tel: 724-628-6840 (Bus. Office); Fax: 724-628-0838.
See Conn-Area Catholic School, Connellsville under Elementary Schools, Inter-Parochial located in the Institution section.
Catechesis/Religious Program—Sr. Mary Agnes Kirsch, S.C., D.R.E. Students 63.
Chapel—Dawson, Sacred Heart Chapel, Suppressed April 16, 2007.
3—ST. JOHN THE EVANGELIST, (Slovak), [CEM] Rev. Joseph E. Bonafed, Admin.; Deacon William J. Hisker. In Res., Rev. Dennis A. Bogusz.
Res.: 908 W. Crawford Ave., 15425. Tel: 724-628-6840.
See Conn-Area Catholic School, Connellsville under Elementary Schools, Inter-Parochial located in the Institution section.
Catechesis/Religious Program—Students 43.
4—ST. RITA, (Italian), [CEM] Rev. Joseph E. Bonafed, Admin.; Deacon William J. Hisker.
Partner Parishes Offices: 116 S. Second St., 15425. Tel: 724-628-6840.
See Conn-Area Catholic School, Connellsville under Elementary Schools, Inter-Parochial located in the Institution section.
Catechesis/Religious Program—Tel: 724-628-0979. Students 66.

CORAL, INDIANA CO.
1—ST. FRANCIS, [CEM] Merged with St. Louis, Lucernemines to form Our Lady of the Assumption, Coral.
2—OUR LADY OF THE ASSUMPTION Rev. Terry A. Hercik; Sr. Donna Mulligan, Pastoral Min.
Res.: 403 Lucerne Rd., Lucerne, 15754. Tel: 724-479-0983.
Church: 2434 Neal Rd., P.O. Box G, 15731. Tel: 724-479-9542; Fax: 724-479-1130.
Catechesis/Religious Program—Donna Mulligan, D.R.E. Students 157.

CRABTREE, WESTMORELAND CO., ST. BARTHOLOMEW, [CEM] Rev. Leon Hont, O.S.B.
Res.: 2538 State Rte. 119, P.O. Box A, 15624. Tel: 724-834-0709; Fax: 724-832-3768.
Catechesis/Religious Program—Eric Kocian, D.R.E. Students 57.

DELMONT, WESTMORELAND CO., ST. JOHN BAPTIST DE LA SALLE Rev. Michael P. Sikon.
Res.: 497 Athena Dr., 15626. Tel: 724-468-4221; Fax: 724-468-6206.
Catechesis/Religious Program—Sr. Georgia Litzenberg, S.C., Pastoral Min. Students 73.

DERRY, WESTMORELAND CO., ST. JOSEPH, [CEM] Rev. Stephen C. West.
Rectory—117 S. Ligonier St., 15627. Tel: 724-694-5359; Fax: 724-694-6215.
Catechesis/Religious Program—Betty Wechtenhiser, D.R.E. Students 34.

DONEGAL, WESTMORELAND CO., ST. RAYMOND OF THE MOUNTAINS, [CEM] Rev. Anthony W. Ditto.
Res.: 170 School House Ln., P.O. Box 330, 15628. Tel: 724-593-7479; Fax: 724-593-5934.
Catechesis/Religious Program—Toni T. Terretti, D.R.E. Students 68.

DUNBAR, FAYETTE CO., ST. ALOYSIUS, [CEM] Rev. Msgr. J. Edward McCullough.
Res.: 459 Ranch Rd., 15431. Tel: 724-277-4236; Fax: 724-277-0192.
Catechesis/Religious Program—Jane Laurion, D.R.E. Students 81.

EAST VANDERGRIFT, WESTMORELAND CO., OUR LADY, QUEEN OF PEACE Rev. John T. Euker, Admin. In Res., Rev. Michael J. Sciberras.
Res.: 400 Kennedy Ave., P.O. Box 429, 15629. Tel: 724-567-7603; Fax: 724-568-3365.
Catechesis/Religious Program—Fax: 724-568-3365. Carol Hollenbaugh, D.R.E. Students 45.

ERNEST, INDIANA CO., CHURCH OF THE ASSUMPTION, Closed. For inquiries for parish records contact Church of the Resurrection, Clymer.

EVERSON, FAYETTE CO., ST. JOSEPH, (Polish), [CEM] Rev. John A. Sedlak.
Mailing Address: P.O. Box 3, 15631.
Res.: 201 Painter St., 15631. Tel: 724-887-6714; Fax: 724-887-8180.
Catechesis/Religious Program—Students 52.

EXPORT, WESTMORELAND CO., ST. MARY Rev. Michael P. Sikon, Admin.; Maureen Wygonik, Dir. Liturgy & Music.
Res.: 5900 Kennedy Ave., 15632. Tel: 724-327-0647; Fax: 724-325-3784.
Catechesis/Religious Program—Tel: 724-733-4976. Students 75.

FAIRCHANCE, FAYETTE CO., SS. CYRIL AND METHODIUS, [CEM] Rev. Andrew M. Kawecki.
Res.: 50 Morgantown St., 15436. Tel: 724-564-7436; Fax: 724-564-7435.
Catechesis/Religious Program—Tel: 724-438-5271. Rita Kennison, C.R.E. Students 15.
Chapel—Shoaf, Chapel of SS. Cyril & Methodius, Fairchance, Suppressed Oct. 1, 2007.

FARMINGTON, FAYETTE CO., ST. JOAN OF ARC, [CEM] Rev. James L. Popochock.
Res.: 3521 National Pike, P.O. Box 92, 15437. Tel: 724-329-4522; Fax: 724-329-4955.
Catechesis/Religious Program—Mary Judd, D.R.E. Students 39.

FAYETTE CITY, FAYETTE CO., HOLY SPIRIT, Closed. For inquiries for parish records, see Saint Sebastian, Belle Vernon.

FOOTEDALE, FAYETTE CO., ST. THOMAS, (Polish), [CEM] Rev. Peter L. Peretti, Admin.
Res.: 528 Footedale Rd., P.O. Box 547, New Salem, 15468. Tel: 724-245-9244; Fax: 724-245-9289.
Catechesis/Religious Program—Students 40.

FORBES ROAD, WESTMORELAND CO., ST. MARY, Closed. For inquiries for parish records, see St. Bartholomew, Crabtree.

FORD CITY, ARMSTRONG CO.
1—CHRIST, PRINCE OF PEACE PARISH Rev. Thomas S. Trupkovich.
718 Fourth Ave., 16226.
Res.: 736 Fifth Ave., 16226. Tel: 724-763-9141; Fax: 724-763-9142.
Catechesis/Religious Program—Tel: 724-763-2521. Joann Kochman, D.R.E. Students 59.
2—ST. FRANCIS OF PAOLA, (Polish), Merged with St. Mary and Holy Trinity, Ford City to form Christ, Prince of Peace Parish, Ford City.
3—HOLY TRINITY, (Slovak), Merged St. Mary and St. Francis of Paola, Ford City to form Christ, Prince of Peace Parish, Ford City.
4—ST. MARY, Merged with St. Francis of Paola and Holy Trinity, Ford City to form Christ, Prince of Peace Parish, Ford City.

FREEPORT, ARMSTRONG CO., ST. MARY, [CEM] Rev. Edward Volz, O.S.P.P.E.
Res.: 608 High St., 16229. Tel: 724-295-2281; Fax: 724-295-3090.
Catechesis/Religious Program—610 High St., 16229. Students 168.

GLEN CAMPBELL, INDIANA CO., ST. MICHAEL, Closed. For inquiries for parish records contact Church of the Resurrection, Clymer.

GRINDSTONE, FAYETTE CO., ST. CECILIA, (Slovak), Rev. Vincent J. Gigliotti, Admin.
Mailing Address: P.O. Box 251, Smock, 15480. Tel: 724-785-7781; Fax: 724-785-0844.
Catechesis/Religious Program—Anita Lamendola, D.R.E. Students 5.

HARRISON CITY, WESTMORELAND CO., ST. BARBARA, [CEM] Very Rev. Kenneth G. Zaccagnini; Rev. Douglas E. Dorula.
Mailing Address: 111 Raymaley Rd., 15636.
Res.: 91 Raymaley Rd., 15636. Tel: 724-744-7474; Fax: 724-744-3056.
Catechesis/Religious Program—Tel: 724-744-4885. Kenneth M. Meyer, D.R.E. Students 603.

HEILWOOD, INDIANA CO., ST. JOHN THE BAPTIST, Closed. For inquiries for parish records contact Church of the Resurrection, Clymer.

HERMINIE, WESTMORELAND CO., ST. EDWARD Rev. John J. Harrold.
Res.: 120 St. Edward Ln., 15637. Tel: 724-446-5197; Fax: 724-446-1433.
Catechesis/Religious Program—Mrs. Kathleen Topolosky, D.R.E. Students 169.

INDIANA, INDIANA CO.
1—ST. BERNARD, [CEM] Rev. William J. Kiel.
Res.: 200 Clairvaux Dr., 15701. Tel: 724-465-2210; Fax: 724-465-0422.
School—300 Clairvaux Dr., 15701. Tel: 724-465-7139; Fax: 724-465-0803. Denise Swope, Prin. Lay Teachers 12; Students 116.
Catechesis/Religious Program—Tel: 724-349-9145. Students 159.
2—ST. THOMAS MORE UNIVERSITY PARISH, (Newman Center) Rev. William J. Lechnar; Lynne Jones, Coord. Liturgy & Music; Bill Mrozowski, Business & Office Mgr.; Cindy Schillinger, Pastoral Assoc.
Catechesis/Religious Program—Patty DeBiasio, Dir. Camp Ministry & Faith Formation. Students 156.
Indiana University of PA—1200 Oakland Ave., 15701. Tel: 724-463-2277; Fax: 724-463-7116.

IRWIN, WESTMORELAND CO., IMMACULATE CONCEPTION, [CEM] Rev. John A. Moineau.
Res.: 308 Second St., 15642. Tel: 724-863-9550; Fax: 724-863-9552.
See Queen of Angels Regional Catholic School, under Elementary Schools, Inter-Parochial located in the Institution section.
Catechesis/Religious Program—Ginny McConnell, D.R.E. Students 345.

ISELIN, INDIANA CO., HOLY CROSS, Closed. For inquiries for parish records contact Church of the Good Shepherd, Kent.

JEANNETTE, WESTMORELAND CO.
1—ASCENSION, (Italian), Rev. John M. Foriska, Admin.
Res.: 615 Division St., 15644. Tel: 724-523-6567; 724-523-6568; Fax: 724-523-5199.
504 Cowan Ave., 15644. Tel: 724-523-2560.
Catechesis/Religious Program—John Ridilla, D.R.E. Students 80.
2—SACRED HEART, [CEM] Rev. John M. Foriska.
Office: 504 Cowan Ave., 15644. Tel: 724-523-2560; Fax: 724-523-9400.
Catechesis/Religious Program—Students 116.

KENT, INDIANA CO., CHURCH OF THE GOOD SHEPHERD Rev. Charles P. Esposito.
Res.: 100 Good Shepherd Dr., P.O. Box 99, 15752. Tel: 724-479-3881; Fax: 724-479-3882.
Catechesis/Religious Program—Mrs. Denise Pencola, Coord. Faith Formation; Mrs. Ella Zagurskie, Coord. Faith Formation. Students 133.

KITTANNING, ARMSTRONG CO., ST. MARY, OUR LADY OF GUADALUPE, [CEM] Rev. Daniel L. Blout; Deacon F. Daniel Frescura.
Office: 348 N. Water St., 16201.
Res.: 101 W. High St., 16201. Tel: 724-548-7649; Fax: 724-543-2938.
Catechesis/Religious Program—Sr. Mary Hall, C.S.J., D.R.E. Students 104.

LATROBE, WESTMORELAND CO.
1—ST. BONIFACE, (Chestnut Ridge) Rev. Anthony W. Ditto, Admin. Tel: 724-593-7479.
Res.: c/o 170 School House Ln., P.O. Box 330, Donegal, 15628. Tel: 724-593-7479.
See Christ the Divine Teacher School, Latrobe under Elementary Schools, Inter-Parochial located in the Institution section.
Catechesis/Religious Program—Fax: 724-593-5934. Toni T. Terretti, D.R.E. Students 68.
2—HOLY FAMILY, [CEM] Very Rev. Daniel C. Mahoney.
Res.: 1200 Ligonier St., 15650. Tel: 724-539-9751; Fax: 724-539-8044.
See Christ the Divine Teacher School, Latrobe under Elementary Schools, Inter-Parochial located in the Institution section.
Catechesis/Religious Program—Tel: 724-539-3638. Elizabeth Wechtenhiser, D.R.E. Students 90.
3—ST. JOHN THE EVANGELIST Rev. Anthony J. Carbone.
Res.: 306 St. John Dr., 15650. Tel: 724-537-8909; Fax: 724-537-2788.
See Christ the Divine Teacher School, Latrobe under Elementary Schools, Inter-Parochial located in the Institution section.
Catechesis/Religious Program—Erin Colcombe, D.R.E. Students 52.
4—ST. ROSE, [CEM] Rev. William P. Donahue.
Res.: 4969 Rte. 982, 15650. Tel: 724-537-3709.
See Christ the Divine Teacher School, Latrobe under Elementary Schools, Inter-Parochial located in the Institution section.
Catechesis/Religious Program—Eva Japalucci, D.R.E. Students 63.
5—ST. VINCENT BASILICA, [CEM] Revs. Thomas P. Curry, O.S.B.; Daniel Paul O'Keefe, O.S.B.

Res.: 300 Fraser Purchase Rd., 15650. Tel: 724-539-8629; Fax: 724-539-3810.
See Christ the Divine Teacher School, Latrobe under Elementary Schools, Inter-Parochial located in the Institution section.
Catechesis/Religious Program—Tel: 724-539-8629, Ext. 16. Darlene Argall, D.R.E. Students 208.

LECKRONE, FAYETTE CO., OUR LADY OF PERPETUAL HELP (ST. MARY), [CEM] Rev. John M. Butler.
Res.: 304 Leckrone High House Rd., P.O. Box 248, 15454. Tel: 724-737-5736; Fax: 724-737-1042.
Catechesis/Religious Program—Anita Olesh, D.R.E. Students 12.

LEECHBURG, ARMSTRONG CO.
1—ST. CATHERINE OF ALEXANDRIA, Closed. For inquiries for parish records contact Christ the King, Leechburg.
2—CHRIST THE KING, [CEM] Rev. Joseph V. Trupkovich.
Administrative Center—630 Second St., 15656. Tel: 724-845-8191; 724-842-1791; Fax: 724-845-5480.
Catechesis/Religious Program—Jim Peterman, D.R.E. Students 57.
3—CHURCH OF THE ASSUMPTION, Closed. For inquiries for parish records contact Christ the King, Leechburg.
4—ST. MARTHA, (Slovak), Closed. For inquiries for parish records contact Christ the King, Leechburg.

LEISENRING, FAYETTE CO., ST. VINCENT DE PAUL, [CEM] Closed. For inquiries for parish records, see Saint Aloysius, Dunbar.

LIGONIER, WESTMORELAND CO., HOLY TRINITY, [CEM] Rev. Msgr. William G. Charnoki; Mrs. Carol A. Serafin, Pastoral Assoc.
Res.: 342 W. Main St., 15658. Tel: 724-238-6434; Fax: 724-238-6688.
School—327 W. Vincent St., 15658. Tel: 724-238-6430; Fax: 724-238-6402. Mrs. Barbara Sabo, Prin. Lay Teachers 11; Students 103.
Catechesis/Religious Program—Tel: 724-238-6341. Students 56.

LOWER BURRELL, WESTMORELAND CO., ST. MARGARET MARY Rev. Msgr. James T. Gaston; Mr. John Kane, Coord. Ministry.
Mailing Address: 3055 Leechburg Rd., 15068. Tel: 724-335-2336; Fax: 724-335-1945.
Res.: 231 Park Dr., 15068.
Catechesis/Religious Program—Joan Duncan, Dir. Faith Formation. Students 466.

LUCERNEMINES, INDIANA CO., ST. LOUIS, [CEM] Merged with St. Francis, Coral to form Our Lady of the Assumption, Coral.

MARGUERITE, WESTMORELAND CO., ST. BENEDICT Revs. Martin R. Bartel, O.S.B., Admin.; Alan N. Polczynski, Parochial Vicar.
Mailing Address: 260 Bruno Rd., 15601. Tel: 724-834-9045; Fax: 724-834-1880.
Res.: 1715 Poplar St., 15601.
Catechesis/Religious Program—Tel: 724-537-9750; 724-837-8473; Fax: 724-537-9750. Lynette DiDonato, D.R.E. Students 70.

MASONTOWN, FAYETTE CO., ALL SAINTS, [CEM] Rev. John M. Butler.
Res.: 101 W. Church Ave., 15461. Tel: 724-583-7866; Fax: 724-583-0373.
School—100 S. Washington St., 15461. Tel: 724-583-2141; Fax: 724-583-2141. Mr. Steven J. Dorko, Prin. Lay Teachers 8; Students 70.
Catechesis/Religious Program—Ms. Wanda Wokulich, D.R.E. Students 45.
Chapel—McClellandtown, Chapel of All Saints, Masontown

MAXWELL, FAYETTE CO., ST. JAMES, Closed. For inquiries for parish records, see Saint Peter, Brownsville.

MONESSEN, WESTMORELAND CO., THE EPIPHANY OF OUR LORD, [CEM 2] Rev. David Nazimek.
Res.: 618 Knox Ave., 15062. Tel: 724-684-7661; Fax: 724-684-8981.
Catechesis/Religious Program—Mr. Scott J. Martin, D.R.E. Students 25.

MOUNT PLEASANT, WESTMORELAND CO.
1—ST. PIUS X, [CEM] Rev. Richard J. Kosisko; Cindy Copeland, Pastoral Assoc.
Res.: 216 Spruce St., 15666. Tel: 724-547-1911; Fax: 724-547-2630.
Catechesis/Religious Program—Students 66.
2—TRANSFIGURATION, (Polish), [CEM] Closed. For inquiries for parish records contact the chancery.
3—VISITATION OF THE BLESSED VIRGIN MARY, (Slovak), [CEM] Rev. Richard J. Kosisko, Admin.
Mailing Address: 740 Walnut St., 15666. Tel: 724-547-1911; Fax: 724-547-2630.
Res.: 216 Spruce St., 15666.
Catechesis/Religious Program—Students 50.

MURRYSVILLE, WESTMORELAND CO., MOTHER OF SORROWS Revs. Thaddeus J. Kaczmarek; Thomas S. Trupkovich.
Res.: 4202 Old William Penn Hwy., 15668. Tel: 724-733-8870; Fax: 724-733-8108. Email: pastoralcenter2@mosparish.org. Web: www.mosparish.org.
School—3264 Evergreen Dr., 15668. Tel: 724-733-8840; Fax: 724-325-1144. Email: jrice@mosschool.org. Web: www.mosschool.org. Joseph J. Rice, Prin. Lay Teachers 21; Students 280.
Catechesis/Religious Program—Jason Stanislaw, D.R.E. Tel: 724-733-1887. Students 575.

NEW ALEXANDRIA, WESTMORELAND CO., ST. JAMES Rev. Msgr. Lawrence T. Persico.
Res.: 306 Saint James Ln., 15670. Tel: 724-668-2829; Fax: 724-668-7327.
Catechesis/Religious Program—William J. D'Angelo, D.R.E. Students 31.

NEW DERRY, WESTMORELAND CO., ST. MARTIN, [CEM] Rev. Stephen C. West, Admin.
Res.: 5684 Rte. 982, 15671-1008. Tel: 724-694-5716; Fax: 724-694-5716.
Catechesis/Religious Program—Betty Wechtenhiser, D.R.E. Students 9.

NEW KENSINGTON, WESTMORELAND CO.
1—ST. JOSEPH Revs. Richard P. Karenbauer; Alan W. Grote, Parochial Vicar.
Res.: 1125 Leishman Ave., 15068. Tel: 724-337-6412; Fax: 724-337-4022.
See Mary Queen of Apostles, New Kensington, located under Inter-Parochial Schools in the Institution Section.
Catechesis/Religious Program—Mrs. Denise Pencola, Dir. Min.
2—ST. MARY OF CZESTOCHOWA, (Polish), [CEM] Revs. Richard P. Karenbauer, Admin.; Alan W. Grote, Parochial Vicar; Sr. Mary Carol Kardell, C.S.S.F., Pastoral Min.
Res.: 857 Kenneth Ave., 15068. Tel: 724-335-8212; Fax: 724-335-1314.
Catechesis/Religious Program—Deborah Discello, D.R.E. Students 95.
3—MT. ST. PETER, (Italian), Rev. Msgr. Michael J. Begolly.
Res.: 100 Freeport Rd., 15068. Tel: 724-335-9877; Fax: 724-335-9138.
Catechesis/Religious Program—Sisters Susan Jenny, S.C., Faith First Coord.; Valerie Zottola, Coord. Youth & Young Adult Ministry. Students 210.

NEW SALEM, FAYETTE CO., ST. PROCOPIUS, [CEM] Rev. Peter L. Peretti.
Res.: 20 Church St., P.O. Box 547, 15468. Tel: 724-245-9244; Fax: 724-245-9289.
Catechesis/Religious Program—Students 49.

NORTH HUNTINGDON, WESTMORELAND CO.
1—ST. AGNES Rev. Msgr. V. Paul Fitzmaurice.
Res.: 11400 St. Agnes Ln., 15642. Tel: 724-863-2626; 724-863-2630; Fax: 724-863-1057.
See Queen of Angels Regional Catholic School, North Huntingdon under Elementary Schools, Inter-Parochial located in the Institution section.
Catechesis/Religious Program—Tel: 724-864-5393. Mary Blythe, D.R.E. Students 293.
2—ST. ELIZABETH ANN SETON Rev. Leonard W. Stoviak.
Res.: 200 Leger Rd., 15642. Tel: 724-864-6364; Fax: 724-864-4580.
Catechesis/Religious Program—Sr. Charlene Ozanick, C.S.S.F., D.R.E. Students 205.

PALMER, FAYETTE CO., ST. ALBERT, Closed. For inquiries for parish records, see St. Mary, Our Lady of Perpetual Help, Leckrone.

PARKER, ARMSTRONG CO., ST. MARY, OUR LADY OF THE SNOWS, Closed. For inquiries for parish records, see Saint Patrick, Brady's Bend.

PENN, WESTMORELAND CO., ST. BONIFACE, [CEM] Closed. For inquiries for parish records, see Sacred Heart, Jeannette.

PERRYOPOLIS, FAYETTE CO., ST. JOHN THE BAPTIST, [CEM] Rev. Robert T. Lubic.
Res.: P.O. Box 606, 15473. Tel: 724-736-4442; Fax: 724-736-8403.
Catechesis/Religious Program—Tel: 724-736-0158; Fax: 724-736-0158. Sr. Loretta Topper, D.R.E. Students 120.

POINT MARION, FAYETTE CO., ST. HUBERT Rev. Andrew M. Kawecki, Admin.
Res.: c/o 50 N. Morgantown St., Fairchance, 15436. Tel: 724-725-3655; Fax: 724-564-7435.
Catechesis/Religious Program—Students 6.

REPUBLIC, FAYETTE CO., HOLY ROSARY, [CEM] Rev. Stephen R. Bugay.
Res.: 1043 Main St., P.O. Box 400, 15475. Tel: 724-246-9639; Fax: 724-246-8081.
Catechesis/Religious Program—Kathleen Dunlevy, D.R.E. Students 44.

ROSSITER, INDIANA CO., ST. FRANCIS OF ASSISI, Closed. For inquiries for parish records contact the Church of the Resurrection, Clymer.

ROSTRAVER, WESTMORELAND CO., ST. ANNE Rev. Ronald L. Simboli.
Res.: 1870 Rostraver Rd., Belle Vernon, 15012. Tel: 724-872-3555; Fax: 724-872-3373.
Catechesis/Religious Program—Tel: 724-872-3486. Barbara Zucconi, D.R.E. Students 180.

SAGAMORE, ARMSTRONG CO., SACRED HEART, [CEM] Closed. Parish closed Oct. 1, 2007. For inquiries for parish records, see St. Mary, Yatesboro.

SALTSBURG, INDIANA CO., ST. MATTHEW, (Italian), [CEM] Rev. Salvatore R. Lamendola, Admin.
Mailing Address: 505 Cambria Ave., P.O. Box 617, Avonmore, 15618.
Res.: 505 Cambria Ave., Avonmore, 15618. Tel: 724-697-4129; Fax: 724-697-4484.
Catechesis/Religious Program—703 Indiana Ave., 15687. Students 41.

SCOTTDALE, WESTMORELAND CO., ST. JOHN THE BAPTIST, [CEM] Rev. E. George Saletrik; Sr. Susanne Chenot, O.S.B., Pastoral Assoc.
Res.: 416 S. Broadway, 15683. Tel: 724-887-6321; Fax: 724-887-6324.
School—504 S. Broadway, 15683. Tel: 724-887-9550; Fax: 724-887-9553. Dr. Joseph Dreliszak, Prin. Lay Teachers 14; Students 134.
Catechesis/Religious Program—Dr. Joseph Dreliszak, D.R.E. Students 50.
Convent—Benedictine Sisters, 408 S. Broadway, 15683. Tel: 724-887-6612.

SEWARD, WESTMORELAND CO., HOLY FAMILY, [CEM 3] Rev. Robert M. Washko.
Res.: 425 Bridge St., Box 481, 15954. Tel: 814-446-5759.
Catechesis/Religious Program—Gail Smyder, D.R.E. Students 111.

SLICKVILLE, WESTMORELAND CO., ST. SYLVESTER Rev. Salvatore R. Lamendola, Admin. In Res., Rev. James M. Goldberg, Senior Priest.
Res.: 3028 Rt. 819, Box 307, 15684. Tel: 724-468-5794; Fax: 724-468-5765.
Catechesis/Religious Program—Students 12.

SMITHTON, WESTMORELAND CO., ST. TIMOTHY, [CEM] Closed. For inquiries for parish records, see St. Ann, Rostraver.

SMOCK, FAYETTE CO., ST. HEDWIG, (Slovak), [CEM 2] Revs. Robert T. Lubic, Admin.; James F. Petrovsky, Sr. Priest.
Res.: Box 251, 15480. Tel: 724-677-2110; Fax: 724-677-0146.
Catechesis/Religious Program—Students 16.

STARFORD, INDIANA CO., ST. ELIZABETH, Closed. For inquiries for parish records contact Church of the Resurrection, Clymer.

SUTERSVILLE, WESTMORELAND CO., ST. CHARLES BORROMEO, Closed. For inquiries for parish records, see Holy Family, West Newton.

TRAFFORD, WESTMORELAND CO., ST. REGIS Rev. James D. Tringhese.
Res.: 517 Homewood Ave., 15085. Tel: 412-372-4577; Fax: 412-373-5979.
Catechesis/Religious Program—Tel: 412-372-7609. Kathy Wawrzeniak, D.R.E. Students 135.

TRAUGER, WESTMORELAND CO., FORTY MARTYRS, (Hungarian), [CEM] Closed. For inquiries for parish records, see St. Florian, United.

UNIONTOWN, FAYETTE CO.
1—ST. JOHN THE EVANGELIST Rev. Michael J. Crookston.
Res.: 50 Jefferson St., 15401. Tel: 724-437-7569; Fax: 724-437-6277.
School—52 Jefferson St., 15401. Tel: 724-438-8598; Fax: 724-438-8585. Christine Roskovensky, Prin. Lay Teachers 12; Students 208.
Catechesis/Religious Program—Students 127.
2—ST. JOSEPH, (Polish), [CEM] Rev. Alexander L. Pleban.
Res.: 180 Old Walnut Hill Rd., 15401. Tel: 724-437-3927; Fax: 724-437-5354.
Catechesis/Religious Program—Tel: 724-438-2236. Patricia Neel, D.R.E. Students 80.
3—NATIVITY OF THE BLESSED VIRGIN MARY, (Slovak), [CEM] Rev. Micah E. Kozoil; Nancy Blake, Pastoral Min.
Res.: 61 N. Mount Vernon Ave., 15401. Tel: 724-437-1513; Fax: 724-437-7482.
School—17 Gilmore St., 15401. Tel: 724-438-8471; Fax: 724-438-8338. Melvyn Sepic, Prin. Lay Teachers 12; Students 146.
Catechesis/Religious Program—Students 61.
Convent—Vincentian Sisters of Charity, 7 Gilmore St., 15401. Tel: 724-437-5478.
4—ST. THERESE, THE LITTLE FLOWER OF JESUS, (Italian), Rev. Msgr. Michael W. Matusak.
Res.: 61 Mill St., 15401. Tel: 724-438-2341; Fax: 724-438-2361.
Catechesis/Religious Program—Marlene Bandzuch, D.R.E. Students 245.

UNITED, WESTMORELAND CO., ST. FLORIAN, [CEM] Rev. William C. McGuirk.
Res.: 4261 Rt. 981, P.O. Box 187, 15689. Tel: 724-423-4431; Fax: 724-423-4438.
School—(Grades PreSchool), 4257 Rt. 981, Mount Pleasant, 15666. Tel: 724-423-4437. Lay Teachers 2; Students 30.
Catechesis/Religious Program—Toni Chovanec, D.R.E. Students 43.

VANDERGRIFT, WESTMORELAND CO., ST. GERTRUDE, [CEM] Rev. James Loew, O.S.B.

Res.: 303 Franklin Ave., 15690. Tel: 724-568-2331; Fax: 724-568-2030.
School—(Grades PreSchool-7), 315 Franklin Ave., 15690. Tel: 724-568-3304; Fax: 724-567-1900. Karen McClarnom, Prin. Lay Teachers 13; Students 122.
Catechesis/Religious Program—James Peterman, D.R.E. Students 60.

WEST NEWTON, WESTMORELAND CO., HOLY FAMILY Rev. John T. Sweeney.
Res.: 225 N. Second St., 15089. Tel: 724-872-6123; Fax: 724-872-6133.
Catechesis/Religious Program—Tel: 724-872-2106. Michalene Lovato, D.R.E. Students 86.

WHITNEY, WESTMORELAND CO., ST. CECILIA Rev. Peter Augustine H. Pierjok, O.S.B., Admin.
Res.: 218 St. Cecilia Rd., P.O. Box 80, 15693. Tel: 724-423-3777; 724-423-2289; Fax: 724-423-3778.
Catechesis/Religious Program—William Smith, C.R.E. Students 48.

YATESBORO, ARMSTRONG CO., ST. MARY, [CEM] Rev. Daniel L. Blout, Admin.; Deacon F. Daniel Frescura.
Mailing Address: 111 Second St., P.O. Box 327, 16263.
Res.: 109 Second St., P.O. Box 327, 16263. Tel: 724-783-7191; Fax: 724-783-7783.
Catechesis/Religious Program—Students 85.

YOUNGSTOWN, WESTMORELAND CO., SACRED HEART Rev. Peter Augustine H. Pierjok, O.S.B.
Res.: c/o 218 St. Cecelia Rd., P.O. Box 80, Whitney, 15693. Tel: 724-537-7358; Fax: 724-537-6988.
Catechesis/Religious Program—William Smith, C.R.E. Students 31.

YOUNGWOOD, WESTMORELAND CO., HOLY CROSS Rev. John S. Szczesny.
Res.: 711 Depot St., 15697. Tel: 724-925-7811; Fax: 724-925-6170.
Catechesis/Religious Program—Tel: 724-925-8206. Michele Ligus, D.R.E. Students 40.

YUKON, WESTMORELAND CO., SEVEN DOLORS, [CEM] Rev. Emil S. Payer.
Res.: 102 Center St., P.O. Box 308, 15698. Tel: 724-722-3141; 724-722-3150 (Hall); Fax: 724-722-3140.
Catechesis/Religious Program—Martha Hazlinsky, D.R.E. Partner Parishes of Seven Dolors & St. Timothy. Students 31.

Chaplains of Public Institutions

GREENSBURG. *Excela Health - Westmoreland Hospital*, Tel: 724-832-4000; 724-832-4447 (Chaplain's Office). Revs. Jacques de Paul Daley, O.S.B., Chap., Robert R. Byrnes, Assoc. Chap., Justin Withrow, O.S.B., Assoc. Chap.

BROWNSVILLE. *Brownsville General Hospital*. Attended by St. Peter, Brownsville, Tel: 724-785-7200; 724-785-7781 (Res.).

CONNELLSVILLE. *Highlands Hospital & Health Center*, Tel: 724-628-1500. Rev. Dennis A. Bogusz, Chap. Tel: 724-626-0736.

INDIANA. *Indiana Hospital*, Tel: 724-465-7000. Rev. Timothy J. Kruthaupt, Chap. Tel: 724-254-3041. Attended by St. Bernard, Indiana, Tel: 724-465-3900 (Hospital); 724-254-3041 (Res.).

KITTANNING. *Armstrong County Hospital*, Tel: 724-543-8500. Rev. Raphael K. Glinkowski, O.S.P.P.E., Chap. Tel: 724-763-1375 (Res.).

LATROBE. *Excela Health - Latrobe Area Hospital*, Tel: 724-537-1000. Revs. Justin Withrow, O.S.B., Assoc. Chap. Tel: 734-532-6600, John Mary Tompkins, O.S.B., Assoc. Chap. Tel: 724-532-6600 (Res.).

MOUNT PLEASANT. *Frick Community Health Center*, Tel: 724-547-1500 (Hospital). Rev. Dennis A. Bogusz, Chap. Tel: 724-626-0736.

NEW KENSINGTON. *Citizens General Hospital*, Tel: 724-337-3541. Attended by St. Mary, New Kensington, Tel: 724-335-8212 (Res.); St. Joseph, New Kensington, Tel: 724-337-6412 (Res.); Mount St. Peter, New Kensington, Tel: 724-335-9877 (Res.).

TORRANCE. *Torrance State Hospital*, Tel: 724-459-8000. Rev. Chester J. Raimer, Chap. Tel: 724-459-7103 (Res.).

UNIONTOWN. *Uniontown Hospital*, Tel: 724-430-5000 (Res.); 724-246-9657. Rev. James W. Clark, Chap. Tel: 724-246-9657.

On Duty Outside the Diocese:
Rev.—
Wisneski, Jonathan J., DeSales Hall, Catholic University of America, 721 Lawrence St. NE, Washington, DC 20017.

Retired:
Rev. Msgrs.—
Conway, John L., V.F., St. Margaret Mary Church, 3055 Leechburg Rd., Lower Burrell, 15068.
McCarren, Stephen A., 307 Avenue of Dukes, Nokomis, FL 34275.
Revs.—
Bratus, Walter N., 723 E. Pittsburgh St., 15601.
Bucci, Michael J., 1319 Walnut St., South Connellsville, 15425.
Cheatham, Louis W., Neumann House, 2900 Seminary Dr., 15601.
Dylag, Michael R., 1 Kenberton Dr., Pleasant Ridge, MI 48069.
Higgins, Edward F., Neumann House, 2900 Seminary Dr., 15601.
Kacinko, Elmer A., 1987 Centurion Dr., Apt. 601, Pittsburgh, 15221.
Lukac, Thomas M., St. Anne Home, 685 Angela Dr., 15601.
Mandock, Patrick H., P.O. Box 497, Elephant Butte, NM 87935.
Minsterman, Joseph, 510 S. Chestnut St., Scottdale, 15683.
Murphy, Harry J., 203 Nazareth House-St. Michael's, 6333 Rancho Mission Rd., San Diego, CA 92108-2099.
O'Connor, Patrick J., Villa Anyela, 685 Anyela Dr., 15601.
Rutkowski, Ronald J., 231 Rocky Branch Rd., Blountville, TN 37617.
Sweeney, Denis, 900 Washington Rd., Apt. 105, Pittsburgh, 15228.
Trongo, Nicholas M., 207 N. Hamilton Ave., 15601.
Weiksner, Jerome M., P.O. Box 667, New Smyrna Beach, FL 32170-0667.
Whalen, Paul A., Villa Anyela, 685 Anyela Dr, 15601.

INSTITUTIONS LOCATED IN THE DIOCESE

[A] SEMINARIES, RELIGIOUS OR SCHOLASTICATES

LATROBE. *St. Vincent Seminary*, 300 Fraser Purchase Rd., 15650. Tel: 724-805-2592; Fax: 724-532-5052. Email: justin.matro@email.stvincent.edu. Web: www.benedictine.stvincent.edu/seminary. Very Rev. Justin M. Matro, O.S.B., Rector; Revs. Matthias Martinez, O.S.B., Asst. to Rector & Dean of Students; Lester Knoll, O.F.M.Cap, Dir. Spiritual Formation; Cyprian G. Constantine, O.S.B., Liturgy Director; David Brzoska (CHL), Vice Rector & Dir. of Pastoral Formation; Patrick T. Cronauer, O.S.B., Dir. Rel. Ordination Students; Bro. David Kelly, O.S.B., Dir. Library; Dr. Michel Therrien, S.T.D., Academic Dean; Ms. Denise A. Hegeman, Lattimer Family Library Public Svcs. Librarian. Professors 28; Lay Students 11; Seminarians 76; Benedictines 23; Other Religious 2.

[B] COLLEGES AND UNIVERSITIES

GREENSBURG. *Seton Hill University* 15601. Tel: 724-834-2200; Fax: 724-830-4611. Email: admit@setonhill.edu. Web: www.setonhill.edu. Dr. JoAnne W. Boyle, Pres.; Mary Ann Gawelek, Ed.D., Provost & Dean of Faculty; Mr. David Stanely, Librarian. Sisters of Charity of Seton Hill. Sisters 3; Lay Teachers 75; Students 1,946.

LATROBE. *Saint Vincent College*, 300 Fraser Purchase Rd., 15650-2690. Tel: 724-532-6600; Fax: 724-537-4587. Rt. Rev. Douglas R. Nowicki, O.S.B., Chancellor; H. James Towey, Pres.; Bros. Norman W. Hipps, O.S.B., Exec. Vice Pres.; David Kelly, O.S.B., Dir. of Libraries.
Saint Vincent College Corporation Priests 18; Brothers 7; Lay Teachers 98; Students 1,984.

[C] HIGH SCHOOLS, DIOCESAN

GREENSBURG. *Greensburg Central Catholic High School*, 911 Armory Dr., 15601. Tel: 724-834-0310; Fax: 724-834-2472. Email: info@gcchs.org. Web: www.gcchs.org. Rev. Alan N. Polczynski, Chap. & Rel. Instructor; Mr. Donald M. Favero, Prin.; Carol Whalen, Librarian. Priests 1; Sisters 2; Lay Teachers 37; Students 499.

CONNELLSVILLE. *Geibel Catholic (Middle-High School)*, 611 E. Crawford Ave., 15425. Tel: 724-628-5600; Fax: 724-626-5700. Web: www.geibelcatholic.org. Rev. Robert T. Lubic, Chap. & Rel. Instructor; Mr. John J. Lipchik, Prin. Priests 1; Lay Teachers 18; Students 201.

[D] ELEMENTARY SCHOOLS, INTER-PAROCHIAL

GREENSBURG. *Aquinas Academy*, (Grades PreK-8), 340 N. Main St., 15601. Tel: 724-834-7940; Fax: 724-836-0497. Email: info@aquinasacademy.org. Mrs. Cherie L. Rullo, M.Ed, Prin.; Mr. Daniel Mahoney, Vice Prin.; Mrs. Michelle Finoli, Librarian. Lay Teachers 31; Students 381.

CONNELLSVILLE. *Conn-Area Catholic School*, 110 N. Prospect St., 15425. Tel: 724-628-5090; Fax: 724-628-1745. Email: connarea@cvzoom.net. Web: www.connareacatholic.org. Mrs. Cecilia Solan, Prin. Lay Teachers 11; Students 91.

FORD CITY. *Divine Redeemer School*, 726 Fourth Ave., 16226. Tel: 724-763-3761; Fax: 724-763-4112. Nicalena Cartesi, Prin. Lay Teachers 8; Students 88.

LATROBE. *Christ the Divine Teacher School*, (Grades PreK-8), 323 Chestnut St., 15650. Tel: 724-539-1561; Fax: 724-532-3873. Email: cdt@cdtschool.org. Web: www.cdtschool.org. Timothy Larouere, Prin.; Faith Kerr, Librarian. Lay Teachers 22; Students 241.

NEW KENSINGTON. *Mary Queen of Apostles* (Regional School), 1129 Leishman Ave., 15068. Tel: 724-339-4411; Fax: 724-337-6457. Catherine M. Collett, Prin. Lay Teachers 14.

NORTH HUNTINGDON. *Queen of Angels School/The Bishop Anthony G. Bosco Center*, One Main St., 15642. Tel: 724-978-0144; Fax: 724-978-0171. Email: info@queenofangelssch.org. Web: www.queenofangelssch.org. Mrs. Linda L. Holsopple, Prin. Lay Teachers 22; Students 344.

[E] SPECIAL EDUCATION

GREENSBURG. *Clelian Heights School for Exceptional Children*, 135 Clelian Heights Ln., 15601. Tel: 724-837-8120; Fax: 724-837-6480. Email: clelian@aol.com. Web: www.clelianheights.org. Sisters Ritamary Schulz, A.S.C.J., Exec. Dir.; Charlene Celli, A.S.C.J., Prin.; Rev. Bernard Survil, Chap. Apostles of the Sacred Heart of Jesus. Sisters 13; Lay Teachers 12; Students 89.
Elizabeth Seton Montessori School of Westmoreland County, Inc., 294 Frye Farm Rd., P.O. Box 268, 15601. Tel: 724-837-8500; Fax: 724-836-0772. Email: esmontessori@comcast.net. Sr. Anita Schulte, S.C., Admin.; Mrs. Linda M. Fidazzo, Dir. & Teacher in Charge. Sisters of Charity. Sisters 1; Lay Teachers 3; Students 40.

MOUNT PLEASANT. *Verna Montessori School*, 268 Prittstown Rd., 15666. Tel: 724-887-8810; Fax: 724-887-2977. Email: vmsami@zoominternet.net. Sisters M. Letizia Tribuzio, S.C.I.C., Prin.; Donatella Garreffa, Admin. Ivrea Sisters of Charity of the Immaculate Conception. Sisters 9; Lay Teachers 9; Students 140.

[F] HOMES FOR AGED

GREENSBURG. *St. Anne Home*, 685 Angela Dr., 15601. Tel: 724-837-6070; Fax: 724-837-6099. Email: bfiedor@stannehome.org. Web: www.stannehome.org. Rev. Leonard J. McAlpin, Chap.; Sr. Bernice M. Fiedor, C.S.S.F., Admin. Felician Sisters 5; Daughters of Mary 4; Assisted Living 55; Capacity for Intermediate Skilled Care 125.
Neumann House, 2900 Seminary Dr., 15601. Tel: 724-834-7350; Fax: 724-834-7351. Email: jbertig@dioceseofgreensburg.org. Residence for retired Priests. In Res. Rev. Msgrs. Lawrence R. Kiniry; Donald J. Mondello; John A. Regoli (Retired); Revs. Louis W. Cheatham (Retired). Tel: 724-850-7619; Edward F. Higgins (Retired); Lawrence Hoppe; Richard E. Mackiewicz (Retired); Henry S. Preneta (Retired); Donald P. Trexler; Anthony A. Wozniak.

[G] MONASTERIES AND RESIDENCES OF PRIESTS AND BROTHERS

BOLIVAR. *Mount Carmel Hermitage*, 244 Baileys Rd., 15923. Tel: 724-238-0423; Fax: 724-238-0423. Revs. Bede J.K. Mulligan, O.Carm., Prior; Simeon D. Marro, O.Carm., Procurator. Email: smarr@winbeam.com; Bro. Robert Ryba, O.Carm. Priests 2; Brothers 1.

KITTANNING. *Pauline Fathers Monastery*, 543 Bunker Hill Rd., P.O. Box 66, 16201. Tel: 724-763-1375; Fax: 724-763-8100. Revs. Edward Volz, O.S.P.P.E.; Raphael K. Glinkowski, O.S.P.P.E., Admin. Priests 2.

LATROBE. *Saint Vincent Archabbey*, 300 Fraser Purchase Rd., 15650-2690. Tel: 724-532-6600; Fax: 724-539-2110. Email: douglas.nowicki@email.stvincent.edu. Web: benedictine.stvincent.edu. Rt. Revs. Paul R. Maher, O.S.B., Archabbot (Retired); Douglas R. Nowicki, O.S.B., Archabbot; Rev. Edward M. Mazich, O.S.B., Master of Novices; Very Rev. Earl J. Henry, O.S.B., Prior; Bro. Anthony Kirsch, O.S.B., Subprior; Revs. Sebastian A. Samay, O.S.B.; Philip M. Kanfush, O.S.B., Procurator; Thomas Acklin, O.S.B.; Joseph M. Adams, O.S.B.; Benoit Alloggia, O.S.B.; Jeremy J. Bolha, O.S.B.; Brian D. Boosel, O.S.B., Admin. Asst. to Archabbot; Gilbert J. Burke, O.S.B., Dir. Alumni St. Vincent Seminary & St. Vincent Devel. Club;

Aaron N. Buzzelli, O.S.B.; Frederick Byrne, O.S.B., Dir. Vocations; Andrew S. Campbell, O.S.B.; Athanasius C. Cherry, O.S.B.; Richard Chirichiello, O.S.B.; Wulfstan F. Clough, O.S.B.; Cyprian G. Constantine, O.S.B.; Patrick T. Cronauer, O.S.B., Master of Juniors, St. Vincent Archabbey; Vincent R. Crosby, O.S.B.; Thomas P. Curry, O.S.B., Pastor, St. Vincent Basilica, Latrobe; Jacques de Paul Daley, O.S.B., Chap., Excela Health, Greensburg; Alvin T. Downey, O.S.B.; Demetrius R. Dumm, O.S.B.; Wilfred M. Dumm, O.S.B.; Conan E. Feigh, O.S.B.; Chad R. Ficorilli, O.S.B.; Augustine A. Flood, O.S.B.; Michael J. Gabler, O.S.B.; Campion P. Gavaler, O.S.B.; Joseph U. Gerg, O.S.B.; Anthony J. Grossi, O.S.B.; Mark F.X. Gruber, O.S.B.; Thomas M. Hart, O.S.B.; Bede J. Hasso, O.S.B.; Boniface Hicks, O.S.B.; Vernon A. Holtz, O.S.B.; Cuthbert A. Jack, O.S.B., Admin., Church of the Protection of Mary, Homer City, PA; Myron M. Kirsch, O.S.B.; Omer U. Kline, O.S.B.; Rene M. Kollar, O.S.B.; Stanley T. Markiewicz, O.S.B.; Matthias Martinez, O.S.B.; Very Rev. Justin M. Matro, O.S.B., Rector of Seminary; Revs. Nathan J. Munsch, O.S.B., Admin., St. Mary Parish, West Salisbury, PA; Jonathan J. Murrman, O.S.B.; Warren D. Murrman, O.S.B.; John Murtha, O.S.B.; Justin Nolan, O.S.B.; Daniel Paul O'Keefe, O.S.B., Parochial Vicar, St. Vincent Basilica, Latrobe; Dominic J. Petroy, O.S.B., Chap., Mercy Jeannette Hospital, Jeannette; Peter Augustine H. Pierjok, O.S.B., Pastor, Sacred Heart Church, Youngstown; Admin., St. Cecilia Church, Whitney; Jerome J. Purta, O.S.B.; Donald Raila, O.S.B.; Blane L. Resko, O.S.B.; Leo P. Rothrauff, O.S.B.; Noel H. Rothrauff, O.S.B., Dir. of Foreign Missions; Paul E. Rubadue, O.S.B.; Sebastian A. Samay, O.S.B.; Chrysostom V. Schlimm, O.S.B.; Paul-Alexander Shutt, O.S.B.; Thomas More Sikora, O.S.B.; Paul R. Taylor, O.S.B.; John Mary Tompkins, O.S.B., Chap., Latrobe Area Hospital, Latrobe; Damian J. Warnock, O.S.B.; Mark Edward Wenzinger, O.S.B.; Justin Withrow, O.S.B.; Flavian G. Yelinko, O.S.B.

The Benedictine Society of Westmoreland County
Saint Vincent College Corporation
The Wimmer Corporation
The Saint Vincent Cemetery Corporation Priests in Archabbey 66; Priests in Community 115; Brothers 3; Deacons 3; Solemn Professed Choir-Monks 32; Junior Professed Monks 9; Choir Novices 6.

Priests of the Archabbey Serving Abroad: Rt. Rev. Joaquim de Arruda Zamith, O.S.B. (Retired); Very Rev. Lucas Torrell deAlmeida Costa, O.S.B.; Revs. Felipe R.J. del Almeida, O.S.B.; Paulo Sergio Panza, O.S.B., Prior.

Priests on Leave: Revs. Michael A. McIlwain, O.S.B., Pastor, Forty Martyrs, Trauger; Michael McKay, O.S.B.; Richard B. Michel, O.S.B.; Cajetan P. Homick, O.S.B.; Mauro de Souza Fernandes, O.S.B.; Claudio Moraes, O.S.B.; Becket G. Senchur, O.S.B.

Priests on Loan: Revs. Cornelius P. Chang, O.S.B., Archdiocese of New York; Meinrad J. Lawson, O.S.B., St. Mary Church, St. Mary's, PA (Erie Diocese); Lee R. Yoakam, O.S.B., US Army: Active Duty, 3600 South, Pentagon, Washington, DC.

Priests on Leave for Study and Teaching: Revs. Shawn Matthew Anderson, O.S.B., Virginia Commonwealth University, Richmond, VA; Kurt J. Belsole, O.S.B., North American College, Rome, Italy; Brian D. Boosel, O.S.B., Catholic University, Washington, DC; Maurus Mount, O.S.B., University of Illinois, Champaign, IL; Liang D. Ho, O.S.B., Loyola University, Baltimore, MD.

UNIONTOWN. *St. Anthony Friary*, 115 Oakland Ave., 15401-2818. Tel: 724-438-0500; Fax: 724-438-4251. Revs. Matthew R. Brozovic, O.F.M., Guardian & Sacramental Min.; John Joseph Gonchar, O.F.M., Sacramental Min.; Bros. Damien Murkley, O.F.M., Vicar; Bill Spond, O.F.M., Asst. Fraternal Ministry.

[H] CONVENTS AND RESIDENCES FOR SISTERS

GREENSBURG. *Apostles of the Sacred Heart of Jesus, Clelian Heights Convent*, 135 Clelian Heights Ln., 15601-6665. Tel: 724-837-8120; Fax: 724-837-6480. Email: clelian@aol.com. Web: www.clelianheights.org. Sr. Ritamary Schulz, A.S.C.J., Local Supr.; Rev. Bernard Survil, Chap. Sisters 13.

Benedictine Nuns, St. Emma Monastery, 1001 Harvey Ave., 15601-1494. Tel: 724-834-3060; Fax: 724-834-5772. Email: benedictinenuns@stemma.org. Web: www.stemma.org. Sr. Mary Anne Noll, O.S.B., Prioress; Rev. Joseph L. Sredzinski, M.Div. Sisters 11; Novices 1.

Doran Hall, 441 Mount Thor Rd., 15601. Tel: 724-837-8645. Web: www.scsh.org. Sisters of Charity 14.

Ennis Hall, 443 Mount Thor Rd., 15601. Tel: 724-836-7940. Sisters of Charity 8.

Regina House (Sisters of Charity), 469 Mt. Thor Rd., 15601. Tel: 724-836-0406; Fax: 724-836-8280. Web: www.scsh.org. Sr. Vivien Linkhauer, S.C., Prov. Supr.

Sisters of Charity, Caritas Christi, Motherhouse, 129 DePaul Center Rd., 15601. Tel: 724-853-7948; Fax: 724-838-1512. Web: www.scsh.org. Sr. Jane Mary Kelly, Sister Servant. Sisters 83.

Sisters of Charity, Marian Hall, 449 Mount Thor Rd., 15601. Tel: 724-837-5863. Web: www.scsh.org. Sisters of Charity 2.

Sisters of Charity of Seton Hill, Greensburg, Pennsylvania (DePaul Center), 144 DePaul Center Rd., 15601. Tel: 724-836-0406; Fax: 724-836-8280. Web: www.scsh.org.

Regina House, Regina House: 469 Mt. Thor Rd., 15601. Tel: 724-836-0406; Fax: 724-836-8280.

DePaul Center, 144 DePaul Center Rd., 15601. Tel: 724-836-0406; Fax: 724-836-8280. Administrative offices.

Caritias Christi Tel: 724-853-7948; Fax: 724-838-1512.

Doran Hall Tel: 724-837-8645.

Ennis Hall Tel: 724-836-7940.

Marian Hall Tel: 724-837-5863.

Bayley House Tel: 724-836-6398. A Pennsylvania nonprofit corporation. Sisters 440; Novices 13; Postulants 5.

LATROBE. *Discalced Carmelite Nuns, Carmel of the Assumption*, 5206 Center Dr., 15650. Tel: 724-539-1056; Fax: 724-539-0752. Email: carmelite.monastery@verizon.net. Professed Nuns of Solemn Vows 13.

LEECHBURG. *Catechist Sisters of Mary Immaculate Help of Christians*, 118 Park Rd., 15656. Tel: 724-845-2828; Fax: 724-845-1658. Email: lbgsmi@windstream.net. Sisters 6.

MOUNT PLEASANT. *Ivrea Sisters of Charity of the Immaculate Conception*, Immaculate Virgin of Miracles Convent, 268 Prittstown Rd., 15666. Tel: 724-887-6753; Fax: 724-887-0220. Email: scicusa@zoominternet.net. Sr. M. Letizia Tribuzio, S.C.I.C., Local Supr. Sisters 9.

[I] RETREAT HOUSES

GREENSBURG. *St. Emma Retreat House*, 1001 Harvey Ave., 15601. Tel: 724-834-3060; Fax: 724-834-5772. Email: benedictinenuns@stemma.org. Web: www.stemma.org. Sr. Mary Anne Noll, O.S.B., Prioress. Benedictine Nuns.

[J] MISCELLANEOUS LISTINGS

GREENSBURG. *The Bishop William G. Connare Center*, 2900 Seminary Dr., 15601. Tel: 724-834-7350; Fax: 724-834-7351. Email: jbertig@dioceseofgreensburg.org. Web: www.bishopconnarecenter.org. Mr. Gerald R. Bertig, Dir. Facilities Mgmt. In Res. Revs. Robert R. Byrnes; John R. Cindric; Very Rev. Msgr. Richard G. Curci, V.F.

Congregations of Religious Women Charitable Trust, 144 DePaul Center Rd., 15601. Tel: 724-836-0406; Fax: 724-836-8280. Email: rhildenbrand@scsh.org. Robert M. Hildenbrand, Chm.

Gilbert Straub Plaza, 620 Reamer Ave., 15601. Tel: 724-832-2280; Fax: 724-832-9511. Email: jgrindle@scsh.org. Sr. Mary Janice Grindle, S.C., Mgr. Sisters of Charity. Sisters 1.

INDIANA. *Clairvaux Commons*, 100 Clairvaux Dr., 15701. Tel: 724-349-2920; Fax: 724-349-1355. Sisters of St. Joseph 2.

LOWER BURRELL. *Bishop Morrow Personal Care Home, Inc.*, 118 Park Rd., 15068. Tel: 724-845-2828; Fax: 724-845-1658. Email: lbgsmi@windstream.net. Sr. Mercy F. Anchalakal, S.M.I. Sisters of Mary Immaculate.

NEW SALEM. *Rendu Services, Inc.*, 453 Pechin Rd., Dunbar, 15431. Tel: 724-277-8680; Fax: 724-277-8681. Email: maryfranb@yahoo.com. Web: www.renduservices.org. Sr. Mary Francis Bassick, D.C., Exec. Dir.

SMOCK. *Ladies of Charity*, c/o St. Joseph Church, P.O. Box 3, Everson, 15631. Tel: 724-887-6714; Fax: 724-887-8180. Email: jsedlak@dioceseofgreensburg.org. Rev. John A. Sedlak, Spiritual Advisor; Sr. Mary Price, S.C., Sister Moderator.

RELIGIOUS INSTITUTES OF MEN REPRESENTED IN THE DIOCESE

For further details refer to the corresponding bracketed number in the Religious Institutes of Men or Women section.

[0200]—*Benedictine Monks* (St. Vincent Archabbey)—O.S.B.

[0270]—*Carmelite Fathers and Brothers*—O.Carm.

[0520]—*Franciscan Friars*—O.F.M.

[1010]—*Pauline Fathers*—O.S.P.P.E.

RELIGIOUS INSTITUTES OF WOMEN REPRESENTED IN THE DIOCESE

[0130]—*Apostles of the Sacred Heart of Jesus*—A.S.C.J.

[0190]—*Benedictine Sisters*—O.S.B.

[0230]—*Benedictine Sisters of Pontifical Jurisdiction*—O.S.B.

[0420]—*Discalced Carmelite Nuns*—O.C.D.

[1070]—*Dominican Sisters, St. Mary of the Springs* (Columbus, OH)—O.P.

[1170]—*Felician Sisters*—C.S.S.F.

[2575]—*Institute of the Sisters of Mercy of the Americas* (Pittsburgh, PA)—R.S.M.

[1690]—*School Sisters of the Third Order of St. Francis*—O.S.F.

[0570]—*Sisters of Charity of Seton Hill, Greensburg, Pennsylvania*—S.C.

[0450]—*Sisters of Charity of the Immaculate Conception of Ivrea*—S.C.I.C.

[0990]—*Sisters of Divine Providence* (St. Peter Prov.)—C.D.P.

[2440]—*Sisters of Mary Immaculate*—S.M.I.

[1660]—*Sisters of Saint Francis of the Providence of God*—O.S.F.

[1620]—*Sisters of Saint Francis, Millvale, Pennsylvania*—O.S.F.

[3830-13]—*Sisters of St. Joseph*—C.S.J.

[2040]—*Sisters of the Holy Spirit*—S.H.S.

[3730]—*Sisters of the Order of St. Basil the Great*—O.S.B.M.

[4160]—*Vincentian Sisters of Charity*—V.S.C.

NECROLOGY

† Ramellini, Rev. Msgr. P. Lino, (Retired)—Died Aug. 28, 2009
† Kretz, Edward J., (Retired)—Died Aug. 3, 2009
† Pierce, George R., (Retired)—Died Nov. 17, 2009
† Rivi, Geno G., (Retired)—Died March 15, 2009
† Vasil, James, (Retired)—Died Jan. 24, 2009

An asterisk (*) denotes an organization that has established tax-exempt status directly with the IRS and is not covered by the USCCB Group Ruling.

Diocese of Harrisburg

(Dioecesis Harrisburgensis)

(VACANT SEE)

Diocesan Center: 4800 Union Deposit Rd., Harrisburg, PA 17111-3710. Tel: 717-657-4804; Fax: 717-657-2453.

Web: www.hbgdiocese.org

Email: general@hbgdiocese.org

ESTABLISHED MARCH 3, 1868.

Square Miles 7,660.

Comprises the Counties of Dauphin, Lebanon, Lancaster, York, Adams, Franklin, Cumberland, Perry, Juniata, Mifflin, Snyder, Northumberland, Union, Montour and Columbia in the State of Pennsylvania.

Patron of Diocese: St. Patrick, Bishop and Confessor.

For legal titles of parishes and diocesan institutions, consult the Office of the Vicar General.

STATISTICAL OVERVIEW

Personnel	
Priests: Diocesan Active in Diocese	98
Priests: Diocesan Active Outside Diocese	7
Priests: Retired, Sick or Absent	37
Number of Diocesan Priests	142
Religious Priests in Diocese	32
Total Priests in Diocese	174
Extern Priests in Diocese	11
Ordinations:	
Diocesan Priests	4
Transitional Deacons	1
Permanent Deacons in Diocese	46
Total Brothers	1
Total Sisters	359
Parishes	
Parishes	89
With Resident Pastor:	
Resident Diocesan Priests	75
Resident Religious Priests	11
Without Resident Pastor:	
Administered by Priests	3
Missions	8
Professional Ministry Personnel:	
Brothers	1
Sisters	16
Lay Ministers	77
Welfare	
Catholic Hospitals	1
Total Assisted	254,408
Homes for the Aged	3
Total Assisted	396
Residential Care of Children	1
Total Assisted	30
Specialized Homes	4
Total Assisted	349
Special Centers for Social Services	18
Total Assisted	2,844
Educational	
Diocesan Students in Other Seminaries	27
Total Seminarians	27
High Schools, Diocesan and Parish	7
Total Students	3,819
Elementary Schools, Diocesan and Parish	38
Total Students	8,563
Elementary Schools, Private	1
Total Students	24
Catechesis/Religious Education:	
High School Students	1,624
Elementary Students	16,402
Total Students under Catholic Instruction	30,459
Teachers in the Diocese:	
Priests	1
Sisters	34
Lay Teachers	778
Vital Statistics	
Receptions into the Church:	
Infant Baptism Totals	2,075
Minor Baptism Totals	614
Adult Baptism Totals	321
Received into Full Communion	390
First Communions	3,549
Confirmations	3,030
Marriages:	
Catholic	385
Interfaith	371
Total Marriages	756
Deaths	2,245
Total Catholic Population	232,117
Total Population	2,156,331

Former Bishops—Rt. Revs. JEREMIAH F. SHANAHAN, D.D., ord. July 3, 1859; cons. July 12, 1868; died Sept. 24, 1886; THOMAS MCGOVERN, D.D., ord. Dec. 27, 1861; cons. March 11, 1888; died July 25, 1898; JOHN W. SHANAHAN, D.D., ord. Jan. 2, 1869; cons. May 1, 1899; died Feb. 19, 1916; Most Revs. PHILIP R. MCDEVITT, D.D., cons. Sept. 21, 1916; died Nov. 11, 1935; GEORGE L. LEECH, D.D., J.C.D., appt. Auxiliary of Harrisburg July 6, 1935; cons. Oct. 17, 1935; succeeded to See Dec. 19, 1935; retired Oct. 19, 1971; died March 12, 1985; JOSEPH T. DALEY, D.D., cons. Jan. 7, 1964; appt. Coadjutor Bishop July 31, 1967; succeeded to See Oct. 19, 1971; died Sept. 2, 1983; WILLIAM H. KEELER, ord. July 17, 1955; cons. Sept. 21, 1979; appt. Bishop of Harrisburg, Nov. 10, 1983; succeeded to See Jan. 4, 1984; transferred to Baltimore May 23, 1989; NICHOLAS C. DATTILO, D.D., ord. May 31, 1958; appt. Eighth Bishop of Harrisburg Nov. 21, 1989; cons. Jan. 26, 1990; died March 5, 2004; KEVIN C. RHOADES, ord. July 9, 1983; appt. Ninth Bishop of Harrisburg Oct. 14, 2004; cons. Dec. 9, 2004; appt. Bishop of Fort Wayne-South Bend Nov. 14, 2009; installed Jan. 13, 2010.

Diocese of Harrisburg Officials

Vicar General—Rev. Msgr. WILLIAM J. KING, J.C.D., V.G., 4800 Union Deposit Rd., Harrisburg, 17111-3710. Tel: 717-657-4804; Fax: 717-657-2453.

Assistant to the Vicar General—MARY T. SHRIVER, M.A. Tel: 717-657-4804, Ext. 325. Email: mshriver@hbgdiocese.org.

Moderator of the Curia—Rev. Msgr. WILLIAM J. KING, J.C.D., V.G., Mailing Address: 4800 Union Deposit Rd., Harrisburg, 17111-3710.

Secretary for Catholic Charities—MARK A. TOTARO, Ph.D., MBA, Mailing Address: 4800 Union Deposit Rd., Harrisburg, 17111-3710. Tel: 717-657-4804; Fax: 717-657-8683.

Secretary for Administrative Services—Mr. DONALD J. KAERCHER, CPA, CFO, Mailing Address: 4800 Union Deposit Rd., Harrisburg, 17111-3710. Tel: 717-657-4804; Fax: 717-671-7021.

Secretary for Clergy and Religious Life—Very Rev. WILLIAM J. WALTERSHEID, Mailing Address: 4800 Union Deposit Rd., Harrisburg, 17111-3710. Fax: 717-657-2453.

Office of Communications—Mr. JOSEPH G. APONICK, Dir., Mailing Address: 4800 Union Deposit Rd., Harrisburg, 17111-3710. Tel: 717-657-4804; Fax: 717-657-7673.

Secretary for Education—Very Rev. EDWARD J. QUINLAN, M.Div., M.A., M.S., Mailing Address: 4800 Union Deposit Rd., Harrisburg, 17111-3710. Tel: 717-657-4804; 717-921-2363 (Res.); Fax: 717-657-3790.

Secretary for Catholic Life and Evangelization—Very Rev. JOHN F. BEDNARIK, O.F.M.Cap., M.A., Mailing Address: 4800 Union Deposit Rd., Harrisburg, 17111-3710. Tel: 717-657-4804; Fax: 717-657-4041.

Judicial Vicar—Very Rev. EDWARD C. MALESIC, J.C.L., M.Div., Mailing Address: 4800 Union Deposit Rd., Harrisburg, 17111-3710. Tel: 717-657-4804; Fax: 717-657-1573.

Chancellor—CAROL HOUGHTON, S.T.D., J.C.D., Mailing Address: 4800 Union Deposit Rd, Harrisburg, 17111-3710. Tel: 717-657-4804; Fax: 717-657-1573.

Diocesan Offices, Commissions, Boards and Programs

Adult Education and Catechist Formation, Office of—RYAN BOLSTER, Dir., Mailing Address: 4800 Union Deposit Rd., Harrisburg, 17111-3710. Tel: 717-657-4804, Ext. 225; Fax: 717-657-3790.

Catholic History and Archives, Office of—Rev. Msgr. THOMAS J. KUJOVSKY, Dir.; Dr. LINDA I. ITZOE, Archivist & Asst. Chancellor Archives, 4800 Union Deposit Rd., Harrisburg, 17111-3710. Tel: 717-657-4804.

Black Catholic Apostolate—GWEN SUMMERS, Coord., 4800 Union Deposit Rd., Harrisburg, 17111-3710. Tel: 717-657-4804.

Buildings and Properties—JEFF MCCAUSLIN, Dir., 4800 Union Deposit Rd., Harrisburg, 17111-3710. Tel: 717-657-4804; Fax: 717-657-6208.

Campus Ministry—ROBERT J. WILLIAMS, Dir., Mailing Address: 4800 Union Deposit Rd., Harrisburg, 17111-3710. Tel: 717-657-4804.

Catholic Charities Administration, Department for—MARK A. TOTARO, Ph.D., MBA, Exec. Dir. & CEO; PETER A. BIASUCCI, L.S.W., Asst. Exec. Dir.; CAROLE A. KLINGER, M.B.A., Dir. Admin.; BARBARA SCHREIBER, Dir. Devel.; ERIC BOLTZ, Coord. Grants, Mailing Address: 4800 Union Deposit Rd., Harrisburg, 17111-3710.

Catholic Charities Counseling/Field Services, Department for—Associate Executive Directors: ANNETTE MARTIN, M.H.S.; KIRK REIDER, A.C.S.W, L.C.S.W.; CHRISTOPHER VANDENBERG, M.H.S.; NICHOLAS GIAMPIETRO, M.A.

Catholic Physicians League—Rev. DAVID L. DANNEKER, Ph.D., Liaison, 1840 Marshall Dr., Elizabethtown, 17022.

Catholic Schools, Department for—Mrs. LIVIA ANN RILEY, Supt., Mailing Address: 4800 Union

Deposit Rd., Harrisburg, 17111-3710. Tel: 717-657-4804; Fax: 717-657-3790.

The "Catholic Witness"—Ms. JENNIFER REED, Mng. Editor, 4800 Union Deposit Rd., Harrisburg, 17111-3710. Tel: 717-657-4804; Fax: 717-657-7673.

Catholic Women, Diocesan Council of—Mrs. BARBARA MCCARTHY, 14 Springcreek Manor, Hershey, 17033. Tel: 717-534-1858.

Cemeteries—Mr. DONALD J. KAERCHER, CPA, Diocesan Finance Officer & Sec. for Admin. Svcs., 4800 Union Deposit Rd., Harrisburg, 17111-3710. Tel: 717-657-4804.

Charismatic Renewal—Very Rev. FRANCIS J. KARWACKI, V.F., Liaison, 47 S. Market St., Mount Carmel, 17851. Tel: 570-339-1036.

Consultors, College—Rev. Msgr. WILLIAM J. KING, J.C.D., V.G.; Revs. LAWRENCE J. MCNEIL, D.Min., M.Div.; DANIEL C. MITZEL; Rev. Msgr. HUGH A. OVERBAUGH (Retired); Revs. LOUIS P. OGDEN; PAUL C. HELWIG; Very Rev. KENNETH F. LAWRENCE, V.F.; Revs. JAMES M. LYONS, V.G., M.Div., M.Ed.; DAVID L. DANNEKER, Ph.D.; MICHAEL P. REID II; THOMAS A. SCALA; ROBERT F. SHARMAN, S.T.L.; CHESTER P. SNYDER.

Continuing Formation of Priests, Office of—Dr. MARY ANN BOYARSKI, Ed.D., Dir., 4800 Union Deposit Rd., Harrisburg, 17111-3710. Tel: 717-657-4804; Fax: 717-657-4042.

Cursillo Movement—Rev. Msgr. THOMAS H. SMITH, V.F., Moderator.

Deans—Very Revs. JOSEPH F. GOTWALT, Adams Deanery; WILLIAM C. FORREY, V.F., Cumberland/Perry Deanery; Rev. Msgr. ROBERT E. LAWRENCE, V.F., Dauphin Deanery; Very Revs. JAMES R. O'BRIEN, Franklin Deanery; KENNETH F. LAWRENCE, V.F., North Lancaster Deanery; Rev. Msgr. RICHARD A. YOUTZ, J.C.L., South Lancaster Deanery; Very Revs. PHILIP G. BURGER, V.F., Lebanon Deanery; FRANCIS J. TAMBURRO, V.F., Northern Deanery; FRANCIS J. KARWACKI, V.F., Northumberland Deanery; ROBERT M. GILLELAN JR., V.F., York Deanery.

Diocesan Center—DONNAJOAN MATTIS, Coord., 4800 Union Deposit Rd., Harrisburg, 17111-3710. Tel: 717-657-4804; Fax: 717-671-7146.

Development, Office of—PAULA M. LASECKI, Dir., 4800 Union Deposit Rd., Harrisburg, 17111-3710. Tel: 717-657-4804; Fax: 717-657-8757.

Ecumenical and Interreligious Affairs, Office for—Deacon CHARLES CLARK, Dir., 4800 Union Deposit Rd., Harrisburg, 17111-3710. Tel: 717-657-4804; Fax: 717-657-4041.

Evangelization and Special Ministries, Office of—LUCIA C.R. MURPHY, Ph.D., Dir., 4800 Union Deposit Rd., Harrisburg, 17111-3710. Tel: 717-657-4804; Fax: 717-657-4041.

Family Ministries, Office of—VICTORIA LASKOWSKI, J.D., Dir., 4800 Union Deposit Rd., Harrisburg, 17111-3710. Tel: 717-657-4804; Fax: 717-657-4041.

Finance Council—
Harrisburg Catholic Administrative Services, Inc.—Mr. DONALD J. KAERCHER, CPA, Diocesan Finance Officer & Sec. for Admin., 4800 Union Deposit Rd., Harrisburg, 17111-3710. Tel: 717-657-4804; Fax: 717-671-7021.

Health Care Ministry—LUCIA C.R. MURPHY, Ph.D., Dir., 4800 Union Deposit Rd., Harrisburg, 17111-3710. Tel: 717-657-4804; Fax: 717-657-4041.

Holy Name Societies—THOMAS AUMEN, Liaison, 15 Oak Hill Dr., Hanover, 17331. Tel: 717-637-6491.

Korean Ministry—Rev. THOMAS LEE, 329 Lowther St., Lemoyne, 17043. Tel: 717-774-2728.

Knights of Columbus—Mr. WAYNE S. FREET, State Deputy, 800 North St., Mc Sherrystown, 17344-1609. Tel: 717-637-0546.

Human Resources, Department for—Mrs. JANET E. JACKSON, M.C.I.P.D., 4800 Union Deposit Rd., Harrisburg, 17111-3710. Tel: 717-657-4804.

Legion of Mary—Rev. PAUL R. SHUDA, Moderator (Retired), 675 Rutherford Rd., Harrisburg, 17109. Tel: 717-657-3147.

Mater Dei Community— (Traditional Latin Mass Community) *110 State St., Harrisburg, 17101*. Tel: 717-234-4184. Rev. FRANK PARRINELLO, F.S.S.P.

Mediation Services, Office of—Mrs. BARBARA A. ROTH, Clerk, 4800 Union Deposit Rd., Harrisburg, 17111-3710. Tel: 717-657-4804.

Missions, Office of (Home and Foreign)—Rev. ROBERT F. SHARMAN, S.T.L., Dir., 4800 Union Deposit Rd., Harrisburg, 17111-3710. Tel: 717-657-4804.

Ministry with People with Disabilities, Office for—GINNY DUNCAN, Dir., 4800 Union Deposit Rd., Harrisburg, 17111-3710. Tel: 717-657-4804; Fax: 717-657-4041.

Natural Family Planning, Office of—*4800 Union Deposit Rd., Harrisburg, 17111-3710*. Tel: 717-657-4804; Fax: 717-657-4041.

Pastoral Council, Diocesan—Sr. MARY ANNE BEDNAR, I.H.M.; THOMAS BRADLEY; Very Rev. PHILIP G. BURGER, V.F.; Dr. GREG F. BURKE; PETER A. CICCOCIOPPO; JAMES R. CORBIN; CARMEN CRUZ; BRENDA DANIEL; CHRISTINE DELUCE; MARIA T. DISANTO; GEORGE M. GARBER JR.; Rev. DENNIS GRUMSEY, O.F.M.Conv.; HARRY H. HOLT; WALTER J. LEGENSTEIN; Rev. TIMOTHY D. MARCOE; C. CLAIR MCCORMICK; Deacon JOHN L. PARUSO; YEN PHAN; LINDA WALBORN; EDMUND A. WICKENHEISER; MARY CLARE ZALES; CHARLES L. ZITNICK JR.; JOHN J. ZOGBY.

Diocesan Staff—Mr. JOSEPH G. APONICK; CAROL LEE HOUGHTON, S.T.D., J.C.D.; MARY T. SHRIVER, M.A.; Rev. Msgr. WILLIAM J. KING, J.C.D., V.G.

Permanent Diaconate, Office for—Very Rev. WILLIAM J. WALTERSHEID, Dir., 4800 Union Deposit Rd., Harrisburg, 17111-3710. Tel: 717-657-4804; Fax: 717-657-2453; Deacon MICHAEL A. GRELLA, Ed.D., Dir. Permanent Diaconate Formation. Tel: 717-657-4804; Fax: 717-657-4042.

Presbyteral Council—Revs. LAWRENCE J. MCNEIL, D.Min., M.Div., Adams; STEPHEN D. WEITZEL, Cumberland/Perry; LOUIS P. OGDEN, Dauphin; DAVID A. HILLIER, Franklin; Very Rev. KENNETH F. LAWRENCE, V.F., North Lancaster; Revs. LEO M. GOODMAN, South Lancaster; MICHAEL P. REID II, Lebanon; THOMAS A. SCALA, Northern; Very Rev. FRANCIS J. KARWACKI, V.F., Northumberland; Rev. CHARLES L. PERSING, York.

Appointed—Rev. JOHN B. BATEMAN; Rev. Msgr. HUGH A. OVERBAUGH (Retired); Revs. DANIEL C. MITZEL; DAVID L. DANNEKER, Ph.D.; LOUIS PETRUHA, O.F.M.Cap.; PAUL C. HELWIG; CHESTER P. SNYDER; ROBERT F. SHARMAN, S.T.L.; BENARDO PISTONE; DAVID M. HERESHKO.

Prison Ministry—Very Rev. JOHN F. BEDNARIK, O.F.M.Cap., M.A., Dir., 4800 Union Deposit Rd., Harrisburg, 17111-3710. Tel: 717-657-4804; Fax: 717-657-4041.

Senior Adult Ministry—VICTORIA LASKOWSKI, J.D., Coord., 4800 Union Deposit Rd., Harrisburg, 17111-3710. Tel: 717-657-4804; Fax: 717-657-4041.

Respect Life, Office for—PAUL C.B. SCHENCK, Dir., 4800 Union Deposit Rd., Harrisburg, 17111-3710. Tel: 717-657-4804; Fax: 717-657-2453.

Media Relations—Mr. JOSEPH G. APONICK, 4800 Union Deposit Rd., Harrisburg, 17111-3710. Tel: 717-657-4804; Fax: 717-657-7673.

Religious Education (CCD), Department for—JAMES GONTIS, 4800 Union Deposit Rd., Harrisburg, 17111-3710. Tel: 717-657-4804; Fax: 717-657-3790.

Consecrated Life, Department for—*4800 Union Deposit Rd., Harrisburg, 17111-3710*. Tel: 717-657-4804; Fax: 717-657-2453.

Saint Thomas More Society—ANDREW CLARK, Esq., Pres., 4800 Union Deposit Rd., Harrisburg, 17111-3710. Tel: 717-657-4804, Ext. 305.

Saint Vincent de Paul Society—VACANT.

Hispanic Apostolate—LUCIA C.R. MURPHY, Ph.D., 4800 Union Deposit Rd., Harrisburg, 17111-3710. Tel: 717-657-4804; Fax: 717-657-4041.

Tribunal—*4800 Union Deposit Rd., Harrisburg, 17111-3710*. Tel: 717-657-4804; Fax: 717-657-1573.

Judicial Vicar—Very Rev. EDWARD C. MALESIC, J.C.L., M.Div.

Case Services Administrator—Mrs. BARBARA A. ROTH.

Diocesan Judges—Rev. Msgr. RICHARD A. YOUTZ, J.C.L.; Dr. CAROL L. HOUGHTON, S.T.D., J.C.D.; Rev. JORDAN HITE, T.O.R.

Defender of the Bond—Rev. EDWARD R. LAVELLE.

Promoter of Justice—Rev. WILLIAM J. NESSEL, O.S.F.S., J.C.D. (Retired).

Advocates—Mr. ROBERT F. O'DONNELL; Mrs. BARBARA A. ROTH; Mrs. CONSTANCE T. HESS; Mrs. ANITA M. PAYNTER; Rev. PAUL M. CLARK.

Auditor—Rev. PAUL M. CLARK.

Notaries—Ms. ANNETTE C. EURIECK; Mrs. MARLENE M. RAUDENSKY.

Mediation Services, Office of—Mrs. BARBARA A. ROTH, Clerk.

Victim Assistance Coordinator—MARK A. TOTARO, Ph.D., MBA. Tel: 717-657-4804. Email: mtotaro@hbgdiocese.org.

Vietnamese Ministry—Rev. HOA VAN NGUYEN, Coord., 929 N. Duke St., Lancaster, 17602. Tel: 717-392-2225.

Vocations, Office for—Rev. RAYMOND J. LAVOIE, Dir., 4800 Union Deposit Rd., Harrisburg, 17111-3710. Tel: 717-657-4804; Fax: 717-657-4042.

World Apostolate of Fatima—Rev. JOHN A. SZADA JR., Spiritual Moderator, St. Vincent de Paul, 224 Third St., Hanover, 17331. Tel: 717-637-5190.

Worship, Office of—Rev. NEIL SULLIVAN, Dir., 4800 Union Deposit Rd., Harrisburg, 17111-3710. Tel: 717-657-4804; Fax: 717-657-2453.

Youth and Young Adult Ministry, Office for—ROBERT J. WILLIAMS, Dir., 4800 Union Deposit Rd., Harrisburg, 17111-3710. Tel: 717-657-4804; Fax: 717-657-4041.

Youth Protection Program—Rev. Msgr. WILLIAM J. KING, J.C.D., V.G.; Mrs. JANET E. JACKSON, M.C.I.P.D., Compliance Coord., 4800 Union Deposit Rd., Harrisburg, 17111-3710. Tel: 717-657-4804; Fax: 717-657-2453.

CLERGY, PARISHES, MISSIONS AND PAROCHIAL SCHOOLS

CITY OF HARRISBURG

(DAUPHIN COUNTY)

1—CATHEDRAL PARISH OF ST. PATRICK (1995) Rev. Thomas J. Rozman; Deacon Charles W. Clark. In Res., Revs. Paul M. Clark; Frank Parinello, F.S.S.P.
Res.: 212 State St., 17101. Tel: 717-232-2169; Fax: 717-232-2799. Email: cathedralparish@comcast.net. Web: www.stpatrickcathedral.com.
Catechesis/Religious Program—Students 102.

2—ST. CATHERINE LABOURE (1948), (Shrine of the Miraculous Medal) Revs. Neil S. Sullivan; Jose E. Mera-Vallejos, Parochial Vicar; Deacons Thomas H. Flannery; Thomas A. Fedor. In Res., Rev. Msgr. Vincent J. Topper (Retired).
Res.: 4000 Derry St., 17111. Tel: 717-564-1321; Fax: 717-564-8822. Email: p039stcatherine@hgbdiocese.org. Web: www.saintcatherinelaboure.com.
School—4020 Derry St., 17111. Tel: 717-564-1760; Fax: 717-564-3010. Web: www.stcatherinelaboure.org. Jennifer Wicht, Prin. Sisters of SS. Cyril and Methodius 1; Lay Teachers 28; Students 468.
Catechesis/Religious Program— Fatima Roberge, C.R.E. Students 426.
Convent—4010 Derry St., 17111. Tel: 717-564-0721.

3—ST. FRANCIS OF ASSISI (1901) Revs. Kevin J. Thompson, O.F.M.Cap.; Leon Leitem, O.F.M.Cap.; Deacon Miguel Marroquin. In Res., Very Rev. John F. Bednarik, O.F.M.Cap.; Rev. Gregory Chervenak, O.F.M.Cap.
Res.: 1439 Market St., 17103. Tel: 717-232-1003; Fax: 717-232-4536. Email: cfagan@hbgdiocese.org.
Catechesis/Religious Program—Tel: 717-233-7912. Students 156.

4—HOLY FAMILY (1958) Rev. Bernard P. McGinley.
Church: 555 S. 25th St., 17104. Tel: 717-232-4237; Fax: 717-232-9661.
Rectory—2501 Barkley Ln., 17104. Tel: 717-561-8250.
School—Tel: 717-232-2551. Sr. Margaret Ann Quinn, Prin. Sisters Servants of the Immaculate Heart of Mary 4; Lay Teachers 9; Students 165.
Catechesis/Religious Program—Tel: 717-232-2551. Students 180.
Convent—2473 Adrian St., 17104. Tel: 717-564-7236.

5—HOLY NAME OF JESUS (Lower Paxton Twp.) (1960) Rev. Msgr. Robert E. Lawrence; Rev. Mark M. Speitel, Parochial Vicar; Deacons Jerome T. Foerster; Joseph J. Wrabel; Sr. Helen E. McCormac, Pastoral Assoc.
Res.: 6150 Allentown Blvd., 17112-2603. Tel: 717-652-4211; Fax: 717-652-2033. Email: p036holyname@hbgdiocese.org. Web: www.holynameofjesus.com.
School—(Grades PreK-8), 6190 Allentown Blvd., 17112-2603. Tel: 717-657-1704; Fax: 717-657-9135. Email: s036holyname@hbgdiocese.org. Dr. Ann Marie Licata, Prin.; Mrs. Elaine Tomeck, Librarian. (Lower Paxton Twp.) Sisters of St. Joseph 1; Lay Teachers 34; Students 384.
Catechesis/Religious Program—Tel: 717-545-4357. Sr. Rita Smith, S.S.J., D.R.E. Students 567.
Convent—Tel: 717-545-4357. Email: ssjhnj@ezonline.net. Pastoral Associates 2; Vice Prin. 1.

6—ST. LAWRENCE (1859), (German), Closed. See St. Patrick Cathedral, Harrisburg.

7—ST. MARGARET MARY ALACOQUE (Penbrook) (1948) Rev. Daniel F.X. Powell; Mrs. Karen Hurley, Pastoral Assoc.
Res.: 2848 Herr St., 17103-1817. Tel: 717-233-3062; Fax: 717-238-5633. Email: rectory@stmmparish.org. Web: www.stmmparish.org.
School—Tel: 717-232-3771; Fax: 717-232-0776. Web: school.stmmparish.org. Mrs. Jean Fennessy, Prin. Lay Teachers 25; Students 381.
Catechesis/Religious Program— Bonnie Finnerty, C.R.E. Students 150.

8—OUR LADY OF THE BLESSED SACRAMENT (1906) Rev. Tri M. Luong.
Res.: 2121 N. Third St., 17110-1812. Tel: 717-233-1014; Fax: 717-234-5652.
Catechesis/Religious Program—Students 41.

9—SACRED HEART OF JESUS (1901) Closed. See St. Patrick Cathedral, Harrisburg.

OUTSIDE THE CITY OF HARRISBURG

ABBOTTSTOWN, YORK CO., IMMACULATE HEART OF MARY (1809) [CEM] Rev. David M. Hereshko; Deacon Raymond J. Smith. In Res., Rev. Msgr. Robert C. Gribbin (Retired).
Res.: 6084 W. Canal Rd., 17301. Tel: 717-259-0611; Fax: 717-259-6371.
Catechesis/Religious Program—Tel: 717-259-9426. Students 242.

ANNVILLE, LEBANON CO., ST. PAUL THE APOSTLE (1928) Rev. John J. Peck, O.S.B.; Mary Beazley, Music Min.
Res.: 125 S. Spruce St., 17003. Tel: 717-867-1525; Fax: 717-867-5318. Email: p002stpaul@hbgdiocese.org. Web: www.saintpaulsinannville.org.
Catechesis/Religious Program—Tel: 717-867-7471. Sr. Mary Cronin, D.M., D.R.E. Students 277.
Station—Lebanon Valley College, Miller Chapel, Tel: 717-867-6135.

BERWICK, COLUMBIA CO.
1—IMMACULATE CONCEPTION OF THE BLESSED VIRGIN MARY (1906) [CEM] Very Rev. Francis J. Tamburro.
Res.: 1730 Fowler Ave., 18603-1462. Tel: 570-759-8113; Fax: 570-759-6637.
See Holy Family Consolidated School, Berwick under Consolidated Elementary Schools located in the Institution section.
Catechesis/Religious Program—Tel: 570-759-9225. Students 111.
2—ST. JOSEPH'S (1928) Rev. Dennis G. Dalessandro; Sisters M. Carmel Marie, Pastoral Assoc.; M. Amelia, D.M., Pastoral Assoc.; M. Michael Jean, D.M., Pastoral Assoc.
Res.: 721 Monroe St., 18603. Tel: 570-752-5684; Fax: 570-752-7765.
See Holy Family Consolidated School, Berwick under Consolidated Elementary Schools located in the Institution section.
Catechesis/Religious Program—Students 98.
Convent—Daughters of Mercy, 728 Washington St., 18603. Tel: 570-752-2112. Sisters 4.

BLOOMSBURG, COLUMBIA CO., ST. COLUMBA (1882), (Irish), [CEM] Rev. Paul Fisher.
Mailing Address: P.O. Box 829, 17815. Tel: 570-784-0801; Fax: 570-387-2604. Email: p006stcolumba@hbgdiocese.org.
Res.: 42 E. Third St., 17815. Tel: 570-387-4061.
School—(Grades PreK-8), 40 E. Third St., 17815. Tel: 570-784-5932; Fax: 570-387-1257. Email: principal@saintcolumbaschool.org. Mrs. Mary Ann Venarchick, Prin. Sisters 2; Lay Teachers 12; Students 139.
Catechesis/Religious Program—Tel: 570-784-0801. Students 250.
Mission—Christ the King Mendenhall Ln., Benton, Columbia Co. 17814. Tel: 570-925-6969. P.O. Box 297, Benton, 17814.

BLUE RIDGE SUMMIT, FRANKLIN CO., ST. RITA (1919) [JC] Revs. Michael A. Messaro, M.SS.CC.; Robert Malagesi, M.SS.CC., Parochial Vicar.
Mailing Address: *Immaculate Conception*, P.O. Box 704, Fairfield, 17320. Tel: 717-642-8815; Fax: 717-642-9616. Email: bstaples@hbgdiocese.org.
Catechesis/Religious Program—Tel: 717-794-2067. Students 62.

BONNEAUVILLE, ADAM CO., ST. JOSEPH THE WORKER (1859) [CEM] Rev. Caesar Belchez; Deacon Richard J. Weaver.
Res.: 12 E. Hanover St., Gettysburg, 17325-7750. Tel: 717-334-2510; Fax: 717-337-1968.
Catechesis/Religious Program—Students 50.

BUCHANAN VALLEY, ADAMS CO., ST. IGNATIUS LOYOLA (Orrtanna) (1817) [CEM] Rev. Kenneth G. Smith.
Res.: 1095 Church Rd., Orrtanna, 17353. Tel: 717-677-8012; Fax: 717-677-6350.
Catechesis/Religious Program—Tel: 717-677-8012. Students 60.

CAMP HILL, CUMBERLAND CO., GOOD SHEPHERD (1951) Rev. Paul C. Helwig; Deacon Francis Gorman; Derrick Rosenstein, Parish Mgr.
3435 Trindle Rd., 17011. Tel: 717-761-1167; Fax: 717-761-5313. In Res., Very Rev. William J. Waltersheid.
School—Elementary, 3400 Market St., 17011. Tel: 717-737-7261; Fax: 717-761-4673. Web: www.gss-chpa.org. Mrs. Catherine Gibson, Prin. Lay Teachers 21; Students 286.
Catechesis/Religious Program—3400 Market St., 17011. Tel: 717-737-8216. Amanda Zechman, C.R.E. Students 240.

CARLISLE, CUMBERLAND CO., SAINT PATRICK (1779) [CEM 2] Very Rev. William C. Forrey; Rev. Olusola Adewole, O.P. In Res., Revs. Andre J. Meluskey (Retired); Daniel J. Menniti (Retired); Deacon John Reid Perkins-Buzo.
Res.: 152 E. Pomfret St., 17013. Tel: 717-243-4411; Fax: 717-258-9281. Email: po12stpatrickparishcarlisle@hbgdiocese.org. Web: www.saintpatrickchurch.org.
School—87 Marsh Dr., 17015. Tel: 717-249-4826; Fax: 717-245-0522. Web: www.stpatrickschool.carlisle.pa.us. Lay Teachers 37; Students 354.
Catechesis/Religious Program—Tel: 717-243-4891; Fax: 717-245-0552. Mrs. Helen Richards, D.R.E.; Mr. Joseph Goodman, Dir. Life Teen & Youth Min. Students 413.
Chapel—Pine Grove Furnace, St. Eleanor Regina
Chapel—St. Katherine Drexel Chapel - Perpetual Adoration

CENTRALIA, COLUMBIA CO., ST. IGNATIUS (1869) Closed. See Our Lady of Mount Carmel, Mount Carmel.

CHAMBERSBURG, FRANKLIN CO., CORPUS CHRISTI (1792) [CEM] Very Rev. James R. O'Brien; Revs. Ignacio Palomino, Parochial Vicar; Keith M. Carroll.
Res.: 320 Philadelphia Ave., 17201. Tel: 717-264-6317; Fax: 717-264-1787.
School—305 N. Second St., 17201. Tel: 717-263-5036; Fax: 717-263-6079. Mr. Robert G. Dortenzo, Prin. Lay Teachers 23; Students 260.
Catechesis/Religious Program—Tel: 717-263-9541. Mr. David C. Cheslock, D.R.E. Students 249.
Mission—Our Lady of Refuge 21169 Cross Rd., Doylesburg, Franklin Co. 17219. Tel: 717-349-7953. Rev. John R. Campion, Admin. (Retired).

COAL TOWNSHIP, NORTHUMBERLAND CO.
1—OUR LADY OF HOPE (1995) Revs. Adrian Gallagher, O.F.M.Conv.; David G. Fink, O.F.M.Conv.; Deacon Robert P. Mack.
Res.: 863 W. Chestnut St., 17866-1995. Tel: 570-648-4432; Fax: 570-648-8944. Email: p130ourladyhope@hbgdiocese.org.
Catechesis/Religious Program—Students 7.
2—ST. STEPHEN PROTOMARTYR (1898), (Polish), Closed. See Our Lady of Hope, Coal Township.

COLUMBIA, LANCASTER CO.
1—HOLY TRINITY (1860) [CEM] Very Rev. Kenneth F. Lawrence; Sr. Anna Cosgrave, O.S.F., Pastoral Assoc.
Res.: 409 Cherry St., 17512. Tel: 717-684-2711; Fax: 717-684-9612. Email: jesse@hbgdiocese.org.
School—(Consolidated), 404 Cherry St., 17512. Tel: 717-684-2664; Fax: 717-684-5039. Theresa Burg, Prin. Lay Teachers 14; Students 100.
Catechesis/Religious Program—Tel: 717-684-2232. Students 130.
Convent—Sisters of St. Francis of Philadelphia, 548 Cherry St., 17512. Tel: 717-684-2232.
2—ST. PETER (1828) [CEM 2] Rev. Dominic M. DiBiccaro.
Res.: 121 S. Second St., 17512. Tel: 717-684-7070; Fax: 717-684-3102.
See Our Lady of Angels, Columbia under Consolidated Elementary Schools located in the Institution section.
Catechesis/Religious Program—Tel: 717-684-7070. Corrinne Eck, D.R.E. Students 64.

CONEWAGO TOWNSHIP, ADAMS CO., BASILICA OF THE SACRED HEART OF JESUS (1730) [CEM] Rev. Lawrence J. McNeil.
Res.: 30 Basilica Dr., Hanover, 17331-8924. Tel: 717-637-2721; Fax: 717-637-4569.
School—55 Basilica Dr., Hanover, 17331. Tel: 717-632-8715; Fax: 717-632-6596. Sr. Eileen Kean, Prin. Sisters of St. Joseph 3; Lay Teachers 9; Students 245.
Catechesis/Religious Program—Students 263.
Convent—Sisters of St. Joseph, 55 Basilica Dr., Hanover, 17331. Tel: 717-637-3370. Sisters 5.

CORNWALL, LEBANON CO., SACRED HEART OF JESUS (1886) [CEM] Rev. Rodrigo A. Arrazola; Becky Broderic, Pastoral Assoc.
Res.: 2596 Cornwall Rd., P.O. Box 136, 17016-0136.
Parish Center—Tel: 717-274-3239; Fax: 717-273-9588.
Catechesis/Religious Program—Tel: 717-273-2160. Students 102.

DALLASTOWN, YORK CO., ST. JOSEPH (1850) [CEM] [JC] Rev. Charles L. Persing; Deacons Neil A. Crispo; John Weaver, Emeritus.
Res.: 251 E. Main St., 17313. Tel: 717-246-3007; Fax: 717-244-5278. Email: stjosephdtown@comcast.net. Web: www.sjdchurch.com.
School—271 E. Main St., 17313. Tel: 717-244-9386; Fax: 717-244-9478. Web: www.stjoesdallastown.org. Margaret Snyder, Prin. Lay Teachers 10; Students 190.
Catechesis/Religious Program—Tel: 717-246-9959. Email: psivulka@yahoo.com. Students 365.

DANVILLE, MONTOUR CO., ST. JOSEPH (1848) [CEM 3] Rev. Steven W. Fauser.
Res.: 18 E. Center St., 17821. Tel: 570-275-2512; Fax: 570-275-6840.
School—511 Ferry St., 17821. Tel: 717-275-2435; Fax: 570-275-3947. Lay Teachers 11; Students 140.
Catechesis/Religious Program—Students 177.

DAUPHIN, DAUPHIN CO., ST. MATTHEW, APOSTLE AND EVANGELIST (1976) Very Rev. Edward J. Quinlan; Deacon Richard Aull.
Res.: 420 Stony Creek Rd., P.O. Box 459, 17018. Tel: 717-921-2363; Fax: 717-921-2364.
Catechesis/Religious Program—Students 55.

DOYLESBURG, FRANKLIN CO., OUR LADY OF REFUGE MISSION (1802) [CEM] Rev. John R. Campion, Admin. (Retired).
21169 Cross Rd., 17219-9707. Tel: 717-349-7953; Fax: 717-349-7953.
Catechesis/Religious Program—Students 7.

ELIZABETHTOWN, LANCASTER CO., ST. PETER (1752) [CEM] Rev. David L. Danneker.
Parish Office—1840 Marshall Dr., 17022. Tel: 717-367-1255; Fax: 717-367-1270. Email: secretary@stpeteretown.org. Web: www.stpeteretown.org.
Res.: 1 Saint Peter's Pl., 17022-1956.
School—61 E. Washington St., 17022. Tel: 717-367-1678; Fax: 717-367-1270. Email: spschool@comcast.net. Web: www.stpeteretown.org/school. Mrs. Suzanne Wood, Prin. Lay Teachers 6; Students 77.
Catechesis/Religious Program—Email: cre@stpeteretown.org. Web: www.stpeteretown.org/education.htm. Students 195.

ELYSBURG, NORTHUMBERLAND CO., QUEEN OF THE MOST HOLY ROSARY (1950) [JC] Rev. Alfred P. Sceski.
Res.: 599 W. Center St., 17824. Tel: 750-672-2302; Fax: 570-672-3310. Web: www.qmhr.net.
Catechesis/Religious Program—Students 262.

ENHAUT, DAUPHIN CO., ST. JOHN THE EVANGELIST (1902) Closed. See Prince of Peace, Steelton.

ENOLA, CUMBERLAND CO., OUR LADY OF LOURDES (1926) Rev. Michael J. Grab.
Res.: 225 Salt Rd., 17025. Tel: 717-732-9642; Fax: 717-732-8184. Email: olchurch@comcast.net. Web: www.ololenolapa.org.
Catechesis/Religious Program—Students 360.

EPHRATA, LANCASTER CO., MOTHER OF PERPETUAL HELP (1914) [JC] Revs. Patrick McGarrity, C.Ss.R.; John McLoughlin, C.Ss.R.
Church Office: 320 Church Ave., 17522. Tel: 717-733-9641; Fax: 717-733-2119. Email: perpetualhelp@dejazzd.com. Web: omphchurch.org.
Res.: 300 W. Pine St., 17522. Tel: 717-733-6596; Fax: 717-733-0502.
School—330 Church Ave., 17522. Tel: 717-738-2414; Fax: 717-738-3280. Email: office@omph.org. Web: www.omph.org. Margaret Gardner, Prin. Lay Teachers 10; Students 255.
Catechesis/Religious Program—Tel: 717-738-4517; Fax: 717-733-2119. Students 348.
Convent—310 Church Ave., 17522. Tel: 717-733-1291.

FAIRFIELD, ADAMS CO., IMMACULATE CONCEPTION OF THE BLESSED VIRGIN MARY (1823) [CEM] [JC] Revs. Michael A. Messaro, M.SS.CC.; Robert Malagesi, M.SS.CC., Parochial Vicar.
Res.: 256 Tract Rd., P.O. Box 704, 17320. Tel: 717-642-8815; Fax: 717-642-9616. Email: bstaples@hbgdiocese.org.
Catechesis/Religious Program—Students 95.

GETTYSBURG, ADAMS CO., ST. FRANCIS XAVIER'S (1831) [CEM] Revs. Benardo Pistone; Jonathan P. Sawicki; Deacon James Sneeringer.
Res.: 22 W. High St., 17325. Tel: 717-334-3919; 717-334-7711; Fax: 717-334-3919.
School—45 W. High St., 17325. Tel: 717-334-4221; Fax: 717-334-8883. Sr. Phyllis, R.S.M., Prin. Sisters of Mercy 3; Sisters of St. Joseph 1; Lay Teachers 13; Students 250.
Catechesis/Religious Program—Tel: 717-334-1221. Students 180.
Convent—Sisters of Mercy Convent, Tel: 717-334-4310. Sisters 5.

GREENCASTLE, FRANKLIN CO., ST. MARK THE EVANGELIST (1965) [JC] Rev. Joseph L. Stahura.
Res.: 395 S. Ridge Ave., P.O. Box 218, 17225. Tel: 717-597-2705. Email: stmkstlk@comcast.net.
Catechesis/Religious Program—Tel: 717-597-2705. Students 149.
Mission—St. Luke the Evangelist Overhill Dr. & Black Rd., Mercersburg, Franklin Co. 17236.

HANOVER, YORK CO.
1—ST. JOSEPH (1864) [CEM] Very Rev. Joseph F. Gotwalt; Rev. Timothy D. Marcoe.
Res.: 5055 Grandview Rd., 17331. Tel: 717-637-5236; Fax: 717-637-6615. Web: www.stjosephparishhanover.org.
School—236 Baltimore St., 17331. Tel: 717-632-1335; Fax: 717-632-5147. Web: www.stjosephschool-hanover.org. Mrs. Susan M. Mummert, Prin. Lay Teachers 16; Students 220.
School—Middle School, 5125 Grandview Rd., 17331. Tel: 717-632-0118; Fax: 717-632-0030.
Catechesis/Religious Program—Students 417.
2—ST. VINCENT (1904) [CEM] Rev. John A. Szada Jr.
Res.: 220 Third St., 17331. Tel: 717-637-4625; Fax: 717-637-6650. Email: dklinedinst@hbgdiocese.org. Web: www.stvincentdepaulparish.org.
School—224 Third St., 17331. Tel: 717-637-5190;

Fax: 717-637-0666. Email: office@svschool.net. Lay Teachers 12; Students 107.
Catechesis/Religious Program—Students 69.
HERSHEY, DAUPHIN CO., ST. JOAN OF ARC (1920) Very Rev. Philip G. Burger; Rev. Walter F. Guzman, Parochial Vicar. In Res., Rev. Chukwubikem Okpechi, O.P., Chap., Hershey Medical Center.
Res.: 359 W. Areba Ave., 17033. Tel: 717-533-7168; Fax: 717-520-0526. Email: sjaoffice@gmail.com. Web: www.stjoanhershey.org.
School—329 W. Areba Ave., 17033. Tel: 717-533-2854; Fax: 717-534-0755. Email: sreileen@stjoanhershey.org. Sr. Eileen M. McGowan, Prin. Daughters of Our Lady of Mercy 1; Lay Teachers 28; Students 250.
Catechesis/Religious Program—Tel: 717-533-8578. Email: stjoanrep@yahoo.com. Students 702.
Convent—Sisters 5.
KULPMONT, NORTHUMBERLAND CO.
1—ASSUMPTION OF THE BLESSED VIRGIN MARY (1909) Closed. See Holy Angels, Kulpmont.
2—ST. CASIMIR (1915) Closed. See Holy Angels, Kulpmont.
3—HOLY ANGELS (1995) [CEM 3] Rev. Andrew J. Stahmer.
Res.: 855 Scott St., 17834. Tel: 570-373-1221; Fax: 570-373-1226.
Catechesis/Religious Program—863 Scott St., 17834. Tel: 570-373-3801. Students 101.
LANCASTER, LANCASTER CO.
1—ST. ANNE (1923) Rev. Norman C. Hohenwarter Jr.; Deacon Joseph L. Anders.
Res.: 929 N. Duke St., 17602. Tel: 717-392-2225; Fax: 717-392-3985. Email: mwelsh@hbgdiocese.org.
School—108 E. Liberty St., 17602. Tel: 717-394-6711; Fax: 717-394-8628. Dr. Christopher Kennedy, Prin.
Catechesis/Religious Program—Tel: 717-509-8554. Mrs. Kelly Townsend, C.R.E. Students 227.
2—ST. ANTHONY OF PADUA (1870) [CEM] Rev. Daniel C. Mitzel. In Res., Rev. John A. Acri (Retired).
Res.: 501 E. Orange St., 17602. Tel: 717-394-0669; Fax: 717-394-4507.
See Resurrection, Lancaster under Consolidated Elementary Schools located in the Institution section.
Catechesis/Religious Program—Tel: 717-392-2930. Patricia Meyer, D.R.E. Students 153.
Station—Lancaster County Prison, Tel: 717-299-7800.
Station—Conestoga View Nursing Home, Tel: 717-299-7850.
3—ASSUMPTION OF THE BLESSED VIRGIN MARY (1741) Rev. Leo M. Goodman; Mrs. Frances Sescilla, Pastoral Assoc.; Deacon Manuel Velazquez.
Res.: 119 S. Prince St., 17603. Tel: 717-392-2578; Fax: 717-394-6549. Email: p049assumptionlanc@hbgdiocese.org. Web: www.stmaryslancaster.org.
See Resurrection, Lancaster under Consolidated Elementary Schools located in the Institution section.
Catechesis/Religious Program—Anne Barnes, C.R.E. Students 191.
4—IGLESIA CATOLICA SAN JUAN BAUTISTA Revs. Allan F. Wolfe; Luis A. Jimenez Vargas (Colombia), Parochial Vicar; Deacons Expedito Santos-Santiago; Manuel Velazquez; Felix Ramos.
425 S. Duke St., 17602. Tel: 717-392-4118; Fax: 717-392-4789. Email: p127sanjuan@hbgdiocese.org.
Catechesis/Religious Program—Megan M. Conti, D.R.E. Students 365.
5—ST. JOHN NEUMANN (1978) Rev. Msgr. Richard A. Youtz; Revs. Paul Theisz; Michael J. Culkin; Rose M. Toole, Pastoral Assoc.; Mrs. Yolanda Larson, Pastoral Assoc.
Res.: 601 E. Delp Rd., 17601. Tel: 717-569-8531; Fax: 717-569-2135.
Catechesis/Religious Program—Tel: 717-569-8533. Mrs. Rose Poet, D.R.E. Students 1,175.
6—ST. JOSEPH (1849) [CEM] Rev. Msgr. Thomas H. Smith; Mrs. Patricia Weaver, Pastoral Assoc. In Res., Rev. Joseph C. Hilbert (Retired).
Res.: 440 St. Joseph St., 17603-5298. Tel: 717-397-6921; Fax: 717-397-2120. Email: msgrtsmith@hbgdiocese.org. Web: www.stjosephslanc.com.
See Resurrection, Lancaster under Consolidated Elementary Schools located in the Institution section.
Catechesis/Religious Program—Students 200.
7—SACRED HEART OF JESUS (1900) Rev. Michael E. Messner. In Res., Rev. Arokiaswamy Samson.
Res.: 558 W. Walnut St., 17603. Tel: 717-394-0757; Fax: 717-394-3589. Email: sacredheartlanc@verizon.net. Web: sacredheartlanc.org.
School—235 Nevin St., 17603. Tel: 717-393-8433; Fax: 717-393-1028. Email: shschool@comcast.net. Web: www.sacredheartschoollancaster.com. Sr. Mary Carmel, I.H.M., Prin. Sisters (Servants of the Immaculate Heart of Mary) 3; Lay Teachers 14; Students 169.
Catechesis/Religious Program—Sr. Mary Elizabeth Schmidt, I.H.M., D.R.E. Students 43.
Convent—565 W. Walnut St., 17603. Tel: 717-392-4522.
LEBANON, LEBANON CO.
1—ASSUMPTION OF THE BLESSED VIRGIN MARY (1812) [CEM] Rev. Michael P. Reid II; Deacon Richard Wentzel, Pastoral Assoc. In Res., Rev. Harold F. Dagle (ALN) (Retired).
Office & Res.: 2 N. Eighth St., 17046-5008. Tel: 717-272-5674; Fax: 717-270-2734. Email: abvmleb@comcast.net.
Catechesis/Religious Program—Students 110.
Mission—Our Lady of Fatima US 22 & N. Mill St., Jonestown, Lebanon Co. 17038. Tel: 717-865-7439.
2—ST. BENEDICT THE ABBOT (1995) Rev. Michael W. Rothan.
Res.: 1300 Lehman St., 17046-3331. Tel: 717-450-4506; Fax: 717-270-6926. Web: www.sbaclpa.com.
Catechesis/Religious Program—Students 103.
3—ST. CECILIA (1995) [CEM] Rev. Joseph T. Scanlin.
Res.: 202 E. Lehman St., 17046. Tel: 717-272-4412; Fax: 717-272-3966. Email: scecilia@nbn.net.
Catechesis/Religious Program—Tel: 717-272-4352. Sisters 1; Students 180.
Convent—202 E. Lehman St., 2nd Fl., 17046.
4—SS. CYRIL AND METHODIUS (1905), (Slovak), Closed. See St. Benedict the Abbot, Lebanon.
5—ST. GERTRUDE (1906) Closed. See St. Cecilia, Lebanon.
6—ST. GREGORY THE GREAT (1965) Closed. See St. Cecilia, Lebanon.
LEWISBURG, UNION CO., SACRED HEART OF JESUS (1935) Rev. Msgr. William M. Richardson.
Res.: 814 St. Louis St., 17837. Tel: 570-523-3104; Fax: 570-523-3157.
Catechesis/Religious Program— Kevin Hilgert, Youth Min.; Sr. Thomas More Dzurnak, SS.C.M., D.R.E., Pastoral Asst. Students 325.
Mission—Saint George Church 775 Forest Hill Rd., Mifflinburg, Union Co. 17844. Tel: 570-966-3088.
LEWISTOWN, MIFFLIN CO., SACRED HEART OF JESUS (1830) [CEM] Very Rev. William M. Weary; Rev. Jeffrey Thoms.
Office: 9 N. Brown St., 17044. Tel: 717-242-2781; Fax: 717-447-0058. Email: mbender@sacredheartlewistown.com. Web: www.sacredheartlewistown.com.
Res.: 106 N. Dorcas St., 17044. Tel: 717-447-0727.
School—110 N. Dorcas St., 17044. Tel: 717-248-5351; 717-447-2002; Fax: 717-248-1516. Email: shsoffice@sacredheartlewistown.com. Web: www.sacredheartschool.com. Lay Teachers 9; Students 74.
Catechesis/Religious Program—Email: p135sacredheartlewtn@hbgdiocese.org. Students 85.
LITITZ, LANCASTER CO., ST. JAMES (1977) [CEM 3] Rev. James O'Blaney, C.Ss.R.
Res.: 505 Woodcrest Ave., 17543. Tel: 717-626-5580; Fax: 717-626-2146. Email: p060stjames@hbgdiocese.org. Web: www.stjameslititz.org.
Catechesis/Religious Program—Tel: 717-626-0244. Email: re060@hbgdiocese.org. Rose Barnas, D.R.E. Students 369.
LITTLESTOWN, ADAMS CO., ST. ALOYSIUS (1884) [CEM] Rev. James M. Sterner.
Res.: 29 S. Queen St., 17340. Tel: 717-359-4513; Fax: 717-359-0683.
Catechesis/Religious Program— Cynthia Baughman, D.R.E. Students 83.
LOCUST GAP, NORTHUMBERLAND CO., ST. JOSEPH (1870) Closed. See Our Lady of Mount Carmel, Mount Carmel.
LOCUSTDALE, COLUMBIA CO., ST. JOSEPH (1913) Closed. See Our Lady of Mount Carmel, Mount Carmel.
LYKENS, DAUPHIN CO., OUR LADY HELP OF CHRISTIANS (1853) [CEM 2] [JC 3] Rev. C. Anthony Miller.
Res.: 732 E. Main St., 17048. Tel: 717-453-7895; Fax: 717-453-9426.
Catechesis/Religious Program—Students 76.
Mission—Sacred Heart of Jesus 140 E. Market St., Williamstown, Dauphin Co. 17098. Tel: 717-647-2645.
MANHEIM, LANCASTER CO., ST. RICHARD (1957) [JC] Rev. Francis Menei; Deacon William J. Jordan.
Res.: 201 Adele Ave., 17545. Tel: 717-665-2465; Fax: 717-665-7119.
Catechesis/Religious Program—Karen Henderson, D.R.E. Students 89.
MARIETTA, LANCASTER CO., PRESENTATION OF THE BLESSED VIRGIN MARY (1869) Closed. See Mary, Mother of the Church, Mount Joy.
MARION HEIGHTS, NORTHUMBERLAND CO., OUR LADY OF PERPETUAL HELP (1905) Closed. See Holy Angels, Kulpmont.
MARYSVILLE, PERRY CO., OUR LADY OF GOOD COUNSEL (1965) Rev. John P. Trigilio Jr.
Res.: 121 William St., 17053. Tel: 717-957-2662; Fax: 717-957-4247. Email: church@olgcsb.org. Web: www.olgcsb.org.
Catechesis/Religious Program—Tel: 717-957-9218. Emily VisLocky, D.R.E. Students 26.
Mission—St. Bernadette (1954) 901 High St., Duncannon, Perry Co. 17020. Tel: 717-834-4519.
Catechesis/Religious Program—Students 39.
MCSHERRYSTOWN, ADAMS CO., ANNUNCIATION OF THE BLESSED VIRGIN MARY (1899) [CEM] Rev. Lawrence W. Sherdel; Deacon Joseph F. Lawrence.
Res.: 26 N. Third St., 17344. Tel: 717-637-1191; Fax: 717-637-1715.
School—316 North St., 17344. Tel: 717-637-3135. Email: abvmbusoff@abvmschool.org. Web: www.abvmschool.org. Sr. Ann Marie Wierman, S.S.J., Prin. Lay Teachers 22; Students 287.
Catechesis/Religious Program—Students 45.
MECHANICSBURG, CUMBERLAND CO.
1—ST. ELIZABETH ANN SETON (1977) Rev. Richard P. Waldron. In Res., Rev. Msgr. William J. King.
Res.: 310 Hertzler Rd., 17055. Tel: 717-697-2614; Fax: 717-795-0800. Email: frrwaldron@hbgdiocese.org. Web: www.steas-mech.org.
Catechesis/Religious Program—Tel: 717-697-3545. Email: cstrakaseas@comcast.net. Candice Straka, C.R.E.; Judy Olinger, C.R.E. Students 402.
2—ST. JOSEPH (1950) Revs. Chester P. Snyder; Joshua R. Brommer; Deacon Jack Paruso; John Durle, Parish Mgr.
410 E. Simpson St., P.O. Box 2012, 17055.
Res.: P.O. Box 2012, 17055. Tel: 717-766-9433 (Office); Fax: 717-795-9123. Email: parishoffice@stjosephmech.org.
Church: 400 E. Simpson St., 17055.
School—420 E. Simpson St., 17055. Tel: 717-766-2564; Fax: 717-766-1226. Sisters of SS. Cyril and Methodius 2; Lay Teachers 24; Students 403.
Catechesis/Religious Program—Tel: 717-766-2472. Sr. Joseph Therese, D.R.E. Students 343.
3—SAINT KATHARINE DREXEL (1988) Rev. Stephen D. Weitzel; Rev. Msgr. Vincent J. Smith (Retired); John Frye III, Music Min.
Mailing Address: One Peter Dr., 17050. Email: skdparish@comcast.net. Web: www.skdparish.com. In Res., Rev. Msgr. Vincent J. Smith (Retired).
Res.: 87 Skyline Dr., 17050. Tel: 717-697-8716; Fax: 717-697-3702.
Catechesis/Religious Program—Tel: 717-795-8572. Kristine Hammar, D.R.E.; Gail Chaudrue, Dir., Youth & Young Adult Ministry. Students 397.
MIDDLETOWN, DAUPHIN CO., SEVEN SORROWS OF THE BLESSED VIRGIN MARY (1855) Rev. Louis P. Ogden. In Res., Rev. Edward R. Lavelle.
Res.: 280 N. Race St., 17057. Tel: 717-944-3133; Fax: 717-944-1170. Email: church@sevensorrows.org. Web: www.sevensorrows.org.
School—(Grades PreK-8), 360 E. Water St., 17057. Tel: 717-944-5371; Fax: 717-944-5419. Mrs. Loretta Miller, Prin. Lay Teachers 16; Students 240.
Catechesis/Religious Program— Ray Kerwin, D.R.E. Students 165.
MIFFLINTOWN, JUNIATA CO., ST. JUDE (1959) Very Rev. William M. Weary; Rev. Jeffrey Thoms, Parochial Vicar.
P.O. Box 187, 17059.
Res.: 106 N. Dorcas St., Lewistown, 17044. Tel: 717-242-2781. Email: rectory@stjudemifflintown.org. Web: www.stjudemifflintown.org.
Catechesis/Religious Program—Students 56.
MILLERSBURG, DAUPHIN CO., QUEEN OF PEACE (1952) Rev. Darius G. C. Moss.
Res.: 202 Zimmerman Rd., 17061. Tel: 717-692-3504.
Catechesis/Religious Program—Tel: 717-692-3504. Mrs. J. Roadcap, D.R.E. Students 115.
MILLERSVILLE, LANCASTER CO., ST. PHILIP THE APOSTLE (1965) Rev. Mark E. Weiss; Deacon Ross Beighley.
Res.: 2111 Millersville Pike, Lancaster, 17603. Tel: 717-872-2166; Fax: 717-872-2587.
Catechesis/Religious Program—Tel: 717-872-5653 (Sundays only). Miss Christine M. Miller, D.R.E. Students 347.
MILTON, NORTHUMBERLAND CO., ST. JOSEPH (1805) [CEM] Rev. Thomas A. Scala.
Res.: 109 Broadway, 17847. Tel: 570-742-4356; Fax: 570-742-3475.
Catechesis/Religious Program—854 Cemetery Rd., 17847. Tel: 570-724-4302. Harold Prentiss, C.R.E. Students 39.
MOUNT CARMEL, NORTHUMBERLAND CO.
1—DIVINE REDEEMER (1995) [CEM 4] Rev. Robert A. Yohe Jr.
Res.: 438 West Ave., 17851. Tel: 570-339-3450; Fax: 570-339-5759. Email: divredeemr@verizon.net.
Catechesis/Religious Program—47 S. Market St., 17851. Tel: 570-339-1317; Fax: 570-339-4814. Students 57.
2—HOLY CROSS (1892), (Lithuanian), Closed. See Divine Redeemer, Mount Carmel.
3—ST. JOHN THE BAPTIST (1892), (Slovak), Closed. See Divine Redeemer, Mount Carmel.

4—ST. JOSEPH (1875), (Polish), Closed. See Our Lady of Mount Carmel, Mount Carmel.
5—OUR LADY OF MOUNT CARMEL (1886) [JC 4] Very Rev. Francis J. Karwacki.
Res.: 47 S. Market St., 17851. Tel: 717-339-1031; Fax: 717-339-4814.
Catechesis/Religious Program—Tel: 717-339-1317. Karen Harris, C.R.E. Students 120.
6—OUR MOTHER OF CONSOLATION (1895), (Polish), Closed. See Divine Redeemer, Mount Carmel.
7—ST. PETER (1905), (Italian), Closed. See Divine Redeemer, Mount Carmel.

MOUNT JOY, LANCASTER CO.
1—ASSUMPTION OF B.V.M. (1979) Closed. See Mary, Mother of the Church, Mount Joy.
2—MARY, MOTHER OF THE CHURCH (1995) Rev. Luis R. Rodriguez.
Mailing Address: 625 Union School Rd., 17552-9712.
Res.: 530 St. Mary Dr., 17552-9712. Tel: 717-653-4903. Email: p138marymother@hbgdiocese.org.
Catechesis/Religious Program—Students 139.

MYERSTOWN, LEBANON COUNTY, MARY, GATE OF HEAVEN (1926) Rev. Robert F. Berger.
Res.: 188 W. McKinley Ave., P.O. Box 227, 17067. Tel: 717-866-5640; Fax: 717-866-5951.
Catechesis/Religious Program—Students 83.

NEW BLOOMFIELD, PERRY CO., ST. BERNARD (1942) Rev. Robert F. Sharman.
Res.: 811 Shermans Valley Rd., P.O. Box 25, 17068. Tel: 717-582-4113; Fax: 717-582-3797.
Catechesis/Religious Program— Alice Vilk, D.R.E. Students 127.

NEW CUMBERLAND, CUMBERLAND CO., ST. THERESA OF THE INFANT JESUS (1928) Revs. James E. Lease; J. Michael McFadden. In Res., Rev. T. Ronald Haney (Retired).
Res.: 1300 Bridge St., 17070. Tel: 717-774-5918; Fax: 717-774-5915.
School—1200 Bridge St., 17070. Tel: 717-774-7464; Fax: 717-774-3154. Mr. Michael Tracy, Prin. (Elementary); Dr. David Bouton, Prin. (Trinity High School). Lay Teachers 32; Students 496.
Catechesis/Religious Program—Tel: 717-774-7296. Students 788.

NEW FREEDOM, YORK CO., ST. JOHN THE BAPTIST (1841) [CEM] Revs. Sylvan P. Capitani; Bernard Wamayose, A.J., Parochial Vicar; Deacon Michael Bahn, Pastoral Assoc. In Res., Rev. C. Robert Nugent, S.D.S.
Res.: 315 N. Constitution Ave., 17349. Tel: 717-235-2156; Fax: 717-235-8595.
Catechesis/Religious Program—Tel: 717-235-2439. Students 504.

NEW HOLLAND, LANCASTER CO., OUR LADY OF LOURDES (1972) Rev. John D. Schmalhofer.
Res.: 737 Walnut St., 17557. Tel: 717-354-2540; Fax: 717-354-4170.
Catechesis/Religious Program—Tel: 717-354-3338. Students 218.

NEW OXFORD, ADAMS CO., IMMACULATE CONCEPTION OF THE BLESSED VIRGIN MARY (1852) [CEM] Rev. Daniel P. O'Brien.
Res.: 106 Carlisle St., 17350. Tel: 717-624-4121; Fax: 717-624-4221.
School—101 N. Peter St., 17350. Tel: 717-624-2061; Fax: 717-624-9711. Dianne Giampietro, Prin. Lay Teachers 14; Students 133.
Catechesis/Religious Program—Tel: 717-321-3939; Fax: 717-624-4221. Kimberly DePaulis, D.R.E. Students 278.

NORTHUMBERLAND, NORTHUMBERLAND CO., ST. THOMAS MORE (1955) Closed. See St. Monica, Sunbury.

PALMYRA, LEBANON CO., CHURCH OF THE HOLY SPIRIT (1955) Rev. James F. Podlesny, O.S.B.
Res.: 245 W. Pine St., 17078. Tel: 717-838-3369; Fax: 717-838-3065. Email: church@holyspiritrcchurch.com. Web: holyspiritrcchurch.com.
Catechesis/Religious Program— Marcie Warner, C.R.E. Students 361.

QUARRYVILLE, LANCASTER CO., ST. CATHERINE OF SIENA (1843) [CEM] Rev. Ronald J. Moratelli.
Res.: 955 Robert Fulton Hwy., 17566-9543. Tel: 717-786-2695; Fax: 717-786-0374. Email: p096stcatherinesiena@hbgdiocese.org.
Catechesis/Religious Program—Mrs. Diane Dalgaard, D.R.E. Students 195.

RANSHAW, NORTHUMBERLAND CO., ST. ANTHONY OF PADUA (1919) Closed. See Mother Cabrini, Shamokin.

ROARING CREEK, COLUMBIA CO., OUR LADY OF MERCY (1923) [CEM] Rev. Thomas Ignatius Mannion.
Res.: 304 Slabtown Rd., Catawissa, 17820. Tel: 570-799-5642.
Catechesis/Religious Program—Mrs. Margaret Jessick, D.R.E. Students 62.

ROHRERSTOWN, LANCASTER CO., ST. LEO THE GREAT (1964) Revs. Peter I. Hahn; Tiburtis Antony Raja; Deacon Eugene Vannucci.
Res.: 2427 Marietta Ave., Lancaster, 17601. Tel: 717-394-1742; Fax: 717-394-1779. Email: secretary@stleos.org. Web: www.stleos.org.
School—(Grades K-8) Tel: 717-392-2441; Fax: 717-392-4080. Email: secretary@stleoschool.org. Web: www.stleoschool.org. Mrs. Georgia Steinbacher, Prin. Lay Teachers 17; Students 252.
Catechesis/Religious Program—Tel: 717-394-7354. Email: psr@stleos.org. Sr. Dorothy Wilkinson, S.S.C., D.R.E. Students 438.

SELINSGROVE, SNYDER CO., ST. PIUS X (1964) Rev. Edward J. Keating Jr.
Res.: 112 Fairview Dr., 17870-9406. Tel: 570-374-4113; Fax: 570-374-0156.
Catechesis/Religious Program—Students 256.
Mission—Susquehanna University, Snyder Co. 17870.
Mission—Selinsgrove Center, Snyder Co. 17870. Tel: 570-374-4113.
Mission—Snyder County Prison, Snyder Co.

SHAMOKIN, NORTHUMBERLAND CO.
1—ASSUMPTION OF THE BLESSED VIRGIN MARY (1892), (Slovak), Closed. See Mother Cabrini, Shamokin.
2—ST. EDWARD (1866) Closed. See Mother Cabrini, Shamokin.
3—ST. JOSEPH (1913) Closed, See Our Lady of Hope, Coal Township.
4—ST. MICHAEL ARCHANGEL (1894), (Lithuanian), Closed. See Mother Cabrini, Shamokin.
5—MOTHER CABRINI (1995) [JC 4] Revs. Dennis Grumsey, O.F.M.Conv.; Adam Ziolkowski, O.F.M.Conv.; Paul Marut, O.F.M.Conv.
Res.: 214 N. Shamokin St., 17872. Tel: 570-648-4512; Fax: 570-648-1209.
Catechesis/Religious Program—Students 92.
6—ST. STANISLAUS KOSTKA (1874), (Polish), Closed. See Mother Cabrini, Shamokin.

SHIPPENSBURG, CUMBERLAND CO., OUR LADY OF THE VISITATION (1950) Rev. David A. Hillier.
Res.: 305 N. Prince St., 17257. Tel: 717-532-2912; Fax: 717-532-3905. Email: ourlady106@yahoo.com.
Catechesis/Religious Program—Students 235.

SOUTH MOUNTAIN, FRANKLIN CO., MOST HOLY ROSARY, Closed. See St. Ignatius, Buchanan Valley.

SPRING GROVE, YORK CO., SACRED HEART (1976) Rev. Thomas C. Marickovic.
Res.: 152 N. Main St., Box 42, 17362. Tel: 717-225-1704; Fax: 717-225-9570. Email: sacredheart07@comcast.net. Web: www.sacredheartsg.org.
Catechesis/Religious Program—Sacred Heart Parish Center, 1031 Sprenkle Rd., 17362. Tel: 717-225-1997. Marianne Harbold, C.R.E.; Kristine Trettel, C.R.E. Students 79.

STEELTON, DAUPHIN CO.
1—ST. ANN (1901), (Italian), Closed. See Prince of Peace, Steelton.
2—ASSUMPTION OF THE BLESSED VIRGIN MARY (1898), (Croatian), Closed. See Prince of Peace, Steelton.
3—ST. JAMES (1878) Closed. See Prince of Peace, Steelton.
4—ST. PETER (1909), (Slovenian), Closed. See Prince of Peace, Steelton.
5—PRINCE OF PEACE (1995) Rev. James M. Lyons; Deacon Michael Grella. In Res., Rev. Raymond J. LaVoie.
Res.: 815 S. Second St., 17113. Tel: 717-985-1330; Fax: 717-985-1333. Email: pop.parish@comcast.net.
School—245 Reynders Ave., 17113. Tel: 717-939-6357; Fax: 717-939-3660. Kimberly DePaulis, Prin. Religious Sisters of Mercy 1; Daughters of Mercy 1; Lay Teachers 10; Students 153.
Catechesis/Religious Program—Students 38.

SUNBURY, NORTHUMBERLAND CO.
1—ST. MICHAEL ARCHANGEL (1863) Closed. See St. Monica, Sunbury.
2—ST. MONICA (1995) Rev. William T. Haviland; Linda Walborn, Pastoral Assoc.
Res.: 20 N. Front St., 17801. Tel: 570-286-0761; Fax: 570-286-8588. Email: p141stmonica@hbgdiocese.org.
School—109 Market St., 17801. Tel: 570-286-5983; Fax: 570-286-7351. Email: office@saintmonica.sunbury.pa.us. Web: saintmonicasunbury.com. Susan Bickhart, Prin. Lay Teachers 13; Students 135.
Catechesis/Religious Program—Email: 141stmonica@hbgdiocese.org. Sherri Scholl, D.R.E. Students 73.

TREVORTON, NORTHUMBERLAND CO., ST. PATRICK (1850) [CEM] Revs. Adrian Gallagher, O.F.M.Conv.; Daniel Fink, O.F.M.Conv., Parochial Vicar.
Res.: 331 W. Shamokin St., 17881-1523. Tel: 570-797-8251; Fax: 570-797-3990. Email: stpats@ptd.net.
Catechesis/Religious Program—Tel: 570-797-3545. Students 55.

WAYNESBORO, FRANKLIN CO., ST. ANDREW (1893) [CEM] Rev. John B. Bateman.
Res.: 12 N. Broad St., 17268. Tel: 717-762-1914; Fax: 717-762-3319. Email: office.standrew@embarqmail.com. Web: www.standrewwbo.org.
School—213 E. Main St., 17268. Tel: 717-762-3221; Fax: 717-762-8474. Email: standrewschool@embarqmail.com. Web: www-.saintandrewschool.org. Mrs. Marilynn Noel, Prin. Lay Teachers 13; Students 113.
Catechesis/Religious Program—Fax: 717-762-3319. Email: peg.standrew@embarqmail.com. Margaret E. Wagaman, D.R.E. Students 114.

WILLIAMSTOWN, DAUPHIN CO., SACRED HEART OF JESUS (1875) [CEM] [JC] Rev. C. Anthony Miller.
Church: 140 E. Market St., 17098. Tel: 717-453-7895; Fax: 717-453-9426.
Res.: 732 Main St., Lykens, 17048.
Catechesis/Religious Program—Tel: 717-647-2645. Earl Roberts, D.R.E. Students 61.

YORK, YORK CO.
1—IMMACULATE CONCEPTION OF THE BLESSED VIRGIN MARY (1852) [CEM] [JC] Very Rev. Robert M. Gillelan Jr.; Rev. Michael C. Letteer; Deacon Catalino Gonzalez, Pastoral Assoc. In Res., Rev. L. Frederick Nkwasibwe, A.J.
Res.: 309 S. George St., 17401. Tel: 717-845-7629; Fax: 717-845-2433. Email: stmarysyork@comcast.net.
Catechesis/Religious Program—Tel: 717-846-6001. Ms. Karen Kreller, D.R.E. Students 275.
2—ST. JOSEPH (1913) [JC] Revs. Louis Petruha, O.F.M.Cap.; Stephen Shin, O.F.M.Cap.; Joseph A. Tuscan, O.F.M.Cap. In Res., Bro. Michael Rubus, O.F.M.Cap.
Res.: 2935 Kingston Rd., 17402-4003. Tel: 717-755-7503; Fax: 717-757-1900. Web: www.sjy.org.
School—2945 Kingston Rd., 17402. Tel: 717-755-1797; Fax: 717-751-0136. Mrs. Patricia A. Byrnes, Prin. Lay Teachers 25; Students 348.
Catechesis/Religious Program— Sr. Jean Holtz, S.S.J., D.R.E.; Bernadette L. Snook, C.R.E. Students 754.
3—ST. PATRICK (1776) [CEM] Rev. Samuel E. Houser; Deacon Sam Moschella; Sr. Monica Imgrund, R.S.M., Pastoral Assoc. In Res., Rev. William M. Cawley (GF).
Res.: 231 S. Beaver St., 17401. Tel: 717-848-2007. Email: rectoryoffice@stpatrickyork.org. Web: www.stpatrickyork.org.
School—235 S. Beaver St., 17401. Tel: 717-854-8263; Fax: 717-846-6049. Email: schooloffice@stpatrickyork.org. Sr. Mary Elizabeth Muir, I.H.M., Prin. Lay Teachers 12; Students 148.
Catechesis/Religious Program—219 S. Beaver St., 17401. Tel: 717-854-6653. Email: stpatrick_re@yahoo.com. Susan Varholy, C.R.E. Students 175.
4—ST. ROSE OF LIMA (1907) [JC] Rev. Thomas R. Hoke. In Res., Rev. Carl T. Tancredi.
Res.: 950 W. Market St., 17401. Tel: 717-846-4935; Fax: 717-699-0715.
School—115 N. Biesecker Rd., Thomasville, 17364. Tel: 717-792-0889; Fax: 717-792-3959. Peggy Rizzuio, Prin. Lay Teachers 14; Students 182.
Catechesis/Religious Program—Tel: 717-843-3043. Sr. Jane Keller, S.S.J., D.R.E. Students 417.
Convent—Sisters of St. Joseph, 944 W. Market St., 17404. Tel: 717-854-0378. Sisters 5.

YORK HAVEN, YORK CO., HOLY INFANT (1972) Very Rev. Edward C. Malesic; Rebecca Papa, Pastoral Asst.; Deacon Joseph J. Kramer.
Res.: 34 Third St., P.O. Box 398, 17370. Tel: 717-266-5286. Email: holyinfantyh@comcast.net. Web: www.holyinfantparish.com.
Catechesis/Religious Program—Students 186.

Chaplains of Public Institutions

HARRISBURG. *Community General Osteopathic Hospital*. Rev. Gregory Chervenak, O.F.M.Cap.
Pinnacle Health System, Tel: 717-782-5208. Rev. Gregory Chervenak, O.F.M.Cap.
Polyclinic Medical Clinic, Tel: 717-782-4141. Rev. Tri M. Luong.

CAMP HILL. *State Correctional Institution*, P.O. Box 200, 17011. Tel: 717-737-4531, Ext. 4439. Deacon Epifanio DeJesus.

DANVILLE. *Geisinger Medical Center*, Tel: 717-275-2512. Vacant.
State Hospital, P.O. Box 219, 17821. Tel: 717-275-7011. Rev. Patrick A. Devine (Retired). Tel: 570-275-7011.

HERSHEY. *Milton J. Hershey Medical Center*, 500 University Blvd., 17033. Tel: 717-534-8177. Rev. Chukwubikem Okpechi, O.P.

LANCASTER. *Lancaster County Prison*, 625 E. King St., 17602. Tel: 717-534-8177. Deacon Expedito Santos-Santiago.
Lancaster General Hospital and Lancaster Community Hospital. Rev. Arokiaswamy Samson.

LEBANON. *Veterans Administration Hospital*, R.D. No. 1, 17042. Tel: 717-272-6621. Rev. Harold Dagle.

LEWISBURG. *U.S. Penitentiary*, Tel: 717-523-1251. Rev. Carl Johnson.

SELINSGROVE. *Selinsgrove Center*, Box 500, 17870. Tel:

717-374-2911, Ext. 425. Rev. Edward J. Keating Jr.

SOUTH MOUNTAIN. *Restoration Center*, Tel: 717-749-5773. Rev. Joseph C. Carolin.

YORK. *York Hospital*, 1001 S. George St., 17405. Tel: 717-771-2345. Rev. L. Frederick Nkwasibwe, A.J.

On Duty Outside the Diocese:
Revs.—
Bennett, Michael X., St. Mary Church, Ottawa ON Canada.
Blackwell, Edward A., 520 N.E. 20th St., #408, Fort Lauderdale, FL 33305-2195.
Hoke, John R., U.S. Navy
Kemper, John C., S.S., Provincial House, 5408 Roland Ave., Baltimore, MD 21210.
Topper, Charles J., 467 Bloomfield Ave., Bloomfield, CT 06002.

On Medical Leave:
Rev.—
Conrad, Brian P.

Retired:
Rev. Msgrs.—
Bierster, Leo N.
Brenner, Thomas R.
Fregapane, Mercurio A.
Gribbin, Robert C.
Kujovsky, Thomas J.
Overbaugh, Hugh A.
Rost, George W.
Smith, Vincent J.
Topper, Vincent J.
Revs.—
Campion, John R.
Devine, Patrick A., Maria Hall, 1 Maria Hall Dr., Danville, 17821-1669.
Farace, Frederick A., P.O. Box 276, Mount Carmel, 17851.
Fennessy, Joseph H.
Fontanella, Andrew J.
Haney, T. Ronald
Heintzelman, Gerard T.
Hilbert, Joseph C.
Kofchock, Joseph T.
Langan, Thomas
Lytle, Gerald A.
Mammarella, Dominick
Marinak, Andrew P.
Meluskey, Andre J.
Menniti, Daniel J.
Olszewski, Clarence A.
Orloski, Raymond J.
Rindos, Paul T., Bishop Dattilo Retirement Residence for Priests.
Sempko, Walter A.
Shuda, Paul R.
Steffan, Carl J.
Sullivan, William J., St. Joseph, Mechanicsburg

Permanent Deacons:
Anders, Joseph L., St. Anne, Lancaster
Aull, Richard H., St. Matthew's, Dauphin
Bahn, Michael P., St. Joseph, York
Beighley, Ross W., St. Catherine of Siena, Quarryville
Bertollo, Edward L., Jr.
Clark, Charles W., St. Patrick, Harrisburg
Eckman, Frank M., St. Anne, Lancaster
Fedor, Thomas A., St. Catherine Laboure, Harrisburg
Flannery, Thomas H., St. Catherine, Harrisburg
Foerster, Jerome T., Holy Name of Jesus, Harrisburg
Gonzales, Catalino, Spanish-Speaking Apostolate, Harrisburg
Gorini, Joseph B., St. Katharine Drexel, Mechanicsburg
Gorman, Francis, Good Shepherd, Camp Hill
Grella, Michael A., Ed.D., Prince of Peace, Steelton
Jordan, William J.
Kenski, Francis G.
Kramer, Joseph J., Holy Infant, York Haven
Lawrence, Joseph F., Annunciation BVM, McSherrystown
Light, Martin C., Sr., St. Philip, Millersville
Mack, Robert P.
Marroquin, Miguel, Spanish-Speaking Apostolate, Harrisburg
Moschella, Sabino E., St. Patrick, York
Mowery, John A.
Parr, Frank J.
Paruso, John L., St. Joseph, Mechanicsburg
Ramos, Felix, San Juan Bautista, Lancaster
Ryan, Richard A.
Santiago, Expidito, San Juan Bautista, Lancaster
Sferrella, Joseph
Smith, Raymond, Immaculate Heart, Abbottstown
Sneeringer, James
Vannucci, Eugene D., St. Leo the Great, Rohrerstown
Velazquez, Manuel
Weaver, Richard J., St. Joseph, Bonneauville
Weaver, Robert E., St. Joseph Hospital, Lancaster
Wentzel, Richard W., Assumption BVM, Lebanon
Wrabel, Joseph J., Holy Name, Harrisburg

INSTITUTIONS LOCATED IN THE DIOCESE

[A] HIGH SCHOOLS

HARRISBURG. *Bishop McDevitt High School*, 2200 Market St., 17103-2499. Tel: 717-236-7973; Fax: 717-234-1270. Email: info@mcdevitt.org. Web: www.bishopmcdevitt.org. Sr. Mary Anne Bedner, I.H.M., Prin.; Rev. Raymond J. LaVoie, Chap.; Ms. Claire Bianchi, Librarian. Sisters 4; Lay Teachers 45; Students 708.

Bishop McDevitt High School of Harrisburg, 4800 Union Deposit Rd., 17111. Tel: 717-657-4804. Email: frequinlan@hbgdiocese.org.

CAMP HILL. *Trinity High School*, 3601 Simpson Ferry Rd., 17011. Tel: 717-761-1116; Fax: 717-761-7309. Email: dbouton@trinityhs.k12.pa.us. Web: www.trinityhs.k12.pa.us. Dr. David Bouton, Prin.; Rev. James E. Lease, Chap.; Mrs. Dolores Kirkpatrick, Librarian. Sisters 3; Lay Teachers 42; Students 694.

COAL TOWNSHIP. *Our Lady of Lourdes Regional School*, (Grades PreK-12), 2001 Clinton Ave., 17866-1699. Tel: 570-644-0375; Fax: 570-644-7655. Email: lourdes@ptd.net. Web: www.lourdes.k12.pa.us. Sr. Margaret McCullough, I.H.M., Prin. Lay Teachers 32; Students 432.

LANCASTER. *Lancaster Catholic High School*, 650 Juliette Ave., 17601. Tel: 717-509-0315; Fax: 717-509-0312. Email: tfertal@lchsyes.org. Mr. Thomas Fertal, Prin.; Miss Susan Martin, Librarian. Lay Teachers 50; Students 792.

LEBANON. *Lebanon Catholic School* (1859) (Grades PreK-12), 1400 Chestnut St., 17042. Tel: 717-273-3731; Fax: 717-274-5167. Email: mambrosia@lebanoncatholicschool.org; lebanoncatholic@hbgdiocese.org. Web: www.lebanoncatholicschool.org. Mrs. Michele Ambrosia, Prin.; Rose Kury, Vice Prin.; Rev. Michael W. Rothan, Chap.; Mrs. Nancy Pelepko, Librarian. Sisters 1; Lay Teachers 37; Students 385.

MCSHERRYSTOWN. *Delone Catholic High School*, 140 S. Oxford Ave., Mc Sherrystown, 17344. Tel: 717-637-5969; Fax: 717-637-0442. Email: sdelone@hbgdiocese.org. Web: www.delonecatholic.org. Dr. Maureen Thiec, Prin.; Sr. Jackie Staub, S.S.J., Librarian. Sisters 1; Lay Teachers 40.

YORK. *York Catholic High School*, 601 E. Springettsbury Ave., 17403. Tel: 717-846-8871; Fax: 717-843-4588. Email: info@yorkcatholic.org. Web: www.yorkcatholic.org. George E. Andrews Jr., Prin.; Revs. William M. Cawley (GF), Teacher; Timothy D. Marcoe, Chap.; Sr. Gilmary Beagle, Teacher. Priests 1; Sisters 1; Lay Teachers 46; Total Staff 87; Students 711.

[B] CONSOLIDATED ELEMENTARY SCHOOLS

HARRISBURG. *Cathedral School* (1873) 212 State St., 17101. Tel: 717-234-3797; Fax: 717-213-2000. Email: cathedralcs@paonline.com. Web: www.cathedralschoolharrisburg.com. Mrs. Suzanne Gausman, Prin. Sisters 1; Lay Teachers 12; Students 170.

Upper School (Grades PreK-8), St. Patrick's Building: Tel: 717-234-3797; Fax: 717-213-2000. Lay Teachers 10.

Lower School, St. Lawrence Bldg.: Tel: 717-234-3797. Mrs. Suzanne Gausman, Prin. Sisters 1; Lay Teachers 3; Students 182.

BERWICK. *Holy Family Consolidated School*, 728 Washington St., 18603. Tel: 570-752-2021; Fax: 570-752-2914. Craig Lehnowsky, Prin.; Elaine Miknich, Librarian. Lay Teachers 6.

COLUMBIA. *Our Lady of the Angels School* (1998) *Primary Bldg.*, 215 Union St., 17512. Tel: 717-684-2433; Fax: 717-684-5039. *Elementary Bldg.*, 404 Cherry St., 17512. Tel: 717-684-2664. Email: tburg@ourladyoftheangels.org. Mrs. Theresa M. Burg, Prin.

LANCASTER. *Resurrection Catholic School, Primary Bldg.*, 32 W. Vine St., 17603. Tel: 717-397-3136; Fax: 717-295-8475. *Elementary Bldg.*, 521 E. Orange St., 17602. Tel: 717-392-3083; Fax: 717-735-7793. Email: bweaver@resurrectioncatholicschool.net. Miss Brenda Weaver, Prin.; Mrs. Mary Weaver, Librarian. Lay Teachers 10.

[C] PRESCHOOLS AND DAY NURSERIES

MCSHERRYSTOWN. *St. Joseph Academy Preschool*, 90 Main St., 17344. Tel: 717-630-9990. Email: sjaprek@netrax.net. Sr. Anne Leonard Freed, S.S.J., M.S.Ed., Dir. Sisters of St. Joseph. Sisters 1; Students 36; Aides 1.

[D] CATHOLIC CHARITIES COUNSELING & FIELD SERVICES

HARRISBURG. *Department for Catholic Charities Administrative Office*, 4800 Union Deposit Rd., 17111-3710. Tel: 717-657-4804; Fax: 717-657-8683. Web: www.hbgdiocese.org. 4800 Union Deposit Rd., 17105. Mark A. Totaro, Ph.D., MBA, Exec. Dir. & CEO; Peter A. Biasucci, L.S.W., Asst. Exec. Dir.

Adoption Services, 806-C S. 29th St., 17111. Tel: 717-564-7115; Fax: 717-238-6050. Kelly M. Bolton, M.S.W., L.S.W., Dir. Adoption & Specialized Foster Care.

Capital Region Office, 223 North St., 17101. Tel: 717-233-7978; Fax: 717-233-4194. Kirk Reider, A.C.S.W, L.C.S.W., Assoc. Exec. Dir. of Behavioral Health Svcs.

Evergreen House Program, 100 Evergreen St., 17104. Tel: 717-238-6343; Fax: 717-238-4161. Lydia Porter, M.S., CCDP-DIP, Prog. Dir.

Specialized Foster Care, 806-C S. 29th St., 17111. Tel: 717-654-7115; Fax: 717-564-7180. Kelly M. Bolton, M.S.W., L.S.W., Prog. Mgr.

Immigration and Refugee Services, 900 N. 17th St., 17103. Tel: 717-232-0568; Fax: 717-234-1742. Mira Lukic, Assoc. Exec. Residential Svcs.

English As A Second Language Tel: 717-232-0568; Fax: 717-234-7142. Sara Beck, B.A., Mgr.

Employment Services Tel: 717-232-0568; Fax: 717-234-7142. Jonathon Witmer, B.S.

Resettlement Services Tel: 717-232-0568; Fax: 717-909-0968. Mira Lukic, Mgr.

Interfaith Shelter for Homeless Families, 1002 Hemlock Dr., 17110-3588. Tel: 717-236-6783; Fax: 717-236-3271. Linda Grudi, M.S., Prog. Dir.

Lourdeshouse Maternity Services, 1611 Boas St., 17103. Tel: 717-236-3417; Fax: 717-236-4548. Annette Martin, M.H.S., Assoc. Exec. Residential Svcs.

Paradise School, 6156 West Canal Rd., Abbottstown, 17301. Tel: 717-259-9537; Fax: 717-259-9262. Michael Langley, M.P., S.Sc., Prog. Dir.

Chambersburg Office, 533 S. Main St., Chambersburg, 17201. Tel: 717-263-3765; Fax: 717-263-3226. Kirk Reider, A.C.S.W, L.C.S.W., Prog. Dir.

Chambersburg Family Outreach, 336 Philadelphia Ave., Chambersburg, 17201. Tel: 717-264-2332; Fax: 717-264-0654. Christopher Vandenberg, M.H.S., Assoc. Exec. Dir.

Lancaster Office, 925 N. Duke St., Lancaster, 17602. Tel: 717-299-3659; 717-392-2113 (Spanish); Fax: 717-299-1328. Michelle Maddon, M.Ed., Prog. Dir.

Intensive Day Treatment, 47 S. Mulberry St., Lancaster, 17603. Tel: 717-295-9630; Fax: 717-295-9525. Rebecca Diamondstone, M.S., Prog. Dir.

Lancaster In-Home Intensive Services, 417 Poplar St., Lancaster, 17603. Tel: 717-392-3619; Fax: 717-392-4198. Christopher Vandenberg, M.H.S., Assoc. Exec. Dir.

Lebanon Office, 503 Cumberland St., Lebanon, 17042. Tel: 717-273-8514; Fax: 717-273-7518. Kirk Reider, A.C.S.W, L.C.S.W., Dir.

Lebanon Family FOCUS, 503 Cumberland St., Lebanon, 17042. Tel: 717-273-3011; Fax: 717-273-8518. Jan Edwards, M.A., Prog. Dir.

Northern Offices, 815 W. Chestnut St., Coal Township, 17872. Tel: 570-648-6431; Fax: 570-648-9610. Michael McGranaghan, M.S., Prog. Dir.

Northern Offices, One Maria Hall Dr., Danville, 17821. Tel: 570-275-3667 (Voice); Fax: 570-275-6015. Michael McGranaghan, M.S., Prog. Dir.

York Office, 253 E. Market St., York, 17403. Tel: 717-845-2696; Fax: 717-843-3941. Kirk Reider, A.C.S.W, L.C.S.W., Assoc. Exec. Dir. Behavioral Health Svcs.

York/Adams Family Based Program, c/o Paradise School, 6156 W. Canal Rd., Abbottstown, 17301. Tel: 717-845-3373; Fax: 717-845-4101. Christopher Vandenberg, M.H.S., Prog. Dir.

York Intensive Family Services, 26 E. College Ave., York, 17403. Tel: 717-843-7986; Fax: 717-699-0020. Ann Elicker, M.S., Prog. Dir.

HOPE House, 1509 Cresent Ave., Lancaster, 17601. Tel: 717-293-9089; Fax: 717-293-1425. Carol Carp, Prog. Dir.

Dauphin/Cumberland/Perry County Family Based Program, 806-A S. 29th St., 17111. Tel: 717-564-9450; Fax: 717-564-9456. Sandra Holland, M.Div., Prog. Dir.

[E] GENERAL HOSPITALS

CAMP HILL. *Holy Spirit Health Systems*, 503 N. 21st St., 17011-2288. Tel: 717-763-2100; Fax: 717-763-2183. Email: jfegan@hsh.org. Web: www.hsh.org. Sr. Romaine Niemeyer, S.C.C., Pres. & CEO.
Sisters of Christian Charity Health Care Corporation.
Comfort Care of Holy Spirit Hospital, Inc.
Holy Spirit Ventures, Inc.
Holy Spirit Corporation.
West Shore ALS, Inc.
Holy Spirit Hospital.
Spirit Physician Services, Inc. Sisters of Christian Charity. Inpatient Admissions 15,486; Outpatient Visits 242,563; Bed Capacity 328; Bassinets 15; Sisters 26; Total Staff 2,482.

[F] CONVALESCENT & RETIREMENT HOMES

HARRISBURG. *Bishop Dattilo Retirement Residence for Priests* (2001) 675 Rutherford Rd., 17109. Tel: 717-657-3147; Fax: 717-657-3167. Email: retirementresidence@hbgdiocese.org.

COLUMBIA. *St. Anne's Retirement Community* (1954) 3952 Columbia Ave., 17512-9715. Tel: 717-285-5443; Fax: 717-285-5950. Email: mturnbaugh@stannesrc.org. Mary Turnbaugh, Pres. Adorers of the Blood of Christ. Sisters 1; Total Staff 260; Personal Care Staff 20; Residents 121; Cottages 35; Apartments 34; Bed Capacity 243; Residents in Retirement Village 32; Residents in Apartments 40; Personal Care 52; Total Assisted Annually 73.

DANVILLE. *Holy Family Convent and Infirmary*, One Montour St., 17821. Tel: 570-275-3141; Fax: 570-275-9511. Email: sccbronxsb@juno.com. Web: www.scceast.org. Sr. Barbara Armstrong, S.C.C., Local Coord.; Rev. Michael Laicha, Chap. Tel: 717-275-0103. Home for the Aged Sisters of Christian Charity. Sisters of Christian Charity 59; Bed Capacity 95; Total Staff 44; Patients Assisted Annually 50.
Maria Hall, Inc., Maria Hall Dr., 17821. Tel: 570-275-1120; Fax: 570-275-1134. Email: sscmarhl@aol.com. Sr. Margaret Mary, SS.C.M., Admin.; Rev. Cyril J. Rable (SCR) (Retired). Home for retired Sisters of SS. Cyril and Methodius. Sisters 32; Total Assisted 30; Total Staff 22.
Maria Joseph Manor, 875 Montour Blvd., 17821. Tel: 570-275-4221; Fax: 570-275-4711. Sr. M. Marguerite, SS.C.M., Admin.; Mr. Thomas Conlin Jr., COO. Sisters 9; Religious 10; Bed Capacity 190; Total Assisted Annually 455; Total Staff 220.
The Meadows at Maria Joseph Manor, 875 Montour Blvd., 17821. Tel: 570-271-1000; Fax: 570-271-0848. Sr. Elizabeth Ann Matonak, SS.C.M., Dir. Independent Living Units 112; Total Staff 5; Residents 151.

YORK. *Misericordia Convalescent Home* (1943) 998 S. Russell St., 17402. Tel: 717-755-1964; Fax: 717-840-0010. Email: misericordiaadministrator@comcast.net. Marion Bittner, N.H.A., Admin. Daughters of Our Lady of Mercy. Sisters 6; Bed Capacity 50; Total Assisted 107; Total Staff 75.

[G] MONASTERIES AND RESIDENCES OF PRIESTS AND BROTHERS

EPHRATA. *St. Clement's Mission House*, 300 W. Pine St., 17522-2072. Tel: 717-733-6596; Fax: 717-733-0502. Email: omph@ptd.net. Revs. Patrick McGarrity, C.Ss.R.; James O'Blaney, C.Ss.R.; James Small, C.Ss.R.; Thomas Loftus, C.Ss.R.; John McLoughlin, C.Ss.R.; Gerard Schreiber; Virgil Caskey; Richard Knappik; Bros. Thomas Kuhn; Stephen E. Lendray; Robert P. Skinner. Redemptorist Fathers and Brothers. Total in Residence 12.
Mission Preaching Band: Revs. Paul Bryan, C.Ss.R.; John W. Kelly, C.Ss.R.

[H] CONVENTS AND RESIDENCES FOR SISTERS

HARRISBURG. *Immaculate Heart of Mary Convent*, 603 N. Second St., 17101. Tel: 717-236-4821. Email: ihm603@comcast.net. Sr. Maary L. Birster, I.H.M., Supr. Sisters, Servants of the Immaculate Heart of Mary 6.

COLUMBIA. *Adorers of the Blood of Christ* (1834) *Columbia Center*, 3950 Columbia Ave., 17512-9714. Tel: 717-285-4536; Fax: 717-285-9789. Web: www.adorers.org. Sr. Helen Moore, Dir. Comm. Life & Mission. Columbia Center of the Adorers of the Blood of Christ

DANVILLE. *Discalced Carmelite Nuns of Danville, PA* (1953) One Maria Hall Dr., 17821-1237. Tel: 570-275-4682; Fax: 570-275-4684. Sr. Joan Lundy, O.C.D., Prioress. Discalced Carmelite Nuns. Nuns in Solemn Vows 12.
Sisters of Saints Cyril and Methodius (1909) 17821-1698. Tel: 570-275-3581; 570-275-4929; Fax: 570-275-5997. Email: smtmsscm@hotmail.com. Web: www.sscm.org. Sr. Linda Marie Bolinski, SS.C.M., Gen. Supr. Motherhouse of the Sisters of Saints Cyril and Methodius. Sisters 99.
Villa Sacred Heart Formation Center Tel: 570-275-3702; Fax: 570-275-5997. Web: www.sscm.org.
Vocation Office/SCA Spiritual Center Tel: 570-275-1093; Fax: 570-275-5997. Sr. Deborah Marie, SS.C.M., Vocation Dir.
Villa Sacred Heart Music Conservatory, 17821-1698. Tel: 570-275-5185; Fax: 570-275-5997. Email: smlsscm@hotmail.com. Sr. M. Michaelette, SS.C.M., Dir.
St. Cyril Academy Preschool and Kindergarten, 17821-1698. Tel: 570-275-1505; Fax: 570-275-5997. Email: scpandk@hotmail.com. Web: www.sscm.org; www.stcyril1.vpweb.com. Sr. Donna Marie, SS.C.M., Dir.
St. Cyril Academy Spiritual Center, 17821-1698. Tel: 570-275-0910; Fax: 570-275-5997. Email: jeanholupsscm@yahoo.com. Web: www.sscm.org. Sr. Jean Marie Holup, SS.C.M., Dir.

LANCASTER. *Dominican Nuns of the Perpetual Rosary, Incorporated* (1927) 1834 Lititz Pike, 17601-6585. Tel: 717-569-2104; Fax: 717-569-1598. Email: monlanc@aol.com. Sr. Mary Albert, O.P., Prioress; Rev. Edward M. Gaffney, O.P., Chap. Solemnly Professed Nuns 11.

[I] NEWMAN CENTERS

HARRISBURG. *Catholic Campus Ministry* 4800 Union Deposit Rd., 17111-3710. Tel: 717-657-4804; Fax: 717-657-4041. Email: frbednarik@hbgdiocese.org. Web: www.hbgdiocese.org. Very Rev. John F. Bednarik, O.F.M.Cap., M.A.; Robert J. Williams, Assoc. Dir. Tel: 717-657-4804.
Lebanon Valley College 125 S. Spruce St., Annville, 17003. Tel: 717-867-1525. Rev. John J. Peck, O.S.B.
Bloomsburg University of Pennsylvania 353 College Hill, Bloomsburg, 17815. Tel: 570-784-3123; Fax: 570-784-3123. Rev. Donald W. Cramer; Sr. Deborah Borneman.
Dickinson School of Law 140 E. Pomfret St., Carlisle, 17013. Tel: 717-243-4411; Fax: 717-258-9281. Rev. Olusola Adewole, O.P.
Elizabethtown College 1840 Marshall Dr., Elizabethtown, 17022. Tel: 717-367-1255. Rev. David L. Danneker, Ph.D.; Mrs. Angela Sedun, Asst.
Gettysburg College 300 N. Washington St., Box 427, Gettysburg, 17325-0136. Tel: 717-337-6284; Fax: 717-337-6284. Rev. Caesar Belchez; Susan Collinge.
Hershey Medical Center St. Joan of Arc, 359 W. Areba Ave., 17033. Tel: 717-533-7168. Very Rev. Philip G. Burger, V.F.
Messiah College One College Ave., P.O. Box 3006, Grantham, 17027. Tel: 717-766-2511, Ext. 7192; Fax: 717-796-4791. Cathy Poiesz; Anita Voelker.
Franklin and Marshall College, Lancaster 558 W. Walnut St., Lancaster, 17603. Tel: 717-394-0757. Rev. Michael Messner; Bradley Fischer, Campus Min.
Bucknell University Newman Center, 610 St. George St., Lewisburg, 17837. Tel: 570-577-3766; Fax: 570-577-2760. Rev. Fred Wangwe, A.J. (Africa).
Millersville University Newman Center, 227 N. George St., Millersville, 17551. Tel: 717-872-3350; Fax: 717-872-3668. Rev. Pang S. Tcheou, Campus Min.
Susquehanna University Catholic Campus Ministry 312 Charles Ave., Selinsgrove, 17870. Tel: 570-374-9954. Rev. Edward J. Keating Jr.
Shippensburg University 1817 Old Main, Spiritual Center, Rm. 215, Shippensburg, 17257. Tel: 717-532-2912. Rev. David A. Hillier; Roxanne Dennis.
Penn State University, Mont Alto Campus, South Mountain 12 N. Broad St., Waynesboro, 17268. Tel: 717-762-1914. Rev. John Bateman Jr.
Penn State University, York Campus 950 W. Market St., York, 17401. Tel: 717-846-7591. Rev. Carl T. Tancredi.
York College 950 W. Market St., York, 17401. Tel: 717-846-7591. Rev. Carl T. Tancredi.

[J] MISCELLANEOUS LISTINGS

HARRISBURG. *Harrisburg Catholic Administrative Services, Inc.*, 4800 Union Deposit Rd., 17111. Tel: 717-657-4804.
Kolbe Catholic Publishing, Inc., 4800 Union Deposit Rd., 17111-3710. Tel: 717-657-4804, Ext. 387. Email: pkielwein@hbgdiocese.org. Mr. Patrick Kielwein, Print Broker.
The Neumann Scholarship Foundation, 4800 Union Deposit Rd., 17111-3710. Tel: 717-657-4804; Fax: 717-657-3790. Very Rev. Edward J. Quinlan, M.Div., M.A., M.S., Sec. for Educ.
Pennsylvania Catholic Conference, 223 North St., P.O. Box 2835, 17105. Tel: 717-238-9613; Fax: 717-238-1473. Email: info@pacatholic.org. Web: www.pacatholic.org.
Pennsylvania Catholic Conference Scholarship Foundation, 223 North St., P.O. Box 2835, 17105. Tel: 717-238-9613; Fax: 717-238-1473. Email: info@pacatholic.org. Web: www.pacatholic.org. Dr. Robert J. O'Hara Jr., Exec. Dir.
Pennsylvania Catholic Health Association (1963) 223 North St., P.O. Box 2835, 17105. Tel: 717-238-9613; Fax: 717-238-1473. Email: PCHA@pacatholic.org. Web: www.pacatholic.org/pcha. Sr. Clare Christi Schiefer, O.S.F., Pres.
Roman Catholic Diocese of Harrisburg Charitable Trust, 4800 Union Deposit Rd., 17111. Tel: 717-657-4804.
Roman Catholic Diocese of Harrisburg Real Estate Trust, 4800 Union Deposit Rd., 17111. Tel: 717-657-4804.

DANVILLE. *Carmelite Monastery of Wheeling Corp.* (1913) One Maria Hall Dr., 17821-1237. Tel: 570-275-4682; Fax: 570-275-4684. Sr. Joan Lundy, O.C.D., Pres.

ELYSBURG. *Carmel of Jesus, Mary and Joseph in Elysburg, PA, Inc.*, 430 Monastery Rd., 17824. Tel: 570-672-2122.

FAIRFIELD. *Missionaries of the Sacred Hearts of Jesus & Mary House of Studies*, 350 Tract Rd., 17320. Tel: 717-642-5755; Fax: 717-642-5966. Email: msscc5@yahoo.com. Rev. Robert Malagesi, M.SS.CC., Rector & Formation Dir.

LANCASTER. *St. Joseph Health Ministries*, 1929 Lincoln Hwy. E., Ste. 150, 17602. Tel: 717-397-7625; Fax: 717-397-6057. Email: sjhm@catholichealth.net. Web: www.sjhm.org. (An affiliate of Catholic Health Initiatives)
St. Joseph Health Ministries Foundation, 1929 Lincoln Hwy. E., Ste. 150, 17602. Tel: 717-397-7625; Fax: 741-397-6057. Email: sjhm@catholichealth.net. Web: www.sjhm.org. (An affiliate of Catholic Health Initiatives)
St. Joseph Health Services, Inc., 1929 Lincoln Hwy. E., Ste. 150, 17602. Tel: 717-397-7625; Fax: 717-397-6057. Email: sjhm@catholichealth.net. Web: www.shjm.org. (An affiliate of Catholic Health Initiatives)

MCSHERRYSTOWN. *St. Joseph Village Corporation* Sisters of St. Joseph., Residence for Senior Citizens
Village Location (1995) 50 Academy St., 17344. Tel: 717-637-4441; Fax: 717-637-2441. Sr. Joanne Fehrenbach, S.S.J., Gen. Sec. Total Staff 3; Total in Residence 40.

RELIGIOUS INSTITUTES OF MEN REPRESENTED IN THE DIOCESE

For further details refer to the corresponding bracketed number in the Religious Institutes of Men or Women section.

[]—*Apostles of Jesus*
[]—*Benedictine Monks of Saint Vincent Archabbey, Latrobe*
[]—*Capuchin Franciscan Fathers* (Prov. of Saint Augustine)
[]—*Conventual Franciscans* (Prov. of Saint Anthony of Padua)
[1120]—*Missionaries of the Sacred Hearts of Jesus and Mary*—M.SS.CC.
[]—*Order of Preachers* (Prov. of Nigeria)
[]—*Order of Preachers* (Prov. of Saint Joseph)—O.P.
[]—*Priestly Fraternity of Saint Peter*
[1070]—*Redemptorist Fathers* (Baltimore Prov.)—C.SS.R.
[]—*Society of Jesus*
[]—*Society of Our Lady of the Most Holy Trinity*
[]—*Society of the Divine Savior*
[1060]—*Society of the Precious Blood* (Cincinnati Prov.)—C.PP.S.
[0560]—*Third Order Regular of Saint Francis* (Prov. of the Most Sacred Heart of Jesus)—T.O.R.

RELIGIOUS INSTITUTES OF WOMEN REPRESENTED IN THE DIOCESE

[0100]—*Adorers of the Blood of Christ*—A.S.C.
[ ]—*Bernardine Franciscan Sisters*—
[]—*Carmel of Jesus, Mary and Joseph* (Elysburg)
[0890]—*Daughters of Our Lady of Mercy*—D.M.
[ ]—*Discalced Carmelite Nuns of Danville*—
[ ]—*Dominican Nuns of the Perpetual Rosary*—
[]—*Dominican Sisters, Congregation of Saint Catherine de Ricci*
[ ]—*Guadalupan Missionaries of the Holy Spirit*—
[ ]—*Holy Union Sisters*—
[]—*Missionary Servants of the Most Holy Trinity*
[]—*Missionary Sisters of Saint Benedict*
[0660]—*Sisters of Christian Charity*—S.C.C.
[2575]—*Sisters of Mercy of the Americas*—R.S.M.
[]—*Sisters of Saint Joseph of Chestnut Hill*
[3780]—*Sisters of Saints Cyril and Methodius*—SS.C.M.
[1650]—*The Sisters of St. Francis of Philadelphia*—O.S.F.

[]—*Sisters of St. Joseph* (Baden)—C.S.J.
[]—*Sisters, Servants of the Immaculate Heart of Mary* (Philadelphia)—I.H.M.
[]—*Sisters, Servants of the Immaculate Heart of Mary* (Scranton)
[]—*Society of the Sisters of the Church*

NECROLOGY

† Kumontis, Rev. Msgr. Francis M.—Died Jan. 27, 2009
† Greaney, John, (Retired)—Died March 31, 2009
† Gross, Lawrence C., (Retired)—Died March 24, 2009
† McLernon, Thomas M., (On Duty Outside the Diocese)—Died Dec. 25, 2009
† Sheetz, Steven, (Retired)—Died Oct. 17, 2009
† Slough, Charles R., (Retired)—Died Aug. 8, 2009

An asterisk (*) denotes an organization that has established tax-exempt status directly with the IRS and is not covered by the USCCB Group Ruling.

Archdiocese of Hartford

(Archidioecesis Hartfortiensis)

Most Reverend

HENRY J. MANSELL, D.D.

Archbishop of Hartford; ordained December 19, 1962; appointed Titular Bishop of Marazane and Auxiliary of New York November 24, 1992; ordained January 6, 1993; appointed Bishop of Buffalo April 18, 1995; installed June 12, 1995; appointed Archbishop of Hartford October 20, 2003; installed December 18, 2003. *Office:* . Fax: 860-541-6293. *Res.: 1109 Prospect Ave., West Hartford, CT 06105.*

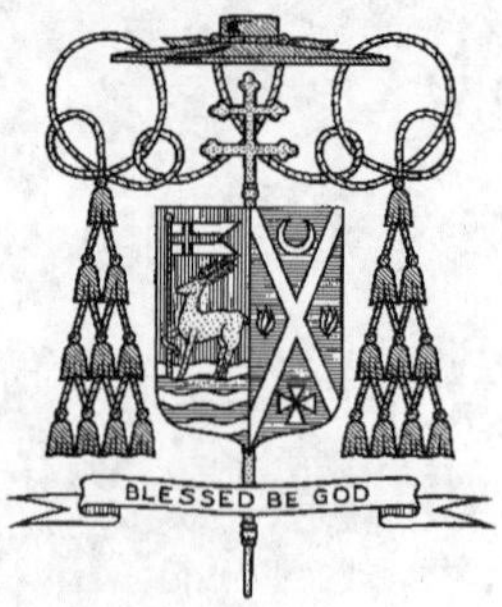

Most Reverend

DANIEL A. CRONIN, D.D., S.T.D.

Archbishop Emeritus of Hartford; ordained December 20, 1952; appointed Titular Bishop of Egnatia and Auxiliary Bishop of Boston June 10, 1968; ordained Bishop September 12, 1968; appointed Bishop of Fall River October 30, 1970; installed December 16, 1970; appointed Archbishop of Hartford December 10, 1991; installed January 28, 1992; retired October 20, 2003. *Office: 469 Bloomfield Ave., Bloomfield, CT 06002.*

Most Reverend

PETER A. ROSAZZA, D.D., V.G.

Auxiliary Bishop of Hartford; ordained June 29, 1961; appointed Auxiliary Bishop of Hartford and Titular Bishop of Oppido Nuovo February 28, 1978; ordained Bishop June 24, 1978. *Office & Res.: 1450 Chapel St., New Haven, CT 06511.* Tel: 203-789-5970; Fax: 203-789-5971.

The Hartford Roman Catholic Diocesan Corporation- Chancery Office: 134 Farmington Ave., Hartford, CT 06105-3784. Tel: 860-541-6491; Fax: 860-541-6309.

Web: www.archdioceseofhartford.org

Most Reverend

CHRISTIE ALBERT MACALUSO, D.D., V.G.

Auxiliary Bishop of Hartford; ordained May 22, 1971; appointed Auxiliary Bishop of Hartford and Titular Bishop of Grassy Valley March 18, 1997; ordained Bishop June 10, 1997. *Office: 134 Farmington Ave., Hartford, CT 06105-3784.* Tel: 860-541-6491; Fax: 860-541-6293.

Square Miles 2,288.

Established November 28, 1843; created Archdiocese August 6, 1953.

Corporate Title: "The Hartford Roman Catholic Diocesan Corporation."

Comprises the Counties of Hartford, Litchfield and New Haven in the State of Connecticut.

For legal titles of parishes and archdiocesan institutions, consult the Chancery Office.

STATISTICAL OVERVIEW

Personnel	
Archbishops	1
Retired Archbishops	1
Auxiliary Bishops	2
Priests: Diocesan Active in Diocese	193
Priests: Diocesan Active Outside Diocese	13
Priests: Retired, Sick or Absent	105
Number of Diocesan Priests	311
Religious Priests in Diocese	96
Total Priests in Diocese	407
Extern Priests in Diocese	43
Ordinations:	
Diocesan Priests	2
Transitional Deacons	4
Permanent Deacons in Diocese	272
Total Brothers	28
Total Sisters	715
Parishes	
Parishes	213
With Resident Pastor:	
Resident Diocesan Priests	164
Resident Religious Priests	13
Without Resident Pastor:	
Administered by Priests	36
Missions	1
Professional Ministry Personnel:	
Brothers	3
Sisters	36
Lay Ministers	107
Welfare	
Catholic Hospitals	3
Total Assisted	889,526
Health Care Centers	2
Total Assisted	4,901
Homes for the Aged	6
Total Assisted	2,946
Day Care Centers	9
Total Assisted	350
Specialized Homes	2
Total Assisted	173
Special Centers for Social Services	86
Total Assisted	52,000
Residential Care of Disabled	9
Total Assisted	33
Educational	
Seminaries, Diocesan	1
Diocesan Students in Other Seminaries	46
Seminaries, Religious	1
Students Religious	150
Total Seminarians	196
Colleges and Universities	2
Total Students	4,349
High Schools, Diocesan and Parish	4
Total Students	2,000
High Schools, Private	5
Total Students	2,677
Elementary Schools, Diocesan and Parish	56
Total Students	11,680
Elementary Schools, Private	2
Total Students	216
Catechesis/Religious Education:	
High School Students	13,499
Elementary Students	45,807
Total Students under Catholic Instruction	80,424
Teachers in the Diocese:	
Priests	9
Brothers	12
Sisters	23
Lay Teachers	1,052
Vital Statistics	
Receptions into the Church:	
Infant Baptism Totals	6,236
Minor Baptism Totals	292
Adult Baptism Totals	228
Received into Full Communion	308
First Communions	7,773
Confirmations	7,192
Marriages:	
Catholic	1,214
Interfaith	213
Total Marriages	1,427
Deaths	7,827
Total Catholic Population	624,230
Total Population	1,911,158

Former Bishops—Rt. Revs. WILLIAM TYLER, D.D., ord. June 3, 1829; first Bishop; cons. March 17, 1844; died June 18, 1849; BERNARD O'REILLY, D.D., ord. Oct. 13, 1831; second Bishop; cons. Nov. 10, 1850; perished at sea, Jan., 1856.; FRANCIS P. MCFARLAND, D.D., ord. May 18, 1845; third Bishop; cons. March 14, 1858; died Oct. 12, 1874; THOMAS GALBERRY, D.D., ord. Dec. 20, 1856; fourth Bishop; cons. March 19, 1876; died Oct. 10, 1878; LAWRENCE S. MCMAHON, D.D., ord. March 24, 1860; fifth Bishop; cons. Aug. 10, 1879; died Aug. 21, 1893; MICHAEL TIERNEY, D.D., ord. May 1866; sixth Bishop; cons. Feb. 22, 1894; died Oct. 5, 1908; Most Revs. JOHN J. NILAN, D.D., ord. Dec. 2, 1878; seventh Bishop; cons. April 28, 1910; died April 13, 1934; MAURICE F. MCAULIFFE, D.D., eighth Bishop; ord. July 29, 1900; appt. Auxiliary to the Bishop of Hartford, Dec. 17, 1925; cons. April 28, 1926; appt. Bishop of Hartford, April 25, 1934; installed May 29, 1934; died Dec. 15, 1944; HENRY J. O'BRIEN, D.D., ninth Bishop, first Archbishop; ord. July 8, 1923; appt. Titular Bishop of Sita and Auxiliary to Bishop of Hartford, March 19, 1940; cons. May 14, 1940; appt. Bishop of Hartford, April 7, 1945; appt. Archbishop of Hartford, Aug. 6, 1953; appt. at Pontifical Throne, April 29, 1955; resigned and appt. Titular Archbishop of Utina, Nov. 20, 1968; Given title "Former Archbishop of Hartford", Nov. 14, 1970; died July 23, 1976; JOHN F. WHEALON, D.D., S.T.L., S.S.L., tenth Bishop, second Archbishop; ord. May 26, 1945; appt. Titular Bishop of Andrapa and Auxiliary of Cleveland, June 2, 1961; consecrated July 6, 1961; appt. Bishop of Erie, Nov. 30, 1966; installed March 7, 1967; appt. Archbishop of Hartford, Dec. 28, 1968; installed March 19, 1969; died Aug. 2, 1991; DANIEL A. CRONIN, D.D., S.T.D., ord. Dec. 20, 1952; appt. Titular Bishop of Egnatia and Auxiliary Bishop of Boston June 10, 1968; ord. Bishop Sept. 12, 1968; appt. Bishop of Fall River Oct. 30, 1970; installed Dec. 16, 1970; appt. Archbishop of Hartford Dec. 10, 1991; installed Jan. 28, 1992; retired Oct. 20, 2003.

Vicars General—Most Revs. PETER A. ROSAZZA, D.D., V.G.; CHRISTIE ALBERT MACALUSO, D.D., V.G.

Episcopal Vicars—Most Rev. PETER A. ROSAZZA, D.D., V.G., Vicar for Hispanics; Rev. Msgrs. JOHN P. CONTE, New Haven Vicariate; JAMES G. COLEMAN, Waterbury Vicariate (Retired); Rev. LAWRENCE R. BOCK, Hartford Vicariate.

Chancery Office—134 Farmington Ave., Hartford, 06105-3784. Tel: 860-541-6491; Fax: 860-541-6293 (Bishop's Office); 860-541-6309 (Chancery). All applications for dispensations and correspondence on diocesan business should be sent to this address. Office Hours: Mon.-Fri. 8:30-4:30.

Moderator of the Curia—Most Rev. CHRISTIE ALBERT MACALUSO, D.D., V.G.

Chancellor—Rev. Msgr. JOHN J. MCCARTHY, J.C.D., J.D.
Assistant Chancellor—Rev. JEFFREY V. ROMANS.
Archdiocesan Liturgical Consultant—Sr. MARY KATHLEEN RONAN, R.S.M. Fax: 860-541-6521.
Archivist—F. MARIA MEDINA, M.L.S.
Finance Office—
Finance Officer—Most Rev. CHRISTIE A. MACALUSO, D.D.
Director of Finance—MATTHEW A. BYRNE, CPA, M.B.A.; LINDA CARROLL, Administrative Asst.
Assistant Director of Finance—TIMOTHY F. DERBY, CPA. *Accounting Manager*, THERESA MROCZKOWSKI. *Accounts Payable*, DONNA SHREVE. *Accounts Receivable*, CHERYL ROAIX. *Accounting Manager - Offices & Corporations*, KEVIN L. BEECHER. *Offices and Corporations Support, Staff Accountants*, ELAINE RUFFINO; DEAN WALFORD. *Risk Management, Workers Compensation, General Insurance, Claims Processing*, BRENDA ROCK.
Director of Parish Financial Services—NANCY H. STUPIK, CPA. *Parish Support Administrator*, PATRICK EGAN. *Assurance Review Coordinator*, ROBERT KEATING.
Director of Facilities & Construction—KEN MUCHERINO.
Development Office—
Director—ROBERT MCTIERNAN.
Associate—COLLEEN CORRIVEAU.
Secretary to the Archbishop—Rev. JEFFREY V. ROMANS.
Assistant—GINGER VENDRILLO.
Human Resources—
Director—KAREN A. KEAN. *Employee and Priest Benefits, Pension, and Payroll*, LESLI ANDERSON.
Metropolitan Tribunal—467 Bloomfield Ave., Bloomfield, 06002-2999. Tel: 860-541-6491.
Judicial Vicar (Officialis)—Rev. ROBERT B. VARGO, J.C.L.
Adjutant Judicial Vicar—Rev. JAMES F. KINNANE, J.C.L.
Defender of the Bond—Rev. M. JUAN-DIEGO BRUNETTA, O.P., J.C.D.
Promoter of Justice—Rev. Msgr. JOHN J. MCCARTHY, J.C.D., J.D.
Judges—Rev. Msgr. WILLIAM J. MULLEN, J.C.D. (Retired); Revs. CHRISTOPHER M. FORD, J.C.L.; JAMES F. KINNANE, J.C.L.; ALVIN J. LEBLANC, J.C.L.; JOHN M. SANTONE, J.C.L.; M. JUAN-DIEGO BRUNETTA, O.P., J.C.D.
Experts—Deacon RONALD BIAMONTE, M.A. (NCC Bd. Eligible); DONALD PAGLIA, M.S., C.A.G.S.; ROBERT SWORDS, M.D.
Assessor—Sr. PATRICK MARIE DOHERTY, I.H.M.
Secretary—NANCY C. SCOTT.
Notary—CAROL M. HATTEN.
College of Consultors—Most Revs. PETER A. ROSAZZA, D.D., V.G.; CHRISTIE ALBERT MACALUSO, D.D., V.G.; Rev. Msgrs. JAMES G. COLEMAN (Retired); JOHN P. CONTE; JOHN J. MCCARTHY, J.C.D., J.D.; Rev. LAWRENCE R. BOCK.
Consultors - Canon 1742—Rev. Msgrs. JAMES G. COLEMAN (Retired); JOHN P. CONTE; Revs. LAWRENCE R. BOCK; WILLIAM J. BRENZA; JOHN J. GEORGIA; GENE E. GIANELLI; JOHN S. GOLAS; THOMAS R. MITCHELL; LAWRENCE S. SYMOLON.
Deans—Hartford Vicariate: Rev. JOHN S. GOLAS, Farmington Valley; Rev. Msgr. DANIEL J. PLOCHARCZYK, New Britain; Revs. JOSEPH T. DEVINE, Hartford; JAMES F. LEARY, Suburban Hartford; KEVIN P. CAVANAUGH, Manchester; ROBERT A. O'GRADY, Enfield. New Haven Vicariate: Rev. DANIEL G. KEEFE, Hamden-North Haven; Rev. Msgr. DAVID M. WALKER, East Shore Line; Revs. SHAWN T. DALY, Meriden; GENE E. GIANELLI, West Shore Line; DANIEL J. MCLEAREN, New Haven. Waterbury Vicariate: Revs. ROBERT M. KWIATKOWSKI, Suburban Waterbury; LEONARD J. KVEDAS, Ansonia-Derby; PAUL J. PACE, Waterbury; CHRISTOPHER M. TIANO, Litchfield; JOHN J. GEORGIA, Bristol; EUGENE J. CHARMAN, Naugatuck-Cheshire.
Presbyteral Council—
Ex Officio Members—Most Revs. PETER A. ROSAZZA, D.D., V.G.; CHRISTIE A. MACALUSO, D.D., Auxiliary Bishop; Rev. Msgrs. JOHN J. MCCARTHY, J.C.D., J.D., Chancellor; JAMES G. COLEMAN, Vicar for Waterbury (Retired); JOHN P. CONTE, Vicar for New Haven; Rev. LAWRENCE R. BOCK, Vicar for Hartford.
Elected Members—
Ansonia-Derby Deanery—Rev. STEPHEN H. BZDYRA.
Bristol Deanery—Rev. JOHN J. GEORGIA.
Cheshire-Naugatuck Deanery—Rev. MICHAEL J. SLUSZ.
East Shore Deanery—Rev. Msgr. DAVID M. WALKER.
Enfield Deanery—Rev. MICHAEL C. DEVITO.
Farmington Valley Deanery—Rev. AIDAN N. DONAHUE.
Hamden-North Haven Deanery—Rev. VINCENT J. CURRAN.
Hartford Deanery—Rev. THOMAS R. MITCHELL.
Litchfield Deanery—Rev. JOHN L. LAVORGNA.
Manchester Deanery—Rev. KEVIN P. CAVANAUGH.
Meriden Deanery—Rev. SHAWN T. DALY.
New Britain Deanery—Rev. RONALD T. SMITH.
New Haven Deanery—Rev. THOMAS B. SHEPARD.
Suburban Hartford Deanery—Rev. JAMES F. LEARY.
Suburban Waterbury Deanery—Rev. JOSEPH T. DONNELLY.
Waterbury Deanery—Rev. Msgr. THOMAS M. GINTY.
West Shore Line Deanery—Rev. GENE E. GIANELLI.
Appointed Members—Revs. M. JUAN-DIEGO BRUNETTA, O.P., J.C.D.; DAVID C. CAREY; DAIRO E. DIAZ; GERALD H. DZIEDZIC; Rev. Msgr. JOHN D. REGAN (Retired); Rev. JACK HOAK, O.F.M.
Ecumenical Affairs, Commission for—Rev. AIDAN N. DONAHUE, Ecumenical Officer, Sacred Heart Church, 26 Wintonbury Ave., Bloomfield, 06002-2488. Tel: 860-242-4142.
Office of Stewardship—COLLEEN B. CORRIVEAU, Dir., 467 Bloomfield Ave., Bloomfield, 06002-2999. Tel: 860-242-4777; Fax: 860-242-4553. Email: stewardshipoffice@stseminary.org.
Holy Childhood Association—Rev. BRIAN W. MONNERAT, Dir.; MARY CHRISTINAT, Assoc. Dir., 467 Bloomfield Ave., Bloomfield, 06002-2999. Tel: 860-761-7440; Fax: 860-243-0661.
Office for Divine Worship—Rev. DAVID J. BARANOWSKI, Dir.; LUCY ZOCCO, Assoc. Dir., 467 Bloomfield Ave., Bloomfield, 06002-2999. Tel: 860-761-7442; Fax: 860-243-0661.
Newspaper— "The Catholic Transcript" Most Rev. HENRY J. MANSELL, D.D., Pres. & Publisher; Rev. Msgr. DAVID Q. LIPTAK, Exec. Editor, 467 Bloomfield Ave., Bloomfield, 06002-2999. Tel: 860-286-2828; 800-726-2391; Fax: 860-726-0000. Email: info@catholictranscript.org; ROBERTA TUTTLE, Mng. Editor; JACK SHEEDY, News Editor; MARY CHALUPSKY, Staff Reporter; JEFFREY GUERRETTE, Advertising Representative; CAROLE CRONSELL, Business Mgr. Graphic Designers: LESLIE DIVENERE; JOSEPH BROWN; JOYCE H. BOUDREAU, Circulation Supvr.
Office for Black Catholic Ministries—Deacon ARTHUR L. MILLER, Dir St. Thomas Seminary, 467 Bloomfield Ave., Bloomfield, 06002-2999. Tel: 860-243-0648; Fax: 860-243-0649.
Office of Ministry Enrichment for Priests—Rev. THOMAS J. SAS, Dir., St. Peter Claver Church, 47 Pleasant St., West Hartford, 06107-1625. Tel: 860-561-4235, Ext. 5; Fax: 860-561-0552.
Office of Radio and Television—Rev. JOHN P. GATZAK, Exec. Dir., 15 Peach Orchard Rd., Prospect, 06712-1052. Tel: 203-758-7367; Fax: 203-758-7371. Web: www.ortv.org. Email: ortv@ortv-hartford.org. Radio Stations: WJMJ-FM 88.9 Hartford, 93.1 Hamden, 107.1 New Haven. Tel.: 860-242-8800. Licensed by St. Thomas Seminary, Bloomfield (Hartford).
Office of WJMJ-FM—Rev. JOHN P. GATZAK, Gen. Mgr. Fax: 860-242-5556. Web: www.wjmj.org. Email: wjmj@ortv-hartford.org.
Office of Family Life, Marriage and Family Apostolate—Co-Directors: DONALD PAGLIA, M.S., C.A.G.S.; CHRISTINE PAGLIA, 412 Ridge Rd., Hamden, 06517-2941. Tel: 203-230-2460; Fax: 203-230-2472.
Archbishop's Annual Appeal—Rev. Msgr. JAMES G. COLEMAN, Pastors' Advisory Committee Chm. (Retired); COLLEEN B. CORRIVEAU, Appeal Coord., Mailing Address: P.O. Box 28, Hartford, 06141. Tel: 860-243-3800; Fax: 860-242-4553. Email: aaa@stseminary.org.
Office of Religious Education—Rev. Msgr. MICHAEL J. MOTTA, Dir.; Ms. PATRICIA KECK, Asst. Dir., St. Thomas Seminary, 467 Bloomfield Ave., Bloomfield, 06002-2999. Tel: 860-243-9465; Fax: 860-243-9690. Web: www.orehartford.org.
Catholic Biblical School—Ms. BARBARA JEAN DALY HORELL, Coord.
Catechesis for Hispanics—Mr. CARLOS AEDO, Coord.
Lay Ministry, RCIA, Adult Formation—Ms. MARY E. MARSAN, Coord.
Youth and Young Adult Ministry—Ms. SHAWNEE BALDWIN, Coord.
Catholic Scouting—Ms. SHANNON PERZAN, Coord.
Evangelization—Rev. Msgr. MICHAEL J. MOTTA, Dir.
Commission for Priests' Retreats—Revs. DAVID CINQUEGRANI, C.P.; RONALD P. MAY; THOMAS J. SAS.
Ministry for Healing and Assistance—Sr. MARY KELLY, C.S.J., Dir., 134 Farmington Ave., Hartford, 06105-3784. Tel: 860-541-6491; Fax: 860-541-6293.
Safe Environment Program—Sr. MARY KELLY, C.S.J., Victims' Assistance Coord.; THERESA HATFIELD, Background Check Coord.; DOLORES SKOVICH, VIRTUS Prog. Coord.; KIMBERLEE DONAHUE, Child Lures Prevention Prog. Coord.; TRACEY MILLER.
Office of Ministry for Priests—Rev. JOSEPH V. DISCIACCA, Min. for Priests, St. Joseph Rectory, 149 Goodwin St., Bristol, 06010-5115. Tel: 860-202-6013; Fax: 860-589-5374.
Mission Cooperative Planning Office—Rev. BRIAN W. MONNERAT, Dir.; MARY CHRISTINAT, Assoc. Dir., 467 Bloomfield Ave., Bloomfield, 06002-2999. Tel: 860-761-7440; Fax: 860-243-0661.
Priests Retirement Plan for Secular Priests of the Archdiocese of Hartford— The Secular Priests of the Archdiocese of Hartford Retirement Trust. 134 Farmington Ave., Hartford, 06105-3784. Tel: 860-541-6491. Ex Officio: Rev. Msgr. GERARD G. SCHMITZ; Rev. JOSEPH V. DISCIACCA. Appointed: Revs. THOMAS E. BERBERICH; JOHN C. BLACKALL (Retired); ARTHUR J. DUPONT (Retired); RONALD P. MAY; ROBERT P. ROY; RONALD R. YELLE; MATTHEW A. BYRNE, CPA, M.B.A.
Pro-Life Activities—Rev. JAMES J. CRONIN, Dir., 70 Gulf St., P.O. Box 230, Milford, 06460-0230. Tel: 203-878-3571; Fax: 203-877-8741; Sr. SUZANNE GROSS, F.S.E., Prog. Coord., 271 Finch Ave., Meriden, 06451-2715. Tel: 203-639-0833. Email: prolife@flcenter.org. Web: www.prolifeministry.org.
Mission Office, The— (The Catholic Mission Aid Society of Hartford, Holy Childhood Assoc., Mission Cooperative Planning Office, Propagation of the Faith) Rev. BRIAN W. MONNERAT, Dir.; MARY CHRISTINAT, Assoc. Dir., 467 Bloomfield Ave., Bloomfield, 06002-2999. Tel: 860-761-7440; Fax: 860-243-0661; Sr. LORETTA FRANCIS MANN, O.S.F., Mission Coord. for Educ.
Office of Catholic Schools—Mr. DALE R. HOYT, Supt. Assistant Superintendents: Sr. KATHLEEN FITZSIMONS, C.N.D.; Mrs. MARIA T. MAYNARD, 467 Bloomfield Ave., Bloomfield, 06002-2999. Tel: 860-242-4362; Fax: 860-242-8683. Web: catholicschoolshartford.org.
Diocesan Labor Institute—Rev. DANIEL E. JOHNSON, Dir. (Retired).
Social Service—ROSE ALMA SENATORE, Dir., 839-841 Asylum Ave., Hartford, 06105. Tel: 860-493-1841; Fax: 860-548-1930.
Vocations—Rev. MICHAEL J. DOLAN, Dir.; MEGHAN JACKSON, Administrative Asst., St. Thomas Seminary, 467 Bloomfield Ave., Bloomfield, 06002-2999. Tel: 860-761-7456; Fax: 860-243-0661.
Office of the Permanent Diaconate—Deacon ROBERT M. PALLOTTI, Dir., 467 Bloomfield Ave., Bloomfield, 06002-2999. Tel: 860-761-7445; Fax: 860-243-0661. Email: deaconofc@aol.com.
Office for Religious—Rev. JAMES F. KINNANE, J.C.L., Vicar; Sr. MARY KELLY, C.S.J., Dir., 134 Farmington Ave., Hartford, 06105-3784. Tel: 860-541-6491; Fax: 860-541-6293.
Office of Vicar For Priests—Rev. Msgr. GERARD G. SCHMITZ, 467 Bloomfield Ave., Bloomfield, 06002-2999. Tel: 860-242-2510; Fax: 860-242-3785. Email: vicar@stseminary.org.
Office of Coordinator for Retired Priests—Rev. Msgr. GERARD G. SCHMITZ, Dir., 467 Bloomfield Ave., Bloomfield, 06002-2999. Tel: 860-242-2510; Sr. CECELIA MARIE SCADUTO, R.S.M., Coord. Retired Priests. Tel: 860-761-7449; Fax: 860-242-3785.
Censor Librorum—Rev. Msgr. DAVID Q. LIPTAK.

Archdiocesan Offices and Directors

Archdiocesan Dispute Resolution Office—Most Rev. CHRISTIE ALBERT MACALUSO, D.D., V.G., Moderator of the Curia, 134 Farmington Ave., Hartford, 06105-3784. Tel: 860-541-6491.
Office for Catholic Social Justice Ministry—Ms. CORI THIBODEAU, Exec. Dir., 81 Saltonstall Ave., New Haven, 06513-4356. Tel: 203-777-7279; Fax: 203-776-3233. Email: ocsjm@catholicsocialjustice.org. Web: www.catholicsocialjustice.org.
Office for Hispanic Evangelization—Most Rev. PETER A. ROSAZZA, D.D., V.G., Vicar; Rev. JOSE A. MERCADO, Dir.; LUZ YUNEZ, Dir. Asst., 467 Bloomfield Ave., Bloomfield, 06002-2999. Tel: 860-243-0940; Fax: 860-286-2797.
Cana Conferences—DONALD PAGLIA, M.S., C.A.G.S.; CHRISTINE PAGLIA, 412 Ridge Rd., Hamden, 06517-2941. Tel: 203-230-2460; Fax: 203-230-2472.
Catholic Cemeteries Association—Rev. Msgr. DAVID M. WALKER, Dir.; CRAIG S. NEAL, Exec. Dir., 700 Middletown Ave., P.O. Box 517, North Haven, 06473-0517. Tel: 203-239-2557; Fax: 203-239-5035.
Catholic Deaf Apostolate—VACANT, Dir., Contact the Office for People with Disabilities, 467 Bloomfield Ave., Bloomfield, 06002-2999. Tel: 860-761-7444.
Catholic Library and Information Center - Catholic Book Store—Rev. EDWARD J. MCLEAN, Dir. (Retired); DONNA DOUTNEY, Mgr., 125 Market St., Hartford, 06103-1397. Tel: 860-522-0602; 860-246-5628; 800-308-3300; Fax: 860-247-3490. Email: catholicbkstore@aol.com; 467 Bloomfield Ave., Bloomfield, 06002-2999. Tel: 860-242-2799.
Connecticut Catholic Conference—MICHAEL C. CULHANE, Exec. Dir.; Deacon DAVID W. REYNOLDS, Legislative Liaison; LI-LING LAM WALLER, Administrative Asst., 134 Farmington Ave.,

Hartford, 06105-3784. Tel: 860-524-7882; Fax: 860-525-0750. Email: ccc@ctcatholic.org.

Coordinator of the Hospital Apostolate—Rev. RICHARD C. BOLLEA, Chap., Waterbury Hospital, 64 Robbins St., Waterbury, 06721-2600. Tel: 203-573-7213; Fax: 203-573-6716.

Office for People with Disabilities—Co-Directors: GEORGE DUCHARME, Ph.D.; MARY N. MCGRATH, 467 Bloomfield Ave., Bloomfield, 06002-2999. Tel: 860-761-7444.

Small Christian Communities Pastoral Department—Bro. ROBERT K. MORIARTY, S.M., Ph.D., Dir., 467 Bloomfield Ave., Bloomfield, 06002-2999. Tel: 860-761-7450; Fax: 860-760-6116. Email: info@sccquest.org.

Cursillo Movement, Archdiocesan Director of—Rev. JOHN M. COONEY, Dir., St. John the Evangelist, 21 Academy Hill, Watertown, 06795-2101. Tel: 860-274-8836; Fax: 860-274-0667.

Victim Assistance Coordinator—Sr. MARY KELLY, C.S.J., 134 Farmington Ave., Hartford, 06105-3784. Tel: 860-541-6491.

CLERGY, PARISHES, MISSIONS AND PAROCHIAL SCHOOLS

CITY OF HARTFORD

(HARTFORD COUNTY)

1—CATHEDRAL OF ST. JOSEPH (1872) Rev. Msgr. John J. McCarthy, Rector; Rev. Collins I. Anaeche, Parochial Vicar; Sr. Ann Marie Strileckis, C.N.D., Pastoral Assoc. In Res., Rev. Lawrence G. Wrenn (Retired); Rev. Msgr. David Q. Liptak; Rev. Daniel Akho, Ministry to the Burmese Community.
Res.: 140 Farmington Ave., 06105-3708. Tel: 860-249-8431; Fax: 860-249-5910. Web: cathedralofsaintjoseph.com.
Catechesis/Religious Program—Students 60.

2—ST. ANNE (1889), (French), Closed. For inquiries for sacramental records contact St. Anne-Immaculate Conception, Hartford.

3—ST. ANNE-IMMACULATE CONCEPTION (2000), (French—Spanish), Rev. Zacarias Pushpanathan; Deacon Carmelo Hernandez.
Res.: 820 Park St., 06106-2388. Tel: 860-728-7445; 860-525-1522; Fax: 860-728-1973.
Catechesis/Religious Program—Students 70.

4—ST. AUGUSTINE (1902) Revs. Jose A. Mercado; Robert J. Grant; Deacon Ramon A. Rosado. In Res., Rev. James O. Ibekwe (Nigeria); Bro. Minlib Dallh, O.P.
Res.: 10 Campfield Ave., 06114-1832. Tel: 860-522-7128; Fax: 860-246-1753. Email: staugust@staugustinehtfd.org. Web: staugustinehtfd.org.
School—(Grades PreK-8), 20 Clifford St., 06114-1798. Tel: 860-249-5661; Fax: 860-293-2981. Mrs. Cynthia Niedbala, Prin. Lay Teachers 9; Students 124.
Catechesis/Religious Program—Tel: 860-249-3430; Fax: 860-246-1753. Students 92.

5—SS. CYRIL AND METHODIUS (1902), (Polish), Revs. Adam C. Subocz; Kazimierz Heisig (Poland).
Res.: 55 Charter Oak Ave., 06106-1902. Tel: 860-522-9157; Fax: 860-524-9433.
School—(Grades PreK-8), 35 Groton St., 06106-2799. Tel: 860-522-8490; Fax: 860-493-7409. Dolores Ungerer, Prin. Sisters 5; Lay Teachers 10; Students 155.
Catechesis/Religious Program—Tel: 860-527-3775. Students 157.
Convent—Felician Sisters, 45 Groton St., 06106-2798. Tel: 860-527-3775.

6—HOLY TRINITY (1900), (Lithuanian), Rev. Charles E. Jacobs.
Res.: 53 Capitol Ave., 06106-1798. Tel: 860-246-4162; Fax: 860-246-5662. Email: holytrinity53@yahoo.com.
Catechesis/Religious Program—Mary Beth Murphy, D.R.E. Students 4.

7—IMMACULATE CONCEPTION (1899) Closed. For inquiries for sacramental records contact St. Anne-Immaculate Conception, Hartford.

8—ST. JUSTIN (1924), (African American—West Indian), Linked with Sacred Heart Parish and St. Michael Parish. Rev. Emmanuel I. Ihemedu; Deacons Isidro DeJesus; Arthur L. Miller.
Res.: 230 Blue Hills Ave., 06112-1836. Tel: 860-246-6897; Fax: 860-246-6898. Email: stjustinsrectory@sbcglobal.net.
Catechesis/Religious Program—Tel: 860-522-6184. Students 34.

9—ST. LAWRENCE O'TOOLE (1885) Revs. Joseph T. Devine; William L. Burns (Retired); Deacon Domingo Delgado. In Res., Rev. Joseph Tran, (Vietnamese Ministry).
Res.: 494 New Britain Ave., 06106-3797. Tel: 860-522-1129; Fax: 860-549-4261. Email: 494slot@sbcglobal.net.
Catechesis/Religious Program—Students 259.

10—ST. LUKE (1930) Rev. A. Waine Kargul.
Res.: 66 Bolton St., 06114. Tel: 860-296-8681; Fax: 860-296-1983. Email: saintlukechurch@comcast.net.
Catechesis/Religious Program—Tel: 860-296-2233.

11—ST. MICHAEL (1900), (African American—Hispanic), Linked with Sacred Heart Parish and St. Justin Parish. Rev. Emmanuel I. Ihemedu; Deacons Isidro DeJesus; Arthur L. Miller.
Res.: 98 Capen St., 06120-2010. Tel: 860-522-6184; Fax: 860-278-8410. Email: stmichaelsrectory@sbcglobal.net.
Catechesis/Religious Program—Tel: 860-522-6184; Fax: 860-278-8410. Students 33.

12—OUR LADY OF FATIMA (1958), (Portuguese), Rev. Antonio Jorge Tchinqui (Angola).
Res.: 22 Madison Ave., 06106. Tel: 860-236-1443; Fax: 860-232-4455. Email: olfchurch1958@yahoo.com. Web: www.ourladyoffatima.us.
Church: Fatima Sq., 50 Kane St., 06106.
Catechesis/Religious Program—Email: olfcatequese@yahoo.com. Students 200.

13—OUR LADY OF SORROWS (1895) Revs. Francis C. Cooney, M.S.; Thomas J. Huhn, M.S.; Deacon Victor Bilbraut. In Res., Rev. Brian D. Schloth, M.S.
Res.: 16 Greenwood St., 06106-2109. Tel: 860-233-4424; Fax: 860-236-0149. Email: olsparish@aol.com. Web: ourladyofsorrowsparish.homestead.com.
Church: 79 New Park Ave., 06106-2109.
Catechesis/Religious Program—Students 60.

14—ST. PATRICK-ST. ANTHONY (1829) Revs. Thomas M. Gallagher, O.F.M.; Andrew Giardino, O.F.M.; Michael P. Jones, O.F.M.; Bro. Erick Lopez, O.F.M.; Patricia Curtis, Pastoral Assoc.
Franciscan Center for Urban Ministry—285 Church St., 06103. Tel: 860-756-4034; Fax: 860-249-6487.
Catechesis/Religious Program—Students 460.

15—ST. PETER (1859), (Irish), Rev. Dairo E. Diaz; Deacon Ramon A. Rosado, Pastoral Assoc.
Res.: 160 Main St., 06106-1894. Tel: 860-525-2683; Fax: 860-548-0202. Email: stpeterhartford@gmail.com.
Catechesis/Religious Program—Tel: 860-525-2684. Students 87.
Convent—Sisters of Mercy, 11 Charter Oak Pl., 06106. Tel: 860-522-8428.

16—SACRED HEART (1872), (Spanish), Linked with St. Justin Parish and St. Michael Parish. Rev. Carlos M. Zapata; Deacon Isidro DeJesus.
Res.: 49 Winthrop St., 06103-1030. Tel: 860-527-6459; Fax: 860-527-6450. Email: shparishhartford@comcast.net.
Catechesis/Religious Program—Students 167.

OUTSIDE THE CITY OF HARTFORD

ANSONIA, NEW HAVEN CO.

1—ST. ANTHONY (1915), (Lithuanian), Linked with Holy Rosary Parish. Rev. Joseph V. Napolitano.
Res.: 10 Father Salemi Dr., 06401-3296. Tel: 203-735-7874; Fax: 203-735-7875.
Catechesis/Religious Program—Tel: 203-736-0242. Students 8.

2—ASSUMPTION (1870) Revs. Robert F. Condron; George P. Burnett (Retired).
Res.: 61 N. Cliff St., 06401-1698. Tel: 203-735-7857; Fax: 203-734-8302. Email: chofaspt@aol.com. Web: assumptionansonia.org.
School—(Grades PreK-8) Tel: 203-734-0855; Fax: 203-734-5521. Web: assumption.eduk12.net. Mrs. Kathleen Molner, Prin. Lay Teachers 11; Students 253.
Catechesis/Religious Program—51 N. Cliff St., 06401-1698. Tel: 203-735-2701; Fax: 203-734-5521. Email: gmiller@assumptionschool.net. Students 257.

3—HOLY ROSARY (1908), (Italian), Linked with St. Anthony Parish. Rev. Joseph V. Napolitano; Deacon Richard W. Renker.
Res.: Fr. Salemi Dr., 06401-2396. Tel: 203-735-7874.
Catechesis/Religious Program—Tel: 203-736-0242; Fax: 203-732-2212. Margaret Vernassa, D.R.E. Students 224.

4—ST. JOSEPH (1925), (Polish), Rev. Mitchell Wanat, C.M. In Res., Rev. Waclaw Hlond, C.M. (Retired).
Res.: 32 Jewett St., 06401-2499. Tel: 203-734-0402; Fax: 203-734-4884. Email: josephansonia@snet.net. Web: rc.net/hartford/stjoseph.
Catechesis/Religious Program—Students 73.

AVON, HARTFORD CO., ST. ANN'S (1917) [CEM] Rev. John W. McHugh; Deacons John J. Mylott, (Retired); Jeffrey B. Sutherland. In Res., Rev. Joseph Cheah, O.S.M.
Res.: 289 Arch Rd., 06001-4209. Tel: 860-673-9858; Fax: 860-675-4350.
Catechesis/Religious Program—Tel: 860-673-2137; Fax: 860-675-4350. Claudine A. Meaney, D.R.E. Students 1,016.

BANTAM, LITCHFIELD CO., OUR LADY OF GRACE (1970) [CEM] Rev. John H. McCann, S.M.M.
Res.: Rte. 202, 715 Bantam Rd., P.O. Box 427, 06750. Tel: 860-567-9522; Fax: 860-567-5540. Email: ourladyofgrace@optonline.net.
Catechesis/Religious Program—Students 52.

BEACON FALLS, NEW HAVEN CO., ST. MICHAEL (1899) Rev. Leonard J. Kvedas; Deacon Victor M. Lembo. In Res., Rev. Richard C. Bollea.
Res.: 25 Maple Ave., 06403-1145. Tel: 203-729-2504. Email: saint_michaels@sbcglobal.net. Web: www.saintmichaelsonline.org.
Catechesis/Religious Program—Tel: 203-729-2504. Students 284.

BETHLEHEM, LITCHFIELD CO., CHURCH OF THE NATIVITY (1921) Rev. Joseph E. Looney; Deacon Daniel W. Polansky.
Res.: 48 East St., Box 192, 06751-0192. Tel: 203-266-5211; Fax: 203-266-7543. Email: churchofnativity@att.net. Web: churchofnativity-ct.org.
Catechesis/Religious Program—Tel: 203-266-5212. Students 229.

BLOOMFIELD, HARTFORD CO.

1—CHRIST THE KING (1936) Closed. For inquiries for sacramental records contact Sacred Heart, Bloomfield.

2—SACRED HEART (1878) Rev. Aidan N. Donahue; Deacons Barry T. Skipp; James F. Papillo; Bro. Paul L. Gauvin, S.C., Pastoral Assoc.
Rectory—35 Cold Spring Dr., 06002. Tel: 860-242-1942.
Church: 26 Wintonbury Ave., 06002. Tel: 860-242-4142; Fax: 860-286-0044.
Catechesis/Religious Program—Students 67.

BRANFORD, NEW HAVEN CO.

1—ST. ELIZABETH (1966), Linked with St. Clare Parish, East Haven. Rev. Kevin G. Donovan; Deacon George G. Sartor.
Res.: 65 Burban Dr., 06405. Tel: 203-488-1661; Fax: 203-483-9248. Email: secretary@st-elizabethparish.org.
Catechesis/Religious Program—Tel: 203-483-1997; Fax: 203-483-9248. Students 82.

2—ST. MARY (1868) [CEM 2] Revs. Christopher M. Ford; John Kuzhikottayil, S.D.B., Parochial Vicar. In Res., Rev. Robert J. Burbank (Retired).
Res.: 731 Main St., 06405-3693. Tel: 203-488-1607; Fax: 203-483-9208.
School—(Grades PreK-8) Tel: 203-488-8386; Fax: 203-488-2347. Donna Binkoski, Prin. Lay Teachers 20; Students 161.
Catechesis/Religious Program—Tel: 203-488-7412. Email: stmarybranford@yahoo.com. Web: stmary-branford.org. Students 511.

3—ST. THERESE (1947) Rev. Msgr. David M. Walker; Deacon Gerald S. Walton.
Office: 105 Leetes Island Rd., 06405. Tel: 203-488-2998; Fax: 203-488-8542. Email: sttheresebfd@comcast.net. Web: www.sttheresebranford.4lpi.com.
Res.: 39 Acorn Rd., 06405. Tel: 203-483-9304.
Catechesis/Religious Program—Students 205.

BRISTOL, HARTFORD CO.

1—ST. ANN (1908), (French), Rev. Alvin J. LeBlanc; Deacons Roger R. Albert; Joseph R. Levesque; John J. Lovett.
Mailing Address: *Parish Center*, 180 Laurel St., 06010.
Res.: 215 West St., 06010-5754. Tel: 860-589-9080; Fax: 860-585-7139. Email: saintann180@comcast.net. Web: stann-bristolct.org.
Catechesis/Religious Program—Tel: 860-582-8169. Students 123.

2—ST. ANTHONY (1920), (Italian), Rev. Alphonso R. Fontana; Deacon James P. McCluskey.
Res.: 111 School St., 06010-6078. Tel: 860-583-1349; Fax: 860-582-3861. Email: rectorystanthony@gmail.com. Web: stanthonybristolct.com.
School—(Grades PreK-8), 30 Pleasant St., 06010. Tel: 860-582-7874; Fax: 860-582-2440. Sr. Frances Stavalo, M.P.F., Prin. Lay Teachers 12; Students 202.
Catechesis/Religious Program—20 Pleasant St., 06010. Tel: 860-583-4495; Fax: 860-582-3861. Students 182.

3—ST. GREGORY THE GREAT (1957) Rev. John J. Georgia; Deacon Stanley J. Piotrowski Jr. In Res., Revs. Carmine B. Raneri (Retired); Arthur J. DuPont (Retired).
Res. & Mailing Address: St. Gregory Rectory, 235 Maltby St., 06010-3892. Tel: 860-589-2295; Fax: 860-589-6692. Email: st.gregory.rectory@comcast.net. Web: stgregorys-bristol.ct.41pi.com.
Catechesis/Religious Program—1043 Stafford Ave., 06010. Tel: 860-589-4232; Fax: 860-584-4786. Claudia Larson, D.R.E. Students 952.

4—ST. JOSEPH (1864) [CEM] Revs. Joseph V. DiSciacca; Isreal Rivera, Parochial Vicar; Deacon Neil B. Richter.
Res.: 149 Goodwin St., 06010-5115. Tel: 860-583-1369; Fax: 860-589-5374. Email: stjoseph@snet.net. Web: www.rc.net/hartford/st_joseph.
School—(Grades PreK-8), 335 Center St., 06010. Tel: 860-582-8696; Fax: 860-584-9907. Email: stjosephschool@comcast.net. Web: www.schoolstjosephbristol.org. Mark J. Monnerat, Prin. Lay Teachers 12; Students 238.
Catechesis/Religious Program—Tel: 860-582-2888. Web: faithformation.stjosephbristol.org. Students 307.

5—ST. STANISLAUS (1919), (Polish), Rev. Raymond S. Smialowski; Deacon Leonard R. Lewandoski.
Res.: 510 West St., P.O. Box 1860, 06011-1860. Tel: 860-583-4242; Fax: 860-583-9464.
Catechesis/Religious Program—Tel: 860-584-5378. Mary Ann Miecznikowski, D.R.E. Students 230.

BROAD BROOK, HARTFORD CO., ST. CATHERINE (1886) [CEM], Linked with St. Philip Parish, East Windsor. Rev. Emilio P. Padelli; Deacon John Abdalla, (Retired).
Res.: 6 Windsorville Rd., P.O. Box 359, 06016-0359. Tel: 860-623-4636; Fax: 860-292-8550.
Catechesis/Religious Program—7 Rye St., 06016. Tel: 860-623-1974. Robert Nadler, D.R.E. Students 275.

CANAAN, LITCHFIELD CO., ST. JOSEPH (1920) [CEM] [JC], Linked with Immaculate Conception Parish, Norfolk. Rev. Brian E. Jeffries.
Mailing Address: P.O. Box 897, 06018-2459.
Res.: 4 Main St., 06018-2459. Tel: 860-824-7078; Fax: 860-824-4925. Email: sacrament@sbcglobal.net. Web: www.rc.net/hartford/saintjoseph.
Catechesis/Religious Program—Denise Dubay, D.R.E. Students 69.

CHESHIRE, NEW HAVEN CO.

1—ST. BRIDGET (1871) [CEM] Rev. Robert P. Ricciardi; Deacon Richard Wilber.
Res.: 175 Main St., 06410-2446. Tel: 203-272-3531; Fax: 203-271-3356.
Parish Center—Tel: 203-271-9994.
School—(Grades PreK-8), 171 Main St., 06410. Tel: 203-272-5860; Fax: 203-271-7031. Web: www.stbridgetcheshire.org. Mrs. Margaret Whalen, Prin.; Lorriane Mikolinski, Librarian. Lay Teachers 34; Students 407.
Catechesis/Religious Program—Tel: 203-272-6504. Students 1,066.

2—CHURCH OF THE EPIPHANY (1967) Rev. John L. Williams.
Res.: 1777 Old Waterbury Rd., 06410-1399.
Church & Parish Center: 1750 Huckins Rd., 06410. Tel: 203-272-4355; Fax: 203-272-4878. Email: church@epiphany.necoxmail.com.
Catechesis/Religious Program—Tel: 203-272-4355, Ext. 2. Students 242.

3—ST. THOMAS BECKET (1971) Rev. Eugene J. Charman.
Res.: 435 N. Brooksvale Rd., 06410. Tel: 203-272-3324; Fax: 203-271-9210. Email: stboffice1@cox.net. Web: www.stthomasbecket.org.
Catechesis/Religious Program—Tel: 203-272-5777. Mrs. Phyllis Provost McNeil, C.R.E. Students 447.

COLLINSVILLE, HARTFORD CO., ST. PATRICK (1856) [CEM] [JC 2] Rev. John P. McHugh; Deacon Timothy E. Healy; Marguerite Janelle, Pastoral Assoc.
Res.: 7 Burlington Ave., P.O. Box 287, 06022-0287. Tel: 860-693-8727; Fax: 860-693-4538.
Catechesis/Religious Program—Fax: 860-693-4538. Peter Fortier, C.R.E. Students 822.

CORNWALL BRIDGE, LITCHFIELD CO., ST. BRIDGET (1883) [CEM], Linked with St. Bernard Parish, Sharon. Rev. Francis R. Fador; Deacon Stephen M. Beecher.
Church: 7 River Rd., 06754. Tel: 860-672-6515; Fax: 860-364-9893.
Res. & Mailing Address: 52 New St., P.O. Box 218, Sharon, 06069-0218. Tel: 860-364-5244; Fax: 860-364-9893. Email: pastor@snet.net. Web: stbridgetschurch.org.
Catechesis/Religious Program—Email: stbern.rel.ed@snet.net. Mrs. Patricia Beecher, D.R.E. Students 25.

DERBY, NEW HAVEN CO.

1—ST. JUDE (1961) Rev. Salvatore J. Rosa.
Res.: 71 Pleasant View Rd., 06418-2455. Tel: 203-735-8725; Fax: 203-735-4402. Email: stjudechurch0640@att.net.
Catechesis/Religious Program—Tel: 203-735-8725; Fax: 203-735-4402. Karen Blake, D.R.E. Students 38.

2—ST. MARY THE IMMACULATE CONCEPTION (1851) Rev. Janusz Kukulka, S.T.L.; Deacon Robert C. Johnson.
Res.: 212 Elizabeth St., 06418-1834. Tel: 203-735-3341; Fax: 203-736-6492. Email: st_mary_s_church@sbcglobal.net. Web: stmaryderbyct.org.
School—St. Mary-St. Michael, (Grades PreK-8), *St. Mary Campus*, 14 Seymour Ave., 06418. Tel: 203-735-6471; Fax: 203-732-9009. Mrs. Donna Doherty, Prin. Lay Teachers 8; Students 113.
Catechesis/Religious Program—Students 209.

3—ST. MICHAEL THE ARCHANGEL (1905), (Polish), [CEM] Rev. Roman Gorowski, C.M.
Res.: 75 Derby Ave., 06418-2098. Tel: 203-734-0005.
School—St. Mary-St. Michael, 14 Seymour Ave., 06418-1491. Tel: 203-735-6471; Fax: 203-732-9099. Mrs. Donna Doherty, Prin. Lay Teachers 8; Students 113.
Catechesis/Religious Program—Fax: 203-736-2044. Students 183.

EAST BERLIN, HARTFORD CO., SACRED HEART (1896) Rev. Edmund S. Nadolny.
Res.: 48 Cottage St., 06023. Tel: 860-828-0154; Fax: 860-828-5305. Email: fngoodnews@aol.com. Web: www.sacredheartchurchct.com.
Church: 66 Cottage St., 06023.
Catechesis/Religious Program—Students 184.

EAST HARTFORD, HARTFORD CO.

1—BLESSED SACRAMENT (1948), Linked with Our Lady of Peace Parish. Rev. James J. Nock; Deacons Raymond A. Parenteau; Leo R. LaRocque.
Mailing Address: 36 Cambridge Dr., 06118. Tel: 860-568-2747; Fax: 860-568-4133. In Res., Rev. Michael S. Galasso.
Catechesis/Religious Program—Linked with Our Lady of Peace, East Hartford. Students 250.

2—ST. CHRISTOPHER (1965) Rev. Vincent J. Curran; Deacons William J. Gilles; Edward J. Giard.
Res.: 538 Brewer St., 06118-2305. Tel: 860-568-5240; Fax: 860-568-0673. Email: stchris-eh@sbcglobal.net. Web: stchris-eh.org.
School—(Grades PreK-8), 570 Brewer St., 06118-2305. Tel: 860-568-4100; Fax: 860-568-1070. Web: saintchristopherschool.org. Mrs. Kathleen Madej, Prin. Lay Teachers 17; Students 250.
Catechesis/Religious Program—580 Brewer St., 06118-2305. Tel: 860-895-8692; Fax: 860-568-0242. Students 173.

3—ST. ISAAC JOGUES (1964), Linked with St. Mary Parish and St. Rose Parish. Revs. John P. Rohan; Robert P. Roy; Deacon Julio C. Maturana.
Parish Center & Mailing Address: 15 Maplewood Ave., 06108. Tel: 860-289-7916; Fax: 860-289-3224.
Church: 1 Community St., 06108-2808. Tel: 860-528-6749.
Res.: 33 Church St., 06108. Tel: 860-289-8616; Fax: 860-289-3966.
Catechesis/Religious Program—Mrs. Judy Craig, D.R.E. Students 21.

4—ST. MARY (1873), Linked with St. Isaac Jogues Parish and St. Rose Parish. Revs. John P. Rohan; Robert P. Roy; Joseph Savino-Gyimah, (Min. to Ghanainan Catholic Community); Deacon Julio C. Maturana. In Res., Rev. Louis D. Cremonie.
Res.: 15 Maplewood Ave., 06108-4021. Tel: 860-289-7916; Fax: 860-289-3224. Email: stmaryschurcheasthartford@comcast.net.
Parish Center—30 Maplewood Ave., 06108. Tel: 860-289-7510.
Catechesis/Religious Program—Students 27.

5—OUR LADY OF PEACE (1971), Linked with Blessed Sacrament Parish. Rev. James J. Nock; Deacons Leo R. LaRocque; Raymond A. Parenteau.
Res.: 370 May Rd., 06118-3496. Tel: 860-568-4414.
Catechesis/Religious Program— Twinned with Blessed Sacrament. Students 250.

6—ST. ROSE (1920), Linked with St. Isaac Jogues Parish and St. Mary Parish. Revs. John P. Rohan; Robert P. Roy; Deacon Julio C. Maturana.
Parish Center & Mailing Address: 15 Maplewood Ave., 06108. Email: strosechurcheasthartford@comcast.net.
Res.: 33 Church St., 06108-3794. Tel: 860-289-8616; 860-289-7916; Fax: 860-289-3224.
School—(Grades PreK-8) Tel: 860-528-4169; Fax: 860-528-4160. Mrs. Mary Macunas, Prin. Lay Teachers 11; Students 101.
Catechesis/Religious Program—Mrs. Judy Craig, D.R.E. Students 197.

EAST HAVEN, NEW HAVEN CO.

1—ST. CLARE (1947), Linked with St. Elizabeth Parish, Branford. Rev. Kevin G. Donovan; Deacon George G. Sartor.
Parish Office: 234 Coe Ave., 06512-4112. Tel: 203-467-5136; Fax: 203-469-0241. Web: www.st-clareparish.org.
Catechesis/Religious Program—Tel: 203-467-0600. Email: faithformation@st-clareparish.org. Students 171.

2—OUR LADY OF POMPEII (1947) Rev. James A. Shanley; Deacon Norman H. Singer, (Retired).
Res.: 355 Foxon Rd., 06513. Tel: 203-469-0764; Fax: 203-469-3645. Email: ourladyofpompeii@snet.net. Web: ourladyofpompeii.com.
Catechesis/Religious Program—Email: olopreled@snet.net. Students 700.

3—ST. VINCENT DE PAUL (1915) Revs. Thomas A. Sievel; Thomas J. Kelly; Deacon Robert J. Macaluso.
Res.: 80 Taylor Ave., 06512. Tel: 203-467-6394; Fax: 203-467-6716.
School—(Grades PreK-8), 35 Bishop St., 06512. Tel: 203-467-1606; 203-467-1607; Fax: 203-467-8851. Email: svdp@snet.net. Web: stvincentdepaulschool.org. Mr. Pasquale Guido, Prin. Lay Teachers 11; Students 172.
Catechesis/Religious Program—Mrs. Carol Silva, D.R.E. Students 325.

EAST WINDSOR, HARTFORD CO., ST. PHILIP'S (1959), Linked with St. Catherine Parish, Broad Brook. Rev. Emilio P. Padelli.
Res.: 150 S. Main St., 06088-9760. Tel: 860-623-0408; Fax: 860-623-8937 (Call ahead to fax).
Catechesis/Religious Program—Students 19.

ENFIELD, HARTFORD CO.

1—ST. ADALBERT'S (1915), (Polish), [CEM] Rev. Edmund M. O'Brien; Deacon Robert E. Lambert. In Res., Rev. Anthony J. Bruno. Tel: 860-745-9966.
Res.: 90 Alden Ave., 06082-2865. Tel: 860-745-4837; Fax: 860-745-1787.
School—(Grades PreK) Tel: 860-745-6135; Fax: 860-741-7358. Lay Teachers 2; Students 60.
Catechesis/Religious Program—Students 105.

2—ST. BERNARD (1870) [CEM] Rev. John P. Melnick; Deacons Hobart Stadtlander, (Retired); Donald H. Pond.
Res.: 426 Hazard Ave., 06082-4719. Tel: 860-749-8353; Fax: 860-749-6456. Email: st.bernards@snet.net.
School—(Grades K-8), 232 Pearl St., 06082-4399. Tel: 860-745-5275; Fax: 860-745-0167. Sr. Marie JoAnn Lewko, C.S.S.F., Prin. Sisters 3; Lay Teachers 18; Students 227.
Catechesis/Religious Program—Tel: 860-749-2993; Fax: 860-749-6456. Email: stbernardccd@yahoo.com. Beth Chase, C.R.E. (Grades 1-6); Jennifer St. Sauveur-Dandurand, C.R.E. (Grades 7-10). Students 205.

3—HOLY FAMILY (1965) Revs. Francis T. Kerwan; Thomas Oppong Mensah; Deacon Arthur J. Dickman.
Res.: 23 Simon Rd., 06082-5903. Tel: 860-741-2101; Fax: 860-741-7411.
Catechesis/Religious Program—Elizabeth McGivney, D.R.E.; Carole Frappier, D.R.E. Students 757.

4—ST. MARTHA (1961) Rev. J. Daniel McElheron; Deacons Robert E. Bernd; Joseph S. Sloan.
Res.: 214 Brainard Rd., 06082-2609. Tel: 860-745-5616; Fax: 860-741-6731. Email: rectory@stmartha.necoxmail.com.
School—(Grades K-8) Tel: 860-745-3833; Fax: 860-745-3329. Email: saintmartha.school@snet.net. Web: stmarthaschool-ct.org. Sr. Theresa Marie Grochowski, C.S.S.F., Prin. Felician Sisters 1; Lay Teachers 9; Students 185.
Catechesis/Religious Program—Tel: 860-745-5616. Brian LeMay, D.R.E. Students 158.

5—ST. PATRICK (1866) [CEM] Rev. John G. Weaver; Deacon Vincent J. Motto.
Church: 64 Pearl St., 06082-3594. Tel: 860-745-2411; Fax: 860-253-9483. Email: stpatricc@aol.com. Web: www.stpartricks-enfield.41pi.com.
Catechesis/Religious Program—Tel: 860-741-0572. Carolyn Dague, D.R.E. Students 160.

FARMINGTON, HARTFORD CO., ST. PATRICK (1871) Revs. Mark F. Flynn; Thomas R. Mitchell; Deacon William A. Farrell.
Res.: 110 Main St., P.O. Box 523, 06034-0523. Tel: 860-677-2639; Fax: 860-677-2672. Email: rectory@stpatsfarm.com. Web: stpatsfarm.com.
Catechesis/Religious Program—Tel: 860-676-0253; Fax: 860-677-2672. Email: religioused@stpatsfarm.com. Eileen Dignazio, D.R.E. Students 460.

FORESTVILLE, HARTFORD CO., ST. MATTHEW (1891) Revs. Brian W. Monnerat; Charles Ikwuegbu; Deacons John E. Pahl; Michael P. Szumigala.
Res.: 120 Church Ave., Box 9216, 06011-9216. Tel: 860-583-1833; Fax: 860-582-6152. Web: stmatthewrcc.com.
School—(Grades PreK-8), Welch Dr., 06010. Tel: 860-583-5214; Fax: 860-314-1541. Web: stmatthewschool.com. Sr. Christina Joseph Dolan, I.H.M., Prin.; Lynn Delfino, Librarian. Sisters 5; Lay Teachers 14; Students 265.
Parish Resource Center—101 Church Ave., 06010. Tel: 860-583-1241.
Catechesis/Religious Program—Tel: 860-583-7806. Sr. Lorraine Gondkofski, I.H.M., D.R.E. Students 562.
Convent—Sisters, Servants of the Immaculate Heart of Mary, 119 Church Ave., 06010. Tel: 860-583-2004.

GLASTONBURY, HARTFORD CO.

1—ST. DUNSTAN (1971) Revs. George M. Couturier; Thomas E. Ptaszynski, Temporary Admin.; Sr. Mary O'Neill, R.S.M., Pastoral Assoc.; Deacon

Peter J. Klein.
Mailing Address: 1345 Manchester Rd., 06033. Tel: 860-633-3317.
Res.: 1150 Neipisc Rd., 06033. Tel: 860-633-8159; Fax: 860-659-8611. Email: stdunstanchurch@aol.com. Web: stdunstanchurch.org.
Catechesis/Religious Program—Tel: 860-633-6876. Debbie Brinckman, C.R.E. (K-5); Kathy Dahlem, C.R.E. (6-8); Kara Nelson, C.R.E. (6-8); Gina Raymond, C.R.E. Students 859.

2—St. Paul (1954), Linked with St. Augustine Parish, South Glastonbury. Revs. John P. Gwozdz; Joseph Moonnanappallil; Deacon Stephen L. Weaver. In Res., Rev. Edward J. McLean (Retired).
Res.: 2577 Main St., 06033-2023. Tel: 860-633-9419; Fax: 860-633-0040.
Catechesis/Religious Program—Tel: 860-659-3029. Students 744.

Goshen, Litchfield Co., St. Thomas of Villanova (1877) [CEM] Rev. Richard M. Taberski; Deacon Kenneth Dos Santos.
Res.: 71 North St., P.O. Box 177, 06756-0177. Tel: 860-491-2756; Fax: 860-491-3780. Email: stthomaschurch@optonline.net. Web: stthomasofvillanovachurch.com.
Catechesis/Religious Program—Tel: 860-491-9276. Students 125.

Granby, Hartford Co., St. Therese (1958) Rev. Ronald R. Yelle; Deacon Robert D. Navickas.
Res.: 120 W. Granby Rd., P.O. Box 600, 06035-2907. Tel: 860-653-3371; Fax: 860-653-5780. Email: srectory4180@sbcglobal.net. Web: www.rc.net/hartford/st_therese.
Catechesis/Religious Program—Tel: 860-844-8627. Students 348.

Guilford, New Haven Co., St. George (1870) [CEM] Rev. Lawrence S. Symolon; Deacons Adam J. Michaele; William A. Elder.
Res.: 33 Whitfield St., 06437-2698. Tel: 203-453-2788; Fax: 203-453-1707.
School—Our Lady of Mercy, School for Guilford and Madison., 149 Neck Rd., Madison, 06443-2728. Tel: 203-245-4393; Fax: 203-245-3498. Dr. John R. Alfone, Prin. Students 196.
Catechesis/Religious Program—Tel: 203-453-3496. Students 1,131.

Hamden, New Haven Co.

1—St. Ann (1919), (Italian), Linked with St. John the Baptist Parish, New Haven. Rev. John J. Keane.
Res.: 930 Dixwell Ave., 06514-4990. Tel: 203-865-0886; Fax: 203-865-4502.
Catechesis/Religious Program—Linked with St. John the Baptist, New Haven. Students 38.

2—Ascension (1964) Rev. Thomas J. O'Rourke.
Res.: 1040 Dunbar Hill Rd., 06514-1410. Tel: 203-288-7516; Fax: 203-288-7516 (Call first).
Catechesis/Religious Program—Tel: 203-288-7516. Donna Olsen, D.R.E. Students 17.

3—Blessed Sacrament (1939) Rev. Donald J. French; Deacon Joseph R. Ryzewski.
Res.: 321 Circular Ave., 06514-3428. Tel: 203-288-1652; Fax: 203-248-0873. Email: bsrectory322@yahoo.com.
Catechesis/Religious Program—306 Circular Ave., 06514. Tel: 203-288-5228. Barbara Gode, C.R.E. Students 157.

4—St. Joan of Arc (1971) Rev. Daniel G. Keefe; Deacon Stephen J. Yatcko.
Res.: 450 W. Todd St., 06518. Tel: 203-288-4543; Fax: 203-288-1130. Email: stjofa@comcast.net. Web: www.sjarc.us.
Catechesis/Religious Program—Tel: 203-230-1926. Students 230.

5—Our Lady of Mt. Carmel (1869) [CEM] Revs. Daniel James Sullivan; Faron Calumba (Philippines); Deacons James H. Stanley, (Retired); John O'Donovan, (Retired).
Res.: 2819 Whitney Ave., 06518-2598. Tel: 203-248-0141; Fax: 203-248-8658. Email: olmtcarmel@sbcglobal.net. Web: www.olomc.org.
Parish Center—2809 Whitney Ave., 06518. Tel: 203-287-9017.
Catechesis/Religious Program—Tel: 203-287-9017. Sr. Ann O'Neill, R.S.M., D.R.E. Students 763.

6—St. Rita (1928) Revs. Philip J. Sharkey; Paul A. Gotta; Deacon Ronald B. Gurr. In Res., Rev. Geoffrey C. Smith.
Res.: 1620 Whitney Ave., 06517. Tel: 203-248-5513; Fax: 203-248-2684. Email: stritachurchct@sbcglobal.net. Web: stritachurch.org.
School—(Grades PreK-8), 1601 Whitney Ave., 06517. Tel: 203-248-3114; Fax: 203-248-1016. Web: stritaschool.org. Sr. Maureen Fitzgerald, A.S.C.J., Prin.; Linda Kiley, Librarian. Priests 1; Apostles of the Sacred Heart 2; Lay Teachers 26; Students 431.
Catechesis/Religious Program—Tel: 203-281-7522; Fax: 203-248-2684. Mrs. Dianne Breen, D.R.E. Students 387.

7—St. Stephen (1953) Rev. Robert G. Heffernan; Deacon George E. McCarroll.
Res.: 400 Ridge Rd., 06517-2941. Tel: 203-288-6439; Fax: 203-288-4152. Email: rectory@ststephenparishhamden.com. Web: ststephenparishhamden.com.
School—(Grades PreK-8) Tel: 203-288-6792; Fax: 203-287-9158. Web: saintstephenschool.net. Mrs. Maria Testa, Prin. Lay Teachers 13; Students 210.
Catechesis/Religious Program—Tel: 203-288-1305. Denise Szczech, C.R.E. Students 49.

Harwinton, Litchfield Co., Immaculate Heart of Mary (1956) Rev. Allan J. Hill; Deacon John H. Charles.
Res.: 78 Litchfield Rd., P.O. Box 127, 06791-2230. Tel: 860-485-1588; Fax: 860-485-1004. Web: www.immaculatehearthartwinton.org.
Catechesis/Religious Program—Tel: 860-485-9264. Mrs. Christine Rousseau, C.R.E. Students 235.

Kensington, Hartford Co., St. Paul (1878) Revs. Mark Curesky, O.F.M.Conv.; Martin Kobos, O.F.M-.Conv.; Michael Miller, O.F.M.Conv.; Deacon Carmen Guzzardi; Sr. Ellen Shea, R.S.M., Pastoral Care.
467 Alling St., 06037-2170. Email: stpaulschurch479@yahoo.com.
Res.: 479 Alling St., 06037-2170. Tel: 860-828-0331; Fax: 860-828-7620.
Parish Center—467 Alling St., 06037.
School—(Grades PreK-8), 461 Alling St., 06037-2170. Tel: 860-828-4343; Fax: 860-828-1226. Email: stpaul461@yahoo.com. Web: www.stpaulschoolkens.org. Robert Biancamano, Prin. Lay Teachers 24; Students 242.
Catechesis/Religious Program—Tel: 860-828-1934; Fax: 860-828-7620. Email: stpaulreled@yahoo.com. Students 922.

Kent, Litchfield Co., Sacred Heart (1970) [CEM] Rev. Thomas E. Berberich.
Res.: 90 Cobble Rd., P.O. Box 186, 06757-0186. Tel: 860-927-3003; Fax: 860-927-3985.
Church: 17 Bridge St., 06757.
Catechesis/Religious Program—Students 51.

Lakeville, Litchfield Co., St. Mary (1874) [CEM] Rev. Joseph G.M. Kurnath.
Res.: 76 Sharon Rd., P.O. Box 466, 06039-0466. Tel: 860-435-2659; Fax: 860-435-1042. Email: churchofstmary@snet.net. Web: stmarylakeville.org.
Catechesis/Religious Program—Nancy Hodgkins, D.R.E. Students 41.

Litchfield, Litchfield Co., St. Anthony of Padua (1882) [CEM] Rev. Robert F. Tucker; Deacon John R. Maffeo.
Res.: 49 South St., P.O. Box 97, 06759-0097. Tel: 860-567-5209; Fax: 860-567-2052. Email: stanthonypadua@optonline.net. Web: stanthonyofpaduachurch.org.
Catechesis/Religious Program—Tel: 860-567-4188. Ken Dos Santos, D.R.E. Students 345.

Madison, New Haven Co., St. Margaret (1937) Rev. Msgr. John P. Conte; Rev. Gerard G. Masters; Deacons Joseph M. Regan; P. Terrence Moran; Paul Prete.
Res.: 24 Academy St., P.O. Box 814, 06443-2647. Tel: 203-245-7301; Fax: 203-245-8568.
School—Our Lady of Mercy, (Grades PreK-8), 149 Neck Rd., 06443-2728. Tel: 203-245-4393; Fax: 203-245-3498. Dr. John R. Alfone, Prin.
Catechesis/Religious Program—Tel: 203-245-7971; Fax: 203-245-3387. Lauri Sturwold, D.R.E.; Monica Piombino, Youth Min. Students 1,233.

Manchester, Hartford Co.

1—Assumption (1955), Linked wtih St. James Parish. Revs. Kevin P. Cavanaugh; Grzegorz Jaworowski (Poland); Honore M. Kombo (Congo).
Res.: 285 W. Center St., 06040-4898. Tel: 860-643-2195; Fax: 860-646-4360. Web: www.assumption-parish.com.
Church: 29 S. Adams St., 06040.
School—(Grades PreK-8) Tel: 860-649-0889; Fax: 860-643-0559. Marguerite Ouellette, Prin. Sisters 2; Lay Teachers 8; Students 146.
Catechesis/Religious Program—Tel: 860-643-7596. Sr. Colleen Doyle, R.S.M., D.R.E. Students 161.
Convent—Sisters of Charity of Our Lady, Mother of the Church, 21 S. Adams St., 06040. Tel: 860-643-0452.

2—St. Bartholomew (1958) Revs. Stephen M. Sledesky; Marcin P. Pluciennik; Deacon William H. Bartlett; Vicky Rispoli, Youth Min.; Diane Gluhosky, Business Mgr.
Res.: 45 Ludlow Rd., 06040-4542. Tel: 860-646-1613; Fax: 860-646-7121. Web: stbartparish.org.
Catechesis/Religious Program—Tel: 860-643-9178. Denise Bartlett, D.R.E. Students 387.

3—St. Bridget (1870) Revs. Stephen M. Sledesky; Marcin P. Pluciennik; Sr. Marilyn Canning, R.S.M., Pastoral Assoc.; John Ryan, Pastoral Assoc.
Res.: 80 Main St., 06042-3140. Tel: 860-643-2403; Fax: 860-646-6936. Email: parishoffice@saintbridget.com. Web: www.saintbridget.com.
School—(Grades PreK-8), 74 Main St., 06042-3140. Tel: 860-649-7731; Fax: 860-646-6936. Web: www.school.saintbridget.com. Mary Alice Nadaskay, Prin. Lay Teachers 18; Students 158.
Catechesis/Religious Program—Tel: 860-643-5454. Kathleen Sinnamon, D.R.E. Students 245.

4—St. James (1874), Linked with Church of the Assumption, Manchester. Revs. Kevin P. Cavanaugh; Grzegorz Jaworowski (Poland); Honore M. Kombo (Congo).
Res.: 896 Main St., 06040-6079. Tel: 860-643-4129; Fax: 860-643-4130. Email: stjamesmanchester@cox.net. Web: saint-james-church.org.
School—(Grades PreK-8), 73 Park St., 06040. Tel: 860-643-5088; Fax: 860-649-6462. Mrs. Patricia Kanute, Prin. Lay Teachers 26; Students 417.
Catechesis/Religious Program—73 Park St., 06040. Tel: 860-643-9605. Students 130.

Marlborough, Hartford Co., St. John Fisher (1972) Rev. Arthur J. Audet; Deacon John W. McKaig.
Res. & Mailing Address: 24 Cheney Rd., 06447-1327. Tel: 860-295-0067. Email: stjohnfisher@yahoo.com.
Church: 30 Jones Hollow Rd., 06447. Tel: 860-295-0001 (Parish Office); Fax: 860-295-8682.
Catechesis/Religious Program—Tel: 860-805-6997. Email: stjohnfisherccd@yahoo.com. Students 317.

Meriden, New Haven Co.

1—The Corporation of the Church of the Holy Angels (1887) Rev. Roland M. LaPlante; Deacons Joseph S. Mazurek; George A. Kraussman, (Retired).
Res.: 915 Main St., 06451-4940. Tel: 203-235-5311 (Rectory); 203-235-3822 (Office); Fax: 203-630-3041. Email: hangels@snet.net. Web: www.holyangelschurch.org.
Catechesis/Religious Program—585 Main St. Tel: 203-237-8697. Email: hared@holyangelschurch.org. Geralyn Kogut, D.R.E. Students 153.

2—St. Joseph (1900), Linked with St. Mary Parish. Revs. Shawn T. Daly; Augustine Okoroafor; Deacon John T. Nugent; Sr. Georgeann Vumbaco, R.S.M., Pastoral Assoc.
Res.: 22 Goodwill Ave., 06451. Tel: 203-237-5593.
School—(Grades K-8) Tel: 203-237-6800; Fax: 203-238-2963. Mrs. Katherine A. Spencer, Prin. Lay Teachers 9; Students 178.
Catechesis/Religious Program—Tel: 203-237-5593. Students 188.

3—St. Laurent (1880), (French), Linked with Our Lady of Mt. Carmel Parish. Rev. David C. Carey; Deacons Donald H. Smith; George W. Frederick; Sr. Gertrude Goldman, O.S.U., Pastoral Assoc.
Mailing: *c/o Mt. Carmel*, 109 Goodwill Ave., 06451.
Res.: 121 Camp St., 06450-3279. Tel: 203-634-1583; Fax: 203-238-3629.
Catechesis/Religious Program—Deborah Haggett, D.R.E. Students 146.

4—St. Mary (1890), (German), [CEM], Linked with St. Joseph Parish. Revs. Shawn T. Daly; Augustine Okoroafor; Deacon John T. Nugent.
Res.: 5 Sherman Pl., 06451. Tel: 203-235-0519.
Catechesis/Religious Program—Students 5.

5—Our Lady of Mount Carmel (1894), (Italian), Linked with St. Laurent Parish. Rev. David C. Carey; Deacons Donald H. Smith; George W. Frederick; Sr. Gertrude Goldman, O.S.U., Pastoral Assoc.
Parish: 109 Goodwill Ave., 06451-3000. Tel: 203-235-6381.
Res.: 17 North St., 06451. Fax: 203-238-3629.
School—(Grades PreK-8), 115 Lewis Ave., 06451. Tel: 203-235-2959. Norine McDermott, Prin. Lay Teachers 10; Students 202.
Catechesis/Religious Program— Deborah Haggett, D.R.E. Students 146.

6—St. Rose of Lima (1848) Revs. Jack Hoak, O.F.M.; Isaac J. Calicchio, O.F.M.; Deacons Charles E. Cunniff Jr.; Raul Cardona.
Res.: 35 Center St., 06450-5685. Tel: 203-235-1644; Fax: 203-235-1360. Email: strosechurch@cox.net.
Catechesis/Religious Program—Tel: 203-235-6887. Students 309.

7—St. Stanislaus (1891), (Polish), [CEM] Rev. Edward Ziemnicki.
Res.: 82 Akron St., 06450-5796. Tel: 203-235-6341; Fax: 203-235-6342. Email: ststanislaus@cox.net.
School—(Grades PreK-8), 81 Akron St., 06450. Tel: 203-235-1005; Fax: 203-630-3424. Email: info@ststanislausschool.org. Web: ststanislausschool.org. George Claffey, Prin. Lay Teachers 20; Students 181.
Catechesis/Religious Program—Tel: 203-235-6341. Students 121.

Middlebury, New Haven Co., St. John of the Cross (1904) Rev. Thomas J. Barry; Deacon Robert F. Wallin.
Res.: 1089 Whittemore Rd., P.O. Box 361, 06762-0361. Tel: 203-758-2659; Fax: 203-758-1121. Email: st.john@snet.net.
Catechesis/Religious Program—Village Sq., 530

Middlebury Rd., 06762. Tel: 203-758-1326; Fax: 203-758-1852. Mrs. Annette Williams, D.R.E. Students 581.

MILFORD, NEW HAVEN CO.

1—ST. AGNES (1906) Rev. Francis X. Callahan; Deacon Nicholas A. Genovese.
Res.: 400 Merwin Ave., 06460-7198. Tel: 203-878-1617; Fax: 203-878-5545.
Catechesis/Religious Program—Students 378.

2—ST. ANN (1924) Rev. Brian A. Shaw.
Res.: 501 Naugatuck Ave., 06460-5095. Tel: 203-874-0634; Fax: 203-874-1919. Web: www.saintann-parish.com.
School—64 Ridge St., 06460. Tel: 203-878-2738; Fax: 203-878-5473. Carol Schweitzer, Prin. Lay Teachers 11; Students 80.
Catechesis/Religious Program—Tel: 203-878-8130. Students 135.

3—CHRIST THE REDEEMER (1966) Rev. Cyriac Maliekal; Deacon George A. Puskas.
Res.: 325 Oronoque Rd., 06461. Tel: 203-878-7431; Fax: 203-878-0677. Web: www.ctrmilford.net.
Catechesis/Religious Program—Students 205.

4—ST. GABRIEL (Wildemere Beach) (1946) Rev. Maurice J. Maroney; Deacons Calvin Croll, (Retired); Henry Doyle, (Retired).
Business Office: 26 Broadway, 06460-5968. Tel: 203-877-6096; Fax: 203-878-9700. Email: stgabchurch@aol.com. Web: stgabchurch.4lpi.com.
School—(Grades PreK-8), 1 Tudor Rd., 06460. Tel: 203-874-3811; Fax: 203-874-0416. Dr. Gail Kingston, Prin. Lay Teachers 17; Students 226.
Catechesis/Religious Program—Students 258.

5—ST. MARY (1874) [CEM] Revs. James J. Cronin; Nathaniel C. Labarda; Chacko K. Kumplam (India); Deacons Richard M. Sennett; John H. Hoffman.
Res.: 70 Gulf St., Box 230, 06460-0230. Tel: 203-878-3571; Fax: 203-877-8741. Email: kelleystmarymfd@optonline.net.
School—(Grades PreK-8) Tel: 203-878-6539; Fax: 203-878-1866. Frank Lacerenza, Prin. Lay Teachers 25; Students 305.
Catechesis/Religious Program—Tel: 203-877-5874. Sue Marra, D.R.E. Students 830.

NAUGATUCK, NEW HAVEN CO.

1—ST. FRANCIS OF ASSISI (1866) Rev. Michael J. Slusz; Deacon Nicholas Iassogna.
Res.: 318 Church St., 06770. Tel: 203-729-4543; Fax: 203-729-6216.
School—(Grades PreK-8) Tel: 203-729-2247; Fax: 203-729-0512. Mr. Thomas Fuller, Prin. Lay Teachers 10; Students 165.
Catechesis/Religious Program—Mrs. Joyce Luzio; Jessica Mulligan, D.R.E. Students 448.

2—ST. VINCENT FERRER (1975) Rev. Kevin J. Forsyth.
Res.: 1006 New Haven Rd., 06770-4731. Tel: 203-723-7497; Fax: 203-729-2978. Email: stvincentfer@sbcglobal.net.
Catechesis/Religious Program—Tel: 203-723-0782. Stephen Kenny, D.R.E.; Helen Northrup, Youth Min. Students 307.

NEW BRITAIN, HARTFORD CO.

1—ALL SAINTS (1918), (Slovak), Closed. For inquiries for sacramental records, contact St. Ann, New Britain.

2—ST. ANDREW (1895), (Lithuanian), Linked with St. John the Evangelist Parish. Rev. Ronald T. Smith.
Res.: 396 Church St., Box 515, 06050-0515. Tel: 860-223-3667; Fax: 860-826-6201.
Catechesis/Religious Program—Tel: 860-223-3667. Students 17.

3—ST. ANN (1938), (Italian), Linked with St. Mary Parish. Revs. J. Thomas Walsh; Donald Anyagwa (Nigeria).
Res.: 47 Clark St., 06051-1903. Tel: 860-225-7625; Fax: 860-224-4283.
Catechesis/Religious Program—Tel: 860-229-1929; Fax: 860-229-1929. Fran Caron, D.R.E. Students 66.

4—ST. FRANCIS OF ASSISI (1941) Revs. Paul R. Guido, O.F.M.; Paul Rotondi, O.F.M.; Deacon Michael E. Cassella.
Res.: 1755 Stanley St., 06053-2099. Tel: 860-225-6449; Fax: 860-225-2315.
Catechesis/Religious Program—Elizabeth Arena, D.R.E. Students 56.
Convent—1757 Stanley St., 06053-2027. Tel: 860-225-7143. School Sisters of Notre Dame 2.

5—HOLY CROSS (1927), (Polish), Revs. Dariusz Gosciniak; Szymon Kurpios, Sch.P.
Res.: 31 Biruta St., 06053-2899. Tel: 860-229-2011; Fax: 860-826-5887.
Church: 220 Farmington Ave., 06053.
School—Pope John Paul II School, (Grades PreK-8), 221 Farmington Ave., P.O. Box 1810, 06050-1810. Tel: 860-225-4275; Fax: 860-225-5073. Email: principal@pjp2school.org. Web: www.pjp2school.org. Mr. Donald Bellizzi, Prin. Lay Teachers 12; Students 172.
Catechesis/Religious Program—Pope John Paul II School of Religion Eva Fadgyas, D.R.E. Students 268.

6—ST. JEROME (1958), Linked with St. Maurice Parish. Rev. Thomas J. Cieslikowski; Deacon Reginald Roy.
Res.: 1010 Slater Rd., 06053-1698. Tel: 860-224-2411; Fax: 860-224-6838. Email: st.jerome.church@snet.net. Web: www.stjeromenb.org.
Catechesis/Religious Program—Students 126.

7—ST. JOHN THE EVANGELIST (1916), Linked with St. Andrew Parish. Rev. Ronald T. Smith.
Res.: 655 East St., 06051-2108. Tel: 860-223-3667; 860-223-3668; Fax: 860-348-1488.
Catechesis/Religious Program—Cheryl Rusczyk, D.R.E. Students 20.

8—ST. JOSEPH'S (1896), Linked with St. Peter Parish. Rev. Joseph P. Crowley; Deacon Gerald S. Geraci.
Res.: 195 S. Main St., 06051-3199. Tel: 860-229-4851; Fax: 860-225-1403.
Catechesis/Religious Program—Students 74.

9—ST. MARY'S (1848), Linked with St. Ann Parish. Revs. J. Thomas Walsh; Donald Anyagwa (Nigeria); Deacons Pedro Rivera; Adolfo Carrero.
Res.: 544 Main St., 06051-1814. Tel: 860-229-4894; Fax: 860-223-2756.
Catechesis/Religious Program—Students 247.

10—ST. MAURICE (1946), Linked with St. Jerome Parish. Rev. Thomas J. Cieslikowski.
Res.: 100 Wightman Rd., 06052-1597. Tel: 860-225-8419; Fax: 860-224-1947.
Catechesis/Religious Program—Tel: 860-225-4477. Linda E. Tower, D.R.E. Students 106.

11—ST. PETER (1873), (German—French), Linked with St. Joseph Parish. Rev. Joseph P. Crowley.
Res.: 98 Franklin Sq., 06051-2607. Tel: 860-224-1446; Fax: 860-223-8717.
Catechesis/Religious Program—Students 8.

12—SACRED HEART OF JESUS (1894), (Polish), [CEM] Rev. Msgr. Daniel J. Plocharczyk; Revs. Stanislaus Dudek (Poland); Andrzej Pogorzelski.
Res.: 158 Broad St., 06053-4195. Tel: 860-229-0081. Email: sercaj@aol.com.
School—(Grades PreK-8), 35 Orange St., 06053. Tel: 860-229-7663; Fax: 860-832-6098. Katherine Muller, Prin. Daughters of Mary of the Immaculate Conception 3; Lay Teachers 22; Students 368.
Catechesis/Religious Program—Students 245.

NEW HARTFORD, LITCHFIELD CO., IMMACULATE CONCEPTION (1869) [CEM] Rev. Timothy A. O'Brien; Deacon Robert N. Blair.
Res.: 60 Town Hill Rd., P.O. Box 285, 06057-0285. Tel: 860-379-5215; Fax: 860-379-9587. Email: immaculate.parish@snet.net. Web: immaculate-conceptionnhct.org.
Catechesis/Religious Program—Students 350.

NEW HAVEN, NEW HAVEN CO.

1—ST. AEDAN (1900), Linked with St. Brendan Parish. Rev. Thomas B. Shepard; Deacons William H. Parkinson; Robert J. Brunell.
Res.: 112 Fountain St., 06515-0156. Tel: 203-389-2619; Fax: 203-389-1235. Email: staedan@sbcglobal.net.
School—St. Aedan-St. Brendan Catholic School, (Grades PreK-8) Tel: 203-387-5693; Fax: 203-387-1609. Michael Votto, Prin. Lay Teachers 11; Students 204.
Catechesis/Religious Program—Students 66.

2—ST. ANTHONY (1904), (Italian), Rev. Ralph M. Colicchio; Deacons Richard L. Santello; Rene J. Kieda.
Res.: 25 Gold St., 06519. Tel: 203-624-1418; Fax: 203-624-3420.
Catechesis/Religious Program—Students 52.

3—ST. BERNADETTE (1938), (Italian), Rev. Francis T. Carter; Deacon Martin J. O'Connor.
Res.: 385 Townsend Ave., 06512-3998. Tel: 203-467-1007; Fax: 203-467-3719. Email: stberndtchurch@sbcglobal.net. Web: www.saintbernadettechurch.org.
School—(Grades PreK-8) Tel: 203-469-2271; Fax: 203-469-4615. Email: sbsoffice@sbcglobal.net. Web: www.saintbernadette.org. Sherry Steines, Prin.; Mrs. Eileen Steele, Librarian. Lay Teachers 10; Students 131.
Catechesis/Religious Program—Tel: 203-467-8763; Fax: 203-467-3719. Tammie Tinari, C.R.E. Students 141.

4—ST. BONIFACE (1868), (German), Closed. For inquiries for sacramental records contact St. Bernadette Parish, New Haven.

5—ST. BRENDAN (1913), Linked with St. Aedan Parish. Rev. Thomas B. Shepard; Deacons Robert Brunell; William H. Parkinson.
Res.: 455 Whalley Ave., 06511-3080. Tel: 203-865-0561; Fax: 203-865-0562.
School—St. Aedan-St. Brendan Catholic School, (Grades K-8), 351 McKinley Ave., 06515. Tel: 203-387-5693. Michael Votto, Prin. Sisters 1; Lay Teachers 8; Students 201.
Catechesis/Religious Program—Students 29.

6—ST. CASIMIR (1912), (Lithuanian), Closed. For inquiries for sacramental records, contact St. Bernadette, New Haven.

7—ST. DONATO (1915), (Italian), Closed. For inquiries for sacramental records, contact St. Francis Parish, New Haven.

8—ST. FRANCIS (1868) Rev. Daniel J. McLearen.
Res.: 397 Ferry St., 06513-3698. Tel: 203-777-5356; Fax: 203-777-0874.
School—(Grades PreK-8) Tel: 203-777-5352; Fax: 203-865-1271. Mr. Victor Vessicchio, Prin.; Marie D'Amato, Librarian. Lay Teachers 18; Students 259.
Catechesis/Religious Program—Tel: 203-865-5179. Students 37.

9—ST. JOHN THE BAPTIST (1893), Linked with St. Ann Parish, Hamden. Rev. John J. Keane. In Res., Rev. Daniel J. Scott, M.S.
Res.: 782 Dixwell Ave., 06511-1098. Tel: 203-624-3097; Fax: 203-562-0433. Email: info@sjbrcchurch.org. Web: www.sjbrcchurch.org.
Parish Center—20 Elizabeth St., 06511. Tel: 203-562-3908.
Catechesis/Religious Program—Tel: 203-562-0433. Sheila Spilka, D.R.E. Students 31.

10—ST. JOHN THE EVANGELIST, Closed. For inquiries for sacramental records contact Sacred Heart, New Haven.

11—ST. JOSEPH'S (1900) Rev. John P. Sullivan.
Res.: 129 Edwards St., 06511-2299. Tel: 203-777-2548. Email: st.josephnh@att.net.

12—SAINT MARTIN DE PORRES (1942), (African American), Rev. Joseph M. Elko.
Res.: 136 Dixwell Ave., 06511-3400. Tel: 203-624-9944.
Catechesis/Religious Program—Students 41.

13—ST. MARY'S PRIORY (1832) Very Rev. Joseph P. Allen, O.P., Prior.
Mailing Address: P.O. Box 1202, 06505-1202. Email: church@stmarys-priory.com. Web: www.stmarys-priory.com. In Res., Revs. Bernard T. Confer, O.P.; Janusz Pyda, O.P. (Poland); Peter John Cameron, O.P.; Albert A. Caprio, O.P. (Retired); M. Juan-Diego Brunetta, O.P.; Henry A. Camacho, O.P.; Hugh Vincent Dyer, O.P.; Bro. Patrick Foley, O.P.
Res.: *St. Mary's Priory*, 5 Hillhouse Ave., 06511. Tel: 203-562-6193; Fax: 203-562-1273.
Catechesis/Religious Program—Sr. Georgiana Miller, S.M.M.I, D.R.E. Students 73.
Shrine—The Shrine of the Infant Prague (Inc.), Tel: 203-562-9326; Fax: 203-562-1273.

14—ST. MICHAEL (1889), (Italian), Rev. Ralph M. Colicchio; Deacon Richard L. Santello.
Res.: 29 Wooster Pl., 06511-6998. Tel: 203-562-7178; Fax: 203-752-0157.
Catechesis/Religious Program—Sharon Tartaris, D.R.E.

15—ST. PETER (1902) Closed. For inquiries for sacramental records contact Sacred Heart, New Haven.

16—ST. ROSE OF LIMA (1907) Rev. James C. Manship; Deacon Emilio Gonzalez; Sr. Rose Yanase, A.S.C.J., Pastoral Assoc.
Res.: 115 Blatchley Ave., 06513-4298. Tel: 203-865-6149; Fax: 203-865-6140. Email: strosechurch@sbcglobal.net.
Catechesis/Religious Program—Students 300.

17—SACRED HEART (1876) Revs. Francis Snell; James Richardson, S.C.
Res.: 25 Gold St., 06519-1601. Tel: 203-562-7592; Fax: 203-562-1737. Email: sacredheart74@snet.net.
School—St. Martin de Porres Academy, (Grades 5-8), 208 Columbus Ave., 06519. Tel: 203-772-2424; Fax: 203-772-2425. Web: www.saintmartinacademy.org. Jay Bowes, Pres.; Mary Surowiecki, Prin. Lay Teachers 13; Students 106.
Catechesis/Religious Program—Students 106.

18—ST. STANISLAUS (1901), (Polish), Revs. Roman Kmiec, C.M.; Marek Sadowski, C.M.; Stanley Miekina, C.M.
Res.: 9 Eld St., 06511-3815. Tel: 203-562-2828; Fax: 203-752-0217. Email: stanislausnewhaven@comcast.net.
Catechesis/Religious Program—Students 70.
Convent—Sisters Minor of Mary Immaculate, 15 Eld St., 06511. Tel: 203-562-2751.

NEW MILFORD, LITCHFIELD CO.

1—ST. FRANCIS XAVIER (1871) [CEM] Revs. Michael MacInnis, O.F.M.; Philip Pacheco, O.F.M.; Deacon Roland G. Miller.
Mailing Address: 1 Elm St., 06776-4009. Tel: 860-354-2202; Fax: 860-355-9485.
Res.: 48 Old Park Lane Rd., 06776-2508. Tel: 860-350-1611; Fax: 860-350-3214. Web: www.sfxnewmilford.org.
Catechesis/Religious Program—Tel: 860-354-5372. Mary Vannucci, C.R.E. Students 898.

2—OUR LADY OF THE LAKES (1990) Rev. Frederick M. Langlois; Deacon Robert E. Muro Sr. Tel: 860-354-9062.
Res.: 3 Old Town Park Rd., 06776-4212. Tel:

860-354-5239; Fax: 860-354-2968. Email: ololnm@sbcglobal.net.
Catechesis/Religious Program—Tel: 860-355-5365. Karen O'Donnell, D.R.E. Students 273.

NEWINGTON, HARTFORD CO.

1—CHURCH OF THE HOLY SPIRIT (1964) Revs. Lawrence R. Bock; James F. Kinnane; Michael A. Carlson; Deacons James H. Shiels; Joseph Guzauckas.
Res.: 183 Church St., 06111-4898. Tel: 860-666-5671; Fax: 860-666-9784. Web: www.holyspirit.41pi.com.
Catechesis/Religious Program—Tel: 860-666-3562. Susan Skipp, D.R.E. Students 595.

2—ST. MARY (1924) Revs. Joseph F. Keough; Dennis J. Vincenzo; Deacons Bruce R. Thompson; Andrew Moemeka; Sr. Rosemary Spodnick, S.S.N.D., Pastoral Min. In Res., Rev. Nicholas J. Cesaro (Retired).
Res.: 626 Willard Ave., 06111. Tel: 860-666-1591; Fax: 860-666-5720.
School—(Grades PreK-8), 652 Willard Ave., 06111-2692. Tel: 860-666-3844; Fax: 860-666-5570. Thomas Maynard, Prin. Lay Teachers 12; Students 200.
Catechesis/Religious Program—Tel: 860-666-6347. Mrs. Joan Guerrera, D.R.E. Students 608.

NORFOLK, LITCHFIELD CO., IMMACULATE CONCEPTION (1889) [CEM], Linked with St. Joseph Parish, Canaan. Rev. Brian E. Jeffries.
Mailing Address: P.O. Box 897, Canaan, 06018.
Church: 2 North St., 06058-0583. Tel: 860-542-5442; Fax: 860-824-4925. Email: imconception@sbcglobal.net.
Catechesis/Religious Program—Robin Gundlach, D.R.E. Students 45.

NORTH BRANFORD, NEW HAVEN CO., ST. AUGUSTINE (1941) Rev. Robert J. Rousseau; Deacons John Hart; William J. Lovelace.
Res.: 30 Caputo Rd., 06471-1027. Tel: 203-484-0403; Fax: 203-484-0132. Email: staugustinenobfdct@sbcglobal.net. Web: staugustine.catholicweb.com.
Catechesis/Religious Program—Bernadette Lysaght, D.R.E. Students 523.

NORTH HAVEN, NEW HAVEN CO.

1—ST. BARNABAS (1922) Revs. Hugh J. MacDonald; John J. Daly (Retired); Deacon Anthony P. Solli.
Res.: 44 Washington Ave., 06473-1799. Tel: 203-239-5378; Fax: 203-239-3510.
Catechesis/Religious Program—Tel: 203-239-3804. Mrs. Karin Tierney, D.R.E. Students 240.

2—ST. FRANCES CABRINI (1967) Rev. Edward G. Pfnausch; Deacon George R. Stephens, (Retired).
Res.: 6 Welch Rd., 06473-2896. Tel: 203-239-5700; Fax: 203-239-6463. Email: st_frances_rector@sbcglobal.net.
Church & Parish Center: 57 Pond Hill Rd., 06473. Tel: 203-239-5644.
Catechesis/Religious Program—94 Chapel Hill Rd., 06473. Tel: 203-985-0424; Fax: 203-985-0236. Students 331.
Nursery School—90 Chapel Hill Rd., 06473. Tel: 203-239-8012.
Convent—Sisters of the Sacred Heart of Jesus of Ragusa

3—ST. THERESE (1925) Rev. Timothy A. Meehan; Deacon Louis J. Florio. In Res., Rev. John D. Casey (Retired).
Res.: 555 Middletown Ave., 06473-4000. Tel: 203-239-1671; Fax: 203-234-2220. Web: www.sttheresenoh.com.
School—St. Therese Nursery School, Tel: 203-234-9971; Fax: 203-907-0545. Michele Adinolfi-Lucibello, Dir. Students 93.
Catechesis/Religious Program—Tel: 203-234-9287; Fax: 203-907-0545. Terry Raffone, D.R.E. Students 674.

NORTHFORD, NEW HAVEN CO., ST. MONICA (1964) Rev. Joseph Parel; Deacons Louis P. Fusco; William B. Bergers, (Retired); Joseph P. Marenna; Mrs. Judith Derbacher, Pastoral Assoc. Tel: 203-484-2434.
Res.: 1331 Middletown Ave., Box 160, 06472-0160. Tel: 203-484-9226; Fax: 203-484-1189.
Catechesis/Religious Program—Tel: 203-484-2434. Students 279.

OAKVILLE, LITCHFIELD CO., ST. MARY MAGDALEN (1900) Rev. James T. Gregory; Deacon George M. Pettinico.
Res.: 145 Buckingham St., 06779-1728. Tel: 860-274-9273; Fax: 860-274-2013.
School—(Grades PreK-8), 140 Buckingham St., 06779. Tel: 860-945-0621; Fax: 860-945-6162. Web: www.smmsoakville.org. Julie Pilon, Prin. Lay Teachers 13; Students 290.
Catechesis/Religious Program—Kelly A. Shamansky, D.R.E. Students 322.

ORANGE, NEW HAVEN CO., HOLY INFANT (1952) Revs. Peter S. Dargan; Francois-Xavier Eale; Deacon Joseph D. Sullivan.
Res.: 450 Race Brook Rd., 06477. Tel: 203-799-2379; Fax: 203-799-9720.
Catechesis/Religious Program—Tel: 203-777-2417. Connie Gustafson, D.R.E. Students 885.

OXFORD, NEW HAVEN CO., ST. THOMAS THE APOSTLE (1966) Rev. Dominic J. Valla; Sr. Mary Elizabeth Preston, O.S.U., Pastoral Assoc.
Res.: 733 Oxford Rd., 06478. Tel: 203-888-2382; Fax: 203-881-5518.
Catechesis/Religious Program—Christine Troia, Dir. Faith Formation. Students 288.

PLAINVILLE, HARTFORD CO., OUR LADY OF MERCY (1881) [CEM] Revs. John F. Brinsmade; Sebastian Kochupurackal, C.M.I. (India); Deacon Robert A. Berube; Bryan Knorr, Pastoral Assoc.
Res.: 19 S. Canal St., 06062-2756. Tel: 860-747-6825; Fax: 860-747-5407.
Catechesis/Religious Program— Jeanne Gionfriddo, D.R.E. Students 171.

PLANTSVILLE, HARTFORD CO.

1—ST. ALOYSIUS (1961) [JC] Rev. Kevin M. Dillon; Deacons Angelo J. Coppola; James V. Arena.
Res.: 254 Burritt St., 06479-1426. Tel: 860-276-9208; Fax: 860-628-7650.
Catechesis/Religious Program—Tel: 860-621-2454. Students 787.

2—MARY OUR QUEEN (1961) Rev. William J. Brenza; Deacon John L. Crowley.
Res.: 248 Savage St., P.O. Box 46, 06479-0046. Tel: 860-628-4901; Fax: 860-621-0610.
Catechesis/Religious Program—Tel: 860-628-0437. Annelise Fusco, D.R.E. Students 455.

POQUONOCK, HARTFORD CO., ST. JOSEPH'S (1874) [CEM] Rev. Robert B. Vargo; Deacon Ronald Biamonte.
Res.: 1747 Poquonock Ave., P.O. Box 253, 06064-0253. Tel: 860-688-9566; Fax: 860-683-2225. Email: stjoepoquonock@aol.com. Web: home.catholicweb.com/stjosephwinct.
Catechesis/Religious Program—Tel: 860-683-0366. Cyndie Glick, D.R.E. Students 208.

PROSPECT, NEW HAVEN CO., ST. ANTHONY'S (1939) Rev. Mark S. Suslenko; Deacons Domenic Stolfi; George J. Dinkle.
Res.: 4 Union City Rd., P.O. Box 7117, 06712-0117. Tel: 203-758-4056; Fax: 203-758-4594.
Catechesis/Religious Program—Tel: 203-758-4848. Students 372.

ROCKY HILL, HARTFORD CO.

1—ST. ELIZABETH SETON (1985) Rev. Stuart H. Pinette; Deacon Michael A. Shelto.
Res.: 280 Brook St., 06067-0485. Tel: 860-529-3222; Fax: 860-529-6421. Email: churchoffice@stesetonchurch.org. Web: www.stesetonchurch.org.
Catechesis/Religious Program—Students 662.

2—ST. JAMES (1880) Rev. David J. Baranowski; Deacon Robert M. Pallotti.
Res.: 767 Elm St., 06067-1902. Tel: 860-529-8655; Fax: 860-257-1754. Web: stjamesrh.org.
Catechesis/Religious Program—Tel: 860-529-1274. Thomas Sacerdote, D.R.E.; Joyce O'Sullivan, Music Min. Tel: 860-529-8655, Ext. 17. Students 523.

SEYMOUR, NEW HAVEN CO.

1—ST. AUGUSTINE (1866) [CEM] Rev. Stephen H. Bzdyra; Deacons Mario DiRienzo; Frank J. Bevvino Jr.
Res.: 35 Washington Ave., 06483-3124. Tel: 203-888-2081; Fax: 203-888-9681. Email: staugustine@snet.net.
Catechesis/Religious Program—Tel: 203-888-7003. Students 162.

2—GOOD SHEPHERD (1967) Rev. Edward S. Jaksina; Deacons Frank J. Krasnicki; Kenneth E. Ewaskie.
Res.: 135 Mountain Rd., 06483-2038. Tel: 203-888-9243; Fax: 203-888-6016.
Catechesis/Religious Program—Tel: 203-735-3190. Glenn Durette, D.R.E.; Debra Durette, D.R.E. Students 412.

SHARON, LITCHFIELD CO., ST. BERNARD (1885) [CEM], Linked with St. Bridget, Cornwall Bridge. Rev. Francis R. Fador; Deacon Stephen Beecher.
Res.: 52 New St., Box 218, 06069-0218. Tel: 860-364-5244; Fax: 860-364-9893. Email: pastor@snet.net.
Catechesis/Religious Program—Mrs. Patricia Beecher, D.R.E. Students 43.

SIMSBURY, HARTFORD CO., ST. MARY (1921) Revs. William R. Metzler; John M. Santone; Deacons Thomas P. Scanlon, (Retired); Joseph Gabriele, (Retired).
Res.: 940 Hopmeadow St., P.O. Box 575, 06070-0575.
Parish Office—3 Massaco St., P.O. Box 575, 06070-0575. Tel: 860-658-7627; Fax: 860-658-7626. Web: stmarysimsbury.org.
School—St. Mary School, (Grades PreK-8), 946 Hopmeadow St., 06070. Tel: 860-658-9412; Fax: 860-658-1737. Web: stmarysschoolsimsbury.org. Mrs. Marie Gannatti, Prin.; Dorothy Marks, Librarian. Lay Teachers 13; Students 232.
Catechesis/Religious Program—Tel: 860-658-5919. Judy Eagen, C.R.E.; Jeannie Carpenter, C.R.E. Students 982.

SOUTH GLASTONBURY, HARTFORD CO., ST. AUGUSTINE (1877) [CEM], Linked with St. Paul Parish, Glastonbury. Revs. John P. Gwozdz; Joseph Moonnanappallil; Deacon Stephen L. Weaver.
Res.: 55 Hopewell Rd., P.O. Box 175, 06073-0175. Tel: 860-633-9505; Fax: 860-633-1341.
Catechesis/Religious Program—Tel: 860-657-9121. Students 330.

SOUTH WINDSOR, HARTFORD CO.

1—ST. FRANCIS OF ASSISI (1941) Rev. Jeremiah N. Murasso.
Res.: 600 Ellington Rd., 06074-4166. Tel: 860-528-8288 (Parish Office); Fax: 860-528-1685. Email: pastorsfoac@aol.com. Web: www.stfrancisofassisisw.org.
Catechesis/Religious Program—Mark F. Cerrato, D.R.E. Students 330.

2—ST. MARGARET MARY (1961) Rev. Daniel Jeremiah Sullivan; Deacons Thomas J. Conklin; Michael D. Haines.
Res.: 80 Hayes Rd., 06074-1499. Tel: 860-644-2411; Fax: 860-644-5765. Email: office@smm.necoxmail.com. Web: stmargaretmary-sowindsor-ct4lpi.com.
Catechesis/Religious Program—Tel: 860-644-2549; Fax: 860-644-5765. Email: re@smm.necoxmail.com. Louise Bridge, D.R.E.; Michael Ryba, C.R.E. Students 800.

SOUTHBURY, NEW HAVEN CO., SACRED HEART (1884) [CEM] Rev. Joseph T. Donnelly; Deacon Charles Dietsch, Pastoral Assoc.; Sr. Patricia Torre, D.W., Pastoral Assoc.
Church: 910 Main St. S., 06488. Tel: 203-264-5071; Fax: 203-264-9562.
Res.: 91 Old Waterbury Rd., 06488.
Catechesis/Religious Program—Tel: 203-264-5065; Fax: 203-264-4271. Anne Sharkey, D.R.E. Students 710.

SOUTHINGTON, HARTFORD CO.

1—ST. DOMINIC (1971) Rev. Ronald P. May; Deacons Paul J. Kulas; Eugene P. Nebiolo.
Res.: 1050 Flanders Rd., 06489-1344. Tel: 860-628-0349; Fax: 860-276-8390. Web: saintdominicchurch.com.
School—(Grades PreK-5) Tel: 860-628-4678; Fax: 860-628-6572. Mrs. Patricia O'Neil Tiezzi, Prin.; Johanna Needham, Librarian.
Catechesis/Religious Program—Tel: 860-628-5159; Fax: 860-620-9246. Jacqueline Marenholz, D.R.E. Students 867.

2—IMMACULATE CONCEPTION (1915), (Polish), [CEM] Rev. Daniel T. Wojtun; Deacon Wayne F. Griffin.
Res.: 130 Summer St., 06489. Tel: 860-628-2181; Fax: 860-628-0341. Email: immaculateconception06489@gmail.com. Web: www.immaculateconception06489.4lpi.com.
Catechesis/Religious Program—Judy Telesmanick, D.R.E. Students 152.
Father Kolbe Catechetical Center—152 Summer St., Plantsville, 06479. Tel: 860-628-6973.

3—ST. THOMAS (1860) [CEM] Rev. Nicholas P. Melo; Deacon Wesley F. Baxter.
Res.: 99 Bristol St., 06489-4599. Tel: 860-628-4713; Fax: 860-628-7341. Email: stchurch@snet.net.
School—(Grades PreK-8), 133 Bristol St., 06489. Tel: 860-628-2485. Mrs. Mary Pat Wirkus, Prin. Lay Teachers 13; Students 157.
Catechesis/Religious Program—Tel: 860-628-9679. Sr. Marie Roccapriore, M.P.F., D.R.E. Students 197.
Convent—Religious Sisters Filippini, 20 Eden Pl., 06489-4599. Tel: 860-621-1904.

SUFFIELD, HARTFORD CO.

1—ST. JOSEPH (1916), (Polish), [CEM] Rev. William L. Baldyga.
Res.: 140 S. Main St., 06078-2218. Tel: 860-668-2880.
Catechesis/Religious Program—Students 8.

2—SACRED HEART (1884) [JC] Rev. Michael C. DeVito; Deacon Richard F. Boucher; Sr. Dorothy Connelly, S.N.D.deN., Pastoral Assoc. In Res., Rev. Theodore T. Raczynski (Retired).
Res.: 446 Mountain Rd., P.O. Box 626, 06078-0626. Tel: 860-668-4246; Fax: 860-668-1337. Email: sheart.church@sbcglobal.net. Web: www.sacredheartct.com.
Catechesis/Religious Program—Tel: 860-668-7766; Fax: 860-668-7811. Students 600.

TARIFFVILLE, HARTFORD CO., ST. BERNARD (1878) [CEM] Rev. Thomas A. Flower.
Res.: 7 Maple St., P.O. Box 85, 06081-0085. Tel: 860-658-5142; Fax: 860-658-2804. Email: stbernardschurch@comcast.net. Web: www.stbernardschurch.net.
Catechesis/Religious Program—Students 124.

TERRYVILLE, LITCHFIELD CO.

1—ST. CASIMIR (1906), (Polish), Linked with Immaculate Conception Parish. Rev. Gerald H. Dziedzic; Deacon Leo B. Conard III.
Res.: 21 Maple St., 06786. Tel: 860-583-4697; Fax: 860-584-8656. Email: immclte.cncptn.chrch@snet.net. Web: rc.net/hartford/stcasimir.

Catechesis/Religious Program—Students 104.

2—IMMACULATE CONCEPTION (1882) [CEM 2], Linked with St. Casimir Parish. Rev. Gerald H. Dziedzic; Deacon Leo B. Conard III.
Res. & Mailing Address: 21 Maple St., 06786-1197. Tel: 860-583-4697. Email: immclte.cncptn.chrch@snet.net. Web: rc.net/hartford/icc.
Church: 170 Main St., 06786.
Catechesis/Religious Program—Fax: 860-584-8656. Students 201.

THOMASTON, LITCHFIELD CO., ST. THOMAS (1869) [CEM] Rev. William F. O'Keefe; Deacons Jose L. Dlugokinski; Victor C. Mitchell Jr.
Parish Center—19 Electric Ave., 06787-1651. Tel: 860-283-5817; Fax: 860-283-1009. Email: stc-office@sbcglobal.net. Web: www.stthomasthomaston.org.
Catechesis/Religious Program—Tel: 860-283-4296. Students 368.

TORRINGTON, LITCHFIELD CO.

1—ST. FRANCIS OF ASSISI (1877) Revs. Christopher M. Tiano; Gustavo Lopez; John L. Lavorgna; Sisters Helen Marie Clark, R.S.M., Pastoral Assoc.; Eleanor Rathburn, R.S.M., Pastoral Assoc.; Deacons John L. Dembishack; Roy C. Dungan; David W. Reynolds; James M. Sullivan.
Church: Pope John Paul II Pastoral Center, 160 Main St., 06790-5201. Tel: 860-482-5571; Fax: 860-489-4070. Email: torringtoncatholicparishes@yahoo.com. Web: www.torringtoncatholics.org.
School—(Grades PreK-8) Tel: 860-489-4177; Fax: 860-489-1590. Web: spsfschool.org. Mrs. Jo-Anne Gauger, Prin. Lay Teachers 14; Students 163.
Catholic Youth Ministry of Torrington—
Catechesis/Religious Program— 06790. Tel: 860-482-3121. Anthony Smith, D.R.E.; Lisa Kelsey, C.R.E. Students 153.

2—ST. MARY (1919), (Polish), Revs. Christopher M. Tiano; John L. Lavorgna; Gustavo Lopez; Sisters Eleanor Rathburn, R.S.M., Pastoral Assoc.; Helen Marie Clark, R.S.M., Pastoral Assoc.; Deacons David W. Reynolds; John L. Dembishack; Roy C. Dungan; James M. Sullivan.
Mailing Address: Pope John Paul II Pastoral Center, 160 Main St., 06790-5201. Tel: 860-482-5047; Fax: 860-482-1972. Email: torringtoncatholicparishs@yahoo.com. Web: www.torringtoncatholics.org.
Church: 85 Pulaski St., 06790-5201.
Catechesis/Religious Program—360 Prospect St., 06790. Tel: 860-482-3121. Anthony Smith, D.R.E.; Lisa Kelsey, C.R.E. Students 23.

3—ST. PETER (1910), (Italian), Revs. Christopher M. Tiano; Gustavo Lopez; John L. Lavorgna, Parochial Vicar; Sisters Helen Marie Clark, R.S.M., Pastoral Assoc.; Eleanor Rathburn, R.S.M., Pastoral Assoc.; Deacons Roy C. Dungan; John L. Dembishack; David W. Reynolds; James M. Sullivan.
Mailing Address: Pope John Paul II Pastoral Center, 160 Main St., 06790-5201.
Church: 107 E. Main St., 06790-5493. Tel: 860-482-4433; Fax: 860-489-4070.
School—(Grades PreK-8), 360 Prospect St., 06790. Tel: 860-489-4177; Fax: 860-489-1590. Mrs. Jo-Anne Gauger, Prin. Sisters (Maestre Pie Filippini) 1; Lay Teachers 14; Students 163.
Catechesis/Religious Program—360 Prospect St., 06790. Tel: 860-482-3121. Anthony Smith, D.R.E.; Lisa Kelsey, C.R.E. Students 135.

4—SACRED HEART (1910), (Slovak), Revs. Christopher M. Tiano; John L. Lavorgna; Gustavo Lopez; Deacons John L. Dembishack; Roy C. Dungan; David W. Reynolds; Sisters Helen Marie Clark, R.S.M., Pastoral Assoc.; Eleanor Rathburn, R.S.M., Pastoral Assoc.
Mailing Address: Pope John Paul II Pastoral Center, 160 Main St., 06790-5047.
Church: 116 Grove St., 06790-5047. Tel: 860-482-8246; Fax: 860-489-4070. Email: torringtoncatholicparishes@yahoo.com. Web: www.torringtoncatholics.org.
Catechesis/Religious Program—360 Prospect St., 06790. Tel: 860-482-3121. Anthony Smith, D.R.E.; Lisa Kelsey, C.R.E. Students 20.

UNION CITY, NEW HAVEN CO.

1—ST. HEDWIG (Naugatuck) (1906), (Polish), Linked with St. Mary Parish, Union City. Rev. Adam Hurbanczuk (Poland); Deacons Thomas J. Clifford; Earle A. Kimball.
Res.: 32 Golden Hill St., 06770-3099. Tel: 203-729-2490; Fax: 203-720-2161. Email: sthedwig.unioncity@gmail.com. Web: www.sthedwigschool.org.
School—(Grades PreK-8), 32 Golden Hill St., 06770-3099. Tel: 203-729-2403; Fax: 203-723-7954. Dr. John Salatto, Prin. Lay Teachers 10; Students 160.
Catechesis/Religious Program—Students 98.

2—ST. MARY (Naugatuck) (1907), Linked with St. Hedwig, Union City. Rev. Adam Hurbanczuk (Poland); Deacons Earle A. Kimball; Thomas J. Clifford.
Res.: 338 N. Main St., 06770-3235. Tel: 203-729-2279; Fax: 203-729-1392.
Catechesis/Religious Program—Linked with St. Hedwig, Union City.

UNIONVILLE, HARTFORD CO., ST. MARY (1874) [CEM] Rev. John S. Golas; Deacon Thomas S. Sutak. In Res., Rev. Robert J. St. Martin (Retired).
Res.: 16 Bidwell Sq., 06085-1116. Tel: 860-673-2422; Fax: 860-673-2001. Web: www.stmary-unionville.org.
Catechesis/Religious Program—Tel: 860-675-8522. Email: st.mary.re@sbcglobal.net. Students 672.

WALLINGFORD, NEW HAVEN CO.

1—HOLY TRINITY (1869) Rev. Gary F. Simeone; Deacons Eugene C. Riotte; Tullio V. Ossa; Joseph Cretella.
Res.: 68 N. Colony St., 06492-3696. Tel: 203-269-8791; Fax: 203-269-0880.
School—(Grades K-8), 11 N. Whittlesey Ave., 06492. Tel: 203-269-4476; Fax: 203-294-4983. Sr. Kathleen Kelly, R.S.M., Prin. Sisters of Mercy 1; Lay Teachers 9; Students 216.
Catechesis/Religious Program—Tel: 203-265-6300. Frances Selmecki, D.R.E. Students 791.
Convent—*Sisters of Mercy*, 247 S. Main St., 06492-3619. Tel: 203-265-6999.

2—SS. PETER AND PAUL (1924) [CEM] Rev. Ronald P. Zepecki.
Res.: 139 N. Orchard St., 06492-3617. Tel: 203-269-4617; Fax: 203-265-6751. Email: st_peter_paul@sbcglobal.net. Web: www.stpeterpaulwallingford.org.
Catechesis/Religious Program—Tel: 203-269-0271. Jennifer Perrin, C.R.E. Students 72.

3—RESURRECTION (1963) Rev. Joseph T. Kaminsky; Joseph Tatta, Pastoral Assoc.
Res.: 115 Pond Hill Rd., 06492-4836. Tel: 203-265-1694; Fax: 203-284-9766.
Catechesis/Religious Program—Tel: 203-269-4683; Fax: 203-269-4683. Mrs. Mary Ann Marchitto, D.R.E. Students 476.

WASHINGTON DEPOT, LITCHFIELD CO., OUR LADY OF PERPETUAL HELP (1893) [CEM] Revs. Thomas F. Bennett; Mathew T. Kappalumakkel; Deacon George H. Streib.
Res.: 34 Green Hill Rd., P.O. Box 303, 06794. Tel: 860-868-2600; Fax: 860-868-7252 (Call First).
Catechesis/Religious Program—Students 101.
Mission—*St. Patrick's* Church St., Roxbury, Litchfield Co. 06783.

WATERBURY, NEW HAVEN CO.

1—BASILICA OF THE IMMACULATE CONCEPTION (1847) Revs. John J. Bevins; Alexander J. Cherukarakunnel (India); Stanley Grove, M.S.A.; John R. Lyons, M.S.A.; Emmanuel Okechukwu; Susith Silva; Charles Bak, M.S.A.
Res.: 74 W. Main St., 06721-1670. Tel: 203-574-0017; Fax: 203-756-8748.
School—*St. Mary*, (Grades PreK-8), 55 Cole St., 06706-1291. Tel: 203-753-2574; Fax: 203-796-2498. Joseph Kenny, Prin.; Patricia Greene, Librarian. Lay Teachers 16; Students 375.
Catechesis/Religious Program—Students 230.

2—BLESSED SACRAMENT (1911) Rev. Michael F.X. Hinkley, S.T.D.; Deacon Carl H. Gerstung. In Res., Rev. John P. Gatzak.
Res.: 182 Robbins St., 06708. Tel: 203-753-3149; Fax: 203-596-0740.
School—(Grades K-8), 386 Robinwood Rd., 06708-2750. Tel: 203-756-5313; Fax: 203-756-5313. Debora Mainstruck, Prin. Lay Teachers 9; Students 279.
Catechesis/Religious Program—Students 90.

3—ST. CECILIA (1893), (German), Closed. For inquiries for sacramental records, contact Sacred Heart-Sagrado Corazon, Waterbury.

4—ST. FRANCIS XAVIER (1896) Rev. Paul J. Pace.
Res.: 625 Baldwin St., 06706-1597. Tel: 203-756-7804.
School—(Grades PreK-8), 605 Baldwin St., 06706. Tel: 203-753-3197; Fax: 203-574-0128. Mrs. Pamela Belury, Prin. Lay Teachers 6; Students 98.
Catechesis/Religious Program—Tel: 203-754-6996. Mrs. Laurie Ciarello, D.R.E. Students 94.

5—ST. JOSEPH (1894), (Lithuanian), Linked with St. Patrick Parish. Revs. Joseph F. Gorman, Temporary Admin. (Retired); Edward J. Tissera (Sri Lanka).
50 Charles St., P.O. Box 271, 06708. Tel: 203-756-8837; Fax: 203-756-4690.

6—ST. LEO THE GREAT (1974), Linked with SS. Peter and Paul Parish. Rev. Msgr. James G. Coleman (Retired); Rev. Cornelius Kelechi Anyanwu; Deacon Modesto A. Rosello, (Retired). In Res., Rev. Joseph F. Gorman (Retired).
Res.: 14 Bentwood Dr., 06705-3612. Tel: 203-573-0572; Fax: 203-573-9642. Email: ssppchurchI@juno.com.
Catechesis/Religious Program—Students 80.

7—ST. LUCY (1926), (Italian), Linked with Our Lady of Lourdes Parish. Rev. Ronald A. Ferraro; Deacon Paul Lauer.
Res.: 24 Branch St., 06704-3626. Tel: 203-574-5903.
Catechesis/Religious Program—At Our Lady of Lourdes Parish. Students 6.

8—ST. MARGARET (1910), (Hispanic), Revs. Robert Villa; Will-Roger Malave (Retired); Deacon Paul P. Iadarola.
Res.: 289 Willow St., 06710. Tel: 203-754-6101; Fax: 203-754-2006. Email: stmargarets@snet.net.
Catechesis/Religious Program—Tel: 860-567-2394. Jaqueline Boulier Tiul, D.R.E. (Elem & Middle School). Students 150.

9—ST. MICHAEL (1902) Rev. Roger L. Hall, O.F.M.; Deacon George D. Hajjar.
Res.: 62 St. Michael Dr., 06704-1295. Tel: 203-753-0689; Fax: 203-573-9101.
Catechesis/Religious Program—Students 116.

10—OUR LADY OF FATIMA (1971), (Portuguese), Rev. Francisco Eurico.
Res.: 2071 Baldwin St., 06706. Tel: 203-753-1424; Fax: 203-573-1914. Email: fatimachurchwaterbury@yahoo.com.
Catechesis/Religious Program—Students 245.

11—OUR LADY OF LORETO (1971), Linked with St. Stanislaus Kostka. Rev. Msgr. Thomas M. Ginty.
Res.: 12 Ardsley Rd., 06708-1825. Tel: 203-757-6112; Fax: 203-756-9656.
Catechesis/Religious Program—Students 104.

12—OUR LADY OF LOURDES (1899), (Italian), Linked with St. Lucy Parish. Rev. Ronald A. Ferraro; Deacon Paul Lauer.
Res.: 309 S. Main St., 06706-1014. Tel: 203-754-4134; Fax: 203-755-0456.
Catechesis/Religious Program—Students 62.

13—OUR LADY OF MT. CARMEL (1923), (Italian), Rev. Frederick M. Aniello; Deacon Nicholas J. Diorio.
Res.: 785 Highland Ave., 06708-4116. Tel: 203-756-8981; Fax: 203-756-2074.
School—(Grades PreK-8), 645 Congress Ave., 06708-4198. Tel: 203-755-6809; Fax: 203-755-5850. Joaquim (Jack) Taveras, Prin.; Karen Kleinschmidt, Librarian. Lay Teachers 10; Students 203.
Catechesis/Religious Program— Sr. Georgia E. Wright, S.S.C., Dir. Faith Formation. Students 170.

14—ST. PATRICK (1880), (Irish), Linked with St. Joseph Parish. Revs. Joseph F. Gorman, Temporary Admin. (Retired); Edward J. Tissera (Sri Lanka).
Mailing Address: 50 Charles St., 06708. Tel: 203-756-8837; Fax: 203-756-4690.
Res.: 50 Charles St., 06708. Tel: 203-756-8837; Fax: 203-756-4690.

15—SS. PETER AND PAUL (1920), Linked with St. Leo the Great Parish. Rev. Msgr. James G. Coleman (Retired); Rev. Cornelius Kelechi Anyanwu; Deacon Charles Colella.
Res.: 67 Southmayd Rd., 06705. Tel: 203-756-7919; Fax: 203-755-3535. Email: ssppchurch@juno.com.
School—(Grades PreK-8), 116 Beecher Ave., 06705. Tel: 203-755-0881. Mrs. Janet Curry, Prin. Lay Teachers 11; Students 250.
Catechesis/Religious Program—116 Beecher Ave., 06705. Tel: 203-753-4242. Frances Walsh, D.R.E. Students 227.

16—SACRED HEART-SAGRADO CORAZON (1885) Rev. Kevin J. Gray.
Office: 13 Wolcott St., 06702-1790. Tel: 203-757-8737; Fax: 203-754-5862. Email: sacredheartsagradocorazon@yahoo.com.
Catechesis/Religious Program—Students 365.

17—SHRINE OF SAINT ANNE FOR MOTHERS (1886), (French), Rev. Michael F.X. Hinkley, S.T.D., Admin.; Deacon Carl H. Gerstung.
Res.: 515 S. Main St., 06706-1089. Tel: 203-756-4439; Fax: 203-754-3244. Web: www.shrineofsaintanne.org.

18—ST. STANISLAUS KOSTKA (1913), (Polish), Linked with Our Lady of Loreto Parish. Rev. Msgr. Thomas M. Ginty.
Mailing Address: Parish Office, 12 Ardsley Rd., 06708. Tel: 203-757-6112; Fax: 203-756-9656.
Church: 86 E. Farm St., 06704.

19—ST. THOMAS (1898) Closed. For inquiries for sacramental records contact St. Michael, Waterbury.

WATERTOWN, LITCHFIELD CO., ST. JOHN THE EVANGELIST (1878) [CEM] Revs. John M. Cooney; James George (India); Deacons Robert D. Gordon; Daniel Camerota.
Res. & Mailing Address: 21 Academy Hill, 06795-2101. Tel: 860-274-8836; Fax: 860-274-0667. Web: www.stjohns-wtnct.4lpi.com.
Church: 574 Main St., 06795.
School—(Grades PreK-8), 760 Main St., 06795. Tel: 860-274-9208; Fax: 860-945-1082. Web: www-.stjohnwtn.org. John Petto, Prin. School Sisters of Notre Dame 1; Lay Teachers 13; Students 191.
Catechesis/Religious Program—Theresa N. Morgado, D.R.E. Students 436.
Convent—*School Sisters of Notre Dame*, 9 Academy

Hill, 06795-2101. Tel: 860-274-1820.

WEST HARTFORD, HARTFORD CO.

1—ST. BRIGID (1919) Rev. Msgr. Douglas P. Clancy; Rev. Robert A. Morgewicz II; Deacon Richard D. Santos.
Res.: 1088 New Britain Ave., 06110-2426. Tel: 860-236-5965; Fax: 860-233-8016. Email: stbrigidchurchwhct@sbcglobal.net.
School—(Grades PreK-8), 100 Mayflower St., 06110-1420. Tel: 860-561-2130; Fax: 860-561-0011. Web: www.saintbrigidschool.org. Susan B. O'Brien, Prin. Lay Teachers 19; Students 199.
Catechesis/Religious Program—Tel: 860-521-8523. Mrs. Penny Hickey, D.R.E. Students 178.

2—THE CHURCH OF ST. TIMOTHY (1958) Rev. Henry P. Cody; Deacon Anthony Nwankwo; Patricia A. Piano, Pastoral Assoc. Tel: 860-232-8594; Patricia L. Pruitt, Business Mgr.
Res.: 1116 N. Main St., 06117-1209. Tel: 860-233-5131; Fax: 860-232-2189.
School—St. Timothy Middle School, 225 King Philip Dr., 06117. Tel: 860-236-0614; Fax: 860-920-0293. Dr. Stephen Balkun, Prin. Lay Teachers 10; Students 148.
Catechesis/Religious Program—Tel: 860-232-3952. Bobbi Moran, D.R.E. (Grades 6-10); Jayne O'Donnell, D.R.E. (Grades PreK-5). Students 317.

3—ST. HELENA (1966) Rev. Msgr. Douglas P. Clancy; Revs. Francis P. Johnson, Pastor Emeritus (Retired); Robert A. Morgewicz II; Thomas Puthiyadom (India), Ministry for the Syro-Malabar Catholic Community.; Deacon Robert J. Hilliard. In Res., Revs. Eugene M. Kilbride (Retired); Zigford J. Kriss (Retired). Tel: 860-521-1908.
Res.: 30 Echo Ln., 06107-3698. Tel: 860-521-1921.
Catechesis/Religious Program—Tel: 860-521-3661. Students 230.

4—ST. JOHN THE EVANGELIST (1942) Closed. For inquiries for sacramental records contact St. Lawrence O'Toole, Hartford.

5—ST. MARK THE EVANGELIST (1942) Rev. Msgr. Michael J. Motta; Deacon Raymond J. Fugere. In Res., Rev. Thomas E. Ptaszynski.
Res.: 467 S. Quaker Ln., 06110-1042. Tel: 860-233-1269; Fax: 860-233-5791. Email: st_marks_church@snet.net.
Catechesis/Religious Program—Tel: 860-236-3545. Lou Ann Warren, D.R.E. Students 248.

6—ST. PETER CLAVER (1966) Revs. James F. Leary; Thomas J. Sas; Deacon James E. Hickey Jr.
Res.: 47 Pleasant St., 06107-1625. Tel: 860-561-4235; Fax: 860-561-0552. Email: st.peterclaver@sbcglobal.net. Web: www.stpeterclaverparish.com.
Catechesis/Religious Program—Tel: 860-521-2904. Email: spcreled@sbcglobal.net. Janine Cote, D.R.E. Students 479.

7—ST. THOMAS THE APOSTLE (1921) Revs. Arthur J. Murphy; Edward M. Moran; Richard P. Okiria (Africa); Deacons Dennis R. Ferguson; Kevin M. Monahan.
Res.: 872 Farmington Ave., 06119-1499. Tel: 860-233-8269; Fax: 860-523-8794. Email: stawh@comcast.net.
School—(Grades PreK-5), 25 Dover Rd., 06119-1298. Tel: 860-236-6257; Fax: 860-236-8865. Mrs. Colleen DiSanto, Prin.; Janet Cashman, Librarian; Tracy Aszkler, Librarian. Lay Teachers 22; Students 209.
Catechesis/Religious Program—Tel: 860-523-4209; Fax: 860-570-0273. Mrs. Elizabeth B. Kiselica, D.R.E. Students 305.

WEST HAVEN, NEW HAVEN CO.

1—ST. JOHN VIANNEY (1965), Linked with Our Lady of Victory Parish. Rev. Joseph R. Cronin; Deacons Paul E. Sabo; Robert P. Tartaris; Sr. Ellen McNulty, O.P., Pastoral Assoc. In Res., Rev. Gregory M. Altermatt.
Parish Office: 600 Jones Hill Rd., 06516.
Res.: 300 Capt. Thomas Blvd., 06516-5974. Tel: 203-934-6000; Fax: 203-932-3315.
Catechesis/Religious Program—Attended at Our Lady of Victory., Tel: 203-933-0044.

2—ST. LAWRENCE (1886), Linked with St. Paul, West Haven. Rev. Mark R. Jette; Deacon Edward J. Mancini.
Res.: 207 Main St., 06516-4599. Tel: 203-934-8351; Fax: 203-937-7858.
School—(Grades PreK-8), 231 Main St., 06516. Tel: 203-933-2518; Fax: 203-932-2058. Mr. Paul De Fronzo, Prin. Lay Teachers 11; Students 200.
Catechesis/Religious Program—231 Main St., 06516. Tel: 203-933-2519. Students 200.

3—ST. LOUIS (1886), (French Territorial), Rev. Jeffrey Gubbiotti; Deacon Salvatore DeFilippo.
Res.: 89 Bull Hill Ln., 06516-3998. Tel: 203-934-5249; Fax: 203-934-1055. Email: st.louischurch@catholicweb.com. Web: www.saintlouischurch.catholicweb.com.
Catechesis/Religious Program—Students 242.

4—OUR LADY OF VICTORY (1935), Linked with St. John Vianney Parish. Rev. Joseph R. Cronin; Deacons Paul E. Sabo; Robert P. Tartaris; Sr. Ellen McNulty, O.P., Pastoral Assoc. In Res., Rev. Gregory M. Altermatt.
Res.: 600 Jones Hill Rd., 06516-6399. Tel: 203-934-6357; Fax: 203-932-3315. Email: olovrectory@yahoo.com. Web: www.olov.org.
School—(Grades PreK-8), 620 Jones Hill Rd., 06516-6397. Tel: 203-932-6457; Fax: 203-932-6456. Ardell Bartolotta, Prin. Lay Teachers 14; Students 184.
Catechesis/Religious Program—Twinned with St. John Vianney Parish., Tel: 203-933-0044. Email: olovore@sbcglobal.net. Angela Petrowski, D.R.E. Students 616.
Convent—Ursuline Sisters of Tildonk, 634 Jones Hill Rd., 06516-6398. Tel: 203-934-8601.

5—ST. PAUL'S (1916), (Italian), Linked with St. Lawrence, West Haven. Rev. Mark R. Jette; Deacon Edward J. Mancini. In Res., Revs. Titus Ibe; Augustine Mangalath (India).
Parish Office & Rectory: 41 Alling St., 06516-2799. Tel: 203-933-1024; Fax: 203-931-9416.
Parish Center: 45 Alling St., 06516-2798.
Catechesis/Religious Program—Tel: 203-934-1357. Sr. Cora Lombardo, A.S.C.J., D.R.E. Students 242.

WEST SIMSBURY, HARTFORD CO., ST. CATHERINE OF SIENA (1971) Rev. Michael G. Whyte.
Res.: Box 184, 06092. Tel: 860-658-1642; Fax: 860-658-0668. Email: stcathy@comcast.net.
Catechesis/Religious Program—Tel: 860-658-4737; Fax: 860-658-0668. Mrs. Kathi Bonner, D.R.E. Students 633.

WETHERSFIELD, HARTFORD CO.

1—CORPUS CHRISTI (1941), Linked with Sacred Heart Parish. Revs. Thomas B. Campion; David W. Lonergan; Deacon Seth M. English.
Res.: 84 Somerset St., 06109-3068. Tel: 860-529-2545; Fax: 860-529-5861. Email: corpuschristi1@cox.net. Web: www.corpuschristiparish.net.
Church: 601 Silas Deane Hwy., 06109.
School—(Grades PreK-8), 581 Silas Deane Hwy., 06109. Tel: 860-529-5487; Fax: 860-257-9106. Email: corpuschristisch@yahoo.com. Web: corpuschristis-choolct.com. Mrs. Eileen Sampiere, Prin. Lay Teachers 27; Students 425.
Catechesis/Religious Program—581 Silas Deane Hwy., 06109. Tel: 860-721-9419; Fax: 860-721-9418. Students 830.

2—INCARNATION (1963) Rev. James M. Moran.
Res.: 544 Prospect St., 06109-3696. Tel: 860-529-2533; Fax: 860-721-6595. Email: cincarnation@sbcglobal.net.
Catechesis/Religious Program—Tel: 860-529-6765. Noranne Wamester, D.R.E. Students 687.

3—SACRED HEART (1876), Linked with Corpus Christi Parish. Revs. Thomas B. Campion; David W. Lonergan; John Hoon Gyeom Kim (Korea, South) (Korean Catholic Community); Deacons Cornelius D. O'Connell; James H. Toner.
Res.: 56 Hartford Ave., 06109-1805. Tel: 860-529-1991 (Office & Rectory).
Catechesis/Religious Program—Tel: 860-257-0740. Barbara Davis, C.R.E.; Candace Detrich, C.R.E. Students 143.

WINDSOR, HARTFORD CO.

1—ST. GABRIEL (1894) Revs. Richard J. Neumann; Edmund K. Karwowski, Parochial Vicar; Deacon R. Carl Lickwar.
Res.: 379 Broad St., 06095-3004. Tel: 860-688-4905; Fax: 860-688-2638. Email: gabrielchurch@comcast.net. Web: www.stgabes.org.
School—(Grades K-8), 77 Bloomfield Ave., 06095. Tel: 860-688-6401; Fax: 860-298-8668. Web: www-.stgabrielschool.org. Patricia Martin, Prin. Lay Teachers 11; Students 195.
Catechesis/Religious Program—Mrs. Janet Alampi, D.R.E. Students 163.

2—ST. GERTRUDE (1947) Rev. Maurice J. Barry.
Res.: 550 Matianuck Ave., 06095-3599. Tel: 860-522-6163; Fax: 860-525-2320. Email: stgertrudechurch@sbcglobal.net.
Catechesis/Religious Program—Keva Griggs, D.R.E. Students 95.

WINDSOR LOCKS, HARTFORD CO.

1—ST. MARY (1852) [CEM] Revs. Robert A. O'Grady; George Vellaplackil (India); Deacons Donald Norton; Benedict L. Winiarski. In Res., Rev. Francis P. McDonnell (Retired).
Res.: 42 Spring St., 06096-2311. Tel: 860-623-2524; Fax: 860-623-5684.
Parish Center—45 Church St., 06096. Tel: 860-627-9469.
Catechesis/Religious Program—Marilyn Stratton, D.R.E. Students 458.

2—ST. ROBERT BELLARMINE (1962) Revs. Robert A. O'Grady; George Vellaplackil (India); Deacons Donald Norton; Benedict L. Winiarski.
Office: 52 S. Elm St., P.O. Box 315, 06096-0315. Tel: 860-623-0240.
Catechesis/Religious Program—Twinned with St. Mary, Windsor Locks, *St. Mary Parish Center*, 45 Church St., Enfield, 06082. Tel: 860-627-9469.

WINSTED, LITCHFIELD CO., ST. JOSEPH (1853) [CEM] Rev. Dennis Arambasick, O.F.M.; Friar Christopher Gaffrey, O.F.M.; Deacon William H. Wilcox.
Res.: 66 Oak St., 06098. Tel: 860-379-3369; Fax: 860-379-4194.
School—St. Anthony, (Grades PreK-8), 55 Oak St., 06098. Tel: 860-379-7521; Fax: 860-379-7522. Mrs. Patricia Devanney, Prin. Lay Teachers 10; Students 226.
Catechesis/Religious Program—Tel: 860-379-5968. Students 166.

WOLCOTT, NEW HAVEN CO.

1—ST. MARIA GORETTI (1973) Rev. William R. Sokolowski.
Res.: 1300 Woodtick Rd., P.O. Box 6291, 06716-0291. Tel: 203-879-4608; Fax: 203-879-4609. Email: smariagoretti@sbcglobal.net.
Catechesis/Religious Program—Tel: 203-879-5242. Angela Clement, D.R.E. Students 341.

2—ST. PIUS X (1955) Rev. Henry A. Balchunas; Deacon Emil P. Croce.
Res.: 525 Woodtick Rd., 06716-2898. Tel: 203-879-2544; Fax: 203-879-2545.
Catechesis/Religious Program—Tel: 203-879-9030. Kari-Beth Yashenko, D.R.E. Students 432.

WOODBRIDGE, NEW HAVEN CO., CHURCH OF THE ASSUMPTION (1924) Rev. Gene E. Gianelli; Deacons William J. Sayles; John J.M. Conte Jr., (Retired).
Res.: 81 Center Rd., 06525-1699. Tel: 203-387-7119; Fax: 203-387-4281. Email: gassumptionchurch@sbcglobal.com. Web: www.assumptionchurch.com.
Catechesis/Religious Program—Tel: 203-389-9863. Sr. Dorellen Sullivan, R.S.M., D.R.E. Students 617.

WOODBURY, LITCHFIELD CO., ST. TERESA (1902) Rev. Robert M. Kwiatkowski; Deacons Ralph Rescildo; Terence M. Nolan; Horace Hamor; Sr. Marilyn Cullina, C.N.D., Pastoral Min. Tel: 203-263-2882.
Res.: 11 Washington Ave., P.O. Box 5001, 06798-5001. Tel: 203-263-2008; Fax: 203-263-7259. Email: saintteresas@aol.com. Web: www.saintteresaofavila.org.
Catechesis/Religious Program—Tel: 203-263-0608. Mrs. Carol Moriarty, D.R.E. Students 510.

YALESVILLE, NEW HAVEN CO., OUR LADY OF FATIMA (1956) Rev. Salvatore F. Cavagnuolo; Deacon James P. Taylor.
Res.: 382 Hope Hill Rd., 06492-2270. Tel: 203-265-0961; Fax: 203-269-9386.
Catechesis/Religious Program—Tel: 203-265-6818; Fax: 203-269-5343. Tracy Blum, D.R.E. Tel: 203-265-6426; Corinne Sommo, Youth Min. Students 515.

Chaplains of Public Institutions

HARTFORD. *Hartford Correctional Institution*, 177 Weston St., 06120. Tel: 860-240-1857. Rev. Robert A. O'Grady, Chap., Sr. Jerilyn Hunihan, A.S.C.J., Chap.
Hartford Hospital, 80 Seymour St., 06102-5037. Tel: 860-545-2251; Fax: 860-545-3594. Rev. James O. Ibekwe (Nigeria), Chap.

BRISTOL. *Bristol Hospital*, Brewster Rd., 06011-0977. Tel: 860-585-3431. Rev. J. Richard Fowler, Interfaith Chap. (United Church of Christ).

CHESHIRE. *Cheshire Correctional Institution*, 900 Highland Ave., 06410-1698. Tel: 203-250-2787. Rev. Stephen A. Krugel, Chap., Deacons George Hajjar, Chap., Rene Kieda, Chap., Carl Vecca, Chap.
Manson Youth Institution, 42 Jarvis St., 06410-1545. Tel: 203-806-2508. Rev. Dariusz Gosciniak, Chap., Deacon Carl Vecca, Chap.
Webster Correctional Institute, 111 Jarvis St., 06410. Tel: 203-271-5902. Rev. Stephen A. Krugel, Chap., Deacons George D. Hajjar, Chap., Rene Kieda, Chap.

ENFIELD. *Carl Robinson Correctional Institution*, P.O. Box 1400, 06083-1400. Tel: 860-763-6387. Deacon Robert E. Lambert, Chap., Rev. Thomas Plathottam, C.S.T.
Enfield Correctional Institute, 289 Shaker Rd., 06083. Tel: 860-763-7318. Rev. Thomas Plathottam, C.S.T., Deacon Benedict L. Winiarski.
Willard-Cybulski Correction Institute, 391 Shaker Rd., P.O. Box 2400, 06082. Tel: 860-763-6140. Rev. Stephen A. Krugel, Chap., Deacon Leo B. Conard III, Chap.

MANCHESTER. *Manchester Memorial Hospital*, 71 Haynes St., 06040-4188. Tel: 860-646-1222, Ext. 2137. Rev. Louis D. Cremonie, Chap.

NEW BRITAIN. *The Hospital of Central Connecticut (New Britain General Hospital)*, 100 Grand St., 06050-2016. Tel: 860-224-5011; Fax: 860-224-5740. Rev. Ronald T. Smith, Chap.
Res.: 396 Church St., P.O. Box 515, 06050-0515. Tel: 860-224-0341.

NEW HAVEN. *Yale-New Haven Hospital*, 20 York St., 06504-1001. Tel: 203-688-2151; Fax: 203-688-3478.

Rev. Geoffrey C. Smith, Chap. Tel: 203-688-7031, Sr. Carole Hermann, O.P. Tel: 203-688-7032.

ROCKY HILL. *Veterans' Home and Hospital*, 287 West St., 06067-3902. Tel: 860-529-2571, Ext. 2386. Rev. Francis J. Kulas, M.S. Tel: 860-257-3368.

SUFFIELD. *Macdougall - Walker Correctional Institute*, 1153 E. St. S., 06080-0002. Tel: 860-627-2148 Mac Dougall; 860-292-3429 Walker; Fax: 860-627-2152 Mac Dougall. Deacon Richard F. Boucher, Rev. Stephen A. Krugel, Chap.

WATERBURY. *Waterbury Hospital*, 64 Robbins St., 06721-2600. Tel: 203-573-7213; Fax: 203-573-7326; 203-573-6000. Revs. Richard C. Bollea, Chap., Cosmos Archibong, Chap.

Res.: 25 Maple Ave., Seymour, 06483. Tel: 203-729-2504.

WEST HAVEN. *V.A. CT Health Care System*, 950 Campbell Ave., 06516-2700. Tel: 203-932-5711, Ext. 2422. Revs. Daniel V. Scott, M.S., Cosmas Archibong.

WETHERSFIELD. *Connecticut Department of Correction*, 24 Wolcott Hill Rd., 06109-1152. Tel: 860-692-7577; Fax: 860-692-6263. Rev. Anthony J. Bruno, Dir. Religious Svcs.

Res.: 90 Alden Ave., Enfield, 06082-2865. Tel: 860-745-9966.

Special and other Archdiocesan Assignment:

Rev. Msgrs.—

Liptak, David Q., Editor, "The Catholic Transcript", 467 Bloomfield Ave., Bloomfield, 06002.

McCarthy, John J., J.C.D., J.D., Chancellor & Rector, 134 Farmington Ave., 06105. Cathedral of St. Joseph, 140 Farmington Ave., 06105.

Motta, Michael J., Dir., Office of Religious Education, 467 Bloomfield Ave., Bloomfield, 06002.

Schmitz, Gerard G., St. Thomas Seminary, 467 Bloomfield Ave., Bloomfield, 06002. Vicar for Priests and Pres./Rector.

Walker, David M., Dir., Catholic Cemeteries Association, P.O. Box 517, North Haven, 06473-0517.

Revs.—

Altermatt, Gregory M., Hospital of St. Raphael, 1450 Chapel St., New Haven, 06511.

Baranowski, David J. Office for Divine Worship 467 Bloomfield Ave., Bloomfield, 06002.

Beloin, Robert L., Ph.D., More House, Yale University, 268 Park St., New Haven, 06511-4714.

Bollea, Richard C., Waterbury Hospital, 64 Robbins St., Waterbury, 06721.

Brockett, Norman L., St. Mary Home, 2021 Albany Ave., West Hartford, 06117-2796.

Bruno, Anthony J., Connecticut Department of Correction, 24 Wolcott Hill Rd., 06109-1152.

Bzdyra, Stephen H., MacDougall-Walker Correctional Institution, 1153 East St. S., Suffield, 06080-0002.

Cremonie, Louis D., Manchest Memorial Hospital, 71 Haynes St., Manchester, 06040.

Cronin, James J., Pro-Life Activities, 271 Finch Ave., Meriden, 06451-2715.

DiSciacca, Joseph V., Office of Minister for Priests, 467 Bloomfield Ave., Bloomfield, 06002-2999.

Dolan, Michael J., Campus Min. & Dir. Vocations, 467 Bloomfield Ave., Bloomfield, 06002. Tel: 860-297-2015. Email: mjdofr@aol.com

Donahue, Aidan N., Diaconate Continuing Formation, 35 Cold Spring Dr., Bloomfield, 06002.

Gatzak, John P., Exec. Dir., 15 Peach Orchard Rd., Prospect, 06712-1052. Office of Communications (Radio/Television).

Halovatch, Paul J., Southern Connecticut State University, New Haven, 06515.

Kinnane, James F., J.C.L., 134 Farmington Ave., 06105-3784. Vicar for Religious and Adjutant Judicial Vicar.

Krugel, Stephen A., Cheshire Correctional Institution, P.O. Box 3260, Milford, 06460.

McLean, Edward J. (Retired), Catholic Library and Information Center, 125 Market St., 06103. Dir.

Monnerat, Brian W., Propagation of the Faith, 467 Bloomfield Ave., Bloomfield, 06002-2999.

O'Brien, Timothy A., Coord. Restructuring Committee, P.O. Box 285, New Hartford, 06057-0285.

O'Grady, Robert A., Hartford Correctional Institution, 117 Weston St., 06120.

Romans, Jeffrey V., Asst. Chancellor & Sec. Archbishop, 134 Farmington Ave., 06105-3784.

Sas, Thomas J., Office of Ministry Enrichment, 467 Bloomfield Ave., Bloomfield, 06002-2999.

Smith, Geoffrey C., Yale - New Haven Hospital, 20 York St., New Haven, 06510-3202.

Smith, Ronald T., The Hospital of Central Connecticut, 100 Grand St., New Britain, 06050-2016.

Staron, Stanley R., St. Mary Hospital, 56 Franklin St., Waterbury, 06706-1200.

Vargo, Robert B., J.C.L., Judicial Vicar (Officialis), Chancery, 134 Farmington Ave., 06105-3784.

On Duty Outside the Archdiocese:

Rev. Msgrs.—

Guerrera, Vittorio, 25 E. 39th St., New York, NY 10016.

Sokolowski, Robert S., Catholic University of America, School of Philosophy, Washington, DC 20064.

Revs.—

Couturier, George M., St. Patrick Seminary, 320 Middlefield Rd, Menlo Park, CA 94025.

Cwiekowski, Frederick J., S.S., St. Patrick Seminary, 320 Middlefield Rd., Menlo Park, CA 94025.

Dietrich, John J., Mt. St. Mary Seminary, Emmitsburg, MD 21727-7797.

Leavitt, Robert F., S.S., St. Mary Seminary, 5400 Roland Ave., Baltimore, MD 21210.

Matera, Frank J., M.A., Ph.D., Catholic University of America, Dept. of Theology, Washington, DC 20064.

McBrien, Richard P., University of Notre Dame, Notre Dame, IN 46556.

McKearney, James L., S.S., St. Patrick Seminary, 320 Middlefield Rd., Menlo Park, CA 94025.

Smolenski, Stanley, 300C Ashton Ave., Kingstree, SC 29556.

Thayer, David D., S.S., Theological College of Catholic University of America, 401 Michigan Ave., N.E., Washington, DC 20064.

Military Chaplains:

Rev. Msgr.—

Charbonneau, William R., HGB/HC, 1411 Jefferson Davis Hwy., Ste. 9502, Arlington, VA 22202-3231. U.S. Air National Guard

Revs.—

Hanley, Dennis P., PSC 2, Box 15047, Apo, AE 09012. U.S. Air Force

Hellwig, Lee W., RELMIN Dept., USS Peleliu (LHA 5), FPO, AP 99624-1620. Tel: 619-556-4200 U.S. Navy

---

Medical Leave:

Revs.—

Bennett, Thomas F.

Lonergan, David W.

Mangiafico, Paul J.

Mitchell, Thomas R.

Leave of Absence:

Rev.—

Manna, David

Unassigned:

Revs.—

Gingras, Dennis C.

Van Nguyen, Thanh, (Retired), Portland in Maine, 115 F Beachwood Dr., Bristol, 06010. Tel: 860-585-6663

Retired:

Rev. Msgrs.—

Daly, Charles W., Archbishop Daniel A. Cronin Retirement Residence, 467 Bloomfield Ave., Bloomfield, 06002.

Johnson, Charles B., Archbishop Daniel A. Cronin Retirement Residence, 467 Bloomfield Ave., Bloomfield, 06002.

Mullen, William J., J.C.D., Archbishop Daniel A. Cronin Retirement Residence, 467 Bloomfield Ave., Bloomfield, 06002.

Regan, John D., Archbishop Daniel A. Cronin Retirement Residence, 467 Bloomfield Ave, Bloomfield, 06002.

Revs.—

Ahern, John S., The Village of Mariner's Point, 111 South Shore Dr., East Haven, 06512.

Archambault, James H., 2003 49th St. W., Bradenton, FL 34209.

Barry, Raymond J., P.O. Box 257, Westbrook, 06498.

Baylis, Thomas J., 7 Jensen Ct., Southington, 06489.

Berkery, Patrick J., P.O. Box 971, North Branford, 06471.

Birmingham, Robert F., P.O. Box 177, Shenorock, NY 10587.

Blackall, John C., 1027 Farmington Ave., West Hartford, 06107.

Blackall, Randall L., 1027 Farmington Ave., West Hartford, 06107.

Bonadies, Kenneth P., 5402 Glenn Ivy Place, Pinellas Park, FL 33782.

Borino, David J., 45 Francis St., East Haven, 06512-2808.

Burbank, Robert J., St. Mary Rectory, 731 Main St., Branford, 06405-3693.

Burnett, George P., Assumption Rectory, 61 N. Cliff St., Ansonia, 06401-1698.

Burns, William L., St. Lawrence O'Toole Rectory, 494 New Britain Ave., 06106-3735.

Casey, John D., St. Therese Rectory, 555 Middletown Ave., North Haven, 06473-4000.

Cesaro, Nicholas J., St. Mary Rectory, 626 Willard Ave., Newington, 06111-2614.

Chow, Louis Y., 4 E. 5th St., Corning, NY 14830.

Cockayne, John E., P.O. Box 716, Southington, 06489.

Connaghan, Daniel H.

Daly, John J., St. Barnabas Rectory, 44 Washington Ave., North Haven, 06473-1799.

DeCarolis, Joseph R., P.O. Box 1325, Naugatuck, 06770.

DeCarolis, Vito C., Box 1325, Naugatuck, 06770.

Dery, Henry R., Archbishop Daniel A. Cronin Retirement Residence, 467 Bloomfield Ave., Bloomfield, 06002.

Dilion, Joseph A., 13 Leeway Dr., Westbrook, 06498.

DuPont, Arthur J., St. Gregory the Great Rectory, 235 Maltby St., Bristol, 06010-3892.

Evangelisto, Louis Anthony, 37 Cairo Ave., Northport, NY 11768.

Fanelli, James G., Archbishop Daniel A. Cronin Retirement Residence, 467 Bloomfield Ave., Bloomfield, 06002.

Farrell, Thomas F., Archbishop Daniel A. Cronin Retirement Residence, 467 Bloomfield Ave., Bloomfield, 06002.

Frascadore, Henry C., Bushnell Towers, 1 Gold St., Apt. 4C, 06103. Tel: 860-904-7817

Genua, Ronald L., Archbishop Daniel A. Cronin Retirement Residence, 467 Bloomfield Ave, Bloomfield, 06002.

Gorman, Joseph F., St. Leo the Great Rectory, 14 Bentwood Dr., Waterbury, 06705.

Gunnoud, James B., 34 Hobart St., #205, Southington, 06489.

Hagearty, Charles B., 39 Carriage Dr., Naugatuck, 06770. Tel: 203-592-7749. Email: liturgy@cisbek.net

Heinrich, Harold D., 216 Bristol St., Southington, 06489.

Jaenicke, Alfred J., St. Mary Home, 2021 Albany Ave., West Hartford, 06117.

Johnson, Daniel E., 67 Crumpstone Rd., Hamden, 06518-2424.

Johnson, Francis P., St. Helena Rectory, 30 Echo Ln., West Hartford, 06107-3698.

Karpiey, Daniel J., Archbishop Daniel A. Cronin Retirement Residence, 467 Bloomfield Ave., Bloomfield, 06002.

Karvelis, Francis V., 14 Deepwood Dr., Southington, 06489-3442.

Kearns, Harold M., Visitation Plaza, 100 Jefferson Sq., Apt. 4F, Waterbury, 06706.

Kenefick, Paul F., Archbishop Daniel A. Cronin Retirement Residence, 467 Bloomfield Ave., Bloomfield, 06002.

Kilbride, Eugene M., St. Helena Rectory, 30 Echo Ln., West Hartford, 06107-3698.

Killeen, Bernard D., St. Mary Home, 2021 Albany Ave., West Hartford, 06117-2701.

Killeen, William J., 185 Ridge Rd., Hamden, 06517-3511.

Kriss, Zigford J., St. Helena Rectory, 30 Echo Ln., West Hartford, 06107.

Krupnik, Marion I., 548 Eddy Glover Blvd., New Britain, 06053.

Ladamus, Robert G., 38 Marshall St., Milford, 06460.

Ladish, Robert W., 255 W. Shore Rd., New Preston, 06777.

Laliberte, George G., 948 Villeroy Greens Dr., Sun City Center, FL 33573.

Lauretti, George F., 6 Father Crudele Dr., Bristol, 06010.

LeClair, Lawrence J., 208 Summer Hill Dr., South Windsor, 06074.

Lewandowski, David J., 24 Woodhaven Rd., Bristol, 06010.

Lord, Robert J., P.O. Box 4097, Milford, 06460-4097.

Malave, Will-Roger, St. Margaret Rectory, 289 Willow St., Waterbury, 06710-1515.

Maynard, Leo E., Hebrew Home, 1 Abrahms Blvd., West Hartford, 06117-1508.

McDonnell, Francis P., St. Mary Rectory, 42 Spring St., Windsor Locks, 06096-2311.

McLean, Edward J., St. Paul Rectory, 2577 Main St., Glastonbury, 06033-2023.

Mitchell, Peter G., 275 Steele Rd., Apt. B322, West Hartford, 06117.

Montgomery, Joseph T., 30 Royal Oak Rd., 06053.

Morrison, Douglas A., 24 Courthouse Sq., Apt. 805, Rockville, MD 20850.

Moskus, John T., 42 Maplewood Ave., Storrs, 06268.

Murphy, Joseph G., The McAuley, 275 Steele Rd., #8310, West Hartford, 06117. Tel: 860-236-8333

Parzymies, Joseph K., 140 Poland Brook Rd., Terryville, 06786.

Pettit, Joseph H., 433 Lakeview Dr., Southington, 06489.
Pilon, James F., 331 Songbird Ln., Southington, 06489.
Proulx, Raymond G., Apple Rehab, 269 Farmington Ave., Plainville, 06062.
Raczynski, Theodore T., Sacred Heart Rectory, 446 Mountain Rd., P.O. Box 626, Suffield, 06078-0626.
Raffaeta, George J., c/o Atty Gerry Farrell, 54 N. Elm St., Wallingford, 06492.
Raneri, Carmine B., St. Gregory the Great Rectory, 235 Maltby St., Bristol, 06010-3892.
Rush, James C., 161 Brunswick Ave., West Hartford, 06107-1715.
Russell, Richard R., Archbiship Daniel A. Cronin Retirement Residence, 467 Bloomfield Ave., Bloomfield, 06002.
Russo, Robert T., Archbishop Daniel A. Cronin Retirement Residence, 467 Bloomfield Ave, Bloomfield, 06002.
Shaw, Charles E., P.O. Box 10158, Phoenix, AZ 85064.
Shellman, Richard L., Archbishop Daniel A. Cronin Retirement Residence, 467 Bloomfield Ave., Bloomfield, 06002.
Sherer, Richard B., 40 Niantic River Rd., Waterford, 06385.
Sheridan, Philip A., 20 Carmel Ridge Estates, Trumbull, 06611-2072.
Sikora, Stanley J., Archbishop Daniel A. Cronin Retirement Residence, 467 Bloomfield Ave., Bloomfied, 06002-2999.
Smith, James H., 117 Elmfield St., West Hartford, 06110.
Sobiecki, Peter S., 49 Hillhurst Ave., New Britain, 06053.
Spodnik, A. Leo, P.O. Box 456, Higganum, 06441.
St. Martin, Robert J., St. Mary Rectory, 16 Bidwell Sq., Unionville, 06085-1116.
Stack, John J., St. Mary Home, 2021 Albany Ave., West Hartford, 06117-2701.
Testa, Genaro J., 2179 Herman Drake Rd., Young Harris, GA 30582.
Thuer, William J., Archbishop Daniel A. Cronin Retirement Residence, 467 Bloomfield Ave., Bloomfield, 06002.
Toscano, Pasquale A., St. Joseph Residence, 1365 Enfield St., Enfield, 06082-4900.
Tracy, John P., Archbishop Daniel A. Cronin Retirement Residence, 467 Bloomfield Ave., Bloomfield, 06002.
Traxl, William L., P.O. Box 1031, Westbrook, 06498.
Ventura, Anthony C., St. Mary Home, 2021 Albany Ave., West Hartford, 06117-2701.
Vujs, Joseph E., 14 Hawley St., Newington, 06111.
Wrenn, Lawrence G., 8941 Veranda Way, #522, Sarasota, FL 34238-3372.
Ziezulewicz, George F., 5 Whitewood Rd., Killingworth, 06419.

Permanent Deacons:
Abdalla, John, (Retired)
Albert, Roger R., St. Ann, Bristol
Arena, James V., St. Aloysius, Plantsville
Bailey, Thomas
Bandeira, Francis, (Retired)
Bartlett, William, Jr., (Retired)
Bartlett, William H., St. Bartholomew, Manchester; St. Bridget, Manchester
Battiston, Donald, (Retired)
Beecher, Stephen M., St. Bridget, Cornwall Bridge; St. Bernard, Sharon
Bergers, William B., (Retired)
Bernd, Robert E., St. Martha, Enfield
Berube, Robert A., Our Lady of Mercy, Plainville
Bevvino, Frank J., Jr., St. Augustine, Seymour
Biamonte, Ronald, M.A., St. Joseph, Poquonock
Bichi, Americo, (Retired)
Bilbrault, Victor C., Our Lady of Sorrows, Hartford
Blair, Robert N., Immaculate Conception, New Hartford
Borland, Joseph P., (Retired)
Boucher, Richard F., Sacred Heart, Suffield
Brady, John F., Jr., (Retired)
Breen, Thomas F., III, Assumption, Manchester
Brown, George S., (Retired)
Brunell, Robert J., St. Brendan, New Haven; St. Aedan, New Haven
Camerota, Daniel A., (Retired)
Campbell, Alan D., (Retired)
Cardona, Raul, St. Rose of Lima, Meriden
Carrero, Adolfo G., St. Mary, New Britain
Cassella, Michael E., St. Francis of Assisi, New Britain
Cassidy, Vincent, (Retired)
Charles, John H., Immaculate Heart of Mary, Harwinton
Chope, Robert C.
Clifford, Thomas J., St. Hedwig & St. Mary, Union City
Colella, Charles, SS. Peter and Paul, Waterbury; St. Leo the Great, Waterbury
Conard, Leo B., III, Immaculate Conception & St. Casmir, Terryville
Conklin, Thomas J., St. Margaret Mary, South Windsor
Conte, John J.M., Jr., (Retired)
Cooke, Joseph J., (Retired)
Coppola, Angelo J., St. Aloysius, Plantsville
Cornell, Thomas
Cote, Laurent L., (Retired)
Coyne, Joseph F., (Retired)
Cretella, Joseph J., Jr., Most Holy Trinity, Wallingford
Croce, Emil P., St. Pius X, Wolcott
Croll, Calvin S., (Retired)
Crowley, John, Mary Our Queen, Plantsville
Cruess, Donald E., (Retired)
Culhane, Neil, (Retired)
Cunniff, Charles E., Jr., (Retired)
D'Efemia, Robert J., (Retired)
Daigle, Ronald R., St. Francis of Assisi, South Windsor
DeFilippo, Salvatore A., St. Louis, West Haven
DeHippolytis, Albert J., (Retired)
DeJesus, Isidiro, Sacred Heart, St. Justin and St. Michael, Hartford
Delehanty, Thomas F., (Retired)
Delgado, Domingo, St. Lawrence O'Toole, Hartford
Delmonte, Richard F., (Retired)
Dembishack, John L., (Retired)
Dempsey, John F., (Retired)
Dickman, Arthur J., Holy Family, Enfield
Dietsch, Charles C., Sacred Heart, Southbury
Dinkle, George J., (Retired)
Diorio, Nicholas J., Our Lady of Mt. Carmel, Waterbury
DiPiro, Joseph L., (Retired)
DiRienzo, Mario, St. Augustine, Seymore
Dlugokinski, Jose L., St. Thomas, Thomaston
DosSantos, Kenneth, St. Thomas Villanova, Goshen
Doyle, Henry, (Retired)
Driscoll, Frank M., (Inactive)
Dudzic, Anthony
Dungan, Roy C., Torrington Clustered Parishes
Elder, William A., St. George, Guilford
English, Seth M., (Retired)
Eschrich, Paul C., (Retired)
Ewaskie, Kenneth E., Good Shepherd, Seymour
Eyles, William H., (Retired)
Falbo, Anthony
Farrell, William A., St. Patrick, Farmington
Ferguson, Dennis R., St. Thomas the Apostle, West Hartford
Florio, Louis J., St. Therese, North Haven
Fracasso, Robert G., (Retired)
Frederick, George W., St. Laurent & Our Lady of Mt. Carmel, Meriden
Fugere, Raymond J., St. Mark the Evangelist, West Hartford
Fusco, Louis P., St. Monica, Northford
Gabriele, Joseph G., (Retired)
Gallucci, Donald
Genovese, Nicholas A., St. Agnes, Milford
Geraci, Gerald S., (Medical Leave)
Gerstung, Carl H., St. Anne & Blessed Sacrament, Waterbury
Giaimo, Thomas
Giard, Edward J., St. Christopher, East Hartford
Gilles, William J., St. Christopher, East Hartford
Giusto, Oreste M., (Retired)
Gluhosky, Frank
Godlewsky, Robert H., (Retired)
Gonzalez, Emilio, St. Rose of Lima, New Haven
Gonzalez, Ricardo
Gordon, Robert D., St. John the Evangelist, Watertown
Grant, Frederick M., (Retired)
Griffin, Wayne F., Immaculate Conception, Southington
Gurr, Ronald B., St. Rita, Hamden
Guzauckas, Joseph, Holy Spirit, Newington
Guzzardi, Carmelo A., St. Paul, Kensington
Haines, Michael D., St. Margaret Mary, South Windsor
Hajjar, George D., St. Michael, Waterbury
Hamor, Horace, St. Teresa, Woodbury
Hart, John L., St. Augustine, North Branford
Healy, Timothy E., St. Patrick, Collinsville
Hernandez, Carmelo, St. Anne - Immaculate Conception, Hartford
Hickey, James E., Jr., St. Peter Claver, West Hartford
Higgs, Kenneth
Hilliard, Robert J., (Retired)
Hoffman, Harold, St. Mary, Milford
Iadarola, Paul P., St. Margaret, Waterbury
Iassogna, Nicholas J., Jr., St. Francis of Assisi, Naugatuck
Jacobs, James M., (Retired)
Jacques, J. Martin, (Retired)
Johnson, Robert C., St. Mary, Derby
Johnson, Thomas F., St. Maria Goretti, Wolcott
Kane, Joseph E., (Retired)
Kelly, Stephen J., (Retired)
Kieda, Rene J., (Leave of Absence)
Kimball, Earle A., St. Mary & St. Hedwig, Union City
Klein, Peter J., Jr., St. Dunstan, Glastonbury
Klimanowski, Peter J.
Krasnicki, Frank J., Good Shepherd, Seymour
Kraussman, George A., (Retired)
Krikawa, Joseph F., (Retired)
Kulas, Michael J., (Retired)
Kulas, Paul J., St. Dominic, Southington
Lafleur, Carl
Lambert, Robert E., St. Adalbert, Enfield
LaPierre, Joseph W., (Retired)
LaRocque, Leo R., Blessed Sacrament & Our Lady of Peace, East Hartford
Lauer, Paul B., (Retired)
Lavoie, Joseph V., (Retired)
Lawson, Thomas L., (Retired)
LeBlanc, Gaspard D., (Retired)
Lembo, Victor M., St. Michael, Beacon Falls
Lepkowski, Henry M., (Retired)
Levesque, Joseph J., (Retired)
Lewandoski, Leonard R., St. Stanislaus, Bristol
Lickwar, R. Carl, St. Gabriel, Windsor
Linehan, F. Robert, (Retired)
Lovelace, William, St. Augustine, North Branford
Lovetre, Arthur
Lozier, Albert J., (Retired)
Macaluso, Robert J., St. Vincent de Paul, East Haven
Maffeo, John R., St. Anthony of Padua, Litchfield
Mahoney, Patrick
Makara, John W., (Leave of Absence)
Mancini, Edward J., St. Lawrence, West Haven; St. Paul, West Haven
Marcarelli, Julius R., (Retired)
Marenna, Joseph P., St. Monica, Northford
Maturana, Julio C., St. Rose of Lima, East Hartford; St. Isaac Jogues, East Hartford; St. Mary Parishes, East Hartford
Mazurek, Joseph S., Holy Angels, Meriden
McCarroll, George E., St. Stephen, Hamden
McCluskey, James P., St. Anthony, Bristol
McGivney, Raymond J., Jr., (Inactive)
McGrath, William M., (Retired)
McInnis, John P., (Retired)
McKaig, John W., St. John Fisher, Marlborough
Michaele, Adam J., St. George, Guilford
Miller, Arthur L., St. Michael, St. Justin & Sacred Heart, Hartford; Dir., Office for Black Catholic Ministry; Campus Min., Capital Community College.
Miller, Roland G., St. Francis Xavier, New Milford
Mitchell, Richard
Mitchell, Victor C., Jr., St. Thomas, Thomaston
Moemeka, Andrew A., St. Mary, Newington
Monahan, William
Morales, Jose A.
Moran, Patrick T., St. Margaret, Madison; Campus Min., Southern Connecticut State University
Motto, Vincent J., St. Patrick, Enfield
Muro, Robert E., Sr., Our Lady of the Lakes, New Milford
Murray, Thomas A.
Mylott, John J., (Retired)
Navickas, Robert D., (Retired)
Nebiolo, Eugene, (Retired)
Neris, Susano, (Retired)
Newbery, Robert D., (Retired)
Nolan, Terence M., St. Teresa, Woodbury
Norton, Donald E., St. Mary, Windsor Locks
Nugent, John T., St. Joseph, Meriden
Nwankwo, Anthony, St. Timothy, West Hartford
O'Connell, Cornelius D., Sacred Heart, Wethersfield
O'Connor, Martin J., St. Bernadette, New Haven; Campus Min., Univ. of New Haven
O'Donovan, John, (Retired)
O'Neill, James F., (Retired)
O'Toole, Michael J., (Retired)
Ortiz, Edwin, St. Michael, St. Justin, & Sacred Heart, Hartford
Ortiz, Jacinto
Ossa, Tullio V., Most Holy Trinity, Wallingford
Pahl, John E., St. Matthew, Forestville
Pallotti, Robert M., St. James, Rocky Hill; Dir Office for Permanent Diaconate
Pantalena, Edward J., (Retired)
Papillo, James F., Sacred Heart, Bloomfield
Parenteau, Raymond A., (Retired)
Parkinson, William H., St. Aedan and St. Brendan, New Haven
Parlee, Charles, (Retired)
Perez, Valentin, (Unassigned)
Pettinico, George, St. Mary Magdalen, Oakville
Phaneuf, Eugene E., (Retired)

Philip, Donald, Franciscans Sisters of the Eucharist, Meridan
Piotrowski, Stanley J., Jr., St. Gregory the Great, Bristol
Poland, James K., (Retired)
Polansky, Daniel W., Nativity, Bethlehem
Pond, Donald H., Jr., St. Bernard, Enfield
Poulin, Gerald L.
Prete, Paul V., St. Margaret, Madison
Probulis, Gerard J.
Puskas, George A., Christ the Redeemer, Milford
Quinn, James P., (Retired)
Ramos, Edmund J., (Retired)
Regan, Joseph M., Jr., St. Margaret, Madison
Renker, Richard W., Holy Rosary, Ansonia; St. Anthony, Ansonia
Rescildo, Ralph, St. Teresa, Woodbury
Reynolds, David W., Sacred Heart, St. Francis of Assisi, St. Mary & St. Peter, Torrington
Richter, Neil B., St. Joseph, Bristol
Riotte, Eugene C., (Retired)
Rivera, José A., (Retired)
Rivera, Pedro L., St. Ann & St. Mary, New Britain
Rogers, Joseph K., (Retired)
Rosado, Ramon A., St. Augustine, Hartford
Rosello, Modesto A., (Retired)
Roy, Reginald, St. Jerome, New Britain
Rubitz, Michael, St. Joseph & St. Mary, Meriden
Ryan, Richard
Ryzewski, Joseph R., Blessed Sacrament, Hamden
Sabo, Paul E., Our Lady of Victory & St. John Vianney, West Haven
Sandford, Wayne E., Our Lady of Pompeii, East Haven
Santello, Richard L., St. Michael & St. Anthony, New Haven
Santos, Richard D., St. Brigid, West Hartford
Sartor, George G., St. Clare, East Haven; St. Elizabeth, Branford
Sayles, William J., Church of the Assumption, Woodbridge
Scanlon, Thomas P., (Retired)
Sennett, Richard M., (Retired)
Shelto, Michael A., St. Elizabeth Seton, Rocky Hill
Shiels, James H., Holy Spirit, Newington
Singer, Norman H., Our Lady of Pompeii, East Haven
Skipp, Barry T., Sacred Heart, Bloomfield
Sloan, Daniel A., (Retired)
Sloan, Joseph S., St. Martha, Enfield
Smith, Donald H., Our Lady of Mt. Carmel and St. Laurent, Meriden
Solli, Anthony P., St. Barnabas, North Haven
Sponzo, Michael T., (Retired)
Stadtlander, Hobart, (Retired)
Stanley, James H., Our Lady of Mt. Carmel, Hamden
Stephens, George R., (Retired)
Stolfi, Domenic N., St. Anthony, Prospect
Streib, George H., Our Lady of Perpetual Help, Washington Depot
Sullivan, James M., St. Peter, Sacred Heart, St. Francis Assisi & St. Mary, Torrington
Sullivan, Joseph, Holy Infant, Orange
Sutak, Thomas S., St. Mary, Unionville
Sutherland, Jeffrey B., St. Ann, Avon
Suzio, John J., (Retired)
Sweeney, John M., (Leave of Absence)
Szewczyk, Edward J., (Retired)
Szumigala, Michael P., St. Matthew, Forestville
Taddei, Edward D., (Retired)
Talbot, Oral A., (Retired)
Tartaris, Robert P., Our Lady of Victory & St. John Vianney, West Haven
Taylor, James P., Our Lady of Fatima, Yalesville
Thayer, John E.
Thompson, Bruce R., (Retired)
Thorney, Vincent M., (Retired)
Tolassi, Bernard, (Retired)
Toner, James H., Corpus Christi & Sacred Heart, Wethersfield
Tripp, James A., Sr., (Retired)
Twerago, John P., (Retired)
Vazquez, Julio, (Retired)
Vecca, Carl M., Chaplain, Cheshire Correctional Facility
Violette, Carroll, (Inactive)
Wallin, Robert F., St. John of the Cross, Middlebury
Walsh, Maurice J., (Retired)
Walton, Gerald S., St. Therese, Branford
Weaver, Stephen L., St. Augustine, South Glastonbury; St. Paul Glastonbury
Wheeler, John E., (Retired)
Wilber, Richard, St. Bridget, Cheshire
Wilcox, William H., (Retired)
Winiarski, Benedict L., St. Mary & St. Robert Bellarmine, Windsor Locks
Yatcko, Stephen J., St. Joan of Arc, Hamden

INSTITUTIONS LOCATED IN THE ARCHDIOCESE

[A] SEMINARIES, ARCHDIOCESAN

BLOOMFIELD. *St. Thomas Seminary*, 467 Bloomfield Ave., 06002-2999. Tel: 860-242-5573; Fax: 860-242-4886. Email: info@stseminary.org. Web: stseminary.org. Rev. Msgr. Gerard G. Schmitz, Rector & Contact; Karen Lesiak, Library Dir. Priests 20; Candidates for Diaconate Studies 18. In Res. Most Rev. Christie A. Macaluso, D.D.; Revs. Michael J. Dolan; Dario E. Diaz In Res. at the Archbishop Daniel A. Cronin Retirement Residence at St. Thomas Seminary Rev. Msgrs. Charles W. Daly (Retired); Charles B. Johnson (Retired); William J. Mullen, J.C.D. (Retired); John D. Regan (Retired); Revs. Henry R. Dery (Retired); James G. Fanelli (Retired); Thomas F. Farrell (Retired); Ronald L. Genua (Retired); Daniel J. Karpiey (Retired); Paul F. Kenefick (Retired); Richard R. Russell (Retired); Robert T. Russo (Retired); Richard L. Shellman (Retired); Stanley J. Sikora (Retired); William J. Thuer (Retired).

[B] SEMINARIES, RELIGIOUS OR SCHOLASTICATES

CHESHIRE. *Novitiate of the Legion of Christ*, 475 Oak Ave., 06410. Tel: 203-271-0805; Fax: 203-271-3845. Email: cheshire@legionaries.org. Web: www.legionofchrist.org. Revs. Christopher Brackett, L.C., Rector; Oscar Capilla, L.C., Chap.; Joseph Burtka, L.C.; Joseph Brickner, L.C., Novice Instructor; Kevin Meehan, L.C.; Christopher O'Connor, L.C., Prof.; Tarsicio Samaniego, L.C., Prof. Priests 8; Religious 11; Students 150.

Studies: Revs. Owen Kearns, L.C.; Andreas Kramarz, L.C., Dean Studies; Walter Schu, L.C., Prof.

[C] COLLEGES AND UNIVERSITIES

HAMDEN. *Mt. Sacred Heart College*, 295 Benham St., 06514-2801. Tel: 203-248-4225; Fax: 203-230-8341. Email: semmerich@ascjus.org. Sisters Maureen Martin, A.S.C.J., Pres.; Susan Emmerich, A.S.C.J., Dean. Chartered by the State of Connecticut for Sisters of Community of Apostles of the Sacred Heart of Jesus.

CHESHIRE. *Legion of Christ College, Inc.*, 475 Oak Ave., 06410. Tel: 203-271-0805; Fax: 203-271-3845. Rev. Jose Felix Ortega, L.C., Contact Person.

NEW HAVEN. *Albertus Magnus College* (1925) 700 Prospect St., 06511-1189. Tel: 203-773-8550; Fax: 203-773-9539. Email: admissions@albertus.edu. Web: www.albertus.edu. Dr. Julia M. McNamara, Pres.; Dr. William C. Schulz, Vice Pres. Academic Affairs; Sr. Patricia Thomas, O.P., Dir., Campus Ministry; Jeanne Mann, Treas.; Eileen Perillo, Registrar; Maureen Morrison, Dean Student Svcs. Dominican Sisters (St. Mary of the Springs, Columbus, OH). Sisters 7; Lay Teachers 35; Total Enrollment 2,407.

WEST HARTFORD. *Saint Joseph College* (1932) 1678 Asylum Ave., 06117. Tel: 860-232-4571; Fax: 860-233-5695. Email: admissions@sjc.edu. Web: www.sjc.edu. Pamela Trotman Reid, Ph.D., Pres.; Robert Madden, Vice Pres. Academic Affairs; Christine Bell, Vice Pres. Enrollment Mgmt.; Carol Descak, Vice Pres. Enrollment Mgmt.; Mary Kate Cox, Vice Pres. Inst. Advancement; Charles Mann, Vice Pres. Finance; Jennifer Washington, Registrar; Linda Geffner, Dir. Library. Sisters of Mercy., Women's College-Undergraduates; Graduate School-Co-ed.; Chartered by the State of Connecticut. Priests 1; Sisters 2; Lay Teachers 80; Students 1,942; Undergraduates Women 963; Graduates Coed Women 972; Men 7; School for Young Children 139; Gengras Center for Exceptional Children 127.

[D] HIGH SCHOOLS, ARCHDIOCESAN

BRISTOL. *St. Paul Catholic High School*, 1001 Stafford Ave., 06010-3894. Tel: 860-584-0911; Fax: 860-585-8815. Web: www.spchs.com. Mr. Cary Dupont, Pres.; Sharon Mielcarz, Dean of Academic Life; Albert Wallace, Dean of Student Life; Rev. Michael A. Carlson, Campus Min.; Dawn Zillich, Librarian. Faculty 27; Lay Teachers 27; Students 318.

MANCHESTER. *East Catholic High School*, 115 New State Rd., 06042. Tel: 860-649-5336; Fax: 860-649-7191. Web: ECHS.com. Christian J. Cashman, Prin. & Chief Admin.; Geoffrey Andrews, Vice Prin., Student Life; Elena Gostic, Vice Prin., Academics; Constance Jurczak, Library/Media Dir. Sisters of Notre Dame de Namur 3; Lay Teachers 53; Students 684.

WATERBURY. *Sacred Heart High School*, 142 S. Elm St., 06706. Tel: 203-753-1605; Fax: 203-597-1686. Email: jc.jennings@snet.net; eileenregan@snet.net. Web: sacredhearthighschool.org. Mrs. Jacqueline C. Jennings, Prin.; Mrs. Eileen Regan, Dir. Devel. & Interim Pres.; Debra Taylor, Dir. Student Activities; Rev. James T. Gregory; Jane Scully-Parshall, Librarian. Priests 1; Lay Teachers 30; Students 381.

WEST HARTFORD. *Northwest Catholic High School* (1961) 29 Wampanoag Dr., 06117. Tel: 860-236-4221; Fax: 860-586-0911. Email: callahan@nwcath.org. Web: www.nwcath.org. Mrs. Margaret R. Williamson, Prin. & Chief Admin.; Mr. Richard Callahan, Vice Prin.; Mr. John Cusson, Academic Dean; Kristina Gillespie, Dir., Campus Ministry; Rev. Joseph P. Crowley, Chap.; Mrs. Helga Phillips, Librarian. Priests 2; Sisters 1; Lay Teachers 53; Students 652.

[E] HIGH SCHOOLS, PRIVATE

HAMDEN. *Sacred Heart Academy*, 265 Benham St., 06514-2833. Tel: 203-288-2309; Fax: 203-230-9680. Email: Principal@SHA-Excelsior.org. Web: www.sha-excelsior.org. Sr. Colleen Smith, A.S.C.J., Prin. & Contact; Maureen Hayes, Librarian. Apostles of the Sacred Heart of Jesus. Sisters 7; Lay Teachers 45; Students 494.

MILFORD. *Academy of Our Lady of Mercy*, Lauralton Hall, 200 High St., 06460. Tel: 203-877-2786; Fax: 203-876-9760. Email: cmonk@lauraltonhall.org. Web: www.lauraltonhall.org. Antoinette Iadarola, Ph.D., Pres. & Contact; Ann Pratson, Prin.; Theresa Lawler, Librarian. Sisters of Mercy of the Americas. Sisters 2; Lay Teachers 43; Students 431.

NEW MILFORD. *Canterbuck School*, Aspetuck Ave., 06776-1739. Tel: 860-210-3800; Fax: 860-350-4425. Email: tsheehy@cbury.org. Web: www.cbury.org. Thomas J. Sheehy III, Headmaster; Patricia L. Hiro, Headmaster's Asst. & Contact; Rev. Sebastian Leonard, O.S.B., Chap. Coed. Boarding and day students Priests 1; Lay Teachers 75; Students 350.

WATERBURY. *Holy Cross High School* (1968) 587 Oronoke Rd., 06708. Tel: 203-757-9248; Fax: 203-757-3423. Email: tmcdonald@holycrosshs-ct.com. Web: HolyCrosshs-ct.com. Mr. Timothy McDonald, Pres. & Contact; Mrs. Margaret Leger, Prin.; James Carroll, Dir. Campus Min.; Michael Phelan, Library & Media. Brothers of the Congregation of Holy Cross, conducted in cooperation with Sisters of the Congregation of Notre Dame. Brothers 1; Sisters 2; Lay Teachers 64; Students 800.

WEST HAVEN. *Notre Dame High School*, 24 Ricardo St., 06516-2499. Tel: 203-933-1673; Fax: 203-933-2474. Email: pclifford@notredamehs.com. Web: www.notredamehs.com. Bro. James J. Branigan, C.S.C., B.A., M.S., Pres.; Mr. Patrick Clifford, Prin.; Mr. Ralph Proto, Exec. Vice. Pres., Faculties Mgmt. & Planning; Mr. Thomas Marcucci, Athletic Dir.; Adam Laput, Asst. Prin.; Mr. Joseph Ramirez, Asst. Prin.; Mrs. Gail Bellucci, Campus Min.; Lisa Mierzejewski, Librarian. Congregation of Holy Cross. Brothers 4; Sisters 2; Lay Teachers 55; Students 650.

Notre Dame Loyalty & Endowment Fund, Inc., 24 Ricardo St., 06516. Tel: 203-933-1673; Fax: 203-933-2474.

[F] SPECIALIZED CHILD CARING HOME

NEW HAVEN. *St. Francis Home for Children, Inc.* (1852) 651 Prospect St., 06511-2003. Tel: 203-777-5513; Fax: 203-777-0644. Email: psalerno1@aol.com. Mr. Peter T. Salerno, Exec. Dir. & Contact. Provides an array of residential programs for youth and community-based services for families and youth including preschool, extended day treatment, life skills, and family support center. Lay Staff 135; Children 52; Extended Day Treatment 25; Preschool 25; Special Education School 70.

[G] DAY CARE CENTER

HAMDEN. *Clelian Adult Day Center* (1988) 261 Benham St., 06514-2898. Tel: 203-288-4151; Fax: 203-288-0551. Email: cleliancenter@juno.com. Web: www.clelianadultdaycenter.com. Doreen Mosko, Dir. & Contact. Apostles of the Sacred Heart of Jesus., A day health care facility for elderly and disabled adults (interdenominational). Total Assisted 175; Total Staff 20; Capacity 60.

Sacred Heart Manor Nursery and Kindergarten, 261 Benham St., 06514. Tel: 203-230-4889. Email: sealat@yahoo.com. Sr. Elaine Ann Lattanzi, A.S.C.J., Prin. & Contact. Apostles of the Sacred

Heart of Jesus 1; Lay Teachers 4; Students 70; Total Assisted 70.

[H] GENERAL HOSPITALS

HARTFORD. *Saint Francis Hospital and Medical Center*, 114 Woodland St., 06105-1299. Tel: 860-714-4000; Fax: 860-714-7809. Email: pastoralcare@stfranciscare.org. Web: www.stfranciscare.com. Christopher M. Dadlez, Pres. & CEO; Sr. Judith A. Carey, R.S.M., Ph.D., Vice Pres. Mission Integration; Suzanne Nolan, Dir. Pastoral Care/Chap.; Sr. Nancy Ahern, C.S.J., Chap.; Rev. Mark Bonsignore, Chap.; Roy McAlpin, Chap.; Tina Varona, Media Rels. Mgr. Licensed Beds 617; Bassinets 65; Outpatient Visits 325,972; Inpatient Visits 32,807; Observation 771; Staff 3,841. In Res. Revs. Elias Menuba, Chap.; Thomas Puthiyadom (India), Chap.

The Women's Auxiliary of Saint Francis Hospital and Medical Center Tel: 860-714-4558; Fax: 860-714-7809. Janet Newman, Pres.

Asylum Hill Family Medicine Center, Inc. Tel: 860-714-4212; Fax: 860-714-8079. Web: stfranciscare.org.

Woodland Physician Associates, Inc. Web: stfranciscare.org.

Camillus Corporation

The One Thousand Corporation Tel: 860-714-4793.

One Thousand One Corporation

Saint Francis Hospital and Medical Center Foundation, Inc., 95 Woodland St., 06105-1299. Tel: 860-714-4900; Fax: 860-714-8069. Web: stfranciscare.org. Paul Pendergast, Pres. & Chief Devel. Officer.

Mount Sinai Rehabilitation Hospital, Inc., 480 Blue Hills Ave., 06112. Tel: 860-714-3500; Fax: 860-714-8550. Web: stfranciscare.org.

NEW HAVEN. *Hospital of St. Raphael* (1907) 1450 Chapel St., 06511. Tel: 203-789-3000; Fax: 203-789-3328. Email: jgranville@srhs.org. Web: www.srhs.org. Christopher M. O'Connor, Pres. & CEO; Sr. Joan Granville, S.C., Vice Pres. Missions & Contact; Revs. Gregory M. Altermatt, Chap.; Augustine Mangalath (India), Chap.; Steven Voytovich, Orthodox Church in America & Chap.; William West, UCC & Chap.; Rev. Sandy Alves Belcher, Episcopal Priest & Chap.; Rabbi Steve Steinberg, Chap. Sisters of Charity of St. Elizabeth., Legal Holdings: Saint Raphael Healthcare System; Saint Raphael Foundation, Inc.; DePaul Health Services Corporation; Saint Regis Health Center, Inc. (Nonprofit charitable corporations affiliated with the Hospital of Saint Raphael). Chaplains 9; Sisters 3; Bed Capacity 511; Bassinets 22; Patients Assisted Annually 300,000; Total Staff 3,500; CPE Residents 5.

Saint Regis Health Center, Inc. dba Sister Anne Virginia Grimes Health Center 1354 Chapel St., 06511. Tel: 203-867-8300; Fax: 203-867-8370. Email: jtarutis@srhs.org. Web: www.srhs.org. John Tarutis, Exec. Dir. 122-bed skilled nursing facility. Total Assisted Annually 800; Total Staff 152.

WATERBURY. *Saint Mary's Hospital*, 56 Franklin St., 06706. Tel: 203-709-6000; Fax: 203-709-3238. Email: community@stmh.org. Web: stmh.org. Revs. Joseph Pullikattil, Chap.; Stanley R. Staron, Chap.; Deacon Paul B. Lauer, Chap. Saint Mary's Health System, Inc., Saint Mary's Hospital Foundation, Inc., (Nonprofit corporations for the exclusive benefit of Saint Mary's Hospital). Sisters 2; Bed Capacity 202; Licensed 347; Bassinets 32; Neonatal ICU 8; Patients Assisted Annually 230,000; Total Staff 1,600.

Saint Mary's Hospital Foundation, Inc., 56 Franklin St., 06706. Tel: 203-709-6390; Fax: 203-709-3272. Pea Lawlor, Pres.

Saint Mary's Health System, Inc., 56 Franklin St., 06706. Tel: 203-709-6000; Fax: 203-709-3238. Email: community@stmh.org. Chad W. Wable, Pres. & CEO.

Saint Mary's Hospital Auxiliary, 56 Franklin St., 06706. Tel: 203-709-3732; Fax: 203-709-3703.

[I] SPECIAL HOSPITALS

HARTFORD. **Malta House of Care, Inc.*, One State St., Ste. 2400, 06103. Tel: 860-808-0195. Web: www.maltahouseofcare.org. Peter G. Kelly, Chm.; Luis Diez-Morales, M.D., Board Pres. To deliver charitable primary and/or preventative medical health care to the needy uninsured of the Greater Hartford region.

WEST HARTFORD. *Saint Agnes Home, Inc.* (1914) 104 Mayflower St., 06110. Tel: 860-521-7516; Fax: 860-521-6160. Email: info@stagneshome.org. Web: www.stagneshome.org. Lorna Little, M.S.W., Exec. Dir. For adolescent single mothers and their infants. Bed Capacity 16; Patients Assisted Annually 53; Total Staff 40.

[J] HOMES FOR AGED

ENFIELD. *The Home for the Aged of the Little Sisters of the Poor* (1839) Incorporated Operating as St. Joseph's Residence, 1365 Enfield St., 06082-4900. Tel: 860-741-0791; Fax: 860-265-1891. Email: enmothersuperior@littlesistersofthepoor.org. Sr. Mary Bernard Nettle, L.S.P., Supr. & Contact; Rev. Lech Kuna (Poland), Chap. Little Sisters of the Poor 11; Lay Staff 209; Residents 79; Bed Capacity 80; Total Assisted Annually 98.

NEW BRITAIN. *St. Lucian's Residence, Inc.*, 532 Burritt St., 06053-3699. Tel: 860-223-2123; Fax: 860-612-0321. Email: stlucian.res.inc@snet.net. Halina A. Marut, Admin. & Contact; Rev. Augustine Pilatowski, O.F.M.Conv., Chap. Daughters of Mary of the Immaculate Conception. Residents 42; Total Staff 24; Total Assisted Annually 42.

Monsignor Bojnowski Manor, Inc. (1974) 50 Pulaski St., 06053. Tel: 860-229-0336; Fax: 860-229-3252. Carol Ann E. Salvietti, Admin. Owned and operated by the Daughters of Mary of the Immaculate Conception. Skilled Nursing Beds 60; Total Staff 85.

WEST HARTFORD. *Saint Mary Home*, 2021 Albany Ave., 06117. Tel: 860-570-8200; Fax: 860-570-8205. Web: www.saintmaryhome.org. Peter Madden, Admin.; Christopher Johnson, Asst. Admin.; Mrs. Aysha Kuhlor, Dir. Nursing Svcs. Sisters of Mercy 19; Sisters in Residence 9; Residents (Frances Warde Apts.) 97; Patients Assisted Annually 652; Bed Capacity 256; Personnel 355; Skilled Nursing 256; Total Staff 355. In Res. Rev. Norman L. Brockett, Resident Chap.

[K] HEALTH CARE CENTERS FOR AGED

WEST HARTFORD. *McAuley Center, Inc.* (1988) 275 Steele Rd., 06117. Tel: 860-920-6300; Fax: 860-232-4077. Stephen Surprenant, Exec. Dir. & Contact. Continuing care retirement community; Sisters of Mercy. 229 residential apartment units for individuals age 62 and over. Nursing care at St. Mary's Home included.

[L] MONASTERIES AND RESIDENCES OF PRIESTS AND BROTHERS

HARTFORD. *Missionaries of LaSalette Province of Mary, Mother of the Americas*, 915 Maple Ave., 06114-2330. Tel: 860-956-8870; Fax: 860-956-8849. Email: mlsadmin@aol.com. Web: www.lasalette.org. Very Rev. Joseph G. Bachand, M.S., Prov. Supr.; Revs. Denis A. Kolumber, M.S.; James H. Kuczynski, M.S., Vicar; Phil M. Negley, M.S., Asst.; Brian D. Schloth, M.S., Pro. Treas.

The Missionaries of La Salette Corporation.

MLS Religious Trust Province of Mary, Mother of the Americas. Priests 5. *Missionaries of LaSalette*, 85 New Park Ave., 06106-2184. Tel: 860-523-8275; Fax: 860-586-0754. Revs. Salvatore D. Altavista, M.S.; Gerald Biron, M.S.; Richard R. Boucher, M.S.; James D. Caffery, M.S.; Emery N. DesRochers, M.S.; Emile C. Dusseault, M.S.; Frederick R. Flaherty, M.S.; Michael J. Flanagan, M.S.; Rene Gelinas, M.S.; Stanley T. Kennedy, M.S.; Francis J. Kula, M.S.; Maurice F. Linehan, M.S.; James T. Lowery, M.S.; Normand F. Mailloux, M.S.; John J. McCarthy, M.S.; Patrick R. McCarthy, M.S.; Alan B. McGuirk, M.S.; William W. Mulcair, M.S.; Joseph J. Nolan, M.S.; Claudius S. Nowinski, M.S.; Joseph M. O'Neil, M.S., Local Supr.; Louis M. Ouellette, M.S.; Daniel J. Scott, M.S.; Donald D. Simonds, M.S.; Donald K. Thomas, M.S.; Roland G. Vandal, M.S.; Bros. Jean Paul Champagne, M.S., (Retired); G. Peter Collins, M.S.; David J. Cook, M.S.; Mark L. Gallant, M.S.; Andre J. Hamel, M.S.; Paul Maceyka, Oblate; Leonard Melanson, M.S.; Thomas C. Murphy, M.S.; Edmund A. Normantowicz, M.S. Priests 40; Brothers 9; Oblates 1.

Priests-Brothers of Province Serving Abroad: Missionaries in Argentina: Revs. Norman H. Butler, M.S.; Robert R. Butler, M.S.; John M. Garvey, M.S. Bolivia: Revs. John F. Higgins, M.S.; James M. Weeks, M.S. *Our Lady of Sorrows Rectory*, 16 Greenwood St., 06106-2109. Tel: 860-233-4424; Fax: 860-236-0149. Revs. Francis C. Cooney, M.S.; Thomas J. Huhn, M.S.; Brian D. Schloth, M.S. Rome, Italy: Rev. Paul A. Roy, M.S. *North American La Salette Mission Center*, 915 Maple Ave., 06114-2330. Tel: 860-956-8870; Fax: 860-956-8849. Rev. John R. Nuelle, M.S., Dir.; Mrs. Connie Evans, Sec.

St. Patrick-St. Anthony Friary (Holy Name Prov.), 285 Church St., 06103-1105. Tel: 860-756-4034; Fax: 860-249-6487. Web: stpatrick-stanthony.org. Franciscan Friars. Priests 3.

BLOOMFIELD. *Brothers of the Sacred Heart* (1821) 1153 Blue Hills Ave., 06002-1971. Tel: 860-242-3342. Email: plgauvinsc@hotmail.com. Total in Residence 4.

CHESHIRE. *Legionaries of Christ*, 475 Oak Ave., 06410. Tel: 203-271-0805; Fax: 203-271-3845. Email: cheshire@legionaries.org. Web: www.legionofchrist.org. 393 Derby Ave., Orange, 06477. Tel: 203-974-6000; Fax: 203-795-2808.

LITCHFIELD. *Montfort Missionaries*, 83 Montfort Rd., P.O. Box 667, 06759. Tel: 860-567-8434; Fax: 860-567-9670. Email: lourdesshrinect@gmail.com. Web: www.shrinect.org. Revs. James Brady, S.M.M., Admin.; Bernard Brault, S.M.M.; William Considine, S.M.M., Supr. Priests 3. *Lourdes in Litchfield* Tel: 860-567-1041; Fax: 860-567-9670.

Lourdes Shrine Guild, Inc. Montfort House (Center for Spiritual Renewal) Tel: 860-567-8434; Fax: 860-567-9670.

MANCHESTER. *DePaul Provincial Residence* (1995) 234 Keeney St., 06040-7048. Tel: 860-643-2828; Fax: 860-533-9462. Email: nepcm1@cox.net. Revs. A. Rafal Kopystynski, C.M., Prov. & Contact; Edmund Gutowski, C.M.; Chester R. Mrowka, C.M.; Stanley Staniszewski, C.M.; Bro. Joseph S. Zurowski, C.M.

The New England Province of the Congregation of the Mission Incorporated Congregation of the Mission, New England Province., (Vincentian Fathers and Brothers)

Charitable Trust of the New England Province of the Congregation of the Mission

Special Assignments: Revs. George J. Dabrowski, C.M. (Retired); Julian Szumilo, C.M.; Ronald A. Wiktor, C.M. *St. Joseph Rectory* (1926) 32 Jewett St., Ansonia, 06401-2499. Tel: 203-734-0402; Fax: 203-734-4884. *St. Michael the Archangel*, 75 Derby Ave., Derby, 06418-2098. Tel: 203-734-0005; Fax: 203-736-2044. *St. Stanislaus Rectory* (1904) 9 Eld St., New Haven, 06511-3899. Tel: 203-562-2828; Fax: 203-752-0217.

MERIDEN. *Franciscan Brothers of the Eucharist*, 173 Goodspeed Ave., 06451. Tel: 203-237-3601; Fax: 203-237-4217. Email: brothers@fbecommunity.org. Web: www.fbecommunity.org. Bro. Leo Maneri, F.B.E., Pres.

NEW BRITAIN. *Conventual Franciscans* (1979) 548 Burritt St., 06053-2869. Tel: 860-225-5786. Rev. Augustine Pilatowski, O.F.M.Conv., Supr., Delegate & Contact. Daughters of Mary Motherhouse. *St. Paul Friary* (1985) 479 Alling St., Kensington, 06037-2100. Tel: 860-828-0331; Fax: 860-828-7620.

NEW HAVEN. *St. Mary Priory*, 5 Hillhouse Ave., 06511. Tel: 203-562-6193; Fax: 203-562-1273. Email: church@stmarys-priory.com. Web: www.stmarys-priory.com. Order of Preachers (Dominicans). Total in Residence 9.

Priests of the Congregation of Holy Cross, 203 Maple St., 06511. Tel: 203-776-2405. Email: jlmyoung@pol.net. Rev. John L. Young, C.S.C.

NORTH GUILFORD. *Our Lady of Grace Monastery* (1947) 11 Race Hill Rd., 06437-1099. Tel: 203-457-0599; Fax: 203-457-1248. Web: www.ourladyofgracemonastery.org. Sr. Claire, O.P., Prioress & Contact. Order of Preachers (Dominicans). Total in Residence 33.

WATERBURY. *Immaculate Conception Rectory*, 74 W. Main St., 06702. Tel: 203-574-0017; Fax: 203-756-8748. Email: iccsdms@aol.com. Web: www.TheImmaculate.com. Missionaries of the Holy Apostles

St. Michael Rectory (1902) 62 St. Michael Dr., 06704-1295. Tel: 203-753-0689; Fax: 203-573-9101. Web: www.stmichaelwtby.com. Rev. Roger L. Hall, O.F.M. (Immaculate Conception Prov.)

WEST HARTFORD. *Holy Family Monastery/Retreat*, 303 Tunxis Rd., 06107. Tel: 860-521-0440; Fax: 860-521-0883 (Community); 860-521-1929 (Retreat Center). Email: holyfamilyretreat@cpprov.org. Web: www.holyfamilyretreat.org. Very Rev. Terence J. Kristofak, C.P., Prov. Vicar; Rev. Ronan Callahan, C.P. Congregation of the Passion of Jesus Christ.

Monastery Staff: Retreat Center. Revs. Quentin Amrhein, C.P.; Cajetan Bendernagel, C.P.; Daniel Free, C.P.; Henry Free, C.P.; Stephen Haslach, C.P.; Clement Kasinskas, C.P.; Julian Morgan, C.P.; Columkille O'Grady, C.P.; Gregory Paul, C.P.; John Baptist Pesce, C.P.; Owen Sharkey, C.P.; Simon Paul Wood, C.P.; Bros. Frederick Barton, C.P.; Charles Dell, C.P.; William Drotar, C.P.; Conrad Federspiel, C.P.

Retreat Center: Rev. David Cinquegrani, C.P., Retreat Dir.

WEST HAVEN. *Brothers of Holy Cross*, 24 Ricardo St., 06516-2499. Tel: 203-932-2101. Bro. Thomas Gorman, C.S.C. Brothers of Holy Cross.

[M] CONVENTS AND RESIDENCES FOR SISTERS

HARTFORD. *SS. Cyril & Methodius Convent*, 45 Groton St., 06106. Tel: 860-527-3775; Fax: 860-493-7409. Rev. Adam C. Subocz. Felician Sisters of the Order of St. Francis of Connecticut.

Dominican Oblates of Jesus (1958) 510 New Britain Ave., 06106. Tel: 860-249-2912; 860-249-3735. Sr. Teresa Landa, D.O.-O.P., Supr. & Contact. Sisters 3.

Medical Mission Sisters (1925) 92 Sherman St., 06105. Tel: 860-233-0875; Fax: 860-509-9509. Email: mtwinter@hartsem.edu; mms@hartsem.edu. Web: mtwinter.hartsem.edu. Sisters Mary Elizabeth Johnson, M.M.S.; Miriam Therese Winter, M.M.S., Ph.D.

Mercyhouse (2002) 102 Putnam St., 06106-1324. Tel: 860-560-9590. Email: mercyhouse@juno.com. Sisters of Mercy of the Americas.

St. Peter Convent, 11 Charter Oak Pl., 06106. Tel: 860-522-8428. Email: rsmstpeter@aol.com. Sisters of Mercy of the Americas - Northeast Community

Sisters of Mercy of the Americas Northeast Community (1831) *Mercyhouse*, 102 Putnam St., 06106-1324. Tel: 860-560-9590.

Sisters of St. Joseph of Chambery (1650) West Hartford, 06119. Tel: 860-233-5126; Fax: 860-232-4649. Email: csjusa@sbcglobal.net. Web: sistersofsaintjoseph.org. 27 Park Rd., West Hartford, 06119. Tel: 860-233-5126; Fax: 860-232-4649. 145 Elizabeth St., 06105. Tel: 860-523-5704. 73 Cannon Rd., East Hartford, 06108. Tel: 860-291-8998. *Formation House*, 40 Clifford St., 06114. Tel: 860-246-4083.

Shalom Community, 33 Freeman St., 06114. Tel: 860-956-9247. 14 Ringgold St., West Hartford, 06119. Tel: 860-231-8272. 35B Freeman St., 06114. Tel: 860-956-1939.

Spirit of Mercy Community, 410 Campfield Ave., 06114-2807. Tel: 860-956-3030. Sisters of Mercy.

BETHLEHEM. *Abbey of Regina Laudis* (1946) 237 Flanders Rd., 06751. Tel: 203-266-7727; Fax: 203-266-5915. Web: www.abbeyofreginalaudis.com. Sr. David Serna, O.S.B., Abbess & Mailing Contact. Benedictine Nuns of the Primitive Observance. Professed Nuns 30; In First Vows 4; Novices 3.

St. Catherine's Convent of Mercy, 63 Crane Hollow Rd., 06751. Tel: 203-266-5411; Fax: 203-266-5421. Sisters Maureen McDonald, R.S.M.; Mary Kathleen Ronan, R.S.M., Supr. & Contact; Mary Rachel Nerbun, R.S.M.; Cecelia Marie Scaduto, R.S.M. Religious Sisters of Mercy (Alma, MI). Sisters 7.

BLOOMFIELD. *Sisters of Mercy of the Americas Northeast Community*, 5 Garrison Ter., 06002-3005. Tel: 860-243-8524. Sr. Irene Holowesko, R.S.M., Contact.

Sisters of Notre Dame de Namur (Connecticut Province), 5 Garrison Ter., 06002. Tel: 860-243-8524; Fax: 860-683-1351. Email: sndbloom@aol.com. Total in Residence 3.

BRANFORD. *Benedictines of Jesus Crucified, Monastery of the Glorious Cross*, 61 Burban Dr., 06405-4003. Tel: 203-315-9964; Fax: 203-483-5829. Email: monasterygc@juno.com. Sisters Marie Rita Syn, O.S.B., Prioress. Tel: 203-483-4235; Mary Zita Wenker, O.S.B., Vocation Dir.

BRISTOL. *Queen of Apostles Provincial House*, 474 East Rd., 06010. Tel: 860-584-2138; Fax: 860-582-1119. Email: Ltflower@Erols.com. Web: queenofapostles.com. Sisters Regina Arena, M.F.P., Prov. Supr.; Guytina Campisi, M.P.F., Community Archivist & Contact. Religious Teachers Filippini. Sisters in Diocese 16.

CHESHIRE. *Sisters of St. Joseph of Chambery*, 441 E. Mitchell Ave., 06410. Tel: 203-699-9421; Fax: 203-272-2807. Email: luscata@aol.com. Sr. Lucy Scata, C.S.J., 145 Main St., 06410. Tel: 203-272-6504; Fax: 203-271-3356.

EAST HARTFORD. *Sisters of Notre Dame de Namur*, 21 Highview St., 06108-2983. Tel: 860-289-5295. Sr. Marion Raymond Hurley, S.N.D., Contact. 50 Larrabee St., #G, 06108. Tel: 860-289-2421. 908 Forbes St., 06118. Tel: 860-568-6958.

Sisters of Notre Dame de Namur, 908 Forbes St., 06118-1924. Tel: 860-568-6958. Email: ellisnd@aol.com. Sr. Mary Rose Crowley, S.N.D., Contact. Total in Residence 4.

EAST HAVEN. *Provincial House*, 32 Tuttle Pl., 06512. Tel: 203-469-7872; Fax: 203-469-8819. Email: scmm@comcast.net. Web: www.sistersofcharity.net. Sr. Barbara Connell, S.C.M.M., Contact. 87 Gerrish Ave., 06512. Tel: 203-468-9112.

ENFIELD. *Felician Sisters - Our Lady of the Angels Provincial House*, 1315 Enfield St., 06082-4929. Tel: 860-745-7791; 860-745-4946; Fax: 860-741-0819. Email: provcssfct@feliciansenfield.org. 1315 Enfield St, 06082-4929. Tel: 860-745-4946; Fax: 860-741-7871. Sr. Mary Bernardine Mucha, C.S.S.F., Prov. Min. Felician Sisters of the Order of St. Francis of Connecticut.

Provincial House (1932) Tel: 860-745-7791; Fax: 860-741-0819. Sr. Mary Bernardine Mucha, C.S.S.F., Prov. Min.; Rev. Jerzy Puguscik, O.F.M.Conv. Felician Sisters. Professed Sisters 73.

Felician Adult Day Care (1990) 1333A Enfield St., 06082-4929. Tel: 860-745-2542; Fax: 860-745-2542. Email: fadcmail@juno.com. Sr. Patricia Marie Iagrosso, C.S.S.F., Dir. Felician Sisters., A day respite health care facility for Caregivers of the Frail, elderly and Alzheimer Clients. Total Assisted 22; Total Staff 10.

Felician Sisters Infirmary (1938) 1315 Enfield St., 06082-4929. Tel: 860-745-0217; Fax: 860-741-6474. Email: snancy@feliciansenfield.org.

Mother Angela Residence (1964) 1333-B Enfield St., 06082-4929. Tel: 860-745-5705. Email: maresidence@sbcglobal.net.

Child Jesus Convent (1965) 1370 Enfield St., 06082-5526. Tel: 860-745-5847; Fax: 860-745-2010.

Enfield Montessori School (1965) 1370 Enfield St., 06082-5526. Tel: 860-745-5847; Fax: 860-745-2010. Email: montessorischool@cox.net. Sr. Francine Mary Sousa, C.S.S.F., Dir. & Contact. Students 113.

Little Sisters of the Poor (1839) 1365 Enfield St., 06082-4925. Tel: 860-741-0791; Fax: 860-741-3982. Email: enmothersuperior@littlesistersofthepoor.org. Sr. Mary Bernard Nettle, L.S.P., Pres., Supr. & Contact. Sisters 11.

FARMINGTON. *Maryknoll Sisters of St. Dominic* (1920) 275 Main St. #A1, 06032-2930. Tel: 860-678-1971. Email: kmageemm@yahoo.com. Web: sisters.maryknoll.org.

Sisters of the Cross and Passion (1852) St. Gabriel's House, 31 Colton St., 06032. Tel: 860-678-7274; Fax: 860-677-2873. Web: www.cptryon.org/scp; passionistsisters.org. Sr. Mary O'Brien, C.P., Contact. Sisters 4.

FORESTVILLE. *St. Matthew Convent*, 119 Church Ave., 06010-6799. Tel: 860-583-2004; Fax: 860-314-1541 (School). Email: matthewct1@home.com. Sisters, Servants of the Immaculate Heart of Mary.

Sisters of St. Joseph of the Third Order of St. Francis, 82 Kenney St., 06010. Tel: 860-584-2985.

HAMDEN. *Mary, Mother of the Church Convent*, 115 Denslow Hill Rd., 06514. Tel: 203-407-1042. Sr. Sheila O'Neill, A.S.C.J., Religious Supr. Sisters 5.

Mount Sacred Heart Provincial House and Formation House, 295 Benham St., 06514-2801. Tel: 203-248-4225; Fax: 203-230-8341. Email: semmerich@ascjus.org. Web: www.ascjus.org. Sisters Maureen Martin, A.S.C.J., Prov. Supr.; Anne Walsh, A.S.C.J., Vicaress; Susan Emmerich, A.S.C.J., Sec. & Contact. Sisters in Province 134; Professed 131; Novices 3.

Sisters of Mercy of the Americas Northeast Community, 2809 Whitney Ave., 06518-2544. Tel: 203-287-9017. Sr. Ann O'Neill, R.S.M., Contact, D.R.E.

LITCHFIELD. *Daughters of Wisdom* (1949) 229 E. Litchfield Rd., 06759. Tel: 860-567-3163; Fax: 860-567-3166. Email: rg@wisdomhouse.org. Web: www.wisdomhouse.org. Sisters Rosemarie Greco, D.W., Contact; Jo-Ann Iannotti, O.P.

Daughters of Wisdom, 12 Clark Rd., 06759-2808. Tel: 860-529-8419; Fax: 860-529-8419. Web: daughtersofwisdom.org. Sisters 3.

MADISON. *Sisters of Mercy of the Americas Northeast Community*, 149 Neck Rd., 06443. Tel: 203-245-4261. Email: emmanuel115@juno.com. Sr. Lillian Pannozza, R.S.M., Contact.

MANCHESTER. *Assumption Convent* (1961) 21 S. Adams St., 06040. Tel: 860-643-0452; Fax: 860-643-0559. Email: assumption.school@snet.net. Web: www.assumption-parish.com. Sisters Mary Bernard, S.C.M.C., Supr. & Contact; Joan Marie, S.C.M.C.; Joan Clare, S.C.M.C. Sisters of Charity of Our Lady, Mother of the Church.

Sisters of Notre Dame de Namur, 9 Plano Pl., 06040-4907. Tel: 860-647-8544; Fax: 860-647-8544. Email: frandall01@aol.com. Web: www.snadden.org. Sr. Frances Randall, S.N.D., Contact.

Sisters of St. Joseph of Chambery, 572F Hilliard St., 06042. Tel: 860-645-9750. Email: jarcsj@aol.com. Sr. Joan Reilly, C.S.J., Contact.
572 F Hilliard St., 06042. Tel: 860-645-9750.

MERIDEN. *Generalate of the Franciscan Sisters of the Eucharist* (1973) Mailing Address: *Motherhouse of the Franciscan Sisters of the Eucharist*, 405 Allen Ave., 06451. Tel: 203-238-2243; Fax: 203-237-3734. Email: fseinfo@fsecommunity.org. Web: fsecommunity.org. Sisters Shaun Vergauwen, F.S.E., Mother Gen.; Suzanne Gross, F.S.E., Sec. & Contact.

Franciscan Sisters of the Eucharist, Inc. The Institute of the Franciscan Sisters of the Eucharist. Professed 21; Novices 2. 275 Finch Ave., 06451. Tel: 203-238-2400; Fax: 203-237-3739.
269 Finch Ave., 06451. Tel: 203-630-1771; Fax: 203-630-1776.

St. Joseph Convent, 19 Goodwill Ave., 06451. Tel: 203-686-0559. Email: sr.georgeann@cox.net. Sr. Georgeann Vumbaco, R.S.M., Contact.

Mt. Carmel Convent, 109 Goodwill Ave., 06451. Tel: 203-235-3622.

Ursuline Sisters of the Congregation of Tildonk, Belgium, 64 Springdale Ave., 06451. Tel: 203-686-1702. Sr. Gertrude Goldman, O.S.U., Contact.

MILFORD. *Sisters of Mercy of the Americas Northeast Community*, 23 Jones Ct., 06460. Tel: 203-877-1171. Email: Patsio@sbcglobal.net. Sisters Madeline Follachio, R.S.M., Contact; Patricia J. Rooney, R.S.M., Fundraising Consultant.

NEW BRITAIN. *Cana*, 1190 Slater Rd., 06053-1614. Tel: 860-826-1655. Sisters of St. Joseph of Chambery. Total in Residence 2.

St. Francis of Assisi Convent, School Sisters of Notre Dame, 1757 Stanley St., 06053. Tel: 860-225-7143. Email: stfrancis@snet.net. Sisters 2.

Motherhouse of Daughters of Mary of the Immaculate Conception (1904) 643 Burritt St., 06053. Tel: 860-225-9406; Fax: 860-225-4321. Web: www.crossfire.org/daughtersofmary/. Sisters Mary Jennifer Carroll, D.M., Supr. Gen.; Mary Clare, D.M., Sec. Daughters of Mary of the Immaculate Conception. Sisters in Community 38.

Sacred Heart Convent (1904) 23 Orange St., 06053. Tel: 860-225-3989.

Msgr. Bojnowski Manor (1974) 50 Pulaski St., 06053. Tel: 860-229-0336; Fax: 860-229-3252.

St. Lucian's Residence, 532 Burritt St., 06053. Tel: 860-223-2123; Fax: 860-612-0321.

Sisters of Mercy of the Americas Northeast Community, 37 Carlton St., 06053. Tel: 860-229-7575. Sr. Barbara Kowalski, R.S.M., Contact.

Sisters of the Cross and Passion (1849) 25 Streamside Ln., 06052. Tel: 860-224-1193. Sr. Ann Rodgers, C.P., Contact.

NEW HARTFORD. *Missionary Servants of the Most Blessed Trinity*, 595 Town Hill Rd., 06057. Tel: 860-379-4329; Fax: 860-379-4329. Email: trinita@charter.net. Total in Residence 4.

NEW HAVEN. *St. Brendan Convent*, 455 1/2 Whalley Ave., 06511. Tel: 203-787-4631; Fax: 203-785-1781. Email: marineap@hotmail.com. Sisters of Our Lady of the Garden.

Dominican Sisters of Peace (1901) *St. Mary's Convent*, 15 Lincoln St., 06511. Tel: 203-865-7305. Sisters Barbara DeCrosta, O.P., Contact; Mary Ellen Boyle, O.P.; Ellen McNulty, O.P.; Maureen O'Brien, O.P.

St. Joseph Convent, 135 Edwards St., 06511. Tel: 203-562-9202. Email: chermann8@juno.com. Web: www.columbusdominicans.org. Sisters Helen Kieran, O.P., Contact; Melanie Hannigan, O.P., Dominican Sister, St. Mary of the Springs; Sheila O'Brien, O.P. 15 Lincoln St., 06511. Tel: 203-865-7305. Email: melboyle1@juno.com. 1914 Chapel St., 06515. Tel: 203-389-9428.

Sisters Minor of Mary Immaculate, 15 Eld St., 06511. Tel: 203-562-2751. Sisters Maria Elisabetta Patrizi, Foundress, (Resides in Italy); Kathleen Howard, S.M.M.I., Delegate.

Sisters of Charity of St. Elizabeth, Convent Station, 1450 Chapel St., 06511. Tel: 203-789-3000. 450 Central Ave., 06515. Tel: 203-397-5243. 80 Whittier Ave., 06515. Tel: 203-389-4400.

Sisters of Notre Dame de Namur 311 Eastern St., 1916 E., 06513. Tel: 203-469-8385.

St. Mary's Convent, 15 Lincoln St., 06511. Tel: 203-865-7305. Email: melboylel@juno.com. Dominican Sisters of Peace (Columbus, OH).

NORTH GUILFORD. *Monastery of Our Lady of Grace* (1947) 11 Race Hill Rd., 06437-1099. Tel: 203-457-0599; Fax: 203-457-1248. Web: www.ourladyofgracemonastery.org. Dominican Contemplative Nuns (Cloistered). Professed Sisters 33.
A contemplative community with solemn vows and papal enclosure. Perpetual Adoration. Sr. Claire, O.P., Prioress & Contact; Rev. Thomas B. Confer, O.P., Chap.
Dominican Contemplative Nuns (Cloistered). Sr. Claire, O.P., Prioress & Contact; Rev. Thomas B. Confer, O.P., Chap. Tel: 203-562-6193.

NORTH HAVEN. **St. Frances Cabrini Convent*, 94 Chapel Hill Rd., 06473. Tel: 203-239-8012; Fax: 203-985-0236. Sisters of the Sacred Heart of Jesus of Ragusa. Total in Residence 4.

TORRINGTON. *St. Francis of Assisi Convent*, 248 McKinley St., 06790. Tel: 860-489-7405; Fax: 860-482-1972. Email: shmclark@att.net; elrrsm@att.net. Sisters of Mercy of the Americas of the Northeast. Sisters 2.

St. Peter Convent, 25 St. John Pl., 06790. Tel: 860-489-4035. Email: spsweb@snet.net. Sisters Pietrina Mazzola, M.P.F., Sister in Charge; Carmela DiMauro, M.P.F., Pastoral Min. Religious Teachers Filippini.

WALLINGFORD. *Holy Trinity Convent*, 247 S. Main St., 06492. Tel: 203-265-6999; Fax: 203-294-4983. Sisters of Mercy of the Americas of Connecticut.

WATERBURY. *Holy Land Convent*, 60 Slocum St., 06706. Tel: 203-755-2456. Religious Teachers Filippini.

St. Mary Hospital, 56 Franklin St., 06706-1200. Tel: 203-574-6455. Sr. Patricia Corcoran, C.S.J., Contact. Sisters of St. Joseph of Chambery. 284 Windy Dr., 06705-2543. Tel: 203-574-6374. 31 Marita Dr., 06705-2527. Tel: 203-574-6482.

Notre Dame Convent, 119 Southmayd Rd., 06705. Tel: 203-753-1095; Fax: 203-754-4431. Sr. Edith Laflamme, C.N.D., Contact. Sisters of the Congregation of Notre Dame. Sisters 5. 587 Oronoke Rd., 06708. Tel: 203-755-8828. Sisters 7.

Sisters of Notre Dame de Namur (1804) 131 Herschel Ave., 06708. Tel: 203-757-1444. Sr. Mary Beth Johnson, S.N.D., Contact. 38 Summer St., 06704. Tel: 203-755-0012.

Visitation Plaza, 100 Jefferson Sq., #7J, 06706. Tel: 203-755-7236.

WATERTOWN. *St. John the Evangelist Convent*, 9 Academy Hill, 06795-2101. Tel: 860-274-1820; Fax: 860-945-6418. Email: bvaluckas@gmail. com. School Sisters of Notre Dame. Sisters 2.

WEST HARTFORD. *Convent of Mary Immaculate, Provincial House of the Sisters of St. Joseph of Chambery* (1650) (North American Province), 27 Park Rd., 06119. Tel: 860-233-5126; Fax: 860-232-4649. Email: csjusa@sbcglobal.net. Web: www.sistersofsaintjoseph.org. Sr. Dolores Lahr, C.S.J., Prov.; Mrs. Mary D'Arcangelo, Admin. Asst. & Contact.

The Sisters of St. Joseph Corporation Sisters of St. Joseph of Chambery., In Community: Professed Sisters 119.

Religious Trust of the Sisters of St. Joseph of Chambery (the "Trust")

Dominican Sisters, 78 Westpoint Ter., 06107. Tel: 860-521-8296; Fax: 860-521-8296. Sr. Magdalene Nguyen, O.P., Supr. & Contact. Total in Residence 2.

Saint Mary Home, 2021 Albany Ave., 06117. Tel: 860-570-8200; Fax: 860-570-8205. Web: www.saintmaryhome.org. Peter Madden, Admin. & Contact.

Sisters of Mercy of the Americas - Northeast Community, Inc., 55 E. Cedar St., Newington, 06111. Tel: 860-594-8619; Fax: 860-665-0532. Sr. Mary Etta Higgins, R.S.M., Life & Min. Admin.

Life and Ministry Office, 55 E. Cedar St., Newington, 06111. Tel: 860-594-8619; Fax: 860-665-0532. Sr. Mary Etta Higgins, R.S.M., Life & Ministry Admin. Sisters in Community 203.

Sisters of Mercy of the Americas of Connecticut, 132 Milton St., 06119-1218. Tel: 860-523-0707.

St. Joseph College, Lourdes Hall, 1678 Asylum Ave., 06117-2791. Tel: 860-232-6730.

St. Paul Convent, 243 Steele Rd., 06117-2741. Tel: 860-232-7745.

Trocaire, 243 Steele Rd., 06117-2796. Tel: 860-233-2195.

Sacred Heart Convent, 243 Steele Rd., 06117-2797. Tel: 860-236-3503.

Maranatha, 243 Steele Rd., 06117-2797. Tel: 860-236-9448. 54 Boulanger Ave. #1, 06110-1103. Tel: 860-231-8472. 54 Boulanger Ave. #2, 06110-1103. Tel: 860-233-6679.

Sisters of Mercy of the Americas of Vermont, 54 Clifford Dr., 06107-1208. Tel: 860-586-8402.

WEST HAVEN. *Our Lady of Victory Convent*, 634 Jones Hill Rd., 06516-6398. Tel: 203-934-8601. Sr. Denise Farrands, O.S.U. Ursuline Sisters of the Congregation of Tildonk, Belgium.

WINCHESTER CENTER. *Villa Ferretti, Religious Teachers Filippini*, 438 Winchester Rd., Box 55, 06094. Tel: 860-379-3279; Fax: 860-379-6479.

WINDSOR. *Sisters of Notre Dame de Namur*, Province Center, 468 Poquonock Ave., 06095-2473. Tel: 860-688-1832; Fax: 860-683-1741. Email: sndct@aol.com. Web: www.sndden.org. Sisters Mary Rose Crowley, S.N.D., Leadership Team & Contact. Tel: 860-285-8901; Maureen O'Brien, S.N.D., Leadership Team. Tel: 860-285-8441; Marie Verrilli, S.N.D., Leadership Team.

Community, 468 Poquonock Ave., 06095-2473. Tel: 860-285-0038; Fax: 860-683-1741.

Julie House Residential Care Home, 425 Poquonock Ave., 06095-2465. Tel: 860-298-8320; Fax: 860-683-1351. Assisted living home for S.N.D.'s only. Residents 16; Total Staff 4.

Sisters of St. Joseph of Chambery, 67 Bloomfield Ave., 06095. Tel: 860-285-0890. Email: windwomen@att.net.

WOLCOTT. *Contemplative Sisters of the Good Shepherd*, 5 Carriage Hill Dr., 06716. Tel: 203-879-6330; Fax: 203-879-5920. Email: gdshep620@sbcglobal.net. Web: www.goodshepherdsisters.org. Sr. Mary Edith Olaguer, C.G.S., Contact Person & Coord.

Daughters of Wisdom, 18 Munson Rd., #2, 06716. Tel: 203-879-3432. Email: dguerettedw@comcast.net.

[N] COUNSELING CENTERS

MERIDEN. *Franciscan Life Center*, 271 Finch Ave., 06451. Tel: 203-237-8084; Fax: 203-639-1333. Web: www.flcenter.org. Sr. Barbara Johnson, F.S.E., Exec. Dir.

Franciscan Life Center Network, Inc. Franciscan Sisters of the Eucharist 7; Total Assisted 3,000; Total Staff 20.

[O] ADOPTION SERVICES-HOME CARE

MERIDEN. *Franciscan Family Care Center* (1979) 267 Finch Ave., 06451. Tel: 203-238-1441; Fax: 203-686-0807. Email: ssuzanne@franciscanhc.org. Sr. Suzanne Gross, F.S.E., Admin. Franciscan Home Care & Contact. Tel: 203-237-8084; Fax: 203-639-1333.

Franciscan Family Care Center, Inc. (dba Franciscan Home Care and Hospice Care) Franciscan Sisters of the Eucharist 6; Total Assisted 650; Total Staff 93.

[P] RETREAT HOUSES-RENEWAL CENTERS

FARMINGTON. *Our Lady of Calvary Retreat House*, 31 Colton St., 06032. Tel: 860-677-8519; Fax: 860-677-2873. Email: olcretreat@sbcglobal.net. Web: www.ourladyofcalvary.com. Conducted by the Sisters of the Cross and Passion for Religious and Lay Persons.

Staff: Sisters Mary O'Brien, C.P.; Ann Rodgers, C.P., Prog. Dir.; Pauline Semkow, R.S.M.; Theresina Scully, C.P., Admin. & Contact; Nancy Babcock, Retreat Team; Maria Descy, Retreat Team.

LITCHFIELD. *Wisdom House Retreat Center* (1949) 229 E. Litchfield Rd., 06759-3002. Tel: 860-567-3163; Fax: 860-567-3166. Email: rg@wisdomhouse.com. Web: www.wisdomhouse.org. Sisters Rosemarie Greco, D.W., Admin. & Contact; Jo-Ann Iannotti, O.P., Art & Spirituality Coord. A retreat center which presents programs in spirituality, education & the arts. Use of space is available for nonprofit organizations when their purpose corresponds to the Mission of Wisdom House. The Center is a sponsored ministry of the Daughters of Wisdom.

MADISON. *Mercy Center, Incorporated*, 167 Neck Rd., P.O. Box 191, 06443. Tel: 203-245-0401; Fax: 203-245-8718. Email: info@mercybythesea.org. Web: www.mercybythesea.org. Krista May, Interim Exec. Dir. & Contact. Sisters of Mercy. Sisters 3; Total in Residence 3; Total Staff 10.

WEST HARTFORD. *Holy Family Passionist Retreat Center*, 303 Tunxis Rd., 06107. Tel: 860-521-0440; Fax: 860-521-1929. Email: holyfamilyretreat@cpprov.org. Web: www.holyfamilyretreat.org. Rev. David Cinquegrani, C.P., Retreat Dir.; Very Rev. Terence J. Kristofak, C.P., Retreat Team; Rev. Gregory Paul, C.P., Retreat Team; Sisters Sally Hodgdon, C.S.J., Retreat Team; Elissa Rinere, C.P., Retreat Team; Theresa Wiss, Dir. & Youth Ministry; Brandon Nappi, Assoc. Dir.; Joan Kelly, D.Min., Retreat Team. For laymen and laywomen. Conducted by the Passionist Community Priests 3; Sisters 2; Lay Staff 3.

[Q] NEWMAN CENTERS

HARTFORD. *Capital Community College* 950 Main St., 06103. Tel: 860-906-5000. Web: www.ccc.commnet.edu. Deacon Arthur L. Miller, Chap.

University of Hartford Newman Center 200 Bloomfield Ave., 06117-1599. Tel: 860-768-4899. Email: campusministry4@aol.com. Web: www.myspace.com/uha_newman_club. Rev. Michael J. Dolan, Chap.

Trinity College Chapel 300 Summit St., 06106-3186. Tel: 860-297-2015. Email: campusministry5@aol.com. Web: www.trincoll-edu/orgs/newman-club.

HAMDEN. *Catholic Community at Quinnipiac University* 275 Mt. Carmel Ave., 06518-1908. Tel: 203-582-8257. Web: www.qubranches.org. Rev. Jonathan Kalisch, O.P., Chap. & Contact, Res.: St. Mary's Priory, 5 Hillhouse Ave., New Haven, 06505. Tel: 203-562-6193; Fax: 203-562-1273.

St. Mary's Priory, 5 Hillhouse Ave., New Haven, 06505. Tel: 203-562-6193; Fax: 203-562-1273.

NEW BRITAIN. *Central Connecticut State University Newman House* 145 Paul J. Manafort Dr., 06053-2552. Tel: 860-832-3795; Fax: 860-225-2315. Rev. Paul Rotondi, O.F.M. Total Staff 1.

St. Francis of Assisi Friary 1755 Stanley St., 06053-2099. Tel: 860-225-6449; Fax: 860-225-2315.

NEW HAVEN. *Southern Connecticut State University Catholic Center* 129 Edwards St., 06511. Tel: 203-392-5331; 203-624-5297. Email: furlongj1@southernct.org. Rev. Paul A. Gotta, Chap.; Deacon Patrick T. Moran, Campus Min.; James Furlong, Inter Faith Office.

Yale University-St. Thomas More Catholic Center and Chapel (1957) 268 Park St., 06511-4714. Tel: 203-777-5537; Fax: 203-777-0144. Email: morehouse@yale.edu. Web: www.yale.edu/stm. Revs. Robert L. Beloin, Ph.D., Chap. & Contact; Peter J. Walsh, C.S.C.; Kathleen Byrnes, Campus Minister.

[R] ORGANIZED CHARITIES

HARTFORD. *Catholic Charities, Inc. (Archdiocese of Hartford)* Administrative Office, 839-841 Asylum Ave., 06105. Web: www.ccaoh.org. Alyson Karpiej, Contact.

839-841 Asylum Ave., 06105. Tel: 860-493-1841; Fax: 860-548-1930. Rose Alma Senatore, CEO.

Network Connecticut, Inc., c/o Catholic Charities, 839-841 Asylum Ave., 06105. Tel: 860-493-1841; Fax: 860-548-1930. Rose Alma Senatore, CEO.

Ansonia Office, 205 Wakelee Ave., Box 364, Ansonia, 06401. Tel: 203-735-7481; Fax: 203-735-5021.

Guilford Office, 652 Boston Post Rd., Guilford, 06437. Tel: 203-453-5746; Fax: 203-773-3626.

Hartford Office, 896 Asylum Ave., 06105. Tel: 860-522-8241; Fax: 860-527-1919.

Meriden Office, 61 Colony St., Meriden, 06451. Tel: 203-235-2507; Fax: 203-639-6509.

Milford Office, 203 High St., Milford, 06460. Tel: 203-874-6270; Fax: 203-874-3301.

New Britain Office, 90 Franklin Sq., New Britain, 06051. Tel: 860-225-3561; Fax: 860-225-2558.

New Haven Office, 501 Lombard St., New Haven, 06511. Tel: 203-787-2207; Fax: 203-773-3626.

Torrington Office, 132 Grove St., Torrington, 06790. Tel: 860-482-5558; Fax: 860-489-2984.

Waterbury Office, 56 Church St., Waterbury, 06702. Tel: 203-755-1196; Fax: 203-575-9675.

13 Wolcott St., Waterbury, 06702. Tel: 203-596-9359; Fax: 203-757-9753.

Migration and Refugee Service, 125 Market St., 06103. Tel: 860-548-0059; Fax: 860-549-8697. Lorna Little, M.S.W., Exec. Dir.

St. Agnes Family Center, St. Agnes Home, 104 Mayflower St., West Hartford, 06110-1425. Tel: 860-521-7516; Fax: 860-521-6160. Email: info@stagneshome.org. Web: www.stagneshome-.org. Residential Home for teen mothers and babies.

St. Francis Home for Children, Inc., 651 Prospect St., New Haven, 06511-2003. Tel: 203-777-5513; Fax: 203-777-0644. Paula Moody, Exec. Dir.

[S] SOCIAL SERVICE CENTERS FOR SPANISH-SPEAKING AND BLACK PEOPLE

BLOOMFIELD. *Office for Hispanic Evangelization*, 467 Bloomfield Ave., 06002-2999. Tel: 860-243-0940; Fax: 860-286-2797. Email: hispanic.off@hotmail.com. Most Rev. Peter A. Rosazza, Vicar for Hispanics; Rev. Jose A. Mercado, Dir.; Luz Yunes, Office Mgr. & Asst. to Dir.

WATERBURY. *Spanish-Speaking Center*, 13 Wolcott St., 06702-1790. Tel: 203-757-8737. Rev. Kevin J. Gray, Contact. Total Assisted 350; Total Staff 1.

[T] SOCIETY OF ST. VINCENT DE PAUL

WATERBURY. **St. Vincent de Paul Mission of Waterbury, Inc.*, P.O. Box 1612, 06721. Tel: 203-754-0000; Fax: 203-756-0865. Email: st.vincent.depaul@snet.net. Deacon Paul P. Iadarola, Exec. Dir. & Contact Person.

[U] MISCELLANEOUS

HARTFORD. *Cathedral Green, Inc.*, 839-841 Asylum Ave., 06105. Tel: 860-728-2562. Rose Alma Senatore, Contact Person. Providing housing opportunities for low income and homeless persons, potentially homeless persons or elderly, disabled or otherwise disadvantaged persons.

**Connecticut Federation of Catholic School Parents, Inc.*, 134 Farmington Ave., 06105-3784. Tel: 860-541-6310. John L. Cattelan, Dir.

Hartford Educational Broadband, Inc., 134 Farmington Ave., 06105-3784. Tel: 860-541-6491; Fax: 860-541-6309. Matthew A. Byrne, CPA, M.B.A., Dir. Finance. Purpose: to provide broadband capacity to archdiocesan educational institutions, license the excess broadband capacity and provide funds generated for the support of the Archdiocesan educational mission.

**Malta House of Care Foundation, Inc.*, One State St., Ste. 2400, 06103. Tel: 860-808-0195. Web: www.maltahouseofcare.org. Jean-Pierre van Rooy, Board Chm. & Hospitaller of Hartford of the Federal Assn. of the Order of Malta; Filomena Soyster, Board Pres.; Barbara "Bobbie" Bartucca, Dir. Philanthropy & Organizational Advancement.

Mercy Housing and Shelter Corporation, 211 Wethersfield Ave, 06114. Tel: 860-808-2040; Fax: 860-548-0692. Email: pmckeon@mercyhousingct.org. Web: www.mercyhousingct.org. Patricia McKeon, R.S.M., Pres. & Exec. Dir.; Carl Rodenhizer, Vice Pres. Assoc. Exec. Dir.; Stephen Abshire, Treas. & Dir. Finance; Henrietta Rand, Sec. & Exec. Asst. Homeless Services Total Assisted 9,700; Total Staff 84.

MLS Religious Trust MLS Trust, 915 Maple Ave., 06114-2330. Tel: 860-956-8870; Fax: 860-956-8849. Sr. Katherine Baker, C.S.J., Contact.

North American La Salette Mission Center, Inc. (1996) 915 Maple Ave., 06114-2330. Tel: 860-956-8870; Fax: 860-956-8849. Email: lsmc2@charter.net. Web: www.lsmc.org. Rev. John R. Nuelle, M.S., Exec. Dir. & Contact; Mrs. Connie Evans, Sec.

The Archdiocese of Hartford Investment Trust, 134 Farmington Ave., 06105-3784. Tel: 860-541-6491; Fax: 860-541-6309. Email: mab@aohct.org. Matthew A. Byrne, CPA, M.B.A., Dir. Fin. & Investment Officer.

The Benevolent Association for Priests of The Archdiocese of Hartford, Incorporated, 134 Farmington Ave., 06105-3784. Tel: 860-541-6491; Fax: 860-541-6309. Email: mab@aohct.org. Matthew A. Byrne, CPA, M.B.A., Dir. Finance.

HAMDEN. *Helping Hand Investments, Inc.*, 33 Rossotto Dr., 06514. Tel: 203-288-6898; Fax: 203-288-3229. Rev. Jose Felix Ortega, L.C., Sec.

Horizons Institute, Inc., 33 Rossotto Dr., 06514. Tel: 203-288-6898; Fax: 203-288-3229. Rev. Jose Felix Ortega, L.C., Contact.

Logos, Inc., 33 Rossotto Dr., 06514. Tel: 203-288-6898; Fax: 203-288-3229. Email: sellis@legionaries.org. Rev. Jose Felix Ortega, L.C., Sec.

LUX ET VITA, INC., 33 Rossotto Dr., 06514. Tel: 203-288-6898; Fax: 203-288-3229. Rev. Jose Felix Ortega, L.C., Contact Person.

Racebrook, Inc., 33 Rossotto Dr., 06514. Tel: 203-288-6898; Fax: 203-288-3229. Rev. Jose Felix Ortega, L.C., Sec.

Rossotto, Inc. (1992) 33 Rossotto Dr., 06514. Tel: 203-288-6898; Fax: 203-288-3229. Rev. Jose Felix Ortega, L.C.

The Legion of Christ, Incorporated (1971) 33 Rossotto Dr., 06514. Tel: 203-288-6898; Fax: 203-288-3229. Email: mbrisson@legionaries.org. Rev. Jose Felix Ortega, L.C., Contact. Priests 4; Religious 4.

U.S. Apostolic Visitation Corporation, P.O. Box 4328, 06514-9998. Tel: 203-287-5467. Web: www.apostolicvisitation.org. Sr. Mary Clare Millea, A.S.C.J., Pres.

BLOOMFIELD. *Foundation for the Advancement of Catholic Schools*, 467 Bloomfield Ave., 06002-2999. Tel: 860-761-7499; Fax: 860-242-8683. Cynthia Basil Howard, Dir. Devel.

BRISTOL. *Magnificat-Mother of Divine Mercy Corporation, Bristol, CT*, 12 Pleasant St., 06010. Tel: 860-584-8803. Ms. Gloria Brophy, Pres. Purpose: to foster the work of intercession; to conduct prayer focused meetings and to serve the needy.

LITCHFIELD. *Lourdes Shrine Guild, Inc.* (1946) 83 Montfort Rd., 06759. Tel: 860-567-1041; Fax: 860-567-9670. Email: lourdesshrinect@gmail.com. Revs. William Considine, S.M.M., Supr., Dir. & Contact Person; James Brady, S.M.M., Admin. Priests 3.

MERIDEN. *Franciscan Life Center Network, Incorporated*, 405 Allen Ave., 06451. Tel: 203-237-8084; Fax: 203-639-1333. Web: www.flcenter.org.

Franciscan Life Center, 271 Finch Ave., 06451. Tel: 203-237-8084; Fax: 203-639-1333. Sr. Barbara Johnson, F.S.E., Exec. Dir.

Franciscan Life Process Center, 11650 Downes St., Lowell, MI 49331. Tel: 616-897-7842; Fax: 616-897-7054. Sr. Colleen Ann Nagle, F.S.E., Dir.

Franciscan Montessori Earth School, 14750 S.E. Clinton St., Portland, OR 97236. Tel: 503-760-8220; Fax: 503-760-8333. Sr. Kathleen Ann Cieslak, F.S.E., Admin.

Franciscan Northwoods Computer Center, 5601 Lilac Hill Rd., Duluth, MN 55810. Tel: 218-624-5478; Fax: 218-624-4649.

John S. Duss Memorial Music Center, 2211 Greysolon Rd., Duluth, MN 55812. Tel: 203-724-6912; Fax: 218-724-3318.

Franciscan Cre-Act School, 526 Grant St., P.O. Box 723, Pocatello, ID 83204. Tel: 208-233-4747; Fax: 208-233-4114. Sr. Janice Otis, F.S.E., Prin.

Franciscan Family Life Center, 1745 Pocatello Creek Rd., Pocatello, ID 83201. Tel: 208-233-9383; Fax: 208-233-2707. Sr. Mary Paul Moller, F.S.E., Dir.

Franciscan Cre-Act School, 526 S. Grant St., Pocatello, ID 83204. Tel: 208-233-4747.

NEW BRITAIN. *Marian Heights, Incorporated*, 314 Osgood Ave., 06053. Tel: 860-225-9406. Web: www.crossfire.org. Sr. Mary Jennifer Carroll, D.M., Contact Person. Purpose: home is limited for low income elderly, adult day care, child day care, convent.

NEW HAVEN. *The Children's Foundation at St. Francis Home, Inc.*, 651 Prospect St., 06511. Tel: 203-777-5513; Fax: 203-777-0644. Email: psalerno1@aol.com. Mr. Peter T. Salerno, Exec. Dir.

NEW MILFORD. *Our Lady of the Lakes Corporation* (1990) 3 Old Town Park Rd., 06776-4212. Tel: 860-354-5239; Fax: 860-354-2968. Email: ololnm@sbcglobal.net. Rev. Frederick M. Langlois, Pastor & Contact.

WEST HARTFORD. *Mercy Community Health, Inc.*, 2021 Albany Ave., 06117-2796. Tel: 860-570-8300; Fax: 860-233-8849. Web: www.mchct.org. William J. Fiocchetta, Pres. & CEO.

Mercy Community Home Care Services, Inc., 275 Steele Rd., 06117. Tel: 860-586-8318; Fax: 860-586-8418. Email: lstpierre.mchc@mchct.org. Web: www.mercycommunityhomecare.org. Linda St. Pierre, Admin.

Mercy Services, Inc., 2021 Albany Ave., 06117-2796. Tel: 860-570-8300; Fax: 860-233-8849. Web: www.mchct.org. William J. Fiocchetta, Pres. & CEO.

Sisters of St. Joseph of Chambery, Business Office & Mailing, 27 Park Rd., 06119. Tel: 860-233-5126; Fax: 860-232-4649. Email: csjusa@sbcglobal.net. Web: www.sistersofstjoseph.org.

WINDSOR. *The Connecticut Province of the Sisters of Notre Dame de Namur, Inc.*, 468 Poquonock Ave., 06095-2473. Tel: 860-688-1832; Fax: 860-683-1741. Email: sndct@aol.com. Web: www.sndden.org. Sisters Mary Rose Crowley, S.N.D., Contact & Leadership Team; Maureen O'Brien, S.N.D., Leadership Team.

RELIGIOUS INSTITUTES OF MEN REPRESENTED IN THE ARCHDIOCESE

For further details refer to the corresponding bracketed number in the Religious Institutes of Men or Women section.

[0200]—*Benedictine Monks*—O.S.B.
[0600]—*Brothers of Holy Cross* (Notre Dame, IN)—C.S.C.
[1100]—*Brothers of the Sacred Heart*—S.C.
[0275]—*Carmelites of Mary Immaculate*—C.M.I.
[0610]—*Congregation of the Holy Cross*—C.S.C.
[1330]—*Congregation of the Mission (Vincentian Fathers)*—C.M.
[1000]—*Congregation of the Passion* (Prov. of St. Paul of the Cross)—C.P.
[0480]—*Conventual Franciscans* (St. Anthony of Padua Prov.)—O.F.M.Conv.
[]—*Franciscan Brothers of the Eucharist*—F.B.E.
[0520]—*Franciscan Friars* (Immaculate Conception, Holy Name Provs.)—O.F.M.
[0690]—*Jesuit Fathers and Brothers*—S.J.
[0730]—*Legionaries of Christ*—L.C.
[0780]—*Marist Fathers*—S.M.
[0800]—*Maryknoll*—M.M.
[0720]—*The Missionaries of Our Lady of La Salette* (Prov. O.L. of Seven Dolors)—M.S.
[0590]—*Missionaries of the Holy Apostles*—M.S.A.
[0870]—*Montfort Missionaries*—S.M.M.
[0910]—*Oblates of Mary Immaculate*—O.M.I.
[093]—*Oblates of St. Joseph*—O.S.J.
[0430]—*Order of Preachers-Dominicans* (Eastern Prov.)—O.P.
[1190]—*Salesians of St. John Bosco*—S.D.B.
[1240]—*Servites (Order of Friar Servants of Mary)*—O.S.M.
[0760]—*Society of Mary (Marianists)*—S.M.
[]—*Sons of Charity*—S.C.

RELIGIOUS INSTITUTES OF WOMEN REPRESENTED IN THE ARCHDIOCESE

[0130]—*Apostles of the Sacred Heart of Jesus*—A.S.C.J.
[0180]—*Benedictine Nuns of the Primitive Observance*—O.S.B.
[2250]—*Congregation of Benedictines of Jesus Crucified*—O.S.B.
[1830]—*Contemplative Sisters of the Good Shepherd*—C.G.S.
[0860]—*Daughters of Mary of the Immaculate Conception*—D.M.
[]—*Daughters of Our Lady of the Garden*—O.L.G.
[0820]—*Daughters of the Holy Spirit*—D.H.S.
[0960]—*Daughters of Wisdom*—D.W.
[1050]—*Dominican Contemplative Nuns*—O.P.
[]—*Dominican Oblates of Jesus* (Madrid, Spain)—D.O-O.P.
[]—*Dominican Sisters (Congregation of St. Catherine of Siena)*—O.P.
[]—*Dominican Sisters of Fatima*—O.P.
[1070-15]—*Dominican Sisters of Hope*—O.P.
[1115]—*Dominican Sisters of Peace*—O.P.
[1170]—*Felician Sisters* (Our Lady of the Angels Province)—C.S.S.F.
[1250]—*Institutes of the Franciscan Sisters of the Eucharist*—F.S.E.
[2340]—*Little Sisters of the Poor*—L.S.P.
[2470]—*Maryknoll Sisters of St. Dominic*—M.M.
[2490]—*Medical Mission Sisters*—M.M.S.
[2790]—*Missionary Servants of the Most Blessed Trinity*—M.S.B.T.
[]—*Missionary Servants of the Word* (Mexico)—H.M.S.P.
[]—*Missionary Servants of the Word (Sisters/ Mexico)*—H.M.S.P.
[2519]—*Religious Sisters of Mercy of Alma* (MI)—R.S.M.
[3430]—*Religious Teachers Filippini*—M.P.F.
[2970]—*School Sisters of Notre Dame*—S.S.N.D.
[]—*Sisters Minor of the Mary Immaculate*—S.M.M.I.
[0520]—*Sisters of Charity of Our Lady, Mother of Mercy*—S.C.M.M.
[0530]—*Sisters of Charity of Our Lady, Mother of the Church*—S.C.M.C.
[0590]—*Sisters of Charity of Saint Elizabeth, Convent Station*—S.C.
[2575]—*Sisters of Mercy of the Americas* (Albany, Vermont, Detroit & Connecticut)—R.S.M.
[3000]—*Sisters of Notre Dame de Namur* (Connecticut, Boston, California & Base Community)—S.N.D.deN.
[1650]—*Sisters of St. Francis of Philadelphia*—O.S.F.
[3850]—*Sisters of St. Joseph of Chambery*—C.S.J.
[3930]—*Sisters of St. Joseph of the Third Order of St. Francis*—S.S.J.-T.O.S.F.
[2980]—*Sisters of the Congregation de Notre Dame*—C.N.D.
[3180]—*Sisters of the Cross and Passion*—C.P.
[]—*Sisters of the Sacred Heart of Jesus of Ragusa*—S.S.H.J.
[2170]—*Sisters, Servants of the Immaculate Heart of Mary*—I.H.M.
[4060]—*Society of the Holy Child Jesus*—S.H.C.J.
[4130]—*Ursuline Sisters of The Congregation of Tildonk, Belgium*—O.S.U.

ARCHDIOCESAN CEMETERIES

HARTFORD. *Catholic Cemeteries Association of the Archdiocese of Hartford, Inc.*, 700 Middletown Ave., P.O. Box 517, North Haven, 06473-0517. Tel: 203-239-2557; Fax: 203-239-5035. Email: ccahart@aol.com. Web: cathcemhartford.com. Rev. Msgr. David M. Walker, Dir.

Holy Trinity
St. Patrick

ANSONIA. *St. Mary*
Old St. Mary

BLOOMFIELD. *Mount Saint Benedict*

DERBY. *Mount St. Peter*
Old St. Mary Cemetery

EAST HARTFORD. *St. Mary*

GLASTONBURY. *Holy Cross*

MANCHESTER. *St. Bridget*
St. James

MERIDEN. *St. Patrick*
Sacred Heart

NAUGATUCK. *St. Francis* (New Haven Region)
St. James

NEW BRITAIN. *St. Mary*
Old St. Mary

NEW HAVEN. *St. Bernard*

NORTH HAVEN. *All Saints*

TORRINGTON. *St. Francis*
Old St. Francis
St. Peter

WALLINGFORD. *Holy Trinity*
St. John

WATERBURY. *Calvary*
St. Joseph
Old St. Joseph

WATERTOWN. *Mount Olivet*

WEST HAVEN. *St. Lawrence*

NECROLOGY

† Colton, Bradford, (Retired)—Died Oct. 5, 2009
† Daily, Leo J., (Retired)—Died May 30, 2009
† Donahue, Joseph P., (Retired)—Died Jan. 1, 2009
† Frisbie, Kenneth J., (Retired)—Died Jan. 17, 2009
† Graziani, Joseph A., (Retired)—Died May 3, 2009
† Kaminski, Ladislaus J., (Retired)—Died Aug. 21, 2009
† Pepe, Mario P., (Retired)—Died Sept. 17, 2009
† Ptaszynski, Stephen F., (Retired)—Died Jan. 5, 2009
† Scholsky, Martin J., (Retired)—Died July 5, 2009

An asterisk (*) denotes an organization that has established tax-exempt status directly with the IRS and is not covered by the USCCB Group Ruling.

Diocese of Helena

(Dioecesis Helenensis)

Most Reverend

GEORGE LEO THOMAS, D.D., PH.D.

Bishop of Helena; ordained May 22, 1976; appointed Auxiliary Bishop of Seattle November 19, 1999; appointed Bishop of Helena March 23, 2004; installed June 4, 2004.

Chancery: 515 N. Ewing, P.O. Box 1729, Helena, MT 59624-1729. Tel: 406-442-5820; Fax: 406-442-5191.

Web: www.diocesehelena.org

Email: chancery@diocesehelena.org

ERECTED MARCH 7, 1884.

Square Miles 51,922.

Comprises the western part of the State of Montana, and is made up of the following Counties: Lewis and Clark, Glacier, Pondera, Flathead, Lake, Lincoln, Missoula, Mineral, Sanders, Powell, Granite, Ravalli, Deer Lodge, Silver Bow, Jefferson, Broadwater, Gallatin, Madison, Beaverhead, Meagher, Wheatland and parts of Teton and Toole.

Diocesan Legal Title--Roman Catholic Bishop of Helena, Montana, a Corporation Sole.

For legal titles of parishes and diocesan institutions, consult the Chancery Office.

STATISTICAL OVERVIEW

Personnel	
Retired Archbishops	1
Bishop	1
Priests: Diocesan Active in Diocese	40
Priests: Diocesan Active Outside Diocese	5
Priests: Diocesan in Foreign Missions	1
Priests: Retired, Sick or Absent	32
Number of Diocesan Priests	78
Religious Priests in Diocese	6
Total Priests in Diocese	84
Extern Priests in Diocese	5
Permanent Deacons in Diocese	28
Total Brothers	3
Total Sisters	31
Parishes	
Parishes	57
With Resident Pastor:	
Resident Diocesan Priests	40
Resident Religious Priests	3
Without Resident Pastor:	
Administered by Priests	5
Administered by Deacons	4
Administered by Religious Women	2
Administered by Lay People	2
Missions	39
Pastoral Centers	14
Professional Ministry Personnel:	
Sisters	7
Welfare	
Catholic Hospitals	2
Total Assisted	284,212
Day Care Centers	3
Total Assisted	129
Educational	
Seminaries, Diocesan	1
Diocesan Students in Other Seminaries	12
Total Seminarians	12
Colleges and Universities	1
Total Students	1,428
High Schools, Diocesan and Parish	2
Total Students	334
Elementary Schools, Diocesan and Parish	4
Total Students	960
Catechesis/Religious Education:	
High School Students	867
Elementary Students	2,759
Total Students under Catholic Instruction	6,360
Teachers in the Diocese:	
Priests	1
Brothers	2
Sisters	1
Lay Teachers	121
Vital Statistics	
Receptions into the Church:	
Infant Baptism Totals	573
Minor Baptism Totals	192
Received into Full Communion	140
First Communions	719
Confirmations	742
Marriages:	
Catholic	140
Interfaith	54
Total Marriages	194
Deaths	817
Total Catholic Population	54,460
Total Population	551,627

Former Bishops—Rt. Revs. JOHN B. BRONDEL, cons. Bishop of Victoria, V.I., Dec. 14, 1879; appt. Vicar Apostolic of Montana, April 17, 1883; Bishop of Helena, March 7, 1884; died Nov. 3, 1903; JOHN P. CARROLL, D.D., cons. Bishop of Helena, Dec. 21, 1904; died Nov. 4, 1925; Most Revs. GEORGE J. FINNIGAN, C.S.C., D.D., cons. Bishop of Helena, Aug. 1, 1927; died Aug. 14, 1932; RALPH L. HAYES, D.D., cons. Bishop of Helena, Sept. 21, 1933; transferred to Rectorship North American College, Rome, Italy, Sept. 11, 1935; transferred to Titular See of Hierapolis, Oct. 26, 1935; transferred to Davenport, Nov. 16, 1944; appt. Assistant at the Pontifical Throne, April 30, 1958; transferred to Titular See of Naraggara and retired, Oct. 20, 1966; died July 4, 1970; JOSEPH M. GILMORE, S.T.D., cons. Bishop of Helena, Feb. 19, 1936; died April 2, 1962; RAYMOND G. HUNTHAUSEN, ord. June 1, 1946; appt. July 8, 1962; cons. Bishop of Helena, Aug. 30, 1962; transferred to Archdiocese of Seattle, Feb. 25, 1975; installed Archbishop of Seattle, May 22, 1975; retired Aug. 21, 1991; ELDEN F. CURTISS, D.D., ord. May 24, 1958; appt. March 4, 1976; cons. Bishop of Helena, April 28, 1976; transferred to Archdiocese of Omaha, May 4, 1993; installed Archbishop of Omaha, June 25, 1993; ALEXANDER J. BRUNETT, Ph.D., ord. July 13, 1958; appt. April 19, 1994; cons. Bishop of Helena, July 6, 1994; transferred to Archdiocese of Seattle Oct. 28, 1997; installed Archbishop of Seattle Dec. 18, 1997; ROBERT C. MORLINO, ord. June 1, 1974; cons. Bishop of Helena Sept. 21, 1999; transferred to Diocese of Madison May 23, 2003; installed Bishop of Madison Aug. 1, 2003.

Vicar General—Rev. Msgr. KEVIN S. O'NEILL, V.G. Email: koneill@diocesehelena.org.

Episcopal Vicar for Clergy—Rev. GARY W. RELLER, Mailing Address: 217 Tremont St., Missoula, 59801. Tel: 406-543-3129. Email: greller@diocesehelena.org.

Director for Ministry to Priests—Rev. THOMAS P. HAFFEY, 2100 Farragut, Butte, 59701. Tel: 406-723-4303. Email: thaffey@diocesehelena.org.

Episcopal Vicar for Senior Status Priests—Rev. Msgr. JOSEPH D. HARRINGTON (Retired), Carroll College, 1601 N. Benton Ave., Helena, 59625. Tel: 406-447-4459.

Episcopal Vicar for Canonical Services—Rev. JOHN W. ROBERTSON, Mailing Address: P.O. Box 1729, Helena, 59624. Tel: 406-442-5820; Fax: 406-442-1085. Email: jrobertson@diocesehelena.org.

Chancery Services—515 N. Ewing St., P.O. Box 1729, Helena, 59624. Tel: 406-442-5820; Fax: 406-442-5191. Email: chancery@diocesehelena.org. Web: www.diocesehelena.org.

Director—Sr. RITA MCGINNIS, S.C.L.

Chancellor—Rev. JOHN W. ROBERTSON.

Pastoral and Renewal Services—MARK FREI.

Pastoral Planning Services—Sr. RITA MCGINNIS, S.C.L.

Archivist—Sr. DOLORES BRINKEL, S.C.L.

Financial Services—PETER MCNAMEE, Diocesan Financial Svcs. Officer, 515 N. Ewing St., P.O. Box 1729, Helena, 59624. Tel: 406-442-5820; Fax: 406-442-5191.

Development and Stewardship Services—GLENDA SEIPP, Dir. Stewardship & Annual Giving, Mailing Address: P.O. Box 1729, Helena, 59624. Tel: 406-442-5820; Fax: 406-442-5191.

Foundation for the Diocese of Helena, Inc.—ROBERT PEARCE JR., Pres.; BETH YEAKEL, Exec. Dir., Mailing Address: P.O. Box 1729, Helena, 59624. Tel: 406-442-5820; Fax: 406-442-5191.

Diocesan Tribunal—Rev. JOHN W. ROBERTSON, Mailing Address: P.O. Box 1729, Helena, 59624. Tel: 406-442-5820; Fax: 406-442-1085.

Judicial Vicar—Rev. JOHN W. ROBERTSON.

Associate Judges—Revs. THOMAS P. HAFFEY; MATTHEW P. HUBER; PATRICK C. MCGURK (Retired).

Promoter of Justice—Rev. ROBERT GROSCH, J.C.L.

Defenders of the Bond—Revs. JEFFREY M. FLEMING; ROBERT C. NOONAN (Retired); GARY W. RELLER.

Notaries—PEGGY PETRINO; MARY MICHAEL SZADERA; VICKI LAFOND-SMITH.

Diocesan Consultors—Rev. Msgr. KEVIN S. O'NEILL, V.G.; Rev. JEFFREY M. FLEMING; Rev. Msgr. JOSEPH D. HARRINGTON (Retired); Rev. EDWARD HISLOP; Rev. Msgr. DONALD SHEA; Revs. ANDREW MADDOCK, S.J.; LEO J. PROXELL; GARY W. RELLER.

Presbyteral Council—Rev. Msgr. KEVIN S. O'NEILL, V.G.; Revs. RUDOLPH BULLMAN; JEFFREY M. FLEMING; ROBERT HALL; MARC J. LENNEMAN; DOUGALD MCCALLUM; RICHARD PERRY, S.J.; VALENTINE D. ZDILLA; GARY W. RELLER; Rev. Msgr. DONALD SHEA.

Diocesan Pastoral Council—Most Rev. GEORGE LEO THOMAS; Rev. Msgr. KEVIN S. O'NEILL, V.G.; STEPHEN BARRY; MARY JEAN BROPHY; SYLVIA BRYCE; VINCENT CHRIS BURGMEIER; LAURIE CROGHAN; DANIEL DOYLE; Rev. JEFFREY M. FLEMING; VIRGINIA HANSON; RON JOHNSON; Deacon THOMAS MCCARTHY; JAMES MCDEVITT; Sr. MARY JO MCDONALD, S.C.L.; JAMES MCNEELY; TIMOTHY NORBECK; SEANEEN PRENDERGAST; Rev. JOHN W. ROBERTSON; DONALD SHAUGHNESSY; CHUCK TELLIER; DOUG TOOKE; MARGARET WALSH; LAWRENCE WHITE JR.; BEVERLY YORK; SUSAN ZEZEUS.

Diocesan Finance Council—PETER MCNAMEE; SUSAN BJERKE; MARK CROSS; CHUCK TURNER; LORI MURPHY-MOULLET; Rev. Msgrs. KEVIN S. O'NEILL, V.G.; JOSEPH HARRINGTON; MAUREEN STOHL; MICHAEL HOLLAND; DENNIS LOVELESS; Rev. JOHN W. ROBERTSON; SHERI BROUDY, Chm.; Sr. RITA MCGINNIS, S.C.L.

Deaneries—Rev. EDWARD KOHLER, Conrad; Rev. Msgr. KEVIN S. O'NEILL, V.G., Helena; Revs. EDWARD HISLOP, Missoula; RUDOLPH BULLMAN, Kalispell; THOMAS P. HAFFEY, Butte; LEO J. PROXELL, Bozeman.

Personnel Board—Rev. Msgr. KEVIN S. O'NEILL, V.G.; Revs. GARY W. RELLER; JOHN J. DARRAGH; TIMOTHY J. MORIARTY; THOMAS M. O'DONNELL; DANIEL B. SHEA; MARC J. LENNEMAN; THOMAS HAFFEY.

Interdiocesan Organizations

Montana Catholic Conference—Mailing Address: 1301 11th Ave., P.O. Box 1708, Helena, 59624. Tel: 406-442-5761; Fax: 406-442-9047. Email: director@montana.cc.org. Web: www.montanacc.org. MOE WOSEPKA, Exec. Dir.; SUZANNE JOHNSON, Exec. Sec.; JAMES ZIEGLER, Bd. Pres.

Catholic Social Services for Montana, Inc.—ROSEMARY MILLER, Exec. Dir., 1301 11th Ave., P.O. Box 907, Helena, 59624. Tel: 406-442-4130; Fax: 406-442-4192. Email: rosemary@cssmt.org. Web: www.cssmt.org. Coordinates and supervises all Catholic Social welfare in the State of Montana; JAMES ZIEGLER, Bd. Pres.

Helena Office—ROSEMARY MILLER, Dir., Adoptions; HELEN BEAUSOLEIL, Social Worker; LESLIE MARTIN, Social Worker; SHIRLEY COLE, Mailing Address: P.O. Box 907, Helena, 59624. Tel: 406-442-4130; SUSAN GLIKO, Rachel's Hope Prog. Coord.

Billings Office—1048 N. 30th St., Billings, 59101. Tel: 406-252-3399. Social Workers: BECKY HUBBERT, (Billings); LINDA CLADIS, (Billings); SAM HUBBERT, (Columbus).

Great Falls Office—Social Workers: DALJEAN WADSWORTH; KYLA WRIGHT, 401 Central Ave., #601, Great Falls, 59401. Tel: 406-771-7805.

Missoula Office—BETSY ROBEL, Social Worker, 420 W. Pine St., Missoula, 59802. Tel: 406-728-5429.

Montana Association of Churches—LYLE HAMILTON, Pres., 25 S. Ewing St., Ste. 408, Helena, 59601. Tel: 406-449-6010; Fax: 406-449-6657. Email: macexecutivedirector@montana-churches.net. Web: www.montana-churches.net; Rev. RUDOLPH BULLMAN, Diocesan Ecumenical Officer, Mailing Address: 65 W. Evergreen, Kalispell, 59901. Tel: 406-752-4219. Email: rbullman@diocesehelena.org.

Diocesan Offices and Organizations

Borromeo Pre-Seminary Program—Rev. MARC J. LENNEMAN, Carroll College, 1601 N. Benton Ave., Helena, 59625. Tel: 406-447-4869.

Catholic Campaign for Human Development—MARK FREI, Mailing Address: Diocese of Helena, P.O. Box 1729, Helena, 59624. Tel: 406-442-5820.

Catholic Committee on Scouting—MIKE MORGAN, Mailing Address: 23 Laurin Loop, Sheridan, 59749. Tel: 406-842-5085.

Catholic Youth Coalition—DOUG TOOKE, Contact, Mailing Address: P.O. Box 1729, Helena, 59624. Tel: 406-442-5820.

Charismatic Renewal—MARK FREI, Mailing Address: Diocesan Pastoral Office, P.O. Box 1729, Helena, 59624. Tel: 406-442-5820.

Christian Family Movement—MARK FREI, Contact, Diocesan Pastoral Office, P.O. Box 1729, Helena, 59624.

Continuing Formation of the Clergy—Rev. THOMAS P. HAFFEY, Dir., 2100 Farragut, Butte, 59701. Tel: 406-723-4303.

Assembly of Women Religious—Sr. RITA MCGINNIS, S.C.L., Delegate for Rel., Mailing Address: P.O. Box 1729, Helena, 59624. Tel: 406-442-5820.

Cursillo Movement, Journey and Search—MARK FREI, Mailing Address: Diocesan Pastoral Office, P.O. Box 1729, Helena, 59624. Tel: 406-442-5820.

Daughters of Isabella—ANTOINETTE ALEXANDER, Regent, Mailing Address: P.O. Box 603, Bonner, 59823. Tel: 406-258-5378.

Diocesan Attorney—WILLIAM DRISCOLL, Mailing Address: Franz & Driscoll, P.L.L.P., P.O. Box 1155, Helena, 59624. Tel: 406-442-0005.

Diocesan Buildings—Mr. SCOTT FITZPATRICK, Mgr., Mailing Address: P.O. Box 1729, Helena, 59624.

Diocesan Council of Catholic Women—MILLIE MITCHKE, Pres., 14193 Grandview Ter., Bigfork, 59911. Tel: 406-837-1032.

Diocesan Ecumenical Officer—Rev. RUDOLPH BULLMAN, 65 W. Evergreen, Kalispell, 59901. Tel: 406-752-4219. Email: rbullman@diocesehelena.org.

Friends of The Catholic University—Rev. Msgr. JOSEPH HARRINGTON, Chm., Carroll College, 1601 N. Benton Ave., Helena, 59625. Tel: 406-447-4459.

Guatemala Missions—MARK FREI, Mailing Address: P.O. Box 1729, Helena, 59624. Tel: 406-442-5820.

Holy Childhood Association—Rev. JOSEPH L. BYRNE, Dir., Mailing Address: P.O. Box 610, Townsend, 59644. Tel: 406-266-4811.

Legendary Lodge (Diocesan Summer Camp)—JOHN FENCIK, Mailing Address: P.O. Box 1729, Helena, 59624. Tel: 406-442-5820.

Marriage Encounter—BILL OLSEN; LYNNE OLSEN, 9825 Cougar Dr., Bozeman, 59718.

Office of Due Process—Rev. JOHN W. ROBERTSON, Mailing Address: P.O. Box 1729, Helena, 59624. Tel: 406-442-5820.

Permanent Deacons—Rev. JOHN W. ROBERTSON, Dir., Mailing Address: P.O. Box 1729, Helena, 59624. Tel: 406-442-5820.

Program of Formation for Lay Ministry—JAMES TUCKER, Mailing Address: P.O. Box 1729, Helena, 59624. Tel: 406-442-5820.

Program of Formation for the Permanent Diaconate—Rev. JOHN W. ROBERTSON, Mailing Address: P.O. Box 1729, Helena, 59624. Tel: 406-442-5820.

Liturgical Commission—Rev. EDWARD HISLOP, Chm., 1475 Eaton St., Missoula, 59801. Tel: 406-721-2405. Members: JOSEPH BEAUSOLEIL; Deacon JAMES BUTTS; DALE FLECK; Rev. JEFFREY M. FLEMING; Sr. MARY AGNES HOGAN, S.C.L.; LORRAINE TUCKER; KATHY WALTER; Sr. MARY JO QUINN, S.C.L. Consultant: Rev. MICHAEL DRISCOLL.

Propagation of the Faith—Rev. JOSEPH L. BYRNE, Diocesan Dir., Mailing Address: P.O. Box 610, Townsend, 59644. Tel: 406-266-4811.

Christian Formation Department—JOHN FENCIK, Dir., 515 N. Ewing St., P.O. Box 1729, Helena, 59624. Tel: 406-442-5820.

Resource Center—KATHY WARD, Mgr., 515 N. Ewing St., P.O. Box 1729, Helena, 59624. Tel: 406-442-5820.

Superintendent of Schools—PATRICK HAGGARTY, Ed.D., Supt., 515 N. Ewing St., P.O. Box 4851, Missoula, 59806. Tel: 406-594-1461; Fax: 406-442-5191.

Third Order of St. Francis—TONY POELMAN, 1702 Peosta, Helena, 59601.

Victim Assistance Coordinator—HELEN BEAUSOLEIL. Tel: 406-442-4130. Mailing Address: P.O. Box 1729, Helena, 59624. Tel: 406-442-5820, Ext. 77. Email: victimassistant@diocesehelena.org.

Vocations Office—Mailing Address: P.O. Box 1729, Helena, 59624. Tel: 406-442-5820. Rev. THOMAS M. O'DONNELL, Dir., Mailing Address: P.O. Box 1110, East Helena, 59635. Tel: 406-227-5334.

"The Montana Catholic" (Diocesan Newspaper)—RENEE ST. MARTIN-WIZEMAN, Editor; M. CATHERINE TILZEY, Sr. Staff Writer & Copy Editor; SUSAN GALLAGHER, Staff Writer & Copy Editor, 515 N. Ewing St., P.O. Box 1729, Helena, 59624. Tel: 406-442-5820; Fax: 406-442-5191.

CLERGY, PARISHES, MISSIONS AND PAROCHIAL SCHOOLS

CITY OF HELENA

(LEWIS AND CLARK COUNTY)

1—CATHEDRAL OF ST. HELENA (1866) Rev. Msgr. Kevin S. O'Neill; Rev. Daniel Madigan, Parochial Vicar; Deacon Gerald Kuhl; Michael Vreeberg, Pastoral Assoc.; Valarie Krause, Pastoral Assoc.
Office: 530 N. Ewing St., 59601. Tel: 406-442-5825; Fax: 406-449-5113. Email: koneill@sthelenas.org.
Catechesis/Religious Program—Bob Fishman, D.R.E.; Joannie Volesky, D.R.E. (High School). Students 278.
Good Samaritan Thrift Store—3067 N. Montana Ave., 59601. Tel: 406-442-0780. Theresa Ortega, Dir. (Assistance to those in need.)
Mission—St. Theodore Avon, Powell Co. 59713.

2—ST. MARY (1910) Rev. William Barton Tolleson, Pastoral Admin.
Office: 1700 Missoula Ave., 59601. Tel: 406-442-5268; Fax: 406-449-0860. Email: smcc@stmaryhelena.org.
Catechesis/Religious Program—Deb Kralicek, D.R.E. Students 65.

3—OUR LADY OF THE VALLEY Rev. Daniel B. Shea; Deacon Randy Fraser.
Office: 1502 Shirley Rd., 59602. Tel: 406-458-6114; Fax: 406-458-8179. Email: olv@mt.net.
Catechesis/Religious Program—Students 141.
Mission—Sacred Heart Wolf Creek, Lewis and Clark Co.

OUTSIDE THE CITY OF HELENA

ANACONDA, DEER LODGE CO.

1—ANACONDA CATHOLIC COMMUNITY (1980), Serves the entire community of Anaconda. Revs. Timothy J. Moriarty; Stuart Long; Sr. Eileen Johnson, S.C.L., Pastoral Assoc.; Mr. John McKenna, Admin.
Office:—217 W. Pennsylvania, 59711. Tel: 406-563-8406; Fax: 406-563-5912. Email: anacondacatholic@questoffice.net.
Holy Family: 217 W. Pennsylvania, 59711.
St. Peter: 405 Alder St., 59711.
Catechesis/Religious Program—Students 131.
Station—Georgetown Lake

2—ST. JOSEPH'S (1957) Closed. 1977. For inquiries for parish records contact Anaconda Catholic Community, Anaconda.

3—ST. PAUL'S (1888) Closed. 1980. For inquiries for parish records contact Anaconda Catholic Community, Anaconda.

4—ST. PETER'S (1898) Closed. 1980. For inquiries for parish records contact Anaconda Catholic Community, Anaconda.

BIGFORK, FLATHEAD CO., POPE JOHN PAUL II (1958) Rev. Msgr. Donald Shea; Deacons James Butts, Pastoral Assoc.; Anthony Martin.
Res.: P.O. Box 277, 59911. Tel: 406-837-4846; Fax: 406-755-5591. Email: johnpaul2@centurytel.net.
Church: 195 Coverdell Rd., 59911.
Catechesis/Religious Program—Deacon James Butts, D.R.E. Students 51.

BONNER, MISSOULA CO., ST. ANN (1940) Rev. Michael P. Poole.
Res.: P.O. Box 1008, 59823. Tel: 406-258-6815; Fax: 406-258-2943. Email: stannparishbonner@diocesehelena.org.
Catechesis/Religious Program—Colleen Frohlich, D.R.E. Students 32.
Mission—Living Water 3195 Hwy. 93 N., P.O. Box 995, Seeley Lake, Missoula Co. 59868.

BOULDER, JEFFERSON CO., ST. CATHERINE (1894) Rev. William Greytak.
Res.: 214 S. Elder St., P.O. Box 205, 59632. Tel: 406-225-3222; Fax: 406-225-9152.
Catechesis/Religious Program—Students 37.
Mission—St. John the Evangelist Boulder Valley, Jefferson Co.

BOZEMAN, GALLATIN CO.

1—HOLY ROSARY (1885) Rev. Leo J. Proxell.
Office: 220 W. Main St., P.O. Box 96, 59771-0096. Tel: 406-587-4581; Fax: 406-582-0248. Email: hrp@bridgeband.com.
Catechesis/Religious Program—Chris Cichon, Parish Elementary Coord.; Cecilia Hanson, Parish Youth Ministry Coord. Students 179.

2—RESURRECTION (1965), (Newman Parish) Rev. Valentine D. Zdilla; Diane Dwyer, Admin.
Office:—1725 S. 11th Ave., 59715. Tel: 406-586-9243; Fax: 406-586-2886. Email: resparadmin@bresnan.net.
Catechesis/Religious Program—Students 141.

BROWNING, GLACIER CO., CHURCH OF THE LITTLE FLOWER (1904) Rev. Edward Kohler; Deacons John Gobert; Ronald Running Crane.
Office: P.O. Box 529, 59417. Tel: 406-338-5775; Fax: 406-338-5506. Email: lfp@3rivers.net.
Church: 204 First St. N.W., 59417.
School—De La Salle Blackfeet Middle School, (Grades 4-8), P.O. Box 1489, 59417. Tel: 406-338-5290. Bro. Paul Ackerman, F.S.C., Pres.; Mr. Neal Wedum, Prin.
Catechesis/Religious Program—Toni Running Fisher, D.R.E. Students 81.
Mission—St. Mary, Queen of the World Babb, Glacier Co.
Mission—Sacred Heart Starr School.
Mission—Chapel of the Ascension East Glacier, Glacier Co.

BUTTE, SILVER BOW CO.

1—ST. ANN (1917) Rev. Thomas P. Haffey; Sr. Mary Jo McDonald, S.C.L., Pastoral Admin.; Deacon H. J. Johnson.
Res.: 2100 Farragut Ave., 59701. Tel: 406-723-4303; Fax: 406-723-5172. Email: stannparish@bresnan.net.
Catechesis/Religious Program—Rosie Stimatz-Richards, D.R.E. Students 61.

2—BUTTE CATHOLIC COMMUNITY NORTH, Includes Immaculate Conception, St. Joseph, and St. Patrick Parishes. See individual listings. Rev. Robert Hall.
Office & Res.: 102 S. Washington St., 59701. Tel: 406-723-5407; Fax: 406-782-8082. Email: bccn@diocesehelena.org.
Catechesis/Religious Program—Fax: 406-723-5408. Seaneen Prendergast, D.R.E. Students 26.

3—ST. HELENA (1921) Closed. 1966. For inquiries for parish records contact Butte Catholic Community North, Butte.

4—HOLY SAVIOR (1904) Closed. Closed in 1974. For inquiries for parish records contact Butte Catholic Community North, Butte.

5—HOLY SPIRIT (1978) Revs. William Dornbos; Thomas P. Haffey, Sacramental Min.; Deacon Dan McGrath, Pastoral Admin.
Office:—3930 East Lake St., 59701. Tel: 406-494-5078; Fax: 406-494-5726. Email: holyspirit@theglobal.net.
Catechesis/Religious Program—Students 47.

6—IMMACULATE CONCEPTION (1907), (Butte Catholic Community North) Rev. Robert Hall.
Office & Res.: 102 S. Washington, 59701. Tel: 406-723-5407; Fax: 406-723-5408.
Church: Western & Caledonia St., 59701.

7—ST. JOHN THE EVANGELIST (1917) Revs. Thomas P. Haffey, Pastoral Admin.; Frank Wright, S.M.A., Sacramental Min.
Office: 1500 Cobban St., 59701. Tel: 406-782-8349. Email: stjohnparish@bresnan.net.
Church: 1500 Majors Ave., 59701.
Catechesis/Religious Program—Kathy Walter, D.R.E.

8—ST. JOSEPH (1905), (Butte Catholic Community North) Rev. Robert Hall.
Office & Res.: 102 S. Washington, 59701. Tel: 406-723-5407 (Office); Fax: 406-723-5408.
Church: Utah & Second St., 59701.
Catechesis/Religious Program—Seaneen Prendergast, D.R.E. Students 84.

9—ST. MARY (1903) Closed. 1986. For inquiries for parish records contact Butte Catholic Community North, Butte.

10—ST. PATRICK (1881), (Butte Catholic Community North) Rev. Robert Hall.
Mailing Address: 102 S. Washington St., 59701.
Church: 329 W. Mercury, 59701. Tel: 406-723-5407; Fax: 406-723-5408.

11—SACRED HEART PARISH (1903) Closed. 1970. For inquiries for parish records contact Butte Catholic Community North, Butte.

CHOTEAU, TETON CO., ST. JOSEPH (1898) Rev. Dougald McCallum.
Res.: P.O. Box 640, 59422. Tel: 406-466-2961; Fax: 406-466-5157.
Church: 320 Main St., 59422.
Catechesis/Religious Program—Julienne Gramm, D.R.E. Students 38.

COLUMBIA FALLS, FLATHEAD CO., ST. RICHARD (1941) Rev. John P. Miller; Deacon Robert Pearce; Floyd McCubbins, Pastoral Assoc.; Doug Cordier, Pastoral Assoc.
Mailing Address: P.O. Box 2073, 59912. Church: 1210 9th St. W., 59912. Tel: 406-892-5142; Fax: 406-892-2147. Email: strichards@bresnan.net.
Catechesis/Religious Program—Students 54.
Mission— West Glacier, Flathead Co.
Station—Apgar

CONRAD, PONDERA CO., ST. MICHAEL (1909) Rev. Stanislaw Rog, Pastoral Admin.
Res.: 106 S. Maryland St., 59425. Tel: 406-278-7517; Fax: 406-278-9106. Email: stmike@3rivers.net.
Catechesis/Religious Program—Kathy Hauer, D.R.E. Students 83.

CUT BANK, GLACIER CO., ST. MARGARET (1914) Rev. Michael Drury.
Res.: 129 Second Ave., S.E., P.O. Box 207, 59427. Tel: 406-873-4413; Fax: 406-873-5002. Email: stmarg207@gmail.com.
Catechesis/Religious Program—Juanita Meeks, D.R.E. Students 42.

DEER LODGE, POWELL CO., IMMACULATE CONCEPTION (1911) Rev. Robert G. Porter; Chris Dubay, Pastoral Assoc.
Res.: 605 Clark St., P.O. Box 786, 59722. Tel: 406-846-1444; Fax: 406-846-1999. Email: icchurch_2@msn.com.
Catechesis/Religious Program—Karen Phillips, D.R.E. Students 16.

DILLON, BEAVERHEAD CO., ST. ROSE OF LIMA (1901) Rev. Herbert J. Pins.
Office: 226 S. Atlantic St., 59725. Tel: 406-683-4391; Fax: 406-683-6244. Email: strosedillon@gmail.com.
Catechesis/Religious Program—Paul Rust, D.R.E.; Denice Rust, D.R.E. Students 36.
Mission—St. John The Apostle Melrose, Silver Bow Co.
Mission—Our Lady of Wisdom Wisdom, Beaverhead Co.
Station— Lima, Beaverhead Co.

DRUMMOND, GRANITE CO., ST. MICHAEL (1919) Vickie Burgmeier, Parish Admin.
Res.: P.O. Box 329, 59832. Tel: 406-288-3463. Email: vburgmeier@blackfoot.net.
Catechesis/Religious Program—Students 16.
Mission—St. Mary Goldcreek, Powell Co.

DUTTON, TETON CO., ST. WILLIAM (1962) Rev. Stanislaw Rog, Pastoral Admin.; Frank Loch, Pastoral Assoc.; Marie Loch, Pastoral Assoc.
Church: 20 1st Ave., N.E., P.O. Box 18, 59433. Tel: 406-476-3327.
Catechesis/Religious Program—Students 13.
Mission—Guardian Angel Power, Teton Co.

EAST HELENA, LEWIS AND CLARK CO., SS. CYRIL AND METHODIUS (1907) Rev. Thomas M. O'Donnell; Deacon Robert J. Miller.
Res.: 120 W. Riggs St., P.O. Box 1110, 59635. Tel: 406-227-5334; Fax: 406-227-5891. Email: denice@sscyril.org.
Catechesis/Religious Program—Marie Moran, D.R.E. Students 203.
Mission—Our Lady of the Lake Canyon Ferry, Lewis and Clark Co.
Mission—St. John's Clancy, Jefferson Co.

EUREKA, LINCOLN CO., OUR LADY OF MERCY (1916) Rev. Gregory Lively; Deacon Dan Casazza, Pastoral Admin.
Res.: 500 Dewey Ave., P.O. Box 626, 59917. Tel: 406-297-2118; Fax: 406-297-5247. Email: olm@interbel.net.
Catechesis/Religious Program—Students 35.

FAIRFIELD, TETON CO., ST. JOHN THE EVANGELIST (1941) Rev. Dougald McCallum.
Res.: 519 First Ave. S., P.O. Box 397, 59436. Tel: 406-466-2961; Fax: 406-466-5157.
Catechesis/Religious Program—Cindy Luoma, D.R.E. Students 20.
Mission—St. Matthias Augusta, Lewis and Clark Co.

FRENCHTOWN, MISSOULA CO., ST. JOHN THE BAPTIST (1884) [CEM] Rev. Kevin Christofferson.
Mailing Address: P.O. Box 329, 59834.
Res.: 16680 Main St., P.O. Box 329, 59834. Tel: 406-626-4492; Fax: 406-626-1970. Email: rhoward@montana.com.
Catechesis/Religious Program—Students 56.
Mission—St. Mary Queen of Heaven Superior, Mineral Co.
Mission—St. Albert the Great Alberton, Mineral Co.

HAMILTON, RAVALLI CO., ST. FRANCIS (1896) Rev. John J. Darragh; Sr. Margaret Hogan, S.C.L., Pastoral Assoc.
Mailing Address: P.O. Box 593, 59840.
Res.: 411 S. 5th St., 59840. Tel: 406-363-1385; Fax: 406-363-1451. Email: francis@montana.com.
Catechesis/Religious Program—Sara Morin, D.R.E. Students 114.
Mission—St. Philip Benizi 312 Miles Ave., Darby, Ravalli Co. 59829.

HARLOWTON, WHEATLAND CO., ST. JOSEPH (1909) Rev. Jeffrey M. Benusa.
Res.: 26 Third St., N.W., Box 286, 59036. Tel: 406-632-5538. Email: jbenusa@diocesehelena.org.
Catechesis/Religious Program—Kristi Lane, D.R.E. Students 16.
Mission—Immaculate Conception Judith Gap, Wheatland Co.
Mission—Blessed Sacrament Shawmut, Wheatland Co.

HEART BUTTE, GLACIER CO., ST. ANNE (BLACKFEET RESERVATION) (1911) Rev. Daniel Powers, S.J.; Bev Bullshoe, Pastoral Assoc.; Deacon Melvin Rutherford, Pastoral Assoc.
Mailing Address: P.O. Box 160, 59448. Tel: 406-338-2312; Fax: 406-338-2362. Email: dpowers@3rivers.net.
Mission—Holy Family Mission [CEM], Glacier Co.

HELMVILLE, POWELL CO., ST. THOMAS (1889) [CEM] Rev. John Robertson.
Res.: 108 Main St., P.O. Box 90, 59843. Tel: 406-793-5697. Email: hlm5843@blackfoot.net.
Catechesis/Religious Program—Maureen Mannix, D.R.E. Students 30.
Mission—St. Jude's P.O. Box 802, Lincoln, Lewis and Clark Co. 59639.

KALISPELL, FLATHEAD CO.

1—ST. MATTHEW (1895) Rev. Victor E. Langhans.
Office: 602 S. Main St., 59901. Tel: 406-752-6788; Fax: 406-756-8248. Email: parish@stmatthewskalispell.org.
Catechesis/Religious Program—Kristen Fausey, D.R.E. Students 20.

2—RISEN CHRIST (1978) Rev. Rudolph Bullman.
Res.: 65 W. Evergreen Dr., 59901. Tel: 406-752-4219; Fax: 406-752-4226. Email: rcparish@montanasky.us.
Catechesis/Religious Program—Cristy Ghekiere, D.R.E. Students 110.

LIBBY, LINCOLN CO., ST. JOSEPH (1911) Rev. Jozef Perehubka (Poland).
Res.: 719 Utah Ave., P.O. Box 1467, 59923. Tel: 406-293-4322; Fax: 406-293-7231. Email: stjosephparishlibby@montanasky.us.
Catechesis/Religious Program—Helen Barnett, D.R.E. Students 36.
Mission—Immaculate Conception Troy, Lincoln Co.

MISSOULA, MISSOULA CO.

1—ST. ANTHONY (1921) Rev. Gary W. Reller; Terry Jimmerson, Pastoral Assoc.; Deacon Van Wolverton.
Office: 217 Tremont St., 59801. Tel: 406-543-3129; Fax: 406-549-6009. Email: office@saintanthonyparish.com.
Catechesis/Religious Program— Robin L. Hall, D.R.E. Students 65.

2—BLESSED TRINITY PARISH (1971) Rev. Edward Hislop; Sr. Helen Dobell, M.M., Pastoral Assoc.; Deacon Thomas McCarthy.
Office: 1475 Eaton St., 59801. Tel: 406-721-2405; Fax: 406-721-0025. Email: blessedtrinity@montana.com.
Catechesis/Religious Program—Students 41.
Mission—Spirit of Christ 5475 Farm Ln., Lolo, Missoula Co. 59847.

3—CHRIST THE KING (1966), (Newman Parish) Rev. Jeffrey M. Fleming; Sr. Doris Faber, O.P., Pastoral Assoc.; Suzanne A. Monroe, Office Mgr.
Office: 1400 Gerald Ave., 59801. Tel: 406-728-3845; Fax: 406-829-8797. Email: ctkccm@christthekingccm.org.
Catechesis/Religious Program—Patti Cassidy, D.R.E. Students 91.

4—ST. FRANCIS XAVIER (1881) Revs. Richard Perry, S.J.; Sean Raftis, S.J.; Deacons Michael Bloomdahl, Parish Admin.; Carlton Quamme. In Res., Revs. Thomas F. Healy, S.J.; George J. Dumais, S.J.
Office:—420 W. Pine St., 59802. Tel: 406-542-0321; Fax: 406-327-8537. Email: sfx@montanadsl.net.
Catechesis/Religious Program—Debra Johnson, D.R.E. Students 83.

5—HOLY FAMILY (1972) Closed. For inquiries for parish records contact the chancery.

PHILIPSBURG, GRANITE CO., ST. PHILIP (1892) Vickie Burgmeier, Parish Admin.
Mailing Address: P.O. Box 329, Drummond, 59832.
Church: 308 W. Kearney, 59858. Tel: 406-241-3604.
Catechesis/Religious Program—Students 15.

PLAINS, SANDERS CO., ST. JAMES (1889) Rev. Kenneth E. Fortney; Deacon Lynn F. McAtee.
Res.: 109 W. Meany St., P.O. Box 745, 59859. Tel: 406-826-3668. Email: sccc@blackfoot.net.
Catechesis/Religious Program—Tel: 406-741-3026 (Sacred Heart Mission).
Mission—Sacred Heart Hot Springs, Sanders Co.

POLSON, LAKE CO., IMMACULATE CONCEPTION (1909) [CEM 3] Rev. James Connor; Deacons Wesley Vert; Daniel Gullotta.
Res. & Church: 1002 4th Ave. E., P.O. Box 1477, 59860. Tel: 406-883-2506 (Office); Fax: 406-883-4649. Email: icparish59860@gmail.com.
Catechesis/Religious Program—Marjorie Shrider, D.R.E. Students 50.

RONAN, LAKE CO., SACRED HEART (1911) Rev. James Connor; Sr. Barbara Brown, O.P., Pastoral Assoc.
Res.: 35933 Round Butte Rd. W., 59864. Tel: 406-676-4511; Fax: 406-676-4515. Email: sacredheart@ronan.net.
Catechesis/Religious Program—Students 31.
Mission—St. Joseph's Charlo, Lake Co.

ST. IGNATIUS, LAKE CO., ST. IGNATIUS MISSION (1854) Rev. Andrew Maddock, S.J.; Sr. Mary Stauder, O.P., Pastoral Assoc.
Res.: P.O. Box 667, 59865. Tel: 406-745-2768; Fax: 406-745-0010. Email: mission7@blackfoot.net.
Catechesis/Religious Program—Students 134.
Mission—Sacred Heart 112 Taelman, Arlee, Lake Co. 59821. Tel: 406-726-3450; Fax: 406-726-3540.
Mission—St. John Berchman's Jocko, Lake Co.

SHELBY, TOOLE CO., ST. WILLIAM (1924) Rev. Michael Drury; Diane Abrahamson, D.R.E.; Lore Sisk, D.R.E.
Res.: 531 Main St., 59474. Tel: 406-434-2988; Fax: 406-434-9133. Email: saintwm@3rivers.net.
Catechesis/Religious Program—Students 73.
Mission—St. Thomas Aquinas (1917) 120 1st St., S., Sunburst, 59482.

SHERIDAN, MADISON CO., MADISON COUNTY CATHOLIC COMMUNITY, Comprised of St. Mary of the Assumption, Laurin; St. Joseph, Sheridan; and St. Patrick, Ennis. Deacon Andrew Dorrington, Pastoral Admin.
Res.: 105 Poppleton, P.O. Box 17, 59749. Tel: 406-842-5588; Fax: 406-842-7433. Email: kootenai@catholic.org.
Catechesis/Religious Program—Margaret Stecker, D.R.E. Students 28.

STEVENSVILLE, RAVALLI CO., ST. MARY (1842) [CEM] Rev. Matthew P. Huber.
Res.: 333 Charlos St., 59870. Tel: 406-777-5257; Fax: 406-777-1032. Email: st_marys_stevi@g.com.
Catechesis/Religious Program—Students 96.
Mission—St. Joseph Florence, Ravalli Co.

SWAN VALLEY, LAKE CO., OUR LADY OF SWAN VALLEY MISSION Michelle Jenkins, Pastoral Assoc.
Mailing Address: *The Sycamore Tree*, 21592 Sycamore Tree Ln., Swan Lake, 59911. Tel: 406-754-2429; Fax: 406-754-2429. Email: sycamoretree@blackfoot.net.
Church: 201 E. Beck Rd., Condon, 59826.

THOMPSON FALLS, SANDERS CO., ST. WILLIAM (1955) Rev. Kenneth E. Fortney; Deacon Ronald Kazmierczak.
Res.: 416 Preston Ave., P.O. Box 186, 59873. Tel: 406-827-4433; Fax: 406-827-4433. Email: stwilliam@blackfoot.net.
Catechesis/Religious Program—Students 8.

Mission— Noxon.

THREE FORKS, GALLATIN CO., HOLY FAMILY (1886) Rev. Eric C. Gilbaugh; Deacon Robert Lane.
Church: 104 E. Birch St., P.O. Box 99, 59752. Tel: 406-285-3592; Fax: 406-388-2321.
Catechesis/Religious Program—Students 106.
Mission—Valley of Flowers 609 Quaw Blvd., Belgrade, Gallatin Co. 59714.

TOWNSEND, BROADWATER CO., HOLY CROSS (1903) Rev. Joseph L. Byrne.
Res.: 101 S. Walnut, P.O. Box 610, 59644. Tel: 406-266-4811. Email: holycrossparish@mt.net.
Catechesis/Religious Program—Students 37.

VALIER, PONDERA CO., ST. FRANCIS (1909) Rev. Michael Drury; Mary Jean Brophy, Pastoral Assoc.
Res.: 616 4th St., P.O. Box 338, 59486. Tel: 406-279-3327.
Catechesis/Religious Program— Leslie Majerus, D.R.E. Students 52.
Mission—Holy Cross Dupuyer, Pondera Co.

WALKERVILLE, SILVER BOW CO., ST. LAWRENCE O'TOOLE (1896) Closed. 1986. For inquiries for parish records contact Butte Catholic Community North, Butte.

WEST YELLOWSTONE, GALLATIN CO., OUR LADY OF THE PINES Rev. Joseph B. Oblinger (Retired); Sr. Patricia Toeckes, S.C.L., Pastoral Admin.
Res.: 437 Madison Ave., P.O. Box 577, 59758. Tel: 406-646-7755. Email: ptoeckes@mcn.net.
Catechesis/Religious Program—Students 11.
Mission—St. Joseph of Big Sky Big Sky, Gallatin Co.

WHITE SULPHUR SPRINGS, MEAGHER CO., ST. BARTHOLOMEW (1916) Rev. Jeffrey M. Benusa; AnnaLee Kiff, Pastoral Assoc.
Res.: 407 Second Ave., S.E., P.O. Box 422, 59645. Tel: 406-547-3737. Email: jbenusa@diocesehelena.org.
Catechesis/Religious Program—Gail Weitz, D.R.E. Students 18.

WHITEFISH, FLATHEAD CO., ST. CHARLES BORROMEO (1890) Rev. Patrick G. Patton.
Res.: 230 Baker Ave., P.O. Box 128, 59937. Tel: 406-862-2051; Fax: 406-862-9897. Email: stcharles@bresnan.net.
Catechesis/Religious Program—Lynn Beck, D.R.E. Students 58.

WHITEHALL, JEFFERSON CO., ST. TERESA OF AVILA (1911) Rev. Daniel Driscoll.
Res.: 107 Second Ave. E., P.O. Box 430, 59759. Tel: 406-287-3893; Fax: 406-287-9213. Email: stteresa6@q.com.
Catechesis/Religious Program—Students 38.
Mission—Notre Dame Twin Bridges, Jefferson Co.

DIOCESAN MISSIONS

GUATEMALA, SANTO TOMAS Rev. James Hazelton; Sisters Mary Waddell, B.V.M.; Anna Priester, B.V.M., D.R.E.; Sheila McShane, Clinic Dir.
Guatemula Missions, P.O. Box 1729, 59624.

HELENA, LEWIS AND CLARK CO.
GUATEMALA MISSION MEDICAL FUND—P.O. Box 1729, 59624.

Chaplains of Public Institutions

HELENA. *U.S. Veteran's Hospital*, Fort Harrison, 59626. Served by Helena Area Parishes.

BOULDER. *Boulder River School and Hospital*. Rev. William Greytak. Attended from St. Catherine, Boulder.

DEER LODGE. *Montana State Prison*. Attended from Immaculate Conception Parish, Deer Lodge. Rev. Robert G. Porter.

WARM SPRINGS. *Warm Springs State Hospital*. Rev. Herbert J. Pins.

Special Assignments:
Revs.—
Dornbos, William, 100 E. Broadway, Butte, 59701.
Dumais, George J., S.J., Dir., Loyola Sacred Heart High School, 1700 Madeline, Missoula, 59801.
Malnar, Stan, 4220 W. Fremont Rd., Spokane, WA 99204.
Robertson, John W., Vicar for Canonical Svcs., Chancellor & Judicial Vicar, P.O. Box 1729, 59624.

On Duty Outside the Diocese:
Rev. Msgr.—
McCarthy, John F., P.A., Oblates of Wisdom, P.O. Box 13230, St. Louis, MO 63157.
Revs.—
Driscoll, Michael, Notre Dame University, Department of Theology, South Bend, IN 46617.
Flynn, Thomas, Emory University, 1278 Oakdale Rd., N.E., Atlanta, GA 30307.
Hazelton, James, Santo Tomas La Union, Departmento Suchitepuez 10017 Guatemala.

Military Chaplains:
Rev.—
Diphe, Juan M., U.S. Air Force

Health Leave:
Rev.—
Moran, Joseph P., 4307 Gharrett, Missoula, 59803.

Leave of Absence:
Rev.—
Popowski, Stanley, P.O. Box 1729, 59624-1729.

Retired:
Rev. Msgrs.—
Brown, Anthony M., 30 Penny Ln., Butte, 59701.
Harrington, Joseph D., 1726 Cannon St., 59601.
Revs.—
Burke, Gregory, 105 Rampart Dr., Butte, 59701.
Courtney, Edward, 242 Waterford Dr., Butte, 59701.
Finnegan, Joseph, P.O. Box 503, Whitehall, 59759.
Hannigan, Raymond, 848 S. 79th Pl., Mesa, AZ 85208.
Hogan, James J., 1400 Gerald Ave., Missoula, 59801.
Hunthausen, John F., Carroll College, 59625.
Lowney, Jeremiah, 1601 N. Benton Ave., 59625.
Lynam, Gerald J., 915 Saddle Dr., #115, 59601.
McGurk, Patrick C., 534 Gold Creek Rd., Gold Creek, 59733.
Murray, John E., 901 Pennsylvania Ave., Deer Lodge, 59722.
Noonan, Robert C., 720A Missy's Way, Missoula, 59801.
O'Sullivan, Sarsfield, 410 N. Western Ave., Butte, 59701.
Oblinger, Joseph B., 2400 Durston Rd., #37, Bozeman, 59718.
Okorn, Dusan A., Sycamore Tree, Swan Lake, 59911.
Roman, Charles, 2250 Merganser Dr., Kalispell, 59901.
Smith, Michael M., 4309 Gharrett St., Missoula, 59803.
Sodja, Richard H., 915 Saddle Dr., 59601.
Strom, Charles W., 1001 River Lake Pkwy., Apt. 233, Whitefish, 59937.
Stupca, Edward L., 100 E. Broadway, Butte, 59701.
Sullivan, James M., 1100 Le Grande Cannon Blvd., 59601.
Sullivan, Jeremiah, 1601 N. Benton, 59625.
Tallman, Stephen, 5630 Lower Woodchuck Rd., Florence, 59833.
Wang, John, 425 Ford St., Missoula, 59801.

Permanent Deacons:
Bloomdahl, Michael, St. Francis Xavier, Missoula
Bremner, Robert, Little Flower, Browning
Britton, Michael, (Retired)
Butts, James, Pope John Paul II, Bigfork
Casazza, Dan, Our Lady of Mercy, Eureka
Dorrington, Andrew, Madison County Catholic Community
Duvernay, J. Anthony, (Retired)
Fournier, Ronald, St. John Parish, Butte
Fraser, Randall, Our Lady of the Valley, Helena
Gobert, John, Little Flower, Browning
Gullotta, Daniel, Immaculate Conception, Polson
Johnson, H. J., St. Ann's, Butte
Kazmierczak, Ronald, St. William, Thompson Falls
Kuhl, Gerald, Cathedral of St. Helena
Lane, Robert, Holy Family, Three Forks
Marks, Donald, Holy Cross, Townsend
Martin, Anthony, Pope John Paul II, Bigfork
McAtee, Lynn F., St. James, Plains
McCarthy, Thomas, Blessed Trinity, Missoula
McGrath, Daniel, Holy Spirit, Butte
Miller, Richard, Helena
Miller, Robert J., Sts. Cyril and Methodius, East Helena
Pearce, Robert, St. Richard, Columbia Falls
Quamme, Carlton, St. Francis Xavier, Missoula
Running Crane, Ronald, Little Flower, Browning
Rutherford, Melvin, Little Flower, Browning
Vert, Wesley, Immaculate Conception, Polson
Wolverton, Van, St. Anthony, Missoula

INSTITUTIONS LOCATED IN THE DIOCESE

[A] SEMINARIES, DIOCESAN

HELENA. *Carroll College*, 1601 N. Benton Ave., 59625. Tel: 406-447-4300; Fax: 406-447-4533. Email: mlenneman@carroll.edu. Rev. Marc J. Lenneman, Dir. Diocesan Pre-Seminary Prog.

[B] COLLEGES AND UNIVERSITIES

HELENA. *Carroll College* (1909) 1601 N. Benton Ave., 59625. Tel: 406-447-4300; Fax: 406-447-4533. Web: www.carroll.edu. Rev. Marc J. Lenneman, Chap. & Campus Min.; Dr. Thomas Trebon, Pres.; Ms. Lynn Etchart, Vice Pres. Finance & Admin.; Mr. Thomas J. McCarvel, Vice Pres. Community Rels.; Dr. James Hardwick, Vice Pres. Student Life; Dr. Paula McNutt, Sr. Vice Pres. Academic Affairs & Dean College; Colleen Dunne, Dir. Campus Ministry Programs; Rev. Daniel B. Shea; Christian Frazza, Librarian, Acting Dir. Four-year Diocesan College of Liberal Arts and Sciences. Priests 2; Lay Professors 81; Students 1,428; Total Staff 144. In Res. Rev. Msgr. Joseph D. Harrington (Retired); Revs. John F. Hunthausen (Retired); Richard H. Sodja (Retired).

[C] HIGH SCHOOLS, DIOCESAN

BUTTE. *Central High School* (1924) 9 S. Idaho St., 59701. Tel: 406-782-6761; Fax: 406-723-3873. Email: tim.norbeck@buttecentralschools.org. Timothy Norbeck, Prin. Lay Teachers 18; Students 129.

MISSOULA. *Loyola Sacred Heart High School* (Missoula Catholic Schools), 320 Edith St., 59801. Tel: 406-549-6101; Fax: 406-542-1432. Email: info@missoulacatholicschools.org. Web: www.missoulacatholicschools.org. Patrick Haggarty, Ed.D., Supt., Schools; Jeremy Beck, Prin.; Patrice Schwenk, Librarian. Priests 1; Lay Teachers 20; Students 205.

[D] SCHOOLS, ELEMENTARY

BROWNING. *De La Salle Blackfeet School*, (Grades 4-8), P.O. Box 1489, 59417. Tel: 406-338-5290; Fax: 406-338-7900. Email: info@dlsbs.org. Web: www.dlsbs.org. Bro. Paul Ackerman, F.S.C., Pres.; Mr. Neal Wedum, Prin. Brothers 2; Lay Teachers 8; Students 63.

BUTTE. *Butte Central Elementary Junior High School*, (Grades PreK-8), 1100 Delaware, 59701. Tel: 406-782-4500; Fax: 406-723-4845. Email: carolyn.trudnowski@buttecentralschools.org. Carolyn Trudnowski, Prin. Sisters 1; Lay Teachers 21; Students 267.
After School Care Students (Ages 5-12), Tel: 406-782-4500; Fax: 406-723-4845.
Central Junior High School, (Grades 6-8), 1100 Delaware, 59701. Tel: 406-782-4500; Fax: 406-723-4845. Carolyn Trudnowski, Prin.; Colleen Stillwagon, Librarian. Sisters 1; Lay Teachers 18; Students 129.

KALISPELL. *St. Matthew School* (1917) (Grades PreSchool-8), 602 S. Main St., 59901. Tel: 406-752-6303; Fax: 406-756-8248. Email: office@stmattsaints.org. Web: www.digisys.net. Joanna Eichner, Prin.; Myrna Matulevich, Librarian. Clergy 1; Sisters 1; Lay Teachers 27; Preschool (Age 4) 59; Students 314.
Day Care Center Tel: 406-756-6807; Fax: 406-756-8248. Marlene Stephens, Dir. (Ages 2-6) Students 60.

MISSOULA. *St. Joseph Elementary School* (1873) (Grades K-8), (Missoula Catholic Schools), 503 Edith St., 59801. Tel: 406-549-1290; Fax: 406-543-4034. Email: rhyland@missoulacatholicschools.org. Web: www.missoulacatholicschools.org. Rich Hyland, Prin.; Jennifer Hossack, Librarian. Religious 1; Lay Teachers 21; Students 319.
Child Care Center Tel: 406-549-1290; Fax: 406-543-4034. Evalie Hankinson, Dir. (Ages 2-12) Students 45.

[E] GENERAL HOSPITALS

BUTTE. *St. James Health Care, Sisters of Charity of Leavenworth Health System*, 400 S. Clark St., 59701. Tel: 406-723-2500; Fax: 406-723-2443. Web: www.sj-mt.org. P.O. Box 3300, 59702. Charles Wright, CEO; Sr. Mary Agnes Hogan, S.C.L., Dir. Spiritual Care & Mission Svcs.; Rev. Gregory Burke, Chap. & Pastoral Care (Retired). Bed Capacity 100; Sisters of Charity of Leavenworth 2; Lay Staff 575; Patients Assisted Annually 86,122.

MISSOULA. *St. Patrick Hospital and Health Sciences Center, Sisters of Providence of Montana Corporation*, 500 W. Broadway, 59802. Tel: 406-543-7271; Fax: 406-329-5693. Email: lsconce@saintpatrick.org. Web: www.saintpatrick.org. P.O. Box 4587, 59806. Jeff Fee, Pres. & CEO; Rev. Frank McCormick; Sr. Elizabeth Olsen, B.V.M., Pastoral Care. Sisters 1; Lay Staff 1,600; Bed Capacity 237; Patients Assisted Annually 160,000.

POLSON. *St. Joseph Hospital Corporation* (1916) #6 Thirteenth Ave. E., P.O. Box 1010, 59860. Tel: 406-883-5377; Fax: 406-883-8488. Email:

dwhealon@saintjoes.org. Web: saintjoes.org. Steve McNeece, CEO; Rev. James Connor, Chap.; Deacon Wes Vert; John Payne, Pastoral Care. Bed Capacity 22; Lay Staff 213; Patients Assisted Annually 38,090.

[F] HOUSES OF PRAYER

SWAN LAKE. *The Sycamore Tree Contemplative Prayer Center*, 21592 Sycamore Tree Ln., 59911. Tel: 406-754-2429; Fax: 406-754-2429. Email: sycamoretree@blackfoot.net. Michelle Jenkins, Contact Person.

[G] NEWMAN CHAPLAINS

BOZEMAN. *Montana State University* , (Newman Program), Office: 1725 S. Eleventh, 59715-4218. Tel: 406-586-9243; Fax: 406-586-2886. Web: www.resurrectionbozeman.org. Rev. Valentine D. Zdilla.

BUTTE. *Montana College of Mineral Science and Technology* Office: 102 S. Washington St., 59701. Tel: 406-723-5407; Fax: 406-723-5408. Email: bccn@diocesehelena.org. Web: www.diocesehelena.org. Rev. Robert Hall, Chap.; Seaneen Prendergast, Campus Min.

DILLON. *University of Montana - Western* 226 S. Atlantic St., 59725. Tel: 406-683-4391; Fax: 406-683-6244. Email: strosedillon@gmail.com. Rev. Herbert J. Pins.

MISSOULA. *University of Montana* , (Christ the King Parish), 1400 Gerald Ave., 59801-4230. Tel: 406-728-3845; Fax: 406-829-8797. Email: ctkccm@christthekingccm.org. Web: www.christthekingccm.org. Rev. Jeffrey M. Fleming; Sr. Doris Faber, O.P., Pastoral Assoc.; Suzanne A. Monroe, Admin. Asst.

[H] FOUNDATIONS

HELENA. *Cathedral of St. Helena Historic Preservation Trust*, 530 N. Ewing St., 59601-4001. Tel: 406-442-5825; Fax: 406-449-5113. Terry B. Cosgrove, Chmn.

BUTTE. *St. James Healthcare Foundation*, 425 W. Porphyry, 59701. Tel: 406-782-5640; Fax: 406-782-5643. Email: kevin.dennehy@sjh-mt.org. Kevin P. Dennehy, Exec. Dir.

MISSOULA. *St. Patrick Hospital and Health Foundation*, 500 W. Broadway, 59806. Tel: 406-329-5640; Fax: 406-329-5693. Email: lankford@stpatrick.org. Kelly Williams, Pres.; Joel Lankford, Exec. Dir.

[I] MISCELLANEOUS

BROWNING. *St. Vincent de Paul Thrift Store*, 112 First Ave., N.W., P.O. Box 974, 59417. Tel: 406-338-5403. Mona Kipling, Mgr.

BUTTE. *Central Education Foundation*, P.O. Box 634, 59703-0634. Tel: 406-723-6706; Fax: 406-782-4026. Email: buttecentraldev@yahoo.com. Don Peoples Jr., Exec. Dir.

**Maternal Life International* (1996) 326A S. Jackson St., 59701-8804. Tel: 406-782-1719; Fax: 406-782-1719 (Call First). Email: usacares@in-tch.com. Web: www.MLIonline.org. Dr. George Mulcaire-Jones, Medical Dir. & Bd. Pres.; Cortlandt L. Freeman, Exec. Dir.

MISSOULA. *Loyola Sacred Heart High School Foundation* (1960) Serving Missoula Catholic Schools., 300 Edith St., 59801. Tel: 406-728-2367; Fax: 406-542-9900. Email: jgeer@missoulacatholicschools.org. Tom Stergios, Pres.; Judy Geer, Exec. Dir.

STEVENSVILLE. *Historic St. Mary's Mission*, P.O. Box 211, 59870-0211. Tel: 406-777-5734; Fax: 406-777-5734. Email: stmary@cybernet1.com. Web: saintmarysmission.org. Colleen Meyer, Dir.

RELIGIOUS INSTITUTES OF MEN REPRESENTED IN THE DIOCESE

For further details refer to the corresponding bracketed number in the Religious Institutes of Men or Women section.

[0330]—*Brothers of the Christian Schools* (Midwest Prov.)—F.S.C.

[0690]—*Jesuit Fathers and Brothers* (Oregon Prov.)—S.J.

RELIGIOUS INSTITUTES OF WOMEN REPRESENTED IN THE DIOCESE

[1070-03]—*Dominican Sisters*—O.P.

[1070-11]—*Dominican Sisters*—O.P.

[1070-13]—*Dominican Sisters*—O.P.

[2575]—*Institute of the Sisters of Mercy of the Americas* (Cedar Rapids, IA)—R.S.M.

[0440]—*Sisters of Charity of Cincinnati, Ohio*—S.C.

[0480]—*Sisters of Charity of Leavenworth, Kansas*—S.C.L.

[0430]—*Sisters of Charity of the Blessed Virgin Mary*—B.V.M.

[3550]—*Sisters of Providence - Mother Joseph Province*

[3840]—*Sisters of St. Joseph of Carondelet*—C.S.J.

[1720]—*Sisters of the Third Order Regular of St. Francis of the Congregation of Our Lady of Lourdes*—O.S.F.

DIOCESAN CEMETERIES

HELENA. *Resurrection Cemetery*, 3700 N. Montana Ave., P.O. Box 5029, 59604. Tel: 406-442-1782; Fax: 406-443-7036. Mr. Scott Fitzpatrick, Dir. Cemeteries; Kathy Redd, Office Mgr.

Resurrection Cemetery Association, 3700 N. Montana Ave., P.O. Box 5029, 59604. Tel: 406-442-1782; Fax: 406-443-7036. Mr. Scott Fitzpatrick, Exec. Dir.; Kathy Redd, Office Mgr. (Corporate Name for Diocesan Cemeteries)

BUTTE. *Holy Cross Cemetery*, Office: 4700 Harrison Ave., 59701. Tel: 406-494-3812. Kenny Martz, Mgr.

St. Patrick Cemetery, Office: 4700 Harrison Ave., 59701. Tel: 406-494-3812. Kenny Martz, Mgr.

MISSOULA. *St. Mary Cemetery*, Office: 641 Turner St., 59802. Tel: 406-543-7951. Mike Hamlin, Mgr.

NECROLOGY

† Fenlon, Thomas J., (Retired)—Died April 21, 2009

† Gilmore, Raymond V., (Retired)—Died May 25, 2009

† Koenig, Bernard, (Retired)—Died Dec. 28, 2009

An asterisk (*) denotes an organization that has established tax-exempt status directly with the IRS and is not covered by the USCCB Group Ruling.

Diocese of Honolulu

(Dioecesis Honoluluensis)

Most Reverend

CLARENCE R. SILVA

Bishop of Honolulu; ordained May 2, 1975; appointed Bishop of Honolulu May 17, 2005; ordained July 21, 2005. *Bishop's Office: 1184 Bishop St., Honolulu, HI 96813.*

Chancery Office: 1184 Bishop St., Honolulu, HI 96813. Tel: 808-585-3300; Fax: 808-521-8428.

Web: www.catholichawaii.org

Square Miles 6,435.

Corporate Title: The Roman Catholic Church In The State Of Hawaii.

Comprises all of the Hawaiian Islands.

The Hawaiian Islands were annexed as a Territory of the United States in 1898. Hawaii became the 50th State of the Union on August 21, 1959.

In 1826, a Prefecture-Apostolic was erected for the Hawaiian Islands, then called Sandwich Islands, and entrusted to the Fathers of the Sacred Hearts of Jesus and Mary (Picpus). The Very Rev. Alexis Bachelot, SS.CC., was the first Prefect-Apostolic. He arrived with his companions at Honolulu on the 7th of July, 1827. In 1844, the Islands were erected a Vicariate. Diocese erected Sept. 10, 1941.

For legal titles of parishes and diocesan institutions, consult the Chancery Office.

STATISTICAL OVERVIEW

Personnel	
Bishop	1
Priests: Diocesan Active in Diocese	38
Priests: Diocesan Active Outside Diocese	7
Priests: Retired, Sick or Absent	13
Number of Diocesan Priests	58
Religious Priests in Diocese	58
Total Priests in Diocese	116
Extern Priests in Diocese	27
Ordinations:	
Diocesan Priests	1
Religious Priests	1
Permanent Deacons	62
Permanent Deacons in Diocese	67
Total Brothers	33
Total Sisters	165
Parishes	
Parishes	66
With Resident Pastor:	
Resident Diocesan Priests	36
Resident Religious Priests	26
Without Resident Pastor:	
Administered by Priests	4
Missions	24
Professional Ministry Personnel:	
Brothers	2
Sisters	8
Lay Ministers	51
Welfare	
Health Care Centers	2
Total Assisted	1,687
Day Care Centers	1
Total Assisted	440
Specialized Homes	1
Total Assisted	29
Special Centers for Social Services	1
Total Assisted	242
Educational	
Seminaries, Diocesan	2
Students from This Diocese	2
Diocesan Students in Other Seminaries	6
Total Seminarians	8
Colleges and Universities	1
Total Students	2,688
High Schools, Diocesan and Parish	3
Total Students	893
High Schools, Private	4
Total Students	2,107
Elementary Schools, Diocesan and Parish	23
Total Students	5,705
Elementary Schools, Private	4
Total Students	772
Catechesis/Religious Education:	
High School Students	2,365
Elementary Students	5,039
Total Students under Catholic Instruction	19,577
Teachers in the Diocese:	
Priests	5
Brothers	12
Sisters	46
Lay Teachers	846
Vital Statistics	
Receptions into the Church:	
Infant Baptism Totals	2,542
Minor Baptism Totals	163
Adult Baptism Totals	121
Received into Full Communion	210
First Communions	1,774
Confirmations	1,097
Marriages:	
Catholic	403
Interfaith	132
Total Marriages	535
Deaths	1,603
Total Catholic Population	237,206
Total Population	1,285,498

Former Prelates—Very Revs. ALEXIS BACHELOT, SS.CC., Pref. Apost.; died Dec. 5, 1837; LOUIS MAIGRET, SS.CC. ord. Sept. 23, 1828; Pref. Apost. till 1844; Rt. Revs. VINCENT FERRIER DUBOIZE, SS.CC., resigned before he was consecrated; LOUIS MAIGRET, SS.CC., ord. Sept. 23, 1828; Titular Bishop of Arathia; consecrated at Santiago, Nov. 28, 1847; died June 11, 1882; HERMAN KOECKEMANN, SS.CC., ord. May 31, 1862; Titular Bishop of Olba; cons. at San Francisco Aug. 21, 1881; died Feb. 22, 1892; GULSTAN ROPERT, SS.CC., ord. May 26, 1866; Titular Bishop of Panopolis; cons. at San Francisco, Sept. 25, 1892; died Jan. 4, 1903; LIBERT H. BOEYNAEMS, SS.CC., ord. Sept. 11, 1881; Titular Bishop of Zeugma; cons. at San Francisco, July 25, 1903; died May 13, 1926; Most Revs. STEPHEN P. ALENCASTRE, SS.CC., ord. April 5, 1902; Titular Bishop of Arabissus; cons. at Los Angeles, Aug. 24, 1924; died Nov. 9, 1940; JAMES J. SWEENEY, D.D., ord. June 20, 1925; appt. May 20, 1941; cons. at San Francisco, July 25, 1941; died June 19, 1968; JOHN J. SCANLAN, D.D., Retired Bishop of Honolulu; ord. June 22, 1930; succeeded to see March 6, 1968; retired June 30, 1981; died Jan. 31, 1997; JOSEPH A. FERRARIO, D.D., Retired Bishop of Honolulu; ord. May 19, 1951; succeeded to see June 25, 1982; retired Oct. 12, 1993; died Dec. 12, 2003; FRANCIS X. DILORENZO, ord. May 18, 1968; appt. Titular Bishop of Tigia and Auxiliary Bishop of Scranton Jan. 26, 1988; cons. March 8, 1988; appt. Apostolic Admin. Oct. 12, 1993; succeeded to See November 29, 1994; appt. Bishop of Richmond March 31, 2004; installed May 24, 2004.

Office of the Bishop

Office of the Bishop—1184 Bishop St., Honolulu, 96813-2858. Tel: 808-585-3300; Fax: 808-521-8428. Office Hours: Mon.-Fri. 8-4.

Administrative Assistant to the Bishop—JOY BULOSAN, M.P.A.

Vicar General, Moderator of the Curia, Diocesan Theologian, and Censor Liborum—Very Rev. MARC R. ALEXANDER, S.T.D., V.G.

Administrative Secretary/Public Notary—ELINA SIMON.

Episcopal Vicar for Clergy—Rev. KHANH HOANG.

Vocations Director—Rev. PETER DUMAG.

Administrative Secretary—DARLENE CACHOLA.

Master of Ceremonies for Episcopal Functions and Coordinator of Diocesan Major Events—Rev. Msgr. TERRENCE WATANABE.

Diocesan Ecumenical Interfaith Officer—Rev. WILLIAM J. KUNISCH II.

College of Consultors—Very Rev. MARC R. ALEXANDER, S.T.D., V.G.; Revs. KONELIO FALETOI; MANUEL A. HEWE; WILLIAM J. KUNISCH II; DENNIS KOSHKO; THOMAS PURAYIDATHIL, Ph.D.; WILLIAM SHANNON; SCOTT BUSH; EFREN A. TOMAS, M.S.

Vicars Forane—Revs. GARY L. SECOR, East Oahu; WILLIAM J. KUNISCH II, West Oahu; MANUEL A. HEWE, Central Oahu; SCOTT BUSH, Leeward Oahu; DENNIS KOSHKO, Windward Oahu; KONELIO FALETOI, West Hawaii; MICHAEL G. SCULLY, S.J., East Hawaii; WILLIAM SHANNON, Kauai; EFREN A. TOMAS, M.S., Maui, Molokai, Lanai.

Business Office—1184 Bishop St., Honolulu, 96813-2858. Tel: 808-585-3300; Fax: 808-521-8428. Office Hours: Mon.-Fri. 8-4.

Diocesan Finance Officer—LISA SAKAMOTO.

Hawaii Catholic Herald—1184 Bishop St., Honolulu, 96813-2858. Tel: 808-533-1791; Fax: 808-585-3381. Most Rev. CLARENCE R. SILVA, Publisher; PATRICK DOWNES, Editor.

St. Stephen Diocesan Center—6301 Pali Hwy., Kaneohe, 96744-5224. Tel: 808-203-6700; Fax: 808-261-7022. Office Hours: Mon.-Fri. 8-4.

Chancellor and Archivist—Deacon WALTER H. YOSHIMITSU. Tel: 808-203-6735.

Ecclesiastical Notary and Secretary for the Chancellor/Archives—NETTIE LOU PEILER.

Administrator's Assistant for St. Stephen Diocesan Center—SABRINA IZAGUIRRE. Tel: 808-203-6724.

Tribunal and Canonical Affairs—

Judicial Vicar and Director of Canonical Affairs—Very Rev. MARVIN SAMIANO, J.C.L. Tel: 808-203-6766; Fax: 808-263-8518.

Defender of the Bond and Promoter of Justice—Rev. MARK J. GANTLEY, J.C.L.; ANNE KIRBY; Rev. HERMAN LEONG, J.C.L.

Moderator of the Tribunal Chancery—MARY L. DUDDY. Email: mary_duddy@rcchawaii.org.

Ecclesiastical Notary and Secretary—LORI J. GRESS.

Judge—Rev. STEVEN NGUYEN, J.C.L.

Hawaii Catholic Schools—CARMEN HIMENES, Ed.D., Supt. Tel: 808-203-6764. Associate Superintendents: LOUISE WONG. Tel: 808-203-6760; Mrs. LOVEY ANN DEREGO. Tel: 808-203-6755.

Office of Worship—Sr. HELENE WOOD, SS.CC., Dir. Tel: 808-203-6728.

Administrative Secretary—JONILLA KIM. Tel: 808-203-6727.

Office of Religious Education—JAYNE MONDOY, M.A., P.L., Dir. Tel: 808-203-6745.

Office for Youth & Young Adult Ministry—LISA GOMES, Dir. Tel: 808-203-6743.

Diocesan Development Office—CYNTHIA LALLO, Dir. Tel: 808-203-6723.

Capital Campaign—GARY HAWKINS, Dir. Tel: 808-203-6748.

Office for Parish Resources—SHARON CHIARUCCI, Dir. Tel: 808-203-6733.

Facilities Management—VINCENT A. VERNAY, Diocesan Facilities Svcs. Mgr., 1184 Bishop St., Honolulu, 96813. Tel: 808-585-3334.

Real Estate Office—MARLENE DECOSTA, Diocesan Dir., 1184 Bishop St., Honolulu, 96813. Tel: 808-585-3332.

Prison Ministry—Tel: 808-203-6735. Deacon WALTER H. YOSHIMITSU, Diocesan Rep.

Missionary Coopertive Program—Very Rev. MARVIN SAMIANO, J.C.L., Dir. Tel: 808-203-6741. Email: msamiano@rcchawaii.org.

Victim Assistance Program—JOE BLOOM, Coord. Tel: 808-535-0159.

Respect Life Office—Deacon WALTER H. YOSHIMITSU, Dir. Tel: 808-203-6735.

Administrative Secretary—PAULETTE VERNAY. Tel: 808-203-6722.

Natural Family Planning—EDWARD CODA; BETTY CODA; Deacon WALTER H. YOSHIMITSU; FRANCES YOSHIMITSU; Deacon RONALD NELSON; LUCI NELSON.

Office for Social Ministry—140 B Holomua St., Hilo, 96720. Tel: 808-935-3050; 877-935-3050 (Toll Free); Fax: 808-935-3794. CAROL IGNACIO, Diocesan Dir.

Catholic Relief Services—IWIE TAMASHIRO, Diocesan Dir.

Office of Affordable Housing—CAROL IGNACIO, Diocesan Dir.

Care-a-Van Homeless—BRANDEE MENINO, Prog. Admin.

Mobile Care Health Project - Big Island—KAYE LUNDBURG, Prog. Dir.

Parish Social Ministry—St. Stephen Diocesan Center, 6301 Pali Hwy., Kaneohe, 96744-5224. Tel: 808-203-6702. Program Directors: IWIE TAMASHIRO; Sr. ROSELANI ENOMOTO, C.S.J. Tel: 808-203-6734.

Catholic Campaign for Human Development—Sr. ROSELANI ENOMOTO, C.S.J., Dir. Tel: 808-203-6734.

Councils, Committees and Commissions

Presbyteral Council—Very Rev. MARC R. ALEXANDER, S.T.D., V.G.; Revs. LANE AKIONA, SS.CC.; SCOTT BUSH; GARY P. COLTON; MICHEL DALTON, O.F.M.Cap.; KONELIO FALETOI; HERMAN GOMES, SS.CC.; MANUEL A. HEWE; KHANH HOANG; GREGORIO S. HONORIO, M.S.; DONG MIN (PAUL) LI; ALAPAKI KIM; DENNIS KOSHKO; WILLIAM J. KUNISCH II; JACK RYAN; GARY L. SECOR; MICHAEL G. SCULLY, S.J.; WILLIAM SHANNON; EFREN A. TOMAS, M.S.

Diocesan Finance Council—Very Rev. MARC R. ALEXANDER, S.T.D., V.G.; LISA SAKAMOTO; Sr. DAVILYN AHCHICK, O.S.F., Sec.; MARLENE DE COSTA; MARILYN FISCHER; ROBERT BRUCE GRAHAM JR., ESQ.; ROBERT HARRISON, Chm.; LAWRENCE LASUA; TARYN SCHUMAN; MELVIN VENTURA, Co Chm.

Diocesan Pastoral Council—Mr. MICHAEL WEAVER, Chm., Windward Oahu Representative; Deacon JERRY L. TOKARS, M.A., Deacon Representative; DALLAS CARTER JR., Central Oahu Vicariate Representative; Mr. NATHANIEL CHANG, East Hawaii Vicariate Representative; Mr. WALTER CLUR, Maui Vicariate Representative; Mr. DOUGLAS DICK, West Hawaii Vicariate Representative; Rev. ALAPAKI KIM, Presbyteral Council Representative; Sr. EVA JOSEPH MESINA, C.S.J., Rel. Women Representative; Ms. KIM-DUNG NGUYEN, West Honolulu Vicariate Representative; Bro. DENNIS SCHMITZ, S.M., Rel. Men Representative; Mr. THOMAS PANGILINAN, East Honolulu Vicariate Representative; JANEEL T. T. HEW, Molokai/Lanai Vicariate Representative; ELIZABETH FREITAS, Kauai Vicariate Representative; Rev. GERONIMO CASTRO, M.S., Priest Representative; BERNADETTE GALANG, Leeward Oahu Vicariate Representative; MARIA LISA IGNACIO, Youth Representative; GABRIEL GANIBE, Young Adults Representative; SHARON CHIARUCCI, Staff Representative.

Bishops Administrative Advisory Council—Very Rev. MARC R. ALEXANDER, S.T.D., V.G.; Revs. MICHEL DALTON, O.F.M.Cap.; KHANH HOANG; Deacon WALTER H. YOSHIMITSU; DARA PERREIRA; JAYNE MONDOY, M.A., P.L.; LISA SAKAMOTO.

Clergy Personnel Board—Very Rev. MARC R. ALEXANDER, S.T.D., V.G.; Revs. KHANH HOANG, Chm.; THOMAS L. GROSS; GORDIAN CARVALHO; PATRICK FREITAS; ADRIAN R. GERVACIO; DENNIS KOSHKO.

Deacon Council—Deacons CLARENCE DECAIRES, Chm.; THOMAS P. CONTRADES, Vice Chm.; EFRAIN ANDREWS, Treas.; BERNIE GALANG, Sec. Members: Deacons JAMES BOSTICK; LEROY ANDREWS; CORA CONSTANTINO; EVIE ADAMS; ROSE NUNOGAWA; ALICIA BORJA; Deacons STEPHEN MAGLENTE; THOMAS J. ADAMS; MODESTO R. CORDERO; KEITH GALANG; ANDREW GERAKAS; HENRY MINER; JERRY L. TOKARS, M.A.; GEORGE THORP JR.; BILLY WHITFIELD; Rev. KHANH HOANG.

Permanent Diaconate Formation Core Team—Co Directors: Deacon JOHN A. COUGHLIN; KATHLEEN COUGHLIN. Members: Deacon EFRAIN ANDREWS; PAMELA ANDREWS; Deacon THOMAS P. CONTRADES; JACQUELYN CONTRADES; Deacon MODESTO R. CORDERO; NYDIA-AILEEN CORDERO; Deacon FREDERICO CARAHASEN JR.; LINA CARAHASEN; Rev. KHANH HOANG.

Office of Clergy Priest Retirement Committee—Very Rev. MARC R. ALEXANDER, S.T.D., V.G.; Rev. GARY L. SECOR, Chm.; DARA PERREIRA, Co Chm.; STELLA M. WONG, M.S.W.; Revs. LANE AKIONA, SS.CC.; GORDON COMBS, O.F.M.Cap. (Retired); CLARENCE L. FISCHER; DENNIS KOSHKO; THOMAS PURAYIDATHIL, Ph.D.; KHANH HOANG; Sr. PATTY CHANG, C.S.J.

Office of Clergy: Diocesan Screening Committee—Rev. KHANH HOANG, Chm.; Very Rev. MARC R. ALEXANDER, S.T.D., V.G.; Dr. ALFRED M. ARENSDORF, M.D., F.A.A.C.A.P.; Revs. CLARENCE L. FISHER (Retired); WILLIAM SHANNON; MARK DEL ROSARIO, S.S.S.; GARY L. SECOR.

Hawaii Catholic Conference Board—Most Rev. CLARENCE R. SILVA, Chm. Members: Very Rev. MARC R. ALEXANDER, S.T.D., V.G.; Deacon WALTER H. YOSHIMITSU; Sr. EARNEST CHUNG, M.M.; DAVID COLEMAN, M.A., Ph.D.; JERRY CORREA JR.; PATRICK DOWNES; Rev. TIMOTHY EDEN, S.M.; JEROME E. RAUCKHORST; CARMEN HIMENES, Ed.D.; ANNE HARPHAM; BETTY LOU LARSON; PEGGY LEONG; EVA MARIE ANDRADE; CAROL IGNACIO; PAMELA WITTY-OAKLAND.

Saint Damien/Blessed Mother Marianne Commission—Most Rev. CLARENCE R. SILVA, Chm. Members: Sisters DAVILYN AHCHICK, O.S.F.; WILLIAM MARIE ELENIKI, O.S.F.; MARION KIKUKAWA, O.S.F., M.Ed.; ALICIA DAMIEN LAU, O.S.F.; Very Rev. CHRISTOPHER KEAHI, SS.CC.; Revs. CLYDE L. GUERREIRO, SS.CC.; LANE AKIONA, SS.CC.; Sr. HELENE WOOD, SS.CC.; PATRICK BOLAND; Ms. MARIA SULLIVAN, Esq.; VENNY VILLAPANDO; BARBARA OKAMOTO; JULIE-ANN BICOY.

Diocesan Development Committee—JOAN BICKSON; R. CHARLES BOCKEN; JOHN BROGAN, Chm.; ROBERT BRUCE GRAHAM JR., ESQ.; STANLEY HONG; JON THOMAS HUNTER; LILA MARANTZ; Very Rev. MARC R. ALEXANDER, S.T.D., V.G.; LISA SAKAMOTO; CYNTHIA LALLO.

Diocesan Liturgical Commission—Deacon CLARENCE DECAIRES JR. Ex Officio: Most Rev. CLARENCE R. SILVA; Sr. HELENE WOOD, SS.CC.; JONILLA KIM. Members: ROSE BRITO; DARLENE AH YO; CALVIN LIU, Chm.; CECIL FARIN; Deacon WALLACE MITSUI; GWEN MITSUI; MARINA PASCUA; Deacon RONALD PAGLINAWAN; CORA BUNO.

Bishop's Advisory Board for Persons with Disabilities—Members: VALERY O'BRIEN; IWIE TAMASHIRO, Staff Rep.; CAROL IGNACIO, Staff Rep.; Dr. DARRYL SALVADOR; LINDA DEVERA; BERNIE HARRISON; NIP HO; NANI FIFE; MICHAEL PAEKUKUI; Dr. DARRYL SALVADOR; Sr. ROSELANI ENOMOTO, C.S.J.; SHARON CHIARUCCI.

Diocesan Board of Education—Most Rev. CLARENCE R. SILVA, Ex Officio; Very Rev. MARC R. ALEXANDER, S.T.D., V.G., Ex Officio; CARMEN HIMENES, Ed.D.; LOUISE WONG; Mrs. LOVEY ANN DEREGO.

Chairman—ANDREA KAUMEHEIWA. Members: WILLIAM BRILHANTE JR.; LISA COLUCCIO; MARY JEAN BUZA-SIMS; DANELLE GERONA; SUSAN CAINDEE-RANCHEZ; Ms. BRIDGET OLSEN; Revs. GARY L. SECOR; LANE AKIONA, SS.CC.; Dr. EDWARD KLEIN; ANTONINETTE MARTINEZ; Mrs. CINDY OLASO; URSULA KUIEE.

Diocesan Ecumenical Commission—Revs. WILLIAM J. KUNISCH II, Ecumenical & Interfaith Officer; CLARENCE L. FISHER (Retired); JACK RYAN; REGINA PFEIFFER, D.Min.; PETER STEIGER, Ph.D.; GAIL SUGIMOTO-LEONG.

Diocesan Theological Commission—Very Rev. MARC R. ALEXANDER, S.T.D., V.G.; DAVID COLEMAN, M.A., Ph.D.; LISA DAHM, M.A.; JAYNE MONDOY, M.A., P.L.; Deacon FERNANDO V. ONA, M.D.; REGINA PFEIFFER, D.Min.; PETER STEIGER, Ph.D.; Rev. THOMAS PURAYIDATHIL, Ph.D.; Deacon JERRY L. TOKARS, M.A.; Sr. MALIA DOMINICA WONG, O.P., D.Min.

Catholic Campaign for Human Development Commission—Sr. ROSELANI ENOMOTO, C.S.J., Dir. Members: Sr. ROSALINDA BARROZO, M.M.; LUIS CAMPO; TRINI JONES; Deacon MANUEL PASCUA; JASMINE HIGA; ALLEN PACQUING; Deacon LAUREN S. WONG; MARGARET UIAGALELEI; Deacon JERRY H. NUNOGAWA.

Diocesan Planning and Building Commission—Deacon WALTER H. YOSHIMITSU; Very Rev. MARC R. ALEXANDER, S.T.D., V.G.; Rev. Msgr. TERRENCE WATANABE; Sr. HELENE WOOD, SS.CC.; GARY BATCHELLER; LISA SAKAMOTO; EDWARD ANDRADE; Rev. WILLIAM SHANNON; VINCENT A. VERNAY, Chm.; ANNE KUSAO; MARK LIVELY; FRANK FELIX JR.; Mr. DOUGLAS DICK; STEPHEN FONG; Mr. WALTER CLUR; MARLENE DE COSTA.

Diocesan Youth and Young Adult Board—Advisors: DOMINIC OLASO, East Honolulu; JEFF CHANG, West Honolulu; EULERSON PAJIMULA, Leeward Oahu; CHARLESTON UNCIANO, Central Oahu; LISA GOMES, Windward Oahu; EDWINA FUJIMOTO, West Hawaii; KRISLYN PAKELE-VILLENA, East Hawaii; CHARLIE SILVA, Kauai; MAKA SECRETARIO, Maui.

Implementation Commission of Diocesan Road Map for Pastoral Program and Facility Needs—COLLEEN SATHRE, Chm.; Very Rev. MARC R. ALEXANDER, S.T.D., V.G., Co Chm.; RIANE ASHLEY CARDENAS; SHARON CHIARUCCI; JEANETTE CASTILLO; Rev. MICHEL DALTON, O.F.M.Cap.; PATRICK DOWNES; CARMEN HIMENS, Ed.D.; Rev. KHANH HOANG; CAROL IGNACIO; Deacon WALLACE MITSUI; DARA PERREIRA; JAYNE MONDOY, M.A., P.L.; Bro. BERNARD PLOEGER, S.M.; Sr. FLORENCE REMATA, O.S.F.; LISA SAKAMOTO; Ms. MARIA SULLIVAN, Esq.; VINCENT A. VERNAY; Mr. MICHAEL WEAVER.

Hawaii Catholic Community Foundation—Most Rev. CLARENCE R. SILVA; Very Rev. MARC ALEXANDER, S.T.D., V.G.; LISA SAKAMOTO; IRENE LEE, Pres.; JOHN BROGEN, Vice Pres.; GEORGE FONTAINE, Sec.; MARK PILLORI, Treas.; LINDA NISHIGAYA; CHUCK FURR.

St. Anthony Jr./Sr. High School Board of Education (Maui)—Rev. Msgr. TERRENCE WATANABE, Ex Officio; Dr. ALFRED M. ARENSDORF, M.D., F.A.A.C.A.P.; CATHERINE NOBRIGA-KIM; ELDON MATTOS; GAIL MITCHELL; DANIEL L. ORNELLAS; ROY SILVA.

CLERGY, PARISHES, MISSIONS AND PAROCHIAL SCHOOLS

ISLAND OF OAHU

CITY OF HONOLULU

1—CATHEDRAL OF OUR LADY OF PEACE (1843) Most Rev. Clarence R. Silva; Rev. John W. Berger, Rector. In Res., Revs. Khanh Hoang; Gordon Combs, O.F.M.Cap. (Retired).
Office: 1184 Bishop St., Honolulu, 96813-2838. Tel: 808-536-7036; Fax: 808-585-3383. Email: coolop@rcchawaii.org. Web: www.cathedralofourladyofpeace.com.
School—Cathedral Catholic Academy, (Grades K-8), 1728 Nuuanu Ave., Honolulu, 96817. Tel: 808-533-2069; Fax: 808-533-2069. Mrs. Jaydee Wagner, Interim Prin. Lay Teachers 13; Students 135.
Catechesis/Religious Program—Mr. Mike Bauer, D.R.E. Students 42.

2—ST. ANTHONY (1916) Revs. Manuel C. Dela Cruz, M.S.; Napoleon Andres, M.S., Parochial Vicar; Deacon George W. Thorp Jr. In Res., Rev. Teodulo Gaquit.
Office: 640 Puuhale Rd., Honolulu, 96819. Tel: 808-845-3255; Fax: 808-842-3664.
School—Tel: 808-845-2769; Fax: 808-853-2234. Sr. Eleonor Amante, S.P.C., Prin. Sisters 4; Lay Teachers 6; Students 102.
Catechesis/Religious Program—Students 132.
Convent—702 Puuhale Rd., Honolulu, 96819. Tel: 808-845-4888. St. Paul of Chartres 5.

3—ST. AUGUSTINE BY THE SEA (1854) Revs. Lane Akiona, SS.CC.; Lusius Nimu, SS.CC., Parochial Vicar; Deacon Andres J. Calunod.
Office: 130 Ohua Ave., Honolulu, 96815. Tel: 808-923-7024; Fax: 808-922-4086.
Catechesis/Religious Program—Students 26.

4—BLESSED SACRAMENT (1938) Rev. Khanh Pham Nguyen, Admin.; Deacon Ronald Choo. In Res., Rev. Michael J. Owens.
Office: 2124 Pauoa Rd., Honolulu, 96813. Tel: 808-531-6980. Email: bscpauoa@rcchawaii.org.
Catechesis/Religious Program—Students 43.

5—CO-CATHEDRAL OF ST. THERESA OF THE CHILD JESUS (1931) Rev. William J. Kunisch II, Rector; Deacon Roy T. Matsuo. In Res., Rev. Peter Dumag (Philippines).
Office: 712 N. School St., Honolulu, 96817. Tel:

808-521-1700; Fax: 808-599-3629.
School—(Grades K-8) Tel: 808-536-4703; Fax: 808-524-6861. Mr. Robert Gallagher, Headmaster. Sisters 3; Lay Teachers 22; Students 397.
Catechesis/Religious Program—Students 300.
Convent—Sisters of St. Joseph of Carondelet, Tel: 808-533-3101.
Vietnamese Catholic Community—Tel: 808-536-0046. Email: vietholymartyrs@gmail.com. Web: www.vietmartyrs-honolulu.net. Rev. Vincent Kien Nguyen, Chap.

6—HOLY FAMILY (1950) Rev. Conrado J. Lomibao, Admin.
Office: 830 Main St., Honolulu, 96818. Tel: 808-422-1135. Email: stphilomena@rcchawaii.org; hfspadmin@hotmail.com.
School—(Grades PreK-8) Tel: 808-423-9612; Fax: 808-422-5030. Email: cmalins@hfca-hawaii.org. Christina Malins, Prin.; Denise Kaono, Librarian. Lay Teachers 21; Students 485.
Catechesis/Religious Program—Tel: 808-839-1876, Ext. 226; Fax: 808-634-6888. Diane Fujinaga, C.R.E.; Cherry Dolak, C.R.E. Students 103.

7—HOLY TRINITY (1939) Rev. Gary L. Secor; Deacons Samuel Taylor; Daniel R. Guinaugh; Santiago Gorospe. In Res., Rev. George Busto, C.O.
Office: 5919 Kalanianaole Hwy., Honolulu, 96821. Tel: 808-396-0551; Fax: 808-396-1380.
School—(Grades K-8) Tel: 808-396-8466; Fax: 808-396-3310. Sr. Rose Miriam Schillinger, C.S.J., Prin. Sisters 4; Lay Teachers 9; Students 70.
Catechesis/Religious Program—Tel: 808-396-0551, Ext. 11; Fax: 808-396-1380. Students 102.

8—ST. JOHN THE BAPTIST (1844) [CEM] Rev. Jack Ryan; Deacons Modesto R. Cordero; Peter Soumwei. In Res., Rev. Mario Raquepo.
Office: 2324 Omilo Ln., Honolulu, 96819. Tel: 808-845-0984; Fax: 808-841-6643. Email: sjbkalihi@gmail.com.
School—(Grades PreK-8) Tel: 808-841-5551; Fax: 808-842-6104. Web: sjbhawaii.net. Sr. Laurencia Camayudo, O.P., Acting Prin. Dominican Sisters 7; Lay Teachers 15; Students 225.
Catechesis/Religious Program—Tel: 808-845-3304. Students 224.
Convent—2330 Omilo Ln., Honolulu, 96819. Tel: 808-551-3309. Web: www.ophawaiiregion.com. Dominican Sisters of the Most Holy Rosary 7.

9—LATIN MASS COMMUNITY Rev. Francis Nakagawa, S.M., Chap.
P.O. Box 30285, Honolulu, 96813.

10—NEWMAN CENTER-HOLY SPIRIT PARISH (1981) Revs. Russell J. Roide, S.J.; John Chandler, S.J., Parochial Vicar.
Mailing Address: 1941 East West Rd., Honolulu, 96822-2321. Tel: 808-988-6222; Fax: 808-988-1752. Jesuit House: 2727 Pamoa Rd., Honolulu, 96822-1838. Tel: 808-988-3464; Fax: 808-988-7627. Web: www.newmanhawaii.org.
Catechesis/Religious Program—Students 50.

11—OUR LADY OF THE MOUNT (1870) [CEM] Rev. Adrian R. Gervacio.
Office: 1614 Monte St., Honolulu, 96819. Tel: 808-845-0828; Fax: 808-845-0826. Email: olmount@aol.com. Web: www.olmount.org.
Catechesis/Religious Program—Tel: 808-845-0828. Students 92.

12—ST. PATRICK (1929) Revs. Clarence L. Guerreiro, SS.CC.; Thomas Choo, SS.CC., Parochial Vicar. Please refer to the listing for St. Patrick Monastery under Monasteries and Residences for Priests and Brothers for additional residents.
Office: 1124 Seventh Ave., Honolulu, 96816. Tel: 808-732-5565; Fax: 808-737-2477.
School—(Grades K-8), 3320 Harding Ave., Honolulu, 96816. Tel: 808-734-8979; Fax: 808-732-2851. Sr. Anne Clare De Costa, SS.CC., Parish Dir. Educ. Sisters 1; Lay Teachers 22; Students 342.
Catechesis/Religious Program—Students 75.

13—SS PETER AND PAUL (1969) Revs. David O. Travers, S.J., Admin.; Romeo C. Nietes, Parochial Vicar; Deacons Richard Port; Richard Abel.
Mailing Address: 800 Kaheka St., Honolulu, 96814. Tel: 808-941-0675; Fax: 808-945-0689. Email: sspeterpaul@hawaii.rr.com. Web: www.sspeterpaulhawaii.org.
Res.: 1561 Kanunu St., #1006, Honolulu, 96814. Tel: 808-955-8830.
Catechesis/Religious Program—Students 65.

14—ST. PHILOMENA (1942) Rev. Marino Angostura, Admin.
Office: 3300 Ala Laulani St., Honolulu, 96818-2837. Tel: 808-839-1876; Fax: 808-834-6888. Email: stphilomena@rcchawaii.org; sp.hawaii.church@gmail.com. Web: www.stphilomena.net.
School & Early Learning Center—Tel: 808-833-8080; Fax: 808-834-3438. Angeline A.V. Thomas, Prin. Lay Teachers 12; Students 200.
Catechesis/Religious Program—Tel: 808-839-1876, Ext. 226. Email: reledsphf@hotmail.com. Diane Fujinaga, C.R.E.; Cherry Dolak, C.R.E. Students 84.

15—ST. PIUS X (1958) Revs. Gordian Carvalho; Jovito Niniel, Parochial Vicar; Deacons Sidney Townsley, (Retired); Vince Wozniak; Ronald Nelson; Julio Naich.
Res. & Mailing Address: 2821 Lowrey Ave., Honolulu, 96822-1644. Tel: 808-988-3308; Fax: 808-973-2209. Email: general@mp-cc.net. Web: www.mp-cc.net.
Catechesis/Religious Program—Students 38.
Korean Catholic Community—2949 Kahawai St., Honolulu, 96822. Tel: 808-988-9678; Fax: 808-988-6047. Revs. Peter Kim, Chap.; Kwang Seog Han.

16—SACRED HEART (1914) Revs. Gordian Carvalho; Jovito Niniel, Parochial Vicar; Deacons Sidney Townsley, (Retired); Vince Wozniak; Ronald Nelson; Julio Naich.
Office: 1701 Wilder Ave., Honolulu, 96822. Tel: 808-973-2211; Fax: 808-973-2209. Email: general@mp-cc.net. Web: www.mp-cc.net.
School—Maryknoll School, (Grades PreK-12), 1526 Alexander St., Honolulu, 96822. Tel: 808-952-8400; 808-952-7100; Fax: 808-972-7101. Shana Tong, Grade School Prin.; Christopher Casupang, Grade School Vice Prin.; Ms. Betsey H. Gunderson, High School Prin.; Darcie Kawamura, High School Vice Prin.; Virginia Koo, Librarian (Grade School); Jennifer Tseu, Librarian (High School). Lay Teachers 88; Students 1,392.
Catechesis/Religious Program—Tel: 808-952-7120; Fax: 808-952-7121. Stephanie Couching, D.R.E. Students 124.

17—STAR OF THE SEA (1946) Revs. Mark del Rosario, S.S.S.; Paterno B. Labasano, S.S.S., Parochial Vicar; Bro. Salvador Yanzon, S.S.S.; Deacons Andrew Gerakas; Henry Miner; Leslie Victor; Fernando V. Ona.
Office: 4470 Aliikoa St., Honolulu, 96821. Tel: 808-734-0396; Fax: 808-735-6017.
School—4469 Malia St., Honolulu, 96821. Tel: 808-734-0208; Fax: 808-735-9790. Email: star@starofthesea.org. Web: www.starofthesea.org. Carola A. Souza, Prin. Lay Teachers 22; Students 235.
Early Learning Center—4470 Aliikoa St., Ste. 100, Honolulu, 96821. Tel: 808-734-3840; Fax: 808-732-1738. Email: elc@starofthesea.org. Web: www.starofthesea elc.org. Lisa Foster, Prin. Lay Teachers 12; Students 190.
Catechesis/Religious Program—Tel: 808-735-0259. Darlene Ah Yo, D.R.E. Students 101.

18—ST. STEPHEN (1932) Rev. Khanh Pham Nguyen, Admin.; Deacon Lauren S. Wong.
Office: 2747 Pali Hwy., Honolulu, 96817. Tel: 808-595-3105. Email: ssccpali@rcchawaii.org.
Catechesis/Religious Program—Students 35.

OUTSIDE THE CITY OF HONOLULU

County of Honolulu

AIEA, ST. ELIZABETH (1926) Revs. Thomas Purayidathil; Jon Cabico, Parochial Vicar; Deacons Joaquin Borja; Frederico Carahasen Jr.
Office: 99-312 Moanalua Rd., 96701. Tel: 808-487-2414; Fax: 808-487-2168. Web: www.stelizabethaiea.org.
School—(Grades K-8), 99-310 Moanalua Rd., 96701. Tel: 808-488-5322; Fax: 808-486-0856. Email: info@steliz-hi.org. Web: www.steliz-hi.org. Sr. Bernarda Sindol, O.P., Prin. Sisters 5; Lay Teachers 13; Students 232.
Catechesis/Religious Program—Tel: 808-487-7994; Fax: 808-487-2168. Manette Kokubun, D.R.E. Students 223.
Convent—Dominican Sisters of the Most Holy Rosary 5.

EWA, IMMACULATE CONCEPTION CHURCH (1929), (Filipino), Rev. Michel Dalton, O.F.M.Cap.
Office: 91-1298 Renton Rd., 96706. Tel: 808-681-3701; Fax: 808-681-3117. Web: parishesonline.com/scripts/hostedsites/org.asp?ID=4286.
Catechesis/Religious Program—Students 185.

EWA BEACH, OUR LADY OF PERPETUAL HELP (1969) Revs. Scott Bush; Cosmenio Rosimo Jr., Parochial Vicar; Deacon Ron Paglinawan.
Res.: 91-1004 North Rd., 96706-2796. Tel: 808-689-8681; Fax: 808-689-1954.
School—(Grades K-8), 91-1010 North Rd., 96706. Tel: 808-689-0474; Fax: 808-689-4847. Sr. Davilyn AhChick, O.S.F., Prin. Lay Teachers 9; Students 185.
Catechesis/Religious Program—Remi Cabrera, C.R.E.; Julia Torres, D.R.E. Students 52.

KAHUKU, ST. ROCH (1928) [CEM] Rev. Sydney Fernandes, Admin.
Mailing Address: P.O. Box 295, 96731.
Res.: 56-350 Kamehameha Hwy., 96731. Tel: 808-293-5026; Fax: 808-293-1737. Email: saintrocc001@hawaii.rr.com. Web: saintrochkahuku.com.
Catechesis/Religious Program—Tel: 808-293-5026. Students 51.
Mission—St. Joachim (1917) P.O. Box 295, Honolulu Co. 96731.

KAILUA

1—ST. ANTHONY OF PADUA (1933) Revs. Dennis Koshko; Steve Nguyen, Parochial Vicar; Deacon Ernest F. Carlbom.
Office: 148 Makawao St., Ste. A, 96734-2334. Tel: 808-266-2222; Fax: 808-266-2229. Web: www.stanthonyskailua.org.
Res.: 116 Makua St., 96734.
School—(Grades K-8), 148 Makawao St., 96734-2334. Tel: 808-261-3331; Fax: 808-263-3518. Ms. Bridget Olsen, Prin. Sisters 1; Lay Teachers 22; Students 303.
Early Learning Center—Lay Teachers 4; Students 68.
Catechesis/Religious Program—Tel: 808-791-6525. Donna Estomago, C.R.E. Students 130.

2—ST. JOHN VIANNEY (1962) Rev. Thomas L. Gross; Deacons Walter H. Yoshimitsu; Clarence DeCaires; Jerry L. Tokars; Lauren S. Wong.
Office: 920 Keolu Dr., 96734-3842. Tel: 808-262-8317; Fax: 808-772-5634. Email: sjv920@hawaii.rr.com. Web: www.sjvhawaii.org.
School—(Grades PreK-8), 940 Keolu Dr., 96734-3842. Tel: 808-261-4651; Fax: 808-263-0505. Email: achee@hawaii.rr.com. Mr. Michael Busekrus, Prin. Lay Teachers 28; Students 260.
Catechesis/Religious Program—Students 183.

KANEOHE, ST. ANN (1841) [CEM] Revs. Herman Gomes, SS.CC.; Benny Kosasih, SS.CC., Parochial Vicar; Deacon Billy Whitfield.
Office: 46-129 Haiku Rd., 96744. Tel: 808-247-3092; Fax: 808-235-0717.
School & Early Learning Center—46-125 Haiku Rd., 96744. Tel: 808-247-3092; Fax: 808-235-0717. Email: dkauhane@hawaii.rr.com; vdesilva@stannshi.org. Daphne Kauhane, Parish Dir. Educ.; Victoria DeSilva, Prin. (School); Clarie Thompson, Prin. (Early Learning Center). Sisters 1; Lay Teachers 33; Students 385.
Catechesis/Religious Program— Malu Pangilinan, D.R.E. Students 286.

KAPOLEI, ST. JUDE (1988) Rev. Joseph A. Diaz, Admin.; Rev. Msgr. John Mbinda, Parochial Vicar; Deacons Edward Vargas; John A. Coughlin.
Res.: 92-104 Leipapa Way, 96707. Tel: 808-672-9041. Church: 92-455 Makakilo Dr., 96707. Tel: 808-672-8669; Fax: 808-672-3779. Email: info@stjudehawaii.org; pastor@stjudehawaii.org. Web: www.stjudehawaii.org.
Catechesis/Religious Program—Tel: 808-672-8669, Ext. 212. Bonnie Boquer, D.R.E. Students 241.

MILILANI TOWN, ST. JOHN APOSTLE AND EVANGELIST (1969) Revs. Manuel A. Hewe; Cletus Mooya, Parochial Vicar; Deacons Wally Mitsui; Modesto R. Cordero.
Office: 95-370 Kuahelani Ave., 96789. Tel: 808-623-3332, Ext. 100; Fax: 808-623-3286. Email: info@sjmililani.com. Web: www.sjmililani.com.
St. John Catholic Preschool—Tel: 808-623-3332, Ext. 200; Fax: 808-623-6496. Email: preschool@sjmililani.com. Catherine Awong, Dir. Lay Teachers 3; Students 66.
Catechesis/Religious Program—Tel: 808-623-3332, Ext. 204,. Gwen Mitsui, D.R.E. Students 423.

NANAKULI, ST. RITA (1963) Rev. Alapaki Kim; Deacon Harold S. Levy Jr.
Office: 89-318 Farrington Hwy., 96792. Tel: 808-668-7833; Fax: 808-668-7716. Email: strita_nanakuli@rcchawaii.org. Web: www.stritananakuli.org.
Catechesis/Religious Program—Tel: 808-668-5634. Brenda Levy, D.R.E. Students 65.

PEARL CITY, OUR LADY OF GOOD COUNSEL (1958) [CEM] Revs. Pascual Abaya, Admin.; Dong Min (Paul) Li, Parochial Vicar; Deacons Thomas Miyashiro; Efrain Andrews.
Office & Rectory: 1525 Waimano Home Rd., 96782. Tel: 808-455-3012; 808-455-9039; Fax: 808-456-9443. Email: olgc@hawaii.rr.com. Web: www.olgc.moki.org.
School—(Grades PreSchool-8), 1530 Hoolana St., 96782. Tel: 808-455-4533; Fax: 808-455-5587. Mrs. Cindy Olaso, Prin. Lay Teachers 15; Students 285.
Catechesis/Religious Program—Eulerson Pajimula, Coord., Youth Min. Students 184.

WAHIAWA, OUR LADY OF SORROWS (1939) Rev. Edgar B. Brillantes; Rev. Msgr. Thaddeus F. Mercado, Parochial Vicar; Deacon Benjamin A. Awana.
Office: 1403-A California Ave., 96786-2595. Tel: 808-621-5109; Fax: 808-622-5073. Email: ourladyofsorrows@rcchawaii.org; ols@hawaiiantel.net.
Catechesis/Religious Program— Mr. Jack Kampfer, D.R.E. Students 129.

WAIALUA, ST. MICHAEL (1853) [CEM] Revs. Bertram Lock, SS.CC.; Johnathan Hurrell, SS.CC., Parochial Vicar.

Office: 67-390 Goodale Ave., 96791. Tel: 808-637-4040; Fax: 808-637-4287. Email: stsmichaelpeter_paul@hawaii.rr.com. Web: www.stsmichaelpeterpaul.com.
School—(Grades PreK-8), 67-340 Haona St., 96791. Tel: 808-637-7772; Fax: 808-637-7722. Deanna Arecchi, Prin. Sisters 1; Lay Teachers 13; Students 240.
Catechesis/Religious Program—Tel: 808-637-4040. Students 90.
Convent—Sisters 2.
Mission—*SS. Peter and Paul* 67-390 Goodale Ave., Honolulu Co. 96791.

WAIANAE, SACRED HEART (1838) [CEM] Rev. Carmelo Rey Lim; Deacons Jerome Vito; Misa Sewen.
Office: 85-786 Old Government Rd., 96792. Tel: 808-696-3773; Fax: 808-696-2242. Email: shcwaianae@hawaii.rr.com.
Catechesis/Religious Program—Tel: 808-696-2242. Students 110.

WAIKANE, OUR LADY OF MT. CARMEL (1850) [CEM] Rev. Paulo R. Kosaka, O.F.M.Cap., Admin.
Office: P.O. Box 6581, 96744.
Res.: 48-422 Kamehameha Hwy., 96744. Tel: 808-239-9269; Fax: 808-239-8561. Email: olmc001@hawaii.rr.com. Web: www.mtcarmelhawaii.wordpress.com.
Catechesis/Religious Program—Students 55.

WAIMANALO, ST. GEORGE (1954) Rev. Robert Maher, O.F.M.Cap., Admin.; Deacon Edward Cho. In Res., Rev. Marvin Bearis, O.F.M.Cap.
Office: 41-1323 Kalanianaole Hwy., 96795. Tel: 808-259-7188; Fax: 808-259-0169. Email: stgeorge96795@aol.com. Web: www.stgeorgechurchwaimanalo.com.
Catechesis/Religious Program—Tel: 808-259-8979. Students 105.

WAIPAHU, ST. JOSEPH (1940) [CEM] Revs. Gregorio S. Honorio, M.S.; Ronaldo Guzman, M.S.; Deacon Keith Galang.
Office: 94-675 Farrington Hwy., 96797. Tel: 808-677-4276; Fax: 808-671-3215.
School—(Grades PreK-8), 94-651 Farrington Hwy., 96797. Tel: 808-677-4475; Fax: 808-677-8937. Email: sjs@stjosephwaipahu.org. Web: www.stjosephwaipahu.org. Miss Beverly Sandobal, Prin.; Vivian Sua, Librarian. Sisters 2; Lay Teachers 31; Students 438.
Catechesis/Religious Program—Tel: 808-676-3493; Fax: 808-676-3493. Geraldine Simbahon, D.R.E. Students 542.

WAIPIO, RESURRECTION OF THE LORD (1986) Rev. Paul L. Minchak, O.F.M.Cap., Admin.; Deacon Ernest Libarios Sr.
Mailing Address: 94-1260 Lumikula St., Waipahu, 96797. Tel: 808-676-4700; Fax: 808-676-4534. Email: resurrect001@hawaii.rr.com.
Catechesis/Religious Program— Yuko D. Ornellas, D.R.E. Students 142.

ISLAND OF HAWAII

County of Hawaii

HAWI, SACRED HEART (1926) [CEM 2] Rev. Maurice Cardinal, M.S., Admin.; Deacon Thomas J. Adams.
Mailing Address: P.O. Box 220, 96719. Email: sacredhearthawi@hawaiiantel.net.
Res.: 55-3374 Akonipule Hwy., 96719. Tel: 808-889-6436; Fax: 808-889-5698. Email: sacredhearthawi@hawaiiantel.net.
Catechesis/Religious Program—Tel: 808-889-0674; Fax: 808-880-5698. Students 75.

HILO, ST. JOSEPH (1839) [CEM] Revs. Samuel E. Loterte, S.S.S., Admin.; Joseph Hennen, Parochial Vicar; Deacons Don Aanavi; Jerry H. Nunogawa.
Office: 43 Kapiolani St., 96720. Tel: 808-935-1465; Fax: 808-969-1665. Email: stjosephchurch@stjoehilo.com. Web: stjoehilo.org.
School—(Grades PreK-12), 1000 Ululani St., 96720. Tel: 808-935-4935 (Elementary); 808-935-4936 (High School); Fax: 808-935-6894 (Elementary); 808-969-9019 (High School). Victoria Torcolini, Prin.; Janin Malinowski, Elem. School Librarian; Miri Sumida, Jr./Sr. High School Librarian. Sisters 1; Deacons 1; Lay Teachers 26; Students 312.
Catechesis/Religious Program—Tel: 808-935-1202. Sr. Lusika Sangma, M.S.M.H.C., C.R.E. Students 176.
Convent—315 Oln St., 96720. Tel: 808-959-5803. Sisters 4.

HONAUNAU, ST. BENEDICT (1899) [CEM 5] [JC 5] Rev. Alfred Rebuldela.
Office: 84-5140 Painted Church Rd., Captain Cook, 96704. Tel: 808-328-2227; Fax: 808-328-8482.
Catechesis/Religious Program—Cheryline Ono, D.R.E. Students 78.
Mission—*St. John the Baptist* Kealakekua, Hawaii Co.
Mission—*St. Peter* Milolii, Honaunau Co.

HONOKAA, OUR LADY OF LOURDES (1870) [CEM 6] Rev. Raymund Ellorin, Admin.
Mailing Address: P.O. Box 129, 96727. Tel: 808-775-9591; Fax: 808-775-0591. Email: ourladyof001@hawaii.rr.com.
Res.: 45-5028 Plumeria St., 96727.
Catechesis/Religious Program—

KAILUA-KONA, ST. MICHAEL THE ARCHANGEL (1840) [CEM 4] Revs. Konelio Faletoi; John Fredy Quintero, Parochial Vicar. In Res., Rev. John B. Stawasz (Retired).
Office: 75-5769 Alii Dr., 96740. Tel: 808-326-7771; Fax: 808-326-7096. Email: info@onecatholicohana.org. Web: www.onecatholicohana.org.
Catechesis/Religious Program—Students 131.
Mission—*Holy Rosary* Kalaoa, Hawaii Co.
Mission—*Immaculate Conception* Holualoa, Hawaii Co.
Mission—*St. Paul* Honalo, Hawaii Co.
Mission—*St. Peter by the Sea* Kahaluu, Hawaii Co.

KAMUELA, CHURCH OF THE ANNUNCIATION (1965) [CEM] Rev. Robert W. Schwarzhaupt; Deacons William McPeek; Larry Ignacio.
Mailing Address: P.O. Box 301, 96743.
Res.: 65-1235 Kawaihae Rd., 96743. Tel: 808-885-4196; Fax: 808-887-1220.
Catechesis/Religious Program—Tel: 808-887-1203. Students 120.
Mission—*Church of the Ascension, Puako* Puako, Hawaii Co. 96743.

KEAUKAHA, HILO, MALIA PUKA O' KALANI (MARY GATE OF HEAVEN) (1929) Revs. Samuel E. Loterte, S.S.S., Admin.; Joseph Hennen, Parochial Vicar.
Office: 326 Desha Ave., Hilo, 96720. Tel: 808-935-9338; Fax: 808-935-3865.
Catechesis/Religious Program—Students 13.

LAUPAHOEHOE, ST. ANTHONY (1926) [CEM 2] Rev. Michael G. Scully, S.J., Admin.
Office: P.O. Box 339, 96764. Tel: 808-962-6538; Fax: 808-962-6971.
Catechesis/Religious Program—Dorothy DeConte, D.R.E. Students 10.

MOUNTAIN VIEW, ST. THERESA (1930) Rev. Salvador Bringas Jr., Admin.
Office: P.O. Box 37, 96771. Tel: 808-968-6233; Fax: 808-968-6215. Email: stcmv@hawaii.rr.com.
Catechesis/Religious Program—Students 62.
Mission—*Holy Rosary* Keaau, Hawaii Co.

NAALEHU, SACRED HEART (1846) [CEM] Rev. Joel Barut, Admin.
Office: P.O. Box 760, Pahala, 96772. Tel: 808-929-7474 (Rectory); 808-928-8208 (Office); Fax: 808-928-8208. Email: hrc.shc@gmail.com.
Street Address: 95-5558 Mamalahoa Hwy., 96772.
Catechesis/Religious Program— 96772. Tel: 808-929-7686. JoAnn Moseley, C.R.E. Students 29.

PAHALA, HOLY ROSARY (1885) [CEM] Rev. Joel Barut, Admin.
Office: P.O. Box 760, 96777. Tel: 808-928-8208; Fax: 808-928-8208. Email: hrc.shc@gmail.com.
Church: 96-3143 Pikake St., 96777.
Catechesis/Religious Program—Students 30.

PAHOA, SACRED HEART (1882) [CEM 2] Rev. Carlito Ranjo, Admin.; Deacons Robert Cyr; Julio Akapito.
Mailing Address: P.O. Box 17, 96778. Tel: 808-965-8202; Fax: 808-965-5144. Email: shpahoa@hotmail.com.
Catechesis/Religious Program—Debra Bulosan, C.R.E. Students 99.

PAPAIKOU, IMMACULATE HEART OF MARY (1923) [CEM] Rev. Michael G. Scully, S.J., Admin.; Deacon LeRoy Andrews.
Church: P.O. Box 79, 96781. Tel: 808-964-1240; 808-963-5434; Fax: 808-964-5313.
Catechesis/Religious Program—Louise Isherwood, D.R.E. Students 49.
Mission—*Good Shepherd* [CEM] Honomu, Hawaii Co. 96728.

ISLAND OF KAUAI

County of Kauai

KALAHEO, HOLY CROSS (1909) [CEM] Rev. Edison Pamintuan, M.S.
Mailing Address: P.O. Box 487, 96741. Tel: 808-332-8011; Fax: 808-332-7749.
Res.: 2-2370 Kaumualii Hwy., 96741. Tel: 808-332-8011; Fax: 808-332-7749.
Catechesis/Religious Program—Students 110.
Mission—*Sacred Heart* P.O. Box 487, Eleele, Kauai Co. 96741.

KAPAA, ST. CATHERINE (1887) [CEM 2] Revs. Romelo Somera, Admin.; Peter Miti, Parochial Vicar; Deacon Manuel Pascua.
Office: 5021-A Kawaihau Rd., 96746. Tel: 808-822-4804; 808-822-7900 (Office); Fax: 808-822-3014. Email: stcatherine.kauai@hawaiiantel.net. Web: www.stcatherinekauai.org.
School—(Grades PreK-8) Tel: 808-822-4212; Fax: 808-823-0991. Celina Haigh, Prin.; Gloria Aqui, Librarian. Lay Teachers 10; Students 135.
Catechesis/Religious Program—Students 83.
Mission—*St. Sylvester* 2390 Kolo Rd., Kilauea, Kauai Co. 96754.
Mission—*St. William* 5292 Kuhio Hwy., Hanalei, Kauai Co. 96714. Tel: 808-822-7900.

KEKAHA, ST. THERESA (1944) [JC] Rev. Danilo C. Galang, M.S.
Mailing Address: P.O. Box 159, 96752. Tel: 808-337-1548 (Office); Fax: 808-337-1548. Email: sttheresac@yahoo.com.
School—(Grades PreK-8), 8320 Elepaio Rd., 96752. Tel: 808-337-1351; Fax: 808-337-1714. Email: sttheresa_kekaha@yahoo.com. Mary Jean Buza-Sims, Prin.; Adela Chavez, Librarian. Sisters 4; Lay Teachers 6; Students 121.
Catechesis/Religious Program—Tel: 808-338-1725. Beverly Johnston, C.R.E. Students 42.
Convent—P.O. Box 489, 96752. Tel: 808-337-9661. Sr. Marie Bernadette Dorn, Supr. Franciscan Sisters of Christian Charity 5.
Mission—*Sacred Hearts of Jesus & Mary* 9496 Kaumualii Hwy., Waimea, Kauai Co. 96796.

KOLOA, ST. RAPHAEL (1841) [CEM 2] Rev. Augustine Uthuppu; Deacon Thomas P. Contrades, Parochial Vicar. In Res., Rev. Rene Bisaillon, M.S. (Retired).
Office: 3011 Hapa Rd., 96756. Tel: 808-742-1955; Fax: 808-742-1845. Email: st.raphael@hawaiiantel.net.
Catechesis/Religious Program—Students 86.

LIHUE, IMMACULATE CONCEPTION (1884) [CEM 2] Rev. William Shannon; Deacon William A. Farias.
Mailing Address: 4453 Kapaia Rd., 96766. Tel: 808-245-2432; Fax: 808-246-2571.
Catechesis/Religious Program—Tel: 808-632-0638. Sr. Florence Remata, O.S.F., D.R.E. Students 147.

ISLAND OF LANAI

LANAI CITY, SACRED HEARTS OF JESUS AND MARY PARISH (1930) [JC] Rev. Reginald Paul S. Pira, Admin.
Mailing Address: P.O. Box 630784, 96763. Tel: 808-565-6837; Fax: 808-565-9052. Email: sacredheartslanai@yahoo.com.
Catechesis/Religious Program—Tel: 808-565-6051. Jessie Myers, D.R.E.; Wilma Koep, Asst. D.R.E. Students 60.

ISLAND OF MAUI

County of Maui

HAIKU, ST. RITA (1922) Rev. Patrick Freitas.
Office: 655 Haiku Rd., 96708. Tel: 808-575-2601; Fax: 808-575-2063.
Catechesis/Religious Program—Sandra Silva, D.R.E. Students 41.
Mission—*St. Gabriel*, Keanae.

HANA, ST. MARY (1859) [CEM] [JC 2] Rev. Jose Macoy.
Church: 5065 Hana Hwy., 96713.
Office: P.O. Box 219, 96713. Tel: 808-248-8030; Fax: 808-248-8042.
Catechesis/Religious Program—Tel: 808-248-7417. Esse Sinenci, D.R.E. Students 62.
Mission—*St. Peter* Puuiki, Maui Co.
Mission—*St. Paul* Kipahulu, Maui Co.
Mission—*St. Joseph* Kaupo, Maui Co.

KAHULUI, CHRIST THE KING (1932) [CEM] Revs. Efren A. Tomas, M.S.; Adondee Arrellano, Parochial Vicar; Deacons Cornelio Pulido; Kenneth Bissen Jr.
Office: 20 W. Wakea Ave., 96732. Tel: 808-877-6098; Fax: 808-871-6296. Web: www.ctkchurchmaui.org.
School—(Grades PreK-6), 211 S. Kaulawahine St., 96732. Tel: 808-877-6618; Fax: 808-871-8101. Bernadette Lopez, Prin.; Sr. Catherine Acain, C.S.J., Librarian. Sisters 2; Lay Teachers 7; Students 131.
Catechesis/Religious Program—Tel: 808-877-3674. Sr. Angela Laurenzo, C.S.J, D.R.E. Students 255.
Convent—*Sisters of St. Joseph of Carondelet*

KIHEI, MAUI CO., ST. THERESA (1908) Rev. Msgr. Terrence A.M. Watanabe; Rev. Jose Augusto Cadavid, Hispanic Ministry; Deacon Lawrence S. Franco; Sr. Candelaria Angela Pinula, F.S.P., D.R.E.
Office: 25 W. Lipoa St., 96753. Tel: 808-879-4844; Fax: 808-879-0045. Email: info@saint-theresa.com. Web: www.saint-theresa.com.
Catechesis/Religious Program—Students 183.

KULA, HAWAII CO., OUR LADY QUEEN OF THE ANGELS (1944) [CEM 2] Rev. Arthur Amian.
Office: 9177 Kula Hwy., 96790-9464. Tel: 808-878-1261; Fax: 808-878-3105. Email: kcchurch@hawaii.rr.com. Web: www.kulacathliccommunity.org.
Catechesis/Religious Program—Tel: 808-878-3838. Mary Jean Bega, D.R.E. Students 73.
Mission—*Holy Ghost* 4300 Lower Kula Rd., Waiakoa, Maui Co. 96790-9464. Tel: 808-878-1091.
Mission—*St. James the Less* Ulupalakua, Maui Co.

LAHAINA, MAUI CO., MARIA LANAKILA (1846) [CEM] Revs. Gary P. Colton; Louis Hoang, Parochial Vicar.
Office: 712 Wainee St., 96761-1511. Tel: 808-661-0552; Fax: 808-661-1670. Email: info@marialanakila.org. Web: www.marialanakila.org.
School—*Sacred Hearts School*, (Grades PreK-8), 239 Dickenson St., 96761. Tel: 808-661-4720; Fax:

808-667-5363. Email: principal@sacredheartschool.net. Web: www.sacredheartsschool.net. Susan Hendricks, Interim Prin. Lay Teachers 19; Students 221.
Catechesis/Religious Program—Students 125.
Mission—Sacred Hearts of Jesus and Mary Office Rd., Honokahua (Kapalua), Maui Co. 96761.
MAKAWAO, HONOLULU, ST. JOSEPH (1851) [CEM] Rev. Geronimo Castro, M.S.
Res. & Office: 1294 Makawao Ave., 96768. Tel: 808-572-7652; Fax: 808-573-2278.
School—(Grades PreK-5) Tel: 808-572-8675; Fax: 808-572-0748. Beth Fobbe-Wills, Prin. Sisters 1; Lay Teachers 13; Students 81.
Catechesis/Religious Program— Sr. Georgina Delgado, O.P., D.R.E. Students 131.
Convent—Dominican Sisters of the Most Holy Rosary 2.
PAIA, MAUI CO., HOLY ROSARY (1866) [CEM] Rev. Elias Escanilla, Admin.; Deacon Patrick Constantino.
Church: 954 Baldwin Ave., 96779-9605. Tel: 808-579-9551; Fax: 808-575-2063.
Catechesis/Religious Program—Tel: 808-579-9551. Students 14.
WAIHEE , HONOLULU, ST. ANN (1935) [CEM] [JC] Rev. Ramon J. Francisco, Admin.
Office: 40 Kuhinia St., 96793-9216. Tel: 808-244-3284; Fax: 808-244-3284.
Catechesis/Religious Program—Students 63.
Mission—St. Joseph [CEM] [JC] Waikapu, Maui Co. 96793.
Mission—St. Francis Xavier [CEM] [JC] Kahakuloa, Maui Co. 96793.
WAILUKU, MAUI CO., ST. ANTHONY OF PADUA (1846) [CEM] Revs. Roland Bunda, S.M.; Gerald Pleva, S.M., Parochial Vicar; Deacons Hiram Haupu; Stephen Maglente.
Office: 1627 B Mill St., 96793-1999. Tel: 808-244-4148; Fax: 808-242-9375.
School—(Grades PreK-6) Tel: 808-244-4976; 808-242-9024 (PreK); Fax: 808-244-7950. Winona Martinez, Prin.; Carlene Santos, Dir. (PreK). Lay Teachers 13; Students 180.
Catechesis/Religious Program—Tel: 808-242-6040. Sr. Eva Joseph Mesina, C.S.J., D.R.E. Students 354.

ISLAND OF MOLOKAI

KALAUPAPA, KALAWAO LAHAINA CO., ST. FRANCIS (1873) Rev. Felix J. Vandebroek, SS.CC.
Mailing Address: P.O. Box 9, 96742. Tel: 808-567-6238.
Mission—St. Philomena
KAUNAKAKAI, MAUI CO., SAINT DAMIEN CATHOLIC PARISH (1874) [CEM 2] Attended by Our Lady of Sorrows, Kalua'aha; St. Joseph, Kamalo (Shrine); St. Sophia, Kaunakakai; and St. Vincent Ferrer, Maunaloa. Rev. Clyde L. Guerreiro, SS.CC.; Deacon Michael K. Shizuma.
Mailing Address: P.O. Box 1948, 96748-1948. Tel: 808-553-5220; Fax: 808-553-3534. Email: molocathl@hawaiiantel.net. Web: www.blesseddamienchurch.org.
Office: 115 Ala Malama St., 96748.
Catechesis/Religious Program—Students 76.

Chaplains of Public Institutions

HONOLULU. *Diocesan Hospital Ministry*, 1330 Ala Moana Blvd., #2602, 96814. Tel: 808-591-8160; Fax: 808-591-8160. Revs. Paul Smith, Dir., Teodulo Gaquit, Deacon Vincent Wozniak.
Prison Ministry, 6301 Pali Hwy, 96744. Tel: 808-203-6735. Deacon Walter H. Yoshimitsu, Diocesan Representative.

Military Chaplains:
Revs.—
Fleury, Joseph M., S.M., U.S. Army
Kloak, David, U.S. Navy
Koester, Timothy, U.S. Navy
McCormick, Patrick J., U.S. Marines
Voyt, Steve, U.S. Air Force
Weber, Mike, U.S. Air Force

On Duty Outside the Diocese:
Revs.—
Blazek, Eugene
Butler, John
Coughlin, Thomas
Evers, Paul H., U.S. Marines
Grimaldi, Joseph A., J.C.L., M.A.
Lanuevo, Victor
Mamo, Nathan
Santry, Robert

Retired:
Rev. Msgrs.—
Dever, Daniel J., 6301 Pali Hwy., 96744.
Nagai, Alan A., 801 S. King St., #1001, 96813.
Revs.—
Bolger, Anthony
Burke, Ronald
Carroll, Joseph, 801 S. King St. #1007, 96813.
Ching, Herbert, 86-660 Lualualei Homestead, Maili, 96792.
DeCosta, George
Fisher, Clarence L., 99-727 Malae Pl., Aiea, 96701.
Ky, Joseph T., S.S., The Congregation of the Mother Co-Redemptrix, 1900 Grand Ave., Carthage, MO 64836-3500.
McNichol, Daniel, 1738 Elua St., 96817.
Peterson, Francis, 801 S. King St., #1003, 96813.
Sabog, Henry, 2909 Kalihi St., 96819.
Siu, Robert K.C., P.O. Box 1047, Lander, WY 82520.
Stawasz, James, 75-5769 Alii Dr., Kailua-Kona, 96740.
Yim, Louis H., 801 S. King St. #1002, 96813.

Permanent Deacons:
Aanavi, Don, St. Joseph-Hilo, P.O. Box 165, Ninole, 96773.
Abel, Richard, Sts. Peter and Paul, 2116 Lime St. #202, 96826.
Adams, Thomas J., Sacred Heart-Hawi, P.O. Box 1048, Kapaau, 96755.
Akapito, Julio, Sacred Heart, Pahoa
Andrews, Efrain, Our Lady of Good Counsel, 98-1366 Oni Kiniki Pl., Aiea, 96701.
Andrews, LeRoy, Immaculate Heart of Mary, 136 Ululani St., Hilo, 96720.
Awana, Benjamin A., 89-104 A Haleakala Ave., Nannakuli, 96792. Our Lady of Sorrows, Wahiawa
Bissen, Kenneth, Jr., Christ the King, P.O. Box 331208, Kahului, 96732.
Borja, Joaquin, St. Elizabeth, 98-1613 Hoomaike St., Pearl City, 96782.
Bostick, James E., (Retired), P.O. Box 894, Kekaha, 96752.
Calunod, Andres J., St. Augustine By the Sea, 1434 Gregory St., 96817.
Carahasen, Frederico, Jr., St. Elizabeth, 98-1040 Moanalua Rd. #1-101, Aiea, 96701.
Carlbom, Ernest F., St. Anthony, Kailua, 41-865 Mahailua St., Waimanalo, 96795.
Cho, Edward, St. George, 41-1403 Kumuula St., Waimanalo, 96795.
Choo, Ronald T.Y., Blessed Sacrament, 46-144 Hilinama St., Kaneoha, 96744.
Cobb, Robert C., (Retired), 2500 Kalakaua Ave., #1003, 96815.
Constantino, Patrick R., 3188 Kilani Pl., Pukalani, 96734.
Contrades, Thomas P., 171 A Lani Alii Pl., Kapaa, 96746.
Cordero, Modesto R., St. John Baptist, 91-1015 Keoneula Blvd., Ewa Beach, 96706.
Coughlin, John A., St. Jude, 92-1041 Makakilo Dr. #80, Kapolei, 96707.
Cyr, Robert, 15-2811 Opakapaka St., Pahoa, 96778-8611. Sacred Heart, Pahoa
DeCaires, Clarence, Jr., St. John Vianney, 1131 Kupau St., Kailua, 96734.
Farias, William A., Immaculate Conception, 4696 Hoomana Rd., Lihue, 96766.
Franco, Lawrence Stanley, St. Theresa - Maui, 452 Kaiola Pl., Kihei, Maui 96753.
Galang, Keith, St. Joseph, 94-595 Kaiewa St., Waipahu, 96797.
Gerakas, Andrew J., Star of the Sea, 4524 Waikui St., 96821.
Gorospe, Santiago, Holy Trinity
Guinaugh, Daniel R., Holy Trinity, 520 Lunalilo Home Rd., 96825.
Haupu, Hiram B., St. Anthony, 4 Nakea Way, Wailuku, 96793.
Ignacio, Lawrence, Annunciation Parish, Kamuela, P.O. Box 317, Paauilo, 96776.
Levy, Harold S., Jr., St. Rita, 87-2214 Farrington Hwy., Waianae, 96792.
Libarios, Ernest, Sr., Resurrection of the Lord, 98-1470 Kaonohi St., Aiea, 96701.
Maglente, Stephen, St. Anthony Maui, 50 E. Waiko Rd., Wailuku, 96793-9319.
Matsuo, Roy T., Co-Cathedral, 1755 Mahani Loop, 96819.
McPeek, William, Anunciation Parish, Kamuela, P.O. Box 278, Kapaau, 96755.
Miner, Henry, Star of the Sea, 1438 Hunakai St., 96816.
Mitsui, Wallace M., St. John Apostle & Evangelist, 95-690 Lewanuu St., Mililani, 97689.
Miyashiro, Thomas H., Our Lady of Good Counsel, 2054 Hoohai St., Pearl City, 96782.
Naich, Julio, Sacred Heart-Punahou and St. Pius X-Manoa, Honolulu
Nelson, Ronald, 66 Queen St., #2301, 96813. Sacred Heart, Honolulu; St. Pius X
Nunogawa, Jerry H., 1673 Haleloke St., Hilo, 96720. St. Joseph, Hilo; Malia Puka O'Kalani
Ona, Fernando V., M.D., Star of the Sea, 1350 Ala Moana Blvd., 96814.
Paglinawan, Ronald, Our Lady of Perpetual Help, 94-348 Kioele Pl., Miliani, 96789.
Pascua, Manuel, 380 Kaima Pl., Kapaa, 96746. St. Catherine, Kauai
Phillips, Albert C., (Retired), 3297 Haleakala Hwy., Makawao, 96768.
Port, Richard J., Sts. Peter and Paul, 1600 Ala Moana Blvd., #3100, 96815.
Pulido, Cornelio, Christ the King, 624 Molokai Hema St., Kahului, 96732.
Rienzi, Thomas M., (Retired), 4389 Malia St., #531, 96821.
Sewen, Misa, Sacred Heart, 85-186 McArthur St., G-304, Waianae, 96792.
Shizuma, Michael K., Saint Damien Catholic Parish, P.O. Box 1311, Kaunakakai, 96748.
Soumwei, Peter, St. John the Baptist, Honolulu
Taylor, Samuel, Holy Trinity, 7218 Pikoni Pl., 96825.
Thorp, George, Jr., St. Anthony-Kalihi, 1459 Akamai St., Kailua, 96734.
Tokars, Jerry L., M.A., St. John Vianney, 748 Iana St., Kailua, 96734.
Townsley, Sidney J., (Retired), 4389 Malia St., Apt. 225, 96821. Sacred Heart, Honolulu; St. Pius X
Vargas, Edward, 92-1051 Makakilo Dr. #96, Kapolei, 96707.
Victor, Leslie, Star of the Sea, 7255 Kuhono St., 96825.
Vito, Jerome, Sacred Heart-Waianae, 87-150 Helelua St.#6, Waianae, 96792.
Whitfield, Billy, P.O. Box 530, Kaaawa, 96730. St. Ann, Kaneohe
William, Chitaro, Our Lady of Sorrows, Wahiawa
Wong, Lauren S.F., St. John Vianney, 1309 Kupau St., Kailua, 96734.
Wozniak, Vincent, Sacred Heart; St. Pius X, 1524 Halekula Way #D, 96822-4918.
Yoshimitsu, Walter H., St. John Vianney, 681 Akoakoa St., Kailua, 96734.

INSTITUTIONS LOCATED IN THE DIOCESE

[A] COLLEGES AND UNIVERSITIES

HONOLULU. **Chaminade University of Honolulu* (1955) 3140 Waialae Ave., 96816. Tel: 808-735-4711; Fax: 808-735-7748. Email: admissions@chaminade.edu. Web: www.chaminade.edu. Revs. Timothy E. Eden, S.M., Chap.; Kenneth A. Templin, S.M., Dir. Campus Ministry (Retired); Timothy E. Eden, S.M., Chap.; Bros. Bernard Ploeger, S.M., Pres.; Jerome Bommer, S.M., Rector; Sharon LePage, Librarian. Priests 4; Brothers 11; Lay Teachers 95; Students 2,688; Total Staff 167; Total Enrollment 2,688.

[B] SCHOOLS-LOWER EDUCATION

ISLAND OF OAHU. *Blessed Marianne Cope Preschool* (1999) (Grades PreSchool), 2707 Pamoa Rd., Honolulu, 96822. Tel: 808-988-6528; Fax: 808-988-5497. Email: sjasouza@stfrancis-oahu.org. Sr. Joan of Arc Souza, O.S.F., Prin. Students 49; Teachers 4.
Damien Memorial School (1962) (Grades 7-12), 1401 Houghtailing St., Honolulu, 96817. Tel: 808-841-0195; Fax: 808-847-1401. Email: weaver@damien.edu; bho@damien.edu; tomita@damien.edu. Web: www.damien.edu. Mr. Bernard A.K.S. Ho, Pres. & CEO; Mr. Michael Weaver, Prin. (High School); Burton Tomita, Prin. (Middle School); Ms. Cheryle O'Brien, Librarian.
The Congregation of Christian Brothers of Hawaii, Inc. Christian Brothers of Ireland, Inc. Priests 1; Brothers 1; Lay Teachers 37; Students 460.
St. Francis School (1924) (Grades PreK-12), 2707 Pamoa Rd., Honolulu, 96822. Tel: 808-988-4111; Fax: 808-988-5497. Email: admin@stfrancis-oahu.org; lgerboc@stfrancis-oahu.org. Web: www.stfrancis-oahu.org. Sr. Joan of Arc Souza, O.S.F., Prin.; Louise Gerboc, Contact Person; Jennifer Mylett, Librarian. Sisters 6; Lay Teachers 35; Girls 323; Boys 86.
Holy Family Catholic Academy Early Learning Center, 830 Main St., Honolulu, 96818. Tel: 808-421-1265; Fax: 808-422-5030. Email: ELC@holyfamilycatholicacademy.org. Kalei DeMello, Dir. Lay Teachers 4; Students 96.
St. John's Catholic Preschool (1979) 95-370 Kuahelani Ave., Mililani Town, 96789. Tel: 808-623-3332, Ext. 200; Fax: 808-623-6496. Email: preschool@sjmililani.com. Web: sjmililani.com. Catherine Awong, Dir. Total Staff 14; Lay

Teachers 4; Students 75.

Saint Louis School, (Grades 4-12), 3142 Waialae Ave., Honolulu, 96816-1578. Tel: 808-739-7777; Fax: 808-739-4853. Email: info@saintlouishawaii.org. Web: www.saintlouishawaii.org. Walter Kirimitsu, Pres.; Derrick Ligsay, Dir. Middle School; John Rizzo, Prin.; Kevin Allen, Librarian. Lay Teachers 50; Boys 765.

Maryknoll Grade School, (Grades PreK-8), 1526 Alexander St., Honolulu, 96822. Tel: 808-952-7100; Fax: 808-952-7101. Email: admission@maryknollschool.org. Web: www.maryknollschool.org. Perry K. Martin, Pres.; Shana Tong, Prin.; Virginia Koo, Librarian. Students 817; Lay Teachers 44.

Maryknoll High School, 1526 Alexander St., Honolulu, 96822. Tel: 808-952-7200; Fax: 808-952-7201. Email: admission@maryknollschool.org. Web: www.maryknollschool.org. Perry K. Martin, Pres.; Ms. Betsey H. Gunderson, Prin. Lay Teachers 44; Students 575.

St. Philomena Early Learning Center (1978) 3300 Ala Laulani St., Honolulu, 96818. Tel: 808-833-8080; Fax: 808-834-3438. Email: admin@stphilomenaelc.com. Angie A. Thomas, Prin. Lay Teachers 12; Teacher Aides 25; Students 200.

Sacred Hearts Academy (1909) (Grades PreK-12), 3253 Waialae Ave., Honolulu, 96816. Tel: 808-734-5058; Fax: 808-737-7867. Email: bwhite@sacredhearts.org. Web: www.sacredhearts.org. Mrs. Betty White, Head of School; Linde Debo, Vice Prin.; Mary Roy, Librarian; Christina Abelardo, Librarian. Sisters 2; Lay Teachers 95; Girls 1,100; Support Staff, Counselors, Administrators 30.

Star of the Sea Early Learning Center, 4470 Aliikoa St., Ste. 100, Honolulu, 96821. Tel: 808-734-3840; Fax: 808-732-1738. Email: postmaster@staroftheseaelc.org. Web: www.staroftheseaelc.org. Lisa Foster, Dir. Lay Teachers 12; Students 190.

ISLAND OF HAWAII. *St. Joseph Montessori Based Preschool and Elementary School* (1948) (Grades PreK-6), 999 Ululani St., Hilo, 96720. Tel: 808-935-4935; Fax: 808-935-6894. Email: sjshilo.principal@gmail.com. Web: www.sjeshilo.org. Victoria Torcolini, Prin.; Janan Malinowski, Librarian. Sisters 1; Lay Teachers 15; Students 181; Total Staff 6.

St. Joseph Jr.-Sr. High School (1949) (Grades 7-12), 1000 Ululani St., Hilo, 96720. Tel: 808-935-4936; Fax: 808-969-9019. Email: sjshilo.principal@gmail.com. Web: www.sjhshilo.org. Victoria Torcolini, Prin.; Miri Sumida, Librarian. Deacons 1; Lay Teachers 11; Students 131; Total Staff 8.

ISLAND OF MAUI. *St. Anthony Grade School*, (Grades PreK-6), 1622-A Mill St., Wailuku, 96793. Tel: 808-244-4976; Fax: 808-244-7950. Email: office@sagsmaui.com. Winoa Martinez, Prin. Lay Teachers 13; Students 180.

St. Anthony Junior-Senior High School, (Grades 7-12), 1618 Lower Main St., Wailuku, 96793. Tel: 808-244-4190; Fax: 808-242-8081. Email: sas@sasmaui.org. Web: www.sasmaui.org/. Rev. James Orsini, Prin.; Andrew Izutsu, Librarian. Sisters 1; Lay Teachers 17; Students 183.

St. Anthony Pre-School, 1627-B Mill St., Wailuku, 96793. Tel: 808-242-9024; Fax: 808-986-0654. Email: sap@hawaii.rr.com. Carlene Santos, Dir. Lay Teachers 7; Students 46.

[C] HEALTHCARE INSTITUTES

HONOLULU. *St. Francis Healthcare System of Hawaii*, 2226 Liliha St., Ste. 227, 96817. Tel: 808-547-6883; Fax: 808-547-8018. Web: www.sfhs.hi.org. Sr. Agnelle Ching, CEO; Revs. Mario Raquepo, Chap.; Joseph E. Specht, S.J., Chap.; George Busto, C.O., Chap.; Sisters Patricia Schofield, O.S.F., Chap.; Candida Oroc, O.S.F., Chap.; Miriam Dionise Cabacungan, O.S.F., Chap.; Jovita Agustin, O.S.F., Chap. Total Staff 284.

St. Francis Home Care Services, 2228 Liliha St., Ste. 106, 96817. Tel: 808-534-0777; Fax: 808-676-1300. Corinne Suzuki, Exec. Dir.

St. Francis Home Care Services-Kauai, 4472 Pahee St., Ste. N, Lihue, 96766. Tel: 808-245-6430; Fax: 808-246-8620. Dardanelle Kaauwai, Dir.

Mobile Care Health Project, 140-B Holomua St., Hilo, 96720. Tel: 808-935-3050; Fax: 808-935-3794.

St. Francis Residential Care Community dba Franciscan Vistas 91-2135 Ft. Weaver Rd., #502, Ewa Beach, 96706. Tel: 808-676-1200; Fax: 808-676-1208. Total Staff 3.

St. Francis Healthcare Foundation of Hawaii, 2228 Liliha St., Ste. 205, 96817. Tel: 808-547-8030; Fax: 808-547-8034. Sr. William Marie Eleniki, O.S.F., Chief Admin. Total Staff 4.

St. Francis Community Health Services, 2251 Mahalo St., 96817. Tel: 808-595-7566; Fax: 808-547-8149. Sr. Agnelle Ching, CEO.

The Sister Maureen Keleher Center (Hospice), 24 Puiwa Rd., 96817. Tel: 808-595-7566; Fax: 808-595-6996. Joy Yadao, Exec. Dir. Bed Capacity 12; Patients Assisted Annually 85.

Sister Maureen Intergenerational Learning Environment aka Franciscan Adult Day Center 2715 Pamoa Rd., 96822. Tel: 808-988-5678; Fax: 808-988-1179. Theresa Basta, Dir. Total Staff 8; Capacity 35; Patients Assisted Annually 130.

The Maurice J. Sullivan Family Hospice Center, 91-2127 Fort Weaver Rd., Ewa Beach, 96706. Tel: 808-678-7580; Fax: 808-678-7597. Joy Yadao, Exec. Dir. Bed Capacity 24; Patients Assisted Annually 146.

Health Services for Senior Citizens, 2251 Mahalo St., 96817. Tel: 808-547-8065; Fax: 808-547-8149. Patients Assisted Annually 440.

St. Francis Hospice Home Setting Program Patients Assisted Annually 1,141.

Healthy Lifestyles Program Tel: 808-547-6035; Fax: 808-595-6996.

St. Francis Lifeline Tel: 808-547-8060; Fax: 808-547-8149. Persons Served Annually 163.

Our Lady of Kea'au, P.O. Box 1475, Waianae, 96792. Tel: 808-696-7255; Fax: 808-696-5672. Sr. Beatrice Tom, O.S.F., Chief Admin.

St. Francis Development Corporation, 91-2135 Fort Weaver Rd., Ste. 502, Ewa Beach, 96706. Tel: 808-676-1200; Fax: 808-676-1202. Email: pwittyoakland@stfrancishawaii.org. Web: stfrancishawaii.org. Pamela Witty-Oakland, Cheif Admin.

KALAUPAPA. *Kalaupapa Nursing Facility* (Molokai), P.O. Box 3333, 96742. Tel: 808-567-6911; Fax: 808-567-6916. Email: knfcef@aloha.net. Carol Franko, Nursing Supvr.; Dr. Kalani Brady, Settlement Medical Dir.; Dr. John Buzanoski, Dept. Medical Dir. Operated by the State Dept. of Health for Hansen's Disease Branch. Franciscan Sisters of the Third Order 1; Bed Capacity 16; Patients Assisted Annually 22; Total Staff 15.

[D] MONASTERIES AND RESIDENCES OF PRIESTS AND BROTHERS

HONOLULU. *The Christian Brothers of Ireland, Inc.*, 1401 Houghtailing St., 96817. Tel: 808-845-2330; Fax: 808-847-1401. Email: cullerton@damien.edu. Bros. B. John Cullerton, C.F.C., Contact Person; F. Louis Frick, C.F.C., (Retired); Liam V. Nolan, C.F.C., School Counselor; W. Greg O'Donnell, C.F.C., (Retired); Patrick L. O'Hare, C.F.C., (Retired); F. M. Popish, C.F.C., (Retired); K. J. Reilly, C.F.C.; T. Patrick Rowland, C.F.C., (Retired). Brothers 8.

Jesuit Fathers House, 2727 Pamoa Rd., 96822-1838. Tel: 808-988-3464; Fax: 808-988-7627. Email: jchandler@calprov.org. Web: www.newmanhawaii.org. Revs. John Chandler, S.J., Regl. Supr.; Joseph E. Specht, S.J.; Russell J. Roide, S.J.

California Province of the Society of Jesus

Marianist Communities 3140 Waialae Ave., 96816-1578. Rev. Francis Nakagawa, S.M.; Bro. Robert G. Hoppe, S.M., Vice Pres., Marianist Center of Hawaii. *Center Marianist Community*, 3140 Waialae Ave., 96816. Tel: 808-739-8500; 808-739-8517; Fax: 808-739-8501. Bro. Dennis Schmitz, S.M., Community Dir.; Revs. Timothy Eden, S.M.; Kenneth A. Templin, S.M. (Retired). Priests 2; Brothers 8; Total in Residence 10. *Marianist Hall Community*, 3140 Waialae Ave., 96816. Tel: 808-739-8300; Fax: 808-739-8320. Revs. Joseph Priestly, S.M.; John Klobuka, S.M.; James Bartlett, S.M.; Bro. Frank Damm, Community Dir. Priests 3; Brothers 5. *Chaminade Pohaku Marianist Community*, 3140 Waialae Ave., 96816. Tel: 808-735-4857; Fax: 808-739-8333. Bro. Gary Morris, Dir.; Rev. Robert Bouffier, S.M. Priests 1; Brothers 2. *Wailuku Marianist Community*, 1627 B Mill St., Wailuku, 96793. Tel: 808-244-4148; Fax: 808-242-9375. Revs. Roland Bunda, S.M.; Gerald Pleva, S.M.; Bro. Jim Vorndran, S.M., Community Dir. Priests 2; Brothers 1.

KANEOHE. *Congregation of the Sacred Hearts of Jesus and Mary (Hawaii Province SS.CC.)* (1800) P.O. Box 1365, 96744-1365. Tel: 808-247-5035; Fax: 808-235-8849. Email: sacredhearts@hawaii.rr.com. Very Rev. Christopher Keahi, SS.CC., Pres. Prov. Priests 16; Brothers 6.

Sacred Hearts Center, P.O. Box 1365, 96744-1365. Tel: 808-247-5035; Fax: 808-235-8849. Email: sacredhearts@hawaii.rr.com. Very Rev. Christopher Keahi, SS.CC., Prov. Supr.; Revs. James Anguay, SS.CC., (Philippines); Albert Garcia, SS.CC., Supr.; Paul Zaccone, SS.CC.; Bros. George Apo, SS.CC.; Charles Kaahanui, SS.CC., (Molokai). Total in Residence 6; Total Staff 2. *St. Patrick's Monastery*, 1124-A Seventh Ave., Honolulu, 96816. Tel: 808-732-0281. Revs. Thomas Choo, SS.CC.; Clarence Guerreiro, SS.CC.; Albert Miechielsen, SS.CC.; Stephen Van den Eynde, SS.CC.; Bros. Richard Kupo, SS.CC.; Leo Vendiola, SS.CC.; Patrick Hughes, SS.CC; William Dunn, SS.CC. Total in Residence 8; Total Staff 6.

WAIALUA, OAHU. *Benedictine Monastery of Hawaii/Retreat Center* (1984) 67-290 Farrington Hwy., P.O. Box 490, 96791. Tel: 808-637-7887; Fax: 808-637-8601. Email: monastery@hawaiibenedictines.org. Web: www.hawaiibenedictines.org. Revs. Michael Sawyer, O.S.B., Treas.; Timothy Ottman, O.S.B.; David Barfknecht, O.S.B., Supr. & Pres.; Sisters Mary Jo McEnany, O.S.B., Vice Pres.; Celeste Cabral, O.S.B.; Geralyn Spaulding, O.S.B.; Bros. Gregory Foret, O.S.B., Sec.; Isidore Derouen, O.S.B. Benedictine Congregation of Our Lady of Mounte Oliveto, O.S.B.

[E] CONVENTS AND RESIDENCES FOR SISTERS

HONOLULU. *Congregation of the Sacred Hearts and of Perpetual Adoration* (1800) 1120 Fifth Ave., 96816. Tel: 808-737-5822; Fax: 808-735-0878. Web: www.ssccpicpus.com. (Sisters of the Congregation of the Sacred Hearts of Jesus and Mary of Perpetual Adoration, SS.CC.).

Regina Pacis Community, 1120 Fifth Ave., 96816. Tel: 808-737-5822; Fax: 808-735-0878. Sisters Helene Wood, SS.CC., Pres. & Prov. Supr.; Regina Mary Jenkins, SS.CC., Vice Pres., Vicar Prov., Supr., & Contact Person; Anne Clare DeCosta, SS.CC., Sec.; Irene Barboza, SS.CC., Treas. Sisters 5.

Puawakea Community, 3351 Kalihi St., 96819. Tel: 808-845-4353; Fax: 808-848-2696. Sr. Rose Kathleen Lenchanko, SS.CC., Contact Person. Sisters 3.

Paewalani Community, 45-901 Wailele Rd., 96744. Tel: 808-247-3688; Fax: 808-235-0717. Sisters Rose Kathleen Lenchanko, SS.CC., Supr.; Anne Clare DeCosta, SS.CC., Contact Person. Sisters 4.

Malia o ka Malu Community, 1117 Fourth Ave., 96816. Tel: 808-734-2048. Sr. Anne-Marie Tamanaha, SS.CC., Supr. & Contact Person. Sisters 14.

Na Leo Ho'onani Community, 2151 Kauhana St., 96816. Tel: 808-739-5566. Sisters Katherine Francis Miller, SS.CC., Supr.; Irene Barboza, SS.CC., Contact Person. Sisters 3.

Maryknoll Sisters of St. Dominic Central Pacific Region 125 Ainoni St., Kailua, 96734-2138. Tel: 808-261-6356 (Res.); 808-261-0267. Email: mkainoni@lava.net. Sr. Sandra Galazin, M.M., Contact Person. Sisters 2. 2880 Oahu Ave., 96822-1732. Tel: 808-988-6540; Fax: 808-988-8089. Email: mkmanoa@hawaii.rr.com. Sisters 4. 1570 Mokulua Dr., Kailua, 96734-3254. Tel: 808-261-1674. Email: mksrslan@hawaiiantel.net. Sisters 2. 87-204 Holomalia Pl., Nanakuli, 96792-3706. Tel: 808-668-1603. Email: mkskkp@hawaiiantel.net. Sisters 2.

The Sisters of St. Francis of the Neumann Communities (1883) St. Francis Convent, 2715 Pamoa Rd., 96822-1885. Tel: 808-988-4432; Fax: 808-687-8695. Email: mkikukawa@sosf.org. Sr. Marion Kikukawa, O.S.F., M.Ed., Contact Person & Region Admin. Sisters of St. Francis of the Neumann Communities (O.S.F.); St. Francis Healthcare System of Hawaii; St. Francis School. Sisters 45.

Sisters of St. Joseph of Carondelet CSJ, Hawaii Vice-Province, Administration Center, 5311 Apo Dr., 96821-1829. Tel: 808-373-3850; Fax: 808-373-5341. Email: smlp@hawaiiantel.net. Sr. Margaret L. Perreira, C.S.J., Dir.

The following are listings of residences and the number of sisters residing at each:

Carondelet Community, 5311 Apo Dr., 96821-1829. Tel: 808-373-3850; Fax: 808-373-5341. Email: pachang@verizon.net. Sisters 5.

Holy Trinity Community, 6590 Hawaii Kai Dr., 96825-1112. Tel: 808-396-9182. Email: htcsj@juno.com.

Mana'olana Community, 1046 6th Ave., 96816-1644. Tel: 808-737-2130; Fax: 808-732-2851. Email: rsm@hawaii.rr.com. Sisters 3.

St. Joseph by the Sea Community, 206 Kailua Rd., Kailua, 96734-2398. Tel: 808-262-0575. Email: sjbts@hawaii.rr.com. Sisters 3.

St. Theresa Community, 712 N. School St. B, 96817-3098. Tel: 808-533-3101. Email: stccsj@pixi.com. Sisters 3.

Christ the King Community, 211 A. South Kaulawahine St., Kahului, 96732-2200. Tel: 808-877-0790. Email: LePuycsj@aol.com. Sisters 4.

KANEOHE. *Carmel of the Holy Trinity (Carmelite Monastery)*, 6301 Pali Hwy., 96744-5224. Tel: 808-261-6542. Sr. Agnes Marie Wong, Prioress. Order of Discalced Carmelite Nuns of Our Lady of Mount Carmel (O.C.D.). Sisters 5.

WAIPAHU. *Dominican Center Hawaii*, 94-1249 Lumikula St., 96797. Tel: 808-676-1452; 808-677-1202; Fax: 808-677-1202. Email: srmauraliaop@juno.com. Web: www.ophawiiregion.com. Sisters

M. Aurelia Sanchez, O.P., Regl. Sec. & Councilor; Dominica Wong, O.P., Contact Person. Please refer to the following parish convents for additional residences: St. Elizabeth, Aiea; St. John, Honolulu; St. Joseph, Makawao; House of Aloha Convent, Waianae. Sisters 24.

St. Elizabeth Convent, 99-310 Moanalua Rd., Aiea, 96701. Tel: 808-487-3131. Sr. Delia Obenza, O.P., Contact Person. Sisters 5.

St. John the Baptist Convent, 2330 Omilo Ln., Honolulu, 96819. Tel: 808-845-2622; Fax: 808-842-6104. Email: srmaryloup@juno.com. Sr. Maria Genovena Binas, O.P., Contact Person. Sisters 7.

St. Joseph Convent, 57 Dominican Way, Makawao, 96768. Tel: 808-572-8454. Sr. Georgina Delgado, O.P., Contact Person. Sisters 2.

[F] CATHOLIC CHARITIES

HONOLULU. **Catholic Charities Hawaii*, 1822 Keeaumoku St., 96822. Tel: 808-524-4673; Fax: 808-599-8761. Members of the Corporation: Most Rev. Clarence R. Silva; Very Rev. Marc R. Alexander, S.T.D., V.G.; Roger J. Wall; Lisa Sakamoto; Marianita Lopez, Esq. Board of Directors: Rix Maurer III, Chm.; Dr. Leslie Correa, Ed.D., Vice Pres.; Mary Fastenau, Sec.; Gregg Robertson, Treas.; Very Rev. Marc R. Alexander, S.T.D., V.G., Dir.; Ruth Ann Becker, Dir.; Clementine Ceria-Ulep, Ph.D., Dir.; Dan Colin, Dir.; Dr. Leslie Correa, Ed.D.; Christopher R. Dang, Esq., Dir.; James E. Dannemiller, Dir.; Phyllis B. Dendle, Dir.; Koren Dreher, Dir.; Brandt Farias, Dir.; Bonnie Fong, Dir.; Wesley Fong; James Hasselman, Dir.; Elsa Honma, Dir.; Alan Ito, Dir.; Chuck Jones; Ted Jung Jr.; Dew-Anne Langcaon; Jeffrey Loo, Dir.; Richard E. Meiers, Dir.; Leigh-Ann Miyasato, Dir.; Debbie Ng-Furuhashi, Dir.; Quin Ogawa, Dir.; Jan Ohtani; Jerry Rauckhorst, Dir.; Gregg Robertson; Antonio J. Saguibo Jr., Dir.; Rev. Gary L. Secor, Dir.; Mary Sheridan, Ph.D., Dir.; Kim Tomlinson; David Waldron, Dir.; Roger J. Wall, Dir.; Dara Young, Dir.

Catholic Charities Housing Development Corporation, 1822 Keeamoku St., 96822. Tel: 808-524-4673; Fax: 808-527-4849. Email: eddieontai@catholiccharitieshawaii.org. Web: www.catholiccharitieshawaii.org. Edward C. Ontai, Vice Pres.

[G] RETREAT AND SPIRITUAL CENTERS

HONOLULU. *St. Anthony Retreat Center* (1909) 3351 Kalihi St., 96819. Tel: 808-845-4353; Fax: 808-848-2696. Sr. Rose Kathleen Lenchanko, SS.CC., Contact. Sisters 2.

**Marianist Center of Hawaii* (1986) 3140 Waialae Ave., 96816. Tel: 808-738-5887; Fax: 808-732-3374. Email: brohoppe@aol.com. Bros. Robert G. Hoppe, S.M., Vice Pres.; Dennis Schmitz, S.M., Dir. Special Ministry. Total Staff 2.

Our Lady the Mystical Rose Chapel , (Oratory), c/o Marianist Center of Hawaii, 3140 Waialae Ave., 96816. Tel: 808-739-4738; 808-738-5887 (direct line); Fax: 808-732-3374. Email: brohoppe@aol.com. Rev. Timothy Eden, S.M., Chap.; Bro. Robert G. Hoppe, S.M., Contact Person. Tel: 808-738-5887.

KANEOHE. *Saint Stephen Diocesan Center*, 6301 Pali Hwy., 96744-5298. Tel: 808-203-6700; Fax: 808-261-7022. Email: sizaguirre@rcchawaii.org. Deacon Walter H. Yoshimitsu, Admin.

WAIALUA, OAHU. *Benedictine Monastery of Hawaii / Retreat Center* (1984) 67-290 Farrington Hwy., P.O. Box 490, 96791. Tel: 808-637-7887; Fax: 808-637-8601. Rev. Michael Sawyer, O.S.B., Treas. Benedictine Congregation of Our Lady of Mounte Oliveto, O.S.B.

[H] ASSOCIATIONS OF THE FAITHFUL

HONOLULU. *Hawaii Catholic Charismatic Renewal Services*, 620 Lunalilo Home Rd., #6215, 96825. Deacon Daniel Guinaugh, Contact Person; Rita Guinaugh, Contact Person.

Nocturnal Adoration Society, 1018 11th Ave., 96819. Leonard Letoto, Contact Person.

KAILUA. *Catholic Women's Guild*, 925 Alapapa Dr., 96734. Alice Secor, Contact Person.

KANEOHE. **INHIM Ministries, Inc.*, 6301 Pali Hwy., 96744. Tel: 808-497-7451. Email: information@inhimhawaii.org.

Legion of Mary, P.O. Box 17, 96744. Nettie Lou Peiler, Contact Person.

KAPOLEI. *Diocesan Catholic Congress of Filipino Catholic Clubs*, P.O. Box 700606, 96709. Tel: 808-672-8100. Estrella Estillore, Contact Person.

MILILANI. *Missionary Basic Christian Community*, 95-761 Pulehulehu St., 96789. Rodney Kekina, Contact Person.

PEARL CITY. *Society of St. Vincent DePaul Honolulu District Council*, 920 Keolu Dr., Kailua, 96734-3842. Tel: 808-262-8317. Dennis Sasaki, Contact Person.

WAIALUA. *Basic Christian Community of Hawaii, Benedictine Monastery*, P.O. Box 490, 96791. Tel: 808-674-1853. Raul Perez, Contact Person; Annabelle Perez, Contact Person.

[I] FOUNDATIONS

KANEOHE. *Augustine Educational Foundation* (1984) St. Stephen Diocesan Center, 6301 Pali Hwy., 96744. Tel: 808-203-6736; Fax: 808-230-2441. Email: aef@aloha.net. Web: www.augustinefoundation.org. Most Rev. Clarence R. Silva, Pres.; Very Rev. Marc R. Alexander, S.T.D., V.G., Vice Pres.; Susan Ferandin, Exec. Dir.

WAILUKU. *Maui Helio Endowment Fund*, 1885 Main St., Ste. 404, 96793. Patrick Wong, Pres. & Contact Person; John Kim, Vice Pres.; Kara Shimizu, Treas.; Paul Harikawa, Sec.

RELIGIOUS INSTITUTES OF MEN REPRESENTED IN THE DIOCESE

For further details refer to the corresponding bracketed number in the Religious Institutes of Men or Women section.

[0200]—*Benedictine Monks* (Olivetan)—O.S.B.

[]—*Blessed Sacrament Fathers*—S.S.S.

[0470]—*The Capuchin Friars*—O.F.M.Cap.

[0310]—*Congregation of Christian Brothers*—C.F.C.

[]—*Congregation of the Blessed Sacrament*—S.S.S.

[1140]—*Fathers of the Sacred Hearts* (Hawaii Prov.)—SS.CC.

[0690]—*Jesuit Fathers*—S.J.

[]—*La Salette Fathers*—M.S.

[0800]—*Maryknoll*—M.M.

[0720]—*The Missionaries of Our Lady of La Salette* (Pacific Region)—M.S.

[0950]—*Oratorians*—C.O.

[0760]—*Society of Mary* (Prov. of the Pacific)—S.M.

RELIGIOUS INSTITUTES OF WOMEN REPRESENTED IN THE DIOCESE

[]—*Benedictine Congregation of Our Lady of Mounte Oliveto*—O.S.B.

[0950]—*Daughters of Saint Paul*—F.S.P.

[0420]—*Discalced Carmelite Nuns*—O.C.D.

[1070-03]—*Dominican Sisters of the Most Holy Rosary*—O.P.

[1230]—*Franciscan Sisters of Christian Charity*—O.S.F.

[2470]—*Maryknoll Sisters of St. Dominic*—M.M.

[]—*Missionary Sisters of Mary Help of Christians*—M.S.M.H.C.

[]—*Sinsinawa Dominicans*—O.P.

[]—*Sisters for Christian Community*—S.F.C.C.

[0430]—*Sisters of Charity of the Blessed Virgin Mary*—B.V.M.

[]—*Sisters of Divine Providence*—C.D.P.

[]—*Sisters of St. Paul of Chartres*—S.C.P.

[]—*Sisters of St. Francis of the Neumann Communities*—O.S.F.

[3840]—*Sisters of St. Joseph of Carondelet*—C.S.J.

[1960]—*Sisters of the Holy Family*—S.H.F.

[3690]—*Sisters of the Sacred Hearts and of Perpetual Adoration*—SS.CC.

[1490]—*Sisters of the Third Franciscan Order* (Syracuse, NY)—O.S.F

NECROLOGY

† Eikmeier, Rev. Msgr. Bernard J., (Retired)—Died July 8, 2009

† Duffy, Edwin J., (Retired)—Died March 19, 2009

† Halloran, John, (Retired)—Died May 5, 2009

An asterisk (*) denotes an organization that has established tax-exempt status directly with the IRS and is not covered by the USCCB Group Ruling.

Diocese of Houma-Thibodaux

(Dioecesis Humensis-Thibodensis)

Most Reverend

SAM G. JACOBS, D.D.

Bishop of Houma-Thibodaux; ordained June 6, 1964; appointed Bishop of Alexandria July 1, 1989; ordained and installed August 24, 1989; appointed third Bishop of Houma-Thibodaux August 1, 2003; installed October 10, 2003. *Office: 2779 Hwy. 311, Schriever, LA 70395.*

Chancery: P.O. Box 505, Schriever, LA 70395. Tel: 985-868-7720; Fax: 985-868-7727.

Email: jbaker@htdiocese.org

ERECTED JUNE 5, 1977.

Square Miles 3,440.

Comprises the parishes of Lafourche, Terrebonne, parts of St. Mary and Jefferson.

For legal titles of parishes and diocesan institutions, consult the Chancery Office.

STATISTICAL OVERVIEW

Personnel	
Bishop	1
Priests: Diocesan Active in Diocese	43
Priests: Diocesan Active Outside Diocese	1
Priests: Retired, Sick or Absent	18
Number of Diocesan Priests	62
Religious Priests in Diocese	7
Total Priests in Diocese	69
Permanent Deacons in Diocese	31
Total Brothers	6
Total Sisters	29
Parishes	
Parishes	39
With Resident Pastor:	
Resident Diocesan Priests	37
Without Resident Pastor:	
Administered by Priests	2
Missions	3
Professional Ministry Personnel:	
Brothers	5
Sisters	9
Lay Ministers	15
Welfare	
Homes for the Aged	1
Total Assisted	60
Day Care Centers	1
Total Assisted	116
Specialized Homes	1
Total Assisted	60
Educational	
Diocesan Students in Other Seminaries	12
Total Seminarians	12
High Schools, Diocesan and Parish	3
Total Students	1,919
Elementary Schools, Diocesan and Parish	10
Total Students	3,955
Catechesis/Religious Education:	
High School Students	2,552
Elementary Students	4,901
Total Students under Catholic Instruction	13,339
Teachers in the Diocese:	
Brothers	4
Sisters	4
Lay Teachers	373
Vital Statistics	
Receptions into the Church:	
Infant Baptism Totals	1,310
Minor Baptism Totals	33
Adult Baptism Totals	50
Received into Full Communion	55
First Communions	1,233
Confirmations	992
Marriages:	
Catholic	293
Interfaith	30
Total Marriages	323
Deaths	1,272
Total Catholic Population	105,836
Total Population	202,000

Former Bishops—Most Revs. WARREN L. BOUDREAUX, J.C.D., D.D., First Bishop of Houma-Thibodaux; ord. May 30, 1942; retired Dec. 29, 1992; died Oct. 6, 1997; MICHAEL JARRELL, D.D., Second Bishop of Houma-Thibodaux; ord. June 3, 1967; appt. Dec. 29, 1992; cons. and installed March 4, 1993; appt. 6th Bishop of Lafayette, Louisiana Nov. 8, 2002.

Chancery

Chancery—Address all correspondence to: P.O. Box 505, Schriever, 70395. Office: 2779 Hwy. 311, Schriever, 70395. Tel: 985-868-7720; Fax: 985-868-7727. Office Hours: Mon.-Fri. 8:30-4:30.

Vicar General—Very Rev. JAY BAKER.

Chancellor—VACANT.

Finance Officer—Rev. Msgr. FREDERIC J. BRUNET.

Judicial Vicar—Very Rev. VICENTE DELA CRUZ.

Director of Tribunal—VACANT.

Diocesan Tribunal— Address all correspondence to: VERONICA SONGE, Mailing Address: P.O. Box 505, Schriever, 70395. Office: 2779 Hwy. 311, Schriever, 70395. Tel: 985-850-3126.

Departments of the Diocesan Curia

Department of Administration Ministries

Judges—Very Revs. VICENTE DELA CRUZ; JAY BAKER.

Defender of the Bond—Very Rev. DANIEL M. POCHE.

Counselor—Mrs. NANCY DIEDRICH, L.P.C., L.M.F.T.

Priests Council—Revs. DOMINGO CRUZ; JOSEKUTTY VARGHESE; Very Rev. CHARLES J. PERKINS, V.F.; Revs. SHENAN J. BOQUET; JEROD DUET; Very Rev. DANIEL M. POCHE; Rev. JOSHUA JOHN RODRIGUE; Very Rev. CARL COLLINS; Rev. ROBERT C. ROGERS; Very Rev. JAY BAKER, Ex Officio, Mailing Address: P.O. Box 505, Schriever, 70395. 2779 Hwy. 311, Schriever, 70395.

College of Consultors—Very Rev. CHARLES J. PERKINS, V.F.; Revs. JOSEKUTTY VARGHESE; SHENAN J. BOQUET; Very Revs. CARL COLLINS; DANIEL M. POCHE; JAY BAKER, Ex-Officio.

Deans—

Upper Lafourche Deanery—Very Rev. DANIEL M. POCHE, Mailing Address: P.O. Box 2623, Morgan City, 70381.

South Lafourche Deanery—Very Rev. CHARLES J. PERKINS, V.F., Mailing Address: 3500 Hwy. 1, Raceland, 70394.

Terrebonne Deanery—Very Rev. CARL COLLINS, 8594 Main St., Houma, 70363.

Diocesan Finance Council—GLENN J. LANDRY; Rev. Msgr. FREDERIC J. BRUNET; Very Revs. PATRICK O'BRIEN; JAY BAKER; ANGELIQUE BARKER; RODNEY WHITNEY; LARRY CALLAIS; PHILIP MCMAHON; A. J. CHAMPAGNE JR.; ROBERT NAQUIN.

Coordinator—GLENN J. LANDRY, 2779 Hwy. 311, Schriever, 70395. Mailing Address: P.O. Box 505, Schriever, 70395. Tel: 985-850-3122.

Accounting, Business Office, Finance—GLENN J. LANDRY, Business Mgr., 2779 Hwy. 311, Schriever, 70395. Mailing Address: P.O. Box 505, Schriever, 70395. Tel: 985-868-7720.

Archives and Historical Research Center—KEVIN ALLEMAND, 205 Audubon St., Thibodaux, 70301. Tel: 985-446-2383.

Building Commission—JAMES J. DANOS, Dir., 2779 Hwy. 311, Schriever, 70395. Mailing Address: P.O. Box 505, Schriever, 70395. Tel: 985-868-7720.

Cemeteries—GEORGE COOKE, Dir., 949 Menard St., Thibodaux, 70301. Tel: 985-446-0280.

Legal Services—Very Rev. JAY BAKER, Dir., 2779 Hwy. 311, Schriever, 70395. Mailing Address: P.O. Box 505, Schriever, 70395. Tel: 985-868-7720. Attorneys: KENNETH WATKINS; DANIEL WALKER, Mailing Address: 501 Roussell St., P.O. Box 5095, Houma, 70361. Tel: 985-868-2333.

Stewardship and Development—JEREMY PUNCH, Dir., 2779 Hwy. 311, Schriever, 70395. Mailing Address: P.O. Box 505, Schriever, 70395. Tel: 985-868-7720.

Human Resources & Employment Benefits—KATHLEEN THERIOT, Dir., 2779 Hwy. 311, Schriever, 70395. Mailing Address: P.O. Box 505, Schriever, 70395. Tel: 985-868-7720.

Insurance - Property, Casualty & Liability—SHEILA LEBOUEF, Dir., 2779 Hwy. 311, Schriever, 70395. Mailing Address: P.O. Box 505, Schriever, 70395. Tel: 985-868-7720.

Operations - Computers & Technology—HOLLY BECNEL, Dir., 2779 Hwy. 311, Schriever, 70395. Mailing Address: P.O. Box 505, Schriever, 70395. Tel: 985-868-7720.

Department for Clergy and Religious

Coordinator—Very Rev. JAY BAKER, 2779 Hwy. 311, Schriever, 70395. Mailing Address: P.O. Box 505, Schriever, 70395. Tel: 985-868-7720.

Clergy Personnel—Very Rev. JAY BAKER, Mailing Address: P.O. Box 505, Schriever, 70395. Tel: 985-868-7720.

Continuing Education of the Clergy-Ministry to Priests Program—Rev. GLENN LECOMPTE, Mailing Address: P.O. Box 505, Schriever, 70395. Tel: 985-868-7720.

Vicar for Priests—Rev. ROGER VILLARRUBIA JR. (Retired), 8594 Main St., Houma, 70363. Tel: 985-876-7652.

Permanent Diaconate—Deacon DOUGLAS AUTHEMENT, 123 Fane St., Houma, 70364. Tel: 985-876-0842. 2779 Hwy. 311, Schriever, 70395. Mailing Address: P.O. Box 505, Schriever, 70395. Tel: 985-868-7720.

Vocations—Rev. JOSEPH PILOLA, Dir., NSU Box 2051, Thibodaux, 70310. Tel: 985-446-2606.

Seminarians—Rev. MARK TOUPS, P.O. Box 1436, Larose, 70373. Tel: 985-414-9717.

Women Religious—VACANT, Mailing Address: P.O. Box 505, Schriever, 70395. Tel: 985-850-3122.

Department of Formation Ministries

Coordinator—LOUIS G. AGUIRRE, 2779 Hwy. 311, Schriever, 70395. Mailing Address: P.O. Box 505, Schriever, 70395. Tel: 985-868-7720.

Campus Ministry—Rev. JOSEPH PILOLA, Dir., N.S.U., Mailing Address: Box 2051, Thibodaux, 70310. Tel: 985-446-6201.

Catholic Schools—Sr. IMMACULATA PAISANT, M.S.C., Supt., 2779 Hwy. 311, Schriever, 70395. Mailing

Address: P.O. Box 505, Schriever, 70395. Tel: 985-868-7720.

Communications, Public Relations, Publications, Radio & Television—LOUIS G. AGUIRRE, Dir., 2779 Hwy. 311, Schriever, 70395. Mailing Address: P.O. Box 505, Schriever, 70395. Tel: 985-868-7720.

Religious Education—Dr. FAITH ANN SPINELLA, Dir., 2779 Hwy. 311, Schriever, 70395. Mailing Address: P.O. Box 505, Schriever, 70395. Tel: 985-868-7720.

New Evangelization and Pastoral Services—PAUL GEORGE, Dir., 2779 Hwy. 311, Schriever, 70395. Mailing Address: P.O. Box 505, Schriever, 70395. Tel: 985-868-7720.

"The Bayou Catholic"— (Diocesan Newspaper)-- LOUIS G. AGUIRRE, Editor, 2779 Hwy. 311, Schriever, 70395. Mailing Address: P.O. Box 505, Schriever, 70395. Tel: 985-868-7720.

Youth Ministries—MICHAEL DISALVO, 2779 Hwy. 311, Schriever, 70395. Mailing Address: P.O. Box 505, Schriever, 70395. Tel: 985-868-7720.

Family Ministries—CATHERINE KLINGMAN, 2779 Hwy. 311, Schriever, 70395. Mailing Address: P.O. Box 505, Schriever, 70395. Tel: 985-868-7720.

Worship—Rev. GLENN LECOMPTE, 2779 Hwy. 311, Schriever, 70395. Mailing Address: P.O. Box 505, Schriever, 70395. Tel: 985-868-7720.

Rite of Chiristian Initiation of Adults—CAROLYN DUPRE; Deacon DENNIS DUPRE, 1001 Wright St., Houma, 70364. Tel: 985-872-2816.

Young Adult Ministries—PAUL GEORGE, Dir., Mailing Address: 265 Corporate Dr., Houma, 70361. Tel: 985-876-4132.

Conference Office—1181 W. Tunnel Blvd., Ste. D, Houma, 70360. Tel: 985-872-1810; Fax: 985-872-5268. SALLY DUBROC, Coord.; MELANIE WEEKS, Asst. Coord.

Department of Social Ministries

Coordinator—VACANT, 2779 Hwy. 311, P.O. Box 505, Schriever, 70395. Tel: 985-850-3122.

Assisi Bridge House—Mr. ROBERT GORMAN, A.C.S.W., B.C.S.W., Dir., 600 Bull Run Rd., Schriever, 70395. Tel: 985-872-5529.

Catholic Campaign for Human Development—Mr. ROBERT GORMAN, A.C.S.W., B.C.S.W., Diocesan Dir., 1220 Aycock St., P.O. Box 3894, Houma, 70361. Tel: 985-876-0490.

Catholic Relief Service Director—KATHRYN ANDERSON.

Catholic Social Services; Justice & Peace—ROBERT D. GORMAN, A.C.S.W., B.C.S.W., Dir.; GERMAINE JACKSON, Assoc. Dir., 1220 Aycock St., P.O. Box 3894, Houma, 70361. Tel: 985-876-0490.

Disaster Relief—ROBERT D. GORMAN, A.C.S.W., B.C.S.W., Exec. Dir.; GERMAINE JACKSON, Dir., 1220 Aycock St., P.O. Box 3894, Houma, 70361. Tel: 985-876-0490.

St. Lucy's Day Care Center—MARSHALL GULLAGE, Admin., 1224 Aycock St., P.O. Box 3894, Houma, 70361. Tel: 985-876-1246.

Other Offices and Commissions

Charismatic Renewal—PAUL MACLEAN, Charismatic Renewal Liaison, Mailing Address: P.O. Box 3620, Houma, 70361. Tel: 985-856-5345.

Cursillo—Rev. ROCH R. NAQUIN, Dir., 539 Island Rd., Montegut, 70377. Tel: 985-594-5144; Fax: 985-594-6960.

Ecumenism—VACANT, P.O. Box 505, Schriever, 70395. Tel: 985-868-7720; Fax: 985-868-7727.

Pontifical Societies for the Propagation of the Faith—Holy Childhood Association; Society of St. Peter the Apostle. Rev. ROBERT JOEL CRUZ, Dir., 1220 Aycock St., Houma, 70360. Tel: 985-850-0035; Fax: 985-850-0063.

Scouting—MICHAEL J. DISALVO, Dir., 2779 Hwy. 311, Schriever, 70395. Mailing Address: P.O. Box 505, Schriever, 70395. Tel: 985-868-7720; Fax: 985-850-3215.

Organizations

Catholic Daughters of the Americas—Rev. JEROD DUET, Spiritual Advisor, 409 Funderburk Ave., Houma, 70364.

Diocesan Council of St. Vincent de Paul Societies—NORMAN SIMON, Pres., 901 Liberty St., Houma, 70360. Tel: 985-851-2432.

Knights of Columbus—Rev. CLYDE MAHLER, Diocesan Chap., Mailing Address: 246 Corporate Dr., Houma, 70360. Tel: 985-876-3313.

Legion of Mary—Mrs. JERRALINE SERPAS, Pres.; VACANT, Spiritual Dir.

St. Vincent de Paul Store—Mr. PETE CAVALIER, Pres.; Mr. ROY BURNS, Vice Pres.; Mr. CULLEN BOUDREAUX, Treas. Store Managers: JIM LAGARDE; PHYLLIS LAGARDE, 107 Point St., Houma, 70360. Tel: 985-872-9373; Fax: 985-223-1931.

Serra Club of South Lafourche—Mr. BOBBY CHERAMIE, Pres.

Serra Club of Thibodaux—Rev. JOSEPH PILOLA, Spiritual Advisor; Mr. DON HARRIS, Pres.

Anawim—EVELYN RUCKSTUHL, Pres., 501 Grinage St., Houma, 70360. Tel: 985-850-3129.

Victim Assistance Coordinator—Mrs. NANCY DIEDRICH, L.P.C., L.M.F.T. Tel: 985-850-3129. Email: ndiedrich@htdiocese.org.

CLERGY, PARISHES, MISSIONS AND PAROCHIAL SCHOOLS

CITY OF HOUMA

(PARISH TERREBONNE)

1—CATHEDRAL OF ST. FRANCIS DE SALES (1847) [CEM 2] Very Rev. Vicente DeLa Cruz, Rector; Revs. Elmer Villamayor; Glenn LeCompte; Deacons Douglas Authement; Joseph Weigand Jr.
Res.: 500 Goode St., Houma, 70360. Tel: 985-876-6904; Fax: 985-851-4204.
School—(Grades PreSchool-7), 300 Verret St., Houma, 70360. Tel: 985-868-6646; Fax: 985-851-5896. Brenda Tanner, Prin.; Celeste Cancienne, Asst. Prin. Lay Teachers 34; Students 803.
Catechesis/Religious Program—Students 241.
Convent—501 Grinage St., Houma, 70360. Tel: 985-876-7260.

2—ANNUNZIATA (1963) Rev. Michael A. Bergeron; Sr. Paula Richard, O.P., Pastoral Assoc.; Deacons Raymond Bourg Jr.; Connely Duplantis. In Res., Rev. Msgr. Donald Ledet (Retired).
Res.: 2011 Acadian Dr., Houma, 70363. Tel: 985-876-2971; Fax: 985-868-6414.
Catechesis/Religious Program—Students 223.

3—ST. BERNADETTE (1958) Very Rev. Patrick O'Brien; Rev. Jerod Duet; Kathy Lirette, Pastoral Assoc.; Deacon Gerald Rivette.
Res.: 409 Funderburk Ave., Houma, 70364. Tel: 985-851-6629; Fax: 985-876-9654.
School—(Grades PreSchool-7), 309 Funderburk Ave., Houma, 70364. Tel: 985-872-3854. Angie Adams, Prin.; Lydia Landry, Asst. Prin.; Dale Ford, Librarian. Lay Teachers 37; Students 477.
Catechesis/Religious Program—Wanda Fos, C.R.E. Students 614.

4—ST. GREGORY BARBARIGO (1963) Rev. Shenan J. Boquet; Deacon Dennis Dupre.
Res.: 439 Sixth St., Houma, 70364. Tel: 985-873-7770.
Administration Bldg.—1005 Williams Ave., Houma, 70364. Tel: 985-876-2047; Fax: 985-876-0628.
School—(Grades PreSchool-7), 441 Sixth St., Houma, 70364. Tel: 985-876-2038; Fax: 985-879-2789. Elizabeth Scurto, Prin. Lay Teachers 10; Students 167.
Catechesis/Religious Program—Students 97.

5—ST. LOUIS (1965) [CEM] Rev. Carlos Talavera.
Res.: 2226 Bayou Blue Rd., Houma, 70364. Tel: 985-876-3449.
Catechesis/Religious Program—Tel: 985-876-6686; Fax: 985-876-6810. Catherine Butler, D.R.E. Students 281.

6—ST. LUCY Rev. Mark Toups.
Mailing Address: P.O. Box 3508, Houma, 70361. Tel: 985-879-2632; Fax: 985-879-2402.
Res.: 430 E. 1st St., Thibodaux, 70301. Tel: 985-414-9717.
Church: 1220 Aycock St., Houma, 70360.
Catechesis/Religious Program—Bernadette Travis, D.R.E. Students 36.

7—MARIA IMMACOLATA (1963) Revs. Clyde Mahler; Nilo Batausa.
Administration Office—246 Corporate Dr., Houma, 70360. Tel: 985-876-3313; Fax: 985-879-2137.
Res.: 326 Estate Dr., Houma, 70364. Tel: 985-868-4915.
School—(Grades PreSchool-7), 324 Estate Dr., Houma, 70364. Tel: 985-876-1631; Fax: 985-876-1608. Sr. Theresa Gossen, Prin.; Karen DeBlieux, Librarian. Lay Teachers 12; Students 210.
Catechesis/Religious Program—Students 285.

8—OUR LADY OF THE MOST HOLY ROSARY (1948) [CEM], (Holy Rosary Church) Very Rev. Carl Collins. In Res., Rev. Roger Villarrubia Jr. (Retired).
Res.: 8594 Main St., Houma, 70363. Tel: 985-876-7652; Fax: 985-876-7647.
Catechesis/Religious Program—Tel: 985-879-2815; Fax: 985-876-0591. Students 117.

CITY OF THIBODAUX

(LAFOURCHE PARISH)

1—ST. CHARLES BORROMEO (1912) [CEM] Rev. Michael Manase.
Res.: 1027 Hwy. 308, Thibodaux, 70301. Tel: 985-446-6663; Fax: 985-447-3348.
Catechesis/Religious Program—Students 154.

2—CHRIST THE REDEEMER (1983) [CEM] Rev. John Gallen; Deacon Charles Giroir.
Res.: 720 Talbot Ave., Thibodaux, 70301. Tel: 985-447-2013; Fax: 985-447-4422.
Catechesis/Religious Program—Students 209.

3—ST. GENEVIEVE (1959) Rev. Dean F. Danos; Deacon Irving Daigle.
Res.: 815 Barbier Ave., Thibodaux, 70301. Tel: 985-446-5571; Fax: 985-449-1939.
School—(Grades K-7), 807 Barbier Ave., Thibodaux, 70301. Tel: 985-447-9291; Fax: 985-447-9883. Chris Knobloch, Prin.; Cheryl Thibodaux, Asst. Prin.; Jere Shields, Librarian. Lay Teachers 30; Students 476.
Catechesis/Religious Program—Tel: 985-446-5127. Students 139.

4—ST. JOHN THE EVANGELIST (1919) [CEM] Rev. Guy Zeringue; Sheryl Chauvin, Pastoral Assoc.
Res.: 2085 St. Mary St., Thibodaux, 70301. Tel: 985-447-3995; Fax: 985-447-2092.
Catechesis/Religious Program—Fax: 985-447-2092. Susie Richard, C.R.E. Students 140.

5—ST. JOSEPH CO-CATHEDRAL (1817) Very Rev. Jay Baker; Revs. Jacinto Beltran; Renerio Dayanan; Deacons Ambrose J. Ayzinne; Pedro Pujals. In Res., Rev. Philip Vathyiakaril-Eapen.
Res.: 721 Canal Blvd., P.O. Box 966, Thibodaux, 70302. Tel: 985-446-1387; Fax: 985-446-6571.
School—(Grades PreSchool-7), 501 Cardinal Dr., Thibodaux, 70301. Tel: 985-446-1346; Fax: 985-449-0760. Gerard Rodrigue, Prin.; Nadine Delatte, Librarian. Lay Teachers 42; Students 680.
Catechesis/Religious Program—Students 136.

6—ST. LUKE (1923), (African American), Rev. Mark Toups.
Office:—300 E. 11th St., Thibodaux, 70301. Tel: 985-446-0487; Fax: 985-446-0480.
Catechesis/Religious Program—Students 30.

7—ST. THOMAS AQUINAS (1970) Rev. Joseph Pilola. Nicholls Sta.: NSU Box 2051, Thibodaux, 70310. Tel: 985-446-6201; Fax: 985-449-0710.
Catechesis/Religious Program—Tel: 985-446-6201; Fax: 985-449-0710. Students 70.

OUTSIDE THE CITIES OF HOUMA AND THIBODAUX

AMELIA, ST. MARY PARISH

1—ST. ANDREW (1965) [CEM] Rev. Evelio Buenaflor Jr.
Res.: 833 Julia St., 70340. Tel: 985-631-2333; Fax: 985-631-2334.
Catechesis/Religious Program—Students 123.

2—THANH GIA (1981), Personal Parish for Vietnamese Community. Revs. Anthony Lap Nguyen; Dominic Dieu Tran.
Res.: 711 Magnolia St., Morgan City, 70380. Tel: 985-631-3194; Fax: 985-631-2634.
Catechesis/Religious Program—Students 104.

BAYOU BLACK, TERREBONNE PARISH, ST. ANTHONY OF PADUA (1876) Rev. Joshua John Rodrigue; Deacon Jesse LeCompte.
Res.: 3897 Bayou Black Dr., Houma, 70360. Tel: 985-872-0922; Fax: 985-872-2001.
Catechesis/Religious Program—Students 211.

BOURG, TERREBONNE PARISH, ST. ANN (1908) [CEM] Rev. Ty Van Nguyen; Deacon Gerald Belanger.
Res.: 4355 Hwy. 24, 70343. Tel: 985-594-3548; Fax: 985-594-3570.
Catechesis/Religious Program—Tel: 985-594-5088. Students 402.

CHACAHOULA, TERREBONNE PARISH, ST. LAWRENCE (1858) [CEM 2] Rev. Josekutty Varghese.
Res.: 2128 Bull Run Rd., 70395. Tel: 985-448-2165; Fax: 985-448-2166.
Catechesis/Religious Program—Students 40.

CHACKBAY, LAFOURCHE PARISH, OUR LADY OF PROMPT SUCCOR (1892) [CEM 2] Rev. Robert Joel Cruz.
Res.: 529 Hwy. 20, Thibodaux, 70301. Tel: 985-633-2903; Fax: 985-633-9225.
Catechesis/Religious Program—Students 357.

CHAUVIN, TERREBONNE PARISH, ST. JOSEPH (1948) [CEM] Rev. Msgr. Frederic J. Brunet.
Res.: 5232 Hwy. 56, 70344. Tel: 985-594-5859; Fax: 985-594-2116. Email: saintjosephchurch@charter.net. Web: stjosephchauvin.parishesonline.com.
Catechesis/Religious Program—Jamie Robichaux, D.R.E. Students 403.

CUT-OFF, LAFOURCHE PARISH, SACRED HEART (1923) [CEM] Rev. Wilfredo Decal; Deacons Sam J. Burregi; Eldon Frazier.
Res.: 15300 W. Main, 70345. Tel: 985-632-3858; Fax: 985-632-4452.
Catechesis/Religious Program—Tel: 985-632-6322; Fax: 985-632-4452. Students 449.

GALLIANO, LAFOURCHE PARISH, ST. JOSEPH (1958) [CEM] Rev. Joseph Pereira.
Res.: P.O. Box 519, 70354. Tel: 985-632-7321; Fax: 985-632-7345.
Catechesis/Religious Program—Students 165.

GHEENS, LAFOURCHE PARISH, COMMUNITY OF ST. ANTHONY (1987) [CEM], (Quasi Parish) Revs. Sabino B. Rebosura II; Thankachan (John) Nambusseril.
Res.: 333 Twin Oaks Dr., Raceland, 70394. Tel: 985-537-6002; Fax: 985-537-4408.

Catechesis/Religious Program—Tel: 985-537-6002; Fax: 985-337-4408. Students 50.
GIBSON, TERREBONNE PARISH
1—MOST BLESSED SACRAMENT FAITH COMMUNITY Rev. Van Constant, Chap.
P.O. Box 587, 70356.
2—ST. PATRICK (1920) Merged with St. Lawrence, Chacahoula.
GOLDEN MEADOW, LAFOURCHE PARISH, OUR LADY OF PROMPT SUCCOR (1916) [CEM] Rev. Ronilo Villamor.
Res.: 723 N. Bayou Dr., 70357. Tel: 985-475-5428; Fax: 985-475-7699.
Catechesis/Religious Program—Tel: 985-475-5886; Fax: 985-475-7699. Students 229.
GRAND CAILLOU, TERREBONNE PARISH, HOLY FAMILY (1952) [CEM 2] Rev. Ronald Yee-Mon; Deacon Bernard A. Harold Fanguy.
Res.: P.O. Box 87, Dulac, 70353. Tel: 985-563-2325; Fax: 985-563-4980.
Catechesis/Religious Program—Students 122.
GRAND ISLE, WEST JEFFERSON PARISH, OUR LADY OF THE ISLE (1933) [CEM] Rev. Mike Tran.
Res.: P.O. Box 885, 70358. Tel: 985-787-2385; Fax: 985-787-4530.
Catechesis/Religious Program—Tel: 985-787-2385. Students 48.
KRAEMER, LAFOURCHE PARISH, ST. LAWRENCE THE MARTYR (1962) [JC 2] Rev. Baby V. Kuruvilla.
Res.: 3723 Hwy. 307, Thibodaux, 70301. Tel: 985-633-9431; Fax: 985-633-5706.
Mission—St. James [CEM] Thibodaux. 3086 Choctaw Rd., Choctaw, Lafourche Parish 70301. Tel: 985-633-9855.
Catechesis/Religious Program—Tel: 985-633-5714. Students 190.
LAROSE, LAFOURCHE PARISH, OUR LADY OF THE ROSARY (1873) [CEM] Revs. Francis Quyet Bui; Alberto Santiago; Deacon Michael Cantrelle.
Res.: 12937 E. Main, P.O. Box 10, 70373. Tel: 985-693-3433; Fax: 985-693-7551.
School—Holy Rosary, (Grades PreK-8), P.O. Box 40, 70373. Tel: 985-693-3342; Fax: 985-693-3348. Joan LeBouef, Prin.; Connie Callais, Librarian. Lay Teachers 16; Students 243.
Catechesis/Religious Program—Jennifer Sanamo, D.R.E. Students 282.
LOCKPORT, LAFOURCHE PARISH, HOLY SAVIOR (1850) [CEM] Rev. Robert C. Rogers.
Res.: 612 Main St., 70374. Tel: 985-532-3533; Fax: 985-532-2010.
School—(Grades N-8), 201 Church St., 70374. Tel: 985-532-2536; Fax: 985-532-2269. Annette Parfait, Prin.; Christy Kern, Librarian. Lay Teachers 16; Students 299.
Catechesis/Religious Program—Tel: 985-532-6111; Fax: 985-532-2010. Students 246.
MONTEGUT, TERREBONNE PARISH, SACRED HEART (1864) [CEM 2] Rev. Caesar Silva.
Res.: P.O. Box 2, 70377. Tel: 985-594-5856; Fax: 985-594-8087.
Catechesis/Religious Program—Tel: 985-594-5856; Fax: 985-594-8087. Students 76.
MORGAN CITY, ST. MARY PARISH
1—HOLY CROSS (1964) Very Rev. Daniel M. Poche; Deacons Andrew Dragna; Vic Bonnaffee.
Res.: 2100 Cedar St., Unit 3, 70380. Tel: 985-384-3551; Fax: 985-384-5790.
School—(Grades PreSchool-6), 2100 Cedar St., Unit 2, 70381. Tel: 985-384-1933; Fax: 985-384-3270. Mamie Bergeron, Prin.; Marion Collins, Librarian. Lay Teachers 18; Students 343.
Catechesis/Religious Program—Tel: 985-384-3551; Fax: 985-384-5970. Students 253.
Mission—St. Rosalie 1315 Stephensville Rd., St. Mary Parish 70380. Tel: 985-385-5713.
2—SACRED HEART OF JESUS (1859) Rev. Gregory Fratt.
Res.: 415 Union St., P.O. Box 632, 70381. Tel: 985-385-0770; Fax: 985-384-7176.
Catechesis/Religious Program—Tel: 985-384-8108. Students 260.
POINTE-AUX-CHENES, LAFOURCHE PARISH, ST. CHARLES BORROMEO (1971) [CEM] Rev. Thomas Kuriakose.
Mailing Address: P.O. Box 54, Montegut, 70377.
Res.: 1237 Hwy. 665, Montegut, 70377. Tel: 985-594-6801; Fax: 985-594-6802.
Catechesis/Religious Program—Fax: 985-594-6802. Students 95.
RACELAND, LAFOURCHE PARISH
1—ST. HILARY OF POITIERS (1965) Revs. Sabino B. Rebosura II; Thankachan (John) Nambusseril.
Res.: 333 Twin Oaks, 70394. Tel: 985-537-6002; Fax: 985-537-4408.
Catechesis/Religious Program—Fax: 985-537-4408. Students 300.
2—ST. MARY'S NATIVITY (1850) [CEM] Very Rev. Charles J. Perkins, Admin.; Deacon Brent P. Bourgeois.
Res.: 3500 Hwy. 1, 70394. Tel: 985-537-3204; Fax: 985-537-3235.
School—(Grades PreK-8), 3492 Nies St., 70394. Tel: 985-537-7544; Fax: 985-537-4020. Marissa Bagala, Prin.; Judy Watts, Librarian. Lay Teachers 13; Students 257.
Catechesis/Religious Program—Students 133.
SCHRIEVER, TERREBONNE PARISH, ST. BRIDGET (1911) [CEM] Rev. Domingo Cruz; Deacon Lloyd Duplantis.
Res.: 100 Hwy. 311, 70395. Tel: 985-446-6801; Fax: 985-448-2764.
Catechesis/Religious Program—Tel: 985-446-1985. Students 135.
THERIOT, TERREBONNE PARISH, ST. ELOI (1875) [CEM] Rev. Florentino F. Santiago; Deacons Daniel Bascle; Glenn Porche.
Res.: 1335 Bayou Dularge Rd., 70397. Tel: 985-872-2946; Fax: 985-872-9961.
Catechesis/Religious Program—Tel: 985-851-6893. Students 112.

Chaplains of Public Institutions

HOUMA. *Chabert Medical Center*. Deacon Linwood Liner, Chap.
Terrebonne General Medical Center. Rev. Joseph Tu Tran.
Terrebonne Parish Sheriff Police and Fire Departments. Deacon Linwood Liner, Chap.
THIBODAUX. *Lafourche Parish Sheriff, Police and Fire Departments*. Vacant.
Thibodaux Regional Medical Center. Rev. Philip Vathyiakaril-Eapen.

On Duty Outside the Diocese:
Rev.—
Bouterie, Thomas

Administrative Leave:
Revs.—
Cavell, Lawrence Arthur
Cheramie, Lonnie
Dugas, Scott
Le, Peter Tai Thanh
Morrison, James

Retired:
Rev. Msgrs.—
Amedee, Francis, 725 St. Philip St., 70301.
Bergeron, Albert G., Hollywood Park Apartments, 546 Ave. B, Marrero, 70072.
Ledet, Donald, 2011 Acadian Dr., Houma, 70363.
Songy, James B., 410 Ninth St., Lockport, 70374.
Revs.—
Broussard, Hubert C., Chateau Creole, 273 Monarch Dr., Apt. J13, Houma, 70364.
Chassaniol, Warren F., 4642 Highway 1, Raceland, 70394.
Foley, Brendan P., 182 E. 110th St., Galliano, 70354.
Hayes, Gerard C., 316 Hawthorne Dr., Houma, 70360.
LeBlanc, Etienne
Naquin, Roch, 539 Island Rd., Montegut, 70377.
Nguyen, Joseph Luu, P.O Box 29451, New Orleans, 70189.
Ruiz, John, Audubon Guest House, 2110 Audubon Ave., 70301.
Timbre, Roland
Todd, Wilmer, 267 Klondyke Rd., Bourg, 70343.
Villarrubia, Roger, Jr., 8594 Main St., Houma, 70363.

Permanent Deacons:
Authement, Douglas, Cathedral of St. Francis de Sales, Houma
Ayzinne, Ambrose Joseph, St. Joseph, Thibodaux
Bascle, Daniel, St. Eloi, Theriot
Belanger, Gerald, St. Ann, Bourg
Bonnaffee, Vic, Holy Cross, Morgan City
Bourg, Raymond, Annunziata, Houma
Bourgeois, Brent P., St. Mary's Nativity, Raceland
Burregi, Sam J., Sacred Heart, Cut-Off
Cantrelle, Michael, Holy Rosary, Larose
Daigle, Irving, St. Genevieve, Thibodaux
Doucet, Davis, Our Lady of the Rosary, Larose
Dragna, Andrew J., Holy Cross, Morgan City
Dufrene, Roland, St. Hilary of Poitiers, Mathews
Duplantis, Connely, Annunzita, Houma
Duplantis, Lloyd, St. Bridget, Schriever
Dupre, Dennis, St. Gregory, Houma
Duthu, James, Houma
Fanguy, Bernard A. Harold, Holy Family, Grand Caillou
Frazier, Eldon, Cut-Off; Sacred Heart
Giroir, Charles, Christ the Redeemer, Thibodaux
Landry, Alduce, St. Charles, Thibodaux
LeCompte, Jesse, St. Anthony of Padua, Bayou Black
Liner, Linwood Paul, Sr., St. Lucy, Houma
Marts, Melvin, Shalom Catholic Ministries
Porche, Glenn, St. Eloi, Theriot
Prestenback, Chris A., St. Bernadette, Houma
Pujals, Pedro P., St. Joseph Co-Cathedral, Thibodaux
Rabalais, Bertrand A.
Rivette, Gerald, St. Bernadette, Houma
Uzee, Dickey, Raceland; St. Mary's Nativity
Weigand, Joseph, Jr., Cathedral of St. Francis de Sales, Houma
Haddad, Gregory, Gray

INSTITUTIONS LOCATED IN THE DIOCESE

[A] HIGH SCHOOLS, DIOCESAN

HOUMA. *Vandebilt Catholic High*, (Grades 8-12), 209 S. Hollywood Rd., 70360. Tel: 985-876-2551; Fax: 985-868-9774. Email: vandebilthi@htdiocese.org. Web: www.vandebiltcatholic.org. Mr. James Reiss, Prin.; Bro. Harold Harris, Counselor; Patricia Chiasson, Librarian. Brothers of the Sacred Heart. Brothers 1; Lay Teachers 67; Students 945.

THIBODAUX. *Edward Douglas White Catholic High*, (Grades 8-12), (Coed), 555 Cardinal Dr., 70301. Tel: 985-446-8486; Fax: 985-448-1275. Email: edwhitehi@htdiocese.org. Myra Luft, Prin.; Mr. David Boudreaux, Pres.; Lozia Richard, Librarian. Brothers of the Sacred Heart. Brothers 3; Lay Teachers 54; Students 752.
E.D. White Catholic High School Foundation, Inc. Tel: 985-446-8486; Fax: 985-446-5444.
E.D. White Catholic High School Alumni Assn. Tel: 985-446-8486; Fax: 985-448-1275.

MORGAN CITY. *Central Catholic High*, (Grades 7-12), 2100 Cedar St., Unit 1, 70380. Tel: 985-385-5372; Fax: 985-385-3444. Email: centcathi@htdiocese.org. Web: www.cchseagles.com. Deacon Vic Bonnaffee, Prin.; Karen Tycer, Senior High & Guidance Counselor; Anna Saleme, Librarian. Lay Teachers 24; Students 222.

[B] DAY CARE CENTERS

HOUMA. *St. Lucy Child Development Center*, P.O. Box 3894, 70361. Tel: 985-876-1246; Fax: 985-876-7751. Email: mgullage@htdiocese.lorg. Marshall Gullage, Asst. Dir. Total Staff 10; Children 61.

[C] RETREAT CENTERS

SCHRIEVER. *Lumen Christi Retreat Center*, 100 Lumen Christi Ln., Hwy. 311, 70395. Tel: 985-868-1523; Fax: 985-868-1525.

[D] CONVENTS

LOCKPORT. *Monastery of the Heart of Jesus*, 155 Church St., 70374. Tel: 985-532-2411. Sr. Mary Valerie Dupree, O.P. Dominican Contemplative Sisters of the Heart of Jesus of the Diocese of Houma-Thibodaux.

[E] PRIVATE ASSOCIATIONS OF THE FAITHFUL

THIBODAUX. *Marian Servants of the Word*, 506 Cardinal Dr., 70301. Tel: 985-447-6564; Fax: 985-447-5734. Email: marianservants@att.net. Very Rev. Michael Bergeron, Chap.; Claire Joller, Dir.; Brenda Fremin, Sec.; Mrs. Sally Sobert, Treas.

[F] PIUS ASSOCIATION

THIBODAUX. *Daughters of St. Joseph - Pius Association*, 113 Lafaye Ave., 70301. Tel: 985-446-7525. Debra McCullough, Contact Person. Daughters 4.

[G] MISCELLANEOUS

THIBODAUX. **Adore Ministries, Inc.*, P.O. Box 4174, Houma, 70361. Tel: 985-876-4132.
The Diocese of Houma-Thibodaux Historical Research Center, 205 Audubon Ave., 70301. Tel: 985-446-2383; Fax: 985-449-0574. Email: kallemand@htdiocese.org.
St. Joseph Manor (Retirement Community), 1201 Cardinal Dr., 70301. Tel: 985-446-9050; Fax: 985-449-0047. Email: annt@stjosephmanor.org. Web: www.stjosephmanor.org. Ann Thibodaux, Admin.
Magnificat of the Houma-Thibodaux Diocese, 830 Laurel Valley Rd., 70301. Tel: 985-446-5001; Fax: 985-447-4261. Mrs. Mina McKee, Coord., Bayou River Chapter.

SCHRIEVER. *Cemeteries Trust*, P.O. Box 505, 70395. Tel: 985-850-3112; Fax: 985-868-7727. Email: glandry@htdiocese.org.

RELIGIOUS INSTITUTES OF MEN REPRESENTED IN THE DIOCESE

For further details refer to the corresponding bracketed number in the Religious Institutes of Men or Women section.

[1100]—*Brothers of the Sacred Heart*—S.C.

RELIGIOUS INSTITUTES OF WOMEN REPRESENTED IN THE DIOCESE

[]—*Congregation of Divine Providence*

[0400]—*Congregation of Our Lady of Mount Carmel*—O.Carm.

[2410]—*Congregation of the Marianites of Holy Cross*—M.S.C.

[3832]—*Congregation of the Sisters of St. Joseph*—C.S.J.

[]—*Daughters of Our Lady of the Holy Rosary*

[]—*Dominican Contemplative Sisters*—O.P.

[1115]—*Dominican Sisters of Peace*—O.P.

[]—*Dominican Sisters of St. Rose of Lima*

[2970]—*School Sisters of Notre Dame*—S.S.N.D.

[]—*Sisters for Christian Community*

[]—*Sisters of Emanuel*

[3830]—*Sisters of St. Joseph*—C.S.J.

[2050]—*Sisters of the Holy Spirit and Mary Immaculate*—S.H.Sp.

NECROLOGY

† Legendre, Rev. Msgr. Francis, (Retired)—Died Jan. 15, 2009

† Sevigny, Robert J., (Retired)—Died Dec. 27, 2008

An asterisk (*) denotes an organization that has established tax-exempt status directly with the IRS and is not covered by the USCCB Group Ruling.

Archdiocese of Indianapolis

(Archidioecesis Indianapolitana)

SEEK THE FACE OF THE LORD

Most Reverend

DANIEL MARK BUECHLEIN, O.S.B., D.D.

Archbishop of Indianapolis; ordained May 3, 1964; appointed to Memphis January 16, 1987; consecrated Bishop March 2, 1987; installed March 2, 1987; appointed Archbishop of Indianapolis July 14, 1992; installed September 9, 1992.

The Archbishop Edward T. O'Meara Catholic Center: 1400 N. Meridian St., P.O. Box 1410, Indianapolis, IN 46206. Tel: 317-236-1400; Fax: 317-236-1401.

Web: www.archindy.org

Email: chancery@archindy.org

Square Miles 13,758.

Established a Diocese in 1834; established an Archdiocese December 19, 1944 by decree of Pope Pius XII.

Comprises the Counties of Bartholomew, Brown, Clark, Clay, Crawford, Dearborn, Decatur, Fayette, Floyd, Franklin, Hancock, Harrison, Hendricks, Henry, Jackson, Jefferson, Jennings, Johnson, Lawrence, Marion, Monroe, Morgan, Ohio, Orange, Owen, Parke, Perry, Putnam, Ripley, Rush, Scott, Shelby, Switzerland, Union, Vermillion, Vigo, Washington and Wayne, and the township of Harrison in Spencer County, in the southern part of Indiana.

For legal titles of parishes and archdiocesan institutions, consult the Chancery Office.

STATISTICAL OVERVIEW

Personnel	
Archbishops	1
Abbots	1
Retired Abbots	3
Priests: Diocesan Active in Diocese	101
Priests: Diocesan Active Outside Diocese	2
Priests: Retired, Sick or Absent	48
Number of Diocesan Priests	151
Religious Priests in Diocese	87
Total Priests in Diocese	238
Extern Priests in Diocese	20
Ordinations:	
Diocesan Priests	5
Religious Priests	3
Permanent Deacons in Diocese	26
Total Brothers	29
Total Sisters	621
Parishes	
Parishes	139
With Resident Pastor:	
Resident Diocesan Priests	95
Resident Religious Priests	10
Without Resident Pastor:	
Administered by Priests	16
Administered by Deacons	1
Administered by Religious Women	9
Administered by Lay People	1
Completely Vacant	2
Missions	12
Professional Ministry Personnel:	
Brothers	2
Sisters	43
Lay Ministers	286
Welfare	
Catholic Hospitals	2
Total Assisted	1,237,087
Homes for the Aged	3
Total Assisted	372
Day Care Centers	1
Total Assisted	93
Specialized Homes	2
Total Assisted	909
Special Centers for Social Services	16
Total Assisted	140,000
Educational	
Seminaries, Diocesan	1
Students from This Diocese	13
Students from Other Diocese	12
Diocesan Students in Other Seminaries	13
Seminaries, Religious	1
Students Religious	111
Total Seminarians	137
Colleges and Universities	2
Total Students	3,820
High Schools, Diocesan and Parish	7
Total Students	3,641
High Schools, Private	4
Total Students	2,237
Elementary Schools, Diocesan and Parish	61
Total Students	16,937
Elementary Schools, Private	1
Total Students	75
Catechesis/Religious Education:	
High School Students	3,431
Elementary Students	12,311
Total Students under Catholic Instruction	42,589
Teachers in the Diocese:	
Priests	5
Brothers	2
Sisters	18
Lay Teachers	1,749
Vital Statistics	
Receptions into the Church:	
Infant Baptism Totals	4,064
Minor Baptism Totals	385
Adult Baptism Totals	428
Received into Full Communion	506
First Communions	3,914
Confirmations	3,194
Marriages:	
Catholic	624
Interfaith	386
Total Marriages	1,010
Deaths	2,007
Total Catholic Population	226,216
Total Population	2,430,606

The Diocese of Vincennes (now Indianapolis) was established by decree of Pope Gregory XVI, May 6, 1834, and the See was fixed at Vincennes. The territory then comprised the entire State of Indiana and the eastern third of Illinois. By decree of Pope Pius IX, January 8, 1857, the northern half of the State became the Diocese of Fort Wayne. The southern half of the State remained the Diocese of Vincennes.

The second Bishop of Vincennes, by Apostolic Brief, was permitted to establish his residence either at Vincennes, Madison, Lafayette or Indianapolis; the See City, however, was to remain at Vincennes. This permission was renewed to the fourth Bishop, with the exception of Lafayette. On the appointment of the fifth Bishop, he was directed to fix his residence at Indianapolis, but the Cathedral and title of the See were continued at Vincennes. By an Apostolic Brief dated March 28, 1898, the title of the Diocese was changed to that of "Diocese of Indianapolis" with the city of Indianapolis as the Episcopal See. By the same Brief the Patron Saint of the Diocese was to remain St. Francis Xavier, the title of the old Cathedral in Vincennes.

On December 19, 1944, Most Reverend Amleto Giovanni Cicognani, Apostolic Delegate to the United States, solemnly proclaimed the Papal Decree of Pope Pius XII in SS. Peter and Paul Cathedral, Indianapolis, elevating Indianapolis to the status of an Archdiocese, the State of Indiana being the Metropolitan Area. The Dioceses of Evansville and Lafayette-in-Indiana were created by the same decree and were made Suffragan Sees of Indianapolis. Upon the establishment of the Diocese of Gary on December 17, 1956, it too became a Suffragan See.

Former Bishops—Rt. Revs. SIMON GUILLAUME GABRIEL BRUTE DE REMUR, S.S., D.D., ord. 1808; cons. 1834; died 1839; CELESTIN DE LA HAILANDIERE, D.D., ord. 1825; cons. 1839; resigned 1847; died in France, 1882; JOHN S. BAZIN, D.D., ord. 1822; cons. 1847; died 1848; MAURICE DE SAINT PALAIS, D.D., ord. 1836; cons. Jan. 14, 1849; died June 28, 1877; FRANCIS SILAS CHATARD, D.D., ord. 1862; cons. May 12, 1878; died Sept. 7, 1918; Most Revs. JOSEPH CHARTRAND, D.D., ord. Sept. 24, 1892; cons. Titular Bishop of Flavias and Coadjutor Bishop, Sept. 15, 1910; succeeded to the See of Indianapolis, Sept. 7, 1918; died Dec. 8, 1933; JOSEPH ELMER RITTER, S.T.D., ord. May 30, 1917; cons. Titular Bishop of Hippo and Auxiliary Bishop, March 28, 1933; succeeded to the See March 24, 1934; installed as Archbishop Dec. 19, 1944; transferred to Metropolitan See of St. Louis, July 20, 1946; named Cardinal, Jan. 16, 1961; died June 10, 1967; PAUL C. SCHULTE, D.D., ord. June 11, 1915; cons. Bishop of Leavenworth, Sept. 21, 1937; appt. Archbishop of Indianapolis, July 20, 1946; installed Oct. 10, 1946; resigned Jan. 14, 1970; died Feb. 17, 1984; GEORGE J. BISKUP, ord. March 19, 1937; cons. Titular Bishop of Hemeria and Auxiliary of Dubuque, April 24, 1957; transferred to Des Moines Feb. 3, 1965; transferred to Indianapolis "cum jure successionis," July 26, 1967; succeeded to See Jan. 14, 1970; resigned March 26, 1979; died Oct. 17, 1979; EDWARD T. O'MEARA, S.T.D., ord. Dec. 21, 1946; appt. Titular Bishop of Thisiduo and Auxiliary of St. Louis Jan. 28, 1972; consecrated in the Basilica of St. Peter, Rome, Feb. 13, 1972; appt. Archbishop of Indianapolis Nov. 27, 1979; installed Jan. 10, 1980; died Jan. 10, 1992.

Archdiocesan Administration— Secretariats/Vicariates/Agencies and Offices can be contacted through The Archbishop Edward T. O'Meara Catholic Center. *1400 N. Meridian St., Indianapolis, 46202. Address all mail, unless otherwise indicated, to: P.O. Box 1410, Indianapolis, 46206-1410.* Tel: 317-236-1400; Fax: 317-236-1401.

Vicar General and Moderator of the Curia—Rev. Msgr. JOSEPH F. SCHAEDEL, M.S., M.Div., V.G.

Chancellor—ANNETTE "MICKEY" LENTZ.

Assistant Chancellor—Rev. STEPHEN GIANNINI, M.Div., M.A., M.S.

Chief Financial Officer—JEFFREY D. STUMPF.

Board of Consultors—Most Rev. DANIEL M. BUECHLEIN, O.S.B., D.D., Chm.; Rev. Msgr. JOSEPH F. SCHAEDEL, M.S., M.Div., V.G.; Revs. WILLIAM F. STUMPF, V.F.; CLIFFORD R. VOGELSANG, S.T.B., M.Div. (Retired); STEPHEN GIANNINI, M.Div., M.A., M.S.; Rev. Msgr. PAUL KOETTER, V.F.; Revs. GERALD KIRKHOFF, V.F.; DANIEL MAHAN; DANIEL J. STAUBLIN.

Deaneries and Deans—Rev. GERALD J. KIRKHOFF, V.F., Indianapolis North; Rev. Msgr. PAUL KOETTER, V.F., Indianapolis East; Revs. JAMES R. WILMOTH, V.F., Indianapolis South; KENNETH TAYLOR, V.F., Indianapolis West; DENNIS M. DUVELIUS, V.F., Batesville; WILLIAM F. STUMPF, V.F., Bloomington; STANLEY J. HERBER, M.A., V.F., Connersville; WILFRED E. DAY, V.F., New Albany; JOHN A. MEYER, V.F., Seymour; VACANT, Tell City; Rev. JOSEPH KERN, V.F., Terre Haute.

Council of Priests—Most Rev. DANIEL M. BUECHLEIN, O.S.B., D.D., Pres.; Rev. Msgr. JOSEPH F. SCHAEDEL, M.S., M.Div., V.G.; ANNETTE "MICKEY" LENTZ, Chancellor; Revs. JOSEPH M. FELTZ, V.F.; ROBERT J. GILDAY, S.T.B.; JOSEPH F. RAUTENBERG; WILLIAM F. STUMPF, V.F.; CARLTON BEAVER; STEPHEN JARRELL; DAVID LAWLER; GEORGE PLASTER; GERALD KIRKHOFF, V.F.; CLIFFORD R. VOGELSANG, S.T.B., M.Div. (Retired); DANIEL ATKINS; STEPHEN GIANNINI, M.Div., M.A., M.S.; TODD MICHAEL GOODSON; JEFFREY H. GODECKER; JOHN M. HALL; ROBERT JASON HANKEE.

Finance Council—Most Rev. DANIEL M. BUECHLEIN, O.S.B., D.D., Chm.; Rev. Msgr. JOSEPH F. SCHAEDEL, M.S., M.Div., V.G.; JEFFREY D. STUMPF, CFO; CLARK BYRUM; DANIEL DEBARD, Sec.; DALE GETTELFINGER; KENNETH J. HEDLUND, Vice Pres.; TIMOTHY ROBINSON; MARY HORN, Pres.; PHILIP B. MCKEIRNAN; SCOTT NICKERSON; JERRY WILLIAMS.

Priests' Personnel Board—Most Rev. DANIEL M. BUECHLEIN, O.S.B., D.D.; Revs. NOAH J. CASEY; JAMES M. FARRELL; H. MICHAEL HILDERBRAND, M.A., M.Div., M.S., Ed.S.; GERALD J. KIRKHOFF, V.F., Chm.; Rev. Msgr. PAUL KOETTER, V.F.; Revs. PAUL M. SHIKANY, J.C.L.; STEPHEN GIANNINI, M.Div., M.A., M.S.; KENNETH TAYLOR, V.F.; GEORGE F. PLASTER.

Archdiocesan Review Board—ANN M. DELANEY; CATHLEEN GRAHAM; RICHARD K. GRANA; Rev. PAUL D. ETIENNE; JOHN "JACK" M. WHELAN; MICHAEL H. ZUNK.

Bishop Simon Brute College Seminary—Rev. ROBERT J. ROBESON, Rector. Tel: 317-955-6126.

Secretariat for Catholic Charities and Family Ministries—DAVID J. SILER, L.C.S.W., Exec. Dir. Tel: 317-236-7325.

Catholic Campaign for Human Development—DAVID J. SILER, L.C.S.W., Dir. Tel: 317-236-7325.

Deaf Ministry—DAVID BETHURAM, M.A., M.Min, Contact Person. Tel: 317-236-1595.

Office of Family Ministries—VACANT, Dir. Tel: 317-236-1595.

Commission for Multicultural Ministry—Rev. KENNETH TAYLOR, V.F., Dir. Tel: 317-236-1562.

Office for Pro-Life Ministry—Sr. DIANE CAROLLO, S.G.L., Dir. Tel: 317-236-1569.

Catholic Charities Indianapolis—DAVID BETHURAM, M.A., M.Min, Indianapolis Agency Dir. Tel: 317-236-1500.

Catholic Charities Terre Haute—JOHN C. ETLING, Terre Haute Agency Dir. Tel: 812-232-1447.

Catholic Charities New Albany—MARK CASPER, New Albany Agency Dir. Tel: 812-949-7305.

Catholic Charities Bloomington—MARSHA MCCARTY, Bloomington Agency Dir. Tel: 812-332-1262.

Catholic Charities Tell City—JOAN HESS, Tell City Agency Dir. Tel: 812-547-0903.

St. Elizabeth Coleman Pregnancy and Adoption Services—DAVID BETHURAM, M.A., M.Min, Agency Dir. Tel: 317-787-3412.

St. Elizabeth's Regional Maternity Center—MARK CASPER, Agency Dir. Tel: 812-949-7305.

Secretariat for Catholic Education and Faith Formation—ANNETTE "MICKEY" LENTZ, Exec. Dir. Tel: 317-236-1440.

Catholic Education—G. JOSEPH PETERS, Assoc. Exec. Dir. Tel: 317-236-1430.

Faith Formation—KEN OGOREK, Dir. Catechesis. Tel: 317-236-1446.

Catholic Education, School Improvement—RONALD COSTELLO, Supt. Catholic Schools. Tel: 317-236-1486.

SPRED—RONI WYLD, Coord. Tel: 317-236-1448.

Mother Theodore Catholic Academies—CONNIE ZITTNAN, Dir. Tel: 317-236-7322; DENNIS SPONSEL, Chm. Bd. Tel: 317-236-1421.

Catholic Youth Organization—EDWARD TINDER, Dir., 580 E. Stevens St., Indianapolis, 46203. Tel: 317-632-9311.

Youth Ministry—KAY SCOVILLE, Dir. Tel: 317-236-1477.

Young Adult and College Campus Ministry—Rev. RICK NAGEL.

St. Mary's Child Center—CONSTANCE SHERMAN, Dir., 901 Dr. Martin Luther King, Jr. St., Indianapolis, 46202. Tel: 317-635-1491.

Secretariat for Communications—GREG A. OTOLSKI, Exec. Dir. Tel: 317-236-1585.

Archdiocesan Newspaper, "The Criterion"—Most Rev. DANIEL M. BUECHLEIN, O.S.B., D.D., Publisher; GREG A. OTOLSKI, Assoc. Publisher; MICHAEL A. KROKOS, Editor. Tel: 317-236-1570.

Catholic Communications Center—GREG A. OTOLSKI, Dir. Tel: 317-236-1585.

Secretariat for Finance and Administrative Services—JEFFREY D. STUMPF, CFO & Exec. Dir. Tel: 317-236-1410.

Accounting Services—JULIE SHEWMAKER, Controller. Tel: 317-236-1410.

Information Services—TOM O'DROBINAK, Dir. Tel: 317-236-1420.

Management Services—ERIC L. ATKINS, Dir. Tel: 317-236-1452.

Purchasing Office—STEPHEN M. JAMES, Dir. Tel: 317-236-1451.

Catholic Cemeteries Assoc.—TONY LLOYD, Buchanan Group, 9001 N. Haverstick Rd., Indianapolis, 46240. Tel: 317-574-8898.

Roman Catholic Archdiocese of Indianapolis Properties—Most Rev. DANIEL M. BUECHLEIN, O.S.B., D.D., Pres.; Rev. Msgr. JOSEPH F. SCHAEDEL, M.S., M.Div., V.G., Vice Pres.; JEFFREY D. STUMPF, Sec. Tel: 317-236-1410.

Secretariat for Lay Ministry and Pastoral Services—ANNETTE "MICKEY" LENTZ, Dir.

Archives—KAREN ODDI, Assoc. Archivist. Tel: 317-236-1429; TERESA LAW, Records Mgmt. Coord.

Archdiocesan Historian—Rev. JACK W. PORTER (Retired).

Human Resources—ED ISAKSON, Dir. Tel: 317-236-1594.

Lay Ministry—ED ISAKSON, Dir.

Parish Planning and Organizational Development—ANNETTE "MICKEY" LENTZ, Dir.

Secretariat for Spiritual Life and Worship—CHARLES GARDNER, Exec. Dir. Tel: 317-236-1483.

Archdiocesan Cathedral—Rev. DANIEL B. DONOHOO, Pastor & Rector.

Evangelization Commission—VACANT, Coord.

Office of Worship—CHARLES GARDNER, Dir. Tel: 317-236-1483.

Retreat & Renewal Ministries and Fatima Retreat House—Rev. JAMES M. FARRELL, Dir., 5353 E. 56th St., Indianapolis, 46226. Tel: 317-545-7681; Fax: 317-545-0095.

Secretariat for Stewardship and Development—DAVID MILROY, Exec. Dir. Tel: 317-236-1415.

Office of Stewardship and Development—KENT J. GOFFINET, Dir. Stewardship & Devel. Tel: 317-236-1465; RON GREULICH, Dir. Stewardship Educ. Tel: 317-236-1426; JOLINDA MOORE, Dir. Annual Major Giving. Tel: 317-236-1462; DENA PERRY, Dir. Communications. Tel: 317-236-1578; DANA TOWNSEND, Dir., Donor Svcs. Tel: 317-236-1498; MICHAEL KIRK, Assoc. Dir. Annual Major Giving. Tel: 317-236-1546.

Catholic Community Foundation, Inc.—Most Rev. DANIEL M. BUECHLEIN, O.S.B., D.D., Chm.; VACANT, Dir. Gift Planning. Tel: 317-236-1427.

Mission Office—Rev. Msgr. JOSEPH F. SCHAEDEL, M.S., M.Div., V.G., Dir. Tel: 317-236-1485.

Vicariate for Clergy and Parish Life Coordinators: Formation and Personnel—Rev. STEPHEN GIANNINI, M.Div., M.A., M.S., Vicar. Tel: 317-236-1495.

Deacon Formation—Rev. BEDE CISCO, O.S.B., Dir. Tel: 317-236-1491.

Vicariate for Advocacy to Priests—Revs. GERALD J. KIRKHOFF, V.F., Vicar. Tel: 317-236-1489; JOSEPH F. RAUTENBERG, Ethics & Bioethics Consultant. Tel: 317-236-1449.

Personnel: Priests and Parish Life Coordinators—Rev. STEPHEN GIANNINI, M.Div., M.A., M.S., Dir. Tel: 317-236-1495.

Priestly and Religious Vocations—Revs. ERIC MATTHEW JOHNSON, Dir. Tel: 317-236-1490; AARON M. JENKINS, Assoc. Dir.

Vicariate Judicial Metropolitan Tribunal—Rev. Msgr. FREDERICK EASTON, J.C.L., Vicar Judicial. Tel: 317-236-1460.

Adjunct Vicars Judicial—Revs. ROBERT J. GILDAY, S.T.B.; PAUL M. SHIKANY, J.C.L.

Judge Instructors and Assessors—Ms. ANN TULLY, B.S., M.T.S.; Ms. MARY ELLEN HAUCK, B.A.

Defenders of the Bond—Revs. JAMES R. BONKE, J.C.L.; PATRICK COONEY, O.S.B., J.C.L.; Ms. PATRICIA JEFFERS, B.A.; Rev. STANLEY PONDO, J.D., J.C.D., M.Div.; LYNDA ROBITAILLE, J.C.D.

Promoter of Justice—Rev. JAMES R. BONKE, J.C.L.

Archdiocesan Judges—Revs. CLIFFORD R. VOGELSANG, S.T.B., M.Div. (Retired); FRANCIS E. BRYAN (Retired); CLEMENT T. DAVIS, M.Div.; NICHOLAS J. DANT, M.Div., S.T.L.; MICHAEL C. FRITSCH, M.Div.; VINCENT LAMPERT, M.Div.; LAWRENCE J. RICHARDT, M.A., S.T.L.; HERMAN LUTZ, S.T.L., J.C.L. (Retired); SEVERIN MESSICK, O.S.B., M.Div.; RICHARD MUELLER, S.T.L. (Retired); STEPHEN GIANNINI, M.Div., M.A., M.S.

Auditor—Rev. ROBERT E. MAZZOLA, S.T.B.

Notaries—Ms. KAY SUMMERS, B.A.; NANCY THOMPSON; Ms. ROSEANNE L. HUCKLEBERRY, B.A.

Victim Assistance Coordinator—JAN LINK. Tel: 317-236-1548; 800-382-9836, Ext. 1548.

CLERGY, PARISHES, MISSIONS AND PAROCHIAL SCHOOLS

CITY OF INDIANAPOLIS

(MARION COUNTY)

1—SS. PETER AND PAUL CATHEDRAL (1892) [JC] Rev. Daniel B. Donohoo, Rector. In Res., Rev. James R. Bonke; Rev. Msgr. Joseph F. Schaedel; Rev. Michael W. Magiera, F.S.S.P.
Res.: 1347 N. Meridian St., 46202. Tel: 317-634-4519; Fax: 317-630-9621. Web: www.ssppc.org.

2—ST. ANDREW THE APOSTLE (1946) Deacon Robert W. Decker, Parish Life Coord.; Revs. Gerald J. Kirkhoff, Priest Mod.; Clifford Vogelsang, Sacramental Min.
Parish Office—4052 E. 38th St., 46218-1444. Tel: 317-546-1571; Fax: 317-549-6311. Email: wnowicki@standrewstrita.org. Web: www.standrewindy.org.
School—St. Andrew & St. Rita Catholic Academy, (Grades PreK-8), 4050 E. 38th St., 46218. Tel: 317-549-6305; Fax: 317-549-6306. Yolanda D. McCormick, Prin. School & Daycare Lay Teachers 15; Students 203.
Catechesis/Religious Program—Email: rdecker@standrewstrita.org. Students 17.

3—ST. ANN (1917) [JC] Rev. Glenn L. O'Connor.
Office & Mailing Address: 6350 S. Mooresville Rd., 46221-4519. Tel: 317-821-2909; Fax: 317-821-2929. Email: saintannchurc@aol.com. Web: www.st-ann-rcindy.org.
Catechesis/Religious Program—Email: saintannindy@sbcglobal.net. Kelly O'Brien, C.R.E. Students 37.

4—ST. ANTHONY (1891), (Irish—German), [JC] Rev. John Patrick McCaslin.
337 N. Warman Ave., 46222. Tel: 317-636-4828; Fax: 317-636-3140.
School—St. Anthony, (Grades PreK-6), 349 N. Warman Ave., 46222-4145. Tel: 317-636-3739; Fax: 317-636-1928. Cynthia L. Greer, Prin. Lay Teachers 9; Students 93.
Catechesis/Religious Program—Students 204.

5—ST. BARNABAS (1965) Revs. Randall R. Summers; Peter A. Marshall; Deacon Patrick Bower.
Res.: 8300 Rahke Rd., 46217. Tel: 317-882-0724; Fax: 317-887-8932.
School—(Grades K-8) Tel: 317-881-7422; Fax: 317-887-8933. Debra Perkins, Prin. Lay Teachers 33; Students 624.
Catechesis/Religious Program—Students 336.

6—ST. BERNADETTE (1952) [CEM] Rev. J. Nicholas Dant.
Church & Parish Office: 4838 Fletcher Ave., 46203. Tel: 317-356-5867; Fax: 317-356-4184. Email: parishoffice@stb-indy.org. Web: www.stb-indy.org.
Res.: 4720 E. 13th St., 46203. Tel: 317-357-8352.
Catechesis/Religious Program—Students 20.

7—CHRIST THE KING (1939) Revs. Anthony R. Volz; James R. Bonke. In Res., Rev. Jeff Godecker.
Parish Office—5884 Crittenden Ave., 46220. Tel: 317-255-3666; Fax: 317-475-6579. Email: ctk@ctk-indy.org. Web: www.christtheking-indy.org.
Res.: 1827 E. Kessler Blvd., 46220.
School—5858 Crittenden Ave., 46220. Tel: 317-257-9366; Fax: 317-475-6581. Lay Teachers 25; Students 375.
Catechesis/Religious Program—Tel: 317-255-3666; Fax: 317-475-6579. Students 89.

8—ST. CHRISTOPHER (Speedway City) (1937) Revs. D. Michael Welch; David Lawler, Assoc. Pastor; Sisters Sue Bradshaw, O.S.F., Pastoral Assoc.; Kathleen Morrissey, O.P., Pastoral Assoc.; Mary DeFazio, S.P., Pastoral Assoc. Faith Formation; Mr. Bill Szolek Van Valkenburgh, Pastoral Assoc.
Res.: 5301 W. 16th St., 46224. Tel: 317-241-6314; Fax: 317-241-6587.
School—5335 W. 16th St., 46224. Fax: 317-244-6678. Vincent Schurgar, Prin. Lay Teachers 16; Students 222.
Catechesis/Religious Program—Mr. Joseph E. Fey, D.R.E. Students 312.

9—St. Gabriel the Archangel (1963) Rev. Larry P. Crawford; Deacon Oscar Morales, Pastoral Assoc. In Res., Rev. Msgr. Frederick Easton.
Parish Center:—6000 W. 34th St., 46224. Tel: 317-291-7014; Fax: 317-297-6455. Email: info@stgabrielindy.org. Web: www.stgabrielindy.org.
School—(Grades PreK-8) Tel: 317-297-1414; Fax: 317-297-6453. Ms. Sarah Watson, Prin. Teachers 24; Students 124.
Catechesis/Religious Program—Tel: 317-299-9924. Mrs. Teresa Keith, Dir. Faith Formation. Students 159.

10—Good Shepherd (1993) [JC], (St. Catherine, 1909, and St. James the Greater, 1951, were closed, merged, and renamed in 1993.) David R. Wilson, Parish Life Coord.
Church & Parish Office: 2905 S. Carson Ave., 46203. Tel: 317-783-3158; Fax: 317-781-5961. Email: plcdavewilson@sbcglobal.net.
School—Central Catholic School, (Grades K-8), 1155 E. Cameron St., 46203. Tel: 317-783-7759; Fax: 317-781-5964. Sara Browning, Prin. Students 177.
Catechesis/Religious Program—Students 21.

11—Holy Angels (1903), (African American), Rev. Kenneth Taylor.
Res.: 740 W. 28th St., 46208-5099. Tel: 317-926-3324; Fax: 317-926-3325. Email: holyangelsbulletin@hotmail.com. Web: www.holyangelsindy.org.
School—(Grades K-6), 2822 Dr. Martin Luther King, Jr. St., 46208. Tel: 317-926-5211; Fax: 317-926-5219. Cynthia L. Greer, Prin.; Michael Joseph, Campus Dir.; Mrs. Jude Mitchell, Librarian. Sisters of I.H.M. Reparatrix 1; Lay Teachers 12; Students 156.
Catechesis/Religious Program—Students 30.

12—Holy Cross (1895) Rev. Lawrence Voelker.
Church: 125 N. Oriental St., 46202. Tel: 317-637-2620; Fax: 317-637-0112. Email: parish@holycrossindy.org. Web: www.holycrossindy.org.
School—Tel: 317-638-9068; Fax: 317-638-0116. Email: school@holycrossindy.org. Ruth Tinsley, Prin. Lay Teachers 14; Students 143.
Catechesis/Religious Program—Email: epaige@holycrossindy.org. Eileen Page, Dir. Faith Formation. Students 26.

13—Holy Rosary (1909), (Italian), [JC] Rev. Msgr. Joseph F. Schaedel; Rev. Michael W. Magiera, F.S.S.P.
Office: 520 Stevens St., 46203. Tel: 317-636-4478; Fax: 317-636-2522. Email: holyrosary@cs.com. Web: www.holyrosaryindy.org.

14—Holy Spirit (1946) Revs. Paul D. Koetter; Christopher Wadelton.
Res.: 7243 E. 10th St., 46219. Tel: 317-353-9404; Fax: 317-351-1707. Web: www.holyspirit-indy.org.
School—(Grades PreK-8), 7241 E. 10th St., 46219. Tel: 317-352-1243; Fax: 317-351-1822. Rita Parsons, Prin. Lay Teachers 23; Students 371.
Catechesis/Religious Program—Tel: 317-357-6915. Students 500.

15—Holy Trinity (1906) [JC] Rev. John Patrick McCaslin, Admin.
Parish Office: 337 N. Warman Ave., 46222.
Church: N. Holmes Ave. & W. St. Clair St., 46222.
Res.: 379 N. Warman Ave., 46222. Tel: 317-631-2939; Fax: 317-636-3140. Email: holytrinityindy@catholicweb.com. Web: www.holytrinityindy.catholicweb.com.
See All Saints Consolidated, Indianapolis under St. Anthony Indianapolis for details.
Catechesis/Religious Program—Students 6.

16—Immaculate Heart of Mary (1946) [JC] Rev. Robert W. Sims.
Parish Center—5692 N. Central Ave., 46220. Tel: 317-257-2266; Fax: 317-475-7380. Web: ihmindy.org.
School—317 E. 57th St., 46220. Tel: 317-255-5468; Fax: 317-475-7379. Peggy Elson, Prin. Lay Teachers 32; Students 424.
Catechesis/Religious Program—Students 90.

17—St. Joan of Arc (1921) [JC] Rev. Guy R. Roberts.
Res.: 4217 Central Ave., 46205. Tel: 317-283-5508; Fax: 317-283-5511.
School—(Grades PreK-8), 500 E. 42nd St., 46205. Tel: 317-283-1518; Fax: 317-931-3380. Mary Pat Sharpe, Prin. Lay Teachers 9; Students 152.
Catechesis/Religious Program—Fax: 317-283-5511. Students 87.

18—St. John the Evangelist (1837), (Irish), Rev. Stephen W. Giannini.
Res.: 126 W. Georgia St., 46225. Tel: 317-635-2021; Fax: 317-635-2014. Email: office@stjohnsindy.com. Web: www.stjohnsindy.com.
Catechesis/Religious Program—Students 9.

19—St. Joseph (1949) [JC] Rev. Glenn L. O'Connor.
Res.: 1375 S. Mickley Ave., 46241. Tel: 317-244-9002; Fax: 317-244-0278. Email: glo1375@aol.com.
See St. Anthony School under St. Anthony Indianapolis for details.
Catechesis/Religious Program—Students 65.

20—St. Jude (1959) Rev. Stephen Banet; Deacon Wesley Jones.
Res.: 5353 McFarland Rd., 46227. Tel: 317-786-4371; Fax: 317-780-7592. Web: www.stjudeindy.org.
School—5375 McFarland Rd, 46227. Tel: 317-784-6828; Fax: 317-780-7594. Sr. James Michael Kesterson, S.P., Prin. Sisters of Providence 2; Lay Teachers 26; Students 518.
Catechesis/Religious Program—Tel: 317-780-7591. Students 176.

21—St. Lawrence (1949) Revs. John Beitans; Jae Peter Choi, Korean Community.
Office: 6944 E. 46th St., 46226-3704. Tel: 317-546-4065; Fax: 317-543-4926.
Res.: 4650 N. Shadeland Ave., 46226.
School—6950 E. 46th St., 46226. Tel: 317-543-4923; Fax: 317-543-4929. Betty Popp, Prin. Lay Teachers 22; Students 360.
Catechesis/Religious Program—Students 120.

22—St. Luke (1961) [JC] Revs. Noah J. Casey; Joseph L. Newton.
Res.: 7550 Holliday Dr. E., 46260. Tel: 317-259-4373; Fax: 317-254-3210. Web: www.stluke.org.
School—7650 N. Illinois St., 46260. Tel: 317-255-3912. Stephen Weber, Prin. Lay Teachers 35; Students 589.
Catechesis/Religious Program—Students 151.

23—St. Mark the Evangelist (1946) Rev. George F. Plaster; Deacon Kerry Blanford.
Res.: 535 E. Edgewood, 46227. Tel: 317-787-8246; Fax: 317-781-6466. Email: ksweeney@stmarkindy.org. Web: www.stmarkindy.org.
School—541 E. Edgewood Ave., 46227. Tel: 317-786-4013; Fax: 317-783-9574. Rusty Albertson, Prin. Lay Teachers 19; Students 238.
Catechesis/Religious Program—Tel: 317-784-7155. Email: mlcav@stmarkindy.org. Students 167.

24—St. Mary/Immaculate Conception (1858), (Hispanic), [JC] Rev. Michael E. O'Mara; Mr. Juan Antonio Guzman, Pastoral Assoc.
Res.: 317 N. New Jersey St., 46204-2174. Tel: 317-637-3983; Fax: 317-637-0111. Email: parish@saintmarysindy.org. Web: www.saintmarysindy.org.
Catechesis/Religious Program—The Marian Center, 311 N. New Jersey St., 46204. Students 105.

25—St. Matthew (1958) Rev. Paul M. Shikany. In Res., Rev. Robert E. Mazzola.
Res.: 4100 E. 56th St., 46220. Tel: 317-257-4297; Fax: 317-479-2381. Email: pwitt@saintmatt.org. Web: www.saintmatt.org.
School—(Grades K-8) Tel: 317-251-3997. Email: principal@saintmatt.org. Web: www.saint-matthew-school.org. P. Martin Erlenbaugh, Prin. Religious 1; Lay Teachers 29; Students 375.
Catechesis/Religious Program—Tel: 317-257-4297, Ext. 1005. Email: jnoll@saintmatt.org. Students 90.

26—St. Michael the Archangel (1948) Rev. Varghese Maliakkal, Admin.
Res.: 3354 W. 30th St., 46222. Tel: 317-926-7359; Fax: 317-921-3282. Email: rectory@indyarchangel.org. Web: www.stmichaelindy.com.
School—3352 W. 30th St., 46222. Tel: 317-926-0516; Fax: 317-921-3280. Steven M. Padgett, Prin. Lay Teachers 18; Students 217.
Catechesis/Religious Program—Tel: 317-921-3284. Email: b.ldanner@juno.com. Students 48.

27—St. Monica (1956) Revs. Todd Michael Goodson; Jeremy M. Gries.
Res.: 6131 N. Michigan Rd., 46228. Tel: 317-253-2193; Fax: 317-253-3342. Email: stmonica@indyweb.net. Web: stmonicaparishindy.org.
School—Tel: 317-255-7153; Fax: 317-259-5570. Lay Teachers 33; Students 507.
Catechesis/Religious Program—Students 454.

28—Nativity of Our Lord Jesus Christ (1947) [JC] Rev. Patrick Doyle.
7225 Southeastern Ave., 46239. Tel: 317-357-1200. Email: tmarlin@nativityindy.org. Web: www.nativityindy.org.
School—3310 S. Meadow Dr., 46239. Tel: 317-357-1459; Fax: 317-357-9175. Lay Teachers 20; Students 274.
Catechesis/Religious Program—Tel: 317-359-6075. Email: rhawthorne@nativityindy.org. Students 160.

29—Our Lady of Lourdes (1909) Rev. J. Nicholas Dant.
5333 E. Washington St., 46219. Tel: 317-356-7291; Fax: 317-356-2358. Email: parishsecretary@ollindy.org. Web: www.lourdesparish.com.
School—30 S. Downey Ave., 46219. Tel: 317-357-3316; Fax: 317-357-0980. Lay Teachers 19; Students 282.
Catechesis/Religious Program—Email: bhansberry@ollindy.org. Beverly Hansberry, D.R.E. & Pastoral Assoc. Students 25.

30—St. Patrick (1865), (Irish—Hispanic), Rev. Arturo M. Ocampo, O.F.M.
Church: 950 Prospect St., 46203. Tel: 317-631-5824; Fax: 317-631-5828.
See Central Catholic Consolidated, Indianapolis under Good Shepherd, Indianapolis for details.
Catechesis/Religious Program—Students 174.

31—St. Philip Neri (1909), (Irish—Hispanic), [JC] Rev. Carlton J. Beever.
Res.: 550 N. Rural St., 46201. Tel: 317-631-8746; Fax: 317-632-8161.
School—545 Eastern Ave., 46201. Tel: 317-636-0134; Fax: 317-636-3231. Mary McCoy, Prin. Lay Teachers 14; Students 160.
Catechesis/Religious Program—Students 155.

32—St. Pius X (1955) Revs. Gerald J. Kirkhoff; Robert T. Hausladen.
Res.: 7200 Sarto Dr., 46240. Tel: 317-255-4534; Fax: 317-466-3354. Web: www.spxparish.org.
School—Tel: 317-466-3361. Bill Herman, Prin. Lay Teachers 28; Students 429.
Catechesis/Religious Program—Tel: 317-257-1085; Fax: 317-466-3377. Students 131.

33—St. Rita (1919), (African American), [JC] Rev. Eusebius Mbidoaka; Deacon Donald Dearman.
1733 Dr. Andrew J. Brown Ave., 46202. Web: www.stritachurch-indy.org.
See St. Andrew & St. Rita Catholic Academy, Indianapolis under St. Andrew the Apostle, Indianapolis for details.
Catechesis/Religious Program—Students 27.

34—St. Roch (1922) [JC] Rev. James R. Wilmoth.
Res.: 3600 S. Pennsylvania St., 46227. Tel: 317-784-1763; Fax: 317-783-9617.
School—3603 S. Meridian St., 46217. Tel: 317-784-9144. Lay Teachers 21; Students 261.
Catechesis/Religious Program—Students 78.

35—Sacred Heart of Jesus (1875), (German), [CEM 2] [JC] Rev. Frank Kordek, O.F.M. In Res., Revs. Thomas Fox, O.F.M.; Dennis Bosse, O.F.M.; Justin Belitz, O.F.M., The Hermitage, P.O. Box 30248, 46230.
Res.: 1530 S. Union St., 46225. Tel: 317-638-5551; Fax: 317-637-9741.
See Central Catholic School, Indianapolis under Good Shepherd, Indianapolis for details.
Catechesis/Religious Program—Students 35.

36—St. Simon the Apostle (1961) Rev. William G. Marks; Deacon Thomas Ward.
Church & Office: 8155 Oaklandon Rd., 46236-8578. Tel: 317-826-6000; Fax: 317-826-6010.
School—(Grades PreSchool-8) Tel: 317-826-6000, Ext. 107; Fax: 317-826-6020. Kathleen Wright, Prin. Lay Teachers 37; Students 759.
Catechesis/Religious Program—Tel: 317-826-6000, Ext. 113. Students 420.

37—St. Therese of the Infant Jesus (Little Flower) (1925) [JC] Rev. Robert J. Gilday.
Res.: 4720 E. 13th St., 46201. Tel: 317-357-8352; Fax: 317-357-5316. Web: www.littleflowerparish.org.
School—(Grades PreSchool-8), 1401 N. Bosart Ave, 46202. Tel: 317-353-2282; Fax: 317-322-7702. Web: www.littleflowerparish.org/school. Kevin Gawrys, Prin. Lay Teachers 16; Students 220.
Catechesis/Religious Program—Students 60.

38—St. Thomas Aquinas (1939) Rev. Steven C. Schwab.
Office: 4625 N. Kenwood Ave., 46208. Tel: 317-253-1461; Fax: 317-253-1410. Email: mcrain@staindy.org. Web: www.staindy.org.
Res.: 4650 N. Illinois St., 46208.
School—4600 N. Illinois St., 46208. Tel: 317-255-6244; Fax: 317-255-6106. Email: rsochacki@staschool-indy.org. Web: www.staschool-indy.org. Jerry Flynn, Prin. Lay Teachers 21; Students 221.
Catechesis/Religious Program—Students 40.

OUTSIDE THE CITY OF INDIANAPOLIS

Aurora, Dearborn Co., St. Mary of the Immaculate Conception (1857) Rev. Stephen D. Donahue.
Parish Office—203 Fourth St., 47001. Tel: 812-926-0060; Fax: 812-926-4439. Email: stmarychurch@uswebmail.biz. Web: www.stmarychurchaurora.com.
School—(Grades K-8), 211 Fourth St., 47001. Tel: 812-926-1558; Fax: 812-926-4439. Email: stmary@uswebmail.biz. Web: www.stmaryschoolaurora.com. James Tush, Prin. Lay Teachers 9; Students 146.
Catechesis/Religious Program—Email: carolynmeyer@uswebmail.biz.

Batesville, Ripley Co., St. Louis (1868), (German), [CEM] Revs. Bernard Varghese, O.F.M.Cap. (India), Temporary Admin.; Stephen Akange (Nigeria).
Res.: 13 St. Louis Pl., 47006. Tel: 812-934-3204; Fax: 812-933-0667. Web: www.stlouis-batesville.org.
School—Preschool, 200 S. Walnut St., 47006. Tel: 812-932-1731.
School—17 St. Louis Pl., 47006. Tel: 812-934-3310; Fax: 812-934-6202. Chad M. Moeller, Prin. Lay

Teachers 26; Students 489.
Catechesis / Religious Program—Tel: 812-934-3204, Ext. 249. Email: tmeyer@stlouisschool.org. Terri Meyer, D.R.E. Students 195.

BEDFORD, LAWRENCE CO., ST. VINCENT DE PAUL (1864) Rev. Richard W. Eldred; Deacon David Reising.
Parish/Mailing Office: 1723 I St., 47421.
Rectory—St. Mary of the Assumption: 777 S. 11th St., Mitchell, 47446. Tel: 812-275-6539; Fax: 812-275-3493.
School—(Grades PreK-8), 923 18th St., 47421. Tel: 812-279-2540; Fax: 812-276-4880. Katherine Sleva, Prin. Lay Teachers 11; Students 184.
Catechesis / Religious Program—Students 65.

BEECH GROVE, MARION CO., HOLY NAME (1908) [JC] Rev. Stanley Pondo; Deacon David Reising.
Res.: 89 N. 17th Ave., 46107. Tel: 317-784-5454 (Parish Office); Fax: 317-784-1834 (Parish Office). Email: frstan@holyname.cc. Web: www.holyname.cc.
School—21 N. 17th Ave., 46107. Tel: 317-784-9078 Office; 317-788-3617; 317-788-3618; Fax: 317-788-3616. Email: gfleming@holyname.cc. Web: www.holyname.cc/school.htm. Gina Kuntz Fleming, Prin. Lay Teachers 22; Students 239.
Catechesis / Religious Program—Tel: 317-784-5454, Ext. 4. Email: jchamblee@holyname.cc. Web: www.holyname.cc. Students 55.

BLOOMINGTON, MONROE CO.
1—ST. CHARLES BORROMEO (1864) [JC] Revs. William F. Stumpf; Don Davison, C.P.P.S.; Deacon Marc Kellams.
Res.: 2001 Southdowns St., 47401. Tel: 812-339-9180; Fax: 812-331-6732.
School—(Grades PreK-8), 2224 E. Third St., 47401. Tel: 812-336-5853; Fax: 812-349-0300. Alec Mayer, Prin. Lay Teachers 32; Students 456.
Catechesis / Religious Program—2222 E. Third St., 47401. Tel: 812-334-1664. Students 277.
2—ST. JOHN THE APOSTLE (1970) Rev. Michael C. Fritsch.
Res.: 4607 W. State Rd. 46, 47404-9255. Tel: 812-876-1974; Fax: 812-876-9494. Email: info@sjabloomington.org. Web: sjabloomington.org.
Catechesis / Religious Program—Tel: 812-876-0718, Ext. 203. Lynn Hansen, D.R.E. Students 145.
3—ST. PAUL CATHOLIC CENTER (1969) Revs. Robert Keller, O.P.; Stanley Drongowski, O.P.; Richard Litzau, O.P.; Stephanie Hudson, Business Mgr.
Res.: 1413 E. 17th St., 47408. Tel: 812-339-5561; Fax: 812-333-4846. Web: www.hoosiercatholic.org.
Catechesis / Religious Program—Email: faithformation@hoosiercatholic.org. Students 215.

BRADFORD, HARRISON CO., ST. MICHAEL (1835) [CEM] Rev. John L. Fink.
Mailing Address: 11400 Farmers Ln., N.E., P.O. Box 22, 47107. Tel: 812-364-6646; Fax: 812-364-6614. Web: saintmichaelschurch.net.
Catechesis / Religious Program—Tel: 812-364-6173. Email: johnjacobi@insightbb.com. Students 195.

BRAZIL, CLAY CO., ANNUNCIATION OF THE BLESSED VIRGIN MARY (1865) Rev. Harold W. Rightor II.
Office: 19 N. Alabama St., 47834. Tel: 812-448-1901; Fax: 812-448-1901. Email: annunciationchurch@msn.com.
School—(Grades PreSchool), 415 E. Church St., 47834. Fax: 812-443-3089. Jane Osborn, Admin.
Catechesis / Religious Program—Students 26.

BRIGHT, DEARBORN CO., ST. TERESA BENEDICTA OF THE CROSS (2000) Rev. Thomas G. Kovatch; Deacon Tim Heller.
Parish Office: 23455 Gavin Ln., Lawrenceburg, 47025-8372. Tel: 812-656-8700; Fax: 812-656-8777.
Catechesis / Religious Program—Students 187.

BROOKVILLE, FRANKLIN CO., ST. MICHAEL (1845), (German), [CEM] Rev. William M. Williams, Admin.
Church: 145 St. Michael Blvd., 47012. Tel: 765-647-5462; Fax: 765-647-1634.
School—Tel: 765-647-4961; Fax: 765-647-4961. Gary Ferguson, Prin. Sisters of the Third Order Regular of St. Francis 2; Lay Teachers 13; Students 199.
Catechesis / Religious Program—Students 48.

BROWNSBURG, HENDRICKS CO., ST. MALACHY (1869), (Irish), [CEM 2] Revs. Joseph M. Feltz; John J. Hollowell, Sacramental Min.
Parish Center—326 N. Green St., 46112. Tel: 317-852-3195; Fax: 317-852-8939.
Church: 9833 E. Co. Rd. 750 N., 46112. Web: www.saintmalachyparish.org.
School—(Grades K-8), 330 N. Green St., 46112. Tel: 317-852-2242; Fax: 317-852-3604. Mary Sullivan, Prin. Lay Teachers 30; Students 427.
Catechesis / Religious Program—Tel: 317-852-8476. Students 781.

BROWNSTOWN, JACKSON CO., OUR LADY OF PROVIDENCE (1934) Attended by St. Ambrose, Seymour. Rev. Scott E. Nobbe, Admin.
Mailing Address: c/o St. Ambrose Church, 325 S. Chestnut St., Seymour, 47274. Tel: 812-522-5304; Fax: 812-522-8959.
Church: 1500 S. C.R. 150 W., 47220.
Catechesis / Religious Program—Students 22.

CAMBRIDGE CITY, WAYNE CO., ST. ELIZABETH OF HUNGARY (1852) Rev. Joseph F. Rautenberg.
333 W. Maple St., 47327. Tel: 765-478-3242; Fax: 765-478-3585.
Catechesis / Religious Program—Email: meekerchristine@yahoo.com. Students 70.

CANNELTON, PERRY CO., ST. MICHAEL (1859) [CEM] Rev. Barnabas Gillespie, O.S.B.
Parish Office—c/o Catholic Ministry Center, 824 Jefferson St., Tell City, 47586-2114. Tel: 812-547-7994; Fax: 812-547-6985. Email: stpaulch@psci.net.
Res.: 814 Jefferson St., Tell City, 47586. Tel: 812-547-9901.
Church: Eighth St., 47520.
Catechesis / Religious Program—Students 10.

CEDAR GROVE, FRANKLIN CO., HOLY GUARDIAN ANGELS (1874), (German), [CEM] Rev. William M. Williams.
Mailing Address: 145 St. Michael Blvd., Brookville, 47012. Tel: 765-647-6981; Fax: 765-647-1634. Email: churchhga@verizon.net.
Church: 405 U.S. Hwy. 52, 47016.
Catechesis / Religious Program—Students 115.

CHARLESTOWN, CLARK CO., ST. MICHAEL (1860) [CEM] Rev. Steven Schaftlein.
Res.: 101 St. Michael Dr., 47111. Tel: 812-256-3200; Fax: 775-307-6142. Email: michaelsecretary@insightbb.com.
Child Care Center—102 St. Michael Dr., 47111. Tel: 812-256-3503; Fax: 775-307-6142. (PreK-K) Students 125.
Catechesis / Religious Program—Students 79.

CLARKSVILLE, CLARK CO., ST. ANTHONY OF PADUA (1851) [CEM] Rev. Regis Schlagheck, O.F.M.Conv.
In Res., Bro. Bruno Nemcosky, O.F.M.Conv., (Retired); Revs. John Curran; John Elmer, O.F.M.Conv.; Tom Smith, O.F.M.Conv.
Res.: 310 N. Sherwood Ave., 47129. Tel: 812-282-8515. Web: www.stanthonchurch.us.
School—320 N. Sherwood Ave., 47129. Tel: 812-282-2144; Fax: 812-282-2169. Sheila Noon, Prin. Ursuline Sisters 2; Lay Teachers 26; Students 350.
Catechesis / Religious Program—Email: stadre@insightbb.com. Students 38.

CLINTON, VERMILLION CO., SACRED HEART (1891) Rev. Joseph L. Villa.
619 S. Fifth St., 47842-2016. Tel: 765-832-8468; Fax: 765-832-5092. Email: sacredheartclinton@sbcglobal.net.
Rectory—558 Nebeker St., 47842.
Catechesis / Religious Program—Students 64.
Mission—St. Joseph (1920) 270 E. Wood Ave., Universal, Vermillion Co. 47884.

COLUMBUS, BARTHOLOMEW CO., ST. BARTHOLOMEW (1994), St. Bartholomew (1841) and St. Columba (1963) were closed, merged, and renamed St. Bartholomew. Rev. Clement T. Davis.
Mailing Address: 1306 27th St., 47201. Tel: 812-379-9353; Fax: 812-375-0720. Web: www.saintbartholomew.org.
School—(Grades K-8), 1306 27th St., 47201. Fax: 812-376-0377. Kathy Schubel, Prin. Lay Teachers 26; Students 409.
Catechesis / Religious Program—Students 980.

CONNERSVILLE, FAYETTE CO., ST. GABRIEL (1851) [JC] Rev. Stanley J. Herber; Pamela S. Rader, Business Mgr.
Res.: 232 W. Ninth St., 47331-2099. Tel: 765-825-8578; Fax: 765-825-7060.
School—(Grades PreK-6), 224 W. Ninth St., 47331. Tel: 765-825-7951; Fax: 765-827-4347. Email: stgab@ydial.net. Web: www.stgabriel.k12.in.us. Sue Barth, Prin. Lay Teachers 8; Students 133.
Catechesis / Religious Program—Students 55.

CORYDON, HARRISON CO., ST. JOSEPH (1896) [CEM] Rev. J. Daniel Atkins.
Res.: 312 E. High St., 47112. Tel: 812-738-2742; Fax: 812-738-2718. Email: joecorydon@yahoo.com. Web: www.triparishcommunity.com.
School—512 N. Mulberry St., 47112. Tel: 812-738-4549; Fax: 812-738-2722. Lay Teachers 12; Students 110.
Catechesis / Religious Program—Tel: 812-738-2759. Students 140.
Mission—Most Precious Blood (1880) [CEM] Corydon-New Middletown Rd., New Middletown, Harrison Co. 47160.
Mission—St. Peter (1849) [CEM] Buena Vista Rd., Elizabeth, Harrison Co. 47117.

DANVILLE, HENDRICKS CO., MARY QUEEN OF PEACE (1939) Rev. Bernard Cox; Austin Rahill, Youth Min.
Res.: 1005 W. Main St., 46122. Tel: 317-745-4284; Fax: 317-745-7090. Web: www.maryqueenofpeacedanville.org.
Catechesis / Religious Program—Tel: 317-745-4284, Ext. 13. Email: polycarp11@iquest.net. Peg Klein, D.R.E. Students 245.

DOVER, DEARBORN CO., ST. JOHN THE BAPTIST (1824) [CEM] Rev. C. Ryan McCarthy.
Church & Mailing Address: 25743 State Rd. 1, Guilford, 47022. Tel: 812-576-4302; Fax: 812-576-2324.
Catechesis / Religious Program—Students 49.

EDINBURGH, JOHNSON CO., HOLY TRINITY (1851) Rev. Thomas L. Schliessmann.
100 Keeley St., P.O. Box 216, 46124.
Res.: 114 Lancelot Dr., Franklin, 46131. Tel: 317-738-3929; Fax: 812-526-2477. Email: hilltop3@sbcglobal.net.
Catechesis / Religious Program—Tel: 812-526-9470. Students 39.

ENOCHSBURG, DECATUR CO., ST. JOHN THE EVANGELIST (1844), (German), [CEM] Rev. George Joseph Nangachiveettil (India).
Mailing Address: 5267 N. Hamburg Rd., Oldenburg, 47036. Tel: 812-934-2880; Fax: 812-934-2880.
Church: 9995 E. Base Rd., Greensburg, 47240.
Catechesis / Religious Program—Fax: 812-934-2880. Students 80.

FORTVILLE, HANCOCK CO., ST. THOMAS THE APOSTLE (1869) Rev. Joseph G. Pesola.
Res.: 523 S. Merrill St., 46040. Tel: 317-485-5101; Fax: 317-485-0022. Email: stthomas@iquest.net. Web: www.stthomasfortville.org.
Catechesis / Religious Program—Tel: 317-485-5103; Fax: 317-485-0022. Students 174.

FRANKLIN, JOHNSON CO., ST. ROSE OF LIMA (1868) Rev. Thomas L. Schliessmann; Jean Martin, Pastoral Assoc. Tel: 317-738-2965.
Res.: 114 Lancelot Dr., 46131. Tel: 317-738-3929; Fax: 317-738-3583.
School—(Grades PreK-8) Tel: 317-738-3451. Kelly England, Prin.; Shelley Sorgent, Librarian.
Catechesis / Religious Program—Tel: 317-736-6754. Students 150.

FRENCH LICK, ORANGE CO., OUR LADY OF THE SPRINGS (1887) Revs. Joseph B. Moriarty; John M. Hall, Admin.
Res.: 8796 W. State Rd. 56, 47432. Tel: 812-936-4568; Fax: 812-936-4561. Email: ols936@bluemarble.net.
Catechesis / Religious Program—Tel: 812-936-9331. Students 12.
Mission—Our Lord Jesus Christ the King (1948) Hwy 150, E., Paoli, Orange Co. 47454.
Catechesis / Religious Program—Students 22.

FRENCHTOWN, HARRISON CO., ST. BERNARD (1849) [CEM] Rev. John L. Fink.
Church: 7600 Hwy. 337. Tel: 812-347-2326; Fax: 812-347-2172.
Res.: 7600 Hwy. 337 N.W., Depauw, 47115.
Res.: 11400 Farmers Ln., Bradford, 47107. Tel: 812-364-6646; Fax: 812-364-6614.
Catechesis / Religious Program—Students 38.
Mission—St. Joseph (1855) State Road 66, Marengo, Crawford Co. 47140.

FULDA, SPENCER CO., ST. BONIFACE (1847) [CEM] Rev. Anthony Vinson, O.S.B., Admin.
Mailing Address: P.O. Box 8, St. Meinrad, 47577. Tel: 812-357-5533; Fax: 812-357-2862.
Church: 15529 N. State Rd. 545, 47536.
Catechesis / Religious Program—Students 48.

GREENCASTLE, PUTNAM CO., ST. PAUL THE APOSTLE (1853) Rev. Stephen Jarrell.
Res.: 202 E. Washington St., 46135. Tel: 765-653-5678; Fax: 765-653-4377.
Catechesis / Religious Program—Students 118.

GREENFIELD, HANCOCK CO., ST. MICHAEL (1860) Rev. Severin Messick, O.S.B.
Res.: 519 Jefferson Blvd., 46140. Tel: 317-462-4240; Fax: 317-462-2571. Email: lnewett@stmichaelsgrfld.org. Web: www.stmichaelsgrfld.org.
School—(Grades PreK-8), 515 Jefferson Blvd., 46140. Tel: 317-462-6380; Fax: 317-467-2864. Theresa Slipher, Prin.; Emily Capen, Librarian. Lay Teachers 19; Students 287.
Catechesis / Religious Program—Email: prichey@stmichaelsgrfld.org. Students 320.

GREENSBURG, DECATUR CO., ST. MARY (1858) [CEM] Rev. Msgr. Harold L. Knueven, Admin. (Retired).
Res.: 302 E. McKee St., 47240. Tel: 812-663-8427; Fax: 812-663-6088.
School—(Grades PreK-6), 210 S. East St., 47240. Tel: 812-663-2804. Nancy Buening, Prin. Lay Teachers 16; Students 221.
Catechesis / Religious Program—Students 273.

GREENWOOD, JOHNSON CO.
1—SS. FRANCIS AND CLARE OF ASSISI (1993) Rev. Vincent Lampert.
Church & Parish Office: 5901 Olive Branch Rd., 46143. Tel: 317-859-4673; Fax: 317-859-4678. Web: www.francisandclare.org.
School—(Grades PreK-3) Sandra Patel, Prin.
Catechesis / Religious Program—Students 510.
2—OUR LADY OF THE GREENWOOD (1948) [JC] Rev. Msgr. Mark Svarczkopf; Revs. Donald A. Quinn, Sacramental Min.; Mauro G. Rodas, Hispanic Min. (Retired).
Res.: 101 Orchard Ave., 46143. Tel: 317-888-2861; Fax: 317-885-5006. Email: info@olgreenwood.org. Web: www.olgreenwood.org.
School—(Grades PreK-8), 399 S. Meridian St.,

46143. Tel: 317-881-1300. Kent Clady, Prin. Lay Teachers 27; Students 447.
Catechesis/Religious Program—Students 275.

HAMBURG, FRANKLIN CO., ST. ANNE (1869) [CEM] Rev. George Joseph Nangachiveettil (India).
5267 N. Hamburg Rd., Oldenburg, 47036.
Res.: 9995 E. Base Rd., Greensburg, 47240. Tel: 812-934-5854; Fax: 812-934-5854. Email: stanne@seidata.com.
Catechesis/Religious Program—Students 36.

HENRYVILLE, CLARK CO., ST. FRANCIS XAVIER (1869), Attended from St. Michael, 101 St. Michael Dr., Charlestown, IN 47111. Tel: 812-256-3200; Fax: 775-307-6142. Rev. Steven Schaftlein.
Church: Hwy. 31 & Hwy. 160, 47126. Fax: 775-307-6142. Email: michaelsecretary@insightbb.com.
Catechesis/Religious Program—Students 50.

JEFFERSONVILLE, CLARK CO.

1—ST. AUGUSTINE (1851) [CEM] Rev. Thomas E. Clegg.
Res.: 315 E. Chestnut St., P.O. Box 447, 47131. Tel: 812-282-2677; Fax: 812-282-8821. Email: saintaug@insightbb.com. Web: www.saintaug.org.
Catechesis/Religious Program—316 E. Maple St. Tel: 812-282-1231; Fax: 812-282-1605. Students 118.

2—SACRED HEART (1953) Rev. Thomas E. Clegg.
Church & Parish Office: 1840 E. 8th St., 47103. Tel: 812-282-0423; Fax: 812-284-6673.
School—1842 E. 8th St., 47130. Tel: 812-283-3123. Becky Spitznagel, Prin. Lay Teachers 15; Students 210.
Catechesis/Religious Program—Students 67.

KNIGHTSTOWN, HENRY CO., ST. ROSE (1872) Sr. Shirley Gerth, O.S.F., Parish Life Coord.; Revs. Joseph F. Rautenberg, Sacramental Min.; Stanley J. Herber, Priest Mod.
Mailing Address: P.O. Box 209, 46148. Tel: 765-345-5595.
Church: 8144 W. U.S. Hwy. 40, 46148. Tel: 765-345-5595; Fax: 765-345-5595. Email: strose@ktownonline.net.
Catechesis/Religious Program—Students 29.

LANESVILLE, HARRISON CO., ST. MARY (1843), (German), [CEM] Rev. H. Michael Hilderbrand.
Res.: 2500 St. Mary's Dr., 47136. Tel: 812-952-2853 (Parish Office); 812-952-0060; Fax: 812-952-2852. Email: stmarys@insightbb.com. Web: stmaryslanesville.org.
Catechesis/Religious Program—Tel: 812-952-2854. Email: smlff@insightbb.com. Students 124.

LAWRENCEBURG, DEARBORN CO., ST. LAWRENCE (1842), (German), Rev. J. Peter Gallagher.
Parish Office—542 Walnut St., 47025. Tel: 812-537-3992.
Rectory—526 Walnut St., 47025. Tel: 812-537-1297.
School—524 Walnut St., 47025. Tel: 812-537-3690; Fax: 812-537-9685. Karen White, Prin. Lay Teachers 18; Students 281.
Catechesis/Religious Program—Tel: 812-537-1112. Students 94.

LEOPOLD, PERRY CO., ST. AUGUSTINE (1837) [CEM] Rev. Aaron Pfaff.
Res.: 18020 Lafayette St., 47551. Tel: 812-843-5143.
Catechesis/Religious Program—Students 45.

LIBERTY, UNION CO., ST. BRIDGET (1854) [CEM] Rev. Stanley J. Herber, Admin.
Mailing Address: P.O. Box 112, 47353.
Res.: 404 E. Vine St., 47353.
Catechesis/Religious Program—Tel: 765-458-5412. Students 25.

MADISON, JEFFERSON CO., PRINCE OF PEACE (1993) [CEM 3], St. Michael (1837), St. Mary (1851), St. Patrick (1853), Madison, and St. Anthony, China (1861) were closed, merged and renamed Prince of Peace. Rev. John A. Meyer.
Mailing Address: *Catholic Community Center*, 305 W. State St., 47250. Tel: 812-265-4166; Fax: 812-273-3427. Web: www.popeace.org.
Res.: 415 E. Second St., 47250. Tel: 812-265-4166.
School—Pope John XXIII, (Grades PreSchool-6), 221 State St., 47250. Tel: 812-273-3957; Fax: 812-265-4566.
High School—Shawe Memorial Junior-Senior High School, Tel: 812-273-2150; Fax: 812-273-2013. See High Schools, Inter-Parochial, under Institutions Located in the Archdiocese.
Catechesis/Religious Program—Students 31.

MARENGO, CRAWFORD CO., ST. JOSEPH (1855) [CEM] Attended by St. Bernard, Frenchtown. Rev. John L. Fink, Admin.
Mailing Address: 7600 Hwy. 337 N.W., Depauw, 47115. Tel: 812-347-2326.
Church: State Rd. 66, 47140.
Catechesis/Religious Program—Students 20.

MARTINSVILLE, MORGAN CO., ST. MARTIN OF TOURS (1848) [CEM] Rev. John M. Hall.
Res.: 1709 E. Harrison St., 46151. Tel: 765-342-6379.
Catechesis/Religious Program—Tel: 765-352-0602; Fax: 765-342-1263. Students 157.

MILAN, RIPLEY CO., ST. CHARLES BORROMEO (1908) Rev. Gregory D. Bramlage, Admin.
Mailing Address: *c/o St. Nicholas*, 6457 E. St. Nicholas Dr., Sunman, 47041. Fax: 812-934-5936.
Church: 213 Ripley St., 47031. Tel: 812-623-8007.
Catechesis/Religious Program—Tel: 812-744-3882. Ed King, D.R.E. Students 82.

MILLHOUSEN, DECATUR CO., IMMACULATE CONCEPTION (1834) [CEM] Sr. Christine Ernstes, O.S.F., Parish Life Coord.; Revs. Robert Jason Hankee, Sacramental Min.; Paul E. Landwerlen, Priest Mod.
Mailing Address: 2081 E. County Rd., 820 S., Greensburg, 47240-9636. Tel: 812-591-2362; Fax: 812-591-2362. Email: icchurch@voyager.net. Web: icsdchurches.com.
Mission—St. Denis (1894) [CEM] Church: 12155 N. County Rd., 600 E., St. Denis, Jennings Co. 47283.
Catechesis/Religious Program—Students 106.

MITCHELL, LAWRENCE CO., ST. MARY/ASSUMPTION (1869) Rev. Richard W. Eldred.
Res.: 777 S. 11th St., 47446. Tel: 812-849-3570; Fax: 812-849-6024. Email: stmarysmitchell@verizon.net. Web: www.catholiccommunityoflawrencecounty.com.
Catechesis/Religious Program—Fax: 812-849-6024. Students 24.

MOORESVILLE, MORGAN CO., ST. THOMAS MORE (1967) Rev. Mark Gottemoeller.
Res.: 1200 N. Indiana St., 46158. Tel: 317-831-4142; Fax: 317-834-2947. Email: stmkphillips@sbcglobal.net.
Catechesis/Religious Program—Students 256.

MORRIS, RIPLEY CO., ST. ANTHONY OF PADUA (1856) [CEM] Rev. Pascal E. Nduka, Admin.; Deacon John J. Chlopecki.
Mailing Address: P.O. Box 3, 47033. Tel: 812-934-6218; Fax: 812-934-5936.
Parish Office:—4781 E. Morris Church St., 47033.
Catechesis/Religious Program—Students 112.

NAPOLEON, RIPLEY CO., ST. MAURICE (1848) [CEM] Rev. Robert Jason Hankee.
Mailing Address: 8874 Harrison St., P.O. Box 17, 47034. Tel: 812-852-4237.
Catechesis/Religious Program—Fax: 812-852-4237. Students 125.

NASHVILLE, BROWN CO., ST. AGNES (1940) [JC] Sr. Eileen Flavin, C.S.C., Parish Life Coord.; Rev. Eric Johnson, Sacramental Min.
Mailing Address: 1008 McLary Rd., 47448. Tel: 812-988-2778; Fax: 812-988-2778. Email: stagnes5@iquest.net. Web: www.stagneschurchnashville.org.
Catechesis/Religious Program—Tel: 812-988-1432. Students 104.

NAVILLETON, FLOYD CO., ST. MARY (1845), (German), [CEM] Rev. Pius Poff, O.F.M.Conv.
Res.: 7500 Navilleton Rd., Floyds Knobs, 47119. Tel: 812-923-5419; Fax: 812-923-3430. Email: stmarynavilleton@insightbb.com. Web: www.stmarysnavilleton.com.
Catechesis/Religious Program—Students 128.

NEW ALBANY, FLOYD CO.

1—HOLY FAMILY (1954) [JC] Rev. Wilfred E. Day.
Res.: 129 W. Daisy Ln., 47150. Tel: 812-944-8283; Fax: 812-945-0180. Web: www.holyfamilynewalbany.org. Email: hfna@insightbb.com.
School—(Grades PreSchool-8), 217 W. Daisy Ln., 47150. Tel: 812-944-6090; Fax: 812-944-7299. Web: www.school.holyfamilyeagles.com. Gerald Ernstberger, Prin. Lay Teachers 23; Students 303.
Catechesis/Religious Program—Students 119.

2—ST. MARY (1858), (German), [CEM] [JC] Rev. Henry F. Tully.
Res.: 415 E. Eighth St., 47150. Tel: 812-944-0417; Fax: 812-944-9557. Email: info@stmarysna.org. Web: www.stmarysna.org.
School—(Grades PreSchool-8), 420 E. 8th St., 47150. Tel: 812-944-0888; Fax: 812-945-4770. Email: cougars@iglou.com. Web: www.smconline.com. Kimberly C. Hartlage, Prin. Lay Teachers 14; Students 159.
Catechesis/Religious Program—Students 57.

3—OUR LADY OF PERPETUAL HELP (1950) Rev. Eric Augenstein; Tom Yost, Pastoral Assoc. In Res., Rev. Mathew Choorapanthiyil, O.C.D. (India).
Res.: 1752 Scheller Ln., 47150. Tel: 812-944-1184; Fax: 812-944-3326. Email: lslusser@olphna.org. Web: olphna.org.
School—Tel: 812-944-7676; Fax: 812-948-2944. Theresa Horton, Prin. Lay Teachers 28; Students 355.
Catechesis/Religious Program—Tel: 812-948-0185. Students 135.

NEW ALSACE, DEARBORN CO., ST. PAUL (1833) [CEM] Rev. Brian Esarey.
Mailing Address: 8044 Yorkridge Rd., Guilford, 47022. Tel: 812-623-3408; Fax: 812-623-4879.
Res.: 9798 N. Dearborn Rd., Guilford, 47022. Tel: 812-623-3408.
School—(Grades PreSchool-6), 9788 N. Dearborn Rd., Guilford, 47022. Tel: 812-623-2631. Michael Monnig, Prin. Lay Teachers 5; Students 55.
Catechesis/Religious Program—Tel: 812-623-2662. Students 50.

NEW CASTLE, HENRY CO., ST. ANNE (1873) [CEM] Sr. Shirley Gerth, O.S.F., Parish Life Coord.; Revs. Joseph F. Rautenberg, Sacramental Min.; Stanley J. Herber, Priest Mod.
Parish Office—102 N. 19th St., 47362. Tel: 765-529-0933; 765-529-3395. Email: stannechurch@hotmail.com. Web: saintanne.us.to.
Church: 1904 Broad St., 47362. Tel: 765-529-7413; Fax: 765-529-2879.
Catechesis/Religious Program—Tel: 765-529-8976. Email: lwelch.st.anne@hotmail.com. Students 74.

NEW MARION, RIPLEY CO., ST. MARY MAGDALEN (1847) [CEM] Attended by St. John, Osgood. Rev. Shaun P. Whittington.
Office & Rectory: 331 S. Buckeye St., Osgood, 47037. Tel: 812-689-4244; Fax: 812-689-5035. Email: secretary@stjohnsosgood.org.
Church: 4613 S. Old Michigan Rd., Holton, 47023.
Catechesis/Religious Program—Tel: 812-689-6670. Jessica Gorman, D.R.E. Students 9.

NEW MIDDLETOWN, HARRISON CO., MOST PRECIOUS BLOOD (1880) [CEM], Attended from St. Joseph, 312 E. High St., Corydon, IN 47112. Tel: 812-738-2742. Rev. Daniel Atkins.
Mailing Address: *c/o St. Joseph*, 312 E. High St., Corydon, 47112.
Church: Corydon-New Middletown Rd., 47160. Tel: 812-738-2742; Fax: 812-738-2718. Email: joecorydon@yahoo.com. Web: www.triparishcommunity.com.
Catechesis/Religious Program—Tel: 812-738-2759. Combined with St. Joseph, Corydon Students 10.

NORTH VERNON, JENNINGS CO., ST. MARY/NATIVITY OF THE BLESSED VIRGIN MARY (1861) [CEM] Rev. Jonathan P. Meyer.
212 Washington St., 47265. Tel: 812-346-3604; Fax: 812-346-3506. Web: www.stmaryscc.org.
School—(Grades K-8), 209 Washington St., 47265. Tel: 812-346-3445; Fax: 812-346-5930. Email: stmarys@seidata.com. Web: www.stmarysnv.com. Sr. Joanita Koors, O.S.F., Prin. Lay Teachers 8; Students 207.
Catechesis/Religious Program—Students 97.

OLDENBURG, FRANKLIN CO., HOLY FAMILY (1837) [CEM] Rev. David Kobak, O.F.M. In Res., Rev. Carl Hawver, O.F.M., Chap., Sisters of St. Frances; Bro. Tim Lamb, O.F.M.
Res.: 3027 Pearl St., P.O. Box 98, 47036. Tel: 812-934-3013; Fax: 812-933-0728.
Catechesis/Religious Program—Students 189.

OSGOOD, RIPLEY CO., ST. JOHN (1867) [CEM] Rev. Shaun P. Whittington.
Res.: 331 S. Buckeye St., 47037. Tel: 812-689-4244; Fax: 812-689-5035. Email: secretary@stjohnsosgood.org. Web: www.stjohnsosgood.org.
Mission—St. Mary Magdalen (1847) [CEM] Holton, Ripley Co. 47023.
Catechesis/Religious Program—Tel: 812-689-6670; Fax: 812-689-6670. Email: cre@stjohnsosgood.org. Students 60.

PAOLI, ORANGE CO., OUR LORD JESUS CHRIST THE KING (1948), Attended from Our Lady of the Springs, French Lick. Revs. John M. Hall, Admin.; Joseph B. Moriarty, Sacramental Min.
Mailing Address: 8796 W. State Rd. 56, French Lick, 47432.
Church: Hwy. 150 E., 47454. Tel: 812-936-4568.
Catechesis/Religious Program—Tel: 812-723-5506. Jim O'Connell, D.R.E. Students 18.

PLAINFIELD, HENDRICKS CO., ST. SUSANNA (1953) Rev. Kevin Morris.
Res.: 1210 E. Main St., 46168. Tel: 317-839-3333; Fax: 317-839-0732. Web: www.saintsusannachurch.org.
School—(Grades PreSchool-8), 1212 E. Main St., 46168. Tel: 317-839-3713; Fax: 317-838-7718. Krista Keith, Prin. Lay Teachers 21; Students 348.
Catechesis/Religious Program—Tel: 317-838-7722; Fax: 317-838-7720. Email: klcrouse@saintsusanna.com. Students 402.

RICHMOND, WAYNE CO.

1—ST. ANDREW (1846) [JC] Revs. Todd M. Riebe; Gerald Okeke (Nigeria).
Res.: 720 A North St., 47374. Tel: 765-962-3569.
Church: 235 S. 5th St., 47374.
Parish Center & Mailing Address: 240 S. 6th St., 47374. Tel: 765-966-0916; Fax: 765-966-0820.
School—St. Elizabeth Ann Seton, (Grades 7-12), 801 W. Main, 47374. Tel: 765-965-6956; Fax: 765-935-9930. Cynthia Johnson, Prin. Lay Teachers 20; Students 293.
See Seton Catholic High School, Richmond under High Schools, Inter-Parochial in the Institution section.
Catechesis/Religious Program—Tel: 765-966-0916. Marcy Valentini, D.R.E. Students 49.

2—HOLY FAMILY (1953) Revs. Todd M. Riebe; Gerald Okeke (Nigeria).
Mailing Address: 240 S. 6th St., 47374. Tel: 765-962-3902; Fax: 765-966-0820.
Res.: 720 N. A St., 47374. Tel: 765-962-3569.
Church: 815 W. Main St., 47374.
School—St. Elizabeth Ann Seton, (Grades 3-6), 801 W. Main St., 47374. Tel: 765-962-4877; Fax: 765-962-5381. Cynthia Johnson, Prin. Lay Teachers 11; Students 293.
See Seton Catholic High School, Richmond under High Schools, Inter-Parochial in the Institution section.
Catechesis/Religious Program—233 S. 5th St., 47374. Marcy Valentini, D.R.E. Students 25.

3—ST. MARY (1859) [JC] Revs. Todd M. Riebe; Gerald Okeke (Nigeria).
Mailing Address: 240 S. 6th St., 47374. Tel: 765-962-3902; Fax: 765-966-0820. Email: rcco@richmondcatholiccommunity.com.
Church & Res.: 720 N. A St., 47374. Tel: 765-962-3569.
School—St. Elizabeth Ann Seton, (Grades PreK-2), 700 N. A St., 47374. Tel: 765-962-5010; Fax: 765-962-3692. Cynthia Johnson, Prin. Lay Teachers 7; Students 293.
See Seton Catholic High School, Richmond under High Schools, Inter-Parochial in the Institution section.
Catechesis/Religious Program—233 S. 5th St., 47374. Tel: 765-966-0916. Marcy Valentini, D.R.E. Students 61.

ROCKVILLE, PARKE CO., ST. JOSEPH (1867) Rev. Joseph L. Villa.
Res.: 217 E. Ohio St., 47872. Tel: 765-569-5406. Email: stjoerockville@yahoo.com.
Catechesis/Religious Program—Tel: 765-597-2474. Twinned with Sacred Heart, Clinton. Students 18.

RUSHVILLE, RUSH CO., IMMACULATE CONCEPTION/ST. MARY (1857) [CEM] Rev. William J. Turner.
Res.: 512 N. Perkins St., 46173. Tel: 765-932-2588; Fax: 765-932-2458. Email: stmarys512@comcast.net.
School—(Grades PreK-6), 226 E. 5th St., 46173. Tel: 765-932-3639; Fax: 765-938-1322. Web: www.st-marys-school.org. Stephanie Hasecuster, Prin. Lay Teachers 11; Students 100.
Catechesis/Religious Program—Students 141.

ST. ANNE, JENNINGS CO., ST. ANNE (1841) [CEM], Attended from St. Joseph, North Vernon. Rev. Jonathan P. Meyer, Admin.
Mailing Address: 1875 S. County Rd. 700 W., North Vernon, 47265.
Church: 4570 N. Co. Rd. 150 E., North Vernon, 47265. Tel: 812-346-4783; Fax: 812-352-9033. Email: rectory@stjoefourcorners.org. Web: www.stjoefourcorners.org.
Catechesis/Religious Program—Rita Bott, D.R.E. Students 50.

ST. CROIX, PERRY CO.

1—HOLY CROSS (1860) [CEM] Rev. Aaron Pfaff.
Mailing Address: 12239 State Rd. 62, 47576.
Res.: 824 Jefferson St., Tell City, 47586. Tel: 603-289-8119. Web: www.catholic-church.org/holycrossparish.
Catechesis/Religious Program—Students 27.

2—ST. ISIDORE THE FARMER (1968) [CEM], St. John, (1875), and St. Joseph, (1891), Perry Co., were closed, merged and renamed St. Isidore in 1968. Rev. Guy Mansini, O.S.B.
Res.: 6501 St. Isidore Rd., Bristow, 47515. Tel: 812-843-5713; Fax: 812-843-3103. Email: saintisidore@psci.net.
Catechesis/Religious Program—Students 99.

ST. DENIS, JENNINGS CO., ST. DENIS (1894) [CEM] Attended by Immaculate Conception, Millhousen. Revs. Robert Jason Hankee, Sacramental Min.; Paul E. Landwerlen, Priest Mod.; Sr. Christine Ernstes, O.S.F., Parish Life Coord.
Mailing Address: 2081 E. County Rd. 820S, Greensburg, 47240. Tel: 812-591-2362. Email: icchurch@voyager.net. Web: www.icsdchurches.com.
Church: 12155 N. County Rd. 600E, Westport, 47283.
Catechesis/Religious Program— Clustered with Immaculate Conception, Milhousen.

ST. JOSEPH, JENNINGS CO., ST. JOSEPH (1850) [CEM 2] Rev. Jonathan P. Meyer, Admin.
Mailing Address: 1875 S. County Rd. 700 W., North Vernon, 47265. Tel: 812-346-4783; Fax: 812-352-9033. Email: rectory@stjoefourcorners.org. Web: www.stjoefourcorners.org.
Mission—St. Anne (1841) 150 E. 450 N., North Vernon, Jennings Co. 47265.
Catechesis/Religious Program—Students 69.

ST. JOSEPH HILL, CLARK CO., ST. JOSEPH (1853) [CEM] Rev. John W. Curran, O.F.M.Conv.
Res.: 2605 St. Joe Rd. W., Sellersburg, 47172. Tel: 812-246-2512; Fax: 812-246-2671. Email: parishoffice@stjoehill.org. Web: www.stjoehill.org.
Catechesis/Religious Program—Tel: 812-246-3969. Lisa Whitaker, C.R.E. Students 145.

ST. LEON, DEARBORN CO., ST. JOSEPH (1841) [CEM] Rev. C. Ryan McCarthy.
Res.: 7536 Church Ln., West Harrison, 47060. Tel: 812-576-3593; Fax: 812-576-2304.
Catechesis/Religious Program—29060 State Rte. 1, West Harrison, 47060. Tel: 812-576-3234. Students 98.

ST. MARK, PERRY CO., ST. MARK (1863), (German), [CEM] [JC] Rev. Dennis M. Duvelius.
Res.: 5377 Acorn Rd., Tell City, 47586. Tel: 812-836-2481. Email: stmark@psci.net.
Catechesis/Religious Program—Students 40.

ST. MARY-OF-THE-KNOBS, FLOYD CO., ST. MARY-OF-THE-KNOBS (1823) [CEM] Rev. John F. Geis.
Res.: 3033 Martin Rd., Floyds Knobs, 47119. Tel: 812-923-3011; Fax: 812-923-1431. Web: www.stmaryoftheknobs.org.
School—(Grades PreSchool-6) Tel: 812-923-1630; Fax: 812-923-0310. Students 129.
Catechesis/Religious Program—Students 201.

ST. MARY-OF-THE-ROCK, FRANKLIN CO., ST. MARY-OF-THE-ROCK (1844) [CEM] Sr. Margie Niemer, O.S.F., Parish Life Coord.
Office: 17440 St. Mary's Rd., Batesville, 47006. Tel: 812-934-4165; Fax: 812-934-0111.
Catechesis/Religious Program—Students 49.
Oratory—SS. Philomena and Cecilia (1844) 16194 St. Mary's Rd., Brookville, 47012. Tel: 765-647-0310.

ST. MARY-OF-THE-WOODS, VIGO CO., ST. MARY-OF-THE-WOODS (1837) [CEM] Sr. Joan Slobig, S.P., Parish Life Coord.; Rev. Bernard Head, Sacramental Min. & Priest Mod. (Retired).
Mailing Address: P.O. Box 155, 47876. Tel: 812-535-1261; Fax: 812-535-1561.
Catechesis/Religious Program—Diana Bird, D.R.E. Students 69.

ST. MAURICE, DECATUR CO., ST. MAURICE (1859) [CEM] Rev. George Joseph Nangachiveettil (India), Admin.
Church: 1963 N. St. John St., Greensburg, 47240. Tel: 812-663-4754; Fax: 812-663-4754. Email: stmauricechrch@yahoo.com.
Catechesis/Religious Program—Students 156.

ST. MEINRAD, SPENCER CO., ST. MEINRAD (1854) [CEM] Rev. Anthony Vinson, O.S.B.
Mailing Address: P.O. Box 8, 47577. Tel: 812-357-5533; Fax: 812-357-2862.
Church: 19630 N. 4th St., 47577.
Catechesis/Religious Program—Students 58.

ST. NICHOLAS, RIPLEY CO., ST. NICHOLAS (1836) [CEM] Rev. Gregory D. Bramlage.
Res.: 6461 E. St. Nicholas Dr., Sunman, 47041. Tel: 812-623-2964 (Office); 812-623-8007 (Rectory); Fax: 812-623-2964.
School—(Grades K-8), 6459 E. St. Nicholas Dr., Sunman, 47041. Tel: 812-623-2348. Judy Luhring, Prin.; Laura Kraus, Librarian. Lay Teachers 11; Students 154.
Catechesis/Religious Program—Students 73.

ST. PETER, FRANKLIN CO., ST. PETER (1838), (German), [CEM] Sr. Margie Niemer, O.S.F., Parish Life Coord.; Revs. William F. Stumpf, Priest Mod.; Humbert Moster, O.F.M., Sacramental Min.
Res.: 1207 East Rd., Brookville, 47012. Tel: 812-623-3670; Fax: 812-623-5261. Email: stpeter@nalu.net.
Catechesis/Religious Program—Tel: 812-623-3670. Students 78.

ST. PETER, HARRISON CO., ST. PETER (1849) [CEM], Attended from St. Joseph, Corydon, St. Peter, 312 E. High St., Corydon, Harrison Co., IN 47112. Rev. Daniel Atkins.
Mailing Address: *c/o St. Joseph*, 312 E. High St., Corydon, 47112. Tel: 812-738-2742; Fax: 812-738-2718. Email: joecorydon@yahoo.com. Web: www.triparishcommunity.com.
Church: Buena Vista Rd., Elizabeth, 47117.
Catechesis/Religious Program—Tel: 812-738-2759. Religious education program held at St. Joseph, Corydon. Students 13.

ST. PIUS, RIPLEY CO., ST. PIUS (1859) [CEM], Attended from St. Charles Borromeo, Milan. Rev. Gregory D. Bramlage, Admin.
Mailing Address: *c/o St. Nicholas*, 6457 E. St. Nicholas Dr., Sunman, 47041. Tel: 812-623-8007.
Catechesis/Religious Program—Ed King, D.R.E.

ST. VINCENT DE PAUL, SHELBY CO., ST. VINCENT DE PAUL (1837) Rev. Paul E. Landwerlen.
Res.: 4218 E. Michigan Rd., Shelbyville, 46176. Tel: 317-398-4028.
Catechesis/Religious Program—Tel: 317-392-3879; Fax: 317-392-3879. Students 71.

SALEM, WASHINGTON CO., ST. PATRICK (1942) [CEM] Rev. Louis Manna.
208 S. Shelby St., P.O. Box 273, 47167. Tel: 812-752-3693.
Catechesis/Religious Program—Tel: 812-883-3589. Students 41.

SCOTTSBURG, SCOTT CO., AMERICAN MARTYRS (1938) Rev. Louis Manna.
Mailing Address: 270 S. Bond St., 47170-2009. Tel: 812-752-3693; Fax: 812-752-0969. Email: amartyrs@verizon.net. Web: www.amartyrs.org.
Parish Office: 262 W. Cherry St., 47170-2013.
Catechesis/Religious Program—Students 42.
Mission—St. Patrick (1942) 208 S. Shelby St., P.O. Box 273, Salem, Washington Co. 47167. Tel: 812-883-3589.

SEELYVILLE, VIGO CO., HOLY ROSARY (1908) Rev. Harold W. Rightor II.
Church & Mailing Address: 2585 N. Main, P.O. Box 151, 47878. Tel: 812-877-1279.
Catechesis/Religious Program—Students 35.

SELLERSBURG, CLARK CO., ST. PAUL (1949) Rev. Paul F. Richart.
Church: 218 Scheller Ave., 47172. Tel: 812-246-3522; Fax: 812-246-7635. Email: parsec.stpaul@insightbb.com. Web: www.stpaulsellersburg.org.
School—(Grades K-6), 105 St. Paul St., 47172. Tel: 812-246-3266; Fax: 812-246-7632. Email: stpauls.school@insightbb.com. Web: www.stpaulk6.org. Donna Francis Matusky, Prin. Lay Teachers 20; Students 290.
Catechesis/Religious Program—216 Scheller Ave., 47172. Tel: 812-246-5088. Email: reled.stpaul@insightbb.com. Students 80.

SEYMOUR, JACKSON CO., ST. AMBROSE (1860) [CEM] Rev. Scott E. Nobbe; Deacon Michael East.
Res.: 325 S. Chestnut St., 47274. Tel: 812-522-5304; Fax: 812-522-8959.
School—(Grades PreK-7), 301 S. Chestnut St., 47274. Tel: 812-522-3522. Sr. Anna Rose Lueken, O.S.B., Prin. Lay Teachers 13; Students 137.
Catechesis/Religious Program—Tel: 812-522-2686. Students 80.
Mission—Our Lady of Providence (1934) 325 S. Chestnut St., Brownstown, Jackson Co. 47274.

SHELBYVILLE, SHELBY CO., ST. JOSEPH (1868) [CEM] [JC] Rev. Christopher A. Craig.
Res.: 125 E. Broadway, 46176. Tel: 317-398-8227; Fax: 317-392-7820. Web: www.stjosephshelby.org.
School—(Grades PreK-5), 127 E. Broadway, 46176. Tel: 317-398-4202; Fax: 317-398-0270. Email: stjoe@lightbound.com. Lay Teachers 10; Students 138.
Catechesis/Religious Program—Tel: 317-398-0530; Fax: 317-392-7820. Students 214.

SIBERIA, PERRY CO., ST. MARTIN OF TOURS (1869) [CEM] Rev. Aaron Pfaff.
Mailing Address: P.O. Box 8, St. Meinrad, 47577. Tel: 812-357-5533; Fax: 812-357-2862.
Church: 27246 Perry St., 47515.
Catechesis/Religious Program—Students 6.

SPENCER, OWEN CO., ST. JUDE THE APOSTLE (1951) Rev. William L. Ehalt.
300 W. Hillside Ave., P.O. Box 317, 47460. Tel: 812-829-3082; Fax: 812-829-0888. Email: stjudespencer@sbcglobal.net.
Catechesis/Religious Program—Students 23.

STARLIGHT, CLARK CO., ST. JOHN THE BAPTIST (1861), (German), [CEM] [JC] Rev. Frederick J. Denison.
Res.: 8310 St. John Rd., Floyds Knobs, 47119. Tel: 812-923-5785; Fax: 812-923-2015.
Catechesis/Religious Program—Tel: 812-923-0445; Fax: 812-923-5785. Students 45.

TELL CITY, PERRY CO., ST. PAUL (1859) [CEM] Rev. Dennis M. Duvelius.
Parish Office—Catholic Ministry Center, 824 Jefferson St., 47586. Tel: 812-547-7994; Fax: 812-547-6985. Email: stpaulch@psci.net. In Res., Rev. Barnabas Gillespie, O.S.B.
Church: 814 Jefferson St., 47586. Tel: 812-547-9901.
Catechesis/Religious Program—Tel: 812-547-7102. Students 288.

TERRE HAUTE, VIGO CO.

1—ST. ANN (1876) [JC] Sr. Constance Kramer, S.P., Parish Life Coord.; Rev. Darvin E. Winters, Sacramental Min.
Res.: 1440 Locust St., 47807. Tel: 812-232-6832; Fax: 812-232-2444. Email: stannchurch@stannchurchth.org.
Catechesis/Religious Program—Students 27.

2—ST. BENEDICT (1865), (German), [JC] Rev. Joel Burget, O.F.M.Conv.
Church & Parish Office: 111 S. Ninth St., 47807. Tel: 812-232-8421; Fax: 812-238-9203. Email: joel@stbenedictth.org. Web: www.stbenedictth.org.
Catechesis/Religious Program—Students 98.

3—ST. JOSEPH UNIVERSITY PARISH (1838) [JC] Revs. Richard Kaley, O.F.M.Conv.; John Bammon, O.F.M.
Res.: 118 S. 9th St., 47807. Tel: 812-232-5075. Web: www.stjoeup.org.
Catechesis/Religious Program—Email: reled@stjoeup.org. Students 280.

4—ST. MARGARET MARY (1920) [JC] Rev. Richard Ginther; Deacon Michael Stratman.
Res.: 2421 S. Seventh St., 47802. Tel: 812-232-3512; Fax: 812-232-6921.
Catechesis/Religious Program—Students 96.

5—ST. PATRICK (1881) Rev. Richard Ginther; John

Fuller, Business Mgr.
Church: 1807 Poplar St., 47803. Tel: 812-232-8518; Fax: 812-234-3312. Web: www.saintpat.org.
School—(Grades PreK-8), 449 S. 19th St., 47803. Tel: 812-232-2157; Fax: 812-478-9384. Amy McClain, Prin. Lay Teachers 19; Students 290.
Catechesis/Religious Program—Tel: 812-232-2827. Students 185.

6—SACRED HEART OF JESUS (1924) Rev. Darvin E. Winters.
Res.: 2322 N. 13 1/2 St., 47804. Tel: 812-466-1231; Fax: 812-466-9683.

TROY, PERRY CO., ST. PIUS (1849) [CEM 2] Rev. Barnabas Gillespie, O.S.B.
Parish Office & Mailing Address: Catholic Ministry Center, 824 Jefferson St., Tell City, 47586. Tel: 812-547-7994; Fax: 812-547-6985. Email: stpaulch@psci.net.
Church: State Rd. 66, 47588.
Catechesis/Religious Program—Students 29.

UNIVERSAL, VERMILLION CO., ST. JOSEPH (1920), Attended from Sacred Heart, 619 S. Fifth St., Clinton, IN 47842-2016. Tel: 765-832-8468. Rev. Joseph L. Villa, Admin.
Church: 270 E. Wood Ave., 47884.
Catechesis/Religious Program—Students 4.

VEVAY, SWITZERLAND CO., MOST SORROWFUL MOTHER OF GOD (1876) Rev. John A. Meyer.
Mailing Address: *Catholic Community Center*, 305 W. State St., Madison, 47250. Tel: 812-265-4166; Fax: 812-273-3427.
Church: Ferry St., 47043.

WEST TERRE HAUTE, VIGO CO., ST. LEONARD OF PORT MAURICE (1912) Sr. Joan Slobig, S.P., Parish Life Coord.; Rev. Bernard Head, Sacramental Min. & Priest Mod. (Retired).
126 N. Eighth St., 47885. Tel: 812-535-1261.
Catechesis/Religious Program—Diana Bird, D.R.E. Combined with St. Mary's, St. Mary-of-the-Woods Students 3.

YORKVILLE, DEARBORN CO., ST. MARTIN (1850) [CEM] Rev. Brian Esarey.
Res.: 8044 Yorkridge Rd., Guilford, 47022. Tel: 812-487-2096; 812-623-3408; Fax: 812-623-4879. Email: flobraun@etczone.com.
Catechesis/Religious Program—Tel: 812-623-2662. Email: paquette5@comcast.net. Donn Paquette, D.R.E.; Michelle Paquette, D.R.E. Students 48.

Chaplains of Public Institutions

INDIANAPOLIS. *Indiana Women's Prison*. Rev. Lawrence Voelker.
Indianapolis Fire Department. Rev. James R. Wilmoth, V.F.
Indianapolis International Airport. Rev. Glenn L. O'Connor.
Indianapolis Metropolitan Police Department. Rev. Steven C. Schwab.
Veterans' Administration Hospital. Rev. Joachim Kiene, O.F.M.Conv.

PUTNAMVILLE. *Indiana State Farm*. Rev. Stephen Jarrell.

RICHMOND. *Richmond State Hospital*. Rev. Todd M. Riebe.

Unassigned:
Revs.—
Ashmore, Ronald M.
Maung, John S.
Schafer, Raymond E.

Graduate Studies:
Revs.—
Danda, Sean, Pontifical North American College 00120 Vatican City State.
Kappes, Christiaan W.

On Special or Other Archdiocesan Assignment:
Revs.—
Mazzola, Robert E., S.T.B., Auditor, Metropolitan Tribunal
Porter, Jack W., Archdiocesan Historian (Retired)

On Disability Leave:
Revs.—
Buckel, John
Mader, Joseph

Retired:
Rev. Msgrs.—
Kavanagh, Richard T., St. Paul Hermitage, 501 N. 17th Ave., Beech Grove, 46107-1196.
Knueven, Harold L., 1339 Indiana Ave., Connersville, 47331.
Moran, Lawrence J., 89 Allendale, Terre Haute, 47802.
Wright, John M., CHC, USN, 5385 Toscana Way, Apt. 348, San Diego, CA 92122.
Revs.—
Ajamie, Albert, St. Augustine Home, 2345 W. 86th St., 46206.
Arneson, James E., 1868 Shore Dr. S., #114, South Pasadena, FL 33707.
Bryan, Francis E., 1746 W. Morris St., 46221.
Buchanan, Donald E., LCDR, CHC, USN, P.O. Box 367, Austin, 47102-0367.
Burkert, Gerald F., 501 N. 17th Ave., Beech Grove, 46107.
Burwinkel, Elmer J., M.Ed., M.Div., 3991 W.C.R. 925 S., Madison, 47250.
Ciano, Kenneth J., 922 Springdale Ln., Terre Haute, 47803.
Commons, Patrick M., St. Paul Hermitage, 501 N. 17th Ave., Beech Grove, 46107.
Dede, Paul M., 2442 Stonelake Cir., Bloomington, 47404.
Eckstein, Francis J., P.O. Box 336, Milan, 47031.
Ernst, William W., V.F., 2210 Charlestown Rd., New Albany, 47150.
Evard, Paul A., Casilla 6804, Guayaqil, Equador.
Hartzer, John, 909 Ridge Ave., Lawrenceburg, 47025.
Head, Bernard, P.O Box 116, Saint Mary Of The Woods, 47876.
Kern, Joseph R., 936 Springdale Ln., Terre Haute, 47802.
Kraeszig, Charles J., 7901 Castle Dr., Lakewood Estates, New Port Richey, FL 34653.
Luerman, John H., 823 S.W. 15th St., 47374.
Lutz, Herman, S.T.L., J.C.L., St. Paul Hermitage, 501 N. 17th Ave., Beech Grove, 46107-1196.
McNally, Joseph J., 219 E. Eagle Dr., Ninevah, 46164.
Meny, Hilary G., 111 N. Race St., Haubstadt, 47639.
Mueller, Richard J., 8140 Township Line Rd., Apt. 314, 46260.
Munshower, William G., 5353 E. 56th St., 46226.
Murphy, Thomas J., St. Paul Hermitage, 501 N. 17th Ave., Beech Grove, 46107.
Peter, Martin A., 12935 Sawmill Rd., Columbus, 47201.
Porter, Jack W., 7432-D Lions Head Dr., 46260-3445.
Reidman, Joseph G.
Richardt, J. Lawrence, 2026 N. Erin Ct., Huntingburg, 47542-9520.
Ripperger, William, 8310 St. John Rd., Floyds Knobs, 47119.
Rodas, Mauro G., 4002 Oakfield Dr., 46237.
Sheets, Joseph B., 436 Mutton Creek Dr., Seymour, 47274.
Stepanski, Thomas K., 3 Hickory Ln., Danville, 46122.
Vogelsang, Clifford R., S.T.B., M.Div., 9140 Cinnebar Dr., 46268.

Permanent Deacons:
Deacons—
Alunday, Arthur, St. Mary, Greensburg
Blandford, Kerry, Assoc Dir. Deacon Formation, St. Mark the Evangelist, Indianapolis; Village Oaks at Greenwood
Bower, Patrick, St. Barnabas; Methodist Hospital, Indianapolis
Chlopecki, John J., St. Anthony of Padua, Morris
Collier, Daniel, St. Malachy, Brownsburg; Indianapolis Juvenile Correction Facility
Davis, Wayne, St. Michael, Greenfield; Hancock Regional Hospital
Dearman, Donald, St. Rita, Marion County Jail #1, Indianapolis
Decker, Robert W., PLC of St. Andrew the Apostle, Indianapolis
East, Michael, Assoc. Dir. Deacons, St. Ambrose, Seymour; Our Lady of Providence, Brownstown; Jackson County Jail
Ferrer-Soto, Emilio, St. Patrick; Wishard Hopsital, Indianapolis
French, Lawrence, St. Maurice, Napoleon; Manderley Health Center and Buckeye Village, Osgood
Gardner, Michael, Prince of Peace, Madison; Most Sorrowful Mother of God, Vevay; Madison State Hospital
Gretencord, Steven, Sacred Heart; Ryves Youth Center of Catholic Charities Terre Haute, Terre Haute
Heller, Timothy, St. Teresa Benedicta of the Cross, Bright; Dearborn County Jail, Lawrenceburg
Henn, David, Our Lady of the Greenwood; Kindred Hospital Indianapolis South, Greenwood
Hilger, Edward, St. Bartholomew, Columbus
Hodges, Stephen, St. Rose of Lima, Franklin; Johnson County Jail
Jones, Wesley, Ph.D., St. Jude, Indianapolis; Catholic Charities Indianapolis
Jones, William, St. Bartholomew, Columbus; Substance Addiction Ministry
Kellams, Marc, JD, St. Charles Borromeo, Bloomington
Morales, Oscar, St. Gabriel the Archangel; Marion County Jail #2, Indianapolis
Reimer, Ronald, SS. Francis and Clare of Assisi, Greenwood
Reising, David, St. Vincent de Paul, Bedford; St. Mary, Mitchell; Lawrence County Jail, Bedford
Stratman, Michael, St. Patrick, St. Margaret Mary, Union Hospital, Terre Haute
Thompson, John, St. Augustine, Jeffersonville; Clark County Jail
Ward, Thomas, St. Simon the Apostle, St. Vincent New Hope, Indianapolis

INSTITUTIONS LOCATED IN THE ARCHDIOCESE

[A] SEMINARIES, RELIGIOUS OR SCHOLASTICATES

ST. MEINRAD. *Saint Meinrad School of Theology*, 200 Hill Dr., 47577. Tel: 812-357-6611; Fax: 812-357-6964. Email: rector@saintmeinrad.edu. Web: www.saintmeinrad.edu. Revs. Denis Robinson, O.S.B., Pres. & Rector; Bede Cisco, O.S.B., Dir. Inst. Research; Patrick Cooney, O.S.B., J.C.L., Dir. Human Formation; Cyprian Davis, O.S.B., Prof. Church History; Guerric DeBona, O.S.B.; Damian Dietlein, O.S.B., (Assumption Abbey); Jonathan Fassero, O.S.B., Dir.; Harry Hagan, O.S.B.; Eugene Hensell, O.S.B.; Columba Kelly, O.S.B.; Gabriel Kim, Assoc. Dir. of Spir. of Formation, (Busan, Korea); J. Ronald Knott, D.Min. (L), Dir. Institute for Priests & Presbyterates; Guy Mansini, O.S.B.; Joseph B. Moriarty, Assoc. Dir. Spiritual Formation; Brendan Moss, O.S.B., M.Div., Dir. Pastoral Formation; Godfrey Mullen, O.S.B., Vice Rector & Provost; Paul Nord, O.S.B.; Mark O'Keefe, O.S.B.; Thomas Richstatter, O.F.M., (Province of St. John the Baptist); Kurt Stasiak, O.S.B., Dir. Spiritual Formation; Very Rev. Charles C. Thompson, J.C.L. (L); Revs. Timothy Sweeney, O.S.B.; Julian Peters, O.S.B., Dir. Permanent Deacon Prog.; Bros. Zachary Wilberding, O.S.B., Assoc. Dir. Pastoral Formation; John Mark Falkenham, O.S.B.; Sisters Diane Pharo, S.C.N., Dir. Counseling Ctr.; Clare Smith, R.S.M., Dir. Mader Learning Ctr.; Bernardone Rock, F.S.E., Dir. Liturgical Music; Dan Kolb, Ph.D., Library Dir. School of Theology. Other Faculty and Staff 32; Seminarians 121; Lay Degree Students 97.

[B] COLLEGES AND UNIVERSITIES

INDIANAPOLIS. *Marian University* (Coed), 3200 Cold Spring Rd., 46222. Tel: 317-955-6000; Fax: 317-955-6448. Email: admit@marian.edu. Web: www.marian.edu. Sr. Jean Marie Cleveland, O.S.F., Vice Pres. Mission Effectiveness; Dr. Thomas Enneking, Ph.D., Provost; Daniel J. Elsener, Pres.; Revs. Dennis Bosse, O.F.M.; Leopold Keffler, O.F.M.Conv.; Ms. Kelley Griffith, Librarian. Sisters of the Third Order Regular of St. Francis. Priests 2; Sisters 3; Lay Teachers 95; Students 2,276.

SAINT MARY-OF-THE-WOODS. *Saint Mary-of-the-Woods College* (1840)St. Mary-of-the-Woods, 47876. Tel: 812-535-5151; Fax: 812-535-5005. Email: smeier@smwc.edu. Web: www.smwc.edu. Dr. David Behrs, Ph.D., Pres.; Judy Tribble, Librarian. Sponsored by the Sisters of Providence, St. Mary-of-the-Woods. Priests 1; Sisters 4; Lay Teachers 64; Lay Staff 87; Students 1,677.

[C] HIGH SCHOOLS, INTER-PAROCHIAL

INDIANAPOLIS. *Bishop Chatard High School* (1961) 5885 Crittenden Ave., 46220. Tel: 317-251-1451; Fax: 317-254-5427. Email: president@bishopchatard.org. Web: www.bishopchatard.org. William "Bill" Sahm, Pres.; Al Holok, Prin.; Rev. Robert T. Hausladen, Chap. Priests 1; Sisters of St. Benedict 3; Lay Teachers 59; Students 669.
Cardinal Ritter High School, 3360 W. 30th St., 46222. Tel: 317-924-4333; Fax: 317-927-7822. Paul Lockard, Pres.; E. Jo Hoy, B.S., M.S., Prin.; Rev. John J. Hollowell, Chap.; Elizabeth Jessen, Librarian. Priests 1; Sisters 1; Lay Teachers 42; Students 571.
Father Thomas Scecina Memorial High School, 5000 Nowland Ave., 46201-1836. Tel: 317-356-6377; Fax: 317-322-4287. Email: tdavis@scecina.org. Web: www.scecina.org. Mr. Joseph Therber, Pres.; Mr. Thomas W. Davis, Prin.; Rev. Aaron M. Jenkins, Chap.; Sr. Sheila Hackett, Librarian. Priests 1; Lay Teachers 28; Students 333.
Roncalli High School, 3300 Prague Rd., 46227. Tel: 317-787-8277; Fax: 317-788-4095. Email: cweisenbach@roncallihs.org. Web: www.roncalli.org. Mr. Joseph D. Hollowell, Pres.;

Charles Weisenbach, Prin.; Rev. James R. Wilmoth, V.F., Chap. Priests 1; Lay Teachers 75; Students 1,142.

CLARKSVILLE. *Our Lady of Providence Junior - Senior High School*, 707 Providence Way, 47129. Tel: 812-945-2538; Fax: 812-945-3460. Email: mernstberger@providencehigh.net. Web: www.providencehigh.net. Mrs. Melinda Ernstberger, Prin.; Joan Hurley, Pres.; Rev. Mathew Choorapanthiyil, O.C.D. (India), Chap. Priests 1; Sisters 1; Lay Teachers 37; Students (9-12) 452; Students (7-12) 524.

MADISON. *Shawe Memorial Junior-Senior High School* (1954) 201 W. State St., 47250. Tel: 812-273-2150; Fax: 812-273-2013. Email: shaweprincipal@popeace.org. Jerome Bomholt, Prin.; Rev. John A. Meyer, V.F., Chap. Priests 1; Chaplains 1; Lay Teachers 18; Students 162.

RICHMOND. *Seton Catholic High School*, 233 S. 5th St., 47374. Tel: 765-965-6956; Fax: 765-966-0820. Email: dmusial@setoncatholichighschool.org. Rick Ruhl, Prin.; Rev. Todd Riebe. Priests 1; Lay Teachers 10; Students 155.

[D] HIGH SCHOOLS, PRIVATE

INDIANAPOLIS. *Brebeuf Jesuit Preparatory School, Inc.* (1962) 2801 W. 86th St., 46268-1926. Tel: 317-524-7050; Fax: 317-524-7142. Web: www.brebeuf.org. Dr. Matthew Hayes, Pres.; Mrs. LaTonya Turner, Prin.; Revs. Thomas C. Widner, S.J., Rector; Frederick J. Deters, S.J., A.B., M.A., S.T.D.; George R. Menke, S.J.; Paul Peterson, S.J.; Bro. John F. Buchman, S.J.; Mrs. Ann Sharp, Librarian. Society of Jesus Community. Priests 4; Brothers 1; Lay Teachers 70; Students 810.

Cathedral High School (Cathedral Trustees, Inc.) (1918) 5225 E. 56th St., 46226. Tel: 317-542-1418; Fax: 317-542-1484. Email: dworland@cathedral-irish.org. Web: www.cathedral-irish.org. Rev. William G. Munshower, Chap. (Retired); Stephen J. Helmich, M.S., Pres.; David Worland, Prin.; Melinda Bundy, Librarian. Priests 1; Sisters 2; Staff 1; Lay Teachers 96; Students 1,256.

Providence Cristo Rey Corporate Work Study Program, Inc., 75 N. Belleview Pl., 46222-4145. Tel: 317-236-1430. Email: jhagelskamp@archindy.org. Sr. Jeanette Hagelskamp, S.P., Pres.; Ellen Jose, Ph.D., Prin.

Providence Cristo Rey High School, Inc., 75 N. Belleview Pl., 46222-4145. Tel: 317-860-1000; Fax: 317-860-1004. Web: www.pcrhs.org. Paul F. Madden, Pres.; Sr. Jeanette Hagelskamp, S.P., Prin.

OLDENBURG. *Oldenburg Academy of the Immaculate Conception*, One Twister Cir., P.O. Box 200, 47036-0200. Tel: 812-934-4440; Fax: 812-934-4838. Email: tgillman@oldenburgacademy.org. Web: www.oldenburgacademy.org. Sr. Therese Gillman, O.S.F., Pres.; Mrs. Bettina Rose, Prin. Lay Teachers 19; Students 214.

[E] DAY CARE

SAINT MARY-OF-THE-WOODS. *Woods Day Care/ Preschool, Inc.* (1987) St. Mary-of-the-Woods, 47876-1099. Tel: 812-535-4610; Fax: 812-535-4674. Children 93; Total Staff 38.

[F] RELIGIOUS EDUCATION CENTERS

CLARKSVILLE. *Aquinas Center for Continuing Religious Education*, 707 Providence Way Side, 47129. Tel: 812-945-0354; Fax: 812-945-2929. Email: dcmnad@sbcglobal.net. Web: aquinascenter.org. Ms. Christina Flum, Dir. Catechetical Ministry.

TERRE HAUTE. *Terre Haute Deanery Pastoral Center*, 2931 Ohio Blvd., 47803. Tel: 812-232-8400; Fax: 812-234-2665. Email: director@thdeanery.org. Web: www.thdeanery.org. Sr. Mary Montgomery, S.P., Dir. Total Staff 2.

[G] GENERAL HOSPITALS

INDIANAPOLIS. *Central Indiana Health System Cardiac Services, Inc.* (1991) 8425 N. Harcourt Rd., 46260. Tel: 317-583-3289; Fax: 317-583-3285. Email: jbford@stvincent.org. Mailing Address: 10330 N. Meridian St., 46290. Vincent C. Caponi, Chm.

St. Vincent Hospital and Health Care Center, Inc. (1884) 2001 W. 86th St., 46260. Tel: 317-583-3289; Fax: 317-583-3285. Email: jbford@stvincent.org. Web: www.stvincent.org. Mailing Address: 10330 N. Meridian St., 46290. J. Albert Smith Jr., Chairperson; Vincent C. Caponi, CEO, St. Vincent Health, Inc.; Kyle DeFur, Pres.; Ron L. Mead, Vice Pres. Mission Svcs.; Rev. Ben Okonkwo; Ms. Joan M. Bumpus, Dir. Pastoral Care. Daughters of Charity of St. Vincent de Paul. Sisters 8; Chaplains 22; Bed Capacity 810; Total Staff 5,264; Inpatient Admissions 34,088; Outpatient Visits 754,999; Emergency Visits 62,209.

**St. Vincent New Hope, Inc.* (1988) 8450 N. Payne Rd., 46268. Tel: 317-872-4210; Fax: 317-338-4585. Email: jbford@stvincent.org. Web: www.stvincent.org. Daughters of Charity of St. Vincent de Paul. Bed Capacity 73; Total Assisted Annually 322; Total Staff 486.

**St. Vincent Pediatric Rehabilitation Center, Inc.* (A member of St. Vincent Health & Ascension Health.), 1707 W. 86th St., 46260. Tel: 317-415-5500; Fax: 317-415-5595. Email: akmott@stvincent.org. Jeff Poltawski, CEO; Andrea Mott, CFO.

BEECH GROVE. *St. Francis Hospital and Health Centers* (1914) 1600 Albany St., 46107. Tel: 317-787-3311; Fax: 317-782-6731. Web: www.stfrancishospitals.org. Mr. Robert J. Brody, B.A., M.H.A., Pres. & CEO; Sr. Marlene Shapley, B.S., R.N., Vice Pres., Mission Integration Svcs.; Revs. Frederick J. Deters, S.J., A.B., M.A., S.T.D., Chap.; Ruta A. Cabazi (Tanzania), Chap.; John H. Mannion, B.S., M.Div. (LFT), Chap.; Constantine L. Silayo, Chap. Sisters of St. Francis Health Services, Inc. Sisters 4; Priests 4; Staff 4,414; Bed Capacity 600; Patients Assisted Annually 448,000.

(1995) 8111 S. Emerson Ave., 46237. Tel: 317-865-5000; Fax: 317-865-5061. Web: www.stfrancishospitals.org.

1201 Hadley Rd., Mooresville, 46158. Tel: 317-834-1160; Fax: 317-831-9315. Web: www.stfrancishospitals.org.

BRAZIL. **St. Vincent Clay Hospitals, Inc.* (A member of St. Vincent Health & Ascension Health.), 1206 E. National Ave., P.O. Box 489, 47834. Tel: 812-442-2500; Fax: 812-442-2605. Email: jrlau@stvincent.org. Jerry R. Laue, CEO. Bed Capacity 25; Total Staff 158.

NORTH VERNON. *St. Vincent Jennings Hospital Foundation, Inc.*, 301 Henry St., 47265. Tel: 812-352-4200; Fax: 812-352-4201.

**St. Vincent Jennings Hospital, Inc.* (A member of St. Vincent Health & Ascension Health.), 301 Henry St., 47265. Tel: 812-352-4200; Fax: 812-352-4201. Email: jclines@stvincent.org. Joseph E. Roche, CEO; John Lines, CFO. Inpatients 603; Outpatients 76,539; Total Staff 197.

[H] PROTECTIVE INSTITUTIONS

TERRE HAUTE. *Gibault Children's Services*, 6301 S. U.S. Hwy. 41, P.O. Box 2316, 47802-0316. Tel: 812-299-1156; Fax: 812-298-3044. Email: gibault@gibault.org. Web: www.gibault.org. Mr. James M. Sinclair, M.S.S.W., J.D., Pres. & C.E.O. Residential treatment facility for males and females between the ages of 8 and 18, sponsored by the Knights of Columbus of Indiana. Licensed Youth 147; Total Staff 287; Total Assisted Annually 302.

[I] HOMES FOR AGED

INDIANAPOLIS. *St. Augustine Home, Little Sisters of the Poor* (1873) 2345 W. 86th St., 46260. Tel: 317-872-6420; Fax: 317-875-9883. Sr. Judith Meredith, Supr. & Admin.; Rev. Msgr. Joseph Duncan, Chap. Sisters 11; Bed Capacity 94; Residents 94; Total Staff 108; Total Assisted Annually 208.

BEECH GROVE. *St. Paul Hermitage*, 501 N. 17th Ave., 46107. Tel: 317-786-2261; Fax: 317-782-1411. Email: sharonbierman@benedictine.com. Rev. Msgr. Richard Kavanaugh (Retired); Revs. Herman Lutz, S.T.L., J.C.L., Chap. (Retired); Patrick M. Commons (Retired); James Rogers, (Evansville Diocese); Gerald F. Burkert, Chap. (Retired); Sr. Sharon Bierman, O.S.B., Admin.

Sisters of St. Benedict of Beech Grove, Ind., Inc. Sisters 6; Bed Capacity 122; Total Assisted Annually 128; Residents 100; Total Staff 108.

NEW ALBANY. *Mercy Long Term Care Initiatives dba Providence Retirement Home* 4915 Charlestown Rd., 47150. Tel: 812-945-5221; Fax: 812-945-2614. Email: ttodd@lourdes-pad.org. Web: www.prhonline.org. Yvonne Cook, Admin. Sisters of Mercy. Priests 1; Sisters 1; Total Staff 186; Residents 172; Adult Day Care clients 32.

Providence Retirement Home Auxiliary, Inc., 4915 Charlestown Rd., 47150.

[J] RETREAT HOUSES

INDIANAPOLIS. *Our Lady of Fatima Retreat House, Inc.* (1950) 5353 E. 56th St., 46226. Tel: 317-545-7681; Fax: 317-545-0095. Email: fatima@archindy.org. Web: www.archindy.org/fatima. Rev. James M. Farrell, Dir. Used by both clergy and laity. Priests 1; Total in Residence 1; Served 9,542; Total Staff 21.

BEECH GROVE. *Benedict Inn Retreat & Conference Center* (1981) 1402 Southern Ave., 46107-1197. Tel: 317-788-7581; Fax: 317-782-3142. Email: benedictinn@benedictinn.org. Web: www.benedictinn.org. Sr. Mary Luke Jones, O.S.B., Admin. Retreats and workshops for clergy, religious, and laity. Sisters 6.

MOUNT SAINT FRANCIS. *Mount Saint Francis Friary and Retreat Center* (1896) 101 St. Anthony Dr., Mount St. Francis, 47146-9999. Tel: 812-923-8444; Fax: 812-923-8145. Rev. Wayne Hellmann, O.F.M.Conv., Prof., St. Louis Univ. In Res. Rev. John Elmer, O.F.M.Conv., Prov. Devel. Office; Bro. Robert Baxter, O.F.M.Conv., Sec. of the Province & Guardian; Rev. Conrad Sutter, O.F.M.Conv.

Province of Our Lady of Consolation, Inc., Mount St. Francis. Tel: 812-923-8444; Fax: 812-923-8145. Rev. James Kent, O.F.M.Conv., Vicar; Bro. Robert Baxter, O.F.M.Conv., Sec. of Prov. (Provincial Office) Total Staff 5; Total in Residence 14.

ST. MEINRAD. *Archabbey Guest House & Retreat Center*, 200 Hill Dr., 47577. Tel: 812-357-6585; 800-581-6905; Fax: 812-357-6841. Email: mzoeller@saintmeinrad.edu. Web: www.saintmeinrad.edu. Bro. Maurus Zoeller, O.S.B., Retreat Dir. & Guest Master. Retreat House for Men, Women, Couples Rooms 31.

[K] MONASTERIES AND RESIDENCES OF PRIESTS AND BROTHERS

BLOOMINGTON. *Marian Friary of Our Lady Coredemptrix, Franciscan of the Immaculate*, 8210 W. State Rd. 48, 47404. Tel: 812-825-4642, Ext. 232. Revs. Elias Mary Mills, F.I., Father Guardian; Jacinto Mary Chapin, F.I., Vocation Dir.; Joachim Mary Mudd, F.I. Priests 3.

MOUNT SAINT FRANCIS. *Provincial Headquarters for the Conventual Franciscan Province*, 101 Anthony Dr., Mount St. Francis, 47146. Tel: 812-923-8444; Fax: 812-923-8145. Email: ProvOffOLC@aol.com. Web: www.franciscansusa.org. Rev. James Kent, O.F.M.Conv., Vicar Prov.; Bro. Robert B. Baxter, O.F.M.Conv., Sec. of Prov.

Province of Our Lady of Consolation Priests 2.

Development Office, 103 St. Francis Blvd., Mount St. Francis, 47146. Tel: 812-923-5250; Fax: 812-923-3200. *Vocation Office of the Province* Tel: 502-933-4439; Fax: 502-933-7747. *St. Paul Friary*, 6901 Dixie Hwy., Pleasure Ridge Park, KY 40258. Tel: 502-933-4439; Fax: 502-933-7747. Rev. Paul Schloemer, O.F.M.Conv., Dir. Vocation. *Curia Generalizia*, Generalate: Piazza Ss. Apostoli, 51, Rome 00187 Italy. Tel: 0113906699571; Fax: 011390669957321. Rev. Marco Tasca, O.F.M.Conv., Min. General.

ST. MEINRAD. *St. Meinrad Archabbey* (1854) 100 Hill Dr., 47577-1010. Tel: 812-357-6611; Fax: 812-357-6551. Email: abbot@saintmeinrad.edu. Web: www.saintmeinrad.edu. Rt. Revs. Justin DuVall, O.S.B., Archabbot; Lambert Reilly, O.S.B., Resigned Archabbot; Bonaventure Knaebel, O.S.B., Resigned Archabbot; Revs. Tobias Colgan, O.S.B., Prior; Guerric DeBona, O.S.B., Subprior, Master of Novices & Junior Master; Gavin Barnes, O.S.B.; Aurelius Boberek, O.S.B.; Meinrad Brune, O.S.B.; Adrian Burke, O.S.B., V.F., P.O. Box 8, Saint Meinrad, 47577. Tel: 812-357-5533; Fax: 812-357-2862; Bede Cisco, O.S.B., St. Michael Parish, 3354 W. 30th St., 46222; Aelred Cody, O.S.B.; Patrick Cooney, O.S.B., J.C.L.; Joseph Cox, O.S.B.; Simeon Daly, O.S.B.; Augustine Davis, O.S.B.; Cyprian Davis, O.S.B.; Jonathan Fassero, O.S.B.; Colman Grabert, O.S.B.; Harry Hagan, O.S.B.; Warren Heitz, O.S.B.; Eugene Hensell, O.S.B.; Richard Hindel, O.S.B.; Gabriel Hodges, O.S.B.; Sean Hoppe, O.S.B., St. Augustine Church, General Delivery, Leopold, 47551; Columba Kelly, O.S.B.; Jeremy King, O.S.B.; Pius Klein, O.S.B., St. Mary Rectory, 313 Washington St., Huntingburg, 47542; Eric Lies, O.S.B.; Guy Mansini, O.S.B.; Benedict Meyer, O.S.B.; Brendan Moss, O.S.B., M.Div.; Noel Mueller, O.S.B.; Louis Mulcahy, O.S.B.; Godfrey Mullen, O.S.B.; Paul Nord, O.S.B.; Rupert Ostdick, O.S.B.; Julian Peters, O.S.B.; Denis Robinson, O.S.B., Pres. & Rector, School Theology; Timothy Sweeney, O.S.B., Parish of the Immaculate, 2516 Christie Pl., Owensboro, KY 42301; Germain Swisshelm, O.S.B.; Vincent Tobin, O.S.B.; Donald Walpole, O.S.B. Archabbey of the Order of St. Benedict, including School of Theology (St. Meinrad Seminary). Priests 67; Brothers 28.

Priests of the Archabbey Teaching, Studying at Universities, or on Special Assignment: Revs. Ephrem Carr, O.S.B., Collegio Sant' Anselmo, Piazza Cavalieri di Malta 5, Rome I-00153 Italy; Gregory D. Chamberlin, O.S.B., St. Benedict Church, 1328 Lincoln Ave., Evansville, 47714-1598; Cassian Folsom, O.S.B., Monastero San Benedetto, Comunita di Maria Sedes Sapientias, Via Reguardati, 22, Norcia (pg) 06046 Italy; Barnabas Gillespie, O.S.B., St. Paul Church, 802 Ninth St., Tell City, 47586; Harold Hammerstein, O.S.B., 701 S. Boeke, Evansville, 47714; Boniface Hardin, O.S.B., 2171 Avondale Pl., P.O. Box 18567, 46218; Micheas Langston, O.S.B., The Hollows, 1300 Longcreek Dr., Apt. 713, Columbia, SC 29210; Sebastian

Leonard, O.S.B., Canterbury School, Aspetuck Ave., New Milford, CT 06776; Edward Linton, O.S.B., St. James Parish, 2942 S. Wabash, Chicago, IL 60616; Severin Messick, O.S.B., M.Div., St. Michael Church, 519 Jefferson Blvd., Greenfield, 46140; Matthias Neuman, O.S.B., 1414 Southern Ave., Beech Grove, 46107; Mark O'Keefe, O.S.B.; Mel Patton, O.S.B., Sacred Heart Monastery, 1005 W. Eighth St., Yankton, SD 57078; David Rabenecker, O.S.B., P.O. Box 3394, Terre Haute, 47803; Anselm Russell, O.S.B., Jesuit Community, 6525 Sheridan Rd., Chicago, IL 60626-5385; Damian Schmelz, O.S.B., St. Henry Parish, 1311 W. 1100 S., Ferdinand, 47532; Stephen Snoich, O.S.B.; Raymond Studzinski, O.S.B., Curley Hall, Catholic University of America, Washington, DC 20064; Anthony Vinson, O.S.B.; Samuel Weber, O.S.B., Wake Forest Divinity School, P.O. Box 7719, Winston Salem, NC 27109-7719.

[L] CONVENTS AND RESIDENCES FOR SISTERS

INDIANAPOLIS. *F.I.H. Convent* (1998) 514 E. Merrill St., 46203. Tel: 317-917-0306; Fax: 317-917-0306. Email: njgansis@hotmail.com. Sr. Ushatta Mary, F.I.H., Supr. Franciscan Sisters of the Immaculate Heart of Mary. Sisters 13.

Servants of the Gospel of Life, Inc., 1400 N. Meridian St., 46202. Tel: 317-236-1521. Email: dcarollo@archindy.org. Sr. Diane Carollo, S.G.L., Sister Servant.

BEECH GROVE. *Our Lady of Grace Monastery*, 1402 Southern Ave., 46107-1197. Tel: 317-787-3287; Fax: 317-780-2368. Email: olgprioress@benedictine.com. Web: www.benedictine.com.

Sisters of St. Benedict of Beech Grove, Ind., Inc. 1414 Southern Ave., 46107-1197. Tel: 317-786-0338; Fax: 317-780-2368. Email: mneuman204@att.net. Rev. Matthias Neuman, O.S.B., Chap. Sisters 70.

OLDENBURG. *Motherhouse of the Congregation of the Sisters of the Third Order of St. Francis* 47036. Tel: 812-934-2475; Fax: 812-933-6403. Email: osf@oldenburgosf.com. Web: www.oldenburgfranciscans.org. Sr. Barbara Piller, O.S.F., Congregational Min.; Rev. Carl Hawver, O.F.M. Professed Sisters in Congregation 255; Professed Sisters in Archdiocese 174; Total in Residence 119.

Sisters of St. Francis Community Support Trust Tel: 812-934-2475.

Sisters of Our Lady of Mount Carmel Carmelite Monastery (1922) *Carmelite Sisters*, P.O. Box 260, 47036. Tel: 812-932-2075; Fax: 812-932-2076. Email: indycarmelites@yahoo.com. Sr. Jean Alice McGoff, O.C.D., Prioress. Professed Religious 9.

SAINT MARY-OF-THE-WOODS. *Sisters of Providence General Administration*, St. Mary Of The Woods, 47876-1007. Tel: 812-535-4193; Fax: 812-535-1011. Web: www.sistersofprovidence.org. Sr. Denise Wilkinson, S.P., Gen. Supr.; Rev. Daniel R. Hopcus, Chap. Professed in Congregation 401; Professed Residing in Archdiocese 258; Novices 1; Postulants 1; In Transfer Process 1.

TERRE HAUTE. *Sisters of Our Lady of Mount Carmel of Terre Haute, Carmelite Monastery* (1947) Carmelite Monastery, 59 Allendale, 47802-4751. Tel: 812-299-1410; Fax: 812-299-5820. Email: carmelth@heartsawake.org. Web: www.heartsawake.org. Sr. Anne Brackmann, O.C.D., Prioress. Solemnly Professed 12.

[M] ARCHDIOCESAN CHARITIES

INDIANAPOLIS. *Adult Day Services*, 1400 N. Meridian, P.O. Box 1410, 46206. Tel: 317-466-0015; Fax: 317-261-3375. Email: sdinnin@fairviewpresbyterian.org. Sr. Susan Dinnin, Prog. Dir.

A Caring Place - Adult Day Services, c/o Fairview Presbyterian Church, 4609 N. Capitol Ave., 46208. Tel: 317-466-0015; Fax: 317-475-3093. Sr. Susan Dinnin, Prog. Dir.

Catholic Charities Indianapolis, The Catholic Center, 1400 N. Meridian St., P.O. Box 1410, 46206. Tel: 317-236-1500; Fax: 317-261-3375. Email: vsperka@archindy.org. Web: www.catholiccharitiesindpls.org. David Bethuram, M.A., M.Min, Agency Dir.

St. Elizabeth/Coleman Pregnancy & Adoption Services, 2500 Churchman Ave., 46203. Tel: 317-787-3412; Fax: 317-787-0482. Email: stelizabeths@stelizabeths.org. Web: www.stelizabeths.org. David Bethuram, M.A., M.Min, Agency Dir.

Holy Family Services, 907 N. Holmes Ave., 46222. Tel: 317-635-7830; Fax: 317-684-9702. Email: bbickel@archindy.org. Web: www.catholiccharitiesindpls.org. Bill Bickel, M.T.S., Dir. Total Staff 16; Total Assisted 1,000.

BLOOMINGTON. *Catholic Charities Bloomington*, 631 N. College Ave., 47404. Tel: 812-332-1262; Fax: 812-334-8464.

NEW ALBANY. *St. Elizabeth's Regional Maternity Center*, 601 E. Market St., 47150. Tel: 812-949-7305; Fax: 812-941-7008. Email: info@stelizabethcatholiccharities.org. Web: www.stelizabethcatholiccharities.org. Mark Casper, Dir. Full-range maternity home and adoption agency offering residential and outreach services. Total Staff 26; Total Assisted 607.

St. Elizabeth - Catholic Charities, 601 E. Market St., 47150. Tel: 812-949-7305; Fax: 812-941-7008. Email: info@stelizabethcatholiccharities.org. Web: www.stelizabethcatholiccharities.org. Total Staff 26; Total Assisted 607.

TELL CITY. *Catholic Charities Tell City*, 802 9th St., 47586. Tel: 812-547-0903; Fax: 812-547-0903. Email: info@catholiccharitiestellcity.org. Web: www.catholiccharitiestellcity.org. Joan Hess, Agency Dir.

TERRE HAUTE. *Catholic Charities Terre Haute*, Corporate Square Annex, 2931 Ohio Blvd., 47803. Tel: 812-232-1447; Fax: 812-478-1363. Email: jetling@catholiccharitiesterrehaute.org. Web: www.catholiccharitiesterrehaute.org. John C. Etling, Dir. Total Staff 25.

Catholic Charities Terre Haute, Corporate Square Annex, 2931 Ohio Blvd., 47803. Tel: 812-232-1447; Fax: 812-478-1363. John C. Etling, Agency Dir.

Bethany House, 1402 Locust Ave., 47807. Tel: 812-232-4978. Dottye Crippen, Prog. Dir. Total Staff 5; Total Assisted 13,000.

Christmas House, 829 N. 14th St., 47807. Tel: 812-234-7242. George Nardini, Prog. Dir. Total Staff 1; Total Assisted 3,740.

Household Exchange, 829 N. 14th St., 47807. Tel: 812-234-1132. George Nardini, Prog. Dir. Total Staff 1; Total Assisted 3,140.

Ryves Youth Center at Etling Hall, 1356 Locust St., 47807. Tel: 812-235-1265. Jim Edwards, Prog. Dir. Total Staff 6; Total Assisted 1,917.

Terre Haute Catholic Charities Foodbank, 1356 Locust St., 47807. Tel: 812-235-3424. Pat Etling, Prog. Dir. Total Staff 7; Total Assisted 82,000.

[N] CATHOLIC YOUTH ORGANIZATIONS

INDIANAPOLIS. *Catholic Youth Organization*, Related Ministries, 580 E. Stevens St., 46203. Tel: 317-632-9311. Web: www.cyoarchindy.org. Mr. Edward J. Tinder, Exec. Dir.; Mr. Gerald R. Ross, Asst. Exec. Dir. Monsignor Downey Athletic Field Perkins & Raymond St., 46203.

NASHVILLE. *C.Y.O. Camp Rancho Framasa* (1946) 2230 N. Clay Lick Rd., 47448-8638. Tel: 888-988-2839; Fax: 812-988-4842. Email: info@campranchoframasa.org. Web: www.campranchoframasa.org. Mr. Kevin Sullivan, Camp Dir.

[O] CAMPUS MINISTRIES

INDIANAPOLIS. *Butler University c/o Center for Faith and Vocation*, 4600 Sunset Ave., 46208. Tel: 317-509-6012. Rev. Jeffrey H. Godecker.

University of Indianapolis Newman Center c/o Good Shepherd Parish, 2905 S. Carson Ave., 46203. David R. Wilson.

BLOOMINGTON. *Indiana University, Bloomington c/o St. Paul Catholic Center*, 1413 E. 17th St., 47408. Tel: 812-339-5561; Fax: 812-333-4846. Web: www.hoosiercatholic.org. Rev. Robert Keller, O.P.

FRANKLIN. *Franklin College* (1834) *c/o St. Rose of Lima Parish*, 114 Lancelot Dr., 46131. Tel: 317-738-3929. Rev. Thomas L. Schliessmann, M.N.

GREENCASTLE. *DePauw University c/o St. Paul the Apostle Parish*, 202 E. Washington St., 46135. Tel: 765-653-5678. Rev. Stephen Jarrell.

MADISON. *Hanover College c/o Prince of Peace Parish*, 415 E. Second St., 47250. Tel: 812-265-4166; Fax: 812-273-3427. Rev. John A. Meyer, V.F.

RICHMOND. *Earlham College c/o St. Andrew Parish*, 240 S. 6th St., 47374. Tel: 765-962-3902. Rev. Todd M. Riebe.

TERRE HAUTE. *Indiana State University/Rose-Hulman Institute c/o St. Joseph University Parish*, 113 Fifth St., 47807. Tel: 812-232-8088. Sr. Carmen Gillick, S.F.C.C., Pastoral Assoc. for College Students.

[P] MISCELLANEOUS

INDIANAPOLIS. *Hearts and Hands Corporation of Indiana*, 1400 N. Meridian St., 46202-2367. Rev. Msgr. Joseph Schaedel.

**Inter Mirifica, Inc.*, 7340 E. 82nd St., Ste. A, 46256. Tel: 317-598-6700; Fax: 317-598-6701. Email: bob@teipencpa.com. Web: www.catholicradioindy.org. Robert C. Teipen, Chm.

Society of St. Vincent de Paul, Archdiocesan Council of Indianapolis, Inc., 3001 E. 30th St., 46218. Tel: 317-924-5769; Fax: 317-924-5781. Web: www.svdpindy.org. Mr. Jake Asher, Pres. Total Assisted 67,000.

SVSM, Inc. (2001) 2001 W. 86th St., 46260. Tel: 317-583-3289; Fax: 317-583-3285. Email: jbford@stvincent.org. Web: www.stvincent.org. Mailing Address: 10330 N. Meridian St., 46290. Vincent Caponi, CEO, St. Vincent Health, Inc.

**St. Vincent Health, Inc.*, 8425 Harcourt Rd., 46260. Tel: 317-583-3289; Fax: 317-583-3285. Email: jbford@stvincent.org. Web: www.stvincent.org. Mailing Address: 10330 N. Meridian St., 46290. Vincent Caponi, CEO; Joseph B. Ford, Mgr. Finance & Contact Person.

BEECH GROVE. *Alverno Information Services*, 1300 Albany St., 46107. Tel: 317-532-7800; Fax: 317-532-7801. Email: william.laker@ssfhs.org. Web: www.alverno.org. Mr. William G. Laker, Senior Vice Pres. & CIO. Sponsored by Sisters of St. Francis Health Services, Inc.

Charitable Trust of the Monastery of Our Lady of Grace (1989) 1402 Southern Ave., 46107-1197. Tel: 317-787-3287; Fax: 317-780-2368. Email: olgprioress@benedictine.com. Web: www.benedictine.com.

Charitable Trust of the Monastery of Our Lady of Grace, Sisters of the Order of St. Benedict

CLARKSVILLE. *New Albany Deanery-Catholic Youth Ministries*, 707 Providence Way Side, 47129. Tel: 812-945-2000; Fax: 812-945-2995. Email: marlene@nadyouth.org. Web: www.nadyouth.org.

GEORGETOWN. *Providence Self-Sufficiency Ministries, Inc.* (1994) 8037 Unruh Dr., 47122-8759. Tel: 812-951-1878; Fax: 812-951-1659. Email: sbarannz@insightbb.com. Web: www.pssm.org. Sr. Barbara Ann Zeller, Pres. & CEO. Sponsored by The Sisters of Providence, Saint Mary-of-the-Woods. Total Assisted 2008-2009 12,416; Total Assisted Historically 87,061; Volunteers 79.

MADISON. *Mary's King's Village Schoenstatt Center, Inc.*, 3991 WCR 925 S., 47250. Tel: 812-689-3551. Rev. Elmer J. Burwinkel, M.Ed., M.Div., Pres. & Dir. (Retired).

MOORESVILLE. *St. Thomas More Free Clinic, Inc.*, 410 N. Monroe St., Ste. 16, POB 935, 46158. Tel: 317-831-1697. Email: jbuckner@crowntech.com. Jeff Buckner, Bd. Member.

MOUNT SAINT FRANCIS. *Mount Saint Francis Sanctuary, Inc., Marian College*, 3200 Cold Spring Rd., 46222. Tel: 812-923-8817; Fax: 812-923-0177. Samuel L. Smith, Pres.; Chris Jones, Vice Pres.; Thomas A. Smith, O.F.M.Conv., Treas.; Rev. Leopold Keffler, O.F.M.Conv., Sec.

NORTH VERNON. *St. Vincent Jennings Hospital Foundation Inc.*, 301 Henry St., 47265.

OLDENBURG. *Association of Contemplative Sisters, Carmelite Sisters*, P.O. Box 260, 47036-0260. Tel: 812-932-2075; Fax: 812-932-2076. Email: jalicemcgoff@yahoo.com. Web: www.laycontemplative.org/thesites/ACS.htm. Mary Lyons, Pres. Membership 363.

ST. MARY OF THE WOODS. **Guerin Outreach Ministries, Inc., Sisters of Providence, Owens Hall*, 1 Sisters of Providence Rd., Saint Mary Of The Woods, 47876.

Providence Health Care, Inc., Owens Hall, 1 Sisters of Providence, 47876-1007. Tel: 812-535-2864; Fax: 812-535-1011. Sponsored by the Sisters of Providence of Saint Mary-of-the-Woods.

Sisters of Providence Community Support Trust 47876-1007. Tel: 812-535-4193; Fax: 812-535-1011. Web: www.sistersofprovidence.org. Sr. Rosemary Schmalz, S.P., Gen. Sec.

Women of Providence in Collaboration, Inc., 1 Sisters of Providence Rd., Saint Mary Of The Woods, 47876.

ST. MEINRAD. *Swiss-American Benedictine Congregation, Inc.*, Saint Meinrad Archabbey, 100 Hill Dr., 47577. Tel: 503-845-3304. Email: peter.eberle@mtangel.edu. Web: www.osb.org/swissamFax: 503-895-3202. Rt. Rev. Peter Eberle, O.S.B., Abbot Pres.

TERRE HAUTE. *St. Ann Community Outreach Services of Terre Haute*, 1440 Locust St., 47807. Tel: 812-232-6832; Fax: 812-232-2442. Email: stannchurch@gmail.com. Mailing Address: 1440 Locust St., 47807. Sr. Constance Kramer, S.P., Dir.

[Q] CLOSED PARISHES, SCHOOLS AND OTHER INSTITUTIONS

INDIANAPOLIS. *Archives of the Archdiocese of Indianapolis*, 1400 N. Meridian St., 46202. Tel: 317-236-1429; Fax: 317-236-1406. Email: archives@archindy.org. Sacramental and other records may be found where indicated.

Closed Parishes and Missions:

Indianapolis:

Assumption (1894-1994) Merged with St. Anthony, where sacramental records are kept.

St. Bridget (1880-1994) Merged with SS. Peter & Paul, where sacramental records are kept.

St. Catherine of Siena (1909-1993) Merged with St. James and renamed Good Shepherd, where sacramental records are kept.

St. Francis de Sales (1881-1983) Merged with four neighboring parishes. Sacramental records are located in the archives.
St. James the Greater (1951-1993) Merged with St. Catherine and renamed Good Shepherd, where sacramental records are kept.
St. Joseph (1873-1949) Sacramental records kept at the new St. Joseph parish.
Acton:
St. John the Evangelist (1855-1936) Sacramental records are located in the archives.
Adyeville:
St. Jude Thaddeus (1889-1898)
Bainbridge:
St. Patrick (1865-1973)
Blanford:
Queen of the Most Holy Rosary (1917-1942)
Cannelton:
St. Patrick (1847-1902) Merged with St. Michael, Cannelton, where sacramental records are kept.
Carbon:
St. Joseph (1870-1970) Sacramental records are located in the archives.
Centenary:
St. Anthony (1917-1942)
China:
St. Anthony (1861-1993) Merged with Prince of Peace, Madison, where sacramental records are kept.
Columbus:
St. Columba (1963-1994) Merged with St. Bartholomew, Columbus, where sacramental records are kept.
Cypress Dale:
Sacred Heart (1868-1918)
Derby:
St. Mary (1824-1973) Sacramental records kept at St. Augustine, Leopold.
Diamond:
St. John Baptist (Greek Uniate Catholic) (1897-1926) Sacaramental records are located in the archives.
St. Mary (1897-1991) Sacramental records are located in the archives.
Dogwood:
St. Michael (1820-1928)
Dugger:
Our Lady of Perpetual Help (1911-1982) Sacramental records kept at St. Mary, Sullivan Co., Diocese of Evansville.
Ellsworth:
St. John (1910-1912)
Eureka:
Mattingly Chapel (1874-1886)
Fontanet:
St. Augustine (1891-1980) Sacramental records are located in the archives.
Hovey:
All Souls Chapel (1900-1915)
Indian Creek:
St. Columban (1848-1868)
Knightsville:
St. Patrick (1868-1890)
Laconia:
Sacred Heart of Mary (1854-1922)
Laurel:
St. Raphael (1869-1958) Sacramental records kept at St. Gabriel, Connersville.
Lexington:
Mother of God (1854-1941)
Locust Point:
St. Joachim (1888-1930)
Madison:
St. Mary (1851-1993) Merged with St. Patrick (1853-1993) and St. Michael (1837-1993) and renamed Prince of Peace, where sacramental records are kept.
Magnet:
Sacred Heart Sacramental records kept at St. Augustine, Leopold.
McCutcheonville:
St. Patrick (1842-1881)
Mecca:
St. Mary (1905-1936)
Milltown:
St. Joseph (1855-1974) Sacramental records kept at St. Joseph, Crawford Co.
Montezuma:
Parke Co., Immaculate Conception (1867-2001) Sacramental records kept at St. Joseph, Rockville.
Mount Erin:
St. John the Baptist (1852-1885)
Mount Pleasant:
St. Rose (1821-1883)
Nebraska:
St. Bridget (1845-1936)
New Albany:
Holy Trinity (1836-1975) Merged with St. Mary, New Albany, where sacramental records are kept.
Oak Forest:
Franklin Co., St. Cecilia of Rome (Formerly St. Philomena) (1844-2000) Sacramental records are kept at St. Mary of the Rock.
Rome:
St. Peter (1868-1885) Sacramental records are located in the archives.
St. Catherine (1841-1871) Sacramental records are located in the archives.
St. James (1844-1850) Merged with St. Joseph, Perry Co. (1891-1968) and renamed St. Isidore, Perry Co., where sacramental records are kept.
St. Magdalen (1847-1941) Sacramental records kept at St. John, Osgood.
St. Paul (1859-1996) Sacramental records kept at St. Vincent, Shelby Co.
Perry Co.:
St. Peter (See Rome, IN St. Peter.)
St. Rose (1840-1903) Merged with St. Thomas, Knox Co., Diocese of Evansville, where sacramental records are kept.
Salem
St. Mary (1871-1902)
Scipio:
St. Patrick (1841-1958) Sacramental records are located in the archives.
Shelburn:
St. Ann (1909-1978) Sacramental records kept at St. Mary, Sullivan, Diocese of Evansville.
Shirley:
Mother of God (1900-1920) Sacramental records are located in the archives.
Taylorsville (Selvin):
St. Thomas (1845-1875)
Valley Mills:
St. John the Baptist (1855-1903) Sacramental records are located in the archives.
West Baden Springs:
Our Lady of Lourdes (1900-1929)
Willow Valley:
St. Stephen (1906-1944)
Closed Parish Grade Schools:
Indianapolis:
Assumption, St. Anthony (Consolidated) School, 75 N. Belleview Pl., 46222. Tel: 317-636-3739.
Cathedral, Holy Cross Central School, 125 N. Oriental St., 46201. Tel: 317-638-9068.
Holy Rosary, Holy Rosary Rectory, 520 Stevens St., 46203. Tel: 317-636-4478.
Holy Trinity, St. Anthony (Consolidated) School, 75 N. Belleview Pl., 46222. Tel: 317-636-3739.
Sacred Heart, Sacred Heart Rectory, 1530 Union St., 46225. Tel: 317-638-5551.
St. Ann, St. Ann Rectory, 2862 S. Holt Rd., 46241. Tel: 317-244-3750.
St. Anthony, All Saints Catholic School, 75 N. Belleview Pl., 46222. Tel: 317-636-3739.
St. Bernadette
St. Bridget Sacramental records are located in the archives.
St. Catherine, Central Catholic School, 1155 Cameron St., 46203. Tel: 317-783-7759.
St. Francis de Sales Sacramental records are located in the archives.
St. James the Greater, Central Catholic School, 1155 Cameron St., 46203. Tel: 317-783-7759.
St. Joseph, St. Anthony (Consolidated) School, 75 N. Belleview Pl., 46222. Tel: 317-636-3739.
St. Mary, Holy Cross Central School, 125 N. Oriental St., 46201. Tel: 317-638-9068.
St. Patrick, Central Catholic School, 1155 Cameron St., 46203. Tel: 317-783-7759.
Madison:
St. Mary; St. Michael, Pope John XXIII Grade School, 221 State St., Madison, 47250. Tel: 812-273-3957.
Morris:
St. Anthony, St. Anthony Rectory, P.O. Box 3, Morris, 47033. Tel: 812-934-6218.
New Castle:
St. Anne, St. Anne Rectory, 102 N. 19th St., New Castle, 47362. Tel: 765-529-0933.
Richmond:
Holy Family; St. Andrew; St. Mary, Elizabeth Ann Seton School, 801 W. Main St., Richmond, 47374. Tel: 765-962-4877.
Terre Haute:
St. Ann; St. Joseph, Student Services, Vigo County School Corp., P.O. Box 3703, Terre Haute, 47803. Tel: 812-462-4224.
St. Benedict, Terre Haute. Sacramental records are located in the archives.
St. Margaret Mary, St. Margaret Mary Rectory, 2405 S. Seventh St., Terre Haute, 47802. Tel: 812-232-3512.
Closed High Schools and Academies.
Indianapolis:
Bruté Latin School School records are located in the archives.
Chartrand; Kennedy; Sacred Heart, Roncalli High School, 3300 Prague Rd., 46227. Tel: 317-787-8277.
St. John; St. Agnes; Ladywood; Ladywood / St. Agnes Academies, Sisters of Providence, Records Office - Owens Hall, St. Mary-of-the-Woods, 47876. Tel: 812-535-3131.
St. Mary Academy, Registrar, Franciscan Motherhouse. Tel: 812-934-2475.
Beech Grove:
Our Lady of Grace Academy, Our Lady of Grace Monastery, 1402 Southern Ave., Beech Grove, 46107. Tel: 317-787-3287.
Terre Haute:
Central Catholic High School for Girls
St. Patrick High School for Girls
St. Vincent Academy Renamed St. Joseph Academy.
Schulte High School, Student Services, Vigo County School Corp., P.O. Box 3703, Terre Haute, 47803. Tel: 812-462-4224.
Other Closed Institutions:
Indianapolis:
Sisters of the Good Shepherd Convent Sacramental records are located in the archives.
Angel Guardian School for Orphans Entrance records, 1924-1937, are located in the archives.
Marydale School For Girls Sacramental records, 1875-1953, are located in the archives. School records are located in the archives of the Archdiocese of Indianapolis.
New Albany:
St. Edward Hospital, New Albany, Box 766, Mishawaka, 46546. Tel: 219-259-5427.
Terre Haute:
St. Anthony Hospital Baptismal records are located in the archives.

RELIGIOUS INSTITUTES OF MEN REPRESENTED IN THE ARCHDIOCESE

For further details refer to the corresponding bracketed number in the Religious Institutes of Men or Women section.

[0200]—*Benedictine Monks of St. Meinrad*—O.S.B.
[]—*Congregation of Christian Brothers* (Edmund Rice Oceania Province, Australia)—C.F.C.
[0480]—*Conventual Franciscans* (Our Lady of Consolation Prov.)—O.F.M.Conv
[0520]—*Franciscan Friars (St. John the Baptist & Sacred Heart Province)*—O.F.M.
[]—*Franciscans of the Immaculate*—F.I.
[0690]—*Jesuit Fathers and Brothers* (Chicago Prov.)—S.J.
[]—*Missionary Oblates of Mary Immaculate*—O.M.I.
[]—*Order of Friar Minor Capuchin* (Kerala, India)—O.F.M.Cap.
[0430]—*Order of Preachers Central Province*—O.P.
[1065]—*Priestly Fraternity of Saint Peter*—F.S.S.P.
[0420]—*Society of the Divine Word* (Chicago Province)—S.V.D.
[1060]—*Society of the Precious Blood* (Cincinnati Province)—C.PP.S.

RELIGIOUS INSTITUTES OF WOMEN REPRESENTED IN THE ARCHDIOCESE

[0230]—*Benedictine Sisters of Pontifical Jurisdiction* (Ferdinand, IN)—O.S.B.
[]—*Congregation of St. Joseph*—C.S.J.
[1920]—*Congregation of the Sisters of the Holy Cross*—C.S.C.
[1730]—*Congregation of the Sisters of the Third Order of St. Francis, Oldenburg, IN*—O.S.F.
[0760]—*Daughters of Charity of St. Vincent De Paul* (Evansville, IN)—D.C.
[]—*Daughters of Mary Mother of Mercy* (Umuahia, Abia State, Nigeria)—D.M.M.M.
[0420]—*Discalced Carmelite Nuns*—O.C.D.
[1070-03]—*Dominican Sisters*—O.P.
[]—*Evangelization Sisters of Mother of Perpetual Help*—N.E.S.
[]—*Franciscan Sisters of the Immaculate Heart of Mary* (Kerala, India)—F.I.H.
[2340]—*Little Sisters of the Poor* (Baltimore, MD)—L.S.P.
[2710]—*Missionaries of Charity*—M.C.
[2820]—*Missionary Sisters of Our Lady of Africa* (American Headquarters, Winooski, VT)—M.S.O.L.A.
[]—*Servants of the Gospel of Life*—S.G.L.
[0440]—*Sisters of Charity of Cincinnati, Ohio* (Central Region)—S.C.
[0500]—*Sisters of Charity of Nazareth* (Nazareth, KY)—S.C.N.
[]—*Sisters of Loretto at the Foot of the Cross* Nerinx, KY—S.L.
[2990]—*Sisters of Notre Dame* (Toledo, Ohio)—S.N.D.
[3360]—*Sisters of Providence of Saint Mary-of-the-Woods*—S.P.
[]—*Sisters of St. Benedict of Our Lady of Grace Monastery* (Beech Grove, IN)—O.S.B.
[1640]—*Sisters of St. Francis of Perpetual Adoration*—O.S.F.
[3840]—*Sisters of St. Joseph Carondelet* (St. Louis, MO)—C.S.J.
[]—*Sisters Of The Immaculate Heart of Mary Reparatrix* (Kisubi, Uganda)—(I.H.M.R.)

[1720]—*Sisters of the Third Order Regular of St. Francis of the Congregation of Our Lady of Lourdes*—O.S.F.

ARCHDIOCESAN CEMETERIES

INDIANAPOLIS. *Catholic Cemeteries*, 9001 Haverstick Rd., 46240.
Indianapolis South Deanery
Holy Cross Indianapolis
St. Joseph Indianapolis
Calvary Indianapolis
Indianapolis North Deanery
Our Lady of Peace Indianapolis
Indianapolis West Deanery
St. Malachy Brownsburg
St. Malachy Pittsboro

BATESVILLE. *Batesville Deanery*
St. Ann Hamburg
St. Anthony Morris
St. Cecilia Oak Forest
Cemetery (North end of Brookville) Brookville
St. Charles Milan
Holy Family Oldenburg
Holy Family Shrine Oldenburg
Holy Guardian Angels Cedar Grove
Immaculate Conception Millhousen
St. John Dover
St. John Enochsburg
St. John Osgood
St. Joseph St. Leon
St. Joseph Shelbyville
St. Louis Batesville
St. Martin Yorkville
St. Mary Greensburg
St. Mary of the Rock St. Mary of the Rock
St. Maurice Napoleon
St. Maurice St. Maurice
St. Michael Brookville
St. Paul New Alsace
St. Paul St. Paul
St. Peter St. Peter
St. Pius St. Pius
St. Raphael Laurel
St. Vincent de Paul St. Vincent de Paul

BLOOMINGTON. *Bloomington Deanery*
Catholic South of Martinsville
St. Martin Martinsville
Our Lady of Springs French Lick

CONNERSVILLE. *Connersville Deanery*
St. Anne New Castle
St. Andrew Richmond
St. Bridget Liberty
Calvary Rushville
St. Mary Richmond

NEW ALBANY. *New Albany Deanery*
St. Anthony Jeffersonville
St. Bernard Frenchtown
St. Bernard, Old Frenchtown
Cemetery Southwest of Bradford
St. Francis Henryville
Holy Trinity New Albany
St. Joachim Locust Point
St. John Starlight
St. Joseph Corydon
St. Joseph St. Joseph Hill
St. Mary Lanesville
St. Mary New Albany
St. Mary Navilleton
St. Mary of the Knobs Floyds Knobs
Mary, Queen of Heaven Jeffersonville
St. Michael Bradford
St. Michael Charlestown
St. Michael Dogwood
Most Precious Blood New Middleton
St. Peter Taylor Township

SEYMOUR. *Seymour Deanery*
St. Ambrose Seymour
St. Anne Jennings Co.
St. Anthony China
St. Bridget Nebraska
St. Catherine of Siena St. Catherine
St. Dennis Jennings Co.
St. Joseph Madison
St. Joseph St. Joseph
St. Magdalen Madison
St. Mary North Vernon
Old St. James St. James
St. Patrick Madison
St. Patrick Salem
St. Patrick Scipio

TELL CITY. *Tell City Deanery*
St. Augustine Leopold
St. Boniface Fulda
Cemetery, St. Croix. Cemetery on original parish site. St. Croix
Holy Cross St. Croix
St. Isidore Bristow
St. John St. John
St. Joseph Milltown
St. Joseph St. Croix
St. Joseph St. Joseph
St. Martin Siberia
St. Mary Derby
St. Mary Tell City
St. Meinrad St. Meinrad
St. Michael Cannelton
Old St. Patrick Cannelton
St. Paul Cemetery Tell City
St. Peter Cannelton

TERRE HAUTE. *Terre Haute Deanery*
Annunciation Brazil
Catholic Armiesburg
Calvary Terre Haute
Greek Catholic Perth
Immaculate Conception Montezuma
St. John Greek Diamond
St. Joseph Terre Haute
St. Mary-of-the-Woods St. Mary-of-the-Woods

NECROLOGY

† Brown, Henry P., Beech Grove, IN St. Paul Hermitage—Died June 21, 2009
† Schmidlin, Donald L., Indianapolis, IN St. Andrew the Apostle—Died Feb. 5, 2009

An asterisk (*) denotes an organization that has established tax-exempt status directly with the IRS and is not covered by the USCCB Group Ruling.

Diocese of Jackson

(Dioecesis Jacksoniensis)

Most Reverend

WILLIAM R. HOUCK, D.D.

Retired Bishop of Jackson; ordained May 19, 1951; appointed Auxiliary Bishop of Jackson and Titular Bishop of Allessano on March 28, 1979; consecrated May 27, 1979; appointed Bishop of Jackson April 24, 1984; installed June 5, 1984; retired January 3, 2003. *Mailing Address: Catholic Diocese of Jackson, P.O. Box 2248, Jackson, MS 39225-2248.*

Most Reverend

JOSEPH N. LATINO

Bishop of Jackson; ordained May 25, 1963; appointed Bishop of Jackson January 3, 2003; consecrated March 7, 2003. *Mailing Address: P.O. Box 2248, Jackson, MS 39225-2248.*

Chancery Office: 237 E. Amite St., P.O. Box 2248, Jackson, MS 39225-2248. Tel: 601-969-1880; Fax: 601-960-8455.

Web: www.jacksondiocese.org

Email: chancery@jacksondiocese.org

Square Miles 37,643.

Established July 28, 1837 as Diocese of Natchez. Name changed to Diocese of Natchez-Jackson, March 7, 1957. Name changed to Diocese of Jackson, June 6, 1977.

Comprises 65 Counties in the State of Mississippi, namely: Adams, Alcorn, Amite, Attala, Benton, Bolivar, Calhoun, Carroll, Chickasaw, Choctaw, Claiborne, Clarke, Clay, Coahoma, Copiah, De Soto, Franklin, Grenada, Hinds, Holmes, Humphreys, Issaquena, Itawamba, Jasper, Jefferson, Kemper, Lafayette, Lauderdale, Leake, Lee, Leflore, Lincoln, Lowndes, Madison, Marshall, Monroe, Montgomery, Neshoba, Newton, Noxubee, Oktibbeha, Panola, Pike, Pontotoc, Prentiss, Quitman, Rankin, Scott, Sharkey, Simpson, Smith, Sunflower, Tallahatchie, Tate, Tippah, Tishomingo, Tunica, Union, Warren, Washington, Webster, Wilkinson, Winston, Yalobusha and Yazoo.

Legal Title: "Catholic Diocese of Jackson".

STATISTICAL OVERVIEW

Personnel	
Bishop	1
Retired Bishops	1
Priests: Diocesan Active in Diocese	36
Priests: Diocesan Active Outside Diocese	1
Priests: Retired, Sick or Absent	18
Number of Diocesan Priests	55
Religious Priests in Diocese	29
Total Priests in Diocese	84
Ordinations:	
Transitional Deacons	1
Permanent Deacons in Diocese	7
Total Brothers	9
Total Sisters	172
Parishes	
Parishes	75
With Resident Pastor:	
Resident Diocesan Priests	31
Resident Religious Priests	12
Without Resident Pastor:	
Administered by Priests	16
Administered by Deacons	1
Administered by Professed Religious Men	1
Administered by Religious Women	5
Administered by Lay People	5
Administered by Pastoral Teams, etc.	4
Missions	26
New Parishes Created	1
Closed Parishes	1
Professional Ministry Personnel:	
Brothers	2
Sisters	8
Lay Ministers	36
Welfare	
Catholic Hospitals	1
Total Assisted	119,754
Health Care Centers	2
Total Assisted	9,142
Homes for the Aged	1
Total Assisted	450
Residential Care of Children	3
Total Assisted	352
Day Care Centers	2
Total Assisted	227
Specialized Homes	7
Total Assisted	6,513
Special Centers for Social Services	17
Total Assisted	21,488
Residential Care of Disabled	3
Total Assisted	63
Other Institutions	3
Total Assisted	78
Educational	
Diocesan Students in Other Seminaries	10
Total Seminarians	10
Colleges and Universities	3
Total Students	42
High Schools, Diocesan and Parish	4
Total Students	1,198
Elementary Schools, Diocesan and Parish	15
Total Students	3,102
Catechesis/Religious Education:	
High School Students	1,120
Elementary Students	3,753
Total Students under Catholic Instruction	9,225
Teachers in the Diocese:	
Brothers	3
Sisters	9
Lay Teachers	353
Vital Statistics	
Receptions into the Church:	
Infant Baptism Totals	924
Minor Baptism Totals	66
Adult Baptism Totals	66
Received into Full Communion	209
First Communions	742
Confirmations	439
Marriages:	
Catholic	134
Interfaith	123
Total Marriages	257
Deaths	416
Total Catholic Population	50,114
Total Population	2,111,593

Former Bishops—Rt. Revs. JOHN J. CHANCHE, S.S., D.D., ord. June 5, 1819; cons. March 14, 1841; died July 22, 1852; J. O. VAN DE VELDE, S.J., D.D., ord. Sept. 25, 1827; appt. Bishop of Chicago Dec. 1, 1848; ord. Feb. 11, 1849; appt. Bishop of Natchez July 29, 1853; died Nov. 13, 1855.; Most Revs. WILLIAM HENRY ELDER, D.D., cons. May 3, 1857; transferred to Cincinnati, 1880; died Oct. 31, 1904; FRANCIS JANSSENS, D.D., cons. May 1, 1881; transferred to New Orleans, Aug. 7, 1888; died June 9, 1897; Rt. Revs. THOMAS HESLIN, D.D., ord. Sept. 18, 1869; cons. June 18, 1889; died Feb. 22, 1911; JOHN EDWARD GUNN, S.M., D.D., ord. Feb. 2, 1890; cons. Aug. 29, 1911; died Feb. 19, 1924; Most Revs. RICHARD OLIVER GEROW, LL.D., S.T.D., ord. June 5, 1909; appt. June 25, 1924; cons. Oct. 15, 1924; retired Dec. 2, 1967; died Dec. 20, 1976; JOSEPH B. BRUNINI, D.D., LL.D., J.C.D., ord. Dec. 5, 1933; cons. Jan. 29, 1957; appt. Bishop, Dec. 2, 1967; installed Jan. 29, 1968; retired Jan. 24, 1984; died Jan. 7, 1996; WILLIAM R. HOUCK, D.D. (Retired), ord. May 19, 1951; appt. Auxiliary Bishop of Jackson and Titular Bishop of Allessano on March 28, 1979; cons. May 27, 1979; appt. Bishop of Jackson April 24, 1984; installed June 5, 1984; retired Jan. 3, 2003.

Chancery Office—237 E. Amite St., P.O. Box 2248, Jackson, 39225-2248. Tel: 601-969-1880; Fax: 601-960-8455. The telephone number for all Diocesan Offices is 601-969-1880, unless otherwise listed. Office Hours: 8:30-4:30.

Office of the Bishop—Most Rev. JOSEPH N. LATINO, 237 E. Amite St., P.O. Box 2248, Jackson, 39225-2248.

Office of Vicar General—Rev. Msgrs. ELVIN SUNDS; MICHAEL FLANNERY, J.C.L.

Department of Ecclesiastical Affairs—

Chancellor—Rev. Msgr. ELVIN SUNDS, 237 E. Amite St., P.O. Box 2248, Jackson, 39225-2248.

Vice Chancellor—Very Rev. JEFFREY WALDREP, S.T.L., J.C.L.

Office of Child Protection—Mrs. VICKIE CAROLLO.

Office of Vocations—Revs. KENT BOWLDS, Dir.; LENIN VARGAS, Asst. Dir.

Youth Ministry—Ms. KATHIE CURTIS, Diocesan Dir.

Campus Ministry—FRAN LAVELLE, Dir.

Parish Pastoral Councils—Rev. Msgr. ELVIN SUNDS, Dir.

Black Catholic Ministry—Mr. WILL JEMISON, Dir.

Hispanic Ministry—Bro. THEODORE DAUSCH, C.F.C., Dir.

Director of Permanent Diaconate—VACANT.

Propagation of the Faith—Very Rev. JEFFREY WALDREP, S.T.L., J.C.L., Dir., Mailing Address: P.O. Box 2248, Jackson, 39225-2248.

Archivist—Miss MARY WOODWARD.

Judicial Vicar—Very Rev. JEFFREY WALDREP, S.T.L., J.C.L.

Adjutant Judicial Vicar—Rev. KEVIN SLATTERY, J.C.L.

Engaged Encounter—Very Rev. JEFFREY WALDREP, S.T.L., J.C.L., Dir.

Ecumenism—Miss MARY WOODWARD.

Continuing Formation Committee—Co Chairmen: Revs. DAVID O'CONNOR; RICARDO M. PHIPPS; GERARD HURLEY; LINCOLN DALL; GREGORY PLATA, O.F.M.; LENIN VARGAS; Rev. Msgr. ELVIN SUNDS, Ex Officio; Mrs. PAMELA MINNINGER; Miss MARY WOODWARD.

Promoter of Justice—Rev. Msgr. MICHAEL FLANNERY, J.C.L.

Defenders of the Bond—Rev. Msgr. ELVIN SUNDS; Revs. DANIEL GALLAGHER; THOMAS MCGING, J.C.L. at First Instance; RICARDO M. PHIPPS; Sr. JOYCE HOBEN, S.N.D.N., J.C.L.

Notaries—Rev. MICHAEL O'BRIEN; MARYBETH RABERT; JUDY CANNON.

Diocesan Judges—Very Rev. JEFFREY WALDREP, S.T.L., J.C.L.; Revs. KEVIN SLATTERY, J.C.L.; XAVIER COLAVECHIO, O.Praem., S.T.D.

Approved Advocate and Auditors—Revs. JOHN BOHN; CHARLES BUCCIANTINI; FRANCIS J. COSGROVE; ROBERT GOODYEAR, S.T.; BRIAN KASKIE; JOSEPH TONOS; MATTHEW P. SIMMONS.

Priests' Council—Most Rev. JOSEPH N. LATINO, Pres.; Rev. Msgr. ELVIN SUNDS, Sec.; Very Rev. JEFFREY WALDREP, S.T.L., J.C.L., Treas.; Revs. MICHAEL O'BRIEN; JOSEPH DYER; LINCOLN DALL; THOMAS LALOR; DAVID O'CONNOR; SAMUEL MESSINA, Chm.; GREGORY PLATA, O.F.M.; EDWARD J. ZEMLIK, S.C.J.; DARRELL C. KELLY, S.V.D.; LENIN VARGAS; FRANCIS J. COSGROVE.

Diocesan Consultors—Most Rev. JOSEPH N. LATINO, Pres.; Rev. Msgr. MICHAEL FLANNERY, J.C.L.; Revs. FRANCIS J. COSGROVE; THOMAS LALOR; MICHAEL O'BRIEN; KEVIN SLATTERY, J.C.L.; Rev. Msgrs. ELVIN SUNDS, (Ex Officio); PATRICK FARRELL.

Association of Priests—Most Revs. JOSEPH N. LATINO, Co-Chm.; ROGER P. MORIN, Co-Chm.; Rev. Msgrs. PATRICK FARRELL, Pres.; MICHAEL THORNTON, Sec., Treas. & Pres.-Elect. Trustees: Revs. CHARLES BUCCIANTINI; THOMAS CONWAY; THOMAS MCGING, J.C.L.; PATRICK MOCKLER.

Diocesan Pastoral Council—Most Rev. JOSEPH N. LATINO, Pres.

Personnel Board—Rev. Msgrs. ELVIN SUNDS, Personnel Dir.; PATRICK FARRELL; Revs. WILLIAM HENRY; MICHAEL O'BRIEN; KEVIN SLATTERY, J.C.L.; MATTHEW P. SIMMONS.

Department of Administration & Finance—Mr. WILLIAM P. DUNNING, Dir., Admin. Affairs, 237 E. Amite St., P.O. Box 2248, Jackson, 39225-2248.

Department of Stewardship - Development—Mrs. REBECCA HARRIS, Dir.

Catholic Foundation—Mrs. REBECCA HARRIS, Dir., 237 E. Amite St., P.O. Box 2248, Jackson, 39225-2248.

Department of Catholic Charities and Community Services—

Catholic Charities, Inc.—Mr. GREGORY PATIN, Dir., 200 N. Congress, Ste. 100, Jackson, 39201. Tel: 601-355-8634; Fax: 601-960-8493. Mailing Address: P.O. Box 2248, Jackson, 39225-2248.

Parish-Based Ministries—MICHAEL ANN OROPEZA, Dir. Parish Social Ministry. Tel: 601-355-8634; Mrs. LOUISE DILLON, Dir. Family Ministry.

Peace and Justice—Mr. GREGORY PATIN, Dir., Mailing Address: P.O. Box 2248, Jackson, 39225-2248.

Victim Assistance Coordinator—Mrs. LOUISE DILLON. Tel: 601-326-3728. Email: louise.dillon@catholiccharitiesjackson.org.

Department of Formational Ministries—Sr. DEBORAH HUGHES, S.S.J., Dir., 237 E. Amite St., P.O. Box 2248, Jackson, 39225-2248.

Superintendent of Schools—Sr. DEBORAH HUGHES, S.S.J.

Assistant Superintendent—Ms. CATHERINE D. COOK.

Director of Faith Formation—Mrs. ALICE HUGHES.

Director of Spring Hill Theology Program—Mrs. ALICE HUGHES.

Holy Childhood Pontifical Association—Ms. CATHERINE D. COOK, Dir.

Early Child Development, Health and Education Projects—Sr. DEBORAH HUGHES, S.S.J.

Department of Evangelization—Miss MARY WOODWARD, Dir.

Charismatic Renewal—Rev. WILLIAM F. HENRY.

Cursillo Movement—Rev. DANIEL GALLAGHER, Spiritual Dir.

"Mississippi Catholic"—JANNA AVALON, Editor.

CLERGY, PARISHES, MISSIONS AND PAROCHIAL SCHOOLS

CITY OF JACKSON

(HINDS COUNTY)

1—ST. PETER CATHEDRAL (1846) Very Rev. Jeffrey Waldrep, Rector.
Res.: 123 N. West St., P.O. Box 57, 39205-0057. Tel: 601-969-3125; Fax: 601-969-3130. Web: cathedralsaintpeter.org.
Catechesis/Religious Program—Ferrell Tadlock, D.R.E. Students 44.

2—CHRIST THE KING (1945) Rev. Ricardo M. Phipps.
Res.: 2303 John R. Lynch St., 39209. Tel: 601-948-8867.
School—Sister Thea Bowman School, (Grades PreK-6), 1217 Hattiesburg St., 39209-7411. Tel: 601-352-5441; Fax: 601-352-5136. Gladys Shae Goodman-Robinson, Prin. Students 70.
Catechesis/Religious Program—Mrs. Frankie Bradley, D.R.E. Students 60.

3—HOLY FAMILY (1957) Revs. Michael O'Brien; Lincoln Dall; Sr. Eileen Hauswald, O.S.F., Pastoral Assoc.
Church: 820 Forest Ave., 39206-3299. Tel: 601-362-1888; Fax: 601-362-1134. Email: holyfamilycc@comcast.net. Web: www.holyfamilycjackson.org.
Catechesis/Religious Program—Joyce Adams, C.R.E.; Gladys Russell, C.R.E. Students 28.

4—HOLY GHOST (1908) Rev. Darrell C. Kelly, S.V.D.
Res.: 1151 Cloister St., 39202. Tel: 601-353-1339; Fax: 601-353-9607.

5—ST. MARY (1948) Rev. Ricardo M. Phipps.
Res.: 653 Claiborne Ave., 39209. Tel: 601-353-2292; Fax: 601-354-3716.
Catechesis/Religious Program—Mrs. Frankie Bradley, D.R.E. Students 14.

6—ST. RICHARD OF CHICHESTER (1953) Revs. Michael O'Brien; Lincoln Dall. In Res., Rev. Msgr. Elvin Sunds.
Church: 1242 Lynnwood Dr., P.O. Box 16547, 39206. Tel: 601-366-2335; Fax: 601-366-0438. Web: www.saintrichard.com.
School—(Grades PreK-6), 100 Holly Dr., 39206. Tel: 601-366-1157; Fax: 601-366-4344. Web: www-.strichardschool.com. Jules Michel, Prin.; Paulette Cockrell, Librarian. Lay Teachers 31; Students 470.
St. Richard's School Special Kids Program— Lay Teachers 1; Students 3.
Catechesis/Religious Program—Allyson Harris, D.R.E. Students 291.

7—ST. THERESE (1955) Rev. William Henry.
Church: 309 McDowell Rd., P.O. Box 8642, 39284-8642. Tel: 601-372-4481; Fax: 601-376-0094.
School—(Grades PreK-6) Tel: 601-372-3323; Fax: 601-372-3365. Karla Luke, Co-Prin.; Carol McWilliams, Co-Prin. Lay Teachers 10; Students 101.

OUTSIDE THE CITY OF JACKSON

ABERDEEN, MONROE CO., ST. FRANCIS OF ASSISI (1977) Rev. Vincent Burns; Susan Sweet, Pastoral Assoc.
Res. & Church: 108 S. James St., P.O. Box 134, 39730-0134. Tel: 662-319-6657. Email: stfa@juno.com.
Catechesis/Religious Program—Students 8.
Mission—Immaculate Heart of Mary (1942) P.O. Box 309, Houston, Chickasaw Co. 38851. Tel: 662-456-5450. Sr. Pat Hinton, O.S.F., Pastoral Min.
Mission—St. Theresa 116 N. Fleming St., Okolona, Chickasaw Co. 38860. Tel: 662-447-3008. Sr. Elizabeth Brown, C.S.J., Lay Ecclesial Min.

ACKERMAN, CHOCTAW CO., ST. MARK (2001) Sr. Alies Therese, Lay Ecclesial Min.
Mailing Address: 181 E. Main St., P.O. Box 1293, 39735. Tel: 662-285-3347.
Catechesis/Religious Program—Students 8.

AMORY, MONROE CO., ST. HELEN (1977) Sr. Florita Rodman, C.D.P., Lay Ecclesial Min.
Res.: 401 Eighth Ave. S., P.O. Box 97, 38821-0097. Tel: 662-256-8392; Fax: 662-256-8392 (call first).
Catechesis/Religious Program—Nancy Hoang, D.R.E. Students 35.

BATESVILLE, PANOLA CO., ST. MARY (1960) Rev. Samuel Messina.
Res.: 120 Hwy. 35 N., P.O. Box 569, 38606-0569. Tel: 662-563-2273; Fax: 662-563-9788. Email: saintmarycc@bellsouth.net. Web: www.stmarysstjohn.org.
Catechesis/Religious Program—Tel: 662-563-1197. Sharon Hodge, D.R.E. Students 39.
Mission—St. John the Baptist 110 N. Main St., Sardis, Panola Co. 38666.

BELZONI, HUMPHREYS CO., ALL SAINTS (1953) Rev. Walter Brown.
Church: 200 Bowles St., 39038-3602. Tel: 662-247-1408; Fax: 662-247-1504.
Catechesis/Religious Program—Paul Alleman, D.R.E. Students 7.

BOONEVILLE, PRENTISS CO., ST. FRANCIS OF ASSISI (1962) Rev. Richard Smith, Sacramental Min.; Sr. Colette Fahrner, S.L.W., Lay Ecclesial Min.
Church: 721 N. College St., P.O. Box 654, 38829. Tel: 662-728-7509; Fax: 662-728-7509. Email: stfrancischurch@shsm.org. Web: stfrancisbooneville.com.
Res.: 200 Washington St., 38829. Tel: 662-728-2257.
Catechesis/Religious Program—Students 22.
Mission—St. Mary 205 Eastport St. E., P.O. Box 651, Iuka, Tishomingo Co. 38852. Tel: 662-423-9358; Fax: 662-423-9358. Email: stmarycath078710@bellsouth.net.

BROOKHAVEN, LINCOLN CO., ST. FRANCIS (1887) Rev. Matthew P. Simmons.
Res.: 227 E. Cherokee St., P.O. Box 196, 39602. Tel: 601-833-1799. Web: www.stfrancisbrookhaven.org.
Catechesis/Religious Program—Tel: 601-833-2709. Sue Jun Kin, D.R.E. Students 76.
Mission—St. Ann Meadville, Franklin Co.

BRUCE, CALHOUN CO., ST. LUKE THE EVANGELIST (1997) Sr. Mary Jean Morris, O.S.F., Lay Ecclesial Min.
Church: 209 W. Calhoun St., P.O. Box 230, 38915-0230. Tel: 662-983-4600; Fax: 662-983-4600. Email: stluke@tycom.net. Web: catholicweb.com.
Catechesis/Religious Program—Students 18.

CAMDEN, MADISON CO., SACRED HEART (1850) Rev. Michael Barth, S.T.
Res.: 1493 Hwy. 17, 39045-9524. Tel: 662-468-2354; 662-468-0550; Fax: 662-468-2488. Web: www.sacredheartcamden.com.
Parish Center - Sacred Heart Family Center: 1493 Hwy. 17, 39045.

CANTON, MADISON CO.

1—HOLY CHILD JESUS (1946) Revs. Kevin Slattery; Onwuham Akpa, O.Praem.
Church: 315 Garrett St., P.O. Box 366, 39046. Tel: 601-859-2957; Fax: 601-859-8011. Email: schccanton@bellsouth.net.
School—(Grades PreK-1), 315 Garrett St., 39046. Tel: 601-859-4168; Fax: 601-859-4140. Mrs. Felicia Stewart, Prin. Sisters 1; Lay Teachers 3; Students 50.
Catechesis/Religious Program—Sacred Heart Parish Center, 238 E. Center St., 39046. Sr. Mary Anne Poeschl, R.S.M., D.R.E.

2—SACRED HEART (1859) Revs. Kevin Slattery; Onwuham Akpa, O.Praem.
Res.: 238 E. Center St., P.O. Box 361, 39046-0361. Tel: 601-859-3749; Fax: 601-859-8011. Email: schccanton@bellsouth.net.
Catechesis/Religious Program—Sr. Mary Anne Poeschl, R.S.M., D.R.E. Students 26.

CARTHAGE, LEAKE CO., ST. ANNE (1954) [CEM] Sr. Patricia Godri, S.C., Lay Ecclesial Min.; Rev. Jeremy Tobin, O.Praem., Sacramental Min.
Res.: 207 Red Dog Rd., 39051. Tel: 601-267-7190; Fax: 601-267-7190.
Catechesis/Religious Program—Students 40.

CHARLESTON, TALLAHATCHIE CO., ST. JOHN (1973) Bro. Senan Gallagher, S.T., Deacon Ecclesial Min.
Church: 304 W. Cypress St., P.O. Box 30, 38921-0030. Tel: 662-647-3170.
Catechesis/Religious Program—Students 2.

CHATAWA, PIKE CO., ST. TERESA (1868) Rev. Brian Kaskie.
Church: P.O. Box 67, 39632-0067. Tel: 601-684-5648.
Mission—St. James Bay St., Magnolia, Pike Co. 39652.

CLARKSDALE, COAHOMA CO.

1—ST. ELIZABETH (1891) Rev. John Vollor.
Res.: 130 Florence Ave., 38614-2720. Tel: 662-624-4301; Fax: 662-627-7856.
School—(Grades PreK-6), 150 Florence Ave., 38614-2720. Tel: 662-624-4239; Fax: 662-624-2072. Mrs. Elizabeth Scarbrough, Prin.; Georgette Sabbatini, Librarian. Lay Teachers 9; Students 114.
Catechesis/Religious Program—Maria Fyfe, D.R.E. Students 78.

2—IMMACULATE CONCEPTION (1945) Rev. John Vollor; Bro. Matt Connors, S.V.D., Pastoral Min.
Res.: 510 Ritchie Ave., 38614. Tel: 662-624-4029.

CLEVELAND, BOLIVAR CO., OUR LADY OF VICTORIES (1924) Rev. Sean Atkinson.
Res.: 215 Bishop Rd., P.O. Box 1450, 38732-1450. Tel: 662-846-6273; Fax: 662-846-6270. Email: olvcc@tecinfo.ocm.
Catechesis/Religious Program—Melanie Bray, D.R.E. Students 134.
Station—Delta State University

CLINTON, HINDS CO., HOLY SAVIOR (1966) Rev. Thomas McGing.
Church: 714 Lindale St., P.O. Box 85, 39060-0085. Tel: 601-924-6344; Fax: 601-924-6344. Email: holysavior@exceedtech.net.
Catechesis/Religious Program—Tel: 601-924-6344; Fax: 601-924-6344. Dena Kinsey, D.R.E. Students 128.
Mission—Immaculate Conception Raymond, Hinds Co. Rev. Richard P. Chiles, O.Praem.

COLUMBUS, LOWNDES CO., ANNUNCIATION (1863) Rev. Robert Dore.
Res.: 823 College St., 39701. Tel: 662-328-2927; Fax: 662-329-8270.
School—(Grades K-6), 223 N. Browder St., 39702-5236. Tel: 662-328-4479; Fax: 662-328-0430. Mrs. Barbara Calland, Prin. Lay Teachers 14; Students 128.

CORINTH, ALCORN CO., ST. JAMES (1956) Rev. Richard Smith.

Church: 3189 Harper Rd., P.O. Box 660, 38835-0660. Tel: 662-287-1051; Fax: 662-287-1051 (call ahead). Email: stjamesc@comcast.net.
Res.: 3187 Harper Rd., P.O. Box 660, 38835-0660. Tel: 662-287-1385.
Catechesis/Religious Program—Linda Gunther, D.R.E.; Peggie Clapp, C.R.E. Students 60.

CRYSTAL SPRINGS, COPIAH CO., ST. JOHN THE EVANGELIST (1953) Rev. Thomas Delaney; Janice Stansell, Pastoral Min.
Church: 221 E. Georgetown St., P.O. Box 167, 39059-0167. Tel: 601-892-1717; Fax: 601-892-0746.
Rectory—221 E. Georgetown St., 39059.
Catechesis/Religious Program—Students 21.
Mission—St. Martin Hazlehurst, Copiah Co.

EUPORA, WEBSTER CO., ST. JOHN NEUMANN (1990) Sr. Alies Therese, Lay Ecclesial Min.; Mr. Lorenzo Aju, Pastoral Min.
Church: 2620 W. Roane Ave., 39744. Tel: 662-258-7539; Fax: 662-258-7539 (call ahead). Email: stjohnseupora@yahoo.com.
Catechesis/Religious Program—Mr. Lorenzo Aju, D.R.E. Students 20.

FAYETTE, JEFFERSON CO., ST. ANNE (1969) Rev. John O'Hallaran, S.S.J.
Church: 89 Harriston Rd., P.O. Box 159, 39069. Tel: 601-445-5700; Fax: 601-442-6030.
Catechesis/Religious Program—Belinda Nickels, D.R.E. Students 12.

FLOWOOD, RANKIN CO., ST. PAUL (1978) Rev. Brian Carroll.
Church: 5971 Hwy. 25, 39232-7101. Tel: 601-992-9547; Fax: 601-992-9972. Email: saintpaulchurch@hotmail.com. Web: www.saintpaulcatholicchurch.com.
Res.: 108 Twin Oaks Dr., Brandon, 39047. Tel: 601-992-3222.
Learning Center—5969 Hwy. 25, 39232. Tel: 601-992-2876; Fax: 601-992-8741. Darlene Scanlon, Dir. Students 115.
Catechesis/Religious Program—Sarah O'Donnell, C.R.E. Students 240.

FOREST, SCOTT CO., ST. MICHAEL (1957) Rev. Joseph Dyer.
Church: P.O. Box 388, 39074. Tel: 601-469-1916; Fax: 601-469-1815.
Res.: 1352 E. Third St., 39074.
Catechesis/Religious Program—Students 40.
Mission—St. Anne 608 Decatur St., Newton, Newton Co. 39045.
Station—Centro San Martin De Porres Hwy. 80 W., Morton, 39117.

GLUCKSTADT, MADISON CO., ST. JOSEPH (1905) Rev. Kevin Slattery, Sacramental Min.; Mrs. Pamela Minninger, Lay Ecclesial Min.
127 Church Rd., 39110. Tel: 601-856-2054; Fax: 601-856-2054. Email: stjoegluckstadt@bellsouth.net. Web: stjosephgluckstadt.com.
Catechesis/Religious Program—Stephanie Word, C.R.E. Students 133.

GREENVILLE, WASHINGTON CO.

1—ST. JOSEPH (1868) Rev. Richard Somers. In Res., Rev. Frank Corcoran (Retired).
Res.: 410 Main St., P.O. Box 1220, 38702-1220. Tel: 662-335-5251; Fax: 662-332-1178.
School—Our Lady of Lourdes, (Grades PreK-6), 1600 E. Reed St., 38703-7229. Tel: 662-334-3287; Fax: 662-332-9877. Mrs. Michelle Gardiner, Prin. Sisters 2; Lay Teachers 23; Students 285.
High School—Junior & Senior High School, (Grades 7-12), 1501 VFW Rd., 38701-5841. Tel: 662-378-9711; Fax: 662-378-3496. Mr. Paul Artman, Prin. Students 245.

2—SACRED HEART (1913) Revs. Thomas A. Mullally, S.V.D.; Tarsisius Puling, S.V.D.
Res.: 560 E. Gloster St., 38701-3836. Tel: 662-332-0891; Fax: 662-332-0891. Email: mullally42@yahoo.com. Web: www.shcc-greenville.org.
Catechesis/Religious Program—Students 25.

GREENWOOD, LEFLORE CO.

1—ST. FRANCIS OF ASSISI (1951) Revs. Gregory Plata, O.F.M.; Robert Konopa, O.F.M. In Res., Rev. William Stout, O.F.M.
Res.: 2613 Hwy. 82 E., 38930-5966. Tel: 662-453-0623; Fax: 662-453-9060. Email: themission@bellsouth.net.
School—(Grades PreK-6), 2607 Hwy. 82 E., 38930-5966. Tel: 662-453-9511; Fax: 662-453-9060. Email: stfran@bellsouth.net. Web: www.stfrancisassisi.com. Sr. Carol Seidl, O.S.F., Prin. Sisters 6; Lay Teachers 9; Students 120.
Catechesis/Religious Program—Sr. Elaine Turba, D.R.E. Students 25.
Convent—Franciscan Sisters of Christian Charity, 2603 Hwy. 82 E., 38930-5966. Tel: 662-453-1221; Fax: 662-453-9060.

2—IMMACULATE HEART OF MARY (1909) Revs. Gregory Plata, O.F.M.; William Stout, O.F.M.
Church: 511 W. Washington St., P.O. Box 313, 38935-0313. Tel: 662-453-3980.
Parish Center/Church Office—310 Henderson St., 38935-0313. Fax: 662-453-0399.
Catechesis/Religious Program—Students 67.

GRENADA, GRENADA CO., ST. PETER (1943) Rev. Martin Ruane.
Res.: 320 College Blvd., 38901-3808. Tel: 662-226-2490.
Catechesis/Religious Program—Donna Mumme, D.R.E. Students 85.

HERNANDO, DESOTO CO., HOLY SPIRIT (1961) Revs. Robert Tucker, S.C.J., Moderator; Timothy Gray, S.C.J.; Edward J. Zemlik, S.C.J.
Church: 545 E. Commerce St., P.O. Box 424, 38632-0424. Tel: 662-429-7851; Fax: 662-429-7882. Email: holyspiritchurch@shsm.org. Web: www.holyspirit-catholic.com.
Catechesis/Religious Program—Tel: 662-429-3467. Amanda Ready, C.R.E. Students 124.

HOLLY SPRINGS, MARSHALL CO., ST. JOSEPH (1857) Rev. Leonard F. Elder, S.C.J.
Church: 305 E. Van Dorn Ave., P.O. Box 430, 38635-0430. Tel: 662-252-3138; Fax: 662-252-3138.
School—Holy Family School, (Grades PreK-8), 395 N. West St., 38635-1922. Tel: 662-252-1612; Fax: 662-252-3694. Clara Isom, Prin. Sisters 1; Lay Teachers 20; Students 135.
Catechesis/Religious Program—Students 10.

INDIANOLA, SUNFLOWER CO.

1—ST. BENEDICT THE MOOR (1953) Revs. Thomas A. Mullally, S.V.D.; Tarsisius Puling, S.V.D.
Res.: 403 Church Ave., P.O. Box 407, 38751. Tel: 662-887-4659.
Catechesis/Religious Program—Rosemary Miller, D.R.E. Students 11.

2—IMMACULATE CONCEPTION (1955) Revs. Thomas A. Mullally, S.V.D.; Tarsisius Puling, S.V.D.
Res.: 700 N. Sunflower Ext. Hwy. 448, P.O. Box 944, 38751-9665. Tel: 662-887-4659.
Catechesis/Religious Program—Rosemary Miller, D.R.E. Students 26.

KOSCIUSKO, ATTALA CO., ST. THERESE (1956) Barbara A. Sturbaum, Lay Ecclesial Min.
Res.: 108 Bell St., P.O. Box 628, 39090. Tel: 662-289-1193.
Catechesis/Religious Program—Students 25.

LELAND, WASHINGTON CO., ST. JAMES (1944) Rev. Charles Bucciantini.
Res.: 312 E. Third St., P.O. Box 352, 38756-0352. Tel: 662-686-7352; Fax: 662-686-7352. Email: stjamesch@yahoo.com.
Mission—Immaculate Conception Hwy. 12 E., Hollandale, Washington Co. 38748.
Mission—Our Mother of Mercy 119 Jefferson St., Anguilla, Sharkey Co. 38721.

LEXINGTON, HOLMES CO., ST. THOMAS (1966) Rev. Gregory Plata, O.F.M., Admin.
Church: 200 Boulevard St., 39095. Tel: 662-453-0623; Fax: 662-453-9060.
Catechesis/Religious Program—Students 11.
Mission—Sacred Heart 304 Jones St., Winona, Montgomery Co. 38967. Tel: 662-453-0623. Rev. Gregory Plata, O.F.M.

LOUISVILLE, WINSTON CO., SACRED HEART (1966) Barbara A. Sturbaum, Lay Ecclesial Min.
Res.: 410 Spring Ave., 39339. Tel: 662-773-6062.
Catechesis/Religious Program—Students 1.

MADISON, MADISON CO., ST. FRANCIS OF ASSISI (1983) Rev. Msgr. Michael Flannery; Rev. Kent Bowlds. In Res., Rev. Alfred L. Camp (Retired).
Office: 4000 W. Tidewater Ln., 39110-8942. Tel: 601-856-5556; Fax: 601-856-2849. Web: www.stfrancismadison.org.
School—St. Anthony Catholic School, (Grades PreK-6), 1585 Old Mannsdale Rd., 39110. Tel: 601-607-7054. Angela Brunini, Prin. Lay Teachers 25; Students 160.
Learning Center—Tel: 601-856-9494. Sr. Paula Blouin, S.S.N.D., Dir. Students 168.
Catechesis/Religious Program—Mary Catherine George, D.R.E. Students 585.

MAGEE, SIMPSON CO., ST. STEPHEN (1968) Mrs. Eula Purvis, Lay Ecclesial Min.
Res.: 594 Simpson Hwy. 149, P.O. Box 427, 39111-0427. Tel: 601-849-3237; Fax: 601-849-3398.
Catechesis/Religious Program—Alicia Keith, D.R.E. Tel: 601-849-3539. Students 24.

MCCOMB, PIKE CO., ST. ALPHONSUS (1876) Rev. Brian Kaskie.
Church: 509 Delaware Ave., P.O. Box 1105, 39649. Tel: 601-684-5648; Fax: 601-684-1924.
Elementary and Preschool—(Grades PreK-6), 104 S. 5th St., 39648. Tel: 601-684-1843; Fax: 601-684-1831. Mrs. Tammy Mabile, Prin. Students 200.
Catechesis/Religious Program—Annette Gabler, D.R.E. Students 231.

MERIDIAN, LAUDERDALE CO.

1—ST. JOSEPH (1910) Revs. Francis J. Cosgrove; Lenin Vargas; Edgar Hernandez, Pastoral Min.
Church & Mailing Address: 1914 18th Ave., P.O. Box 532, 39302-0532. Tel: 601-485-5349; Fax: 601-484-8953. Web: www.stpatsofmeridian.org.
Catechesis/Religious Program—Students 21.

2—ST. PATRICK (1865) Revs. Francis J. Cosgrove; Lenin Vargas; Edgar Hernandez, Pastoral Min.
Church & Mailing Address: 2601 Davis St., P.O. Box 529, 39302. Tel: 601-693-1321; Fax: 601-484-8953. Web: www.stpatsofmeridian.org.
Res.: 204-39th Ct., 39301. Tel: 601-693-2574.
School—(Grades PreK-6), 2700 Davis St., 39301. Tel: 601-482-6044; Fax: 601-485-2762. Email: jaxsp@people.com. Web: www.stpatrickcatholicschool.org. Julie Bordelon, Prin.; Sheri Wall, Librarian. Lay Teachers 9; Students 123.
Catechesis/Religious Program—Students 185.

MOUND BAYOU, BOLIVAR CO., ST. GABRIEL (1949) [CEM] Rev. John Vollor, Sacramental Min.; Bro. Pius Kamphefner, F.S.C., Lay Ecclesial Min.
Mailing Address: P.O. Box 53, 38762-0053.
Res. & Church: 501 Martin Luther King St., 38762-0053. Tel: 662-741-2439.

NATCHEZ, ADAMS CO.

1—ASSUMPTION OF THE B.V.M. (1957) Rev. David O'Connor.
Res.: 10 Morgantown Rd., 39120-2788. Tel: 601-442-7250; Fax: 601-442-7250.
Catechesis/Religious Program—Students 17.

2—HOLY FAMILY (1891) Rev. John O'Hallaran, S.S.J.
Res.: 16 Orange Ave., 39120. Tel: 601-445-5700; Fax: 601-442-6030.
School—(Grades PreK-K), 8 Orange Ave., 39120-3647. Tel: 601-442-3947; Fax: 601-442-3973. Mrs. Ira Young, Co-Dir.; Sr. Bernadette McNamara, Co-Dir. Sisters 3; Lay Teachers 5; Students 95.
Catechesis/Religious Program—Sr. Kathleen Higgins, S.H.Sp., D.R.E. Students 44.
Convent—Sisters of the Holy Spirit, 26 Orange Ave., 39120. Tel: 601-445-6785; Fax: 601-442-3973.
Mission—St. John the Baptist Cranfield, Adams Co.

3—ST. MARY BASILICA (1842) Rev. David O'Connor.
Res.: 107 S. Union St., P.O. Box 1044, 39121-1044. Tel: 601-445-5616; Fax: 601-445-9631. Email: stmarybasilica@cableone.net. Web: www.stmarybasilica.org.
Catechesis/Religious Program—Ruth Powers, D.R.E. Students 623.

NEW ALBANY, UNION CO., ST. FRANCIS OF ASSISI (1949) Rev. Mario Solorzano.
Res.: 1507 S. Central Ave., P.O. Box 887, 38652-0887.
Church: 650 Hwy. 15 S., P.O. Box 887, 38652-0887. Tel: 662-534-4654; Fax: 662-534-4654.
Mission—St. Christopher 431 Pineridge Dr., P.O. Box 67, Pontotoc, Pontotoc Co. 38863-0067. Tel: 662-489-7749. Rev. Timothy Murphy.

OLIVE BRANCH, DESOTO CO., QUEEN OF PEACE (1983) Rev. Terence Langley, S.C.J.; Deacon Henry Babin.
Res.: 8455 Germantown Rd., P.O. Box 65, 38654-0065. Tel: 662-895-5007; Fax: 662-895-5036.
Catechesis/Religious Program—Mrs. Victoria Stirek, D.R.E. Students 212.

OXFORD, LAFAYETTE CO., ST. JOHN THE EVANGELIST (1943) Rev. Joseph Tonos.
Church: 416 S. 5th St., 38655-3806. Tel: 662-234-6073; Fax: 662-234-6079.
Catechesis/Religious Program—Susan Kelly, D.R.E. Students 134.

PAULDING, JASPER CO., ST. MICHAEL (1843) Rev. Joseph Dyer.
Mailing Address: P.O. Box 388, Forest, 39074-0388. Tel: 601-469-1916.
Church: Star Rte., P.O. Box 15, 39348. Tel: 601-469-1916.
Catechesis/Religious Program—

PEARL, RANKIN CO., ST. JUDE (1962) Rev. Gerard Hurley.
Rectory—399 Barrow St., P.O. Box 5526, 39288-5526. Tel: 601-939-3181 (Office); 601-939-1863; Fax: 601-939-3160. Email: stjudescatholicc@bellsouth.net. Web: www.saintjudecatholicchurch.org.
Catechesis/Religious Program—Virginia Brown, D.R.E. Students 129.
Station—Mississippi State Mental Hospital Whitfield.

PHILADELPHIA, NESHOBA CO.

1—HOLY CROSS (1860) Rev. Kenan Ryan, S.T.
Res.: 406 Wilson St., 39350-2906. Tel: 601-656-1841; Fax: 601-650-9098.

2—HOLY ROSARY (Tucker Community) (1884) Rev. Robert Goodyear, S.T.
Res.: 10131 Holy Rosary Rd., P.O. Box 37, 39350. Tel: 601-656-2880; Fax: 601-656-2829.
Catechesis/Religious Program—Students 52.
Mission—St. Catherine 9857 Hwy. 489, Conehatta, Newton Co. 39057.
Mission—St. Theresa, Neshoba Co.

PORT GIBSON, CLAIBORNE CO., ST. JOSEPH (1849) Rev. Faustin Misakabo, O.Praem.
Church: 411 Coffee St., P.O. Box 1012, 39150. Tel: 601-437-5790.
Catechesis/Religious Program—Students 2.

RIPLEY, TIPPAH CO., ST. MATTHEW (1997) Sr. Kate Regan, C.S.J., Lay Ecclesial Min.

Res.: 103 Hospital St., P.O. Box 452, 38663. Tel: 662-837-8391; Fax: 662-837-8391.
Catechesis/Religious Program—Students 63.

ROBINSONVILLE, TUNICA CO., GOOD SHEPHERD CATHOLIC CHURCH (2009) Revs. Robert Tucker, S.C.J., Moderator; Timothy Gray, S.C.J.; Edward Zemlik, S.C.J.
Church: 1329 Casino Center Dr. Ext., P.O. Box 70, 38664. Tel: 662-357-0250; 662-342-1073 (Southaven); Fax: 662-342-7733 (Southaven).
Convent—School Sisters of St. Francis, P.O. Box 237, Walls, 38680. Tel: 662-781-0807. School Sisters of St. Francis 1; Sisters of Mercy 1.
Mission—Sacred Heart 6473 Hwy. 161 N., P.O. Box 60, Walls, DeSoto Co. 38680-0060. Tel: 662-781-0450; Fax: 662-429-8423.

ROSEDALE, BOLIVAR CO., SACRED HEART (1968) Sisters Celia Evers, O.P., Pastoral Min.; Catherine Leamy, S.N.J.M., Lay Ecclesial Min.; Rev. Sean Atkinson.
Res.: 113 Railroad St., P.O. Box 307, 38769. Tel: 662-759-6341.
Catechesis/Religious Program—Students 2.
Station—Mississippi State Penitentiary Parchman, 38738. Tel: 662-745-6611.

SENATOBIA, TATE CO., ST. GREGORY THE GREAT (1978) Revs. Robert Tucker, S.C.J., Moderator; Timothy Gray, S.C.J.; Edward J. Zemlik, S.C.J.
Church: 705 Strayhorn St., P.O. Box 129, 38668-0129. Tel: 662-562-5318; Fax: 662-429-8423.

SHAW, BOLIVAR CO., ST. FRANCIS OF ASSISI (1949) Revs. Thomas A. Mullally, S.V.D.; Tarsisius Puling, S.V.D.; Dr. Florence Louise Ouzts, Pastoral Min.
Res.: 303 Dean Blvd., P.O. Box 239, 38773. Tel: 662-754-5561; Fax: 662-754-5561.

SHELBY, BOLIVAR CO., ST. MARY (1905) Sr. Jo Ann Villademoras, S.S.N.D., Lay Ecclesial Min.
Church: 700 Second St., P.O. Box 208, 38774-0208. Tel: 662-398-7964.

SOUTHAVEN, DESOTO CO., CHRIST THE KING (1974) Revs. Robert Tucker, S.C.J., Moderator; Timothy Gray, S.C.J.; Edward J. Zemlik, S.C.J.
Office: 785 Church Rd. W., 38671. Tel: 662-342-1073; Fax: 662-342-7733. Email: ctkshaven@aol.com. Web: www.ctkshaven.com.
School—Sacred Heart Elementary School, (Grades PreK-8), 5150 Tchulahoma Rd., 38671. Tel: 662-349-0900; Fax: 662-349-0690. Ms. Catherine Warwick, Prin.
Catechesis/Religious Program—Donna Williamson, D.R.E.

STARKVILLE, OKTIBBEHA CO., ST. JOSEPH (1930) Rev. John Bohn.
Res.: 607 University Dr., 39759. Tel: 662-323-2257; Fax: 662-323-2258.
Catechesis/Religious Program—Geraldine Orgler, D.R.E. Students 186.
Mission—Corpus Christi P.O. Box 533, Macon, Noxubee Co. 39341.
Chaplaincy—Mississippi State University, 39760.

TUPELO, LEE CO., ST. JAMES (1908) Rev. Thomas Lalor.
Church: 845 Lakeshire Dr., P.O. Box 734, 38802. Tel: 662-842-4881; Fax: 662-844-0327. Email: st_james_parish@comcast.net. Web: www.saint-james.net.
Res.: 757 Lakeshire Dr., 38804. Tel: 662-840-7628.
Catechesis/Religious Program—Dawn Steinman, D.R.E.; Mary Ann Plasensia, D.R.E. Students 281.
Mission—St. Thomas Aquinas Saltillo, Lee Co.
Mission—Christ the King 100 E. Main St., P.O. Box 614, Fulton, Itawamba Co. 38843-0614. Tel: 662-862-2239; Fax: 662-862-2239. Don Stephan, Lay Ecclesial Min.

VICKSBURG, WARREN CO.

1—ST. MARY (1906) Rev. Malcolm O'Leary, S.V.D., Admin.
Res.: 1512 Main St., 39183. Tel: 601-636-0115; Fax: 601-661-0677.
Catechesis/Religious Program—Tel: 601-638-3890; Fax: 601-638-3822. Leona Barnes Stringer, D.R.E. Students 43.

2—ST. MICHAEL (1966) Rev. Patrick Curley.
Res.: 100 St. Michael Pl., 39180-8246. Tel: 601-636-3445; Fax: 601-636-3534.

3—ST. PAUL (1848) [CEM] Rev. Msgr. Patrick Farrell.
Res.: 713 Crawford St., 39180-0646. Tel: 601-636-0140; Fax: 601-638-5021. Email: stpaulvick@att.net.
High School—Vicksburg Catholic School, (Grades PreK-12) Tel: 601-636-2256; Fax: 601-631-0430. Ms. Michele Townsend, Prin. See High Schools, Inter-Parochial under Institutions Located in the Diocese.
Catechesis/Religious Program—Terri Booth, D.R.E. Students 84.

WALLS, DESOTO CO., SACRED HEART (1944), See Good Shepherd, Robinsville.
Res.: *St. Michael Cummunity House*, P.O. Box 38, Nesbit, 38651.
Church: 6473 Hwy. 161 N., P.O. Box 60, 38680-0060. Tel: 662-781-0450; Fax: 662-429-8423.
Convent—School Sisters of St. Francis, P.O. Box 237, 38680. Tel: 662-781-0807. School Sisters of St. Francis 1; Sisters of Mercy 1.
Mission—Sacred Heart P.O. Box 60, DeSoto Co. 38680-0060.

WEST POINT, CLAY CO., IMMACULATE CONCEPTION (1965) Rev. Robert Dore, Sacramental Min.
Res.: 617 E. Main, 39773-3007. Tel: 662-494-3486. Email: immaculatecon904@bellsouth.net.
Catechesis/Religious Program—Students 35.

WOODVILLE, WILKINSON CO., ST. JOSEPH (1873) Rev. Patrick Smith.
Res.: 338 Church St., P.O. Box 668, 39669. Tel: 601-888-3261; Fax: 601-888-3129. Email: stjoewms@bellsouth.net.
Mission—St. Patrick Fort Adams, Wilkinson Co.
Mission—Holy Family P.O. Box 548, Gloster, Amite Co. 39638. Tel: 601-225-4171.

YAZOO CITY, YAZOO CO.

1—ST. FRANCIS (1940) Rev. Walter Brown.
Res.: 735 E. Powell St., 39194-4398. Tel: 662-746-1680.

2—ST. MARY (1851) Rev. Walter Brown.
Church: 129 N. Washington St., P.O. Box 27, 39194-0027. Tel: 662-746-1680.

Chaplains of Public Institutions

JACKSON. *Institute for the Blind, Institute for the Deaf and Speech Impaired*. Rev. Michael O'Brien.
University of Mississippi Medical Center. Vacant.
Veterans Administration Hospital. Rt. Rev. E. Thomas DeWane, O.Praem.

MERIDIAN. *East Mississippi State Hospital*. Rev. Francis J. Cosgrove.

PARCHMAN. *Mississippi State Penitentiary*. Sr. Catherine Leamy, S.N.J.M.

PEARL. *Rankin County Prison*. Rev. Gerard Hurley.

SANATORIUM. *Boswell Retardation Center*. Rev. Joseph P. Keenan, S.T., Mrs. Eula Purvis, Chap.

WHITFIELD. *Mississippi State Hospital*. Rev. Gerard Hurley.

On Leave for Studies:
Rev.—
Quyet, Anthony

On Leave:
Rev.—
Daniels, Jerrell Michael

Retired:
Most Rev.—
Houck, William R., D.D.
Rev. Msgrs.—
Harkins, Thaddeus, St. Catherine's Village, 200 Dominican Dr. #S-247, Madison, 39110.
Koury, Joseph A., 105 Abby Oak Dr., Clinton, 39056.
Revs.—
Balser, Edward, 381 St. Augustine Dr., Madison, 39110.
Brock, John, 306 Briarwood Rd., #3-B, Natchez, 39120.
Camp, Alfred L., St. Francis of Assisi, 4000 W. Tidewater Ln., Madison, 39110-8942.
Corcoran, Frank, St. Joseph Church, P.O. Box 1220, Greenville, 38702-1220.
Cullen, William
Derivaux, Donald F., 2440 Ballground Rd., Vicksburg, 39183.
Johnson, Howard, St. Joseph Seminary, 1200 Varnum St., N.E., Washington, DC 20017.
Lopez, Jose
Niemira, Thomas, 3600 Fox Ridge, Lorena, TX 76655.
Noonan, Patrick
O'Riordan, James
Pentony, Liam, Parochia House, Dundalk, Co. Louth, Ireland.
Prendergast, Noel
Rietti, John, 1607 42nd Ave., Gulfport, 39501-3833.
Shelton, Henry

Permanent Deacons:
Agosta, Frank, (Retired)
Babin, Henry, Queen of Peace, Olive Branch
Baglioni, Victor, (Retired)
Baker, Sam, (Retired)
Campbell, Lawrence M., (Retired)
Klingen, Dr. Theodore, (Retired)
Pancratz, Arnold, (Retired)

INSTITUTIONS LOCATED IN THE DIOCESE

[A] HIGH SCHOOLS, INTER-PAROCHIAL

GREENVILLE. *St. Joseph Catholic School* (1888) (Grades 7-12), (Coed), 1501 VFW Road, 38701. Tel: 662-378-9711; Fax: 662-378-3496. Web: stjoeirish.com. Mr. Paul Artman, Prin.; Donna Goss, Librarian/Media Specialist. Lay Teachers 22; Students 225.

MADISON. *St. Joseph Catholic School* (1870) (Grades 7-12), (Coed), 308 New Mannsdale Rd., P.O. Box 2027, 39130-2027. Tel: 601-898-4800; Fax: 601-898-4689. Email: info@stjoebruins.com. Web: www.stjoebruins.com. Mr. William M. Heller, Prin.; Connie Machado, Librarian. Brothers 3; Sisters 2; Lay Teachers 63; Students 473.

NATCHEZ. *Cathedral School*, (Grades PreK-12), (Coed), 701 Martin Luther King, Jr. St., 39120. Tel: 601-442-2531; Fax: 601-442-0960. Mr. Patrick Sanguinetti, Prin. Lay Teachers 57; Students 666.

VICKSBURG. *Vicksburg Catholic School*, (Grades PreK-12), (Coed), 1900 Grove St., 39183. Tel: 601-636-2256; Fax: 601-631-0430. Web: www.vicksburgcatholic.org. Ms. Michele Townsend, Prin. Lay Teachers 47; Students 638.

[B] ELEMENTARY SCHOOLS INTER-PAROCHIAL

JACKSON. *Sister Thea Bowman School*, (Grades PreK-5), 1217 Hattiesburg St., 39209-7411. Tel: 601-352-5441; Fax: 601-352-5136. Mrs. Shae Robinson, Prin.; Sarah Walton, Librarian.

SOUTHAVEN. *Sacred Heart School* (1947) (Grades PreK-8), 5150 Tchulahoma Rd., 38671. Tel: 662-349-0900; Fax: 662-349-0690. Email: cwarwick@shsm.org. Ms. Catherine Warwick, Prin. Sisters 2; Lay Teachers 23; Students 338.

[C] GENERAL HOSPITALS

JACKSON. *St. Dominic-Jackson Memorial Hospital* (1946) 969 Lakeland Dr., 39216. Tel: 601-200-2000; Fax: 601-200-6800. Email: charbarger@stdom.com. Web: www.stdom.com. Sr. Kristin Rever, Prioress; Mr. Claude W. Harbarger, Pres.; Rev. Daniel Gallagher, Resident Chap. Sisters of St. Dominic of Springfield, IL 7; Bed Capacity 535; Patients Assisted Annually 119,754.

GLENDORA. *Glendora Clinic (Satellite of Tutwiler Clinic)* (1995) Gipson & Westbrook Sts., P.O. Box 189, 38928. Tel: 662-375-8878; Fax: 662-375-8878. Patients Assisted Annually 1,077.

TUTWILER. *Tutwiler Clinic, Inc.* (1983) 205 Alma St., P.O. Box 462, 38963-0462. Tel: 662-345-8334; Fax: 662-345-8336. Sr. Anne Brooks, S.N.J.M., D.O., Dir. Patients Assisted Annually 8,065.

[D] ORPHANAGES AND INFANT HOMES

JACKSON. *D'Evereaux Hall Home, Inc.*, P.O. Box 2248, 39225. Tel: 601-355-8634; Fax: 601-960-8493. Email: greg.patin@catholiccharitiesjackson.org. Mr. Gregory Patin, Exec. Dir.
St. Mary Orphan Home, Inc., P.O. Box 2248, 39225. Tel: 601-355-8634; Fax: 601-960-8493. Email: greg.patin@catholiccharitiesjackson.org. Mr. Gregory Patin, Exec. Dir.

[E] MONASTERIES AND RESIDENCES OF PRIESTS AND BROTHERS

JACKSON. *Christian Brothers Residence*, 625 Claiborne Ave., 39209. Bros. John Brennan, C.F.C.; Theodore Dausch, C.F.C.; Daniel Lauber, C.F.C.; Dennis Gunn, C.F.C. Congregation of Christian Brothers.
Priory of St. Moses the Black, 7100 Midway Rd., Raymond, 39154. Tel: 601-857-0157; Fax: 601-857-5076. Rt. Rev. E. Thomas DeWane, O.Praem., Abbot/Prior; Revs. Onwuham Akpa, O.Praem.; Richard P. Chiles, O.Praem.; Norbert N'Zilamba, O.Praem.; Jeremy Tobin, O.Praem.; Sebastian Schalk, O.Praem. Canons Regular of Premontre (The Premonstratensian Fathers). Priests 5.

NESBIT. *St. Michael Community House*, 1360 Nesbit Rd., P.O. Box 38, 38651. Tel: 662-429-8424; Fax: 662-429-8423. Email: fatherlen@juno.com. Revs. Leonard F. Elder, S.C.J., Coord.; Jack Kurps, S.C.J., Exec. Dir.; Timothy Gray, S.C.J.; Thomas Lind, S.C.J.; Robert Tucker, S.C.J.; Edward J. Zemlik, S.C.J.

[F] CONVENTS AND RESIDENCES FOR SISTERS

JACKSON. *St. Dominic Convent*, 969 Lakeland Dr., 39216. Tel: 601-200-6729; Fax: 601-944-0096. Email: strinita@stdom.com. Web: www.stdom.com. Dominican Sisters (Springfield, IL) 7.
St. Elizabeth Ann Seton (2001) Daughters of Charity., 4642 Trawick Dr., 39211-5834. Fax: 601-982-5183; 601-982-5183. Email: easdc@comcast.net. Web: www.doc-ecp.org. Daughters of Charity 2.
Our Lady of Mount Carmel and Little Flower Monastery (1951) 2155 Terry Rd., 39204. Tel: 601-373-1460; Fax: 601-372-1369. Email: jm2155jt@

aol.com. Sr. Margaret Mary Flynn, O.C.D., Prioress. Discalced Carmelites. Nuns with Solemn Vows 6.

CHATAWA. *St. Mary of the Pines*, 3167 Old Hwy. 51 S., P.O. Box 38, 39632. Tel: 601-783-3494; Fax: 601-783-5758. Sr. Georgiann Wildhaber, S.S.N.D., Admin.; Rev. Thomas Potts, S.V.D., Chap. Home for the Retired Sisters of the Dallas Province of the School Sisters of Notre Dame. Retreat Center for Lay and Religious Groups. Sisters in Residence 53.

GREENVILLE. *Our Lady of Lourdes Convent* (1964) 1600 E. Reed Rd., 38703-7229. Tel: 662-334-4337; 662-334-3287 (School); Fax: 662-332-9877. Email: alspaughm@tecinfo.com. Web: lourdes.greenville.ms.us. Sisters of St. Joseph.

GREENWOOD. *St. Francis Convent*, 2603 Hwy. 82 E., 38930-5966. Tel: 662-453-1221; Fax: 662-453-9060. Email: sjnorwick@hotmail.com. Web: www.stfrancisassisi.com. Franciscan Sisters of Christian Charity 4.

[G] RETREAT CENTERS

BROOKSVILLE. *The Dwelling Place*, 2824 Dwelling Place Rd., 39739-9796. Tel: 662-738-5348; Fax: 662-738-5345. Email: dwellpl@crawdat.com. Web: www.dwellingplace.com. Clare Van Lent, Dir.

CHATAWA. *St. Mary of the Pines*, 3167 Old Hwy. 51 S., P.O. Box 38, 39632. Tel: 601-783-3494; Fax: 601-783-5758. Sr. Georgiann Wildhaber, S.S.N.D., Admin.; Rev. Thomas Potts, S.V.D., Chap. Home for the Retired Sisters of the Dallas Province of the School Sisters of Notre Dame. Retreat Center for Lay and Religious Groups. Sisters in Residence 56.

[H] NEWMAN CENTERS

JACKSON. *Belhaven College Newman Center* P.O. Box 57, 39205-0057. Very Rev. Jeffrey Waldrep, S.T.L., J.C.L.

Jackson State University Newman Center c/o Christ the King, 2303 J.R. Lynch St., 39209-7498. Rev. Ricardo M. Phipps.

Millsaps College Newman Center P.O. Box 57, 39205-0057. Very Rev. Jeffrey Waldrep, S.T.L., J.C.L.

Tougaloo College Newman Center Holy Ghost Church, 1151 Cloister St., 39202. Tel: 601-353-1339. Rev. Darrell C. Kelly, S.V.D.

University of Mississippi Medical Center - Newman Center P.O. Box 57, 39205-0057. Very Rev. Jeffrey Waldrep, S.T.L., J.C.L.

BOONEVILLE. *Northeast Mississippi Community College Catholic Student Center St. Francis of Assisi*, P.O. Box 654, 38829. Tel: 662-728-7509; Fax: 662-728-7503. Email: stfrancischurch@shsm.org. Web: www.stfrancisbooneville.com. Sr. Colette Fahrner, S.L.W.

BROOKHAVEN. *Lincoln Junior College Newman Center* P.O. Box 196, 39602-0196. Tel: 601-833-1799. Rev. Matthew P. Simmons.

CLEVELAND. *Delta State University Newman Center Our Lady of Victories*, 215 Bishop Rd., P.O. Box 1450, 38732-1450. Tel: 662-846-6273. Rev. Sean Atkinson.

CLINTON. *Mississippi College Newman Center Holy Savior Church*, P.O. Box 85, 39060. Tel: 601-924-6344. Email: holysavior@att.net. Rev. Thomas McGing, J.C.L.

COLUMBUS. *Mississippi University for Women Student Center* Annunciation Church, 823 College St., 39701. Tel: 662-328-2927; Fax: 662-329-8270. Email: annunchr@bellsouth.net. Web: www.annunciationcatholicchurch.com. Rev. Robert Dore.

FOREST. *East Central Community College Newman Center St. Michael's Church*, P.O. Box 388, 39074. Tel: 601-469-1916; Fax: 601-469-1815. Rev. Joseph Dyer.

GOODMAN. *Holmes Community College Newman Center St. Thomas*, 200 Boulevard St., Lexington, 39095. Tel: 662-453-0623; Fax: 662-453-9060. Rev. Gregory Plata, O.F.M.

HOLLY SPRINGS. *Rust College Newman Center St. Joseph's*, P.O. Box 430, 38635. Tel: 662-252-3138; Fax: 662-252-3138. Mr. James Rayford Sr.

OXFORD. *Ole Miss Campus Ministries St. John Church*, 416 S. 5th St., 38655. Tel: 662-234-6073; Fax: 662-234-6079. Email: office@stjohnoxford.org. Rev. Joseph Tonos.

RAYMOND. *Hinds Community College Catholic Student Organization* 7100 Midway Rd., 39154. Tel: 601-857-0157. Rev. Jeremy Tobin, O.Praem.

STARKVILLE. *Mississippi State University Catholic Student Association* St. Joseph Church, 607 University Dr., 39759. Tel: 662-323-2257; Fax: 662-323-2258. Email: falavelle@hotmail.com. Web: www.msstate.edu/org/csa. Rev. John Bohn; Fran Lavelle, Campus Min.

[I] MISCELLANEOUS

JACKSON. *Jackson Diocese Educational Services, Inc.*, P.O. Box 2248, 39225-2248. Tel: 601-969-2742; Fax: 601-960-8469. Email: education.office@jacksondiocese.org. Sr. Deborah Hughes, S.S.J., Dir. Formational Ministries, Supt. Schools.

Parroquia De San Miguel Arcangel, P.O. Box 2248, 39225-2248. Saltillo Mission Sponsored by Dioceses of Jackson and Biloxi.
Av. Central 4649 y Calle 44, Col. Vista Hermosa, Saltillo, Coahuila C.P. 25010 Mexico. Tel: 011-52-84-44-82-2207. Rev. Benjamin Piovan.

Pax Christi Franciscans (1952) LaVerna House, 2108 Alta Woods Blvd., 39204. Tel: 601-373-4463. Kathleen Feyen, Pres.; Rhoda Kalscheur, House Dir. A Private Association of the Christian faithful, living a consecrated life, engaged in social and educational works. Consecrated Members 6.

ABERDEEN. *Catholic Committee of the South, Inc., St. Christopher Church*, P.O. Box 67, Pontotoc, 38863. Tel: 662-489-7749. Email: stchristopher@juno.com. Sr. Mary Priniski, O.P., Coord.

CANTON. *Notre Dame Education Center, Inc.*, 3390 N. Liberty St., Ste. C, P.O. Box 505, 39046. Tel: 601-859-6826; Fax: 601-859-6898. Email: ndec@netdoor.com.

GREENWOOD. *Pax Christi Franciscans*, St. Francis Information Center, 709 Ave. I, 38930. Tel: 662-453-1465; Fax: 662-453-1465. Email: stfrancis_center@bellsouth.net. Genevieve Feyen, Pres.; Bessie Willburn, Center Dir. A Private Association of the Christian faithful, living a consecrated life, engaged in social and educational works. Consecrated Members 6.

JONESTOWN. *Jonestown Family Center for Education and Wellness*, 401 Main St., P.O. Box 248, 38639. Tel: 662-358-4335; Fax: 662-358-4671. Sr. Teresa Shields, S.N.J.M., Exec. Dir.

MADISON. **St. Catherine's Village, Inc.* (1988) 200 Dominican Dr., 39110. Tel: 601-856-0100; Fax: 601-200-0823. Web: www.stcatherinesvillage.com. Assisted Annually 450.

MOUND BAYOU. *St. Gabriel Mercy Center*, P.O. Box 0824, 38762-0824. Tel: 662-741-3255; Fax: 662-741-3494. Email: moundbayou@tecinfo.com. Sr. Donald Mary Lynch, R.S.M., Dir., Coord. Parenting Prog.; Ms. La Toya Lee, Development Dir.; Sr. Cleo Heinrich, R.S.M., Coord. Cottage Industry; Dwana Lyles, Coord., Senior Outreach Prog.; Myrtle Lucas, Coord. GED Classes. Outreach Program of the Sisters of Mercy Health System (Mercycare) and Educational Services, Inc; Mercy Computer Learning Lab, Mound Bayou, MS 38762, Eliza Jackson-Williams, Coord.

ROSEDALE. *Delta Catholic Ministries*, 113 Railroad St., P.O. Box 307, 38769-0307. Tel: 662-759-6341. Email: dcmsh@juno.com. Sisters Catherine Leamy, S.N.J.M., Pres. & Dir.; Kay Burton, S.N.J.M., Vice Pres. & Dir.; Celia Evers, O.P., Sec., Treas. & Dir.; Joanne Blomme, O.P., Bd. Member; Jo Ann Villademoras, S.S.N.D., Bd. Member; Manette Durand, C.S.J., Bd. Member.

WALLS. *Sacred Heart League* (1955) 6050 Hwy. 161 N., P.O. Box 300, 38680-0300. Tel: 662-781-1360; Fax: 662-781-3340. Email: jkurps@shsm.org. Web: www.shl.org. Rev. Jack Kurps, S.C.J., Exec. Dir.; Mr. Stephen Koepke, Dir. Devel.

Sacred Heart Southern Missions Housing Corporation, P.O. Box 365, 38680-0365. Tel: 662-781-1516; Fax: 662-781-0886. Sr. Ruthann Williams, Dir. Programs; Rev. Jack Kurps, S.C.J., Pres.

Sacred Heart Southern Missions, Inc. (1942) 6050 Hwy. 161 N., P.O. Box 190, 38680-0190. Tel: 662-781-1360; Fax: 662-342-3390. Email: jkurps@shsm.org. Rev. Jack Kurps, S.C.J., Exec. Dir.

RELIGIOUS INSTITUTES OF MEN REPRESENTED IN THE DIOCESE

For further details refer to the corresponding bracketed number in the Religious Institutes of Men or Women section.

[0330]—*Brothers of the Christian Schools* (Prov. of St. Louis, MO)—F.S.C.
[0900]—*Canons Regular of Premontre*—O.Praem.
[0310]—*Congregation of Christian Brothers*—C.F.C.
[1130]—*Congregation of the Priests of the Sacred Heart*—S.C.J.
[0520]—*Franciscan Friars* (Pulaski, WI)—O.F.M.
[0570]—*Glenmary Home Missioners*—G.H.M.
[0840]—*Missionary Servants of the Most Holy Trinity*—S.T.
[0420]—*Society of the Divine Word*—S.V.D.
[0700]—*St. Joseph's Society of the Sacred Heart*—S.S.J.

RELIGIOUS INSTITUTES OF WOMEN REPRESENTED IN THE DIOCESE

[2410]—*Congregation of the Marianites of the Holy Cross*—M.S.C.
[3710]—*Congregation of the Sisters of Saint Agnes*—C.S.A.
[3832]—*Congregation of the Sisters of St. Joseph* (La Grange Park, IL)—C.S.J.
[1780]—*Congregation of the Sisters of the Third Order of St. Francis of Perpetual Adoration*—F.S.P.A.
[0760]—*Daughters of Charity of St. Vincent de Paul*—D.C.
[0420]—*Discalced Carmelite Nuns*—O.C.D.
[1070-03]—*Dominican Sisters* (Sinsinawa, WI)—O.P.
[1070-09]—*Dominican Sisters* (Racine, WI)—O.P.
[1070-06]—*Dominican Sisters* (Newburgh, NY)—O.P.
[1070-10]—*Dominican Sisters* (Springfield, IL)—O.P.
[1070-13]—*Dominican Sisters* (Adrian, MI)—O.P.
[1115]—*Dominican Sisters of Peace*—O.P.
[1230]—*Franciscan Sisters of Christian Charity*—O.S.F.
[1310]—*Franciscan Sisters of Little Falls, Minnesota*—O.S.F.
[2575]—*Institute of the Sisters of Mercy of the Americas* (St. Louis, MO)—R.S.M.
[]—*Literary Society of St. Catherine of Sienna Kentucky Dominican*—O.P.
[2800]—*Missionary Sisters of the Most Sacred Heart of Jesus*—M.S.C.
[2970]—*School Sisters of Notre Dame* (Baltimore & Dallas Provs., Mankato)—S.S.N.D.
[1680]—*School Sisters of St. Francis*—O.S.F.
[0500]—*Sisters of Charity of Nazareth* (Kentucky)—S.C.N.
[0430]—*Sisters of Charity of the Blessed Virgin Mary* (Dubuque, IA)—B.V.M.
[]—*Sisters of Christian Community*—S.F.C.C.
[0990]—*Sisters of Divine Providence*—C.D.P.
[2100]—*Sisters of Humility of Mary*—C.H.M.
[]—*Sisters of Mercy of Mississippi, Inc.*—R.S.M.
[3360]—*Sisters of Providence of Saint Mary-of-the-Woods, Indiana*—S.P.
[3893]—*Sisters of Saint Joseph of Chestnut Hill, Philadelphia*—S.S.J.
[]—*Sisters of St. Francis of Dubuque*
[]—*Sisters of St. Francis of Sylvania, Ohio*—O.S.F.
[1570]—*Sisters of St. Francis of the Holy Family* (Dubuque)—O.S.F.
[3830-15]—*Sisters of St. Joseph* (Concordia, KS)—C.S.J.
[3840]—*Sisters of St. Joseph of Carondelet* (St. Louis & St. Paul Provs.)—C.S.J.
[3930]—*Sisters of St. Joseph of the Third Order of St. Francis* (Marymount Prov.)—S.S.J.-T.O.S.F.
[1030]—*Sisters of the Divine Savior*—S.D.S.
[1990]—*Sisters of the Holy Names of Jesus and Mary* (Albany, NY; Spokane, WA; Los Gatos, CA; Marylhurst, OR)—S.N.J.M.
[2050]—*Sisters of the Holy Spirit and Mary Immaculate*—S.H.Sp.
[2350]—*Sisters of the Living Word*—S.L.W.
[2160]—*Sisters, Servants of the Immaculate Heart of Mary*—I.H.M.
[4120-03]—*Ursuline Nuns of the Congregation of Paris*—O.S.U.

NECROLOGY

† Jones, Patrick M., (Retired)—Died Nov. 16, 2009

An asterisk (*) denotes an organization that has established tax-exempt status directly with the IRS and is not covered by the USCCB Group Ruling.

Diocese of Jefferson City

(Dioecesis Civitatis Jeffersoniensis)

Most Reverend

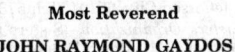

JOHN RAYMOND GAYDOS

Bishop of Jefferson City; ordained December 20, 1968; appointed June 25, 1997; consecrated August 27, 1997. *Res.: P.O. Box 104900, Jefferson City, MO 65110-4900.*

Catholic Center: Alphonse J. Schwartze Memorial, 2207 W. Main St., P.O. Box 104900, Jefferson City, MO 65110-4900. Tel: 573-635-9127; Fax: 573-635-0386.

Web: www.diojeffcity.org

ESTABLISHED JULY 2, 1956.

Square Miles 22,127.

Comprises the Counties of Adair, Audrain, Benton, Boone, Callaway, Camden, Chariton, Clark, Cole, Cooper, Crawford, Gasconade, Hickory, Howard, Knox, Lewis, Linn, Macon, Maries, Marion, Miller, Moniteau, Monroe, Montgomery, Morgan, Osage, Pettis, Phelps, Pike, Pulaski, Putnam, Ralls, Randolph, Saline, Schuyler, Scotland, Shelby and Sullivan in the State of Missouri.

For legal titles of parishes and diocesan institutions, consult the Chancery Office.

STATISTICAL OVERVIEW

Personnel	
Bishop	1
Priests: Diocesan Active in Diocese	60
Priests: Diocesan Active Outside Diocese	2
Priests: Retired, Sick or Absent	31
Number of Diocesan Priests	93
Religious Priests in Diocese	12
Total Priests in Diocese	105
Extern Priests in Diocese	13
Ordinations:	
Transitional Deacons	2
Permanent Deacons in Diocese	47
Total Brothers	1
Total Sisters	62
Parishes	
Parishes	95
With Resident Pastor:	
Resident Diocesan Priests	49
Resident Religious Priests	6
Without Resident Pastor:	
Administered by Priests	28
Administered by Deacons	3
Administered by Religious Women	3
Administered by Lay People	1
Missions	15
Professional Ministry Personnel:	
Brothers	1
Sisters	14
Lay Ministers	120
Welfare	
Catholic Hospitals	1
Total Assisted	258,234
Health Care Centers	16
Total Assisted	130,171
Special Centers for Social Services	2
Educational	
Diocesan Students in Other Seminaries	18
Total Seminarians	18
High Schools, Diocesan and Parish	2
Total Students	956
Elementary Schools, Diocesan and Parish	37
Total Students	6,494
Catechesis/Religious Education:	
High School Students	2,350
Elementary Students	3,575
Total Students under Catholic Instruction	13,393
Teachers in the Diocese:	
Priests	8
Brothers	1
Sisters	11
Lay Teachers	605
Vital Statistics	
Receptions into the Church:	
Infant Baptism Totals	1,168
Minor Baptism Totals	132
Adult Baptism Totals	134
Received into Full Communion	303
First Communions	1,279
Confirmations	1,096
Marriages:	
Catholic	285
Interfaith	222
Total Marriages	507
Deaths	826
Total Catholic Population	80,708
Total Population	876,490

Former Bishops—Most Revs. JOSEPH M. MARLING, C.PP.S., D.D., ord. Feb. 21, 1929; appt. Auxiliary of Kansas City, June 9, 1947; cons. Aug. 6, 1947; appt. Bishop of Jefferson City, Aug. 24, 1956; retired July 2, 1969; died Oct. 2, 1979; MICHAEL F. MCAULIFFE, S.T.D., ord. May 31, 1945; appt. July 2, 1969; cons. Aug. 18, 1969; retired Aug. 27, 1997; died Jan. 9, 2006.

Vicar General—Rev. Msgr. GREGORY L. HIGLEY, V.G., Mailing Address: P.O. Box 104900, Jefferson City, 65110-4900.

Episcopal Vicars—Rev. Msgrs. MICHAEL T. FLANAGAN, E.V.; MICHAEL J. WILBERS, E.V.

Chancery Office—2207 W. Main St., P.O. Box 104900, Jefferson City, 65110-4900. Tel: 573-635-9127; Fax: 573-635-0386. All offices are at this address unless noted otherwise.

Chancellor—SR. KATHLEEN WEGMAN, S.S.N.D.

Secretary to the Bishop—Rev. JEREMY A. SECRIST.

Vice-Chancellors—Rev. Msgr. ROBERT A. KURWICKI; Revs. BRENDAN DOYLE; JEREMY A. SECRIST.

Moderator of the Curia—Rev. Msgr. GREGORY L. HIGLEY, V.G.

Diocesan Tribunal— All marriage papers should be sent to the attention of Diocesan Tribunal Office.

Judicial Vicar—Rev. BRENDAN DOYLE.

Adjutant Judicial Vicar—Rev. Msgr. GREGORY L. HIGLEY, V.G.

Defenders of the Bond—Rev. ROBERT W. DUESDIEKER; Deacon JAMES R. BUTLER; Mrs. CONSTANCE SCHEPERS.

Promoter of Justice—Rev. MARK A. PORTERFIELD, J.C.L.

Judges—Revs. J. JAMES OFFUTT; MARK A. PORTERFIELD, J.C.L.; MICHAEL F. QUINN; P. GREGORY OLIGSCHLAEGER; MARK S. SMITH.

Notary—SHERYL NOVOTNEY.

Diocesan Consultors—Rev. Msgrs. MICHAEL T. FLANAGAN, E.V.; GREGORY L. HIGLEY, V.G.; DAVID D. COX; Revs. MICHAEL P. MURPHY; PHILIP E. NIEKAMP; P. GREGORY OLIGSCHLAEGER; Rev. Msgr. MICHAEL J. WILBERS, E.V.

Deans—I. Columbia: Rev. ROBERT W. DUESDIEKER Dean: Boonville, Columbia, Fayette, Moberly, Pilot Grove, Brunswick, Glasgow, Indian Grove, Salisbury, Slater, Marshall. II. Hannibal: Rev. PAUL M. HARTLEY Dean: Canton (La Grange), Ewing, Hannibal, Indian Creek, Kahoka (Wayland), Louisiana (Clarksville), Monroe City, Palmyra, Perry (Paris), St. Clement, St. Patrick, Vandalia (Laddonia). III. Jefferson City: Rev. J. DAVID MAHER Dean: California, Holts Summit, Jefferson City, Russellville, St. Martins, Taos, Wardsville. IV. Kirksville: Rev. MICHAEL P. MURPHY Dean: Baring, Edina, Kirksville (Novinger), Memphis, Milan (Unionville), Brookfield, Clarence, Macon (Bevier), Marceline, Shelbina. V. Mexico: Rev. P. GREGORY OLIGSCHLAEGER Dean: Centralia, Fulton, Hermann, Jonesburg, Martinsburg, Mexico, Mokane, Montgomery City, Rhineland, Wellsville. VI. Rolla: Rev. Msgr. DAVID D. COX Dean: Belle, Bourbon, Brinktown, Crocker, Cuba, Dixon, Owensville, Richland, Rolla, Rosati, St. James, Steelville, Vienna, St. Robert. VII. Sedalia/Lake Ozark: Rev. EDWIN J. COLE Dean: Camdenton, Eldon, Laurie (Versailles), Hermitage (Climax Springs), Lake Ozark, Mary's Home, St. Anthony, St. Elizabeth, Sedalia, Tipton, Warsaw. VIII. Westphalia: Rev. IGNAZIO C. MEDINA Dean: Argyle (Koeltztown), Bonnots Mill, Chamois, Folk, Frankenstein, Freeburg, Linn, Loose Creek, Meta, Rich Fountain, Westphalia, Morrison, Osage Bend, St. Thomas.

Masters of Ceremonies—

To The Bishop—Revs. MICHAEL W. PENN; JEREMY A. SECRIST; BENJAMIN NWOSU.

Personnel Board—Most Rev. JOHN RAYMOND GAYDOS; Revs. J. DAVID MAHER; ROBERT W. DUESDIEKER; Rev. Msgrs. MICHAEL T. FLANAGAN, E.V.; ROBERT A. KURWICKI; GREGORY L. HIGLEY, V.G.; DONALD W. LAMMERS; MICHAEL J. WILBERS, E.V.

Presbyteral Council—Most Rev. JOHN RAYMOND GAYDOS, Pres. Senators: Rev. MICHAEL P. MURPHY, Vice Chm.; Rev. Msgr. DAVID D. COX, Sec.; Revs. JOHN J. SCHMITZ, Treas.; MICHAEL W. PENN; LOUIS E. DORN; Rev. Msgr. ROBERT A. KURWICKI; Revs. PATRICK J. SHORTT; MARK A. PORTERFIELD, J.C.L.; LINUS EVERS, C.PP.S., Rel. Rep. Appointed Members: Rev. EDWIN J. COLE; Rev. Msgr. RAPHAEL P. KEYES, Chm.; Revs. P. GREGORY OLIGSCHLAEGER; PHILIP E. NIEKAMP. Ex Officio Members: Rev. Msgrs. MICHAEL J. WILBERS, E.V.; MICHAEL T. FLANAGAN, E.V.; GREGORY L. HIGLEY, V.G.

Diocesan Offices and Directors

Buildings and Properties—Rev. Msgr. MICHAEL J. WIBERS, E.V.; Mr. BARRY VOLLMER, Coord.

Campus Ministry—Mrs. BETTIE LESZENSKI, Dir.

Catholic Relief Overseas Fund—Ms. BARBARA ROSS, Dir. & Coord.

Cemeteries—Rev. JEREMY A. SECRIST, Dir.

Charismatic Renewal Program—Deacon KENNETH BERRY, Diocesan Representative, 201 N. Cottey, Edina, 63537. Tel: 660-397-2636.

Communication—Mr. MARK D. SAUCIER, Dir., 600 Clark Ave., P.O. Box 1022, Jefferson City, 65102.

Cursillo Movement—Mr. P. KEVIN HUNTON, Lay Dir.; Rev. JOSEPH S. COREL, Spiritual Dir.

Chief Financial Officer—Deacon JOSEPH M. BRADDOCK.

Diaconate Office—Rev. FREDERICK J. ELSKAMP, Vicar; Deacon RAYMOND L. PURVIS.

Engaged Encounter—Coordinators: BURDETT WILSON; JOYCE WILSON, 1408 Rosewood Terr., Macon, 63552; Rev. MICHAEL F. QUINN, Spiritual Dir.

Family Life—Mr. MICHAEL A. VAN GUNDY, Dir.; Dr. STEPHANA LANDWHER, Pro-Life.

Finance—Deacon JOSEPH BRADDOCK, CFO.

Stewardship—Mrs. E. JANE RUTTER, Dir.

Finance Committee—Most Rev. JOHN RAYMOND GAYDOS; Deacon JOSEPH M. BRADDOCK; Mr. CHARLES CASSMEYER; Mrs. E. JANE RUTTER; Rev. Msgr. MICHAEL T. FLANAGAN, E.V.; Mr. GEORGE CASEY; Rev. Msgr. GREGORY L. HIGLEY, V.G.; Mr. MICHAEL KELLY; Mr. RODNEY LOESCH; Mr. MATTHIAS TOLKSDORF; Mr. JAMES E. WESTBROOK; Mrs. HELEN VOSSEN; Rev. Msgr. MICHAEL J. WILBERS, E.V.; Mrs. BETTY ZIMMER; Sr. KATHLEEN WEGMAN, S.S.N.D.

Hispanic Ministry—JUSTO GONZALEZ II, Chap. & Dir.

El Puente—Sisters PEGGY BONNOT, C.C.V.I.; BERTHA FLORES, C.C.V.I.; MARGARET SNYDER, C.C.V.I., 403A S. Cooper, California, 65018. Tel: 573-796-3071.

Historical Archives—Rev. JEREMY A. SECRIST, Dir.

Human Development Campaign—Ms. BARBARA ROSS.

Leadership Services—Sr. KATHLEEN WEGMAN, S.S.N.D., Chancellor; Mr. RONALD VESSELL, Assoc. to Chancellor.

Legion of Mary—Rev. WILLIAM L. KORTE, 301 W. Williams, Salisbury, 65281. Tel: 660-388-5590.

Liturgical Commission—Rev. DANIEL J. MERZ.

Mediation and Arbitration Board—Rev. LOUIS E. DORN.

Marriage Encounter—Chair Couple: Mr. DALE EMBRY; Mrs. ANGEL EMBRY, 301 W. Versailles Ave., California, 65018. Tel: 573-796-2767; Rev. GREGORY C. MEYSTRIK, Spiritual Dir., 6410 Rt. W, Jefferson City, 65101. Tel: 573-636-4925.

Marriage Tribunal—Mrs. CONSTANCE SCHEPERS, Admin.

Ministry Formation—Rev. JOSEPH S. COREL.

Ministry to Priests—Most Rev. JOHN RAYMOND GAYDOS; Revs. FRANK A. BUSSMANN; JOSEPH S. COREL, Chm.; Rev. Msgr. DAVID D. COX; Rev. PATRICK G. DOLAN; Rev. Msgr. MARION J. MAKAREWICZ; Revs. JEREMY A. SECRIST, Sec.; GERALD J. KAIMANN; GREGORY C. MEYSTRIK.

Mission Office—Mr. MARK D. SAUCIER, Dir., Mailing Address: 600 Clark Ave., P.O. Box 1022, Jefferson City, 65102.

Newspaper--"The Catholic Missourian"—Mr. JAY NIES, Editor, Mailing Address: P.O. Box 104900, Jefferson City, 65110-4900.

Priestly and Religious Vocations Committee—Revs. JOSEPH S. COREL, Chair; DAVID J. VEIT; MARK S. SMITH; JOHN J. SCHMITZ; R. WILLIAM PECKMAN; CHRISTOPHER L. CORDES; WAYNE M. BOYER; Rev. Msgrs. DAVID D. COX; GREGORY L. HIGLEY, V.G.

Priests' Mutual Benefit Society—Board of Trustees: Most Rev. JOHN R. GAYDOS; Revs. CHRISTOPHER L. CORDES; GREGORY C. MEYSTRIK; Rev. Msgrs. MICHAEL T. FLANAGAN, E.V.; RAPHAEL P. KEYES; GREGORY L. HIGLEY, V.G., Sec. & Treas.; MICHAEL J. WILBERS, E.V.

Religious Education Office—Mr. JAMES M. KEMNA, Dir.; Mrs. CAROLYN A. SAUCIER, Assoc.

Refugee and Immigration Services—Ms. LORNA TRAN, Dir.

Columbia Office—201 W. Broadway, Bldg. 3, Columbia, 65203. Tel: 573-442-7568. Mr. SENAD MUSIC, Office Mgr.

Residents Encounter Christ—Ms. BARBARA ROSS, Diocesan Liaison; Rev. LOUIS E. DORN, Spiritual Dir.

School Office—Mr. DONALD F. NOVOTNEY, Supt.

Diocesan Schools Technology Foundation—Mr. DONALD F. NOVOTNEY, Supt., 2207 W. Main St., P.O. Box 104900, Jefferson City, 65110-4900. Tel: 573-635-9127; Fax: 573-635-2286.

Scouting—Rev. GREGORY C. MEYSTRIK, Chap., 6410 Rt. W, Jefferson City, 65101. Tel: 573-636-4925.

Diocesan Sisters' Organization—Sisters EVELYN MARIE PETERMAN, F.S.M., Pres.; NADINE FLOTT, C.P.P.S., Sec.

Social Concerns Office—Ms. BARBARA ROSS, Dir.

Prison Ministry—Rev. LOUIS E. DORN.

Stewardship—Mrs. E. JANE RUTTER, Dir.

Teens Encounter Christ (TEC)—Mr. STEVE MAXWELL, Lay Dir., 1801 Miami Ave., Marshall, 65340; Rev. MICHAEL A. COLEMAN, Spiritual Dir., P.O. Box 310, Moberly, 65270.

Risk Management Administer—VACANT.

Victim Assistance Coordinator—Mr. RONALD VESSELL. Tel: 573-635-9127, Ext. 224. Email: review@diojeffcity.org.

Youth Ministry—Rev. JOSEPH S. COREL, Dir.

CLERGY, PARISHES, MISSIONS AND PAROCHIAL SCHOOLS

JEFFERSON CITY

(COLE COUNTY)

1—ST. JOSEPH CATHEDRAL (1959) [JC] Rev. Msgr. Robert A. Kurwicki; Rev. Benjamin Nwosu; Deacons Robert J. Rackers, (Retired); Joseph M. Braddock; Dana K. Joyce; James L. Kliethermes.
2305 W. Main St., 65109.
Tel: 573-635-7991; Fax: 573-635-0842. Email: stjosephb@juno.com. Web: www.cathedraljc.org.
School—(Grades PreK-8), 2303 W. Main St., 65109. Tel: 573-635-5024; Fax: 573-635-5238. Email: spencer.allen@cathedralschooljc.com. Web: www.cathedralschooljc.com. Spencer L. Allen, Prin.; Cheryl Kosmatka, Librarian. Lay Teachers 27; Students 480.
Catechesis/Religious Program—Students 93.

2—IMMACULATE CONCEPTION (1913) [JC] Revs. Patrick G. Dolan; Hillary Andebo; David J. Veit. In Res., Rev. Brendan Doyle; Deacons Mark Albur; Raymond L. Purvis.
Res.: 1206 E. McCarty St., 65101. Tel: 573-635-6143; 573-635-6144; Fax: 573-635-6036. Email: icchurch@mchsi.com. Web: www.icparishjc.com.
School—(Grades PreK-8), 1208 E. McCarty St., 65101. Tel: 573-636-7680; Fax: 573-635-1833. Email: jstruemph@icangels.com. Web: www.icangels.com. Jill Struemph, Prin. Sisters 1; Lay Teachers 34; Students 440.
Catechesis/Religious Program—Students 100.

3—ST. PETER (1846) [JC] Revs. J. David Maher; Basil Eruo; Deacons Robert L. Dulle; Anthony J. Valdes; Thomas M. Whalen; Fred Schmitz.
Res.: 216 Broadway, 65101. Tel: 573-636-8159; Fax: 573-634-6079. Email: parish@stpeterjc.org. Web: www.stpeterjc.org.
School—(Grades K-8) Tel: 573-636-8922; Fax: 573-636-8410. Email: spsmc@socket.net. Dr. Joseph Gulino, Prin.; Megan Cline, Librarian. Sisters 2; School Sisters of Notre Dame 1; Sisters of Charity of the Incarnate Word 1; Lay Teachers 30; Students 457.
Catechesis/Religious Program—Students 105.

OUTSIDE JEFFERSON CITY

ARGYLE, OSAGE CO., ST. ALOYSIUS (1910) [CEM 2] Rev. Msgr. Marion J. Makarewicz.
Mailing Address: P.O. Box 6, 65001. Tel: 573-728-6212; Fax: 573-728-6217.
Catechesis/Religious Program—Students 73.
Mission—St. Boniface (1866) P.O. Box 53, Koeltztown, 65048. Tel: 314-728-6919.

BARING, KNOX CO., ST. ALOYSIUS (1894) [CEM] Attended by Edina Rev. Joseph Hoi; Deacon Kenneth Berry.
Res.: 509 N. Main St., Edina, 63537-1239. Tel: 660-397-2183; Fax: 660-397-3680. Email: stjoeal@marktwain.net. Web: knoxcountycatholic.org.
Catechesis/Religious Program—Twinned with St. Joseph, Edina. Students 9.

BELLE, MARIES CO., ST. ALEXANDER (1910) [CEM] Attended by Immaculate Conception, Owensville. Rev. Jeremy A. Secrist.
Mailing Address: 400 W. Third St., P.O. Box 606, 65013. Tel: 573-859-6231.
Catechesis/Religious Program—Students 15.

BONNOTS MILL, OSAGE CO., ST. LOUIS (1905) [CEM] Rev. Thomas J. Seifner.
Mailing Address: P.O. Box 8, 65016. Tel: 573-897-2922.
Church: 211 Church Hill, P.O. Box 8, Loose Creek, 65054. Tel: 573-897-2922; Fax: 573-897-4271.
Catechesis/Religious Program—Students 20.

BOONVILLE, COOPER CO., SS. PETER AND PAUL (1856) [CEM] Rev. Robert W. Duesdieker; Deacon David Miller. In Res., Rev. M. Brendan Griffey.
Res.: 322 7th St., 65233. Tel: 660-882-6468; Fax: 660-882-7920. Email: ssppchurch@socket.net. Web: www.catholic-forum.com/churches/0865sspeterpaul.
School—(Grades PreK-8), 502 7th St., 65233. Tel: 660-882-2589; Fax: 660-882-2476. Mr. Alan Lammers, Prin. Lay Teachers 11; Students 176.
Catechesis/Religious Program—Email: sspprelед@socket.net. Students 101.

BOURBON, CRAWFORD CO., ST. FRANCIS (1915) [CEM 2] Rev. James Finder.
Mailing Address: 415 W. School, Cuba, 65453.
Church: 1098 Old Hwy. 66 W., 65441. Tel: 573-885-3520; Fax: 573-885-3501. Email: stf@fidnet.com.

BRINKTOWN, MARIES CO., HOLY GUARDIAN ANGELS (1891) [CEM] Attended by Visitation, Vienna. Rev. Msgr. Marion J. Makarewicz.
Res. & Mailing Address: P.O. Box 226, Vienna, 65582. Tel: 573-422-3950; Fax: 573-422-3950.
Church: 37515 Hwy., 65443. Tel: 573-422-3105.
Catechesis/Religious Program—Students 13.

BROOKFIELD, LINN CO., IMMACULATE CONCEPTION (1859) [CEM] Rev. Gerald J. Kaimann, Canonical Pastor; Sr. Donna Eggering, O.S.F., Pastoral Admin.
Res.: 313 N. Livingston St., 64628. Tel: 660-258-2507; Fax: 660-258-5637. Email: icp0011@sbcglobal.net.
Catechesis/Religious Program—Students 87.

BRUNSWICK, CHARITON CO., ST. BONIFACE (1860) [CEM] Rev. Leonard S. Misey.
Res.: 203 E. Harrison St., P.O. Box 5, 65236. Tel: 660-548-3267.
Catechesis/Religious Program—Students 33.
Mission—St. Joseph (1870) Hurricane Branch, Chariton Co.

CALIFORNIA, MONITEAU CO., ANNUNCIATION (1872) [CEM] Rev. Frederick J. Elskamp; Sr. Mary Ruth Wand, S.S.N.D., Pastoral Min.
Res.: 310 S. Mill St., 65018. Tel: 573-796-4842; Fax: 573-796-4842 (*51). Email: annunciati@socket.net.
Catechesis/Religious Program—Tel: 573-796-4842. Students 150.

CAMDENTON, CAMDEN CO., ST. ANTHONY (1946) Rev. Msgr. Raphael P. Keyes; Rev. Robert H. Fields; Deacon Richard A. Von Gunten.
Church & Mailing: 1874 N. Business Rte. 5, 65020. Tel: 573-346-2716; Fax: 573-346-0625. Email: stanthonys@sbcglobal.net.
Catechesis/Religious Program—Students 264.
Mission—Our Lady of the Snows (1990)Tel: 573-345-4548.

CANTON, LEWIS CO., ST. JOSEPH (1865) Rev. Richard W. Frank.
Res.: 812 Lewis St., 63435. Tel: 573-288-3198; Fax: 573-288-3198. Email: stjosephcanton@centurytel.net.
Catechesis/Religious Program—Students 45.
Mission—Notre Dame (1868) Rte. C, La Grange, Lewis Co. 63448. Tel: 573-655-4296.
Catechesis/Religious Program—Students 7.

CENTRALIA, BOONE CO., HOLY SPIRIT (1897) Rev. J. James Offutt.
Res.: 404 S. Rollins St., 65240. Tel: 573-682-2815. Email: hsoffice@socket.net. Web: members.socket.net/~holyspirit.
Catechesis/Religious Program—Students 70.

CHAMOIS, OSAGE CO., MOST PURE HEART OF MARY (1865) [CEM 2] Rev. David A. Means, Canonical Admin.
Res.: P.O. Box 156, 65024. Tel: 573-763-5345. Email: mphparish@centurytel.net.
Catechesis/Religious Program—Students 24.

CLARENCE, SHELBY CO., ST. PATRICK (1884) [CEM] Rev. Donardo S. Bermejo, Canonical Admin.
Res. & Mailing Address: 307 E. Chestnut, P.O. Box 306, Shelbina, 63468. Tel: 573-588-4498; Fax: 573-588-4728. Email: marypat@socket.net.
Church: 201 Grand St., 63437. Tel: 573-699-3805.

COLUMBIA, BOONE CO.

1—OUR LADY OF LOURDES (1958) Rev. Msgr. Michael T. Flanagan; Rev. Joseph L. Shetler; Deacons Fred Fritsch, (Retired); Joseph Puglis; James Leyden; Thomas Miller.
Res.: 903 Bernadette Dr., 65203. Tel: 573-445-7915; Fax: 573-446-7402. Email: office2@ourladyoflourdes.org. Web: www.ourladyoflourdes.org.
School—(Grades K-8), 817 Bernadette Dr., 65203. Tel: 573-445-6516; Fax: 573-445-9887. Web: ccsk8.org. Linda Garner, Prin.; Julie Barnett, Librarian. Lay Teachers 41; Students 606.
Catechesis/Religious Program—Tel: 573-445-9602. Email: redirector@ourladyoflourdes.org. Students 385.

2—SACRED HEART (1876) Rev. Steven Kuhlmann, O.P.; Deacon John D. Weaver.
Mailing Address: 105 Waugh St., 65201.
Office: 1115 Locust St., 65201. Tel: 573-443-3470; Fax: 573-442-1082. Email: sbauer@sacredheart-church.org. Web: sacredheart-church.org.
Catechesis/Religious Program—Students 69.

3—ST. THOMAS MORE NEWMAN CENTER, UNIVERSITY OF MISSOURI (1963) Revs. Thomas Saucier, O.P.; Simon Felix Michalski, O.P.; Deacons Francis Ruggiero; Gene Kazmierczak.
Res.: 905 S. Greenwood, 65203. Tel: 573-442-6044. Email: chris.temporal@newmancentercolumbia.org. Web: www.newmancentercolumbia.org.
Church: 701 Maryland, 65201. Tel: 573-449-5514; 573-449-5424; Fax: 573-874-2777.
Catechesis/Religious Program—Students 195.

CROCKER, PULASKI CO., ST. CORNELIUS (1966) [CEM] Attended by Dixon. Rev. Walter J. Reisinger, C.M.
Res.: P.O. Box 310, Dixon, 65459. Tel: 573-759-7521.
Catechesis/Religious Program—Students 4.

CUBA, CRAWFORD CO., HOLY CROSS (1880) [CEM] Rev. James Finder.
Res.: 415 W. School Ave., 65453. Tel: 573-885-3520; Fax: 573-885-3501. Email: hccc@fidmail.com.
School—(Grades PreK-8), 407 W. School Ave., 65453. Tel: 573-885-4727. Cate Sanazaro, Prin. Lay

Teachers 6; Students 63.
Catechesis/Religious Program—Students 53.
DIXON, PULASKI CO., ST. THERESA (1928) [CEM] Rev. Walter J. Reisinger, C.M.
Res.: 506 Oak St., P.O. Box 310, 65459. Tel: 573-759-7521.
Catechesis/Religious Program—Students 4.
EDINA, KNOX CO., ST. JOSEPH (1844) [CEM 2] Rev. Joseph Hoi; Deacon Kenneth Berry.
Res.: 509 N. Main St., 63537-1239. Tel: 660-397-2183; Fax: 660-397-3680. Email: stjoeal@marktwain.net. Web: www.knoxcountycatholic.org.
Catechesis/Religious Program—Fax: 660-397-3680. Students 78.
ELDON, MILLER CO., SACRED HEART (1910) Rev. Patrick J. Shortt; Deacon Gary Christoff, Pastoral Admin.; Rev. Patrick Dowling, Sacramental Min.
Res.: 540 N. Mill St., 65026. Tel: 573-392-5334; Fax: 573-392-3493. Email: sacred540@sbcglobal.net.
Catechesis/Religious Program—Students 73.
EWING, LEWIS CO., QUEEN OF PEACE (1887) [CEM 2] Rev. Richard W. Frank.
Res.: P.O. Box 347, 63440. Tel: 573-209-3343. Email: qofpeace@marktwain.net.
Catechesis/Religious Program—Students 30.
FAYETTE, HOWARD CO., ST. JOSEPH (1956) Rev. Robert W. Duesdieker.
Res.: 300 S. Cleveland Ave., 65248. Tel: 660-248-2439; Fax: 660-248-2439. Email: stjoseph-fayette@socket.net. Web: www.stjosephcath.org.
Catechesis/Religious Program—Students 37.
FOLK, OSAGE CO., ST. ANTHONY OF PADUA (1905) [CEM] Rev. Mark S. Smith.
Mailing Address: P.O. Box 157, Westphalia, 65085. Tel: 573-455-2888. Email: folkchurch@osageconnect.net.
Catechesis/Religious Program—Students 48.
FRANKENSTEIN, OSAGE CO., OUR LADY HELP OF CHRISTIANS (1863) [CEM 3] Rev. Ignazio C. Medina.
Church & Mailing Address: 1665 Hwy. C, Bonnots Mill, 65016. Tel: 573-897-2587.
School—Tel: 573-897-2567; Fax: 573-897-4143. Sr. Celly Ann Amparano, S.S.N.D., Prin. Sisters 2; Lay Teachers 2; Students 42.
Catechesis/Religious Program—Students 16.
FREEBURG, OSAGE CO., HOLY FAMILY (1904) [CEM] Rev. Philip E. Niekamp.
Res.: 104 Oliver St., P.O. Box 9, 65035. Tel: 573-744-5254; Fax: 573-744-9201. Email: cathedralofozark@juno.com.
School—(Grades K-8) Tel: 573-744-5200. Email: djcc05@earthlink.net. Debbie Reinkemeyer, Prin. Sisters 1; Lay Teachers 5; Students 72.
Catechesis/Religious Program—Students 40.
FULTON, CALLAWAY CO., ST. PETER (1875) Rev. Karl Barman, O.S.B.; Deacon John L. Nuedecker.
Parish Center—700 State Rd. Z, 65251. Tel: 573-642-5562; Fax: 573-642-2839. Email: stpeterparishoffice@stpeterfultonmo.org.
School—(Grades K-8) Tel: 573-642-2839; Fax: 573-642-2839. Email: mrsloftus@stpeterfultonmo.org. Cynthia Loftus, Prin. Lay Teachers 7; Students 83.
Catechesis/Religious Program—Students 76.
GLASGOW, HOWARD CO., ST. MARY (1866) [CEM] Rev. Michael W. Penn.
Res.: 421 Third St., P.O. Box 44, 65254. Tel: 660-338-2053; Fax: 660-338-2598. Email: glasgowcatholicchurch@yahoo.com.
School—(Grades K-8), 501 3rd St., 65254. Tel: 660-338-2258; Fax: 660-338-9930. Email: kentmonnig@att.net. Kent Monnig, Prin.; Melissa Morrison, Librarian. Lay Teachers 11; Students 115.
Catechesis/Religious Program—Students 9.
HANNIBAL, MARION CO., HOLY FAMILY (1845) [JC] Rev. Michael F. Quinn; Deacons Eugene Pierceall; Robert Leake.
Office: 2103 Broadway, 63401. Tel: 573-221-1078; Fax: 573-248-1662. Email: hfparish@sbcglobal.net. Web: www.myholyfamily.com.
School—(Grades PreK-8), 1113 Broadway, 63401. Tel: 573-221-0456; Fax: 573-221-6357. Melissa Millan, Prin. Lay Teachers 18; Students 183.
Catechesis/Religious Program—Students 65.
HERMANN, GASCONADE CO., ST. GEORGE (1845) [CEM] Rev. William D. Debo.
Res.: 128 W. 4th St., 65041-1099. Tel: 573-486-2723; Fax: 573-486-3062. Email: bdd@stgeorge-hermann.com. Web: www.stgeorge-hermann.com.
School—(Grades PreK-8) Tel: 573-486-5914; Fax: 573-486-2434. Email: jclingman@stgeorge-hermann.com. Web: www.school.stgeorge-hermann.com. Julie Clingman, Prin. Lay Teachers 13; Students 148.
Catechesis/Religious Program—Students 60.
HERMITAGE, HICKORY CO., ST. BERNADETTE (1973) Rev. Msgr. Raphael P. Keyes; Rev. Robert H. Fields.
Church: Hwy. 254, P.O. Box 167, 65668. Tel: 417-745-6361.
Catechesis/Religious Program—Students 3.
HOLTS SUMMIT, CALLAWAY CO., ST. ANDREW (1975) [CEM] Rev. Msgr. Gregory L. Higley; Deacons Daniel J. Ramsay; David Thompson.
Church: 400 St. Andrew Dr., 65043. Tel: 573-896-5010. Email: standrew@embarqmail.com. Web: www.standrewholtssummit.com.
Catechesis/Religious Program—Students 110.
ILASCO, RALLS CO., HOLY CROSS, Closed. For inquiries for parish records please see Holy Family, Hannibal.
INDIAN CREEK, MONROE CO., ST. STEPHEN (1833) [CEM] Rev. Donald J. Antweiler.
Res.: 27519 Monroe Rd. 533, Monroe City, 63456. Tel: 573-735-4033. Email: swinkeypat@gmail.com. Web: www.missouri.edu/~tmk5f7/swinkey.
Catechesis/Religious Program—
INDIAN GROVE, CHARITON CO., ST. RAPHAEL (1886) [CEM] Attended by St. Boniface, Brunswick. Rev. Leonard S. Misey.
Mailing Address: 203 E. Harrison St., P.O. Box 5, Brunswick, 65236-0005. Tel: 660-548-3267.
JONESBURG, MONTGOMERY CO., ST. PATRICK (1862) [CEM] Rev. Frank A. Bussmann, Canonical Pastor; Ms. Kristin Roth, Pastoral Admin.
Res.: 505 First St., 63351. Tel: 636-488-5623; Fax: 636-488-5629. Email: stpats@centurytel.net.
Catechesis/Religious Program—Students 30.
KAHOKA, CLARK CO.
1—ST. MICHAEL THE ARCHANGEL (1891) Rev. Paul M. Hartley.
Church: 622 W. Exchange St., 63445. Tel: 660-727-3472. Email: stmichel@centurytel.net.
Catechesis/Religious Program—Students 6.
Mission—St. Martha (1887) 202 S. Main St., Wayland, Clark Co. 63472.
Catechesis/Religious Program—Students 24.
2—THE SHRINE OF ST. PATRICK (1839) [CEM] Attended by Canton. Rev. Paul M. Hartley.
Res.: 622 W. Exchange, 63445. Tel: 660-727-3472. Email: stmichel@centurytel.net.
Catechesis/Religious Program—Students 8.
KIRKSVILLE, ADAIR CO., MARY IMMACULATE (1888) [CEM] Rev. Christopher L. Cordes; Deacon David D. Ream.
716 E. Washington St., 63501. Tel: 660-665-2466; Fax: 660-665-8955. Email: marie.wiskirchen@miparish.org. Web: www.miparish.org.
School—(Grades K-8), 712 E. Washington St., 63501. Tel: 660-665-1006; Fax: 660-665-3621. Email: srklauser@miparish.org. Web: www.parish.org/school. Sr. Ruth Ann Klauser, S.S.N.D., Prin. Lay Teachers 8; Students 76.
Catechesis/Religious Program—Tel: 660-665-2466. Students 130.
Mission—St. Rose of Lima (1903) Hwy. 149, Novinger, Adair Co. 63559.
LAKE OZARK, MILLER CO., OUR LADY OF THE LAKE (1940) Rev. Msgr. Michael J. Wilbers.
Church: 2411 Bagnell Dam Blvd., P.O. Box 2390, 65049. Tel: 573-365-2241; Fax: 573-365-4458. Email: ourladylake@sbcglobal.net.
Catechesis/Religious Program—Students 108.
LAURIE, MORGAN CO., SHRINE OF ST. PATRICK (1870) [CEM] Rev. Edwin J. Cole.
Office: 176 Marian Dr., P.O. Box 1098, 65038-1098. Tel: 573-374-7855; Fax: 573-374-0627. Email: stpats@charterinternet.com.
Catechesis/Religious Program—Students 32.
Mission—St. Philip Benizi (1963) 17034 Hwy. D, Versailles, Morgan Co. 65084. Tel: 573-378-5958; Fax: 573-374-4825. Email: stphilip@yhti.net. Rev. C. Duane Ryan.
Catechesis/Religious Program—(Combined with Shrine of St. Patrick, Laurie)
Shrine—The National Shrine of Mary, Mother of the Church P.O. Box 1250, 65038. Tel: 573-374-6279; Fax: 573-374-0627.
LINN, OSAGE CO., ST. GEORGE (1866) [CEM] Rev. Ignazio C. Medina.
Res.: 613 E. Main St., P.O. Box 49, 65051. Tel: 573-897-2293. Email: stglinn@osageconnect.net.
School—(Grades PreK-8) Tel: 573-897-3645; Fax: 573-897-2148. Sr. Celly Ann Amparano, S.S.N.D., Prin. Religious 2; Lay Teachers 11; Students 175.
Catechesis/Religious Program—Tel: 573-897-3203. Students 50.
LOOSE CREEK, OSAGE CO., IMMACULATE CONCEPTION (1845) [CEM 2] Rev. Thomas J. Seifner.
Res.: 121 County Rd. 402, P.O. Box 8, 65054. Tel: 573-897-2922. Email: frtjs1@gmail.com.
School—(Grades K-8) Tel: 573-897-3516; Fax: 573-897-4271. Rita Stiefermann, Prin. School Sisters of Notre Dame 1; Lay Teachers 9; Students 95.
Catechesis/Religious Program—Students 48.
LOUISIANA, PIKE CO., ST. JOSEPH (1865) [CEM] Rev. Louis E. Dorn; Deacon Mark J. Dobelmann.
Res.: 508 N. 3rd St., 63353. Tel: 573-754-4757.
Catechesis/Religious Program—Tel: 573-754-6609. Students 45.
Mission—Mary Queen of Peace (1951) South Second St., Clarksville, Pike Co. 63336. Tel: 573-242-3730.
MACON, MACON CO., IMMACULATE CONCEPTION (1857) [CEM] Rev. Michael P. Murphy; Deacons Bernhard Toll; Lloyd Collins.
Res.: 402 N. Rollins St., 63552. Tel: 660-385-3792; Fax: 660-385-3792. Email: imchurch2004@yahoo.com.
School—(Grades K-8) Tel: 660-385-2711; Fax: 660-385-2839. Sr. Barbara Rose Koch, C.P.P.S., Prin. Lay Teachers 5; Students 66.
Catechesis/Religious Program—Students 40.
Mission—Sacred Heart (1880) Bevier, Macon Co. 63532.
MARCELINE, LINN CO., ST. BONAVENTURE (1888) [CEM 2] Revs. Gerald J. Kaimann; Daniel P. Ewald, Senior Asst. Priest.
Res.: 409 S. Kansas Ave., 64658-1301. Tel: 660-376-3239. Email: stbon@mcmsys.com. Web: www.stbon.org.
School—Fr. McCartan Memorial School, (Grades PreK-8), 327 S. Kansas Ave., 64658. Tel: 660-376-3580; Fax: 660-376-2836. Kelly Ott, Prin. Lay Teachers 6; Students 43.
Catechesis/Religious Program—Students 37.
MARSHALL, SALINE CO., ST. PETER (1870) [CEM] Revs. Kevin Gormley; Thomas L. Alber, Senior Priest; Deacons Richard H. Luebbering; Joseph R. Mitchell.
Res.: 1801 S. Miami Ave., P.O. Box 220, 65340. Tel: 660-886-7960; Fax: 660-831-1723. Email: stpeter.office@att.net. Web: www.stpeterchurch-marshallmo.org.
School—(Grades PreK-8), 368 S. Ellsworth St., 65340. Tel: 660-886-6390; Fax: 660-866-6606. Gary Littrell, Prin. Lay Teachers 12; Students 180.
Catechesis/Religious Program—Students 120.
Mission—Holy Family (1945) 200 Ruby St., Sweet Springs, Saline Co. 65351.
MARTINSBURG, AUDRAIN CO., ST. JOSEPH (1876) [CEM] Rev. P. Gregory Oligschlaeger.
Res.: 408 E. Kellett, 65264. Tel: 573-492-6595; Fax: 573-492-6105. Email: joseph@socket.net.
School—(Grades K-8) Tel: 573-492-6283. Email: stjoeschool@socket.net. Kathleen Robnett, Prin. Lay Teachers 7; Students 64.
Catechesis/Religious Program—Students 34.
MARY'S HOME, MILLER CO., OUR LADY OF THE SNOWS (1883) [CEM] Rev. Patrick J. Shortt.
Res.: 274 Hwy. H, Eugene, 65032-4231. Tel: 573-498-3820; Fax: 573-498-3779. Email: frpshortt@gmail.com.
School—(Grades PreK-8) Tel: 573-498-3574; Fax: 573-498-3776. Email: gaylet@radiowire.net. Web: www.oloscougars.com. Gayle Trachsel, Prin. Lay Teachers 7; Students 96.
Catechesis/Religious Program—Students 134.
MEMPHIS, SCOTLAND CO., ST. JOHN (1952) [CEM] Rev. Joseph Hoi.
Mailing Address: Rt. 3, Box 34-H, 63555.
Res.: 509 N. Main St., Edina, 63537. Tel: 660-465-7130. Email: stjohns@nemr.net.
Catechesis/Religious Program—Students 23.
META, OSAGE CO., ST. CECILIA (1904) [CEM] Rev. Mark A. Porterfield.
Res.: P.O. Box 146, St. Thomas, 65076. Tel: 573-477-3315; Fax: 573-477-0177. Email: stthomasoffice@embarqmail.com.
Catechesis/Religious Program—Students 73.
MEXICO, AUDRAIN CO., ST. BRENDAN (1857) [CEM] Rev. John J. Schmitz.
Res.: 615 S. Washington St., 65265-2658. Tel: 573-581-4720; Fax: 573-581-7711. Email: stbrendn@swbell.net.
School—(Grades PreK-8) Tel: 573-581-2443; Fax: 573-581-2571. Email: bgleeson@saintbrendans.org. Bill Gleeson, Prin. Lay Teachers 12; Students 150.
Catechesis/Religious Program—Students 30.
MILAN, SULLIVAN CO., ST. MARY (1868) [CEM 2] Revs. Gerald J. Kaimann, Canonical Pastor; Daniel P. Ewald, Sacramental Min.; Sr. Ellen Orf, C.P.P.S., Pastoral Admin.
Res.: 101 W. Baker St., P.O. Box 147, 63556. Tel: 660-265-4110; Fax: 660-265-4110. Email: stmarys@nemr.net. Web: www.stmarymilan.parishesonline.com.
Catechesis/Religious Program—Tel: 660-265-4110. Students 57.
Mission—St. Mary (1868) 1118 Main St. Hwy. 136 E., Unionville, Putnam Co. Tel: 660-947-2599.
Catechesis/Religious Program—Students 22.
MOBERLY, RANDOLPH CO., ST. PIUS X (1870) [CEM] Rev. Michael A. Coleman; Deacon David F. Ritter.
Res.: 209 S. Williams St., P.O. Box 310, 65270. Tel: 660-263-5243; Fax: 660-263-0101. Web: www.stpiuschurch.com.
School—(Grades PreK-8), 210 S. Williams St., 65270. Tel: 660-263-5500; Fax: 660-263-5744. Email: office@st-pius.com. Web: st-pius.com. Mr. William Hagdorn, Prin. Lay Teachers 19; Students 168.
Catechesis/Religious Program—Students 90.

MOKANE, CALLAWAY CO., ST. JUDE THADDEUS (1900) Rev. Karl Barmann, O.S.B.; Deacon Lawrence A. Weber.
Rectory—700 State Hwy. Z, Fulton, 65251.
Church: 401 Adams St., 65059. Tel: 573-676-3238.
Catechesis/Religious Program—Students 18.

MONROE CITY, MONROE CO., HOLY ROSARY (1884) [CEM] Rev. Donald J. Antweiler.
Res.: 405 S. Main St., 63456. Tel: 573-735-4718; Fax: 573-735-0713. Email: hrosary@mywdo.com. Web: www.holyrosaryschool.com.
School—(Grades K-8) Tel: 573-735-2422; Fax: 573-735-3091. Email: hrssw@socket.net. Sr. Suzanne Walker, O.P., Prin. Sisters 2; Lay Teachers 10; Students 155.
Catechesis/Religious Program—Students 79.

MONTGOMERY CITY, MONTGOMERY CO., IMMACULATE CONCEPTION (1861) [CEM 2] Rev. Frank A. Bussmann.
Res.: 307 N. Walker, 63361. Tel: 573-564-2375; Fax: 573-564-2375. Email: imm-con@sbcglobal.net.
School—(Grades PreK-8), 407 W. Third St., 63361. Tel: 573-564-2679; Fax: 573-564-2305. Email: lgruenefeld@ic-school.org. Web: www.ic-school.org. Lisa Gruenefeld, Interim Prin.; Bernice Reagan, Librarian; Aggie Baldetti, Librarian. Lay Teachers 5; Students 30.
Catechesis/Religious Program—Students 53.

MORRISON, GASCONADE CO., ASSUMPTION (1875) [CEM 2] Attended by Chamois. Rev. David A. Means, Canonical Admin.
Mailing Address: P.O. Box 156, Chamois, 65024. Tel: 573-763-5345. Email: mphparish@centurytel.net.
Catechesis/Religious Program—Students 9.

OSAGE BEND, COLE CO., ST. MARGARET OF ANTIOCH (1907) [CEM] Rev. Gregory C. Meystrik, Canonical Pastor; Deacon Robert Smerek, Pastoral Admin. 12025 Rte. W., 65101. Tel: 573-496-3404. Email: rssmerek@aol.com.
Catechesis/Religious Program—Students 40.

OWENSVILLE, GASCONADE CO., IMMACULATE CONCEPTION (1893) [CEM 2] Rev. Jeremy A. Secrist.
Res.: 404 S. First St., 65066. Tel: 573-437-2494; Fax: 573-437-7494. Email: icchurch@fidnet.com. Web: icowensville.org.
Catechesis/Religious Program—Tel: 573-437-3086. Students 144.

PALMYRA, MARION CO., ST. JOSEPH (1866) Rev. M. Christopher Smith.
Res.: 400 S. Lane St., P.O. Box 606, 63461. Tel: 573-769-3270; Fax: 573-769-4702. Email: stjoepalmyra@yahoo.com.
Catechesis/Religious Program—Students 72.

PERRY, RALLS CO., ST. WILLIAM (1901) [CEM] Rev. John A. Henderson.
Res.: P.O. Box 339, 63462. Tel: 573-565-2852; Fax: 573-565-8012. Email: stwill@rallstech.com.
Catechesis/Religious Program—Students 19.
Mission—St. Frances Cabrini (1953) 25560 Business Hwy. 24, Paris, Monroe Co. 65275.
Mission—St. Paul (Historic Church) 22520 St. Paul Dr., Center, Ralls Co. 63436. Email: stwill@rallstech.com.

PILOT GROVE, COOPER CO., ST. JOSEPH (1894) [CEM 3] Rev. Philip M. Kane.
Res.: 407 Harris St., 65276. Tel: 660-834-5600; Fax: 660-834-5601. Email: secretarypg@catholicweb.com. Web: www.stjosephparishpg.catholicweb.com.
School—405 Harris St., 65276. Tel: 660-834-5600; Fax: 660-834-5601. Email: principalpg@catholicweb.com. Kent Monnig, Prin. Lay Teachers 6; Students 38.
Catechesis/Religious Program—Students 48.
Station—St. John the Baptist (1840) Clear Creek, 65276. (Mass)
Station—St. Joseph Otterville, 65348. (Mass)

RHINELAND, MONTGOMERY CO., CHURCH OF THE RISEN SAVIOR (1979) [CEM 2] Rev. William D. Debo; Deacons Joseph E. Horton; Gerald W. Korman.
Res.: 605 Bluff St., 65069. Tel: 573-236-4390. Email: risensav@ktis.net. Web: www.historicshrine.org.
Catechesis/Religious Program—Students 6.
Pilgrimage Site— (1888) Shrine of Our Lady of Sorrows, 65069. Tel: 573-236-4390.

RICH FOUNTAIN, OSAGE CO., SACRED HEART (1838) [CEM] Rev. Philip E. Niekamp.
Church: 4277 Hwy. U, 65035. Tel: 573-744-5987. Email: shrf1838@earthlink.net. Web: www.sacredheartrf.com.
School—4309 Hwy. U, 65035. Tel: 573-744-5898; Fax: 573-744-5761. Email: shsrf@sacredheartrf.com. Web: www.sacredheartrf.com. Linda Neuner, Prin. Sisters of Notre Dame 1; Lay Teachers 5; Students 69.
Catechesis/Religious Program—Students 55.

RICHLAND, PULASKI CO., ST. JUDE (1972) Rev. John W. Groner.
Res. & Mailing Address: 367 Old Hwy. 66, St. Robert, 65584. Tel: 573-336-3662.

ROLLA, PHELPS CO., ST. PATRICK (1862) [CEM] Rev. Msgr. David D. Cox; Deacons Michael S. Brooks; Thomas C. Manion; Matthew McLaughlin.
Res.: 17 St. Patrick Ln., 65401. Tel: 573-364-1435; Fax: 573-364-2073. Email: stpats@stpatsrolla.org. Web: www.rollanet.org/~stpats.
School—(Grades PreK-8), 19 St. Patrick Ln., 65401. Tel: 573-364-1162; Fax: 573-364-0679. Deacon Michael Brooks, Prin. Lay Teachers 16; Students 152.
Catechesis/Religious Program—Students 128.

ROSATI, PHELPS CO., ST. ANTHONY (1906) [CEM] Rev. Charles D. Pardee, Canonical Pastor; Sr. Mary Rost, S.S.N.D., Pastoral Admin.
Res.: 21670 County Rd. 3640, St. James, 65559. Tel: 573-265-7247. Email: sttony@socket.net.

RUSSELLVILLE, COLE CO., ST. MICHAEL (1906) [CEM 2] Rev. Msgr. Donald W. Lammers, Canonical Pastor; Deacon Robert DePyper, Pastoral Admin.
Res.: 13321 Railroad Ave., 65074-1214. Tel: 573-782-4503; Fax: 573-782-3171. Email: stmrussellville@yahoo.com.
Catechesis/Religious Program—Tel: 573-782-3171. Students 62.

ST. ANTHONY, MILLER CO., ST. ANTHONY (1906) [CEM] Rev. Daniel I.J. Lueckenotte.
Church: 132 Main St., Iberia, 65486. Tel: 573-793-6550; Fax: 573-793-6550. Email: stanthonyofpaduachurch@hotmail.com.
Catechesis/Religious Program—Students 49.

ST. CLEMENT, PIKE CO., ST. CLEMENT (1871) [CEM 2] Rev. R. William Peckman.
Res.: 21509 Hwy. 161, Bowling Green, 63334. Tel: 573-324-5545; Fax: 573-324-5155. Email: clement@dishmail.net.
School—(Grades K-8) Tel: 573-324-2166; Fax: 573-324-6159. Email: stclement@socket.net. Larry Twellman, Prin. Lay Teachers 6; Students 80.
Catechesis/Religious Program—Students 122.

ST. ELIZABETH, MILLER CO., ST. LAWRENCE (1871) [CEM] Rev. Daniel I.J. Lueckenotte.
Res.: 246 Main, P.O. Box 128, 65075. Tel: 573-493-2301; Fax: 573-793-6550. Email: stlawrencegridiron@hotmail.com.
Catechesis/Religious Program—Tel: 573-793-6550. Students 121.

ST. JAMES, PHELPS CO., IMMACULATE CONCEPTION (1870) Rev. Charles D. Pardee.
Rectory—316 E. Scioto, 65559. Tel: 573-265-7250; Fax: 573-265-7269. Email: icchurch@socket.net. Web: www.icchurchstjames.org.
Catechesis/Religious Program—Students 56.

ST. MARTINS, COLE CO., ST. MARTIN (1885) [CEM] Rev. Edwin A. Schmidt; Deacons Francis J. Butel; Stephan J. Kliethermes.
Res.: 7148 St. Martins Ave., 65109. Tel: 573-893-2923; Fax: 573-893-3865. Email: stmartin@socket.net.
School—(Grades K-8), 7206 St. Martins Ave., 65109. Tel: 573-893-3519; Fax: 573-893-7404. Email: cwolters3@embarqmail.com. Cathy Wolters, Prin. Lay Teachers 14; Students 218.
Catechesis/Religious Program—Tel: 573-893-2352; Fax: 573-893-9587. Email: BAWasinger@aol.com. Students 31.

ST. ROBERT, PULASKI CO., ST. ROBERT BELLARMINE (1941) [CEM] Rev. John W. Groner.
Res.: 367 Old Hwy. 66, 65584. Tel: 573-336-3662. Email: strobert@fidmail.com.
Catechesis/Religious Program—Students 85.

ST. THOMAS, COLE CO., ST. THOMAS THE APOSTLE (1869) [CEM] Rev. Mark A. Porterfield.
Res.: 14814 Rt. B, P.O. Box 146, 65076. Tel: 573-477-3315; Fax: 573-477-0177. Email: stthomasoffice@embargmail.com.
School—(Grades PreK-8), P.O. Box 211, 65076. Tel: 573-477-3322; Fax: 573-477-3700. Email: lboessen@embarqmail.com. Web: www.stthomasmo-.com. Lora Boessen, Prin. Lay Teachers 9; Students 110.
Catechesis/Religious Program—Students 62.

SALISBURY, CHARITON CO., ST. JOSEPH (1870) [CEM] Rev. William L. Korte; Deacon John DeGraff.
Res.: 301 W. Williams, 65281. Tel: 660-388-5590; Fax: 660-388-5590. Email: stjosephchurch@mcmsys.com.
School—(Grades K-8) Tel: 660-388-5518; Fax: 660-388-5518. Email: stjoe@mcmsys.com. Jan Dubbert, Prin. Lay Teachers 11; Students 100.
Catechesis/Religious Program—Tel: 660-388-6180. Students 32.

SEDALIA, PETTIS CO.
1—ST. PATRICK (1866) Revs. James G. Betzen, C.PP.S.; Linus Evers, C.PP.S.; Deacon Jerome Connery. In Res., Rev. William Miller, C.PP.S.
Rectory—415 E. Fourth St., 65301. Tel: 660-826-2062; Fax: 660-829-1085. Email: stpatricks@charter.net.
Catechesis/Religious Program—Students 85.
2—SACRED HEART (1882) [CEM] Revs. James G. Betzen, C.PP.S.; Linus Evers, C.PP.S.; Deacon Jerome Connery. In Res., Rev. William Miller, C.PP.S.
Res.: 421 W. Third St., 65301. Tel: 660-827-2311; Fax: 660-827-3941. Email: shparish@charter.net.
School—(Grades K-8), 416 W. Third St., 65301. Tel: 660-827-3800; Fax: 660-827-3806. Dr. Mark Register, Prin.; Jinny O'Donnell, Librarian. Lay Teachers 12; Students 190.
High School—Dr. Mark Register, Prin. Lay Teachers 25; Students 240.
Catechesis/Religious Program—Students 106.
Mission—St. John (1845) Bahner, Pettis Co.
Station—St. Patrick (1876) Spring Fork. (Mass)

SHELBINA, SHELBY CO., ST. MARY (1879) [CEM] Rev. Donardo S. Bermejo, Canonical Admin.
Mailing Address: 307 E. Chestnut St., P.O. Box 306, 63468. Tel: 573-588-4498; Fax: 573-588-4498. Email: marypat@socket.net.
Catechesis/Religious Program—Students 87.

SLATER, SALINE CO., ST. JOSEPH (1882) Attended by Glasgow. Rev. Michael W. Penn.
Res.: 325 W. Emma St., 65349. Tel: 660-529-2588. Email: stjoseph1927@sbcglobal.net.
Catechesis/Religious Program—Students 16.

STEELVILLE, CRAWFORD CO., ST. MICHAEL (1949) Rev. James Finder.
Res.: 415 W. School St., Cuba, 65453. Tel: 573-885-3520; Fax: 573-885-3501. Email: stmich@fidmail.com.
Church: Hwy. 8 E., 65565.
Catechesis/Religious Program—Students 25.

TAOS, COLE CO., ST. FRANCIS XAVIER (1838) [CEM] Rev. Wayne M. Boyer; Deacon James E. Skahan. In Res., Rev. Roberto Ike.
Res.: 7319 Rte. M, 65101. Tel: 573-395-4401; Fax: 573-395-4302. Email: sfxchurch1@embarqmail.com. Web: www.members.socket.net/~SFXschool.
School—(Grades K-8), 7307 Rt. M., 65101. Tel: 573-395-4612. Donna Frazier, Prin. Lay Teachers 19; Students 182.
Catechesis/Religious Program—Students 94.

TIPTON, MONITEAU CO., ST. ANDREW (1857) [CEM] Rev. Frederick J. Elskamp.
Res.: 106 W. Cooper St., 65081-8210. Tel: 660-433-2162. Email: standrewchurch@embarqmail.com. Web: www.standrewtipton.org.
School—(Grades K-8), 118 E. Cooper St., 65081-0617. Tel: 660-433-2232; Fax: 660-433-5432. Email: standr34@embarqmail.com. Helen J. Franken, Prin. Lay Teachers 13; Students 125.
Catechesis/Religious Program—Students 64.

VANDALIA, AUDRAIN CO., SACRED HEART (1891) Rev. Russell R. Judge.
Res.: 203 W. Home, 63382. Tel: 573-594-2717. Email: shccastj@windstream.net.
Catechesis/Religious Program—Students 31.
Mission—St. John (1889) 7th & Elm, Laddonia, Audrain Co. 63352. Tel: 573-373-5351.

VIENNA, MARIES CO., VISITATION OF THE BLESSED VIRGIN MARY (1867) [CEM] Rev. Msgr. Marion J. Makarewicz.
Res.: 105 N. Main St., P.O. Box 171, 65582. Tel: 573-422-3950; Fax: 573-422-3950. Email: bvmchurch@att.net.
School—(Grades K-8), 105 N. Coffey St., P.O. Box 269, 65582. Tel: 573-422-3375; Fax: 573-422-3375. Web: www.vi-ps.org. Linda Stuckenschneider, Prin. Lay Teachers 5; Students 62.
Catechesis/Religious Program—Students 23.

WARDSVILLE, COLE CO., ST. STANISLAUS (1880) [CEM] Rev. Gregory C. Meystrik.
Res.: 6418 Rte. W., 65101. Tel: 573-636-4925; Fax: 573-636-2534. Web: www.ststan.net. Email: ststan@socket.net.
School—(Grades PreK-8), 6410 Rte. W., 65101. Tel: 573-636-7802; Fax: 573-635-4782. Email: nancyh@ststan.net. Web: www.ststan.net. Nancy Heberlie, Prin. Lay Teachers 19; Students 246.
Catechesis/Religious Program—Students 115.

WARSAW, BENTON CO., ST. ANN (1945) [CEM] Rev. Keith Branson, C.PP.S.
Res.: 30455 W. Dam Access Rd., 65355. Tel: 660-438-3844; Fax: 660-438-3844. Email: stannwarsaw1@yahoo.com. Web: stannwarsaw.org.
Catechesis/Religious Program—Tel: 660-438-3843. Students 48.
Mission—SS. Peter & Paul (1878) P.O. Box 248, Cole Camp, Benton Co. 65325. Tel: 660-668-3468. Email: spap@iliand.net.

WELLSVILLE, MONTGOMERY CO., CHURCH OF THE RESURRECTION (1873) [CEM] Rev. P. Gregory Oligschlaeger.
Church: 409 E. Bates, 63384.
Res. & Mailing Address: 408 E. Kellett, Martinsburg, 65264. Tel: 573-492-6595; Fax: 573-492-6105. Email: joseph@socket.net.
Catechesis/Religious Program—Students 10.

WESTPHALIA, OSAGE CO., ST. JOSEPH (1835) [CEM 2] Rev. Mark S. Smith.
Res.: P.O. Box 116, 65085-0116. Tel: 573-455-2320; Fax: 573-455-2984. Email: stjo1835@socket.net. Web:

www.stjo1835.org.
School—(Grades K-8) Tel: 573-455-2339; Fax: 573-455-2287. Email: sjsw1838@att.net. Deacon James E. Skahan, Prin. Lay Teachers 16; Students 217.
Catechesis/Religious Program—Students 94.
WIEN, CHARITON CO., ST. MARY OF THE ANGELS (1876) [CEM 2] Rev. William L. Korte.
Res.: 12520 St. Mary's Ave., New Cambria, 63558-3418. Tel: 660-226-5243.
Catechesis/Religious Program—Students 52.

Chaplains of Public Institutions
Prisons

JEFFERSON CITY. *Algoa Correctional Center*, Algoa Rd., P.O. Box 538, 65102. Tel: 573-751-3911. Rev. Patrick Dowling, Chap. Tel: 660-433-2162.
Jefferson City Correctional Center, 8200 Fenceline Rd., 65101. Tel: 573-751-3224. Rev. Charles D. Pardee, Chap. Tel: 573-897-4528.
BOONVILLE. *Boonville Correctional Center*.
E. Morgan St., 65233. Tel: 660-882-6521. Deacon David Miller, Chap. Tel: 660-882-2131.
BOWLING GREEN. *Northeast Correctional Center*, 13698 Pike 46, Airport Rd., 63334. Tel: 573-324-9975. Rev. Louis E. Dorn, Chap. Tel: 573-754-4757.
FULTON. *Diagnostic and Reception Center*, P.O. Box 581, 65251. Tel: 573-592-4040. Rev. Patrick Dowling, Chap. Tel: 660-433-2162, Deacon Robert L. Dulle, Chap. Tel: 573-896-8620.
MOBERLY. *Moberly Correctional Center*, P.O. Box 7, 65270. Tel: 660-263-3778. Rev. Michael A. Coleman, Chap. Tel: 660-263-5243.
TIPTON. *Tipton Treatment Center*, 619 N. Osage Ave., 65081. Tel: 660-433-2031. Rev. Patrick Dowling, Chap. Tel: 660-433-2162.
VANDALIA. *Women's Eastern Missouri Reception, Diagnostic and Correctional Center*, P.O. Box 300, 63382. Tel: 573-594-6686. Rev. Russell R. Judge, Chap. Tel: 573-594-2556.

Hospitals and Schools

JEFFERSON CITY. *Capital Region Medical Center*, 1125 Madison St., 65101. Tel: 573-635-5035. Rev. Hillary Andebo, Chap. Tel: 573-635-9143.
COLUMBIA. *Boone Hospital Center*, 1600 E. Broadway, 65201. Tel: 573-815-8000.
Columbia Catholic Hospital Ministry. Eleanor S. Braddock, M.D., Justo Gonzalez II, Dir. Tel: 573-999-0166, Deacon Gene Kazmierczak, Volunteer. Tel: 573-446-0387, Revs. Steven Kuhlmann, O.P., Chap. Tel: 573-874-2138, Thomas Saucier, O.P., Chap. Tel: 573-874-2138, Simon Felix Michalski, O.P., Chap. Tel: 573-874-2138, Joseph L. Shetler, Chap. Tel: 573-445-3815, M. Brendan Griffey, Chap. Tel: 573-338-2199.
Columbia Regional Hospital, 404 Keene St., 65201. Tel: 573-875-9000.
Ellis Fischel State Cancer Hospital, 115 Business Loop 70 W., 65201. Tel: 573-882-2100.
Mid-Missouri Mental Health Center, Three Hospital Dr., 65201. Tel: 573-884-1300.
Rusk Rehabilitation Center, 315 Business Loop 70 W., 65203. Tel: 573-817-2703.
University Hospital & Clinics, One Hospital Dr., 65201. Tel: 573-882-4141.
Veterans' Administration Medical Center, 800 Stadium Rd., 65201. Tel: 573-814-6000. Rev. Patrick Adejoh, Chap. Tel: 573-819-1872. (Harry S. Truman Memorial).
FULTON. *Fulton State Hospital*, 600 Fifth St., 65251. Tel: 573-592-4100. Rev. Patrick Dowling, Chap. Tel: 660-433-2162, Deacon Robert L. Dulle, Chap. Tel: 573-896-8620.
Missouri School for the Deaf, 505 E. Fifth St., 65251. Tel: 573-592-4000.
MARSHALL. *Marshall State School-Hospital*, E. Slater St., 65340. Tel: 660-886-2202. Rev. Kevin Gormley, Chap. Tel: 660-886-7960.
ST. JAMES. *Missouri Veterans' Home*, 620 N. Jefferson St., 65559. Tel: 573-265-3271. Rev. Charles D. Pardee, Chap. Tel: 573-265-7250.

On Duty Outside the Diocese:
Revs.—
Merz, Daniel J.
Steinhauser, Kenneth B.

Absent on Leave:
Revs.—
Behan, Hugh F.
Hereford, Thomas D.
Schlachter, Eric A.
Tatro, Timothy M.

Retired:
Rev. Msgrs.—
McCorkle, Louis W., 107 Shepherd Dr., Hannibal, 63401. Tel: 573-221-0947
Patterson, Charles, 321 S. Hickman St., Centralia, 65240.
Sommer, Jerome, Regina Cleri, 10 Archbishop May Dr., St. Louis, 63119. Tel: 314-918-8216
Revs.—
Barnett, Fred J., Jeanne Jugan Center, 8745 James A. Reed Rd., Kansas City, 64138. Tel: 816-761-4744
Bauer, Sylvester W., 23 Bauer Ln., Freeburg, 65035. Tel: 573-744-5913
Breaker, Donald J., P.O. Box 627, Fort Leonard Wood, 65473. Tel: 573-759-2595
Buescher, David G., 708 Marshall, 65101. Tel: 573-635-8845
Buhman, Leo T., LaVerna Village, P.O. Box 279, Savannah, 64485. Tel: 816-324-3185
Calasara, Mansuelo, P.O. Box 448, Dixon, 65459. Tel: 573-759-6381
Cronin, Richard, PO Box 44, Westphalia, 65085. Tel: 573-455-2151
Daly, Manus P.
Degnan, John F.
Doyle, Edward F., #9 Garden Place, Montgomery City, 63361. Tel: 573-564-2497
Flanagan, William F., 27519 Monroe Rd. 533, Monroe City, 63456. Tel: 573-735-4033
Fuemmeler, James R., 1567 Resorts Rd., Camdenton, 65020. Tel: 573-873-3263
Jones, Paul W., HC 77, P.O. Box 536, Pittsburg, 65724.
Konrad, Erwin, 12440 S. Benck Dr., Apt. 2, Alsip, IL 60803. Tel: 703-388-6803
Kramer, George, P.O. Box 68, Bonnots Mills, 65018. Tel: 573-897-2061
Lawless, P. Brendan, Sarah Community, Rm. 106, 12284 DePaul Dr., Bridgeton, 63044. Tel: 314-298-3899
Lawlor, Joseph G.
Long, John, c/o Owens Tara Curaheed Rd., Bishopstown 1, Cork, Ireland. Tel: 011-353-21-4831103
McGrath, Thomas E., 207 Norris Dr., 65109. Tel: 573-761-9180
Pierceall, Patrick L., P.O. Box 561, Hannibal, 63401. Tel: 573-406-1043
Schutty, John J.
Starmann, Joseph W., 25 Ackermann Rd., Winfield, 63389-3106. Tel: 636-566-8420
Stockman, Gerald W., 718 Randolph St., Glasgow, 65254. Tel: 660-338-2188
Stuart, Francis, O.S.B., St. Elizabeth Care Ctr., 649 S. Walnut St., Saint Elizabeth, 65075.
Waickman, Thomas L., Little Flower Rectory, 1264 Arch Ter., Richmond Heights, 63117. Tel: 314-645-1445
Wallace, Donald L.
Walsh, Peter, Friars Lodge Nursing Home, Convent Rd., Ballinrobe, Co. Mayo, Ireland.
Wheeler, Clarence, M.S., M.S., 612 Norris, 65109. Tel: 573-635-0648
Wiederholt, Clarence E., 1818 Almarie Ct., 65101. Tel: 573-636-4303

Permanent Deacons:
Anderberg, Peter K., (Retired)
Aulbur, Mark
Berry, Kenneth
Bilgrien, Kenneth D., (On Duty Outside the Diocese)
Braddock, Joseph M.
Breazile, James E., (On Duty Outside the Diocese)
Brooks, Michael
Brucks, Jerome C., (Retired)
Butel, Francis J.
Capuano, Tom, (Retired)
Chaplin, Mark, (On Duty Outside the Diocese)
Chavaux, Paul, (Leave of Absence)
Christoff, Gary
Collins, Lloyd
Connery, Jerome
Daly, Michael M., (Leave of Absence)
Davis, Howard E., (On Duty Outside the Diocese)
DeGraff, John
DePyper, Robert
Dobelman, Mark J.
Dulle, Robert L.
Fritsch, Frederick, (Retired)
Heidlage, Walter F., (Retired)
Hildebrand, Larry, (On Duty Outside the Diocese)
Horsefield, Earl R.
Horton, Joseph E.
Houston, John D., (Retired)
Joyce, Dana K.
Kazmierczak, Eugene S.
Kliethermes, James L.
Kliethermes, Stephan J.
Korman, Gerald W.
Leake, Robert
Leyden, James
Linhardt, Wayne
Lovell, David
Luebbering, Richard H., (Retired)
Manion, Thomas C.
McLaughlin, Matthew
Miller, David
Miller, Thomas
Mitchell, Joseph R.
Neudecker, John L.
Orscheln, Donald W., (Retired)
Parn, Harold L., (Retired)
Pierceall, Eugene E., (Retired)
Poulter, Paul
Puglis, Joseph
Purvis, Raymond L.
Rackers, Robert J., (Retired)
Ramsay, Daniel J.
Ream, David D.
Reibenspies, Terence L., (On Duty Outside the Diocese)
Ritter, David F.
Rohan, Peter
Ruggiero, Frank
Schmitz, Fred
Shumake, Lindell P., (Retired)
Skahan, James E.
Smerek, Robert
Stahl, Theodore E., (Retired)
Thompson, David
Toll, Bernhard F.
Valdes, Anthony J.
Visot, Luis R., (On Duty Outside the Diocese)
Von Gunten, Richard A.
Warden, Donald E., (Retired)
Watson, G. Robert, (Leave of Absence)
Weaver, John D.
Weber, Lawrence A.
Weisel, Fred M., (Leave of Absence)
Whalen, Tom

INSTITUTIONS LOCATED IN THE DIOCESE

[A] HIGH SCHOOLS, DIOCESAN

JEFFERSON CITY. *Helias High School*, 1305 Swift's Hwy., 65109. Tel: 573-635-6139; Fax: 573-635-5615. Email: info@heliashighschool.com. Web: www.heliashighschool.com. Mr. Didier Aur, Pres.; Sr. Jean Dietrich, Prin.; Mr. Stan Ochsner, Dean of Students; Rev. Brendan Doyle, Spiritual Dir.; Mrs. Christina Bockwinkel-Baker, Campus Ministry; Shelley Swoyer, Librarian. Brothers of the Christian Schools 2; School Sisters of Notre Dame 1; Lay Teachers 54; Students 822.

[B] CATHOLIC HOSPITALS

JEFFERSON CITY. *St. Mary Health Center*, 100 St. Mary's Medical Plaza, 65101. Tel: 573-761-7000; Fax: 573-636-5733. Web: www.stmarys-jeffcity.com. Brent VanConia, Pres.; Rev. James Carter, American Baptist Min., APC Certified Chap.; Mrs. Peggy Van Gundy, Dir., Mission Effectiveness, Certified Chap.; Revs. James Gearhart, Chap.; Paul Deutsch, Chap.; Bart Larson, Chap.; Mark Steffen, Chap.; Randall Bunch, Chap. Member of SSM Health Care. Bed Capacity 167; Patients Assisted Annually 258,234; Clinics 16; Clinic Visits 130,171.

[C] CONVENTS AND RESIDENCES FOR SISTERS

JEFFERSON CITY. *Discalced Carmelite Monastery*, 2201 W. Main St., 65109. Tel: 573-636-3364. Sr. Marie Therese Dubois, O.C.D., Prioress. Professed of Solemn Vows 6.
Franciscan Sisters of Mary, 827-R Southwest Blvd., 65109-2698. Tel: 573-644-8055. Sisters 3.
COLUMBIA. *Our Lady of Peace Monastery*, 3710 W. Broadway, 65203-0116. Tel: 573-446-2300; Fax: 573-446-2312. Email: smeek37@gmail.com. Web: www.benedictinesister.org. Sr. Sandra Meek, O.S.B., Admin. Benedictine Sisters of Pontifical Jurisdiction 7.

[D] NEWMAN CENTERS

COLUMBIA. *St. Thomas More Newman Center* 701 Maryland, 65201. Tel: 573-449-5424; Fax: 573-874-2777. Email: chris.temporal@newmancentercolumbia.org. Web: www.newmancentercolumbia.org. Revs. Thomas Saucier, O.P., Pastor; Simon Felix Michalski, O.P.
KIRKSVILLE. *Catholic Newman Center, Truman State University* 709 S. Davis, 63501. Tel: 660-665-4357; Fax: 660-665-3592. Email: tsnewman@socket.net. Web: newman.truman.edu. Mrs. Bettie Lesczynski, Dir.; Rev. William P. Kottenstette, Chap.
ROLLA. *Catholic Newman Center, Missouri University of Science and Technology* formerly University of Missouri-Rolla 1607 N. Rolla St., P.O. Box 838, 65402. Tel: 573-364-2133; Fax: 573-368-3560. Email: newman@mst.edu. Web: www.rollanewman.org. Rev. Msgr. David D. Cox,

Chap.; Sr. Laura Spaeth, S.S.N.D., Campus Min.

[E] SOCIAL SERVICES

JEFFERSON CITY. *Samaritan Center*, 1310 E. McCarty St., P.O. Box 1687, 65102. Tel: 573-634-7776; Fax: 573-761-5948. Email: samaritan@midmosamaritan.org. Web: midmosamaritan.org. Marylyn DeFeo, Exec. Dir.

[F] MISCELLANEOUS

JEFFERSON CITY. *Catholic Diocese of Jefferson City Fund, Inc.*, P.O. Box 104900, 65110-4900. Tel: 573-635-9127; Fax: 573-635-0386.

Columbia Catholic High School Fund, P.O. Box 104900, 65110-4900. Tel: 573-635-9127; Fax: 573-635-0386.

Diocesan Excellence in Education Fund, Inc., P.O. Box 104900, 65110-4900. Tel: 573-635-9127; Fax: 573-635-0386.

Diocese of Jefferson City Jubilee Fund, P.O. Box 104900, 65110-4900. Teletype: 573-635-9127; Fax: 573-635-0386.

Diocese of Jefferson City Real Estate Corporation, P.O. Box 104900, 65110-4900.

Diocese of Jefferson City Real Estate Trust, P.O. Box 104900, 65110-4900.

Jefferson City Diocese Chancery Building Fund, P.O. Box 104900, 65110-4900. Tel: 573-635-9127; Fax: 573-635-0386.

St. Mary's Health Center, Jefferson City, Missouri, Foundation, 100 St. Mary's Medical Plaza, 65101. Tel: 573-761-7198; Fax: 573-659-2106. Web: www.LetHealingBegin.com. Member of SSM Health Care.

Missouri Catholic Conference, 600 Clark Ave., P.O. Box 1022, 65102. Tel: 573-635-7239; Fax: 573-635-7431. Email: mocatholic@mocatholic.org. Web: www.mocatholic.org. Michael Hoey, Interim Dir.

St. Peter School Foundation, P.O. Box 104900, 65110-4900. Tel: 573-635-9127; Fax: 573-635-0386.

Regional Catholic High School in Columbia Foundation, P.O. Box 104900, 65110-4900.

Residents Encounter Christ, P.O. Box 104900, 65110-4900.

LINN. *Good Shepherd Center*, 1117 Adams St., P.O. Box 763, 65051. Tel: 573-897-0525. Bill Voss, Volunteer Dir.

ST. JAMES. *Boys and Girls Town of Missouri*, 13160 County Rd. 3610, 65559. Tel: 800-737-3251. Web: www.bgtm.org.

RELIGIOUS INSTITUTES OF MEN REPRESENTED IN THE DIOCESE

For further details refer to the corresponding bracketed number in the Religious Institutes of Men or Women section.

[0330]—*Brothers of the Christian Schools* (Midwest Prov.)—F.S.C.

[1330]—*Congregation of the Mission* (Midwest Prov.)—C.M.

[]—*Dominican Order of St. Albert the Great* (Central Province)—O.P.

[0720]—*The Missionaries of Our Lady of La Salette* (Prov. of Mary Queen)—M.S.

[]—*Order of St. Benedict* (Conception Abbey)—O.S.B.

[1060]—*Society of the Precious Blood* (Kansas City Prov.)—C.PP.S.

RELIGIOUS INSTITUTES OF WOMEN REPRESENTED IN THE DIOCESE

[0230]—*Benedictine Sisters of Pontifical Jurisdiction* (Columbia, MO)—O.S.B.

[0460]—*Congregation of the Sisters of Charity of the Incarnate Word* (San Antonio, TX)—C.C.V.I.

[1730]—*Congregation of the Sisters of the Third Order of St. Francis* (Oldenburg, IN)—O.S.F.

[0420]—*Discalced Carmelite Nuns (Second Order of the Carmel)* Jefferson City, MO—O.C.D.

[1070-11]—*Dominican Sisters* (Sparkill, NY)—O.P.

[1415]—*Franciscan Sisters of Mary* (St. Louis, MO)—F.S.M.

[2970]—*School Sisters of Notre Dame* (St. Louis Prov.)—S.S.N.D.

[1680]—*School Sisters of St. Francis* (Milwaukee, WI)—O.S.F.

[]—*Sisters of Mercy of the Americas* (Omaha, NE)—R.S.M.

[3840]—*Sisters of St. Joseph of Carondelet* (St. Paul, MN)—C.S.J.

[3270]—*Sisters of the Most Precious Blood* (O'Fallon, MO)—C.PP.S.

DIOCESAN CEMETERIES

JEFFERSON CITY. *St. Peter's Catholic Cemetery Association*, c/o Resurrection Cemetery, 3015 W. Truman Blvd., 65109. Tel: 573-893-2751; Fax: 573-893-5026. Mr. Lawrence Hasenbeck, Pres.

NECROLOGY

† Poelker, Rev. Msgr. Gerard L., (Retired)—Died Aug. 3, 2009

† Duggan, Thomas J., (Retired)—Died Sept. 29, 2009

† Forst, William, (Retired)—Died Sept. 13, 2009

† Moriarty, Philip M., Wien, MO St. Mary of the Angels—Died June 18, 2009

† Reichert, Henry J., Tipton, MO St. Andrew & California, MO Annunciation—Died June 20, 2009

An asterisk (*) denotes an organization that has established tax-exempt status directly with the IRS and is not covered by the USCCB Group Ruling.

Diocese of Joliet in Illinois

(Dioecesis Joliettensis in Illinois)

Most Reverend

JAMES PETER SARTAIN, D.D., S.T.L.

Bishop of Joliet; ordained July 15, 1978; appointed Bishop of Little Rock January 4, 2000; consecrated and installed March 6, 2000; appointed Bishop of Joliet May 16, 2006; installed June 27, 2006. *Chancery: 425 Summit St., Joliet, IL 60435.* Tel: 815-722-6606; Fax: 815-722-6632.

Most Reverend

JOSEPH L. IMESCH, D.D.

Retired Bishop of Joliet; ordained December 16, 1956; ordained Auxiliary Bishop of Detroit April 3, 1973; appointed Bishop of Joliet June 30, 1979; installed August 28, 1979; retired June 21, 2006. *Res.: 425 Summit St., Joliet, IL 60435.*

OF YOU MY HEART HAS SPOKEN

Chancery: 425 Summit St., Joliet, IL 60435. Tel: 815-722-6606; Fax: 815-722-6602.

Web: www.dioceseofjoliet.org

Email: jdavies@dioceseofjoliet.org

Most Reverend

JOSEPH M. SIEGEL

Auxiliary Bishop of Joliet; ordained June 4, 1988; appointed Auxiliary Bishop of Joliet and Titular Bishop of Pupiana October 28, 2009; ordained January 19, 2010. *Chancery: 425 Summit St., Joliet, IL 60435.*

ESTABLISHED BY BULL DATED DECEMBER 11, 1948.

Square Miles 4,218.

Canonically Erected March 24, 1949.

Comprises the Counties of Du Page, Kankakee, Will, Grundy, Ford, Iroquois and Kendall in the State of Illinois.

Patron of Diocese: St. Francis Xavier.

For legal titles of parishes and diocesan institutions, consult the Chancery.

STATISTICAL OVERVIEW

Personnel	
Bishop	1
Auxiliary Bishops	1
Retired Bishops	1
Abbots	1
Retired Abbots	1
Priests: Diocesan Active in Diocese	119
Priests: Diocesan Active Outside Diocese	4
Priests: Diocesan in Foreign Missions	1
Priests: Retired, Sick or Absent	58
Number of Diocesan Priests	182
Religious Priests in Diocese	110
Total Priests in Diocese	292
Extern Priests in Diocese	10
Ordinations:	
Diocesan Priests	3
Transitional Deacons	5
Permanent Deacons	18
Permanent Deacons in Diocese	209
Total Brothers	63
Total Sisters	496
Parishes	
Parishes	120
With Resident Pastor:	
Resident Diocesan Priests	98
Resident Religious Priests	13
Without Resident Pastor:	
Administered by Priests	9
Missions	10
Professional Ministry Personnel:	
Sisters	34
Lay Ministers	268
Welfare	
Catholic Hospitals	3
Total Assisted	759,596
Homes for the Aged	16
Total Assisted	84,001
Day Care Centers	4
Total Assisted	1,630
Specialized Homes	1
Total Assisted	1,904
Special Centers for Social Services	5
Total Assisted	33,651
Residential Care of Disabled	1
Total Assisted	124
Educational	
Diocesan Students in Other Seminaries	28
Total Seminarians	28
Colleges and Universities	3
Total Students	14,619
High Schools, Diocesan and Parish	3
Total Students	1,823
High Schools, Private	4
Total Students	3,584
Elementary Schools, Diocesan and Parish	54
Total Students	17,151
Catechesis/Religious Education:	
High School Students	4,561
Elementary Students	47,873
Total Students under Catholic Instruction	89,639
Teachers in the Diocese:	
Priests	23
Brothers	21
Sisters	31
Lay Teachers	2,295
Vital Statistics	
Receptions into the Church:	
Infant Baptism Totals	8,075
Minor Baptism Totals	196
Adult Baptism Totals	205
Received into Full Communion	598
First Communions	9,638
Confirmations	8,268
Marriages:	
Catholic	1,259
Interfaith	333
Total Marriages	1,592
Deaths	3,460
Total Catholic Population	655,415
Total Population	1,888,772

Former Bishops—Most Revs. MARTIN D. MCNAMARA, D.D., appt. first Bishop of Joliet; ord. Dec. 3, 1922; appt. Dec. 17, 1948; cons. March 7, 1949; died May 23, 1966; ROMEO BLANCHETTE, D.D., appt. Auxiliary Bishop of Joliet and Titular Bishop of Maxita Feb. 8, 1965; cons. April 3, 1965; appt. Bishop of Joliet July 19, 1966; installed Aug. 31, 1966; resigned Jan. 30, 1979; died Jan. 10, 1982; JOSEPH J. IMESCH, D.D., ord. Dec. 16, 1956; ord. Auxiliary Bishop of Detroit April 3, 1973; appt. Bishop of Joliet June 30, 1979; installed Aug. 28, 1979; retired May 16, 2006.

Chancery—425 Summit St., Joliet, 60435. Tel: 815-722-6606; Fax: 815-722-6602. Office Hours: Mon.-Thurs. 8-4:30, Fri. 8-1.

Vicar General—Very Rev. JOSEPH TAPELLA, J.C.L.

Chancellor—Sr. JUDITH A. DAVIES, O.S.F.

Moderator of the Curia—Very Rev. JOSEPH TAPELLA, J.C.L.

Director of Buildings and Properties—Mr. CHRISTOPHER NYE.

Chief Financial Officer—Mr. MICHAEL BAVA.

Matrimonial Tribunal—310 Bridge St., Joliet, 60435. Tel: 815-722-2256.

Judicial Vicar—Very Rev. JOSEPH TAPELLA, J.C.L.

Adjutant Judicial Vicar—VACANT.

Notaries—Mrs. BETTY JOUTRAS; Mrs. HELEN MILCHERSKA; Mrs. DELORES AICHELE.

Defender of the Bond—Sr. MARILYN PHILLIPS, O.S.F., Ph.D., J.C.D.

Judges—Very Rev. JOSEPH TAPELLA, J.C.L.; Mr. THOMAS E. KERBER, J.C.L.

Advocates—Mrs. VIRGINIA L. LAUTZ; Sr. CLARE VAN VOOREN, O.S.F.

Diocesan Offices and Directors

Board of Conciliation and Arbitration—425 Summit St., Joliet, 60435. Mr. ROBERT WHEELER, Chm.

Campaign for Human Development—Ms. MARIBETH MEAUX, St. Charles Borromeo Pastoral Center, 402 S. Independence Blvd., Romeoville, 60441. Tel: 815-834-4027.

Catholic Cemeteries—Mr. RICHARD TAPELLA, Dir., St. Charles Borromeo Pastoral Center, 402 S. Independence Blvd., Romeoville, 60441. Tel: 815-838-0395.

Catholic Charities— Legal Title: Catholic Charities of the Diocese of Joliet. Ms. KATHLEEN MCGOWAN, Exec. Dir., 203 N. Ottawa St., Joliet, 60432. Tel: 815-723-3405.

The Catholic Education Foundation of the Diocese of Joliet—Mrs. JANE LAGGER, Dir., St. Charles Borromeo Pastoral Center, 402 S. Independence Blvd., Romeoville, 60441. Tel: 815-834-4033.

Diocesan Educational Endowment Fund—Chancery, 425 Summit St., Joliet, 60435. Tel: 815-722-6606.

Catholic Relief Services—Mr. THOMAS GARLITZ, Dir., St. Charles Center, 402 S. Independence Blvd., Romeoville, 60441. Tel: 815-834-4026.

Council of Catholic Women—Mrs. CARLOTTA LAWTON, Office: St. Charles Borromeo Pastoral Center, 402 S. Independence Blvd., Romeoville, 60441. Tel: 815-834-4070.

Communications Office—Mr. DOUG DELANEY, Chancery, 425 Summit St., Joliet, 60435. Tel: 815-722-6606.

Continuing Formation for Priests—Rev. JOHN BALLUFF, Dir.

Cursillo Movement—Rev. MARK JENDRYSIK, Moderator, St. Philip Parish, 1223 W. Holtz, Addison, 60101. Tel: 630-628-0900.

Deans—Revs. WILLIAM DESALVO, East Dupage; GERALD RIVA, West Dupage Kendall; MICHAEL LANE, East Will; VACANT, West Will (incl. Grundy); Revs. CHARLES WHEELER, Kankakee; ROBERT J. COLEMAN, Ford-Iroquois.

Development—Mr. TONY BRANDOLINO, Chief Devel. Officer, St. Charles Borromeo Pastoral Center, 402 S. Independence Blvd., Romeoville, 60441. Tel: 815-838-8515.

Coordinator for Health Affairs—Sr. JUDITH A. DAVIES, O.S.F., Chancery, 425 Summit St., Joliet, 60435. Tel: 815-722-6606.

Vicar for Religious—Sr. THERESA GALVAN, C.N.D., St. Charles Borromeo Pastoral Center, 402 S. Independence Blvd., Romeoville, 60441. Tel: 815-834-4009.

Vicar for Priests—Rev. WILLIAM G. DEWAN.

Diaconate—Deacon JOSEPH DALPIAZ, Dir., St. Charles Borromeo Pastoral Center, 402 S. Independence Blvd., Romeoville, 60441. Tel: 815-834-4091.

Divine Worship—Sr. SHARON MARIE STOLA, O.S.B., Dir., St. Charles Borromeo Pastoral Center, 402 S. Independence Blvd., Romeoville, 60441. Tel: 815-834-4010.

Ecumenism—VACANT.

Family Ministry—Dr. JAMES HEALY, Dir., St. Charles Borromeo Pastoral Center, 402 S. Independence Blvd., Romeoville, 60441. Tel: 815-838-5334.

Hispanic Ministry—Mr. MIGUEL MORENO, Dir., St. Charles Borromeo Center, 402 S. Independence Blvd., Romeoville, 60441. Tel: 815-834-4037.

"Christ Is Our Hope" Magazine—Mr. CARLOS BRICENO, Editor, Office: 402 S. Independence Blvd., Romeoville, 60441. Tel: 815-834-4060; Fax: 815-834-4068.

Diocesan Life Office—Rev. THOMAS MILOTA, Dir., Sts. Peter & Paul Parish, 36 N. Ellsworth Ave., Naperville, 60540. Tel: 630-718-2121; Fax: 630-355-1179.

Marriage Encounter—Leadership Couple: ANDY JOBST; BRIDGET JOBST, 6 Camden Ct., Cary, 60013. Tel: 847-516-0005.

Marriage Preparation—Dr. JAMES HEALY, Dir., St. Charles Borromeo Pastoral Center, 402 S. Independence Blvd., Romeoville, 60441. Tel: 815-838-5334.

Ministry Formation—VACANT, Dir., St. Charles Borromeo Pastoral Center, 402 S. Independence Blvd., Romeoville, 60441. Tel: 815-834-4001.

College Campus Ministry—Mr. KEVIN O'DONNELL, 402 S. Independence Blvd., Romeoville, 60446-2264. Tel: 815-834-4022.

Peace and Social Justice Ministry—Mr. THOMAS GARLITZ, Dir. Tel: 815-834-4026. St. Charles Borromeo Pastoral Center, 402 S. Independence Blvd., Romeoville, 60441.

Human Resources—Mrs. NANCY SIEMERS, Dir. Tel: 815-834-4077.

Presbyteral Council—Rev. JEFFERY STONEBERG, Pres., 425 Summit, Joliet, 60435. Tel: 815-722-6606.

Propagation of the Faith—Rev. DAMIEN GRAZIANO, Dir., 1 S 314 Summit Ave., Oakbrook Terrace, 60181. Tel: 630-629-5810.

Religious Education—Mr. THOMAS QUINLAN, Dir., 402 S. Independence Blvd., Romeoville, 60446. Tel: 815-838-6475.

Rural Life—VACANT.

Catholic Schools—Sr. HELEN JEAN KORMELINK, O.S.B., Supt., St. Charles Borromeo Pastoral Center, 402 S. Independence Blvd., Romeoville, 60441. Tel: 815-838-2181.

Scouts—Deacon SCOTT BRECHTEL, Office: Corpus Christi, 1415 Lies Rd., Carol Stream, 60188-4841. Tel: 630-483-4673.

Victim Assistance Coordinator—Mrs. JUDITH SPECKMAN. Tel: 815-263-6467.

Vocations—Rev. BURKE MASTERS, Dir., St. Charles Borromeo, 402 S. Independence Blvd., Romeoville, 60441. Tel: 815-834-4002.

CLERGY, PARISHES, MISSIONS AND PAROCHIAL SCHOOLS

CITY OF JOLIET

(WILL COUNTY)

1—THE CATHEDRAL OF ST. RAYMOND (1917) Revs. Brad Baker, Rector; Nathan Gohlke, Parochial Vicar. In Res., Very Rev. Joseph Tapella.
Res.: 604 N. Raynor Ave., 60435. Tel: 815-722-6653. Email: bulletin@straymond.net. Web: www.straymond.net.
School—(Grades PreSchool-8), 608 N. Raynor Ave., 60435. Tel: 815-722-6626; Fax: 815-727-4668. Email: straymond60435@yahoo.com. Dr. Jennifer Groves, Prin.; Melody Grizzle, Librarian. Lay Teachers 24; Students 520.
Catechesis/Religious Program—Tel: 815-726-0947; Fax: 815-722-3137. Students 310.

2—ST. ANTHONY (1902), (Italian), Rev. Vytas Memenas, Admin. (Retired).
Res.: 100 N. Scott St., 60432-4210. Tel: 815-722-1057; Fax: 815-722-9805. Email: saintanthonyjoliet@hotmail.com.

3—ST. BERNARD (1921) Rev. Richard Ross; Deacon Frank Juricic.
Res.: 1313 Ridgewood Ave., 60432. Tel: 815-726-4474; Fax: 815-726-4520.
Catechesis/Religious Program—Tel: 815-722-7653; Fax: 815-724-1720. Clustered with St. Mary Magdalene, Joliet. Students 28.

4—SS. CYRIL AND METHODIUS (1900), (Slovak), Closed. For inquiries for parish records contact the chancery.

5—ST. FRANCIS XAVIER (2002) [CEM] Rev. Kevin J. Spiess (CHI).
Mailing Address: 2500 Arbeiter Rd., 60431. Tel: 815-609-8077; Fax: 815-609-8078. Email: missionlands@aol.com. Web: www.st-francis-xavier.com.

6—HOLY CROSS (1893), (Polish), [JC] Revs. Christopher Groh; Julian Kaczowka, S.Ch.
901 Elizabeth St., 60435. Tel: 815-722-0785; Fax: 815-723-0679.
School—Please see St. Mary Nativity, Joliet
School—Polish School of Religion, (Grades K-8) Dominik Nestorowicz, Dir. Students 160.
Catechesis/Religious Program—Please see St. Mary Nativity, Joliet.

7—ST. JOHN THE BAPTIST (1852) [CEM] Revs. John Dombrowski, O.F.M.; Fred Radtke, O.F.M., Parochial Vicar; Deacons Jose Lopez; James Janousek. In Res., Revs. Dennis Schafer, O.F.M., Dir. Postulancy Guardian; Rogelio Martinez Ruteaga, O.F.M., Asst. Dir. Postulancy; J. Derran Combs, O.F.M.; Allan DeCorte, O.F.M.
Res.: 404 N. Hickory St., 60435. Tel: 815-727-4788. Email: stjohnbap@church404.comcastbiz.net. Web: www.stjohnsjoliet.org.
Catechesis/Religious Program—403 N. Hickory St., 60435. Tel: 815-727-9077; Fax: 815-727-1729. Students 700.

8—ST. JOSEPH (1891), (Slovenian), [CEM] Rev. Roger Kutzner.
Res.: 416 N. Chicago St., 60432. Tel: 815-727-9378; Fax: 815-727-9580. Email: stjoseph416@stjosephjoliet.org.
School—(Grades K-8), 409 N. Scott St., 60432. Tel: 815-722-1005; Fax: 815-722-1213. Mr. David Spesia, Prin.; Tina Dodge, Librarian. Lay Teachers 13; Students 180.
Catechesis/Religious Program—Students 75.

9—ST. JUDE (1954) Rev. Michael Lane; Deacons Raymond Clark, Business Mgr.; William Hetzel.
Res.: 2212 McDonough St., 60436. Tel: 815-725-2209; Fax: 815-741-8844. Email: mlane@catholicexchange.com. Web: www.stjudejoliet.org.
School—(Grades K-8), 2204 McDonough St., 60436. Tel: 815-729-0288; Fax: 815-729-0344. Sr. Rita Mandella, O.S.F., Prin. Sisters of St. Francis of Mary Immaculate 1; Lay Teachers 11; Students 180.
Catechesis/Religious Program—Email: jfrato@catholicexchange.com. Students 173.

10—ST. MARY, Closed. For inquiries for parish records contact the chancery.

11—ST. MARY MAGDALENE (1953) Rev. Ron P. Neitzke.
Res.: 127 S. Briggs St., 60433. Tel: 815-722-7653; Fax: 815-724-1720.
Catechesis/Religious Program—Students 105.

12—ST. MARY NATIVITY (1906), (Croatian), [JC] Revs. Christopher Groh; Julian Kaczowka, S.Ch.; Lee F. Bacchi, Parochial Vicar; Margaret Trepal, Pastoral Assoc.; Deacon Daniel Mahoney Sr.
Res.: 706 N. Broadway, 60435. Tel: 815-726-4031; Fax: 815-727-4393. Web: www.stmarynativity.com.
School—(Grades PreSchool-8), 702 N. Broadway, 60435. Tel: 815-722-8518. Mrs. Joan Matejka, Prin. Sisters of St. Francis of Christ the King 1; Lay Teachers 14; Students 149.
Catechesis/Religious Program—Tel: 815-726-4073. Michael Hoyt, D.R.E. Students 160.
Convent—700 N. Hickory St., 60435. Tel: 815-722-0416.

13—MOUNT CARMEL (1939), (Mexican-American), Revs. Jose Cilia, O.Carm.; Enrique Varela-Nungaray, O.Carm., Parochial Vicar.
Church Office: 407 Irving St., 60432. Tel: 815-727-7187; Fax: 815-727-7187. Email: montecarmelo@prodigy.net. Web: www.ourladymtcarmel.net.
Weekend Svcs.: 205 E. Jackson St., 60432. Daily Mass: 405 E. Irving St., 60432.
Res.: 409 Irving St., 60432. Tel: 815-726-5208; Fax: 815-727-7225.
Catechesis/Religious Program—Tel: 815-727-0899; Fax: 815-531-8201. Students 700.

14—ST. PATRICK (1838) Rev. Peter G. Jankowski; Deacons Paul Kolodziej; Charles Peterson.
Res.: 710 W. Marion St., 60436-1556. Tel: 815-727-4746; Fax: 815-727-4798. Email: stpatrectory0710@sbcglobal.net. Web: www.stpatsjoliet.com.
School—(Grades PreSchool-8), 110 Willow Ave., 60436. Tel: 815-726-2924; Fax: 815-726-9289. Dr. Lonnie Hughes, Prin.; Karen Hughes, Librarian; Nancy Seeman, Librarian. Lay Teachers 20; Students 200.
Catechesis/Religious Program—Tel: 815-727-4746; Fax: 815-727-4746. Students 200.

15—ST. PAUL THE APOSTLE (1950) Revs. Gregory Rothfuchs; George Klepec, Pastor Emeritus; Deacon William Bevan.
Res.: 18 Woodlawn Ave., 60435. Tel: 815-725-1527; Fax: 815-730-9907. Email: stpauljoliet@sbcglobal.net. Web: www.stpauljoliet.com.
School—(Grades PreSchool-8), 130 Woodlawn Ave., 60435. Tel: 815-725-3390; Fax: 815-725-3180. Web: www.thestpaulschool.org. Mrs. Mary Kay Robbins, Prin. Lay Teachers 23; Students 393.
Catechesis/Religious Program—120 Woodlawn Ave., 60435. Tel: 815-725-6927. Students 217.

16—SACRED HEART (1886), (African American), Rev. Raymond C. Lescher; Deacon Ralph Bias.
Res.: 337 S. Ottawa St., 60436. Tel: 815-722-0295; Fax: 815-722-6088.
Catechesis/Religious Program—Students 24.

17—ST. THADDEUS (1927), (Polish), Closed. For inquiries for parish records contact the chancery.

OUTSIDE THE CITY OF JOLIET

ADDISON, DU PAGE CO.

1—ST. JOSEPH (1956), (Hispanic), Rev. Luis Gutierrez; Deacons Gabriel Gamboa; Philip Marrow.
Res.: 330 E. Fullerton, 60101. Tel: 630-279-6553; Fax: 630-279-4925. Email: stjoes@catholic.org. Web: www.stjoeaddison.com.
See Holy Family Catholic School, Bensenville under St. Charles Borromeo, Bensenville for details.
Catechesis/Religious Program—Tel: 630-832-5514. Ms. Dolly Matthews, C.R.E. Students 539.

2—ST. PHILIP THE APOSTLE (1963) Rev. Mark Jendrysik; Deacon Philip Heitz.
Res.: 1223 W. Holtz Ave., 60101. Tel: 630-628-0900; Fax: 630-543-9858.
School—(Grades PreSchool-8), 1233 W. Holtz Ave., 60101. Tel: 630-543-4130; Fax: 630-458-8750. Denise Sedlak, Prin. Lay Teachers 15; Students 330.
Catechesis/Religious Program—Tel: 630-543-1754; Fax: 630-543-4672. Mr. Frank Giangrego, D.R.E. Students 300.

ASHKUM, IROQUOIS CO., ASSUMPTION OF THE BLESSED VIRGIN MARY (1903) [CEM] [JC 2] Rev. James Holup.
Res.: 208 N. Second St., Box 218, 60911. Tel: 815-698-2262; Fax: 815-698-2262.
Mission—St. John the Baptist (1856) Box 218, L'Erable, Iroquois Co. 60911. Tel: 815-698-2262.
Catechesis/Religious Program—Students 114.

AURORA, DU PAGE CO., OUR LADY OF MERCY (1988) Rev. Hugh Fullmer; Deacons Robert Vavra; Philip Rehmer; Timothy Kueper; Arturo Tiongson.
Res.: 701 S. Eola Rd., 60504. Tel: 630-851-3444; Fax: 630-851-3468.
Catechesis/Religious Program—Tel: 630-851-3444, Ext. 222. Students 1,472.

BEAVERVILLE, IROQUOIS CO., ST. MARY (1857), (French), [CEM] [JC] Rev. Robert J. Coleman.
Res.: 308 St. Charles St., P.O. Box 152, 60912. Tel: 815-435-2432. Email: stmarys@dioceseofjoliet.org.
Catechesis/Religious Program—Ryan Loy, D.R.E. Students 24.

BENSENVILLE, DU PAGE CO.

1—ST. ALEXIS (1926) Rev. Agustin Ortega-Ruiz; Sr. Laurina Kahne, C.S.J., Pastoral Assoc.
Res.: 400 W. Wood St., 60106. Tel: 630-766-3530; Fax: 630-766-3536.
Catechesis/Religious Program—410 W. Wood St., 60106. Tel: 630-766-4417. Dr. Donna Cascino, D.R.E. Students 344.

2—ST. CHARLES BORROMEO (1959) Rev. John Klein; Deacon Timothy Taylor.
Res.: 1135 Daniel, 60106-3467. Tel: 630-860-1120; Fax: 630-860-5029. Web: www.stcbchurch.org.
School—Holy Family Catholic School, (Grades PreK-8), 145 E. Grand Ave., 60106. Tel: 630-766-0116; Fax: 630-766-0181. Email: officeeast@hfcatholic.org. Web: www.hfcatholic.org. Mrs. Corrine Alimento, Prin.; Dannette Kimmel, Librarian. Lay Teachers 18; Students 155.
Catechesis/Religious Program—Tel: 630-766-8822; Fax: 630-766-3481. Students 166.

BLOOMINGDALE, DUPAGE CO., ST. ISIDORE (1920) [CEM] Revs. Gerald Simonelli; Mark Cote, Parochial Vicar; Dennis Paul, Parochial Vicar; Deacons John Freund; Terry Cummiskey; Lawrence Migliorato; Don Randolph; Lupe Villarreal; Tom Norton, Parish Admin.
Res.: 427 W. Army Trail Rd., 60108-1390. Tel: 630-529-3045; Fax: 630-529-2940. Email: general@stisidoreparish.org. Web: www.stisidoreparish.org.
School—(Grades PreSchool-8) Tel: 630-529-9323; Fax: 630-529-8882. Email: school@stisidoreparish.org. Mrs. Cyndi Collins, Prin. Lay Teachers 26; Students 313.
Catechesis/Religious Program—Tel: 630-529-9191. Students 1,255.

BOLINGBROOK, WILL CO.
1—ST. DOMINIC (1964) Revs. David Lawrence; Marek Jurzyk (Poland) (CHI), Parochial Vicar; Deacons Lorenzo Chaidez; David Ritter; Robert Wallace; Paul Walen.
Res.: 408 E. Briarcliff Rd., 60440. Tel: 630-739-5703; Fax: 630-739-2036. Email: stdominic@comcast.net. Web: www.stdombb.org.
School—(Grades PreSchool-8), 420 E. Briarcliff Rd., 60440. Tel: 630-739-1633; Fax: 630-739-5989. Email: stdominicschool@comcast.net. Mr. William Eggebrecht, Prin. Lay Teachers 15; Students 276.
Catechesis/Religious Program—Tel: 630-739-5703, Ext. 21; 630-739-5703, Ext. 23. Students 641.
2—ST. FRANCIS OF ASSISI (1980) Rev. Herbert Essig; Deacons John Blumenstein; Raymond Hamilton; Marco Lovero; Michael McGuire; Genaro Mempin; Gregory Gresik, Pastoral Assoc.
Res.: 1501 W. Boughton Rd., 60490. Tel: 630-759-7588; Fax: 630-759-5257. Web: www.stfrancisbb.org.
Catechesis/Religious Program— Theresa Palicka, D.R.E. Students 931.

BOURBONNAIS, KANKAKEE CO., MATERNITY OF THE BLESSED VIRGIN MARY (1847) [CEM] Rev. Richard Pighini, C.S.V.; Deacons Euchrist J. Marcotte; Francis Chamness; Patrick Skelly. In Res., Revs. James E. Michaletz, C.S.V.; Kenneth Yarno, C.S.V. (Retired).
Res.: 308 E. Marsile St., 60914. Tel: 815-933-8285; Fax: 815-933-8289. Email: maternitybvm1847@yahoo.com. Web: www.mbvm.org.
School—(Grades PreSchool-8), 324 E. Marsile St., 60914. Tel: 815-933-7758; Fax: 815-933-1884. Mr. Terry Granger, Prin.; Teresa Rigney, Librarian. Lay Teachers 17; Students 312.
Catechesis/Religious Program—Tel: 815-933-8226; Fax: 815-933-1884. Email: mpallissard@mbvm.org. Students 252.

BRADLEY, KANKAKEE CO., ST. JOSEPH (1904) Rev. Anthony A. Nugent; Deacons Leon Fritz; Jerome Gregoire. In Res., Rev. John Antczak.
Res.: 211 N. Center Ave., 60915. Tel: 815-939-3573; Fax: 815-939-3138. Email: rraymond@stjosephbradley.org. Web: www.stjosephbradley.org.
School—(Grades PreSchool-8), 247 N. Center Ave., 60915. Tel: 815-933-8013; Fax: 815-933-2775. Email: mmeier@stjosephbradley.org. Web: www.stjosephbradley.org/school. Sr. Mary Ann Hettel, S.S.C.M., Prin.; Kelly Carroll, Librarian. Sisters 2; Lay Teachers 16; Students 207.
Catechesis/Religious Program—247 N. Center Ave., 60915. Tel: 815-937-9340. Email: mmarcotte@stjosephbradley.org. Students 200.
Convent—235 N. Center Ave., 60915. Tel: 815-932-0112.

BRAIDWOOD, WILL CO., IMMACULATE CONCEPTION (1869), (Irish—Italian), [CEM] Rev. Danilo Soriano.
Res.: 110 S. School St., 60408. Tel: 815-458-2125; Fax: 815-458-2836. Email: imu359@aol.com.
Catechesis/Religious Program—Students 136.
Mission—St. Lawrence O'Toole Essex, Kankakee Co.

CABERY, FORD CO., ST. JOSEPH (1867), (German), [CEM] Rev. Richard F. Kostelz (Retired).
Res.: 112 W. Main St., P.O. Box 77, 60919. Tel: 815-949-1568.
Catechesis/Religious Program—Students 16.
Mission—St. Mary (1899) Reddick, Kankakee Co. 60961.

CAROL STREAM, DU PAGE CO.
1—CORPUS CHRISTI (1989) Rev. Robert A. Hoffenkamp; Deacon Thomas R. Thiltgen, Pastoral Assoc.; Mrs. Kathleen A. Brewer, Pastoral Assoc.; Deacon William Thomas.
Res.: 1415 W. Lies Rd., 60188. Tel: 630-483-4673; Fax: 630-483-4679. Email: corpuschristicc@sbcglobal.net. Web: www.corpuschristicarolstream.org.
Catechesis/Religious Program—Tel: 630-483-4222 (RE); 630-483-4226 (YM). Email: ccedu@sbcglobal.net. Students 631.
2—ST. LUKE (1963) Rev. Thomas Schutter; Sr. Barbara Rowan, S.S.S.F., Pastoral Assoc.
Res.: 421 Cochise Ct., 60188. Tel: 630-668-1325; Fax: 630-668-1356.
Catechesis/Religious Program—Tel: 630-665-2322. Students 122.

CHANNAHON, WILL CO., ST. ANN PARISH (1990) Rev. Jeffery Stoneberg.
Church: 24500 S. Navajo Dr., 60410. Tel: 815-467-6962; Fax: 815-467-2320. Email: stannparish@cbcast.com.
Rectory—25658 Cherokee Tr., 60410.
Catechesis/Religious Program—Tel: 815-467-6992. Students 548.

CHEBANSE, IROQUOIS CO., SS. MARY AND JOSEPH (1869) [CEM] Rev. Vernon Arseneau.
Res.: 525 S. Chestnut, P.O. Box 5, 60922-0005. Tel: 815-697-2654; Fax: 815-694-3507. Email: vern950@comcast.net.
Catechesis/Religious Program—Students 22.

CLARENDON HILLS, DU PAGE CO., NOTRE DAME (1954) Revs. Robert J. Schuler; Venard Kommer, O.F.M.; Sundar Raj Kocherla (India); Deacons Frank Foys; David Lifka; Alex McConnell; Alan Symonanis.
Res.: 64 Norfolk Ave., 60514. Tel: 630-654-3365; Fax: 630-654-8701. Web: www.notredameparish.org.
School—(Grades PreSchool-8) Tel: 630-323-1642; Fax: 630-654-3255. Ms. Mary Ann Feeney, Prin. Lay Teachers 17; Students 266.
Catechesis/Religious Program—Tel: 630-654-3365, Ext. 237. Students 609.

CLIFTON, IROQUOIS CO., ST. PETER'S (1869) [CEM] [JC] Rev. Vernon Arseneau.
Res.: 450 E. Third Ave., P.O. Box 25, 60927-0025. Tel: 815-694-2027; Fax: 815-694-3507.
Catechesis/Religious Program—Tel: 815-694-2970. Email: vern950@comcast.net. Students 101.

COAL CITY, GRUNDY CO., ASSUMPTION OF THE BLESSED VIRGIN MARY (1889) Rev. Robert Noesen.
Res.: 245 S. Kankakee St., 60416. Tel: 815-634-4171; Fax: 815-634-4186. Web: www.ccassumption.org.
Catechesis/Religious Program—Tel: 815-634-8020. Pam Middleton, C.R.E. Students 259.

CREST HILL, WILL CO.
1—ST. AMBROSE (1965) Rev. John J. Doyle.
Res.: 1711 Burry Cir., 60403. Tel: 815-722-3748; Fax: 815-722-4950. Email: st.ambrose@sbcglobal.net.
Catechesis/Religious Program—Tel: 815-722-9193. Students 125.
2—ST. ANNE (1953) Rev. John J. Doyle.
Res.: 1702 N. Dearborn St., 60403. Tel: 815-722-3222; Fax: 815-722-1955. Email: stannech@comcast.net.
Catechesis/Religious Program—Students 125.

DARIEN, DU PAGE CO.
1—OUR LADY OF KOREAN MARTYRS MISSION (1999), (Korean), Rev. Minkee Ju.
7121 Clarendon Hills Rd., 60561. Tel: 630-794-0203; Fax: 630-887-0991.
Catechesis/Religious Program—Email: olkm7121@hotmail.com. Students 15.
2—OUR LADY OF MOUNT CARMEL (1970) Revs. Michael O'Keefe, O.Carm.; Edward Ward, O.Carm.; Deacon John Farrell.
Res.: 8404 Cass Ave., 60561. Tel: 630-852-3303; Fax: 630-852-5227. Web: www.ourladyofmtcarmel.org.
Catechesis/Religious Program—Tel: 630-963-3053. Students 1,372.
3—OUR LADY OF PEACE (1970) Revs. Walter Dziordz, M.I.C.; James Enin, M.I.C., Parochial Vicar; David Lord, M.I.C., Parochial Vicar; Deacons Frank Bina; Paul Brachle; Larry Fudacz; Dennis Stolarz.
Res.: 701 Plainfield Rd., 60561. Tel: 630-323-4333; Fax: 630-323-4354.
School—(Grades K-8), 709 Plainfield Rd., 60561. Tel: 630-325-9220; Fax: 630-325-1995. Mickey Tovey, Prin.; Nancy Kobylarcik, Librarian. Lay Teachers 28; Students 422.
Catechesis/Religious Program—Tel: 630-986-8430; 630-986-8446; Fax: 630-986-1214. Students 318.

DOWNERS GROVE, DU PAGE CO.
1—DIVINE SAVIOR (1968) Rev. William Conway; Deacon Paul S. Newey.
Res.: 6700 Main St., 60516. Tel: 630-969-1532; Fax: 630-969-1724. Email: parish@divinesavior.net. Web: www.divinesavior.net.
Catechesis/Religious Program—Tel: 630-969-1673. Students 439.
2—ST. JOSEPH (1907) Revs. Jerome Kish; Matthew Nathan, Parochial Vicar.
Res.: 4824 Highland, 60515. Tel: 630-964-0216; Fax: 630-964-0867.
School—(Grades K-8), Franklin & Highland, 60515. Tel: 630-969-4306; Fax: 630-969-3946. Sr. Dorothy Randall, C.S.J., Pres.; Rita Stasi, Prin. Lay Teachers 25; Students 405.
Catechesis/Religious Program—Tel: 630-971-1740; Fax: 630-964-0867. Students 402.
3—ST. MARY OF GOSTYN (1891) Revs. Ernest Norbeck; John Phan, Parochial Vicar.
Res.: 444 Wilson St., 60515. Tel: 630-969-1063; Fax: 630-969-1259. Email: parish@stmarygostyn.org. Web: www.stmarygostyn.org.
School—(Grades PreSchool-8), 440 Prairie Ave., 60515. Tel: 630-968-6155; Fax: 630-968-6208. Email: school@stmarygostyn.org. Mrs. Dolores Mielzynski, Prin. Felician Sisters 2; Lay Teachers 24; Students 549.
Catechesis/Religious Program—445 Prairie Ave., 60515. Tel: 630-960-3565; Fax: 630-969-1289. Email: religiouseducation@stmarygostyn.org. Students 660.

ELMHURST, DU PAGE CO.
1—IMMACULATE CONCEPTION (1876) Revs. James Murphy; Raymond Garbin; Show Reddy Allam (India), Parochial Vicar; Deacons Thomas Goebel; John Feely.
Res.: 134 Arthur St., 60126. Tel: 630-530-8515; Fax: 630-530-9346. Web: www.icelmhurst.org.
School—(Grades PreSchool-8), Grade School., 132 Arthur St., 60126. Tel: 630-530-3490; Fax: 630-530-9787. Mrs. Cathy Linley, Prin. Lay Teachers 26; Students 567.
High School—217 Cottage Hill Ave., 60126. Tel: 630-530-3460; Fax: 630-530-2290. Ms. Pamela M. Levar, Prin. Lay Teachers 25; Students 251.
Catechesis/Religious Program—Tel: 630-530-3483; Fax: 630-530-9346. Students 723.
2—MARY, QUEEN OF HEAVEN (1956) Rev. Anthony Taschetta.
Res.: 426 N. West Ave., 60126-2128. Tel: 630-279-5700; Fax: 630-279-4667. Web: www.maryqueen.org.
Catechesis/Religious Program—442 N. West Ave., 60126. Tel: 630-832-8962. Email: mqhreo@juno.com. Students 590.
3—VISITATION (1953) Rev. Matthew Pratscher, Parochial Vicar; Deacons Jay Janousek; Anthony Spatafore; James Eaker.
Res.: 779 S. York St., 60126. Tel: 630-834-6700; Fax: 630-834-6711.
School—(Grades PreSchool-8), 851 S. York, 60126. Tel: 630-834-4931; Fax: 630-834-4936. Sr. Thomas Leo Monahan, O.P., Prin. Sisters of St. Dominican Adrian 3; Lay Teachers 25; Students 540.
Catechesis/Religious Program—851 S. York, 60126. Tel: 630-279-7058; Fax: 630-279-9340. Students 615.

FRANKFORT, WILL CO., ST. ANTHONY (1929) Rev. Greg Skowron; Deacons Donald Berkey; Daniel Danahey, Business & Facilities Mgr.; Richard Rosko; William Boucek; Joseph Johnson, Liturgy Dir.
Res.: 7659 W. Sauk Tr., 60423. Tel: 815-469-3750; Fax: 815-469-6514. Web: www.stanthonyfrankfort.com.
Catechesis/Religious Program—Tel: 815-469-6072; Fax: 815-806-9421. Kathleen Littleton, D.R.E.; Sophie Follenweider, D.R.E. Students 1,133.

GIBSON CITY, FORD CO., OUR LADY OF LOURDES (1875) [JC] Rev. Dennis Spies; Deacon Jeffrey Volker.
Res.: 534 N. Wood St., 60936. Tel: 217-784-4671; Fax: 217-784-4671. Email: pastor@ololgc.org. Web: www.ololgc.org.
Catechesis/Religious Program—Alyce Hafer, D.R.E. Students 54.
Mission—St. George Melvin, Ford Co.
Mission—Immaculate Conception Roberts, 60962.

GILMAN, IROQUOIS CO., IMMACULATE CONCEPTION (1872) [CEM] Revs. Michael Pennock; John Balluff.
Res.: 224 N. Secor St., 60938. Tel: 815-265-7236; Fax: 815-265-7236.
Catechesis/Religious Program—Students 190.

GLEN ELLYN, DU PAGE CO.
1—ST. JAMES THE APOSTLE (1965) Rev. John J. Ouper; Deacons John W. Moeller; Matthew Pidgeon.
Res.: 579 Prince Edward Rd., 60137. Tel: 630-469-7540; Fax: 630-469-7590.
School—(Grades PreK-8) Tel: 630-469-8060; Fax: 630-469-1107. Mrs. Constance Schwab, Prin. Lay Teachers 17; Students 256.
Catechesis/Religious Program—490 S. Park Blvd., 60137. Tel: 630-858-5646; Fax: 630-858-5687. Students 900.
2—ST. PETRONILLE (1925) Revs. James Dougherty; Patrick Mulcahy, Parochial Vicar; Deacons Ronald Yurcus; John Spiezio; Bob Cassey. In Res., Rev. John D. Sullivan (Retired).
Res.: 420 Glenwood Ave., 60137. Tel: 630-469-0404; Fax: 630-469-0412. Email: office@stpetschurch.org. Web: www.stpetschurch.org.
School—(Grades K-8), 425 Prospect Ave., 60137. Tel: 630-469-5041; Fax: 630-469-5071. Email: office@stpetschool.org. Web: www.stpetschool.org. Dr. Mary Kelly, Prin.; Mrs. Linda Lohr, Librarian. Lay Teachers 33; Students 548.
Catechesis/Religious Program—Tel: 630-858-3796, Ext. 4000; Fax: 630-858-6232. Susan Tutaj, D.R.E.; Therese Stahl, Assoc. Dir. Students 975.
3—QUEENSHIP OF MARY (1993), (Vietnamese), [JC]
Church: 219 Armitage, 60137. Tel: 630-668-2333; Fax: 630-752-0332.
Catechesis/Religious Program—Tel: 630-752-0332. Students 178.

GLENDALE HEIGHTS, DU PAGE CO., ST. MATTHEW (1960) Revs. Kevin McBrien, O.Carm.; Kevin Lafey, O.Carm; Deacon Robert Malek; Mr. Michael Ruddle, Pastoral Assoc.
Res.: 1555 Glen Ellyn Rd., 60139. Tel: 630-469-6300; Fax: 630-469-6302. Web: www.stmatthewchurch.org.
School—(Grades PreSchool-8) Tel: 630-858-3112; Fax: 630-858-0623. Mrs. Neoma Mastruzzo, Prin. Lay Teachers 17; Students 352.
Catechesis/Religious Program—Tel: 630-469-5178; Fax: 630-469-6302. Mr. Alan Bucek, D.R.E. Students 300.

GOODRICH, KANKAKEE CO., SACRED HEART (1895) [CEM] Revs. Douglas L. Hauber; Richard Jacklin, Sacramental Min.; Thomas G. Henry, Business Mgr.
Res.: 588 S. 10000 W. Road, Bonfield, 60913-7019. Tel: 815-426-2221.
Catechesis/Religious Program—Students 19.

HERSCHER, KANKAKEE CO., ST. MARGARET MARY, [CEM] Rev. Douglas L. Hauber.
Res.: 207 E. Fifth St., 60941. Tel: 815-426-2153; Fax: 801-751-8793.
Catechesis/Religious Program—Tel: 815-426-2550. Students 73.

HINSDALE, DU PAGE CO., ST. ISAAC JOGUES (1930), (Irish—Italian), Revs. William Donnelly; Patrick Murphy.
Res.: 306 W. Fourth St., 60521. Tel: 630-323-1248; Fax: 630-323-6373. Web: www.sij.net.
School—(Grades K-8), 421 S. Clay St., 60521. Tel: 630-323-3244; Fax: 630-655-6676. Mr. Richard Cronquist, Prin.; Vickie Maxwell, Librarian. Religious 1; Lay Teachers 39; Students 585.
Catechesis/Religious Program—427 S. Clay St., 60521. Tel: 630-323-0265. Students 934.

HOMER GLEN, WILL CO.

1—ST. BERNARD (1978) Rev. Martin M. Gabel.
Res.: 14135 Parker Rd., 60491. Tel: 708-301-3020; Fax: 708-301-0738. Email: st.bernardsrectory@comcast.net.
Catechesis/Religious Program—14724 S. Arboretum Dr., 60491. Tel: 708-301-6952; Fax: 708-301-8870. Students 405.

2—OUR MOTHER OF GOOD COUNSEL (1996) Rev. John M. Ohner, O.S.A.
Church: 16043 S. Bell Rd., 60491. Tel: 708-301-6246; Fax: 708-301-6356. Email: omgcc@comcast.net. Web: omgc.org.
Catechesis/Religious Program—Tel: 708-301-0214. Email: janet.litterio@comcast.net. Students 726.

HOPKINS PARK, KANKAKEE CO., SACRED HEART (1939), (African American), Rev. Daniel Hessling.
Res. & Mailing Address: P.O. Box 557, 60944. Tel: 815-944-5562; Fax: 815-472-3043. Email: srmarybeth1@sbcglobal.net.
Catechesis/Religious Program—16485 E. Birch, P.O. Box 557, 60944. Students 2.

IRWIN, KANKAKEE CO., ST. JAMES THE APOSTLE, [CEM] Rev. Douglas L. Hauber.
Res.: 4372 Main St., Kankakee, 60901. Tel: 815-426-2550.
Catechesis/Religious Program—Tel: 815-933-5443. Students 59.

ITASCA, DU PAGE CO.

1—ST. ANDREW KIM (1981), (Korean), [JC] Rev. Andrew Soo Hong Jeon (Korea, South).
Res.: 1275 N. Arlington Hts. Rd., 60143. Tel: 630-250-0576; Fax: 630-250-2502. Email: info@standrewkimchicago.org. Web: www.standrewkimchicago.org.

2—ST. PETER THE APOSTLE (1956) Rev. Slawomir Ignasik.
Office: 524 N. Rush St., 60143-1698. Tel: 630-773-1272; Fax: 630-773-1720. Email: frslawek@gmail.com.
School—(Grades PreSchool-8), 500 N. Cherry St., 60143-1699. Tel: 630-773-1979; Fax: 630-773-2826. Email: mbillmeyer@stpeteritasca.org. Mary Ellen Billmeyer, Prin. Lay Teachers 13; Students 139.
Catechesis/Religious Program—Tel: 630-773-1272, Ext. 216. Students 28.

KANKAKEE, KANKAKEE CO.

1—ST. MARTIN OF TOURS (1950) [JC] Rev. Dennis F. Settles.
Res.: 953 S. Ninth Ave., 60901. Tel: 815-933-7177; Fax: 815-933-2171.
School—St. Martin of Tours Religious Education, (Grades PreSchool-4), Consolidated with Aquinas Catholic Academy., 907 S. Ninth Ave., 60901. Tel: 815-932-7911; Fax: 815-932-7296.
Catechesis/Religious Program—Students 212.

2—ST. PATRICK (1893), (Irish), Rev. John N. Peeters, C.S.V.; Sr. Theresa Galvan, C.N.D., Pastoral Min.; Marilyn Mulcahy, Pastoral Assoc. In Res., Rev. Donald R. Wehnert, C.S.V. (Retired).
Res.: 428 S. Indiana Ave., 60901. Tel: 815-932-6716; Fax: 815-932-2585. Email: stpatskan@ameritech.net. Web: stpatrickkankakee.org.
School—Aquinas Catholic Academy, Consolidated with St. Patrick, St. Teresa & St. Martin, Kankakee, 366 E. Hickory St., 60901. Tel: 815-932-8124; Fax: 815-932-0485. Sr. Nancy Gannon, S.F.C.C., Prin. Lay Teachers 16; Students 208.
Catechesis/Religious Program—Tel: 815-932-0314. Students 295.

3—ST. ROSE OF LIMA (1857) Rev. Charles Wheeler.
Res.: 486 W. Merchant St., 60901-3631. Tel: 815-933-9391; Fax: 815-933-9393. Email: stroslima@sbcglobal.net.
Catechesis/Religious Program—Students 109.

4—ST. STANISLAUS, (Polish), Closed. For inquiries for parish records contact the chancery.

5—ST. TERESA (1949) [CEM] Rev. Thomas Cargo; Sisters Dolores McKinney, C.N.D., Hispanic Pastoral Min.; Karen Bricher, S.S.C.M., Pastoral Min.; Deacons Ronald Whitman; David Marlowe; Barbara Staniszeski, Pastoral Assoc.; Silvia Barajas, Hispanic Pastoral Min.
Res. & Parish Office: 361 N. St. Joseph Ave., 60901. Tel: 815-933-7683; Fax: 815-933-7692.
Lisieux Pastoral Center—371 St. Joseph Ave., 60901. Tel: 815-939-2913. Kathy Wade, Dir.
Azzarelli Outreach Clinic—341 St. Joseph Ave., 60901. Tel: 815-928-6093. Mrs. Helen Chigaros, Dir.
School—(Grades PreSchool-8), Consolidated with Aquinas Catholic Academy.
Catechesis/Religious Program—Mrs. Virginia Wayer, D.R.E. Twinned with St. Patrick, Kankakee.

KINSMAN, GRUNDY CO., SACRED HEART (1880) Rev. John Joseph Hornicak.
Res.: c/o 165 Rice St., P.O. Box 190, South Wilmington, 60474. Tel: 815-237-2230; Fax: 815-237-2201.
Catechesis/Religious Program—Students 45.

LISLE, DU PAGE CO., ST. JOAN OF ARC (1924) Revs. Gabriel Baltes, O.S.B.; Scaria T. Thoppil, C.M.I. (India); Kenneth Zigmond, O.S.B.; Donald Kocher, Senior Priest (Retired); Deacons Denis Stucko; Joseph Dalpiaz; Thomas Richardt; George Soloy.
820 Division St., 60532. Tel: 630-963-4500; Fax: 630-963-4568. Email: info@sjalisle.org.
School—(Grades PreSchool-8), 4913 Columbia, 60532. Tel: 630-969-1732; Fax: 630-963-9070. Email: stjoanofarcschool@sjalisle.org. Web: www.sjalisle-.org. Sr. Carolyn Sieg, O.S.B., Prin. Religious 4; Lay Teachers 27; Students 640.
Catechesis/Religious Program—Email: mbarouski@sjalisle.org. Students 330.

LOCKPORT, WILL CO.

1—ST. DENNIS (1846) Rev. Jim Curtin; Sr. Joanne Vallaro, C.S.J., Pastoral Assoc.; Deacon Rob Weierman, Pastoral Assoc.; Jackie Bedore, Pastoral Assoc. In Res., Rev. Thomson Panakal.
Res.: 1214 Hamilton St., 60441. Tel: 815-838-2592; Fax: 815-838-2401. Email: church@saint-dennis.org. Web: www.saint-dennis.org.
School—(Grades PreSchool-8), 1201 S. Washington St., 60441. Tel: 815-838-4494; Fax: 815-838-5435. Email: school@saint-dennis.org. Mrs. Lisa Smith, Prin. Lay Teachers 20; Students 230.
Catechesis/Religious Program—Generations of Faith Program Email: jbedore@saint-dennis.org. Web: generationsfsoffaith.us. Participants 361.

2—ST. JOHN VIANNEY (1958) Rev. Stanley Drewniak (Poland), Admin.
Res.: 401 Brassel, 60441. Tel: 815-723-3291; Fax: 815-724-0566.
Catechesis/Religious Program—Students 17.

3—ST. JOSEPH (1868) Rev. Thomas McGivney Jr.; Dr. Jeanne M. Cosgrove, Pastoral Assoc.
Res.: 410 S. Jefferson St., 60441. Tel: 815-838-0187; Fax: 815-838-5379.
School—(Grades PreSchool-8), 529 Madison, 60441. Tel: 815-838-8173; Fax: 815-838-0504. Miss Lynne Scheffler, Prin. Lay Teachers 14; Students 282.
Catechesis/Religious Program—529 Madison St., 60441. Tel: 815-838-2112. Sr. Mary Therese Forst, D.R.E. Students 235.
Convent—531 E. Fourth St., 60441. Tel: 815-838-0186.

LOMBARD, DU PAGE CO.

1—CHRIST THE KING (1960) Rev. Peter Jarosz; Deacons Fred Francl; Frank Lillig, Pastoral Assoc.; Wayne Storrs.
Res.: 1501 S. Main St., 60148. Tel: 630-629-1717; Fax: 630-705-0692. Email: office@ctklombard.org. Web: www.christthekingjolietdiocese.org.
School—(Grades PreSchool-K), 115 E. 15th St., 60148. Tel: 630-627-0640; Fax: 630-705-0139. Email: ckslombard@comcast.net. Jill Placey, Academy Dir. Lay Teachers 2; Students 32.
Catechesis/Religious Program—Tel: 630-629-1717, Ext. 6076. Email: eileen@ctklombard.org. Students 250.

2—DIVINE MERCY POLISH MISSION (1997) Revs. Adam Bobola, S.Ch.; Tomasz Ludwicki, S.Ch.; Rafal Dygula.
21W411 Sunset Ave., 60148. Tel: 630-268-8766; Fax: 630-268-8712. Email: polishmission@comcast.net. Web: www.misjamilosierdziabozego.org.
Catechesis/Religious Program—Tel: 630-830-2669. Mrs. Fryderyka Kubica, D.R.E. Students 1,000.

3—ST. PIUS X (1954) Rev. Thomas A. Corbino; Sr. Pauline Schutz, O.S.F., Pastoral Assoc.; Deacons John Chan; Thomas Rachubinski; Ron Knecht; Larry Lissak.
Res.: 1025 E. Madison, 60148. Tel: 630-627-4526; Fax: 630-495-5926. Email: parishoffice@stpiuslombard.org. Web: www.stpiuslombard.org.
School—(Grades PreSchool-8), 601 S. Westmore, 60148. Tel: 630-627-2353; Fax: 630-627-1810. Web: www.stpiusknights.org. Mr. Daniel Flaherty, Prin. Lay Teachers 34; Students 476.
Catechesis/Religious Program—Tel: 630-627-1551. Gina Weidman, Dir. Faith Formation. Students 446.

4—SACRED HEART (1912) Rev. Thomas Botheroyd; Deacons Frank Annerino; Thomas Bailey; William H. Crane.
Res.: 114 S. Elizabeth St., 60148. Tel: 630-627-0687; Fax: 630-627-0688.
School—(Grades PreSchool-8), 322 W. Maple St., 60148. Tel: 630-629-0536; Fax: 630-629-4752. Mr. Joseph Benning, Prin. Lay Teachers 11; Students 251.
Catechesis/Religious Program—Tel: 630-495-0843; Fax: 630-627-0688. Students 321.

MANHATTAN, WILL CO., ST. JOSEPH (1891) [CEM 2] Rev. John T. McGeean; Deacons Patrick Forsythe; John Putman.
Res.: 235 W. North, P.O. Box 25, 60442. Tel: 815-478-3341; Fax: 815-478-7046. Web: www.stjoemanhattanil.org.
School—(Grades PreSchool-8) Tel: 815-478-3951; Fax: 815-478-7412. Mrs. Eileen Ramsay, Prin. Lay Teachers 14; Students 151.
Catechesis/Religious Program—Tel: 815-478-4452. Students 471.

MANTENO, KANKAKEE CO., ST. JOSEPH (1855) [CEM] Rev. Albert J. Heidecke; Deacons Richard Balgeman; John Leonas, (Retired).
Res.: 207 S. Main St., 60950. Tel: 815-468-3403; Fax: 815-468-7089. Email: stjoemanteno@sbcglobal.net. Web: www.stjosephmanteno.com.
Catechesis/Religious Program—Tel: 815-468-8116. Email: annie619@sbcglobal.net. Students 380.

MARTINTON, IROQUOIS CO., ST. MARTIN (1899) [CEM] Rev. Robert J. Coleman.
Mailing Address: P.O. Box 152, Beaverville, 60912.
Res.: 308 St. Charles, Beaverville, 60912. Tel: 815-435-2432.
Catechesis/Religious Program—Ryan Loy, D.R.E. Students 8.

MINOOKA, GRUNDY CO., ST. MARY (1862), (Irish), [CEM] Rev. Mark A. Fracaro.
Res.: 303 W. St. Mary St., P.O. Box 456, 60447. Tel: 815-467-2233; Fax: 815-467-1760.
Catechesis/Religious Program—Tel: 815-467-2769; Fax: 815-521-0266. Students 593.

MOKENA, WILL CO., ST. MARY CHURCH (1864) [CEM] Rev. James Dvorscak; Sisters Dolores Zemont, O.S.F., Pastoral Assoc.; Rose Marie Surwilo, O.S.F., Pastoral Assoc.; Deacons Robert Kaminski; Gary Bednar.
Res.: P.O. Box 2, 60448-0002. Tel: 708-326-9300; Fax: 708-326-9301. Email: mail@stmarymokena.com. Web: www.stmarymokena.com.
School—(Grades K-8), 11409 W. 195th St., 60448. Tel: 708-326-9330; Fax: 708-326-9331. Mrs. Judy Rozgo, Prin. Franciscan Sisters of the Sacred Heart 1; Lay Teachers 22; Students 439.
Catechesis/Religious Program—11409 W. 195th St., 60448. Tel: 708-326-9350; Fax: 708-326-9351. Kathy Kowalewski, D.R.E. Students 1,600.

MOMENCE, KANKAKEE CO., ST. PATRICK (1859) [CEM] Rev. Daniel Hessling.
Res.: 119 Market St., 60954. Tel: 815-472-2864; Fax: 815-472-3043. Email: stpatsrectory@mchsi.com.
School—(Grades PreSchool-8), 404 W. Second St., 60954. Tel: 815-472-2469. Web: saintpatrickacademy.net. Ken Fox, Prin. Lay Teachers 6; Students 71.
Catechesis/Religious Program—Students 125.
Mission—Sacred Heart P.O. Box 557, Hopkins Park, Kankakee Co. 60944. Tel: 815-944-5562.

MONEE, WILL CO., ST. BONIFACE (1868), (Irish—Polish), [JC] Rev. Mark Menezes.
Church: 5304 W. Main St., P.O. Box 217, 60449. Tel: 708-534-9682; Fax: 708-534-9683. Email: stboniface@dioceseofjoliet.org.
Rectory—25942 S. Middlepoint Ln., 60449.
Catechesis/Religious Program—Students 103.

MORRIS, GRUNDY CO., IMMACULATE CONCEPTION OF THE BLESSED VIRGIN MARY (1852) [CEM] Rev. Richard Smith; Deacons Robert Stansberry Jr.; Dennis Kobs.

516 E. Jackson St., 60450.
Res.: 411 E. Jackson St., 60450. Tel: 815-942-0620; Fax: 815-942-3171. Web: ic-morris.e-paluch.com.
School—(Grades PreSchool-8) Tel: 815-942-4111; Fax: 815-942-5094. Web: www.ics1.org. Mr. Kim DesLauriers, Prin. Lay Teachers 11; Students 218.
Catechesis/Religious Program—505 E. North St., 60450. Tel: 815-942-4177; Fax: 815-942-4177. Students 275.

NAPERVILLE, DUPAGE CO.

1—ST. ELIZABETH SETON (1986) Rev. Thomas Paul; Sr. Karen Nykiel, O.S.B., Pastoral Assoc.; Deacons Bart Federici; Thomas Ross; Gary Swauger; Andrew Cirmo; Scott Pace.
Res.: 2220 Lisson Rd., 60565. Tel: 630-416-3325; Fax: 630-416-3642. Web: www.sesnaperville.org.
Catechesis/Religious Program—Tel: 630-416-1992; Fax: 630-416-4086. Students 1,318.

2—HOLY SPIRIT CATHOLIC COMMUNITY (1998) Rev. Dennis Lewandowski; Deacon Tom Schroeder.
Res.: 2003 Hassert Blvd., 60564. Tel: 630-922-0081; Fax: 630-922-0085.
Rectory—2228 Snow Creek Rd., 60564.
Catechesis/Religious Program—Students 2,313.

3—ST. MARGARET MARY (1980) Revs. Paul Hottinger; William J. O'Shea, Pastor Emeritus (Retired); Sr. Madelyn Gould, S.S.S.F., Pastoral Assoc.; Deacons Kenneth J. Miles; Terry Taylor.
1450 Green Trails Dr., 60540. Tel: 630-369-0777; Fax: 630-369-1493.
Catechesis/Religious Program—Tel: 630-369-0833. Students 1,110.

4—STS. PETER AND PAUL (1856) [CEM] Revs. Thomas Milota; Ryan Larson, Parochial Vicar; Dong Bui, Parochial Vicar; Deacons Ronald Brown; Richard Yarshen; Roger Novak. In Res., Rev. Joseph Valentine, F.S.S.P.
Res.: 36 N. Ellsworth St., 60540. Tel: 630-355-1081; Fax: 630-355-1179.
School—(Grades K-8), 201 E. Franklin, 60540. Tel: 630-355-0113; Fax: 630-355-9803. Mr. Frank Glowaty, Prin. Lay Teachers 33; Students 622.
Catechesis/Religious Program—36 N. Ellsworth St., Ste. 104, 60540. Tel: 630-357-2436; Fax: 630-357-2458. Students 907.

5—ST. RAPHAEL (1963) Revs. Theodore Weitzel; Dindo Billote, Parochial Vicar; Deacons Andrew Repak; Charles Woods; Thomas Marciani.
Mailing Address: 1215 Modaff Rd., 60540-7818. Tel: 630-355-4545; Fax: 630-355-7470. Web: www.st-raphael.com.
School—(Grades K-8) Tel: 630-355-4545, Ext. 135; Fax: 630-428-4974. Mrs. Karen Udell, Prin.; Mary Beth Boland, Librarian. Lay Teachers 19; Students 315.
Catechesis/Religious Program—Tel: 630-355-4545, Ext. 121; Fax: 630-355-7470. Web: www.st-raphael.com. Students 1,981.

6—ST. THOMAS THE APOSTLE (1984) Rev. Joel Fortier; Deacons William Worden; Charles Lane; James Breen; Lawrence Kearney; Michael Barrett. Email: mbarrett@stapostle.org.
Res.: 1500 Brookdale Rd., 60563. Tel: 630-355-8980; Fax: 630-355-0521. Email: mainoffice@stapostle.org. Web: www.stapostle.org.
Catechesis/Religious Program—Tel: 630-305-6318. Email: pdougherty@stapostle.org. Students 1,219.

NEW LENOX, WILL CO., ST. JUDE (1934) Revs. Donald R. Lewandowski, O.S.A.; R. William Sullivan, O.S.A.; Donald J. Bates, O.S.A.; Deacons Robert Fitt; William Ciston; Dennis Theriault.
Res.: 241 W. Second Ave., 60451. Tel: 815-485-8049; Fax: 815-485-7754.
School—(Grades K-8) Tel: 815-485-2549; Fax: 815-485-0234. Mrs. Luanne Watson, Prin.; Cheryl Meyer, Librarian. Lay Teachers 10; Students 141.
Catechesis/Religious Program—Tel: 815-485-4852; Fax: 815-485-2623. Students 1,687.

OAKBROOK TERRACE, DUPAGE CO., ASCENSION OF OUR LORD (1967) Rev. J. Damien Graziano; Deacons William J. Tansey; Peter Rooney.
Res.: 1 S. 314 Summit Ave., 60181. Tel: 630-629-5810; Fax: 630-953-8251. Email: nlonis@ascensionofourlord.net.
Catechesis/Religious Program—Tel: 630-629-5810, Ext. 215. Students 87.

OSWEGO, KENDALL CO., ST. ANNE (1963) Rev. David J. Hankus; Deacons David Brockman; Duane Wozek.
Res.: 551 Boulder Hill Pass, P.O. Box 670, 60543. Tel: 630-554-3331; Fax: 630-554-0530. Email: stanne@stanneparish.org. Web: www.stanneparish.org.
Catechesis/Religious Program—Tel: 630-554-1425; Fax: 630-554-9797. Email: reo@stanneparish.org. Students 1,627.

PARK FOREST, WILL CO., ST. MARY (1959) Rev. Tri Van Tran; Deacons John Drechny; Edward Szymanski.
Rectory—212 Monee Rd., 60466. Tel: 708-747-1600; Fax: 708-748-6907.
Church: 227 Monee Rd., 60466. Tel: 708-748-6686. Web: www.stmaryparkforest.org.
School—(Grades PreK-8) Mr. John Prevost, Prin. Lay Teachers 10; Students 130.
Catechesis/Religious Program—Students 31.

PAXTON, FORD CO., ST. MARY (1910) Rev. Scott Huggins.
Res.: 407 W. Pells, 60957-1290. Tel: 217-379-4033.
Mission—St. Joseph
Catechesis/Religious Program—Tel: 217-379-2983. Students 150.

PEOTONE, WILL CO., ST. PAUL THE APOSTLE (1961) Rev. Daniel Hoehn.
Res.: 501 N. Conrad St., 60468. Tel: 708-258-6917. Email: stpauloffice@att.netFax: 708-258-3061.
Catechesis/Religious Program—Tel: 708-258-9580. Students 197.

PIPER CITY, FORD CO., ST. PETER (1887) [CEM] Rev. Michael Pennock.
Res. & Mailing Address: 212 Pine St., P.O. Box 186, 60959. Tel: 815-686-2595.
Catechesis/Religious Program—1245 E. 2800 N., 60959. Tel: 815-686-9270. Students 10.
Mission—Immaculate Conception [CEM 2] Roberts, Ford Co.

PLAINFIELD, WILL CO., ST. MARY IMMACULATE (1908) [CEM] Revs. David Medow; Daniel Bachner, Parochial Vicar; Mark Rosenbaum, Parochial Vicar; Deacons James Sossong; Terry Sakfo; Patrick Lombardo; Thomas O'Connell; Manuel Guerrero; Thomas Sagenbrecht; Patricia Widlowski, Office Mgr. & Admin. Asst.; Janice Gregoire, Business Mgr.; David Bachtel, Community Dir.
Res.: 15626 S. Frederick Ave., 60544. Tel: 815-436-2651; Fax: 815-436-5017.
School—(Grades PreSchool-8) Tel: 815-436-3953; Fax: 815-439-8045. Mr. John Garvey, Prin.; Jennifer Erthum, Asst. Prin.; Lisa Kissel, Librarian. Lay Teachers 27; Students 554.
Catechesis/Religious Program—Tel: 815-436-4501; Fax: 815-439-2304. Students 1,851.

PLANO, KENDALL CO., ST. MARY (1885) [CEM] Revs. Diego Maximino, M.I.C.; Daniel Cambra, M.I.C.; Matthew Lamoureux, M.I.C.; Deacons Santos Martinez; William Dunn.
Res.: 901 N. Center St., 60545. Tel: 630-552-3448; Fax: 630-552-3450. Email: stmary_plano@sbcglobal.net.
School—(Grades K-8), 817 N. Center Ave., 60545. Tel: 630-552-3345; Fax: 630-552-4385. Mr. Ed Condon, Prin. Lay Teachers 20; Students 219.
Catechesis/Religious Program—810 N. Center Ave., 60545. Tel: 630-552-1505. Students 235.

ROCKDALE, WILL CO., ST. JOSEPH (1914) Rev. Joseph Kudilil (India), Admin.
Res.: 1329 Belleview Ave., 60436. Tel: 815-725-4469; Fax: 815-725-1820.
Catechesis/Religious Program—Tel: 815-729-9149. Students 50.

ROMEOVILLE, WILL CO., ST. ANDREW THE APOSTLE (1959) Revs. Gregor Gorsic; Grzegorz Podwysocki, Parochial Vicar; Deacons Herb Waldron; Rich Ford; Jerry Clark; Tom Powers. In Res., Rev. John Driscoll (Retired).
Parish Offices: 530 Glen Ave., 60446. Tel: 815-886-4165; Fax: 815-886-6119. Email: office@standrewromeoville.com.
School—(Grades PreSchool-8), 505 Kingston Dr., 60446. Tel: 815-886-5953; Fax: 815-293-2016. Web: www.standrewromeoville.com. Joseph Leppert, Prin. Lay Teachers 10; Students 186.
Catechesis/Religious Program—505 Kingston Dr., 60446. Tel: 815-886-5962; Fax: 815-886-6624. Students 499.

ROSELLE, DU PAGE CO., ST. WALTER (1946) Revs. James Schwab; Daniel F. Stempora, Admin. (Retired); Francis B. McDonald, Pastor Emeritus (Retired); Mario S. Quejadas, Parochial Vicar; Deacons Ron Searls; Michael Kowalchik; Richard Foy.
Res.: 130 W. Pine Ave., 60172. Tel: 630-894-2461; Fax: 630-582-4206. Web: www.stwalterchurch.com.
School—(Grades PreSchool-8), 201 W. Maple Ave., 60172. Tel: 630-529-1721; Fax: 630-529-9290. Email: stwalterinfo@sbcglobal.net. Web: www.stwalter-school.com. Mrs. Mary Lloyd, Prin. Lay Teachers 29; Students 702.
Catechesis/Religious Program—140 W. Pine, 60172. Tel: 630-894-5880; Fax: 630-582-5192. Kenneth Ortega, D.R.E. Students 930.

ST. ANNE, KANKAKEE CO., ST. ANNE (1865), (French-Canadian), [CEM] Rev. James Fanale, C.S.V.
Res.: 230 N. Sixth Ave., P.O. Box 470, 60964. Tel: 815-427-8265; Fax: 815-427-8267.
Catechesis/Religious Program—Students 47.

ST. GEORGE, KANKAKEE CO., ST. GEORGE (1853), (French-Canadian), [CEM] Rev. Daniel R. Belanger, C.S.V.; Deacon Joseph Cotugno.
Res.: 5272 E. 5000 North Rd., Bourbonnais, 60914-9725. Tel: 815-939-1851; Fax: 815-939-2777.
Catechesis/Religious Program—Students 41.

SHOREWOOD, WILL CO., HOLY FAMILY (1959) Revs. William G. Dewan; John L. Dennerlein, Pastor Emeritus (Retired); Alejandro Flores, Parochial Vicar; Deacons Fred Straub; Karl Huebner; Thomas Paluch; Paul Schneider.
Church: 600 Brook Forest Ave., 60404. Tel: 815-725-6880; Fax: 815-725-2311. Web: www.holyfamilyshorewood.org.
School—(Grades PreSchool-8) Tel: 815-725-8149. Mrs. Judith Strohschein, Prin. Lay Teachers 15; Students 337.
Catechesis/Religious Program—Tel: 815-730-8691. Students 1,000.

SOUTH WILMINGTON, GRUNDY CO., ST. LAWRENCE (1904) Rev. John Joseph Hornicak; Deacon Steven Frazier.
Res.: 165 Rice St., Box 190, 60474. Tel: 815-237-2230; Fax: 815-237-2201. Email: stlawrenceswilm@yahoo.com.
Catechesis/Religious Program—Students 68.

STEGER, WILL CO., ST. LIBORIUS (1902) Rev. Reynaldo B. Treyes; Deacon Len Olszak.
Res.: 71 W. 35th St., 60475. Tel: 708-754-1363; Fax: 708-754-7577. Email: stliborius@yahoo.com.
School—(Grades PreSchool-8), 3436 Halsted Blvd., 60475. Tel: 708-754-0192; Fax: 708-755-3982. Mary Jane Bartley, Prin. (Steger Campus) Lay Teachers 11; Students 206.
Catechesis/Religious Program—Tel: 708-754-3460. Students 213.

VILLA PARK, DU PAGE CO.

1—ST. ALEXANDER (1924) Rev. Tuan Van Nguyen; Deacons John Boyle; Christopher Cochran; James Krueger; John Gibbons.
Res.: 300 S. Cornell Ave., 60181. Tel: 630-833-7730; Fax: 630-833-3127. Email: stavpark@aol.com. Web: www.stalexanderparish.org.
School—(Grades K-8), 136 S. Cornell Ave., 60181. Tel: 630-834-3787; Fax: 630-834-1961. Web: www-.stalexanderschool.org. Glenn Purpura, Prin. Lay Teachers 9; Students 139.
Catechesis/Religious Program—130 S. Cornell Ave., 60181. Tel: 630-832-0506. Students 200.

2—ST. JOHN THE APOSTLE (1959), (Italian—Polish), Rev. Robert Duda.
Res.: 330 N. Westmore, 60181. Tel: 630-279-7404; Fax: 630-530-9910.
Catechesis/Religious Program—Tel: 630-832-7588; Fax: 630-832-7588. Students 93.

WARRENVILLE, DU PAGE CO., ST. IRENE (1927) Rev. James Antiporek; Deacons William Murphy, Pastoral Assoc.; Robert True, Pastoral Assoc.; Joseph Urso, Pastoral Assoc.; Annette Kubalanza, Pastoral Assoc.
Res.: 28 W. 441 Warrenville Rd., 60555. Tel: 630-393-2400; Fax: 630-393-9680. Email: parishoffice@st-irene.org. Web: www.st-irene.org.
School—(Grades PreSchool-8), 3S601 Warren Ave., 60555. Tel: 630-393-9303; Fax: 630-393-7009. Email: school@st-irene.org. Web: www.st-ireneschool.org. Mrs. Maureen White, Prin. Lay Teachers 14; Students 139.
Catechesis/Religious Program—Tel: 630-393-2400, Ext. 22. Sr. Nancy Ulrich, O.S.F., D.R.E. Students 200.

WATSEKA, IROQUOIS CO., ST. EDMUND (1872) Rev. F. Lee Ryan.
Church: 219 E. Locust St., 60970. Tel: 815-432-3274; Fax: 815-432-3275.
Catechesis/Religious Program—Tel: 815-432-5569. Students 120.
Mission—St. Joseph P.O. Box 173, Crescent City, Iroquois Co. 60928.

WAYNE, DU PAGE CO., RESURRECTION CATHOLIC COMMUNITY (1964) Rev. John Sponder.
Res.: 30W350 Army Trail Rd., 60184. Tel: 630-289-5400, Ext. 203; Fax: 630-289-5407. Email: ressec@sbcglobal.net. Web: www.rescatholiccom.com.
Catechesis/Religious Program—Tel: 630-289-5400, Ext. 215. Email: resff@sbcglobal.net. Students 292.

WEST CHICAGO, DU PAGE CO., ST. MARY (1894) [CEM] Revs. John Balluff; Felipe Legarreta, Parochial Vicar; Sr. Rocio Castillo, Pastoral Assoc., Hisp. Min.; Deacons Bruce Carlson; Luis Saltigerald.
Res.: 140 N. Oakwood Ave., 60185. Tel: 630-231-0013; Fax: 630-293-2671. Email: parish.office@stmarywc.org. Web: www.stmarywc.org.
School—(Grades PreSchool-8), 147 Garden St., 60185. Tel: 630-231-1776. Ms. Nancy Coughlin, Prin. Lay Teachers 10; Students 153.
Catechesis/Religious Program—Tel: 630-231-5704. Sr. Maria Romero, D.R.E. Students 486.

WESTMONT, DU PAGE CO., HOLY TRINITY (1938) Revs. William DeSalvo; Jan Krutewicz, Parochial Vicar; Deacons William Casey; Thomas Jagielo.
Res.: 111 S. Cass Ave., 60559. Tel: 630-968-1366; Fax: 630-968-7846. Email: smccowan@holytrinitywestmont.org. Web: www.holytrinitywestmont.org.
School—(Grades PreSchool-8), 108 S. Linden,

60559. Tel: 630-971-0184; Fax: 630-971-1175. Email: cterry@holytrinitywestmont.org. Dr. Charles Terry, Prin.; Marie Wagner, Librarian. Lay Teachers 17; Students 214.
Catechesis/Religious Program—Tel: 630-968-5978. Students 460.

WHEATON, DU PAGE CO.
1—ST. DANIEL THE PROPHET CHURCH (1989) Revs. Tom Sularz; Thomas J. White, Pastor Emeritus (Retired); Deacons Ken Jackson, Pastoral Assoc.; James Perry; Anne Sinclair, Dir. Music & Liturgist.
Res.: 101 West Loop Rd., 60189. Tel: 630-682-5003; Fax: 630-682-5004. Web: www.stdaniel.org.
Catechesis/Religious Program—Tel: 630-682-5003, Ext. 121. Diane Ahlemeyer, D.R.E. Students 354.
2—ST. MARK (1962) Rev. John Ducaji.
Res.: 303 E. Parkway Dr., 60187. Tel: 630-665-0030; Fax: 630-665-0303.
Catechesis/Religious Program—300 E. Cole St., 60187. Tel: 630-668-4614. Students 92.
3—ST. MICHAEL (1882) [CEM] Revs. Don E. McLaughlin; Santos Castillo, Parochial Vicar; Deacons John Cozzens; William Stroner; David Meador; Kenneth Kubica.
Res.: 310 S. Wheaton Ave., 60187. Tel: 630-665-2250; Fax: 630-510-8891. Web: www.stmichaelcommunity.org.
School—(Grades PreSchool-8), 314 W. Willow Ave., 60187. Tel: 630-653-1454; Fax: 630-665-1491. Marcia Opal, Prin. Lay Teachers 34; Students 597.
Catechesis/Religious Program—317 Willow Ave., 60187. Tel: 630-682-3650; Fax: 630-690-3324. Students 950.

WILMINGTON, WILL CO., ST. ROSE (1855) [CEM] Rev. Steven Bondi; Sr. Ann Ellen Quirk, B.V.M., Pastoral Assoc.; Deacon Don Dyer.
Res.: 603 S. Main St., 60481. Tel: 815-476-7491; Fax: 815-476-1085.
School—(Grades PreSchool-8), 626 Kankakee St., 60481. Tel: 815-476-6220; Fax: 815-476-2154. Linda Bland, Prin. Lay Teachers 8; Students 151.
Catechesis/Religious Program—Students 132.

WILTON CENTER, WILL CO., ST. PATRICK (1905), (Irish), [CEM] Rev. Daniel Hoehn.
Res.: 14936 Wilmington Peotone Rd., Manhattan, 60442. Tel: 815-478-3440; Fax: 815-478-4186.
Catechesis/Religious Program—Students 28.

WINFIELD, DU PAGE CO., ST. JOHN THE BAPTIST (1867) [CEM] [JC 2] Revs. Frank Vitus; Thomas Theneth, C.M.I., Parochial Vicar; Deacons Andrew Nielo; Rod Accardi. In Res., Rev. Henry Wilkening (Retired).
Res.: O.S. 233 Church St., 60190. Tel: 630-668-0918; Fax: 630-668-1074. Web: www.stjohnwinfield.org.
School—(Grades PreSchool-8), O.S. 259 Church St., 60190. Tel: 630-668-2625; Fax: 630-668-7176. Julie Tobin, Prin. Lay Teachers 21; Students 222.
Catechesis/Religious Program—Tel: 630-682-4400; Fax: 630-668-1074. Maureen Brennan, D.R.E. Students 442.

WOOD DALE, DU PAGE CO., HOLY GHOST (1946) Rev. Kevin R. Farrell; Deacon Dino Franch.
Res.: 254 N. Wood Dale Rd., 60191. Tel: 630-860-2975; Fax: 630-860-9482. Email: secy@holyghostparish.org. Web: www.holyghostparish.org.
School—(Grades PreSchool-8) Tel: 630-766-4508; Fax: 630-860-7697. Mrs. Diana Mendez, Prin. Lay Teachers 14; Students 198.
Catechesis/Religious Program—Tel: 630-766-1045. Sheri Abel, D.R.E. Students 95.

WOODRIDGE, DU PAGE CO.
1—CHRIST THE SERVANT PARISH (1990) Rev. Philip Danaher; Deacon Thomas Fricke.
Mailing Address: 8700 Havens Dr., 60517. Tel: 630-910-0770; Fax: 630-910-6060. Email: ctsoffice@ctswoodridge.org. Web: www.ctswoodridge.org.
Catechesis/Religious Program—Students 226.
2—ST. SCHOLASTICA (1962) Rev. Gerald Riva; Deacons Gerald G. Christensen; Roger Schmith; Terry Zarembka.
Res.: 7800 S. Janes Ave., 60517. Tel: 630-985-2351; Fax: 630-985-8770. Email: archabbess@aol.com. Web: www.stscholasticaparish.org.
School—(Grades K-8) Tel: 630-985-2515; Fax: 630-985-2395. Gail Kueper, Prin.; Barbara Stance, Librarian. Lay Teachers 11; Students 273.
Catechesis/Religious Program—7720 Janes Ave., 60517. Tel: 630-985-9255. Chris Hannigan-Wiehn, Dir. Faith Formation. Students 509.

YORKVILLE, KENDALL CO., ST. PATRICK (1885) [CEM] [JC] Revs. Matthew Lamoureux, M.I.C.; Andy Davy, M.I.C., Parochial Vicar; Deacons Dale Metcalfe; Donald Cyr.
406 Walnut St., 60560. Tel: 630-553-6671; Fax: 630-553-2695. Email: info@stpatrickyorkville.org. Web: www.stpatrickyorkville.org.
Catechesis/Religious Program— Justin Frato, D.R.E. & RCIA Dir. Students 834.

Chaplains of Public Institutions

JOLIET. *Dept. of Corrections*, 2848 McDonough St., 60432. Rev. Richard Ross.
Illinois State Penitentiary, P.O. Box 112, 60434. Deacon Charles Peterson.
Illinois Youth Commission, Reception and Diagnostic Center, McDonough St., 60435. Deacon Joseph O'Connor.
Silver Cross Hospital, 1200 Maple Rd., 60432. Vacant.

DOWNERS GROVE. *Good Samaritan Hospital*, 3821 Highland Ave., 60515. Vacant.

ELMHURST. *Elmhurst Memorial Hospital*, 200 Berteau Ave., 60126. Rev. Michael McMillen, S.C.J.

HINSDALE. *Hinsdale Hospital*, 120 N. Oak, 60521. Rev. James Walton, O.F.M.

KANKAKEE. *Riverside Medical Center*, 350 N. Wells, 60901. Rev. John Antczak.
Shapiro Development Center, 100 E. Jeffery, 60901. Rev. Richard Jacklin.

NAPERVILLE. *Edward Hospital*, S. Washington St., 60540. Rev. Stanley Tabor.

WINFIELD. *Central DuPage Hospital*, 0N025 Winfield Rd., 60190. Rev. Henry Wilkening (Retired), Deacon Rod Accardi.

On Duty Outside the Diocese:
Revs.—
Butters, Joseph, 13140 Nassau Dr., Apt. 214B, Seal Beach, CA 90740.
Dieter, Thomas M.
Hemrick, Eugene F.
Martis, Douglas, Ph.D., S.T.D., Mundelein Seminary, Mundelein, 60060.
Schoenstene, Robert L., M.A., S.S.L., St. Mary of the Lake Seminary, Mundelein, 60060.

Absent on Leave:
Revs.—
Bennett, Richard
Buczyna, Andrew L.
Burnett, James
Collogan, Robert
Dennerlein, Arno A.
Heramb, James
La Pore, Arthur
McCawley, Scott M.
Pozen, Matthew
Radek, James
Regan, John

Retired:
Most Rev.—
Imesch, Joseph L., 425 Summit St., 60435.
Revs.—
Barrett, John, 460 Raintree Ct. #1H, Glen Ellyn, 60137.
Best, Richard
Bowden, Lloyd, 115 N. May St., 60435.
Carlin, Warren, O.Carm.
Corkery, Raymond, O.Carm.
Corley, Thomas
Cullen, William, 6267 Trinity Dr., #2D, Lisle, 60532.
Dennerlein, John L.
Dillon, David, O.Carm.
Driscoll, John, St. Andrew the Apostle, 530 Glen Ave., Romeoville, 60446.
Fleming, Thomas, Carmelite Carefree Village, Darien, 60561.
Guiney, John, S.M.A., 256 Forest, Glen Ellyn, 60137.
Guz, Leonard J.
Hurley, George, 5 Oak Brook Club Dr., Oakbrook, 60521-1314.
Kelpsas, A., M.I.C.
Kenny, Donald, Quito, Ecuador
Kloepfer, John S., Box 1742, Clarksville, VA 23927.
Kocher, Donald
Kostelz, Richard F.
Lennon, James M., Fiat House, 113 Ottawa, 60432.
Maher, Arthur, 1115 Lorraine Rd., #32, Wheaton, 60189.
Maher, Francis, 965-B Tenderfoot Hill Rd., Colorado Springs, CO 80906.
Mahoney, Gordon, St. John Vianney Villa, Naperville, 60540.
Maternoski, Robert
Meis, Anthony
Memenas, Vytas, St. Anthony Parish, 100 Scott St., 60432.
Micka, A., M.I.C.
Moriarty, John J.
Morrissette, Dominic, Nazareth House, 6333 Rancho Mission Rd., San Diego, CA 92108.
Mumper, Edward, 4515 Sawdust Rd., Bruce, WI 54819.
O'Connor, Donald
O'Shea, William J.
Orlikiewicz, Stanley
Pietras, Robert E.
Poff, Edward
Prodehl, Richard B.
Rowland, Edward P.
Ryan, William
Schubert, Gerold, O.F.M.
Sebahar, John, St. John Vianney Villa, Naperville.
Stalzer, Joseph
Stempora, Daniel F.
Sullivan, John D.
Testa, Jess
Tivy, Gerald
Valente, Michael, 3633 N. Pacific Ave., Chicago, 60634.
Wehnert, Donald R., C.S.V.
White, Denis
White, Thomas J.
Wilkening, Henry, St. John the Baptist Parish, OS233 Church St., 60190.
Wolter, Thomas
Yarno, Kenneth, C.S.V.
Zanoni, John
Zulkie, Lambert, O.Carm.

Permanent Deacons:
Accardi, Rodger F., Central DuPage Hospital and St. John the Baptist, Winfield
Agurkis, Albert, St. Mary of Gostyn, Downers Grove
Anchor, Robert, (On Duty Outside the Diocese)
Anderson, Roy D., (On Duty Outside the Diocese)
Annerino, Frank, Sacred Heart, Lombard
Bailey, Thomas, Sacred Heart, Lombard
Balgeman, Richard, St. Joseph, Manteno
Barrett, Michael, St. Thomas, Naperville
Beabout, Norman, (On Duty Outside the Diocese)
Bednar, Gary, St. Mary, Mokena
Berkey, Donald, St. Anthony, Frankfort
Bernardin, Donald, (Leave of Absence)
Bevan, William F., III, St. Paul the Apostle, Joliet
Bias, Ralph, Sacred Heart, Joliet
Bina, Frank, Our Lady of Peace, Darien
Blumenstein, John, St. Francis of Assisi, Bolingbrook
Borkowicz, Leo M., (Retired)
Boucek, William, St. Anthony, Frankfort
Bowns, Loren, St. Liborius, Steger
Boyle, John R., St. Alexander, Villa Park
Brachle, Paul L., Jr., Our Lady of Peace, Darien
Brechtel, Scott, (Leave of Absence)
Breen, James, St.Thomas the Apostle, Naperville
Brockman, David, St. Anne, Oswego
Brown, Ronald, Sts. Peter & Paul, Naperville
Bumble, John, St. James Manor, Crete
Carlson, Bruce, St. Mary, West Chicago
Carson, Neill, (Retired)
Casey, William, Holy Trinity, Westmont
Cassey, Robert, St. Petronille, Glen Ellyn
Chaidez, Lorenzo, St. Dominic, Bolingbrook
Chambers, Frank A., (On Duty Outside the Diocese)
Chamness, Francis J., Maternity BVM, Bourbonnais
Chan, John, St. Pius X, Lombard
Christensen, Gerald G., St. Scholastica, Woodridge
Cirmo, Andrew, St. Elizabeth Seton, Naperville
Ciston, William, St. Jude, New Lenox
Clark, Gordon, St. Andrew, Romeoville
Clark, Raymond, St. Jude, Joliet
Clodi, Gregory, St. Martin of Tours, Kankakee
Cochran, Christopher, St. Alexander, Villa Park
Cole, John, (Leave of Absence)
Cook, Michael, (On Duty Outside the Diocese)
Cooley, Stephen, (On Duty Outside the Diocese)
Cotugno, Joseph, St. George, St. George
Cozzens, John, St. Michael, Wheaton
Crane, William H., St. Pius X, Lombard
Cummiskey, Terry, St. Isidore, Bloomingdale
Cyr, Donald, St. Patrick, Yorkville
Dalpiaz, Joseph C., St. Joan of Arc, Lisle
Dalton, James, Cathedral of St. Raymond, Joliet
Danahey, Daniel, St. Anthony, Frankfort
Darschewski, Ronald, (On Duty Outside the Diocese)
Dennison, James, (Between Assignments)
Dixon, James A., (On Duty Outside the Diocese)
Drechny, John, St.Mary, Park Forest
Duncan, Robert, St. Ann, Channahon
Dunn, William, St. Mary, Plano
Dyer, Donald L., St. Rose, Wilmington
Eaker, James, Visitation, Elmhurst
Eastburn, Lloyd D., (Leave of Absence)
Ellman, Edward, (On Duty Outside the Diocese)
Farrell, John, Our Lady of Mt. Carmel, Darien
Federici, Bart, St. Elizabeth Seton, Naperville
Feely, John, Immaculate Conception, Elmhurst
Fitt, Robert, St. Jude, New Lenox
Ford, Richard, St. Andrew, Romeoville
Forsythe, Patrick, St. Joseph, Manhattan
Fox, Steven A., (On Duty Outside the Diocese)
Foy, Richard, St. Walter, Roselle

Foys, Frank F., Notre Dame, Clarendon Hills
Franch, Dino J., Holy Ghost, Wood Dale
Francl, Frederick, Christ the King, Lombard
Frazier, Steven, St. Lawrence, South Wilmington
Freund, John, St. Isidore, Bloomington
Fricke, Thomas E., Christ the Servant, Woodridge
Fritz, Leon P., St. Joseph, Bradley
Fudacz, Larry, Our Lady of Peace, Darien
Gagnon, Ronnie, St. Patrick, Kankakee
Gamboa, Gabriel, St. Joseph, Addison
Gatons, Edwin, St. James Manor, Crete
Gavin, Philip, (Retired)
Gibbons, John, St. Alexander, Villa Park
Girard, William, (Retired)
Goebel, Thomas, Immaculate Conception, Elmhurst
Gregoire, Jerome, St. Joseph, Bradley
Guerrero, Manuel, St. Mary Immaculate, Plainfield
Hahn, Duane, (Leave of Absence)
Hamilton, Raymond, St. Francis of Assisi, Bolingbrook
Heitz, Philip, St. Philip, Addison
Henrissey, Francis R., (Leave of Absence)
Hetzel, William, St. Jude, Joliet
Huebner, Karl, Holy Family, Shorewood
Jackson, Kenneth, St. Daniel the Prophet, Wheaton
Jagielo, Thomas, Holy Trinity, Westmont
Janousek, James, St. John the Baptist, Joliet
Janousek, Jay, Visitation, Elmhurst
Jazdzewski, Melvin J., (Leave of Absence)
Jimenez, Julio, St. Alexander, Villa Park
Johnson, Joseph, St. Anthony, Frankfort
Jossey, Robert, (Retired)
Juricic, Frank, St. Bernard, Joliet
Kaminski, Robert, St. Mary, Mokena
Kearney, Lawrence, St. Thomas, Naperville
Kelly, William, (On Duty Outside the Diocese)
Kim, Paul, St. Andrew Kim, Itasca
Kinsella, James, Cathedral of St. Raymond, Joliet
Knecht, Ronald, St. Pius X, Lombard
Kobs, Dennis, Immaculate Conception, Morris
Kolodziej, Paul, St. Patrick, Joliet
Kowalchik, Michael, St. Walter, Roselle
Kowalski, Henry, (Retired)
Koza, Joseph, (On Duty Outside the Diocese)
Kozar, Francis, St. Joseph, Downers Grove
Krueger, James, St. Alexander, Villa Park
Kubica, Kenneth, St. Michael, Wheaton
Kueper, Timothy, Our Lady of Mercy, Aurora
Lamon, John D., (On Duty Outside the Diocese)
LaMotte, Robert, St. Martin of Tours, Kankakee
Lane, Charles, St. Thomas, Naperville
Lange, Kurt, St. Raphael, Naperville
Legner, Neil, (On Duty Outside the Diocese)
Leonard, John, Our Lady of Lourdes, Gibson City
Leonas, John, (Retired)
Leppert, Milton, St. Patrick, Wilton Center
Lifka, David, Notre Dame, Clarendon Hills
Lillig, Francis, Christ the King, Lombard
Lissak, Lawrence, St. Pius X, Lombard
Lombardo, Patrick, St. Mary Immaculate, Plainfield
Lopez, Jose L., St. John the Baptist, Joliet
Lovero, Marco, St. Francis of Assisi, Bolingbrook
Lysaght, Evan, (On Duty Outside the Diocese)
Mahoney, Daniel, Sr., St. Mary Nativity, Joliet
Malek, Robert, St. Matthew, Glendale Heights
Maloney, John R., (Retired)
Marciani, Thomas, St. Raphael, Naperville
Marcotte, Euchrist, Maternity B.V.M., Bourbonnais
Marlowe, David, St. Theresa, Kankakee
Marrow, Philip, St. Joseph, Addison
Martinez, Santos H., St. Mary, Plano
McConnell, Alexander, Notre Dame, Clarendon Hills
McGuire, Michael, St. Francis of Assisi, Bolingbrook
Meador, David, St. Michael, Wheaton
Mele, John, St. Mary Magdalene, Joliet
Mempin, Genaro, St. Francis of Assisi, Bolingbrook
Metcalfe, Dale R., St. Patrick, Yorkville
Miciunas, Robert, St. Mary of Gostyn, Downers Grove
Migliorato, Lawrence, St. Isidore, Bloomingdale
Miles, Kenneth J., St. Margaret Mary, Naperville
Moeller, John, St. James, Glen Ellyn
Molinaro, Serafin, Resurrection, Wayne
Monahan, Kevin, (On Duty Outside the Diocese)
Murphy, William E., St. Irene, Warrenville
Neher, Norman, (Retired)
Newey, Paul, Divine Savior, Downers Grove
Nguyen, Anthony, Queenship of Mary, Glen Ellyn
Nielo, Andrew, St. John the Baptist, Winfield
Nolan, Thomas J., Mary, Queen of Heaven, Elmhurst
Novak, Roger, Sts. Peter and Paul, Naperville
Nowak, Richard, (Retired), (On Duty Outside the Diocese)
Nunez, Charles, (Retired)
O'Connell, Thomas, St. Mary Immaculate, Plainfield
O'Connor, Joseph, St. Joseph, Downers Grove
Olszak, Leonard, St. Liborius, Steger
Otten, Mark, St. Boniface, Monee
Ouska, Gregory, St. Joseph Downers Grove
Pace, Scott, St. Elizabeth Seton, Naperville
Pagliaro, Jesse, St. Joseph, Lockport
Pallo, Daniel, (On Duty Outside the Diocese)
Paluch, Thomas, Holy Family, Shorewood
Perry, James, St. Daniel the Prophet, Wheaton
Petak, Edwin, Cathedral of St. Raymond, Joliet
Peterson, Charles M., St. Patrick, Joliet
Pidgeon, Matthew, St. James, Glen Ellyn
Pistorio, Charles, St. Ambrose, Crest Hill
Powers, Thomas, St. Andrew, Romeoville
Principe, Michael, (Retired)
Putman, John, St. Joseph, Manhattan
Rachubinski, Thomas, St. Pius X, Lombard
Randolph, Donald, St. Isidore, Bloomingdale
Raskowski, David, St. Joseph, Joliet
Rehmer, Philip, Our Lady of Mercy, Aurora
Repak, Andrew, (Retired)
Richardt, Thomas, St. Joan of Arc, Lisle
Riggi, Joseph, (Retired)
Rittenhouse, Daniel, Our Mother of Good Counsel, Homer Glen
Ritter, David, St. Dominic, Bolingbrook
Robinson, Peter, Christ the King, Lombard
Rooney, Peter, Ascension, Oakbrook Terrace
Rosko, Richard, St. Anthony, Frankfort
Ross, Thomas, St. Elizabeth Seton, Naperville
Ryan, Kevin, St. Bernard, Homer Glen
Safko, Terry L., St. Mary Immaculate, Plainfield
Sagenbrecht, Thomas, St. Mary Immaculate, Plainfield
Saltigerald, Luis, St. Mary, West Chicago
Schaper, Ed, (On Duty Outside the Diocese)
Schlund, James, (On Duty Outside the Diocese)
Schmith, Roger, St. Scholastica, Woodridge
Schneider, Paul A., Holy Family, Shorewood
Schroeder, Thomas, Holy Spirit Catholic Community, Naperville
Schubert, Anthony, (On Duty Outside the Diocese)
Schumacher, Carl N.J., St. Joseph, Downers Grove
Searls, Ronald, St. Walter, Roselle
Sebastian, John, St. Isaac Jogues, Hinsdale
Sheridan, Thomas, (Leave of Absence)
Siwek, Raymond, (Retired)
Skelly, Patrick, Maternity BVM, Bourbonnais
Solis, Joseph, (On Duty Outside the Diocese)
Soloy, George, St. Joan of Arc, Lisle
Sossong, James R., St. Mary Immaculate, Plainfield
Spatafore, Anthony, Visitation, Elmhurst
Spiezio, John, St. Petronille, Glen Ellyn
Stansberry, Robert T., Jr., Immaculate Conception, Morris
Stevens, Richard R., (On Duty Outside the Diocese)
Stolarz, Dennis, Our Lady of Peace, Darien
Storrs, Wayne, Christ the King, Lombard
Straub, Fred, Holy Family, Shorewood
Stroner, William, St. Michael, Wheaton
Stucko, Denis, St. Joan of Arc, Lisle
Sullivan, Robert, St. Joseph, Downers Grove
Swauger, Gary, St. Elizabeth Seton, Naperville
Symonanis, Alan, Notre Dame, Clarendon Hills
Szymanski, Edward, St. Mary, Park Forest
Tagle, Jesse, St. Andrew, Romeoville
Tansey, William, Ascension, Oakbrook Terrace
Taylor, Terrance, St. Margaret Mary, Naperville
Taylor, Timothy, St. Charles Borromeo, Bensenville
Tetrault, Robert L., (On Duty Outside the Diocese)
Theriault, Dennis, St. Jude, New Lenox
Thiltgen, Thomas R., Corpus Christi, Carol Stream
Thomas, William, Corpus Christi, Carol Stream
Tiongson, Arturo, Our Lady of Mercy, Aurora
Troy, Daniel, (Retired)
True, Robert, St. Irene, Warrenville
Uffmann, William, (Leave of Absence)
Urso, Joseph, St. Irene, Warrenville
Valdez, George, (Leave of Absence)
Vavra, Robert, Our Lady of Mercy, Aurora
Villarreal, Guadalupe, St. Isidore, Bloomingdale
Volker, Jeffrey, Our Lady of Lourdes, Gibson City
Waldron, Herbert, St. Andrew, Romeoville
Walen, Paul J., Sr., St. Dominic, Bolingbrook
Wallace, Robert, St. Dominic, Bolingbrook
Weierman, Robert, St. Dennis, Lockport
Wharry, James, (On Duty Outside the Diocese)
Whitman, Ronald, St. Teresa, Kankakee
Winblad, Joseph, Marian Village, Homer Glen
Woods, Charles, St. Raphael, Naperville
Worden, William, St. Thomas the Apostle, Naperville
Wozek, Duane, St. Anne, Oswego
Yarshen, Richard, Sts. Peter & Paul, Naperville
Yurcus, Ronald J., St. Petronille, Glen Ellyn
Zarembka, Terrance, St. Scholastica, Woodridge
Ziomek, Robert, St. Peter the Apostle, Itasca

INSTITUTIONS LOCATED IN THE DIOCESE

[A] COLLEGES AND UNIVERSITIES

JOLIET. *University of St. Francis* (1920) 500 N. Wilcox, 60435. Tel: 800-735-7500; Fax: 815-740-4285. Email: information@stfrancis.edu. Web: www.stfrancis.edu. Dr. Michael J. Vinceguerra, B.S., M.S., Ph.D., Pres.; Sisters Rosemary Small, O.S.F., B.A., M.Ed., Vice Pres., Mission Integration and Ministry; Sharon Frederick, O.S.F., B.A., M.S., Dir. University Ministry; Mr. Terry Cottrell, B.A., M.S., Librarian; Rev. J. Derran Combs, O.F.M., B.A., M.Div., Th.M., Special Asst. to Provost. A coed residence and commuter school. Priests 1; Sisters of St. Francis of Mary Immaculate 2; Lay Teachers 96; Students 3,172; Total Staff 349.

LISLE. *Benedictine University*, 5700 College Rd., 60532-0900. Tel: 630-829-6600; Fax: 630-960-1126. Web: www.ben.edu. Rt. Rev. Dismas B. Kalcic, O.S.B., Chancellor; Dr. William J. Carroll, Pres.; Dr. Donald Taylor, Provost & Vice Pres. Academic Affairs; Mr. Charles Gregory, Exec. Vice Pres.; Rev. David Turner, O.S.B., Asst. Provost for Mission; Dr. Maria De La Camara, Dean, College of Liberal Arts; Dr. Ralph D. Meeker, Dean, College of Sciences; Dr. Sandra Gill, Dean, College Business; Dr. Alan Gorr, Dean, College Educ. & Health Svcs.; Michael Carroll, Dean, College of Adult & Professional Studies; Jack Fritts, Librarian; Rt. Rev. Hugh R. Anderson, O.S.B., Dir. of Univ. Ministry; Revs. Thomas Becket Franks, O.S.B., Asst. Campus Min.; Robert Sum, O.S.B., Asst. Campus Min.; Bro. Richard Poro, O.S.B., Asst. Campus Min.; Revs. Theodore D. Suchy, O.S.B.; Philip S. Timko, O.S.B.; John Palmer, C.S.V.; Julian von Duerbeck, O.S.B.; James Flint, O.S.B.; Bro. Augustine Mallak, O.S.B. Fathers 10; Brothers 2; Sisters 1; Lay Teachers 112; Administrators 273; Students 5,600.

Founders Woods, Ltd., 5700 College Rd., 60532.

ROMEOVILLE. *Lewis University* (Coed University), One University Pkwy., 60446-2200. Tel: 815-838-0500; Fax: 815-838-5979. Email: brjgaff@lewisu.edu. Web: www.lewisu.edu/. Bros. James Gaffney, F.S.C., Pres.; Philip Johnson, F.S.C., Dir. University Ministry; Rev. Daniel L. Torson, C.PP.S., Chap.; Mary Hollerich, Dir. Library Svcs. Priests 2; De La Salle Christian Brothers 15; Lay Teachers 196; Students 5,847.

[B] HIGH SCHOOLS, DIOCESAN

KANKAKEE. *Bishop McNamara Catholic High School* (1922) 550 W. Brookmont Blvd., 60901. Tel: 815-932-7413; Fax: 815-932-0926. Email: glamore@bishopmac.com. Web: www.bishopmac.com. Kurt Weigt, Prin.; Sharon M. Jackson, Dir. Fundraising & Special Events; Gina La More, Dir. Admissions. Priests 1; Deacons 1; Lay Teachers 30; Students 404; Total Staff 53.

[C] HIGH SCHOOLS, PRIVATE

JOLIET. *Joliet Catholic Academy* (Coed), 1200 N. Larkin Ave., 60435. Tel: 815-741-0500; Fax: 815-773-0690. Email: faith@jca-online.org. Web: www.jca-online.org. Sr. Faith Szambelanczyk, O.S.F., Pres. & CEO; Jeffrey Budz, Prin. & COO; William Pender, Asst. Prin.; Mary Ann Hartnett, Librarian. Carmelites & Joliet Franciscans. Priests 1; Sisters 1; Lay Teachers 61; Students 780.

LISLE. *Benet Academy* (1887) 2200 Maple Ave., 60532. Tel: 630-719-2782; Fax: 630-719-2790. Email: webmaster@benet.org. Web: www.benet.org. Rt. Rev. Dismas B. Kalcic, O.S.B., Chancellor; Rev. Jude D. Randall, O.S.B., Pres.; Mr. Stephen A. Marth, Prin.; Mr. James Brown, Asst. Prin.; Mr. Joseph Cannizzaro, Dir. Devel.; Mrs. Barbara Sloan, Business Mgr.; Deborah Sola, Librarian. Priests 3; Brothers 3; Lay Teachers 76; Students 1,332.

LOMBARD. *Montini Catholic High School* (1996) 19 W. 070 16th St., 60148-4797. Tel: 630-627-6930; Fax: 630-627-0537. Web: www.montini.org. James F. Segredo, Pres.; Mrs. Maryann O'Neill, Prin.; Mrs. Estelle Soger, Librarian. De La Salle Christian Brothers 1; Lay Teachers 58; Students 700.

NEW LENOX. *Providence Catholic High School* (1918) (Coed), 1800 W. Lincoln Hwy., 60451. Tel: 815-485-2136; Fax: 815-485-2709. Web: www.providencecatholic.org. Rev. Richard J. McGrath, O.S.A., Ph.D., Pres.; Mr. Donald E. Sebestyen, Prin.; Mrs. Janlyn Auld, Asst. Prin.; Revs. John D. Merkelis, O.S.A., Pastoral Dir.; John J. Sotak, O.S.A., Prior, Augustinian Province & Teacher; Ms. Soteria Papagiannopoulos,

Librarian. Priests 4; Lay Teachers 78; Students 1,168. In Res. Revs. John A. Kret, O.S.A.; Raymond R. Ryan, O.S.A.; Michael J. Slattery, O.S.A.

WHEATON. *St. Francis High School* (1956) 2130 W. Roosevelt Rd., 60187. Tel: 630-668-5800; Fax: 630-668-5893. Email: rhuhn@sfhsnet.org. Web: www.sfhsnet.org. Raeann Huhn, Prin.; Judi Rath, Librarian. Sisters 1; Lay Teachers 51; Students 772.

[D] ELEMENTARY SCHOOLS, DIOCESAN

NAPERVILLE. *All Saints Catholic Academy*, (Grades PreK-8), 1155 Aurora Ave., 60540. Tel: 630-961-6125; Fax: 630-961-3771. Email: srrenehan@yahoo.com. Web: ascacademy.org. Revs. Paul Hottinger; Joel Fortier; Thomas Paul; Sandy R. Renehan, Ed.D., Prin.; Nancy Kries, Librarian. Teachers 43; Students 509.

[E] AGENCIES AND INSTITUTIONS OF THE CHARITIES OF THE DIOCESE

JOLIET. *Catholic Charities*, 203 N. Ottawa St., 60432. Tel: 815-723-3405; Fax: 815-723-3452. Email: kmcgowan@cc-doj.org. Web: www.cc-doj.org. Ms. Kathleen McGowan, Exec. Dir. Diocesan Administrative Office and Regional Office for Will, Grundy and Kendall Counties.

KANKAKEE. *Catholic Charities*, 270 N. Schuyler Ave., 60901. Tel: 815-933-7791; Fax: 815-932-3030. Web: www.cc-doj.org. Regional Office for Kankakee, Ford, and Iroquois Counties.

LOMBARD. *Catholic Charities*, 26 W. St. Charles Rd., 60148. Tel: 630-495-8008; Fax: 630-495-9854. Email: kmcgowan@cc-doj.org. Web: www.cc-doj.org. Regional Office for DuPage County.

[F] PROTECTIVE INSTITUTIONS

JOLIET. *Guardian Angel Community Services*, 1550 Plainfield Rd., 60435. Tel: 815-729-0930; Fax: 815-744-6087. Email: Sheila@guardianangelhome.org. Web: www.guardianangelhome.org. Sponsored by the Sisters of St. Francis of Mary Immaculate; Child and family welfare agency: therapeutic school, foster care, domestic violence shelter, child abuse prevention center, counseling, transitional living program, and Rape Crisis Program.

MOMENCE. *Good Shepherd Manor* (1971) P.O. Box 260, 60954. Tel: 815-472-6492; 815-472-3700; Fax: 815-472-2160. Email: gsmanor@mchsi.com. Web: www.goodshepherdmanor.org. Mr. Bruce Fitzpatrick, Pres.; Rev. Wolf Werling, Asst. Chap.; Bro. Alphonsus Brown, B.G.S., Asst. Admin. Adult Male DD-MR. Brothers of the Good Shepherd 4; Brother/Priest 1; Bed Capacity 124; Permanent Residents 124.

[G] DAY CARE

JOLIET. *Vilaseca Josephine Center* (1974) 351 N. Chicago St., 60432. Tel: 815-727-1467; Fax: 815-727-1480. Email: josemvilaseca@hotmail.com. Sisters Araceli Perez, Dir.; Judith Perez, Sub-Dir. Josephine Sisters. Students 88.

[H] LEARNING CENTERS

JOLIET. *Franciscan Learning Center* (1979) (Grades PreSchool-K), 1734 Theodore St., 60435. Tel: 815-744-7634; Fax: 815-744-2152. Email: FLC1734@aol.com. Sr. Margaret McGuckin, Co-Dir., Prin. & Teacher. Sisters 3; Lay Staff 3; Students 84.

KANKAKEE. *Provena Fortin Villa*, 1025 N. Washington Ave., 60901. Tel: 815-932-8411; Fax: 815-936-3275. Email: jessica.christie@provena.org. Jessica Christie, Dir. Childcare with Preschool for children 6 weeks to 12 years. Total Staff 30; Students 129.

[I] GENERAL HOSPITALS

JOLIET. *Provena Saint Joseph Medical Center*, 333 N. Madison St., 60435-6595. Tel: 815-725-7133; 708-478-7678; Fax: 815-741-7579; 708-478-6332. Web: www.provenasaintjoe.org. Jeffrey Brickman, System Sr. Vice Pres. & CEO; Deacon Ed Petak, Vice Pres. Mission Svcs.

Provena Hospitals dba Provena St. Joseph Medical Center Sisters 4; Chaplains 8; Bed Capacity 480; Patients Assisted Annually 529,908; Total Staff 2,517.

Provena Industrial Rehabilitation Center, Joliet Tel: 815-741-7416; Fax: 815-741-0774.

Provena Physical Rehab & Sports Injury Center, Joliet Tel: 815-741-7114; Fax: 815-725-6997.

KANKAKEE. *Provena St. Mary's Hospital*, 500 W. Court St., 60901. Tel: 815-937-2400; Fax: 815-937-3535. Web: www.provena.org/stmarys. Sr. Anne Jaeger, S.S.C.M., Dir. Mission Svcs.; Michael Arno, Pres. & CEO; Rev. Michael Powell, Priest Chap.

Provena Hospitals dba Provena St. Mary Hospital Chaplains 5; Sisters (SSCM) 2; Bed Capacity 186; Patients Assisted Annually 223,256; Total Staff 864.

MOKENA. *Provena Health (Jol)* (1997) 19065 Hickory Creek Dr., Ste. 300, 60448. Tel: 708-478-6300; Fax: 708-478-5960. Web: www.provena.org. Priests 1; Total Staff 220.

Provena Hospitals (Jol) (1997) 19065 Hickory Creek Dr., Ste. 300, 60448. Tel: 708-478-6300; Fax: 708-478-5960. Web: www.provena.org.

[J] REHABILITATION CENTERS

WHEATON. *Marianjoy Rehabilitation Hospital & Clinics, Inc.* (1969) 26 W. 171 Roosevelt Rd., P.O. Box 795, 60189. Tel: 630-462-4000; Fax: 630-462-0112. Web: www.marianjoy.org. Kathleen Yosko, Pres. & CEO. Franciscan Sisters, Daughters of the Sacred Hearts of Jesus and Mary (Wheaton, IL). Bed Capacity 120; Patients Assisted Annually 6,432.

[K] HOMES FOR AGED

JOLIET. *Our Lady of Angels Retirement Home*, 1201 Wyoming Ave., 60435. Tel: 815-725-6631; Fax: 815-725-1451. Rev. Benet Fonck, O.F.M., Chap.; Sr. Maria Pesavento, O.S.F., CEO & Village Dir. Sisters of St. Francis of Mary Immaculate. Sisters 4; Lay Staff 151; (Retired) 38; Residents 97; Total Staff 155. In Res. Sr. Sandra Salois, O.S.F., Local Coord.

Provena Villa Franciscan, 210 N. Springfield Ave., 60435. Tel: 815-725-3400; Fax: 815-725-2160. Ann Dodge, Admin.; Paul Kselman, Dir. Pastoral Care.

Provena Senior Services, Extended, Intermediate, and Skilled Care, Respite Care. Bed Capacity 176.

BOURBONNAIS. *Provena Our Lady of Victory*, 20 Briarcliff Ln., 60914. Tel: 815-937-2022; Fax: 815-936-3231. Email: Robin.Gifford@provena.org. Robin Gifford, Admin.; Sr. Martha Harrington, Dir. Pastoral Care.

Provena Senior Services Bed Capacity 107.

CLIFTON. *Merkle-Knipprath Countryside Home* (1975) 1190 E. 2900 N Rd., 60927-7103. Tel: 815-694-2306. Bro. Damien DeBraekeleer, O.S.F., Admin. Apartment Community and Nursing Center. Religious 4; Total in Nursing Care 100; Apartment Living 30.

DARIEN. *Carmelite Carefree Retirement Village* (1979) 8419 Bailey Rd., 60561-5361. Tel: 630-960-4060; Fax: 630-960-4071. Email: susan.hiles@provena.org. Web: carmelitecarefree.org. *Society of Mt. Carmel*, 1317 Frontage Rd., 60561. Tel: 630-971-0050; Fax: 630-971-0195. Sandra Kariotis, Dir.; Revs. John Hertel, O.Carm.; John Maisonneuve, O.Carm.; Xavier McEachern; Raphael Sutherland; Lambert Zulkie, O.Carm. (Retired). Residents 96.

HOMER GLEN. *Franciscan Communities, Inc. dba Marian Village* 15624 Marian Dr., 60491. Tel: 708-226-3780; Fax: 708-226-3781. Web: www.franciscancommunities.com. 1055 W. 175th St., Ste. 202, Homewood, 60430. Daniel Bannon, Exec. Dir.

KANKAKEE. *Provena Heritage Lodge*, 995 N. Entrance Ave., 60901. Tel: 815-939-4506; Fax: 815-939-4761. Email: carol.mcintyre@provena.org. Carol McIntyre, Admin.

Provena Senior Services dba Provena Heritage Lodge Bed Capacity 26.

Provena Senior Services (Jol), Kankakee Tel: 815-939-4506; Fax: 815-939-4761.

Provena Heritage Village, 901 N. Entrance Ave., 60901. Tel: 815-939-4506; Fax: 815-939-4761. Email: carol.mcintyre@provena.org. Carol McIntyre, Admin.; Patricia Dennison, Dir. Pastoral Care.

Provena Senior Services dba Provena Heritage Village Bed Capacity 130.

LISLE. *Villa St. Benedict*, 1920 Maple Ave., 60532. Tel: 630-725-7000; Fax: 630-852-3196. Email: gtrembley@villastben.org. Web: www.villastben.org. Mr. Glenn Trembley, Admin. Continuing Care Retirement Lay Staff 117; Residents 239.

NAPERVILLE. *St. John Vianney Villa*, 1464 Green Trails Dr., 60540-8372. Tel: 630-983-0533; Fax: 630-983-6375. Revs. Ronald Hart; Gordon Mahoney (Retired); James Nowak (Retired); Robert E. Pietras (Retired); Edward P. Rowland (Retired); John Sebahar (Retired); Daniel F. Stempora (Retired); Jess Testa (Retired); Thomas Wolter (Retired); John Zanoni (Retired). Retirement home for priests. Residents 10.

St. Patrick's Residence, 1400 Brookdale Rd., 60563-2126. Tel: 630-416-6565; Fax: 630-416-8755. Email: info@stpatricksresidence.org. Web: www.stpatricksresidence.org. Sr. Jeanne Francis Haley, Admin. Carmelite Sisters 6; Bed Capacity 210; Residents 205; Total Staff 247.

OAKBROOK. *Franciscan Tertiary Province of the Sacred Heart, Inc. dba Mayslake Village Inc.* 1801 35th St., Oak Brook, 60523. Tel: 630-850-8232; Fax: 630-850-8233. Email: mayslakevillage@comcast.net. Web: www.mayslake.com. Mr. Michael A. Frigo, Vice Pres., Admin. Senior Citizen Retirement Community.

Mayslake Annex II, NFP, 1801 35th St., Oak Brook, 60523. Tel: 630-850-8232; Fax: 630-850-8233. Email: mayslakevillage@comcast.net. Web: www.mayslake.com. Rev. Larry Dreffein, O.F.M., M.Div., M.P.S., Pres. & Contact Person; Mr. Michael A. Frigo, Vice Pres., Admin.

Mayslake East Wing, Inc., 1801 35th St., Oak Brook, 60523. Tel: 630-850-8232; Fax: 630-850-8233. Email: mayslakvillage@comcast.net. Web: www.mayslake.com. Mr. Michael A. Frigo, Vice Pres., Admin.

PLAINFIELD. *Mayslake Village- Plainfield Campus, Inc. dba Cedarlake Village* 14800 S. Van Dyke Rd., 60544. Tel: 815-254-3564; Fax: 815-439-9651. Email: cedarlakevillage@comcast.net. Web: www.cedarlakevillage.com. Rev. Larry Dreffein, O.F.M., M.Div., M.P.S., Pres.; Mr. Michael A. Frigo, Vice Pres., Admin. Senior Citizen Retirement Community. Total Staff 5.

WHEATON. *Marian Park, Inc.* (1972) 2126 W. Roosevelt Rd., 60187. Tel: 630-665-9100; Fax: 630-665-9357. Web: www.wfs-inc.org. *Mailing Address*, 26 W. 171 Roosevelt Rd., P.O. Box 667, 60189-0667. Units 209.

[L] MONASTERIES AND RESIDENCES OF PRIESTS AND BROTHERS

JOLIET. *St. Elias Carmelites*, 3504 Lake Shore Dr., 60431-8819. Tel: 815-439-8246; Fax: 815-439-8633. Email: steliascarmelites@comcast.net. Revs. Robert Boley, O.Carm.; John J. Comerford, O.Carm.; Raymond Foster, O.Carm.; Bros. Lawrence Fidelus, O.Carm.; Dominic Saganich. Priests 3; Brothers 2.

St. John the Baptist Friary, 404 N. Hickory St., 60435. Tel: 815-727-9783; Fax: 815-740-1521. Revs. J. Derran Combs, O.F.M., B.A., M.Div., Th.M., Faculty, Univ. of St. Francis.; John Dombrowski, O.F.M.; Fred Radtke, O.F.M., Parochial Vicar; Rogelio Martinez Ruteaga, O.F.M., Vicar & Assoc. Dir. Postulancy; Ildephonse Skorup, O.F.M., Chap. at Franciscan Sisters of the Sacred Heart, Frankfort; Gerold Schubert, O.F.M. (Retired); Dennis Schafer, O.F.M., Dir. Postulancy & Guardian. Priests 5; Brothers 1.

BURR RIDGE. *Christian Brothers Provincial Office (Midwest Province)* (1995) 7650 S. County Line Rd., 60527-7959. Tel: 630-323-3725; Fax: 630-323-3779. Email: info@cbmidwest.org. Web: www.cbmidwest.org. Bros. Bede Baldry, F.S.C., Prov. Special Projects; Francis Carr, F.S.C., Prov.; Larry Schatz, F.S.C., Auxiliary Prov.; Thomas Hetland, F.S.C., Dir. Devel.; Tina Bonacci, Formation & Accompaniment; Bros. Joseph Saurbier, F.S.C., Dir. Finance; Patrick Conway, F.S.C., Dir. Vocations & Formation; Nicholas Schumer, F.S.C., Dir. St. La Salle Auxiliary; William Clarey, F.S.C., Dir. Senior Brothers; Kevin Convey, F.S.C., Dir. Education & Mission.

DARIEN. *Carmelite Provincial Office*, 1317 Frontage Rd., 60561. Tel: 630-971-0050; Fax: 630-971-0195. Email: provincial@carmelnet.org. Web: www.carmelnet.org. Very Rev. John F. Welch, O.Carm., Prior Prov.; Revs. Bernhard Bauerle, O.Carm., Prov. Procurator; David L. Simpson, O.Carm., Commissary Prov.; Bro. Charles Kwiatkowski, O.Carm.

The Society of Mt. Carmel

Carmelites Serving in Italy: Revs. Raul Maravi, O.Carm. Email: rmaravi@carmelnet.org; Craig Morrison, O.Carm.; Joachim Smet, O.Carm.

Carmelites Serving in Canada: Revs. Roger Bonneau, O.Carm.; Thomas Hakala, O.Carm.; Leo Huard, O.Carm.; Stanley Makacinas, O.Carm., Acting Dir. Mt. Carmel Spiritual Center; Anthony McNamara, O.Carm.; Gerard Power, O.Carm.; Jordon Rooney, O.Carm.; Bruce Taggart, O.Carm.; John-Benedict Weber, O.Carm.; Bro. Gabriel Murray, O.Carm.

Carmelites Serving in Peru: Most Rev. Michael LaFay, O.Carm.; Revs. Salvador Bartolo, O.Carm., Prelate Nullius, Sicuani, Peru. Tel: 011-51-8-435-11611; Fax: 011-51-8-435-1089; Alban Quinn, O.Carm., Prelate Nullius, Sicuani, Peru. Tel: 011-51-8-435-11611; Fax: 011-51-8-435-1089; Enrique Laguna-Vargas, O.Carm., Prelate Nullius, Sicuani, Peru. Tel: 011-51-8-435-11611; Fax: 011-51-8-435-1089; Edward Adelmann, O.Carm., Prelate Nullius, Sicuani, Peru. Tel: 011-51-8-435-11611; Fax: 011-51-8-435-1089; Eduardo Rivero, O.Carm., Prelate Nullius, Sicuani, Peru. Tel: 011-51-8-435-11611; Fax: 011-51-8-435-1089; Jorge Remuzgo, O.Carm., Prelate Nullius, Sicuani, Peru. Tel: 011-51-8-435-11611; Fax: 011-51-8-435-1089; Gerald Payea, O.Carm., Prelate Nullius, Sicuani,

Peru. Tel: 011-51-8-435-11611; Fax: 011-51-8-435-1089; Michael Sgarioto, O.Carm.; Jorge Villegas, O.Carm., Prelate Nullius, Sicuani, Peru. Tel: 011-51-8-435-11611; Fax: 011-51-8-435-1089; Deacon Miguel Bacigalupo, Prelate Nullius, Sicuani, Peru. Tel: 011-51-8-435-11611; Fax: 011-51-8-435-1089; Bros. Carlos Valdez, O.Carm., Prelate Nullius, Sicuani, Peru. Tel: 011-51-8-435-11611; Fax: 011-51-8-435-1089; Rodolfo Aznaran, O.Carm.; Adolfo Medrano, O.Carm.

Carmelites Serving in Australia: Bro. Sean Keefe, O.Carm.

Carmelites Serving in Mexico: Revs. Peter Hinde, O.Carm.; Thomas Jordan, O.Carm.; Mario Loya, O.Carm.; Bros. Emilio Rodriguez, O.Carm.; Jose Luis Torres P., O.Carm.

Carmelites Serving in El Salvador: Rev. David Blanchard, O.Carm.; Bros. Mario Cadena, O.Carm.; Rogelio Garcia, O.Carm.; Floristar Guerrero, O.Carm.; Alfredo Guillen, O.Carm.; Alejandro Muro, O.Carm.; Luis Jesus Paz, O.Carm.; Fabio Rajas, O.Carm.; Benjamin Salas, O.Carm.; Alberto Seminario, O.Carm.

Carmelites Serving in France: Rev. Terrence Cyr, O.Carm.

Carmelites Serving Elsewhere: Revs. Emil Agostino, O.Carm. (Retired); Benjamin Aguilar, O.Carm.; Tim Andres, O.Carm.; Joseph Atcher, O.Carm.; Nelson Belizario, O.Carm.; Peter Byrth, O.Carm.; Kyrin Caggiano, O.Carm. (Retired); Warren Carlin, O.Carm. (Retired); Emeric Carmody, O.Carm. (Retired); Michael Flynn, O.Carm., Pastor; Michael Greenwell, O.Carm.; Ashley Harrington, O.Carm.; Gregory Houck, O.Carm.; Myron Judy, O.Carm.; Anton Kollar, O.Carm.; Albert P. Koppes, O.Carm.; James Lewis, O.Carm.; Bernard Lickteig, O.Carm.; Joseph Maisonneuve, O.Carm. (Retired); Joseph McCarthy, O.Carm.; Blaise McInerney, O.Carm.; Zachary Monet, O.Carm.; James Mueller, O.Carm.; Henry Ormond, O.Carm.; Paul Robinson, O.Carm.; John Russell, O.Carm.; Enrique Varela, O.Carm.; Frank Weil, O.Carm.; Bros. David McGinnis, O.Carm.; Daryl Moresco, O.Carm.

St. Simon Stock Priory (1959) 8501 Bailey Rd., 60561. Tel: 630-241-1802; Fax: 630-969-7519. Very Rev. John F. Welch, O.Carm.; Bro. Charles Kwiatkowski, O.Carm.; Revs. Bernhard Bauerle, O.Carm.; Robert E. Colaresi, O.Carm., Prior; John Knoernschild, O.Carm.; David L. Simpson, O.Carm. Priests 5; Brothers 1.

LISLE. *St. Procopius Abbey*, 5601 College Rd., 60532. Tel: 630-969-6410; Fax: 630-969-6426. Email: stprocopius@hotmail.com. Web: www.procopius.org. Rt. Revs. Dismas B. Kalcic, O.S.B., Abbot; Hugh R. Anderson, O.S.B., Retired Abbot; Bro. Columban Trojan, O.S.B., Subprior; Very Rev. Anthony J. Jacob, O.S.B., Prior; Revs. Thomas Chisholm, O.S.B., Novice Master; Joseph Chang, O.S.B.; Odilo Crkva, O.S.B.; Julian von Duerbeck, O.S.B.; James Flint, O.S.B.; T. Becket Franks, O.S.B.; Zachary Hrisko, O.S.B.; Edward J. Kucera, O.S.B.; Timothy R. Marceau, O.S.B.; Austin Murphy, O.S.B.; Jude D. Randall, O.S.B., Pres., Benet Academy; Theodore D. Suchy, O.S.B.; Robert Sum, O.S.B.; Philip S. Timko, O.S.B.; David Turner, O.S.B.; Kenneth Zigmond, O.S.B.; Most Rev. Daniel W. Kucera, O.S.B., Archbishop of Dubuque, IA (Retired). Benedictine Monks. Monks 33; Priests 21; Brothers 11; Archbishops 1; Oblates 1. *Benedictine Chinese Mission*, 5601 College Rd., 60532. Tel: 630-969-6410; Fax: 630-969-6426. *Slav Missions*, 5601 College Rd., 60532. Tel: 630-969-6410; Fax: 630-969-6426. *Benedictine University*, 5700 College Rd., 60532. Tel: 630-829-6000; Fax: 630-829-6242. Web: www.ben.edu. *Benet Academy*, 2200 Maple Ave., 60532. Tel: 630-969-6550; Fax: 630-719-0929. Web: www.benet.org. *St. Procopius Abbey Endowment*, 5601 College Rd., 60532. Tel: 630-969-6410; Fax: 630-969-6426.

MOMENCE. *Brother Mathias Barrett Inc. of Illinois*, P.O. Box 736, 60954. Tel: 815-472-3700; Fax: 815-472-2160. Bro. Alphonsus Brown, B.G.S., Pres. Brothers 4.

NEW LENOX. *Augustinian Friary*, 1800 W. Lincoln Hwy., 60451. Tel: 815-485-6880; Fax: 815-485-2709. Rev. Richard M. Jacobs, O.S.A. (See separate listing for Providence High School) In Res. Revs. John A. Kret, O.S.A.; John D. Merkelis, O.S.A.; Richard J. McGrath, O.S.A., Ph.D., Pres.; Raymond R. Ryan, O.S.A.; Michael J. Slattery, O.S.A.; John J. Sotak, O.S.A.

ROMEOVILLE. *La Salle House Community* (1996) 100 Faculty Lane, 60446-1178. Tel: 815-836-5530; Fax: 815-836-5858. Email: johnsoph@lewisu.edu. Bros. Philip Johnson, F.S.C., Dir.; Pierre St. Raymond, Sub-Dir.; Joel Dolan; Thomas Dupre; James Gaffney, F.S.C.; Leo Jones, F.S.C. Email: LJones9911@aol.com; Augustine Kossuth; Joseph Martin; Raphael Mascari; Raymond McManaman; Regis Morgan; Lawrence Oelschlegel; Bernard Rapp; John Vietoris; William Walz, F.S.C.; Robert Wilsbach. Brothers 16.

WESTMONT. *Westmont North Community* (2002) 222 S. Cass Ave., 60559. Tel: 630-724-1976; Fax: 630-724-1978. Bro. Fred Dillenburg, Dir. Brothers 4.

[M] CONVENTS AND RESIDENCES FOR SISTERS

JOLIET. *St. Clare House of Prayer* (1968) 3208 Indianwood Ln., 60431-4119. Tel: 815-630-5431. Email: stclarehouse@aol.com. Sisters of St. Francis of Mary Immaculate 3.

Josephine Sisters (1872) 351 N. Chicago St., 60432. Tel: 815-727-1467; Fax: 815-727-1480. Email: josephinesis@hotmail.com. Josephine Sisters of Mexico (Hermanas Josefinas). Sisters 6.

Sisters of St. Francis of Mary Immaculate (1865) 1433 Essington Rd., 60435-2873. Tel: 815-725-8735; Fax: 815-725-8648. Web: www.jolietfranciscans.org. Sr. Mary Rose Lieb, O.S.F., M.S.Ed., M.S.A., Pres. & Gen. Supr.

Congregation of the Third Order of St Francis of Mary Immaculate, Joliet, IL.

FRANKFORT. *Franciscan Sisters of the Sacred Heart* (1866) St. Francis Woods, 9201 W. St. Francis Rd., 60423-8335. Tel: 815-469-4895; Fax: 815-464-3809. Email: judith.plumb@provena.org. Web: www.fssh.com. Sr. Mary Elizabeth Imler, O.S.F., Gen. Supr.

An Association of Franciscan Sisters of the Sacred Heart and Franciscan Foundation. Sisters 95.

KANKAKEE. *Servants of the Holy Heart of Mary, Holy Family Prov., U.S.A.* (1889) *Provincial Administration*, 15 Elmwood Dr., 60901. Tel: 815-937-2380; Fax: 815-937-5520. Email: linda.hatton@provena.org. Web: www.sscm-usa.org. Sr. Linda K. Hatton, S.S.C.M., Prov. Supr.

Servants of the Holy Heart of Mary Charitable Trust, Provena Health including 7 hospitals and 13 long term care institutions. Professed Sisters 40.

LISLE. *Benedictine Sisters of the Sacred Heart, Sacred Heart Monastery* (1895) 1910 Maple Ave., 60532-2164. Tel: 630-725-6000; Fax: 630-969-5814. Email: jheble@shmlisle.org. Web: www.shmlisle.org. Sr. Judith Ann Heble, O.S.B., Prioress.

Benedictine Sisters of the Sacred Heart Charitable Trust Professed Sisters 29.

MINOOKA. *The Poor Clares of Joliet, Annunciation Monastery*, 6200 E. Minooka Rd., 60447. Tel: 815-467-0032; Fax: 815-467-0032. Email: paxbonvm@aol.com. Web: www.poorclaresjoliet.org. Sr. M. Dorothy Urschalitz, P.C.C., Contact Person. Cloistered Sisters 12; Extern Sisters 2.

NEW LENOX. *Mother of Good Counsel Monastery*, 440 N. Marley Rd., 60451. Tel: 815-463-9662. Sr. Mary Villar, O.S.A., Prioress. Augustinian Nuns. Solemnly Professed Sisters 4; Postulants 1.

PLAINFIELD. *Mantellate Sisters Servants of Mary of Plainfield*, 16949 S. Drauden Rd., 60586. Tel: 815-436-5796; Fax: 815-436-7486. Sr. Louise Staszewski, O.S.M., Regl. Supr. Homes for the Aged and Foreign Missions.; Yr. Founded: Italy-1861; USA-1916; Plainfield-1977; Ministry in the field of Academic Educ., Parish Ministry, Social Work, Nursing, Homes for the Aged, and Foreign Missions. Sisters 7.

WHEATON. *St. Clara Province Charitable Trust*, 26 W. 171 Roosevelt Rd., P.O. Box 667, 60189-0667. Tel: 630-462-7422; Fax: 630-909-6615.

Convent of Our Lady of the Angels Motherhouse and Novitiate (1860) Franciscan Sisters, Daughters of the Sacred Hearts of Jesus and Mary (Wheaton, IL), P.O. Box 667, 60187. Tel: 630-909-6600; Fax: 630-462-7148. Email: danderson@wheatonfranciscan.org. Web: www.wheatonfranciscan.org. Sr. Beatrice Hernandez, O.S.F., Prov. Dir.

Wheaton Franciscan Sisters Corp. Sisters 73.

Loretto Convent, Religious of the Institute of the Blessed Virgin Mary, P.O. Box 508, 60187. Tel: 630-653-6113; Fax: 630-653-4886. Email: ibvmjfrye1@aol.com. Web: www.ibvm.us. Sisters 20.

Loretto Center Tel: 630-653-7918; Fax: 630-653-0845. Email: IBVMLC@aol.com. Web: www.lorettocenter.org.

Office of Development Tel: 630-682-9097; Fax: 630-868-8258. Email: development@ibvm.org.

Loretto Extension Service Tel: 630-462-3860; Fax: 630-784-9544. Email: IBVMMBRML@aol.com.

Loretto Early Childhood Center Tel: 630-690-8410; Fax: 630-868-2764. Email: IBVMJULIES@hotmail.com.

Children of God Retreats Tel: 630-588-8501; Fax: 630-653-4886. Email: IBVMMCG@aol.com.

United States Province Administration Tel: 630-665-3814 (Superior); 630-653-6113 (Treas.); 630-868-2904 (Sec.); Fax: 630-868-2852. Email: IBVMRosemary@aol.com.

[N] HOUSES OF RETREAT/PRAYER

DARIEN. *Carmelite Spiritual Center*, 8433 Bailey Rd., 60561. Tel: 630-969-4141; Fax: 630-969-3376. Email: cscretreat@aol.com. Revs. Robert E. Colaresi, O.Carm., Dir.; David L. Simpson, O.Carm., Spiritual Dir. Total Staff 16.

FRANKFORT. *Portiuncula Center for Prayer* (1990) 9263 W. St. Francis Rd., 60423-8330. Tel: 815-464-3880; Fax: 815-469-4880. Email: info@portforprayer.org. Web: www.portforprayer.org.

LOMBARD. *Mayslake Ministries, Inc.* (1991) 450 E. 22nd St., Ste. 170, 60148. Tel: 630-268-9000; Fax: 630-268-9001. Email: mamore@mayslakeministries.org. Web: mayslakeministries.org. Rev. Jonathan D. Foster, O.F.M.; Mary Amore, Exec. Dir. Priests 1; Lay Staff 6.

PLANO. *La Salle Manor Christian Brothers Retreat House* (1957) 12480 Galena Rd., 60545. Tel: 630-552-3224; Fax: 630-552-9160. Email: info@lasallemanor.org. Web: www.lasallemanor.org. Robert Dressel, Pres.

WARRENVILLE. *Congregation of Our Lady of the Retreat in the Cenacle* (1939) 3S. 230 Warren Ave., P.O. Box 797, 60555-0797. Tel: 630-393-2976; Fax: 630-393-2646. Web: www.cenacle.org. Sr. Joyce Kemp, r.c. Sisters 1; Personnel 4.

[O] MISCELLANEOUS

JOLIET. *Diocesan Educational Endowment Fund*, 425 Summit St., 60435.

Fiat House of Discernment, 113 N. Ottawa, 60432. Tel: 815-724-0034; Fax: 815-724-0632. Email: frburke@dioceseofjoliet.org. Web: www.vocations.com. Rev. Burke Masters, Dir. Vocations.

**The Upper Room Crisis Hotline (TURCH)*, P.O. Box 3572, 60434. Tel: 815-727-4367; 888-808-8724 (Hotline); Fax: 815-726-5004. Email: turch@sbcglobal.net. Web: www.theupperroomcrisishotline.org. Rev. Dennis Schafer, O.F.M., Pres.; Sr. Mary Frances Seeley, O.S.F., Ph.D., CEO.

AURORA. *Assisi Homes - Constitution House, Inc.* (1995)Mailing Address: 26 W. 171 Roosevelt Rd., P.O. Box 667, Wheaton, 60187-0667. 401 N. Constitution Dr., 60506. Tel: 630-896-2100; Fax: 630-896-0313. Web: www.wfhealthcare.org. Units 232.

BURR RIDGE. *Christian Brothers Fund, Inc.*, 7650 S. County Line Rd., 60527-4718. Tel: 630-323-3725; Fax: 630-323-3779. Email: info@cbmidwest.org. Web: cbmidwest.org. Bros. Thomas Hetland, F.S.C., Pres.; Fred Dillenburg, Treas.

CAROL STREAM. *Assisi Homes - Colony Park, Inc.* (1995) 550 E. Thornhill Dr., 60188. Tel: 630-682-9000; Fax: 630-682-9008. Web: www.wfhealthcare.org. Mailing Address: 26 W. 171 Roosevelt Rd., P.O. Box 667, Wheaton, 60187-0667. Tel: 630-462-6900. Units 284.

DARIEN. *Carmelite Mission Office*, 8501 Bailey Rd., 60561. Tel: 630-969-5220; Fax: 630-969-5266. Email: jemalley@juno.com. Web: www.carmelitemissions.org. Rev. John Malley, O.Carm., Dir.

National Shrine of St. Therese, 8501 Bailey Rd., 60561. Tel: 630-969-3311; Fax: 630-969-5536. Email: webmaster@saint-therese.org. Web: www.saint-therese.org. Rev. Robert E. Colaresi, O.Carm., Dir.

Provincial Office of Lay Carmelites and Scapular Center, 8501 Bailey Rd., 60561. Tel: 630-969-5050; Fax: 630-969-7519. Email: laycarmelites@carmelnet.org. Web: carmelnet.org. Sisters Libby Dahlstrom, O.Carm., Assoc. Dir.; Mary Martin, O.Carm., Prov. Delegate; Very Rev. John F. Welch, O.Carm., Prior Prov.

Society of the Little Flower (1923) 1313 Frontage Rd., 60561-5341. Tel: 630-968-9400; Fax: 630-968-9542. Email: webmaster@littleflower.org. Web: www.littleflower.org. Rev. Robert E. Colaresi, O.Carm., Dir.

FRANKFORT. *Provena Care @ Home Inc.*, 9223 W. St. Francis Rd., 60423-8334. Tel: 815-806-2300; Fax: 815-806-0409. Email: margaretcgleason@provenahealth.com. Web: www.provenahealth.com. Margaret C. Gleason, Pres. & Contact Person.

Provena Home Health, Inc., 9223 W. St. Francis Rd., 60423-8334. Tel: 815-806-2300; Fax: 815-806-0409. Email: margaretcgleason@provenahealth.com. Web: www.provenahealth.com. Margaret C. Gleason, Pres. & Contact Person.

KANKAKEE. *Lisieux Pastoral Outreach Center*, 371 N. St. Joseph Ave., 60901-2741. Tel: 815-939-2913.

Provena St. Mary's Adult Day Center, 1025 E. Washington, 60901. Tel: 815-937-2447; Fax: 815-936-3245. Email: rebecca.barney@provena.org.

Web: www.provena.org. 19065 Hickory Creek Dr., #300, Mokena, 60448. Rebecca Barney, Admin.

LISLE. *Catholic CEO Healthcare Connection (CCHC)* (1985) 3333 Warrenville Rd, Ste. 200, 60532. Tel: 630-799-8315; Fax: 630-799-8316. Email: roger.butler@cchcforum.org. Mr. Roger N. Butler, Exec. Dir.

National Association of Catholic Nurses-U.S.A., P.O. Box 3016, 60532-8016. Tel: 508-776-5556; 630-852-1049. Email: capekirkpatrick@verizon.net. Web: www.nacn-usa.org. Kathleen Kirkpatrick, B.A., Pres.

MOKENA. *Provena Senior Services*, 19065 Hickory Creek Dr., Ste. 310, 60448-8507. Tel: 708-478-7900; Fax: 708-478-5143. Email: connie.march@provena.org. Web: www.provena.org. Ms. Connie March, Pres. & CEO.

MOMENCE. *B.G.S. Charitable Trust*, P.O. Box 736, 60954-0736. Tel: 815-472-3131; Fax: 815-472-6914. Michael Brown, Contact Person.

Little Brothers of the Good Shepherd, Inc. of Illinois, 4129 N. State Rt. I-17, P.O. Box 736, 60954. Tel: 815-472-3131; Fax: 815-472-6914. Email: judy@lbgs.org. Web: www.lbgs.org. Bro. Richard MacPhee, Treas. Gen.; Judy Brinkmann, Dir. of Finance.

OAK BROOK. *Mayslake Center II, N.F.P.*, 1801 35th St., 60523. Tel: 630-850-8232; Fax: 630-850-8233.

MV Benevolent Fund, Inc. (2003) 1801 35th St., 60523. Tel: 630-214-1858; Fax: 630-850-8233.

PLAINFIELD. *Housing Options for Religious, Clergy and Laity, NFP*, 15555 Mt. Carmel Dr., Apt. 141, Homer Glen, 60491. Tel: 708-590-8141. Email: SMDMV141@yahoo.com. Sr. Marcian Deisenroth, R.S.M., Chm., Year of final profession: 1953.

ROMEOVILLE. *The Catholic Education Foundation of the Diocese of Joliet*, 402 S. Independence Blvd., 60441.

Charitable Trust of the Brothers of the Christian Schools, 1205 Windham Pkwy., 60446-1679. Tel: 630-378-2900; Fax: 630-378-2501. Email: info@cbservices.org. Web: www.cbservices.org.

Christian Brothers Employee Benefit Trust, 1205 Windham Pkwy., 60446-1679. Tel: 630-378-2900; Fax: 630-378-2501. Email: info@cbservices.org. Web: www.cbservices.org.

Christian Brothers Employee Retirement Plan Trust, 1205 Windham Pkwy., 60446-1679. Tel: 630-378-2900; Fax: 630-378-2501. Email: info@cbservices.org. Web: www.cbservices.org.

Christian Brothers Religious Community Deductible Trust, 1205 Windham Pkwy., 60446-1679. Tel: 630-378-2900; Fax: 630-378-2501. Email: info@cbservices.org. Web: www.cbservices.org.

Christian Brothers Religious Comprehensive Trust, 1205 Windham Pkwy., 60446-1679. Tel: 630-378-2900; Fax: 630-378-2501. Email: info@cbservices.org. Web: www.cbservices.org.

Christian Brothers Retirement Savings Plan Trust, 1205 Windham Pkwy., 60446-1679. Tel: 630-378-2900; Fax: 630-378-2501. Email: info@cbservices.org. Web: www.cbservices.org.

**Christian Brothers Services*, 1205 Windham Pkwy., 60446-1679. Tel: 630-378-2900; Fax: 630-378-2501. Email: info@cbservices.org. Web: www.cbservices.org. Bro. Michael Quirk, F.S.C., Pres. & CEO.

Religious & Charitable Risk Pooling Trust of the Brothers of the Christian Schools, 1205 Windham Pkwy., 60446-1679. Tel: 630-378-2900; Fax: 630-378-2501. Email: info@cbservices.org. Web: www.cbservices.org.

WEST CHICAGO. **The Society of St. Vincent de Paul of the Joliet Diocesan Council, Inc.*, 231 Main St., 60185.

WHEATON. *Assisi Homes of Illinois, Inc.* (1974)Mailing Address: 26 W. 171 Roosevelt Rd., P.O. Box 667, 60187-0667. 2126 W. Roosevelt Rd., 60187-0667. Tel: 630-909-6900; Fax: 630-665-9357. Web: www.wfhealthcare.org. Units 65.

Canticle Ministries, Inc., 26 W. 171 Roosevelt Rd., P.O. Box 667, 60189. Tel: 630-588-9165; Fax: 630-588-9167. Email: info@canticleministries.org. Web: www.canticleministries.org. Jeana Stewart, Co-Dir. Tel: 630-784-2722.

Canticle Place, Inc. (1994) 26 W. 171 Roosevelt Rd., 60187. Tel: 630-588-9165; Fax: 630-588-9167. Web: www.wfhealthcare.org. Mailing Address: 26 W. Roosevelt Rd., P.O. Box 667, 60187-0667. Units 12.

Clara Pfaender Fund, Inc. (1984) 26 W. 171 Roosevelt Rd., P.O. Box 667, 60187. Tel: 630-909-6900; Fax: 630-462-4977. Sr. Patricia Norton, Chairperson & Pres. Franciscan Sisters, Daughters of the Sacred Hearts of Jesus and Mary (Wheaton, IL).

Franciscan Health & Education Corp., Inc., 26 W. 171 Roosevelt Rd., P.O. Box 667, 60187. Tel: 630-462-7422; Fax: 630-909-6615.

**Franciscan Ministries Community Foundation, Inc.* (2001) 26 W. 171 Roosevelt Rd., 60189. Tel: 630-462-9271; Fax: 630-462-4977. Web: www.wfhealthcare.org.

Franciscan Ministries, Inc. (1983)Property & Mailing Address: 26 W. 171 Roosevelt Rd., P.O. Box 667, 60187-0667. Tel: 630-909-6900; Fax: 630-784-2485. Web: www.wfhealthcare.org.

Institute of the Blessed Virgin Mary Charitable Trust, P.O. Box 508, 60187. Tel: 630-653-6113; Fax: 630-653-4886. Email: ibvmjfryel@aol.com. Web: www.ibvm.us.

**Marianjoy Foundation, Inc.* (1986) 26 W. 171 Roosevelt Rd., P.O. Box 1620, 60187. Tel: 630-462-7514; Fax: 630-462-4440. Web: www.marianjoy.org.

Marianjoy Rehabilitation Center Auxiliary, 26 W. 171 Roosevelt Rd., 60187. Web: www.marianjoy.org.

**Marianjoy, Inc.*, 26 W. 171 Roosevelt Rd., P.O. Box 667, 60187.

**Rehabilitation Medicine Clinic, Inc.* (1997) 26 W. 171 Roosevelt Rd., 60187. Tel: 630-462-9271; Fax: 630-462-0112. Web: www.marianjoy.org.

Wheaton Franciscan Services, Inc. (1983) 26 W. 171 Roosevelt Rd., P.O. Box 667, 60187. Tel: 630-909-6900; Fax: 630-462-4977. Web: www.mywheaton.org. Joseph Lewis, Chm.; John D. Oliverio, Pres. & CEO; Rev. Thomas Borkowski (KC), Chap.

RELIGIOUS INSTITUTES OF MEN REPRESENTED IN THE DIOCESE

For further details refer to the corresponding bracketed number in the Religious Institutes of Men or Women section.

[0140]—*The Augustinians* (Mother of Good Counsel Prov.)—O.S.A.
[0200]—*Benedictine Monks*—O.S.B.
[0330]—*Brothers of the Christian Schools* (Midwest Prov.)—F.S.C.
[0580]—*Brothers of the Good Shepherd*—B.G.S.
[0270]—*Carmelite Fathers & Brothers* (Prov. of Pure Heart of Mary)—O.Carm.
[0275]—*Carmelites of Mary Immaculate*—C.M.I.
[0360]—*Claretian Missionaries*—C.M.F.
[1320]—*Clerics of St. Viator*—C.S.V.
[0310]—*Congregation of Christian Brothers*—C.F.C.
[1130]—*Congregation of the Priests of the Sacred Heart*—S.C.J.
[0430]—*Dominicans* (Prov. of Albert the Great)—O.P.
[0520]—*Franciscan Friars* (Sacred Heart Prov.)—O.F.M.
[0540]—*Franciscan Missionary Brothers of the Sacred Heart of Jesus*—O.S.F.
[0520]—*Franciscans* (Order of Friars Minor, Sacred Heart Prov.)—O.F.M.
[0740]—*Marian Fathers* (Prov. of St. Casimer)—M.I.C.
[1065]—*Priestly Fraterity of St. Peter*—F.S.S.P.
[0610]—*Priests of the Congregation of Holy Cross*—C.S.C.
[0110]—*Society of African Missions*—S.M.A.
[1260]—*Society of Christ*—S.Ch.
[0690]—*Society of Jesus* (Chicago and St. Louis Prov.)—S.J.
[2010]—*Society of the Precious Blood*—C.PP.S.

RELIGIOUS INSTITUTES OF WOMEN REPRESENTED IN THE DIOCESE

[160]—*Augustinian Nuns of Contemplative Life*—O.S.A.
[0230]—*Benedictine Sisters of Pontifical Jurisdiction* (Lisle, IL; Ferdinand, IN)—O.S.B.
[0330]—*Carmelite Sisters for the Aged and Infirm* (Germantown, NY)—O.Carm.
[0400]—*Congregation of Our Lady of Mount Carmel* (Lacombe, LA)—O.Carm.
[3110]—*Congregation of Our Lady of the Retreat in the Cenacle*—R.C.
[1070]—*Congregation of St. Cecilia*—O.P
[3710]—*Congregation of the Sisters of Saint Agnes*—C.S.A.
[3832]—*Congregation of the Sisters of St. Joseph*—C.S.J.
[1920]—*Congregation of the Sisters of the Holy Cross*—C.S.C.
[1710]—*Congregation of the Third Order of St. Francis of Mary Immaculate, Joliet, IL*—O.S.F.
[1070-03]—*Dominican Sisters* (Sinsinawa)—O.P.
[1070-13]—*Dominican Sisters* (Adrian)—O.P.
[1070-10]—*Dominican Sisters* (Springfield)—O.P.
[1170]—*Felician Sisters*—C.S.S.F.
[1450]—*Franciscan Sisters of the Sacred Heart*—O.S.F.
[1240]—*Franciscan Sisters, Daughters of the Sacred Hearts of Jesus and Mary*—O.S.F.
[1910]—*Hermanas Josefinas*—H.J.
[2370]—*Institute of the Blessed Virgin Mary (Loretto Sisters)*—I.B.V.M.
[2575]—*Institute of the Sisters of Mercy of the Americas* (Chicago, IL)—R.S.M.
[3570]—*Mantellate Sisters, Servants of Mary* (Plainfield, IL)—O.S.M.
[2865]—*Missionaries of the Sacred Heart of Jesus & Our Lady of Guadalupe*—M.S.C.Gpe.
[2084]—*Missionary Sisters of Christ the King*—M.Ch.R.
[]—*Missionary Sisters of the Holy Family* (Komorrow-Warsaw, Poland)—M.S.F.
[3760]—*Order of St. Clare*—P.C.C.
[3230]—*Poor Handmaids of Jesus Christ*—P.H.J.C.
[2970]—*School Sisters of Notre Dame* (Chicago Prov.)—S.S.N.D.
[1680]—*School Sisters of St. Francis* (U.S. Prov.)—O.S.F.
[3590]—*Servants of Mary* (Ladysmith, WI)—O.S.M.
[3520]—*Servants of the Holy Heart of Mary*—S.S.C.M.
[0460]—*Sisters of Charity of Incarnate Word*—C.C.V.I.
[0430]—*Sisters of Charity of the Blessed Virgin Mary*—B.V.M.
[1890]—*Sisters of Helpers*—H.H.S.
[]—*Sisters of Korean Martyrs*—S.K.M.
[2350]—*Sisters of Living Word*—S.L.W.
[3000]—*Sisters of Notre Dame de Namur* (Cincinnati Prov.)—S.N.D.deN.
[3360]—*Sisters of Providence of Saint Mary-of-the-Woods, IN*—S.P.
[1540]—*Sisters of St. Francis* (Clinton, IA)—O.S.F.
[1705]—*The Sisters of St. Francis of Assisi* (St. Francis)—O.S.F.
[1520]—*Sisters of St. Francis of Christ the King*—S.S.F.C.R.
[1570]—*Sisters of St. Francis of Dubuque* (Iowa)—O.S.F.
[3930]—*Sisters of St. Joseph of the Third Order of St. Francis* (Prov. of Immaculate Conception)—S.S.J.-T.O.S.F.
[2980]—*Sisters of the Congregation de Notre Dame*—C.N.D.
[1920]—*Sisters of the Holy Cross*—C.S.C.
[1720]—*Sisters of the Third Order Regular of St. Francis of the Congregation of Our Lady of Lourdes* (Rochester, MN)—O.S.F.
[2150]—*Sisters Servants of the Immaculate Heart of Mary*—I.H.M.
[]—*Third Order Regular Common Franciscan Novitiate*

DIOCESAN CEMETERIES

JOLIET. *SS. Cyril and Methodius Cemetery*, Rte. 6 Maple Rd., 60432. Tel: 815-838-0395.

Holy Cross Cemetery, Theodore St., Crest Hill, 60403. Tel: 815-838-0395.

St. John the Baptist Cemetery, 402 S. Independence Blvd., 60435. Tel: 815-838-0395.

St. Mary Nativity Cemetery, Caton Farm Rd. & Oakland Ave., Crest Hill, 60435. Tel: 815-838-0395.

Mount Olivet Cemetery, 1320 E. Cass St., 60432. Tel: 815-838-0395.

St. Patrick Cemetery, 710 W. Marion St., Hunter St. & Jefferson St., 60436. Tel: 815-838-0395; Fax: 815-834-4069.

BOURBONNAIS. *All Saints Cemetery*, *All Saints Cemetery*, 1839 W. Rte. 102, 60914. Tel: 815-936-9378.

Maternity/BVM Cemetery, Canterberry Ln., 60914. Tel: 815-933-2342. 1839 W. Rt. 102, 60914.

CAROL STREAM. *St. Stephen Cemetery*, St. Charles Rd., 60188. Tel: 630-668-3313.

DOWNERS GROVE. *St. Bernard Cemetery*, Hobson & Belmont Roads, 60517. Tel: 630-668-3313.

ELMHURST. *St. Mary Cemetery*, Alexander Blvd., 60126. Tel: 630-668-3313.

KANKAKEE. *Mt. Calvary Cemetery*, 2000 E. Court St., 60901. Tel: 815-933-2342.

St. Rose Cemetery, Rte. 50, 60901. Tel: 815-933-2342.

LOCKPORT. *Calvary Cemetery*, Rte. 171 & High Rd., 60441. Tel: 815-838-0395.

LOCKPORT SOUTH. *Lockport South Cemetery*, 16th St. & Washington St., 60441. Tel: 815-838-0395.

LOMBARD. *St. Mary Cemetery*, Finley Rd., 60148. Tel: 630-668-3313.

NAPERVILLE. *SS. Peter & Paul Cemetery*, Columbia St. & North Ave., 60563. Tel: 630-668-3313.

OSWEGO. *Risen Lord Cemetery*, 1501 Simons Rd., 60543. Tel: 630-554-7590.

ROMEOVILLE. *Catholic Cemeteries Monument Sales*, 402 S. Independence Blvd., 60446-2264. Tel: 815-838-0395.

Resurrection, 135th St. & Rte. 53, 60446. Tel: 815-838-0395.

WHEATON. *Assumption Cemetery*, One S. 510 Winfield Rd., 60187. Tel: 630-668-3313.

WINFIELD. *St. John the Baptist*, OS233 Church St., 60190. Tel: 630-668-0918; Fax: 630-668-1074.

NECROLOGY

✠ Kaffer, Most Rev. Roger L., Retired Auxiliary Bishop of Joliet—Died May 28, 2009

† Dugal, William, (Absent on Sick Leave)—Died April 4, 2009

An asterisk (*) denotes an organization that has established tax-exempt status directly with the IRS and is not covered by the USCCB Group Ruling.

Diocese of Juneau

(Dioecesis Junellensis)

Most Reverend

EDWARD J. BURNS

Bishop of Juneau; ordained June 25, 1983; appointed Bishop of Juneau January 19, 2009; ordained March 3, 2009; installed April 2, 2009. *Office: 415 Sixth St., #300, Juneau, AK 99801.*

Chancery: 415 Sixth St., #300, Juneau, AK 99801. Tel: 907-586-2227; Fax: 907-463-3237.

Web: www.dioceseofjuneau.org

Email: junodio@gci.net

ESTABLISHED JUNE 23, 1951.

Square Miles 37,566.

Corporate Title: "Corporation of the Catholic Bishop of Juneau."

Comprises the entire southeastern part of the State of Alaska known legally as The First Judicial District.

For legal titles of parishes and diocesan institutions, consult the Chancery Office.

STATISTICAL OVERVIEW

Personnel	
Bishop	1
Priests: Diocesan Active in Diocese	6
Priests: Diocesan Active Outside Diocese	1
Priests: Retired, Sick or Absent	3
Number of Diocesan Priests	10
Religious Priests in Diocese	2
Total Priests in Diocese	12
Permanent Deacons in Diocese	3
Total Sisters	3
Parishes	
Parishes	9
With Resident Pastor:	
Resident Diocesan Priests	5
Resident Religious Priests	3
Without Resident Pastor:	
Administered by Religious Women	1
Missions	17
Professional Ministry Personnel:	
Sisters	3
Lay Ministers	11
Welfare	
Catholic Hospitals	1
Total Assisted	45,000
Day Care Centers	1
Total Assisted	100
Special Centers for Social Services	1
Total Assisted	10,000
Other Institutions	1
Total Assisted	15,000
Educational	
Diocesan Students in Other Seminaries	1
Total Seminarians	1
Elementary Schools, Diocesan and Parish	1
Total Students	125
Catechesis/Religious Education:	
High School Students	452
Elementary Students	82
Total Students under Catholic Instruction	660
Teachers in the Diocese:	
Lay Teachers	10
Vital Statistics	
Receptions into the Church:	
Infant Baptism Totals	60
Minor Baptism Totals	14
Adult Baptism Totals	8
Received into Full Communion	7
First Communions	86
Confirmations	74
Marriages:	
Catholic	9
Interfaith	4
Total Marriages	13
Deaths	28
Total Catholic Population	10,000
Total Population	75,000

Former Bishops—Most Revs. DERMOT O'FLANAGAN, D.D., ord. Aug. 27, 1929; appt. Bishop July 9, 1951; cons. Oct. 3, 1951; resigned June 19, 1968; appt. Titular Bishop of Trecalae; died Dec. 31, 1972; FRANCIS T. HURLEY, D.D., ord. June 16, 1951; appt. Titular Bishop of Daimlaig and Auxiliary of Juneau, Feb. 4, 1970; cons. March 19, 1970; Ordinary of See, July 20, 1971; appt. Archbishop of Anchorage, May 4, 1976; MICHAEL H. KENNY, D.D., ord. March 30, 1963; appt. March 20, 1979; cons. May 27, 1979; installed June 15, 1979; died Feb. 19, 1995; MICHAEL W. WARFEL, ord. April 26, 1980; appt. Nov. 19, 1996; installed Dec. 17, 1996; appt. Bishop of Great Falls-Billings Nov. 20, 2007.

Diocesan Pastoral Center

Bishop of Juneau—Most Rev. EDWARD J. BURNS.

Chancery—415 Sixth St., #300, Juneau, 99801. Tel: 907-586-2227; Fax: 907-463-3237.

Episcopal Delegate of the Apostolic Administrator—Rev. PATRICK J. TRAVERS, J.C.L., J.D.

Chancellor—Rev. PATRICK J. TRAVERS, J.C.L., J.D.

Diocesan Consultors—Revs. PETER GORGES (Retired); JEAN-PAULIN LOCKULU; PERRY KENASTON; SCOTT R. SETTIMO; PATRICK J. TRAVERS, J.C.L., J.D.; EDMUND J. PENISTEN; THOMAS L. WEISE.

Tribunal—433 Jackson St., Ketchikan, 99901. Tel: 907-247-2755; Fax: 907-225-2571.

Judicial Vicar—Rev. PATRICK J. TRAVERS, J.C.L., J.D.

Defender of the Bond—Sr. CAROLYN ROEBER, O.P., J.C.L., J.D.

Auditor—Ms. ALETHEA JOHNSON.

Notaries—Mrs. LINDA K. KELLEY; Ms. ALETHEA JOHNSON.

Administration—415 Sixth St., #300, Juneau, 99801. Tel: 907-586-2227; Fax: 907-463-3237.

Business Manager and Finance Officer—JAMES DONAGHEY.

Director of Administrative Services/Assistant to the Bishop—ROBERTA IZZARD.

Assistant to the Finance Officer—DENISE GRANT.

Finance Council—HUGH GRANT; Rev. PATRICK J. TRAVERS, J.C.L., J.D.; JAMES DONAGHEY; Mr. WILLIAM PETERS; DENISE GRANT; Most Rev. EDWARD J. BURNS.

Miscellaneous

Apostleship of the Sea—Port Chaplains: Revs. THOMAS L. WEISE, 416 Fifth St., Juneau, 99801; EDMUND J. PENISTEN, 433 Jackson St., Ketchikan, 99801.

Catholic Community Service, Inc.—ROSEMARY HAGEVIG, Exec. Dir., 419 Sixth St., Juneau, 99801. Tel: 907-463-6151.

Board of Directors—Most Rev. EDWARD J. BURNS, Pres.; VICKI SOBOLEFF; JOHN GREELY; LISA PUSICH; LOREN JONES; DOUG SMITH, M.D.; PATRICIA ATKINSON; KEVIN RITCHIE; JAMES CARROLL; TONY YORBA; JEFF DUVERNAY; BILL DIEBELS; Dr. LINDY JONES; LEON VANCE.

Catholic Community Service—Program Directors: Ms. MARIANNE MILLS, Southeast Sr. Svcs. (SESS) (seniors and adults with disabilities); Ms. HELEN KALK, Child Care & Family Resources (CCFR) (children and families); VACANT, Hospice & Home Care of Juneau (HHCJ) (people who need in-home care and end-of-life services).

Diocesan Publication "Inside Passage"—KARLA DONAGHEY, Editor, 415 Sixth St., #300, Juneau, 99801. Tel: 907-586-2237, Ext. 32.

Office of Ministries & Missions—Deacon CHARLES ROHRBACHER, Dir., 415 Sixth St., #300, Juneau, 99801. Tel: 907-586-2227.

Permanent Deacon Program—Deacon GARY HORTON, 415 6th St., #300, Juneau, 99801. Tel: 907-586-2227, Ext. 36.

School—CONNIE WINGREN, Prin., Holy Name School, 433 Jackson St., Ketchikan, 99901. Tel: 907-225-2400.

Shrine of St. Therese—RUTH VINCENT, 419 6th St., #300, Juneau, 99801. Tel: 907-780-6112. Caretakers: JOHN JORDAN; JEANNE JORDAN.

St. Vincent de Paul Society—DAN AUSTIN, 8617 Teal St., Juneau, 99801. Tel: 907-789-5535.

Special Collections and Archivist—Deacon GARY HORTON, 415 6th St., #300, Juneau, 99801. Tel: 907-586-2227, Ext. 36.

Victim Assistance Coordinator and Safe Environment Coordinator—ROBERTA IZZARD. Tel: 907-586-2227, Ext. 25. Email: robbiei@gci.net.

Vocations—Rev. EDMUND J. PENISTEN, 433 Jackson St., Ketchikan, 99901-5715. Tel: 907-225-2570.

CLERGY, PARISHES, MISSIONS AND PAROCHIAL SCHOOLS

CITY AND BOROUGH OF JUNEAU

1—CATHEDRAL OF THE NATIVITY OF THE BLESSED VIRGIN MARY Rev. Thomas L. Weise.

Res.: 416 Fifth St., 99801. Tel: 907-586-1513; Fax: 907-586-8091.

Catechesis/Religious Program—Katherine Rice, D.R.E. Students 79.

2—ST. PAUL THE APOSTLE Rev. Patrick J. Travers.

Res.: 9055 Atlin Ave., 99801. Tel: 907-789-2648 (Rectory); 907-789-7307 (Office); Fax: 907-790-3430.

Catechesis/Religious Program—Tel: 907-789-7303. Marilyn Monagle, D.R.E. Students 220.

OUTSIDE THE CITY AND BOROUGH OF JUNEAU

HAINES, SACRED HEART Rev. James Blaney, O.M.I.
Res.: Box 326, 99827. Tel: 907-766-2241.
Mission—St. Therese of the Child Jesus P.O. Box 496, Skagway, 99840. Tel: 907-983-2271.
Mission— Kluckwan.

KETCHIKAN, KETCHIKAN GATEWAY CO., HOLY NAME Rev. Edmund J. Penisten.
Res.: 433 Jackson St., 99901. Tel: 907-225-2570; 907-247-2728 (Rectory); Fax: 907-225-2571.
School—(Grades PreSchool-8) Tel: 907-247-0041. Connie Wingren, Prin. Lay Teachers 10; Students 119.
*Catechesis/Religious Program—*Tel: 907-225-2120; Fax: 907-225-2570. Mrs. Linda K. Kelley, D.R.E. Students 142.
Mission—Holy Family

KLAWOCK, ST. JOHN BY THE SEA Rev. Perry Kenaston.
Res.: P.O. Box 245, 99925. Tel: 907-755-2345; Fax: 907-755-2350.
Mission— Thorne Bay, 99919. Tel: 907-828-3324.
Mission— Coffman Cove.
Mission— Hydaburg.
Mission— Naukati.
Mission— Hollis.
Mission— Meyers Chuck.

PETERSBURG, WRANGELL-PETERSBURG(CA) CO., ST. CATHERINE OF SIENA Rev. Patrick T. Casey, O.M.I.
Res.: P.O. Box 508, 99833. Tel: 907-772-3257; Fax: 907-772-3020.

SITKA, SITKA CO., ST. GREGORY OF NAZIANZEN Rev. Scott R. Settimo, Admin.
Res.: P.O. Box 495, 99835. Tel: 907-747-8371; 907-747-6997; Fax: 907-747-8401.
Mission— Kake.

SKAGWAY, SKAGWAY-HOONAH-ANGOON (CA) CO., ST. THERESE OF THE CHILD JESUS, Closed. Now a mission of Sacred Heart, Haines, AK.

WRANGELL, WRANGELL-PETERSBURG (CA) CO., ST. ROSE OF LIMA Rev. Patrick T. Casey, O.M.I.
Res.: Box 469, 99929. Tel: 907-874-3771; Fax: 907-874-3744.

YAKUTAT, YAKUTAT CO., ST. ANN Sr. Josephine Aloralrea, O.S.U., Parish Admin.
Res.: P.O. Box 323, 99689. Tel: 907-784-3406.
Mission— Elfin Cove.
Mission— Gustavus.
Mission— Pelican.
Mission— Tenakee Springs.
Mission— Hoonah.
Mission— Kake.
Mission— Excursion Inlet.

Chaplains of Public Institutions Hospitals

KETCHIKAN. *Ketchikan General Hospital.* 3100 Tongass, 99901. Tel: 907-225-5171; Fax: 907-228-8322. Sr. Arnadene Bean, C.S.J.P., Chap.
New Horizons Transitional Care Unit

On Duty Outside the Diocese:
Rev.—
Saba, Joseph, 5660 W. Placita Del Risco, Tucson, AZ 85745.

Retired:
Revs.—
Frister, Jerome, Arcadia Place, 1080 Arcadia Ave., Rm. 116, Vista, CA 92084.
Gorges, Peter, St. Gregory, P.O. Box 495, Sitka, 99835-0495.
Konda, Bernard, Priests Retirement Center, 6900 E. 45th St. N. F-1, Bel Aire, KS 67226.

Permanent Deacons:
Hansen, Vincent G, Sacred Heart, Haines
Horton, Gary, Cathedral of the Nativity of the Blessed Virgin Mary, Juneau
Rohrbacher, Charles, Cathedral of the Nativity of the Blessed Virgin Mary, Juneau

INSTITUTIONS LOCATED IN THE DIOCESE

[A] CONVENTS AND RESIDENCES FOR SISTERS

JUNEAU. *St. Joseph Convent,* Mailing Address: c/o 415 6th St., 99801. 2971 Douglas Hwy., 99801. Tel: 907-586-2085. Intercommunity residence of various religious orders of women.

KETCHIKAN. *Sisters of St. Joseph of Peace, Ketchikan General Hospital,* 3100 Tongass Ave., 99901. Tel: 907-225-5171; Fax: 907-228-8322.

RELIGIOUS INSTITUTES OF WOMEN REPRESENTED IN THE DIOCESE

For further details refer to the corresponding bracketed number in the Religious Institutes of Men or Women section.

[1070]—*Dominican Sisters*—O.P.
[3890]—*Sisters of St. Joseph of Peace*—C.S.J.P.
[]—*Ursuline Sisters of the Roman Union*—O.S.U.

NECROLOGY

† Ryan, James Patrick, (Retired)—Died Feb. 15, 2009

An asterisk (*) denotes an organization that has established tax-exempt status directly with the IRS and is not covered by the USCCB Group Ruling.

Diocese of Kalamazoo

(Dioecesis Kalamazuensis)

Most Reverend

PAUL J. BRADLEY

Bishop of Kalamazoo; ordained May 1, 1971; appointed Titular Bishop of Afufenia and Auxiliary Bishop of Pittsburgh December 16, 2004; ordained February 2, 2005; appointed Bishop of Kalamazoo April 6, 2009; installed June 5, 2009.

Most Reverend

JAMES A. MURRAY

Retired Bishop of Kalamazoo; ordained June 7, 1958; appointed Bishop of Kalamazoo November 18, 1997; ordained and installed January 27, 1998; retired April 6, 2009. Email: jmurray@dioceseofkalamazoo.org.

Most Reverend

PAUL V. DONOVAN, D.D.

Former Bishop of Kalamazoo; ordained May 20, 1950; appointed Bishop of Kalamazoo June 15, 1971; ordained and installed July 21, 1971; resigned November 22, 1994. *Mailing Address: 1700 Bronson Way, #166, Kalamazoo, MI 49009-3317.*

ESTABLISHED JULY 21, 1971.

Square Miles 5,337.

Comprises the following nine Counties in the State of Michigan: Allegan, Barry, Berrien, Branch, Calhoun, Cass, Kalamazoo, St. Joseph and Van Buren.

For legal titles of parishes and diocesan institutions, consult the Chancery.

Chancery: 215 N. Westnedge Ave., Kalamazoo, MI 49007-3760. Tel: 269-349-8714; Fax: 269-349-6440.

Web: dioceseofkalamazoo.org

STATISTICAL OVERVIEW

Personnel	
Bishop	1
Retired Bishops	2
Priests: Diocesan Active in Diocese	44
Priests: Diocesan Active Outside Diocese	4
Priests: Retired, Sick or Absent	18
Number of Diocesan Priests	66
Religious Priests in Diocese	8
Total Priests in Diocese	74
Extern Priests in Diocese	6
Ordinations:	
Diocesan Priests	4
Permanent Deacons in Diocese	36
Total Brothers	2
Total Sisters	217
Parishes	
Parishes	46
With Resident Pastor:	
Resident Diocesan Priests	39
Resident Religious Priests	5
Without Resident Pastor:	
Administered by Priests	1
Administered by Deacons	3
Administered by Religious Women	1
Missions	13
Pastoral Centers	1
Professional Ministry Personnel:	
Brothers	2
Sisters	1
Welfare	
Catholic Hospitals	3
Total Assisted	467,065
Health Care Centers	5
Total Assisted	623,455
Homes for the Aged	4
Total Assisted	450
Day Care Centers	16
Total Assisted	430
Specialized Homes	4
Total Assisted	283
Special Centers for Social Services	7
Total Assisted	40,469
Educational	
Diocesan Students in Other Seminaries	13
Total Seminarians	13
High Schools, Diocesan and Parish	3
Total Students	651
Elementary Schools, Diocesan and Parish	19
Total Students	2,656
Catechesis/Religious Education:	
High School Students	1,443
Elementary Students	6,050
Total Students under Catholic Instruction	10,813
Teachers in the Diocese:	
Sisters	2
Lay Teachers	230
Vital Statistics	
Receptions into the Church:	
Infant Baptism Totals	1,277
Adult Baptism Totals	194
Received into Full Communion	195
First Communions	1,203
Confirmations	1,116
Marriages:	
Catholic	226
Interfaith	114
Total Marriages	340
Deaths	828
Total Catholic Population	105,844
Total Population	949,063

Former Bishops—Most Revs. PAUL V. DONOVAN, D.D., ord. May 20, 1950; appt. Bishop of Kalamazoo June 15, 1971; installed July 21, 1971; resigned Nov. 22, 1994; ALFRED J. MARKIEWICZ, D.D., ord. June 6, 1953; appt. Titular Bishop of Afufenia and Auxiliary to the Bishop of Rockville Centre, July 7, 1986; ord. Bishop, Sept. 17, 1986; appt. Bishop of Kalamazoo, Nov. 22, 1994; installed Jan. 31, 1995; died Jan. 9, 1997; JAMES A. MURRAY, ord. June 7, 1958; appt. Bishop of Kalamazoo Nov. 18, 1997; ord. and installed Jan. 27, 1998; retired April 6, 2009.

Vicar General—Rev. Msgr. MICHAEL D. HAZARD, V.G., St. Joseph Church, 936 Lake St., Kalamazoo, 49001. Tel: 269-343-6256; Fax: 269-343-1214.

Diocesan Pastoral Center—215 N. Westnedge Ave., Kalamazoo, 49007-3760. Tel: 269-349-8714, Ext. 122; Fax: 269-349-6440. Web: dioceseofkalamazoo.org. Office Hours: 8:30-4.

Chancellor— Direct all matters to the Bishop's Office. Rev. Msgr. THOMAS A. MARTIN, J.C.D., 215 N. Westnedge Ave., Kalamazoo, 49007. Tel: 269-349-8714, Ext. 122; Fax: 269-349-6440.

Direct Communications regarding Marriage Dispensations to Chancellor's Office *Diocese of Kalamazoo, 215 N. Westnedge Ave., Kalamazoo, 49007-3760.* Tel: 269-349-8714, Ext. 122; Fax: 269-349-6440.

Diocesan Tribunal—215 N. Westnedge Ave., Kalamazoo, 49007-3760. Tel: 269-349-8714, Ext. 115; Fax: 269-349-6440.

Judicial Vicar—Rev. Msgr. THOMAS A. MARTIN, J.C.D.

Defender of the Bond—Rev. MICHAEL A. HACK, J.C.D.

Promoter of Justice—Deacon HAL BOHAN.

Judges—Rev. EDWARD A. HANKIEWICZ, J.C.L.; Sr. JOYCE HOBEN, S.N.D.deN., J.C.L.; Rev. KENNETH W. SCHMIDT, J.C.D., M.A., L.P.C.

Advocates—Revs. ROBERT E. FLICKINGER; LAWRENCE M. FARRELL; CHARLES H. FISCHER.

Chief Notary and Administrative Assistant—Mrs. MARLENE J. PRANSKATIS.

Ecclesiastical Notaries—Mrs. NANCY L. BOOTHBY; Mrs. DENISE ABRAHAM.

Address communications regarding Marriage Dispensations to The Chancellor's Office *Diocese of Kalamazoo, 215 N. Westnedge, Kalamazoo, 49007-3760.* Tel: 269-349-8714, Ext. 122; Fax: 269-349-6440.

Diocesan Consultors—Revs. DAVID ADAMS (Retired); JAMES L. BARRETT (Retired); ROBERT E. FLICKINGER; Rev. Msgrs. MICHAEL D. HAZARD, V.G.; THOMAS A. MARTIN, J.C.D.; Rev. MARK J. VYVERMAN.

Presbyteral Council Members—Most Rev. PAUL J. BRADLEY; Revs. DAVID ADAMS (Retired); JAMES L. BARRETT (Retired); ROBERT E. FLICKINGER; Rev. Msgrs. MICHAEL D. HAZARD, V.G.; THOMAS A. MARTIN, J.C.D.; Revs. MARK J. VYVERMAN; CHRISTOPHER DERDA; JOHN FLECKENSTEIN; FABIO H. GARZON, S.D.B.; JOSEPH MCCORMICK, O.S.A.; DONALD G. POTTS; Rev. Msgr. EUGENE A. SEARS (Retired).

Diocesan Offices and Directors

Campaign for Human Development—Sr. SUSAN RIDLEY, O.P., Dir., 215 N. Westnedge Ave., Kalamazoo, 49007-3760. Tel: 269-349-8714, Ext. 238; Fax: 269-349-6440.

Catholic Family Services—Mrs. FRANCES H. DENNY, M.B.A., M.S.W., Exec. Dir., 1819 Gull Rd., Kalamazoo, 49001. Tel: 269-381-9800; Fax: 269-381-2932.

Catholic Relief Services—Sr. SUSAN RIDLEY, O.P., Dir., 215 N. Westnedge Ave., Kalamazoo, 49007-3760. Tel: 269-349-8714, Ext. 238; Fax: 269-349-6440.

Cemeteries—Rev. JOHN FLECKENSTEIN, St. Catherine of Siena, 1150 W. Centre St., Portage, 49024. Tel: 269-327-5165; Fax: 269-327-7266.

Diocesan Cemetery - Kalamazoo—Mt. Olivet.

Evangelization, Catechesis & Initiation—Mr. D. J. FLORIAN, Dir. Tel: 269-349-8714, Ext. 227. Assoc. Directors: LISA IRWIN. Tel: 269-349-8714, Ext. 228; Deacon KURT LUCAS. Tel: 269-349-8714, Ext. 234. 215 N. Westnedge Ave., Kalamazoo, 49007-3760. Tel: 269-349-8714, Ext. 227; Fax: 269-349-6440.

Christian Service—Sr. SUSAN RIDLEY, O.P., Dir., 215

N. Westnedge Ave., Kalamazoo, 49007-3760. Tel: 269-349-8714, Ext. 238; Fax: 269-349-6440.

Communications—Ms. VICKIE CESSNA, Dir., 215 N. Westnedge Ave., Kalamazoo, 49007-3760. Tel: 269-349-8714, Ext. 350.

Audiovisual Resources—Mr. D. J. FLORIAN, Coord., 215 N. Westnedge Ave., Kalamazoo, 49007-3760. Tel: 269-349-8714, Ext. 227.

Diocesan Council of Catholic Women (D.C.C.W.)—Rev. DONALD P. KLINGLER, Spiritual Dir., St. Margaret's Church, 245 Court St., Otsego, 49078. Tel: 269-694-6311; Mrs. JOAN WALSH, Pres., 406 Crandall St., Albion, 49224. Tel: 517-629-9273.

Diocesan Development and Stewardship Office—VACANT, Dir., 215 N. Westnedge Ave., Kalamazoo, 49007-3760. Tel: 269-349-8714, Ext. 349.

Delegate for Ecumenical and Interreligious Concerns—Rev. Msgr. THOMAS A. MARTIN, J.C.D., Dir., 215 N. Westnedge Ave., Kalamazoo, 49007-3760. Tel: 269-349-8714, Ext. 118.

Diocesan Pastoral Council—VACANT, 215 N. Westnedge Ave., Kalamazoo, 49007-3760. Tel: 269-349-8714.

Diocesan-Parish Council Ministry—VACANT, 215 N. Westnedge Ave., Kalamazoo, 49007-3760. Tel: 269-349-8714.

Education—Mrs. MARGARET ERICH, Supt. of Schools. Tel: 269-349-8714, Ext. 239; VACANT, Assoc. Supt., 215 N. Westnedge Ave., Kalamazoo, 49007-3760. Tel: 269-349-8714, Ext. 248; Fax: 269-349-6440.

Diocesan Finance Council—Mr. LEO A. SWIAT, Pres., Olmsted & Mulhall, Inc.; Mr. LEN AMAT, Vice Pres. & Regl. Mgr., Chemical Bank/Shoreline; Mr. EDWARD BAUMAN, Retired Sr. Dir. Mktg. Procurement, Kellogg Company, Battle Creek, MI; Mr. T. EDWARD CAREY JR., CFO, Vice Chancellor, Diocese of Grand Rapids; Revs. JOHN D. FLECKENSTEIN, Pastor, St. Catherine Catholic Church, Portage; WILLIAM JACOBS, Pastor, SS John - Bernard Catholic Church, Benton Harbor, MI; Mr. JERRY B. LOVE, CPA, Arcadia Investment Mgmt. Corp., Kalamazoo; Rev. Msgr. THOMAS A. MARTIN, J.C.D., Rector St. Augustine Cathedral, Chancellor Diocesan Pastoral Center; Mrs. BOBBIE OTTO, CPA, South Haven, MI; Rev. JAMES RICHARDSON, M.A., Asst. Pastor, St. Thomas More Church, Kalamazoo.

Diocesan Finance Office—Mr. BRUCE D. RAGAN, Dir. Tel: 269-349-8714, Ext. 353; Fax: 269-349-6440; Mrs. SANDY L. BOOTHBY, Accounting Mgr., 215 N. Westnedge Ave., Kalamazoo, 49007-3760. Tel: 269-349-8714, Ext. 349. Email: sboothby@dioceseofkalamazoo.org.

Holy Childhood Association and Propagation of the Faith—Rev. LAWRENCE FARRELL, Dir., 215 N. Westnedge Ave., Kalamazoo, 49007-3760. Tel: 269-349-8714, Ext. 119.

Inner City Ministry—Sisters RITA SCHAFER, S.S.J.; MARY PUNG, S.S.J., Catholic Community Center, 589 Pearl St., Benton Harbor, 49022. Tel: 269-926-6424; Fax: 269-926-2870.

Jail Ministry—Sr. SUSAN RIDLEY, O.P., Coord., 215 N. Westnedge Ave., Kalamazoo, 49007-3760. Tel: 269-349-8714, Ext. 238.

Knights of Columbus—Rev. ROBERT F. CREAGAN, Diocesan Chap., 150 Taylor St., Coldwater, 49036.

Marriage and Family Ministry, Office of—Mr. JOE SCHMITT, Dir. Tel: 269-349-8714, Ext. 112; Mrs. JANE BODWAY, Asst. Dir. Tel: 269-349-8714, Ext. 113. 215 N. Westnedge Ave., Kalamazoo, 49007-3760. Fax: 269-349-6440.

Ministry with Persons with Disabilities—Miss ANN SHERZER, Dir., 215 N. Westnedge Ave., Kalamazoo, 49007-3760. Tel: 269-349-7276, Ext. 229.

Missions—Rev. LAWRENCE FARRELL, Dir., 215 N. Westnedge Ave., Kalamazoo, 49007-3760. Tel: 269-349-8714, Ext. 119; Fax: 269-349-6440.

Natural Family Planning Center of Southwestern Michigan—Mrs. LYNN BRUNNER, Diocese of Kalamazoo, 215 N. Westnedge, Kalamazoo, 49007-3760. Tel: 269-349-8714, Ext. 113.

Permanent Diaconate—Deacons EUGENE HAAS, Dir. Deacon Personnel; JOHN BODWAY, Dir. Deacon Formation; Rev. JOHN PETER AMBROSE, M.S.F.S., Dir. Deacon Spiritual Formation, 215 N. Westnedge Ave., Kalamazoo, 49007-3760. Tel: 269-349-8714, Ext. 227; Fax: 269-349-6440.

Presbyteral Council Members—Most Rev. PAUL J. BRADLEY; Revs. DAVID ADAMS (Retired); JAMES L. BARRETT (Retired); ROBERT E. FLICKINGER; Rev. Msgrs. MICHAEL D. HAZARD, V.G.; THOMAS A. MARTIN, J.C.D.; Revs. MARK J. VYVERMAN; CHRISTOPHER DERDA; JOHN FLECKENSTEIN; FABIO H. GARZON, S.D.B.; JOSEPH MCCORMICK, O.S.A.; DONALD G. POTTS; Rev. Msgr. EUGENE A. SEARS (Retired).

Priestly Life and Ministry Office—Rev. KENNETH W. SCHMIDT, J.C.D., M.A., L.P.C., Dir., 421 Monroe St., Kalamazoo, 49006. Tel: 269-381-8917; Fax: 269-381-0195.

Respect Life—Sr. SUSAN RIDLEY, O.P., Dir., 215 N. Westnedge Ave., Kalamazoo, 49007-3760. Tel: 269-349-8714, Ext. 238; Fax: 269-349-6440.

St. Vincent DePaul Society—Sr. SUSAN RIDLEY, O.P., 215 N. Westnedge, Kalamazoo, 49007-3760. Tel: 269-349-8714, Ext. 238; Fax: 269-349-6440.

Office of Immigration Services—Ms. KISH ENSTICE, Dir., 1128 Race St., Kalamazoo, 49001. Tel: 269-385-1019; Fax: 269-344-6602.

Office of Strategic Planning—VACANT, Dir., 215 N. Westnedge Ave., Kalamazoo, 49007-3760. Tel: 269-349-8714.

Scouting Apostolate—Rev. RICHARD L. ALTINE, Chap., 402 S. Nottawa St., Sturgis, 49091. Tel: 269-651-5200.

Spanish-Speaking Apostolate—Ms. FANNY TABARES, Dir., 215 N. Westnedge Ave., Kalamazoo, 49007-3760. Tel: 269-349-8714, Ext. 236; Fax: 269-349-6440.

Victim Assistance Coordinator—Deacon PATRICK HALL, B.A. Tel: 269-349-8714, Ext. 246. Email: phall@dioceseofkalamazoo.org.

Vocations—Revs. JOHN D. FLECKENSTEIN, Dir.; CHRISTOPHER DERDA, Assoc. Dir., 215 N. Westnedge Ave., Kalamazoo, 49007-3760. Tel: 269-349-8714, Ext. 242; Fax: 269-349-6440.

Office of Christian Worship—Mr. DAVID J. REILLY, Dir., 215 N. Westnedge Ave., Kalamazoo, 49007-3760. Tel: 269-349-8714, Ext. 245; Fax: 269-349-6440.

Address communications for all other offices to Diocesan Pastoral Center *Diocese of Kalamazoo, 215 N. Westnedge Ave., Kalamazoo, 49007-3760.* Tel: 269-349-8714, Ext. 122; Fax: 269-349-6440.

CLERGY, PARISHES, MISSIONS AND PAROCHIAL SCHOOLS

CITY OF KALAMAZOO

(KALAMAZOO COUNTY)

1—ST. AUGUSTINE CATHEDRAL (1856) Rev. Msgr. Thomas Martin; Rev. Harold G. Potter, Parochial Vicar.
Res.: 542 W. Michigan Ave., 49007. Tel: 269-345-5147; Fax: 269-349-0166.
School—600 W. Michigan Ave., 49007. Tel: 269-349-1945; Fax: 269-349-1085. Lay Teachers 22; Students 268.
Catechesis/Religious Program—Students 58.

2—ST. JOSEPH (1904) Rev. Msgr. Michael D. Hazard; Rev. Anthony Bitchapogu, Parochial Vicar.
Res.: 936 Lake St., 49001. Tel: 269-343-6256; Fax: 269-343-1214. Email: stjosephkazoo@tds.net.
Catechesis/Religious Program—Students 367.

3—ST. MARY (1935) Revs. Robert Sirico; David Grondz.
Res.: 939 Charlotte, 49007. Tel: 269-385-9933.
Catechesis/Religious Program—Mrs. Anne Holewa, D.R.E. Students 29.

4—ST. MONICA (1955) Revs. Lawrence M. Farrell; Arthur Howard; Deacons Robert Stevens; Kurt Lucas. In Res., Revs. Robert E. Consani; Wieslaw Lipka (Poland).
Res.: 534 W. Kilgore Rd., 49008. Tel: 269-345-4389.
Church Office: 4408 S. Westnedge, 49008. Fax: 269-345-5211.
School—530 W. Kilgore Rd., 49008. Tel: 269-345-2444; Fax: 269-345-8534. Web: sms.csgk.org. Lay Teachers 27; Students 382.
Catechesis/Religious Program—Students 541.

5—ST. THOMAS MORE STUDENT PARISH (1956) Rev. Kenneth W. Schmidt; Sr. Susan McCrery, S.S.J., Pastoral Assoc.; Mrs. Marian Nelson, Pastoral Assoc.; Deacons Patrick Hall, Pastoral Assoc.; Joe Schmitt, Pastoral Assoc.
Office: 421 Monroe St., 49006. Tel: 269-381-8917; Fax: 269-381-0195. Email: sttoms@sttomskazoo.org. Web: www.sttomskazoo.org.
Catechesis/Religious Program—936 Lake St., 49001. Tel: 269-343-6258; Fax: 269-343-1214. Students 90.

OUTSIDE THE CITY OF KALAMAZOO

ALBION, CALHOUN CO., ST. JOHN THE EVANGELIST (1873) [CEM] Rev. Carl F. Peltz.
Office: 1020 Irwin Ave., 49224-9713. Tel: 517-629-4532; Fax: 517-629-5462. Web: stjohn-church.org.
Res.: 879 Finley Dr., 49224. Tel: 517-629-8678.
Catechesis/Religious Program—Students 54.

ALLEGAN, ALLEGAN CO., BLESSED SACRAMENT (1934) [CEM] Rev. Alan P. Jorgensen.
Res.: 422 Hubbard St., 49010-1246. Tel: 616-673-4455; Fax: 616-673-5869. Email: blsacch@allegan.net.
Church: 110 Cedar St., 49010-1244. Tel: 269-673-4455; Fax: 269-673-5869.
Catechesis/Religious Program—Students 100.
Mission—*Sacred Heart* 2036 20th St., 49010.

AUGUSTA, KALAMAZOO CO., ST. ANN (1958) Rev. Christopher Derda.
Res.: 12648 E. D Ave., 49012. Tel: 269-731-4721; Fax: 269-731-4147. Email: stann_gl@comcast.net. Web: saintanngl.googlepages.com.
Catechesis/Religious Program—Tel: 269-731-0295. Students 200.

BANGOR, VAN BUREN CO., SACRED HEART OF JESUS (1932) [CEM] Rev. John Peter Ambrose, M.S.F.S. (India), Admin.
Res.: 201 S. Walnut St., 49013. Tel: 269-427-7514; Fax: 269-302-0133. Email: secretary@sacredheartbangor.org. Web: www.sacredheartbangor.com.
Catechesis/Religious Program—Students 28.
Chapel—*Grand Junction, St. Cyril*, (Summer)

BATTLE CREEK, CALHOUN CO.

1—ST. JEROME (1955) [JC] Rev. John Tuyen Kim Tran.
Res.: 242 Collier Ave., 49037. Tel: 269-968-2218; 269-441-2309; Fax: 269-968-2233. Email: stjeromechurch22@aol.com.
Catechesis/Religious Program—Students 25.

2—ST. JOSEPH (1942) [JC] Revs. Robert F. Creagan; Joseph B. Grey, Parochial Vicar; Craig Lusk.
Res.: 61 N. 23rd St., 49015. Tel: 269-962-0165; Fax: 269-962-5937. Web: www.stjosephchurchonline.org.
School—47 N. 23rd, 49015. Tel: 269-965-7749; Fax: 269-965-0790. Web: bcacs.org. Lay Teachers 26; Students 465.
Catechesis/Religious Program—Tel: 269-965-4079. Students 212.

3—ST. PHILIP (1869) [CEM] Rev. Charles H. Fischer; Deacons Hal Bohan; Bernie Mileski.
Office: 112 Capital Ave., N.E., 49017. Tel: 269-968-6645; Fax: 269-968-0632. Email: stpchurch@ctsmail.net. Web: stphilipchurch-bc.org.
Res.: 126 Capital Ave., N.E., 49017.
School—20 Cherry St., 49017. Tel: 269-963-4503; Fax: 269-963-5590. Lay Teachers 15; Students 146.
Catechesis/Religious Program—Tel: 269-962-9506. Students 136.

BENTON HARBOR, BERRIEN CO.

1—ST. BERNARD, Merged with St. John, Benton Harbor.

2—SS. JOHN & BERNARD (1996) [CEM] Revs. William Jacobs; Michael Revent; Deacon Al Lazaga.
Res.: 600 Columbus Ave., 49022. Tel: 616-925-2425; Fax: 616-925-4678. Email: ssjandb@sbcglobal.net.
Catechesis/Religious Program—220 Church St., St. Joseph, 49085. Tel: 616-983-1575. Students 529.

3—ST. JOHN THE EVANGELIST, Merged with St. Bernard, Benton Harbor.

BRIDGMAN, BERRIEN CO., OUR LADY QUEEN OF PEACE (1939) Rev. German Perez-Diaz.
Res.: 3903 Lake St., 49106-0747. Tel: 269-465-6252; Fax: 269-465-4930. Email: pastor@queenofpeaceb.org. Web: www.queenofpeaceb.org.
Catechesis/Religious Program—Students 70.
Mission—*St. Gabriel Mission Church* 429 Rose Hill, Berrien Springs, Berrien Co. 49103. Tel: 269-471-2424.

BRONSON, BRANCH CO., ST. MARY'S (1867), (Polish), [CEM] Revs. Richard A. Fritz; Carlos Portela (Colombia); Deacon Gerald Smoker.
Res.: 602 W. Chicago, 49028. Tel: 517-369-2120; Fax: 517-369-9012.
School—204 Albers Rd., 49028. Tel: 517-369-4625; Fax: 517-369-1652. Lay Teachers 6; Students 100.
Mission—*St. Barbara* Colon, St. Joseph Co. Tel: 616-432-2109.
Catechesis/Religious Program—Tel: 517-278-5408. Students 50.

BUCHANAN, BERRIEN CO., ST. ANTHONY (1941) [JC] Rev. Mathew Manalel.
Res.: 509 W. 4th St., 49107. Tel: 269-695-3863; Fax: 269-697-8187. Email: stanthonychurch@gmail.com.
Catechesis/Religious Program—Students 53.

BYRON CENTER, KENT CO., ST. MARY'S VISITATION (1866), (German), [CEM 2] [JC 2] Rev. Stephen Rodrigo, S.J. (India).
Res.: 2459 146th Ave., 49315. Tel: 616-681-9701; Fax: 616-681-9919. Email: gandres@smvchurch.org. Web: www.smvchurch.org.
School—2455 146th Ave., 49315. Email: mmaclachlan@smvschool.org. Web: smvschool.org. Lay Teachers 7; Students 89.
Catechesis/Religious Program—Tel: 616-681-9701, Ext. 203. Email: plaperna@smvchurch.org. Students 101.

CASSOPOLIS, CASS CO., ST. ANN (1915) Rev. Donald G. Potts.
Church & Mailing Address: 421 N. Broadway, P.O. Box 247, 49031. Tel: 269-445-3000; Fax: 269-445-5787.

Res.: 312 N. Disbrow, P.O. Box 247, 49031. Tel: 269-445-3140.
Catechesis/Religious Program—Email: stanncass@verizon.net. Students 15.

COLDWATER, BRANCH CO., ST. CHARLES BORROMEO (1849) Rev. Daniel E. Doctor.
Res.: 150 Taylor St., 49036. Tel: 517-278-2650; Fax: 517-278-5800.
School—79 Harrison St., 49036. Tel: 517-279-0404; Fax: 517-278-0505. Lay Teachers 7; Students 75.
Catechesis/Religious Program—Students 75.
Mission—Our Lady of Fatima Union City, Branch Co. Tel: 517-741-7275.

DECATUR, VAN BUREN CO., HOLY FAMILY (1938) Rev. Patrick H. Craig.
Res.: 500 W. St. Mary St., 49045. Tel: 269-783-4223; Fax: 269-783-4668. Email: holyfamilydecatur@comcast.net.
Catechesis/Religious Program—Students 46.

DELTON, BARRY CO., ST. AMBROSE (1950) Sr. Constance Fifelski, O.P., Parish Coord.
11137 Floria Rd., 49046. Tel: 269-623-2490; Fax: 269-623-2498. Email: stambrose@mei.net.
Res.: 11252 Floria Rd., 49046.
Catechesis/Religious Program—Students 50.
Mission—Our Lady of Great Oak Lacey, Barry Co.

DORR, ALLEGAN CO., ST. STANISLAUS (1892), (Polish), [CEM] Rev. Stanley Witek (Poland).
Res.: 1871 136th Ave., 49323. Tel: 269-793-7268; Fax: 269-793-3325.
School—(Grades PreSchool-8), 1861 136th Ave., 49323. Tel: 269-793-7204; Fax: 269-793-3264. Lay Teachers 7; Students 100.
Catechesis/Religious Program—Students 34.

DOUGLAS, ALLEGAN CO., ST. PETER (1894) [CEM] Rev. W. Timothy Cuny, O.S.A. In Res., Bro. John J. Stobba, O.S.A.
Res.: 100 St. Peter's Dr., P.O. Box 248, 49406-0248. Tel: 269-857-7951; 269-857-8175; Fax: 269-857-8164.
Catechesis/Religious Program—Students 96.

DOWAGIAC, CASS CO., HOLY MATERNITY OF MARY (1892) [CEM] Rev. Leo A. Taubitz.
Res.: 210 N. Front St., 49047. Tel: 269-782-2808; Fax: 269-782-3558.
Catechesis/Religious Program—Students 68.

EDWARDSBURG, CASS CO., OUR LADY OF THE LAKE (1923) Rev. Joseph McCormick, O.S.A.
Res.: 24832 U.S. 12 E., 49112. Tel: 269-699-5870; Fax: 269-699-5474.
Catechesis/Religious Program—Students 147.

GOBLES, VAN BUREN CO., ST. JUDE (1985) Rev. Joseph Xavier, M.S.F.S.; Deacon John R. Bodway, Parish Coord.
Church and Mailing: 13809 M-40 N., P.O. Box 102, 49055. Tel: 269-628-2219; Fax: 269-628-2219. Email: st.judeparish@verizon.net.
Res.: 2802 Nichols Rd., 49004. Tel: 269-382-2379.
Catechesis/Religious Program—Students 22.

HARTFORD, VAN BUREN CO., IMMACULATE CONCEPTION (1946), (Hispanic), Rev. Fabio H. Garzon, S.D.B.; Deacons Arthur Morsaw; James Rauner.
Res.: 63559 60th Ave., 49057. Tel: 269-621-4106; Fax: 269-621-2138.
Catechesis/Religious Program—Students 126.

HASTINGS, BARRY CO., ST. ROSE OF LIMA (1873) [CEM] Rev. Alfred J. Russell.
Res.: 805 S. Jefferson Ave., 49058. Tel: 269-945-4246; Fax: 269-945-0005.
School—707 S. Jefferson St., 49058. Tel: 269-945-3164. Lay Teachers 7; Students 85.
Catechesis/Religious Program—Students 91.
Mission—St. Cyril 203 N. State St., Nashville, Barry Co. 49073.

MARSHALL, CALHOUN CO., ST. MARY (1852) [CEM] Rev. Stephen Naas.
Mailing Address: 212 W. Hanover St., 49068.
Res.: 214 S. Eagle St., 49068. Tel: 269-781-3949.
Catechesis/Religious Program—Tel: 269-781-5656. Students 175.

MATTAWAN, VAN BUREN CO., ST. JOHN BOSCO (1953) Rev. Mathew Illikattil.
Res.: 23830 Front Ave., 49071. Tel: 269-668-3312, Ext. 21; Fax: 269-668-3313. Web: www.stjohnbosco.com.
Catechesis/Religious Program—Tel: 269-668-3312, Ext. 13. Email: kellyepoage@yahoo.com. Students 131.
Mission—St. Margaret Mary 296 E. Dibble St., Marcellus, Cass Co. 49067. Tel: 269-668-3312, Ext. 10; Fax: 269-668-3313. Web: www.stjohnbosco.com.

MENDON, ST. JOSEPH CO., ST. EDWARD (1872) [CEM] Rev. James Vinh Le.
Res.: 332 W. State, P.O. Box 368, 49072. Tel: 269-496-3525; Fax: 269-496-8640. Email: stedwardchurch@msn.com.
Catechesis/Religious Program—Students 47.

NEW BUFFALO, BERRIEN CO., ST. MARY OF THE LAKE (1857) Rev. James A. Morris.
Res.: 718 W. Buffalo St., 49117. Tel: 269-469-2637; Fax: 269-469-7393. Email: sml-parish@comcast.net.
School—704 W. Merchant St., 49117. Tel: 269-469-1515; Fax: 269-469-3772. Lay Teachers 10; Students 84.
Catechesis/Religious Program—Students 18.

NILES, BERRIEN CO.

1—ST. MARK (1955) Rev. Thomas King, C.S.C.
Res.: 3 N. 19th St., 49120-2117. Email: stmark319@yahoo.com.
Catechesis/Religious Program—Tel: 269-683-8650; Fax: 269-683-9314. Students 32.

2—ST. MARY OF THE IMM. CONCEPTION CHURCH (1870) [CEM 2] Rev. David C. Otto; Deacon Roger Gregorski.
Res.: 211 S. Lincoln Ave., 49120. Tel: 269-683-5087, Ext. 12.
203 S. Lincoln Ave., 49120.
Parish Center—219 S. State St., 49120. Tel: 269-683-5087; Fax: 269-683-5089.
School—(Grades PreK-5), 217 S. Lincoln Ave., 49120. Tel: 269-683-9191; Fax: 269-683-8118. Lay Teachers 7; Students 97.
Catechesis/Religious Program—Email: stmaryniles@sbcglobal.net. Students 83.

OTSEGO, ALLEGAN CO., ST. MARGARET (1887) [CEM] Rev. Donald P. Klingler.
Res.: 766 S. Farmer St., 49078. Tel: 269-694-9369 (Rectory); 269-694-6311 (Church); Fax: 269-694-5415. Email: stmsec@yahoo.com. Web: www.stmargaret-otsego.org.
School—736 S. Farmer, 49078. Tel: 269-694-2951; Fax: 269-694-4520. Email: cheidelber@yahoo.com. Lay Teachers 12; Students 116.
Catechesis/Religious Program—Tel: 269-694-6311, Ext. 264. Email: reen@bedl.net. Students 96.

PARCHMENT, KALAMAZOO CO., ST. AMBROSE (1955) Rev. James S. O'Leary.
Res.: 1628 E. G Ave., 49004. Tel: 269-385-4152; Fax: 269-385-2527. Email: ambroseparchment@sbcglobal.net.
Catechesis/Religious Program—Tel: 269-343-0099. Email: ambrosedre@sbcglobal.net. Students 98.

PAW PAW, VAN BUREN CO., ST. MARY (1887) [CEM] Rev. Joseph Xavier, M.S.F.S.
Mailing Address: 500 Paw Paw St., 49079.
Res.: 214 S. Brown St., 49079. Tel: 269-657-4459; Fax: 269-657-4260. Email: stmarypawpawoffice@verizon.net. Web: home.catholicweb.com/stmarypawpaw.
School—508 Paw Paw St., 49079. Tel: 269-657-3750. Email: stmarypp@i2k.com. Lay Teachers 6; Students 107.
Catechesis/Religious Program—Students 149.
Mission—St. Jude's Church 13809 N. M-40, Gobles, Van Buren Co. 49055. Tel: 269-628-2219; Fax: 269-628-7479. Email: stjudeparish@verizon.net.

PEARL, ALLEGAN CO., SAN FELIPE DE JESUS (1986), (Hispanic), Rev. Fabio H. Garzon, S.D.B.; Mr. Joseph Marble, Parish Coord.; Deacon Maximino Rodriguez.
Mailing Address: P.O. Box 588, Fennville, 49408. Tel: 269-561-5029; Fax: 269-561-5029.
Res.: 63559 60th Ave., Hartford, 49057. Tel: 269-621-4106; Fax: 269-621-2138.
Catechesis/Religious Program—Students 80.

PORTAGE, KALAMAZOO CO., ST. CATHERINE OF SIENA (1966) Revs. John D. Fleckenstein; Christopher Ankley, Parochial Vicar; Angela Garcia, Admin.; Peg Klitch, Sec.
Res.: 1150 W. Centre St., 49024-5385. Tel: 269-327-5165; Fax: 269-327-7266. Email: info@stcatherinesiena.org. Web: www.stcatherinesiena.org.
Catechesis/Religious Program—Tel: 269-327-0861. Paula Mathieu, D.R.E. Students 651.

ST. JOSEPH, BERRIEN CO., ST. JOSEPH (1720) [CEM] Rev. Msgr. Michael A. Osborn; Deacon Michael Gallagher.
Res.: 211 Church St., 49085. Tel: 269-983-1575. Email: sjcath1@att.net. Web: www.stjoestjoe.com.
Catechesis/Religious Program—220 Church St., 49085. Tel: 269-983-1575, Ext. 10 (Rel. Educ. & Sacramental Prep.); Fax: 269-983-7798. Email: rciaandfamilyministry@hotmail.com. Students 517.

SILVER CREEK, CASS CO., SACRED HEART OF MARY (1838), (Native American), [CEM] Deacon Frank Wesolowski, Parish Coord.
Res.: 51841 Leach Rd., Dowagiac, 49047. Tel: 269-782-5740; Fax: 269-782-5692; 269-783-0192. Email: shm@i2k.com.
Catechesis/Religious Program—Tel: 269-782-8048. Students 41.

SOUTH HAVEN, VAN BUREN CO., ST. BASIL (1900) [CEM] Rev. Robert E. Flickinger.
Res.: 634 Kentucky Ave., 49090. Email: stbasil@i2k.com.
Rectory—513 Monroe Blvd., 49090. Tel: 269-637-2404; Fax: 269-637-8374. Email: stbasil@i2k.com.
School—94 Superior St., 49090. Tel: 269-637-3529; Fax: 269-639-1242. Lay Teachers 9; Students 97.
Catechesis/Religious Program—Tel: 269-637-4732. Students 50.

STURGIS, ST. JOSEPH CO., HOLY ANGELS (1879) Rev. Richard L. Altine.
Res.: 402 S. Nottawa St., 49091. Tel: 269-651-5200; Fax: 269-659-8366.
Mission—St. Joseph P.O. Box 344, White Pigeon, St. Joseph Co. 49099. Tel: 269-483-7621; Fax: 269-483-7891.
Catechesis/Religious Program—Students 211.

THREE OAKS, BERRIEN CO., ST. MARY OF THE ASSUMPTION (1880) Rev. Donald Suberlak, C.R.
Res.: 28 W. Ash St., 49128. Tel: 269-756-2041; Fax: 269-756-2212.
Catechesis/Religious Program—Students 33.
Mission—St. Agnes Sawyer, Berrien Co.

THREE RIVERS, ST. JOSEPH CO., IMMACULATE CONCEPTION (1885) Rev. Mark J. Vyverman.
Res.: 645 S. Douglas Ave., 49093. Tel: 269-273-8953; Fax: 269-273-2114. Email: icchurch@verizon.net.
School—601 S. Douglas Ave., 49093-2044. Tel: 269-273-2085. Lay Teachers 5; Students 50.
Catechesis/Religious Program—Tel: 269-273-8953; Fax: 269-273-2114. Deacon Rick Demars, D.R.E. Students 106.
Mission—St. Clare 229 N. Dean, Centreville, St. Joseph Co. 49032. Tel: 269-273-8953. Email: icchurch@verizon.net.

VICKSBURG, KALAMAZOO CO., ST. MARTIN (1951) Rev. James Vinh Le.
Res.: 5855 E. W Ave., P.O. Box 264, 49097. Tel: 269-649-1629; Fax: 269-649-0199. Web: www.stmartinvicksburg.org.
Catechesis/Religious Program—Tel: 269-649-3626. Email: stmartinreleducation@stmartinvicksburg.com. Students 152.

WATERVLIET, BERRIEN CO., ST. JOSEPH (1896) [CEM] Rev. Gordon L. Greene.
Mailing Address: 157 Lucinda Ln., 49098.
Res.: 179 Lucinda Ln., 49098. Tel: 269-463-5470; Fax: 269-463-4642. Email: church@sjcatholic.com. Web: www.sjcatholic.com.
School—Tel: 269-463-3941; Fax: 269-463-4525. Lay Teachers 6; Students 74.
Catechesis/Religious Program—Tel: 269-463-5470, Ext. 101. Students 30.

WAYLAND, ALLEGAN CO.

1—SS. CYRIL AND METHODIUS (1917) [CEM] Rev. Christian R. Johnston.
Church: 159 131st Ave., 49348. Tel: 269-792-3543; Fax: 269-792-9062. Email: sscm@triton.net. Web: sscmcc.triton.net.
Catechesis/Religious Program—Students 48.

2—ST. THERESE OF LISIEUX (1942) Rev. Christian R. Johnston.
Res.: 128 Cedar St., 49348. Tel: 269-792-2138; 269-792-9315; Fax: 269-792-2908. Web: www.sttheresewayland.org.
School—430 S. Main St., 49348. Tel: 269-792-2016; Fax: 269-792-6778. Email: sttoffice@sbcglobal.net. Web: www.sttschool.com. Lay Teachers 6; Students 82.
Catechesis/Religious Program—Tel: 269-792-2016, Ext. 27. Email: bg14all-dre@yahoo.com. Web: www-.stl.catholicweb.com. Students 79.

WHITE PIGEON, ST. JOSEPH CO., ST. JOSEPH (1832) [CEM] Deacon Lawrence M. Kasuboski, Parish Coord.
Office: 702 E. Chicago Rd., P.O. Box 344, 49099-0344. Tel: 269-483-7621; Fax: 269-483-7891. Email: saintjoewp@comcast.net.
Res.: 315 S. Maple St., Sturgis, 49091. Tel: 269-651-4071.
Catechesis/Religious Program—Tel: 269-483-7622. Students 43.

Chaplains of Public Institutions

COLDWATER. *Camp Branch*. Rev. Brian L. Stanley, Volunteer Chap.
St. Charles Church, 150 Taylor St., 49036. Tel: 517-278-2650; Fax: 517-278-5800.
Florence Crane Correctional Facility for Women. Rev. Brian L. Stanley, Volunteer Chap.
Lakeland Correctional Facility for Men. Rev. Brian L. Stanley, Volunteer Chap.

Graduate Studies:
Rev.—
Adams, James, Rome

On Leave of Absence:
Rev.—
Kassian, Jeffery

Retired:

Rev. Msgrs.—

Bogdan, Leonard A., P.O. Box 5753, Sun City Center, AZ 85376-5753.

Fitzgerald, William (LAN), 602 South St., 49007.

Sears, Eugene A., 302 Anchor's Way, Saint Joseph, 49085.

Revs.—

Adams, David, 9160 East D Ave, #601, Richland, 49083.

Barrett, James L., "F" Dr., Marshall, 49068.

Barth, Raymond J., P.O. Box 186, Baroda, 49101.

Consani, Robert E., 1604 Laughton Pl., Sun City Center, FL 33573.

Grathwohl, John M., 2065 Arrowhead Dr., Traverse City, 49686.

Limbert, William G., 11859 Marquette Dr., New Buffalo, 49117.

Pohl, Leon H., St. Charles Church, 150 Taylor St., 49036.

Sonefeld, Raymond G., 814 Engleman St., Manistee, 49660.

Thachet, Joseph, St. Joseph Home, Kenala 686008 India.

Valls, Richard, 10552 Rancho Carmel, San Diego, CA 92128.

Weller, Joseph W., Meadows at Worcester, 463 Founders Village, Lansdale, PA 19446-5869.

Wieber, Donald A., P.O. Box 360, Coloma, 49038.

Young, John, 15485 Blue Star Hwy., South Haven, 49090.

Permanent Deacons:

Barbosa, Juan, Diocese of Brownsville, TX

Bartholomew, David, St. Augustine Cathedral, Kalamazoo

Bell, Alfred, St. Catherine of Sienna, Portage

Bodway, John, St. Jude Mission, Gobles

Bohan, Hal, St. Philip, Battle Creek

Connelly, Bart, Immaculate Conception, Three Rivers

DeMars, Richard, Immaculate Conception, Three Rivers

DeStazio, John, Diocese of Winona, MN

Gallagher, Michael, St. Joseph, St. Joseph

Gregorski, Roger, St. Mary, Niles

Guido, David, St. Martin of Tours, Vicksburg; St. Edwards, Mendon

Haas, Eugene, St. Rose of Lima, Hastings; St. Margarets, Ostego

Hall, Patrick, B.A., St. Thomas More, Kalamazoo

Herrera, Manuel, Diocese of Grand Rapids, MI

Kasuboski, Lawrence M., St. Joseph Mission, White Pigeon

Lavelline, James, St. Charles Borromeo, Coldwater

Lazaga, Alfred C., SS John & Bernard, Benton Harbor

Lohstorfer, John, St. Augustine Cathedral, Kalamazoo

Lucas, Kurt, St. Monica, Kalamazoo

Mellen, James, St. Rose of Lima, Hastings

Middleton, Allan, Diocese of Grand Rapids, MI

Mileski, Bernie, St. Philip, Battle Creek

Moreno, Michael, St. Joseph, Battle Creek

Morsaw, Arthur, Immaculate Conception, Hartford

Nelson, James, St. Joseph, Battle Creek

Nethercott, Anthony, St. Peter, Douglas

Patrick, Albert, St. Philip, Battle Creek

Prendergast, Jack, St. Catherine of Sienna, Portage

Radford, Alfred, St. Joseph, Battle Creek

Rauner, James, Immaculate Conception, Hartford

Rodriguez, Maximino, San Felipe de Jesus, Fennville

Schmitt, Joe, M.A., St. Thomas More, Kalamazoo

Smoker, Gerald, St. Mary of the Assumption, Bronson

Stevens, Robert, St. Monica, Kalamazoo

Thamann, Thomas, St. Martin of Tours, Vicksburg

Van Dril, William, (Retired)

Vogel, Richard, Appalachian Mission Center, Louisa, KY

Wesolowski, Frank, Sacred Heart Mission, Dowagiac

Whitehouse, Howard, (Retired)

Wright, Gary, St. Jerome, Battle Creek

INSTITUTIONS LOCATED IN THE DIOCESE

[A] HIGH SCHOOLS, DIOCESAN

KALAMAZOO. *Msgr. Hackett Catholic Central High School* (1964) 1000 W. Kilgore Rd., 49008. Tel: 269-381-2646; Fax: 269-381-3919. Email: hackett@hackettcc.org. Web: www.hackettcc.org. Rev. James Richardson, M.A., Chap.; Mr. Tim Eastman, Prin.; Terri Luzenske, Librarian. Priests 1; Lay Teachers 24; Students 350.

BATTLE CREEK. *St. Philip Catholic Central High School*, 20 Cherry St., 49017. Tel: 616-963-4503; Fax: 616-963-5590. Kathy Grosso, Prin.; Laura Miller, Librarian. Total Staff 9; Students 134.

ST. JOSEPH. *Lake Michigan Catholic Middle and High School*, (Grades 6-12), 915 Pleasant St., 49085. Tel: 616-983-2511; Fax: 616-983-0883. Email: jberlin@lmclakers.com. Web: www.lmclakers.org. John Berlin, Prin. Priests 1; Adrian Dominican Sisters of Immaculate Conception Province 1; Sisters of St. Casimir 1; Lay Teachers 17; Students 274.

[B] GRADE SCHOOLS, INTERPAROCHIAL

ST. JOSEPH. *Lake Michigan Catholic Schools*, (Grades PreK-5), 3165 Washington Ave., 49085. Tel: 269-429-0227; Fax: 269-429-1461. Email: catholicprincipal@yahoo.com. Web: lmclakers.org. Mrs. Jody G. Maher, Prin.; Janice Mathews, Librarian. Lay Teachers 17; Students 293.

[C] CATHOLIC SOCIAL AGENCIES

KALAMAZOO. *Catholic Family Services*, 1819 Gull Rd., 49048. Tel: 269-381-9800; Fax: 269-381-2932. Email: frandenny@catholicfamilyservices.org. Web: www.catholicfamilyservices.org. Mrs. Frances H. Denny, M.B.A., M.S.W., Exec. Dir.

[D] GENERAL HOSPITALS

KALAMAZOO. *Borgess Medical Center*, 1521 Gull Rd., 49048-1640. Tel: 269-226-7000; Fax: 269-226-7396. Paul Spaude, Pres. & CEO. Bed Capacity 422; Total Staff 2,757; Patients Assisted Annually (Inpatient Discharges plus Outpatient Visits) 467,065.

BATTLE CREEK. *Battle Creek Health System*, 300 North Ave., 49016. Tel: 269-966-8000; Fax: 269-966-8008. Web: www.bchealth.com. Mr. Patrick R. Garrett, Pres. & CEO. Div. of Trinity Health. Bed Capacity 172; Patients Assisted Annually 174,000; Total Staff 1,500.

DOWAGIAC. *Lee Memorial Hospital*, 420 W. High St., 49047. Tel: 269-782-8681; Fax: 269-783-3044. Web: www.borgesslee.com. Joy A. Strand, Admin./COO. Bed Capacity 25; Total Staff 238; Patients Assisted Annually 96,688.

[E] RESIDENCES OF PRIESTS AND BROTHERS

KALAMAZOO. *St. Philip Neri House*, 219 Woodward Ave., 49007. Tel: 269-385-9933; Fax: 269-553-9497. Email: frrobert@stphilipnerihouse.org. Web: www.stphilipnerihouse.org. Revs. David Grondz; Robert Sirico; James Richardson, M.A.

DOUGLAS. *Order of St. Augustine* (Chicago Prov.), 100 St. Peter Dr., Box 248, 49406-0248. Tel: 269-857-8175; 269-857-7951 (Parish); Fax: 269-857-8164. Rev. W. Timothy Cuny, O.S.A. In Res. Bro. John J. Stobba, O.S.A.

[F] HOMES FOR SENIOR CITIZENS

KALAMAZOO. *Borgess Nursing Home*, 3057 Gull Rd., 49048. Tel: 269-552-6500; Fax: 269-552-6510. Email: bartcarrel@borgess.com. Web: www.borgess.com. Bart Carrel, Admin. Bed Capacity 101; Total Assisted 261; Total Staff 150.

Dillon Complex for Independent Living, Inc., Dillion Hall, 3301 Gull Rd., P.O. Box 308, 49048. Tel: 269-342-0263; Fax: 269-342-1814. Email: tmacintyre@csjoseph.org. Sr. Theresa MacIntyre, C.S.J., Vice Pres. Bd. Directors, Sec. Sponsored by the Congregation of the Sisters of St. Joseph. Total in Residence 77; Total Staff 4; Apartments 72.

BATTLE CREEK. *Mercy Pavilion Skilled Nursing Home and Senior Care Residence*, 80 N. 20 St., 49015. Tel: 269-964-5400; Fax: 269-964-5559. Mr. Robert M. Irwin, Admin. Sub. of Battle Creek Health System. Bed Capacity 77; Senior Care Residence Beds 64.

OTSEGO. *Otsego Senior Apts., Inc.*, Baraga Manor, 301 Washington St., 49078. Tel: 269-694-9711; Fax: 269-694-5857. Email: dianejones@catholicfamilyservices.org. Web: catholicfamilyservices.org. Managed by Catholic Family Services, Diocese of Kalamazoo. Rental Units 48; Total Staff 5; Total Assisted Annually 65.

1819 Gull Rd., 49048. Apartments 48.

[G] CONVENTS AND RESIDENCES FOR SISTERS

NAZARETH. *Congregation of the Sisters of St. Joseph* (1889) 49074. Tel: 269-381-6290; Fax: 269-381-4909. Web: www.csjoseph.org. Sr. Mary Joan Walsh, C.S.J., Admin. Ministry in the field of Education; Social Services; Parish and Church-related Ministries; Healthcare, Spirituality Sisters in Community 217.

[H] NEWMAN CENTERS

KALAMAZOO. *Western Michigan University, Kalamazoo College, Kalamazoo Valley Community College* St. Thomas More Catholic Student Parish, 421 Monroe St., 49006. Tel: 269-381-8917; Fax: 269-381-0195. Email: sttoms@sttomskazoo.org. Web: www.sttomskazoo.org. Rev. Kenneth W. Schmidt, J.C.D., M.A., L.P.C.; Sr. Sue McCrery, S.S.J., M.A., D.Min., Pastoral Assoc.; Mrs. Marian Nelson, M.A., Pastoral Assoc.; Deacons Patrick Hall, B.A., Pastoral Assoc.; Joe Schmitt, M.A., Pastoral Assoc. Davenport University, Kalamazoo Center for Medical Studies.

[I] MISCELLANEOUS LISTINGS

KALAMAZOO. *Borgess Health* (1889) 1521 Gull Rd., 49048. Tel: 269-226-4800; Fax: 269-226-7396. Web: www.borgess.com. Paul Spaude, Pres. & CEO; Michael Alfred, Exec. Dir., Business Devel. & Public Rels.; Shirley A. Larkins, Trustee; Larry D. Lueth, Chm.; Joni Knapper, Sec.; Michael L. Chojnowski, Treas. Borgess Health Care is a Health Care System sponsored by Ascension Health which operates Borgess Ambulatory Care, Inc., Borgess Foundation, Borgess Medical Center, Borgess Nursing Home, Borgess-Pipp Hospital, CareLink of Jackson, Borgess-Lee Memorial Hospital, ProMed Healthcare, Borgess Visiting Nurse Services, Borgess Home Care, Borgess Hospice, Textile Systems, Inc. and other related companies. Incorporated in the State of Michigan. Inpatients 21,286; Outpatients 602,169; Personnel 2,350.

Catholic Schools of Greater Kalamazoo, 215 N. Westnedge Ave., 49007-3760. Tel: 269-349-8714, Ext. 235; Fax: 269-349-6440.

Diocesan Council of St. Vincent dePaul, 5227 EFG Ave., 49004. Tel: 269-660-9579; Fax: 269-372-0908. Email: MFC7@home.com. Walter Brockmeyer, Pres. Total Assisted 150.

Kalamazoo Regional Catholic Schools Foundation, 1000 W. Kilgore Rd., 49008. Tel: 269-381-2646; Fax: 269-381-3919. Email: teastman@hackettcc.org. Web: hackettcc.org.

BATTLE CREEK. *BCACS Foundation, Inc.* (Battle Creek Area Catholic Schools Foundation, Inc.), 63 N. 24th St., 49015. Tel: 269-963-4771; Fax: 269-963-3917. Email: kgallagher@bcacs.org.

HASTINGS. *St. Rose Lima Trust Fund*, 805 S. Jefferson St., 49058. Tel: 269-945-4246; Fax: 269-945-0005.

ST. JOSEPH. *Twin-City Area Catholic School Fund, Inc.* (1971) P.O. Box 32, 49085. Tel: 269-861-3108; Fax: 269-983-5520. Email: tcacsf@comcast.net. Martin Golob, Exec. Dir.

SOUTH HAVEN. *St. Basil Educational Endowment Fund*, 94 Superior St., 49090. Tel: 269-637-3529; Fax: 269-639-1242. Email: ceciliawondergem@saintbasilcatholic.org. Web: www.saintbasilcatholic.org.

STURGIS. **Holy Angels School Foundation, Inc.*, P.O. Box 24, 49091-0024. Tel: 616-467-8114.

Secular Franciscan Order, 25580 Waneta Way, 49091. Tel: 269-467-8114. Mr. James Goethals, Pres.

RELIGIOUS INSTITUTES OF MEN REPRESENTED IN THE DIOCESE

For further details refer to the corresponding bracketed number in the Religious Institutes of Men or Women section.

[0140]—*The Augustinians*—O.S.A.

[0140]—*Benedictine Monks* (Stafford)—O.S.B.

[1330]—*Congregation of the Mission*—C.M.

[1080]—*Congregation of the Resurrection*—C.R.

[0730]—*Legionaries of Christ* (Ruede)—L.C.

[]—*Missionaries of St. Frances de Sales*—M.S.F.S.

[0920]—*Oblates of St. Francis deSales* (Toledo-Detroit Prov.)—O.S.F.S.

[0610]—*Priests of the Congregation of the Holy Cross* (Indiana Prov.)—C.S.C.

[1190]—*Salesians of Don Bosco* (Garzon)—S.D.B.

[]—*Society of Jesus*—S.J.

RELIGIOUS INSTITUTES OF WOMEN REPRESENTED IN THE DIOCESE

[3832]—*Congregation of the Sisters of St. Joseph*—C.S.J.

[1920]—*Congregation of the Sisters of the Holy Cross*—C.S.C.

[1070-05]—*Dominican Sisters*—O.P.

[1070-13]—*Dominican Sisters*—O.P.

[1070-14]—*Dominican Sisters*—O.P.

[2575]—*Sisters of Mercy of the Americas*—R.S.M.

[3930]—*Sisters of St. Joseph of the Third Order of St. Francis*—S.S.J.-T.O.S.F.

[3260]—*Sisters of the Precious Blood* (Dayton, OH)—C.PP.S.

[2150]—*Sisters, Servants of the Immaculate Heart of Mary* (Monroe, MI)—I.H.M.

NECROLOGY

(No Deaths)

An asterisk (*) denotes an organization that has established tax-exempt status directly with the IRS and is not covered by the USCCB Group Ruling.

Archdiocese of Kansas City in Kansas

(Archidioecesis Kansanopolitana in Kansas)

Most Reverend

JOSEPH F. NAUMANN

Archbishop of Kansas City in Kansas; ordained May 24, 1975; appointed Titular Bishop of Caput Cilla and Auxiliary Bishop of St. Louis July 9, 1997; consecrated September 3, 1997; appointed Coadjutor Archbishop of Kansas City in Kansas January 7, 2004; installed March 19, 2004; succeeded to See January 15, 2005.

Most Reverend

JAMES P. KELEHER, S.T.D.

Archbishop Emeritus of Kansas City in Kansas; ordained April 12, 1958; appointed Bishop of Belleville October 23, 1984; consecrated December 11, 1984; appointed Archbishop of Kansas City in Kansas June 28, 1993; installed September 8, 1993; retired January 15, 2005.

Catholic Chancery Offices: 12615 Parallel Pkwy., Kansas City, KS 66109. Tel: 913-721-1570; Fax: 913-721-1577.

Web: www.archkck.org

Email: archkck@archkck.org

Square Miles 12,524.

Established Vicariate Apostolic July 19, 1850. Diocese of Leavenworth established May 22, 1877. See changed to Kansas City in Kansas May 10, 1947; created Archdiocese August 9, 1952.

Comprises the following 21 Counties of Kansas: Anderson, Atchison, Brown, Coffey, Doniphan, Douglas, Franklin, Jackson, Jefferson, Johnson, Leavenworth, Linn, Lyon, Marshall, Miami, Nemaha, Osage, Pottawatomie, Shawnee, Wabaunsee and Wyandotte.

Patrons of the Diocese: I. Blessed Virgin Mary (Immaculate Conception); II. St. John Baptist Vianney.

For legal titles of institutions, please contact the Catholic Chancery Offices.

STATISTICAL OVERVIEW

Personnel	
Archbishops	1
Retired Archbishops	1
Abbots	1
Retired Abbots	2
Priests: Diocesan Active in Diocese	71
Priests: Diocesan Active Outside Diocese	2
Priests: Diocesan in Foreign Missions	1
Priests: Retired, Sick or Absent	28
Number of Diocesan Priests	102
Religious Priests in Diocese	56
Total Priests in Diocese	158
Extern Priests in Diocese	16
Ordinations:	
Diocesan Priests	3
Transitional Deacons	1
Permanent Deacons in Diocese	3
Total Brothers	14
Total Sisters	510
Parishes	
Parishes	110
With Resident Pastor:	
Resident Diocesan Priests	59
Resident Religious Priests	10
Without Resident Pastor:	
Administered by Priests	41
Closed Parishes	1
Professional Ministry Personnel:	
Sisters	13
Lay Ministers	86
Welfare	
Catholic Hospitals	3
Total Assisted	577,426
Health Care Centers	4
Total Assisted	21,540
Homes for the Aged	3
Total Assisted	647
Day Care Centers	2
Total Assisted	164
Special Centers for Social Services	5
Total Assisted	33,292
Educational	
Diocesan Students in Other Seminaries	26
Students Religious	2
Total Seminarians	28
Colleges and Universities	3
Total Students	4,611
High Schools, Diocesan and Parish	6
Total Students	3,355
High Schools, Private	1
Total Students	178
Elementary Schools, Diocesan and Parish	38
Total Students	12,017
Elementary Schools, Private	3
Total Students	160
Catechesis/Religious Education:	
High School Students	2,359
Elementary Students	14,197
Total Students under Catholic Instruction	36,905
Teachers in the Diocese:	
Sisters	15
Lay Teachers	1,106
Vital Statistics	
Receptions into the Church:	
Infant Baptism Totals	3,730
Minor Baptism Totals	239
Adult Baptism Totals	270
Received into Full Communion	498
First Communions	3,742
Confirmations	3,593
Marriages:	
Catholic	626
Interfaith	386
Total Marriages	1,012
Deaths	1,438
Total Catholic Population	202,006
Total Population	1,300,373

Predecessors—Most Revs. J. B. MIEGE, S.J., cons. Bishop of Messenia, Vicar-Apostolic, March 25, 1851; resignation accepted by Pope Pius IX Nov. 8, 1874; died July 21, 1884; LOUIS M. FINK, O.S.B., D.D., cons. Bishop of Eucarpia June 11, 1871; appt. first Bishop of Leavenworth May 22, 1877; died March 17, 1904; THOMAS F. LILLIS, O.D., cons. Bishop of Leavenworth, Dec. 27, 1904; appt. Coadjutor Bishop of Kansas City, with right of succession March 14, 1910; succeeded to the See of Kansas City, Feb. 21, 1913; JOHN WARD, D.D., ord. July 17, 1884; appt. Bishop of Leavenworth Nov. 25, 1910; cons. Feb. 22, 1911; died April 20, 1929; FRANCIS JOHANNES, D.D., LL.D., cons. May 1, 1928; succeeded to the See, April 20, 1929; died March 13, 1937; PAUL C. SCHULTE, D.D., ord. June 11, 1915; appt. Bishop of Leavenworth May 29, 1937; cons. Sept. 21, 1937; appt. Archbishop of Indianapolis July 20, 1946; installed Oct. 10, 1946; GEORGE J. DONNELLY, S.T.D., ord. June 12, 1921; appt. Titular Bishop of Coela and Auxiliary of St. Louis March 19, 1940; cons. April 23, 1940; appt. Bishop of Leavenworth Nov. 9, 1946; died Dec. 13, 1950; EDWARD J. HUNKELER, D.D., ord. June 14, 1919; appt. Bishop of Grand Island March 10, 1945; cons. May 1, 1945; transferred to Kansas City March 28, 1951; elevated to Archiepiscopal dignity Aug. 9, 1952; retired Sept. 10, 1969; died Oct. 1, 1970; IGNATIUS J. STRECKER, D.D., S.T.D., ord. Dec. 19, 1942; appt. Bishop of Springfield-Cape Girardeau April 7, 1962; cons. June 20, 1962; transferred to Kansas City Sept. 10, 1969; retired Sept. 8, 1993; died Oct. 16, 2003; JAMES P. KELEHER, S.T.D., ord. April 12, 1958; appt. Bishop of Belleville Oct. 23, 1984; cons. Dec. 11, 1984; appt. Archbishop of Kansas City in Kansas June 28, 1993; installed Sept. 8, 1993; retired Jan. 15, 2005.

Catholic Chancery Offices—12615 Parallel Pkwy., Kansas City, 66109. Tel: 913-721-1570; Fax: 913-721-1577. Office Hours: 8:30-5.

Vicars General—Revs. GARY PENNINGS; BRIAN SCHIEBER.

Chancellor—Rev. JOHN A. RILEY.

Vice-Chancellor—Rev. Msgr. RAYMOND BURGER (Retired).

Metropolitan Tribunal—12615 Parallel Pkwy., Kansas City, 66109. Tel: 913-721-1570; Fax: 913-721-1577.

Judicial Vicar—Rev. Msgr. GARY APPLEGATE, J.C.L.

Judges—Rev. GEORGE BERTELS, J.C.L. (Retired); Rev. Msgr. GARY APPLEGATE, J.C.L.; Rev. DENIS MEADE, O.S.B., J.C.D.

Defenders of the Bond—Rev. Msgr. RAYMOND BURGER (Retired); Rev. PHILIP KENDALL, C.S.V., J.C.D.

Advocates— Selected priests, Sr. MARY ANN BARTOLAC, S.C.L., selected Lay Advocates.

Notary—LUCIA DAVIS.

Archdiocesan Consultors—Rev. Msgr. THOMAS TANK; Rev. GARY PENNINGS; Rt. Rev. BARNABAS SENECAL, O.S.B.; Rev. BRIAN SCHIEBER; Rev. Msgrs. MICHAEL MULLEN; CHARLES MCGLINN; Revs. WILLIAM PORTER; MICHAEL KOLLER; JOHN A. RILEY; Rev. Msgr. GARY APPLEGATE, J.C.L.; Rev. FRANCIS BURGER.

Archdiocesan Council on Finances—Rev. JOHN A. RILEY, Chancellor; Mr. L. JOSEPH BAUMAN; Mr. FRANK J. BECKER; Mr. GARY DAVIS; Mr. RUSS JENKINS; Mr. MICHAEL EASTERDAY; Mr. FRED FOSNACHT; Mr. JERRY MAYNE; Mr. JAMES HEINTZ; Mr. JOHN GILLCRIST; Mr. KEVIN KELLY; Mr. MICHAEL MORRISSEY; Mr. L. TRAVIS HICKS; Mr. MEL LAVERY; Mrs. JODY OLBERDING; Ms. KATHLEEN LUSK; Mr. MAL ROBINSON; Revs. RICHARD HALVORSON; GARY PENNINGS; Mrs. LESLE KNOP; Ms. JEANNE GORMAN; Mr. JOHN SEITZER;

Mr. GEORGE REBECK.

Archdiocesan Finance Officer—Mr. JERRY MAYNE.

Regional Pastoral Leaders—Revs. GERARD SENECAL, O.S.B., Atchison; MICHAEL HAWKEN, Johnson Co.; PATRIC RILEY, Lawrence; PHILLIP J. WINKELBAUER, Leavenworth; GERALD VOLZ, Topeka; WILLIAM FISHER, Southern; JAMES SHAUGHNESSY, Nemah-Marshall; DANIEL GARDNER, Wyandotte Co.

Archdiocesan Pastoral Council—Most Rev. JOSEPH NAUMANN; MARGARET BLEVINS; DARYL CURRIE; Sr. MARY RACHEL FLYNN; JEFF FOLEY; LAURA FORTMEYER; GERALD FRIETCHEN; JEAN HINMAN; JERRY JEWELL; MARK JIRAK; KATE JIRON; GEORGE KARNAZE; GARY LAMMERS; Revs. KEITH LUNSFORD; MARK MERTES; Sr. ELENA MORCELLI; DENISE OGILVIE; CARMEN OREGEL; MARY ELLEN REESE; MIGUEL SANCHEZ; CAROL SHOMIN; SCOTT WAGNER; SHARON WILLIAMS. Ex Officio: Revs. GARY PENNINGS, Vicar Gen.; JOHN RILEY, Chancellor; Mr. CARROLL MACKE, Dir. Communications & Planning.

Archdiocesan Administrative Team—Mrs. LESLE KNOP; Rev. JOHN RILEY; Dr. KATHLEEN O'HARA; Mr. JERRY MAYNE; Rev. BRIAN SCHIEBER; Mrs. JAN LEWIS; Mr. CARROLL MACKE; Rev. GARY PENNINGS.

Catholic Foundation of Northeast Kansas—12615 Parallel Pkwy., Kansas City, 66109.

Catholic Education Foundation—12615 Parallel Pkwy., Kansas City, 66109.

Minister to Priests—Rev. JAMES WHITE, S.J., 12600 Hollingsworth Rd., Kansas City, 66109. Tel: 913-721-3966.

Archdiocesan Archivist—Mr. MICHAEL PODREBARAC.

Archdiocesan Offices and Directors

Savior Pastoral Center—12601 Parallel, Kansas City, 66109. Tel: 913-721-1097; Fax: 913-721-2339. Web: www.saviorpastoralcenter.org. Email: savior@archkck.org. Rev. GARY PENNINGS, Dir.; Mrs. EILEEN MANZA, Prog. Dir.

Black Catholics—BARBARA BAILEY, 2203 Parallel, Kansas City, 66104. Tel: 913-321-1958.

Department of Parish Ministries—Rev. GARY PENNINGS, Dir., 12615 Parallel Pkwy., Kansas City, 66109. Tel: 913-721-1570.

Evangelization and Catholic Formation of Youth—Mr. DANA NEARMYER, Consultant; Mr. RICK CHEEK, Assoc. Consultant.

Evangelization & Catholic Formation of Adults—Consultants: Mr. MATT KARR; Ms. KIMBERLY RODE.

Prairie Star Ranch—12615 Parallel Pkwy., Kansas City, 66109. Tel: 913-721-1570; Fax: 913-721-2680. Mr. DANA NEARMYER, Dir.; Mr. SHAWN MADDEN, Prog. Coord.

Deaf Ministry—Mrs. PAT RICHEY.

Family Life—Mrs. JACKI CORRIGAN, Consultant; Mrs. BETH MEIER, Assoc. Consultant.

Liturgy—Mr. MICHAEL PODREBARAC.

My House (Freedom from Pornography)—Mr. SAM MEIER.

Pro-life/Respect Life—Mr. RON KELSEY.

Social Justice—Mr. BILL SCHOLL.

Hispanic Ministry—Revs. PATRICK MURPHY, C.S.; JESUS OLIVARES, C.S., Assoc.

Administrative Services—Mrs. RITA HERKEN.

Human Resources—Ms. KATHLEEN THOMAS.

Stewardship and Development Office—Mrs. LESLE KNOP, Dir., 12615 Parallel Pkwy., Kansas City, 66109. Tel: 913-721-1570.

Catholic Youth Organization—DAVE NICK, Athletic Dir., 5041 Reinhardt Dr., Mission, 66205. Tel: 913-384-7377.

Catholic Charities of Northeast Kansas, Inc.— See Institution section H.

Council for Catholic Charismatic Renewal—Rev. MARK MERTES.

Archdiocesan Council of Catholic Women (ACCW)—Rev. JOSEPH CRAMER, Spiritual Moderator.

Catholic Charities Foundation of Northeast Kansas—See Institution section H.

Catholic Neighborhood Outreach, Inc.— See Institution section H.

Communications—Mr. CARROLL MACKE, Dir., 12615 Parallel Pkwy., Kansas City, 66109. Tel: 913-721-1570.

Catholic Scouts—Rev. MARK BROSKI, O.S.B., Chap.

Holy Childhood Association—Rev. NORBERT LICKTEIG (Retired), 12615 Parallel Pkwy., Kansas City, 66109. Tel: 913-721-1570.

Hospitals—Rev. JEREMIAH L. SPENCER, Dir., 16 S. Iowa, Kansas City, 66103.

Kansas Catholic Conference—MICHAEL SCHUTTLOFFEL, Exec. Dir., 6301 Antioch, Shawnee Mission, 66202. Tel: 913-722-6633.

Legion of Mary—Rev. BRIAN KLINGELE, Spiritual Moderator, 514 E. 4th St., Garnett, 66032.

Missions—Rev. NORBERT LICKTEIG (Retired), 12615 Parallel Pkwy., Kansas City, 66109.

Newspaper "The Leaven"—Rev. MARK GOLDASICH, Editor, Mailing Address: 12615 Parallel Pkwy., Kansas City, 66109. Tel: 913-721-1570; Fax: 913-721-5276.

Nurses Association—Rev. JEREMIAH L. SPENCER, Dir., 16 S. Iowa, Kansas City, 66103.

Priests' Council—Rev. FRANK BURGER, Chm.

Pontifical Mission Societies in the United States—Rev. NORBERT LICKTEIG (Retired), 12615 Parallel Pkwy., Kansas City, 66109.

Schools—Dr. KATHLEEN O'HARA, Supt.; Mrs. KARLA LEIBHAM, Assoc. Supt.; Mrs. KAREN KROH, Asst. Supt. for Special Needs, 12615 Parallel Pkwy., Kansas City, 66109. Tel: 913-721-1570.

Victim Assistance Coordinator—Dr. DENNIS SCHEMMEL, Ph.D. Tel: 913-909-2740.

Vocations Office—Rev. MITCHEL ZIMMERMAN, Dir. Vocations. Co Directors Seminarians: Rev. Msgr. MICHAEL MULLEN; Rev. MITCHEL ZIMMERMAN, 12615 Parallel Pkwy., Kansas City, 66109. Tel: 913-721-1570.

CLERGY, PARISHES, MISSIONS AND PAROCHIAL SCHOOLS

CITY OF KANSAS CITY

(WYANDOTTE COUNTY)

1—CATHEDRAL OF ST. PETER THE APOSTLE (1907) Rev. Harold F. Schneider.
Office & Res.: 409 N. 15th St., 66102. Tel: 913-371-0840 (Business Office); 913-371-2345; Fax: 913-371-2345.
See Resurrection Catholic School at the Cathedral under Elementary Schools, Interparochial in the Institution Section
Catechesis/Religious Program—Students 7.

2—ALL SAINTS (2007) Revs. Daniel Gardner; Ciro Gonzalez.
229 S. 8th St., 66101.
Office: 229 S. 8th St., 66101. Tel: 913-371-1837; Fax: 913-621-2709. Email: allsaintsparish@sbcglobal.net.
Res.: 801 Vermont, 66101. Tel: 913-621-3521.
See Resurrection Catholic School at the Cathedral under Elementary Schools, Interparochial in the Institution Section
Catechesis/Religious Program—Marielena Aguilar, D.R.E. Students 287.

3—BLESSED SACRAMENT (1899) Rev. William McEvoy.
Res.: 2203 Parallel Ave., 66104. Tel: 913-321-1958; Fax: 913-321-1997.
Catechesis/Religious Program—1416 N. 62nd St., 66102. Tel: 913-299-9344; Fax: 913-321-1997. Franchiel Nyakatura, D.R.E.; Miguel Sanchez, C.R.E. Hispanic Ministry. Students 79.

4—CHRIST THE KING Rev. William McEvoy. In Res., Rev. Roger Schmit, O.S.B.
Res.: 3024 N. 53rd St., 66104. Tel: 913-287-8823; Fax: 913-287-8711. Web: www.ctkkckedulz.net.
School—(Grades PreK-8), 3027 N. 54th St., 66104. Tel: 913-287-8883; Fax: 913-287-7409. Web: www.ctkcatholicschool.org. Cathy Fithian, Prin. Lay Teachers 14; Students 287.
Catechesis/Religious Program—Franchiel Nyakatura, D.R.E. Students 23.

5—SS. CYRIL AND METHODIUS (1904), (Slovak), Merged with St. Joseph and St. Benedict, Kansas City to form All Saints, Kansas City.

6—HOLY FAMILY, (Slovenian), Revs. Peter Jaramillo, Admin.; John Melnick.
Res.: 274 Orchard Ave., 66101. Tel: 913-371-1561.
See Resurrection Catholic School at the Cathedral under Elementary Schools, Interparochial in the Institution Section

7—HOLY NAME (1876) Rev. Jeremiah L. Spencer.
Res.: 16 S. Iowa St., 66103. Tel: 913-236-9219; Fax: 913-403-8834. Email: holynamechurchkck@sbcglobal.net.
School—(Grades PreSchool-8), 1007 S.W. Blvd., 66103. Tel: 913-722-1032; Fax: 913-722-4175. Email: holyname@archkckcs.org. Web: www.archkckcs.org/holyname. Kathy Rhodes, Prin. Lay Teachers 11; Students 156.
Catechesis/Religious Program—Tel: 913-236-9219; Fax: 913-404-8834. Maureen McGill, D.R.E. Students 20.

8—ST. JOHN THE BAPTIST, (Croatian), Rev. Francis Horvat.
Res.: 708 N. Fourth St., 66101. Tel: 913-371-0627; Fax: 913-342-3324.
See Resurrection Catholic School at the Cathedral under Elementary Schools, Interparochial in the Institution Section

9—ST. JOHN THE EVANGELIST, Merged with Sacred Heart, Kansas City to form Our Lady of Unity, Kansas City.

10—ST. JOSEPH AND ST. BENEDICT, Merged with SS. Cyril and Methodius, Kansas City to form All Saints, Kansas City.

11—ST. MARY-ST. ANTHONY Revs. Peter Jaramillo; John Melnick.
Res.: 615 N. Seventh St., 66101. Tel: 913-371-1408; Fax: 913-371-4177. Email: smsakcks@sbcglobal.net.
Catechesis/Religious Program—Miguel Sanchez, D.R.E. Students 38.

12—OUR LADY AND ST. ROSE, Attended by Blessed Sacrament, Kansas City. Rev. William McEvoy.
Office: 2203 Parallel, 66101.
Church: 2300 N. Eighth St., 66101.
Catechesis/Religious Program—Tel: 913-321-1958; Fax: 913-321-1997. Students 18.

13—OUR LADY OF UNITY (2007) Rev. Kent O'Connor.
2910 Strong Ave., 66106.
Res.: 2910 Strong Ave., 66106. Tel: 913-677-4621; Fax: 913-677-4625. Email: oluparish@gmail.com.
See Our Lady of Unity School, Kansas City under Elementary Schools, Interparochial located in the Institution section.
Catechesis/Religious Program—Tel: 913-262-7022. Karen Robinson, D.R.E. Students 270.

14—ST. PATRICK'S (1873) Rev. Msgr. Michael Mullen; Rev. Jojaiah Mandagiri, M.S.F.S.
Res.: 1086 N. 94th St., 66112. Tel: 913-299-3370; Fax: 913-299-3422.
School—(Grades K-8), 1066 N. 94th, 66112. Tel: 913-299-8131; Fax: 913-299-2845. Mary Staley, Prin.; Rosemary Bratkovic, Librarian. Lay Teachers 20; Students 352.
Catechesis/Religious Program—Tel: 913-299-3728. Susan Buck, D.R.E. Students 200.

15—SACRED HEART, Merged with St. John the Evangelist, Kansas City to form Our Lady of Unity, Kansas City.

16—ST. THOMAS THE APOSTLE, Closed. For inquiries for parish records contact the chancery.

OUTSIDE THE CITY OF KANSAS CITY

ALMA, WABAUNSEE CO., HOLY FAMILY (1874) [CEM] Attended by St. Bernard, Wamego. Rev. John Pilcher.
Mailing Address: *c/o St. Bernard*, 1006 Eighth, Wamego, 66547.
Church: 1st & Kansas. Tel: 785-456-7869.
Catechesis/Religious Program—Tel: 785-765-2316. Dan Deiter, D.R.E. Students 27.

ATCHISON, ATCHISON CO.

1—ST. BENEDICT'S (1866) [JC] Rev. Gerard Senecal, O.S.B.
Res.: 1001 N. Second St., 66002. Tel: 913-367-0671; Fax: 913-367-0797.
Church: 1000 N. Second St., 66002. Tel: 913-360-8543.
See Atchison Catholic Elementary, Atchison under Elementary Schools, Interparochial located in the Institution section.
Catechesis/Religious Program—Tel: 913-367-3503. Students 38.
Mission—St. John the Baptist Doniphan, Doniphan Co. (Stational Church)

2—ST. JOSEPH'S (1949) [JC] Rev. Bertrand LaNoue, O.S.B.
Res.: 705 Spring Garden St., 66002. Tel: 913-367-4271.
See Atchison Catholic Elementary, Atchison under Elementary Schools, Interparochial located in the Institution section.
Catechesis/Religious Program—Tel: 913-367-3503; Fax: 913-367-0797. Students 67.

3—SACRED HEART (1892) [JC] Rev. Gerard Senecal, O.S.B.
Office: 1001 N. 2nd St., 66002. Tel: 913-367-0387; Fax: 913-367-0797.
Church: 1439 Kansas Ave., 66002.
See Atchison Catholic Elementary, Atchison under Elementary Schools, Interparochial located in the Institution section.
Catechesis/Religious Program—Rick Weber, D.R.E. Students 25.

AXTELL, MARSHALL CO., ST. MICHAEL'S Rev. Albert Hauser, O.S.B.
Mailing Address: 504 6th St., P.O. Box K, 66403. Tel: 785-736-2220; Fax: 785-736-2230.
School—(Grades 1-6), 605 Elm St., 66403. Tel: 785-736-2257. Todd Leonard, Prin. Lay Teachers 3; Students 35.
Catechesis/Religious Program—Tel: 785-736-2260. Janice Koch, D.R.E. Students 38.

BAILEYVILLE, NEMAHA CO., SACRED HEART (1912) [CEM] Rev. Edward J. Oen, C.PP.S.
Church: 357 Third St., Box 36, 66404. Tel: 785-336-6464.
Catechesis/Religious Program—Tel: 785-336-6415.

Debbie Waller, D.R.E. Students 108.

BALDWIN, DOUGLAS CO., ANNUNCIATION, [CEM] Attended by Assumption, Edgerton Rev. Brandon Farrar.
Church Mailing: P.O. Box 293, 66006. Tel: 785-594-3700.
Catechesis/Religious Program—Ginny Meinen, D.R.E. Students 95.

BASEHOR, LEAVENWORTH CO., HOLY ANGELS (1866) [CEM] Rev. Alfred Rockers.
Office: 15438 Leavenworth Rd., 66007. Tel: 913-724-1665. Email: holyangelscatholicchurch@hotmail.com.
Res.: 15440 Leavenworth Rd., 66007. Tel: 913-724-3122; Fax: 913-724-4148. Web: www.HolyAngelsBasehor.org.
Catechesis/Religious Program— Marilyn Hauschild, D.R.E. Students 208.

BEATTIE, MARSHALL CO., ST. MALACHY'S (1880) Attended by St. Gregory, Marysville. Rev. Anthony Putti (India).
Church: 1012 Main St., 66406. Tel: 785-353-2280.
Catechesis/Religious Program—Tel: 785-292-4576. Judy Studer, D.R.E. Students 21.

BENDENA, DONIPHAN CO., ST. BENEDICT (1855) [CEM] Attended by St. Joseph, Wathena. Rev. Roderic Giller, O.S.B.
Church & Mailing: 676 St. Benedict Rd., P.O. Box 128, 66008. Tel: 785-359-6725; Fax: 785-989-2313.
Catechesis/Religious Program—Tel: 785-359-6725. Amy Joyce, D.R.E. Students 41.

BLAINE, POTTAWATOMIE CO., ST. COLUMBKILLE, Attended by St. Vincent de Paul, Onaga. Rev. Arul Carasala.
Mailing Address: *c/o St. Vincent de Paul*, Box 396, Onaga, 66521.
Church: 66480.
Catechesis/Religious Program—Sally Olson, D.R.E. Students 26.

BLUE RAPIDS, MARSHALL CO., ST. MONICA - ST. ELIZABETH, Attended by Annunciation, Frankfort. Rev. James Shaughnessy.
Mailing Address: *c/o Annunciation*, 213 E. 5th St., Frankfort, 66427.
Catechesis/Religious Program—Brenda Hendrickson, D.R.E. Students 26.

BURLINGTON, COFFEY CO., ST. FRANCIS XAVIER (1871) [CEM] Rev. Marianand Mendem.
Res.: 214 Juniatta, 66839. Tel: 620-364-2416; Fax: 620-364-5671.
Catechesis/Religious Program—Tel: 316-364-5220. Leslie Mahoney, D.R.E. Students 103.

CORNING, NEMAHA CO., ST. PATRICK'S (1928) [CEM] Attended by St. Vincent de Paul, Onaga. Rev. Arul Carasala.
Mailing Address: 1387 56th Rd., 66417.
Catechesis/Religious Program—Ann Stallbaumer, D.R.E. Students 122.

DELIA, JACKSON CO., SACRED HEART OF JESUS, (Stational Church)

DONIPHAN, DONIPHAN CO., ST. JOHN'S, (Stational Church), *c/o St. Benedict's*, 1001 N. 2nd St., Atchison, 66002.

EASTON, LEAVENWORTH CO.

1—ST. JOSEPH-ST. LAWRENCE Revs. Phillip J. Winkelbauer, Admin.; Paul Dao Dou.
Res. & Church: 211 W. Riley St., P.O. Box 129, 66020. Tel: 913-773-5712; Fax: 913-773-8401. Web: home.catholicweb.com/triparish.
St. Joseph of the Valley Church: 31151 207th St., Leavenworth, 66048.
Catechesis/Religious Program—Tel: 913-773-8546. Rita Oatney, D.R.E.; Barbara Ernzen, D.R.E. Students 80.

2—ST. LAWRENCE (1878) [CEM] Consolidated with St. Joseph of the Valley, Leavenworth to form St. Joseph-St. Lawrence, Easton.

EDGERTON, JOHNSON CO., ASSUMPTION (1857) [CEM] Rev. Brandon Farrar.
Church: P.O. Box 74, 66021. Tel: 913-893-6272.
Catechesis/Religious Program—Tel: 913-893-6731; Fax: 913-893-6061. Barb Lewis, D.R.E. Students 28.

EFFINGHAM, ATCHISON CO., ST. ANN, [CEM] Rev. Benjamin Tremmel, O.S.B.
Res.: 301 Williams St., Box 54, 66023. Tel: 913-833-5660.
Catechesis/Religious Program—Julie Baker, D.R.E. Students 38.

EMERALD, ANDERSON CO., ST. PATRICK'S, Served by St. Francis Xavier, Burlington. Rev. Marianand Mendem.
Mailing Address: *c/o St. Francis Xavier*, 214 Juniatta, Burlington, 66839.
Church: 66095. Tel: 620-364-2416; Fax: 620-364-5671.
Catechesis/Religious Program—Cindy Rubick, D.R.E. Students 14.

EMMETT, POTTAWATOMIE CO., HOLY CROSS, Consolidated with Immaculate Conception, St. Marys.

EMPORIA, LYON CO.

1—ST. CATHERINE, [CEM] Attended by Didde Catholic Campus Center, Emporia. Rev. Raymond May Jr.
Church: 205 S. Lawrence St., 66801. Tel: 620-342-1368.
Catechesis/Religious Program—Tel: 620-342-1368. Sr. Aurora Villamar, D.R.E. Students 250.

2—SACRED HEART (1874) [CEM] Rev. Richard Warsnak.
Office: 101 Cottonwood St., 66801. Tel: 620-342-1061; Fax: 620-342-0450. Email: parish@sacredheartemporia.org. Web: www.sacredheartemporia.org.
School—(Grades K-6), 102 Cottonwood St., 66801. Tel: 620-343-7394. Email: school@sacredheartemporia.org. Web: www.shsemporia.eduk12.net. Theresa Lein, Prin.; Brelana DeLong, Librarian. Lay Teachers 7; Students 54.
Rectory—1811 Deerbrook Ln., 66801. Tel: 620-342-1708.
Catechesis/Religious Program—Tel: 620-342-1061. Linda DeDonder, D.R.E. Students 198.

ESKRIDGE, WABAUNSEE CO., ST. JOHN VIANNEY, Closed.

EUDORA, DOUGLAS CO., HOLY FAMILY, [CEM] Rev. Patric Riley.
Res.: 311 E. 9th St., 66025. Tel: 785-542-2788; Fax: 785-542-1908. Email: hfceudora@sunflower.com. Web: www.holyfamilyeudora.com.
Catechesis/Religious Program—Students 206.

FIDELITY, BROWN CO., ST. AUGUSTINE'S, [CEM] Attended by Sacred Heart, Sabetha. Rev. Balachandra Miriyala.
Church: 1948 Acorn Rd., Sabetha, 66534. Tel: 785-467-3130; Fax: 785-467-3817.
Catechesis/Religious Program—Tel: 785-284-3152. Denise Plattner, D.R.E. Students 16.

FLUSH, POTTAWATOMIE CO., ST. JOSEPH, Attended by St. Bernard, Wamego. Rev. John Pilcher. Tel: 785-456-7869.
Mailing Address: *c/o St. Bernard*, 1006 8th St., Wamego, 66547. Web: www.sbc-sjc.com. In Res., Rev. Carl Dekat (Retired). Tel: 785-494-8234.
Church: 8965 Flush Rd., Saint George, 66535.
Catechesis/Religious Program—Tel: 785-456-2431. Students 54.

FORT LEAVENWORTH, LEAVENWORTH CO., ST. IGNATIUS CHAPEL Rev. Joseph Hannon, Military Services Army Chap. (Major).
Mailing Address: 600 Thomas Ave., Unit 13, 66027. Tel: 913-684-8991; Fax: 913-684-8994.

FRANKFORT, MARSHALL CO., ANNUNCIATION (1880) [CEM] Rev. James Shaughnessy.
Office: Tel: 785-292-4462; Fax: 785-292-5095.
Res.: 213 E. Fifth St., 66427. Tel: 785-292-4170; Fax: 785-292-5095.
Catechesis/Religious Program—Tel: 785-292-4462. Linda Roeder, D.R.E.; Jan Stallbaumer, D.R.E. (Elementary). Students 70.

GARDNER, JOHNSON CO., SACRED HEART, [CEM] Rev. Joseph Cramer.
Office: 555 W. Main, 66030. Tel: 913-856-7781; Fax: 913-856-8893. Web: www.catholicgardnerks.com.
Res.: 122 E. Warren, 66030. Tel: 913-856-7780; 913-884-7788 (Parish Center).
Church: 155 W. Main, 66030.
Catechesis/Religious Program—Tel: 913-884-7788. Judy Orth, D.R.E. Students 345.

GARNETT, ANDERSON CO., HOLY ANGELS, [CEM] Rev. Brian Klingele.
Res.: 514 E. Fourth, 66032. Tel: 785-448-3846.
See St. Rose Philippine Duchesne School under Elementary Schools, Interparochial located in the Institution Section
Catechesis/Religious Program—Linda Huettenmueller, D.R.E. Students 35.

GREELEY, ANDERSON CO., ST. JOHN THE BAPTIST'S (1881) [CEM] Attended by Holy Angels, Garnett. Rev. Brian Klingele.
Mailing Address: P.O. Box 94, 66033.
Res.: 66033. Tel: 785-867-2170.
See St. Rose Philippine Duchesne School under Elementary Schools, Interparochial located in the Institution Section
Catechesis/Religious Program—Tel: 785-867-2821. Betty Gellhaus, D.R.E. Students 25.

HARTFORD, LYON CO., ST. MARY'S, Attended by St. Joseph's, Olpe. Rev. Anthony C. Williams.
Mailing Address: *c/o St. Joseph*, P.O. Box 165, Olpe, 66865.
Catechesis/Religious Program—Students 25.

HIAWATHA, BROWN CO., ST. ANN'S Rev. Gabriel Landis, O.S.B.
Res.: 800 Hiawatha Ave., 66434. Tel: 785-742-3010.
Catechesis/Religious Program— Brian Lillie, D.R.E.; Kim Lillie, D.R.E.; Kevin Hill, D.R.E.; Ellen Hill, D.R.E. Students 116.

HOLTON, JACKSON CO., ST. DOMINIC (1870) [CEM] Rev. William Bruning, Admin.
Res.: 416 Ohio Ave., 66436. Tel: 785-364-3262; Fax: 785-364-1499.
Catechesis/Religious Program—Tel: 785-364-3621. Students 146.
Mission—Our Lady of the Snows Shrine Potawatomie Reservation, Mayetta, Jackson Co. 66509.

HORTON, BROWN CO., ST. LEO'S, [CEM 3] Rev. Earl Dekat.
Res.: 1340 First Ave. E., 66439. Tel: 785-486-3971; Fax: 785-486-3971.
Catechesis/Religious Program—Ronda Smith, D.R.E. Students 85.

KELLY, NEMAHA CO., ST. BEDE (1901) [CEM] Attended by St. Vincent de Paul, Onaga. Rev. Arul Carasala. Tel: 785-336-3189.
Mailing Address: 7344 Drought St., 66538.
Catechesis/Religious Program—Colette Allen, D.R.E.; Kim Henry, D.R.E.; Angie Lueger, D.R.E. Students 74.

LACYGNE, LINN CO., OUR LADY OF LOURDES (1982) Attended by St. Philip Neri, Osawatomie. Rev. Reginald Saldanha.
Mailing Address: *c/o St. Philip Neri*, P.O. Box 4, Osawatomie, 66064. Tel: 913-755-2652.
Church: 819 N. 5th St., 66040.
Catechesis/Religious Program—Eric Victor, D.R.E. Students 20.

LANSING, LEAVENWORTH CO., ST. FRANCIS DE SALES, [JC] Rev. Michael C. Stubbs.
Res.: 119 Woodland Rd., 66043. Tel: 913-727-3768. Email: sfds@prodigy.net. Web: pages.prodigy.net/sfds.
Church: 900 Ida St., 66043. Tel: 913-727-3742; Fax: 913-727-1281.
Catechesis/Religious Program—Tel: 913-727-3742; Fax: 913-727-1281. Sr. Roberta O'Leary, D.R.E. Students 149.

LAPEER, DOUGLAS CO., ST. FRANCIS OF ASSISI, [CEM] Attended by St. Patrick, Osage City. Rev. Anthony Ouellette.
Mailing Address: *c/o St. Patrick*, 309 S. 6th St., Osage City, 66523.
Catechesis/Religious Program—Tel: 785-256-2752; Fax: 785-528-3381. Joy Schmidt, D.R.E.; Rock Turner, Youth Dir. Students 80.

LAWRENCE, DOUGLAS CO.

1—CORPUS CHRISTI (1981) [JC] Rev. Michael Mulvany.
Church & Office: 6001 Bob Billings Pkwy., 66049-5200. Tel: 785-843-6286; Fax: 785-865-3933. Web: www.corpuschristilks.org. Email: christi@corpuschristilks.org.
School—(Grades PreK-6) Tel: 785-331-3374. Mary Mattern, Prin. Lay Teachers 15; Students 222.
Catechesis/Religious Program—Nancy Nelson, D.R.E. Students 229.

2—ST. JOHN THE EVANGELIST, [CEM] Revs. John Schmeidler, O.F.M.Cap.; Earl Meyer, O.F.M.Cap.
Office: 1229 Vermont St., 66044. Tel: 785-843-0109; Fax: 785-749-5064. Email: churchoffice@saint-johns.net. Web: www.saint-johns.net.
School—(Grades PreK-6), 1208 Kentucky, 66044. Tel: 785-843-9511; Fax: 785-843-7143. Web: www.saint-johns.net/school. Patricia Newton, Prin.; Karen Rinke, Librarian. Religious Teachers 1; Lay Teachers 19; Students 290.
Catechesis/Religious Program—Students 262.

LEAVENWORTH, LEAVENWORTH CO.

1—ST. CASIMIR'S, (Polish), Merged with Sacred Heart, Leavenworth to form Sacred Heart-St. Casimir, Leavenworth.

2—IMMACULATE CONCEPTION (1855) Merged with St. Joseph's, Leavenworth to form Immaculate Conception-St. Joseph's, Leavenworth.

3—IMMACULATE CONCEPTION-ST. JOSEPH (2007), (Old Cathedral) Revs. David McEvoy, O.Carm.; Christopher Kulig, O.Carm, Parochial Vicar; Deacons Timothy McEvoy, Pastoral Assoc.; Terrance Mulcare, Pastoral Assoc.
Office & Mailing: 747 Osage, 66048. Tel: 913-682-3953; Fax: 913-682-5599. Web: www.icsj.org.
Immaculate Conception Church: 711 N. 5th St., 66048.
St. Joseph Church: 306 N. Broadway, 66048.
Rectory—300 N. Broadway, 66048. Tel: 913-682-0809.
See Xavier Elementary School, Leavenworth under Elementary Schools, Interparochial located in the Institution section.
Catechesis/Religious Program—Students 128.
Mission—Sacred Heart, Kickapoo Twp. 66048.

4—ST. JOSEPH OF THE VALLEY (1863) [CEM] Consolidated with St. Lawrence, Easton to form St. Joseph-St. Lawrence, Easton.

5—ST. JOSEPH'S (1858) Merged with Immaculate Conception, Leavenworth to form Immaculate Conception-St. Joseph's, Leavenworth.

6—SACRED HEART OF JESUS, [CEM] Merged with St. Casimir, Leavenworth to form Sacred Heart-St. Casimir, Leavenworth.

7—SACRED HEART-ST. CASIMIR (2007) Rev. Phillip J. Winkelbauer; Robert D. Zbylut, D.R.E.
Office: 521 Linn St., 66048. Tel: 913-772-2424. Web:

www.shsc.org.
Res.: 1401 Second Ave., 66048. Tel: 913-772-1787; Fax: 913-651-2150.
Sacred Heart Church: 1405 2nd Ave., 66048.
St. Casimir Church: 715 Pennsylvania, 66048.
See Xavier Elementary School, Leavenworth under Elementary Schools, Interparochial located in the Institution section.
Catechesis/Religious Program—Tel: 913-772-2424; Fax: 913-651-2150. Students 46.

LEAWOOD, JOHNSON CO.
1—CHURCH OF THE NATIVITY (1986) Rev. Francis Hund. In Res., Rev. Michael Hermes.
Church: 3800 W. 119th St., 66209. Tel: 913-491-5017; Fax: 913-491-5065. Email: info@kcnativity.org. Web: www.kcnativity.org.
School—(Grades K-8), 3700 W. 119th St., 66209. Tel: 913-338-4330; Fax: 913-338-2050. Email: nativityparishschool@kcnativity.org. Maureen Huppe, Prin.; Amy Sells, Librarian; Ann Anderson, Librarian. Lay Teachers 37; Students 465.
Catechesis/Religious Program—Peggy Schrick, D.R.E. Students 342.
Christian Formation Office—Tel: 913-338-4367; Fax: 913-338-0285.
2—CURÉ OF ARS (1959) Rev. Msgr. Charles McGlinn; Rev. Gregory Hammes.
Res.: 9401 Mission Rd., 66206. Tel: 913-649-1337; Fax: 913-649-1339.
School—(Grades K-8), 9403 Mission Rd., 66206. Tel: 913-648-2620; Fax: 913-648-3810. Web: www.archkckcs.org/curears. Marlene Rowe, Prin. Lay Teachers 35; Students 606.
Catechesis/Religious Program—Sandy Hawekotte, D.R.E. Students 610.
3—ST. MICHAEL THE ARCHANGEL (1999) Rev. William Porter. In Res., Rev. Gary Pennings.
Church: 14251 Nall Ave., Overland Park, 66223. Tel: 913-402-3900; Fax: 913-851-8220.
School—(Grades K-8), 14201 Nall Ave., 66223. Tel: 913-402-3950; Fax: 913-851-8221. Michael Cullinan, Prin. Lay Teachers 46; Students 654.
Catechesis/Religious Program—Denise Ogilvie, D.R.E. Students 1,300.

LENEXA, JOHNSON CO., HOLY TRINITY (1880) Revs. Thomas Dolezal; Patrick Sullivan, Parochial Vicar.
Office: 9150 Pflumm Rd., 66215. Tel: 913-888-2770; Fax: 913-888-4403. Email: holytrinity@htlenexa.org. Web: www.htlenexa.org.
School—(Grades K-8), 13600 W. 92nd St., 66215. Tel: 913-888-3250; Fax: 913-438-2572. Gary Lammers, Prin.; Kelly Kinnan, Librarian. Lay Teachers 36; Students 696.
Catechesis/Religious Program—Tel: 913-492-6068. Stuart Holland, D.R.E. Students 338.

LILLIS, MARSHALL CO., ST. JOSEPH'S, [CEM] Attended by Annunciation, Frankfort. Rev. James Shaughnessy. Tel: 785-292-4170.
Mailing Address: *c/o Annunciation*, 213 E. 5th St., Frankfort, 66427.
Catechesis/Religious Program—Students 10.

LOUISBURG, MIAMI CO., IMMACULATE CONCEPTION (1887) [CEM] Rev. Msgr. Robert Bergman.
Office: Box 118, 66053. Tel: 913-837-2295; Fax: 913-837-3309. Email: iccc@mokancomm.net.
Res.: 602 S. Elm, 66053.
Catechesis/Religious Program—Lynne Moore, D.R.E. Students 124.

MARYSVILLE, MARSHALL CO., ST. GREGORY'S (1862) [CEM] Rev. Anthony Putti (India).
Office: 207 N. 14th St., Ste. B, 66508. Tel: 785-562-3302. Email: parishoffice@stgregorychurch.org. Web: www.stgregorychurch.org.
Res.: 206 N. 14th, 66508. Tel: 785-562-2989; Fax: 785-562-4039.
School—(Grades PreK-6), 207 N. 14th, 66508. Tel: 785-562-2831; Fax: 785-562-4039. Barbara Hawkins, Prin. Lay Teachers 10; Students 142.
Catechesis/Religious Program—Rick McCormack, D.R.E. Students 115.

MAYETTA, JACKSON CO., ST. FRANCIS XAVIER, [CEM] Attended by St. Dominic, Holton. Rev. William Bruning, Admin.
Mailing Address: *c/o St. Dominic*, 416 Ohio Ave., Holton, 66436. Tel: 785-364-3262.
Catechesis/Religious Program—Tel: 785-966-2690. Barbara Berg, D.R.E. Students 55.

MERIDEN, JEFFERSON CO., ST. ALOYSIUS, [CEM] Attended by St. Theresa, Perry. Rev. Tom Aduri.
Res. & Mailing Address: P.O. Box 364, 66512. Tel: 785-484-3312; Fax: 785-484-3338. Email: stalsmer@yahoo.com.
Church: 615 Wyandotte, 66512. Tel: 785-597-5656.
Catechesis/Religious Program—Heather Roenne, D.R.E. (Grades PreK-5); Mary Naumann, D.R.E. (Grades 6-12). Students 135.

MISSION, JOHNSON CO., ST. PIUS X (1954) Rev. Kenneth W. Kelly.
Res.: 5601 Woodson Ave., 66202. Tel: 913-432-4855; Fax: 913-432-2086.
See John Paul II School under Elementary Schools, Interparochial located in the Institution Section
Catechesis/Religious Program— Deborah Alexander, D.R.E. Students 81.

MOONEY CREEK, JEFFERSON CO., CORPUS CHRISTI, [CEM] Attended by St. Joseph, Nortonville. Rev. John C. Reynolds.
Mailing Address: 18760 Rogers Rd., Atchison, 66002. Tel: 913-774-2385.
Catechesis/Religious Program— Charles Noll, D.R.E.; Sara Noll, D.R.E. Students 38.

MOUND CITY, LINN CO., SACRED HEART SHRINE TO ST. PHILIPPINE DUCHESNE (1942) [CEM] Attended by St. Philip Neri, Osawatomie. Rev. Reginald Saldanha.
Mailing Address: *c/o St. Philip Neri*, P.O. Box 4, Osawatomie, 66064. Tel: 913-755-2652.
Church Site: 729 W. Main St., 66056. Tel: 913-795-2724.
Catechesis/Religious Program—Melinda Dent, D.R.E. Students 35.

NORTONVILLE, JEFFERSON CO., ST. JOSEPH'S, [CEM] Rev. John C. Reynolds.
Church: 221 N. Sycamore St., 66060. Tel: 913-886-2030.
Catechesis/Religious Program—Shawn Gigstad, D.R.E. Students 67.

OLATHE, JOHNSON CO.
1—ST. PAUL (1868) [JC] Revs. John Torrez; Clement Cobb.
Office: 900 S. Honeysuckle, 66061. Tel: 913-764-0323; Fax: 913-764-1584. Web: www.stpaulolathe.org.
Res.: 840 Larkspur, 66061. Tel: 913-782-8999.
School—(Grades PreK-8), 920 W. Honeysuckle, 66061. Tel: 913-764-0619; Fax: 913-768-6040. Web: www.stpaulsolathe.com. Stephanie Hill, Prin.; Ana Escobar, Librarian. Lay Teachers 12; Students 125.
Catechesis/Religious Program—Tel: 913-764-0323, Ext. 119. Mary Mashek, C.R.E. Students 490.
2—PRINCE OF PEACE (1979) Revs. Frank Burger; Andrew Strobl, Parochial Vicar.
Office: Tel: 913-782-8864; Fax: 913-780-9658. Web: www.princeofpeace.info.
School—(Grades K-8), 16000 W. 143rd St., 66062. Tel: 913-764-0650; Fax: 913-393-0819. Email: school@princeofpeace.info. Jane Shriver, Prin.; Pam Schuetz, Librarian. Lay Teachers 36; Students 623.
Catechesis/Religious Program—Tel: 913-829-1147; Fax: 913-747-7747. Mark Schuetz, D.R.E. (Elementary); Polly Holmes, D.R.E. (Jr. High); Phyllis Mills, D.R.E. (High School). Students 1,528.

OLPE, LYON CO., ST. JOSEPH'S (1885) [CEM] Rev. Anthony C. Williams.
Res.: 306 Iowa, P.O. Box 165, 66865. Tel: 620-475-3326.
School—(Grades PreK-6) Tel: 620-475-3416. Theresa Lein, Prin. Lay Teachers 6; Students 45.
Catechesis/Religious Program—Rose Redeker, D.R.E. Students 94.

ONAGA, POTTAWATOMIE CO., ST. VINCENT DE PAUL Revs. Arul Carasala; Mathew Francis.
Res.: Box 396, 66521. Tel: 785-889-4896.
Church Site: 308 E. 3rd St.
Catechesis/Religious Program—Lisa Meyer, D.R.E. Students 73.

OSAGE CITY, OSAGE CO., ST. PATRICK, [CEM 3] Rev. Anthony Ouellette.
Mailing Address: 309 S. 6th St., 66523. Tel: 785-528-3424; Fax: 785-528-3381.
Catechesis/Religious Program—Tel: 785-528-3424. Michelle Ehrhart, D.R.E.; Rock Turner, Youth Dir. Students 39.

OSAWATOMIE, MIAMI CO., ST. PHILIP NERI (1889) Rev. Reginald Saldanha.
Church: 500 Parker Ave., 66064. Tel: 913-755-2652.
Catechesis/Religious Program—Brenda Minden, D.R.E. Students 45.
Chaplaincy—State Hospital for Mentally Ill, 66064.

OTTAWA, FRANKLIN CO., SACRED HEART, [CEM] Rev. William Fisher.
Res.: 408 S. Cedar St., 66067. Tel: 785-242-2174; Fax: 785-242-0820.
School—(Grades K-5), 426 S. Cedar, 66067. Tel: 785-242-4297; Fax: 785-242-0820. Diane Chapman, Prin.; Megan Dickinson, Librarian. Lay Teachers 8; Students 65.
Catechesis/Religious Program—Tel: 785-242-7258. Anne Madden, D.R.E. Students 120.

OVERLAND PARK, JOHNSON CO.
1—CHURCH OF THE ASCENSION (1991) Rev. Msgr. Thomas Tank; Rev. Matthew Schiffelbein, Parochial Vicar.
9510 W. 127th St., 66213. Tel: 913-681-3348; Fax: 913-681-3517. Email: ascensionchurch@kcascension.org. Web: www.kcascension.org.
School—(Grades K-8) Tel: 913-851-2531; Fax: 913-851-2518. Email: info@acseagles.org. Web: www.acseagles.org. Margaret Sachs, Prin. Lay Teachers 35; Students 620.
Catechesis/Religious Program—Tel: 913-681-7683; Fax: 913-681-7634. William O'Leary, D.R.E. Students 1,149.
2—HOLY CROSS (1968) Rev. Mark Mertes, Pastor. In Res., Rev. Thomas Kearns (Retired).
Office: 8311 W. 93rd St., 66212. Tel: 913-381-2755; Fax: 913-381-2766.
Res.: 8315 W. 93rd St., 66212. Tel: 913-341-5618; Fax: 913-381-2766. Email: churchoffice@holycrossopks.org. Web: www.holycrossopks.org.
School—(Grades K-8), 8101 W. 95th, 66212. Tel: 913-381-7408; Fax: 913-381-1312. Email: gradeschool@hccsmail.com. Mary Jo Gates, Prin. Lay Teachers 25; Students 326.
Catechesis/Religious Program—Tel: 913-381-2757. Julie Dresser, D.R.E. Students 287.
3—HOLY SPIRIT Revs. Richard Storey; Anthony Lickteig (Retired).
Office: 11300 W. 103rd St., 66214. Tel: 913-492-7318; Fax: 913-492-7370. Web: www.holyspiritcatholicchurch.org.
School—(Grades PreK-8) Tel: 913-492-2582; Fax: 913-492-9613. Web: www.hsschool.net. Michele Watson, Prin. Lay Teachers 28; Students 414.
Catechesis/Religious Program—Tel: 913-492-7382; Fax: 913-492-7370. Joyce Strain, D.R.E. Students 200.
4—QUEEN OF THE HOLY ROSARY (1944) Rev. Donald Cullen.
Res.: 7023 W. 71st St., 66204. Tel: 913-432-4616; Fax: 913-432-0620.
See John Paul II School under Elementary Schools, Interparochial located in the Institution Section
Catechesis/Religious Program—Tel: 913-722-2206; Fax: 913-432-0620. Denise Godinez, D.R.E. Students 187.

PAOLA, MIAMI CO., HOLY TRINITY, [CEM] Rev. Richard Halvorson.
Office: 400 S. East St., 66071. Tel: 913-557-2067; Fax: 913-557-2067. Email: htchurch@catholic.org. Web: www.holytrinity.4lpi.com.
School—(Grades K-8), 601 E. Chippewa, 66071. Tel: 913-294-3286; Fax: 913-294-5286. Eric White, Prin. Lay Teachers 9; Students 130.
Catechesis/Religious Program—Tel: 913-294-5492. Gina Sallman, D.R.E. Students 83.

PAXICO, WABAUNSEE CO., SACRED HEART (1884) [CEM], Served from St. Bernard, Wamego. Rev. John Pilcher.
Res.: *c/o St. Bernard*, 1006 W. 8th, Wamego, 66547. Tel: 785-456-7869.
Office: 22298 Newbury Rd., 66526. Tel: 785-636-5578; Fax: 785-636-5572.
Catechesis/Religious Program— Michelle Stuhlsatz, D.R.E. Students 85.

PERRY, JEFFERSON CO., ST. THERESA'S, [CEM 2] Rev. Tom Aduri.
Res.: P.O. Box 42, 66073. Tel: 785-597-5656.
Catechesis/Religious Program—Tel: 785-597-5138. Lisa Whitechair-Carver, D.R.E. Students 104.

PRAIRIE VILLAGE, JOHNSON CO., ST. ANN (1949) [CEM] Rev. Keith Lunsford.
Office: 7231 Mission Rd., 66208. Tel: 913-660-1182; Fax: 913-660-1194. Web: www.stannpv.org.
School—(Grades K-8), 7241 Mission Rd., 66208. Tel: 913-660-1101; Fax: 913-660-1132. Becky Akright, Prin.; Janet Postlewait, Librarian. Lay Teachers 26; Students 455.
Catechesis/Religious Program—Tel: 913-660-1195. Betsy Rushton, D.R.E. Students 167.

PURCELL, DONIPHAN CO., ST. MARY'S, [CEM] Attended by St. Leo's, Horton. Rev. Earl Dekat.
c/o St. Leo 1340 First Ave. E., Horton, 66439.
Church Site: 446 Hwy. 137, 66041. Tel: 785-486-3971; Fax: 785-486-3971.
Catechesis/Religious Program—Ronda Smith, D.R.E. Students 35.

READING, LYON CO., ASSUMPTION, Closed. For inquiries for parish records contact the chancery.

RICHMOND, FRANKLIN CO., ST. THERESE (1929) Attended by St. Boniface, Scipio. Rev. J. Gerald Williams, O.Carm. In Res., Rev. Clyde Ozminkowski, O.Carm. (Retired).
Res.: 32292 N.E. Norton Rd., Garnett, 66032. Tel: 785-835-6273; Fax: 785-835-6112.

ROELAND PARK, JOHNSON CO., ST. AGNES Revs. Gerardo Arano-Ponce; John H. Wisner.
Res.: 5250 Mission Rd., 66205. Tel: 913-262-2400; Fax: 913-262-1050. Email: stagnesparish@stagneskc.org. Web: www.stagneskc.org.
School—(Grades PreK-8), 5130 Mission Rd., 66205. Tel: 913-262-1686; Fax: 913-384-1567. Kim Hammers, Prin. Lay Teachers 32; Students 395.
Catechesis/Religious Program—Sarah Sullivan, D.R.E. Students 148.

ROSSVILLE, SHAWNEE CO., ST. STANISLAUS, Attended by Immaculate Conception, St. Marys. Rev. Benedict Gomes.
Mailing Address: P.O. Box 794, 66533.
Catechesis/Religious Program—Tel: 785-584-6612.

Connie Fischer, D.R.E. Students 143.
ST. BENEDICT, NEMAHA CO., ST. MARY'S (1859) [CEM] Attended by Sacred Heart, Baileyville. Rev. Edward J. Oen, C.PP.S.
Res.: 9208 Main St., 66538. Tel: 785-336-3174.
Catechesis/Religious Program—Tel: 785-336-3957. Diane Schmitz, D.R.E. (Elementary); Anita Schmitz, D.R.E. (Jr. High & High School). Students 79.
ST. LOUIS, ATCHISON CO., ST. LOUIS, [CEM] Attended by St. Ann's, Effingham. Rev. Benjamin Tremmel, O.S.B.
Mailing Address: 301 William, Box 54, Effingham, 66023. Tel: 913-833-5660.
Church: 11321 Morton Rd., Atchison, 66002. Tel: 913-847-6849.
Catechesis/Religious Program—Tel: 913-874-5191. Jennifer Miller, D.R.E. Students 41.
ST. MARYS, POTTAWATOMIE CO., IMMACULATE CONCEPTION (1849) [CEM] Rev. Benedict Gomes.
Res.: 208 W. Bertrand, 66536. Tel: 785-437-2408; Fax: 785-437-2938. Email: unity-general@oct.net.
Catechesis/Religious Program—Peggy Wehner, D.R.E. Students 183.
ST. PATRICK, ATCHISON CO., ST. PATRICK'S (1857) [CEM] Attended by St. Joseph. Rev. Bertrand LaNoue, O.S.B.
Mailing Address: *c/o St. Joseph*, 705 Spring Garden, Atchison, 66002.
Catechesis/Religious Program—Students 7.
SABETHA, NEMAHA CO., SACRED HEART Rev. Balachandra Miriyala.
Office: 1031 S. 12th, 66534. Tel: 785-284-0888; Fax: 785-284-2913. Email: sacredheartsabetha@sbcglobal.net.
Res.: 1042 S. 14th, 66534. Tel: 785-284-3068.
Catechesis/Religious Program—Christine Krebs, D.R.E. Students 133.
SCIPIO, ANDERSON CO., ST. BONIFACE (1858) [CEM] Revs. J. Gerald Williams, O.Carm.; Clyde Ozminkowski, O.Carm. (Retired).
Res.: 32292 N.E. Norton Rd., Garnett, 66032. Tel: 785-835-6273; Fax: 785-835-6112.
Catechesis/Religious Program—Nancy Hermreck, D.R.E. Students 60.
SCRANTON, OSAGE CO., ST. PATRICK'S, [CEM] Attended by St. Patrick's, Osage City. Rev. Anthony Ouellette.
Mailing Address: *c/o St. Patrick*, 309 S. 6th St., Osage City, 66523.
Catechesis/Religious Program—Tel: 785-793-2149. Joy Schmidt, D.R.E.; Rock Turner, Youth Dir. Students 65.
SENECA, NEMAHA CO., SS. PETER AND PAUL'S (1869) [CEM] Rev. Michael Koller.
Res.: 411 Pioneer, 66538. Tel: 785-336-2128; Fax: 785-336-2307. Email: sppchurch@carsoncomm.com.
School—(Grades PreK-8), 409 Elk St., 66538. Tel: 785-336-2727; Fax: 785-336-3817. Todd Leonard, Prin.; Rosalie Divelbiss, Librarian. Benedictine Sisters 1; Lay Teachers 12; Students 157.
Catechesis/Religious Program—Susan Stallbaumer, D.R.E. Students 151.
SHAWNEE, JOHNSON CO.
1—GOOD SHEPHERD (1973) Rev. James E. Ludwikoski.
Office: 12800 W. 75th St., 66216. Tel: 913-631-7116; Fax: 913-631-3539. Email: church@goodshepherdshawnee.org. Web: www.goodshepherdshawnee.org.
Res.: 12509 W. 73rd Ter., 66216. Tel: 913-631-5661.
Parish Center:—12800 W. 75th St., 66216. Tel: 913-631-7116; Fax: 913-631-3539.
School—(Grades K-8), 12800 W. 75th St., 66216. Tel: 913-631-0400; Fax: 913-631-3539. Ann Mc Guff, Prin.; Staci Rueter, Librarian. Lay Teachers 32; Students 413.
Catechesis/Religious Program—Tel: 913-563-5303. Deb Carmody, D.R.E. Students 220.
2—ST. JOSEPH Revs. Michael Hawken; John Riley.
Office: 5901 Flint St., 66203. Tel: 913-631-5983; Fax: 913-631-5973.
School—(Grades K-8), 11505 Johnson Dr., 66203. Tel: 913-631-7730; Fax: 913-631-3608. Web: www.archkckcs.org/stjoe. Sue Carter, Prin.; Jane Goodell, Librarian. Lay Teachers 35; Students 548.
Early Education Center—11525 Johnson Dr., 66203. Tel: 913-631-0004; Fax: 913-631-4362. (Day Care & Preschool) Auxiliary Teachers 31; Students 204.
Catechesis/Religious Program—Tel: 913-631-8923; Fax: 913-631-5973. Beth Bracken, D.R.E. Students 172.
3—SACRED HEART (1900) Rev. Craig Maxim.
Office & Mailing Address: 5501 Monticello Rd., 66226. Tel: 913-422-5700; Fax: 913-422-5723. Web: www.shoj.org.
School—(Grades PreK-8), 21801 Johnson Dr., 66218. Tel: 913-422-5520; Fax: 913-745-0290. Nick Antista, Prin. Lay Teachers 30; Students 392.
Catechesis/Religious Program—Tel: 913-422-5700; Fax: 913-422-5723. Tracie Kersey, D.R.E. (Elementary); Kyle Kuckelman, Youth Min. (Grades 6-12). Students 514.
SUMMERFIELD, MARSHALL CO., HOLY FAMILY, Attended by St. Michael's, Axtell. Rev. Albert Hauser, O.S.B.
Church & Mailing: P.O. Box 136, 66541. Tel: 785-736-2220.
Catechesis/Religious Program—Rosalie Meybrunn, D.R.E. Students 26.
TONGANOXIE, LEAVENWORTH CO., SACRED HEART, [JC] Rev. Mark Goldasich.
Office: 1100 West St., P.O. Box 539, 66086-0539. Tel: 913-369-2851; Fax: 913-369-2851 (call first). Email: catholicbetty@sunflower.com. Web: www.shcct.org.
Catechesis/Religious Program—Tel: 913-369-8697. Students 221.
TOPEKA, SHAWNEE CO.
1—ASSUMPTION (1862) Consolidated with Holy Name, Topeka to form Mater Dei, Topeka.
2—CHRIST THE KING (1977) Rev. Peter O'Sullivan.
Res.: 5972 S.W. 25th St., 66614. Tel: 785-273-0710; 785-273-0715; Fax: 785-273-4766.
Church: 5973 S.W. 25th St., 66614. Web: ctkparish.net.
School—(Grades K-8) Tel: 785-272-2220; Fax: 785-272-9255. Relynn Reynoso, Prin. Lay Teachers 22; Students 422.
Catechesis/Religious Program—Tel: 785-273-2917. Chris Henderson, D.R.E. Students 329.
3—HOLY NAME, Consolidated with Assumption, Topeka to form Mater Dei, Topeka.
4—ST. JOSEPH'S (1887) Consolidated with Sacred Heart, Topeka to form Sacred Heart-St. Joseph, Topeka.
5—MATER DEI (2006) Rev. Jon Hullinger. In Res., Rev. John F. Rossiter (Retired).
Office: 1114 W. 10th Ave., 66604. Tel: 785-232-7744; Fax: 785-232-2341. Web: www.materdeiparish.org.
School—Elementary, (Grades K-8), 934 S.W. Clay St., 66606. Tel: 785-233-1727; Fax: 785-233-1728. Andrea Hillebert, Prin. (Elementary & Middle School). Lay Teachers 21; Students 285.
Catechesis/Religious Program—Tel: 785-233-3727. Linda Mlynek, D.R.E. Students 75.
6—ST. MATTHEW (1955) Rev. Jerry Volz.
Res.: 2700 S.E. Virginia Ave., 66605. Tel: 785-232-5012; Fax: 785-232-0028. Web: www.saintmatthews.org.
School—(Grades K-8), 1000 S.E. 28th, 66605. Tel: 785-235-2188; Fax: 785-235-2207. Web: stmatthew.eduk12.net. Heather Huscher, Prin.; Debbie Otting, Librarian. Lay Teachers 12; Students 143.
Catechesis/Religious Program—Cheryl Byrne, Dir. Christian Formation. Students 225.
7—MOST PURE HEART OF MARY (1946) [JC] Revs. Brian Schieber; Shawn Tunink.
Office: 1800 S.W. Stone, 66604. Tel: 785-272-5590; Fax: 785-272-2801. Web: www.mphm.com.
Church: 3601 S.W. 17th St., 66604.
School—(Grades K-8), 1750 S.W. Stone, 66604. Tel: 785-272-4313; Fax: 785-272-1138. William Hund, Prin.; Judy Desetti, Librarian. Lay Teachers 29; Students 461.
Catechesis/Religious Program—Tel: 785-272-4727; Fax: 785-272-2801. Lucas Tappan, D.R.E. Students 106.
8—MOTHER TERESA OF CALCUTTA (2004) Revs. William Bruning; Christopher Rossman.
Mailing Address: 2014 N.W. 46th St., 66618. Tel: 785-286-2188; Fax: 785-286-2803. Email: mtcctopeka@att.net.
Res.: 4609 N.W. Kendall Dr., 66618. Tel: 785-286-2113.
Catechesis/Religious Program—Beth Mercer, D.R.E. Students 400.
9—OUR LADY OF GUADALUPE (1814), (Mexican), [CEM] Revs. John Cordes; Robert Conroy, M.C.
Office: 134 N.E. Lake St., 66616. Tel: 785-232-5088; Fax: 785-232-8834. Email: olg134@sbcglobal.net. Web: www.olg-parish.org.
Consolidated with Sacred Heart School and renamed Holy Family School. See Elementary Schools Interparochial located in the Institution section.
Catechesis/Religious Program—Tel: 785-233-4593. Sr. Rebecca Granado, D.R.E. Students 350.
10—SACRED HEART (1919) Consolidated with St. Joseph, Topeka to form Sacred Heart-St. Joseph, Topeka.
11—SACRED HEART-ST. JOSEPH (2006) Rev. Timothy A. Haberkorn.
Res. & Church: 227 S.W. VanBuren, 66603. Tel: 785-232-2863.
Church Site: *Sacred Heart*, 312 N.E. Freeman Ave., 66616.
See Holy Family School under Elementary Schools, Interparochial located in the Institution Section
Catechesis/Religious Program—Tel: 785-357-0293. Lori Price, D.R.E. Students 80.
TROY, DONIPHAN CO., ST. CHARLES, [CEM] Attended by St. Joseph's, Wathena. Rev. Roderic Giller, O.S.B.
Mailing Address: P.O. Box 456, 66087.
Church: 133 S. Park, P.O. Box 456, 66087. Tel: 785-985-2271.
Catechesis/Religious Program—Barb Greaser, D.R.E. Students 23.
VALLEY FALLS, JEFFERSON CO., ST. MARY'S IMMACULATE CONCEPTION, [CEM] Attended by St. Joseph's, Nortonville. Rev. John C. Reynolds.
Mailing Address: *c/o St Joseph Church*, 221 N. Sycamore, Nortonville, 66060. Tel: 913-886-2030.
Church: 905 Broadway, P.O. Box 176, 66088. Tel: 913-945-3544.
Catechesis/Religious Program—Tel: 785-945-3787; Fax: 785-945-4021. Sharon Lindteigen, D.R.E. Students 81.
WAMEGO, POTTAWATOMIE CO., ST. BERNARD'S (1898) [CEM] Rev. John Pilcher.
Res.: 1006 8th St., 66547. Tel: 785-456-7869; Fax: 785-456-7862. Email: saintb@wamego.net. Web: www.sbc-sjc.com.
Catechesis/Religious Program—Students 162.
WATERVILLE, MARSHALL CO., ST. MONICA'S, Closed. For inquiries see St. Monica - St. Elizabeth, Blue Rapids.
WATHENA, DONIPHAN CO., ST. JOSEPH'S (1869) [CEM] Rev. Roderic Giller, O.S.B.
Res.: 102 S. 7th St., P.O. Box 159, 66090. Tel: 785-989-4818; Fax: 785-989-2313.
Catechesis/Religious Program— Mary Kay Nold, D.R.E. Students 49.
WAVERLY, COFFEY CO., ST. JOSEPH'S, Attended by St. Francis Xavier, Burlington. Rev. Marianand Mendem.
Mailing Address: *c/o St. Francis Xavier*, 214 Juniatta, Burlington, 66839. Tel: 316-364-2416; Fax: 316-364-2416.
Catechesis/Religious Program—Tel: 785-733-2278. Michelle Lee, D.R.E. Students 29.
WEA, MIAMI CO., QUEEN OF THE HOLY ROSARY (Bucyrus P.O.) [CEM] Rev. Lawrence Albertson.
Office: 22705 Metcalf Rd., Bucyrus, 66013. Tel: 913-533-2462; Fax: 913-533-2460. Email: holyrosarywea@yahoo.com. Web: www.holyrosarywea.org.
School—(Grades PreK-8), 22705 Metcalf Rd., Bucyrus, 66013. Tel: 913-533-2462; Fax: 913-533-2460. Rebecca Sachen, Prin. Lay Teachers 25; Students 253.
Catechesis/Religious Program—Kathy O'Bryan, Adult Faith Formation & D.R.E. Students 220.
WESTPHALIA, ANDERSON CO., ST. TERESA'S, Attended by St. Francis Xavier, Burlington. Rev. Marianand Mendem.
Mailing Address: *c/o St. Francis Xavier*, 214 Juniatta, Burlington, 66839. Tel: 316-364-2416; Fax: 316-364-2416.
Catechesis/Religious Program—Tel: 785-489-2324. Jan Biggs, D.R.E. Students 42.
WETMORE, NEMAHA CO., ST. JAMES, Attended by Sacred Heart, Sabetha. Rev. Balachandra Miriyala.
Catechesis/Religious Program—Louise Tanking, D.R.E. Students 42.
WHEATON, POTTAWATOMIE CO., ST. MICHAEL'S, Closed. For inquiries for parish records contact the chancery.

Chaplains of Public Institutions

KANSAS CITY. *K.U. Medical Center and Chapel*, Holy Name Church, 66160. Rev. Jeremiah L. Spencer, Chap.
LAWRENCE. *Haskell Institute*. Rev. Duane F. Reinert, O.F.M.Cap. (Government Indian School)

Special Assignment:
Revs.—
Chontos, Joseph, 901 N. 52nd St., 66102.
Wait, Dennis, Sanctuary of Hope, 2601 Ridge Ave., 66102-4617.

On Duty Outside the Archdiocese:
Rev.—
Tillia, Marc, Bahia, Brazil

Further Studies:
Revs.—
Ansems, Bruce
McDonald, Richard

On Sabbatical:
Rev.—
Ziegler, Michael Tod

On Leave of Absence:
Rev.—
Henson, Darren

Retired:
Rev. Msgrs.—
Burger, Raymond, Olathe, KS

Krische, Vincent E., Lawrence, KS
Revs.—
Bertels, George, J.C.L., Leavenworth, KS
Blaufuss, Tony, Garnett, KS
Burger, Robert, Olathe, KS
Cooper, Leo, Olathe, KS
Cornish, Ron, Overland Park, KS
Dekat, Carl, St. George, KS
Dunnivan, John, Overland Park, KS
Hasenkamp, Robert, Lecompton, KS
Hayes, Edward, Leavenworth, KS
Hesse, Thomas, Lecompton, KS
Horvat, Matthew, Olathe, KS
Kearns, Thomas, Overland Park, KS
Klasinski, George, Topeka, KS
Krische, Francis, Topeka, KS
Lickteig, Anthony, Overland Park, KS
Lickteig, Norbert, Shawnee, KS
Livojevich, Ronald, Overland Park, KS
Melchior, Thomas, Topeka, KS
Pflumm, Robert, Overland Park, KS
Rossiter, John F., Topeka, KS
Schwalm, Donald, Minnesota
Seuferling, George, Meriden, KS
Sheeds, Gerald E., Kansas City, KS
Wempe, Richard C., Kansas City, KS

INSTITUTIONS LOCATED IN THE ARCHDIOCESE

[A] COLLEGES AND UNIVERSITIES

KANSAS CITY. *Donnelly College*, 608 N. 18th St., 66102. Tel: 913-621-6070; Fax: 913-621-8719. Email: admissions@donnelly.edu. Web: www.donnelly.edu. Steve LaNasa, Ph.D., Pres.; Kevin Kelley, Dean Instruction; Sr. Fran Cross, Registrar; Jane Ballagh de Tovar, Librarian. Benedictine Sisters 3; Sisters of Charity 1; Lay Teachers 57; Students 1,232.

ATCHISON. *Benedictine College*, 1020 N. 2nd St., 66002. Tel: 913-367-5340; Fax: 913-367-6566. Web: www.benedictine.edu. Stephen D. Minnis, J.D., Pres.; Ron Olinger, CFO; Pete Helgesen, Dean Enrollment Mgmt.; Kimberly C. Shankman, Ph.D., Dean of College; Joseph Wurtz, Dean of Students; Phil Baniewicz, Vice Pres. College Relations; Linda Henry, Vice Pres. Student Life; Kelly J. Vowels, Vice Pres. Advancement; Charlie Gartenmayer, Dir. Athletics; Raquel Huntington, Registrar; Revs. Denis Meade, O.S.B., J.C.D., Religious Studies Dept.; Meinrad Miller, O.S.B., Chap. & Religious Studies Dept.; Brendan Rolling, O.S.B., Dir. Mission & Min.; Blaine Schultz, O.S.B., Prof. Emeritus Music; Sisters Thomasita Homan, O.S.B., Prof. Emeritus English; Linda Herndon, O.S.B., Assoc. Dean & Dir. Academic Records; Angela Osterman, O.S.B., Health, Phys. Ed. & Recreation; Deborah Peters, O.S.B., English Dept.; Bro. Lawrence Bradford, O.S.B., Biology Dept.; Rev. Marion Charboneau, O.S.B., History Dept.; Steven Gromatzky, Librarian. Coed College of St. Benedict's & Mount St. Scholastica. Priests 5; Brothers 1; Benedictine Sisters 4; Lay Persons 75; Students 1,877.

LEAVENWORTH. *University of Saint Mary*, 4100 S. 4th St. Trafficway, 66048. Tel: 913-682-5151; Fax: 913-758-6140. Email: admis@stmary.edu. Web: www.stmary.edu. Sr. Diane Steele, S.C.L., Ph.D., Pres.; Dr. Bryan LeBeau, Academic Vice Pres.; Penelope Lonergan, Librarian. Sisters of Charity of Leavenworth 5; Lay Teachers 40; Students 1,502.

[B] HIGH SCHOOLS, INTERPAROCHIAL

KANSAS CITY. *Bishop Miege High School* (1958) 5041 Reinhardt Dr., Shawnee Mission, 66205. Tel: 913-262-2700; Fax: 913-262-3754. Email: lgerard@bishopmiege.com. Web: www.bishopmiege.com. Joseph Passantino, Ed.D., Pres.; Stanley Herbic, Prin.; Rev. Greg Hammes, Chap.; Judi Wollenziehn, Library Media Specialist. Sisters 1; Lay Teachers 55; Students 730.

Bishop Miege High School Foundation Tel: 913-262-2700; Fax: 913-262-3754.

Bishop Ward High School, 708 N. 18th St., 66102. Tel: 913-371-1201; Fax: 913-371-2145. Email: wardhigh@wardhigh.org. Web: www.wardhigh.org. Rev. Michael Hermes, Pres.; Mr. Dennis Dorr, Prin. Sisters of Charity of Leavenworth 1; Benedictines 1; Lay Teachers 25; Students 303.

Bishop Ward High School Foundation Tel: 913-371-1201; Fax: 913-371-2145.

LEAVENWORTH. *Immaculata High School*, 600 Shawnee St., 66048. Tel: 913-682-3900; Fax: 913-682-9036. Email: lcsadmin@archkckcs.org. Mrs. Helen Schwinn, Prin. Lay Teachers 15; Students 123.

LENEXA. *Saint James Academy* (2005) 24505 Prairie Star Pkwy., 66227. Tel: 913-254-4200; Fax: 913-254-4221. Web: www.sjakeepingfaith.org. Andy Tylicki, Prin. Sisters 2; Lay Teachers 38; Students 605.

OVERLAND PARK. *Saint Thomas Aquinas High School, Inc.* (1988) 11411 Pflumm Rd., 66215. Tel: 913-345-1411; Fax: 913-345-2319. Email: wpford@stasaints.net. Web: www.stasaints.net. Dr. William P. Ford, Pres.; Rev. Andrew Strobl, Chap.; Dr. Michael Sullivan, Prin.; Dr. Rebecca Heidlage, Prin.; Barbara Summerson, Librarian. Priests 1; Lay Teachers 79; Students 1,063.

St. Thomas Aquinas High School Foundation Tel: 913-345-1411; Fax: 913-345-2319.

TOPEKA. *Hayden High School* (1911) 401 Gage Blvd., 66606. Tel: 785-272-5210; Fax: 785-272-2975. Email: streckerr@haydenhigh.org. Web: www.haydenhigh.org. Mr. Rick Strecker, Pres.; Mr. Mark Madsen, Prin.; Karen Scheopner, Librarian. Lay Teachers 36; Students 527.

Hayden High School Foundation Tel: 785-272-5210; Fax: 785-272-2975.

[C] HIGH SCHOOLS, PRIVATE

ATCHISON. *Maur Hill - Mount Academy*, 1000 Green St., 66002. Tel: 913-367-5482; Fax: 913-367-5096. Email: admissions@mh-ma.com. Web: www.mh-ma.com. Mrs. Sharon Pruett, Prin.; Courtney Laurie, Librarian. Lay Teachers 20; Students 178.

[D] ELEMENTARY SCHOOLS, INTERPAROCHIAL

KANSAS CITY. *Our Lady of Unity School*, (Grades K-8), 2646 S. 34th, 66106. Tel: 913-262-7022; Fax: 913-262-7836. Email: luv2teach1@hotmail.com. Karen Davis, Prin. Lay Teachers 13; Students 148.

Resurrection Catholic School at the Cathedral, (Grades PreK-8), (Merger of Cathedral, St. John/Holy Family and All Saints Schools), 425 N. 15th St., 66102. Tel: 913-371-8101; Fax: 913-371-2151. Ann Connor, Prin.; Donna O'Connor, Librarian. Lay Teachers 18; Students 224.

ATCHISON. *Atchison Catholic Elementary*, (Grades K-8), 201 Division, 66002. Tel: 913-367-3503; Fax: 913-367-9324. Email: rweber@benedictine.edu. Rick Weber, Prin. Lay Teachers 18; Students 206.

GARNETT. *St. Rose Philippine Duchesne School*, (Grades K-8), 530 E. Fourth, 66032. Tel: 785-448-3423; Fax: 785-448-3164. Nancy Butters, Prin. Lay Teachers 7; Students 55.

LEAVENWORTH. *Xavier Elementary School*, (Grades PreK-8), Admin. Office, 320 N. Broadway, 66048. Tel: 913-682-7801; Fax: 913-682-6021. Email: lcsadmin@archkckcs.org. Scott Hulshoff, Prin. Consolidation of the following parishes: St. Casimir (PreK); Sacred Heart (Grades K-2); St. Joseph (Grades 6-8); and Immaculate Conception (Grades 3-5), St. Ignatius, St. Francis de Sales, St. Lawrence, and St. Joseph of the Valley. Religious Teachers 3; Lay Teachers 21; Students 319.

OVERLAND PARK. *John Paul II School*, (Grades PreK-8), 6915 W. 71st., 66204. Tel: 913-432-6350; Fax: 913-432-5081. Web: johnpaul2.eduk12.net. Susie English, Prin.; Jenny Yankovich, Librarian. Lay Teachers 18; Students 254.

TOPEKA. *Holy Family School*, (Grades PreSchool-8), (East): 1725 N.E. Seward Ave., 66616. Tel: 785-234-8980; Fax: 785-234-6778. (West): 210 N.E. Branner, 66616. Tel: 785-233-9171. Lee Schmidt, Prin.; Nancy Walker, Librarian. Religious 4; Lay Teachers 14; Students 254.

[E] ELEMENTARY AND SECONDARY SCHOOLS, PRIVATE

MAPLE HILL. *St. John Vianney Preparatory School* (2000) 14611A Waterman Crossing Rd., 66507. Tel: 785-256-4500; Fax: 785-256-4611. Email: school@stjohnv.com. Rev. James Gordon, F.S.S.P., Chap.; Judy Keyes, Prin. Priests 2; Lay Teachers 11; Students 81.

SHAWNEE. **Padre Pio Academy*, (Grades K-8), 5901 Flint, 66203. Tel: 913-268-3155. Email: info@padrepioacademy.org. Web: www.padrepioacademy.org. Joanne Hanson, Prin. Lay Teachers 6; Students 47.

[F] GENERAL HOSPITALS

KANSAS CITY. *Providence Medical Center*, 8929 Parallel Pkwy., 66112. Tel: 913-596-4000; Fax: 913-596-4098. Email: george.noonan@providence-health.org. Web: www.providence-health.org. Mr. Mike Dorsey, Pres. & CEO. An affiliate of the Sisters of Charity of Leavenworth Health System, Inc. Bed Capacity 400; Bassinets 16; Employees 1,285; Physicians 311; Patients Assisted Annually 116,380.

LEAVENWORTH. *Saint John Hospital*, 3500 S. 4th St., 66048. Tel: 913-680-6000; Fax: 913-680-6013. Mr. Bain Farris, Admin.; Mr. Mike Dorsey, Pres. & CEO. Physicians 164; Employees 266; Bassinets 8; Bed Capacity 76; Patients Assisted Annually 26,046.

TOPEKA. *St. Francis Health Center, Inc.*, 1700 W. 7th St., 66606. Tel: 785-295-8000; Fax: 785-295-5479. Mr. Grant Wicklund, Interim Pres. & CEO. Bed Capacity 378; Total Staff 1,940; Patients Assisted Annually 435,000.

[G] NURSING AND REST HOMES

OLATHE. *Villa St. Francis, Inc.* (1945) 16600 W. 126th St., 66062. Tel: 913-829-5201; Fax: 913-829-5399. Email: villa_st_francis@msn.com. Web: www.villastfrancis.com. Mr. John May, Admin. Owned and operated by Villa St. Francis, Inc.; Skilled nursing care; independent boarding - nuns & priests. Live-in Priest Chaplain 1; Sisters of Charity of Leavenworth 1; Bed Capacity 170; Total Staff 203; Total in Residence 155; Total Assisted 284.

OVERLAND PARK. *Villa St. Joseph Nursing Home*, 11901 Rosewood, 66209. Tel: 913-345-1745; Fax: 913-345-1346. Email: kensign@carondelet.com. Ms. Katharine Ensign, Admin. Bed Capacity 120; Total Staff 150; Total Assisted 268.

[H] CATHOLIC CHARITIES

KANSAS CITY. *Catholic Charities of Northeast Kansas, Inc.*, 2220 Central Ave., 66102. Tel: 913-433-2100; Fax: 913-621-4507. Email: info@ccsks.org. Web: www.CatholicCharitiesKS.org. Mrs. Jan Lewis, Pres. & CEO.

Emporia: 702 Commercial, Ste. 3A, Emporia, 66801. Tel: 620-343-2296; Fax: 620-343-9517.

Leavenworth: 716 N. 5th St., Leavenworth, 66048. Tel: 913-651-8060; Fax: 913-651-9350.

North Johnson County: 9806 W. 87th St., Overland Park, 66212. Tel: 913-384-6608; Fax: 913-384-6610.

South Johnson County: 333 E. Poplar, Olathe, 66061. Tel: 913-782-4077; Fax: 913-782-0983.

Topeka: 234 S. Kansas Blvd., Topeka, 66603. Tel: 785-233-6300; Fax: 785-233-7234. Email: ccs@cjnetworks.com.

Wyandotte County: 2220 Central Ave., 66102. Tel: 913-621-3445; Fax: 913-621-6586.

Catholic Charities Foundation of Northeast Kansas, 9720 W. 87th St., Overland Park, 66212. Tel: 913-433-2086.

Catholic Neighborhood Outreach, Inc. (2004) 2220 Central Ave., 66102. Tel: 913-648-6795.

Shalom House Men's Shelter (1971) 2100 N. 13th St., 66104. Tel: 913-321-2206.

St. Benedict's Early Education Center, 220 S. 9th St., 66101. Tel: 913-621-7403.

[I] MONASTERIES AND RESIDENCES FOR PRIESTS AND BROTHERS

ATCHISON. *St. Benedict's Abbey* (1857) 1020 N. 2nd St., 66002. Tel: 913-367-7853; Fax: 913-367-6230. Email: bsenecal@kansasmonks.org. Web: www.kansasmonks.org. Rt. Revs. Barnabas Senecal, O.S.B., Abbot; Ralph Koehler, O.S.B., Abbott (Retired); Owen Purcell, O.S.B., (Retired Abbot); Most Rev. Herbert Hermes, O.S.B. Bishop, Prelacy of Cristalandia; Very Rev. James R. Albers, O.S.B., Prior; Rev. Meinrad Miller, O.S.B., Subprior; Very Rev. Maurice C. Haefling, O.S.B., Business Mgr.; Revs. Jude Burbach, O.S.B. (Retired); Joaquim Carvalho, O.S.B.; Marion Charboneau, O.S.B.; Josias Dias da Costa, O.S.B.; Roderic Giller, O.S.B.; Matthew Habiger, O.S.B.; Albert Hauser, O.S.B.; Hugh Keefer, O.S.B.; Louis Kirby, O.S.B.; Gabriel Landis, O.S.B.; Bertrand LaNoue, O.S.B.; Daniel McCarthy, O.S.B.; Kieran McInerny, O.S.B.; Denis Meade, O.S.B., J.C.D.; Rodrigo Perissinotto, O.S.B.; Aaron Peters, O.S.B.; Donald Redmond, O.S.B (Retired); Brendan Rolling, O.S.B.; Duane Roy, O.S.B.; Michael Santa, O.S.B. (Retired); Blaine Schultz, O.S.B.; Gerard Senecal, O.S.B.; Ignatius Smith, O.S.B.; Paul Steingreaber, O.S.B.; Bruce Swift, O.S.B.; Benjamin Tremmel, O.S.B.; Camillus Wurtz, O.S.B. (Retired); Michael Zoellner, O.S.B.; Bros. Lawrence Bradford, O.S.B.; Martin Burkhard, O.S.B., (Retired); Dominic Cason, O.S.B.; Gregory Dulmes, O.S.B.; Haraldo Ferreira; Leven Harton; Robert Heiman, O.S.B.; Jeremy Heppler, O.S.B.; Kaio Maluf, O.S.B.; Diego Oliviera; John Peto, O.S.B.; Joseph Ryan, O.S.B.; Anthony Vorwerk, O.S.B.; Simon Baker, O.S.B. Bishops 1; Priests 35; Brothers 14.

LAWRENCE. *St. Conrad's Friary* (1990) (Capuchins), 745 Tennessee, 66044. Tel: 785-843-0188; Fax: 785-843-2214. Web: www.capuchins.org. Total in Residence 4. In Res. Revs. James Moster, O.F.M.Cap., Guardian; Earl Meyer, O.F.M.Cap.; Duane F. Reinert, O.F.M.Cap.; John Schmeidler, O.F.M.Cap.

[J] CONVENTS AND RESIDENCES FOR SISTERS

KANSAS CITY. *Little Sisters of the Lamb*, Provincial House: 36 S. Boeke St., 66101. Tel: 913-621-1727; Fax: 913-621-2823. Sr. Benedicte Bertrand, Prioress.

Servants of Mary, Ministers to the Sick, 800 N. 18th St., 66102. Tel: 913-371-3423; 913-621-1147; Fax: 913-621-4962. Email: mprovincialsdemkc@yahoo.com. Ministers to the Sick, Motherhouse of the Congregation for the United States.; Nurses, private duty, and visiting nursing in the homes. St. Peters Cathedral: Sisters Carmela Sanz, S.deM., Prov. Supr.; Claudia Rodriguez, S.deM., Local Supr.; Rev. Daniel Gardner, Chap. Professed 33.

ATCHISON. *Dooley Center, Inc.* (1993) 801 S. Eighth St., 66002. Tel: 913-360-6200; Fax: 913-360-6275. Benedictine Sisters of Mount St. Scholastica, Inc., Atchison, KS., Nursing care facility for the aged/infirm members of this religious community.

Mount St. Scholastica (1863) 801 S. 8th St., 66002. Tel: 913-360-6200; Fax: 913-360-6190. Email: anne@mountosb.org. Web: www.mountosb.org. Sr. Anne Shepard, O.S.B., Prioress. Motherhouse of the Sisters of St. Benedict. Professed Sisters 163; Novices 1; Postulants 1.

LEAVENWORTH. *Motherhouse of the Sisters of Charity of Leavenworth*, 4200 S. 4th St., 66048-5054. Tel: 913-758-6501; Fax: 913-682-2128. Email: smiller@scls.org. Web: www.scls.org. Sisters Joan Sue Miller, S.C.L., Community Dir.; Lucy Walter, S.C.L., Local Coord.; Rita Smith, S.C.L., Local Admin.; Rev. Michael Zoellner, O.S.B., Chap. Sisters 297; Total in Residence 103.

OVERLAND PARK. *Association of the Apostles of the Interior Life*, 10300 Cody St., 66214. Tel: 913-261-9692. Email: susanmarie.avi@gmail.com. Web: www.apostlesofil.org. Sr. Susan Pieper, Supr. Sisters 6.

[K] PRIVATE ASSOCIATIONS OF THE FAITHFUL

KANSAS CITY. *Society of St. Augustine - Public Association of the Faithful* (2000) 3008 S. 34th St., 66106. Tel: 913-384-3583. Email: pmjaramillo@msn.com. Web: www.angelfire.com/pa5/augustinian. Rev. Peter Jaramillo, Spiritual Moderator.

SHAWNEE MISSION. *Franciscan Servants of the Holy Family - Public Association of the Faithful* (2001) P.O. Box 7251, 66207. Tel: 816-729-7065. Email: srdoris@aol.com. Sr. Doris Engeman, Sister Servant. Mission: Helping families grow in holiness and unity.

[L] CAMPUS MINISTRY

EMPORIA. *Didde Catholic Campus Center, Emporia State University* Office: 1415 Merchant St., 66801. Tel: 620-343-6765; Fax: 620-343-6792. Email: dccc-emp@sbcglobal.net. Web: www.emporia.edu/dccc. 1102 Neosho St., 66801. Tel: 620-342-8727. Rev. Raymond May Jr., Chap. Total Staff 7.

LAWRENCE. *Haskell Catholic Campus Center* (1985) 2301 Barker Ave., 66046-4813. Tel: 785-842-2401. Rev. Duane F. Reinert, O.F.M.Cap., Chap.; Ms. Monica Olivera, Dir. Total Staff 1.

St. Lawrence Catholic Campus Center at the University of Kansas and Residence 1631 Crescent Rd., 66044. Tel: 785-843-0357; Fax: 785-842-2203. Email: slccc@st-lawrence.org. Web: www.st-lawrence.org. Rev. Steven Beseau, S.T.L., Dir. Total Staff 15.

St. Lawrence Center Foundation

TOPEKA. *Catholic Campus Center at Washburn University* 1633 S.W. Jewell, 66604. Tel: 785-233-2204; Fax: 785-233-2205. Email: wucatholic@hotmail.com. Web: www.wucatholic.com. Patti Lyon, Dir.

[M] MISCELLANEOUS LISTINGS

KANSAS CITY. *Catholic Care Campus, Inc. dba Santa Marta* (2004) 13800 W. 116th St., Olathe, 66215. Tel: 913-906-0990; Fax: 913-906-0911. Web: www.santamartaretirement.com. Total Assisted 235; Total Staff 163.

The Catholic Foundation of Northeast Kansas, 12615 Parallel, 66109. Tel: 913-647-0325; Fax: 913-647-0333. Email: stewdev@archkck.org. Web: www.archkck.org. (Formerly known as Archdiocesan Foundation)

Catholic Housing of Wyandotte County, 2 S. 14th St., 66101. Tel: 913-342-7580; Fax: 913-342-7581. Web: www.chwconline.com.

Duchesne Clinic (1989) 636 Tauromee, 66101. Tel: 913-321-2626; Fax: 913-321-2651. Email: caritas@kc.rr.com. Web: www.duchesneclinic.org. Amy Falk, Exec. Dir.; Gloria Guerra, Mgr. A division of Caritas Clinics, Inc., Leavenworth, KS. Total Staff 15; Total Patient Visits 10,416; Patients Assisted Annually 1,500.

**El Centro, Inc.*, 650 Minnesota Ave., 66101. Tel: 913-677-0100; Fax: 913-362-8513. Web: www.elcentroinc.com. Ms. Mary Lou Jaramillo, Pres. & CEO.

Academy for Children, 608 N. 18th St., 66102.

Academy for Children Child Care Center, 1330 S. 30th St., 66106. Tel: 913-677-1115; Fax: 913-677-7090.

Academy for Children, Choo Choo Child Care, 219 S. Mill St., 66101. Tel: 913-371-1744; Fax: 913-371-1866.

ECI Development, Inc., 2100 Metropolitan Ave., 66106. Tel: 913-677-1120; Fax: 913-677-0051.

El Centro, Inc. Argentine, 1333 S. 27th St., 66106. Tel: 913-677-0177; Fax: 913-362-8250.

El Centro, Inc. Family Center, Johnson County, 9525 Metcalf Ave., Overland Park, 66212. Tel: 913-381-2861; Fax: 913-381-2914.

St. Joseph Adoption Referral Service, Inc. (2001) 8160 Parallel Pkwy., Ste. 103, 66112. Tel: 913-299-5222; 800-752-1737; Fax: 913-299-5111. Email: apeacefulblessing@yahoo.com. Web: www.catholicadoption.info. Sisters Helene Lentz, Pres. & Contact Person; Dolora May, Dir. Staff 3; Total Assisted Annually 15.

Lay Employee's Retirement Plan of the Archdiocese of Kansas City in Kansas (1978) 12615 Parallel Pkwy., 66109. Tel: 913-721-1570; Fax: 913-721-2680. Email: kthomas@archkck.org. Web: www.archkck.org.

Priest's Retirement Plan of the Archdiocese of Kansas City in Kansas (1978) 12615 Parallel Pkwy., 66109. Tel: 912-721-1570; Fax: 912-721-2680. Email: kthomas@archkck.org. Web: www.archkck.org.

Providence Saint John Foundation, 8929 Parallel Pkwy., 66112. Tel: 913-596-4151; Fax: 913-596-3418. Email: karla.kimerer@providence-health.org. Web: www.providence-health.org.

ATCHISON. *The Maur Hill Prep School Endowment Association, Inc.*, 1000 Green St., 66002. Tel: 913-367-5482.

EASTON. *Shantivanam Archdiocesan House of Prayer* (1972) 22019 Meagher Rd., 66020. Tel: 913-773-8255. Total in Residence 4; Total Staff 5.

LEAVENWORTH. *Caritas Clinics, Inc.*, 818 N. 7th St., 66048. Tel: 913-651-8860; Fax: 913-682-4409. Email: caritas@kc.rr.com. Web: www.sclhs.org. Amy Falk, Exec. Dir. Sisters of Charity of Leavenworth., Administrative structure for St. Vincent Clinic, Leavenworth, Duchesne Clinic, Kansas City. Total Staff 5.

Catholic School Foundation of the Leavenworth Region, Inc., 320 N. Broadway, 66048. Tel: 913-682-7801; Fax: 913-682-6019. Email: lcsdev@archkckcs.org. Barbara Ferrara, Dir.

Saint Vincent Clinic (1986) 818 N. 7th St., 66048. Tel: 913-651-8860; Fax: 913-682-4409. Email: caritas@kc.rr.com. Web: www.sclhs.org. Amy Falk, Exec. Dir. (A division of Caritas Clinics, Inc., Leavenworth, KS.) Total Staff 5; Total Patients 654; Total Patient Visits 4,884.

LENEXA. *Sisters of Charity of Leavenworth Health System, Inc.*, 9801 Renner Blvd., Ste. 100, 66219. Tel: 913-895-2800; Fax: 913-895-2900. Web: www.sclhealthsystem.org. Mr. William M. Murray, Pres.

MAYETTA. *Our Lady of the Snows Catholic Shrine* Potawatomi Reservation, 66509. Mailing Address: c/o St. Dominic, 416 Ohio Ave., Holton, 66436. Tel: 785-364-3262; Fax: 785-364-1499. Attended by: St. Dominic, Holton, KS.

OVERLAND PARK. *Holy Family School of Faith Institute*, 11020 W. 101st St., 66214. Tel: 913-991-2424. Email: support@schooloffaith.com. Web: www.schooloffaith.com. Michael Scherschligt, Exec. Dir.

TOPEKA. *The Cursillo Movement of the Archdiocese of Kansas City in Kansas* (1974) 124 N.E. Chandler St., 66616. Tel: 785-235-9200. Email: wpickering@cox.net. Web: www.kccursillo.org. Bill Pickering, Lay Dir.

El Centro de Servicios Para Hispanos dba El Centro of Topeka (1971) 134 N.E. Lake, 66616. Tel: 785-232-8207; Fax: 785-232-8834. Email: lalo@elcentrooftopeka.org.

St. Francis Health Center Foundation, 1700 W. 7th St., 66606. Tel: 785-295-5356; Fax: 785-295-5479. Email: wsnodgrass@stfrancistopeka.org. Web: www.stfrancistopeka.org.

Marian Clinic, Inc., 1001 S.W. Garfield Ave., 66604. Tel: 785-233-8081; Fax: 785-233-8952. Email: btrepinski@marianclinic.org. Web: www.marianclinic.org. Mr. William M. Murray, Pres., SCLHS; Robert Trepinski, Exec. Dir. Affiliate of Sisters of Charity of Leavenworth Health System Total Patients 5,217.

RELIGIOUS INSTITUTES OF MEN REPRESENTED IN THE ARCHDIOCESE

For further details refer to the corresponding bracketed number in the Religious Institutes of Men or Women section.

[0200]—*Benedictine Monks* (St. Benedict's Abbey)—O.S.B.

[0200]—*Benedictine Monks* (Conception Abbey)—O.S.B.

[0470]—*The Capuchin Friars* (Holy Family)—O.F.M.Cap.

[0270]—*Carmelite Fathers & Brothers* (American Prov.)—O.Carm.

[1000]—*Congregation of the Passion*—C.P.

[]—*Missionaries of Charity*—M.C.

[1210]—*Missionaries of St. Charles-Scalabrinians*—C.S.

[]—*Missionaries of St. Francis de Sales*—M.S.F.S.

[1065]—*Priestly Fraternity of St. Peter*—F.S.S.P.

[]—*Society of Jesus*—S.J.

[0975]—*Society of Our Lady of the Most Holy Trinity*—S.O.L.T.

[1060]—*Society of the Precious Blood*—C.PP.S.

RELIGIOUS INSTITUTES OF WOMEN REPRESENTED IN THE ARCHDIOCESE

[0100]—*Adorers of the Blood of Christ*—A.S.C.

[0230]—*Benedictine Sisters of Pontifical Jurisdiction*—O.S.B.

[3832]—*Congregation of the Sisters of St. Joseph of Wichita*—C.S.J.

[0760]—*Daughters of Charity of St. Vincent de Paul*—D.C.

[1115]—*Dominican Sisters of Peace*—O.P.

[]—*Franciscan Servants of Holy Family (Public Association of the Faithful)*

[1430]—*Franciscan Sisters of Our Lady of Perpetual Help*—O.S.F.

[]—*Little Sisters of the Lamb*—O.P.

[2500]—*Medical Sisters of St. Joseph*—M.S.J.

[]—*Missioneras Guadalupanos de Cristo Rey*

[0480]—*Sisters of Charity of Leavenworth, Kansas*—S.C.L.

[0990]—*Sisters of Divine Providence*—C.D.P.

[2575]—*Sisters of Mercy of the Americas*—R.S.M.

[]—*Sisters of St. Anne*—C.S.S.A.

[]—*Sisters of St. Francis of the Martyr St. George*—F.S.G.M.

[]—*Sisters of St. Joseph* (Concordia, KS)—C.S.J.

[3840]—*Sisters of St. Joseph of Carondelet* (St. Louis, MO)—C.S.J.

[]—*Sisters of the Apostles of the Interior Life*—A.V.I.

[3600]—*Sisters, Servants of Mary*—S.M.

[4120-05]—*Ursuline Nuns, of the Congregation of Paris*—O.S.U.

ARCHDIOCESAN CEMETERIES

KANSAS CITY. *Gate of Heaven*

St. John's, Mount Calvary, Resurrection, St. Joseph's, Shawnee, and St. John, Lenexa

ATCHISON. *Mount Calvary*

LEAVENWORTH. *Mount Calvary*

LENEXA. *Holy Trinity*

TOPEKA. *Mount Calvary*

NECROLOGY

† Andalikiewicz, Charles, Louisburg, KS Immaculate Conception—Died April 2, 2009

† Finnerty, William, (Retired)—Died Oct. 7, 2009

An asterisk (*) denotes an organization that has established tax-exempt status directly with the IRS and is not covered by the USCCB Group Ruling.

Diocese of Kansas City-St. Joseph

(Dioecesis Kansanopolitanae Sancti Josephi)

Most Reverend

ROBERT W. FINN, D.D.

Bishop of Kansas City-St. Joseph; born April 2, 1953; ordained July 7, 1979; appointed Coadjutor Bishop of Kansas City-St. Joseph March 9, 2004; installed May 3, 2004; succeeded to See May 24, 2005. *Mailing Address: P.O. Box 419037, Kansas City, MO 64141-6037.*

Most Reverend

RAYMOND J. BOLAND, D.D.

Retired Bishop of Kansas City-St. Joseph; born February 8, 1932; ordained June 16, 1957; appointed Bishop of Birmingham February 2, 1988; consecrated March 25, 1988; appointed Bishop of Kansas City-St. Joseph June 22, 1993; installed September 9, 1993; retired May 24, 2005. *Mailing Address: P.O. Box 419037, Kansas City, MO 64141-6037.*

Square Miles 15,429.

Diocese of Kansas City Established September 10, 1880; Diocese of St. Joseph Established March 3, 1868.

Redesignated Diocese of Kansas City-St. Joseph August 29, 1956.

Comprises the Counties of Andrew, Atchison, Bates, Buchanan, Caldwell, Carroll, Cass, Clay, Clinton, Daviess, DeKalb, Gentry, Grundy, Harrison, Henry, Holt, Jackson, Johnson, Lafayette, Livingston, Mercer, Nodaway, Platte, Ray, St. Clair, Vernon and Worth in the State of Missouri.

For legal titles of parishes and diocesan institutions, consult the Chancery Office.

Chancery: P.O. Box 419037, Kansas City, MO 64141-6037. Tel: 816-756-1850; Fax: 816-756-0878.

Web: www.diocese-kcsj.org

STATISTICAL OVERVIEW

Personnel	
Bishop	1
Retired Bishops	1
Abbots	1
Priests: Diocesan Active in Diocese	65
Priests: Diocesan Active Outside Diocese	3
Priests: Diocesan in Foreign Missions	1
Priests: Retired, Sick or Absent	27
Number of Diocesan Priests	96
Religious Priests in Diocese	87
Total Priests in Diocese	183
Extern Priests in Diocese	5
Ordinations:	
Diocesan Priests	2
Religious Priests	1
Transitional Deacons	4
Permanent Deacons	3
Permanent Deacons in Diocese	58
Total Brothers	34
Total Sisters	242
Parishes	
Parishes	86
With Resident Pastor:	
Resident Diocesan Priests	60
Resident Religious Priests	18
Without Resident Pastor:	
Administered by Priests	6
Administered by Deacons	1
Administered by Lay People	1
Missions	12
Professional Ministry Personnel:	
Brothers	2
Sisters	3
Lay Ministers	93
Welfare	
Catholic Hospitals	3
Total Assisted	307,377
Homes for the Aged	11
Total Assisted	2,338
Day Care Centers	8
Total Assisted	1,663
Special Centers for Social Services	7
Total Assisted	223,949
Residential Care of Disabled	1
Total Assisted	32
Other Institutions	2
Total Assisted	173
Educational	
Seminaries, Diocesan	1
Students from This Diocese	6
Students from Other Diocese	110
Diocesan Students in Other Seminaries	21
Total Seminarians	27
Colleges and Universities	2
Total Students	5,609
High Schools, Diocesan and Parish	4
Total Students	1,209
High Schools, Private	4
Total Students	2,367
Elementary Schools, Diocesan and Parish	28
Total Students	7,766
Elementary Schools, Private	1
Total Students	320
Catechesis/Religious Education:	
High School Students	1,901
Elementary Students	6,672
Total Students under Catholic Instruction	25,871
Teachers in the Diocese:	
Priests	5
Brothers	5
Sisters	18
Lay Teachers	1,548
Vital Statistics	
Receptions into the Church:	
Infant Baptism Totals	2,159
Minor Baptism Totals	215
Adult Baptism Totals	242
Received into Full Communion	412
First Communions	2,510
Confirmations	1,823
Marriages:	
Catholic	440
Interfaith	341
Total Marriages	781
Deaths	1,109
Total Catholic Population	135,966
Total Population	1,489,890

Former Bishops—Most Revs. JOHN JOSEPH HOGAN, D.D., ord. April 10, 1852; cons. Bishop of St. Joseph, MO, Sept. 13, 1868; transferred to Kansas City, Sept. 10, 1880; died Feb. 21, 1913; THOMAS F. LILLIS, D.D., ord. Aug. 15, 1885; cons. Bishop of Leavenworth, Dec. 27, 1904; appt. Coadjutor to the Bishop of Kansas City, "cum jure successionis," March 14, 1910; Bishop of Kansas City, Feb. 21, 1913; appt. assistant at the Pontifical Throne, Aug. 19, 1935; died Dec. 29, 1938; EDWIN V. O'HARA, D.D., ord. June 10, 1905; appt. Bishop of Great Falls, MT, August 1, 1930; cons. Oct. 28, 1930; transferred to the See of Kansas City, April 15, 1939; made assistant at the Pontifical Throne, Jan. 5, 1949; appt. Archbishop "ad personam," June 29, 1954; died Sept. 11, 1956; His Eminence JOHN CARDINAL CODY, D.D., S.T.D., ord. Dec. 8, 1931; appt. Titular Bishop of Appollonia and Auxiliary Bishop of St. Louis, May 14, 1947; cons. July 2, 1947; promoted to coadjutor of St. Joseph "cum jure successionis," Jan. 27, 1954; appt. to Diocese of Kansas City-St. Joseph, Aug. 24, 1956; succeeded to See Sept. 11, 1956; transferred to Archdiocese of New Orleans as Coadjutor Archbishop "cum jure successionis," Aug. 10, 1961; acceded to the See of New Orleans, Nov. 8, 1964; transferred to the Archdiocese of Chicago, June 16, 1965; created Cardinal Priest, June 26, 1967; died April 25, 1982; Most Revs. CHARLES H. HELMSING, D.D., ord. June 10, 1933; appt. Titular Bishop of Axomis and Auxiliary Bishop of St. Louis, March 17, 1949; cons. April 19, 1949; appt. Bishop of Springfield-Cape Girardeau, Aug. 24, 1956; transferred to Diocese of Kansas City-St. Joseph, Jan. 27, 1962; retired Aug. 17, 1977; died Dec. 20, 1993; JOHN J. SULLIVAN, D.D., ord. Sept. 23, 1944; appt. Bishop of Grand Island, July 25, 1972; cons. Sept. 19, 1972; installed Grand Island, Sept. 21, 1972; appt. Bishop of Kansas City-St. Joseph, June 27, 1977; installed Aug. 17, 1977; retired Sept. 9, 1993; died Feb. 8, 2001; RAYMOND J. BOLAND, D.D., born Feb. 8, 1932; ord. June 16, 1957; appt. Bishop of Birmingham Feb. 2, 1988; cons. March 25, 1988; appt. Bishop of Kansas City-St. Joseph June 22, 1993; installed Sept. 9, 1993; retired May 24, 2005.

Former Bishops of Diocese of St. Joseph, MO—Most Revs. JOHN J. HOGAN, D.D., ord. April 10, 1852; appt. first Bishop of St. Joseph, March 3, 1868; consecrated Sept. 13, 1868; transferred to See of Kansas City, Sept. 10, 1880; administrator of St. Joseph until 1893; died Feb. 21, 1913; MAURICE F. BURKE, D.D., born May 5, 1844; ord. May 22, 1875; appt. first Bishop of Cheyenne, WY, Aug. 9, 1887; consecrated Oct. 28, 1887; transferred to St. Joseph, June 19, 1893; died March 17, 1923; FRANCIS GILFILLAN, D.D., born Feb. 16, 1872; ord. June 24, 1895; appt. Titular Bishop of Spigas and Coadjutor with the right of succession to the See of St. Joseph, July 8, 1922; consecrated Nov. 8, 1922; succeeded to the See of St. Joseph, March 17, 1923; died Jan. 13, 1933; CHARLES H. LEBLOND, D.D., ord. Oct. 27, 1909; appt. Bishop of St. Joseph, July 21, 1933; consecrated Sept. 21, 1933; resigned as Bishop of St. Joseph and appointed Titular Bishop of Orcistus, Aug. 24, 1956; died Dec. 30, 1958.

Vicar General—Rev. Msgr. A. ROBERT MURPHY.

Chancery—Mailing Address: P.O. Box 419037, Kansas City, 64141-6037. Tel: 816-756-1850; Fax: 816-756-0878. All official matters should be sent to this address.

Chancellor—Rev. Msgr. BRADLEY S. OFFUTT.

Vice Chancellors—CLAUDE SASSO, Ph.D.; PAULA MOSS.

Finance Officer—DAVID A. MALANOWSKI.

Tribunal—Mailing Address: P.O. Box 419037, Kansas City, 64141-6037. Tel: 816-756-1850.

Judicial Vicar and Tribunal Director—Rev. JOSEPH H. MATT, J.C.L.

Judge—Rev. C. MICHAEL COLEMAN, J.C.L.

Defender of the Bond—Sr. RITA KILLACKEY, O.S.B., J.C.L.

Procurators—DONETTA K. SHAW; ALLISON TOWNLEY.

Consultors—Revs. J. KENNETH CRIQUI; RONALD J. ELLIOTT; DONALD P. FARNAN; Rev. Msgr. ROBERT S. GREGORY; Rev. THOMAS W. HERMES; Rev. Msgrs. A. ROBERT MURPHY; BRADLEY S. OFFUTT; Rev. ALEXANDER B. SINCLAIR (Retired); Very Rev. JOHN J. VOWELLS, S.J.

Presbyteral Council—Rev. Msgr. ROBERT S. GREGORY, Chm.; Revs. MICHAEL E. TIERNEY, Vice Chm.; THOMAS LUDWIG, Sec. & Treas.; Rev. Msgr. JOHN E. LEITNER, Senior Priests (Retired); Revs. JUSTIN E. HOYE, Ordained Ten Years & Under; MARTIN DEMEULENAERE, O.S.B.; JOSEPH MILLER, C.PP.S.; Very Rev. JOHN J. VOWELLS, S.J.

Deans—Rev. TERRELL FINNELL, Deanery I; Rev. Msgr. ROBERT S. GREGORY, Deanery II; Revs. JOSEPH CISETTI, Deanery III; TERRY BRUCE, Deanery IV; CHARLES P. TOBIN, Deanery V; MICHAEL E. TIERNEY, Deanery VI; PHILIP EGAN, Deanery VII; J. KENNETH CRIQUI, Deanery VIII; THOMAS W. HERMES, Deanery IX; MARTIN DEMEULENAERE, O.S.B., Deanery X; JAMES TARANTO, Deanery XI; THOMAS LUDWIG, Deanery XII; CHARLES ROWE, Deanery XIII; THOMAS HAAKE, O.M.V., S.T.D., Deanery XIV.

Diocesan Offices and Directors

Archivist—Rev. C. MICHAEL COLEMAN, J.C.L.

Bishop Helmsing Institute—SCOTT MCKELLAR, Dir.

Bishop's Representative for Health Care Issues—Rev. THOMAS HAAKE, O.M.V., S.T.D.

Building Commission—JOSEPH W. HARRIS, Chm.; PAUL BOSCHI; FRANK COHALLA; BOB DRAKE; BERNARD J. GRAM; BERNARD JACQUINOT; ROBERT JONES; DAVE KOPEK; DAVID A. MALANOWSKI; Rev. Msgr. BRADLEY S. OFFUTT; WAYNE ROY; THOMAS STRAHAN; Deacon RALPH L. WEHNER.

Catholic Charities Foundation—ROZANNE PRATHER, Exec. Dir, 301 E. Armour Blvd., Ste. 620, Kansas City, 64111. Tel: 816-756-1850, Ext. 563; Fax: 816-756-5022.

Catholic Charities of Kansas City-St. Joseph, Inc.—1112 Broadway, Kansas City, 64105-1574. Tel: 816-221-4377; Fax: 816-221-9116. MICHAEL W. HALTERMAN, CEO; GEORGE HANS, CFO.

Catholic Charities Caritas Center—SUSAN ENGEL, Dir. Community Svcs., 301 E. Armour Blvd., Ste. 650, Kansas City, 64111. Tel: 816-931-9399; 877-931-9399, Ext. 111. Northwest Missouri Branch Office: Deacon MARTIN J. GOEDKEN, Assoc. Dir., 902 Edmond, Ste. 204, St. Joseph, 64501. Tel: 816-232-2885. Heart of Missouri Office: JUDY THOMPSON, Assoc. Dir., 118 W. Hout St., Ste. F, Warrensburg, 64093. Tel: 660-747-2241.

The "Catholic Key" Diocesan Newspaper—JACK SMITH, Editor.

Cemeteries (Catholic Cemeteries Associated, Diocese of Kansas City-St. Joseph, Inc.)—JOSEPH W. HARRIS, 7601 Blue Ridge, Kansas City, 64138. Cemeteries: Kansas City, Mt. Olivet; Mt. St. Mary; Resurrection; St. Joseph, Mt. Olivet.

Censor Librorum—Rev. Msgr. WILLIAM J. BLACET, P.A., J.C.L.

Communications—REBECCA SUMMERS, Dir.

Hispanic Ministry—JOANN ROA, Dir.

Religious Education—CLAUDE SASSO, Ph.D.

Central City School Fund Office—DAN RYAN, Exec. Dir.

Consecrated Life Office—Sr. CONNIE BOULCH, O.S.F., Dir.

Ecumenical Officer—Rt. Rev. GREGORY POLAN, O.S.B.

Family Life Office—Deacon KENNETH GREENE, Dir.

Finance Council—Most Rev. ROBERT W. FINN; VINCE ANCH; MICHAEL BROSNAHAN; MARYELLEN CONNOR; JOHN CROWE; JOHN DESTEFANO; Rev. Msgr. ROBERT S. GREGORY; JOHN HOULEHAN; THERESA HUPP; RON JURY; THOMAS A. MCCULLOUGH; ED MCSHANE; JERRY MEINERS; PAULA MOSS, Non-voting Member; MARGO SHEPARD; Rev. RONALD VERHAEGHE. Staff Representatives: MONICA ADAMS; DAVID A. MALANOWSKI.

Finance Office—DAVID A. MALANOWSKI, Finance Officer; MONICA ADAMS, Internal Auditor; DAVID GATELY, Mgr. Accounting Svcs.

Holy Childhood Association—Rev. ROBERT M. CAMERON, Dir.

Human Resources—RHONDA STUCINSKI, Dir.; ROSALEE WIETHARN, Benefits Coord.

Human Rights Office—JUDE HUNTZ, Dir.

Insurance Office—MONICA ADAMS, Risk Mgr.

Legion of Mary—Rev. DONALD E. STURM, Dir.

Ministry for Persons With Disabilities—JUDY SHUTE, Coord., 4101 E. 105th Ter., Kansas City, 64137. Tel: 816-765-9805.

Permanent Diaconate—Rev. Msgr. A. ROBERT MURPHY, Vicar for Deacons; Rev. JOSEPH I. CISETTI, Dir. Spiritual Formation; Deacon DWAYNE KATZER, Dir. Diaconate Formation; Rev. RONALD J. ELLIOTT, Dir. Deacons.

Priestly Life and Ministry—Rev. ERNEST P. DAVIS, Dir.

Priests' Pension Plan—Administrative Committee: Revs. WILLIAM A. BAUMAN, Chm. (Retired); ERNEST P. DAVIS; DONALD P. FARNAN; GAYLE LAPLANTE; DAVID A. MALANOWSKI; Rev. Msgr. A. ROBERT MURPHY; RHONDA STUCINSKI.

Priests' Purgatorial Society—Rev. ROBERT M. CAMERON, Sec.

Propagation of the Faith— (Pontifical Society for the Propagation of the Faith, Missionary Union of the Clergy and Religious, The Pontifical Society of St. Peter the Apostle for Native Clergy, and Daily World missionaries) Rev. ROBERT M. CAMERON, Dir.

Property Management—WAYNE ROY, Diocesan Property Mgr.; GERI SIRNA, Property Mgmt. Coord.; ROBERT JONES, A.I.A., Construction Mgr. Fax: 816-756-5572.

Respect Life Office—BILL FRANCIS, Dir.

Safe Environment Program-Protecting God's Children for Adults and Touching Safety for Children—MARY FRANCES HORTON, Coord. Email: mfhorton@kc.rr.com.

St. Vincent De Paul Particular Council—FRANK SCHLOEGEL, Moderator.

School Office—Mr. MARLON DE LA TORRE, Supt. Associate Superintendents: PAT BURBACH; SHERI DISHONG.

Stewardship and Development—PAULA MOSS, Dir.; GREG VRANICAR, Assoc. Dir.

Victim Assistance Coordinator—LESLIE GUILLOT.

Vocations—Rev. RICHARD ROCHA, Dir. Vocations.

Worship Office—Deacon RALPH L. WEHNER, Dir. & Master of Ceremonies; Sr. CLAUDETTE SCHIRATTI, R.S.M., Assoc. Dir.

Young Adult and Campus Ministry—CARRIE KAFKA, Dir.

Youth Office—JON SCHAFFHAUSEN, Dir.

CLERGY, PARISHES, MISSIONS AND PAROCHIAL SCHOOLS

KANSAS CITY

(JACKSON COUNTY)

1—CATHEDRAL OF IMMACULATE CONCEPTION (1882) Rev. Msgr. Robert S. Gregory, Rector; Deacon Stephen W. Livingston. In Res., Rev. Msgr. Bradley S. Offutt, Chancellor.
Res.: 416 W. 12th St., 64105. Tel: 816-842-0416; 816-842-0416, Ext. 112 Cathedral Social Services; Fax: 816-842-3849.

2—ST. ALOYSIUS (1886), (Hispanic), Closed. For inquiries for parish records contact Archives, Catholic Chancery.

3—ST. ANTHONY (1991) Rev. Joseph Cisetti; Deacon Michael Elsey.
Res.: 318 Benton Blvd., 64124. Tel: 816-231-5445; Fax: 816-231-5446.
Catechesis/Religious Program—Students 62.

4—ST. BERNADETTE'S (1958) Rev. David L. Holloway; Deacons Emory Corrigan, (Retired); David Townley.
Res.: 9020 E. 51st Ter., 64133. Tel: 816-356-3700; Fax: 816-737-3447. Email: stbernadette@kc.rr.com. Web: www.stbernadettekcmo.com.
Catechesis/Religious Program—Students 15.

5—BLESSED SACRAMENT, Closed. For inquiries for parish records contact Archives, Catholic Chancery.

6—ST. CATHERINE OF SIENA (1926) Rev. Robert Kerr; Deacon William Markey, (Retired); Veronica Ward, Pastoral Assoc. Tel: 816-761-5483, Ext. 110.
Res.: 4101 E. 105th Ter., 64137-1649. Tel: 816-761-5483; Fax: 816-761-8795. Web: www.saintcatherine.com.
Catechesis/Religious Program—Tel: 816-761-5483, Ext. 110.

7—ST. CHARLES BORROMEO (1947) Rev. Kenneth A. Riley; Deacons Jerry Williams; Frank Peak.
Res.: 900 N.E. Shady Lane Dr., 64118-4742. Tel: 816-436-0880; Fax: 816-436-0103. Web: www.stcharleskc.com.
School—804 N.E. Shady Lane Dr., Oakview, 64118. Tel: 816-436-1009; Fax: 816-436-6293. Lay Teachers 48; Students 460.
Catechesis/Religious Program—Students 183.

8—CHRIST THE KING (1938) Rev. Michael E. Tierney.
Res.: 8510 Wornall Rd., 64114. Tel: 816-363-4888; Fax: 816-363-2315. Web: www.ctkkcmo.org.
School—(Grades K-8), 425 W. 85th St., 64114. Tel: 816-363-1113; Fax: 816-363-2889. Lay Teachers 11; Students 106.
Preschool—Tel: 816-363-5313. (Infant/Toddler & Preschool) Lay Teachers 15; Students 54.

9—CHURCH OF THE HOLY MARTYRS (1991), (Vietnamese), Rev. Joseph Phan Trong Hanh.
Res.: 7801 Paseo, 64131. Tel: 816-333-3214; Fax: 816-523-8168. Email: hphan43@sbcglobal.net.
Catechesis/Religious Program—Tel: 816-333-5349. Students 300.

10—ST. ELIZABETH'S (1917) Revs. Terry Bruce; Christian Malewski; Deacons Donald Schmit; Mike McClean; Charles Cecil.
Office: 2 E. 75th St., 64114. Tel: 816-523-2405; Fax: 816-444-9858.
Rectory—7444 Main St., 64114. Tel: 816-523-2155.
School—14 W. 75th St., 64114. Tel: 816-523-7100; Fax: 816-523-2566. Email: info@stelizabethkc.org. Lay Teachers 34; Students 383.
Catechesis/Religious Program—Students 23.

11—ST. FRANCIS SERAPH, Closed. For inquiries for parish records contact St. Anthony, Kansas City.

12—ST. FRANCIS XAVIER (1909) Revs. Matthew D. Ruhl, S.J.; A. James Blumeyer, S.J.; Thomas G. Cwik, S.J.
Res.: 1001 E. 52nd St., 64110. Tel: 816-523-5115; Fax: 816-333-0082. Email: parish@sfx-kc.org. Web: www.sfx.kc.org.
Catechesis/Religious Program—Tel: 816-523-5115, Ext. 204. Students 75.

13—ST. GABRIEL ARCHANGEL (1956) Rev. Joseph M. Sharbel; Deacon Larry West.
Res.: 4737 N. Cleveland Ave., 64117. Tel: 816-453-1183; Fax: 816-453-6254. Web: saintgabrielparish.4lpi.com.
School—Tel: 816-453-4443. Lay Teachers 15; Students 190.
Early Childhood Learning Center—Tel: 816-453-4555. Lay Teachers 26; Students 110.
Catechesis/Religious Program—Tel: 816-453-1183, Ext. 217. Students 155.

14—GUARDIAN ANGELS (1909) Margaret Lima, Pastoral Admin.; Rev. Glenn R. Mueller, S.J.
Parish Office—1310 Westport Rd., 64111. Tel: 816-931-4351; Fax: 816-531-6396. Web: guardianangelsparish.ws.
School—Our Lady of the Angels School, 4232 Mercier, 64111. Tel: 816-931-1693; Fax: 816-931-6713. Email: mcdelac@yahoo.com.
School—Our Lady of Guadalupe School, 2310 Madison, 64108. Tel: 816-221-2539; Fax: 816-283-3315. Email: wdejbowman@everestkc.com. Web: olgkc.org.
Catechesis/Religious Program—Students 29.

15—HOLY CROSS (1902) Revs. Joseph I. Cisetti; Arnulfo Contreras (Mexico), Hispanic Ministry.
Res.: 5106 St. John Ave., 64123. Tel: 816-231-4845; Fax: 816-483-0900.
Catechesis/Religious Program—Students 127.

16—HOLY FAMILY (1980) Rev. Matthew Brumleve.
Res.: 919 N.E. 96th St., 64155. Tel: 816-436-9200; Fax: 816-436-8049. Web: www.holyfamily.com.
Catechesis/Religious Program—Students 261.

17—HOLY ROSARY (1891), (Italian), Rev. Joseph Vicentini, C.S. In Res., Revs. Patrick Murphy, C.S.; Jesus Olivares, C.S.
Res.: 911 Missouri Ave., 64106. Tel: 816-842-5440; Fax: 816-474-3806. Web: www.holyrosarykc.org.
Catechesis/Religious Program—Tel: 816-842-5440. Students 11.

18—HOLY TRINITY, Closed. For inquiries for parish records contact Our Lady of Peace, Kansas City.

19—ST. JAMES (1906) Rev. Garry Richmeier, C.PP.S.; Deacon Philip Ross Beaudoin, Pastoral Admin.
Res.: 3909 Harrison St., 64110. Tel: 816-561-8512; Fax: 816-561-7950. Email: stjames.kc@sbcglobal.net. Web: www.stjkc.org.
Catechesis/Religious Program—Students 29.

20—ST. JOHN FRANCIS REGIS (1964) Rev. Thomas Holder.
Res.: 8941 James A. Reed Rd., 64138. Tel: 816-761-1608; Fax: 816-966-1350. Email: cmelchior@regischurch.org. Web: www.regischurch.org.
School—Tel: 816-763-5837. Email: mbachkora@regischurch.org. Lay Teachers 20; Students 290.
Catechesis/Religious Program—Tel: 816-763-1366. Email: sduerr@regischurch.org. Students 64.

21—St. John the Baptist, Closed. For inquiries for parish records contact St. Anthony, Kansas City, Tel: 816-231-5445.

22—St. Louis (1919), (African American), Rev. Carlos Saligumba, S.O.L.T.
Church & Rectory: 5930 Swope Pkwy., 64130. Tel: 816-444-6535; Fax: 818-444-6027. Email: saint.louis@sbcglobal.net. Web: www.solt3.org.
Catechesis/Religious Program—Fax: 816-444-6027.

23—St. Matthew The Apostle (1964) Rev. Lloyd E. Opoka.
Res.: 8001 Longview Rd., 64134. Tel: 816-763-0208; Fax: 816-765-2617. Web: www.stmatthewapostle.com.
Catechesis/Religious Program—Students 32.

24—St. Michael Archangel, Closed. For inquiries for parish records contact Our Lady of Peace, Kansas City, Tel: 816-231-0953.

25—St. Monica (1995), (African American), Rev. Terrell Finnell; Deacons Kenneth Greene; Darwin Dupree.
Res.: 1616 The Paseo, 64108. Tel: 816-471-3696; Fax: 816-471-1111. Email: stmonica1616kc@hotmail.com. Web: stmonicacatholicchurch.net.
Catechesis/Religious Program—Maxine G. Myers, D.R.E.

26—Oratory of Old St. Patrick (1869), Traditional Latin Mass Community. Rev. William E. Avis, I.C.R.S.S., Rector.
Mailing Address: P.O. Box 414237, 64141-4237. 806 Cherry St., 64106. Tel: 816-931-5612. Email: oldstpatrick@institute-christ-king.org. Web: www.institute-christ-king.org/kansascity/.

27—Our Lady of Good Counsel (1866) Rev. Msgr. William J. Blacet.
Res.: 3934 Washington, 64111-2904. Tel: 816-561-0400; Fax: 816-561-1551.

28—Our Lady of Guadalupe, Closed. For inquiries for parish records contact Sacred Heart - Guadalupe, Kansas City, Tel: 816-842-6146.

29—Our Lady of Peace (1991), (Hispanic), Revs. Francisco Guianan, S.O.L.T.; Lauro Bejo, S.O.L.T.; Deacon Donald L. McCandless.
Res.: 1029 Bennington Ave., 64126-2299. Tel: 816-231-0953; Fax: 816-231-8911. Email: admin@olopkc.org. Web: www.olopkc.org.
See St. Stephen's Academy, Kansas City under Consolidated Schools located in the Institution section.
Catechesis/Religious Program—Students 97.

30—Our Lady of Perpetual Help (1878) Revs. Stephen Benden, C.Ss.R.; Terry McCloskey, C.Ss.R.; Robert Lindsey, C.Ss.R.; Bros. Charles Long, C.Ss.R.; John Matthys, C.Ss.R. In Res., Revs. Frank Kriski, C.Ss.R.; Edward Morgan, C.Ss.R.; Patrick Power, C.Ss.R.; John Willett, C.Ss.R.; Richard Quinn, C.Ss.R; Vincent Aggeler, C.Ss.R.
Res.: 3333 Broadway, 64111. Tel: 816-561-3771; Fax: 816-561-3704.
School—Cristo Rey, 211 W. Linwood Blvd., 64111. Tel: 816-457-6044; Fax: 816-457-6046. Mary Kallman, Prin. Sisters 8; Brothers 1; Lay Teachers 7; Students 300.
Catechesis/Religious Program—Students 82.

31—Our Lady of Sorrows (1890) Revs. Stephen Benden, C.Ss.R.; John Willett, C.Ss.R.; Edward Morgan, C.Ss.R.
Res.: 2552 Gillham Rd., 64108. Tel: 816-421-2112; Fax: 816-421-6037. Email: olos@kc.rr.com.
Catechesis/Religious Program—Students 4.

32—St. Patrick (1924) Rev. Shawn Ratigan; Deacon Michael Lewis, Pastoral Assoc.
1357 N.E. 42nd Ter., 64116. Tel: 816-453-5510; Fax: 816-453-4458. Email: stpat1@mindspring.com. Web: saintpatrick-kc.com.
Res.: 4505 NE Carolane, 64116.
School—1401 N.E. 42nd Ter., 64116. Tel: 816-453-0971; Fax: 816-453-5451. Web: stpatrickkc.com. Lay Teachers 10; Students 120.
Catechesis/Religious Program—Students 60.

33—St. Peter's (1925) Rev. Stephen M. Cook. In Res., Rev. Richard Rocha.
Res.: 6415 Holmes Rd., 64131. Tel: 816-363-2320; Fax: 816-363-8157. Web: www.stpetersparishkcmo.org.
School—6400 Charlotte St., 64131. Tel: 816-523-4899; Fax: 816-523-1248. Sisters 2; Lay Teachers 58; Students 585.
Catechesis/Religious Program—Students 10.

34—St. Raphael the Archangel (1963) Closed. For inquiries for parish records contact Archives, Catholic Chancery.

35—Sacred Heart-Guadalupe (1887), (Hispanic), Rev. Aloys Ebach, C.PP.S.
Res.: 907 Cesar Chavez Ave., 64108. Tel: 816-842-6146; Fax: 816-471-7540.
Catechesis/Religious Program—Students 39.

36—St. Stanislaus, Closed. For inquiries for parish records contact Our Lady of Peace, Kansas City, Tel: 816-231-0953.

37—St. Therese Little Flower (1925) Rev. Ernest P. Davis.
Res.: 5814 Euclid Ave., 64130. Tel: 816-444-5406; Fax: 816-444-9345. Email: edavis@sttheresekc.org. Web: www.sttheresekc.org.
Catechesis/Religious Program—Students 30.

38—St. Therese Parish (Kansas City North) (1949) Revs. Michael Roach; Duc Nguyen. In Res., Rev. Patrick Tobin (Retired).
Res.: 7207 Hwy. 9, N.W., 64152. Tel: 816-741-2800; Fax: 816-741-4959.
School—7277 Hwy. 9 N.W., 64152. Tel: 816-741-5400; Fax: 816-741-0533. Email: sttheresenorth@sttheresenorth.org. Web: www.sttheresenorth.org. Lay Teachers 41; Students 749.
Catechesis/Religious Program—Tel: 816-741-5400, Ext. 107. Students 689.

39—St. Thomas More (1964) Rev. Donald P. Farnan. In Res., Rev. Michael G. O'Connor.
Res.: 11822 Holmes St., 64131. Tel: 816-942-2492; Fax: 816-942-8803. Email: information@stmkc.com. Web: www.stmkc.com.
School—Tel: 816-942-5581; Fax: 816-941-2450. Web: www.stmcyclones.org. Lay Teachers 42; Students 615.
Catechesis/Religious Program—Students 61.

40—Visitation of the Blessed Virgin Mary (1909), (Irish), Rev. Patrick J. Rush.
Mailing Address: 5141 Main St., 64112. Tel: 816-753-7422; Fax: 816-753-5505. Email: vis@visitation.org. Web: www.visitation.org.
Res.: 2 E. 51st, 64112. Tel: 816-756-2663.
School—Tel: 816-531-6200; Fax: 816-531-8045. Lay Teachers 35; Students 545.
Catechesis/Religious Program—Students 72.

CITY OF ST. JOSEPH

(Buchanan County)
St. Joseph

1—Co-Cathedral of St. Joseph (1845) Rev. Joseph Powers; Deacon Steven Welsh.
Res.: 519 N. 10th St., 64501. Tel: 816-232-7763; Fax: 816-232-2460. Web: www.cathedralofstjoe.com.
School—518 N. 11th St., 65401. Tel: 816-232-8486; Fax: 816-232-8793. Web: www.cathedralschool-stjoseph.org. Lay Teachers 18; Students 241.
Catechesis/Religious Program—Students 38.

2—St. Francis Xavier (1890) Rev. Ronald L. Will, C.PP.S. In Res., Rev. William Walter.
Res.: 2618 Seneca St., 64507. Tel: 816-232-8449; Fax: 816-364-5174. Email: eford@sfxstjoe.com. Web: sfxstjoe.com.
School—2614 Seneca St., 64507. Tel: 816-232-4911; Fax: 816-364-0263. Lay Teachers 24; Students 359.
Catechesis/Religious Program—Students 106.

3—St. James (1900) Rev. Joseph Totton.
Res.: 5814 King Hill Ave., 64504. Tel: 816-238-0853; Fax: 816-238-1758.
School—120 Michigan Ave., 64504. Tel: 816-238-0281. Lay Teachers 9; Students 196.
Catechesis/Religious Program—Students 40.

4—St. Mary's (1891) Rev. Douglas Langner.
Res.: 1606 N. 2nd St., 64505. Tel: 816-279-1154; Fax: 816-279-4078. Email: stmarys91@yahoo.com.
Catechesis/Religious Program—Students 42.

5—Our Lady of Guadalupe (1982) Rev. Thomas K. Ludwig.
Church: 4503 Frederick Blvd., 64506. Tel: 816-232-2847; Fax: 816-232-0269. Web: www.olog.org.
Catechesis/Religious Program—Tel: 816-232-0112. Students 207.

6—St. Patrick (1869) Rev. Jorge Ramirez, Admin.
Office:—1813 S. 12th St., 64503. Tel: 816-279-2594; Fax: 816-232-7904. Email: stpatrickchurch@stjoelive.com. Web: www.parishesonline.com.
Catechesis/Religious Program—Students 25.

7—Queen of the Apostles, Closed. For inquiries for parish records contact the Co-Cathedral of St. Joseph, Kansas City, Tel: 816-232-7763.

OUTSIDE THE CITIES OF KANSAS CITY AND ST. JOSEPH

Belton, Cass Co., St. Sabina's (1944) Rev. Charles P. Tobin.
Res.: 700 Trevis Ave., 64012. Tel: 816-331-4713; Fax: 816-322-6196. Web: www.stsabina.org.
Catechesis/Religious Program—Students 213.

Bethany, Harrison Co., Blessed Sacrament (1945) [JC 2] Rev. Isaac True, O.S.B.
Res.: 1208 S. 25th St., 64424. Tel: 660-425-8160; Fax: 660-425-3109. Email: cathlc@grm.net. Web: www.blessedsacramentbethany.parishesonline.com.
Catechesis/Religious Program—Students 16.

Blue Springs, Jackson Co.
1—St. John La Lande (1938) Revs. Ronald J. Elliott; Angelo Bartulica.
Res.: 805 NW R.D. Mize Rd., 64015. Tel: 816-229-3378; Fax: 816-229-1362. Web: www.stjohnlalande.com.
School—801 NW R.D. Mize Rd., 64015. Tel: 816-228-5895; Fax: 816-228-8979. Lay Teachers 23; Students 288.
Catechesis/Religious Program—Students 185.

2—St. Robert Bellarmine (1983) Rev. James E. Healy.
Res.: 4112 S.W. 9th St., 64015. Tel: 816-229-5168; Fax: 816-229-3981. Web: www.robertbellarmine.org.
Catechesis/Religious Program—Students 225.

Buckner, Jackson Co., Church of the Santa Fe (1965) Rev. Msgr. Ralph L. Kaiser.
231 Sibley St., 64016.
Res.: P.O. Box 317, 64016. Tel: 816-650-9341.
Catechesis/Religious Program—Students 26.

Butler, Bates Co., St. Patrick's (1882) Rev. John J. Bolderson.
Res.: 400 W. Nursery St., 64730. Tel: 660-679-4482.
Catechesis/Religious Program—Students 50.

Cameron, Clinton Co., St. Munchin (1867), (German—Irish), [CEM 2] Rev. Paul Turner.
Res.: 301 N. Cedar St., 64429. Tel: 816-632-2768; Fax: 816-632-7997. Email: munchin@cameron.net. Web: www.munchin.net.
Catechesis/Religious Program—Tel: 816-632-6276. Students 101.
Mission—St. Aloysius 301 S. Water, Maysville, DeKalb Co. 64469.

Carrollton, Carroll Co., St. Mary's (1867) [CEM] Rev. J. Kenneth Criqui.
Res.: 211 E. Shanklin St., 64633. Tel: 660-542-1259. Email: stmary2007@sbcglobal.net. Web: www.carolnet.com/smcp.
Catechesis/Religious Program—Students 84.
Mission—Sacred Heart 403 S. Walnut, Norborne, Carroll Co. 64668. Tel: 660-593-3536.

Chillicothe, Livingston Co., St. Columban (1857) [CEM 2] Revs. Thomas W. Hermes; Michael Diochi; Deacons Lawrence Schneider, (Retired); Jerry Davis, (Retired).
Res.: 1111 Trenton St., 64601-1499. Tel: 660-646-0190; Fax: 660-646-1802. Web: www.stcolumbanonline.org.
School—Bishop Hogan Memorial School, 1114 Trenton St., 64601. Tel: 660-646-0705. Web: www.bishophogan.org. Lay Teachers 8; Students 55.
Catechesis/Religious Program—Students 158.

Clinton, Henry Co., Holy Rosary (1875) Rev. Philip Egan; Deacon Steven Carter.
Res.: 610 S. 4th St., 64735. Tel: 660-885-4523; Fax: 660-885-3959.
School—400 E. Wilson, 64735. Tel: 660-885-4412. Lay Teachers 10; Students 112.
Catechesis/Religious Program—Students 67.
Mission—St. Catherine's Hwy. WW, Osceola, St. Clair Co. 64776. Tel: 417-646-2217.
Mission—St. Bartholomew 504 E. Benton, Windsor, Henry Co. 65360. Tel: 660-647-2613.

Conception Junction, Nodaway Co., St. Columba (1860) [CEM] Rev. Allan Stetz, O.S.B.; Deacon Martin Goedken.
Res.: 311 Roosevelt, P.O. Box 127, 64434. Tel: 660-944-2301.
Catechesis/Religious Program—Students 129.

Easton, Buchanan Co., St. Joseph's (1830), (Irish—German), [CEM] Rev. M. Jeffrey Stephan.
Rectory—107 N. Shortridge, P.O. Box 197, 64443. Tel: 816-473-2011. Email: stjosephchurch@centurytel.net.
Catechesis/Religious Program—Students 21.

Excelsior Springs, Clay Co., St. Ann (1889) Rev. Msgr. William Caldwell.
Res.: 1503 Tracy, 64024. Tel: 816-630-6659.
Catechesis/Religious Program—Tel: 816-630-5874; 816-630-7790. Connie Davis, D.R.E. (Elementary); Chris Sanders, Youth Min. Students 171.

Gladstone, Clay Co., St. Andrew the Apostle (1964) Rev. Msgr. Joseph A. Mancuso; Rev. Thomas Haake, O.M.V.
Res.: 6415 N.E. Antioch Rd., 64119. Tel: 816-453-2089; Fax: 816-453-2442. Email: spalmarine@sataps.com. Web: www.sataps.com.
School—(Grades PreK-8) Tel: 816-454-7377; Fax: 816-453-6393. Email: wwinkler@sataps.com. Sisters 1; Lay Teachers 11; Students 258.
Catechesis/Religious Program—Tel: 816-454-7377, Ext. 107. Students 124.

Grandview, Jackson Co., Coronation of Our Lady (1958) Rev. Alexander B. Sinclair, Temporary Admin. (Retired); Deacon Kenneth Fuenfhausen.
Res.: 13000 Bennington Ave., 64030. Tel: 816-761-8811; Fax: 816-761-8812. Email: coronation@kc.rr.com. Web: www.coronationofourlady.com.
Catechesis/Religious Program—Students 84.

Hamilton, Caldwell Co., Sacred Heart (1921) Rev. Robert Rost.
Res.: P.O. Box 188, 64644-0188. Tel: 816-583-4413. Email: shchurch@cameron.net.
Catechesis/Religious Program—Students 32.
Mission—Mary Immaculate 409 S. Main, Gallatin, Daviess Co. 64640. Tel: 816-583-4413. Rev. Robert Kerr.

HARRISONVILLE, CASS CO., OUR LADY OF LOURDES (1941) Rev. Paw Tun Lwin; Deacon Ronald F. Strong.
Res.: 2700 E. Mechanic, P.O. Box 247, 64701. Tel: 816-380-5744; Fax: 816-380-5132. Email: ollmclark@embarqmail.com. Web: www.ololharrisonville.parishesonline.com.
Catechesis/Religious Program—Students 197.

HIGGINSVILLE, LAFAYETTE CO., ST. MARY'S (1879), (German—Irish), [CEM] Rev. Thomas J. D. Hawkins.
Res.: 401 W. Broadway, 64037. Tel: 660-584-3038. Email: smhigg@ctcis.net.
Catechesis/Religious Program—Students 49.

HIRLINGEN, BUCHANAN CO., SEVEN DOLORS (1872), (German), [CEM] [JC] Rev. Donald E. Sturm.
Res.: 2830 Angelique, 64501. Tel: 816-671-1510.
Catechesis/Religious Program—Students 6.

HOLDEN, JOHNSON CO., ST. PATRICK'S (1869) [CEM 2] Rev. Peter M. Savidge.
Res.: 703 S. Olive St., 64040-1443. Tel: 816-850-4999. Email: stpatsholden@embarqmail.com.
Catechesis/Religious Program—Kathleen Bryant, D.R.E. Students 41.
Mission—Holy Trinity 1372 N.W. Graham Rd., Urich, Henry Co. 64788. Tel: 660-638-4715; Fax: 816-773-2674.

INDEPENDENCE, JACKSON CO.

1—ST. ANN'S (1917) Rev. Bernard E. Branson; Deacon James Reynolds III.
Res.: 10113 E. Lexington Ave., 64053. Tel: 816-252-1160; Fax: 816-252-1161. Email: saintanns64053@yahoo.com.
Catechesis/Religious Program—Students 5.

2—ST. JOSEPH THE WORKER (1976) Rev. Joseph H. Matt.
Res.: 2102 N. Blue Mills Rd., 64058. Tel: 816-796-6877; Fax: 816-796-6876. Email: stjosephtheworker@hotmail.com. Web: www.sjtw.catholicweb.com.
Catechesis/Religious Program—Barbara Ganz, D.R.E. Students 41.

3—ST. MARK (1965) Rev. James Taranto.
Res.: 3736 S. Lees Summit Rd., 64055. Tel: 816-373-2600; Fax: 816-373-3816. Web: www.stmarksparish.com.
Catechesis/Religious Program—Joyce Arthur, D.R.E. Students 476.

4—ST. MARY'S (1823) [CEM] Rev. Matthew Rotert; Deacon Thomas D. Powell.
Res.: 600 N. Liberty St., 64050. Tel: 816-252-0121; Fax: 816-461-8153. Web: saintmarysparish.org.
Catechesis/Religious Program—Email: debbie@saintmarysparish.org. Students 68.

5—NATIVITY OF MARY PARISH (1938) Rev. Robert Stone.
10017 E. 36th Ter., 64052.
Res.: 10015 E. 36th Ter., 64052. Tel: 816-353-2184; Fax: 816-358-4155. Email: parish@nativityofmary.org. Web: www.nativityofmary.org.
School—(Grades PreK-8), 10021 E. 36th Ter., 64052. Tel: 816-353-0284; Fax: 816-356-0286. Email: school@nativityofmary.org. Lay Teachers 28; Students 277.
Catechesis/Religious Program—Students 31.

KEARNEY, CLAY CO., CHURCH OF THE ANNUNCIATION (1980) Rev. John Wolf, C.PP.S.
Mailing Address: 701 N. Jefferson, P.O. Box 599, 64060-0599. Tel: 816-628-5030; Fax: 816-628-4279. Web: annunciationkearney.com.
Catechesis/Religious Program—Tel: 816-628-5030; Fax: 816-628-4279. Students 260.

LEE'S SUMMIT, JACKSON CO.

1—HOLY SPIRIT (1979) Rev. Ronald Verhaeghe; Ann Hayles, Pastoral Assoc.; Deacon Richard Akins.
1800 SW State Rte. 150, 64082.
Res.: 1137 S.W. Georgetown, 64082. Tel: 816-537-6990; Fax: 816-537-8104. Email: parish@holyspiritcatholicchurch.net. Web: www.holyspiritcatholicchurch.net.
Catechesis/Religious Program—Tel: 816-537-6990. Students 489.

2—ST. MARGARET OF SCOTLAND CATHOLIC CHURCH (1999) Rev. Robert H. Stewart; Sue Nichols, Parish Mgr.
Res.: 777 N.E. Blackwell Rd., 64086. Tel: 816-246-6800; Fax: 816-246-9858. Email: snichols@stmargaretsparish.org. Web: www.stmargaretsparish.org.
Catechesis/Religious Program—Email: cliccar@stmargaretsparish.org. Cathie Liccar, D.R.E. Students 203.

3—OUR LADY OF THE PRESENTATION (1896) Rev. Michael Clary; Deacons Joseph Stueve; Del Wilkinson; Mark Fountain; Mike Peterson.
Parish Office—130 N.W. Murray Rd., 64081. Tel: 816-251-1100; Fax: 816-251-1199. Web: www.presentation-parish.org.
School—150 N.W. Murray Rd., 64081. Tel: 816-251-1150; Fax: 816-251-1155. Web: www.presentation-parish.org. Lay Teachers 28; Students 460.
Catechesis/Religious Program—Tel: 816-251-1135. Jo Engert, D.R.E. Students 309.

LEXINGTON, LAFAYETTE CO., IMMACULATE CONCEPTION (1842) [CEM] Rev. Stephen Hansen.
Res.: 107 N. 18th St., 64067. Tel: 660-259-3043; Fax: 660-259-3043. Email: icccpastor@embarqmail.com.
Catechesis/Religious Program—Students 19.

LIBERTY, CLAY CO., ST. JAMES (1840) Revs. Thomas Albers, C.PP.S.; Timothy Armbruster, C.PP.S.
Res.: 309 S. Stewart Rd., 64068. Tel: 816-781-4343; Fax: 816-792-8691.
School—Tel: 816-781-4428; Fax: 816-781-0747. Lay Teachers 55; Students 427.
Catechesis/Religious Program—Students 640.

MARYVILLE, NODAWAY CO., ST. GREGORY BARBARIGO (1858) [CEM 2] [JC] Rev. Martin DeMeulenaere, O.S.B.; Deacon Roy Seipel.
333 S. Davis St., 64468. Tel: 660-582-3833; Fax: 660-582-5914. Web: www.asde.net/~stgreg.
Res.: 825 E. Edwards St., 64468. Tel: 660-582-2051.
School—315 S. Davis St., 64468. Tel: 660-582-2462; Fax: 660-582-2496. Email: gregory@asde.net. Susan Martin, Prin. Lay Teachers 16; Students 161.
Newman Center— 606 College Ave., 64468. Tel: 660-582-7373. Email: catholic@nwmissouri.edu.
Catechesis/Religious Program—Tel: 660-582-5914. Students 159.

MONTROSE, HENRY CO., IMMACULATE CONCEPTION (1876), (German), [CEM] [JC 2] Rev. John J. Bolderson.
Res.: 606 Kansas Ave., 64770-9601. Tel: 660-693-4651; Fax: 660-693-4713.
School—St. Mary School, 608 Kansas Ave., 64770. Tel: 660-693-4502. Lay Teachers 4; Students 46.
Catechesis/Religious Program—Students 25.

NEVADA, VERNON CO., ST. MARY (1887) [CEM] Rev. Justin E. Hoye.
330 N. Main St., 64772. Tel: 417-667-5604. Email: stmarysnevada@sbcglobal.net. Web: www.stmarysnevada.parishesonline.com.
School—Tel: 417-667-7517; Fax: 417-667-7517. Lay Teachers 3; Students 29.
Catechesis/Religious Program—Students 46.
Mission—St. Bridget's Rich Hill, Bates Co.

ODESSA, LAFAYETTE CO., ST. GEORGE (1882) Rev. John Schuele.
Res.: 716 S. Third, 64076. Tel: 816-230-4127. Email: stgeorge7@hotmail.com.
Mission—St. Jude the Apostle 2001 S. Broadway, P.O. Box 590, Oak Grove, Jackson Co. 64075. Tel: 816-690-3165.
Catechesis/Religious Program—Tel: 816-230-7475. Email: stj2515@earthlink.net. Students 67.

PARNELL, NODAWAY CO., ST. JOSEPH'S (1891) [CEM] [JC] Rev. Aidan McSorley, O.S.B.
Res.: 411 S. Main, P.O. Box 78, 64475. Tel: 660-986-3305.
Catechesis/Religious Program—Students 73.

PLATTE CITY, PLATTE CO., TWELVE APOSTLES PARISH (2008) Rev. Charles Rowe.
700 Branch St., 64079. Mailing Address: 407 Cherry St., Weston, 64098. Tel: 816-640-2206.
Catechesis/Religious Program—Students 123.

PLATTSBURG, CLINTON CO., ST. ANN'S (1866), (Irish), [CEM] Rev. M. Jeffrey Stephan.
Res.: 700 W. Maple St., 64477. Tel: 816-539-2634. Email: stann001@centurytel.net. Web: www.stannplattsburg.parishesonline.com.
Catechesis/Religious Program—Students 37.

PLEASANT HILL, CASS CO., ST. BRIDGET (1884) Rev. Msgr. Robert Murphy; Deacon Gary Kappler.
Mailing Address: 2103 N. Lexington, P.O. Box 43, 64080. Tel: 816-540-4563; Pager: 816-540-2162. Email: stbridgetparish@embarqmail.com. Web: stbridgetcatholicchurch.org.
Catechesis/Religious Program—Cathy Vogel, D.R.E. Students 124.

RAYTOWN, JACKSON CO., OUR LADY OF LOURDES (1948) Rev. Steven C. Rogers; Deacon Samuel Adams.
8812 E. Gregory Blvd., 64133.
Res.: 7009 Blue Ridge Blvd., 64133. Tel: 816-353-2380; Fax: 816-353-5737.
School—8812 E. Gregory Blvd., 64133. Tel: 816-353-7062; Fax: 816-353-7650. Lay Teachers 15; Students 138.
Catechesis/Religious Program—Students 50.

RICHMOND, RAY CO., IMMACULATE CONCEPTION (1869) [CEM] Rev. George Ssebadduka.
Res.: 602 S. Camden, 64085. Tel: 816-776-6870.
Catechesis/Religious Program—Students 37.

SAVANNAH, ANDREW CO., ST. ROSE OF LIMA (1898) Rev. Peter Ullrich, O.S.B.
Mailing Address: 707 Hall Ave., 64485. Tel: 816-324-5700; Fax: 816-324-5726. Email: srlp@stjoelive.com.
Res.: 705 S. Hall Ave., 64485. Tel: 816-324-3231.
Catechesis/Religious Program—Students 110.
Mission—St. Patrick 303 Grand Ave., Forest City, Holt Co. 64451. Tel: 660-446-2045.

SMITHVILLE, CLAY CO., CHURCH OF THE GOOD SHEPHERD (1974) Rev. Gregory Haskamp.
Res.: 1103 S. Commercial, P.O. Box 653, 64089. Tel: 816-532-4344 (Church); Fax: 816-532-0019. Email: goodshepherd653@sbcglobal.net. Web: www.goodshepherdmo.org.
Catechesis/Religious Program—Tel: 816-734-8925. Email: gsccpsr@sbcglobal.net. Students 190.

STANBERRY, GENTRY CO., ST. PETER'S (1880) [CEM] Rev. Sebastian Allgaier, O.S.B.
Res.: 614 N. Alanthus Ave., 64489. Tel: 660-783-2159. Email: stpetersparish@sbcglobal.net.
Catechesis/Religious Program—Students 74.
Mission—St. Patrick's Ford City, MO. 4201 State Hwy. AA, King City, Gentry Co. 64463.

SUGAR CREEK, JACKSON CO., ST. CYRIL (1912), (Croatian—Slovak), Rev. Francis Schuele.
Res.: 11231 Chicago Ave., 64054. Tel: 816-252-9564; Fax: 816-252-1161.
Catechesis/Religious Program—Deacon James Reynolds III, D.R.E. Students 1.

TARKIO, ATCHISON CO., ST. PAUL THE APOSTLE (1890) [JC] Rev. Reginald Sander, O.S.B.
Res.: 908 Elm St., 64491. Tel: 660-736-4342.
Catechesis/Religious Program—Students 17.
Mission—St. Benedict Catholic Church Burlington Junction, Nodaway Co. 64428. Tel: 660-725-4407.

TRENTON, GRUNDY CO., ST. JOSEPH'S (1872) [CEM] Rev. Vince Rogers.
Res.: 1728 St. Joseph St., 64683. Tel: 660-359-2841. Email: st.joe@cebridge.net.
Mission—Immaculate Heart of Mary Church 1728 St. Joseph St., Princeton, Mercer Co. 64683.
Catechesis/Religious Program—Students 69.

WARRENSBURG, JOHNSON CO., SACRED HEART (1865) Rev. James A. Urbanic, C.PP.S.
300 S. Ridgeview Dr., 64093. Email: sacredheartparish@embarqmail.com.
Res.: 109 E. Hale Lake Rd., 64093. Tel: 660-747-6154; Fax: 660-747-7623.
Catechesis/Religious Program—Students 209.

WESTON, PLATTE CO., HOLY TRINITY (1842) [JC] Rev. Charles Rowe.
Res.: 407 Cherry St., 64098. Tel: 816-640-2206.
Catechesis/Religious Program—Students 67.

Special Assignment:
Rev. Msgrs.—
Murphy, A. Robert, V.G., P.O. Box 419037, 64141-6037.
Offutt, Bradley S., Chancellor & Moderator of the Curia, P.O. Box 419037, 64141-6037.
Revs.—
Cameron, Robert M., Mission Office Dir., 7601 Blue Ridge, 64138.
Coleman, C. Michael, J.C.L., Adjutant Judicial Vicar & Diocesan Archivist, P.O. Box 419037, 64141-6037.
Matt, Joseph H., J.C.L., Judicial Vicar, P.O. Box 419037, 64141-6037.
Rocha, Richard, Dir. of Vocations, P.O. Box 419037, 64141-6037.

On Duty Outside the Diocese:
Revs.—
Borkowski, Thomas, Wheaton, IL
Pileggi, Anthony, Washington, D.C.
Reardon, Daniel, Military Chap.

Mission Duty:
Rev.—
Gillgannon, Michael, Casilla 12162, La Paz, Bolivia.

Retired:
Rev. Msgrs.—
Bauer, Henry, 6425 Woodson, 64133.
Leitner, John E., 12100 Wornall Rd. #357, 64145.
Revs.—
Bauman, William A., P.O. Box 5278, 64112-0278.
Blaes, Paul, M.A., Ph.D., 7130 Beneva Rd., Apt. 206, Sarasota, FL 34238.
Cleary, Donald R., 411 E. 79th St., 64131.
Cronin, Thomas, 143 Desert Lakes Rd., Fernley, NV 89408.
Deming, Robert N., 9415 Terrace St., 64114.
Eldringhoff, John P., 16504 E. 54th St., Independence, 64055.
Gauthier, Ernest, L.C.S.W., 2920 S.E. Bingham Ct., Lee's Summit, 64063.
Hart, James, 616 E. 120th St., 64145.
Jones, Charles F., 2120 Norton, Independence, 64052.
Karels, Ambrose G., P.O. Box 410834, 64141.
Mahoney, Robert J., 4550 Warwick, #905, 64111.
McCormack, John, 8300 E. 88th Ter., #2010, 64138-4490.
Moscaritolo, Mario, 4019 Warwick, 64111.
Mullin, Hugh J., 10901 Johnson Blvd. J 712, Seminole, FL 33772.
Rice, Michael D., 1650 Shawnee Bend Rd., Sunrise

Beach, 65079.
Rotert, Norman, 121 W. 48th St., Apt. 305, 64112.
Ryan, C. Duane, 310 No Return Rd., Sunrise Beach, 65079.
Saale, Richard T., 8300 E. 88th Ter., #3006, 64138.
Sinclair, Alexander B., 4545 Wornall Rd., #608, 64111.
Tobin, Patrick, 7207 Hwy. 9 N.W., 64152.
Walker, Michael, 67008 E. Miami Rd., Montrose, CO 81401.
Wandless, John H., 5426 Wyandotte St., 64112.
Ward, Thomas, 127 S. W. Hillcrest Ln., Lees Summit, 64063.
Waris, Gerald R., 11710 Jefferson St., 64114.
Wiederholt, Thomas W., 514 W. 26th, 4-N, 64108.

Permanent Deacons:
Adams, Samuel
Akins, Richard
Albers, Kenneth
Beaudoin, Philip Ross
Browning, Melvin, (Retired)
Carter, Steven
Cecil, Charles
Corrigan, Emory S., (Retired)
Davis, F. Jerry, (Retired)
Dennis, Michael
Dupree, Darwin
Elsey, Michael
Falcon, Francis L., (Retired)
Fountain, J. Mark, (Retired)
Fuenfhausen, Kenneth
Goedken, Martin J.
Greene, Kenneth
Henggeler, Francis J., (Retired)
Kappler, Gary
Katzer, Dwayne
Koch, John J., (Retired)
Kopp, George C., Jr., (Retired)
Kopp, Harold G., Sr., (Retired)
Langdon, Harry, (Retired)
Lauhoff, John D., (Retired)
LeMay, Joseph
Lewis, Michael
Livingston, Stephen W.
Madden, Donald
Markey, William R., (Retired)
McCandless, Donald L.
McKay, Clarence W., (Retired)
McLean, Michael
McMenamy, Justin M., (Retired)
Muller, Paul
Muraski, Richard J., (Retired)
Myler, Douglas
Ohmes, Albert J., (Retired)
Peak, Frank L.
Peterson, Mike
Pham, Tuyen
Powell, D. Thomas
Reynolds, James, III
Riead, John T., (Retired)
Rodman, Harold M., (Retired)
Schieber, Martin L., (Retired)
Schmit, Donald A., (Retired)
Schneider, Lawrence, (Retired)
Seipel, Leroy, (Retired)
Strong, Ronald F.
Stueve, Joseph E., (Retired)
Thompson, John R., (Retired)
Townley, David
Tran, Doan
Van Pham, Hao
Welsh, Steven
West, Larry
Williams, Jerry
Zimmerman, Tony

INSTITUTIONS LOCATED IN THE DIOCESE

[A] SEMINARIES, RELIGIOUS OR SCHOLASTICATES

KANSAS CITY. *Gaspar Mission House*, 5221 Rockhill Rd., 64110. Tel: 816-333-7980. Revs. Richard Bayuk, C.PP.S.; Aloys Ebach, C.PP.S.; Garry Richmeier, C.PP.S. Priests 3.

CONCEPTION. *Conception Seminary College*, 37174 State Hwy., P.O. Box 502, 64433. Tel: 660-944-3105; Fax: 660-944-2829. Email: seminary@conception.edu. Web: conceptionabbey.org. Rt. Rev. Gregory Polan, O.S.B., Chancellor; Very Rev. Samuel Russell, O.S.B., Pres. & Rector; Revs. Daniel J. Merz (JC), Vice Rector & Dean of Students; Thomas Bailey, O.S.B., Marmion Abbey; Albert Bruecken, O.S.B.; Patrick Caveglia, O.S.B.; Donald Grabner, O.S.B.; Aidan McSorley, O.S.B.; Pachomius Meadw, O.S.B.; Xavier Nacke, O.S.B.; Benedict Neenan, O.S.B.; Daniel Petsche, O.S.B.; Duane F. Reinert, O.F.M.Cap.; John Rini (ELP) (Retired); Adam Ryan, O.S.B.; Timothy Schoen, O.S.B.; Francis Tran, C.M.C., Congregation of Mother Coredemptrix; Isaac True, O.S.B.; Bro. Thomas Sullivan, O.S.B. Priests 23; Brothers 10; Sisters 1; Lay Professors 8; Total Staff 49; Students 116.

LIBERTY. *Precious Blood Center* (1991) (Kansas City Province), 2110-2140 Saint Gaspar Way, 64068-7941. Tel: 816-781-4344; Fax: 816-781-3639. Email: sec@kcprov.org. Rev. Michael Goode, C.PP.S., Local Dir. Priests 4; Brothers 3.

Society of the Precious Blood Provincial Offices (1965) P.O. Box 339, 64069-0339. Tel: 816-781-4344; Fax: 816-781-3639. Email: sec@kcprov.org. Revs. Aloys Ebach, C.PP.S., 3rd Councilor & Prov. Sec.; James A. Urbanic, C.PP.S., Prov. Dir.; Joseph Nassal, C.PP.S., Vice Provincial; Richard Bayuk, C.PP.S., 2nd Councilor; Garry Richmeier, C.PP.S., 4th Councilor; Thomas A. Conway, C.PP.S., Librarian (Retired). Bishops 1; Priests 48; Brothers 3; Candidates 5.

[B] COLLEGES AND UNIVERSITIES

KANSAS CITY. *Avila University*, 11901 Wornall Rd., 64145-1698. Tel: 816-942-8400; Fax: 816-501-2451. Email: ron.slepitza@avila.edu. Web: www.avila.edu. Ronald A. Slepitza, Ph.D., Pres.; Edwin B. Harris, Ph.D., Vice Pres. Enrollment & Student Devel.; Sr. Marie Joan Harris, C.S.J., Ph.D., Provost & Vice Pres. for Academic Affairs; Paul G. Bookmeyer, B.S., Vice Pres. for Finance & Admin. Svcs.; Sue King, Vice Pres. Information Svcs. & Vice Provost; David Armstrong, Dir. Campus Ministry & Mission Effectiveness; Greg Reichart, Vice Pres. for Advancement; Darby Peoples, Dean of Students. Sisters 2; Lay Teachers 208; Students 1,893.

Rockhurst University (1910) 1100 Rockhurst Rd., 64110-2561. Tel: 816-501-4000; Fax: 816-501-4293. Email: kathy.soloducha@rockhurst.edu. Web: www.rockhurst.edu. Clyde F. Wendel, Chm. Bd. of Trustees; Rev. Thomas B. Curran, O.S.F.S., Pres.; Thomas N. Dart, Vice Pres. Inst. Advancement; William Haefele, Vice Pres., Academic Affairs & Student Devel.; Guy Swanson, Vice Pres. Finance & Admin; Laurie Hathman, Dir. of the Library; Rachael Lierz, Controller; Rev. Kevin L. Cullen, S.J., Vice Pres. for Mission & Ministry; Matthew Quick, Assoc. Vice Pres., Student Devel., Athletics, & Campus Ministry & Dean of Students; Matt Heinrich, Assoc. Vice Pres., Admin.; David Melton, Assoc. Vice Pres., Enrollment. Priests 3; Lay Professors 227; Students 3,047.

College of Arts and Sciences Tel: 816-501-4075; Fax: 816-501-4169. Web: www.rockhurst.edu/academic/deansoffice/index.asp. Timothy L. McDonald, Interim Dean.

School of Graduate and Professional Studies Tel: 816-501-4686; Fax: 816-501-4615. Web: www.rockhurst.edu/academic/SGPS/index.asp. Jeffrey R. Breese, Interim Dean.

Helzberg School of Management Tel: 816-501-4087; Fax: 816-501-4650. Web: www.rockhurst.edu/HSOM/index.asp. James Daley, Dean.

Research College of Nursing, 2525 E. Meyer Blvd., 64132. Tel: 816-995-2800; Fax: 816-995-2817. Web: www.researchcollege.edu. Nancy DeBasio, Pres. & Dean.

[C] HIGH SCHOOLS, DIOCESAN

KANSAS CITY. *Archbishop O'Hara High School* (Coed), 9001 James A. Reed Rd., 64138. Tel: 816-763-4800; Fax: 816-765-5008. Email: postmaster@oharahs.org. Web: www.oharahs.org. James C. Redd, Ed.D., Prin.; Denise Crawford, Librarian. Christian Brothers 3; Lay Teachers 34; Students 415.

St. Pius X High School, 1500 N.E. 42nd Ter., 64116. Tel: 816-453-3450; Fax: 816-452-7099. Email: jmonachino@stpiusxhs-kc.com. Web: www.stpiusxhs-kc.com. Joseph Monachino Jr., Prin.; Sue Johnson, Librarian. Lay Teachers 34; Students 407.

ST. JOSEPH. *Bishop LeBlond High School*, 3529 Frederick Ave., 64506. Tel: 816-279-1629; Fax: 816-279-5488. Email: shaynes@bishopleblondhs.com. Web: bishopleblond.com. Dr. Solon Haynes, Prin.; Rev. Donald Langner, Chap. Priests 1; Sisters 1; Lay Teachers 20; Students 232.

INDEPENDENCE. *St. Mary's Diocesan High School-Bundschu Memorial* (1853) 622 N. Main St., 64050. Tel: 816-252-8733; Fax: 816-252-2780. Email: jlynch@stmhs.org. Web: www.stmhs.org. Mr. Jeff Lynch, Prin. Lay Teachers 13; Students 155.

[D] HIGH SCHOOLS, PRIVATE

KANSAS CITY. *Cristo Rey Kansas City High School*, 211 W. Linwood Blvd., 64111. Tel: 816-457-6044; Fax: 816-457-6046. Email: vperkins@cristoreykc.org. Web: www.cristoreykc.org. Sr. Vickie Perkins, S.C.L., Pres.; Mary Kallman, Prin. Brothers 1; Sisters 5; Lay Staff 40; Students 330.

Notre Dame de Sion High School (1912) 10631 Wornall Rd., 64114-5096. Tel: 816-942-3282; Fax: 816-942-4052. Email: general@ndsion.edu. Web: www.ndsion.edu. Alice Munninghoff, Head of School; Michelle Olson, Prin.; Kathleen Geldhof, Librarian. Affiliated with Sisters of Notre Dame de Sion. Lay Teachers 39; Students 434.

Rockhurst High School (1910) 9301 State Line Rd., 64114-3229. Tel: 816-363-2036; Fax: 816-363-3764. Web: www.rockhursths.edu. Revs. Terrence A. Baum, S.J., Pres.; Ian R. Gibbons, S.J.; William T. Sheahan, S.J.; Mr. Larry Ruby, Prin.; Mrs. Jessica Tipton, Librarian. Jesuit Priests 3; Lay Teachers 73; Students 1,073.

St. Teresa's Academy, 5600 Main St., 64113-1298. Tel: 816-501-0011; Fax: 816-523-0232. Email: bmccormick@stteresasacademy.org. Web: www.stteresasacademy.org. Mrs. Nan Bone, Pres.; Mary Anne Hoecker, M.A., Prin.; Barbara McCormick, M.A., Prin.; Jackie Hershewe, Librarian. Affiliated with Sisters of St. Joseph of Carondelet. Sisters 1; Lay Teachers 45; Students 530.

[E] CONSOLIDATED SCHOOLS

KANSAS CITY. *Holy Cross School*, 121 N. Quincy, 64123-1399. Tel: 816-231-8874; Fax: 816-231-7258. Jean T. Ferrara, Prin. Lay Teachers 11; Students 175.

Our Lady of Guadalupe School (1915) 2310 Madison, 64108. Tel: 816-221-2539; Fax: 816-283-3315. Email: wdcjbowman@everestkc.net. Web: olgkc.net. Connie Bowman, Prin. Lay Teachers 7; Total Staff 12; Students 97.

Our Lady of the Angels School, (Grades PreK-8), 4232 Mercier, 64111. Tel: 816-931-1693; Fax: 816-931-6713. Email: mcdelac@yahoo.com. Mary Delac, Prin. Sisters 1; Lay Teachers 11; Students 173.

St. Stephen's Academy (1888) 1001 Bennington Ave., 64126. Tel: 816-231-5227; Fax: 816-231-2824. Email: richard@ststephensacademy.org. Web: www.ststephensacademy.org. Richard C. Stoetaert, Prin. Consolidation of Our Lady of Peace, St. Anthony's, Holy Cross & Holy Rosary. Lay Teachers 8; Students 68.

[F] ELEMENTARY SCHOOLS, PRIVATE

KANSAS CITY. *Notre Dame de Sion Elementary School* (1912) 3823 Locust St., 64109-2697. Tel: 816-753-3810; Fax: 816-753-0806. Email: general@ndsion.edu. Web: www.ndsion.edu. Alice Munninghoff, Head of School; Catherine Butel, Prin.; Kathy Parker, Librarian. Affiliated with Sisters of Notre Dame de Sion. Lay Teachers 29; Students 320.

[G] GENERAL HOSPITALS

KANSAS CITY. *St. Joseph Medical Center*, 1000 Carondelet Dr., 64114. Tel: 816-942-4400; Fax: 816-943-2840. Web: www.stjosephkc.com. Scott Kashman, CEO. Sponsored by the Sisters of St. Joseph of Carondelet. Sisters 3; Bed Capacity 300; Nurses 539; Total Staff 1,286; Patients Assisted Annually 149,984.

Parent Corporation:

Carondelet Health, 1000 Carondelet Dr., 64114. Tel: 816-943-5678; Fax: 816-943-2840. Web: www.carondelethealth.org. Fleury Yelvington, Pres. & CEO. Parent Co. Sponsored by the Sisters of St. Joseph of Carondelet.

Divisions:

St. Joseph Medical Center Foundation, 1000 Carondelet Dr., 64114. Tel: 816-942-4400; Fax: 816-943-2786. Web: www.carondelethealth.org. Dorene Shipley, Exec. Dir.; Fleury Yelvington, Pres. & CEO. Sponsored by the Sisters of St. Joseph of Carondelet.

11050 Roe Ave., Ste. 120, Overland Park, KS 66211. Tel: 816-529-4800; Fax: 913-345-9129. Web: www.carondelethealth.org. Home health agency affiliated with Carondelet Health.

BLUE SPRINGS. *St. Mary's Medical Center*, 201 NW R.D. Mize Rd., 64014. Tel: 816-228-5900; Fax: 816-655-5408. Web: www.stmarykc.com. Annette Small, CEO. Sponsored by the Sisters of St. Joseph of Carondelet. Acute care facility, having medical, surgical and obstetrical. Sisters 1; Nurses 258; Bed Capacity 146; Patients Assisted Annually 99,393; Total Staff 637.

MARYVILLE. *St. Francis Hospital & Health Services* (1894) 2016 S. Main, 64468. Tel: 660-562-2600; Fax: 660-562-7911. Web:

www.stfrancismaryville.com. H. Gray Cox, Pres. Member of SSM Health Care. Sponsored by Franciscan Sisters of Mary, St. Louis, MO. Acute care facility. Bed Capacity 81; Total Staff 500; Patients Assisted Annually 58,000.

[H] SPECIAL CARE UNITS

KANSAS CITY. *Carondelet Manor*, 621 Carondelet Dr., 64114. Tel: 816-943-4777. Rick Blim, Admin.

Carondelet Long Term Care Facilities, Inc., Owned and operated by Carondelet Long Term Care Facilities, Inc. Sponsored by Sisters of St. Joseph of Carondelet and Benedictine Health System. Bed Capacity 162.

BLUE SPRINGS. *St. Mary's Manor* (1987) 111 Mock Ave., 64014. Tel: 816-228-5655; Fax: 816-228-8480. Email: pkelley@carondelet.com. Patricia Kelley, Admin.

Carondelet Long Term Care Facilities, Inc., Long term care facility with skilled nursing care and residential care. Sponsored by Benedictine Health System and Sisters of St. Joseph of Carondelet. Skilled Care 132; Residential Care 57; Total Assisted 189; Total Staff 250; Bed Capacity 827,820; Total Assisted Annually 696,420.

LIBERTY. *Immacolata Manor* (1981) 2135 Manor Way, 64068-9397. Tel: 816-781-4332; Fax: 816-781-8820. Email: info@imanor.org. Dale R. Herrick, Exec. Dir.; Karen Sage, Pres. Residential and day habilitation services for people with developmental disabilities; Operated by the Immacolata Board of Directors. Residents 30; Total Staff 63; Total Assisted Annually 32.

[I] HOMES FOR THE ELDERLY

KANSAS CITY. *Brighton Place*, 1905 Hardesty, 64127. Tel: 816-483-6233; Fax: 816-483-1142. Email: nowlin01@kc.rr.com. 32 units 236, S/8 housing for family. Total Assisted 32; Total Staff 3.

Cathedral Square Towers, 444 W. 12th St., 64105. Tel: 816-471-6555; Fax: 816-421-1279. Email: cathedral01@kc.rr.com. Jan Carson, Mgr.; Michael W. Halterman, Diocesan Liaison. Apartment residence for the elderly and handicapped. Units 156; Total in Residence 164; Total Staff 10.

Columbus Park Plaza, 801 Pacific, 64106. Tel: 816-472-0887; Fax: 816-472-6105. Catherine Huntsucker, Mgr.; Mike W. Halteman, Diocesan Liaison. Apartment residence for elderly and handicapped. Units 56; Total in Residence 55; Total Staff 4.

Jeanne Jugan Center, 8745 James A. Reed Rd., 64138. Tel: 816-761-4744; Fax: 816-761-8313. Email: mskansascity@littlesistersofthepoor.org. Sr. Therese Marie Minerich, Pres.; Rev. John McCormack, Chap. (Retired).

Little Sisters of the Poor Little Sisters of the Poor. Apartments 33; Bed Capacity 73; Total in Residence 106; Total Staff 94; Total Assisted 113; Sisters 13.

Marlborough Manor, 1818 E. 79th St., 64132. Tel: 816-333-7761; Fax: 816-523-2388. Email: marlborough01@kc.rr.com. Louise Shepherd, Mgr. Rental housing for low income (a 31-unit apartment residence for the elderly and disabled). Total in Residence 31; Total Staff 3.

Red Bridge Place, 11300 Colorado, 64137. Tel: 816-761-4667; Fax: 816-761-4769. Email: redbridge01@kc.rr.com. Linda Barber, Mgr. Total Staff 3; Total Assisted 45.

Tremont Place (1994) 6161 N. Chatham, 64151. Tel: 816-587-7707; Fax: 816-587-7637. Email: tremont01@kc.rr.com. Donna Quick, Mgr.; Michael W. Halterman, CEO & Diocesan Liaison. A 50-unit apartment residence for the elderly and disabled. Must be sixty-two or over.

ST. JOSEPH. *The Living Community of St. Joseph* (2004) 1202 Heartland Rd., 64506. Tel: 816-671-8500; Fax: 816-671-8571. Email: chris.kerns@bhshealth.org. Web: www.lcosj.com. Christine Kerns, Admin./CEO. Bed Capacity 131; Total Assisted Annually 970; Total Staff 230.

CAMERON. *St. Patrick's Manor*, 514 Northland Dr., 64429. Tel: 816-632-1684; Fax: 816-632-7624. Email: cpp61587@centurytel.net. Nancy Williams, Property Mgr.; Michael W. Halterman, Diocesan Dir. A 31-unit apartment residence for the elderly and disabled. Total Staff 3.

LIBERTY. *Our Lady of Mercy Country Home*, 2115 Maturana Dr., 64068. Tel: 816-781-5711; Fax: 816-781-7276. Email: dtrimmer@ourladyofmercy.net. Web: ourladyofmercy.net. Sr. Sandra Thibodeaux, M.M.B., Regl. Moderator. Mercedarian Missionaries of Berriz. Guest Capacity 106; Sisters 15; Bed Capacity 106; Total Assisted Annually 525; Total Staff 54.

[J] MONASTERIES AND RESIDENCES OF PRIESTS

KANSAS CITY. *Redemptorists Fathers of Kansas City, Missouri*, 3333 Broadway Blvd., 64111. Tel: 816-561-3771; Fax: 816-561-3704. Email: tmccssr@yahoo.com. Revs. Frank Kriski, C.Ss.R.; J. Terrence McCloskey, C.Ss.R.; John Willett, C.Ss.R.; Patrick Power, C.Ss.R.; Edward Morgan, C.Ss.R.; Stephen Benden, C.Ss.R.; Richard Quinn, C.Ss.R; Vincent Aggeler, C.Ss.R; Bros. Charles Long, C.Ss.R.; John Matthys, C.Ss.R.; Rev. Bob Lindsey, C.Ss.R. Priests 9; Brothers 2.

Rockhurst Jesuit Community, 5133 Forest Ave., 64110-2513. Tel: 816-501-3300; Fax: 816-501-3250. Web: www.rockhurst.edu/jesuitcommunity. Very Rev. John J. Vowells, S.J., Rector; Revs. Terrence A. Baum, S.J.; A. James Blumeyer, S.J.; Martin J. Bredeck, S.J.; Luke J. Byrne, S.J.; Kevin L. Cullen, S.J.; Thomas B. Curran, O.S.F.S.; Thomas G. Cwik, S.J.; Dirk J. Dunfee, S.J.; Ian R. Gibbons, S.J.; Gregg H. Grovenburg, S.J.; Vernon R. Heinsz, S.J.; Wilfred L. LaCroix, S.J.; Glenn R. Mueller, S.J.; Louis J. Oldani, S.J.; Matthew D. Ruhl, S.J.; William T. Sheahan, S.J.; James D. Wheeler, S.J. Total in Residence 19.

Society of Our Lady of the Most Holy Trinity, 3738 Tracy Ave., 64109. Tel: 816-561-8849; Fax: 816-753-3068. Email: soltlaity@gmail.com. Web: www.solt3.org. Priests 2; Brothers 1; Deacons 1; Sisters 4; Laity 50.

CONCEPTION. *Conception Abbey* 64433. Tel: 660-944-3100; Fax: 660-944-2800. Email: communications@conception.edu. Web: www.ConceptionAbbey.org. Rt. Rev. Gregory Polan, O.S.B., Abbot; Rev. Kenneth Reichert, O.S.B.; Bro. Bernard Montgomery, O.S.B., Subprior; Revs. Sebastian Allgaier, O.S.B.; Albert Bruecken, O.S.B.; Patrick Caveglia, O.S.B.; Anthony Shidler, O.S.B.; Hugh Tasch, O.S.B.; Paschal Thomas, O.S.B.; Isaac True, O.S.B.; Peter Ullrich, O.S.B. Benedictine Monks. Priests 38; Brothers 21. St. Gregory Barbarigo: 333 S. Davis, Maryville, 64468. Tel: 660-582-3833. Revs. Donald Grabner, O.S.B.; Martin DeMeulenaere, O.S.B. *St. Joseph Parish*, P.O. Box 78, Parnell, 64475. Tel: 660-986-3305. Revs. Aidan McSorley, O.S.B.; Xavier Nacke, O.S.B.; Benedict Neenan, O.S.B. *St. Peter Parish*, 614 N. Alanthus Ave., Stanberry, 64489. Tel: 660-783-2159. Very Rev. Samuel Russell, O.S.B., Seminary Pres. & Rector; Revs. Allan Stetz, O.S.B.; Adam Ryan, O.S.B.; Norbert Schappler, O.S.B.; Joachim Schieber, O.S.B.; Timothy Schoen, O.S.B.

INDEPENDENCE. *Vincentian Parish Mission Center*, 2100 N. Noland Rd., 64050. Tel: 816-254-3000; Fax: 816-254-2204. Email: mm@vpmc.net. Web: www.vpmc.net. Revs. Richard Gielow, C.M., Supr. Tel: 816-254-3700; Michael Mulhearn, C.M.; Carl G. Schulte, C.M.; Thomas Cawley, C.M. Total in Residence 6.

LIBERTY. *Precious Blood Center* (1991) 2130 Saint Gaspar Way, 64068-7941. Tel: 816-781-4344; Fax: 816-781-3639. Email: sec@kcprov.org. Revs. Thomas A. Conway, C.PP.S. (Retired); Michael Goode, C.PP.S.; Richard Colbert, C.PP.S.; James A. Urbanic, C.PP.S.; James Schrader, C.PP.S; Bros. Stephen Ohnmacht, C.PP.S.; Daryl Charron, C.PP.S.; Robert Herman, C.PP.S.

Precious Blood Society Provincial Office (1965) P.O. Box 339, 64069-0339. Tel: 816-781-4344; Fax: 816-781-3639. Email: sec@kcprov.org. Revs. James A. Urbanic, C.PP.S., Prov. Dir.; Aloys Ebach, C.PP.S., Prov. Sec.; Richard Bayuk, C.PP.S., Prov. Treas.; Joseph Miller, C.PP.S., Vocation Dir. Priests 4; Brothers 3.

[K] CONVENTS AND RESIDENCES FOR SISTERS

KANSAS CITY. *Benedictines of Mary, Queen of Apostles* Priory of Our Lady of Ephesus, 1400 N.E. 42nd Ter., 64116. Tel: 816-455-2065; 816-455-2067 Chaplain; Fax: 816-455-2063. Web: benedictinesofmary.org. Sr. Therese McNamara, O.S.B., Prioress of Our Lady of Ephesus. Professed 13; Novices 4; Postulants 4.

Sisters of the Society of Our Lady of the Most Holy Trinity (1958) 3738 Tracy, 64109. Tel: 816-561-8849. Society of Apostolic Life. Sisters 5.

CLYDE. *Benedictine Convent of Perpetual Adoration* (1874) 31970 State Hwy. P, 64432. Tel: 660-944-2221; Fax: 660-944-2152. Email: sister@benedictinesisters.org. Web: www.benedictinesisters.org. Sr. Patricia Nyquist, Prioress Gen. Attended by Conception Abbey; Two other interdependent monasteries: Tucson, AZ; and Dayton, WY. Membership in Clyde Community 59; Total in Congregation 86; Sisters 83.

INDEPENDENCE. *St. Francis Convent Novitiate and Prayer Center* (Switzerland 1378, U.S. 1892) 2100 N. Noland Rd., 64050. Tel: 816-252-1673; Fax: 816-252-5574. Email: STFRAN2100@aol.com. Web: www.osfholyeucharist.org. Sr. M. Lucy Lang, O.S.F., Supr. Motherhouse of the Sisters of St. Francis of the Holy Eucharist. Sisters 16; Postulants 1.

LIBERTY. *Mercedarian Missionaries of Berriz*, U.S. Regional Headquarters, 2115 Maturana Dr., #101B, 64068-7985. Tel: 816-781-8202; Fax: 816-781-8205. Email: mmbus@sbcglobal.net. Web: mmberriz.com. Sr. Sandra Thibodeaux, M.M.B., Regl. Coord. Mercedarian Mission. Mercedarian Missionaries of Berriz 14.

Mercedarian Missionaries of Berriz (M.M.B.), 2116 Maturana Dr., 64068. Tel: 816-415-3024. Sr. Linda Teegarden, M.M.B., Local Coord. Mercedarian Mission. Sisters 3.

Mercedarian Missionaries of Berriz (M.M.B.), 2120 Maturana Dr., 64068. Tel: 816-415-3133. Email: thibfay@sbcglobal.net. Sr. Sandra Thibodeaux, M.M.B., Local Coord. Mercedarian Mission. Sisters 2.

Queen of Angels Monastery - Benedictine Sisters, 23615 N.E. 100th St., 64068-8716. Tel: 816-750-4618; Fax: 816-750-4620. Email: sisters@libertyosb.org. Web: libertyosb.org. Sr. Agnes Helgenberger, O.S.B., Prioress. Sisters 6; Total in Residence 9.

SAVANNAH. *Sisters of St. Francis Provincial House* (1922) 104 E. Park, Box 488, 64485-0488. Tel: 816-324-3179; Fax: 816-324-7264. Email: osf@stjoelive.com. Web: sistersofstfrancis.org. Rev. Hugh Tasch, O.S.B. Sisters of St. Francis of Savannah, MO. Motherhouse and Novitiate. Sisters 12.

Maintenance and Custodial Care Trust of the Franciscan Sisters of Savannah, MO Tel: 816-324-3179; Fax: 816-324-7264.

[L] SERVICES

KANSAS CITY. *Bishop Sullivan Center* (1972) 6435 Truman Rd., 64126. Tel: 816-231-0984; Fax: 816-231-3096. Email: tturner@bishopsullivan.org. Web: www.bishopsullivan.org. Rev. Thomas W. Turner, Dir. Total Assisted 17,000; Total Staff 14.

Redemptorist Social Services Center, Inc., 207 Linwood Blvd., 64111-1327. Tel: 816-931-9942; Fax: 816-531-0583. Email: info@kcsocialservices.org. Web: www.kcsocialservices.org. Diana Kennedy, Dir. Total Assisted 4,100; Total Staff 7.

**Seton Center Family & Health Services*, 2816 E. 23 St., 64127. Tel: 816-231-3955; Fax: 816-231-7455. Web: www.setonkc.org. Sr. Loretto Marie Colwell, S.C.L., Exec. Dir. Total Assisted 12,696; Total Staff 20.

[M] NEWMAN CENTERS

KANSAS CITY. *Avila University Campus Ministry* 11901 Wornall Rd., 64145. Tel: 816-501-2423; Fax: 816-501-2454. Email: david.armstrong@avila.edu. Web: www.avila.edu. David Armstrong, Dir. Campus Ministry. Total Assisted 1,200; Staff 1.

MARYVILLE. *Newman Catholic Center, Northwest Missouri State University* 606 College Ave., 64468. Tel: 660-582-7373; Fax: 660-582-7397. Email: newman@nwmissouri.edu.

WARRENSBURG. *Newman Center Catholic Campus Ministry for University of Central Missouri* 106 Broad St., 64093. Tel: 660-747-6997; Fax: 660-747-6997. Email: ucmnewman@gmail.com. Michael McCormick, Campus Min. Total Assisted 200; Total Staff 1.

[N] MISCELLANEOUS

KANSAS CITY. *St. Anthony's Home*, 300 E. 36th St., P.O. Box 419037, 64141-6037. Tel: 816-756-1850.

Bishop Boland Institute for Housing and Community Development, 1112 Broadway, 64105. Tel: 816-756-1850; Fax: 816-756-5221. Email: mgoedken@ccharities.com. Web: www.catholiccharities-kcsj.org. Martin Goedken, Dir.

Camp Little Flower, 300 E. 36th St., P.O. Box 419037, 64141. Tel: 816-756-1850. Rose-Mary Montemore, Pres.

Catholic Charities Foundation, 301 E. Armour Blvd., Ste. 620, 64111. Tel: 816-756-1858, Ext. 563; Fax: 816-756-5022. Email: rprather@ccharities.com. Web: www.catholiccharities-kcsj.org. Rozanne Prather, Exec. Dir.

Cristo Rey Kansas City Corporate Internship Program, 211 W. Linwood Blvd., 64111. Tel: 816-457-6044; Fax: 816-457-6046. Email: vperkins@cristoreykc.org. Web: www.cristoreykc.org. Sr. Vickie Perkins, S.C.L., Pres. & Contact Person; Mary Kallman, Prin.

Cursillo, 300 E. 36th St., 64111. Tel: 816-756-1850; Fax: 816-756-5221. Email: greene@diocesekcsj.org. Web: www.diocese-kcsj.org/igm/familylife/index.htm. Deacon Kenneth Greene, Spirtual Advisor.

De La Salle Academy, 3732 Paseo, 64109. Tel: 816-531-6561; Fax: 816-756-3916. Email: mooney81@hotmail.com. Christian Brothers, F.S.C. and LaSallian Volunteers., Special Lasallion Volunteer Program. Christian Brothers 2; LaSallian Volunteers 2.

**De La Salle Alumni Association*, P.O. Box 380083, 64138. Tel: 816-767-9800; Fax: 816-767-9800.

Diocesan Council of Catholic Women, 300 E. 36th St., P.O. Box 419037, 64141. Tel: 816-756-1850. Email: kcdietch@aol.com. Rev. Msgr. Joseph A. Mancuso, Diocesan Moderator; Elizabeth Dietrich, Contact Person.

Diocesan Education Endowment Trust Fund (1989) 300 E. 36th St., P.O. Box 419037, 64111. Tel: 816-756-1850; Fax: 816-756-5089. Email: moss@diocesekcsj.org. Web: www.diocese-kcsj.org. Paula Moss, Contact Person.

Friends, Inc., 300 E. 36th St., P.O. Box 419037, 64141-6037. Tel: 816-756-1850.

Immacolata Retreat Center, 300 E. 36th St., P.O. Box 419037, 64141-6037. Tel: 816-756-1850.

St. John's Seminary, Inc., P.O. Box 419037, 64141-6037.

Knights of St. Peter Claver (K.P.C.), 1600 Paseo, St. Monica Parish, 64108. Tel: 816-471-3696; Fax: 816-471-1100. Ladies Auxiliary of St. Peter Claver.

Ladies of Charity of Metropolitan Kansas City (1952) P.O. Box 480753, 64148-0753. Web: www.lockc.org. Gwen Brooks, Pres. A group of volunteers who work and raise money to help the poor and those in need through Seton Center and other agencies in the greater Kansas City area.

Marillac Home for Children, P.O. Box 419037, 64141-6037.

Our Lady of Perpetual Help Charitable Trust (1978) 3333 Broadway, 64111. Tel: 816-561-3771; Fax: 816-561-3704. Email: sbenden12us@yahoo.com. Web: www.redemptoristkc.org. Rev. Stephen Benden, C.Ss.R., Contact Person.

**R.J. Stukenborg Corporation, c/o Rev. Michael Goode, C.PP.S.*, 2130 Saint Gaspar Way, P.O. Box 339, Liberty, 64069. Tel: 816-781-4344; Fax: 816-781-3639. Rev. Michael Goode, C.PP.S., Pres.; Bro. Stephen Ohnmacht, C.PP.S., Sec.

Siena Club, 300 E. 36th St., P.O. Box 419037, 64141. Tel: 816-756-1850.

CONCEPTION. **The St. Benedict Education Foundation, Conception Abbey Office*, P.O. Box 16, 64433. Tel: 660-944-2820; Fax: 660-944-2885. Email: patrick@conception.edu. Web: www.santanselmo.us. Rev. Patrick Caveglia, O.S.B.

LEE'S SUMMIT. *Mercy Midwest Properties*, 920 Northeast Ridgeview Dr. #A, Lees Summit, 64086. Tel: 816-525-0990; Fax: 816-524-0078. Email: thustedde@mercyhousing.org. Affordable service enriched housing for individuals and families who are economically poor. Total Assisted 141; Total Staff 3.

LIBERTY. **St. Gaspar Society* (1991) P.O. Box 339, 64069. Tel: 816-781-4344; Fax: 816-781-3639. Email: sec@kcprov.org. Revs. James A. Urbanic, C.PP.S., Pres.; Michael Goode, C.PP.S., Treas.; Bro. Stephen Ohnmacht, C.PP.S., Sec.

Our Lady of Mercy Home, 2115 Maturana Dr., 64068-9469. Tel: 816-781-5711; Fax: 816-781-7276.

**Queen of Angels Foundation, Inc.*, 23615 N.E. 100th St., 64068. Tel: 816-750-4618; Fax: 816-750-4620. Email: sisters@libertybenedicdinesisters.org.

**R.J. Stukenborg Corporation*, 2130 St. Gaspar Way, 64068. Tel: 816-781-4344; Fax: 816-781-3639.

MARYVILLE. *St. Francis Hospital Foundation*, 2016 S. Main, 64468. Tel: 660-562-7933; Fax: 660-562-7982. Web: www.stfrancismaryville.com.

RELIGIOUS INSTITUTES OF MEN REPRESENTED IN THE DIOCESE

For further details refer to the corresponding bracketed number in the Religious Institutes of Men or Women section.

[0200]—*Benedictine Monks* (Conception Abbey)—O.S.B.

[]—*Benedictine Monks* (St. Gregory's Abbey)—O.S.B.

[0330]—*Christian Brothers of the Midwest, Burr Ridge*—F.S.C.

[1330]—*Congregation of the Mission* (Western Province)—C.M.

[1210]—*Congregation of the Missionaries of St. Charles*—C.S.

[0305]—*Institute of Christ the King-Sovereign Priest*—I.C.

[0690]—*Jesuit Fathers and Brothers* (Missouri Prov.)—S.J.

[0920]—*Oblates of St. Francis de Sales*—O.S.F.S.

[]—*Oblati di Maria Vergine* (Rome, Italy)—O.M.V.

[]—*Priestly Fraternity of St. Peter*—F.S.S.P.

[1070]—*Redemptorist Fathers of Kansas City, Missouri* (Denver Prov.)—C.SS.R.

[0975]—*Society of Our Lady of Most Holy Trinity*—S.O.L.T.

[1060]—*Society of the Precious Blood* (Kansas City Prov.)—C.PP.S.

RELIGIOUS INSTITUTES OF WOMEN REPRESENTED IN THE DIOCESE

[0230]—*Benedictine Sisters of Pontifical Jurisdiction* (Atchinson, KS; Liberty, MO)—O.S.B.

[]—*Benedictines of Mary, Queen of Apostles*—O.S.B.

[0397]—*Congregation of Mary Queen* (Springfield, MO)—C.M.R.

[0220]—*Congregation of the Benedictine Sisters of Perpetual Adoration of Pontifical Jurisdiction*—O.S.B.

[3832]—*Congregation of the Sisters of St. Joseph* (Wichita, KS)—C.S.J.

[1115]—*Dominican Sisters of Peace* (Columbus, OH)—O.P.

[2575]—*Institute of the Sisters of Mercy of the Americas* (Omaha, NE)—R.S.M.

[2340]—*Little Sisters of the Poor*—L.S.P.

[2510]—*Mercedarian Missionaries of Berriz*—M.M.B.

[2960]—*Notre Dame Sisters* (Omaha, NE)—N.D.

[]—*School Sisters of Christ the King*—C.K.

[2150]—*Sister Servants of Immaculate Heart of Mary* (Monroe, MI)—I.H.M.

[0480]—*Sisters of Charity of Leavenworth, Kansas*—S.C.L.

[0430]—*Sisters of Charity of the Blessed Virgin Mary*—B.V.M.

[2360]—*Sisters of Loretto at the Foot of the Cross*—S.L.

[1670]—*Sisters of St. Francis of Savannah, MO*—O.S.F.

[1560]—*Sisters of St. Francis of the Holy Eucharist* (Independence, MO)—O.S.F.

[]—*Sisters of St. Francis of the Holy Eucharist Foundation*

[3830-15]—*Sisters of St. Joseph* (Concordia, KS)—C.S.J.

[3840]—*Sisters of St. Joseph of Carondelet*—C.S.J.

[3105]—*Society of Our Lady of the Most Holy Trinity*—S.O.L.T.

[4120-05]—*Ursuline Sisters* (Maple Mount, KY)—O.S.U.

DIOCESAN CEMETERIES

KANSAS CITY. *Mount Olivet & Mount St. Mary*

ST. JOSEPH. *Mount Olivet*

KANSAS CITY NORTH. *Resurrection*

NECROLOGY

† Paa, Donald R., (Retired)—Died July 25, 2009

An asterisk (*) denotes an organization that has established tax-exempt status directly with the IRS and is not covered by the USCCB Group Ruling.

Diocese of Knoxville

Most Reverend

RICHARD F. STIKA

Third Bishop of Knoxville; ordained December 14, 1985; appointed third Bishop of Knoxville January 12, 2009; ordained and installed March 19, 2009. *Office: 805 Northshore Dr., S.W., Knoxville, TN 37919.*

Chancery Office: 805 Northshore Dr., S.W., Knoxville, TN 37919. Tel: 865-584-3307.

ESTABLISHED SEPTEMBER 8, 1988.

Square Miles 14,242.

Comprises the Counties of Anderson, Bledsoe, Blount, Bradley, Campbell, Carter, Claiborne, Cocke, Cumberland, Fentress, Grainger, Greene, Hamblen, Hamilton, Hancock, Hawkins, Jefferson, Johnson, Knox, Loudon, McMinn, Marion, Meigs, Monroe, Morgan, Pickett, Polk, Rhea, Roane, Scott, Sequatchie, Sevier, Sullivan, Unicoi, Union and Washington in the State of Tennessee.

For legal titles of parishes and diocesan institutions, consult the Chancery Office.

STATISTICAL OVERVIEW

Personnel	
Bishop	1
Priests: Diocesan Active in Diocese	48
Priests: Diocesan Active Outside Diocese	4
Priests: Retired, Sick or Absent	10
Number of Diocesan Priests	62
Religious Priests in Diocese	11
Total Priests in Diocese	73
Extern Priests in Diocese	5
Ordinations:	
Diocesan Priests	2
Permanent Deacons in Diocese	53
Total Brothers	10
Total Sisters	27
Parishes	
Parishes	45
With Resident Pastor:	
Resident Diocesan Priests	35
Resident Religious Priests	3
Without Resident Pastor:	
Administered by Priests	7
Missions	2
Pastoral Centers	2
Professional Ministry Personnel:	
Sisters	2
Lay Ministers	20
Welfare	
Catholic Hospitals	2
Total Assisted	388,772
Health Care Centers	1
Total Assisted	310
Homes for the Aged	1
Total Assisted	600
Specialized Homes	2
Total Assisted	1,069
Special Centers for Social Services	7
Total Assisted	50,455
Educational	
Diocesan Students in Other Seminaries	9
Total Seminarians	9
High Schools, Diocesan and Parish	2
Total Students	1,135
Elementary Schools, Diocesan and Parish	8
Total Students	2,170
Catechesis/Religious Education:	
High School Students	1,375
Elementary Students	3,581
Total Students under Catholic Instruction	8,270
Teachers in the Diocese:	
Priests	2
Sisters	6
Lay Teachers	203
Vital Statistics	
Receptions into the Church:	
Infant Baptism Totals	1,203
Minor Baptism Totals	75
Adult Baptism Totals	105
Received into Full Communion	259
First Communions	1,074
Confirmations	742
Marriages:	
Catholic	135
Interfaith	124
Total Marriages	259
Deaths	308
Total Catholic Population	60,295
Total Population	2,330,795

Former Bishops—Most Revs. ANTHONY J. O'CONNELL, ord. 1963; appt. Bishop of Knoxville May 27, 1988; installed Sept. 8, 1988; appt. Bishop of Palm Beach Nov. 11, 1998; JOSEPH E. KURTZ, ord. 1972; appt. Bishop of Knoxville Oct. 26, 1999; ord. and installed Dec. 8, 1999; appt. Archbishop of Louisville June 12, 2007.

Vicar General—Rev. Msgr. FRANCIS XAVIER MANKEL, S.T.L., V.G.

Episcopal Vicar—Very Rev. DAVID BOETTNER, V.E.

Deans of the Diocese—Revs. G. PATRICK GARRITY, Five Rivers Deanery; GEORGE E. SCHMIDT JR., Chattanooga Deanery; MICHAEL SWEENEY, Cumberland Mtn. Deanery; Rev. Msgr. T. ALLEN HUMBRECHT, Smoky Mtn. Deanery.

Chancery Office—805 Northshore Dr., S.W., Knoxville, 37919. Tel: 865-584-3307; Fax: 865-584-7538. Office Hours: Mon.-Fri. 9-5; All official business should be directed to this office.

Moderator of the Curia—Very Rev. DAVID BOETTNER, V.E.

Chancellor—Deacon SEAN K. SMITH.

Assistant to the Bishop—Deacon SEAN K. SMITH.

Auditors— All priests on assignment in the diocese.

Presbyteral Council—Revs. BEDE C. ABOH; KWAKU JOHN APPIAH; Very Rev. DAVID BOETTNER, V.E.; Revs. PATRICK P. BROWNELL; DAVID CARTER; JOSEPH A. CICCONE, C.S.P., Recording Sec.; GILBERT M. DIAZ; G. PATRICK GARRITY, Dean, Chm.; ROBERT J. HOFSTETTER; Rev. Msgrs. T. ALLEN HUMBRECHT, Dean; FRANCIS XAVIER MANKEL, S.T.L., V.G.; Revs. WILLIAM L. MCKENZIE, Vice Chm.; CHRIS MICHELSON; GEORGE E. SCHMIDT JR., Dean; MICHAEL SWEENEY, Dean.

Diocesan Consultors—Revs. PATRICK P. BROWNELL; G. PATRICK GARRITY, Dean; ROBERT J. HOFSTETTER; Rev. Msgrs. T. ALLEN HUMBRECHT, Dean; FRANCIS XAVIER MANKEL, S.T.L., V.G.; Rev. MICHAEL F. NOLAN.

Diocesan Finance Council—HERBERT ADAMS; DORMAN BLAINE; J. MICHAEL CONNOR, Chm.; Very Rev. DAVID BOETTNER, V.E., Ex-Officio, Episcopal Vicar; Deacon DAVID J. LUCHEON, Ex Officio, Diocesan Finance Officer; SHARON FOLK; GEORGE HAGGARD; RUDY HOGAN; SUZANNE P. ERPENBACH, Ex Officio, Diocesan Dir., Stewardship & Devel.; Rev. Msgr. FRANCIS XAVIER MANKEL, S.T.L., V.G., Ex Officio; Rev. CHRIS MICHELSON; JOHN T. O'CONNOR, Ex Officio, Diocesan Attorney; PAUL PREMO; SOCRATES SABATER; DAVE SANTI; Rev. GEORGE E. SCHMIDT JR., Dean; SUZANNE SCHRIVER; Deacon SEAN K. SMITH, Ex Officio; BILL SWAIN; FRAN THIE, Vice Chm.

Diocesan Offices and Directors

Archives—Deacon SEAN K. SMITH, 805 Northshore Dr., S.W., Knoxville, 37919. Tel: 865-584-3307.

Campus Ministries—

East Tennessee State University—Rev. MICHAEL E. CUMMINS, Chap., Catholic Center, 734 W. Locust St., Johnson City, 37604. Tel: 423-926-7061.

University of Tennessee-Chattanooga—Rev. JAMES MALLETT, Dir., 514 Palmetto St., Chattanooga, 37403. Tel: 423-267-3064.

University of Tennessee-Knoxville—Rev. CHARLES DONOHUE, C.S.P., Dir., 1710 Melrose Pl., Knoxville, 37916. Tel: 865-523-7931.

Catholic Schools Office—Dr. SHERRY G. MORGAN, Supt., 805 Northshore Dr., S.W., Knoxville, 37919. Tel: 865-584-3307.

Catholic Charities of East Tennessee, Inc.—Rev. RAGAN SCHRIVER, Exec. Dir., 3009 Lake Brook Blvd., Knoxville, 37909. Tel: 865-524-9896; Fax: 865-971-3575. Email: info@ccetn.org. The umbrella agency for all Catholic Charities of the diocese.

Catholic Campaign for Human Development—Rev. RAGAN SCHRIVER, Dir., 3009 Lake Brook Blvd., Knoxville, 37909. Tel: 865-524-9896.

Catholic Charities (Chattanooga Area)—LIBBY SCHLEIFER, Site Admin., 859 McCallie Ave., Chattanooga, 37403. Tel: 423-267-1297.

Catholic Charities (Knoxville Area)—TONIA GRAF, Site Admin., 3009 Lake Brook Blvd., Knoxville, 37909. Tel: 865-524-9896.

Catholic Charities (Upper East Tennessee Area)—BRENDA DUNN, Site Admin., 703 E. Jackson Blvd., P.O. Box 323, Jonesborough, 37659. Tel: 423-753-3002.

Cemeteries—Deacon SEAN K. SMITH, Dir., 805 Northshore Dr., S.W., Knoxville, 37919. Tel: 865-584-3307; Revs. GEORGE E. SCHMIDT JR., Dean, Contact, Mt. Olivet Cemetery in Chattanooga. Tel: 423-266-1618; JOSEPH J. CICCONE, C.S.P., Contact, Calvary Cemetery in Knoxville, 2000 Martin Luther King, Jr. Blvd., Knoxville, 37915. Mailing Address: c/o Immaculate Conception Church, 414 W. Vine Ave., Knoxville, 37902-1327. Tel: 865-522-1508.

Chancellor—Deacon SEAN K. SMITH, 805 Northshore Dr., S.W., Knoxville, 37919. Tel: 865-584-3307.

Censor Librorum—Rev. ROBERT J. HOFSTETTER, 308 Lou Ellen St., Newport, 37821. Tel: 423-237-6419.

Christian Formation—Sr. MARY TIMOTHEA ELLIOTT, R.S.M., Dir.; Rev. RICHARD G. ARMSTRONG JR., Asst. Dir., 805 Northshore Dr., S.W., Knoxville, 37919. Tel: 865-584-3307.

Deaf Ministry—Rev. MICHAEL E. CUMMINS, Dir., Office: ETSU - Catholic Center, 734 W. Locust St., Johnson City, 37604. Tel: 423-926-7061.

Diaconate—Deacon TIM ELLIOTT, Dir., Mailing Address: 620 N. Cedar Bluff Rd., Knoxville, 37923. Tel: 865-531-0770.

Ongoing Formation of Deacons—Deacon TIM ELLIOTT, Coord., Mailing Address: 620 N. Cedar Bluff Rd., Knoxville, 37923. Tel: 865-531-0770.

Diocesan Council of Catholic Women—Rev. Msgr. FRANCIS XAVIER MANKEL, S.T.L., V.G., Diocesan Spiritual Moderator, 111 Hinton Ave., Knoxville, 37927. Tel: 865-522-2205.

Ecumenism—Rev. Msgr. T. ALLEN HUMBRECHT, Dean & Dir., 805 Northshore Dr., S.W., Knoxville, 37919. Tel: 865-584-3307.

Finance Office—Deacon DAVID J. LUCHEON, Diocesan Finance Officer, 805 Northshore Dr., S.W., Knoxville, 37919. Tel: 865-584-3307.

Hispanic Ministry—LOURDES GARZA, Dir., Chancery Office: 805 Northshore Dr., S.W., Knoxville, 37919. Tel: 865-584-3307.

Justice and Peace Office—PAUL SIMONEAU, Dir., Chancery Office: 805 Northshore Dr., S.W., Knoxville, 37919. Tel: 865-584-3307.

Marriage Tribunal—Rev. DEXTER BREWER, J.C.L., J.V., 2400 21st Ave. S., Nashville, 37212-5387. Tel: 615-383-6393 Diocesan marriage tribunal is shared with the Diocese of Nashville.

Ministries of the Chattanooga Deanery—Rev. GEORGE E. SCHMIDT JR., Dean; JANE HUBBARD, Deanery Coord., 859 McCallie Ave., Ste. 302, Chattanooga, 37403. Tel: 423-267-9878.

Ministries of the Five Rivers Deanery—Rev. G. PATRICK GARRITY, Dean, 2518 W. Andrew Johnson Hwy., Morristown, 37814. Tel: 423-586-9174.

Ministries of the Cumberland Mtn. Deanery—Rev. MICHAEL SWEENEY, Dean, 535 Margrave Dr., Harriman, 37748. Tel: 865-882-9838.

Ministries of the Smoky Mtn. Deanery—Rev. Msgr. T. ALLEN HUMBRECHT, Dean, 711 Northshore Dr., S.W., Knoxville, 37919. Tel: 865-588-0249.

Moderator of the Curia—Very Rev. DAVID BOETTNER, V.E., 805 Northshore Dr., S.W., Knoxville, 37919. Tel: 865-584-3307.

Priestly Life and Ministry—Rev. PETER J. IORIO, Dir., 900 Clingan Ridge Dr., N.W., Cleveland, 37312. Tel: 423-476-8123.

Propagation of the Faith—PAUL SIMONEAU, Dir., 805 Northshore Dr., S.W., Knoxville, 37919. Tel: 865-584-3307.

Scouting—Deacon OTTO PRESKE, Scout Chap., 535 Buckhorn Rd., Gatlinburg, 37738. Tel: 865-436-5339.

Diocesan Catholic Committee on Scouting—GEORGE C. LECRONE SR., Chm., 10700 Leeward Lane, Knoxville, 37934. Tel: 865-974-0050.

Stewardship and Development—SUZANNE P. ERPENBACH, Dir., 805 Northshore Dr., S.W., Knoxville, 37919. Tel: 865-584-3307. Email: serpenbach@dioknox.org.

"The East Tennessee Catholic"— (Diocesan Newspaper). MARY C. WEAVER, Editor, 805 Northshore Dr., S.W., Knoxville, 37919. Tel: 865-584-3307. Email: mweaver@dioknox.org.

Victim Assistance Coordinator—MARLA LENIHAN, 400 Laboratroy Rd., Ste. 103, Oak Ridge, 37830. Tel: 865-482-1388.

Vocations—Rev. PETER J. IORIO, Vocation Dir., 805 Northshore Dr., S.W., Knoxville, 37919. Tel: 865-584-3307; Sr. MARY YVETTE GILLEN, R.S.M., Coord. Vocation Promotion for Rel. Tel: 865-457-4073.

Vocation Discernment Office—Rev. MICHAEL E. CUMMINS, Dir., 734 W. Locust St., Johnson City, 37604. Tel: 423-926-7061.

Worship and Liturgy—Rev. RANDY STICE, Dir., 805 Northshore Dr., S.W., Knoxville, 37919. Tel: 865-584-3307.

Youth and Young Adult Ministry—AL FORSYTHE, Diocesan Coord., 805 Northshore Dr., S.W., Knoxville, 37919. Tel: 865-584-3307; DONNA L. JONES, Coord. Chattanooga Deanery, 859 McCallie Ave., Ste. 302, Chattanooga, 37403. Tel: 423-267-9878; Deacons G. JAMES FAGE II, Coord., Five Rivers Deanery, 780 Roddy Dr., Morristown, 37814. Tel: 423-587-4925; DAN HOSFORD, Coord. Cumberland Mtn. and Smoky Mtn. Deanery, 102 Pheasant Rd., Clinton, 37716. Tel: 865-603-9682.

CLERGY, PARISHES, MISSIONS AND PAROCHIAL SCHOOLS

CITY OF KNOXVILLE

(KNOX COUNTY)

1—CATHEDRAL OF THE SACRED HEART OF JESUS (1956) [JC] Rev. Msgr. T. Allen Humbrecht; Rev. Jose Manuel Perez (Mexico); Very Rev. David Boettner; Rev. Christopher Riehl; Deacons James Lawson, Pastoral Assoc.; Ben Johnston; David J. Lucheon; Joe Stackhouse.
Res.: 711 Northshore Dr., S.W., 37919. Tel: 865-588-4132; Fax: 865-558-9671. Web: www.shcathedral.org.
School—(Grades PreK-8) Tel: 865-588-0415; Fax: 865-558-4139. Web: www.shcschool.org. Sedonna Prater, Prin. Lay Teachers 41; Students 604.
Catechesis/Religious Program—Tel: 865-584-4528. Brigid Johnson, D.R.E. Students 183.

2—ST. ALBERT THE GREAT CHURCH (2007) Rev. Chris Michelson; Deacons Michael Eiffe; Patrick Murphy-Racey.
7200 Brickey Ln., 37918. Email: office@satgknox.org. Web: www.satgknox.org.
Catechesis/Religious Program—Kristen Lehman, D.R.E. Students 137.

3—ALL SAINTS CATHOLIC CHURCH (1994) [JC] Revs. Michael Woods; Jesus Antonio Giraldo (Colombia); Deacons Tim Elliott; Kenneth Long.
Mailing Address: 620 N. Cedar Bluff Rd., 37923. Tel: 865-531-0770; Fax: 865-531-1009. Email: allsaintsknox@bellsouth.net. Web: www.all-saintsknoxville.org. In Res., Rev. Anthony E. Dickerson.
Catechesis/Religious Program—Students 509.

4—HOLY GHOST (1908) [JC] Rev. Msgr. Francis Xavier Mankel; Rev. John Arthur Orr.
1041 N. Central St., 37917.
Res.: 111 Hinton Ave., 37917. Tel: 865-522-2205; Fax: 865-525-6051. Email: hgchurch@bellsouth.net. Web: www.discoveret.org/holyghst.
School—St. Joseph, (Grades PreK-8), 1810 Howard Rd., 37918. Tel: 865-689-3424; Fax: 865-687-7885. Web: www.stjoseph-knoxville.org. Dr. Aurelia Montgomery, Prin.; Charles Walden, Librarian. Lay Teachers 21; Students 217.
Catechesis/Religious Program—Kathleen Kramer, D.R.E. Students 65.

5—IMMACULATE CONCEPTION (1852), (Irish), [CEM] Rev. Joseph A. Ciccone, C.S.P.; Deacon Joseph Hieu Vinh.
Office: 414 W. Vine Ave., 37902-1327. Tel: 865-522-1508; Fax: 865-524-8514. Email: icoffice@bellsouth.net. Web: www.icknoxville.org.
Res.: 707 E. Scott Ave., 37917. Tel: 865-637-6451.
Catechesis/Religious Program— Kathleen Kramer, D.R.E. Students 74.

6—ST. JOHN NEUMANN (1977) Rev. John R. Dowling; Deacons Donald Amelse, M.P.S., Pastoral Assoc.; Marquis Syler; Michael Gouge.
Church: 645 St. John Ct., 37934-1555. Tel: 865-966-4540; Fax: 865-675-6815. Email: neumanncc@tds.net. Web: www.sjn-knox.org.
School—(Grades K-8), 625 St. John Ct., 37934-1555. Tel: 865-777-0077; Fax: 865-777-0087. Web: www.sjncs-knox.org. Bill Derbyshire, Prin.; Nancy Sanford, Librarian. Lay Teachers 25; Students 321.
Catechesis/Religious Program—Students 274.

7—JOHN XXIII UNIVERSITY PARISH/CATHOLIC CENTER (1968) [CEM], (Non-territorial parish for the University of Tennessee at Knoxville). Rev. Charles Donahue, C.S.P.; Ruth Queen Smith, Pastoral Assoc.
Res.: 1710 Melrose Pl., 37916. Tel: 865-523-7931; Fax: 865-523-7979.
Catechesis/Religious Program—Students 47.

OUTSIDE THE CITY OF KNOXVILLE

ALCOA, BLOUNT CO., OUR LADY OF FATIMA (1950) Revs. Bede C. Aboh (Nigeria); James Brent Allen Shelton; Deacon W. Joseph Armento.
Res. & Rectory: 860 Louisville Rd., 37701.
Office: 858 Louisville Rd., 37701. Tel: 865-982-3672; Fax: 865-977-4183. Web: www.ourladyoffatima.org.
Catechesis/Religious Program—Fax: 865-983-3563. Joyce McCormick, D.R.E. Students 298.
Mission—St. Francis of Assisi 7719 River Rd., Townsend, Blount Co. 37882. Tel: 865-448-6070. Email: saintfrancis@netzero.com. Deacon Michael G. Nestor.
Catechesis/Religious Program—

ATHENS, MCMINN CO., ST. MARY (1968) Rev. William Dickson Oruko, A.J. (Kenya).
Office: 1291 E. Madison Ave., 37303. Tel: 423-745-4277; Fax: 423-745-4277 (Call First). Email: stmaryathens@comcast.net. Web: www.stmaryathenstn.org.
Catechesis/Religious Program—Tel: 423-263-1217. Lee Ann Moates, D.R.E. Students 111.

CHATTANOOGA, HAMILTON CO.

1—ST. JUDE (1958) [JC] Revs. Charles Burton; Miguel Velez-Cardona; Deacons Gaspar DeGaetano; Brian Gabor; Thomas McConnell.
Res.: 930 Ashland Ter., 37415. Tel: 423-870-2386; Fax: 423-876-8960. Email: info@stjudechattanooga.org. Web: www.stjudechattanooga.org.
School—(Grades PreSchool-8) Tel: 423-877-6022; Fax: 423-875-8920. Jamie Goodhard, Prin.; Jane Ray, Librarian. Lay Teachers 34; Students 361.
Catechesis/Religious Program—Marilyn Derbyshire, D.R.E. Students 108.

2—OUR LADY OF PERPETUAL HELP (1937) Revs. James L. Vick; Augustine Idra, A.J. (Kenya); Deacon Mark Gang Jr.
Res.: 501 S. Moore Rd., 37412. Tel: 423-622-7232; Fax: 423-624-2686. Web: www.myolph.com.
School—(Grades K-8), 505 S. Moore Rd., 37412. Tel: 423-622-1418; Fax: 423-622-2016. Mrs. Jeri McInturff, Prin.; Patsy Duenas, Librarian. Lay Teachers 26; Students 290.
Catechesis/Religious Program—Tel: 423-622-7232; Fax: 423-624-2686. Lois Colosia, D.R.E. Students 135.

3—SS. PETER AND PAUL (1852) [JC] Rev. George E. Schmidt Jr.; Deacon James Wilson. In Res., Rev. Bertin Glennon, S.T.
Res.: 214 E. 8th St., 37402. Tel: 423-266-1618.
Catechesis/Religious Program—Tel: 706-935-4518. Ann May, D.R.E. Students 63.

4—ST. STEPHEN (1961) [JC] Rev. Gilbert M. Diaz; Deacon Gary Brinkworth.
Res. & Office: 7111 Lee Hwy., 37421. Tel: 423-892-1261; Fax: 423-892-3242. Email: catholicstephen@comcast.net. Web: www.dioceseofknoxville.org.
Catechesis/Religious Program—Tel: 423-892-2957. Anna Anthony, D.R.E. Students 150.

CLEVELAND, BRADLEY CO., ST. THERESE OF LISIEUX (1914) Revs. Peter J. Iorio; Michael R. Maples.
Res.: 900 Clingan Ridge Dr., N.W., 37312. Tel: 423-476-8123; Fax: 423-479-3339.
Catechesis/Religious Program—Email: sttherese@charter.net. Gerri Toeller, D.R.E. Students 237.

CLINTON, ANDERSON CO., ST. THERESE (1971) Rev. William H. Gahagan; Sr. Yvette Gillen, R.S.M., Pastoral Assoc. & D.R.E.
Church & Res.: 701 S. Charles G. Seivers Blvd., 37716. Tel: 865-457-4073 (Church); 865-457-1317 (Res.); Fax: 865-463-9734.
Catechesis/Religious Program—Students 45.

COPPERHILL, POLK CO., ST. CATHERINE LABOURE (1977) Rev. William Patrick Resen.
Mailing Address: 115 E. Main St., P.O. Box 1165, 37317. Tel: 423-496-3498. Email: sclc@bellsouth.net.
Catechesis/Religious Program— Mary Jane Uhlik, D.R.E.

CROSSVILLE, CUMBERLAND CO., ST. ALPHONSUS (1948) Rev. James P. Harvey II.
Res.: 151 St. Alphonsus Way, 38555. Tel: 931-484-2358 (Office); 931-456-5005 (Res.); Fax: 931-484-7407. Email: stalphonsus@frontiernet.net. Web: www.stalphonsuscrossville.org.
Catechesis/Religious Program—Tel: 931-456-5227; Fax: 931-484-7407. Sara Carey, D.R.E. Students 115.

DAYTON, RHEA CO., ST. BRIDGET (1968) Rev. Samuel L. Sturm; Deacon Tom Kiefer.
Res.: 320 Walnut Grove Church Rd., P.O. Box 106, 37321. Tel: 423-775-2664 (Church); 423-775-5542 (Rectory); Fax: 423-775-2664. Email: rosa@saintbridget.net. Web: www.saintbridget.net.
Catechesis/Religious Program—Christina Mugridge, D.R.E. Students 54.

DUNLAP, SEQUATCHIE CO., SHEPHERD OF THE VALLEY (1997) Rev. Mark A. Scholz.
Res.: 6191 Hwy. 28, 37327. Tel: 423-949-6903; Fax: 423-837-7793.
Catechesis/Religious Program—Students 5.

ELIZABETHTON, CARTER CO., ST. ELIZABETH (1923) Rev. Dennis Kress.
Res.: 510 W. C St., P.O. Box 7, 37644-0007. Tel: 423-543-3412; Fax: 423-542-2961. Email: stelizabeth@chartertn.net.
Catechesis/Religious Program—Students 26.

FAIRFIELD GLADE, CUMBERLAND CO., ST. FRANCIS OF ASSISI (1983) [CEM] Rev. John B. Charles O'Neill; Deacons Mark A. Fredrick; Mark F. White; Keith S. Farber. In Res., Rev. Msgr. Philip F. Thoni, CH (LTC) (Retired).
Res.: 7505 Peavine Rd., 38558. Tel: 931-456-0415; Fax: 931-707-0186. Email: stfrancis@frontiernet.net. Web: www.stfrancisfairfield.com.
Church: 7503 Peavine Rd., 38558. Tel: 931-484-3628.
Catechesis/Religious Program—Students 10.

GATLINBURG, SEVIER CO., ST. MARY (1935) Very Rev. David Boettner, Parochial Admin.
Res.: 304 Historic Nature Tr., 37738. Tel: 865-436-4907; Fax: 865-430-3623.
Catechesis/Religious Program—Students 13.

GREENEVILLE, GREENE CO., NOTRE DAME (1955) Rev. Kwaku John Appiah.
Res.: 212 Mt. Bethel Rd., 37745. Tel: 423-639-9381; Fax: 423-638-5219. Email: notredametn@embarqmail.com. Web: notredamechurchtn.org.
Catechesis/Religious Program—Tel: 423-639-9382. Susan Collins, D.R.E. Students 110.

HARRIMAN, ROANE CO., BLESSED SACRAMENT (1908) Rev. Michael Sweeney.
Res.: 535 Margrave Dr., 37748. Tel: 865-882-9838; Fax: 865-882-3786 (Rectory); 865-882-5491 (Sec.). Email: blessedsacrament@juno.com.
Catechesis/Religious Program—Students 74.
Mission—Saint Christopher 204 Tinch Ave., Jamestown, Fentress Co. 38556-5221. Tel: 931-879-8144; Fax: 931-879-8145. 160 Holt Spur Rd.,

Jamestown, 38556-5221.
Catechesis/Religious Program—
Station—Brushy Mountain Prison Wartburg. Tel: 865-346-6641.
Station—Morgan County Regional Correctional Facility Wartburg.

HELENWOOD, SCOTT CO., ST. JUDE PARISH (1982) Rev. William H. Gahagan; Sr. Patricia Soete, R.S.M., Pastoral Assoc.
Mailing Address: 13067 Scott Hwy., P.O. Box 555, 37755. Tel: 423-569-9584 (Church).
Catechesis/Religious Program—

JEFFERSON CITY, JEFFERSON CO., HOLY TRINITY CATHOLIC CHURCH (1997) Rev. Dan G. Whitman; Deacons Gordon Lowery; Jim Prosak; John Riehl.
475 N. Hwy. 92, P.O. Box 304, 37760. Tel: 865-471-0347; Fax: 865-471-0349.
Catechesis/Religious Program—Students 64.

JOHNSON CITY, WASHINGTON CO., ST. MARY (1906) Revs. Anietie Akata (Nigeria); Michael Cummins. In Res., Deacons Richard Carner; George Fredericks III; Michael Jacobs.
Res.: 2211 E. Lakeview Dr., 37601. Tel: 423-282-6367; Fax: 423-282-6145. Web: www.stmarysjc.org.
School—(Grades K-8) Tel: 423-282-3397; Fax: 423-282-0224. Randi McKee, Prin.; Polly Theobald, Librarian. Lay Teachers 20; Students 175.
Catechesis/Religious Program—Anne DeVeaux, D.R.E. Students 365.

KINGSPORT, SULLIVAN CO., ST. DOMINIC (1941) Revs. Michael F. Nolan; Paul J. Valleroy; Deacons Robert Lange; Frank Fischer; Laurent Legault.
Res.: 2517 John B. Dennis Hwy., 37660. Tel: 423-288-8101; Fax: 423-288-7183. Web: www.saintdominicchurch.org.
School—(Grades K-5) Tel: 423-245-0362; Fax: 423-245-2907. Debbie DePollo, Prin.; Harry Arnold, Librarian. Lay Teachers 15; Students 52.
Catechesis/Religious Program—Tel: 423-288-8101. Sheila Eanes, D.R.E.; Suzanne Payne, Youth Min. Students 264.

LAFOLLETTE, CAMPBELL CO., OUR LADY OF PERPETUAL HELP (1904) Rev. Joe Campbell.
Mailing Address: 1142 E. Elm St., 37766. Tel: 423-562-0312.
Catechesis/Religious Program—Students 15.

LANCING, MORGAN CO., ST. ANN (1982) Attended by Blessed Sacrament, Harriman. Rev. Michael Sweeney; Deacon Norman Amero.
Mailing Address: P.O. Box 77, 37770-0077. Tel: 865-346-6260; Fax: 865-882-5491.
Catechesis/Religious Program—Tel: 865-882-9838; Fax: 865-882-3786. Students 4.

LENOIR CITY, LOUDON CO., ST. THOMAS THE APOSTLE (1973) Revs. Christian Mathis; Thomas W. Moser; Deacons Jose Rivera; Sean K. Smith.
Res.: 1580 St. Thomas Way, 37772. Tel: 865-986-9885; Fax: 865-988-8230. Email: ourparish@sthomaslc.com. Web: www.sthomaslc.com.
Catechesis/Religious Program—Email: jill@sthomaslc.com. Students 242.

MADISONVILLE, MONROE CO., ST. JOSEPH THE WORKER (1992) Revs. P. J. McGinnity; William Patrick Resen.
Mailing Address: 649 Old Tellico Hwy. N., 37354. Tel: 423-442-7273; Fax: 423-442-7272. Email: sjtwrcc@bellsouth.net.
Catechesis/Religious Program—Students 60.

MORRISTOWN, HAMBLEN CO., ST. PATRICK (1959) Revs. G. Patrick Garrity; Joseph Hammond (Ghana); Deacons Gerald James Fage; Robert Smearing.
Res.: 2518 W. Andrew Johnson Hwy., 37814. Tel: 423-586-9174; Fax: 423-318-7044. Email: saintpat@charter.net. Web: www.stpatrickmorristown.net.
Catechesis/Religious Program—Tel: 423-586-4091. Kathleen DeAngelis, D.R.E.; Colleen Jacobs, Youth Minister (Elementary & Middle School). Students 213.

MOUNTAIN CITY, JOHNSON CO., ST. ANTHONY OF PADUA CATHOLIC CHURCH (1995), (Quasi Parish) Rev. Dennis Kress, Parochial Admin.; Deacons Donald F. Hathaway; John Hackett.
Res.: 513 Hickory, 37683. Tel: 423-543-3412; Fax: 423-542-2961.
Church: 833 W. Main St., 37683. Tel: 423-727-5156; Fax: 423-727-5017.
Catechesis/Religious Program—Students 10.

NEWPORT, COCKE CO., GOOD SHEPHERD (1967) Rev. Robert J. Hofstetter; Mr. Dennis H. Bible, Parish Coord.; Deacon Otto Preske.
Mailing Address: 2361 Cosby Hwy., P.O. Box 1894, 37822. Tel: 423-623-5051.
Catechesis/Religious Program—Students 4.

NORRIS, ANDERSON CO., ST. JOSEPH (1949) Rev. William H. Gahagan; Deacon Dan Hosford.
Res.: P.O. Box 902, 37828. Tel: 865-494-9964; Fax: 865-494-7702. Email: stjosephnorris1@comcast.net. Web: www.rc.net/knoxville/stjoseph/index.htm.
Church: 3425 Andersonville Hwy. 61, P.O. Box 387, 37828. Tel: 865-494-7746.
Catechesis/Religious Program—Lynnette Currie, D.R.E. Students 52.

OAK RIDGE, ANDERSON CO., ST. MARY (1943) Revs. William L. McKenzie; Jorge Andres Cano Ramirez (Colombia); Deacon Gary Sega.
Res.: 327 Vermont Ave., 37830. Tel: 865-482-2875; Fax: 865-766-8435. Email: office@smcor.org. Web: www.stmarysoakridge.org.
School—(Grades K-8), 323 Vermont Ave., 37830. Tel: 865-483-9700; Fax: 865-483-8305. Web: www.stmarysoakridge.org. Sr. Andrea Marie Graham, O.P., Prin.; Cheryl Kress, Librarian. Sisters 4; Lay Teachers 21; Students 227.
Catechesis/Religious Program—Tel: 865-766-8386. Karen Wilkins-Butz, D.R.E. Students 281.

PIGEON FORGE, SEVIER CO., HOLY CROSS (1992) Rev. Jay M. Flaherty; Deacon James Larry West.
Church: 144 Wears Valley Rd., 37863. Tel: 865-429-5587; Fax: 865-453-8951. Web: www.holycrossinthesmokies.org.
Catechesis/Religious Program—Students 123.

ROGERSVILLE, HAWKINS CO., ST. HENRY (1981) Rev. Michael T. Jennings.
Res.: 112-114 Hwy. 70 N., 37857. Tel: 423-272-6897.
Catechesis/Religious Program—Students 12.

SEYMOUR, SEVIER CO., HOLY FAMILY (1984) Rev. Ragan Schriver; Deacons Ronald J. Volek; Dean Burry.
Mailing Address: 307 Black Oak Ridge Rd., 37865. Tel: 865-609-1081; Fax: 865-579-3645.
Catechesis/Religious Program—Tel: 865-573-1203. Carol Idol, D.R.E. Students 96.

SIGNAL MOUNTAIN, HAMILTON CO., ST. AUGUSTINE (1938) [CEM] Rev. Patrick P. Brownell; Deacon Gordon Kilburn.
Res.: 1716 Anderson Pike, P.O. Box 10, 37377. Tel: 423-826-0429; Fax: 423-886-3451. Email: parishoffice@staugustinecatholic.org. Web: www.staugustinecatholic.org.
Catechesis/Religious Program—Students 170.

SNEEDVILLE, HANCOCK CO., ST. JAMES THE APOSTLE (1982) Attended by St. Henry, Rogersville. Rev. Michael T. Jennings.
Res. & Mailing Address: P.O. Box 93, 37869. Tel: 423-272-6897.

SODDY DAISY, HAMILTON CO., HOLY SPIRIT CATHOLIC CHURCH (1999) Revs. Michael Creson; Alex J. Waraksa; Deacons Michael Kucharzak; Noel W. Spencer Jr.
Mailing Address: P.O. Box 1015, 37384.
Church: 10768 Dayton Pike, 37379. Tel: 423-332-5300; Fax: 423-332-5391. Email: forhscc@yahoo.com. Web: www.holyspirittn.com.
Res.: 10812 Dayton Pike, 37379. Tel: 423-332-8283.
Catechesis/Religious Program—Students 99.

SOUTH PITTSBURG, MARION CO., OUR LADY OF LOURDES (1899) Rev. Mark A. Scholz.
Res.: 700 Holly Ave., P.O. Box 288, 37380. Tel: 423-837-7068; Fax: 423-837-7793.
Mission—Virgin of the Poor Shrine New Hope, Marion Co.
Catechesis/Religious Program—Students 12.

TAZEWELL, CLAIBORNE CO., CHRIST THE KING (1990) Attended by Our Lady of Perpetual Help Church, LaFollette Rev. Joseph Campbell.
Res. & Mailing Address: 1142 E. Elm St., LaFollette, 37766. Tel: 423-562-0312.
Catechesis/Religious Program—Students 27.

TOWNSEND, BLOUNT CO., ST. FRANCIS OF ASSISI (1961) Attended by Our Lady of Fatima, Alcoa. Revs. Bede C. Aboh (Nigeria); James Brentshelton; William J. McNeeley; Deacon Michael Nestor.
Mailing Address: 7719 River Rd., 37882. Tel: 423-448-6070.
Catechesis/Religious Program—

Retired:
Rev. Msgr.—
Thoni, Philip F., CH (LTC), 7503 Pearvine Rd., Fairfield Glade, 38558.
Revs.—
Brando, Joseph J., 2146 Floyd Porter Rd., Maryville, 37803.
Brett, Frank X., P.O. Box 510401, Melbourne Beach, FL 32951.
Casey, William, 740 Shake Rag Rd., Greeneville, 37743.
Demers, Bertrand, 1239 Chelsea Rd., 37922.
Hostettler, Paul A., Villa Maria Manor, 32 White Bridge Rd., Apt. 225, Nashville, 37205.
Neuzil, Gregory, 10510 Buckeye Rd., Cleveland, OH 44104.
O'Connell, Thomas P., 806 Villa View Way, 37920.

Permanent Deacons:
Amelse, Donald, M.P.S., St. John Neumann, Knoxville
Amero, Norman, St. Ann, Lancing
Armento, W. Joseph, Our Lady of Fatima, Aloca
Bresler, Thomas, St. Augustine Chapel, Signal Mountain; Alexian Village
Brinkworth, Gary, St. Stephen, Chattanooga
Burry, Dean, Holy Family, Seymour
Carner, Richard, St. Mary, Johnson City
DeGaetano, Gaspar, St. Jude, Chattanooga
Diesing, William
Eiffe, Michael, St. Albert the Great, Knoxville
Elliott, Tim, All Saints, Knoxville
Fage, G. James, II, St. Patrick, Morristown
Farber, Keith S., St. Francis of Assisi, Fairfield Glade
Fischer, Frank, St. Dominic, Kingsport
Fischer, Robert W., (Retired)
Fredericks, George, III, St. Mary, Johnson City
Fredrick, Mark A., (Retired)
Gabor, Brian, St. Jude, Chattanooga
Gang, Mark, Jr., Our Lady of Perpetual Help, Chattanooga
Gouge, Mike, St. John Neumann, Knoxville
Hackett, John, St. Anthony of Padua, Mountain City
Hathaway, Donald F., St. Anthony, Mountain City
Hosford, Dan, St. Joseph, Norris
Jacobs, Michael, St. Mary, Johnson City
Johnston, Ben, Cathedral of the Sacred Heart of Jesus, Knoxville
Kiefer, Thomas, St. Bridget, Dayton
Kilburn, Gordon, St. Augustine, Signal Mountain
Kucharzak, Michael, Holy Spirit, Soddy Daisy
Lange, Robert, St. Dominic, Kingsport
Lawson, James, Cathedral of the Sacred Heart of Jesus
Legault, Laurent, St. Dominic, Kingsport
Long, Kenneth, All Saints, Knoxville
Lowery, Gordon, Holy Trinity, Jefferson City
Lucheon, David J., Cathedral of the Sacred Heart of Jesus, Knoxville
McConnell, Thomas, St. Jude, Chattanooga
Murphy-Racey, Patrick, St. Albert the Great, Knoxville
Nelson, Paul, (Inactive)
Nestor, Michael, St. Francis of Assisi, Townsend
Oleck, William A., (Retired)
Preske, Otto F., Good Shepherd, Newport
Prosak, Jim, Holy Trinity, Jefferson City
Riehl, John, Holy Trinity, Jefferson City
Rivera, Jose, (Retired), St. Thomas the Apostle, Lenoir City
Sega, Gary, St. Mary, Oak Ridge
Smearing, Robert, St. Patrick, Morristown
Smith, Sean K., St. Thomas the Apostle, Lenoir City
Solis, Joseph, St. Alphonsus, Crossville
Spencer, Noel W., Jr., Ph.D., (Inactive)
Stackhouse, Joe, Cathedral of the Sacred Heart of Jesus, Knoxville
Syler, Marquis E., St. John Neumann, Knoxville
Vinh, Joseph, Immaculate Conception, Knoxville
Volek, Ronald J., Holy Family, Seymour
West, James Larry, Holy Cross, Pigeon Forge
White, Mark F., St. Francis of Assisi, Fairfield Glade
Wilson, James E., SS. Peter and Paul, Chattanooga

INSTITUTIONS LOCATED IN THE DIOCESE

[A] HIGH SCHOOLS, DIOCESAN

KNOXVILLE. *Knoxville Catholic High School* (1932) 9245 Fox Lonas Rd., 37923. Tel: 865-560-0313; Fax: 865-560-0314. Email: info@knoxvillecatholic.com. Web: knoxvillecatholic.com. Mr. Dickie Sompayrac, Prin. Tel: 865-560-0518; Fax: 865-560-0591; Mr. Mark Balog, Campus Min./Rel. Teacher. Tel: 865-560-0529; Fax: 865-560-0314; Rev. Anthony E. Dickerson, Chap.; Deacon Patrick Murphy-Racey. Tel: 865-560-0527; Fax: 865-560-0314; Dawn Harbin, Librarian. Tel: 865-560-0313; Fax: 865-560-0314. Priests 2; Sisters 2; Lay Teachers 47; Total Staff 51; Students 665.

Knoxville Catholic High School Development Board of Trust Tel: 865-560-0509; Fax: 865-560-0314.

CHATTANOOGA. *Notre Dame High School* (1876) 2701 Vermont Ave., 37404. Tel: 423-624-4618; Fax: 423-624-4621. Email: storeyp@myndhs.com. Web: www.myndhs.com. Mr. Perry Storey, Prin.; Nancy Trice, Librarian; Rev. Augustine Idra, A.J. (Kenya), Spiritual Dir. Priests 1; Lay Teachers 38; Students 471; Total Staff 19.

Notre Dame High School Financial Board of Trustees

[B] GENERAL HOSPITALS

KNOXVILLE. *St. Mary's Health System, Inc.* (1930) 900 E. Oak Hill Ave., 37917. Tel: 865-545-8000; Fax: 865-545-7682. Web: www.mercy.com. A. David Jimenez, CEO; Rev. Evan Eckhoff, O.F.M., Chap. Conducted by Sisters of Mercy of the Americas. Sisters 6; Bed Capacity 472; Patients Assisted Annually 291,320; Total Staff 3,064.

St. Mary's Health System, Inc. Tel: 865-545-8000; Fax: 865-545-7682. Web: www.mercy.com.

CHATTANOOGA. *Memorial Health Care System, Inc.* (1952) 2525 deSales Ave., 37404. Tel: 423-495-2525; Fax: 423-495-7726. Web: memorial.org. James M. Hobson, Pres. & CEO. (Member of Catholic Health Initiatives) Sisters 2; Bed Capacity 405; Patients Assisted Annually 97,452; Total Staff 4,001.

Memorial Health Care System Foundation, Inc. (2001) 2525 deSales Ave., 37404. Tel: 423-495-4438; Fax: 423-495-6235.

[C] SPECIAL HOSPITALS

SIGNAL MOUNTAIN. *Alexian Village Health Care Center* (1938) 671 Alexian Way, 37377. Tel: 423-886-0338; Fax: 423-886-0488. Email: lkrueger@alexianbrothers.net. Web: www.alexianvillage.com. Bro. John Howard, C.F.A., Dir. Community; Revs. Joseph Kuzhupil, M.S.F.S. (India), Chap.; Augustine Joseph, M.S.F.S. (India), Assoc. Chap.; Bro. Lawrence Krueger, C.F.A., Healthcare Admin. Licensed Skilled & Intermediate Care Nursing Home. Brothers 8; Bed Capacity 114; Patients Assisted Annually 278; Assisted Living 32; Total Staff 105.

[D] HOMES FOR THE AGED

SIGNAL MOUNTAIN. *Alexian Village of Tennessee* (1983) 437 Alexian Way, 37377. Tel: 423-886-0100; Fax: 423-886-0470. Email: kmulhearn@alexianbrothers.net. Web: www.alexianvillage.com. Kevin Mulhearn, Pres. & CEO; Revs. Joseph Kuzhupil, M.S.F.S. (India), Chap.; Valerie Carnes, Chap.; Augustine Joseph, M.S.F.S. (India), Assoc. Chap.; Maro Cannon, C.F.A., Assoc. Chap.; Camilius Blazek, Assoc. Chap. Retirement Community & Healthcare Center. Life Care Units 328; Total in Residence 600; Total Staff 300.

[E] PROTECTIVE INSTITUTIONS

KNOXVILLE. *Columbus Home, Inc.*, 3227 Division St., 37919. Tel: 865-971-3560; Fax: 865-546-0433. Total Assisted Annually 22; Total Staff 12.

[F] MONASTERIES AND RESIDENCES OF PRIESTS AND BROTHERS

SIGNAL MOUNTAIN. *Alexian Brothers*, 198 James Blvd., 37377. Tel: 423-886-0380; Fax: 423-886-0381. Email: jhoward@alexianbrothers.net. Web: www.alexianbrothers.org/. Bros. Edward Walsh, C.F.A., Supr. Gen.; John Howard, C.F.A., Provincial Councilor & Community Dir.; Simeon Pytel, C.F.A., Sec. (Generalate); Andrew Thome, C.F.A., Patient Visitor: Alexian Brothers PACE Program; Philip Kennedy, C.F.A., (Retired); Rev. Maro Cannon, C.F.A., Chap.; Bros. Lawrence Krueger, C.F.A., Admin., Health Care Center, Alexian Village TN & Provincial Councilor; James Darby, C.F.A., (Retired); Exequiel Mata, C.F.A.; Ronald Ruberg, C.F.A. Brothers 9.

[G] CONVENTS AND RESIDENCES FOR SISTERS

KNOXVILLE. *Sisters of Mercy* (1831) (South Central Region), Tel: 865-545-8128; 865-545-8265; Fax: 865-545-7915. Email: snaber@mercy.com. Web: www.mercy.com.

St. Mary's Medical Center (1930) 900 E. Oak Hill Ave., 37917. Tel: 865-545-8000; Fax: 865-545-7915. Sisters 6.

CLINTON. *St. Therese Convent*, 701 S. Charles G. Seivers Blvd., 37716. Tel: 865-463-8935; Fax: 865-463-9734. Email: ygillen@bellsouth.net. Sr. Mary Yvette Gillen, R.S.M., Pastoral Assoc. & D.R.E.

COPPERHILL. *Monastery of Our Lady of Little Citeaux* (1997) 255 Golf Course Rd., 37317. Tel: 423-496-7373.

HELENWOOD. *Sisters of Mercy*, 13071 Scott Hwy., P.O. Box 555, 37755. Tel: 423-569-3492.

St. Jude Church, 13067 Scott Hwy., 37755. Tel: 423-569-9584. Email: pasoete@highland.net. Sr. Patricia Soete, R.S.M., Pastoral Assoc. Tel: 423-569-3492.

OAK RIDGE. *Dominican Sisters (St. Cecilia Congregation)* (1860) St. Mary's Convent, 323 Vermont Ave., 37830. Tel: 865-483-9700; Fax: 865-483-8305. Web: nashvilledominican.org. Sisters 7.

[H] NEWMAN CENTERS

KNOXVILLE. *UT-Knoxville, Newman Foundation, Inc.* (1968) *John XXIII University Parish/Catholic Center*, 1710 Melrose Pl., 37916. Tel: 865-523-7931; Fax: 865-523-7979. Email: john23@utk.edu. Web: www.john23rd.org. Rev. Charles Donahue, C.S.P.

CHATTANOOGA. *Newman Foundation of Chattanooga, Inc.* Catholic Student Center, 514 Palmetto St., 37403. Tel: 423-267-3064. Email: cathstudentctr@chattanooga.net. Web: www.catholicdeaneryofchattanooga.org/utcx.html. Rev. James Mallet. Total Staff 2.

JOHNSON CITY. *ETSU-Catholic Center* 734 W. Locust St., 37604. Tel: 423-926-7061. Email: etsucatholiccenter@yahoo.com. Web: www.etsu.edu/newman. Rev. Michael Cummins. Total Staff 1.

[I] HEALTH CARE SYSTEMS

KNOXVILLE. *Mercy Health Partners, Inc.*, 900 E. Oak Hill Ave., 37917. Tel: 865-545-8000; Fax: 865-545-7682.

[J] FOUNDATIONS AND ENDOWMENTS

KNOXVILLE. *The Catholic Diocese of Knoxville Foundation, Inc.*, 805 Northshore Dr., S.W., 37919. Tel: 865-584-3307; Fax: 865-584-7538.

Catholic Foundation of East Tennessee, 805 Northshore Dr., S.W., 37919. Tel: 865-584-3307; Fax: 865-584-7538.

Mercy Health Partners Foundation, Inc., 900 E. Oak Hill Ave., 37917. Tel: 865-632-5678; Fax: 865-549-4690.

[K] MISCELLANEOUS

KNOXVILLE. *Diocesan Council of Catholic Women*, 805 Northshore Dr., S.W., 37919. Tel: 865-482-7449. Rev. Msgr. Francis Xavier Mankel, S.T.L., V.G., Diocesan & Deanery Spiritual Moderator; Revs. Dan G. Whitman, Deanery Spiritual Moderator, Five Rivers; Peter J. Iorio, Deanery Spiritual Moderator, Chattanooga; Michael Woods, Deanery Spiritual Moderator, Cumberland Mountain.

Ladies of Charity (1942) 1031 N. Central Ave., 37917. Tel: 865-522-6341; 865-524-0538; Fax: 865-524-0538. Rev. Msgr. Francis Xavier Mankel, S.T.L., V.G., Spiritual Moderator. Total Assisted Annually 32,476; Total Staff 9.

Ladies of Charity- Pantry, 119 Dameron Ave., 37917. Tel: 865-522-6341.

CHATTANOOGA. *Ladies of Charity*, 2821 Rossville Blvd., 37407. Tel: 423-624-3222; Fax: 423-698-8048. Emergency assistance through referrals from area churches and social service agencies in the form of food, medicine, clothing, Lifeline, meals on wheels, layettes for newborns, payment on utilities, rent, glasses, dental work, etc. Total Assisted Annually 4,832.

RELIGIOUS INSTITUTES OF MEN REPRESENTED IN THE DIOCESE

For further details refer to the corresponding bracketed number in the Religious Institutes of Men or Women section.

[0120]—*Alexian Brothers*—C.F.A.

[]—*Apostles of Jesus*—A.J.

[0600]—*Brothers of the Congregation of Holy Cross*—C.S.C.

[]—*Crusaders of the Holy Spirit*—C.H.S.

[0520]—*Franciscan Friars*—O.F.M.

[0570]—*The Glenmary Home Missioners*—Glmy.

[0840]—*Missionary Servants of the Most Holy Trinity*—S.T.

[]—*Order of Missionaries of St. Francis de Sales*—M.S.F.S.

[1030]—*Paulist Fathers*—C.S.P.

RELIGIOUS INSTITUTES OF WOMEN REPRESENTED IN THE DIOCESE

[1920]—*Congregation of Sisters of Holy Cross*—C.S.C.

[1070-07]—*Dominican Sisters (St. Cecilia Congregation)*—O.P.

[2575]—*Institute of the Sisters of Mercy of the Americas* (South Central)—R.S.M.

[]—*Missionary Sisters of the Sacred Heart of Jesus "Ad Gentes"*—M.A.G.

[2519]—*Religious Sisters of Mercy of Alma, Michigan*—R.S.M.

[0500]—*Sisters of Charity of Nazareth*—S.C.N.

[3930]—*Sisters of St. Joseph, Third Order of St. Francis*—S.S.J.-T.O.S.F.

[0970]—*Sisters of the Divine Compassion*—R.D.C.

INTERPAROCHIAL CEMETERIES

KNOXVILLE. *Calvary Cemetery*, 2000 Martin Luther King Jr. Blvd., 37915. Tel: 865-522-1508. *c/o Immaculate Conception Church*, 414 West Vine Ave., 37902-1327. Rev. Joseph A. Ciccone, C.S.P.

CHATTANOOGA. *Mount Olivet Cemetery*, One Mount Olivet Dr., 37412. Tel: 423-622-0728; Fax: 423-894-7893. Rev. George E. Schmidt Jr.; David E. Hale, Supt.

NECROLOGY

† Prescott, Herbert W., (Retired)—Died Nov. 26, 2009

An asterisk (*) denotes an organization that has established tax-exempt status directly with the IRS and is not covered by the USCCB Group Ruling.

Diocese of La Crosse

(Dioecesis Crossensis)

(VACANT SEE)

Chancery Office: 3710 East Ave. S., P.O. Box 4004, La Crosse, WI 54602-4004. Tel: 608-788-7700; Fax: 608-788-8413.

Web: www.dioceseoflacrosse.com

Email: mailbox@dioceseoflacrosse.com

Square Miles 15,078.

Erected March 3, 1868. Subdivided May 3, 1905. Subdivided January 15, 1946.

Comprises the following 19 Counties in the State of Wisconsin: Adams, Buffalo, Chippewa, Clark, Crawford, Dunn, Eau Claire, Jackson, Juneau, La Crosse, Marathon, Monroe, Pepin, Pierce, Portage, Richland, Trempealeau, Vernon and Wood.

For legal titles of parishes and diocesan institutions, consult the Chancery Office.

STATISTICAL OVERVIEW

Personnel	
Priests: Diocesan Active in Diocese	98
Priests: Diocesan Active Outside Diocese	7
Priests: Diocesan in Foreign Missions	3
Priests: Retired, Sick or Absent	58
Number of Diocesan Priests	166
Religious Priests in Diocese	18
Total Priests in Diocese	184
Extern Priests in Diocese	40
Permanent Deacons in Diocese	42
Total Brothers	4
Total Sisters	393
Parishes	
Parishes	165
With Resident Pastor:	
Resident Diocesan Priests	106
Resident Religious Priests	6
Without Resident Pastor:	
Administered by Priests	53
Professional Ministry Personnel:	
Sisters	13
Lay Ministers	40
Welfare	
Catholic Hospitals	9
Total Assisted	608,548
Homes for the Aged	10
Total Assisted	1,047
Day Care Centers	2
Total Assisted	144
Specialized Homes	6
Total Assisted	9,874
Special Centers for Social Services	2
Total Assisted	3,085
Educational	
Seminaries, Diocesan	1
Students from This Diocese	7
Students from Other Diocese	1
Diocesan Students in Other Seminaries	27
Total Seminarians	34
Colleges and Universities	1
Total Students	3,088
High Schools, Diocesan and Parish	7
Total Students	1,565
Elementary Schools, Diocesan and Parish	63
Total Students	7,138
Catechesis/Religious Education:	
High School Students	3,798
Elementary Students	12,471
Total Students under Catholic Instruction	28,094
Teachers in the Diocese:	
Priests	10
Sisters	17
Lay Teachers	832
Vital Statistics	
Receptions into the Church:	
Infant Baptism Totals	2,307
Adult Baptism Totals	150
Received into Full Communion	227
First Communions	2,529
Confirmations	2,491
Marriages:	
Catholic	548
Interfaith	270
Total Marriages	818
Deaths	1,983
Total Catholic Population	196,246
Total Population	849,626

Former Bishops—Most Rev. MICHAEL HEISS, D.D., cons. Sept. 6, 1868; appt. Titular Archbishop of Hadrianople, and coadjutor to the Metropolitan of Milwaukee March 14, 1880; promoted to Milwaukee, Sept. 1881; died March 26, 1890; Rt. Revs. KILIAN CASPAR FLASCH, D.D., cons. Aug. 24, 1881; died Aug. 3, 1891; JAMES SCHWEBACH, D.D., cons. Feb. 25, 1892; died June 6, 1921; Most Revs. ALEXANDER J. MCGAVICK, D.D., LL.D., cons. Titular Bishop of Marcopolis and Auxiliary Bishop of Chicago, May 1, 1899; transferred to See of La Crosse, Nov. 21, 1921; died Aug. 25, 1948; JOHN P. TREACY, S.T.D., cons. Titular Bishop of Metelis and Coadjutor of La Crosse "cum jure successionis," Oct. 2, 1945; succeeded to the See, July 23, 1946; died Oct. 11, 1964; FREDERICK W. FREKING, D.D., J.C.D., cons. Bishop of Salina, KS, Nov. 30, 1957; transferred to the See of La Crosse, Dec. 30, 1964; installed La Crosse, Feb. 24, 1965; retired May 10, 1983; died Nov. 28, 1998; JOHN J. PAUL, appt. Titular Bishop of Lambese and Auxiliary Bishop of La Crosse, May 17, 1977; cons. Aug. 4, 1977; appt. to the Residential See of La Crosse, Oct. 18, 1983; installed as Bishop of La Crosse, Dec. 5, 1983; retired Dec. 10, 1994; died March 5, 2006; RAYMOND L. BURKE, D.D., J.C.D., appt. to the Residential See of La Crosse Dec. 10, 1994; cons. Jan. 6, 1995; installed as Eighth Bishop of La Crosse Feb. 22, 1995; appt. Archbishop of the Archdiocese of St. Louis Dec. 2, 2003; installed Jan. 26, 2004; JEROME E. LISTECKI, D.D., J.C.D., ord. May 14, 1975; appt. Auxiliary Bishop of Chicago and Titular Bishop of Nara Nov. 7, 2000; cons. Jan. 8, 2001; appt. Bishop of La Crosse Dec. 29, 2004; installed March 1, 2005; appt. Archbishop of Milwaukee Nov. 14, 2009; installed Jan. 4, 2010.

Chancery Office—3710 East Ave. S., P.O. Box 4004, La Crosse, 54602-4004. Tel: 608-788-7700; Fax: 608-788-8413. Office Hours: Mon.-Fri. 8-4:30.

Chancellor—Mr. BENEDICT T. NGUYEN, M.T.S., J.D., J.C.L.

Vice-Chancellor—Rev. LEON A. POWELL.

Diocesan Administrator and Moderator of the Curia—Rev. Msgr. RICHARD W. GILLES, J.C.L.

Archivist—Rev. ROBERT T. ALTMANN (Retired).

Finance Officer—SONDRA RIEDER.

Ecclesiastical Notaries—Rev. Msgr. RICHARD W. GILLES, J.C.L.; Rev. LEON A. POWELL; Mr. BENEDICT T. NGUYEN, M.T.S., J.D., J.C.L.; KELLY MCCARTHY; SUSAN VLASAK, Mailing Address: P.O. Box 4004, La Crosse, 54602-4004.

Diocesan Tribunal—3710 East Ave. S., P.O. Box 4004, La Crosse, 54602-4004. Tel: 608-788-7700. (Address all rogatory commissions to the Chancellor).

Judicial Vicar—Rev. Msgr. ROBERT P. HUNDT, J.C.L.

Promoter of Justice—Rev. Msgr. RICHARD W. GILLES, J.C.L.

Defensor Vinculi—Mr. BENEDICT T. NGUYEN, M.T.S., J.D., J.C.L.; Rev. FRANCIS ABUAH-QUANSAH, J.C.D.

Auditor—AARON NIELSEN.

Diocesan Judges—Rev. Msgr. ROBERT P. HUNDT, J.C.L.; Very Rev. MICHAEL J. GORMAN; Rev. Msgr. RICHARD W. GILLES, J.C.L.

Deans—Very Revs. MICHAEL E. KLOS, Arcadia; DONALD J. BAUER, Chippewa Falls; THOMAS J. KRIEG, Durand; EUGENE A. KLINK, Eau Claire; MICHAEL J. GORMAN, La Crosse; DONALD L. MEURET, Marshfield; EUGENE J. WOLF, Prairie du Chien; ROBERT J. COOK, Richland Center; STEVEN J. KACHEL, Mauston-Sparta; JOHN A. POTACZEK, Stevens Point; WOODROW H. PACE, Thorp; CHARLES J. HIEBL, Wausau; R. JOHN SWING, Wisconsin Rapids.

Diocesan Offices and Directors

Apostolate for Native Americans—ELEANOR ST. JOHN, Coord.

Boy Scouts—Rev. JAMES T. ALTMAN; Mr. ROBERT J. COOPER, Chm., Mailing Address: P.O. Box 4004, La Crosse, 54602-4004. Tel: 608-791-2667.

Building Commission—CHRISTOPHER CARSTENS; Rev. Msgr. RICHARD W. GILLES, J.C.L.; Mr. BENEDICT T. NGUYEN, M.T.S., J.D., J.C.L.; SONDRA RIEDER; TRAVIS J. SIMPSON.

Catholic Women, Diocesan Council of—VACANT.

Department of Catholic Education—ANN C. LANKFORD, Dir. Catechesis & Evangelization; DIANA L. ROBERTS, Dir. Schools; SUSAN HOLMAN, Asst. Dir. Schools; MARY ANN JOHNSON, Fiscal Controller; VACANT, La Crosse Area Hmong Catechist, 3710 East Ave. S., P.O. Box 4004, La Crosse, 54602-4004. Tel: 608-788-7707.

Office of Family Life—JEFFREY HEINZEN, Dir.; Deacon MARK C. ARNOLD, Asst. Dir., Mailing Address: P.O. Box 4004, La Crosse, 54602-4004. Tel: 608-791-2665.

Natural Family Planning Program—JEFFREY HEINZEN, Educator; ALICE HEINZEN, Coord., 711 24th St. N.E., Menomonie, 54751. Tel: 715-235-6226.

Holy Childhood Association—Rev. ROGER J. SCHECKEL, Dir., Mailing Address: P.O. Box 4004, La Crosse, 54602-4004. Tel: 608-788-7700.

Hospitals and Health Affairs—Rev. Msgr. EDMUND J.

KLIMEK, Coord., Sacred Heart Hospital, 900 W. Clairemont Ave., Eau Claire, 54701. Tel: 715-839-4121; Rev. LAWRENCE G. DUNKLEE, Coord., P.O. Box 4004, La Crosse, 54602-4004. Tel: 608-791-2689.

International Priests—Tel: 608-791-2679. Rev. Msgr. RICHARD W. GILLES, J.C.L. On Behalf of the Diocesan Bishop, responsible for the recruitment and retention of international priests who serve in the Diocese; Oversees all legal aspects of hosting international priests including visas, travel documents and residency; Facilitates initial and ongoing orientation within parishes and the Diocese; Maintains relationships with foreign bishops and religious superiors to ensure fruitful, pastoral rapport.

Newman Campus Ministry—Rev. MARK R. PIERCE, Coord., 1732 State St., La Crosse, 54601. Tel: 608-784-4994.

Office of Communications and Public Relations—Mr. BENEDICT T. NGUYEN, M.T.S., J.D., J.C.L., Dir., Mailing Address: P.O. Box 4004, La Crosse, 54602-4004. Tel: 608-791-2655.

Office of Diocesan Buildings and Grounds—TRAVIS J. SIMPSON, Dir., Mailing Address: P.O. Box 4004, La Crosse, 54602-4004. Tel: 608-791-2692.

Office of the Consecrated Life—Sr. M. STEPHANIA NEWELL, F.S.G.M., Dir., Mailing Address: P.O. Box 4004, La Crosse, 54602-4004. Tel: 608-791-2655.

Office of Ecumenism—Rev. SAMUEL A. MARTIN, Diocesan Officer, Ecumenical Questions, P.O. Box 4004, La Crosse, 54602-4004. Tel: 608-788-9095.

Office of Ministries and Social Concerns—CHRISTOPHER J. RUFF, Dir.; Deacon MATTHEW LUDDICK, Asst. Dir., Mailing Address: P.O. Box 4004, La Crosse, 54602-4004. Tel: 608-791-2667 Office of Ministries consists of Permanent Diaconate, Lay Ministries.

Office of Sacred Worship—Mr. CHRISTOPHER J. CARSTENS, Dir., Mailing Address: P.O. Box 4004, La Crosse, 54602-4004. Tel: 608-791-2675 Sacred Worship Commission-Confer Office.

Office of Youth Ministry—CHRISTOPHER J. ROGERS, Dir., Mailing Address: P.O. Box 4004, La Crosse, 54602-4004.

Pastoral Council—Rev. Msgr. RICHARD W. GILLES, J.C.L., Exec. Sec., Mailing Address: P.O. Box 4004, La Crosse, 54602-4004.

Personnel Council—Revs. DAVID C. KUNZ, Chm.; THOMAS J. DONALDSON (Retired); ALLEN F. JAKUBOWSKI; Very Rev. WOODROW H. PACE, Mailing Address: P.O. Box 4004, La Crosse, 54602-4004. Tel: 608-788-7700. Ex Officio: Rev. Msgr. RICHARD W. GILLES, J.C.L.; Rev. JOSEPH W. HIRSCH.

Presbyteral Council—VACANT, Pres. Appointed Members: Revs. JOSEPH J. RAFACZ; LAWRENCE B. BERGER; MARK R. PIERCE, Chm.; THOMAS F. LINDNER; BRIAN D. KONOPA; DANIEL H. HACKEL; JAMES C. WEIGHNER; JOHN MARY GILBERT; PETER M. MANICKAM.

Ex Officio—Rev. Msgr. RICHARD W. GILLES, J.C.L.; Revs. JOSEPH W. HIRSCH; DELBERT J. MALIN (Retired); WILLIAM N. GREVATCH; Very Revs. EUGENE A. KLINK; JOHN A. POTACZEK; Revs. JOHN W. STEINER; ALAN P. WIERZBA. Consultors: Rev. Msgr. RICHARD W. GILLES, J.C.L., Sec.; Rev. JOSEPH W. HIRSCH; Very Rev. EUGENE A. KLINK; Revs. WILLIAM N. GREVATCH; JOHN W. STEINER; Very Rev. JOHN A. POTACZEK.

Propagation of the Faith—Rev. ROGER J. SCHECKEL, Dir., Mailing Address: P.O. Box 4004, La Crosse, 54602-4004. Tel: 608-788-7700.

St. Joseph's Priest Fund, Inc., (Benevolent Society)—Very Revs. STEVEN J. KACHEL, Pres.; MICHAEL J. GORMAN, Exec. Sec., Mailing Address: P.O. Box 4004, La Crosse, 54602-4004. Tel: 608-788-7700.

"Catholic Times" Diocesan Newspaper—STANTON GOULD, Editor; DENNIS DOWNEY, Asst. Editor, Mailing Address: P.O. Box 4004, La Crosse, 54602-4004. Tel: 608-788-1524.

Victim Assistance Coordinator—VACANT.

CLERGY, PARISHES, MISSIONS AND PAROCHIAL SCHOOLS

CITY OF LA CROSSE

(LA CROSSE COUNTY)

1—ST. JOSEPH THE WORKMAN CATHEDRAL (1860) [CEM 2] Very Rev. Michael J. Gorman, Rector. In Res., Rev. Todd A. Mlsna; Deacon Joseph Richards.
Res.: 530 Main St., 54601. Tel: 608-782-0322; Fax: 608-782-8228. Email: ejones@centurytel.net. Web: www.cathedralsjworkman.org.
See Coulee Catholic Schools, LaCrosse under Unified Catholic School Systems located in the Institution section.
Catechesis/Religious Program—Tel: 608-782-2953; Fax: 608-785-1064. Students 195.

2—BLESSED SACRAMENT (1937) [CEM 2] Rev. David P. Olson.
Res.: 130 Losey Blvd. S., 54601. Tel: 608-782-2953; Fax: 608-785-1064.
See Coulee Catholic Schools, LaCrosse under Unified Catholic School Systems located in the Institution section.

3—HOLY CROSS, Closed. For inquiries for parish records contact the Diocesan Archive, P.O. Box 4004, La Crosse, WI 54602-4004 Tel: 608-788-7700.

4—HOLY TRINITY (1887) [JC] Rev. Lawrence B. Berger.
Res.: 1333 S. 13th St., 54601. Tel: 608-782-2028; Fax: 608-784-2029.
Catechesis/Religious Program—Fax: 608-784-2029. Jeannie M. Weber, D.R.E. Students 220.

5—ST. JAMES THE LESS (1886) Rev. Roger J. Scheckel.
Res.: 1032 Caledonia St., 54603. Tel: 608-782-7557; Fax: 608-796-0086. Email: rscheckel@charter.net. Web: www.saintjameschurch.net.
Catechesis/Religious Program—Students 64.

6—ST. JOHN THE BAPTIST, Closed. For inquiries for parish records contact Diocesan Archives, P.O. Box 4004, La Crosse, WI 54602-4004 Tel: 608-788-7700.

7—ST. MARY, Closed. For inquiries for parish records contact The Diocesan Archives, P.O. Box 4004, La Crosse, WI 54602-4004 Tel: 608-788-7700.

8—MARY, MOTHER OF THE CHURCH (2000) Rev. Douglas C. Robertson.
Res.: 2006 Weston St., 54601. Tel: 608-788-5483; Fax: 608-788-4070. Email: mmoc@centurytel.net.
See Coulee Catholic Schools, LaCrosse under Unified Catholic School Systems located in the Institution section.

9—ST. PIUS X, Closed. For inquiries for parish records contact Mary, Mother of the Church, La Crosse, WI 54602-4004 Tel: 608-788-7700.

10—RONCALLI NEWMAN PARISH (1976) Rev. Mark R. Pierce; Deacon Kevin Ray.
Res.: 1732 State St., 54601. Tel: 608-784-4994; Fax: 608-784-0230. Email: roncallinewman@charterinternet.com. Web: www.roncallinewman.com.
Catechesis/Religious Program—Kathleen M. Nicklaus, D.R.E. Students 177.

11—ST. THOMAS MORE, Closed. For inquiries for parish records contact Mary, Mother of the Church, La Crosse, WI 54602-4004. Tel: 608-788-7700.

12—ST. WENCESLAUS, Closed. For inquiries for parish records contact The Diocesan Archives, P.O. Box 4004, La Crosse, WI 54602-4004 Tel: 608-788-7700.

OUTSIDE THE CITY OF LA CROSSE

ABBOTSFORD, CLARK CO., ST. BERNARD (1904) [JC] Revs. Sahayanathan Nathan; I. Enrique Castro Cuba (Peru), Hispanic Min.
Res.: 101 W. Cedar St., 54405. Tel: 715-223-3331; Fax: 715-229-4548. Email: catholiccentral@gmail.com.
Catechesis/Religious Program—Therese Geiger, D.R.E. Students 171.

ADAMS, ADAMS CO., ST. JOSEPH (1884) [CEM], Also serves St. Ann, Brooks. Rev. James P. McNamee; Deacon David Kennedy.
Res.: 166 N. Main, P.O. Box 310, 53910. Tel: 608-339-3485; Fax: 608-339-3485. Email: stjosephcc@verizon.net.
Catechesis/Religious Program—Students 84.

ALMA CENTER, JACKSON CO., IMMACULATE CONCEPTION (1882) [CEM] Rev. Jude T. Dioka (Nigeria).
Mailing Address: Box 188, 54611. Tel: 715-964-5201.
Res.: 341 W. Main, 54611.

ALMA, BUFFALO CO., ST. LAWRENCE (1867), Served from Immaculate Conception, Fountain City. Rev. G. Richard Roberts.
Res.: One Wall St., P.O. Box 218, Fountain City, 54629. Tel: 608-687-3496.
Catechesis/Religious Program—Bernice Semling, C.R.E. Students 30.

ALMOND, PORTAGE CO., HOLY GUARDIAN ANGELS, Closed. For inquiries for parish records contact St. Maximilian Maria Kolbe, Southeastern Portage County.

ALTDORF, WOOD CO., ST. JOSEPH, Closed. For inquiries for parish records contact St. Joachim, Pittsville.

ALTOONA, EAU CLAIRE CO., ST. MARY (1902) [JC] Rev. Damian Joseph Redfern.
Rectory—1827 Lynn Ave., 54720. Tel: 715-835-8813; Fax: 715-855-8664.
Church & Office: 1812 Lynn Ave., 54720. Tel: 715-855-1294. Email: stmary@charterinternet.net.
See Catholic Area Schools of the Eau Claire Deanery (C.A.S.E.), Eau Claire under Unified Catholic School Systems located in the Institution section.
Catechesis/Religious Program—Tel: 715-855-1294. Mary Kneer, D.R.E. Students 136.

AMHERST, PORTAGE CO., ST. JAMES (1905) [CEM], Also serves St. Mary of Mount Carmel, Fancher.
Res.: 453 S. Main, Box 280, 54406-0280. Tel: 715-824-3455; Fax: 715-824-3455. Email: sjsm@triver.com.
Catechesis/Religious Program—Barbara Lepak, D.R.E.; Dorene Stolpa, D.R.E. Students 157.

ARCADIA, TREMPEALEAU CO.

1—HOLY FAMILY (2000) [CEM], Also serves St. Boniface, Waumandee. Very Rev. Michael E. Klos; Sr. Rosemary Rombalski, Pastoral Min.
Res.: 223 E. Maple St., 54612. Tel: 608-323-7116; Fax: 608-323-8346. Email: secretary@holyfamily.com. Web: www.holyfam.com.
School—*Holy Family Catholic School*, (Grades K-8), 341 S. Washington St., 54612. Tel: 608-323-3676; Fax: 608-323-7386.
Catechesis/Religious Program—Students 166.

2—OUR LADY OF PERPETUAL HELP, Closed. For inquiries for parish records contact Holy Family, Arcadia.

3—ST. STANISLAUS, Closed. For inquiries for parish records contact Holy Family, Arcadia.

ARKANSAW, PEPIN CO., ST. JOSEPH (1913) [CEM 2] Rev. Jerome G. Hoeser.
Res.: N. 460 Cty. Rd. D, Eau Galle, 54737. Tel: 715-283-4448. Email: saintjoseph@nelson-tel.net.
Church: W7805 City Rd. 2, 54721.
Catechesis/Religious Program—Tel: 715-285-5849. Darlene Huppert, C.R.E. Students 82.

ARPIN, WOOD CO., ST. FRANCIS, Closed. For inquiries for parish records contact St. James, Vesper.

ATHENS, MARATHON CO., ST. ANTHONY DE PADUA (1881) [JC], Also serves Holy Family, Poniatowski and St. Thomas, Milan. Very Rev. Charles J. Hiebl.
Res.: 417 Caroline St., P.O. Box 206, 54411-0206. Tel: 715-257-7684; Fax: 715-257-7791. Email: stanthonyathens@gmail.com.
School—Tel: 715-257-7541. Sisters 1; Lay Teachers 8; Students 112.

AUBURNDALE, WOOD CO., NATIVITY OF THE BLESSED VIRGIN MARY (1886) [CEM 2], Also serves St. Michael, Hewitt. Rev. Eric G. Linzmaier.
Res.: 5866 Main St., P.O. Box 177, 54412-0177. Tel: 715-652-2806; Fax: 715-652-8020.

AUGUSTA, EAU CLAIRE CO., ST. ANTHONY DE PADUA, Closed. For inquiries for Parish Records contact St. Raymond of Penafort, Southern Eau Claire County.

BABCOCK, WOOD CO., ALL SAINTS, Closed. For inquiries for Parish Records contact Sacred Heart of Jesus, Nekoosa.

BAKERVILLE, WOOD CO., CORPUS CHRISTI, Attended by Sacred Heart, Marshfield. Rev. Peter M. Manickam.
Res. & Mailing Address: 112 E. 11th St., Marshfield, 54449. Tel: 715-676-3658 (Mail); 715-384-3213 (Res.).
Church: 10075 Hwy. BB, Marshfield, 54449.
See Marshfield Area Catholic Schools (MACS), Marshfield under Unified Catholic School Systems located in the Institution section.

BANGOR, LA CROSSE CO., ST. MARY (1899) [CEM] Attended by St. Leo the Great, West Salem. Rev. Robert S. Hegenbarth.
Mailing Address: 303 16th Ave. S., P.O. Box 290, 54614. Tel: 608-786-0610.

BEAR VALLEY, RICHLAND CO., ST. KILIAN, Closed. For inquiries for parish records contact Nativity, B.V.M., Keyesville.

BEVENT, MARATHON CO., ST. LADISLAUS (1886) [CEM] Attended by St. Joseph, Galloway. Rev. Rex A. Zimmerman; Sr. Mary Ellen Diermeier, S.S.J.-T.O.S.F., Pastoral Assoc.; Deacon David Ashenbrenner.
Mailing Address: 6455 State Hwy. 153, Hatley, 54440. Tel: 715-446-3060; Fax: 715-446-2668.

BIG RIVER, PIERCE CO., NATIVITY OF THE BLESSED VIRGIN MARY (1872) [CEM 2] Rev. William J. Matzek.
Res.: W10137 570th Ave., River Falls, 54022. Tel: 715-425-5806; Fax: 715-425-5806.

BLACK RIVER FALLS, JACKSON CO., ST. JOSEPH (1857) [CEM] Rev. John W. Steiner.
Res.: 507 Main St., 54615-1647. Tel: 715-284-5613; Fax: 715-284-8159.
Catechesis/Religious Program— Denise Cook, C.R.E. Students 88.

BLAIR, TREMPEALEAU CO., ST. ANSGAR (1961) Attended by St. Bridget, Ettrick Rev. Irudaya Nathan Thainase, O.F.M. Cap., Parochial Admin.
Mailing Address: 22650 Washington St., Ettrick, 54627. Tel: 715-538-4607; Fax: 715-538-2224.
Catechesis/Religious Program—Paula Glynn, D.R.E. Students 32.

BLENKER, WOOD CO., ST. KILIAN (1882) [CEM] Attended by St. Wenceslaus, Milladore. Rev. Augustine Kofi Bentil.

Mailing Address: Box 100, Milladore, 54454. Tel: 715-457-2314.

BLOOMER, CHIPPEWA CO., ST. PAUL (1902) [CEM 3] Rev. James K. Arthur; Deacon Richard Kostner.
Res.: 1222 Main St., 54724. Tel: 715-568-3255.
School—1210 Main St., 54724. Tel: 715-568-3233; Fax: 715-568-3244. Sisters 2; Lay Teachers 11; Students 187.
Catechesis/Religious Program—Tel: 715-568-3256. Barbara Kostner, D.R.E. Students 192.
Convent—1205 13th Ave., 54724. Tel: 715-568-3266.

BOYCEVILLE, DUNN CO., ST. LUKE (1964) [JC] Attended by St. Joseph, Rockfalls Rev. Victor Inbaraj.
Mailing Address: 919 Center St., P.O. Box 316, 54725. Tel: 715-643-3081. Email: stlukebv@yahoo.com.

BOYD, CHIPPEWA CO., SACRED HEART OF JESUS-ST. JOSEPH (1996) [CEM 2] Attended by Holy Family, Stanley. Rev. Joseph Raja. In Res., Rev. Eugene P. Smith (Retired). Tel: 714-667-3038.
Res.: 719 Patten St., P.O. Box 10, 54726-0010. Tel: 715-667-3341.

BRACKETT, EAU CLAIRE CO., HOLY GUARDIAN ANGELS, Closed. For inquiries for Parish Records contact St. Raymond of Penafort, Southern Eau Claire County.

BROOKS, ADAMS CO., ST. ANN, [CEM] Attended by St. Joseph, Adams. Rev. James P. McNamee.
Mailing Address: P.O. Box 132, Oxford, 53952. Tel: 608-584-4900.

BUENA VISTA, PORTAGE CO., ST. MARTIN, Closed. For inquiries for parish records contact St. Maximilian Maria Kolbe, Southeastern Portage County.

CADOTT, CHIPPEWA CO., ST. ROSE OF LIMA, [CEM], Also serves Sacred Heart, Jim Falls. Very Rev. Donald J. Bauer.
Res.: 415 N. Maple St., P.O. Box 160, 54727. Tel: 715-289-4551; Fax: 715-289-4551.
School—Tel: 715-289-4985. Lay Teachers 6; Students 48.

CAMP DOUGLAS, JUNEAU CO., ST. JAMES (1857) [CEM], Also serves St. Michael, Indian Creek. Rev. John Ofori-Domah.
Res.: 100 Bartell St., Box 289, 54618. Tel: 608-427-6762.

CASHTON, MONROE CO., SACRED HEART OF JESUS (1918) [CEM 3] Attended by Nativity of the Blessed Virgin Mary, St, Mary's Ridge. Rev. John L. Parr; Deacon Samuel Schmirler.
Res.: 1205 Front St., 54619-9757. Tel: 608-645-5955; Fax: 608-823-7272. Email: smr1856@centurytel.net.
School—Sacred Heart of Jesus School, 710 Kenyon St., 54619. Tel: 608-654-7733; Fax: 608-654-7733. Lay Teachers 5; Students 50.

CASSEL, MARATHON CO., SACRED HEART, [CEM], Served from St. Patrick, Halder Rev. Barnabas Kyeah.
Rectory—3372 County Rd. S., Marathon, 54448. Tel: 715-443-3675.

CASTLE ROCK LAKE, JUNEAU CO., OUR LADY OF THE LAKE, [CEM] Attended by St. Paul, New Lisbon. Rev. George Nelson Graham.
Res.: 408 W. River St., New Lisbon, 53950. Tel: 608-562-3125.

CAZENOVIA, RICHLAND CO., ST. ANTHONY DE PADUA (1857) [CEM] [JC], Also serves Sacred Heart, Lone Rock and St. Mary, Keyesville. Rev. Andrezej K. Panek.
Res.: 32505 CTH V, 53924. Tel: 608-983-2367.

CHILI, CLARK CO., ST. STEPHEN, Closed. For inquiries for Parish Records contact St. Mary's Parish, Neillsville, WI.

CHIPPEWA FALLS, CHIPPEWA CO.

1—ST. CHARLES BORROMEO (1884) [JC], Also serves St. Peter, Tilden. Rev. William P. Felix; Deacons Thomas Kinnick; Daniel Rider.
Res.: 810 Pearl St., 54729. Tel: 715-723-4088; Fax: 715-723-2195.
See Chippewa Falls Area Catholic Schools, Chippewa Falls under Unified Catholic School Systems located in the Institution section.

2—HOLY GHOST (1886) [JC], Also serves St. Bridget, Springfield. Revs. V. Arul Joseph; Justin Kizewski.
Res.: 412 S. Main St., 54729. Tel: 715-723-4890; Fax: 715-723-7358. Email: hgparish@charter.net.
See Chippewa Falls Area Catholic Schools, Chippewa Falls under Unified Catholic School Systems located in the Institution section.
Catechesis/Religious Program—Tel: 715-723-4890. Sr. Donna Snyder, D.R.E. Students 466.

3—NOTRE DAME (1856) [JC] Rev. Brian J. Jazdzewski. In Res., Rev. Daniel B. DuChez, O.S.
Res.: 117 Allen St., 54729-2899. Tel: 715-723-7108; Fax: 715-723-7523. Email: cfnotredame@yahoo.com.
See Chippewa Falls Area Catholic Schools, Chippewa Falls under Unified Catholic School Systems located in the Institution section.
Catechesis/Religious Program—Dori Loomis, D.R.E. Students 79.

COLBY, CLARK CO., ST. MARY HELP OF CHRISTIANS (1877) [CEM] Rev. Daniel H. Hackel.
Res.: 205 S. 2nd St., P.O. Box 436, 54421. Tel: 715-223-3048; Fax: 715-223-0223.
School—Tel: 715-223-3033. Lay Teachers 11; Students 86.
Catechesis/Religious Program—Tel: 715-223-4926. Diane Feiten, D.R.E. Students 106.

COOKS VALLEY, CHIPPEWA CO., ST. JOHN THE BAPTIST (1884) [CEM] Rev. James K. Arthur.
Mailing Address: 4540 State Hwy. 40, Bloomer, 54724. Tel: 715-568-3778; Fax: 715-568-9778. In Res., Rev. Albert W. Sonnberger (Retired).
Res.: 1222 Main St., Bloomer, 54724. Tel: 715-568-3255.

COON VALLEY, VERNON CO., ST. MARY, [CEM] Rev. Wayne R. Kidd.
Res.: 904 Central Ave., 54623. Tel: 608-452-3841.
Catechesis/Religious Program—Beverly Dwyer, D.R.E. Students 56.

CORNELL, CHIPPEWA CO., HOLY CROSS (1915) [CEM 2] Rev. Jeremiah Cashman; Deacon Dennis Rivers.
Res.: 107 S. 8th St., P.O. Box 68, 54732. Tel: 715-239-6826.
Catechesis/Religious Program—Tel: 715-239-6759. Pamela Herrell, D.R.E.; Betty Rivers, C.R.E. Students 60.

CUSTER, PORTAGE CO., IMMACULATE CONCEPTION (1875) [CEM] Rev. Rajendran Anandan.
Res.: 7176 Esker Rd., 54423. Tel: 715-592-4330; Fax: 715-344-6277.

CZESTOCHOWA, CLARK CO., ST. MARY OF CZESTOCHOWA, Closed. For inquiries for parish records contact Holy Family, Stanley.

DE SOTO, CRAWFORD CO., SACRED HEART, Closed. For inquiries for parish records contact St. Charles Borromeo, Genoa.

DILLY, VERNON CO., ST. JOHN NEPOMUCENE, Closed. For inquiries for parish records contact Diocesan Archives, P.O. Box 4004, La Crosse,WI 54602-4004 Tel: 608-788-7700.

DORCHESTER, CLARK CO., ST. LOUIS (1878) [JC], Served from St. Bernard, Abbotsford. Rev. Sahayanathan Nathan.
Res.: 101 W. Cedar St., Abbotsford, 54405. Tel: 715-223-3331; Fax: 715-229-4548.
Catechesis/Religious Program—Tel: 715-654-5467. Therese Geiger, D.R.E. Students 67.

DRYWOOD, CHIPPEWA CO., ST. ANTHONY (1886) [CEM] Attended by St. Rose of Lima, Cadott. Very Rev. Donald J. Bauer.
Mailing Address: P.O. Box 160, Cadott, 54727.

DURAND, PEPIN CO., ST. MARY'S ASSUMPTION (1860) [CEM] Revs. Allen F. Jakubowski; David G. Rybicki; Deacons James Weingart; Robert Hansen.
Mailing Address: 911 W. Prospect St., P.O. Box 188, 54736-1049. Tel: 715-672-5640; Fax: 715-672-4193. Web: www.triparish.41pi.com.
School—901 W. Prospect St., 54736. Tel: 715-672-5617; Fax: 715-672-3931. Lay Teachers 10; Students 90.

EASTMAN, CRAWFORD CO., ST. WENCESLAUS (1883) [CEM] Rev. Thomas M. Huff.
Res.: P.O. Box 109, 54626-0109. Tel: 608-874-4151; Fax: 608-874-4151.
Catechesis/Religious Program—Tel: 608-874-4221. Barbara Martin, D.R.E. Students 71.

EAU CLAIRE, EAU CLAIRE CO.

1—IMMACULATE CONCEPTION (1945) Very Rev. Eugene A. Klink.
Res.: 1712 Highland Ave., 54701. Tel: 715-835-9935; Fax: 715-835-9459.
See Catholic Area Schools of the Eau Claire Deanery (C.A.S.E.), Eau Claire under Unified Catholic School Systems located in the Institution section.
Catechesis/Religious Program—Tel: 715-835-7721; Fax: 715-830-9846. Linda Corey, D.R.E.; Barb Brandner, D.R.E. Students 264.

2—ST. JAMES THE GREATER (1948) [JC] Rev. John A. Schultz; Sr. Judie Wagener, S.S.N.D., Pastoral Assoc.
Res.: 2502 Eleventh St., 54703-2700. Tel: 715-835-5887; Fax: 715-835-3110. Email: stjameseac@aol.com. Web: www.stjameseauclaire-.catholicweb.com.
See Catholic Area Schools of the Eau Claire Deanery (C.A.S.E.), Eau Claire under Unified Catholic School Systems located in the Institution section.
Catechesis/Religious Program—Tel: 715-834-8921. Jan Legge, D.R.E.; Terri Kannel, D.R.E. Students 154.

3—NEWMAN COMMUNITY (1969) [JC] Rev. George R. Szews; Rev. Msgr. Edmund J. Klimek.
Res.: 110 Garfield Ave., 54701-4042. Tel: 715-834-3399.
Catechesis/Religious Program—Tel: 715-834-3399. Flo Sheridan, D.R.E. Students 82.

4—ST. OLAF, [JC] Rev. Brian D. Konopa; Deacon Robert Chittendon.
Mailing Address: P.O. Box 1203, 54702-1203. Tel: 715-832-2504; Fax: 715-832-0742.
Church: 3220 Monroe St., 54703.
See Catholic Area Schools of the Eau Claire Deanery (C.A.S.E.), Eau Claire under Unified Catholic School Systems located in the Institution section.

5—ST. PATRICK, Merged with Sacred Heart of Jesus, Eau Claire to form Sacred Heart of Jesus-St. Patrick, Eau Claire. For inquiries for parish records contact Sacred Heart of Jesus-St. Patrick, Eau Claire.

6—SACRED HEART OF JESUS, Merged with St. Patrick, Eau Claire to form Sacred Heart of Jesus-St. Patrick, Eau Claire. For inquiries for parish records contact Sacred Heart of Jesus-St. Patrick, Eau Claire.

7—SACRED HEART OF JESUS-ST. PATRICK (1999) [CEM 2] Rev. William A. Dhein; Deacon Larry Agema. In Res., Rev. James R. Kurzynski.
Res.: 416 N. Dewey St., 54703. Tel: 715-832-0925; Fax: 715-832-0366. Email: sacrdhrt@charter.net. Web: www.sacredheartsaintpatrick.org.
Parish Office: 322 Fulton St., 54703.
Rectory—318 Fulton St., 54703.

EAU GALLE, DUNN CO., ST. HENRY (1856) [CEM], Also serves St. Joseph, Arkansaw. Rev. Jerome G. Hoeser.
Res.: N460 CTH D, 54737. Tel: 715-283-4448.
Catechesis/Religious Program—Tel: 715-283-4255. Orpha Baier, C.R.E. Students 34.

EDGAR, MARATHON CO., ST. JOHN THE BAPTIST (1900), (German—Polish), [CEM] Rev. Robert A. Streveler.
Res.: 207 N. 3rd Ave., 54426-0386. Tel: 715-352-3444.
Church: 103 N. Fourth Ave., P.O. Box 35, 54426.
School—125 N. 4th Ave., P.O. Box 66, 54426-0066. Tel: 715-352-3000; Fax: 715-352-7517. Lay Teachers 9; Students 77.
Catechesis/Religious Program—Tel: 715-352-2216. Susan Schraufnagel, C.R.E. Students 156.

EDSON, CHIPPEWA CO., SACRED HEART OF JESUS, Merged with St. Joseph, Boyd to form Sacred Heart of Jesus-St. Joseph, Boyd.

ELK MOUND, DUNN CO., ST. JOSEPH (1959) [CEM] Rev. Victor Inbaraj. In Res., Rev. Henry R. Hoerburger (Retired).
Res.: P.O. Box 275, 54739. Tel: 715-879-5332. Email: stjosephem@centurytel.net.
Catechesis/Religious Program—Sharon Biegel, D.R.E. Students 71.

ELLSWORTH, PIERCE CO., ST. FRANCIS OF ASSISI (1897) [CEM] [JC 4] Rev. Roy R. Witucki.
Res.: 264 S. Grant St., P.O. Box 839, 54011. Tel: 715-273-4774; Fax: 715-723-4066.
School—Box 250, 54011. Tel: 715-273-4391; Fax: 715-273-4066. Lay Teachers 7; Students 145.

ELMWOOD, PIERCE CO., SACRED HEART, [CEM], Also serves Sacred Heart of Jesus, Spring Valley. Rev. Varkey V. Joseph.
114 W. Wilson Ave., 54740. Tel: 715-639-2741; Fax: 715-639-6031.

ELROY, JUNEAU CO., ST. PATRICK (1877) [CEM] Attended by St. Joseph, Kendall. Rev. Richard C. Dickman.
Res.: 307 Spring St., Box 155, Kendall, 54638. Tel: 608-463-7120; Fax: 608-462-5876. Email: stjosephkendall@centurytel.net.
Catechesis/Religious Program—Tel: 608-462-5067. Jayne Beaver, C.R.E. Students 36.

ETTRICK, TREMPEALEAU CO., ST. BRIDGET (1869) [CEM], Also serves St. Ansgar, Blair. Rev. Irudaya Nathan Thainase, O.F.M. Cap.
Res.: 22650 Washington St., 54627. Tel: 608-525-3811; Fax: 608-525-2909. Email: stbridgets@centurytel.net.

FAIRCHILD, EAU CLAIRE CO., ST. JOHN CANTIUS, Attended by St. Joseph, Fairview. Rev. Jude T. Dioka (Nigeria).
Res.: N13740 Fairview Rd., 54741-8514. Tel: 715-334-2202; Fax: 715-334-2202.
Church: 306 2nd St., 54741.

FAIRVIEW, EAU CLAIRE CO., ST. JOSEPH, Also serves Immaculate Conception, Alma Center; and St. John Cantius, Fairchild. Rev. Jude T. Dioka (Nigeria).
Res.: N13740 Fairview Rd., Fairchild, 54741-8514. Tel: 715-334-2202; Fax: 715-334-2202.

FALL CREEK, EAU CLAIRE CO.

1—ST. JOHN THE APOSTLE, Closed. For inquiries for Parish Records contact St. Raymond of Penafort, Southern Eau Claire County.

2—ST. RAYMOND OF PENAFORT (1998) [CEM] Rev. John P. Hogan; Deacon Larry Agema.
S10444 Hwy. 53, 54742. Tel: 715-878-4183.

FANCHER, PORTAGE CO., ST. MARY OF MOUNT CARMEL (1884) [CEM] Attended by St. James, Amherst.
Res.: 3995 Cty. K, P.O. Box 280, Amherst, 54406. Tel: 715-824-3455; Fax: 715-824-3455.
Catechesis/Religious Program—Cindy Klish, D.R.E. Students 144.

FOUNTAIN CITY, BUFFALO CO., IMMACULATE CONCEPTION (1857) [CEM], Also serves St. Lawrence, Alma. Rev. G. Richard Roberts.
Res.: 1 Wall St., P.O. Box 218, 54629-0218. Tel: 608-687-3496.

GALESVILLE, TREMPEALEAU CO., ST. MARY (1904) Attended by St. Bartholomew, Trempealeau. Rev. Edmund J. Doerre.
Res. & Mailing Address: 11646 South St., Trempealeau, 54461-8238. Tel: 608-534-6652. Web: www.saintbartholomew.net.

GALLOWAY, MARATHON CO., ST. JOSEPH (1921) [CEM], Also serves St. Ladislaus, Bevent. Rev. Rex A. Zimmerman; Sr. Mary Ellen Diermeier, S.S.J.-T.O.S.F., Pastoral Assoc.; Deacon David Ashenbrenner.
Res.: 8846 CTH C, Wittenberg, 54499-8936. Tel: 715-454-6431.
Catechesis/Religious Program—Tel: 715-454-6432. Dorothy Ashenbrenner, D.R.E. Students 51.

GAYS MILLS, CRAWFORD CO., ST. MARY (1908) [JC], Also serves St. Philip, Rolling Ground.
Res.: 115 E. School St., 54631. Tel: 608-735-4420.
Catechesis/Religious Program—Tel: 608-734-3054. Students 23.

GENOA, VERNON CO., ST. CHARLES BORROMEO, [CEM], Served from St. James the Less, LaCrosse. Rev. Robert Weighner, L.C.
Mailing Address: 100 Walnut St., P.O. Box 130, 54632. Tel: 608-689-2646; Fax: 608-689-2811.
School—Tel: 608-689-2642; Fax: 608-689-2811. Lay Teachers 6; Students 48.

GREENWOOD, CLARK CO., ST. MARY HELP OF CHRISTIANS (1903) [CEM], Also serves Holy Family, Willard. Rev. A. Joseph Follmar.
Res.: 123 N. Main St., P.O. Box 129, 54437. Tel: 715-267-6282.
School—Tel: 715-267-6477; Fax: 715-267-6477. Lay Teachers 3; Students 27.

HALDER, MARATHON CO., ST. PATRICK, [CEM], Also serves Sacred Heart, Cassel. Rev. Barnabas Kyeah.
Rectory—3158 Halder Dr., Mosinee, 54455. Tel: 715-693-2765. Email: stpats@mtc.net.

HATLEY, MARATHON CO., ST. FLORIAN (1885) [CEM] Rev. Jerzy Rebacz.
Res.: 500 Church Ln., P.O. Box 100, 54440. Tel: 715-446-2252; 715-446-3085 (Office); Fax: 715-446-2756.

HEFFRON, PORTAGE CO., ST. JOHN THE BAPTIST, Closed. For inquiries for parish records contact St. Maximilian Maria Kolbe, Southeastern Portage County.

HEWITT, WOOD CO., ST. MICHAEL (1888) [JC] Attended by St. Mary, Auburndale. Rev. Eric G. Linzmaier.
Parish Office: 11100 Main St., 54441. Tel: 715-384-7676; Fax: 715-384-7675. Email: stmichaelhewitt@gmail.com.
Res.: 5866 Main St., Box 177, Auburndale, 54412. Tel: 715-652-2806; Fax: 715-652-8020. Email: revlinz@tds.net.

HILLSBORO, VERNON CO., ST. ALOYSIUS (1905) [JC] Rev. Joseph C. Nakwah; Deacon John Nusse.
Res.: 545 Prairie Ave., P.O. Box 466, 54634. Tel: 608-489-2580; Fax: 608-489-2580.
Catechesis/Religious Program—Tel: 608-489-3544; Fax: 608-489-2580. Students 56.

HOLMEN, LA CROSSE CO., ST. ELIZABETH ANN SETON (1983) Rev. Robert A. Schaller; Sr. Bridget Donaldson, O.S.B., Pastoral Assoc.; Deacon Matthew Luddick.
Office: 515 N. Main St., 54636-9745. Tel: 608-526-4424; Fax: 608-526-3177.
Res.: 704 Hillcrest Dr., 54636-9745.
Catechesis/Religious Program—Students 467.

INDEPENDENCE, TREMPEALEAU CO., SS. PETER AND PAUL (1875) [CEM], Also serves St. John the Apostle, Whitehall. Rev. David C. Kunz.
Res.: 36028 Osseo Rd., P.O. Box 430, 54747-0430. Tel: 715-985-2227; Fax: 715-985-2649.
School—Tel: 715-985-3719. Lay Teachers 9; Students 113.

INDIAN CREEK, MONROE CO., ST. MICHAEL (1869) [CEM] Attended by St. James, Camp Douglas. Rev. John Ofori-Domah.
Mailing Address: P.O. Box 199, Camp Douglas, 54618. Tel: 608-427-6762.

JIM FALLS, CHIPPEWA CO., SACRED HEART OF JESUS Rev. Brian J. Jazdzewski; Deacon Mark C. Arnold.
Res.: 13989 195th St., Box 68, 54748. Tel: 715-382-4422.

JUNCTION CITY, PORTAGE CO., ST. MICHAEL (1884) [CEM] Attended by St. Wenceslaus, Milladore. Rev. Augustine Kofi Bentil.
Res.: P.O. Box 100, Milladore, 54454. Tel: 715-457-2314; Fax: 715-457-6255.
Church: 324 Main St., 54443.

KENDALL, MONROE CO., ST. JOSEPH (1883) [CEM], Also serves St. Patrick, Elroy, and St. John the Baptist, Wilton. Rev. Richard C. Dickman.
Res.: 307 Spring St., P.O. Box 155, 54638. Tel: 608-463-7120. Email: stjosephkendall@centurytel.net.
Catechesis/Religious Program—Tel: 608-463-7649. Mary Skolos, C.R.E. Students 35.

KEYESVILLE, RICHLAND CO., NATIVITY OF THE BLESSED VIRGIN MARY, [CEM] Attended by St. Anthony, Cazenovia. Rev. Andrezej K. Panek.
Mailing Address: 32605 Durst Ln., Richland Center, 53581. Tel: 608-585-4846.
Res.: 32505 Hwy. V, Cazenovia, 53924. Tel: 608-983-2367.

KNOWLTON, MARATHON CO., ST. FRANCIS XAVIER (1853) [CEM], Also serves St. John the Baptist, Peplin. Rev. Joseph A. Grassl.
Res.: 651 Mead Ln., Mosinee, 54455. Tel: 715-693-3120; Fax: 715-693-3120. Email: sfknowl@mtc.net.

LANARK, PORTAGE CO., ST. PATRICK, Closed. For inquiries for parish records contact St. Maximilian Maria Kolbe, Southeastern Portage County.

LIMA, PEPIN CO., HOLY ROSARY, [CEM], Served from: St. Mary's Assumption, Durand. Revs. Allen F. Jakubowski; David G. Rybicki; Deacons James Weingart; Robert Hansen.
Mailing Address: 911 W. Prospect St., Box 188, Durand, 54736-1048. Tel: 715-672-5640; Fax: 715-672-4193.
School—Tel: 715-672-4276. Lay Teachers 4; Students 57.

LONE ROCK, RICHLAND CO., SACRED HEART, Attended by St. Anthony, Cazenovia. Rev. Andrezej K. Panek.
Mailing Address: 32505 Hwy. V, Cazenovia, 53924. Tel: 608-983-2367.

LOYAL, CLARK CO., ST. ANTHONY OF PADUA (1893) [CEM] Rev. Jerome Naduvathaniyil, O.S.B.
Res.: 407 N. Division St., P.O. Box 69, 54446-0069. Tel: 715-255-8017; Fax: 715-255-8017.
School—212 W. Spring St., 54446. Tel: 715-255-8636; Fax: 715-255-8636. Lay Teachers 7; Students 76.
Catechesis/Religious Program—Tel: 715-255-9938. Mary Ann Olson, D.R.E. Students 112.

LYNDON STATION, JUNEAU CO., ST. MARY, [CEM] Rev. Valentine Joseph.
Res.: 117 Juneau St. N., P.O. Box 303, 53944. Tel: 608-666-2421; Fax: 608-666-2421. Email: stmaryslyndon@charter.net.
Catechesis/Religious Program—Vicki McGowan, C.R.E. Students 22.

MARATHON CITY, MARATHON CO., NATIVITY OF THE BLESSED VIRGIN MARY (1856) [CEM] Rev. Joseph Diermeier.
Res.: 712 Market St., Box 7, 54448-0007. Tel: 715-443-2045; Fax: 715-443-3045. Email: bvmparish@stmarymara.org.
School—Tel: 715-443-3430. Lay Teachers 14; Students 180.
Catechesis/Religious Program—Tel: 715-443-2433; Fax: 715-443-2575. Students 90.

MARSHFIELD, WOOD CO.

1—ST. JOHN THE BAPTIST (1877) [JC], Also serves Christ the King, Spencer. Revs. Charles D. Stoetzel; Victor C. Feltes.
Res.: 201 W. Blodgett St., 54449-2400. Tel: 715-384-3252; Fax: 715-384-3252. Web: www.stjohnsmarshfield.org.
See Marshfield Area Catholic Schools (MACS), Marshfield under Unified Catholic School Systems located in the Institution section.
Catechesis/Religious Program—Tel: 715-384-3919. Richard Hoffman, D.R.E. Students 155.

2—OUR LADY OF PEACE (1947) [JC] Very Rev. Donald L. Meuret.
Res.: 1414 W. 5th St., 54449. Tel: 715-384-9414; Fax: 715-384-6606.
See Marshfield Area Catholic Schools (MACS), Marshfield under Unified Catholic School Systems located in the Institution section.
Catechesis/Religious Program—Tel: 715-676-2549; Fax: 715-384-6606. Corinne Johnson, D.R.E. Students 217.

3—SACRED HEART OF JESUS (1916) [JC], Also serves Corpus Christi, Bakerville. Rev. Peter M. Manickam.
Res.: 112 E. 11th St., 54449-4216. Tel: 715-384-3213; Fax: 715-384-6929. Email: sacred_heart@verizon.net. Web: www.sacredheartmarshfield.org.
See Marshfield Area Catholic Schools (MACS), Marshfield under Unified Catholic School Systems located in the Institution section.

MAUSTON, JUNEAU CO., ST. PATRICK (1901) [CEM 2] Rev. Eric R. Berns.
Res.: 401 Mansion St., 53948-1393. Tel: 608-847-6054; Fax: 608-847-3288. Email: stpatsparish@btsmailbox.com. Web: www.stpatricksmauston.com.
School—325 Mansion St., 53948. Tel: 608-847-5844; Fax: 608-847-4103. Lay Teachers 14; Students 172.

MELROSE, JACKSON CO., ST. KEVIN, [JC] Attended by St. Joseph, Black River Falls Rev. John W. Steiner. 813 N. Washington St., 54642.

MENOMONIE, DUNN CO., ST. JOSEPH (1861) [CEM] Very Rev. Thomas J. Krieg.
Res.: 910 Wilson Ave., 54751. Tel: 715-232-4922; Fax: 715-232-4923.
School—Tel: 715-232-4920. Lay Teachers 13; Students 178.
Catechesis/Religious Program—Emily Revak, D.R.E.; Pam Sirinek, Youth Min. Students 260.

MIDDLE RIDGE, LA CROSSE CO., ST. PETER (1869) [CEM], Also serves St. Joseph, St. Joseph Ridge. Rev. Francis Abuah-Quansah.
Res.: W697 State Rd. 33, #101M, Rockland, 54653. Tel: 608-486-2180.

MILAN, MARATHON CO., ST. THOMAS (1913) [CEM] Attended by St. Anthony, Athens. Very Rev. Charles J. Hiebl.
Mailing Address: 417 Caroline St., P.O. Box 206, Athens, 54411. Tel: 715-257-7684; Fax: 715-257-7791.

MILL CREEK, PORTAGE CO., ST. BARTHOLOMEW, [CEM] Attended by St. Stephen, Stevens Point. Very Rev. John A. Potaczek; Deacon Richard Rozumalski.
Res.: 2493 County Rd. M, Stevens Point, 54481. Tel: 715-344-3003; Fax: 715-344-0331. Email: stbartholomew@g29.net.

MILLADORE, WOOD CO., ST. WENCESLAUS (1883) [CEM], Also serves St. Kilian, Blenker & St. Michael, Junction City. Rev. Augustine Kofi Bentil.
Res.: 146 Main St., Box 100, 54454. Tel: 715-457-2314; Fax: 715-457-6255.

MONDOVI, BUFFALO CO., SACRED HEART OF JESUS (1896) [JC] Attended by St. Mary's Assumption, Durand Revs. Allen F. Jakubowski; David G. Rybicki; Deacon Robert Hansen.
Mailing Address: P.O. Box 188, Durand, 54736. Tel: 715-672-5640; Fax: 715-672-4193.

MOSINEE, MARATHON CO., ST. PAUL (1878) [CEM] Rev. Donald L. Przybylski.
Res.: 603 Fourth St., 54455. Tel: 715-693-2650; Fax: 715-692-2650. Email: stpaulch@mtc.net. Web: stpauls-mosinee.org.
School—404 High St., 54455. Tel: 715-693-2675; Fax: 715-693-1332. Lay Teachers 8; Students 62.
Catechesis/Religious Program—Tel: 715-693-4030; Fax: 715-693-1332. Kathryn Lesniak, D.R.E. Students 281.

NECEDAH, JUNEAU CO., ST. FRANCIS OF ASSISI (1876) [CEM] Rev. Hector C. Moreno; Deacon Glen Heinzl.
Res.: 2001 S. Main St., 54646-8273. Tel: 608-565-2488; Fax: 608-565-6722.

NEILLSVILLE, CLARK CO., ST. MARY (1878) [CEM] Very Rev. Woodrow H. Pace.
Res.: 1813 Black River Rd., 54456. Tel: 715-743-3840; Fax: 715-743-7963. Email: stmaryneillsville@tds.net.

NEKOOSA, WOOD CO., SACRED HEART OF JESUS (1900) [JC], Also serves St. Alexander, Port Edwards. Very Rev. R. John Swing.
Res.: 711 Prospect Ave., 54457. Tel: 715-886-3422; Fax: 715-886-3954.
See Wisconsin Rapids Area Catholic Schools, Wisconsin Rapids under Unified Catholic School Systems located in the Institution section.

NEW AUBURN, CHIPPEWA CO., ST. JUDE, Closed. For inquiries for parish records contact the chancery.

NEW LISBON, JUNEAU CO., ST. PAUL (1862) [CEM], Also serves Our Lady of the Lake, Castle Rock Lake. Rev. George Nelson Graham.
Res.: 408 W. River St., 53950. Tel: 608-562-3125; Fax: 715-562-6225. Email: st.paul@mwt.net.
Catechesis/Religious Program—Tel: 608-562-5482. Leta Nelson, C.R.E. Students 48.

NORTH CREEK, TREMPEALEAU CO., ST. MICHAEL (1875) Closed. For inquiries for parish records contact the chancery.

NORWALK, MONROE CO., ST. AUGUSTINE OF HIPPO (1903) [CEM] Attended by Nativity of the Blessed Virgin Mary, St. Mary's Ridge. Rev. Keith Kitzhaber; Deacon Samuel Schmirler. In Res., Rev. James H. Miller (Retired).
Res.: 26400 CTH U, Cashton, 54619-8621. Tel: 608-823-7906; Fax: 608-823-7272. Email: smr1856@centurytel.net.

ONALASKA, LA CROSSE CO., ST. PATRICK (1949) [JC] Rev. Patrick A. Umberger; Deacon Frank Abnet.
Res.: 1031 Main St., 54650. Tel: 608-783-5535.
See Coulee Catholic Schools, LaCrosse under Unified Catholic School Systems located in the Institution section.
Catechesis/Religious Program—Tel: 608-783-1099. Cathryn Olson, D.R.E.; Nina Long, D.R.E. Students 533.

OWEN, CLARK CO., HOLY ROSARY (1953), Served from: St. Bernard, Abbotsford. Rev. Sahayanathan Nathan.
Parish Office: 415 W. 3rd St., P.O. Box 309, 54460-0309. Tel: 715-229-2348; Fax: 715-229-4548. Email: catholiccentral@gmail.com.

PEPLIN, MARATHON CO., ST. JOHN THE BAPTIST (1916) [CEM] Attended by St. Francis Xavier, Knowlton.

Rev. Joseph A. Grassl.
Mailing Address: 651 Mead Ln., Mosinee, 54455. Tel: 715-693-3120. In Res., Rev. Wladyslaw J. Kowalski (SUP) (Retired).

PINE CREEK, TREMPEALEAU CO., MOST SACRED HEART (1864) [CEM] Rev. Amalraj Arockiam.
Res.: N20555 CTH G, Dodge, 54625-9721. Tel: 608-539-3704; Fax: 608-539-3704. Email: sacredheartparis@centurytel.net.

PITTSVILLE, WOOD CO., ST. JOACHIM, [CEM], Also serves St. James, Vesper and Holy Rosary, Sigel. Rev. Robert W. Nelson.
Res.: 5312 Third Ave., P.O. Box 69, 54466-0069. Tel: 715-884-6815; Fax: 715-884-6160.
Catechesis/Religious Program—Tel: 715-884-2115. Judy Gachnang, D.R.E. Students 129.

PLOVER, PORTAGE CO., ST. BRONISLAVA (1896) [JC] Rev. James F. Trempe.
Res.: 3200 Plover Rd., P.O. Box 158, 54467-0158. Tel: 715-344-4326; Fax: 715-344-6121.
School—3301 Willow Dr., 54467. Tel: 715-342-2015; Fax: 715-342-2016.
Catechesis/Religious Program—Tel: 715-341-6700. Jody Cieslewicz, D.R.E.; Julie Studinski, Youth Min. Students 445.

PLUM CITY, PIERCE CO., ST. JOHN THE BAPTIST (1872) [JC] Rev. Ambrose J. Blenker.
Res.: 212 Church Rd., P.O. Box 206, 54761-0206. Tel: 715-647-2301; Fax: 715-647-2901.

POLONIA, PORTAGE CO., SACRED HEART, [CEM] Attended by St. Adalbert, Rosholt Rev. Marcin Mankowski, O.P.; Deacon James Maciejewski.
Res.: 7375 Church St., Custer, 54423. Tel: 715-592-4221; Fax: 715-592-4189.
School—7379 Church St., Custer, 54423. Tel: 715-592-4902. Lay Teachers 4; Students 48.
Convent—7381 Church St., Custer, 54423. Tel: 715-592-4213.

PONIATOWSKI, MARATHON CO., HOLY FAMILY (1877) [CEM 2] Attended by St. Anthony de Padua, Athens. Very Rev. Charles J. Hiebl; Deacon LeRoy Knauf, Pastoral Assoc.
Mailing Address: 417 Caroline St., P.O. Box 206, Athens, 54411-0206.
Church: R444 CTHU, Edgar, 54426. Tel: 715-443-2527.
Catechesis/Religious Program—Deacon LeRoy Knauf, D.R.E. Students 73.

PORT EDWARDS, WOOD CO., ST. ALEXANDER (1941) [JC], Served from: Sacred Heart, Nekoosa Very Rev. R. John Swing. In Res., Sr. Catherine Kaiser, F.S.P.A., Pastoral Assoc.
Church & Res.: 880 First St., 54469. Tel: 715-887-3012; Fax: 715-887-3748. Email: stalex@wctc.net.

PRAIRIE DU CHIEN, CRAWFORD CO.
1—ST. GABRIEL (1817) [CEM 2], Served from: St. Nepomucene, Prairie du Chien Rev. James C. Weighner.
Office: 506 N. Beaumont Rd., P.O. Box 176, 53821-0176. Tel: 608-326-2404.
School—Prairie Catholic Schools, 515 N. Beaumont Rd., 53821. Tel: 608-326-8624. Lay Teachers 22; Students 240.
2—ST. JOHN NEPOMUCENE (1891), Also Serves: St. Gabriel, Prairie du Chien Revs. James C. Weighner; Amaldas Kulandaisamy, O.S.B.Cam.
Res.: 710 S. Wacouta St., P.O. Box 28, 53821-0028. Tel: 608-326-6511; Fax: 608-326-4876.
School—Prairie Catholic Schools, 720 S. Wacouta St., 53821. Tel: 608-326-4400.

PRESCOTT, PIERCE CO., ST. JOSEPH, [CEM] Rev. Edward J. Shuttleworth; Deacon Gerald Rynda.
Res.: 269 Dakota St. S., P.O. Box 245, 54021-0245. Tel: 715-262-5310; Fax: 715-262-4543. Email: stjosephprescott@comcast.net. Web: stjosephprescott.com.
School—281 Dakota St. S., 54021. Tel: 715-262-5912; Fax: 715-262-5901. Franciscan Sisters of Perpetual Adoration 2; Lay Teachers 10; Students 120.
Convent—268 Dakota St. S., 54021. Tel: 715-262-5105.

RICHLAND CENTER, RICHLAND CO., ST. MARY (ASSUMPTION OF B.V.M.), [CEM] Very Rev. Emmanuel Famiyeh; Deacon Edward Wendt.
160 W. 4th St., P.O. Box 456, 53581. Tel: 608-647-2621; Fax: 608-647-6029.
School—155 W. 5th St., 53581. Tel: 608-647-2422. Lay Teachers 12; Students 124.
Catechesis/Religious Program—Tel: 608-647-4210. Denise Gainor, D.R.E. Students 180.
Convent—789 N. Central Ave., 53581. Tel: 608-647-4210.

RISING SUN, CRAWFORD CO., ST. JAMES, Closed. For inquiries for parish records contact The Diocesan Archive, P.O. Box 4004, La Crosse, WI, 54602-4004.

ROCK FALLS, DUNN CO., ST. JOSEPH (1905) [CEM] Rev. Victor Inbaraj.
Res.: E. 9265 State Rd. 85, Mondovi, 54755-8857. Tel: 715-875-4539; Fax: 715-875-4539. Email: stjosephrf@yahoo.com.
Catechesis/Religious Program—Amy Mayer, C.C.D. Coord. Tel: 715-875-4527. Students 23.

ROLLING GROUND, CRAWFORD CO., ST. PHILIP (1857) [CEM] Attended by St. Mary, Gays Mills., Mailing Address: 115 E. School St., Gays Mills, 54631-7211. Tel: 608-735-4420; Fax: 608-735-4520.
Catechesis/Religious Program—Students 35.

ROSHOLT, PORTAGE CO., ST. ADALBERT, [CEM], Also serves Sacred Heart, Polonia. Rev. Marcin Mankowski, O.P.; Deacon James Maciejewski.
Res.: 3315 St. Adalbert Rd., 54473. Tel: 715-677-4519; Fax: 715-677-6943.
School—3314 St. Adalbert Rd., 54473. Tel: 715-677-4517. Lay Teachers 5; Students 41.
Catechesis/Religious Program—Patty Lawson, D.R.E. Students 63.

ROTHSCHILD, MARATHON CO.
1—ST. MARK (1937) Rev. Allan L. Slowiak; Deacon Patrick McKeough.
Res.: 602 Military Rd., 54474-1523. Tel: 715-359-5206; Fax: 715-355-8904. Email: stmarkroths@smproths.org.
See Newman Area Catholic Schools, Wausau under Unified Catholic School Systems located in the Institution section.
Catechesis/Religious Program—Fax: 715-355-8904. Mary Hart, D.R.E. Students 236.
2—ST. THERESE OF THE CHILD JESUS, [CEM] Rev. Janusz Kowalski.
Res.: 113 W. Kort St., 54474-1094. Tel: 715-359-2421; Fax: 715-355-3088.
See Wausau Area Catholic Schools, Wausau under Unified Catholic School Systems located in the Institution section.
Catechesis/Religious Program—112 W. Kort St., Schofield, 54476. Tel: 715-359-9006. Students 223.

ROZELLVILLE, MARATHON CO., ST. ANDREW, [CEM] Attended by St. Joseph, Stratford. Rev. Thomas J. Rudolph. In Res., Rev. Arthur S. Redmond (Retired). Tel: 715-384-7932.
Res.: Box 106, Stratford, 54484. Tel: 715-687-2404.
Rectory—D 1876 CTH C., Stratford, 54484.

RUDOLPH, WOOD CO., ST. PHILIP, [CEM] Attended by St. Lawrence, Wisconsin Rapids. Rev. Timothy J. Welles.
Parish Office: 6957 Grotto Ave., Box 165, 54475. Tel: 715-435-3286.
Res.: 530 Tenth Ave. N., Wisconsin Rapids, 54495. Tel: 715-421-5777.
See Wisconsin Rapids Area Catholic Schools, Wisconsin Rapids under Unified Catholic School Systems located in the Institution section.

SAINT JOSEPH RIDGE, LA CROSSE CO., ST. JOSEPH (1866) [CEM] Attended by St. Peter, Middle Ridge. Rev. Francis Abuah-Quansah.
Res.: W2601 Hwy. 33, 54601. Tel: 608-788-1646.

SAINT MARY'S RIDGE, MONROE CO., NATIVITY OF THE BLESSED VIRGIN MARY (1856) [CEM], Also serves St. Augustine, Norwalk; St. John the Baptist, Summit. Rev. Keith Kitzhaber; Deacon Samuel Schmirler.
Res.: 26400 CTH U, Cashton, 54619-9157. Tel: 608-823-7906; Fax: 608-823-7272.
School—Tel: 608-823-7577. Lay Teachers 5; Students 27.

SENECA, CRAWFORD CO., ST. PATRICK (1872) [CEM] Very Rev. Eugene J. Wolf.
Res.: 21150 State Hwy. 27, P.O. Box 18, 54654. Tel: 608-734-3931.

SIGEL, WOOD CO., HOLY ROSARY (1881) [CEM] Attended by Joachim, Pittsville. Rev. Robert W. Nelson.
Mailing Address: P.O. Box 69, Pittsville, 54466-0069.

SOUTHEASTERN PORTAGE COUNTY, PORTAGE CO., ST. MAXIMILIAN MARIA KOLBE (1996) [CEM 4] Rev. Daniel H. Farley.
Mailing Address: 8611 State Hwy. 54, Almond, 54909. Tel: 715-824-3380.

SPARTA, MONROE CO., ST. PATRICK (1876) [CEM] Rev. James Leary, O.F.M.Cap.
Res.: 319 W. Main St., 54656-2143. Tel: 608-269-2655; Fax: 608-269-3084. Web: www.stpatricksparish.41pi.com.
School—100 S. L St., 54654. Tel: 608-269-4748; Fax: 608-269-4748. Lay Teachers 11; Students 150.
Catechesis/Religious Program—Tel: 608-269-7500. Students 253.

SPAULDING-CITY POINT, JACKSON CO., NORTH AMERICAN MARTYRS, Closed. For inquiries for parish records contact St. Joachim, Pittsville.

SPENCER, MARATHON CO., CHRIST THE KING (1938) [JC] Attended by St. John, Marshfield. Revs. Charles D. Stoetzel; Victor C. Feltes.
Res.: 201 W. Blodgett, Marshfield, 54449-2004. Tel: 715-659-4480; Fax: 715-384-3252.
Catechesis/Religious Program—101 Wendell St., P.O. Box 156, 54479-0156. Fax: 715-384-3252. Students 126.

SPRING VALLEY, PIERCE CO., SACRED HEART OF JESUS (1884) [CEM 2] Attended by Sacred Heart, Elmwood. Rev. Varkey V. Joseph.
Res.: S. 105 Sabin Ave., P.O. Box 456, 54767-0456. Tel: 715-778-5519; Fax: 715-778-5599. Email: shp@svtel.net.

SPRINGFIELD, EAU CLAIRE CO., ST. BRIDGET (1859) [CEM] Attended by Holy Ghost, Chippewa Falls. Revs. V. Arul Joseph; Justin Kizewski.
Office: 412 S. Main, Chippewa Falls, 54729. Tel: 715-723-4890. Email: hgparish@charter.net.

STANLEY, CHIPPEWA CO., HOLY FAMILY (1896) [CEM], Also serves Sacred Heart of Jesus-St. Joseph, Boyd. Rev. Joseph Raja.
Office: 226 E. 3rd Ave., P.O. Box 125, 54768. Tel: 715-644-5435; Fax: 715-644-5433.
Res.: 239 S. Franklin St., P.O. Box 125, 54768. Tel: 715-644-3561.

STEVENS POINT, PORTAGE CO.
1—ST. CASIMIR (1871) [CEM], Also serves St. Mary, Torun. Rev. Wesley Janowski (Poland).
Res.: 203 W. Casimir Rd., 54481. Tel: 715-344-9582. Email: stcasimir@localnet.com.
2—ST. JOSEPH (1884) [JC] Rev. Alan T. Burkhardt.
Res.: 1709 Wyatt Ave., 54481-3699. Tel: 715-341-1617; Fax: 715-341-2623. Web: www.togetherinfaith.org.
See Stevens Point Area Catholic Schools, Stevens Point under Unified Catholic School Systems located in the Institution section.
Catechesis/Religious Program—1901 Lincoln Ave., 54481. Tel: 715-341-1617, Ext. 115; Fax: 715-341-2623. Lynn Meyer, C.R.E.; Teresa Geib, Youth Min.; Kris Hansen, Pastoral Min. Students 179.
3—NEWMAN UNIVERSITY PARISH (1970) [JC] Rev. Thomas F. Lindner.
Office: 2108 Fourth Ave., 54481. Tel: 715-345-6500; Fax: 715-345-5303.
Catechesis/Religious Program—Bonnie Seidl Bauman, D.R.E. Students 101.
4—ST. PETER (1876) [JC] Rev. Kevin C. Louis. In Res., Rev. Robert M. Letona.
Res.: 800 4th Ave., 54481-1627. Tel: 715-344-6115; Fax: 715-344-6277. Web: www.saintpetercatholic.com.
See Stevens Point Area Catholic Schools, Stevens Point under Unified Catholic School Systems located in the Institution section.
5—ST. STANISLAUS (1917) [JC] Rev. George Kutty Thayilkuzhithottu, M.S.F.S.; Deacon Donald Borski.
Res.: 838 Fremont St., 54481. Tel: 715-344-9117; Fax: 715-344-1771. Email: ststans@charter.net. Web: www.saintstans.net.
See Stevens Point Area Catholic Schools, Stevens Point under Unified Catholic School Systems located in the Institution section.
6—ST. STEPHEN (1852) [CEM], Also serves St. Bartholomew, Mill Creek. Very Rev. John A. Potaczek; Deacons Robert Hensen; Arthur Schaller; Richard Rozumalski.
Res.: 1401 Clark St., 54481. Tel: 715-344-3319; Fax: 715-344-6101. Email: ststephenparish@att.net. Web: www.saintstephenparish.com.
See Stevens Point Area Catholic Schools, Stevens Point under Unified Catholic School Systems located in the Institution section.
Catechesis/Religious Program—1335 Clark St., 54481. Tel: 715-344-6433. Students 130.

STRATFORD, MARATHON CO., ST. JOSEPH (1900) [CEM 3], Also serves St. Andrew, Rozellville. Rev. Thomas J. Rudolph.
Res.: 420 Larch St., P.O. Box 6, 54484. Tel: 715-687-2404.
School—P.O. Box 6, 54484. Tel: 715-687-4145; Fax: 715-687-4343. Lay Teachers 13; Students 130.
Catechesis/Religious Program—Tel: 715-687-3392. Ruth Gawlikoski, D.R.E. Students 189.

SUMMIT, MONROE CO., ST. JOHN THE BAPTIST (1877) [CEM] Attended by Nativity of the Blessed Virgin Mary, St. Mary's Ridge. Rev. Keith Kitzhaber; Deacon Samuel Schmirler.
Mailing Address: 26400 CTH U, Cashton, 54619-9757. Tel: 608-823-7906; Fax: 608-823-7272.

THORP, CLARK CO., ST. BERNARD-ST. HEDWIG PARISH (1884) [CEM] Rev. Keith B. Apfelbeck.
Res.: 109 N. Church St., Box 329, 54771. Tel: 715-669-5526; Fax: 715-669-5754.
School—411 E. School St., Box 369, 54771. Tel: 715-669-5530. Lay Teachers 10; Students 77.
Catechesis/Religious Program—Tel: 715-669-7302. Leeann Klapatauskas, D.R.E. Students 229.

TILDEN, CHIPPEWA CO., ST. PETER (1869) [CEM], Attended by St. Charles Borromeo, Chippewa Falls. Rev. William P. Felix; Deacons Thomas Kinnick; Daniel Rider.
Mailing Address: 11358 CTH Q, Chippewa Falls, 54729-6115. Tel: 715-288-6484; Fax: 715-723-2195.
Res.: 11358 CTU Q, Chippewa Falls, 54729-6115. Tel: 715-723-4088; Fax: 715-723-2195.
School—11370 CTH Q, Chippewa Falls, 54729. Tel: 715-288-6250; Fax: 715-288-6250. Lay Teachers 6; Students 60.

TOMAH, MONROE CO., ST. MARY (IMMACULATE CONCEPTION) (1867) [CEM], Also serves St. Andrew,

Warrens. Very Rev. Steven J. Kachel.
Office: 303 W. Monroe St., 54660. Tel: 608-372-4516.
Res.: 516 W. Foster, 54660.
School—315 W. Monroe St., 54660. Tel: 608-372-5765; Fax: 608-372-4440. Lay Teachers 15; Students 180.
Catechesis/Religious Program—Tel: 608-372-0825. Wanda Thorson, D.R.E. Students 179.

TORUN, PORTAGE CO., ST. MARY, [CEM] Attended by St. Casimir, Stevens Point. Rev. Wesley Janowski, C.R., Parochial Admin.
Res.: 5589 Dewey Dr., Stevens Point, 54481. Tel: 715-344-2599; Fax: 715-345-1377.

TREMPEALEAU, TREMPEALEAU CO., ST. BARTHOLOMEW (1869) [CEM 2], Also serves St. Mary, Galesville. Rev. Edmund J. Doerre.
Res.: 11646 South St., 54661-8238. Tel: 608-534-6652. Web: www.saintbartholomew.net.

UNION CENTER, JUNEAU CO., ST. THERESA OF AVILA, Closed. For inquiries for parish records contact St. Jerome, Wonewoc.

VESPER, WOOD CO., ST. JAMES, [CEM] Attended by St. Joachim, Pittsville. Rev. Robert W. Nelson.
6623 N. Church St., Box 68, 54489. Tel: 715-569-4412.
Res.: P.O. Box 69, Pittsville, 54489.
Catechesis/Religious Program—Annette Molepske, D.R.E. Students 58.

VIROQUA, VERNON CO., ANNUNCIATION OF THE BLESSED VIRGIN MARY (1906) Very Rev. Robert J. Cook.
Res.: 400 Congress Ave., 54665-1309. Tel: 608-637-7711; Fax: 608-637-6914. Email: rjc1965@frontiernet.net. Web: www.saintmaryviroqua.org.
Catechesis/Religious Program—Tel: 608-634-3033. Dennis Olson, C.R.E. Students 211.

WARRENS, MONROE CO., ST. ANDREW, Attended by St. Mary (Immaculate Conception), Tomah. Very Rev. Steven J. Kachel.
Mailing Address: 24798 Atlas Ave., 54666. Tel: 608-378-4397.
Res.: 203 W. Monroe St., Tomah, 54660. Tel: 608-372-4516.

WAUMANDEE, BUFFALO CO., ST. BONIFACE (1867) [CEM 2], Served from Holy Family, Arcadia Very Rev. Michael E. Klos.
Res.: 52026 Cty. Rd. U, 54622-0962. Tel: 608-626-2621.
School—Tel: 608-626-2611. Students 39.

WAUSAU, MARATHON CO.

1—ST. ANNE (1949) [JC] Rev. Steven J. Brice; Deacon Robert G. Anderson.
Res.: 700 W. Bridge St., 54401. Tel: 715-849-3930; Fax: 715-849-4679. Email: frsteve@stanneswausau.org. Web: www.stanneswausau.org.
See Newman Catholic Schools, Wausau under Unified Catholic School Systems located in the Institution section.
Catechesis/Religious Program—Tel: 715-849-3520. Barbara Ceranski, D.R.E. Students 755.

2—CHURCH OF THE RESURRECTION (1998) [JC] Revs. William N. Grevatch; Gregory A. Michaud; Deacon Peter Burek.
Mailing Address: 621 2nd St., 54403. Tel: 715-845-6715; 715-845-5379; Fax: 715-845-4120.

3—HOLY NAME OF JESUS (1946) Rev. Gerald Pehler, O.F.M.Cap.
Res.: 1104 S. 9th Ave., 54401. Tel: 715-842-4543; Fax: 715-845-5059. Email: hnoffice@charter.net.
See Wausau Area Catholic Schools, Wausau under Unified Catholic School Systems located in the Institution section.

4—ST. JAMES THE GREATER, Closed. For inquiries for Parish Records contact Resurrection of Our Lord Jesus Christ, Wausau.

5—ST. MARY (IMMACULATE CONCEPTION), Closed. For inquiries for Parish Records contact Resurrection of Our Lord Jesus Christ, Wausau.

6—ST. MATTHEW (1958) Rev. Robert C. Thorn.
Res.: 229 S. 28th Ave., 54401. Tel: 715-842-3148; Fax: 715-842-3209.
See Newman Area Catholic Schools, Wausau under Unified Catholic School Systems located in the Institution section.
Catechesis/Religious Program—Sandy Grabko, D.R.E. Students 139.
St. Matthew Parish Center—221 S. 28th Ave., 54401. Tel: 715-842-3148.

7—ST. MICHAEL (1887) [CEM] Revs. William N. Grevatch; Gregory A. Michaud.
611 Stark St., 54403-3577.
Res.: Tel: 715-842-4283; 715-842-2344; Fax: 715-849-2509.
See Wausau Area Catholic Schools, Wausau under Unified Catholic School Systems located in the Institution section.
Convent—Tel: 715-845-6885; Fax: 715-849-2509.

WAUZEKA, CRAWFORD CO., SACRED HEART (1881) [CEM] Attended by Prairie du Chien. Rev. James C. Weighner.
Mailing Address: 711 E. Main St., P.O. Box 237, 53826.

WEST SALEM, LA CROSSE CO., ST. LEO THE GREAT (1957), Also serves St. Mary, Bangor. Rev. Robert S. Hegenbarth.
Res.: 210 W. Hamlin St., 54669. Tel: 608-786-0610.

WESTON, MARATHON CO., ST. AGNES (1910) [CEM] Rev. Joseph J. Rafacz.
Res.: 6101 Zinser St., Schofield, 54476. Tel: 715-359-5675; Fax: 715-359-4392.
Catechesis/Religious Program—Students 215.

WHITEHALL, TREMPEALEAU CO., ST. JOHN THE APOSTLE (1948), Served from SS Peter & Paul, Independence. Rev. David C. Kunz.
Office: 35900 Lee St., 54773. Tel: 715-538-4607; Fax: 715-538-2224.

WILLARD, CLARK CO., HOLY FAMILY (1912) [CEM] Attended by St. Mary Help of Christians, Greenwood. Rev. A. Joseph Follmar.
Res.: 123 N. Main St., Greenwood, 54437. Tel: 715-267-6905.

WILSON, EAU CLAIRE CO., ST. PETER, Closed. For inquiries for parish records contact Sacred Heart-St. Joseph, Boyd.

WILTON, MONROE CO., ST. JOHN THE BAPTIST (1875) [CEM] Attended by St. Joseph, Kendall. Rev. Richard C. Dickman.
Res.: Box 155, Kendall, 54638. Tel: 608-463-7120.
Catechesis/Religious Program—Tel: 608-463-7649. Mary Skolos, D.R.E. Students 50.

WISCONSIN RAPIDS, WOOD CO.

1—ST. LAWRENCE, [JC], Also serves St. Philip, Rudolph. Rev. Timothy J. Welles; Deacon James L. Landry.
Res.: 530 10th Ave. N., 54495. Tel: 715-421-5777; 715-424-2651; Fax: 715-421-2478.
See Wisconsin Rapids Area Catholic Schools, Wisconsin Rapids under Unified Catholic School Systems located in the Institution section.

2—OUR LADY, QUEEN OF HEAVEN (1947) [JC] Revs. Alan P. Wierzba; Zacharie B. Tshingimba.
Res.: 750 10th Ave. S., 54495. Tel: 715-423-1251; Fax: 715-423-9407. Email: ourladyqueenofheaven@hotmail.com. Web: www.our-lady.org.
See Wisconsin Rapids Area Catholic Schools, Wisconsin Rapids under Unified Catholic School Systems located in the Institution section.

3—SS. PETER AND PAUL (1837) [CEM], Served from Our Lady Queen of Heaven, Wisconsin Rapids. Rev. Alan P. Wierzba.
Mailing Address: 1150 2nd St. N., 54494.
Catechesis/Religious Program—Tel: 715-423-6045. Charles Peeters, D.R.E. Students 240.

4—ST. VINCENT DE PAUL (1956) Rev. William G. Menzel.
Res.: 820 13 St. S., 54494-5336. Tel: 715-423-2111; Fax: 715-423-4227.
See Wisconsin Rapids Area Catholic Schools, Wisconsin Rapids under Unified Catholic School Systems located in the Institution section.
Catechesis/Religious Program—Tel: 715-423-2540; Fax: 715-423-4227. Mary Jo Sigourney, D.R.E. Students 128.

WONEWOC, JUNEAU CO., ST. JEROME, [CEM] Attended by St. Aloysius, Hillsboro. Rev. Joseph C. Nakwah; Deacon John Nusse.
Office:—528 N. Center St., R.R. 2, Box 87A, 53968. Tel: 608-464-7713; 608-462-5875.

WUERZBURG, MARATHON CO., ST. JOHN THE BAPTIST (1904) Closed. For inquiries for parish records contact the Diocesan Archives.

YUBA, RICHLAND CO., ST. WENCESLAUS, Closed. For inquiries for parish records contact The Diocesan Archives.

Chaplains of Public Institutions

OXFORD. *Federal Correctional Institute*, Tel: 608-584-5511. Vacant.

TOMAH. *Veterans Administration Medical Center* 54660. Tel: 608-372-3971.

WAUSAU. *Wausau Hospital Center*, 333 Pine Ridge Blvd., 54401. Tel: 715-847-2121; 715-847-2840.
Res.: 4303 Lake Shore Dr., 54401. Tel: 715-355-4499.

Special Assignment:
Rev. Msgr.—
Gilles, Richard W., J.C.L., Vicar General & Moderator of the Curia, P.O. Box 4004, 54602-4004. Tel: 608-788-7700
Revs.—
Apfelbeck, Keith B., Chap. of Hmong Catholics of the Diocese of LaCrosse, St. Bernard-St. Hedwig Parish, P.O. Box 329, Thorp, 54771-0329. Tel: 715-669-5526
Hirsch, Joseph W., Liaison for Clergy, P.O. Box 4004, 54602-4004. Tel: 608-788-7700
Malin, Delbert J., Liaison for Senior Priests (Retired), Holmen, 54636.
Martin, Samuel A., Dir. of Holy Cross, Seminary House of Formation, P.O. Box 4004, 54602-4004. Tel: 608-788-9095
Powell, Leon A., Vice Chancellor, P.O. Box 4004, 54602-4004. Tel: 608-788-7700
Thorn, Robert C., Diocesan Chap. of Spanish Speaking Catholics, St. Matthew Rectory, 2700 Westwood Dr., 54403. Tel: 715-842-3148; 608-788-6594

On Duty Outside the Diocese:
Revs.—
Czerwonka, Paul G., Naamestraat 100, B-3000 Leuven, Belgium.
Fliss, Richard L. (Retired), 8531 S.W. 185th Ter., Miami, FL 33157. Tel: 305-969-9964
Heagle, John L., P.O. Box 510, Lincoln City, OR 97367. Tel: 541-764-2982
Sakowski, Derek (WH), Casa Santa Maria, Via Del'Umilta 30, Rome 00187 Italy.

Foreign Missions:
Revs.—
Flock, Robert H., Parroquia de la Santa Cruz, Casilla 713, Santa Cruz, Bolivia. Tel: 011-591-332-6302
Kolodziejczyk, Sebastian J., Casa Hogar Juan Pablo II, Lurin 16, Peru. Tel: 011-5114-30-5646

Leave of Absence:
Revs.—
Apfelbeck, Kurt J.
Bauer, Scott A.
Benzmiller, James T.
Kiedinger, Daniel J.
Konopacky, Joseph R.
McHugh, John T.
Neis, William P.
O'Hara, Joseph M.
Olson, Randy G.
Stashek, Brian E.
Waldbilling, Brian T.
Wolf, Anthony J.

Retired:
Rev. Msgrs.—
Blecha, Charles A., 420 Heller Rd., Apt. 322, Menomonie, 54751. Tel: 715-235-1860
Malik, John E., 510 W. Wausau St., Colby, 54421.
McGarty, Bernard O., 109 S. 9th St., 54601. Tel: 608-784-4473
Revs.—
Altmann, Robert T., 10080 County Rd. F, P.O. Box 103, Blenker, 54415.
Beckfelt, John W., Westwood Benedictine Health Center, 925 Kenwood Ave., Apt. 2142, Duluth, MN 55811. Tel: 218-279-7654
Berg, Donald M., Renaissance Rm. 224, 4602 Barbican Ave., Weston, 54476. Tel: 715-352-3444
Blazewicz, William J., Holy Cross Diocesan Center, 3710 East Ave., S., P.O. Box 4004, 54602-4004.
Cassidy, John V., 3325 Solaris Ln., 54601. Tel: 608-788-1196
Donaldson, Thomas J., W7805 Co. Rd. Z, Arkansaw, 54721.
Faber, Emmet N., 162 Cynthia Dr., Bastrop, TX 78602.
Finucan, J. Thomas, Holy Cross Diocesan Center, 3710 East Ave. S., P.O. Box 4004, 54602-4004. Tel: 608-785-3167
Fliss, Richard L., 16843 S. Octillo View Pl., Corona De Tucson, AZ 85641.
Gerum, Jerome G., 1601 N. Palmetto Ave., P.O. Box 673, Marshfield, 54449-0673. Tel: 715-387-4783
Greatorex, Robert W., 1300 Maria Dr., Stevens Point, 54481.
Herrmann, Richard J., 309 W. Blodgett St., Marshfield, 54449. Tel: 715-384-5039
Hoerburger, Henry R., St. Joseph Rectory, P.O. Box 275, Elk Mound, 54739. Tel: 715-879-5332
Keating, Joseph R., 811 W. 1st Ave., Parkesburg, PA 19365.
Kelly, Daniel J., 1547 Raymond Dr., Naperville, IL 60563.
Lesczynski, James J., 2882 City Rd. Z., Adams, 53910. Tel: 608-565-2488
Logan, James J., 706 S. Palmetto Ave., Marshfield, 54449.
Malin, Delbert J., 909 Western Ave., Holmen, 54636.
McInnis, Thomas J., 19660 Bluffview Pl., P.O. Box 368, Galesville, 54630-6085.
Mertens, Michael G., Holy Cross Diocesan Center, 3710 East Ave. S., P.O. Box 4004, 54602-4004. Tel: 608-788-0311
Miller, James H., 109 CTH U W., Norwalk, 54648. Tel: 608-823-7643
Mish, Roy L., 107 4th Ave., Apt. 2, Strum, 54770.
Monti, Robert M., 804 Cypress Grove Ln. #302, Pompano Beach, FL 33069.
Osowski, Chester J., St. Philip Rectory, 6597 Grotto

Ave., P.O. Box 165, Rudolph, 54475. Tel: 715-569-4412

Pedretti, Raymond J., St. Mary of Mt. Carmel Rectory, 3995 Cty. Rd. K, Amherst, 54406. Tel: 715-824-3455

Pedretti, Robert F., 491 Red Tail Dr., Amherst, 54406.

Penchi, Edward J., Casilla 713, Santa Cruz, Bolivia. Tel: 011-591-343-0302

Raschke, Bernard L., Corpus Christi Rectory, 10075 City Hwy. BB, Marshfield, 54449.

Redmond, Arthur S., St. Andrew Rectory, D1868 CTHC, P.O. Box 106, Stratford, 54484-0106.

Reuter, Arnold F., Holy Cross Diocesan Center, 3710 East Ave. S., P.O. Box 4004, 54602-4004. Tel: 608-788-0717

Sankoorikal, Paul L., c/o Karla Hansen, 3428 Kinney Coulee Rd., Onalaska, 54650.

Schaefer, James F., P.O. Box 1552, 54402-1552.

Schelble, T. Michael, Holy Cross Diocesan Center, P.O. Box 4004, 54602-4004. Tel: 608-787-8283

Schulte, Lyle L., 234 Main St., P.O. Box 287, Junction City, 54443.

Smith, Eugene P., St. Joseph Rectory, P.O. Box 10, Boyd, 54726-0010. Tel: 715-667-3038

Smith, Thomas J., Holy Cross Diocesan Center, 3710 East Ave., P.O. Box 4004, 54602-4004. Tel: 608-788-4555

Sonnberger, Albert W., St. John the Baptist Rectory, 4540 State Hwy. 40, Bloomer, 54724. Tel: 715-568-3778

Stanchik, Dennis P., St. Bartholomew Rectory, 2493 CTHM, Stevens Point, 54481. Tel: 715-344-3003

Thome, Edwin J., Holy Cross Diocesan Center, P.O. Box 4004, 54602-4004. Tel: 608-783-5535

Wagner, Robert J., Holy Cross Diocesan Center, P.O. Box 4004, 54602-4004.

Wilger, Norbert J., St. Mary Rectory, 1827 Lynn Ave., Altoona, 54720. Tel: 715-835-8813

Wisneski, John A., 1775 N. First Ave., 54401-1985.

Ziegelmaier, David A., N3180 Vista Ct. N., 54601.

Zoromski, Herbert P., 8490 Padre Dr., Wittenberg, 54499. Tel: 715-454-6994

Permanent Deacons:

Abnet, Frank, St. Patrick, Onalaska

Agema, Larry, Sacred Heart, St. Patrick, Eau Claire

Anderson, Robert, St. Anne, Wausau

Arnold, Mark C., Asst. Dir., Office of Family Life, Diocesan Curia, La Crosse

Ashenbrenner, David, St. Joseph, Galloway, St. Ladislaus, Bevent

Borski, Donald, St. Stanislaus, Stevens Point

Brunner, Norbert, St. Vincent de Paul, Wisconsin Rapids

Burek, Peter, Church of the Resurrection, Wausau, WI

Chittendon, Robert, St. Olaf, Eau Claire

Delgado, Juan, Mauston

Hansen, Robert, N5904 Albany N., Mondovi, 54755.

Heinzl, Glen, St. Francis of Assisi, Necedah

Hensen, Robert, (Retired)

Hurrish, Florian, (Retired), Mesa, AZ

Jansing, Richard, 5625 Sandpiper Dr., Stevens Point, 54481.

Jirous, Thomas, St. James, Amherst, St. Mary of Mt. Carmel, Fancher

Jolliffe, Garry, Chandler, AZ

Kennedy, David, St. Joseph, Adams

Kinnick, Thomas, St. Charles Borromeo, Chippewa Falls; St. Peter, Tilden

Knauf, LeRoy, Holy Family, Poniatowski

Kostner, Richard, St. Paul, Bloomer, St. Jude, New Auburn

Koza, J. Michael, La Crescent, MN

Landry, James, St. Lawrence, Wisconsin Rapids

Ludick, Matthew, St. Elizabeth Ann Seton, Holmen

Maciejewski, James, Sacred Heart, Polonia; St. Adalbert, Rosholt

McKeough, Patrick, St. Mark, Rothschild

Nusse, John, St. Aloysius, Hillsboro; St. Jerome, Wonewoc

Ray, Kevin, Roncalli Newman Parish, Hillsboro

Richards, Joseph, St. Joseph the Workman Cathedral, La Crosse

Rider, Daniel, St. Charles Borromeo, Chippewa Falls; St. Peter, Tilden

Rivers, Dennis, Holy Cross, Cornell

Rozumalski, Richard, St. Stephen, Stevens Point; St. Bartholomew, Mill Creek

Rynda, Gerald, St. Joseph, Prescott

Sage, Richard, Exec. Dir., Catholic Charities of The Diocese of La Crosse

Schaller, Arthur, St. Maximilian Kolbe, Southeastern Portage County.

Schaper, Edward, Black River Falls, WI

Schmirler, Samuel, Sacred Heart, Cashton; Nativity of the BVM, St. Mary's Ridge; St. Augustine, Norwalk; St. John the Baptist, Summit Ridge

Slason, Stillman, Volin, SD

Walker, Hugh, (Retired)

Weingart, James, St. Mary's Assumption, Durand; Holy Rosary, Lima; Sacred Heart, Mondovi

Wendt, Edward, 29445 Town Hall Rd., Muscoda, 53573.

INSTITUTIONS LOCATED IN THE DIOCESE

[A] SEMINARIES, DIOCESAN

LA CROSSE. *Holy Cross Seminary House of Formation*, 3710 East Ave. S., P.O. Box 4004, 54602-4004. Tel: 608-788-9095; Fax: 608-788-8413. Rev. Samuel A. Martin, Dir.; Rev. Msgr. Richard W. Gilles, J.C.L., Spiritual Dir.; Mr. Adam Husing, Prefect. Tel: 608-787-8978. Students 5.

[B] COLLEGES AND UNIVERSITIES

LA CROSSE. *Viterbo University*, 900 Viterbo Dr., 54601-8804. Tel: 608-796-3000; Fax: 608-796-3050. Email: admission@viterbo.edu. Web: www.viterbo.edu. Dr. Richard Artman, Pres.; Barbara Gayle, Vice Pres. Academic Affairs; Diane Brimmer, Vice Pres. Student Devel.; Todd M. Ericson, C.P.A., Vice Pres. Finance; Patrick G. Kerrigan, Vice Pres. Communications & Mktg.; Amy Gleason, Registrar; Roland Nelson, Ph.D., Vice Pres. Admission; Gary Klein, Vice Pres. Institutional Advancement. Founded in 1890 by the Franciscan Sisters of Perpetual Adoration, Viterbo Univ. is a Catholic, Franciscan Univ. Comprised of Five Undergraduate Schools, A Graduate School, and a School of Graduate, Professional, and Adult Learning. Priests 1; Sisters 4; Lay Teachers 113; Students 3,287.

[C] UNIFIED CATHOLIC SCHOOL SYSTEMS

LA CROSSE. *Aquinas Catholic Schools*, 521 S. 13th St., 54601. Tel: 608-784-8585; Fax: 608-784-9988. Web: www.aquinascatholicschools.org. Very Rev. Michael J. Gorman, Dean; Kurt Nelson, Pres.

Aquinas Middle School (1999) 315 S. 11th St., 54601. Tel: 608-784-0156; Fax: 608-784-0229. Web: www.aquinascatholicschools.org/aquinasms/. Mrs. Patricia A. Gallagher-Kosmatka, Prin. Lay Teachers 16; Students 158.

Aquinas High School, 315 S. 11th St., 54601. Tel: 608-784-0287; Fax: 608-782-8851. Web: www.aquinascatholicschools.org/aquinashs/. Ted Knutson, Prin. Priests 1; Religious 1; Lay Teachers 29; Students 345.

Blessed Sacrament School (Grades 3-6), 2404 King St., 54601. Tel: 608-782-5564; Fax: 608-782-7765. Email: kayberra@pvt.k12.wi.us. Web: www.aquinascatholicschools.org/blessedsacrament/. Kay Berra, Prin. Lay Teachers 18; Students 167.

Mary, Mother of the Church Early Childhood Center (Grades PreK-K), 2000 Weston St., 54601. Tel: 608-788-5225; Fax: 608-788-5230. Web: www.aquinasschools.org/ecc/. Val Breidel, Dir. Students 99.

St. Joseph Cathedral School (Grades PreK-2), 1319 Ferry St., 54601. Tel: 608-782-5998; Fax: 608-784-9933. Web: www.aquinascatholicschools.org/cathedral/. John Stellflue, Prin. Lay Teachers 14; Students 130.

St. Patrick School (Grades PreK-6), 127 11th Ave. N., Onalaska, 54650. Tel: 608-783-5483; Fax: 608-783-5483. Web: www.aquinasschools.org/stpats/. Greg Wesely, Prin. Lay Teachers 19; Students 195.

CHIPPEWA FALLS. *Chippewa Falls Area Catholic Schools* Central Office, 1316 Bel Air Blvd., 54729. Tel: 715-723-0538; Fax: 715-723-1501. Web: www.cacs.k12.wi.us. Dr. Chad Ronnander, Pres.

Holy Ghost Elementary School (Grades 4-6), 436 S. Main St., 54729. Tel: 715-723-6478; Fax: 715-723-8990. Mary Selz, Prin. Lay Teachers 8; Students 96.

McDonell Central Catholic High School, 1316 Bel Air Blvd., 54729. Tel: 715-723-9126; Fax: 715-723-1501. Bro. Roger Betzold, Prin.; Rev. Justin Kizewski, Chap. & Instructor. Priests 1; Christian Brothers 1; Lay Teachers 18; Students 175.

Notre Dame Middle School (Grades 7-8), 1316 Bel Air Blvd., 54729. Tel: 715-723-4777; Fax: 715-723-3353. Bro. Roger Betzold, Prin. Lay Teachers 2; Students 50.

St. Charles Primary School (Grades PreK-3), 429 W. Spruce St., 54729. Tel: 715-723-5827; Fax: 715-723-2109. Mary Selz, Prin. Lay Teachers 12; Students 112.

EAU CLAIRE. *Catholic Area Schools of the Eau Claire Deanery (C.A.S.E.)* Central Office:, 448 N. Dewey St., 54703. Tel: 715-830-2273; Fax: 715-835-4658. Email: chofacker@case.kiz.wi.us. Web: www.case.kiz.wi.us. Cynthia Hofacker, Pres.

Genesis Child Development Center, 418 N. Dewey St., 54701. Tel: 715-830-2275. Gayle Flaig, Dir.

Immaculate Conception School (Grades K-6), 1703 Sherwin Ave., 54701. Tel: 715-830-5816; Fax: 715-835-9459. Sr. Dorothy Brenner, F.S.P.A., Prin. Lay Teachers 18; Students 270.

Regis Child Devel. Center, 2100 Fenwick Ave., 54701. Tel: 715-830-2274; Fax: 715-830-2270. Gayle Flaig, Dir.

Regis Middle School (Grades 7-8), 2100 Fenwick Ave., 54701. Tel: 715-830-1327; Fax: 715-835-4658. Renee Cassidy, Prin.; Rev. William A. Dhein, Chap. Lay Teachers 10; Students 125.

Regis High School, 2100 Fenwick Ave., 54701. Tel: 715-830-2271; Fax: 715-830-5461. Thomas Saporito, Prin.; Rev. William A. Dhein, Chap. Priests 1; Lay Teachers 17; Students 209.

St. James School (Grades K-6), 2502 Eleventh St., 54703. Tel: 715-830-2277; Fax: 715-830-9861. Lay Teachers 9; Students 116.

St. Mary School (Grades K-5), 1828 Lynn Ave., Altoona, 54720. Tel: 715-830-2278; Fax: 715-830-9573. Lay Teachers 9; Students 73.

St. Olaf School (Grades K-6), 2407 North Ln., 54703. Tel: 715-830-2279; Fax: 715-832-0742. Faculty 10; Students 123.

MARSHFIELD. *Marshfield Area Catholic Schools (MACS)*, 710 S. Columbus Ave., 54449. Tel: 715-387-1177; Fax: 715-384-4535. Email: catalanog@mfldacs.net. Mr. David Eaton, Pres.

Columbus High School, 710 S. Columbus Ave., 54449-3413. Tel: 715-387-1177; Fax: 715-384-4535. Email: catalanog@mfldacs.net. Web: www.columbus.marshfield.wi.us. Barbara Billings, Prin.; Rev. Victor C. Feltes, Chap. Priests 1; Lay Teachers 27; Students 150.

Columbus Catholic Middle School, 710 S. Columbus Ave., 54449. Tel: 715-384-7184; Fax: 715-384-4535. Email: hfms@wctc.net. Web: www.columbus.marshfield.wi.us/hfms. Barbara Billings, Prin.; Rev. Victor C. Feltes, Chap. Priests 1; Lay Teachers 8; Students 110.

Our Lady of Peace School (Grades 4-6), 1300 W. Fifth St., 54449. Tel: 715-384-5474; Fax: 715-387-8697. Sr. Mary Ann Wutkowski, S.S.N.D., Prin. Students 153.

St. John the Baptist School (Grades PreK-3), 307 Walnut Ave., 54449. Tel: 715-384-4989; Fax: 715-384-5131. Sr. Mary Ann Wutkowski, S.S.N.D., Prin. Students 115.

STEVENS POINT. *Stevens Point Area Catholic Schools* Central Office:, 1004 First St., 54481. Tel: 715-341-2445; Fax: 715-342-2001. Email: jdyer@spacs.k12.wi.us. Web: www.spacs.k12.wi.us. Mr. James Dyer, Pres.

St. Bronislava School (Grades PreK-5), 3301 Willow Dr., Plover, 54467. Tel: 715-342-2015; Fax: 715-342-2016. Mr. James Dyer, Prin. Lay Teachers 7; Students 127.

Pacelli High School, 1301 Maria Dr., 54481. Tel: 715-341-2442; Fax: 715-341-6799. Mr. Jeff Brengman, Prin.; Rev. Robert M. Letona, Chap. & Instructor. Priests 1; Sisters 2; Lay Teachers 25; Students 241.

St. Joseph School Early Childhood Center, 1901 Lincoln Ave., 54481. Tel: 715-341-2878; Fax: 715-342-2013. Lori Shafranski, Dir. Lay Teachers 1; Students 89.

St. Peter Middle School (Grades 6-8), 708 First St., 54481. Tel: 715-344-1890; Fax: 715-342-2005. Ellen Lopas, Prin.; Rev. Robert M. Letona, Chap. Lay Teachers 15; Students 168.

St. Stanislaus School (Grades K-2), 2150 High St., 54481. Tel: 715-344-3086; Fax: 715-342-2014. Mr. Gregg Hansel, Prin. Lay Teachers 10; Students 115.

St. Stephen School (Grades 3-5), 1335 Clark St., 54481. Tel: 715-344-3751; Fax: 715-342-2013. Mr. Gregg Hansel, Prin. Lay Teachers 9; Students 152.

WAUSAU. *Newman Catholic Schools*, 619 Stark St., 54403. Tel: 715-845-5735; Fax: 715-848-3582. Web: www.newmancatholicschools.com. Janet M. Klosinski, Pres. Central Office:

Newman Catholic High School, 1130 W. Bridge St., 54401. Tel: 715-845-8274; Fax: 715-842-1302. Lawrence Theiss, Prin.; Rev. Gregory A. Michaud, Chap. Priests 1; Lay Teachers 20; Students 188.

Newman Catholic Elementary School at St. Anne Parish (Grades PreK-5), 604 N. 6th Ave., 54401. Tel: 715-845-5754; Fax: 715-842-4021. Emily Miller, Prin. Sisters 1; Lay Teachers 16; Students 239.

Newman Catholic Elementary School at St. Mark Parish, 602 Military Rd., Rothschild, 54474. Tel: 715-359-9662; Fax: 715-355-8904. Jeanne Lang, Prin. Sisters 1; Lay Teachers 19; Students 118.

Newman Catholic Middle School at St. Matthew Parish, 225 S. 28th Ave., 54401. Tel: 715-842-4857; Fax: 715-845-2937. Tina Meyer, Prin.; Rev. Robert C. Thorn, Chap. Lay Teachers 15; Students 149.

Newman Catholic Elementary School at St. Michael

Parish (Grades PreK-5), 615 Stark St., 54403. Tel: 715-848-0206; Fax: 715-845-6852. Jeanne Lang, Prin. Felician Sisters 1; Lay Teachers 8; Students 85.

WISCONSIN RAPIDS. *Wisconsin Rapids Area Catholic Schools* Central Office, 1120 Lincoln, Ste. B, 54494. Tel: 715-422-0900; Fax: 715-422-0903. Email: colson@wracs.org. Web: wracs.org. Carol Olson, Pres.

Assumption Middle School, 440 Mead, 54494. Tel: 715-422-0950; Fax: 715-422-0955. Joan Bond, Prin.; Rev. James T. Altman, Chap. Students 103.

Assumption High School, 445 Chestnut St., 54494. Tel: 715-422-0910; Fax: 715-422-0912. Email: jbond@wracs.org. Joan Bond, Prin.; Rev. James T. Altman, Chap. Priests 1; Lay Teachers 21; Students 186.

Our Lady Queen of Heaven School, 750 Tenth Ave. S., 54495. Tel: 715-422-0980; Fax: 715-424-2972. Email: pfochs@wracs.org. Pam Fochs, Prin. Lay Teachers 9; Students 94.

St. Lawrence Early Childhood Center, 551 Tenth Ave. N., 54495. Tel: 715-422-0990; Fax: 715-422-0993. Lay Teachers 5; Students 87.

St. Vincent de Paul School, 831 12th St. S., 54494. Tel: 715-422-0960; Fax: 715-422-0963. Brenda Walczak, Prin. Lay Teachers 16; Students 142.

[D] GENERAL HOSPITALS

LA CROSSE. *Franciscan Skemp Healthcare, Mayo Health System, La Crosse Campus Medical Center*, 700 West Ave. S., 54601-4796. Tel: 608-785-0940; Fax: 608-791-9429. Web: www.mayohealthsystem.org. Robert Nesse, Pres. & CEO; Rev. Todd A. Mlsna, Chap. Franciscan Sisters of Perpetual Adoration and Mayo Foundation. Sisters 1; Total Staff 2,734; Bed Capacity 298; Patients Assisted Annually 29,867.

ARCADIA. **Arcadia Campus Hospital (Franciscan Skemp Healthcare, Mayo Health System)*, 464 S. St. Joseph Ave., 54612. Tel: 608-323-3341; Fax: 608-323-3694. Email: tracey.Robert@mayo.edu. Web: www.mayohealthsystem.org. 700 West Ave., S., 54601. Robert Tracey, Admin.; Sr. Rose Grabowski, S.S.J.-T.O.S.F., Chap. Pastoral Care. Franciscan Sisters of Perpetual Adoration and Mayo Foundation. Total Staff 63; Bed Capacity 25; Patient Days 686.

CHIPPEWA FALLS. *St. Joseph's Hospital* (1888) 2661 County Hwy. I, 54729. Tel: 715-726-3200; Fax: 715-726-3204. Web: www.stjoeschipfalls.com. David B. Fish, Exec. Vice Pres.; Revs. Daniel B. DuChez, O.S., Chap.; Frank Corradi, Mission Educator & Chap.; William Jablonske. Hospital Sisters of the Third Order of St. Francis., Hospital Sisters Health System. Total Staff 625; Bed Capacity 217; Patients Assisted Annually 78,554.

EAU CLAIRE. *Sacred Heart Hospital*, 900 W. Clairemont Ave., 54701-6122. Tel: 715-839-4121; Fax: 715-839-8417. Web: www.sacredhearthospital-ec.org. Stephen F. Ronstrom, Exec. Vice Pres.; Rev. Msgr. Edmund J. Klimek, Chap.; Rev. Lawrence G. Dunklee, Dir. Center for Spiritual Care. Hospital Sisters of the Third Order of St. Francis 3; Bed Capacity 344; Patients Assisted Annually 128,751.

MARSHFIELD. *Saint Joseph's Hospital of Marshfield, Inc.*, 611 St. Joseph Ave., 54449. Tel: 715-387-1713; Fax: 715-387-8601. Web: www.ministryhealth.org. Michael Schmidt, Pres.; Michael Kryda, CEO. Corporate Sponsor: Ministry HealthCare, Inc. (Milwaukee, WI); Sponsored by the Sisters of the Sorrowful Mother., Training School for Nurses (Affiliated with U.W.-Eau Claire).

Spiritual Services Dept. Tel: 715-387-7753. Michael Adamson, Dir. Mission Svcs.; Rita Austin, Pastoral Care Staff; Robert Cassidy, Pastoral Care Staff; Rev. Steven E. Sutterer, Protestant Chap.; Revs. Linden Nelson, Protestant Chap.; Pius Akajiufor, Chap.; Anselm Ibe, Chap.; Mary Jane Lipinski, Pastoral Care Staff. Priests 2; Sisters of the Sorrowful Mother 1; Bed Capacity 504; Patients Assisted Annually 104,100; Total Staff 1,848.

SPARTA. **Sparta Campus Hospital (Franciscan Skemp Healthcare, Mayo Health System)*, 310 W. Main St., 54656-2142. Tel: 608-269-2132; Fax: 608-269-4562. Web: www.mayohealthsystem.org. 700 West Ave., S., 54601. Robert M. Tracey, Admin.; Curtis Miller, Chap. Pastoral Care. Franciscan Sisters of Perpetual Adoration and Mayo Foundation. Total Staff 125; Bed Capacity 25; Patient Days 927.

STANLEY. **Our Lady of Victory Hospital*, 1120 Pine St., P.O. Box 220, 54768-0220. Tel: 715-644-5571; Fax: 715-644-6221. Email: eichmanc@olvh.org. Web: www.ministryhealth.org. Mrs. Cynthia Eichman, Pres.; Sr. Pat Belongia, Dir. Spiritual Svcs. Corporate Sponsor: Ministry Healthcare, Inc. (Milwaukee, WI); Sponsored by Sisters of the Sorrowful Mother. Hospital 24; Total Staff 160; Patients Assisted Annually 47,000.

STEVENS POINT. *St. Michael's Hospital of Stevens Point, Inc.*, 900 Illinois Ave., 54481. Tel: 715-346-5000; Fax: 715-346-5088. Email: jeff.martin@ministryhealth.org. Web: www.ministryhealth.org. Jeffrey L. Martin, FACHE, Pres. & CEO; Rev. Dennis J. Lynch, Chap.; Mr. David C. Baker, Dir. Spiritual Svcs.; Mrs. Janet Jacoby, Spiritual Svcs. & Chap.; Martin Lieber, Spiritual Svcs. & Chap. Corporate Sponsor: Ministry Health Care, Inc. (Milwaukee, WI); Sponsored by Sisters of the Sorrowful Mother. Licensed Bed Capacity 181; Patients Assisted Annually 183,564; Total Staff 1,219.

Ministry Medical Group, Inc., 824 Illinois Ave., 54481. Tel: 715-342-7500; Fax: 715-346-5088. Email: chuck.fehring@ministryhealth.org. Web: www.ministryhealth.org. Mark L. Fenlon, M.D., Regl. Vice Pres.; Charles F. Fehring, Regl. Admin. Total Staff 400; Patients Assisted Annually 250,000.

WESTON. *Saint Clare's Hospital of Weston, Inc.* (2002) 3400 Ministry Pkwy., 54476. Tel: 715-393-2501; Fax: 715-359-1087. Web: www.ministryhealth.org. Mary Krueger, Pres. (Ministry Health Care)Tel: 715-393-2500. Corporate Sponsor: Ministry Health Care, Inc. (Milwaukee, WI). Sponsored by Sisters of the Sorrowful Mother.

[E] REHABILITATION FACILITIES

CHIPPEWA FALLS. *L.E. Phillips Libertas Treatment Center* (1977) 2661 County Hwy. I, 54729. Tel: 715-723-5585; 800-680-4578; Fax: 715-726-3504. Email: ddachel@sjcf.hshs.org. Web: www.stjoeschipfalls.com. David B. Fish, Exec. Vice Pres.; Dr. Shawna T. Kovach, Prog. Coord. Hospital Sisters Health System, Hospital Sisters of the Third Order of St. Francis. Bed Capacity 48; Patients Assisted Annually 1,200; Total Staff 60.

[F] HOMES FOR AGED

LA CROSSE. *Bethany St. Joseph Care Center*, 2501 Shelby Rd., 54601. Tel: 608-788-5700. Eric Jacobson, Admin. Bed Capacity 172; Patients Assisted Annually 350.

Franciscan Skemp Healthcare, Mayo Health System, La Crosse Campus Nursing Home, 700 West Ave. S. 9th, 54601. Tel: 608-785-0940, Ext. 2494; Fax: 608-791-7823. Richard Berendes, Admin. Bed Capacity 23; Patient Days 3,619.

St. Joseph's Rehabilitation Center, 2902 East Ave. S., 54601. Tel: 608-788-9870; Fax: 608-787-8889. Daniel Meyer, Admin. Operated by Catholic Residential Services, Inc., Diocese of La Crosse. Units 80; Patients Assisted Annually 205.

ARCADIA. *Arcadia Campus Nursing Home (Franciscan Skemp Healthcare, Mayo Health System)*, 464 S. St. Joseph Ave., 54612. Tel: 608-323-3341; Fax: 608-323-3694. 700 West Ave., S., 54601. Darlene Goehner, Admin.; Sisters Rose Grabowski, S.S.J.-T.O.S.F., Chap.; Arlene Melder, F.S.P.A., Chap. Franciscan Sisters of Perpetual Adoration and Mayo Foundation. Bed Capacity 75; Total Staff 62; Patient Days 26,975.

EAU CLAIRE. *St. Francis Apartments* (1986) 851 University Dr., 54701. Tel: 715-834-1388; Fax: 715-858-1602. Email: cwerner@shec.hshs.org. Cathy Werner, Managing Agent.

Hospital Sisters Health Care-West, Inc. Units 60; Total in Residence 75.

WAUSAU. *Marywood Convalescent Center*, 1821 N. 4th Ave., 54401. Tel: 715-675-9451; Fax: 715-675-9051. Scott W. Rusch, Admin. Operated by Catholic Residential Services, Inc. Units 90; Patients Assisted Annually 131.

[G] RETREAT HOUSES

LA CROSSE. *Franciscan Spirituality Center*, 920 Market St., 54601-8809. Tel: 608-791-5295; Fax: 608-782-6301. Email: fscenter@fspa.org. Web: www.franciscanspiritualitycenter.org. Vince Hatt, Dir. Sisters of the Third Order of St. Francis of Perpetual Adoration.

EAU CLAIRE. *Saint Bede Retreat and Conference Center*, 1190 Priory Rd., P.O. Box 66, 54702-0066. Tel: 715-834-8642; Fax: 715-834-4292. Email: center@saintbede.org. Web: www.saintbede.org. Sr. Judith Kramer, O.S.B., Dir.; Mary Traynor, Admin. Asst. Benedictine Sisters.

MARATHON CITY. *St. Anthony Spirituality Center*, 300 E. 4th St., 54448-9602. Tel: 715-443-2236; Fax: 715-443-2235. Email: info@sarcenter.com. Web: www.sarcenter.com. Rev. Dan Crosby, O.F.M.Cap., Dir. The Province of St. Joseph of the Capuchin Order, Inc. Priests 2.

[H] MONASTERIES AND RESIDENCES OF PRIESTS AND BROTHERS

LA CROSSE. *Holy Cross (Seminary) Diocesan Center*, 3710 East Ave. S., P.O. Box 4004, 54602-4004. Tel: 608-788-7700; Fax: 608-788-8413. Mr. John J. Newman, Dir. In Res. Revs. Robert T. Altmann (Retired); William J. Blazewicz (Retired); Peter Cops. Tel: 608-787-8739; J. Thomas Finucan (Retired); Joseph W. Hirsch. Tel: 608-343-0627; Rev. Msgr. Robert P. Hundt, J.C.L.; Revs. Samuel A. Martin. Tel: 608-788-9095; Michael G. Mertens (Retired). Tel: 608-788-0311; Leon A. Powell. Tel: 608-788-4625; Arnold F. Reuter (Retired). Tel: 608-788-0717; Michael T. Schelble; Thomas J. Smith (Retired). Tel: 608-788-4555; Edwin J. Thome (Retired); Robert J. Wagner (Retired).

SPARTA. *Our Lady of Spring Bank, Cistercian Abbey*, 17304 Havenwood Rd., 54656-9536. Tel: 608-269-8138; Fax: 608-269-1992. Email: Porter@MonksOnline.org. Web: www.MonksOnline.org. Rev. Robert Keffer, O.Cist., Subprior; Very Rev. Bernard McCoy, O.Cist., Prior & Steward of Temporal Affairs; Bros. David Klecker, O.Cist.; Adam Mathews, O.Cist.; Stephen Treat, O.Cist.; Rev. Joseph Watson, O.Cist. Solemnly Professed 5; Simple Professed 1.

SPRING VALLEY. *Brothers of St. Pius X*, S. 105 Sabin, P.O. Box 284, 54767. Tel: 715-778-4999. Bro. Charles Bisenius, C.S.P.X. Dir.

WAUSAU. *St. Mary's Roman Catholic Oratory*, 26384 County Hwy. U, Cashton, 54646. Tel: 715-842-9995; Fax: 715-842-9995. Email: stmarysoratory@aol.com. Web: www.institute-christ-king.org. Institute of Christ the King-Sovereign Priest.

[I] CONVENTS AND RESIDENCES FOR SISTERS

LA CROSSE. *St. Rose Convent*, 912 Market St., 54601-4782. Tel: 608-782-5610; Fax: 608-782-6301. Email: fspa@fspa.org. Web: www.fspa.org. Sr. Marlene Weisenbeck, F.S.P.A., Pres. Motherhouse and Novitiate of the Congregation of the Franciscan Sisters of Perpetual Adoration. In Community: Professed 312; In Motherhouse 74.

Villa St. Joseph, W2658 State Rd. 33, 54601-2625. Tel: 608-788-5100; Fax: 608-788-7360. Email: jmtreba@charter.net. Web: www.fspa.org. Sr. Jean Michael Treba, F.S.P.A., Admin. Franciscan Sisters of Perpetual Adoration., A Retirement home for aged and convalescent Franciscan Sisters of Perpetual Adoration. Sisters 10; Lay Staff 130; Under Care 103.

CUSTER. *St. Clare Convent* (1874) 7381 Church St., Polonia, 54423. Tel: 715-592-4213; Fax: 715-592-4099. Felician Sisters 3.

EAU CLAIRE. *St. Bede Monastery* (1848) 1190 Priory Rd., P.O. Box 66, 54702-0066. Tel: 715-834-3176; Fax: 715-834-4292. Email: sisters@saintbede.org. Web: www.saintbede.org. Sr. Michaela Hedican, O.S.B., Prioress; Rev. John P. Hogan, Chap. Motherhouse of Sisters of the Order of St. Benedict. Retreat and Conference Center. Professed 29.

Sisters of St. Benedict, The Clairemont, 2120 Heights Dr., 54701. Tel: 715-852-6221. Sr. Margaret Michaud, O.S.B., Prioress. Residence for Sisters of the Order of St. Benedict. Sisters 8.

STEVENS POINT. *St. Joseph Motherhouse* (1901) 1300 Maria Dr., 54481. Tel: 715-344-2830; Fax: 715-344-2380. Email: jsmolinski@ssj-tosf.org. Rev. Robert W. Greatorex, Chap. (Retired). Tel: 715-344-8346; Sr. Janet Smolinski, S.S.J.-T.O.S.F., Coord. Residence of the Sisters of St. Joseph of the Third Order of St. Francis. Sisters 54.

[J] SOCIAL SERVICE AGENCIES

LA CROSSE. *Catholic Charities of the Diocese of La Crosse, Inc.* (1932) 3710 East Ave. S., P.O. Box 266, 54602-0266. Tel: 608-782-0710; Fax: 608-782-0702. Email: info@catholiccharitieslax.org. Web: www.cclse.org. Mr. Benedict T. Nguyen, M.T.S., J.D., J.C.L., Chm.; Rev. Msgr. Richard W. Gilles, J.C.L., Treas.; Deacon Richard Sage, Exec. Dir. Fin. Counseling, Pregnancy & Parenting Svcs., Adoption Placement, Emergency Svcs., Immigration Svcs, In Home Support Svcs. Total Staff 74.

Catholic Residential Services, Inc., 3710 East Ave., S., P.O. Box 2394, 54602-2394. Tel: 608-784-5323; Fax: 608-784-7522. Mr. Robert A. Laubach, Exec. Dir.; John Prince, Bd. Pres.; Glenn Horessi, Bd. Vice Pres.; Barbara Smith, Bd. Sec. Total Staff 300; Patients Assisted Annually 420.

WAUSAU. *Northland House*, 102 McClellan St., 54402-0231. Tel: 715-845-4898; Fax: 715-848-0498. Email: nhgh@dwave.net. Web: www.crsinc.org/northland. Janet R. Nissen, Admin. Operated by Catholic Residential Services, Inc., Diocese of La Crosse.; Residential Care of Children.

[K] NEWMAN CAMPUS MINISTRY

LA CROSSE. *Roncalli Newman Parish* 1732 State St., 54601. Tel: 608-784-4994; Fax: 608-784-0230. Email: roncallinewman@charterinternet.com.

Web: www.roncallinewman.com. Rev. Mark R. Pierce, Pastor; Jon Stuttgen, Campus Min. Serving Univ. of Wisconsin-La Crosse and Western Technical College.

EAU CLAIRE. *Newman Parish* 110 Garfield Ave., 54701-4042. Tel: 715-834-3399. Email: georgeszews@charterinternet.com. Web: www.newmanec.com. Rev. George R. Szews, Pastor; Rev. Msgr. Edmund J. Klimek, Assoc. Serving Univ. of Wisconsin-Eau Claire and Chippewa Valley Technical College.

MENOMONIE. *The Ministry to the University of Wisconsin-Stout* 108 3rd Ave. W., 54751. Tel: 715-235-4258; Fax: 715-235-4258. Very Rev. Thomas J. Krieg, Chap.; Sr. Kathy Wiesneski, S.C.S.C., M.A., Dir. Campus Min.

STEVENS POINT. *Newman University Parish* 2108 Fourth Ave., 54481. Tel: 715-345-6500. Email: TomLNewman@aol.com. Web: www.newmanuwsp.org. Rev. Thomas F. Lindner, Pastor. Serving Univ. of Wisconsin-Stevens Point.

[L] FOUNDATIONS, FUNDS & TRUSTS

LA CROSSE. *Aquinas High School and Aquinas Schools Foundation*, 315 S. 11th St., 54601. Tel: 608-784-0287; 608-784-0707 (Foundation); Fax: 608-782-8851.

Bishop John J. Paul Scholarship Endowment Trust, P.O. Box 4004, 54602-4004.

Bishop's Education Endowment Trust, P.O. Box 4004, 54602-4004. Tel: 608-788-7700.

Blessed Sacrament Parish Endowment Trust, 130 S. Losey Blvd., 54601. Tel: 608-782-2953; Fax: 608-785-1064. Email: blessedsacrament@centurytel.net. Web: www.blessedsacramentlacrosse.com.

Caritas Endowment Trust, 3710 East Ave. S., P.O. Box 266, 54602-0266. Tel: 608-782-0710; Fax: 608-782-0702.

Cathedral of St. Joseph the Workman Endowment Trust, 530 Main St., 54601. Tel: 608-782-0322; Fax: 608-782-8228.

Diocese of La Crosse Youth Ministry Endowment Trust, Office of Youth Ministry, P.O. Box 4004, 54602-4004.

Father Joseph Walijewski Orphanage Endowment Trust, 3710 E. Ave S., 54601. Tel: 608-788-7700; Fax: 608-788-8413. Rev. Roger J. Scheckel, Exec. Sec.

Franciscan Skemp Foundation, Inc., 700 West Ave. S., 54601-4796. Tel: 608-784-6449; Fax: 608-791-9799. Email: grabow.peter@mayo.edu. Web: www.mayohealthsystem.org. Peter Grabow, Dir.

Holy Cross Seminary Education Fund Endowment Trust, P.O. Box 4004, 54602-4004. Tel: 608-788-7700; Fax: 608-788-8413.

Holy Trinity Catholic Church Endowment Trust, 1333 S. 13th St., 54601. Tel: 608-782-2028; Fax: 608-784-2029.

St. James Parish Endowment Trust, 1032 Caledonia St., 54603. Tel: 608-782-7557; Fax: 608-796-0086. Email: scheckel@charter.net.

La Crosse Deanery Catholic Education Endowment Trust, P.O. Box 4004, 54602-4004.

Mary, Mother of the Church Parish Endowment Trust, 2006 Weston St., 54601. Tel: 608-788-5483; Fax: 608-788-4070.

Roncalli Newman Parish Student Endowment Trust, 1732 State St., 54601. Tel: 608-784-4994; Fax: 608-784-0230. Email: roncallinewman@charterinternet.com. Web: www.roncallinewman.com.

ALMOND. *St. Maximilian Kolbe Church Endowment Trust*, 8611 State Hwy. 54, 54909.

ALTOONA. *St. Mary Parish Endowment Trust*, 1812 Lynn Ave., 54720. Tel: 715-855-1294; Fax: 715-855-8664. Email: stmary@charterinternet.net.

ARCADIA. *Arcadia Catholic School Endowment Trust Fund*, 341 S. Washington St., 54612. Tel: 608-323-3676; Fax: 608-323-3786. Email: acs@triwest.net. Web: www.holyfam.com.

Franciscan Skemp Foundation of Arcadia, Inc., 464 S. St. Joseph Ave., 54612. Tel: 608-323-3341; Fax: 608-323-3694. Email: tracey.Robert@mayo.edu. Web: www.mayohealthsystem.org. 700 West Ave., S., 54601. Robert Tracey, Ex-Officio.

ATHENS. *Saint Anthony Parish Endowment Trust*, 417 Caroline St., P.O. Box 206, 54411. Tel: 715-257-7684; Fax: 715-257-7791.

AUBURNDALE. *St. Mary Education Endowment Trust*, Box 177, 54412-0177. Tel: 715-652-2806; Fax: 715-652-8020.

BIG RIVER. *The St. Mary's-Big River Endowment Trust*, W10137 570th Ave., River Falls, 54022. Tel: 715-425-5806.

BLAIR. *The St. Ansgar Catholic Church Endowment Trust*, 35900 Lee St., Whitehall, 54773. Tel: 715-538-4607; Fax: 715-538-2224.

BLOOMER. *St. Paul Catholic Parish of Bloomer Wisconsin Endowment Trust*, 1222 Main St., 54724. Tel: 715-568-3255.

CADOTT. *St. Rose of Lima Catholic Church Endowment Trust*, Box 160, 54727. Tel: 715-289-4551.

CASHTON. *Sacred Heart of Jesus Education Endowment Trust*, 26400 CTH U, 54619-8627. Tel: 608-823-7906; Fax: 608-823-7272.

CHIPPEWA FALLS. *St. Charles Future Fund Trust*, 810 Pearl St., 54729. Tel: 715-723-4088; Fax: 715-723-2195.

The Chippewa Area Catholic Schools Endowment Trust, 1316 Bel Air Blvd., 54729. Tel: 715-723-0538; Fax: 715-723-1501.

The Education/Sustaining Endowment Trust, 412 Main St., 54729. Tel: 715-723-4890; Fax: 715-723-7358.

Friends of St. Joseph's, 2661 County Hwy. I, 54729. Tel: 715-723-3392; Fax: 715-726-3302. Email: bgiles@sjcf.hshs.org. Web: www.stjoeschipfalls.com.

Notre Dame Children's Endowment Trust, 117 Allen St., 54729-2899. Tel: 715-723-7108; Fax: 715-723-7523. Email: cfnotredame@gmail.com.

Notre Dame Parish Endowment Trust, 117 Allen St., 54729-2899. Tel: 715-723-7108; Fax: 715-723-7523. Email: cfnotredame@gmail.com.

COLBY. *St. Mary's Catholic School, Colby Endowment Trust*, P.O. Box 436, 54421. Tel: 715-223-3033; Fax: 715-223-0223.

CUSTER. *Sacred Heart School, Polonia Endowment Trust*, 7379 Church St., 54423.

DURAND. *St. Mary Catholic School Endowment Trust*, 901 W. Prospect St., 54736-1049. Tel: 715-672-5617.

EAU CLAIRE. *Catholic Area Schools of Eau Claire Deanery Foundation*, 2100 Fenwick Ave., 54701.

Catholic Area Schools of the Eau Claire Deanery Endowment Fund (Case Endowment Fund), 2100 Fenwick Ave., 54701. Tel: 715-830-2273; Fax: 715-835-4658.

Friends of St. James the Greater Catholic School at Eau Claire Tuition Endowment Trust, 2502 11th St., 54703-2700. Tel: 715-835-5887; Fax: 715-835-3110. Email: stjameseac@aol.com.

Hospital Sisters of St. Francis Foundation, Inc., 901 University Dr., 54701. Friends of St. Joseph's Hospital (a division of Hospital Sisters of St. Francis Foundation, Inc.)

The St. James the Greater Catholic Church Endowment Trust, 2502 11th St., 54703-2700. Tel: 715-835-5887; Fax: 715-835-3110. Email: stjameseac@aol.com. Web: www.stjameseauclaire.catholicweb.com.

The Newman Parish - Eau Claire Endowment Trust, 110 Garfield Ave., 54701-4042. Tel: 715-834-3399. Email: georgeszews@charterinternet.com. Web: www.newmanec.com.

St. Olaf Parish Endowment Trust, 3220 Monroe St., P.O. Box 1203, 54703-1203. Tel: 715-832-2504; Fax: 715-832-0742. Email: solaf@execpc.com. Web: www.saintolafparish.com.

St. Patrick Parish of Eau Claire Endowment Trust, 322 Fulton St., 54703-5323. Tel: 715-832-0925; Fax: 715-832-0366. Email: sacrdhrt@charter.net.

Regis High School Foundation, 2100 Fenwick Ave., 54701-4498. Tel: 715-830-2271; Fax: 715-830-5461.

The Sacred Heart Parish Endowment Trust, 322 Fulton St., 54703. Tel: 715-832-0925; Fax: 715-832-0366. Email: sacrdhrt@charter.net.

ELLSWORTH. *The St. Francis Parish Endowment Trust*, 264 S. Grant, Box 839, 54011. Tel: 715-273-4774; Fax: 715-273-4066. Email: francis@warpdriveonline.com.

HATLEY. *St. Ladislaus Parish Bevent Endowment Trust*, 6455 State Rd. 153, 54440. Tel: 715-446-3060; Fax: 715-446-2668.

HOLMEN. *St. Elizabeth Ann Seton Endowment Trust*, 515 N. Main St., 54636. Tel: 608-526-4424; Fax: 608-526-3177. Email: seas883@charter.net.

INDEPENDENCE. *The SS. Peter & Paul Parish-Independence Education Endowment Trust*, 36028 Osseo Rd., P.O. Box 430, 54747-0430. Tel: 715-985-2227; Fax: 715-985-2649.

LYNDON STATION. *Troy Quasi-Endowment Trust*, P.O. Box 303, 53944. Tel: 608-666-2421.

MARATHON CITY. *Nativity of the Blessed Virgin Mary, Marathon Endowment Trust*, 712 Market, Box 7, 54448-0007. Tel: 715-443-2045.

MARSHFIELD. *Columbus High School Foundation*, 710 S. Columbus Ave., 54449. Tel: 715-387-2444; Fax: 715-384-4535. Email: kefferm@mfldacs.net. Web: www.marshfieldareacatholicschools.org. Michelle Keffer, Devel. Coord.

Foundation of Saint Joseph's Hospital of Marshfield, Inc., 611 St. Joseph Ave., 54449. Tel: 715-389-4072; Fax: 715-389-3993. Email: ann.boson@ministryhealth.org. Web: www.ministryhealth.org.

St. John the Baptist Educational Endowment Trust, 201 W. Blodgett, 54449. Tel: 715-384-3252; Fax: 715-384-3252.

St. John the Baptist Maintenance Endowment Trust, 201 W. Blodgett, 54449. Tel: 715-384-3252; Fax: 715-384-3252.

Marshfield Area Catholic Schools Endowment Trust, 710 S. Columbus Ave., 54449.

The Our Lady of Peace Endowment Trust, 1414 W. 5th St., 54449. Tel: 715-384-9414; Fax: 715-384-6606. Email: peacerectory@charter.net. Web: www.olpmarshfield.org.

MAUSTON. *St. Patrick's Congregation Trust*, 401 Mansion St., 53948-1393. Tel: 608-847-6054; Fax: 608-847-3288. Email: stpatsparish@btsmailbox.com. Web: www.stpatrickmauston.com.

MENOMONIE. *The St. Joseph School at Menomonie Endowment Trust*, 910 Wilson Ave., 54751. Tel: 715-232-4920; Fax: 715-232-4923.

MOSINEE. *St. Paul Parish Endowment Trust*, 603 4th St., 54455. Tel: 715-693-2650; Fax: 715-692-2650.

NEILLSVILLE. *The St. Mary's Catholic Church Endowment Trust*, 1813 Black River Rd., 54456. Tel: 715-743-3840; Fax: 715-743-7963. Email: stmaryneillsville@tds.net.

ONALASKA. *Charles Simpson of St. Patrick Parish, Onalaska Endowment Trust*, 1031 Main St., 54650.

Father John Rossiter and Friends Endowment Trust of St. Patrick Parish, 1031 Main St., 54650. Tel: 608-783-5535.

PITTSVILLE. *St. Joachim's Parish Endowment Trust*, P.O. Box 69, 54466-0069. Tel: 715-884-6815.

PLOVER. *St. Bronislava Parish, Plover Endowment Trust*, 3200 Plover Rd., P.O. Box 158, 54467-0158. Tel: 715-344-4326; Fax: 715-344-6121. Web: stbrons.com.

PORT EDWARDS. *St. Alexander's Church, Port Edwards Endowment Trust*, 880 First St., 54469. Tel: 715-887-3012; Fax: 715-887-3748. Very Rev. R. John Swing.

PRAIRIE DU CHIEN. *The St. Gabriel's Endowment Trust*, 506 N. Beaumont Rd., P.O. Box 176, 53821-0176. Tel: 608-326-2404.

The St. John's Endowment Trust, 710 S. Wacouta St., P.O. Box 28, 53821-0028. Tel: 608-326-6511; Fax: 608-326-4876.

RICHLAND CENTER. *The Assumption of the Blessed Virgin Mary Parish Endowment Trust*, 160 W. 4th St., Box 456, 53581. Tel: 608-647-2621; Fax: 608-647-6029. Email: parishsec@mwt.net. Web: www.stmarysrc.4LPI.COM.

ROTHSCHILD. *The St. Mark Catholic Parish Endowment Trust*, 602 Military Rd., 54474-1523. Tel: 715-359-5206; Fax: 715-355-8904.

St. Therese Catholic Church Endowment Fund, 113 W. Kort St., 54474. Tel: 715-359-2421; Fax: 715-355-3088.

ST. JOSEPH RIDGE. *St. Joseph Endowment Trust*, W2602 Hwy. 33, 54601. Tel: 608-788-1646.

ST. MARY'S RIDGE. *Holy Family Endowment Trust Fund*, Rectory: 26400 CTH U, Cashton, 54619-9757. Tel: 608-823-7906; Fax: 608-823-7272. Email: SMR1856@centurytel.com.

SPARTA. *Endowment Trust of the Friends and Parishioners of St. Patrick Parish*, 319 W. Main St., 54656-2143. Tel: 608-269-2655.

Franciscan Skemp Foundation of Sparta, Inc., 310 W. Main St., 54656-2142. Tel: 608-269-2132; Fax: 608-269-4562. Web: www.mayohealthsystem.org. 700 West Ave., S., 54601. Robert M. Tracey, Admin.

STEVENS POINT. *Catholic Schools Endowment Trust in Portage County, Wisconsin*, 1004 Fiest St., 54481. Tel: 715-341-2445; Fax: 715-342-2001. Email: jdyer@spacs.k12.wi.us. Web: www.spacs.k12.wi.us.

Community Foundation of Saint Michael's Hospital of Stevens Point, Inc., 900 Illinois Ave., 54481. Tel: 715-346-5337; Fax: 715-343-3330. Email: stmichaelsfoundation@ministryhealth.org. Kristin Duckart, Dir.

St. Joseph's Congregation, Stevens Point Endowment Trust, 1709 Wyatt Ave., 54481-3699. Tel: 715-341-1617; Fax: 715-341-2623. Web: www.togetherinfaith.org. Rev. Alan T. Burkhardt, Exec. Sec.

Newman Campus Ministry Endowment Trust, 2108 Fourth Ave., 54481.

Pacelli High School Foundation, 1301 Maria Dr., 54481. Tel: 715-341-2445; Fax: 715-342-2001.

St. Stanislaus Kostka Congregation, Stevens Point Endowment Trust, 838 Fremont St., 54481. Tel: 715-344-9117; Fax: 715-344-1771. Email: ststans@charter.net.

St. Stephen Parish Endowment Trust, 1401 Clark St., 54481. Tel: 715-344-3319; Fax: 715-344-6101. Email: ststephenparish@att.net. Web: www.saintstephenparish.com.

STRATFORD. *St. Joseph Parish Endowment Trust*, Box 6, 54484. Tel: 715-687-2404; Fax: 715-687-4343.

TILDEN. *St. Peter Parish Endowment Trust*, 11358 CTH Q, 54729. Tel: 715-288-6484; Fax: 715-723-2195.

TOMAH. *The St. Mary's Catholic Church Educational Endowment Trust*, 303 W. Monroe St., 54660. Tel: 608-372-4516; Fax: 608-372-4440.

VIROQUA. *St. Mary's Parish Viroqua Endowment Trust*, 400 Congress Ave., 54665. Tel: 608-637-7711; Fax: 608-637-6914.

WAUMANDEE. *St. Boniface Parish Catholic School Endowment Trust Fund*, 52026 Cty. Rd. U., 54622-8111. Tel: 608-626-2621. Email: stbon@mwt.net. Web: www.mwt.net/~stbon.

WAUSAU. *Church of the Resurrection Parish Church Building Endowment Trust*, 621 Second St., 54403. Tel: 715-845-6715; Fax: 715-845-4120.

St. Michael Parish Endowment Trust, 611 Stark St., 54403-3577. Tel: 715-842-4283; Fax: 715-849-2509. Email: frbill@eastsideparishes.org.

**Newman Catholic Schools Endowment Trust*, 619 Stark St., 54403. Tel: 715-845-5735; Fax: 715-848-3582. Janet M. Klosinski, Pres.

WESTON. *Foundation of Saint Clare's Hospital of Weston, Inc.*, 3400 Ministry Pkwy., 54476. Tel: 715-393-2604; Fax: 715-393-2645. Web: www.ministryhealth.org. Matt Ruppert, Foundation Dir.

WHITEHALL. *St. John Parish Endowment Trust*, 35900 Lee St., 54773. Tel: 715-538-4607; Fax: 715-538-2224. Email: bettyhalama@tcc.coop.

WILLARD. *Holy Family Parish, Willard Endowment Trust* 54493. Tel: 715-267-6905.

WISCONSIN RAPIDS. *St. Lawrence Parish, Wisconsin Rapids Endowment Trust*, 530 10th Ave. N., 54495-2566. Tel: 715-421-5777.

Our Lady Queen of Heaven Parish Endowment Trust, 750 10th Ave. S., 54495. Tel: 715-423-1251; Fax: 715-423-9407. Email: ourladyqueenofheaven@hotmail.com.

St. Vincent de Paul Parish, Wisconsin Rapids Endowment Trust, 820 13th St., S., 54494-5336. Tel: 715-423-2111; Fax: 715-423-4227. Email: stvin@wctc.net.

Wisconsin Rapids Area Catholic Schools Endowment Trust, 711 Hill St., 54494.

[M] ASSOCIATIONS OF THE FAITHFUL

EASTMAN. *Marian Academy of the Oblates of Holy Tradition*, P.O. Box 109, 54626. Very Rev. Msgr. John F. McCarthy, P.A., Contact Person.

Society of the Oblates of Wisdom, P.O. Box 109, 54626-0109. Tel: 608-874-4733.

TILDEN. *Institute of St. Joseph*, 11386 CTH Q, Chippewa Falls, 54729-6115. Tel: 715-288-6272. Email: srpetra@centurytel.net. Revs. William P. Felix, Moderator Gen.; John Mary Gilbert, Chap., 11358 Cty. Hwy. Q, Chippewa Falls, 54729.

[N] MISCELLANEOUS LISTINGS

LA CROSSE. **Franciscan Skemp Healthcare, Inc., Mayo Health System, Corporate Office*, 700 West Ave. S., 54603. Tel: 608-785-9710; Fax: 608-791-9429. Web: www.mayohealthsystem.org. Robert E. Nesse, Pres. & CEO, Integrated Healthcare Delivery System. Sponsored by the Congregation of the Sisters of the Third Order of St. Francis of Perpetual Adoration (Franciscan Sisters of Perpetual Adoration) and Mayo Foundation.

**Franciscan Skemp Medical Center, Inc.*, 700 West Ave. S., 54601-4796. Tel: 608-785-0940; Fax: 608-791-9429. Robert E. Nesse, Pres. & CEO; Rev. Todd A. Mlsna, Chap. Sisters 1; Total Staff 1,169; Bed Capacity 248.

Gerard Hall Tel: 608-791-3985; Fax: 608-791-7802. 8 bed home for women with AODA, MH, or Pregnancy and Parenting Issues. Total Staff 5; Patients Days 1,862.

Mens LAAR House Tel: 608-782-7700; Fax: 608-791-9431. 18 bed home for chemically dependent adults. Total Staff 4; Patient Days 2,106.

Scarseth House Tel: 608-785-1270; Fax: 608-784-7084. 8 bed home for chemically dependent male adolescents. Total Staff 4; Patient Days 1,785.

Siena Hall Tel: 608-784-6010; Fax: 608-784-7084. 20 bed home for mentally ill adults. Total Staff 11; Patient Days 5,861.

Village on Cass, 225 S. 24th St., 54601. Tel: 608-791-9487; Fax: 608-782-2779. 30 bed assisted living unit for elderly. Total Staff 7.

Village on 9th, 621 S. 9th St., 54601. Tel: 608-791-9505; Fax: 608-782-2779. 24 bed independent living unit for elderly

Villa Succes, Prairie du Chien, 53821. Tel: 608-326-8424; Fax: 608-326-8638. 12 bed halfway house for AODA and AODA outpatient and Detox programs. Total Staff 7; Patient Days 2,316.

Womens LAAR House Tel: 608-791-6147; Fax: 608-791-9511. 9 bed home for chemically dependent adults. Total Staff 5; Patient Days 2,817.

La Crosse Guild of the Catholic Medical Association, W5560 County Rd. MM, 54601. Tel: 608-788-5052.

The Marian Catechist Apostolate, 1032 Caledonia St., 54603. Tel: 608-782-0011; Fax: 608-796-0086. Theresa Ann Knothe, National Coord.

Mater Redemptoris House of Formation, 3730 East Ave. S., 54601. Tel: 608-788-4530; Fax: 608-788-4571. Email: snewell@dioceseoflacrosse.com. Sr. M. Stephania Newell, F.S.G.M., Dir.

Shrine of Our Lady of Guadalupe, Inc., 5250 Justin Rd., P.O. Box 1237, 54602-1237. Tel: 608-782-5440; Fax: 608-782-3104. Email: smchrista@shrineofourlady.com. Web: www.guadalupeshrine.org. Sr. Christa Marie Halligan, F.S.G.M., Exec. Dir.

We Belong To Christ Campaign, Inc., P.O. Box 4004, 54602-4004. Tel: 608-791-2685; Fax: 608-788-3854. Email: agaertner@dioceseoflacrosse.com. Andy Gaertner, Dir. Stewardship & Devel.

CHIPPEWA FALLS. *Northern Wisconsin Center for the Developmentally Disabled*, East Park Ave., 54729. Tel: 715-723-5542. State Institution for the Developmentally Disabled.

EAU CLAIRE. *Hospital Sisters Health Care-West, Inc.*, St. Francis Apartments, 851 University Dr., 54701. Tel: 715-834-1338; Fax: 715-858-1602. Email: cwerner@shec.hshs.org.

GENOA. *The Hermitage of St. Mary, Inc.* (1997) W1498 Spring Coulee Rd., 54632. Tel: 608-689-2753; Fax: 608-689-2753. Email: godshermitess@hotmail.com. Sr. Mary Dawiczyk, Pres. & Treas.

HILLSBORO. *St. Joseph's Community Health Services*, 400 Water Ave., P.O. Box 527, 54634. Tel: 608-489-8000; Fax: 608-489-8181. Email: k.coblentz.stjoseph@wmt.net. Web: stjhealthcare.org. Deb Warthan, Pastoral Care Dir. Franciscan Sisters of Perpetual Adoration

St. Joseph's Family Clinic, 504 Water Ave., P.O. Box 527, 54634. Tel: 608-489-8280; Fax: 608-489-8189.

St. Joseph's Nursing Home, 400 Water St., P.O. Box 527, 54634. Tel: 608-489-8000; Fax: 608-489-8187. 1705 Omaha St., Elroy, 53929. Tel: 608-489-8720; Fax: 608-489-8188.

St. Joseph's Family Clinic, 103 Railroad, Wonewoc, 53968. Tel: 608-464-3575.

St. Joseph's Memorial Hospital Tel: 608-489-8000; Fax: 608-489-8186.

MARSHFIELD. **Ministry Home Care*, 611 St. Joseph Ave., 54449. Tel: 715-389-3802; Fax: 715-387-9950. Web: www.ministryhomecare.org.

STEVENS POINT. *Ministry Behavioral Health of St. Michael's Hospital, Inc.*, 209 Prentice St. N., 54481. Tel: 715-344-4611; Fax: 715-344-8127. Email: giffinj@smhosp.org. Web: www.ministrybehavioralhealth.org. JoAnne Griffin, Exec. Dir. Corporate Sponsor: Ministry Health Care, Inc. (Milwaukee, WI); Sponsored by Sisters of the Sorrowful Mother.

TOMAH. *Assisi Homes - Eldr Manor, Inc.*, 1500 Lincoln Ave., 54660. Tel: 608-372-5890. Sr. Susan Dillberg, O.S.F., Pres. Franciscan Sisters, Daughters of the Sacred Hearts of Jesus and Mary of Wheaton, IL., Purpose: to acquire or develop and operate housing projects for low income families and elderly persons.

WILLARD. *The Christine Center*, W8303 Mann Rd., 54493. Tel: 715-267-7507; Fax: 715-267-7512. Email: christinecenter@ceas.cood. Web: www.christinecenter.org. Sr. Cecilia Corcoran, F.S.P.A., Pres.

RELIGIOUS INSTITUTES OF MEN REPRESENTED IN THE DIOCESE

For further details refer to the corresponding bracketed number in the Religious Institutes of Men or Women section.

[1180]—*Brothers of Saint Pius X* (La Crosse)—C.S.P.X.

[0470]—*The Capuchin Friars* (St. Joseph's Prov., Detroit)—O.F.M.Cap.

[0340]—*Cistercian Fathers* (Sparta, WI)—O.Cist.

[]—*Congregation of the Blessed Sacrament*

[0180]—*Congregation of the Resurrection* (Poland)—C.R.

[0690]—*Jesuit Fathers and Brothers* (Missouri Prov. & Wisconsin Prov.)—S.J.

[]—*Missionaries of St. Francis de Sales*

[0430]—*Order of Preachers* Cracow, Poland Province)—O.P.

RELIGIOUS INSTITUTES OF WOMEN REPRESENTED IN THE DIOCESE

[]—*Benedictine Sisters of Mother of God Monastery*

[0230]—*Benedictine Sisters of Pontifical Jurisdiction* (Eau Claire, WI)—O.S.B.

[1010]—*Congregation of Divine Providence* (San Antonio, TX)—C.D.P.

[0470]—*Congregation of Sisters of Charity of the Incarnate Word* (San Antonio, TX)—C.C.V.I.

[1170]—*Congregation of the Sisters of St. Felix of Cantalice, of the III Order of St. Francis* (Chicago, IL)—C.S.S.F.

[1780]—*Congregation of the Sisters of the Third Order of St. Francis of Perpetual Adoration* (La Crosse, WI)—F.S.P.A.

[]—*Daughters of the Redeemer* (Zambia)

[1310]—*Franciscan Sisters of Little Falls, Minnesota*—O.S.F.

[1820]—*Hospital Sisters of the Third Order of St. Francis* (Springfield, IL)—O.S.F.

[]—*Presentation Sisters of the Blessed Virgin Mary* (Philippines)

[2970]—*School Sisters of Notre Dame* (Milwaukee Prov.)—S.S.N.D.

[1680]—*School Sisters of St. Francis* (Milwaukee, WI)—O.S.F.

[3590]—*Servants of Mary* (Ladysmith, WI)—O.S.M.

[1070-03]—*Sinsinawa Dominican Congregation of the Most Holy Rosary*—O.P.

[2630]—*Sisters of Mercy of the Holy Cross* (Merrill, WI)—S.C.S.C.

[]—*Sisters of Our Lady of Good Counsel* (Uganda)

[1620]—*Sisters of St. Francis of Millvale* (Pittsburgh, PA)—O.S.F.

[]—*Sisters of St. Francis of the Martyr St. George* (Alton, IL, Prov. of St. Elizabeth)—O.S.F.

[1720]—*Sisters of St. Francis of the Third Order Regular of St. Francis of the Congregation of Our Lady of* (Rochester, MN)—O.S.F.

[3930]—*Sisters of St. Joseph - Third Order Regular* (Stevens Point, WI)—S.S.J.-T.O.S.F.

[1030]—*Sisters of the Divine Savior* (Milwaukee, WI)—S.D.S.

[4100]—*Sisters of the Sorrowful Mother* (U.S./Caribbean Prov.)—S.S.M.

[1705]—*Sisters of the Third Order of St. Francis of Assisi of Penance and Charity* (Milwaukee, WI)—O.S.F.

[]—*Tertiary Sisters of St. Francis* (Cameroon Province)

DIOCESAN CEMETERIES

LA CROSSE. *Catholic Cemetery*, 519 Losey Blvd. S., 54601. Tel: 608-782-0238. Jeffrey Reinhart, Supt. Gate of Heaven Cemetery; French Island Cemetery.

Woodlawn, 3636 Mormon Coulee Rd., 54601. Tel: 608-788-0980. John Reinhart, Supt.

CHIPPEWA FALLS. *Hope Cemetery and Mausoleum*, 418 N. State St., 54729. Tel: 715-723-0792. Walter Hurt, Supt.

EAU CLAIRE. *Calvary Cemetery and Mausoleum*, P.O. Box 633, 54702-0633. Tel: 715-552-8195. Peter J. Wagemen, Mgr.

MARSHFIELD. *Gate of Heaven*, 1803 S. Maple Ave., 54449. Tel: 715-384-5815. Marvin Fait, Pres.; Monica Herman, Sec.

STEVENS POINT. *Stevens Point Area Catholic Cemetery Association, Inc.*, P.O. Box 497, 54481. Tel: 715-341-3236. Jack Okonek, Supt.; Shirley Suplicki, Exec. Sec. & Treas.

NECROLOGY

† Finucan, Rev. Msgr. James P., (Retired)—Died June 12, 2009
† Knauf, Rev. Msgr. Edwin L., (Retired)—Died Oct. 27, 2009
† O'Neill, Thomas M., Chap., La Cross, WI Viterbo Univ.—Died Sept. 2, 2009
† Reardon, Thomas J., (Retired)—Died Jan. 10, 2010
† Theisen, Donald J., (Retired)—Died Oct. 4, 2009
† Wagner, Raymond J., (Retired)—Died Oct. 14, 2009

Diocese of Lafayette

(Dioecesis Lafayettensis)

Most Reverend

MICHAEL JARRELL, D.D.

Bishop of Lafayette; ordained June 3, 1967; ordained to the episcopacy and installed as second Bishop of Houma-Thibodaux March 4, 1993; appointed sixth Bishop of Lafayette November 8, 2002; installed December 18, 2002. *Office: 1408 Carmel Dr., Lafayette, LA 70501.*

ESTABLISHED JANUARY 11, 1918.

Square Miles 5,777.

Comprises the civil parishes (Counties) of Acadia, Evangeline, Iberia, Lafayette, St. Landry, St. Martin and St. Mary (west of Atchafalaya River) and Vermilion in the south central part of the State of Louisiana.

For legal titles of Diocese, parishes and diocesan institutions, consult the Chancery Office.

Administrative Offices: Diocesan Office Building, 1408 Carmel Dr., Lafayette, LA 70501. Tel: 337-261-5500; Fax: 337-261-5635.

Web: www.dol-louisiana.org

Email: robins@dol-louisiana.org

STATISTICAL OVERVIEW

Personnel

Bishop	1
Priests: Diocesan Active in Diocese	111
Priests: Diocesan Active Outside Diocese	1
Priests: Diocesan in Foreign Missions	1
Priests: Retired, Sick or Absent	43
Number of Diocesan Priests	156
Religious Priests in Diocese	40
Total Priests in Diocese	196
Extern Priests in Diocese	9
Ordinations:	
Diocesan Priests	3
Transitional Deacons	3
Permanent Deacons in Diocese	79
Total Brothers	16
Total Sisters	158

Parishes

Parishes	121
With Resident Pastor:	
Resident Diocesan Priests	83
Resident Religious Priests	17
Without Resident Pastor:	
Administered by Priests	16
Administered by Deacons	5
Missions	29
Professional Ministry Personnel:	
Brothers	1
Sisters	6
Lay Ministers	49

Welfare

Catholic Hospitals	1
Total Assisted	107,667
Homes for the Aged	28
Total Assisted	3,600
Specialized Homes	15
Total Assisted	7,873
Special Centers for Social Services	6
Total Assisted	100,445

Educational

Diocesan Students in Other Seminaries	32
Seminaries, Religious	1
Students Religious	15
Total Seminarians	47
High Schools, Diocesan and Parish	9
Total Students	3,553
High Schools, Private	1
Total Students	120
Elementary Schools, Diocesan and Parish	30
Total Students	10,699
Elementary Schools, Private	2
Total Students	781
Catechesis/Religious Education:	
High School Students	6,834
Elementary Students	14,525
Total Students under Catholic Instruction	36,559
Teachers in the Diocese:	
Sisters	2
Lay Teachers	995

Vital Statistics

Receptions into the Church:	
Infant Baptism Totals	4,094
Minor Baptism Totals	151
Adult Baptism Totals	65
Received into Full Communion	307
First Communions	3,885
Confirmations	3,068
Marriages:	
Catholic	920
Interfaith	152
Total Marriages	1,072
Deaths	3,442
Total Catholic Population	322,507
Total Population	568,154

Former Bishops—Most Revs. JULES B. JEANMARD, D.D., LL.D., ord. June 11, 1903; appt. first Bishop of Lafayette, July 18, 1918; cons. Dec. 8, 1918; installed as first Bishop of Lafayette, Dec. 12, 1918; appt. Assistant at the Pontifical Throne, Dec. 8, 1943; resigned and named Titular Bishop of Bareta, March 13, 1956; died Feb. 23, 1957; ROBERT E. TRACY, D.D., LL.D., Auxiliary Bishop of Lafayette, March 18, 1959; appt. first Bishop of Baton Rouge, Aug. 10, 1961; died April 4, 1980; WARREN L. BOUDREAUX, D.D., J.C.D., Auxiliary Bishop of Lafayette, May 19, 1962; appt. second Bishop of Beaumont, Texas, June 4, 1971; died Oct. 6, 1997; MAURICE SCHEXNAYDER, D.D., ord. April 11, 1925; appt. Titular Bishop of Tuscamia and Auxiliary of Lafayette, Dec. 11, 1950; cons. Feb. 22, 1951; appt. second Bishop of Lafayette, March 13, 1956; installed May 24, 1956; resigned Nov. 7, 1972; died Jan. 23, 1981; GERARD L. FREY, D.D., appt. third Bishop of Lafayette, Nov. 7, 1972; installed Jan. 7, 1973; resigned May 13, 1989; died Aug. 16, 2007; HARRY J. FLYNN, D.D., ord. May 28, 1960; appt. Coadjutor Bishop of Lafayette, April 19, 1986, fourth Bishop of Lafayette, May 13, 1989; appt. Coadjutor Archbishop of St. Paul and Minneapolis, Feb. 22, 1994; EDWARD JOSEPH O'DONNELL, D.D. (Retired), ord. April 6, 1957; appt. Titular Bishop of Britonia and Auxiliary Bishop of St. Louis Dec. 6, 1983; cons. Feb. 10, 1984; appt. fifth Bishop of Lafayette Nov. 8, 1994; installed Dec. 16, 1994; retired Nov. 8, 2002; died Feb. 1, 2009.

Bishop's Office—Mailing Address: Diocesan Office Building, P.O. Box 3387, Lafayette, 70502-3387. Tel: 337-261-5614; Fax: 337-261-5603.

Administrative Offices—Diocesan Office Building, 1408 Carmel Dr., Lafayette, 70501-5298. Tel: 337-261-5500; Fax: 337-261-5635.

Vicar General—Very Rev. Msgr. H. ALEXANDRE LARROQUE, J.C.D., V.G. Tel: 337-261-5613.

Chancellor & Vicar for Priests—Very Rev. Msgr. RUSSELL J. HARRINGTON, V.E., Mailing Address: P.O. Box 3387, Lafayette, 70502-3387. Tel: 337-261-5611; Fax: 337-261-5603.

Council of Priests—Rev. JAMES L. LAMBERT, S.J., St. Charles Borromeo, P.O. Drawer A, Grand Coteau, 70541.

Diocesan Pastoral Council—Mailing Address: 1408 Carmel Dr., Lafayette, 70501. Tel: 337-261-5551.

Clergy Personnel Advisory Board—Very Rev. Msgr. ROBIE E. ROBICHAUX, J.C.L., Mailing Address: P.O. Box 3387, Lafayette, 70502-3387. Tel: 337-261-5623; Fax: 337-261-5646.

Finance Officer—Deacon JEFF TRUMPS, Diocesan Finance Officer & Dir., Mailing Address: P.O. Box 3387, Lafayette, 70502-3387. 1408 Carmel Dr., Lafayette, 70501-5298. Tel: 337-261-5632.

Victims Assistance Coordinator—Ms. CARMER FALGOUT, R.N., M.S.W., L.C.S.W., B.C.D., 100 Coulee Shore Dr., Lafayette, 70503. Tel: 337-235-5749.

Abuse Review Board—Mailing Address: P.O. Box 3387, Lafayette, 70502-3387. Tel: 337-261-5611.

Tribunal

Tribunal—Mailing Address: P.O. Box 3387, Lafayette, 70502-3387. Tel: 337-261-5623; Fax: 337-261-5646.

Judicial Vicar—Very Rev. Msgr. ROBIE E. ROBICHAUX, J.C.L. Tel: 337-261-5623; Fax: 337-261-5646.

Adjutant Judicial Vicar—VACANT.

Assessors—Rev. KEN BROUSSARD, O.S.B.; Mrs. JANE JOY. Instructors: Rev. Msgr. RICHARD VON PHUL MOUTON (Retired); Mr. PHIL LIZOTTE.

Promoter of the Justice—Very Rev. Msgr. H. ALEXANDRE LARROQUE, J.C.D., V.G. Tel: 337-261-5613.

Judges—Very Rev. Msgr. H. ALEXANDRE LARROQUE, J.C.D., V.G. Tel: 337-261-5613; Rev. HERBERT J. MAY, J.C.L.

Defenders of the Bond—Revs. OVERTON JOSEPH BREAUX; W. CURTIS MALLET, J.C.L.

Notary—Mrs. LINDA W. SAVOY.

Diocesan Consultors—Very Rev. Msgrs. RUSSELL J. HARRINGTON, V.E.; H. ALEXANDRE LARROQUE, J.C.D., V.G.; Rev. Msgr. RICHARD VON PHUL MOUTON (Retired); Revs. JOHN G. BREAUX; MICHAEL CHAMPAGNE; GARY SCHEXNAYDER; BRYCE SIBLEY; Rev. Msgr. HARRY E. BENEFIEL (Retired); Revs. M. KEITH LABOVE; KEVIN BORDELON; THOMAS VOORHIES; JAMES BRADY, J.C.L.

Diocesan Secretaries, Offices, and Directors

Secretariat of Community Services—MAUREEN K. FONTENOT, Dir.

"Acadiana Catholic" Newspaper—Deacon THOMAS SOMMERS, Editor, 1408 Carmel Dr., Lafayette, 70501-5298. Tel: 337-261-5513.

Archives - Research and Information—BARBARA C. DEJEAN, Dir., 1408 Carmel Dr., Lafayette,

70501-5298. Tel: 337-261-5639; 337-261-5667.
Catholic Schools—ANNA LARRIVIERE, Supt., 1408 Carmel Dr., Lafayette, 70501-5298. Tel: 337-261-5529.
Christian Formation and Adult Catechesis—ANN BROUSSARD, Dir., 1408 Carmel Dr., Lafayette, 70501-5298. Tel: 337-261-5550.
College Ministry—Rev. CHESTER ARCENEAUX, Pastor & Dir., Mailing Address: Our Lady of Wisdom Catholic Student Center, P.O. Box 42371, Lafayette, 70504-2371. Tel: 337-232-8742.
Human Resources - Safe Environment—MAUREEN K. FONTENOT, Dir., 1408 Carmel Dr., Lafayette, 70501-5298. Tel: 337-261-5526.
Pro-Life Issues—KAROL MEYNARD, Dir., 1408 Carmel Dr., Lafayette, 70501-5298. Tel: 337-261-5607.
Radio-TV—DAVID MERGIST, Producer & Dir., 1408 Carmel Dr., Lafayette, 70501-5298. Tel: 337-261-5626.
Youth Ministry - Project Wellsprings—ROSIE BROWN, 1408 Carmel Dr., Lafayette, 70501-5298. Tel: 337-261-5551.
Secretariat of Pastoral Services—Deacon JAMES KINCEL, Dir.
Black Catholic Ministry—STEPHANIE BERNARD, Dir., 1408 Carmel Dr., Lafayette, 70501-5298. Tel: 337-261-5694.
Catholic Social Services—PAULA MILNER, Dir., 1408 Carmel Dr., Lafayette, 70501-5298. Tel: 337-261-5654.
Family Life Ministry—Rev. JUDE HALPHEN, Ph.D., Dir., Mailing Address: 1408 Carmel Dr., Lafayette, 70501-5298. Tel: 337-261-5653.
Hispanic Ministry—CRISTINA LEBLANC, Interim Dir., 1408 Carmel Dr., Lafayette, 70501-5298. Tel: 337-261-5544.
Office of Justice and Peace—VACANT, Dir., 1408 Carmel Dr., Lafayette, 70501-5298. Tel: 337-261-5545.
Migration and Refugee Services—TINA QUESADA, Dir., 1408 Carmel Dr., Lafayette, 70501-5298. Tel: 337-261-5535.
Persons with Disabilities and Deaf Apostolate—MYRA MOUTON, Dir., 1408 Carmel Dr., Lafayette, 70501-5298. Tel: 337-232-3463; 337-261-5548.
Vietnamese Catholic Ministry—Rev. LOUIS LAM VU, Dir., Mailing Address: P.O. Drawer 219, Patterson, 70392. Tel: 985-395-3616.
Office of Worship—Rev. Msgr. KEITH J. DEROUEN, Dir.; FAYE DROBNIC, Asst. Dir., 1408 Carmel Dr., Lafayette, 70501-5298. Tel: 337-261-5554.
Secretariat of Religious Personnel—Very Rev. Msgr. RUSSELL J. HARRINGTON, V.E., Dir.
Continuing Education of Priests—Rev. KEVIN BORDELON, Dir., 7166 Roberts Cove Rd., Rayne, 70578-9726. Tel: 337-334-5056; Fax: 337-334-0832.
Minister to Priests—Rev. MICHAEL GUIDRY, Mailing Address: P.O. Box 319, Morrow, 71356-0319. Tel: 318-346-7010.
Permanent Diaconate—Deacon JAMES KINCEL, Dir., 1408 Carmel Dr., Lafayette, 70501-5298. Tel: 337-261-5607.
Religious Brothers and Sisters—Sr. JUDITH COREIL, M.S.C., Dir., 1408 Carmel Dr., Lafayette, 70501-5298. Tel: 337-261-5430.
Seminarians—Rev. J. AARON MELANCON, Dir., 1408 Carmel Dr., Lafayette, 70501-5298. Tel: 337-261-5690.
Vicar for Priests—Very Rev. Msgr. RUSSELL J. HARRINGTON, V.E., 1408 Carmel Dr., Lafayette, 70501-5298. Tel: 337-261-5611; Fax: 337-261-5603.
Vocations—Rev. J. AARON MELANCON, Dir., 1408 Carmel Dr., Lafayette, 70501-5298. Tel: 337-261-5690.
Secretariat of Stewardship—Deacon JEFF TRUMPS, Dir. & Diocesan Finance Officer, 1408 Carmel Dr., Lafayette, 70501-5298. Tel: 337-261-5632.
Building & Renovations—AIA, Coordinators: GERALD GOSSEN, A.I.A.; AL LANDRY, 1408 Carmel Dr., Lafayette, 70501-5298. Tel: 337-261-5606.
General Manager—ANTHONY BOUDREAUX, 1408 Carmel Dr., Lafayette, 70501-5298. Tel: 337-261-5605.
Community Development—J. BERNEL FONTENOT, Dir., 1408 Carmel Dr., Lafayette, 70501-5298. Tel: 337-261-5650.
Information Technology—ROBIN STEVENSON, Dir., 1408 Carmel Dr., Lafayette, 70501-5298. Tel: 337-261-5613.
Financial Affairs—Deacon JEFF TRUMPS, Diocesan Finance Officer & Dir., Mailing Address: P.O. Box 3387, Lafayette, 70502-3387. 1408 Carmel Dr., Lafayette, 70501-5298. Tel: 337-261-5632.
Auxiliary Services—PATSY ARWOOD, Dir., 1408 Carmel Dr., Lafayette, 70501-5298. Tel: 337-261-5600.
Bishop's Services Appeal—CONNIE B. BABIN, Dir., 1408 Carmel Dr., Lafayette, 70501-5298. Tel: 337-261-5641.
Controller—TOM LANDRY, CPA, 1408 Carmel Dr., Lafayette, 70501-5298. Tel: 337-261-5627.
Development Office—CONNIE B. BABIN, Dir., 1408 Carmel Dr., Lafayette, 70501-5298. Tel: 337-261-5641.

Miscellaneous

Catholic Charismatic—Rev. ALBERT G. NUNEZ, Liaison, Office: 1408 Carmel Dr., Lafayette, 70501. Tel: 337-265-3733.
Catholic Daughters of America—Diocesan Co Chaplains: Revs. HERBERT BENNERFIELD. Tel: 337-685-4426; CEDRIC SONNIER. Tel: 337-457-8107.
Knights of Columbus—Rev. MARK DERISE, State Chap., Mailing Address: P.O. Box 10110, New Iberia, 70562-0110. Tel: 337-365-5481.
Catholic Relief Services—VACANT, Diocesan Coord., 1408 Carmel Dr., Lafayette, 70501. Tel: 337-261-5545.
Credit Union—*St. Jules Credit Union, 1600 N. Bertrand Dr., Lafayette, 70506*. Tel: 337-261-1151.
Cursillo—Rev. THEODORE BROUSSARD JR., Spiritual Dir. to Secretariat of the Cursillo & Dir. Women's Cursillo. Tel: 337-543-7425; 337-543-2100.
Ecumenism—Rev. CHARLES LANGLOIS, Mailing Address: St. Peter Church, P.O. Box 12507, New Iberia, 70562-2507. Tel: 337-369-3816.
Hospitals—Rev. M. KEITH LABOVE, Coord. Health Affairs, Mailing Address: 406 E. Pinhook Rd., Lafayette, 70501. Tel: 337-237-0988.
Pontifical Mission Societies—Rev. Msgr. RICHARD VON PHUL MOUTON (Retired), 1408 Carmel Dr., Lafayette, 70501-5298. Tel: 337-261-5536.
Holy Childhood—Rev. Msgr. RICHARD VON PHUL MOUTON (Retired), 1408 Carmel Dr., Lafayette, 70501. Tel: 337-261-5536.
Retreats—Rev. WARREN J. BROUSSARD, S.J. Our Lady of the Oaks Retreat House, Grand Coteau, LA. Mailing Address: P.O. Box D, Grand Coteau, 70541-1003. Tel: 337-662-5410.
Scouting—Rev. GARY SCHEXNAYDER, Chap., Mailing Address: St. Michael Church, P.O. Box 406, Crowley, 70527-0406. Tel: 337-783-7394; ROBERT T. CLEMENTS, Lay Chm., 204 Crawford, Lafayette, 70506-6028. Tel: 337-981-2519.

CLERGY, PARISHES, MISSIONS AND PAROCHIAL SCHOOLS

CITY OF LAFAYETTE

(LAFAYETTE PARISH)

1—CATHEDRAL OF ST. JOHN THE EVANGELIST (1821) [CEM] Rev. Msgr. Keith J. DeRouen, Rector. In Res., Rev. Joseph Kurian Kanat (India); Rev. Msgr. Richard von Phul Mouton (Retired).
Res. & Mailing Address: P.O. Drawer V, 70502. Tel: 337-232-1322; Fax: 337-232-1379. Email: sjclaf@bellsouth.net. Web: www.saintjohncathedral.org.
Church: 914 St. John St., 70501. Email: sjc@bellsouth.net.
School—*Cathedral-Carmel Elementary*, (Grades PreK-8), 848 St. John St., 70501. Tel: 337-235-5577; Fax: 337-261-9493. Web: cathedralcarmel.com. Mary Catherine "Kay" Aillet, Prin. Sisters of Mt. Carmel 2; Lay Teachers 65; Students 805.
Catechesis/Religious Program—Tel: 337-232-1325. Email: sjcreligiouseducation@yahoo.com. Students 186.

2—ST. ANTHONY (1955), (African American), [JC] Rev. Michael M. Sucharski, S.V.D.; Deacon Albert Marcel.
Mailing Address: P.O. Box 92708, 70509. Tel: 337-234-5855; Fax: 327-264-1507.
Church: 615 Edison St., 70501.
Catechesis/Religious Program—Students 146.

3—ST. EDMOND (1974) Rev. Timothy Richard; Deacons Frank Cormier; Randy Hyde; Paul D. Matte.
Res.: 4131 W. Congress St., 70506. Tel: 337-981-0874; Fax: 337-989-1417. Web: www.st-edmond.org. Email: frichard@st-edmond.org.
Catechesis/Religious Program—Carol Broglio. Students 406.

4—ST. ELIZABETH SETON (1975) Rev. Martin Borcherding; Deacon Nelson Joseph Schexnayder Jr.
Office: 610 Raintree Tr., 70507. Tel: 337-235-1483; Fax: 337-235-9645. Email: pastor@setonchurch.org. Web: www.setonchurch.org.
Catechesis/Religious Program—Students 169.

5—ST. GENEVIEVE (1929) [CEM] Revs. W. Curtis Mallet; Salvino Primor.
Res.: 417 E. Simcoe St., 70501. Tel: 337-234-5147; Fax: 337-234-8654. Email: stgenevieve@cox.net.
School—*Elementary School*, (Grades PreK-5), 201 Elizabeth St., 70501. Tel: 337-234-5257; Fax: 337-237-6065. Email: sgscardinals@stgen.net. Web: www.stgen.net. Becky Trouille, Prin. Lay Teachers 18; Students 355.
School—*Middle School*, (Grades 6-8), 1500 E. Willow St., 70501. Tel: 337-266-5553; Fax: 337-266-5775. Mrs. Julie Champagne, Prin. Lay Teachers 10; Students 179.
See Teurlings Catholic High under High Schools, Interparochial located in the Institution section.
St. Genevieve School Foundation, Inc.—
Catechesis/Religious Program—Tel: 337-234-5147, Ext. 104; Fax: 337-234-8654. Students 115.
Mission—*Gift of Mary Chapel*, Lafayette Parish.

6—HOLY CROSS (1965) Rev. Howard Blessing; Deacons Michael Clark; Richard Picard.
Res.: 415 Robley Dr., 70503. Tel: 337-984-9636; Fax: 337-988-3790. Email: hocross@bellsouth.net. Web: www.holycrosschurch.net.
Catechesis/Religious Program—Tel: 337-984-9643. Students 754.

7—IMMACULATE HEART OF MARY (1934), (African American), [CEM] Very Rev. Thomas James, S.V.D.; Rev. Michael Long Vu, S.V.D.; Deacon Anthony Ozene.
Res.: 818-12th St., P.O. Box 2398, 70502. Tel: 337-235-4618; Fax: 337-235-4775. Email: ihm818@bellsouth.net. Web: www.ihmch.homestead.com.
School—(Grades K-8), 800-12th St., 70502. Tel: 337-235-7843; Fax: 337-233-0070. Mr. Thomas H. Brown, Prin. Sisters of the Holy Family 3; Lay Teachers 12; Students 151.
Catechesis/Religious Program—Tel: 337-235-6323. Students 349.

8—ST. JULES (1962) Rev. J. Daniel Edwards.
Res.: 116 St. Jules St., 70506. Tel: 337-234-2727; Fax: 337-232-1544. Email: stjuleschurch@bellsouth.net.
Catechesis/Religious Program—Students 42.

9—ST. LEO THE GREAT (1960) [CEM] Very Rev. Msgr. Robie E. Robichaux.
Res.: 300 W. Alexander St., 70501. Tel: 337-232-2404; Fax: 337-261-0801.
School—*Sts. Leo-Seton*, (Grades PreK-8), 502 St. Leo St., 70501. Tel: 337-234-5510; Fax: 337-234-3676. Ebrar Reaux, Prin. Sisters 1; Lay Teachers 35; Students 556.
Catechesis/Religious Program—Tel: 337-257-2132. Students 51.

10—ST. MARY, MOTHER OF THE CHURCH (1975) Rev. Harold Trahan.
Res.: 419 Doucet Rd., 70503. Tel: 337-981-3379; Fax: 337-981-5445. Email: stmary@cox-internet.com. Web: www.stmarych.com.
St. Mary Early Learning Center—Tel: 337-984-3750. Amy Robideaux, Prin. Students 174.
Catechesis/Religious Program—Tel: 337-984-5396. Students 250.

11—OUR LADY OF FATIMA (1949) Rev. Michael Russo; Deacon Timothy Maragos.
Res.: 2319 Johnston St., 70503. Tel: 337-232-8945; Fax: 337-232-0323. Web: fatimalafayette.org.
School—(Grades K-8), 2315 Johnston St., 70503. Tel: 337-235-2464; Fax: 337-235-1320. Web: www-.fatimawarrior.com. Mr. Herb Boasso, Prin.; Mrs. Lois Sellers, Asst. Prin.; Mr. David Hamilton, Asst. Prin. Special Ed. offered Lay Teachers 65; Students 910.
Catechesis/Religious Program—Email: education@fatimalafayette.org. Students 42.

12—OUR LADY OF WISDOM, UNIVERSITY OF LOUISIANA (1942) Rev. Chester Arceneaux.
Mailing Address: P.O. Box 42371, 70504-2371. Tel: 337-232-8741; Fax: 337-236-6737. Email: wisdom@ourladyofwisdom.org. Web: www.ourladyofwisdom.org.
Catechesis/Religious Program—Students 30.

13—OUR LADY QUEEN OF PEACE (1969), (African American), [CEM] Rev. F. Hampton Davis III.
Mailing Address: P.O. Box 90740, 70509-0740.
Church: 145 Martin Luther King Jr. Dr., 70501. Tel: 337-233-1591; Fax: 337-232-5961. Email: QueenofPeace1969@bellsouth.net.
Rectory—415 Cooper St., 70501. Tel: 337-233-0598.
Catechesis/Religious Program—Students 179.

14—ST. PATRICK (1952) Rev. M. Keith LaBove, (Chap. to Hospital Ministry).
Res.: 406 E. Pinhook Rd., 70501. Tel: 337-237-0988; Fax: 337-233-8868.

15—ST. PAUL THE APOSTLE (1911), (African American), Rev. Robert Seay; Bro. Juniper Crouch, O.F.M.
Res.: 326 S. Washington St., 70501. Tel: 337-235-0272; Fax: 337-235-3100.
Catechesis/Religious Program—Students 175.
Mission—*Our Lady of Good Hope*, Lafayette Parish. Tel: 337-235-0272; Fax: 337-235-3100.

16—ST. PIUS X (1968) [JC] Revs. Steven C. LeBlanc; J. Aaron Melancon.
Res.: 200 E. Bayou Pkwy., P.O. Box 80489, 70598-0489. Tel: 337-232-4656; Fax: 337-233-9468.

Web: www.stpiusxchurch.org.
School—(Grades PreK-8), 205 E. Bayou Pkwy., 70508. Tel: 337-237-3139; Fax: 337-232-3455. Web: www.stpiuselementary.org. Miss Donna Lemaire, Prin. Lay Teachers 63; Students 745.
Catechesis/Religious Program—Tel: 337-232-4672. Students 226.

OUTSIDE THE CITY OF LAFAYETTE

ABBEVILLE, VERMILION PARISH

1—ST. MARY MAGDALEN (1844) [CEM 2] Revs. William C. Blanda; Brad D. Guillory; Deacon Tom Tran.
Mailing Address: P.O. Box 1507, 70511. Tel: 337-893-0244; 337-893-0245; Fax: 337-893-0427. Web: www.stmarymagdalenparish.org.
School—Mt. Carmel Elementary, (Grades K-8), 405 Park Ave., 70510. Tel: 337-898-0859; Fax: 337-893-5968. Email: carmel@mceschool.org. Web: www.mceschool.org. Sr. Janet LeBlanc, O.Carm., Prin.; Tiffany Abshire, Librarian. Sisters 2; Lay Teachers (K-8) 27; Lay Teachers (PreK) 3; Students (K-8) 437; Students (PreK) 37.
High School—Vermilion Catholic, 425 Park Ave., 70510. Tel: 337-893-6636; Fax: 337-898-0394. Web: www.vermilioncatholic.com. Joseph L. Steepleton, Prin. Lay Teachers 17; Students 169.
St. Mary Magdalen Christian Service Center—701 Chevis St., 70510. Tel: 337-893-9756; Fax: 337-893-1532. Greg Mitchell, Dir.
Catechesis/Religious Program—Tel: 337-893-0244; Fax: 337-893-0427. Students 283.

2—ST. THERESA OF THE CHILD JESUS (1959) Rev. Kenneth Mayne.
Mailing Address: P.O. Box 609, 70511. Tel: 337-893-5631; Fax: 337-893-9168.
Catechesis/Religious Program—Students 222.

ARNAUDVILLE, ST. LANDRY PARISH

1—ST. CATHERINE (1949), (African American), Rev. Keenan Wynn Brown; Deacon James B. Davis, Pastoral Assoc.
Mailing Address: P.O. Box 53, 70512. Tel: 337-754-7754; Fax: 337-754-7754.
Catechesis/Religious Program—Tel: 337-754-5912; Fax: 337-754-7754.

2—ST. JOHN FRANCIS REGIS (1853) [CEM] Rev. Keenan Wynn Brown.
Mailing Address: P.O. Box 649, 70512. Tel: 337-754-5912; Fax: 337-754-7203. Email: johnfrancisregis@hotmail.com.
Catechesis/Religious Program—Tel: 337-754-5912; Fax: 337-754-7203. Students 273.

BALDWIN, ST. MARY PARISH, SACRED HEART (1906) [CEM] Rev. Gregory P. Cormier; Deacons Harry Darce; Gerald Bourg.
Mailing Address: P.O. Box 308, 70514. Tel: 337-923-7781; Fax: 337-923-4966.
Catechesis/Religious Program— Joland Charpentier, D.R.E. Students 65.

BASILE, EVANGELINE PARISH, ST. AUGUSTINE (1921) [CEM] Rev. Brian Taylor.
Res.: 2717 Third St., 70515. Tel: 337-432-6817; Fax: 337-432-5203. Web: www.geocities.com/st_augustine_basile.
Catechesis/Religious Program—Tel: 337-432-5608. Students 277.
Mission—Assumption, Evangeline Parish. Tel: 337-432-6817; Fax: 337-432-5203.

BAYOU VISTA, ST. MARY PARISH, ST. BERNADETTE (1963) [CEM] Rev. William G. Rogalla.
Res.: 1112 Saturn Rd., Morgan City, 70380. Tel: 985-395-2470; Fax: 985-395-6514. Email: stbern@teche.net. Web: stbern-bv.org.
Catechesis/Religious Program—Tel: 985-395-6517. Students 191.

BERWICK, ST. MARY PARISH, ST. STEPHEN (1950) Rev. Mathew Mullamangalam (India); Deacon Joseph Comeaux.
Res.: 3217 Second St., 70342. Tel: 985-385-1280; Fax: 985-385-1279.
Catechesis/Religious Program—Tel: 985-385-1283. Students 190.

BREAUX BRIDGE, ST. MARTIN PARISH

1—ST. BERNARD (1847) [CEM 2] [JC 2] Revs. Paul J. LaFleur; Neil McNeill; Deacons Jim Davis; Marcel P. Hebert Jr.; Bob McDonner.
Mailing Address: *Admin. Bldg.*, 219 E. Bridge St., 70517.
Res.: 204 N. Main St., 70517. Tel: 337-332-2159; Fax: 337-332-2276. Web: stbernardch.net.
School—(Grades PreK-8), 251 E. Bridge St., 70517. Tel: 337-332-5350; Fax: 337-332-5894. Robin Couvillon, Prin. Lay Teachers 21; Students 500.
Catechesis/Religious Program—219 E. Bridge St., 70517. Tel: 337-332-4488; Fax: 337-332-4488. Students 294.

2—ST. FRANCIS OF ASSISI (1923), (African American), [CEM] Rev. James P. Fallon, S.S.J.; Deacon Lawrence V. Jacobs Jr.
Res.: 610 N. Main St., 70517. Tel: 337-332-2250; Fax: 337-332-5026.
Catechesis/Religious Program—Students 235.

BROUSSARD, LAFAYETTE PARISH

1—ST. JOSEPH (1952), (African American), [CEM 2] Rev. Lambert Lein, S.V.D.
Mailing Address: P.O. Box 278, 70518.
Res.: 232 St. DePorres St., 70518. Tel: 337-837-6218; Fax: 337-837-2072.
Catechesis/Religious Program—Students 97.
Mission—St. Anthony Cade, St. Martin Parish.

2—SACRED HEART OF JESUS (1883) [CEM] Revs. Louis J. Richard; Keith Landry; Deacon Joseph I. Trahan, Admin.
Mailing Address: 200 W. Main St., P.O. Box 737, 70518. Tel: 337-837-1864; Fax: 337-837-1703. Email: pastor@shbroussard.org. Web: shbroussard.org.
School—St. Cecilia, (Grades PreK-8), P.O. Box 309, 70518. Tel: 337-837-6363; Fax: 337-837-3688. Web: scsbluejays.org. Mr. George Fontenot, Prin.; Helen Wofford, Librarian. Lay Teachers 31; Students 492.
Catechesis/Religious Program—Students 398.

CANKTON, ST. LANDRY PARISH, ST. JOHN BERCHMANS (1925) [CEM] Rev. Henry J. Broussard.
Res.: 552 Main St., 70584-9722. Tel: 337-668-4413; Fax: 337-668-4505. Email: stjb@centurytel.net.
Catechesis/Religious Program—Students 173.

CARENCRO, LAFAYETTE PARISH

1—OUR LADY OF THE ASSUMPTION (1925), (African American), [CEM] Rev. Peter Emusa; Deacon James Kincel.
Res.: 410 N. Michaud St., P.O. Box 130, 70520-0130. Tel: 337-896-8304; Fax: 337-896-5874. Email: officemanager@assumptiononline.com. Web: www.assumptiononline.com.
Catechesis/Religious Program—Tel: 337-896-8370. Students 75.

2—ST. PETER (1874) [CEM] Rev. Bill John Melancon; Deacons Eugene Waguespack; Ken Arnaud.
Mailing Address: P.O. Box 40, 70520. Tel: 337-896-9408; Fax: 337-896-9414. Web: www.sprcc.org.
School—Carencro Catholic, (Grades PreK-8), 200 W. St. Peter St., 70520. Tel: 337-896-8973; Fax: 337-896-1931. Web: www.carencrocatholic.org. Andrea Angelle, Acting Prin.; Sandie Enland, Librarian. Lay Teachers 27; Students 456.
Catechesis/Religious Program—Tel: 337-896-8488. Students 395.

CATAHOULA, ST. MARTIN PARISH, ST. RITA (1952) [CEM] Rev. Richard Fabre.
Res.: 1006 St. Rita Hwy., St. Martinville, 70582. Tel: 337-394-4679; Fax: 337-394-7020. Email: church@st.rita.brcoxmail.com.
Catechesis/Religious Program—Students 191.

CECILIA, ST. MARTIN PARISH

1—ST. JOSEPH (1893) [CEM] [JC] Rev. Michael L. Delcambre.
Mailing Address: P.O. Box 279, 70521. Tel: 337-667-6344; Fax: 337-667-7073.
Catechesis/Religious Program—Fax: 337-667-7073. Students 278.

2—ST. ROSE OF LIMA (1944), (African American), [CEM] Rev. Michael L. Delcambre.
Mailing Address: P.O. Box 126, 70521. Tel: 337-667-6555; Fax: 337-667-6686.
Catechesis/Religious Program—Students 117.

CENTERVILLE, ST. MARY PARISH, ST. JOSEPH (1953) [CEM] Rev. Thomas E. Habetz.
Mailing Address: P.O. Box 280, 70522. Tel: 337-836-5659; Fax: 337-836-4600.
Catechesis/Religious Program—P.O. Box 280, 70522.

CHARENTON, ST. MARY PARISH, IMMACULATE CONCEPTION (1844) [CEM] Rev. William Crumley, C.S.C.
Mailing Address: P.O. Box 278, 70523. Tel: 337-923-4281.
Catechesis/Religious Program—

CHATAIGNIER, EVANGELINE PARISH, OUR LADY OF MOUNT CARMEL (1869), (French), [CEM] Rev. Lawrence N. Abara, Sacramental Min.; Deacon Thomas J. Richard, Parish Life Coord.
Mailing Address: P.O. Box 100, 70524. Tel: 337-885-3223; Fax: 337-885-3223.
Catechesis/Religious Program—Students 17.

CHURCH POINT, ACADIA PARISH

1—OUR LADY OF THE SACRED HEART (1873) [CEM 3] [JC] Very Rev. Msgr. Jefferson J. DeBlanc Jr.; Rev. Gregory S. Chauvin; Deacons James G. Cormier; Byrne Winn. In Res., Rev. Wilbur Joseph Brown.
Res.: 118 N. Rogers St., P.O. Box 403, 70525. Tel: 337-684-5494; Fax: 337-684-2133.
School—Our Mother of Peace, (Grades K-8), 218 N. Rogers St., 70525. Tel: 337-684-5780; Fax: 337-684-5780. Donald Courville, Prin. Lay Teachers 17; Students 326.
Catechesis/Religious Program—Students 286.
Chapel—Lewisburg, St. John, Tel: 337-684-5494; Fax: 337-684-2133.

2—OUR MOTHER OF MERCY (1941), (African American), [JC] Rev. Francis Butler, S.S.J.
Res.: 693 N. Main St., P.O. Box 237, 70525. Tel: 337-684-2319; Fax: 337-684-3086.
Catechesis/Religious Program—Students 52.

COTEAU HOLMES, ST. MARTIN PARISH, ST. ELIZABETH (1956) [CEM] Rev. Joseph L.F. Padinjarepeedika, C.M.I. (India).
Office: 1006 St. Elizabeth St., St. Martinville, 70582. Tel: 337-394-6684; Fax: 337-394-6684.
Catechesis/Religious Program—Students 44.

COTEAU, IBERIA PARISH, OUR LADY OF PROMPT SUCCOR (1934) [CEM] Rev. Barry F. Crochet.
Res.: 2409 Coteau Rd., New Iberia, 70560. Tel: 337-369-6993; Fax: 337-560-4475. Email: olps2409@bellsouth.net.
Catechesis/Religious Program—Students 309.

COW ISLAND, VERMILION PARISH, ST. ANNE (1933) [CEM] [JC 3] Rev. Randall Moreau; Deacon David L. Vaughn.
Res.: 17315 Lionel Rd., Abbeville, 70510. Tel: 337-643-7714; Fax: 337-643-1021.
Catechesis/Religious Program—Students 124.
Mission—Sacred Heart Pecan Island, Vermilion Parish.

CROWLEY, ACADIA PARISH

1—IMMACULATE HEART OF MARY (1959) Rev. Matthew P. Higginbotham.
Res.: 825 E. Elm St., 70526.
Rectory—901 E. Elm St., 70526. Tel: 337-783-3498; Fax: 337-783-7444. Email: ihmcatholicchurch@cox-internet.net.
School—Redemptorist Catholic Elementary School, (Grades PreK-8), 606 South Ave. N., 70526. Tel: 337-783-4466; Fax: 337-788-0961. Web: rcsraiders.org. Carl Lejeune, Prin. Lay Teachers 15; Students 215.
Catechesis/Religious Program—Tel: 337-783-7444. Students 121.

2—ST. MICHAEL ARCHANGEL (1895) Revs. Gary Schexnayder; Avelino Vale.
Mailing Address: P.O. Box 406, 70527. Tel: 337-783-7394; Fax: 337-788-0237.
School—(Grades PreK-8), 805 E. Northern Ave., 70526. Tel: 337-783-1410; Fax: 337-783-8547. Mrs. Myra Broussard, Prin. Lay Teachers 29; Students 436.
Catechesis/Religious Program—Tel: 337-783-7393. Students 107.

3—ST. THERESA (1920), (African American), Rev. James P. Fallon, S.S.J.
Res.: 417 W. 3rd St., 70526. Tel: 337-783-1880; Fax: 337-783-9676.
Catechesis/Religious Program—Tel: 337-783-1311; Fax: 337-783-9676. Students 100.

DELCAMBRE, VERMILION PARISH

1—SAINT MARTIN DE PORRES (1948), (African American), [JC] Rev. Herbert Bennerfield.
Res.: 206 W. Church St., 70528. Tel: 337-685-4426; Fax: 337-685-4426.
Catechesis/Religious Program—Castel School of Religion, 208 S. Peter St., 70528. Tel: 337-685-2549. Students 9.

2—OUR LADY OF THE LAKE (1897) [CEM] Rev. Herbert Bennerfield.
Res.: 206 W. Church St., 70528. Tel: 337-685-4426; Fax: 337-685-4426.
Catechesis/Religious Program—Castel School of Religion, 208 South St. Peter St., 70528. Tel: 337-685-2549. Students 282.

DURALDE, EVANGELINE PARISH, ANNUNCIATION OF THE B.V.M. (1964), (Acadian), Rev. Gilbert J. Dutel; Deacon Chuck Ortego, Pastoral Assoc.
Res.: 4476 Duralde Hwy., Eunice, 70535. Tel: 337-457-4849; Fax: 337-457-4502.
Catechesis/Religious Program—Students 76.

DUSON, LAFAYETTE PARISH

1—ST. BENEDICT THE MOOR, (African American), [CEM] Rev. Martin C. Leonards.
Mailing Address: P.O. Box 8, 70529. Tel: 337-873-6772; Fax: 337-873-3023.
Catechesis/Religious Program—Tel: 337-873-6772; Fax: 337-873-3023. Students 118.

2—ST. THERESA OF THE CHILD JESUS (1928) [CEM] Rev. Martin C. Leonards; Deacon Steve Simon.
Mailing Address: P.O. Box 8, 70529. Tel: 337-873-4962; Fax: 337-873-3023.
Catechesis/Religious Program—Tel: 337-873-4488. Students 157.

ERATH, VERMILION PARISH, OUR LADY OF LOURDES (1928) [CEM 2] Rev. Paul Broussard.
Res.: 700 S. Broadway, 70533. Tel: 337-937-6888; Fax: 337-937-8650. Email: beth@ololcatholic.com. Web: ololcatholic.com.
Catechesis/Religious Program—Email: ftoups@ololcatholic.com. Students 496.

EUNICE, ST. LANDRY PARISH

1—ST. ANTHONY OF PADUA (1902) [CEM] Revs. Gilbert J. Dutel; Edward J. Duhon Jr.; Deacon Chuck Ortego.
Mailing Address: 310 W. Vine Ave., P.O. Box 31, 70535. Tel: 337-457-5285; Fax: 337-457-7904. Email: stanthonypaduaeunice@charter.net.
School—St. Edmund Elementary, (Grades PreK-6), 331 N. 3rd St., 70535. Tel: 337-457-5988; 337-457-3777; Fax: 337-457-5989. Email:

elementary@stedmund.com. Web: stedmund.com. Mrs. Elizabeth Christ, Prin.; Mr. James Wallett, Asst. Prin.
High School—St. Edmund High, (Grades PreK-12), 351 W. Magnolia St., 70535. Tel: 337-457-2592; Fax: 337-457-2510. Leon Estes, Asst. Prin. Lay Teachers 45; Students 587.
Catechesis/Religious Program—Tel: 337-457-7505; Fax: 337-457-7904. Students 210.

2—St. Mathilda (1939), (African American), [CEM] Rev. Darren J. Eldridge.
Mailing Address: P.O. Box 346, 70535. Tel: 337-457-3286; Fax: 337-457-3274. Email: stmathildaeunice@gmail.com.
Res.: 800 E. Laurel Ave., 70535.
Catechesis/Religious Program—Tel: 337-457-0108. Students 83.

3—St. Thomas More (1967) Rev. Cedric Sonnier; Deacon David Guillory.
Mailing Address: P.O. Box 1022, 70535. Tel: 337-457-8107; Fax: 337-457-1735. Email: stmeu@charterinternet.com.
Catechesis/Religious Program—Tel: 337-457-8101. Email: stm-eunice@charterinternet.com. Students 240.

Evangeline, Acadia Parish, St. Joseph (1938) [CEM 2] Rev. Theodore Broussard Jr.
Mailing Address: P.O. Box 183, 70537. Tel: 337-824-4995; Fax: 337-824-4995.
Catechesis/Religious Program—Tel: 337-824-8352. Students 106.
Mission—St. Jules Petit Mamou, Acadia Parish 70537.

Four Corners, St. Mary Parish, St. Peter the Apostle (1960) Rev. Gregory P. Cormier.
Mailing Address: P.O. Box 308, Baldwin, 70514. Tel: 337-923-7781; Fax: 337-923-4966.
Catechesis/Religious Program—Lou Pearl Washington, D.R.E.
Mission—St. Joan of Arc, (Closed), Glencoe, St. Mary Parish.

Franklin, St. Mary Parish
1—Assumption B.V.M. (1852) Rev. Lloyd F. Benoit Jr.; Deacon Douglas Hebert.
Mailing Address: 211 Iberia St., 70538. Tel: 337-828-3869; Fax: 337-828-3872. Email: marysassumption@yahoo.com. Web: www.churchofassumption.com.
School—St. John Elementary, (Grades PreK-5), 924 Main St., 70538. Tel: 337-828-2648; Fax: 337-828-2112. Email: stjohn@msis.net. Web: www-.stjohnelem.com. Mrs. Sheri Higdon, Prin. Lay Teachers 7; Students 196.
High School—Hanson High School, (Grades 6-12), 903 Anderson St., 70538. Tel: 337-828-3487; Fax: 337-828-7431. Web: www.hansonmemorial.com. Dr. Vincent Maholic, Prin. Lay Teachers 20; Students 261.
Catechesis/Religious Program—Tel: 337-828-9499. Students 81.

2—St. Jules (1950) [CEM] Rev. Thomas Hein Vu; Deacon Joseph Thomas.
Res.: 601 Magnolia St., 70538. Tel: 337-828-1714; Fax: 337-828-1734. Email: stjules1943@yahoo.com.
Catechesis/Religious Program—Students 164.
Mission—Immaculate Conception 601 Magnolia, Verdunville, St. Mary Parish.

Grand Coteau, St. Landry Parish, St. Charles Borromeo (1819) [CEM] [JC] Revs. James L. Lambert, S.J.; Ferdinand Derrera, S.J.; Clair M. Cazayoux, S.J.; Deacons Samuel Henry; Herd Guilbeau.
Mailing Address: P.O. Box A, 70541. Tel: 337-662-5279; Fax: 337-662-5270. Web: www.st-charles-borromeo.org.
Res.: 174 Church St., 70541.
School—St. Ignatius, (Grades K-8), P.O. Drawer J, 70541. Tel: 337-662-3325; Fax: 337-662-3349. Web: stignatiusschool.us. Mrs. Cindy Prather, Prin. Lay Teachers 25; Students 300.
Catechesis/Religious Program—Tel: 337-662-5271. Students 269.
Mission—Christ the King Opelousas. 369 Christ the King Rd., Opelousas, St. Landry Parish 70570.

Grand Prairie, St. Landry Parish, St. Peter (1951) [CEM 2] [JC] Rev. Mark F. Melaneon.
Res. & Mailing Address: 1074 Hwy. 748 (Grand Prairie), Washington, 70589-4541. Tel: 337-826-3870; Fax: 337-826-5635.
Catechesis/Religious Program—Students 117.

Gueydan, Vermilion Parish, St. Peter the Apostle (1907) [JC] Rev. Jason Vidrine.
Res.: 603 Main St., P.O. Box 28, 70542. Tel: 337-536-9258; Fax: 337-536-0071.
School—(Grades PreK-8), 513 6th St., 70542. Tel: 337-536-7930; Fax: 337-536-9460. Sr. Ann Arno, M.S.C., Prin. Sisters 2; Lay Teachers 9; Students 125.
Catechesis/Religious Program—Students 121.
Mission—St. David Mulvey, Vermilion Parish.

Henderson, St. Martin Parish, Our Lady of Mercy (1962) [CEM] [JC] Rev. Lawrence N. Abara.
Mailing Address: P.O. Box 587, Breaux Bridge, 70517. Tel: 337-228-2352; Fax: 337-228-2372.
Res.: 1454 Henderson Hwy., 70517.
Catechesis/Religious Program—Tel: 337-228-2234. Students 151.
Mission—Sacred Heart Butte La Rose, St. Martin Parish.

Henry, Vermilion Parish, St. John (1939), (French-Acadian), [CEM] Rev. Emmanuel Fernandez.
Res.: 18534 La. Hwy. 689, Erath, 70533. Tel: 337-937-5108; Fax: 337-937-0002.
Catechesis/Religious Program—Students 129.
Mission—St. James 21125 LA Hwy. 333, Abbeville, 70510.

Iota, Acadia Parish, St. Joseph (1892) [CEM] Rev. Mikel Anthony Polson.
Mailing Address: 604 St. Joseph Ave., 70543. Tel: 337-779-2627; Fax: 337-779-2632. Email: stjosephiota@charter.net.
School—St. Francis, 490 St. Joseph Ave., 70543. Tel: 337-779-2527. Louis Cramer, Prin. Lay Teachers 12; Students 202.
Catechesis/Religious Program—Students 306.
Mission—St. Michael Egan, Acadia Parish. Tel: 337-788-0529.

Jeanerette, Iberia Parish
1—St. John the Evangelist (1879) [CEM] Rev. Jody Simoneaux.
Res.: 1510 Church St., 70544. Tel: 337-276-4576; Fax: 337-276-5804. Email: stjohnev@yahoo.com. Web: www.stjohnjeanerette.com.
School—St. Joseph, (Grades K-8), 10917 Old Jeanerette Rd., 70544. Tel: 337-276-3615; Fax: 337-276-7659. Mr. Earl Price, Prin. Lay Teachers 14; Students 105.
Catechesis/Religious Program—Tel: 337-276-6944. Students 112.

2—Our Lady of the Rosary (1945), (African American), [CEM] [JC] Rev. Ryszard Kalinowski, S.V.D.
Res.: 11200 Old Jeanerette Rd., 70544. Tel: 337-276-6900; Fax: 337-276-6931.
Catechesis/Religious Program—Students 85.

Judice, Lafayette Parish, St. Basil (1970) [CEM 2] Rev. A. Rex Broussard Jr.
Res.: 1803 Duhon Rd. (Judice), Duson, 70529. Tel: 337-984-2179.
Catechesis/Religious Program—Tel: 337-988-2655. Email: stbasil@cox.net. Students 166.

Kaplan, Vermilion Parish, Our Lady of the Holy Rosary (1896) [JC] Rev. F. David Broussard; Deacons Paul R. Eleazar; David L. Vaughn.
Mailing Address: 603 N. Herbert Ave., 70548. Tel: 337-643-6472; Fax: 337-643-2516.
School—Maltrait Memorial, (Grades PreK-8), One Crusader Square, 70548. Tel: 337-643-7765; Fax: 337-643-7765. Mrs. Renee C. Meaux, Prin. Lay Teachers 14; Students 136.
Catechesis/Religious Program—701 N. Boudreaux Ave., P.O. Box 429, 70548. Students 590.
Mission—St. Frances Xavier Cabrini 901 N. Frederick Ave., Vermilion Parish 70548.

Krotz Springs, St. Landry Parish, St. Anthony of Padua (1958) Rev. Mark Ledoux.
Mailing Address: 219 Eighth Ave., P.O. Box 425, 70750. Tel: 337-566-3527; Fax: 337-566-2803.
Catechesis/Religious Program—Students 75.

Lawtell, St. Landry Parish
1—St. Bridget (1920) [CEM 2] Rev. Daniel Picard.
Mailing Address: P.O. Box 156, 70550. Tel: 337-543-7591; Fax: 337-543-7593.
Catechesis/Religious Program—Students 96.
Mission—Sacred Heart Prairie Ronde, St. Landry Parish.

2—Holy Family (1953), (African American), Rev. Denis A. Osuagwu (Nigeria).
Mailing Address: P.O. Box 310, 70550. Tel: 337-543-2366; Fax: 337-543-8281. 283 Thibodeaux St., 70550.
Catechesis/Religious Program—Twinned with St. Ann, Mallet.

Lebeau, St. Landry Parish, Immaculate Conception (1897), (African American), [CEM] Rev. Walter Cerbin, S.S.J., Admin.
Mailing Address & Office: 103 Lebeau Church Rd., 71345. Tel: 337-623-0838 (Rectory); 337-623-0303 (Office); Fax: 337-623-0675.
Rectory—P.O. Box 6, 71345.
Catechesis/Religious Program—Students 50.

Leonville, St. Landry Parish
1—St. Catherine (1952), (African American), [JC] Rev. Kenneth J. Domingue.
Mailing Address: P.O. Box 547, 70551. Tel: 337-879-2365; Fax: 337-879-3050.
Catechesis/Religious Program—Tel: 337-879-2347; Fax: 337-879-9717.
Mission—St. Jules Prairie Laurent, St. Landry Parish.

2—St. Leo the Great (1896) [CEM] [JC] Rev. Kenneth J. Domingue.
Mailing Address: P.O. Box 544, 70551. Tel: 337-879-2365; Fax: 337-879-3050.
Catechesis/Religious Program—Students 416.

Leroy, Vermilion Parish, Our Lady of Perpetual Help (1922) [CEM] Rev. Gregory M. Simien.
Res.: 12995 Louisiana Hwy. 699, Maurice, 70555. Tel: 337-893-0610; Fax: 337-893-6412.
Catechesis/Religious Program—Students 130.

Loreauville, Iberia Parish
1—St. Joseph (1873) [CEM] [JC 2] Rev. John G. Breaux.
Mailing Address: P.O. Box 365, 70552. Tel: 337-229-4254; Fax: 337-229-4255. In Res., Rev. Paul Onuegbe.
Catechesis/Religious Program—Tel: 337-229-6728. Students 325.

2—Our Lady of Victory (1953), (African American), [CEM 2] [JC] Rev. Paul Onuegbe.
Mailing Address: 120 Daigre St., P.O. Box 387, 70552. Tel: 337-229-8284; Fax: 337-229-8254. Email: olv-loreauville@yahoo.com.
Catechesis/Religious Program—Tel: 337-229-6329. Students 105.

Louisa, St. Mary Parish, St. Helena (1890) [CEM] Rev. Thomas Thanh Nguyen.
Res.: 108 St. Helen's Church Ln., Franklin, 70538. Tel: 337-867-4378; Fax: 337-867-5223.
Chapel—St. Francis Cypremort Point.

Lydia, Iberia Parish, St. Nicholas (1867) [CEM 2] Rev. Donavan J. Labbe.
Mailing Address: P.O. Box 369, 70569. Tel: 337-364-5228; Fax: 337-364-5251.
Catechesis/Religious Program—Tel: 337-367-0562; Fax: 337-364-5251. Students 298.

Lyons Point, Acadia Parish, St. John the Baptist (1952) [CEM] Rev. Donald Pousson.
Mailing Address: 8021 Lyons Point Hwy., Crowley, 70526. Tel: 337-783-2457; Fax: 337-783-9015.
Catechesis/Religious Program—Tel: 337-783-2457. Students 73.

Mallet, St. Landry Parish, St. Ann (1856), (African American), [CEM] Rev. Denis A. Osuagwu (Nigeria).
Mailing Address: P.O. Box 310, Lawtell, 70550. Tel: 337-543-2385; Fax: 337-543-8281. 8348 Hwy. 190, Lawtell, 70550.
Catechesis/Religious Program—Combined with Holy Family, Lawtell., Tel: 337-543-2366. Students 116.

Mamou, Evangeline Parish, St. Ann (1914) [CEM] Revs. Bryce Sibley; Jude W. Thierry.
Parish Center—716 Sixth St., 70554. Tel: 337-468-3159; Fax: 337-468-3427.
Catechesis/Religious Program—Students 273.
Mission—Holy Spirit

Maurice, Vermilion Parish
1—St. Alphonsus (1893) [CEM] Rev. O. Joseph Breaux.
Res.: 8700 Maurice Ave., P.O. Box 190, 70555. Tel: 337-893-4099; Fax: 337-893-2474. Email: stalphonsus@cox-internet.com. Web: www.stalphonsus-maurice.org.
Catechesis/Religious Program—Tel: 337-893-0923; Fax: 337-893-2474. Students 458.

2—St. Joseph (1946), (African American), [JC] Rev. Arockiam Arockiam, S.V.D. (India).
Mailing Address: P.O. Box 250, 70555. Tel: 337-893-5428; Fax: 337-893-5441. Email: stjosephchurchmaurice@yahoo.com. Web: www.stjoseph-maurice.org. 8005 Maurice Ave., 70555.
Catechesis/Religious Program—Students 107.

Melville, St. Landry Parish, St. John the Evangelist (1931) [CEM] Rev. James Bam Nguyen.
Mailing Address: 318 First St., P.O. Box 256, 71353-0256. Tel: 337-623-4957; Fax: 337-623-4970. Email: stjohndioceselaf@att.net.
Catechesis/Religious Program—Students 28.
Mission—St. Thomas, the Apostle Palmetto, St. Landry Parish.

Mermentau, Acadia Parish, St. John the Evangelist (1882) [CEM] Rev. Donald Pousson.
Mailing Address: P.O. Box 340, 70556. Tel: 337-824-2278; Fax: 337-824-9624.
Catechesis/Religious Program—Tel: 337-824-2278; Fax: 337-824-9624. Students 129.
Mission—St. Margaret 311 Miller St., Estherwood, Acadia Parish 70534.

Milton, Lafayette Parish, St. Joseph (1977) [CEM] Rev. William J. Gearheard; Deacon Cody Miller.
Mailing Address: P.O. Box 299, 70558. Tel: 337-856-5997; Fax: 337-856-5955. Email: bg1960@cox.net. Web: www.stjo-milton.org.
Catechesis/Religious Program—Tel: 337-856-5997; Fax: 337-856-5955. Email: dre@stjo-milton.org. Students 468.

Mire, Acadia Parish, Assumption of the Blessed Virgin Mary (1954) [CEM] Very Rev. Msgr. Russell J. Harrington.

Res.: 6080 Mire Hwy., Church Point, 70525. Tel: 337-873-6574; Fax: 337-873-3777.
Catechesis / Religious Program—Tel: 337-873-3777. Students 279.

MORROW, ST. LANDRY PARISH, ST. PETER (1947), (French), [CEM] Rev. Michael Guidry.
Mailing Address: P.O. Box 319, 71356. Tel: 318-346-7010. Email: stpeters319@att.net.
Catechesis / Religious Program—Students 3.
Mission—Resurrection Whiteville.

MORSE, ACADIA PARISH, IMMACULATE CONCEPTION (1956) Rev. Donald Pousson.
Mailing Address: P.O. Box 297, 70559-0297. Tel: 337-783-2968; Fax: 337-783-2965.
Catechesis / Religious Program—Tel: 337-783-2968. Students 113.
Mission—St. Aloysius Midland. Tel: 337-783-2968.

MOWATA, ACADIA PARISH, ST. LAWRENCE (1905) [CEM 2] Rev. Joseph T. Sai Tran, S.V.D.
Res.: 29031 Crowley-Eunice Hwy., Eunice, 70535. Tel: 337-457-2739; Fax: 337-457-2739.
Catechesis / Religious Program—Students 67.

NEW IBERIA, IBERIA PARISH

1—ST. EDWARD (1917) [CEM] [JC] Very Rev. Msgr. Ronald Broussard.
Mailing Address: 175 Ambassador W. Lemelle Dr., 70560. Tel: 337-369-3101; Fax: 337-369-3118. Email: stedwardcc@cox.net.
School—(Grades K-3), 175 Porter St., 70560. Tel: 337-369-6764; Fax: 337-369-9534. Dave Cavalier Jr., Prin. Lay Teachers 15; Students 378.
Catechesis / Religious Program—Tel: 337-365-3762. Students 103.
Mission—St. Jude, Iberia Parish 70560.

2—NATIVITY OF OUR LADY (1964) [CEM] Rev. Michael Arnaud.
Res.: Richelieu Circle, 70560. Tel: 337-364-8360; Fax: 337-364-1509. Email: nativity@cox.net.
Catechesis / Religious Program—Tel: 337-365-3759; Fax: 337-364-1509. Students 260.

3—OUR LADY OF PERPETUAL HELP (1949) [JC] Revs. Mark Derise; D. Blaine Clement.
Res.: 1303 St. Jude Ave., 70560. Tel: 337-365-5481; Fax: 337-365-5483. Email: olphni@bellsouth.net.
Catechesis / Religious Program—Students 238.

4—ST. PETER (1838), (Hispanic—Acadian), [CEM] [JC] Revs. Charles Langlois; Jude Halphen; Deacons Wade Joseph Broussard; Patrick D. Burke.
Mailing Address: P.O. Box 12507, 70562. Tel: 337-369-3816; Fax: 337-369-3192. Email: stpeter@cox-internet.com.
Catechesis / Religious Program—Students 222.

5—SACRED HEART OF JESUS (1960) Very Rev. Msgr. Richard Greene. In Res., Rev. Juan Luis Gandara (Mexico) Office of Hispanic Ministry.
Res.: 2514 Old Jeanerette Rd., 70563. Tel: 337-364-4439; Fax: 337-364-4474.
Catechesis / Religious Program—Students 383.

OPELOUSAS, ST. LANDRY PARISH

1—HOLY GHOST (1920), (African American), [JC] Revs. Jaison Mangalath, S.V.D.; Stanley Jawa, S.V.D.; Anthony A. Anala, S.V.D.
Mailing Address: P.O. Box 1785, 70571-1785. Email: holyghostchurch@bellsouth.net.
Res.: 747 N. Union St., 70570. Tel: 337-942-2732; Fax: 337-948-4108.
Catechesis / Religious Program—Students 217.

2—ST. LANDRY (1776) [CEM] [JC] Very Rev. Msgr. J. Robert Romero; Deacon John W. Miller.
Res.: 1020 N. Main St., 70570. Tel: 337-942-6552; Fax: 337-948-1295. Email: stlandrychurch@charter.net. Web: www.stlandrycatholicchurch.org.
Catechesis / Religious Program—Students 40.

3—OUR LADY OF MERCY (1942) Rev. Paul G. Bienvenu; Deacons Ulysse Joubert; Thomas Lindsey.
Res.: 207 N. Camille St., 70570. Tel: 337-942-4174; Fax: 337-942-1476. Email: ourladymercy@aol.com. Web: ourladymercy.org.
Catechesis / Religious Program—Tel: 337-942-9404. Students 136.

4—OUR LADY QUEEN OF ANGELS (1967) [JC] Rev. Angelo Cremaldi; Deacons Jerome Collins; Sammy Diesi.
Mailing Address: P.O. Box 508, 70571-0508. Email: qoacremaldi@charter.net. Web: www.queenofangelschurch.org. In Res., Rev. Msgr. Louis J. Melancon.
Res.: 2125 S. Union St., 70570. Tel: 337-942-5628; Fax: 337-942-9708.
Catechesis / Religious Program—Tel: 337-942-7831; Fax: 337-942-9708. Email: qoajerome@charter.net. Students 290.

PARKS, ST. MARTIN PARISH, ST. JOSEPH (1938) Rev. Stephen Ugwu.
Mailing Address: 1034 Bridge St., 70582. Tel: 337-845-4168; Fax: 337-845-5079. Email: parkscatholic@gmail.com. Web: www.parkscatholic.com.
Catechesis / Religious Program—Students 290.
Mission—St. Louis, Tel: 337-845-4168.

PATTERSON, ST. MARY PARISH, ST. JOSEPH (1848) [CEM] Rev. Louis Lam Vu.
Res.: P.O. Box 219, 70392-0219. Tel: 985-395-3616; Fax: 985-395-9129. Email: stjoepat@cox-internet.com.
Catechesis / Religious Program—Students 173.

PINE PRAIRIE, EVANGELINE PARISH, ST. PETER (1924) [CEM 2] Rev. Richard Dale Broussard.
Mailing Address: 1325 1st St., P.O. Box 709, 70576. Tel: 337-599-2224; Fax: 337-599-3003.
Mission—St. Theresa 2117 St. Landry Hwy., Evangeline Parish, LA.
Catechesis / Religious Program—Students 225.

PLAISANCE, ST. LANDRY PARISH, ST. JOSEPH (1949), (African American), [CEM] Rev. Jude M. Obiechina, C.M.F. (Nigeria).
Res.: 3283 Hwy. 167, Opelousas, 70570. Tel: 337-826-3395; Fax: 337-826-3550.
Catechesis / Religious Program—Students 29.
Mission—St. Ann Frilot Cove, Evangeline Parish.

PORT BARRE, ST. LANDRY PARISH

1—ST. MARY (1952), (African American), [CEM] [JC] Rev. Godwin Nzehi, C.M.F., Sacramental Min.; Deacon Alvin DeJean, Parish Life Coord.
Mailing Address: P.O. Box 338, 70577. Tel: 337-585-2315; Fax: 337-585-2315.
Catechesis / Religious Program—Tel: 337-585-2863; Fax: 337-585-5860.

2—SACRED HEART OF JESUS (1871) [CEM] [JC] Rev. Charles N. Trahan.
Mailing Address: P.O. Box 129, 70577. Tel: 337-585-2279; Fax: 337-585-5377.
Catechesis / Religious Program—Fax: 337-585-2215. Students 320.

RAYNE, ACADIA PARISH

1—ST. JOSEPH (1872) [CEM 2] [JC 2] Revs. William Paul Ruskoski; Clint James Trahan.
Mailing Address: P.O. Box 199, 70578. Tel: 337-334-2193; Fax: 337-334-2199.
School—Rayne Catholic Elementary, (Grades PreK-8), 407 S. Polk St., 70578. Tel: 337-334-5657; 337-334-5658; Fax: 337-334-3301. Email: raynecatholicelem@bellsouth.net. Web: www.raynecatholic.org. Fred Menard, Prin.; Sharon Chatelain, Librarian. Lay Teachers 25; Students 440.
Catechesis / Religious Program—Tel: 337-334-9849. Students 289.

2—OUR MOTHER OF MERCY (1924), (African American), [CEM] Rev. Richard F. Wagner, S.S.J. In Res., Rev. Daniel P. Bastianelli, S.S.J.
Res. & Mailing Address: 707 Lyman Ave., 70578. Tel: 337-334-3516.
Catechesis / Religious Program—Students 100.

RICHARD, ACADIA PARISH, ST. EDWARD (1939) [CEM] [JC] Unassigned.
Res.: 1463 Charlene Hwy., Church Point, 70525. Tel: 337-684-5991; Fax: 337-684-0189.
Catechesis / Religious Program—Students 205.
Mission—St. Thomas Savoy, St. Landry Parish.

ROBERTS COVE, ACADIA PARISH, ST. LEO IV (1883), (German), [CEM] Rev. Kevin Bordelon.
Res.: 7166 Roberts Cove Rd., Rayne, 70578-8912. Tel: 337-334-5056; Fax: 337-334-0832.
Catechesis / Religious Program—Tel: 337-334-7458. Students 77.
Mission—St. Edmund Chapel Branch, Acadia Parish.

RYNELLA, IBERIA PARISH, ST. MARCELLUS (1960) [CEM] Deacon Theo Landry, Parish Life Coord.; Rev. Donavan J. Labbe, Sacramental Min.
Res.: 6100 Avery Island Rd., New Iberia, 70560. Tel: 337-364-0818; Fax: 337-364-0824. Email: stmarcellusc@aol.com.
Catechesis / Religious Program—Tel: 337-364-9419. Students 190.

ST. MARTINVILLE, ST. MARTIN PARISH

1—ST. MARTIN OF TOURS (1765) [CEM] Rev. Msgr. J. Douglas Courville; Rev. Kenneth A. Bienvenu (Retired).
Res.: 133 S. Main St., P.O. Drawer 10, 70582. Tel: 337-394-6021; Fax: 337-394-6020.
Catechesis / Religious Program—Tel: 337-394-4203. Students 185.

2—NOTRE DAME DE PERPETUEL SECOURS (1938), (African American), [CEM] [JC] Revs. Augustinus Seran, S.V.D.; Justin Arockiasamy, S.V.D.; Deacon David Chambers.
Res.: 201 Gary St., 70582. Tel: 337-394-3084; Fax: 337-394-5380.
Catechesis / Religious Program—Tel: 337-394-3084. Students 368.

SCOTT, LAFAYETTE PARISH

1—SAINT MARTIN DE PORRES (1961), (African American), [CEM] Rev. Peter Emusa, Sacramental Min.; Deacon Louis J. Lloyd, Parish Life Coord.
Mailing Address: P.O. Box 1347, 70583-1347. Tel: 337-232-1968; Fax: 337-266-8922. Email: deporres@bellsouth.net.
Catechesis / Religious Program—Students 83.

2—STS. PETER AND PAUL (1904) [CEM] Revs. Thomas P. Voorhies; Louis Allen Breaux.
Mailing Address: P.O. Box 610, 70583. Tel: 337-235-2433; Fax: 337-233-4868. Email: stpeterandpaulscott@hotmail.com. 110 Old Spanish Tr., 70583.
School—Sts. Peter and Paul Catholic School, (Grades PreK-3), P.O. Box 640, 70583. Tel: 337-504-3400. Ms. Patricia Sonnier, Prin.
Catechesis / Religious Program—Tel: 337-232-6167. Students 452.

VILLE PLATTE, EVANGELINE PARISH

1—ST. JOSEPH (1947), (African American), [CEM] Revs. Eugene R. Tremie; Joshua P. Guillory; Clinton M. Sensat; Sr. Rita Darensbourg, S.S.F., Pastoral Assoc.
Res.: 1107 Martin L. King Dr., 70586. Tel: 337-363-1051.
Catechesis / Religious Program—Students 32.

2—OUR LADY QUEEN OF ALL SAINTS (1969) Rev. Marion P. Romero; Deacon Eugene Le Boeuf.
1220 W. Dardeau St., 70586.
Rectory—1135 Parkview St., P.O. Drawer E, 70586. Tel: 337-363-5167; Fax: 337-363-5179.
Catechesis / Religious Program—Students 150.

3—SACRED HEART OF JESUS (1854) [CEM] Revs. Eugene R. Tremie; Clinton M. Sensat.
Res.: 708 E. Main St., 70586. Tel: 337-363-2989; Fax: 337-363-3500. Email: sacredheart-vp@centurytel.net. Web: www.geocities.com/sacredheart-vp.
School—Sacred Heart Elementary, (Grades K-8), 532 E. Main St., 70586. Tel: 337-363-3445; Fax: 337-363-2318. Diane Fontenot, Admin. Elementary & High School; Mrs. Evelyn G. Fontenot, Asst. Prin. Lay Teachers 27; Students 598.
High School—Sacred Heart High, 114 Trojan Ln., 70586. Tel: 337-363-1475; Fax: 337-363-0348. Mr. Andrew Ducote, Prin.; Mrs. Dawn C. Shipp, Asst. Prin. Lay Teachers 15; Students 243.
Catechesis / Religious Program—Tel: 337-363-7788; Fax: 337-363-3500. Students 45.
Chapel—Belarie Cove Chapel 2003 Belaire Cove Rd., 70586. Tel: 337-363-2989; Fax: 337-363-3500.

WASHINGTON, ST. LANDRY PARISH

1—HOLY TRINITY (1950), (African American), Rev. Albert Gayle Nunez; Deacon Alvin R. DeJean, Parish Life Coord.
Mailing Address: P.O. Box 186, 70589. Tel: 337-826-3376; Fax: 337-826-3376.
Catechesis / Religious Program—Students 21.

2—IMMACULATE CONCEPTION (1756), (French—German), Rev. Albert G. Nunez.
Mailing Address: P.O. Box 116, 70589. Tel: 337-826-7396; Fax: 337-826-0099. Email: immaculate123@charterinternet.com.
Catechesis / Religious Program—Tel: 337-826-0099. Students 50.

YOUNGSVILLE, LAFAYETTE PARISH, ST. ANNE (1859) [CEM] Rev. Thomas Jason Mouton.
Mailing Address: P.O. Box 410, 70592. Tel: 337-856-8212; Fax: 337-856-8277. Email: stanne@bellsouth.net.
Catechesis / Religious Program—Tel: 337-856-8242. Students 562.

On Special Assignment:
Revs.—
Akalawa, Ambrose, Chap., Our Lady of Lourdes.
Boyer, Millard G., Chap., Lafayette General Medical Center, 210 X Long Plantation Blvd., 70508. Tel: 337-289-7483
Broussard, Ken, O.S.B.
Castano, Jairo, Hispanic Ministry.
Eze, Cyprian, Hospital Ministry - Central Region.
Finley, John Thomas, Chap., Bethany Health Care, 417 E. Simcoe, 70501.
Gandara, Juan Luis (Mexico), Hispanic Ministry.
Kanat, Kurian, Cathedral St. John the Evangelist.
Mauk, Dismas, S.V.D., Hospital Ministry.
Richard, Rusty P., Austin, TX.

Graduate Studies:
Rev.—
Guillory, Joshua P., Rome.

Absent on Sick Leave:
Revs.—
Delauney, Herbert C.
Downs, Gregory Todd, P.O. Box 432, Natchitoches, 71458-0432.
Guidry, Mitchell
Vidrine, Richard

On Leave:
Rev. Msgr.—
Herpin, Michael
Revs.—
Alexander, Joseph
Arceneaux, Jules

Retired:
Rev. Msgrs.—
Angelle, Robert G., 205 N. Anita St., 70501.
Benefiel, Harry E., 301 Eraste Landry Rd., 70506-2321. Tel: 337-235-4373
Mallet, Charles J., 40 Audobon Oaks Blvd., 70506.
Metrejean, Paul, 136 Metrejean Ln., Opelousas, 70570.
Mouton, Richard von Phul, P.O. Drawer V, 70502.
Revs.—
Bergeron, C. Paul, 402 Wayside Dr., Houma, 70360.
Betrand, Conley, 1804 W. University Ave., 70506.
Bienvenu, Kenneth A., 1017 Alan Dr., St. Martinville, 70582.
Bourgeois, Francis L., P.O. Box 52, Mamou, 70554.
Brennan, Joseph F., 203 Bocage Circle, 70503.
Brown, Wilbur J., Eunice, LA
Calais, Floyd J., 313 Rue Louis XIV, Apt. H, 70508. Tel: 318-988-6278
Courville, Robert, 111 Greenbriar St., Alexandria, 71301.
Degeyter, Edward, P.O. Box 923, Saint Martinville, 70582.
DeLeeuw, John, 526 Raintree Tr., 70507.
Dugas, Willard, 520 Dugas Rd., 70507-3010.
Dutra, Luis C., 1522 Carmel Dr., 70501. (Extern-Diocesan)
Estilette, Grady J., P.O. Box 82315, 70598-2315.
Frey, Jerome V.
Hebert, T. J., 411 Hanover Sq., 70508.
Landry, Oneil Anthony, P.O. Box 202, Centerville, 70522.
Landry, Ralph James, 2603 Bodin Rd., New Iberia, 70560.
Ledoux, Louis Vernon, (Retired Armed Forces), 205-21 115th Rd., Jamaica, NY 11412-2907.
Leger, Austin, 1906 George Dr., Opelousas, 70570.
Matt, J. Wilson, 2319 E. Main St., New Iberia, 70560.
Montelaro, Thomas, 5485 Charleston Blvd., Las Vegas, NV 89142.
Pelous, Donald
Robitaille, Raymond, 2319 Main St., New Iberia, 70560-4096.
Simon, George Howard, 503 Mount Vernon Dr., 70503.
Spekschate, John, De Gauden, 49, 5801 BX Venray, The Netherlands.
Speyrer, Jules, 1530 White St., Basile, 70515. Tel: 337-432-5054
Stemmann, Joseph, 2319 Main St., New Iberia, 70560.
Theriot, Donald C., 2006 W. Summer Dr., Abbeville, 70510.
Thibodeaux, Paul, 222 Bombardier Ln., Eunice, 70535.
Thychery, George, India.
Warren, Arthur, Tribunal Office, 1408 Carmel Dr., 70501.

Permanent Deacons:
Arnaud, John Kenneth, St. Francis Regis, Arnaudville
Bakeler, Arthur Francis, Jr., Sts. Peter & Paul, Scott
Bergeron, Harris, St. Rita, Catahoula
Besse, Daniel Lee, St. Joseph, Rayne
Bollich, Reginald Anthony, St. Jules, Lafayette
Borbas, Timothy, Houston, TX
Boudreaux, Ulysse, (Retired)
Bourg, Gerald J., Exec. Asst. to Regl. Vicar, South, Sacred Heart, Baldwin
Broussard, Wade, St. Peter, New Iberia
Burke, Patrick Douglas, St. Peter, New Iberia
Chambers, David Brodrick, Notre Dame, St. Martinville
Clark, Michael, Holy Cross, Lafayette
Collins, Jerome, Our Lady Queen of Angels, Opelousas
Cormier, Frank Alex, St. Edmond, Lafayette
Cormier, James, Our Lady of the Sacred Heart, Church Point
Darce, Harry, Sacred Heart, Baldwin
Davis, James, St. Catherine, Arnaudville
DeJean, Alvin Ray, St. Mary, Port Barre; Holy Trinity, Washington
Derouen, Raymond Charles, St. Edward, New Iberia
Diesi, Samuel Charles, Our Lady Queen of Angels, Opelousas
Doumit, Christopher, St. Joseph, Loreauville
Faulk, Kendal, Our Lady of the Holy Rosary, Kaplan (Seminary)
Gaudin, Gary Michael, St. Anthony, Eunice
Guilbeau, Joseph Herd, St. Charles Borromeo, Coteau
Guillory, David, St. Thomas More, Eunice
Hebert, Clifford Mitchell, Jr., Sacred Heart of Jesus, Port Barre
Hebert, Marcel, St. Bernard, Breaux Bridge
Henry, Samuel, St. Charles, Grand Coteau
Hyde, Randy Eugene, St. Edmond, Lafayette
Jacobs, Lawrence, St. Francis of Assisi, Breaux Bridge
Joubert, Ulysse, Our Lady of Mercy, Opelousas
Kincel, James, Our Lady of Assumption, Carencro
Landry, Theodule, St. Marcellus, Rynella
Lebouef, Eugene J., Queen of All Saints, Ville Platte
Ledet, Timothy Francis, St. Joseph, Rayne
Lee, Carlton J., Sr., Notre Dame, St. Martinville
Leger, Robert Lee, St. Augustine, Basile
Lejeune, Joseph L., St. Peter, Gueydan
Leleux, Rodless, St. Michael, Crowley
Lindsey, Thomas, Our Lady of Mercy, Opelousas
Lloyd, Louis, St. Martin de Porres, Scott
Maragos, Timothy Alan, Our Lady of Fatima, Lafayette
Marcel, Albert, St. Anthony, Lafayette
Matte, Paul, St. Edmond, Lafayette
McDonner, Robert, St. Bernard, Breaux Bridge
Melancon, J. Douglas, St. Martin de Tours, St. Martinville
Miller, Cody, St. Joseph, Milton
Miller, John W., St. Landry, Opelousas
Mouton, Chris, (Leave of Absence)
Nguyen, Tuan Anh, Vietnamese Ministry, Lafayette
Ortego, Charles, St. Anthony of Padua, Eunice
Ozene, Anthony, Immaculate Heart of Mary, Lafayette
Perron, Roderick P., (Retired)
Picard, Richard, Holy Cross, Lafayette
Richard, Thomas, Our Lady of Mount Carmel, Chataignier
Schexnayder, Nelson Joseph, Jr., St. Elizabeth Seton, Lafayette
Senegal, Nolton, St. Edwards, New Iberia
Sikes, George, Our Lady of Perpetual Help, New Iberia
Simon, Steve, St. Theresa, Duson
Soignier, Kenneth Earl, Cathedral of St. John the Evangelist, Lafayette
Soileau, Harris, (Retired)
Sommers, Thomas Richard, St. John the Baptist, Lyons Point
Thibodeaux, John, (Retired)
Thomas, Joseph, St. Jules, Franklin
Trahan, Joseph, Sacred Heart, Broussard
Tran, Hieu Van, Vietnamese Ministry, Lafayette
Tran, Tam, St. Mary Magdalen, Abbeville
Trumps, Jeffrey Paul, Diocesan Finance Officer; Sacred Heart, Broussard
Vaughn, David Lee, St. Anne, Cow Island
Waguespack, Eugene, (Retired)
Wilson, James, St. Peter, New Iberia
Winn, Byrne James, Our Lady of the Sacred Heart, Church Point
Yenik, Michael Robert, Immaculate Conception, Washington

INSTITUTIONS LOCATED IN THE DIOCESE

[A] SEMINARIES, RELIGIOUS OR SCHOLASTICATES

GRAND COTEAU. *St. Charles College*, P.O. Box C, 70541-1003. Tel: 337-662-5251; Fax: 337-662-3187. Revs. Mark E. Thibodeaux, S.J., Novice Dir.; Daniel White, S.J., Asst. Novice Dir. Novitiate of Missouri and New Orleans Provinces of the Society of Jesus. Priests 2; Novices 14.

[B] HIGH SCHOOLS, INTERPAROCHIAL

LAFAYETTE. *Teurlings Catholic High* (1955) 139 Teurlings Dr., 70501. Tel: 337-235-5711; Fax: 337-234-8057. Email: mboyer@tchs.net. Web: www.tchs.net. Mr. Michael H. Boyer, Prin.; Mrs. Toni Dueitt, Librarian. Lay Teachers 52; Students 682.

St. Thomas More, 450 E. Farrel Rd., 70508. Tel: 337-988-3700; Fax: 337-988-2911. Web: www.stmcougars.com. Mr. Ray Simon, Prin. Lay Teachers 86; Students 1,048.

CROWLEY. *Notre Dame High School of Acadia Parish*, 910 N. Eastern Ave., 70526. Tel: 337-783-3519; Fax: 337-788-2115. Email: cistre@ndpios.com. Web: www.ndpios.com. Ms. Cindy M. Istre, Prin.; Donna R. Fruge, Librarian. Lay Teachers 36; Students 433.

NEW IBERIA. *Catholic High School*, (Grades 4-12), 1301 DeLaSalle Dr., 70560. Tel: 337-364-5116; Fax: 337-364-5041. Email: tuhl@chspanthers.com. Web: chspanthers.com. Dr. Tim Uhl, Prin.; Roberta Landry, Librarian. Lay Teachers 56; Total Staff 69; Students 859.

OPELOUSAS. *Opelousas Catholic School* (1971) (Grades PreK-12), Elementary: (PreK-5); High School: (6-12), 428 E. Prudhomme St., 70570. Tel: 337-942-5404; Fax: 337-942-5922. Email: ocsvikings@yahoo.com. Mr. Perry Fontenot, Prin.; Leslie Carlos, Librarian. Lay Teachers 50; Students 715.

[C] ELEMENTARY SCHOOLS, INTERPAROCHIAL

LAFAYETTE. *Holy Family School* (1903) (Grades PreK-6), 200 St. John St., 70501. Tel: 337-235-0267; Fax: 337-235-0558. Email: hfs98@aol.com. Roger Griffin, Prin.; Dorothy Navarre, Librarian. Sisters of the Holy Family. Sisters 1; Lay Teachers 14; Students 224.

ST. MARTINVILLE. *Trinity Catholic School* (1971) (Grades PreK-8), 242 Gary St., 70582. Tel: 337-394-6693; Fax: 337-394-3394. Email: rpierre@trinitycatholicschoolla.org. Miss Rosemary Pierre, Prin.; Karen Olivier, Librarian. Lay Teachers 19; Total Staff 28; Students 283.

[D] ELEMENTARY SCHOOLS, PRIVATE

ABBEVILLE. *Mt. Carmel Elementary School* (1885) (Grades K-8), 405 Park, 70510. Tel: 337-898-0859; Fax: 337-893-5968. Email: srjanet@mceschool.com. Web: www.mceschool.org. Sr. Janet LeBlanc, O.Carm., Prin.; Tiffany Abshire, Librarian. Sisters of Mt. Carmel 2; Lay Teachers 24; Students 453.

[E] HIGH AND ELEMENTARY SCHOOLS, PRIVATE

GRAND COTEAU. *Academy of the Sacred Heart*, (Grades PreK-12), P.O. Box 310, 70541. Tel: 337-662-5275; Fax: 337-662-3011. Email: llieux@sshcoteau.org. Web: www.sshcoteau.org. Sisters Lynne Lieux, R.S.C.J., Head Mistress; Maureen Little, R.S.C.J., Prin. (Elementary); Sheila Kurtz, Prin. (High School); Mae Ludeau, Librarian. Day School for girls. Boarding facilities for girls 7th-12th grade. Religious of the Sacred Heart 2; Lay Teachers 47; Students 390.

[F] GENERAL HOSPITALS

LAFAYETTE. *Our Lady of Lourdes Regional Medical Center, Inc.* (1949) 611 St. Landry St., P.O. Box 4027, 70502. Tel: 337-289-2100; Fax: 337-289-2574. Email: padgettd@lourdesrmc.com. Web: www.lourdes.net. Henry C. Perret Jr., Chm. of the Governing Bd.; Mr. W.F. "Bud" Barrow, Pres. & CEO. Bed Capacity 263; Total Staff 1,285; Patients Assisted Annually 107,667.

[G] HOMES FOR THE AGED INFIRM

LAFAYETTE. *Bethany M.H.S. Health Care Center* (1962) P.O. Box 2308, 70502. Tel: 337-234-2459; Fax: 337-234-9483. Sisters of the Most Holy Sacrament 5; Total Staff 55; Bed Capacity 42; Total Assisted 49.

Village du Lac, Inc., 1404 Carmel Ave., 70501. Tel: 337-234-5106; Fax: 337-234-2630. J. Bernel Fontenot, Dir. Community housing for the handicapped and elderly with low income. Sponsored by the Diocese. Residents 200.

NEW IBERIA. *Consolata Home* (1960) 2319 E. Main St., 70560. Tel: 337-365-8226; Fax: 337-365-8626. Email: chasdel@cox-internet.com. Mr. David Landry, Admin.; Rev. Joseph Stemmann, Chap. (Retired). Tel: 337-365-7477. Clergy Apartments 6; Residents 98; Bed Capacity 120; Total Staff 108.

OPELOUSAS. *C'est La Vie Center of the Sisters Marianites of Holy Cross*, 960 E. Prudhomme St., 70570. Tel: 337-942-8154; Fax: 337-942-8279. Email: promptsuccor@bellsouth.net. Web: www.promptsuccor.com. Harriet Fisher, Coord.; Michael Purser, Admin. Independent living for the elderly and handicapped. Sisters 2; Total Staff 6; Bed Capacity 34; Patients Assisted Annually 50.

Our Lady of Prompt Succor Home, 954 E. Prudhomme St., 70570. Tel: 337-948-3634; Fax: 337-942-8279. Email: mike@promptsuccor.com. Web: www.promptsuccor.com. Michael Purser, Admin. Sisters 30; Patients Assisted Annually 200; Bed Capacity 120; Total Staff 125.

[H] MONASTERIES AND RESIDENCES PRIESTS AND BROTHERS

LAFAYETTE. *De La Salle Christian Brothers*, 1522 Carmel Dr., 70501. Tel: 337-235-3576; Fax: 337-261-0765. Email: arthurcsf@aol.com. Bro. Arthur Carroll, F.S.C.; Rev. Luis C. Dutra, Chap. (Retired). Retired Brothers Home. Brothers 13.

De La Salle Christian Brothers Provincialate, 1522 Carmel Dr., 70501. Tel: 337-234-1973; Fax: 337-261-1014. Email: coldwellnosf@cox.net. Bros. Timothy Coldwell, F.S.C., Prov.; Arthur Carroll, F.S.C., Local Supr.; David Sinitiere, F.S.C., Auxiliary Prov. & Ed. Dir.; Clarence Fioke, F.S.C., Prov. Bookkeeper & Fin. Dir.

Brothers of the Christian Schools of Lafayette LA,

Inc., Headquarters for the New Orleans-Santa Fe District.

OPELOUSAS. *Mother of the Redeemer Monastery* (1990) 168 Monastery Ln., 70570. Tel: 337-543-2237; Fax: 337-543-7752. Revs. James Liprie, O.S.B., Supr.; Bernard V. Lebiedz, O.S.B.; Jeremy O'Neill, O.S.B.; Bros. Mark Bordelon; Lawrence Kirn, O.S.B.; Deacon Joseph Brasseaux, O.S.B.; Thomas Reilly, Postulant. Priests 3; Brothers 3; Deacons 1.

[I] CONVENTS AND RESIDENCES FOR SISTERS

LAFAYETTE. *Discalced Carmelites* Monastery of Mary, Mother of Grace., 1250 Carmel Dr., 70501-5299. Tel: 337-232-4651; Fax: 337-232-3540. Sr. Regina Mullins, O.C.D., Prioress; Very Rev. Msgr. H. Alexandre Larroque, J.C.D., V.G., Chap. Cloistered Nuns 14; Extern Sisters 2.

Franciscan Missionaries of Our Lady, 611 St. Landry St., 70506. Tel: 337-289-2110; Fax: 337-289-2574.

Marianites of Holy Cross, 1417 St. John St., 70506. Tel: 337-234-5454. Email: judithmsc@cs.com. Sisters 3.

Missionaries of Charity, 904 Jack St., 70501. Tel: 337-233-3929. Sisters 4.

School Sisters of Notre Dame, 105 Dogwood, 70501. Tel: 337-504-4360. Email: landrylor@cox.net.

Sisters of Divine Providence (1866) 317 Guilbeau Rd., Apt. 101-E, 70506. Tel: 337-984-8520. Email: mildredleonards@peoplepc.com. Sisters 2.

Sisters of Mt. Carmel (1846) 309 Evangeline Dr., 70501. Tel: 337-235-8687. Sisters 4.

Sisters of the Most Holy Sacrament (1872) *Convent, Generalate & Administrative Offices*, 313 Corona Dr., P.O. Box 90037, 70509-0037. Tel: 337-981-8475; Fax: 337-981-9128. Sr. Judine Theriot, M.H.S., Major Supr. Sisters 28.

CROWLEY. *Marianites of the Holy Cross*, 516 N. Ave. E, 70526. Tel: 337-783-1550; Fax: 337-783-1550. Marianites of Holy Cross 2.

DUSON. *Eucharistic Missionaries of St. Dominic*, P.O. Box 725, 70529. Tel: 337-873-4159; Fax: 337-873-4159. Sisters 11.

GRAND COTEAU. *Religious of the Sacred Heart*, P.O. Box 438, 70541. Tel: 337-662-5526. Email: tdowney@rscj.org. Web: www.rscj.org. Sisters 12.

Sisters of the Holy Spirit, P.O. Box 115, Lebeau, 71345. Tel: 337-623-5540.

NEW IBERIA. *Sisters of Providence*, 213 Oak Hill Rd., 70563. Tel: 337-364-3142.

Sisters of the Blessed Sacrament, 720 Providence St., 70560. Tel: 337-369-9534; Fax: 337-369-9534. Email: stedwards@cox-internet.com. Sisters also reside in Rayne 5.

OPELOUSAS. *Sisters of the Holy Family*, 317 Congress, 70570. Tel: 337-942-2052; Fax: 337-942-2052. Email: sr.antonia@charter.net. Sisters 4.

[J] RETREAT HOUSES

GRAND COTEAU. *Jesuit Spirituality Center (St. Charles College)*, P.O. Box C, 70541-1003. Tel: 337-662-5251; Fax: 337-662-3187. Email: office@jesuitspiritualitycenter.org. Web: jesuitspiritualitycenter.org. Revs. Thomas J. Madden, S.J.; Hernando J. Ramirez, S.J.; Anthony H. Ostini, S.J., Supr. of St. Charles & Dir.; Sr. Consuelo Champagne, M.S.C.; Rev. Carlos de la Cruz, S.J.; Sr. Marlene Labbe, M.S.C.; Bro. A. Joseph Martin, S.J. Year-round directed retreats of 3, 5, 8, or 30 days plus a variety of weekend retreats and/or programs open to men and women. Priests 4; Brothers 1; Sisters 2.

Our Lady of the Oaks Retreat House, P.O. Box D, 70541. Tel: 337-662-5410; Fax: 337-662-5331. Email: olorhgcla@centurytel.net. Web: www.ourladyoftheoaks.com. Deacon Robert Furlow, Dir.; Rev. Jerome H. Neyrey, S.J. Jesuit Fathers., Preached retreats for men, women and married couples.

[K] CURSILLO CENTERS

OPELOUSAS. *Cursillo Center*, 3651 Hwy. 104 (Prairie Ronde), 70570. Tel: 337-543-7425; Fax: 337-543-2100. Email: rctomlinson@bellsouth.com. Web: www.whowillsit.com. Rev. Theodore Broussard Jr., Dir.

[L] NEWMAN CENTERS

LAFAYETTE. *Our Lady of Wisdom Catholic Student Center Univ. of Louisiana*, P.O. Box 43271, 70504. Tel: 337-232-8741; 337-232-8742; Fax: 337-236-6737. Email: wisdom@ourladyofwisdom.org. Web: ourladyofwisdom.org. Revs. Chester Arceneaux; Jason Vidrine.

EUNICE. *Catholic Student Center-Louisiana State Univ.* P.O. Box 1129, 70535. Tel: 337-457-8668; 337-580-1129; Fax: 337-457-7298. Email: yogisittig@dialdat.com. Deborah "Yogi" Sittig, Dir. Total Staff 1; Total in Residence 1.

[M] MISCELLANEOUS

LAFAYETTE. *Magnolia Lafayette, Inc.*, 1522 Carmel Dr., 70501. Tel: 504-899-4567. Bro. Timothy Caldwell.

St. Augustine Trust Fund, P.O. Box 90037, 70509-0037. Tel: 337-981-8475; Fax: 337-981-9128. Sisters of the Most Holy Sacrament.

Brothers of the Christian Schools of Lafayette - Retirement Trust (1988) 1522 Carmel Dr., 70501. Tel: 337-234-1973; Fax: 337-261-1014. Email: coldwellnosf@cox.net; bacomb@joneswalker.com.

Come Lord Jesus! Inc. (1974) 1804 W. University Ave., 70506. Tel: 337-233-6277; Fax: 337-233-6144. Email: comelord@BellSouth.net. Web: www.comelordjesus.com. Rev. Conley Bertrand, Dir. Priests 3; Total Staff 4.

Community of Jesus Crucified, 421 1/2 Carmel Dr., 70501. Tel: 337-232-7491; Fax: 337-261-5294. Email: cjc_ols@att.net. Revs. Jerome V. Frey, Spiritual Dir. (Retired); Michael Champagne.

St. La Salle Auxiliary (1921) 1522 Carmel Dr., 70501. Tel: 337-234-1973; Fax: 337-261-1014. Email: coldwellnosf@cox.net. The St. LaSalle Auxiliary is a development project of "De La Salle Christian Brothers," a nonprofit organization.

Lourdes Foundation, Inc., 611 St. Landry St., 70506. Tel: 337-289-4024; Fax: 337-289-2278. Web: www.lourdes.net. Jeigh O. Stipe, Exec. Dir.; James Prince, Chm. & Pres. of Governing Board.

Sisters of the Eucharistic Covenant, 105 Upperline Ave., 70501. Tel: 337-233-2226; Fax: 337-233-2226. Sr. Celeste D. Larroque, S.E.C., Pres.

NEW IBERIA. *Progressive Education Program, Inc.* (1976) P.O. Box 10237, 70562-0237. Tel: 337-365-0933; Fax: 337-364-2555. Email: pepi1990@att.net. Sr. Barbara Kraus, S.S.N.D., Dir.

[N] CATHOLIC SOCIAL SERVICE CENTERS

LAFAYETTE. *Lafayette Catholic Service Centers, Inc.* (1973) 405 St. John St., P.O. Box 3177, 70502-3177. Tel: 337-235-4972; Fax: 337-234-0953. Web: www.catholicservice.org. Total Assisted Annually 89,976.

Service Centers: Kimberly James Boudreaux, Exec. Dir.

Bishop O'Donnell Transitional Housing Tel: 337-233-7788; Fax: 337-234-0953. Web: www.catholicservice.org. Cynthia Herring, Dir.

Msgr. A. O. Sigur Service Center, 401 St. John St., 70501. Tel: 337-233-7788; Fax: 337-234-0953. Web: www.catholicservice.org. Rita Landry, Dir.

St. Joseph Shelter for Men, 425 St. John St., 70501. Tel: 337-233-6816; Fax: 337-233-6829. Web: www.catholicservice.org. Eric Gammons, Dir.

St. Joseph Diner, 403 W. Simcoe, 70501. Tel: 337-232-8434; Fax: 337-233-8475. Web: www.catholicservice.org. Carlene Seamon, Dir.

St. Bernadette Clinic Tel: 337-264-6292.

New Life Center, 411 E. Landry, Opelousas, 70570. Tel: 337-948-3161; Fax: 337-948-0011. Web: www.catholicservice.org. Angella Angelle, Dir. Total Assisted Annually 333.

St. Michael Center for Veterans, 425 St. John St., 70501. Tel: 337-233-6816; Fax: 337-233-6829. Web: www.catholicservice.org. Daniel Foster, Dir.

CROWLEY. *Crowley Christian Care Center* (1987) 726 W. 7th St., P.O. Box 686, 70527-0686. Tel: 337-783-5811; Fax: 337-783-5811. Total Staff 50; Total Assisted 4,800.

NEW IBERIA. *Social Service Center* (1975) 432 Bank Ave., 70560. Tel: 337-369-6384; Fax: 337-369-7522. Shirley DeClouet, Dir. Total Staff 30; Total Families Assisted 5,000.

OPELOUSAS. *New Life Center*, 411 E. Landry St., P.O. Box 3177, 70502. Tel: 337-948-3161; Fax: 337-948-0011. Web: www.catholicservice.org. Angella Angelle, Dir. Emergency Shelter Transitional Housing and Child Care Center for women & children operated under the direction of the Lafayette Catholic Services Centers, Inc. Staff 18; Total Assisted 383.

VILLE PLATTE. *Christian Care and Share Center* (1985) 129 W. Main St., P.O. Box 901, 70586. Tel: 337-363-8041. Mr. Eugene S. Fontenot, Chm. Total Staff 12.

RELIGIOUS INSTITUTES OF MEN REPRESENTED IN THE DIOCESE

For further details refer to the corresponding bracketed number in the Religious Institutes of Men or Women section.

[0200]—*Benedictines (Olivetan, Subiaco Congregation)*—O.S.B.

[0330]—*Brothers of the Christian Schools* (New Orleans Prov.)—F.S.C.

[]—*Carmelites of Mary Immaculate*—C.M.I.

[]—*Claretians*—C.M.F.

[]—*Congregation of St. Theresa of the Child Jesus*—C.S.T.

[0520]—*Franciscan Friars*—O.F.M.

[]—*Holy Ghost Fathers*—C.S.Sp.

[0690]—*Jesuit Fathers and Brothers* (New Orleans Prov.)—S.J.

[]—*Missionaries of St. Paul* (Nigeria)—M.S.P.

[0610]—*Priests of the Congregation of Holy Cross*—C.S.C.

[]—*Society of the Divine Savior*—S.D.S.

[0420]—*Society of the Divine Word*—S.V.D.

[0700]—*St. Joseph's Society of the Sacred Heart* (Baltimore Prov.)—S.S.J.

[]—*Vincentians*—C.M.

RELIGIOUS INSTITUTES OF WOMEN REPRESENTED IN THE DIOCESE

[0400]—*Congregation of Our Lady of Mount Carmel*—O.Carm.

[2410]—*Congregation of the Marianites of Holy Cross*—M.S.C.

[3832]—*Congregation of the Sisters of St. Joseph*—C.S.J.

[1950]—*Congregation of the Sisters of the Holy Family*—S.S.F.

[0420]—*Discalced Carmelite Nuns*—O.C.D.

[]—*Dominican Rural Missionaries*—O.P.

[1115]—*Dominican Sisters of Peace*—O.P.

[1380]—*Franciscan Missionaries of Our Lady*—O.S.F.

[2710]—*Missionaries of Charity* (Bronx, NY)—M.C.

[]—*Pontifical Secular Institute Oblate Missionaries of Mary Immaculate*

[4070]—*Religious of the Sacred Heart*—R.S.C.J.

[2970]—*School Sisters of Notre Dame* (South Central)—S.S.N.D.

[0990]—*Sisters of Divine Providence* (San Antonio, TX)—C.D.P.

[]—*Sisters of Our Lady of Sorrows*—O.L.S.

[]—*Sisters of Providence*—S.P.

[2050]—*Sisters of the Holy Spirit and Mary Immaculate*—S.H.Sp.

[2940]—*Sisters of the Most Holy Sacrament*—M.H.S.

NECROLOGY

(No Deaths)

An asterisk (*) denotes an organization that has established tax-exempt status directly with the IRS and is not covered by the USCCB Group Ruling.

Diocese of Lafayette in Indiana

(Dioecesis Lafayettensis in Indiana)

Most Reverend

WILLIAM L. HIGI, D.D.

Bishop of Lafayette in Indiana; ordained May 30, 1959; appointed Bishop of Lafayette in Indiana April 7, 1984; consecrated and installed June 6, 1984. *Res.: 610 Lingle Ave., P.O. Box 260, Lafayette, IN 47902-0260.*

PRAISED BE JESUS CHRIST

Office of Bishop and Chancery: P.O. Box 260, Lafayette, IN 47902-0260. Tel: 765-742-0275; Fax: 765-742-7513.

Web: www.dioceseoflafayette.org

CANONICALLY ERECTED OCTOBER 21, 1944.

Square Miles 9,832.

Comprises the Counties of Benton, Blackford, Boone, Carroll, Cass, Clinton, Delaware, Fountain, Fulton, Grant, Hamilton, Howard, Jasper, Jay, Madison, Miami, Montgomery, Newton, Pulaski, Randolph, Tippecanoe, Tipton, Warren and White in the State of Indiana.

For legal titles of parishes and diocesan institutions, consult the Bishop's Office (Chancery).

STATISTICAL OVERVIEW

Personnel	
Bishop	1
Priests: Diocesan Active in Diocese	64
Priests: Diocesan Active Outside Diocese	28
Priests: Retired, Sick or Absent	29
Number of Diocesan Priests	121
Religious Priests in Diocese	14
Total Priests in Diocese	135
Extern Priests in Diocese	6
Ordinations:	
Diocesan Priests	1
Transitional Deacons	4
Permanent Deacons in Diocese	18
Total Brothers	3
Total Sisters	67
Parishes	
Parishes	63
With Resident Pastor:	
Resident Diocesan Priests	45
Resident Religious Priests	6
Without Resident Pastor:	
Administered by Priests	12
Professional Ministry Personnel:	
Brothers	3
Sisters	18
Lay Ministers	90
Welfare	
Catholic Hospitals	9
Total Assisted	1,074,224
Homes for the Aged	1
Total Assisted	590
Educational	
Diocesan Students in Other Seminaries	30
Total Seminarians	30
Colleges and Universities	3
Total Students	6,121
High Schools, Diocesan and Parish	2
Total Students	838
Elementary Schools, Diocesan and Parish	18
Total Students	4,116
Catechesis/Religious Education:	
High School Students	3,103
Elementary Students	9,637
Total Students under Catholic Instruction	23,845
Teachers in the Diocese:	
Priests	1
Brothers	3
Sisters	8
Lay Teachers	392
Vital Statistics	
Receptions into the Church:	
Infant Baptism Totals	1,860
Minor Baptism Totals	148
Adult Baptism Totals	191
Received into Full Communion	359
First Communions	2,291
Confirmations	1,639
Marriages:	
Catholic	260
Interfaith	182
Total Marriages	442
Deaths	761
Total Catholic Population	100,691
Total Population	1,296,384

Former Bishops—Most Rev. JOHN GEORGE BENNETT, D.D., LL.D., ord. June 27, 1914; appt. First Bishop of Lafayette Nov. 11, 1944; cons. Jan. 10, 1945; died Nov. 20, 1957; His Eminence JOHN CARDINAL CARBERRY, D.D., S.T.D., J.C.D., Ph.D., ord. July 28, 1929; appt. Coadjutor with Right of Succession Aug. 22, 1956; appt. Bishop of Lafayette in Indiana Nov. 20, 1957; transferred to Diocese of Columbus, Jan. 20, 1965; transferred to the Archdiocese of St. Louis March 24, 1968; created Cardinal April 28, 1969; retired July 31, 1979; died June 17, 1998; Most Revs. RAYMOND J. GALLAGHER, D.D., ord. March 25, 1939; appt. Bishop of Lafayette in Indiana June 23, 1965; cons. Aug. 11, 1965; installed Aug. 23, 1965; resigned Oct. 26, 1982; retired April 13, 1983; died March 7, 1991; GEORGE A. FULCHER, S.T.D., D.D., ord. Feb. 28, 1948; appt. Auxiliary Bishop of Columbus, OH and Titular Bishop of Morosbido May 24, 1976; cons. July 18, 1976; appt. Bishop of Lafayette in Indiana Feb. 8, 1983; installed April 14, 1983; died Jan. 25, 1984.

Vicar General—Rev. Msgr. ROBERT L. SELL III, J.C.L., V.G.

Chancellor and Moderator of the Curia—Rev. Msgr. ROBERT L. SELL III, J.C.L., V.G.

Office of Bishop and Chancery—Mailing Address: P.O. Box 260, Lafayette, 47902-0260. Tel: 765-742-0275; Fax: 765-742-7513.

Deans—Revs. DANIEL B. GARTLAND, V.F., Lafayette Deanery; ROBERT L. WILLIAMS, V.F., Anderson Deanery; DONALD L. GROSS, V.F., Fowler Deanery; THEODORE D. ROTHROCK, V.F., Carmel Deanery; FRANCIS I. KILCLINE III, V.F., Logansport Deanery; ROBERT E. MORAN, V.F., Muncie Deanery.

Diocesan Consultors—Rev. Msgr. ROBERT L. SELL III, J.C.L., V.G.; Revs. DANIEL B. GARTLAND, V.F.; THEODORE D. ROTHROCK, V.F.; PAUL W. COCHRAN; DONALD L. GROSS, V.F.; FRANCIS I. KILCLINE III, V.F.; ROBERT L. WILLIAMS, V.F.

Diocesan Pastoral Office for Administration—Mr. ROBERT H. QUINN, Finance Officer; EILEEN HATKE, Financial Svcs. Mgr.; MARILYN DEHNE, Accounts Coord.; KATHY ASKINS, Admin. Asst.; KENT MIKESELL, Maintenance; ANDREW A. GULJAS, Facilities Mgmt. Coord., Mailing Address: P.O. Box 260, Lafayette, 47902-0260. Tel: 765-742-4852. Email: aguljas@dioceseoflafayette.org. Conducts the financial affairs of the diocese; oversees employee benefit program.

Diocesan Pastoral Office for Planning and Communication—KEVIN CULLEN, Dir., Mailing Address: P.O. Box 1603, Lafayette, 47902-1603. Tel: 765-742-2050. Shipping Address: 610 Lingle Ave., Lafayette, 47901-1740.

Publisher- "The Catholic Moment"—KEVIN CULLEN, Editor; LAURIE CULLEN, Asst. Editor; CAROLINE MOONEY, Contributing Editor; CAROLYN MCKINNEY, Advertising/Circulation, Coordinates pastoral planning; serves the communications needs of the diocese primarily through "The Catholic Moment"; maintains the diocesan web page on the world wide web.

Pastoral Office for Family Life—Catholic Pastoral Center, 2300 S. Ninth St., Lafayette, 47909-2400. Tel: 765-474-6644; Fax: 765-474-3403. VACANT, Dir.

Associates for Hispanic Ministry—Deacons DOMINGO CASTILLO; JOSE MUNOZ. Tel: 888-544-1684.

Administrative Assistant—CHARLENE KUHN, Promotes the dignity of the family and all human life through promotion and coordination of programs dealing with family life, marriage preparation and pro-life activities.

Pastoral Office for Worship & RCIA—Catholic Pastoral Center, 2300 S. Ninth St., Lafayette, 47909-2400. Tel: 765-474-6644; Fax: 765-474-3403. JULIE MALES, Dir.; JUDY HANSELL, Receptionist, Provides direction, consultation and staff development opportunities for pastors, principals, directors of religious education, teachers and catechists of the schools and parishes.

Associate Director for Music—ROSE HALLBERG.

Associate Director for Liturgical Resources—ANNE HATTON.

Pastoral Office for Adult Catechesis—Dr. ANNE D. ROAT, Dir.; PAUL SHIREMAN, Assoc. Dir.; LINDA HARMON, Admin. Asst., Provides formational opportunities for adults; prepares men and women for lay ministry in the diocese and the catholic church through human, spiritual, pastoral and intellectual formation.

Adult Formation Associate Director—EVELYN BURTON, Assoc. Dir. Faith Formation; TRICIA MULLER, Administrative Asst.; ERIC LECHER, Assoc. Dir. Youth & Young Adult Formation.

Pastoral Office for Stewardship and Development—ROBERT MCCREARY, Dir. Planned Giving; KATHY WALDREP, Assoc. Dir., Oversees the Biennial Fruitful Harvest Appeal; organizes and presents estate planning programs, the Annual Seminary Fund Appeal and Diocesan Capital Campaigns.

Pastoral Office for Education and Youth Catechesis—Dr. MARIE WILLIAMS, Supt.; MARY BANTA, Assoc. for Educ.; LOUISE SMITH, Admin. Asst.

Diocesan Tribunal—Catholic Pastoral Center, 2300 S. Ninth St., Lafayette, 47909-2400. Tel: 765-474-0506.

Officialis—Rev. DAVID L. RASNER, J.C.L.

Vice Officialis—Rev. TIMOTHY M. ALKIRE, J.C.L.

First Instance—

Presiding Judges—Revs. DAVID L. RASNER, J.C.L.; TIMOTHY M. ALKIRE, J.C.L.

Associate Judges—Revs. PETER J. VANDERKOLK; SAMUEL KALU, J.C.L.
Defenders of the Bond—Revs. DONALD L. GROSS, V.F.; DAVID J. BUCKLES, J.C.L.; WILLIAM R. VATH, Appelate Court.
Ecclesiastical Notary—VERNA S. MEEK.
Full-Time Advocates—BRIDGET O'BRIEN; LOU CUFFING.
Periti—VERONICA GIBBS, M.S.
Second Instance—
Presiding Judge—Rev. DAVID J. BUCKLES, J.C.L.
Associate Judges—Rev. Msgrs. JOHN C. DUNCAN; FRED E. POTTHOFF (Retired); Very Rev. GERALD J. BORAWSKI; Revs. MELVIN J. BENNETT; JAMES R. GOODRUM (Retired); PAUL W. COCHRAN; EDWARD F. DHONDT (Retired); THOMAS J. ZIMMER (Retired); DAVID J. NEWTON.
Defender of the Bond—Rev. WILLIAM R. VATH.
Ecclesiastical Notary—VERNA S. MEEK.
Advocates— See the Archdiocese of Indianapolis.
Lay Advocates— See the Archdiocese of Indianapolis.
Periti— See the Archdiocese of Indianapolis.
Administrative Causes—Rev. Msgr. ROBERT L. SELL III, J.C.L., V.G.

Diocesan Offices and Directors

Archivist—VACANT.
Building Commission—NORBERT STRANSKY, Chm.; Rev. THEODORE D. ROTHROCK, V.F.; Rev. Msgr. ROBERT L. SELL III, J.C.L., V.G., Ex Officio; ANDREW A. GULJAS, Ex Officio; MICHAEL GIBSON; EUGENE HATKE; STEPHAN GOFFINET; Dr. DOUGLAS SUTTON; WILL WRIGHT; DANIEL MADER; DENNIS G. PAGE; ANDRE MAUE.
Office of the Permanent Diaconate—Rev. THEODORE C. DUDZINSKI, Episcopal Vicar. Associate Directors: Deacons STEPHEN MILLER, Dir. Formation; JOHN JEZIERSKI, Assoc. Dir. Formation; MIKE GRAY, Assoc. Dir. Personnel; Dr. ANNE D. ROAT, Coord. Academics; Deacon WILLIAM REID, Coord. Pastoral Field Educ. & Vocation Recruitment; Rev. DALE W. EHRMAN, Spiritual Formation; SUZANNE KEARNEY, Administrative Asst., Mailing Address: 3155 S. County Rd., 200 W., Kokomo, 46902-9611. Tel: 765-865-6688; Fax: 765-865-6683.
Office of the Ecclesial Lay Ministry Program—Dr. ANNE D. ROAT, Dir.; PAUL SHIREMAN, Assoc.; LINDA HARMON, Administrative Asst., Mailing Address: 2300 S. 9th St., Lafayette, 47909-2400. Tel: 765-474-6644; 888-544-1684; Fax: 765-474-3403.
Finance Officer—Mr. ROBERT H. QUINN, Mailing Address: P.O. Box 260, Lafayette, 47902-0260. Tel: 765-742-4852.
Administration— Refer to Diocesan Pastoral Office.
Corporation— Roman Catholic Diocese of Lafayette in Indiana, Inc. (Incorporated, March 21, 1958). Most Rev. WILLIAM LEO HIGI, D.D., Pres. & Treas.; Rev. Msgr. ROBERT L. SELL III, J.C.L., V.G., Vice Pres. & Sec.; Mr. ROBERT H. QUINN, Asst. Sec. & Treas.
Director of Planned Giving—ROBERT MCCREARY, Mailing Address: Bishop's Office, P.O. Box 1687, Lafayette, 47902-1687. Tel: 765-742-7000; Fax: 765-742-7513.
Fruitful Harvest Office—Mailing Address: P.O. Box 1687, Lafayette, 47902. Tel: 765-742-4852.
Finance Council—Most Rev. WILLIAM LEO HIGI, D.D.; Rev. Msgr. ROBERT L. SELL III, J.C.L., V.G.; Mr. ROBERT H. QUINN, Dir. Pastoral Office for Admin.; LEON CYR; LEO DIERCKMAN; LYNN LAYDEN; MARIANNE MCLEAN; LEE SNIDER; DON GOETZ; EDWARD LOPKE; MARY PIANTEK; TOM PARENT, Legal Advisor.
Human Resources Department—HELEN BENDER, Dir.; CAROL MALLETT, Administrative Asst., Mailing Address: P.O. Box 260, Lafayette, 47902-0260. Tel: 765-742-4852.
Legal Council—JOHN C. DUFFEY, Mailing Address: Life Building, P.O. Box 1010, Lafayette, 47902. Tel: 765-423-1561; Fax: 765-742-8175.
Presbyteral Council—Revs. PAUL W. COCHRAN, Chm.; ROBERT L. WILLIAMS, V.F., Vice Chm.
Members—Rev. Msgr. ROBERT L. SELL III, J.C.L., V.G.; Revs. BRIAN A. DUDZINSKI; THEODORE D. ROTHROCK, V.F.; MICHAEL MCKINNEY; DANIEL C. DAVIS, O.P.; DANIEL B. GARTLAND, V.F.; DONALD L. GROSS, V.F.; ROBERT E. MORAN, V.F.; ROBERT J. BERNOTAS; PAUL W. COCHRAN; DAVID A. HOYING, C.PP.S.
Catholic Relief Services—VACANT.
Censor Librorum—Rev. DAVID L. RASNER, J.C.L., Catholic Pastoral Center, 2300 S. Ninth St., Lafayette, 47909-2400. Tel: 765-474-0506.
Aquinas Educational Foundation, Inc.—Rev. DANIEL C. DAVIS, O.P., Res. Agent, 535 State St., West Lafayette, 47906. Tel: 765-743-4653.
Catholic Charities Central Office— Refer to Diocesan Pastoral Office.
Superintendent for Catholic Schools—Dr. MARIE WILLIAMS, The Catholic Pastoral Center, 2300 S. Ninth St., Lafayette, 47909-2400. Tel: 765-474-6644.
Liturgical Commission— Refer to Diocesan Pastoral Office.
Eucharistic League—The Chancery, P.O. Box 260, Lafayette, 47902.
Greater Lafayette Catholic School Board—Rev. TIMOTHY M. ALKIRE, J.C.L. Tel: 765-742-5064.
Greater Lafayette Catholic School Foundation, Inc.—WILLIAM BURNS, P.O. Box 1493, Lafayette, 47902.
Holy Childhood Association—VACANT.
Diocesan Board of Education— In process of reorganization & formation.
D.C.C.W.—VACANT.
Ministry to Priests' Program—Rev. DONALD L. GROSS, V.F., Dir., Sacred Heart Church, 107 E. Main St., Fowler, 47944-1148. Tel: 765-884-1818.
Newman Apostolate, Purdue University—Rev. DANIEL C. DAVIS, O.P., Dir., 535 State St., West Lafayette, 47906. Tel: 765-743-4652.
Newman Foundation, Ball State, Inc.—Rev. JOHN J. KEIFER, Dir., 800 Riverside Ave., Muncie, 47303. Tel: 765-288-6180.
Newspaper "The Catholic Moment"—KEVIN CULLEN, Editor; LAURIE CULLEN, Asst. Editor; CAROLINE MOONEY, Contributing Editor; CAROLYN MCKINNEY, Advertising, Editorial Office, P.O. Box 1603, Lafayette, 47902. Tel: 765-742-2050.
Office of the Apostolate to the Spanish Speaking—Deacon DOMINGO CASTILLO, Assoc. Dir., 1404 Ironwood Dr., Marion, 46952. Tel: 317-662-6078. Res.: Guadalupe Center. Tel: 765-664-3710.
Propagation of the Faith—Rev. Msgr. ROBERT L. SELL III, J.C.L., V.G., Refer to the Bishop's Office.
Religious Education Dept.— Refer to Pastoral Office for Formation.
Rural Life Program—VACANT, Dir.
Schools— See Superintendent listing.
St. Joseph Memorial Hospital Foundation, Inc.—PEGGY CALDWELL, Exec. Dir., 1907 W. Sycamore St., Kokomo, 46901. Tel: 765-456-5425.
Vicar for Clergy—VACANT.
Vicar for Hispanic Ministry in White County—Rev. CHRISTOPHER T. MILLER, 600 St. Mary's Ave., Frankfort, 46041-2735.
Vicar for Religious—VACANT.
Victim Assistance Coordinator—TIMOTHY HECK, Ph.D. Tel: 800-533-7018.
Conduct in Ministry Officer—CHARLES "MAX" LAYDEN. Tel: 765-463-2242.
Vocation Director—Rev. BRIAN M. DOERR, Dir., St. Elizabeth Ann Seton, 10655 Haverstick Rd., Carmel, 46033-3800. Tel: 317-846-3850, Ext. 149.

CLERGY, PARISHES, MISSIONS AND PAROCHIAL SCHOOLS

CITY OF LAFAYETTE

(TIPPECANOE COUNTY)

1—ST. MARY CATHEDRAL (1843) [JC] Revs. Daniel B. Gartland, Rector; Eric Christopher Underwood; Christopher R. Shocklee; Dennis Faker.
Res.: 1207 Columbia St., 47901-1522. Tel: 765-742-4440; Fax: 765-742-8933.
School—(Grades PreK-3) Tel: 765-742-6302. Lay Teachers 11; Students 164.
Catechesis/Religious Program—Tel: 765-742-8336. Students 174.

2—ST. ANN (1884) [JC] Rev. Dominic G. Young. In Res., Rev. Maurice R. Miller (Retired).
Res.: 612 Wabash Ave., 47905-1096. Tel: 765-742-7031; Fax: 765-429-5690. Email: dom.parishofstanns@insightgg.com.
Catechesis/Religious Program—Tel: 765-423-4635. Students 73.

3—ST. BONIFACE (1853), (German), [CEM] Rev. Timothy M. Alkire; Deacon Ron Nevinger. In Res., Revs. William R. Vath; Gustavo Lopez (Mexico).
Res.: 318 N. Ninth St., 47904-2597. Tel: 765-742-5063; Fax: 765-742-5018. Email: bonioffice@comcast.net. Web: www.stboniface.org.
School—Lafayette Catholic School, (Grades 4-6) Tel: 765-742-7913; Fax: 765-423-4988. Email: srlenore@lcss.org. Web: lcss.org. Sr. M. Lenore Schwartz, O.S.F., Prin. Sisters 1; Lay Teachers 5; Students 112.
Catechesis/Religious Program—Tel: 765-742-1351. Email: religioused@maxkolbe.net. Students 516.

4—ST. LAWRENCE (1895) Revs. Daniel B. Gartland; Christopher R. Shocklee; Eric Christopher Underwood; Dennis Faker; Michael Gray; John Jezierski.
Res.: 1916 Meharry St., 47904-1442. Tel: 765-742-2107; Fax: 765-742-1347.
School—1902 Meharry St., 47904-1497. Tel: 765-742-4450. Jody Williams, Prin. Lay Teachers 16; Students 272.
Catechesis/Religious Program—Tel: 765-423-2396. Carl Wagner, D.R.E. Students 372.

OUTSIDE THE CITY OF LAFAYETTE

ALEXANDRIA, MADISON CO., ST. MARY (1896) Rev. Paul W. Cochran.
Res.: 820 W. Madison St., 46001-1520. Tel: 765-724-2483; 765-724-4459; Fax: 765-724-9711.
School—Tel: 765-724-4459. Sisters 1; Lay Teachers 6; Students 81.
Catechesis/Religious Program—Students 44.

ANDERSON, MADISON CO.

1—ST. AMBROSE (1947) Rev. Robert L. Williams. In Res., Rev. Edward F. Dhondt (Retired).
Res.: 2801 Lincoln St., 46016-5067. Tel: 765-644-5956; Fax: 765-642-9439. Web: www.st.ambrosechurch.com.
School—2825 Lincoln St., 46016. Tel: 765-642-8428; Fax: 765-642-7348. Email: stan.warner@ambrosechurch.com. Lay Teachers 15; Students 140.
Catechesis/Religious Program—Students 100.

2—ST. MARY (1858) [CEM] Rev. Robert L. Williams; Andrew Lykens, Pastoral Min.
Res.: 1115 Pearl St., 46016-1789. Tel: 765-644-8467; Fax: 765-648-4000. Email: stoner@catholicweb.com. Web: www.stmary.catholicweb.com.
School—Tel: 765-642-1848; Fax: 765-642-1828. Email: stmarys.school@catholicweb.com. Web: www.smschool.catholicweb.com. Ms. Elizabeth Richards, Prin. Lay Teachers 19; Students 140.
Station—St. John Medical Center Chapel 46016. Tel: 765-649-2511.
Catechesis/Religious Program—Tel: 765-644-8467. Email: stmarys.minister@catholicweb.com. Students 150.

ATTICA, FOUNTAIN CO., ST. FRANCIS XAVIER (1863) [CEM] Rev. David L. Rasner.
Res.: 407 S. Perry St., P.O. Box 55, 47918-0001. Tel: 765-762-3330.
Catechesis/Religious Program—Students 63.

BRYANT, JAY CO., HOLY TRINITY (1861), (German), [CEM] Rev. David A. Hoying, C.PP.S.
Res.: 7321 E. SR 67, 47326-9636. Tel: 219-997-6450. Email: dahht@watchtv.net.
Catechesis/Religious Program—Tel: 219-997-6450. Students 149.

CARMEL, HAMILTON CO.

1—ST. ELIZABETH ANN SETON (1981) Revs. Theodore D. Rothrock; Brendan O. Mbagwu; Melvin J. Bennett; Brian M. Doerr; Deacon William Reid.
Res.: 10655 Haverstick Rd., 46033-3800. Tel: 317-846-3850; Fax: 317-846-3710. Email: parish@seas-carmel.org. Web: www.seas-carmel.org.
Catechesis/Religious Program—Tel: 317-816-0045. Students 731.

2—OUR LADY OF MOUNT CARMEL (1955) Rev. Richard J. Doerr; Rev. Msgr. John C. Duncan; Rev. Christopher George Roberts; Deacon William Rahill.
Office: 14598 Oak Ridge Rd., 46032-1198. Tel: 317-846-3475; Fax: 317-846-3477. Web: www.olmc1.org.
School—14596 Oak Ridge Rd., 46032-1198. Tel: 317-846-1118; Fax: 317-582-2375. Web: www.olmc-school.org. Dominican Sisters of St. Cecilia 3; Lay Teachers 40; Students 687.
Catechesis/Religious Program—Tel: 317-846-3878. Students 1,074.

CICERO, HAMILTON CO., SACRED HEART (1898), (German—Irish), Rev. W. Michael Kettron.
Res.: 429 S. Main St., 46034-9680. Tel: 317-984-5117; Fax: 317-984-5117. Web: www.sacredheartcicero.org.
Catechesis/Religious Program—Tel: 317-984-2115. Students 79.

COVINGTON, FOUNTAIN CO., ST. JOSEPH (1861) [CEM] Rev. David L. Rasner.
Res.: 308 Pearl St., 47932-1062. Tel: 765-793-3289.
Catechesis/Religious Program—Tel: 765-793-4628. Students 27.

CRAWFORDSVILLE, MONTGOMERY CO., ST. BERNARD (1859) [CEM] Rev. David E. Hellmann.
Res.: 1306 E. Main St., 47933-0719. Tel: 765-362-6121; Fax: 765-361-0796. Email: stbernardchurch@sbcglobal.net.
Catechesis/Religious Program—Tel: 765-362-6121, Ext. 17. Email: amy.huff@sbcglobal.net. Amy Huff, D.R.E. & Youth Min. Students 136.

DE MOTTE, JASPER CO., ST. CECILIA (1952) [CEM] Rev. Msgr. Robert L. Sell III.
Mailing Address: P.O. Box 700, 46310-0700.
Res.: 334 Fifteenth St., S.W., 46310-9269. Tel: 219-987-3511.
Catechesis/Religious Program—Tel: 219-987-3514. Students 156.

DELPHI, CARROLL CO., ST. JOSEPH (1859) [CEM] Rev. Peter J. Vanderkolk.

Res.: 207 N. Washington St., 46923-1297. Tel: 765-564-2407.
Catechesis/Religious Program—Tel: 765-564-3601. Students 165.

DUNKIRK, JAY CO., ST. MARY (1896) Rev. David J. Newton.
Res.: 346 S. Broad St., P.O. Box 286, 47336-0286. Tel: 765-768-6157.
Catechesis/Religious Program—Students 30.

DUNNINGTON, BENTON CO., ST. MARY (1876) [CEM] Rev. Donald L. Gross.
Mailing Address: 2961 South SR71, Ambia, 47917. Tel: 765-884-1818.
Catechesis/Religious Program—Students 30.

EARL PARK, BENTON CO., ST. JOHN THE BAPTIST (1888) [CEM] Rev. Robert J. Bernotas.
Mailing Address: P.O. Box 131, Kentland, 47951-0131.
Catechesis/Religious Program—Students 27.

ELWOOD, MADISON CO., ST. JOSEPH (1889), (Irish—German), [CEM] [JC] Rev. Paul W. Cochran.
Res.: 1306 S. A St., 46036-1941. Tel: 765-552-6753.
Catechesis/Religious Program—Tel: 765-552-6753. Elaine Bowers, D.R.E. Students 75.

FISHERS, HAMILTON CO.

1—HOLY SPIRIT CHURCH (1991) Rev. Phillip T. Bowers.
Res.: 10350 Glaser Way, 46037. Tel: 317-849-9245; Fax: 317-849-9388.
Catechesis/Religious Program—Tel: 317-849-8016. Students 2,043.

2—ST. JOHN VIANNEY PARISH (2005) Rev. Brian A. Dudzinski.
14500 E. 136th St., 46037. Tel: 317-485-0150; Fax: 317-598-9477. Web: stjohnvianney-fishers.com.
Catechesis/Religious Program—Margie Crooks, D.R.E.; Jim Stroud, D.R.E. Students 95.

3—ST. LOUIS DE MONTFORT (1978) Rev. Patrick R. Click.
Res.: 11441 Hague Rd., 46038-1876. Tel: 317-842-6778; Fax: 317-576-1932. Email: info@sldmfishers.org. Web: sldmfishers.org.
School—11421 Hague Rd., 46038. Tel: 317-842-1125; Fax: 317-842-1126. Email: ajones@sldmfishers.org. Annette Jones, Prin. Lay Teachers 30; Students 464.
Catechesis/Religious Program—Students 651.

FOWLER, BENTON CO., SACRED HEART OF JESUS (1872) [CEM] Rev. Donald L. Gross.
Res.: 107 E. Main St., 47944-1148. Tel: 765-884-1818; Fax: 765-884-1583.
School—Tel: 765-884-0710; Fax: 765-884-0710. Mrs. Terri Goodman, Prin. Lay Teachers 10; Students 95.
Catechesis/Religious Program—Students 72.
Mission—St. Mary's Church 2961 S. State Rd. 71, Ambia, 47917-8516.

FRANCESVILLE, PULASKI CO., ST. FRANCIS SOLANO (1867) Rev. Paul R. White, C.PP.S., Admin. (Retired).
St. Joseph's College: P.O. Box 852, Rensselaer, 47978. Tel: 219-866-6271.
Catechesis/Religious Program—Students 5.

FRANKFORT, CLINTON CO., ST. MARY (1875) [CEM] Rev. Christopher T. Miller.
Res.: 600 St. Mary's Ave., 46041-2735. Tel: 765-654-5796; Fax: 765-654-6589. Email: stmarysfkt@sbcglobal.net.
Preschool—Tel: 765-659-3914.
Catechesis/Religious Program—Tel: 765-654-2913. Email: stmarysjohnpaul@sbcglobal.net. Students 312.

GAS CITY, GRANT CO., HOLY FAMILY (1908) Rev. Richard J. Weisenberger.
Res.: 325 E. North A St., 46933-1431. Tel: 765-674-2605; Fax: 765-674-3875. Email: hcatholicchurch@indy.rr.com.
Catechesis/Religious Program—Students 52.

GOODLAND, NEWTON, SS. PETER AND PAUL (1880) [CEM] Rev. Robert J. Bernotas.
Church: 421 S. Newton St., 47948-8156.

HARTFORD CITY, BLACKFORD CO., ST. JOHN THE EVANGELIST (1865) Rev. David J. Newton.
Res.: 209 S. Spring St., 47348-2551. Tel: 765-348-3123; Fax: 765-348-4399.
Catechesis/Religious Program—Students 46.

KENTLAND, NEWTON, ST. JOSEPH (1864) [CEM] Rev. Robert J. Bernotas.
P.O. Box 131, 47951-1322.
St. Joseph School Foundation, Inc.—Tel: 219-474-5514.
Catechesis/Religious Program—Students 55.

KEWANNA, FULTON CO., ST. ANN (1857) [CEM] Rev. Herbert Woolson, Admin.
Mailing Address: 1310 Main St., Rochester, 46975.
Catechesis/Religious Program—Tel: 574-223-2808; Fax: 574-224-2808.

KOKOMO, HOWARD CO.

1—ST. JOAN OF ARC (1927) Revs. Theodore C. Dudzinski; Daniel Joseph Duff; Thomas Obiatuegwu (Nigeria); David Joseph Hasser.
3155 S. 200 W., 46902-9611.
School—Sts. Joan of Arc & Patrick, (Grades PreSchool-8) Jan Underwood, Librarian. (Consolidated School) Lay Teachers 25; Students 307.
Catechesis/Religious Program—Students 282.

2—ST. PATRICK (1859) [JC] Revs. Theodore C. Dudzinski; Thomas Obiatuegwu (Nigeria); Daniel Joseph Duff; David Joseph Hasser.
Office & Mailing Address: 320 W. Broadway, 46901-2898. Tel: 765-452-6021; Fax: 765-868-8384. Web: www.stpatrick-kokomo.org.
Res.: 1229 N. Washington, 46901-2898.
School—Sts. Joan of Arc & Patrick, 1230 N. Armstrong St., 46901. Tel: 765-459-4769; Fax: 765-457-3096. Web: www.stsjp.org. Lay Teachers 19; Students 178.
Catechesis/Religious Program—Students 119.

LAKE VILLAGE, NEWTON, ST. AUGUSTA (1947) [JC] Rev. Stephen Snoich, O.S.B.
Res.: 3228 W. St. Rd. 10, 46349-9706. Tel: 219-992-3220; Fax: 219-992-9332. Email: staugusta@sbcglobal.net.
Catechesis/Religious Program—Students 52.

LEBANON, BOONE CO., ST. JOSEPH (1862) [CEM] Rev. Timothy Kroeger; Norma DeLaRosa, Youth Min.
Mailing Address: P.O. Box 309, 46052-0309. Tel: 765-482-5558; Fax: 765-482-1436. Email: stjoe@stjoeleb.org. Web: www.stjoeleb.org.
Res.: 310 E. Pearl St., 46052-2684. Tel: 765-482-5558.
Catechesis/Religious Program—Email: religioused@stjoeleb.org. Caroline VanAtter, D.R.E. Students 204.

LOGANSPORT, CASS CO., ALL SAINTS (1985) [JC], Consolidation of the following three parishes (Legal Titles): St. Bridget (1875); St. Joseph (1868); and St. Vincent de Paul (1838). Revs. Michael McKinney; Jeffrey D. Martin; Deacon Juan Rodriguez.
Parish Office—112 E. Market St., 46947-3428. Tel: 574-722-4080; Fax: 574-722-5426. Web: www.allsaintslogansport.com.
School—All Saints Elementary, (Grades PreSchool-6), 121 Eel River Ave., 46947-3188. Tel: 574-753-3410; Fax: 574-753-1608. Lay Teachers 10; Students 166.
Catechesis/Religious Program—Tel: 574-722-4080; Fax: 574-722-5426. Students 294.

LUCERNE, CASS CO., ST. ELIZABETH (1953) Closed. For inquiries for parish records, please see All Saints Church, Logansport.

MARION, GRANT CO.

1—OUR LADY OF GUADALUPE, (Hispanic), Closed. For inquiries for parish records contact St. Paul, Marion.

2—ST. PAUL (1868) Rev. Richard J. Weisenberger.
Res.: 1031 W. Kem Rd., 46952-2048. Tel: 765-664-6345; Fax: 765-668-3518. Email: stpaul@stpaulcatholicmarion.com. Web: www.stpaulcatholicmarion.com.
School—1009 Kem Rd., 46952. Tel: 765-662-2883; Fax: 765-664-5953. Email: jpcertain@stpaulcatholicmarion.com. Mrs. Jackie Certain, Prin. Lay Teachers 10; Students 97.
Catechesis/Religious Program—Email: nreynolds@stpaulcatholicmarion.com. Students 170.

MEDARYVILLE, PULASKI CO., ST. HENRY (1868) [CEM] Rev. Paul R. White, C.PP.S., Admin. (Retired).
St. Joseph's College: P.O. Box 852, Rensselaer, 47978. Tel: 219-866-6271.
Catechesis/Religious Program—Students 5.

MONTEREY, PULASKI CO., ST. ANNE (1851), (German), [CEM 2] Rev. Herbert Woolson.
Mailing Address: 6894 N. Walnut St., P.O. Box 96, 46960-0096.
Res.: 2122 E. 250 N., Winamac, 46996. Tel: 574-946-3453; Fax: 574-946-3563. Email: woolson@winamac.tv. Web: www.parishesonline.com/holytrinitycluster.
Catechesis/Religious Program—Tel: 219-542-4711. Students 11.

MONTICELLO, WHITE CO., OUR LADY OF THE LAKES (1948) Very Rev. Gerald J. Borawski; Deacon Edward Cleary.
Res.: 543 S. Main St., 47960-2948. Tel: 574-583-5724; Fax: 574-583-4112.
Catechesis/Religious Program—Tel: 574-583-6790. Students 197.

MONTPELIER, BLACKFORD CO., ST. MARGARET OF SCOTLAND (1864) [CEM] Rev. David J. Newton.
Res.: 207 W. Huntington St., P.O. Box 247, 47359. Tel: 765-728-5757.

MUNCIE, DELAWARE CO.

1—ST. FRANCIS OF ASSISI (1973), (Ball State University Parish) Rev. John D. Kiefer.
Res.: 1200 W. Riverside Ave., 47303-3650. Tel: 765-288-6180; Fax: 765-288-7777. Email: admin.stfrancis@comcast.net. Web: www.stfrancisnewman.org.
Catechesis/Religious Program—Students 130.

2—ST. LAWRENCE (1869) Rev. Dennis J. Goth.
Res.: 820 E. Charles St., 47305-2699. Tel: 765-288-9223; Fax: 765-289-9262. Email: parish@stlawrence.com. Web: www.stlawrencemuncie.com.
School—2801 E. 16th St., 47302. Tel: 765-282-9353; Fax: 765-282-0457. Lay Teachers 7; Students 86.
Catechesis/Religious Program—Tel: 765-284-2673. Students 42.

3—ST. MARY (1930) Rev. Andrew J. Dudzinski; Deacon Gary Kuenz, Pastoral Assoc.; Carol Kuenz, Pastoral Assoc.; Molly Ellsworth, Business Mgr. In Res., Rev. James T. Keane.
Res.: 2300 W. Jackson St., 47303-4797. Tel: 765-288-5308; Fax: 765-288-6357. Web: www.stmarymuncie.org.
School—(Grades K-5), 2301 W. Gilbert St., 47303-4797. Tel: 765-288-5878; Fax: 765-284-3685. Lay Teachers 13; Students 148.
School—Pope John Paul II Middle School, (Grades 6-8)
Catechesis/Religious Program—Mary Burford, C.R.E. Students 133.

NOBLESVILLE, HAMILTON CO., OUR LADY OF GRACE (1944) Revs. Thomas H. Metzger; John H. Zahn; Michael J. Witka, Dir. Business & Devel.; Barb Leap, Music & Liturgy Coord.
Res.: 9900 E. 191st St., 46060-1520. Tel: 317-773-4275; Fax: 317-773-9344. Web: www.ologn.org.
School—Tel: 317-770-5660; Fax: 317-770-5663. Web: www.ologs.org. Maureen Clerkin, Prin. Lay Teachers 30; Students 365.
Catechesis/Religious Program—Tel: 317-773-0297. Stacy Costa, Youth Ministry Coord.; Jake Teitgen, Youth Ministry Coord.; Becky Hampton, C.R.E. Students 465.

OTTERBEIN, BENTON CO., ST. CHARLES (1902) [JC] Rev. Robert Klemme.
Res. & Mailing: 502 S. Michigan St., Oxford, 47971-8562. Tel: 765-385-2587; Fax: 765-385-0225. Church: 108 N. Meadow St., 47970-0661. Tel: 765-583-4641.
Catechesis/Religious Program—Students 81.

OXFORD, BENTON CO., ST. PATRICK (1867), (Irish), [CEM] [JC] Rev. Robert Klemme.
Res.: 502 S. Michigan St., 47971-8562. Tel: 765-385-2587; Fax: 765-385-0225. Email: spchurch@localline.com.
Catechesis/Religious Program—Students 67.

PERU, MIAMI CO., ST. CHARLES BORROMEO (1860) [CEM] Rev. Francis I. Kilcline III; Deacon Truman Stevens.
Church & Office: 58 W. Fifth St., 46970-2100. Tel: 765-473-5543; Fax: 765-472-2692. Web: www.stcharlesperu.org.
Catechesis/Religious Program—Tel: 765-473-5544; Fax: 765-472-2692. Students 100.

PORTLAND, JAY CO., IMMACULATE CONCEPTION (1876), (German), Rev. Robert E. Moran.
Res.: 506 E. Walnut St., 47371-1599. Tel: 260-726-7341.
Catechesis/Religious Program—Tel: 260-726-7055. Students 194.

REMINGTON, JASPER CO., SACRED HEART (1875), (German—French), [CEM] Rev. Thomas E. Fox.
Res.: 124 New York St., P.O. Box 159, 47977-0159. Tel: 219-261-2302; Fax: 219-261-2934. Email: shremin@embarqmail.com.
Catechesis/Religious Program—Tel: 219-279-2910. Students 35.

RENSSELAER, JASPER CO., ST. AUGUSTINE (1883) [CEM] Rev. Timothy Knepper, C.PP.S.
Res.: 318 N. McKinley Ave., 47978-2599. Tel: 219-866-5351; Fax: 219-866-4310. Email: stachurch@nwiis.com.
School—328 N. Mckinley Ave., 47978. Tel: 219-866-5480; Fax: 219-866-5663. Religious 1; Lay Teachers 7; Students 118.
Catechesis/Religious Program—Tel: 219-866-5351. Students 70.

REYNOLDS, WHITE CO., ST. JOSEPH (1866) [CEM] Rev. John J. Cummings, Admin.
Res.: 601 S. Kenton St., 47980-8098. Tel: 219-984-5401; Fax: 219-984-5443.
Catechesis/Religious Program—Students 50.

ROCHESTER, FULTON CO., ST. JOSEPH (1900) Rev. Herbert Woolson, Pastor & Admin.
Rectory—1310 Main St., 46975-2108. Tel: 574-223-2808; Fax: 574-224-2808. Web: www.parishesonline.com/holytrinitycluster.
Catechesis/Religious Program—Tel: 574-223-3246. Students 78.
Mission—St. Ann Kewanna, Fulton Co.

STAR CITY, PULASKI CO., ST. JOSEPH (1851) [CEM 2] Rev. Ronald J. Schiml, C.PP.S.
Res.: 5895 S. SR 119, 46985-8826. Tel: 574-595-7198.
Catechesis/Religious Program—Students 21.

TIPTON, TIPTON CO., ST. JOHN THE BAPTIST (1866) [CEM] Rev. Leroy G. Kinnaman.
Res.: 340 N. Mill St., 46072-1403. Tel: 765-675-2422. Email: baptizer@tiptontel.com. Web: www.stjohnstipton.com.
School—(Grades PreK-5), 323 Mill St., 46072. Tel: 765-675-4741; Fax: 765-675-2163. Email: principal@stjohnstipton.com. Web: www.stjohnstipton.com/school/school.htm. Lay

Teachers 7; Students 80.
Catechesis/Religious Program—Email: joericeglass@insightbb.com. Students 103.

UNION CITY, RANDOLPH CO., ST. MARY (1865), (Irish—German), [CEM] Rev. Michael J. McKinley.
Rectory—425 W. Hickory St., 47390-1301. Tel: 765-964-4202. Email: www.stmaryuc@embarqmail.com.
Catechesis/Religious Program—Tel: 937-968-3642. Ida Hall, D.R.E. Students 52.

WEST LAFAYETTE, TIPPECANOE CO.
1—BLESSED SACRAMENT (1957) Rev. David J. Buckles.
Res.: 2224 Sacramento Dr., 47906-1998. Tel: 765-463-5733; Fax: 765-497-7866. Email: info@blessedsacramentwl.org. Web: www.bscwl.org.
Catechesis/Religious Program—Students 242.
Station—Indiana Veterans' Home, Tel: 765-463-1502.

2—ST. THOMAS AQUINAS (1951), (Purdue University Parish) Revs. Daniel C. Davis, O.P.; Tom Poulsen, O.P.; Patrick Baikauskas, O.P.
Office: 535 State St., 47906-3592. Tel: 765-743-4652; Fax: 765-743-0426. Email: sttoms@sttoms-purdue.org. Web: www.sttoms-purdue.org.
Catechesis/Religious Program—Katy Argadine, D.R.E. Students 332.

WESTFIELD, HAMILTON CO., ST. MARIA GORETTI (1995) Rev. Kevin J. Haines; Deacon Steve Miller, Pastoral Assoc.; Pat Gorman, Financial Controller. In Res., Rev. Dale W. Ehrman.
Res.: 17102 Spring Mill Rd., 46074. Tel: 317-867-5694 (Rectory); Fax: 317-867-3263. Web: www.smgonline.org.
School—(Grades PreK-8), 17104 Spring Mill Rd., 46074. Tel: 317-896-5582; Fax: 317-867-0783. Rebecca Hammel, Prin. Lay Teachers 23; Students 416.
Catechesis/Religious Program—Connie Anderson, D.R.E.; Jeff Stankovsky, Youth Min. Students 853.

WHEATFIELD, JASPER CO., SORROWFUL MOTHER (1887) [CEM] Rev. Alejandro Paternoster.
Res.: 165 Grace St., P.O. Box 248, 46392-0248. Tel: 219-956-3343; Fax: 219-956-3343.
Church Hall: Tel: 219-956-4648.
Catechesis/Religious Program—Tel: 219-956-3347. Students 62.

WINAMAC, PULASKI CO., ST. PETER (1859) [CEM] Rev. Martin J. Sandhage.
Res.: 401 N. Monticello St., 46996-1327. Tel: 574-946-4906; Fax: 574-946-4962. Email: stpete4906@embarqmail.com.
Catechesis/Religious Program—424 N. Market St., 46996. Tel: 574-946-6804. Email: spreo@pwrt.com. Students 130.

WINCHESTER, RANDOLPH CO., ST. JOSEPH (1952) Rev. Michael J. McKinley.
St. Mary's Rectory: 425 W. Hickory St., Union City, 47390-1301. Tel: 765-964-4202. Email: www.stmaryuc@embarqmail.com.
Church: 514 W. Washington St., 47394.
Catechesis/Religious Program—Tel: 765-886-5614. Janice Wiwi, D.R.E. Students 27.

ZIONSVILLE, BOONE CO., ST. ALPHONSUS (1945) [JC] Revs. Dennis J. O'Keeffe; Joshua Moran Janko. In Res., Rev. Raymond A. Akeriwe.
Res.: 1870 W. Oak St., 46077-1894. Tel: 317-873-2885; Fax: 317-873-8746. Email: stalphonsuszvill@indy.rr.com.
Catechesis/Religious Program—Students 697.

Chaplains of Public Institutions

LAFAYETTE. *Indiana Veterans' Home, Queen of the Universe Chapel.* Attended from Blessed Sacrament Church, West Lafayette.

GRISSOM. *Grissom Air Force Base, St. Michael's Chapel* 46971. Tel: 765-688-2191. Rev. Philip S. Hascinger, Auxiliary Civilian Chap.

LOGANSPORT. *Logansport State Hospital*. Vacant.

MARION. *U.S. Veteran's Hospital*. Revs. James Rose (FTW), Chap. (Retired), Joseph W. Grace, Auxiliary Chap. (Retired).

PENDLETON. *Correctional Industrial Complex Ecumenical Chapel*, P.O. Box 601, 46064. Tel: 765-778-8011. Rev. Joseph Pesola.
Indiana State Reformatory, St. Christopher Chapel, P.O. Box 28, 46064. Tel: 765-778-2107. Rev. Joseph Pesola.

Special Assignment:
Rev. Msgr.—
Sell, Robert L., III, J.C.L., V.G., Vicar Gen., Chancellor & Moderator of the Curia, 1128 E. State St., 47905. Tel: 765-742-1665
Revs.—
Buckles, David J., J.C.L., Diocesan Tribunal, 2300 S. 9th St., 47905. Tel: 765-474-0506
Doerr, Brian M., Vocation Dir., 900 S. Purdum St., Kokomo, 46901-5598. Tel: 765-457-9371
Miller, Christopher T., Vicar for Hispanics, 600 St. Mary's Ave., Frankfort, 46041-2735. Tel: 765-654-5796. Email: frchris93@yahoo.com
Vath, William R., Diocesan Tribunal, 2300 S. 9th St., 47905. Tel: 765-474-0506; 317-742-4440

On Duty Outside the Diocese:
Revs.—
Clegg, Timothy, 3635 Westchester Dr., Holiday, FL 34691.
Comeau, Ronald R., 6 Johnson Rd., Aurora ON L4C 2A2 Canada. Tel: 416-772-1965
Cover, Phillip B., 1600 S. Eads St., #923-S, Arlington, VA 22202.
Gross, Barry, 1601 Georgia Ave., Wheaton, MD 20902.
Holbrook, William M. (Retired), 6210 W. Bell Plaine, Chicago, IL 60634.
Mannion, John H., B.S., M.Div., 1600 Albany St., Beechgrove, 46107. Tel: 317-787-3311 St. Francis Hospital, Pastoral Care Department
Westfall, Joseph B., P.O. Box 45715, Kansas City, MO 64171.

Military Chaplains:
Rev.—
Kinney, John M., 2520 Crested Hills, Schertz, TX 78154. Tel: 210-658-6825

Unassigned:
Revs.—
Courtney, Patrick E.
Hagan, Paul

Retired:
Rev. Msgr.—
Potthoff, Fred E., 37 Wea Oaks St., 47905-3406. Tel: 765-474-7152
Revs.—
Askar, George F., 901 Edison Blvd., Port Huron, MI 48060-2117. Tel: 810-982-0516
Bach, John A., 155 Durkee Run Dr., 47905-5561. Tel: 765-423-4861
Bates, James R., 5016 Allisonville Rd., Apt. D, Indianapolis, 46205-1536. Tel: 317-257-5569
Bruetsch, Joseph J., St. Mary Cathedral, 1212 South St., 47901-1576. Tel: 765-742-4440
Cox, Alan B., 56 Fulton Rd., Salmon, ID 83467-5099.
Dhondt, Edward F., St. Ambrose, 2801 Lincoln St., Anderson, 46016. Tel: 765-644-5956
Douglas, David M., 1700 Lindberg Rd., Apt. 1130, West Lafayette, 47906-7317.
Eder, Donald, 3056 N. State Rd. 17, Logansport, 46947-8746. Tel: 574-732-1509
Goodrum, James R., 112B Williams St., Monticello, 47960-1675. Tel: 574-583-5755
Grace, Joseph W., Bishop Gallagher Manor, 100 N. Celia Ave., Muncie, 47303-4607. Tel: 765-289-7415
Heitz, Louis S., 120 Red Oak Dr., Cridersville, OH 45806. Tel: 419-645-4157
Holbrook, William M., 5900 W. Barry Ave., Chicago, IL 60634-5728. Tel: 773-622-5900, Ext. 6
Hosey, P. Keith, St. Joseph Center, 1440 W. Division Rd., Tipton, 46072-8584. Tel: 765-675-4146
Jacob, Joseph E., 920 Sunflower Ln., Rochester, 46975-2450. Tel: 574-223-3939
Matuszak, Edward S., 400 E. Gord Rd., Erie, PA 16509-3726. Tel: 814-455-1166
McCormack, Douglas, 17973 Candlewood Ct., Noblesville, 46062-7258. Tel: 317-861-2951
Miller, Maurice R., St. Ann, 612 Wabash Ave., 47905-1096. Tel: 765-742-2604
Ondo, Michael A., 6765 State Rd., Parma, OH 44134-4581. Tel: 440-663-1296
Puetz, Richard W., St. Elizabeth Healthcare Center, 701 Armory Rd., Rm. 409, Delphi, 46923-1915. Tel: 765-564-2182
Ruffing, Joseph R., 317 E. Pinetree Blvd., Thomasville, GA 31792-6858. Tel: 229-228-7356
Schiavone, Jeldo J., 1701 Pinehurst Rd., Apt. 20E, Dunedin, FL 34698-3627.
Schultz, John C., University Place, 1750 Lindberg Rd., West Lafayette, 47906-4956. Tel: 765-463-3928
Wicklum, Paul R., 11385 N. 540 E., Roselawn, 46310-8945.
Ziegler, Ambrose M., 3118 Longlois Rd., 47904-1716. Tel: 765-447-5458
Zimmer, Thomas J., 3814 Sunray Dr., Holiday, FL 34691-3239. Tel: 813-943-5112

Permanent Deacons:
Cain, Jerry, Blessed Sacrament, West Lafayette
Castillo, Domingo, St. Paul, Marion
Cleaver, Edward, Our Lady of the Lakes, Monticello
Gallagher, Patrick, St. Joseph, Lebanon
Gray, D. Michael, St. Lawrence, Lafayette
Jezierski, John, Cathedral, Lafayette
Kuenz, Gary, St. Mary, Muncie
MacDongall, James, St. Lawrence, Muncie
Miller, Mark, Our Lady of Grace, Noblesville
Miller, Stephen, St. Maria Goretti, Westfield
Morrow, Ronald, St. Patrick, Kokomo
Munoz, Jose, St. Boniface, Lafayette
Nevinger, Ronald, St. Boniface, Lafayette
Rahill, William, Our Lady of Mount Carmel, Carmel
Reid, William, St. Elizabeth Seton, Carmel
Rodriguez, Juan, All Saints, Logansport
Stevens, Truman, St. Patrick, Kokomo
Van Schepen, Joe, St. Cecilia, DeMotte

INSTITUTIONS LOCATED IN THE DIOCESE

[A] COLLEGES AND UNIVERSITIES

RENSSELAER. *Saint Joseph's College* (1889) P.O. Box 909, 47978. Tel: 219-866-6000; Fax: 219-866-6100. Web: www.saintjoe.edu. F. Dennis Riegelnegg, Ed.D., Pres.; Revs. Philip F. Gilbert, C.PP.S., M.S.; Jeffrey S. Kirch, C.PP.S., Graduate Studies; Leonard J. Kostka, C.PP.S., J.C.L. (Retired); Timothy D. McFarland, C.PP.S., Ph.D., Assoc. Vice Pres. Academics; William J. Stang, C.PP.S., M.D., Rel. Supr.; Paul R. White, C.PP.S., M.A. (Retired); Kevin Scalf, C.PP.S., M.A., M.Div., Chap.; Bros. Timothy P. Hemm, C.PP.S.; Robert Reuter, C.PP.S., Ph.D.; Sr. Patricia Robinson, B.V.M., Ph.D.; Cathy Salyers, Librarian. The Society of the Precious Blood. Priests 5; Brothers 2; Sisters 1; Lay Teachers 88; Students 1,171; Total Staff 201.

[B] HIGH SCHOOLS, INTER-PAROCHIAL

LAFAYETTE. *Central Catholic Junior-Senior High School*, 2410 S. Ninth St., 47909-2499. Tel: 765-474-2496; Fax: 765-474-8752. Email: musial@lcss.org. Web: www.lcss.org. Mr. Dennis A. Musial, Prin.; Grant Freeman, Campus Min. Sister-Campus Minister 1; Lay Teachers 40; Administrators 4; Lay Staff 9; Students 342.

NOBLESVILLE. *Saint Theodore Guerin High School*, 15300 N. Gray Rd., 46062. Tel: 317-582-0120; Fax: 317-582-0140. Email: dehrman@guerincatholic.org. Web: www.guerincatholic.org. Rev. Dale W. Ehrman, Vice Pres. Faculty 38; Students 421.

[C] GENERAL HOSPITALS

LAFAYETTE. *St. Elizabeth Central* (1874) 1501 Hartford St., P.O. Box 7501, 47903. Tel: 765-423-6011; Fax: 765-423-6364. Email: ste.pr@ssfhs.org. Web: www.ste.org. Terrance E. Wilson, Pres. & CEO; Sr. M. Ann Kathleen Magiera, O.S.F., Vice Pres. Mission Integration; Revs. Paul Graf; Cajetan Ebuziem. Sisters of St. Francis Health Services, Inc. Sisters 4; Operational Beds 116; Patients Assisted Annually 185,000; Total Staff 668.
St. Elizabeth School of Nursing Tel: 765-423-6408; Fax: 765-423-6364. Web: www.ste.org. Students 230.
St. Elizabeth East, 1701 S. Creasy Ln., 47905. Tel: 765-502-4000; Fax: 765-423-6364. Email: ste.pr@ssfhs.org. Web: ww.ste.org. Terrance E. Wilson, Pres. & CEO. Owned by the Sisters of St. Francis Health Services, Inc. ("SSFHS"). Operational Beds 150; Patients Assisted Annually 188,000; Total Staff 902.
St. Vincent Seton Specialty Hospital (1996) 1501 Hartford St., 47904. Tel: 765-423-6650; Fax: 765-423-6648. Email: cxschech@stvincent.org. Web: seton.stvincent.org. Sr. Raphael Kochert, O.S.F., Certified Chap. (A member of St. Vincent Health, Inc. and Ascension Health.) Bed Capacity 30; Total Patient Visits Per Year 400; Total Staff 95.

ANDERSON. *Saint John's Health System*, 2015 Jackson St., 46016. Tel: 765-646-8373; Fax: 765-646-8504. Email: tjvanosd@sjhsnet.org. Web: www.stjohnshealthsystem.org. Mr. Tom VanOsdol, Pres.; Sr. Kathleen Reilly, C.S.C., Vice Pres. Mission. Sisters of the Holy Cross 4; Bed Capacity 252; Total Assisted 303,744; Total Staff 1,346.

CARMEL. *St. Elizabeth Ann Seton Hospital of Central Indiana, Inc.* (1996) Tel: 317-582-8500; Fax: 317-582-8565. Email: phalexan@stvincent.org.
St. Elizabeth Ann Seton Hospital of Carmel, 13500 N. Meridian St., 46032. Tel: 317-582-8560; Fax: 317-582-8565. Email: phalexan@stvincent.org. Peter H. Alexander, Exec. Dir. Bed Capacity 38; Patients Assisted Annually 411; Total Staff 150; Bed Capacity 29; Patients Assisted Annually 32; Total Staff 50.
St. Vincent Carmel Hospital, Inc. (1985) 13500 N. Meridian St., 46032-1903. Tel: 317-582-7137; Fax:

317-582-7744. Web: www.stvincent.org. Email: jclandry@stvincent.org. Carey Landry, Certified Chap. (A member of St. Vincent Health, Inc. and Ascension Health.) Bed Capacity 135; Total Assisted Annually by Pastoral Care 5,000; Total Pastoral Care Staff 1; Total Hospital Staff 850.

CRAWFORDSVILLE. *St. Clare Medical Center,* 1710 Lafayette Rd., 47933. Tel: 765-362-2800; Fax: 765-364-3189. Email: jim.siemers@ssfhs.org. Web: www.stclaremedical.org. Jim Siemers, Exec. Dir. Sisters of St. Francis Health Services, Inc. Sisters of St. Francis of Perpetual Adoration 1; Bed Capacity 71; Licensed Beds 103; Patients Assisted Annually 43,080; Total Staff 474.

ELWOOD. *St. Vincent Mercy Hospital, Inc.* (1926) 1331 South A St., 46036-1942. Tel: 765-552-4600; Fax: 765-552-4700. Email: ACYates@stvincent.org. Web: mercy.stvinent.org. Ann C. Yates, R.N., Dir., Patient Care. Bed Capacity 25; Total Assisted Annually 67,741; Total Staff 256.

(1999) Tel: 765-552-4600; Fax: 765-552-4700. Bed Capacity 25; Patients Assisted Annually 71,989; Total Staff 2.

KOKOMO. *St. Joseph Hospital & Health Center,* 1907 W. Sycamore St., 46901. Tel: 765-452-5611; 765-456-5300 (Administration); Fax: 765-456-5038. Email: vlmason@stjoseph.stvincent.org. Web: www.stjoseph.stvincent.org. P.O. Box 9010, 46904-9010. Kathlene Young, M.S., F.A.C.H.E., Pres. & CEO; Sr. Catherine Kelly, D.C., M.T.S., M.S.-H.S., Vice Pres., Mission Integration, Clinical Leader, & Palliative Care; Luann Young, Mgr., Pastoral Care. Sisters 1; Total Staff 865; Bed Capacity 167; Patients Assisted Annually 188,078.

Saint Joseph Foundation of Kokomo, Indiana, Inc. Tel: 765-456-5406; Fax: 765-456-5387. Email: tmoser@stjoseph.stvincent.org. Web: stjoseph.stvincent.org. Todd Moser, Dir./St. Joseph Foundation.

WILLIAMSPORT. *St. Vincent Williamsport Hospital,* 412 N. Monroe St., 47993-1097. Tel: 765-762-4000; Fax: 765-762-4126. Web: www.stvincent.org. Jane Craigin, CEO. Priests 1; Bed Capacity 16; Patients Assisted Annually 76,000; Total Staff 176.

[D] NURSING HOMES

LAFAYETTE. *St. Anthony Health Care,* 1205 N. 14th St., 47904. Tel: 765-423-4861; Fax: 765-742-8790. Email: admin@sahc.net. Web: www.sahc.net. Rev. John A. Bach, Chap. (Retired). Bed Capacity 120; Residents 115; Total Assisted Annually 590; Total Staff 147.

[E] MONASTERIES AND RESIDENCES OF PRIESTS AND BROTHERS

LAFAYETTE. *Emmaus House,* 2500 S. Ninth St., 47909. Tel: 765-477-6441. Revs. Cajetan Ebuziem, Hospital Chap.; Donald Vernon (Retired). Priests 2.

[F] CONVENTS AND RESIDENCES FOR SISTERS

ANDERSON. *Congregation of the Sisters of the Holy Cross,* 2115 Meridian St., 46016. Tel: 765-642-2427.

Sisters of the Holy Cross, Inc. Sisters 3.

KOKOMO. *Maria Regina Mater Monastery* (1959) 1175 N. 300 W., 46901-1799. Tel: 765-457-5743. Web: www.thepoorclares.org. Sr. Miriam, P.C.C., Abbess; Rev. Thomas Obiatuegwu (Nigeria), Chap. Monastery of Poor Clares of the Reform of St. Colette. Solemnly Professed Nuns in Cloister 7; Perpetually Professed Extern Sisters 1; Canonical Novice 1.

TIPTON. *St. Joseph Center: Congregation of the Sisters of St. Joseph* (1888) 1440 W. Division Rd., 46072-8584. Tel: 765-675-4146; 765-675-6203; Fax: 765-675-7471. Email: tmacintyre@csjoseph.org. Web: www.csjoseph.org. Sr. Theresa MacIntyre, C.S.J., Asst. Sec. Sisters Resident at Motherhouse 18; Total in Residence 18; Total Staff 40.

Sisters of St. Joseph of Tipton, Indiana, Inc., 1440 W. Division Rd., 46072. Tel: 765-675-4146; Fax: 765-675-7471.

[G] RETREAT HOUSES

HARTFORD CITY. *John XXIII Center,* 407 W. McDonald St., 47348. Tel: 765-348-4008; Fax: 765-348-5819. Email: john23rd@sbcglobal.net. Web: www.john23rdretreatcenter.com. Sr. Joetta Huelsmann, P.H.J.C., Dir.; Dorothy Stewart, Office Mgr.

[H] NEWMAN CENTERS

MUNCIE. *Newman Foundation-Ball State University* (1973) 1200 W. Riverside Ave., 47303. Tel: 765-288-6180; Fax: 765-288-7777. Email: frjohnkiefer@juno.com. Web: www.stfrancisnewman.org. Rev. John D. Kiefer.

WEST LAFAYETTE. *St. Thomas Aquinas Parish and Foundation for Catholic Students Attending Purdue University* (1951) 535 State St., 47906-3592. Tel: 765-743-4652; Fax: 765-743-0426. Email: sttoms@sttoms-purdue.org. Web: www.sttoms-purdue.org. Revs. Daniel C. Davis, O.P., Pastor & Dir., Newman Apostolate; Tom Poulsen, O.P., Assoc. Pastor; Patrick Baikauskas, O.P., Assoc. Pastor.

Katy Argadine, D.R.E. Students 3,000.

[I] MISCELLANEOUS

LAFAYETTE. *Catholic Foundation of Northcentral Indiana, Inc.,* P.O. Box 1687, 47902-1687. Tel: 765-742-7000; Fax: 765-742-7513. Email: bmccreary@dol-in.org. Web: www.dioceseoflafayette.org/staff-development.html. Robert McCreary, Dir., Pastoral Office for Stewardship & Devel.; Joseph Bonner, Chm. Bd. Total Staff 3.

ANDERSON. *Saint John's Foundation, Inc.,* 2015 Jackson St., 46016. Tel: 765-646-8373; Fax: 765-646-8504. Email: tjvanosd@sjhsnet.org. Web: www.stjohnshealthsystem.org. Mr. Tom VanOsdol, Pres.

CARMEL. *Our Lady of Mount Carmel Parochial School,* 14596 Oak Ridge Rd., 46032. Tel: 317-846-1118; Fax: 317-582-2375. Email: OLMCprincipal@olmc1.org. Web: olmc1.org. Rev. Richard J. Doerr, Contact Person.

NOBLESVILLE. *Hamilton County Catholic High School Corporation,* 15300 Gray Rd., 46062. Tel: 317-582-0120; Fax: 317-582-0140. Email: dehrman@guerincatholic.org. Web: www.guerincatholic.org. Most Rev. William Leo Higi, D.D., Bishop, Diocese of Lafayette in Indiana Board Members: Rev. Msgr. Robert L. Sell III, J.C.L., V.G.; Dr. Marie Williams; G. Gary Malone; Robert Quinn.

Hamilton County Catholic High School Corporation, Blessed Theodore Guerin High School, 15300 N. Gray Rd., 46062. Tel: 317-582-0120; Fax: 317-582-0140. Web: www.guerincatholic.org. Rev. Dale W. Ehrman, Vice Pres.; Steve Hood, Business Mgr. Priests 1; Total Staff 50.

PERU. *St. Charles Conference of the Society of St. Vincent DePaul, Inc.,* P.O. Box 1332, 46970. Tel: 317-472-1855.

WEST LAFAYETTE. *Dominicans, Community of St. Thomas Aquinas, Inc.,* 2535 Newman Rd., 47906-4537. Tel: 765-743-3795. Rev. Thomas R. Poulsen, O.P., Pres.

RELIGIOUS INSTITUTES OF MEN REPRESENTED IN THE DIOCESE

For further details refer to the corresponding bracketed number in the Religious Institutes of Men or Women section.

[0520]—*Order of St. Francis Minors*—O.F.M.

[1060]—*Society of the Precious Blood*—C.PP.S.

RELIGIOUS INSTITUTES OF WOMEN REPRESENTED IN THE DIOCESE

[3832]—*Congregation of the Sisters of St. Joseph*—C.S.J.

[1920]—*Congregation of the Sisters of the Holy Cross*—C.S.C.

[1070-09]—*Dominican Sisters*—O.P.

[1780]—*Franciscan Sisters of Peace*—F.S.P.A.

[4150]—*Irish Ursuline Union*—O.S.U.

[0240]—*Olivetan Benedictine Sisters*—O.S.B.

[3230]—*Poor Handmaids of Jesus Christ*—P.H.J.C.

[2970]—*School Sisters of Notre Dame*—S.S.N.D.

[0110]—*Sisters Adorers of the Precious Blood*—A.P.B.

[0430]—*Sisters of Charity of the Blessed Virgin Mary*—B.V.M.

[2990]—*Sisters of Notre Dame* (Toledo Prov.)—S.N.D.

[3000]—*Sisters of Notre Dame de Namur*—S.N.D.deN.

[3360]—*Sisters of Providence of Saint Mary-of-the-Woods, IN*—S.P.

[]—*Sisters of St. Francis* (Sylvania, OH)—O.S.F.

[1640]—*Sisters of St. Francis of Perpetual Adoration*—O.S.F.

[3260]—*Sisters of the Precious Blood* (Dayton, Ohio)—C.PP.S.

NECROLOGY

† Remaklus, Charles W., (Retired)—Died Aug. 23, 2009

† Schott, Victor P., (Retired)—Died Dec. 15, 2008

An asterisk (*) denotes an organization that has established tax-exempt status directly with the IRS and is not covered by the USCCB Group Ruling.

Diocese of Lake Charles

Most Reverend

GLEN JOHN PROVOST

Bishop of Lake Charles; ordained June 29, 1975; appointed Bishop of Lake Charles March 6, 2007; ordained April 23, 2007. *Chancery Office: 414 Iris St., P.O. Box 3223, Lake Charles, LA 70602.* Tel: 337-439-7400; Fax: 337-439-7413.

Chancery Office: 414 Iris St., P.O. Box 3223, Lake Charles, LA 70602. Tel: 337-439-7400; Fax: 337-439-7413.

Web: lcdiocese.laol.net

Email: lcdiocese@laol.net

ESTABLISHED APRIL 25, 1980.

Square Miles 5,313.

Comprises the civil parishes (or counties) of Allen, Beauregard, Calcasieu, Cameron and Jefferson Davis in the State of Louisiana.

For legal titles of parishes and diocesan institutions, consult the Chancery Office.

STATISTICAL OVERVIEW

Personnel	
Bishop	1
Retired Bishops	1
Priests: Diocesan Active in Diocese	37
Priests: Diocesan Active Outside Diocese	2
Priests: Retired, Sick or Absent	8
Number of Diocesan Priests	47
Religious Priests in Diocese	12
Total Priests in Diocese	59
Extern Priests in Diocese	8
Ordinations:	
Transitional Deacons	1
Permanent Deacons in Diocese	25
Total Brothers	1
Total Sisters	16
Parishes	
Parishes	38
With Resident Pastor:	
Resident Diocesan Priests	29
Resident Religious Priests	6
Without Resident Pastor:	
Administered by Priests	3
Administered by Professed Religious Men	6
Missions	8
Professional Ministry Personnel:	
Brothers	1
Sisters	16
Welfare	
Catholic Hospitals	1
Total Assisted	79,988
Homes for the Aged	1
Total Assisted	118
Day Care Centers	2
Total Assisted	74
Special Centers for Social Services	3
Total Assisted	2,402
Educational	
Diocesan Students in Other Seminaries	9
Total Seminarians	9
High Schools, Diocesan and Parish	1
Total Students	656
Elementary Schools, Diocesan and Parish	7
Total Students	2,066
Catechesis/Religious Education:	
High School Students	2,124
Elementary Students	4,979
Total Students under Catholic Instruction	9,834
Teachers in the Diocese:	
Sisters	1
Lay Teachers	233
Vital Statistics	
Receptions into the Church:	
Infant Baptism Totals	1,055
Adult Baptism Totals	49
Received into Full Communion	49
First Communions	1,105
Confirmations	902
Marriages:	
Catholic	219
Interfaith	75
Total Marriages	294
Deaths	1,080
Total Catholic Population	75,983
Total Population	284,611

Former Bishops—Most Revs. JUDE SPEYRER, D.D., ord. July 25, 1953; appt. First Bishop of Lake Charles Jan. 29, 1980; ord. and installed April 25, 1980; resigned Dec. 12, 2000; EDWARD K. BRAXTON, ord. May 13, 1970; appt. Auxiliary Bishop of St. Louis March 28, 1995; ord. Auxiliary Bishop of St. Louis May 17, 1995; appt. Bishop of Lake Charles Dec. 12, 2000; installed Feb. 22, 2001; appt. Bishop of Belleville March 15, 2005.

Diocesan Board of Administration— (Legal Title - Society of the Roman Catholic Church of the Diocese of Lake Charles, LA) Deacon GEORGE A. STEARNS; Rev. Msgr. JACE F. ESKIND.

Bishop's Office—414 Iris St., P.O. Box 3223, Lake Charles, 70602. Tel: 337-439-7400, Ext. 204.

Chancery Office—414 Iris St., P.O. Box 3223, Lake Charles, 70602. Tel: 337-439-7400; Fax: 337-439-7413. Office Hours: Mon.-Fri. 8:30-4:30.

Bishop Perry Building—411 Iris St., Lake Charles, 70601. Tel: 337-439-7426; Fax: 337-439-7428. Office Hours: Mon.-Fri. 8:30-4:30.

Vicar General and Moderator of the Curia—Very Rev. DANIEL A. TORRES, V.G., Mailing Address: P.O. Box 3223, Lake Charles, 70602. Tel: 337-439-7400.

Chancellor—Deacon GEORGE STEARNS, Mailing Address: P.O. Box 3223, Lake Charles, 70602. Tel: 337-439-7400, Ext. 22.

Vicar Judicial—Rev. Msgr. JACE F. ESKIND, Mailing Address: P.O Box 3223, Lake Charles, 70602. Tel: 337-439-7400, Ext. 210.

Tribunal—414 Iris St., P.O. Box 3223, Lake Charles, 70602. Tel: 337-439-7400, Ext. 210.

Judges—Rev. Msgrs. JACE F. ESKIND; VINCENT SEDITA (Retired); Ms. BONNIE LANDRY, J.C.L.; Rev. ALBERT BOREL, J.C.L.

Advocates—Revs. JOHN POERIO (Retired); THEOPHILUS L. HERLONG (Retired); Deacon GEORGE CARR.

Defenders of the Bond—Rev. Msgr. HARRY D. GREIG II; Rev. JAMES DOYLE.

Notary—Mrs. DEBRA FOREMAN.

Promoter of Justice—Rev. Archimandrite HERBERT J. MAY, J.C.L.

Deans—Very Rev. AUBREY V. GUILBEAU, West Deanery; Rev. Archimandrite HERBERT J. MAY, J.C.L., East Deanery; Very Rev. MARCUS JOHNSON, Central Deanery.

Presbyteral Council—Revs. ANTHONY FONTENOT, Chm.; TIMOTHY GOODLY; Very Rev. MARCUS JOHNSON; Revs. ROMMEL P. TOLENTINO, Vice Chm.; THOMAS VELLAPALLIL; Rev. Msgr. RONALD GROTH; Rev. SUSIL FERNANDO; Very Rev. AUBREY V. GUILBEAU; Revs. FRED RUSSI (Retired); DON PIRARO; Very Rev. DANIEL A. TORRES, V.G.; Rev. Msgr. JACE F. ESKIND; Rev. Archimandrite HERBERT MAY, J.C.L.

Diocesan Consultors—Rev. FRED RUSSI (Retired); Very Revs. AUBREY V. GUILBEAU; MARCUS JOHNSON; Revs. SUSIL FERNANDO; TIMOTHY GOODLY; DON PIRARO; ROMMEL P. TOLENTINO; Rev. Archimandrite HERBERT J. MAY, J.C.L.; Rev. Msgr. RONALD GROTH; Very Rev. DANIEL A. TORRES, V.G.; Rev. Msgr. JACE F. ESKIND; Rev. ANTHONY FONTENOT.

Offices, Boards, Commissions, Committees

Black Catholics—Deacon EDWARD LAVINE, Mailing Address: P.O. Box 3223, Lake Charles, 70601. Tel: 337-439-7436, Ext. 11.

Clergy Formation—Rev. WHITNEY MILLER, 411 Iris St., Lake Charles, 70601. Tel: 337-439-7400.

Communications—MORRIS LEBLEU, Mailing Address: P.O. Box 3223, Lake Charles, 70601. Tel: 337-439-7400, Ext. 304.

Counseling—Rev. WHITNEY MILLER, 411 Iris St., Lake Charles, 70601. Tel: 337-439-7400.

Deaf Apostolate—Very Rev. AUBREY V. GUILBEAU, 418 Iris St., Lake Charles, 70601. Tel: 337-439-4373.

Development Office—MORRIS LEBLEU, Mailing Address: P.O. Box 3223, Lake Charles, 70602. Tel: 337-439-7400, Ext. 304.

Diocesan Building Commission—Deacon GEORGE STEARNS, Chm., Mailing Address: P.O. Box 3223, Lake Charles, 70602. Tel: 337-439-7400, Ext. 204.

Director of Seminarians—Very Rev. DANIEL A. TORRES, V.G., Vocation Dir. & Dir. Seminarians, 414 Iris St., Lake Charles, 70601. Tel: 337-439-7400.

Education—Mrs. KIMBERLEE GAZZOLO, Supt., Mailing Address: P.O. Box 3223, Lake Charles, 70602. Tel: 337-439-7426, Ext. 18.

Evangelization—BERNEL EZELL, 411 Iris St., Lake Charles, 70601. Tel: 337-439-7426, Ext. 300.

Fiscal Administration—Ms. PATRICIA MYERS, Mailing Address: P.O. Box 3223, Lake Charles, 70602. Tel: 337-439-7400, Ext. 203.

Hispanic Ministry—Rev. ARTURO LOZANO, S.J., Dir. & Hispanic Chap., Mailing Address: St. Henry Catholic Church, 1021 8th Ave., Lake Charles, 70601. Tel: 337-436-7223; Fax: 337-436-4614.

Office For Worship—Rev. Msgr. JACE F. ESKIND, 414 Iris St., Lake Charles, 70601. Tel: 337-439-7400, Ext. 210.

Parish Boundaries Commission—Very Rev. DANIEL A. TORRES, V.G., Chm., Mailing Address: P.O. Box 3223, Lake Charles, 70602. Tel: 337-439-7400, Ext. 204.

Permanent Diaconate—Deacon GEORGE CARR, 617 W. Claude St., Lake Charles, 70605. Tel: 337-477-1236.

Personnel Board—Very Rev. DANIEL A. TORRES, V.G., Vicar Gen.

Propagation of the Faith & Holy Childhood Association—Rev. WAYNE LEBLEU, Dir., Mailing

Address: 7680 Gulf Hwy., Lake Charles, 70607. Tel: 337-478-0213; Fax: 337-478-0793.

Religious Education—Mrs. DENISE DONAHOE, 411 Iris St., Lake Charles, 70601. Tel: 337-439-7426, Ext. 302.

Relief Services Catholic—Rev. WAYNE LEBLEU.

St. Charles Retreat Center—Revs. DON PIRARO, Dir.; WHITNEY MILLER, Asst. Dir., 2151 Sam Houston Jones Pkwy., Lake Charles, 70611. Tel: 337-855-1232.

Sea, Apostleship of the—Deacon PATRICK LAPOINT, 160 Marine St., Lake Charles, 70601. Tel: 337-436-1315.

Catholic Charities—Mrs. TRISH TREJO, Dir., 612 Louisiana Ave., Lake Charles, 70601. Tel: 337-439-7436.

Pastoral Services, Catholic—Rev. WAYNE LEBLEU.

Scouting—Rev. NATHAN LONG, Our Lady Queen of Heaven, Lake Charles, 70601.

Seminary Advisory Board—Very Rev. DANIEL A. TORRES, V.G., Vicar Gen.

Vocation Director—Very Rev. DANIEL A. TORRES, V.G., Vicar Gen. Vocation Recruiters: Revs. ANTHONY FONTENOT; NATHAN LONG; RUBEN J. BULLER; SUSIL FERNANDO; Very Rev. MARCUS JOHNSON, 411 Iris St., Lake Charles, 70601. Tel: 337-439-7400, Ext. 308.

CLERGY, PARISHES, MISSIONS AND PAROCHIAL SCHOOLS

LAKE CHARLES

(CALCASIEU PARISH)

1—IMMACULATE CONCEPTION CATHEDRAL (1869) [CEM] Rev. Msgr. Jace F. Eskind.
Mailing Address: P.O. Box 1029, 70602. Tel: 337-436-7251; Fax: 337-436-7240. In Res., Rev. Timothy Goodly.
Church: 935 Bilbo, 70601. Tel: 337-439-7400.
School—(Grades PreK-8), 1536 Ryan St., 70601. Tel: 337-433-3497; Fax: 337-433-5056. Mrs. Dinah Bradford, Prin. Lay Teachers 28; Students 401.

2—CHRIST THE KING (2002) Rev. V. Wayne LeBleu.
Res.: 7680 Gulf Hwy., 70607. Tel: 337-478-0213; Fax: 337-478-0793.
Catechesis/Religious Program—Students 141.

3—ST. HENRY (1958) [JC] Very Rev. Daniel A. Torres; Revs. Ruben J. Buller, Parochial Vicar; Arturo Lozano, S.J., Hispanic Chap.; Deacon Ray Granger.
Res.: 1021 Eighth Ave., 70601. Tel: 337-436-7223; Fax: 337-436-4614.
Catechesis/Religious Program—Tel: 337-433-6119. Phyllis Kittling, D.R.E. Students 174.

4—IMMACULATE HEART OF MARY (1953), (African American), Very Rev. Marcus Johnson; Deacon Joseph Bushnell. In Res., Rev. Arturo Lozano, S.J., Hispanic Chap.
Res.: 2031 Opelousas St., 70601. Tel: 337-436-8093; Fax: 337-436-8033. Email: ihmchurch@cox_internet.com.
Catechesis/Religious Program—Tel: 337-433-0158. Students 231.
Mission—Our Lady of Fatima Chapel 1700 Graham St., Calcasieu Parish 70601.

5—ST. MARGARET (1940) Very Rev. William Miller; Rev. Emanuel Tanu, S.V.D.; Deacons Dan Landry; Raymond Menard.
Res.: 2500 Enterprise Blvd., 70601. Tel: 337-439-4585; Fax: 337-433-3186.
School—Tel: 337-436-7959; Fax: 337-436-9932. Mrs. Brenda Dufrene, Prin. Lay Teachers 28; Students 287.
Catechesis/Religious Program—Tel: 337-436-6358. Myrtle Wren, D.R.E.; Joanne Schwem, D.R.E. Students 168.

6—ST. MARTIN DEPORRES (2002) Rev. Keith Pellerin. 5326 Elliott Rd., 70605. Mailing Address: P.O. Box 4386, 70606.
Res.: 2503 Vogue Dr., 70605. Tel: 337-478-3845; Fax: 337-477-2828.
Catechesis/Religious Program—Students 55.

7—OUR LADY OF GOOD COUNSEL (1957) Rev. Alan P. Trouille; Deacon Glenn Viau.
Res.: 221 Aqua Dr., 70605. Tel: 337-477-1434; Fax: 337-479-2129. Web: www.mcneesecatholic.com.
Catechesis/Religious Program—Students 118.

8—OUR LADY QUEEN OF HEAVEN (1957) [CEM] Rev. Msgr. James Gaddy; Rev. Nathan Long, Parochial Vicar.
Mailing Address: P.O. Box 5940, 70606.
Res.: 617 W. Claude St., 70605. Tel: 337-477-1236; Fax: 337-478-3451. Email: olqh@lcdiocese.org.
School—(Grades PreK-8), 3908 Creole St., 70605. Tel: 337-477-7349; Fax: 337-477-7384. Ms. JoAnn Wallwork, Prin. Tel: 337-477-8438; Jackie Bohdan, Librarian. Lay Teachers 49; Students 693.
Catechesis/Religious Program—3909 Creole St., 70605. Tel: 337-477-3937. Pamela Alston, D.R.E. (Grades 7-12); Mrs. Robin Suire, D.R.E. (Grades 1-6). Students 658.

9—SACRED HEART OF JESUS (1919), (African American), [CEM] Revs. Henry Mancuso, Admin.; Joseph Angadiath, C.M.I.; Deacon Ed Lavine.
Res.: 1102 Mill St., 70601. Tel: 337-439-2646; Fax: 337-439-2650.
School—Tel: 337-436-3588; Fax: 337-433-1761. Dr. Kathleen Dorsey Bellow, Prin.; Rev. Ruben J. Buller, Chap. Lay Teachers 15; Students 115.
Catechesis/Religious Program—Tel: 337-439-9923. Jacqueline Mathews, D.R.E. Students 133.

10—ST. THEODORE (1974) Rev. Msgr. Charles J. Dubois; Deacon Jack Reynolds, (Retired).
Mailing Address: 785 Sam Houston Jones Pkwy., 70611. In Res., Rev. James Doyle.
Res.: 713 Longleaf Dr., 70611. Tel: 337-855-6662; Fax: 337-855-6663.
School—(Grades PreK-8) Tel: 337-855-9465; Fax: 337-855-2809. Mrs. Jennifer Bellon, Interim Prin. Lay Teachers 16; Students 131.
Catechesis/Religious Program—Tel: 337-855-6664. Students 514.
Mission—St. Pius X Mission 16816 Hwy. 171, Ragley, 70657. Tel: 337-725-3719; Fax: 337-725-6248.

OUTSIDE THE CITY OF LAKE CHARLES

BELL CITY, CALCASIEU PARISH, ST. JOHN VIANNEY (1939) [CEM] Rev. Augustine Mulanjanany.
Res.: 7120 Hwy. 14 E., 70630. Tel: 337-622-3255; Fax: 337-622-3337.
Catechesis/Religious Program—Paige Myers, D.R.E. Students 182.

BIG LAKE, CAMERON PARISH, ST. MARY OF THE LAKE (1938) Rev. Msgr. Harry D. Greig II.
Res.: 11054 Hwy. 384, 70607. Tel: 337-598-3101; Fax: 337-598-4298.
Catechesis/Religious Program—Students 175.
Mission—St. Patrick's Sweet Lake, Cameron Parish.

CAMERON, CAMERON PARISH, OUR LADY STAR OF THE SEA (1961) Rev. Richard U. Adiukwu.
Church: 135 Our Lady's Rd., 70631. Tel: 337-538-2245; Fax: 337-538-2246.
Res.: 5035 Grand Chenier Hwy., Grand Chenier, 70643.
Catechesis/Religious Program—Students 55.

CREOLE, CAMERON PARISH, SACRED HEART OF JESUS (1890) [CEM 3] Rev. Richard U. Adiukwu.
Res.: 5035 Grand Chenier Hwy., Grand Chenier, 70643. Tel: 337-538-2245; Fax: 337-538-2246.
Church: 5250 W. Creole Hwy., Cameron, 70631.
Catechesis/Religious Program—Stephanie Rodrigue, D.R.E. Students 100.

DEQUINCY, CALCASIEU PARISH, OUR LADY OF LA SALETTE (1955) Rev. Edward J. Brunnert, M.S.
Res.: 203 S. Grand, 70633. Tel: 337-786-3500; Fax: 337-786-4222. Email: ourladyoflasalette@centurytel.net.
Catechesis/Religious Program—Tel: 337-786-3205. Students 76.

DE RIDDER, BEAUREGARD PARISH, ST. JOSEPH'S (1938) Rev. Jude Brunnert, M.S.; Deacon Sumner Kohlhund.
Res.: 1125 Blankenship Dr., 70634. Tel: 337-463-6878; Fax: 337-463-6875.
Catechesis/Religious Program—Mrs. Theresa Pendley, D.R.E. Students 172.

ELTON, JEFFERSON DAVIS PARISH

1—ST. JOSEPH'S (1951), (African American), [CEM] Rev. Maxwell Okolie; Deacon John Eaves.
Res.: P.O. Box 789, 70532. Tel: 337-584-2038; Fax: 337-584-3997.
Catechesis/Religious Program—Tel: 337-584-2642. Carroll Sue Gobert, D.R.E. Students 7.

2—ST. PAUL (1913) [CEM] Rev. Marshall Boulet; Deacon John Eaves.
Res.: P.O. Box 129, 70532. Tel: 337-584-2818; Fax: 337-584-3246. Web: www.saintpaul-elton.com.
Catechesis/Religious Program—Cathy Hollingsworth, D.R.E. Students 144.

FENTON, JEFFERSON DAVIS PARISH, ST. CHARLES BORROMEO (1980) Rev. Roland G. Vaughn. In Res., Rev. E. Joseph McGrath.
Res.: P.O. Box 309, 70640. Tel: 337-756-2529; Fax: 337-756-2706.
Catechesis/Religious Program—Beverly Cormier, D.R.E. Students 61.
Mission—St. John the Evangelist Lacassine, Jefferson Davis Parish 70647.
Catechesis/Religious Program—Cindy Scharff, D.R.E. Students 131.

GRAND CHENIER, CAMERON PARISH, ST. EUGENE (1962) [CEM 3] Rev. Richard U. Adiukwu.
Res.: 5035 Grand Chenier Hwy., 70643. Tel: 337-538-2245; Fax: 337-538-2246.
Catechesis/Religious Program—Students 45.

HACKBERRY, CAMERON PARISH, ST. PETER APOSTLE (1955) [CEM] Rev. Rommel P. Tolentino.
Res.: 1210 Main St., P.O. Box 372, 70645. Tel: 337-762-3365; Fax: 337-762-3160.
Catechesis/Religious Program—Tel: 337-762-3160. Tamra Welch, D.R.E. Students 127.
Mission—Our Lady of the Assumption Johnson Bayou.

IOWA, CALCASIEU PARISH, ST. RAPHAEL (1931) [CEM] Revs. Andreas A. Kedati, S.V.D.; Emanuel Tanu, S.V.D., Parochial Vicar.
Res.: P.O. Drawer 849, 70647. Tel: 337-582-3503; Fax: 337-582-6326.
Catechesis/Religious Program—Students 284.
Mission—St. Joseph P.O. Box 849, Le Bleu Settlement, Calcasieu Parish 70647-0849. Tel: 337-582-3483.

JENNINGS, JEFFERSON DAVIS PARISH

1—IMMACULATE CONCEPTION (1956) Rev. Anthony Fontenot; Deacon Bennett McNeal.
Res.: 515 Bryan St., P.O. Box 358, 70546. Tel: 337-824-1164; Fax: 337-824-1717.
Catechesis/Religious Program—Deacon Bennett McNeal, D.R.E. Students 135.

2—OUR LADY HELP OF CHRISTIANS (1891) [CEM] Rev. Charles McMillin; Deacon Edward McNally.
Res.: 710 State St., P.O. Drawer 1170, 70546. Tel: 337-824-0168; Fax: 337-824-7597. Web: www.olhc.catholicweb.com.
School—600 Roberts Ave., 70546. Tel: 337-824-1743; Fax: 337-824-1752. Nicole Reeves, Prin. Lay Teachers 24; Students 269.
Catechesis/Religious Program—Tel: 337-824-0168. Florence McNally, C.R.E. Students 362.

3—OUR LADY OF PERPETUAL HELP (1941) [CEM] Rev. Celsius Offor (Nigeria).
Res.: 920 S. Broadway, P.O. Box 1331, 70546. Tel: 337-824-3182; 337-824-3186; Fax: 337-824-3186.
Catechesis/Religious Program—Tel: 337-824-3703. Sharolyn S. Cormier, D.R.E.; Ada Williams, D.R.E. Students 98.

KINDER, ALLEN PARISH, ST. PHILIP NERI (1937), (Acadian—French), [CEM] Rev. Carlos Garcia Cardona; Deacon Roy Nash.
Res.: P.O. Box 146, 70648. Tel: 337-738-5612; Fax: 337-738-2728.
Catechesis/Religious Program—Troy Fuselier, D.R.E. Students 312.

LAKE ARTHUR, JEFFERSON DAVIS PARISH, OUR LADY OF THE LAKE (1922) [CEM] [JC 3] Rev. Clyde Thomas.
Res.: 203 Commercial Ave., P.O. Drawer P, 70549. Tel: 337-774-2614; Fax: 337-774-3793.
Catechesis/Religious Program—203 Commercial St., 70549. Tel: 337-774-2675. Students 170.

OAKDALE, ALLEN PARISH, SACRED HEART (1948) [CEM] Rev. Jose Vattakunnel.
Mailing Address: P.O. Box 926, 71463-0926.
Res.: 1208 E. Seventh Ave., 71463. Tel: 318-335-3780; Fax: 318-335-0708.
Catechesis/Religious Program—Students 62.
Mission—St. Frances 204 Poplar St., P.O. Box 926, Elizabeth, Allen Parish 70638.

OBERLIN, ALLEN PARISH, ST. JOAN OF ARC (1920) [CEM] Rev. Felix Anyikwa, Admin.; Deacons Norris Chapman, (Retired); James Dale Deshatel.
Res.: 110 W. Fifth Ave., P.O. Box 479, 70655. Tel: 337-639-4399; 337-639-4798; Fax: 337-639-4799.
Catechesis/Religious Program—Freddy Gorman, D.R.E. Students 196.

RAYMOND, JEFFERSON DAVIS PARISH, ST. LAWRENCE (1951) Rev. Msgr. Ronald Groth.
Res.: 5505 Pine Island Hwy., Jennings, 70546. Tel: 337-584-2700.
Catechesis/Religious Program—Tel: 337-584-2002; Fax: 337-584-3990. Students 196.

SULPHUR, CALCASIEU PARISH

1—IMMACULATE CONCEPTION OF THE B.V.M. (1959) Very Rev. Aubrey V. Guilbeau.
Res.: 2700 Maplewood Dr., 70663. Tel: 337-625-3364; Fax: 337-625-9547.
Catechesis/Religious Program—Tel: 337-625-9719. Vicki Cordell, D.R.E. (Elementary); Sherry Miller, D.R.E. (Middle & H.S.). Students 342.

2—OUR LADY OF LASALETTE (1961) Rev. James M. Winiarski, M.S.; Deacons Johnny Mounce; Maurice Serice. In Res., Rev. Lawrence A. Kohler, M.S.; Bro. Donald V. Smith, M.S.
Res.: 602 N. Claiborne St., 70663. Tel: 337-527-6722; Fax: 337-527-0909.
Catechesis/Religious Program—Tel: 337-527-8307. Elise LeBoeuf, D.R.E. Students 206.

3—OUR LADY OF PROMPT SUCCOR (1919) Revs. Joseph Gosselin, M.S.; Gerard J. Boulanger, M.S. In Res., Rev. Ernest Corriveau, M.S.
Res.: 1109 Cypress St., 70663. Tel: 337-527-5261; Fax: 337-528-2991.
School—1111 Cypress St., 70663. Tel: 337-527-7828; Fax: 337-528-3778. Lana Cooley, Prin. Lay Teachers 18; Students 180.

Catechesis/Religious Program—1029 Lasalette Dr., 70663. Tel: 337-527-9964. Adrienne Poncho, D.R.E.; Terry Sittig, D.R.E. Students 239.

4—ST. THERESA (1971) Rev. Thomas Vellappallil, M.S.; Mary Little, Admin. In Res., Rev. Donald P. Jeffrey.
Res.: 4822 Carlyss Dr., 70665. Tel: 337-583-4800; Fax: 337-583-4818.
Catechesis/Religious Program—Tel: 337-583-4010. Angie Clark, D.R.E. Students 380.

VINTON, CALCASIEU PARISH, ST. JOSEPH (1920) Rev. Susil Fernando.
Res.: 1502 Industrial, 70668. Tel: 337-589-7358; Fax: 337-589-7843.
Catechesis/Religious Program—Tel: 337-589-2982. Students 155.

WELSH, JEFFERSON DAVIS PARISH

1—ST. JOSEPH (1941), (African American), [JC] Rev. Celsius Offor (Nigeria).
Res.: P.O. Box 607, 70591. Tel: 337-734-3673.
Mission—St. Peter Claver 400 W. 2nd St., Iowa, Calcasieu Parish 70547. Fax: 337-734-4435.
Catechesis/Religious Program—Students 18.

2—OUR LADY OF SEVEN DOLORS (1904) [CEM] [JC] Rev. Archimandrite Herbert J. May; Deacons Richard Hinchee; Wayne Chapman.
Res.: P.O. Box 515, 70591. Tel: 337-734-3446; Fax: 337-734-3697.
Catechesis/Religious Program—Tel: 337-734-3848. Betty LaBouve, D.R.E. Students 257.

WESTLAKE, CALCASIEU PARISH, ST. JOHN BOSCO (1955) Rev. Albert Borel; Deacons Fred Reed Jr.; Garrett Caraway Jr. In Res., Rev. Michael J. Barras.
Res.: 1301 Sampson St., 70669. Tel: 337-433-2467; Fax: 337-436-9766.
Catechesis/Religious Program—Tel: 337-439-6585; Fax: 337-493-8579. Fred Reed, D.R.E.; Judy Reed, D.R.E. Students 345.

Chaplains of Public Institutions

LAKE CHARLES. *Lake Charles Memorial Hospital*. Rev. Joseph Angadiath, C.M.I.

DEQUINCY. *Phelps Correctional Facility*. Deacon Edward Lavine.

SULPHUR. *West Calcasieu Cameron Hospital*. Rev. Michael J. Barras.

On Duty Outside the Diocese:
Rev.—
Harris, Whitney G.

On Leave:
Revs.—
Fuselier, Karl
Mancuso, Henry, 858 Kirby St., 70601.
Miles, James, 115 Gladys Ave., Lansdowne, MD 21227.

Retired:
Rev. Msgrs.—
Bourque, Joseph A., 2960 Lake St., Apt. 142, 70601.
Melancon, Louis, P.O. Box 508, Opelousas, 70571.
Revs.—
Alers, Juan, P.O. Box 722, Oakdale, 71463.
Herlong, Theophilus L., 5635 B Welcome Rd., 70611.
Poerio, John
Russi, Fred
Smit, Gerard C., 105 Justice Way, Elkton, MD 21921.
Soileau, Charles, 1017 Rose Ann St., Opelousas, 70570.

Permanent Deacons:
Broussard, Gordon, (Retired), St. Raphael, IA
Bushnell, Joseph, Immaculate Heart of Mary, LC
Caraway, Julius G., Jr., St. John Bosco Church, Westlake
Carr, George, Our Lady Queen of Heaven, LC
Chapman, Norris, St. Joan of Arc, Oberlin
Chapman, Wayne, Our Lady of Seven Dolors, Welsh
Deshotel, Dale, St. Joan of Arc, Oberlin
Eaves, John, St. Paul, Elton
Granger, James R., St. Henry, Lake Charles
Harmon, Glenn, St. Theodore, LC
Hinchee, Richard, Our Lady of Seven Dolors, Welsh
Kohlhund, Sumner, St. Joseph's, De Ridder
Landry, Dan, St. Margaret, Lake Charles
LaPoint, Frederick, St. Philip Neri, Kinder
LaPoint, Patrick Our Lady of Prompt Succor, Sulpher
Lavine, Edward, Sacred Heart, Lake Charles
McNally, Edward, Immaculate Conception, Jennings
McNeal, Bennett, Immaculate Conception, Jennings
Menard, Raymond, St. Margaret, LC
Mounce, Johnny, Our Lady of LaSalette, Sulphur
Nash, Roy, Our Lady Star of the Sea, Cameron; Sacred Heart, Creole
Reed, Frederick, (Retired), St. John Bosco, Westlake
Reynolds, Jack J., (Retired), St. Theodore's, Lake Charles
Serice, Maurice, Our Lady of LaSalette, Sulphur
Stearns, George, Chancellor & Archivist
Tramel, Michael, St. Lawrence, Jennings
Viau, Glenn, Our Lady of Good Counsel, Lake Charles
Wagner, Harry E., Jr., Lake Charles

INSTITUTIONS LOCATED IN THE DIOCESE

[A] HIGH SCHOOLS, INTERPAROCHIAL

LAKE CHARLES. *St. Louis High School*, 1620 Bank St., 70601. Tel: 337-436-7275; Fax: 337-436-6792. Web: www.slchs.org. Very Rev. Marcus Johnson, Rector; Ms. Deborah Frank, Pres. Lay Teachers 56; Students 656.

[B] GENERAL HOSPITALS

LAKE CHARLES. *CHRISTUS Health Southwestern Louisiana*, 524 Dr. Michael DeBakey Dr., 70601. Tel: 337-436-2511; Fax: 337-430-4300. Email: brian.king@christushealth.org. Web: www.sph.christushealth.org. Ms. Ellen Jones, CEO; Revs. Brian Madison King, Dir. Pastoral Care & Vice Pres. Mission Integration; Charles Okorougo. Sponsored by Christus Health System, Dallas, TX. Sisters 1; Bed Capacity 266; Patients Assisted Annually 79,988; Total Staff 1,400.

[C] RETREAT HOUSES

LAKE CHARLES. *Holy City Community*, 5611 Welcome Rd., 70611. Tel: 337-855-2871. Email: selma01@localnet.com. Deacon Edward McNally, Moderator & Admin.; Selma Thompson, Sec. & Treas.

MOSS BLUFF. *St. Charles Center*, 2151 Sam Houston Jones Pkwy., 70611. Tel: 337-855-1232; Fax: 337-855-9062. Revs. Don Piraro, Dir.; Whitney Miller, Asst. Dir.

[D] MONASTERIES AND RESIDENCES OF PRIESTS AND BROTHERS

OAKDALE. **Herald of Good News, Inc.*, P.O. Box 926, 71463. Tel: 318-335-3780; Fax: 318-335-0708. Rev. Jose Vattakunnel.

[E] SPECIAL RESIDENCES

LAKE CHARLES. *Our Lady Queen of Heaven Manor*, Villa Maria, 3905 Kingston St., 70605. Tel: 337-478-4780; Fax: 337-474-8822. Email: villamaria@suddenlink.net. Units 61; Bed Capacity 118; Total Staff 32.

[F] NEWMAN CENTERS

LAKE CHARLES. *Catholic Student Center* McNeese State University, 221 Aqua Dr., 70605. Tel: 337-477-1434; Fax: 337-479-2129. Web: www.mcneesecatholic.com. Rev. Alan P. Trouille; Sr. Shirley Gobert, S.E.C., Campus Min.; Deacon Glenn Viau, Pastoral Assoc.

[G] SOCIAL SERVICE CENTERS

LAKE CHARLES. *Catholic Service Center*, 612 Louisiana Ave., 70601. Tel: 337-439-7436; Fax: 337-439-7435. Mrs. Trish Trejo, Dir.

[H] MISCELLANEOUS

LAKE CHARLES. *Catholic Daughters of America*, 2117 Constance Ln., 70605.
CHRISTUS St. Patrick Home Care, 4444 Lake St., 70605. Tel: 337-480-3000; Fax: 337-480-3050. Ms. Ellen Jones, Pres./CEO; Mr. Bernard Leger, Admin.
School Food Services of Lake Charles, Inc., 1112 Bilbo St., 70601. Tel: 337-433-9640, Ext. 202; Fax: 337-433-9685. Email: edrie.durio@lcdiocese.org.

RELIGIOUS INSTITUTES OF MEN REPRESENTED IN THE DIOCESE

For further details refer to the corresponding bracketed number in the Religious Institutes of Men or Women section.

[0275]—*Carmelites of Mary Immaculate*—C.M.I.
[0690]—*Jesuit Fathers and Brothers*—S.J.
[]—*Missionaries of Compassion*
[0720]—*The Missionaries of Our Lady of La Salette* (Prov. of Mary Queen)—M.S.

RELIGIOUS INSTITUTES OF WOMEN REPRESENTED IN THE DIOCESE

[0470]—*Congregation of the Sisters of Charity of the Incarnate Word, Houston, Texas*—C.C.V.I.
[]—*Daughters of Mary, Mother of Mercy*
[]—*Sisters of Emanuel*—S.E.
[]—*Sisters of the Eucharistic Covenant*—S.E.C.

NECROLOGY

(No Deaths)

An asterisk (*) denotes an organization that has established tax-exempt status directly with the IRS and is not covered by the USCCB Group Ruling.

Diocese of Lansing

(Dioecesis Lansingensis)

Most Reverend

EARL A. BOYEA

Bishop of Lansing; ordained May 20, 1978; appointed Auxiliary Bishop of Detroit and Titular Bishop of Siccenna July 22, 2002; consecrated September 13, 2002; appointed Bishop of Lansing February 27, 2008; installed April 29, 2008. *Chancery: 300 W. Ottawa, Lansing, MI 48933.* Tel: 517-342-2452; Fax: 517-342-2505.

Most Reverend

CARL F. MENGELING, D.D., S.T.D.

Retired Bishop of Lansing; ordained May 25, 1957; appointed Bishop of Lansing November 7, 1995; consecrated and installed January 25, 1996; retired February 27, 2008. *Chancery, 300 W. Ottawa St., Lansing, MI 48933.* Tel: 517-342-2452; Fax: 517-342-2505.

Chancery: 300 W. Ottawa, Lansing, MI 48933. Tel: 517-342-2440; Fax: 517-342-2527.

Web: www.dioceseoflansing.org

Email: chancery@dioceseoflansing.org

ESTABLISHED MAY 22, 1937.

Square Miles 6,218.

Canonically Erected August 4, 1937.

Comprises the Counties of Clinton, Eaton, Genesee, Hillsdale, Ingham, Jackson, Lenawee, Livingston, Shiawassee and Washtenaw, in the State of Michigan.

For legal titles of parishes and diocesan institutions, consult the Chancery Office.

STATISTICAL OVERVIEW

Personnel	
Bishop	1
Retired Bishops	1
Priests: Diocesan Active in Diocese	90
Priests: Diocesan Active Outside Diocese	9
Priests: Retired, Sick or Absent	50
Number of Diocesan Priests	149
Religious Priests in Diocese	42
Total Priests in Diocese	191
Extern Priests in Diocese	19
Ordinations:	
Diocesan Priests	1
Transitional Deacons	5
Permanent Deacons	13
Permanent Deacons in Diocese	102
Total Brothers	8
Total Sisters	429
Parishes	
Parishes	86
With Resident Pastor:	
Resident Diocesan Priests	68
Resident Religious Priests	9
Without Resident Pastor:	
Administered by Priests	5
Administered by Deacons	1
Administered by Religious Women	2
Administered by Lay People	1
Pastoral Centers	2
Closed Parishes	4
Professional Ministry Personnel:	
Sisters	23
Lay Ministers	331
Welfare	
Catholic Hospitals	5
Total Assisted	1,511,775
Health Care Centers	6
Total Assisted	20,967
Homes for the Aged	3
Total Assisted	332
Day Care Centers	1
Total Assisted	100
Specialized Homes	3
Total Assisted	173
Special Centers for Social Services	11
Total Assisted	290,083
Residential Care of Disabled	1
Total Assisted	60
Educational	
Diocesan Students in Other Seminaries	36
Seminaries, Religious	6
Total Seminarians	36
Colleges and Universities	1
Total Students	2,365
High Schools, Diocesan and Parish	4
Total Students	2,123
High Schools, Private	1
Total Students	40
Elementary Schools, Diocesan and Parish	33
Total Students	7,165
Elementary Schools, Private	2
Total Students	347
Catechesis/Religious Education:	
High School Students	3,526
Elementary Students	18,249
Total Students under Catholic Instruction	33,851
Teachers in the Diocese:	
Priests	2
Brothers	1
Sisters	8
Lay Teachers	555
Vital Statistics	
Receptions into the Church:	
Infant Baptism Totals	2,687
Minor Baptism Totals	237
Adult Baptism Totals	266
Received into Full Communion	464
First Communions	3,482
Confirmations	3,298
Marriages:	
Catholic	455
Interfaith	332
Total Marriages	787
Deaths	1,991
Total Catholic Population	217,672
Total Population	1,790,849

Former Bishops—Most Revs. JOSEPH H. ALBERS, D.D., J.C.D., appt. Titular Bishop of Lunda and Auxiliary to the Archbishop of Cincinnati, Dec. 16, 1929; cons. Dec. 27, 1929; appt. first Bishop of Lansing, Aug. 4, 1937; died Dec. 1, 1965; ALEXANDER M. ZALESKI, D.D., S.S.L., appt. Titular Bishop of Lyrbe and Auxiliary of Detroit, March 28, 1950; cons. May 23, 1950; transferred to Lansing Oct. 7, 1964; acceded to the See Dec. 1, 1965; died May 16, 1975; KENNETH J. POVISH, D.D., appt. Bishop of Crookston, July 28, 1970; cons. Sept. 29, 1970; appt. Bishop of Lansing, Oct. 8, 1975; installed Dec. 11, 1975; retired Nov. 7, 1995; died Sept. 5, 2003; CARL F. MENGELING, D.D., S.T.D., ord. May 25, 1957; appt. Bishop of Lansing Nov. 7, 1995; cons. and installed Jan. 25, 1996; retired Feb. 27, 2008.

Chancery—300 W. Ottawa St., Lansing, 48933. Tel: 517-342-2440; Fax: 517-342-2519. (see Diocesan Departments for additional Fax numbers); Office Hours: Mon.-Fri. 8-12 & 1-4:30; Address all communications to this office.

Bishop's Office—300 W. Ottawa St., Lansing, 48933. Tel: 517-342-2452; Fax: 517-342-2505. Rev. Msgrs. STEVEN J. RAICA, J.C.D., Chancellor & Administrative Asst. to the Bishop. Tel: 517-342-2454; MICHAEL D. MURPHY, Moderator of the Curia. Tel: 517-342-2450; GEORGE C. MICHALEK, J.C.L., Vice Chancellor. Tel: 517-485-9902.

Vicar General—Rev. Msgr. RICHARD GROSHEK (Retired), 4381 Springbrook Dr., Swartz Creek, 48473. Tel: 810-630-2042.

Regional Vicars—Revs. JOHN P. KLEIN, Lansing; DENNIS J. HOWARD, Clinton/Shiawassee; ANDREW A. CZAJKOWSKI, Genesee; JAMES R. SHAVER, Jackson; DANIEL WHEELER, Lenawee; DAVID HOWELL, Livingston; BRENDAN J. WALSH, Washtenaw.

College of Consultors—Rev. Msgrs. MICHAEL D. MURPHY; STEVEN J. RAICA, J.C.D.; Revs. JAMES F. EISELE; KARL L. PUNG; DAVID HOWELL; CHARLES IRVIN (Retired); ROBERT H. MCGRAW; THOMAS D. NENNEAU; FREDERICK H. TAGGART, O.S.A.; BRENDAN J. WALSH; DANIEL WHEELER.

Vicar for Charismatic Communities—Rev. PETER J. CLARK, St. Mary Church, 157 High St., Williamston, 48895. Tel: 517-655-2620; Fax: 517-655-3933.

Vicar for Religious—Sr. MARY ANN FOGGIN, S.G.L., 300 W. Ottawa St., Lansing, 48933. Tel: 517-342-2506; Fax: 517-342-2468.

Ecumenical Officer—Rev. WILLIAM WEGHER, St. Mary, 10601 Dexter Pinckney Rd., Pinckney, 48169. Tel: 734-878-3161; Fax: 734-878-2383.

Commissions and Councils—

Presbyteral Council—Rev. Msgr. GEORGE C. MICHALEK, J.C.L., St. Mary Cathedral, 219 Seymour St., Lansing, 48933. Tel: 517-484-5331; Fax: 517-484-0475.

Board of Education and Catechesis—MICHAEL MCCARTHY, Pres. Tel: 810-519-4056.
Building Commission—Rev. JONATHAN WEHRLE, St. Martha Church, 1100 W. Grand River, Okemos, 48864. Tel: 517-349-1763; Fax: 517-347-3536.
Cursillo—Rev. Msgr. SYLVESTER L. FEDEWA, Spiritual Dir. (Retired), 120 N. Willow St., Box 412, Westphalia, 48894. Tel: 989-587-4379.
Finance Council—Rev. DANIEL WHEELER, St. Elizabeth, 506 N. Union St., Tecumseh, 49286. Tel: 517-423-2447; Fax: 517-424-7706.
Priest Pension Board—Rev. JONATHAN WEHRLE, St. Martha, 1100 W. Grand River, Okemos, 48864. Tel: 517-349-1763.
Priests' Assignment Commission—Revs. ROBERT H. MCGRAW; JAMES F. EISELE; MARK INGLOT; JOHN FAIN; THOMAS BUTLER; KARL PUNG; TIMOTHY NELSON; STEVEN M. MATTSON; CHARLES CANOY; GORDON P. REIGLE.

Diocesan Offices And Departments

Moderator of the Curia—Rev. Msgr. MICHAEL D. MURPHY. Tel: 517-342-2450; Fax: 517-342-2505.
Safe Environment Office—SALLY ELLIS, Coord. Tel: 517-342-2551; Fax: 517-481-2260.
Diocesan Archivist—Rev. Msgr. GEORGE C. MICHALEK, J.C.L., 300 W. Ottawa St., Lansing, 48933. Tel: 517-485-9902; Fax: 517-484-8880.
Diocesan Mission Office— (Includes Propagation of the Faith, Holy Childhood Assoc., Inter-Parish Sharing) Rev. MICHAEL J. WILLIAMS, Dir., 300 W. Ottawa St., Lansing, 48933. Tel: 517-342-2541; Fax: 517-342-2519.
Legal Advisor—Deacon MICHAEL MURRAY. Tel: 517-342-2456; Fax: 517-342-2527.
Diocesan Tribunal—
Judicial Vicar—Rev. Msgr. RAYMOND J. GOEHRING, J.C.L., 300 W. Ottawa St., Lansing, 48933. Tel: 517-342-2560; Fax: 517-342-2561 (Address all rogatory commissions to the Diocesan Tribunal).
Tribunal Judges—Rev. Msgrs. RAYMOND J. GOEHRING, J.C.L.; STEVEN J. RAICA, J.C.D.; EILEEN JARAMILLO, J.C.L.; Rev. Msgr. GEORGE C. MICHALEK, J.C.L.; Rev. PHILLIP SCHWEDA, J.C.L.
Defenders of the Bond—Rev. BENNETT P. CONSTANTINE, J.C.D.; Deacon JOHN CAMERON, J.C.L.
Promoter of Justice—Rev. CHARLES IRVIN (Retired).
Court Experts—RICHARD G. STRIFE, Ph.D.; LINDA BLOHM, Ph.D.
Notary—AVA JO PUNG.
Victim Assistance Coordinator—Rev. Msgrs. MICHAEL D. MURPHY. Tel: 517-342-2450. Email: mmurphy@dioceseoflansing.org; STEVEN J. RAICA, J.C.D. Tel: 517-342-2454. Email: sraica@dioceseoflansing.org.
Office of Pastoral Planning—Sr. RITA WENZLICK, O.P., Dir. Tel: 517-342-2502; Fax: 517-342-2468.
Christian Initiation Advisory Committee—MICHAEL ANDREWS, Chm. Tel: 517-342-2479.
Faith Magazine— See Miscellaneous Listings: Faith Publishing Service.
Liturgical Commission Publishings— See Miscellaneous Listings.
Department of Catholic Charities—CHRISTOPHER ROOT, Chm. Tel: 517-342-2562; Fax: 517-342-2446.
Bishop's Council on Alcoholism-Chemical Dependency—VINCENT GALE. Tel: 517-342-2471.
Befriender Ministry—VINCENT GALE. Tel: 517-342-2471.
Campaign for Human Development—VINCENT GALE. Tel: 517-342-2471.
Catholic Relief Services—VINCENT GALE. Tel: 517-342-2471.
Courage and Encourage—VINCENT GALE. Tel: 517-342-2471.
Family Life—VINCENT GALE. Tel: 517-342-2471.
Natural Family Planning—CHRISTINE BACKLUND. Tel: 517-342-2587.
Life Justice—VACANT. Tel: 517-342-2469.
Restorative Justice—TIM METTS, Dir. Tel: 517-342-2495.
Separated & Divorced Ministry—VINCENT GALE. Tel: 517-342-2471.
Project Rachel (Post-Abortion Counseling)—VINCENT GALE. Tel: 517-342-2471.
Multicultural Evangelization—RONALD LANDFAIR, Dir. Tel: 517-342-2496.
Ministry with Persons with Disabilities—JOANN DAVIS, Ph.D., Dir. Tel: 517-342-2497.
Catholic Deaf Ministry—ROSE SMITH, Dir. Tel: 517-342-2532; Rev. BOSCO PADAMATTUMMAL, Chap. Tel: 810-629-2251.
Hispanic/Migrant Ministry—RONALD LANDFAIR, Dir. Tel: 517-342-2496.
Department of Communication—MICHAEL DIEBOLD, Chm. Tel: 517-853-7660; Fax: 517-853-7616.
Department of Education and Catechesis—Rev. STEVEN M. MATTSON, Chm. Tel: 517-342-2481; Fax: 517-342-2515.
Superintendent of Schools—Rev. STEVEN M. MATTSON. Tel: 517-342-2481.
Instructional Programs PreK-12—SALLY AMMAN, Dir. Tel: 517-342-2483.
Evangelization—PATRICK RINKER. Tel: 517-342-2485.
Catechesis—MICHAEL ANDREWS, Dir. Tel: 517-342-2479.
Youth Ministry and Young Adult Ministry—PATRICK RINKER. Tel: 517-342-2485.
Campus Ministry—PATRICK RINKER. Tel: 517-342-2485.
Worship Office—RITA THIRON, Dir. Tel: 517-342-2480.
Worship Commission—Rev. WILLIAM R. LUGGER. Tel: 517-482-1346.
Department of Finance—THOMAS PASTULA, Chm. & Finance Officer. Tel: 517-342-2442; Fax: 517-342-2527.
Accounting Services—ANDREA RATHWELL. Tel: 517-342-2445; Fax: 517-342-2519.
Diocesan Services Appeal and Development—PATRICIA O'HEARN. Tel: 517-342-2503; Fax: 517-342-2519.
Property & Cemeteries—PAUL GARRIEPY. Tel: 517-342-2534; Fax: 517-342-2519.
Technology Administrator—SHARON BYERS. Tel: 517-342-2538; Fax: 517-342-2519.
Department of Formation and Lay Ministry—Rev. GERALD L. VINCKE, Chm. Tel: 517-342-2507; Fax: 517-342-2468.
Director of Seminarians—Rev. GERALD L. VINCKE. Tel: 517-342-2507.
Joseph H. Albers Trust Fund for Diocesan Vocations—Rev. GERALD L. VINCKE. Tel: 517-342-2507.
Lay Ecclesial Ministry—NANCY JOSEPH, Dir. Tel: 517-342-2512.
Permanent Diaconate—Deacon GERALD BRENNAN. Tel: 517-342-2451.
Priestly Life and Ministry—Rev. KARL L. PUNG, Dir. Tel: 810-229-9863; Fax: 810-220-0730.
Vocation Services—Sr. MARY ANN FOGGIN, S.G.L., Dir. Tel: 517-342-2506.
Discernment Houses—
Emmaus House—Rev. GERALD L. VINCKE, Dir., 320 M.A.C. Ave., East Lansing, 48823. Tel: 517-351-1543.
Father McGiveny House—Rev. WILLIAM A. ASHBAUGH, Dir., St. Thomas the Apostle Church, 530 Elizabeth St., Ann Arbor, 48104. Tel: 734-761-8606.
St. Catherine House—Rev. WILLIAM A. ASHBAUGH, Dir., St. Thomas the Apostle Church, 530 Elizabeth St., Ann Arbor, 48104. Tel: 734-761-8606.

CLERGY, PARISHES, MISSIONS AND PAROCHIAL SCHOOLS

CITY OF LANSING

(INGHAM COUNTY)

1—ST. MARY CATHEDRAL (1866) Revs. Bernard Reilly; Jeffrey Njus. In Res., Rev. Msgrs. George C. Michalek, Vice Chancellor, Diocese of Lansing; Steven J. Raica, Chancellor, Diocese of Lansing.
Res.: 219 Seymour, 48933. Tel: 517-484-5331; Fax: 517-484-0475. Web: http://stmarycathedrallansing.catholicweb.com.
Catechesis/Religious Program—Jennifer Nelson, D.R.E. Students 15.

2—ST. ANDREW DUNG-LAC (1998), (Vietnamese), Rev. Joseph Tran.
5430 S. Washington Ave., 48911. Tel: 517-882-8205; Fax: 517-882-8209. Email: s_lac@sbcglobal.net. Web: www.giaoxudunglac.org.
Res.: 820 Mel Ave., 48911. Tel: 517-272-3276.
Catechesis/Religious Program—Chuong Thanh Nguyen, D.R.E. Students 79.

3—ST. CASIMIR (1921) Rev. William R. Lugger.
Mailing Address: 815 Sparrow Ave., 48910-8003. Tel: 517-482-1346; Fax: 517-482-1313. Email: office@stcas.org. Web: www.stcas.org.
Catechesis/Religious Program—Students 108.

4—CRISTO REY (1961), (Hispanic), Rev. Frederick L. Thelen; Deacon Rogelio Alfaro.
Office: 201 W. Miller Rd., 48911. Tel: 517-394-4639; Fax: 517-394-8090. Web: www.cristoreychurch.org.
Res.: 6121 Rosedale Rd., 48911. Tel: 517-394-0676.
Catechesis/Religious Program—Students 225.

5—ST. GERARD (Delta Township, Eaton Co.) (1958) [JC] Revs. John P. Klein; Prabhu Lakra; Deacons Richard Savage; Jim Corder.
Res.: 1304 Maycroft, 48917. Tel: 517-323-2379; Fax: 517-886-1394. Web: stgerard.org.
School—4433 W. Willow, 48917. Tel: 517-321-6126; Fax: 517-323-8046. Email: mpiecuch@stgerard.org. Web: stgerardlansing.org. Michelle Piecuch, Prin. Lay Teachers 30; Students 561.
Catechesis/Religious Program—Tel: 517-321-4179. Students 414.

6—HOLY CROSS (1924) Closed. For inquiries for parish records contact the chancery.

7—IMMACULATE HEART OF MARY (1949) Revs. John Byers; George Daisy; Deacons William Fudge III; John Cameron.
Office:—3815 S. Cedar, 48910. Tel: 517-393-3030; Fax: 517-393-0855. Email: smithb@ihmlansing.org. Web: immaculateheartofmarylansing.catholicweb.com.
School—Tel: 517-882-6631; Fax: 517-882-5536. Email: shewchuckj@ihmlansing.org. Web: www.ihmlansing.org. Angela Johnston, Prin. Lay Teachers 8; Students 160.
Catechesis/Religious Program—Tel: 517-393-3033. Students 255.

8—RESURRECTION (1922) Revs. William J. Koenigsknecht; Pankratius Kerketta. In Res., Rev. Msgr. Raymond J. Goehring.
Res.: 1531 E. Michigan Ave., 48912. Tel: 517-482-4749; Fax: 517-484-4740. Email: resurrection1531@sbcglobal.net. Web: resurrectionlansing.org.
School—1527 E. Michigan Ave., 48912. Tel: 517-487-0439; Fax: 517-487-3198. Email: resurrectionschool@comcast.net. Web: resschool-.com. Jack Von Achen, Prin. Lay Teachers 12; Students 141.
Catechesis/Religious Program—1527 E. Michigan Ave., 48912. Tel: 517-482-2605. Students 82.

9—ST. THERESE (1949) [CEM] Rev. Michael J. Williams; Deacon David Borzenski; Anthony Sperendi, Adult Faith Formation Dir.
Res.: 102 W. Randolph St., 48906. Tel: 517-487-3749; Fax: 517-487-3755. Email: staff@sttherese.org. Web: www.sttherese.org.
School—2620 N. Turner St., 48906. Tel: 517-482-1634; Fax: 517-482-1634. Web: www.sttherese.org/school. Mr. R. Thomas Derengoski, Prin. Lay Teachers 9; Students 121.
Catechesis/Religious Program—Tel: 517-487-3730. Ms. Patricia Droste, D.R.E. Students 82.

OUTSIDE THE CITY OF LANSING

ADRIAN, LENAWEE CO.

1—ST. JOSEPH (1863) [CEM] Rev. David William Hudgins.
Res.: 415 Ormsby St., 49221. Tel: 517-265-8938; Fax: 517-265-1987. Email: office@stjosephadrian.com. Web: www.stjosephadrian.com.
Catechesis/Religious Program—Email: aimee@stjosephadrian.com. Students 136.

2—ST. MARY OF GOOD COUNSEL (1853) [CEM] Rev. Robert Schramm, O.S.F.S.; Deacons Richard Bayes Jr.; Calistro Torres. In Res., Rev. Louis A. Komorowski, O.S.F.S.
Office: 305 Division St., 49221. Tel: 517-263-4681; Fax: 517-263-4682. Email: stmarys@tc3net.com. Web: www.stmarysadrian.com.
Res.: 320 Division St., 49221. Tel: 517-265-6543.
Catechesis/Religious Program—Tel: 517-265-4160; Fax: 517-263-4682. Students 162.

ANN ARBOR, WASHTENAW CO.

1—CHRIST THE KING (1981) Rev. Edward O. Fride; Deacons Daniel R. Foley; Gerald P. Holowicki; Louis J. Russello, Pastoral Assoc.; Larry Randolph. 4000 Ave Maria Dr., 48105. Tel: 734-665-5040; Fax: 734-663-3735. Email: thofer@ctkcc.net. Web: www.ctkcc.net.
Catechesis/Religious Program—Tel: 734-663-2388; Fax: 734-663-3735. Email: bbenjamin@ctkcc.net. Students 300.

2—ST. FRANCIS OF ASSISI (1950) [CEM] Revs. James G. McDougall; John Linden.
Res.: 2150 Frieze Ave., 48104. Tel: 734-769-2550; Fax: 734-821-2102. Email: stfrancis@rc.net. Web: www.stfrancisa2.com. In Res., Rev. Terrence J. Dumas (Retired).
School—(Grades K-8) Tel: 734-821-2200; Fax: 734-821-2202. Email: stf@stfrancisaa.org. Sara Collins, Prin.; Mary Hendricks, Librarian; Laurie Ruselowski, Librarian. Lay Teachers 39; Students 444.
Catechesis/Religious Program—Tel: 734-821-2130. Email: stfreled@stfrancisa2.org. Students 750.

3—ST. MARY STUDENT PARISH (1915), Serving students, faculty, and staff at the University of Michigan. Revs. J. Thomas McClain, S.J.; Dennis T. Dillon, S.J.; Dennis T. Glasgow, S.J.; Dan Reim, S.J., Campus Min.; Rachel Brennan, Devel. Dir.; Susan L. Waters, Admin.; Sr. Catherine Morgan, O.P., Campus Min.; Anita M. Bohn, Music Min.; Patrick J. Waters, Pastoral Assoc.; Sr. Dorothy Ederer, O.P., Campus Min.; Deacon Romolo J. Leone, Pastoral Assoc.; Michael Bayer, Campus Min.

Office: 331 Thompson St., 48104-2295. Tel: 734-663-0557; 734-663-0558; Fax: 734-663-2756. Email: stmarys@umich.edu. Web: www.stmarystudentparish.org.
Catechesis/Religious Program—Students 265.

4—St. Patrick (1831) [CEM] Rev. Gerald Gawronski.
Res.: 5671 Whitmore Lake Rd., 48105. Tel: 734-662-8141; 734-663-1851; Fax: 734-994-9136. Email: carlap@parishmail.com. Web: www.oldstpatrick-annarbor.com.
Catechesis/Religious Program—Students 31.

5—St. Thomas the Apostle (1835) [CEM] Revs. William A. Ashbaugh; Nithyaselvam Arokiaselvam; Glen D. Johnston, Business Mgr.; Deacons James Miles; Warren Hecht.
Mailing Address: 530 Elizabeth St., 48104. Tel: 734-761-8606; Fax: 734-997-8432. Web: www.sta2.org.
School—Tel: 734-769-0911; Fax: 734-769-9078. Tony Moskus, Prin. Lay Teachers 21; Students 272.
Catechesis/Religious Program—Tel: 734-761-8606; Fax: 734-997-8432. Monica Pope, Dir. Faith Formation; Beth Montgomery, Coord., Youth Ministry. Students 202.

Bellevue, Eaton Co., St. Ann (1923) Rev. Francis D. Mossholder, Parochial Admin.; Rev. Msgr. Raymond J. Goehring, Sacramental Min.
Res.: 312 S. Main St., P.O. Box 33, 49021. Tel: 269-763-9372; Fax: 269-763-0067.
Catechesis/Religious Program—Students 19.

Blissfield, Lenawee Co., St. Peter the Apostle (1910) Rev. John Loughran, O.S.F.S.
Res.: 309 S. Lane St., 49228. Tel: 517-486-2156; Fax: 517-486-2157. Email: djensen.stpeter@tc3net.com.
Catechesis/Religious Program—Email: kbriggs.stpeter@tc3net.com. Students 105.

Brighton, Livingston Co.

1—Holy Spirit (1979) Rev. John George Rocus; Deacon Gerald Brennan.
Res.: Tel: 810-231-9199, Ext. 212; Fax: 810-231-6129. Email: holyspiritchurch@chartermi.net. Web: www.hsrcc.net.
School—9565 Musch Rd., 48116. Tel: 810-231-9199, Ext. 214. Email: holyspiritschool@chartermi.net. Anna Piccirillo-Loewe, Prin.
Catechesis/Religious Program—Tel: 810-231-9199, Ext. 209. Katherine Jean, Dir. Faith Formation. Students 65.

2—St. Mary Magdalen Church (1993) Rev. David Howell; Deacons H. David Scharf; James Chevalier; Gary Prise.
Res.: 2201 Old U.S. 23, 48114. Tel: 810-229-0646; 810-229-8624; Fax: 810-229-6471. Email: info@saintmarymagdalen.org. Web: www.saintmarymagdalen.org.
Catechesis/Religious Program—Students 725.

3—St. Patrick (1832), (Irish), [CEM] Revs. Karl L. Pung; Mark J. Rutherford; Deacons David Lawrence; Patrick A. McDonald; Sr. Theresa M. Fifer, O.S.F., Pastoral Min.; Margaret Mullally-Henne, Pastoral Min.; Glenna Diskin, Pastoral Min.; Robert Wolf, Pastoral Min.; Martha Goode, Pastoral Min.; H. William Smeal, Pastoral Min.
711 Rickett Rd., 48116.
Res.: 129 Becker, 48116-9863. Tel: 810-229-9863; Fax: 810-220-0730. Web: http://home.catholicweb.com/stpatchurch.
School—1001 Orndorf Dr., 48116. Tel: 810-229-7946; Fax: 810-229-6206. Jeanine Kenny, Prin. Lay Teachers 27; Students 455.
Catechesis/Religious Program—710 Rickett Rd., 48116. Tel: 810-229-4221; Fax: 810-229-6206. Email: secre@stpatchurch.org. Sr. Theresa M. Fifer, O.S.F., D.R.E. Students 1,015.

Brooklyn, Lenawee Co., St. Joseph Shrine (Irish Hills) (1854) [CEM] Rev. Carl A. Simon; Deacon Gene Hausmann.
Office: 8743 U.S. 12, 49230. Tel: 517-467-2183; Fax: 517-467-4285. Email: sjshrine@frontiernet.net. Web: www.stjosephshrinebrooklyn.catholicweb.com.
Catechesis/Religious Program—Tel: 517-467-2106. Students 115.

Burton, Genesee Co.

1—Blessed Sacrament (1957) Rev. Joseph Sy Kim.
Res.: 6340 Roberta, 48509. Tel: 810-742-3151; Fax: 810-742-1409. Email: blesssacrament@comcast.net.
Catechesis/Religious Program—Rev. Joseph Sy Kim, D.R.E. Students 43.

2—Holy Redeemer (1940) Rev. Timothy E. MacDonald; Deacon Rodney Amon, Business Mgr.
Res.: 1227 E. Bristol Rd., 48529. Tel: 810-743-3050; Fax: 810-743-4381. Email: hrcatholic@yahoo.com. Web: www.holyredeemerburton.com.
Catechesis/Religious Program—Tel: 810-742-9460; Fax: 810-743-9102. Email: play_stairway@hotmail.com. Jacki Popadich, D.R.E. Students 189.

Charlotte, Eaton Co., St. Mary (1868) Rev. Francis D. Mossholder; Deacons Thomas Fogle; Gregory Poole.
807 St. Mary Blvd., 48813. Tel: 517-543-4319; Fax: 517-543-9078. Email: stmaryschurch807@att.net. Web: stmarycharlotte.catholicweb.com.
Res.: 812 St. Mary Blvd., 48813. Tel: 517-541-2755; Fax: 517-543-9078.
School—905 St. Mary Blvd., 48813. Tel: 517-543-3460; Fax: 517-541-9798. Email: smschar@sbcglobal.net. Web: stmaryschoolcharlotte.catholicweb.com. Nancy Gibson, Prin. Lay Teachers 4; Students 60.
Catechesis/Religious Program—Tel: 517-541-8223. Email: stmarydre@sbcglobal.net. Students 104.

Chelsea, Washtenaw Co., St. Mary (1845) [CEM] [JC] Rev. William J. Turner; Deacon Thomas Franklin.
Res.: 14200 E. Old U.S. Hwy. 12, 48118. Tel: 734-475-7561; Fax: 734-475-3207. Email: smcch@aol.com. Web: www.stmarychelsea.org.
Catechesis/Religious Program—Tel: 734-475-8164; Fax: 734-475-5835. Students 500.

Clarklake, Jackson Co., St. Rita (1916) [JC] Rev. Lehr Barkenquest, O.S.F.S.; Deacon Louis Weitzel.
Res.: 10720 Hayes Rd., 49234. Tel: 517-592-5470; Fax: 517-592-5470 (Call First). Email: stritascatholicchurch@frontiernet.net. Web: catholicweb.com/stritaclarklake.
Catechesis/Religious Program—Tel: 517-592-5718. Students 252.

Clinton, Lenawee Co., St. Dominic Oratory (1853) [CEM] Revs. Daniel Wheeler; Paul Ruddy, O.S.F.S., Sacramental Min.
Res.: 506 N. Union, Tecumseh, 49286. Tel: 517-423-2447; Fax: 517-424-7706.
Catechesis/Religious Program—Tel: 517-456-4501. Students 32.

Clio, Genesee Co., SS. Charles and Helena (1953) Rev. Gerald Ploof.
Res.: 230 E. Vienna St., 48420-1423. Tel: 810-686-9861; Fax: 810-686-8070. Email: sscharlesandhelena@catholicweb.com. Web: www.sscharlesandhelena.org.
Catechesis/Religious Program—Tel: 810-686-6720. Students 201.

Concord, Jackson Co., St. Catherine Laboure (1953) Rev. Denis R. Spitzley; Deacon Carol Franssen.
211 Harmon Ave., 49237.
Res.: 312 Kryst St., 49237. Tel: 517-524-7578; Fax: 517-524-7518. Web: http://home.catholicweb.com/stcatherinelaboureconcord.
Catechesis/Religious Program—Students 104.

Davison, Genesee Co., St. John the Evangelist (1871) [CEM] Revs. Andrew A. Czajkowski; George Varkey, M.S.F.S.; Deacon Dan Fairweather.
404 N. Dayton St., 48423-1397.
Res.: 316 N. Dayton St., 48423-1397. Tel: 810-653-2377; 810-653-8015; 810-658-4776 (Voice Mail); Fax: 810-658-1123. Web: www.stjohndavison.org.
Catechesis/Religious Program—505 N. Dayton, 48423. Tel: 810-653-4056. Elaine Davis, D.R.E.; Elaine Ouellette, D.R.E.; Paul Schlegelmilch, D.R.E., Youth Ministry. Students 636.

DeWitt, Clinton Co., St. Jude (1971) Rev. Dwight M. Ezop.
Res.: 409 Wilson, De Witt, 48820. Tel: 517-669-8335; Fax: 517-669-8343. Email: catholic.stjude@comcast.net. Web: www.stjudedewitt.com.
Catechesis/Religious Program—Tel: 517-669-8341. Students 515.

Deerfield, Lenawee Co., St. Alphonsus (1864) [CEM] Rev. John Loughran, O.S.F.S.
Church Office: 222 Carey St., 49238. Tel: 517-447-3500; 517-447-3766 (Rectory); Fax: 517-447-3210. Email: stalphon@cass.net.
Catechesis/Religious Program—Tel: 517-447-3500; Fax: 517-447-3210. Students 104.

Dexter, Washtenaw Co., St. Joseph (1840) [CEM] Rev. Brendan J. Walsh; Deacon Romolo Leone.
Office: 3430 Dover St., 48130. Tel: 734-426-8483; Fax: 734-426-6451. Email: info@stjos.com. Web: www.stjos.com.
Church: 6805 Mast Rd., 48130.
Catechesis/Religious Program—Tel: 734-426-2674; Fax: 734-426-6451. Email: marinell_high@stjos.com. Students 624.

Durand, Shiawassee Co., St. Mary (1900) Rev. Msgr. Steven J. Raica.
Res.: 700 Columbia Dr., 48429. Tel: 989-288-6704; Fax: 989-288-0295. Web: www.stmarydurand.catholicweb.com.
Catechesis/Religious Program—Tel: 989-288-6704. Students 220.

East Lansing, Ingham Co.

1—St. John the Evangelist Church and Student Center (1958) Revs. Mark Inglot; Joseph J. Krupp; Linda Pivarnik, Dir. Devel.; Denise Waytes, Campus Min.; Stephen Kasperick-Postellon, Dir. Worship; Al Weilbaecher, Dir. Formation & Family Min.; Katie Cervenak, Dir. Communications & Special Events; Keith Tharp, Business Mgr.
327 M.A.C. Ave., 48823.
Res.: 915 Alton Rd., 48823. Tel: 517-351-7215; Fax: 517-337-8358. Email: stjohnsp@msu.edu. Web: www.stjohnmsu.org.

2—St. Thomas Aquinas (1940) Revs. Mark Inglot; Michael O'Brien, Parochial Vicar; Joseph J. Krupp, Dir. Campus Min.; Deacons James Kasprzak; Michael Murray.
Res.: 955 Alton Rd., 48823. Tel: 517-351-7215; Fax: 517-351-7271. Web: www.elcatholics.org.
School—915 Alton Rd., 48823. Tel: 517-332-0813; Fax: 517-332-9490. Rod Murphy, Prin. Lay Teachers 24; Students 318.
Catechesis/Religious Program—Tel: 517-351-5460. Students 620.

Eaton Rapids, Eaton Co., St. Peter (1891) Rev. Bennett P. Constantine; Deacon Gideon Marsal.
Res.: 405 Knight St., 48827. Tel: 517-663-4735; Fax: 517-663-7110. Email: cspc2001@sbcglobal.net. Web: www.stpetereatonrapids.catholicweb.com.
School—515 E. Knight St., 48827. Tel: 517-663-1799; Fax: 517-663-3799. Email: kchristesen@stpeterknight.com. Web: www.stpeterknights.com. Kathleen Christensen, Prin. Students 35.
Catechesis/Religious Program—Tel: 517-663-2088; Fax: 517-663-7110. Email: gideonmar@sbcglobal.net. Web: www.stpetereatonrapids.catholicweb.com. Students 122.

Fenton, Genesee Co., St. John (1843) [CEM 2] Revs. David W. Harvey; Bosco Padamattummal (India); Deacon Ronald Kenney.
Res.: 600 N. Adelaide St., 48430. Tel: 810-629-2251; Fax: 810-629-2302. Web: www.stjohnfenton.org.
School—514 Lincoln St., 48430. Tel: 810-629-6551; Fax: 810-629-2213. Ted Havens, Prin. Lay Teachers 31; Students 475.
Catechesis/Religious Program—512 N. Adelaide St., 48430. Tel: 810-629-1850. Students 665.

Flint, Genesee Co.

1—St. Agnes (1928) Closed. For inquiries for parish records contact St. John Vianney, Flint.

2—All Saints (1910), (Polish), [CEM] Rev. Anthony P. Majchrowski.
Res.: G-4063 W. Pierson Rd., 48504. Tel: 810-787-0491.
Catechesis/Religious Program—Students 34.

3—Christ the King (1929), (African American), Rev. Philip Schmitter.
1811 Seymour Ave., 48503. Tel: 810-233-0402; Fax: 810-233-0466. Email: ccatholic@att.net. Web: www.christthekingflint.catholicweb.com.
Res.: G-2381 E. Carpenter Rd., 48505.
Catechesis/Religious Program—Students 16.

4—St. Francis of Assisi, Closed. For inquiries for parish records contact the diocesan archives.

5—Holy Rosary (1951) Rev. George Puthenpeedika (India), Parochial Admin.; Deacon Michael Dear.
Res.: 5199 Richfield Rd., 48506. Tel: 810-736-4040; Fax: 810-736-9129. Email: holyrosarysecretary@yahoo.com. Web: www.holyrosaryflint.catholicweb.com; www.holyrosaryflint.org.
School—5191 Richfield Rd., 48506. Tel: 810-736-4220; Fax: 810-736-0164. Email: hrschool@comcast.net. Deborah Hodges, Admin. Lay Teachers 5; Students 87.
Catechesis/Religious Program—Tel: 810-736-4040, Ext. 30. Students 70.

6—St. John Vianney (1941) Rev. Thomas Firestone.
Res.: 2415 Bagley St., 48504-4613. Tel: 810-235-1812; Fax: 810-235-4911.
School—2319 Bagley St., 48504. Tel: 810-235-5687; Fax: 810-235-2811. Web: www.sjvkids.com. Mrs. Kathleen Slattery, Prin. Lay Teachers 14; Total Staff 14; Students 250.
Catechesis/Religious Program—Students 84.

7—St. Leo the Great (1957) Closed. For inquiries for parish records contact Holy Rosary, Flint.

8—St. Luke (1950) Closed. For inquiries for parish records contact St. John Vianney, Flint.

9—St. Mary (1919) Rev. Santhiyagu Arockiyasamy, M.S.F.S. (India).
Res.: 2500 N. Franklin Ave., 48506. Tel: 810-232-4012; Fax: 810-232-3889. Email: stmaryflint@hotmail.com.
Catechesis/Religious Program—Sr. Mary McCarron, S.S.J., D.R.E. & Pastoral Assoc. Students 20.

10—St. Matthew (1911) Revs. Frederick H. Taggart, O.S.A.; John F. Flynn, O.S.A.; James G. Ryan, O.S.A.
Res.: 706 Beach St., 48502. Tel: 810-232-0880; Fax: 810-232-4148. Web: www.stmatthewflint.org.
Catechesis/Religious Program—Students 15.

11—St. Michael (1843) Rev. Arockiyasamy Santhiyagu, M.S.F.S. (India); Deacon Ronald Rowe.
Res.: 609 E. Fifth Ave., 48503. Tel: 810-238-2679; Fax: 810-232-6820. Email: rxrowe@hotmail.com.
Catechesis/Religious Program—Tel: 810-238-7931; Fax: 810-232-6820. Students 66.

12—Our Lady of Guadalupe (1957), (Spanish), Rev. Timothy Nelson.

Res.: G-2316 W. Coldwater Rd., 48505. Tel: 810-787-5701; Fax: 810-787-3198. Email: olog-flint@rc.net. Web: www.ologflint.org.
Catechesis/Religious Program—Tel: 810-744-4241. Email: smetzler@sbcglobal.net. Students 121.
13—ST. PIUS X (1955) Rev. Robert F. Copeland; Deacon Gary A. Gallagher.
Res.: G-3139 Hogarth Ave., 48532. Tel: 810-235-8574. Email: stpiuschurch@comcast.net. Web: www.saintpiusxparish.com.
School—Tel: 810-235-8572; Fax: 810-235-2675. R.J. Kaplan, Prin. Sisters 1; Lay Teachers 13; Students 212.
Catechesis/Religious Program—Students 68.
Convent—G-3165 Hogarth Ave., 48532. Tel: 810-233-8956.
14—SACRED HEART (1928) Closed. For inquiries for parish records contact St. John Vianney, Flint.
FLUSHING, GENESEE CO., ST. ROBERT (1875) [CEM] Revs. Roy Theodore Horning; Louis T. Ekka; Deacon Dennis Pennell.
Res.: 310 N. Cherry St., 48433. Tel: 810-659-2501; Fax: 810-659-2564. Email: jrymar@parishmail.com. Web: www.strobertparish.org.
School—St. Robert School, 214 E. Henry, 48433. Tel: 810-659-2503; Fax: 810-659-4002. Email: srsoffice@aol.com. Web: www.strobertschool.com. Susan C. Sharp, Prin. Lay Teachers 21; Students 253.
Catechesis/Religious Program—Tel: 810-659-8556. Students 276.
FOWLER, CLINTON CO., MOST HOLY TRINITY (1881), (German), [CEM] Rev. Dennis J. Howard; Deacon Mark Simmon.
Res.: 545 N. Maple St., 48835. Tel: 989-593-2162; Fax: 989-593-2171. Email: mhtchurch@edzone.net. Web: www.mhtparish.com.
School—11144 Kent St., 48835. Tel: 517-593-2616; Fax: 989-593-2801. Email: annehufn@edzone.net. Anne K. Hufnagel, Prin. Lay Teachers 7; Students 81.
Catechesis/Religious Program—Tel: 517-593-3174; Fax: 517-593-2801. Email: halfmanandrew@hotmail.com. Students 278.
FOWLERVILLE, LIVINGSTON CO., ST. AGNES (1891) [CEM] Rev. James W. Lothamer, S.S.; Deacons Roger Cahaney; Peter Guditas.
Res.: 855 E. Grand River Ave., 48836. Tel: 517-223-8684; Fax: 517-223-0813. Email: stagnesfowlerville@sbcglobal.net. Web: www.stagnesfowlerville.parishesonline.com.
Catechesis/Religious Program—Tel: 517-223-8684. Students 340.
GAINES, GENESSEE CO., ST. JOSEPH (1871) [CEM] Revs. David Harvey, Canonical Pastor; Robert McKeon, Sacramental Min. (Retired); Sr. Ann Marie Petri, O.P., Pastoral Coord.
Res.: 9450 Duffield Rd., P.O. Box 145, 48436. Tel: 989-271-8434; Fax: 989-271-3017. Email: stjosephgaines@gmail.com. Web: stjosephgaines.catholicweb.com.
Catechesis/Religious Program—Tel: 989-288-0548; Fax: 989-288-6130. Sandy Corrion, D.R.E. Students 110.
GOODRICH, GENESEE CO., ST. MARK THE EVANGELIST (1978) Rev. Michael W. Kuchar.
Church: 7296 Gale Rd., P.O. Box 131, 48438. Tel: 810-636-2216; Fax: 810-636-7319. Email: stmarkslink@hotmail.com. Web: home.catholicweb.com/stmarktheevangelistgoodrich.
Catechesis/Religious Program—Email: stmarksdre@hotmail.com. Students 195.
GRAND BLANC, GENESEE CO., HOLY FAMILY (1946) Revs. Kenneth F. Coughlin; Kusitino Cobona; Deacons Jack Daunt; Terry Carsten.
Res.: 11824 S. Saginaw, 48439. Tel: 810-694-4891; Fax: 810-694-1583. Email: info@holyfamilygrandblanc.org. Web: www.holyfamilygrandblanc.catholicweb.com.
School—(Grades PreK-8), 215 Orchard St., 48439. Tel: 810-694-9072; Fax: 810-694-9405. Michele Jahn, Prin. Lay Teachers 24; Students 461.
Catechesis/Religious Program—Tel: 810-694-9072, Ext. 101; Fax: 810-695-0063. Students 399.
GRAND LEDGE, EATON CO., ST. MICHAEL (1901) Rev. James F. Eisele.
Res.: 405 Edwards St., 48837. Tel: 517-627-8493, Ext. 26; Fax: 517-627-1289. Web: www.stmichaelgl.org.
Church: 345 Edwards St., 48837.
School—325 Edwards St., 48837. Tel: 517-627-2167. Mitzi Luttrull, Prin. Lay Teachers 11; Students 186.
Catechesis/Religious Program—Tel: 517-627-8493. Students 287.
HILLSDALE, HILLSDALE CO., ST. ANTHONY (1853) [CEM] Rev. Thomas W. Butler.
Res.: 11 N. Broad St., 49242. Tel: 517-437-3305; Fax: 517-437-0034. Email: sharista@dmcibb.net. Web: http://home.catholicweb.com/stanthonypadua.
Catechesis/Religious Program—Tel: 517-437-2777. Students 216.
HOWELL, LIVINGSTON CO.
1—ST. AUGUSTINE (1843) [CEM], (Quasi Parish) Rev. Gregg A. Pleiness; Deacon William Sirl.
Church: 6481 Faussett Rd., 48855. Tel: 517-546-9807.
Res.: 8011 Faussett Rd., Fenton, 48430.
Parish House—Tel: 810-750-0354.
Catechesis/Religious Program—Students 182.
2—ST. JOHN THE BAPTIST (1843), (Irish—German), [CEM] Rev. Francis M. George; Deacon David Piggot.
Res.: 2099 Hacker Rd., 48855. Tel: 517-546-7200; Fax: 517-546-0403. Web: www.stjohnthebaptisthowell.catholicweb.com.
Catechesis/Religious Program—Tel: 517-548-2540; Fax: 517-546-0403. Students 565.
3—ST. JOSEPH (1888) [CEM] Revs. David J. Speicher; Kurian Kollapallil, M.S.F.S., Parochial Vicar; Deacons Endre Doran; Frank Wines Sr., Stewardship Dir.; Ray Kunik.
Res.: 456 Livingston St., 48843. Tel: 517-546-0090; Fax: 517-546-3126. Web: www.stjosephhowell.com.
School—425 E. Washington, 48843. Tel: 517-546-0090, Ext. 200; Fax: 517-546-8939. Kathleen Freeman, Prin. Lay Teachers 21; Students 330.
Catechesis/Religious Program—Tel: 517-546-0090, Ext. 200. Deacon Frank Wines Sr., D.R.E. Students 411.
HUDSON, LENAWEE CO., SACRED HEART (1846) [CEM] Rev. Richard Eberle, O.S.F.S.
Res.: 207 S. Market St., 49247. Tel: 517-448-3811; Fax: 517-448-2401. Email: rteberle@tc3net.com. Web: www.laforestnet.com/church.
School—Tel: 517-448-6405. Web: www.sacredhearthudson.com. April McCaskey, Prin. Lay Teachers 7; Students 86.
Catechesis/Religious Program—Web: www.sacredhearthudson.com/catechism. Students 63.
JACKSON, JACKSON CO.
1—ST. JOHN THE EVANGELIST (1856) [CEM] [JC] Revs. James R. Shaver; Randall J. Miller; Deacon Joseph A. Kratofil; Patricia Willson, Pastoral Assoc.
Res.: 711 N. Francis St., 49201. Tel: 517-784-0553; Fax: 517-788-5381. Email: stjohnjackson@catholicweb.com. Web: www.stjohntheevangelistjackson.catholicweb.com.
School—405 E. North St., 49202. Tel: 517-784-1714; Fax: 517-788-5382. Kathy Tarnacki, Prin. Lay Teachers 16; Students 183.
Catechesis/Religious Program—717 N. Waterloo at St. Joseph, 49202. Tel: 517-784-5746. Students 290.
2—ST. JOSEPH (1902), (Polish—Lithuanian), [JC] Revs. James Shaver; Randall J. Miller; Robert J. Pienta.
Rectory—705 N. Waterloo Ave., 49202. Tel: 517-784-9716; Fax: 517-784-5411.
Catechesis/Religious Program—Students 45.
3—ST. MARY STAR OF THE SEA (1881) Rev. Cecilio C. Reyna; Deacons Vincent C. Genco; Matthew Shannon.
Res.: 301 S. Mechanic St., 49201. Tel: 517-784-7184; Fax: 517-783-2571. Web: www.stmaryjackson.catholicweb.com.
School—116 E. Wesley St., 49201. Tel: 517-784-8811; Fax: 517-788-3425. Email: stmaryschool@tds.net. Julia Hurlburt, Prin. Lay Teachers 13; Students 125.
Catechesis/Religious Program—Tel: 517-788-6153. Email: stmaryjacksondre@tds.net. Students 85.
Oratory—St. Stanislaus Kosta 608 S. Elm Ave., 49203.
4—QUEEN OF THE MIRACULOUS MEDAL (1934) Revs. Robert H. McGraw; Jeff A. Poll; Deacons David Barrett; Ken Spaulding; Jack Kowalski.
Res.: 606 S. Wisner, 49203. Tel: 517-783-2748; Fax: 517-788-4528. Web: www.queenschurch.com.
School—811 S. Wisner, 49203. Tel: 517-782-2664; Fax: 517-782-3570. Ruth A. Benner, Prin. Lay Teachers 15; Students 310.
Catechesis/Religious Program—Students 137.
5—ST. STANISLAUS KOSTKA (1920), Now an oratory of St. Mary Star of the Sea, Jackson.
LAINGSBURG, SHIAWASSEE CO., ST. ISIDORE (1902) [CEM] Rev. Duaine H. Pamment.
Res.: 310 Crum St., 48848. Tel: 517-651-6617; 517-651-6722 (Office); Fax: 517-651-6617. Web: www.stisidorelaingsburg.catholicweb.com. Email: parishhq1@juno.com.
Catechesis/Religious Program—Tel: 517-651-6722. Students 115.
LESLIE, INGHAM CO., SS. CORNELIUS AND CYPRIAN (Bunker Hill) (1863) [CEM] Rev. Michael A. Petroski; Deacon Tom Rea.
Res.: 1320 Catholic Church Rd., 49251. Tel: 517-589-8492; Fax: 517-589-8470. Email: bnkrhlch@acd.net. Web: sscorneliusandcyprianleslie.catholicweb.com.
Catechesis/Religious Program—Students 71.
MANCHESTER, WASHTENAW CO., ST. MARY (1871) [CEM] Rev. Timothy D. Krzyzaniak; Deacon R. Dennis Walters.
Res.: 210 W. Main St., P.O. Box 249, 48158. Tel: 734-428-8811; Fax: 734-428-1393. Email: stmaryofc@rc.net. Web: www.stmarymanchester.catholicweb.com.
Catechesis/Religious Program—Students 61.
MANITOU BEACH, LENAWEE CO., ST. MARY ON THE LAKE (1956) Mrs. Jean Schaub, Pastoral Coord.; Revs. Paul F. Grehl, O.S.F.S., Sacramental Min.; Richard Eberle, O.S.F.S., Canonical Pastor.
Res.: 450 Manitou Rd., 49253. Tel: 517-547-7496; Fax: 517-547-4162.
Catechesis/Religious Program—Students 27.
MASON, INGHAM CO., ST. JAMES (1942) Rev. Alan J. Wakefield; Deacon Thomas Feiten.
Office: 1010 S. Lansing St., 48854. Tel: 517-676-9111; Fax: 517-676-1343.
Catechesis/Religious Program—Rose Robertson, D.R.E. Students 211.
MICHIGAN CENTER, JACKSON CO., OUR LADY OF FATIMA (1954) Rev. Jeffrey Robideau.
Res.: 913 Napoleon Rd., 49254. Tel: 517-764-2088; 517-764-2112; Fax: 517-764-0461. Email: olf_parish@tds.net.
School—911 Napoleon Rd., 49254. Tel: 517-764-2563; Fax: 517-764-5411. Email: olf_principal@tds.net. Colleen McNeal, Prin. Lay Teachers 6; Students 71.
Catechesis/Religious Program—Tel: 517-764-1321. Email: olf_reled@tds.net. Students 126.
MILAN, WASHTENAW CO., IMMACULATE CONCEPTION (1854) Rev. Vincent VanDoan; Deacon John Flanagan.
Church: 420 North St., 48160. Tel: 734-439-2030; Fax: 734-439-5659.
Catechesis/Religious Program—Tel: 734-439-2030. Students 204.
MONTROSE, GENESEE CO., GOOD SHEPHERD (1979) Rev. Steven D. Anderson, Parochial Admin.
400 N. Saginaw, P.O. Box 3274, 48457-0974.
Res.: 314 Genesee, 48457-0974. Fax: 810-639-3245. Email: goodshep@centurytel.net. Web: www.goodshepherdmontrose.catholicweb.com.
Catechesis/Religious Program—Students 92.
MORRICE, SHIAWASSEE CO., ST. MARY (1875) [CEM] Rev. John M. Bosco (India).
Res.: 509 N. Main St., P.O. Box 310, 48857. Tel: 517-625-4260; Fax: 517-625-3050. Email: cgarrison@catholicweb.com; lnebo@catholicweb.com. Web: www.stmarymorrice.catholicweb.com.
Catechesis/Religious Program—Tel: 517-625-6140. Students 107.
MOUNT MORRIS, GENESEE CO., ST. MARY (1867) [CEM] Rev. Thomas D. Nenneau.
Res.: 11110 Saginaw St., 48458. Tel: 810-686-3920; Fax: 810-686-0759. Web: stmarymountmorris.catholicweb.com.
School—11208 N. Saginaw, 48458. Tel: 810-686-4790; Fax: 810-686-4749. Web: www.saintmaryscatholic.com. Dennis Winchester, Prin. Lay Teachers 12; Students 131.
Catechesis/Religious Program—Students 87.
OKEMOS, INGHAM CO., ST. MARTHA (1988) Rev. Jonathan Wehrle; Deacon Vince Guarnaccia. In Res., Rev. Phillip Schweda.
Church: 1100 W. Grand River, 48864. Tel: 517-349-1763; Fax: 517-347-3536.
School—Tel: 517-349-3322; Fax: 517-349-3322. Francie Herring, Prin. Sisters of Charity 2; Lay Teachers 9; Students 182.
Catechesis/Religious Program—Students 323.
OTISVILLE, GENESEE CO., ST. FRANCIS XAVIER (1947) Revs. Gerald Ploof, Canonical Pastor; Francis Faraci, Sacramental Min. (Retired); Sr. Elaine LaBell, O.P., Pastoral Coord.
212 Center St., 48463. Tel: 810-631-6305; Fax: 810-631-4412. Email: sfranotisville@aol.com. Web: stfrancisxavierotisville.catholicweb.com.
Catechesis/Religious Program—Email: dre_grace@yahoo.com. Students 92.
OVID, SHIAWASSEE CO., HOLY FAMILY (1966) Rev. Raymond J. Urbanek; Deacon Michael F. Barrett.
Res.: 510 N. Mabbitt Rd., P.O. Box 612, 48866. Tel: 989-834-5855; Fax: 989-834-1208. Email: holy_family_church@verizon.net. Web: http://holyfamilyovid.catholicweb.com.
Catechesis/Religious Program—Tel: 989-834-2138. Students 104.
OWOSSO, SHIAWASSEE CO.
1—ST. JOSEPH (1923) Rev. David E. Fisher.
Res.: 915 E. Oliver St., 48867. Tel: 989-725-5215; Fax: 989-725-1519. Email: nancyann@sjowosso.com. Web: www.catholicweb.com.
St. Joseph Child Care Services—Child Care 129.
Catechesis/Religious Program—811 E. Oliver St., 48867. Tel: 989-723-4765. Email: hrdnbrgh@verizon.net. Students 95.
2—ST. PAUL (1871) [CEM 2] Revs. John Fain; Nonatus Lakra, Parochial Vicar; Deacon Gary Edington.
Res.: 111 N. Howell St., 48867. Tel: 989-723-4277; Fax: 989-723-9503. Email: spcowosso@aol.com. Web:

www.stpaulowosso.org.
School—738 W. Main St., 48867. Tel: 989-725-7766; Fax: 989-725-9824. Email: spsowosso@aol.com. Merry Jane Robertson, Prin. Lay Teachers 12; Students 144.
Catechesis/Religious Program—718 W. Main St., 48867. Tel: 989-723-1400. Students 190.

PINCKNEY, LIVINGSTON CO., ST. MARY (1867) [CEM] Rev. William Wegher.
Res.: 10601 Dexter-Pinckney Rd., 48169. Tel: 734-878-3161; Fax: 734-878-2383. Email: hshamp@stmarypinckney.org. Web: www.stmarypinckney.org.
School—Tel: 734-878-5616. Email: mrskinsey@stmarypinckey.org. Web: www.stmarypinckney.org/school. Veronica Kinsey, Prin. Lay Teachers 16; Students 152.
Catechesis/Religious Program—Tel: 734-878-2217. Email: rkeiser@stmarypinckney.org. Students 312.

ST. JOHNS, CLINTON CO., ST. JOSEPH (1874) Rev. Eoin Murphy (Ireland); Deacons Marvin Robertson; Gerald Fust.
Res.: 109 Linden St., 48879. Tel: 989-224-8994; Fax: 989-224-3475. Email: stjoechurch@mutualdata.com. Web: www.stjoecatholic.com.
School—201 E. Cass St., Saint Johns, 48879. Tel: 989-224-2421; Fax: 989-224-1900. Web: www.stjoecatholic.com. Tomi Ann Schultheiss, Prin. Lay Teachers 13; Students 273.
Catechesis/Religious Program—Tel: 989-224-8537. Students 299.

SALINE, WASHTENAW CO., ST. ANDREW (1968) Revs. William J. Stevenson; Charles Canoy; Deacons Paul Ellis; Douglas Cummings; Jon Krueger, Music Dir.
Res.: 910 Austin Dr., 48176. Tel: 734-429-5210; Fax: 734-429-0680. Email: standrew@comcast.net. Web: www.standrewsaline.parishesonline.com.
Catechesis/Religious Program—Tel: 734-429-7776. Margaret Greca, D.R.E.; Nancy Carter, Coord. Youth Ministry, Grades 7-8; Chellsy Brereton, Coord. Youth Ministry, Grades 9-12. Students 815.

SWARTZ CREEK, GENESEE CO., ST. MARY (1912), (Czech), [CEM] Rev. Steven M. Mattson; Deacon Rodney Amon.
Res.: 7563 Mary St., 48473. Tel: 810-635-3476; Fax: 810-630-1630.
Catechesis/Religious Program—Tel: 810-635-3240. Students 130.

TECUMSEH, LENAWEE CO., ST. ELIZABETH (1947) Rev. Daniel Wheeler; Deacons James Nicholson; Ray Pizana.
Res.: 506 N. Union St., 49286. Tel: 517-423-2447; Fax: 517-424-7706. Email: steliz50@aol.com. Web: www.stelizabethparishesonline.com.
Catechesis/Religious Program—512 N. Union St., 49286. Tel: 517-423-4501. Mary Kirby, D.R.E.; Kimberly Bauer, Youth Min. Students 293.

WESTPHALIA, CLINTON CO., ST. MARY (1836), (German), [CEM] Rev. James P. Conlon; Deacons Bernard Pohl; Chuck Thelen.
Res.: 201 N. Westphalia St., P.O. Box 267, 48894. Tel: 989-587-4201; Fax: 989-587-3838. Email: office@stmarychurch.net. Web: www.stmarychurch.net.
School—209 N. Westphalia St., P.O. Box 270, 48894. Tel: 989-587-3702; Fax: 989-587-3706. Raymond Rzepecki, Prin. Lay Teachers 13; Students 268.
Catechesis/Religious Program—Tel: 989-587-4201. Students 277.

WILLIAMSTON, INGHAM CO., ST. MARY (1869) [CEM] Rev. Peter J. Clark.
Res.: 157 High St., 48895. Tel: 517-655-2620; Fax: 517-655-3933.
School—220 Cedar St., 48895. Tel: 517-655-4038; Fax: 517-655-3855. Katherine White, Prin. Lay Teachers 6; Students 86.
Catechesis/Religious Program—Tel: 517-655-2520. Adam Janke, D.R.E. Students 193.

YPSILANTI, WASHTENAW CO.

1—ST. ALEXIS, Closed. For inquiries for parish records contact Transfiguraton Catholic Church.

2—HOLY TRINITY STUDENT PARISH (1965) Rev. Phillip Mayfield, P.I.M.E.; Deacon Stanley Kukla.
Res.: 315 Benjamin Dr., 48198. Tel: 734-480-4392. Church: 511 W. Forest, 48197. Tel: 734-482-1400; Fax: 734-482-0542. Email: holytrinity@emich.edu. Web: www.catholicsoncampus.org.
Catechesis/Religious Program—Students 35.

3—ST. JOHN (1858) [CEM] Rev. Robert Roggenbuck; Deacons Wayne Charlton; Stephen A. Thomashefski.
Res.: 410 W. Cross St., 48197. Tel: 734-483-3360; Fax: 734-483-0712. Email: stjohnypsilanti@parishmail.com. Web: www.ypsilanticatholic.com.
Catechesis/Religious Program—Students 168.
Convent—411 Florence St., 48197. Tel: 734-483-0742.

4—ST. JOSEPH (1889) [CEM] Rev. Edmond L. Ertzbischoff.
Res.: 9425 Whittaker Rd., 48197. Tel: 734-461-6555; Fax: 734-461-1444.
Catechesis/Religious Program—Tel: 734-461-1800. Students 115.

5—TRANSFIGURATION CATHOLIC CHURCH (1994) Closed. For inquiries for parish records contact the chancery.

6—ST. URSULA, Closed. For inquiries for parish records contact Transfiguration Catholic Church.

Chaplains of Public Institutions

Hospitals

LANSING. *Ingham Regional Medical Center, Sparrow Hospital*, Tel: 517-646-6850. Jane Vatter, Chap. Tel: 517-364-2902.

ANN ARBOR. *University of Michigan Hospitals/Pastoral Dept.* Rev. Lewis Eberhart, Deacon Wayne Charlton. Tel: 734-434-2546.
Veterans' Hospital. Rev. Quang Minh Tran.

FLINT. *Hurley Regional Medical Center*. Rev. Paul Schwermer. Tel: 810-252-6979.
McLaren Regional Medical Center. Rev. Paul Schwermer. Tel: 810-252-6979.

GRAND BLANC. *Genesys Regional Medical Center*. Vacant.

JACKSON. *Foote Hospital*. Vacant.

Prisons

ADRIAN. *Gus Harrison Regional Facility*. Rev. Carl A. Simon. Tel: 517-467-2183, Deacons Calistro Torres. Tel: 517-265-8927, Gene Hausmann. Tel: 517-423-7451.
Parr Hwy. Correctional Facility. Rev. Thomas J. Helfrich, O.S.F.S., Deacons Ray Pizana. Tel: 517-467-7621, Jim Nicholson. Tel: 517-467-2072, Gene Hausmann. Tel: 517-423-7451.

JACKSON. *Cotton Facility*. Rev. James R. Shaver. Tel: 517-784-0553.
Egeler Correctional Facility. Rev. Gary McInnis. Tel: 810-232-3639.
Parnall Facility. Deacons Vincent Genco. Tel: 517-750-3759, Matthew Shannon. Tel: 517-789-6260.

MILAN. *Federal Correctional Institution*. Deacons Calistro Torres. Tel: 517-265-8927, James Hashman. Tel: 517-486-2083.

Special Alternative Incarceration

CHELSEA. *Camp Cassidy Lake*. Revs. Fortunato Turati, S.C. Tel: 734-475-8430, William J. Turner. Tel: 734-475-1697.

WHITMORE LAKE. *W. J. Maxey Boys Training School*. Rev. John George Rocus. Tel: 810-231-9199, Deacon Joseph Lennon. Tel: 734-663-7213.

On Duty Outside the Diocese:
Revs.—
Bui, Vincent, S.S., Laframboise Hall, 249 Main St., Ottawa ON KIS 1C5 Canada.
Gerl, Robert, P.O. Box 19225, Kalamazoo, 49019.
Irish, Robert, 8280 W. Warm Springs Rd., Las Vegas, NV 89113.
Kersten, Jay J., Navy Chap.
Kropf, Richard, Star Rte. 1, P.O. Box 629, Johannesburg, 49751.
Madey, Louis, Ss. Cyril & Methodius Seminary, 3535 Indian Trail, Orchard Lake, 48324.
Sessions, Phillip D., St. Catherine Laboure, 4124 Mt. Abraham Ave., San Diego, CA 92111.
Sokol, Nathaniel, 341 MacLaren St., Ottawa ON K2P 2E2 Canada.
Weber, Eric Christopher, Sacred Heart Major Seminary, 2701 Chicago Blvd., Detroit, 48206.

On Leave of Absence:
Revs.—
Carlos, Miguel
Dehetre, Mark
McKean, Dan
Munley, J. Thomas
Thomsen, Steven (New Zealand)

Retired:
Rev. Msgrs.—
Fedewa, Sylvester L., 120 N. Willow St., Box 412, Westphalia, 48894.
Groshek, Richard, 4381 Springbrook Dr., Swartz Creek, 48473.
Howard, Vincent, 1849 Pierce Rd., Chelsea, 48118.
Lunsford, Robert D., 401-A E. Madison, Dewitt, 48820.
Revs.—
Aubin, Joseph, 402 E. Madison, #B, Dewitt, 48820.
Beiter, Eugene J., 402 E. Madison #D, Dewitt, 48820.
Bettendorf, James B., 1139 Creekside Ct., Burton, 48509.
Brennan, Thomas, 468 Lancaster Ct., Saline, 48176.
Cummings, Paul J., 3505 Cherry Blossom Dr., Jackson, 49201.
Czarnota, Stanislaus, 401 Madison, Apt. C, Dewitt, 48820.
Dougherty, C. Peter, P.O. Box 14062, 48901.
Dumas, Terrence J., 2150 Frieze Ave., Ann Arbor, 48104.
Dupuis, Philip, 13280 Friendly Dr., Wolverine, 49799.
Eder, Donald, 6290 Oak Creek Dr., Swartz Creek, 48473.
Faraci, Francis, 2214 Blackthorn, Burton, 48509.
Fedewa, Matthew, 4437 W. Willow, 48917.
Foglio, John, P.O. Box 4098, East Lansing, 48826.
Gallagher, Philip P., 1473 Amy St., Burton, 48509.
Irvin, Charles, 402 E. Madison, Apt. A, Dewitt, 48820.
Kolenski, Robert D., 3375 N. Linden Rd., #205, Flint, 48504.
Ledwidge, Brendan, The Village Woodland, 7533 Grand River Ave., Apt. 201, Brighton, 48114.
Lesniak, Marian, 2497 Redwood Dr., Flushing, 48433.
Lorenzo, Eduardo, 6073 Ballard, Flint, 48505.
Makranyi, Steven F., 3096 Vineyard Ln., Flushing, 48433.
Martin, Francis, 4437 W. Willow, 48917.
McDevitt, Thomas, 5700 Bayonne Ave., Haslett, 48840.
McDonald, Kenneth, 401-D E. Madison, DeWitt, 48820.
McKeon, Robert, 10018 Lehring Rd., Box 132, Byron, 48418-0132.
Murray, Francis J., 2146-3 Robinson Rd., Jackson, 49203-8620.
Osborn, Douglas, 402-C E. Madison, Dewitt, 48820.
Ritter, Nicholas J., 500 E. University Dr., Rochester, 48307.
Robert, Darin T., 620 Oakdale, Chelsea, 48116.
Rusch, Donald, P.O. Box 399, East Pointe, 48021.
Schmitt, James, Jr., 215 Banberry North, 48906.
Swiat, James R., 3903 Ruthin Rd., Kalamazoo, 49008.
Taylor, Jon, 5594 Livingston Ave., Eugene, OR 97402.
Thompson, Thomas W., 10317 Lakeside Dr., P.O. Box 187, Perrinton, 48871.
Tyler, Bernard L. (GAY), 112 McKee St., Houghton, 48629.
Werner, Benjamin, 620 Oakdale Dr., Chelsea, 48118.
Williams, Francis, 401-B E. Madison, DeWitt, 48820.
Wyszynski, Darius W., 2235 Cascade Ridge, Jackson, 49203.

Permanent Deacons:
Alfaro, Rogelio, Cristo Rey, Lansing
Amon, Rodney, St. Mary Queen of Angels, Swartz Creek
Arquette, Lester, St. Thomas the Apostle, Ann Arbor
Barrett, David, Queen of the Miraculous Medal, Jackson
Barrett, Michael, Holy Family, Ovid
Bayes, Richard, St. Mary of Good Counsel, Adrian
Borzenski, David, St. Therese, Lansing
Brennan, Gerald, Director of Deacons; Holy Spirit, Hamburg
Cahaney, Roger, St. Agnes, Fowlerville
Cameron, John, J.C.L., Diocese of Lansing Tribunal; Immaculate Heart of Mary, Lansing
Carsten, Terry, St. John, Fenton
Charlton, Wayne, St. John the Baptist, Ypsilanti
Chevalier, James, St. Mary Magdalen, Brighton
Coffelt, Randy, St. Mary, Pinckney
Corder, James, St. Gerard, Lansing
Cummings, Doug, St. Andrew, Saline
Daunt, Jack, Holy Family, Grand Blanc
Dear, Michael, Holy Rosary, Flint
Doran, Endre, St. Joseph, Howell
Edington, Gary, St. Paul, Owosso
Ellis, Paul, St. Andrew, Saline
Epley, John, St. John the Evangelist, Jackson
Fairweather, Daniel, St. John the Evangelist, Davison
Feiten, Thomas, St. James, Mason
Flanagan, John, Immaculate Conception, Milan
Fogle, Thomas, St. Mary, Charlotte
Foley, Daniel R., Christ the King, Ann Arbor
Franklin, Thomas, St. Mary, Chelsea
Franssen, Carol, St. Catherine Laboure, Concord
Fudge, William, Immaculate Heart of Mary, Lansing
Fust, Gerald, St. Joseph, St. Johns
Gallagher, Gary, St. Pius X, Flint
Genco, Vincent, St. Mary Star of the Sea, Jackson
Giesige, Richard, St. Joseph, Ypsilanti
Guarnaccia, Vincent, St. Martha, Okemos
Gudaitis, Peter, St. Agnes, Fowlerville
Hashman, James, St. Peter, Blissfield
Hausmann, Gene, St. Joseph Shrine, Brooklyn
Hecht, Warren, St. Thomas the Apostle, Ann Arbor

Heutsche, Ted, St. Jude, Dewitt
Hilker, Stephen, St. Mary, Williamston
Holowicki, Gerry, Christ the King, Ann Arbor
Kazprzak, James, St. Thomas Aquinas, East Lansing
Kenney, Ronald, St. John, Fenton
Kowalski, John, Queen of the Miraculous Medal, Jackson
Kratofil, Joseph, St. John the Evangelist, Jackson
Krieger, Albert, St. Joseph, Jackson
Kukla, Stanley, Holy Trinity, Ypsilanti
Kunik, Ray, St. Joseph, Howell
Lawrence, Dave, St. Patrick, Brighton
Leone, Romolo, St. Joseph, Dexter
Marsal, Gideon, St. Peter, Eaton Rapids
McCarthy, John, St. Michael, Grand Ledge
McDonald, Patrick, St. Patrick, Brighton
Michael, Donald, St. Anthony, Hillsdale
Middleton, Greg, St. Mary, Durand
Miles, James, St. Thomas the Apostle, Ann Arbor
Murray, Michael, St. Thomas Aquinas, East Lansing
Nicholson, James, St. Elizabeth, Tecumseh
Papp, Frank, St. Patrick, Ann Arbor
Pennell, Dennis, St. Robert Bellarmine, Flushing
Petersen, Aaron, St. Anthony of Padua, Hillsdale
Piggot, David, St. John the Baptist, Hartland
Pigott, David, SS. Charles & Helena, Clio
Pizana, Eulalio, St. Elizabeth, Tecumseh
Pohl, Bernard, St. Mary, Westphalia
Poole, Gregory, St. Mary, Charlotte
Prise, Gary, St. Mary Magdalen, Brighton
Randolph, Larry, Christ the King, Ann Arbor
Rea, Tom, SS. Cornelius & Cyprian, Leslie
Robertson, Marvin, St. Joseph, St. Johns
Rowe, Ronald, St. Michael, Flint
Russello, Lou, Christ the King, Ann Arbor
Savage, Richard, St. Gerard Majella, Lansing
Scharf, David, St. Mary Magdalen, Brighton
Shaneyfelt, Richard, St. Mary, Chelsea
Shannon, Matthew, St. Mary Star of the Sea, Jackson
Simmon, Mark, Most Holy Trinity, Fowler
Sirl, William, St. Augustine, Deerfield Twp.
Spaulding, Kenneth, Queen of the Miraculous Medal, Jackson
Stanford, Richard, St. Mary Cathedral, Lansing
Sullivan, Michael, St. Francis of Assisi, Ann Arbor
Sundwick, John, St. John Vianney, Flint; Our Lady of Guadalupe, Flint
Tardif, Andy, St. Michael, Grand Ledge
Thelen, Chuck, St. Mary, Westphalia
Thomashefski, Stephen A., St. John the Baptist, Ypsilanti
Torres, Calistro, St. Mary, Adrian
Turkovich, Al, St. Casimir, Lansing
Verdun, Anthony, St. John Vianney, Flint
Walters, Dennis, St. Mary, Manchester
Washington, Oliver
Weitzel, Louis, St. Rita, Clarklake
Wines, Frank, Sr., St. Joseph, Howell

INSTITUTIONS LOCATED IN THE DIOCESE

[A] COLLEGES AND UNIVERSITIES

ADRIAN. *Siena Heights University*, 1247 E. Siena Heights Dr., 49221-1796. Tel: 517-263-0731; Fax: 517-264-7702. Web: www.sienaheights.edu. Sisters Peg Albert, O.P., Ph.D., Pres.; Sharon R. Weber, O.P., Ph.D., Academic Dean; Robert Gordon, Ph.D., Dir. Library. Sponsored by the Adrian Dominican Sisters. Sisters 8; Faculty 70; Total Staff 145; Students 2,365.

[B] HIGH SCHOOLS, DIOCESAN

LANSING. *Lansing Catholic Central High School*, 501 N. Marshall St., 48912. Tel: 517-267-2100; Fax: 517-267-2135. Email: draminsk@lcchs.org. Web: www.lansingcatholic.org. Thomas P. Maloney, Prin.; Rev. Gordon P. Reigle, Chap.; Liz Webster, Librarian. Lansing Catholic Central Board of Education Priests 1; Lay Teachers 33; Students 525.

ANN ARBOR. *Father Gabriel Richard High School* (1867) 4333 Whitehall Dr., 48105. Tel: 734-662-0496; Fax: 734-662-4133. Email: fgoffice@fgrhsaa.org. Web: www.fgrhsaa.org. Brian Wolcott, Prin.; Catherine Weber, Librarian; Rev. Richard C. Lobert, Chap. Gabriel Richard Board of Education Priests 1; Sisters 1; Lay Teachers 38; Students 497.

FLINT. *Luke M. Powers Catholic High School*, G-2040 W. Carpenter Rd., 48505. Tel: 810-591-4741; Fax: 810-591-0383. Email: tfurnas@powerscatholic.org. Web: www.powerscatholic.org. Mr. Thomas Furnas, M.A., Prin.; Dana Bolle, Librarian; Rev. Steven Anderson, Chap. Powers Catholic Board of Education Priests 2; Sisters 1; Lay Teachers 31; Total Staff 32; Other 26; Students 603.

JACKSON. *Lumen Christi Catholic High School*, 3483 Spring Arbor Rd., 49203. Tel: 517-787-0630; Fax: 517-787-1066. Web: www.jcslumenchristi.org. Patrick R. Kalahar, M.S., Prin.; Revs. Paul F. Grehl, O.S.F.S.; Geoff Rose, O.S.F.S.; Bro. John W. Bailey, O.S.F.S.; Martha Artz, Librarian. Oblates of St. Francis de Sales. Priests 2; Brothers 1; Lay Teachers 39; Students 500.

[C] ELEMENTARY & MIDDLE SCHOOLS, DIOCESAN

JACKSON. *Jackson Catholic Middle School*, 915 Cooper, 49202. Tel: 517-784-3385; Fax: 517-782-7883. Email: jacksoncatholicms@jcmjcms.org. Web: www.jcsjcms.org. Anthony Shaughnessy, Prin.; Mrs. Elizabeth Norkey, Librarian. Lay Teachers 15; Students 211.

[D] SCHOOLS, PRIVATE

ADRIAN. **St. Joseph Academy* (1896) (Grades K-8), 1267 E. Siena Heights Dr., 49221. Tel: 517-263-4898; Fax: 517-265-6240. Email: info@sjaschool.org. Web: sjaschool.org. Sr. Patricia Fischer, O.P., Prin.; Valorie Veld, Librarian. Sisters of St. Dominic, Congregation of the Most Holy Rosary (Adrian, MI). Sisters 1; Lay Teachers 15; Assistants 8; Administrators 2; Students 162; Total Staff 26.

ANN ARBOR. **Spiritus Sanctus Academy*, (Grades K-8), 4101 E. Joy Rd., 48105. Tel: 734-996-3855; Fax: 734-996-4270. Web: www.spiritussanctus.org. Sr. John Dominic Rasmussen, O.P., Prin.; Rev. Charles Kibirige, Chap. Priests 1; Sisters 4; Lay Teachers 10; Students 152; Staff 16.

BURTON. *St. Thomas More Academy* (1989) (Grades K-12), 6456 E. Bristol Rd., 48519. Tel: 810-742-2411; Fax: 810-742-4803. Email: stma2003@sbcglobal.net. Web: stma-mi.org. Dan Le Blanc, Prin. Priests 1; Lay Teachers 12; Administrators 4; Students (K-8) 68; (9-12) 40 108; Total Staff 17.

PLYMOUTH. **Spiritus Sanctus Academy*, 10450 Joy Rd., 48170. Tel: 734-414-8430; Fax: 734-414-8495. Email: srmarysamuel@sistersofmary.org. Web: www.spiritussanctus.org. Sr. Mary Samuel Handwerker, O.P., M.A., Prin.; Rev. Charles Muwonge, Chap. Priests 1; Sisters 4; Lay Teachers 12; Students 188.

YPSILANTI. **HVS Corp. (Huron Valley Catholic School)* (2000) (Grades PreK-8), 1300 N. Prospect, 48198-3087. Tel: 734-483-0366; Fax: 734-483-0372. Timothy F. Kotyuk, Prin.; Barb Oas, Librarian. Sisters 2; Lay Teachers 10; Students 188; Total Staff 15.

[E] SPECIALIZED CHILD CARE FACILITIES & SCHOOLS

CHELSEA. *St. Louis Center for Exceptional Children & Adults*, 16195 Old U.S. 12, 48118. Tel: 734-475-8430; Fax: 734-475-0310. Email: frjoe@stlouiscenter.org. Web: www.stlouiscenter.org. Revs. Joseph Rinaldo, S.C., Prov. Treas.; Satheesh C. Alphonse, Asst. Admin.; Fortunato Turati, S.C., Chap.; Enzo Addari, M.Div., M.Ed, Admin.; David Stawasz, S.C., R.N., Medical Program. Operated by the Servants of Charity. Priests 5; Total Staff 51; Residents 60.

CLINTON. *Boysville of Michigan, Inc./Holy Cross Children's Services*, 8744 Clinton-Macon Rd., 49236. Tel: 517-423-6500; Fax: 517-423-5442. Email: fboylan@hccsnet.org. Web: www.hccsnet.org. Bro. Francis Boylan, C.S.C., Pres.; Mr. Loren P. Brown, Exec. Dir.; Mr. Jesse Cox, Pastoral Min.; Mr. William Geddes, Regl. Dir. Residential and community based treatment programs for troubled youth and their families with facilities located throughout the state of Michigan under the auspices of the Brothers of Holy Cross & Notre Dame. Brothers 1; Boys 100; Total Staff 160.

St. Thomas More High-Boysville, 8744 Clinton-Macon Rd., 49236. Tel: 517-423-7451; Fax: 517-423-5214. Email: fboylan@hccsnet.org. Web: www.hccsnet.org. Mr. James Chludzinski, Prin. Lay Teachers 22; Total Staff 25; Students 125.

JACKSON. *St. Joseph Home for Children, Inc.*, 1000 E. Porter, 49202. Tel: 517-787-3320; Fax: 517-787-3704. Sr. Mary Bertha Stamm, C.S.S.F., Admin.; Lezlie Bowles, Prog. Dir. Felician Sisters (C.S.S.F.)., Retreats, Conferences, Day Care Center for Children Pre-school. Children 100; Sisters 3; Lay Teachers 1; Lay Caregivers 22.

MOUNT MORRIS. *Boysville of Michigan/Holy Cross Children's Services: Corcoran House*, 8212 N. Jennings Rd., 48458. Tel: 810-687-5100; Fax: 810-687-5020. Email: fboylan@hccsnet.org. Web: www.hccsnet.org. Bro. Francis Boylan, C.S.C., Pres.; Mr. Loren P. Brown, Exec. Dir.; Ms. Sharon Berkobien, Regl. Dir. A day treatment program for 13 boys and girls; residential treatment for 15 girls. Total Assisted 33; Total Staff 27; Total in Residence 6.

[F] CATHOLIC CHARITIES & SERVICE AGENCIES

LANSING. **Cristo Rey Community Center*, 1717 N. High St., 48906. Tel: 517-372-4700; Fax: 517-372-8499. Email: castillojohnroycrcc@earthlink.net. Web: www.cristo-rey.org. John Roy Castillo, J.D., Exec. Dir. Total Assisted 25,500; Total Staff 54.

St. Vincent Catholic Charities (1948) 2800 W. Willow, 48917. Tel: 517-323-4734; Fax: 517-886-1150. Email: kitchep@stvcc.org. Web: www.stvcc.org. Andrea E. Seyka, CEO. Total Assisted 4,367; Total Staff 177.

Adoption, 2800 W. Willow, 48917. Tel: 517-323-4734; Fax: 517-886-1168. Email: villasg@stvcc.org.

Children's Home, 2828 W. Willow St., 48917. Tel: 517-323-4734; Fax: 517-323-0257. Email: radzill@stvcc.org. Residents 40.

Counseling Services, 2800 W. Willow, 48917. Tel: 517-323-4734; Fax: 517-886-1158. Email: millerk@stvcc.org.

Family Preservation, 2800 W. Willow, 48917. Tel: 517-323-4734; Fax: 517-886-1168. Email: villasg@stvcc.org.

Foster Care Includes case management and licensing., 2800 W. Willow, 48917. Tel: 517-323-4734; Fax: 517-886-1168. Email: villasg@stvcc.org.

Immigration Law Clinic, 2800 W. Willow, 48917. Tel: 517-323-4734; Fax: 517-886-1150. Email: glennol@stvcc.org. Lesley Glennon, Dir.

Volunteer Opportunities, 2800 W. Willow, 48917. Tel: 517-323-4734; Fax: 517-886-1150. Email: leee@stvcc.org.

Refugee Resettlement, 2800 W. Willow, 48917. Tel: 517-323-4734; Fax: 517-853-0031. Email: aldridg@stvcc.org. (Includes Reception, Placement, Health & Employment).

Housing Services for the Homeless, 2800 W. Willow St., 48917. Tel: 517-323-4734; Fax: 517-853-0031. Email: aldridg@stvcc.org.

ADRIAN. *Catholic Social Services of Lenawee County* (1958) 199 N. Broad St., 49221. Tel: 517-263-2191; Fax: 517-264-6080. Email: cssdir@tc3net.com. Web: www.catholiccharitieslenawee.com. Sue Lewis, B.A., Exec. Dir. Total Assisted Annually 1,000; Total Staff 24.

ANN ARBOR. *C.S.S. of Washtenaw County*, 4925 Packard Rd., 48108. Tel: 734-971-9781; Fax: 734-971-2730. Email: info@csswashtenaw.org. Web: www.csswashtenaw.org. Lawrence J. Voight, A.C.S.W. Total Assisted Annually 8,500; Total Staff 130.

Catholic Charities of Michigan (2000) 4925 Packard St., 48108. Tel: 734-223-1844; Fax: 734-973-2138. Email: ceo@catholiccharities-mi.org. Web: www.catholiccharities-mi.org. Roberto M. Javier, M.H.A., CEO.

DAVISON. *Outreach East*, 425 N. Genesee St., P.O. Box 61, 48423. Tel: 810-653-7711; Fax: 810-658-0891. Jan Lebert, Dir. Total Assisted 7,012; Total Staff 1.

FLINT. *Catholic Charities of Shiawassee & Genessee Counties - North End Soup Kitchen*, 901 Chippewa St., 48503. Tel: 810-232-9950; Fax: 810-232-9110. Email: vschultz@catholiccharitiessg.org. Web: www.catholiccharitiesSG.org. Vicky L. Schultz, Pres. & CEO. Total Meals 155,487; Total Assisted Daily 595; Total Staff 9.

Catholic Charities of Shiawassee and Genesee Counties (1941) 901 Chippewa St., 48503. Tel: 810-232-9950; Fax: 810-232-9110. Email: vschultz@ccsgc.org. Web: www.catholiccharitiesSG.org. Vicky L. Schultz, Pres. & CEO. Total Assisted Annually 9,615; Total Staff 79.

Catholic Outreach, 509 N. Grand Traverse, P.O. Box 815, 48501. Tel: 810-234-4693; Fax: 810-234-1717. Gregg T. Berent, Dir. Total Assisted Annually 8,944; Total Staff 34.

HOWELL. *Livingston County Catholic Social Services* (1985) 2020 E. Grand River Ave., Ste. 104, 48843. Tel: 517-545-5944; Fax: 517-545-7390. Email: lccss@sbcglobal.net. Mark T. Robinson, A.C.S.W., Exec. Dir. Total Assisted Annually 2,300; Total Staff 23.

JACKSON. *Catholic Charities of Jackson* (1966) 1522 Joy Ave., 49203. Tel: 517-782-2551; Fax: 517-783-1986. Email: ccoj@comcast.net. Web: www.ccjax.org. Sue Lewis, B.A., Exec. Dir. Total Assisted Annually 3,574; Total Staff 28.

OWOSSO. *Catholic Charities of Shiawassee & Genesee County*, 120 W. Exchange, Ste. 300, 48867. Tel: 989-723-8239; Fax: 989-723-8230. Email: vschultz@ccsgc.org. Web: www.catholiccharitiesSG.org. Vicky L. Schultz, Pres. & CEO. Total Assisted Annually 2,096; Total Staff 10.

[G] GENERAL HOSPITALS

LANSING. **Migrant Clinic-Cristo Rey Community Center*, 1717 N. High St., 48906. Tel: 517-371-1700; Fax: 517-371-4245. Email: castillojohnroycrcc@earthlink.net. Web: www.cristo-rey.org. Dr. Peter Cooke, Medical Dir. Total Assisted 100; Total Staff 2.

ANN ARBOR. *Catherine McAuley Health Services Corporation* (Subsidiary of Trinity Health), 5305 E. Huron River Dr., P.O. Box 992, 48106. Tel: 734-712-4986; Fax: 734-712-5459. Health Care Center, Ancillary Care Systems: (Primary Care Physician Practices) Total Staff 94; Total Assisted Annually 55,664.

Saint Joseph Mercy Health System (A Member of Trinity Health), 5305 E. Huron River Dr., Box 992, 48106. Tel: 734-712-4986; Fax: 734-712-5459. Garry C. Faja, Pres. & CEO. General Hospitals 3; Bed Capacity 747; Total Staff 5,102; Total Assisted Annually 1,304,386.

St. Joseph Mercy Hospital, 5301 E. Huron River Dr., P.O. Box 995, 48106. Tel: 734-712-4986; Fax: 734-712-5459. Email: soler@trinityhealth.org. Garry C. Faja, Pres. & CEO; Rev. Timothy Dombrowski, Chap. General Hospitals 1; Bed Capacity 537; Total Staff 3,736; Patients Assisted Annually 895,962.

CHELSEA. *Chelsea Community Hospital* (A member of Trinity Health), 775 S. Main, 48118. Tel: 734-475-3812; Fax: 734-475-4066. Email: soler@trinity-health.org. Web: trinity-health.org. Kathleen Griffiths, Pres. & CEO; Kathy Schell, Chap. Bed Capacity 113; Patients Assisted Annually 154,000; Total Staff 1,058.

FLINT. *Center for Gerontology* An affiliate of Genesys Health System., 3919 Beecher Rd., 48532. Tel: 810-606-7781; Fax: 810-606-7758. Email: marcia.billingsley@genesys.org. Web: genesys.org. *Corporate Responsibility*, One Genesys Pkwy., Grand Blanc, 48439. Linda Gibson, Dir. Provides adult day care, care management programs, and educational training. Adult Day Care Days 11,426; Total Assisted 76; Total Staff 18.

Genesys Ambulatory Health Services, Inc. (1981) An affiliate of Genesys Health System., 3935 Beecher Rd., 48532. Tel: 810-606-7781; Fax: 810-606-7758. Email: marcia.billingsley@genesys.org. Web: genesys.org. Jo Anne Herman, Vice Pres. Provides private duty home care services and manages shared services. Total Staff 172; Total Assisted Annually 5,320.

GRAND BLANC. *Genesys Health System, Corporate Responsibility*, One Genesys Pkwy., 48439. Tel: 810-606-7781; Fax: 810-606-7758. Email: marcia.billingsley@genesys.org. Web: genesys.org. Mark Taylor, Pres. & CEO. Total Staff 4,096.

Genesys Regional Medical Center An affiliate of Genesys Health System. Acute care hospital., *Corporate Responsibility*, One Genesys Pkwy., 48439. Tel: 810-606-7781; Fax: 810-606-7758. Email: marcia.billingsley@genesys.org. Web: www.genesys.org. Betsy Aderholdt, Pres. Bed Capacity 410; Total Staff 3,477; Total Assisted Annually 266,475.

HOWELL. *Saint Joseph Mercy Livingston Hospital* (A member of Trinity Health), 620 Byron Rd., 48843-1093. Tel: 517-545-6000; Fax: 517-545-6192. Email: edemad@trinity-health.org. Web: trinity-health.org. Kathleen Rhine, M.B.A., Vice Pres. & COO. Bed Capacity 136; General Hospitals 1; Patients Assisted Annually 114,735; Total Staff 824.

SALINE. *Saint Joseph Mercy Saline Hospital*, 400 W. Russell, 48176. Tel: 734-429-1600; Fax: 734-429-4662. Garry Faja, Pres. & CEO. (A unit of Saint Joseph Mercy Health System) General Hospitals 1; Bed Capacity 74; Patients Assisted Annually 80,603; Total Staff 174.

[H] HOMES FOR THE AGED & CONVALESCENT

ANN ARBOR. *Servants of God's Love Ministries: Emmanuel House* (1999) 475 Evergreen, 48103. Tel: 734-669-8825; Fax: 734-669-8261. Email: emmanuelhse@juno.com. Sr. Fran DePuydt, S.G.L., Admin. Bed Capacity 7; Total Assisted 7; Volunteers 90.

GRAND BLANC. *Genesys Convalescent Center-Grand Blanc, Inc.* (1980) An affiliate of Genesys Health System., 8481 Holly Rd., 48439-1899. Tel: 810-606-7781; Fax: 810-606-7758. Email: marcia.billingsley@genesys.org. Web: genesys.org. One Genesys Pkwy., 48439. Robert Stevens, Admin. Skilled Nursing Facility Bed Capacity 140; Patients Assisted Annually 321; Total Staff 197.

YPSILANTI. *Emmanuel House II* (2002) 3341 Hillside Dr., 48197. Tel: 734-528-9031; Fax: 734-528-9086. Email: ehypsi@juno.com. Sr. Mary Zielinski, Admin. Bed Capacity 4; Total Assisted 5; Total Staff 45.

[I] HOSPICES

LANSING. **Mother Teresa House for the Care of the Terminally Ill*, 308 N. Walnut St., 48933. Tel: 517-484-5494. Web: motherteresahouse.org. Karen Bussey, Dir. & Contact Person. Total Staff 4; Total Assisted 24.

FLINT. *Genesys Home Health & Hospice* (1997) An affiliate of Genesys Health System., 3933 Beecher Rd., 48532. Tel: 810-762-4600; Fax: 810-767-1741. Email: rstevens@genesys.org. Web: www.genesys.org. Robert Stevens, Vice Pres. Continuum Care Svcs. Provides professional home care and rehabilitation services. Home Health Staff 110; Total Assisted 3,350.

GOODRICH. *Genesys Hospice* (Affiliate of Genesys Health System), 7280 S. State Rd., 48438. Tel: 810-636-5000; Fax: 810-636-5019. Email: lmccombs@genesys.org. LaVerne McCombs, Admin. & Contact Person. Provides in-home and residential hospice care. Inpatient hospice care for symptom management and respite care. Bed Capacity 22; Care Center Patients Assisted Annually 278; Home Program Patients Assisted Annually 469; Total Staff 86.

[J] MONASTERIES AND RESIDENCES OF PRIESTS AND BROTHERS

ANN ARBOR. *Detroit Province of the Society of Jesus - Jesuit Residence*, 1250 Ferdon Rd., 48104. Tel: 734-663-0557; Fax: 734-663-2756. Revs. Daniel T. Reim, S.J., Supr.; Dennis T. Dillon, S.J.; Dennis T. Glasgow, S.J.; J. Thomas McClain, S.J.

BROOKLYN. *Oblate Fathers of St. Francis De Sales, Inc.*, 1124 Ventura Dr., 49230. Tel: 517-592-8218; Fax: 517-592-8218. Email: mckenna@desales.org. Web: www.desales.org. Total in Residence 4.

Thorrez Vocational Trust, Ltd., 1124 Ventura Dr., 49230. Tel: 517-592-8218. Email: mckenna@desales.org. Web: www.desales.org. Rev. Kenneth N. McKenna, O.S.F.S., Contact Person.

[K] CONVENTS AND RESIDENCES FOR SISTERS

LANSING. *Congregation of the Passion* (1984) St. Therese Convent, 109 E. Randolph, 48906-4042. Tel: 517-372-5849; Fax: 517-372-1099. Email: mavialfaro@hotmail.com. Sr. Marcella Oloarte, C.F.P., Prioress. Sisters 4.

ADRIAN. *Adrian Dominican Office of Development* (1987) 1257 E. Siena Heights. Dr., 49221-1793. Tel: 517-266-3400; Fax: 517-266-3545. Email: devoffad@aol.com. Web: www.adriandominicans.org. Adrian Dominican Sisters.

Dominican Sisters of Adrian, MI, Inc. (1998) 1257 E. Siena Heights Dr., 49221. Tel: 517-266-3570. Sr. Donna Markham, O.P., Pres.

Motherhouse of the Sisters of St. Dominic, Congregation of the Most Holy Rosary (1923) 1257 E. Siena Heights Dr., 49221-1793. Tel: 517-266-3400; Fax: 517-266-3545. Web: www.adriandominicans.org. Sr. Donna Markham, O.P., Prioress; Rev. Robert Kelly, O.P., Dir. Liturgy & Chap. Total in Congregation 828.

Adrian Rea Literacy Center, 1257 E. Siena Heights Dr., 49221-1793. Tel: 517-266-4260; Fax: 517-266-4235. Sr. Carleen Maly, O.P., Dir.

Dominican Life Center (1926) 1277 E. Siena Heights Dr., 49221-1755. Tel: 517-266-3650; Fax: 517-266-3656. Sr. Rosemary Abramovich, O.P., Admin.

ANN ARBOR. *Benedictine Sisters of Corpus Christi Monastery*, 4485 Earhart Rd., 48105-9710. Tel: 734-995-3876; Fax: 734-930-9471. Email: benedictines@sbcglobal.net. Sr. Regina Mary Kust, O.S.B., Supr.

Dominican Sisters of Mary, Mother of the Eucharist (1997) 4597 Warren Rd., 48105. Tel: 734-994-7437; Fax: 734-994-7438. Email: sjab@sistersofmary.org. Web: www.sistersofmary.org. Sr. Mary Assumpta Long, O.P., Prioress Gen. Final Professed 26; Temporary Professed 39; Novices 17; Postulants 17.

Dominican SMME Corporation (2002) c/o *Dominican Sisters of Mary, Mother of the Eucharist*, 4597 Warren Rd., 48105. Tel: 734-994-7437; Fax: 734-994-7438. Email: sjab@sistersofmary.org. Sr. Mary Assumpta Long, O.P., Pres.

**Servants of God's Love* (1975) 4399 Ford Rd., 48105. Tel: 734-663-6128; Fax: 734-663-6128. Email: sgl@att.net. Web: www.servantsofgodslove.catholicweb.net. Sr. Dorcee Clarey, Supr.

DE WITT. *St. Albert the Great House of Studies*, 217 Schavey Rd., 48820. Tel: 517-669-2277; Fax: 517-669-8123. Email: saintalberts@rsmofalma.org. Web: rsmofalma.org. Sr. Mary Raphael Paradis, R.S.M., Supr. Religious Sisters of Mercy, Alma Michigan 4.

[L] PASTORAL CENTERS

FLUSHING. *Mt. Zion Catholic Community* (1988) 8228 N. McKinley Rd., 48433. Tel: 810-639-7175; Fax: 810-639-5262. Email: mtzion@centurytel.net. Web: youthtoyouthcatholic.com.
Res.: 8236 N. McKinley Rd., 48433. Tel: 810-639-3563.

JACKSON. *Sacred Heart Chapel c/o St. Stanislaus Oratory*, 608 Elm Ave., 49203. Tel: 517-783-2772. Email: sacredchapel@aol.com. Sr. Marcella Oloarte, C.F.P., Pastoral Assoc.; Angela Medina, Treas.

[M] RETREAT CENTERS

ADRIAN. *Weber Retreat Center* (1970) 1257 E. Siena Heights Dr., 49221-1793. Tel: 517-266-4000; Fax: 517-266-4004. Email: webercenter@adriandominicans.org. Web: www.adriandominicans.org/weber. Sr. Margaret O'Flynn, O.P., Dir.

BROOKLYN. *Lake Vineyard Camps, Inc., (De Sales Center)*, 1124 Ventura, 49230-9078. Tel: 517-592-8218; Fax: 517-592-8218. Email: mckenna@desales.org. Web: www.desales.org. Rev. Kenneth N. McKenna, O.S.F.S., Dir. De Sales Center is a Catholic Retreat Center operated by Lake Vineyard Camps, Inc. for the Oblates of St. Francis de Sales, Inc. Also on the property is the Novitiate House for the Toledo-Detroit Province of the Oblates of St. Francis de Sales. Priests 3; Total Staff 40; Total Assisted 1,160.

DE WITT. *St. Francis Retreat Center*, 703 E. Main St., 48820. Tel: 517-669-8321; 866-669-8321 (Toll Free); Fax: 517-669-2708. Email: information@stfrancis.ws. Web: www.stfrancis.ws. Rev. Lawrence Delaney, Dir.; Deacon Richard Savage, Operations Mgr. Total in Residence 1; Total Staff 35.

Bethany House (Spiritual Life Center for Youth) (2001) St. Francis Retreat Center, 703 E. Main St., DeWitt, 48820. Tel: 517-669-8321; Fax: 517-669-2708.

[N] CAMPUS MINISTRY

ADRIAN. *Siena Heights University* 1247 E. Siena Heights Dr., 49221. Tel: 517-264-7192; Fax: 517-264-7745. Email: tpuszcze@sienaheights.edu. Web: www.sienaheights.edu. Tom Puszczewicz, Dir. Campus Ministry; Rev. Thomas J. Helfrich, O.S.F.S., Chap. Tel: 517-264-7198. Email: thelfric@sienaheights.edu. Campus Ministry.

ANN ARBOR. *St. Mary Student Parish* 331 Thompson St., 48104-2295. Tel: 734-663-0557; Fax: 734-663-2756. Email: stmarys@umich.edu. Web: www.stmarystudentparish.org. Rev. J. Thomas McClain, S.J. Serving the University of Michigan. Total Staff 18.
Refer to the parish section for complete campus ministry staff.

BELLEVUE. *St. Ann* (1923) 312 S. Main St., P.O. Box 38, 49021. Tel: 269-763-9372; Fax: 269-763-0067. Web: stannbellevue.catholicweb.com. Serving Olivet College. (Refer to parish section for complete ministry staff.)

EAST LANSING. *St. John the Evangelist Church and Student Center* 327 M.A.C. Ave., 48823-4388. Tel: 517-337-9778; Fax: 517-337-8358. Email: stjohnsp@msu.edu. Web: www.elcatholics.org. Rev. Mark Inglot. Serving Michigan State University
Refer to the parish section for complete campus ministry staff.

HILLSDALE. *St. Anthony Family Center* 11 Broad St., 49242. Tel: 517-439-1316; Fax: 517-437-0034. Email: stanthony@dmci.net. (Serving Hillsdale College and all of Hillsdale Co.) Total Assisted 1,500; Total Staff 1.

YPSILANTI. *Holy Trinity Student Parish* (1965) 511 W. Forest, 48197. Tel: 734-482-1400; Fax: 734-482-0542. Email: holytrinity@emich.edu. Web: www.catholicsoncampus.org. Rev. Phillip Mayfield, P.I.M.E.; Bill Alt, Asst. Dir., Campus Ministry. Serving Eastern Michigan University and Washtenaw Community College.

[O] ENDOWMENTS AND TRUSTS

LANSING. *Chancery Office*, 300 W. Ottawa, 48933. Tel: 517-342-2440.

Blessed Sacrament Educational Trust Fund Tel: 810-742-3151; Fax: 810-742-1409. Rev. Joseph Sy Kim. (Blessed Sacrament Parish, Burton)

Camilla Madden Charitable Trust (Adrian)
Church of the Resurrection Educational Trust Fund (Church of the Resurrection, Lansing) Tel: 517-482-4749; Fax: 517-484-4740.
Father Al Miller Educational Trust Fund (St. Mary Parish, Westphalia) Tel: 517-587-4201; Fax: 517-587-3838.
Father Gabriel Richard High School Trust Fund (Fr. Gabriel Richard H.S., Ann Arbor) Tel: 734-662-0496; Fax: 734-662-4133.
Greater Lansing Catholic Education Foundation (Lansing) Tel: 517-485-8333; Fax: 517-484-8880.
Immaculate Heart of Mary St. Casimir School Mary Goeddeke Educational Trust Fund Tel: 517-882-6631. (IHM-St. Casimir School, Lansing)
Luke M. Powers Educational Trust Fund (Flint) Tel: 810-591-4741; Fax: 810-591-0383.
Lumen Christi High School Endowment Fund (Lumen Christi H.S., Jackson) Tel: 517-787-0630; Fax: 517-787-1066.
Most Holy Trinity Educational Trust Fund (Most Holy Trinity Church, Fowler) Tel: 517-593-2616; Fax: 517-593-2801.
Msgr. Lawrence H. Soest Educational Trust Fund (St. Mary Parish, Flint) Tel: 810-232-4012; Fax: 810-232-4013.
Rev. Joseph R. Robb Educational Trust Fund (Holy Rosary Parish, Flint) Tel: 810-736-4040; Fax: 810-736-9129.
Sacred Heart Educational Fund (Sacred Heart Parish, Hudson) Tel: 517-448-3811.
St. Francis of Assisi Educational Trust Fund (St. Francis of Assisi Parish, Ann Harbor) Tel: 734-821-2200; Fax: 734-821-2202.
St. John the Evangelist Parish Educational Trust Fund (St. John the Evangelist Parish, Jackson) Tel: 517-784-0553; Fax: 517-788-5381.
St John School Educational Foundation, Inc. (St. John Parish, Fenton) Tel: 810-629-2251; Fax: 810-629-2302.
St. John Vianney Educational Trust Fund (St. John Vianney Parish, Flint) Tel: 810-235-1812; Fax: 810-235-4911.
St. Joseph Church of Howell Trust Fund (St. Joseph Church, Howell) Tel: 517-546-0090.
St. Joseph Educational Trust Fund (St. Joseph Church, Owosso) Tel: 517-725-5215; Fax: 517-725-1519.
St. Joseph Educational Trust Fund (St. Joseph Church, St. Johns) Tel: 517-224-8994; Fax: 517-224-3475.
St. Louis Center for Exceptional Children & Adults Endowment Trust Agreement (St. Louis Center, Chel Tel: 734-475-8430; Fax: 734-475-0310.
St. Mary Educational Trust Fund (St. Mary Parish, Mt. Morris) Tel: 810-686-3920; Fax: 810-686-0759.
St. Mary Parish Educational Trust Fund (St. Mary Parish, Charlotte) Tel: 517-543-4319; Fax: 517-543-9078.
St. Mary Star of the Sea Educational Trust Fund (St. Mary Star of the Sea Parish, Jackson) Tel: 517-784-7184; Fax: 517-783-2571.
St. Michael's School Endowment Fund Policy (St. Michael School, Grand Ledge) Tel: 517-627-2167.
St. Paul's School Education Trust Fund (St. Paul Parish, Owosso) Tel: 517-723-4277; Fax: 517-723-9503.
St. Pius X Church Educational Trust Fund (St. Pius X Church, Flint) Tel: 810-235-8574; Fax: 810-235-8580.
St. Robert Bellarmine/Fr. Charles Jacobs Educational Trust Fund (St.Robert Bellarmine Parish, Flushing Tel: 810-659-2501; Fax: 810-659-2564. (St. Robert Bellarmine Parish, Flushing)
St. Therese Educational Trust Fund (St. Therese Parish, Lansing) Tel: 517-487-3749; Fax: 517-487-3755.
St. Thomas Aquinas Educational Foundation Trust (St. Thomas Aquinas Parish, East Lansing) Tel: 517-351-7215; Fax: 517-351-7271.
St. Thomas Grade School Trust Agreement (St. Thomas the Apostle Parish, Ann Arbor) Tel: 734-761-8606; Fax: 734-997-8432.
St. Thomas Scholarship Trust for Father Gabriel Richard H.S., 517 Elizabeth St., Ann Arbor, 48104. Tel: 734-769-0911; Fax: 734-997-8432. (St. Thomas the Apostle Parish, Ann Arbor)
St. Patrick Parish Educational Trust Fund (St. Patrick Parish, Brighton) Tel: 810-229-9863; Fax: 810-220-0730.
St. Gerard Educational Trust Fund (St. Gerard Parish, Lansing) Tel: 517-323-2379; Fax: 517-886-1394.
Holy Redeemer Educational Trust Fund (Holy Redeemer Parish, Burton) Tel: 810-743-3050; Fax: 810-743-4381.

[P] MISCELLANEOUS LISTINGS

LANSING. *Catholic Lawyers Guild* (1985) 300 W. Ottawa St., 48933. Tel: 517-484-5331; Fax: 517-484-0475.
Diocesan Service Committee (Catholic Charismatic Renewal), 835 Maycroft Rd., 48917. Tel: 517-321-8661. Email: rstamford@hotmail.com. Rev. Peter J. Clark, Bishop's Liaison, St. Mary, Williamston; Ralph Stamford, Assoc. Liaison & Treas.; Patricia Stamford, Sec. Communications & Assoc. Liaison; Jack Karr, Representative to Michigan Svc. Committee; Olga Ortiz, Ann Arbor Representative; Debbie Hawley, Flint Area Representative; Kathy Pamman, Livingston Co. Area Representative.
FAITH Publishing Service, 1500 E. Saginaw St., 48906. Tel: 517-853-7600; Fax: 517-853-7616. Email: pobrien@faithcatholic.com. Web: www.faithcatholic.com. Patrick O'Brien, Pres. & Managing Editor.
Diocesan Communications Tel: 517-853-7660. Michael Diebold, Dir.
FAITH Magazine Rev. Dwight M. Ezop, Editor; Patrick O'Brien, Mng. Editor; Elizabeth Solsburg, Editorial Dir.
Liturgical Products Michael Marshall, Dir.
Ministry Marketing Joanne Eason, Dir.
Michigan Catholic Conference (1963) 510 S. Capitol Ave., 48933. Tel: 517-372-9310; Fax: 517-372-3940. Email: srmonica@micatholicconference.org. Web: www.micatholicconference.org. Sr. Monica Kostielney, R.S.M., Pres. & CEO.
ADRIAN. *Adrian Dominican Montessori Teacher Education Institute*, 1257 E. Siena Heights Dr., 49221. Tel: 517-266-3415; Fax: 517-266-3545. Email: info@admtei.org. Web: www.admtei.org. Sr. Leonor J. Esnard, O.P., Ph.D., Dir.
ANN ARBOR. *Catholic Men's Movement* (1997) 1 Ave Maria Dr., P.O. Box 466, 48106. Tel: 734-930-4524. Email: cmmdesk@catholic-men.org. Web: www.catholic-men.org. Peter Ziolkowski, Dir.; Bob Roleke, Admin. Tel: 734-930-4524; Rev. Patrick Egan, M.A., M.S., S.T.B., Chap. Tel: 734-930-3246.
The Marnee and John DeVine Foundation, 4925 Packard, 48108. Tel: 734-971-9781; Fax: 734-971-2730. Email: info@csswashtenaw.org. Web: www.csswashtenaw.org. Jan Wisniewski, Contact Person. Philanthropic arm of Catholic Social Services of Washtenaw County.
Renewal Ministries Inc. (1980) 230 Collingwood Blvd., Ste. 250, 48103. Tel: 734-662-1730; Fax: 734-662-4697. Email: gseromik@renewalministries.net. Web: www.renewalministries.net. Ralph Martin, Pres. Total Staff 13.
CHELSEA. *The Franciscan Project, Inc.*, Office: 14228 E. Old U.S. Hwy. 12, 48118. Tel: 734-475-9005. Mailing Address: P.O. Box 9, 48118-0009. Sr. Patricia Mary Hackett, S.A., Pres. & Treas.
FENTON. *Alma Redemptoris Mater*, 7381 Turner Rd., 48430. Tel: 810-735-6578; Fax: 734-663-2756. Email: tmf734@netzero.com. Rev. Thomas Firestone, Contact Person; Bro. Gary Pearce.
FLINT. *St. Luke N.E.W. Life Center*, 3115 Lawndale Ave., 48504.
GRASS LAKE. *The Pious Union of St. Joseph*, 953 E. Michigan Ave., 49240-9210. Tel: 517-522-8017 (Voice/TDD); Fax: 517-522-8387. Email: piousunion@pusj.org. Web: www.piousunionofstjoseph.org. Revs. Joseph Rinaldo, S.C., Dir.; Fortunato Turati, S.C.; Sr. Margaret Mary Schissler, D.S.M.P., Prog. Dir.
"Now and at the Hour" Magazine: Tel: 517-522-8017; Fax: 517-522-8387. Email: piousunion@pusj.org. Web: www.piousunionofstjoseph.org.

RELIGIOUS INSTITUTES OF MEN REPRESENTED IN THE DIOCESE

For further details refer to the corresponding bracketed number in the Religious Institutes of Men or Women section.
[]—*Alma Redemptoris Mater*—A.R.M.
[0140]—*The Augustinians*—O.S.A.
[0480]—*Conventual Franciscans*—O.F.M.Conv.
[]—*Detroit Province of the Society of Jesus*—S.J.
[0920]—*Oblates of St. Francis de Sales*—O.S.F.S.
[1050]—*Pontifical Institute for Foreign Missions, Inc.*—P.I.M.E.
[]—*Priests of the Congregation of Holy Cross*—C.S.C.
[1220]—*Servants of Charity*—S.C.
[]—*Society of the Priests of Saint Sulpice*—S.S.

RELIGIOUS INSTITUTES OF WOMEN REPRESENTED IN THE DIOCESE

[]—*Benedictine Nuns of Corpus Christi*—O.S.B.
[]—*Congregation of the Passion*—C.F.P.
[3832]—*Congregation of the Sisters of St. Joseph*—C.S.J.
[1070-13]—*Dominican Sisters*—O.P.
[1070-14]—*Dominican Sisters* (Grand Rapids)—O.P.
[1170]—*Felician Sisters*—C.S.S.F.
[2575]—*Institute of the Sisters of Mercy of the Americas*—R.S.M.
[]—*Mercy Sisters of Holy Cross*—C.S.C.S.
[]—*Servants of God's Love*—S.G.L.
[3580]—*Servants of Mary*—O.S.M.
[0440]—*Sisters of Charity of Cincinnati, Ohio*—S.C.
[]—*Sisters of Mary, Mother of the Eucharist*—S.M.M.E.
[1560]—*Sisters of St. Francis of the Holy Eucharist*—O.S.F.
[3830]—*Sisters of St. Joseph*—C.S.J.
[2110]—*Sisters of the Humility of Mary*—H.M.
[2260]—*Sisters of the Lamb of God*—A.D.
[2350]—*Sisters of the Living Word*—S.L.W.
[3260]—*Sisters of the Precious Blood (Dayton, OH)*—C.PP.S.
[3320]—*Sisters of the Presentation of the Blessed Virgin Mary*—P.B.V.M.
[2150]—*Sisters Servants of the Immaculate Heart of Mary*—I.H.M.

DIOCESAN CEMETERIES

LANSING. *St. Joseph*
LAINGSBURG. *St. Patrick*
FLINT. *St. Michael Byzantine*
New Calvary
Old Calvary

NECROLOGY

† Prokop, Roger, (Retired)—Died May 22, 2009

An asterisk (*) denotes an organization that has established tax-exempt status directly with the IRS and is not covered by the USCCB Group Ruling.

Diocese of Laredo

Most Reverend

JAMES A. TAMAYO, D.D.

Bishop of Laredo; ordained Priest June 11, 1976; appointed Titluar Bishop of Ita and Auxiliary Bishop of Galveston-Houston January 26, 1993; consecrated March 10, 1993; appointed first Bishop of Diocese of Laredo July 3, 2000; installed August 9, 2000. *Office: 1901 Corpus Christi St., Laredo, TX 78043.* Tel: 956-727-2140; Fax: 956-727-2777.

Chancery Office: 1901 Corpus Christi St., Laredo, TX 78043. Tel: 956-727-2140; Fax: 956-727-2777. *Mailing Address: P.O. Box 2247, Laredo, TX 78044-2247*

ESTABLISHED AUGUST 9, 2000.

Square Miles 10,905.

Comprises the Counties of Webb, Zapata, Jim Hogg, La Salle, Maverick, Zavala and Dimmitt.

STATISTICAL OVERVIEW

Personnel	
Bishop	1
Priests: Diocesan Active in Diocese	28
Priests: Retired, Sick or Absent	2
Number of Diocesan Priests	30
Religious Priests in Diocese	19
Total Priests in Diocese	49
Extern Priests in Diocese	27
Permanent Deacons in Diocese	34
Total Brothers	6
Total Sisters	6
Parishes	
Parishes	32
With Resident Pastor:	
Resident Diocesan Priests	22
Resident Religious Priests	10
Missions	17
Professional Ministry Personnel:	
Brothers	4
Sisters	17
Lay Ministers	12
Welfare	
Residential Care of Children	1
Total Assisted	57
Specialized Homes	1
Total Assisted	762
Special Centers for Social Services	2
Total Assisted	151,685
Other Institutions	1
Total Assisted	65
Educational	
Diocesan Students in Other Seminaries	5
Total Seminarians	5
High Schools, Diocesan and Parish	1
Total Students	436
Elementary Schools, Diocesan and Parish	5
Total Students	1,209
Elementary Schools, Private	1
Total Students	580
Catechesis/Religious Education:	
High School Students	2,586
Elementary Students	6,458
Total Students under Catholic Instruction	11,274
Teachers in the Diocese:	
Priests	1
Brothers	1
Sisters	7
Lay Teachers	147
Vital Statistics	
Receptions into the Church:	
Infant Baptism Totals	2,692
Minor Baptism Totals	255
Adult Baptism Totals	55
Received into Full Communion	56
First Communions	3,100
Confirmations	1,450
Marriages:	
Catholic	410
Interfaith	18
Total Marriages	428
Deaths	1,056
Total Catholic Population	279,046
Total Population	328,290

Chancery—1901 Corpus Christi St., Laredo, 78043. Tel: 956-727-2140; Fax: 956-727-2777. *Mailing Address: P.O. Box 2247, Laredo, 78044-2247.*

Vicar General—Rev. Msgr. STANLEY A. SLIWIAK, V.G., Ph.D., Blessed Sacrament, 2219 Galveston St., Laredo, 78043. Tel: 956-722-1231; Fax: 956-722-2823.

Chancellor—MARIA DE LA LUZ R. CARDENAS, 1201 Corpus Christi St., Laredo, 78043. Tel: 956-727-2140; Fax: 956-764-7842.

Vice Chancellor—Rev. IDEN JOSE BELLO MIQUILENA, 1201 Corpus Christi St., Laredo, 78040. Tel: 956-727-2140; Fax: 956-764-7842.

Tribunal—Rev. OLIVER ANGEL, J.C.L., Judicial Vicar, 1901 Corpus Christi St., Laredo, 78043. Tel: 956-727-2140; Fax: 956-712-1343.

Fiscal Officer—LOURDES MARTINEZ, CPA, 1901 Corpus Christi St., Laredo, 78043. Tel: 956-727-2140; Fax: 956-523-0828.

Presbyteral Council—Most Rev. JAMES ANTHONY TAMAYO, D.D., Pres.; VACANT, Chm.; Rev. Msgr. JAMES E. HARRIS; Revs. WOJCIECH PRZYSTASZ; JERZY KRZYWDA; LESZEK J. WACLAWIK; JAMES A. LOIACONO, O.M.I.; JACINTO OLGUIN; ALIRIO CORRALES; JOHN JESUS MOLONEY, C.S.J. Ex Officio Members: Rev. Msgr. STANLEY A. SLIWIAK, V.G., Ph.D., Vicar Gen.; Revs. R. ANTHONY MENDOZA, Dean/Northern; RICHARD HALL, O.M.I., Dean/Central; FRANCISCO LEON, O.S.A., Dean/San Agustin; JAN ZIEMNIAK, Dean/Southern.

College of Consultors—Revs. IDEN JOSE BELLO MIQUILENA; JOSE MARIA GUEVARA; RICHARD HALL, O.M.I.; R. ANTHONY MENDOZA; Rev. Msgr. STANLEY A. SLIWIAK, V.G., Ph.D., Ex Officio; Rev. JAN ZIEMNIAK.

Diocesan Offices and Directors

Campus Ministry— Congregation of St. John; Laredo Community College; Texas A&M International University. Rev. MICHAEL THERESE SCHEERGER, C.S.J., 505 Century Dr. S., Laredo, 78046. Tel: 956-722-3399, Ext. 26. Web: www.newmanclub.us.

Laredo Catholic Communications, Inc.—BENNETT MCBRIDE, Exec. Vice Pres. & Gen. Mgr., 1901 Corpus Christi St., Laredo, 78043. Tel: 956-722-4167; Fax: 956-722-4464. Email: khoy@khoy.org. Web: www.khoy.org.

Communications Department—BENNETT MCBRIDE, Dir.; GREGORIO M. LOPEZ, Editor, La Fe Magazine, 1901 Corpus Christi St., Laredo, 78043. Tel: 956-722-4167; Fax: 956-722-4464. Email: glopez@dioceseoflaredo.org.

Stewardship and Development—REBECCA C. SEPULVEDA, Dir., 1901 Corpus Christi St., Laredo, 78043. Tel: 956-727-2140; Fax: 956-523-0828.

Catholic Social Services—REBECCA SOLLOA, Dir., 1919 Cedar St., Laredo, 78043. Tel: 956-722-2443; Fax: 956-725-2238.

Emergency Assistance Program—CHRISTINA RODRIGUEZ. Tel: 956-722-2443.

Immigration Services—MYRNA GONZALEZ, Servicios Para Inmigrantes, 1919 Cedar St., Laredo, 78040. Tel: 956-722-2443. Email: mgonzalez@csslaredo.org.

Catholic Social Services Senior Center—Sr. CARMEL RANGEL, O.S.U., 1717 Callaghan Ave., Laredo, 78040. Tel: 956-722-3629.

Calvary Catholic Cemetery—ROSA ALDAPE, Mgr., 3600 McPherson, P.O. Box 2366, Laredo, 78040. Tel: 956-723-6811; Fax: 956-723-8726.

Charismatic Renewal—Deacon ANASTACIO BERNAL, Mailing Address: P.O. Box 671, Laredo, 78042. Tel: 956-724-2659.

Cursillo Movement—Rev. TORIBIO C. GUERRERO, Spiritual Dir., 1510 Matamoros St., Laredo, 78040. Tel: 956-723-3850; Fax: 956-725-6544.

Finance Council—J. PAT HEARN, Chm.; SABAS ZAPATA III; Rev. Msgr. STANLEY A. SLIWIAK, V.G., Ph.D.; HECTOR GARCIA; Rev. WOJCIECH KOSOWICZ, Ph.D.; HECTOR J. CERNA; SAUL FERNANDEZ.

Human Resources—MELINDA MENDOZA, Dir., 1901 Corpus Christi St., Laredo, 78043. Tel: 956-727-2140; Fax: 956-523-0828.

Natural Family Planning and Understanding Sexuality—Family Life Office, 1201 Corpus Christi St., Laredo, 78040. Tel: 956-727-2140; Fax: 956-764-7842.

Religious Education for Children—Sr. KAREN SCHWANE, O.S.U., Interim Part Time, 1201 Corpus Christi St., Laredo, 78040. Tel: 956-727-2140; Fax: 956-764-7842.

Religious Education for Adults—REYNALDO MONTEMAYOR, Dir., 1201 Corpus Christi St., Laredo, 78040. Tel: 956-727-2140; Fax: 956-764-7842.

Office of Respect Life—Rev. R. ANTHONY MENDOZA, Spiritual Dir., 1201 Corpus Christi St., Laredo, 78040. Tel: 956-727-2140; Fax: 956-764-7842.

Persons with Disabilities—Rev. DANIEL RAMIREZ-PORTUGAL, Dir.; MARY MACIAS, Prog. Coord., 1201 Corpus Christi St., Laredo, 78040. Tel: 956-727-2140; Fax: 956-764-7842.

Priests Personnel Board—Revs. RICHARD HALL, O.M.I.; FRANCISCO LEON, O.S.A.; R. ANTHONY MENDOZA; JAN ZIEMNIAK.

Youth Ministry—JOHNNY HERRERA, Interim Dir., 1201 Corpus Christi St., Laredo, 78040. Tel: 956-727-2140; Fax: 956-764-7842.

Archives—MARIA DE LA LUZ R. CARDENAS, Dir.; ESTHER DELGADILLO, Asst. Archivist, 1919 Cedar St., Laredo, 78040. Tel: 956-727-0700; Fax: 956-727-1530.

Family Life Ministry—MARTHA E. MILLER, Dir., 1201 Corpus Christi St., Laredo, 78040. Tel: 956-727-2140; Fax: 956-764-7842.

Victim Assistance Coordinator—MARIA DE LA LUZ R. CARDENAS, Dir., 1201 Corpus Christi St., Laredo, 78040. Tel: 956-764-7825; Fax: 956-764-7842. Email: mchancellor3@dioceseoflaredo.org.

Vocation Office—Rev. IDEN JOSE BELLO MIQUILENA, Dir., 2302 Corpus Christi St., Laredo, 78043. Tel: 956-568-0463; Fax: 956-764-7842.

Other Offices and Organizations

Catholic Daughters of the Americas—ANNA CHAPMAN, District Deputy #15: Court St. Joan of Arc #1224, 202 Silver Sage Dr., Del Rio, 78840. Tel: 830-774-7081.

International Order of the Alhambras-Zahana Caravan No. 64—JORGE DE LA GARZA, Grand Commander, 1117 Laredo St., Laredo, 78040. Tel: 956-724-8644.

Catholic Schools—

Superintendent's Office—Dr. ROSA MARIA VIDA, Ph.D., Supt.

Sultanas—ROSA IMELDA DE LA GARZA, Sultana, 1117 Laredo St., Laredo, 78040. Tel: 956-724-8644.

CLERGY, PARISHES, MISSIONS AND PAROCHIAL SCHOOLS

CITY OF LAREDO

(WEBB COUNTY)

1—SAN AGUSTIN CATHEDRAL (1762), (Hispanic), Revs. Francisco J. Hernandez, Admin.; Oscar Martinez Ramirez, Parochial Vicar; Deacon Miguel Vallarta.
200 San Agustin Ave., 78040. Tel: 956-722-1382; Fax: 956-722-0441. Email: san_agustine@sbcglobal.net.
Parish Office: 214 San Bernardo Ave., 78040.
Catechesis/Religious Program—Students 380.

2—BLESSED SACRAMENT (1950), (Hispanic), [CEM 2] Rev. Wojciech Przystasz, Admin.; Rev. Msgr. Stanley A. Sliwiak, Pastor Emeritus; Deacons David Vargas; Larry Sandlin.
2219 Galveston St., 78043. Tel: 956-722-1231; Fax: 956-722-2823. Email: blessedsacrament@prodigy.net.
Catechesis/Religious Program—Students 197.

3—SAN CARLOS MISSION (1993) Unassigned. Attended by Christ the King, Laredo., c/o 146 Northpoint Dr., 78041.
Catechesis/Religious Program—Laura Villalobos, D.R.E. Students 114.

4—CHRIST THE KING (1954) Rev. Jose Luis Balderas.
1105 Tilden Ave., 78040. Tel: 956-723-4267; Fax: 956-791-8034.
Catechesis/Religious Program—Tel: 956-722-7821. Students 306.

5—DIVINE MERCY (1998) Rev. Michael De Leon.
Parish Office: 9350 Amber Ave., 78045. Tel: 956-726-9972; Fax: 956-726-1286.
Catechesis/Religious Program—Students 423.

6—ST. FRANCES CABRINI (1958), (Hispanic), [CEM] Rev. Jose Alfredo Gaytan, S.O.L.T.
3018 Davis Ave., 78040. Tel: 956-722-2919; Fax: 956-724-5232. Email: mothercabrinichurch@bizlaredo.rr.com.
Catechesis/Religious Program—Tel: 956-722-8315; Fax: 956-724-5232. Students 98.

7—HOLY FAMILY (1984), (Hispanic), Rev. P. Nolasco Hinojosa Jr.; Deacon Hector D. Hernandez.
2705 McPherson, 78040. Tel: 956-724-6881; Fax: 956-724-5581. Email: hfccl_oc@yahoo.com.
Catechesis/Religious Program—Tel: 956-724-5581. Students 150.

8—HOLY REDEEMER (1940), (Hispanic), [JC] Rev. Francisco Leon, O.S.A.; Deacon Edmundo Lopez Jr.
Mailing Address: P.O. Box 1087, 78040. 1602 Garcia St., 78040. Tel: 956-723-7171; Fax: 956-723-7194. Email: holyredeemer@laredohrc.org. Web: www.laredohrc.org.
Mission—Santa Cruz 2002 Lee Ave., Webb Co. 78040.
Catechesis/Religious Program—Students 174.

9—ST. JOHN NEUMANN (1979) Rev. Daniel Ramirez-Portugal; Rev. Msgr. James E. Harris, Parochial Vicar.
102 W. Hillside Rd., 78041. Tel: 956-726-9488; Fax: 956-726-0540.
Catechesis/Religious Program—Tel: 956-726-9452. Students 90.

10—ST. JOSEPH (1953) Rev. Leszek J. Waclawik; Deacon Crispin O. Soto.
109 N. Meadow, 78040. Tel: 956-723-4172; Fax: 956-728-8824.
Catechesis/Religious Program—Tel: 956-791-6664; Fax: 956-728-8824. Students 152.

11—ST. JUDE (1984) Rev. Jose Maria Guevara.
Mailing Address: 2031 Lowry Rd., 78045. 2031 Lowry Rd., 78045. Tel: 956-722-2280; Fax: 956-722-0209.
Catechesis/Religious Program—Students 550.

12—NUESTRA SENORA DEL ROSARIO INDEPENDENT MISSION (2000) Revs. Jan Ziemniak; Mario Flores Meza, O.F.M., Parochial Vicar.
420 Sierra Vista Blvd., 78046. Tel: 956-753-8764; Fax: 956-753-9972.
Catechesis/Religious Program—Diana Salazar, D.R.E. Students 480.

13—OUR LADY OF GUADALUPE (1926) [JC] Revs. Richard Hall, O.M.I.; Edward J. Vrazel, O.M.I.; Deacon Anastacio Bernal.
Mailing Address: P.O. Box 671, 78042. 1718 San Jorge Ave., 78040. Tel: 956-723-6954; Fax: 956-723-6047. Email: petraolog@sbcglobal.net. Web: www.ologlaredo.com.
Catechesis/Religious Program—Students 140.

14—ST. PATRICK (1970) Revs. Wojciech Kosowicz, Admin.; Jacinto Olguin, Parochial Vicar.
555 E. Del Mar Blvd., 78041. Tel: 956-722-6215; Fax: 956-764-7842. Email: stpatlaredotx@yahoo.com.
Catechesis/Religious Program—Tel: 956-722-8451. Students 500.
Mission—Apostolate Missions in Northern Mexico

15—ST. PETER THE APOSTLE (1897) Rev. Toribio C. Guerrero.
Mailing Address: 1510 Matamoros St., P.O. Box 26, 78040. Tel: 956-723-6301; Fax: 956-729-1229.
Catechesis/Religious Program—Students 51.

16—SAGRADO CORAZON DE JESUS MISSION (1994) Rev. Mario Flores Meza, O.F.M.
Res.: 420 Sierra Vista, 78046. Tel: 956-753-8764; 956-417-3325; Fax: 956-417-3325.
Catechesis/Religious Program—Students 51.

17—SAN FRANCISCO JAVIER (1966), (Hispanic), Rev. William Davis, O.M.I.; Deacon Ignacio Valdez.
Mailing Address: P.O. Box 1175, 78042-1175. 2502 Zaragoza St., 78042-1175. Tel: 956-723-3850; Fax: 956-725-6544. Email: chaqui6@aol.com.
Catechesis/Religious Program—Students 83.

18—SAN LUIS REY (1958), (Hispanic), Revs. Juan Francisco Munoz, S.D.B.; Thomas Juarez, S.D.B., Vicar; Deacon Jose Rodriguez.
Church: 3502 Sanders Ave., P.O. Box 2294, 78044. Tel: 956-723-6587; Fax: 956-723-6825. Email: sanluisreychurch@yahoo.com.
Catechesis/Religious Program—Tel: 956-722-3323. Students 280.

19—SAN MARTIN DE PORRES (1979), (Hispanic), Rev. Msgr. Alejandro Salazar; Deacon Leonel San Miguel.
Mailing Address: 1704 Sandman St., P.O. Box 2666, 78041. Tel: 956-723-5215; Fax: 956-723-9443. Web: www.san-martin.org.
Catechesis/Religious Program—Tel: 956-725-2440; Fax: 956-725-2440. Email: smartinccd@hotmail.com. Students 460.

20—SANTA ANITA MISSION, Closed.

21—SANTA MARGARITA DE ESCOCIA (1991), (Hispanic), Rev. Alirio Corrales, Admin.
320 Segovia Dr., 78046. Tel: 956-724-9669; Fax: 956-791-2167. Email: stmargaritachurch@att.net.
Catechesis/Religious Program—Students 173.

22—SANTO NINO (1985), (Hispanic), Rev. Santiago Domingo, Admin.
2717 Cross St., 78046. Tel: 956-724-6638; Fax: 956-712-8096.
Catechesis/Religious Program—Students 282.

23—SANTA TERESITA MISSION (1996) Rev. Msgr. Alejandro Salazar.
109 N. Meadow Ave., 78040. Tel: 956-723-4172; Fax: 956-728-8824. P.O. Box 2666, 78044. Tel: 956-723-5215; Fax: 956-723-9443.
Catechesis/Religious Program—Students 28.

24—ST. VINCENT DE PAUL (1969), (Hispanic), Revs. Pastor Martinez, O.S.A.; Leonel Martinez, O.S.A., Parochial Vicar; Deacon Leonardo Aguillon.
2710 Boulanger St., 78043. Tel: 956-722-3034; Fax: 956-722-4829.
Catechesis/Religious Program—Tel: 956-726-4134. Students 759.

OUTSIDE THE CITY OF LAREDO

ASHERTON, DIMMIT CO., IMMACULATE CONCEPTION (1918), (Hispanic), Rev. Salvador Pedroza.
Mailing Address: 579 Crocket & 6th St., P.O. Box 8, 78827.
Mission—St. Michael P.O. Box 266, Big Wells, Dimmit Co. 78830-0266. Tel: 830-457-2693; Fax: 830-457-0100.
Mission—St. Henry P.O. Box 15, Catarina, Dimmit Co. 78836. Tel: 830-468-3343.
Catechesis/Religious Program—Students 101.

CARRIZO SPRINGS, DIMMIT CO., OUR LADY OF GUADALUPE (1881) Rev. Jerzy Krzywda; Deacon Jose F. Perez.
Mailing Address: 1003 N. 6th St., 78834. Tel: 830-876-2239; Fax: 830-876-5023.
Catechesis/Religious Program—Tel: 830-876-0153; Fax: 830-876-5023. Students 355.

COTULLA, LA SALLE CO., SACRED HEART (1917) [JC] Rev. Francisco Stodola; Deacon Jose Patterson.
Mailing Address: 307 S. Main St., P.O. Box 560, 78014. Tel: 830-879-2658; Fax: 830-879-4916. Email: sagradocorazon@sbcglobal.net.
Catechesis/Religious Program—Tel: 930-879-3196. Students 115.

CRYSTAL CITY, ZAVALA CO., SACRED HEART (1917), (Hispanic), Rev. Jozef Glabinski, Admin.
115 E. Kinney St., 78839. Tel: 830-374-3148; Fax: 830-374-2211. Email: sacredheartchurchcc@yahoo.com.
Catechesis/Religious Program—Students 175.

EAGLE PASS, MAVERICK CO.

1—ST. JOSEPH (1967), (Hispanic), Rev. Richard Kulwiec, O.M.I.
Mailing Address: 800 Comal St., 78852-4029. Tel: 830-773-6114; Fax: 830-773-6608.
Catechesis/Religious Program—Tel: 830-773-6515; Fax: 830-773-6608. Students 330.

2—OUR LADY OF REFUGE (1859) [CEM] Revs. James A. Loiacono, O.M.I.; James Erving, O.M.I.; Deacon Efren Maldonado.
Mailing Address: 815 Webster, 78852. Tel: 830-773-8451 (Office); 830-773-8421 (Res.).
Mission—Our Lady of Lourdes Seco Mines, Maverick Co. Tel: 830-773-8288.
Mission—Our Lady of Guadalupe Quemado, Maverick Co. Tel: 830-758-1888.
Catechesis/Religious Program—Tel: 830-773-8915 (Res.); 830-773-7744 (Office). Students 596.

3—SACRED HEART (1966), (Hispanic), Revs. Paul Whelan, O.M.I.; Roberto Pena, O.M.I.; Deacons Manuel Rene Cardona; Victor Carrillo Jr.; Leandro Contreras Jr.; Hector Ricardo Martinez.
Church: 2055 Williams St., 78852. Tel: 830-773-2451; Fax: 830-773-0643.
Catechesis/Religious Program—Tel: 830-758-1681. Students 520.
Mission—Our Lady of San Juan El Indio, Maverick Co.

ENCINAL, LA SALLE CO., IMMACULATE HEART OF MARY (1898), (Hispanic), Rev. Noel Davis.
Mailing Address: P.O. Box 5, 78019-0005. 400 Santa Fe St., 78019-0005. Tel: 956-948-5328; Fax: 956-948-5328. Email: ihmcce@yahoo.com.
Catechesis/Religious Program—Students 65.

HEBBRONVILLE, JIM HOGG CO., OUR LADY OF GUADALUPE (1926) [CEM] Revs. Francisco Javier Aceves Aguilar, O.F.M.; Gustavo Ortega Rodriguez, O.F.M., Parochial Vicar; Guillermo Ulises Ortrz Flores, O.F.M., Parochial Vicar.
504 E. Santa Clara St., 78361. Tel: 361-527-3865; Fax: 361-527-5548. Email: gpeheb@hotmail.com.
Mission—St. Agnes Mirando City, Jim Hogg Co.
Mission—St. Bridget Oilton, Jim Hogg Co.
Mission—Sacred Heart Bruni, Jim Hogg Co.
Catechesis/Religious Program—Tel: 361-231-0003 (After 6:00 P.M.); Fax: 361-527-5548. Clemencia Villanueva, D.R.E. Students 140.

LA PRYOR, ZAVALA CO., ST. JOSEPH (1917), (Hispanic), Rev. R. Anthony Mendoza; Deacons Gene Corrigan; Juan Gallegos.
Mailing Address: 628 Burton St., P.O. Box 436, 78872-0436. Tel: 830-365-4107; Fax: 830-365-9367.
Mission—St. Patrick P.O. Box 83, Batesville, Zavala Co. 78829.
Catechesis/Religious Program—Students 181.

RIO BRAVO, WEBB CO., SANTA RITA DE CASIA INDEPENDENT MISSION (1986) Rev. Janusz Glabinski.
1001 Espejo Molina, 78046. Tel: 956-725-7215; Fax: 956-728-8539.
Catechesis/Religious Program—Students 90.
Mission—Santa Monica Mission 507 Morales (El Cenizo), Webb Co. 78046. Tel: 956-724-4413.

ZAPATA, ZAPATA CO., OUR LADY OF LOURDES (1940), (Spanish), Revs. Agustin Escalante, Admin.; Gerardo Silos, Parochial Vicar.
Mailing Address: 1609 Gleen St., Box 3213 Stop 32A, 78076.
Res.: 1609 Glenn St., 78076. Tel: 956-765-4216; Fax: 956-765-6188.
Catechesis/Religious Program—Students 427.
Mission—Ntra. Sra. De Lourdes Box 3213 Stop 32A, Zapata Co. 78076.
Mission—Our Lady of Refuge San Ignacio, Zapata Co. Tel: 950-765-4940.
Mission—San Pedro Lopeno, Zapata Co.
Mission—Santa Ana Falcon, Zapata Co.

Chaplains of Public Institutions

LAREDO. *Webb County Jail*, 4402 Tilden Ave., 78041. Tel: 956-723-5029. Deacon Jose Rodriguez, Prison Chap. Chaplaincy Apostolate to Refugees & Jail Ministry.

INSTITUTIONS LOCATED IN THE DIOCESE

[A] HIGH SCHOOLS

LAREDO. *St. Augustine High School* (Diocesan), 1300 Galveston St., 78040. Tel: 956-724-8131; Fax: 956-724-8770. Email: ogentry@st-augustine.org. Web: st-augustine.org. Mrs. Olga P. Gentry, Prin.; Ms. Graciela Noyola, Librarian. Lay Teachers 27; Students 436; Administration 3.

[B] JUNIOR HIGH AND ELEMENTARY SCHOOLS

LAREDO. *St. Augustine (Elementary School)* (1927) (Diocesan), 1300 Galveston St., 78040. Tel: 956-724-1176; Fax: 956-724-9891. Email: cortez@st-augustine.org. Web: www.st-augustine.org. Slyvia F. Cortez, Prin. Lay Teachers 28; Students 446.

Blessed Sacrament School, 1501 N. Bartlett St., 78043. Tel: 956-722-1222; Fax: 956-712-2002. Email: ebgutierrezbss@yahoo.com. Esther B. Gutierrez, Prin.; Maria Del Carmen Alaniz, Librarian. Lay Teachers 13; Students 219.

Mary Help of Christians School (Private) , 10 E. Del Mar Blvd., 78045. Tel: 956-722-3966; Fax: 956-722-1413. Web: www.mhsoul.org. Sr. Suzanne Miller, F.M.A., Prin. Sisters 6; Lay Teachers 45; Students 580.

Our Lady of Guadalupe School (1904) 400 Callaghan St., 78040-3834. Tel: 956-722-3915; Fax: 956-727-2840. Email: hrlndmartinez@yahoo.com. Herlinda Martinez, Prin. Lay Teachers 9; Other Personnel 4; Students 116.

St. Peter Memorial (Diocesan), 1519 Houston St., P.O. Box 520, 78040. Tel: 956-723-6302; Fax: 956-725-2671. Linda G. Mitchell, Ed.D., Prin. Sisters 1; Lay Teachers 12; Students 152.

EAGLE PASS. *Our Lady of Refuge* (1950) 577 Washington St., 78852. Tel: 830-773-3531; 830-773-1800; Fax: 830-773-7310. Email: aolivares@olorschool.org. Web: oloroschool.org. Adolfo Olivares Jr., Prin. Sisters 1; Lay Teachers 12; Students 276.

[C] ORPHANAGES AND INFANT HOMES

LAREDO. *Sacred Heart Children's Home* (1907) 3310 S. Zapata Hwy., 78046. Tel: 956-723-3343; Fax: 956-723-3409. Sr. Maria Teresa Grajeda, S.S.H.J.P., Supr. Sisters 17; Children 55.

[D] MONASTERIES AND RESIDENCES OF PRIESTS AND BROTHERS

LAREDO. *St. John Priory, F.J.* Congregation of St. John, 505 Century Dr., South, 78046. Tel: 956-242-6623; Fax: 956-242-6623. Email: laredo@stjean.com. Web: www.communityofstjohn.com. Revs. John Jesus Moloney, C.S.J., Prior; Marie Joseph Weyne; Michael T. Sheerger, Vicar Accountant; Bros. Joachim Arnold; Michael W. Paul. Priests 4; Brothers 3; Total in Residence 7.

Marist Brothers, 1511 Cherry Hill Dr., 78041-3807. Tel: 956-724-2651; Fax: 956-724-1963. Email: fmslaredo@prodigy.net. Bros. Philip R. Degagne, F.M.S., Dir.; Joseph E. Herrera, F.M.S.; Thomas W. Coyne, F.M.S. Marist Brothers 3.

[E] CONVENTS AND RESIDENCES FOR SISTERS

LAREDO. *Eucharistic Missionary Society (EMS)*, 1101 Cortez St., 78040. Tel: 956-726-4085; Fax: 956-726-4085. Email: emisoc@laredo.globalpc.net. Sr. Maria Manuela Susana Pedroza, E.M.S.

Mary Help of Christians Convent (1935) 10 E. Del Mar Blvd., 78045. Tel: 956-791-8617; Fax: 956-722-1413. Email: msmiller@mhsoul.org. Web: www.mhsoul.org. Sr. Marie Gannon, F.M.A., Supr. Daughters of Mary Help of Christians (Salesian Sisters). Sisters 6.

Misioneras del Rosario de Fatima, 1802 San Francisco, 78040. Tel: 956-723-5598; Fax: 956-764-7342.

Mother of the Eucharist Convent Felician Sisters (1855) 705 Dellwood Dr., 78045. Tel: 956-568-1502. Email: feliciansisters@stx.rr.com. Web: www.southwestfeliciansisters.org. Sisters 3.

Sacred Heart Children's Home Convent (1907) 3310 S. Zapata Hwy., 78046. Tel: 956-723-3343; Fax: 956-723-3409. Sr. Maria Yolanda Fernandez, S.S.H.J.P., Regl. Supr. Servants of the Sacred Heart of Jesus and of the Poor. Sisters 17.

Sisters of Mercy Convent, 1120 E. Guerrero St., 78040-6543. Tel: 956-724-5512. Email: livorsm@sbcglobal.net; ktinnel@mercysc.org. Sr. Kathleen Marie Tinnel, R.S.M., Contact Person.

Sisters of Our Lady of the Most Holy Trinity, 2454 Colonia Loop, 78046. Tel: 956-727-3965. Sisters Ma. Esperanza Lopez, S.O.L.T., Migrant Min. Dir.; Mary Teresa Pacheco, S.O.L.T., American Region Sister Servant.

Sisters of St. John (1992) 504 Century Dr., S., 78046. Tel: 956-727-1028; Fax: 956-727-1028. Sisters Jean Marthe, Local Supr.; Belinda Mary Caballero. Total in Residence 9.

Ursuline Sisters, 136 Palencia, 78046. Tel: 956-722-1101. Sr. Carmel Rangel, O.S.U., Treas.

EAGLE PASS. *Benedictine Sisters* Nurse Employed by Fort Duncan Regional Medical Center., 1080 Vista Hermosa, 78852. Tel: 830-758-0812.

Missionary Sisters of Our Lady of Perpetual Help (1934) 895 Webster, 78852. Tel: 956-727-2140; Fax: 956-764-7842. Sisters Sanolra Lerma Montanez, M.P.S., Office Supr.; Irene Mejia, M.P.S.

[F] RETREAT HOUSES

LAREDO. *Holy Spirit Retreat and Conference Center*, 501 Century Dr., S., 78046. Tel: 956-242-6223; Fax: 956-242-6623. Email: lhsrc@sbcglobal.net. Web: www.communityofstjohn.com. Revs. John Jesus Moloney, C.S.J., Prior; Mary Joseph Weyne; Michael T. Sheerger, Accountant/Vicar; Bros. Joachim Arnold, Guest Master; Michael W. Paul.

[G] MISCELLANEOUS

LAREDO. *St. Augustine School Endowment Fund, Inc.*, 1300 Galveston, 78040. Tel: 956-724-8131; Fax: 956-724-8770. Email: ogentry@st-augustine.org. Web: www.st-augustine.org. Mrs. Olga P. Gentry, Prin.

Bethany House (1982) 819 Hidalgo St., 78040. Tel: 956-722-4152; Fax: 956-791-1102. Email: info@bethanyhouseoflaredo.org. Web: bethanyhouseoflaredo.org. Barbara Kazen, Pres.; Jerri Lynn Ortiz, Exec. Dir.

Casa de Misericordia (1998) P.O. Box 430175, 78043-0175. Tel: 956-712-9590; 877-782-2722; Fax: 956-791-1364. Email: misericordia@stx.rr.com. Maria Elena Arambula, Shelter Admin. Domestic Violence Shelter for Women and Children.

Diocese of Laredo Deposit and Loan Fund, Inc., 1901 Corpus Christi St., 78043. Tel: 956-727-2140; Fax: 956-523-0828.

Diocese of Perpetual Benefit Endowment Fund, Inc., 1901 Corpus Christi St., 78043. Tel: 956-727-2140; Fax: 956-523-0828.

Mercy Ministries of Laredo (2003) 2500 Zacatecas, 78046. Tel: 956-718-6810; Fax: 956-721-7405. Email: mercy.laredo@mercy.net. Web: mercylaredo.com. Sr. Maria Luisa Vera, R.S.M., CEO.

San Agustin Historical Preservation & Restoration Society, Inc., 201 San Agustin Ave., 78040. Tel: 956-722-1382; Fax: 956-722-0441. Email: san_agustine@sbcglobal.net. Deacon Miguel Vallarta, Contact Person.

NECROLOGY

(No Deaths)

An asterisk (*) denotes an organization that has established tax-exempt status directly with the IRS and is not covered by the USCCB Group Ruling.

Diocese of Las Cruces

(Dioecesis Las Cruces)

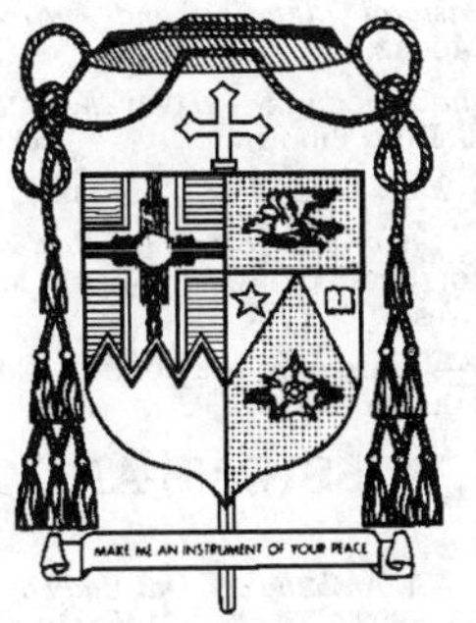
MAKE ME AN INSTRUMENT OF YOUR PEACE

Most Reverend

RICARDO RAMIREZ, C.S.B., D.D.

Bishop of Las Cruces; ordained December 10, 1966; appointed Titular Bishop of Vatarba and Auxiliary of San Antonio October 27, 1981; consecrated December 6, 1981; appointed First Bishop of Las Cruces August 31, 1982; installed October 18, 1982. *Res.: 5625 Spanish Pointe Rd., Las Cruces, NM 88007.*

The Pastoral Center: 1280 Med Park Dr., Las Cruces, NM 88005. Tel: 575-523-7577; Fax: 575-524-3874.

Web: www.dioceseoflascruces.org

Email: pastoralcenter@dioceseoflascruces.org

ESTABLISHED OCTOBER 18, 1982.

Square Miles 44,483.

Comprises the Counties of Dona Ana, Hidalgo, Grant, Luna, Sierra, Otero, Lincoln, Chaves, Eddy and Lea in the State of New Mexico.

For legal titles of parishes and diocesan institutions, consult The Pastoral Center.

STATISTICAL OVERVIEW

Personnel	
Bishop	1
Priests: Diocesan Active in Diocese	24
Priests: Retired, Sick or Absent	9
Number of Diocesan Priests	33
Religious Priests in Diocese	44
Total Priests in Diocese	77
Extern Priests in Diocese	6
Ordinations:	
Diocesan Priests	2
Transitional Deacons	1
Permanent Deacons in Diocese	40
Total Brothers	3
Total Sisters	41
Parishes	
Parishes	45
With Resident Pastor:	
Resident Diocesan Priests	16
Resident Religious Priests	18
Without Resident Pastor:	
Administered by Priests	10
Administered by Deacons	1
Missions	46
Pastoral Centers	1
Professional Ministry Personnel:	
Brothers	2
Sisters	3
Lay Ministers	59
Welfare	
Day Care Centers	1
Total Assisted	50
Special Centers for Social Services	1
Total Assisted	8,000
Educational	
Diocesan Students in Other Seminaries	6
Total Seminarians	6
Elementary Schools, Private	5
Total Students	597
Catechesis/Religious Education:	
High School Students	2,487
Elementary Students	5,540
Total Students under Catholic Instruction	8,630
Teachers in the Diocese:	
Lay Teachers	53
Vital Statistics	
Receptions into the Church:	
Infant Baptism Totals	1,892
Minor Baptism Totals	159
Adult Baptism Totals	57
Received into Full Communion	259
First Communions	1,691
Confirmations	1,055
Marriages:	
Catholic	300
Interfaith	29
Total Marriages	329
Deaths	822
Total Catholic Population	132,646
Total Population	498,308

The Pastoral Center—1280 Med Park Dr., Las Cruces, 88005. Tel: 575-523-7577; Fax: 575-524-3874. Office Hours: Mon.-Fri. 8:00-12:00 & 1:00-5:00.

Bishops Administrative Council—Most Rev. RICARDO RAMÍREZ, C.S.B., D.D.; Very Rev. Msgr. JOHN E. ANDERSON, V.G., P.A.; DEBBIE ISHAM MOORE; Dr. WAYNE E. PRIBBLE; DAVID MCNAMARA; GRACE CASSETTA.

Vicar General—Very Rev. Msgr. JOHN E. ANDERSON, V.G., P.A.

Episcopal Vicar for Clergy and Personnel—Very Rev. Msgr. ROBERT L. GETZ, P.A.

Chancellor—Dr. WAYNE E. PRIBBLE.

Vice Chancellor—DEBBIE ISHAM MOORE.

Director of Clergy Personnel—Very Rev. Msgr. JOHN E. ANDERSON, V.G., P.A.

Diocesan Tribunal—Rev. JOHN S. WEBER, J.C.L., Judicial Vicar, 1280 Med Park Dr., Las Cruces, 88005.

Promoter of Justice—Rev. ENRIQUE LOPEZ.

Judges—Revs. GILES CARIE, O.F.M.Conv.; JOHN S. WEBER, J.C.L.; JOSE ROGELIO MARTINEZ, J.C.L.; IRENE VALLES.

Defenders of the Bond—Very Rev. Msgr. JOHN E. ANDERSON, V.G., P.A.; Revs. RICHARD CATANACH; MICHAEL P. LINDSAY.

Administrative Director for Tribunal—IRENE VALLES.

Assesor—NORMA SPINA, M.A.

Advocate—IRENE VALLES.

Notaries—VELIA SALINAS; DOROTHY MEDINA.

Vicars—Revs. RICHARD CATANACH; ROBERT L. BECERRA; VALENTINE M. JANKOWSKI, O.F.M.Conv.; ANDRES ALAVA, O.A.R.; PAUL MURTAGH, SS.CC.; ALFRED GALVAN.

Diocesan Consultors—Most Rev. RICARDO RAMIREZ, C.S.B.; Very Rev. Msgrs. JOHN E. ANDERSON, V.G., P.A.; ROBERT L. GETZ, P.A.; Revs. VALENTINE M. JANKOWSKI, O.F.M.Conv.; MARCOS REYNA.

Presbyteral Council—Rev. MIGUEL BRISENO, O.F.M.Conv., Pres.; Very Rev. Msgr. JOHN E. ANDERSON, V.G., P.A.; Revs. RICHARD CATANACH; MARCOS REYNA; ROBERT L. BECERRA; RAYMOND J. FLORES; VALENTINE M. JANKOWSKI, O.F.M.Conv.; ANDRES ALAVA, O.A.R.; ALFRED GALVAN; RUBEN ROMERO RUIZ; PAUL MURTAGH, SS.CC.; JUAN CARLOS RAMIREZ; CYPRIAN ULINE, O.F.M.Conv.; Most Rev. RICARDO RAMIREZ, C.S.B.; Revs. ENRIQUE LOPEZ; JOHN WEBER, J.C.L.; EDWARD HERRERA; BRYANT HAUSFELD, O.F.M.; WILLIAM MCCANN; PAUL BOTENHAGEN, O.F.M.; Dr. WAYNE E. PRIBBLE.

Clergy Personnel Board—Very Rev. Msgrs. JOHN E. ANDERSON, V.G., P.A.; ROBERT L. GETZ, P.A.; Most Rev. RICARDO RAMIREZ, C.S.B.; Revs. RICHARD CATANACH; WILLIAM MCCANN; MARCOS REYNA; MANUEL IBARRA; ENRIQUE LOPEZ; EDWARD HERRERA; RAYMOND J. FLORES; Dr. WAYNE E. PRIBBLE.

Priestly Life and Ministry Committee—Revs. RICHARD CATANACH, Chm.; MARCOS REYNA; PAUL BOTENHAGEN, O.F.M.; RAYMOND J. FLORES.

Priests Retirement Fund Committee—Very Rev. Msgr. ROBERT L. GETZ, P.A.; Revs. MICHAEL LINDSAY; WILLIAM MCCANN; Very Rev. Msgr. JOHN E. ANDERSON, V.G., P.A.; Rev. RICHARD CATANACH; Mr. DANIEL DOLAN; FELIPE SALCIDO JR.

Permanent Deacon Council—Deacons RICHARD RODRIGUEZ, Chm.; MARIANO MELENDREZ, Sec.; PAUL LEDERMAN; ANTONIO DOMINGUEZ; HOWARD HERRING.

Director of Deacon Formation—Rev. MICHAEL P. CERRETTO, C.S.B.; Deacon LOUIS ROMAN.

Director of Deacons—Deacon PAUL LEDERMAN, Interim Dir.

Comptroller—FELIPE SALCIDO JR.

Human Resources—DEBBIE ISHAM MOORE, Dir.; PATRICIA RAMOS, HR Asst. & Office Mgr.

Finance Council—Most Rev. RICARDO RAMÍREZ, C.S.B., D.D.; Judge MANUEL SAUCEDO; Very Rev. Msgr. JOHN E. ANDERSON, V.G., P.A.; Dr. WAYNE E. PRIBBLE; Rev. WILLIAM MCCANN; DAN DOLAN, Diocesan Attorney; Rev. RICARDO BAUZA; TIM FLYNN; DAVID MCNAMARA; TOM MCCARTY; Rev. JOHN S. WEBER, J.C.L.; SUSAN ROBERTS; FELIPE SALCIDO, Comptroller; BILL QUINONES; CONNIE PRIETO; LEONARD MURPHY; ROSE MARY HINDES; PAM HESTER; GEMMA FERGUSON; MARGARET FLORES.

Office of Development, Stewardship and Foundation—SUSAN ROBERTS, Exec. Dir.; CHRISTINA VILLEGAS, Devel. Assoc.

Office of Insurance—MARTA ROMERO, Insurance Dir.

Office of Buildings and Properties—MANUEL LEYVA, Dir.

Diocesan Ministries Offices and Directors

Office of Education and Formation—DAVID MCNAMARA, Dir.

Office of Adult Catechesis—DAVID MCNAMARA, Dir.

Office of Vocations—Revs. MARCOS REYNA; RAYMOND J. FLORES.

Art and Environment Committee—Sr. LUCY MEISSEN, C.PP.S.

Attorneys—Mr. DANIEL DOLAN; MIKE LILLEY; DAVID MCNEILL; Mr. CARLOS MARTINEZ.

Campus Ministry—Revs. MITCHELL DOWALGO, C.S.B.; MARCOS REYNA.

Judicial Vicars—Revs. JOHN S. WEBER, J.C.L.; JOSE ROGELIO MARTINEZ, J.C.L.

Office of Catholic Social Ministry—CLAUDIA I. MONCADA-TRUEBLOOD, Dir.

Colonias Development Council—DIANA BUSTAMANTE, Dir.

Cursillo Secretariat—VICTOR RODRIGUEZ, Pres.; BLANCA LUNA, Treas.; VICENTE LUNA, Sec.

Office of Elementary Catechesis—MARY HELEN LLANEZ, Dir.

Lay Ministry Formation—DAVID MCNAMARA, Dir.

Ecumenical Liaison—VACANT.

Hispanic Ministry—VACANT.

Holy Childhood Association—Very Rev. Msgr. JOHN E. ANDERSON, V.G., P.A.

Office of Liturgical Education—Sr. LUCY MEISSEN, C.PP.S.

Propagation of the Faith—Very Rev. Msgr. JOHN E. ANDERSON, V.G., P.A.

Order of Christian Initiation—Sr. LUCY MEISSEN, C.PP.S., Adult; DAVID MCNAMARA, Children; ROMELIA ENRIQUEZ; VENITA CHELGREN; SALLY HARPER.

Office of Adolescent Catechesis and Youth Ministry—GRACE CASSETTA, Dir.

Diocesan Pastoral Council—Most Rev. RICARDO RAMIREZ, C.S.B. Members: EZEQUIO NAVARETTE; LYNNE YBARRA; LUCIANO MONTES; Deacon DAVID MCNEIL; JESSE SANCHEZ, Vice Chm.; Rev. MARCOS REYNA; Sr. ROBERT ANN HECKER, O.S.F.; Rev. BRIAN GUERRINI; JAN SETTLES; GARY MONTOYA; MARY SALAZAR-HIGHTOWER; LOUIS A. ROMAN, Chm.; DEBBIE ISHAM MOORE, Sec.

Office of Pastoral Planning and Outreach—DEBBIE ISHAM MOORE.

Catholic Lending Library—DAVID MCNAMARA, Coord.; DOLORES DIAZ, Librarian.

Diocesan Archives—Dr. WAYNE E. PRIBBLE, Archivist.

Charismatic Renewal Liaisons—Rev. MARTIN G. CORDERO; Mr. SAM TOME, (West); Mrs. ENEDINA TOME, (West).

Agua Viva—CHRISTINA ANCHONDO, Editor; DAVID MCNAMARA, Special Projects.

Agua Viva Editorial Advisory Board—Most Rev. RICARDO RAMIREZ, C.S.B.; CHRISTINA ANCHONDO; MANUEL LEYVA; DAVID MCNAMARA; MARY CARTER; Dr. WAYNE E. PRIBBLE; DEBBIE ISHAM MOORE; LOURDES RAMOS; CHRISTINA VILLEGAS; Rev. MICHAEL P. CERRETTO, C.S.B.; Deacon LOUIS ROMAN.

Office of Prison and Jail Ministry—Deacon EMILIO RAMOS.

Office of Marriage and Family Life—MARY HELEN LLANEZ, Coord.

Office of Catholic Schools—BEN TRUJILLO, Supt.

Pro-Life Coordinators—JOSEPH BEHNKE; ELIZABETH BEHNKE.

Victim Assistance Coordinator—Dr. WAYNE E. PRIBBLE. Tel: 575-523-7577. Email: wpribble@dioceseoflascruces.org.

CLERGY, PARISHES, MISSIONS AND PAROCHIAL SCHOOLS

CITY OF LAS CRUCES

(DONA ANA COUNTY)

1—CATHEDRAL OF THE IMMACULATE HEART OF MARY (1953) Revs. Sean M. Garrity, C.S.B., Rector; Rene Espejel, C.S.B., Parochial Vicar; Deacons Louis Roman, Pastoral Assoc.; Edward Misquez. In Res., Revs. Michael P. Cerretto, C.S.B.; Arthur Roberts, C.S.B.
1240 S. Espina St., 88001. Tel: 575-524-8563; Fax: 575-523-2252.

2—ST. ALBERT THE GREAT NEWMAN PARISH (1986), Serving New Mexico State University. Rev. Mitchell G. Dowalgo, C.S.B.; Deacon David McNeill Jr.
Res.: 2615 S. Solano, 88001. Tel: 575-522-6202; Fax: 575-521-3453.

3—ST. GENEVIEVE (1859) [CEM] Rev. Ricardo Bauza. In Res., Rev. Juan Moreno.
Res.: 100 S. Espina, 88001. Tel: 575-524-9649; Fax: 575-524-3263.

4—HOLY CROSS (1970) Very Rev. Msgr. John E. Anderson; Deacons Paul Lederman, Pastoral Assoc.; Steve Apodaca, Pastoral Assoc.
Office: 1327 N. Miranda St., 88005. Tel: 575-523-0167; Fax: 575-523-8023.

5—OUR LADY OF HEALTH (1956) Revs. Ricardo Hinojal, O.A.R.; Jesus Martinez de Espronceda, O.A.R., Parochial Vicar.
Res.: 1178 N. Mesquite, 88001. Tel: 575-526-9545; Fax: 575-526-9545.
Catechesis/Religious Program—Sr. Marie-Paule Willem, F.M.M., D.R.E. Students 255.

6—SANTA ROSA DE LIMA (1982) Rev. Francisco Oviedo, O.A.R.
Church: 5035 Holsome Rd., 88011. Tel: 575-382-8123; Fax: 575-382-5481.

OUTSIDE THE CITY OF LAS CRUCES

ALAMOGORDO, OTERO CO.

1—IMMACULATE CONCEPTION (1900) [CEM] Revs. Bryant Hausfeld, O.F.M.; Bruce Hausfeld, O.F.M., Admin.; Deacons Donald Dickman; Peter Schumacher; Bro. Bill Spirk, Pastoral Assoc.
Res.: 705 Delaware Ave., 88310. Tel: 575-437-3291; Fax: 575-437-3239.
Mission—Our Lady of the Desert, (Closed), Boles Acres, Otero Co.
Mission—Our Lady of the Light La Luz, Otero Co. Tel: 575-434-9460.
Mission—Sacred Heart Cloudcroft, Otero Co. Tel: 575-682-2228.

2—ST. JUDE (1965) Revs. Wayne D. Herpin, S.J.; Thomas W. Hoffman, S.J., Parochial Vicar.
Office: 1404 College Ave., 88310-4860. Tel: 575-437-0238; Fax: 575-437-0267.

ANTHONY, DONA ANA CO., ST. ANTHONY'S (1899) [CEM] Revs. Andres Alava, O.A.R.; Juan Almarza, O.A.R., Parochial Vicar.
Church: 224 Lincoln St., P.O. Box 2624, 88021. Tel: 575-882-2239; Fax: 575-882-7343.
Convent—Hermanas Dominicas de la Doctrina Cristiana, 124 Tornillo, Chaparral, 88081. Tel: 575-824-0508.
Mission—Our Lady of Refuge 1320 Mercantil, La Union, Dona Ana Co. 88021. Tel: 505-589-0542. Rodolfo Franco, Pastoral Team Coord.
Mission—Immaculate Conception San Benito Rd., P.O. Box 155, Berino, Dona Ana Co. 88024.

ARTESIA, EDDY CO.

1—ST. ANTHONY (1905) Rev. Paul Murtagh, SS.CC.
Res.: 502 S. Ninth St., 88210. Tel: 575-746-4471; Fax: 575-748-1049.

2—OUR LADY OF GRACE (1942) Revs. Paul Murtagh, SS.CC.; Brian Guerrini, Parochial Vicar.
Res.: 709 N. Roselawn, 88210.
Church: 1111 N. Roselawn Ave., 88210. Tel: 575-748-1356; Fax: 575-748-1049.

BAYARD, GRANT CO., OUR LADY OF FATIMA (1950) Rev. Paulus Kao.
Church: 340 Mayo St., P.O. Box 1425, 88023. Tel: 575-537-2421.
Mission—St. Anthony c/o Our Lady of Fatima, P.O. Box 1425, 88023. Fierro, NM, Grant Co.
Mission—Holy Family P.O. Box 67, Hanover, Grant Co. 88043.
Mission—San Lorenzo-Black Range Station San Lorenzo, Grant Co. Tel: 575-313-4126.

CARLSBAD, EDDY CO.

1—ST. EDWARD (1893) Rev. Cyprian Uline, O.F.M.Conv. In Res., Rev. Maurus Hauer, O.F.M.Conv.; Deacon Antonio Dominguez.
Office:—209 N. Guadalupe St., 88220. Tel: 575-885-6600; Fax: 575-885-9992.
Res.: 610 W. Stevens, 88220. Tel: 575-887-6486.

2—SAN JOSE (1902) Rev. Valentine M. Jankowski, O.F.M.Conv.; Deacons Melvin Balderrama; Emilio Ramos.
Church: 1002 DeBaca, 88220. Tel: 575-885-5792; Fax: 575-887-3553.
Religious Education Center—Tel: 575-887-1346. Patsy Grantner, D.R.E.

CARRIZOZO, LINCOLN CO., ST. RITA (1850) [CEM] Rev. Franklin Eichhorst, O.F.M.Cap.
Church: 213 Birch St., Box 727, 88301. Tel: 575-648-2853; Fax: 575-648-2833.
Mission—Sacred Heart Capitan, Lincoln Co.
Mission—St. Therese of the Little Flower Corona, Lincoln Co.

CHAMBERINO, DONA ANA CO., SAN LUIS REY (1959) Rev. Robert Villegas, C.S.C.
Church: 206 S. San Luis Ave., P.O. Box 230, 88027. Tel: 505-882-2045.

CHAPARRAL, DONA ANA CO., ST. THOMAS MORE CHURCH (1977) Rev. Miguel Echeverria, O.A.R.
112 Lisa Dr., PMB 119, 88081. Tel: 575-824-4433; Fax: 575-842-4433.

DEMING, LUNA CO.

1—ST. ANN'S (1918) Rev. Enrique Lopez.
Res.: 400 S. Ruby St., 88030. Tel: 575-546-3343; Fax: 575-546-3444.
Catechesis/Religious Program—Tel: 575-546-3905. Alexandra Vigil, D.R.E. Students 493.

2—HOLY FAMILY (1905) Revs. Enrique Lopez; James Joshe Duplissey (CC), Parochial Vicar.
Res.: 612 S. Copper St., 88030-4114. Tel: 575-546-9783; Fax: 575-546-9815.
Catechesis/Religious Program—615 S. Copper St., 88030. Students 93.
Mission— P.O. Box 1498, Columbus, Luna Co. Tel: 575-531-2373; Fax: 575-546-8192.

DEXTER, CHAVEZ CO., IMMACULATE CONCEPTION (1953) Deacon Jesus Herrera, Admin.
Church: 400 W. Sixth St., P.O. Box 189, 88230. Tel: 575-734-5478.
Mission—Our Lady of Guadalupe 204 Broadway, Lake Arthur, Chavez Co. 88253.
Mission—St. Catherine 200 S. Texas, Hagerman, Chavez Co. 88232.

DONA ANA, DONA ANA CO., OUR LADY OF THE PURIFICATION (1860) [JC] Rev. Miguel Macaya; Deacon Daniel Check.
Mailing Address: 5525 Cristo Rey, P.O. Box 706, 88032. Tel: 575-526-2114. In Res., Deacon Rigoberto Chavez.
Mission—San Isidro San Isidro, Dona Ana Co.

GARFIELD, DONA ANA CO., SAN ISIDRO (1945) Rev. Carlos Espinoza, O.F.M.
Res.: 2003 Loma Parda, HC 31, Box 43, 87936-9701. Tel: 575-267-5111; Fax: 575-267-1887.
Mission—San Jose Arrey, Sierra Co.
Mission—Our Lady of Guadalupe Hillsboro, Sierra Co.

HATCH, DONA ANA CO., OUR LORD OF MERCY (1889) Rev. Raymond J. Flores.
Church: 117 Hartman St., Box 321, 87937. Tel: 575-267-4983; Fax: 575-267-4299.
Mission—Our Lady of All Nations Rincon, Dona Ana Co.

HOBBS, LEA CO.

1—ST. HELENA (1951) Rev. Juan Carlos Ramirez, Admin. In Res., Rev. Joseph Pacquing.
Office: 100 E. Bender Blvd., 88240. Tel: 575-392-7551; 575-392-7552; Fax: 575-392-3333.

2—OUR LADY OF GUADALUPE (1981) Rev. Ruben Romero, Admin.; Deacon Samuel Navarrette.
Office: 914 S. Selman, 88240. Tel: 575-393-4991; Fax: 575-397-1480.

HURLEY, GRANT CO., INFANT JESUS (1916) Revs. Paulus Kao; Robert L. Becerra, Admin.
Church: 204 Cortez St., Box 97, 88043. Tel: 575-537-3691; Fax: 575-537-3514.
Mission—San Juan San Juan, Grant Co.
Mission—San Jose Faywood, Luna Co.

JAL, LEA CO., ST. CECILIA (1941) Rev. Jose Rogelio Martinez.
Res.: 300 W. Merryman St., P.O. Box 430, 88252. Tel: 575-395-2431; Fax: 575-395-2238.

LA MESA, DONA ANA CO., SAN JOSE, [JC] Rev. Martin G. Cordero.
Church: 353 Josephine St., P.O. Box 278, 88044. Tel: 575-233-3191; Fax: 575-233-2204.
Mission—San Pedro (Del Cerro) P.O. Box 278, Dona Ana Co. 88044.

LORDSBURG, HIDALGO CO., ST. JOSEPH (1900) Rev. Michael Williams (CC), Parochial Vicar.
Res.: 416 E. Second St., 88045. Tel: 575-542-3268.
Mission—St. Jude Cotton City, Hidalgo Co.
Mission—San Felipe Rodeo, Hidalgo Co.
Mission—St. Catherine Hachita, Grant Co.
Mission—St. Augustine Playas, Hidalgo Co.

LOVING, EDDY CO., OUR LADY OF GRACE (1937) Rev. Valentine M. Jankowski, O.F.M.Conv.
Office: 301 4th St., P.O. Box 428, 88256. Tel: 575-745-3341.
Res.: 610 W. Stevens, Carlsbad, 88220. Tel: 575-887-6486.
Mission—Cristo Rey P.O. Box 69, Malaga, Eddy Co. 88263.

LOVINGTON, LEA CO., ST. THOMAS AQUINAS (1919) Rev. Manuel Ibarra.
Res.: 1301 N. Ninth St., 88260. Tel: 575-396-4206; Fax: 575-396-4116.
Mission—Our Lady of the Holy Rosary Tatum, Lea Co.

MESCALERO, OTERO CO., ST. JOSEPH (1895), (Native American), Rev. Paul Botenhagen, O.F.M.; Sr. Robert Ann Hecker, O.S.F.
Res.: Box 187, 88340. Tel: 575-464-4473; Fax: 575-464-1511.
Mission—Our Lady of Guadalupe Hwy. 70, Bent, Otero Co. 88340.
Mission—St. Patrick Three Rivers, Otero Co.

MESILLA PARK, DONA ANA CO., SHRINE AND PARISH OF OUR LADY OF GUADALUPE Rev. Vincent Petersen, O.F.M.Conv.
Church: 3600 Parroquia St., Box 298, 88047. Tel: 575-526-8171; Fax: 575-523-1175.

MESILLA, DONA ANA CO., BASILICA OF SAN ALBINO (1852) Rev. Richard Catanach.
Church: 2280 Calle Principal, P.O. Box 26, 88046. Tel: 575-526-9349; Fax: 575-647-1619.
Mission—San Jose Mission P.O. Box 502, Fairacres, Dona Ana Co. 88033. Tel: 505-647-1979. Rev. John S. Weber, Parochial Vicar.

ROSWELL, CHAVES CO.

1—ASSUMPTION OF THE BLESSED VIRGIN MARY (1963) Rev. William McCann.
Res.: 2808 N. Kentucky, 88201. Tel: 575-622-9895; Fax: 575-622-6845.

2—ST. JOHN THE BAPTIST (1903), (Hispanic), Rev. Juan Antonio Gutierrez, O.F.M.; Deacons Louis Romero; Enrique Salas.
Res.: 506 S. Lincoln, 88203. Tel: 575-622-3531; Fax: 575-623-8933.

3—ST. PETER (1903) Rev. Joseph Nelson, O.F.M.; Deacon Howard Herring, Pastoral Assoc.
Church: 111 E. Deming, 88203. Tel: 575-622-5092; Fax: 575-623-9228.

RUIDOSO, LINCOLN CO., ST. ELEANOR (1939) Rev. Alfred Galvan; Deacon Robert G. Racicot.
Res.: 207 Junction Rd., P.O. Box 8300, 88345. Tel: 575-257-2330; Fax: 575-257-7062.
Mission—St. Jude Thaddeus [CEM] San Patricio, Lincoln Co.
Mission—San Juan Lincoln, Lincoln Co.
Mission—Sacred Heart Fort Stanton, Lincoln Co.
Mission—St. Joseph Picacho, Lincoln Co.
Mission—San Ysidro Glencoe, Lincoln Co.

SAN MIGUEL, DONA ANA CO., SAN MIGUEL (1927) Rev. Jose Pedro Valdez, Admin.
Res.: Drawer E, 88058. Tel: 575-233-2453; Fax: 575-233-2453.
Mission—Our Lady of Perpetual Help P.O. Box 48, Mesquite, Dona Ana Co. 88048. Tel: 575-233-4695.

SANTA CLARA, GRANT CO., SANTA CLARA (1888) Rev. Robert L. Becerra; Deacons Richard Rodriguez; David M. Castanon.
Church: 207 S. Bayard, P.O. Box 215, 88026. Tel: 575-537-3713; Fax: 575-537-3517.

SILVER CITY, GRANT CO.
1—ST. FRANCIS NEWMAN CENTER PARISH (1964), Serving Western New Mexico University. Rev. Marcos Reyna.
Res.: 914 W. 13th St., 88061. Tel: 575-538-3662; Fax: 575-534-1059.
2—ST. VINCENT DE PAUL (1874) Rev. Roderick Nichols; Deacons William Holguin; Johnnie Perez; Jeremiah Bustillos.
Res.: 414 Bayard St., P.O. Box 1189, 88062. Tel: 575-538-9373; Fax: 575-388-0870.
Mission—St. Isidore Gila, Grant Co.
Mission—Holy Cross Pinos Altos, Grant Co.
Parish Retreat Center: *St. Mary Theotokos Retreat Center*, 5202 Hwy. 152, 88062. Tel: 575-537-4839.

SUNLAND PARK, DONA ANA CO., ST. MARTIN DE PORRES (1964) Rev. Edward Herrera; Deacons Jesus Favela; Rogelio Montes.
Res.: 1885 McNutt Rd., 88063. Tel: 575-589-2106.
Mission—Santa Teresa de Avila Santa Teresa, Dona Ana Co.

TRUTH OR CONSEQUENCES, SIERRA CO., OUR LADY OF PERPETUAL HELP (1916) Revs. Anthony Basso, S.D.V., Admin.; Donald Hyatt, C.S.B., Parochial Vicar; Deacon Adam L. Sanchez.
Res.: 103 E. Sixth Ave., 87901. Tel: 575-894-7804; Fax: 575-894-0451.
Mission—St. Joseph Cuchillo, Sierra Co.
Mission—San Ysidro Las Palomas, Sierra Co.
Mission—St. Ignatius Montecello, Sierra Co.
Mission—San Lorenzo Placitas, Sierra Co.
Chapel—St. Gregory, Chapels Chise
Chapel—San Miguel, Rancho de San Miguel
Station—St. James
Station—St. Jude Winston.

TULAROSA, OTERO CO., ST. FRANCIS DE PAULA (1868) [CEM] [JC] Rev. Maximilian J. Hottle, O.F.M.; Deacon Mariano Melendrez. In Res., Revs. John W. Peterson, O.F.M.; Peter A. Verheggen, O.F.M.; Clifford Herle, O.F.M.
Res.: 303 Encino, 88352. Tel: 575-585-2793; Fax: 575-585-3005.
Mission—Santo Nino

Absent On Leave:
Revs.—
Amezaga, Louis
Beggane, Thomas

Retired:
Rev. Msgr.—
Getz, Robert, P.A.
Revs.—
Bergs, David
Burke, Ronald
Clark, Anthony
Colgan, John
Lafrenz, James
Reitmeyer, Larry

Permanent Deacons:
Albin, Richard, Dir. of Deacon Formation
Apodaca, Steve, Holy Cross, Las Cruces
Baca, Tom, San Jose, La Mesa
Balderrama, Mel L.
Brotherton, Bob, IHM, Las Cruces
Bustillos, Jeramiah Gomes, St. Vincent de Paul, Silver City
Castanon, David M., Santa Clara, Santa Clara
Chavez, Rigoberto, Our Lady of Purification, Dona Ana
Check, Daniel
Dickman, Donald, Our Lady of the Light, La Luz
Dominguez, Antonio, St. Edward, Carlsbad
Favela, Jesus, San Martin de Porres, Sunland Park
Herrera, Jesus, Immaculate Conception, Dexter
Herring, Howard, St. Peter, Roswell
Holguin, William, St. Vincent de Paul, Silver City
Lederman, Paul, Holy Cross, Las Cruces; Interim Dir. Deacons
Lucero, Levy, Immaculate Conception, Alamogordo
Mata, Roberto, St. Thomas More, Chaparral
McNeill, David, Jr., Albert the Great Newman Center, Las Cruces
Melandrez, Mariano C., St. Francis de Paula, Tularosa
Merjil, Pablo, Our Lady of Grace, Artesia
Miller, Jerry Our Lady of Fatima, Bayard
Misquez, Edward, IHM, Las Cruces
Montes, Rogelio, San Martin de Porres, Sunland Park
Moreno, Leopoldo, St. Peter, Roswell
Narvaez, Arthur, (Retired)
Navarrette, Sam, Our Lady of Guadalupe, Hobbs
Padilla, Luis, St. Anthony, Anthony
Perez, Johnnie, St. Vincent de Paul, Silver City
Racicot, Robert G., St. Eleanor, Ruidoso
Ramos, Emilio, San Jose, Carlsbad
Rodriguez, Richard Alires, Santa Clara, Santa Clara
Roman, Louis, IHM, Las Cruces
Romero, Louis, St. John the Baptist, Roswell
Sanchez, Adam L., St. Jude, Alamogordo
Sanchez, Jesse, Our Lady of Refuge, La Union
Schretlen, Frank, (Retired)
Schumacher, Peter
Shuster, John, St. Joseph, Mescalero
Wheeler, John C.

INSTITUTIONS LOCATED IN THE DIOCESE

[A] ELEMENTARY SCHOOLS, PRIVATE

LAS CRUCES. *Las Cruces Catholic School*, (Grades PreK-10), 1331 N. Miranda, 88005. Tel: 575-526-2517; Fax: 575-524-0544. Web: www.lascrucescatholicschool.org. Karen Trujillo, Prin. Lay Teachers 30; Students 291.

ALAMOGORDO. *Fr. James B. Hay, Inc.* (1956) (Grades PreK-8), 1000 E. Eighth St., 88310. Tel: 575-437-7821; Fax: 575-443-6129. Email: jbhay@zianet.com. Web: www.fatherhay.org. Mr. Wallace Moore, Admin.; Ms. Blaza Madrid, Librarian. Lay Teachers 7; Students 50.

CARLSBAD. *St. Edward School, Inc.*, (Grades PreK-5), 805 Walter, 88220. Tel: 575-885-4620; Fax: 575-885-7706. Rita London, Prin.; Jack Litschke, Prin. Lay Teachers 6; Students 98.

HOBBS. *St. Helena School of Hobbs, Inc.*, (Grades PreK-6), 105 E. St. Anne St., 88240. Tel: 575-392-5405; Fax: 575-392-0128. Mrs. Sheila Fuentes, Prin. Students 78.

ROSWELL. *All Saints Catholic School*, (Grades PreK-8), 2808 N. Kentucky, 88201. Tel: 575-627-5744; Fax: 575-622-6845. Email: principal@allsaintsschool.us. Web: www.allsaintsschool.us. Veronica Ortega, Lead Teacher; Rosella Romero, Librarian. Lay Teachers 10; Students 80.

[B] MONASTERIES & RESIDENCES OF PRIESTS AND BROTHERS

LAS CRUCES. *Basilian Fathers*, 1682 Alta Vista Pl., 88011. Tel: 575-521-4269. Web: www.basilian.org. Revs. Sean M. Garrity, C.S.B., Supr.; Michael P. Cerretto, C.S.B., 1st Councilor; Mitchell G. Dowalgo, C.S.B.; Rene Espejel, C.S.B.; Arthur Roberts, C.S.B.

MESILLA. *Augustinian Recollect Fathers* Province of St. Nicholas of Tolentine, Provincial Delegation in the South of U.S.A., *San Alypius House*, P.O. Box 310, 88046. Tel: 575-523-7030. Revs. Ricardo Hinojal, O.A.R., Supr.; Jesus Martinez de Espronceda, O.A.R.; Antonio Martinez, O.A.R.; Francisco Oviedo, O.A.R.

[C] CONVENTS AND RESIDENCES FOR SISTERS

LAS CRUCES. *Franciscan Missionaries of Mary*, 2119 Laredo Ave., 88011. Tel: 575-523-9083.

CHAPARRAL. *Dominicas De La Doctrina Cristiana*, 124 Tornillo, 88081. Tel: 575-824-0508. Professed 5; Novices 2.
Religious of the Assumption (2001) 300-2 McCombs Rd., PMB #43, 88081. Tel: 575-824-2850. Email: rachaparral@juno.com. Sr. Maria Isabel Galbe Sada, R.A., Contact Person, Supr.

DEMING. *Daughters of the Heart of Mary*, P.O. Box 1531, 88030. Tel: 575-546-7599. Email: nazhouse@swnm.com.

ROSWELL. *The Community of Poor Clares of New Mexico, Inc.* (1948) 809 E. 19th St., 88201. Tel: 575-622-0868; Fax: 575-627-2184. Web: www.poorclaresroswell.com. Sisters Angela Kelly, P.C.C., Abbess; Mary Jeannine, P.C.C., Vicaress. Professed Nuns 22.

SILVER CITY. *Sisters of St. Joseph*, St. Mary's Center, 1801 N. Alabama, 88061. Tel: 575-538-3350. Email: rplante@zianet.com.

[D] RETREAT CENTERS

MESILLA PARK. *Holy Cross Retreat and Friary*, P.O. Box 158, 88047. Tel: 575-524-3688; Fax: 575-524-3811. Email: programs@holycrossretreat.org. Web: www.holycrossretreat.org. Revs. Donald Adamski, O.F.M.Conv.; Miguel Briseno, O.F.M.Conv.; Giles Carie, O.F.M.Conv.; Peter Nickels, O.F.M.Conv.; Vincent Petersen, O.F.M.Conv.

[E] MISCELLANEOUS

LAS CRUCES. *Catholic Charities of the Diocese of Las Cruces, Inc.*, 1280 Med Park Dr., 88005. Tel: 575-523-7577; Fax: 575-524-3874. Claudia I. Moncada-Trueblood, Exec. Dir.
Catholic Diocese of Las Cruces Foundation, Inc., 1280 Med Park Dr., 88005. Tel: 575-523-7577; Fax: 575-524-3874. Email: cvillegas@dioceseoflascruces.org. Web: dioceseoflascruces.org. Susan Roberts, Exec. Dir.
**Order of Secular Discalced Carmelites* (1989) 6100 Robledo Rd., 88012-9566. Tel: 575-382-3795. Email: annunez@zianet.com. Carolyn Nunez, Pres.; Therese Mastrantuono, Contact Person.
Our Lady of Guadalupe Prayer Center, Inc., 5480 Lassiter Rd., P.O. Box 1135, Mesilla Park, 88047. Tel: 575-647-1117. Email: olgpclc@aol.com.
The Priests' Retirement Plan of the Catholic Diocese of Las Cruces, Inc., 1280 Med Park Dr., 88005. Tel: 575-523-7577; Fax: 575-524-3874.

ALAMOGORDO. *Shroud Exhibit and Museum, Inc.*, 3199 N. White Sands Blvd., Ste. D-1, 88310.

ANTHONY. *Family Unity and Citizenship Program*, 880 Anthony Dr., Ste. 13, 88021. Tel: 575-525-6779; Fax: 575-525-6589. Claudia I. Moncada-Trueblood, Dir.

CLOUDCROFT. **Mount Subasio Hermitage* (1997) 603-16 Springs Canyon, 88317. Tel: 575-687-2507. Email: mtsubasio@yahoo.com. Ms. Helen Riegger, Dir. & Trustee.

MESILLA. *Magnificat-Our Lady of the Cross Chapter, Inc.*, P.O. Box 1387, 88046. Tel: 575-541-1625. Olivia McDonald, Chapter Coord.

SAN PATRICIO. *Benedictine Center*, 123 La Mancha, P.O. Box 102, 88348. Tel: 575-653-4415.

RELIGIOUS INSTITUTES OF MEN REPRESENTED IN THE DIOCESE

For further details refer to the corresponding bracketed number in the Religious Institutes of Men or Women section.

[0170]—*Basilian Fathers*—C.S.B.
[0200]—*Benedictine Monks*—O.S.B.
[]—*Capuchin Friars* (St. Bonaventure)—O.F.M.Cap.
[1140]—*Congregation of the Sacred Hearts of Jesus and Mary*—SS.CC.
[0480]—*Conventual Franciscans* (Our Lady of Guadalupe Custody)—O.F.M.Conv
[0520]—*Franciscan Friars* (St. John the Baptist, Our Lady of Guadalupe, St. Barbara Provs.)—O.F.M.
[0690]—*Jesuit Fathers and Brothers* (New Orleans, Wisconsin Provs.)—S.J.
[0150]—*Order of the Augustinian Recollects*—O.A.R.
[0610]—*Priests of the Congregation of Holy Cross* (Southwest Prov.)—C.S.C.

RELIGIOUS INSTITUTES OF WOMEN REPRESENTED IN THE DIOCESE

[0810]—*Daughters of the Heart of Mary*—D.H.M.
[]—*Discalced Carmelites*
[1110]—*Dominican Sisters of Our Lady of the Rosary and of Saint Catherine of Siena, Cabra*—O.P.
[1115]—*Dominican Sisters of Peace*—O.P.
[1070]—*Dominicas de la Doctrina Cristiana*—O.P.
[]—*ECCE Franciscan Sisters*
[1370]—*The Franciscan Missionaries of Mary*—F.M.M.
[]—*Franciscan Sisters*
[1430]—*Franciscan Sisters of Our Lady of Perpetual Help*—O.S.F.
[]—*Los Consagrados, dba Mission Helpers of the Holy Savior*
[2490]—*Medical Mission Sisters*—M.M.S.
[3760]—*Poor Clares Monastery of Our Lady of Guadalupe*—P.C.C.
[]—*Religious of the Assumption*—R.A.
[]—*Sisters of Loretto*—S.L.
[2575]—*Sisters of Mercy of the Americas* (Omaha, Vermont, Cincinnati, New Jersey)—R.S.M.
[3830-15]—*Sisters of St. Joseph*—C.S.J.

[1990]—*Sisters of the Holy Name of Jesus and Mary*—S.N.J.M.

[3270]—*Sisters of the Most Precious Blood (O'Fallon, MO)*—C.PP.S.

[]—*Sisters of the Sacred Hearts of Jesus and Mary*—SS.CC.

[4100]—*Sisters of the Sorrowful Mother*—S.S.M.

NECROLOGY

† Flores, Virgilio M., Deming, NM St. Ann's—Died Nov. 5, 2009

An asterisk (*) denotes an organization that has established tax-exempt status directly with the IRS and is not covered by the USCCB Group Ruling.

Diocese of Las Vegas

(Dioecesis Campensis)

Most Reverend

JOSEPH A. PEPE

Bishop of Las Vegas; ordained May 16, 1970; appointed Bishop of Las Vegas April 6, 2001; ordained and installed May 31, 2001. *Mailing Address: P.O. Box 18316, Las Vegas, NV 89114-8316*. Tel: 702-735-3500; Fax: 702-735-8941.

Catholic Center: 336 Cathedral Way, Las Vegas, NV 89109. Mailing Address: P.O. Box 18316, Las Vegas, NV 89114-8316. Tel: 702-735-3500; Fax: 702-735-8941.

Square Miles 39,688.

Erected by His Holiness Pope Pius XI March 27, 1931.

Redesignated Diocese of Reno-Las Vegas by Pope Paul VI, October 13, 1976.

Redesignated Diocese of Las Vegas by His Holiness Pope John Paul II March 21, 1995.

For legal titles of parishes and diocesan institutions, consult the Chancery Office.

STATISTICAL OVERVIEW

Personnel	
Bishop	1
Priests: Diocesan Active in Diocese	22
Priests: Diocesan Active Outside Diocese	4
Priests: Retired, Sick or Absent	13
Number of Diocesan Priests	39
Religious Priests in Diocese	19
Total Priests in Diocese	58
Extern Priests in Diocese	32
Ordinations:	
Diocesan Priests	1
Permanent Deacons in Diocese	16
Total Brothers	4
Total Sisters	3
Parishes	
Parishes	28
With Resident Pastor:	
Resident Diocesan Priests	12
Resident Religious Priests	3
Without Resident Pastor:	
Administered by Priests	13
Missions	6
Professional Ministry Personnel:	
Brothers	4
Sisters	3
Lay Ministers	31
Welfare	
Special Centers for Social Services	24
Total Assisted	6,300,000
Other Institutions	1
Total Assisted	3,575
Educational	
Diocesan Students in Other Seminaries	6
Total Seminarians	6
High Schools, Diocesan and Parish	1
Total Students	1,169
Elementary Schools, Diocesan and Parish	7
Total Students	2,649
Catechesis/Religious Education:	
High School Students	2,996
Elementary Students	10,442
Total Students under Catholic Instruction	17,262
Teachers in the Diocese:	
Priests	2
Lay Teachers	225
Vital Statistics	
Receptions into the Church:	
Infant Baptism Totals	5,965
Minor Baptism Totals	264
Adult Baptism Totals	341
Received into Full Communion	876
First Communions	4,590
Confirmations	1,835
Marriages:	
Catholic	541
Interfaith	112
Total Marriages	653
Deaths	804
Total Catholic Population	716,000
Total Population	1,925,000

Former Bishop—Most Rev. DANIEL F. WALSH, D.D., ord. March 30, 1963; appt. Titular Bishop of Tigia and Auxiliary of San Francisco Sept. 24, 1981; appt. Bishop of Reno-Las Vegas June 9, 1987; installed Aug. 6, 1987; appt. Bishop of Las Vegas March 21, 1995; installed July 28, 1995; appt. Bishop of Santa Rosa in California, April 11, 2000; installed May 22, 2000.

Catholic Center—336 Cathedral Way, Las Vegas, 89109. Tel: 702-735-3500; Fax: 702-735-8941. Web: www.lasvegas-diocese.org. *Mailing Address: P.O. Box 18316, Las Vegas, 89114-8316*. Office Hours: Mon.-Fri. 8-12 & 1-4.

Chancellor and Moderator of the Curia—Rev. Msgr. KEVIN W. MCAULIFFE, J.C.L., V.G. Tel: 702-697-3903; Fax: 702-735-8941.

Vicar General—Rev. Msgr. KEVIN W. MCAULIFFE, J.C.L., V.G. Tel: 702-697-3903.

Diocesan Tribunal Office-Judicial Vicar—Rt. Rev. Archimandrite FRANCIS M. VIVONA, S.T.M., J.C.L. Tel: 702-735-1210; Fax: 702-735-5146.

Notary-Secretary—Mrs. PAM MORLEY, A.A.

Promoters of Justice—Rev. Msgr. KEVIN W. MCAULIFFE, J.C.L., V.G.; Rev. THOMAS J. FRANSISCUS, C.SS.R., J.C.L.

Defender of the Bond—Rev. KURT BURNETTE, J.C.D.

Diocesan Judges—Rev. Msgrs. KEVIN W. MCAULIFFE, J.C.L., V.G.; THOMAS F. DONOVAN, J.C.D.; Very Rev. LANGES J. SILVA, J.C.D.; Revs. KURT BURNETTE, J.C.D.; DAVID H. SCHUYLER, S.M., J.C.D.

Diocesan Advocates—Mr. ROBERT HANDCOX, J.D.; Mrs. PAM MORLEY, A.A.; Revs. ROLANDO RIVERA, M.Div.; THOMAS J. FRANSISCUS, C.SS.R., J.C.L.; MARCUS GOMORI, M.A., M.S.; Mr. PAUL KILROY, A.A.

Presbyteral Council for the Diocese of Las Vegas—Rt. Rev. Archimandrite FRANCIS M. VIVONA, S.T.M., J.C.L., Ex Officio; Rev. Msgr. KEVIN W. MCAULIFFE, J.C.L., V.G., Ex Officio; Very Revs. PATRICK W. RENDER, C.S.V., V.E.; TIMOTHY WEHN, V.E.; Rev. Msgr. PATRICK LEARY; Revs. GUSTAVO CRUZ; MARC C. HOWES; WILLIAM KENNY; DAVID E. CASALEGGIO; BEDE WEVITA; ALBERT FELICE-PACE, O.P.; RON ZANONI.

Diocesan Offices and Directors

Building Committee—Revs. RON ZANONI; STEVEN R. HOFFER; Bro. JOHN J. DODD, C.S.V.; Rev. Msgr. KEVIN W. MCAULIFFE, J.C.L., V.G.; GIA NGUYEN; HARRY SHULL.

Catholic Charities of Southern Nevada—

Executive Director—Rev. Msgr. PATRICK LEARY, 1501 Las Vegas Blvd. N., Las Vegas, 89101. Tel: 702-385-2662.

Chief Financial Officer—Bro. JOHN J. DODD, C.S.V. Tel: 702-735-7865.

Director of Clergy Education—Rev. Msgr. KEVIN W. MCAULIFFE, J.C.L., V.G.

St. Thomas Aquinas Catholic Newman Community at UNLV—Rev. ALBERT FELICE-PACE, O.P., Dir. & Campus Minister, 4765 Brussels St., Las Vegas, 89119. Tel: 702-736-0887; Fax: 702-891-0615. Email: info@unlvnewman.com. Web: newman.unlv.edu.

Human Resources Department—Tel: 702-735-4570. JUDITH KOHL, Esq.

Legal Department—Tel: 702-735-2512. JUDITH KOHL, Esq., Gen. Counsel.

Department of Faith & Ministry Formation

Director for Faith and Ministry Formation—MARC GONZALEZ, D.Min. Tel: 702-735-6044.

Catholic Campaign for Human Development, Catholic Relief Services, Social Action Ministry—Mr. TIM O'CALLAGHAN, 1420 W. Bartlett Ave., Las Vegas, 89106. Tel: 702-631-5393; Fax: 702-631-5393.

Home and Foreign Missions—Rev. Msgr. KEVIN W. MCAULIFFE, J.C.L., V.G. Tel: 702-697-3903.

Hospital Apostolate—Revs. REY SALDITOS. Tel: 702-870-2767; VICENTE PANALIGAN. Tel: 702-870-2767; SABINO LATTANZIO, O.F.M.Cap., Ph.D. Tel: 702-561-5323.

Information, Communications and Media—Rev. Msgr. KEVIN W. MCAULIFFE, J.C.L., V.G. Tel: 702-697-3903.

Italian Catholic Federation—Rev. RON ZANONI.

Native American and Colored People Commission—Rev. Msgr. KEVIN W. MCAULIFFE, J.C.L., V.G.

Pontifical Association of the Holy Childhood—VACANT.

Propagation of the Faith—Very Rev. TIMOTHY WEHN, V.E. Tel: 702-697-3903.

Priests' Pension Board—Bro. JOHN J. DODD, C.S.V.; Rev. Msgr. KEVIN W. MCAULIFFE, J.C.L., V.G., Ex Officio; Revs. ROBERT W. PUHLMAN; GUSTAVO CRUZ; MANUEL QUINTERO; RON ZANONI.

Property Management—Bro. JOHN J. DODD, C.S.V.

Vocations—Rev. MUGAGGA LULE, Dir.

Respect Life Liaison—Mrs. KATHLEEN MILLER, 3510 Leor Ct., Las Vegas, 89121. Tel: 702-212-6472; 702-737-1672.

Natural Family Planning/Fertility Care—MICKEY BACHMAN, R.N., C.N.F.P.P. Tel: 702-616-7550.

Diocesan Finance Committee Members—PATRICIA MULROY; LEO FALKENSAMMER; CHUCK KERZETSKI; TED ATENCIO; ED SKONICKI.

Diocesan Loan Committee—PAT MULROY; RANDY GARCIA; ARTHUR DEJOYA; ED SKONICKI.

Catholic Charities of Southern Nevada—Board of Trustees: Most Rev. JOSEPH ANTHONY PEPE, D.D., J.C.D.; Rev. Msgrs. PATRICK LEARY, Exec. Dir. Catholic Charities, 1501 Las Vegas Blvd. N., Las Vegas, 89101. Tel: 702-385-2662; KEVIN W. MCAULIFFE, J.C.L., V.G.; DENISE MAULER, Pres.; JEANNE KILDUFF; Rev. MARC C. HOWES; KEVIN J. HIGGINS; T. J. MATTHEWS; VICTORIA FOUCE-OTTER; TOM MCCORMICK; LARRY BROWN; JILL BLANCHETTE; FRANK GARGANO; JOHN PAGE; SHAUNDELL NEWSOME; JOHN D. SELI; JENNIFER LOGAN; PATRICIA MORRISSEY.

Victim Advocate & Safe Environment Coordinator—Mr. RONALD VALLANCE. Tel: 702-235-7723.

Archivist—TONY MCGILTON. Tel: 702-735-2744.

Diocesan Liturgy Committee—Rev. Msgr. KEVIN W. MCAULIFFE, J.C.L., V.G.; ARGIA KOPA; MAREK RACHELSKI; MICHAEL LAROCCA.

CLERGY, PARISHES, MISSIONS AND PAROCHIAL SCHOOLS

CITY OF LAS VEGAS

(CLARK COUNTY)

1—GUARDIAN ANGEL CATHEDRAL (1963) Rev. Lawrence Lentz, C.S.V., Rector.
Office: 336 Cathedral Way, 89109. Tel: 702-735-5241; Fax: 702-734-7086.
Rectory—

2—ST. ANNE (1948) Revs. David E. Casaleggio; Gregorio Leon.
Office & Res.: 1901 S. Maryland Pkwy., 89104. Tel: 702-735-0510; Fax: 702-735-5582.
School—(Grades PreK-8), 1813 S. Maryland Pkwy., 89104. Tel: 702-735-2586; Fax: 702-735-8357. Dr. James Machinski, Prin.; Linda Niles, Librarian. Lay Teachers 13; Students 317.
Catechesis/Religious Program—Tel: 702-866-0008; Fax: 702-866-0006. Students 1,139.

3—ST. ANTHONY OF PADUA (2006) Revs. Samuel J. Falbo, Admin.; Gerald Grupczynski, S.Ch., Parochial Vicar.
5081 N. Rainbow Blvd., Ste. 107, 89130. Fort Apache & Centennial.
Rectory—5605 Rainbow Springs, 89149. Tel: 702-399-6897; Fax: 702-645-9975. Email: stanthony@saplv.org.
Catechesis/Religious Program—Patti Shovlin, D.R.E. Students 397.

4—ST. BRIDGET CATHOLIC CHURCH (1945) Revs. Jesse Cortes, Admin.; Frank Yncierto; Deacon Sonny Laqui.
Office: 220 N. 14th St., 89101-4312. Tel: 702-384-3382; Fax: 702-382-9467. Email: sbcclv@earthlink.net. Web: sbcclv.e-paluch.com.
Res.: 215 N. 14th St., 89101. Tel: 702-489-2877.
Catechesis/Religious Program—Students 340.

5—CHRIST THE KING (1978) Rev. William J.M. Kenny.
Mailing Address: 4925 S. Torrey Pines, 89118. Tel: 702-871-1904; Fax: 702-251-4935.
Catechesis/Religious Program—Tel: 702-871-1904, Ext. 230. Beth Thompson, D.R.E. Students 457.
Mission—St. Catherine of Siena Jean. P.O. Box 19789, Sandy Valley, Clark Co. 89019. Tel: 702-723-5454.

6—ST. ELIZABETH ANN SETON (1992) Rev. Msgr. Kevin W. McAuliffe; Revs. Marcus Gomori (VNN); Steven R. Hoffer; Deacons Joseph Deegan; Francis Pemper.
In Res., Rt. Rev. Archimandrite Francis M. Vivona.
Office & Mailing Address: 1811 Pueblo Vista Dr., 89128. Tel: 702-228-8311; Fax: 702-228-8310. Email: seas@dioceseoflasvegas.org.
Res.: 2109 Golden Lotus Dr., 89134.
School—(Grades K-8), 1807 Pueblo Vista Dr., 89128. Tel: 702-804-8328; Fax: 702-228-8906. Email: school@seaslv.org. Dr. Cary Roybal-Benson, Prin. Lay Teachers 25; Students 478.
Catechesis/Religious Program—Tel: 702-228-8311; Fax: 702-228-2154. Students 771.

7—ST. FRANCIS DE SALES (1964) Revs. Manuel Quintero; Rolando Rivera (Mexico).
Mailing Address: 1111 Michael Way, 89108. Tel: 702-647-3440; Fax: 702-646-3587.
Res.: 1628 Desert Fort, 89128. Tel: 702-341-7009.
School—(Grades K-8) Tel: 702-647-2828; Fax: 702-647-0284. Web: www.sfdslv.org. Mrs. Catherine Thompson, Prin. Lay Teachers 20; Students 305.
Catechesis/Religious Program—Tel: 702-646-2266; Fax: 702-647-6701. Students 678.

8—HOLY FAMILY (1975) Revs. M. Eugene Kinney, Admin.; Innocent Anyanwu.
Mailing Address: 4490 Mountain Vista, 89121.
Res.: 4528 E. Harmon Ave., 89121-6548. Tel: 702-458-2211 (Office); Fax: 702-458-0966 (Office).
Catechesis/Religious Program—Tel: 702-458-3575. Students 528.

9—HOLY SPIRIT CATHOLIC CHURCH (2007) Rev. William J.M. Kenny, Admin.
5959 S. Hualapai Way, 89148. Tel: 702-459-7778; Fax: 702-437-9548. Email: holyspiritlv@embarqmail.com. Web: www.holyspiritlv.org.
Catechesis/Religious Program—Len Urso, D.R.E. (K-8); Louie Latina, D.R.E. (9-12). Students 260.

10—ST. JAMES THE APOSTLE (1942), (African American), Rev. Henry Salditos, Admin.
Office & Church: 1920 N. Martin Luther King Blvd., 89106. Tel: 702-648-6606; Fax: 702-648-0352. Email: stjameschurch@lvcoxmail.com.
Catechesis/Religious Program—Tel: 702-648-6606; Fax: 702-648-0352. Arsenia Eagan, D.R.E. Students 162.

11—ST. JOAN OF ARC (1908) Very Rev. Timothy Wehn.
Office & Res.: 315 S. Casino Center Blvd., 89101. Tel: 702-382-9909; Fax: 702-382-6655.
School—(Grades K-8), 1300 Bridger Ave., 89101. Tel: 702-384-6909; Fax: 702-386-0249. Mrs. Lynda Ballard, Prin. Lay Teachers 15; Students 153.
Catechesis/Religious Program—Clustered with St. Bridget's, Las Vegas.

12—ST. JOSEPH, HUSBAND OF MARY (1989) Revs. Marc C. Howes; Thomas E. Gallenbach; Clarence J. Savial, Parochial Vicar; Deacon Tom Bast; Rob Holman, Youth Min.; Barbara Finn, Music Min.; Vince Murone, Finance.
Office & Mailing Address: 7260 W. Sahara Ave., 89117. Tel: 702-363-1902; Fax: 702-363-7976. Web: www.stjosephhom.org.
Res.: 7761 Via Olivero Ave., 89117.
Catechesis/Religious Program—Fax: 702-363-0142. Cynthia O'Connell, D.R.E. Students 795.

13—ST. MARY THE VIRGIN (1983) Closed. For inquiries for parish records contact the chancery.

14—OUR LADY OF LAS VEGAS (1957) Revs. Peter A. Romeo; Rey Salditos; Vicente Panaligan.
Office: 3050 Alta Dr., 89107. Tel: 702-870-2767; Fax: 702-870-1267. Email: ollvparish@ollv.org. Web: www.ollv.org.
Res.: 3104 Alta Dr., 89107.
School—(Grades PreK-8), 3046 Alta Dr., 89107. Tel: 702-878-6841; Fax: 702-880-5758. Phyllis Joyce, Prin. Lay Teachers 26; Students 610.
Catechesis/Religious Program—Tel: 702-870-1882. Email: lizwilliams1234@hotmail.com. Students 595.

15—ST. PAUL JUNG-HA-SANG (1987), (Korean), Rev. Hee Ook Chung, Chap.
Korean Community, 6080 S. Jones Blvd., 89118. Tel: 702-222-4349; Fax: 702-227-8817.
Catechesis/Religious Program—Eun-Mi Park, D.R.E.

16—PRINCE OF PEACE (1981) Revs. Gustavo Cruz; Ruben D. Bedoya Sanchez; Deacon James B. Whittle.
Office: 5485 E. Charleston Blvd., 89142. Tel: 702-431-2233; Fax: 702-431-2234. Web: www.lasvegas-diocese.org.
Res.: 653 Los Feliz, 89110.
Catechesis/Religious Program—Students 1,475.

17—SHRINE OF OUR LADY OF LA VANG (2003), (Vietnamese), Rev. Joseph Trong Nguyen.
Vietnamese Community, 4835 S. Pearl St., 89121. Tel: 702-821-1459. Web: www.lavang-lasvegas.com.
Catechesis/Religious Program—Mai Le Tran, D.R.E.; Ron Tran, D.R.E. Students 100.

18—SHRINE OF THE MOST HOLY REDEEMER (1991)
Office: 55 E. Reno Ave., 89119. Tel: 702-891-8600; Fax: 702-891-0339. Email: mostholyredeemer3@embarqmail.com.

19—ST. VIATOR (1954) Revs. Richard A. Rinn, C.S.V.; William F. Haesaert, C.S.V.; Bro. Michael Rice, C.S.V.; Anita Taylor, Business Mgr.
Office: 2461 E. Flamingo Rd., 89121. Tel: 702-733-8323; Fax: 702-733-8154. Web: www.stviator.org.
School—(Grades PreK-8), 4246 S. Eastern Ave., 89119-5426. Tel: 702-732-4477; Fax: 702-732-4418. Mrs. Kathleen Daulton, Prin. Lay Teachers 32; Students 660.
Catechesis/Religious Program—Tel: 702-732-0459. Judie Dawson, D.R.E. Students 202.

OUTSIDE THE CITY OF LAS VEGAS

AMARGOSA VALLEY, NYE CO., CHRIST OF THE DESERT CATHOLIC CHURCH (1984), (Hispanic), Mission of Our Lady of the Valley, Pahrump. Rev. John McShane.
Whitesands Ave., H 69 Box 450 E, 89020.
Catechesis/Religious Program—Students 24.

BOULDER CITY, CLARK CO., ST. ANDREW'S (1931) [JC] Rev. Robert E. Stoeckig.
1399 San Felipe Dr., 89005. Tel: 702-293-7500; Fax: 702-293-4419. Email: church@standrewbc.org.
Catechesis/Religious Program— Jenifer Jefferies, D.R.E. Students 102.

CALIENTE, LINCOLN CO., HOLY CHILD (1870) [CEM] Rev. John McShane, Chap.
Mailing Address: P.O. Box 748, 89008-0748. Tel: 775-726-3669; Fax: 775-726-3669.
Church: 80 Tennille St., 89008.
Catechesis/Religious Program—Students 24.

ELY, WHITE PINE CO., SACRED HEART (1869) Rev. Paul Oye, O.P., Admin.; Nancy Marich, Office Manager.
Mailing Address & Office: 900 E. 11th St., P.O. Box 151026, 89315. Tel: 775-289-2201; Fax: 775-289-2207.
Res.: 515 Murry St., 89301. Tel: 775-289-3606.
Catechetical Ministry Center—Tel: 775-289-2200.
Catechesis/Religious Program—Email: srsandy@yahoo.com. Sr. Sandy DiCianno, D.R.E. Students 102.
Mission—St. Michael's

HENDERSON, CLARK CO.

1—ST. FRANCIS OF ASSISI (2003) Revs. Mark J. Gantley, Admin.; John T. Assalone, Parochial Vicar.
2300 Sunridge Heights, 89052. Tel: 702-914-2175; Fax: 702-914-2178. Email: sfa@sfahdnv.org. Web: www.sfahdnv.org.
Rectory—725 Waltham Hills St., 89052.
Catechesis/Religious Program—Tel: 702-914-3529; Fax: 702-914-3563. Email: king@sfahdnv.org. Students 950.

2—ST. PETER THE APOSTLE (1943) Revs. Bruno Mauricci (Peru); Mugagga Lule, Parochial Vicar; Donald A. Casey (Retired); Deacons Daniel De Pozo; Bill Davis.
Office: 204 S. Boulder Hwy., 89015. Tel: 702-565-8406; Fax: 702-565-8731. Email: info@stpahend.org.
Rectory—179 Mount St. Helen Dr., 89012.
Catechesis/Religious Program—Tel: 702-565-0284; Fax: 702-565-3809. Students 455.

3—ST. THOMAS MORE (1986) Very Rev. Patrick W. Render, C.S.V.; Revs. Michael P. Keliher, C.S.V.; Robert T. Bolser, C.S.V.; Deacons Eugene Krzeminski; Richard Daluga.
130 N. Pecos Rd., 89074. Tel: 702-361-3022; Fax: 702-361-7784. Email: stmlv02@aol.com. Web: www.stmlv.org.
Catechesis/Religious Program—Tel: 702-361-8840; Fax: 702-361-5992. Juliann Dwyer, D.R.E.; Dorothy Distel, D.R.E. Students 1,416.

LAUGHLIN, CLARK CO., ST. JOHN THE BAPTIST CATHOLIC MISSION (1992) Rev. Charles B. Urnick, Admin.; Deacon Daniel McHugh.
Office & Mailing Address: 3055 El Mirage Way, P.O. Box 31230, 89028. Tel: 702-298-0440. Email: stjohn@cmaaccess.com. Web: www.stjohncatholic-laughlin.e-paluch.com.
Res.: 3115 Terrace View, 89029.
Catechesis/Religious Program—Students 20.

MESQUITE, CLARK CO., LA VIRGEN DE GUADALUPE (1992) Rev. Robert W. Puhlman; Deacon John Lawrence Smith.
Mailing Address: 401 Canyon Crest Blvd., P.O. Box 300, 89024.
Office & Chapel: 312 W. Mesquite Blvd., #116, 89027. Fax: 702-345-2280. Email: lvdgoffice@mesquiteweb.com.
Catechesis/Religious Program—Fax: 702-346-6077. Students 146.

NORTH LAS VEGAS, CLARK CO.

1—ST. CHRISTOPHER (1953) [JC] Revs. Ron Zanoni; Alberto Alzate (Colombia).
Mailing Address: 1840 N. Bruce St., 89030. Tel: 702-642-1154; Fax: 702-642-0719. Email: cfierro@stchrisnlv.org.
Res.: 1401 Flower Ave., 89030.
School—(Grades K-8) Tel: 702-657-8008; Fax: 702-642-2461. Email: pmertzman@stchrisnlv.org. Web: www.schris.org. Paul Mertzman, Prin. Lay Teachers 13; Students 129.
Catechesis/Religious Program—Tel: 702-657-6779; Fax: 702-657-8406. Victoria Gonzales, D.R.E. Students 1,391.

2—ST. JOHN NEUMANN (1999) Rev. Bede Wevita; Deacon Frank Oettinger.
Mailing Address: 2575 W. El Campo Grande Ave., 89031. Tel: 702-657-0200; Fax: 702-648-2327. Email: secretary@sjnc.org. Web: www.sjnc.org.
Res.: 912 Whitehollow Ave., 89031. Tel: 702-642-6750.
Catechesis/Religious Program—Tel: 702-657-0200, Ext. 210. Email: dre@sjnc.org. Students 658.

OVERTON, CLARK CO., ST. JOHN THE EVANGELIST (1959) Rev. Robert W. Puhlman, Admin.
Mailing Address: P.O. Box 457, 89040.
Church & Office: 2955 St. Joseph St., Logandale, 89021. Tel: 702-398-3998; Fax: 702-398-3995. Email: stjohn@mvdsl.com.
Res.: 3228 Taylor St., Logandale, 89021. Tel: 702-398-7275.
Catechesis/Religious Program—Students 48.

PAHRUMP, NYE CO., OUR LADY OF THE VALLEY (1985) Rev. Anthony Hughes, Admin.
Mailing Address: 781 E. Gamebird, 89048.
Rectory—3031 S. Blagg Rd., 89048.
Catechesis/Religious Program—Students 156.

TONOPAH, NYE CO., ST. PATRICK (1902) Rev. Antony P. Poovakulam.
Mailing Address: P.O. Box 325, 89049.
Res.: 144 South St., 89049. Fax: 775-482-8446. Email: stpatrickstonopah@frontier.com.
Catechesis/Religious Program—Students 47.
Mission—St. Barbara 91 Hadley Cir., Round Mountain, 89045.
Mission—Our Lady of Guadalupe SR 264, Fish

Lake Community Center, Dyer, Esmeralda Co. 89010.

On Duty Outside the Diocese:
Rev. Msgr.—
Gordon, Gregory W., Apostolic Nunciature, 3339 Massachusetts Ave., N.W., Washington, DC 20008.
Revs.—
Anthony, Joseph, P.O. Box 295042, Kerrville, TX 78029.
Vercellone, Anthony, Our Lady of the Snows, 1138 Wright St., Reno, 89509.

Military Chaplains:
Rev.—
Amaliri, Paul, Wing Chap., Our Lady of the Skies, 4302 N. Washington Blvd., Nellis AFB, 89191.

Unassigned:
Revs.—
Petekiewicz, Robert P.
Waters, Bernard F. (New Zealand)

Administrative Leave:
Rev.—
Chaanine, George

Retired:
Revs.—
Annese, Joseph P.
Bevan, James J., Jr.
Caviglia, Caesar J.
Franzinell, Benjamin
Lavoy, Elwood
McVeigh, John J.
O'Donnell, Philip
Slatterie, Leo
Timoney, Francis

Permanent Deacons:
Bast, Thomas
Daluga, Richard
Davis, William
Deegan, Joseph
Depozo, Dan
Dineen, Terry Paul
Favela, Jacobo, Jr.
Green, Richard
Halt, Tom
Krzeminski, Eugene
Laqui, Sonny
McHugh, Daniel
Oettinger, Frank F.
Pemper, Frank
Smith, John Lawrence
Whittle, James

INSTITUTIONS LOCATED IN THE DIOCESE

[A] HIGH SCHOOLS, DIOCESAN

LAS VEGAS. *Bishop Gorman High School* (1954) 5959 S. Hualapai, 89148. Tel: 702-732-1945; Fax: 702-732-8830. Web: www.bishopgorman.org. Rev. Edward Wagner, O.SS.T., Chap., Campus Ministry; Aggie Evert, Prin.; Mr. John Kilduff, Pres. Priests 2; Lay Teachers 79; Students 1,169.

[B] GENERAL HOSPITALS

HENDERSON. *St. Rose Dominican Hospital, Rose de Lima Campus dba Catholic Healthcare West* (1947) 102 E. Lake Mead Pkwy., 89015. Tel: 702-564-2622; Fax: 702-616-4699. Web: www.strosehospitals.org. Renato V. Baciarelli, Pres. Sponsored by Sisters of St. Dominic, Congregation of the Most Holy Rosary Adrian, MI. Priests 1; Sisters 5; Beds 145; Patients Assisted Annually 52,765; Total Staff 849.

St. Rose Dominican Hospital, San Martin Campus dba Catholic Healthcare West 8280 W. Warm Springs Rd., 89113. Tel: 702-492-8000; Fax: 702-492-8511. Web: www.strosehospitals.org. Vicky VanMeetren, Pres. Sisters of St. Dominic, Congregation of the Most Holy Rosary, Adrian, MI. Priests 1; Bed Capacity 147; Patients Assisted Annually 34,404; Total Staff 702.

St. Rose Dominican Hospital, Siena Campus dba Catholic Healthcare West (2000) 3001 St. Rose Pkwy., 89052-6178. Tel: 702-616-5000; Fax: 702-616-5511. Web: www.strosehospitals.org. Rod Davis, Pres., Southern NV Market Area. Sponsored by Sisters of St. Dominic, Congregation of the Most Holy Rosary Adrian, MI. Sisters 2; Bed Capacity 219; Patients Assisted Annually 85,781; Total Staff 1,764.

[C] MONASTERIES AND RESIDENCES OF PRIESTS AND BROTHERS

LAS VEGAS. *Clerics of St. Viator Retirement Home*, 4219 Pinecrest Cir. E., 89121. Tel: 702-456-8512. Revs. Patrick J. Durkin, C.S.V.; Edward C. Anderson, C.S.V; William F. Haesaert, C.S.V. Priests 3.

Dominican Rectory, Fra Angelico House (1998) 1701 Chapman Dr., 89104-3516. Tel: 702-369-1215; Fax: 702-369-3742. Rev. Albert Felice-Pace, O.P., Supr.; Bro. Frederick W. Narbares, O.P., Prof.; Revs. Joseph O'Brien, O.P.; Donald Bramble, O.P., On Sabbatical. (Western Dominican Province) Priests 3; Brothers 1.

[D] CONVENTS AND RESIDENCES FOR SISTERS

LAS VEGAS. *The Franciscan Sisters of Perpetual Adoration* (1979) 1304 E. St. Louis Ave., 89104-3466. Email: lorforster1@aol.com. Sr. Lorraine Forster, Contact Person.

Holy Family Convent, 5276 S. Lookout St., 89120. Tel: 702-435-1526; Fax: 702-435-1526. Sisters of the Holy Family 3.

[E] NEWMAN CENTERS

LAS VEGAS. *St. Thomas Aquinas Catholic Newman Community at UNLV*, 4765 Brussels St., 89119. Tel: 702-736-0887; Fax: 702-891-0615. Email: info@unlvnewman.com. Web: newman.unlv.edu. Rev. Albert Felice-Pace, O.P., Dir. & Campus Min.; David Zeamer, Assoc. Dir. & Devel. Dir.

[F] MISCELLANEOUS

LAS VEGAS. *Bishop Gorman Development Corp.*, P.O. Box 18316, 89114-8316. Tel: 702-735-7865; Fax: 702-735-2996. Email: witkowski@dioceseoflasvegas.org. Bro. John J. Dodd, C.S.V., Exec. Dir.

Catholic Charities of Southern Nevada (1941) 1501 Las Vegas Blvd., N., 89101. Tel: 702-385-2662; Fax: 702-384-0677. Web: www.catholiccharities.com. Rev. Msgr. Patrick Leary, Exec. Dir.

Adoption Program (1941) Tel: 702-385-3351; Fax: 702-388-8723. Web: www.catholiccharities.com.

Crossroads Transitional Program for Senior Men (1995) Tel: 702-387-2282; Fax: 702-383-8243. Web: www.catholiccharities.com.

Deferred Giving Program (1994) Tel: 702-385-2662; Fax: 702-384-0677. Web: www.catholiccharities-.com.

Immigration Services (1984) Tel: 702-387-2229; Fax: 702-436-1579. Web: www.catholiccharities.com.

Marian Transitional Program for Senior Women (1995) Tel: 702-565-5388; Fax: 702-565-7711. Web: www.catholiccharities.com.

Migration and Refugee Services (1975) Tel: 702-387-2229; Fax: 702-436-1579. Web: www.catholiccharities.com.

Respite Care Referral Service (1995) Tel: 702-382-0721; Fax: 702-385-3206. Web: www.catholiccharities.com.

RSVP (Retired & Senior Volunteer Program) (1975) Tel: 702-382-0721; Fax: 702-307-1203. Web: www-.catholiccharities.com.

Senior Community Employment Service (1977) Tel: 702-215-4701; Fax: 702-366-2066. Web: www-.catholiccharities.com.

Senior Companion (1974) Tel: 702-382-0721; Fax: 702-307-1203. Web: www.catholiccharities.com.

Senior Foster Grandparent Program Tel: 702-647-1515; Fax: 702-307-1203. Web: www.catholiccharities.com.

Senior Nutrition & Meals-on-Wheels (1975) Tel: 702-385-5284; Fax: 702-385-3206. Web: www-.catholiccharities.com.

Social Ministry (1996) Tel: 702-385-2662; Fax: 702-384-0677. Web: www.catholiccharities.com.

Social Services (1941) Tel: 702-387-2291; Fax: 702-383-9031. Web: www.catholiccharities.com.

St. Vincent Lied Dining Facility (1965) Tel: 702-366-2072; Fax: 702-385-1173. Web: www.catholiccharities.com.

St. Vincent Resident Work Program (1985) Tel: 702-387-2282; Fax: 702-366-2066. Web: www-.catholiccharities.com.

Employment Services Center

Catholic Charities Thrift Stores (1961) Tel: 702-385-2662; Fax: 702-384-0677. Web: www.catholiccharities.com.

NCWB Housing, Inc. (1978) Tel: 702-878-5398; Fax: 702-878-4579.

CCSN Mojave Project, Inc. (1985) Tel: 702-384-2643; Fax: 702-384-8759.

CCSN-CTS Annex, Inc. (1988) Tel: 702-384-2643; Fax: 702-384-8759.

CCSN McFarland Housing Development Corporation, Inc. (1997) Tel: 702-736-9596; Fax: 702-736-9597.

Women, Infants, and Children (WIC) Tel: 702-366-2069; Fax: 702-366-9551. Web: www.catholiccharities.com.

HENDERSON. *Diocesan Residence* (1999) 507 Chestnut View Pl., 89052-2821. Tel: 702-735-7865; Fax: 702-735-2996. Lee Liguori, Vice Chancellor.

St. Rose Dominican Health Foundation, 3001 St. Rose Pkwy., 89052. Tel: 702-616-5750; Fax: 712-616-5751. Web: www.strosehospitals.org.

Saint Therese Center (1998) HIV/AIDS Outreach Program, 100 E. Lake Mead Pkwy., 89015. Tel: 702-564-4224; Fax: 702-564-0604. Email: aidsproject@dioceseoflasvegas.org. Web: sainttheresecenter.org. Rev. Joseph O'Brien, O.P., Exec. Dir.; Bro. Frederick Naberes, O.P.

Central Las Vegas Satellite, 1120 Almond Tree Ln., #201, 89104. Tel: 702-360-9276; Fax: 702-564-0604.

West Las Vegas Satellite, 8280 W. Warm Springs Rd., San Martin Hospital G3022, 89113. Tel: 702-564-4224; Fax: 702-564-0604.

Laughlin Satellite, 3055 El Mirage Way, St. John the Baptist Mission Church, Laughlin, 89028. Tel: 702-564-4224; Fax: 702-564-0604.

RELIGIOUS INSTITUTES OF MEN REPRESENTED IN THE DIOCESE

For further details refer to the corresponding bracketed number in the Religious Institutes of Men or Women section.

[]—*Capuchin Friars*—O.F.M.Cap.
[1320]—*Clerics of St. Viator*—C.S.V.
[]—*Congregation of the Holy Spirit*—C.S.Sp
[]—*Order of the Holy Trinity*—O.SS.T.
[]—*Western Dominican Province*—O.P.

RELIGIOUS INSTITUTES OF WOMEN REPRESENTED IN THE DIOCESE

[]—*Community of the Holy Spirit*—C.H.S.
[1780]—*Congregation of the Sisters of the Third Order of St. Francis of Perpetual Adoration*—F.S.P.A.
[1070-04]—*Dominican Sisters*—O.P.
[]—*Franciscan Sisters*—O.S.F.
[]—*Sisters of Mercy*—R.S.M.
[1960]—*Sisters of the Holy Family*—S.H.F.

NECROLOGY

† Sullivan, John Andrew, Office of the Tribunal—Died June 10, 2009

An asterisk (*) denotes an organization that has established tax-exempt status directly with the IRS and is not covered by the USCCB Group Ruling.

Diocese of Lexington

FROM HIS FULLNESS GRACE UPON GRACE

Most Reverend

RONALD W. GAINER

Bishop of Lexington; ordained May 19, 1973; appointed Bishop of Lexington December 13, 2002; consecrated February 22, 2003. *Office: The Catholic Center, 1310 W. Main St., Lexington, KY 40508-2048.*

The Catholic Center: 1310 W. Main St., Lexington, KY 40508-2048. Tel: 859-253-1993; Fax: 859-254-6284.

Web: www.cdlex.org

Email: webmaster@cdlex.org

ESTABLISHED MARCH 2, 1988.

Square Miles 16,423.

Comprises the counties of Anderson, Bath, Bell, Bourbon, Boyd, Boyle, Breathitt, Carter, Clark, Clay, Elliott, Estill, Fayette, Floyd, Franklin, Garrard, Greenup, Harlan, Jackson, Jessamine, Johnson, Knott, Knox, Laurel, Lawrence, Lee, Leslie, Letcher, Lincoln, McCreary, Madison, Magoffin, Martin, Menifee, Mercer, Montgomery, Morgan, Nicholas, Owsley, Perry, Pike, Powell, Pulaski, Rockcastle, Rowan, Scott, Wayne, Whitley, Wolfe and Woodford.

For legal titles of parishes and diocesan institutions, consult the Chancellor.

STATISTICAL OVERVIEW

Personnel	
Bishop	1
Retired Bishops	1
Priests: Diocesan Active in Diocese	36
Priests: Diocesan Active Outside Diocese	3
Priests: Retired, Sick or Absent	11
Number of Diocesan Priests	50
Religious Priests in Diocese	24
Total Priests in Diocese	74
Ordinations:	
Diocesan Priests	1
Transitional Deacons	1
Permanent Deacons in Diocese	57
Total Brothers	3
Total Sisters	91
Parishes	
Parishes	50
With Resident Pastor:	
Resident Diocesan Priests	38
Resident Religious Priests	14
Without Resident Pastor:	
Administered by Deacons	2
Administered by Professed Religious Men	1
Administered by Religious Women	7
Administered by Lay People	1
Missions	13
Closed Parishes	1
Professional Ministry Personnel:	
Sisters	28
Lay Ministers	43
Welfare	
Catholic Hospitals	11
Total Assisted	777,247
Health Care Centers	4
Total Assisted	54,000
Homes for the Aged	1
Total Assisted	209
Special Centers for Social Services	1
Total Assisted	8,000
Educational	
Diocesan Students in Other Seminaries	10
Total Seminarians	10
High Schools, Diocesan and Parish	1
Total Students	842
High Schools, Private	1
Total Students	68
Elementary Schools, Diocesan and Parish	14
Total Students	2,928
Elementary Schools, Private	1
Total Students	142
Catechesis/Religious Education:	
High School Students	717
Elementary Students	3,265
Total Students under Catholic Instruction	7,972
Teachers in the Diocese:	
Priests	2
Sisters	9
Lay Teachers	345
Vital Statistics	
Receptions into the Church:	
Infant Baptism Totals	861
Minor Baptism Totals	25
Adult Baptism Totals	85
Received into Full Communion	188
First Communions	843
Confirmations	848
Marriages:	
Catholic	118
Interfaith	92
Total Marriages	210
Deaths	299
Total Catholic Population	46,798
Total Population	1,567,853

Former Bishop—Most Rev. JAMES K. WILLIAMS, D.D., ord. May 25, 1963; appt. Titular Bishop of Catula and Auxiliary Bishop of Covington on April 15, 1984; cons. June 19, 1984; appt. Bishop of Lexington Jan. 14, 1988; installed March 2, 1988; resigned June 11, 2002.

The Catholic Center—1310 W. Main St., Lexington, 40508-2048. Tel: 859-253-1993; Fax: 859-254-6284. Office Hours: Mon.-Fri. 8:30-4:30.

Vicar General—Very Rev. MARK DREVES.

Chancellor—KAREN ABBEY.

Chief Administrative Officer—Deacon JIM PARIS.

Executive Administrative Assistant To The Bishop—KAREN ABBEY.

Secretariat for Stewardship—Deacon BILL WAKEFIELD, CFO, 1310 W. Main St., Lexington, 40508-2048.

College of Consultors—Revs. JOHN MORIARTY; THOMAS P. FARRELL; MICHAEL CHOWNING, O.F.M.; TERENCE E. HOPPENJANS; DANIEL J. NOLL; FRANK C. OSBURG (Retired), 1310 W. Main St., Lexington, 40508-2048.

Regional Councillors—Fayette: Rev. JOHN MORIARTY. Bluegrass West: Rev. THOMAS P. FARRELL. Bluegrass East: Rev. JACOB ORAVANAMTHADATHIL, H.G.N. Mountain West: Rev. MICHAEL J. RAMLER. Mountain East: Rev. MICHAEL CHOWNING, O.F.M. Big Sandy/Licking: Rev. TERENCE E. HOPPENJANS.

Diocesan Tribunal—1310 W. Main St., Lexington, 40508-2048. Tel: 859-253-1993; Fax: 859-259-0951.

Judicial Vicar—Rev. JOHN E. LIST, J.C.L. Email: jlist@cdlex.org.

Tribunal Director—RENATA BABICZ-BARATTO, J.U.D., J.C.L. Email: ribabicz@cdlex.org.

Associate Judges—Revs. THOMAS P. KOONS, J.C.L.; VICTOR FINELLI, J.C.L.; BARRY WINDHOLTZ, J.C.L.

Defenders of the Bond—Revs. THOMAS V. THAI, Ph.D. (Retired); MICHAEL WEGLICKI; PAUL PRABELL; MARCO RAJKOVICH, J.D.

Case Instructors—CAROLYN G. SNOWDEN; FRANCES GOODFRIEND.

Promoter of Justice—Rev. PAUL PRABELL.

Notaries—CAROLYN G. SNOWDEN; FRANCES GOODFRIEND.

Ministry Admissions Board—Most Rev. RONALD WILLIAM GAINER.

Priests' Retirement Board—Revs. DENNIS KNIGHT; LAWRENCE W. HEHMAN (Retired); FRANK C. OSBURG (Retired); MICHAEL J. RAMLER; CHRIS CLAY; CHARLES J. MCDONALD (Retired); Mr. JOHN D. PRICE; WILLIAM TOZER; JOB D. TURNER; Deacon BILL WAKEFIELD.

Diocesan Offices And Directors

Secretariat of the Vicar General—Very Rev. MARK DREVES, Vicar Gen., 1310 W. Main St., Lexington, 40508. Tel: 859-253-1993. Email: mdreves@cdlex.org.

Archives—KAREN ABBEY, 1310 W. Main St., Lexington, 40508-2048. Tel: 859-253-1993.

Campus Ministry— Newman Center Dir., Contact The Catholic Center, *1310 W. Main St., Lexington, 40508-2048.* Tel: 859-253-1993. Ms. JOAN ROOT, Dir.

Catholic Scouting—Rev. MICHAEL WEGLICKI, Diocesan Dir. Tel: 606-464-3357.

Secretariat for Social Services—Tel: 859-253-1993. Mrs. RUSLYN CASE-COMPTON, Dir., Lexington. Tel: 859-253-1993. Email: cssb@cdlex.org.

Catholic Charities of Lexington—Mrs. RUSLYN CASE-COMPTON, Dir., 1310 W. Main St., Lexington, 40508-2048. Tel: 859-253-1993, Ext. 215. Email: charities@cdlex.org.

Father Beiting Appalachian Mission Center—Rev. Msgr. RALPH BEITING, Founder; Mr. PHILLIP TEAGUE, Dir. Oper., 502 Lacey Ave., Louisa, 41230. Tel: 606-638-0219. Mailing Address: P.O. Box 885, Louisa, 41230-0885.

Deaf Ministry— Masses: Sun. 11 am every other week at Mary, Queen of the Holy Rosary, Lexington; Sun. 11:15 am at Sts. Peter and Paul, Danville.

Secretariat for Stewardship—Deacon BILL WAKEFIELD, CFO, 1310 W. Main St., Lexington, 40508-2048. Tel: 859-253-1993, Ext. 238.

Mission Office, Propagation of the Faith and The Holy Childhood—Deacon BILL WAKEFIELD, Propagation of the Faith Coord., 1310 W. Main St., Lexington, 40508-2048. Tel: 859-253-1993, Ext. 238.

Ecumenical Liaison—Deacon MARK STAUFFER, 4505 Thornbridge Lane, Lexington, 40515. Tel: 859-272-8545.

R.C.I.A.—KAREN ROOD, Coord., 1310 W. Main St., Lexington, 40508-2048. Tel: 859-253-1993, Ext. 251.

Healthcare—Deacon BILL WAKEFIELD, Diocesan Coord., 1310 W. Main St., Lexington, 40508-2048. Tel: 859-253-1993, Ext. 238.

Secretariat for Pastoral Life—Deacon JIM PARIS, Sec., 1310 W. Main St., Lexington, 40508-2048. Tel: 859-253-1993, Ext. 220.

Superintendent of Schools—Mr. WILLIAM A. FARNAU, 1310 W. Main St., Lexington, 40508-2048. Tel: 859-253-1993, Ext. 219.

Catechetical Service & Adult Faith Formation—DOUG CULP, Dir., 1310 W. Main St., Lexington, 40508-2048. Tel: 859-253-1993, Ext. 221.

Cliffview Retreat Center—Co-Directors: DAVID WELLS; SHARLA WELLS. Tel: 859-792-3333.

Communications—THOMAS SHAUGHNESSY, Dir., 1310 W. Main St., Lexington, 40508-2048. Tel: 859-253-1993, Ext. 258.

Hispanic Ministry—Sr. SANDRA DELGADO, O.P., Dir.; Rev. JOSEPH VON HANDORF.

Buen Pastor - Centro Catolico—1310 W. Main St., Lexington, 40508. Tel: 859-254-5507. Staff: DANNY HERNANDEZ-SILVA, Youth Min.; YOLANDA PINILLA, Prog. Coord.; LINNETTE HACKER, Families & Youth Activities Coord.

Peace & Justice—VACANT, Dir., 1310 W. Main St., Lexington, 40508. Tel: 859-253-1993, Ext. 224.

Director of Family Life—MICHAEL ALLEN. Tel: 859-253-1993, Ext. 212.

Director of Youth Ministry—Ms. JOAN ROOT, The Catholic Center, 1310 W. Main St., Lexington, 40508-2048. Tel: 859-253-1993, Ext. 218.

HIV/AIDS Ministry—Rev. JOHN C. CURTIS, Diocesan Coord.

Commission for African American Catholic Concerns—Contacts: Mrs. BARBARA DEHAAN; Mrs. CHRISTINA WEATHERS, Mailing Address: 410 Jefferson St., Lexington, 40508. Tel: 859-223-3703; 859-254-0030.

Rural Life—The Catholic Center, 1310 W. Main St., Lexington, 40508-2048. Tel: 859-253-1993.

Regina Pacis Community— (Traditional Latin Mass Community) *177 St. Ann Dr., Lexington, 40502.* Tel: 859-983-6729; 859-268-5159. Rev. VALENTINE YOUNG, O.F.M., Chap. Email: fr.valentineyoung.ofm@hotmail.com.

Liturgy—KAREN ROOD, Dir., 1310 W. Main St., Lexington, 40508-2048. Tel: 859-253-1993, Ext. 251.

Newspaper "Cross Roads"—THOMAS F. SHAUGHNESSY, Editor, 1310 W. Main St., Lexington, 40508-2048. Tel: 859-253-1993, Ext. 258; Fax: 859-259-0951.

Permanent Diaconate—Co-Directors: ARDEN WOLTERMAN; BETTY WOLTERMAN, 3 Lansdowne Estate, Lexington, 40502-3321. Tel: 859-276-4123.

Ministry for Persons with Disabilities—JOE PETRY; Mrs. MARY PETRY, 124 Rolling Hills, Danville, 40422. Tel: 859-936-8656.

Priests' Personnel—Rev. DANIEL J. NOLL, 295 Huntertown Rd., Versailles, 40383-9183. Tel: 859-983-2643.

Prison Ministry—Mrs. RUSLYN CASE-COMPTON, Diocesan Coord., 1310 W. Main St., Lexington, 40508. Tel: 859-253-1993, Ext. 215. Email: rcasecompton@cdlex.org.

Religious—Sr. MARIA GORETTI BROWNE, O.P., Delegate, 327 Duke Rd., No. 2, Lexington, 40502. Tel: 859-266-9809.

Respect Life—Deacon JIM PARIS, Diocesan Coord.

Victim Assistance Coordinator—Mrs. NELDA JACKSON. Tel: 859-253-1993, Ext. 214. Email: njackson@cdlex.org.

Vocations—Rev. STEPHEN ROBERTS, Dir. Tel: 859-253-1993, Ext. 249. Email: sroberts@cdlex.org; Mr. ERICK SANDSTAD, Dir. Vocational Discernment, 1310 W. Main St., Lexington, 40508-2048. Tel: 859-253-1993, Ext. 275. Email: esandstad@cdlex.org.

CLERGY, PARISHES, MISSIONS AND PAROCHIAL SCHOOLS

CITY OF LEXINGTON

(FAYETTE COUNTY)

1—CATHEDRAL OF CHRIST THE KING (1945) Very Rev. Mark Dreves, Rector; Revs. Daniel Fister, Parochial Vicar; Gino Donatelli, S.J., Parochial Vicar; Deacons Arden Wolterman; Mark Stauffer; Fred Fugazzi Jr.; Raoul Ouellette; Paul Root; Timothy Weinmann; Patricia Dimon, Business Mgr.; Joseph Cipriano, Youth Min.; Josette Garstka, Event & Facilities Mgr.; Deborah Goonan, Outreach Min.; Robert Whitaker, Music Min.; Brian Hunt, Asst. Music Min.
Res.: 299 Colony Blvd., 40502. Tel: 859-268-2861; Fax: 859-268-8061. Web: cathedral.cdlex.org.
School—(Grades K-8), 412 Cochran Rd., 40502. Tel: 859-266-5641; Fax: 859-266-4547. Karen Thomas, Prin. Lay Teachers 33; Students 455.
Catechesis/Religious Program—Rod Stearn, D.R.E. Students 224.

2—ST. ELIZABETH ANN SETON (1980) Rev. John Moriarty; Sr. Eileen Golby, O.S.F., Pastoral Assoc.; Deacons Thomas Waken; Robert S. Joice; Matthew C. Coriale; Mark T. Woelfel.
Res.: 1750 Summerhill Dr., 40515. Tel: 859-273-0134.
Parish Center—Tel: 859-273-1318; Fax: 859-272-6988. Email: seasparish@cdlex.org. Web: seas.cdlex.org.
School—Seton Catholic School, (Grades PreK-8), 1740 Summerhill Dr., 40515. Email: lcoomer@cdlex.org. Web: setonschool.cdlex.org. Lee Coomer, Prin. Lay Teachers 34; Students 457.
Education Office—Tel: 859-273-7827. Jayne Morris, D.R.E.

3—MARY, QUEEN OF THE HOLY ROSARY (1960) Revs. Robert Nieberding, Admin. (Retired); Nicholas A. Pagano, Parochial Vicar; Eulices Godinez-Ramos, Parochial Vicar; Deacons Jim Paris; James Horine; Bob Kotzbauer; Bill Rood.
Church & Res.: 601 Hill'N Dale Rd., 40503. Tel: 859-278-7432; Fax: 859-278-2453.
School—(Grades PreK-8), 605 Hill 'N Dale Rd., 40503. Tel: 859-277-3030; Fax: 859-277-1784. Email: lkeeney@mq.cdlex.org. Web: maryqueenschool.cdlex.org. Rebecca Brown, Prin.; Betsy Tibe, Librarian. Lay Teachers 38; Students 450.
Catechesis/Religious Program—Students 944.

4—THE NEWMAN CENTER, HOLY SPIRIT (1963), Parish for Students, Faculty and Staff of the University of Kentucky. Revs. Albert J. DeGiacomo; Emmanuel F. Zamora, Parochial Vicar.
Res.: 320 Rose Ln., 40508. Tel: 859-255-8566; Fax: 859-254-7519.
Catechesis/Religious Program—Sr. Ellen Kehoe, S.P., D.R.E. Students 138.

5—ST. PAUL (1865) [JC] Rev. Charles W. Niehaus, S.J.; Sr. Clara Fehringer, O.S.U., Parish Life Dir.; Deacons Michael Rupinen; Raymond D. Martorano.
Res.: 501 W. Short St., 40507-1254. Tel: 859-252-0738; Fax: 859-225-6127. Email: saintpaul@cdlex.org. Web: saintpaul.cdlex.org.
Catechesis/Religious Program—Carey Parker, D.R.E. Students 94.
See Inter-Parish Elementary - Sts. Peter and Paul, Lexington under St. Peter, Lexington for details.

6—PAX CHRISTI CATHOLIC CHURCH (1994) [CEM] Rev. Richard D. Edelen; Deacon Ralph B. Jahnige; Melissa Holland, Pastoral Assoc.; Elena Beauregard, Children & Youth Min.
Res.: 460 Fox Harbour, 40517. Tel: 859-273-2465; Fax: 859-245-8123.

7—ST. PETER (1812) [JC] Rev. John E. List; Deacon Bill Wakefield; Pam Berger, Pastoral Assoc. In Res., Revs. Theodore A. Keller (Retired); Henry Kenney, S.J. (Retired).
Res.: 153 Barr St., 40507. Tel: 859-252-7551; Fax: 859-252-1853.
School—Inter-Parish Elementary - Sts. Peter and Paul School, (Grades PreK-8) Tel: 859-254-9257; Fax: 859-254-9050. Julie Wright, Prin. Lay Teachers 34; Students 395.
Catechesis/Religious Program—Students 55.

8—ST. PETER CLAVER (1887) Rev. Norman Fischer; Deacons James Weathers, Parish Life Dir.; Paul E. Olson, Prison Ministry.
Res.: 410 Jefferson St., 40508-1319. Tel: 859-254-0030; Fax: 859-253-6740.
Catechesis/Religious Program—Tel: 859-257-6802; Fax: 859-253-6740. Martha Crumbie, C.R.E. Students 35.

OUTSIDE THE CITY OF LEXINGTON

ASHLAND, BOYD CO., HOLY FAMILY (1860) [CEM] Rev. John P. Noe; Deacon Bob Maher.
Res.: 900 Winchester Ave., 41101-7497. Tel: 606-329-1607; Fax: 606-329-1806.
School—(Grades PreK-8), 932 Winchester Ave., 41101. Tel: 606-324-7040; Fax: 606-324-6288. Mrs. Mary Lou Chandler, Prin. Lay Teachers 13; Students 130.
Catechesis/Religious Program—Students 80.
Mission—St. Lawrence Greenup.

BARBOURVILLE, KNOX CO., ST. GREGORY (1910) Rev. Peter Joseph, H.G.N.
Church: 329 N. Sycamore Dr., 40906-1540. Tel: 606-546-4461; Fax: 606-546-4461.
Catechesis/Religious Program—Kathy Greene, D.R.E. Students 15.

BEATTYVILLE, LEE CO., QUEEN OF ALL SAINTS (1965) Rev. Michael Weglicki; Sr. Alice Retzner, O.S.F., Pastoral Assoc.
Mailing Address: P.O. Box 563, 41311-0563. Tel: 606-464-8695; Fax: 606-464-3357 (Call First).
Res.: 90 Railroad St., 41311. Tel: 606-464-3357. Email: queenas1@bellsouth.net.
Mission—Booneville Catholic Church of the Holy Family (1984) R.R. 2, Box 221, Booneville, Owsley Co. 41314. Tel: 606-593-6948; Fax: 606-593-6948. Email: meilermanosf@yahoo.com. Sr. Marge Eilerman, O.S.F, Pastoral Assoc.
Catechesis/Religious Program—Tel: 606-593-6948. Students 6.
Oratory—St. Therese (1948) P.O. Box 563, Heidelberg, Lee Co. 41311. Tel: 606-464-3357.

BEREA, MADISON CO., ST. CLARE (1950) Revs. Frank Brawner; John Agapito, C.P.M., Parochial Vicar; Sr. Theresa Bowman, C.D.P., Pastoral Assoc.
Res.: 655 Scaffold Cane Rd., 40403. Tel: 859-228-0937; Fax: 859-985-8413. Email: stclare@cdlex.org.
Catechesis/Religious Program—Students 80.
Mission—Our Lady of Mt. Vernon (1954) P.O. Box 1006, Mt. Vernon, Rockcastle Co. 40456. Tel: 859-985-8413.
Mission—St. Paul (1973) P.O. Box 189, McKee, Jackson Co. 40447. Tel: 606-287-7601. Email: stpaulmk@prtnet.org. Mr. John Roche, Pastoral Assoc.; Ms. Emily Gerke, C.R.E.

CARLISLE, NICHOLAS CO., SHRINE OF OUR LADY OF GUADALUPE (1962) Rev. John C. Curtis.
Church: 617 E. Main St., 40311. Tel: 859-289-5502.
Res.: 1007 Main St., Paris, 40361-1709. Tel: 859-987-1571; Fax: 859-987-7367.
Catechesis/Religious Program—Tel: 859-289-5586. Sr. Dorothy Bondi, O.S.U., D.R.E. Students 10.

CORBIN, KNOX CO., SACRED HEART (1902) Rev. Joseph N. Koury Jr.
Res.: 703 Masters St., P.O. Box 455, 40702. Tel: 606-528-5222; Fax: 606-523-9901. Email: sacredheartparish@newwavecomm.net. Web: corbin.cdlex.org.
Catechesis/Religious Program—Students 84.

CUMBERLAND, HARLAN CO., ST. STEPHEN (1940) Rev. Edward H. Lammert, O.F.M. In Res., Rev. Maynard Tetreault, O.F.M.
Res.: 304 Central St., 40823. Tel: 606-589-5616; Fax: 606-589-4549. Email: sstephen@windstream.net.

DANVILLE, BOYLE CO., SS. PETER & PAUL (1807) Rev. Thomas P. Farrell; Deacon Jeremiah Noe.
Res.: 117 W. Main St., 40422. Tel: 859-236-2111; Fax: 859-236-2922. Email: ssppchurch@cdlex.org. Web: denville.cdlex.org.
Catechesis/Religious Program—Students 163.

FRANKFORT, FRANKLIN CO., GOOD SHEPHERD (1845) Rev. Charles W. Howell; Deacon Thomas Snyder.
Office: 310 Wapping St., 40601-2060. Tel: 502-227-4511; Fax: 502-875-9854.
Church: 1050 Leestown Rd., 421 S., 40601.
School—(Grades K-8), 316 Wapping St., 40601. Tel: 502-223-5041; Fax: 502-223-2755. Debbie Pack, Prin. Lay Teachers 22; Students 216.
Catechesis/Religious Program—Students 84.

GEORGETOWN, SCOTT CO., SS. FRANCIS & JOHN CATHOLIC CHURCH (1869) [CEM] Rev. Linh Nguyen; Deacon John Calandrella.
Res.: 604 E. Main St., 40324. Tel: 502-863-3404; Fax: 502-863-3402. Email: georgetown@cdlex.org.
School—(Grades PreK-8), 106 Military St., 40324. Tel: 502-863-2607; Fax: 502-863-2259. Kathleen Boothe, Prin. Religious 2; Lay Teachers 14; Students 212.
Catechesis/Religious Program—Tel: 502-863-1213. Carmen Garcia, D.R.E. Students 163.

GRAYSON, CARTER CO., SS. JOHN & ELIZABETH (1964) Sr. Marie Colette Gerry, O.S.F., Parish Life Dir.; Rev. Laurence B. Goulding, G.H.M.
Church: 799 State Hwy. 1947, 41143. Tel: 606-474-9979; Fax: 606-474-9979. Email: sje1947@gmail.com.
Res.: P.O. Box 841, 41143. Tel: 606-474-9897.
Catechesis/Religious Program—Tel: 606-474-6440. Nancy Kozee, D.R.E. Students 11.

HARLAN, HARLAN CO., HOLY TRINITY (1948) Marjorie D. Grieshop, Parish Life Dir.; Rev. Edward H. Lammert, O.F.M.
Res.: 2536 S. U.S. Hwy. 421, 40831-1798. Tel: 606-573-6311; Fax: 606-574-0093. Email: holytrinity@bellsouth.net.
The Learning Center—Tel: 606-573-3570. Email: tlcholytrinity@harlanonline.net.
Catechesis/Religious Program—Students 33.

HARRODSBURG, MERCER CO., ST. ANDREW (1858) [CEM] Rev. Daniel P. Schwendeman; Deacon Richard L. Abbey.
Res.: 1125 Danville Rd., P.O. Box 648, 40330-0648. Tel: 859-734-4270; Fax: 859-733-9770. Email: standrewschurch2@bellsouth.net.
Catechesis/Religious Program—Mary Jane Trimble, D.R.E. Students 118.
Mission—St. Mary (1949) 307 S. Buell St., Perryville, Boyle Co. 40468.

HAZARD, PERRY CO., MOTHER OF GOOD COUNSEL (1913) Rev. Michael Chowning, O.F.M.; Ms. Patricia Riestenberg, Pastoral Assoc.
Res.: 329 Poplar St. & Cedar St., 41701. Tel: 606-436-2533; Fax: 606-435-0171.
Catechesis/Religious Program—Students 28.

JACKSON, BREATHITT CO., HOLY CROSS (1923) Bro. Jerome Beetz, O.F.M., Parish Life Dir.; Rev. Reynolds Garland, O.F.M.
Church: 51 Brewers Dr., 41339-9616. Tel: 606-666-7871; Fax: 606-666-7370.

Mission—Catholic Church of the Good Shepherd (1987) P.O. Box 742, Campton, Wolfe Co. 41301. Tel: 606-668-3731. (A Mission of Holy Cross, Jackson, KY).

JELLICO, WHITLEY CO., KY & CAMPBELL CO., TN, ST. BONIFACE (1886) [CEM] Rev. Joseph N. Koury Jr.; Sr. Margaret Verhoff, C.D.P., Parish Life Dir.
Res.: 76 W. Sycamore St., Williamsburg, 40769. Tel: 606-549-2156.
Catechesis/Religious Program—Students 3.

JENKINS, LETCHER CO., ST. GEORGE (1912) Rev. Santosh Madanu, H.G.N.
Res.: P.O. Box 787, 41537. Tel: 606-832-2409.
Catechesis/Religious Program—Sr. M. Sujaya, M.C., D.R.E. Students 2.
Mission—Holy Angels (1960) McRoberts, Letcher Co.

LANCASTER, GARRARD CO., ST. WILLIAM (1951) Rev. Thobias Sabariar, M.C.
Res.: 224 Lexington St., P.O. Box 269, 40444. Tel: 859-792-4009; Fax: 859-792-4009. Email: stwlcath@windstream.net.
Catechesis/Religious Program—Tel: 859-792-4578. Joni Jordan, D.R.E. Students 15.

LAWRENCEBURG, ANDERSON CO., ST. LAWRENCE (1873) Rev. Catesby Clay Jr.
Res.: 120 Gatewood Ave., 40342. Tel: 502-839-6381; Fax: 502-859-2419. Email: stlawrencecathol@bellsouth.net. Web: lawrenceburg.cdlex.org.
Catechesis/Religious Program—Angela Pike, D.R.E. Students 97.

LONDON, LAUREL CO., ST. WILLIAM (1905) [CEM] Rev. Patrick F. Stewart.
Res.: 521 W. 5th St., 40741. Tel: 606-864-7500; Fax: 606-864-8263. Email: stwilliam@windstream.net. Web: london.cdlex.org.
Rectory—
Catechesis/Religious Program—Sr. Marjorie Manning, C.S.C. Students 71.
Mission—St. Ann (1952) 222 Town Branch Rd., Manchester, Clay Co. 40962-1322. Tel: 606-598-2718; Fax: 606-598-2718. Email: saint_ann@windstream.net.
Oratory—St. Sylvester, East Bernstadt

LOUISA, LAWRENCE CO., ST. JUDE (1982) Rev. Msgr. Ralph Beiting; Rev. Anthony Muthu, H.G.N., Parochial Vicar.
Res.: 120 Chaplin Ln., 41230. Tel: 606-638-0418; Fax: 606-638-0220. Email: churchstjude@yahoo.com. Web: www.louisa.cdlex.org.
Catechesis/Religious Program—Chris Howard, C.R.E. Students 25.
Mission—St. John Neumann (1980) Rte. 292, Hode, Martin Co. 41223. Tel: 606-395-5316. Mailing Address: P.O. Box 290, Warfield, 41267.

LYNCH, HARLAN CO., CHURCH OF THE RESURRECTION (1917) Rev. Edward H. Lammert, O.F.M.
Res.: 304 Central St., Cumberland, 40823. Tel: 606-589-5616; Fax: 606-589-4549. Email: sstephen@windstream.net.
Catechesis/Religious Program—Mrs. Anna Carruba, D.R.E.

MIDDLESBORO, BELL CO., ST. JULIAN (1890) Rev. Chinnappan Amalanathan, H.G.N.
Res.: 118 E. Chester Ave., 40965-1256. Tel: 606-248-2068; Fax: 606-248-2207. Email: saintjuliancatho@bellsouth.net.
School—(Grades K-6), 116 E. Chester Ave., 40965. Tel: 606-248-8309; Fax: 606-248-8309. Tom Keleman, Prin.; Kim Honeycutt, Vice Prin. Lay Teachers 3; Students 49.
Catechesis/Religious Program—Theresa Tanner, D.R.E. Tel: 423-869-9555; Barry Tanner, D.R.E. Tel: 423-869-9255. Students 38.
Mission—St. Anthony (1889) P.O. Box 628, Pineville, Bell Co. 40977-0628. Rosemary Combs, D.R.E.

MONTICELLO, WAYNE CO., ST. PETER (1967) Deacon Thomas Wagner, Parish Life Dir.; Rev. John L. Kieffer, S.J.
Office: P.O. Box 669, 42633. Tel: 606-348-9416. Web: monticello.cdlex.org.
Res.: 455 Michigan Ave., 42633. Tel: 606-348-0086.
Catechesis/Religious Program—Students 13.

MOREHEAD, ROWAN CO., CHURCH OF JESUS OUR SAVIOR (1961) Rev. Paul Prabell; Deacon William T. Buelterman.
Res.: 315 Battson-Oates, P.O. Box 307, 40351. Tel: 606-784-4392; Fax: 606-783-0190.
Catechesis/Religious Program—Sr. Rosemary McCormack, D.R.E. Students 85.
Chapel—Morehead, St. Claire Medical Center, Tel: 606-783-6500.

MT. STERLING, MONTGOMERY CO., ST. PATRICK (1868) [CEM] Rev. Jacob Oravanamthadathil, H.G.N.
Office: 139 W. Main St., 40353. Tel: 859-498-0300; Fax: 859-499-1742. Email: stpatmtsterling@bellsouth.net.
Catechesis/Religious Program—Diana Ingram, C.R.E. Students 64.

MT. VERNON, ROCKCASTLE CO., OUR LADY OF MT. VERNON (1954) Closed. Now a mission of St. Clare, Berea.

NICHOLASVILLE, JESSAMINE CO., ST. LUKE (1867) Rev. William C. Bush; Deacons Michael Burns; Frank Keller.
Res.: 304 S. Main St., 40356. Tel: 859-885-4892; Fax: 859-885-6762. Email: nicholasville@catholicweb.com. Web: nicholasville.cdlex.org.
Catechesis/Religious Program—Theresa Kemp, D.R.E. Students 100.

OTTENHEIM, LINCOLN CO., ST. SYLVESTER (1885) [CEM] Rev. Thobias Sabariar, M.C.
Res.: 224 Lexington St., P.O. Box 269, Lancaster, 40444. Tel: 859-792-4009; Fax: 859-792-4009. Email: stwlcath@windstream.net.
Catechesis/Religious Program—Tel: 606-365-2902. Jenny Schuler, D.R.E. Students 8.

PAINTSVILLE, JOHNSON CO., ST. MICHAEL CATHOLIC CHURCH (1941) Rev. Terence E. Hoppenjans; Deacons John M. Lewis; Paul David Brown.
Res.: 720 Washington Ave., 41240. Tel: 606-789-4455; Fax: 606-789-4455. Email: stmike@bellsouth.net.
School—Our Lady of the Mountains, (Grades PreK-8), 405 Third St., 41240. Tel: 606-789-3661; Fax: 606-789-3661. Catherine Cybriwsky, Prin. Lay Teachers 7; Students 52.
Catechesis/Religious Program—Cathy Brown, D.R.E. Students 41.

PARIS, BOURBON CO., ANNUNCIATION OF THE BLESSED VIRGIN MARY (1856) [CEM] Rev. John C. Curtis.
Res.: 1007 Main St., 40361. Tel: 859-987-1571; Fax: 859-987-7367.
School—St. Mary, (Grades PreK-8), 1121 Main St., 40361. Tel: 859-987-3815; Fax: 859-987-3815. Rich Martinez, Prin. Lay Teachers 10; Students 108.
Catechesis/Religious Program—Jennifer Frye, D.R.E. Students 125.

PIKEVILLE, PIKE CO., ST. FRANCIS OF ASSISI (1949) Rev. Wilfred Fraenzle.
Office: 132 Bryan St., 41501.
Res.: 139 Keel St., 41501-6822. Tel: 606-437-6822; Fax: 606-437-6822.
Church: 136 S. College St., 41501.
School—(Grades K-6), 147 Bryan St., 41501. Tel: 606-437-6117. Theresa Dawahare, Prin. Lay Teachers 7; Students 69.
Catechesis/Religious Program—Linda Justice, D.R.E. Students 25.
Mission—St. Joseph the Worker (1985) P.O. Box 55, Elkhorn City, Pike Co. 41522. Tel: 606-754-5225; Fax: 606-754-5225. Sr. Margie Zureick, C.P.P.S., Pastoral Assoc.
Mission—Jesus of the Mountains Catholic Church (1988) 38 Birch Ct., Phelps, Pike Co. 41553. Tel: 606-456-7907. Sr. Beth Carrender, O.S.F., Pastoral Assoc.

PRESTONSBURG, FLOYD CO., ST. MARTHA (1984) Rev. Robert Damron.
Res.: 60 Martha Vineyard, 41653. Tel: 606-874-9526. Email: stmarthas@bellsouth.net. Web: www.prestonsburg.cdlex.org.
Catechesis/Religious Program—Patty McBride, D.R.E. Students 30.
Chapel—Martin, St. Joseph Hospital, Tel: 606-285-6400.

RAVENNA, ESTILL CO., ST. ELIZABETH OF HUNGARY (1932) Rev. Albert Fritsch, S.J.
Res.: 316 5th St., 40472-1812. Tel: 606-723-4705.
Catechesis/Religious Program—Students 8.

RICHMOND, MADISON CO., ST. MARK (1867) Rev. James W. Sichko; Deacon James D. Bennett.
Res.: 608 W. Main St., 40475. Tel: 859-623-2989; Fax: 859-623-4652.
School—(Grades PreK-3) Tel: 859-623-2989, Ext. 4; Fax: 859-623-9947. Sr. Cecilia Clare Werle, C.D.P., Librarian. Sisters 2; Lay Teachers 15; Students 56.
Mission—St. Stephen the Martyr (1977) 405 University Dr., Madison Co. 40475. Tel: 859-623-9400. Brian Walsh, Campus Min. (Eastern Kentucky University, Newman Center).

SALYERSVILLE, MAGOFFIN CO., ST. LUKE (1982) Rev. Robert Damron.
1221 Parkway Dr., 41465. Tel: 606-349-5320. Email: stluke41465@hotmail.com. Mailing Address: P.O. Box 129, 41465.
Catechesis/Religious Program—Students 4.

SOMERSET, PULASKI CO., ST. MILDRED (1887) Rev. Michael J. Ramler; Deacons G. A. Weigel; Vincent E. Cheshire; Larry Cranfill.
203 S. Central Ave., 42501. Tel: 606-678-5051. Email: saintmildred@windstream.net. Web: somerset.cdlex.org.
Catechesis/Religious Program—Students 86.

STANTON, POWELL CO., OUR LADY OF THE MOUNTAINS (1984) Rev. Albert Fritsch, S.J.; Sr. Mary Jane Kreidler, Parish Life Dir.
1093 E. College Ave., P.O. Box 727, 40380-2354. Tel: 606-663-5919.
Catechesis/Religious Program—Fax: 606-663-5919. Students 18.

VERSAILLES, WOODFORD CO., ST. LEO (1891) Rev. Daniel J. Noll; Sr. Mary Ann Warner, H.M., Parish Life Dir.
Res. & Church: 295 Huntertown Rd., 40383. Tel: 859-879-8481; 859-873-4573 (Church); Fax: 859-873-1495 (Church). Email: stleo@cdlex.org. Web: versailles.cdlex.org.
School—(Grades K-8), 239 N. Main St., 40383. Tel: 606-873-4591. Email: stleoschool@catholicweb.com. Web: stleoschool.cdlex.org. Catherine Nuno, Prin. Lay Teachers 11; Students 154.
Catechesis/Religious Program—Pat Newell, D.R.E. Students 129.

WEST LIBERTY, MORGAN CO., PRINCE OF PEACE (1963) Rev. Mark D. Edelen.
Res.: Pine Acres Dr., P.O. Box 393, 41472. Tel: 606-743-3266.
Rectory—Tel: 606-743-4817.
Mission—St. Julie Catholic Church (1969) P.O. Box 382, Owingsville, Bath Co. 40360. Tel: 606-674-3261; 606-743-3266. Deacon William R. Grimes, D.R.E.

WHITLEY CITY, MCCREARY CO., GOOD SHEPHERD CHAPEL (1974) Rev. Michael J. Ramler; Sr. Nancy Sutton, Parish Life Dir.
Res.: 130 N. Main St., P.O. Box 427, 42653. Tel: 606-376-8728. Email: gshepherd31@gmail.com. Web: www.cdlex.org.
Catechesis/Religious Program—Students 1.

WILLIAMSBURG, WHITLEY CO., OUR LADY OF PERPETUAL HELP (1963) Rev. Peter Joseph, H.G.N.; Sr. Margaret Verhoff, C.D.P., Parish Life Dir.
Office: 76 W. Sycamore St., 40769. Tel: 606-549-2156. Email: olph.boniface@gmail.com. Web: williamsburg.cdlex.org.
Catechesis/Religious Program—Students 6.

WINCHESTER, CLARK CO., ST. JOSEPH (1872) Rev. Jacob Oravanamthadathil, H.G.N.; Deacon Anthony R. Fritz.
Office: 248 S. Main St., 40391.
Res.: 254 S. Main St., 40391. Tel: 859-744-4917; Fax: 859-744-0994. Email: stjoseph@cdlex.org.
School—St. Agatha Academy, (Grades K-8), 244 S. Main St., 40391. Tel: 859-744-6484; Fax: 859-744-0268. Email: stagatha@bellsouth.net. Christine Rickert, Prin. (Montessori) Lay Teachers 17; Students 156.
Catechesis/Religious Program—Rose Watt, D.R.E. Students 40.

Chaplains of Public Institutions

LEXINGTON. *Federal Medical Center*, 3301 Leestown Rd., 40507. Vacant.
Veterans' Administration Hospital, Leestown Pk., 40511. Tel: 859-233-4511. Rev. W. Henry Kenney, S.J., Chap.

ASHLAND. *Federal Correctional Institution.*
900 Winchester Dr., 41101-7497. Rev. John P. Noe, Chap.

MANCHESTER. *Federal Correction Institute*. Vacant.

Special Assignment:
Revs.—
Aduaka, Anthony, (On Duty Outside of Diocese)
Fedders, William, (On Administrative Leave)
Fitzsimons, Patrick, (On Administrative Leave)
Johnson, Carl, Allenwood Correctional Complex, Allenwood, PA
Kenney, Henry, S.J. (Retired), Spiritual Dir., Lexington, KY.
Molina, Arturo, (On Duty Outside of Diocese)
Muench, Joseph N., (On Administrative Leave)
Sichko, James W., Asst. to the Bishop, Special Projects

Retired:
Rev. Msgr.—
Rolf, John J., 15 Lemans Dr., Naples, FL 34112.
Revs.—
Dane, John, 193 Barnsley Rd., Wombwell, Barnsley, South Yorkshire S73 8DR, England.
Hehman, Lawrence W., 1332 Viley Rd., 40504.
Imfeld, Thomas J., 200 Red Oak St., Corbin, 40702.
Keller, Theodore A., 153 Barr St., 40507.
McDonald, Charles J., 2725 Bay Cedar Cove, 40511.
Nieberding, Robert, 2716 Green Vally Ct., 40511.
Osburg, Frank C., 2717 Bay Cedar Cove, 40511.
Poole, William G., 2724 Green Valley Ct., 40511.
Stratman, Raymond, 2720 Green Valley Ct., 40511.
Thai, Thomas V., Ph.D., 4698 Long Dr., Hamilton, OH 45011.

Permanent Deacons:
Abbey, Richard L.
Agnoli, Frank
Alessio, Joseph J.
Bennett, James D.

Boduch, Robert
Brown, David
Buelterman, William
Burns, Michael
Calandrella, John
Cheshire, Vincent
Coe, John C.
Coriale, Matthew C.
Cox, James H.
Cranfill, Larry
Daukas, Michael R.
Downey, Richard C.
Flowers, Don K.
Fritz, Anthony R.
Fugazzi, Frederick E., Jr.
Greenwell, William
Grimes, William R.
Horine, James
Jahnige, Ralph B.
Joice, Robert S.
Keller, William F.
Kotzbauer, Robert N.
Lackney, Robert R.
Lewis, John M.
Maher, Robert J.
Marshall, Boyd, (Retired)
Martorano, Raymond D.
Mellenger, Karl, (Retired)
Noe, Jeremiah
O'Neil, Dennis J., (Retired)
Olson, Paul E.
Ouellette, Guy R.
Paris, Jim
Rich, Robert M.
Rohan, Thomas, (Retired)
Rood, William A.
Root, Paul S.
Ross, Carter, Jr., (Retired)
Rupinen, Michael
Schueneman, Joseph T., (Retired)
Snyder, Thomas, (Retired)
Strauffer, Mark B.
Wagner, Thomas
Wakefield, Bill
Waken, Thomas J.
Watson, Richard
Weathers, James
Weigel, Gerard A.
Weinmann, Timothy E.
Woelfel, Mark T.
Wolterman, Arden J.
Young, Melvin
Zeigler, John F.

PARISH PILGRIMAGE SHRINES

CARLISLE. *Our Lady of Guadalupe Shrine*, 617 E. Main St., 40311.

INSTITUTIONS LOCATED IN THE DIOCESE

[A] HIGH SCHOOLS, DIOCESAN

LEXINGTON. *Lexington Catholic High School*, 2250 Clays Mill Rd., 40503. Tel: 859-277-7183; Fax: 859-276-5086. Web: www.lexingtoncatholic.com. Dr. Steven Angelucci, Pres.; Mrs. Sally Stevens, Prin.; Karen McDavid, Librarian. Lay Teachers 68; Students 841.

[B] HIGH SCHOOLS, PRIVATE

MARTIN. *The Piarist School* (1990) Rte. 80, P.O. Box 870, 41649. Tel: 606-285-3950; Fax: 606-285-3950. Email: piarist@bellsouth.net. Web: www.geocities.com/piarist. Rev. Thomas R. Carroll, Sch.P., Prin. College Prep High School. Priests 2; Lay Teachers 9; Students 70.

[C] ELEMENTARY SCHOOLS, PRIVATE

CORBIN. *St. Camillus Academy* (1914) (Grades PreK-8), 709 Roy Kidd Ave., 40701. Tel: 606-528-5077; Fax: 606-526-0106. Email: stcam@bellsouth.net. Web: homeforangels.org. Ms. Patty Beckert, Prin. Sisters of Divine Providence of KY., Coed Day School. Sisters 4; Lay Teachers 8; Students 160.

[D] GENERAL HOSPITALS

LEXINGTON. *Continuing Care Hospital, Inc.* (2001) 150 N. Eagle Creek Dr., 40509. Tel: 859-967-5744; Fax: 859-967-5616. Email: willto@sje.sjhlex.org. Tonja Williams, Pres. & CEO.

St. Joseph Health Care, Inc. dba St. Joseph East 150 N. Eagle Creek Dr., 40509. Tel: 859-967-5000; Fax: 859-967-5766. Web: www.saintjosephhealthcare.org. Gene Woods, Pres. & CEO. Bed Capacity 166; Patients Assisted Annually 28,702.

St. Joseph Hospital, One St. Joseph Dr., 40504. Tel: 859-313-1000; Fax: 859-313-3000. Gene Woods, Pres. & CEO. (Member of Catholic Health Initiatives). Sisters of Charity of Nazareth 1; Sister Servants of the Immaculate Heart of Mary 1; Bed Capacity 445; Patients Assisted Annually 75,000.

ASHLAND. *Our Lady of Bellefonte Hospital, Inc.*, St. Christopher Dr., 41101. Tel: 606-833-3333; Fax: 606-833-3593. Web: www.careyoucantrust.com. Kevin Halter, Interim CEO; Sharon McDonald, Pastoral Care; Revs. John P. Noe, Chap.; Martha H Rucker, B.C.C., Chap.; Sandy Adams, PRN Chap. (Member of Bon Secours Kentucky Health System, Inc.) Bed Capacity 214; Patients Assisted Annually 206,904.

BEREA. *Saint Joseph-Berea*, 305 Estill St., 40403. Tel: 859-986-3151; Fax: 859-986-6768. Email: greggerard@catholichealth.net. A member of Catholic Health Initiatives. Bed Capacity 25.

IRVINE. *Marcum and Wallace Memorial Hospital*, 60 Mercy Ct., 40336. Tel: 606-723-2115; Fax: 606-723-2951. Email: sstarling@marcumandwallace.org. Web: www.marcumandwallace.org. Susan Starling, Pres. & CEO. (Member of Mercy Health System, Cincinnati, OH). Bed Capacity 25; Patients Assisted Annually 53,354.

LONDON. *Saint Joseph-London*, 310 E. Ninth St., 40741. Tel: 606-878-6520; Fax: 606-878-4319. Email: vbdempsey@sj-london.org. Web: saintjoseph-london.org. Virginia B. Dempsey, Pres. (Member of Catholic Health Initiatives). Bed Capacity 89; Patients Assisted Annually 139,262.

MARTIN. *Saint Joseph-Martin*, Box 910, 41649. Tel: 606-285-6400; Fax: 606-285-6422. Email: jparsons@sj-martin.org. Web: www.saintjoseph-martin.org. Ms. Kathy Stumbo, Pres. Member of Catholic Health Initiatives. Bed Capacity 25; Patients Assisted Annually (Patient Visits) 57,538.

MOREHEAD. *Saint Claire Regional Medical Center* 40351. Tel: 606-783-6500; Fax: 606-783-6503. Email: mjneff@st-claire.org. Web: st-claire.org. Mr. Mark Neff, Pres. & CEO. Sisters of Notre Dame. Sisters 5; Bed Capacity 159; Bassinets 10; Patients Assisted Annually 342,881; Patients with Primary Care Centers 76,230.

MT. STERLING. *St. Joseph Hospital Mt. Sterling*, 50 Sterling, 40353. Tel: 859-497-7701. Email: bak@flaget.com. Mr. Bruce A. Klockars, Pres. Bed Capacity 63.

[E] PRIMARY HEALTH CARE SERVICES

FRENCHBURG. *St. Claire Regional Family Medicine-Frenchburg*, 732 Hwy. 36, 40322. Tel: 606-768-2191; Fax: 606-768-6130. Email: mjgulley@st-claire.org. Web: st-claire.org. Rachel Short, M.D., Medical Dir. (Div. of St. Claire Regional Medical Center). Patients Assisted Annually 10,000.

OLIVE HILL. *St. Claire Regional Family Medicine-Olive Hill*, 155 Bricklayer St., P.O. Box 1268, 41164. Tel: 606-286-4152; Fax: 606-286-2385. Janie Zornes, Clinic Coord. (Div. of St. Claire Medical Center). Patients Assisted Annually 15,000.

OWINGSVILLE. *St. Claire Regional Family Medicine - Owingsville*, 632 Slate Ave., P.O. Box 1120, 40360. Tel: 606-674-6386; Fax: 606-674-3096. Levonda Thomas, Clinic Coord. (Div. of St. Claire Medical Center). Patients Assisted Annually 14,500.

SANDY HOOK. *St. Claire Regional Family Medicine-Sandy Hook*, P.O. Box 748, 41171. Tel: 606-738-5155; Fax: 606-738-5420. Amy Conley, M.D., Clinic Medical Dir. (Div. of St. Claire Medical Center). Patients Assisted Annually 14,000.

[F] NURSING HOMES

VERSAILLES. *Taylor Manor Nursing Home*, 300 Berry Ave., 40383. Tel: 859-873-4201; Fax: 859-873-4856. Email: tmnh1958@msn.com. Sr. Mary Christina Murray, S.J.W., Admin. Sisters of St. Joseph the Worker 8; Patients Assisted Annually 209.

[G] RESIDENCES OF PRIESTS

PRESTONSBURG. *Piarist Fathers* (1989) P.O. Box 870, Martin, 41649. Tel: 606-285-3950; Fax: 606-285-3950. Rev. Thomas R. Carroll, Sch.P. Priests 2.

[H] MONASTERIES FOR SISTERS

MARTIN. *Mt. Tabor Benedictines-The Dwelling Place Monastery* (1982) 150 Mt. Tabor Rd., 41649. Tel: 606-886-9624; Fax: 606-886-9624. Email: mtabor150@hotmail.com. Web: www.geocities.com/athens/9871. Sr. Judy Yunker, O.S.B., Prioress. Total number in Community (Perpetually Professed) 5.

[I] SECULAR INSTITUTES

LEXINGTON. *Society of St. Vincent de Paul*, 1730 Summerhill Dr., 40515. Tel: 859-266-8003. Email: svdp_seas@hotmail.com. Tim Lewis, Pres. District Council of Lexington.

[J] SOCIAL SERVICES

MOUNT VERNON. **Appalachia Science in the Public Interest*, 50 Lair St., 40456. Tel: 606-256-0077; Fax: 606-256-2779. Email: aspi@a-spi.org. Web: www.a-spi.org. Rev. John L. Kieffer, S.J.

[K] RENEWAL CENTERS

HAZARD. *Father Farrell Spiritual Life Center*, 329 Poplar at Cedar, 41701. Tel: 606-436-2533; Fax: 606-435-0171. Email: mike.chowning@mgccc.org. Rev. Michael Chowning, O.F.M., Dir.; Pat Riestenberg, Assoc. Dir.

LANCASTER. *Cliffview Retreat Center*, 789 Bryants Camp Rd., 40444. Tel: 859-792-3333; 877-792-3330; Fax: 859-792-1223. Email: cliffctr@cdlex.org. Web: www.cliffview.org. David Wells, Co-Dir.; Sharla Wells, Co-Dir.

MARTIN. *Mt. Tabor Retreat Center*, 150 Mt. Tabor Rd., 41649. Tel: 606-886-9624; Fax: 606-886-7070. Email: mtabor150@hotmail.com. Staff Sisters 5.

[L] NEWMAN CENTERS

LEXINGTON. *The Newman Center Holy Spirit Parish University of Kentucky* 320 Rose Ln., 40508. Tel: 859-255-8566; Fax: 859-254-7519. Email: timenewman@aol.com. Revs. Albert J. DeGiacomo; Emmanuel F. Zamora.

BARBOURVILLE. *St. Gregory Church-Union College* 329 N. Sycamore St., 40906-1540. Tel: 606-546-4461; Fax: 606-546-4461. Email: stgreg@barbourville.com. Web: barbourville.catholicweb.com. Rev. Peter Joseph, H.G.N.

BEREA. *St. Clare Church-Berea College* 711 Chestnut St., Ste. 3, 40403. Tel: 859-986-4633; Fax: 859-756-3408. Email: stclare@cdlex.org. Rev. Frank Brawner; Sr. Theresa Bowman, C.D.P., Campus Min.

MOREHEAD. *Catholic Student Center-Morehead State University* P.O. Box 307, 40351. Tel: 606-784-4392; Fax: 606-783-0190. Email: joscc@roadrunner.com. Web: www.cdlex.org/morehead. Rev. Paul Prabell.

RICHMOND. *St. Stephen Newman Center-St. Mark Church* Eastern Kentucky University, 405 University Dr., 40475-2154. Tel: 859-623-2989 (Center); Fax: 859-623-4652. Email: ekunewman@kih.net. Web: stmark-richmond.org/newman. Revs. James W. Sichko; P. Brian Walsh, Campus Min.

[M] MISCELLANEOUS

LEXINGTON. *Catholic Way Bible Study*, P.O. Box 22324, 40522-2324. Email: teachingleader@cwbs.org. Web: www.cwbs.org. Lavinia Spirito, Teaching Leader.

ASHLAND. *Bon Secours Kentucky Health System Foundation, Inc. dba Our Lady of Bellefonte Hospital Foundation* 1000 St. Christopher Dr., 41101. Tel: 606-833-3333. Web: www.careyoucantrust.com. Mr. Chuck Charles, Vice Pres., Foundation.

Bon Secours Kentucky Health System, Inc., St. Christopher Dr., 41101. Tel: 606-833-3333. Web: www.careyoucantrust.com. Kevin Halter, Int. CEO.

IRVINE. *Marcum & Wallace Memorial Hospital Foundation Inc.*, 60 Mercy Ct., 40336. Tel: 606-723-2115, Ext. 152; Fax: 606-723-2951. Email: sstarling@marcumandwallace.org. Web: www.marcumandwallace.org.

MIDDLESBORO. *Herald of Good News Missionary Society, Inc.* (2004) 118 E. Chester Ave., 40965. Tel: 606-248-2068; Fax: 606-248-2207. Rev. Chinnappan Amalanathan, H.G.N., Dir. & Contact Person. Priests 17.

STANTON. *The Catholic Committee of Appalachia* (1970) 150 Mt. Tabor Rd., Martin, 41649. Tel: 606-886-9624. Email: janibosb@hotmail.com. Rev. John Rausch, G.H.M., Dir.

RELIGIOUS INSTITUTES OF MEN REPRESENTED IN THE DIOCESE

For further details refer to the corresponding bracketed number in the Religious Institutes of Men or Women section.

[0820]—*Congregation of the Fathers of Mercy*—C.P.M.

[0520]—*Franciscan Friars* (St. John Baptist Prov.)—O.F.M.

[0570]—*Glenmary Home Missioners*—G.H.M.

[0585]—*Heralds of Good News* (India)—H.G.N.

[0690]—*Jesuit Fathers and Brothers* (Chicago & Detroit Provs.)—S.J.

[1040]—*Piarist Fathers* (U.S. Prov.)—Sch.P.

RELIGIOUS INSTITUTES OF WOMEN REPRESENTED IN THE DIOCESE

[0230]—*Benedictine Sisters of Pontifical Jurisdiction* (Pittsburgh, PA; Covington, KY; Martin, KY)—O.S.B.

[2100]—*Congregation of Humility of Mary*—C.H.M.

[2230]—*Congregation of the Infant Jesus*—C.I.J.

[3832]—*Congregation of the Sisters of St. Joseph*—C.S.J.

[1920]—*Congregation of the Sisters of the Holy Cross*—C.S.C.

[1730]—*Congregation of the Sisters of the Third Order of St. Francis* (Oldenburg, IN)—O.S.F.

[1070-13]—*Dominican Sisters* (Adrian, MI)—O.P.

[1070-14]—*Dominican Sisters* (Grand Rapids, MI)—O.P.

[2080]—*Home Mission Sisters of America (Glenmary)*—G.H.M.S.

[2710]—*Missionaries of Charity*—M.C.

[2850]—*Missionary Sisters of the Precious Blood*—C.P.S.

[2070]—*Religious of the Holy Union of the Sacred Hearts*—S.U.S.C.

[2970]—*School Sisters of Notre Dame* (Baltimore)—S.S.N.D.

[1680]—*School Sisters of St. Francis*—O.S.F.

[0430]—*Sisters of Charity of Blessed Virgin Mary* (Dubuque, IA)—B.V.M.

[0440]—*Sisters of Charity of Cincinnati, OH*—S.C.

[0500]—*Sisters of Charity of Nazareth*—S.C.N.

[0580]—*Sisters of Charity of St. Augustine* (Rienfield, OH)—C.S.A.

[1000]—*The Sisters of Divine Providence of Kentucky*—C.D.P.

[2990]—*Sisters of Notre Dame* (Covington Prov.)—S.N.D.

[3360]—*Sisters of Providence of St. Mary-of-the-Woods, Indiana*—S.P.

[3893]—*Sisters of Saint Joseph of Chestnut Hill, Philadelphia*—S.S.J.

[1540]—*Sisters of St Francis* (Clinton, IA)—O.S.F.

[3830-05]—*Sisters of St. Joseph* (Brentwood, NY)—C.S.J.

[3850]—*Sisters of St. Joseph of Chambery*—C.S.J.

[3920]—*Sisters of St. Joseph the Worker*—S.J.W.

[2110]—*Sisters of the Humility of Mary* (Villa Maria, PA)—H.M.

[1760]—*Sisters of the Third Order of St. Francis of Penance and Charity* (Tiffin, OH)—O.S.F.

[2150]—*Sisters, Servants of the Immaculate Heart of Mary*—I.H.M.

[4120-04]—*Ursuline Sisters of the Immaculate Conception* (Cleveland, OH)—O.S.U.

DIOCESAN CEMETERIES

LEXINGTON. *Calvary*

ASHLAND. *Calvary*

MT. STERLING. *St. Thomas*

NECROLOGY

(No Deaths)

An asterisk (*) denotes an organization that has established tax-exempt status directly with the IRS and is not covered by the USCCB Group Ruling.

Diocese of Lincoln

(Dioecesis Lincolnensis)

Most Reverend

FABIAN W. BRUSKEWITZ, D.D., S.T.D.

Bishop of Lincoln; ordained July 17, 1960; appointed Bishop of Lincoln March 24, 1992; consecrated May 13, 1992. *Mailing Address: P.O. Box 80328, Lincoln, NE 68501-0328.*

Chancery: P.O. Box 80328, Lincoln, NE 68501-0328. Tel: 402-488-0921; Fax: 402-488-3569.

ERECTED AUGUST 2, 1887.

Square Miles 23,844.

Comprises that part of the State of Nebraska south of the Platte River.

Legal Title: "The Catholic Bishop of Lincoln." For legal titles of parishes and diocesan institutions, consult the Chancery.

STATISTICAL OVERVIEW

Personnel	
Bishop	1
Priests: Diocesan Active in Diocese	121
Priests: Diocesan Active Outside Diocese	6
Priests: Retired, Sick or Absent	25
Number of Diocesan Priests	152
Religious Priests in Diocese	10
Total Priests in Diocese	162
Extern Priests in Diocese	3
Ordinations:	
Diocesan Priests	4
Religious Priests	3
Transitional Deacons	4
Permanent Deacons in Diocese	3
Total Sisters	137
Parishes	
Parishes	133
With Resident Pastor:	
Resident Diocesan Priests	82
Resident Religious Priests	1
Without Resident Pastor:	
Administered by Priests	50
Missions	1
Pastoral Centers	5
Closed Parishes	1
Professional Ministry Personnel:	
Sisters	137
Lay Ministers	2
Welfare	
Catholic Hospitals	3
Total Assisted	218,396
Homes for the Aged	3
Total Assisted	256
Day Care Centers	1
Total Assisted	29
Special Centers for Social Services	21
Total Assisted	26,748
Residential Care of Disabled	1
Total Assisted	13
Other Institutions	1
Total Assisted	3,229
Educational	
Seminaries, Diocesan	1
Students from This Diocese	29
Students from Other Diocese	14
Diocesan Students in Other Seminaries	14
Seminaries, Religious	1
Students Religious	75
Total Seminarians	118
High Schools, Diocesan and Parish	6
Total Students	1,764
Elementary Schools, Diocesan and Parish	25
Total Students	5,302
Non-residential Schools for the Disabled	1
Total Students	13
Catechesis/Religious Education:	
High School Students	1,941
Elementary Students	5,019
Total Students under Catholic Instruction	14,157
Teachers in the Diocese:	
Priests	30
Sisters	38
Lay Teachers	442
Vital Statistics	
Receptions into the Church:	
Infant Baptism Totals	1,088
Minor Baptism Totals	187
Adult Baptism Totals	121
Received into Full Communion	148
First Communions	1,487
Confirmations	1,526
Marriages:	
Catholic	263
Interfaith	182
Total Marriages	445
Deaths	677
Total Catholic Population	95,445
Total Population	580,275

Former Bishops—Most Revs. THOMAS BONACUM, D.D., Bishop of Lincoln; cons. Nov. 20, 1887; died Feb. 4, 1911; J. HENRY TIHEN, D.D., cons. Bishop of Lincoln, July 6, 1911; transferred to the See of Denver, Sept. 21, 1917; died Jan. 14, 1940; CHARLES J. O'REILLY, D.D., cons. Bishop of Baker City, Aug. 24, 1903; transferred to the See of Lincoln, March 20, 1918; died Feb. 4, 1923; FRANCIS J. L. BECKMAN, S.T.D., D.D., cons. Bishop of Lincoln, May 1, 1924; elevated to the Metropolitan See of Dubuque, Jan. 17, 1930; died Oct. 17, 1948; LOUIS B. KUCERA, D.D., cons. Bishop of Lincoln, Oct. 28, 1930; died May 9, 1957; JAMES V. CASEY, appt. Auxiliary of Lincoln April 5, 1957; cons. April 24, 1957; appt. Bishop of Lincoln June 14, 1957; promoted to Archbishop of Denver, Feb. 22, 1967; died March 14, 1986; GLENNON P. FLAVIN, D.D., appt. Titular Bishop of Joannina and Auxiliary Bishop of St. Louis April 24, 1957; cons. May 30, 1957; promoted to See of Lincoln, May 29, 1967; retired March 24, 1992; died Aug. 27, 1995.

Chancery—3400 Sheridan Blvd., Lincoln, 68506. Mailing Address: P.O. Box 80328, Lincoln, 68501-0328. Tel: 402-488-0921; Fax: 402-488-3569. Office Hours: 8:30-5.

Moderator of the Curia—Rev. Msgr. TIMOTHY J. THORBURN, J.C.L.

Vicar General—Rev. Msgr. TIMOTHY J. THORBURN, J.C.L.

Chancellor—Rev. DANIEL J. RAYER, J.C.L.

Diocesan Tribunal—3400 Sheridan Blvd., Lincoln, 68506. Mailing Address: P.O. Box 80328, Lincoln, 68501-0328.

Officialis—Rev. Msgr. MARK D. HUBER, J.C.L.

Adjutant Judicial Vicars—Revs. MAURICE H. CURRENT, J.C.L.; CRAIG A. DOTY, J.C.L.

Promoters Justitiae—Rev. Msgr. TIMOTHY J. THORBURN, J.C.L.; Rev. GARY COULTER, J.C.L.; Rev. Msgr. DANIEL J. SEIKER, J.C.L.

Defensores Vinculi—Rev. Msgr. TIMOTHY J. THORBURN, J.C.L.; Rev. GARY COULTER, J.C.L.

Judge—Rev. DANIEL J. RAYER, J.C.L.

Advocates—Very Rev. THOMAS Y. AU; Revs. THOMAS D. MCGUIRE; MICHAEL J. MORIN; RAFAEL RODRIGUEZ-FUENTES; BENJAMIN P. HOLDREN; CHRISTOPHER J. MILLER; MICHAEL K. HOULIHAN; JAMES W. COOPER; ANDREW J. KURZ; JOSEPH J. FAULKNER; SEAN P. KILCAWLEY; BRENDAN R.J. KELLY; ANTHONY O. STAMMITTI; DAVID F. BOUREK; THOMAS M. BUSH; ANDREW V. MENKE; SCOTT M. COURTNEY; RAMON E. DECAEN; MATTHEW J. VANDEWALLE; JEREL A. SCHOLL; JAMIE S. HOTTOVY; THOMAS S. MACLEAN; JOSEPH C. BERNARDO; DAVID A. OLDHAM; SEAN M. TIMMERMAN; JAY M. BUHMAN; MARK L. CYZA; CHRISTOPHER P. GOODWIN; PAUL G. FRANK; LEE T. JIROVSKY; NICHOLAS A. KIPPER; LOTHAR M. GILDE; JONATHAN J. HASCHKE; ANDREW J. HEASLIP; DOMINIC T.H. PHAN; STEVEN SNITILY.

Notaries—Rev. Msgr. JOHN T. FOLDA; Rev. CHRISTOPHER L. BARAK; Sr. COLLETTE BRUSKEWITZ, O.S.F.; Mrs. MARILYN L. FRIESEN.

Diocesan Consultors—Rev. Msgr. TIMOTHY J. THORBURN, J.C.L.; Revs. DANIEL J. RAYER, J.C.L.; MARK L. CYZA; THOMAS S. BROUILLETTE; Rev. Msgr. JOHN J PERKINTON; Rev. HARLAN D. P. WASKOWIAK; Rev. Msgr. MARK D. HUBER, J.C.L.; Rev. ROBERT A. MATYA.

Presbyteral Council—Rev. Msgrs. TIMOTHY J. THORBURN, J.C.L.; MYRON J. PLESKAC; Revs. JAMES W. COOPER; THOMAS D. MCGUIRE; THOMAS KUFFEL; THOMAS BROUILLETTE; MARK L. CYZA; ROBERT FROMAGEOT, F.S.S.P.; BRIAN P. KANE; HARLAN D. P. WASKOWIAK; Rev. Msgr. JOHN J PERKINTON; Revs. RAYMOND L. JANSEN; DANIEL J. RAYER, J.C.L.; Rev. Msgr. MARK D. HUBER, J.C.L.; Rev. ROBERT A. MATYA.

Vicars For Religious—Rev. Msgrs. JOHN T. FOLDA; DANIEL J. SEIKER, J.C.L.

Deaneries and Deans—Rev. Msgr. MYRON J. PLESKAC, Crete; Very Revs. JOHN C. ROONEY, V.F., David City; RUDOLF F. OBORNY, V.F., Fairbury; Rev. Msgr. ROBERT A. ROH, V.F., M.A., S.T.L., Falls City; Very Revs. MARK E. SEIKER, M.Div., Indianola; VALERIAN BARTEK, Grant; THOMAS Y. AU, Hastings; JAMES C. SCHRADER JR., V.F., Lawrence; Rev. Msgr. LIAM M. BARR, Lincoln; Very Rev. NICHOLAS J. BAKER, V.F., Orleans; Rev. Msgrs. PAUL K. WITT, V.F., Plattsmouth; DANIEL J. SEIKER, J.C.L., Wahoo; Very Rev. M. JAMES DIVIS, S.T.L., V.F., York.

Diocesan Offices and Directors

Apostleship of Prayer—Rev. MICHAEL J. MORIN, Dir.

Apostolate to the Elderly—Rev. ANTHONY O. STAMMITTI, Asst.

Apostolate to the Spanish Speaking—Revs. JOHN J. KEEFE, Dir.; BERNARD A. LORENZ, Asst. Dir.; THOMAS B. DUNAVAN; JAMES BENTON; JULIUS TVRDY; MARK L. CYZA; WILLIAM D. GRANT; RAMON E. DECAEN.

Apostolate of Suffering—Rev. CHRISTOPHER K. KUBAT, 3700 Sheridan Blvd., Lincoln, 68506. Tel: 402-489-1834; Fax: 402-489-2046.

Archivist—Sr. KATHRYN MANEY, M.S.

Bishop's Lay Committee for Vocations—Rev. ROBERT A. MATYA, Chap.

Bishop's Pastoral Plan for Pro-Life Activities—GREG SCHLEPPENBACH, State Dir., 215 Centennial Mall S., Ste. 310, Lincoln, 68508.

Building Commission—Rev. Msgrs. JOHN J PERKINTON, Chm.; ADRIAN F. HERBEK, V.F. (Retired); IVAN F. VAP (Retired); TIMOTHY J. THORBURN, J.C.L.; Rev. LEO V. SEIKER; Rev. Msgr. MARK D. HUBER, J.C.L.; Revs. JAMIE S. HOTTOVY; THOMAS S. MACLEAN; Very Rev. JOHN C. ROONEY, V.F.

Catholic Relief Services—Rev. DANIEL J. RAYER, J.C.L., Dir.

Cemeteries—Rev. Msgr. DAVID R. HINTZ, Dir.

Censores Librorum—Very Rev. M. JAMES DIVIS, S.T.L., V.F.; Rev. Msgrs. JOHN T. FOLDA; TIMOTHY J. THORBURN, J.C.L.

Catholic Social Services—Rev. CHRISTOPHER K. KUBAT, Dir., Catholic Social Services: Pregnancy & Counseling Services, 3700 Sheridan Blvd., Lincoln, 68506. Tel: 402-489-1834. Administrative, Food Pantry, Housing Refugee & Emergency Services, 2241 O St., Lincoln, 68510. Tel: 402-474-1600. Email: curtkrueger@csshope.org; Catholic Social Services, 515 W. 3rd St., Hastings, 68901. Tel: 402-463-2112. Counseling Services, 229 N. St. Joseph Ave., Hastings, 68901. Tel: 402-463-1119. Email: pgibson@csshope.org; Catholic Social Services, 1014 Central Ave., Auburn, 68305. Tel: 402-274-4818.

Clergy Relief Society--The Saint John Vianney Association—Rev. Msgr. TIMOTHY J. THORBURN, J.C.L., Sec. & Treas., Mailing Address: P.O. Box 80328, Lincoln, 68501-0328.

Commission on Alcohol and Drug Abuse—Very Revs. M. JAMES DIVIS, S.T.L., V.F., Dir.; JOHN C. ROONEY, V.F., 3400 Sheridan Blvd., Lincoln, 68506. Tel: 402-483-1941.

Commission for Sacred Liturgy and Sacred Music—Rev. Msgr. JOSEPH J. NEMEC, Chm.; Revs. CHRISTOPHER L. BARAK; ROBERT K. BARNHILL; MAURICE H. CURRENT, J.C.L.; LAWRENCE STOLEY; MATTHEW EICKHOFF; LEO D. KOSCH; ANDREW V. MENKE; Sr. COLLETTE BRUSKEWITZ, O.S.F.

Catholic Lawyers Guild—Rev. Msgr. DANIEL J. SEIKER, J.C.L., Spiritual Dir.

Catholic Planned Giving Office—Mr. MICHAEL L. HENKENIUS, Dir., Mailing Address: P.O. Box 80328, Lincoln, 68501-0328. Tel: 402-488-2142.

Catholic Physicians Guild—Rev. Msgr. JOHN T. FOLDA, Spiritual Dir., 800 Fletcher Rd., Seward, 68434-7541. Tel: 402-643-4052.

Office of Religious Education (CCD)—Rev. CHRISTOPHER L. BARAK, Diocesan Dir. Tel: 402-488-2040. Diocesan Area CCD Directors: Very Revs. THOMAS Y. AU; NICHOLAS J. BAKER, V.F.; Revs. LORAS K. GRELL; JAMIE S. HOTTOVY; THOMAS KUFFEL; THOMAS D. MCGUIRE; MICHAEL J. MORIN; Very Rev. RUDOLF F. OBORNY, V.F.; Revs. SEAN M. TIMMERMAN; MICHAEL S. STEC; RAMON E. DECAEN.

Cursillo—Very Rev. MARK E. SEIKER, M.Div., Dir.; MARK PRIBYL, Asst.

Deaf Ministry—Revs. ROBERT K. BARNHILL, Dir. Tel: 402-488-2040 (TTY); MICHAEL S. STEC, Asst. Dir.

Diocesan Council of Catholic Women—Mrs. KATHERINE BROZ; Revs. THOMAS J. LUX, Moderator; THOMAS D. MCGUIRE, Asst. Moderator.

Diocesan Director of Liturgy—Rev. Msgr. JOSEPH J. NEMEC, 735 S. 36th St., Lincoln, 68510.

Bishop Bruskewitz Charity and Stewardship Appeal (DDP)—Rev. KENNETH A. BOROWIAK, Dir., Mailing Address: P.O. Box 80328, Lincoln, 68501-0328.

Diocesan Finance Council—Most Rev. FABIAN WENDELIN BRUSKEWITZ, D.D., S.T.D.; Rev. Msgr. TIMOTHY J. THORBURN, J.C.L.; Rev. JOHN R. SULLIVAN, Finance Officer. Members: Rev. Msgrs. ADRIAN F. HERBEK, V.F. (Retired); JOHN T. FOLDA; Rev. MICHAEL G. MCCABE.

Diocesan Health Ministries, Inc.—Most Rev. FABIAN WENDELIN BRUSKEWITZ, D.D., S.T.D., Pres.; Rev. Msgrs. TIMOTHY J. THORBURN, J.C.L., Vice Pres.; JOHN T. FOLDA, Sec., Mailing Address: P.O. Box 80328, Lincoln, 68501-0328. Tel: 402-488-0921; Fax: 402-488-3569.

Diocesan Housing Ministries, Inc.—Most Rev. FABIAN WENDELIN BRUSKEWITZ, D.D., S.T.D., Pres.; Rev. Msgrs. TIMOTHY J. THORBURN, J.C.L.; JOHN T. FOLDA; JOHN J PERKINTON; Revs. DANIEL J. RAYER, J.C.L.; CHRISTOPHER K. KUBAT, Mailing Address: P.O. Box 80328, Lincoln, 68501-0328. Tel: 402-488-0921.

Ecumenical Affairs, Commission for—Revs. PETER M. MITCHELL, Chm.; MATTHEW EICKHOFF; Very Rev. M. JAMES DIVIS, S.T.L., V.F., Chm.; Rev. Msgr. PAUL K. WITT, V.F.; Rev. MAURICE H. CURRENT, J.C.L.

Engaged Encounter—Rev. MATTHEW EICKHOFF.

Evangelization Office—Rev. MATTHEW EICKHOFF, Chm.

Evangelization Committee—Rev. MATTHEW EICKHOFF, Chm. Tel: 402-488-2040; Rev. Msgrs. TIMOTHY J. THORBURN, J.C.L.; MYRON J. PLESKAC; JAMES D. DAWSON (Retired); PAUL K. WITT, V.F.; Revs. CHRISTOPHER L. BARAK; WILLIAM D. GRANT; Rev. Msgr. JOSEPH J. NEMEC.

Family Life Office—Rev. MATTHEW EICKHOFF, Dir., Mailing Address: P.O. Box 80328, Lincoln, 68501-0328. Tel: 402-488-2040.

Holy Childhood, Pontifical Association—Rev. K. WILLIAM HOLOUBEK, Dir., Mailing Address: P.O. Box 80328, Lincoln, 68501-0328.

Health Care Facilities—Revs. STEPHEN A. COONEY, 5401 South St., Lincoln, 68506; EDWIN L. STANDER, Mailing Address, 555 S. 70th St., Lincoln, 68510; JOSEPH P. FINN; CASEY PORADA; ANTHONY O. STAMMITTI; THOMAS S. MACLEAN.

Office of Information and Media—Rev. KENNETH A. BOROWIAK, Dir., Mailing Address: P.O. Box 80329, Lincoln, 68501. Tel: 402-488-0090.

Insurance—Rev. Msgr. TIMOTHY J. THORBURN, J.C.L., Dir.; Mrs. MARSHA BARTEK, Mailing Address: P.O. Box 80328, Lincoln, 68501-0328.

Legion of Mary—Revs. PETER J. GADIENT, Spiritual Dir. (Retired); JEREMY L. HAZUKA, Asst. Spiritual Dir.; MARK L. CYZA; JOYCE RICHTER, Pres.

Liturgical Ministries—Rev. DANIEL J. RAYER, J.C.L.

Marriage Encounter—Rev. MATTHEW EICKHOFF, Dir.

Missionary Union of the Clergy—Rev. K. WILLIAM HOLOUBEK.

Natural Family Planning—Rev. MATTHEW EICKHOFF, Diocesan Dir.; MICHELLE CHAMBERS, Diocesan Coord. Tel: 402-488-2040.

Nebraska Catholic Conference—215 Centennial Mall S., Ste. 310, Lincoln, 68508-1813. JAMES R. CUNNINGHAM, Exec. Dir., 215 Centennial Mall S., Ste. 310, Lincoln, 68508. Tel: 402-477-7517; Fax: 402-477-1503.

Newman Center University of Nebraska—Rev. ROBERT A. MATYA, Chap., 320 N. 16th St., Lincoln, 68508. Tel: 402-474-7914.

Newspaper— "The Southern Nebraska Register" Revs. KENNETH A. BOROWIAK, Editor; NICHOLAS A. KIPPER, Asst. Editor, 3700 Sheridan Blvd., Lincoln, 68506. Tel: 402-488-0090. Mailing Address: P.O. Box 80329, Lincoln, 68501.

Office of Stewardship & Development—Rev. Msgr. LIAM M. BARR, Delegate; Mrs. JODY PAULSEN, Asst., Mailing Address: P.O. Box 80328, Lincoln, 68501. Tel: 402-488-0921; Fax: 402-488-3569.

Permanent Deacon Continuing Education Committee—Revs. DANIEL J. RAYER, J.C.L.; LEO V. SEIKER; DOUGLAS D. DIETRICH.

PREP—Rev. MATTHEW EICKHOFF.

Priests' Continuing Education Committee—Rev. Msgrs. MYRON J. PLESKAC; TIMOTHY J. THORBURN, J.C.L.; JOHN T. FOLDA; Revs. DANIEL J. RAYER, J.C.L.; CHRISTOPHER L. BARAK; MAURICE H. CURRENT, J.C.L.; Rev. Msgrs. JOHN J PERKINTON; DANIEL J. SEIKER, J.C.L.; MARK D. HUBER, J.C.L.; Revs. ROBERT A. MAYTA; JOHN R. SULLIVAN.

Pro Life—Revs. JEFFREY R. EICKHOFF, Dir.; LEO V. SEIKER, Asst. Dir.

Project Rachel—*Catholic Social Services*. Tel: 800-964-3787.

Propagation of the Faith—Rev. K. WILLIAM HOLOUBEK, Dir., Mailing Address: P.O. Box 80328, Lincoln, 68501-0328.

Retreat Program—Rev. LAWRENCE STOLEY, Dir., Our Lady of Good Counsel Retreat House. Tel: 402-786-2705.

Rural Life Conference—Rev. DAVID F. BOUREK, Mailing Address: P.O. Box 80328, Lincoln, 68501-0328. Tel: 402-488-0921.

Serra Club—Rev. ROBERT A. MATYA, Chap. & Spiritual Dir. Tel: 402-474-7914.

Schools—Rev. Msgr. JOHN J PERKINTON, Supt.; Rev. LAWRENCE STOLEY; Sr. COLLETTE, O.S.F., Asst. Supt., 3400 Sheridan Blvd., Lincoln, 68506. Mailing Address: P.O. Box 80328, Lincoln, 68501-0328.

Scouting—Rev. ROBERT K. BARNHILL.

Society of St. Vincent de Paul - Lincoln Council—Rev. THOMAS R. WALSH, Spiritual Advisor; Mr. RONALD LEE, Pres.; JOYCE BURGESS, Council Sec. & Res. Agent, Sacred Heart Church, 3128 S St., Lincoln, 68503. Tel: 402-476-2610.

Teens Encounter Christ (TEC)—Rev. MATTHEW EICKHOFF.

1962 Mass Apostolate—Rev. ROBERTO CANO, F.S.S.P., St. Francis of Assisi Church, 1145 South St., Lincoln, 68502. Tel: 402-477-5145.

Victim Assistance Coordinator—Rev. Msgr. DANIEL J. SEIKER, J.C.L. Tel: 402-784-2511.

Vocations—Revs. ROBERT A. MATYA, Dir.; BENJAMIN P. HOLDREN, Asst., St. Thomas Aquinas Church, 320 N. 16th St., Lincoln, 68508. Tel: 402-474-7914.

CLERGY, PARISHES, MISSIONS AND PAROCHIAL SCHOOLS

CITY OF LINCOLN

(LANCASTER COUNTY)

1—CATHEDRAL OF THE RISEN CHRIST (1932) [JC] Rev. Msgr. Robert G. Tucker; Rev. Jay M. Buhman. In Res., Rev. Andrew V. Menke.
Res.: 3500 Sheridan Blvd., 68506. Tel: 402-488-0948; Fax: 402-488-7895.
School—(Grades PreK-8) Tel: 402-489-9621. Lay Teachers 24; Students 378.
Catechesis/Religious Program—Students 113.

2—BISHOP BONACUM CHANCERY (1961) Rev. Msgr. Timothy J. Thorburn, Moderator of the Curia.
Res.: 3400 Sheridan Blvd., P.O. Box 80328, 68501. Tel: 402-488-0921; Fax: 402-488-3569.

3—BLESSED SACRAMENT (1922) [JC] Revs. John R. Sullivan; Brendan R.J. Kelly. In Res., Rev. Casey Porada.
Res.: 1720 Lake St., 68502. Tel: 402-474-4249; Fax: 402-474-4258.
School—(Grades PreK-8) Tel: 402-476-6202; Fax: 402-476-0232. Priests 2; Sisters 3; Lay Teachers 15; Students 213.
Catechesis/Religious Program—Students 77.

4—CRISTO REY (2002), (Hispanic), Revs. John J. Keefe; William David Grant.
4245 J St., 68510. Tel: 402-327-2170. In Res., Rev. Anthony O. Stammitti.
Catechesis/Religious Program—Students 310.

5—IMMACULATE HEART OF MARY (1979), (Vietnamese), Rev. Jim Ngo-Hoang Khoi, C.M.C. (Vietnam).
Res.: 6345 Madison Ave., 68507. Tel: 402-464-0111; Fax: 402-464-0111.
Catechesis/Religious Program—Students 176.

6—ST. JOHN THE APOSTLE (1959) [JC] Revs. Lyle Johnson; Lee T. Jirovsky.
Res.: 731 Skyway Rd., 68505. Tel: 402-489-1946; Fax: 402-489-2048. Email: stjohn@inebraska.com.
School—(Grades PreK-8) Tel: 402-486-1860; Fax: 402-486-4732. Lay Teachers 20; Students 278.
Catechesis/Religious Program—Students 196.

7—ST. JOSEPH (1976) [JC] Rev. Msgr. Liam M. Barr; Rev. Christopher J. Miller, Parochial Vicar. In Res., Rev. William David Grant.
Res.: 7900 Trendwood Dr., 68506. Tel: 402-483-2288; Fax: 402-483-2336. Web: www.stjosephlnk.org.
School—(Grades PreK-8), 1940 S. 77th St., 68506. Tel: 402-489-0341; Fax: 402-489-3260. Sisters 3; Lay Teachers 39; Students 583.
High School—Pius X High School, 6000 A St., 68510. Students 166.
Catechesis/Religious Program—Students 178.

8—ST. MARY (1867) [JC] Rev. Douglas D. Dietrich. In Res., Revs. Joseph P. Finn; Thomas S. MacLean.
Res.: 1420 K St., 68508. Tel: 402-435-2125. Web: www.stmarylincoln.org.
School—(Grades K-8) Tel: 402-476-3987; Fax: 402-476-0838. Lay Teachers 10; Students 144.
Catechesis/Religious Program—Students 16.

9—NORTH AMERICAN MARTYRS (1993) [JC] Revs. Brian P. Connor; Steven P. Snitily, Parochial Vicar.
Res.: 1101 Isaac Dr., 68521. Tel: 402-476-8088. Email: julie-crawford@cdolinc.net.
School—(Grades PreK-8), 1101 Issac Dr., 68521. Tel: 402-476-7373. Web: www.namartyrs.org. Sr. Patricia Heirigs, O.S.B., Prin. Priests 2; Sisters 4; Lay Teachers 20; Students 570.
Catechesis/Religious Program—Students 239.

10—ST. PATRICK'S (1893) [JC] Rev. Msgr. David R. Hintz; Rev. Nicholas A. Kipper. In Res., Rev. James J. Meysenburg.
Res.: 6126 Morrill Ave., P.O. Box 29106, 68507. Tel: 402-466-2752; Fax: 402-466-3572.
School—Tel: 402-466-3710; Fax: 402-466-3752. Marian Sisters (Waverly, NE) 3; Lay Teachers 12; Students 160.
Catechesis/Religious Program—Students 151.

11—ST. PETER (1990) [JC] Revs. Michael R. Christensen; Joseph J. Faulkner.
Res.: 4500 Duxhall Dr., 68516. Tel: 402-423-1239; Fax: 402-421-6507. Web: www.saintpeterslincoln.com.
School—(Grades PreK-8) Tel: 402-421-6299. Priests 2; School Sisters of Christ the King 3; Lay Teachers 25; Students 476.
Catechesis/Religious Program—Students 301.

12—SACRED HEART (1919) [JC] Rev. Thomas R. Walsh. In Res., Very Rev. John A. Cooper.
Res.: 3128 S St., 68503. Tel: 402-476-2610.
School—Tel: 402-476-1783; Fax: 402-476-3040. Sisters 2; Lay Teachers 12; Students 200.
Catechesis/Religious Program—Students 115.

13—ST. TERESA'S (1926) [JC] Rev. Msgr. Joseph J. Nemec; Rev. Jonathan J. Haschke, Parochial Vicar.

Res.: 735 S. 36th St., 68510. Tel: 402-477-3979.
School—(Grades PreK-8), 616 S. 36th St., 68510. Tel: 402-477-3358; Fax: 402-477-3361. Sisters 3; Lay Teachers 16; Students 311.
Catechesis/Religious Program—Students 75.
14—St. Thomas Aquinas (1958) [JC] Revs. Robert A. Matya; Benjamin P. Holdren.
Res.: 320 N. 16th St., 68508. Tel: 402-474-7914; Fax: 402-476-2620.

OUTSIDE THE CITY OF LINCOLN

Ashland, Saunders Co., St. Mary's (1900) Rev. Gary Coulter.
Res.: 1625 Adams St., 68003. Tel: 402-944-3554; Fax: 402-944-3554. Email: stmaryashland@alltel.net.
Catechesis/Religious Program—Students 85.
Mission—St. Joseph's Greenwood, Cass Co.

Auburn, Nemaha Co., St. Joseph's (1881) [CEM] Rev. Gregory P. Pawloski.
Res.: 1306 23rd St., P.O. Box 406, 68305. Tel: 402-274-3733; Fax: 402-274-3733. Email: stjoseph@windstream.net.
Catechesis/Religious Program—Students 111.
Mission—St. Clara Peru, Nemaha Co.

Aurora, Hamilton Co., St. Mary's (1888) Rev. Dennis M. Hunt.
Res.: 1419 10th St., P.O. Box 291, 68818. Tel: 402-694-3427; Fax: 402-694-2455. Email: stmarys@hamilton.net.
Catechesis/Religious Program—Students 145.
Mission—St. Joseph's [CEM] Giltner, Hamilton Co.

Beatrice, Gage Co., St. Joseph's (1869) [CEM] Rev. Steven P. Major.
Res.: 612 High St., 68310. Tel: 402-223-2923.
School—Tel: 402-223-5033. Lay Teachers 9; Students 90.
Catechesis/Religious Program—Students 218.

Beaver Crossing, Seward Co., Sacred Heart (1890) Rev. Maurice H. Current.
Res.: 401 Dimery, P.O. Box 208, 68313. Tel: 402-532-2545.
Catechesis/Religious Program—Students 84.
Mission—St. Patrick's [CEM 2] Utica, Seward Co.

Bellwood, Butler Co.
1—St. Peter's (1889) [JC] Rev. Scott M. Courtney.
Res.: 211 Esplanade St., 68624-2402. Tel: 402-538-3135.
Catechesis/Religious Program—Students 24.
Mission—St. Joseph's, Butler Co.
2—Presentation (1874) [JC] Rev. Joseph S. Steele.
Res.: 1291 41 Rd., 68624. Tel: 402-367-3666.
Catechesis/Religious Program—Students 50.

Benkelman, Dundy Co., St. Joseph's (1911) [CEM] Rev. Christopher P. Goodwin, Admin.
Res.: 817 Cheyenne St., P.O. Box 447, 69021. Tel: 308-423-2329.
Catechesis/Religious Program—Students 61.
Mission—St. Joseph's Stratton, Hitchcock Co.

Brainard, Butler Co., Holy Trinity (1888) [CEM] Rev. Matthew Eickhoff.
Res.: P.O. Box 39, 68626. Tel: 402-545-2691.
Catechesis/Religious Program—Students 63.

Bruno, Butler Co., St. Anthony (1899) [CEM] Rev. Ronald G. Homes.
Res.: 405 Pine St., 68014. Tel: 402-543-2233.
Catechesis/Religious Program—Tel: 402-543-2465. Students 49.
Mission—SS. Peter and Paul [CEM 2] Abie, Butler Co.

Cambridge, Furnas Co., St. John's (1883) [CEM] Rev. Robert K. Barnhill.
Res.: 815 Nelson, P.O. Box F, 69022. Tel: 308-697-3722.
Catechesis/Religious Program—Students 57.
Mission—St. Germanus Arapahoe, Furnas Co.

Campbell, Franklin Co., St. Anne (1880) [CEM] Very Rev. James C. Schrader Jr.
Res.: 518 S. Stewart, P.O. Box 156, 68932-0156. Tel: 402-756-8006.
Catechesis/Religious Program—Students 59.
Mission—Holy Trinity 513 S. Liberty, Blue Hill, Webster Co. 68930.

Cheney, Lancaster Co., St. Michael (1909) [CEM] Rev. Kenneth A. Borowiak. In Res., Rev. Joseph C. Bernardo.
Res.: 9230 First St. (Cheney), 68526. Tel: 402-328-8480. Web: www.stmichaelcheney.org.
Catechesis/Religious Program—Students 171.

Colon, Saunders Co., St. Joseph's (1919) [CEM] Rev. Matthew J. Vandewalle.
Res.: 111 Cherry St., P.O. Box 58, 68018. Tel: 402-647-4901.
Catechesis/Religious Program—Students 65.
Mission—St. Mary [CEM] Cedar Bluffs, Saunders Co.

Cortland, Gage Co., St. James (1882) [CEM] Rev. Leo V. Seiker.
Res.: 255 W. First St., 68331. Tel: 402-798-7335. Email: leoseiker@windstream.net.
Catechesis/Religious Program—Students 86.

Crete, Saline Co., Sacred Heart (1873) [CEM] Rev. Julius Tvrdy. In Res., Rev. Paul York.
Res.: 515 E. 14th St., 68333. Tel: 402-826-2044; Fax: 402-826-2318.
School—(Grades K-6) Tel: 402-826-2318. Sisters 3; Lay Teachers 6; Students 129.
Catechesis/Religious Program—Students 137.

Curtis, Frontier Co., St. James (1914) Rev. Ferdinand Boehme.
Res.: 313 E. 6th St., P.O. Box 144, 69025. Tel: 308-367-4280.
Catechesis/Religious Program—Students 16.
Mission—St. Joseph's Farnam, Dawson Co.
Mission—St. William's Wellfleet, Lincoln Co.

Davey, Lancaster Co., St. Mary's (1876) [CEM] Rev. Leo D. Kosch.
Res.: 17630 N. 3rd St., P.O. Box 37, 68336. Tel: 402-785-3445.
Catechesis/Religious Program—Students 93.

David City, Butler Co.
1—St. Francis (Center) (1878) [CEM] Rev. Kenneth F. Hoesing.
Res.: 3071 P Rd., 68632. Tel: 402-367-4202.
Catechesis/Religious Program—Students 27.
2—St. Mary's (1877) [CEM] Revs. Bernard Kimminau; Lawrence Ejiofo.
Res.: 580 I St., 68632. Tel: 402-367-3579; Fax: 402-367-3570.
School—(Grades K-5) Tel: 402-367-3669. Priests 1; Sisters 3; Lay Teachers 13; Students 209.
Catechesis/Religious Program—Students 25.
Mission—Assumption (1878), Butler Co. 68632.

Dawson, Richardson Co., St. Mary's (1873) [CEM] Rev. Ramon E. Decaen.
Res.: 312 4th St., P.O. Box 96, 68337. Tel: 402-855-3595.
Catechesis/Religious Program—Students 22.
Mission—St. Anne's [CEM 2] Shubert, Richardson Co.

Denton, Lancaster Co., St. Mary's (1906) Rev. Msgr. Mark D. Huber.
Res.: 7105 Cass, P.O. Box 406, 68339. Tel: 402-797-2105. Email: stmary@inebraska.com.
Catechesis/Religious Program—Students 82.

Doniphan, Hall Co., St. Ann's (1888) [CEM] Rev. Andrew Kurz.
Res.: 404 Cedar, Box 407, 68832. Tel: 402-845-2707.
Catechesis/Religious Program—Students 102.

Dwight, Butler Co., Assumption (1899) [CEM] Rev. Sean M. Timmerman.
Res.: 336 W. Pine, P.O. Box 70, 68635. Tel: 402-566-2765.
Catechesis/Religious Program—Students 88.
Mission—St. Wenceslaus [CEM] 350 Elm St., Bee, Seward Co. 68314.

Exeter, Fillmore Co., St. Stephen's (1871) [JC] Rev. Thomas Kuffel.
Res.: 207 N. Union Ave., P.O. Box 57, 68351. Tel: 402-266-5581.
Catechesis/Religious Program—Students 42.
Mission—St. Patrick's [CEM] 305 E. M St., Mc Cool Junction, York Co. 68401.
Catechesis/Religious Program—Students 20.

Fairbury, Jefferson Co., St. Michael's (1885) [CEM] Rev. John B. Birkel.
Res.: 807 F St., P.O. Box 406, 68352. Tel: 402-729-2058.
Catechesis/Religious Program—Students 68.
Mission—St. Mary's 511 Amanda, Alexandria, Thayer Co. 68303.

Falls City, Richardson Co., SS. Peter and Paul (1871) [CEM 2] Rev. Msgr. Robert A. Roh.
Res.: 1820 Fulton St., 68355. Tel: 402-245-3002; Fax: 402-245-3002. Email: raroh@sentco.net.
School—(Grades PreK-12) Tel: 402-245-4151; Fax: 402-245-5217. Lay Teachers 18; Students 215.
Catechesis/Religious Program—Students 37.

Friend, Saline Co., St. Joseph's (1874) [CEM] Rev. David F. Bourek.
Res.: 405 S. Main St., 68359. Tel: 402-947-3651.
Catechesis/Religious Program—Tel: 402-947-3657. Students 72.
Mission—St. Wenceslaus (1874) Milligan, Fillmore Co.

Geneva, Fillmore Co., St. Joseph's (1898) [CEM 2] Rev. Michael J. Morin.
Res.: 831 E St., P.O. Box 383, 68361. Tel: 402-759-3225; Fax: 402-759-3225. Email: saint_joseph@alltel.net.
Catechesis/Religious Program—Students 101.
Mission—St. Mary Shickley, Fillmore Co.

Grant, Perkins Co., Mother of Sorrows (1928) Rev. Mark S. Pfeiffer.
Res.: 739 Garfield Ave., P.O. Box 536, 69140. Tel: 308-352-4803.
Catechesis/Religious Program—Students 23.

Harvard, Clay Co., St. Joseph's (1878) Rev. James Benton, Admin.
Res.: 605 N. Kearney, P.O. Box 70, 68944. Tel: 402-772-3511.
Catechesis/Religious Program—Students 70.

Hastings, Adams Co.
1—St. Cecilia's (1878) [JC] Revs. Joseph M. Walsh; Andrew J. Heaslip, Parochial Vicar. In Res., Rev. Troy J. Schweiger.
Res.: 301 W. 7th St., 68901. Tel: 402-463-1336; Fax: 402-463-1336.
Catechesis/Religious Program—Hastings Catholic Schools, Tel: 402-462-2105; Fax: 402-462-2106. Students 282.
2—St. Michael's (1945) [JC] Revs. Michael K. Houlihan; Dominic T.H. Phan, Parochial Vicar.
Res.: 715 Creighton Ave., 68901. Tel: 402-463-1023.
Catechesis/Religious Program—Hastings Catholic Schools, 721 Creighton Ave., 68901. Tel: 402-462-6310; Fax: 402-462-6035. Students 659.

Hebron, Thayer Co., Sacred Heart (1878) [CEM] Very Rev. Rudolf F. Oborny.
Res.: 436 N. 3rd St., 68370. Tel: 402-768-6293. Email: robornyhebron@yahoo.com.
Catechesis/Religious Program—Students 80.

Holdrege, Phelps Co., All Saints (1902) Rev. Thomas J. Lux, Pastor.
Res.: 1308 Logan St., 68949. Tel: 308-995-9561.
School—(Grades PreK-4), 1206 Logan St., 68949. Tel: 308-995-8931. Lay Teachers 4; Students 71.
Catechesis/Religious Program—Tel: 308-995-4590. Students 89.
Mission—St. John's Smithfield, Gosper Co.

Imperial, Chase Co., St. Patrick's (1903) Rev. Bernard A. Lorenz.
Res.: 126 E. 7th St., P.O. Box 96, 69033. Tel: 308-882-4995; Fax: 308-882-4995.
Catechesis/Religious Program—Students 81.

Indianola, Red Willow Co., St. Catherine's (1888) [CEM] Rev. Thomas D. McGuire.
Res.: 815 D St., P.O. Box O, 69034. Tel: 308-364-2428; Fax: 308-364-2428.
Catechesis/Religious Program—Students 71.

Kenesaw, Adams Co., Sacred Heart (1908) Rev. Andrew Kurz.
Res.: 404 Cedar, Box 407, Doniphan, 68832. Tel: 402-845-2707 (Pastor).
Catechesis/Religious Program—Tel: 402-752-8149. Students 13.

Lawrence, Nuckolls Co., Sacred Heart (1893) [CEM 3] Rev. Loras K. Grell.
Res.: 141 E. 2nd St., P.O. Box 247, 68957. Tel: 402-756-7393.
School—Tel: 402-756-7043. Lay Teachers 3; Students 23.
Catechesis/Religious Program—Students 171.
Mission—Assumption 506 Liberty St., Deweese, Clay Co. 68934.
Mission—St. Stephen's 1838 Road 2600, Nuckolls Co. 68957.

Loma, Butler Co., St. Luke's Czech Catholic Shrine (1912), (Czech), [CEM], Mailing Address: *c/o Rev. Msgr. Myron J. Pleskac, Admin.*, 4100 S.W. 56th St., 68522. Email: msgr.myron-pleskac@cdolinc.net.

Manley, Cass Co., St. Patrick's (1881) [CEM] Rev. Patrick F. Murphy.
Res.: 101 N. Broadway, P.O. Box 27, 68403. Tel: 402-234-3595.
Catechesis/Religious Program—Students 140.
Mission—St. Mary's [CEM] 505 W. G St., Elmwood, Cass Co. 68349. Tel: 402-994-2485.

McCook, Red Willow Co., St. Patrick (1886) [CEM] Rev. Gary G. Brethour.
Res.: 612 E. 4th St., P.O. Box 1040, 69001. Tel: 308-345-6734; Fax: 308-345-6734.
School—(Grades PreK-8), 401 E. F St., 69001. Tel: 308-345-4546; Fax: 308-345-5542. Priests 2; Lay Teachers 15; Students 149.
Catechesis/Religious Program—Students 75.
Mission—Sacred Heart, Red Willow Co.
Mission—St. Ann's [CEM], Red Willow Co.

Mead, Saunders Co., St. James (1882) [CEM 2] Rev. Jerel A. Scholl.
Res.: 213 E. 8th St., 68041. Tel: 402-624-3555.
Catechesis/Religious Program—Students 94.

Minden, Kearney Co., St. John the Baptist (1882) Very Rev. Nicholas J. Baker.
Res.: 624 N. Garber Ave., P.O. Box 245, 68959. Tel: 308-832-1245; Fax: 308-832-1626. Email: stjohnbaptist@charter.net.
Catechesis/Religious Program—Tel: 308-832-1626. Students 90.
Mission—Holy Family Heartwell, Kearney Co.

Morse Bluff, Saunders Co., St. George (1945) Rev. Brian P. Kane.
Res.: 260 Short St., P.O. Box 98, 68648. Tel: 402-666-5280.
Catechesis/Religious Program—Students 20.
Mission—Sacred Heart [CEM] Cedar Hill, Saunders Co.

Nebraska City, Otoe Co.
1—St. Benedict's (1856) [CEM] Rev. Jeremy L. Hazuka.
Res.: 411 5th Rue, 68410. Tel: 402-873-3047.
See Lourdes Elementary and Lourdes Primary, Nebraska City under Elementary Schools, Interparochial located in the Institution section.

Catechesis/Religious Program—Students 19.
2—St. Mary's (1869) [CEM] Revs. Michael G. McCabe; Mark L. Cyza; Rayappa Konka.
Res.: 218 N. 6th St., 68410. Tel: 402-873-3024.
Catechesis/Religious Program—Students 74.

North Platte, Lincoln Co., St. Elizabeth Ann Seton (1994) Very Rev. Mark E. Seiker.
Res.: 3301 Echo Dr., 69101. Tel: 308-534-5461; Fax: 308-534-0914.
Catechesis/Religious Program—Students 40.

Orleans, Harlan Co., St. Mary's (1878) [CEM] Rev. Harlan D. P. Waskowiak.
Res.: 109 W. Linn, P.O. Box 446, 68966. Tel: 308-473-3475.
Catechesis/Religious Program—Students 45.
Mission—St. Michael's Oxford, Furnas Co.
Mission—St. Joseph's (1909) 810 4th, P.O. Box 764, Alma, Harlan Co. 68920. Tel: 308-928-2575. Rev. Jesuraj Savarimuthu.
Catechesis/Religious Program—Students 24.

Osceola, Polk Co., St. Vincent Ferrer (1946) Rev. James W. Cooper.
Res.: 751 S. Nance, P.O. Box 212, 68651. Tel: 402-747-3491; Fax: 402-747-4221.
Catechesis/Religious Program—Students 101.
Mission—St. Mary's (1893), Polk Co.

Palmyra, Otoe Co., St. Leo's (1874) [CEM 2] Rev. Christopher L. Barak.
Res.: 330 W. 8th St., 68418-2537. Tel: 402-780-5535.
Catechesis/Religious Program—Students 40.
Mission—St. Martin's Douglas, Otoe Co.

Paul, Otoe Co., St. Joseph's (1871) [CEM] Rev. Thomas M. Bush.
Res.: 5592 O Rd., Nebraska City, 68410. Tel: 402-873-4569.
Catechesis/Religious Program—Students 14.
Mission—St. Bernard's [CEM] Julian, Nemaha Co.

Plattsmouth, Cass Co., Church of the Holy Spirit (1862) [CEM] Rev. Msgr. Paul K. Witt.
Res.: 520 S. 18th St., 68048. Tel: 402-296-3139; Fax: 402-296-2408.
School—(Grades K-8) Tel: 402-296-6230. Lay Teachers 12; Students 184.
Catechesis/Religious Program—Students 34.

Prague, Saunders Co., St. John's (1901) [CEM] Rev. Jamie S. Hottovy.
Res.: 122 Center Ave., P.O. Box 96, 68050. Tel: 402-663-4615.
Catechesis/Religious Program—Students 52.
Mission—SS. Cyril and Methodius [CEM] Plasi, Saunders Co.

Red Cloud, Webster Co., Sacred Heart (1883) [CEM] Rev. Paul G. Frank.
Res.: 413 N. Seward St., 68970. Tel: 402-746-3750.
Catechesis/Religious Program—Students 21.
Mission—St. Kathrine Drexel Franklin, Franklin Co. 68939.

Roseland, Adams Co., Sacred Heart (1921) Very Rev. Thomas Y. Au.
Res.: 11818 W. Alexander, P.O. Box 67, 68973. Tel: 402-756-6251.
Catechesis/Religious Program—Students 66.
Mission—Assumption [CEM] Juniata, Adams Co.

Rulo, Richardson Co., Immaculate Conception (1863) [CEM] Rev. David A. Oldham.
Res.: 601 W. Rouleau St., 68431. Tel: 402-245-4731.
School—Tel: 402-245-4151. Priests 1; Lay Teachers 6; Students 35.
Catechesis/Religious Program—Tel: 402-245-3002. Students 7.
Mission—St. Mary's Arago, Richardson Co.

Seward, Seward Co., St. Vincent de Paul (1878) Revs. Randall L. Langhorst; Rafael Rodriguez-Fuentes.
Res.: 152 Pinewood Ave., 68434. Tel: 402-643-3421; Fax: 402-643-2594.
School—(Grades K-4) Tel: 402-643-9525. Students 94.
Catechesis/Religious Program—Tel: 402-643-3521. Students 241.

Shelby, Polk Co., Sacred Heart (1898) [CEM] Very Rev. John C. Rooney.
Res.: 200 S. Walnut St., P.O. Box 340, 68662. Tel: 402-527-5425; Fax: 402-527-5849. Web: www.shelbysacredheart.com.
Catechesis/Religious Program—Students 59.

Steinauer, Pawnee Co., St. Anthony (1882) [CEM] Rev. Thomas L. Wiedel.
Res.: 310 Hickory St., 68441. Tel: 402-869-2256.
Catechesis/Religious Program—Students 78.
Mission—Sacred Heart [CEM] Burchard, Pawnee Co.

Superior, Nuckolls Co., St. Joseph's (1934) Rev. Bradley Zitek.
Res.: 1415 California, 68978-1019. Tel: 402-879-3735; Fax: 402-879-4495.
Catechesis/Religious Program—Students 66.
Mission—Sacred Heart Nelson, Nuckolls Co.

Sutton, Clay Co., St. Mary's (1876) [CEM] Rev. K. William Holoubek.
Res.: 312 S. Saunders Ave., P.O. Box 406, 68979. Tel: 402-773-5346.
Catechesis/Religious Program—Students 90.
Mission—St. Helena's 172 Jackson St., Grafton, Fillmore Co. 68365.

Syracuse, Otoe Co., St. Paulinus (1906) Rev. Michael S. Stec.
Mailing Address: 863 5th St., 68446-9504. Tel: 402-269-3382.
Catechesis/Religious Program—Students 104.
Mission—Holy Trinity [CEM] 4456 Arbor Rd., Avoca, Cass Co. 68307.

Tecumseh, Johnson Co., St. Andrew's (1866) [CEM] Rev. Thomas B. Dunavan.
Res.: 186 N. 5th St., P.O. Box 656, 68450. Tel: 402-335-3742; Fax: 402-335-2234.
School—(Grades K-6) Tel: 402-335-2234. Sisters 1; Lay Teachers 2; Students 22.
Catechesis/Religious Program—Students 40.
Mission—St. Mary's [CEM] St. Mary, Johnson Co.

Trenton, Hitchcock Co., St. James (1894) [CEM] Very Rev. Valerian Bartek.
Res.: 117 W. B St., P.O. Box 488, 69044. Tel: 308-334-5328.
Catechesis/Religious Program—Students 40.
Mission—Holy Family Palisade, Hitchcock Co.
Mission—St. John's [CEM] Wauneta, Chase Co. Tel: 308-394-5440 (Church).

Ulysses, Butler Co., Immaculate Conception (1915) [CEM] Rev. Raymond L. Jansen.
Res.: 215 S. 6th St., P.O. Box 128, 68669. Tel: 402-549-2437.
Catechesis/Religious Program—Students 24.

Valparaiso, Saunders Co., Sts. Mary and Joseph's (1975) [CEM] Rev. Msgr. Daniel J. Seiker.
Res.: 601 Iver St., P.O. Box 248, 68065. Tel: 402-784-2511.
Catechesis/Religious Program—Students 100.

Wahoo, Saunders Co., St. Wenceslaus (1877) [CEM 2] Revs. Charles L. Townsend; Lothar M. Gilde. In Res., Rev. John L. Copenhaver.
Res.: 214 E. 2nd St., 68066. Tel: 402-443-4235; Fax: 402-443-4275.
School—(Grades K-6), 108 N. Linden, 68066-1953. Tel: 402-443-3336; Fax: 402-443-5551. Sisters 1; Lay Teachers 13; Students 291.
Catechesis/Religious Program—Students 615.

Wallace, Lincoln Co., St. Mary's (1909) Rev. Mark S. Pfeiffer.
Res.: 221 N. Commercial Ave., P.O. Box 191, 69169. Tel: 308-387-4441. Email: stmary@nebnet.net.
Catechesis/Religious Program—Students 26.
Mission—Resurrection of Our Lord Elsie, Perkins Co.

Weston, Saunders Co., St. John Nepomucene (1885) [CEM 2] Rev. Thomas Brouillette.
Res.: 110 Front St., P.O. Box 10, 68070. Tel: 402-642-5245.
School—(Grades PreK-6) Tel: 402-642-5234. Lay Teachers 7; Students 98.
Mission—St. Vitus [CEM] Touhy, Saunders Co.

Wilber, Saline Co., St. Wenceslaus (1878) Rev. Craig A. Doty.
Res.: 501 N. Wilson, P.O. Box 706, 68465. Tel: 402-821-2689.
Catechesis/Religious Program—Students 100.
Mission—St. Joseph's Tobias, Saline Co.

Wymore, Gage Co., St. Mary's (1881) [CEM 3] Rev. Dennis W. Hotovy.
Res.: 107 N. 11th St., P.O. Box 295, 68466. Tel: 402-645-3051.
Catechesis/Religious Program—Students 53.
Mission—St. Joseph's Barneston, Gage Co.
Mission—St. Mary's [CEM] Odell, Gage Co.

York, York Co., St. Joseph's (1878) [CEM] Rev. Mark A. Tasler. In Res., Rev. Melvin Rempe.
Res.: 505 N. East Ave., 68467. Tel: 402-362-4595.
School—(Grades K-8) Tel: 402-362-3021; Fax: 402-362-4067. Franciscan Apostolic Sisters 2; Lay Teachers 12; Students 105.
Catechesis/Religious Program—Students 192.

Shrines

Crete, Saline Co., Schoenstatt Shrine (2001) Sr. M. Veronica Muniz, I.S.S.M., Supr.
Shrine— 340 Hwy. 103, 68333. Tel: 402-826-3346. Web: www.schoenstattne.org.

Loma, Butler Co., St. Luke's Czech Catholic Shrine Rev. Msgr. Myron J. Pleskac, Dir.
P.O. Box 80328, 68501.

Chaplains of Public Institutions

Lincoln. *Nebraska Penal Complex*, 1420 K St., 68508. Tel: 402-742-4421. Rev. Msgr. Myron J. Pleskac, Revs. Thomas B. Dunavan, Thomas S. MacLean, Michael J. Morin, Mark A. Tasler.

On Duty Outside the Diocese:
Rev. Msgrs.—
Fucinaro, Thomas J., Villa Stritch, Via della Nocetta, 63, 00164 Rome, Italy.
Reinert, James M., Villa Stritch, Via della Nocetta, 63, Rome 00164 Italy.
Revs.—
Gross, Gary, Military Duty, 14 St. LO Dr., Fort Carson, CO 80902.
Panzer, Joel, Military Duty, 265 Fernander Ave., Unit 101, Wahiawa, HI 96786-4142.

Graduate Studies:
Revs.—
Gyhra, Richard A., (Pontifica Accademia Ecclesiastica)
Kilcawley, Sean P., (Casa Santa Maria)

Retired:
Rev. Msgrs.—
Dawson, James D., Bonacum House, 3301 Sheridan Blvd., 68506.
Hain, Raymond B., Bonacum House, 3301 Sheridan Blvd., 68506.
Herbek, Adrian F., V.F., Bonacum House, 3301 Sheridan Blvd., 68506.
Holoman, Thomas L., 566 N. Maple Ave., Greensburg, PA 15601.
Keenan, Charles J., Madonna Hospital, 5401 South St., 68506.
Pohl, Daniel J., Bonacum House, 3301 Sheridan Blvd., 68506.
Vap, Ivan F., 1301 E. 9th, Hastings, 68901.
Very Rev.—
O'Byrne, Patrick J., West End Millstreet, Co. Cork Ireland.
Revs.—
Danko, Michael S., 1100 E. Montclair, Rm. 116, Springfield, MO 65807.
Gadient, Peter J., Bonacum House, 3301 Sheridan Blvd., 68506.
Glaves, John J., Madonna Hospital, 5401 South St., 68506.
Hebert, John M., 9 Perralena Ln., Hot Springs, AR 71909.
Kalin, William A., Bonacum House, 3301 Sheridan Blvd., 68506.
Lyons, Patrick J., Bonacum House, 3301 Sheridan Blvd., 68506.
Mroczkowski, Joseph A., P.O. Box 238, Cedar Creek, 68016.
Murphy, Francis J., #1 West End, Millstreet, Co. Cork Ireland.
O'Connor, James M., 2110 30th Ave., #32, Kearney, 68845.
Rauth, Philip J., 13305 William Cir., Omaha, 68144.
Rutten, Paul J., Bonacum House, 3301 Sheridan Blvd., 68506.
Thomas, Milton, J.C.L., Grand Island Veteran's Home, 2300 W. Capital Ave., Grand Island, 68803.
Zastrow, John A., Bonacum House, 3301 Sheridan Blvd., 68506.

INSTITUTIONS LOCATED IN THE DIOCESE

[A] SEMINARIES, RELIGIOUS OR SCHOLASTICATES

Denton. *Our Lady of Guadalupe Seminary*, 7880 W. Denton Rd., P.O. Box 147, 68339. Tel: 402-797-7700; Fax: 402-797-7705. Email: seminary@fsspolgs.org. Very Rev. Josef Bisig, F.S.S.P., Rector; Revs. William Lawrence, F.S.S.P.; Robert Fromageot, F.S.S.P.; Charles Van Vliet, F.S.S.P.; Calvin R. Goodwin, F.S.S.P.; James B. Buckley, F.S.S.P.; Robert Ferguson, F.S.S.P.; Joseph Portzer, F.S.S.P.; Sr. Stephen Larson, O.S.B., Librarian. Priests 8; Sisters 1; Lay Staff 11; Adjunct 3; Students 74.

Seward. *St. Gregory the Great Seminary*, 800 Fletcher Rd., 68434. Tel: 402-643-4052; Fax: 402-643-6964. Email: sggs@stgregoryseminary.edu. Web: www.stgregoryseminary.edu. Rev. Msgr. John T. Folda, Rector; Very Rev. M. James Divis, S.T.L., V.F., Spiritual Dir.; Revs. Jeffrey R. Eickhoff, Academic Dean; Peter M. Mitchell; Dr. Terrence Nollen, Ph.D., Librarian. Priests 11; Sisters 3; Lay Staff 5; Students 43.

[B] ELEMENTARY SCHOOLS, INTERPAROCHIAL

Hastings. *St. Michael's Elementary, Hastings Catholic Schools*, 721 Creighton Ave., 68901. Tel: 402-462-6310; Fax: 402-462-6035. Email: smb@esu9.org. Sr. M. Bernard Simmons, F.S.G.M., Prin. Priests 6; Sisters 2; Lay Teachers 21; Students 255.

NEBRASKA CITY. *Lourdes Elementary*, (Grades PreK-5), 412 2nd Ave., 68410. Tel: 402-873-6154; Fax: 402-873-3154. Mrs. Valerie Able, Prin. Lay Teachers 9; Students 174.
Lourdes Primary, (Grades K-3), 411 5th Rue, 68410. Tel: 402-873-3739. Lay Teachers 6; Students 80.

[C] HIGH SCHOOLS, INTERPAROCHIAL

LINCOLN. *Pius X Catholic High School*, 6000 A St., 68510. Tel: 402-488-0931; Fax: 402-488-1061. Email: webmaster@piusx.net. Web: www.piusx.net. Revs. James J. Meysenburg, B.A., M.A., M.Div., M. ED., Supt.; Andrew V. Menke, Asst. Supt.; Mr. Tom Korta, Prin.; Mr. Greg Lesiak, Asst. Prin.; Mrs. Jan Frayser, Dir. of Guidance; Mr. Tim Aylward, Dir. Activities. Priests 13; Sisters 4; Lay Teachers 60; Students 1,065.

DAVID CITY. *Aquinas/St. Mary's Schools* (1899) (Grades PreK-12), 3420 MN Rd., P.O. Box 149, 68632. Tel: 402-367-3175; Fax: 402-367-3176. Email: fr.kenneth-hoseing@cdolinc.net. Web: www.aquinas.esu7.org. Rev. Kenneth F. Hoesing, Supt.; Mr. David G. McMahon, Prin. (Aquinas High School); Miss Carmelita Fiala, Prin. (St. Mary's); Rev. Joseph S. Steele, Guidance Dir.; Bobbi Schmid, Career Counselor. Priests 6; Sisters 3; Lay Teachers 34; Students 500.

FALLS CITY. *Sacred Heart School*, 1820 Fulton St., 68355. Tel: 402-245-4151; Fax: 402-245-5217. Email: doug-goltz@fcsacredheart.org. Web: www.sacredheart.esu6.org/. Rev. Msgr. Robert A. Roh, V.F., M.A., S.T.L., Supt.; Mr. Douglas Goltz, M.A., Prin.; Rev. David A. Oldham, Dir., Guidance; Linda Barnhill, Librarian.
High School Email: robert.roh@fcsacredheart.org. Web: www.sacredheart.esu6.org/. Priests 3; Lay Teachers 9; Students 66.
Elementary School Priests 3; Lay Teachers 18; Students 180.

HASTINGS. *St. Cecilia's Middle School/High School*, (Grades 6-12), 521 N. Kansas, 68901. Tel: 402-462-2105; Fax: 402-462-2106. Email: mbutler@esu9.org. Web: www.esu9.org/~hcs.esu9.org. Rev. Troy J. Schweiger, Supt.; Mrs. Marie Butler, Prin.; Mrs. Marilyn Zysset, Librarian. Priests 5; Sisters 2; Lay Teachers 30; Students 296.

NEBRASKA CITY. *Lourdes Central Catholic Schools*, (Grades K-12), 412 2nd Ave., 68410. Tel: 402-873-6154; Fax: 402-873-3154. Email: lourdes-office@cdolinc.net. Revs. Michael G. McCabe, Supt.; Jeremy L. Hazuka, High School Prin.; Mrs. Valerie Able, Elementary Prin. Priests 5; Sisters 3; Lay Teachers 26; Students 330.

WAHOO. *Bishop Neumann Jr.-Sr. High School*, 202 S. Linden, 68066. Tel: 402-443-4151; Fax: 402-443-5551. Web: bishopneumann.com. Revs. Charles L. Townsend, Supt.; Brian P. Kane, Prin. Priests 6; Sisters 1; Lay Teachers 22; Students 323.

[D] GENERAL HOSPITALS

LINCOLN. *St. Elizabeth Regional Medical Center* (1889) 555 S. 70th St., 68510. Tel: 402-219-8000; Fax: 402-219-8973. Email: blanik@stez.org. Web: www.saintelizabethonline.com. Mr. Robert Lanik, Pres.; Rev. Edwin L. Stander, Chap. Affiliate of Catholic Health Initiatives. Priests 1; Sisters 2; Bed Capacity 257; Total Staff 2,288; Patients Assisted Annually 129,526.

NEBRASKA CITY. *St. Mary's Hospital*, 1314 3rd Ave., 68410. Tel: 402-873-3321; Fax: 402-873-9033. Email: dkelly@stez.org. Web: www.stmaryshospitalnecity.org. Daniel J. Kelly, Pres., C.E.O., Admin. Affiliate of Catholic Health Initiatives. Bed Capacity 18; Total Staff 147; Patients Assisted Annually 31,647.

[E] HOMES FOR AGED

LINCOLN. *Bonacum House* (1987) 3301 Sheridan Blvd., 68506. Tel: 402-483-0391; Fax: 402-483-0391. Rev. Msgrs. Raymond B. Hain (Retired); Adrian F. Herbek; James D. Dawson (Retired); Daniel J. Pohl (Retired); Revs. Peter J. Gadient (Retired); William A. Kalin (Retired); Patrick J. Lyons (Retired); Paul J. Rutten (Retired); John A. Zastrow (Retired). Residence for retired priests.
Madonna Rehabilitation Hospital, 5401 South St., 68506. Tel: 402-489-7102; Fax: 402-483-9460. Email: feedback@madonna.org. Web: www.madonna.org. Physical Medicine and Rehabilitation, Outpatient Services, Long-Term Care, Adult Day Care and Supportive Inpatient Hospice, Alzheimers Care. Sisters 7; Bed Capacity 303; Patients Assisted Annually 33,218.

DAVID CITY. *St. Joseph's Court, Inc.* (2000) 646 I St., 68632. Tel: 402-367-4337; Fax: 402-367-4345. Email: stoutva@hotmail.com. Web: saintjosephsvilla.org. Assisted Living Residents 26; Total Assisted 28.
St. Joseph's Villa, Inc., 927 7th St., 68632. Tel: 402-367-3045; Fax: 402-367-3730. Email: stoutva@hotmail.com. Joyce Stewart, Admin.; Vicki Stout, Admin. Sisters Adorers of the Blood of Christ (St. Louis, MO). Residents 58; Total Assisted 72; Total Staff 103.

[F] RETREAT HOUSES

WAVERLY. *Our Lady of Good Counsel Retreat House*, 7303 N. 112th St., 68462. Tel: 402-786-2705; Fax: 402-786-7211. Email: goodcounsel@cdolinc.net. Web: www.goodcounselretreat.com. Rev. Lawrence Stoley, Dir. Private Rooms 50. In Res. Rev. Msgr. John J Perkinton.

[G] CONVENTS AND RESIDENCES FOR SISTERS

LINCOLN. *Adoration Convent and Church of Christ the King*, 1040 S. Cotner Blvd., 68510. Tel: 402-489-0765; Fax: 402-489-0864. Sr. Mary Henrita Robillard, Supr.; Rev. Msgr. Joseph J. Nemec, Chap. Sister Servants of the Holy Spirit of Perpetual Adoration. Professed Sisters 7.
St. Agnes Convent, 3405 Sheridan Blvd., 68506. Tel: 402-484-7348. Professed Sisters 2.
Congregation of Missionary Sisters of the Blessed Virgin Mary, Queen of Mercy, P.O. Box 30917, 68503. 1313 Eldon Dr., 68503. Tel: 402-421-1704; Fax: 402-421-1704. Email: srsqueenmercy@hotmail.com. Professed Sisters 10.
Guadalupan Missionaries of the Holy Spirit (1924) Hispanic Apostolate, 110 W. "E" St., 68508-3087. Tel: 402-477-1190 (U.S. Delegation Headquarters, Miami, FL). Email: hijasespsto@alltel.net. Sr. Manuela de Jesus Gutierrez, Supr. Sisters 4.
School Sisters of Christ the King, Villa Regina Motherhouse & Novitiate (1976) 4100 S.W. 56th St., 68522-9201. Tel: 402-477-5232; Fax: 402-477-0464. Email: M.Joan-Paul@cdolinc.net. Web: www.rc.net/lincoln/schoolsisters. Sr. Joan Paul, C.K., Supr. Sisters 23; Novices 3; Postulants 3. In Res. Rev. Msgr. Myron J. Pleskac. Tel: 402-477-1768.

CRETE. *Secular Institute of the Schoenstatt Sisters of Mary, ISSM*, 340 Hwy. 103, 68333. Tel: 402-826-3346; Fax: 402-826-3346. Sr. M. Veronica Muniz, I.S.S.M., Supr.

NEBRASKA CITY. *The Franciscan Sisters of the Sorrowful Mother*, 1503 4th Corso, 68410. Tel: 402-873-3052. Email: fs93813@alltel.net. Sr. Ana Maria Solis, O.S.F., Supr.

TECUMSEH. *Benedictine Sisters of Mt. Scholastica - Atchison, KS, St. Andrew Convent*, 179 N. 6th, P.O. Box 386, 68450. Tel: 402-335-2034. Email: sr.mary-ellen@standrewtecumseh.org. Sr. Mary Ellen Auffert, Contact Person.

VALPARAISO. *Carmel of Jesus, Mary, and Joseph*, 9300 Agnew Rd., 68065. Tel: 402-784-0375; Fax: 402-784-0375. Sr. Teresa of Jesus, O.C.D., Prioress.

WAVERLY. *Marian Sisters of the Diocese of Lincoln Motherhouse and Novitiate*, 6765 N. 112th St., 68462-9762. Tel: 402-786-2750; Fax: 402-786-7256. Sr. Jacquelyn Darner, M.S., Supr. Professed 34; Postulants 2.

[H] SPECIAL EDUCATION

LINCOLN. *Villa Marie School and Home for the Educable Mentally Handicapped* (1964) P.O. Box 80328, 68501. Tel: 402-786-3625; Fax: 402-488-6525. Sr. Peggy Kucera, M.S., Prin.; Rev. Msgr. John J Perkinton, Dir. Marian Sisters (Waverly, NE). Sisters 3; Students 4.

[I] NEWMAN CENTERS

LINCOLN. *University of Nebraska, Newman Club* 320 N. 16th St., 68508. Tel: 402-474-7914; Fax: 402-476-2620. Email: newmancenter@unl.edu. Web: newmancenter.unl.edu. Revs. Robert A. Matya, Vocation Dir.; Benjamin P. Holdren. See also: St. Thomas Aquinas, Lincoln, NE.

[J] FUNDS, FOUNDATIONS AND TRUSTS

LINCOLN. *Chancery*, 3400 Sheridan Blvd., P.O. Box 80328, 68501. Tel: 402-488-0921; Fax: 402-488-3569.
Mass Stipends Rev. Daniel J. Rayer, J.C.L.
Mission Office Fund
The Catholic Foundation of the Diocese of Lincoln, P.O. Box 80328, 68501-0328. Tel: 402-488-0921; Fax: 402-488-3569. Rev. Msgr. Timothy J. Thorburn, J.C.L.
Crossing the Threshold Campaign, Crossing the Threshold Campaign, 3400 Sheridan Blvd., 68506. Tel: 402-488-0921; Fax: 402-488-3569. Rev. Msgr. Timothy J. Thorburn, J.C.L.
Charity and Stewardship Appeal (DDP), Charity and Stewardship Appeal (DDP), 3400 Sheridan Blvd., 68506. Tel: 402-488-0921; Fax: 402-488-3569. Rev. Msgr. Timothy J. Thorburn, J.C.L.

[K] CATHOLIC SOCIAL SERVICES

LINCOLN. *Catholic Social Services*, Admin. Offices 2241 O St., 68510. Tel: 402-474-1600; Fax: 402-474-1612. Email: frckubat@cssisus.org. Web: www.cssisus.org. Rev. Christopher K. Kubat, Dir. (Housing Services & Social Services)
Other Addresses:
Apostolate of Suffering, 1313 Eldon Dr., 68510. Tel: 402-474-1600; Fax: 402-474-1612. Email: frckubat@cssisus.org.
Counseling Svcs. 3700 Sheridan Blvd., 68506. Tel: 402-489-1834; 800-961-6277; Fax: 402-489-2046.
Catholic Social Svcs. 515 W. Third St., Hastings, 68901. Tel: 402-463-2112; 888-826-9629; Fax: 402-463-2322. Email: tschik@csshope.org.
1014 Central Ave., Auburn, 68305. Tel: 402-274-4818.

[L] MISCELLANEOUS LISTINGS

LINCOLN. *Blessed John XXIII Diocesan Center* (2001) 3700 Sheridan Blvd., 68506. Tel: 402-488-2040; Fax: 402-488-6525. Email: joan-penn@cdolinc.net. Rev. Msgr. John J Perkinton.
Calvary Cemetery and Mausoleum, 145 S. 40th St., 68510. Tel: 402-476-8787. Rev. Msgr. David R. Hintz, Dir. Joint cemetery for Lincoln parishes.
Camp Kateri, P.O. Box F, Mc Cool Junction, 68401. Tel: 402-499-4082. Rev. Robert K. Barnhill, Dir.
Catholic Social Services (1932) 2241 O St., 68510. Tel: 402-474-1600; Fax: 402-474-1612. Email: frckubat@cssisus.org. Rev. Christopher K. Kubat, Dir. St. Thomas Orphanage.
Cristo Rey Catholic Hispanic Center, 4245 J St., 68510. Tel: 402-488-5087; Fax: 402-488-8370.
St. Francis of Assisi Church, 3400 S. 17th St., 68502. Tel: 402-477-5145; Fax: 402-477-5159. Rev. Roberto Cano, F.S.S.P., Chap. In Res. Rev. Robert Fromageot, F.S.S.P.
Holy Family Convent, 5720 A St., 68510. Tel: 402-486-3706.
Magnificat-Lincoln, 7221 South St. #4, 68506. Tel: 402-476-1880. Email: mharper55@yahoo.com. Mary Harper, Coord.
Pius X Foundation and Pius X Endowment Fund, 6000 A St., 68510. Tel: 402-488-1046; Fax: 402-488-1061. Email: michelle.birkel@piusx.net. Web: www.piusx.net. Rev. James J. Meysenburg, B.A., M.A., M.Div., M. ED., Sec. & Treas.

CRETE. *Schoenstatt Shrine* 340 State Hwy. 103, 68333. Tel: 402-826-3346; Fax: 402-826-3346. Web: www.schoenstattne.org.

DAVID CITY. *Aquinas High School Endowment Fund*, 3420 MN Rd., 68632. Tel: 402-367-3175; Fax: 402-367-3176. Email: fr.kenneth-hoesing@cdolinc.net. Web: aquinas.esu7.org. Rev. Kenneth F. Hoesing.

FALLS CITY. *Sacred Heart High School Endowment Fund*, 1820 Fulton St., 68355. Tel: 402-245-4151; Fax: 402-245-3002. Email: raroh@sentco.net. Rev. Msgr. Robert A. Roh, V.F., M.A., S.T.L., Sec. & Treas.

HASTINGS. *St. Cecilia High School Endowment Fund* (1981) 521 N. Kansas, 68901. Tel: 402-462-2105; Fax: 402-462-2106. Email: faterson1@yahoo.com. Web: www.esu9.org/~hcs. Rev. Troy J. Schweiger, Sec. & Treas.

NEBRASKA CITY. *Lourdes Central High School Endowment Fund*, 412 Second Ave., 68410. Tel: 402-873-6154; Fax: 402-873-3154. Email: sm22100@navix.net. Rev. Michael G. McCabe, Sec. & Treas.

WAHOO. *Bishop Neumann High School Endowment Fund*, 202 S. Linden, 68066. Tel: 402-443-4151; Fax: 402-443-5551. Email: fr.chrles-townsend@cdolinc.net. Web: bishopneumann.com. Revs. Charles L. Townsend, Sec. & Treas.; Brian P. Kane, Contact Person.

RELIGIOUS INSTITUTES OF MEN REPRESENTED IN THE DIOCESE

For further details refer to the corresponding bracketed number in the Religious Institutes of Men or Women section.

[]—*Congregation of the Mother Coredemptrix* (Vietnamese)—C.M.C.

[1065]—*Priestly Fraternity of St. Peter*—F.S.S.P.

RELIGIOUS INSTITUTES OF WOMEN REPRESENTED IN THE DIOCESE

[0100]—*Adorers of the Blood of Christ*—A.S.C.

[]—*Benedictine Sisters of Mount St. Scholastica*—O.S.B.

[0230]—*Benedictine Sisters of Pontifical Jurisdiction* (Yankton)—O.S.B.

[]—*Benedictine Sisters of the Sacred Hearts* (Tulsa, OK)—O.S.B.

[0420]—*Carmelite Monastery of Jesus, Mary, and Joseph*—O.C.D.

[]—*Congregation of Missionary Sisters of the Blessed Virgin Mary, Queen of Mercy* (Vietnam)

[1115]—*Dominican Sisters of Peace*—O.P.

[]—*Franciscan Apostolic Sisters*—F.A.S.

[]—*Franciscan Sisters of Christian Charity* (Manitowoc, WI)—O.S.F.
[]—*Franciscan Sisters of the Sorrowful Mother*—O.S.F.
[1845]—*Guadalupan Missionaries of the Holy Spirit*—M.G.Sp.S.
[]—*Handmaids of the Holy Child of Jesus* (Ikot Ekpene, Nigeria)—H.H.C.J.
[]—*Holy Family Sisters of the Needy*—H.F.S.N.
[2575]—*Institute of the Sisters of Mercy of the Americas*—R.S.M.
[2400]—*Marian Sisters of the Diocese of Lincoln*—M.S.
[2960]—*Notre Dame Sisters*—N.D.
[]—*Schoenstatt Sisters of Mary*
[]—*School Sisters of Christ the King*—C.K.
[1680]—*School Sisters of St. Francis*—O.S.F.
[3540]—*Sister Servants of the Holy Spirit of Perpetual Adoration*—S.Sp.S.deA.
[1600]—*Sisters of St. Francis of Martyr St. George*—O.S.F.
[1640]—*Sisters of St. Francis of Perpetual Adoration* (Prov. of St. Joseph)—O.S.F.

NECROLOGY

† Gyhra, Lawrence J., (Retired)—Died May 17, 2009

An asterisk (*) denotes an organization that has established tax-exempt status directly with the IRS and is not covered by the USCCB Group Ruling.

Diocese of Little Rock

(Dioecesis Petriculana)

Most Reverend

ANTHONY BASIL TAYLOR

Bishop of Little Rock; ordained August 2, 1980; appointed seventh Bishop of Little Rock March 18, 2008; consecrated & installed June 5, 2008. *Res.: 30 Sherrill Rd., Little Rock, AR 72202.* Tel: 501-664-0340. *Mailing Address: P.O. Box 7565, Little Rock, AR 72217. Office: 2500 N. Tyler St., Little Rock, AR 72207.*

Most Reverend

ANDREW J. McDONALD, D.D., J.C.D.

Bishop Emeritus of Little Rock; ordained May 8, 1948; appointed Bishop of Little Rock July 4, 1972; consecrated September 5, 1972; installed September 7, 1972; retired January 4, 2000. *Res.: St. Joseph's Home for the Elderly, 80 W. Northwest Hwy., Palatine, IL 60067.* Tel: 847-358-5700; Fax: 847-934-6979.

THE HUMBLE SHALL INHERIT THE EARTH

Chancery: 2500 N. Tyler St., P.O. Box 7565, Little Rock, AR 72217. Tel: 501-664-0340.

Web: www.dolr.org

ESTABLISHED NOVEMBER 28, 1843.

Square Miles 52,068.

Comprises the State of Arkansas.

For legal titles of parishes and diocesan institutions, consult the Chancery Office.

STATISTICAL OVERVIEW

Personnel	
Bishop	1
Retired Bishops	1
Abbots	1
Priests: Diocesan Active in Diocese	52
Priests: Retired, Sick or Absent	15
Number of Diocesan Priests	67
Religious Priests in Diocese	37
Total Priests in Diocese	104
Extern Priests in Diocese	25
Ordinations:	
Diocesan Priests	2
Transitional Deacons	5
Permanent Deacons in Diocese	81
Total Brothers	27
Total Sisters	181
Parishes	
Parishes	88
With Resident Pastor:	
Resident Diocesan Priests	55
Resident Religious Priests	14
Without Resident Pastor:	
Administered by Priests	18
Administered by Deacons	1
Missions	38
Pastoral Centers	1
Professional Ministry Personnel:	
Brothers	1
Sisters	16
Lay Ministers	72
Welfare	
Catholic Hospitals	12
Total Assisted	862,562
Health Care Centers	5
Total Assisted	42,029
Homes for the Aged	26
Total Assisted	969
Day Care Centers	27
Total Assisted	1,329
Specialized Homes	1
Total Assisted	133
Special Centers for Social Services	5
Total Assisted	46,875
Other Institutions	9
Total Assisted	22,191
Educational	
Diocesan Students in Other Seminaries	27
Total Seminarians	27
High Schools, Diocesan and Parish	4
Total Students	1,011
High Schools, Private	2
Total Students	665
Elementary Schools, Diocesan and Parish	28
Total Students	5,556
Catechesis/Religious Education:	
High School Students	2,105
Elementary Students	9,484
Total Students under Catholic Instruction	18,848
Teachers in the Diocese:	
Priests	3
Brothers	4
Sisters	9
Lay Teachers	544
Vital Statistics	
Receptions into the Church:	
Infant Baptism Totals	2,733
Minor Baptism Totals	250
Adult Baptism Totals	228
Received into Full Communion	510
First Communions	2,638
Confirmations	1,649
Marriages:	
Catholic	347
Interfaith	240
Total Marriages	587
Deaths	863
Total Catholic Population	122,842
Total Population	2,855,390

Former Bishops—Rt. Revs. ANDREW BYRNE, D.D., cons. March 10, 1844; died in Helena, June 10, 1862; EDWARD FITZGERALD, D.D., preconized June 22, 1866; cons. Feb. 3, 1867; died in Hot Springs, Feb. 21, 1907; Most Revs. JOHN B. MORRIS, D.D., ord. June 11, 1892; cons. June 11, 1906; died in Little Rock, Oct. 22, 1946; ALBERT L. FLETCHER, D.D., ord. June 4, 1920; cons. April 25, 1940; appt. Bishop of Little Rock Dec. 7, 1946; retired July 3, 1972; died Dec. 6, 1979; ANDREW J. McDONALD, D.D., J.C.D. (Retired), ord. May 8, 1948; appt. Bishop of Little Rock July 4, 1972; cons. Sept. 5, 1972; installed Sept. 7, 1972; retired Jan. 4. 2000; JAMES PETER SARTAIN, D.D., S.T.L., ord. July 15, 1978; appt. Bishop of Little Rock Jan. 4, 2000; cons. and installed March 6, 2000; appt. Bishop of Joliet May 16, 2006.

Pastoral Center—2500 N. Tyler St., P.O. Box 7565, Little Rock, 72217. Tel: 501-664-0340; Fax: 501-664-9075. Office Hours: Mon.-Fri. 8:30-5.

Vicar General—Rev. Msgr. R. SCOTT FRIEND, V.G.

Chancellor for Ecclesial Affairs—Very Rev. Msgr. FRANCIS I. MALONE, J.C.L., V.F.

Chancellor for Canonical Affairs—Deacon JOHN M. McALLISTER, J.D., J.C.L., This office also handles Archives.

Chancellor for Administrative Affairs—Mr. DENNIS P. LEE.

Vice Chancellors—Rev. Msgr. SCOTT L. MARCZUK, J.C.L.; Revs. JOHN K. ANTONY, J.C.L.; GREGORY T. LUYET, J.C.L.; Rev. Msgr. ROYCE R. THOMAS, J.C.L., J.V.

Finance Officer—Mr. GREGORY C. WOLFE, CFO.

Diocesan Tribunal—Fax: 501-664-4583.

Judicial Vicar—Rev. Msgr. ROYCE R. THOMAS, J.C.L., J.V. Adjutant Judicial Vicars: Revs. JOHN K. ANTONY, J.C.L.; GREGORY T. LUYET, J.C.L.

Judges—Revs. JOHN K. ANTONY, J.C.L.; GREGORY T. LUYET, J.C.L.; Deacon JOHN M. McALLISTER, J.D., J.C.L.

Defenders of the Bond—Rev. Msgr. JOHN KORDSMEIER (Retired); CATHERINE A. GILLIGAN, J.C.L.; Mrs. BARBARA ANHALT.

Promoter of Justice—CATHERINE A. GILLIGAN, J.C.L.

Notaries—Mrs. LIZ PARKER; JAN BRASS; LAZETH NOVAK; TERI TRIBBY; SUSI BLANCO.

Vicars for Religious—Very Rev. Msgr. FRANCIS I. MALONE, J.C.L., V.F.; Very Revs. JOHN E. MARCONI, V.F.; MARK WOOD; GREGORY G. HART, V.F.; VINCENT FLUSCHE, V.F.; WARREN HARVEY, V.F.; Rt. Rev. JEROME KODELL, O.S.B., V.F.; Very Rev. Msgr. DAVID LESIEUR, V.F.

Diocesan Consultors—Rev. Msgr. R. SCOTT FRIEND, V.G.; Very Rev. Msgr. FRANCIS I. MALONE, J.C.L., V.F.; Rev. Msgr. SCOTT L. MARCZUK, J.C.L.

Deans—Very Rev. Msgr. FRANCIS I. MALONE, J.C.L., V.F., Central Deanery; Very Revs. VINCENT FLUSCHE, V.F., Ouachita Deanery; JOHN E. MARCONI, V.F., North Delta Deanery; GREGORY G. HART, V.F., North Ozark Deanery; Rt. Rev. JEROME KODELL, O.S.B., V.F., River Valley Deanery; Very Rev. WARREN HARVEY, V.F., South Delta Deanery; Very Rev. Msgr. DAVID LESIEUR, V.F., West Ozark Deanery.

Diocesan Offices and Directors

Unless otherwise indicated all Diocesan Offices and Directors are located at: *St. John Pastoral Center, 2500 N. Tyler St., Little Rock, 72207.* Tel: 501-664-0340; Fax: 501-664-9075. *Mailing Address: P.O. Box 7565, Little Rock, 72217-7565.*

Catholic Adoption Services, Inc.—Ms. ANTJE HARRIS, Dir. Fax: 501-664-9186.

Diocesan Council for Black Catholics—Very Rev. WARREN HARVEY, V.F., Bishop's Liaison, P.O. Box 7434, Pine Bluff, 71611. Tel: 870-534-4701.

Building Commission—Mr. JIM DRIEDRIC, Exec. Sec. Fax: 501-664-1310.

Catholic Charities of Arkansas—Sr. MARY LOU STUBBS, D.C., Dir. This office also handles: Alcohol and Chemical Addiction Ministry; Catholic Adoption Services; Catholic Campaign for Human Development; Catholic Immigration Services, N.W. Arkansas; Catholic Immigration Services - Little Rock; Catholic Relief Services; Disaster Response; Parish Social Ministries; Prison Ministry; Refugee Resettlement; Social Action; Westside Free Medical Clinics.Fax: 501-664-9186.

Catholic Campus Ministry—Mrs. LIZ TINGQUIST, Dir.

Catholic Immigration Services - Little Rock Office—MARICELLA GARCIA, Dir. Fax: 501-664-9186.

Catholic Immigration Services - NW Arkansas Office—Mr. FRANK HEAD JR., Dir. Refugee Resettlement Program 2022 W. Sunset Ave., Springdale, 72762. Tel: 479-927-1996; Fax: 479-927-2979.

Catholic Women, Diocesan Council of—VACANT, Moderator. Contact: KEM DRAKE, Pres., 115 S. 14th St., Paragould, 72450. Tel: 870-236-2937.

Catholic Youth Ministry—Mrs. LIZ TINGQUIST, Dir.

Calvary Cemetery, Greater Little Rock—MICHAEL CAGLE, Supt., W. Charles Bussey Ave. & S. Woodrow St., Little Rock, 72207. Mailing Address: Calvary Cemetery, Diocese of Little Rock, 2500 N. Tyler St., Little Rock, 72207. Tel: 501-664-0340; Fax: 501-664-1310. Email: smullins@dolr.org.

Charismatic Movement—Rev. Msgr. JAMES E. MANCINI, Bishop's Liaison, St. Bernard of Clairvaux Chu, 1 St. Bernard Ln., Bella Vista, 72715. Tel: 479-855-9069. Email: jammanci@aol.com.

Clergy Welfare Board—Rev. Msgr. ROYCE R. THOMAS, J.C.L., J.V., Chm.

Continuing Education for the Clergy—Very Rev. Msgr. DAVID LESIEUR, V.F., Dir.

Cursillo Movement—Sr. JOSELINA CEDENO, C.M.S.T., Spiritual Dir., Spanish Cursillo Office; Deacon WILLIAM G. BRANDON JR., Spiritual Dir., English Cursillo Office; VACANT, Dir. English Cursillo Office; JOSE DIONICIO "NICHO" VAZQUEZ, Dir. Spanish Cursillo Office. Fax: 501-664-9075.

Information Systems—Rev. Msgr. THOMAS SEBAUGH, Dir.

Stewardship and Development Office—DIANNE BRADY, Interim Dir.

Diaconate Office—Deacon JOHN JACOB MARSCHEWSKI, Min. to Permanent Deacons.

Diaconate Formation (English)—Deacon ROBERT E. WANLESS.

Diaconate Formation (Spanish)—Deacon MARCELINO LUNA.

Ecumenical and Interreligious Affairs Office—Deacon JOHN JACOB MARSCHEWSKI, Dir., 9 Arles Dr., Little Rock, 72223. Tel: 501-664-0340; Fax: 501-664-9075.

Family Life Office: (Pre-Cana, Marriage Encounter, Retrouvaille, Natural Family Planning)—ELIZABETH REHA, Dir.

Hispanic Ministry—Deacon J. MARCELINO LUNA, Dir.

Hospitals—Very Rev. Msgr. FRANCIS I. MALONE, J.C.L., V.F.

Library—Mrs. TERESA HAYDEN, Librarian.

Office of Worship—Rev. SHAUN C. WESLEY.

Minister to Priests—Very Rev. Msgr. DAVID LESIEUR, V.F.

Newspaper "Arkansas Catholic"—Mrs. MALEA HARGETT, Editor, P.O. Box 7417, Little Rock, 72217.

Presbyteral Council—Most Rev. ANTHONY B. TAYLOR; Rev. Msgr. R. SCOTT FRIEND, V.G.; Very Rev. Msgr. FRANCIS I. MALONE, J.C.L., V.F.; Revs. JOHN M. CONNELL; GREGORY T. LUYET, J.C.L.; Very Revs. GREGORY G. HART, V.F.; VINCENT FLUSCHE, V.F.; Rev. RICHARD P. DAVIS; Very Rev. WARREN HARVEY, V.F.; Revs. THOMAS A. ELLIOTT; PIUS A. IWU, J.C.D.; Rev. Msgrs. SCOTT L. MARCZUK, J.C.L.; JACK D. HARRIS, D.Min.; J. GASTON HEBERT; Rev. LEONARD WANGLER, O.S.B.; Very Rev. MARK WOOD; Rt. Rev. JEROME KODELL, O.S.B., V.F.; Very Rev. Msgr. DAVID LESIEUR, V.F.

Priests Personnel Board (Diocesan)—Most Rev. ANTHONY B. TAYLOR; Rev. Msgr. R. SCOTT FRIEND, V.G.; Very Rev. Msgrs. FRANCIS I. MALONE, J.C.L., V.F.; DAVID LESIEUR, V.F.; Rev. Msgr. ROYCE R. THOMAS, J.C.L., J.V.; Very Rev. MARK WOOD; Rev. Msgr. JACK D. HARRIS, D.Min.; Very Rev. WARREN HARVEY, V.F.; Rev. GREGORY T. LUYET, J.C.L.; Rev. Msgrs. J. GASTON HEBERT; SCOTT L. MARCZUK, J.C.L.

Project Rachel—Mrs. ANNE DIERKS, Dir., 2500 N. Tyler St., Little Rock, 72207. Tel: 501-664-0340, Ext. 357.

Propagation of the Faith—Very Rev. Msgr. FRANCIS I. MALONE, J.C.L., V.F. Fax: 501-664-5835.

Refugee Resettlement Program—Mr. FRANK HEAD JR., Dir.

Religious Education Department/Christian Initiation—VACANT.

Respect Life Office—MARIANNE LINANE, Dir.

St. John's Catholic Center/Office Services—VACANT.

Schools—Mrs. VERNELL BOWEN, Supt. Fax: 501-603-0518.

Little Rock Scripture Study—Ms. CACKIE UPCHURCH, Dir.; Ms. LILLY HESS, Assoc. Dir., Administration & Production; Mr. CLIFF YEARY, Assoc. Dir., Devel. of Study Materials.

Monsignor James E. O'Connell Diocesan Seminarian Fund, Inc.—Rev. Msgr. R. SCOTT FRIEND, V.G., Dir.

Social Action and Prison Ministry, Catholic Campaign for Human Development Alcohol and Chemical Addiction Ministry—TOM NAVIN, Dir. Fax: 501-664-9186.

Parish Social Ministry and Disaster Response—Ms. JAMIE DEERE, Dir., 2500 N. Tyler St., Little Rock, 72207. Tel: 501-664-0340; Fax: 501-664-9186.

Victim Assistance Coordinator—Dr. GEORGE SIMON; Dr. SHERRY SIMON. Cell: 501-766-6001. Email: vacoord@dolr.org.

Vocations—Rev. Msgr. R. SCOTT FRIEND, V.G., Dir. Assistant Directors: Very Rev. ERIK POHLMEIER, V.F.; Rev. Msgr. JOHN F. O'DONNELL (Retired).

Westside Free Medical Clinic—Mrs. KAREN DIPIPPA, Dir. Fax: 501-664-9186.

CLERGY, PARISHES, MISSIONS AND PAROCHIAL SCHOOLS

GREATER LITTLE ROCK

(PULASKI COUNTY)

1—CATHEDRAL OF ST. ANDREW (1845) [JC] Rev. G. Matthew Garrison, Rector; Deacon William J. Bowen.
617 Louisiana St., 72201. Tel: 501-374-2794; Fax: 501-375-3292. Email: cathedralstandrew@sbcglobal.net. Web: www.cathedralsaintandrew.org.
Catechesis/Religious Program—Andrea Cordell, D.R.E. Students 60.

2—ST. ANNE (North Little Rock) (1935) [JC] Rev. Thomas Stehlik, C.M.
Mailing Address: 6150 Remount Rd., North Little Rock, 72118. Tel: 501-753-3977; Fax: 501-753-3991. Email: info@saintannenlr.org. Web: www.saintannenlr.org.
Catechesis/Religious Program—Belinda Kaye Ortner, D.R.E. Students 343.

3—ST. AUGUSTINE (1929), (African American), [JC] Rev. Frank V. DuPreez.
1421 E. Second, North Little Rock, 72114. Tel: 501-375-9617; Fax: 501-375-9617.
Catechesis/Religious Program—Rosalyn G. Pruitt, D.R.E. Students 23.

4—ST. BARTHOLOMEW (1907), (African American), Rev. Ryszard Zawadzki, S.V.D. (Poland); Deacon Kirke Leo Herman.
1622 Marshall St., 72202. Tel: 501-372-4682. Email: nev_pastor@sbcglobal.net.
Catechesis/Religious Program—Students 29.

5—CHRIST THE KING (1966) [JC] Very Rev. Msgr. Francis I. Malone; Revs. Udochukwu Vincent Ogbuji (Nigeria); Michael E. Bass; Deacons William Melville Hartmann, (Retired); John M. McAllister; Richard Lewis Patterson; Dan Charles Cashman; Curtis Don Greenway; William Johnson; John Jacob Marschewski.
4000 N. Rodney Parham Rd., 72212. Tel: 501-225-6774; Fax: 501-225-7169. Web: www.ctkLr.org.
School—(Grades PreK-8) Tel: 501-225-7883; Fax: 501-225-1315. Mrs. Kathy House, Prin. Lay Teachers 40; Students 727.
Catechesis/Religious Program—Students 170.
Msgr. Hebert Endowment Fund—Tel: 501-225-7883; Fax: 501-225-1315.

6—ST. EDWARD (1884) [JC] Rev. Jason Tyler; Deacons Daniel James Hennessey III; J. Marcelino Luna.
815 Sherman St., 72202. Tel: 501-374-5767; Fax: 501-374-5839. Email: office@saintedwards.net. Web: www.saintedwards.net.
School—(Grades PreK-8), 805 Sherman St., 72202. Tel: 501-374-9166. Jason Pohlmeier, Prin.; Karen Stoltz, Librarian. Lay Teachers 17; Students 180.
Catechesis/Religious Program— Lilia Hernandez, D.R.E. Students 371.

7—IMMACULATE CONCEPTION (1948) [JC] Rev. James P. West; Deacons Chuck Arthur Farrar; Ron Stager.
7000 John F. Kennedy Blvd., North Little Rock, 72116. Tel: 501-835-4323; Fax: 501-834-5598. Email: secretary@iccnlr.org. Web: www.iccnlr.org.
School—(Grades PreK-8) Tel: 501-835-0771; Fax: 501-834-8652. Email: dwolfe@icsnlr.org. Web: icsnlr.org. Mrs. Diane Wolfe, Prin. Lay Teachers 42; Students 386.
Catechesis/Religious Program—Tel: 501-835-4323, Ext. 30. Phyllis Eubanks, D.R.E. Students 100.
Immaculate Conception School Endowment Fund—Fax: 501-834-0165.

8—IMMACULATE HEART OF MARY (Marche) (1878), (Polish), [CEM] Rev. Robert T. Dienert; Deacon Brunon John Strozyk.
7006 Jasna Gora Dr., North Little Rock, 72118. Tel: 501-851-2763; Fax: 501-851-4769. Email: ihmparish@ihmparishschool.org. Web: www.ihmparishschool.org.
School—(Grades PreK-8) Tel: 501-851-2760; Fax: 501-851-4769. Email: ihmschool@sbcglobal.net. Maureen Pettei, Prin. Lay Teachers 17; Students 178.
Catechesis/Religious Program—Students 20.
Immaculate Heart of Mary Educational Trust Fund for Immaculate Heart of Mary School—Tel: 501-851-2763.

9—ST. MARY (North Little Rock) (1897), (Polish), Rev. Jose Uppani.
1516 Parker St., North Little Rock, 72114. Tel: 501-374-7123; Fax: 501-372-2995. Email: stmaryschurchlr@comcast.net.
School—North Little Rock Catholic Academy, (Grades PreK-8), 1518 Parker St., North Little Rock, 72114. Tel: 501-374-5237; Fax: 501-374-5237. Denise Troutman, Admin.; Sandra Naylor, Librarian. Lay Teachers 15; Students 232.
Catechesis/Religious Program—Denise Troutman, D.R.E. Students 287.
St. Mary's School Endowment Fund—Tel: 501-758-2220; Fax: 501-753-6623.

10—OUR LADY OF GOOD COUNSEL (1894) Rev. Ryszard Zawadzki, S.V.D. (Poland); Deacon John Augustine Hartnedy.
1321 S. Van Buren St., 72204. Tel: 501-666-5073; Fax: 501-664-1964. Email: olgc_parishoffice@sbcglobal.net. Web: www.goodcounselchurch.org.
Msgr. Scheper Endowment Fund for Our Lady of Good Counsel Catholic School—
Catechesis/Religious Program—Email: olgc_debbie@sbcglobal.net. Debbie King, C.R.E. Students 46.

11—OUR LADY OF THE HOLY SOULS (1947) Rev. Msgr. Royce R. Thomas; Rev. John Azu (Nigeria); Deacons William Cranford; Lawrence H. Jegley; Timothy Massanelli.
Church & Office: 1003 N. Tyler St., 72205. Tel: 501-663-8632; Fax: 501-663-8699. Email: office@holysouls.org. Web: www.holysouls.org.
School—(Grades PreK-8), 1001 N. Tyler St., 72205. Tel: 501-663-4513; Fax: 501-663-1014. Email: hss@holysouls.org. Web: arcathsch.org/hs/. Ileana Dobbins, Prin.; Ellie Stewart, Librarian. Lay Teachers 41; Students 515.
Catechesis/Religious Program—Anne Thomisee, D.R.E. Students 90.

12—ST. PATRICK (1880) [JC] Rev. Frank V. DuPreez.
211 W. 19th St., North Little Rock, 72114. Tel: 501-758-1155; Fax: 501-753-8251. Email: saintpatrick@sbcglobal.net. In Res., Rev. Do Duy Nho.
Catechesis/Religious Program—Students 16.
St. Patrick School Endowment Fund—Tel: 501-605-0008; Fax: 501-753-8251.

13—ST. THERESA (1954) [JC] Rev. D. Mark Wood; Deacon Donald Joseph Francis.
6219 Baseline Rd., 72209. Tel: 501-565-9198; Fax: 501-565-3949. Email: parishoffice@sttheresaschurch.org. Web: www.sttheresaschurch.org.
School—(Grades PreK-8) Tel: 501-565-3855; Fax: 501-565-9522. Marguerite Olberts, Prin. Lay Teachers 16; Students 184.
St. Theresa Catholic School Endowment Fund—
Catechesis/Religious Program—Tel: 501-565-5647. Students 331.

OUTSIDE THE CITY OF LITTLE ROCK

ADONA, CONWAY CO., ST. ELIZABETH (Oppelo) (1884), (German), [CEM] Attended by St. Boniface Church, New Dixie. Rev. Richard P. Davis.
Mailing Address: 20 St. Boniface Dr., Bigelow, 72016. Tel: 501-354-0631; Fax: 501-759-2152.
Catechesis/Religious Program—Students 48.

ALTUS, FRANKLIN CO., ST. MARY (1879) [CEM] Rev. Hilary Filiatreau, O.S.B.; Deacon Matthew Joseph Post.
5118 St. Mary's Ln., 72821. Tel: 479-468-2585.
Catechesis/Religious Program—Students 72.

ARKADELPHIA, CLARK CO., ST. MARY (1971) Rev. Linus Ukomadu; Deacon Edward Carl "Bud" Daven.
Church: P.O. Box 26, 71923. Tel: 870-246-7575.
Catechesis/Religious Program—Students 45.

ASHDOWN, LITTLE RIVER CO., ST. ELIZABETH ANN SETON CHURCH (1991) Attended by St. Edward, Texarkana. Very Rev. Vincent Flusche.
Mailing Address: 1910 Rankin St., P.O. Box 966, 71822. Tel: 870-898-8529.
Catechesis/Religious Program—Students 3.

ATKINS, POPE CO., ASSUMPTION B.V.M. (1878), (German), [CEM] Rev. Ernest L. Hardesty.
Mailing Address: P.O. Box 337, 72823. Tel: 479-641-7179.
Catechesis/Religious Program—Students 11.

BALD KNOB, WHITE CO., ST. RICHARD CHURCH, Attended by St. James, Searcy. Rev. John O. Agbakwuo.
Mailing Address: P.O. Box 172, Searcy, 72145. Tel: 501-268-5252 (Searcy).
Church: 101 W. Cleveland St., 72010.

BARLING, SEBASTIAN CO., SACRED HEART OF MARY (1902) [CEM] Revs. Henry B. Mischkowiuski; Peter Quang Le, (Vietnamese Catholic Community).
1301 Frank St., 72923. Tel: 479-452-1795; Fax: 479-452-0571.
Catechesis/Religious Program—Edwina Schwarz, D.R.E.; Dottie Hunter, D.R.E. Students 30.
Mission—SS. Sabina & Mary Church, (See listing under Fort Smith), Jenny Lind. Dr. Thomas Bonin, D.R.E.

BATESVILLE, INDEPENDENCE CO., ST. MARY (1909) Rev. Paul F. Worm; Deacon Mike Comnock.
3800 Harrison St., 72501. Tel: 870-793-7717 (Office); 870-793-7464 (Rectory); Fax: 870-793-7717. Email: stmarys@suddenlinkmail.com.
Catechesis/Religious Program—Patricia Hinds, D.R.E.
Mission—St. Cecilia 2475 Galleria Dr., Newport, Jackson Co. 72112. Tel: 870-523-6542.

BELLA VISTA, BENTON CO., ST. BERNARD OF CLAIRVAUX (1980) [CEM] Rev. Msgr. James E. Mancini; Deacon Raymond Edward Brust.
Office: One St. Bernard Ln., 72715. Tel: 479-855-9069; Fax: 479-855-9069. Email: office@bvstbernard.org. Web: www.bvstbernard.org.
Catechesis/Religious Program—Tel: 479-855-3416. Irene Harold Wallace, C.R.E. Students 60.

BENTON, SALINE CO., OUR LADY OF FATIMA (1942) Rev. William Elser; Deacons John Charles Duke; Gilbert Paul Morgan.
900 W. Cross St., 72015. Tel: 501-315-5186. Email: olfchurch@swbell.net. In Res., Rev. Joseph Ejimofor (Nigeria).
School—(Grades K-8), 818 W. Cross St., 72015. Tel: 501-315-3398; Fax: 501-315-1479. Web: www.ourladyoffatimaschool.com. Jan Cash, Prin. Lay Teachers 11; Students 92.
Our Lady of Fatima School Endowment Trust Fund—
Catechesis/Religious Program—Cecelia Patton, D.R.E. Students 146.
Station—Arkansas Health Center, Tel: 501-860-0500.

BENTONVILLE, BENTON CO., ST. STEPHEN (1989) [CEM] Rev. Msgr. Scott L. Marczuk.
Mailing Address: 1300 N.E. J St., 72712. Tel: 479-273-1240; Fax: 479-464-0969. Email: ststephen@cox-internet.com. Web: www.ststephenbentonville.com.
Rectory—1208 N.E. J St., 72712. Tel: 479-273-1240; Fax: 479-464-0969.
Catechesis/Religious Program—Students 537.

BERRYVILLE, CARROLL CO., ST. ANNE (1958) Attended by St. Elizabeth of Hungary, Eureka Springs. (See listing for Eureka Springs). Rev. Shaun C. Wesley.
614 S. Main, 72616. Tel: 870-423-3927. Email: stannes@mynewroads.com. Web: www.stanneschurchberryville.org.
Res.: 30 Crescent Dr., Eureka Springs, 72632. Tel: 479-253-9853.
Catechesis/Religious Program—Students 106.

BIGELOW, PERRY CO., ST. BONIFACE (1879), (German), [CEM] Rev. Richard P. Davis.
20 St. Boniface Dr., 72016. Tel: 501-759-2371; Fax: 501-759-2152.
Catechesis/Religious Program—Students 46.
Mission—St. Francis of Assisi Little Italy, Pulaski Co.
Mission—St. Elizabeth Adona, Conway Co.

BLYTHEVILLE, MISSISSIPPI CO., IMMACULATE CONCEPTION (1894) Very Rev. Joseph L. Pallo; Deacons William G. Brandon Jr.; Kenneth Klinger.
Mailing Address: 1301 W. Main St., P.O. Box 747, 72316.
Office: 1301 Main St., 72315. Tel: 870-762-2506; Fax: 870-762-2506.
Catechesis/Religious Program—Tel: 870-561-4120. Students 30.
Mission—St. Matthew S. Ermen St., P.O. Box 583, Osceola, Mississippi Co. 72370.

BOONEVILLE, LOGAN CO., CHURCH OF OUR LADY OF THE ASSUMPTION (1953) Rev. Don Tranel, G.H.M.
Mailing Address: P.O. Box 298, 72927. Tel: 479-675-3371.
Church: 616 N. Cherry Ave., 72927.
Catechesis/Religious Program—Students 55.

BRINKLEY, MONROE CO., ST. JOHN THE BAPTIST (1875) [CEM] Rev. Athanasius N. Okeiyi (Nigeria).
203 W. Ash, 72021-3201. Tel: 870-734-1202.
Catechesis/Religious Program—Tel: 870-734-3392. Carl Frein, D.R.E. Students 6.
Mission—St. Francis of Assisi Forrest City.
Mission—St. Mary of the Lake, See St. St. Mary of the Lake, Horseshoe Lake for complete listing., Horseshoe Lake, Crittenden Co. 72348.

CAMDEN, OUACHITA CO., ST. LOUIS (1923) Rev. Thomas Joseph Hart.
Mailing Address: 202 Adams, N.W., 71701. Tel: 870-836-2426.
Res.: 2114 N. Jackson St., Magnolia, 71753. Email: stlouiscc6674@sbcglobal.net.
Catechesis/Religious Program—Tel: 870-231-4554. Mrs. Deb Murray, D.R.E. Students 33.
Mission—Immaculate Heart of Mary 2114 N. Jackson St., Magnolia, Columbia Co. 71753. Tel: 870-234-2710. Mailing Address: P.O. Box 365, Magnolia, 71754.

CARLISLE, LONOKE CO., ST. ROSE OF LIMA CHURCH (1895) Rev. Thomas W. Keller; Deacon William Cunningham Jr.
603 E. Park, P.O. Box M, 72024. Tel: 870-552-3601. Email: strose011@centurytel.net. Mailing Address: P.O. Box M, 72024.
Catechesis/Religious Program—Beth Plafcan, D.R.E. Students 29.
Mission—Holy Trinity, (See listing under England), England, Lonoke Co.

CENTER RIDGE, CONWAY CO., ST. JOSEPH (1881), (Italian), [CEM] Rev. John L. Yates, C.S.Sp.
Mailing Address: 343 Catholic Point Rd., 72027. Tel: 501-893-2887; Fax: 501-893-2887. Email: stjoseph343@hotmail.com.
Catechesis/Religious Program—Annette May, D.R.E. Students 36.

CHARLESTON, FRANKLIN CO., SACRED HEART (1879) [CEM] Rev. Peter Sharum, O.S.B.
18 Prairie St., 72933-9334. Tel: 479-965-2432. Email: shchurch@centurytel.net. Web: www.sacredheartcharleston.com.
Catechesis/Religious Program—Tel: 479-965-2771. Anita Collier, D.R.E. Students 92.

CHEROKEE VILLAGE, SHARP CO., ST. MICHAEL (1939) Very Rev. Thomas C. Marks.
Mailing Address: P.O. Box 970, 72525. Tel: 870-257-2850; Fax: 870-257-2200. Email: stmichaelcv@yahoo.com. Web: www.stmichaelscv.org.
49 Tekakwitha Dr., 72529.
Res.: 12 Micanopy Circle, 72529. Tel: 870-257-4456.
Catechesis/Religious Program—Students 33.
Mission—St. Mary of the Mount Church 401 E. Church St., Horseshoe Bend, Izard Co. 72512. Tel: 870-670-5896.
St. Michael Memorial Garden (Columbarium)—Hwy. 62/167 S. Tekakwitha Dr., 72529. Tel: 870-257-2850.

CLARKSVILLE, JOHNSON CO., HOLY REDEEMER (1879) [CEM] Rev. William Wewers, O.S.B.
103 E. Main St., 72830. Tel: 479-754-3610. Email: wgwosb@suddenlinkmail.com. Web: www.magicinterludes.net/holyredeemer/.
Catechesis/Religious Program—Students 263.

CLINTON, VAN BUREN CO., ST. JUDE CHURCH (1988) Attended by St. Francis of Assisi, Fairfield Bay. Rev. Oliver Ochieze (Nigeria).
Mailing Address: P.O. Box 526, 72031. Tel: 501-745-5716; Fax: 501-745-5716. Email: grakme@clinton.cable.
Catechesis/Religious Program—David Adams, D.R.E. Students 30.

CONWAY, FAULKNER CO., ST. JOSEPH (1878) [CEM] Rev. George Spangenberg, C.S.Sp.; Deacons David Kirby Westmoreland; Richard John Papini; Gerald Joseph Harrison.
Parish Business Office: 1115 College Ave., 72032. Tel: 501-327-5528; 501-327-6568; Fax: 501-327-6607. Email: sjbusoff@hotmail.com. Web: www.sjparish.org.
School—(Grades PreK-12), 502 Front St., 72032. Tel: 501-329-5741; Fax: 501-513-6804. Web: www-.stjosephconway.org. Joe Mallett, Prin.; Matt Tucker, Asst. Prin. (PreK-3); Susie Freyaldenhoven, Asst. Prin. (Grades 4-6); Karen Wilson, Librarian; Myra Book, Librarian. Lay Teachers 48; Students 505.
Catechesis/Religious Program—Tel: 501-513-6812. Jean Leffler, D.R.E. Students 386.

CORNING, CLAY CO., ST. JOSEPH THE WORKER CHURCH (1968) Attended by St. Paul the Apostle, Pocahontas Very Rev. John E. Marconi.
Mailing Address: c/o 2CR 186, 72422. Tel: 870-857-6607.
Church Site: 1415 Harb S., 72422.

CRAWFORDSVILLE, CRITTENDEN CO., SACRED HEART CHURCH, Attended by St. Michael, West Memphis. Rev. Leslie A. Farley.
Mailing Address: *c/o St. Michael*, P.O. Box 899, West Memphis, 72303. Tel: 870-733-1212 (West Memphis); Fax: 870-732-4808. Email: stmichaels899@sbcglobal.net.
Church: 216 S. Main St., 72327.

CROSSETT, ASHLEY CO., HOLY CROSS, Attended by St. Mary, McGehee. Rev. Chuma P. Ibebuike (Nigeria).
Mailing Address: 2400 S. Main St., 71635.
Catechesis/Religious Program—1309 Hickory, 71635. Tel: 870-364-7073. Vickie McMahan, D.R.E. Students 16.

DANVILLE, YELL CO., SAINT ANDREW CHURCH (1996) Attended by St. Jude Thaddeus, Waldron. Rev. Neil Pezzulo, G.H.M.
Mailing Address: c/o P.O. Box 1688, Waldron, 72958.
Catechesis/Religious Program—David Henley, D.R.E. Students 148.

DARDANELLE, YELL CO., ST. AUGUSTINE (1925) Rev. Clayton Gould, Admin.
P.O. Box 460, 72834.
Church: 1001 N. 2nd., 72834. Tel: 479-229-3972.
Catechesis/Religious Program—Students 105.

DE QUEEN, SEVIER CO., ST. BARBARA (1911) [CEM] [JC] Rev. Jose Orellara.
Mailing Address: P.O. Box 86, 71832. Tel: 870-642-2256; Fax: 870-642-3426. Email: st.barbar@hotmail.com.
Catechesis/Religious Program—Students 359.

DUMAS, DESHA CO., HOLY CHILD CHURCH, (Hispanic), Attended by St. Mark, Monticello. Rev. Phillip A. Reaves.
Mailing Address: *c/o St. Mark*, 1016 N. Hyatt St., Monticello, 71655. Tel: 870-367-2848 (Monticello); Fax: 870-367-5868.
Church: 807 E. Waterman St., 71639.
Catechesis/Religious Program—Students 8.

EL DORADO, UNION CO., HOLY REDEEMER (1923) Rev. Gregory Pilcher, O.S.B.
Church: 440 W. Main St., 71730-5757. Tel: 870-863-3620; Fax: 870-863-7537. Email: holyredeemer@suddenlinkmail.com. Web: www.holyredeemereldorado.org.
Catechesis/Religious Program—Students 104.
El Dorado Holy Redeemer School Endowment Fund—1103 W. Cedar St., 71730. Tel: 870-863-8677; Fax: 870-863-7779.

ENGELBERG, RANDOLPH CO., ST. JOHN THE BAPTIST (Pocahontas P.O.) (1885), (German), [CEM] Attended by St. Paul the Apostle, Pocahontas. Very Rev. John E. Marconi.
4650 Engelberg Rd., Pocahontas, 72455. Tel: 870-892-3319.
Catechesis/Religious Program—Tel: 870-647-1141. Sr. Elizabeth Love, O.S.B., D.R.E. Students 27.

ENGLAND, LONOKE CO., HOLY TRINITY CHURCH (1976) Attended by St. Rose of Lima, Carlisle Rev. Thomas W. Keller.
Mailing Address: P.O. Box 243, 72046.
Church: 1240 AR Hwy 161 W., 72046. Tel: 870-552-3601 (Carlisle).

EUREKA SPRINGS, CARROLL CO., ST. ELIZABETH OF HUNGARY (1909) Rev. Shaun C. Wesley.
Mailing Address: 232 Passion Play Rd., 72632. Tel: 479-253-2222; Fax: 479-253-6616. Email: stelizabeth@mynewroads.com.
Res.: #30 Crescent Dr., 72632. Tel: 479-253-9853.
Catechesis/Religious Program—Tel: 479-253-6742. Margaret Bartell, D.R.E.; Kathy Tromburg, D.R.E. Students 16.
Mission—St. Anne, (See listing for Berryville), 614 S. Main St., Berryville, 72616. Tel: 870-423-3927.

FAIRFIELD BAY, VAN BUREN CO., ST. FRANCIS ASSISI (1976) Rev. Oliver Ochieze (Nigeria); Deacon Frank Joseph Zanoff.
Res.: 250 Woodlawn Dr., 72088. Tel: 501-884-3349; Fax: 501-884-4852. Email: stfrancis@artelco.com.
Catechesis/Religious Program—Tel: 501-884-7272. Deacon Frank Joseph Zanoff, D.R.E. Students 9.
Mission—St. Jude, (See listing under Clinton), Clinton, Van Buren Co.

FAYETTEVILLE, WASHINGTON CO.

1—ST. JOSEPH (1844) [CEM] Rev. John K. Antony; Deacon Bud Baldwin III.
Church & Office: 1722 N. Starr Dr., 72701. Tel: 479-442-0890; Fax: 479-442-7887. Email: bbarber@sjfay.com. Web: www.sjfay.com.
School—(Grades PreK-7) Tel: 479-442-4554. Web: www.sjfay.com. Ann Finch, Prin.; Jenny Long, Librarian. Lay Teachers 21; Students 286.
St. Joseph Endowment and Educational Trust Fund—1722 N. Starr Dr., 72701. Tel: 479-442-4554.
Catechesis/Religious Program—Tel: 479-442-0890, Ext. 256. Email: skrumpelman@sjfay.com. Suzanne Krumpelman, D.R.E. Students 512.

2—ST. THOMAS AQUINAS UNIVERSITY PARISH (1960) Revs. Joseph Patrick Marconi; Lourduswamy Dhanraj Narla (India).
603 N. Leverett Ave., 72701-3220. Tel: 479-444-0223; Fax: 479-442-2633.

FORDYCE, DALLAS CO., GOOD SHEPHERD (1977) Attended by Holy Cross, Sheridan. Rev. Joseph

Ejimofor (Nigeria).
Mailing Address: 5 Holly St., 71742. 410 W. Oak St., 71742. Tel: 870-352-2328.
Catechesis/Religious Program—Tami Strickland, D.R.E. Students 7.

FOREMAN, LITTLE RIVER CO., SACRED HEART CHURCH, A mission of St. Edward, Texarkana. Very Rev. Vincent Flusche.
Mailing Address: P.O. Box 43, 71836. Tel: 870-542-6574; Fax: 870-542-6715.
Catechesis/Religious Program—Students 14.

FORREST CITY, ST. FRANCIS CO., ST. FRANCIS OF ASSISI (1876) [JC] Rev. Athanasius N. Okeiyi (Nigeria).
621 S. Washington St., P.O. Box 786, 72336-0786. Tel: 870-633-1665; Fax: 870-633-6307. Email: stfrancis@arkansas.net.
Catechesis/Religious Program—Students 8.

FORT SMITH, SEBASTIAN CO.

1—ST. BONIFACE (1886) [JC] Rev. H. Jon McDougal; Deacon John Joseph Burns.
1820 North B St., 72901. Tel: 479-783-6711; Fax: 479-783-7423. Email: stbface@aol.com. Web: www.saintboniface.com.
School—(Grades PreK-6), 201 N. 19th St., 72901. Tel: 479-783-6601; Fax: 479-783-6605. Web: www.stbonifaceschool.org. Karen Hollenbeck, Prin. Lay Teachers 15; Students 174.
Catholic Education Endowment Trust of Fort Smith, Arkansas—
Catechesis/Religious Program—Rowena Gran, D.R.E. Students 43.

2—CHRIST THE KING (1928) [CEM] [JC] Rev. Thomas A. Elliott.
2112 S. Greenwood Ave., 72901. Tel: 479-783-7745; Fax: 479-783-7075. Email: ctkpastor@christ-king.org. Web: www.christ-king.org.
School—(Grades PreK-6), 1918 S. Greenwood, 72901. Tel: 479-782-0614; Fax: 479-782-1098. Email: principal@christ-king.org. Web: www.ctk-school.com. Marna Boltuc, Prin. Lay Teachers 20; Students 263.
Christ the King Catholic School Trust and Endowment Fund—Tel: 479-783-1937.
Catechesis/Religious Program—Tel: 479-783-5305. Wendy Lorenz, Youth Min.; Beth Roberts, D.R.E. Students 168.

3—IMMACULATE CONCEPTION (1849) [JC] Revs. Gregory T. Luyet; Edward P. D'Almeida; Deacons Greg Pair; Tony Picciano.
Mailing Address: P.O. Box 1866, 72902-1866.
Church: 22 North 13th, 72901. Tel: 479-783-7963; Fax: 479-783-7865.
School—(Grades K-6), 223 South 14th St., 72901. Tel: 479-783-6798; Fax: 479-783-0510. Web: www.ic-schoolfs.org. Sharon Blentlinger, Prin.; Sr. Mary Sarto Gaffrey, Librarian. Sisters of Mercy 1; Lay Teachers 29; Students 354.
Immaculate Conception School Educational Trust—
Catechesis/Religious Program—Tel: 479-783-7497. Surennah Werley, D.R.E. Students 700.
Mission—St. Leo's P.O. Box 1866, Hartford, Sebastian Co. 72902.

4—SS. SABINA & MARY CHURCH, Attended by Sacred Heart of Mary, Barling. Rev. Henry B. Mischkowiuski.
Mailing Address: 14304 Old Jenny Loop Rd., 72919. Tel: 479-452-1795 (Barling); Fax: 501-452-0571.
Catechesis/Religious Program—Dr. Thomas Bonin, D.R.E. Students 36.

GLENWOOD, PIKE CO., OUR LADY OF GUADALUPE CHURCH, Closed. Now a mission of St. Agnes, Mena.

GRADY, LINCOLN CO., BLESSED SACRAMENT CHURCH, (Hispanic), Attended by St. Justin, Star City. Sr. Kathleen Miles, D.C., Pastoral Admin.
Mailing Address: P.O. Box 128, Star City, 71667.
Res.: 1207 S. Main, 71644. Tel: 870-628-3092; Fax: 870-628-3092.

HAMBURG, ASHLEY CO., HOLY SPIRIT CHURCH (1987), (Hispanic), Attended by Our Lady of the Lake, Lake Village. Rev. Theophilus Okpara (Nigeria).
Mailing Address: P.O. Box 272, Lake Village, 71653. Tel: 870-265-5439; Fax: 870-265-5439.
Church: 110 E. Franklin, 71646. Tel: 870-853-8991.

HARRISON, BOONE CO., MARY, MOTHER OF GOD (1919) Very Rev. Gregory G. Hart.
Mailing Address: P.O. Box 2150, 72602. Tel: 870-741-5234; Fax: 870-741-4234.
Church: Hwy. 43 E. & Maplewood Rd., 72602.
Catechesis/Religious Program—Fax: 870-741-4234. Roz Slavik, D.R.E. Students 108.
Mission—St Andrews Catholic Church, (See listing under Yellville), Yellville, Marion Co.

HARTFORD, SEBASTIAN CO., ST. LEO'S (1901), A mission of Immaculate Conception, Fort Smith. Revs. Gregory T. Luyet; Edward P. D'Almeida.
Mailing Address: P.O. Box 1866, Fort Smith, 72902. Tel: 479-783-7963; Fax: 479-783-7865.
Catechesis/Religious Program—

HEBER SPRINGS, CLEBURNE CO., ST. ALBERT CHURCH, Attended by St. James, Searcy. Rev. John O. Agbakwuo; Deacon Robert L. Morris.
Mailing Address: 21 Park Rd., 72543. Tel: 501-362-2914; Fax: 501-362-8942. Email: stalbert21@suddenlinkmail.com.
Catechesis/Religious Program—Students 50.

HELENA, PHILLIPS CO., ST. MARY (1858) [CEM] Rev. Charles U. Kanu (Nigeria).
123 Columbia St., 72342. Tel: 870-338-6990; Fax: 870-338-6990.
Catechesis/Religious Program—Students 33.
Mission—St. Andrew, (See listing for Marianna), 54 W. Tennessee St., P.O. Box 724, Marianna, Lee Co. 72360.

HOPE, HEMPSTEAD CO., OUR LADY OF GOOD HOPE (1875) [CEM] Rev. Kevin O. Atunzu; Deacon Robert V. Regan, (Retired).
Mailing Address: P.O. Box 517, 71802-0517.
Office: 315 S. Walker St., 71802-0517. Tel: 870-777-3202; Fax: 870-777-8533. Email: ourladyofgoodhope@sbcglobal.net.
Catechesis/Religious Program—Karen Barham, D.R.E. Students 93.

HORSESHOE BEND, IZARD CO., ST. MARY OF THE MOUNT (1974) [CEM] Attended by St. Michael, Cherokee Village. Very Rev. Thomas C. Marks.
1002 First St., 72512. Tel: 870-670-5896. Email: mounts@centurytel.net.
Catechesis/Religious Program—

HORSESHOE LAKE, CRITTENDEN CO., ST. MARY OF THE LAKE CHURCH, Attended by St. John the Baptist, Brinkley Rev. Athanasius N. Okeiyi (Nigeria).
Mailing Address: *c/o St. John the Baptist*, 203 W. Ash, Brinkley, 72021-3201. Tel: 870-734-1202.
Church: 1713 Horseshoe Cr., 72348.

HOT SPRINGS NATIONAL PARK, GARLAND CO.

1—ST. JOHN THE BAPTIST (1907) Very Rev. Erik Pohlmeier; Revs. Alan Rosenau; Innocent Okore (Nigeria); Deacons David Lee Briselden; Patrick McCruden.
Res.: 589 W. Grand Ave., 71901. Tel: 501-623-6201; Fax: 501-318-0328.
School—(Grades PreK-8), 583 W. Grand Ave., 71901. Tel: 501-624-3141; Fax: 501-624-3141. Mrs. Elizabeth Shackelford, Prin. Sisters of Mercy 3; Lay Teachers 15; Students 116.
St. John's School Endowment—Tel: 501-624-3171.
Catechesis/Religious Program—Students 111.

2—ST. MARY OF THE SPRINGS (1869) [JC] Very Rev. Erik Pohlmeier; Revs. Alan Rosenau; Innocent Okore (Nigeria); Deacons Joe Dale Harrison; Lee Leckner.
100 Central Ave., 71901. Tel: 501-623-3233. Email: stmcc@hotsprings.net.
Catechesis/Religious Program—Students 71.

HOT SPRINGS VILLAGE, GARLAND CO., SACRED HEART OF JESUS (1979) Rev. Msgr. Bernard G. Malone; Deacons Bernard Louis Bauer; Larry Lipsmeyer; William Friedman.
Rectory—293 Balearic Rd., 71909. Tel: 501-922-4024.
Church & Mailing Address: 295 Balearic Rd., 71909. Tel: 501-922-2062; Fax: 501-922-4153. Email: sacredheart@hsvsacredheart.com. Web: www.hsvsacredheart.com.

HUNTSVILLE, MADISON CO., ST. JOHN THE EVANGELIST (1963) [JC], Attended from St. Joseph, Tontitown Revs. Joseph Patrick Marconi; Lourduswamy Dhanraj Narla (India); George Lowe, Business Mgr.
Mailing Address: P.O. Box 755, 72740.
Church: 411 Crossbow Rd., 72740. Tel: 479-559-2826.
Catechesis/Religious Program—Tel: 479-232-5790. Susan Rivera, D.R.E. Students 25.

JACKSONVILLE, PULASKI CO., ST. JUDE THE APOSTLE (1966) Rev. W. Andrew Smith; Deacons James M. Alberson; Max R. Elliott.
2403 McArthur Dr., 72076. Tel: 501-982-4891; Fax: 501-982-0821. Email: stjude982@aol.com.
Catechesis/Religious Program—Tel: 501-843-9467. Paula Porce, D.R.E. Students 287.

JONESBORO, CRAIGHEAD CO.

1—BLESSED JOHN NEWMAN UNIVERSITY PARISH, Attended by Blessed Sacrament, Jonesboro Rev. Jack Vu; Deacon David Emory England; Mary Ruth Stuadt, Dir.
Mailing Address: 2800 E. Johnson Ave., 72401. Tel: 870-972-1888; Fax: 870-972-6294. Email: cnc28@sbcglobal.net. Web: www.clt.astate.edu/cnc.

2—BLESSED SACRAMENT (1885) [CEM] Deacons Victor J. Stepka; David Emory England.
614 S. Church St., P.O. Box 1735, 72401. Tel: 870-932-2529. Email: office@catholicjonesboro.com. Web: www.catholicjonesboro.com.
School—(Grades K-6), 720 S. Church St., 72401. Tel: 870-932-3684. Email: pillow@tdn.to. Lee Ann Graddy, Prin. Lay Teachers 8; Students 114.
Catechesis/Religious Program—Tel: 870-931-7079. Students 295.
Blessed Sacrament Educational Endowment Fund—Tel: 870-935-2871.
Mission—St. Norbert, See St. Norbert, Marked Tree for complete listing., Marked Tree, 72365.
Mission—St. Anthony, See St. Anthony, Weiner for complete listing.

LAKE VILLAGE, CHICOT CO., OUR LADY OF THE LAKE (1869), (Italian), [CEM 2] Rev. Theophilus Okpara (Nigeria).
Mailing Address: P.O. Box 272, 71653. Tel: 870-265-5439; Fax: 870-265-5663.
School—(Grades PreK-6) Tel: 870-265-2921; Fax: 870-265-2921. Kelly Pieroni, Prin. Lay Teachers 9; Students 94.
Catechesis/Religious Program—Deborah Vaughn, D.R.E.; Terry Lee, D.R.E. Students 35.
St. Mary's Educational Trust Fund—
Mission—Holy Spirit, See Holy Spirit, Hamburg for complete listing., Hamburg, Ashley Co. 71646.

LEOLA, GRANT CO., BLESSED JUAN DIEGO CHURCH, Closed. For inquiries for parish records contact the chancery.

LITTLE ITALY, PULASKI CO., ST. FRANCIS OF ASSISI CHURCH (1922) Attended by St. Boniface, Bigelow. Rev. Richard P. Davis.
Mailing Address: *c/o St. Boniface*, 20 St. Boniface, Bigelow, 72016. Tel: 501-759-2371.
Catechesis/Religious Program—

MAGNOLIA, COLUMBIA CO., IMMACULATE HEART OF MARY (1946) Attended by St. Louis Church, Camden. Rev. Thomas Joseph Hart.
Mailing Address: P.O. Box 365, 71754. Tel: 870-234-2710.
Catechesis/Religious Program—Students 27.

MALVERN, HOT SPRING CO., ST. JOHN THE BAPTIST (1949) Rev. Linus Ukomadu.
Mailing Address: 1121 McBee St., P.O. Box 6, 72104. Tel: 501-332-6244; Fax: 501-332-7100.
Catechesis/Religious Program—Carolyn Paul, D.R.E. Students 12.

MARIANNA, LEE CO., ST. ANDREW, Attended by St. Mary's, Helena. Rev. Charles U. Kanu (Nigeria).
54 W. Tennessee St., P.O. Box 724, 72360. Tel: 870-338-6990 (Helena); Fax: 870-338-6990 (Helena).

MARKED TREE, POINSETT CO., ST. NORBERT (1947) Rev. Jack Vu.
Mailing Address: 42 Frisco St., 72365. Tel: 870-358-2135; Fax: 870-358-4055.
Church: 501 Normandy St., 72365.

MCCRORY, WOODRUFF CO., ST. MARY CHURCH, Attended by St. Peter, Wynne. Very Rev. Edwin Graves.
Mailing Address: c/o 1695 N. Falls Blvd., P.O. Box 517, Wynne, 72396. Tel: 870-731-0048; Fax: 870-238-2613 (Wynne).
Catechesis/Religious Program—

MCGEHEE, DESHA CO., ST. MARY (1906) Attended by Holy Cross, Crossett. Rev. Chuma P. Ibebuike (Nigeria).
401 N. 3rd St., 71654. Tel: 870-222-3389 (call for fax).

MENA, POLK CO., ST. AGNES (1896) [CEM] Rev. Norbert F. Rappold; Deacon Larry Hatch.
203 8th St., 71953. Tel: 479-394-1017; Fax: 479-394-2088. Email: saintagnesmena@sbcglobal.net.
Catechesis/Religious Program—Students 70.
Mission—All Saints, (See listing Mount Ida), Mount Ida, Montgomery Co.
Mission—Our Lady of Guadalupe Glenwood, Pike Co.

MONTICELLO, DREW CO., ST. MARK (1975) Rev. Phillip A. Reaves.
Mailing Address: 1016 N. Hyatt St., 71655. Tel: 870-367-2848; Fax: 870-367-5868.
Rectory—452 W. Jefferson, 71655. Tel: 870-367-5974.
Catechesis/Religious Program—Tel: 870-460-9919. Amanda Kuttenkuler, D.R.E. Students 65.
Mission—St. Luke, (See listing under Warren), Warren, Bradley Co.
Mission—Holy Child, (See listing under Dumas), Dumas, Desha Co.

MORRILTON, CONWAY CO., SACRED HEART (1879) [CEM] Rev. Charles Thessing.
506 E. Broadway, 72110. Tel: 501-354-4181; Fax: 501-354-4181. Email: sacred_heart@hotmail.com.
School—(Grades K-6) Tel: 501-354-8113; Fax: 501-354-2001. Brian Bailey, Prin.; Katherine Etris, Librarian. Lay Teachers 8; Students 137.
High School—(Grades 7-12), 106 N. St. Joseph, 72110. Brian Bailey, Prin.; Katherine Etris, Librarian. Lay Teachers 12; Students 101.
Catechesis/Religious Program—Students 95.
Sacred Heart School Endowment—

MORRISON BLUFF, LOGAN CO., SS. PETER AND PAUL (1878) Rev. Barnabas Maria Susai, I.M.S.
Res. & Mailing Address: 108 E. Main St., Scranton, 72863. Tel: 479-938-2821.
Catechesis/Religious Program—Ruth Beshoner, D.R.E. Students 23.

MOUNT IDA, MONTGOMERY CO., ALL SAINTS CHURCH, Attended by St. Agnes, Mena. Rev. Norbert F. Rappold.

Mailing Address: P.O. Box 724, 71957. Tel: 479-867-4644; Fax: 479-867-4644 (Mena).
Catechesis/Religious Program—Students 3.

MOUNTAIN HOME, BAXTER CO., ST. PETER THE FISHERMAN (1959) Revs. James M. Fanrak; Stan Swiderski; Deacons John Thomas Krug, (Retired); Richard Linstad; Robert Crawford; Paul Poulosky.
249 Dyer St., P.O. Box 298, 72654. Tel: 870-425-2832; Fax: 870-424-5172.
Catechesis/Religious Program—Rev. James M. Fanrak, D.R.E. Students 105.
Mission—St. Mary Church (1983), (See listing under Mountain View), Mountain View, Stone Co.

MOUNTAIN VIEW, STONE CO., ST. MARY CHURCH (1982) Attended by St. Peter the Fisherman, Mountain Home. Revs. James M. Fanrak; Stan Swiderski.
Mailing Address: P.O. Box 926, Stone Co. 72560.
Res.: 17068 Hwy. 66 W., 72560. Tel: 870-269-5194; Fax: 870-269-5194. Email: stmarychurch@mvtel.net.
Catechesis/Religious Program—Loreena Hegenbart, D.R.E. Students 16.

NASHVILLE, HOWARD CO., ST. MARTIN CHURCH, Attended by Our Lady of Good Hope, Hope. Rev. Kevin O. Atunzu.
Mailing Address: 1011 Leslie St., P.O. Box 1039, 71852. Tel: 870-845-1271.
Catechesis/Religious Program—Nona Broussard, D.R.E. Students 38.

NEWPORT, JACKSON CO., ST. CECILIA, Attended by St. Mary's, Batesville. Rev. Paul F. Worm.
Church: 2475 Galeria Subdivision, 72112. Tel: 870-793-7464; 870-523-6542; Fax: 870-793-7717.
St. Mary Church: 3800 Harrison St., Batesville, 72501. Tel: 870-793-7717.
Catechesis/Religious Program—

OSCEOLA, MISSISSIPPI CO., ST. MATTHEW (1879) Attended by Immaculate Conception, Blytheville. Very Rev. Joseph L. Pallo.
Mailing Address: P.O. Box 583, 72370.
Res.: 1301 W. Main St., Blytheville, 72315. Tel: 870-762-2506; Fax: 870-762-2506.
Church: S. Ermen St., 72370.
Catechesis/Religious Program—800 Betty Lynn, 72370. Tel: 870-563-4889. Students 6.

PARAGOULD, GREENE CO., ST. MARY (1883) [CEM] Rev. Michael Sinkler; Deacon Rex A. Bouldin.
Church, Office & Mailing Address: 220 N. Second St., 72450. Tel: 870-236-2568; Fax: 870-236-8675. Email: stmoff@grno.net. Web: www.stmarysparagould.org.
School—(Grades PreK-6) Tel: 870-236-3681; Fax: 870-236-1073. Sharon Warren, Prin. Lay Teachers 8; Students 55.
Catechesis/Religious Program—Tel: 870-239-3976. Karen Ussery, D.R.E. Students 47.
Mission—St. Joseph the Worker, (See listing under Corning), Corning, Clay Co. Tel: 870-857-6607.
St. Mary Educational Trust Fund—

PARIS, LOGAN CO., ST. JOSEPH (1879), (German), [CEM] Rev. Eugene Luke, O.S.B.; Deacon Thomas J. Pohlmeier.
15 S. Spruce St., 72855. Tel: 479-963-2131. Web: www.stjosephsweb.org.
School—(Grades PreK-8), 25 S. Spruce St., 72855. Tel: 479-963-2119; Fax: 479-963-8039. Vivian Fox, Prin. Lay Teachers 6; Students 63.
Catechesis/Religious Program—Students 15.
St. Joseph Endowment Fund—

PINE BLUFF, JEFFERSON CO.
1—ST. JOSEPH (1858) [CEM 5] [JC] Rev. L. Warren Harvey; Deacon Noel F. "Bud" Bryant.
412 W. 6th Ave., P.O. Box 7434, 71611. Tel: 870-534-4701; Fax: 870-534-4703. Web: www.sbjosephpinebluff.org.
See St. Joseph Catholic Jr./Sr. High School, Pine Bluff under High Schools, Diocesan located in the Institution section.
Catechesis/Religious Program—Tel: 870-536-6699. Brynn Koschel, D.R.E. Students 109.
Mission—St. Mary Plum Bayou P.O. Box 7434, Jefferson Co. 71611-7434.
St. Joseph's Education Fund—Tel: 870-879-4217. David Schimmel, Pastoral Council Pres.
Junior High Endowment Fund—
Senior High Trust Fund—
2—ST. PETER (1894), (African American), Rev. Donald L. Murrin, S.V.D.; Deacon Elton Harrison.
207 E. 16th Ave., 71601. Tel: 870-534-6418. Email: dmsppb@aristotle.net.
School—(Grades K-6) Tel: 870-535-4017; Fax: 870-535-4017. Carol A. Beeman, Prin. Daughters of Charity 1; Lay Teachers 8; Students 69.
Convent—Tel: 870-534-2316.
Mission—St. Raphael, Jefferson Co.
St. Peter Catholic School Foundation—

POCAHONTAS, RANDOLPH CO., ST. PAUL THE APOSTLE (1868) [CEM], Attended from St. John the Baptist, Engelberg (see listing for Engelberg); St. Joseph the Worker, Corning (see listing for Corning). Very Rev. John E. Marconi; Deacon George Joseph Edwards.
1002 Convent St., 72455. Tel: 870-892-3319. Email: saintpaul@suddenlink.net. Web: saintpaulscatholic.com.
School—(Grades PreK-6), 311 Cedar St., 72455. Tel: 870-892-5639. Email: stpaulsch@suddenlink.net. Karla Thielmeier, Prin. Lay Teachers 12; Students 134.
Catechesis/Religious Program—Sr. Elizabeth Love, O.S.B., D.R.E. Students 95.

PRAIRIE VIEW, LOGAN CO., ST. MEINRAD CHURCH (1913) Attended by St. Ignatius, Scranton. Rev. Barnabas Maria Susai, I.M.S.
Mailing Address: 108 Main St., P.O. Box 87, Scranton, 72863.
35 Saint Meinrad Loop, Scranton, 72863. Tel: 479-938-2821; Fax: 479-938-2821 (Scranton).
Catechesis/Religious Program—Susie Koenigseder, D.R.E. Students 35.

RATCLIFF, LOGAN CO., ST. ANTHONY (1879), (German), [CEM] Rev. Don Tranel, G.H.M., Sacramental Min.; Deacon Bob Grierson Cowie, Pastoral Admin.
470 W. Wilson St., 72951. Mailing Address: c/o N. Carbon City Rd., Paris, 72855. Tel: 479-963-3990.
Catechesis/Religious Program—Jana Stengel, D.R.E. Students 21.

ROGERS, BENTON CO., ST. VINCENT DE PAUL (1941) [CEM] Very Rev. Msgr. David LeSieur; Rev. Salvador Vega-Alvarenga (El Salvador); Deacons William Renee Cook; Clarence Arthur Leis; John Ray Pate.
Church: 1416 W. Poplar St., 72758. Tel: 479-636-4020. Web: www.st-vincent-depaul.com.
School—(Grades PreK-8), 1315 W. Cypress St., 72758. Tel: 479-636-4421; Fax: 479-636-5812. Web: www.svdpschool.net. Ann Morrison, Interim Prin.; Carolyn Pio, Asst. Prin.; Alice Stautzenberger, Librarian. Lay Teachers 24; Students 325.
St. Vincent de Paul Endowment Fund—Tel: 479-621-1723; Fax: 479-621-1723.
Catechesis/Religious Program—Students 1,074.

RUSSELLVILLE, POPE CO.
1—ST. JOHN (1950) Rev. William F. Thomas.
Mailing Address: 1900 W. Main St., 72801. Tel: 479-967-3699; Fax: 479-967-6215. Email: stjcatholic@suddenlinkmail.com. Web: www.saintjohnrussellville.org.
School—(Grades PreK-5), 1912 W. Main St., 72801. Tel: 479-967-4644; Fax: 479-967-6215. Karen Thomas, Librarian. Lay Teachers 10; Students 55.
Catechesis/Religious Program—Patricia Joselin, D.R.E. Students 110.
St. John's Educational Trust—1912 W. Main St., 72801.
2—ST. LEO THE GREAT UNIVERSITY PARISH, Attended by Assumption of the Blessed Virgin Mary, Atkins. Rev. Ernest L. Hardesty.
Mailing Address: P.O. Box 9033, 72811. 509 W. "L" St., 72801. Tel: 479-968-8249. Email: stleos@hotmail.com. Web: www.stleoatu.homestead.com.

ST. VINCENT, CONWAY CO., ST. MARY (1880) [CEM] Rev. James Burnie, C.S.Sp.
11 Kaufman Ln., Hattieville, 72063. Tel: 501-354-3206; Fax: 501-354-4132.
Catechesis/Religious Program—Students 64.

SCRANTON, LOGAN CO., ST. IGNATIUS (1913), (German), [CEM] Rev. Barnabas Maria Susai, I.M.S.
Mailing Address: P.O. Box 87, 72863.
Church: 108 E. Main St., 72863. Tel: 479-938-2821.
Catechesis/Religious Program—Tel: 479-938-7474. Students 49.
Mission—St. Meinrad, (See listing under Prairie View), Prairie View, Logan Co.
Mission—SS. Peter & Paul Church Hwy. 109, Morrison Bluff, Logan Co. Tel: 479-938-2200.

SEARCY, WHITE CO., ST. JAMES (1915) Rev. John O. Agbakwuo; Deacon Robert L. Morris.
1102 Pioneer Rd., P.O. Box 172, 72143. Tel: 501-268-5252 (Office); Fax: 501-268-2388. Email: stjames172@sbcglobal.net. Web: www.stjamescatholicsearcy.org.
Catechesis/Religious Program—Theresa Gillram, D.R.E. Students 170.
Mission—St. Albert, (See listing under Heber Springs), Heber Springs, Cleburne Co.
Mission—St. Richard, (See listing under Bald Knob), Bald Knob, White Co.

SHERIDAN, GRANT CO., HOLY CROSS (1949) Rev. Joseph Ejimofor (Nigeria).
Res.: 910 W. Vine St., P.O. Box 624, 72150-0624.
Catechesis/Religious Program—Tel: 870-942-8366. Mary Hale, D.R.E.

SHOAL CREEK, LOGAN CO., ST. SCHOLASTICA (New Blaine) (1878), (German), Rev. Denis Soerries, O.S.B.
288 St. Scholastica Rd., New Blaine, 72851. Tel: 479-938-7566.
Catechesis/Religious Program—Students 16.

SILOAM SPRINGS, BENTON CO., ST. MARY (1963) Rev. Salvador Marquez-Munoz.
Mailing Address: P.O. Box 118, 72761. Tel: 479-524-8526 (rectory); Fax: 479-524-5677.
Catechesis/Religious Program—Tel: 479-524-3120. Leticia Zavala, D.R.E. Students 236.

SLOVAK, PRAIRIE CO., SS. CYRIL AND METHODIUS, [CEM] Attended by Holy Rosary, Stuttgart. Rev. Msgr. Jack D. Harris.
Mailing Address: 1852 Hwy. 86 W., Stuttgart, 72160. Tel: 870-241-3359; Fax: 870-673-6701.
Catechesis/Religious Program—Students 28.

SPRINGDALE, WASHINGTON CO., ST. RAPHAEL (1949) [JC] Revs. John M. Connell; James P. Melnick; Jose Y. Lozano-Burgos; Deacon Chuck Marino.
Church: 1386 S.West End St., 72764. Tel: 479-756-6711; Fax: 479-756-8818. Email: info@straphaelcc.org. Web: www.straphaelcc.org.
School—(Grades PreSchool), 1721 W. Sunset St., 72762. Tel: 479-756-5411. Karen LaMendola, Prin. Staff 17; Students 116.
Catechesis/Religious Program—Students 1,519.

STAMPS, LAFAYETTE CO., ST. VINCENT DE PAUL, Closed. For inquiries for parish records contact the chancery.

STAR CITY, LINCOLN CO., ST. JUSTIN (1986) [CEM] [JC] Sr. Kathleen Miles, D.C., Admin.
Mailing Address: 400 N. Drew St., P.O. Box 128, 71667. Tel: 870-628-3092; Fax: 870-628-3092.
Catechesis/Religious Program—Students 17.
Mission—Blessed Sacrament, (See listing under Gary), Grady, Lincoln Co.

STUTTGART, ARKANSAS CO., HOLY ROSARY (1887) [CEM] Rev. Msgr. Jack D. Harris.
1815 S. Prairie St., 72160. Tel: 870-673-8351; Fax: 870-673-6701.
School—(Grades PreK-6), 920 W. 19th St., 72160. Tel: 870-673-3211. Kathy Lorince, Prin. Lay Teachers 7; Students 38.
Catechesis/Religious Program—Polly Franzen, D.R.E. Students 20.

SUBIACO, LOGAN CO., ST. BENEDICT (1878) [CEM] Rev. Aaron Pirrera, O.S.B.
Church & Res.: 81 W. Parish Dr., 72865. Tel: 479-934-4321. Email: stbensubi@yahoo.com.
Catechesis/Religious Program—Tel: 479-934-4106. Donna Forst, D.R.E. Students 89.

TEXARKANA, MILLER CO., ST. EDWARD (1903) [CEM] Very Rev. Vincent Flusche; Deacons Joe Lawrence Bruick; David Fowler.
Mailing Address: P.O. Box 1186, 71854.
Office: 410 Beech St., 71854. Tel: 870-772-1115; Fax: 870-773-2890. Email: office@saintedwardstexarkana.com. Web: www.saintedwardstexarkana.com.
Rectory—407 Beech St., P.O. Box 1186, 71854.
Catechesis/Religious Program—Tel: 870-772-7098. Kelli Nugent, D.R.E. Students 165.
Mission—St. Elizabeth Ann Seton, (See listing under Ashdown), Ashdown, Little River Co.
Mission—Sacred Heart, (See listing under Foreman), Foreman, Little River Co.

TONTITOWN, WASHINGTON CO., ST. JOSEPH (1898), (Italian), [CEM] Revs. Joseph Patrick Marconi; Lourduswamy Dhanraj Narla (India).
Mailing Address: P.O. Box 39, 72762. Tel: 479-361-2612; Fax: 479-361-9271. Email: stjoetontitown1@att.net. Web: www.stjoetontitown.org. 154 E. Henri de Tonti Blvd., 72770.
Catechesis/Religious Program—Tel: 479-521-4978. Shannon Stowe, D.R.E. Students 221.

VAN BUREN, CRAWFORD CO., ST. MICHAEL (1872) Rev. Timothy Donnelly, O.S.B.
1019 Pointer Tr. E., 72956. Tel: 479-471-1211; Fax: 479-471-1219. Email: stmichael@sbcglobal.net. Web: www.stmichaelcatholicchurch.com.
Catechesis/Religious Program—Tel: 479-471-1211. Students 237.
Shrine—Our Lady of the Ozarks Shrine 22741 N. Hwy. 71, Winslow, Crawford Co. 72959.

WALDRON, SCOTT CO., ST. JUDE THADDEUS CHURCH (1947) Rev. Neil Pezzulo, G.H.M.; Kathy O'Brien, Pastoral Assoc.
Mailing Address: P.O. Box 1688, 72958. Tel: 479-637-5063. Web: www.waldronar.catholicweb.com.
Catechesis/Religious Program—Michael Luongo, D.R.E.; Marianne Luongo, D.R.E. Students 92.
Mission—St. Andrew Danville, Yell Co. 72833.

WALNUT RIDGE, LAWRENCE CO., IMMACULATE HEART OF MARY (1925) Rev. Michael Sinkler; Deacon Marlyn Glenn Tate.
320 Free St., P.O. Box 70, 72476. Tel: 870-886-2119.
Catechesis/Religious Program—Students 13.

WARREN, BRADLEY CO., ST. LUKE CHURCH, Attended by St. Mark, Monticello. Rev. Phillip A. Reaves.
508 W. Pine St., 71671. Tel: 870-367-2848 (Monticello); Fax: 870-367-5868 (Monticello). Mailing Address: c/o St. Mark, 1016 N. Hyatt, Monticello, 71656.
Catechesis/Religious Program—Students 42.

WEINER, POINSETT CO., ST. ANTHONY (1902) [CEM] Rev. Jack Vu.
Mailing Address: P.O. Box 76, 72479. Tel: 870-684-2656; Fax: 870-684-2656.
Church: 407 Kings Hwy., 72479.

Catechesis/Religious Program—Tel: 870-578-4255. Mary Beth Wallace, D.R.E. Students 48.

WEST MEMPHIS, CRITTENDEN CO., ST. MICHAEL (1914) Rev. Leslie A. Farley.
Mailing Address: P.O. Box 899, 72303.
Res.: 208 W. Cooper Ave., 72301.
Church: 411 Missouri, P.O. Box 899, 72303. Tel: 870-733-1212; 870-735-7983; Fax: 870-732-4808. Email: stmichaels899@sbcglobal.net. Web: www.stmichaelsparish.org.
School—(Grades PreK-6), 405 Missouri, P.O. Box 899, 72303. Tel: 870-735-1730; Fax: 870-735-3017. Michael Beauregard, Prin. Olivetan Benedictine Sisters 2; Lay Teachers 13; Students 90.
Catechesis/Religious Program—Libby Burroughs, D.R.E. Students 36.
St. Michael's School Endowment and Charitable Trust—Tel: 870-735-2683. Robert Gross, CPA.
Mission—Sacred Heart, (See listing under Crawfordsville), Crawfordsville, Crittenden Co.

WINSLOW, CRAWFORD CO., OUR LADY OF THE OZARKS SHRINE (1946) [CEM] Rev. Timothy Donnelly, O.S.B.; Deacon Dan Joseph Daily, Pastoral Admin.
Mailing Address: 22741 N. Hwy. 71, 72959. Tel: 479-634-2181.
Catechesis/Religious Program—1832 Seminole Ct., Fayetteville, 72701. Tel: 479-521-4536. Students 7.

WYNNE, CROSS CO., ST. PETER (1921) Very Rev. Clarence Edwin Graves.
Mailing Address: P.O. Box 517, 72396. Tel: 870-238-2613; Fax: 870-238-2613. Email: stpeterswynne@sbcglobal.net.
Church: 1695 N. Falls Blvd., 72396.
Catechesis/Religious Program—Students 50.
Mission—St. Mary, (See listing under McCrory), McCrory, Woodruff Co.

YELLVILLE, MARION CO., ST. ANDREW CHURCH (1980) Attended by Mary Mother of God, Harrison. Very Rev. Gregory G. Hart.
Mailing Address: P.O. Box 197, 72687. Tel: 870-449-4850; Fax: 870-741-4234 (Harrison).
Church: 1486 Hwy. 62 W., 72687.
Catechesis/Religious Program—Pat Goulet, D.R.E. Students 20.

Chaplains of Public Institutions

LITTLE ROCK. *John L. McClellan Memorial Hospital, VA Medical Center*, 4300 W. 7th St., 72205. Tel: 501-257-2151; Fax: 501-257-2157. Vacant.

FAYETTEVILLE. *U.S. Veterans Administration Hospital*. Attended from St. Joseph Church.

NORTH LITTLE ROCK. *Fort Roots VA Medical Center*, Tel: 501-257-2151; Fax: 501-257-2157. Vacant.

On Special or Other Diocesan Assignment:
Rev. Msgr.—
Sebaugh, Thomas, Dir. Information Systems, 2500 N. Tyler St., P.O. Box 7565, 72217. Tel: 501-664-0340; Fax: 501-664-9075
Rev.—
Iwu, Pius A., J.C.D.

Leave of Absence:
Rev.—
Kerr, John W.

Retired:
Rev. Msgrs.—
Kordsmeier, John, St. John Manor, Apt. 306, 2414 N. Tyler St., 72207.
O'Donnell, John F., St. John Manor, 2414 N. Tyler St., 72207.
Revs.—
Cheney, Jesse C., St. John Manor, Apt. #201, 2414 N. Tyler St., 72207.
Enderlin, Joseph J., St. John Manor, Apt. #309, 2414 N. Tyler St., 72207.
Esposito, Ralph J., 220 Hillcrest Ave., New Castle, PA 16105.
Lange, Milton R., P.O. Box 6037, Springdale, 72766.
Oswald, John, St. John Manor, Apt. 304, 2414 N. Tyler St., 72207.
Preske, Venantius, 1716 Court Loop, Horseshoe Bend, 72512.
Rossi, Raymond R., P.O. Box 21817, Hot Springs, 71913.
Savary, James, 6720 Brentwood Rd., 72205.
Strock, Richard M., St. John Manor, 2414 N. Tyler St., 72207.

Permanent Deacons:
Deacons—
Alberson, James M., St. Jude the Apostle, Jacksonville
Anderson, Arthur John, (On Duty Outside the Diocese)
Baldwin, Warren Thomas, St. Joseph & St. Thomas Aquinas, Fayetteville
Bauer, Bernard Louis, (Retired)
Bouldin, Rex A., St. Mary, Paragould
Bowen, William Joseph, Cathedral of St. Andrew, Little Rock
Brandon, William G., Jr., Immaculate Conception, Blytheville
Briselden, David Lee, St. John the Baptist, Hot Springs
Bruick, Joe Lawrence, St. Edward, Texarkana
Brust, Raymond Edward, St. Bernard, Bella Vista
Bryant, Noel F. "Bud", St. Joseph, Pine Bluff
Burns, John Joseph, St. Boniface, Fort Smith
Cashman, Dan Charles, Christ the King, Little Rock
Connell, John Michael, (Retired)
Cook, William Renee, (Retired)
Cowie, Bob Grierson, St. Anthony, Ratcliff
Cumnock, Thomas Michael, St. Mary, Batesville; St. Cecelia, Newport
Cunningham, William Wayne, St. Rose, Carlisle
Daily, Dan Joseph, Our Lady of the Ozarks, Winslow
Daven, Edward Carl "Bud", St. John the Baptist, Malvern; St. Mary, Arkadelphia
Duke, John Charles, (Retired)
Edwards, George Joseph, (Retired)
Elliott, Max Robert, St. Jude the Apostle, Jacksonville; Little Rock Air Force Base
England, David Emory, Blessed Sacrament, Jonesboro
Farrar, Chuck Arthur, Immaculate Conception, North Little Rock
Fowler, David, St. Edward, Texarkana
Francis, Donald Joseph, St. Theresa, Little Rock
Genna, Albert, (Unassigned)
Gieringer, Wallace Arnold, (Retired)
Goetz, Roy E., St. Benedict, Subiaco
Greenway, Curtis Don, Christ the King, Little Rock
Hankins, Chuck Elden, (Leave of Absence)
Harrison, Elton Clement, St. Peter, Pine Bluff
Harrison, Gerald Joseph, St. Joseph, Conway
Harrison, Joe Dale, St. Mary of the Springs, Hot Springs
Hartmann, William Melville, (Retired)
Hartnedy, John Augustine, Our Lady of Good Counsel, Little Rock
Hennessey, Daniel James, III, St. Edward, Little Rock
Herman, Kirke Leo, (Retired)
Jegley, Lawrence H., (Retired)
Johnson, Robert Joseph, St. Michael, Van Buren
Johnson, William Albert, Christ the King, Little Rock
Klingler, Kenneth Arlie, Immaculate Conception, Blytheville
Krug, John Thomas, (Retired)
Leckner, Leland Paul, St. Mary of the Springs, Hot Springs
Leis, Clarence Arthur, (Retired)
Lipsmeyer, Lawrence Joseph, Sacred Heart of Jesus, Hot Springs Village
Luna, J. Marcelino, St. Edward, Little Rock
Marino, Charles, Jr., St. Raphael, Springdale
Marschewski, John Jacob, Christ the King, Little Rock
Massanelli, Garland Edward, (Retired)
Mattingly, Johnson Smith, (Retired)
McAllister, John M., J.D., J.C.L., Christ the King, Little Rock
Miller, Thomas Ervin, (Out of Diocese)
Morgan, Gilbert Paul, Our Lady of Fatima, Benton
Morris, Robert L., (Retired)
Pair, Greg, Immaculate Conception, Fort Smith
Papini, Richard John, St. Joseph, Conway
Pate, John Ray, St. Vincent de Paul, Rogers
Patterson, Richard Lewis, Christ the King, Little Rock
Pohlmeier, Thomas J., St. Joseph, Paris
Post, Matthew Joseph, (Retired)
Regan, Robert V., (Retired)
Rohlman, Oscar Aloys, (Retired)
Smith, James, (On Duty Outside the Diocese)
Stager, Ronald F., Immaculate Conception, North Little Rock
Stepka, Victor J., (Retired)
Strozyk, Brunon John, Immaculate Heart of Mary, North Little Rock
Tate, Marlyn Glenn, Immaculate Heart of Mary, Walnut Ridge
Westmoreland, David Kirby, St. Joseph, Conway
Wrape, William Robert, (Retired)
Zanoff, Frank Joseph, St. Francis of Assisi, Fairfield Bay; St. Jude, Clinton

INSTITUTIONS LOCATED IN THE DIOCESE

[A] SEMINARIES, RELIGIOUS OR SCHOLASTICATES

LITTLE ROCK. *Marylake - Carmelite Novitiate* (1952) 5151 Marylake Dr., 72206. Tel: 501-888-3052; Fax: 501-888-3080. Revs. John Michael Payne, O.C.D., Supr.; Raphael Kitz, O.C.D., Novice Master; John Magdalene Suenram, O.C.D., Dir. Devel.; Marion Joseph Bui, O.C.D. Discalced Carmelite Friars of the Province of St. Therese, Little Rock. Priests 4.

SUBIACO. *Subiaco Abbey*, 405 N. Subiaco Ave., 72865. Tel: 479-934-1000; Fax: 479-934-4328. Web: www.subi.org. Rev. Richard Walz, O.S.B., Novice Master, Formation Dir.; Rt. Rev. Jerome Kodell, O.S.B., V.F., Abbot; Revs. David Bellinghausen, O.S.B., Prior; Hugh Assenmacher, O.S.B.; Placidus Eckart, O.S.B.; Bruno Fuhrman, O.S.B.; Brendan Miller, O.S.B.; Camillus Cooney, O.S.B.; Nicholas Fuhrmann, O.S.B.; Leonard Wangler, O.S.B.; Mark Stengel, O.S.B.; Sebastian Beshoner, O.S.B.; Victor Gillespie, O.S.B.; Bro. Ephrem O'Bryan, O.S.B., Subprior. Abbots 1; Priests 22; Brothers 21; Novices 4.

[B] HIGH SCHOOLS, DIOCESAN

LITTLE ROCK. *Catholic High School*, 6300 Father Tribou St., 72205. Tel: 501-664-3939; Fax: 501-664-6549. Email: chs@lrchs.org. Mr. Steve Straessle, Prin.; Rev. Msgr. Lawrence A. Frederick, Rector.
Catholic High School of Little Rock, AR Priests 1; Brothers 1; Lay Teachers 37; Total Staff 39; Students 675.
Catholic High School Foundation, Inc. Tel: 501-664-3939; Fax: 501-664-6549.

CONWAY. *St. Joseph High School*, (Grades 7-12), 502 Front St., 72032-5408. Tel: 501-329-5741; Fax: 501-513-6804. Web: www.stjosephconway.org. Joe Mallett, Prin.; Matthew Tucker, Asst. Prin. (Grades K-3); Susie Freyaldenhoven, Asst. Prin. (Grades 4-6); Myra Book, Librarian (Grades K-6); Karen Wilson, Librarian (Grades 7-12). Lay Teachers 19; Students 246.

FORT SMITH. *Trinity Junior High*, (Grades 7-9), 1205 S. Albert Pike, 72903. Tel: 479-782-2451; Fax: 479-782-7263. Email: cdoss@trinitycatholicjh.org. Web: www.trinitycatholicjh.org. Rev. Thomas A. Elliott, Admin.; Mrs. Chandler Doss, Prin.; Bonnie Gondolfi, Librarian. Lay Teachers 23; Total Staff 23; Students 263.
Trinity Educational Trust Fund Tel: 479-782-2451; Fax: 479-782-7263.

MORRILTON. *Sacred Heart Catholic School*, 106 N. St. Joseph St., 72110. Tel: 501-354-8113; Fax: 501-354-2001. Email: shcsbailey@cox-internet.com. Brian Bailey, Prin. Lay Teachers 13; Total Staff 13; Students 72.

PINE BLUFF. *St. Joseph Catholic Jr./Sr. High School*, (Grades 7-12), 1501 W. 73rd Ave., 71603. Tel: 870-540-0413; Fax: 870-540-0345. Email: stjosephhighschool@cablelynx.com. Web: www.stjosephschool.cc. Very Rev. Warren Harvey, V.F.; Brenda Costello, Prin.; Debbie Ogg, Librarian. Total Staff 11; Students 66.

[C] HIGH SCHOOLS, PRIVATE

LITTLE ROCK. *Mount St. Mary Academy* (Girls), 3224 Kavanaugh Blvd., 72205. Tel: 501-664-8006; Fax: 501-666-4382. Web: www.mtstmary.edu. Sr. Deborah Troillett, R.S.M., Pres.; Mrs. Diane Wolfe, Prin.; Sr. Lisa Griffith, R.S.M., Dean Academics; Alice W. Jones, Librarian. Priests 1; Sisters of Mercy 3; Lay Teachers 33; Students 492.
Mount St. Mary Academy Endowment and Scholarship Fund Tel: 501-664-8006; Fax: 501-664-4382.

SUBIACO. **Subiaco Academy*, 405 N. Subiaco Ave., 72865. Tel: 479-934-1005; Fax: 479-934-1033; 800-364-7824. Web: www.subi.org. Michael Burke, Headmaster; Bro. Vincent Klein, O.S.B., Librarian. Priests 2; Brothers 3; Lay Teachers 27; Students 172.

[D] GENERAL HOSPITALS

LITTLE ROCK. *St. Vincent Doctors Hospital*, 6101 St. Vincent Cir., 72205. Tel: 501-552-3664; Fax: 501-552-8614. Email: pneedham@stvincenthealth.com. Bed Capacity 282; Total Assisted Annually 19,903; Total Staff 164.
St. Vincent Infirmary Medical Center (1888) No. 2 St. Vincent Circle, 72205. Tel: 501-552-3664; Fax: 501-552-8614. Sisters 1; Total Staff 1,881; Bed Capacity 615; Patients Assisted Annually 190,538.

FORT SMITH. *St. Edward Mercy Medical Center* (1905) 7301 Rogers Ave., 72917. Tel: 479-314-6000; Fax: 479-314-1188. Web: www.StEdwardMercy.com. P.O. Box 17000, 72917-7000. Sr. Chabanel

Finnegan, R.S.M., Dir. Pastoral Svcs,; Jeffrey A. Johnston, Pres. & CEO; Jill E. McCormick, Dir. Mktg & Planning. Total Staff 1,829; Bed Capacity 349; Patients Assisted Annually 85,289.

St. Edward Mercy Foundation, 5401 Ellsworth Rd., 72903. Tel: 479-314-1133.

HOT SPRINGS NATIONAL PARK. *St. Joseph's Mercy Health Center*, P.O. Box 29001, 71903-9001. Tel: 501-622-1000; Fax: 501-622-1199. Email: patrickmccruden@mercy.net. Web: www.saintjosephs.com. Timothy J. Johnsen, Pres. & CEO; Rev. Alan Rosenau, Priest Chap.; Deacon Patrick McCruden, Vice Pres. Mission & Ethics, Contact Person. Sisters of Mercy 3; Lay Staff 1,950; Total Staff 1,954; Patients Assisted Annually 45,000; Bed Capacity 279.

Sisters of Mercy of St. Joseph Convent of Hot Springs, Arkansas, Inc. Tel: 501-321-1554.

JONESBORO. *St. Bernard Medical Center* (1900) 225 E. Jackson #84, 72401. Tel: 870-972-4100; Fax: 870-974-7040. Email: hhutchison@SBRmc.org. Web: stbernards.info. Ben E. Owens, Pres. & CEO. Olivetan Benedictine Sisters 13; Total Staff 2,119; Patients Assisted Annually 243,842; Bed Capacity 438.

MORRILTON. *St. Anthony's Hospital Association* (1925) #4 Hospital Dr., 72110-4510. Tel: 501-977-2300; Fax: 501-977-2400. Email: fgottsponer@stvincenthealth.com. Christy Hockaday, Admin. & CEO.

St. Anthony's Hospital Association, Sponsored by St. Vincent Health System, a division of Catholic Health Initiatives. Total Staff 189; Patients Assisted Annually 27,077; Bed Capacity 25.

OZARK. *St. Edward Health Facilities of Franklin County dba Mercy Hospital/Turner Memorial* 801 W. River St., 72949. Tel: 479-667-4138; Fax: 479-667-4751; 479-667-9778 (Asst. Admin.). Email: ron.summerhill@mercy.net. Doug Gantier, Vice Pres. Total Staff 57; Patients Assisted Annually 11,000; Bed Capacity 25.

PARIS. *St. Edward Health Facilities of Logan Co. dba North Logan Mercy Hospital* 500 E. Academy, 72855. Tel: 479-963-6101; Fax: 479-963-6155. Email: j.maddox@mercy.net. Doug Gantier, Vice Pres.; Deacon Chuck Elden Hankins, Dir. Pastoral Svcs. Total Staff 40; Patients Assisted Annually 11,445; Bed Capacity 16.

ROGERS. *St. Mary-Rogers Memorial Hospital dba Mercy Medical Center* 2710 Rife Medical Ln., 72756. Tel: 479-338-2903; Fax: 479-338-2906. Email: nancy.king@mercy.net. Web: www.mercy4u.com. George Flynn, CEO. Total Staff 750; Bed Capacity 165; Patients Assisted Annually 124,902.

St. Mary Hospital Foundation Tel: 479-338-8000; Fax: 479-338-2906.

SHERWOOD. *St. Vincent Medical Center/Sherwood* (1999) 2215 Wildwood Ave., 72120. Tel: 501-552-3664; Fax: 501-552-8614. Bed Capacity 69; Total Assisted Annually 52,392; Total Staff 220.

WALDRON. *St. Edward Health Facilities of Scott County dba Mercy Hospital* 1341 W. 6th St., 72958. Tel: 479-637-4135; Fax: 479-637-3523. Email: j.maddox@mercy.net. Doug Gantier, Vice Pres.; Dorothy "Dede" O'Bar, Asst. Admin.; Jerry Stevenson, CEO; Deacon Chuck Elden Hankins, Dir. Pastoral Svcs. Total Staff 58; Patients Assisted Annually 30,956; Bed Capacity 24.

WYNNE. *St. Bernard Community Hospital Corporation dba Crossridge Community Hospital* 310 S. Falls Blvd., 72396. Tel: 870-238-3300; Fax: 870-238-7432. Email: gsparks@sbrmc.org. P.O. Box 590, 72396. Bed Capacity 25; Total Staff 152; Patients Assisted Annually 20,208.

[E] PROTECTIVE INSTITUTIONS

LITTLE ROCK. *ABBA House, Missionaries of Charity*, 1014 S. Oak St., 72204. Tel: 501-666-9718 (Abba House); 501-663-3596 (convent). Home for expectant mothers, homeless women & children. Missionaries of Charity 4; Staff 4; Bed Capacity 13; Monthly food distribution assisted 9,012; Total Assisted 133.

[F] HOMES FOR AGED

BARLING. *Mercy Crest Housing, Inc. aka Mercy Crest Retirement Living* 1300 Strozier Ln., 72923. Tel: 479-478-3000; Fax: 479-452-8382. Web: www.mercycrest.com. Sandra Presson, R.N., Admin. Sponsored by the Religious Sisters of Mercy. Total Staff 47; Bed Capacity 47; Assisted & Independent Living 102; Patients Assisted Annually 142.

BERRYVILLE. *St. John's Home Care of Berryville, Inc.*, 214 Carter St., 72616. Tel: 866-433-6078 (toll free); Fax: 870-423-4367. Total Staff 13; Total Assisted Annually 330.

JONESBORO. *Benedictine Manor I*, 312 Bridge St., 72401. Bed Capacity 20.

Benedictine Manor II, 312 Bridge St., 72401. Bed Capacity 20.

St. Bernard Village, Inc., 1606 Heern Dr., 72401. Tel: 870-932-8141; Fax: 870-933-5563. Web: www.stbernards.info. Kevin Hodges, Vice Pres., Senior Svcs.; Mr. Brian Rega, Dir. (Affiliated with Olivetan Benedictine Sisters, Inc., Jonesboro, AR) Patients Assisted Annually 250; Total Staff 38; Bed Capacity 142.

[G] RESIDENCES FOR PRIESTS

LITTLE ROCK. *St. John Manor*, 2414 N. Tyler St., 72207. Tel: 501-664-0340; Fax: 501-664-9075. Email: wfallon@dolr.org. Rev. Msgrs. John Kordsmeier (Retired); John F. O'Donnell (Retired); Revs. Jesse C. Cheney (Retired); John Oswald (Retired); Mr. Jinho Zyung, Mgr.; Rev. Joseph J. Enderlin (Retired); Very Rev. Msgr. Richard Oswald, V.F., (Sick Leave); Rev. Richard M. Strock (Retired). Priests 6.

[H] CONVENTS AND RESIDENCES FOR SISTERS

LITTLE ROCK. *Discalced Carmelite Nuns*, 7201 W. 32nd St., 72204-4716. Tel: 501-565-5121; Fax: 501-565-3877. Email: Lrcarmel@comcast.net. Web: www.littlerockcarmel.org. Sr. Cecilia Chun, O.C.D., Prioress.

Discalced Carmelite Nuns of Little Rock, Attended from Catholic High School, Little Rock. Sisters 13; Nuns with Solemn Vows 13.

Mt. St. Mary's Convent (1851) 3508 Kavanaugh Blvd., 72205. Tel: 501-664-5977; Fax: 501-666-4382. Email: srjkonecny@mercysc.org. Sisters 6.

BARLING. *McAuley Convent and Retirement Residence*, 1300 Strozier Ln., 72923. Tel: 479-478-3002; Fax: 479-478-3006. Email: dallen@mercystl.org. Sisters of Mercy 21; Bed Capacity 30; Number Served 21.

FORT SMITH. *St. Scholastica Monastery-Motherhouse* (1879) 1301 S. Albert Pike, P.O. Box 3489, 72913. Tel: 479-783-4147; Fax: 479-782-4352. Email: monastery@stscho.org. Web: www.stscho.org. Sisters Maria Goretti DeAngeli, O.S.B., Prioress; Catherine Markey, Archivist; Rev. David McKillin, O.S.B., Chap. Benedictine Professed Sisters 63.

Sisters of Mercy of St. Edward Convent (1905) 7315 Riviera Dr., 72903. Tel: 479-314-6097; Fax: 479-452-1699. Email: srsjm@yahoo.com. Sisters of Mercy 2.

JONESBORO. *Holy Angels Convent-Motherhouse* 72403-0130. Tel: 870-935-5810; Fax: 870-935-4210. Email: olivben@olivben.org. Web: www.olivben.org. Sr. Mary Anne Nuce, O.S.B., Prioress; Rev. Richard Cleary, O.S.B. Olivetan Benedictine Sisters. Sisters 43; Postulants 1.

[I] NEWMAN CENTERS

LITTLE ROCK. *Catholic Campus Ministry* 2500 N. Tyler St., 72207. Tel: 501-664-0340; Fax: 501-664-0119. Email: ltingquist@dolr.org.

Univ. of Arkansas at Little Rock Catholic Campus Ministry 10 Castle Hill Ct., 72227. Tel: 501-772-2512. Email: ualrcatholic@aol.com. Web: http://ualr.edu/catholic/. Mrs. Diane Hanley, Campus Min.

CLARKSVILLE. *University of Ozarks Catholic Campus Ministry (Clarksville)* 1068 CR 2305, Hartman, 72840. Tel: 479-979-1434. Email: mlstickl@ozarks.edu. Melodye Stickley, Campus Min.

CONWAY. *University of Central Arkansas & Hendrix College Catholic Campus Ministry* 2204 Bruce St., 72034. Tel: 501-336-9091; Fax: 501-336-9091. Email: catholic@cyberback.com. Web: www.uca.edu/org/ccm. Deacon Richard John Papini, Campus Min. (Conway)

FAYETTEVILLE. *University of Arkansas, St. Thomas Aquinas University Parish* 603 N. Leverett Ave., 72701. Tel: 479-444-0223; Fax: 479-442-2633. Email: ccm@uark.edu. Rev. Joseph Patrick Marconi; Nora Bryant, Administrative Asst.; Laurie Schuler, Campus Min.; Jay Carney, Campus Min.

FORT SMITH. *University of Arkansas at Fort Smith, Catholic Campus Ministry* 1301 S. Albert Pike, 72903. Tel: 479-783-4147. Email: kimberly@stscho.org.

JONESBORO. *Arkansas State University, Blessed John Newman University Parish* 2800 E. Johnson Ave., 72401. Tel: 870-972-1888; Fax: 870-972-6294. Email: cnc28@sbcglobal.net. Web: www.clt.astate.edu/cnc. Rev. Jack Vu; Mary Ruth Staudt, Dir. & Campus Min.; Terry Brimhall, Asst. Admin.; Deacon David Emory England.

RUSSELLVILLE. *St. Leo the Great University Parish* 509 W. L St., 72801. Tel: 479-968-8249. Email: stleos@hotmail.com. Web: www.stleoatu.homestead.com/homepage. P.O. Box 9033, 72811. Rev. Ernest L. Hardesty, Pastor; Mrs. Pat Buford, Dir. Campus Ministry.

SEARCY. *Harding University In Searcy/Arkansas State University at Beebe, Campus Ministry* 109 Campbell Dr., Beebe, 72012. Tel: 501-882-6299; Fax: 501-882-5465. Email: flo.fitch@badger.k12.ar.us. Flo Fitch, Campus Min.

[J] RETREAT CENTERS

BERRYVILLE. *Little Portion Hermitage* (Public Association of the Faithful), 350 CR 248, 72616-8505. Tel: 479-253-7710; Fax: 479-888-5678. Email: info@littleportion.org. Web: www.LittlePortion.org. John Michael Talbot, B.S.C., Gen. Min.; Viola Talbot, B.S.C., Vicar Gen. Min.

Brothers and Sisters of Charity at Little Portion, Inc.

EUREKA SPRINGS. *Little Portion Retreat and Training Center at MORE Mt.*, 171 Hummingbird Ln., 72632. Tel: 479-253-7379; Fax: 479-253-8227. Email: retreatinfo@littleportion.org. Web: www.littleportion.org. John Michael Talbot, B.S.C., Exec. Dir.; Peggy Lodewyks, B.S.C.D., Contact Person & Mgr.

FORT SMITH. *St. Scholastica Center*, 1205 S. Albert Pike, P.O. Box 3489, 72913. Tel: 479-783-1135; Fax: 479-783-8138. Email: retreats@stscho.org. Web: www.scholasticafortsmith.org. Sisters Hilary Decker, O.S.B., Center Dir.; Madeline Bariola, O.S.B., Dir. Maintenance & Hospitality; Macrina Wiederkehr, O.S.B., Retreats & Spiritual Dir. Conducted by Benedictine Sisters.

SHOAL CREEK. *Hesychia House of Prayer* (1981) 204 St. Scholastica Rd., New Blaine, 72851. Tel: 479-938-7375. Email: hesychia@centurytel.net. Web: www.scholasticafortsmith.org. Sr. Louise Sharum, O.S.B., Dir.; Rev. Denis Soerries, O.S.B. Attended from New Subiaco Abbey, Subiaco, AR. Benedictine Sisters 3.

[K] MISCELLANEOUS LISTINGS

LITTLE ROCK. *"Arkansas Catholic"* (1911) Published by Arkansas Catholic, Inc. of the Diocese of Little Rock., 2500 N. Tyler St., P.O. Box 7417, 72217. Tel: 501-664-0340; 501-664-0125; Fax: 501-664-6572. Email: mhargett@dolr.org. Web: www.arkansas-catholic.org. Mrs. Malea Hargett, Editor.

Christopher Homes of Arkansas, Inc., 2417 N. Tyler St., 72207. Tel: 501-664-1881; Fax: 501-664-1631. Email: jmckinnon@dolr.org. Jimmy McKinnon, Exec. Dir. Total in Residence 549.

Christopher Homes, Inc.

Christopher Homes of Augusta, Inc. (1989) Tel: 870-347-2388; Fax: 870-347-2388. Units 20.

Christopher Homes of Brinkley, Inc. (1987) Tel: 870-734-2201; Fax: 870-734-2201. Units 20.

Christopher Homes of Camden, Inc. (1988) Tel: 870-837-1911; Fax: 870-837-1911. Units 20.

Christopher Homes of Clarendon, Inc. (1989) Tel: 870-747-5441; Fax: 870-747-5441. Units 20.

Christopher Homes of DeQueen, Inc. (1986) Tel: 870-642-6211; Fax: 870-642-6211. Units 20.

Christopher Homes of DeValls Bluff, Inc. (1990) Tel: 870-998-7280; Fax: 870-998-7280. Units 15.

Christopher Homes of Elaine, Inc. (1988) Tel: 870-827-3705; Fax: 870-827-3705. Units 20.

Christopher Homes of El Dorado, Inc. (1985) Tel: 870-862-9711; Fax: 870-862-9711. Units 40.

Christopher Homes of Forrest City, Inc. (1986) Tel: 870-633-4804; Fax: 870-633-4804. Units 20.

Christopher Homes of Horatio, Inc. (1988) Tel: 870-832-4014; Fax: 870-832-4014. Units 19.

Christopher Homes of Jonesboro, Inc. (1988) Tel: 870-931-9575; Fax: 870-931-9575. Units 20.

Christopher Homes of Marianna, Inc. (1986) Tel: 870-295-6345; Fax: 870-295-6345. Units 20.

Christopher Homes of Paragould, Inc. (1990) Tel: 870-239-8609; Fax: 870-239-8609. Units 18.

Christopher Homes of Parkin, Inc. (1990) Tel: 870-755-2939; Fax: 870-755-2939. Units 20.

Christopher Homes of Searcy, Inc. (1985) Tel: 501-268-7804; Fax: 501-268-7804. Units 40.

Christopher Homes of West Helena, Inc. (1984) Tel: 870-572-9433; Fax: 870-572-9433. Units 62.

Christopher Homes of Wynne, Inc. (1991) Tel: 870-238-3388; Fax: 870-238-3388. Units 20.

Christopher Homes of Hot Springs, Inc. (1997) Tel: 501-318-1317; Fax: 501-318-1317. Units 20.

Christopher Homes of Monette, Inc. (1993) Tel: 870-486-2748; Fax: 870-486-2748. Units 20.

Christopher Homes of North Little Rock, Inc. (1996) Tel: 501-758-8582; Fax: 501-758-8582. Units 55.

Christopher Homes of Palestine, Inc. (1993) Tel: 870-581-2023; Fax: 870-581-2023. Units 20.

Christopher Homes of Strong, Inc. (1994) Tel: 870-797-7525; Fax: 870-797-7525. Units 20.

Clergy Welfare Fund, Inc., P.O. Box 7565, 72217-7565. Tel: 501-664-0340; Fax: 501-664-1310. Email: gwolfe@dolr.org. Mr. Gregory C. Wolfe, Dir. Finance.

Diocese of Little Rock Catholic Schools Education

Trust, 2500 N. Tyler St., 72207. Tel: 501-664-0340. Email: vbowen@dolr.org. Mrs. Vernell Bowen, Supt.

John Gazzola Trust, P.O. Box 7565, 72217. Tel: 501-664-0340; Fax: 501-664-1310. Mr. Gregory C. Wolfe, Trustee; Mr. Charles Baker, Trustee; Mr. Dale Wintroath, Trustee.

Ladies of Charity of Arkansas, 2500 N. Tyler St., 72207. Tel: 501-664-0340; Fax: 501-664-9075.

Little Rock Scripture Study (1974) 2500 N. Tyler St., P.O. Box 7565, 72217. Tel: 501-664-0340; 501-664-6102; Fax: 501-664-9075. Email: lrss@dolr.org. Web: www.littlerockscripture.org. Ms. Cackie Upchurch, Dir.

The Mary Raymond Trust, P.O. Box 7565, 72217-7565. Tel: 501-664-0340; Fax: 501-664-1310. Email: gwolfe@dolr.org. Mr. Gregory C. Wolfe, Dir. Finance.

Monsignor James E. O'Connell Diocesan Seminarian Fund, Inc., P.O. Box 7565, 72217. Tel: 501-664-0340, Ext. 331; Fax: 501-664-9075. Email: sfriend@dolr.org.

St. Thomas More Society of Arkansas, Inc., 4801 North Hills Blvd., Ste. 1550, North Little Rock, 72116. Tel: 501-753-4800; Fax: 501-753-7477. Email: haleyoung@aristotle.net. Milas "Butch" Hale III, Pres.

BERRYVILLE. **Society of St. Vincent De Paul, St. Anne's Conference Inc.*, 1844 Hwy. 62 W., 72616.

BLYTHEVILLE. *Immaculate Conception Trust Fund* (1894) 1301 W. Main St., 72315. Tel: 870-762-2506; Fax: 870-762-2506. P.O. Box 747, 72316. Very Rev. Joseph L. Pallo, V.F.

DUMAS. *Daughters of Charity Services*, 145 W. Waterman, P.O. Box 158, 71639. Tel: 870-382-4878; Fax: 870-382-4895. Email: kmusholt@dcsark.org. *Administrative Offices*, 161 S. Main St., P.O. Box 158, 71639. Tel: 870-382-3080; Fax: 870-382-3085. Kathryn Musholt, CEO. Patients Assisted Annually 4,200; Total Staff 35.

Clinics:

St. Elizabeth Health Center, P.O. Drawer 370, Gould, 71643. Tel: 870-263-4317; Fax: 870-263-4782.

DePaul Health Center, P.O. Box 158, 71639. Tel: 870-382-4878; Fax: 870-382-4895.

Wellness Center, Hwy. 65 S., P.O. Box 473, Gould, 71643. Tel: 870-263-4748; Fax: 870-263-4233.

JONESBORO. *St. Bernard Healthcare*, 225 E. Jackson Ave., 72401. Tel: 870-972-4284; Fax: 870-974-7040. Web: www.stbernards.info. Mr. Robert S. Jones, Attorney.

Jonesboro Real Estate Holding Company, Inc., 225 E. Jackson St., 72401. Tel: 870-972-4301; Fax: 870-974-7040. Email: bowens@sbrmc.org. Ralph Waddell, Legal Counsel.

Total Life Healthcare, Inc., 225 E. Jackson #92, 72401. Tel: 870-336-5000; Fax: 870-336-5001. Staff 10; Total Assisted 29.

NORTH LITTLE ROCK. *Priestly Fraternity of St. Peter*, 1921 Maple St., 72114. Tel: 501-812-9155; Fax: 501-812-9155. Email: fssp_arkansas@sbcglobal.net. Web: www.arkansaslatinmass.org. Revs. Laurent Demets, F.S.S.P., Chap.; Robert Novokowsky, Asst. Chap.

POCAHONTAS. *St. Paul the Apostle Catholic Church - Capital Improvement Trust Fund*, 1002 Convent St., 72455. Tel: 870-892-3319; Fax: 870-892-5199. Email: saintpaul@suddenlink.net. Web: saintpaulcatholic.com. Very Rev. John E. Marconi, V.F., Pastor.

STUTTGART. *Holy Rosary Catholic School "Vision 2000" Educational Trust Fund*, 1815 S. Prairie St., 72160. Tel: 870-673-8351; Fax: 870-673-6701. Email: holyrose@centurytel.net. Rev. Msgr. Jack D. Harris, D.Min.

RELIGIOUS INSTITUTES OF MEN REPRESENTED IN THE DIOCESE

For further details refer to the corresponding bracketed number in the Religious Institutes of Men or Women section.

[0200]—*Benedictine Monks* (Conception Abbey, MO)—O.S.B.

[0200]—*Benedictine Monks* (Subiaco Abbey)—O.S.B.

[0460]—*Brothers of the Poor of St. Francis*—C.F.P.

[1330]—*Congregation of the Mission*—C.M.

[0260]—*Discalced Carmelite Friars* (St. Therese Prov.)—O.C.D.

[0570]—*Glenmary Home Missioners*—G.H.M.

[0650]—*Holy Ghost Fathers* (Western Vice Prov.)—C.S.Sp.

[]—*Indian Missionary Society*—I.M.S.

[1065]—*Priestly Fraternity of St. Peter*—F.S.S.P.

[0420]—*Society of the Divine Word* (Techny, IL)—S.V.D.

RELIGIOUS INSTITUTES OF WOMEN REPRESENTED IN THE DIOCESE

[0230]—*Benedictine Sisters of Pontifical Jurisdiction* (Fort Smith, AR)—O.S.B.

[1855]—*Congregation of the Handmaids of the Holy Child Jesus*—H.H.C.J.

[0470]—*Congregation of the Sisters of Charity of the Incarnate Word, Houston, Texas*—C.C.V.I.

[0760]—*Daughters of Charity of St. Vincent de Paul* (West Central Prov.)—D.C.

[]—*Daughters of Mary of the Cross*—D.M.C.

[0420]—*Discalced Carmelite Nuns* (Little Rock, AR)—O.C.D.

[1070-10]—*Dominican Sisters*—O.P.

[2575]—*Institute of the Sisters of Mercy of the Americas* (St. Louis, MO)—R.S.M.

[2710]—*Missionaries of Charity*—M.C.

[0390]—*Missionary Carmelites of St. Teresa*—C.M.S.T.

[2860]—*Missionary Sisters of the Sacred Heart*—M.S.C.

[]—*Missioneras Catequestas de los Pobres*—M.C.P.

[0240]—*Olivetan Benedictine Sisters* (Jonesboro, AR)—O.S.B.

[0500]—*Sisters of Charity of Nazareth*—S.C.N.

[3830-13]—*Sisters of St. Joseph*—C.S.J.

[3840]—*Sisters of St. Joseph of Carondelet*—C.S.J.

CEMETERIES

LITTLE ROCK. *Calvary*

FORT SMITH. *Calvary*

NECROLOGY

† Janesko, Rev. Msgr. John A., Stuttgart, AR Holy Rosary—Died June 19, 2009

† Gunti, Frederick W., (On Duty Outside Diocese)—Died Jan. 29, 2009

An asterisk (*) denotes an organization that has established tax-exempt status directly with the IRS and is not covered by the USCCB Group Ruling.

Archdiocese of Los Angeles

(Archidioecesis Angelorum in California)

His Eminence

ROGER CARDINAL MAHONY, D.D.

Archbishop of Los Angeles; ordained May 1, 1962; appointed Titular Bishop of Tamascani and Auxiliary Bishop of Fresno January 7, 1975; consecrated March 19, 1975; appointed Bishop of Stockton February 26, 1980; installed as the third Bishop of Stockton April 17, 1980; appointed Archbishop of Los Angeles July 16, 1985; installed as the fourth Archbishop of Los Angeles September 5, 1985; Created Cardinal June 28, 1991. *Res.: 555 W. Temple St., Los Angeles, CA 90012. Office: 3424 Wilshire Blvd., Los Angeles, CA 90010-2241.* Tel: 213-637-7288; Fax: 213-637-6510.

Archdiocesan Catholic Center Office: 3424 Wilshire Blvd., Los Angeles, CA 90010-2241. Tel: 213-637-7000; Fax: 213-637-6000.

Web: www.LA-Archdiocese.org

Email: info@LA-Archdiocese.org

Most Reverend

JOSE H. GOMEZ

Coadjutor Archbishop of Los Angeles; ordained August 15, 1978; appointed Auxiliary Bishop of Denver and Titular See of Belali January 23, 2001; ordained March 26, 2001; appointed Archbishop of San Antonio December 29, 2004; installed February 15, 2005; Pallium conferred June 29, 2005; appointed Coadjutor Archbishop of Los Angeles April 6, 2010.

Most Reverend

JOHN J. WARD, D.D., J.C.L., V.G.

Retired Auxiliary Bishop of Los Angeles; ordained May 4, 1946; appointed Titular Bishop of Bria and Auxiliary Bishop of Los Angeles October 16, 1963; consecrated December 12, 1963; Assigned Titular Bishop of California, June 15, 1996; retired July 1, 1996. *Office: 3424 Wilshire Blvd., Los Angeles, CA 90010-2241.*

Most Reverend

THOMAS J. CURRY, D.D., PH.D.

Auxiliary Bishop of Los Angeles; ordained June 18, 1967; appointed Titular Bishop of Ceanannus Mor and Auxiliary Bishop of Los Angeles February 8, 1994; ordained Bishop March 19, 1994. *Office: Santa Barbara Pastoral Region, 3240 Calle Pinon, Santa Barbara, CA 93105.*

Most Reverend

JOSEPH M. SARTORIS, D.D., V.G.

Retired Auxiliary Bishop of Los Angeles; ordained May 30, 1953; appointed Titular Bishop of Oliva and Auxiliary Bishop of Los Angeles February 8, 1994; ordained Bishop March 19, 1994; retired December 31, 2002. *1988 Rolling Vista Dr., #21, Lomita, CA 90717.*

Most Reverend

GABINO ZAVALA, D.D., J.C.L., V.G.

Auxiliary Bishop of Los Angeles; ordained May 28, 1977; appointed Titular Bishop of Tamascani and Auxiliary Bishop of Los Angeles February 8, 1994; ordained Bishop March 19, 1994. *Office: San Gabriel Pastoral Region, 16009 E. Cypress Ave., Irwindale, CA 91706.*

Most Reverend

GERALD E. WILKERSON, D.D.

Auxiliary Bishop of Los Angeles; ordained May 1, 1965; appointed Titular Bishop of Vincennes and Auxiliary Bishop of Los Angeles November 5, 1997; ordained Bishop January 21, 1998. *Office: San Fernando Pastoral Region, 15101 San Fernando Mission Blvd., Mission Hills, CA 91345-1109.*

Most Reverend

EDWARD W. CLARK, D.D.

Auxiliary Bishop of Los Angeles; ordained May 27, 1972; appointed Titular Bishop of Gardar and Auxiliary Bishop of Los Angeles January 16, 2001; ordained March 26, 2001. *Office: Regional Bishop, Our Lady of the Angels Pastoral Region, 5835 W. Slauson, Culver City, CA 90230.*

Most Reverend

OSCAR AZARCON SOLIS, D.D., V.G.

Auxiliary Bishop of Los Angeles; ordained April 28, 1979; appointed Titular Bishop of Urci and Auxiliary Bishop of Los Angeles December 11, 2003; installed February 10, 2004. *Office: San Pedro Pastoral Region, 3555 St. Pancratius Pl., Lakewood, CA 90712-1416.*

Most Reverend

ALEXANDER SALAZAR

Auxiliary Bishop of Los Angeles; ordained June 16, 1984; appointed Titular Bishop of Nesqually and Auxiliary Bishop of Los Angeles September 7, 2004; installed November 4, 2004. *Office of Ethnic Ministry; and Office of Justice and Peace, 3424 Wilshire Blvd., Los Angeles, CA 90010-2241.*

Square Miles 8,762.

Diocese Established 1840; an Archbishopric July 11, 1936.

Comprises the Counties of Los Angeles, Santa Barbara and Ventura in the State of California.

Patroness of the Diocese: St. Vibiana.

Legal Titles:
The Roman Catholic Archbishop of Los Angeles, a Corporation Sole.
Archdiocese of Los Angeles Education and Welfare Corporation.
Our Lady Queen of Angels.
St. John's Seminary College.
St. John's Seminary in California.
The Cardinal McIntyre Fund for Charity.
Catholic Charities of Los Angeles, Inc.
Catholic Charities Community Development Corporation.
The Tidings.
Vida Nueva.
Catholic Education Foundation.
Opus Caritatis.
Cathedral of Our Lady of the Angels.
For legal titles of parishes and archdiocesan institutions, consult the Chancery Office.

STATISTICAL OVERVIEW

Personnel	
Cardinals	1
Archbishops	1
Auxiliary Bishops	6
Retired Bishops	2
Retired Abbots	1
Priests: Diocesan Active in Diocese	342
Priests: Diocesan Active Outside Diocese	13
Priests: Retired, Sick or Absent	176
Number of Diocesan Priests	531
Religious Priests in Diocese	548
Total Priests in Diocese	1,079
Extern Priests in Diocese	124
Ordinations:	
Diocesan Priests	6
Religious Priests	3
Transitional Deacons	7
Permanent Deacons	9
Permanent Deacons in Diocese	315
Total Brothers	103
Total Sisters	1,956
Parishes	
Parishes	287
With Resident Pastor:	
Resident Diocesan Priests	173
Resident Religious Priests	58
Without Resident Pastor:	
Administered by Priests	41
Administered by Deacons	1
Administered by Religious Women	2
Administered by Lay People	4
Administered by Pastoral Teams, etc.	8
Missions	9
Pastoral Centers	15
Professional Ministry Personnel:	
Brothers	13
Sisters	139
Lay Ministers	691
Welfare	
Catholic Hospitals	14
Total Assisted	2,500,227
Health Care Centers	5
Total Assisted	9,127
Homes for the Aged	5
Total Assisted	2,628
Residential Care of Children	1
Total Assisted	250
Day Care Centers	19
Total Assisted	1,053
Specialized Homes	1
Total Assisted	95
Special Centers for Social Services	29
Total Assisted	272,617
Residential Care of Disabled	6
Total Assisted	823
Other Institutions	4
Total Assisted	289
Educational	
Seminaries, Diocesan	1
Students from This Diocese	52
Students from Other Diocese	39
Diocesan Students in Other Seminaries	1
Seminaries, Religious	11
Students Religious	12
Total Seminarians	65
Colleges and Universities	5

Total Students	12,999
High Schools, Diocesan and Parish	26
Total Students	14,908
High Schools, Private	24
Total Students	13,467
Elementary Schools, Diocesan and Parish	214
Total Students	50,010
Elementary Schools, Private	9
Total Students	2,320
Catechesis/Religious Education:	
High School Students	37,103
Elementary Students	89,119
Total Students under Catholic Instruction	219,991
Teachers in the Diocese:	
Priests	30
Scholastics	2
Brothers	15
Sisters	217
Lay Teachers	3,612
Vital Statistics	
Receptions into the Church:	
Infant Baptism Totals	82,432
Minor Baptism Totals	3,648
Adult Baptism Totals	1,597
Received into Full Communion	6,315
First Communions	47,220
Confirmations	27,799
Marriages:	
Catholic	6,927
Interfaith	849
Total Marriages	7,776
Deaths	11,834
Total Catholic Population	4,180,859
Total Population	11,669,322

Former Bishops—Rt. Revs. FRANCIS GARCIA DIEGO Y MORENO, O.F.M., D.D., cons. Oct. 4, 1840; Bishop of both Californias; died at Santa Barbara, April 30, 1846; JOSEPH SADOC ALEMANY, O.P., D.D., cons. June 30, 1850; Bishop of Monterey; transferred to San Francisco, July 29, 1853; died in Valencia, Spain, April 14, 1888; THADDEUS AMAT, C.M., D.D., cons. March 12, 1854; died May 12, 1878; FRANCIS MORA, D.D., cons. Titular Bishop of Mosynopolis and Coadjutor to Bishop Amat, Aug. 3, 1873; resigned May 6, 1896; died Aug. 3, 1905 in Sarria, Barcelona, Spain; GEORGE MONTGOMERY, D.D., cons. April 8, 1894, Bishop of Tmul and Coadjutor-Bishop of Monterey and Los Angeles cum jure successionis; succeeded to May 6, 1896; appt. Coadjutor-Archbishop of San Francisco, Jan. 1, 1903; died in San Francisco, Jan. 10, 1907; THOMAS JAMES CONATY, D.D., ord. 1872; cons. Nov. 24, 1901, Titular-Bishop of Samos; appt. Bishop of Monterey and Los Angeles, March 27, 1903; died at Coronado, CA, Sept. 18, 1915; Most Rev. JOHN J. CANTWELL, D.D., LL.D., appt. Bishop of Monterey-Los Angeles, Sept. 21, 1917; cons. Dec. 5, 1917; appt. Assistant to the Pontifical Throne, Sept. 30, 1929; transferred to Los Angeles, June 1, 1922; elevated to Archepiscopal dignity, July 11, 1936; installed Dec. 3, 1936; died Oct. 30, 1947, at Los Angeles, CA; His Eminence JAMES FRANCIS MCINTYRE, D.D., appt. Auxiliary Bishop of New York, Nov. 16, 1940; cons. Jan. 8, 1941; promoted to Coadjutor Archbishop, July 20, 1946; appt. Archbishop of Los Angeles, Feb. 7, 1948; installed March 19, 1948; created Cardinal Priest, Jan. 12, 1953; resigned Jan. 21, 1970; died July 16, 1979; TIMOTHY CARDINAL MANNING, D.D., J.C.D., appt. Titular Bishop of Lesvi and Auxiliary Bishop of Los Angeles, Aug. 3, 1946; cons. Oct. 15, 1946; installed as first Bishop of Fresno, Dec. 15, 1967; appt. Titular Bishop of Capri and Coadjutor Archbishop of Los Angeles, May 26, 1969; appt. Archbishop of Los Angeles, Jan. 21, 1970; created a Cardinal Priest, March 5, 1973; retired Sept. 4, 1985; died June 23, 1989 at Los Angeles, CA.

Archdiocesan Catholic Center Office—3424 Wilshire Blvd., Los Angeles, 90010-2241. Tel: 213-637-7000; Fax: 213-637-6000.

Office of the Cardinal—His Eminence ROGER CARDINAL MAHONY, D.D., 3424 Wilshire Blvd., Los Angeles, 90010-2241. Tel: 213-637-7288; Fax: 213-637-7510.

Priest Secretary/Master of Ceremonies—Rev. Msgr. MARC V. TRUDEAU. Tel: 213-637-7261.

Master of Ceremonies for Stational Liturgies—Rev. Msgr. KEVIN J. KOSTELNIK. Tel: 213-680-5208.

Cardinal's Theologian—Dr. MICHAEL DOWNEY. Tel: 213-637-7447.

Canonical Services, Vicar for—Rev. THOMAS C. ANSLOW, C.M., J.C.L. Tel: 213-637-7888.

Director of Special Services—Sr. MARY JEAN MEIER, R.S.M. Tel: 213-637-7520.

General Counsel—MARGARET G. GRAF. Tel: 213-637-7511.

Chief Financial Officer—RANDOLPH E. STEINER. Tel: 213-637-7218.

Auxiliary Bishops-Vicars General—Most Revs. JOHN J. WARD, D.D., J.C.L., V.G. (Retired), 3424 Wilshire Blvd., Los Angeles, 90010-2241. Tel: 213-637-7265; Fax: 213-637-6265; THOMAS J. CURRY, D.D., Ph.D., V.G., Santa Barbara Region, 3240 Calle Pinon, Santa Barbara, 93105-2760. Tel: 805-682-0442; Fax: 805-682-7509; JOSEPH M. SARTORIS, D.D., V.G. (Retired), Mailing Address: 3424 Wilshire Blvd., Los Angeles, 90010-2241; GABINO ZAVALA, D.D., J.C.L., V.G., San Gabriel Pastoral Region, Office, 16009 E. Cypress Ave., Irwindale, 91706-2122. Tel: 626-960-9344; Fax: 626-962-0455; GERALD E. WILKERSON, D.D., V.G., San Fernando Pastoral Region, 15101 San Fernando Mission Blvd., Mission Hills, 91345-1109. Tel: 818-361-6009; Fax: 818-361-6270; EDWARD W. CLARK, D.D., S.T.D., V.G., Our Lady of the Angels Pastoral Region, 5835 Slauson Ave., Culver City, 90230-6528. Tel: 310-215-0703; Fax: 323-938-1190; ALEXANDER SALAZAR, D.D., V.G., Office of Ethnic Ministry and Office of Justice and Peace, 3424 Wilshire Blvd., Los Angeles, 90010-2241. Tel: 213-637-7356; Fax: 213-637-6356; OSCAR A. SOLIS, D.D., V.G., San Pedro Pastoral Region, 3555 St. Pancratius Pl., Lakewood, 90712-1416. Tel: 562-634-0456; Fax: 562-531-4783.

Moderator of the Curia and Vicar General—Rev. Msgr. ROYALE M. VADAKIN, V.G., P.A. Tel: 213-637-7255.

Chancellor—Sr. MARY ELIZABETH GALT, B.V.M. Tel: 213-637-7460.

Vice Chancellor—Rev. Msgr. JOSEPH F. HERNANDEZ. Tel: 213-637-7426.

Archdiocesan Pastoral Regions

Santa Barbara Region—Most Rev. THOMAS J. CURRY, D.D., Ph.D., V.G., 3240 Calle Pinon, Santa Barbara, 93105-2760. Tel: 805-682-0442; Fax: 805-682-7509.

Deanery 1—Very Rev. CHARLES HOFSCHULTE, C.J., St. Louis de Montfort, Santa Maria, 93455. Tel: 805-922-7099.

Deanery 2—Rev. RAFAEL MARIN-LEON, V.F., Our Lady of Guadalupe, Santa Barbara, 93103.

Deanery 3—Rev. JON F. MAJARUCON, V.F., Santa Clara, Oxnard, 93030.

Deanery 4—Rev. Msgr. PAUL A. ALBEE, Holy Cross, Moorpark, 93021.

San Fernando Region—Most Rev. GERALD E. WILKERSON, D.D., V.G., Mailing Address: P.O. Box 7608, Mission Hills, 91346-7608. 15101 San Fernando Mission Blvd., Mission Hills, 91345-1109. Tel: 818-361-6009; Fax: 818-361-6270.

Deanery 5—Rev. ROBERT L. MILBAUER, St. John Baptist de la Salle, Granada Hills, 91344.

Deanery 6—Rev. Msgr. JAMES C. GEHL, St. Bede the Venerable, La Canada Flintridge, 91011.

Deanery 7—Rev. Msgr. ROBERT J. GALLAGHER, V.F., St. Charles Borromeo, North Hollywood, 91602.

Deanery 8—Rev. THOMAS E. BAKER, V.F., Sacred Heart, Lancaster, 93534.

San Gabriel Region—Most Rev. GABINO ZAVALA, D.D., J.C.L., V.G., 16009 E. Cypress Ave., Irwindale, 91706-2122. Tel: 626-960-9344; Fax: 626-962-0455.

Deanery 9—Rev. Msgr. JOHN T. MORETTA, V.F., Resurrection, Los Angeles, 90023.

Deanery 10—Rev. RICHARD G. KREKELBERG, V.F., St. Rita, Sierra Madre, 91024.

Deanery 11—Rev. NESTOR REBONG, St. Christopher, West Covina, 91790. Tel: 626-918-8314.

Deanery 12—Rev. Msgr. JAMES J. LOUGHNANE, V.F., P.A., St. Denis, Diamond Bar, 91765.

Our Lady of the Angels Pastoral Region—Most Rev. EDWARD W. CLARK, D.D., S.T.D., V.G., 5835 Slauson Ave., Culver City, 90230-6505. Tel: 310-215-0703; Fax: 310-215-0749.

Deanery 13—Rev. KEVIN L. NOLAN, V.F., St. Augustine, Culver City, 90232.

Deanery 14—Rev. MICHAEL J. MANDALA, S.J., Blessed Sacrament, Los Angeles, 90028.

Deanery 15—Rev. Msgr. JARLATH CUNNANE, V.F., St. Thomas the Apostle, Los Angeles, 90006.

Deanery 16—Rev. Msgr. TIMOTHY J. DYER, V.F., St. Columbkille, Los Angeles, 90003.

San Pedro Pastoral Region—Most Rev. OSCAR A. SOLIS, D.D., V.G., 3555 St. Pancratius Pl., Lakewood, 90712-1416. Tel: 562-634-0456; Fax: 562-531-4783.

Deanery 17—Rev. ANTONIO GARNICA, M.S.C., V.F., Sagrado Corazon y Santa Maria de Guadalupe, Cudahy, 90201.

Deanery 18—Rev. PEDRO J. LOPEZ, V.F., St. Pius X, Santa Fe Springs, 90670.

Deanery 19—Rev. Msgr. JOHN BARRY, V.F., American Martyrs, Manhattan Beach, 90266.

Deanery 20—Rev. Msgr. BERNARD LEHENY, E.V., St. Bartholomew, Long Beach, 90803.

Archdiocesan Catholic Center

Unless otherwise listed, all ACC offices are located at: *3424 Wilshire Blvd., Los Angeles, 90010-2241.* Tel: 213-637-7000; Fax: 213-637-6000.

African-American Catholic Center for Evangelization—ANDERSON SHAW, 9505 Haas Ave., Los Angeles, 90047-3439. Tel: 323-777-2106; Fax: 323-777-2151. Email: aaccfe@shcglobal.net.

AIDS/HIV Ministry—Rev. CHRISTOPHER D. PONNET, Liaison, 1911 Zonal Ave., Los Angeles, 90033. Tel: 323-223-9047. Email: cponnet@stcamillus.ftml.net. Web: www.stcamilluscenter.org.

Alcohol and Substance Abuse—Rev. Msgr. TERRENCE RICHEY, Dir. (Retired). Tel: 213-637-7644.

Annual Catholic Appeal—Mr. JOSEPH HINDLEY, Dir. Tel: 213-637-7673; Fax: 213-637-6111.

Apostleship of Prayer—Rev. DOAN T. HOANG, S.J., Dir., 5322 Franklin Ave., Los Angeles, 90027-1613. Tel: 323-871-1518.

Apostleship of the Sea—Rev. HENRY L. HERNANDO, Maritime Chap., 870 W. Eighth St., San Pedro, 90731-3091. Tel: 310-833-3541.

Applied Technology—DAVID SCHMITT, Dir. Tel: 213-637-7526; QUI TRAN, Network Admin. Tel: 213-637-7784; JAMES R. CELONI, Technology Evangelist. Tel: 213-637-7271.

Archives—Rev. Msgr. FRANCIS J. WEBER, Archivist; KEVIN FEENEY, Adjunct Archivist, 15151 San Fernando Mission Blvd., Mission Hills, 91345-2617. Tel: 818-365-1501; Fax: 818-361-3276.

Brothers Council, Religious—Bro. WILLIAM NICK, C.S.C. Tel: 818-933-3610.

ACC Liaison to Brothers' Council—Rev. Msgr. JOSEPH HERNANDEZ, Vice Chancellor. Tel: 213-637-7426.

Canonical Services, Vicar for—Rev. THOMAS C. ANSLOW, C.M., J.C.L. Tel: 213-637-7888; Fax: 213-637-6178.

Canonical Services Coordinator—Rev. PATRICK J. HILL, J.C.L. Tel: 213-637-7888.

Legal Secretary—ELVIA MACDONALD. Tel: 213-637-7888.

Cardinal Manning House of Prayer for Priests—Rev. JOHN D. STOEGER, Dir., 3441 Waverly Dr., Los Angeles, 90027-2526. Tel: 323-662-7966; Fax: 323-953-4802.

Cardinal McIntyre Fund for Charity—Rev. FRANCIS J. HICKS, Dir. Tel: 213-637-7438; Fax: 213-637-6438.

Cathedral of Our Lady of the Angels Mausoleum—FRED BALAK, Dir. Tel: 213-680-5226.

Catholic Campaign for Human Development—JOAN HARPER, Coord. Tel: 213-637-7560.

Catholic Charities of Los Angeles, Inc.—1531 James M. Wood Blvd., P.O. Box 15095, Los Angeles, 90015-0095. Tel: 213-251-3400; Fax: 213-380-4603.

Executive Director—Rev. Msgr. GREGORY A. COX, M.S.W., M.B.A., M.Div. Tel: 213-251-3464.

Chief Administrative Officer—RONALD G. LOPEZ, M.S.W. Tel: 213-251-3413.

Chief Financial Officer—JAMES E. BATHKER, M.B.A. Tel: 213-251-3410.

Department of Resource Development—ALEXANDRIA "SANDI" ARNOLD, M.S., Dir. Tel: 213-251-3495.

Department of Human Resources—JOSEPH W. PAULICIVIC JR., S.P.H.R., Dir. Tel: 213-251-3414.

Adeste--Child Care Services—ARMINE LALAIAN, Mgr. Tel: 213-251-3468.

Central Intake Unit—BRENDA THOMAS, Dir. Tel: 818-502-2002.

Immigration and Refugee Services—LOC NAM NGUYEN, Dir. Tel: 213-251-3489.

CCLA Continuous Quality Improvement—EDWARD NELSON, Ph.D., Dir.

Youth Employment Services—ROBERT L. GUTIERREZ, Prog. Dir., 3250 Wilshire Blvd., Ste. 1010, Los Angeles, 90010. Tel: 213-736-5456.

Esperanza Immigrant Rights Project—JULIANNE DONNELLY, J.D., Project Dir. Tel: 213-251-3505.

Regional Offices and Community Centers—

Our Lady of the Angels: Metro (Los Angeles Inner City)—HECTOR MANUEL BRIONES, J.D., Regl. Dir. Tel: 310-392-8701.

Our Lady of the Angels: Western—HECTOR MANUEL BRIONES, J.D., Regl. Dir. Tel: 310-392-8701.

San Fernando Pastoral Region—MOEED KHAN, M.S.W., Regl. Dir. Tel: 818-883-6015.

San Gabriel Pastoral Region—MARY ROMERO, Regl. Dir. Tel: 323-266-3130.

San Pedro Pastoral Region—ANNA R. TOTTA, M.S., Regl. Dir. Tel: 562-591-1641.

Santa Barbara County—FRANK BOGNAR, D.P.A., Regl. Dir. Tel: 805-965-7045.

Ventura County—MICHAEL E. PERRY, M.A., Regl. Dir. Tel: 805-643-4694.

Catholic Education Foundation—KATHLEEN ANDERSON, Exec. Dir. Tel: 213-637-7576.

Catholic Relief Services—JOAN HARPER, Coord. Tel: 213-637-7560.

Cemeteries, Catholic—Tel: 213-637-7801; Fax: 213-637-6800.

Pastoral Relations—Deacon SAM FRIAS. Tel: 213-637-7807.

Director of Information Services—BRIAN MCMAHON. Tel: 213-637-7815.

Associate Director—SOFIA V. SANDRU. Tel: 213-637-7812.

Censores Librorum—Dr. MICHAEL DOWNEY, Coord. Tel: 213-637-7447.

Clergy, Vicar for—Rev. Msgr. MICHAEL W. MEYERS, V.F., Vicar; Rev. LORENZO MIRANDA, Assoc. Vicar. Tel: 213-637-7284.

Priest Personnel Board of the Archdiocese—Chair: Rev. Msgr. JAMES J. LOUGHNANE, V.F., P.A. Tel: 909-861-7106; Fax: 909-861-2697. Ex Officio: Rev. Msgr. MICHAEL W. MEYERS, V.F., Vicar for Clergy; Rev. LORENZO MIRANDA, Assoc. Vicar for Clergy. Members: Rev. Msgrs. GREGORY A. COX, M.S.W., M.B.A., M.Div.; ROBERT J. GALLAGHER, V.F.; Revs. PEDRO J. LOPEZ, V.F.; JON F. MAJARUCON, V.F.; Sr. MARY ELIZABETH GALT, B.V.M.; Revs. FRANCIS MENDOZA; KEVIN L. NOLAN, V.F.; SAL A. PILATO; LOUIS VELASQUEZ; Ms. KATHERINE RUSSELL. Vicar for Clergy: Rev. Msgr. MICHAEL W. MEYERS, V.F. Associate Vicar for Clergy: Rev. LORENZO MIRANDA.

Continuing Formation for Clergy—Rev. Msgr. JOSEPH F. HERNANDEZ, Dir. Tel: 213-637-7426.

Director of Deacons—Deacon MANUEL MARTINEZ, F.S.P. Tel: 213-637-7734.

Alcohol and Substance Abuse Ministry—Rev. Msgr. TERRENCE RICHEY, Dir. (Retired). Tel: 213-637-7644.

Ministry to Retired and Ill Priests—Tel: 213-637-7680. Sr. CARMEN ARENAS, S.deM. Tel: 213-637-7238.

Orientation and Support Programs—LOUIS VELASQUEZ. Tel: 213-637-7575; LUCILLE MILLER, Exec. Asst. Tel: 213-637-7284; MARGARITA FRANCO, Admin. Asst. Tel: 213-637-7573.

Continuing Formation—Rev. Msgr. JOSEPH F. HERNANDEZ, Dir. Tel: 213-637-7426; MARIA IBARRA, Exec. Sec. Tel: 213-637-7219.

Construction—JOHN CHEE, Dir. Tel: 213-637-7858; CECILIA URIBE, Asst. Dir. Tel: 213-637-7855; RICHARD VILLACORTA, Construction Project Supvr. Tel: 213-637-7860.

Council of Catholic Women, Archdiocesan—Tel: 213-637-7394.

Cursillo Movement—Rev. MODESTO LEWIS PEREZ, J.C.D., Archdiocesan Spiritual Dir. Tel: 626-281-0466; Rev. Msgr. JUAN MATAS, Spanish Spiritual Advisor. Tel: 323-722-5861; Deacon PETER CHU, Chinese Spiritual Advisor. Tel: 909-598-4710; Revs. JOSE FERNANDO LAMBELHO, Portugese Spiritual Advisor. Tel: 213-637-7482; PETER THANG NGO, J.C.L., Vietnamese Spiritual Advisor. Tel: 909-626-9513; NESTOR D. REBONG, Filipino Spiritual Advisor. Tel: 626-960-1805; GAEL SULLIVAN, S.D.B., English Spiritual Advisor. Tel: 323-920-7796; BRIAN CHUNG, Korean Spiritual Advisor.

Deacons—Deacon MANUEL MARTINEZ, F.S.P., Dir. Tel: 213-637-7734.

Diaconate, Formation Office—Deacons CRAIG SIEGMAN, Dir. Tel: 213-637-7282; VALENTIN SAUCEDO, Assoc. Dir. Tel: 213-637-7754. Coordinators: Rev. FRANK FERRANTE, C.M.F. Tel: 213-637-7536; Dr. WILLIAM SHAULES. Tel: 213-637-7738; Mrs. JENNIFER OCEGUEDA-REYNOSA. Tel: 213-637-7747.

Ecumenical and Interreligious Affairs—Rt. Rev. ALEXEI R. SMITH, Dir., c/o St. Andrew's Church, 538 Concord St., El Segundo, 90245. Tel: 310-322-1892; Fax: 310-322-1919.

Ethnic Ministry—Most Rev. ALEXANDER SALAZAR, D.D., V.G., Vicar. Email: asalazar@la-archdiocese.org; MARIA GUADALUPE GARRIDO, Exec. Sec. Tel: 213-637-7356.

Family Life Office—JOAN T. VIENNA, Dir. Tel: 213-637-7227; Fax: 213-637-6681. Email: familylife@la-archdiocese.org.

Coordinators, Marriage Preparation and Natural Family Planning—CANDY METOYER. Tel: 213-637-7250 (English); GRACIELA VILLALOBOS. Tel: 213-637-7561 (Spanish).

Filipino Ministry—4954 Santa Monica Blvd., Los Angeles, 90029-2539. Tel: 323-662-8480; Fax: 323-664-9391. Spiritual Moderator: Rev. ALBERT H. AVENIDO, St. Pancratius, 3519 St. Pancratius Pl., Lakewood, 90712. Tel: 562-634-6111.

Financial Services—Information Desk. Tel: 213-637-7500. SANDRA SMITH, CPA, M.B.A., Controller. Tel: 213-637-7622; ELISITA LANDRY, Accounts Receivable & Payable. Tel: 213-637-7291; EDNA CRISTOBAL, CPA, M.B.A., Investments. Tel: 213-637-7292; ROSA R. PADILLA, Payroll. Tel: 213-637-7544; DOREEN RODRIGUEZ, Exec. Asst. Tel: 213-637-7267.

Government Funded Programs—LILIA CHAVEZ, Dir. Tel: 213-637-7915; Fax: 213-637-6900.

Pre-School Director—PATRICIA S. ACEVEDO. Tel: 213-637-7902; Fax: 213-637-6902.

Youth Employment Programs—ROBERT L. GUTIERREZ, Dir., 3250 Wilshire Blvd., #1010, Los Angeles, 90010. Tel: 213-736-5456.

Health Affairs—Sr. ANGELA HALLAHAN, C.H.F., Dir. Tel: 213-637-7531.

Holy Childhood Association— (See Mission Office)

Holy Name Union—JESUS MENDEZ, Pres., Mailing Address: Archdiocesan Union of Holy Name Societies, 430 S. Fresno St., Los Angeles, 90063-3160. Tel: 323-265-1740.

Moderator—Rev. Msgr. PAUL M. MONTOYA. Tel: 661-259-2276.

Human Resources—WILLIAM HEINEN, Dir. Tel: 213-637-7596; Fax: 213-637-6116; MARGARET M. ANTCZAK, ACC Human Resources Mgr. Tel: 213-637-7625; MARGIE RODRIGUEZ, H.R. Specialist. Tel: 213-637-7371.

Human Resources Representative—TERESA BARRY. Tel: 213-637-7242.

Information—MARIA VARGAS, ACC Switchboard. Tel: 213-637-7000.

Instructional Television—DAVID G. MOORE, Dir. Tel: 213-637-7312; FERNANDO DIAZ, Studio Technician. Tel: 213-637-7399.

Insurance—LEVONTINE TOMACAN, Dir. Tel: 213-637-7279; GUADALUPE A. GARIBAY, Priests' Pension. Tel: 213-637-7320; BERTHA MIER, Benefits Admin. Tel: 213-637-7671.

Justice and Peace—Most Rev. ALEXANDER SALAZAR, D.D., V.G., Dir. Tel: 213-637-7690; JOAN HARPER, Prog. Consultant. Tel: 213-637-7560; Sr. GAIL YOUNG, S.S.S., Prog. Coord. Tel: 213-637-7690.

Knights of Columbus—California State Council Office, 15808 Arrow Blvd., Ste. A, Fontana, 92335. Tel: 909-434-0460; Fax: 909-434-0465.

State Deputy—ROBERT J. VILLALABOS. Email: state.deputy@kofc-california.org.

State Chaplain—Rev. CHUCK FULD. Tel: 858-490-8279. Email: frchuckfuld@aol.com.

Ladies of Charity of St. Vincent de Paul—2131 W. Third St., Seton Hall, Los Angeles, 90057-0992. Tel: 213-413-3688.

Marriage Encounter—Contacts: BOON HAZBOUN; GINNY HAZBOUN, 12506 Dolan Ave., Downey, 90242. Tel: 562-861-7562. Web: www.geocities.com/melawest. Marriage Encounter Weekends are offered in English, Spanish and Korean in the Archdiocese of Los Angeles.

Marriage Tribunal— (See Tribunal)

Media Relations—Mr. TOD TAMBERG, Dir. Tel: 213-637-7215; Fax: 213-637-6215; CAROLINA GUEVARA, Assoc. Dir. Tel: 213-637-7253; MARIA RODRIGUEZ, Sec. Tel: 213-637-7215.

Mission Office—Rev. Msgr. TERRANCE L. FLEMING, V.G., S.T.D., Dir.; LYDIA GAMBOA, Assoc. Dir. Tel: 213-637-7223; Fax: 213-637-6223. Email: missionoffice@la-archdiocese.org.

Holy Childhood Association—Rev. KEN DEASEY. Tel: 213-637-7229.

Mission Circles—Tel: 213-637-7223.

Propagation of the Faith—Rev. Msgr. TERRANCE L. FLEMING, V.G., S.T.D. Tel: 213-637-7223.

Operations—Director of Archdiocesan Catholic Center Facilities and Operations: EILEEN O'BRIEN. Tel: 213-637-7618.

Parish Life Office—Ms. KATHERINE RUSSELL, Dir. Tel: 213-637-7533.

Priest Pension Plan—GUADALUPE A. GARIBAY. Tel: 213-637-7320.

Project Rachel—CONNIE MARTIN, 1028 N. Lake, Ste. 207, Pasadena, 91104. Tel: 626-398-6100.

Purchasing/Mail Center—SANDY B. VILLAREAL, Purchasing Agent. Tel: 213-637-7535.

Real Estate—MICHAEL T. DAVITT, Dir. Tel: 213-637-7273; Fax: 213-637-6273.

Escrows—MARIE A. URBACH. Tel: 213-637-7505.

Leases—BEATRIZ VELASQUEZ. Tel: 213-637-7270.

Property Taxes—ALICIA PINKLEY. Tel: 213-637-7516.

Religious Education—Sr. EDITH PRENDERGAST, R.S.C., Dir. Tel: 213-637-7309; Fax: 213-637-6574. Web: ore.la-archdiocese.org.

Adult Education—Rev. DAVID C. LOFTUS. Tel: 213-637-7654.

Adult Education, Spanish—MARTHA NUNEZ. Tel: 213-637-7705; ERNESTO VEGA. Tel: 213-637-7345.

Advanced Cathechetical Ministries and Formation—English—Rev. DAVID C. LOFTUS. Tel: 213-637-7654. *Spanish*—LOURDES GONZALES-RUBIO. Tel: 213-637-7344.

Confirmation, Junior High and Youth Ministry—J. MICHAEL NORMAN, Assoc. Dir. Tel: 213-637-7674; HEATHER MACDONALD, Santa Barbara Region. Tel: 805-682-5500; CHRISTINA LUJAN. Tel: 213-637-7616; THERESA THIBODEAUX, (Spanish). Tel: 213-637-7498.

Early Childhood—JAN PEDROZA, Congress Prog. Coord. Tel: 213-637-7352.

Elementary—DIONE GRILLO, (English). Tel: 213-637-7410; MARTHA NUNEZ, (Spanish). Tel: 213-637-7705.

Ministry to the Spanish Speaking—ERNESTO VEGA. Tel: 213-637-7345.

Religious Education Congress—Coordinators: PAULETTE SMITH. Tel: 213-637-7332; JAN PEDROZA. Tel: 213-637-7352. Web: recongress.org.

Ministry with Young Adults—THERESA THIBODEAUX, (English). Tel: 213-637-7498; ALBERTO EMBRY, (Spanish). Tel: 213-637-7355.

ORE Regional Offices—Our Lady of the Angels Region: Mr. DAVID LARA, 5835 W. Slauson Ave., Culver City, 90230. Tel: 310-216-9587. San Fernando Region: MARGARET SARDO, San Fernando Pastoral Region, 15101 San Fernando Mission Blvd., Mission Hills, 91345. Tel: 818-365-5123; Fax: 818-361-4133. Mailing Address: P.O. Box 7608, Mission Hills, 91346. San Gabriel Region: EILEEN GATELEY, San Gabriel Pastoral Region, 16009 E. Cypress Ave., Irwindale, 91706. Tel: 626-962-7707; Fax: 626-962-0455. San Pedro Region: KARINA PLASCENCIA, San Pedro Pastoral Region, 3555 St. Pancratius Pl., Lakewood, 90712. Tel: 562-630-6272; Fax: 562-531-4783. Santa Barbara Region: SUE SPIES, Santa Barbara Pastoral Region, Bishop Garcia Diego Center, 4032 La Colina Rd., Santa Barbara, 93110. Tel: 805-569-1135; Fax: 805-569-2746.

Respect Life Office—Rev. Msgr. TIMOTHY P. O'CONNELL, Coord. (Retired), 2100 S. Western Ave., Apt. 9, San Pedro, 90732-4331. Tel: 310-547-1930. Email: respectlife1@aol.com.

Restorative Justice—Co Directors: Rev. GEORGE E. HORAN. Tel: 213-438-4820, Ext. 14; JAVIER E. STAURING. Tel: 213-438-4820, Ext. 15.

Safeguard the Children—JOAN T. VIENNA, Dir. Tel: 213-637-7227.

Schools, Department of Catholic—Tel: 213-637-7300; Fax: 213-637-6140.

Superintendent Elementary Schools—Dr. KEVIN BAXTER. Tel: 213-637-7328.

Elementary School Supervisors—CARLA COTTON. Tel: 213-637-7315; WENDY MCLAUGHLIN. Tel: 213-637-7584; LELANA MORAN. Tel: 213-637-7322; NANCY NICHOLAS. Tel: 213-637-7317; Dr. NINA RUSSO. Tel: 213-637-7319.

WASC Certification for Elementary Schools—PATRICIA LIVINGSTON. Tel: 213-637-7318.

Director of Personnel (K-8)—LOU ANNE INSPRUCKER. Tel: 213-637-7436.

Superintendent Secondary Schools—Rev. SABATO A. PILATO. Tel: 213-637-7265.

Secondary Supervisor/WCEA/WASC—JAMES MCCLUNE, Secondary Regl. Supvr. Tel: 213-637-7325; MARIROSE DRISTINE, Secondary Supvr. Tel: 213-637-7701.

Finance Consultant: Secondary—LOURDES "LUDY" SANTA MARIA. Tel: 213-637-7701.

High School Religion Certification Director—Sr. ANGELA HALLAHAN, C.H.F. Tel: 213-637-7324.

Federal and State Programs—Sr. PATRICIA SUPPLE, C.S.J., Dir. Tel: 213-637-7436.

Scouting, Camp Fire Ministry—Web: www.ccsala.org. DENNIS SWINK, Chm., Los Angeles Catholic Committee on Scouting, 1417 E. Leadora Ave., Glendora, 91741. Tel: 626-963-6769; Rev. JAMES J. MAHER, Chap. Tel: 818-991-3915; SHARON SHELLMAN, Chm. Girls & Camp Fire Groups. Tel: 626-967-1815.

Society of St. Vincent de Paul—JAMES R. WEISS, Pres., 210 N. Ave. 21, Los Angeles, 90031-1713. Tel: 323-224-6287; 800-974-3571; JOSE J. ROSSIER, Exec. Dir. Tel: 800-974-3571.

Synod Implementation/Stewardship—Tel: 213-637-7542. Deacon DAVID ESTRADA, Exec. Dir. Tel: 213-637-7474.

Theologian, Cardinal's—Dr. MICHAEL DOWNEY. Tel: 213-637-7447.

"The Tidings" (Archdiocesan Newspaper)—Tel: 213-637-7360; Fax: 213-637-6360.

Executive Publisher—DAVID G. MOORE. Tel: 213-637-7312.

Editor—MICHAEL NELSON, Editor. Tel: 213-637-7543; MARY TRUDEAU-MOTTOLA, Circulation Mgr. Tel: 213-637-7599; JOSE VELASQUEZ, Production Mgr. Tel: 213-637-7380; HERMINE LEES, Directory. Tel: 213-637-7392; CORA LEUTERIO, Business Mgr. Tel: 213-637-7391.

Tribunal—Main Office, 3424 Wilshire Blvd., Los Angeles, 90010-2241. Tel: 213-637-7245; Fax: 213-637-6245. *Santa Barbara/Ventura Branch, P.O. Box 2215, Oxnard, 93034.* Tel: 805-486-6553; Fax: 805-486-3884.

Judicial Vicar—Rev. Msgr. CHARLES J. CHAFFMAN, J.C.D. Tel: 213-637-7209.

Adjutant Judicial Vicar—Rev. REYNALDO B. MATUNOG, J.C.L. Tel: 213-637-7220.

Canonical Staff—Revs. WHARREN BANICO; TRUC NGUYEN, J.C.L.

Judges—Rev. Msgrs. CHARLES J. CHAFFMAN, J.C.D.; TERRANCE L. FLEMING, V.G., S.T.D.; Rev. REYNALDO B. MATUNOG, J.C.L.; Deacon HAROLD "HAL" PARISH, J.C.D.

Promoter of Justice—Rev. Msgr. FRANCIS T. WALLACE, J.C.L. Tel: 213-637-7631.

Defenders of the Bond—Revs. TRUC NGUYEN, J.C.L.; REYNALDO B. MATUNOG, J.C.L.; JAMES SHIFFER, S.S.C., J.C.L.

Advocate and Auditor—LOUIS A. SHAPIRO.

Notaries and Other Officials—Sr. ROSA GONZALEZ, F.M.I.; HELEN GULLIVER; Sr. M. DOMNIC JONES, S.N.D.; BOBBIE LOPEZ; SARAH FIERRO; Sr. TRACY SHARP, S.C.R.H.; OLIVIA ALVAREZ; ESPERANZA IZQUIERDO; Rev. JOHN G. MONTEJANO.

Trusts and Estate Programs—H. RICHARD CLOSSON, Dir. Tel: 213-637-7472.

Victim Assistance Ministry—SUZANNE HEALY. Tel: 800-355-2545 (Hotline); 213-637-7650 (Office). Email: sdhealy@la-archdiocese.org.

"Vida Nueva" (Archdiocesan Spanish Newspaper)—Tel: 213-637-7360; Fax: 213-637-6360. DAVID G. MOORE, Exec. Publisher. Tel: 213-637-7599; VICTOR ALEMAN, Editor. Tel: 213-637-7310; MARY TRUDEAU-MOTTOLA, Circulation Mgr. Tel: 213-637-7599; JOSE VELASQUEZ, Production Dir. Tel: 213-637-7380.

Vocations—Tel: 213-637-7248. Web: www.vocations.la-archdiocese.org. Revs. JAMES FORSEN, Dir. Email: frjrforsen@la-archdiocese.org; JAMES M. ANGUIANO, Dir. House of Formation. Tel: 310-516-6671.

Women Religious, Vicar for—Sr. M. ANNCARLA COSTELLO, S.N.D., Ex Officio. Tel: 213-637-7592; Fax: 213-637-6592.

Association of Women Religious—3424 Wilshire Blvd., Los Angeles, 90010-2241. Tel: 213-637-7592.

Special Projects Coordinator—Sr. MIRIAM JOSEPH, E.F.M.S. Tel: 213-637-7559.

Coordinating Council—Sisters M. ANNCARLA COSTELLO, S.N.D.; JOAN HENEHAN, C.S.J.; ADA LOCATELLI, F.K.M.; Sisters CAROLYN MCCORMACK, O.P.; CARMEN MALDONADO, S.S.C.; MARY ELIZA MARTIN, C.S.C.; JEAN MORNINGSTAR, S.N.J.M.; REINA PEREA, O.P.; JANE RANDOLPH, O.P.; MARGARET SPILLER, S.N.J.M.; MARY JOSEPH SUTER, D.C.; DARLENE YOUNG, S.C.R.H.

Worship—Sr. ROSANNE BELPEDIO, C.S.J., Dir. Tel: 213-637-7262. Email: worship@la-archdiocese.org.

Hispanic Liturgy and Ministry Coordinator—Rev. MANUEL SANAHUJA, Sch.P. Tel: 213-637-7588.

Archdiocesan Advisory Boards

Unless otherwise indicated, mailing address for all offices is: *3424 Wilshire Blvd., Los Angeles, 90010-2241.*

AIDS/AIDS Council—Rev. CHRISTOPHER D. PONNET, Dir., St. Camillus Center, 1911 Zonal Ave., Los Angeles, 90033. Tel: 323-225-4461, Ext. 221. Executive Committee: CAROL CLARK; MANUEL TORREZ; RENEE STAMPOLIS; FRANK GALVAN; EDNA WILLIAMS, (with Advisory Committee); NICK ROCCA.

AIDS/HIV Ministry—Director & Cardinal Liaison: Rev. CHRIS PONNET, St. Camillus Center, 1911 Zonal Ave., Los Angeles, 90033-1032. Tel: 323-225-4461, Ext. 221. Web: www.stcamilluscenter.org. Email: cponnet@stcamillus.ftml.net. Executive Committee: CAROL CLARK; MANUEL TORREZ; RENEE STAMPOLIS; FRANK GALVAN; NICK ROCCA.

Cardinal McIntyre Fund for Charity—Director: Rev. FRANK HICKS, 3424 Wilshire Blvd., Los Angeles, 90010-2241. Tel: 213-637-7438. Email: frfjhicks@la-archdiocese.org. Chairman: His Eminence ROGER CARDINAL MAHONY, D.D. President: Rev. Msgr. ROYALE M. VADAKIN, V.G., P.A. Secretary: Sr. MARY ELIZABETH GALT, B.V.M. Treasurer: Rev. JOSEPH P. SHEA, V.F Board of Directors: Rev. ANTONIO CACCIAPUOTI; Rev. Msgr. GREGORY A. COX, M.S.W., M.B.A., M.Div.; Sr. MARY ELIZABETH GALT, B.V.M.; Rev. Msgr. BERNARD M. LEHENY; Rev. JOSEPH QUAN NGUYEN; Rev. Msgr. GUSTAVO J. RAMON; Rev. JOSEPH P. SHEA, V.F. Executive Director: Rev. Msgr. JOSEPH HERNANDEZ.

Clergy Misconduct Oversight Board—Administrator: ROSE ANN RASIC, 3424 Wilshire Blvd., Los Angeles, 90010-2241. Tel: 213-637-7548. Chair: DANIEL R. KOENIG. Vice Chair: Judge RICHARD P. BYRNE. Members: FERNANDO L. AENLLE-ROCHA; Rev. JAMES M. ANGUIANO; JUDI ARNOLD; ADRIENNE CEDRO-HAMENT; ILEGRA EVANS; JACK HOURIGAN; JAMES J. MCGOUGH, M.D.; Dr. INES MONGUIO; TERRY SEIDLER; Rev. Msgr. DAVID A. SORK; Mr. GEORGE K. TAKAHASHI; Sr. GENEVIEVE VIGIL, S.J.C.

Commission for Catholic Life Issues—Chairman and Coordinator of Activities: Rev. Msgr. TIMOTHY P. O'CONNELL (Retired), 2100 S. Western Ave., Apt. 9, San Pedro, 90732-4331. Tel: 310-547-1930. Email: respectlife1@aol.com. Commission Members: WILLIAM ANDERSON, Esq.; DENNIS DE PIETRO; RACHEL DI PIETRO; ASTRID BENNETT GUTIERREZ; DAN MANSUETO; LICIA NICASSIO; BETTY ODELLO, R.N., M.S.N.; ROSALINDA TANDOC; JENNIFER SHAW; Sr. PAULA VANDEGAER, S.S.S., L.C.S.W. Advisory Members to the Commission: ANDREA BURMAN, M.A.; MARIAN BURMAN, M.A.; VINCENT FORTANASCE, M.D.; Revs. MARCOS GONZALEZ; SABATO A. PILATO; KATHERINE DOWLING SCHLAERTH, M.D.; MARY V. SHERIDAN; GERMAINE WENSLEY, R.N.; MARLENE WILSON, M.S.W., L.C.S.W.

College of Consultors—President: His Eminence CARDINAL ROGER MAHONY. Members: Most Revs. EDWARD W. CLARK, D.D., S.T.D., V.G., Our Lady of the Angels Pastoral Region; THOMAS J. CURRY, D.D., Ph.D., V.G., Santa Barbara Pastoral Region; OSCAR A. SOLIS, D.D., V.G., San Pedro Pastoral Region; ALEXANDER SALAZAR, D.D., V.G., Office of Ethnic Ministry, and Office of Justice and Peace; GERALD E. WILKERSON, D.D., V.G., San Fernando Pastoral Region; GABINO ZAVALA, D.D., J.C.L., V.G., San Gabriel Pastoral Region; Rev. Msgrs. ROYALE M. VADAKIN, V.G., P.A., Vicar General/ Moderator of the Curia; TIMOTHY E. NICHOLS, Chair, Council of Priests; TIMOTHY J. DYER, V.F., Dean, Our Lady of the Angels Pastoral Region.

Commission for Ecumenical and Interreligious Affairs—Rt. Rev. ALEXEI R. SMITH, Dir., 538 Concord St., El Segundo, 90245. Tel: 310-322-1892; Fax: 310-322-1919.

Council of Deacons—Director of Deacons: Deacon MANUEL MARTINEZ, F.S.P., 3424 Wilshire Blvd., Los Angeles, 90010-2202. Tel: 213-637-7734. Council Chair: Deacon RALPH ULIBARRI. Council Secretary: Deacon ED MILLS.

Regional Representatives and Alternates—San Gabriel Region: Deacon JIM CROWLEY, Regl. Representative; ANNETTE CROWLEY, Regl. Representative; Deacon AL AUSTIN, Alternate Representative; RITA AUSTIN, Alternate Representative. San Pedro Region: Deacon RALPH ULIBARRI, Regl. Representative; MAXINE ULIBARRI, Regl. Representative; Deacon TIMOTHY J. ROBERTO, Alternate Representative; PAT ROBERTO, Alternate Representative. Santa Barbara Region: Deacon ED MILLS, Regl. Representative; KATE MILLS, Regl. Representative; VACANT, Alternate Representative. San Fernando Region: Deacon DOUGLAS JONES, Regl. Representative; DOLORES JONES, Regl. Representative; Deacon RAY GUIAO, Alternate Representative; LALLY GUIAO, Alternate Representative. Our Lady of the Angels Region: Deacon MARK RACE, Regl. Representative; VICKY RACE, Regl. Representative; Deacon JOSEPH GIRARD, Alternate Representative; JUDITH GIRARD, Alternate Representative.

Spiritual Growth Committee—Chairpersons: Deacon GARY PATTERSON; MARGE PATTERSON.

Continuing Education Committee—Deacon ROBERT SEIDLER, Chm.

Council of Priests—President: His Eminence ROGER CARDINAL MAHONY, D.D. Chairman: Rev. RICHARD MARTINI. Tel: 213-637-7479. Vice Chairman: Rev. EDWARD DOVER. Secretary & Treasurer: Rev. ALEX ACLAN.

Elected Members—Santa Barbara Region: Revs. JON F. MAJARUCON, V.F.; STEVE V. DAVOREN; Rev. Msgr. MICHAEL J. JENNETT, S.T.D. San Fernando Region: Revs. THOMAS E. BAKER, V.F.; ALBERT BAHHUTH; EDWARD DOVER. San Gabriel Region: Rev. Msgr. JOHN T. MORETTA, V.F.; Revs. ALEX ACLAN; GUSTAVO CASTILLO. San Pedro Region: Rev. ANTONIO GARNICA, M.S.C., V.F.; Rev. Msgrs. JOSEPH BRENNAN; JOHN S. WOOLWAY. Our Lady of the Angels Region: Rev. Msgr. TIMOTHY J. DYER, V.F.; Revs. BRIAN CASTANEDA; RICHARD MARTINI. Ex Officio Members: Most Revs. EDWARD W. CLARK, D.D., S.T.D., V.G.; THOMAS J. CURRY, D.D., Ph.D., V.G.; ALEXANDER SALAZAR, D.D., V.G.; OSCAR A. SOLIS, D.D., V.G.; Rev. Msgr. ROYALE M. VADAKIN, V.G., P.A.; Most Revs. GERALD E. WILKERSON, D.D., V.G.; GABINO ZAVALA, D.D., J.C.L., V.G.

Archdiocesan Finance Council Members—Chairman: PAUL WATSON, Retired Chm. Wells Fargo Bank. Tel: 213-637-7218. Vice Chairman: MICHAEL ENRIGHT, Exec. Vice Pres. Chartwell Partners, LLC. Members: ALBERTO G. ALVARADO, District Dir., U.S. Small Business; ROBERT BERRY, Retired Exec. Vice Pres., Lockheed Federal Credit Union; RICHARD CORGEL, Exec. Dir., Ernst & Young, LLP; DAVID S. DEVITO, Mng. Dir. & CFO, Trust Company of the West; THOMAS LARKIN, Pres., COO, Trust Company of the West; ALLEN LUND, Pres. & CEO, Allen Lund Co.; WILLIAM WARDLAW, Esq., Freeman Spogli & Co.; SUSAN WEGLEITNER, Mng. Dir., J.P. Morgan Chase & Co.; JOHN T. WHOLIHAN, Retired Dean, College of Business Admin., Loyola Marymount University; DIANA NISHIURA, Sr. Counsel, California Dept. of Financial Institutions, Legal Div.; Rev. Msgrs. PAUL M. ALBEE, V.F., Pastor, Holy Cross, Moorpark; JOHN BARRY, V.F., Pastor, American Martyrs, Manhattan Beach; JARLATH CUNNANE, V.F., Pastor, St. Thomas the Apostle, LA; ROBERT J. GALLAGHER, V.F., Pastor, St. Charles Borromeo, North Hollywood; Rev. NESTOR REBONG, Pastor, St. Christopher, West Covina; Most Rev. ALEXANDER SALAZAR, D.D., V.G., Vicar, Ethnic Ministries/Director of Justice & Peace. Ex Officio: His Eminence ROGER CARDINAL MAHONY, D.D., Archbishop of Los Angeles; Rev. Msgr. ROYALE M. VADAKIN, V.G., P.A., Moderator of the Curia & Vicar Gen.; RANDOLPH STEINER, CFO, Archdiocese of Los Angeles.

Justice and Peace Commission—Chair: ALLIS DRUFFEL. Vice Chair: TONY FADALE. Members: ALICE LINSMEIER; ANDERSON SHAW; BERNADETTE ROBERT; CHRISTOPHER GABRIELE; Deacon JAIME ABRERA; FRANCES JONTE; Rev. FRANCISCO VALDOVINOS, S.T.; GEORGE CROOK; JOE DOMOND; JOE ESSEFF; JOE LUSNIA; JUANNA TORRES; KURT ORZECK; LUCY BOUTTE; RAMON POSADA; ROCKY T. DOMINGO; Sr. MARILYN RUDY, C.S.J.; TONY FADALE. Ex Officio Member: Most Rev. ALEXANDER SALAZAR, D.D., V.G., Dir.; CAMBRIA SMITH; AQUILINA SORIANO; Sr. GAIL YOUNG, S.S.S., Prog. Coord.; JOAN HARPER, Prog. Consultant.

Spirituality Commission—Chair: Rev. JAMES CLARKE, Ph.D. Tel: 805-482-2755, Ext. 1056. Members: Rt. Rev. ALEXEI R. SMITH; Dr. MICHAEL DOWNEY; Sisters LAURA GORMLEY, S.S.L.; THOMAS BERNARD MACCONNELL, C.S.J.; Ms. FE MUSGRAVE; JUDY ALVAREZ.

Theological Commission—Co Chairmen: Dr. MICHAEL DOWNEY; Rev. THOMAS P. RAUSCH, S.J., Ph.D. Secretary: Sr. KAREN WILHELMY, C.S.J., M.A. Tel: 562-942-7300, Ext. 219.

Members—Rev. RICHARD B. BENSON, C.M., S.T.D.; Most Rev. EDWARD W. CLARK, D.D., S.T.D., V.G.; Rev. Msgr. CRAIG A. COX, J.C.D.; Revs. LUKE DYSINGER, O.S.B., M.D., D.Phil.; GUILLERMO C. GARCIA, Ph.D.; ELIZABETH DIVELY LAURO, Ph.D.; Sr. MARY MCKAY, C.S.J., Ph.D. Consultant: DANIEL SMITH-CHRISTOPHER, Ph.D.

Liturgical Commision—Mr. VINCENT ADAMS (2011) St. Jude, 32032 W. Lindero Canyon Rd., Westlake Village, 91361. Cell: 310-713-0726. Email: vpa323@aol.com; Ms. DONNA BARNES (2011) Holy Trinity, 209 N. Hanford Ave., San Pedro, 90732. Tel: 310-548-6535, Ext. 306. Email: dbarnes@holytrinitysp.org; Deacon ARTURO BARRAGAN (2009) (St. Gregory the Great), 11547 Cecilia St., Santa Fe Springs, 90670. Tel: 562-863-1232 (Home); Cell: 562-441-1444. Email: turito1947@aol.com; Rev. CHRISTOPHER BAZYOUROS (2011) St. Albert the Great, 804 E. Compton Blvd., Rancho Dominguez, 90220. Tel: 310-329-7548; Fax: 310-484-8666; Cell: 626-485-3564. Email: frchrisbaz90220@live.com; Mr. FRANK BROWNSTEAD (2010) Cathedral of Our Lady of the Angels. Tel: 213-680-5205. Email: fbrownstead@olacathedral.org; Ms. SYLVIA DEVILLERS, Acting Chm. (2009) Padre Serra. Tel: 805-484-7428 (Home). Email: devillers@roadrunner.com; Mr. JAMES DROLLINGER (2010) St. Charles Borromeo & St. Jerome. Cell: 310-617-2465; Tel: 310-642-9162 (Home). Email: hjames81@earthlink.net; Ms. GABRIELA ESPARZA-REITZELL (2011) Cathedral of Our Lady of the Angels. Tel: 213-680-5201. Email: greitzell@olacathedral.org; Dr. PAUL F. FORD, Ph.D. (2010) St. John Seminary, 5012 Seminary Rd., Camarillo, 93012-2598. Tel: 805-482-2755, Ext. 1066; Fax: 805-482-3470. Email: paulfford@stjohnsem.edu. Web: www.pford.stjohnsem.edu; Home: 5246 Creekside Rd., Camarillo, 93012-5420. Tel: 805-484-0681. Email: paulfford@verizon.net; companion_to_narnia@hotmail.com; Rev. Msgr. HELMUT A. HEFNER, J.C.L. (2011) St. Mel, 20870 Ventura Blvd., Woodland Hills, 91364-2318. Tel: 818-340-6020, Ext. 1014. Email: pastor@stmel.org; Rev. JOEL HENSON (2011) St. John's Seminary, 5012 Seminary Rd., Camarillo, 93012. Tel: 805-482-2755, Ext. 6739. Email: jhenson@stjohnsem.edu; Ms. ROSE M. HERNANDEZ (2009) Our Lady of Peace, 15444 Nordhoff St., North Hills, 91343. Tel: 818-894-1176, Ext. 203; Cell: 323-854-7792. Email: rhernandez@olpeace.org; Ms. LILIANA HSUEH-GUTIERREZ (2010) Mailing Address: St. Elizabeth Ann Seton, P.O. Box 5426, Hacienda Heights, 91745-0426. Tel: 626-369-0533 (Home); Cell: 626-475-1215. Email: lilianahg77@yahoo.com; Mr. DAVID LARA (2011) Our Lady of Angels Pastoral Office, 5835 W. Slauson Ave., Los Angeles, 90230. Tel: 310-216-9587 (Office); Fax: 310-215-0749. Email: dlara@olapr.org; Revs. PEDRO J. LOPEZ, V.F. (2009) St. Pius X, Santa Fe Springs, 10827 Pioneer

Blvd., Santa Fe Springs, 90670-4216. Tel: 562-863-8734. Email: frpedro@aol.com; KEVIN MCCRACKEN, C.M. (2011) St. John's Seminary, 5012 Seminary Rd., Camarillo, 93012. Tel: 805-482-2755, Ext. 1028; 805-389-2006. Email: kmccracken@stjohnsem.edu; Ms. FE MUSGRAVE (2009) St. Elizabeth Ann Seton. Tel: 626-964-3629 (Work); 626-912-6474 (Home). Email: stafel143@aol.com; Ms. JANIS NELSON, Sec. (2010) 1039 Nina Dr., Oxnard, 93030. Cell: 818-516-8308; Tel: 805-485-8934 (Home). Email: janismnelson@aol.com; Ms. KIM NGUYEN (2011) Maria Regina, 3855 W. 181st St., Torrance, 90504. Tel: 310-354-6954 (Home); Cell: 310-429-6573. Email: mrliturgy@yahoo.com; Ms. MARY LOU VANDERLIP (2011) St. John Eudes. Cell: 818-314-0005; Tel: 818-998-3613 (Home). Email: louiestarr@yahoo.com; Rev. Msgr. THOMAS WELBERS (2010); Mr. DAN WHITE (2009) (St. John Vianney), 15437 Newton St., Hacienda Heights, 91745. Cell: 626-893-0689. Email: dwhite.ddwa@verizon.net. Ex Officio: Sr. ROSANNE BELPEDIO, C.S.J., Office for Worship: 3424 Wilshire Blvd., Los Angeles, 90010. Tel: 213-637-7513 (Office); Rev. MANUEL SANAHUJA, Sch.P., Office for Worship: 3424 Wilshire Blvd., Los Angeles, 90010. Tel: 213-637-7588 (Office); 323-223-4153, Ext. 21 (Residence). Email: frmsanahuja@la-archdiocese.org; Most Rev. ALEXANDER SALAZAR, D.D., V.G. Email: asalazar@la-archdiocese.org.

CLERGY, PARISHES, MISSIONS AND PAROCHIAL SCHOOLS

CITY OF LOS ANGELES

(LOS ANGELES COUNTY)

1—CATHEDRAL OF OUR LADY OF THE ANGELS (2002) His Eminence Cardinal Roger Mahony; Rev. Msgrs. Kevin J. Kostelnik; Marc V. Trudeau; Rev. Francis Mendoza; Deacon Manny Martinez.
Church: 555 W. Temple St., 90012. Tel: 213-680-5200; Fax: 213-620-1982. Email: ebonaduce@olacathedral.org. Web: www.olacathedral.org.
Catechesis/Religious Program—Michelle-Marie Youssef, D.R.E.

2—ST. AGATHA (1923) Sr. M. Karen Collier, S.S.L., Parish Life Dir. In Res., Revs. William Axe, O.SS.T.; Frank Whatley, O.SS.T.
Res.: 2610 S. Mansfield Ave., 90016. Tel: 323-935-8127; Fax: 323-939-3547. Email: st.agatha@stagathas.org. Web: www.stagathas.org.
Catechesis/Religious Program—Tel: 323-933-0963. Email: religioused@stagathas.org. Students 423.

3—ST. AGNES (1903), (Hispanic—Korean), Revs. John Franck, C.PP.S.; William J. Delaney, C.PP.S., Senior Priest; Stephen dos Santos, C.PP.S., Parochial Vicar. In Res., Rev. Young Chan Lee, S.J., Chap., Korean Catholic Community.
Res.: 2625 S. Vermont Ave., 90007. Tel: 323-731-2464, Ext. 100; Fax: 323-731-6186.
School—1428 W. Adams Blvd., 90007. Tel: 323-731-2464, Ext. 140; Fax: 323-735-7719. Lay Teachers 11; Students 260.
Catechesis/Religious Program—Mrs. Miriam Oliva, D.R.E. Students 452.

4—ALL SAINTS (1926), (Hispanic), Revs. Jose L. Vega, O.M.; Gino Vanzillotta, O.M.; Mario Pisano, O.M.; Deacon Pedro Rojas.
Rectory—3431 Portola Ave., 90032-2215. Tel: 323-223-1101; Fax: 323-223-9592.
School—(Grades K-8), 3420 Portola Ave., 90032. Tel: 323-225-7264; Fax: 323-225-1240. Lay Teachers 9; Students 100.
Catechesis/Religious Program—Tel: 323-225-5193; Fax: 323-225-5193. Students 380.

5—ST. ALOYSIUS GONZAGA (1908), (Hispanic), [CEM] Rev. Ramon Palomera.
Res.: 7814 Crocket Blvd., 90001. Tel: 323-585-4485; Fax: 323-589-8485.
School—2023 E. Nadeau St., 90001. Tel: 323-582-4965; Fax: 323-585-4938. Mrs. Nicole Johnson, Prin. Lay Teachers 9; Students 225.
Catechesis/Religious Program—2023 E. Nadeau St. Tel: 323-277-7824. Students 535.

6—ST. ALPHONSUS (1935), (Hispanic), Revs. Enrique De Los Rios, Admin.; Benito Armenta.
Res.: 5223 Hastings St., 90022-2625. Tel: 323-264-3353; Fax: 323-264-4858.
School—552 S. Amalia Ave., 90022-2625. Tel: 323-268-5165; Fax: 323-268-7784. Web: www.stalphonsusschool.org. Lay Teachers 9; Students 225.
Catechesis/Religious Program—552 South Amalia Ave., 90022. Tel: 323-266-0855. Students 508.

7—ST. ANASTASIA (1953) Rev. Thomas F. King; Rev. Msgr. Royale M. Vadakin, Pastor Emeritus. In Res., Rev. Msgr. Gregory A. Cox.
Res.: 7390 W. Manchester Ave., 90045. Tel: 310-670-2243; Fax: 310-670-5052. Email: parish@st-anastasia.org. Web: www.st-anastasia.org.
School—8631 S. Stanmoor Dr., 90045. Tel: 310-645-8816; Fax: 310-645-6923. Mrs. Rosemary Connolly, Prin. Lay Teachers 12; Students 292.
Catechesis/Religious Program—Students 175.

8—ST. ANN (1937) Revs. Theodore Ley, S.M., Admin. Pro Tem; Hugh Crowe, Pastor Emeritus (Retired).
Office: 1365 Blake Ave., 90031.
Res.: 2302 Riverdale Ave., 90031. Fax: 323-222-6871.
Catechesis/Religious Program—Tel: 323-222-9749. Ramona Lopez, D.R.E. Students 137.

9—ST. ANSELM (1924) Rev. Lawrence Shelton.
Res.: 2222 W. 70th St., 90043. Tel: 323-758-6729; Fax: 323-758-8455. Email: tcanselm@aol.com.
Catechesis/Religious Program—Students 100.

10—ST. ANTHONY (1910), (Croatian), [CEM] Revs. Mate Bizaca, Admin.; Vlatko Poljicak, Senior Priest.
Res.: 712 N. Grand Ave., 90012. Tel: 213-628-2938; Fax: 213-628-1635. Email: croatsvantela@sbcglobal.net. Web: croatianchurch.org/la.
Catechesis/Religious Program—Students 75.

11—ASCENSION (1923), (Hispanic—African American), Rev. Humberto Bernabe.
Res.: 517 W. 112th St., 90044. Tel: 323-754-2978; Fax: 323-754-3905. Email: ascens@pacbell.net.
School—500 W. 111th Pl., 90044. Tel: 323-756-4064; Fax: 323-756-1060. Dr. Karen Kallay, Prin. Lay Teachers 10; Students 261.
Catechesis/Religious Program—Tel: 323-777-6356. Students 350.

12—ASSUMPTION (1926), (Hispanic), Rev. Msgr. Gustavo J. Ramon. In Res., Rev. Diosdado Martin (Retired).
Res.: 2832 Blanchard St., 90033. Tel: 323-269-8171; Fax: 323-269-0106. Email: assumptionchurch@sbcglobal.net.
School—(Grades K-8), 3016 Winter St., 90063. Tel: 323-269-4319; Fax: 323-269-2434. Carolina Gomez, Prin. Lay Teachers 8; Students 182.
Catechesis/Religious Program—Tel: 213-269-5920; Fax: 323-269-7786. Students 54.
Mission—Assumption 414 N. Fresno St., Old Co. 90063.

13—ST. BASIL'S (1920) Revs. Francis J. Hicks; Ki-Jun Lawrence Pak. In Res., Rev. Msgr. Terrence Richey (Retired); Revs. Jerome Anthony Bouska (Retired); Cornelius Noel Phelan (Retired); Dennis P. Marrell.
Res.: 637 S. Kingsley Dr., 90005. Tel: 213-381-6191; Fax: 213-382-5883.
Catechesis/Religious Program—Students 47.

14—ST. BERNADETTE (1947), (African American), Rev. Allan Roberts; Deacons Emile Adams; Mark Race.
Res.: 3825 Don Felipe Dr., 90008. Tel: 323-293-4877; Fax: 323-293-2838. Email: stbernadette@earthlink.net.
School—4196 Marlton Ave., 90008. Tel: 323-291-4284; Fax: 323-291-0839. Mrs. Barbara M. Davis, Prin. Lay Teachers 10; Students 215.
Catechesis/Religious Program—Students 65.

15—ST. BERNARD (1924) Rev. Gerald McSorley; Rev. Msgr. Patrick McNulty, Pastor Emeritus (Retired).
Res.: 2500 W. Ave. 33, 90065. Tel: 323-255-6142; Fax: 323-255-2351. Email: stbla@aol.com. Web: stbernardla.cc.
School—3254 Verdugo Rd., 90065. Tel: 323-256-4989; Fax: 323-256-4963. Email: sstbernard3@aol.com. Mrs. Margaret Samaniego, Prin. Lay Teachers 10; Students 170.
Catechesis/Religious Program—2515 W. Ave. 33, 90065. Tel: 323-478-0001; Fax: 323-256-6242. Students 315.

16—BLESSED SACRAMENT (1904) Revs. Michael J. Mandala, S.J.; Wayne Negrete, S.J.; James A. Doogan, S.J.; Yolanda Lichtman, Dir. Social Svcs.
Res.: 6657 Sunset Blvd., 90028. Tel: 323-462-6311; Fax: 323-462-0113. Email: church@blessedsacramenthollywood.org. Web: www.blessedsacramenthollywood.org.
School—6641 Sunset Blvd., 90028. Tel: 323-467-4177; Fax: 323-467-6099. Email: blesacsch@juno.com. Lay Teachers 13; Students 86.
Catechesis/Religious Program—Tel: 323-463-9820. Email: religioused@blessedsacramenthollywood.org. Virginia Cipres, D.R.E. Students 200.

17—ST. BRENDAN (1915) Rev. Msgr. Terrance L. Fleming; Rev. Kenneth Deasy; Deacon Eric Stoltz.
Res.: 310 S. Van Ness Ave., 90020. Tel: 323-936-4656; Fax: 323-936-9058. Email: info@stbrendanchurch.org. Web: www.stbrendanchurch.org.
School—238 S. Manhatten Pl., 90004. Tel: 213-382-7401; Fax: 213-382-8918. Sisters 3; Lay Teachers 18; Students 300.
Catechesis/Religious Program—Students 115.

18—ST. BRIDGET'S CHINESE CATHOLIC CHURCH (1940), (Chinese), [JC] Rev. John Lam, S.D.B.
445 Cottage Home St., 90012-1418. Tel: 323-222-5518. Web: www.stbridgetccc.com.
Res.: 448 Cottage Home St., 90012. Tel: 323-276-8587; Fax: 323-222-0814.
Church: 510 Cottage Home, 90012-1418.

19—ST. BRIGID'S (1920), (African American—Hispanic), Rev. Thomas Frank, S.S.J.
Res.: 5214 S. Western Ave., 90062. Tel: 323-292-0781; Fax: 323-290-1254. Email: stbrigidchurch@sbcglobal.net.
Catechesis/Religious Program—Students 95.

20—ST. CAMILLUS DE LELLIS (1954), (Center for Pastoral Care). Rev. Christopher D. Ponnet, Pastor, Dir. & Chap.; His Eminence Cardinal Roger Mahony, Chap.; Rev. Robert J. Jones, C.M., Chap.; Sisters Mary Jean Ferry, B.V.M., Chap.; Angela Pacheco, C.S.J., Chap.; Martha Vega, S.S.S., Chap.; Rev. Tony Diaz, C.M.F., Chap.; Sisters Theresa Hann, O.S.F., Chap.; Yolanda Vega, S.S.S., Chap.; Deacon Walter J. Hanson, Chap.; Leticia Delgado, Chap.; Mr. Rene Valle, Chap.
Res.: 1911 Zonal Ave., 90033-1032. Tel: 323-225-4461; Fax: 323-225-9096. Web: www.circlesofhope.org.
Catholics Against the Death Penalty Center—Tel: 323-225-4461, Ext. 221.
Catholic HIV/AIDS Office—Tel: 323-225-4461, Ext. 221.
Pax Christi Los Angeles—Tel: 323-225-4461, Ext. 221.
Ministry with Gay & Lesbian Catholics—Tel: 323-225-4461, Ext. 221.
Consistent Life Ethics Institute—Tel: 323-225-4461, Ext. 221.

21—ST. CASIMIR (1946), (Lithuanian), Rev. Tomas Karanauskas, Admin.
Res.: 2718 St. George St., 90027. Tel: 323-664-4660; Fax: 323-664-8729.
Catechesis/Religious Program—Tel: 818-248-4046. Students 125.

22—CATHEDRAL CHAPEL (1927) Revs. Truc Q. Nguyen, Admin.; Earl Gordon Walker, Pastor Emeritus (Retired); Most Rev. Edward W. Clark, Auxiliary Bishop OLA Region.
Mailing Address: 927 S. La Brea Ave., 90036.
Office: 926 S. Detroit St., 90036. Tel: 323-930-5976; 323-930-5977; Fax: 323-935-7308. Email: parish@cathedralchapel.org. Web: cathedralchapel.org.
Church: 923 S. La Brea Ave., 90036.
Res.: 922 S. Detroit St., 90036. Tel: 323-930-5978; Fax: 323-935-7308.
School—755 S. Cochran Ave., 90036. Tel: 323-938-9976; Fax: 323-938-9930. Web: cathedralchapelschool.org. Lay Teachers 12; Students 285.
Catechesis/Religious Program—Students 54.

23—ST. CECILIA (1909), (African American—Hispanic), Revs. Joseph Forlani, M.C.C.J. (Italy), Admin.; Xavier Colleoni, M.C.C.J. (Italy).
Res.: 4230 S. Normandie Ave., 90037. Tel: 323-294-6628; Fax: 323-294-3310. Email: parish@stcecilia-la.org.
School—4224 S. Normandie Ave., 90037. Tel: 323-293-4266; Fax: 323-293-5556. Lay Teachers 9; Students 290.
Catechesis/Religious Program—Students 618.

24—CHRIST THE KING (1926) Rev. Antonio Cacciapuoti. In Res., Rev. Msgr. Charles J. Chaffman.
Res.: 624 N. Rossmore Ave., 90004. Tel: 323-465-7605; Fax: 323-463-4895. Email: christtheking@sbcglobal.net. Web: www.ctk-ca.org.
School—617 N. Arden Blvd., 90004. Tel: 323-462-4753; Fax: 323-462-8475. Lay Teachers 9; Students 232.
Catechesis/Religious Program—Tel: 323-465-7084. Students 314.

25—ST. COLUMBAN (1945), (Filipino), Rev. John Brannigan, S.S.C.; Deacon Felix Dumlao.
Res.: 125 Loma Dr., 90026-5712. Tel: 213-250-8818; Fax: 213-975-9398.
Catechesis/Religious Program—Students 60.

26—ST. COLUMBKILLE (1921), (Hispanic—African American), Rev. Msgr. Timothy J. Dyer; Rev. Angel Castro. In Res., Rev. James Forsen.
Res.: 6315 S. Main St., 90003. Tel: 323-758-5540; Fax: 323-758-8108.
School—145 W. 64th St., 90003. Tel: 323-758-2284; Fax: 323-750-7141. Sisters 1; Lay Teachers 8; Students 240.
Catechesis/Religious Program—Tel: 323-789-3344. Students 475.

27—CRISTO REY (1954), (Hispanic), [CEM] Revs. Galo Espinoza, O.A.R. (Mexico); Euben Capacillo, O.A.R. (Philippines); Michael Stechmann, O.A.R.
Res.: 4343 Perlita Ave., 90039. Tel: 323-245-4585; Fax: 818-247-8831.
Catechesis/Religious Program—Students 183.

28—DIVINE SAVIOUR (1907), (Hispanic), Rev. Federico (Rene) Juarez, O.F.M.

Res.: 610 Cypress Ave., 90065. Tel: 323-225-9181; Fax: 323-225-1099. Email: office@divinesaviour.com. Web: www.divinesaviour.e-paluch.com.
School—Tel: 323-222-6077; Fax: 323-222-6494. Email: principaldss@yahoo.com. Lay Teachers 9; Students 133.
Catechesis/Religious Program—Tel: 323-225-9181, Ext. 115. Email: reled@divinesaviour.com. Sr. Estela Pina, E.E.P., D.R.E. Students 332.

29—DOLORES MISSION (1945), (Hispanic), Revs. Scott Santarosa, S.J.; Joseph G. Spieler, S.J.; Yolanda S. Brown, Pastoral Assoc.; Ellie Hidalgo, Pastoral Assoc.; Errol Briggs, Business Mgr.; Dana Valenzuela, Devel. Dir.; Paula Charboneau, Youth Min. In Res., Revs. Robert Dolan, S.J.; Gregory Boyle, S.J.; Mark Torres.
Res.: 1901 E. 4th St., 90033. Tel: 323-881-0039 (Church); 323-780-8859; Fax: 323-881-0034. Web: www.dolores-mission.org.
School—Tel: 323-881-0001; Fax: 323-881-0003. Karina Moreno, Prin. Lay Teachers 9; Students 210.
Catechesis/Religious Program—Students 170.

30—ST. DOMINIC (1921) Very Revs. Raymond Finerty, O.P.; La Salle Hallissey, O.P.; David Geib, O.P.; John Evans, O.P. In Res., Very Rev. Judi Eli, O.P.; Rev. Dominic DeLay, O.P.
Res.: 2002 Merton Ave., 90041. Tel: 323-254-2519; Fax: 323-255-3067. Email: st.dominic@sbcglobal.net. Web: dominicla.org.
School—Tel: 323-255-5803; Fax: 323-255-2817. Ms. Elida Lujan, Prin. Sisters of Notre Dame 2; Lay Teachers 9; Students 220.
Catechesis/Religious Program—Tel: 323-255-6373. Students 168.

31—ST. EUGENE (1942) Mailing Address: 9505 Haas Ave., 90047. Pastoral Team:, Rev. Jude Umeobi, Admin.; Martin Hicks, Dir. Pastoral Svcs.
Church: 9506 S. Van Ness Ave., 90047. Tel: 323-757-3121; Fax: 323-757-8872. Email: steugenechurch@sbcglobal.net.
Catechesis/Religious Program—Students 70.

32—FORMER CATHEDRAL OF ST. VIBIANA (1876) Closed. For inquiries for Sacramental Records contact 555 W. Temple St., Los Angeles, CA 90012.

33—ST. FRANCES XAVIER CABRINI (1946), (African American—Latino), Rev. Cesar Raffo.
Res.: 1440 W. Imperial Hwy., 90047. Tel: 323-757-0271; Fax: 323-757-9267.
School—1428 W. Imperial Hwy., 90047. Tel: 323-756-1354; Fax: 323-756-1157. Email: cabrini@pacbell.net. Web: www.sfxcla.org. Michelle Sarmiento, Prin. Lay Teachers 7; Students 200.
Catechesis/Religious Program—Students 330.

34—ST. FRANCIS OF ASSISI (1920) Revs. Richard Juzix, O.F.M.; Alberto Villafan, O.F.M. In Res., Bro. Hajime Okuhara, O.F.M.
Res.: 1523 Golden Gate Ave., 90026. Tel: 323-664-1305; Fax: 323-664-4975.
School—1550 Maltman Ave., 90026. Tel: 323-665-3601; Fax: 323-665-4143. Lay Teachers 11; Students 215.
Catechesis/Religious Program—Tel: 323-662-3345. Students 124.

35—ST. FRANCIS XAVIER CHAPEL *dba Maryknoll Japanese Catholic Center* (1921), (Japanese), Rev. Richard Hoynes.
Res.: 222 S. Hewitt St., 90012. Tel: 213-626-2279; Fax: 213-628-1757. Email: info@sfxjcc.org. Web: www.sfxjcc.org.
Catechesis/Religious Program—Students 57.

36—ST. GERARD MAJELLA (1952) Rev. Martin Slaughter.
Res.: 4439 Inglewood Blvd., 90066. Tel: 310-390-5034; Fax: 310-397-0964. Email: stgerardmajella@comcast.net. Web: stgerardla.com.
Catechesis/Religious Program—Tel: 310-391-9637. Students 330; High School 120.

37—ST. GREGORY NAZIANZEN (1923) Rev. Alex Chung.
Res.: 900 S. Bronson Ave., 90019. Tel: 323-935-4224; Fax: 323-934-0016.
School—911 S. Norton Ave., 90019. Tel: 323-936-2542; Fax: 323-936-1690. Email: la154e@aol.com. Web: www.stgregorylaschool.com. Zulay Chavez, Prin. Lay Teachers 8; Students 154.
Catechesis/Religious Program—Tel: 323-935-4701. Maria Acosta, C.R.E. Students 98.

38—HOLY CROSS (1906), (African American—Hispanic), Revs. Luis Cananza Cervantes, M.C.C.J. (Mexico); Modi Abil Nairki, M.C.C.J.; Robert Kleiner, M.C.C.J.
Res.: 4705 S. Main St., 90037. Tel: 323-234-5984; Fax: 323-234-0130.
Catechesis/Religious Program—Students 860.

39—HOLY NAME OF JESUS (1921), (African American), Rev. Paul J. Spellman; Deacons Hosea Alexander Sr.; Alejandro Marin; Douglass R. Johnson Sr.
Res.: 2190 W. 31st St., 90018. Tel: 323-734-8888; Fax: 323-734-8430. Web: www.holynameofjesus-la.org.
School—Tel: 323-731-2255; Fax: 323-730-0321. Mrs. Marva Belisle, Prin. Lay Teachers 10; Students 170.
Catechesis/Religious Program—Students 90.

40—HOLY SPIRIT (1926) Rev. Brian Castaneda.
Res.: 1425 S. Dunsmuir Ave., 90019-4031. Tel: 323-935-1333; Fax: 323-935-7741.
School—(Grades K-4), 1418 S. Burnside Ave., 90019. Tel: 323-933-7775; Fax: 323-933-7453. Sisters of the Holy Faith 2; Lay Teachers 4; Students 94.
Catechesis/Religious Program—Students 304.

41—HOLY TRINITY (1925), (Filipino—Hispanic), Revs. Maurice D. Harrigan; Thomas James Peacha, Pastor Emeritus (Retired); John J. Daly, Pastor Emeritus (Retired); James Bong-Won Choe (Korea, South); Deacon Rolando Bautista.
Res.: 3722 Boyce Ave., 90039. Tel: 323-664-4723; Fax: 323-664-2581.
School—3716 Boyce Ave., 90039. Tel: 323-663-2064; Fax: 323-663-0732. Email: holytrinityla@yahoo.com. Lay Teachers 16; Students 270.
Catechesis/Religious Program—Students 295.

42—ST. IGNATIUS OF LOYOLA (1911) Rev. Arturo Velasco.
Res.: 322 N. Ave. 61, 90042. Tel: 323-256-3041; Fax: 323-256-0105.
School—6025 Monte Vista St., 90042. Tel: 323-255-6456; Fax: 323-255-0959. Dominican Sisters, San Jose Mission 1; Lay Teachers 10; Students 269.
Catechesis/Religious Program—Tel: 323-254-9073; Fax: 323-254-9073. Email: stignatiusla@msjdonimicans.org. Students 565.

43—IMMACULATE CONCEPTION (1908), (Hispanic), Revs. Alfonso Amezcua (Mexico); Jose Cruz (Mexico); Rafael Ochoa (Mexico); Octavio Mata.
Res.: 1433 James M. Wood Blvd., 90015. Tel: 213-384-1019; Fax: 213-384-0437. Email: immaconc@sbcglobal.net.
School—830 Green St., 90017. Tel: 213-382-5931; Fax: 213-382-4563. Ms. Mary Ann Murphy, Prin. Lay Teachers 14; Students 200.
Catechesis/Religious Program—832 Green Ave., 90017. Tel: 213-389-7277. Students 625.

44—IMMACULATE HEART OF MARY (1910) Revs. Rodel G. Balagtas; David Ochoa (Mexico); Mateo H. Hicarte (Retired); Deacon George Asmar.
Res.: 4954 Santa Monica Blvd., 90029. Tel: 323-660-0034; Fax: 323-660-0047.
School—1055 N. Alexandria Ave., 90029. Tel: 323-663-4611; Fax: 323-663-6216. Sisters 1; Lay Teachers 11; Students 260.
Catechesis/Religious Program—4954 W. Santa Monica Blvd., 90029. Tel: 323-660-0034, Ext. 17. Students 247.

45—ST. JEROME (1949) Rev. Msgr. Norman F. Priebe.
Res.: 5550 Thornburn St., 90045. Tel: 310-348-8212; Fax: 310-417-3577.
School—Tel: 310-670-1678; Fax: 310-670-2170. Web: www.stjeromewestchester.org. Sisters of St. Joseph of Carondelet 2; Lay Teachers 16; Students 299.
Catechesis/Religious Program—Tel: 310-645-8318; Fax: 310-645-8318. Students 225.
Convent—5570 Thornburn St., 90045. Tel: 310-670-8838.

46—ST. JOAN OF ARC (1943), (Spanish), Revs. James H. Barnes; Frederick Byaruhanga (Uganda).
Res.: 11534 Gateway Blvd., 90064. Tel: 310-479-5111; Fax: 310-479-2513. Email: sjachurchwla@msn.com. Web: www.stjoanofarcla.com.
School—11561 Gateway Blvd., 90064. Tel: 310-479-3607; Fax: 310-478-1398.
Catechesis/Religious Program—Students 194.

47—ST. JOHN, THE EVANGELIST (1909), (Hispanic—African American), Revs. Damian Kabot, S.V.D. (Poland); Anthaiah Madanu, S.V.D. (India). In Res., Deacon Willard Hall.
Res.: 6028 Victoria Ave., 90043. Tel: 323-758-9161; Fax: 323-758-0112. Email: saint_john_evangelist@yahoo.com. Web: www.johnevangelist.org.
School—Tel: 323-751-8545; Fax: 323-751-1651. Email: principal@stjohnevangelistsch.com. Web: www.stjohnevangelistsch.com. Karen Velasquez, Prin. Lay Teachers 7; Students 131.
Catechesis/Religious Program—Students 160.

48—ST. JOSEPH (1888), (Hispanic), Rev. Rafael Casillas.
Res.: 218 E. 12th St., 90015. Tel: 213-748-5394; Fax: 213-748-4793.
School—Tel: 213-749-8894; Fax: 213-749-0424. Claudia Moreno, Prin. Lay Teachers 9; Students 137.
Catechesis/Religious Program—Tel: 213-748-5394; 626-813-0763. Students 197.
Mission—St. Turibius 1524 Essex, Los Angeles Co. 90021. Tel: 213-749-8894; Fax: 213-749-0424.

49—ST. KEVIN (1923), (Hispanic—Filipino), Revs. Melchor Villero, M.J.; Manuel Gacad, M.J.; Melanio Viuya, M.J.; Enrique Ymson, M.J.; Deacon Carlos Magos.
Res.: 4072 Beverly Blvd., 90004. Tel: 213-383-8206; Fax: 213-381-3255.
Catechesis/Religious Program—Students 175.

50—ST. LAWRENCE OF BRINDISI (1908), (African American—Hispanic), Capuchin Franciscan Friary. Revs. Peter Banks, O.F.M.Cap.; James L. Cleary, O.F.M.Cap.; Jesus Vela, O.F.M.Cap.
Res.: 10122 Compton Ave., 90002. Tel: 323-567-1439; Fax: 323-564-4050.
School—10044 Compton Ave., 90002. Tel: 323-564-3051. Lay Teachers 9; Students 285.
Catechesis/Religious Program—Tel: 323-567-4698. Students 830.

51—ST. LUCY (1981), (Hispanic), [CEM] Revs. Ramon Novell, Sch.P.; Miguel Mascorro, Sch.P. In Res., Rev. Vicente Casaus, Sch.P.
Res.: 1419 N. Hazard Ave., 90063. Tel: 323-266-0451; Fax: 323-266-4907.
Catechesis/Religious Program—Tel: 323-266-0456.

52—ST. MALACHY (1926), (Hispanic), Revs. Abel Loera; Victor Raul Ramos.
Res.: 1221 E. 82nd St., 90001. Tel: 323-585-1437; Fax: 323-277-4776. Email: st.malachychurch@gmail.com.
School—Saint Malachy Pre-School, 1232 E. 81st St., 90001. Tel: 323-582-1096; Fax: 323-582-9972. Lay Teachers 2; Students 20.
School—Saint Malachy Elementary School, 1200 E. 81st St., 90001. Tel: 323-582-3112; Fax: 323-582-9340. Email: stmalachyschl@sbcglobal.net. Lay Teachers 9; Students 210.
Catechesis/Religious Program—Tel: 323-582-0203. Sr. Virginia Sandoval, M.J.C., D.R.E. Students 323.
Convent—Missionaries of Jesus Crucified, St. Malachy Convent, 1228 E. 81st St., 90001. Tel: 323-582-2992. Sisters 3.

53—ST. MARCELLINUS (1957) Humberto Ramos, Parish Life Dir.
Res.: 2349 Strong Ave., Commerce, 90040. Tel: 323-269-2733.
Catechesis/Religious Program—Tel: 323-266-4938. Students 215.

54—ST. MARTIN OF TOURS (1946) Rev. Ben Le, Admin.; Rev. Msgr. Lawrence O'Leary, Pastor Emeritus (Retired); Rev. Donal Keohane (Ireland).
Res.: 11967 Sunset Blvd., 90049. Tel: 310-476-7403; Fax: 310-476-0290. Email: info@saintmartinoftours.com. Web: www.saintmartinoftours.com.
Church: 11967 Sunset Blvd., 90049.
School—11955 Sunset Blvd., 90049. Tel: 310-472-7419; Fax: 310-440-2298. Email: coswald@smtschool.net. Web: smtschool.net. Sisters 1; Lay Teachers 27; Students 241.
Catechesis/Religious Program—Tel: 310-472-1757, Ext. 235. Email: smtchurchlady@aol.com. Students 95.

55—ST. MARY (1896) Revs. Joseph A. Farias, S.D.B.; Avelino Lorenzo, S.D.B.; Robert Stein, S.D.B.
Res.: 407 S. Chicago St., 90033. Tel: 323-268-7432; Fax: 323-268-8076. Email: stmarysela@aol.com.
School—(Grades K-8) Tel: 323-262-3395; Fax: 323-262-4738. Email: stmary_la@yahoo.com. Daughters of Mary Help of Christians 2; Lay Teachers 11; Students 208.
Catechesis/Religious Program—Tel: 323-268-2351. Email: stmarysccd@yahoo.com. Students 356.

56—ST. MARY MAGDALEN (1930) Rev. Brian Castaneda.
Res.: 1241 Corning St., 90035. Tel: 310-652-2444; Fax: 310-652-4885. Email: saintmarymagdalen@sbcglobal.net. Web: stmarymagdalenla.org.
School—1223 Corning St., 90035. Tel: 310-652-4723. Sisters of the Holy Faith 1; Lay Teachers 6; Students 141.
Catechesis/Religious Program—Students 493.

57—ST. MICHAEL (1907), (Hispanic—African American), Rev. Msgr. David O'Connell. In Res., Rev. Stan Bosch, S.T.
Res.: 1016 W. Manchester Ave., 90044. Tel: 323-753-2696; Fax: 323-753-3475. Email: stmichaelchurch@hotmail.com.
School—(Grades K-8), 1027 W. 87th St., 90044. Tel: 323-752-6101; Fax: 323-752-6785. Lay Teachers 11; Students 169.
Catechesis/Religious Program—Tel: 323-753-2976. Students 526.

58—MOTHER OF SORROWS (1923), (Hispanic—African American), Revs. Abel Loera; Victor Raul Ramos.
Res.: 114 W. 87th St., 90003. Tel: 323-758-7697; Fax: 323-758-7853.
School—Tel: 323-758-6204; Fax: 323-758-6203. Jennifer Beltramo, Prin. Lay Teachers 12; Students 208.
Catechesis/Religious Program—Tel: 323-789-6316. Sr. Rosa Lidia Orellana, C.S.J., D.R.E. Students 343.

59—NATIVITY (1920), (Hispanic—African American), Rev. Msgr. Timothy J. Dyer.
Res.: 953 W. 57th St., 90037. Tel: 323-759-1562; Fax: 323-759-7716.
School—944 W. 56th St., 90037. Tel: 323-752-0720; Fax: 323-752-1945. Lay Teachers 8; Students 320.

Catechesis/Religious Program—Tel: 323-752-1770. Students 605.
Loretto Literary & Benevolent Institution—

60—NATIVITY OF BLESSED VIRGIN MARY (1947), (Ukrainian—Byzantine), Rev. Myron Mykyta.
Res.: 5154 De Longpre Ave., 90027. Tel: 323-663-6307; Fax: 323-663-0369.

61—ST. ODILIA (1926), (Hispanic—African American), Rev. Francis Eldridge, S.A.
Res.: 5222 Hooper Ave., 90011-4807. Tel: 323-231-5930; Fax: 323-231-9714.
School—5300 S. Hooper Ave., 90011. Tel: 323-232-5449; Fax: 323-233-6154. Ms. Sharon E. Oliver, Prin. Lay Teachers 10; Students 226.
Catechesis/Religious Program—Tel: 323-233-2651. Students 282.
Mission—St. John Bosco 5516 Duarte St., Los Angeles Co. 90058. Tel: 323-581-3345.

62—OUR LADY HELP OF CHRISTIANS (MARIA AUXILIADORA) (1923), (Hispanic), Revs. Jose Sosa, Sch.P., Parish Admin.; Martin Madero, Sch.P. In Res., Rev. Manuel Sanahuja, Sch.P.
Res.: 512 S. Ave. 20, 90031. Tel: 323-223-4153; Fax: 323-223-1427.
School—2024 Darwin Ave., 90031. Tel: 323-222-3913; Fax: 323-222-2561. Maria G. Negrete, Prin. Lay Teachers 7; Students 150.
Catechesis/Religious Program—Tel: 323-225-2846. Students 120.

63—OUR LADY OF GUADALUPE (1923), (Hispanic), Revs. J. Rigoberto Rodriguez; Jose A. Ortiz-Padilla.
Res.: 4018 Hammel St., 90063. Tel: 323-261-8051; Fax: 323-261-1259.
School—436 Hazard Ave., 90063. Tel: 323-269-4998; Fax: 323-780-7001. Lay Teachers 9; Students 170.
Catechesis/Religious Program—Tel: 323-262-7957. Students 270.
Mission—San Felipe 738 N. Geraghty Ave., Los Angeles Co. 90063. Tel: 213-266-1433; Fax: 323-261-1259.

64—OUR LADY OF GUADALUPE (Rosehill) (1928), (Hispanic), Revs. Pedro A. Cobenas; Rio Antonio C. Yllana.
Res.: 4509 Mercury Ave., 90032. Tel: 323-225-4201; Fax: 323-225-3668.
School—4522 Browne Ave., 90032. Tel: 323-221-8187. Lay Teachers 10; Students 140.
Catechesis/Religious Program—Tel: 323-223-1777. Students 350.

65—OUR LADY OF GUADALUPE SANCTUARY (1929), (Hispanic), Rev. Leslie N. Delgado (Panama).
Res.: 4100 E. Second St., 90063. Tel: 323-261-4365; Fax: 323-261-2735.
Catechesis/Religious Program—Students 256.

66—OUR LADY OF LORETTO (1905) Rev. Richard Casillas, S.V.D. In Res., Rev. Frank Drzaic.
Res.: 250 N. Union Ave., 90026. Tel: 213-483-3013; Fax: 213-484-0187. Email: ollsvd@aol.com.
School—258 N. Union Ave., 90026. Tel: 213-483-5251; Fax: 213-483-6709. Web: www.ollalumni.com. Lay Teachers 9; Students 211.
Catechesis/Religious Program—Tel: 213-483-8137. Students 373.

67—OUR LADY OF LOURDES (1910) Revs. Eamonn Donnelly, S.V.D.; Gerard O'Doherty, S.V.D.
Res.: 3772 E. Third St., 90063-2408. Tel: 323-526-3800; Fax: 323-526-3807.
School—315 S. Eastman Ave., 90063. Tel: 323-526-3813; Fax: 323-526-3814. Lay Teachers 9; Students 200.
Catechesis/Religious Program—Tel: 323-526-3804. Students 296.

68—OUR LADY OF SOLITUDE (1925), (Hispanic), Revs. Benito Rojas, M.S.P.; Saul A. Garcia, M.S.P.; Deacon Sergio A. Perez.
Res.: 4561 Cesar Chavez Ave., 90022. Tel: 323-269-7248; Fax: 323-269-3600.
Catechesis/Religious Program—Tel: 323-261-1083. Students 345.

69—OUR LADY OF THE BRIGHT MOUNT (1925), (Polish), Rev. Marek Ciesielski, S.Ch. In Res., Rev. Antoni Bury, S.Ch.
Res.: 3424 W. Adams Blvd., 90018. Tel: 323-734-5249; Fax: 323-734-0046. Email: office@polskaparafiala.org. Web: www.polskaparafiala.org.
Catechesis/Religious Program—Students 80.
Convent—Tel: 323-734-6754. Missionary Sisters of Christ the King for Polonia 2.

70—OUR LADY OF THE ROSARY OF TALPA (1928), (Spanish), Rev. Margarito Severino Martinez.
Res.: 2914 E. Fourth St., 90033. Tel: 323-268-9176; Fax: 323-268-4026. Email: talpachurch@sbcglobal.net.
School—411 S. Evergreen Ave., 90033. Tel: 323-261-0583; Fax: 323-261-0352. Daughters of Charity of St. Vincent de Paul 1; Lay Teachers 9; Students 280.
Catechesis/Religious Program—Tel: 323-264-3345. Students 300.
Convent—427 S. Evergreen St., 90033. Tel: 323-268-7731.
Mission—La Purisima Chapel 3236 Inez St., Los Angeles Co. 90023.

71—OUR LADY OF VICTORY (1966), (Spanish), Rev. Pedro G. Valdez.
Res.: 1316 S. Herbert Ave., 90023. Tel: 323-268-9502; Fax: 323-780-1719. Email: elavictory@adelphia.net.
Catechesis/Religious Program—1317 S. Herbert Ave., 90023. Tel: 323-262-2101.

72—OUR LADY QUEEN OF MARTYRS, (Armenian), Rev. Antoine Panossian, P.I.A.
Res.: 1327 Pleasant Ave., 90033. Tel: 323-261-9898; Fax: 323-261-0522.

73—OUR LADY QUEEN OF THE ANGELS (1781), (Spanish), Very Rev. Roland Lozano, C.M.F.; Revs. Paschal Amagba, C.M.F.; Domingo Zuniga, C.M.F.; Richard Estrada, C.M.F.; Deacon Hernan Ramirez-Chavez.
Res.: 535 N. Main St., 90012. Tel: 213-629-3101; Fax: 213-629-1951. Email: placita@pacbell.net. Web: www.laplacita.org.
Catechesis/Religious Program—Students 256.

74—OUR MOTHER OF GOOD COUNSEL (1925) Revs. James A. Mott, O.S.A.; James P. Retzner, O.S.A. In Res., Rev. Thomas W. Behan, O.S.A.
Res.: 2060 N. Vermont Ave., 90027. Tel: 323-664-2111; Fax: 323-664-0556. Web: www.omogc.org.
School—4622 Ambrose Ave., 90027. Tel: 323-664-2131; Fax: 323-664-1906. Andrea Deebs, Prin. Lay Teachers 9; Students 200.
Catechesis/Religious Program—Students 165.

75—OUR SAVIOUR CATHOLIC CENTER (1957) Rev. Lawrence Seyer.
3207 University Ave., 90007. Email: info@catholictrojan.org. Web: www.catholictrojan.org.
Res.: Transfiguration, 2515 Martin Luther King Jr. Blvd., 90008. Tel: 323-291-1136; Fax: 323-291-1136. Email: frlawrence@catholictrojan.org.

76—ST. PATRICK (1904), (Hispanic), Rev. Francisco X. Ramirez.
Res.: 1046 E. 34th St., 90011. Tel: 323-234-5963; Fax: 323-234-6725. Email: spatricio@aol.com.
Catechesis/Religious Program—Tel: 323-232-5460. Students 720.

77—ST. PAUL (1917) Revs. Jose Navarro Gonzalez, M.G.; Julio Ramos, M.G.; Maurilio Franco, M.G.
Office: 1920 S. Bronson Ave., 90018. Tel: 323-730-9490; Fax: 323-734-5266. Email: stpaulschurch@hotmail.com. Web: www.stpaulla.org.
Res.: 4112 W. Washington Blvd., 90018. Tel: 323-730-9491.
School—1908 S. Bronson Ave., 90018. Tel: 213-734-4022; Fax: 323-734-5057. Mr. Mario Pandy, Prin. Lay Teachers 9; Students 178.
Catechesis/Religious Program—Tel: 323-737-1784. Sr. Antonia Lopez, D.R.E. Students 28.

78—ST. PAUL THE APOSTLE (1928) Revs. John B. Ardis, C.S.P., Supr.; Joe Scott, C.S.P. In Res., Revs. Thomas J. Clerkin, C.S.P., Chap. UCLA Medical Center; Frank Desiderio, C.S.P.; Theodore A. Vierra (Retired); Edward D. Wrobleski, C.S.P. (Retired); Patrick E. Hensy, C.S.P. (Retired); Edward Donovan, C.S.P. (Retired); Ivan Tou, C.S.P., Chap. UCLA Catholic Center; Peter Abdella, C.S.P., Chap. UCLA Catholic Center & Dir. Campus Ministry; Eric Andrews, C.S.P.
Res.: 10750 Ohio Ave., 90024. Tel: 310-474-1527; Fax: 310-474-2897. Email: frontdesk@sp-apostle.org. Web: sp-apostle.org.
School—1536 Selby Ave., 90024. Tel: 310-474-1588; Fax: 310-474-4272. Daughters of Mary and Joseph 3; Lay Teachers 33; Students 540.
Catechesis/Religious Program—Tel: 310-474-1527, Ext. 212. Students 126.

79—ST. PETER (1904), (Italian), Revs. Raniero Alessandrini, C.S.; Esvin Morroquin, C.S.
Res. & Mailing Address: 1039 N. Broadway, 90012-1429. Tel: 323-225-8119; Fax: 323-225-0085. Email: stpeterit@yahoo.com. Web: www.stpeterschurchla.org.
Catechesis/Religious Program—Michele Famara, D.R.E. Students 36.
Mission—San Conrado 1820 Bouett St., Los Angeles Co. 90012. Tel: 323-223-6581.
Scalabrini House of Discernment (Seminary)—
Scalabrini Vocation Center—

80—PRECIOUS BLOOD (1923) Revs. Melchor Villero, M.J.; Manuel Gacad, M.J.; Enrique Ymson, M.J.; Melanio Viuya, M.J.; Deacon Carlos Magos.
Res.: 435 S. Occidental Blvd., 90057. Tel: 213-389-8439; Fax: 213-389-1951. Email: precblchurch@aol.com.
School—307 S. Occidental Blvd., 90057. Tel: 213-382-3345; Fax: 213-382-2078. Email: pbtigers@netscape.net. Web: www.pbschool:us. Lay Teachers 12; Students 200.
Catechesis/Religious Program—Tel: 213-382-3906. Students 163.

81—PRESENTATION OF THE MARY (1925), (Hispanic), Revs. Jose Rafael Lara, Admin.; Sigifredo Martin Roque; Deacon Valentin Saucedo.
Res.: 6406 Parmelee Ave., 90001. Tel: 323-585-0570; Fax: 323-585-8148.
Catechesis/Religious Program—Students 545.

82—ST. RAPHAEL (1924), (Hispanic—African American), Revs. Tracy O'Sullivan, O.Carm.; Thomas John Alkire, O.Carm.; Deacons Hernan Ramirez-Chavez; Miguel Angel Martinez; Bro. Edgar Lopez, O.Carm.; Mr. Harry Wiley, Dir. African American Ministry.
Res.: 942 W. 70th St., 90044. Tel: 323-758-7100; Fax: 323-758-7134.
School—Mrs. Barbara Curtis, Prin. Lay Teachers 11; Students 280.
Catechesis/Religious Program—Tel: 323-752-5965; Fax: 323-752-5955. Mrs. Maria Moran, D.R.E.; Ms. Carolina Hernandez, C.R.E. (Confirmation Coord.). Students 300.

83—RESURRECTION (1923), (Mexican), Rev. Msgr. John T. Moretta; Rev. Gustavo Mejia; Deacon Hernando Rodriguez.
Res.: 3324 E. Opal St., 90023. Tel: 323-268-1141; Fax: 323-268-1143. Email: resurrectionla@yahoo.com. Web: resurrectionla.com.
School—3360 E. Opal St., 90023. Tel: 323-261-5750; Fax: 323-261-1463. Angelica Figueroa, Prin. Franciscan Sisters of Mary Immaculate 2; Lay Teachers 10; Students 230.
Catechesis/Religious Program—Tel: 323-264-1963. Students 570.
Convent—3346 Opal St., 90023. Tel: 323-261-6957.

84—SACRED HEART (1887), (Hispanic), Rev. Tesfaldet Asghedom. In Res., Revs. George E. Horan; Reynaldo B. Matunog (Philippines).
Res.: 2210 Sichel St., 90031. Tel: 323-221-3179; Fax: 323-221-3613. Email: sacredheart2210@sbcglobal.net.
School—2109 Sichel St., 90031. Tel: 323-225-4177; Fax: 323-225-2615. Dominican Sisters of Mission San Jose 2; Lay Teachers 10; Students 253.
Catechesis/Religious Program—Tel: 323-223-7571. Students 460.
Convent—2222 Sichel St., 90031. Tel: 323-222-5157; Fax: 323-276-9431.

85—SAN ANTONIO DE PADUA (1926), (Hispanic), Rev. Msgr. Gustavo J. Ramon; Rev. Abel Loera.
Res.: 555 N. Fairview Ave., 90033. Tel: 323-225-1301; Fax: 323-225-2534.
School—1500 Bridge St., 90033. Tel: 323-221-6970; Fax: 323-343-9183. Solis Rivas, Prin.
Catechesis/Religious Program—Tel: 323-225-1086. Students 95.

86—SAN CONRADO MISSION (1966) See separate listing. (See St. Peter, Los Angeles for details.)

87—SAN FRANCISCO CHURCH (1982), (Hispanic), [CEM] [JC] Rev. Severiano Castaneda.
Res.: 4800 E. Olympic Blvd., 90022. Tel: 323-262-4253; Fax: 323-268-8246. Email: sfchurch@attglobal.net.
Catechesis/Religious Program—Tel: 323-261-2447. Students 572.

88—SAN MIGUEL (1927), (Hispanic), Rev. Jose Valdez Romo, M.S.C.
Res.: 2214 E. 108th St., 90059. Tel: 323-569-5951; Fax: 323-567-1850.
School—2270 E. 108th St., 90059. Tel: 323-567-6892; Fax: 323-567-4065. Lay Teachers 10; Students 189.
Catechesis/Religious Program—Students 229.

89—SANTA ISABEL (1915), (Mexican), Revs. Saul A. Garcia, M.S.P.; Guillermo Martinez, M.S.P.
Res.: 918 S. Soto St., 90023. Tel: 323-268-4065; Fax: 323-268-4180.
School—2424 Whittier Blvd., 90023. Tel: 323-263-3716. Lay Teachers 10; Students 204.
Catechesis/Religious Program—Tel: 323-268-3019. Students 310.
Convent—Tel: 323-262-1711; 323-264-6556; Fax: 323-526-1655.
Mission—Hermanas Misioneras Servidoras de la Palabra 90023. Tel: 323-268-7063.

90—SANTA TERESITA (1923), (Hispanic), Revs. Augustin Arriola, Sch.P.; Ramon Novell, Sch.P.; Miguel Mascorro, Sch.P.; Raymond Farre, Sch.P.
Res.: 2645 Zonal Ave., 90033. Tel: 323-221-2446; Fax: 323-221-2216. Email: steresita38@yahoo.com.
School—(Grades K-8), 2646 Zonal Ave., 90033. Tel: 323-221-1129; Fax: 323-221-6339. Email: santa@msjdominicans.org. Dominican Sisters 1; Lay Teachers 9; Students 235.
Catechesis/Religious Program—Tel: 213-221-2511. Students 121.
Convent—1375 Murchison St., 90033. Tel: 323-221-6663.

91—ST. SEBASTIAN (1924) Rev. German Sanchez, Admin.
Res.: 1453 Federal Ave., 90025-2301. Tel: 310-479-7421.
Church: 1425 Federal Ave., 90025.

Parish Center—11607 Ohio Ave., 90025. Tel: 310-478-0136; Fax: 310-479-5121. Email: office@stsebastian.net.
School—1430 Federal Ave. W., 90025. Tel: 310-473-3337; Fax: 310-473-3178. Email: info@saintsebastian.com. Web: saintsebastianschool.com.
Catechesis/Religious Program—Tel: 310-479-7380. Students 198.

92—ST. STEPHEN OF HUNGARY (1928), (Hungarian—German), Rev. William J. Bonner.
Res.: 3705 Woodlawn Ave., 90011. Tel: 323-234-9246; Fax: 323-234-2455.
Catechesis/Religious Program—Students 150.

93—ST. TERESA OF AVILA (1921) Rev. Msgr. Joseph Hernandez; Rev. David C. Loftus.
Res.: 2216 Fargo St., 90039. Tel: 323-664-8426; Fax: 323-665-3115.
School—(Grades K-8), 2215 Fargo St., 90039. Tel: 323-662-3777; Fax: 323-662-3420. Email: cdbfc@stteresaofavilala.org. Web: www.stteresaofavila.org. Lay Teachers 9; Students 221.
Catechesis/Religious Program—Students 80.
Convent—2223 Fargo St., 90039. Tel: 323-906-2901.

94—ST. THOMAS THE APOSTLE (1903), (Hispanic), Rev. Msgr. Jarlath Cunnane; Revs. William Rodriguez; Leo Ortega; Deacons Juan Bautista Cantillo; Daniel Bernal.
Res.: 2727 W. Pico Blvd., 90006. Tel: 323-737-3325; Fax: 323-737-2665.
Church: 2760 W. Pico Blvd., 90006.
School—Tel: 323-737-4730; Fax: 323-737-6348. Lay Teachers 10; Students 295.
Catechesis/Religious Program—2632 W. 15th St., 90006. Tel: 323-737-5624; Fax: 323-737-2582. Students 779.

95—ST. TIMOTHY (1943) Rev. Paul E. Vigil.
Rectory—10425 W. Pico Blvd., 90064. Tel: 310-474-1216; Fax: 310-475-6047. Email: stc.la@verizon.net. Web: sttimothyla.org.
School—Tel: 310-474-1811; Fax: 310-470-1391. Web: sttimothy.org. Iselda E. Richmond, Prin. Lay Teachers 13; Students 160.
Catechesis/Religious Program—Students 49.

96—TRANSFIGURATION (1923), (African American), Rev. Richard Martini. In Res., Revs. Michael P. McCullough; Lawrence Seyer.
Res.: 2515 W. Martin Luther King Blvd., 90008-2728. Tel: 323-291-1136; Fax: 323-291-8216.
School—4020 Roxton Ave., 90008. Tel: 323-292-3011; Fax: 323-292-1527. Web: transfigeagles.org. Lay Teachers 11; Students 166.
Catechesis/Religious Program—Tel: 323-292-5112. Students 80.

97—ST. VINCENT DE PAUL (1887), (Hispanic), Bro. Anthony B. Wiedemer, C.M., Admin.; Revs. Ruben D. Restrepo, C.M.; Luis Ariel Ramirez, C.M.; Minn J. Pham, C.M.
Res.: 621 W. Adams Blvd., 90007. Tel: 213-749-8950; Fax: 213-749-9137.
School—2333 S. Figueroa St., 90007. Tel: 213-748-5367; Fax: 213-748-5347. Email: svs1911@pacbell.net. Web: home.pacbell.net/svs1911. Sisters 3; Lay Teachers 11; Students 270.
Catechesis/Religious Program—Tel: 213-741-9347. Students 505.
Mission—Santo Nino 601 E. 23rd St., Los Angeles Co. 90011. Tel: 213-748-5246.

98—VISITATION (1943) [JC] Rev. William J. Brelsford. In Res., Revs. James F. O'Grady, Pastor Emeritus (Retired); James L. Kolling (Retired).
Res.: 6561 W. 88th St., 90045. Tel: 310-216-1145; Fax: 310-216-1002. Email: visone@earthlink.net.
School—8740 Emerson Ave., 90045. Tel: 310-645-6620; Fax: 310-645-4407. Lay Teachers 16; Students 246.
Catechesis/Religious Program—Tel: 310-568-9085; Fax: 310-216-1002. Students 103.

OUTSIDE THE CITY OF LOS ANGELES

ALHAMBRA, LOS ANGELES CO.

1—ALL SOULS (1912) Revs. Modesto L. Perez; Joseph Dass.
29 S. Electric Ave., 91801. In Res., Rev. Msgr. William P. O'Toole (Retired).
Res.: 29 S. Electric Ave., 91801. Tel: 626-281-0466; Fax: 626-281-2163. Email: allsoulscc@allsouls-la.org. Web: www.allsouls-la.org.
Pastoral Ministry Center—
School—29 S. Electric Ave., 91801. Tel: 626-282-5695; Fax: 626-282-2260.
Catechesis/Religious Program—29 S. Electric Ave., 91801. Tel: 626-281-0466, Ext. 214. Students 230.

2—ST. THERESE (1924), (Little Flower) Revs. Jan Lundberg, O.C.D.; Robert Barcelos, O.C.D. In Res., Rev. Jerome Lantry, O.C.D.
Res.: 510 N. El Molino St., 91801. Tel: 626-282-2744; Fax: 626-282-7560. Web: sts-alh.org.
School—1106 E. Alhambra, 91801. Tel: 626-289-3364; Fax: 626-284-6700. Web: st-thereseschool.com. Lay Teachers 18; Students 254.
Catechesis/Religious Program—Tel: 626-284-0020. Students 125.

3—ST. THOMAS MORE (1948) Rev. Paul F. Menke (Retired); Mrs. Anne McFee, Business Mgr.; Sisters Margaret Devlin, S.S.C., Pastoral Assoc.; Andrea Johnson, C.S.H., Pastoral Assoc. In Res., Rev. Jeremiah O'Neill, Pastor Emeritus (Retired).
Res.: 2510 S. Fremont Ave., 91803. Tel: 626-284-8333; Fax: 626-282-4459.
School—Tel: 626-284-5778; Fax: 626-284-3303. Mrs. Judith Jones, Co-Prin.; Mrs. Jennifer Schmidt, Co-Prin. Lay Teachers 9; Students 200.
Catechesis/Religious Program—Tel: 626-457-5302. Mrs. Mary Joslyn, D.R.E. Students 300.

ALTADENA, LOS ANGELES CO.

1—ST. ELIZABETH OF HUNGARY (1918) Rev. Edwin C. Duyshart; Deacons Jose Gallegos; Charles A. Mitchell; Julliette Marsh-Williams, Pastoral Assoc. In Res., Rev. Msgr. Michael W. Meyers.
Office:—1879 N. Lake Ave., 91001. Tel: 626-797-1167; Fax: 626-797-9245. Web: saintelizabethchurch.org.
School—1840 N. Lake Ave., 91001. Tel: 626-797-7727; Fax: 626-797-6541. Web: saint-elizabeth.org. Lay Teachers 15; Students 270.
Catechesis/Religious Program—Students 377.

2—SACRED HEART (1935), (African American—Hispanic), Rev. Tovia Lui, Admin.; Rev. Msgr. Jerome Lucien Schmit, Pastor Emeritus (Retired); Rev. Gilbert Cruz.
Church: 2889 N. Lincoln Ave., 91001. Tel: 626-794-2046; Fax: 626-794-8315. Email: sacredheart600@yahoo.com. Web: www.sacredheartaltadena.org.
Catechesis/Religious Program—600 W. Mariposa. Tel: 626-798-6961; Fax: 626-798-2616. Students 515.

ARCADIA, LOS ANGELES CO., HOLY ANGELS (1935) Revs. Michael J. Evans; John Hoa Nguyen; Jay Jay Wu; Deacon Arnaldo Lopez.
Res.: 370 Campus Dr., 91007. Tel: 626-447-1671; Fax: 626-447-7617. Email: ha@holyangelsarcadia.org. Web: www.holyangelsarcadia.org.
School—360 Campus Dr., 91007. Tel: 626-447-6312; Fax: 626-447-2843. Email: admin@holyangelsarcadia.org. Lay Teachers 17; Students 285.
Catechesis/Religious Program—Tel: 626-445-2967. Students 234.

ARTESIA, LOS ANGELES CO., HOLY FAMILY (1931) Revs. Johnny Zulueta, C.M.; Victor Pacheco, C.M.; Antony Gaspar; Faustino Martin, C.M.
Res.: 18708 S. Clarkdale Ave., 90701. Tel: 562-865-2185; Fax: 562-860-0718.
School—Our Lady of Fatima, 18626 S. Clarkdale Ave., 90701. Tel: 562-865-1621; Fax: 562-860-1091. Lay Teachers 9; Students 170.
Catechesis/Religious Program—Tel: 562-860-5973. Students 816.

AVALON, LOS ANGELES CO., ST. CATHERINE OF ALEXANDRIA (1902) Rev. Paul Alcuin Siebenand.
Res.: Box 735, 90704. Tel: 310-510-0192; Fax: 310-510-8360.
Catechesis/Religious Program—Students 160.

AZUSA, LOS ANGELES CO., ST. FRANCES OF ROME (1908), (Hispanic), [CEM] Revs. Gustavo Castillo; Aloysius Ezeonyeka, O.S.B.; Edward Joseph Landreau, Pastor Emeritus (Retired); Roque A.D. Fernandes (Retired).
Res.: 501 E. Foothill Blvd., P.O. Box 637, 91702. Tel: 626-969-1829; Fax: 626-815-2755.
School—734 N. Pasadena Ave., 91702. Tel: 626-334-2018; Fax: 626-815-2760. Lay Teachers 13; Aides 2; Students 190.
Catechesis/Religious Program—508 N. Soldano, 91702. Tel: 626-334-3500. Students 694.

BALDWIN PARK, LOS ANGELES CO., ST. JOHN THE BAPTIST (1946), (Hispanic—Filipino), Revs. John G. Montejano; John Lloyd Ukaegbu; Antonio M. Aldaz.
Res.: 3848 Stewart Ave., 91706. Tel: 626-960-2795; Fax: 626-960-5085.
School—3870 Stewart Ave., 91706. Tel: 626-337-1421; Fax: 626-337-3733. Sisters of the Love of God 5; Lay Teachers 16; Students 489.
Catechesis/Religious Program—Tel: 626-962-1004. Students 848.
Convent—3963 Baldwin Park Blvd., 91706. Tel: 626-337-0527.

BELL GARDENS, LOS ANGELES CO., ST. GERTRUDE (1938) Revs. Guillermo C. Garcia; Rolando A. Sierra, C.Ss.R. (Venezuela).
Res.: 7025 Garfield Ave., 90201. Tel: 562-927-4495; Fax: 562-927-5826. Web: www.saintgertrudechurch.org.
School—6824 Toler Ave., 90201. Tel: 562-927-1216; Fax: 562-927-5607. Lay Teachers 10; Students 240.
Catechesis/Religious Program—Tel: 562-927-3185. Students 933.

BELLFLOWER, LOS ANGELES CO.

1—ST. BERNARD (1923) Revs. Michael Ume; Gaylord Reyes.
Res.: 9647 E. Beach St., 90706. Tel: 562-867-2337; Fax: 562-867-4863.
School—9626 Park St., 90706. Tel: 562-867-9410; Fax: 310-866-2310. Mrs. Melissa Oswald, Prin. Lay Teachers 10; Students 214.
Catechesis/Religious Program—Tel: 562-925-9886. Students 325.

2—ST. DOMINIC SAVIO (1954) Revs. Ted Montemayor, S.D.B.; Jack Gibson, S.D.B.; Thinh Nguyen, S.D.B.
Res.: 13400 Bellflower Blvd., 90706. Tel: 562-920-7796; Fax: 562-920-0149.
School—9750 Foster Rd., 90706. Tel: 562-866-3617; Fax: 562-867-0887. Salesian Sisters of St. John Bosco 7; Lay Teachers 20; Students 385.
Catechesis/Religious Program—Tel: 562-920-7796, Ext. 317. Students 725.

BEVERLY HILLS, LOS ANGELES CO., GOOD SHEPHERD (1924) Rev. Colm O'Ryan (Retired). In Res., Rev. George O'Brien.
Res.: 505 N. Bedford Dr., 90210. Tel: 310-285-5425; Fax: 310-285-5433. Email: shphrd505m@aol.com. Web: shepherd.catholicweb.com.
School—148 S. Linden Dr., 90212. Tel: 310-275-8601; Fax: 310-275-0366. Email: goodshepherddbh@aol.com. Web: www.goodshepherd-beverlyhills.com. Terry Miller, Prin. Lay Teachers 14; Students 191.
Catechesis/Religious Program—Tel: 310-271-9745. Students 83.

BURBANK, LOS ANGELES CO.

1—ST. FINBAR (1938) Rev. Albert Bahhuth.
Res.: 2010 W. Olive Ave., 91506. Tel: 818-846-6251; Fax: 818-846-1703. Web: www.stfinbarburbank.org.
School—2120 W. Olive Ave., 91506. Tel: 818-848-0191; Fax: 818-848-4315. Lay Teachers 17; Students 296.
Catechesis/Religious Program—Students 374.

2—ST. FRANCIS XAVIER (1954) Revs. Richard Albarano; Benny George, C.M.I. (India); Deacon Jaime Abrera. In Res., Rev. John D. Murray (Retired).
Res.: 3801 Scott Rd., 91504. Tel: 818-504-4400; Fax: 818-767-5096. Email: rectory@sfxrccburbank.org. Web: www.sfxrccburbank.org.
School—Tel: 818-504-4422; Fax: 818-504-4424. Lay Teachers 19; Students 280.
Catechesis/Religious Program—Tel: 818-504-4411. Email: religiousd@sfxrccburbank.org. Rosie Roope, C.R.E. Students 264.

3—ST. ROBERT BELLARMINE (1907) Rev. John Collins; Rev. Msgrs. Patrick Reilly (Retired); Francis T. Wallace; Peter C. Healy (Retired).
Ministry Center (Offices):—520 E. Orange Grove Ave., 91501. Email: srbcc@srbburbank.org. Web: srbburbank.org.
Res.: 133 N. Fifth St., 91501. Tel: 818-846-3443; Fax: 818-954-9441.
Church: Fifth St. and E. Orange Grove Ave., 91501.
School—154 N. Fifth St., 91501. Tel: 818-842-5033; Fax: 818-842-9789. Email: info@strobertbellarmineburbank.com. Web: strobertbellarmineburbank.com. Lay Teachers 13; Students 284.
Catechesis/Religious Program—Tel: 818-845-3521. Students 307.

CAMARILLO, VENTURA CO.

1—BLESSED JUNIPERO SERRA (1988), Liturgies celebrated at: Padre Serra Parish, 5205 Upland Rd., Camarillo, CA 93012. Rev. Jarlath Dolan; Deacons Bob Fargo; John Picard; Ludger Adam Gueringer; William Spies; Neil Joseph Kingsley; Arnold Peter Reyes; Jack William Redmond, II; Joseph Felix Torti.
Office & Mailing Address: 5205 Upland Rd., 93012. Tel: 805-482-6417; Fax: 805-987-8100. Email: parish@padreserra.org. Web: www.padreserra.org.
Catechesis/Religious Program—Students 599; Preschool 58.

2—ST. MARY MAGDALEN (1940) Rev. James Stehly; Rev. Msgr. John Charles Hughes, Pastor Emeritus (Retired); Rev. John Neiman; Deacons George Bednar; Johnnie Hammonds; Larry Modugno; Anh Quoc Vu; Ronald Dale Moon. In Res., Rev. John Morgan.
Res.: 2532 Ventura Blvd., 93010. Tel: 805-484-0532; Fax: 805-987-2941.
School—2534 Ventura Blvd., 93010. Tel: 805-482-2611; Fax: 805-987-8211. Lay Teachers 13; Students 248.
Catechesis/Religious Program—Tel: 805-482-1219. Students 457.

CANOGA PARK, LOS ANGELES CO., OUR LADY OF THE VALLEY (1921) Revs. Ikechukwu Ikeocha; Roman Arzate; Leo Del Carmen; Sr. Estela del Bando, C.H.S.
Pastoral Center—22021 Gault St., 91303-1804. Tel: 818-592-2880; Fax: 818-592-0299. Web: www.ourladyofthevalley.org.

School—Tel: 818-592-2894; Fax: 818-592-2896. Web: www.olvcrusaders.org. Lay Teachers 10; Students 213.
Catechesis/Religious Program—Tel: 818-592-2892. Students 475.

CARPINTERIA, SANTA BARBARA CO., ST. JOSEPH (1933) Rev. Adalberto Blanco.
Mailing Address: 1532 Linden Ave., 93013. Tel: 805-684-2181; Fax: 805-684-0534.
Catechesis/Religious Program—Students 176.
Chapel— 7th & Ash, 93013.

CARSON, LOS ANGELES CO., ST. PHILOMENA (1956) [CEM] Revs. Demetrio L. Bugayong; William E. Ruther; Thomas P. Asia, M.M.H.C.; Niko F. Leota.
Res.: 21900 S. Main St., 90745. Tel: 310-835-7161; Fax: 310-830-5494. Email: stphilomenacatholicchurch@yahoo.com.
School—21832 S. Main St., 90745. Tel: 310-835-4827; Fax: 310-835-1655. Email: stphilomenasch@aol.com. Carmelite Sisters 5; Lay Teachers 11; Students 268.
Catechesis/Religious Program—Tel: 310-830-6180; Fax: 310-830-6287. Email: repnarcy@yahoo.com. Students 1,166.
Convent—21832 1/2 S. Main St., 90745. Tel: 310-834-9180.

CHATSWORTH, LOS ANGELES CO., ST. JOHN EUDES (1963) Rev. Msgr. Peter Nugent; Rev. William McLean, Senior Priest; Deacons Robert Seidler, Pastoral Admin.; Michael A. Perez.
Church Office & Res.: 9901 Mason Ave., 91311. Tel: 818-341-3680 (Office); Fax: 818-882-4326 (Office). Web: stjohneudes.org.
School—9925 Mason Ave., 91311. Tel: 818-341-1454; Fax: 818-341-3093. Barbara Danowitz, Prin. Sisters of the Pious Schools 3; Lay Teachers 12; Students 297.
Catechesis/Religious Program—9933 Mason Ave., Chatsworth, 91311. Tel: 818-882-9323; Fax: 818-700-5142. Students 984.
Mission—Blessed Alphonsa Catholic Mission, Los Angeles Co.

CLAREMONT, LOS ANGELES CO., OUR LADY OF THE ASSUMPTION (1947) Revs. Charles J. Ramirez; John Nghi Tran; Christopher Troxell; Deacons Arthur Escovedo, (Retired); Robert Steighner; John Tulluis. In Res., Rev. Msgr. Peter A. O'Reilly (Retired); Rev. José Luis Florez, O.S.A.
Res.: 435 Berkeley Ave., 91711. Tel: 909-626-3596; Fax: 909-624-3680. Email: ola@olaclaremont.org. Web: www.olaclaremont.org.
School—611 E. Bonita Ave., 91711. Tel: 909-626-7135; Fax: 909-398-1395. Web: www.ola-ca.org. Administrators 1; Lay Teachers 21; Students 417.
Catechesis/Religious Program—Tel: 909-624-1360. Email: ffoffice@olaclaremont.org. Students 595; Preschool 20.

COMPTON, LOS ANGELES CO.
1—ST. ALBERT THE GREAT (1949), (Hispanic—African American), [CEM] Revs. Christopher Bazyouros; Cristobal Guardado Gonzalez; Deacon Frank Millholland.
Res.: 804 E. Compton Blvd., Rancho Dominguez, 90220. Tel: 310-329-7548; Fax: 310-464-8666.
School—Tel: 310-323-4559; Fax: 310-323-4825. Lay Teachers 10; Students 215.
School—823 E. Compton Blvd., Rancho Dominguez, 90220. Tel: 310-515-3891. Teachers 8; Students 185.
Catechesis/Religious Program—Tel: 310-323-1599. Arturo Gallardo, D.R.E. Students 377.
2—OUR LADY OF VICTORY (1920), (Hispanic—African American), Revs. Francisco Valdovinos, S.T. (Mexico); Rigoberto Chavez, S.T. In Res., Rev. John Seymour, S.T.
Res.: 519 E. Palmer St., 90221. Tel: 310-631-3233; Fax: 310-886-5681.
School—601 E. Palmer St., 90221. Tel: 310-631-1320; Fax: 310-631-4280.
Catechesis/Religious Program—Tel: 310-631-1831. Students 750.
3—SAGRADO CORAZON, SACRED HEART (1956), (Hispanic), Margarita Flores, Parish Life Dir.; Rev. Msgr. John S. Woolway, Priest Min.
Res.: 1720 North Culver Ave., 90222. Tel: 310-635-5436; Fax: 310-635-2121.
Catechesis/Religious Program—Tel: 310-635-8483. Students 397.

COVINA, LOS ANGELES CO.
1—ST. LOUISE DE MARILLAC (1963) Revs. Lawrence Dowdel Jr.; Robert A. Folbrecht.
Mailing Address: 1720 E. Covina Blvd., 91724.
Res.: 1770 E. Covina Blvd., 91724. Tel: 626-915-7873; Fax: 626-332-4431.
School—1728 E. Covina Blvd., 91724. Tel: 626-966-2317; Fax: 626-967-7947. Lay Teachers 13; Students 308.
Catechesis/Religious Program—Tel: 626-332-5822. Students 501.
2—SACRED HEART (1927) Revs. William T. Easterling; Brian M. Cavanagh (Retired); Jeffrey Deikel; James J. Kelly; Deacons John G. Horn; Ronald Butler; Rodolfo R. Leyva.
Res.: 344 W. Workman St., 91723. Tel: 626-332-3570; Fax: 626-967-4884. Email: admin@sacredheart.cc. Web: www.sacredheart.cc.
School—360 W. Workman St., 91723. Tel: 626-332-7222; Fax: 626-967-8836. Web: www.shs.cc. Lay Teachers 18; Students 285.
Catechesis/Religious Program—Tel: 626-331-7914; Fax: 626-966-7165. Students 596.

CUDAHY, LOS ANGELES CO., SAGRADO CORAZON Y SANTA MARIA DE GUADALUPE (1991), (Hispanic), [JC] Revs. Antonio Garnica Lopez, M.S.C.; Florentino Victorino, M.S.C.
4235 Clara St., 90201. Tel: 323-562-3356; Fax: 323-562-3332. Email: sagrado_cudahy@yahoo.com.
Catechesis/Religious Program—Tel: 323-773-6040; Fax: 323-562-3332. Students 675.

CULVER CITY, LOS ANGELES CO., ST. AUGUSTINE (1919) Revs. Kevin L. Nolan; Richard J. Gleason; Jose Vaughn Banal; Deacon Rafael A. Victorin.
Res.: 3850 Jasmine Ave., 90232. Tel: 310-838-2477; Fax: 310-838-3070.
School—3819 Clarington Ave., 90232. Tel: 310-838-3144; Fax: 310-838-7479. Daughters of Mary and Joseph 1; Lay Teachers 15; Students 313.
Catechesis/Religious Program—Tel: 310-836-6561; Fax: 310-838-2477. Students 685.

DIAMOND BAR, LOS ANGELES CO., ST. DENIS (1971) Rev. Msgr. James J. Loughnane; Revs. Sebastian Vettickal, C.M.I. (India); Dennis Mongrain; Deacon Tom Le Donne. In Res., Rev. Donald William Potthoff, Pastor Emeritus (Retired).
Res.: 2151 S. Diamond Bar Blvd., 91765-2981. Tel: 909-861-7106; Fax: 909-861-2697. Web: stdenis91765.parishworld.net.
Catechesis/Religious Program—Tel: 909-861-8018. Students 940.

DOWNEY, LOS ANGELES CO.
1—OUR LADY OF PERPETUAL HELP (1909) Revs. Mark Warnstedt; Vivian B. Lima; Deacons Charles Denisac; Carlos Origel.
Res.: 10727 S. Downey Ave., 90241. Tel: 562-923-3246; Fax: 562-862-7020. Email: olphoffice@ca.rr.com. Web: olphdowney.parishesonline.com.
School—10441 S. Downey Ave., 90241. Tel: 562-869-9969; Fax: 562-923-0659. Web: ourladyschool.com. Lay Teachers 14; Students 285.
Catechesis/Religious Program—Tel: 562-862-7268. Theresa Nicholas, D.R.E. Students 575.
2—ST. RAYMOND (1956) Revs. John Higgins; Francis Osana Kalathil, O.C.D.; Deacons Ralph Riera; Mario Guerra. In Res., Rev. Joseph Ambrose, O.C.D.
Res.: 12348 Paramount Blvd., 90242. Tel: 562-923-4509; Fax: 562-869-3359. Email: straydny@aol.com. Web: www.st-raymond-downey.org.
School—12320 Paramount Blvd., 90242. Tel: 562-862-3210; Fax: 562-862-6328. Sisters of the Holy Faith 1; Lay Teachers 16; Students 310.
Catechesis/Religious Program—Tel: 562-862-6959. Sr. Paula Strohfus, C.H.F., D.R.E. Students 597.
Convent—12322 Paramount Blvd., 90242.
Mission—Rancho Los Amigos Hospital 7601 Imperial Hwy., Los Angeles Co. 90242. Tel: 562-401-7111.
Mission—Los Padrinos Juvenile Hall 7285 Quill Dr., Los Angeles Co. 90242. Tel: 562-940-8711.

EL MONTE, LOS ANGELES CO.
1—NATIVITY (1923) Revs. Alberto Villalobos; John K. Vo (Vietnam); Fulgencio "Dol" L. Legaspi; Doan The Pham; Randy Raul Campos (La).
Res.: 3743 N. Tyler Ave., 91731. Tel: 626-444-2511; Fax: 626-443-1417. Email: parish@mynativity.org.
School—10907 St. Louis Dr., 91731. Tel: 626-448-2414; Fax: 626-448-2763. Web: www.school.mynativity.org. Sisters of St. Louis 5; Lay Teachers 9; Students 194.
Catechesis/Religious Program—Tel: 626-448-8895; Fax: 626-443-2495. Students 337.
2—OUR LADY OF GUADALUPE (1973), (Hispanic), Revs. Francisco Vitela; Jesus Castrillo, C.M.F. (Spain).
Res.: 11359 Coffield Ave., 91731. Tel: 626-448-1795; Fax: 626-448-9507. Email: ologpe@pacbell.net. Web: ologpeelmonte.org.
Catechesis/Religious Program—Tel: 626-448-7131; Fax: 626-448-8376. Email: ologpe@pacbell.net. Students 1,000.

EL SEGUNDO, LOS ANGELES CO.
1—ST. ANDREW (1936), (Russian—Greek), Rt. Rev. Alexei R. Smith.
Res.: 538 Concord St., 90245. Tel: 310-322-1892; Fax: 310-322-1919.
Catechesis/Religious Program—Students 8.
2—ST. ANTHONY (1925) Rev. Robert Victoria; Deacon Richard Pruitt.
Mailing Address: 215 Lomita St., 90245. In Res., Rev. Manuelito Villas.
Res.: 710 E. Grand Ave., 90245. Tel: 310-322-4392; Fax: 310-322-0797. Email: administration@stanthonyes.com. Web: www.stanthonyes.com.
School—233 Lomita St., 90245. Tel: 310-322-4218; Fax: 310-322-2659. Lay Teachers 13; Students 144.
Catechesis/Religious Program—Tel: 310-322-4392, Ext. 311. Email: stanthonydre@yahoo.com. Students 290.

ENCINO, LOS ANGELES CO.
1—ST. CYRIL (1949) Rev. Msgrs. Carl F. Bell; Cyril Navin, Pastor Emeritus (Retired). In Res., Rev. James J. Melley (MIA) (Retired).
Res.: 4601 Firmament Ave., 91436. Tel: 818-986-8234; Fax: 818-986-3310. Email: st-cyril-encino@sbcglobal.net.
School—4548 Haskell Ave., 91436. Tel: 818-501-4155; Fax: 818-501-8480. Lay Teachers 14; Students 312.
Catechesis/Religious Program—Tel: 818-789-5947. Students 120.
2—OUR LADY OF GRACE (1945) Revs. Austin C. Doran; Thomas Feltz.
Res.: 5011 White Oak Ave., 91316. Tel: 818-342-4686; Fax: 818-342-6579. Web: www.ourladyofgrace.org.
School—Tel: 818-344-4126; Fax: 818-344-1736. Web: www.ourladyofgrace.org. Sisters 2; Lay Teachers 14; Students 271.
Catechesis/Religious Program—Tel: 818-342-4505. Students 337.

FILLMORE, VENTURA CO., ST. FRANCIS OF ASSISI (1926) [JC] Revs. John W. Love; Heriberto Palacios Quiroz (Nicaragua).
Church: 1048 W. Ventura St., 93015. Web: www.stfrancisfillmore.com.
Catechesis/Religious Program—Tel: 805-524-2865. Email: stfrancisoffice@sbcglobal.net. Students 672.
Mission—San Salvador 4045 E. Center St., P.O. Box 508, Piru, Ventura Co. 93040. Rev. Bernard Gatlin, Mission Admin.

GARDENA, LOS ANGELES CO.
1—ST. ANTHONY OF PADUA (1910) Revs. George Aquilera; Alfonso Borgen; Deacons Felix Dumlao; Antonio Huerta.
Res.: 1050 W. 163rd St., 90247. Tel: 310-327-5830; Fax: 310-327-6440.
School—1003 W. 163rd St., 90247. Tel: 310-329-7170; Fax: 310-329-9843. Lay Teachers 14; Students 220.
Catechesis/Religious Program—Tel: 310-323-0860. Students 962.
Mission—St. Francis Korean Catholic Center 2040 W. Artesia Blvd., Los Angeles Co. 90504. Tel: 310-324-8159; Fax: 310-769-1882.
2—MARIA REGINA (1956) [CEM] Rev. Leo W. Alberg; Deacon Phuoc Van Nguyen. In Res., Rev. Thomas M. Acton, Pastor Emeritus (Retired).
Res.: 2150 W. 135th St., 90249. Tel: 310-323-0030; Fax: 310-323-8081. Email: mariaregina56@sbcglobal.net.
School—13510 S. Von Ness, 90249. Tel: 310-327-9133; Fax: 310-327-2636. Lay Teachers 15; Students 245.
Catechesis/Religious Program—Tel: 310-323-0030; Fax: 310-323-8081. Students 450.

GLENDALE, LOS ANGELES CO.
1—CHURCH OF THE INCARNATION (1927) Rev. Paul Hruby; Rev. Msgr. Eugene P. Frilot, Pastor Emeritus (Retired); Rev. Thomas Schweitzer; Deacon Restie Noriega.
Res.: 1001 N. Brand Blvd., 91202-2979. Tel: 818-242-2579; Fax: 818-507-4976.
School—123 W. Glenoaks, 91202-2908. Tel: 818-241-2269; Fax: 818-241-4734. Lay Teachers 14; Students 285.
Pre-School—214 W. Fairview, 91202. Tel: 818-241-2264; Fax: 818-241-0876. Teachers 2; Students 14.
Catechesis/Religious Program—Tel: 818-241-7045. Students 269.
2—HOLY FAMILY (1907) Revs. James M. Bevacqua; Rafael Venegas; Marcial Juan; Deacon John Steele.
Res.: 209 E. Lomita Ave., 91205. Tel: 818-247-2222; Fax: 818-247-4780. Web: www.hfglendale.org.
School—Holy Family Grade School, (Grades K-8), 400 S. Louise, 91205. Tel: 818-243-9239; Fax: 818-243-0976. Web: www.hfgsglendale.org. Lay Teachers 12; Students 292.
High School—(Grades 9-12), (Girls) College Prep, 400 E. Lomita Ave., 91205. Tel: 818-241-3178; Fax: 818-241-7753. Web: hfhsglendale.org. Lay Teachers 20; Girls 260.
Catechesis/Religious Program—Tel: 818-240-6551, Ext. 220; Fax: 818-243-2560. Students 380.

GLENDORA, LOS ANGELES CO., ST. DOROTHY (1958) Rev. John J. Vogel; Deacons William Bolduc; Steve Marsh. In Res., Revs. Lawrence Joseph; Leszek Semik.
Res.: 241 S. Valley Center, 91741-3854. Tel: 626-914-3941; Fax: 626-335-0059. Web: www.stdorothy.org.
School—215 S. Valley Center, 91741. Tel: 626-335-0772. Lay Teachers 14; Students 258.
Catechesis/Religious Program—Tel: 626-335-2811; Fax: 626-335-0057. Students 300.

GOLETA, SANTA BARBARA CO.
1—ST. MARK UNIVERSITY PARISH (1966) [CEM] Rev. Tomas Alfonso Elis (Retired).
Res.: 6550 Picasso Rd., 93117. Tel: 805-968-1078; Fax: 805-968-3965. Email: frtom@saint-marks.net. Web: www.saint-marks.net.
2—ST. RAPHAEL (1896) Revs. Bruce Correio; Mark A. Strader; Deacons Wayne Rascati; Stephen James Montross; Noel Fuentes, Pastoral Assoc.
Res.: 5444 Hollister Ave., Santa Barbara, 93111-2308. Tel: 805-967-5641; Fax: 805-964-2988. Email: raphstgo@yahoo.com. Web: www.straphaelsb.com.
School—160 St. Joseph St., Santa Barbara, 93111. Tel: 805-967-2115; Fax: 805-683-9765. Email: sraph@sbceo.org. Web: www.sbceo.k12.ca.us/~sraph. Ellen Manning, Prin. Lay Teachers 12; Students 295.
Catechesis/Religious Program—Tel: 805-967-1641. Ana Solis-Cervantes, C.R.E. (Bilingual); Karen Froelicher, C.R.E. (English); John Vasellina, Youth Ministry. Students 550.

GRANADA HILLS, LOS ANGELES CO.
1—ST. EUPHRASIA (1963) Rev. Rolly P. Jardiniano, Admin. Pro-Temp.
Res.: 11766 Shoshone Ave., 91344. Tel: 818-360-4611; Fax: 818-360-2755. Email: st.euphrasia@verizon.net. Web: www.steuphrasia.org.
School—Tel: 818-363-5515; Fax: 818-832-6678. Web: www.steuphrasiaschool.org. Lay Teachers 10; Students 247.
Catechesis/Religious Program—Tel: 818-368-4512. Email: religiouseducation@steuphrasiaschool.org. Students 235.
2—ST. JOHN BAPTIST DE LA SALLE (1953) Revs. Robert L. Milbauer; Jozef Mitek; Deacon Samuel Frias.
Res.: 10738 Hayvenhurst Ave., 91344. Tel: 818-363-2535; Fax: 818-360-7407.
School—16535 Chatsworth St., 91344. Tel: 818-363-2270; Fax: 818-832-8950. Web: www.dlsschool.com. Lay Teachers 24; Students 530.
Catechesis/Religious Program—Tel: 818-368-1514. Students 590.

GUADALUPE, SANTA BARBARA CO., OUR LADY OF GUADALUPE (1867), (Hispanic), [JC] Rev. Marco Solis.
Res.: 1164 Obispo St., P.O. Box 897, 93434. Tel: 805-343-2181; Fax: 805-343-6642.
Catechesis/Religious Program—Tel: 805-343-4404. Students 230.

HACIENDA HEIGHTS, LOS ANGELES CO., ST. JOHN VIANNEY (1965) Rev. Msgr. Timothy E. Nichols; Revs. Francis Ilano; Ricardo Henry Viveros; Deacons Jesse Martinez; Richard Noon. In Res., Rev. Michael J. Sezzi.
Res.: 1345 Turnbull Canyon Rd., 91745. Tel: 626-330-2269; Fax: 626-330-0220. Web: sjvhh.org.
Catechesis/Religious Program—Students 850.

HAWAIIAN GARDENS, LOS ANGELES CO., ST. PETER CHANEL (1986), (Mexican—Filipino), Revs. Lawrence T. Darnell, O.M.V.; Edward Broom, O.M.V.; Fernando Cuenca, O.M.V.; Vincenzo Antolini, O.M.V.; Sean Morris, O.M.V.
Res. & Church: 12001 E. 214th St., 90716-1117. Tel: 562-924-7591; Fax: 562-402-9411. Email: spcparish@yahoo.com. Web: www.spcomv.com.
Catechesis/Religious Program—Tel: 562-860-3637 (Spanish); 562-865-6498 (English). Students 1,353.

HAWTHORNE, LOS ANGELES CO., ST. JOSEPH (1915) Revs. Perry D. Leiker; Eugene S. Buhr (Retired); Mario Pacheco; Michael Tang.
Res.: 11901 Acacia Ave., 90250. Tel: 310-679-1139; Fax: 310-679-3034.
School—11886 Acacia Ave., 90250. Tel: 310-679-1014; Fax: 310-679-1310. Lay Teachers 24; Students 500.
Catechesis/Religious Program—Tel: 310-679-1139, Ext. 114. Email: mrivera@stjoseph-haw.org. Students 1,000.

HERMOSA BEACH, LOS ANGELES CO., OUR LADY OF GUADALUPE (1927) [CEM] Revs. Raymond Mallett, O.F.M.Conv.; Lazaro Sandoval, O.F.M.Conv.; Bro. John Fleming, O.F.M.Conv. In Res., Revs. Peter Mallin, O.F.M.Conv.; Kevin Schindler-McGraw, O.F.M.Conv.; Steve Gross, O.F.M.Conv.; Bros. James Reiter, O.F.M.Conv.; Christopher Saindon, O.F.M.Conv.
Res.: 320 Massey Ave., 90254. Tel: 310-372-7077; Fax: 310-798-4051. Web: ourladyofguadalupechurch.org.
School—340 Massey Ave., 90254. Tel: 310-372-7486. Web: ourladyofguadalupeschool.org. Mrs. Cheryl Hunt, Prin. Lay Teachers 13; Students 171.
Catechesis/Religious Program—Students 374.

HUNTINGTON PARK, LOS ANGELES CO.
1—ST. MARTHA (1913), (Hispanic), Revs. Manuel Vazquez, M.Sp.S.; Mario Rodriguez, M.Sp.S.; Enrique Espinosa Ramirez, M.Sp.S.; Deacon Ciro Augusto Garza.
6012 Seville Ave., 90255.
Res.: 6019 Stafford Ave., 90255. Tel: 323-585-5776; Fax: 323-585-4560. Email: stamartha@aol.com. Web: www.christthepriest.org.
Catechesis/Religious Program—Tel: 323-585-4941, Ext. 25 (Confirmation). Students 533.
2—ST. MATTHIAS (1913), (Latino), [JC] Revs. Mario Torres; Peter Thang Ngo, Parochial Vicar. In Res., Revs. Rody Ignatius Gorman (Retired); Ornoldo Cherrez (Ecuador); Victor Vargas (Colombia).
Res.: 7125 Mission Pl., 90255. Tel: 323-588-2134; Fax: 323-588-4519. Email: st_matthias@msn.com.
School—7130 Cedar St., 90255. Tel: 323-588-7253; Fax: 323-588-1136. Email: stmatthiaspanthers@hotmail.com. Lay Teachers 12; Students 208.
Catechesis/Religious Program—7105 Mission Pl., 90255. Tel: 323-277-1188; Fax: 323-277-1192. Students 1,271.

INGLEWOOD, LOS ANGELES CO., ST. JOHN CHRYSOSTOM (1923), (Hispanic), Revs. Marcos Gonzalez, Admin.; Javier Altuna, S.J.; Mark Martinez; Deacon Roberto Vasquez. In Res., Rev. Sal A. Pilato.
Res.: 546 E. Florence Ave., 90301. Tel: 310-677-2736; Fax: 310-677-0584. Email: stjohnchrysostom@sbcglobal.net. Web: www.stjohnchrysostomparish.org.
School—530 E. Florence Ave., 90301. Tel: 310-677-5868; Fax: 310-677-3429. Email: sjcnet@earthlink.net. Religious Teachers 4; Lay Teachers 12; Students 245.
Catechesis/Religious Program—Tel: 310-674-3733. Email: sjreligioused-conf@sbcglobal.net. Students 1,266.

IRWINDALE, LOS ANGELES CO., OUR LADY OF GUADALUPE (1964) Rev. Joseph Canna; Deacons Gary Patterson; Roberto I. Chevez.
Res.: 16025 E. Cypress St., 91706-2199. Tel: 626-962-3649, Ext. 231; Fax: 626-337-3318.
Catechesis/Religious Program—Students 1,178.

LA CANADA FLINTRIDGE, LOS ANGELES CO., ST. BEDE THE VENERABLE (1951) Rev. Msgr. James C. Gehl; Rev. Kevin A. Kester. In Res., Rev. Greg Dongkore.
Res.: 215 Foothill Blvd., 91011. Tel: 818-949-4300; Fax: 818-790-9520. Web: www.bede.org.
School—(Grades K-8), 4524 Crown Ave., 91011. Tel: 818-949-4388; Fax: 818-790-7887. Email: stbedeeducationcenter@yahoo.com. Web: stbedeschool.net. Lay Teachers 17; Students 257.
Catechesis/Religious Program—Tel: 818-949-4322; Fax: 818-949-7887. Moira Arjani, D.R.E.; Rose Banich, Dir Youth Ministry & Teenlife Coord.; Theresa Costanzo, Confirmation Coord. Students 562.

LA CRESCENTA, LOS ANGELES CO., ST. JAMES THE LESS (1955) Rev. Edward Dover; Deacons Joe Hegenbart; Raymond Lim.
Res.: 4625 Dunsmore Ave., 91214. Tel: 818-248-3442; Fax: 818-248-9332. Email: stjameschurch4@hotmail.com. Web: www.saintjamescatholicchurch.net.
School—4635 Dunsmore Ave., 91214. Tel: 818-248-7778; Fax: 818-248-5242. Lay Teachers 12; Students 175.
Catechesis/Religious Program—Students 200.

LA MIRADA, LOS ANGELES CO.
1—BEATITUDES OF OUR LORD (1964) Rev. Anthony J. Page.
Res.: 13013 S. Santa Gertrudes Ave., 90638. Tel: 562-943-1521; Fax: 562-902-7627. Email: beatitudeschurch@ca.rr.com. Web: beatitudesofourlord.org.
School—Tel: 562-943-3218; Fax: 562-943-9718. Web: bolschool.org. Lay Teachers 13; Students 268.
Catechesis/Religious Program—Tel: 562-943-5678; Fax: 562-943-9419. Email: beatitudesreo@ca.rr.com. Students 352.
2—ST. PAUL OF THE CROSS (1956) Revs. Joseph Visperas; George Sullivan; Deacons Mark Orcutt; Timothy J. Roberto.
Res.: 14020 Foster Rd., 90638. Tel: 562-921-2914; Fax: 562-926-1514. Email: splamir@msn.com. Web: www.stpaulofthecross.org.
School—14030 Foster Rd., 90638. Tel: 562-921-2118; Fax: 562-802-2048. Lay Teachers 9; Students 197.
Catechesis/Religious Program—Tel: 562-921-4911. Students 246.

LA PUENTE, LOS ANGELES CO.
1—ST. JOSEPH (1919) Revs. Matthew T. Cumberland; Roberto Pirrone; Deacon Ruben Guerra. In Res., Rev. Msgr. Patrick Joseph Staunton (Retired).
Res.: 550 N. Glendora Ave., 91744. Tel: 626-336-2001; Fax: 626-336-6010.
School—15650 E. Temple Ave., 91744. Tel: 626-336-2821; Fax: 626-369-8921. Carmelite Sisters 4; Lay Teachers 6; Students 204.
Catechesis/Religious Program—15650 E. Temple Ave., 91744. Tel: 626-336-1191; Fax: 626-934-7371. Students 314.
2—ST. LOUIS OF FRANCE (1955) Revs. Cesar A. Fernandez; Miguel B. Java (Philippines); Deacons Oscar Valeriano Jr.; Jaime S. Guerrero; Bernardo Zavala. In Res., Rev. Eric Anthony Lewis.
Res.: 13935 E. Temple, 91746-2098. Tel: 626-918-8314; Fax: 626-917-8413. Email: stlouis91746@roadrunner.com. Web: www.stlouisoffrance.org.
School—13901 E. Temple Ave., 91746-2021. Tel: 626-918-6210; Fax: 626-918-9549. Web: www.saintlouisoffrance.org. Lay Teachers 11; Students 226.
Catechesis/Religious Program—Tel: 626-918-7002; Fax: 626-917-8434. Email: stlouisre@roadrunner.com. Students 1,319.

LAKEWOOD, LOS ANGELES CO., ST. PANCRATIUS (1953) Rev. Msgr. Joseph F. Greeley; Rev. Albert H. Avenido.
Res.: 3519 St. Pancratius Pl., 90712. Tel: 562-634-6111; Fax: 562-634-7817. Email: stpanrectory@sbcglobal.net.
School—3601 St. Pancratius Pl., 90712. Tel: 562-634-6310; Fax: 562-633-0731. Lay Teachers 14; Students 236.
Catechesis/Religious Program—Tel: 562-634-1611; Fax: 562-634-2524. Email: stpanre@sbcglobal.net. Students 271.

LANCASTER, LOS ANGELES CO.
1—BLESSED JUNIPERO SERRA (Quartz Hill) (1987) Revs. Leo Dechant, C.S.J.; Ernest Candelaria, C.S.J., Parochial Vicar; Deacons Gary D. Poole; Paul Schwerdt; Rito R. Lopez. In Res., Rev. Giampietro Gasparin, C.S.J.
Res.: 6122 W. Azalea Dr., 93536-3700. Tel: 661-943-6475 (Res.); Fax: 661-943-6863.
Office: 42121 60th St. W., 93536-3767. Tel: 661-943-9314. Email: serra@qnet.com. Web: www.fatherserra.org.
School—*Father Serra Mission Bell Preschool*, 42121 60th St. W., 93536-3767. Tel: 661-943-8094; Fax: 661-943-6863.
Catechesis/Religious Program—Students 655.
Mission—*St. Elizabeth* 13845 Johnson Rd., Lake Hughes, Los Angeles Co. 93532. Tel: 661-724-9911.
2—SACRED HEART (1886) Revs. Thomas E. Baker; Hieu Chi Tran; Deacons John Charters; Ron Routolo; Dale Reynolds. In Res., Rev. Michael Ohanete (Nigeria).
Res.: 45007 N. Cedar Ave., 93534. Tel: 661-942-7122; Fax: 661-945-4255. Web: www.sacredheartlancaster.org.
School—45002 N. Date Ave., 93534. Tel: 661-948-3613; Fax: 661-948-4486. Web: www.shsav.org. Lay Teachers 11; Students 308.
Catechesis/Religious Program—45027 N. Cedar Ave., 93534. Tel: 661-948-3011; Fax: 661-948-2697. Students 1,079.

LOMITA, LOS ANGELES CO., ST. MARGARET MARY ALACOQUE (1937) Rev. Msgr. Patrick Thompson; Revs. Esteban Marquez; Raymond Decipeda, M.M.H.C.; Deacons Craig Siegman; Rick Soria; Dan Wallace.
Res.: 25429 Eshelman Ave., 90717.
Parish Center—25511 Eshelman Ave., 90717. Tel: 310-326-3364; Fax: 310-539-1570. Email: smmchur@yahoo.com.
School—(Grades K-8), 25515 Eshelman Ave., 90717. Tel: 310-326-9494; Fax: 310-326-2711. Linda Areyan, Librarian. Lay Teachers 13; Students 306.
Catechesis/Religious Program—Tel: 310-326-3364, Ext. 17. Email: smmreligiouseduc@yahoo.com. Students 741.

LOMPOC, SANTA BARBARA CO.
1—LA PURISIMA CONCEPCION (1787) Rev. Thomas S. Cook.
Pastoral Center: 213 W. Olive Ave., 93436. Tel: 805-735-3068; Fax: 805-735-7649. Email: lapurcon@impulse.net. Web: www.lapurisima.org.
Rectory—324 S. I Street, 93436.
School—219 W. Olive Ave., 93436. Tel: 805-736-6210; Fax: 805-735-4639. Email: marcy.tijerina@lapurisima.org. Lay Teachers 10; Students 135.
Catechesis/Religious Program—Tel: 805-735-3068, Ext. 23. Email: suzann.oseguera@lapurisima.org. Students 350.
2—OUR LADY QUEEN OF ANGELS (1972) Rev. Msgr. John G. Fitzgerald.
Res.: 3495 Rucker Rd., 93436. Tel: 805-733-2735; Fax: 805-733-1235.
Catechesis/Religious Program—Tel: 805-733-3155. Students 242.

LONG BEACH, LOS ANGELES CO.
1—ST. ANTHONY (1902) Rev. Jose L. Magana.
Mailing Address: 600 Olive Ave., 90802. In Res., Rev. James L. Halley.
Res.: 540 Olive Ave., 90802. Tel: 562-590-9229; Fax: 562-590-9048. Email: community@stanthonylb.org. Web: stanthonylb.org.
School—855 E. 5th St., 90802. Tel: 562-432-5946; Fax: 562-435-8606. Email: elementary@stanthonylb.org. Lay Teachers 12;

Students 215.
High School—620 Olive Ave., 90802. Tel: 562-432-4496; Fax: 562-437-3055. Lay Teachers 19; Students 300.
Catechesis/Religious Program—Tel: 562-590-9229, Ext. 34. Email: religioused@stanthonylb.org. Students 960.
Mission—Our Lady of Mt. Carmel Cambodian Catholic Center 600 Olive Ave., Los Angeles Co. 90806.

2—ST. ATHANASIUS (1933) Rev. Jose Luis Cuevas.
Res.: 5390 Linden Ave., 90805. Tel: 562-423-7986; Fax: 562-422-0306. Email: athanasius@charter.net. Web: www.stathanasius.us.
School—5369 Linden Ave., 90805. Tel: 562-428-7422. St. Francis Mission Community 3; Lay Teachers 9; Students 190.
Catechesis/Religious Program—Tel: 562-428-3494. Students 1,440.

3—ST. BARNABAS (1939) Rev. Msgr. Loreto Gonzales; Rev. George Reynolds; Deacons Carlito De Los Reyes; Alden Bohlig.
Res.: 3955 Orange Ave., 90807. Tel: 562-424-8595; Fax: 562-595-7875. Email: stbarnabaschurch@verizon.net. Web: www.stbarnabaslb.org.
School—(Grades PreK-8), 3980 Marron Ave., 90807. Tel: 562-424-7476; Fax: 562-981-3351. Lay Teachers 11; Students 245.
Catechesis/Religious Program—Tel: 562-988-6855; Fax: 562-981-8792. Email: religioused@sblb.org. Students 570.

4—ST. BARTHOLOMEW (1937) Rev. Msgr. Bernard M. Leheny.
Rectory—252 Granada Ave., 90803. Tel: 562-438-3826; Fax: 562-438-2227. Email: stbarts@sblb.org. Web: www.sblb.org.
Church: 5100 E. Broadway, 90803.
Catechesis/Religious Program—Tel: 562-439-1802. Students 365.

5—ST. CORNELIUS (1951) Revs. Michael Gleeson (Ireland); Pat Sheary, S.J.; Deacon Richard Boucher.
Res.: 5500 Wardlow Rd., 90808. Tel: 562-421-8966; Fax: 562-421-5096.
School—3330 Bellflower Blvd., 90808. Tel: 562-425-7813; Fax: 562-425-2743. Lay Teachers 14; Students 313.
Catechesis/Religious Program—Tel: 562-420-7613; Fax: 562-420-7613. Students 313.

6—ST. CYPRIAN (1945) Revs. Jason Souza; Alfonso A. Scott (Retired).
Res.: 4714 Clark Ave., 90808. Tel: 562-421-9487; Fax: 562-496-1024.
School—5133 Arbor Rd., 90808. Tel: 562-425-7341; Fax: 562-421-1642. Email: info@stcyprianschool.org. Web: www.stcyprianschool.org. Lay Teachers 11; Students 245.
Catechesis/Religious Program—Tel: 562-420-6885; Fax: 562-421-1422. Students 334.

7—HOLY INNOCENTS (1923) Revs. G. Peter Irving III; Raphael Davis, O.Praem., Parochial Vicar.
Res.: 425 E. 20th St., 90806. Tel: 562-591-6924; Fax: 562-685-0556. Email: holyinnocents@gmail.com. Web: www.holyinnocentslongbeach.blogspot.com.
School—2500 Pacific Ave., 90806. Tel: 562-424-1018; Fax: 562-424-9250. Carmelite Sisters of the Most Sacred Heart 4; Lay Teachers 7; Students 182.
Catechesis/Religious Program—Students 295.

8—ST. JOSEPH (1955) Rev. William J. O'Connor; Deacons Don Gath; Thomas L. Halliwell. In Res., Rev. Harold LeRoy Ford (Retired).
Res.: 6220 E. Willow St., 90815. Tel: 562-594-4657; Fax: 562-431-7424.
School—6200 E. Willow St., 90815. Tel: 562-596-6115; Fax: 562-596-6725. Lay Teachers 14; Students 303.
Catechesis/Religious Program—6180 E. Willow St., 90815. Tel: 562-598-0519; Fax: 562-598-8720. Email: religioused@stjosephparishcommunity.com. Students 310.

9—ST. LUCY (1944) Revs. Michael Roebert; John Quy V. Tran; Antonio Rodriguez; Deacon Victor Cepero Lopez.
Res.: 2344 Cota Ave., 90810. Tel: 562-424-9051; Fax: 562-988-0376. Email: lucy2344@gmail.com.
School—2320 Cota Ave., 90810. Tel: 562-424-9062; Fax: 562-424-8572. Lay Teachers 9; Students 180.
Catechesis/Religious Program—Tel: 562-997-0511. Students 498.

10—ST. MARIA GORETTI (1955) Rev. Msgr. Douglas Wm. Saunders.
Res.: 3954 Palo Verde Ave., 90808-2298. Tel: 562-425-7459; Fax: 562-421-0475.
School—3950 Palo Verde Ave., 90808-2298. Tel: 562-425-5112. Email: principal@smgschool.com. Web: www.smgschool.com. Lay Teachers 10; Students 128.
Catechesis/Religious Program—3950 Palo Verde Ave., 90808-2298. Tel: 562-420-1321. Students 100.

11—ST. MATTHEW (1920) Revs. Guillermo Rodriguez (El Salvador); Gerald A. Meisel, Pastor Emeritus (Retired).
Res.: 672 Temple Ave., 90814. Tel: 562-439-0931; Fax: 562-434-7621. Email: stmatt@stmatthewlb.org. Web: stmatthewlb.org.
Catechesis/Religious Program—Tel: 562-434-6402. Students 430.

12—OUR LADY OF REFUGE (1948) Rev. Raymond D. Morales; Rev. Msgr. William J. O'Keeffe, Pastor Emeritus; Rev. Thomas Joseph Glynn (Retired); Deacon Roger Faubert.
Res.: 5195 Stearns St., 90815. Tel: 562-498-6641; Fax: 562-498-3344. Email: parish@olrs.org. Web: www.ourladyofrefuge.org.
School—5210 Los Coyotes Diagonal, 90815. Tel: 562-597-0819; Fax: 562-597-1419. Email: admin@olrs.org. Web: www.olrs.org. Lay Teachers 10; Students 144.
Catechesis/Religious Program—Tel: 562-597-3102; Fax: 562-494-4381. Email: sre@olrs.org. Students 289.

LOS NIETOS, LOS ANGELES CO., OUR LADY OF PERPETUAL HELP (1958), (Hispanic), Revs. Michael Sears; Josef Draugialis.
Res.: 8545 S. Norwalk Blvd., 90606. Tel: 562-692-3758; Fax: 562-695-4068.
Catechesis/Religious Program—Tel: 562-463-3389. Students 810.

LYNWOOD, LOS ANGELES CO.

1—ST. EMYDIUS (1924) Rev. Msgr. Emigdio Herrera; Revs. Mario F. Cabrera; Long Nguyen; Marco D. Reyes; Sr. Margaret Bannan, Pastoral Assoc.
Res.: 10900 California Ave., P.O. Box 100, 90262-2094. Tel: 310-637-7095; Fax: 310-637-3319.
School—10990 California Ave., 90262. Tel: 310-635-7184; Fax: 310-605-3041. Sisters of the Holy Faith 1; Lay Teachers 14; Students 300.
Catechesis/Religious Program—Tel: 310-639-1249. Students 1,525.
Convent—10950 California Ave., 90262. Tel: 310-635-3264. Missionaries of Charity 6.

2—ST. PHILIP NERI (1948), (Hispanic), Revs. Juan Enriquez; Gilberto Monico Soltero; Deacon Joe T. Battle. Tel: 310-632-4745.
Res.: 4311 Olanda St., 90262. Tel: 310-632-7179; Fax: 310-632-5119. Email: info@st-philipneri.org. Web: www.st-philipneri.org.
Pastoral Center—12435 Cookacre Ave., 90262.
School—12522 Stoneacre Ave., 90262. Tel: 310-638-0341; Fax: 310-638-9805. Lay Teachers 9; Students 322.
Catechesis/Religious Program—Tel: 310-632-7893. Students 1,570.

MALIBU, LOS ANGELES CO., OUR LADY OF MALIBU (1946) Rev. William F. Kerze. In Res., Rev. Msgr. John Virgilius Sheridan, Pastor Emeritus (Retired).
Res.: 3625 Winter Canyon Rd., 90265. Tel: 310-456-2361; Fax: 310-456-3942. Email: parish@olmalibu.org. Web: www.olmalibu.org.
School—Tel: 310-456-8071; Fax: 310-456-7767. Lay Teachers 14; Students 122.
Catechesis/Religious Program—Tel: 310-456-8813. Students 140.

MANHATTAN BEACH, LOS ANGELES CO., AMERICAN MARTYRS (1930) Rev. Msgr. John F. Barry; Revs. Nicholas Assi; Mark Villano, C.S.P.; Deacons Fred Rose; Derek A. Brown.
Res.: 624 15th St., P.O. Box 3639, 90266. Tel: 310-545-5651; Fax: 310-546-9209. Email: rectory@americanmartyrs.org. Web: www.americanmartyrs.org.
School—1701 Laurel Ave., 90266-4805. Tel: 310-545-8559; Fax: 310-546-7219. Email: ams@americanmartyrs.org. Web: americanmartyrsschool.org. Lay Teachers 29; Students 645.
Catechesis/Religious Program—1701 Laurel Ave., 90266-4805. Tel: 310-546-4734; Fax: 310-546-9104. Students 1,374.
Spirituality Center—770 17th St., 90266-4805.

MAYWOOD, LOS ANGELES CO., ST. ROSE OF LIMA (1922), (Hispanic), Revs. David M. Velazquez; Edward P. Soto (Retired); Primitivo Gonzalez; J. Jesus Garcia (Mexico).
Res.: *Rectory Office*, 4430 E. 60th St., 90270. Tel: 323-560-2381; Fax: 323-560-8537.
School—4422 E. 60th St., 90270. Tel: 323-560-3376; Fax: 323-560-8539. Lay Teachers 8; Students 160.
Catechesis/Religious Program—4430 E. 60th St., 90270. Tel: 323-560-0187. Students 750.

MISSION HILLS, LOS ANGELES CO., SAN FERNANDO REY MISSION (1797) Rev. Msgr. Francis J. Weber, Admin.; Kevin Feeney, Business Mgr.
Res.: 15151 San Fernando Mission Blvd., 91345. Tel: 818-361-0186; Fax: 818-361-3276.

MONROVIA, LOS ANGELES CO.

1—ANNUNCIATION (1949) Rev. Eugene Herbert; Deacon Gilbert Chavez. In Res., Rev. Msgr. Roland George Zimmerman (Retired), Pastor Emeritus; Revs. Ramon Marti, Sch.P.; Michael G. Callanan, M.M. (Retired).
Church Office & Mailing Address: 2701 S. Peck Rd., 91016. Tel: 626-447-6202; Fax: 626-447-9834.
Res.: 1307 E. Longden Ave., Arcadia, 91006.
School—(Grades K-8) Tel: 626-447-8262; Fax: 626-447-3841. Lay Teachers 14; Students 221.
Catechesis/Religious Program—Tel: 626-447-9834. Mrs. Patricia Taylor, D.R.E. Students 146.

2—IMMACULATE CONCEPTION (1904) Revs. Juan Francisco Gonzalez; Hung Ba Tran; Deacons Fred Conrey; Michael Salcido; Ronald Sanchez; Neomi H. Torres, Admin. In Res., Rev. Francis J. Cassidy (Retired).
Res.: 740 S. Shamrock Ave., 91016. Tel: 626-358-1166; Fax: 626-358-6466. Web: www.icmonrovia.org.
School—726 S. Shamrock Ave., 91016. Tel: 626-358-5129; Fax: 626-358-3933. Web: www.icsmonrovia.org. Lay Teachers 9; Students 141.
Catechesis/Religious Program—Tel: 626-357-3010; Fax: 626-357-5299. Students 640.

MONTEBELLO, LOS ANGELES CO.

1—ST. BENEDICT (1906) Revs. Domingos A. Machado, O.A.R.; James D. McGuire, O.A.R.; Felizardo J. Daganta, O.A.R.; Michael Rafferty, O.A.R.; Deacons David J. Estrada; Alfonso Castillo.
Res.: 1022 W. Cleveland Ave., 90640. Tel: 323-721-1184; Fax: 323-721-5075.
School—Tel: 323-721-3348; Fax: 323-721-8698. Frank Loya, Prin. Lay Teachers 21; Students 557.
Catechesis/Religious Program—1009 W. Madison Ave., 90640. Tel: 323-720-5760, Ext. 100. Raymundo Garcia, D.R.E. Students 539.

2—OUR LADY OF THE MIRACULOUS MEDAL (1950) Rev. Msgr. Juan Matas; Revs. Jude Umeobi; Roland Astudillo; Deacons Fred Rios; Frederick Peter Lara. In Res., Rev. Brian Delaney.
Res.: 820 N. Garfield Ave., 90640. Tel: 323-725-7578; Fax: 323-722-2654. Web: olmmparish.com.
School—840 N. Garfield Ave., 90640. Tel: 323-728-5435; Fax: 323-728-8038. Web: olmmschool.com. Daughters of Charity of St. Vincent de Paul 2; Lay Teachers 21; Aides 7; Students 491.
Catechesis/Religious Program—Tel: 213-725-6962; Fax: 323-722-2654. Email: maria@olmmparish.com. Students 41.

MONTEREY PARK, LOS ANGELES CO.

1—ST. STEPHEN MARTYR (1921) Rev. Lawrence E. Estrada, Priest Min.; Sr. Susan M. Slater, S.H.C.J., Parish Life Coord. In Res., Rev. Stephanus Heruyanto Widiatmojo (Indonesia), Indonesian Community Chap.
Res.: 320 W. Garvey Ave., 91754. Tel: 626-573-0427; Fax: 626-288-0260.
School—119 S. Ramona, 91754. Tel: 626-573-1716; Fax: 626-573-3251. Lay Teachers 12; Students 241.
Catechesis/Religious Program—Tel: 626-573-4517. Students 80.
Convent—122 S. Ramona Ave., 91754. Tel: 626-573-2417.

2—ST. THOMAS AQUINAS (1960) Revs. Gabriel Lui; Ming Yu "Vincent" Lin (China).
Res.: 1501 S. Atlantic Blvd., 91754. Tel: 323-264-4447; Fax: 323-264-2524. Email: saintthomasaquinas@sbcglobal.net.
School—Tel: 323-261-6563; Fax: 323-261-5972. Email: sta-eagles@yahoo.com.
Catechesis/Religious Program—Tel: 323-264-1338. Students 116.

MONTROSE, LOS ANGELES CO., HOLY REDEEMER (1925) Rev. Edward Dover; Rev. Msgr. John Kieran Foley, Pastor Emeritus (Retired).
Res.: 2411 Montrose Ave., 91020. Tel: 818-249-2008; Fax: 818-249-5642. Email: hrcoffice@aol.com.
School—2361 Del Mar Rd., 91020. Tel: 818-541-9005; Fax: 818-541-9006. Web: holyredeemerschool.net. Lay Teachers 12; Students 176.
Catechesis/Religious Program—Tel: 818-249-2008, Ext. 443. Students 285.

MOORPARK, VENTURA CO., HOLY CROSS (1982) Rev. Msgr. Paul M. Albee; Rev. Joseph Quan Nguyen; Deacons Jerry Heyer; J. Trinidad Andrade; Kevin Barry Mauch.
Res., Parish Church & Administration Bldg.: 13955 Peach Hill Rd., 93021. Tel: 805-529-1397; Fax: 805-529-3939.
Catechesis/Religious Program—Tel: 805-529-0283; Fax: 805-529-5897. Students 799.

NEW CUYAMA, SANTA BARBARA CO., IMMACULATE CONCEPTION (1969) Deacon Ricardo Barragan, Parish Dir.
Res.: 4793 Cebrian St., P.O. Box 265, 93254. Tel: 661-766-2741; Fax: 661-766-2919.
Catechesis/Religious Program—Students 16.

NEWBURY PARK, VENTURA CO., ST. JULIE BILLIART (1969) Rev. Msgr. Michael Bunny; Rev. Michael Carrol; Deacons Louis Henschel; Barry Harper; David Nicholas Smith.
Res. & Church: 2475 Borchard Rd., 91320. Tel: 805-498-3602; Fax: 805-376-2332. Email: parish@stjuliesnp.org. Web: www.stjuliesnp.org.
Catechesis/Religious Program—Tel: 805-499-0979. Email: heather@stjuliesnp.org. Students 364.

NORTH HILLS, LOS ANGELES CO., OUR LADY OF PEACE (1944) Revs. Alexander Lewis; Brian Delaney; Peter Ha; John Bosco Musinguzi; Deacons Doug Jones; Rey Guiao; Ms. Rose M. Hernandez, Pastoral Assoc.
Res.: 15444 Nordhoff St., 91343. Tel: 818-894-1176; Fax: 818-894-3838. Email: olpeace@olpeace.org. Web: www.olpeace.org.
School—9022 Langdon Ave., 91343. Tel: 818-894-4059; Fax: 818-894-6759. Email: school@olpeace.org. Lay Teachers 10; Students 210.
Catechesis/Religious Program—Tel: 818-891-3578; Fax: 818-894-5498. Email: religioused@olpeace.org. Students 404.

NORTH HOLLYWOOD, LOS ANGELES CO.

1—ST. CHARLES BORROMEO (1921) Rev. Msgr. Robert J. Gallagher; Revs. Robert E. J. Garon; Preston P. Passos; Julio Gonzalez. In Res., Rev. Msgr. Gabriel Gonzales; Rev. James Aloysius Toal (Retired).
Res.: 10828 Moorpark St., 91602. Tel: 818-766-3838.
Parish Center—10834 Moorpark St., 91602. Tel: 818-766-3838; Fax: 818-766-5711. Email: generalinfo@scbnh.com.
School—10850 Moorpark St., 91602. Tel: 818-508-5359; Fax: 818-508-4511. Email: scbsoffice@pacbell.net. Web: www.stcharlescatholicschool.org. Sisters 1; Lay Teachers 15; Students 254.
Catechesis/Religious Program—Tel: 818-980-1826. Students 415.

2—ST. JANE FRANCES DE CHANTAL (1948) Rev. Ferdinand Lansang, O.Carm.; Deacon Richard Morgan; Miss Gladys S. Rodriguez, Pastoral Assoc. In Res., Revs. Thomas Batsis, O.Carm.; Brian Henden, O.Carm.
Res.: 13001 Victory Blvd., 91606.
Parish Center—12930 Hamlin St., 91606. Tel: 818-985-8600; Fax: 818-985-0606. Web: www.dechantalparish.org.
School—12950 Hamlin St., 91606. Tel: 818-766-1714. Mr. Edgar Sedano, Prin. Lay Teachers 10; Students 250.
Catechesis/Religious Program—Students 294.

3—ST. PATRICK (1948) Rev. Gregory C. King.
Res. & Office: 6153 Cahuenga Blvd., 91606-5117. Tel: 818-752-3240; Fax: 818-769-6174.
School—10626 Erwin St., 91606. Tel: 818-761-7363; Fax: 818-761-6349. Email: razar@stpatrickcatholicschool.com. Web: stpatrickcatholicschool.com. Lay Teachers 11; Students 281.
Catechesis/Religious Program—Tel: 818-769-0263. Students 396.

4—ST. PAUL ASSYRIAN-CHALDEAN (1980), (Assyrian-Chaldean), [JC] Revs. Noel Gorgis; Tomy Tomikeh (SPA).
Res.: 13050 Vanowen St., 91605. Tel: 818-765-3665; Fax: 818-765-0493.

5—SACRED HEART SYRIAC CATHOLIC PARISH (1996), (Jesus Sacred Heart Antiochene Syrian Catholic Mission, Antiochean Syriac Rite). Chorbishop Yousif Habash.
10837 Collins St., 91601. Tel: 818-766-7001; Fax: 818-766-7254.
Catechesis/Religious Program—Layla Toma, D.R.E. Students 42.

NORTHRIDGE, LOS ANGELES CO., OUR LADY OF LOURDES (1958) Rev. Msgr. Peter C. Moran; Revs. Jeremiah E. O'Keeffe, Senior Priest; Ramon G. Valera; Deacon Juan Galido.
Church: 18405 Superior St., 91325. Tel: 818-349-1500; Fax: 818-349-2516. Email: parishcenter@ollnr.org. Web: www.ollnr.org/parish.
Res.: 9800 Canby Ave., 91325.
School—18437 Superior St., 91325. Tel: 818-349-0245; Fax: 818-349-4156. Web: ollnr.org/school. Lay Teachers 14; Students 300.
Catechesis/Religious Program—Tel: 818-349-1285. Email: lourdesreligioused@yahoo.com. Students 275.

NORWALK, LOS ANGELES CO.

1—ST. JOHN OF GOD (1950) Revs. Edward J. Dober; John-Paul Gonzalez; John Moloney.
Res.: 13819 S. Pioneer Blvd., 90650. Tel: 562-863-5721; Fax: 562-406-3927. Web: www.sjogparish.org.
School—13817 S. Pioneer Blvd., 90650. Tel: 562-863-5721, Ext. 228; Fax: 562-406-3928. Web: www.sjogschool.com. Lay Teachers 14; Students 240.
Catechesis/Religious Program—Tel: 562-863-5721, Ext. 231. Students 793.

2—ST. LINUS (1961) Revs. Anthony J. Gomez; Huy Nguyen; Deacons Chuck Baker; John T. Cunneen.
Mailing Address: 13915 Shoemaker Ave., 90650.
Res.: 13921 Shoemaker Ave., 90650. Tel: 562-921-6649; Fax: 562-921-5150. Email: stlinus@stlinus.org. Web: www.stlinus.org. In Res., Revs. Paul Vung Le, S.V.D.; Mark Choi.
School—13913 Shoemaker Ave., 90650. Tel: 562-921-0336; Fax: 562-926-9077. Lay Teachers 16; Students 286.
Catechesis/Religious Program—Tel: 562-921-5179. Students 262.

OJAI, VENTURA CO., ST. THOMAS AQUINAS (1919) Rev. Michael J. McFadden, O.S.A.; Deacon Chris Gorman. In Res., Rev. Patrick J. Keane, O.S.A., Pastor Emeritus (Retired).
Res.: 185 St. Thomas Dr., 93023. Tel: 805-646-4338; Fax: 805-646-5928.
Catechesis/Religious Program—Tel: 805-646-0307. Students 228.

OXNARD, VENTURA CO.

1—ST. ANTHONY (1959) Revs. Albert Sang V. Tran; Porfirio Alvarez; Deacons James Henry; Jon McPheeters; Oscar Duke; George Angel Garcia; Joe Kennedy; Donald Pinedo; Roy Edward Sadowski.
Res.: 2511 S. C St., P.O. Box 2215, 93034. Tel: 805-486-7301; Fax: 805-486-3142.
School—2421 S. C. St., 93033. Tel: 805-487-5317; Fax: 805-486-1537. Lay Teachers 9; Students 166.
Catechesis/Religious Program—Students 74.

2—MARY STAR OF THE SEA (1963), (Filipino—Mexican), Rev. Fidel Hernandez, O.A.R.; Deacon Harold "Hal" Parish; Revs. Ricardo Copon; Marlon Beof, O.A.R.; Frank T. Wilder, O.A.R.; Deacons Dante Tibor Manalo; Noe Morales.
Res.: 463 W. Pleasant Valley Rd., 93033. Tel: 805-486-6133; Fax: 805-483-6913.
Catechesis/Religious Program—Tel: 805-483-9313. Students 866.

3—OUR LADY OF GUADALUPE PARISH (1958), (Hispanic), Revs. Roberto Saldivar, M.Sp.S.; Agustin Rodriguez, M.Sp.S.; Guillermo Flores, M.Sp.S.; Deacons Arturo Godinez; Francisco Lopez; Henry Barajas; Alejandro Zendejas Marron.
Res.: 500 N. Juanita Ave., P.O. Box 272, 93030. Tel: 805-483-0987; 805-483-1481; Fax: 805-486-2434. Email: olgpar@aol.com.
School—530 N. Juanita Ave., 93030. Tel: 805-483-5116; Fax: 805-385-7242. Lay Teachers 12; Students 339.
Catechesis/Religious Program—Tel: 805-487-4737; Fax: 805-486-2434. Students 747.
Mission—Christ the King 535 Cooper Rd., Ventura Co. 93030. Tel: 805-483-3499.

4—SANTA CLARA (1885) Rev. Jon F. Majarucon; Rev. Msgr. Charles Francis O'Gorman, Senior Priest (Retired); Revs. Michael S. Grieco; Marco Antonio Durazo; Deacons Milton Rosenberg; John G. Castorena; Fidel Ramirez; Lawrence James Lopez; Michael Holguin; Raymond Vasquez Jr.; Vincent Charles Kelch; Dano L. Ramos.
Res.: 323 S. E St., 93030. Tel: 805-487-3891; Fax: 805-487-4733. Email: parish@santaclaraparish.org. Web: www.santaclaraoxnard.parishesonline.com.
School—324 S. E St., 93030. Tel: 805-483-6935; Fax: 805-487-6686. Lay Teachers 15; Students 250.
Catechesis/Religious Program—Tel: 805-487-6742. Students 1,021.
Mission—Santa Clara Chapel 1333 Ventura Blvd., El Rio, Ventura Co. 93030. Tel: 805-485-7335; Fax: 805-981-1183.

PACIFIC PALISADES, LOS ANGELES CO., CORPUS CHRISTI (1950) Rev. Msgr. Liam J. Kidney; Rev. Laurence Gallagher, C.Ss.R.; Deacon John Paul Allen. In Res., Rev. Dominic Arputham.
Parish Office: 880 Toyopa Dr., 90272. Tel: 310-454-1328; Fax: 310-573-5021. Email: parishmail@corpuschristichurch.com. Web: corpuschristichurch.com.
Rectory—887 Toyopa Dr., 90272.
School—890 Toyopo Dr., 90272. Tel: 310-454-9411; Fax: 310-454-3776. Sisters of St. Louis (Monaghan) 1; Lay Teachers 25; Students 262.
Catechesis/Religious Program—Tel: 310-454-1328, Ext. 226. Students 154.
Convent—875 Toyopa Dr., 90272.

PACOIMA, LOS ANGELES CO.

1—GUARDIAN ANGEL (1956), (Hispanic), Rev. Steven Guitron. In Res., Rev. Pedro G. Valdez.
Res.: 10886 Lehigh Ave., 91331. Tel: 818-899-2345; Fax: 818-899-2537. Email: guardianangelchurch@yahoo.com.
School—10919 Norris Ave., 91331. Tel: 818-896-1113; Fax: 818-834-4014. Religious of Jesus and Mary 1; Lay Teachers 8; Students 206.
Catechesis/Religious Program—Tel: 818-899-8907. Students 450.

2—MARY IMMACULATE (1954), (Spanish), Revs. John A. Lasseigne, O.M.I.; Leo J. LeBlanc, O.M.I.; John M. Curran, O.M.I.
Res.: 10390 Remick Ave., 91331. Tel: 818-899-0278; Fax: 818-890-9878. Email: maryimmaculateparish@yahoo.com.
School—Tel: 818-834-8551; Fax: 818-896-7996. Web: miseagles.org. Lay Teachers 10; Students 252.
Catechesis/Religious Program—Tel: 818-899-2111. Students 1,270.

PALMDALE, LOS ANGELES CO., ST. MARY (1890) Revs. Vaughn P. Winters; Fidelis C. Omeaku; Loji C. Pilones; Christopher Fagan; Deacons Elvys C. Perez; Ed Caputo. In Res., Rev. Thomas White, State Prison Chap.
Res.: 1600 E. Ave., R-4, 93550. Tel: 661-947-3306; Fax: 661-947-8687.
School—Tel: 661-273-5555; Fax: 661-273-3845. Carolyn Gries, Prin. Lay Teachers 12; Students 294.
Catechesis/Religious Program—Tel: 661-273-5554; Fax: 661-273-5525. Students 1,708.
Mission—Our Lady of the Desert 35647 87th St. E, Littlerock, Los Angeles Co3620 Antelope Valley Rd., Acton, 93543. Tel: 661-269-8837.

PANORAMA CITY, LOS ANGELES CO., ST. GENEVIEVE (1950) Revs. Alden J. Sison; John Kyebasuuta; Patrick Mbazuigwe; Ricardo Henry Viveros.
Res.: 14061 Roscoe Blvd., 91402. Tel: 818-894-2261; Fax: 818-893-4284. Web: www.stgenevievechurch.org.
School—St. Genevieve Elementary School, 14024 Community St., 91402. Tel: 818-892-3802; Fax: 818-893-8143. Web: spartansonline.org. Sisters 3; Lay Teachers 25; Students 625.
High School—13967 Roscoe Blvd., 91402. Tel: 818-894-6417; Fax: 818-892-9853. Lay Teachers 35; Students 560.
Catechesis/Religious Program—Tel: 818-892-7177. Students 652.

PARAMOUNT, LOS ANGELES CO., OUR LADY OF THE ROSARY (1913), (Hispanic—Tongan), Rev. Jesse C. Galaz; Deacons Oscar A. Corcios; Jorge Perez. In Res., Revs. Alojzy Gryszko, S.D.B.; William A. Gil Londono.
Res.: 14815 S. Paramount Blvd., 90723. Tel: 562-633-1126; Fax: 562-633-3192. Email: olrspr@aol.com.
School—Our Lady of the Rosary School, 14813 S. Paramount Blvd., 90723. Tel: 562-633-6360; Fax: 562-633-2641. Sisters of the Daughters of Mary and Joseph 5; Lay Teachers 5; Students 198.
Catechesis/Religious Program—Tel: 562-602-0086. Students 1,114.

PASADENA, LOS ANGELES CO.

1—ST. ANDREW (1886), (Hispanic), Revs. Paul A. Sustayta; Paul Gerard Griesgraber. In Res., Rev. Msgr. Tobias P. English, Pastor Emeritus (Retired).
Res.: 311 N. Raymond Ave., 91103. Tel: 626-792-4183; Fax: 626-792-4456. Email: standrewpasadena@sbcglobal.net.
School—(Grades K-8) Tel: 626-796-7697; Fax: 626-796-1931. Sisters of the Holy Names of Jesus and Mary 1; Lay Teachers 9; Students 276.
Catechesis/Religious Program—42 Chestnut St., 91103. Tel: 626-577-1770; Fax: 626-792-4456. Students 450.

2—ASSUMPTION OF THE BLESSED VIRGIN MARY (1950) Rev. Gerard O'Brien; Rev. Msgr. Robert W. Gipson, Senior Priest; Deacon Jim Crowley.
Res.: 2640 E. Orange Grove Blvd., 91107. Tel: 626-792-1343; Fax: 626-792-0052. Web: assumptionchurch.net.
School—2660 E. Orange Grove Blvd., 91107. Tel: 626-793-2089; Fax: 626-793-4070. Web: abvmschool.net. Ms. Christine Hunter, Prin. Lay Teachers 16; Students 307.
Catechesis/Religious Program—Tel: 626-792-6844; Fax: 626-792-6844. Email: abvmre@yahoo.com. Students 163.

3—ST. PHILIP THE APOSTLE (1921) Revs. Joseph V. Moniz; David Whorton; Deacons William Landa; Richard J. Medina.
Res.: 151 S. Hill Ave., 91106. Tel: 626-793-0693; Fax: 626-793-0733. Email: cjurecki@stphiliptheapostle.org. Web: www.stphiliptheapostle.org.
School—161 S. Hill Ave., 91106. Tel: 626-795-9691; Fax: 626-795-9946. Email: jramirez@stphiliptheapostle.org. Web: www.stphiliptheapostle.org/school. Lay Teachers 27; Students 531.
Catechesis/Religious Program—Students 322.

PICO RIVERA, LOS ANGELES CO.

1—ST. FRANCIS XAVIER (1939) Revs. Enrique Huerta; Jorge A. Penaloza, Pastor Emeritus (Retired); Arturo Valadez; Deacon Carlos R. Rivas.
Res.: 4245 S. Acacia Ave., 90660. Tel: 562-699-7517; 562-699-8527; Fax: 562-699-5331.
Catechesis/Religious Program—Students 747.

2—ST. HILARY (1950) Revs. Joshua Peter Lee; Nelson Trinidad.
Res.: 5465 Citronell Ave., 90660. Tel: 562-942-7300; Fax: 562-948-3760.
School—Tel: 562-942-7361; Fax: 562-801-9131. Web: sthilaryschool.org. School Sisters of Notre Dame 1; Lay Teachers 13; Students 270.
Catechesis/Religious Program—5401 S. Citronell Ave., 90660. Tel: 562-942-7018. Email: st.hilarydre@yahoo.com. Students 263.
Convent—5333 S. Citronell Ave., 90660. Tel: 562-942-7151.

3—ST. MARIANA DE PAREDES (1951), (Hispanic), Revs. David Gallardo; Paul Jesus Velazquez.
Res.: 7922 S. Passons Blvd., 90660. Tel: 562-949-8240; Fax: 562-942-2405. Email: parish@stmariana.org. Web: www.stmariana.org.

School—7911 Buhman Ave., 90660. Tel: 562-949-1234; Fax: 562-948-3855. Web: www.smschargers.org. Karen Lloyd, Prin. Lay Teachers 11; Students 250.
Catechesis/Religious Program—Tel: 562-949-5653; Fax: 562-949-9277. Rebecca Salcido, D.R.E. Students 500.

POMONA, LOS ANGELES CO.

1—ST. JOSEPH (1886) Revs. Roberto Jaranilla Jr.; Anh-Tuan Dominic Nguyen. In Res., Rev. Richard Van De Water.
Res.: 1150 W. Holt Ave., 91768. Tel: 909-629-4101; Fax: 909-623-0265. Email: stjosephpomona@verizon.net. Web: mysite.verizon.net/stjosephpomona.
School—1200 W. Holt Ave., 91768. Tel: 909-622-3365; Fax: 909-469-5146. Lay Teachers 11; Students 217.
Catechesis/Religious Program—Tel: 909-629-1404. Students 900.
Convent—1180 W. Holt Ave., 91768-3429. Tel: 909-639-1308.

2—ST. MADELEINE (1963) Rev. Alejandro Aclan; Rev. Msgr. Andrew Stanislaus Tseu, Pastor Emeritus (Retired).
Res.: 931 E. Kingsley Ave., 91767. Tel: 909-629-9495; Fax: 909-623-7148.
Catechesis/Religious Program—Tel: 909-620-1300; Fax: 909-623-7148. Students 460.

3—SACRED HEART (1935) Revs. Juan Silva; Alberto Arreola, O.M.I.; Deacon Carlos Madrigal; Marta McBride, Business Mgr.
Res.: 1215 S. Hamilton Blvd., 91766. Tel: 909-622-4553; Fax: 909-623-0841.
Catechesis/Religious Program—Ruth Ibarra, D.R.E. Students 1,165.

RANCHO PALOS VERDES, LOS ANGELES CO., ST. JOHN FISHER (1961) Rev. Msgrs. David A. Sork; Eugene A. Gilb, Pastor Emeritus (Retired); Rev. Keith Byrne.
Res.: 5448 Crest Rd., 90275. Tel: 310-377-5571; Fax: 310-377-6303. Email: info@sjf.org. Web: www.sjf.org.
School—5446 Crest Rd., 90275. Tel: 310-377-2800; Fax: 310-377-3863. Email: principal@sjf.org. Lay Teachers 21; Students 250.
Catechesis/Religious Program—5400 Crest Rd., 90275. Tel: 310-377-4573. Email: religioused@sjf.org. Margaret Johnson, C.R.E. Students 797.

REDONDO BEACH, LOS ANGELES CO.

1—ST. JAMES (1892) Revs. James F. Kavanagh; Joseph Kammerer; Brendan Kearney, S.J.; Deacons Richard Shinkle; Robert J. Miller.
Parish Office & Mailing Address: 124 N. Pacific Coast Hwy., 90277. Tel: 310-372-5228; Fax: 310-379-5552.
Res.: 415 Vincent St., 90277.
School—4625 Garnet St., Torrance, 90503. Tel: 310-371-0416; Fax: 310-371-8377. Sisters of St. Joseph of Carondelet 3; Lay Teachers 12; Students 316.
Catechesis/Religious Program—Tel: 310-379-3221. Diana Holly, D.R.E. Students 325.

2—ST. LAWRENCE MARTYR (1955) Rev. Msgrs. Paul J. Dotson; Michael Lenihan, Pastor Emeritus (Retired); Revs. Richard Sunwoo; Kevin Schindler-McGraw, O.F.M.Conv.; Deacons Frank Dieter; James A. Egnatuk; Dale Sheckler.
Res.: 1900 S. Prospect Ave., 90277-6099. Tel: 310-540-0329; Fax: 310-540-8999.
School—1950 Prospect Ave., 90277-6003. Tel: 310-540-3049; Fax: 310-316-0888. Lay Teachers 14; Students 315.
Catechesis/Religious Program—Tel: 310-316-4460. Students 590.

RESEDA, LOS ANGELES CO., ST. CATHERINE OF SIENA (1949) Revs. Paul Gerard Griesgraber; Raul Cortes; Hernan Canete; Deacon Pedro Lira.
Res.: 18115 Sherman Way, 91335. Tel: 818-343-2110; Fax: 818-343-1018.
School—18125 Sherman Way, 91335. Tel: 818-343-9880; Fax: 818-343-6851. Lay Teachers 13; Students 194.
Catechesis/Religious Program—Tel: 818-996-4588. Students 631.

ROWLAND HEIGHTS, LOS ANGELES CO., ST. ELIZABETH ANN SETON (1981) Revs. John H. Keese; Alejandro A. Amayun (Philippines); Peter Zhai, S.V.D.; Rev. Msgr. Michael F. Killeen, Pastor Emeritus (Retired); Deacons Steven V. Hillman; Peter K. Chu.
Res.: 18090 Via Amorosa, 91748. Tel: 626-964-3629. Email: stelizabethannseton@yahoo.com.
Church & Mailing Address: 1835 Larkvane Rd., 91748. Tel: 626-964-3629; Fax: 626-913-2209.
Catechesis/Religious Program—Tel: 626-965-5792; Fax: 626-513-0580. Students 573.

SAN DIMAS, LOS ANGELES CO., HOLY NAME OF MARY (1957) Revs. John Roche, SS.CC.; Peadar Cronin, SS.CC.; Martin P. O'Loghlen, SS.CC.; Deacons Marv Estey; Mario Lopez; Alfred H. Austin; Robert Fleming, Business Mgr.
724 E. Bonita Ave., 91773.
Res.: 764 Dickens Ln., La Verne, 91750. Tel: 909-592-4613. Web: holynamemary.org.
School—Tel: 909-542-0449, Ext. 224; Fax: 909-592-3884. Web: holynamemaryschool.org. Lay Teachers 17; Students 302.
Catechesis/Religious Program—Tel: 909-599-1243, Ext. 232. Melanie Bailey, D.R.E. Students 612.

SAN FERNANDO, LOS ANGELES CO.

1—ST. FERDINAND (1902) Revs. Stephen Conserva, O.M.I.; Manuel "Meme" Villarreal, O.M.I.
Office: 1109 Coronel St., 91340. Tel: 818-365-3967; Fax: 818-365-0067.
School—1012 Coronel St., 91340. Tel: 818-361-3264; Fax: 818-361-5894. Sisters of St. Joseph of Carondelet 1; Religious Sisters of Charity 1; Lay Teachers 9; Students 200.
Catechesis/Religious Program—Tel: 818-361-1813. Students 349.

2—SANTA ROSA (1927), (Hispanic), Revs. Stanislaw Zowada, O.M.I. (Poland); Harold Fisher, O.M.I.; Juan Ayala, O.M.I.
Res.: 668 S. Workman St., 91340. Tel: 818-361-4617; Fax: 818-365-8599.
School—1309 Mott St., 91340. Tel: 818-361-5096; Fax: 818-361-2259. Franciscan Missionary Sisters of the Immaculate Conception 6; Lay Teachers 5; Students 165.
Catechesis/Religious Program—Tel: 818-361-4617, Ext. 450. Students 362.

SAN GABRIEL, LOS ANGELES CO.

1—ST. ANTHONY (1945), (Hispanic—Filipino), Revs. Jerome Schmit; Luis R. Lucchetti (Peru); Leszek Mielechowicz (Poland).
Res.: 1901 S. San Gabriel Blvd., 91776. Tel: 626-288-8912; Fax: 626-288-3730. Email: saintanthonychurch@hotmail.com.
School—1905 S. San Gabriel Blvd., 91776. Tel: 626-280-7255; Fax: 626-280-3870. Mrs. Pauline Ortega, Prin. Lay Teachers 13; Students 193.
Catechesis/Religious Program—Tel: 626-288-5511; Fax: 626-288-5210. Stephanie Ramos, D.R.E.; Luz Garcia, Confirmation Coord. Students 474.
Convent—626 E. Marshall St., 91776. Tel: 626-288-2200.

2—SAN GABRIEL MISSION (1771) [CEM], (Old Mission) Revs. Stephen Niskanen, C.M.F.; Theo Fuentes, C.M.F.; Arnold J. Gonzalez, C.M.F.; Tony Diaz, C.M.F.; Anthony Quyen Nguyen, C.M.F.; Fernando Vega, C.M.F.
Church and Res.: 428 S. Mission Dr., 91776. Tel: 626-457-3035; Fax: 626-282-5308.
School—San Gabriel Mission Elementary School, 416 S. Mission Dr., 91776. Tel: 626-281-2454; Fax: 626-281-4817. Dominican Sisters 2; Lay Teachers 13; Students 240.
High School—San Gabriel Mission High School, 254 S. Santa Anita St., 91776. Tel: 626-282-3181; Fax: 626-282-4209. Girls College Prep. Parish School Sisters 4; Lay Teachers 17; Girls 249.
Catechesis/Religious Program—Tel: 626-457-3041. Students 360.
Convent—412 S. Mission Dr., 91776. Tel: 626-284-9585.

SAN MARINO, LOS ANGELES CO., SAINTS FELICITAS AND PERPETUA (1938) Rev. Paul K. Fitzpatrick; Sr. Mary Ann Martin, C.S.J.
Res.: 1190 Palomar Rd., 91108. Tel: 626-796-0432; Fax: 626-796-0363. Web: www.ssfp.org.
School—2955 Huntington Dr., 91108. Tel: 626-796-8223. Lay Teachers 14; Students 250.
Catechesis/Religious Program—Students 155.

SAN PEDRO, LOS ANGELES CO.

1—HOLY TRINITY (1924) Rev. Msgr. Joseph Brennan; Revs. Edward C. Benioff; Joseph Van Vu.
Parish Center:—209 N. Hanford Ave., 90732. Tel: 310-548-6535; Fax: 310-833-1134.
Church: 1292 W. Santa Cruz St., 90732.
School—1226 W. Santa Cruz St., 90732. Tel: 310-833-0703; Fax: 310-833-5219. Mrs. Linda Wiley, Prin. Lay Teachers 30; (incl. preschool) 575.
Catechesis/Religious Program—Tel: 310-833-3500. Students 610.

2—MARY, STAR OF THE SEA (1889) Revs. John F. Provenza; Lorenzo De Dominici (Retired); Brian Nunes; Deacon William Garcia.
Res.: 870 W. 8th St., 90731. Tel: 310-833-3541; Fax: 310-833-9254. Email: office@marystar.org. Web: www.marystar.org.
School—Tel: 310-831-0875; Fax: 310-831-0877. Email: marystarelementary@sbcglobal.net. Priests 1; Lay Teachers 10; Students 238.
High School—Tel: 310-547-1138; Fax: 310-547-1827. Email: marystarhigh@aol.com. Web: www.marystarhigh.com. Priests 6; Lay Teachers 24; Students 510.
Catechesis/Religious Program—810 W. 8th St., 90731. Tel: 310-833-3933; Fax: 310-832-1257. Students 435.

3—ST. PETER (1965), (Hispanic), Revs. Claudio De Agostini, C.S.J.; Bruno De Santi, C.S.J.; Sylvan Schiavo, C.S.J.
Res.: 338 N. Grand Ave., 90731-2006. Tel: 310-831-5360; Fax: 310-831-0415.
Catechesis/Religious Program—Tel: 310-832-6731. Students 600.

SANTA BARBARA, SANTA BARBARA CO.

1—HOLY CROSS (1973) Revs. Ludo DeClippel, C.J. (Belgium); Alfred Verstreken, C.J. (Belgium); Deacons Nicholas Curran; Randy Saake.
Res.: 1740 Cliff Dr., 93109. Tel: 805-962-0411; Fax: 805-564-6921. Email: parish@holycross.sbcoxmail.com. Web: www.rc.net/losangeles/holycross.
Catechesis/Religious Program—Tel: 805-962-7311. Email: dirreled@holycross.sbcoxmail.com. Students 162.

2—OLD MISSION SANTA BARBARA (1786) [CEM] Rev. Daniel Barica, O.F.M.
Res.: 2201 Laguna St., 93105. Tel: 805-682-4151; Fax: 805-687-7841. Email: stbabs@yahoo.com. Web: www.saintbarbaraparish.org.
Catechesis/Religious Program—Tel: 805-682-4713, Ext. 140. Students 75.

3—OUR LADY OF GUADALUPE (1928), (Hispanic), Rev. Rafael Marin-Leon.
Mailing Address: 227 N. Nopal St., 93103.
Res.: 801 Jennings Ave., 93103. Tel: 805-965-4060; Fax: 805-965-3386.
Catechesis/Religious Program—Tel: 805-962-4441. Students 220.

4—OUR LADY OF MOUNT CARMEL (1856) Revs. Maurice K. O'Mahony (Retired); Carrol O'Sullivan (Retired).
Res.: 1300 E. Valley Rd., 93108. Tel: 805-969-6868; Fax: 805-565-5959. Email: dellastrada@aol.com. Web: www.olmc-montecito.com.
School—530 Hot Springs Rd., Montecito, 93108. Tel: 805-969-5965; Fax: 805-565-9841. Lay Teachers 16; Students 203.
Catechesis/Religious Program—Tel: 805-969-4868. Students 175.

5—OUR LADY OF SORROWS (1856) Revs. Paul Devot, S.J.; Denis E. Collins, S.J.; Michael W. Ravenkamp, S.J.; Joseph Morris, S.J.; Augusto Berrio, S.J.; Deacons William Sangster; Luis Cabello; Gregory Robert Calderon; Arturo Gonzalez; Jose Ascencion Ramirez; Jose Antonio Trujillo. In Res., Rev. Christopher Soh, S.J.
Res.: 21 E. Sola St., 93101. Tel: 805-963-1734; Fax: 805-965-6461.
School—Notre Dame, 33 E. Micheltorena St., 93101. Tel: 805-965-1033; Fax: 805-965-1034. Deacon Henry Barrajas, Prin. Lay Teachers 11; Students 168.
Catechesis/Religious Program—Tel: 805-966-4941. Students 384.

6—SAN ROQUE (1953) [JC] Rev. Msgr. Michael J. Jennett.
Res.: 325 Argonne Cir., 93105. Tel: 805-687-5215; Fax: 805-682-9778. Email: office@sanroqueparish.org.
Catechesis/Religious Program—Tel: 805-682-1097. Email: education@sanroqueparish.org. Students 146.

SANTA CLARITA, LOS ANGELES CO.

1—BLESSED KATERI TEKAKWITHA (1998) Rev. Msgr. Michael J. Slattery; Rev. Blaise N. Brockman, Admin.; Deacons Edward Littleton; Jay Reiser.
Res.: 22508 Copper Hill Dr., 91350-4299. Tel: 661-296-3180; Fax: 661-296-7854. Email: secretary@blessedkateriparish.org. Web: www.blessedkateriparish.org.
Catechesis/Religious Program—Tel: 661-296-6945. Email: re@blessedkateriparish.org. Students 1,481.

2—ST. CLARE (1977) Rev. Olin Mayfield, Admin.; Rev. Msgr. Edmond M. Renehan, Pastor Emeritus (Retired); Revs. William B. Ustaski, C.R.I.C.; Malcolm Ambrose.
Res.: 27341 Camp Plenty Rd., 91351. Tel: 661-252-3353; Fax: 661-252-1539. Web: www.st-clare.org.
Catechesis/Religious Program—Tel: 661-252-6950; Fax: 661-299-6594. Peggy Pigors, D.R.E.; Nancy Fishwick, Youth Min. Students 840.

3—OUR LADY OF PERPETUAL HELP (1944) Rev. Msgr. Paul M. Montoya; Revs. Donatus Ekenachi (Nigeria); Nicolas Sanchez; Deacon Richard Karl.
Res.: 23233 Lyons Ave., 91321-2632. Tel: 661-259-2276; Fax: 661-259-1873. Email: olphnewhall@la.twcbc.com. Web: www.olph-church.org.
School—Tel: 661-259-1141; Fax: 661-259-8254. Lay Teachers 11; Students 246.
Catechesis/Religious Program—Tel: 661-259-4266; Fax: 661-259-2084. Students 1,025.

SANTA FE SPRINGS, LOS ANGELES CO., ST. PIUS X (1954), (Hispanic), Revs. Pedro J. Lopez; Khoa L. Mai; Francis V. Aguilar.
Res.: 10827 Pioneer Blvd., 90670. Tel: 562-863-8734; Fax: 562-868-0051. Email: stpiusx10@aol.com. Web: www.stpiusx10.org.
School—Tel: 562-864-4818; Fax: 562-864-7120. Lay Teachers 14; Students 247.

Catechesis / Religious Program—Tel: 562-868-2389. Students 783.

SANTA MARIA, SANTA BARBARA CO.

1—ST. JOHN NEUMANN (Santa Barbara) (1986) Revs. Lucio Juarez; Ramon Orozco; Deacons Roberto Lupian Valdez; Ricardo Berumen.
Res.: 966 W. Orchard, 93458-2063. Tel: 805-922-7099; Fax: 805-346-1747.
Catechesis / Religious Program—Tel: 805-922-5288. Students 1,350.

2—ST. LOUIS DE MONTFORT (Santa Barbara) (1963) [JC] Very Rev. Charles Hofschulte, C.J.; Revs. Mark L. Newman, C.J.; John A. Mayhew, C.J.; Campion W. Aspinall, C.J. (Retired); Alidor Mikobi, C.J.; Deacons Richard Carmody; Douglas Halvorsen; Robert Maciel; Shawn Stanley Vedro; Raul Blanco.
Res.: 5075 Harp Rd., 93455. Tel: 805-937-4555; Fax: 805-934-2805. Email: sldmchurch@sldm.org. Web: www.sldm.org.
School—5095 Harp Rd., 93455. Tel: 805-937-5571; Fax: 805-937-3181. Email: sldmschool@sbceo.org. Web: www.sldmschool.org. Lay Teachers 11; Students 255.
Catechesis / Religious Program—Tel: 805-937-8363. Email: ckuhbander@sldm.org. Students 700.
Mission—St. Anthony's Church 270 Helena St., Los Alamos, 93440. Tel: 805-344-1604.

3—ST. MARY OF THE ASSUMPTION (1905) [JC] Rev. Riz Carranza; Rev. Msgr. James Philip Colberg, Pastor Emeritus (Retired); Deacons Francisco Javier Lopez; Zenon Nawrocik.
Res.: 414 E. Church St., 93454. Tel: 805-922-5826; Fax: 805-922-1986. Email: parish@stmary-sm.org. Web: www.stmary-sm.org.
School—424 E. Cypress St., 93454. Tel: 805-925-6713; Fax: 805-925-3815. Email: stmsch@verizon.net. Web: stmarysm.ca.campusgrid-.net.home. Lay Teachers 10; Students 210.
Preschool—209 S. School St., 93454. Tel: 805-346-6541; Fax: 805-347-7658. Email: stmpresch@verizon.net. Teachers 7; Students 42.
Catechesis / Religious Program—Tel: 805-922-5826, Ext. 20 (temporary #); 805-925-2007 (Confirmation I & II). Email: rep@stmary-sm.org. Students 245.

SANTA MONICA, LOS ANGELES CO.

1—ST. ANNE (1951) Rev. Michael D. Gutierrez.
Res.: 2011 Colorado Ave., 90404. Tel: 310-829-4411; Fax: 310-829-9006. Email: stanshrn@verizonmail.net. Web: www.stanneshrine.org.
School—2015 Colorado Ave., 90404. Tel: 310-829-2775; Fax: 310-829-3945. Lay Teachers 9; Students 237.
Catechesis / Religious Program—Tel: 310-829-4040. Students 185.

2—ST. CLEMENT (1904) Rev. Anthony Gonzalez.
Res.: 3102 Third St., 90405. Tel: 310-396-2679; Fax: 310-396-4239. Email: stclements@verizon.net.
Catechesis / Religious Program—Students 99.

3—ST. MONICA (1886) Rev. Msgr. Lloyd A. Torgerson; Rev. Timothy Clement Klosterman; Deacon Frank Vargas.
725 California Ave., 90403. Tel: 310-393-9287; Fax: 310-319-9758. Email: info@stmonica.net. Web: www.stmonica.net. In Res., Revs. Willie Raymond, C.S.C.; David Guffey, C.S.C.; Venantius Yikore (Ghana).
School—Elementary School., 1039 Seventh St., 90403. Tel: 310-451-9801; Fax: 310-394-6001. Email: lynda.auer@stmonicaelem.com. Web: www.stmonica.net/ele. Lay Teachers 11; Students 284.
High School—1030 Lincoln Blvd., 90403. Tel: 310-394-3701; Fax: 310-458-1353. Web: www.stmonicahs.org. Sisters 2; Lay Teachers 50; Students 600.
Catechesis / Religious Program—Tel: 310-395-8903. Students 635.

SANTA PAULA, VENTURA CO.

1—OUR LADY OF GUADALUPE (1929), (Hispanic), [CEM] Rev. Charles R. Lueras, C.R.I.C.
Res.: 427 N. Oak St., 93060. Tel: 805-525-3716; Fax: 805-525-3788.
Catechesis / Religious Program—423 N. Oak St., 93060. Tel: 805-525-2225. Students 591.
Convent—432 N. Oak St., 93060. Tel: 805-525-9207; Fax: 805-933-2729. Email: opolgs@aol.com. Web: crmsdusadelegation.org.

2—ST. SEBASTIAN (1896) Revs. Pasquale Vuoso, C.R.I.C.; Thomas J. Dome, C.R.I.C.; Deacon Alfonso A. Guilin.
Res.: 235 N. Ninth St., 93060. Tel: 805-525-2149; Fax: 805-933-5520.
School—325 E. Santa Barbara St., 93060. Tel: 805-525-1575; Fax: 805-933-0190. Lay Teachers 20; Students 176; Preschool 44.
Catechesis / Religious Program—Tel: 805-225-3201. Email: stsebastianccd@verizon.net. Students 130.

SHERMAN OAKS, LOS ANGELES CO., ST. FRANCIS DE SALES (1938) Revs. Michael Wakefield; Kevin John Larkin, Pastor Emeritus (Retired); Rev. Msgr. Richard Affrim. In Res., Rev. Jerome O'Mahony, M.S.C. (Retired).
Res.: 13360 Valleyheart Dr., S., 91423. Tel: 818-784-0105; Fax: 818-784-4807.
Church: Moorpark St. at Dixie Canyon Ave., 91423.
School—13368 Valleyheart Dr., 91423. Tel: 818-784-9573; Fax: 818-784-9649. Sisters 1; Lay Teachers 18; Students 315.
Catechesis / Religious Program—Tel: 818-782-1907. Students 95.

SIERRA MADRE, LOS ANGELES CO., ST. RITA (1908) Rev. Richard G. Krekelberg; Deacon Manuel Valencia.
Res.: 50 E. Alegria Ave., 91024. Tel: 626-355-1292; Fax: 626-355-2290. Web: st-rita.org.
School—322 N. Baldwin Ave., 91024. Tel: 626-355-6114; Fax: 626-355-0713. Lay Teachers 16; Students 289.
Catechesis / Religious Program—Tel: 626-355-3841; Fax: 626-355-3841. Students 153.

SIMI VALLEY, VENTURA CO.

1—ST. PETER CLAVER (1972) Rev. Msgr. Gary P. Bauler; Rev. William R. Crowe; Deacon Brian Clements.
Res.: 5649 E. Pittman St., 93063. Tel: 805-526-6499; Fax: 805-526-7233. Email: saintpeterclaver@aol.com. Web: www.saintpeterclaver.org.
School—(Grades PreSchool-K), 5670 Cochran St, 93063. Tel: 805-526-2244. Lay Teachers 11; Students 81.
Catechesis / Religious Program—Tel: 805-526-0680; Fax: 805-526-3658. Email: pspcre@aol.com. Students 700.

2—ST. ROSE OF LIMA (1921) Revs. Joseph P. Shea; Budi Wardhana; Deacons Peter Wilson Jr.; Terence Reibenspies; Louis Homero Fernandez.
Res.: 1305 Royal Ave., 93065. Tel: 805-526-1732; Fax: 805-526-0067. Email: parish@strosesv.com.
School—1325 Royal Ave., 93065. Tel: 805-526-5304; Fax: 805-526-0939. Web: srls.org. Lay Teachers 18; Students 252.
Catechesis / Religious Program—Tel: 805-526-5513; Fax: 805-520-7638. Students 583.

SOLVANG, SANTA BARBARA CO., OLD MISSION SANTA INES (1804), (Spanish), Revs. Gerald Barron, O.F.M-.Cap.; Daniel Kabat, O.F.M.Cap.; Deacon Ancelmo Aguirre. In Res., Revs. Peter Banks, O.F.M.Cap.; Harold Snider, O.F.M.Cap.
Res.: 1760 Mission Dr., P.O. Box 408, 93464. Tel: 805-688-4815; Fax: 805-686-4468. Email: office@missionsantaines.org. Web: www.missionsantaines.org.
Catechesis / Religious Program—Tel: 805-688-4138. Students 285.

SOUTH EL MONTE, LOS ANGELES CO., EPIPHANY (1956), (Hispanic), Revs. Antonio Esteban; Moises R. Apolinar Jr., Admin. Pro-Tempore; Jose A. Ortiz (El Salvador); Joseph Francis (Sri Lanka); Deacon Doroteo Gonzalez.
Res.: 10911 Michael Hunt Dr., 91733. Tel: 626-442-6262; Fax: 626-575-1738. Email: epiphanysem@earthlink.net. Web: epiphanychurchsem.com.
School—10915 Michael Hunt Dr., 91733. Tel: 626-442-6264; Fax: 626-442-6074. Lay Teachers 9; Students 128.
Catechesis / Religious Program—Tel: 626-448-3636; Fax: 626-448-0894. Students 528.

SOUTH GATE, LOS ANGELES CO., ST. HELEN (1931) Revs. Samuel W. Ward; Edgar Garcia, O.M.I. (Peru); Deacon Cecilio G. Pena.
Res.: 3170 Firestone Blvd., 90280. Tel: 323-563-3522; Fax: 323-563-0161.
School—9329 Madison Ave., 90280. Tel: 323-566-5491; Fax: 323-566-2810. Sisters of Notre Dame 1; Lay Teachers 10; Students 361.
Catechesis / Religious Program—9314 Madison Ave., 90280. Tel: 323-569-9550; Fax: 323-569-5103. Students 948.

SOUTH PASADENA, LOS ANGELES CO., HOLY FAMILY (1910) Rev. Msgr. Clement J. Connolly; Revs. Jose Parathanal; Niall Finbarr O'Leary, Dir. of Spirituality (Retired); Cambia Smith, Parish Life Dir.
Pastoral Center—1527 Fremont Ave., 91030. Tel: 626-799-8908; Fax: 626-799-0423.
School—1301 Rollin St., 91030. Tel: 626-799-4354; Fax: 626-403-6180. Web: www.holyfamily.net/school. Carolyn Strong, Prin. Lay Teachers 16; Students 318.
Catechesis / Religious Program—Tel: 626-403-6118; Fax: 626-403-6199. Students 506.

SUN VALLEY, LOS ANGELES CO., OUR LADY OF THE HOLY ROSARY (1937), (Hispanic—Filipino), Revs. Richard Zanotti, C.S.; Ariel Durian, C.S.
Res.: 7800 Vineland Ave., 91352-4596. Tel: 818-765-3350; Fax: 818-765-3170.
School—7802 Vineland Ave., 91352. Tel: 818-765-4897; Fax: 818-765-5791. Servant Sisters of the Blessed Sacrament 4; Lay Teachers 9; Students 235.
Catechesis / Religious Program—Tel: 818-982-4248. Diana Cruz, D.R.E. Students 650.
Mission—Our Lady of Zapopan 7824 Lankershim Blvd., North Hollywood, Los Angeles Co. 91605. Tel: 818-503-8920.

SYLMAR, LOS ANGELES CO., ST. DIDACUS (1957), (Hispanic), Rev. Msgr. Peter L. Amy; Deacon Raymond Camacho. In Res., Rev. Norman A. Supancheck.
Res.: 14339 Astoria St., 91342. Tel: 818-367-6181; Fax: 818-367-0604. Email: sdoffice@stdidacus.org. Web: www.stdidacus.org.
School—14325 Astoria St., 91342. Tel: 818-367-5886; Fax: 818-364-5486. Lay Teachers 10; Students 218.
Catechesis / Religious Program—Tel: 818-367-4155. Students 810.

TEMPLE CITY, LOS ANGELES CO., ST. LUKE THE EVANGELIST (1946) Revs. Joseph C. Wah; Joseph Yang; Michael W. Meyer.
Mailing Address: *Parish Administrative Center*, 5605 Cloverly Ave., 91780.
Res.: 9451 E. Broadway, P.O. Box 798, 91780. Tel: 626-291-5900; Fax: 626-287-2332. Email: stlukegrace@earthlink.net. Web: www.stluketemplecity.org.
School—5521 Cloverly Ave., 91780. Tel: 626-291-5959; Fax: 626-285-5367. Religious 1; Lay Teachers 9; Students 185.
Catechesis / Religious Program—Tel: 626-291-5925. Students 325.

THOUSAND OAKS, VENTURA CO., ST. PASCHAL BAYLON (1960) Revs. David Heney; Thai Le; Deacons James Robinson; Mitchell Ito.
Res.: 155 E. Janss Rd., 91360. Tel: 805-496-0222; Fax: 805-379-2506. Email: parish@stpaschal.org. Web: www.stpaschal.org.
School—(Grades K-8), 154 E. Janss Rd., 91360. Tel: 805-495-9340; Fax: 805-778-1509. Email: school@stpaschal.org. Donna Howard, Librarian. Lay Teachers 16; Students 350.
Catechesis / Religious Program—Tel: 805-496-0222, Ext. 115. Students 580.

TORRANCE, LOS ANGELES CO.

1—ST. CATHERINE LABOURE (1947) Revs. John O'Byrne; John Vo; Tovia Lui.
Res.: 3846 Redondo Beach Blvd., 90504. Tel: 310-323-8900; Fax: 323-321-0486. Email: pastor@stcatchurch.org. Web: stcatchurch.org.
School—Tel: 310-324-8732; Fax: 310-324-2471. Mrs. Kathleen Gorze, Prin. Lay Teachers 20; Students 400.
Catechesis / Religious Program—16831 Ainsworth, 90504. Tel: 310-515-6033; Fax: 310-515-5619. Students 521.

2—NATIVITY (1924) Revs. Alfred Hernandez; Patrick Joseph McHugh, Pastor Emeritus (Retired); Gerhart Habison.
Res.: 1447 Engracia Ave., 90501-3234. Tel: 310-328-2776; Fax: 310-328-0508.
School—2371 Carson, 90501. Tel: 310-328-5387; Fax: 310-328-5365. Lay Teachers 9; Students 269.
Catechesis / Religious Program—Tel: 310-320-6673. Students 502.

TUJUNGA, LOS ANGELES CO., OUR LADY OF LOURDES (1920) Rev. Freddie T. Chua; Mrs. Pam Wollonciej, Parish Business Mgr.
Res.: 10321 Tujunga Canyon Blvd., 91042.
Parish Business Office: 7344 Apperson St., 91042. Tel: 818-352-3218; Fax: 818-352-2738.
School—Tel: 818-353-1106; Fax: 818-951-4276. Lay Teachers 13; Students 210.
Catechesis / Religious Program—Tel: 818-353-3053. Email: tanker@catholicweb.com. Students 258.

VALINDA, LOS ANGELES CO., ST. MARTHA (1958), (Hispanic—Filipino), Revs. Mauricio O. Goloran III (Philippines); Xavier Alvarez (Mexico); Rolando Clarin, O.S.C. (Philippines). In Res., Rev. Msgr. Aidan M. Carroll.
Res.: 444 N. Azusa Ave., 91744-4299. Tel: 626-964-4313; Fax: 626-913-2953. Email: spirit@stmarthaval.org. Web: www.stmarthaval.org.
School—Tel: 626-964-1093; Fax: 626-912-2014. Sisters of the Love of God 5; Lay Teachers 4; Students 222.
Catechesis / Religious Program—Tel: 626-912-2581. Students 809.
Youth Ministry Confirmation Program—Tel: 626-964-1903; Fax: 626-965-7034. Students 243.

VAN NUYS, LOS ANGELES CO.

1—ST. BRIDGET OF SWEDEN (1955) Rev. Joseph Dass; Deacon Ramon Rivera.
Res.: 16711 Gault St., 91406. Tel: 818-782-7180; Fax: 818-782-7184. Web: www.sbos.org.
School—7120 Whitaker, 91406. Tel: 818-785-4422; Fax: 818-785-0490. Email: stbridgetof1@yahoo.com. Lay Teachers 11; Students 200.
Catechesis / Religious Program—Gloria Romono, D.R.E. Students 250.

2—ST. ELISABETH (1919), (Hispanic), Revs. John Bruno, R.C.J.; Rodolfo D'Agostino, R.C.J.; Vito Di Marzio, R.C.J.; Deacon Salvador Espana.

Res.: 6635 Tobias Ave., 91405. Tel: 818-779-1756; Fax: 818-785-4492.
School—Tel: 818-779-1766; Fax: 818-779-1768. Lay Teachers 10; Students 235.
Catechesis/Religious Program—Tel: 818-779-1772. Students 757.

VENICE, LOS ANGELES CO., ST. MARK (1923) Rev. Michael Rocha. In Res., Rev. Richard Dimler, S.J.
Res.: 940 Coeur d'Alene Ave., 90291. Tel: 310-821-5058; Fax: 310-821-7031. Email: info@st-mark.net. Web: www.st-mark.net.
School—912 Coeur d'Alene Ave., 90291. Tel: 310-821-6612; Fax: 310-822-6101. Lay Teachers 20; Students 230.
Catechesis/Religious Program—Tel: 310-822-1201. Students 40.

VENTURA, VENTURA CO.

1—OUR LADY OF THE ASSUMPTION (1954) Revs. Steve V. Davoren; Robert E. J. Garon; Deacons James M. Farley; Rodger Adams; Ed Mlls; Aurelio Robles Macias; Charles Philip Wessler; Bill Wilson. In Res., Rev. Msgr. Donal Mulcahy, Pastor Emeritus (Retired).
Res.: 3175 Telegraph Rd., 93003-3283. Tel: 805-642-7966; Fax: 805-642-7635. Email: parish@ola-vta.org. Web: olaventura.com.
School—3169 Telegraph Rd., 93003-3282. Tel: 805-642-7198; Fax: 805-642-7110. Lay Teachers 11; Students 280.
Catechesis/Religious Program—Tel: 805-642-7966, Ext. 118. Students 505.

2—SACRED HEART (1966) Revs. Daniel A. O'Sullivan, Pastor Emeritus (Retired); Cyprian Carlo, Admin.; Ernesto Arceo; Deacons Fernando M. Flores; John William Barry.
Res.: 10800 Henderson Rd., 93004. Tel: 805-647-3235; Fax: 805-647-8087. Email: rectory@sacredheartventura.org. Web: www.sacredheartventura.org.
School—(Grades K-8), 10770 Henderson Rd., 93004. Tel: 805-647-6174; Fax: 805-647-2291. Email: school@sacredheartventura.org. Lay Teachers 12; Students 214.
Catechesis/Religious Program—Tel: 805-647-6260. Email: re@sacredheartventura.org. Students 395.

3—SAN BUENAVENTURA MISSION (1782), (Hispanic), Revs. Michael J. Carcerano; Peter Damian Fernando, Senior Priest; Jiwan A. Kim, O.F.M-.Conv.; Deacons Mark Lawrence Banda; Teodoro Landeros; Alfonso Cruz Mendez.
Res.: 211 E. Main St., 93001. Tel: 805-643-4318; Fax: 805-643-7831. Email: mission@sanbuenaventuramission.org. Web: www.sanbuenaventuramission.org.
School—Tel: 805-643-1500. Lay Teachers 10; Students 176.
Catechesis/Religious Program—Students 518.

VERNON, LOS ANGELES CO., HOLY ANGELS PARISH OF THE DEAF (1987) Revs. Thomas Schweitzer; Brian D. Doran, Senior Priest (Retired).
Res.: 4433 Santa Fe Ave., 90058. Tel: 323-587-0397 (TDD); 323-587-2096; Fax: 323-587-7193. Web: hacofthdeaf.org.
Catechesis/Religious Program—Students 60.

WALNUT, LOS ANGELES CO., ST. LORENZO RUIZ (1991) Revs. Tony P. Astudillo; Hyacinth Kalu.
Res.: 747 Meadowpass Rd., 91789. Tel: 909-595-9545; Fax: 909-594-3940.
Catechesis/Religious Program—Tel: 909-468-1812. Students 416.

WEST COVINA, LOS ANGELES CO., ST. CHRISTOPHER (1954) Revs. Nestor D. Rebong; Joseph Magdaong; Francis Dang Hoang, S.J., Chap. (Vietnamese Community); Thomas Han, Chap. (Korean Community); Deacons Douglas Moloney; Loc Nguyen; Ching Dimaculangan, Business Mgr.
Res.: 629 S. Glendora Ave., 91790. Tel: 626-960-1805; Fax: 626-851-0595. Web: www.stchristopher91790.parishworld.net.
School—900 W. Christopher St., 91790. Tel: 626-960-3079; Fax: 626-338-7910. Web: www.saintchristopherparishschool.com. Mrs. Mary Bachman, Prin. Lay Teachers 12; Students 248.
Catechesis/Religious Program—Tel: 626-338-2937. Dolores Zavala, D.R.E. Students 494.
Mission—St. Christopher Korean Catholic Community 833-835 W. Christopher St., Los Angeles Co. 91790. Tel: 626-960-5647; Fax: 626-960-5300.

WEST HOLLYWOOD, LOS ANGELES CO.

1—ST. AMBROSE (1922) Revs. William P. Wolfe; Brian D. Doran (Retired).
Res.: 1281 N. Fairfax Ave., 90046-5205. Tel: 323-656-4433; Fax: 323-656-6634. Email: stambrosech@aol.com. Web: www.st-ambrose.com.

2—ST. VICTOR (1906) Rev. Msgr. Jeremiah Murphy. In Res., Rev. Msgr. George John Parnassas (Retired).
Res.: 8634 Holloway Dr., 90069. Tel: 310-652-6477; Fax: 310-652-6478. Email: info@saintvictor.org. Web: saintvictor.org.
Catechesis/Religious Program—Students 13.

WESTLAKE VILLAGE, LOS ANGELES CO., ST. JUDE (1970) Rev. Peter Foran; Deacons Dick Dornan; Joseph Manion; Bill Smith.
Res.: 32032 W. Lindero Canyon Rd., 91361-4270. Tel: 818-889-1279; Fax: 818-889-3405. Email: stjudeswv@stjudeswv.org. Web: stjudeswv.org.
School—32036 W. Lindero Canyon Rd., 91361-4270. Tel: 818-889-9483. Web: www.stjudeschool.org/school. Lay Teachers 15; Students 245.
Catechesis/Religious Program—Tel: 818-889-0612. Email: cindy@stjudeswv.org. Students 144.

WESTLAKE VILLAGE, VENTURA CO., ST. MAXIMILIAN KOLBE (1992) Revs. Michael Carroll; James J. Maher; Deacons John Kruer; Vince Tomkovicz.
Res.: 5801 Kanan Rd., 91362. Tel: 818-991-3915; Fax: 818-991-7152. Email: kolbe@stmaxchurch.org. Web: www.stmaxchurch.org.
Catechesis/Religious Program—Tel: 818-991-3915, Ext. 112. Students 505.

WHITTIER, LOS ANGELES CO.

1—ST. BRUNO (1955) Revs. Michael Reardon; James Bradley, S.D.S.; Deacons P. Michael Freeman; Bruce Sago, Pastoral Assoc.
Res.: 15740 Citrustree Rd., 90603. Tel: 562-947-5637; Fax: 562-943-3193. Email: stbruno@stbrunochurch.org. Web: www.stbrunochurch.org.
School—15700 Citrustree Rd., 90603. Tel: 562-943-8812; Fax: 562-943-2172. Web: www.saintbrunoschool.com. Lay Teachers 15; Students 314.
Catechesis/Religious Program—Tel: 562-943-2510; 562-947-5637. Email: re@stbrunochurch.org. Students 519.
Convent—10734 S. Widener Ave., 90603. Tel: 562-947-1177.

2—ST. GREGORY THE GREAT (1951) Revs. John S. Schiavonne; Finbarr Divine; Deacon Arturo Barragan.
Res.: 13935 Telegraph Rd., 90604. Tel: 562-941-0115; Fax: 562-941-3785.
School—13925 Telegraph Rd., 90604. Tel: 562-941-0750; Fax: 562-903-7325. Lay Teachers 13; Students 255.
Catechesis/Religious Program—Tel: 562-944-8311; Fax: 562-941-4380. Students 660.

3—ST. MARY OF THE ASSUMPTION (1893) Revs. Jose Luis Chavez, C.Ss.R.; Donald B. Willard, C.Ss.R.; Steven J. Nyl, C.Ss.R. In Res., Revs. Joseph Elliott, C.Ss.R. (Retired); Donald Liberty, C.Ss.R. (Retired); Arthur Frost, C.Ss.R. (Retired); William Adams, C.Ss.R. (Retired); Enrique Lopez, C.Ss.R. (Retired); Michael McAndrew, C.Ss.R.; Anthony Phuc Nguyen, C.Ss.R.
Res.: 7215 S. Newlin Ave., 90602-1266. Tel: 562-698-0107; Fax: 562-696-1617. Web: st-maryschurch.org.
School—7218 S. Pickering Ave., 90602. Tel: 562-698-0253; Fax: 562-698-0206. Lay Teachers 10; Students 190.
Catechesis/Religious Program—Tel: 562-693-3764. Email: drecruces@yahoo.com. Students 860.

WILMINGTON, LOS ANGELES CO.

1—HOLY FAMILY (1929), (Hispanic), Rev. Samuel Rendon (Mexico).
Res. & Pastoral Center: 1011 E. "L" St., 90744. Tel: 310-834-6333; Fax: 310-834-9038. Email: holyfamily@hfamwil.org.
School—1122 E. Robidoux St., 90744. Tel: 310-518-1440; Fax: 310-518-1257. Email: holyfmly@hfswilm.org. Web: www.hfswilm.org. Mrs. Carmen A. Orinoco-Hart, Prin. Lay Teachers 6; Students 110.
Catechesis/Religious Program—Tel: 310-549-0011. Students 588.

2—SS. PETER AND PAUL (1865) Revs. Raymond L. Perez, O.Praem.; Michael U. Perea, O.Praem.; Godfrey Bushmaker, O.Praem.
Res.: 515 W. Opp St., 90744. Tel: 310-834-5215; Fax: 310-834-4685. Email: sppc@sbcglobal.net. Web: www.sppc.us.
School—706 Bayview Ave., 90744. Tel: 310-834-5574; Fax: 310-834-1601. Email: spp_school@yahoo.com. Web: www.sppcatholicschool-.com. Lay Teachers 9; Students 180.
Catechesis/Religious Program—Students 390.

WINNETKA, LOS ANGELES CO., ST. JOSEPH THE WORKER (1956), (Hispanic—Vietnamese), Revs. Kevin E. Rettig; Hugo R. Neyra; Francis Ty Bui; Deacon Heriberto "Ed" Vega; Mike Stafford, Parish Business Mgr.
Res.: 19808 Cantlay St., 91306. Tel: 818-341-6634; Fax: 818-341-3875.
Parish Center—19808 Cantlay St., 91306. Web: www.sjwchurch.com.
School—19812 Cantlay St., 91306. Tel: 818-341-6616; Fax: 818-341-1102. Web: www.saintjosephtheworkerschool.net. Sr. Barbara Joseph Wilson, C.S.J., Prin. Lay Teachers 17; Students 296.
Catechesis/Religious Program—Tel: 818-998-4166. Web: www.sjwchurch.com. Students 591.

WOODLAND HILLS, LOS ANGELES CO.

1—ST. BERNARDINE OF SIENA (1962) Revs. Robert J. McNamara; Daniel A. Fox; Deacons Jerry Cellner; Dale Taufer; Steven Ellms; Jesus S. Pasos. In Res., Rev. Msgr. Richard Hayes Murray, Pastor Emeritus (Retired).
Res.: 24410 Calvert St., 91367. Tel: 818-888-8200; Fax: 818-888-5046. Web: www.stbernardine.org.
School—Tel: 818-340-2130; Fax: 818-340-3417. Lay Teachers 17; Students 317.
Catechesis/Religious Program—6061 Valley Circle Blvd., 91367. Tel: 818-340-1440. Students 419.

2—ST. MEL (1955) Rev. Msgr. Helmut A. Hefner; Revs. Benedict Anthony; Larry Neumeier.
Res.: 20870 Ventura Blvd., 91364. Tel: 818-340-6020; Fax: 818-340-0261. Email: parish@stmel.org. Web: www.stmelparish.org.
School—20874 Ventura Blvd., 91364. Tel: 818-340-1924; Fax: 818-347-4426. Web: www.stmel.org. Lay Teachers 34; Students 501.
Catechesis/Religious Program—Tel: 818-340-6020, Ext. 1022. Email: pandre@stmel.org. Students 270.

Chaplains of Public Institutions
Non-Catholic Hospitals/Institutions

LOS ANGELES. *Cedar Sinai Medical Center*. Vacant, Chap.
8700 Beverly Blvd., Rm. 2508, 90048. Tel: 310-855-5550; Fax: 310-967-0643.
L.A. City Fire Dept., Tel: 818-894-2261. Rev. Msgr. Sean B. Flanagan (Retired). Tel: 562-438-3826.
L.A. County Fire Dept. Rev. Robert A. Folbrecht, Chap. Tel: 626-960-1136.
L.A. County/University of Southern California Hospital.
Norris Cancer and USC University Hospital, St. Camillus Center for Pastoral Care, 1911 Zonal Ave., 90033. Tel: 323-225-4461; 213-223-9047 (AIDS Center); Fax: 323-225-9096. Revs. Christopher D. Ponnet, Chap., Robert J. Jones, C.M., Chap., Mark Martinez, Chap., Deacon Walter J. Hanson, Chap., Bro. Adam Bacerra, F.S.P., Chap., Sisters Mary Jean Ferry, B.V.M., Chap., Theresa Hann, O.S.F., Chap., Angela Pacheco, C.S.J., Chap., Martha Vega, S.S.S., Chap., Yolanda Vega, S.S.S., Chap., Leticia Delgado, Chap., Vu Ngo, Chap., William Rice, Chap., Manuel Torres, Chap.
L.A. Police Dept. Rev. Michael P. McCullough, Chap.
Employee Assistance Unit, 150 N. Los Angeles St., 90012. Tel: 213-485-0703.
Martin Luther King, Jr., Drew Medical Center, 12021 Wilmington Ave., 90059-3019. Rev. Don Richard Kribs, Chap. (Retired).
435 S. Occidental, 90057-1598. Tel: 213-388-3742 (Precious Blood Church).
Metropolitan Detention Center. (Federal Institution), 535 N. Alameda St., 90012. Tel: 213-253-9575. Vacant.

CAMARILLO. *Youth Correctional Facility, California Youth Authority*, 3100 Wright Rd., 93010-8307. Catherine Conneally-Salazar, Chap.

DOWNEY. *Rancho Los Amigos Medical Center*, 7601 E. Imperial Hwy., 90242. Rev. Msgr. John Anthony Fosselman, Chap. (Retired). Tel: 562-940-7257.

DUARTE. *City of Hope Medical Center*, 1500 E. Duarte Rd., 91010. Tel: 626-359-8911. Rev. Ramon Marti, Sch.P., Chap.

LANCASTER. *Immigration and Naturalization Service*, Mira Loma Facility, 45100 N. 60th St. W., 93536. Tel: 661-949-3811. Imelda Bermejo, Chap.

LOMPOC. *Lompoc Federal Correctional Institution*, 3600 Guard Rd., 93436-2705. Tel: 805-736-4154, Ext. 725. Rev. Michael D. Kirkness, Supvr. & Chap., Deacon John Burke, Chap. Federal Intensive Confinement Center.
US Penitentiary, 3901 Klein Rd., 93436. Tel: 805-735-2771, Ext. 450 &. Rev. Michael D. Kirkness, Supvr. & Chap., Deacon John Burke, Chap.
Vandenberg Air Force Base. Rev. David J. Ivey, Chap. Tel: 805-606-5773.
30SW/HC, 587 Utah St., Bldg. 16200, Vandenberg AFB, 93437-6309.

LONG BEACH. *Veterans Affairs Medical Center*. Revs. Leo M. Miller, O.M.I., Chap., Anselm Deehr, S.T., Michael Philen, C.M.F.
5901 E. 7th St., 90822. Tel: 562-494-5418.

NORWALK. *California Youth Authority*. Tom Moletteire, Chap.
Southern Youth Correction Reception, 13200 S. Bloomfield Ave., 90650. Tel: 562-868-9979, Ext. 2467.
Metropolitan State Hospital. Vacant. Tel: 310-863-7011.
11400 S. Norwalk Blvd., 90650. Tel: 562-651-4311.

POINT MUGU. *Naval Air Station*. Rev. Adrian R. Gervacio, LCDR, CHC, USNR.
Bldg. 121, Code NASCG, 93042. Tel: 805-989-7967.

POMONA. *Frank D. Lanterman Developmental Center*, 3530 W. Pomona Blvd., 91768. Tel: 909-595-1221, Ext. 7162. P.O. Box 100, 91769. Tel: 909-444-7162. Sr. Nuala Ryan, S.S.L., Chap.

PORT HUENEME. *Naval Construction Battalion Center*. Rev. Adrian R. Gervacio.
NCBC Code CBCHP, 1000 23rd Ave., 93042. Tel: 805-982-4358.
SAN PEDRO. *Fort MacArthur Annex*. Rev. Michael J. DiRenzo, 61-ABG/HC.
Chaplain's Office, 325 Challenger Way, Ste. 1901, LA AFB, El Segundo, 90245-5677. Tel: 310-363-1956.
Immigration and Naturalization Service, San Pedro Service Processing Center, 2001 Seaside Ave., 90731. Tel: 310-241-2347. Imelda Bermejo.
SEPULVEDA. *Veterans Administration Medical Center*. Rev. Patrick J. O'Hagan, SS.CC. Tel: 818-895-9322.
16111 Plummer St., 91343-2099.
TERMINAL ISLAND. *Federal Correctional Institution*. Rev. Henry L. Hernanco, Contract Chap., 1299 Seaside Ave., San Pedro, 90731. Tel: 626-918-8314.
1299 Seaside Ave., San Pedro, 90731-0207. Tel: 626-918-8314.
TORRANCE. *L.A. County-Harbor-U.C.L.A. Medical Center*, 1000 W. Carson, 90509. Tel: 310-222-2345; 310-222-2167 (Catholic Chap. Office). Vacant, 1000 W. Carson, 90509. Tel: 310-222-2345; 310-222-2167 Catholic Chap. Office.
21900 S. Main St., Carson, 90745. Tel: 310-835-7161 (St. Philomena Parish).
WEST LOS ANGELES. *Chaplain Service*, 11301 Wilshire Blvd. 691/125, 90099-5786. Tel: 310-268-3391. Rev. Max Saldua, Chap.
Veterans Administration Wadsworth Hospital Center. Rev. Francis Kelly (Retired). Tel: 310-824-4312.

Restorative Justice

LOS ANGELES. *L.A. Juvenile Detention Facilities*, Central Juvenile Hall, 1605 Eastlake Ave., 90033. Tel: 323-226-8530. Janne Shirley, Chap.
MacLaren Hall. Vacant.
Dorothy Kirby Center. Dwain Miller, Chap. Tel: 323-981-4301.
L.A. Men's Central Jail, 441 Bauchet St., 90012. Tel: 213-974-8081. Rev. George E. Horan, Chap., Deacon Paulino Jaurez-Ramirez, Chap., Patricia L. Bartlett, Chap., Vincent Colavitti, Chap., Sr. Patricia Geoghegan, D.C., Chap.
Metropolitan Detention Center, 535 N. Alameda St., 90053. Tel: 213-253-9575. Vacant. (Federal Institution)
Office of Restorative Justice, 2049 S. Santa Fe Ave., 90021-2919. Tel: 213-438-4820; Fax: 213-438-4830. Rev. George E. Horan, Co-Dir. Tel: 213-438-4820, Ext. 14, Javier E. Stauring, Co-Dir. Tel: 213-438-4820, Ext. 13.
Twin Towers Correctional Facility I, 450 Bauchet St., 90063. Tel: 213-893-5241; Fax: 213-830-0907. Gerardo F. Gomez, Chap.
CAMARILLO. *Youth Correctional Facility*, 3100 Wright Rd., 93010. Tel: 805-278-3746. Catherine Conneally-Salazar.
Twin Towers Correctional Facility II, 450 Bauchet St., 90063. Tel: 213-893-5152; Fax: 213-830-0907. Dennis Gibbs.
DOWNEY. *Los Padrinos Juvenile Hall*, 7285 Quill Dr., 90242. Tel: 562-940-8711; 562-940-8712. Sr. Teresa Doherty, R.S.C.
LANCASTER. *California State Prison, L.A. County*, 44750 60th St. W., 93536-7620. Tel: 805-729-2000, Ext. 6129. Rev. Thomas White, Chap.
Challenger Youth Memorial Center, 5300 West Ave. I, 93536. Tel: 805-940-4165; 805-940-4166. Samuel Smolinsky, Chap.
LYNWOOD. *Century Regional Detention Facility*, 11705 S. Alameda St., 90262. Tel: 323-357-5114. Sr. Catherine Marie Bazar, O.P., Chap. (Women)
NORWALK. *Southern Youth Correctional Reception*, 13200 S. Bloomfield Ave., 90650. Tel: 562-868-9979, Ext. 2467. Tom Moletteire, Chap.
OJAI. *Ojai Men's Honor Farm*, 370 W. Baldwin Rd., 93023. Tel: 805-649-6020. Margaret Oberon, Chap. Tel: 805-654-5087.
Ojai Women's Jail Farm, 370 W. Baldwin Rd., 93023. Tel: 805-649-3020. Margaret Oberon, Chap. Tel: 805-654-5087.
SANTA BARBARA. *Los Prietos Boy's Camp*, Star Rte., 93105-9722. Tel: 805-898-7008. Marciano Avilla, Chap.
Santa Barbara County Jail, 4436A Calle Real, 93110. Tel: 805-898-7008. Marciano Avilla, Chap.
Santa Barbara Juvenile Hall, 4500 Hollister Ave., 93111. Tel: 805-681-5334. Marciano Avilla, Chap.
SANTA MARIA. *Juvenile Hall*, 812-B W. Foster Rd., 93454. Tel: 805-681-5334. Marciano Avilla, Chap.
SANTA PAULA. *Santa Paula Jail*, 600 S. Todd Rd., 93060. Tel: 805-933-8564. Margaret Oberon, Chap. Tel: 805-654-5087.
SAUGUS. *North County Correctional Facility*, 29340 The Old Rd., 91350. Tel: 661-295-7800, Ext. 5217. Gonzalo De Vivero, Chap.
Pitchess Detention Center, 29300 The Old Rd., 91350.
Medium South. Alexis Quintana, Chap. Tel: 661-295-8805, Ext. 3020.
Medium North. Gonzalo De Vivero, Chap.
Maximum East. Eric Z. Dersom. Tel: 661-295-8815, Ext. 3337.
SYLMAR. *Barry J. Nidorf Juvenile Hall*, 16350 Filbert St., 91342. Tel: 818-364-2021. Janne Shirley, Chap.
THOUSAND OAKS. *East County Jail*, 2101 E. Olsen Rd., 93162. Tel: 805-933-8564. Margaret Oberon, Chap. Tel: 805-654-5087.
VENTURA. *Colston Treatment Center*, 315 N. Hillmont Ave., 93003. Tel: 805-652-5721. Margaret Oberon, Chap.
Ventura County Jail, 800 S. Victoria Ave., 93009. Margaret Oberon, Chap. Tel: 805-654-5087.
Ventura Juvenile Hall-Clifton Tatum Center, 380 N. Hillmont Ave., 93003. Tel: 805-652-5727. Margaret Oberon, Chap.
Ventura Juvenile Restitution Project, 381 Hospital Rd., 93003. Tel: 805-652-6594. Margaret Oberon, Chap.

Camps

LOS ANGELES. *Juvenile Probation Camps*. Thomas Bleich, Coord. Tel: 818-889-0260.
Camp C.B. Afflerbaugh, 6331 N. Stephens Ranch Rd., La Verne, 91750. Tel: 909-596-0686. Connie Arambula, Chap.
Camp Dorothy Kirby Center, 1500 S. McDonnell Ave., 90022. Tel: 323-981-4301. Dwain Miller, Chap.
Camp David Gonzales, 1301 N. Las Virgines Rd., Calabasas, 91302. Tel: 818-222-1192. Ralph Sariego, Chap.
Camp Holton, 12653 N. Little Tujunga Canyon Rd., San Fernando, 91342. Vacant.
Camp Kilpatrick, 427 S. Encinal Canyon Rd., Malibu, 90265. Tel: 818-889-1353. Jim Graham, Chap.
Camp McLaren Children's Center. Closed., 4024 Durfee Rd., El Monte, 91732. Tel: 213-438-4820. Vacant.
Camp Kenyon J. Scudder, 287 N. Bouquet Canyon Rd., Saugus, 91350. Tel: 661-296-9811. Aurora Montejano, Chap.
Camp Mendenhall, 42230 Lake Hughes Rd., Lake Hughes, 93532. Tel: 661-724-1211. Alfred E. Miller, Chap.
Camp Miller, 433 S. Encinal Canyon Rd., Malibu, 90265. Tel: 818-889-0260. Thomas Bleich, Chap.
Camp John Munz, 42220 Lake Hughes Rd., Lake Hughes, 93532. Tel: 661-724-1211. Alfred E. Miller, Chap.
Camp Paige, 6601 N. Stephens Ranch Rd., La Verne, 91750. Tel: 909-593-4921. Frank Cunningham, Chap., Cindy Cunningham, Chap.
Camp Rockey, 1900 N. Sycamore Canyon Rd., San Dimas, 91773. Tel: 909-599-2391. Ron Atkinson, Chap.
Camp Routh, 12500 Big Tujunga Rd., Tujunga, 91042. Tel: 818-352-4407. Bro. Kevin Cunniff, C.F.X., Chap.
Camp Scott, 28700 N. Bouquet Canyon Rd., Saugus, 91350. Tel: 661-296-8500. Deacon Pete Wilson, Chap., Cecilia Smith, Chap., Larry Smith, Chap. (Girls)

On Duty Outside the Archdiocese:
Rev. Msgr.—
Spiteri, Laurence J.
Revs.—
Beck, Lawrence J.
O'Shea, Patrick
Palacios, Joseph M., Ph.D.
Vega, Richard
Young, Gerald A.

Graduate Studies:
Revs.—
Miranda, R. Dario
Ortiz, Marco Antonio
Pham, Thinh Duc
Szkredka, Slawomir

Foreign Mission:
Rev.—
Joy, Laurence (Retired)

Hospital Chaplains:
Rev. Msgrs.—
Hill, Charles E., Chap. (Retired), St. Mary Medical Center CHW Southern California
O'Connell, Timothy P., Chap. (Retired), Jeanne Jugan Residence
Revs.—
Arbelaez, Ernesto, S.J., Chap., Santa Teresita Medical Center
Azu, Edmund (La), Chap., St. Vincent Medical Center
Comerford, Patrick, Chap., St. John of God Hospital, Los Angeles & St. John's Health Center
de Souza, Owen, Chap., St. Mary Medical Center CHW Southern California
Dow, Emanuel, Chap., St. Mary Medical Center CHW Southern California
Gelfer, Peter, Chap., St. John's Regional Medical Center
Halley, James L., Chap., St. Francis Medical Center
Lewis, Eric Anthony, Chap., Citrus Valley Medical Center-Queen of the Valley Hospital, West Corina
Mallin, Peter, O.F.M.Conv., Chap., Providence Little Company of Mary Hospital
Mayor, Paul, Chap., St. Vincent Medical Center
McNulty, Gerard J., Chap., Mike O'Callaghan Federal Hospital, North Las Vegas
Mejia, Jose, Chap. Children's Hospital, Los Angeles
Morris, Joseph, S.J., Chap., St. Joseph's Health & Retirement Center
Nelliparambil, Theophane, O.D.D., Chap., St. Francis Medical Center
Onyenobi, Christopher, Chap., Little Company of Mary-San Pedro
Park, Shin-Hwa, Chap., St. Vincent Medical Center
Ponnet, Christopher D., Chap., Los Angeles County USC Medical Center, Los Angeles
Roman, Julio, Chap. (Retired) St. Vincent Medical Center, Los Angeles
Sigler, John W., Chap. St. Mary Medical Center, Long Beach & St. Mary Medical Center CHW Southern California
Valdez, Pedro G., Chap., Providence Holy Cross Medical Center, Mission Hills
Whatley, Francis, O.Ss.T., Chap., Nazareth House
Sisters—
DeLeon, Grace, S.S.C., Chap., St. Francis Medical Center
Jones, Janice, C.H.S., Chap., St. Francis Medical Center
Nguyen, Van, L.H.C., Chap., St. Francis Medical Center
Rojo, Marth, S.P., Chap., St. Francis Medical Center
Sanchez, Laura Paz, S.S.P., Chap., St. Francis Medical Center
Bros.—
Bui, Thaddeus, O.H., Chap., St. John of God Retirement & Care Center
Hirbe, Richard A., f.s.p., Chap., St. Francis Medical Center
Deacon—
Nawrocik, Zenon, Chap., Marian Medical Center
Bigler, Kelly, Chap., St. Vincent Medical Center
Cosman, Patricia, Chap., Providence Little Company of Mary Hospital
Galan, Cesar, Chap., St. Francis Medical Center
Glynn, Darrah, Chap., Providence Little Company of Mary Hospital
Kiley, Shawn, Chap., Providence Holy Cross Medical Center
Landry, Tom, Chap., Providence St. Joseph Medical Center
Turrentine, Fleeta, Chap., Little Company of Mary Sub Acute Care Center
West, George, Chap., St. John's Pleasant Valley Hospital
Wright, Hillary, Chap., Providence Little Company of Mary Hospital

---

VA Chaplains:
Rev.—
McNulty, Gerard J.

Military Chaplains:
Revs.—
Bautista, Jose A.
Llanos, Philip S.
Lowe, William C.B.

On Sick Leave:
Revs.—
Cavanagh, James
de Souza, Owen
Esteban, Pedro Antonio
Griffin, Noel
McDonnell, Anthony
Nuanez, Anthony
Russo, Frank, Jr.
Wolkovits, Paul Dennis

On Administrative Leave:
Rev. Msgrs.—
Loomis, Richard A.
Van Liefde, Christian M.
Revs.—
Cronin, Sean
Granadino, David F.
Juarez, Robert Jesus
Labonte, Roger
McGowan, Timothy
Messenger, William P.
Prado, Rodolfo

On Active Leave:
Revs.—
Collins, John Michal
Tucker, James
Woodland, Stephen

In Transition:
Rev.—
Thompson, Jerald Wayne

Retired:
Most Revs.—
Sartoris, Joseph M., D.D., V.G., 1988 Rolling Vista Dr., #21, Lomita, 90717.
Ward, John J., Archdiocesan Catholic Center, 3424 Wilshire Blvd., 90010-2202.
Rev. Msgrs.—
Acton, John A., 627 Avenida Sevilla, Unit C, Laguna Woods, 92653.
Cokus, Joseph J., 3 La Serena, Irvine, 92612.
Colberg, James Philip, 414 E. Church St., Santa Maria, 93454.
Cosgrove, Joseph, 7845 Lily Trotter St., North Las Vegas, NV 89084.
Diomartich, Felix S., Nazareth House, 3333 Manning Ave., 90012-2299.
Donnelly, Lawrence Edward, 1065 W. Lomita Blvd., Space 411, Harbor City, 90710.
Doyle, Thomas, 3618 Valihi Way, Glendale, 91208.
English, Tobias P., St. Andrew, 140 Chestnut St., Pasadena, 91103-3896.
Flanagan, Sean B., St. Bartholomew, 252 Granada Ave., Long Beach, 90803-5518.
Foley, John Kieran, Holy Redeemer, 2411 Montrose Ave., Montrose, 91020-1419.
Fosselman, John Anthony, Nazareth House, 3333 Manning Ave., 90064-4804.
Frilot, Eugene P., Incarnation, 1001 N. Brand, Glendale, 91202-2979.
George, Alexander C., P.O. Box 2208, Blue Jay, 92317.
George, Joseph, P.O. Box 2208, Blue Jay, 92317.
Gibson, Lawrence J., 2023 Via Mariposa E., Unit A, Laguna Woods, 92653.
Gilb, Eugene A., St. John the Fisher, 5448 Crest Rd., Rancho Palos Verdes, 90274-5097.
Gomez, Henry, Proto Notary Apostolic, 1401 Pebbledon St., Monterey Park, 91754.
Healy, Peter C., St. Robert Bellarmine, 133 N. Fifth St., Burbank, 91501-2178.
Hernandez, Alfred, P.O. Box 777, Cedar Glen, 92321.
Hill, Charles E., 517 E. 220th St., Carson, 90745.
Howard, Robert E., P.O. Box 2354, Palm Springs, 92263-2354.
Hughes, John Charles, St. Mary Magdelen, 2532 Ventura Blvd., Camarillo, 93010-6649.
Johnson, Edward Joseph, Nazareth House, 3333 Manning Ave., 90064-4804.
Killeen, Michael F., St. Elizabeth Ann Seton, 1835 Larkvane Rd., Rowland Heights, 91748-2501.
Lenihan, Michael, V.F., Proto Notary Apostolic, St. Lawrence Martyr, 1900 S. Prospect Ave., Redondo Beach, 90277-6003.
Leser, William J., C.B., S.T.B., 18550 W. Vincennes St., Apt. 108, Northridge, 91324.
Loftus, Padraic, 22046 Providencia St., Woodland Hills, 91364.
McCabe, Vincent, Santa Teresita Church, 819 Buena Vista St., Duarte, 91010.
McGovern, Thomas, 564 Bellflower Blvd., #309, Long Beach, 90814.
McNulty, Patrick, 2501 W. Ave. 33, 90065-2892.
Mihan, John A., 635 S. Hobart Blvd., Apt. 101, 90005.
Mulcahy, Donal, Our Lady of the Assumption, 3175 Telegraph Rd., Ventura, 93003-3283.
Murray, Richard Hayes, St. Bernardine of Siena, 24410 Calvert St., Woodland Hills, 91367-1099.
Naughton, John Thomas, 2033 Mayorca Dr., Oxnard, 93035.
Navin, Cyril, St. Cyril of Jerusalem, 4601 Firmament Ave., Encino, 91436-3108.
O'Connell, Timothy P., Jeanne Jugan Residence, 2100 S. Western Ave., San Pedro, 90732.
O'Gorman, Charles Francis, Santa Clara Church, 323 S. E St., Oxnard, 93030-5835.
O'Keefe, William Joseph, Our Lady of Refuge, 5195 Stearns St., Long Beach, 90815-2901.
O'Leary, Lawrence, St. Martin of Tours, 11967 Sunset Blvd., 90049-4220.
O'Reilly, Peter A., 722 Alden Rd., Claremont, 91711.
O'Sullivan, Peter, Marycrest Manor, 10664 St. James Dr., Culver City, 90230-5498.
O'Toole, William P., All Souls, 17 S. Electric Ave., Alhambra, 91801-1992.
Parnassas, George John, St. Victor, 8634 Holloway Dr., West Hollywood, 90069-2304.
Rawden, John A., P.O. Box 802, Santa Barbara, 93102.
Reilly, Patrick, St. Robert Bellarmine, 135 N. 5th St., Burbank, 91501-2178.
Renehan, Edmond M., V.F., St. Clare Church, 27341 Camp Plenty Rd., Santa Clarita, 91351-2645.
Richey, Terrence, St. Basil, 637 S. Kingsley Dr., 90005-2392.
Rodriguez, Benigno Antonio, 12103 Bayla St., Norwalk, 90650.
Royer, Ronald Edmund, 40708-B Balch Park Rd., Springville, 93265.
Schmit, Jerome Lucien, St. Anthony, 1901 S. San Gabriel Blvd., San Gabriel, 91776-3992.
Segaric, John, Trg Sv Stosije 1, Zador 23000 Croatia.
Sheridan, John Virgilius, Our Lady of Malibu, 3625 Winter Canyon Rd., Malibu, 90265-4834.
Staunton, Patrick Joseph, St. Joseph Church, 555 N. Glendora Ave., La Puente, 91744-5112.
Tseu, Andrew Stanislaus, St. Madeleine, 931 E. Kingsley Ave., Pomona, 91767-5098.
Van Son, Henry Adrian, 5871 Cathedral Oaks Rd., Goleta, 93117.
Walsh, Michael, Monea, Youghal, County Cork Ireland.
Won, John P. H., KKOP Dongne Center, 37885 Hwy. 76 S., Temecula, 92592.
Young, John Melvin, 3909 Reche Rd., #116, Fallbrook, 92028.
Zimmerman, Roland George, Annunciation, 1307 E. Longdon Ave., Arcadia, 91006-5597.
Revs.—
Acton, Thomas M., St. Maria Regina Church, 2150 W. 135th St., Gardena, 90249-2498.
Bailon, Abelardo B.M., 11764 Broadfield Dr., La Mirada, 90638.
Bebek, Dominic L., 114 Ocean Ave., Seal Beach, 90740.
Belletty, Emile Ignatius, 22039 Mariposa Ave., Torrance, 90502.
Biroschak, Robert V., J.C.L., 70 Parkwood Rd., Stratford, CT 06614.
Boudreau, Thomas Francis, Nazareth House, 3333 Manning Ave., 90064-4804.
Bouska, Jerome Anthony, St. Basil, 637 S. Kingsley Dr., 90005-2392.
Bradley, Robert M., 108 Courtside Dr., Butler, PA 16001-2466.
Brincat, George, 37A Mons. Farrugia St., Victoria Gogo VCT 105 Malta.
Buhr, Eugene S., St. Joseph Church, 11901 S. Acacia Ave., Hawthorne, 90250-3083.
Byrne, Robert Paul, Nazareth House, 3333 Manning Ave., 90064-4804.
Carey, Richard W., P.O. Box 678, Tecate, 91980.
Cassidy, Francis J., Immaculate Conception Church, 740 S. Shamrock Dr., Monrovia, 91016-0510.
Cavanagh, Brian M., Sacred Heart Church, 344 W. Workman St., Covina, 91723-3345.
Ciordia, Pedro M., Resurrection Church, 3324 E. Opal St., 90023-2917.
Colborn, Francis R., S.T.D., 333 Old Mill Rd., #236, Santa Barbara, 93110.
Cooley, John Edward, 31402 Paseo del Mar, Laguna Niguel, 92677-2745.
Coronado, Genero, 2505 W. Foothill Blvd., Apt. 145, San Bernardino, 92410.
Crowe, Hugh, St. Ann Church, 2302 Riverdale Ave., 90031-1133.
Daly, John J., Holy Trinity, 3722 Boyce Ave., 90039-1810.
De Dominici, Lorenzo, Mary Star of the Sea, 870 W. 8th St., San Pedro, 90731-3091.
Delaney, Matthew S., 13700 El Dorado Dr., Seal Beach, 90740.
Doran, Brian D., St. Ambrose Church, 1281 N. Fairfax Ave., West Hollywood, 90046-5205.
Duc Minh, Joseph N., 601 S. Dennis St., Santa Ana, 92704.
Elis, Tomas Alfonso, St. Mark University Parish, 6550 Picasso Rd., Goleta, 93117-4698.
Fahey, John Peter, 1931 Poli St., Ventura, 93001.
Fernandes, Roque A.D., St. Frances of Rome Church, 501 E. Foothill Blvd., Azusa, 91702.
Ferrer, Peter C., 11544 Jerry St., Cerritos, 90703.
Fitzgerald, John B., Nazareth House, 3333 Manning Dr., 90064-4804.
Ford, Harold LeRoy, St. Joseph, 6220 E. Willow St., Long Beach, 90815-2295.
Ford, James Michael, P.O. Box 2231, Palm Springs, 92263.
Fremgen, Edward George, 4849 Hersholt Ave., Long Beach, 90808.
Gaffney, Joseph P., 927 Angelo Dr., National City, 91950.
Gannon, Patrick J., 2075 Paseo de Anza, Vista, 92084.
Glynn, Thomas Joseph, Our Lady of Refuge Church, 5195 Stearns St., Long Beach, 90815-2901.
Gorman, Rody Ignatius, St. Matthias Church, 7125 Mission Pl., Huntington Park, 90255-5299.
Guerrini, Roderic M., Nazareth House, 333 Manning Ave., 90064-4804.
Gutting, John C., Nazareth House, 3333 Manning Ave., 90064-4804.
Haefeli, Joaquin C., St. Ignatius Loyola Church, 322 N. Ave. 61, 90042-3499.
Hicarte, Mateo H., 138 S. Pacific Ave., Glendale, 91204.
Iglesias, Fernando Gonzalez, 23505 Evening Snow, Moreno Valley, 92557.
Janowski, Rock J., 1241 S. Petit Ave., #5, Ventura, 93004.
Johnson, Henry Joseph, 4676 Admiralty Way, Ste. 101, Marina Del Rey, 90292.
Joy, Laurence, P.O. Box 435090, San Ysidro, 92143.
Kelly, Francis, 700 E. Ocean Blvd., Unit 1806, Long Beach, 90802.
Kelly, Paul Maurice, 11660 Church St., Apt. 422, Rancho Cucamonga, 91730.
Kolling, James L., Visitation Church, 6561 W. 88th St., 90045-3716.
Kribs, Don Richard, 22221 S. Bloomfield Ave., #21, Cypress, 90630.
Landreau, Edward Joseph, St. Frances of Rome, 501 E. Foothill Blvd., Azusa, 91702.
Larkin, Kevin John, St. Francis de Sales, 13360 Valleyheart Dr., Sherman Oaks, 91423-3287.
Lee, Joseph P., P.O. Box 1254, Gardena, 90249.
Luck, Robert O., 200 E. Racquet Club Rd., Unit 45, Palm Springs, 92262.
Madrigal, Ildefonso M., Mary Health of the Sick Hospital, 2929 Theresa Dr., Newbury Park, 91320.
Maechler, Edmund Francis, 18401 Delaware St., Huntington Beach, 92648-1415.
Martin, Diosdado, 1808 S. Palm Ave., Alhambra, 91803.
Mayer, Jules Anthony, Nazareth House, 3333 Manning Ave., 90064-4804.
McHugh, Patrick Joseph, Nativity, 1447 Engracia Ave., Torrance, 90501-3234.
Meisel, Gerald A., St. Matthew, 672 Temple Ave., Long Beach, 90814-1297.
Menke, Paul F., St. Thomas More, 2510 S. Fremont Ave., Alhambra, 91803-4398.
Merino, Santiago James, 959 LaDeney Dr., Ontario, 91762.
Meskill, Patrick A., Mary Health of the Sick Hospital, 2929 Theresa Dr., Newbury Park, 91320.
Meskill, Thomas A., Mary Health of the Sick Hospital, 2929 Theresa Dr., Newbury Park, 91320.
Miskella, Richard, Rathimney Gusserane, County Wexford Ireland.
Murray, John D., St. Francis Xavier Church, 3801 Scott Rd., Burbank, 91504-1799.
Nocero, Pascal Francis, P.O. Box 279, Oak View, 93022.
O'Grady, James F., Visitation Church, 6561 W. 88th St., 90045-3716.
O'Grady, James Francis, Glen Keen, Louisburg, County Mayo, Ireland.
O'Leary, Niall Finbarr, Holy Family Church, 1527 Fremont Ave., South Pasadena, 91030-3736.
O'Mahony, Maurice K., Our Lady of Mount Carmel, 1300 E. Valley Rd., Santa Barbara, 93108-1294.
O'Neill, Jeremiah, 2100 W. Carlos Ave., Alhambra, 91803-4321.
O'Ryan, Colm, Good Shepherd, 505 N. Bedford Dr., Beverly Hills, 90210-3298.
O'Shea, Michael, 11 Taobh Lin, Kenmare, County Kerry Ireland.
O'Sullivan, Daniel A., Sacred Heart, 10800 Henderson Rd., Ventura, 93004-1895.
O'Sullivan, Thomas Carrol, Our Lady of Mount Carmel, 1300 E. Valley Rd., Santa Barbara, 93108-1294.
Peacha, Thomas James, 13361 St. Andress Dr., 129 C, Seal Beach, 90740.
Penaloza, Jorge A., St. Francis Xavier Church, 4245 Acaia Ave., Pico Rivera, 90660-1679.
Phelan, Cornelius Noel, St. Basil, 637 S. Kingsley Dr., 90005-2392.
Potthoff, Donald William, St. Denis, 2151 Diamond Bar Blvd., Diamond Bar, 91765-2860.
Raymundo, Gregorio G., 2105 Sylvia St., West Covina, 91792-2441.
Rodriguez, Lawrence, Soto y Amio, Santovenio de San Marcos, Leon CP24125 Spain.
Roman, Julio, P.O. Box 226934, 90022.
Romero, Gilbert Claude, 13220 Southport Ln., #170-E, Seal Beach, 90740-3361.
Romero, Juan R. (SB), 2347 Los Patos Dr., Palm Springs, 92264.
Rothe, James A., P.O. Box 692, Bridgeport, 93517-0692.
Sagardoy, Angel, St. John of God Retirement Center, 2468 S. St. Andrews Pl., 90018.
Scott, Alfonso A., St. Cyprian, 4714 Clark Ave., Long Beach, 90808-1101.

Soto, Edward P., St. Rose of Lima Church, 4450 E. 60th St., Maywood, 90270-3198.
Stehly, Thomas J., 9432 S. Bloomfield Ave., Cypress, 90630.
Steinbock, Leo E., P.O. Box 1950, Covina, 91722.
Suquilvide, Abel, Nazareth House, 3333 Manning Ave., 90064-4804.
Thompson, Jerome H., Windsor Court, 201 Sunrise Way, Palm Springs, 92262.
Toal, James Aloysius, 10908 Moorpark St., North Hollywood, 91602.
Tsang, Peter, 1739 Bolanos Ave., Rowland Heights, 91748.
Walker, Earl Gordon, Cathedral Chapel, 922 S. Detroit St., 90036-4812.
Walker, Gerald Bernard, 2020 Via Mariposa E., Apt. C, Laguna Woods, 92637-0890.
Weible, Thomas C., St. Peter the Apostle, 11 Prince St., Provincetown, MA 02657.

Permanent Deacons:
Abalos, Roland, St. Finbar Church, Burbank
Abrera, Jaime, St. Francis Xavier Church, Burbank
Adams, Emile, St. Bernadette, Los Angeles
Adams, John Rodger, Our Lady of the Assumption Church, Ventura
Aguirre, Ancelmo, Old Mission Santa Ines, Lompoc
Aispuro, Genaro, St. Joseph, Carpinteria
Alexander, Hosea, Sr., Holy Name of Jesus, Los Angeles
Allen, John Paul, (Retired), Corpus Christi, Pacific Palisades
Andrade, J. Trinidad, Holy Cross Church, Moorpark
Aranda, Fernando, Jr., San Gabriel Mission, San Gabriel
Ascencio, Juan Francisco, St. Cecilia, Los Angeles
Asmar, George, Immaculate Heart of Mary, Santa Clarita
Austin, Alfred H., Holy Name of Mary, San Dimas
Baker, Charles, St. Linus, Norwalk
Baker, William F., (Retired)
Banda, Mark Lawrence, San Buenaventura Mission, Ventura
Barajas, Jr., Henry, Our Lady of Guadalupe, Oxnard
Barragan, Arturo, St. Gregory the Great, Whittier
Barragan, Ricardo, Immaculate Conception, Oxnard
Barrera, Jose Oscar, Sagrado Corazon, Compton
Barry, John William, Sacred Heart, Ventura
Bautista, Rolando, Holy Trinity, Los Angeles
Becker, Gary Earle, (Retired), San Roque, Santa Barbara
Bednar, George T., St. Mary Magdalen, Camarillo
Benalcazar, Eudoro G., All Souls, Alhambra
Bernal, Daniel, St. Thomas the Apostle, Los Angeles
Berumen, Ricardo, St. John Neumann, Santa Maria
Betliskey, Michael Joseph, St. Joseph, Carpinteria
Blanco, Raul, St. Louis de Montfort, Santa Maria
Bolduc, William, St. Dorothy, Glendora
Boucher, Richard, St. Cornelius, Long Beach
Brandlin, Thomas E., M.N.A., Chap., Respect Life
Bravo, Anthony J., (Retired)
Brown, Derek A., American Marytrs, Manhattan Beach
Butler, Ronald, Sacred Heart, Covina
Cabello, Luis, Holy Cross, Santa Barbara
Cabello, Rodolfo Naranjo, Holy Cross, Santa Barbara
Calderon, Gregory Robert, Our Lady of Sorrows, Santa Barbara
Camacho, Raymond, St. Didacus, Sylmar
Cantillo Romero, Juan Bautista, St. Thomas the Apostle, Los Angeles
Caputo, Edward E., St Mary, Quartz Hill
Carlson, Dennis Dean, Holy Trinity, San Pedro
Carmody, Richard, St. Louis de Montford, Santa Maria
Castillo, Alfonso, St. Benedict, Montebello
Castorena, John G., Santa Clara, Oxnard
Catipon, Gus, Cathedral of Our Lady of the Angeles, Los Angeles
Cellner, Jerry, St. Bernardine of Siena, Woodland Hills
Charters, John, Sacred Heart, Lancaster
Chavez, Gilbert M., Annunciation, Arcadia
Chavez, Manuel, St. Anthony, San Gabriel
Chavez, Raul, Guardian Angel, Pacoima
Chevez, Roberto I., Our Lady of Guadalupe, Irwindale
Chu, Peter, St. Elizabeth Ann Seton, Rowland Heights
Clements, Brian, St. Peter Claver, Simi Valley
Conenen, Jerry, Our Lady of Malibu, Malibu
Conrey, Fred, Immaculate Conception, Monrovia
Copon, Ricardo Pareja, Jr., Mary Star of the Sea, Oxnard
Corcios, Oscar A., Our Lady of the Rosary, Paramount
Cordero, Ruben A., Guardian Angel, Pacoima
Crisafulli, Nino D., (Retired), Mary Star of the Sea, San Pedro
Crowley, James, Assumption of the Blessed Virgin Mary, Pasadena
Cunneen, John T., St. Linus, Norwalk
Curran, Nicholas P., Holy Cross, Santa Barbara
De Los Reyes, Carlito, St. Barnabas, Long Beach
Denisac, Charles M., Jr., Our Lady of Perpetual Help, Downey
Dieter, Frank, St. Lawrence Martyr, Redondo Beach
Dionne, Ireneaus, (Retired), St. Mary Coptic, Los Angeles
Dornan, Richard, St. Jude, Westlake Village
Duke, Oscar M., (Retired), St. Anthony, Oxnard
Dumlao, Felix, St. Anthony of Padua, Gardena
Egnatuk, James A., St. Lawrence Martyr Church, Redondo Beach
Ellms, Steven, St. Bernardine of Siena, West Hills
Elsey, Ken, Santa Rosa, San Fernando
Escovedo, Arthur, (Retired), Our Lady of the Assumption, Claremont
Espana, Salvador, St. Elisabeth, Van Nuys
Estey, Marvin, Holy Name of Mary, San Dimas
Estrada, Armando, St. Stephen, Monterey Park
Estrada, David J., St. Benedict, Montebello
Fargo, Robert, Blessed Junipero Serra, Camarillo
Farley, James M., (Retired), Our Lady of the Assumption, Ventura
Faubert, Roger, Our Lady of Refuge, Long Beach
Fermin, Gilberto, Our Lady of Guadalupe, Santa Barbara
Fernandez, Louis Homero, St. Rose of Lima, Simi Valley
Fernando, Flores, Sacred Heart, Ventura
Fido, Leonard, Our Lady of Victory, Compton
Finocchiaro, Michael, St. Dominic, Los Angeles
Fitzgerald, James, M.D., St. Mary of the Assumption, Whittier
Flores, Ricardo L., (Retired), St. Gerard Majella, Los Angeles
Freeman, P. Michael, St. Bruno, Whittier
Frias, Sam, St. John the Baptist de la Salle, Granada Hills
Fry, Ralph M., (Retired)
Galido, Juan, Jr., Our Lady of Lourdes, Northridge
Gallardo, Jose Alberto, Our Lady of Guadalupe, Santa Barbara
Gallegos, Jose, St. Elizabeth, Van Nuys
Garcia, George Angel, St. Anthony, Oxnard
Garcia, William J., Mary Star of the Sea, San Pedro
Garcia Bejarano, Marco Antonio, Christ the King, Los Angeles
Garcia Cruz, Juan Rogelio, St. Frances of Rome, Azusa
Garza, Ciro Augusto, St. Martha Catholic Church, Huntington Park
Gath, Don, St. Joseph, Long Beach
Gibboney, Carl, St. Bartholomew Church, Long Beach
Girard, Joseph, St. Mark, Venice
Godinez, Jose Arturo, Our Lady of Guadalupe, Oxnard
Gonzalez, Arturo, Our Lady of Sorrows, Santa Barbara
Gonzalez, Doroteo, Epiphany, South El Monte
Gorman, Christopher, St. Thomas Aquinas, Ojai
Gueringer, Ludger Adam, (Retired), Blessed Junipero Serra, Camarillo
Guerra, Mario, St Raymond, Downey
Guerra, Ruben, St. Joseph, La Puente
Guerrero, Jaime S., St. Louis of France, LaPuente
Guiao, Rey, Our Lady of Peace Church, North Hills
Guilin, Alfonso, St. Sebastian, Los Angeles
Guzman, Francisco, St. Linus, Whittier
Hall, Willard J., Sr., St. John the Evangelist, Los Angeles
Halliwell, Thomas L., St. Joseph, Long Beach
Halvorsen, Douglas A., St. Louis de Montfort, Santa Maria
Hammonds, Johnnie, (Retired), St. Mary Magdalen, Camarillo
Hanson, Walter J., St. Camillus Center for Pastoral Care, Studio City
Harper, John Barry, St. Julie Billiart, Newbury Park
Hegenbart, Joseph, St. James the Less, La Crescenta
Henry, James J., St. Anthony, Oxnard
Henschel, Louis E., St. Julie Billiart, Newbury Park
Hernandez, Roberto, Holy Spirit Church, Los Angeles
Heyer, Jerome, Holy Cross, Moorpark
Hillman, Steven V., St. Elizabeth Ann Seton, Rowland Heights
Holderness, Alan, St. Louise de Marillac, Covina
Holguin, Michael, Santa Clara, Oxnard
Horn, John G., Sacred Heart, Covina
Huerta, Antonio, St. Anthony of Padua, Gardena
Huff, David Warren, (Retired), Holy Cross, Santa Barbara
Ito, Mitchell, St. Pascal Baylon, Thousand Oaks
Johnson, Douglass R., Sr., Holy Name of Jesus, Los Angeles
Jones, Douglas, Our Lady of Peace, North Hills
Juarez, Ernesto Macias, St. Joseph, Carpinteria
Juarez-Ramirez, Paulino, St. Genevieve, Sylmar
Karl, Richard J., Our Lady of Perpetual Help, Santa Clarita
Kelch, Vincent Charles, Santa Clara, Oxnard
Kennedy, Joseph Charles, St. Anthony, Oxnard
Kingsley, Neil Joseph, Blessed Junipero Serra, Camarillo
Kruer, John, St. Maximilian Kolbe, Westlake Village
Landa, William, St. Philip the Apostle, Pasadena
Landeros, Teodoro, San Buenaventura Mission, Ventura
Lanoix, Gilbert, (Retired), St. Brigid, Los Angeles
Lara, Frederick Peter, Our Lady of the Miraculous Medal, Montebello
Lauderdale, Walter John, Holy Trinity, San Pedro
Ledonne, Tom, St. Denis, Diamond Bar
Lee, Paul D., St. Agnes Korean Catholic Community, La Mirada
Leyva, Rodolfo R., Sacred Heart, Covina
Liendo, Manuel, (Retired), St. John Neumann, Santa Maria
Ligot, Romy, St. Pancratius, Lakewood
Lim, Raymond, St. James the Less, Glendale
Lipski, Alexander, (Retired), St. Cornelius, Long Beach
Lira, Pedro, St. Catherine of Siena, Reseda
Littleton, Edward, Blessed Kateri Tekakwitha, Santa Clarita
Lopez, Arnaldo, Holy Angels, Arcadia
Lopez, Francisco Javier, Our Lady of Guadalupe, Oxnard
Lopez, Francisco, St. Mary of the Assumption, Santa Maria
Lopez, Jose R., (Retired), Our Lady of Lourdes, Los Angeles
Lopez, Lawrence James, Santa Clara, Oxnard
Lopez, Mario, Holy Name of Mary, San Dimas
Lopez, Rito R., Blessed Junipero Serra, Lancaster
Lopez, Victor Cepero, St. Lucy, Long Beach
Macias, Aurelio Robles, Sacred Heart, Ventura
Maciel, Robert, Sr., St. Louis de Montfort, Orcutt
Madrigal, Carlos, Sacred Heart, Pomona
Magos, Carlos, Precious Blood, Los Angeles
Manalo, Dante Tibor, Mary Star of the Sea, Oxnard
Manion, Joseph M., Sr., St. Jude, Westlake Village
Marin, Alejandro, Holy Name of Jesus, Los Angeles
Marron, Alejandro Zendejas, Our Lady of Guadalupe Catholic Church, Oxnard
Marsh, Steven R., St. Dorothy, Glendora
Martinez, Jesse, St. John Vianney, Hacienda Heights
Martinez, Manuel J., F.S.P., Cathedral of Our Lady of the Angels, Los Angeles
Martinez, Miguel Angel, St. Raphael, Los Angeles
Mauch, Kevin Barry, Holy Cross, Moorpark
McNamara, Eugene P., (Retired), St. Monica, Santa Monica
McPheeters, Jon C., St. Anthony, Oxnard
Medina, Richard J., San Fernando Pastoral Region Office, Downey
Mejia, J. Guadalupe, Holy Family, Artesia
Mejia, Mario, St. Gertrude, Bell Gardens
Mendez, Alfonso Cruz, San Buenaventura Mission, Ventura
Messer, John, St. Frances of Rome, Azusa
Miller, David, Bishop Arnat High School, Alhambra
Miller, Robert J., St. James, Redondo Beach
Millholland, Frank O., St. Albert the Great, Compton
Mills, Edgar, Our Lady of the Assumption, Ventura
Mitchell, Charles A., St. Elizabeth of Hungary, Altadena
Mizerski, Joseph R., St. Therese, Alhambra
Modugno, Larry, Chap., Camarillo
Molina, Raul, St. Anne, Santa Monica
Moloney, Douglas, St. Christopher, West Covina
Montagna, John, C.S., (Retired)
Montross, Stephen James, St. Raphael, Santa Barbara
Moon, Ronald Dale, St. Mary Magdalen, Camarillo
Morales, Jose Noe, Mary Star of the Sea, Oxnard
Morgan, T. Richard, St. Jane de Chantal, North Hollywood
Moske, Walter Thomas, St. Joseph, Hawthorne
Nawrocik, Zenon, Mary of the Assumption, Santa Maria
Nguyen, Loc, St. Christopher, West Covina
Nguyen, Matthew Van, Maria Regina, Gardena
Noon, Richard, St. John Vianney, Hacienda Heights
Noriega, Restie T., Incarnation, Glendale
O'Malley, Thom, St. Finbar, Burbank
Ochoa, Ruben, Guardian Angel, Pacoima

Orcutt, Mark A., St. Paul of the Cross, La Mirada
Origel, Carlos, Our Lady of Perpetual Help, Downey
Ortiz, Joe, (Retired)
Ortiz Dominguez, David, St. Lawrence of Brindisi, Los Angeles
Palmer, William Scott, Our Lady of Guadalupe, Hermosa Beach
Pardo, Rogelio, Our Lady of Perpetual Help, Los Nietos
Parish, Harold "Hal", J.C.D., (Retired), Mary Star of the Sea, Oxnard
Pasos, Jesus S., St. Bernardine of Siena, West Hills
Patterson, Gary R., Our Lady of Guadalupe, Irwindale
Patterson, Gregory, Transfiguration, Los Angeles
Pena, Cecilio G., St. Helen, Paramount
Pepe, Joseph, (Retired), St. Joseph the Worker, Winnetka
Perez, Elvys C., St. Mary's, Palmdale
Perez, Jorge, Our Lady of the Rosary, Paramount
Perez, Michael A., St. John Eudes, Chatsworth
Perez, Sergio, Our Lady of Solitude Parish, Los Angeles
Pesqueira, Paul, St. Mariana de Paredes, Pico Rivera
Picard, John B., (Retired), Blessed Junipero Serra, Camarillo
Pinedo, Donald, St. Anthony, Oxnard
Pomphrey, Richard, St. Bede the Venerable, La Canada
Poole, Gary D., Blessed Junipero Serra, Lancaster
Pruitt, Richard A., St. Anthony, El Segundo
Rac, Felix, Christ the King, Los Angeles
Race, Mark, St. Bernadette, Los Angeles
Ramirez, Fidel M., Santa Clara, Oxnard
Ramirez, Jose Ascencion, Our Lady of Sorrows, Santa Barbara
Ramirez, Salvador, St. John of God, Norwalk
Ramirez-Chavez, Hernan, St. Raphael, Los Angeles
Ramos, Dano L., Santa Clara, Oxnard
Rascati, Wayne, St. Raphael, Goleta
Recinos, Ricardo, St. Agatha, Los Angeles
Redmond, II, Jack William, Blessed Junipero Serra, Camarillo
Reibenspies, Terence L., St. Rosa of Lima Church, Simi Valley
Reiser, Jay, Blessed Kateri Tekakwitha, Santa Clarita
Reyes, Arnold Peter, Blessed Junipero Serra, Camarillo
Reynolds, Harrell Dale, Jr., Sacred Heart, Lancaster
Riera, Ralph, St. Raymond, Downey
Rios, Fred, Our Lady of the Miraculous Medal, Montebello
Rivas, Carlos R., St. Francis Xavier, Pico Rivera
Rivera, Ramon, St. Bridget of Sweden, Van Nuys
Roberto, Timothy J., St. Paul of the Cross, La Mirada
Robinson, James M., St. Paschal Baylon, Thousand Oaks
Rodriguez, Hernando, Resurrection, Los Angeles
Rodriguez, Jorge Alberto, Our Lady of Guadalupe, Santa Barbara
Rodriguez, Rodrigo, (Retired), St. Mary's, Palmdale
Rojas, Pedro, All Souls, Los Angeles
Rose, David, Holy Angels Church of the Deaf, Vernon
Rose, Frederick, American Martyrs, Manhattan Beach
Rosenberg, Milton, Ph.D., Santa Clara, Oxnard
Ruelas, Hector, St. Lawrence of Brindisi, Los Angeles
Ruotolo, Ronald, Sacred Heart, Lancaster
Ryan, Jack, (Retired), Santa Barbara Mission, Santa Barbara
Sabol, Thomas A., St. Timothy, Los Angeles
Sadowski, Roy Edward, St. Anthony, Oxnard
Sago, Bruce, St. Bruno, Whittier
Sahagun, Luis, St. Ignatius, Los Angeles
Salazar, John Burgos, St. Francis of Assisi, Los Angeles
Salcido, Michael P., Immaculate Conception, Monrovia
Sanchez, Enrique R., St. Mark University Parish, Santa Barbara
Sanchez, Ronald, Immaculate Conception, Monrovia
Sandner, Christopher Alan, Our Lady of Sorrows, Santa Barbara
Sangster, William B., (Retired), Our Lady of Sorrows, Santa Barbara
Saucedo, Valentin, Presentation of Mary, Paramount
Schwerdt, Paul, Blessed Junipero Serra, Lancaster
Sebenius, Wayland "Gus", St. Therese, San Marino
Seidler, Robert, St. John Eudes, Chatsworth
Sheckler, Dale, St. Lawrence Martyr, Redondo Beach
Shinkle, Richard D., (Retired), St. James, Redondo Beach
Shinn, John, Valley Catholic Korean Center, Sherman Oaks
Siegel, Lawrence, St. Joseph, Carpinteria
Siegman, Craig A., St. Margaret Mary Alacoque, Lomita
Skupnik, Raymond P., St. Cyprian, Long Beach
Smith, David Nicholas, St. Julie Billiart, Newbury Park
Smith, William Richard, St. Jude, Westlake Village
Soria, Richard, St. Margaret Mary Alacoque, Lomita
Spies, William, Blessed Junipero Serra, Camarillo
Stalder, Richard, La Purisima Concepcion, Santa Maria
Steele, John, Holy Family, Glendale
Steighner, Robert, Our Lady of the Assumption, Claremont
Stoltz, Eric, St. Brendan, Los Angeles
Suh, Ignatius Jin, Our Lady of Lourdes, Glendale
Taufer, Wm. Dale, St. Bernardine of Siena, West Hills
Tchoi, Francis, The 103 Saints Korean Catholic Center, San Pedro
Tiambeng, Victor, St. Martha, Corona
Tomkovicz, Vincent, St. Maximilian Kolbe, Simi Valley
Torti, Joseph Felix, Blessed Junipero Serra, Camarillo
Trujillo, Jose Antonio, Our Lady of Sorrows, Santa Barbara
Tulluis, John, Our Lady of the Assumption, Claremont
Turner, John, Jr., (Retired)
Ulibarri, Ralph J., Nativity, Torrance
Valdez, Roberto Lupian, St. John Neumann, Santa Maria
Valencia, Manuel, St. Rita, Sierra Madre
Valeriano, Oscar J., Jr., St. Louis of France, La Puente
Valles, Al, St. Louise de Marillac, Covina
Vargas, Frank, St. Monica, Santa Monica
Vasquez, Raymond, Jr., Santa Clara, Oxnard
Vazquez, Roberto L., St. John Chrysostom, Inglewood
Vedro, Shawn Stanley, St. Louis de Montfort, Santa Maria
Vega, Heriberto "Ed", St. Joseph the Worker, Canoga Park
Victorin, Rafael A., St. Augustine Church, Culver City
Villacorta, Ricardo, Christ the King, Los Angeles
Vital, Ernesto, St. Francis of Rome, Los Angeles
Vu, Anh Quoc, St. Mary Magdalen, Camarillo
Wallace, Daniel, St. Margaret Mary Church, Lomita
Wauthy, Guy, St. Jerome Church, Los Angeles
Wessler, Charles Philip, Our Lady of the Assumption, Ventura
Wilson, Peter, Jr., St. Rose of Lima, Simi Valley
Wilson, William Robert, Jr., Our Lady of the Assumption, Ventura
Won, Augustine Y., St. Bede the Venerable, La Canada-Flintridge
Yoque, Leonel, Holy Cross, Los Angeles
Zavala-Dominguez, Bernardo, St. Louis of France, La Puente

INSTITUTIONS LOCATED IN THE ARCHDIOCESE

[A] SEMINARIES, ARCHDIOCESAN

CAMARILLO. *St. John's Seminary*, 5012 Seminary Rd., 93012-2500. Tel: 805-482-2755; Fax: 805-484-4074. Email: ccox@stjohnsem.edu. Web: www.stjohnsem.edu. Rev. Msgr. Craig A. Cox, J.C.D., Rector & Pres.; Revs. John P. Brennan, S.M.A., S.T.D., Vice Rector; James Clarke, Ph.D., Dir. of Spiritual Direction; Leon Hutton, Dir. of Human Formation & Evaluations; Deacon Milton Rosenberg, Ph.D., Dir. Psych. Svcs.; Sisters Leanne Hubbard, S.N.D., Dir. of Pastoral Formation & Field Educ.; Mary Glennon, R.S.M., Assoc. Dir. Spiritual Formation; Rev. Patrick Mullen; Ms. Jacquelein Rotter, Dir. Finance; Mr. Greg Julius, Facilities Mgr.; Mrs. Mary Bissinger, Human Resources Mgr.; Dr. Mark F. Fischer, Ph.D., Dir. Admissions; Dr. Patricia Lyons, M.L.S., Libraries Dir.; Ms. Esme Takahashi, Registrar; Revs. Richard B. Benson, C.M., S.T.D., Academic Dean; Eugenio Cardenas, M.Sp.S.; John Cawley, C.M., Assoc. Dir. of Pastorial Field Educ.; Kevin McCracken, C.M.; Edward Owens, O.SS.T.; Luke Dysinger, O.S.B., M.D., D.Phil.; Joel Henson, Dir. of Students; Steven Thoma, C.R.; Dr. Patrick Mitchell, Dir. Pre-Theology Prog.; Dr. Aurora Mordey, Dir. Language & Cultural Studies; Dr. Alan Vincelette, Dir. Lay Ministry Students. Major Seminary of the Archdiocese of Los Angeles. Priests 12; Sisters 2; Lay Teachers 9; Seminarians 70.

[B] SEMINARIES, RELIGIOUS OR SCHOLASTICATES

LOS ANGELES. *St. Joseph's Novitiate*, 2468 S. St. Andrews Pl., 90018. Tel: 323-734-0233; Fax: 323-731-5987. Email: usaprov-office@sbcglobal.net. Web: hospitallers.org. Bro. Stephen de la Rosa, O.H., Prov. & Formation Dir. Hospitaller Brothers of St. John of God. Brothers 24.

SANTA MARIA. *St. Joseph Seminary (Josephite Fathers' Novitiate)*, 180 Patterson Rd., 93455. Tel: 805-937-5378; Fax: 805-937-5759. Web: www.josephiteweb.org. Revs. Timothy R. Lane, C.J.; John A. Mayhew, C.J.; Edward Jalbert, C.J.; Mark L. Newman, C.J. Priests 4; Total Staff 1.

SANTA PAULA. *Dom Grea House (House of Formation) Canons Regular of the Immaculate Conception, (C.R.I.C.)* (1871) 984 Monte Vista Dr., 93060-1612. Tel: 805-933-5063; Fax: 805-525-5115. Email: domgreahouse@cricusa.com. Web: cricusa.com. Rev. Thomas J. Dome, C.R.I.C., Dir. & Novice Master. Priests 1; Postulants 2.

Dom Grea House (House of Formation and Novitiate)

SANTA YNEZ. *San Lorenzo Seminary - Retreat Center*, Retreat Center: 1802 Sky Dr., P.O. Box 247, 93460-0247. Tel: 805-688-5630; Fax: 805-686-0775. Email: info@sanlorenzo.org. Web: www.sanlorenzo.org. Revs. Evangelist Kelly, O.F.M.Cap., Vicar; Robert A. Barbato, O.F.M.Cap., Guardian & Dir.; Alejandro Magallenes; James Johnson, O.F.M. Cap.; Ronald Talbott, O.F.M.Cap.; Bros. Lance Love, O.F.M.Cap, Vicar & Assoc. Dir.; Joseph Slominski, O.F.M.Cap.; Jim Doyle, O.F.M.Cap. Capuchin Fransiscan Friars. Priests 5; Brothers 3; Total Staff 5.

SUN VALLEY. *Scalabrini House of Discernment (Seminary)*, 10651 Vinedale St., 91352-2825. Tel: 818-504-9561; Fax: 818-504-9562. Revs. Giovanni Bizzotto, C.S., Vocation Dir.; Ramiro V. Sanchez Chan, C.S., Dir. Discernment Program. Seminarians 9.

Scalabrini Vocation Office Tel: 323-216-6278; Fax: 818-504-9562.

[C] COLLEGES AND UNIVERSITIES

LOS ANGELES. *Loyola Marymount University*, One LMU Dr., Ste. 4844, 90045-2659. Tel: 310-338-2700. Web: www.lmu.edu (Including Law School). Revs. Robert B. Lawton, S.J., Pres.; Patrick J. Cahalan, S.J., Chancellor; Dr. Ernest Rose, Senior Vice Pres. & Chief Academic Office; Mr. Thomas O. Fleming Jr., Senior Vice Pres. & CFO; Dennis Slon, Senior Vice Pres. Univ. Rels.; Dr. Lane Bove, Senior Vice Pres. Student Affairs; Rev. Richard A. Robin, S.J., Asst. to the Pres.; Rae Linda Brown, Ph.D., Vice Pres. Undergraduate Educ.; Rev. Robert V. Caro, S.J., Vice Pres. for Mission & Min.; Dr. Abbie Robinson-Armstrong, Vice Pres. for Intercultural Affairs; Ms. Lynne Scarboro, Senior Vice Pres. for Admin.; Mr. David W. Burcham, Provost; Ms. Rosenia St. Onge, Registrar; Kristine Brancolini, Dean, Univ. Libraries; Dr. Birute Vileisis, Dir., Sponsored Projects Office; Anne Prisco, Vice Pres. for Enrollment Mgmt.; Rebecca Chandler, Vice Pres. for Human Resources; Rev. Albert P. Koppes, O.Carm., Assoc. Chancellor; Dr. Dennis W. Draper, Dean of Business Admin.; Dr. Richard G. Plumb, Dean of Science & Engineering; Prof. Barbara Busse, Dean, Communication & Fine Arts; Dr. Stephen V. Duncan, Interim Dean of Film & TV; Dr. Shane P. Martin, Dean, School of Educ.; Mr. Victor Gold, Senior Vice Pres. & Dean Loyola Law School. Students 8,250; Full Time: 498; Part Time 444 942; Loyola Marymount & Loyola Law School Staff 1,150.

Jesuit Community, P.O. Box 45041, 90045-0041. Tel: 310-338-7445; Fax: 310-338-3002. Revs. Robert W. Scholla, S.J., Rector; James Erps, S.J., Dir. Campus Min.; John Galvan, S.J., Min.; Marc Reeves, S.J., Min./Theology; William Rewak, S.J., Min.; Jose Ignacio Badenes, S.J.; Wafik Nasry, S.J.; Rui Nunes, S.J., Scholastic. Priests 40; Brothers 1; Sisters 6; Lay Teachers 451; Total Staff 950; Students 7,645. In Res. Most Rev. Gordon D. Bennett, S.J.; Revs. James Arenz, S.J. (Retired); Mark Bandsuch, S.J.; Patrick J. Cahalan, S.J.; Robert V. Caro, S.J.; Michael Caruso, S.J.; Philip J. Chmielewski, S.J.; Patrick Connolly, S.J.; John P. Daly, S.J.; James Fredericks; William J. Fulco, S.J.; Grant Garinger, S.J.; James H. Keene, S.J.; Albert P. Koppes, O.Carm.; Joseph LaBrie, S.J.; Robert B. Lawton, S.J.; Michael Lee, S.J.; Dorian Llywelyn, S.J.; Terrance L. Mahan, S.J.; John D. Murphy, S.J.; Thomas P. Rausch, S.J., Ph.D.; Thomas Regan, S.J., (Sabbatical); William Rewak, S.J.; Norbert Rigali (Retired); Anastacio Rivera,

S.J., (Sabbatical); Richard A. Robin, S.J.; Randall Roche, S.J.; Richard W. Rolfs, S.J.; Kenneth Rudnick, S.J.; Herbert J. Ryan, S.J.; Robert W. Scholla, S.J.; Ernest S. Sweeney, S.J.; Manh Tran, S.J.; Robert J. Welch, S.J.; Bro. John Grever, C.F.M.M.

The Sacred Heart of Mary and Sisters of St. Joseph of Orange, One LMU Dr., 90045-2659. Tel: 310-338-2700; 310-641-4682.

Communities of the Religious of the Sacred Heart of Mary and Sisters of St. Joseph of Orange

Loyola School of Law (1920) 919 S. Albany St., P.O. Box 15019, 90015. Tel: 213-736-1000. Web: www.lls.edu. Mr. Victor Gold, Sr. Vice Pres. & Dean. Priests 1; Faculty 77; Students 1,281.

Mount St. Mary's College (1925)Tel: 310-954-4010; Fax: 310-954-4019. Email: jpdoud@msmc.la.edu. Web: www.msmc.la.edu. Conducted by the Sisters of St. Joseph of Carondelet., Resident and non-resident students.

Chalon Campus, 12001 Chalon Rd., 90049-1599. Tel: 310-954-4000; Fax: 310-954-4019. Web: www.msmc.la.edu.

Doheny Campus, 10 Chester Pl., 90007. Tel: 213-477-2500; Fax: 213-477-2519. Dr. Jacqueline Powers Doud, Pres.; Dr. Jane Lingua, Vice Pres. Student Affairs; Larry Smith, Vice Pres. Info. Support Svcs. & Enrollment; Dr. Eleanor D. Slebert, Provost & Academic Vice Pres.; Dr. Linda Moody, Graduate Dean; Paul Craft, Vice. Pres. Inst. Advancement; Mr. Dean Kilgour, Asst. Vice Pres. Enrollment Mgmt.; Dr. Karol Dean, Asst. Provost; Chris McAlary, Vice Pres. Admin. & Fin.; Claudia Reed, Librarian. Sisters 3; Priests 1; Lay Teachers 90; Students 2,371.

RANCHO PALOS VERDES. *Marymount College, Palos Verdes, California*, 30800 Palos Verdes Dr., E., 90275-6299. Tel: 310-377-5501; Fax: 310-265-0642. Email: cfausto@marymountpv.edu. Web: www.marymountpv.edu. Michael S. Brophy, Ph.D., M.F.A., Pres.; Dr. June Viley, Dean Academic Affairs; Mr. James Reeves, Vice Pres. College Opers. & Student Svcs.; Mary McMillan, Librarian. An independent and Catholic Co-educational, two-year Liberal Arts College. Priests 1; Sisters 1; Lay Teachers 40; Students 657.

SANTA PAULA. *Thomas Aquinas College* (1969) 10000 N. Ojai Rd., 93060. Tel: 805-525-4417; 800-634-9797; Fax: 805-525-0620. Email: pr@thomasaquinas.edu. Web: www.thomasaquinas.edu. Dr. Thomas E. Dillon, Pres.; Dr. Michael F. McLean, Dean; Mr. Peter L. DeLuca III, Vice Pres. Finance & Admin.; Mr. J. Quincy Masteller, Vice Pres. Devel.; Revs. Charles Willingham, O.Praem., Chap.; Cornelius M. Buckley, S.J., Chap.; Paul Raftery, O.P., Chap.; Viltis Jatulis, Librarian. Four-year undergraduate program in the Liberal Arts leading to the B.A. Degree; Co-educational. Lay Teachers 37; Students 345.

[D] HIGH SCHOOLS, ARCHDIOCESAN

LOS ANGELES. *Bishop Conaty-Our Lady of Loretto High School* (1923) (Girls), 2900 W. Pico Blvd., 90006-3802. Tel: 323-737-0012; Fax: 323-737-1749. Web: www.bishopconatyloretto.org. Richard A. Spicer, Prin.; Marcia Battin, Librarian. Sisters 3; Lay Teachers 23; Students 313; Total Staff 26.

Bishop Mora Salesian High School (Boys), 960 S. Soto St., 90023. Tel: 323-261-7124; Fax: 323-261-9474. Web: salesianmustangs.com. Mr. Samuel Robles, Prin.; Mr. Mark Johnson, Vice Prin. Salesians of Don Bosco. Priests 1; Brothers 2; Lay Teachers 28; Students 420.

Sacred Heart High School (Girls), 2111 Griffin Ave., 90031. Tel: 323-225-2209; Fax: 323-225-5046. Email: angelica@msjdominicans.org. Web: www.shhsla.org. Sr. Angelica Velez, O.P., Prin.; Mrs. Muriel Bourhe, Librarian. Sisters 4; Lay Teachers 22; Students 266; Total Staff 32.

Verbum Dei High School (Boys), 11100 S. Central Ave., 90059-1199. Tel: 323-564-6651; Fax: 323-564-9009. Email: wmuller@verbumdei.us. Web: www.verbumdei.us. Revs. William H. Muller, S.J., Pres.; Luat V. Hoang, S.J., Chap. Students; Bro. Jeffrey R. Allen, S.J., Chap. Adults; Dr. Daniel J. O'Connell, Prin.; Ms. Cristina Cuellar-Villanueva, Vice Pres. Corp. Work Study Prog.; Mr. Victor M. Cancino, S.J., Teacher; Sr. Marilyn Ficht, R.S.H.M., Teacher. Conducted by the Archdiocese of Los Angeles. Priests 2; Brothers 1; Sisters 1; Lay Teachers 22; Students 300; Total Staff 50. Scholastics Rev. Jeff Allen, S.J.

Verbum Dei High School WorkStudy, Inc., 11100 S. Central Ave., 90059-1199. Tel: 323-564-6651, Ext. 21; Fax: 323-564-9009.

BURBANK. *Bellarmine-Jefferson High School* (Coed), 465 E. Olive Ave., 91501. Tel: 818-972-1400 (Main Office); 818-972-1401 (Athletic); 818-972-1402 (Attendance); Fax: 818-559-6387. Web: www.belljeff.net. Sr. Cheryl Milner, S.N.J.M., Prin. Brothers 1; Sisters 1; Lay Teachers 24; Students 295; Total Staff 36.

DOWNEY. *St. Matthias High School*, 7851 E. Gardendale St., 90242. Tel: 562-861-2271; Fax: 562-869-8652. Email: jatencio@stmatthiashs.org. Web: www.stmatthiashs.org. Jane F. Atencio, Prin.; Dave Morek, Librarian. Lay Teachers 19; Students 245.

GARDENA. *Junipero Serra High School* (1950) 14830 S. Van Ness Ave., 90249. Tel: 310-324-6675; Fax: 310-352-4953. Web: www.SerraHighSchool.com. Erick A. Rubalcava, Pres. & Prin.; Mike Wagner, Asst. Prin.; Tamara Shelton, Librarian. Priests 1; Lay Teachers 41; Students 650; Total Staff 14.

LA PUENTE. *Bishop Amat Memorial High School* (Coed), 14301 Fairgrove Ave., 91746. Tel: 626-962-2495; Fax: 626-960-0994. Email: president@bishopamat.org. Web: www.bishopamat.org. Rev. Msgr. Aidan M. Carroll, Pres.; Dr. Merritt V. Hemenway, Prin.; Mr. Richard Beck, Vice Prin.; Ms. Deborah Oswald, Dir. of Finance & Devel.; Mrs. Maria Gover, Asst. Prin.; Mrs. Ivette Salcedo, Asst. Prin. & Student Services; Mrs. Sandra Roberts, Librarian. Conducted by the Archdiocese of Los Angeles. Priests 2; Sisters 1; Lay Teachers 87; Students 1,373; Total Staff 116.

LA VERNE. *Damien High School*, 2280 Damien Ave., 91750. Tel: 909-596-1946; Fax: 909-596-6112. Email: dhstravers@damien-hs.edu. Web: www.damien-hs.edu. Rev. Patrick Travers, SS.CC., Prin.; Mr. Sam Pearsall, Asst. Prin.; Mr. Bob Baiz, Dir. Admissions & Mktg.; Mr. Thomas Carroll, Asst. Prin. Athletic Activities; Mr. Kenneth Kowalewski, Asst. Prin. & Campus Min.; Dr. Michael Williams, Asst. Prin. & Dean Academics; Mrs. Dolores Kowalewski, Fin. Officer.

Congregation of the Sacred Hearts, Inc., Conducted by the Archdiocese of Los Angeles. Priests 1; Lay Teachers 62; Students 1,100; Total Staff 78.

Faculty Res.: 2150 Damien Ave., 91750. Tel: 909-596-1946; Fax: 909-596-6112. Email: dolores@damien-hs.edu. Web: www.damien-hs.edu.

LAKEWOOD. *Saint Joseph High School* (Girls), 5825 N. Woodruff Ave., 90713. Tel: 562-925-5073; Fax: 562-925-3315. Web: www.sj-jester.org. Dr. Terri Mendoza, Ph.D., Prin.; Revs. John Shevlin, S.V.D.; James Henry, S.V.D.; Mrs. Lisa Lindgren, Librarian. Conducted by Archdiocese of Los Angeles. Priests 2; Sisters 2; Lay Teachers 57; Students 754; Total Staff 75.

LANCASTER. *Paraclete High School* (Coed), 42145 N. 30th St., 93536. Tel: 661-943-3255; Fax: 661-722-9455. Email: janson@paracletehs.org. Web: www.paracletehs.org. John W. Anson, M.Ed., Prin.; Mary Ruth Farrell, Librarian. Tel: 661-943-3255, Ext. 116; Rev. Giampietro Gasparin, C.S.J. Conducted by Archdiocese of Los Angeles. Priests 1; Lay Teachers 44; Students 819.

MISSION HILLS. *Bishop Alemany High School*, 11111 N. Alemany Dr., 91345. Tel: 818-365-3925; Fax: 818-365-2064. Email: fferry@alemany.org. Web: www.alemany.org. Mr. Frank Ferry, Prin.; Mr. Keith Murphy, Vice Prin.; Mrs. Jan Galla, Asst. Prin. Student Life; Mike Purnell, Librarian. Priests 1; Sisters 3; Lay Teachers 79; Students 1,637; Total Staff 147.

MONTEBELLO. *Cantwell Sacred Heart of Mary High School* (1946) (Coed), 329 N. Garfield Ave., 90640. Tel: 323-887-2066; Fax: 323-724-4332. Email: cshm@cshm.org. Web: www.cshm.org. David I. Chambers, Prin.; Sr. Rose Marie Wilson, O.S.F., Librarian. Archdiocesan Institution. Sisters 2; Lay Teachers 32; Students 571; Total Staff 43.

OXNARD. *Santa Clara High School*, 2121 Saviers Rd., 93033. Tel: 805-483-9502; Fax: 805-483-1588. Web: www.santaclarahighschool.com. Mrs. Siobhain O'Reilly-Hill, Prin.; Ms. Nancy O'Sullivan, Vice Prin. Lay Teachers 26; Total Faculty & Staff 39; Students 447.

PLAYA DEL REY. *St. Bernard High School* (Coed), 9100 Falmouth Ave., 90293. Tel: 310-823-4651; Fax: 310-827-3365. Email: malvarez@stbernardhs.com. Web: www.stbernardhs.com. Michael Alvarez, Prin. Conducted by Archdiocese of Los Angeles. Brothers 1; Sisters 1; Lay Teachers 23; Students 380; Total Staff 31.

POMONA. *Pomona Catholic High School* (Girls), 533 W. Holt Ave., 91768. Tel: 909-623-5297; Fax: 909-620-6057. Email: storres@pomonacatholichs.org. Web: www.pomonacatholichs.org. Samuel Torres, Prin.; Cara Sultany, Vice Prin.; Mary Smith, Librarian. Sisters 2; Lay Teachers 20; Students 200; Total Staff 4.

ROSEMEAD. *Don Bosco Technical Institute* (Boys), 1151 San Gabriel Blvd., 91770-4299. Tel: 626-940-2000; Fax: 626-940-2001. Email: gcatalano@boscotech.edu. Web: www.boscotech.edu. Sharon J. Morano, Pres.; Gary J. Catalano, Prin.; Revs. Peter Bui, S.D.B.; Mel Trinidad, S.D.B., Campus Youth Min.; Bros. Patrick Barbariol, S.D.B.; Robert Hennings, S.D.B.; Gabriel Gonzalez, Librarian. Secondary Section.; Staffed by Salesians of St. John Bosco. Priests 3; Brothers 2; Administrators 4; Lay Teachers 58; Students 578; Total Staff 84.

SANTA FE SPRINGS. *St. Paul High School* (1956) 9635 S. Greenleaf Ave., 90670. Tel: 562-698-6246; Fax: 562-696-8396. Email: lbarr@stpaulhs.org. Web: www.stpaulhs.org. Ms. Lori Barr, Prin.; Denis O'Sullivan, O.S.F., Librarian. Conducted by Archdiocese of Los Angeles. Brothers 2; Sisters 2; Lay Teachers 40; Students 650; Total Staff 65.

SANTA MARIA. *St. Joseph High School* (1964) (Coed), 4120 S. Bradley Rd., 93455. Tel: 805-937-2038; Fax: 805-937-4248. Email: sjhs@sjhsknights.com. Web: www.sjhsknights.com. Rev. Edward Jalbert, C.J.; Joseph Myers, Prin.; Toni Jetter, Librarian. Conducted by Archdiocese of Los Angeles. Priests 1; Sisters 1; Lay Teachers 35; Students 568.

TORRANCE. *Bishop Montgomery High School* (Coed), 5430 Torrance Blvd., 90503. Tel: 310-540-2021; Fax: 310-543-5102. Email: rlibbon@bmhs-la.org. Web: www.bmhs-la.org. Rosemary Distaso-Libbon, Prin.; William Martinez, Librarian. Conducted by the Archdiocese of Los Angeles. Lay Teachers 90; Students 1,200.

VENTURA. *St. Bonaventure High School* (1963) (Coed), 3167 Telegraph Rd., 93003-3281. Tel: 805-648-6836; Fax: 805-648-4903. Email: office@saintbonaventure.com. Web: www.saintbonaventure.com. Marc Groff, Prin.; Ruth McNamara, Librarian. Conducted by Archdiocese of Los Angeles. Lay Teachers 45; Total Staff 50; Students 610.

[E] HIGH SCHOOLS, PAROCHIAL

High Schools are maintained in the following parishes (for particulars refer to the individual parishes): Glendale: Holy Family; Long Beach: St. Anthony; San Gabriel: San Gabriel Mission; San Pedro: Mary Star of the Sea; Santa Monica, St. Monica; Van Nuys: St. Genevieve

[F] HIGH SCHOOLS, PRIVATE

LOS ANGELES. *Cathedral High School of Los Angeles, Incorporated* (1925) (Boys), 1253 Bishops Rd., 90012. Tel: 323-225-2438; Fax: 323-222-7223. Email: brjohnm@cathedralhighschool.org. Web: www.cathedralhighschool.org. Mr. Martin Farfan, Pres.; Bro. John Montgomery, F.S.C., Prin. Conducted by the Brothers of the Christian Schools (F.S.C.) Brothers 7; Lay Teachers 37; Total Staff 52; Students 700.

Immaculate Heart High School (1906) (Girls), 5515 Franklin Ave., 90028-5999. Tel: 323-461-3651; Fax: 323-462-0610. Email: ihhs1@aol.com. Web: www.immaculateheart.org. Julie Anne McCormick, Pres.; Virginia Hurst, Prin.; Tracie Thomas, Librarian. Conducted by the Immaculate Heart Community. Lay Teachers 48; Students 549.

Loyola High School of Los Angeles, 1901 Venice Blvd., 90006. Tel: 213-381-5121, Ext. 125; Fax: 213-368-1758. Email: ggoethals@loyolahs.edu. Web: loyolahs.edu. Revs. Gregory M. Goethals, S.J., Pres.; Peter F. Filice, S.J., Supr. Jesuit Community; Mr. Frank Kozakowski, Prin.; Revs. John A. Brady, S.J., Pastorial Min.; Jerry Hayes, S.J., Dir. Campus Ministry; Angus Cooper, O.F.M., Teacher; John Quinn, S.J.; Mrs. April Hannah, Librarian; Mr. John Baker, Vice Pres. Advancement; Mr. Joseph O'Keefe, S.J., Scholastic; Mr. Ike Udoh, S.J., Scholastic. Sponsored by the California Province of the Society of Jesus. Priests 4; Lay Teachers 78; Administrators 7; Total Staff 172; Students 1,224. In Res Rev. William H. Muller, S.J., Pres. Verbum Dei High School; Bros. Jeff Allen, S.J.; Joseph Frias, S.J.; Rev. Luat V. Hoang, S.J.

Marymount High School (Girls), 10643 Sunset Blvd., 90077. Tel: 310-472-1205; Fax: 310-476-0910. Email: sstephens@mhs-la.org. Web: www.mhs-la.org. Dr. Mary Ellen Gozdecki, Head. Religious of the Sacred Heart of Mary. Sisters 1; Lay Teachers 51; Total Staff 37; Students 425.

Notre Dame Academy (1949) (Girls), 2851 Overland Ave., 90064. Tel: 310-839-5289; Fax: 310-839-7957. Email: nehrmann@ndala.com. Web: www.ndala.com. Ms. Nancy J. Coonis, Pres.; Joan Gumaer Tyhurst, Prin.; Mrs. Gloria Lukacovic, Librarian. Sisters of Notre Dame of Los Angeles 3; Teachers 34; Students 400.

ALHAMBRA. *Ramona Convent Secondary School, Ramona Convent of the Holy Names* (Girls Grades 7-12), 1701 W. Ramona Rd., 91803-3099. Tel: 626-282-4151; Fax: 626-281-0797. Email: ramona@ramona.pvt.k12.ca.us. Web: www.ramonaconvent.org. Ms. Kathleen Pillon, Prin.; Sr. Kathleen Callaway, S.N.J.M., Pres. Sisters of the Holy Names of Jesus and Mary 3;

Lay Teachers 34; Total Staff 37; Students 400.

BELLFLOWER. *St. John Bosco High School*, 13640 S. Bellflower Blvd., 90706. Tel: 562-920-1734; Fax: 562-867-5322. Email: lbaysinger@bosco.org. Web: www.bosco.org. Rev. Leo Baysinger, S.D.B., Dir.; Bros. Frank Bracchi, S.D.B.; Al Vu, S.D.B.; Barney Hagus, S.D.B.; Noel De Bruton, S.D.B.; Patrick Lee, Prin. (Boys) Priests 2; Brothers 2; Lay Teachers 65; Students 1,096.

BURBANK. *Providence High School* (Coed), 511 S. Buena Vista St., 91505. Tel: 818-846-8141; Fax: 818-843-8421. Email: michele.schulte@providencehigh.org. Web: www.providencehigh.org. Michele Schulte, Prin.; Joanie Fenstermaker, Dir. Campus Ministry; C. Victor LeBreton, Vice Prin. Discipline & Student Activities; Claire Hickey, Dean of Studies; Reece Talley, Dean of Faculty; Jenn Bello, Librarian. Sisters 1; Lay Teachers 41; Total Staff 17; Students 437.

CHATSWORTH. *Chaminade College Preparatory* (1952) Office of the President, 10210 Oakdale Ave., 91311-3533. Tel: 818-366-9284; Fax: 818-363-8492. Email: jadams@chaminade.org. Web: www.chaminade.org. Mr. James V. Adams, Pres.

Chaminade College Preparatory, (Coed Grades 6-12) Priests 2; Brothers 2; Sisters 2; Lay Teachers 132; Total Staff 202; Students 1,975.

Chatsworth Campus (Middle School, Grades 6-8), 19800 Devonshire St., 91311. Tel: 818-363-8127; Fax: 818-363-1219. Mr. Michael Valentine, Prin.; Helen Foster, Librarian.

West Hills Campus (High School, Grades 9-12), 7500 Chaminade Ave., West Hills, 91304. Tel: 818-347-8300; Fax: 818-348-8374. Bro. Thomas Fahy, O.S.F., Prin.; Nancy Saul, Librarian.

Marianist Community Tel: 818-347-8043; Fax: 818-347-2788. Revs. James Mueller, S.M., Chap.; Theodore Ley, S.M., Chap. Priests 1; Brothers 4.

ENCINO. *Crespi Carmelite High School*, 5031 Alonzo Ave., 91316. Tel: 818-345-1672; Fax: 818-705-0209. Web: www.crespi.org. Revs. Thomas Schrader, O.Carm., Pres.; Paul Henson, O.Carm., Prin.; Mr. Jeff Thornton, Vice Prin.; Mr. Jonathan Schild, Vice Prin.; Mr. Brian Banducci, Vice Pres.; Mr. Jason Nevis, Dean; Mrs. Margie Moreno, Dir. Finance; Mr. Greg Cornell, Vice Pres. Inst. Advancement; Mrs. Sharon Barkins-Wasson, Dir. Counseling & Guidance; Mr. Rob Kodama, Dir. Admissions; Mr. Chris Knabenshue, Campus Min.; Mrs. Dona Long, Dir. of Student Activity; Mrs. Janet Nungester, Librarian; Mr. Matthew Luderer, Athletic Dir. For further details about Our Lady of Mount Carmel Priory, Encino please see Monasteries and Residences of Priests and Brothers. Priests 2; Lay Teachers 55; Students 600.

GLENDORA. *St. Lucy's Priory High School* (Girls), 655 W. Sierra Madre Ave., 91741. Tel: 626-335-3322; Fax: 626-335-4373. Email: slphs@aol.com. Web: www.stlucys.com. Sr. Monica Collins, O.S.B., Prin.; Mrs. Marsha Solano, Librarian. Conducted by the Benedictine Sisters. Sisters 2; Lay Teachers 40; Total Staff 46; Students 755.

INGLEWOOD. *St. Mary's Academy* (Girls), 701 Grace Ave., 90301. Tel: 310-674-8470; Fax: 310-674-6255. Email: ymcneal@stmarysacademy.org. Web: www.stmarysacademy.org. Ms. Yvonne McNeal, Prin.; Sr. Maureen Dougherty, Librarian. Sisters of St. Joseph of Carondelet 7; Lay Teachers 22; Total Staff 20; Students 380.

LA CANADA FLINTRIDGE. *Flintridge Sacred Heart Academy* (1931) (Girls), 440 St. Katherine Dr., 91011. Tel: 626-685-8500; Fax: 626-685-8555. Email: cmccormack@fsha.org. Web: www.fsha.org. Sr. Celeste Marie Botello, Prin.

Flintridge Sacred Heart Academy, A Corporation Dominican Sisters of Mission San Jose 5; Lay Teachers 44; Students 406.

St. Francis High School of La Canada-Flintridge (Boys), 200 Foothill Blvd., 91011. Tel: 818-790-0325; Fax: 818-790-5542. Web: sfhs.net. Email: martit@sfhs.net. Rev. Antonio Marti, O.F.M.Cap., Pres. St. Francis High School; Mr. Thomas G. Moran, Prin.; Sr. Barbarine Houdek, O.S.F., Librarian; Rev. Hung Nguyen, O.F.M.Cap., Campus Chap.; Bro. Hai Ho, O.F.M.Cap.; Revs. Chris Thiel, O.F.M.Cap.; Anthony Scannel, O.F.M.Cap.; Michael Walsh; Bro. Tran Vu, O.F.M.Cap.

St. Francis High School of La Canada-Flintridge Priests 3; Brothers 2; Sisters 1; Lay Teachers 49; Teachers 54; Total Staff 69; Students 686.

OJAI. *Villanova Preparatory School*, 12096 N. Ventura Ave., 93023-3999. Tel: 805-646-1464; Fax: 805-646-4430. Email: info@villanovaprep.org. Web: www.villanovaprep.org. Carol Hoffer, Headmaster; Rev. Gregory Heidenblut, O.S.A., Pres.

Villanova Preparatory School of California Conducted by Augustinian Fathers (Order of St. Augustine). Priests 1; Brothers 1; Sisters 3; Lay Teachers 31; Total Staff 67; Students 305.

PASADENA. *La Salle High School* (1956) 3880 E. Sierra Madre Blvd., 91107. Tel: 626-351-8951; Fax: 626-351-0275. Email: principal@lasallehs.org. Web: lasallehs.org. Mr. Patrick Bonacci, Prin.; Dr. Richard Gray, Pres.; Mrs. Delia Swanner, Librarian. Brothers 1; Lay Teachers 74; Total Staff 94; Students 740.

Mayfield Senior School of the Holy Child Jesus, 500 Bellefontaine St., 91105-2439. Tel: 626-799-9121; Fax: 626-799-8576. Email: rita.mcbride@mayfieldsenior.org. Web: www.mayfieldsenior.org. Thomas Wheatley, Dir. Finance & Opers.; Rita C. McBride, Prin.; Ann Pibel, Librarian. Sisters 1; Lay Teachers 36; Students 300.

SANTA BARBARA. *Bishop Garcia Diego High School Inc.* (1959) (Coed), 4000 La Colina Rd., 93110. Tel: 805-967-1266; Fax: 805-964-3178. Email: bishop@bishopdiego.org. Web: www.bishopdiego.org. Rev. Thomas J. Elewaut, C.J., Prin.; Amanda Combs, Librarian. Priests 1; Sisters 2; Lay Teachers 28; Students 275; Total Staff 43.

SHERMAN OAKS. *Notre Dame High School* (1947) 13645 Riverside Dr., 91423. Tel: 818-933-3600; Fax: 818-501-0507. Email: connelly@ndhs.org. Web: www.ndhs.org. Mr. Brett A. Lowart, Pres.; Mrs. Stephanie Connelly, Prin. Priests 1; Brothers 1; Lay Teachers 90; Students 1,195; Total Staff 113.

SIERRA MADRE. *Alverno High School* (Girls), 200 N. Michillinda Ave., 91024. Tel: 626-355-3463; Fax: 626-355-3153. Web: Alverno-hs.org. Ann M. Gillick, M.S., Prin. Lay Teachers 26; Students 285; Total Staff 44.

THOUSAND OAKS. *La Reina High School* (Girls, Grades 7-12), 106 W. Janss Rd., 91360. Tel: 805-495-6494; Fax: 805-494-4966. Email: lareina@lareina.com. Web: www.lareina.com. Cecilia Coe, Prin.; Sr. Mary LaReina Kelly, S.N.D., Pres.; Kristi Balleweg, Dir. Campus Min.; Heather Neidenbach, Library Media Teacher. Sisters of Notre Dame 4; Lay Teachers 43; Students 600; Total Staff 75.

WOODLAND HILLS. *Louisville High School* (1960) (Girls), 22300 Mulholland Dr., 91364. Tel: 818-346-8812; Fax: 818-346-9483. Email: kvercillo@louisvillehs.org. Web: louisvillehs.org. Kathleen Vercillo, Prin.; Sr. Myra McPartland, S.S.L., Pres.; Mrs. Anita Taylor, Librarian. Sisters 4; Lay Teachers 33; Total Staff 22; Students 437.

[G] ELEMENTARY SCHOOLS, PRIVATE

LOS ANGELES. *Notre Dame Academy (Elementary)*, 2911 Overland Ave., 90064. Tel: 310-287-3895; Fax: 310-838-8983. Web: www.ndaes.org. Ms. Nancy J. Coonis, Pres.; Kathleen Nocella, Prin. Sisters of Notre Dame of Los Angeles 1; Lay Teachers 14; Total Staff 27; Students 272.

PASADENA. *Mayfield Junior School*, 405 S. Euclid Ave., 91101. Tel: 626-796-2774; Fax: 626-796-5753. Email: mjs@mayfieldjs.org. Web: www.mayfieldjs.org. Joseph J. Gill, Headmaster; Tatiana Guyer, Librarian. Lay Teachers 65; Total Staff 25; Students 502.

SANTA BARBARA. *Marymount Academy* (1938) (Grades K-8), (Coed), 2130 Mission Ridge Rd., 93103. Tel: 805-569-1811; Fax: 805-682-6892. Email: rwilcox@marymountsb.org. Web: marymountsb.org. Deborah David, Headmaster; Carolyn Gell, Librarian. Lay Teachers 29; Total Staff 47; Students 217.

[H] ORPHANAGES AND INFANT HOMES

ROSEMEAD, LOS ANGELES. *Maryvale* (1953) 7600 E. Graves Ave., P.O. Box 1039, 91770-1003. Tel: 626-280-6510; 323-283-9311; Fax: 626-288-8903. Email: maryvale@maryvalle-ca.org. Web: www.maryvale-ca.org. Steve Gunther, M.S.W., Pres. & Exec. Dir. Daughters of Charity 3; Total Assisted 447; Children: Residential Treatment 85; Mental Health Day Treatment 85; Early Education 257; Aftercare Services 17; Transitional Housing Program 3; Total Staff 228.

The Los Angeles Orphan Asylum (1856) 7600 E. Graves Ave., 91770. Tel: 626-280-6510; Fax: 626-288-8903.

Los Angeles Orphanage Guild (1951) 7600 E. Graves Ave., 91770. Tel: 626-280-6510; Fax: 626-288-8903. Email: maryvale@maryvale-ca.org. Web: www.maryvale-ca.org.

[I] DAY NURSERIES

LOS ANGELES. *Divine Providence Pre-school and Kindergarten* (1954) 2620 Monmouth Ave., 90007. Tel: 213-747-3074; Fax: 213-747-6468. Email: divine_providence@sbcglobal.net. Web: www.companyofmary.us. Sr. Mary Gomez, O.D.N., Dir. & Prin.; Belen Rojas, Co-Prin. Sisters of the Company of Mary 4; Lay Teachers 12; Children 168; Total Staff 4.

St. Jeanne de Lestonnac Preschool and Kindergarten, 4001 Venice Blvd., 90019. Tel: 323-737-1217; Fax: 323-737-3672. Email: sjdlsla@gmail.com. Web: www.companyofmary.us. Sisters Teresa Zapata, O.D.N., Prin. & Dir.; Cecilia Duran, O.D.N., Supvr. (Formerly Little Flower Kindergarten & Day Nursery). Sisters 3; Lay Teachers 15; Children 170; Total Staff 21.

GARDENA. *St. Anthony's Day Nursery*, 1044 W. 163rd St., 90247. Tel: 310-329-8654. Sr. Yadira Villalobos, M.C., Prin. Sisters 10; Total Staff 12; Children 90.

SYLMAR. *Poverello of Assisi Preschool* (1964) 13367 Borden Ave., 91342. Tel: 818-364-7446; Fax: 818-364-8596. Sr. Mary Fatima Guevara, Prin. Franciscan Missionary Sisters of the Immaculate Conception. Sisters 12; Total Staff 15; Children 120.

[J] GENERAL HOSPITALS

LOS ANGELES. *St. Vincent Medical Center*, 2131 W. 3rd St., 90057. Tel: 213-484-7111. Web: www.stvincentmedicalcenter.com. Rev. Julio Roman, Chap. (Retired). Daughters of Charity Health System.; Sponsored by the Daughters of Charity of St. Vincent de Paul, Province of the West. Bed Capacity 366; Patients Assisted Annually 66,463; Total Staff 1,320.

BURBANK. *Providence Health System* (San Fernando Valley Service Area-Spiritual Care Dept.), 501 S. Buena Vista St., 91505. Tel: 818-847-4688; Fax: 818-847-4607. Email: thomas.landry@providence.org (Spiritual Care Manager). Arnold Schaffer, CEO; Sr. Colleen Settles, Regional Dir., Mission Leadership; Mark Zagrando, Mission Leader, Providence St. Joseph & Providence Holy Cross. Sponsored by the Sisters of Providence and the Sisters of the Little Company of Mary.

Providence Saint Joseph Medical Center, 501 S. Buena Vista St., 91505. Tel: 818-843-5111; Fax: 818-525-3444. Web: www.providence.org. Thomas Landry III, Mgr. Spiritual Care; Revs. Luis Antonio Lacson, Chap.; Mark Ciccone, S.J., Chap.; Mr. R. Phillip Kiehl, Chap.; D'vorah McDonald, Chap.; W. Diane Gardner-Slater, Chap.; Jan Hale, Chap.; Samuel Scriven, Chap. Bed Capacity 414; Patients Assisted Annually 35,000; Total Staff 3,000.

Providence St. Elizabeth Care Center, 10425 Magnolia Blvd., North Hollywood, 91601. Tel: 818-980-3872; Fax: 818-980-6349. Bed Capacity 52; Patients Assisted Annually 60; Total Staff 50.

Providence Holy Cross Medical Center, 15031 Rinaldi St., P.O. Box 9600, Mission Hills, 91346-9600. Tel: 818-365-8051; Fax: 818-496-4569. Phil Abraham, Mgr. Spiritual Care Dept.; Rev. John Bosco Musinguzi, Chap.; Sr. Theresa While, Chap.; Kristin Michealson, Chap.; Darlene Montelongo, Chap. Bed Capacity 257; Patients Assisted Annually 107,136; Total Staff 1,250.

Providence Tarzana Medical Center, 18321 Clark St., Tarzana, 91356. Tel: 818-881-0800. Shawn Kiley, Dir. Mission Leadership Dept.; Renee Owen, Mgr. Spiritual Care Dept.; Revs. Paul Kottacka, Chap.; Kenneth Chukwu, Chap.; Sr. Sarah Schmitt, Chap.; Rabbi Sara Berman, Chap.

Providence Little Company of Mary Hospital (Affiliation of the Providence Health System), 4101 W. Torrance Blvd., Torrance, 90503. Tel: 310-540-7676; Fax: 310-540-7659. Web: lcmhs.org; providence.org. Michael Hunn, CEO; Rev. Jason Cusick, Chap. (Protestant); Revs. Peter Mallin, O.F.M.Conv., Chap.; Christopher Onyenobi, Chap. Sponsored by American Province of Little Company of Mary Sisters, Evergreen Park, IL & Sisters of Providence. Total Staff 3,700; Bed Capacity 250; Bassinets 35.

Providence Little Company of Mary San Pedro Hospital, 1300 W. 7th St., San Pedro, 90732. Tel: 310-832-3311; Fax: 310-514-5314. Web: lcmsh.org; providence.org. Nancy Carlson, COO; Rev. Frank Gordillo, Chap. (Protestant); Rev. Francis L. Shigo, S.V.D., Chap. (Affiliate of the Providence Health System); Sponsored by American Province of Little Company of Mary Sisters, Evergreen, IL & Sisters of Providence. Bed Capacity 210; Total Staff 889.

Providence Little Company of Mary Community Health Foundation, 4101 Torrance Blvd., Torrance, 90503. Tel: 310-543-6900; Fax: 310-540-8664. Joseph M. Zanetta, Exec. Dir.

Providence Little Company of Mary Peninsula Diagnostic Center Tel: 310-831-0371; Fax: 310-514-8920.

Providence Little Company of Mary Peninsula Recovery Center Tel: 310-514-5376; Fax: 310-514-5376.

Providence Little Company of Mary San Pedro Peninsula Hospital Pavillion, 1322 W. Sixth St., San Pedro, 90732. Tel: 310-514-5270; Fax: 310-514-5332. Julie Theiring, Admin. Dir.; Rev. Joel R. Buchman, M.A., S.T.B., Dir. Spiritual Care; Rev. Frank Gordillo, Chap. (Protestant); Rev. Francis L.

Shigo, S.V.D., Chap. Skilled Nursing Facility. Bed Capacity 128.

Providence Little Company of Mary Sub-Acute Center-South Bay, 3620 W. Lomita Blvd., Torrance, 90505. Tel: 310-378-8587; Fax: 310-791-4514. La Verna McMiller, Admin. Dir.; Rev. Joel R. Buchman, M.A., S.T.B., Dir. Spiritual Care; Margaret O'Leary, Chap. Skilled Nursing Facility.; Sponsored by American Province of Little Company of Mary Sisters, Evergreen, IL & Sisters of Providence. Bed Capacity 212.

Providence Saint Joseph Medical Center (1944) 501 S. Buena Vista St., 91505. Tel: 818-843-5111; Fax: 818-847-4609. Rev. Mark Ciccone, S.J., Mgr./Spiritual Care; Sr. Mary Prendergast, S.S.L., Chap.; Margaret Burdge, Chap. Conducted by the Sisters of Providence Health System. Bed Capacity 427; Patients Assisted Annually 320,029; Total Staff 2,100.

CAMARILLO. *St. John's Pleasant Valley Hospital*, 2309 Antonio Ave., 93010. Tel: 805-389-5800; Fax: 805-383-7450. Web: www.stjohnshealth.com. T. Michael Murray, Pres. Sponsored by Sisters of Mercy of the Americas West Midwest Community. Sisters 3; Beds 180; Patients Assisted Annually 46,568; Total Staff 537.

DUARTE. *Santa Teresita Medical Center* (1930) 819 Buena Vista St., 91010. Tel: 626-359-3243; Fax: 626-357-7166. Email: administration@santa-teresita.org. Web: www.santa-teresita.org. Sr. Madonna Joseph Seltzer, O.C.D., CEO. Sisters 40; Bed Capacity Skilled Nursing 129; Patients Assisted Annually 48,917; Beds - Assisted Living 44; Total Staff 222.

INGLEWOOD. *Daniel Freeman Memorial Hospital* Division of Daniel Freeman Hospitals, 333 N. Prairie Ave., 90301. Tel: 310-674-7050; 310-678-0361; Fax: 310-419-8273. Web: www.danielfreeman.org. Joseph W. Dunn, Ph.D., CEO; Nancy J. Lee, R.N., M.S.N., COO; Sr. Regina Clare Salazar, C.S.J., Corp. Vice Pres., Sponsorship & Mission; Daniel J. Ahearn, M.D., Vice Pres. & Medical Dir.; Willard F. Worthen, M.D., Chief of Staff; Rev. Francis X. Chrysostom (Sri Lanka), Chap.; Sisters Loretta Flood, C.S.J., Dir. of Pastoral Care; Kathleen Mary McCarthy, C.S.J., Chm. Sponsored by Sisters of St. Joseph of Carondelet in California. Sisters of St. Joseph of Carondelet 11; Sisters from Other Communities 5; Bed Capacity 364; Patients Assisted Annually 102,115; Total Staff 1,643.

Freeman Hospitals Foundation Tel: 310-419-8292; Fax: 310-419-8248. Sr. Mary Esther McCann, C.S.J., Pres. Emeritus; Brian Gauthier, Vice Pres.; Bernie Sklar, Chm.

LONG BEACH. *St. Mary Medical Center dba Catholic Healthcare West* (1924) 1050 Linden Ave., 90813. Tel: 562-491-9000; Fax: 562-436-6378. Web: www.stmarymedicalcenter.org. Christopher DiCicco, Pres.; Sr. Gerard Earls, C.C.V.I., Vice Pres., Mission Integration & Dir. Spirtual Care. Patients Assisted Annually 215,737; Bed Capacity 389; Total Staff 1,467.

St. Mary Medical Center Foundation, P.O. Box 887, 90801. Tel: 562-491-9225; Fax: 562-491-9888. Email: jtwagner@chw.edu. Web: www.stmarymedicalcenter.org/foundation.

St. Mary Professional Building, Inc., 1050 Linden Ave, 90813. Christopher DiCicco, Pres.

LYNWOOD. *St. Francis Medical Center*, 3630 E. Imperial Hwy., 90262. Tel: 310-900-8900; Fax: 310-900-8299 4. Gerald T Kozai, D. Pharm, Pres./CEO; Bro. Richard Hirbe, f.s.p., M.P.C., B.C.C., Division Dir., Spiritual Care & Ethics; Revs. Ambrose Joseph Kadambukatt, O.C.D., Assoc. Chap.; Thomas M. Philip, Assoc. Chap. Sponsored by the Daughters of Charity of St. Vincent de Paul, Province of the West., Daughters of Charity Health System. Patients Assisted Annually 240,000; Bed Capacity 384; Total Staff 2,120.

OXNARD. *St. John's Regional Medical Center*, 1600 N. Rose Ave., 93030. Tel: 805-988-2500; Fax: 805-981-4440. Web: www.stjohnshealth.com. T. Michael Murray, Pres. Sponsored by Sisters of Mercy of the Americas West Midwest Community. Sisters of Mercy 3; Bed Capacity 265; Patients Assisted Annually 88,728; Total Staff 1,376.

St. John's Healthcare Foundation Oxnard and Pleasant Valley, 1600 N. Rose Ave., 93030. Tel: 805-988-2721; Fax: 805-981-4450. Web: stjohnshealth.org. Tony Loren, Exec. Dir. Bed Capacity 445; Total Assisted Annually 70,362; Total Staff 2,001.

SAN PEDRO. *Providence Little Company of Mary Medical Center San Pedro Hospital* (Affiliate of Providence Health Services), 1300 W. Seventh St., 90732. Tel: 310-832-3311; Fax: 310-514-5314. Email: nancy.carlson@providence.org. Web: www.lcmweb.org. Bed Capacity 556; Patients Assisted Annually 60,000; Total Staff 1,000.

SANTA MARIA. *Marian Medical Center dba Catholic Healthcare West* 1400 E. Church St., 93454. Tel: 805-739-3000; Fax: 805-739-3060. Web: www.marianmedicalcenter.org. Charles J. Cova, Pres.; Deacon Zenon L. Nawrocik, Dir. Pastoral Care. Sponsored by Sisters of St. Francis of Penance and Christian Charity. Sisters 5; Bed Capacity 262; Patients Assisted Annually 196,267; Total Staff 1,445.

Marian Medical Center Extended Care Facility Tel: 805-739-3650; Fax: 805-922-9067. Skilled Nursing Facility. Beds 95.

Marian Medical Center Day Care Facility for Children Tel: 805-739-3666; Fax: 805-922-9067. Capacity 52.

Marian Residence Retirement Home, 124 S. College Dr., 93454. Tel: 805-922-7731.

Marian Medical Center Foundation, 1406 E. Main St., Ste. E., 93454. Tel: 805-739-3595; Fax: 805-739-3599. Web: www.marianmedicalcenter.org.

SANTA MONICA. *Saint John's Health Center*, 1328 22nd St., 90404. Tel: 310-829-5511; Fax: 310-315-6134. Web: www.stjohns.org. Sr. Marie Madeleine Shonka, S.C.L., Co-Chair of Legacy Project; Ms. Lou Lazatin, CEO; Rev. Patrick Comerford, Chap. Sisters of Charity of Leavenworth. Sisters 6; Bed Capacity 340; Patients Assisted Annually 225,000; Total Staff 1,500.

Saint John's Health Center Foundation

The Irene Dunne Guild

WEST COVINA. *Citrus Valley Medical Center, Queen of the Valley Campus*, 1115 S. Sunset Ave., P.O. Box 1980, 91790. Tel: 626-962-4011; Fax: 626-814-2428. Email: catherine@cvhp.com. Web: cvhp.org. Rev. Eric Anthony Lewis; Mr. James T. Yoshioka, CEO. Bed Capacity 325; Patients Assisted Annually 125,000; Total Staff 1,500.

[K] SPECIAL HOSPITALS AND SANATORIA FOR INVALIDS

LOS ANGELES. *Order of Malta Los Angeles Clinic, Inc.*, 2222 W. Ocean View, #112, 90057. Tel: 213-384-4323; Fax: 213-384-4097. Email: freemed112@sbcglobal.net. David Frelinger, M.D., K.M., Medical Dir.; David Johnson, Admin. Conducted by Order of Malta Los Angeles Clinic, Inc., Primary Health Care for the frail elderly, the working poor and medically underserved children. Total Assisted 2,217; Total Staff 12.

CULVER CITY. *Marycrest Manor* (1956) 10664 St. James Dr., 90230-5498. Tel: 310-838-2778; 310-838-0016 (Carmelite Sisters); Fax: 310-838-9647; 310-838-0024 (Carmelite Sisters). Email: marycrestocd@yahoo.com. Sisters Noella, O.C.D., Admin.; Veronica Del Carmen, O.C.D., Dir. of Nurses. Carmelite Sisters of the Most Sacred Heart of Los Angeles., Skilled Nursing Facility attended by priests from Loyola Marymount University. Carmelite Sisters of the Most Sacred Heart of Los Angeles 7; Pastoral Care Sisters 2; Bed Capacity 57; Residents 57; Total Assisted Annually 600; Total Staff 85.

NEWBURY PARK. *Mary Health of the Sick Convalescent and Nursing Hospital* (1964) 2929 Theresa Dr., 91320. Tel: 805-498-3644; Fax: 805-498-5112. Web: maryhealth.com. Sr. Maritza Arce, S.de.M., Exec. Dir. Sisters Servants of Mary., Skilled Nursing Facility. Sisters 15; Bed Capacity 61; Residents Assisted Annually 85; Total Staff 86.

OJAI. *St. Joseph's Health and Retirement Center*, 2464 E. Ojai Ave., P.O. Box 760, 93024. Tel: 805-646-1466; Fax: 805-646-1013. Email: brmichaeloh@yahoo.com. Bro. Michael Bassemier, O.H., Admin.; Rev. Thaddeus Bui, O.H., Prior & Chap. Hospitaller Brothers of St. John of God. Capacity 28; Independent Living 25; Total Staff 42.

[L] HANDICAPPED

SANTA MONICA. *Saint John's Child Study Center, Saint John's Hospital & Health Center*, 1339 20th St., 90404. Tel: 310-829-8921; Fax: 310-829-8455. Rev. Patrick Comerford, Chap.; Rebecca Refuerza, L.C.S.W., Dir. Conducted by Sisters of Charity of Leavenworth., Affiliated with Saint John's Hospital. Children Treated Annually 1,800.

SUNLAND. **Tierra del Sol Foundation*, 9919 Sunland Blvd., 91040. Tel: 818-352-1419; Fax: 818-353-0777. Web: tierradelsol.org. Stephen J. Miller, Exec. Dir.; Nancy Bissonette-Andrew, Clinical Dir. Community Program/Supported Employment for Adults with Developmental Disabilities. Licensed Capacity 304.

[M] VISITING NURSE SERVICES

LOS ANGELES. *Servants of Mary, Ministers to the Sick*, 2131 W. 27th St., 90018-3018. Tel: 213-731-5747; Fax: 323-731-4251. Sr. Leticia Rodriguez, S.M., Supr. Sisters 13; Total Assisted 41; Total Staff 7.

[N] PROTECTIVE INSTITUTIONS

LOS ANGELES. *St. Anne's*, 155 N. Occidental Blvd., 90026. Tel: 213-381-2931; Fax: 213-381-7804. Email: stannes@stannes.org. Web: www.stannes.org. Tony Walker, M.A., Pres. & CEO. Sponsored by the Franciscan Sisters of the Sacred Heart., Residential treatment program, Transitional Housing, Mental Health, Family Based Services; Early Learning Center, Services for pregnant and at risk children and families. Beds Licensed for Children Under 18 years of age 50; Children Served Annually in Residential Care 125.

Support groups include:

St. Anne's Foundation

St. Anne's Guild

Mabel Mosler Auxiliary

Loretta Young Auxiliary

Sister Winifred Auxiliary Residential 250; Prevention Education 2,000; Total Staff 220.

Convent of the Good Shepherd-Good Shepherd Shelter (1904) Mailing Address: P.O. Box 19487, 90019. Tel: 323-737-6111; Fax: 323-737-6113. Email: rgsla1@aol.com. Web: www.goodshepherdshelter.org. Conducted by Sisters of the Good Shepherd., Shelter for Battered Women and Their Children. Sisters 10; Women Assisted Annually 24; Children 108; Total Assisted Annually 132.

Little Flower Missionary House (1943) 2434 Gates St., 90031-2824. Tel: 323-221-9248; Fax: 323-221-9831. Email: lflower@catholic.org. Web: www.rc.net/losangeles/littleflower. Sr. Caridad, O.C.D., Supr. & Admin.; Mrs. Catherine Catano, Dir. & Prin. Attended by Salesian priests. Child and Kindergarten Care Center. Sisters 6; Lay Teachers 13; Capacity 135; Kindergarten Capacity 40; Total Staff 26.

CHATSWORTH. *Rancho San Antonio*, 21000 Plummer St., 91311. Tel: 818-882-6400; Fax: 818-882-6404. Bro. John Crowe, C.S.C., Exec. Dir. Directed by the Brothers of Holy Cross., Sponsored by Catholic Archdiocese of Los Angeles. Brothers 1; Boys (13-17 yrs.) 106; Total Staff 168; Families Assisted 257.

SANTA BARBARA. *St. Vincent's* (1858) 4200 Calle Real, 93110-1454. Tel: 805-683-6381; Fax: 805-967-7508. Email: info@sv-sb.org. Web: www.stvincents-sb.org. For single moms on welfare and/or very low income. Daughters of Charity of St. Vincent de Paul 5; Bed Capacity 70; Total Assisted 104; Total Staff 19.

St. Vincent's Casa Alegria Children Center (1999) 4200 Calle Real, 93110-1454. Tel: 805-683-6381, Ext. 211; Fax: 805-967-7508. Email: info@sv-sb.org. Web: www.stvincents-sb.org. For infants, toddlers, and preschoolers. Daughters of Charity of St. Vincent de Paul 5; Day Care 46; Total Staff 14.

[O] HOMES FOR AGED

LOS ANGELES. *St. John of God Retirement and Care Center*, 2468 S. St. Andrews Pl., 90018. Tel: 323-731-0641; Fax: 323-731-1452. Bros. Michael Bassemier, O.H., Admin.; Pablo Lopez, O.H., Provincial; George Tecku, O.H., Prior. Brothers 7; Bed Capacity 287; SNF 131; Residential Care 105; Patients Assisted Annually 280; Total Staff 230; Independent Living 51.

Supporting Organizations:

Hospitaller Foundation of California, Inc. Tel: 323-731-7141; Fax: 323-731-5717. Bro. Patrick Corr, O.H., Pres.

Women's League of St. John of God, Inc., Helpers Club of St. John of God, Inc. Tel: 323-731-7141; Fax: 323-731-5717.

Nazareth House (1946) 3333 Manning Ave., 90064. Tel: 310-839-2361; Fax: 310-839-4204. Email: mbrody@nazarethhouseja.org. Web: www.nazarethouse.org. Sr. Margaret Brody, Supr. & Admin. Congregation of the Sisters of Nazareth. Retired Priests 18; Sisters 8; Total Staff 85; Residents 123.

SAN FERNANDO. *Mother Gertrude Home for Senior Citizens* (Franciscan Missionary Sisters of the Immaculate Conception, Inc.), 11320 Laurel Canyon Blvd., 91340. Tel: 818-898-1546; Fax: 818-365-6646. Capacity 45; Total Staff 19; Total in Residence 36.

SAN PEDRO. *Little Sisters of the Poor* (1979) Jeanne Jugan Residence, 2100 S. Western Ave., 90732. Tel: 310-548-0625; Fax: 310-548-4504. Email: mssanpedro@littlesistersofthepoor.org. Web: www.lspsocal.org. Sr. Marguerite McCarthy, L.S.P., Supr.

Little Sisters of the Poor of Los Angeles. A Corporation Sisters 9; Lay Associates 15; Total Staff 100; Residents 102; Total Assisted Annually 1,260.

SUN VALLEY. *Villa Scalabrini*, 10631 Vinedale St., 91352. Tel: 818-768-6500; Fax: 818-768-0684. Web:

www.villascalabrini.com. Rev. Ermete Nazzani, C.S., Exec. Dir. & Admin. Missionary Fathers of St. Charles., Retirement Center and Special Care Unit; Augustinian Recollect Sisters. Bed Capacity 188; Retirement Center 130; Skilled Nursing Unit 58; Total Staff 115.

[P] MONASTERIES AND RESIDENCES OF PRIESTS AND BROTHERS

LOS ANGELES. *Brothers of John of God, Inc., The,* 2425 S. Western Ave., 90018-2608. Tel: 323-734-0233; Fax: 323-731-5987. Email: usaprov-office@sbcglobal.net. Web: www.hospitallers.org. Bro. Pablo Lopez, O.H., Prov. *Women's League of St. John of God, Inc.,* 90002. Tel: 323-731-7141; Fax: 323-731-5717. *Helper's Club, Inc.* Tel: 323-731-7141; Fax: 323-731-5717. *St. John of God Retirement & Care Center,* 90018. Tel: 323-731-0641; Fax: 323-737-1452. Email: john@stjohnofgodseniors.org. Web: hospitallers.org. *St. Joseph's Health & Retirement Center* Tel: 805-646-1466; Fax: 805-646-1013. Email: igi@ojai.net. Web: hospitallers.org. *Hospitaller Foundation of California, Inc.* Tel: 323-731-7141; Fax: 323-731-5717. Email: arlene@hospitallerfoundation.org. Web: hospitallers.org. *Women's League of St. Joseph's Health & Retirement Center* Tel: 805-646-1466; Fax: 805-646-1013. Web: hospitallers.org. *Grande Apartments-Los Angeles* Tel: 323-730-4100; Fax: 323-737-1452. Email: jpeters@stjohnofgodseniors.org. Web: hospitallers.org. *Hospitaller Brothers Healthcare, Inc.* Tel: 805-734-0233; Fax: 323-737-1452. Email: usaprov-office@sbcglobal.net. Web: hospitallers.org. *St. John of God Health Care Services* Tel: 760-241-4917; Fax: 760-241-8911. Email: brogary@sjghcs.org. Web: hospitallers.org.

Colombiere House Formerly Connolly House., 5322 Franklin Ave., 90027. Tel: 323-466-3723; Fax: 323-466-3826. Email: wdelaney@calprov.org. Revs. Mark Ciccone, S.J.; William K. Delaney, S.J.; Thomas J. Griffin-Smolenski, S.J.; Paul J. Bernadicou, S.J. Jesuit Fathers. Priests 4.

Columban Fathers, Procure House, 2600 N. Vermont Ave., 90027-1245. Tel: 323-665-4289; Fax: 323-664-7160. Email: columbanla@aol.com. Web: www.columban.org. Revs. Peter Kenny, S.S.C., Supr. & Contact Person; Thomas Cusack, S.S.C.; Paul White, S.S.C.; Anthony Mortell, S.S.C.; James Shiffer, S.S.C., J.C.L.; John Wanaurny, S.S.C.; Brendan O'Sullivan, S.S.C.

Divine Word Residence, Divine Word Missionaries, 2181 W. 25th St., 90018. Tel: 323-735-8130; Fax: 323-735-8122. Bro. Andrew Hotchkiss, S.V.D., Rector.

Dominic Savio Salesian Residence (1958) 920 Soto St., 90023-1396. Tel: 323-266-6000; Fax: 323-266-3487. Email: sdblosangeles@hotmail.com. Web: www.donboscowest.org. In Res. Revs. Joseph A. Farias, S.D.B., Pastor St. Mary's & Treas.; John Lam, S.D.B., Pastor St. Bridgit; Lucian B. Lomello, S.D.B. (Retired); Avelino Lorenzo, S.D.B., St. Mary's; James Nieblas, S.D.B., Supr. of Community, Salesian High School; William Schafer, S.D.B., Exec. Dir., Salesian Boys' & Girls' Club, Salesian Family Youth Center; Robert Stein, S.D.B., St. Mary's; Carmen Vairo, S.D.B., Salesian Boy's & Girl's Club & Salesian Family Youth Center; Bro. Tom Mass, S.D.B., Salesian Boy's & Girl's Club, Salesian Family Youth Center & St. Mary's.

Franciscan Brothers of the Third Order Regular, 4522 Gainsborough Ave., 90027-1227. Tel: 323-644-2740; Fax: 323-644-2977. Bro. Paulinus Horkan, O.S.F., Regl. Supr. Brothers 7.

Guadalupe Missioners Procure, 4714 W. 8th St., 90005. Tel: 323-937-2780; Fax: 323-937-2782. Revs. Santiago G. Lara, M.G., Local Supr.; Abraham R. Garcia, M.G., Asst. Priests 2.

Hospitaller Brothers of St. John of God, 2468 S. St. Andrew's Pl., 90018. Tel: 323-731-0641; Fax: 323-731-5987. Email: usaprov-office@sbcglobal.net. Web: www.hospitallers.org. Bro. George Tecku, O.H., Prior. Brothers 10.

St. John of God Retirement and Care Center, 2468 S. St. Andrews Pl., 90018. Tel: 323-731-0641; Fax: 323-737-1452. Email: usaprov-office@sbcglobal.net. Web: www.hospitaller.org. Bros. Pablo Lopez, O.H., Prov.; George Tecku, O.H., Local Supr. Brothers 7.

St. Joseph Friary, 2843 San Fernando Rd., 90065-1320. Tel: 323-254-7764; Fax: 323-259-9833. Revs. Angus Cooper, O.F.M., Guardian; Eugene David Burnett, O.F.M., Vicar; Martial Luebke, O.F.M. (Retired); Robert Pfisterer, O.F.M. (Retired); Bro. Nicholas Ronalter, O.F.M.

Maryknoll Fathers and Brothers (Catholic Foreign Mission Society of America), 222 S. Hewitt St., 90012. Tel: 213-747-9676; Fax: 213-747-8923. Web: www.maryknoll.org. 2701 S. Peck Rd., Monrovia, 91016. Tel: 626-447-6202, Ext. 32 Annunciation Parish, Arcadia. Rev. Michael G. Callanan, M.M. (Retired). 255 S. Grand Ave., #413, 90012-3017. Tel: 213-625-5702. Revs. James P. Colligan, M.M. (Retired); Joseph J. Donovan, M.M. Tel: 213-808-1002; Richard Ouellette, M.M. (Retired), 340 Norumbega Dr., Monrovia, 91016. Tel: 626-358-1825.

Minim Fathers, 3431 Portola Ave., 90032. Tel: 323-223-1101; Fax: 323-223-9592. Email: jvega@earthlink.net. Web: home.earthlink.net/~jvega/. Revs. Mario Pisano, O.M., Supr.; Gino Vanzillotta, O.M.; Jose L. Vega, O.M. Priests 3.

Missionaries of Charity Brothers (1975) Tel: 213-384-6116. *Casa Teresa,* 1316 S. Westlake Ave., 90006. Tel: 213-380-5225. Email: brosla@aol.com. Web: www.lamcbro.com. Hospitality for men. Temporary shelter for sick homeless men. Brothers 5. *Nuestro Hogar,* 1345 Alvarado Ter., 90006. Tel: 213-251-9708. Day Center for young adults. Total Assisted 85; Total Staff 5.

**Missionaries of Jesus, Inc.,* 435 S. Occidental Blvd., 90057. Tel: 213-389-8439, Ext. 19; Fax: 213-389-1951. Email: info@missionariesofjesus.com. Web: www.missionariesofjesus.com. Revs. Manuel Gacad, M.J., Prov. Supr.; Michael Montoya, M.J., Vice Supr.; Melchor Villero, M.J.; Enrique Ymson, M.J.; Melanio Viuya, M.J., Dir. Mission Promotion Office & Treas.

Our Lady of Mount Carmel Priory, 4966 Alonzo Ave., Encino, 91316. Tel: 818-345-6055. Revs. Augustine W. Carter, O.Carm.; John Coleman, O.Carm., Prior; Stephen Cooley, O.Carm.; Matt J. Ewing, O.Carm.; Paul Henson, O.Carm.; Thomas Schrader, O.Carm.; Peter J. Liuzzi, O.Carm.; Barnabas B. Hughes, O.F.M.
Fathers of the Order of Mount Carmel, Corporation Priests 8.

Piarist Fathers, 512 S. Avenue 20, 90031. Tel: 213-223-4153. Revs. Raul Palma, Sch.P.; Juan Trenchs, Sch.P.; Miguel Campos, Sch.P. Priests 4.

The Society of St. Paul (1914) (Mexican Province), 112 Herbert St., 90063. Tel: 323-269-9814; Fax: 323-269-0242. Email: joerelop@hotmail.com. Revs. Valeriano Giachino, S.S.P.; José Refugio López, S.S.P., Supr.; Antonio Francisco Paredes Monjaras, S.S.P., Seminarian; Marco Antonio Vences, S.S.P.

BALDWIN PARK. *Vietnamese Redemptorist Mission,* 3452 N. Big Dalton Ave., 91706. Tel: 626-337-7735; 626-338-3295; Fax: 626-851-1280. Email: chaqhung@yahoo.com. Revs. Ngo Dinh Thoa, C.Ss.R.; Pham Quoc Hung, C.Ss.R.; Doan Trong Son, C.Ss.R.; Nguyen Van Phan, C.Ss.R.; Tran Gia Dien; Bros. John M. Viet Hien, C.Ss.R.; Martin Nguyen Van Moi, C.Ss.R.
In Residence Elsewhere: Revs. Dang Phuoc Hoa, C.Ss.R., 8800 E. 22nd St., Tucson, AZ 85710. Tel: 602-751-2060; Tran Dinh Phuc, C.Ss.R., 22 Stone St., Salinas, 93901. Tel: 408-772-8227; Nguyen Duc Mau, C.Ss.R., 2458 Atlantic Ave., Long Beach, 90806. Tel: 562-424-2041; Fax: 562-424-2152; Phan Phat Huon, C.Ss.R., 2458 Atlantic Ave., Long Beach, 90806. Tel: 562-424-2041; Fax: 562-424-2152; Ngo Van Dao, C.Ss.R., 2458 Atlantic Ave., Long Beach, 90806. Tel: 562-424-2041; Fax: 562-424-2152; Nguyen Ngoc Viet, C.Ss.R., 2458 Atlantic Ave., Long Beach, 90806. Tel: 562-424-2041; Fax: 562-424-2152; Nguyen Tat Hai, C.Ss.R., 2458 Atlantic Ave., Long Beach, 90806. Tel: 562-424-2041; Fax: 562-424-2152; Nguyen Truong Luan, 2458 Atlantic Ave., Long Beach, 90806. Tel: 562-424-2041; Fax: 562-424-2152; Bro. Vo Thanh Ha, C.Ss.R., 2458 Atlantic Ave., Long Beach, 90806. Tel: 562-424-2041; Fax: 562-424-2152; Revs. Dinh Minh Hai, C.Ss.R., 3910 S. Ledbetter Dr., Dallas, TX 75236. Tel: 972-438-4082; Bui Quang Tuan, C.Ss.R., 3910 S. Ledbetter Dr., Dallas, TX 75236. Tel: 972-438-4082; Nguyen Phi Long, C.Ss.R., 3910 S. Ledbetter Dr., Dallas, TX 75236. Tel: 972-438-4082; Chau Xuan Bau, C.Ss.R., 3417 W. Little York Rd., Houston, TX 77091. Tel: 214-321-9493; Fax: 713-686-4589; Le Quang Phung, C.Ss.R., 3417 W. Little York Rd., Houston, TX 77091. Tel: 214-321-9493; Fax: 713-686-4589; Nguyen Duc Thanh, C.Ss.R., 3417 W. Little York Rd., Houston, TX 77091. Tel: 214-321-9493; Fax: 713-686-4589; Nguyen Van Thach, C.Ss.R., 3417 W. Little York Rd., Houston, TX 77091. Tel: 214-321-9493; Fax: 713-686-4589; Nguyen Quoc Dung, C.Ss.R.; Nguyen Dinh Trung, C.Ss.R., 3417 W. Little York Rd., Houston, TX 77091. Tel: 214-321-9493; Fax: 713-686-4589; Bro. Nguyen Tran Duc, C.Ss.R.; Revs. Tung Duc Vu, C.Ss.R.; Dominic Pham, C.Ss.R.; Dinh Ngoc Que, C.Ss.R.; Le Trong Hung, C.S.s.R.; Bros. Nguyen Phuoc Hahn, C.S.s.R.; Nguyen Ngoc Khanh, C.S.s.R.

CUDAHY. *Misioneros del Sagrado Corazon y Santa Maria de Guadalupe* (1938) 4235 Clara St., 90201. Tel: 323-562-3356; Fax: 323-562-3332. Email: sagrado_cudahy@yahoo.com. Tony Vienna, Esq., Contact Person. Tel: 213-485-1555; Fax: 213-689-1004; Rev. Antonio Garnica, M.S.C., V.F., Regl. Supr.

CULVER CITY. *Ignatius House, The Novitiate of the California Province, Society of Jesus,* P.O. Box 5166, 90231-5166. Tel: 310-815-0166; Fax: 310-815-0170. Email: mweiler@calprov.org. Web: www.calprov.org. Revs. Michael F. Weiler, S.J., Dir. of Novices; Christopher T. Nguyen, S.J., Asst. Dir. of Novices; John LeVecke, S.J., Christian Life Community Natl. Ecclesial Asst.; Doan T. Hoang, S.J., Dir. of the Apostleship of Prayer; John W. Clark, S.J.; Edward J. Siebert, S.J.; Bro. Michael E. Breault, S.J., Min. of the Jesuit Community. 10775 Deshire Pl., 90230-5017. Tel: 310-815-0166 (Staff); 310-815-0185 (Novices); Fax: 310-815-0170.

LA VERNE. *Congregation of the Sacred Hearts of Jesus and Mary,* 2150 Damien Ave., 91750-5114. Tel: 909-593-5441 (Provinical Office); Fax: 909-593-3971. Email: ssccwest@cpl.net. Web: www.cpl.net/~ssccwest. Very Rev. Donal McCarthy, SS.CC., Prov. Supr., La Verne, CA; Revs. Michael W. Barry, SS.CC., Dir., Mary's Mercy Center, Inc: Mary's Table & Veronica's Home of Mercy, San Bernardino, CA; Peter K. Dennis, SS.CC., La Verne, CA; Patrick J. Crowley, SS.CC., Hemet House of Prayer, Hemet, CA; Kenneth McCabe, SS.CC., Hemet House of Prayer, Hemet, CA; Michael N. Maher, SS.CC, Pastor, St. Louis Church, Cathedral City, CA; William C. Moore, SS.CC., Ministry of the Arts, Pomona, CA; Patrick J. O'Hagan, SS.CC., Pastor, St. Paul the Apostle, Chino Hills, CA; Thomas J. Mullen, SS.CC., (On Sabbatical); John Roche, SS.CC., Assoc. Pastor, Holy Name of Mary, San Dimas, CA; Richard J. Danyluk, SS.CC., Chap., Sisters of St. Joseph of Carondelet, Los Angeles, CA; Vincent Fallon, SS.CC., Our Lady of the Wisdom, NV; Jeremiah Holland, SS.CC., Pastor, Holy Spirit Catholic Church, Hemet, CA; Pasquale V. Laghezza, SS.CC., Chap., NY Harbor Health Care System, NYC; Henry Paul Murtagh, SS.CC., Pastor, Artesia, NM - Our Lady of Grace; Martin P. O'Loghlen, SS.CC., Assoc. Pastor, Holy Name of Mary, San Dimas, CA; Patrick Travers, SS.CC., Prin., Damien High School, La Verne, CA; Michael J. Brooks, SS.CC., La Verne, CA; Peadar Cronin, SS.CC., Assoc. Pastor, Holy Name of Mary, San Dimas, CA; Patrick Argue, SS.CC. (Retired), Co. Cavan, Ireland; Brian Guerrini, SS.CC., Assoc. Pastor, Artesia, NM - Our Lady of Grace; Patrick P. Coyle, SS.CC. (Retired), Twenty-Nine Palms, CA. Priests in Residence 6; Priests not in Residence 16.

MONTEBELLO. *Congregation of the Mission Western Province,* 1105 Bluff Rd., 90640. Tel: 323-721-6050; Fax: 323-887-1765. Email: cmstlouis@vincentian.org. Web: www.vincentian.org.
DePaul Center, a California Corporation
Congregation of the Mission, Western Province, California
Vincentian Province of the West Support Trust Fund
Vincentian Foreign Mission Society DePaul Evangelization Center, 1105 Bluff Rd., 90640-6198. Tel: 323-721-6060; Fax: 323-887-1765. Revs. Andrew E. Bellisario, C.M., Prov.; James Osendorf, C.M., Supr. & Dir.; Gary S. Landry, C.M., Asst. Vocation Dir.; Binh Van Nguyen, C.M.; Peter J. Diliberto (Retired); Robert J. Jones, C.M.; Thomas J. McIntyre, C.M. (Retired); Bro. Edward D. Graham, C.M., (Retired). Priests 7; Brothers 1.
St. Mary's Evangelization Center, 1964 Las Canoas Rd., Santa Barbara, 93105-2351. Tel: 805-966-4829; Fax: 805-564-1662. Revs. Walter L. Housey, C.M. (Retired); Patrick J. Mullin, C.M., Dir.; Roy A. Persich, C.M. (Retired); John V. Shine, Supr. (Retired). Priests 4. *Amat Residence 1,* 649 W. Adams Blvd., 90007-2546. Tel: 213-747-1227; Fax: 213-749-4504. Email: amathouse@aol.com. Rev. William R. Piletic, C.M., Vocation Dir., Asst. Prov. & Supr. Priests 1. *Amat Residence II,* 641 W. Adams Blvd., 90007-2546. Tel: 213-748-9829; Fax: 213-748-9829. Revs. Pedro Villarroya, C.M.; Thomas C. Anslow, C.M., J.C.L.; Stafford Poole, C.M. (Retired). Priests 3.

OXNARD. *St. Augustine Priory O.A.R.* (1990) 400 Sherwood Way, 93033-7510. Tel: 805-486-7433; Fax: 805-487-2805. Email: saprovince@yahoo.com. Web: augustinianrecollects.org. Revs. Marlon Beof, O.A.R., Prior; Michael Stechmann, O.A.R., Subprior. Total in Residence 9; Priests 6; Brothers 2; Students 1. In Res. Revs. James V. Brown, O.A.R.; Fidel Hernandez, O.A.R.; Robert Huse, O.A.R.; Frank T. Wilder, O.A.R.; Bros. Mario Alvarez, O.A.R.; Raymond Fabrin, O.A.R.

PASADENA. *Legionaries of Christ,* 1041 Rancho Rd., Arcadia, 91006. Tel: 626-445-3511; Fax: 626-792-0475. Web: www.legionofchrist.org. Priests 4. In Res. Revs. Michael Shannon, L.C., Supr.; John

Bullock, L.C.; Mariano de Blas, L.C.; Juan Rivas, L.C.

SANTA BARBARA. *Franciscan Friary, Order of Friars Minor (Old Mission)* (1786) 2201 Laguna St., 93105. Tel: 805-682-4713; Fax: 805-682-6067. Revs. Richard McManus, O.F.M., Guardian; Nevin Ford, O.F.M.; Maurus Kelly, O.F.M.; Howard Hall, O.F.M.; Leo Sprietsma, O.F.M.; Pedro Vasquez, O.F.M.; Thomas Messner, O.F.M.; Daniel Barica, O.F.M.; John Vaughn, O.F.M.; Jack Clark Robinson, O.F.M.; Bros. Timothy Arthur, O.F.M., Prov. Archivist; Joachim Grant, O.F.M.; Philip Morales, O.F.M.; Ernest LuVisi, O.F.M. Priests 11; Brothers 5.

SANTA MARIA. *American Region of the Josephite Fathers Charitable Trust*, 180 Patterson Rd., 93455. Tel: 805-937-4555. Email: frcharles@sldm.org. Web: www.josephiteweb.org. Very Rev. Charles Hofschulte, C.J., Contact Person.

SANTA PAULA. *Canons Regular of the Immaculate Conception* (1871) Dom Grea House of Formation & Novitiate, 984 Monte Vista Dr., 93060-1612. Tel: 805-933-5063; Fax: 805-525-5115. Email: domgreahouse@cricusa.com. Web: cricusa.com. Revs. Pasquale Vuoso, C.R.I.C., Supr. Tel: 805-525-2149; Fax: 805-933-5520; Thomas J. Dome, C.R.I.C., Dir. & Novice Master; Charles R. Lueras, C.R.I.C. Tel: 805-525-2149; Fax: 805-933-5520; William B. Ustaski, C.R.I.C. Tel: 661-252-3353; Fax: 661-252-1539. Priests 4; Postulants 2; Seminarians 2.

SIERRA MADRE. *Passionist Community*, 700 N. Sunnyside Ave., 91024. Tel: 626-355-1740; Fax: 626-355-1744. *Passionist Retreat House*, 700 N. Sunnyside Ave., 91024. Tel: 626-355-7188; Fax: 626-355-0485. Congregation of the Passion, Mater Dolorosa Community. *Passionist Residence*, 700 N. Sunnyside Ave., 91024. Tel: 626-355-1740; Fax: 626-355-1744. Very Rev. Alan Phillip, C.P., Local Supr.; Revs. Alfred Pooler, C.P., Retreat Team; Patrick Brennan, C.P., Retreat Dir.; Michael Hoolahan, C.P., Retreat Team; Bro. John Rockenbach, C.P.; Rev. Tu-Din Paul Kim. Priests 5; Brothers 1.

VALYERMO. *St. Andrew's Abbey*, 31001 N. Valyermo Rd., P.O. Box 40, 93563-0040. Tel: 661-944-2178; Fax: 661-944-1076. Email: monks@valyermo.com. Web: www.saintandrewsabbey.com. Very Rev. Damien Toilolo, O.S.B., Prior Admin.; Rt. Rev. Francis Benedict, O.S.B., Abbot Emeritus; Rev. Simon O'Donnell, O.S.B.; Bro. Patrick Sheridan, O.S.B.; Rev. John Bosco Stoner, O.S.B.; Bros. John Mark Matthews, O.S.B.; Peter Zhou Bang-jiu, O.S.B.; Rev. Philip Edwards, O.S.B.; Bro. Dominic Guillen, O.S.B.; Rev. Gregory Elmer, O.S.B.; Bros. Benedict Dull, O.S.B.; Joseph Iarrobino, O.S.B.; Revs. Luke Dysinger, O.S.B., M.D., D.Phil.; Martin Yslas, O.S.B.; Isaac Kalina, O.S.B.; Carlos Lopez, O.S.B.; Joseph (Dennis) Brennan, O.S.B., Subprior; Aelred Niespolo, O.S.B.; Matthew Rios, O.S.B.; Bros. James Brennan, O.S.B.; Cassian DiRocco, O.S.B.; Bede Hazlet, O.S.B.; Raphael Salandra, O.S.B. Benedictine Monks. Priests 13; Brothers 10.

VAN NUYS. *Rogationist Fathers* (2001) 6635 Tobias Ave., 91405. Tel: 818-782-0184; Fax: 818-782-1794. Email: rogdevoff@aol.com. Web: www.rcj.org; www.vocationsandprayer.org; www.rogationists.org. Revs. John Bruno, R.C.J.; Rodolfo D'Agostino, R.C.J.; Vito Di Marzio, Vocation Dir.

Congregation of Rogationists, Inc.

WHITTIER. *Redemptorists of Whittier*, 7215 S. Newlin Ave., 90602-1266. Tel: 562-698-0107; Fax: 562-696-1617. Web: www.st-maryschurch.org. Revs. Jose Luis Chavez, C.Ss.R.; Donald B. Willard, C.Ss.R.; Joseph Elliott, C.Ss.R. (Retired); Steven J. Nyl, C.Ss.R.; Donald Liberty, C.Ss.R. (Retired); Enrique Lopez, C.Ss.R. (Retired); Arthur Frost, C.Ss.R. (Retired); William Adams, C.Ss.R. (Retired). Priests 11. In Res Revs. Anthony Phuc Nguyen, C.Ss.R.; Michael McAndrew, C.Ss.R.; Tuan Nguyen, C.Ss.R.

[Q] CONVENTS AND RESIDENCES FOR SISTERS

LOS ANGELES. **The Blessed Sacrament Sisters of Charity, Inc.*, 248 S. Mariposa Ave., 90004. Tel: 213-389-7760; Fax: 213-389-1332. Email: ahelga_ahelga@yahoo.com. Sr. Helga S. Rim, Local Supr.

California Institute of the Sisters of the Immaculate Heart Mary (1848) 3431 Waverly Dr., 90027-2526. Tel: 323-664-3357, Ext. 114; Fax: 323-664-2215. Sr. Catherine Rose, I.H.M., Dir. & Treas.

California Institute of the Sisters of the Most Holy and Immaculate Heart of the Blessed Virgin Mary Sisters 9.

Congregation of the Sisters of Nazareth Motherhouse, U.S.A., 3333 Manning Ave., 90064. Tel: 310-839-2361; Fax: 310-839-0648. Email: regional@nazarethhousela.org. Web: www.nazarethhouse.org. Sr. Marie McCormack, C.S.N., Regl. Supr. Sisters 8.

Eucharistic Franciscan Missionary Sisters, Motherhouse: 943 S. Soto St., 90023. Tel: 213-264-6556; Fax: 213-526-1655. Email: efms@earthlink.net. Sr. Rose Seraphim, E.F.M.S., Supr. Gen. Sisters 25.

Eucharistic Franciscan Missionary Sisters of Los Angeles, Nativity Convent: 1421 Cota Ave., Torrance, 90501. Tel: 310-328-6725; Fax: 310-328-5248.

Guadalupanas Missionaries of the Holy Spirit (1930) Novitiate., 758 S. Dunsmuir Ave., 90036. Tel: 323-936-0135; Fax: 323-939-8735. Email: niditomgsps@aol.com. Sr. Maria Julia Lozano, Supr.

Guadalupanas Missionaries of the Holy Spirit, 5467 W. 8th St., 90036. Tel: 323-935-6565; Fax: 323-930-0394. Email: mgspscalal@yahoo.com.

Missionary Guadalupanas of the Holy Spirit, Apostolate House. Sisters 4.

Hermanas Carmelitas de San Jose (1916) 141 W. 87th Pl., 90003. Tel: 323-758-6840; 323-752-2838. Sr. Enedina de Jesus Hernandez, C.S.J., Regl. Supr. US Community. Sisters 4.

Missionary Benedictine Sisters of Tutzing in Los Angeles, Inc. (2002) 912 Bronson Ave., 90019-1935. Tel: 323-939-3977; Fax: 323-937-7971; 323-935-8985. Email: osbgregory@hanmail.net. Sr. Pachomia Kim, O.S.B., Supr. & Contact Person.

Missionary Servants of the Most Blessed Trinity Ascension Missionary Cenacle, 518 W. 111th Pl., 90044. Tel: 213-754-0020.

Missionary Sisters of Christ the King (Poland) (1959) 3424 W. Adams Blvd., 90018. Tel: 323-734-5249; Fax: 323-734-0046. Email: plchurchla@earthlink.net. Sisters Anna Kalinowski, M.S.C.K., Local Supr.; Kinga Hoffman, M.C.H.R., Sec. (Parish Office). Sisters working in Archdiocese of Los Angeles 3.

Monastery of the Angels (Contemplative), 1977 Carmen Ave., 90068. Tel: 323-466-2186; Fax: 323-466-6645. Web: www.op-stjoseph.org/nuns/angels. Sr. Mary Raymond, O.P., Prioress; Rev. Vincent Lopez, O.P., Chap. Nuns of the Order of Preachers. Professed Cloistered Nuns 20.

Pious Disciples of the Divine Master, 501 N. Beaudry, 90012-1509. Tel: 213-250-7962 (Center); 213-977-0893 (Community); Fax: 213-977-0987. Web: www.pddm.us. Sr. M. Lucille Van Hoogmoed, P.D.D.M., Local Supr. Sisters 8.

Presentation Sisters, 10843 Gorman Ave., 90059. Tel: 323-563-3901. Sr. M. Antonio Heaphy, P.B.V.M., Provincial Leader.

Servants of the Immaculate Child Mary, E.I.N. (Esclavas de la Inmaculada Nina) (1901) 5135 Dartmouth Ave., 90032-3323. Tel: 323-225-3279; Fax: 323-225-3279. 350 S. Boyle Ave., 90033-3813. Tel: 323-269-7786; Fax: 323-269-7786. Email: ein-la@hotmail.com.

Sisters of Social Service of Los Angeles (1926) *General Motherhouse*, 4316 Lanai Rd., Encino, 91436. Tel: 818-285-3355; Fax: 818-285-3366. Email: ssocialser@aol.com. Web: www.socialservicesisters.com. Sr. Claire Graham, Gen. Dir.

Sisters of Social Service of Los Angeles, Inc.

Sisters of Social Service Support Trust Fund Sisters 100.

Sisters of Social Service, Formation, 4316 Lanai Rd., Encino, 91436. Tel: 818-285-3355; Fax: 818-285-3366. Email: ssocialser@aol.com. Web: sistersofsocialservice.com. In Formation 2.

Sisters of St. Joseph of Carondelet in California (1850) (St. Mary's Provincialate, Carondelet Center), 11999 Chalon Rd., 90049-1524. Tel: 310-889-2100; Fax: 310-476-8735. Email: provincialate@csjla.org. Web: www.csjla.org. Sisters Mary McKay, C.S.J., Ph.D., Prov. Supr.; Mary Sevilla, Asst. Prov. Supr.; Patricia Ann Nelson, C.S.J., Asst. Prov. Supr. Sisters 357.

Sisters of St. Joseph in California Tel: 310-889-2154; Fax: 310-472-5982.

Sisters of St. Joseph Ministerial Services Tel: 310-889-2157; Fax: 310-472-5982.

Sisters of St. Joseph of Orange, 8000 Regis Way, 90045. Tel: 310-645-2514; 310-645-0718. Email: regishousela@yahoo.com. Sisters 4.

Sisters of the Company of Mary, 2634 Monmouth Ave., 90007. Tel: 213-747-3542; Fax: 213-747-6468. Email: divine_providence@sbcglobal.net. Sisters Maria Elena Minjarez, O.D.N., Supr.; Mary Gomez, O.D.N., Prin. & Dir.; Ruth Henchy, O.D.N., Classroom Aide; Mary Raphael Ybarra, O.D.N., Family Svcs.; Zina Onoro, O.D.N., Teacher. Sisters 6. In Res Sr. Claudia L. Romero, O.D.N., Detention Min.

Sisters of the Good Shepherd (1904) 2561 W. Venice Blvd., 90019. Tel: 323-737-6111; Fax: 323-737-6113. Email: rgsla1@aol.com. Web: www.goodshepherdsisters.org. Sisters 10.

Sisters of the Guardian Angel (1838) 4529 New York St., 90022. Tel: 323-266-4431; Fax: 323-266-4431. Email: rblanco@utla.net.

Sisters of the Immaculate Heart of Mary of Mirinae, I.H.M.M., 423 S. Commonwealth Ave., 90020. Tel: 213-738-1020; Fax: 213-381-6302. Email: laihmm@hanmail.net. Total in Residence 6.

Sisters of the Society Devoted to the Sacred Heart (1940) 869 S. Rimpau Blvd., 90005. Tel: 323-935-2372; Fax: 323-935-5943. Web: www.sacredheartsisters.com. Sisters 4.

ALHAMBRA. *Carmel of St. Teresa of Los Angeles* (1913) 215 E. Alhambra Rd., 91801. Tel: 626-282-2387; Fax: 626-282-2053. Email: momaria@aol.com; teresacarm@aol.com. Web: www.carmelteresa.org. Sr. Brenda Marie, O.C.D., Prioress. Discalced Nuns of the Order of Our Blessed Lady of Mt. Carmel. Sisters 17.

Carmelite Sisters of the Most Sacred Heart of Los Angeles (1941) 920 E. Alhambra Rd., 91801-2799. Tel: 626-289-1353; Fax: 626-308-1913. Email: srines@carmelitesistersocd.com. Web: www.carmelitesistersocd.com. Sisters Regina Marie Gorman, O.C.D., Supr. Gen.; Madonna Joseph Seltzer, O.C.D., Vicar Gen. Professed Sisters 131; Novices 4; Postulants 3.

Carmelite Sisters of the Most Sacred Heart of Los Angeles Tel: 626-289-1353; Fax: 626-308-1913. Email: srines@carmelitesistersocd.com. Web: www-.carmelitesistersocd.com.

Missionary Sisters of St. Columban, 2500 S. Fremont Ave., #E, 91803. Tel: 626-458-1869; Fax: 626-570-6101. Web: www.columbansisters.org.

ALTADENA. *Franciscan Sisters of the Sacred Heart* (1866) *Sacred Heart Convent*, 579 W. Mariposa St., 91001. Tel: 626-791-4359. Email: ruthagee@juno.com. Sr. Mary Elizabeth Imler, O.S.F., Gen. Supr. Sisters 2.

BELLFLOWER. **Sisters of the Blessed Korean Martyrs, S.B.K.M.* (1946) 16276 California Ave., 90706. Tel: 562-461-8100. Sisters 5.

BONITA. *Sister Servants of the Blessed Sacrament*, U.S. Provincial House, 3173 Winnetka Dr., 91902. Tel: 619-267-0720; Fax: 619-267-0920. Email: econ@sjsusprovince.sdcoxmail.com. Sisters in the Province 57.

CHATSWORTH. *Sacred Heart Retreat Apostolate* (2004) 10480 1/2 Winnetka Ave., 91311. Tel: 818-488-1357; Fax: 818-488-1475. Sisters Susan Blaschke, S.D.S.H., Treas. Gen; Jane Stafford, Supr. Gen. Email: mhsdsh2@sbcglobal.net.

CULVER CITY. *Daughters of St. Paul*, 3908 Sepulveda Blvd., 90230. Tel: 310-390-4699; Fax: 310-391-1152. Email: culvercity@paulinemedia.com. Web: pauline.org. Sr. Mary Lea Hill, F.S.P., Supr. Sisters 7.

Religious Sisters of Charity (1815) 10668 St. James Dr., 90230-5461. Tel: 310-559-0176; Fax: 310-559-3530. Email: marshamoon.la@gmail.com. Web: www.rsccaritas.org. Sisters 33.

DOWNEY. *Sisters of the Holy Faith in California*, 12322 S. Paramount Blvd., 90242-3538. Tel: 562-869-6092; Fax: 562-869-4609. Email: shfaith@yahoo.com. Web: www.holyfaithsisters.com. Sisters 31.

GARDENA. *Lovers of the Holy Cross Sisters*, 14700 S. Van Ness Ave., 90249. Tel: 310-516-0271; Fax: 310-352-6435. Email: lhcla@yahoo.com; annetranlhc@yahoo.com. Web: www.lhcla.org.

Queen of Angels Convent, 1650 Rockwood St., 90026. Tel: 213-482-0567; Fax: 310-352-6435. Email: tongalhc@sbcglobal.net. Web: www.lhcla.org. *St. Bruno Convent*, 10734 S. Widener Ave., Whittier, 90603. Tel: 562-947-1177; Fax: 562-947-1177. Email: stellalhc203@yahoo.com. Web: www.lhcla.org. Sisters 60; Postulants 2; Aspirants 11; Novices 4.

Poor Clare Missionary Sisters, Inc., 1050 W. 161st St., 90247. Tel: 310-323-9942. Sr. Elvira Duron, M.C., Supr. Sisters 15.

GLENDORA. *St. Lucy's Priory* (1955) 19045 E. Sierra Madre Ave., 91741. Tel: 626-335-1682; Fax: 626-914-9398. Email: stlucysebrown@aol.com. Web: www.stlucys.com. Sr. Elizabeth Brown, Prioress.

St. Lucy's Priory of Glendora California, Inc. Sisters 12.

HAWAIIAN GARDENS. *Lovers of the Holy Cross Nha Trang* (1950) 21618 Juan Ave., 90716. Tel: 562-809-1570; Fax: 562-809-1570. Sr. Mary Men T. Pham, L.H.C.N.T., Reg. Supr. U.S. Community 5.

LONG BEACH. **Little Handmaids of the Most Holy Trinity, M.A.S.T.* (1988) 3716 Arabella St., 90805. Tel: 562-633-0640; Fax: 562-531-8773. Sr. Monica Bermiso, M.A.S.T., Foundress & Mother Supr.

The Medical Sisters of St. Joseph, 3627 Lemon Ave., 90807. Tel: 562-426-8825. Email: msjnirmala.@aol.com. Web: www.msjnirmala.org. Sr. Dennis Punchakunnel, M.S.J.

MONROVIA. *Maryknoll Sisters of St. Dominic, Inc.* (1912) 340 Norumbega Dr., 91016-2445. Tel: 626-358-1825; Fax: 626-358-1227. Email:

huber_rosemary@yahoo.com. Sr. Rosemary Huber, M.M., Coord. Sisters 39.

MONTEBELLO. *Religious of the Sacred Heart of Mary,* Provincial Center, 441 N. Garfield Ave., 90640-2901. Tel: 323-887-8821; Fax: 323-887-8952. Email: rshmwap@earthlink.net. Web: www.rshm.org.

NORTHRIDGE. *Mother of Mercy Convent,* 9329 Crebs Ave., 91324. Tel: 818-882-4095. Sister of Mercy Burlingame.

Sisters of the Society Devoted to the Sacred Heart (1940) Motherhouse: 9814 Sylvia Ave., 91324. Tel: 818-772-9961; Fax: 818-772-2742. Email: mhsdsh2@sbcglobal.net. Web: www.SDSH.org; www.sacredheartsisters.com. Sr. Jane Stafford, S.D.S.H., Supr. Gen. Sisters 52.

OJAI. *Sisters of Mary Mother of the Church,* 431 Montanna Cir., 93023. Tel: 805-640-1798; Fax: 805-640-1798. Email: SRSMMC@aol.com.

OXNARD. *Servants of Mary, Ministers to the Sick,* 140 North G St., 93030-5214. Tel: 805-486-5502; Fax: 805-486-0663. Email: ssofmary_pro_ox@verizon.net. Sr. Felisa Ripa, Mistress of Novices. Professed Sisters 15; Novices 3.

RANCHO PALOS VERDES. *Daughters of Mary & Joseph, D.M.J.* (1817) 5300 Crest Rd., 90275-5004. Tel: 310-377-9968; Fax: 310-541-5967. Email: leadershipteam@dmjca.org. Web: www.daughtersofmaryandjoseph.org. Sisters 48.

Sisters of Charity of Rolling Hills, 28600 Palos Verdes Dr. E., 90275. Tel: 310-831-4104. Sr. Virginia Buchholz, S.C.R.H., Supr. Gen. Sisters 6.

SAN FERNANDO. *Religious Sisters of Charity,* 1608 Eighth St., 91340. Tel: 818-365-7926; Fax: 818-838-1098. Email: evabryrsc@msn.com. Sisters 3.

SAN PEDRO. *Little Sisters of the Poor* (1979) 2100 S. Western Ave., 90732. Tel: 310-548-0625; Fax: 310-548-4504. Email: mslsppd@attglobal.net. Sr. Marguerite McCarthy, L.S.P., Supr. Priests 4; Sisters 10; Total Staff 90; Total Assisted 102.

SANTA BARBARA. *Monastery of Poor Clares* (1928) Cloistered Contemplative Monastery, 215 E. Los Olivos St., 93105. Tel: 805-682-7670; Fax: 805-682-8041. Web: www.poorclaressantabarbara.org. Sr. Mary Clare of Jesus, Abbess. Attended by Franciscan Fathers of the Old Mission. Professed 12; Postulants 1.

SOLVANG. *Sisters of the Society Devoted to the Sacred Heart* (1940) 1762 Mission Dr., 93463. Tel: 805-688-6158; Fax: 805-688-9247. Sr. Paula Sawhill, S.D.S.H., Supr. Sisters 3.

SYLMAR. *Franciscan Sisters of the Immaculate Conception* (1874) 13367 Borden Ave., Unit A, 91342. Tel: 818-364-6122; 818-364-5557; Fax: 818-362-7536. Email: provstclare@verizon.net.

Franciscan Missionary Sisters of the Immaculate Conception Sisters 100; Novices 2; Postulants 1.

Poor Clare Missionary Sisters, P.O. Box 922046, 91392. Tel: 818-365-8307; Fax: 818-365-8307. Sr. Edelmira Rivera, M.C., Supr. Sisters 7.

THOUSAND OAKS. *Sisters of Notre Dame* (1924) 1776 Hendrix Ave., 91360. Tel: 805-496-3243; Fax: 805-379-3616. Email: kristinsnd@aol.com. Web: www.sndca.org. Sr. Mary Kristin Battles, S.N.D., Prov. Supr. Sisters 64.

TORRANCE. *Little Company of Mary Convent,* 20552 Mansel Ave., 90503. Tel: 310-214-3190; Fax: 310-921-3253. Email: gloria.harper@providence.org. Web: www.lcmglobal.org. Sisters 3. 20562 Mansel Ave., 90503. Tel: 310-370-3992; Fax: 310-370-8452. Email: terrence.landini@providence.org.

VENTURA. *Congregation of the Sisters of the Holy Cross,* 1931 Poli St., 93001. Tel: 805-652-1700; Fax: 805-652-1354.

Sisters of the Holy Cross, (Holy Cross Convent) Sisters 3.

Congregation of the Sisters of the Holy Cross, Saint Catherine-by-the-Sea, 1931 Poli St., 93001-2360. Tel: 805-652-1700; Fax: 805-653-1354. Sr. Linda Bellemore, C.S.C., Supr.

Sisters of the Holy Cross, Inc., Residence for Retired Sisters. Sisters 25.

Handmaids of the Sacred Heart of Jesus, Mary and Joseph, + J.M.J., P.O. Box 2957, 93002-2957. Tel: 805-653-2379. Email: handmaidsjmj@gmail.com; info@handmaids.org. Web: www.handmaidjmj.org.

WINNETKA. *Sisters of St. Louis,* 20253 Ingomar St., 91306-2521. Tel: 818-772-8959. Email: mgtfitzer@yahoo.com. Ursuline Sisters.Presentation Sisters. Sisters 4.

WOODLAND HILLS. *Sisters of St. Louis, Louisville Convent,* 22300 Mulholland Dr., 91364-4933. Tel: 818-883-1678; Fax: 818-346-6109. Email: sslca4@sistersofsaintlouis.com. Web: www.stlouissisters.org. Sr. Bríd Long, S.S.L., Regl. Leader. Sisters 12.

[R] SECULAR INSTITUTES

LOS ANGELES. *Society of Our Lady of the Way,* 2339 N. Catalina St., 90027. Tel: 323-661-3315. Email: jllaca27@msn.com. Web: www.saecimds.com.

Society of Our Lady of the Way of Southern California, Inc.

WEST COVINA. *Fr. Kolbe Missionaries of the Immaculata* (1954) 531 E. Merced Ave., 91790. Tel: 626-917-0040; Fax: 626-917-0900. Email: FkMinCAL@aol.com. Web: www.kolbemission.org.

[S] ASSOCIATIONS OF THE FAITHFUL

LOS ANGELES. **Sisters of the Sick Poor of Los Angeles, Inc.,* 1124 W. Adams Blvd., 90007. Tel: 213-200-2377. Email: sr-ssp@myway.com. Sr. Ellie Alcala, S.S.P., Contact Person.

LONG BEACH. **Friars of the Sick Poor of Los Angeles, Inc.* (2002) 1276 E. Appleton St., 90802-3632. Tel: 562-432-4770. Email: brrichardhirbe@dochs.org. Web: friarsofthesickpoor.org. Bro. Richard A. Hirbe, f.s.p., Min./General-Founder. Friars 7; Novices 1.

TUJUNGA. *Community of the Holy Spirit, C.H.S.,* 10358 Las Lunitas Ave., 91042-1812. Tel: 818-470-2741; 562-596-8423. Email: jjhs106@aol.com.

VENTURA. *Handmaids of the Sacred Heart of Jesus, Mary and Joseph, + J.M.J.,* P.O. Box 2957, 93002-2957. Tel: 805-653-2379. Email: handmaidsjmj@gmail.com; info@handmaidsjmj.org. Web: www.handmaidsjmj.org.

Trinitas, 10332 Darling Rd., 93004-2425. Tel: 805-659-4158; Fax: 805-659-4158. Email: trinitascom@juno.com.

[T] RESIDENCES FOR WOMEN

LOS ANGELES. *St. Anne's,* 155 N. Occidental Blvd., 90026. Tel: 213-381-2931, Ext. 218; Fax: 213-381-7804. Email: stannes@stannes.org. Web: www.stannes.org. Group Home for pregnant, parenting teens and their babies.

Bethany House, 850 N. Hobart Blvd., 90029. Tel: 323-665-6937; Fax: 323-664-0754. Email: imas.bethania@hotmail.com. Sisters 6; Residents 32.

Good Shepherd Center for Homeless Women and Children (1984) Languille Emergency Shelter, 267 N. Belmont Ave., 90026. Tel: 213-250-5241; Fax: 213-250-5073. Email: srjuliamary@sbcglobal.net. Web: www.thegoodshepherdcenter.com. (A Program of Catholic Charities.) Women in Residence 30; Bed Capacity 130; Women Assisted Annually 2,784; Total Staff 26; Total Assisted Annually 3,124.

Mother-Child Transitional Residence Administrative Site (1992) 267 N. Belmont Ave., 90026. Tel: 213-469-6540; Fax: 213-469-0370. Mother-Children in Residence 30; Mother-Children Sheltered Annually 150.

Hawkes Transitional Residence/Women's Village (1998) 1640 Rockwood St., 90026. Tel: 213-482-0281; Fax: 213-482-0299. Women Sheltered Annually 150.

Angel Guardian Home for Homeless Disabled Mothers with Minor Children (2000) 1660 Rockwood St., 90026. Tel: 213-483-6654; Fax: 213-482-0522. Women-Children Sheltered Annually 40.

St. Joseph's Residence (1957) 1124 W. Adams Blvd., 90007. Tel: 213-749-9577; Fax: 213-747-6468. Email: divine_providence@sbcglobal.net. Web: www.companyofmary.com. Sisters of the Company of Mary. Women 60.

[U] RESIDENCES FOR MEN

LOS ANGELES. *"Casa San Juan Diego" Missionaries of Charity Brothers,* 1345 Alvarado Ter., 90006. Tel: 213-251-9708.

Catholic Kolping House, 1225 S. Union Ave., 90015. Tel: 213-388-9438; Fax: 213-388-9438. Email: losangeleskolpinghouse@yahoo.com. Web: www.kolping.org. Alma Tamayo, Mgr. Capacity 60.

Missionaries of Charity Brothers (1975) 1325 S. Westlake Blvd., 90006. Tel: 213-384-6116. Email: brosla@aol.com. Web: www.lamcbro.com. Brothers 5.

[V] RETREAT HOUSES

LOS ANGELES. *Immaculate Heart Retreat House* (1971) (Days of Recollection Only), 3431 Waverly Dr., 90027-2526. Tel: 323-664-3357, Ext. 114; Fax: 323-664-2215. Sr. Catherine Rose, I.H.M., Dir. & Treas. Conducted by the Sisters of the Immaculate Heart. Capacity 60; Sisters 9.

ALHAMBRA. *Sacred Heart Retreat House,* 920 E. Alhambra Rd., 91801. Tel: 626-289-1353; Fax: 626-281-3546. Email: contact@sacredheartretreathouse.com. Web: www.sacredheartretreathouse.com. Sr. Gloria Therese, O.C.D., Retreat Directress. Carmelite Sisters of the Most Sacred Heart of Los Angeles., (See Convents) Capacity 85; Professed Sisters 22; Novices 4; Postulants 3.

ENCINO. *Holy Spirit Retreat Center,* 4316 Lanai Rd., 91436. Tel: 818-784-4515; Fax: 818-784-0409. Email: hsrcenter@earthlink.net. Web: www.hsrcenter.com. Sisters of Social Service.

MALIBU. *Serra Retreat* (1942) 3401 Serra Rd., P.O. Box 127, 90265. Tel: 310-456-6631; Fax: 310-456-9417. Email: frmel@serraretreat.com. Web: www.serraretreat.com. Revs. Melvin A. Jurisich, O.F.M., Dir.; Warren Rouse, O.F.M., Asst. Dir.; Michael Doherty, O.F.M., Retreat Master; Bro. Samuel Cabot, O.F.M. Franciscan Friars. Priests 3; Brothers 1.

MONTEBELLO. *DePaul Evangelization Center* (1987) 1105 S. Bluff Rd., 90640-6143. Tel: 323-721-6060; Fax: 323-887-0765. Email: depaulcenter@att.net. Web: depaulcenter.org. Revs. James Osendorf, C.M., Supr. & Dir.; Andrew E. Bellisario, C.M., Prov.; Peter J. Diliberto (Retired); Robert J. Jones, C.M.; Gary S. Landry, C.M.; Binh Van Nguyen, C.M.; Thomas J. McIntyre, C.M. (Retired); Bro. Edward D. Graham, C.M., (Retired). Formerly St. Vincent's Seminary; Congregation of the Mission (Vincentians); Retreat and Evangelization Center.

RANCHO PALOS VERDES. *Mary and Joseph Retreat Center,* 5300 Crest Rd., 90275-5004. Tel: 310-377-4867; Fax: 310-541-1176. Email: maryjoseph@maryjoseph.org. Web: www.maryjoseph.org. Daughters of Mary and Joseph. Retreat Center Capacity 68.

ROSEMEAD. *St. Joseph's Salesian Youth Renewal Center* (Boys and Girls), 8301 Arroyo Dr., P.O. Box 1639, 91770. Tel: 626-280-8622; Fax: 626-280-0545. Web: stjoescenter.org. Revs. Paul M. Caporali, S.D.B.; Bill Bolton, S.D.B., Dir. Retreat Center; Ted Montemayor, S.D.B., Dir. & Supr.; Mel Trinidad, S.D.B., Youth Min.; Marc Rougeau, S.D.B., Treas. & Vice Dir.; Christian H. Woerz, S.D.B., Vocation Dir.; Bros. Phil Mandile, S.D.B.; Larry King, S.D.B. Conducted by Salesians of St. John Bosco. Priests 6; Brothers 2; Total Staff 4; Total Assisted Annually 6,000.

SAN FERNANDO. *Poverello of Assisi Retreat House* (1962) 1519 Woodworth St., 91340. Tel: 818-365-1071; Fax: 818-361-2751. Email: poverelloretreathouse@verizon.net. Sr. Mary Jesus, O.S.F., Dir. Franciscan Missionary Sisters of the Immaculate Conception., For men and women. Korean groups, Married couples Spanish. Other Denominations workshops seminars, staff meetings. Priests and Sisters retreats, assemblies and chapters, one day retreats for Grammar and High Schools. Capacity 112.

SAN GABRIEL. *Claretian Missionaries - Western Province, Inc.,* 414 S. Mission Dr., 91776. Tel: 626-289-2009; Fax: 626-289-2222. Email: usawestprov@earthlink.net. Web: www.claretian.com. Very Rev. Richard DeTore, C.M.F., Prov. Supr., San Gabriel Mission, 428 S. Mission Dr., 91776. Tel: 626-457-3035; Revs. Daryl Olds, C.M.F., Vicar/Consultor; Paul J. Keller, C.M.F., Consultor/Vocation Dir., Tepeyac House (Novitiate), 6104 York Blvd., 90042. Tel: 323-254-0510; George Whedbee, C.M.F., St. John of God Retirement & Care Center, 2468 S. St. Andrews Pl., 90018. Tel: 323-731-0641; Jose L. Sanchez, C.M.F., Consultor, Tepeyec House, 6104 York Blvd., 90042. Tel: 323-254-0510; Bro. Rene Lepage, C.M.F., Prov. Treas. & Sec., Dominguez Seminary, 18127 S. Alameda St., Rancho Dominguez, 90220. Tel: 323-636-6030. *Tepeyac House (Novitiate),* 6104 York Blvd., 90042. Tel: 323-254-0510. Revs. Paul J. Keller, C.M.F.; John Raab, C.M.F.; Paulson Valiyannoor, C.M.F.; Bro. Larry Moen, C.M.F. *Claretian Tape Ministry, Inc.* Tel: 310-782-6408; Fax: 310-782-8892. *Educational and Renewal Center, Inc.* Tel: 626-289-2009; Fax: 626-289-2222. Email: usawestprov@earthlink.net. Web: www.claretian.com. *Dominguez Seminary Inc.,* 18127 S. Alameda St., Rancho Dominguez, 90220. Tel: 310-631-5981; 310-631-8484; Fax: 310-638-1818. Revs. Robert Billett, C.M.F., Supr.; Robert Bishop, C.M.F., Econome & Treas.; Joseph Daries, C.M.F., Vicar Supr.; Donald Lavelle, C.M.F.; Diego Barrios, C.M.F.; Salvatore Bonano, C.M.F. (Retired); John Corominas, C.M.F.; Albert Connors, C.M.F. (Retired); Alberto Domingo, C.M.F. (Retired); Joseph Gamm, C.M.F.; Isidor Garcia, C.M.F.; Darrin Merlino, C.M.F.; Michael Philen, C.M.F.; Frank Pyka, C.M.F. (Retired); John Hampsch, C.M.F.; Carlos C. Castillo, C.M.F.; Bernard O'Connor, C.M.F.; Christian Ihedoro, C.M.F.; Bros. Paul Roy, C.M.F.; Rene LePage, C.M.F. Congregation of Missionaries, Sons of the Immaculate Heart of Mary (Claretian Missionaries)., Retirement Center, Ministries Community. Priests 20; Brothers 3.

SANTA BARBARA. *St. Mary's Seminary Center,* 1964 Las Canoas Rd., 93105. Tel: 805-966-4829; Fax: 805-564-1662. Email: stmarysseminary@cox.net. Revs. Patrick J. Mullin, C.M., Dir.; Roy A. Persich, C.M. (Retired); James M. Galvin; Walter

L. Housey, C.M. (Retired); John Shine, C.M. Priests 5.

SIERRA MADRE. *Mater Dolorosa Passionist Retreat Center, Inc.*, 700 N. Sunnyside Ave., 91025. Tel: 626-355-7188; Fax: 626-355-0485. Email: materdolorosa@materdolorosa.org. Web: www.passionist.org/materdolorosa. Conducted by the Passionist Community., Lay Retreats for parish men and women. Specialized Retreats. Hosted programs. Priests 3; Brothers 1.
Retreat Team: Revs. Patrick Brennan, C.P., Retreat Dir.; Alfred Pooler, C.P.; Michael Hoolahan, C.P.; Deacons Manuel Valencia; Brian Clements, Weekend Retreat Coord.; Bro. John Rockenbach, C.P.; Elizabeth Welch Velarde, Admin.

VALYERMO. *St. Andrew's Abbey Retreat Center (All Groups)*, 31001 N. Valyermo Rd., P.O. Box 40, 93563. Tel: 661-944-2178, Ext. 0; Fax: 661-944-1076. Email: retreats@valyermo.com. Web: www.valyermo.com. Rt. Rev. Francis Benedict, O.S.B., Retreat Dir. & Abbot Emeritus. Tel: 661-944-2178; Rev. Philip Edwards, O.S.B., Guestmaster. Tel: 661-944-2178, Ext. 0; Bro. Patrick Sheridan, O.S.B., Guestmaster; Rita Jones, Youth Center Contact Person. Tel: 661-944-2734; Cheryl Evanson, Retreat Center Admin. & Youth Center Dir. Conducted by the Benedictine Monks.

[W] PERSONAL PRELATURES

LOS ANGELES. *Prelature of the Holy Cross and Opus Dei*, 655 Levering Ave., 90024. Tel: 310-208-0941; Fax: 310-208-6783. Email: office@tildensc.org. Web: www.tildensc.org. Revs. Paul A. Donlan; Juan Velez; Luke Mata. Tilden Study Center

[X] CATHOLIC CHARITIES OF CALIFORNIA

LOS ANGELES. *Catholic Charities of Los Angeles, Inc.*, 1531 James M. Wood Blvd., P.O. Box 15095, 90015-0095. Tel: 213-251-3400; Fax: 213-380-4603. Web: catholiccharitiesla.org. His Eminence Cardinal Roger Mahony; Rev. Msgr. Gregory A. Cox, M.S.W., M.B.A., M.Div., Exec. Dir. Tel: 213-251-3464.

Central Administrative Offices, 1531 James M. Wood Blvd., P.O. Box 15095, 90015-0095. Tel: 213-251-3400; Fax: 213-380-4603. Web: CatholicCharitiesLA.org. Rev. Msgr. Gregory A. Cox, M.S.W., M.B.A., M.Div., Exec. Dir. Tel: 213-251-3464; Ronald G. Lopez, M.S.W., Chief Admin. Officer. Tel: 213-251-3413; James E. Bathker, M.B.A., CFO. Tel: 213-251-3410; Alexandria "Sandi" Arnold, M.S., Dir. Dept. Resource Devel. Tel: 213-251-3495; Joseph W. Paulicivic Jr., S.P.H.R., Dir. Dept. Human Resources. Tel: 213-251-3414.

Adeste Child Care Services Tel: 213-251-3468; Fax: 213-251-3510. Armine Lalaian, Quality Improvement Mgr. Tel: 213-251-3468.

Archdiocesan Youth Employment Services, 3250 Wilshire Blvd., Ste. 1010, 90010. Tel: 213-736-5456; Fax: 213-736-5654. Robert L. Gutierrez, Prog. Dir.

CYO Athletics Tel: 213-251-3562; Fax: 213-251-3510. Lawrence M. Muno, Prog. Dir. Tel: 213-251-3562.

Esperanza Immigrant Rights Project, 1530 James M. Wood Blvd., 90015. Tel: 213-251-3505; Fax: 213-487-0986. Julianne Donnelly, J.D., Prog. Dir.

Immigration & Refugee Services Tel: 213-251-3489; Fax: 213-251-3444. Loc Nam Nguyen, Prog. Dir. Tel: 213-251-3489; Jo Marcel, Asst. Dir. Tel: 213-251-3470.

Immigration Reception Tel: 213-251-3411; 213-251-3471; Fax: 213-251-3444.

Refugee Resettlement Tel: 213-251-3470.

Central Intake Unit (CIU) Tel: 213-251-3481; Fax: 213-251-3580. Brenda Thomas, Prog. Dir. Tel: 213-251-3445.

CCLA Continuous Quality Improvement Tel: 213-251-3459; Fax: 213-251-3563. Edward Nelson, Ph.D., Continuous Quality Improvement Dir. Tel: 213-251-3459.

Regional Offices and Community Centers:

OUR LADY OF THE ANGELS METRO REGION, 4665 Willowbrook Ave., 90029. Tel: 323-662-1462; Fax: 323-662-2708. Hector Manuel Briones, J.D., Regl. Dir. (Los Angeles Inner City)

Adeste Child Care, 601 E. 23rd St., 90011. Tel: 213-748-5246.

Community Service Centers:

St. Mary's Center, 4665 Willowbrook Ave., 90029. Tel: 323-662-4391; Fax: 323-662-2708.

El Santo Nino Center, 601 E. 23rd St., 90011. Tel: 213-748-5246; Fax: 213-748-9006.

Shelters & Housing Services:

Angels Flight - Runaway/Homeless Youth Shelter, 357 S. Westlake Ave., 90057. Tel: 213-413-2311; 800-833-2499 (Hotline); Fax: 213-413-5690.

Angels Flight Outreach, 357 S. Westlake Ave., 90057. Tel: 213-413-2311.

Sr. Julia Mary Farley House and the Village Kitchen, Women's Village, 1671 Beverly Blvd., 90026. Tel: 213-235-1460.

Good Shepherd Center for Homeless Women, 267 N. Belmont Ave., 90026. Tel: 213-250-5241; Fax: 213-250-5073. Sr. Julia Mary Farley, C.S.J., Prog. Dir.

Good Shepherd Hawkes Transitional Residence, Women's Village, 1650 Rockwood St., 90026. Tel: 213-482-0281; Fax: 213-482-0299.

My Club After School Program, 8701 S. Vermont Ave., Unit A, 90044. Tel: 213-413-2311.

OUR LADY OF THE ANGELS WESTERN REGION, 211 Third Ave., Venice, 90291. Tel: 310-392-8701; Fax: 310-399-4097. Hector Manuel Briones, J.D., Regl. Dir. (Inglewood, Crenshaw District, Korea Town, West Los Angeles, Malibu & Los Angeles Airport region)

Adeste Child Care, 211 Third Ave., Venice, 90291. Tel: 310-392-8701; Fax: 310-399-4097.

Community Service Centers:

St. Margaret's Center, 10217 S. Inglewood Ave., Inglewood, 90304. Tel: 310-672-2208; Fax: 310-672-1841.

St. Peter Claver Center, 4502 W. Washington Blvd., 90016. Tel: 323-297-0292; Fax: 323-737-3649.

St. Robert's Center, 211 Third Ave., Venice, 90291. Tel: 310-392-8701; Fax: 310-399-4097.

Citizenship Services & Classes, St. Margaret's Center, 10217 S. Inglewood Ave., Inglewood, 90304. Tel: 310-672-2208.

Catholic Counseling Services, 211 Third Ave., Venice, 90291. Tel: 310-399-1451; Fax: 310-399-4097.

St. Margaret's Thrift Store, 10505 Hawthorne Blvd., Lennox, 90304. Tel: 310-674-9652.

SAN FERNANDO REGION, 21600 Hart St., Canoga Park, 91303. Tel: 818-883-6015; Fax: 818-883-4122. Moeed Khan, M.S.W., Regl. Dir. (Burbank, Glendale, Eagle Rock, Verdugo Hills, Antelope Valley, San Fernando Valley)

Community Service Centers:

Glendale Community Services Center, 4322 San Fernando Rd., Glendale, 91204. Tel: 818-409-3080; Fax: 818-956-1857.

Temporary Skilled Worker Center, 5101 San Fernando Rd., Glendale, 91204. Tel: 818-548-6495.

Guadalupe Community Center, 21600 Hart St., Canoga Park, 91303. Tel: 818-340-2050.

Loaves and Fishes I, 4322 San Fernando Rd., Glendale, 91204. Tel: 818-409-3080.

Loaves and Fishes II, 14640 Keswick St., Van Nuys, 91405. Tel: 818-997-0943; Fax: 818-497-6980.

Loaves and Fishes IV, 21600 Hart St., Canoga Park, 91303. Tel: 818-340-2050.

Temporary Skilled Worker Center, 1190 S. Flower St., Burbank, 91502. Tel: 818-566-7148.

Immigration & Refugee Department, 4322 San Fernando Rd., Glendale, 91204. Tel: 818-409-0057.

Shelter/Housing Services:

Lancaster Community Shelter, 44611 Yucca Ave., Lancaster, 93534. Tel: 661-945-7524.

SAN GABRIEL REGION, 1307 Warren St., 90033. Tel: 323-266-3130; Fax: 323-266-3269. Mary Romero, Regl. Dir. (San Gabriel Valley, Mt. Baldy, Pomona Valley, East Los Angeles).

Adeste Child Care, 1307 Warren Ave., 90033. Tel: 323-264-4981; Fax: 323-266-3269.

Community Service Centers:

The Art of Parenting (Padua School), 1500 E. Bridge St., 90033. Tel: 323-263-4651.

Brownson House Community Center, 1307 Warren Ave., 90033. Tel: 323-264-8700; Fax: 323-266-3269.

Clinica de Salud-Sagrada Familia, 1215 S. Hamilton Blvd., Pomona, 91766. Tel: 909-622-2824.

McGill Transitional Housing, Administration: 4171 N. Tyler Ave., El Monte, 91731. Tel: 626-350-5867.

Pomona Community Services, 2040 N. Garey Ave., Pomona, 91769. Tel: 909-593-9836.

Youth Employment Services, 5301 Whittier Blvd., 90022. Tel: 323-832-1232.

San Juan Diego Center, 4171 N. Tyler Ave., El Monte, 91731. Tel: 626-575-7652.

SAN PEDRO REGION, 123 E. 14th St., Long Beach, 90813. Tel: 562-591-1641; Fax: 562-591-2481. Anna R. Totta, M.S., Regl. Dir. (Long Beach, South Bay, Compton, Rio Hondo, Vernon, Huntington Park, Whittier, Pico Rivera).

ADESTE Child Care, 10441 S. Downey Ave., Downey, 90241. Tel: 562-862-5750.

Community Service Centers:

Long Beach Community Services, 123 E. 14th St., Long Beach, 90813. Tel: 562-591-1351; Fax: 562-591-2481.

Mahar House Community Center, 1115 Mahar Ave., Wilmington, 90744. Tel: 310-834-7265; Fax: 310-834-8813.

Immigration Services Tel: 310-834-7265.

Pico Rivera Family Resource Center, 5014 Passons Rd., Pico Rivera, 90660. Tel: 562-949-0937.

Elizabeth Ann Seton Homeless Services, 2241 Williams St., Long Beach, 90810. Tel: 562-388-7670.

Oasis Community Center, 2045 St. Gabriel Ave., Long Beach, 90810. Tel: 562-480-2166.

Project Achieve Shelter, 1368 Oregon, Long Beach, 90813. Tel: 562-218-9864.

SANTA BARBARA REGION, 609 E. Haley St., Santa Barbara, 93103. Tel: 805-965-7045; Fax: 805-963-2978. Frank Bognar, D.P.A., Regl. Dir. (Lompoc, Santa Maria, Santa Barbara, Carpinteria).

Community Service Centers:

Santa Barbara Community Services, 609 E. Haley St., Santa Barbara, 93103. Tel: 805-965-7045.

Carpinteria Community Services, 941 Walnut St., Carpenteria, 93013. Tel: 805-684-8621; Fax: 805-684-9771.

Lompoc Community Services & Food Pantry, 903 E. Chestnut, Lompoc, 93436. Tel: 805-736-4886.

Santa Maria Community Services, 607 W. Main, Santa Maria, 93458. Tel: 805-922-2059; Fax: 805-925-1979.

Guadalupe Community Services Tel: 805-922-2059.

New Cuyama Community Services Tel: 805-922-2059.

Thrift Stores:

Thrifty Shopper at Catholic Charities, 609 E. Haley St., Santa Barbara, 93103. Tel: 805-966-9659.

Santa Maria Thrift Store, 605 W. Main St., Santa Maria, 93454. Tel: 805-925-8372.

Older Adult Services, 609 E. Haley St., Santa Barbara, 93103. Tel: 805-965-7045.

Catholic Counseling Services, 609 E. Haley St., Santa Barbara, 93103. Tel: 805-965-7045; Fax: 805-963-2978.

VENTURA COUNTY REGION, 303 N. Ventura Ave., Ste. A, Ventura, 93001. Tel: 805-643-4694; Fax: 805-643-4781. Michael E. Perry, M.A., Regl. Dir. (Camarillo, Moorpark, Oxnard, Thousand Oaks, Simi Valley, Ventura, Conejo Valley)

Adeste Child Care, 303 N. Ventura Ave., Ste. A, Ventura, 93001. Tel: 805-643-4694.

Community Service Centers:

Ventura Community Services, 303 N. Ventura Ave., Ste. C, Ventura, 93001. Tel: 805-643-4694.

Oxnard Community Services, 402 N. "A" St., Oxnard, 93030. Tel: 805-486-2900.

Moorpark Community Services, 609 Fitch Ave., Moorpark, 93021. Tel: 805-529-0720.

Thousand Oaks Community Services, 80 Hillcrest Dr., #120, Thousand Oaks, 91360. Tel: 805-496-1113.

Handicapables Tel: 805-643-4694.

OASIS - Older Adult Services

OASIS - Older Adult Services, 2532 Ventura Blvd., Camarillo, 93010. Tel: 805-987-2083; Fax: 805-383-1318.

Moorpark/Piru/Fillmore, Santa Paula, 93061. Tel: 805-794-5929.

[Y] SUMMER CAMPS

LOS ANGELES. *Scouting and Camp Fire Ministry/ Catholic Youth Camps*, P.O. Box 91764, Long Beach, 90809-1764. Sharon Shellman, Chm. CLGScf. Tel: 626-967-1815; Fax: 626-966-9610; Bill Cole, Vice Chm. Boys, 2972 Canaan Rd., Thousand Oaks, 91360. Tel: 626-732-2831.

St. Vincent dePaul Ranch Camp, 210 N. Ave. 21st, 90031. Tel: 323-224-6213; Fax: 323-226-4997. Raymond P. Lopez, Dir. Camp. (Boys, Ages 7-13); Sponsored by St. Vincent de Paul Society. Capacity 100.

Camp Mariastella, 1120 Manchester Pl., 90019. Fax: 323-266-4139. (Girls). Coed Program for Developmentally Disabled, Ages 7-Adult.; Owned & Operated by Sisters of Social Service.; Located in Wrightwood. Capacity 140.

Sacred Heart Retreat Camp, 869 S. Rimpau Blvd., 90005. Tel: 323-935-2372. Girls & Boys Sessions, Ages 8-17 years.; Owned and operated by the Sisters of the Society Devoted to the Sacred Heart.; Located at Big Bear Lake.

Camp Office, 896 Cienega Rd., P.O. Box 1795, Big Bear Lake, 92315. Tel: 909-866-5696; Fax: 909-866-5650. Capacity 150.

Lions Camp at Teresita Pines, P.O. Box 98, Wrightwood, 92397. Fax: 760-249-1063. Email: teresitapines@snowline.net. Web: www.lionswildcamp.com. (Girls), Ages 7-15 years.; Owned & Operated by Lions.; Located in Big Pines Area near Wrightwood. Capacity 125.

St. Nicholas Camp, 1170 Frontier Rd., Frazier Park, 93225. Tel: 805-245-3571; Fax: 805-245-0710. Available for year round camps & rates.

[Z] ST. VINCENT DE PAUL SOCIETY

LOS ANGELES. *Society of St. Vincent de Paul*, 210 N. Avenue 21, 90031. Tel: 323-224-6288; Fax: 323-225-4997. Email: olreyes@svdpla.org. Web: www.svdpla.org. Jose J. Rossier, Exec. Dir.

St. Vincent de Paul Ranch Camp & Retreat Center, 2550 Hwy. 154, Santa Barbara, 93105. Tel: 323-224-6213; Fax: 323-225-4997. Raymond P. Lopez, Dir.

St. Vincent's Cardinal Manning Center, 231 Winston St., 90013. Tel: 213-229-9963; Fax: 213-620-9141. Joan Sotiros, Dir.

St. Vincent de Paul Stores, 210 N. Avenue 21, 90031. Tel: 323-224-6280; Fax: 323-225-4997.

For Pick Up: 323-224-6280; 800-974-3571. Anthony Terrazas, Store Dir.

[AA] NEWMAN CENTERS

LOS ANGELES. *Campus Ministry c/o Office of the Chancellor* 3424 Wilshire Blvd., 90010-2241. Tel: 213-637-7000; Fax: 213-637-6000.

Loyola Law School 919 S. Albany St., P.O. Box 15019, 90015. Tel: 213-736-1084; Fax: 213-380-3769. Rev. Kenneth Rudnick, S.J., Dir.

Loyola Marymount University One LMU Blvd., 90045. Tel: 310-338-2860; Fax: 310-338-1845. Mr. Anthony Bonta, Dir.

Mount St. Mary College, Chalon Campus 12001 Chalon Rd., 90049. Tel: 310-954-4125; Fax: 310-954-4119. Gail Gresser, Dir.

Mount St. Mary College, Downtown Campus 10 Chester Pl., 90007-2598. Tel: 213-477-2672, Ext. 2672; Fax: 213-477-2669. Gail Krause, Dir.

Occidental College, Catholic Campus Ministry 1600 Campus Rd., 90041. Tel: 323-259-2500; Fax: 323-255-3067. Rev. Raymond J. Finerty, O.P., Dir.

University of California, Los Angeles, University Catholic Center 633 Gayley Ave., 90024. Tel: 310-208-5015; Fax: 310-208-6077. Rev. Peter Abdella, C.S.P., Dir.

University of Southern California Our Saviour University Parish, 3207 University Ave., 90007. Tel: 213-749-5341; Fax: 213-749-3475. Rev. Lawrence Seyer, Dir.

California Institute of Technology I-88, Pasadena, 91125. Tel: 626-395-6212; Fax: 626-792-0475.

Claremont Colleges McAllister Religious Center, 919 N. Columbia, Claremont, 91711. Tel: 909-621-8000, Ext. 8685; Fax: 909-621-8304. Rev. Joe Fenton, S.M.

University of California Santa Barbara St. Mark University Parish, 6550 Picasso Rd., Goleta, 93117. Tel: 805-968-1078; Fax: 805-968-3965. Rev. John W. Love.

University of La Verne (La Verne) Campus Ministry, 1950 Third St., La Verne, 91750. Tel: 909-593-3511, Ext. 4322; Fax: 909-392-2753.

Marymount College (Rancho Palos Verdes) Campus Ministry, 30800 Palos Verdes Dr. E., Palos Verdes Peninsula, 90274. Tel: 310-377-5501; Fax: 310-377-6223. Web: www.marymountpv.edu. Rev. Mark Villano, Chap.

[BB] MISCELLANEOUS LISTINGS

LOS ANGELES. *Catholic Big Brothers Big Sisters, Inc.*, 1530 James M. Wood Blvd., 90015. Tel: 213-251-9800; 213-251-7760 (TTY); Fax: 213-251-9855. Email: info@catholicbigbrothers.org. Web: www.catholicbigbrothers.org. Ken Martinet, Pres. & CEO. Branch offices throughout Los Angeles county.; A mentoring organization for 80 years, its core program matches adult volunteers with children between the ages of 7 and 14. Volunteer mentors provide role modeling and friendship in a one-to-one relationship. Other programs include mentoring among adults, high school youth, and elementary children; school based and site based after-school mentoring.

Catholic Charities Community Development Corporation, Inc., 1531 James M. Wood Blvd., P.O. Box 15095, 90015-0095. Tel: 213-251-3475; Fax: 213-380-4603.

Charisma in Missions, La Porciuncula, 1059 S. Gage Ave., 90023. Fax: 213-260-7221. Catholic Center of Evangelization and renewal ministries. A service for hispanic people through ongoing affirmation and growth seminars and courses; Catholic evangelizers' formation courses; direct evangelization missions; social service programs; prayer hot-line services; television and radio ministries; and a bookstore providing Catholic books, audio and video cassettes.

Collaborative Project for Aging Religious (1992) 2468 S. St. Andrew's Pl., 90018. Tel: 323-735-3625; Fax: 323-737-6320. Email: linkages@cpar.org. Web: www.cpar.org.

Conrad N. Hilton Fund for Sisters, 10100 Santa Monica Blvd., #1000, 90067-4145. Tel: 310-785-0746; Fax: 310-785-0166. Email: info@hiltonfundforsisters.org. Web: www.hiltonfundforsisters.org. Sr. Joyce Meyer, P.B.V.M.

Estrella del Mar de Los Angeles, Inc. dba Regis House Community Center (1949) 2212 W. Beverly Blvd., 90057. Tel: 213-380-8168; Fax: 213-380-8160. Mailing Address: Regis House Community Center, P.O. Box 19787, 90019. Sisters Albertina Morales, S.S.S., Dir.; Teresita Saavedra, S.S.S., Dir. Sisters of Social Service 2.

**Federation of Oases of Koinonia John the Baptist*, 1016 W. Manchester Ave., 90044. Sr. Marie S. Close, Contact Person.

The Focolare Movement, Men's Branch (California) (Work of Mary), 8016 Cowan Ave., 90045-1405. Tel: 310-670-6736; Fax: 310-670-8036. Email: focolare.mla@gmail.com. Web: www.focolare.org. Mr. Carlos Bajo, Dir. West Coast. Formation in the Spirituality of Unity.

The Focolare Movement, Women's Branch, 3138 Glendon Ave., 90034-3404. Tel: 310-470-8505; Fax: 310-470-9239. Email: focolare-fla@att.net. Web: focolare.org. Maria Luise Becker, Co-Dir., Westcoast.

St. Francis Center, 1835 S. Hope St., 90015. Tel: 213-747-5347; Fax: 213-765-8915. Email: info@sfcla.org. Web: www.sfcla.org. Gerard A. Gumbleton, Exec. Dir.; Jill Remelski, Asst. Exec. Dir. A nonprofit, charitable corporation serving the homeless, children and low income families in downtown Los Angeles.

Franciscan Communications, 1530 James M. Wood Blvd., 90015. Tel: 213-251-9800; Fax: 213-251-9855. Kenneth E. Martinet, Pres. & CEO.

Friends of John Paul II Foundation of Southern California, 3424 W. Adams Blvd., 90018. Tel: 626-281-0516. Email: skcybulski@gmail.com. Stanislaw K. Cybulski, Pres.

Hospitaller Foundation of California, Inc., The, 2468 S. St. Andrew's Pl., 90018. Tel: 323-731-7141; Fax: 323-731-5717. Email: info@hospitallerfoundation.org. Web: www.hospitallerfoundation.org. Bro. Patrick Corr, O.H., Pres., Dir. & Moderator. (Fundraising for St. John of God Retirement and Care Center)

Women's League of St. John of God Tel: 323-731-7141; Fax: 323-731-5717.

Helpers Club of St. John of God Tel: 323-731-7141; Fax: 323-731-5717.

**The Institute for Advanced Catholic Studies, University Religious Center*, 835 W. 34th St., Ste. 102, 90089-0751. Tel: 213-740-3055; 213-740-1864; Fax: 213-740-2179. Email: iacss@comcast.net. Web: www.ifacs.com; www.instituteforadvancedcatholicstudies.com. Rev. James L. Heft, S.M., Contact Person.

Korean Catholic Renewal Movement of Southern California, 1230 San Fernando Rd., 90065. Tel: 323-221-8874. Rev. Constantine Kihyen Bae (Korea, South), Chap.

Lay Mission Helpers Association, 3435 Wilshire Blvd., Ste. 1940, 90010-1901. Tel: 213-368-1870; Fax: 213-368-1871. Email: info@laymissionhelpers.org. Web: www.laymissionhelpers.org. Janice England, Program Dir.; Jorenz Campo, Development Dir.

Margaret Aylward Center, 1205 Corning St., 90035.

**Niño Jesus de Belen, Inc.* (2003) 141 W. 87th Pl., 90003-3315. Email: njesusdebelen@yahoo.com. Web: www.ninojesusdebeleninc.org.

Opus Caritatis, Inc., 1531 James W. Wood Blvd., 90015-0095. Tel: 213-251-3464. Paul Smith, Contact Person.

St. Peter Claver Center, 4202 W. Jefferson Blvd., 90016-4113. Tel: 323-737-6036; Fax: 323-737-3649.

Salesian Boys & Girls Club of Los Angeles, 3218 Wabash Ave., 90063. Tel: 323-263-7519; Fax: 323-263-8558. Email: wschafer@salesianclubs-la.org. Web: www.salesianclubs-la.org.

Salesian Family Youth Center, 2228 E. 4th St., 90033. Tel: 323-980-8551; Fax: 323-980-8594. The Salesian Family Youth Center is an outreach site of the Salesian Boys and Girls Club of Los Angeles and forms a single corporate entity with the Salesian Boys and Girls Club of Los Angeles.

Serra Ancillary Care, 3424 Wilshire Blvd., 90010. Tel: 213-637-7531; Fax: 213-637-6531.

Serra Institute, 2060 N. Vermont, 90027. Tel: 323-664-9292. Email: gcrye@aol.com. Web: quantumtheology.org.

Servants of the Immaculate Child Mary, 5135 Dartmouth Ave., 90032. Tel: 323-225-3279; Fax: 323-225-3279. Email: ImmaculateAL@.com. Sr. Raquel Sandoval, Contact Person.

Sisters of Nazareth Foundation, Inc., 3333 Manning Ave., 90064.

Sisters of Nazareth of Los Angeles Real Estate Holdings, Inc., 3333 Manning Ave., 90064.

**South Central Los Angeles Ministry Project aka South Central LAMP* (1993) 892 E. 48th St., 90011. Tel: 323-234-1471; Fax: 323-234-1472. Web: www.southcentrallamp.org. Nina Denise Hernandez, Exec. Dir.

Spirituality Center (1983) 10 Chester Pl., 90007. Tel: 213-747-6508; Fax: 213-477-2649. Email: spircenter@msmc.la.edu. Web: www.archdiocese.la/prayer/spirituality. Sr. Patricia Beirne, R.S.M., Dir.

St. Vincent Senior Citizen Nutrition Program, Inc. aka St. Vincent Meals on Wheels (1977) 2131 W. Third St., 90057. Tel: 213-484-7778; Fax: 213-484-7276. Sr. Alice Marie Quinn, D.C., Prog. Dir. Volunteers 300; Total Staff 98; Meals Served Daily 4,700.

Vincentians Province of the West, Support Trust Fund, 3663 Martin Luther King Blvd., Lynwood, 90262. Tel: 310-603-6007; Fax: 310-638-0075. Robert Issai, Contact Person.

Works in New Directions, Inc. (WIND), 4316 Lanai Rd., Encino, 91436. Tel: 818-285-3355; Fax: 818-285-3366. Sr. Grace Boys, S.S.S., Contact Person.

ALHAMBRA. **Carmelite Educational Centers, Inc.*, 920 E. Alhambra Rd., 91801. Tel: 626-289-1353; Fax: 626-308-1913. Email: srines@carmelitesistersocd.com. Web: www.carmelitesistersocd.com. Sr. Regina Marie Gorman, O.C.D., Dir.

Carmelite Sisters Foundation, Inc., 920 E. Alhambra Rd., 91801. Sr. Ines Sandoval, Gen. Sec.

Flos Carmeli Formation Centers, Inc., 920 E. Alhambra Rd., 91801. Sr. Ines Sandoval, Gen. Sec.

**Little Flower Center, Inc.*, 920 E. Alhambra Rd., 91801. Tel: 626-289-1353; Fax: 626-308-1913. Email: srines@carmelitesistersocd.com. Web: www.carmelitesistersocd.com. Sr. Regina Marie Gorman, O.C.D., Dir.

Mount Carmel Health Ministries, Inc., 920 E. Alhambra Rd., 91801. Sr. Ines Sandoval, Gen. Sec.

ANAHEIM HILLS. *Equestrian Order of the Holy Sepulchre of Jerusalem Western USA Lieutenancy*, 8141 E. Kaiser Blvd., Ste. 300, 92808. Tel: 714-282-9632; Fax: 714-282-1563. Email: awilliams@khswesternusa.org. Web: www.khswesternusa.org. H.E. Patrick D. Powers, Lieutenant.

3424 Wilshire Blvd., 90010-2241. Tel: 213-637-7000; Fax: 213-637-7691. His Eminence Cardinal Roger Mahony, Grand Prior.

ARTESIA. *Filipino Pastoral Ministry*, 18708 S. Clarkdale Ave., 90701. Tel: 562-865-2185; Fax: 562-860-0718. Email: mac3exodus@aol.com. Rev. Johnny Zulueta, C.M.

BALDWIN PARK. *The Redemptorist Vietnamese Mission Corporation*, 3452 N. Big Dalton Ave., 91706. Tel: 626-338-3295; Fax: 626-851-1280. Email: chaqhung@yahoo.com. Rev. Pham Quoc Hung, C.Ss.R., Pres.

BELLFLOWER. *World Apostolate of Fatima, Blue Army, USA, Los Angeles Division*, 15550 Bellflower Blvd., 90706-3819. Tel: 562-867-8661; Fax: 562-867-8661.

BURBANK. **El Sembrador Ministries*, 2636 N. Ontario St., 91504. Tel: 818-260-0222; Fax: 818-557-7796. Noel Diaz, Contact Person; Salvador Hernandez, Office Mgr.

SCRC (Southern California Renewal Communities), 9795 Cabrini Dr., Ste. 208, 91504-1740. Tel: 818-771-1361; Fax: 818-771-1379. Email: spirit@scrc.org. Web: www.scrc.org. Dominic Berardino, Pres.; Rev. William Delaney, S.J., Pastoral Coord. Serving Catholic Charismatic Renewal through annual summer convention, pastoral teaching events, healing masses, retreats, book & tape ministry and a bi-monthly publication.

CARPINTERIA. **International Theological Institute for Studies on Marriage and the Family*, 3299 Padaro Ln., 93013. Tel: 805-649-2346; Fax: 706-867-6216. Betty Hartmann, Contact Person.

COVINA. *Comboni Mission Center*, 645 S. Aldenville Ave., 91723. Tel: 626-339-1914; Fax: 626-974-4238. Email: combonicovin@earthlink.net. Web: www.comboni.com. Revs. Sergio Contran, M.C.C.J. (Italy), Burser; Angelo G. Biancalana, M.C.C.J. (Italy), Community Member; Joseph Forlani, M.C.C.J. (Italy), Community Member.

CULVER CITY. **Loyola Productions, Inc.*, 8511 Washongton Blvd., 90232. Tel: 310-815-8542; Fax: 310-815-8758. Email: esiebert@loyolaproductions.com. Web: www.loyolaproductions.com. Rev. Edward J. Siebert, S.J., Dir.

EL MONTE. *Hombre Nuevo*, 12036 Ramona Blvd., 91732. Tel: 626-444-4442; Fax: 626-444-1435. Email: hn@catolico.com. Web: www.katolico.com. Rev. Juan Rivas, L.C.

GLENDALE. **Together in Christ* (1998) 311 E. Stocker St. Ste. 102, 91207. Tel: 818-246-5582; Fax: 818-246-5582. Email: TogetherChrist1@aol.com. Nancy Barona, Pres.

LA MIRANDA. *World Wide Marriage Encounter*, 16706 Cerise Ave., Torrance, 90504. Tel: 310-515-3522. Web: www.wwme.org. Anthony Mena, Contact; Vel Mena, Contact.

LA VERNE. *Picpus Charitable Trust* (1991) 2150 Damien Ave., 91750. Tel: 909-596-1946; Fax: 909-596-6112. Email: dhstravers@damien-hs.edu.

LANCASTER. *Our Lady of Charity, Conference of St. Vincent de Paul Society*, P.O. Box 412, 93584. Tel: 661-942-3222. Donald Willey, Pres.

LONG BEACH. *St. Mary Catholic Housing Corp. dba St. Mary Tower* 1050 Linden Ave., 90813. Tel: 562-491-9929; Fax: 562-436-6378.

St. Mary Medical Center Foundation (Catholic Healthcare West), 1050 Linden Ave., P.O. Box 887, 90801. Tel: 562-491-9225; Fax: 562-491-9888. Email: jtwagner@chw.edu. Web: stmarymedicalcenter.org. John T. Wagner, Pres.

LYNWOOD. *Daughters of Charity Ministry Services Corp.*, 3663 Martin Luther King Jr. Blvd., 90262. Tel: 310-603-6007; Fax: 310-638-0075.

Hotel Dieu, 3663 Martin Luther King Jr. Blvd., 90262. 265 S. Lake St., 90057. Tel: 213-484-7111; Fax: 213-484-0450. Mary McKenna, CFO.

Rosalie Rendu, Inc. (1998) 1760 Bay Rd., #24, East Palo Alto, 94303. Tel: 650-473-9522. 3663 Martin Luther King Jr. Blvd., 90262. Tel: 310-603-6007; Fax: 310-638-0075. Mary McKenna, CFO.

MONTEREY PARK. *Congregation of St. John the Baptist*, 220 S. Ynez Ave., 91754. Tel: 626-280-3430; Fax: 626-280-1590. Email: csjb@gus.net. Web: www2.gus.net/home/c/csjb. Rev. Antonio Ho, C.S.J.B., Contact Person.

Theresian Sisters, 901 W. El Repetto Dr., 91754. Tel: 323-780-1965; Fax: 323-780-1965. Sr. Felicitas M. Hong, C.S.T., Contact Person.

**United Chinese Apostolate Council*, 1501 S. Atlantic Blvd., 91754. Tel: 323-261-8630.

OJAI. **St. Joseph's H. & RC Foundation* (1996) 2464 Ojai Ave., P.O. Box 760, 93024-0760. Tel: 805-646-1466; Fax: 805-646-1013. Email: igi@ojai.net. Rev. Ignatius Sudol, O.H., CEO/Pres. Priests 2; Total Assisted 50.

PACIFIC PALISADES. *Paulist Pictures* (1985) P.O. Box 1057, 90272. Tel: 310-454-0688; Fax: 310-459-6549. Email: Paulistmail@paulistproduction.org. Web: www.paulistproductions.org.

Paulist Productions (1968) (Insight) 17575 Pacific Coast Hwy., P.O. Box 1057, 90272. Tel: 310-454-0688; Fax: 310-459-6549. Email: Paulistmail@paulistproduction.org. Web: www.paulistproductions.org. Rev. Eric Andrews, C.S.P., Pres.; Barbara Gangi, Vice Pres. Devel.; Enid Sevilla, Gen. Mgr. Financial Officer; Joseph Kim, Vice Pres. Business Affairs.

PASADENA. *Association of Christian Therapists*, 2386 E. Del Mar Blvd., #312, 91107. Tel: 626-795-1233. Email: albert_nyland@msn.com. Web: www.actheals.org.

SAN FERNANDO. *Valley Family Center* (1987) 302 S. Brand Blvd., 91340. Tel: 818-365-8588; Fax: 818-898-3382. Email: info@valleyfamilycenter.org. Web: www.valleyfamilycenter.org. Sr. Carmel Somers, R.S.C., Exec. Dir. Religious Sisters of Charity., All Services are in English and Spanish. Counseling is available for individual, marriage, family, children/teen, victims of sexual and physical abuse, and adults molested as children (AMAC). Special Programs include School Counseling; Parent Education; anger management; violence prevention; victims and perpetrators of domestic violence; at risk youth. Learning Center Programs include tutorials; basic skill building for children and adults; Educational and Psychological Testing, and opportunities for gifted students. Fees on sliding scale basis according to income.

SAN PEDRO. *Apostleship of the Sea, Catholic Maritime Ministry*, Mary, Star of the Sea Parish, 870 W. 8th St., 90731. Tel: 310-833-3541; Fax: 310-833-9254. Email: marystar2@aol.com. Rev. Henry L. Hernando, Dir. of Chap. Svcs.

Center:, Berth 93A, World Cruise Center, Port of Los Angeles, 90731. Tel: 310-521-1041; Fax: 310-521-1046.

SANTA BARBARA. **The Cause of Blessed Junipero Serra*, Old Mission Santa Barbara, 2201 Laguna St., 93105-3611. Tel: 805-682-4713; Fax: 805-682-6067. Email: FriarTim@aol.com. Rev. John Vaughn, O.F.M., Vice Postulator.

St. Clare By The Sea Convent (A California nonprofit corp.), 202 W. Valerio St., 93101-2930. Tel: 805-879-1598; Cell: 805-451-0365; Fax: 805-456-6601. Email: sischris72@hotmail.com. Web: www.fssh.com. Sisters Mary Elizabeth Imler, O.S.F., Gen. Supr.; Christine Bowman, O.S.F., Local Community Leader. Franciscan Sisters of the Sacred Heart, (Frankfort, IL).

SANTA MARIA. *Servants and Handmaids of the Sacred Heart of Jesus, Mary and Joseph*, P.O. Box 2309, 93457-2309. Tel: 805-524-5890. Email: info@theservantsandhandmaids.net. Web: www.theservantsandhandmaids.net.

SANTA SUSANA KNOLLS. *Magnificat, A Ministry to Catholic Women West San Fernando Valley Chapter* (1984) 6202 Wisteria Dr., 93063. Tel: 805-527-3745. Email: terithompson@sbcglobal.net. Web: www.magnificatsfv.com.

STUDIO CITY. **Catholics in Media Associates* (1992) 12400 Ventura Blvd., PMB #228, 91604. Tel: 818-907-2734; Fax: 323-851-8641. Email: catholicsinmedia@aol.com. Web: www.catholicsinmedia.org. Jane Abbott, Pres.

VENICE. *St. Joseph Center* (1976) 204 Hampton Dr., 90291-8633. Tel: 310-396-6468; Fax: 310-392-8402. Email: rmeister@stjosephctr.org. Web: www.stjosephctr.org. Sr. Jill Napier, C.S.J., Contact Person.

VENTURA. *CAREGIVERS: Volunteers Assisting the Elderly* (1984) 1765 Goodyear Ave., #205, 93003. Tel: 805-658-8530; Fax: 805-658-8537. Email: info@caregivers.org. Web: www.vccaregivers.org.

WEST COVINA. *Federation of Filipino Rosary Groups, Inc.*, 2809 Elena Ave., 91792. Eddie B. De Sagun, Contact. Purpose: To provide evangelization of people, particularly the Filipinos, and to aid in building communities of faith through the propagation of the devotion to the Holy Rosary.

Luz De Cristo USA Member of Lumen 2000., 1151 E. Grovecenter St., 91790. Tel: 626-966-7594. Web: www.luzdecristousa.com. Non-profit corporation. Spanish evangelism through modern means of communication.

[CC] LEGAL TITLES

LOS ANGELES. *Archdiocesan Catholic Center*, 3424 Wilshire Blvd., 90010-2241. Tel: 213-637-7000; Fax: 213-637-6000. Email: webmaster@la-archdiocese.org. Web: www.la-archdiocese.org. For further information contact the Chancery. Also see Miscellaneous for additional listings.

Recollect Augustinian Fathers & Brothers, Province of St. Augustine, Inc., O.A.R., Oxnard (1990) Tel: 805-486-7433; Fax: 805-487-2805.

Missionary Oblates of Mary Immaculate Residence, Inc., O.M.I., Arleta Tel: 818-891-0579; Fax: 818-893-9819.

School Sisters of Notre Dame Tel: 314-544-0455; Fax: 314-544-6754. Various Locations in the Archdiocese

Congregation of the Sacred Heart of Jesus & Mary and of Perpetual Adoration, Inc., SS.CC., LaVerne Tel: 909-593-5441; Fax: 909-593-3971.

Sisters of St. Louis Monaghan, Inc., S.S.L., Woodland Hills Tel: 818-883-1678; Fax: 818-346-6109.

Ursulines of the Western Province, Inc., O.S.U., Encino Tel: 650-346-9897.

RELIGIOUS INSTITUTES OF MEN REPRESENTED IN THE ARCHDIOCESE

For further details refer to the corresponding bracketed number in the Religious Institutes of Men or Women section.

[0140]—*The Augustinians*—O.S.A.
[0200]—*Benedictine Monks (Congregation of the Annunciation)*—O.S.B.
[0980]—*Brothers of Our Lady Mother of Mercy*—C.F.M.M.
[1350]—*Brothers of St. Francis Xavier*—C.F.X.
[1160]—*Brothers of St. Patrick*—F.S.P.
[0330]—*Brothers of the Christian Schools*—F.S.C.
[600]—*Brothers of the Congregation of the Holy Cross*—C.S.C.
[0900]—*Canons Regular of Premontre*—O.Praem.
[]—*Canons Regular of the Immaculate Conception*—C.R.I.C.
[0470]—*The Capuchin Friars* (St. Patrick's Custody)—O.F.M.Cap.
[0270]—*Carmelite Fathers & Brothers* (Prov. of the Most Pure Heart of Mary)—O.Carm.
[0275]—*Carmelites of Mary Immaculate*—C.M.I.
[0360]—*Claretian Missionaries* (Western Prov.)—C.M.F.
[0380]—*Comboni Missionaries of the Heart of Jesus* (Verona)—M.C.C.J.
[1150]—*Congregation of St. Joseph*—C.S.J.
[1330]—*Congregation of the Mission* (Prov. of the West)—C.M.
[1210]—*Congregation of the Missionaries of St. Charles*—C.S.
[1000]—*Congregation of the Passion* (Western Prov.)—C.P.
[1140]—*Congregation of the Sacred Hearts of Jesus and Mary*—SS.CC.
[0480]—*Conventual Franciscans* (St. Joseph Cupertino Prov.)—O.F.M.Conv.
[0260]—*Discalced Carmelite Friars*—O.C.D.
[0520]—*Franciscan Friars* (St. Barbara Prov.)—O.F.M.
[0530]—*Franciscan Friars of the Atonement*—S.A.
[]—*Friars of the Sick Poor*—F.S.P.
[]—*Guadalupe Missioners* (Mexico)—M.G.
[0670]—*Hospitaller Brothers of St. John of God*—O.H.
[0690]—*Jesuit Fathers and Brothers* (California Prov.)—S.J.
[0710]—*Josephite Fathers*—C.J.
[0730]—*Legionaries of Christ*—L.C.
[0580]—*Little Brothers of the Good Shepherd*—B.G.S.
[0780]—*Marist Fathers*—S.M.
[0800]—*Maryknoll*—M.M.
[0830]—*Mill Hill Missionaries*—M.H.M.
[]—*Misioneros de la Natividad de Maria*—M.N.M.
[]—*Misioneros de Sagrado Corazon Y Santa Maria de Guadalupe*—M.S.C.
[]—*Misioneros Oblatos de la Sagrada Familia*—O.S.F.
[]—*Misioneros Servidores de la Palabra*—M.S.P.
[]—*Mission Doctors Association*
[]—*Missionaries of Charity Brothers*—M.C.
[]—*Missionaries of Jesus*—M.J.
[]—*Missionaries of St. Francis Xavier*—M.S.F.X.
[0660]—*Missionaries of the Holy Spirit*—M.Sp.S.
[0840]—*Missionary Servants of the Most Holy Trinity*—S.T.
[0910]—*Oblates of Mary Immaculate* (Western Prov.)—O.M.I.
[0930]—*Oblates of St. Joseph*—O.S.J.
[0940]—*Oblates of the Virgin Mary*—O.M.V.
[]—*Operarios del Reino de Cristo*—O.R.C.
[0835]—*Order of Minims*—O.M.
[]—*Order of Our Lady of Mercy*—O.de.M.
[0430]—*Order of Preachers-Dominicans* (Western Prov.)—O.P.
[]—*Order of St. Camillus*—O.S.C.
[0150]—*Order of the Augustinian Recollects*—O.A.R.
[1310]—*Order of the Most Holy Trinity*—O.SS.T.
[1020]—*Pauline Fathers and Brothers, Society of St. Paul*—S.S.P.
[1030]—*Paulist Fathers*—C.S.P.
[1040]—*Piarist Fathers*—Sch.P.
[0610]—*Priests of the Congregation of Holy Cross*—C.S.C.
[1070]—*Redemptorist Fathers* (Denver Prov.)—C.SS.R.
[1090]—*Rogationist Fathers*—R.C.J.
[1190]—*Salesians of Don Bosco*—S.D.B.
[0110]—*Society of African Missions*—S.M.A.
[1260]—*Society of Christ*—S.Ch.
[0760]—*Society of Mary*—S.M.
[0370]—*Society of St. Columban*—S.S.C.
[0420]—*Society of the Divine Word*—S.V.D.
[1060]—*Society of the Precious Blood*—C.PP.S.
[1290]—*Society of the Priests of St. Sulpice*—S.S.
[0700]—*St. Joseph's Society of the Sacred Heart*—S.S.J.

RELIGIOUS INSTITUTES OF WOMEN REPRESENTED IN THE ARCHDIOCESE

[2120]—*Armenian Sisters of the Immaculate Conception*—C.I.C.
[]—*Augustinian Recollect Sisters*—A.R.
[0230]—*Benedictine Sisters of Pontifical Jurisdiction*—O.S.B.
[1810]—*Bernardine Sisters of the Third Order of St. Francis*—O.S.F.
[]—*Blessed Sacrament Sisters of Charity*
[2930]—*California Institute of the Sisters of the Most Holy and Immaculate Heart of the Blessed Virgin Mary*—I.H.M.
[]—*Caritas Sisters of Miyazaki*
[]—*Carmelitas de San Jose*—C.S.J.
[0370]—*Carmelite Sisters of the Most Sacred Heart of Los Angeles*—O.C.D.
[]—*Chinese Dominican Sisters*—O.P.
[]—*Congregation of Hermanitas de la Annunciacion*
[]—*Congregation of Kkottongnae Sisters of Jesus*—C.K.S.J.
[2100]—*Congregation of the Humility of Mary*—C.H.M.
[0470]—*Congregation of the Sisters of Charity for the Incarnate Word*—C.C.V.I.
[3242]—*Congregation of the Sisters of Nazareth*—C.S.N.
[3832]—*Congregation of the Sisters of St. Joseph*—C.S.J.
[3935]—*Congregation of the Sisters of St. Louis, Juilly Monaghan*—S.S.L.
[1920]—*Congregation of the Sisters of the Holy Cross*—C.S.C.
[1940]—*Congregation of the Sisters of the Holy Faith*—C.H.F.
[0760]—*Daughters of Charity of St. Vincent de Paul* (Prov. of the West)—D.C.
[0860]—*Daughters of Mary*—D.M.
[0880]—*Daughters of Mary and Joseph*—D.M.J.
[0850]—*Daughters of Mary Help of Christians*—F.M.A.
[0420]—*Discalced Carmelite Nuns*—O.C.D.
[1050]—*Dominican Comtemplative Nuns (Cloistered)*—O.P.
[1070-03]—*Dominican Sisters*—O.P.
[1070-12]—*Dominican Sisters*—O.P.
[1070-19]—*Dominican Sisters*—O.P.
[1070-21]—*Dominican Sisters*—O.P.
[1070-13]—*Dominican Sisters*—O.P.

[1070-04]—*Dominican Sisters*—O.P.
[]—*Dominican Sisters of Adrian (Pacific West Chapter)*—O.P.
[]—*Dominican Sisters of the Christian Doctrine*—O.P.
[1150]—*Eucharistic Franciscan Missionary Sisters*—E.F.M.S.
[]—*Evangelizadores Eucaristicas de los Pobres*—E.E.P.
[1170]—*Felician Sisters*—C.S.S.F.
[1350]—*Franciscan Missionary Sisters of the Immaculate Conception*—O.S.F.
[1310]—*Franciscan Sisters of Little Falls*—O.S.F.
[1500]—*Franciscan Sisters of Mary Immaculate of the Third Order of St. Francis of Assisi*—F.M.I.
[1780]—*Franciscan Sisters of Perpetual Adoration*—O.S.F.
[1450]—*Franciscan Sisters of the Sacred Heart*—O.S.F.
[1845]—*Guadalupan Missionaries of the Holy Spirit*—M.G.Sp.S.
[]—*Handmaids of the Sacred Heart of Jesus, Mary & Joseph*—J.M.J.
[1895]—*Hermanas Carmelitas de San Jose*—C.S.J.
[]—*Hermanas Misioneras Servidoras de la Palabra*—H.M.S.P.
[2575]—*Institute of the Sisters of Mercy of the Americas* (Burlingame, CA)—R.S.M.
[]—*Little Handmaids of the Most Holy Trinity*—M.A.S.T.
[2340]—*Little Sisters of the Poor*—L.S.P.
[2385]—*Lovers of the Holy Cross Nha Trang*—L.H.C.N.T.
[2390]—*Lovers of the Holy Cross Sisters*—L.H.C.
[2470]—*Maryknoll Sisters of St. Dominic*—M.M.
[2500]—*Medical Sisters of St. Joseph*—M.S.J.
[]—*Misioneras Eucaristicas De Maria Inmaculada*—M.E.M.I.
[2710]—*Missionaries of Charity*—M.C.
[]—*Missionaries of Jesus Crucified*—M.J.C.
[0210]—*Missionary Benedictine Sisters*—O.S.B.
[0390]—*Missionary Carmelites of St. Theresa*—C.M.S.T.
[2715]—*Missionary Sisters of Christ the King*—M.S.C.K.
[2880]—*Missionary Sisters of St. Columban*—S.S.C.
[2750]—*Missionary Sisters of the Immaculate Heart of Mary*—I.C.M.
[3530]—*Missionary Sisters Servants of the Holy Spirit*—S.Sp.S.
[]—*Missionary Sisters, Oblates of the Holy Family*—O.H.F.
[0240]—*Olivetan Benedictine Sisters*—O.S.B.
[3760]—*Order of St. Clare*—P.C.C.
[3130]—*Our Lady of Victory Missionary Sisters*—O.L.V.M.
[0980]—*Pious Disciples of the Divine Master*—P.D.D.M.
[0950]—*Pious Society Daughters of St. Paul*—F.S.P.
[2840]—*Poor Clare Missionary Sisters*—M.C.
[0930]—*Religious Daughters of St. Joseph*—F.S.J.
[1145]—*Religious Missionaries of St. Dominic*—O.P.
[3450]—*Religious of Jesus-Mary*—R.J.M.
[3465]—*Religious of the Sacred Heart of Mary*—R.S.H.M.
[3400]—*Religious Sisters of Charity*—R.S.C.
[2970]—*School Sisters of Notre Dame*—S.S.N.D.
[1680]—*School Sisters of St. Francis*—O.S.F.
[3580]—*Servants of Mary (Servite Order)*—O.S.M.
[3499]—*Servants of the Blessed Sacrament*—S.J.S.
[]—*Servants of the Immaculate Child Mary*—E.I.N.
[3615]—*Servants of the Immaculate Child Mary (Esclavas de la Inmaculada Nina)*—E.I.N.
[]—*Sisters for Christian Community*—S.F.C.C.
[0250]—*Sisters of Bethany*—C.V.D.
[0480]—*Sisters of Charity of Leavenworth, Kansas*—S.C.L.
[]—*Sisters of Charity of Rolling Hills*—S.C.R.H.
[0570]—*Sisters of Charity of Seton Hill, Greensburg, Pennsylvania*—S.C.
[0430]—*Sisters of Charity of the Blessed Virgin Mary*—B.V.M.
[]—*Sisters of Little Jesus*—S.L.J.
[2360]—*Sisters of Loretto At the Foot of the Cross* (Southern Prov.)—S.L.
[]—*Sisters of Mary, Mother of the Church*—M.M.C.
[2575]—*Sisters of Mercy* (New York)—R.S.M.
[2990]—*Sisters of Notre Dame* (Prov. of Los Angeles)—S.N.D.
[3000]—*Sisters of Notre Dame de Namur*—S.N.D.deN.
[]—*Sisters of Our Lady of Perpetual Help*—S.O.L.P.H.
[3350]—*Sisters of Providence*—S.P.
[3360]—*Sisters of Providence of Saint Mary-Of-The-Woods, Indiana*—S.P.
[4080]—*Sisters of Social Service of Los Angeles, Inc.*—S.S.S.
[1705]—*Sisters of St. Francis of Assisi*—O.S.F.
[1710]—*Sisters of St. Francis of Joliet*—O.S.F.
[1620]—*Sisters of St. Francis of Millvale, Pennsylvania*—O.S.F.
[1760]—*Sisters of St. Francis of Oldenburg*—O.S.F.
[1630]—*Sisters of St. Francis of Penance and Christian Charity*—O.S.F.
[1650]—*The Sisters of St. Francis of Philadelphia*—O.S.F.
[1530]—*Sisters of St. Francis of Sylvania*—O.S.F.
[3830-03]—*Sisters of St. Joseph*—C.S.J.
[3860]—*Sisters of St. Joseph Congregation*—S.J.C.
[3840]—*Sisters of St. Joseph of Carondelet*—C.S.J.
[3860]—*Sisters of St. Joseph of Cluny*—S.J.C.
[3830-11]—*Sisters of St. Joseph of Nazareth*—S.S.J.
[3830]—*Sisters of St. Joseph of Orange*—C.S.J.
[3890]—*Sisters of St. Joseph of Peace*—C.S.J.P.
[3930]—*Sisters of St. Joseph to the Third Order of St. Francis*—S.S.J.-T.O.S.F.
[]—*Sisters of the Blessed Korean Martyrs*—B.K.M.
[0700]—*Sisters of the Company of Mary Our Lady*—O.D.N.
[1830]—*Sisters of the Good Shepherd*—R.G.S.
[1850]—*Sisters of the Guardian Angel*—S.A.C.
[]—*Sisters of the Heart of Jesus in the Blessed Sacrament*—H.C.J.S.
[1960]—*Sisters of the Holy Family*—S.H.F.
[1990]—*Sisters of the Holy Names of Jesus and Mary*—S.N.J.M.
[2120]—*Sisters of the Immaculate Conception*—C.I.C.
[]—*Sisters of the Immaculate Heart of Mary at Mirinae*—I.H.M.M.
[2270]—*Sisters of the Little Company of Mary*—L.C.M.
[]—*Sisters of the Love of God*—R.A.D.
[3200]—*Sisters of the Pious Schools*—Sch.P.
[3320]—*Sisters of the Presentation of the B.V.M.* (San Francisco, CA)—P.B.V.M.
[]—*Sisters of the Sacred Heart of Mary*—C.S.C.M.
[4050]—*Sisters of the Society Devoted to the Sacred Heart*—S.D.S.H.
[4100]—*Sisters of the Sorrowful Mother*—S.S.M.
[1490]—*Sisters of the Third Franciscan Order*—O.S.F.
[3600]—*Sisters Servants of Mary*—S.M.
[4060]—*Society of the Holy Child Jesus*—S.H.C.J.
[1505]—*St. Francis Mission Community*—O.S.F.
[]—*Theresian Sisters*—C.S.T.
[3330]—*Union of Sisters of Presentation of the B.B.M.*—P.B.V.M.
[4110]—*Ursuline Nuns (Roman Union)*—O.S.U.
[]—*Verbum Dei Missionary Fraternity*—V.D.M.F.
[4200]—*Visitation Congregation*—S.V.M.

ARCHDIOCESAN CEMETERIES

LOS ANGELES. *Calvary Cemetery and Mausoleum*, 4201 Whittier Blvd., 90023. Tel: 323-261-3106. Maria Orozco, Mgr.

CULVER CITY. *Holy Cross Cemetery & Mortuary*, 5835 W. Slauson Ave., 90230. Tel: 310-836-5500; Fax: 310-836-3560.

LANCASTER. *Good Shepherd Cemetery & Mausoleum*, 43121 70th St. West, 93536. Tel: 661-722-0887; Fax: 661-722-5344. Daniel Rejniak, Mgr.

LONG BEACH. *All Souls Cemetery and Mausoleum*, 4400 Cherry Ave., 90807. Tel: 562-424-8601. Maryann McAdams, Mgr.

MISSION HILLS. *San Fernando Mission Cemetery & Mausoleum*, 11160 Stanwood Ave., 91345. Tel: 818-361-7387. Rosalie Castillo, Mgr.

MONTEBELLO. *Resurrection Cemetery & Mausoleum*, 966 N. Potrero Grande Dr., 90640. Tel: 323-887-2024; Fax: 323-722-0874. Web: www.lacatholiccemeteries.org. Sofia V. Sandru, Mgr.

OXNARD. *Santa Clara Cemetery & Mausoleum*, 2370 North "H" St., 93036. Tel: 805-485-5757. Elizabeth Welsh, Mgr.

POMONA. *Holy Cross Cemetery*, P.O. Box 1145, 91769. Tel: 909-627-3602; Fax: 909-465-0690. Birdie Orta, Mgr.

ROWLAND HEIGHTS. *Queen of Heaven Cemetery*, 2161 S. Fullerton Rd., 91748. Tel: 626-964-1291; Fax: 626-964-4325. Norberta Orta, Mgr.

SANTA BARBARA. *Calvary Cemetery & Mausoleum*, 199 N. Hope Ave., 93110. Tel: 805-687-8811; Fax: 805-569-5814. Gwen Hueston, Mgr.

SIMI. *Assumption Cemetery*, 1380 Fitzgerald Rd., Simi Valley, 93065. Tel: 805-583-5825. Rosalie Castillo, Mgr.

NECROLOGY

† Folliard, Rev. Msgr. John P., (Retired)—Died June 22, 2009
† Kennedy, Rev. Msgr. Christopher J., Long Beach, CA St. Barnabas—Died March 2, 2009
† Kucingis, Rev. Msgr. John A., Los Angeles, CA St. Casimir—Died Jan. 6, 2009
† Moretti, Rev. Msgr. August, Pasadena, CA Assumption of the Blessed Virgin Mary—Died March 14, 2009
† Amengual, Miguel, (Retired)—Died June 17, 2009
† Duffy, Eugene J., (Retired)—Died Jan. 2, 2009
† Gerones, Florencio, Westlake Village, CA St. Jude—Died 2009
† Guillen, Arthur H., (Retired)—Died May 27, 2009
† Hughes, Patrick Michael, (Retired)—Died April 12, 2009
† Murphy, Denis J., (Retired)—Died Jan. 24, 2009
† O'Dwyer, Patrick, Westlake Village, CA St. Maximilian Kolbe—Died July 13, 2009
† Sanchez, Eliseo, (Retired)—Died Dec. 7, 2008
† Vecsey, Stephen N., (Retired)—Died March 9, 2009

Archdiocese of Louisville

(Archidioecesis Ludovicopolitana)

Most Reverend

JOSEPH E. KURTZ

Archbishop of Louisville; ordained 1972; appointed Bishop of Knoxville October 26, 1999; ordained and installed December 8, 1999; appointed Archbishop of Louisville June 12, 2007; installed August 15, 2007. *Office: 212 E. College St., P.O. Box 1073, Louisville, KY 40201.* Tel: 502-585-3291.

Most Reverend

THOMAS C. KELLY, O.P., D.D., J.C.D.

Retired Archbishop of Louisville; ordained June 5, 1958; appointed Titular Bishop of Tusuro July 12, 1977; promoted Archbishop of Louisville December 29, 1981; retired June 12, 2007. *Office: 212 E. College St., P.O. Box 1073, Louisville, KY 40201. Res.: Holy Trinity Parish, 501 Cherrywood Rd., Louisville, KY 40207.*

Chancery: 212 E. College St., P.O. Box 1073, Louisville, KY 40201. Tel: 502-585-3291; Fax: 502-585-2466.

Web: www.archlou.org

Email: chancery@archlou.org

Square Miles 8,124.

Established at Bardstown April 8, 1808; Transferred to Louisville Feb. 13, 1841; created an Archdiocese Dec. 10, 1937.

Comprises the following twenty-four Counties in central Kentucky: Adair, Barren, Bullitt, Casey, Clinton, Cumberland, Green, Hardin, Hart, Henry, Jefferson, Larue, Marion, Meade, Metcalfe, Monroe, Nelson, Oldham, Russell, Shelby, Spencer, Taylor, Trimble and Washington.

For legal titles of parishes and archdiocesan institutions, consult the Chancery.

STATISTICAL OVERVIEW

Personnel	
Archbishops	1
Retired Archbishops	1
Abbots	1
Retired Abbots	2
Priests: Diocesan Active in Diocese	84
Priests: Diocesan Active Outside Diocese	8
Priests: Diocesan in Foreign Missions	2
Priests: Retired, Sick or Absent	56
Number of Diocesan Priests	150
Religious Priests in Diocese	56
Total Priests in Diocese	206
Permanent Deacons in Diocese	120
Total Brothers	59
Total Sisters	697
Parishes	
Parishes	102
With Resident Pastor:	
Resident Diocesan Priests	77
Resident Religious Priests	7
Without Resident Pastor:	
Administered by Priests	14
Administered by Deacons	3
Administered by Lay People	1
Missions	9
New Parishes Created	2
Closed Parishes	6
Professional Ministry Personnel:	
Sisters	13
Lay Ministers	169
Welfare	
Catholic Hospitals	2
Total Assisted	210,500
Health Care Centers	1
Total Assisted	5,689
Homes for the Aged	5
Total Assisted	1,200
Residential Care of Children	2
Total Assisted	850
Day Care Centers	6
Total Assisted	300
Special Centers for Social Services	8
Total Assisted	40,000
Educational	
Diocesan Students in Other Seminaries	14
Total Seminarians	14
Colleges and Universities	3
Total Students	5,595
High Schools, Diocesan and Parish	4
Total Students	2,256
High Schools, Private	5
Total Students	4,181
Elementary Schools, Diocesan and Parish	36
Total Students	13,927
Elementary Schools, Private	3
Total Students	562
Non-residential Schools for the Disabled	1
Total Students	75
Catechesis/Religious Education:	
High School Students	1,009
Elementary Students	6,025
Total Students under Catholic Instruction	33,644
Teachers in the Diocese:	
Priests	7
Brothers	4
Sisters	23
Lay Teachers	1,883
Vital Statistics	
Receptions into the Church:	
Infant Baptism Totals	2,258
Minor Baptism Totals	211
Adult Baptism Totals	195
Received into Full Communion	450
First Communions	2,508
Confirmations	2,657
Marriages:	
Catholic	460
Interfaith	245
Total Marriages	705
Deaths	1,542
Total Catholic Population	192,450
Total Population	1,219,650

Former Bishops—Rt. Revs. BENEDICT JOSEPH FLAGET, S.S., D.D., cons. Bishop of Bardstown, Nov. 4, 1810; died Feb. 11, 1850; JOHN B. DAVID, S.S., D.D., Coadjutor; cons. Aug. 15, 1819; died July 12, 1841; GUY IGNATIUS CHABRAT, S.S., D.D., Coadjutor; cons. July 20, 1834; died Nov. 21, 1868; MARTIN JOHN SPALDING, D.D., Coadjutor with right of succession; cons. Sept. 10, 1848; transferred to Baltimore, May 6, 1864; died Feb. 7, 1872; PETER JOSEPH LAVIALLE, D.D., cons. Sept. 24, 1865; died May 11, 1867; WILLIAM GEORGE MCCLOSKEY, D.D., cons. May 24, 1868; died Sept. 17, 1909; DENIS O'DONAGHUE, D.D., ord. Sept. 6, 1874; cons. Titular Bishop of Pomario and Auxiliary of Indianapolis on April 25, 1900; transferred to Louisville, Feb. 7, 1910; transferred to the Titular See of Lebedus, July 26, 1924; died Nov. 7, 1925; Most Revs. JOHN A. FLOERSH, D.D., ord. June 10, 1911; appt. Titular Bishop of Lycopolis and Coadjutor Bishop of Louisville with right of succession, Feb. 6, 1923; cons. April 8, 1923; succeeded to See July 26, 1924; elevated to Archiepiscopal dignity Dec. 10, 1937; resigned and named to Titular See of Sistroniana, March 1, 1967; died June 11, 1968; THOMAS J. MCDONOUGH, D.D., transferred to Louisville, May 2, 1967; resigned Sept. 29, 1981; died Aug. 4, 1998; THOMAS C. KELLY, ord. June 5, 1958; appt. Titular Bishop of Tusuro July 12, 1977; promoted Archbishop of Louisville Dec. 29, 1981; retired June 12, 2007.

Vicar General—Very Rev. CHARLES C. THOMPSON, J.C.L.

Chancery—212 E. College St., P.O. Box 1073, Louisville, 40201. Tel: 502-585-3291; Fax: 502-585-2466. Office Hours: 8:30-4:30; All applications for dispensations are to be sent to this office.

Chancellor—Dr. BRIAN B. REYNOLDS.

Vice Chancellor—NORMA L. MERRICK.

Secretary to Archbishop—NORMA L. MERRICK.

Archivist—Rev. R. DALE CIESLIK.

Chief Financial Officer—ROBERT L. ASH.

Metropolitan Tribunal—212 E. College St., P.O. Box 1073, Louisville, 40201. Tel: 502-585-3291.

Judicial Vicar and Director—Very Rev. J. MARK SPALDING, J.C.L.

Adjutant Judicial Vicar—Rev. PHILIP LEE ERICKSON, J.C.L.

Promoter of Justice—Very Rev. CHARLES C. THOMPSON, J.C.L.

Defenders of the Bond—Revs. DONALD R. GOETZ; JOHN J. STOLTZ; R. PAUL BEACH; JOHN A. SCHWARTZLOSE; BRIAN A. KENNEY; ANTHONY L. CHANDLER, M.A.; JAMES J. LICHTEFELD (Retired); J. WAYNE MURPHY (Retired); ROBERT E. OSBORNE (Retired); PATRICK J. DOLAN, Ph.D., S.T.D.; Deacon WALTON JONES; Dr. ROBERT L. STENGER, S.T.D., J.D.

Associate Judges—Revs. FREDERICK W. KLOTTER, S.T.L., J.C.L.; KENNETH R. FORTENER; THOMAS A. HOMMRICH (Retired); T. MICHAEL TOBIN, S.T.L., J.C.B.; Ms. JACQUELINE RAPP, J.D., J.C.L.

Assessor and Associate Director—PATRICIA A. NORRIS, Ed.D.

Assessor—VACANT.

Ecclesiastical Notaries—SHARON A. ARCHER; LINDA D. THOMAN; ANN TUMBLIN.

College of Consultors—Very Revs. CHARLES C. THOMPSON, J.C.L.; J. MARK SPALDING, J.C.L.; Revs. TERRY L. BRADSHAW; JOSEPH M. RANKIN; THOMAS A. SMITH; JEFFREY P. SHOONER.

Deans—Revs. WILLIAM D. HAMMER, Bardstown Deanery; GERALD L. BELL, Lebanon Deanery; CHARLES D. WALKER, Elizabethtown Deanery.

Clergy Personnel Commission—Revs. JOSEPH H. VOOR (Retired); R. DALE CIESLIK; WILLIAM S. GRINER (Retired); J. WAYNE JENKINS; BRIAN A. KENNEY; Deacon BRIAN KARLEY, C.R., Dir.

Priests' Council—Most Rev. JOSEPH E. KURTZ, D.D., Presider; Rev. THOMAS A. SMITH, Pres.; NORMA L. MERRICK, Sec., 212 E. College St., Louisville, 40203. Ex Officio: Very Revs. CHARLES C. THOMPSON, J.C.L.; J. MARK SPALDING, J.C.L.; Revs. ROY E. DENTINGER (Retired); WILLIAM D. HAMMER; JEFFREY G. HOPPER; JOHN T. JUDIE; JEFFREY S. NICOLAS; FREDERICK W. KLOTTER, S.T.L., J.C.L.; THOMAS E. GENTILE; LOUIS J. MEIMAN; JOSEPH M. RANKIN; JEFFREY P. SHOONER; TERRY L. BRADSHAW; JOHN J. STOLTZ; JAMES W. GRAF; PETER QUAN DO; KEVIN J. BRYAN; JOSEPH ATCHER, O.Carm.; Very Rev. JAMES M. SULLIVAN, O.P.

Archdiocesan Examiners—Very Rev. WILLIAM L. FICHTEMAN; Revs. THOMAS L. BOLAND; GARY T. PADGETT.

Archdiocesan Offices and Directors

Archdiocesan Communications Center—CECELIA PRICE, Chief Communications Officer, Maloney Center, 1200 S. Shelby St., Louisville, 40203. Tel: 502-636-0296; Fax: 502-636-2379.

Byzantine Rite Faithful—Rev. JOHN W. BIRK, Chap. (Retired), 2082 Douglass Blvd., #1, Louisville, 40205. Tel: 502-451-1555.

Catholic Cemeteries Office—JAVIER FAJARDO, Exec. Dir., 1600 Newburg Rd., P.O. Box 4096, Louisville, 40204. Tel: 502-451-7710; Fax: 502-456-9270.

Catholic Deaf Office— For Deaf Ministry contact St. Stephen Martyr Parish, Louisville, KY

Catholic Charities—Mr. STEVEN E. BOGUS, Exec. Dir., 2911 S. 4th St., Louisville, 40208. Tel: 502-637-9786; Fax: 502-637-9780.

Office of Migration and Refugee Services—Ms. BECKY JORDAN.

Office of Parish Social Ministry—DAVID J. DUTSCHKE.

Respect Life—HELEN ROTHGERBER.

Clergy Personnel Office—Deacon BRIAN KARLEY, C.R., Dir., Mailing Address: P.O. Box 1073, Louisville, 40201. Tel: 502-585-3291; Fax: 502-585-2466.

Clerical Aid Society—212 E. College St., P.O. Box 1073, Louisville, 40201. Tel: 502-585-3291.

Continuing Education for Clergy-Ministry to Priests—Deacon BRIAN KARLEY, C.R., Mailing Address: P.O. Box 1073, Louisville, 40201. Tel: 502-585-3291.

Cursillo Movement—PATRICIA WILLIAMS, Lay Dir.; Rev. JUAN PEREZ, Spiritual Advisor, Flaget Center, 1935 Lewiston Pl., Louisville, 40216. Tel: 502-448-8581.

Due Process Board—JOHN LAUN, Chm., Mailing Address: P.O. Box 1073, Louisville, 40201. Tel: 502-585-3291.

Ecumenical and Interreligious Relations Officer—Rev. MARTIN A. LINEBACH.

Family Ministries Office—SUE BRODFEHRER, Exec. Dir.; THOMAS D. ROBBINS, Ph.D., Clinical Dir., Maloney Center, 1200 S. Shelby St., Louisville, 40203. Tel: 502-636-0296; Fax: 502-636-2379.

Holy Childhood Association—Deacon ROBERT HALL, Dir., 212 E. College St., Box 1073, Louisville, 40201. Tel: 502-585-3291.

Holy Name Society—MICHAEL HEEB, Pres., 2302 Bradford Dr., Louisville, 40218. Tel: 502-454-7151.

L.A.M.P.— (Louisville Archdiocesan Mission Promoters), Most Rev. JOSEPH E. KURTZ, D.D.; Very Rev. CHARLES C. THOMPSON, J.C.L., 212 E. College St., P.O. Box 1073, Louisville, 40201. Tel: 502-585-3291.

Office of the Diaconate—Deacon ROBERT HALL, Dir., Maloney Center, 1200 S. Shelby St., Louisville, 40203. Tel: 502-636-0296; Fax: 502-636-2379.

Office of Lifelong Formation and Education—Rev. JOSEPH ATCHER, O.Carm., Exec. Dir., Flaget Center, 1935 Lewiston Pl., Louisville, 40216. Tel: 502-448-8581; Fax: 502-448-5518.

Superintendent of Schools—LEISA SCHULZ.

Director of Youth Ministry—Dr. CAROLE GOODWIN.

Director of Faith Formation—SAL DELLA BELLA.

Office of Multicultural Ministry—M. ANNETTE TURNER, Dir., Maloney Center, 1200 S. Shelby St., Louisville, 40203. Tel: 502-636-0296.

Office of Pastoral Care—Rev. PAUL A. SCAGLIONE, Dir., Maloney Center, 1200 S. Shelby St., Louisville, 40203. Tel: 502-636-0296; Fax: 502-636-2379. Email: opc@archlou.org.

Office of Worship—Mrs. JUDY BULLOCK, Dir., Maloney Center, 1200 S. Shelby St., Louisville, 40203. Tel: 502-636-0296; Fax: 502-636-2379.

Opportunities for Life—VACANT, Dir., 1042 Burlington Lane, Frankfort, 40601. Tel: 502-223-5330; 800-822-5824; Fax: 502-875-2841.

Personnel and Planning—Dr. BRIAN B. REYNOLDS, Dir., 212 E. College, P.O. Box 1073, Louisville, 40201. Tel: 502-585-3291.

Propagation of the Faith— (Missions Office), Deacon ROBERT HALL, Dir., Mailing Address: P.O. Box 1073, Louisville, 40201. Tel: 502-585-3291.

Sacred Heart Enthronement Center—Rev. LAWRENCE H. LINDLE, Dir. (Retired), 3623 Fern Valley Rd., Louisville, 40219.

Stewardship and Development Office—NICHOLAS K. EVE, Dir., 212 E. College St., P.O. Box 1073, Louisville, 40201. Tel: 502-585-3291; Fax: 502-585-2466.

Vicar for Retired Clergy—Rev. J. ROY STILES (Retired), 2040 Buechel Bank Rd., Louisville, 40218. Tel: 502-499-0868.

Victim Assistance Coordinator—THOMAS D. ROBBINS, Ph.D. Tel: 502-636-1044. Email: trobbins@archlou.org; family@archlou.org.

Vocations—Revs. WILLIAM M. BOWLING, Dir.; JEFFREY P. SHOONER, Assoc. Dir., Maloney Center, 1200 S. Shelby St., Louisville, 40203. Tel: 502-636-0296.

CLERGY, PARISHES, MISSIONS AND PAROCHIAL SCHOOLS

CITY OF LOUISVILLE

(JEFFERSON COUNTY)

1—CATHEDRAL OF THE ASSUMPTION (1852) Very Rev. William L. Fichteman; Rev. Martin A. Linebach; Deacons J. Patrick Wright; P. Stephan Phelps. In Res., Most Rev. Joseph E. Kurtz.
Res.: 433 S. 5th St., 40202. Tel: 502-582-2971; Fax: 502-582-3919.
Catechesis/Religious Program—Students 83.

2—ST. AGNES (1885) Revs. John Conley, C.P.; Albert Schwer, C.P.; Justin Nelson Alphonse, C.P. In Res., Rev. Joseph Mitchell, C.P.
Res.: 1920 Newburg Rd., 40205. Tel: 502-451-2220; Fax: 502-454-8483. Email: jackicecil@yahoo.com. Web: stagneslouisville.org.
School—(Grades K-8), 1800 Newburg Rd., 40205. Tel: 502-458-2850; Fax: 502-459-5215. Carol Meirose, Prin.; Margi Johnstone, Librarian. Lay Teachers 30; Students 431.
Catechesis/Religious Program—Students 45.

3—ST. ALBERT THE GREAT (1959) Revs. Donald M. Hill; Jeffrey D. Gatlin; Deacon Vincent (Jim) G. Stanley.
Res.: 1395 Girard Dr., 40222. Tel: 502-425-3940; Fax: 502-394-9896. Web: www.stalbert.org.
School—(Grades K-8) Tel: 502-425-1804. Jeanne Flowers, Prin. Lay Teachers 42; Students 665.
Catechesis/Religious Program—Tel: 502-423-1590, Ext. 110. Students 136.

4—ST. ALOYSIUS, Closed. For inquiries for parish records contact the chancery.

5—ST. ANDREW, Closed. For inquiries for parish records contact the chancery.

6—ST. ANN, Closed. For inquiries for parish records contact the chancery.

7—ST. ANTHONY (1867) Closed. For inquiries for parish records contact Good Shepherd, Louisville.

8—ASCENSION OF OUR LORD (1965) Rev. Gary T. Padgett; Deacon Michael Edwards.
Res.: 4600 Lynnbrook Dr., 40220. Tel: 502-451-3860; Fax: 502-458-9782. Email: dschabel@ascension-parish.com.
School—(Grades PreK-8) Tel: 502-451-2535; Fax: 502-451-2535. Mary Jo Ellis, Prin.; Elaine Whitehead, Librarian. Lay Teachers 24; Students 280.
Catechesis/Religious Program—Tel: 502-451-3860, Ext. 12. Students 30.

9—ST. ATHANASIUS (1960) Rev. Terry L. Bradshaw.
Res.: 5915 Outer Loop Dr., 40219. Tel: 502-969-3332; Fax: 502-966-8948. Email: rwadell@staparish.com. Web: www.stathanasiuslouisville.com.
School—(Grades PreK-8) Tel: 502-969-2345; Fax: 502-969-8974. Diane Arrow, Prin.; Anne Bainridge, Librarian. Lay Teachers 26; Students 504.
Catechesis/Religious Program—Students 75.

10—ST. AUGUSTINE (1870) Deacon James Turner, Pastoral Admin.; Rev. Patrick D. Delahanty, Sacramental Moderator; Deacon Keith L. McKenzie.
Res.: 1310 W. Broadway, 40203. Tel: 502-584-4602; Fax: 502-581-0893. Email: staugustine@insightbb.com.
Hines Center—Tel: 502-584-5463.

11—ST. BARNABAS (1953) Rev. J. Wayne Jenkins; Deacon James R. Plummer.
Parish Office: 3042 Hikes Ln., 40220. Tel: 502-459-4251; Fax: 502-459-9815. Email: rtemple@stbarnabaslou.org.
Res.: 3700 Mid Dale, 40220. Tel: 502-451-0333.
Catechesis/Religious Program—Students 36.

12—ST. BARTHOLOMEW (1941) Rev. Peter Quan Do; Deacon Thomas E. Box; Mrs. Becky Box, Pastoral Assoc. In Res., Rev. J. Roy Stiles (Retired).
Parish Office: 2042 Buechel Bank Rd., 40218. Tel: 502-499-0883; Fax: 502-499-0877. Web: www.stbarths.org.
Res.: 2040 Buechel Bank Rd., 40218. Tel: 502-499-0876.
Catechesis/Religious Program—2825 Klondike Ln., 40218. Mrs. Becky Box, D.R.E. Students 82.

13—ST. BASIL, Closed. For inquiries for parish records contact the chancery.

14—ST. BENEDICT, Closed. For inquiries for parish records contact the chancery.

15—ST. BERNADETTE PARISH (2008) Deacons Patrick Harris; Danny E. Parker.
Parish Office: 6500 St. Bernadette Ave., Prospect, 40059. Tel: 502-425-2210; Fax: 502-425-0941.
Catechesis/Religious Program—Judy Montgomery, D.R.E. Students 237.

16—ST. BERNARD (1963) Rev. Robert L. Stuempel; Deacon Philip Hettich.
Res.: 7500 Tangelo Dr., 40228. Tel: 502-239-5178; Fax: 502-239-9025. Email: stbernardparish@insightbb.com. Web: stbernardlou.com.
School—(Grades PreK-8) Tel: 502-239-5178; Fax: 502-239-9025. Fred J. Klausing III, Prin. Lay Teachers 27; Students 465.
Catechesis/Religious Program—Tel: 502-239-5178, Ext. 125. Jan Redle, D.R.E. Students 56.

17—BLESSED TERESA OF CALCUTTA (2008) Rev. Robert E. Roy; Deacons Paul J. George; Kenneth J. Mitchell.
903 Fairdale Rd., Fairdale, 40118. Tel: 502-363-9929; Fax: 502-363-9960.
Catechesis/Religious Program—Lynn McDaniel, D.R.E. Students 40.

18—ST. BONIFACE (1836) Rev. Timothy A. Hogan; Deacons David R. Tomes; P. Stephan Phelps.
Parish Office: 531 E. Liberty St., 40202-1107. Tel: 502-584-4279; Fax: 502-584-8659. Email: stboniface@insightbb.com. Web: stbonifacechurch-.com.

19—ST. BRIGID (1873) Revs. Donald R. Goetz; Joseph H. Voor (Retired); Deacon Louis B. Dugan.
Res.: 1520 Hepburn Ave., 40204. Tel: 502-584-5565; Fax: 502-584-1328. Email: stbrigidchlou@bellsouth.net.

20—ST. CECILIA (1873) Closed. For inquiries for parish records contact Good Shepherd, Louisville.

21—ST. CHARLES BORROMEO, Closed. For inquiries for parish records contact the chancery.

22—CHRIST THE KING (1928) Rev. John T. Judie.
Res.: 718 S. 44th St., 40211. Tel: 502-778-5055; Fax: 502-776-5120 (Call first). Email: ctkarchlou@bellsouth.net.
Catechesis/Religious Program—Tel: 502-772-7851. Loueva Moss, D.R.E. Students 36.

23—ST. CLEMENT (1956) Closed. For inquiries for parish records please see St. Peter the Apostle, Louisville.

24—ST. COLUMBA, Closed. For inquiries for parish records contact the chancery.

25—ST. DENIS (1916) Closed. For inquiries for parish records please see Mary Queen of Peace, Louisville.

26—ST. EDWARD (1884) [CEM] Rev. Joseph T. Graffis; Mrs. Betty Deerwester, Pastoral Assoc.
Res.: 9608 Sue Helen Dr., 40299. Tel: 502-267-7494; Fax: 502-267-7495. Email: churchoffice@stedwardchurch.com.
School—(Grades PreK-8), 9610 Sue Helen Dr., 40299. Tel: 502-267-6633; Fax: 502-267-4474. Susan Jones, Prin.; Diane Walsh, Librarian. Lay Teachers 31; Students 458.
Catechesis/Religious Program—Deborah Grisanti, D.R.E. Students 136.

27—ST. ELIZABETH ANN SETON (1975) Rev. R. Dale Cieslik; Deacon James C. Olrich; Margee Joseph, Pastoral Assoc.
Res.: 11507 Maple Way, 40229. Tel: 502-969-0004 Parish; 502-966-3164; Fax: 502-969-0553. Email: parishoffice@bellsouth.net. Web: easeton.com.
Catechesis/Religious Program—Students 105.

28—ST. ELIZABETH OF HUNGARY (1906) Revs. H. Anthony Olges; Robert B. Gray (Retired).
Res.: 1020 E. Burnett Ave., 40217. Tel: 502-636-3706; Fax: 502-636-3707. Email: stemain@iglou.com. Web: germantownwncatholiccluster.org.
Catechesis/Religious Program—2931 Pindell Ave., 40217. Tel: 502-635-5813. Students 14.

29—EPIPHANY (1971) Rev. Jeffrey S. Nicolas; Sr. Mary Gowern, C.S.J., Pastoral Assoc.

Parish Office: 914 Old Harrods Creek Rd., 40223. Tel: 502-245-9733; Fax: 502-245-7658. Email: martha@churchofepiphany.com. Web: churchofepiphany.com.
Catechesis/Religious Program—Students 211.

30—ST. FRANCES OF ROME (1887) Rev. Bernard J. Breen; Sr. Carmelita Dunn, S.C.N., Pastoral Assoc.
Res.: 2119 Payne St., 40206. Tel: 502-896-8401; Fax: 502-895-0310. Email: stfranrome@aol.com. Web: stfrancesofrome.org.
Catechesis/Religious Program—Sr. Mary Jo Gramig, O.S.U., D.R.E. Students 44.

31—ST. FRANCIS OF ASSISI (1886) Rev. Louis J. Meiman; Deacon Lawrence Biven. In Res., Rev. Joseph T. Merkt.
Res.: 1960 Bardstown Rd., 40205-1572. Tel: 502-456-6394; Fax: 502-456-9462. Email: lmeiman@ccsfa.org. Web: ccsfa.org.
School—(Grades K-8), 1938 Alfresco Pl., 40205-1876. Tel: 502-459-3088; Fax: 502-456-9462. Paula Watkins, Prin. Lay Teachers 18; Students 244.
Catechesis/Religious Program—Tel: 502-456-6394. Students 20.

32—ST. GABRIEL THE ARCHANGEL (1953) Revs. John J. Stoltz; James T. Mudd (Retired); Deacons Darryl J. Diemer; T. Stephen Bowling.
Res.: 5505 Bardstown Rd., 40291. Tel: 502-239-5481; Fax: 502-239-7717. Email: parish@stgabriel.net. Web: stgabriel.net.
School—(Grades PreK-8), 5503 Bardstown Rd., 40291. Tel: 502-239-5535; Fax: 502-231-1464. Pamela Huelsman, Prin.; Tammy Herbert, Librarian. Lay Teachers 39; Students 770.
Catechesis/Religious Program—Betsy O'Neill, D.R.E. Students 170.

33—ST. GEORGE, Closed. For inquiries for parish records contact the chancery.

34—GOOD SHEPHERD Rev. John R. Burke; Deacons Paul F. Bissig; Geoffrey Gnau.
Parish Office: 338 N. 25th St., 40212. Tel: 502-772-3694; Fax: 502-772-3695.

35—GUARDIAN ANGELS (1957) Rev. Daniel Lobsinger, C.R.; Deacon Philip Tremblay, C.R.
Res.: 6014 Preston Hwy., 40219. Tel: 502-968-5421; Fax: 502-962-1080. Email: gangelscommunity@bellsouth.net.
Catechesis/Religious Program—Students 10.

36—ST. HELEN (1897) Closed. For inquiries for parish records please see Mary Queen of Peace, Louisville.

37—HOLY CROSS, Closed. For inquiries for parish records contact the chancery.

38—HOLY FAMILY (1929) Rev. H. Anthony Olges; Deacon James H. Abell.
Res.: 3926 Poplar Level Rd., 40213. Tel: 502-459-6066; Fax: 502-456-9198. Email: churchoffice@hofaky.org. Web: hofaky.org.
School—(Grades PreK-8), 3934 Poplar Level Rd., 40213. Tel: 502-458-4531; Fax: 502-456-9188. Gayle Bauch, Prin. Lay Teachers 15; Students 205.
Catechesis/Religious Program—Students 20.

39—HOLY NAME (1891) Rev. David Sanchez.
Res.: 2914 S. 3rd St., 40208. Tel: 502-637-2058; Fax: 502-637-1809. Email: p@holyname.org. Web: oholyname.org.
Catechesis/Religious Program—Students 22.

40—HOLY SPIRIT (1937) Revs. Thomas A. Smith; Paul W. Eve; Deacons Joseph A. Raibert; Robert Hall. In Res., Rev. Joseph Atcher, O.Carm.
Res.: 3345 Lexington Rd., 40206. Tel: 502-893-3982; Fax: 502-893-8287. Email: office@hspirit.org. Web: hspirit.org.
School—(Grades K-8), 322 Cannons Ln., 40206. Tel: 502-893-7700; Fax: 502-893-8078. Doris Swenson, Prin. Lay Teachers 27; Students 409.
Catechesis/Religious Program—Students 25.

41—HOLY TRINITY (1882) Very Rev. Charles C. Thompson; Deacons Walton G. Jones; Jeremiah S. Babin. In Res., Most Rev. Thomas C. Kelly, O.P.
Pastoral Center—501 Cherrywood Rd., 40207. Tel: 502-897-5207; Fax: 502-897-0962. Web: htparish.org.
School—(Grades K-8), 423 Cherrywood Rd., 40207. Tel: 502-897-2785; Fax: 502-896-0990. Mr. Jack Richards, Prin. Lay Teachers 42; Students 701.
Catechesis/Religious Program—Tel: 502-897-5207, Ext. 125. Dinah Tichy, D.R.E. Students 83.

42—ST. IGNATIUS (1963) Rev. Martin A. Linebach, Admin. In Res., Rev. Gerald L. Timmel (Retired).
Res.: 1816 Rangeland Rd., 40219. Tel: 502-964-5904; Fax: 502-964-5905. Email: stignatius@aol.com.
St. Ignatius Child Development Center—1818 Rangeland Rd., 40219. Tel: 502-969-2336; Fax: 502-969-7878. Kathleen Jewell, Dir. Lay Teachers 18; Students 77.
Catechesis/Religious Program—Students 26.

43—IMMACULATE HEART OF MARY (1953) Rev. John T. Judie.
Office: 1545 S. 34th St., 40211. Tel: 502-774-5772; Fax: 502-774-5899. Email: irectory@bellsouth.net.
Catechesis/Religious Program—Students 2.

44—INCARNATION (1966) Rev. Christian Moore, O.F.M.-.Conv.; Deacon Robert Markert; Mary Ann Glaser, Pastoral Assoc.
Res.: 2229 Lower Hunters Trace Rd., 40216. Tel: 502-447-2013; Fax: 502-448-3821. Email: incarnationcatho@bellsouth.net. Web: incarnation-catholicchurch.com.

45—ST. JAMES (1906) Revs. Donald R. Goetz; Joseph H. Voor (Retired); Deacon Louis B. Dugan.
Res.: 1826 Edenside Ave., 40204. Tel: 502-451-1420; Fax: 502-451-1429. Email: stjameschurchlou@bellsouth.net. Web: stjameslou.org.
School—(Grades PreK-8), 1818 Edenside Ave., 40204. Tel: 502-454-0330; Fax: 502-454-0330. Tom Schmitt, Prin. Lay Teachers 16; Students 217.
Catechesis/Religious Program—Students 4.

46—ST. JEROME (1953) Closed. For inquiries for parish records please see Blessed Teresa of Calcutta, Louisville.

47—ST. JOHN, Closed. For inquiries for parish records contact the chancery.

48—ST. JOHN VIANNEY (1951) Rev. Anthony Chinh N'go.
Res.: 4839 Southside Dr., 40214. Tel: 502-366-5517; Fax: 502-366-3544.
Catechesis/Religious Program—Sr. Clare Nguyen, D.R.E.; Mr. Thang Ly, D.R.E. Students 65.

49—ST. JOSEPH (1866) Rev. David Sanchez.
Res.: 1406 E. Washington St., 40206. Tel: 502-583-7401; Fax: 502-589-7465. Email: parish@sjosephcatholic.org. Web: sjosephcatholic.org.
Catechesis/Religious Program—Tel: 502-583-0892. Students 49.

50—ST. LAWRENCE (1953) Rev. Jeffrey P. Shooner, Admin.; Sr. Ann Marie Howard, O.S.B., Pastoral Assoc.; Deacons David Dalton; Kenneth Carter.
Res.: 1925 Lewiston Dr., 40216. Tel: 502-448-2122; Fax: 502-448-2163. Email: stlwendy@gmail.com. Web: lawrencelife.org.
Catechesis/Religious Program— Sr. Ann Marie Howard, O.S.B., D.R.E. Students 157.

51—ST. LEO THE GREAT, Closed. For inquiries for parish records contact the chancery.

52—ST. LEONARD (1953) Rev. Bernard J. Breen; Joy Trimble, Pastoral Assoc.
Res.: 440 Zorn Ave., 40206. Tel: 502-897-2595; Fax: 502-896-8259.
School—(Grades PreK-8) Tel: 502-897-5265; Fax: 502-897-5121. Linda Kinderman, Prin.; Nancy Tomasetti, Librarian. Lay Teachers 24; Students 177.
Catechesis/Religious Program—Students 8.

53—ST. LOUIS BERTRAND (1866) Very Rev. James M. Sullivan, O.P., Prior; Revs. George G. Christian, O.P.; James B. Muller, O.P.; Thomas V. Di Fede, O.P.; Ralph V. Townsend, O.P.
Res.: 1104 S. 6th St., 40203. Tel: 502-583-4448; Fax: 502-589-0056.
Shrine—Lourdes Rosary Shrine, Inc.
Shrine—Blessed Margaret Castello Shrine

54—ST. LUKE (1965) Rev. Joseph M. Rankin.
Res.: 4211 Jim Hawkins Dr., 40229. Tel: 502-969-3291; Fax: 502-969-1718.
Catechesis/Religious Program—Debbie Minton, D.R.E. Students 25.

55—ST. MARGARET MARY (1951) Revs. Stephen A. Pohl; John Miles, C.R.; Theodore R. Sans, Sacramental Assoc. (Retired); Deacon Charles T. Bent.
Res.: 7813 Shelbyville Rd., 40222. Tel: 502-426-1588; Fax: 502-426-1503. Email: grace@stmm.org. Web: stmm.org.
School—(Grades K-8) Tel: 502-426-2635; Fax: 502-426-1304. John Westerfield, Prin. Lay Teachers 36; Students 721.
Catechesis/Religious Program—Students 109.

56—ST. MARTHA (1960) Rev. Donald W. Springman; Deacons Ken Ward, Parish Admin.; John P. Maher.
Res.: 2825 Klondike Ln., 40218. Tel: 502-491-8535; Fax: 502-491-8536. Email: parishof@bellsouth.net.
School—(Grades PreK-8) Tel: 502-491-3171; Fax: 502-495-6107. Sharon Dutton, Prin.; Carolyn Deckelman, Librarian. Lay Teachers 34; Students 531.
Catechesis/Religious Program—Tel: 502-491-5135. Pamela M. Berry, D.R.E. Students 30.

57—ST. MARTIN DE PORRES (1990), Consolidated with St. Benedict, Louisville, St. Charles Borromeo, Louisville, and Holy Cross, Louisville, parishes. Rev. Patrick D. Delahanty, Sacramental Moderator; Sr. Dorothy Jackson, S.C.N., Pastoral Assoc.; Deacon James Turner, Pastoral Admin.
Mailing Address: 3112 W. Broadway, 40211. Tel: 502-778-1118; Fax: 502-778-0148.
Catechesis/Religious Program—Tel: 502-418-3447. M. Annette Mandley-Turner, D.R.E. Students 112.

58—ST. MARTIN OF TOURS (1853) Rev. Frederick W. Klotter; Deacon Jarvis Jackson.
Res.: 639 S. Shelby St., 40202. Tel: 502-582-2827; Fax: 502-582-1780. Email: rectory@louisville-catholic.net.
Catechesis/Religious Program—Students 120.

59—ST. MARY (1968) Closed. For inquiries for parish records please see Blessed Teresa of Calcutta, Louisville.

60—ST. MARY MAGDALEN, Closed. For inquiries for parish records contact the chancery.

61—MARY QUEEN OF PEACE PARISH Rev. Thomas E. Gentile; Deacons Robert M. Kampschaefer; William Niemeier.
Parish Office: 4005 Dixie Hwy., 40216. Tel: 502-448-4008; Fax: 502-448-8546.
Catechesis/Religious Program—Students 18.

62—ST. MATTHIAS (1950) Closed. For inquiries for parish records please see Mary Queen of Peace, Louisville.

63—ST. MICHAEL (1975) Rev. J. Richard Sullivan; Deacon Martin J. Brown.
Res.: 3705 Stone Lakes Dr., 40299. Tel: 502-266-5611; Fax: 502-267-4272. Email: frdick@stmichaellouisville.org. Web: stmichaelchurch.org.
School—(Grades PreK-8) Tel: 502-267-6155; Fax: 502-267-4272. Sheila Marstiller, Prin.; Kathy Geoghegan, Librarian. Lay Teachers 51; Students 579.
Catechesis/Religious Program—Brenda Rickert, D.R.E. Students 186.

64—MOST BLESSED SACRAMENT (1937) Rev. Harry J. Gelthaus.
Mailing Address: 4335 Hazelwood Ave., 40215.
Res.: 3509 Taylor Blvd., 40215. Tel: 502-361-0149; Fax: 502-375-1988. Web: mbsparish.com.
Catechesis/Religious Program—Tel: 502-361-0960. Students 16.

65—MOTHER OF GOOD COUNSEL (1959) Closed. For inquiries for parish records please see St. Bernadette, Louisville.

66—OUR LADY (1839) Closed. For inquiries for parish records contact Good Shepherd, Louisville.

67—OUR LADY HELP OF CHRISTIANS (1957) Closed. For inquiries for parish records please see St. Peter the Apostle, Louisville.

68—OUR LADY OF CONSOLATION (1959) Closed. For inquiries for parish records please see St. Peter the Apostle, Louisville.

69—OUR LADY OF LOURDES (1950) Rev. G. Nicholas Rice; Deacons F. Eugene Waldon; Timothy B. Ayers.
Res.: 508 Breckenridge Ln., 40207. Tel: 502-896-0241; Fax: 502-895-4535. Email: olol@ourlourdes.org. Web: ourlourdes.org.
School—(Grades K-8), 510 Breckenridge Ln., 40207. Tel: 502-895-5122; Fax: 502-893-5051. Laura Glaser, Prin.; Maureen Choate, Librarian. Lay Teachers 26; Students 411.
Catechesis/Religious Program—Tel: 502-896-0241, Ext. 13; Fax: 502-895-4535. Mary Caroline Marchal, S.C., D.R.E.; Ann Pifer, D.R.E. Students 130.

70—OUR LADY OF MOUNT CARMEL (1957) Rev. Philip Lee Erickson.
Parish Office: 5505 New Cut Rd., 40214. Tel: 502-366-5651; Fax: 502-368-9972. Email: parishsecretary@insightbb.com.
Res.: 7333 Southside Dr., 40214.
Catechesis/Religious Program—6105 S. Third St., 40214. Tel: 502-366-1463; Fax: 502-366-1464. Students 73.

71—OUR MOTHER OF SORROWS (1937) Rev. William J. Martin; Deacons Robert C. Bryant; Timothy E. Stewart.
Res.: 747 Harrison Ave., 40217. Tel: 502-637-7442; Fax: 502-637-3794. Email: parishoffice@omos.org. Web: omos.org.

72—ST. PATRICK (1988) Rev. Thomas L. Boland; Deacons Scott R. Haner; Mark J. Rougeux.
Res.: 1000 N. Beckley Station Rd., 40245-4550. Tel: 502-244-6083; Fax: 502-719-0359. Email: ourparish@stpatrick-lou.org. Web: stpatrick-lou.org.
School—(Grades K-8) Tel: 502-244-7083; Fax: 502-719-0369. Elaine M. Wnorowski, Prin.; Adele Koch, Librarian. Lay Teachers 44; Students 693.
Catechesis/Religious Program—Tel: 502-254-9472. Agnes Kovacs, Dir. Formation. Students 211.

73—ST. PAUL (1851) Rev. Dismas J. Veeneman, O.F.M.Conv.; Deacon Charles Beckmann. In Res., Revs. Adam Bunnell, O.F.M.Conv.; Benjamin Knopp, O.F.M.Conv.
Res.: 6901 Dixie Hwy., 40258. Tel: 502-935-1223; Fax: 502-933-7747. Email: dismasv@aol.com.
School—(Grades PreK-8) Tel: 502-935-5511; Fax: 502-935-5596. Kevin Brever, Prin. Lay Teachers 13; Students 183.
Catechesis/Religious Program—Amy Gaekle, D.R.E. Students 57.

74—ST. PETER CLAVER (2008) Closed. For inquiries for parish records contact the chancery.

75—ST. PETER THE APOSTLE PARISH (2008) Revs. Ronald J. Domhoff; Gary G. Davis; Deacons Wayne Thieneman; Steve Smith; Gregory L. Klinglesmith.
Parish Office: 5431 Johnsontown Rd., 40272. Tel: 502-937-5920; Fax: 502-937-5927.
Catechesis/Religious Program—Catherine Blandord,

D.R.E. Students 130.
76—ST. PHILIP NERI, Closed. For inquiries for parish records contact the chancery.
77—ST. PIUS X (1956) Rev. William P. Burks; Sr. Mary Elaine Zehnder, S.C.N., Pastoral Assoc.
Res.: 3521 Goldsmith Ln., 40220. Tel: 502-451-9300 (Office); 502-451-4124 (Rectory); Fax: 502-458-7109.
Catechesis/Religious Program—Kathleen Stout, D.R.E. Students 37.
78—ST. POLYCARP (1960) Closed. For inquiries for parish records please see St. Peter the Apostle, Louisville.
79—ST. RAPHAEL THE ARCHANGEL (1947) Rev. James F. Hackett; Deacon Robert Dever, Pastoral Assoc.
Res.: 2121 Lancashire Ave., 40205. Tel: 502-458-2500.
Parish Offices—2141 Lancashire Ave, 40205. Tel: 502-458-2500; Fax: 502-458-8049.
School—(Grades K-8), 2131 Lancashire Ave., 40205. Tel: 502-456-1541; Fax: 502-451-3632. Paul DeZarn, Prin. Lay Teachers 28; Students 460.
Catechesis/Religious Program—Students 4.
80—RESURRECTION D.N.J.C., Closed. For inquiries for parish records contact the chancery.
81—ST. RITA (1921) Revs. Joseph M. Rankin; Thomas A. Smith, O.F.M.Conv.; Deacon Aurelio A. Puga.
Res.: 8709 Preston Hwy., 40219. Tel: 502-969-4579; Fax: 502-969-3679. Email: lheitz@saintrita.net. Web: saintrita.net.
School—(Grades PreK-8) Tel: 502-969-7067; Fax: 502-969-3679. Mary Lee Lanning, Prin. Lay Teachers 23; Students 298.
Catechesis/Religious Program—Students 150.
82—SS. SIMON AND JUDE (1950) Rev. Harry J. Gelthaus; Deacon David L. McGinty.
Res.: 4335 Hazelwood Ave., 40215. Tel: 502-368-4887; Fax: 502-375-1988.
Catechesis/Religious Program—Students 27.
83—ST. STEPHEN, MARTYR (1948) Rev. J. Randall Hubbard; Deacons Sylvester Nitzken; Stephen J. DaPonte.
Res.: 2931 Pindell Ave., 40217. Tel: 502-635-5813; Fax: 502-635-5888.
School—(Grades PreK-8), 2931 Pindell, 40217. Tel: 502-635-7141. Margaret Bowen, Prin. Lay Teachers 26; Students 380.
Catechesis/Religious Program—Students 100.
84—ST. THERESE (1908) Revs. H. Anthony Olges; Robert B. Gray (Retired).
Res.: 1010 Schiller Ave., 40204. Tel: 502-634-3671; Fax: 502-634-3672.
Catechesis/Religious Program—Twinned with Holy Family, Louisville. Barbara Klump, D.R.E.
85—ST. THOMAS MORE (1944) Rev. Philip Lee Erickson; Deacons Michael A. Tolbert; Terry Maguire.
Res.: 6105 S. Third St., 40214. Tel: 502-366-1463; Fax: 502-366-1464.
Catechesis/Religious Program—Students 73.
86—ST. TIMOTHY (1963) Closed. For inquiries for parish records please see St. Peter the Apostle, Louisville.
87—ST. VINCENT DE PAUL, See separate listing under Oratories.
88—ST. WILLIAM (1901) Rev. John R. Burke; Sharan A. Benton, Pastoral Admin.
Res.: 1226 W. Oak St., 40210. Tel: 502-635-6307; Fax: 502-638-0683 (Call first).
Catechesis/Religious Program—Anne Walter, D.R.E. Students 48.

OUTSIDE THE CITY OF LOUISVILLE

ALBANY, CLINTON CO., EMMANUEL CATHOLIC (1975) Rev. Daniel Whelan, Admin.
Mailing Address: P.O. Box 126, 42602.
Res.: 264 Glasgow Rd., Burkesville, 42717. Tel: 270-864-4107.
Catechesis/Religious Program—Students 3.
Mission—Holy Cross Catholic 264 Glasgow Rd., P.O. Box 197, Burkesville, Cumberland Co. 42717. Fax: 270-864-4107 (Call First).
BARDSTOWN, NELSON CO.
1—BASILICA OF ST. JOSEPH PROTO-CATHEDRAL (1816) [CEM] Revs. William D. Hammer; Troy Overton; Deacons Richard J. Walsh; John Hamilton. In Res., Rev. C. Joseph Batcheldor (Retired).
Res.: 310 W. Stephen Foster Ave., P.O. Box 548, 40004. Tel: 502-348-3126; Fax: 502-349-0941.
School—(Grades PreK-8), 320 W. Stephen Foster Ave., 40004. Tel: 502-348-5994; Fax: 502-348-4694. Michael Bickett, Prin. Lay Teachers 27; Students 357.
St. Joseph Montessori Children's Center—161 West Dr., Nazareth, 40048. Tel: 502-348-1548.
Catechesis/Religious Program—Students 113.
2—ST. MONICA (1956) Rev. John W. Dant; Deacon Scott R. Turner.
Res.: 407 S. Third St., 40004. Tel: 502-348-5250; Fax: 502-348-3635. Email: stmonica@bardstown.com.
Catechesis/Religious Program—Students 31.
BRANDENBURG, MEADE CO., ST. JOHN THE APOSTLE (1892) [CEM] Rev. Anthony L. Chandler; Deacons J. Michael Jones; Robert Caspar.
Res.: 515 Broadway, 40108. Tel: 270-422-2196; Fax: 270-422-2471.
Catechesis/Religious Program—Monica Lucas, D.R.E. Students 291.
CALVARY, MARION CO., HOLY NAME OF MARY (1798) [CEM] Revs. Gerald L. Bell, Admin.; Pablo A. Hernandez.
Mailing Address: 235 S. Spalding Ave., Lebanon, 40033.
Res.: 3295 Hwy. 208, Lebanon, 40033. Tel: 270-692-6491; Fax: 270-692-5708. Email: holymary@windstream.net.
Catechesis/Religious Program—Students 122.
CAMPBELLSVILLE, TAYLOR CO., OUR LADY OF PERPETUAL HELP (1879) [CEM] Rev. James S. Bromwich.
Office: 425 N. Central Ave., 42718. Tel: 270-465-4282; Fax: 270-789-9669.
Catechesis/Religious Program—Students 35.
Mission—Our Lady of Fatima Phillipsburg, Marion Co.
CECILIA, HARDIN CO., ST. AMBROSE (1879) Rev. Charles D. Walker; Deacon William Clark.
Mailing Address: *St. James Church*, 307 W. Dixie Ave., Elizabethtown, 42701. Tel: 270-765-6268.
Church: 609 Main St., 42724.
Catechesis/Religious Program—Students 3.
CLEMENTSVILLE, CASEY CO., ST. BERNARD (1802) Rev. Patrick J. Dolan.
Res.: 5075 KY 551, Liberty, 42539. Tel: 606-787-7570. Email: stbernard@windstream.net.
Catechesis/Religious Program—Tel: 606-787-6600. Sue Goode, D.R.E. Students 14.
Mission—Sacred Heart c/o 5075 KY 551, Liberty, Casey Co. 42539. Tel: 606-787-7324.
CULVERTOWN, NELSON CO., IMMACULATE CONCEPTION Rev. Mark M. Hamilton; Deacon William A. Downs.
Mailing Address: 413 First St., New Haven, 40051-6030. In Res., Rev. Thomas R. Clark (Retired).
Res.: 8191 New Haven Rd., New Haven, 40051-6030. Tel: 502-549-3152; Fax: 502-549-5410.
EDMONTON, METCALFE CO., CHRIST THE HEALER (1975) Rev. Lawrence J. Gelthaus.
Mailing Address: P.O. Box 599, 42129.
Res.: 506 Skyline, 42129. Tel: 270-432-0686.
Catechesis/Religious Program—Tel: 270-678-6280. Students 15.
Mission—Christ the King P.O. Box 518, Tompkinsville, Monroe Co. 42167. Tel: 270-487-8881.
ELIZABETHTOWN, HARDIN CO., ST. JAMES (1851) [CEM] Revs. Charles D. Walker; Jeffrey G. Hopper; Deacons Joseph Chathaparampil; William Clark.
Res.: 307 W. Dixie Ave., 42701. Tel: 270-765-6268; Fax: 270-234-9598. Email: parishoffice@kvnet.org. Web: stjames-etown.org.
School—(Grades PreK-8), 114 N. Miles St., 42701. Tel: 270-765-7011; Fax: 270-769-5745. Sr. Michael Marie Friedman, Prin.; Linda Yates, Librarian. Religious Teachers 1; Lay Teachers 30; Students 361.
Catechesis/Religious Program—Margaret Polin, D.R.E. Students 239.
FAIRFIELD, NELSON CO., ST. MICHAEL (1792) [CEM] Revs. William D. Hammer; Albert J. Hartlage (Retired).
Res.: P.O. Box 27, 40020. Tel: 502-252-8308; Fax: 502-252-0106.
Catechesis/Religious Program—111 Church St., P.O. Box 27, 40020. Tel: 502-252-0106. Gilly Simpson, D.R.E. Students 78.
FINLEY, TAYLOR CO., OUR LADY OF THE HILLS (1908) [CEM] Rev. James S. Bromwich.
Office: 425 N. Central Ave., Campbellsville, 42718. Tel: 270-465-4282; Fax: 270-789-9669.
Catechesis/Religious Program—Students 15.
FLAHERTY, MEADE CO., ST. MARTIN OF TOURS (1848) [CEM] Rev. Anthony L. Chandler; Deacons John R. Whelan; Robert Caspar.
Res.: 440 Saint Martin Rd., Vine Grove, 40175. Tel: 270-828-2552; Fax: 270-828-2562. Email: martinfl@bbtel.com. Web: stmartinfl.org.
Catechesis/Religious Program—Tel: 270-828-8484; Fax: 270-828-8484. Regina Bennett, D.R.E. Students 160.
GLASGOW, BARREN CO., ST. HELEN (1893) Revs. Joel C. Rogers, C.P.M.; Shannon Collins, C.P.M.; Deacons Lee Bidwell; David U. Smith.
Res.: 103 W. Brown St., 42141. Tel: 270-651-5263; Fax: 270-651-1373. Email: sthelen@glasgow-ky.com.
Catechesis/Religious Program—Students 77.
Mission—Our Lady of the Caves Church Rte. 31 W., Horse Cave, Hart Co. 42749. Tel: 270-651-5263.
GOSHEN, OLDHAM CO., TRANSFIGURATION OF OUR LORD (1983) Closed. For inquiries for parish records please see St. Bernadette, Louisville.
GREENSBURG, GREEN CO., HOLY REDEEMER (1969) Rev. Kevin J. Bryan, Admin.
Mailing Address: P.O. Box 247, Jamestown, 42629. Tel: 270-590-1841.
Church: 110 Industrial Rd., 42743.
Catechesis/Religious Program—Students 10.
HODGENVILLE, LARUE CO., OUR LADY OF MERCY (1853) [CEM] Rev. T. Michael Tobin; Deacon Philip Noltemeyer.
Res.: 210 Walters Ave., 42748. Tel: 270-358-4697; Fax: 270-358-3601 (Call First). Email: olmparish@windstream.net.
Catechesis/Religious Program—Tel: 270-325-3801. Students 29.
HOLY CROSS, MARION CO., HOLY CROSS (1785) [CEM] Rev. R. Joseph Hemmerle.
Office: 200 School Dr., Loretto, 40037. Tel: 270-865-2521; Fax: 270-865-2071.
Res.: 3560 N. Saint Francis Rd., Loretto, 40037. Tel: 270-865-2075. Email: sfahc@windstream.net. Web: sf-hc.org.
Catechesis/Religious Program—Carol Blanford, D.R.E. Students 57.
HOWARDSTOWN, NELSON CO., ST. ANN (1916) [CEM] Rev. Kenneth R. Fortener, Admin.
Res.: 7490 Howardstown Rd., 40051. Tel: 502-549-3285.
School—Tel: 502-549-7310. Lois Cecil, Prin. Lay Teachers 3; Students 30.
JAMESTOWN, RUSSELL CO., HOLY SPIRIT (1953) Rev. Kevin J. Bryan, Admin.; Sr. Marian Stenken, S.C.N., Pastoral Assoc.
Res.: 406 N. Main St., P.O. Box 247, 42629. Tel: 270-343-3346.
Catechesis/Religious Program—Students 12.
Mission—Good Shepherd (1964) 1221 Greensburg St., P.O. Box 354, Columbia, Adair Co. 42728. Tel: 270-384-4528. Sr. Marilyn Schatz, O.L.M.V., Pastoral Assoc.
LAGRANGE, OLDHAM CO., IMMACULATE CONCEPTION (1962) Very Rev. J. Mark Spalding; Deacons Charles Brown; Thomas M. McNally.
Res.: 502 N. Fifth St., 40031. Tel: 502-222-0255; Fax: 502-225-9844. Email: office@weareic.org. Web: weareic.org.
Catechesis/Religious Program—Mrs. J.J. Singer, Children's Family Min. Students 370.
Station—Luther Luckett Correctional Center, Tel: 502-222-0363.
Station—Kentucky State Reformatory, Tel: 502-222-9441.
Station—Roederer Farm Prison, Tel: 502-222-0173.
Station—Cedar Lake Lodge La Grange, 40032. Tel: 502-222-7157.
Station—Baptist Hospital Northeast, Tel: 502-222-5388.
Station—Richwood Nursing Home La Grange, 40032. Tel: 502-222-3186.
LEBANON JUNCTION, BULLITT CO., ST. BENEDICT (1907) Revs. David W. Naylor; Ivo E. Cecil (Retired).
Mailing Address: 187 S. Plum St., Shepherdsville, 40165.
Res.: 139 N. Brook St., 40150. Tel: 502-833-4886; Fax: 502-833-4886 (Call first). Email: stbenedictrector@bellsouth.net.
Catechesis/Religious Program—Students 27.
Mission—St. Clare [CEM], See separate listing under Oratories.
LEBANON, MARION CO., ST. AUGUSTINE (1815) [CEM] Revs. Gerald L. Bell; Pablo A. Hernandez; Deacons Tom Mattingly; Joseph R. Dant; Kathy Shannon, Pastoral Assoc.
Res. & Mailing Address: 235 S. Spalding Ave., 40033. Tel: 270-692-3019; Fax: 270-692-5532. Email: staugustinechurch@kyol.net. Web: staugustinechurch.net.
School—(Grades PreK-8), 236 S. Spalding Ave., 40033. Tel: 270-692-2063; Fax: 270-692-6597. Alicia Riggs, Prin.; Molly Bystrek, Librarian. Lay Teachers 13; Students 169.
Catechesis/Religious Program—Mike Luescher, D.R.E. Students 236.
MOUNT WASHINGTON, BULLITT CO., ST. FRANCIS XAVIER (1846) [CEM] Rev. Scott J. Wimsett; Deacon Gerald J. Mattingly.
Res.: 155 Stringer Ln., 40047. Tel: 502-538-4933; Fax: 502-955-0449. Email: sfxfrontoffice@sfxmw.com. Web: sfxmw.com.
Catechesis/Religious Program—Tel: 502-538-0672. Students 220.
Mission—All Saints Church (1830) [CEM] 410 W. Main St., P.O. Box 531, Taylorsville, Spencer Co. 40071. Tel: 502-477-6676.
NEW HAVEN, NELSON CO., ST. CATHERINE (1844) [CEM] Rev. Mark M. Hamilton; Deacon George B. Clark.
Res.: 413 First St., 40051. Tel: 502-549-3152; Fax: 502-549-5410.
School—(Grades PreK-8), 413 First St., 40051. Tel: 502-549-3680; Fax: 502-549-5410. Jo Renee O'Bryan, Prin.; Tonia Greenwell, Librarian. Lay Teachers 6; Students 105.
NEW HOPE, NELSON CO., ST. VINCENT DE PAUL (1820) [CEM] Rev. Kenneth R. Fortener; Deacon Edward J. Hutchins.
Mailing Address: P.O. Box 58, 40052. Tel: 502-549-5559; Fax: 502-549-5572.

Church: 104 Church St., 40052.
Catechesis/Religious Program—Norine Masterson, D.R.E. Students 55.

PAYNEVILLE, MEADE CO., ST. MARY MAGDALEN OF PAZZI (1883) [CEM] Rev. Robert M. Abel; Deacon Gregory A. Beavin.
Res.: 110 Hwy. 376, 40157. Tel: 270-496-4333; Fax: 270-496-4790. Email: stmarymag@insightbb.com.
Catechesis/Religious Program—Tel: 270-422-3345. Rose Etta Pike, D.R.E. Students 45.

PEWEE VALLEY, OLDHAM CO., ST. ALOYSIUS (1871) [CEM] Revs. John A. Caldwell; David W. Harris; Deacons Theodore C. Luckett; Thomas L. Roth.
Res.: 212 Mount Mercy Dr., P.O. Box 468, 40056. Tel: 502-241-8452; Fax: 502-243-1740. Email: parishoffice@staloysiuspwv.org.
School—(Grades PreK-8), 122 Mt. Mercy Dr., 40056. Tel: 502-241-8516; Fax: 502-243-2241. Maryann Hayslip, Prin.; Susan Singer, Librarian. Lay Teachers 28; Students 442.
Catechesis/Religious Program—Tel: 502-241-8452, Ext. 1036. Students 281.
Mission—Korean Catholic Community June Brandenburg, Coord.
Station—Kentucky Correctional Institute for Women, Tel: 502-241-8454.
Station—Friendship Manor Nursing Home, Tel: 502-241-8821.

RADCLIFF, HARDIN CO., ST. CHRISTOPHER (1958) [CEM] Rev. Dennis L. Cousens; Deacons Joseph D. Calvert; Harry Prestwood.
Res.: 1225 S. Wilson Rd., 40160. Tel: 270-351-3706; Fax: 270-351-2843. Email: church@stchristopherparish.org.
Catechesis/Religious Program—Students 60.

RAYWICK, MARION CO., ST. FRANCIS XAVIER CHURCH (1837) [CEM] Rev. James W. Graf; Deacon Edward J. Hutchins.
Res.: 108 Main St., 40060. Tel: 270-692-2245; Fax: 270-692-1138. Email: raywickchurch@kyol.net.
Catechesis/Religious Program—Students 72.

RHODELIA, MEADE CO., ST. THERESA (1818) [CEM] Rev. Robert M. Abel; Deacon Gregory A. Beavin.
Res.: 9245 Rhodelia Rd., Payneville, 40157. Tel: 270-496-4343; Fax: 270-496-4416.
Catechesis/Religious Program—Students 60.

ST. FRANCIS, MARION CO., ST. FRANCIS OF ASSISI (1870) [CEM] Rev. R. Joseph Hemmerle.
Office: 200 School Dr., Loretto, 40037. Tel: 270-865-2521; Fax: 270-865-2071.
Res.: 6785 Hwy. 52, 40062. Tel: 270-865-2075. Email: sfahc@windstream.net. Web: sf-hc.org.
Catechesis/Religious Program—Students 113.

ST. JOHN, HARDIN CO., ST. JOHN THE BAPTIST (1829) [CEM] Rev. Daniel L. Lincoln; Deacon Michael J. Vessels.
Res.: 657 St. John Church Rd., Elizabethtown, 42701. Tel: 270-862-9816.
Catechesis/Religious Program—Tel: 270-862-3005. Lisa Thomas, D.R.E. Students 85.

ST. JOSEPH, MARION CO., ST. JOSEPH, Closed. For inquiries for parish records contact the chancery.

ST. MARY, MARION CO., ST. CHARLES (1786) [CEM] Rev. Brian A. Kenney.
Res.: 675 Hwy. 327, Lebanon, 40033. Tel: 270-692-4513; Fax: 270-692-6204. Email: saintcharles@kyol.net.
Catechesis/Religious Program—Students 68.

ST. THOMAS, NELSON CO., ST. THOMAS (1812) Rev. John W. Dant; Deacons Samuel R. Filiatreau; Scott R. Turner.
Res.: 870 Saint Thomas Ln., Bardstown, 40004. Tel: 502-348-3717; Fax: 502-348-1905. Email: stthomas@bardstown.com. Web: st-thomasparish.org.
Catechesis/Religious Program—Students 90.

SAMUELS, NELSON CO., ST. GREGORY (1845) [CEM] Rev. John A. Schwartzlose; Deacons Joseph E. Livers; Joseph H. Filiatreau.
Parish Office:—330 Samuels Loop, Cox's Creek, 40013. Tel: 502-348-6337; Fax: 502-348-5784. Email: stgreg@bardstown.com.
School—(Grades PreK-8), 350 Samuel's Loop, Cox's Creek, 40013. Tel: 502-348-9583; Fax: 502-348-9597. Paula Cecil, Prin.; Mrs. Peggy Cissell, Librarian. Lay Teachers 11; Students 185.
Catechesis/Religious Program—Students 130.

SHELBYVILLE, SHELBY CO., ANNUNCIATION OF THE BLESSED VIRGIN MARY (1860) Rev. William M. Bowling; Deacons John Shoulta, (Retired); Brendan Kinsella; Robert J. Hart; Francisco J. Villalobos.
Res.: 105 W. Main St., 40065. Tel: 502-633-1547; Fax: 502-633-1547. Email: parishoffice@ourcoa.org.
Catechesis/Religious Program—Tel: 502-633-1547. Debbie Mudd, D.R.E. Students 222.
Mission—St. John Chrysostom (1873) 122 Penn St., P.O. Box 74, Eminence, Henry Co. 40019. Tel: 502-845-7005.

SHEPHERDSVILLE, BULLITT CO., ST. ALOYSIUS (1911) Revs. David W. Naylor; Ivo E. Cecil (Retired).
Res.: 187 S. Plum St., 40165. Tel: 502-543-5918; Fax: 502-543-6615. Email: parish@stafalcons.com.
School—(Grades PreK-8), 197 S. Plum St., 40165. Tel: 502-543-6721; Fax: 502-531-9575. Steve R. Hart, Prin. Lay Teachers 14; Students 167.
Catechesis/Religious Program—Tel: 502-543-5918; Fax: 502-955-6370. Students 12.

SPRINGFIELD, WASHINGTON CO.
1—ST. DOMINIC (1843) [CEM] Rev. Trumie C. Elliott; Deacon Donald K. Flowers.
Res.: 303 W. Main St., 40069. Tel: 859-336-3569; Fax: 859-336-3549. Email: stdom@bellsouth.net.
School—309 W. Main St., 40069. Tel: 859-336-7165; Fax: 859-336-7169. Pamela Breunig, Prin. Lay Teachers 12; Students 211.
Catechesis/Religious Program—Students 50.
2—HOLY ROSARY (1929) Rev. James W. Graf, Sacramental Moderator; Deacon Ernest Cooper, Pastoral Admin.
Mailing Address: Box 146, 40069. Tel: 859-336-3898; Fax: 859-336-3898 (Call first). Email: kyholyrosary@bellsouth.net.
Catechesis/Religious Program—378 Rosary Hgts., 40069. Pamela Grundy, D.R.E. Students 55.
3—HOLY TRINITY (1883) [CEM] Rev. John Christopher Allegra.
Res.: 306 Fredericktown Rd., 40069. Tel: 859-284-5242; Fax: 859-284-5224.
Catechesis/Religious Program—Jill Clements, D.R.E. Students 109.
Mission—Holy Rosary-Manton [CEM] 306 Fredericktown Rd., Washington Co. 40069.
4—ST. ROSE (1806) [CEM] Revs. Stephen Dominic Hayes, O.P.; James Stephen Murray, O.P. In Res., Bro. Peter Osburne, O.P.
Res.: 868 Loretto Rd., P.O. Box 71, 40069. Tel: 859-336-3121; Fax: 859-336-3841. Email: strose3121@att.net.
Catechesis/Religious Program—Students 57.

VINE GROVE, HARDIN CO., ST. BRIGID (1915) [CEM] Rev. Daniel L. Lincoln; Deacons Michael J. Vessels; Joseph M. Dew.
Res.: 306 E. Main St., 40175. Tel: 270-877-2461; Fax: 270-877-2523. Email: brigidvg@bbtel.com. Web: stbrigidvg.org.
Catechesis/Religious Program—Students 82.

WHITE MILLS, HARDIN CO., ST. IGNATIUS (1842) [CEM] Revs. Charles D. Walker; Jeffrey G. Hopper; Deacon William Clark.
Mailing Address: P.O. Box 67, 42788. Tel: 270-369-6279.
Res.: 307 W. Dixie Ave., Elizabethtown, 42701. Tel: 270-765-6268; Fax: 270-737-5661.
Catechesis/Religious Program—Students 10.

ORATORIES

LOUISVILLE, JEFFERSON CO., ST. VINCENT DE PAUL, Closed. For inquiries for parish records contact St. Elizabeth of Hungary, Louisville.

COLESBURG, HARDIN CO., ST. CLARE, Closed. For inquiries for parish records contact St. Benedict, Lebanon Junction.

Chaplains of Public Institutions
For hospitals, contact Office for Pastoral Care, 1200 S. Shelby St., Louisville, KY 40203; Tel: 502-636-0296; Fax: 502-636-2379.

LOUISVILLE. *Norton Audubon Hospital*. Rev. Expedito Muwonge.
Norton Hospitals. Rev. Conrad Sutter, O.F.M.Conv., Chap.

On Duty Outside the Archdiocese:
Revs.—
Branch, Edward B., Catholic Center at Atlanta University Complex, 809 Beckwith St., S.W., Atlanta, GA 30314. Tel: 404-755-2646 Office of Campus Ministry
Dittmeier, Charles R., Maryknoll, P.O. Box 632, Phnom Penh, Cambodia.
Knott, J. Ronald, D.Min., St. Meinrad Seminary, Saint Meinrad, IN 47577.
Langford, Terry L., 712 Anderman Ln., Apt. 102, Darien, IL 60561.
Stevens, Gladstone H., S.S., M.A., S.T.L., Ph.D., St. Patrick Seminary and University, 320 Middlefield Rd., Menlo Park, CA 94025.
Tran, John R., St. Teresa Church, 421 Edgewood Ln., Albany, GA 31707.

Graduate Studies:
Revs.—
Beach, R. Paul, Catholic University of America, De Sales Hall, 721 Lawrence St. N.E., Washington, DC 20017.
Do, Tung Minh, Catholic University of Louvain, Louvain, Belgium.

Unassigned:
Revs.—
Brown, Benedict J.
Lamberson, Bryan
Leger, Jeffrey P.

Retired:
Revs.—
Batcheldor, C. Joseph, St. Joseph Church, P.O. Box 548, Bardstown, 40004.
Bindner, Charles J., 1723 Parkridge Pkwy., 40214.
Birk, John W., 2082 Douglass Blvd., #1, 40205.
Brennan, William J., St. Joseph Home, 15 Audubon Plaza Dr., 40217.
Butler, John J., 3115 Lexington Rd., 40206.
Cecil, Ivo E., 1080 Optimist Rd., Elizabethtown, 42701.
Clark, Thomas R., 8191 New Haven Rd., New Haven, 40051.
Craycroft, Bernard L., 388 University Dr., Radcliff, 40160.
Deatrick, John D., 3806 Village Green Dr., 40299.
Dentinger, Roy E., 3030 Breckenridge Ln., Bldg. 1, Apt. 501, 40220.
Dickman, John W., Sacred Heart Village, 2120 Payne St., 40206.
Eifler, John G., 572 Upland Rd., 40206.
Eimer, Frank J., 3426 Pemaquid Rd., 40218.
Flynn, James E., Masonic Home Dr., #106, Bldg. 290, Masonic Home, 40041.
Fowler, Joseph M., 3509 Taylor Blvd., 40215.
Gephart, John B., Bishop David Apartments, 5146 Dixie Hwy., 40216.
Gray, Robert B., St. Elizabeth, 1020 E. Burnett, 40217.
Griner, William S., 11110 Old Harrods Creek Ct., 40223.
Hall, Joseph S., 4165 Hwy. 52, Loretto, 40037.
Hanrahan, John W., 1170 Castlevale Dr., #3, 40217.
Hartlage, Albert J., P.O. Box 27, Fairfield, 40020.
Hartlage, William C., Sacred Heart Village, 2120 Payne St., 40206.
Hayden, Joseph F., Chimbote, Peru.
Hommrich, Thomas A., St. Joseph Home, 17 Audubon Plaza Dr., 40217.
Howard, Clarence J., 7521 Lanfair Dr., 40241.
Jones, John E., 1697 Taylor Wood Rd., Simpsonville, 40067.
Kamber, Kenneth L., 4029 Busath Ave., 40218.
Lenahan, John B., 1286 Parkway Gardens Ct., #224, 40217.
Lichtefeld, James J., 1278 Parkway Gardens Ct., #227, 40217.
Lindle, Lawrence H., 3623 Fern Valley Rd., Rm. 227, 40219.
Lyon, Joseph A., Doe Valley Park, 37 Pineview Ct., Brandenburg, 40108.
Magel, John E., Sacred Heart Village, 2120 Payne St., 40206.
Miller, William, 3517 Nanz Ave., 40207.
Mudd, James T., 5505 Bardstown Rd., 40291.
Murphy, James Wayne, 7908 Woodfern Way, 40291.
Osborne, Robert E., 3910 Village Green Dr., 40299.
Osborne, Stanley J., 307 W. Dixie Ave., Elizabethtown, 42701.
Reilly, Robert E., Sacred Heart Village, 2120 Payne St., 40206.
Reteneller, Charles E., Nazareth Village, #21, P.O. Box 2000, Nazareth, 40048.
Ryan, Donald P., Bishop David Apts., 5146 Dixie Hwy., 40216.
Sans, Theodore R., 7812 Pine Ridge Rd., 40241.
Scheich, Eugene, 5907 Branden Dunes Dr., 40228.
Smith, F. Harold, 3623 Fern Valley Rd., 40219.
Spalding, Leon C., 626 E. Gray St., 40202.
Stiles, J. Roy, 2042 Buechel Bank Rd., 40218.
Stuecker, Henry C., Sacred Heart Village, 2120 Payne St., 40206.
Timmel, Gerald L., 1816 Rangeland Rd., 40219.
Volpert, Robert C., 3004 Aspenwood Way, 40241.
Voor, Joseph H., St. James Church, 1826 Edenside Ave., 40204.
Wafzig, James E., Sacred Heart Village, 2120 Payne St., 40206.
Wagner, William F., 952 Hinton Hills Loop, Hardinsburg, 40143.
Wilson, Albert L., Bishop David Apts., 5146 Dixie Hwy., 40216.
Zoeller, Eugene, 3920 Manner Dale Dr., 40220.

Permanent Deacons:
Abell, James H., Holy Family, Louisville
Ayers, Timothy B., Our Lady of Lourdes, Louisville
Babin, Jeremiah S., Holy Trinity, Louisville
Beavin, Gregory A., St. Mary Magdalen of Pazzi, Payneville; St. Theresa, Rhodelia
Becker, Gary Earle, (Retired), Santa Barbara, CA
Beckmann, Charles, St. Paul, Louisville
Bell, Kenneth, (On Leave)
Bent, Charles T., St. Margaret Mary, Louisville
Bidwell, Lee G., St. Helen, Glasgow; Our Lady of the Caves, Horse Cave
Bissig, Paul F., Good Shepherd, Louisville
Biven, Lawrence, St. Francis of Assisi, Louisville
Bowling, T. Stephen, St. Gabriel, Louisville

Box, Thomas E., St. Bartholomew, Louisville
Brown, Charles, Immaculate Conception, La Grange
Brown, Martin J., St. Michael, Louisville
Bryant, Robert C., Our Mother of Sorrows, Louisville
Burns, Robert L., Central State Hospital, La Grange
Calvert, Joseph D., St. Christopher, Radcliffe
Carney, Edward P., Nazareth Home, Louisville
Carter, Kenneth, St. Lawrence, Louisville
Caspar, Robert, St. Martin of Tours, Flaherty; St. John the Apostle, Brandenburg
Chathaparampil, Joseph, St. James Church, Elizabethtown
Churchill, John, (Retired)
Clark, George B., St. Catherine, New Haven
Clark, William, St. James, Elizabethtown
Cooper, Ernest A., Holy Rosary, Springfield
Cottrell, Francis E., St. Christopher, Radcliff
Dalton, David, Dismas Charities, St. Lawrence
Dant, Joseph R., St. Augustine, Lebanon
DaPonte, Stephen J., St. Stephen Martyr, Louisville
Dever, Robert, St. Raphael, Louisville
Dew, Joseph M., St. Brigid, Vine Grove
Diemer, Darryl J., St. Gabriel, Louisville
Downs, William A., Immaculate Conception, Culvertown
Dugan, Louis B., St. James & St. Brigid, Louisville
Edwards, Michael, Ascension, Louisville
Filiatreau, Joseph H., St. Gregory, Samuels
Filiatreau, Samuel R., St. Thomas, Bardstown
Flowers, Donald K., St. Dominic, Springfield
George, Paul J., Blessed Teresa, Louisville
Gnau, Geoffrey, Good Shepherd, Louisville
Hall, Robert, Dir., Permanent Diaconate Office, Holy Spirit, Louisville
Hamilton, John, St. Joseph, Bardstown
Haner, Scott R., St. Patrick, Louisville
Harris, Patrick, St. Bernadette, Louisville
Hart, Robert J., Annunciation, Shelbyville; St. John Chrysostom, Eminence
Hasson, Anthony P., (Retired)
Hettich, Philip, St. Bernard, Louisville; Jefferson County Jail
Higgins, Frederick, (Retired)
Houck, Peter L., (Retired)
Hutchins, Joseph E., St. Francis Xavier, Raywick; St. Vincent de Paul, New Hope
Jackson, Jarvis, St. Martin of Tours, Louisville
Jones, J. Michael, St. John the Apostle, Brandenburg
Jones, Walton G., Holy Trinity, Louisville
Kampschaefer, Robert M., Mary Queen of Peace, Louisville
Karley, Brian, C.R., Dir., Office of Clergy Personnel
Kinsella, Brendan, Annunciation, Shelbyville; St. John Chrysostom, Eminence
Klinglesmith, Gregory L., St. Peter the Apostle, Louisville
Klump, William, St. Louis Bertrand, Louisville
Lincoln, Bruce, (Retired)
Livers, Joseph E., St. Gregory, Samuels
Luckett, Theodore C., St. Aloysius, Pewee Valley
Maguire, Terry, Our Lady of Mt. Carmel; St. Thomas More, Louisville
Maher, John P., St. Martha, Louisville
Markert, Robert, Incarnation, Louisville; Catholic Cemeteries Chaplain
Masterson, Donald E., (On Leave)
Mattingly, Gerald J., St. Francis Xavier, Mt. Washington; All Saints, Taylorsville
Mattingly, Tom, (Retired)
McCulloch, Thomas B., (Retired)
McGinty, David L., SS. Simon and Jude, Louisville
McKenzie, Keith L., St. Augustine, Louisville
McNally, Thomas M., Immaculate Conception, La Grange
Miller, Norbert F., (Retired)
Mitchell, Kenneth J., Blessed Teresa, Louisville
Mullins, William L., (Retired)
Murphy, Michael, (On Duty Outside the Diocese)
Nevitt, Charles "Mack", (On Leave)
Niemeier, William, Mary Queen of Peace, Louisville
Nitzken, Sylvester, St. Stephen Martyr, Louisville; Vicar for Senior Deacons
Noltemeyer, Philip, Our Lady of Mercy, Hodgenville
Olrich, James C., St. Elizabeth Ann Seton Church, Louisville
Osborne, Kenneth F., (Retired)
Padgett, Joseph E., (Retired)
Parker, Danny E., St. Bernadette, Louisville
Patterson, Daniel, (Retired)
Phelps, Paul Stephan, Cathedral of the Assumption; St. Boniface, Louisville
Plummer, James R., St. Barnabas, Louisville
Prestwood, Harry, St. Christopher, Radcliff
Puga, Aurelio A., St. Rita, Louisville
Raibert, Joseph A., Holy Spirit, Louisville
Ratterman, Cletus A., (Retired)
Ronald, Edward R., (Retired)
Roth, Thomas L., St. Aloysius, Pewee Valley
Rougeux, Mark J., St. Patrick, Louisville
Ryan, Thomas, (Retired)
Shoulta, John, (Retired)
Simmons, John, (On Leave)
Simpson, John L., (Retired)
Singer, Ernest, (Retired)
Smith, David U., St. Catherine, New Haven; St. Helen, Glasgow; Our Lady of the Caves, Horse Cave
Smith, Steve, St. Peter the Apostle, Louisville
Stanley, Vincent (Jim) G., St. Albert, Louisville
Steinmetz, Richard Earl, St. Joseph Home for the Aged
Stewart, Timothy E., Our Mother of Sorrows, Louisville
Sturgeon, James C., Sr., (Retired)
Thieneman, Wayne, St. Peter the Apostle, Louisville
Thomas, William A., (Retired)
Tolbert, Michael A., St. Thomas More & Our Lady of Mt. Carmel, Louisville
Tomes, David R., St. Boniface, Louisville
Tremblay, Philip, C.R., Guardian Angels, Louisville
Turner, James R., St. Martin de Porres; St. Augustine, Louisville
Turner, Scott R., St. Thomas; St. Monica, Bardstown
Vessels, Michael J., St. John the Baptist, Rineyville; St. Brigid, Vine Grove
Villalobos, Francisco J., Annunciation, Shelbyville; St. John Chrysostom, Eminence
Waldon, F. Eugene, Our Lady of Lourdes, Louisville
Wall, Joseph, (Retired)
Walsh, Richard J., St. Joseph, Bardstown
Ward, Ken, St. Martha, Louisville
Whelan, John R., St. Martin of Tours, Flaherty
Wright, Joseph P., Cathedral of the Assumption, Louisville
Young, R. James, (On Leave)

INSTITUTIONS LOCATED IN THE ARCHDIOCESE

[A] COLLEGES AND UNIVERSITIES

LOUISVILLE. *Bellarmine University*, 2001 Newburg Rd., 40205-0671. Tel: 502-452-8000; Fax: 502-452-8033. Web: www.bellarmine.edu. John Stemmer, Librarian. Priests 5; Sisters 1; Students 3,040.
Administration Officers: Most Rev. Joseph E. Kurtz, D.D., Archbishop of Louisville, Chancellor; Revs. Clyde F. Crews; George A. Kilcourse; Michael Huggins; Isaac McDaniel; Adam Bunnell, O.F.M.Conv.; Dr. Michael Mattei, Dean Continuing & Professional Studies; Dr. Dan Bauer, Dean of the Rubel School of Business; Dr. Susan Davis, Dean of the Lansing School of Nursing; Mr. Glenn Kosse, Vice Pres. Devel. & Alumni Rels.; Dr. Joseph J. McGowan, Pres.; Dr. Carole Pfeffer, Assoc. Vice Pres. Academic Affairs; Dr. Cindy Gnadinger, Dean Thornton School of Education; Dr. Fred W. Rhodes, Vice Pres. Student Affairs; Mr. Tim Sturgeon, Dean of Admissions; Dr. Doris Tegart, Vice Pres. for Academic Affairs; Dr. William Fenton, Interim Dean; Mr. Sean Ryan, Vice Pres. Enrollment Mgmt.; Mr. Robert L. Zimlich, Vice Pres. for Business Affairs; Mr. Hunt Helm, Vice Pres. Communications & Public affairs; John Stemmer, Librarian.

**Spalding University*, 845 S. 3rd St, 40203. Tel: 502-585-9911; Fax: 502-585-7158. Web: www.spalding.edu. Dr. Jo Ann Rooney, L.L.M., J.D., Ed.D., Pres.; Dr. Randy Strickland, Senior Vice Pres. Academic Affairs; Dr. Beverly Keepers, Dean College of Education; Tori Murden McClure, Vice Pres. External Rels., Enrollment Mgmt. & Student Affairs; Dr. John James, Dean College of Social Sciences & Humanities; Dr. Richard Hudson, Assoc. Vice Pres. Student Life & Devel.; Bobbie Rafferty, Dir. Advancement & Philanthropy; Dr. Diane Tobin, Dean College of Business Communication, Accelerated Program; Joanne Berryman, Dean College of Health & Natural Sciences; Michael Ernst, Vice Pres. & CFO; Chris Hart, Dean Enrollment Mgmt.; Rick Barney, Exec. Dir. Mktg. & Public Rels. Sisters 1; Lay Teachers 85; Students 1,712.

ST. CATHARINE. *St. Catharine College*, 2735 Bardstown Rd., 40061. Tel: 859-336-5082; Fax: 859-336-5031. Email: ckays@sccky.edu. Web: www.sccky.edu. Mr. Bill Huston, Pres.; Dr. David Arnold, Vice Pres. & Academic Dean; Roger L. Marcum, Exec. Vice Pres.; Ilona Burdette, Librarian. Dominican Sisters. Priests 1; Sisters 7; Lay Teachers 40; Students 843.

[B] HIGH SCHOOLS, ARCHDIOCESAN

LOUISVILLE. *St. Francis DeSales High School*, 425 Kenwood Dr., 40214. Tel: 502-368-6519; Fax: 502-366-6172. Web: www.desaleshighschool.com. Mr. Douglas Strothman, Pres.; Mr. Chris Walsh, Prin. Sisters 1; Lay Teachers 27; Students 293.

Holy Cross High School, 5144 Dixie Hwy., 40216. Tel: 502-447-4363; Fax: 502-448-1062. Email: holycross@holycrosshs.com. Web: www.holycrosshs.com. Mr. Tim Weihe, Pres.; Ms. Danielle Wiegandt, Prin. Sisters 1; Lay Teachers 23; Students 275.

Trinity High School, 4011 Shelbyville Rd., 40207. Tel: 502-895-9427; Fax: 502-895-6837. Web: trinityrocks.com; www.thsrock.net. Dr. Robert J. Mullen, Pres.; Mr. Daniel J. Zoeller, Prin.; Rev. David H. Zettel, Asst. Prin.; Ms. Charlotte Miller, Librarian. Priests 1; Lay Teachers 100; Students 1,388.

BARDSTOWN. *Bethlehem High School* 40004. Tel: 502-348-8594; Fax: 502-349-1247. Email: BHS@bethlehemhigh.org. Web: www.bethlehemhigh.org. Tom Hamilton, Prin.; Mrs. Susan Simpson, Librarian. Sisters of Charity of Nazareth. Sisters 1; Lay Teachers 23; Students 300.

[C] HIGH SCHOOLS, PRIVATE

LOUISVILLE. *Academy of Our Lady of Mercy*, 5801 Fegenbush Ln., 40228. Tel: 502-671-2010; Fax: 502-499-0661. Email: mike.johnson@mercyacademy.com. Web: www.mercyacademy.com. Mr. Michael C. Johnson, Pres.; Julie H. Crone, Prin.; Karen Alpiger, Asst. Prin.; Angela Kalb, Librarian. Sisters of Mercy 2; Lay Teachers 44; Students 612.

Assumption High School, 2170 Tyler Ln., 40205. Tel: 502-458-9551; Fax: 502-454-8411. Web: www.ahsrockets.org. Elaine Salvo, Pres.; Rebecca Henle, Prin.; Karen Falkenstine, Librarian. Sisters of Mercy. Sisters 1; Lay Teachers 90; Students 935.

Presentation Academy, 861 S. 4th St., 40203. Tel: 502-583-5935; Fax: 502-583-1342. Email: mbruder@presentationacademy.org. Web: www.presentationacademy.org. Sr. Christine Beckett, S.C.N., Pres.; Barbara Wine, Prin.; Terry Roberts, Librarian. Sisters 2; Lay Teachers 37; Students 285.

Sacred Heart Academy, 3175 Lexington Rd., 40206. Tel: 502-897-6097; Fax: 502-893-0120. Email: officesha@sacredheartschools.org. Dr. Beverly McAuliffe, Prin.; Linda Lenahan, Librarian. Ursuline Sisters. Sisters 3; Lay Teachers 78; Students 838.

St. Xavier High School, Xaverian Brothers, 1609 Poplar Level Rd., 40217. Tel: 502-637-4712; Fax: 502-634-2171. Email: psangalli@saintx.com. Web: www.saintx.com. Dr. Perry E. Sangalli, Pres.; Bro. Edward Driscoll, C.F.X., Prin.; Mrs. Elaine Steinberg, Librarian. Sisters 1; Lay Teachers 121; Students 1,461.

[D] ELEMENTARY SCHOOLS, PRIVATE

LOUISVILLE. **Holy Angels Academy, Inc.*, (Grades K-12), 12201 Old Henry Rd., 40223. Tel: 502-254-9440; Fax: 502-254-9907. Joseph M. Norton, Headmaster and Prin., Grade School; Marilyn G. Malone, Prin., High School; Rev. Robert M. Gregor, C.P.M., Chap. Priests 1; Lay Teachers 15; Students 140.

Sacred Heart Model School, (Grades K-8), 3107 Lexington Rd., 40206. Tel: 502-896-3931; Fax: 502-896-3932. Email: mbowling@sacredheartschools.org. Web: www.sacredheartschools.org. Dr. Mary Beth Bowling, Prin.; Mrs. Carol Kraemer, Librarian. Sisters 1; Lay Teachers 36; Students 360.

Sacred Heart Preschool, 3105 Lexington Rd., 40206. Tel: 502-896-3941; Fax: 502-896-3966. Web: www.sacredheartschools.org. Vicki Furlow, Dir. Lay Teachers 40; Students 224.

[E] REGIONAL SCHOOLS

LOUISVILLE. *St. Andrew Academy*, (Grades PreK-8), 7724 Columbine Dr., 40258. Tel: 502-935-4578; Fax: 502-933-2204. Email: office@standrewacademy.com. Suzanne Smith Miller, Prin.; Cathy Wright, Literacy Coord. Lay Teachers 19; Students 324.

St. Nicholas Academy, (Grades K-8) Carol Nord, Head of School.
(Grades K-8), South Campus: 5501 New Cut Rd., 40214. Tel: 502-368-8506; Fax: 502-380-5453. Katherine Schloemer, Prin.
(Grades K-8), North Campus: 4333 Hazelwood

Ave., 40215. Tel: 502-368-8506; Fax: 502-375-8124. Carol Nord, Interim Prin. Lay Teachers 38; Total Enrollment 497.

Notre Dame Academy, (Grades PreK-8), 1927 Lewiston Dr., 40216. Tel: 502-447-3155; Fax: 502-447-5515. Email: ndabernice@gmail.com. Web: nda.myiglou.com. Bernice Scherr, Prin.; Mrs. Daivie Kay, Librarian. Sisters 1; Lay Teachers 25; Students 423.

Pope John Paul II Academy, (Grades PreK-8), 3525 Goldsmith Ln., 40220. Tel: 502-452-1712; Fax: 502-451-2462. Lynn Wilt, Prin.; Nancy Heady, Librarian. Lay Teachers 25; Students 330.

PROSPECT. *St. Mary Academy*, (Grades PreK-8), 11311 St. Mary Ln., 40059. Tel: 502-315-2555; Fax: 502-326-3655. Mrs. Mary Alice Zettel, Prin. Lay Teachers 30; Students 505.

[F] SPECIAL SCHOOLS

LOUISVILLE. *St. Joseph Child Development Center*, 2823 Frankfort Ave., 40206. Tel: 502-893-0241; Fax: 502-896-2394. Email: jennifer@sjkids.org. Web: www.sjkids.org. Leanna Mays, Admin. Students 125; Teachers 28.

**Nativity Academy*, 529 E. Liberty St., 40202. Tel: 502-855-3300; Fax: 502-562-2192. Email: scarson@nativityacademy.org. Sr. Paula Kleine-Kracht, O.S.U., Exec. Dir.; Sheila E. Carson, Prin. (Grades 6-8) Students 62; Staff 19.

Pitt Academy, 6010 Preston Hwy., 40219. Tel: 502-966-6979; Fax: 502-962-8878. Email: sdowney@pitt.com. Web: www.pitt.com. Sherry Downey, Prin. Lay Teachers 10; Students 75.

Sacred Heart School for the Arts, 3105 Lexington Rd., 40206. Tel: 502-897-1816; Fax: 502-896-3927. Email: lslaughter@sacredheartschools.org. Web: www.sacredheartschools.org. Lynn Slaughter, Dir. Students 400.

[G] ORPHANAGES AND INFANT HOMES

LOUISVILLE. *St. Joseph Catholic Orphan Society*, 2823 Frankfort Ave., 40206. Tel: 502-893-0241; Fax: 502-896-2394. Web: www.sjkids.org. Eugene Eckert, Pres. Bd. of Directors.

St. Thomas Orphan Society, Inc., P.O. Box 1073, 40201.

St. Vincent's Orphan Society, Inc., P.O. Box 1073, 40201.

[H] GENERAL HOSPITALS

LOUISVILLE. *SS. Mary and Elizabeth Hospital*, 1850 Bluegrass Ave., 40215. Tel: 502-361-6000; Fax: 502-361-6799. Web: jhsmh.org. Thomas Gessel, Pres. & CEO. Catholic Health Initiatives. Sisters 6; Bed Capacity 331; Patients Assisted Annually 125,945.

BARDSTOWN. *Flaget Memorial Hospital*, 4305 New Shepherdsville Rd., 40004. Tel: 502-350-5000; Fax: 502-350-5039. Email: info@flaget.com. Web: www.flaget.com. Bruce Klockars, Pres. Catholic Health Initiatives., Attended from St. Joseph Church. Sisters 2; Bed Capacity 52; Bassinets 8; Patients Assisted Annually 91,550.

[I] SPECIAL HOSPITALS

LOUISVILLE. *Our Lady of Peace*, 2020 Newburg Rd., 40205. Tel: 502-451-3330; Fax: 502-479-4140. Email: michaelahrens@jhsmh.org. Web: www.jhsmh.org. Thomas Gessel, Interim Pres. & CEO. Catholic Health Initiatives., Hospital for Psychiatric Illness. Sisters 4; Bed Capacity 396; Patients Assisted Annually 5,689.

[J] PROTECTIVE INSTITUTIONS

LOUISVILLE. *Boys' Haven*, 2301 Goldsmith Ln., 40205. Tel: 502-458-1171; Fax: 502-451-2161. Email: vrickert@boyshaven.org. Web: www.boyshaven.org. Mr. Vernon C. Rickert, Exec. Dir. For dependent, neglected, or abused boys and girls, 12 to 23 years of age. Total Assisted 765.

St. Joseph Children's Home, 2823 Frankfort Ave., 40206. Tel: 502-893-0241; Fax: 502-896-2394. Email: barryw@sjkids.org. Web: www.sjkids.org. Barry Walker, Exec. Dir. Ursuline Sisters 1; Children 40.

[K] NURSING HOMES

LOUISVILLE. *St. Joseph Home for the Aged*, 15 Audubon Plaza Dr., 40217. Tel: 502-636-2300; Fax: 502-636-2239. Web: www.littlesistersofthepoor.org. Sr. Isabel Londono-Gomez, Pres.; Rev. Simon Brzozowski, M.S.F., Chap.

Home for the Aged of the Little Sisters of the Poor Sisters 10; Bed Capacity 77.

Nazareth Home, 2000 Newburg Rd., 40205. Tel: 502-459-9681; Fax: 502-456-9077. Email: mhaynes@nazhome.org. Web: nazhome.org. Mary Haynes, CEO & Admin.; Sr. Mary Anne Burkhardt, S.C.N., Dir. Mission & Pastoral Care; Deacon E. Perry Carney, Chap. Sisters of Charity of Nazareth. Staff Sisters 2; Residents 168; Personal Care 33; Total Staff 250.

[L] MONASTERIES AND RESIDENCES OF PRIESTS AND BROTHERS

LOUISVILLE. *Bishop David Apartments*, 5146 Dixie Hwy., 40216. Tel: 502-449-2159. Revs. Albert L. Wilson, Dir. (Retired); John B. Gephart (Retired); Donald P. Ryan (Retired). Priests 3.

St. Francis of Assisi Friary, 2225 Lower Hunters Trace, 40216. Tel: 502-447-5566. Revs. Christian Moore, O.F.M.Conv.; Paul Schloemer, O.F.M.Conv.; Bros. Larry Eberhardt, O.F.M.Conv.; John Mauer, O.F.M.Conv.; Dennis Moses, O.F.M.Conv.

St. Louis Bertrand Priory, 1104 S. Sixth St., 40203. Tel: 502-583-4448; Fax: 502-589-0056. Very Rev. James M. Sullivan, O.P.; Revs. George G. Christian, O.P.; James B. Muller, O.P.; Thomas V. Di Fede, O.P.; Ralph V. Townsend, O.P. Priests: see St. Louis Bertrand Parish Priests 5.

Sacred Heart Retreat, 1924 Newburg Rd., 40205. Tel: 502-451-2330; Fax: 502-451-0192. Web: www.passionist.org. Very Rev. John Schork, C.P., Local Supr. (Corporate Title: Congregation of the Passion, Sacred Heart Community) Priests 7; Brothers 2. In Res. Revs. Justin Nelson Alphonse, C.P.; Rene Champagne, C.P.; John Conley, C.P.; Joachim Gemperline, C.P.; Leon Grantz, C.P.; Philip Schaefer, C.P.; Emmet Linden, C.P.; Joseph Mitchell, C.P.; Albert Schwer, C.P.; Michael Joseph Stengel, C.P.; Frederick Sucher, C.P.; Bernard Weber, C.P.; Bros. Jerome Milazzo, C.P.; John Monzyk, C.P.

Villa Pacis, Resurrectionist Retirement Home, 512 Breckenridge Ln., 40207. Tel: 502-895-3413; Fax: 502-895-3431. Email: crvillapacis@aol.com. In Res. Revs. Raymond Hofmann, C.R.; John Lesousky, C.R.; John Miles, C.R.; Charles Schoenbaechler, C.R.

TRAPPIST. *Abbey of Our Lady of Gethsemani, of the Order of Cistercians of the Strict Observance*, 3642 Monks Rd., 40051. Tel: 502-549-3117; Fax: 502-549-8281. Email: getabbot@iglou.com. Rev. Elias Dietz, O.C.S.O.; Rt. Revs. Damien Thompson, O.C.S.O., Abbot (Retired); Timothy Kelly, O.C.S.O., Abbot (Retired); Revs. James Conner, O.C.S.O.; Alan Gilmore, O.C.S.O.; Matthew Kelty, O.C.S.O.; Michael Casagram, O.C.S.O.; Peter Tong, O.C.S.O.; Joachim Johnson, O.C.S.O.; Seamus Malvey, O.C.S.O.; Andrew McAughan, O.C.S.O.; Anton Rusnak, O.C.S.O.; Carlos Rodriguez, O.C.S.O. Priests 15; Brothers 46.

[M] CONVENTS AND RESIDENCES FOR SISTERS

LOUISVILLE. *Monastery of the Discalced Carmelite Nuns*, 1740 Newburg Rd., 40205. Tel: 502-451-6796; Fax: 502-458-5272. Sr. Katherine, O.C.D., Prioress. Professed Nuns 9; Novices 1; Temporary Professions 1.

Sisters of Mercy St. Catherine Convent, 2169 Tyler Ln., 40205. Tel: 502-451-2245; Fax: 502-452-6988. Email: paulanne@insightbb.com. Sr. Paulanne Diebold, R.S.M., Dir. Sisters in Residence 19.

Sisters of the Good Shepherd, 1819 Newburg Rd., 40205. Tel: 502-742-3744. Email: sistersofthegoodshepherd@insightbb.com. Sisters 4.

Ursuline Motherhouse of the Immaculate Conception, 3105 Lexington Rd., 40206. Tel: 502-896-3914; Fax: 502-896-3913. Email: webmaster@ursulineslou.org. Web: www.ursulineslou.org. Sr. Lynn Jarrel, O.S.U., Pres.; Rev. John J. Butler, Chap. (Retired). Sisters in Motherhouse 28; Total in Congregation 119.

NAZARETH. *Generalate, Motherhouse and Novitiate of the Sisters of Charity of Nazareth*, P.O. Box 172, 40048. Tel: 502-348-1555 (SCN Center & Generalate); 502-348-1500 (Motherhouse); Fax: 502-348-1502. Email: mmiller@scnky.org. Web: www.scnfamily.org. Rev. Gary Young, C.R., Chap., Motherhouse. Sisters at Motherhouse 95; Sisters at David Hall 14; Sisters at SCN Center 2; Nativity Hall 1; Nazareth Villages 7; Nazareth Sadan 2; Guest Houses 3.

NERINX. *Motherhouse and Novitiate of the Sisters of Loretto at the Foot of the Cross*, 515 Nerinx Rd., 40049. Tel: 270-865-5811; Fax: 270-865-2200. Email: maryswain@lorettocommunity.org. Web: www.lorettocommunity.org. Sisters Maria Visse, S.L., Svcs. Coord.; Catherine Mueller, S.L., Pres. Sisters in the Motherhouse 92; Total in Congregation 248.

ST. CATHARINE. *Dominican Sisters of Peace*, 2645 Bardstown Rd., 40061. Tel: 859-336-9303; Fax: 859-336-9306. Email: srpeace@oppeace.org. Web: www.oppeace.org. Sr. Helen O'Sullivan, O.P., Mission Group Coord. Motherhouse of Dominican Sisters. Sisters in Motherhouse 36; Total in Archdiocese 114; Total in Congregation 638.

Sansbury Care Center, Inc., 2625 Bardstown Rd., 40061. Tel: 859-336-3974; Fax: 859-336-0401. Sr. Barbara Ann Fava, O.P., Mission Group Coord.; Darlene Herald, Admin.; Revs. John Christopher Allegra; James Stephen Murray, O.P. Sisters in Infirmary 48.

[N] HOMES FOR MEN AND WOMEN

LOUISVILLE. *Sacred Heart Village I, Inc.* (Senior Housing Apartments), 2110 Payne St., 40206. Tel: 502-895-6409; Fax: 502-895-8166. Bonnie LaTondress, Resident Mgr.

Sacred Heart Village II, Inc. (Senior Housing Apartments), 2108 Payne St., 40206. Tel: 502-895-8085; Fax: 502-895-8039. Bertha Greenwell, Property Mgr.

Sacred Heart Village III, Inc. (Senior Housing Apartments), 3101 Wayside Dr., 40216. Tel: 502-776-5004; Fax: 502-772-7695. James Thompson, Property Mgr.

Sacred Heart Village, Inc. dba Sacred Heart Village 2120 Payne St., 40206. Tel: 502-895-9425; Fax: 502-357-5549. Martha Workman, Pres. & CEO.

Mercy Sacred Heart, Inc. Sisters of Mercy., Mercy Franciscan Health and Housing Services. Sisters 2; Residents 128; Capacity 146.

[O] RETREAT HOUSES

LOUISVILLE. *Catholic Charismatic Renewal*, Flaget Center, 1935 Lewiston Dr., 40216. Tel: 502-448-8581; Fax: 502-448-5518. Tony Doninger, Contact Person. Tel: 502-634-8101.

Flaget Center, 1935 Lewiston Dr., 40216. Tel: 502-448-8581; Fax: 502-448-5518. Email: dmc@archlou.org. Donna M. McHugh, Admin.

CRESTWOOD. *Lake St. Joseph Center*, 5800 Old LaGrange Rd., 40014. Tel: 502-241-4469.

NERINX. *Knobs Haven*, 515 Nerinx Rd., 40049. Tel: 270-865-2621. Email: knobshaven@yahoo.com. Jo Ann Gates, Dir.

NEW HAVEN. *Bethany Spring-Merton Institute Retreat Center*, 115 Dee Head Rd., 40051. Tel: 502-899-1991.

[P] ST. VINCENT DE PAUL SOCIETY

LOUISVILLE. *Society of St. Vincent de Paul, Council of Louisville*, P.O. Box 17126, 40217-0126. Tel: 502-584-2480; Fax: 502-587-1977. Email: ewnorowski@svdplou.org. Web: www.svdplou.org. Edwin Wnorowski, Exec. Dir.; David W. Higgins, Trustee & Bd. Chm.; Rev. Gerald L. Timmel, Spiritual Dir. (Retired).

De Paul Apartments, 1015-A S. Preston St., 40203. Tel: 502-584-2480; Fax: 502-587-1977. (Transitional Shelter for Homeless Single Parent Families)

De Paul Thrift Stores

1029 S. Preston St., 40203. Tel: 502-589-7837; Fax: 502-587-1977.

248 E. Market St., 40202. Tel: 502-583-1370; Fax: 502-587-1977.

2217 Hikes Ln., 40218. Tel: 502-473-8856.

Open Hand Kitchen and Community Center, 1026 S. Jackson St., 40203. Tel: 502-584-2480; Fax: 502-587-1977.

Ozanam Inn, 1034 S. Jackson St., 40203. Tel: 502-584-2480; Fax: 502-587-1977. (Men's Emergency & Transitional Shelter)

Parish Conferences Tel: 502-584-2480; Fax: 502-587-1977.

Roberts Hall, 1032 E. Burnett Ave., 40217. Tel: 502-636-3549; Fax: 502-587-1977. (Women's Housing)

St. Jude Women's Recovery Center, 431 E. St. Catherine St., 40203. Tel: 502-589-6024; Fax: 502-587-1977. (Women's Recovery)

Simon Hall, 1022 S. Jackson St., 40203. Tel: 502-584-2480; Fax: 502-587-1977. (Men's Recovery)

Tranquil House (Housing For Mentally Ill), 1035 S. Preston St., 40203. Tel: 502-584-2480; Fax: 502-587-1977.

[Q] MISCELLANEOUS LISTINGS

LOUISVILLE. *Archdiocesan Marian Committee*, 3623 Fern Valley Rd., #227, 40219. Rev. Lawrence H. Lindle, Dir. (Retired).

Catholic Bicentennial Initiative Fund, Inc., 212 E. College St., 40203. Very Rev. Charles C. Thompson, J.C.L., Dir.; Dr. Brian B. Reynolds, Dir.; Robert L. Ash, Dir.

**Catholic Education Foundation*, 325 W. Main St., Ste. 1806, 40202. Tel: 502-585-2747; Fax: 502-583-4929. Rosemary Bisig Smith, Exec. Dir.

**Center for Interfaith Relations*, 415 W. Muhammad Ali Blvd., Ste. 101, 40202-2334. Tel: 502-583-3100; Fax: 502-583-8524. Web: interfaithrelations.org. Stewart Lussky, Interim Dir.

CHI Kentucky, Inc., 1850 Bluegrass Ave., 40215. Tel: 502-361-6000. Email: peggymartin@catholichealth.net. Sr. Peggy Martin, O.P., Sr. Vice Pres.

The Franciscan Foundation, Inc., 6901 Dixie Hwy., 40258. Tel: 502-935-1223; Fax: 502-933-7747. Email: dismasv@aol.com.

Franciscan Shelter House, 748 S. Preston St., P.O. Box 1673, 40201. Tel: 502-589-0140; Fax: 502-589-1134. Email: fsh748@aol.com. Web: www.franciscanshelterhouse.net. Mrs. Patti L. Thompson, Business Mgr.

Mass of the Air, 508 Breckenridge Ln., 40207. Tel: 502-893-5120; Fax: 502-896-8128. Email: frnick@ourlourdes.org. Rev. G. Nicholas Rice, Dir.

Our Lady's Rosary Makers, 4611 Poplar Level Rd., P.O. Box 37080, 40233. Tel: 502-968-1434; Fax: 502-969-8883. Web: www.olrm.org. Michael Ford, Gen. Mgr.

St. Patrick School Foundation, Inc., 1000 N. Beckley Station Rd., 40245. Tel: 502-244-7083; Fax: 502-719-0359. Web: stpatrick-lou.org. R. Mark Page, Chm.

Perpetual Eucharistic Adoration, 3623 Fern Valley Rd., #227, 40219. Tel: 502-637-5309; 502-968-2933. Rev. Lawrence H. Lindle, Spiritual Dir. (Retired).

Publication: "The Record", Maloney Center, 1200 S. Shelby St., 40203-2600. Tel: 502-636-0296; Fax: 502-636-2379. Email: record@archlou.org. Official newspaper of the Archdiocese of Louisville (Weekly).

Office: Archdiocesan Communications Center Joseph E. Duerr, Editor & Gen. Mgr.

Sacred Heart Schools, Inc., 3177 Lexington Rd., 40206. Tel: 502-896-3910; Fax: 502-895-0989. Email: shs@sacredheartschools.org. Web: www.sacredheartschools.org. Dr. Cynthia Crabtree, Pres. Sponsored by Ursuline Sisters.

**Trinity High School Foundation, Inc* Phillip J. Stuecker, Chm.

Ursuline Society and Academy of Education, 3105 Lexington Rd., 40206. Tel: 502-897-1811; Fax: 502-896-3913. Email: webmaster@ursulineslou.org. Web: www.ursulineslou.org.

World Apostolate of Fatima (Blue Army), 3623 Fern Valley Rd., #227, 40219. Tel: 502-968-2933. Rev. Lawrence H. Lindle, Spiritual Dir. (Retired).

Sacred Heart Apostolate, 3623 Fern Valley Rd., #227, 40219. Tel: 502-968-2933. Rev. Lawrence H. Lindle, Dir. (Retired).

BARDSTOWN. *Flaget Healthcare, Inc.*, 4305 New Shepherdsville Rd., 40004. Tel: 502-350-5040; Fax: 502-350-5039. Email: info@flaget.com. Web: flaget.com. Bruce Klockars, Pres. & CEO.

LEBANON. *The Laura*, 1995 Sam Browning Rd., 40033. Tel: 270-692-1790. Email: mheleneking@windstream.net. Sr. Marilyn King, R.S.M., Dir.

LORETTO. *Holy Cross Cemetery Trust, Inc.*, 7945 Loretto Rd., 40037. Tel: 502-348-5404.

NAZARETH. *Office of Congregational Advancement*, P.O. Box 9, 40048. Tel: 502-348-1578; Fax: 502-348-1587. Email: potoole@scnazarethky.org. Web: www.scnfamily.org. Sisters of Charity of Nazareth.

Sisters of Charity of Nazareth, Inc., Crimmins Hall, 135 West Dr., P.O. Box 187, 40048. Tel: 502-331-4072; Fax: 502-331-4076. Email: jraley@scnazareth.org. Sr. Judy Raley, S.C.N., Provincial.

NERINX. *Sisters of Loretto Charitable Trust*, 515 Nerinx Rd., 40049-9999. Tel: 270-865-3414; Fax: 270-865-2200. Email: maryswain@lorettocommunity.org. Web: www.lorettocommunity.org. Sr. Mary Swain, S.L., Treas.

NEW HOPE. *St. Martin De Porres Lay Dominican Community*, P.O. Box 10, 40052. Tel: 270-325-3061; Fax: 270-325-3091. Email: stmdp@newhope-ky.org. Web: www.newhope-ky.org. Mary Frances Musk, T.O.P., Prioress.

RELIGIOUS INSTITUTES OF MEN REPRESENTED IN THE ARCHDIOCESE

For further details refer to the corresponding bracketed number in the Religious Institutes of Men or Women section.

[1350]—*Brothers of St. Francis Xavier* (American Central Prov.)—C.F.X.

[0270]—*Carmelite Fathers & Brothers* (Pure Heart of Mary Prov.)—O.Carm.

[0350]—*Cistercians Order of the Strict Observance-Trappists*—O.C.S.O.

[0820]—*Congregation of the Fathers of Mercy*—C.P.M.

[1000]—*Congregation of the Passion* (Holy Cross Prov.)—C.P.

[1080]—*Congregation of the Resurrection* (Rome, Italy)—C.R.

[0480]—*Conventual Franciscans* (Prov. of Our Lady of Consolation)—O.F.M.Conv.

[0630]—*Missionaries of the Holy Family*—M.S.F.

[0430]—*Order of Preachers-Dominicans* (St. Joseph Prov.)—O.P.

RELIGIOUS INSTITUTES OF WOMEN REPRESENTED IN THE ARCHDIOCESE

[0230]—*Benedictine Sisters of Pontifical Jurisdiction*—O.S.B.

[2145]—*Congregation of Augustinian Sisters Servants of Jesus and Mary*—O.S.A.

[3832]—*Congregation of the Sisters of St. Joseph*—C.S.J.

[0420]—*Discalced Carmelite Nuns*—O.C.D.

[1070-13]—*Dominican Sisters*—O.P.

[1115]—*Dominican Sisters of Peace*—O.P.

[2575]—*Institute of the Sisters of Mercy of the Americas*—R.S.M.

[2340]—*Little Sisters of the Poor*—L.S.P.

[2470]—*Maryknoll Sisters of St. Dominic*—M.M.

[2490]—*Medical Mission Sisters*—M.M.S.

[0670]—*Order of Trappistines*—O.C.S.O.

[3130]—*Our Lady of Victory Missionary Sisters*—O.L.V.M.

[0440]—*Sisters of Charity of Cincinnati, OH*—S.C.

[0500]—*Sisters of Charity of Nazareth*—S.C.N.

[2360]—*Sisters of Loretto At the Foot of the Cross*—S.L.

[3000]—*Sisters of Notre Dame de Namur*—S.N.D.deN.

[3360]—*Sisters of Providence of Saint Mary-of-the-Woods, IN* (St. Gabriel Prov.)—S.P.

[1630]—*Sisters of St. Francis of Penance and Christian Charity*—O.S.F.

[1830]—*Sisters of the Good Shepherd*—R.G.S.

[4120-03]—*Ursuline Nuns, of the Congregation of Paris*—O.S.U.

[4120-05]—*Ursuline Sisters of Mt. St. Joseph*—O.S.U.

ARCHDIOCESAN CEMETERIES

Offices for all cemeteries: 1600 Newburg Rd., Louisville, KY 40205; Mailing Address: P.O. Box 4096, Louisville, KY 40204. Tel: 502-451-7710; Fax: 502-456-9270.

LOUISVILLE

Calvary, 1600 Newburg Rd., 40205.

St. John, 2601 Duncan St., 40212.

St. Louis, 1215 Barret Ave., 40204.

St. Michael, 1153 Charles St., 40204.

NECROLOGY

† Hendrickson, Frederick, (Retired)—Died April 5, 2009

† Howard, Anthony, (Retired)—Died July 2, 2009

An asterisk (*) denotes an organization that has established tax-exempt status directly with the IRS and is not covered by the USCCB Group Ruling.

Diocese of Lubbock

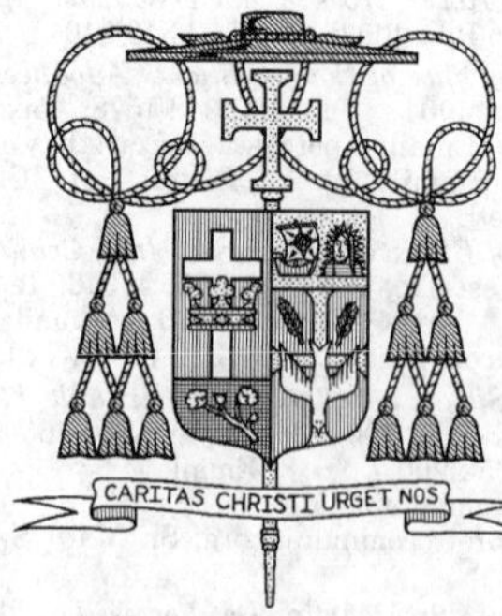
CARITAS CHRISTI URGET NOS

Most Reverend

PLACIDO RODRIGUEZ, C.M.F.

Bishop of Lubbock; ordained May 23, 1968; consecrated December 13, 1983; installed Auxiliary Bishop of Chicago; appointed Second Bishop of Lubbock April 5, 1994; installed June 1, 1994. *Res.: 3505 37th St., Lubbock, TX 79413. Office: The Catholic Pastoral Center, P.O. Box 98700, Lubbock, TX 79499-8700.* Fax: 806-792-2953. Email: prodriguez@catholiclubbock.org.

The Catholic Pastoral Center: P.O. Box 98700, Lubbock, TX 79499-8700. Tel: 806-792-3943; Fax: 806-792-8109.

Web: www.catholiclubbock.org

Email: lbehnke@catholiclubbock.org

ESTABLISHED AND CREATED A DIOCESE, JUNE 17, 1983.

Square Miles 23,382.

Comprises the Counties of Bailey, Lamb, Hale, Floyd, Motley, Cottle, Cochran, Hockley, Lubbock, Crosby, Dickens, King, Yoakum, Terry, Lynn, Garza, Kent, Stonewall, Haskell, Gaines, Dawson, Borden, Scurry, Fisher and Jones.

Legal Title: Roman Catholic Diocese of Lubbock.

STATISTICAL OVERVIEW

Personnel	
Bishop	1
Priests: Diocesan Active in Diocese	33
Priests: Diocesan Active Outside Diocese	3
Priests: Retired, Sick or Absent	11
Number of Diocesan Priests	47
Religious Priests in Diocese	7
Total Priests in Diocese	54
Ordinations:	
Diocesan Priests	1
Permanent Deacons in Diocese	49
Total Sisters	19
Parishes	
Parishes	62
With Resident Pastor:	
Resident Diocesan Priests	52
Resident Religious Priests	10
Professional Ministry Personnel:	
Sisters	10
Lay Ministers	22
Welfare	
Catholic Hospitals	2
Total Assisted	290,800
Health Care Centers	20
Total Assisted	57,600
Special Centers for Social Services	1
Total Assisted	30,000
Educational	
Diocesan Students in Other Seminaries	6
Total Seminarians	6
High Schools, Diocesan and Parish	1
Total Students	49
Elementary Schools, Diocesan and Parish	2
Total Students	411
Catechesis/Religious Education:	
High School Students	1,885
Elementary Students	4,552
Total Students under Catholic Instruction	6,903
Teachers in the Diocese:	
Sisters	2
Lay Teachers	52
Vital Statistics	
Receptions into the Church:	
Infant Baptism Totals	1,163
Minor Baptism Totals	190
Adult Baptism Totals	150
Received into Full Communion	132
First Communions	1,134
Confirmations	860
Marriages:	
Catholic	232
Interfaith	44
Total Marriages	276
Deaths	541
Total Catholic Population	80,742
Total Population	451,995

Former Bishops—Most Rev. MICHAEL J. SHEEHAN, S.T.L., J.C.D., ord. July 12, 1964; cons. and installed as the first Bishop of Lubbock, June 17, 1983; appt. Apostolic Administrator of Santa Fe, April 6, 1993; installed as the 11th Archbishop of Santa Fe, Sept. 21, 1993.

The Catholic Pastoral Center—4620 Fourth St., Lubbock, 79416. Mailing Address: P.O. Box 98700, Lubbock, 79499-8700. Tel: 806-792-3943; Fax: 806-792-8109; 806-792-2953 (Bishop's Office). Office Hours: Mon.-Fri. 8-5.

Chancellor—Rev. Msgr. NICOLAS RENDON.

Moderator of the Curia—Rev. Msgr. NICOLAS RENDON.

Chancellor's Administrative Assistant—BELINDA L. AGUIRRE.

Bishop's Administrative Assistant—JUDY LEOS RODRIGUEZ; PILAR LOPEZ, Receptionist.

Diocesan Tribunal—Mailing Address: P.O. Box 98700, Lubbock, 79499-8700. Tel: 806-792-3943.

Officialis—Rev. JOSE MATTHEW KOCHUPARAMBIL, O.S.B.

Administrative Assistant—RITA ORTIZ.

Promoter of Justice—VACANT.

Defender of the Bond—Very Rev. Msgr. EUGENE J. DRISCOLL.

Defender of the Bond-Appeal—Very Rev. Msgr. EUGENE J. DRISCOLL.

Notaries—RITA ORTIZ; JUDY LEOS RODRIGUEZ; BELINDA L. AGUIRRE.

Presbyteral Council—Rev. Msgr. NICOLAS RENDON; Revs. ANDRES MENDOZA; MARTIN PINA; ARSENIO C. REDULLA; EDUARDO C. TEO; PAUL KARIEAKATT, O.S.B.; MICHAEL MELCHER; JOSEPH THANAVELIL, O.S.B.; Very Rev. Msgr. EUGENE J. DRISCOLL; Rev. RUDY CRASTA.

Priests Personnel Board—Most Rev. PLACIDO RODRÍGUEZ, C.M.F.; Rev. Msgr. NICOLAS RENDON; Revs. ARSENIO C. REDULLA; GERALD LEATHAM; Very Rev. Msgr. EUGENE J. DRISCOLL; Rev. JOSEPH THAVELIL; Deacon JESSIE ESQUIVEL; Rev. Msgr. JAMES O'CONNOR.

Vicars Forane—Revs. JAMES MCCARTNEY, Plainview Deanery; RUDOLF CRASTA, Brownfield Deanery; JOHN CHEROLIKAL, Lubbock Deanery; MICHAEL MELCHER, Snyder Deanery.

Superintendent of Schools—Deacon LEO COTTENOIR, Mailing Address: P.O. Box 98700, Lubbock, 79499; Mrs. CHRISTINE WANJURA, Prin., Christ the King Elementary/Middle School, 4011 54th St., Lubbock, 79413; Mr. JAMES STARKEY, Prin., St. Joseph Elementary School, 20th & W. Division St., Slaton, 79364.

Director of Youth—Sr. MARTHA JANE VENHAUS.

Campus Ministry, Texas Tech University—GREG RAMZINSKI, 2305 Main St., Lubbock, 79401. Tel: 806-762-5225.

Director of Scouting—Rev. Msgr. NICOLAS RENDON.

Priests' Retirement Board—Most Rev. PLACIDO RODRÍGUEZ, C.M.F.; Rev. Msgr. NICOLAS RENDON; Revs. JAMES MCCARTNEY; GERARD KENNEY; GEORGE RONEY; LEONARDO PAHAMTANG; MICHAEL MELCHER; Rev. Msgr. JAMES O'CONNOR; Mr. ANTON BUXKEMPER; Mr. DON BOOK; Mr. DAN CASTRO; Mr. FRED LARA; Mrs. JUANITA PINEDA; Mr. SONNY GARZA.

Diocesan Building Commission—Very Rev. Msgr. EUGENE J. DRISCOLL; Mr. MARC CHAPMAN; Mr. MAX GARZA; Mr. BERNARD GRADEL; Mr. LYLE FETTERLY; Mr. JOSEPH RAPIER; Rev. Msgr. NICOLAS RENDON; JAMES HARGRAVE.

Diocesan Pastoral Liturgy Commission—Most Rev. PLACIDO RODRÍGUEZ, C.M.F.; Rev. ERNESTO LOPEZ; BERNARD MARTIN, Chm.; ALICIA ALVAREZ; Mrs. GLENDA SHAMBURGER, Chm., Mailing Address: P.O. Box 1350, Levelland, 79336. Tel: 806-894-9611, Ext. 2239. Email: gshambur@spc.cc.tx.us; Deacons JESSIE ESQUIVEL; JOE MORIN; Mrs. JANIE HERNANDEZ.

Office of Christian Formation—ALICIA ALVAREZ, Mailing Address: P.O. Box 98700, Lubbock, 79499. Tel: 806-792-3943.

Catholic Family Service, Inc.—VACANT, Dir., 102 Ave. J, Lubbock, 79401. Tel: 806-765-8475.

Director of Hispanic Affairs—Rev. MARTIN PINA, 102 N. Ave. P, Lubbock, 79401. Tel: 806-765-9935.

Ecumenical Affairs—Deacon RICHARD MCCANN.

Diocesan Council of Catholic Women—Rev. GERARD J. KENNEY, Chap.; ANGIE CERVANTES.

Director of Vocations—Rev. MARTIN PINA, Seminarian Formation & Dir. Vocations. Vocation Team Members: Revs. RENE PEREZ; ERNESTO LOPEZ.

Diocesan Attorney—BRIAN E. MURRAY, 913 Texas Ave., Lubbock, 79401.

Diocesan Health Coordinator—VACANT.

Propagation of the Faith—Rev. Msgr. NICOLAS RENDON, Mailing Address: P.O. Box 98700, Lubbock, 79499-8100. Tel: 806-792-3943.

Office of Peace & Justice—VACANT.

Catholic Campaign for Human Development—Deacon DARRIS LINDER, 755 S. 20th St., Slaton, 79364. Tel: 806-828-5662.

Director of the Permanent Diaconate—Deacon CLARKE COCHRAN, Mailing Address: P.O. Box 98700, Lubbock, 79499. Tel: 806-792-3943.

Cursillo Movement—Rev. DAVID CRUZ.

Newspaper— "South Plains Catholic" Deacon LEROY BEHNKE, Editor, Mailing Address: P.O. Box 98700, Lubbock, 79499. Tel: 806-792-3943.

Director of Communications—Deacon LEROY BEHNKE.

Office of Evangelization—VACANT.

Office of Stewardship & Development—Mrs. RENEE UNDERWOOD, M.B.A., Mailing Address: P.O. Box 98700, Lubbock, 79499. Tel: 806-792-3943.

Finance Office—ANNABELLE G. OCANAS, Finance Officer, Mailing Address: P.O. Box 98700, Lubbock, 79499. Tel: 806-797-3943.

Catholic Renewal Center—Mrs. CINDI SIMMONS, Mailing Address: P.O. Box 98700, Lubbock, 79499. Tel: 806-792-1105.

Director of Family Life—Deacon JESSIE ESQUIVEL, P.O. Box 98700, Lubbock, 79499. Tel: 806-792-3943.

Respect Life Office—LAWRENCE D'SOUZA, Mailing Address: P.O. Box 98700, Lubbock, 79499. Tel: 806-792-3943.

Diocesan Rural Life Office—ROGER KITTEN, 20402 CR 3300, Slaton, 79364. Tel: 806-828-6035.

Victim Assistance Coordinator—Mrs. CHARLOTTE AMATO, 4011 54th St., Lubbock, 79413. Tel: 806-792-6168. Email: camato@ctkcathedral.org.

CLERGY, PARISHES, MISSIONS AND PAROCHIAL SCHOOLS

CITY OF LUBBOCK

(LUBBOCK COUNTY)

1—CATHEDRAL CHRIST THE KING (1958) Very Rev. Msgr. Ben Kasteel. In Res., Rev. Anthony Phelps.
Res.: 4011 54th St., 79413-4699. Tel: 806-792-6168; Fax: 806-792-1417.
School—(Grades PreK-12) Tel: 806-795-6477; Fax: 806-795-9715. Mrs. Christine Wanjura, Prin. Lay Teachers 42; Students 372.
Catechesis/Religious Program—Mrs. Charlotte Amato, D.R.E. Students 284.

2—ST. ELIZABETH UNIVERSITY PARISH (1935) Rev. Msgr. James O'Connor; Deacon Richard McCann; Greg Ramzinski, Dir. Campus Min. In Res., Deacon Waldo Martinez.
Res. & Office: 2305 Main St., 79401. Tel: 806-762-5225; Fax: 806-741-1962. Email: stelizabeth@nts-online.net.
Catechesis/Religious Program—Sr. Nancy Palanog, M.S.L.T., D.R.E. Students 410.

3—HOLY SPIRIT (1998) Very Rev. Msgr. Eugene J. Driscoll; Deacons Rick Vasquez; Ralph Rosiles; Gloria Decker, Sec.; Joseph S. Rodriguez, Music Min.; Jerome Larez, Youth Min.; Sam Sparkman, Youth Min.; Tami Sparkman, Youth Min.; Tino Gamueda III, Youth Min.; Katie Gamueda, Youth Min.
Mailing Address: 9821 Frankford Ave., 79424. Tel: 806-698-6400; Fax: 806-798-0646. Email: parish@holyspiritlubbock.org. Web: www.holyspiritcathparish.org.
Res.: 9819 Frankford Ave., 79424. Tel: 806-698-6400; Fax: 806-798-0646.
Catechesis/Religious Program—Rosalinda Erispe, D.R.E.; Jessica Kelly, C.R.E. Students 565.

4—ST. JOHN NEUMANN (1979) Rev. Gerard J. Kenney; Deacons Richard Wood; Kyle Broderson; Clarke Cochran.
Res.: 5802 22nd, 79407-1721. Tel: 806-799-2649; Fax: 806-799-0037.
Catechesis/Religious Program—Sr. Mary Ann Mishurda, RCIA Dir.; Ellie Contreras, D.R.E. Students 415.

5—ST. JOSEPH'S (1924), (Hispanic), Rev. Martin Pina; Deacon Benny Brito.
Res.: 102 N. Ave. P, 79401-1199. Tel: 806-765-9935; Fax: 806-740-0032.
Catechesis/Religious Program—Tel: 806-763-9695. Yolanda Gutierrez, D.R.E. Students 455.

6—OUR LADY OF GRACE (1960), (Hispanic), Rev. David Cruz; Deacons Alfredo Jaime, (Retired); Ernest Hernandez; Joe Morin; Sylvia Rubio, Business Mgr.
Res.: 3111 Erskine St., 79415-1623. Tel: 806-763-4156; Fax: 806-763-2521.
Catechesis/Religious Program—Tel: 806-763-8727. Soyla Castillo, D.R.E.; Liz Lopez, C.R.E. (Elem. School); Maria Trevino, C.R.E. (Elem. School). Students 375.

7—OUR LADY OF GUADALUPE (1980), (Hispanic), [CEM] Rev. Andres Mendoza.
Res.: 1120 52nd St., P.O. Box 3947, 79412. Tel: 806-763-0710; Fax: 806-741-1915.
Catechesis/Religious Program—Tel: 806-763-0732. Tina Narvaiz, D.R.E.; Sr. Mary Jane Alaniz, O.S.F., D.R.E. Students 725.

8—ST. PATRICK (1960) Rev. John Cherolikal.
Res.: 1603 Cherry Ave., 79403-6001. Tel: 806-765-5123; Fax: 806-765-5123. Email: lbksanpatricio@yahoo.com.
Catechesis/Religious Program—Tel: 806-765-6979. Cleta Arrellano, D.R.E. Students 88.
Mission—Our Lady Queen of Apostles Main St. N., New Deal, Lubbock Co. 79403. Tel: 806-765-5123.
Catechesis/Religious Program—Cecelia Villegas, D.R.E. Students 34.

9—ST. THERESA'S (1961), (Hispanic), Rev. Marcos Rene Perez.
Res.: 2202 Upland Ave., 79407. Tel: 806-795-2249; Fax: 806-793-4456. Email: agomez@xanadoo.com.
Catechesis/Religious Program—Nancy Sanchez, D.R.E. Students 56.

OUTSIDE THE CITY OF LUBBOCK

ANSON, JONES CO., ST. MICHAEL (1960), (Hispanic), [JC] Rev. Michael Melcher.
Res.: 2010 County Rd. 477, 79501. Tel: 325-823-2777. Email: mike00777@juno.com.
Catechesis/Religious Program—Terry Ramos, D.R.E.; Eloise Quintanilla, D.R.E. Students 70.
Mission—Holy Trinity (1926) Hwy. 83, Hamlin, Jones Co. 79520. Students 36.

BROWNFIELD, TERRY CO., ST. ANTHONY'S (1952), (Hispanic), Rev. Gerald Leatham; Deacon George Holguin.
Res.: 1902 Levelland Hwy., P.O. Box 671, 79316. Tel: 806-637-6626; 806-637-2344 (Office).
Catechesis/Religious Program—Fax: 806-637-2356. Chris Martinez, D.R.E.; Elsa Martinez, D.R.E. Students 197.
Mission—San Francisco de Asis P.O. Box 92, Ropesville, Hockley Co. 79358.
Catechesis/Religious Program—Anna Ricker, D.R.E. Students 18.

DENVER CITY, YOAKUM CO., ST. WILLIAM (1955) Rev. Joseph Thanavelil, O.S.B. (India).
Res.: 401 Mustang Ave., 79323-2749. Tel: 806-592-2063; Fax: 806-592-2239.
Catechesis/Religious Program— Mr. Angel Hernandez, D.R.E. Students 197.
Mission—Sacred Heart 1305 11th St., Plains, Yoakum Co. 79355. Tel: 806-456-7002.

FLOYDADA, FLOYD CO., ST. MARY MAGDALEN (1928) [JC] Rev. Angelo R. Consemino.
Res.: 309 S. Wall, 79235. Tel: 806-983-5878; Fax: 806-983-2601.
Catechesis/Religious Program—Ellen Enriquez, D.R.E. Students 58.
Mission—Our Lady of Guadalupe 701 Bundy St., Matador, Motley Co. 79244.
Mission—St. Elizabeth Second St. & Clare St., Paducah, Cottle Co. 79348. Tel: 806-492-3053.

HALE CENTER, HALE CO., ST. THERESA'S (1944), (Hispanic), Rev. John K. Smith.
Mailing Address: P.O. Box 528, 79041-0528. Tel: 806-839-2310; Fax: 806-839-2308.
Catechesis/Religious Program—Students 145.
Mission—St. Peter, Apostle (1958) P.O. Box 655, Olton, Lamb Co. 79064. Tel: 806-285-2140; Fax: 806-285-2140.

IDALOU, LUBBOCK CO., ST. PHILIP BENIZI (1979), (Spanish), Rev. Jose Kochuparambil; Deacon Urbano Rodriguez.
Res.: 722 Sixth Pl., Box 1337, 79329-1337. Tel: 806-892-2743; 806-892-2928 (Office); Fax: 806-892-9001.
Catechesis/Religious Program—Manuel Olivarez, D.R.E. Students 121.
Mission—San Lorenzo Jackson & Monroe, P.O. Box 129, Lorenzo, Crosby Co. 79343.

LAMESA, DAWSON CO., ST. MARGARET MARY (1929) [CEM] Rev. Joseph Kurumbel, O.S.B.; Deacon Daniel Valenzuela; Elva Gutierrez, Parish Sec. In Res., Rev. Joseph Kurumbel, O.S.B.
Res.: 911 S. 2nd St., P.O. Box 599, 79331. Tel: 806-872-7100; Fax: 806-872-3630. Email: stmargaretmary@valornet.com.
Catechesis/Religious Program—Ms. Adriana Sauseda, D.R.E.; Ms. Rosa Tijerina, D.R.E. Students 251.
Mission—Our Lady of Guadalupe 407 N. Hartford, P.O. Box 599, Dawson Co. 79331. Fax: 806-872-7100.

LEVELLAND, HOCKLEY CO., ST. MICHAEL'S (1956) Deacons Juan Cavazos; Leo Cottenoir.
Res.: 316 E. Washington St., 79336-2611. Tel: 806-894-2268; Fax: 806-894-9348.
Catechesis/Religious Program—Tel: 806-894-9880. Irma Dominguez, D.R.E. Students 178.
Mission—San Isidro 1306 S. Slaughter, P.O. Box 764, Sundown, Hockley Co. 79372-0764.

LITTLEFIELD, LAMB CO., SACRED HEART (1921) [CEM] Rev. Patrick Maher.
Res.: Eighth & Sunset, P.O. Box 1347, 79339-4234. Tel: 806-385-6043.
Catechesis/Religious Program—Susan Craig, D.R.E. Students 178.

MORTON, COCHRAN CO., ST. ANN (1955) Rev. Heriberto Mercado.
Res.: 105 N.E. Eighth St., 79346-2719. Tel: 806-266-8693; Fax: 806-266-8692.
Catechesis/Religious Program—Christina Ponce, D.R.E. Students 87.
Mission—St. Philip Neri [CEM] Farm Rd. 303, P.O. Box 395, Pep, Hockley Co. 79353. Tel: 806-933-4355.

MULESHOE, BAILEY CO., IMMACULATE CONCEPTION (1956), (Hispanic), [CEM 2] [JC] Rev. Leonardo Pahamtang (Philippines).
Res.: R.R. 3, Box 247, 79347-2460. Tel: 806-272-4384; Fax: 806-272-4384. Email: icchurch@fivearea.com.
Catechesis/Religious Program—Tel: 806-272-4167. Alma Orozco, D.R.E. Students 247.
Mission—St. Mary Magdalen
Catechesis/Religious Program—Patsy Garcia, D.R.E. Students 68.

O'DONNELL, LYNN CO., ST. PIUS X (1959), (Hispanic), [CEM] Rev. Eduardo C. Teo.
Res.: Rte. 1, Box 41-A, 79351. Tel: 806-428-3490; Fax: 806-428-3490.
Catechesis/Religious Program—Tel: 806-428-3691; Fax: 806-428-3691. Students 40.
Mission—St. Jude Thaddeus Catholic Church (1951) P.O. Box 785, Tahoka, Lynn Co. 79373. Tel: 806-561-4436.
Catechesis/Religious Program—Students 98.

PETERSBURG, HALE CO., SACRED HEART (1959) Rev. Jacob P. Puthuparambil, O.S.B. (India).
Mailing Address: P.O. Box 330, 79250-0330. Tel: 806-667-0063.
Res.: R.R. 2, Box 159A, Abernathy, 79311-6921. Tel: 806-298-4278.
Catechesis/Religious Program—Santi Garza, D.R.E. Students 50.
Mission—St. Isidore 510 S. Ave. D, Abernathy, Hale Co. 79311.
Catechesis/Religious Program—Tel: 806-298-4519; Fax: 806-298-4075. Matthew Dole, D.R.E. Students 45.

PLAINVIEW, HALE CO.

1—ST. ALICE (1911) Rev. James McCartney.
Res.: 1114 Houston St., 79072-7124.
Catechesis/Religious Program—Tel: 806-293-2891. Jackie Ball, D.R.E.; Joann Gamez, D.R.E.; Stacey Onta, D.R.E. Students 142.
Mission—San Jose 303 S.E. Fourth, Lockney, Floyd Co. 79241. Tel: 806-652-2321 (Parish Hall).

2—OUR LADY OF GUADALUPE (1946) [CEM] Rev. Raymundo Manriquez.
Mailing Address: P.O. Box 1269, 79072. Tel: 806-291-0195.
Church: 211 W. Seventh St., 79072. Tel: 806-293-0085; Fax: 806-293-4507.
Catechesis/Religious Program—Tel: 806-293-0086. Jonathan Yanez, D.R.E. (Elem.); Belinda Hinojosa, D.R.E. (H.S.). Students 600.

3—SACRED HEART (1964), (Hispanic), Rev. Arsenio C. Redulla.
Res. & Mailing Address: 400 W. 29th St., 79072-2399. Tel: 806-296-2753; Fax: 806-296-6553.
Catechesis/Religious Program—Tel: 806-296-6553. Students 350.

POST, GARZA CO., HOLY CROSS (1955) [JC] Rev. Paul Karieakatt, O.S.B. (India).
Res.: Box 190, 79356-0190. Tel: 806-495-2791.
Catechesis/Religious Program—Susan Collaso, D.R.E. Students 48.
Mission—Blessed Sacrament P.O. Box 119, Wilson, Lynn Co. 79381-0119. Rev. Eduardo C. Teo.

RALLS, CROSBY CO., ST. MICHAEL (1959), (Hispanic), [JC] Rev. Ernesto Lopez.
Mailing Address: P.O. Box 906, 79357-0906. Tel: 806-253-2008.
Catechesis/Religious Program—Students 93.
Mission—St. Joseph P.O. Box 906, Crosby Co. 79357. Tel: 806-253-2008.

ROTAN, FISHER CO., ST. JOSEPH (1929) Rev. Msgr. Timothy Schwertner.
Res.: 303 E. Lee, 79546-3011. Tel: 325-735-3285; 325-735-2935 (Office); Fax: 325-735-2181.
Catechesis/Religious Program— Rosemary Carrillo, D.R.E. Students 33.
Mission—Sacred Heart [CEM] Ranchito, Fisher Co.
Mission—St. Mary Aspermont, Stonewall Co.

SEMINOLE, GAINES CO., ST. JAMES (1958) Rev. Hugh Thekkel, O.S.B.
Res.: P.O. Box 898, 79360-0898. Tel: 432-758-2371; Fax: 432-758-2766. Email: stjamescatholic@sbcglobal.net.
Catechesis/Religious Program—Veronica Rubio, D.R.E.; Wendy Martinez, D.R.E. Students 705.
Mission—St. Paul's P.O. Box 1321, Seagraves, Gaines Co. 79359-1321. Tel: 806-546-2950.

SHALLOWATER, LUBBOCK CO., ST. PHILIP BENIZI (1967), (Hispanic), [JC] Rev. Philip T. Pasupil (Philippines); Deacons Frank Lopez; Tommy Alvarado; Richard Flores.
Res.: 1314 6th St., 79363-0039. Tel: 806-832-5915 (Rectory); 806-832-4088 (Church Hall).
Catechesis/Religious Program—Carmen Behrens, C.R.E.; Natalia Flores, C.R.E. Students 80.
Mission—St. Anthony of Padua (1966) 4th S. Lawrence, Box 545, Anton, Hockley, Co. 79313. Tel: 806-997-2188.

SLATON, LUBBOCK CO.

1—ST. JOSEPH'S (1912), (German), [JC] Rev. Msgr. Nicolas Rendon (Philippines); Deacons Leroy Behnke, Pastoral Assoc.; Darris D. Linder, Pastoral Assoc.
Res.: 205 S. 19th, 79364-3755. Tel: 806-828-3944; Fax: 806-828-4084.
School—(Grades PreK-8), 1305 W. Division St.,

79364. Tel: 806-828-6761; Fax: 806-828-5396. Mr. James Starkey, Prin. Sisters 2; Lay Teachers 4; Students 41.
Catechesis/Religious Program—Students 54.
2—OUR LADY OF GUADALUPE (1952) [JC] Rev. Chacko Thaclathil, O.S.B.; Deacon Phillip Maldonado; Teresa Hernandez, Parish Sec.
Res.: 705 S. Fourth, 79363-5406. Tel: 806-828-5108 (Office).
Catechesis/Religious Program—Tel: 806-828-4573. David Ariaz, Youth Min. (H.S.). Students 124.
SNYDER, SCURRY CO.
1—ST. ELIZABETH'S (1952) [CEM] Rev. Roy Jose Badilles.
Res.: 3005 Ave. A, 79549-3909. Tel: 325-573-2590; Fax: 325-573-1553. Email: steministrydirector@yahoo.com.
Catechesis/Religious Program—Tel: 325-573-0999. Email: royjose@sbcglobal.net. Students 112.
Mission—St. John Hwy. 84, Hermleigh, Scurry Co. 79526.
2—OUR LADY OF GUADALUPE (1955), (Hispanic), [CEM] [JC 2] Rev. Roy Jose Badilles.
Res.: 1311 Ave. K, 79549-9533. Tel: 325-573-3866 (Office); 325-573-1569 (Res.); Fax: 325-573-7142. Email: ologsny@sbcglobal.net.
Catechesis/Religious Program—Tel: 915-573-7142; Fax: 915-573-7142. Irma Guerero, D.R.E.; Melinda Dominguez, Asst. D.R.E. Students 201.
SPUR, DICKENS CO., ST. MARY (1948) Rev. Paul Karieakatt, O.S.B. (India); Deacon Pete Garcia.
Res.: Box 189, 79370-0189. Tel: 806-271-3161; Fax: 806-271-4385.
Catechesis/Religious Program—Students 43.
Mission—Epiphany [JC] Jayton, Kent Co.
STAMFORD, JONES CO., ST. ANN (1952) [CEM] Rev. George Roney.
Res.: 104 New Braunfels, 79553-6415. Tel: 325-773-2659.
Catechesis/Religious Program—Students 93.
Mission—St. George 901 N. 16th St., Haskell, Haskell Co. 79521-3340. Tel: 940-864-3171.
Catechesis/Religious Program—Students 69.
WOLFFORTH, LUBBOCK CO., ST. FRANCIS OF ASSISI MISSION, See separate listing. See San Ramon, Woodrow for details. Rev. Nelson Diaz.
WOODROW, LUBBOCK CO., SAN RAMON (1974) Rev. Nelson Diaz.
Church: 15706 Loop 493, 79423. Tel: 806-863-2201.
Catechesis/Religious Program—Tel: 806-863-3435. Students 145.
Mission—St. Francis of Assisi P.O. Box 785, Wolfforth, Lubbock Co. 79382. Tel: 806-866-9007.

Retired:
Rev. Msgrs.—
Buxkemper, Roland
Comiskey, James
Gonzalez, Antonio, P.O. Box 416, Plainview, 79073.
Halfmann, Curtis T., P.O. Box 94722, 79493.
James, Joseph W., Our Lady of Mercy Retreat Center, P.O. Box 744, Slaton, 79364.
Revs.—
Diebel, Thomas, Box 10753, 79408.
Hayden, Johnrose, 428 E. Loyola Dr., Tempe, AZ 85282.
Hemp, Lawrence, 705 S. 4th St., Slaton, 79364.
Judd, Timothy, Sacred Heart Mission, P.O. Box 530, Petersburg, 79250-0530.
O'Dwyer, Michael, S.A.C., Ireland.
Ramirez, Cornelio C., S.A.C., 8415 Fremont Ave., 79423.
Vazneparambil, Thomas, Desam P.O., Aluva-Kerala 683103, India.

Permanent Deacons:
Aguilar, Francisco, St. Jude, Tahoka
Almager, Ramon, St. James, Seminole
Alvarado, Tommy, St. Anthony, Anton
Behnke, Leroy, St. Joseph, Slaton
Brito, Benny, St. Joseph, Lubbock
Broderson, Kyle, St. John Neumann, Lubbock
Bustamante, Juan, St. Ann, Stamford
Canale, Randy, Christ the King, Lubbock
Cavazos, Juan, St. Michael, Levelland
Cochran, Clarke E., St. John Neumann, Lubbock
Cottenoir, Leo, St. Michael, Levelland
Esquivel, Jessie, Our Lady of Guadalupe, Lubbock
Estrada, Julian, St. George, Haskell
Flores, Richard, St. Anthony, Anton
Garcia, Aureliano, St. Michael, Ralls
Garcia, Doroteo, Sacred Heart, Littlefield
Gracia, Pedro, (Retired), St. Mary, Spur
Hernandez, Ernesto, Our Lady of Grace, Lubbock
Holguin, George, St. Anthony, Brownfield
Key, Billy, On Duty Outside the Diocese
Linder, Darris D., St. Joseph's, Slaton
Lopez, Frank, St. Phillip, Shallowater
Maldonado, Phillip, Our Lady of Guadalupe, Slaton
Martinez, Joe, St. Joseph, Lubbock
Martinez, Waldo, St. Elizabeth, Lubbock
McCann, Richard, St. Elizabeth, Lubbock
McDonald, Isaac, Our Lady of Guadalupe, Lubbock
Morales, Eddie, Church of the Epiphany, Jayton
Morin, Joe, Our Lady of Grace, Lubbock
Ortegon, Frank, (Retired), Our Lady of Guadalupe, Snyder
Ramirez, Robert, Our Lady of Guadalupe, Snyder
Rendon, Dario, (Retired), St. Patrick's, Lubbock
Resendez, Simon, St. Pius X, O'Donnell
Revilla, Nash, (Retired), St. Philip Benizi, Shallowater
Rodriguez, Jose Luis, St. Theresa, Lubbock
Rodriguez, Ramiro, St. Patrick's, Lubbock
Rodriguez, Simon, (Retired)
Rosiles, Ralph, Holy Spirit, Lubbock
Rubalcado, Nasario, St. Joseph, Ralls
Rubio, Jose, St. Phillip Benizi, Idalou
Salazar, Lorenzo, Our Lady of Guadalupe, Lubbock
Saldana, Isidoro, St. Francis, Lubbock
Thompson, Richard, Sacred Heart, Littlefield
Tjia, Steve, Christ the King, Lubbock
Valenzuela, Daniel, St. Margaret Mary, Lamesa
Vasquez, Enrique, St. Mary Magdalen, Floydada
Wood, Richard, St. John Neumann, Lubbock

INSTITUTIONS LOCATED IN THE DIOCESE

[A] CATHOLIC RENEWAL CENTERS

LUBBOCK. *Catholic Renewal Center*, P.O. Box 98700, 79499-8700. Tel: 806-792-3943, Ext. 231 or Ext. 232; Fax: 806-687-8668. Web: www.dioceseoflubbock.org. Mrs. Cindi Simmons, Center Dir. Total Staff 4.
Office for Cursillo Movement, P.O. Box 98303, 79499-8296. Tel: 806-792-4308. Rev. David R. Cruz, Spiritual Dir.

[B] RETREAT HOUSES

SLATON. *Our Lady of Mercy Retreat Center*, 605 S. 19th St., P.O. Box 744, 79364-0744. Tel: 806-828-6428; Fax: 806-828-3856. Email: mercy@door.net. Web: www.catholiclubbock.org/mercycenter. Rev. Msgr. Joseph W. James, Dir. Emeritus (Retired); Deacon Darris D. Linder, Exec. Dir. Total in Residence 1; Total Staff 8.

[C] CONVENTS AND RESIDENCES FOR SISTERS

LUBBOCK. *Our Lady of Grace Convent*, 3101 Erskine, 79415. Tel: 806-747-7472. Missionary Catechists of the Sacred Hearts of Jesus and Mary 3.

PLAINVIEW. *St. Alice Convent*, 1114 Houston, 79072. Tel: 806-296-5426. St. Francis Mission Community 2.

WOLFFORTH. *St. Francis Mission Community* (1981) Our Lady of the Angels Motherhouse, 8202 CR 7700, 79382. Tel: 806-863-4904; Fax: 806-863-4906. Email: franciscan@erfwireless.net. St. Francis Mission Community 17.

[D] MISCELLANEOUS LISTINGS

LUBBOCK. *Catholic Foundation of the Diocese of Lubbock, Inc.*, P.O. Box 98700, 79499-8700. Tel: 806-792-3943, Ext. 206; Fax: 806-771-7660. Email: runderwood@catholiclubbock.org. Web: www.catholiclubbock.org. Mrs. Renee Underwood, M.B.A., Dir.
Christ the King Cathedral School Foundation, 4011 54th St., 79413. Tel: 806-795-8283; Fax: 806-795-9715. Email: cduran@ctkcathedral.org. Web: www.CTKCathederalschool.org. Very Rev. Msgr. Ben Kasteel, V.G., Ex Officio Officer. Total Staff 50.

RELIGIOUS INSTITUTES OF WOMEN REPRESENTED IN THE DIOCESE

For further details refer to the corresponding bracketed number in the Religious Institutes of Men or Women section.

[]—*Adorers of the Blood of Christ*—A.S.C.

[2700]—*Missionary Cathechists of the Sacred Hearts of Jesus and Mary*—M.C.S.S.C.C.J.M.

[]—*Missionary Sisters of the Lord's Table*—M.S.L.T.

[]—*Sisters of Charity of the Incarnate Word*—C.C.V.I.

[2575]—*Sisters of Mercy of the Americas*—R.S.M.

[1620]—*Sisters of Saint Francis the Neumann Communities*—O.S.F.

[]—*St. Francis Mission Community* (Wolfforth, TX)—O.S.F.

NECROLOGY

† Reyes, Reynaldo, Levelland, TX St. Michael—Died Aug. 16, 2009

An asterisk (*) denotes an organization that has established tax-exempt status directly with the IRS and is not covered by the USCCB Group Ruling.

Diocese of Madison

(Dioecesis Madisonensis)

Most Reverend

ROBERT C. MORLINO, D.D., S.T.D.

Bishop of Madison; ordained June 1, 1974; appointed Bishop of Helena July 6, 1999; consecrated and installed September 21, 1999; appointed Bishop of Madison May 23, 2003; installed August 1, 2003. *Chancery: Bishop O'Connor Catholic Pastoral Center, 702 S. High Point Rd., P.O. Box 44983, Madison, WI 53744-4983.*

Most Reverend

WILLIAM H. BULLOCK, D.D., ED.S.

Bishop Emeritus of Madison; ordained June 7, 1952; appointed Auxiliary Bishop of St. Paul and Minneapolis and Titular Bishop of Natchez June 3, 1980; consecrated August 12, 1980; appointed Bishop of Des Moines February 10, 1987; installed April 2, 1987; appointed Bishop of Madison April 13, 1993; installed June 14, 1993; retired May 23, 2003.

Chancery: Bishop O'Connor Catholic Pastoral Center, 702 S. High Point Rd., P.O. Box 44983, Madison, WI 53744-4983. Tel: 608-821-3000; Fax: 608-821-3013.

Web: www.madisondiocese.org

Email: diocese@madisondiocese.org

Most Reverend

GEORGE O. WIRZ, D.D., S.T.L.

Retired Auxiliary Bishop of Madison; ordained May 31, 1952; appointed Auxiliary Bishop of Madison and Titular Bishop of Municipa December 20, 1977; consecrated March 9, 1978; retired February 10, 2004. *Chancery: Bishop O'Connor Center, 702 S. High Point Rd., Madison, WI 53719-4999.*

ESTABLISHED 1946.

Square Miles 8,070.

Corporate Title: "Roman Catholic Diocese of Madison."

Comprises the Counties of Columbia, Dane, Grant, Green, Green Lake, Iowa, Jefferson, Lafayette, Marquette, Rock and Sauk in the State of Wisconsin.

For legal titles of parishes and diocesan institutions, consult the Chancery.

STATISTICAL OVERVIEW

Personnel	
Bishop	1
Retired Bishops	2
Priests: Diocesan Active in Diocese	83
Priests: Diocesan Active Outside Diocese	3
Priests: Retired, Sick or Absent	50
Number of Diocesan Priests	136
Religious Priests in Diocese	18
Total Priests in Diocese	154
Extern Priests in Diocese	16
Ordinations:	
Diocesan Priests	3
Transitional Deacons	2
Permanent Deacons in Diocese	20
Total Brothers	6
Total Sisters	396
Parishes	
Parishes	132
With Resident Pastor:	
Resident Diocesan Priests	75
Resident Religious Priests	1
Without Resident Pastor:	
Administered by Priests	55
Completely Vacant	1
Professional Ministry Personnel:	
Brothers	7
Sisters	22
Lay Ministers	708
Welfare	
Catholic Hospitals	3
Total Assisted	444,437
Health Care Centers	3
Total Assisted	137,095
Homes for the Aged	6
Total Assisted	567
Day Care Centers	23
Total Assisted	909
Special Centers for Social Services	14
Total Assisted	45,588
Residential Care of Disabled	1
Total Assisted	271
Educational	
Diocesan Students in Other Seminaries	25
Total Seminarians	25
Colleges and Universities	1
Total Students	2,550
High Schools, Private	2
Total Students	739
Elementary Schools, Diocesan and Parish	44
Total Students	7,198
Elementary Schools, Private	2
Total Students	313
Catechesis/Religious Education:	
High School Students	6,212
Elementary Students	12,326
Total Students under Catholic Instruction	29,363
Teachers in the Diocese:	
Brothers	2
Sisters	10
Lay Teachers	587
Vital Statistics	
Receptions into the Church:	
Infant Baptism Totals	2,522
Minor Baptism Totals	80
Adult Baptism Totals	81
Received into Full Communion	171
First Communions	2,667
Confirmations	2,146
Marriages:	
Catholic	452
Interfaith	290
Total Marriages	742
Deaths	1,667
Total Catholic Population	278,578
Total Population	996,348

Former Bishops—Most Revs. WILLIAM P. O'CONNOR, D.D., Ph.D., ord. March 10, 1912; appt. Bishop of Superior, Dec. 31, 1941; cons. March 7, 1942; transferred to as first Bishop of Madison, Feb. 22, 1946; resigned Feb. 22, 1967; died July 13, 1973; CLETUS F. O'DONNELL, D.D., J.C.D., ord. May 3, 1941; appt. Titular Bishop of Abrittum and Auxiliary of Chicago, Oct. 26, 1960; cons. Dec. 21, 1960; promoted to Bishop of Madison, Feb. 22, 1967; resigned April 18, 1992; died Aug. 31, 1992; WILLIAM H. BULLOCK, D.D., E.D.S. (Retired), ord. June 7, 1952; appt. Auxiliary Bishop of St. Paul and Minneapolis and Titular Bishop of Natchez June 3, 1980; cons. Aug. 12, 1980; appt. Bishop of Des Moines Feb. 10, 1987; installed April 2, 1987; appt. Bishop of Madison April 13, 1993; installed June 14, 1993; retired May 23, 2003.

Vicars General—Most Revs. WILLIAM H. BULLOCK, D.D., E.D.S. (Retired); GEORGE O. WIRZ, D.D., S.T.L. (Retired); Rev. Msgr. DANIEL T. GANSHERT.

Chancery—Bishop O'Connor Catholic Pastoral Center, 702 S. High Point Rd., P.O. Box 44983, Madison, 53744-4983. Office Hours: Mon.-Fri. 8-4:30.

Chancellor—KEVIN R. PHELAN. Tel: 608-821-3162.

Director of Finance—Mr. JOHN C. PHILIPP. Tel: 608-821-3021.

Diocesan Tribunal—Bishop O'Connor Catholic Pastoral Center, 702 S. High Point Rd., P.O. Box 44983, Madison, 53744-4983. Tel: 608-821-3060; Fax: 608-821-3067. Email: tribunal@straphael.org.

Judicial Vicar—Rev. Msgr. MICHAEL E. HIPPEE, J.C.L.

Director of the Tribunal—VACANT.

Judges—Rev. JAMES W. HINNEN, J.C.L.; Rev. Msgr. MICHAEL E. HIPPEE, J.C.L.; Mrs. MARIA YOUNG, J.U.D.

Promoter of Justice—JAY CONZEMIUS, J.C.L.

Defender of the Bond—JAY CONZEMIUS, J.C.L.

Advocate/Procurator (cc.1481-1490)—Revs. BRIAN J. WILK; ERIC G. STERNBERG; TAIT C. SCHROEDER; MICHAEL R. RADOWICZ.

Notaries—SUSAN STACK; BECCA FISCHER; WILLIAM YALLALY.

Diocesan Consultors—Rev. Msgrs. JAMES R. BARTYLLA; MICHAEL L. BURKE, Sec.; DANIEL T. GANSHERT; KEVIN D. HOLMES; Revs. JOHN M. MEINHOLZ; PATRICK F. NORRIS, O.P.

Presbyteral Council—Most Rev. ROBERT CHARLES MORLINO, Pres.; Rev. Msgr. DANIEL T. GANSHERT, Vicar Gen. & Ex Officio. Elected: Revs. DAVID W. TIMMERMAN; RANDY J. TIMMERMAN; LAWRENCE M. BAKKE; KENNETH J. KLINK; JOHN H. HEDRICK; KENT A. SCHMITT; JAMES H. MURPHY; JOHN M. MEINHOLZ; JAMES M. POSTER; BRIAN J. WILK; RONALD G. KREUL, O.P.; Rev. Msgr. JAMES J. UPPENA; Rev. STEPHEN J. UMHOEFER. Appointed: Rev. PAUL U. ARINZE; Rev. Msgrs. JAMES R. BARTYLLA; MICHAEL L. BURKE; Rev. RICHARD M. HEILMAN; Rev. Msgrs. MICHAEL E. HIPPEE, J.C.L.; KEVIN D. HOLMES; Revs. JARED M. HOOD, S.J.S.; ERIC G. STERNBERG; Rev. Msgr. DELBERT L. SCHMELZER (Retired); Rev. BART D. TIMMERMAN.

Personnel Board—Revs. JOHN R. AUBY; LAWRENCE M. BAKKE; KENNETH J. FRISCH; MICHAEL C. RICHEL; WILLIAM J. SEIPP; Rev. Msgrs. DANIEL T. GANSHERT, Chm.; RAYMOND N. KERTZ.

Vicar for Permanent Deacons—Rev. TAIT C. SCHROEDER, Mailing Address: Diocese of Madison, P.O. Box 44983, Madison, 53744-4983.

Vicar for Priests—Rev. Msgr. DOUGLAS L. DUSHACK, Mailing Address: St. Bernard Parish, 2015

Parmenter St., P.O. Box 620187, Middleton, 53562-0187.

Vicar for Religious—VACANT.

Deaneries—Revs. RAYMOND J. DISCHLER, Columbia Deanery; MICHAEL C. RICHEL, East Dane Deanery; VACANT, Grant Deanery; VACANT, Iowa Deanery; Revs. THOMAS P. MARR, Jefferson Deanery; RANDY J. BUDNAR, Lafayette Deanery; Rev. Msgr. KENNETH J. FIEDLER, Madison Deanery; Rev. DALE W. GRUBBA, Marquette-Green Lake Deanery; VACANT, Rock-Green Deanery; VACANT, Sauk Deanery; Rev. THOMAS L. KELLEY, West Dane Deanery.

Diocesan Offices and Directors

Apostolate to the Handicapped—Rev. Msgr. THOMAS F. CAMPION, Mailing Address: P.O. Box 443, Monroe, 53566. Tel: 608-328-8371.

Apostolate to the Deaf—VACANT.

Archives—Ms. PAT BORN, Archivist, Bishop O'Connor Catholic Pastoral Center, 702 S. High Point Rd., P.O. Box 44983, Madison, 53744-4983. Tel: 608-821-3140; Fax: 608-821-3181.

Catholic Committee on Scouting—Mr. MICHAEL KLECKNER, Chm., 5595 Longford Terr., Madison, 53711. Tel: 608-275-3344. Email: mkleckner@amfam.com.

Building Commission—Rev. Msgrs. MICHAEL E. HIPPEE, J.C.L.; DUANE R. MOELLENBERNDT; DANIEL T. GANSHERT, Chm.; Mr. JOHN C. PHILIPP; Dr. PATRICK GORMAN; Mr. PETER SZOTKOWSKI; Mr. JOHN FELLER.

Camp Gray—Co Directors: JEFF HOEBEN; REBECCA HOEBEN, E10213 Shady Lane Rd., Reedsburg, 53959. Tel: 608-356-8200; Fax: 608-356-5855. Email: bigfun@campgray.com.

Catholic Relief Services—VACANT.

Department of Cemeteries, Diocese of Madison—JOHN MILLER, Diocesan Dir., Central Office, 2705 Regent St., Madison, 53705. Tel: 608-238-5561; Fax: 608-238-5768.

Charities--Catholic Charities of the Diocese of Madison, Inc.—Bishop O'Connor Catholic Pastoral Center, 702 S. High Point Rd., P.O. Box 46550, Madison, 53744-6550. Tel: 608-821-3100. BRIAN A. CAIN, Dir. Fax: 608-821-3125. Madison Area Offices, 30 S. Franklin St., Madison, 53703. Tel: 608-256-2358. 426 S. Yellowstone Dr., Ste. 100, Madison, 53719. Tel: 608-833-4800. Beloit District Office, 3311 Prairie Ave., Beloit, 53511. Tel: 608-365-3665. Janesville District Office, 2020 E. Milwaukee St., Ste. 208, Janesville, 53547. Tel: 608-752-4906.

Office for the Continuing Education of Priests—Rev. Msgr. O. CHARLES SCHLUTER, Dir., Bishop O'Connor Catholic Pastoral Center, 702 S. High Point Rd., P.O. Box 44983, Madison, 53744-4983. Tel: 608-821-3006.

Education—ERIC SCHIEDERMAYER, Exec. Sec. Tel: 608-821-3168; PATRICK DELANEY, Assoc. Dir., Adult & Special Educ. Tel: 608-821-3161; MICHAEL LANCASTER, Supt., Schools. Tel: 608-821-3180; MONICA BISCHOFF, Ed.D., Asst. Supt., Bishop O'Connor Catholic Pastoral Center, 702 S. High Point Rd., P.O. Box 44983, Madison, 53744-4983. Tel: 608-821-3160.

Saint Raphael Society Clergy Retirement Plan—Rev. Msgr. DANIEL T. GANSHERT, Bishop O'Connor Catholic Pastoral Center, 702 S. High Point Rd., P.O. Box 44983, Madison, 53744-4983. Tel: 608-821-3011.

Council of Catholic Women—Rev. Msgr. DUANE R. MOELLENBERNDT, Moderator, Sacred Hearts of Jesus & Mary, 221 Columbus St., Sun Prairie, 53590-2297. Tel: 608-837-7381; Rev. LORIN M. BOWENS, Co-Moderator, Mailing Address: St. Boniface Parish, P.O. Box 60, Lime Ridge, 53942. Tel: 608-986-2101.

Director of Communications—BRENT KING. Tel: 608-821-3033.

Holy Childhood, Pontifical Association—Rev. Msgr. DELBERT L. SCHMELZER, Dir. (Retired), Bishop O'Connor Catholic Pastoral Center, 702 S. High Point Rd., P.O. Box 44983, Madison, 53744-4983. Tel: 608-821-3052.

Information—BRENT KING, Mailing Address: P.O. Box 44983, Madison, 53744-4983.

Office of Worship—Dr. PATRICK GORMAN, Bishop O'Connor Catholic Pastoral Center, 702 S. High Point Rd., P.O. Box 44983, Madison, 53744-4983. Tel: 608-821-3080.

Office of Justice & Pastoral Outreach—VACANT, Bishop O'Connor Catholic Pastoral Center, 702 S. High Point Rd., P.O. Box 44983, Madison, 53744-4983. Tel: 608-821-3086.

Outreach—

Catholic Multicultural Center—ANDREW RUSSELL, Admin. Tel: 608-661-3512. *Centro Pastoral Guadalupano, Catholic Multicultural Center, 1862 Beld St., Madison, 53713.* Tel: 608-661-3512, Ext. 102. VACANT. *St. Martin House, Catholic Multicultural Center, 1862 Beld St., Madison, 53713.* Tel: 608-661-3512, Ext. 200. STEVE MAURICE, Coord.

Hispanic Ministry—Bishop O'Connor Catholic Pastoral Center, 702 S. High Point Rd., P.O. Box 44983, Madison, 53744-4983. Tel: 608-821-3092.

Evangelization and Catechesis Department— (Youth & Young Adult Ministry; Respect Life - Tel: 608-821-3086; Curriculum and Catechist Development; Newman Apostolate - Madison: Rev. Eric H. Nielsen, Dir.; St. Paul Univ. Catholic Center, 723 State St., Madison, WI, 53703. Tel: 608-258-3140. Platteville: Rev. Msgr. O. Charles Schluter; St. Augustine Newman Center, 135 S. Hickory St., Platteville, WI 53818. Tel: 608-348-7530)

Newspaper— "Catholic Herald, Madison Edition" MARY UHLER, Editor, Bishop O'Connor Catholic Pastoral Center, 702 S. High Point Rd., P.O. Box 44983, Madison, 53744-4983. Tel: 608-821-3070.

Diocesan Victim Assistance Program—KEVIN R. PHELAN, Chancellor.

Victim Assistance Coordinator—KEVIN R. PHELAN, Chancellor, Bishop O'Connor Catholic Pastoral Center, 702 S. High Point Rd., P.O. Box 44983, Madison, 53744-4983. Tel: 608-821-3083; Fax: 608-821-3013.

Propagation of the Faith—Rev. Msgr. DELBERT L. SCHMELZER, Dir. (Retired), Bishop O'Connor Catholic Pastoral Center, 702 S. High Point Rd., P.O. Box 44983, Madison, 53744-4983. Tel: 608-821-3052.

St. Vincent de Paul Society—VACANT.

Serra Clubs—Madison: Rev. Msgr. JAMES R. BARTYLLA. Janesville: Rev. RANDY J. TIMMERMAN.

Vigilance Council— (The Very Rev. Deans)

Vocations—Rev. Msgr. JAMES R. BARTYLLA, Dir., Bishop O'Connor Catholic Pastoral Center, 702 S. High Point Rd., P.O. Box 44983, Madison, 53744-4983. Tel: 608-821-3088.

Wisconsin Catholic Conference—JOHN HUEBSCHER, Exec. Sec., 131 W. Wilson St., Ste. 1105, Madison, 53703. Tel: 608-257--0004.

Office of Human Resources—JOHN MILLER, Dir., Bishop O'Connor Catholic Pastoral Center, 702 S. High Point Rd., P.O. Box 44983, Madison, 53744-4983. Tel: 608-821-3047.

Office of Stewardship and Development—DAUN MAIER, Assoc. Dir., Mailing Address: Bishop O'Connor Catholic Pastoral Center, 702 S. High Point Rd., P.O. Box 44983, Madison, 53744-4983. Tel: 608-821-3040.

CLERGY, PARISHES, MISSIONS AND PAROCHIAL SCHOOLS

CITY OF MADISON

(DANE COUNTY)

1—ST. BERNARD (1907) [JC] Rev. Msgr. Michael E. Hippee.
Res.: 2450 Atwood Ave., 53704. Tel: 608-249-9256; Fax: 608-244-3773. Web: www.stbernards.net.
Catechesis/Religious Program—2438 Atwood Ave., 53704. Tel: 608-249-7288, Ext. 230. Email: stb-education@chartermi.net. Students 69.

2—BLESSED SACRAMENT (1922) [JC] Revs. Patrick F. Norris, O.P.; Ronald G. Kreul, O.P.
Mailing Address: 2116 Hollister Ave., 53726-3958. Tel: 608-238-3471; Fax: 608-238-4220. Web: www.blsacrament.org.
Priory: 2131 Rowley Ave., 53726. Tel: 608-238-3472. Rev. Jerome Matthias Walsh, O.P.; Bros. Vincent Dirienzo, O.P.; Terrence Bullock, O.P.; Rev. Joseph A. Fogarty, O.P.
School—2112 Hollister Ave., 53726. Tel: 608-233-6155. Lay Teachers 22; Students 335.
Catechesis/Religious Program—Students 224.

3—CATHEDRAL PARISH OF ST. RAPHAEL (1854), (Merger of St. Raphael, Madison, Holy Redeemer, 128 W. Johnson St., Madison & St. Patrick, 410 E. Main St., Madison) Rev. Msgr. Kevin D. Holmes, Rector; Rev. Jose Luis Vazquez (Mexico); Deacon Raymond Lukesic.
Mailing Address: 404 E. Main St., 53703. Tel: 608-257-5000; Fax: 608-257-5565. Email: cathedral@straphael.org. Web: www.isthmuscatholic.org.
Res.: 120 W. Johnson St., 53703. Tel: 608-255-1658.
Catechesis/Religious Program—Students 213.

4—ST. DENNIS (1956) [JC] Revs. Kent A. Schmitt; Lance J. Schneider, Parochial Vicar; Deacon David Hendrickson.
Res.: 313 Dempsey Rd., 53714. Tel: 608-246-5124; Fax: 608-246-5138. Email: dns@chorus.net. Web: www.st-dennis.org.
School—Tel: 608-246-5121. Dominican Sisters (Sinsinawa, WI) 4; Lay Teachers 18; Students 255.
Catechesis/Religious Program—Tel: 608-246-5123; Fax: 608-246-5138. Judy Hronek, D.R.E. (Pastoral Ministry); Sr. Mary Therese Dolan, O.P., D.R.E. (RCIA); Joanna Gehrmann, D.R.E. (K-3); Lisa Harms, D.R.E. (4-8); David Hendrickson, D.R.E. (H.S.); Pat Hendrickson, Liturgy Director/Pastoral Ministry. Students 890.

5—HOLY REDEEMER (1857) Merged into Cathedral Parish of St. Raphael, Madison.

6—IMMACULATE HEART OF MARY (1950) [JC] Rev. John M. Meinholz.
Res.: 5101 Schofield St., 53716. Tel: 608-221-1521; Fax: 608-221-1794. Web: www.ihmparishmonona.org.
School—4913 Schofield St., 53716. Tel: 608-222-8831; Fax: 608-221-4492. Lay Teachers 16; Students 121.
Catechesis/Religious Program—Students 130.

7—ST. JAMES (1905) [JC], (Linked with St. Joseph, Madison) Rev. Msgr. Thomas F. Baxter.
Res.: 1128 St. James Ct., 53715. Tel: 608-255-1656; Fax: 608-256-6311. Email: madisonstjames@straphael.org. Web: www.stjamesmadison.com.
School—1204 St. James Ct., 53715. Tel: 608-256-3095; Fax: 608-256-6311. Web: www.stjamesschool.org. Lay Teachers 18; Students 179.
Catechesis/Religious Program—Tel: 608-271-5771. Email: zsimon@straphael.org. Sr. Zita Simon, D.R.E. Students 34.

8—SAINT JOSEPH, (Linked with St. James, Madison) Rev. Msgr. Thomas F. Baxter.
Mailing Address: 1905 W. Beltline Hwy., 53713. Tel: 608-271-5771; Fax: 608-271-9366. Email: office@stjosephmadison.org. Web: stjosephmadison.org. In Res., Rev. Manuel Mendez-Cobos, (Latino Ministry).
Catechesis/Religious Program—Students 111.

9—ST. MARIA GORETTI (1959) [JC] Rev. Msgr. Michael L. Burke; Rev. David Greenfield, Parochial Vicar; Deacons Jerome Buhman; Richard Martin.
Res.: 10 Maria Pl., 53711. Tel: 608-271-7421; Fax: 608-275-6621. Email: parish@stmariagoretti.org. Web: www.stmariagoretti.org.
Church: 5313 Flad Ave., 53711.
School—5405 Flad Ave., 53711. Tel: 608-271-7551; Fax: 608-275-6625. Email: admin@stmariagoretti.org. Lay Teachers 31; Students 419.
Catechesis/Religious Program—Tel: 608-271-8081; Fax: 608-268-2974. Students 533.

10—OUR LADY, QUEEN OF PEACE (1945) [JC] Rev. Msgr. Kenneth J. Fiedler; Sr. Sue Hetebrueg, S.S.N.D., Pastoral Assoc.
Res. & Parish Center: 401 S. Owen Dr., 53711. Tel: 608-231-4600; Fax: 608-231-4606. Web: www.qopc.org.
School—418 Holly Ave., 53711. Tel: 608-231-4580; Fax: 608-231-4589. Web: www.qops.k12.wi.us. Lay Teachers 31; Students 473.
Catechesis/Religious Program—Tel: 608-231-4610. Mary Jo Trapani, D.R.E.; Cheryl Horne, Youth Min. Students 409.

11—ST. PATRICK (1888) [JC] Merged into Cathedral Parish of St. Raphael, Madison.

12—ST. PAUL UNIVERSITY PARISH, [JC] Revs. Eric H. Nielsen; Eric G. Sternberg.
Office: 723 State St., 53703. Tel: 608-258-3140; Fax: 608-258-3141.
Catechesis/Religious Program—Students 20.

13—ST. PETER (1967) [JC] Rev. Roger G. Nilles; Deacon Todd Martin.
Res.: 5001 N. Sherman Ave., 53704. Tel: 608-249-6651; Fax: 608-249-6870. Email: mdillon@stpetersofmadison.org. Web: www.stpetersofmadison.org.
Catechesis/Religious Program—Students 245.

14—ST. THOMAS AQUINAS, [JC] Rev. Msgr. Donald J. Heiar Jr.
Res.: 602 Everglade Dr., 53717. Tel: 608-833-2600; Fax: 608-833-1129. Email: parish@stamadison.org. Web: www.stamadison.org.
Catechesis/Religious Program—Tel: 608-833-2606. Holly Irving, D.R.E.; Kay Schachte, D.R.E. Students 252.

OUTSIDE THE CITY OF MADISON

ALBANY, GREEN CO., ST. PATRICK (1868) [CEM], (Linked with St. Rose, Brodhead) Rev. Michael E. Moon.
Res.: 1005 W. 2nd Ave., Brodhead, 53520-1406. Tel: 608-897-2666; Fax: 608-897-4614. Email: stroseoflima@charter.net.
Catechesis/Religious Program—Students 17.

ARGYLE, LAFAYETTE CO., ST. JOSEPH (1898) [CEM 2], (Linked with St. Michael, Yellowstone) Rev. David A. Wanish.
Res.: 313 N. Lafayette St., P.O. Box 76, 53504. Tel: 608-543-3631.
Catechesis/Religious Program— Mrs. Rebecca

Flannery, D.R.E. Students 32.
ASHTON, DANE CO., ST. PETER'S, [CEM], (Linked with St. Martin of Tours, Martinsville) Rev. Eugene F. Hollfelder.
Res.: 7121 Co. Trunk K, Middleton, 53562. Tel: 608-831-4843; Fax: 608-831-5377.
School—Tel: 608-831-4846. Lay Teachers 5; Students 35.
Catechesis/Religious Program—Students 153.
AVOCA, IOWA CO., ST. JOSEPH, [CEM], (Linked with St. John the Baptist, Muscoda and St. Malachy, Clyde) Rev. Robert J. Butz, Admin.
Res.: 341 N. Wisconsin Ave., P.O. Box 35, Muscoda, 53573. Tel: 608-739-3391; Fax: 608-739-9195.
Church: 701 E. Wisconsin St., 53506.
Catechesis/Religious Program—Email: stjohnre@mwt.net. Students 7.
BARABOO, SAUK CO., ST. JOSEPH (1859) [CEM] Rev. Lawrence M. Bakke, Admin.
Mailing Address: 300 2nd St., P.O. Box 70, 53913. Tel: 608-356-4773.
Res.: 314 East St., 53913. Tel: 608-356-3083; Fax: 608-356-4024. Web: stjosephbaraboo.org.
School—Web: www.stjosephbaraboo.org. Lay Teachers 8; Students 115.
Catechesis/Religious Program—Tel: 608-356-5353; Fax: 608-356-4024. Becky Thompson, Dir. Faith Formation. Students 195.
BARNEVELD, IOWA CO., IMMACULATE CONCEPTION (1886) [CEM] [JC], (Linked with St. Bridget, Ridgeway) Rev. Peter Auer, S.O.L.T.
100 Church St., 53507.
Res. & Mailing Address: 803 W. Main St., Ridgeway, 53582-9659. Tel: 608-514-9468.
Catechesis/Religious Program—Students 60.
BELLEVILLE, DANE CO., ST. MARY OF LOURDES, [CEM], (Linked with St. James, Dayton) Rev. Kenneth J. Klink.
Res.: 221 Frederick St., P.O. Box 349, 53508. Tel: 608-424-3681.
Catechesis/Religious Program—Tel: 608-527-2153. Kay Parish, D.R.E.; Dorothy Love, D.R.E. Students 427.
BELMONT, LAFAYETTE CO., ST. PHILOMENA (1957) [CEM], (Linked with St. Michael, Calamine and Immaculate Conception, Truman) Rev. Monte E. Robinson.
Res.: 338 Chestnut St., Box 345, 53510. Tel: 608-762-5446.
Catechesis/Religious Program— Also serves these Missions: St. Michael's at Calamine, WI & Immaculate Conception at Truman, WI Students 62.
BELOIT, ROCK CO.
1—ST. JUDE (1908), (Linked With St. Thomas the Apostle, Beloit) Rev. Steven J. Kortendick; Deacon James Davis.
Res.: 747 Hackett St., 53511. Tel: 608-364-2820; Fax: 608-364-2822. Email: pquinn@stjudebeloit.org. Web: www.stjudebeloit.org.
School—Brother Dutton School, 717 Hackett St., 53511. Tel: 608-364-2825; Fax: 608-364-2827. Web: www.brotherdutton.net. Lay Teachers 10; Students 52.
Catechesis/Religious Program—Students 80.
2—OUR LADY OF THE ASSUMPTION (1953) [JC] Rev. Gary L. Krahenbuhl.
Mailing Address: 2222 Shopiere Rd., 53511. Tel: 608-362-9066. Web: www.olaparish.com.
Res.: 2487 N. Bootmaker Dr., 53511.
School—Tel: 608-365-4015; Fax: 608-368-2832. Lay Teachers 13; Students 155.
Catechesis/Religious Program—Tel: 608-362-1231; Fax: 608-368-2820. Sandy Blevins, Dir. Faith Formation; Dominick Meyer, Youth Min. Students 258.
3—ST. PAUL, Closed. 1988. For inquiries for parish records contact St. Thomas the Apostle, Beloit.
4—ST. THOMAS THE APOSTLE (1851), (Linked with St. Jude, Beloit) Rev. Steven J. Kortendick; John Rowland, Pastoral Assoc.
Church & Office: 822 E. Grand Ave., 53511. Tel: 608-362-1034; Fax: 608-363-9931. Email: parishoffice@stthomasbeloit.org. Web: www.stthomasbeloit.org.
Res.: 747 Hackett St., 53511. Tel: 608-364-2820.
Catechesis/Religious Program—Students 318.
BENTON, LAFAYETTE CO., ST. PATRICK (1845) [CEM], (Linked with St. Rose of Lima, Cube City) Rev. David J. Flanagan.
Res.: 237 E. Main St., P.O. Box 3, 53803-0003. Tel: 608-759-2131.
Catechesis/Religious Program—Students 62.
BERLIN, GREEN LAKE CO.
1—ALL SAINTS (2001) [CEM 2] Rev. Jerome J. Maksvytis.
Church: N8566 State Rd. 49, P.O. Box 269, 54923-0269. Tel: 920-361-5252; Fax: 920-361-5255. Web: allsaintsberlin.org.
Res.: 167 N. Wisconsin, 54923. Tel: 920-361-2354.
School—151 S. Grove St., 54923. Tel: 920-361-1781; Fax: 920-361-7379. Email: szangl@allsaintsberlin.org. Web: www.allsaintsberlin.org/school.html. Lay Teachers 14; Students 154.
Catechesis/Religious Program— 54923. Tel: 920-361-0940. Students 250.
2—ST. JOSEPH, Merged with St. Michael, Berlin and St. Stanislaus, Berlin to form All Saints, Berlin.
3—ST. MICHAEL, Merged with St. Joseph, Berlin and St. Stanislaus, Berlin to form All Saints, Berlin.
4—ST. STANISLAUS, Merged with St. Joseph, Berlin and St. Michael, Berlin to form All Saints, Berlin.
BLANCHARDVILLE, LAFAYETTE CO., IMMACULATE CONCEPTION (1898) [CEM], (Linked with St. Patrick, Hollandale and Holy Redeemer, Perry) Rev. Michael R. Radowicz.
601 Grover St., P.O. Box 37, Hollandale, 53544-0037.
Church: 604 East St., 53516. Tel: 608-967-2344; Fax: 608-967-2344. Email: pastor@tcparishes.org.
Catechesis/Religious Program—Students 17.
BLOOMINGTON, GRANT CO., ST. MARY (1898) [CEM 2], (Linked with St. John, Patch Grove) Rev. Bart D. Timmerman.
Res.: 535 Congress St., P.O. Box 35, 53804-0035. Tel: 608-994-2526; Fax: 608-994-2551. Email: sunday7@grant.tds.net.
School—Lay Teachers 7; Students 69.
Catechesis/Religious Program—P.O. Box 35, 53804. Tel: 608-994-2435. Students 148.
Mission—St. John Parish Patch Grove, Grant Co. 53817.
BOSCOBEL, GRANT CO., IMMACULATE CONCEPTION (1872), Clustered with St. John the Baptist, Muscoda; St. Joseph, Avoca; St. Malachy, Clyde. Rev. Robert J. Butz.
405 E. LeGrand St., 53805.
Res.: 341 N. Wisconsin Ave., P.O. Box 35, Muscoda, 53573. Tel: 608-739-3391.
Catechesis/Religious Program—Mary J. Knoble, C.R.E.; Jan Miller, C.R.E. Students 117.
BRIGGSVILLE, MARQUETTE CO., ST. MARY HELP OF CHRISTIANS (1851) [CEM], (Linked with St. Mary of the Immaculate Conception, Portage) Rev. James H. Murphy; Sr. Jovita Winkel, C.S.A., Pastoral Min.
Res.: 309 W. Cook St., P.O. Box 216, Portage, 53901-0216. Tel: 608-742-6998; Fax: 608-742-1039.
Church: N565 Hwy. A, Box 127, 53920-0127. Tel: 608-981-2282; Fax: 608-981-2282.
Catechesis/Religious Program—Students 51.
BRODHEAD, GREEN CO., ST. ROSE OF LIMA, (Linked with St. Patrick, Albany) Rev. Michael E. Moon.
Res.: 1005 W. 2nd Ave., 53520-1406. Tel: 608-897-2666; Fax: 608-897-4614. Email: stroseoflima@charter.net.
Catechesis/Religious Program—Students 73.
BUFFALO TOWNSHIP, MARQUETTE CO., ST. ANDREW (1860) [CEM], (Linked with St. Mary, Pardeeville) Rev. John H. Hedrick.
Mailing Address: 318 S. Main St., Pardeeville, 53954. Tel: 608-429-3030; Fax: 608-429-3129. Email: stmary@jvlnet.com. Web: www.stmary-standrew.net.
CALAMINE, LAFAYETTE CO., ST. MICHAEL (1916) [CEM], (Linked with St. Philomena, Belmont and Immaculate Conception, Truman) Rev. Monte E. Robinson.
Res.: 338 Chestnut St., Box 345, Belmont, 53510. Tel: 608-762-5446.
Catechesis/Religious Program— Twinned with Holy Rosary, Darlington.; (Included in St. Philomena, Belmont)
CAMBRIDGE, DANE CO., ST. PIUS X (1955) Rev. David W. Timmerman, Admin.
Res.: 701 W. Water St., 53523. Tel: 608-423-3015. Email: stpius@charterinternet.com. Web: www.saintpiusxparish.org.
Catechesis/Religious Program—Tel: 608-423-4699. Bernadette Daggett, C.R.E. Students 140.
CASSVILLE, GRANT CO., ST. CHARLES BORROMEO, [CEM 2], (Linked with St. Mary Help of Christians, Glen Haven) Rev. John Norder.
Res.: 605 E. Dewey St., 53806. Tel: 608-725-5595; Fax: 608-725-2343.
School—521 E. Dewey St., 53806. Tel: 608-725-5173; Fax: 608-725-5179. Lay Teachers 8; Students 49.
Catechesis/Religious Program—Tel: 608-725-2330. Patricia Ballweg, D.R.E. Students 50.
Mission—St. Mary Help of Christians
CASTLE ROCK, GRANT CO., ST. JOHN NEPOMUCENE (1879) [CEM], (Linked with St. Mary's Parish, Fennimore) Rev. George B. Horath.
Mailing Address: 15055 Shemak Rd., Fennimore, 53809.
Res.: 341 N. Wisconsin Ave., Muscoda, 53573. Tel: 608-822-6425.
Catechesis/Religious Program—Students 13.
CLINTON, ROCK CO., ST. STEPHEN (1973) Rev. Sanctus K. Ibe.
Mailing Address: 716 Shular Ln., Box 399, 53525.
Res.: 714 Shular Ln., Box 399, 53525. Tel: 608-676-2241; Fax: 608-676-4981.
Catechesis/Religious Program—716 Shular Ln., 53525. Steve Zahn, D.R.E. Students 88.
CLYDE, DODGE CO., ST. MALACHY (1850) [CEM], (Linked with St. John the Baptist, Muscoda and St. Joseph, Avoca) Rev. Robert J. Butz, Admin.
Mailing Address: P.O. Box 35, Muscoda, 53573-0035. Tel: 608-739-3391; Fax: 608-739-9195.
Res.: 341 N. Wisconsin Ave., Muscoda, 53573.
Church: 5958 County Rd. N., Avoca, 53506.
COLUMBUS, COLUMBIA CO., ST. JEROME (1856) [CEM], (Linked with St. Patrick, Doylestown) Rev. Bruce M. Hennington; Deacon Timothy Byrnes.
Parish Office—1550 Farnham St., 53925. Tel: 920-623-3753; Fax: 920-623-1115. Email: columbussjp@straphael.org.
Res.: 329 Folsom St., 53925. Tel: 920-623-2720.
School—Tel: 920-623-5780. Lay Teachers 13; Students 165.
Catechesis/Religious Program—Students 127.
COTTAGE GROVE, DANE CO., ST. PATRICK (1882) [CEM] Rev. Msgr. Raymond N. Kertz.
Res.: 434 N. Main St., P.O. Box 400, 53527-0400. Tel: 608-251-7857; Fax: 608-839-3593. Email: info@st-patrick-parish.com. Web: www.st-patrick-parish.com.
Catechesis/Religious Program—Karen Meadowcroft, D.R.E.; Lenny Komorowski, Youth Min. Students 304.
CROSS PLAINS, DANE CO., ST. FRANCIS XAVIER (1853) [CEM] Rev. Thomas L. Kelley.
Res.: 2947 Thinnes St., 53528. Tel: 608-798-0800; Fax: 608-798-2976. Email: stfrancis@chorus.net.
School—2939 Thinnes St., 53528. Tel: 608-798-2422; Fax: 608-798-0898. Web: www.sfxschool-cp.org. Lay Teachers 17; Students 192.
Catechesis/Religious Program—Tel: 608-798-4824. Cindy Ballweg, C.R.E. Students 251.
CUBA CITY, GRANT CO., ST. ROSE OF LIMA, [CEM], (Linked with St. Patrick, Benton) Rev. David J. Flanagan.
Res.: 519 W. Roosevelt, 53807. Tel: 608-744-2010; Fax: 608-744-3709.
School—Tel: 608-744-2120; Fax: 608-744-8449. Dominican Sisters (Sinsinawa, WI) 1; Lay Teachers 10; Students 132.
Catechesis/Religious Program—Students 126.
DANE, DANE CO., ST. MICHAEL, [CEM], (Linked with St. Patrick, Lodi) Rev. Francisco Higuera.
Mailing Address: 109 S. Military Rd., 53529.
Res.: 515 Fair St., Lodi, 53555. Tel: 608-592-5711; Fax: 608-592-2078.
School—Tel: 608-848-5619. Lay Teachers 4; Religious Ed. Teachers 3; Students 27.
DARLINGTON, LAFAYETTE CO., HOLY ROSARY (1854) [CEM 2] Rev. Randy J. Budnar.
Mailing Address: 730 Wells St., 53530. Tel: 608-766-4059; Fax: 608-766-4059.
Res.: 104 E. Harriet St., 53530. Tel: 608-776-2251. Email: hrosary@centurytel.net. Web: www.holyrosarycatholicchurch.org.
School—744 Wells St., 53530. Tel: 608-776-3710. Email: hrschool@centurytel.net. Web: www.school-.holyrosarycatholicchurch.org. Diane Smith-Hole, Prin. Lay Teachers 5; Students 60.
Catechesis/Religious Program—Students 223.
DAYTON, GREEN CO., ST. JAMES, [CEM], (Linked with St. Mary of the Lourdes, Belleville) Rev. Kenneth J. Klink.
Res.: 221 Frederick St., P.O. Box 349, Belleville, 53508. Tel: 608-424-3681.
Catechesis/Religious Program—Students 17.
DE FOREST, DANE CO., ST. OLAF (1948) [CEM], (Linked with St. Joseph, East Bristol) Rev. Gary A. Wankerl.
Res.: 623 Jefferson St., 53532. Tel: 608-846-3812.
Catechesis/Religious Program—Tel: 608-846-5726. Paula Hill, D.R.E. Students 380.
DICKEYVILLE, GRANT CO., HOLY GHOST, [CEM], (Linked with Immaculate Conception, Kieler) Rev. Bernard E. Rott; Deacon Lawrence Tranel.
Res.: 305 W. Main St., 53808. Tel: 608-568-7519; Fax: 608-568-3872.
School—325 W. Main St. Tel: 608-568-7790; Fax: 608-568-3872. Rita Hesseling, Prin. Consolidated with Immaculate Conception, Kieler. Lay Teachers 11; Students 145.
Catechesis/Religious Program—Angela Snyder, D.R.E., (Grade School). Tel: 608-568-7925; Tina Tranel, D.R.E., (High School). Tel: 608-568-7530. Students 146.
DODGEVILLE, IOWA CO., ST. JOSEPH, [CEM 3] Rev. Paul Ugo Arinze.
Res.: 405 S. Dacotah St., 53533-1799. Tel: 608-930-3392; Fax: 608-930-1722. Email: sjoffice@charter.net. Web: stjoedodge.org.
School—305 E. Walnut St., 53533. Lay Teachers 12; Students 230.
Catechesis/Religious Program—Students 157.
DOYLESTOWN, COLUMBIA CO., ST. PATRICK (1865) [CEM], (Linked with St. Jerome, Columbus) Rev. Bruce M. Hennington.
Res.: N4085 Bruce St., P.O. Box 40, 53928. Tel: 920-992-3343; Fax: 920-623-1115. Email:

doylestownspp@straphael.org.
Catechesis/Religious Program—Students 51.

DURWARD'S GLEN, COLUMBIA CO., ST. CAMILLUS, [CEM] Closed. For inquiries for parish records contact the chancery.

EAST BRISTOL, DANE CO., ST. JOSEPH (1847) [CEM], (Linked with St. Olaf, De Forest) Rev. Gary A. Wankerl.
Res.: 623 Jefferson St., De Forest, 53532. Tel: 608-846-3812.
Catechesis/Religious Program—1935 Highway V, Sun Prairie, 53590. Students 116.

EDGERTON, ROCK CO., ST. JOSEPH, [CEM 2] Rev. David W. Timmerman.
Res.: 590 S. Saint Joseph's Cir., 53534-1243. Tel: 608-884-3038; Fax: 608-884-3298.
Catechesis/Religious Program—Tel: 608-884-6231. Students 174.

ELK GROVE, LAFAYETTE CO., ST. PETER, [CEM], (Linked with St. Matthew, Shullsburg and Our Lady of Hope, Seymour) Rev. James R. Lins (Retired).
Mailing Address: 344 N. Judgement St., Shullsburg, 53586.
Res.: RFD. 1, Shullsburg, 53586. Tel: 608-965-4518.

EVANSVILLE, ROCK CO., ST. PAUL (1906) [CEM], (Linked with St. Augustine, Footville) Rev. Kevin F. Dooley.
Office: 39 Garfield St., 53536-1110. Tel: 608-882-4138. Email: stpaulevans@sbcglobal.net.
Res.: 35 Garfield Ave., 53536. Tel: 608-882-0490.
Catechesis/Religious Program—Students 160.

FENNIMORE, GRANT CO., ST. MARY (1885) [CEM], (Linked with St. Lawrence O'Toole, Mt. Hope) Rev. George B. Horath; Deacon Patrick Jozefowicz.
Res.: 930 Jefferson St., 53809. Tel: 608-822-6425.
Catechesis/Religious Program—Tel: 608-822-3520. Students 131.

FOOTVILLE, ROCK CO., ST. AUGUSTINE (1869), (Linked with St. Paul, Evansville) Rev. Kevin F. Dooley.
Mailing Address: 280 Haberdale Dr., 53537-0325. Tel: 608-876-6252; Fax: 608-876-6252.
Res.: 35 Garfield Ave., Evansville, 53536. Tel: 608-882-0490; 608-882-4138 (Office); Fax: 608-882-0690.
Catechesis/Religious Program—Tel: 608-876-6311. Email: amazgr8z@ticon.net. Linked with St. Paul, Evansville. Students 56.

FORT ATKINSON, JEFFERSON CO., ST. JOSEPH (1884) [CEM] Rev. James M. Poster.
Mailing Address: 1660 Endl Blvd., 53538. Tel: 920-563-3029. Web: stjosephfort.org.
Res.: 1512 Dommo Dr., 53538.
School—1650 Endl Blvd., 53538. Fax: 920-563-3150. Email: dpodmolik@stjosephfort.org. Mr. David Podmolik, Prin. Lay Teachers 13; Students 154.
Catechesis/Religious Program—Lisa Meitzner, C.R.E. Students 201.

GLEN HAVEN, GRANT CO., ST. MARY HELP OF CHRISTIANS (1864) [CEM 2], (Linked with St. Charles Borromeo, Cassville) Rev. John Norder.
Res.: 605 E. Dewey St., Cassville, 53806. Tel: 608-725-5595; Fax: 608-725-2343.

GRATIOT, LAFAYETTE CO., ST. JOSEPH (1869) [CEM], (Linked with St. John, South Wayne) Rev. David A. Wanish.
Mailing Address: Box 75, Argyle, 53504.
Church: Box 76, Argyle, 53504. Tel: 608-543-3631.
Catechesis/Religious Program—Students 22.

GREEN LAKE, GREEN LAKE CO., OUR LADY OF THE LAKE (1908) Rev. Philip J. Krogman.
Res.: 530 Ruth St., P.O. Box 215, 54941. Tel: 920-294-6440; Fax: 920-294-6550.
Catechesis/Religious Program—Lawrence D. Behlen, D.R.E. Students 69.

HAZEL GREEN, GRANT CO., ST. FRANCIS DE SALES (1845) [CEM], (Linked with St. Joseph, Sinsinawa) Rev. Cyril O. Weisensel.
Parish Center: 2720 N. Percival St., 53811-9681. Tel: 608-854-2391. Email: stfrancisdesales@centurytel.net.
Catechesis/Religious Program—Students 274.

HIGHLAND, IOWA CO., SS. ANTHONY AND PHILIP, [CEM 2], (Linked with St. Thomas, Montfort) Rev. Kenneth J. Frisch.
Res.: 1023 Dodgeville St., P.O. Box 306, 53543. Tel: 608-929-7490; Fax: 608-929-7701. Email: solson@mhtc.net. Web: stsanthonyphilip.com.
Catechesis/Religious Program—Tel: 608-929-7701. Email: deggers@mhtc.net. Delores Eggers, D.R.E. Students 156.

HOLLANDALE, IOWA CO., ST. PATRICK (1844) [CEM], (Linked with Immaculate Conception, Blanchardville and Holy Redeemer, Perry) Rev. Michael R. Radowicz.
Res.: 601 Grover St., P.O. Box 37, 53544. Tel: 608-967-2344; Fax: 608-967-2344. Email: pastor@tcparishes.org.
Catechesis/Religious Program—Students 17.

JANESVILLE, ROCK CO.

1—ST. JOHN VIANNEY (1955) [JC] Rev. Randy J. Timmerman; Deacon John Houseman.
Res.: 1221 Clark St., 53545. Tel: 608-752-8708; Fax: 608-752-1970. Web: www.sjv.org.
School—1250 E. Racine St., 53545. Tel: 608-752-6802. Lay Teachers 19; Students 255.
Catechesis/Religious Program—1238 E. Racine St., 53545. Tel: 608-755-1476; Fax: 608-758-3321. Students 390.

2—NATIVITY OF ST. MARY (1876) [JC] Rev. Stephen Umhoefer; Deacon Steven Hayes.
Res.: 313 E. Wall St., 53545. Tel: 608-752-7861; Fax: 608-758-0720. Email: hrude@nativitymary.org. Web: www.nativitymary.org.
School—Tel: 608-754-5221. Lay Teachers 16; Students 157.
Catechesis/Religious Program— (Family Faith Formation) Students 72.

3—ST. PATRICK (1850) [JC] Rev. James G. Kuhn; Deacon John Houseman, Pastoral Assoc.
Res.: 315 Cherry St., 53548. Tel: 608-754-8193; Fax: 608-754-0357. Email: stpats@straphael.org. Web: www.stpats.org.
School—305 Lincoln St., 53548. Tel: 608-752-0321. Lay Teachers 7; Students 78.
Catechesis/Religious Program—Tel: 608-754-0531. Margaret Clark, D.R.E. Students 99.

4—ST. WILLIAM (1952) [JC] Rev. John R. Auby; Deacon Richard Fischer.
Res.: 1815 Ravine St., 53548. Tel: 608-755-5180; Fax: 608-755-5190. Email: stwill@charterinternet.net. Web: www.stwilliam.net.
School—1822 Ravine St., 53548. Tel: 608-755-5184; Fax: 608-755-5182. Lay Teachers 10; Students 171.
Catechesis/Religious Program—Tel: 608-755-5183. Email: religioused1822@charter.net. Jane Graves, D.R.E. Students 198.

JEFFERSON, JEFFERSON CO.

1—ST. JOHN THE BAPTIST (1859) [CEM], (Linked with St. Lawrence, Jefferson & St. Mary Help of Christians, Sullivan) Rev. Thomas J. Coyle.
Res.: 214 N. Sanborn Ave., 53549. Tel: 920-674-2025; Fax: 920-674-2521.
School—333 E. Church St., 53549. Tel: 920-674-5821. Web: www.stjohnbaptist.net. Lay Teachers 19; Students 190.
Catechesis/Religious Program—Tel: 920-674-5433. Email: stjohnsre@hotmail.com. Julie Endl, C.R.E.; Tiffany Topel, D.R.E. Students 196.

2—ST. LAWRENCE (1850) [CEM], (Linked with St. John the Baptist, Jefferson) Rev. Thomas J. Coyle.
Res.: W. 4975 Hwy. 18, 53549. Tel: 920-674-2822.
Catechesis/Religious Program—W. 4975 Hwy. 18, 53549. Students 80.

JOHNSON CREEK, JEFFERSON CO., ST. MARY MAGDALENE (1906) [CEM], (Linked with St. Francis Xavier, Lake Mills) Rev. Robert W. Hughes.
Res.: 242 Williams St., P.O. Box 202, 53038. Tel: 920-648-2468; Fax: 920-648-2468.
Catechesis/Religious Program—Tel: 920-699-2913. Carol Hunn, D.R.E. Students 73.

KIELER, GRANT CO., IMMACULATE CONCEPTION, [CEM], (Linked with Holy Ghost, Dickeyville) Rev. Bernard E. Rott, Admin.; Deacon Lawrence Tranel.
Res.: Box 57, 53812. Tel: 608-568-7530; Fax: 608-568-3811. Email: icparish@tds.net.
School—Tel: 608-568-7220. Rita Hesseling, Prin. Consolidated with Holy Ghost, Dickeyville. Lay Teachers 13; Students 171.
Catechesis/Religious Program—3685 County HHH. Twinned with Holy Ghost, Dickeyville. Students 70.

KINGSTON, GREENLAKE CO., ST. MARY (1876) [CEM], (Linked with St. Joseph, Markesan) Rev. John H. Hedrick, Admin.
Mailing Address: P.O. Box 370, Markesan, 53946-0370. Tel: 920-398-3146; Fax: 920-398-3147.
Catechesis/Religious Program— Twinned with St. Joseph, Markesan.

LA VALLE, SAUK CO., HOLY FAMILY (1917) [CEM 2], (Linked with St. Boniface, Lime Ridge and St. Patrick, Loreto) Rev. Lorin M. Bowens; Nora Durst, Pastoral Assoc.
Res.: 310 Bluff St., P.O. Box 166, 53941. Tel: 608-985-7558. Email: holyfamily@mwt.net.
Catechesis/Religious Program—Tel: 608-985-7915. Students 85.

LAKE MILLS, JEFFERSON CO., ST. FRANCIS XAVIER (1912), (Linked with St. Mary Magdalene, Johnson Creek) Rev. Robert W. Hughes.
Res.: 602 College St., 53551. Tel: 920-648-2468; Fax: 920-648-2468.
Catechesis/Religious Program—Tel: 920-648-2815. Students 161.

LANCASTER, GRANT CO., ST. CLEMENT (1859) [CEM 2] Rev. William J. Seipp.
Res.: 135 S. Washington St., 53813. Tel: 608-723-4990; Fax: 608-723-4012.
School—330 W. Maple St., 53813. Tel: 608-723-7474; Fax: 608-723-4424. Sisters 2; Lay Teachers 9; Students 119.
Catechesis/Religious Program—Tel: 608-723-7425. Kitty Mumm, D.R.E. Students 153.

LIME RIDGE, SAUK CO., ST. BONIFACE (1912) [CEM], (Linked with Holy Family, La Valle and St. Patrick, Loreto) Rev. Lorin M. Bowens.
Res.: 105 Church St., P.O. Box 60, 53942. Tel: 608-986-2101. Email: boniface@dwave.net.
Catechesis/Religious Program—Tel: 608-985-7915. Rebecca Steiner, D.R.E. (Elementary); Don Seep, D.R.E. (H.S.). Students 56.

LODI, COLUMBIA CO., ST. PATRICK (1857) [CEM], (Linked with St. Michael, Dane) Rev. Francisco Higuera.
521 Fair St., 53555. Tel: 608-592-5711.
Res.: 515 Fair St., 53555. Tel: 608-592-4510; Fax: 608-592-2078. Email: stpats1@verizon.net. Web: www.saintpatrickinlodi.org.
Catechesis/Religious Program—Tel: 608-592-5711. Randy Henderson, Youth Min.; Cynthia Fischer, D.R.E. Students 245.

LORETO, MANITOWOC CO., ST. PATRICK (1866), (Irish—German), [CEM 2], (Linked with Holy Family, LaValle and St. Boniface, Lime Ridge) Rev. Lorin M. Bowens.
Res.: 105 Church St., P.O. Box 60, Lime Ridge, 53942-0060. Tel: 608-986-2101.
Catechesis/Religious Program—E. 3460 McCarville Rd., Plain, 53577. Tel: 608-546-3159. Brenda Faber, D.R.E. Students 81.

MARKESAN, GREEN LAKE CO., ST. JOSEPH (1886), (Linked with St. Mary, Kingston) Rev. John H. Hedrick, Admin.
Res.: 45 St. Joseph St., P.O. Box 370, 53946-0370. Tel: 920-398-3146; Fax: 920-398-3147.
Catechesis/Religious Program— Roland Salter, D.R.E. Students 78.
Mission—St. Mary 177 W. Pearl St., Kingston, Green Lake Co. 53939.

MARSHALL, DANE CO., ST. MARY'S OF THE NATIVITY, [CEM], (Linked with St. Joseph, Waterloo) Rev. Thomas E. Gillespie.
Res.: P.O. Box 250, 53559-0250. Tel: 608-655-3708. Email: smjc@charter.net. Web: www.jefnet.com/sjcs.html.
Catechesis/Religious Program—Tel: 920-478-3232. Eileen Bender, D.R.E. Students 193.

MARTINSVILLE, DANE CO., ST. MARTIN OF TOURS (1850) [CEM], (Linked with St. Peter, Ashton) Rev. Eugene F. Hollfelder.
Res.: 5959 St. Martin Cir., Cross Plains, 53528-9312. Tel: 608-798-2815.
Catechesis/Religious Program—Tel: 608-798-2328. Linda Stafford, D.R.E. Students 98.

MAZOMANIE, DANE CO., ST. BARNABAS (1856) [CEM], (Linked with St. John the Baptist, Mill Creek) Rev. John Del Priore, S.J.S.
113 E. Division St., P.O. Box 68, 53560-0068. Tel: 608-795-9918. Email: parishstbarnabas@charter.net.
Res.: 115 Madison St., Sauk City, 53583. Tel: 608-643-2449.
Catechesis/Religious Program—Tel: 608-795-4321. Students 91.

MCFARLAND, DANE CO., CHRIST THE KING Rev. D. Stephen Smith.
Res.: 5306 Main St., P.O. Box 524, 53558. Tel: 608-838-9797; Fax: 608-838-6449. Email: ctk@myparish.com. Web: www.myparish.com.
Catechesis/Religious Program—Students 300.

MERRIMAC, SAUK CO., ST. MARY, HEALTH OF THE SICK (1948), (Linked with St. Aloysius, Sauk City.) Revs. Jared M. Hood, S.J.S. (Ecuador), Admin.; Faustino Ruiz, S.J.S. (Spain), Parochial Vicar.
231 Main St., P.O. Box 41, 53561.
Res.: 115 Madison St., Sauk City, 53583. Tel: 608-643-2449 (St. Aloysius); 608-742-3364 (Parish Sec.); Fax: 608-742-3364. Email: jmkrejchik@yahoo.com (Parish Sec.).
Catechesis/Religious Program—Students 10.

MIDDLETON, DANE CO., ST. BERNARD (1889) [CEM] Rev. Msgr. Douglas L. Dushack.
Res.: 2015 Parmenter St., P.O. Box 620187, 53562-0187. Tel: 608-831-6531; Fax: 608-831-8101. Email: parish@stbmidd.org. Web: www.stbmidd.org.
Catechesis/Religious Program—Students 540.

MILL CREEK, ST. JOHN THE BAPTIST, (Linked with St. Barnabas, Mazomanie) Revs. Jared M. Hood, S.J.S. (Ecuador); John Del Priore, S.J.S.
Res.: 113 E. Division St., Mazomanie, 53560. Tel: 608-795-4321.
Catechesis/Religious Program—Students 2.

MILTON, ROCK CO., ST. MARY (1891) [CEM] Rev. Msgr. James J. Uppena; Mary Therese Gallagher, Pastoral Assoc. Tel: 608-868-3339.
837 Parkview Dr., 53563. Tel: 608-868-3338; Fax: 608-868-3345. Web: saintmarymilton.org.
Res.: 836 Neumann Ct., 53563. Tel: 608-868-2338. Email: stmarys@centurytel.net.

Catechesis/Religious Program—Tel: 608-868-3336. Sabrina Elsen, Youth Min. Tel: 608-868-3334; Angela McNally, Coord. Liturgy & Music. Tel: 608-868-3335. Students 456.

MINERAL POINT, IOWA CO., CONGREGATION OF ST. MARY-ST. PAUL (1870) [JC 2] Rev. James W. Hinnen.
Res.: 224 Davis St., 53565. Tel: 608-987-2026; Fax: 608-987-3361.
Catechesis/Religious Program—Tel: 608-987-3361. Students 223.

MONROE, GREEN CO., ST. VICTOR, [CEM] Rev. Michael E. Klarer.
Res.: 1760 14th St., 53566. Tel: 608-325-9506; Fax: 608-325-3115. Email: parishcenter@stvictormonroe.org. Web: stvictormonroe.org.
School—Tel: 608-325-3395. Lay Teachers 21; Students 134.
Catechesis/Religious Program—Email: faithcoord@stvictormonroe.org. Students 186.

MONTELLO, MARQUETTE CO., ST. JOHN THE BAPTIST, [CEM], (Linked with Good Shepherd, Westfield) Rev. Michael C. Richel.
Res.: 277 E. Montello St., 53949. Tel: 608-297-2217. Email: sjgs@maqs.net.
Catechesis/Religious Program—Tel: 608-297-7423; Fax: 608-297-8047. Email: sjreled@maqs.net. Students 89.
Mission—Good Shepherd 241 E. 6th St., Westfield, Marquette Co. 53964. Tel: 608-296-3631; Fax: 608-296-2465.

MONTFORT, GRANT CO., ST. THOMAS (1925) [CEM], (Linked with SS. Anthony and Philip, Highland) Rev. Kenneth J. Frisch.
Res.: Box 68, 53569. Tel: 608-943-6944; Fax: 608-943-6944. Email: stthomas@mhtc.net.
Catechesis/Religious Program—Julie Hawes, D.R.E. Students 136.

MOUNT HOPE, GRANT CO., ST. LAWRENCE O'TOOLE (1884) [CEM], (Linked with St. Mary, Fennimore) Rev. George B. Horath.
Res.: 930 Jefferson St., Fennimore, 53809. Tel: 608-822-6425.

MOUNT HOREB, DANE CO., ST. IGNATIUS, [CEM], (Linked with St. Mary of Pine Bluff, Pine Bluff) Rev. Richard M. Heilman.
Mailing Address: 107 S. Seventh St., 53572-2050. Tel: 608-437-5195 (Office); Fax: 608-437-7691.
Res.: 3673 Cty. Tk. P, Cross Plains, 53528. Tel: 608-798-4644; Fax: 608-798-2112.
Catechesis/Religious Program—Tel: 608-437-5348. John Smith, C.R.E. Students 217.

MUSCODA, GRANT CO., ST. JOHN THE BAPTIST (1854) [CEM], (Linked with St. Joseph, Avoca and St. Malachy, Clyde) Rev. Robert J. Butz, Admin.
Res. & Church: 341 N. Wisconsin Ave., P.O. Box 35, 53573. Tel: 608-739-3391; Fax: 608-739-9195. Email: sjb@mwt.net.
Catechesis/Religious Program—Tel: 608-739-3429. Email: stjohnre@mwt.net. Students 65.

NESHKORO, MARQUETTE CO., ST. JAMES, [CEM], (Linked with St. John the Baptist, Princeton) Rev. Dale W. Grubba.
Res.: 1211 W. Main St., Princeton, 54968. Tel: 920-295-6209; Fax: 920-295-0231.
Church: 315 N. Main St., 54960. Tel: 920-293-4211; Fax: 920-293-4211.
Catechesis/Religious Program—Students 25.

OREGON, DANE CO., HOLY MOTHER OF CONSOLATION (1856) [CEM] Rev. William R. Connell.
Res.: 651 N. Main St., 53575. Tel: 608-835-5763; Fax: 608-835-5764. Email: hmoc@charter.net. Web: holymotherchurch.4lpi.com.
Catechesis/Religious Program—Tel: 608-835-5764. Students 626.

PALMYRA, JEFFERSON CO., ST. MARY (1911) [CEM], (Linked with St. Joseph, Fort Atkinson) Rev. James M. Poster.
Res.: 1512 Dommo Dr., Fort Atkinson, 53538. Tel: 920-397-7253.
Church: 919 W. Main St., P.O. Box P, 53156. Tel: 262-495-2395. Email: smarypal@ticon.net.
Catechesis/Religious Program—P.O. Box P, 53156. Tel: 262-495-2395. Sue Peplinksi, C.R.E. Students 22.

PAOLI, DANE CO., ST. WILLIAM, [CEM], (Merged with St. Andrew, Verona) Rev. William F. Vernon.
Res.: 301 N. Main St., Verona, 53593. Tel: 607-845-6613; Fax: 607-848-4293.

PARDEEVILLE, COLUMBIA CO., ST. MARY OF THE MOST HOLY ROSARY (1903), (Linked with St. Andrew, Buffalo) Rev. John H. Hedrick.
Res.: 318 S. Main St., 53954. Tel: 608-429-3030; Fax: 608-429-3129. Email: stmary@jvlnet.com. Web: stmary-standrew.net.
Catechesis/Religious Program—Kristine Radtke, D.R.E. Students 98.
Mission—St. Andrew N117 State Hwy. 22, Buffalo Twp., WI 53949.

PATCH GROVE, GRANT CO., ST. JOHN (1845) [CEM], (Linked with St. Mary, Bloomington) Rev. Bart D. Timmerman.
Res.: 535 Congress St., P.O. Box 35, Bloomington, 53804. Tel: 608-994-2526; Fax: 608-994-2530. Email: sunday7@grant.tds.net.
Catechesis/Religious Program— Twinned with St. Mary, Bloomington.

PERRY, HOLY REDEEMER (1859) [CEM], (Linked with St. Patrick, Hollandale and Immaculate Conception, Blanchardville) Rev. Michael R. Radowicz.
Res.: 601 Grover St., P.O. Box 37, Hollandale, 53544. Tel: 608-967-2344; Fax: 608-967-2344.
Catechesis/Religious Program—111 S. Sixth St., Mount Horeb, 53572. Tel: 608-437-5195; Fax: 608-437-7691.

PINE BLUFF, DANE CO., ST. MARY OF PINE BLUFF (1854) [CEM] [JC], (Linked with St. Ignatius, Mount Horeb) Rev. Richard M. Heilman.
Res. & Parish: 3673 County Road P, Cross Plains, 53528. Tel: 608-798-4644 (Rectory); 608-798-2115 (School); 608-798-2111 (Parish); Fax: 608-798-2112. Email: catholic@tds.net. Web: www.stmarypb.org.
Catechesis/Religious Program—Tel: 608-437-5348. Beth Ptak, C.R.E. (K-5); Steve Davies, C.R.E. (6-12). Students 36.

PLAIN, SAUK CO., ST. LUKE (1857), (German), [CEM 2] [JC 2], (Linked with St. John the Evangelist, Spring Green) Rev. Michael A. Resop; Sr. Lynne Marie Simonich, O.S.F., Pastoral Assoc.
Res.: 1240 Nachreiner Ave., 53577. Tel: 608-546-2482; Fax: 608-546-2616. Email: stlukesplain@charter.net.
School—Tel: 608-546-2963. Web: stlukecatholic-school.catholicweb.com. Lay Teachers 10; Students 96.
Catechesis/Religious Program— Angie Pulvermacher, C.R.E. Students 114.

PLATTEVILLE, GRANT CO.

1—ST. AUGUSTINE UNIVERSITY PARISH (1974), (Linked with St. Mary, Platteville) Rev. Msgr. O. Charles Schluter; Deacon William Bussan, Pastoral Min.
Res.: 130 W. Cedar St., 53818-2457. Tel: 608-348-9735; Fax: 608-348-9920.
Church: 135 S. Hickory St., 53818-3316. Tel: 608-348-7530; Fax: 608-348-7530. Email: thomasl@uwplatt.edu. Web: www.uwplatt.edu/org/catholicnc.
Catechesis/Religious Program—Students 37.

2—ST. MARY (1842), (Linked with St. Augustine University Parish, Platteville) Rev. Msgr. O. Charles Schluter.
Res.: 130 W. Cedar St., 53818-2457. Tel: 608-348-9735; Fax: 608-348-9920.
School—Tel: 608-348-5806; Fax: 608-348-7883. Lay Teachers 10; Students 119.
Catechesis/Religious Program—Students 216.

PORTAGE, COLUMBIA CO., ST. MARY OF THE IMMACULATE CONCEPTION, [CEM], (Linked with St. Mary Help of Christians, Briggsville) Rev. James H. Murphy; Deacon Dennis Sutter.
Mailing Address: 309 W. Cook St., P.O Box 216, 53901-0216.
Res.: 305 W. Cook St., P.O. Box 216, 53901-0216. Tel: 608-742-6998; Fax: 608-742-1039. Email: parish@stmaryotic.com. Web: www.stmaryotic.com.
School—315 W. Cook St., 53901. Tel: 608-742-4998. Email: jhahn@straphael.com. Lay Teachers 15; Students 134.
Catechesis/Religious Program—Sr. Anita Henning, D.R.E. Students 212.

POYNETTE, COLUMBIA CO., ST. THOMAS (1907) [JC], (Linked with St. Joseph, Rio) Rev. Raymond J. Dischler.
Res.: 655 S. Main, P.O. Box 310, 53955-0310. Tel: 608-635-4326.
Catechesis/Religious Program—651 S. Main St., 53955. Tel: 608-635-4326. Julie Cross, C.R.E.; Anna Niemeyer, C.R.E. Students 141.

PRINCETON, GREEN LAKE CO., ST. JOHN THE BAPTIST (1875) [CEM], (Linked with St. James, Neshkoro) Rev. Dale W. Grubba.
Res.: 1211 W. Main, 54968. Tel: 920-295-6209; Fax: 920-295-0231.
School—125 Church St., 54968. Tel: 920-295-3541; Fax: 920-295-0178. Web: stjohnprince.org. Lay Teachers 8; Students 86.
Catechesis/Religious Program—Students 12.

REEDSBURG, SAUK CO., SACRED HEART (1878) [CEM 3] Rev. Thomas J. Monaghan; Deacons Thomas Hale, Pastoral Assoc.; Ronald Pickar.
Res.: 852 8th St., 53959.
Church: 624 N. Willow St., 53959. Tel: 608-524-2412; Fax: 608-524-3831. Email: sheart@rucls.net. Web: www.sacred-heart-online.org.
School—(Grades PreK-8), 545 N. Oak St., 53959. Tel: 608-524-3611. Email: shs@rucls.net. Lay Teachers 8; Religious Ed. Teacher 1; Students 194.
Catechesis/Religious Program—Email: map@rucls.net. Mary Ann Polcyn, D.R.E. Students 280.

RIDGEWAY, IOWA CO., ST. BRIDGET (1850) [CEM] [JC], (Linked with Immaculate Conception, Barneveld) Rev. Peter Auer, S.O.L.T.
Res.: 803 W. Main St., 53582-9659. Tel: 608-514-9468.
Catechesis/Religious Program—
Mission—Immaculate Conception, Barneveld

RIO, COLUMBIA CO., ST. JOSEPH (1902) [CEM 2], (Linked with St. Thomas, Poynette) Rev. Raymond J. Dischler.
Res.: 655 S. Main St., P.O. Box 310, Poynette, 53955-0310. Tel: 608-635-4326.
Catechesis/Religious Program—514 Lincoln Ave., 53960. Tel: 920-992-5185. Janeen Wakeman, C.R.E. Students 32.

ROXBURY, DANE CO., ST. NORBERT (1846) [CEM] Revs. Miguel Galvez, S.J.S. (Spain); Faustino Ruiz, S.J.S. (Spain); Jared M. Hood, S.J.S. (Ecuador); John Del Priore, S.J.S.
Res.: 115 Madison St., Sauk City, 53583. Tel: 608-643-2449.
Church: 8944 County Rd. Y, Sauk City, 53583-9510. Tel: 608-643-3661.
Catechesis/Religious Program—Tel: 608-643-8108. Juanita Wipperfurth, C.R.E.; Ethel Kippley, C.R.E. Students 245.

SAUK CITY, SAUK CO., ST. ALOYSIUS (1845) [CEM 2] Revs. Jared M. Hood, S.J.S. (Ecuador), Admin.; Faustino Ruiz, S.J.S. (Spain), Parochial Vicar; Miguel Galvez, S.J.S. (Spain), Parochial Vicar; John Del Priore, S.J.S., Parochial Vicar; John Patrick Blewett, Parochial Vicar; Osvaldo Enrique Briones Cesped, Parochial Vicar; George Alexander Navarro Saenz, Parochial Vicar.
Res.: 115 Madison St., 53583. Tel: 608-643-2449; Fax: 608-643-2440. Web: www.saint-aloysius.org.
School—608 Oak St., 53583. Tel: 608-643-6868. Lay Teachers 16; Students 104.
Catechesis/Religious Program—Tel: 608-643-4062. John Ramthun, D.R.E.; Sarah Ramthun, D.R.E. Students 199.

SEYMOUR, LAFAYETTE CO., OUR LADY OF HOPE, [CEM] Unassigned. (Linked with St. Peter, Elk Grove and St. Matthew, Shullsburg)
Res.: 344 N. Judgement St., Shullsburg, 53586. Tel: 608-965-4518.

SHULLSBURG, LAFAYETTE CO., ST. MATTHEW (1835) [CEM 2] [JC 2] Unassigned. (Linked with St. Peter, Elk Grove and Our Lady of Hope, Seymour)
Res.: 344 Judgment St., 53586. Tel: 608-965-4518.
Catechesis/Religious Program—Students 130.

SINSINAWA, GRANT CO., ST. JOSEPH, [CEM 2], (Linked with St. Francis de Sales, Hazel Green) Rev. Cyril O. Weisensel.
780 County Hwy. Z, Hazel Green, 53811-9709. Tel: 608-748-4528.
Res.: 2630 N. Main St., Hazel Green, 53811. Tel: 608-748-4528.
Church: 780 CR Z, Hazel Green, 53811.
School—Tel: 608-748-4442. Lay Teachers 7; Students 76.
Catechesis/Religious Program—Students 25.

SOUTH WAYNE, LAFAYETTE CO., ST. JOHN (1898) [CEM], (Linked with St. Joseph, Gratiot) Rev. David A. Wanish.
Res.: 5695 Main St., Box 37, Gratiot, 53541. Tel: 608-543-3631.
Catechesis/Religious Program—Students 28.

SPRING GREEN, SAUK CO., ST. JOHN THE EVANGELIST, [CEM], (Linked with St. Luke, Plain) Rev. Michael A. Resop; Sr. Lynne Marie Simonich, O.S.F., Pastoral Assoc.
209 W. Daley St., 53588. Tel: 608-588-2028; Fax: 608-588-2648.
Office: 1240 Nachreiner Ave., Plain, 53577-0023. Tel: 608-546-2482; Fax: 608-546-2616.
School—P.O. Box 129, 53588. Tel: 608-588-2021; Fax: 608-588-9372. Lay Teachers 10; Students 72.
Catechesis/Religious Program—Tel: 608-546-6436; Fax: 608-588-9372. Angie Pulvermacher, D.R.E. Students 126.

STOUGHTON, DANE CO., ST. ANN, [CEM] Rev. Msgr. Gerard M. Healy.
Res.: 320 N. Harrison St., 53589. Tel: 608-873-7633; Fax: 608-873-6425. Email: weissco@stoughton.k12.wi.us. Web: stannparish.41pi.com.
School—Tel: 608-873-3343. Lay Teachers 13; Students 154.
Catechesis/Religious Program—Students 325.

SULLIVAN, JEFFERSON CO., ST. MARY HELP OF CHRISTIANS (1854) [CEM] Rev. Thomas J. Coyle.
Mailing Address: P.O. Box 418, 53178-0418. Tel: 920-593-2250. Email: smaryhoc@yahoo.com. Web: www.stmaryparishes.org.
Res.: 214 N. Sanborn Ave., Jefferson, 53549. Tel: 920-674-9619.
Catechesis/Religious Program—Tel: 262-593-2721. Edward Paloucek, D.R.E. Students 43.

SUN PRAIRIE, DANE CO.
1—ST. ALBERT THE GREAT Rev. Msgr. Terrence L. Connors; Deacon Joseph Stafford.
Res.: 2420 St. Albert Dr., 53590. Tel: 608-837-3798; Fax: 608-837-8576.
Catechesis/Religious Program—Susan Loet, D.R.E. Students 690.
2—SACRED HEARTS OF JESUS AND MARY, [CEM] Rev. Msgr. Duane R. Moellenberndt; Rev. Brian Dulli, Parochial Vicar; Sr. Anne Raymond Gasser, S.S.N.D., Pastoral Assoc.
221 Columbus St., 53590. Tel: 608-837-7381; Fax: 608-825-9585. Web: www.sacred-hearts.org.
Rectory—227 Columbus St., 53590.
School—219 Columbus St., 53590. Tel: 608-837-8508. Lay Teachers 30; Students 450.
Catechesis/Religious Program—Tel: 608-837-8509; Fax: 608-825-9585. Students 315.

TENNYSON-POTOSI, GRANT CO., SS. ANDREW AND THOMAS (1970) [CEM 2] Rev. Richard J. Leffler.
Res.: 101 Church St., Potosi, 53820. Tel: 608-763-2671. Web: www.ssandrew-thomas.org.
School—100 Hwy. 61 N., P.O. Box 160, Potosi, 53820. Tel: 608-763-2120; Fax: 608-763-4064. Lay Teachers 7; Students 79.
Catechesis/Religious Program—Tel: 608-763-2527 (1-8). Email: ssandrew@pcii.net. Beth Flesch, D.R.E. (1-8); Kathy Schink, D.R.E. (High School). Students 109.

TRUMAN, LAFAYETTE CO., IMMACULATE CONCEPTION (1856) [CEM], (Linked with St. Philomena, Belmont and St. Michael, Calamine) Rev. Monte E. Robinson.
Res.: 338 Chestnut St., Box 345, Belmont, 53510. Tel: 608-762-5446.

VERONA, DANE CO., ST. ANDREW (1917) [CEM], (Merged with St. William, Paoli) Rev. William F. Vernon.
Res.: 301 N. Main St., 53593. Tel: 608-845-6613; Fax: 608-848-4293. Web: www.standrewverona.4Lpi.com.
Catechesis/Religious Program—Ann Princl, D.R.E. Students 498.

WATERLOO, JEFFERSON CO., ST. JOSEPH (1868) [CEM], (Linked with St. Mary's of the Nativity, Marshall) Rev. Thomas E. Gillespie.
Res.: 205 W. Milwaukee Ave., 53594-1329. Tel: 920-478-2032. Email: smjc@charter.net. Web: www.jefnet.com/sjcs.html.
School—387 S. Monroe St., 53594. Tel: 920-478-3221. Lay Teachers 6; Students 94.
Catechesis/Religious Program—Tel: 920-478-3232. Eileen Bender, D.R.E. Students 95.

WATERTOWN, JEFFERSON CO.
1—ST. BERNARD (1843) Rev. Thomas P. Marr; Alan Reinhard, Parish Business Admin.
Res.: 114 S. Church St., 53094-4399. Tel: 920-261-5133; Fax: 920-261-8371. Email: church@stbern.org. Web: www.stbern.org.
School—Email: principal@st.bern.org. Lay Teachers 6; Students 151; Religious Ed. Teacher 1.
Catechesis/Religious Program—111 S. Montgomery St., 53094. Tel: 920-261-2582; Fax: 920-261-7215. Email: faithformation@stbern.org. Students 216.
2—ST. HENRY, [CEM] Rev. Brian J. Wilk.
Res.: 412 N. 4th St., 53094. Tel: 920-261-7273; Fax: 920-261-3681.
School—300 Cady St., 53094. Tel: 920-261-2586. Lay Teachers 12; Students 150.
Catechesis/Religious Program—Tel: 920-261-6332. Todd Weissenborn, D.R.E. Students 160.

WAUNAKEE, DANE CO., ST. JOHN THE BAPTIST (1874) [CEM] Rev. Msgr. James L. Gunn; Rev. Patrick Wendler, Parochial Vicar; Deacon Norbert Brunner.
Res.: 209 South St., 53597. Tel: 608-849-5121; Fax: 608-849-5866. Email: stjohnparishwau@shraphael.org. Web: www.stjb.org.
School—Tel: 608-849-5325; Fax: 608-849-5342. Email: cstark@straphael.org. Conni Stark, Prin. Lay Teachers 24; Students 218.
Catechesis/Religious Program— Paul Margala, C.R.E. Students 468.

WESTFIELD, MARQUETTE CO., GOOD SHEPHERD (1961), (Linked with St. John the Baptist, Montello) Rev. Michael C. Richel.
Res.: 277 E. Montello St., Montello, 53949. Tel: 608-296-2217.
Catechesis/Religious Program—241 E. 6th St., 53964. Tel: 608-296-3631; Fax: 608-296-2465. Darlene Duley, D.R.E. Students 76.

WESTPORT, DANE CO., ST. MARY OF THE LAKE (1866) [CEM] Rev. Daniel P. Finnane.
Res.: 5460 Mary Lake Rd., Waunakee, 53597-9121. Tel: 608-849-4116; Fax: 608-849-4122.
Catechesis/Religious Program—Tel: 608-849-4376. Mary Gartland, D.R.E. Students 80.

WISCONSIN DELLS, COLUMBIA CO., ST. CECILIA, [CEM] Rev. Msgr. Felix G. Oehrlein.
Res. & Office: 1612 Pleasant View Dr., 53965. Tel: 608-253-5107; 608-254-8381 (Office); Fax: 608-254-6217. Email: pastor@dellscatholic.com. Web: www.dellscatholic.com.
Church: 604 Oak St., 53965.
Catechesis/Religious Program—Tel: 608-253-5621. Students 211.

YELLOWSTONE, LAFAYETTE CO., ST. MICHAEL (1870) [CEM], (Linked with St. Joseph, Argyle) Rev. David A. Wanish.
Res.: 313 N. Lafayette St., P.O. Box 76, Argyle, 53504. Tel: 608-543-3631.

Chaplains of Public Institutions

MADISON. *Columbia County Institution*. Attended from St. Mary's Church, Portage.
Dane County Institution. Attended from St. Andrew, Verona.
Grant County Institution. Attended from St. Clement Church, Lancaster.
Green County Institution. Attended from St. Victor Church, Monroe.
Iowa County Institution. Attended from St. Joseph Church, Dodgeville.
Madison-Meriter General Hospital. Attended from St. Raphael Cathedral.
Mendota State Hospital. Vacant.
University Hospitals. Rev. Diego O. Cuevas, Chap. 340 N. Allen St., Apt. #23, 53726-3985.

JANESVILLE. *Jefferson County Institution*. Attended from St. John the Baptist Church, Jefferson.
LaFayette County Institution. Attended from Holy Rosary Church, Darlington.
Mercy Hospital. Attended from Janesville Parishes, Janesville.
Rock County Institution. Attended from Janesville Parishes, Janesville.
Sauk County Institution. Attended from St. Boniface Church, Lime Ridge.
Wisconsin State School for the Blind. Attended from St. Patrick's Church, Janesville.

Graduate Studies:
Rev.—
Schroeder, Tait C.

Leave of Absence:
Revs.—
Clauder, J. Gibbs
Vosen, Gerald P.

Military Chaplains:
Rev.—
Hesseling, Jason E.

Retired:
Rev. Msgrs.—
DeBock, William A., Bishop O'Connor Catholic Pastoral Center, 702 S. High Point Rd., P.O. Box 44983, 53744-4983.
Hastrich, George M., 501 Bram St., 53713.
Hebl, John H., W8595 Fern Rd., Oxford, 53952.
Higgins, Joseph P., 3424 Maple Grove Rd., 53719.
Schmelzer, Delbert L., 7575 Pioneer Pl., Verona, 53593.
Schuster, Wilfred J., Bishop O'Connor Catholic Pastoral Center, 702 S. High Point Rd., P.O. Box 44983, 53744-4983.
Revs.—
Borre, Robert J., 2000 Glenview Rd., Glenview, IL 60025-2850.
Buholzer, Robert E., 300 Silverado Dr., Apt. 204, Stoughton, 53589-5472.
Cassidy, Kevin W., P.O. Box 391, Mauston, 53948.
Conlon, Philip J., 306 Michael Ave., P.O. Box 326, Hollister, MO 65672.
Cox, Joseph C., 2515 Deerfield St., Portage, 53901-1081.
Deitelhoff, Bernard H., 204 Buell St., 53704.
Doheny, Thomas R., 1914 Woodsdale Dr., Durham, NC 27703.
Doherty, Patrick J.
Dominic, Francis J., 2029 Brennan Ct., Cuba City, 53807.
Fitzgerald, Thomas J., All Saints, 8210 Highview Dr., 53719.
Fox, George W., 8202 Highview Dr., Apt. 45, 53719.
Furlong, J. Daryl, 8887 Dwyer Ln., Galena, IL 61036.
Grasso, Philip A., SW Health Center Nursing Home, 808 S Washington St., Cuba City, 53807.
Hower, William J., 1870 Orchard Ln., Oshkosh, 54902.
Kalscheuer, Henry N., 1017 S. Holiday Dr., Waunakee, 53597.
Kieffer, Lawrence J., 4929 Whitcomb Dr., #6, 53711-2650.
Klink, Delbert D.
Lange, Donald F., Academy Apts., Academy Apts., #103, Hazel Green, 53811.
Lesniak, Richard D., 10002 14th Rd., Almond, 54909-9249.
McEnery, James G., 5001 N. Sherman Ave., 53704-1499.
Meier, Laverne G., Bishop O'Connor Pastoral Center, 702 S. Highpoint Rd., P.O. Box 44983, 53744-4983.
Murray, Donald J., 8541 Greenway Blvd., #302, Middleton, 53562.
Nolan, William A., 4007 Sandstone Dr., 53546.
Pickarts, Bernard J., River House, Co. Hwy. Y, #10126, Mazomanie, 53560.
Rank, Ronald G., 700 Rosewood Ave., Marshall, 53559.
Runde, David H., Bishop O'Connor Catholic Pastoral Center, 53719.
Runde, Raymond E.
Schmidt, Francis J., 1934 Dolores Dr., 53716.
Schroeder, Thomas H., Bishop O'Connor Catholic Pastoral Center, 702 S. High Point Rd., P.O. Box 44983, 53744-4983.
Schumacher, Anthony J., 2976 Chapel Valley, #103, 53711.
Steffen, Francis J., Academy Apts. #110, 511 Co. Rd. Z, Hazel Green, 53811.
Taylor, Roger H., Cannery Row, 800 S. Holiday Dr., #302, Waunakee, 53597.
Turner, Jerome R., 5711 N.E., Fox Glove Ln., Poulsbo, WA 98370-8934.
Urban, John L., W 5410 Urban Dr., Johnson Creek, 53038.

Permanent Deacons:
Deacons—
Brunner, Norbert, St. John the Baptist, Waunakee
Brush, Wesley, (Retired)
Buhman, Jerome, St. Maria Goretti, Madison
Bussan, William, St. Augustine Univ., Platteville
Byrnes, Timothy, St. Jerome, Columbus
Davis, James, St. Jude, Beloit
Fernan, John K., Our Lady Queen of Peace, Madison
Fischer, Richard, St. William, Janesville
Hale, Thomas, Sacred Heart, Reedsburg
Hayes, Steven, Nativity of Mary, Janesville
Hendrickson, David, St. Dennis, Madison
Houseman, John, St. Patrick, Janesville
Jozefowicz, Patrick, St. Mary, Fennimore
Kraus, John, (Retired)
Lukesic, Raymond, Cathedral Parish of St. Raphael, Madison
Martin, Richard, St. Maria Goretti, Madison
Martin, Todd, St. Peter, Madison
Pickar, Ronald, Sacred Heart, Reedsburg
Stack, William A., St. Joseph, Madison
Stafford, Joseph, St. Albert the Great, Sun Prairie
Sutter, Dennis, St. Mary of the Immaculate Conception, Portage
Tranel, Lawrence, Holy Ghost, Dickeyville

INSTITUTIONS LOCATED IN THE DIOCESE

[A] COLLEGES

MADISON. *Edgewood College*, 1000 Edgewood College Dr., 53711. Tel: 608-663-4861; Fax: 608-663-6722. Email: edtaylor@edgewood.edu. Web: www.edgewood.edu. Dr. Daniel Carey, Pres.; Mary Klink, Dir. College Ministries; Sr. Margaret Hopkins, O.P., Dir., Office of Dominican Mission; Stephen Bullock, College Ministries; Rev. Anthony J. Schumacher, Chap. (Retired). Dominican Sisters, Sinsinawa, WI. Sisters 9; Lay Teachers 245; Students 2,550.

[B] HIGH SCHOOLS, PRIVATE

MADISON. **St. Ambrose Academy*, 602 Everglade Dr., 53717. Tel: 608-827-5863; Fax: 608-833-1129. Email: info@ambroseacademy.org. Web: www.ambroseacademy.org. David Stiennon, Pres.; Scott Schmiesing, Prin. Lay Teachers 12; Students 56.
Edgewood High School of the Sacred Heart, 2219 Monroe St., 53711. Tel: 608-257-1023; Fax: 608-257-9133. Web: www.edgewoodhs.org. Judd T. Schemmel, Pres.; Mr. Robert Growney, Prin.; Kristin DeLorme, Librarian. Dominican Sisters, Sinsinawa. Lay Teachers 47; Students 661.

[C] ELEMENTARY SCHOOLS, PRIVATE

MADISON. *Edgewood Campus School*, 829 Edgewood College Dr., 53711. Tel: 608-663-4100; Fax: 608-663-4101. Web: www.campus-school.edgewood.edu. Sr. Kathleen Malone, O.P., Pres. & Prin.; Vikki Larson, Librarian. Dominican Sisters, Sinsinawa. Sisters 1; Lay Teachers 22; Students 313.

[D] GENERAL HOSPITALS

MADISON. *St. Mary's Hospital*, 700 S. Park St., 53715. Tel: 608-251-6100; Fax: 608-258-6731. Email: paula_mckenzie@ssmhc.com. Dr. Frank Bryne, M.D., Pres. Franciscan Sisters of Mary (St. Louis, MO)., Member of SSM Health Care. Sisters 2; Total Staff 2,785; Beds 440; Patients Assisted Annually 128,894.

Pastoral Care Department Chaplains: Rev. Gary Hein, Lutheran Min., Evangelical Lutheran Church of America; Sr. Mary Ann Ennis, O.P., Chap.; Rev. Leo Petrimoulx, O.F.M.Cap. (Retired); Rev. Ted Lindquist, Lutheran Min., Evangelical Lutheran Church of America; Sisters Mary Ellen Lewis, F.S.M., Chap. Emeritus; Pamela Moehring, S.S.N.D., Chap.; Clement Sabol, V.S.C., Chap.; Sandra Schmitz, O.P., Chap.; Rev. Janet Summers, United Church of Christ, Chap.; Liz Allen, Chap.; Paula McKenzie, Dir. of Pastoral Care.

BARABOO. *St. Clare Hospital and Health Services*, 707 14th St., 53913. Tel: 608-356-1400; Fax: 608-356-1367. Web: www.stclare.com. Sandra L. Anderson, Pres.; Mary Hess, M.T.S., Chap. Member of SSM Health Care. Bed Capacity 100; Patients Assisted Annually 98,543; Total Staff 477.

MONROE. **The Monroe Clinic, Inc.*, 515 22nd Ave., 53566. Tel: 608-324-1000; Fax: 608-324-1114. Email: mike.sanders@monroeclinic.org. Web: www.monroeclinic.org. Michael B. Sanders, Pres. & CEO; Rev. Msgr. Thomas F. Campion, Chap.; Julie Wilke, CFO, Vice Pres., Contact Person. Congregation of Sisters of St. Agnes. Bed Capacity 61; Nurses 245; Patients Assisted Annually 219,000; Total Staff 1,123.

PORTAGE. *Divine Savior Healthcare, Inc.*, 2817 New Pinery Rd., 53901. Tel: 608-742-4131; Fax: 608-742-6098. Email: mdnelson@dshealthcare.com. Web: dshealthcare.com. Mr. Michael Decker, Pres. & CEO; Levonne Tappa, Dir. Spiritual Care & Chap.; Monica Holden, Chap. Sisters of the Divine Savior. Sisters 2; Bed Capacity 52; Patients Assisted Annually 136,427; Total Staff 598.

[E] HOMES FOR THE AGED

MADISON. *St. Mary's Care Center*, 3401 Maple Grove Dr., 53719. Tel: 608-845-1000; Fax: 608-845-1001. William Bender, Admin.; Pam Norton, Contact Person. Member of SSM Health Care. Total Assisted 668; Total Staff 320; Bed Capacity 184.

BARABOO. *St. Clare Meadows Care Center*, 1414 Jefferson St., 53913. Tel: 608-356-4838; Fax: 608-356-5441. Web: www.stclare.com. Ronnie E. Schaetzl, Admin.; Linda Gamble, Contact Person. Member of SSM Health Care. Total Assisted 20; Total Staff 180; Bed Nursing Home 102.

JANESVILLE. *St. Elizabeth Home*, 109 S. Atwood Ave., 53545. Tel: 608-752-6709; Fax: 608-752-1724. Sr. Marie Julie Saegaert, S.C.M.C., Admin. Aged Residents 43; Bed Capacity 43; Total Assisted Annually 60; Total Staff 85.

PORTAGE. *Divine Savior Healthcare Extended Care*, 715 W. Pleasant St., P.O. Box 387, 53901-0387. Tel: 608-745-5900; Fax: 608-745-5997. Web: dshealthcare.com. (See Divine Savior Healthcare, Portage.) Aged Residents 100; Bed Capacity 110; Total Assisted Annually 247; Total Staff 131.

[F] MONASTERIES AND RESIDENCES OF PRIESTS

MADISON. *Bishop O'Connor Catholic Pastoral Center*, 702 S. High Point Rd., P.O. Box 44983, 53744-4983. Tel: 608-821-3000; Fax: 608-821-3013. Email: o'connorcenter@straphael.org. Web: www.madisondiocese.org. In Res. Most Revs. William H. Bullock, D.D., E.D.S. (Retired); George O. Wirz, D.D., S.T.L. (Retired); Rev. Msgrs. James R. Bartylla, Vocations Dir.; William A. DeBock (Retired); Daniel T. Ganshert; Delbert L. Schmelzer (Retired); Revs. James R. Lins (Retired); Laverne G. Meier (Retired); David H. Runde (Retired); Rev. Msgr. Wilfred J. Schuster (Retired); Revs. Tait C. Schroeder; Thomas H. Schroeder (Retired).

EDGERTON. *Koshkonong Pastoral Center*, 432 Liquori Rd., 53534. Tel: 608-884-3425; Fax: 608-884-9231. Revs. Eugene Gormley, L.C., Supr., Contact Person; Anthony Bailleres, L.C., Asst. to Provincial; Andres Martinez; Jose Felix Ortega, L.C., Sec.; Bros. John Coe, L.C.; Anthony Hale, L.C.; Joao Ricardo Macallo, L.C.; Hoa Nguyen, L.C.

[G] CONVENTS AND RESIDENCES FOR SISTERS

MADISON. *Franciscan Sisters of Mary, St. Joseph of the Lake Community*, 1012 Erin St., 53715-1841. Tel: 608-255-1510; Fax: 608-258-6731. Email: melpw@charter.net. Web: www.fsmonline.org. Sisters 2.

Secular Institute of Schoenstatt Sisters of Mary, 5901 Cottage Grove Rd., 53718-1397. Tel: 608-222-7208. Email: schoenstattheights@sbcglobal.net. Sr. Ellen Marie Baranek, Supr. Sisters 5.

BARABOO. *Franciscan Sisters of Mary*, 1021 Ash St., 53913-2163. Tel: 608-356-8641. Sr. Bridgid McNamara, F.S.M., Contact Person. Sisters 2.

BELOIT. *Blessed Sacrament Convent*, 916 Bluff St., 53511. Tel: 608-362-3326. Sr. Pauline Labrecque, A.B.S., Regl. Supr. Regional House of the Auxiliaries of the Blessed Sacrament. Sisters in Residence 4.

PRAIRIE DU SAC. *Valley of Our Lady Monastery* 53578-9737. Tel: 608-643-3520; 608-643-7986 (Altar Breads). Email: volocist@nunocist.org. Web: www.nunocist.org. Sr. M. Bernarda Seferovich, O.Cist., Prioress, Contact Person. Cistercian Nuns. Solemnly Professed 13; Temporal Professed 7.

SINSINAWA. *Dominican Motherhouse*, 585 County Rd. Z, 53824-9701. Tel: 608-748-4411; Fax: 608-748-4491. Email: spatmul@aol.com. Web: www.sinsinawa.org. Sisters Patricia Mulcahey, O.P., Prioress of the Congregation; Maryann Tranel, O.P., Sec. of the Congregation; Revs. John C. Risley, O.P., Chap.; John Gerlach, O.P., Chap.; Sisters Martha Alken, O.P., Prioress, St. Clara Community; Martha Mary Rohde, O.P., Prioress; Arturo Cranston, O.P., Prioress, St. Dominic Villa. Sinsinawa Dominican Congregation of the Most Holy Rosary. Sisters in the Congregation 595; Sisters 174; Dominican Novitiate: Novices 1.

[H] CHARITABLE INSTITUTIONS

MADISON. *Catholic Charities, Inc.* Diocese of Madison, *Administrative Center*, 702 S. High Point Rd., P.O. Box 46550, 53744-6550. Tel: 608-821-3100; Fax: 608-821-3125. Email: ccharities@ccmadison.org. Web: www.ccmadison.org. Brian A. Cain, Pres.

Central City Counseling Services, 30 S. Franklin St., 53703. Tel: 608-256-2358; Fax: 608-256-2350.

Janesville District Office, 2020 E. Milwaukee St., Janesville, 53545. Tel: 608-752-4906; Fax: 608-752-9699.

Yellowstone Office, 426 S. Yellowstone Dr., Ste. 100, 53719. Tel: 608-833-4800; Fax: 608-833-7897.

Saint Martin House Saint Martin House, 1862 Beld St., 53713. Tel: 608-661-3512, Ext. 200; Fax: 608-661-0363. Email: steve@cmctoday.org. Web: www.cmctoday.org. Rev. Msgr. George M. Hastrich, Spiritual Dir. (Retired); Steve Maurice, Coord.

Society of St. Vincent de Paul (District Council of Madison, Inc.), 1109 Jonathon Dr., 53713-3230. Tel: 608-278-2920; Fax: 608-278-2926. Email: svdpmad@svdpmadison.org. Web: www.svdpmadison.org. Norbert Rabholz, Council Pres.; Ralph B. Middlecamp, Exec. Dir.

BARABOO. *Society of St. Vincent de Paul (Diocesan Council of Madison)*, 408 8th St., 53913. Tel: 608-356-8549; Fax: 608-356-2018. Email: rlpl@centurytel.net. Roger LaMasney, Council Pres.

JEFFERSON. *St. Coletta of Wisconsin, Inc.*, W4955 Hwy. 18, 53549. Tel: 920-674-4330; Fax: 920-674-4603. Web: www.stcolettawi.org. Anthony LoDuca, Pres. & CEO; Andrea Speth, Vice Pres. Mktg. & Community Rels. Sponsored by the Sisters of St. Francis of Assisi. Milwaukee. Sisters 1; Brothers 1; Residents 271; Lay Staff 403.

[I] MISCELLANEOUS

MADISON. *All Saints Assisted Living Center, Inc.*, 702 S. High Point Rd., P.O. Box 46550, 53744-6550. Tel: 608-821-3100; Fax: 608-821-3125. Email: bcain@ccmadison.org. Web: www.ccmadison.org. Brian A. Cain, Sec. & Treas. Bed Capacity 58.

All Saints Retirement Center, Inc., 702 S. High Point Rd., P.O. Box 46550, 53744-6550. Tel: 608-821-3100; Fax: 608-821-3125. Email: bcain@ccmadison.org. Web: www.ccmadison.org. Brian A. Cain, Sec. & Treas. Purpose: To own, operate and maintain apartment homes for the aged in the tradition of the Roman Catholic Church, having a Catholic identity, and serving the physical, mental, emotional and spiritual needs of residents of the Diocese of Madison, Wisconsin. Bed Capacity 144.

The Catholic Diocese of Madison Foundation, Inc., 702 S. High Point Rd., P.O. Box 44983, 53744-4983. Tel: 608-821-3000; Fax: 608-821-3028. Rev. Msgr. Daniel T. Ganshert, Pres. Purpose: to operate at all times hereafter, exclusively for religious charitable and educational purposes within the meaning of 501(c)(3) of the Internal Revenue Code of 1986.....and to exclusively serve the Roman Catholic Diocese of Madison, its Bishop...

Edgewood Incorporated Edgewood College, 1000 Edgewood College Dr., 53711. Tel: 608-663-4861; Fax: 608-663-6722. Email: dcarey@edgewood.edu. Web: www.edgewood.edu. Dr. Daniel Carey, Pres. Sponsored by Sinsinawa Dominican Sisters of Sinsinawa, WI.; Purpose: The education of individuals in such subjects as usually taught in high schools, academies, and colleges.

**The Evangelical Catholic*, 723 State St., 53703. Tel: 608-258-3140, Ext. 107; Fax: 608-258-3141. Mr. Jason J. Simon, M.Div., Exec. Dir.; Mrs. Grace Simon, M.Div., Asoc. Dir.; Mrs. Katelin Cummins, Administrative Asst.

St. Marys Foundation, Inc., 700 S. Park St., 53715. Tel: 608-258-5600; Fax: 608-229-8495. Email: stmarys_foundation@ssmhc.com. Web: www.stmarysmadison.com. Carole Halberg, Contact Person & Exec. Dir.; Sarah E. Coyne, Contact Person & Attorney. Sponsored by the Franciscan Sisters of Mary., Purpose: To solicit, manage, invest and expend endowment funds and other gifts, grants and bequests primarily for the maintenance and benefit of St. Mary's Hospital and St. Mary's Care Center of Madison, WI; to support other medical research, educational or charitable programs or activities of St. Mary's in the Madison, WI area. Member of SSM Health Care.

St. Paul University Catholic Foundation, Inc., 723 State St., 53703-1087. Tel: 608-258-3140; Fax: 608-258-3141. Email: info@stpaulscc.org. Web: www.uwcatholic.org. Most Rev. Robert Charles Morlino, Ex-Officio Pres.; James Stangel, Treas.; Andrew Forecki, Sec.; Jason Strauss, Chm.; Rev. Eric H. Nielsen, Exec. Admin. Purpose: to own and maintain the property on which resides the St. Paul University Parish and St. Paul University Catholic Center. Total Staff 51. In Res. Scott Hackl, Dir. Devel.

San Damiano Friary, 4123 Monona Dr., 53716. Tel: 608-222-6238; Fax: 608-222-6766. Revs. Lester Bach, O.F.M.Cap. (Retired); Augustin Cops, O.F.M.Cap. (Retired); Rupert Dorn, O.F.M.Cap (Retired); Loran Miller, O.F.M.Cap. (Retired); Leo Petrimoulx, O.F.M.Cap. (Retired); William Frigo, O.F.M. Cap. (Retired); Perry McDonald, O.F.M. Cap. (Retired). Capuchin Order-Province of St. Joseph., House of Healing and Hospitality.

SSM Health Care of Wisconsin, Inc., 2901 Landmark Pl., Ste. 300, 53713. Tel: 608-258-6120; Fax: 608-258-6218. Email: msharrison@ssmhc.com. Mary Starmann-Harrison, CEO, Contact Person. Sponsored by: Franciscan Sisters of Mary., Purpose: To provide either directly or in conjunction with other persons or organizations health care, health education and related facilities and services. Member of SSM Health Care.

BARABOO. *St. Clare Health Care Foundation, Inc.*, 707 14th St., 53913. Tel: 608-356-1449; Fax: 608-356-1367. Email: keri_olson@ssmhc.com. Web: www.stclare.com. Keri Olson, Foundation Dir. Sponsored by The Franciscan Sisters of Mary., Purpose: to solicit, manage, invest and expend endowment funds and other gifts, grants and bequests primarily for the maintenance and benefit of St. Clare Hospital & Health Services and St. Clare Meadows Care Center of Baraboo, WI; to support other medical research, educational or charitable programs or activities in the Baraboo, Wisconsin Dells and Lake Delton, Wisconsin Area. Member SSM Health Care.

Saint Vincent de Paul Society-Baraboo (District Council of Baraboo), P.O. Box 233, 53913. Tel: 608-356-4649; Fax: 608-356-4430. Email: svdpbaraboo@centurytel.net. Tim Nolden, Gen. Mgr. Sponsored by: Saint Vincent de Paul Society., Purpose: To help the poor and needy in a Vincentian spirit and manner.

EDGERTON. *Oaklawn Academy*, 432 Liguori Rd., 53534. Tel: 608-884-3425; Fax: 608-884-8175. Email: oaklawnusa@aol.com. Web: www.oaklawnusa.com. Mr. Javier Valenzuela, Prin. & Contact Person.

Oaklawn Incorporated, 432 Liguori Rd., 53534. Tel: 608-884-3425; Fax: 608-884-8175. Email: oaklawnusa@aol.com. Web: www.oaklawnusa.com. Revs. Eugene Gormley, L.C., Chap.; Jose Felix Ortega, L.C., Sec.; Anthony Bailleres, L.C., Asst. to Provincial.

MONROE. **Monroe Clinic and Hospital Foundation, Inc.*, 515 22nd Ave., 53566. Deirdre E. Gruendler, Exec. Dir. Sponsored by Congregation of Sisters of St. Agnes (CSA)

PLATTEVILLE. *St. Augustine Newman Center* 135 S. Hickory, 53818-3316. Tel: 608-348-7530; Fax: 608-348-7530. Email: thomasl@uwplatt.edu. Web: www.uwplatt.edu/org/catholicnc. Rev. Msgr. O. Charles Schluter. Please refer to St. Augustine University Parish, Platteville. Priests 1; Total Assisted 300; Total Staff 3.

130 W. Cedar St., 53818-2457. Tel: 608-348-9735; Fax: 608-348-9920. Email: thomasl@uwplatt.edu.

PRAIRIE DU SAC. *Society of Saint Vincent de Paul, Sauk-Prairie/Roxbury Area*, 815 19th St., 53578.

Tel: 608-643-8905; Fax: 608-643-8905. Email: stvdpmanager@verizon.net. Matt Murphy, Pres. Sponsored by: Saint Vincent de Paul Society., Purpose: To help the poor and needy in a Vincentian spirit and manner.

SINSINAWA. *Mother Samuel Coughlin Charitable Trust,* 585 County Rd. Z, 53824-9701. Tel: 608-748-4411; Fax: 608-748-5501. Email: spatmul@aol.com. Web: www.sinsinawa.org. Sr. Jane Boland, O.P., Contact Person. Sponsored by: Sinsinawa Dominicans., Purpose: To provide financial support to the aged, infirm or disabled vowed members of the Sinsinawa Dominicans.

Sinsinawa Housing, Inc., 585 County Rd. Z, 53824-9701. Tel: 608-748-4411; Fax: 608-748-4491. Email: spatmul@aol.com. Web: www.sinsinawa.org. Sr. Maryann Tranel, O.P., Sec. of the Congregation. Sponsored by the Sinsinawa Dominicans., Purpose: To provide low- to moderate-income housing for senior residents of southwestern Wisconsin.

Sinsinawa Nursing, Inc., 585 County Rd. Z, 53824-9701. Tel: 608-748-4411; Fax: 608-748-4491. Email: spatmul@aol.com. Web: www.sinsinawa.org. Sr. Maryann Tranel, O.P., Sec. of the Congregation. Sponsored by the Sinsinawa Dominicans., To organize, construct, operate and maintain a care center in southwestern Wisconsin for the elderly and infirm.

[J] CLOSED/MERGED PARISHES

Madison Diocesan Archives, 702 S. High Point Rd., P.O. Box 44983, 53744-4983. Tel: 608-821-3140. As the location of sacramental records can change periodically, inquiries for records of parishes on this list should be directed to Madison Diocesan Archives.

Holy Redeemer, Madison Merged. Parish records located at St. Raphael Cathedral Parish, Madison.

Our Lady of Guadalupe, Endeavor Closed. Parish records located at Archives, Diocese of Madison.

Queen of Americas, Cambria Closed. Parish records located at St. Mary, Pardeeville.

St. Andrew, Tennyson Merged. Parish records located at SS. Andrew and Thomas, Potosi.

St. Anthony, Highland Merged. Parish records located at SS. Anthony and Philip, Highland.

St. Camillus, Durward's Glen Closed. Parish records located at St. Mary, Health of the Sick, Merrimac.

St. Francis Xavier, Adams Closed. Parish records located at St. Joseph, Argyle & St. Victor, Monroe.

St. James, Vermont Closed. Parish records located at St. Mary, Pine Bluff.

St. John the Baptist, Union Mills Closed. Parish records located at St. Joseph, Dodgeville.

St. Joseph, Berlin Closed. Parish records located at All Saints, Berlin.

St. Mary, Mineral Point Merged. Parish records located at Cong. of St. Mary's/St. Paul's, Mineral Point.

St. Mary, Monroe Closed. Parish records located at St. Victor, Monroe.

St. Michael, Berlin Merged. Parish records located at All Saints, Berlin.

St. Patrick, Madison Merged. Parish records located at St. Raphael Cathedral Parish, Madison.

St. Patrick, Princeton Closed. Parish records located at St. James, Neshkoro.

St. Paul, Beloit Closed. Parish records located at St. Thomas the Apostle, Beloit.

St. Paul, Mineral Point Merged. Parish records located at Cong. of St. Mary's/St. Paul's, Mineral Point.

SS. Peter & Paul, Pleasant Ridge Closed. Parish records located at St. Joseph, Dodgeville.

St. Philip, Highland Merged. Parish records located at SS. Anthony & Philip, Highland.

St. Raphael Cathedral, Madison Merged. Parish records located at St. Raphael Cathedral Parish, Madison.

St. Stanislaus Kostka, Berlin Merged. Parish records located at All Saints, Berlin.

St. Thomas, Potosi Merged. Parish records located at SS. Andrew and Thomas, Potosi.

RELIGIOUS INSTITUTES OF MEN REPRESENTED IN THE DIOCESE

For further details refer to the corresponding bracketed number in the Religious Institutes of Men or Women section.

[0470]—*The Capuchin Fathers*—O.F.M.Cap.

[0730]—*Legionaries of Christ*—L.C.

[0430]—*Order of Preachers-Dominicans* (Prov. of St. Albert the Great)—O.P.

RELIGIOUS INSTITUTES OF WOMEN REPRESENTED IN THE DIOCESE

[]—*Auxiliaries of the Blessed Sacrament*—A.B.S.

[0230]—*Benedictine Sisters of Pontifical Jurisdiction* (Yorktown, Watertown, SD)—O.S.B.

[3710]—*Congregation of the Sisters of Saint Agnes*—C.S.A.

[1070-03]—*Dominican Sisters*—O.P.

[1070-09]—*Dominican Sisters*—O.P.

[1230]—*Franciscan Sisters of Christian Charity*—O.S.F.

[1415]—*Franciscan Sisters of Mary*—F.S.M.

[2575]—*Institute of the Sisters of Mercy of the Americas*—R.S.M.

[2970]—*School Sisters of Notre Dame*—S.S.N.D.

[1680]—*School Sisters of St. Francis*—O.S.F.

[]—*Secular Institute of Schoenstatt Sisters of Mary*

[3020]—*Sisters Oblates to the Blessed Trinity*—O.B.T.

[0530]—*Sisters of Charity of Our Lady, Mother of the Church*—S.C.M.C.

[3930]—*Sisters of St. Joseph of the Third Order of St. Francis* (Prov. of St. Joseph)—S.S.J.-T.O.S.F.

[1030]—*Sisters of the Divine Savior*—S.D.S.

[1705]—*Sisters of the Third Order of St. Francis of Assisi*—O.S.F.

DEPARTMENT OF CEMETERIES DIOCESE OF MADISON

MADISON. *Resurrection Cemetery,* 2705 Regent St., 53705. Tel: 608-238-5561; Fax: 608-238-5768.

BELOIT. *Calvary Cemetery,* Mailing Address: P.O. Box 1944, Janesville, 53548. Tel: 608-754-3472; Fax: 608-744-8715.

Mount Thabor Cemetery, P.O. Box 1944, Janesville, 53547-1944. Tel: 608-754-3472; Fax: 608-741-8715.

JANESVILLE. *Mount Olivet Cemetery,* P.O. Box 1944, 53547-1944. Tel: 608-754-3472; Fax: 608-744-8715.

NECROLOGY

† Dietzel, Rev. Msgr. Elmer J., (Retired)—Died Oct. 27, 2009

† Koth, Arthur R., (Retired)—Died Nov. 11, 2009

An asterisk (*) denotes an organization that has established tax-exempt status directly with the IRS and is not covered by the USCCB Group Ruling.

Diocese of Manchester

(Dioecesis Manchesteriensis)

Most Reverend

JOHN B. McCORMACK, D.D.

Bishop of Manchester; ordained February 2, 1960; consecrated December 27, 1995; installed September 22, 1998. *Res.: Trudel House, 657 N. River Rd., Manchester, NH 03104.*

Most Reverend

ODORE J. GENDRON, D.D.

Retired Bishop of Manchester; ordained May 31, 1947; appointed December 12, 1974; consecrated February 3, 1975. *Mailing Address: P.O. Box 310, Manchester, NH 03105-0310.*

Chancery Office: 153 Ash St., P.O. Box 310, Manchester, NH 03105. Tel: 603-669-3100; Fax: 603-669-0377.

Web: www.catholicnh.org

Email: webmaster@rcbm.org

Most Reverend

FRANCIS J. CHRISTIAN, PH.D.

Auxiliary Bishop of Manchester; ordained June 29, 1968; appointed April 2, 1996; consecrated May 14, 1996. *Res.: St. Joseph Cathedral, 145 Lowell St., Manchester, NH 03104-6135.*

ESTABLISHED 1884.

Square Miles 9,305.

Comprises the State of New Hampshire.

For legal titles of parishes and diocesan institutions, consult the Chancery Office.

STATISTICAL OVERVIEW

Personnel	
Bishop	1
Auxiliary Bishops	1
Retired Bishops	2
Abbots	1
Priests: Diocesan Active in Diocese	91
Priests: Diocesan Active Outside Diocese	7
Priests: Retired, Sick or Absent	90
Number of Diocesan Priests	188
Religious Priests in Diocese	59
Total Priests in Diocese	247
Extern Priests in Diocese	31
Ordinations:	
Diocesan Priests	2
Permanent Deacons in Diocese	55
Total Brothers	18
Total Sisters	439
Parishes	
Parishes	98
With Resident Pastor:	
Resident Diocesan Priests	86
Resident Religious Priests	12
Missions	14
New Parishes Created	3
Closed Parishes	7
Welfare	
Catholic Hospitals	2
Total Assisted	433,644
Homes for the Aged	9
Total Assisted	1,150
Residential Care of Children	2
Total Assisted	45
Special Centers for Social Services	11
Total Assisted	69,000
Educational	
Diocesan Students in Other Seminaries	7
Total Seminarians	7
Colleges and Universities	4
Total Students	4,338
High Schools, Diocesan and Parish	3
Total Students	1,454
High Schools, Private	2
Total Students	901
Elementary Schools, Diocesan and Parish	20
Total Students	3,956
Elementary Schools, Private	5
Total Students	816
Catechesis/Religious Education:	
High School Students	4,602
Elementary Students	10,816
Total Students under Catholic Instruction	26,890
Teachers in the Diocese:	
Sisters	11
Lay Teachers	391
Vital Statistics	
Receptions into the Church:	
Infant Baptism Totals	2,584
Minor Baptism Totals	120
Adult Baptism Totals	94
Received into Full Communion	271
First Communions	3,341
Confirmations	2,645
Marriages:	
Catholic	403
Interfaith	114
Total Marriages	517
Deaths	2,697
Total Catholic Population	309,987
Total Population	1,315,809

Former Bishops—Rt. Revs. DENIS M. BRADLEY, D.D., ord. June 3, 1871; first Bishop of Manchester; cons. June 11, 1884; died Dec. 13, 1903; JOHN B. DELANY, D.D., ord. May 23, 1891; cons. Sept. 8, 1904; died June 11, 1906; Most Revs. GEORGE ALBERT GUERTIN, D.D., cons. March 19, 1907; died Aug. 6, 1931; JOHN B. PETERSON, D.D., cons. Auxiliary Bishop of Boston, Nov. 10, 1927; transferred to See, May 13, 1932; died March 15, 1944; MATTHEW F. BRADY, D.D., cons. Oct. 26, 1938; transferred to See, Nov. 11, 1944; died Sept. 20, 1959; ERNEST J. PRIMEAU, S.T.D., appt. Nov. 27, 1959; resigned Jan. 30, 1974; died June 15, 1989; ODORE J. GENDRON, D.D. (Retired), ord. May 31, 1947; appt. Dec. 12, 1974; cons. Feb. 3, 1975; retired June 12, 1990; LEO E. O'NEIL, D.D., ord. June 4, 1955; appt. Coadjutor Oct. 17, 1989; succeeded to See June 12, 1990; died Nov. 30, 1997.

Vicar General—Most Rev. FRANCIS J. CHRISTIAN, Ph.D., D.D., 153 Ash St., P.O. Box 310, Manchester, 03105-0310. Tel: 603-669-3100.

Vicar for Priest Personnel—Most Rev. FRANCIS J. CHRISTIAN, Ph.D., D.D.

Vicar for Clergy—Rev. RICHARD B. THOMPSON.

Office of the Permanent Diaconate—Deacon ARNOLD J. GUSTAFSON, Dir.

Institutional Ministries Office—Rev. RICHARD B. THOMPSON.

Vicars Forane—Rev. Msgr. JOHN P. QUINN, V.F.; Very Revs. MARK E. DOLLARD, V.F.; DENNIS J. AUDET, V.F.; DANIEL O. LAMOTHE, V.F.; FREDERICK J. PENNETT JR., V.F.; MICHAEL KERPER, V.F.; AGAPIT H. JEAN JR., V.F.; WILLIAM V. KALIYADAN, M.S., V.F.; RICHARD A. ROBERGE, V.F.

Moderator of the Curia—Rev. ROBERT E. GORSKI.

Propagation of the Faith—Rev. ROBERT E. GORSKI, Dir.

Manchester Mission—CLAIRE AUCOIN, R.N., Dir., Hogarel Buen Samaritano, Calle #20, 6-35, Cartago Valle, Colombia.

Canonical Services and Tribunal—153 Ash St., P.O. Box 310, Manchester, 03105-0310. Tel: 603-669-3101; Fax: 603-669-3102. Mrs. WINIFRED McGRATH, Dir. Canonical Svcs.

Judicial Vicar—Rev. Msgr. DONALD J. GILBERT, J.C.L.

Promoter of Justice—Rev. Msgr. PAUL L. BOUCHARD, S.T.L., J.C.L.

Advocates—Revs. ROGER H. CROTEAU; MICHAEL E. GENDRON; Very Rev. MICHAEL KERPER, V.F.; Rev. ANDRE M. THIBODEAU (Retired).

Defender of the Bond—Rev. Msgr. PAUL L. BOUCHARD, S.T.L., J.C.L.

Diocesan Judges—Revs. FRANCIS L. DEMERS, O.M.I., J.C.D.; JOHN J. MAHONEY JR., J.C.L.; MICHAEL S. TAYLOR, J.C.L.; Rev. Msgr. DONALD J. GILBERT, J.C.L.; Mrs. WINIFRED McGRATH.

Auditors—Rev. JOHN W. FLEMING; JANE COSMO.

Notaries—CHRISTINE MARRA; SHIRLEY PEDRICK; MONIQUE KAMINSKI.

Experts—TOM KELLEY; Dr. DAVID CORRISS.

Presbyteral Council—Most Rev. JOHN B. McCORMACK, D.D., Pres.; Rev. GERALD R. BELANGER; Most Rev. FRANCIS J. CHRISTIAN, Ph.D., D.D.; Rev. Msgr. PAUL L. BOUCHARD, S.T.L., J.C.L.; Revs. PAUL B. BOUDREAU JR.; ROBERT F. COLE; EDWARD J. KELLEY (Retired); DAVID L. KNEELAND; DAVID STEFFY, L.C.; C. PETER DUMONT; Rev. Msgrs. JOHN E. MOLAN, P.A. (Retired); JOHN P. QUINN, V.F.; Revs. ROBERT E. GORSKI, Vice Chm.; RAYMOND J. POTVIN; ROBERT G. BIRON; Very Rev. PETER J. GUERIN, O.S.B.; Rev. CHARLES E. DESRUISSEAUX (Retired); Rev. Msgr. THOMAS J. HANNIGAN (Retired); Revs. RICHARD J. KELLEY; RICHARD B. THOMPSON; JOHN B. MACKENZIE; JOHN W. MICHALOWSKI, S.J.; ANSELM SMEDILE, O.S.B.

College of Consultors—Most Rev. FRANCIS J. CHRISTIAN, Ph.D., D.D.; Revs. GERALD R. BELANGER; ROBERT G. BIRON; PAUL B. BOUDREAU JR.; CHARLES E. DESRUISSEAUX (Retired); C. PETER DUMONT; ROBERT E. GORSKI; Rev. Msgrs. JOHN E. MOLAN, P.A. (Retired); JOHN P. QUINN, V.F.; Rev. RICHARD B. THOMPSON.

Pastoral Council—Most Revs. JOHN B. MCCORMACK, D.D., Pres.; FRANCIS J. CHRISTIAN, Ph.D., D.D., Ex Officio; Sr. MARY ELIZABETH WHALEN, S.N.D.deN.; NICHOLAS BOUDREAU; Rev. THOMAS L. DUSTON; JOSEPH M. HORTON; CINDY OSSOLA; Deacon JAMES E. PATTERSON; INNOCENTUS ALHAMIS; Ms. JO-ANN M. ELLISON; Mr. RONALD CORMIER; Mr. DANIEL TAYLOR; Mr. RICHARD FORCE; Mr. THOMAS LACASCE; Ms. KARLEEN S. DELL'OVA; Mr. JOHN NATALE, Chm.; Mr. LAM TRAN; Mr. WILLIAM WHEELER; Mrs. GLORIA SCHRAUD; Mrs. PAULA A. SMITH.

Finance Council—Most Rev. JOHN B. MCCORMACK, D.D., Chm.; Mr. ALBERT ROMERO, Vice Chm.; Mr. HAROLD ACRES; Rev. JOHN W. FLEMING; Mr. WILLIAM GILES; Mr. STEPHEN J. KANEB; Mr. STEVEN R. MCMANIS; Mr. THOMAS F. PARKS; Mr. RONALD J. RIOUX; Mr. FRANK TOTH; Mr. GUY D. CHAPDELAINE, CPA, Staff.

Diocesan Review Board—Mr. RODNEY H. FOREY; Mr. MARCEL DURETTE; Ms. CAROL J. FURLONG, L.C.M.H.C., M.A.C., M.B.A., Chm.; Rev. Msgr. DONALD J. GILBERT, J.C.L.; Ms. TINA MARIE LEGERE, L.I.C.S.W., M.B.A., C.H.E.; Ms. CHRISTINE O. TREMBLAY; Mr. MARK ATTORRI.

Safe Environment Council—Mr. LOUIS BABIN; Sr. ELIZABETH ROY, C.S.C.; Mrs. TAMMY SAXTON; Ms. PATRICIA BRITTAN; Mr. LEO HART; Mr. BRIAN J. LOANES; Ms. SU MCKINNON, M.Ed.; Ms. DORIS BOUTIN-CYR; Mrs. NANCY WILMOT.

Long Range Planning Committee—Very Rev. DENNIS J. AUDET, V.F.; Deacon LEON E. ABBOTT JR.; Rev. C. PETER DUMONT; AUSTIN FRAIN; Rev. ROBERT E. GORSKI; PAUL F. HARRINGTON; JANET LEROUX; Mr. RONALD J. RIOUX; PATRICK F. MCGEE, A.P.R.

Priest Personnel Board—Most Rev. FRANCIS J. CHRISTIAN, Ph.D., D.D., Chm.; Revs. RICHARD B. THOMPSON, Ex Officio; ROBERT E. GORSKI, Ex Officio; ROBERT G. BIRON; Very Revs. DENNIS J. AUDET, V.F.; RICHARD A. ROBERGE, V.F.; Revs. JEFFREY P. STATZ; GERALD R. BELANGER; ROBERT F. COLE; RICHARD E. ST. LOUIS JR.; ALBERT J. TREMBLAY JR.; Rev. Msgr. JOHN P. QUINN, V.F.

Masters of Ceremonies—Rev. JASON Y. JALBERT. Email: jjalbert@rcbm.org; Mr. ANTHONY J. HALEY. Email: thaley@rcbm.org.

Cabinet Secretary for Evangelization and Education—Sr. MARY ELIZABETH WHALEN, S.N.D.deN. Email: mwhalen@rcbm.org.

Cabinet Secretary for Human Services—THOMAS E. BLONSKI. Email: tblonski@nh-cc.org.

Cabinet Secretary for Administration and Community Affairs—DIANE MURPHY QUINLAN ESQ. Email: dquinlan@rcbm.org.

Cabinet Secretary for Ministry Formation—Very Rev. DENNIS J. AUDET, V.F. Email: daudet@rcbm.org.

Cabinet Secretary for Communication, Planning, and Development—PATRICK F. MCGEE, A.P.R. Email: pmcgee@rcbm.org.

Cabinet Secretary for Real Estate—PAUL F. HARRINGTON. Email: pharrington@rcbm.org.

Chancellor—DIANE MURPHY QUINLAN ESQ., 153 Ash St., P.O. Box 310, Manchester, 03105-0310. Tel: 603-669-3100. Email: dquinlan@rcbm.org.

Secretary to Bishop—LOUANN BRAMANTE. Email: lbramante@rcbm.org.

Secretary to the Auxiliary Bishop—FRANCEEN M. MORASSE. Email: fmorasse@rcbm.org.

Secretariat for Evangelization and Education—Sr. MARY ELIZABETH WHALEN, S.N.D.deN. Email: mwhalen@rcbm.org.

Liaison for Religious Congregations—Sr. MARY ELIZABETH WHALEN, S.N.D.deN., Dir. Email: mwhalen@rcbm.org.

Department of Catholic Schools—MARY MORAN, Supt. Email: mmoran@rcbm.org; GRACE CAVALLO, Asst. Supt. Email: gcavallo@rcbm.org.

Education and Formation of Laity—PATRICIA GABREE, Exec. Dir. Email: pgabree@rcbm.org.

Sacrament of Matrimony Ministry—PATRICIA GABREE, Dir.

Office of Catechetical Formation—MARY ELLEN MAHON, Dir. Email: memahon@rcbm.org.

Office of Youth Ministry—Mr. SHAWN GREGORY.

Catholic Scouting—Rev. RAYMOND A. BALL, Dir.

Catholic Youth Organization Office—CHARLES COOK, Dir.

Office of the Catechumenate and Outreach to Inactive Catholics—EILEEN SMITH, Dir.

Charismatic Renewal—NANCY PARE, Contact.

Cursillo—Mr. DONALD HAMANN, Lay Dir. Tel: 603-332-2977. Co Spiritual Dir.: Revs. PAUL D. MONTMINY. Tel: 603-622-4966; RICHARD E. ST. LOUIS JR. Tel: 603-863-1422.

Diocesan Camps—Mr. GUS PLANCHET, Dir.; MICHAEL DRUMM, Dir. Mktg. & Devel., P.O. Box 206, Gilmanton Iron Works, 03837-0206. Tel: 603-364-5851; Fax: 603-364-5038.

Pastoral Ministry—Sr. MARY ELIZABETH WHALEN, S.N.D.deN., Dir. Email: mwhalen@rcbm.org.

NH Diocesan Council of Catholic Women—EILEEN SMITH; MARILYN AUDET, Pres.

Lay Ministry Formation Commission—Dr. JACQUELINE MARA, Chm.; Deacon PAUL R. BOUCHER; Most Rev. FRANCIS J. CHRISTIAN, Ph.D., D.D.; Mr. RAYMOND J. BILODEAU; Deacon MARK F. HOBSON; Rev. STEVEN G. MONTESANTI; Mrs. JO-ANN FENTON; Rev. BENEDICT M. GUEVIN, O.S.B.; Bro. MARK E. HILTON, S.C.; Sr. AMY HOEY, R.S.M.; Deacon GREGORY MCGINN.

Secretariat for Human Services—

New Hampshire Catholic Charities, Inc.—215 Myrtle St., Manchester, 03104. Tel: 603-669-3030; Fax: 603-626-1252.

Immigration and Refugee Services—CATHY CHESLEY, J.D., Ed.D., Dir.; JEANNE BRENNAN FUNK, Immigration Attorney; MARTHA ELLIS, BIA Accredited Representative; LAN TRUONG, BIA Accredited Rep.; KIMBERLY GEORGE, Immigration Attorney; MARIA EVELETH, BIA Accredited Rep. Tel: 603-893-1971; FRANCIS AGYARE, Immigration Attorney.

Clinical and Family Services Office—JOSEPH P. NAFF, L.I.C.S.W., Dir.

Diocesan Consultation and Counseling Services—JOSEPH P. NAFF, L.I.C.S.W., Clinical Dir.

Elderly Services—SHERYL A. BROOKS, M.S., Social Worker.

Adoption and Maternity Services—JOSEPH P. NAFF, L.I.C.S.W., Adoption Supvr.; ELAINE C. LANGTON, Social Worker.

Project Rachel—JOSEPH P. NAFF, L.I.C.S.W., Coord.

Our Place—JOSEPH P. NAFF, L.I.C.S.W., Dir. & Admin.

Office of Persons with Disabilities—Sr. PAULINE LAFOND, P.M., Coord.

Deaf Ministry—Sr. PAULINE LAFOND, P.M.; Rev. THOMAS L. DUSTON.

Parish Social Ministry Office—Deacon RICHARD J. SHANNON, Dir.

Secretariat for Administration and Community Affairs—

Respect Life Office—PETER J. CATALDO, Ph.D., Dir.

Diocesan Public Policy Office—DIANE MURPHY QUINLAN ESQ., Chancellor.

Public Policy Commission—MEREDITH P. COOK, Chm.; Very Rev. MICHAEL KERPER, V.F.; Revs. THOMAS L. DUSTON; RAYMOND J. POTVIN; Bro. ISAAC S. MURPHY, O.S.B.; Deacon GREGORY R. MCGINN; ELIZABETH FEREN; THOMAS E. BLONSKI; DONALD W. AYRES, M.D.; Bro. PAUL CRAWFORD, O.F.M.Cap.

Ecumenical and Interreligious Affairs—Rev. ROBERT G. BIRON, Dir., Our Lady of Fatima, 724 Main St., New London, 03257-4609. Tel: 603-526-4484.

Ministerial Conduct—Deacon GREGORY R. MCGINN.

Operations & Information Systems—Sr. SHEILA GARVEY, R.S.M., Dir. Email: sgarvey@rcbm.org.

Catholic Campaign for Human Development/ Operation Rice Bowl—PETER J. CATALDO, Ph.D., Coord.

Catholic Relief Services—PETER J. CATALDO, Ph.D.

Victim Assistance Coordinator—JOSEPH P. NAFF, L.I.C.S.W. Tel: 603-668-0014; 800-475-5585 (NH). Email: jnaff@nh-cc.org.

Multicultural Ministries Office—Sr. MARGARET J. CROSBY, S.N.D.deN., Dir.

African Apostolate—VACANT.

Brazilian Apostolate—Rev. CRISTIANO G. BORRO BARBOSA (Diocese of Baura, Brazil); JOSE GONCALVES, Coord. Brazilian Apostolate Pastoral Council, Blessed John XXIII Parish, 121 Allds St., Nashua, 03060-6395. Tel: 603-598-2622.

Hispanic Ministry—Deacon RAMON ANDRADE, Diocesan. *Manchester Hispanic Parish Ministry*, Rev. JOSEPH GURDAK, O.F.M.Cap., Pastor, St. Anne-St. Augustine Church, 382 Beech St., Manchester, 03103. Tel: 603-625-5655; Sr. MARIA LUZ CERVANTES, M.S.C., Pastoral Minister. Pastoral Ministers: SHIRLEY BRIEN; Sisters MARIELA YASMIN GARCIA LOPEZ, H.S.M.P.; MARIA GUADALUPE GRANDOS ABOYTES, H.S.M.P. *Nashua Hispanic Parish Ministry*, Rev. RICHARD H. DION, Pastor, St. Aloysius Rectory, 48 W. Hollis St., Nashua, 03060-3286. Tel: 603-882-4362; LOURDES ULLOA, Pastoral Assoc. Tel: 603-882-4362. Pastoral Ministers: Sisters MARIA ELENA GARCIA RAMIREZ, H.S.M.P.; ELIZABETH CASTRO GONZALES, H.S.M.P.; REBECCA VIDAL CARRANZA, H.S.M.P. *Salem Hispanic Apostolate*, Rev. JORGE REYES, O.S.A.; LEE ALPHEN, Chap. Racetrack Ministry, during race season. Rockingham Park, Salem, 03079. Tel: 603-898-1927.

Indonesian Apostolate—Rev. THOMAS TJAYA, St. Leo Parish, 59 Main St., Gonic, 03839-5220. Tel: 603-332-1863.

Vietnamese Apostolate—Rev. THIEN NGUYEN, St. Christopher Church, 60 Manchester St., Nashua, 03064. Tel: 603-882-0632. St. Anne-St. Augustine Church, 382 Beech St., Manchester, 03103. Tel: 603-625-5655.

Secretariat for Ministry Formation—Very Rev. DENNIS J. AUDET, V.F. Email: daudet@rcbm.org.

Vocations Office—Rev. JASON Y. JALBERT, Dir.

Office of Clergy Formation—Rev. JOHN S. SLEDZIONA, C.M., Dir.

Office for Worship—Rev. JASON Y. JALBERT, Dir. Email: jjalbert@rcbm.org.

Office of Permanent Deacon Formation—Co Directors: Deacon GREGORY R. MCGINN; PATRICIA GABREE.

Secretariat for Communication, Planning and Development—

Communications Office—KEVIN J. DONOVAN, Dir.

Development Office—PATRICK F. MCGEE, A.P.R., Dir.

Secretariat for Finance—Mr. GUY D. CHAPDELAINE, CPA, Cabinet Sec.

Finance Office—Mr. GUY D. CHAPDELAINE, CPA, Finance Officer. Email: gchapdelaine@rcbm.org; DAVID A. GABERT, Dir. Parish & School Financial Svcs. Email: dgabert@rcbm.org; PATRICIA GONEAU, Controller. Email: pgoneau@rcbm.org.

Risk Management and Insurance Office—MARTHA A. KIPP, Dir. Email: mkipp@rcbm.org.

Human Resources Office—CHRISTINE L. HAGEN, Dir.

Secretariat for Real Estate—PAUL F. HARRINGTON, Cabinet Sec. Email: pharrington@rcbm.org. Real Estate Board: JOHN LYONS; ARTHUR W. ROSE, P.E.; Rev. ROBERT E. GORSKI; JOHN E. DOHERTY; FRANCIS X. FRAITZL III; STEPHEN CAMANN; HUGH R. O'NEIL; RAYMOND P. CLEMENT.

Diocesan Cemetery Office—PAUL F. HARRINGTON.

Diocesan Bureau of Housing—Most Rev. JOHN B. MCCORMACK, D.D., Pres.; PAUL F. HARRINGTON, Vice Pres.; MARTHA A. KIPP, Exec. Dir. Email: mkipp@dbhnh.org.

Carpenter Center, Inc.—323 Franklin St., Manchester, 03101. Tel: 603-625-5422; Fax: 603-625-1014. (Apartments 96)

DBH Shelter, III, Inc.—12 W. Broadway, Derry, 03038. Tel: 603-432-0952; Fax: 603-625-1014. (Apartments 28)

DBH Management, Inc.—323 Franklin St., Manchester, 03101. Tel: 603-625-5422; Fax: 603-625-1014. (Total Staff 7; Total Assisted 132)

Censor Librorum—Most Rev. FRANCIS J. CHRISTIAN, Ph.D., D.D.

Society of Saint Vincent de Paul—RAYMOND RIOUX, Pres., NH State Council, 8 Maplewood Ave., Manchester, 03102. Tel: 603-622-1036. Email: riouxr@nationwide.com.

CLERGY, PARISHES, MISSIONS AND PAROCHIAL SCHOOLS

CITY OF MANCHESTER

(HILLSBOROUGH COUNTY)

1—ST. JOSEPH CATHEDRAL (1869) [CEM] Rev. Joseph M. Cooper; Deacon Robert Potvin. In Res., Most Rev. Francis J. Christian; Rev. Msgr. Colin A. MacDonald (Retired); Revs. Jean M. Lemay; Bartholomew Salter, C.S.C.

Res.: 145 Lowell St., 03104-6135. Tel: 603-622-6404; Fax: 603-626-4415.

Chapel—St. Joseph Cathedral Chapel Lowell St., 03104.

Catechesis/Religious Program—Colleen B. Lang, Catechetical Leader.

2—ST. ANNE (1848), Unified in 2004 into St. Anne-St. Augustine, Manchester.

3—ST. ANNE-ST. AUGUSTIN (1871) [CEM] Rev. Joseph Gurdak, O.F.M.Cap.; Sr. Mariella Yasmin Garcia Lopez, H.S.M.P., Pastoral Assoc.; Deacon Ramon Andrade. In Res., Revs. Joseph McCarthy, O.F.M-.Cap.; Bernard J. Campbell, O.F.M.Cap; Patrick Glavin, O.F.M.Cap.; Bro. Paul Crawford, O.F.M.Cap.

Rectory—St. Anne, 231 Merrimack St., 03103.

Office: 383 Beech St., 03103-5397. Tel: 603-623-8809; Fax: 603-626-1517.

Catechesis/Religious Program—Marie Dancy, Catechetical Leader.

4—ST. ANTHONY OF PADUA (1899), (French), Rev. Richard H. Dion; Deacon Harry A. Kram. In Res., Rev. Florent Bilodeau (Retired).

Res.: 172 Belmont St., 03103-4452. Tel: 603-625-6409; Fax: 603-625-0099.

School—(Grades K-6), 148 Belmont St., 03103. Tel: 603-622-0414; Fax: 603-669-5212. Mrs. Saundra T. Stewart, Prin.

Catechesis/Religious Program—Colette Lemarier, Catechetical Leader (K-6); Richard Coulon, Catechetical Leader (7-10).

5—BLESSED SACRAMENT (1907) Revs. John Bavaro, O.F.M.; John Bucchino, O.F.M.; Sisters Olivia Kidney, R.S.M., Pastoral Assoc.; Joan Messier, R.S.M., Pastoral Min.; Anne Martineau, R.S.M., Pastoral Min.
Res.: 14 Elm St., 03103-7242. Tel: 603-622-5445; Fax: 603-627-5983.
Catechesis/Religious Program—Steve Donohue, Catechetical Leader; Martha Donohue, Catechetical Leader.
Perpetual Adoration Chapel: St. Theresa of Lisieux—
6—ST. CATHERINE (1954) Rev. Paul D. Montminy; Sr. Jeannette Landreville, C.S.C., Pastoral Min.; Deacon Edward P. Munz. In Res., Rev. Msgr. Thomas J. Hannigan (Retired); Rev. Ray J. Labrie.
Res.: 207 Hemlock St., 03104-3248. Tel: 603-622-4966; Fax: 603-622-0236.
School—(Grades PreK-6), 206 North St., 03104. Tel: 603-622-1711; Fax: 603-624-4935. Sr. Janet Belcourt, C.S.C., Prin. & Catechetical Leader.
7—ST. EDMUND (1914) Merged in 2002 with St. John the Baptist parish, Manchester and became Parish of the Transfiguration, Manchester.
8—ST. GEORGE (1890), Unified in 2002 with St. Joseph Cathedral, Manchester.
9—ST. HEDWIG (1902), (Polish), [CEM] Rev. Msgr. Alfred Daniszewski.
Res.: 147 Walnut St., 03104-4225. Tel: 603-623-4835.
School—*St. Casimir*, (Grades K-8), 456 Union St., 03103. Tel: 603-623-6411. Sr. Mary Lawrence Lojko, C.S.S.F., Prin.; Mrs. Patricia Farmer, Librarian. Felician Sisters 1; Students 150; Lay Teachers 8.
10—ST. JOHN THE BAPTIST (1914) Merged in 2002 with St. Edward parish, Manchester to form Parish of the Transfiguration, Manchester.
11—STE. MARIE (1880), (French), [CEM 2] Revs. Maurice R. Larochelle; Donald E. Clinton; Deacon Frank Gallinaro, Pastoral Assoc. In Res., Revs. Richard B. Tetu; Wilfred Demers; Marcel M. Allard (Retired).
Office: 133 Wayne St., 03102.
Res.: 378 Notre Dame Ave., 03102-3793. Tel: 603-622-4615; Fax: 603-666-4732.
Catechesis/Religious Program—Terry Bolduc, Catechetical Leader; Michele Allain, Catechetical Leader.
Chapel—*Joseph House* 279 Cartier St., 03102. Tel: 603-627-9493.
Chapel—*Chapel of North American Martyrs* 378 Notre Dame Ave., 03102.
Chapel—*St. Joan of Arc* 378 Notre Dame Ave., 03102.
Chapel—*Mother Rivier Eucharist Adoration Chapel* 133 Wayne St., 03102.
Convent—*Sisters of the Presentation of Mary*, 133 Wayne St., 03102. Tel: 603-623-0815.
12—OUR LADY OF PERPETUAL HELP (1911), Unified in 2006 with St. Anthony of Padua, Manchester.
13—PARISH OF THE TRANSFIGURATION (2002) Rev. John W. Fleming; Sr. Priscilla Lemire, R.J.M., Pastoral Assoc.; Deacon Richard J. Shannon. In Res., Rev. Msgr. James J. Markham (Retired); Revs. Roland P. Cote; John J. Mahoney Jr.
Res.: 107 Alsace St., 03102-3006. Tel: 603-623-4715; Fax: 603-623-4715.
Catechesis/Religious Program—Tel: 603-622-0504. Sr. Bernadette Turgeon, S.N.D.deN., D.R.E.
14—ST. PATRICK (1898) [CEM] Merged Unified in 2007 with Parish of the Transfiguration, Manchester.
15—ST. PIUS X (1955) Rev. Robert E. Gorski; Rev. Msgr. John E. Molan (Retired); Deacon Mark F. Hobson. In Res., Rev. Richard B. Thompson.
Res.: 575 Candia Rd., 03109-4735. Tel: 603-622-6510; Fax: 603-626-1323.
Catechesis/Religious Program—Donna Dukeshire, C.R.E.
16—ST. RAPHAEL (1888) [CEM] Rev. Jerome J. Day, O.S.B.
Res.: 103 Walker St., 03102-4566. Tel: 603-623-2604. Email: raph103@comcast.net.
Catechesis/Religious Program—Tel: 603-647-2283. Therese Dame, D.R.E.; Dorene Turner, Youth Min.
17—SACRED HEART OF JESUS (1911), (French), Revs. Maurice R. Larochelle; Donald E. Clinton; Deacon Frank Gallinaro.
Mailing Address & Office: 247 S. Main St., 03102-4890.
Church: 265 S. Main St., 03102. Tel: 603-625-9525; Fax: 603-666-4732.
Catechesis/Religious Program—Tel: 603-622-3312. Karen Hettrick, Catechetical Leader.
18—ST. THERESA, Unified in 2004 with Blessed Sacrament Manchester.

OUTSIDE THE CITY OF MANCHESTER

ALTON, BELKNAP CO.
1—ST. JOAN OF ARC (1961) Merged in 2003 with St. Cecilia Parish, Wolfelboro to form St. Katharine Drexel, Alton.
2—ST. KATHARINE DREXEL (2003) Rev. Robert F. Cole. Mailing Address: P.O. Box 180, Wolfeboro, 03894-0180. Tel: 603-875-2548; Fax: 603-875-4801.
Res.: 50 Friar Tuck Way, Wolfeboro, 03894.
Church: 40 Hidden Springs Rd., 03809.
ASHLAND, GRAFTON CO., ST. AGNES (1904) Merged in 2006 with St. Matthew, Plymouth and St. Timothy, Bristol to form Holy Trinity Parish, Plymouth.
AUBURN, ROCKINGHAM CO., ST. PETER (1948) Rev. C. Peter Dumont; Deacon George J. Borkush. In Res., Rev. Msgr. John E. Molan (Retired); Rev. William E. Babineau (Retired).
Res. & Church: 567 Manchester Rd., 03032-3123. Tel: 603-623-5429; Fax: 603-669-5598.
Catechesis/Religious Program—Tel: 603-669-5134.
BEDFORD, HILLSBOROUGH CO., ST. ELIZABETH SETON (1964) Rev. Msgr. John P. Quinn; Rev. David L. Kneeland.
Res.: 190 Meetinghouse Rd., 03110-6027. Tel: 603-669-7444; Fax: 603-644-5371.
Catechesis/Religious Program—Deacon Larry Cummins, D.R.E.; Mary Danielson, Catechetical Leader; Carrie Soucy, Catechetical Leader; Susan Foote, Catechetical Leader.
BELMONT, BELKNAP CO., ST. JOSEPH (1949) Rev. Albert J. Tremblay Jr.
Res.: 6 High St., P.O. Box 285, 03220-0285. Tel: 603-267-8174; Fax: 603-267-1170.
Catechesis/Religious Program—Kathy Loiacono, Pastoral Min. Christian Formation.
BENNINGTON, HILLSBOROUGH CO., ST. PATRICK (1936) [CEM] Merged in 2006 with St. Denis, Harrisville and St. Peter, Peterborough in 2006 to form Divine Mercy Parish, Peterborough.
BERLIN, COOS CO.
1—ST. ANNE (1885) Merged in 2000 with Guardian Angel, St. Joseph and St. Kieran to form Good Shepherd Parish, Berlin.
2—GOOD SHEPHERD (2000) Very Rev. Richard A. Roberge; Rev. Jeffrey P. Statz; Sr. Monique Therriault, R.S.M., Pastoral Assoc.; Deacon Merle Albert.
Office: 151 Emery St., P.O. Box 570, 03570-0570. Tel: 603-752-2880; Fax: 603-752-1855.
Res.: 162 Madison Ave., 03570-2065.
Catechesis/Religious Program—140 Blanchard St., 03570. Tel: 603-752-5443; Fax: 603-752-1743. Cecile Labbe, Catechetical Leader; Bridget Goudreau, Youth Min. Students 260.
3—GUARDIAN ANGEL (1917) Merged in 2000 with St. Anne, St. Joseph and St. Kieran to form Good Shepherd parish, Berlin.
4—ST. JOSEPH (1943) Merged in 2000 with Guardian Angel, St. Anne and St. Kieran to form Good Shepherd parish, Berlin.
5—ST. KIERAN (1894) Merged in 2000 with Guardian Angel, St. Anne and St. Joseph to form Good Shepherd parish, Berlin.
BRISTOL, GRAFTON CO., ST. TIMOTHY (1953) Merged in 2006 with St. Agnes, Ashland and St. Matthew, Plymouth to form Holy Trinity Parish, Plymouth.
CANDIA, ROCKINGHAM CO., ST. PAUL (1971) Rev. C. Peter Dumont; Lorette Nault, Pastoral Min.
Res.: 54 Main St., P.O. Box 276, 03034-0276. Tel: 603-483-8481; Fax: 603-483-8481.
Catechesis/Religious Program—Tel: 603-483-5516.
CASCADE, COOS CO., ST. BENEDICT, Closed. in 1991. For Sacramental records contact Good Shepherd, Berlin.
CENTER OSSIPEE, CARROLL CO., ST. JOSEPH (1965) Rev. Edmund A. Babicz; Mary Sullivan, Pastoral Assoc.; Deacon William Rich.
Res.: 23 Moultonville Rd., P.O. Box 248, 03814-0248. Tel: 603-539-5036; Fax: 603-539-6295.
Catechesis/Religious Program—Patricia Swanson, Catechetical Leader; Louis Nardello, Catechetical Leader.
CHARLESTOWN, SULLIVAN CO.
1—ALL SAINTS PARISH (2007) Rev. Michael E. Gendron; Deacon John Blicharz; Sr. Bernadette Ann Bozak, O.S.F., Pastoral Min.
Res. & Office: 285 Main St., P.O. Box 332, 03603-0332. Tel: 603-826-3359; Fax: 603-826-5875.
St. Catherine of Siena Church—290 Main St., 03603-0332.
St. Peter Church—36 Church St., North Walpole, 03609-1715.
Catechesis/Religious Program—Maria Castellano, Catechetical Leader.
Mission—*St. Joseph* Elm St., Walpole, 03608.
2—ST. CATHERINE (1904) Merged in 2007 with St. Peter Parish, North Walpole to form All Saints Parish, Charlestown.
CLAREMONT, SULLIVAN CO.
1—ST. JOSEPH (1920), (Polish), Rev. George Majka.
Res.: 58 Elm St., P.O. Box 824, 03743-0824. Tel: 603-542-5732; Fax: 603-542-5732.
Catechesis/Religious Program—46 Elm St., 03743. Tel: 603-542-9933. Jeanne Brooks, Catechetical Leader.
2—ST. MARY (1823) [CEM] Rev. Shawn M. Therrien; Deacon Paul R. Boucher.
Res.: 32 Pearl St., 03743-2552. Tel: 603-542-9518; Fax: 603-542-9614.
School—(Grades PreK-8), 18 Central St., 03743. Tel: 603-542-6341; Fax: 603-542-5260. Myra Peck, Prin. Lay Teachers 10; Students 100.
Catechesis/Religious Program—32 Pearl St., 03743-2552. Cynthia LaCasce, Catechetical Leader. Students 48.
Mission—*Old St. Mary* Old Church Rd., Sullivan Co. 03743.
COLEBROOK, COOS CO.
1—ST. BRENDAN (1953) [CEM] Merged in 2007 with St. Albert Parish, West Stewartstown to form North American Martyrs Parish, Colebrook.
2—NORTH AMERICAN MARTYRS PARISH (2007) Rev. Craig I. Cheney.
Res. & Office: 55 Pleasant St., 03576-0065. Tel: 603-237-4342; Fax: 603-237-8580.
St. Albert Church—15 Church St., West Stewartstown, 03597.
St. Brendan Church—
Catechesis/Religious Program—
Mission—*St. Pius the Tenth* Main St., Errol, 03579. P.O. Box 65, 03576-0065.
CONCORD, MERRIMACK CO.
1—IMMACULATE HEART OF MARY (1956) Rev. Peter P. Boucher; Deacon John Morrow.
Res.: 180 Loudon Rd., 03301-6028. Tel: 603-224-4393; Fax: 603-224-6229.
Catechesis/Religious Program—Tel: 603-225-2026; Fax: 603-224-6229. Susan Perry, Catechetical Leader; Denise Mainusch, Catechetical Leader.
2—ST. JOHN THE EVANGELIST (1865) Rev. Steven G. Montesanti.
Res. & Church: 72 S. Main St., 03301-4830. Tel: 603-224-2328; Fax: 603-224-2625.
Catechesis/Religious Program—Tel: 603-224-2625; 603-410-6438. Tammy Saxton, Catechetical Leader.
3—ST. PETER (1946) Revs. Anthony Kuzia, C.M.; Luke Sorys, C.M.; Deacon James E. Rock.
Church & Office: 135 N. State St., 03301. Tel: 603-225-2131; Fax: 603-228-4580.
Catechesis/Religious Program—Greta Ernst, Catechetical Coord.
4—SACRED HEART (1892), (French), Revs. Anthony Kuzia, C.M.; Luke Sorys, C.M.; Deacon James E. Rock. In Res., Rev. John S. Sledziona, C.M.
Res.: 52 Pleasant St., 03301-3925. Tel: 603-225-6942; Fax: 603-225-3526.
Catechesis/Religious Program—Cathy Asmar, Catechetical Leader.
DERRY, ROCKINGHAM CO.
1—HOLY CROSS (1989) Rev. Roger H. Croteau.
Church & Office: 187 Hampstead Rd., 03038-4835. Tel: 603-437-9544; Fax: 603-537-1208.
Res.: 4 Belle Brook Ln., 03038.
Catechesis/Religious Program—Tel: 603-537-1208. George Strout, Catechetical Leader.
2—ST. THOMAS AQUINAS (1888) Rev. Bruce Czapla, O.F.M.; Bro. Charles Gingerich, O.F.M.
Res.: 26 Crystal Ave., 03038-1799. Tel: 603-432-5000; Fax: 603-434-0518.
Catechesis/Religious Program—
School—(Grades K-8), 3 Moody St., 03038. Tel: 603-432-2712; Fax: 603-432-2179. Paul Rakiey, Prin. Sisters 1; Lay Teachers 9; Students 217.
DOVER, STRAFFORD CO.
1—ST. CHARLES (1893), (French), [CEM] Merged with St. Joseph & St. Mary, Dover to form Parish of the Assumption, Dover.
2—ST. JOSEPH (1945) Merged with St. Charles & St. Mary, Dover to form Parish of the Assumption, Dover.
3—ST. MARY (1833) Merged with St. Charles & St. Joseph, Dover to form Parish of the Assumption, Dover.
4—PARISH OF THE ASSUMPTION (2009) Revs. Marc R. Gagne; Mark DeVelis, O.C.D.; Deacon Robert J. Gagnon.
Res. & Church: 150 Central Ave., 03820-3464. Tel: 603-742-4837; Fax: 603-749-6779.
St. Charles Borromeo Church: 577 Central Ave., 03820.
St. Mary Church: Chestnut St. at Third St., 03820.
Catechesis/Religious Program—Nancy Watkins, Catechetical Leader; Nancy Gurick, Catechetical Leader; Ileana Hoeing, Catechetical Leader.
Mission—*Chapel of the Nativity* Rte. 9, P.O. Box 163, Barrington, Strafford Co. 03825. Tel: 603-664-9336; Fax: 603-664-2310. Sr. Lorraine G. Choiniere, C.S.C., Pastoral Assoc.
DURHAM, STRAFFORD CO., ST. THOMAS MORE Rev. Andrew W. Cryans; Julie Tracy, Campus Min.
Church & Office: 6 Madbury Rd., Box 620, 03824-0620. Tel: 603-868-2666 (Office); Fax: 603-868-3765.
Catechesis/Religious Program—Kathryn Brunet, Catechetical Leader.
ENFIELD, GRAFTON CO., ST. HELENA (1899) Rev. Johnny Vadakkan, M.S.
Res.: 36 Shaker Hill Rd., 03748-3524. Tel: 603-632-4263; Fax: 603-632-7874.

Catechesis/Religious Program—Lisa Torres, Catechetical Leader.
Mission—St. Mary 1157 Rte. 4, Canaan, Grafton Co. 03741.

EPPING, ROCKINGHAM CO., ST. JOSEPH (1898) [CEM] Rev. Volney J. DeRosia.
Res.: 14 Church St., P.O. Box 337, 03042-0337. Tel: 603-679-8805; Fax: 603-679-5192.
Church: 208 Pleasant St., Rte. 27, P.O. Box 337, 03042-0337.
Catechesis/Religious Program—Lisa Dodge, Catechetical Leader.

EXETER, ROCKINGHAM CO., ST. MICHAEL (1859) Revs. Marc R. Montminy; Christopher M. Martel; Leah Grant, Pastoral Min.
Res.: 9 Lincoln St., 03833-3297. Tel: 603-772-2494; Fax: 603-778-1629.
Church: 93 Front St., 03833.
Catechesis/Religious Program—Mary Howcroft, Catechetical Leader.

FARMINGTON, STRAFFORD CO., ST. PETER (1920) Rev. Daniel J. Sinibaldi; Deacon Richard A. Falardeau; Sr. Madonna M. Kling, C.D.P., Pastoral Assoc.
Res.: 88 Central St., P.O. Box 565, 03835-0565. Tel: 603-755-2280.

FRANKLIN, MERRIMACK CO., ST. PAUL (1884) [CEM] Rev. Raymond E. Gagnon.
Res.: 110 School St., P.O. Box 490, 03235-0490. Tel: 603-934-5013; Fax: 603-934-3469.
Catechesis/Religious Program—Mary Ellen Shaw, Catechetical Leader.

GOFFSTOWN, HILLSBOROUGH CO., ST. LAWRENCE (1955) Rev. Gerard L. Bertin; Gerald Bergeron, Pastoral Min.
Res.: 51 Main St., 03045-1644. Tel: 603-497-2651; Fax: 603-497-3668.
Church: 1 E. Union St., 03045.
Catechesis/Religious Program—Tel: 603-497-4093. Deborah Fatcheric, Catechetical Leader.

GONIC, STRAFFORD CO., ST. LEO (1892) [CEM] Rev. Paul M. Gousse.
Res.: 59 Main St., 03839-5220. Tel: 603-332-1863; Fax: 603-330-0865.
Catechesis/Religious Program—Tel: 603-332-1863; Fax: 603-330-0365. Robin Langlois, Catechetical Leader (K-5); Jerry Gregoire, Catechetical Leader (6-8); Ann McGregor, Catechetical Leader (Confirmation).

GORHAM, COOS CO., HOLY FAMILY (1876) [CEM] Very Rev. Richard A. Roberge; Rev. Jeffrey P. Statz; Deacon Merle M. Albert.
Res.: 9 Church St., 03581-1695. Tel: 603-466-2335; Fax: 603-466-3490.

GREENVILLE, HILLSBOROUGH CO., SACRED HEART OF JESUS (1888) [CEM] Rev. James P. Walsh.
Res.: 15 High St., 03048-3121. Tel: 603-878-1121.
Catechesis/Religious Program—Tel: 603-878-2274. Lisa Kouropoulos, Catechetical Leader.

GROVETON, COOS CO.
1—ST. FRANCIS XAVIER (1899) [CEM] Merged in 2007 with Sacred Heart, North Stratford to form St. Marguerite d'Youville Parish, Groveton., 11 State St., Box 247, 03582-0247.
2—ST. MARGUERITE D'YOUVILLE PARISH (2007) Rev. Daniel R. Deveau; Sisters Marie Mansfield, S.G.M., Pastoral Min.; Helene Georges, S.G.M., Pastoral Min.
Res. & Office: 11 State St., Box 247, 03582-0247. Tel: 603-636-1047; Fax: 603-636-2549.
Sacred Heart Church—59 Main St., North Stratford, 03590.
St. Francis Xavier Church—11 State St., 03582-0247.

HAMPSTEAD, ROCKINGHAM CO., ST. ANNE (1979) Very Rev. Frederick J. Pennett Jr.; Deacon William E. Mullen; Donna Delahanty, Pastoral Assoc.
Church: 26 Emerson Ave., P.O. Box 339, 03841-0339. Tel: 603-329-5886; Fax: 603-329-4468.
Res.: 99 Emerson Ave., P.O. Box 339, 03841-0339. Tel: 603-329-5089.
Catechesis/Religious Program—Donna Delahanty, D.R.E.; Kerri Cornelissen, Youth Ministry.

HAMPTON BEACH, ROCKINGHAM CO., ST. PATRICK (1914), Open in summer months. For all records contact O.L.M.M. Parish, Hampton Tel: 603-926-2206. Church: 5 Williams St., Hampton, NH 03842-2722 Tel: 603-926-2205.

HAMPTON, ROCKINGHAM CO., OUR LADY OF THE MIRACULOUS MEDAL (1949) Rev. Gary J. Kosmowski; Deacons Dennis M. Jacobs; Paul E. Testa; Sisters Doris Ouellette, C.S.C., Pastoral Min.; Theresa Malouin, C.S.C., Pastoral Min. In Res., Rev. Stephen F. Concannon.
Res.: 289 Lafayette Rd., 03842-2109. Tel: 603-926-2206; Fax: 603-926-8602.
School—Sacred Heart School, (Grades PreK-8) Tel: 603-926-3254; Fax: 603-926-2758. Catherine Smith, Prin.; Michelle Ryzewic, Librarian. Sisters 2; Lay Teachers 29; Students 305.
Catechesis/Religious Program—Tel: 603-926-5573. Claudette Dachowski, Catechetical Leader.
Mission—St. Elizabeth of Hungary (1956) 1 Lowell St., Seabrook, Rockingham Co. 03874. Tel: 603-474-3839; Fax: 603-926-8602.

HANOVER, GRAFTON CO., ST. DENIS (1907) Revs. Becket Soule, O.P.; Francis C. Belanger, O.P.
Res.: 8 Sanborn Rd., 03755-2182. Tel: 603-643-2166; Fax: 603-643-9881.
Catechesis/Religious Program—Jannine Walsh, Catechetical Leader.

HARRISVILLE, CHESHIRE CO., ST. DENIS, Merged with St. Patrick, Bennington and St. Peter, Peterborough in 2006 to form Divine Mercy Parish, Peterborough.

HENNIKER, MERRIMACK CO., ST. THERESA (1945) Very Rev. Mark E. Dollard; Deacons Winton P. DeRosia; Joseph P. Borland.
Mailing Address: 158 Old West Hopkinton Rd., P.O. Box 729, 03242-0729. Tel: 603-428-3325; Fax: 603-428-4479.
Catechesis/Religious Program—Mary Corsetti, Catechetical Leader.

HILLSBOROGH, HILLSBOROUGH CO., ST. MARY (1892) [CEM] [JC] Very Rev. Mark E. Dollard; Deacons Joseph P. Borland; Winton P. DeRosia.
Res.: 38 Church St., P.O. Box 907, Hillsborough, 03244-0907. Tel: 603-464-5565; Fax: 603-464-5565.
Catechesis/Religious Program—Michele Greene, Catechetical Leader.
Parish Hall—Tel: 603-464-6021.

HINSDALE, CHESHIRE CO.
1—ST. JOSEPH (1884) [CEM] Merged in 2006 with St. Stanislaus, Winchester to form Mary, Queen of Peace Parish, Hinsdale.
2—MARY, QUEEN OF PEACE PARISH (2006) Very Rev. Daniel O. Lamothe; Revs. Steven M. Kucharski; Paul B. Boudreau Jr.; Deacon Arnold J. Gustafson.
Office: 161 Main St., Ste. 201, Keene, 03431-3790. Tel: 603-352-3525; Fax: 603-352-7472.
Res.: 173 Main St., Keene, 03431-3790.
St. Joseph Church—35 Brattleboro Rd., 03451.
St. Stanislaus Church—80 Richmond St., Winchester, 03470.

HOOKSETT, MERRIMACK CO., HOLY ROSARY (1886) [CEM] Rev. Edmund G. Crowley; Deacon David J. Shrader.
Res.: 21 Main St., 03106-1630. Tel: 603-485-3523; Fax: 603-485-8435.
Catechesis/Religious Program—Tel: 603-485-8567. Donna McCormack, Catechetical Leader.

HUDSON, HILLSBOROUGH CO.
1—ST. JOHN THE EVANGELIST (1949) Merged in 2007 with Infant Jesus, Nashua to form Blessed John XXIII Parish, Nashua.
2—ST. KATHRYN (1968) Rev. Gary J. Belliveau; Deacon Raymond V. Marcotte.
Mailing Address & Church: 4 Dracut Rd., 03051-5006. Tel: 603-882-7793; Fax: 603-595-1465.
Catechesis/Religious Program—Mary Ainley, Catechetical Leader; Nancy Schulz, C.R.E.

JAFFREY, CHESHIRE CO., ST. PATRICK (1885) [CEM] Rev. Wilfred H. Deschamps.
Res.: 87 Main St., 03452-6139. Tel: 603-532-6634; Fax: 603-532-6633.
Church: 89 Main St., 03452.
School—(Grades PreK-8), 70 Main St., 03452. Tel: 603-532-7676; Fax: 603-532-7476. Sr. Cecile Provost, C.S.C., Prin.; Mitzi Turgeon, Librarian. Sisters 2; Lay Teachers 14; Students 94.
Catechesis/Religious Program—Laurie Mathieu, Catechetical Leader.

KEENE, CHESHIRE CO.
1—ST. BERNARD (1862) [CEM] Very Rev. Daniel O. Lamothe; Revs. Steven M. Kucharski; Paul B. Boudreau Jr.; Deacon Arnold J. Gustafson.
Office: 161 Main St., Ste. 204, 03431.
Res.: 173 Main St., 03431-3790. Tel: 603-352-3525; Fax: 603-352-7472.
Church: 185 Main St., 03431.
Catechesis/Religious Program—Tel: 603-352-2861 (Office). Joy Davis, D.R.E. Students 119.
2—ST. MARGARET MARY (1955) Very Rev. Daniel O. Lamothe, Admin.; Revs. Steven M. Kucharski; Paul B. Boudreau Jr.; Deacon Arnold J. Gustafson.
Business Office: 161 Main St., Ste. 201, 03431.
Church: 33-35 Arch St., 03431-2297. Tel: 603-352-2861; Fax: 603-352-7472.
St. Bernard Rectory—173 Main St., 03431.
Catechesis/Religious Program—Tel: 603-357-3781. Joy Davis, D.R.E.

LACONIA, BELKNAP CO.
1—ST. JOSEPH (1871) [CEM] Revs. Marc B. Drouin; Matthew J. Mason; Deacon Russell Morey.
Res.: 30 Church St., 03246-3401. Tel: 603-524-1442; Fax: 603-527-3534.
Catechesis/Religious Program—Tel: 603-524-4196. Kathryn Canfield, Catechetical Leader (K-8); Margaret Gibbs, Catechetical leader (9-10).
2—SACRED HEART (1891), (French-Canadian), [CEM] Revs. Marc B. Drouin; Matthew J. Mason.
Res.: 291 Union Ave., 03246-3122. Tel: 603-524-9609; Fax: 603-524-9620.
Catechesis/Religious Program—Kathryn Canfield, Catechetical leader (K-8); Margaret Gibbs, Catechetical leader (9-10).

LAKEPORT, BELKNAP CO., OUR LADY OF THE LAKES (1905) Revs. Marc B. Drouin; Matthew J. Mason; Deacon William McCarty; Kathryn Canfield, Catechetical Leader.
Res.: 50 Washington St., 03246-2339. Tel: 603-524-1357 (Office); 603-527-0677 (Res.); Fax: 603-524-4524.
Catechesis/Religious Program—Margaret Gibbs, Catechetical Leader.
Mission—St. Helena Rte. 11B, Weirs Beach, Belknap Co.

LANCASTER, COOS CO.
1—ALL SAINTS (1856) [CEM] Merged with St. Matthew, Whitefield to form Gate of Heaven, Lancaster.
2—GATE OF HEAVEN (2009) Rev. Raymond A. Ball; Deacon Joseph A. Polcari.
Res.: 163 Main St., 03584-3032. Tel: 603-788-2083; Fax: 603-788-5553.
All Saints Church: 181 Main St., 03584.
St. Matthew Cemetery Church: 9 Jefferson Rd., Whitefield, 03598-3101.
Mission—St. Agnes 297 Presidential Hwy. (Rte. 2), Jefferson, Coos Co. 03583.
Mission—St. Patrick Twin Mountain. Rte. 3 & 302, Carroll, Coos Co. 03595.
Shrine—Bretton Woods, Our Lady of the Mountains Bretton Woods.

LEBANON, GRAFTON CO., SACRED HEART (1876) Very Rev. William V. Kaliyadan, M.S. In Res., Rev. Richard Delisle, M.S.
Res.: 2 Hough St., P.O. Box 482, 03766-0482. Tel: 603-448-1262; Fax: 603-448-3754.
Catechesis/Religious Program—7 Fairview Ave., 03766. Fax: 603-448-2139. Karen R. Boucher, D.R.E.

LINCOLN, GRAFTON CO., ST. JOSEPH (1902) Rev. John B. MacKenzie.
Res.: 25 Church St., P.O. Box 128, 03251-0128. Tel: 603-745-2266; Fax: 603-745-2888. Email: stjlincoln@hotmail.com.
Catechesis/Religious Program—Barbara Vitale, Catechetical Leader.

LISBON, GRAFTON CO., ST. CATHERINE OF SIENA (1956) Rev. Jeffrey P. Statz.
Res.: c/o 21 Pine St., Woodsville, 03785-1215. Tel: 603-747-2038; Fax: 603-747-8071.
Church: 28 Highland Ave., 03585.
Catechesis/Religious Program—Sandy Perry, Catechetical Leader.

LITCHFIELD, HILLSBOROUGH CO., ST. FRANCIS OF ASSISI (1953) Rev. Ray J. Labrie.
Parish Office—9 St. Francis Way, 03052-8050. Tel: 603-424-3456; Fax: 603-424-8603.
School—(Grades K-6) Tel: 603-424-3312; Fax: 603-424-9128. Shannon Dannible, Prin.; Rose Van Uden, Librarian. Lay Teachers 9; Students 141.
Catechesis/Religious Program—Tel: 603-424-9061. Vicki Isabelle, Catechetical Leader; Jyl Dittbenner, Catechetical Leader.

LITTLETON, GRAFTON CO., ST. ROSE OF LIMA (1882) [CEM] Rev. Marcel I. Martel.
Res.: 77 Clay St., 03561-1205. Tel: 603-444-2593; Fax: 603-444-3126.
Mission—Our Lady of the Snows Main St., Franconia, Grafton Co. 03580.

LONDONDERRY, ROCKINGHAM CO.
1—ST. JUDE (1962) Rev. Robert Couto; Deacon Marc G. Payeur; Sr. Janice Rooney, S.N.D.deN., Pastoral Assoc.
Res.: 435 Mammoth Rd., 03053-2304. Tel: 603-432-3333; Fax: 603-432-1639.
Catechesis/Religious Program—Tel: 603-437-7026. Trish Woodward, Catechetical Leader; Diane Swinarski, Dir. of Youth Ministry.
2—ST. MARK THE EVANGELIST (1981) Rev. Thomas L. Duston; Deacon Leon Abbott Jr.
Res.: One Griffin Rd., 03053.
Church: One South Rd., 03053-3814. Tel: 603-432-8711; Fax: 603-434-6748.
Catechesis/Religious Program—Tel: 603-432-5711. Catherine Kinnon, C.R.E.; Scott Sicard, Youth Min.

MARLBOROUGH, CHESHIRE CO., SACRED HEART (1886) [CEM], Unified in 2006 with St. Bernard, Keene.

MEREDITH, BELKNAP CO., ST. CHARLES BORROMEO (1946) Very Rev. Dennis J. Audet.
Res.: 8 Ridge Rd., P.O. Box 237, 03253-0237.
Church: 300 NH Rte. 25, P.O. Box 237, 03253-0237. Tel: 603-279-4403; Fax: 603-279-9924.
Catechesis/Religious Program—Sr. Harriet Cutting, S.N.D.deN., D.R.E.

MERRIMACK, HILLSBOROUGH CO.
1—ST. JOHN NEUMANN (1982) Very Rev. Agapit H. Jean Jr.; Deacon David C. Hamel.
Res.: 208 Naticook Rd., 03054.
Church: 708 Milford Rd. (Rte. 101A), 03054-4612. Tel: 603-880-4689; Fax: 603-881-9668.
Catechesis/Religious Program—Tel: 603-880-0825. Jennifer Lajoie, Catechetical Leader.

2—OUR LADY OF MERCY (1954) Rev. Msgr. Paul L. Bouchard; Christine Patterson, Pastoral Assoc.; Deacon James E. Patterson.
Res.: 16 Baboosic Lake Rd., 03054-3603. Tel: 603-424-3757; Fax: 603-424-1780.
Catechesis/Religious Program—Tel: 603-424-4477. Elaine Lamb, Catechetical Leader.

MILFORD, HILLSBOROUGH CO., ST. PATRICK (1895) [CEM] Rev. John W. Keegan, S.J.; Patti Sigvardson, Pastoral Assoc.
Res.: 34 Amherst St., P.O. Box 27, 03055-0027. Tel: 603-673-1311; Fax: 603-673-3687.
Catechesis/Religious Program—Tel: 603-673-4797. Sue Pasquale, D.R.E.; Kathy Frye, D.R.E.

NASHUA, HILLSBOROUGH CO.

1—ST. ALOYSIUS (1871), (French), [CEM 3] Rev. Daniel A. St. Laurent.
Res.: 48 W. Hollis St., 03060-3286. Tel: 603-882-4362; Fax: 603-886-8923.
Catechesis/Religious Program—Giselle North, Catechetical Leader.
Convent—5 Green St., 03064.
Chapel—Corpus Christi Chapel 43 Franklin St., 03064.

2—BLESSED JOHN XXIII PARISH (2007) Revs. W. Pierre Baker; Cristiano G. Borro Barbosa (Brazil) (BO); Deacons Edmund C. Hilston; John H. St. George. In Res., Revs. Eric T. Delisle; Andre L. Bedard (Retired).
Res. & Office: 121 Allds St., 03060-6395. Tel: 603-882-2462; Fax: 603-882-7104.
Infant Jesus Church—
Catechesis/Religious Program—Tel: 603-886-9725.
St. John the Evangelist Church—25 Library St., Hudson, 03051-4239.
Catechesis/Religious Program—23 Library St., Hudson, 03051-4239. Tel: 603-882-6541. Dawn Gagnon, Catechetical Leader.
School—(Grades K-6), 3 Crown St., 03060-6366. Tel: 603-889-2649; Fax: 603-594-9117. Mrs. Estelle LaFleur, Prin.
Convent—Infant Jesus Convent
Brazilian Outreach Office—Tel: 603-598-2622.

3—ST. CASIMIR, Unified in 2002 with St. Patrick, Nashua.

4—ST. CHRISTOPHER (1950) Rev. Richard J. Kelley. Church: 60 Manchester St., 03064. In Res., Rev. Bruce W. Collard.
Res.: 62 Manchester St., 03064-6296. Tel: 603-882-0632; Fax: 603-881-8728.
School—(Grades PreK-6), 20 Cushing Ave., 03060. Tel: 603-882-7442; Fax: 603-594-9253. Jack Daniels, Prin. Students 273.
Catechesis/Religious Program—Alana Kocsis, Catechetical Leader; Deacon James Daly, Catechetical Leader.

5—ST. FRANCIS XAVIER (1885) [CEM], Unified in 2003 with St. Aloysius, Nashua.

6—IMMACULATE CONCEPTION (1968) Rev. Robert C. Guillemette; Deacon James Daly; Stephen Kimbell, Pastoral Min./Coord.
Res.: 216 E. Dunstable Rd., 03062-2344. Tel: 603-888-0321; Fax: 603-888-8407.
Catechesis/Religious Program—214 E. Dunstable Rd., 03062-2344. Tel: 603-888-0608; Fax: 603-888-3602. Eileen Bowes, C.R.E.

7—INFANT JESUS (1909) Merged with St. John the Evangelist, Hudson to form Blessed John XXIII Parish, Nashua.

8—ST. JOSEPH (1955) Most Rev. Francis J. Christian. In Res., Rev. Roger P. Bilodeau (Retired).
Church: 777 W. Hollis St., 03062-3553. Tel: 603-883-0757; Fax: 603-883-8057.
Catechesis/Religious Program—Janice Mercure, D.R.E.

9—PARISH OF THE RESURRECTION (1970) Rev. John M. Grace; Ann M. Cormier, Pastoral Min.
Pastoral Center—449 Broad St., 03063-3412. Tel: 603-882-0925; Fax: 603-881-3561.
Catechesis/Religious Program—Tel: 603-889-0012. Terry Root, Co. Coord.; Charlene Tabat, Co. Coord.

10—ST. PATRICK (1855) [CEM 2] Rev. Martin T. Kelly. In Res., Rev. John E. Healey.
Res.: 29 Spring St., 03060-3490. Tel: 603-882-2262; Fax: 603-577-9817.

11—ST. STANISLAUS (1908), Unified in 2002 with St. Aloysius of Gonzaga, Nashua.

NEW LONDON, MERRIMACK CO., OUR LADY OF FATIMA (1952) Rev. Robert G. Biron; Deacon Gregory R. McGinn; Cheryl Fitzgerald, Pastoral Assoc.
Res. & Church: 724 Main St., 03257-7821. Tel: 603-526-4484; Fax: 603-526-8055.
Mission—Immaculate Conception 12 Church Ln., Andover, Merrimack Co. 03216.

NEWMARKET, ROCKINGHAM CO., ST. MARY (1878) [CEM] Revs. Marc R. Montminy; Christopher M. Martel.
Res.: 182 Main St., P.O. Box 337, 03857-0337. Tel: 603-659-3643.
Catechesis/Religious Program—Tel: 603-659-6474. Erin Bajger, Catechetical Leader.

NEWPORT, SULLIVAN CO., ST. PATRICK (1902) [CEM] Rev. Richard E. St. Louis Jr.
Res.: 32 Beech St., 03773-1416. Tel: 603-863-1422; Fax: 603-863-7898.
Catechesis/Religious Program—Assumption Hall, 44 School St., 03773.

NEWTON, ROCKINGHAM CO., MARY, MOTHER OF THE CHURCH (1967) Merged with Holy Angels to form St. Luke the Evangelist Parish, Plaistow.

NORTH CONWAY, CARROLL CO., OUR LADY OF THE MOUNTAINS (1902) [CEM 2] Rev. Donald F. Gauthier Jr.; Deacon John Carey.
Office, Res. & Church: 2905 White Mountains Hwy., 03860. Tel: 603-356-2535; Fax: 603-356-2877.
Catechesis/Religious Program—Kevin Gilbride, Catechetical Leader.

NORTH STRATFORD, COOS CO., SACRED HEART (1888), (French), [CEM 2] Merged with St. Francis Xavier, Groveton to form St. Marguerite d'Youville Parish, Groveton.

NORTH WALPOLE, CHESHIRE CO., ST. PETER (1878) [CEM] Merged with St. Catherine of Siena Parish, Charlestown to form All Saints Parish, Charlestown.

PELHAM, HILLSBOROUGH CO., ST. PATRICK (1946) Rev. Eddy N. Bisson; Deacon John F. Ross. In Res., Rev. Thomas J. Bresnahan (Retired).
Res. & Church: 12 Main St., 03076-3724. Tel: 603-635-3525; Fax: 603-635-3919.
School—(Grades K-8), 16 Main St., 03076. Tel: 603-635-2941; Fax: 603-635-9800. Roger Dumont, Prin.; Traci Gamble, Librarian. Lay Teachers 20; Students 238.
Catechesis/Religious Program—Tel: 603-635-1447. Gael Ouellette, Catechetical Leader; Dawn Paulini, Catechetical Leader.

PENACOOK, MERRIMACK CO., IMMACULATE CONCEPTION (1880) [CEM] Rev. Raymond J. Potvin.
Res.: 9 Bonney St., 03303-1654. Tel: 603-753-4413.
Catechesis/Religious Program—Karen Mead, Catechetical Leader.

PETERBOROUGH, HILLSBOROUGH CO.

1—DIVINE MERCY PARISH (2006) Rev. Gerald R. Belanger.
Res.: 10 Greenfield Rd., Bennington, 03442. Tel: 603-588-2180.
Office: 18 Vine St., 03458-2403. Tel: 603-924-7647 (Church Office); Fax: 603-924-8365.
St. Denis Church—Church St., Harrisville, 03450.
St. Patrick Church—9 Greenfield Rd., Bennington, 03442.
St. Peter Church—18 Vine St., 03458.

2—ST. PETER (1900) [CEM] Merged in 2006 with St. Denis, Harrisville and St. Patrick, Bennington in 2006 to form Divine Mercy Parish, Peterborough.

PITTSFIELD, MERRIMACK CO., OUR LADY OF LOURDES (1889) Rev. John B. Loughnane.
Res.: 20 River Rd., 03263-3314. Tel: 603-435-6242; Fax: 603-435-9398.
Catechesis/Religious Program—Tel: 603-942-8716; Fax: 603-435-8840. Katrina Allan, Catechetical Leader.
Mission—St. Joseph [CEM] 844 1st NH Turnpike (Rte. 4), Northwood, Rockingham Co. 03261. Tel: 603-435-6242; Fax: 603-435-9398.

PLAISTOW, ROCKINGHAM CO.

1—HOLY ANGELS (1892) [CEM] Merged in 2007 with Mary, Mother of the Church, Newton to form St. Luke the Evangelist Parish, Plaistow.

2—ST. LUKE THE EVANGELIST PARISH (2007) Rev. Michael R. Monette.
Office: 8 Atkinson Depot Rd. (Rte. 121), 03865-3103. Tel: 603-382-8324; Fax: 603-382-1113.
Res.: 12 Amesbury Rd., Newton, 03858.
Holy Angels Church—
Mary, Mother of the Church—12 Amesbury Rd., Newton, 03858-3200.
School—St. Luke the Evangelist Pre-School, Tel: 603-382-9783; Fax: 603-382-9783. Jean Lanctot, Prin.
Catechesis/Religious Program—Joyce Szczapa, Catechetical Leader.
Convent—6 Atkinson Depot Rd., 03865. Tel: 603-382-2744.

PLYMOUTH, GRAFTON CO.

1—HOLY TRINITY PARISH (2006) Revs. Leo A. LeBlanc; Eusbio F. Silva; Deacon Michael Guy.
Res. & Office: 46 Langdon St., 03264-1438. Tel: 603-536-4700; Fax: 603-536-4709.
St. Agnes Church—19 Hill Ave., Ashland, 03217.
St. Matthew Church—11 School St., 03264.
St. Timothy Church—119 School St., Bristol, 03222.
Mission—Our Lady of Grace 2 W. Shore Rd., Bristol, 03222.

2—ST. MATTHEW (1916) Merged in 2006 with St. Timothy, Bristol and St. Agnes, Ashland to form Holy Trinity Parish, Plymouth.

PORTSMOUTH, ROCKINGHAM CO.

1—ST. CATHERINE OF SIENA (1951) Merged in 2006 with St. James and Immaculate Conception, Portsmouth to form Corpus Christi Parish, Portsmouth.

2—CORPUS CHRISTI PARISH (2006) Very Rev. Michael Kerper; Rev. Marcos Gonzalez.
Office: 2075 Lafayette Rd., 03801. Tel: 603-436-4555; Fax: 603-433-4401.
Res.: 98 Summer St., 03801. Tel: 603-436-0048; Fax: 603-436-8848.
Immaculate Conception Church—98 Summer St., 03801-4398.
St. Catherine of Siena Church—845 Woodbury Ave., 03801-3294.
St. James Church—2075 Lafayette Rd., 03801-5697.

3—IMMACULATE CONCEPTION (1851) [CEM 2] Merged in 2006 with St. Catherine of Siena and St. James, Portsmouth to form Corpus Christi Parish, Portsmouth.

4—ST. JAMES (1958) [JC] Merged in 2006 with St. Catherine of Siena and Immaculate Conception, Portsmouth to form Corpus Christi Parish, Portsmouth.

ROCHESTER, STRAFFORD CO.

1—ST. MARY (1872) [CEM] Rev. Daniel J. Sinibaldi; Sr. Lucie Ducas, C.S.C., Pastoral Assoc.; Deacon Richard A. Falardeau.
Office: 71 Lowell St., 03867-5002. Tel: 603-332-1869; Fax: 603-332-2040.
Catechesis/Religious Program—Sr. Lucie Ducas, C.S.C., D.R.E.; Anna Ingram, Catechetical Leader.

2—OUR LADY OF THE HOLY ROSARY (1883), (French), [CEM] Rev. Paul M. Gousse.
Res. & Church: 189 N. Main St., 03867-1299. Tel: 603-332-1863; Fax: 603-330-0865.

ROLLINSFORD, STRAFFORD CO., ST. MARY (1856) [CEM] Rev. Michael S. Taylor; Deacon William Brown.
Rectory—Holy Trinity, 404 High St., Somersworth, 03878. Tel: 603-692-4367; Fax: 603-692-4454.
Catechesis/Religious Program—Tel: 603-749-1666. Laurie Lambert, Catechetical Leader.

RYE BEACH, ROCKINGHAM CO., ST. THERESA (1979) Rev. Maurice D. Lavigne.
Res.: 815 Central Rd., P.O. Box 482, 03871-0482. Tel: 603-964-6440; Fax: 603-964-4139.
Catechesis/Religious Program—Tel: 603-964-9878. Gregory Hodsdon, Catechetical Leader; Anne Hoeing, Catechetical Leader.

SALEM, ROCKINGHAM CO.

1—ST. JOSEPH (1910) Revs. John W. Michalowski, S.J.; Thomas J. Fitzpatrick, S.J.; Deacon David Costello, Pastoral Min. In Res., Rev. Arthur Pare, S.J. (Retired).
Res. & Mailing: 33 Main St., 03079-1922. Tel: 603-898-4933; Fax: 603-893-9236.
Church: 40 Main St., 03079.
Catechesis/Religious Program—Tel: 603-893-9692. Gerard Bergeron, D.R.E.

2—MARY, QUEEN OF PEACE (1966) Revs. John W. Michalowski, S.J.; Thomas J. Fitzpatrick, S.J.; Mary Roy, Pastoral Min.
Res.: 200 Lawrence Rd., 03079-3978. Tel: 603-893-8661; Fax: 603-890-0292.
Catechesis/Religious Program—Marie Mullen, C.R.E.; Carol Kater, Catechetical Leader (Jr. High). Students 584.

SANBORNVILLE, CARROLL CO., ST. ANTHONY (1908) [CEM] Rev. Edmund A. Babicz; Mary Sullivan, Pastoral Min.; Deacon William Rich.
Res.: 239 Meadow St., P.O. Box 490, 03872-0490. Tel: 603-522-3304; Fax: 603-522-8273.
Catechesis/Religious Program—Andrea Corso, Catechetical Leader; Beth Kilroy, Catechetical Leader.

SOMERSWORTH, STRAFFORD CO.

1—HOLY TRINITY (1857) [CEM] Merged with St. Martin, Somersworth to form Saint Ignatius of Loyola, Somersworth.

2—SAINT IGNATIUS OF LOYOLA (2009) Rev. Michael S. Taylor; Deacon William Brown.
Res.: 120 Maple St., 03878-1999. Tel: 603-692-2172; Fax: 603-692-2499.
Holy Trinity Church: 404 High St., 03878.
St. Martin Church: 120 Maple St. Ext., 03878.
Catechesis/Religious Program—Janet Jacobson, Catechetical Leader.

3—ST. MARTIN (1882), (French), [CEM] Merged with Holy Trinity, Somersworth to form Saint Ignatius Loyola, Somersworth.

SUNCOOK, MERRIMACK CO., ST. JOHN THE BAPTIST (1873) [CEM 2] Rev. Edmund G. Crowley; Deacon David Shrader. In Res., Revs. John B. Finnigan (Retired); Nicholas P. Rogers (Retired).
Res. & Church: 10 School St., 03275-1917. Tel: 603-485-3113; Fax: 603-485-2113.
Catechesis/Religious Program—Tel: 603-485-3972. Muriel Previe, Catechetical Leader.

TILTON, BELKNAP CO., ST. MARY OF THE ASSUMPTION (1894) [CEM] Rev. Richard M. Giroux.
Res.: 16 Chestnut St., 03276-5546. Tel: 603-286-4445; Fax: 603-286-4663.
Catechesis/Religious Program—Tel: 603-286-4554. Mary Lacroix, Catechetical Leader.

TROY, CHESHIRE CO., IMMACULATE CONCEPTION (1903) [CEM] Very Rev. Daniel O. Lamothe; Revs. Steven M. Kucharski; Paul B. Boudreau Jr.; Deacon

Arnold J. Gustafson.
Mailing Address: 161 Main St., Ste. 204, Keene, 03431.
Catechesis/Religious Program—Joy Davis, D.R.E.

WEST LEBANON, GRAFTON CO., HOLY REDEEMER (1953), Unified in 2003 with Sacred Heart, Lebanon.

WEST STEWARTSTOWN, COOS CO., ST. ALBERT (1926) [CEM] Merged in 2007 with St. Brendan Parish, Colebrook to form North American Martyrs Parish, Colebrook.

WEST SWANZEY, CHESHIRE CO., ST. ANTHONY (1958), Unified in 2004 with St. Bernard Parish, Keene.

WHITEFIELD, COOS CO., ST. MATTHEW (1886) [CEM 2] Merged with All Saints, Lancaster to form Gate of Heaven, Lancaster.

WILTON, HILLSBOROUGH CO., SACRED HEART (1882) [CEM] Rev. James P. Walsh.
Res. & Mailing Address: c/o Sacred Heart of Jesus Rectory, 15 High St., Greenville, 03048-3121. Tel: 603-654-6554 (Parish).
Church: 47 Maple St., 03086.

WINCHESTER, CHESHIRE CO., ST. STANISLAUS (1962) Merged in 2006 with St. Joseph, Hinsdale to form Mary, Queen of Peace Parish, Hinsdale.

WINDHAM, ROCKINGHAM CO., ST. MATTHEW (1962) [JC] Rev. A. Stephen Marcoux III; Deacon Clarence R. Cummins.
Res.: 5 Searles Rd., 03087-1206. Tel: 603-893-3336; Fax: 603-898-4008.
Catechesis/Religious Program—Margaret Donahue-Turner, D.R.E.

WOLFEBORO, CARROLL CO., ST. CECILIA, Merged in 2003 with St. Joan of Arc Parish, Alton to form St. Katharine Drexel, Alton.

WOODSVILLE, GRAFTON CO., ST. JOSEPH (1896) [CEM] Rev. Jeffrey P. Statz.
Res.: 21 Pine St., 03785-1215. Tel: 603-747-2038; Fax: 603-747-8071.
Catechesis/Religious Program—Sandy Perry, Catechetical Leader.

Chaplains of Public Institutions

MANCHESTER. *Catholic Medical Center*. Revs. Donald E. Lafond (Retired), Bartholomew Salter, C.S.C., Sr. Martha Mulligan, R.S.M.
Elliott Hospital. Revs. Donald E. Clinton, Jean M. Lemay.
Hillsborough County Jail. Sr. Andrienne Gendron, P.M., Deacon David Shrader.
Veterans Administration Medical Center. Vacant.
Youth Development Center. Vacant.

BERLIN. *Androscoggin Valley Hospital*. Deacon Merle Albert, Sr. Monique Therriault, R.S.M., P.A., Chap.
Northern New Hampshire Correctional Facility. Very Rev. Richard A. Roberge, V.F.

BRENTWOOD. *Rockingham County House of Corrections*. Very Rev. Michael Kerper, V.F.

CLAREMONT. *Sullivan County House of Corrections*. Rev. Shawn M. Therrien.

CONCORD. *Concord Hospital*. Revs. Robert V. Paskey, S.J., Chap., Paul T. Gilbert, Daniel F. Szopa.
N.H. State Prison. Rev. Bernard J. Campbell, O.F.M-.Cap, Deacon James Daly, Chap., Rev. Anthony Kuzia, C.M.
New Hampshire Hospital. Vacant.

GOFFSTOWN. *New Hampshire State Prison for Women*. Rev. Msgr. John E. Molan, P.A. (Retired), Deacon David J. Shrader.

LACONIA. *Belknap County House of Corrections*. Revs. Gary J. Kosmowski, Albert J. Tremblay Jr.

LEBANON. *Dartmouth-Hitchcock Medical Center*. Revs. Albert A. Agresti, S.J., Christopher Chukwu.

NASHUA. *St. Joseph Hospital*. Revs. Eric T. Delisle, John E. Healey.
Southern N.H. Regional Medical Center and Nursing Homes. Sr. Doris Gagnon, P.M., Chap., Revs. Eric T. Delisle, Chap., John E. Healey.

NORTH HAVERHILL. *Grafton County House of Corrections*. Rev. Jeffrey P. Statz.

OSSIPEE. *Carroll County House of Correction*. Rev. Edmund A. Babicz.

WEST STEWARTSTOWN. *Coos County House of Corrections*. Rev. Craig I. Cheney.

WESTMORELAND. *Cheshire County House of Corrections*. Very Rev. Daniel O. Lamothe, V.F.

On Duty Outside the Diocese:
Revs.—
Arsenault, Edward J., S.T.L. (WDC)
de Laire, Georges F.
Frontiero, Anthony F., Villa Stritch, Via della Nocetta, 63, Rome 00164 Italy.
Mahoney, John J., Jr., J.C.L.

Military Chaplains:
Revs.—
Cody, Kevin W., Major, P.O. Box 52221, Shaw AFB, SC 29152-0221.
Glasgow, Robert K., CH, Major, USA, U.S. Army War College Memorial Chapel, 452 Mara Cir., Carlisle Barracks, PA 17013.

Absent on Sick Leave:
Rev.—
Szopa, Daniel F.

Absent on Leave:
Revs.—
Broussard, Dennis A.
Connor, Kevin T.
Lamy, Raymond J.
Ledoux, Damien C.

Retired:
Rev. Msgrs.—
Blair, Raymond O., 1 Harborside Dr., #4201, Delray Beach, FL 33483.
Burns, Lawrence E., 155 Echo Ave., Unit 1, Portsmouth, 03801.
Crosby, Charles E., 793 Ocean Blvd., Hampton, 03842.
Curran, Francis L., Bishop Peterson Residence, 221 Orange St., 03104-4324.
Desmond, Joseph E., Bishop Peterson Residence, 221 Orange St., 03104-4324.
Hannigan, Thomas J., St. Catherine Parish, 207 Hemlock St., 03104-3248.
MacDonald, Colin A., St. Joseph Cathedral, 145 Lowell St., 03104-6135.
Markham, James J., Parish of The Transfiguration, 107 Alsace St., 03102.
Molan, John E., P.A., St. Peter Rectory, 567 Manchester Rd., Auburn, 03032-3123.
Paradis, Wilfrid H., Bishop Peterson Residence, 221 Orange St., 03104-4324.
Pichette, Fernand L., 164 Boutwell St., 03102.
Revs.—
Allard, Marcel M., Ste. Marie Rectory, 378 Notre Dame Ave., 03102.
Auger, Gerald E., 235 Alsace St., 03102-3008.
Babineau, William E., St. Peter Parish, 567 Manchester Rd., Auburn, 03032-3123.
Bedard, Andre L., Infant Jesus, 121 Allds St., Nashua, 03060-6395.
Bellefeuille, Albert A., 55 Pleasant St., P.O. Box 65, Colebrook, 03576-0065.
Bilodeau, Florent, St. Anthony Parish, 172 Belmont St., 03103-4452.
Bilodeau, Roger P., 1 Gilson Rd., Hollis, 03049.
Blais, Roland O., Bishop Peterson Residence, 221 Orange St., 03104-4324.
Boisvert, Robert G., 6 Faith Ln., Center Barnstead, 03225.
Boucher, Gerard A., Bishop Peterson Residence, 221 Orange St., 03104-4324.
Bresnahan, Thomas J., St. Patrick, 12 Main St., Pelham, 03076-3724.
Bryson, John H., Bishop Peterson Residence, 221 Orange St., 03104-4324.
Coyne, Emmett A., 2606 Hathaway Point Rd., Saint Albans, VT 05478.
Demers, Wilfred G., Ste. Marie Rectory, 378 Notre Dame Ave., 03102-3760.
Desjardins, George A., 6 Pleasant St., E-3, Hooksett, 03106-1421.
Desjardins, Raymond S., Bishop Gendron Apartments, 195 Dover Point Rd., Dover, 03820-4612.
DesRuisseaux, Charles E., 51 River Front Dr., Apt. 3, 03102.
Di Russo, Anthony, St. Aloysius of Gonzaga Parish, 48 W. Hollis St., Nashua, 03060.
Dunn, Gerald R., P.O. Box 7356, Gonic, 03839. Tel: 603-569-5058
Finnigan, John B., St. John the Baptist Parish, 10 School St., Suncook, 03275-1917.
Foisy, Leonard R., Bishop Peterson Residence, 221 Orange St., 03104.
Frechette, Leo L., P.O. Box 68, West Nottingham, 03291-0068.
Gagnon, Andre J., St. Francis Health Care Center, 406 Court St., Laconia, 03246-3600.
Gagnon, Leo G., 4119 Whitford Cir., #401, Glen Allen, VA 23060.
Gallant, Rodrigue J., Parish of the Transfiguration, 107 Alsace St., 03102.
Goggin, Cornelius J., 96 River Rd., 03104.
Goodwin, Robert T., 4851 W. Gandy Blvd., #8-40, Tampa, FL 33611-3016.
Gregoire, Paul L., 377 Wilson St., 03103.
Griffin, Michael J., St. Ann Healthcare Center, 195 Dover Point Rd., Dover, 03820-4693.
Irwin, Patrick F., 77 Israel Head Rd., #17, Ogunquit, ME 03907.
Keenan, Thomas E., 679 Lamoine Beach Rd., Lamoine, ME 04605-4744.
Kelley, Edward J., P.O. Box 416, Dover, 03821-0416.
Kelso, Francis E., 774 Dana Hill Rd., New Hampton, 03256.
Kemmery, Robert J., 2500 Parkview Dr., #621, Hallandale Beach, FL 33009.
Klatka, Joseph S., 53 Claremont Ave., 03103.
Lacroix, Maurice R., 704 Bridge St., 03104-5447.
Lafond, Donald E., 3010 Brown Ave., #1, 03103.
Lampron, Maurice W., P.O. Box 717, Wolfeboro Falls, 03896-0717.
Marchand, Robert A., 419 Coolidge Ave., 03102-3214.
McHugh, Paul F., P.O. Box 3352, Concord, 03302-3352.
O'Connor, Francis J., 15 Pilgrim Cir., Apt. D, Methuen, MA 01844.
Oliviera, Humbert, 9 Hollis St., Cambridge, MA 02140.
Piwowar, Stanley J., 223 Winter St., Claremont, 03743.
Polito, Victor V.J., St. Mary Rectory, 156 E. Main St., Amsterdam, NY 12010. Tel: 518-843-2728
Rogers, Nicholas P., St. John the Baptist Parish, 10 School St., Suncook, 03275.
Rundzio, Mark A., 745 2nd Ave., Berlin, 03570.
Savage, Thomas J., P.O. Box 5531, 03108.
Simoneau, Norman J., 185 Eastern Ave., Unit 202, 03104.
Smith, Richard A., 47 Howard Hill Rd., Apt. 202, Jaffrey, 03452.
Soucey, Louis A., Bishop Paterson Residence, 221 Orange St., 03104-4324.
Thibodeau, Andre M., Bishop Primeau Apts. #304, 519 Bridge St., 03104.
Turgeon, Armand A., 5 Maywood Dr., Nashua, 03064.
Vickery, Richard F., Bishop Peterson Residence, 221 Orange St., 03104-4324.
Wegman, Richard H., 70 Taylor Dr. Back Bay, Wolfeboro, 03894-4356.
Wright, John A., 13 Brandon Ln., Goffstown, 03045.

Permanent Deacons:
Abbott, Leon E., Jr., St. Mark Parish, Londonderry
Albert, Merle M., Good Shepherd, Berlin; Holy Family, Gorham
Anderson, Robert J., Jr., (Retired)
Andrade, Ramon, St. Anne-St. Augustine, Manchester
Blicharz, John, All Saints, Charlestown
Borkush, George J., St. Peter, Auburn; St. Paul, Candia
Borland, Joseph P., St. Mary, Hillsborough; St. Theresa, Henniker
Boucher, Paul R., St. Mary, Claremont
Brown, William, St. Martin and Holy Trinity, Somersworth; St. Mary, Rollinsford
Carey, John J., Our Lady of The Mountains, N. Conway
Cloutier, Richard A., (Retired)
Costello, David T., St. Joseph, Salem
Cummins, Clarence R., St. Matthew, Windham
Daly, James, Immaculate Conception, Nashua
DeRosia, Winton P., St. Theresa, Henniker; St. Mary, Hillsborough
Esposito, Robert, (Retired)
Falardeau, Richard A., St. Mary, Rochester and St. Peter, Farmington
Fitzpatrick, T. Kelly, (Retired)
Gagnon, Robert J., St. Joseph & St. Charles, Dover
Gallinaro, Frank, Ste. Marie and Sacred Heart, Manchester
Gustafson, Arnold J., St. Bernard & St. Margaret Mary, Keene; Mary, Queen of Peace, Hinsdale; Immaculate Conception, Troy
Guy, Michael, Holy Trinity, Plymouth
Hamel, David C., St. John Neumann, Merrimack
Hilston, Edmund C., Blessed John XXIII, Nashua
Hobson, Mark F., St. Pius X, Manchester
Jacobs, Dennis M., Our Lady of the Miraculous Medal, Hampton
Kram, Harry A., St. Anthony Parish, Manchester
LaBonte, Alfred A., Jr., St. Joseph, Nashua
Long, George H. (Gary), Jr., St. Thomas Aquinas, Derry
Marcotte, Raymond V., St. Kathryn, Hudson
Martin, John, St. Joseph Hospital, Nashua
Mazzuchelli, Joseph, St. Elizabeth Seton, Bedford
McCarty, William, Our Lady of the Lakes, Lakeport
McGinn, Gregory R., Our Lady of Fatima, New London
Morey, Russell, St. Joseph, Laconia
Morrow, John, Immacualte Heart of Mary, Concord
Mullen, William E., St. Anne, Hampstead
Munz, Edward P., St. Catherine, Manchester
Patterson, James E., Our Lady of Mercy, Merrimack
Payeur, Marc G., St. Jude, Londonderry
Polcari, Joseph A., St. Matthew, Whitefield
Potvin, Robert R., St. Joseph Cathedral, Manchester
Rich, William, St. Joseph, Center Ossipee and St. Anthony, Sanbornville
Rock, James E., St. Peter & Sacred Heart, Concord
Ross, John F., St. Patrick, Pelham
Schladenhauffen, Charles D., (Retired)

Shannon, Richard J., Parish of the Transfiguration, Manchester
Shrader, David J., Chaplain of New Hampshire State Prison for Women; Goffstown and Hillsborough County Jail, Manchester; Holy Rosary, Hooksett; St. John the Baptist, Suncook
St. George, John H., Blessed John XXIII, Nashua
Testa, Paul E., Our Lady of the Miraculous Medal, Hampton

INSTITUTIONS LOCATED IN THE DIOCESE

[A] SEMINARIES, RELIGIOUS OR SCHOLASTICATES

MANCHESTER. *St. Anselm Abbey Seminary*, 100 St. Anselm Dr., 03102. Tel: 603-641-7115; Fax: 603-641-7116. Email: vocations@anselm.edu. Web: www.anselm.edu. Rev. Anselm Smedile, O.S.B., Dir. Vocations. Order of St. Benedict. Faculty 3; Students 1.

CENTER HARBOR. *Immaculate Conception Apostolic School*, 109 Dane Rd., P.O. Box 936, 03226. Tel: 603-253-7728; Fax: 603-253-8740. Revs. David Steffy, L.C., Prin.; Peter Kim, L.C., Vice Prin.; Victor Franco, L.C.; Steven Licinsky, L.C. Priests 4; Brothers 5; Lay Teachers 10; Students 71.

[B] COLLEGES AND UNIVERSITIES

MANCHESTER. *Saint Anselm College* 03102. Tel: 603-641-7000; Fax: 603-641-7284. Email: jdefelice@anselm.edu. Web: www.anselm.edu. Rt. Rev. Matthew K. Leavy, O.S.B., Ph.D., Chancellor; Rev. Jonathan P. DeFelice, O.S.B., J.C.L., Pres. Admin. & Faculty. Order of St. Benedict. Priests 6; Brothers 2; Sisters 1; Lay Teachers 152; Students 1,900.

MERRIMACK. *The Thomas More College of Liberal Arts* (1978) 6 Manchester St., 03054. Tel: 603-880-8308; Fax: 603-880-9280. Email: info@thomasmorecollege.edu. Web: www.thomasmorecollege.edu. William E. Fahey, Ph.D., Pres.; Thomas Syseskey, Librarian. Total Staff 17; Students 90.

NASHUA. *Rivier College* (1933) 03060-5086. Tel: 603-888-1311; Fax: 603-897-8812. Web: www.rivier.edu. William J. Farrell, Pres.; Rev. Paul R. Demers, S.C., Chap.; Daniel Speidel, Dir. of Library. Sisters of the Presentation of Mary. Presentation Sisters 15; Teaching Sisters 3; Lay Teachers 71; Students 2,187.

WARNER. *Magdalen College* (1973) 511 Kearsarge Mountain Rd., 03278-9206. Tel: 603-456-2656; Fax: 603-456-2660. Email: administration@magdalen.edu. Web: www.magdalen.edu. Jeffrey J. Karls, Pres.; Dr. George Harne, Academic Dean; Marie Lasher, Librarian. Lay Teachers 7; Total Staff 18; Students 69.

[C] HIGH SCHOOLS, DIOCESAN

MANCHESTER. *Trinity High School*, 581 Bridge St., 03104-5395. Tel: 603-668-2910; Fax: 603-668-2913. Email: webmaster@trinity-hs.org. Web: www.trinity-hs.org. Mr. Denis Mailloux, Prin.; Steven Gadecki, Asst. Prin.; Patrick D. Smith, Dean of Students & Admissions Dir.; Joseph Malinowski, Campus Min. Lay Teachers 35; Total Staff 50; Students 480.

CONCORD. *Bishop Brady High School*, 25 Columbus Ave., 03301. Tel: 603-224-7418; Fax: 603-228-6664. Email: info@bishopbrady.edu. Web: www.bishopbrady.edu. Trevor Bonat, Prin.; Greg Roberts, Asst. Prin.; Joy Degnan, Asst. Prin.; Patricia Wilcox, Librarian. Lay Teachers 35; Students 369.

DOVER. *St. Thomas Aquinas High School* (1960) 197 Dover Point Rd., 03820. Tel: 603-742-3206; Fax: 603-749-7822. Email: sta@stalux.org. Web: www.stalux.org. Kevin Collins, Prin.; Mr. James Christie, Librarian. Sisters 1; Lay Teachers 57; Students 676.

[D] HIGH SCHOOLS, PRIVATE

NASHUA. *Bishop Guertin High School* (1963) 194 Lund Rd., 03060. Tel: 603-889-4107; Fax: 603-889-0701. Email: brmark@bghs.org. Web: www.bghs.org. Bro. Mark E. Hilton, S.C., Contact Person, Pres.; Linda Brodeur, Prin.; Bro. Paul Demers, S.C., Chap.; Janis Tunstall, Librarian. Brothers of the Sacred Heart., (Coed) Brothers 7; Lay Teachers 67; Students 882.

SUNAPEE. *Mount Royal Academy*, (Grades PreK-12), 26 Seven Hearths Ln., 03782. Tel: 603-763-9010; Fax: 603-763-5390. Email: dthibault@mountroyalacademy.com. Web: www.mountroyalacademy.com. David A. Thibault, Headmaster. Lay Teachers 12.

[E] REGIONAL AND PAROCHIAL ELEMENTARY SCHOOLS

MANCHESTER. *St. Anthony School* (1904) (Grades PreK-6), 148 Belmont St., 03103. Tel: 603-622-0414; Fax: 603-669-5212. Email: info@stanthonyschool-nh.com. Web: www.stanthonyschool-nh.com. Jerry Bergeron, Prin.; Mrs. Sally Green, Contact Person & Admin. Asst. Lay Teachers 14; Boys 74; Girls 86.

St. Benedict Academy (1989) (Grades PreK-6), 85 Third St., 03102. Tel: 603-669-3932; Fax: 603-669-3932. Email: sbaprincipal@comcast.net. Web: stbenedictacademy.org. Sr. Betty Roy, C.S.C., Prin. Lay Teachers 8; Students 148.

St. Casimir School, (Grades K-8), 456 Union St., 03103. Tel: 603-623-6411; Fax: 603-623-3236. Email: smlcssf@yahoo.com. Web: www.stcasimirnh.org. Sr. Frances Marion Bonczar, C.S.S.F., Prin.; Jennifer Girard, Librarian. Lay Teachers 9; Students 140.

St. Catherine School, (Grades PreK-6), 206 North St., 03104. Tel: 603-622-1711; Fax: 603-624-4935. Email: stcatherinenh@comcast.net. Web: www.saintcatherines.org. Sr. Janet Belcourt, C.S.C., Prin.; Mrs. Alice Gordon, Librarian. Sisters 1; Lay Teachers 20; Students 325.

St. Joseph Regional Junior High, (Grades 7-8), 460 Pine St., 03104-6102. Tel: 603-624-4811; Fax: 603-624-6670. Email: stjoesjrhs@comcast.net. Web: www.stjoesjrhs.org. Pauline D. Martineau, Prin.; Patricia Cote, Librarian. Lay Teachers 14; Students 166.

CONCORD. *St. John Regional School* (1888) (Grades PreK-8), 61 S. State St., 03301. Tel: 603-225-3222; Fax: 603-225-0195. Email: mrsmckenna@stjohnregional.org. Michelle M. McKenna, Prin. Lay Teachers 18; Students 232.

DERRY. *St. Thomas Aquinas School*, (Grades PreK-8), 3 Moody St., P.O. Box 387, 03038. Tel: 603-432-2712; Fax: 603-432-2179. Email: info@staderry.com. Web: www.staderry.com. Paul Rakiey, Prin. Sisters 1; Lay Teachers 9; Students 217.

DOVER. *St. Mary Academy*, (Grades PreK-8), 222 Central Ave., 03820. Tel: 603-742-3299; Fax: 603-743-3483. Email: reese@saintmaryacademy.org. Web: www.saintmaryacademy.org. Cynthia B. Kuder, Interim Prin.; Teresa Zellem, Librarian. Lay Teachers 25; Students 375.

HAMPTON. *Sacred Heart School* (1962) (Grades PreK-8), 289 Lafayette Rd., 03842. Tel: 603-926-3254; Fax: 603-929-1109. Email: prin@shshampton.org. Web: www.OLMMparish.org. Catherine Smith, Prin.; Michelle Ryzewic, Librarian. Sisters 1; Lay Teachers 29; Students 280.

JAFFREY. *St. Patrick School* (1962) (Grades PreK-8), 70 Main St., 03452. Tel: 603-532-7676; Fax: 603-532-7476. Email: principal@saintpatschool.org. Web: www.saintpatschool.org. Sr. Cecile Provost, C.S.C., Prin.; Katie Robbins, Adm. Asst. & Bookkeeper. Sisters 2; Lay Teachers 14; Students 94.

KEENE. *St. Joseph Regional School* (1886) (Grades PreK-8), 92 Wilson St., 03431. Tel: 603-352-2720; Fax: 603-358-5465. Email: ldellasanta@stjosephkeene.org. Web: stjosephkeene.org. Sr. Laura Della Santa, R.S.M., Prin. & Contact; Mrs. Kathy Bill, Librarian. Lay Teachers 14; Students 138; Total Staff 22.

LACONIA. *Holy Trinity* (1971) (Grades PreK-8), 50 Church St., 03246. Tel: 603-524-3156; Fax: 603-524-4454. Email: jfortier@holytrinity.pvt.k12.nh.us. Web: holytrinity.pvt.k12.nh.us. Mr. Jack Fortier, Prin. Lay Teachers 13; Total Staff 21; Students 98.

Litchfield

St. Francis of Assisi School, (Grades PreK-6), 9 St. Francis Way, Litchfield, 03052-8050. Tel: 603-424-3312; Fax: 603-424-9128. Email: sdannible@stfrancisschoolnh.org. Shannon Dannible, Prin.; Rose Van Uden, Librarian. Lay Teachers 9; Students 141.

NASHUA. *St. Christopher School* (1963) (Grades PreK-6), 20 Cushing Ave., 03064. Tel: 603-882-7442; Fax: 603-594-9253. Email: principal@stchrisschoolnh.org. Web: www.stchrisschoolnh.org. Jack Daniels, Prin.; Patricia Riley, Librarian. Lay Teachers 19; Students 300.

Infant Jesus School (1909) (Grades K-6), 3 Crown St., 03060. Tel: 603-889-2649; Fax: 603-594-9117. Email: lafleur@ijschool.org. Web: www.ijschool.org. Estelle LaFleur, Prin.; Mrs. Virginia Dumont, Librarian. Sisters 1; Lay Teachers 20; Students 225.

Nashua Catholic Regional Junior High School (1972) (Grades 7-8), 6 Bartlett Ave., 03064-1602. Tel: 603-883-6707; 603-882-7011; Fax: 603-594-8955. Email: t_kelleher@comcast.net. Web: www.ncrjhs.org. Thomas Kelleher, Prin. Lay Teachers 20; Students 244.

PELHAM. *St. Patrick School*, (Grades K-8), 16 Main St., 03076. Tel: 603-635-2941; Fax: 603-635-9800. Email: stpatsk8@hotmail.com. Web: www.saintpatrickschool.net. Roger Dumont, Prin. & Contact; Traci Gamble, Librarian. Lay Teachers 20; Students 193.

PORTSMOUTH. *St. Patrick* (1888) (Grades PreK-8), 125 Austin St., 03801. Tel: 603-436-0739; Fax: 603-436-1569. Email: office@stpatsweb.com. Web: www.stpatsschool.com. Sr. Mary J. Walsh, O.L.L., Prin.; Mrs. Amanda Norris, Sec.; Melanie Shank, Librarian. Lay Teachers 22; Students 180.

ROCHESTER. *St. Elizabeth Seton School* (1886) (Grades K-8), 16 Bridge St., 03867. Tel: 603-332-4803; Fax: 603-332-2915. Email: stbrochester@metrocast.net. Web: www.sesschool.org. Suzanne T. Boutin, Prin. Lay Teachers 11; Students 137.

SALEM. *St. Joseph Regional Catholic School* (1959) (Grades K-8), 40 Main St., 03079. Tel: 603-893-6811; Fax: 603-893-6811. Email: sjrcsoffice@comcast.net. Web: sjrcs.com. Ruth A. Hassett, Prin.; Lois Powers, Librarian. Lay Teachers 19; Total Staff 34; Students 213.

Kindergarten Marilyn Byron, Dir. Lay Teachers 1; Students 19.

[F] ELEMENTARY SCHOOLS, PRIVATE

MANCHESTER. *St. Augustin Pre-School*, 251 Merrimack St., 03103. Tel: 603-623-8800; Fax: 603-626-1517. Email: sapreschool@comcast.net. Mailing Address: 383 Beech St., 03103. Crystal Elie, Dir. Lay Teachers 6; Boys 26; Girls 9.

Holy Cross Early Childhood Center, 420 Island Pond Rd., 03109-4812. Tel: 603-668-0510. Carol Garhart, Prin. & Admin. Sisters 1; Lay Teachers 3; Students 25.

Mount Saint Mary Academy, (Grades PreK-6), 2291 Elm St., 03104. Tel: 603-623-3155; Fax: 603-621-9254. Email: principal@mtstmary.org. Web: www.mtstmary.org. Patricia Baldissard, Prin.; Sr. Felicia McKone, R.S.M., Contact Person; Jill Archard, Librarian. Sisters 3; Lay Teachers 15; Students 164.

GOFFSTOWN. *Villa Augustina School* (1918) (Grades PreK-8), 208 S. Mast St., 03045. Tel: 603-497-2361; Fax: 603-497-5981. Email: info@villaaugustina.org. Web: www.villaaugustina.org. Mr. Charles Lawrence, Prin.; Mrs. Deidre Angwin, Librarian. Sisters 1; Aides 2; Lay Teachers 19; Students 179.

HUDSON. *Presentation of Mary Academy* (1926) (Grades PreK-8), 182 Lowell Rd., 03051. Tel: 603-889-6054; Fax: 603-595-8504. Web: www.pmaschool.org. Email: pmaprincipal@comcast.net. Sr. Maria Rosa, P.M., Prin.; Denise Babcock, Librarian. Sisters of the Presentation of Mary. Sisters 4; Lay Teachers 30; Students 415.

SUNAPEE. *Mount Royal Academy*, (Grades PreK-12), 26 Seven Hearths Ln., 03782. Tel: 603-763-9010; Fax: 603-763-5390. Email: dthibault@mountroyalacademy.com. Web: www.mountroyalacademy.com. David A. Thibault, Headmaster.

[G] CATHOLIC CHARITIES

MANCHESTER. *Catholic Charities Administration*, 215 Myrtle St., 03104. Tel: 603-669-3030; Fax: 603-626-1252. Web: www.nh-cc.org. Thomas E. Blonski, Pres. & CEO; Mrs. Dominque A. Rust, Vice Pres. & COO; Joanne Hollen, CFO; Joseph P. Naff, L.I.C.S.W., Dir. Clinical & Family Svcs.; Lisa Merrill-Burzak, Vice Pres. Devel.; Mr. Michael D. Lehrman, Vice Pres. Healthcare Svcs.; Deacon Richard J. Shannon, Dir. Parish Social Ministry; Ms. Melanie A. Gosselin, Exec. Dir. of N.H. Food Bank; Cathy Chesley, J.D., Ed.D., Dir. Immigration & Refugee Svcs.

District Offices:

633 Third Ave., P.O. Box 182, Berlin, 03570-0182. Tel: 603-752-1325; Fax: 603-752-6174. Email: berlin@nh-cc.org. Nicole Plourde, Admin. Mgr. & Parish Outreach Coord.

176 Loudon Rd., Concord, 03301-6025. Tel: 603-228-1108; Fax: 603-228-6025. Gertrude F. Bantle, Admin. Mgr. & Parish Outreach Coord.

161 Main St., Suite 200, Keene, 03431-3722. Tel: 603-357-3093; Fax: 603-357-7810. Email: keene@nh-cc.org. Sr. Kathleen Haight, R.C.D., P.A., Admin. Mgr. & Parish Outreach Coord.

17 Gilford Ave, Laconia, 03246-2827. Tel: 603-528-3035; Fax: 603-524-7153. Email: laconia@nh-cc.org. Leonard B. Campbell, Admin. Mgr. & Parish Outreach Coord.

24 Hanover St., #8, Lebanon, 03766-1334. Tel: 603-448-5151; Fax: 603-448-5155. Marc Cousineau, Admin. Mgr. & Parish Outreach Coord.

41 Cottage St., P.O. Box 323, Littleton, 03561-0323. Tel: 603-444-7727; Fax: 603-444-7728. Email:

littleton@nh-cc.org. Anthony Poekert, Admin. Mgr. & Parish Outreach Coord.
325 Franklin St., 03101-1999. Tel: 603-624-4717; Fax: 603-624-4736. Email: manchester@nh-cc.org. Debra Naff, LCMHC, Admin. Mgr., & Clinical Sup.
261 Lake St., Nashua, 03060-4127. Tel: 603-889-9431; Fax: 603-880-4643. Email: nashua@nh-cc.org. Arlene Cody, M.A., LCMHC, Admin. Mgr. & Clinical Sup.
23 Grant St., Rochester, 03867-3001. Tel: 603-332-7701; Fax: 603-332-9629. Email: rochester@nh-cc.org. Debra Naff, LCMHC, Admin. Mgr., & Clinical Sup.
45 Stiles Rd., Ste. 103, Salem, 03079-4808. Tel: 603-893-1971; Fax: 603-898-8661. Email: salem@nh-cc.org. Arlene Cody, M.A., LCMHC, Admin. Mgr., & Clinical Sup.
Other Programs:
Diocesan Consultation & Counseling Services, 215 Myrtle St., 03104. Tel: 603-668-0014; Fax: 603-623-7676. Email: gmckinney@nh-cc.org. Joseph P. Naff, Dir. Clinical & Family Svcs.
Healthcare Services, 215 Myrtle St., 03104. Tel: 603-641-0577; Fax: 603-641-6210. Email: nhcc@nrmail.com. Mr. Michael D. Lehrman, Vice Pres. Healtcare Svcs.
Immigration and Refugee Services, 261 Lake St., Nashua, 03060-4127. Tel: 603-889-9431; Fax: 603-880-4643. Email: kgeorge@nh-cc.org. Cathy Chesley, J.D., Ed.D., Dir. Immigration & Refugee Svcs. Legal and case management services for immigrants and refugees.
New Hampshire Food Bank, 700 E. Industrial Park Dr., 03109. Tel: 603-669-9725; Fax: 603-669-0270. Web: www.nhfoodbank.org. Ms. Melanie A. Gosselin, Exec. Dir. Statewide food distribution to soup kitchens, food pantries and direct service programs.
Our Place, 16 Oak St., 03104-4319. Tel: 603-647-2244; Fax: 603-647-9933. Karen A. Munsell, Admin. Mgr. & Social Worker. Services for pregnant and parenting teens.
St. Charles Children's Home, 19 Grant St., Rochester, 03867-3001. Tel: 603-332-4768; Fax: 603-332-3948. Email: mpm@stcharleshome.net. Sr. Paul Marie Santa Lucia, S.C.M.C., Admin. Residential services for children who have been removed from unsafe home environments. Total Staff 18; Total Assisted 20.
Bishop Peterson Residence, 221 Orange St., 03104-4324. Tel: 603-641-6277; Fax: 603-641-0385. Marlene Makowski, Admin.

[H] CHILD CARE INSTITUTIONS

MANCHESTER. *St. Peter's Home* (1902) 300 Kelley St., 03102-3093. Tel: 603-625-9313; Fax: 603-625-1910. Email: sft@stpeterhome.com. Web: www.stpeterhome.com. Sr. Florence Therrien, S.C.S.H., Dir.; Mrs. Donna M. Vachon, Asst. Dir.; Sr. Rita Beaulieu, S.C.S.H., Treas. Sisters of Charity (Grey Nuns) 4.

ALLENSTOWN. *Pine Haven Boys Center* (1963) 133 River Rd., P.O. Suncook, 03275. Tel: 603-485-7141; Fax: 603-485-7142. Email: fr.john@comcast.net. Revs. Paul Riva, C.R.S., Dir.; John Vitali, C.R.S., M.Ed.; Remo Zanatta, C.R.S. Somascan Fathers. Children 20; Total Staff 40.

ROCHESTER. *St. Charles Children's Home*, 19 Grant St., 03867-3099. Tel: 603-332-4768; Fax: 603-332-3948. Email: mpm@stcharleshome.net. Sr. Paul Marie Santa Lucia, Admin. New Hampshire Catholic Charities. Sisters 7; Dependent Children 25.

[I] GENERAL HOSPITALS

MANCHESTER. *Catholic Medical Center of Manchester, NH, Inc.*, 100 McGregor St., 03102. Tel: 603-668-3545; Fax: 603-663-6850. Web: www.catholicmedicalcenter.org. Alyson Pitman Giles, Pres. & CEO. Sisters 3; Bed Capacity 330; Total Staff 2,081; Inpatient Admissions 9,431; Outpatient Admissions 212,957.
Catholic Medical Center Associates, 100 McGregor St., 03102. Tel: 603-668-3545; Fax: 603-663-6850. Web: www.catholicmedicalcenter.org.
New England Heart Institute Foundation, 100 McGregor St., 03102. Tel: 603-668-3545; Fax: 603-663-6850. Web: www.catholicmedicalcenter.org.

NASHUA. *St. Joseph Hospital*, 172 Kinsley St., 03061. Tel: 603-882-3000; Fax: 603-578-5060. Web: www.stjosephhospital.com. Peter B. Davis, Pres. & CEO; Claudette L. Mahar, Vice Pres. Hospital Svcs.; Deacon John Martin, Staff Chap. Bed Capacity 208; Patients Assisted Annually 211,542; Total Staff 2,000.
Rivier-St. Joseph School of Nursing Fax: 603-897-8813.

[J] HEALTH CARE FACILITIES

MANCHESTER. *Holy Cross Health Center, Inc.* (1984) 357 Island Pond Rd., 03109-4811. Tel: 603-628-3550; Fax: 603-626-6270. Email: bonniehchc@conversent.net. Bonnie McMahon, N.H.A., Admin. Nursing home for women religious.
St. Joseph Residence (1980) 495 Mammoth Rd., 03104. Tel: 603-668-6011; Fax: 603-647-6648. Email: MJMakowski@presmarynh.org. Marlene Makowski, Admin. Sponsored by the Presentation of Mary Sisters., New Hampshire Catholic Charities.
Mt. Carmel Rehabilitation and Nursing Center, 235 Myrtle St., 03104-4399. Tel: 603-627-3811; Fax: 603-626-4696. Email: mtc.administrator@nh-cc.org. New Hampshire Catholic Charities. Residents 122; Total Staff 160; Total Assisted Annually 231.
St. Teresa Rehabilitation and Nursing Center (1948) 519 Bridge St., 03104-5396. Tel: 603-668-2373; Fax: 603-668-0059. Email: stt.administrator@nh-cc.org. Joe Bohunicky, NHA, Admin. New Hampshire Catholic Charities Total Staff 62; Aged Residents 51.
Bishop Primeau Senior Living Community (1986) Tel: 603-668-7703; Fax: 603-668-0059. Linda Illg, Apartment Mgr. Total Staff 3; Apartments 25.

BERLIN. *St. Vincent de Paul Rehabilitation and Nursing Center*, 29 Providence Ave., 03570-3199. Tel: 603-752-1820; Fax: 603-752-7149. Email: stv.administrator@nh-cc.org. Louise Marquis, Admin. New Hampshire Catholic Charities. Residents 80; Total Staff 120.

DOVER. *St. Ann Rehabilitation and Nursing Center* (1958) 195 Dover Point Rd., 03820-4693. Tel: 603-742-2612; Fax: 603-743-3055. Email: sta.administrator@nh-cc.org. Karyn Partin, Admin.; Rev. Donald McAllister, Chap. (Retired). New Hampshire Catholic Charities. Residents 54; Total Staff 90.
Bishop Gendron Senior Living Community (1999) Tel: 603-742-2612; Fax: 603-743-3055. Cathy Meattey-Stawarz, Apartment Mgr. Total Staff 2; Apartments 31.

JAFFREY. *Good Shepherd Rehabilitation and Nursing Center*, 20 Plantation Dr., 03452-1935. Tel: 603-532-8762; Fax: 603-593-0006. Ann Nunn, Admin. & Contact. New Hampshire Catholic Charities. Total Staff 105; Total Assisted 71; Bed Capacity 83.

LACONIA. *Bishop Bradley Senior Living Community*, 406 Court St., 03246. Tel: 603-524-0466; Fax: 603-527-0884. Email: stt.administrator@nh-cc.org. Debra Sturgeon, Apartment Mgr. Apartments 25; Total Staff 4; Total Assisted Annually 36.
St. Francis Rehabilitation and Nursing Center (1948) 406 Court St., 03246-3000. Tel: 603-524-0466; Fax: 603-527-0884. Email: stf.administrator@nh-cc.org. Brenda Buttrick, RNC, NHA, Admin.; Rev. Andre J. Gagnon, Chap. (Retired). New Hampshire Catholic Charities. Residents 51; Total Staff 87; Total Assisted Annually 78.
Bishop Bradley Senior Living Community Total Staff 4; Apartments 25.

WINDHAM. *Warde Health Center*, 21 Searles Rd., P.O. Box 420, 03087-0420. Tel: 603-890-1290; Fax: 603-890-1293. Email: administrator@wardehealthcenter.com. Susan Denopolous, Admin. & Contact. Sisters of Mercy., Managed by New Hampshire Catholic Charities. Total Staff 73; Bed Capacity 64; Total Assisted Annually 106.

[K] MONASTERIES AND RESIDENCES OF PRIESTS AND BROTHERS

MANCHESTER. *St. Anselm Abbey* Of the Order of St. Benedict and St. Anselm College, including Seminary and Formation Program., 100 St. Anselm Dr., 03102-1310. Tel: 603-641-7651; Fax: 603-641-7267. Email: webmaster@anselm.edu. Web: www.anselm.edu/abbey/index.html. Most Rev. Joseph Gerry, O.S.B., D.D. (Retired); Rt. Rev. Matthew K. Leavy, O.S.B., Ph.D., Abbot & Chancellor; Bro. Isaac S. Murphy, O.S.B., Prior; Very Rev. Peter J. Guerin, O.S.B., Subprior; Revs. Bede G. Camera, O.S.B.; Mark A. Cooper, O.S.B.; Jerome J. Day, O.S.B.; Jonathan P. DeFelice, O.S.B., J.C.L.; Bernard Disco, O.S.B.; Cecil J. Donahue, O.S.B.; Mathias D. Durette, O.S.B.; John R. Fortin, O.S.B.; Jude J. Gray, O.S.B.; Benedict M. Guevin, O.S.B.; Augustine G. Kelly, O.S.B.; Iain G. MacLellan, O.S.B.; Benet C. Phillips, O.S.B.; Lawrence Schlegel, O.S.B. (Retired); Anselm Smedile, O.S.B.; Patrick M. Sullivan, O.S.B.; William J. Sullivan, O.S.B.; Bro. Andrew Thornton, O.S.B. Bishops 1; Priests 18; Brothers 3.

CENTER HARBOR. *L.C. Center Harbor, Inc.*, 109 Dane Rd., P.O. Box 936, 03226. Tel: 603-253-7728; Fax: 603-253-8740. Rev. Jose Felix Ortega, L.C., Sec. & Treas.

COLEBROOK. *Shrine of Our Lady of Grace* 03576. Tel: 603-237-5511; Fax: 603-237-8998. Revs. Robert G. Levesque, O.M.I., Supr.; Henri A. DeLisle, O.M.I.; Bros. Donat Daigle, O.M.I.; Paul Ricard, O.M.I. Oblates of Mary Immaculate (United States Province). Priests 2; Brothers 2.

ENFIELD. *Shrine of Our Lady of La Salette*, 410 N.H. Rte. 4A, P.O. Box 420, 03748-0420. Tel: 603-632-4301 (Gift Shop); 603-632-7087 (Business); Fax: 603-632-7648. Email: lasalette-enfield@comcast.net. Revs. Richard Landry, M.S., Shrine Dir.; Leo Maxfield, M.S., Chap. (Retired); Roger J. Plante, M.S., Chap.; Joseph Ross, M.S., Chap. (Retired); Bros. Claude Rheaume, M.S., Chap.; David Carignan, M.S., Chap.
La Salette of Enfield, Inc. Priests 4; Brothers 2; Total Staff 13.

HANOVER. *Order of Preachers, St. Thomas Aquinas House*, 2 Occum Ridge, P.O. Box 147, 03755. Tel: 603-643-2154; Fax: 603-543-9411. Revs. Jonathan Kalisch, O.P., Dir.; C. Francis Belanger, O.P.

NASHUA. *Brothers of the Sacred Heart*, 196 Lund Rd., 03060. Tel: 603-883-3683. Bro. Roger Lemoyne, S.C., Dir. Brothers 9.

[L] CONVENTS AND RESIDENCES OF SISTERS

MANCHESTER. *St. George Manor*, 357 Island Pond Rd., 03109. Tel: 603-624-4557; Fax: 603-645-1516. Sr. Pauline L. Lebel, C.S.C., Local Animator; Rev. Bruce W. Collard, (Non-residential). Sisters 41.
Monastery of the Precious Blood (1898) 700 Bridge St., 03104-5495. Tel: 603-623-4264; Fax: 603-647-8385. Sr. Mary Clare, A.P.B., Supr.; Rev. Maurice R. Lacroix, Chap. (Retired). Sisters Adorers of the Precious Blood. Sisters 27.
Missionary Rosebushes of St. Theresa (1922) 700 Bridge St., 03104-5495. Tel: 603-623-4264; Fax: 603-647-8385.
Regional Office of the Sisters of Holy Cross, 377 Island Pond Rd., 03109. Tel: 603-622-9504; Fax: 603-622-9782. Email: cdcsc@srsofholycross.com. Web: sistersofholycross.org. Sr. Carol J. Descoteaux, C.S.C., Ph.D., Regl. Animator. Total Staff 8.
Sisters of the Presentation of Mary Provincial House, 495 Mammoth Rd., 03104-5494. Tel: 603-669-1080; Fax: 603-622-4953. Email: provincialhouse@presmarynh.org. Web: www.presentationofmary.com. Sisters Suzanne Bourret, P.M., M.A., Prov. Supr.; Marie Christilla, Contact Person. Sisters in the Diocese 127; Sisters of the Presentation of Mary 134. *St. Joseph Residence* (1980) 495 Mammoth Rd., 03104-5494. Tel: 603-627-5831; 603-668-6011. *St. Marie Residence* (1959) 495 Mammoth Rd., 03104-5494. Tel: 603-623-0671. *Bethany House* (1989) 25 Garmon St., 03104. Tel: 603-625-1957. *Presentation of Mary Academy* (1926) 182 Lowell Rd., Hudson, 03051-4987. Tel: 603-883-8192; 603-889-6362; Fax: 603-883-8054. *Presentation of Mary House of Formation*, 186 Lowell Rd., Hudson, 03051-4908. Tel: 603-882-1347; Fax: 603-880-0298. *Presentation of Mary Convent* (1989) 633 Third Ave., Berlin, 03570. Tel: 603-752-1176; Fax: 603-752-4115. *Our Lady of Hope House of Prayer* (1990) 400 Temple Rd., New Ipswich, 03071. Tel: 603-878-2346; Fax: 603-878-4552. *Holy Angels Convent* (1996) 6 Atkinson Depot Rd., Rte. 121, Plaistow, 03865. Tel: 603-382-2744. *Emmaus Convent* (1999) 664 Central St., 03103. Tel: 603-647-4083. *Presentation of Mary Convent* (1998) 135 Ash St., Nashua, 03060. Tel: 603-882-9824.
St. Joseph Mission Center (Religious of Jesus and Mary) (2003) 627 Montgomery St., 03102. Tel: 603-232-4121. Sr. Priscilla Lemire, R.J.M., Pastoral Assoc.

CONCORD. *Monastery of Discalced Carmelites* (1946) 275 Pleasant St., 03301-2590. Tel: 603-225-5791; Fax: 603-223-9670. Sr. Claudette M. Blais, O.C.D., Prioress; Rev. Paul T. Gilbert, Chap. Professed Sisters 6; Novices 3.

LITTLETON. *Daughters of the Charity of the Sacred Heart of Jesus, Provincial House*, 226 Grove St., 03561. Tel: 603-444-5346; Fax: 603-444-5348. Email: srmgagne@roadrunner.com. Web: www.daughters-fcscj-charity-sacredheart.org. Sisters Monique Gagne, F.C.S.C.J., Provincial Supr.; Elaine Voyer, F.C.S.C.J., Supr. Sisters 41.

LONDONDERRY. *Sisters of Holy Cross*, Londonderry House, 68 Mammoth Rd., 03053-4024. Tel: 603-432-2430. Sr. Pauline L. Lebel, C.S.C.

NEW IPSWICH. *Our Lady of Hope House of Prayer*, 400 Temple Rd., 03071. Tel: 603-878-2346; Fax: 603-878-4552. Email: jmleblanc@wildblue.net. Web: presentationofmary.com. Sr. Jacqueline LeBlanc, P.M., Supr. Dir. Sisters 6.

NASHUA. *Holy Infant Jesus Convent*, 3 Crown St., 03060-6366. Tel: 603-882-0553. Email: labcsc@yahoo.com. Sr. Eleanor LaBranche, C.S.C., Local Animator. Sisters 6.

PORTSMOUTH. *Our Lady of Lourdes Convent*, 125

Austin St., #2, 03801. Tel: 603-436-6612; Fax: 603-436-7429. Email: lourdesll@comcast.net. Sr. Mary Joan Walsh, O.L.L., Supr. Sisters of Our Lady of Lourdes (O.L.L.).

WINDHAM. *Sisters of Mercy of the Americas-Northeast Community, Inc., Life & Ministry Office*, 21 Searles Rd., P.O. Box 420, 03087-0420. Tel: 603-893-6550; Fax: 603-893-2413. Email: nhsistersofmercy@comcast.net. Sr. Mary Cronin, R.S.M., Life & Ministry Admin.

Mount Saint Mary Corporation of the Sisters of Mercy, Inc., Nashua. Tel: 603-883-7874; Fax: 603-594-4178.

Manchester Convent of the Sisters of Mercy (1858) Tel: 603-893-6550; Fax: 603-893-2413.

Warde Health Center, Inc. Tel: 603-890-1290; Fax: 603-890-1293.

Mount St. Mary Academy, Inc. Tel: 603-623-3155; Fax: 603-621-9254.

Frances Warde House Tel: 603-893-6550; Fax: 603-893-2413.

McAuley Commons, 03087. Tel: 603-893-6550; Fax: 603-893-2413.

[M] ASSOCIATIONS OF THE CHRISTIAN FAITHFUL

ROCHESTER. **Daughters of Mary, Mother of Healing Love*, 19 Grant St., 03867. Tel: 603-332-4768; Fax: 603-332-3948. Email: smr@stcharleshome.net. Web: www.stcharleshome.org. Sr. Mary Rose Reddy, D.M.M.L., Sec. & Contact Person. (Private Association of the Christian Faithful)

[N] RETREAT HOUSES

ENFIELD. *Shrine of Our Lady of La Salette*, 417 N.H. Rte. 4A, P.O. Box 420, 03748. Tel: 603-632-7087 (Business); 603-632-4301 (Gift Shop); Fax: 603-632-7648. Email: lasalette-enfield@comcast.net. Web: www.lasaletteofenfield.org; www.eco-mission.info. Revs. Leo Maxfield, M.S., Chap. (Retired); Joseph Ross, M.S., Chap. (Retired); Richard Landry, M.S.; Roger J. Plante, M.S.; Bros. David J. Carignan, M.S.; Claude Rheaume, M.S. Priests 4; Brothers 2; Total Staff 13.

PITTSFIELD. *Berakah*, 96 Fairview Rd., 03263-3817. Tel: 603-435-7271; Fax: 603-435-6670. Email: berakah@aol.com. Web: www.berakah.org.

[O] CAMPUS MINISTRY AND NEWMAN CENTERS

DURHAM. *St. Thomas More Catholic Student Center at the University of New Hampshire* 6 Madbury Rd., P.O. Box 620, 03824-0620. Tel: 603-862-1310; Fax: 603-868-3765. Email: stmdurham@aol.com. Rev. Andrew W. Cryans, Chap.; Julie Tracy, Campus Minister; Roberta MacBride, Pastoral Asst.

HANOVER. *The Catholic Student Center at Dartmouth, Aquinas House, Aquinas at Dartmouth, Inc.* (1953) 2 Occom Ridge, P.O. Box 147, 03755. Tel: 603-643-2154; Fax: 603-643-9411. Web: www.dartmouth.edu/~aquinas. Revs. Jonathan Kalisch, O.P., Chap. & Dir.; C. Francis Belanger, O.P., Assoc. Chap.; Eileen Brody, M.Mus., Campus Min. Total Priests in Residence 2; Total Staff 3.

KEENE. *Catholic Newman Center for Keene State College* 161 Main St., Ste. 11, 03431. Tel: 603-357-1444; Fax: 603-352-7472. Email: ksc.newman.ctr@gmail.com. Marika Donders, Campus Min.

PLYMOUTH. *Plymouth State University Catholic Campus Ministry Plymouth State University*, 19 Highland Ave., Ste. A6, 03264. Tel: 603-535-2673. Email: kmtardif@plymouth.edu. Katherine Tardif, Catholic Campus Min. Tel: 603-535-2673.

[P] SPECIAL APOSTOLATE CENTERS

KEENE. *Catholic Faith Formation Center*, 161 Main St., Ste. 118, 03431. Tel: 603-352-7662; Fax: 603-352-7662. Email: cffc-keene@myfairpoint.net. Web: www.catholicfaithformationcenter.org.

LACONIA. *Christian Life Center* (1970) Box 306, 03247. Tel: 603-524-7503; Fax: 603-528-7847. Email: clclakes@verizon.net. Web: www.christianlifecenternh.org. Janet Leroux, Coord.

[Q] CAMPS AND COMMUNITY CENTERS

CENTER OSSIPEE. *Camp Marist* (1949) 22 Abel Blvd., Effingham, 03882. Tel: 603-539-4552; Fax: 603-539-8318. Email: office@campmarist.org. Web: www.campmarist.org. Vincent Gschlecht, Summer Camp Dir. Total Staff 100; Total Assisted 250.

GILMANTON IRON WORKS. *Camp Bernadette (Girls) Camp Fatima (Boys)* (1953) *Winter Business Office*, P.O. Box 206, 03837-0206. Tel: 603-364-5851; Fax: 603-364-5038. Email: info@diocamps.org. Web: www.diocamps.org. Most Rev. John B. McCormack, D.D., Chmn. of the Bd.; Sr. Mary Elizabeth Whalen, S.N.D.deN., Pres.; Mr. Gus Planchet, Dir. Total Assisted Annually 1,000; Total Staff 80.

Summer Business Office for Camp Bernadette, 83 Richards Rd., Wolfeboro, 03894. Tel: 603-569-1692; Fax: 603-569-2560. Total Staff 80; Total Assisted 1,080.

Camp Fatima (1949) (Boys), *Business Office*, P.O. Box 206, 03837-0206. Tel: 603-364-5851; Fax: 603-364-5038. Email: info@diocamps.org. Web: www.diocamps.org. Total Assisted 1,100; Total Staff 80.

[R] MISCELLANEOUS

MANCHESTER. *The Beaumont Trust*, 875 Elm St., 4th Fl., 03101. Tel: 603-634-7752; Fax: 603-634-7788. Marc Mathieu, Vice Pres. & Trust Officer.

Bishop Brady High School Capital Campaign Trust Fund c/o Roman Catholic Bishop of Manchester, a corporation sole., 153 Ash St., 03104. Tel: 603-669-3100, Ext. 117; Fax: 603-669-0377. Email: gchapdelaine@rcbm.org. Web: www.catholicchurchnh.org. Mr. Guy D. Chapdelaine, CPA, Finance Officer & Contact Person.

Bishop's Charitable Assistance Fund (2002) 153 Ash St., 03104. Tel: 603-669-3100; Fax: 603-669-0377. Email: menglish@rcbm.org. Walter Gallo, Chm.

CMC Healthcare System, 100 McGregor St., 03102. Tel: 603-669-3100; Fax: 603-669-0377. Mr. Guy D. Chapdelaine, CPA, Treas., Bd. Dirs., Bishop's Delegate; Alyson Pitman Giles, Pres.

Catholic Medical Center Tel: 603-668-3545; Fax: 603-663-6850.

Alliance Ambulatory Services, Inc., 100 McGregor St., 03102. Tel: 603-668-3545; Fax: 603-663-6850. Alyson Pitman Giles, Pres. & CEO.

Alliance Resources Inc., 100 McGregor St., 03102. Tel: 603-668-3545; 608-663-6850. Alyson Pitman Giles, Pres. & CEO.

St. Peter's Home, 300 Kelly St., 03102. Tel: 603-669-1219. Sr. Florence Therrien, S.C.S.H., Contact Person.

Diocesan Cemetery Office, 153 Ash St., P.O. Box 310, 03105. Tel: 603-669-3100; Fax: 603-669-0377. Email: pharrington@rcbm.org.

St. Patrick Cemetery, Amherst, 03031. Tel: 603-673-1311; Fax: 603-673-3687.

St. Joseph Cemetery, Bartlett, 03812. Tel: 603-356-2535; Fax: 603-356-2877.

St. Joseph Cemetery, Bath, 03740. Tel: 603-747-2038; Fax: 603-747-8071.

St. Joseph Cemetery, Bedford, 03110. Tel: 603-622-9522; Fax: 603-644-0770.

St. Hedwig Cemetery, Bedford, 03110. Tel: 603-623-4835; Fax: 603-623-4835 (Call first).

Mount Calvary Cemetery, Bennington, 03442. Tel: 603-924-7647; Fax: 603-924-8365.

Calvary Cemetery, Berlin, 03570. Tel: 603-752-2880; Fax: 603-752-1855.

St. Anne Cemetery, Berlin, 03570. Tel: 603-752-2880; Fax: 603-752-1855.

St. Kieran Cemetery, Berlin, 03570. Tel: 603-752-2880; Fax: 603-752-1855.

Mount Calvary Cemetery, Berlin, 03570. Tel: 603-752-2880; Fax: 603-752-1855.

Old Parish Cemetery, Bethlehem, 03574. Tel: 603-444-2593.

St. Margaret Cemetery, Carroll, 03598. Tel: 603-837-2558; Fax: 603-837-2558 (Call first).

St. Catherine Cemetery, Charlestown, 03603. Tel: 603-826-3359; Fax: 603-826-5875.

St. Mary Cemetery, Claremont, 03743. Tel: 603-542-9518; Fax: 603-543-3673.

St. Brendan Cemetery, Colebrook, 03576. Fax: 603-237-4342.

St. Charles Cemetery, Dover, 03822. Tel: 603-742-4837; Fax: 603-749-6779.

St. Mary Cemetery, Dover, 03822. Tel: 603-742-4837; Fax: 603-749-6779.

St. Peter Cemetery (Walpole), Drewsville, 03604. Tel: 603-826-3359; Fax: 603-826-5875.

St. Joseph Cemetery, Epping, 03042. Tel: 603-679-8805; Fax: 603-679-5192.

St. Pius Forest Lawn Cemetery, Errol, 03579. Tel: 603-237-4342; Fax: 603-237-8580.

Holy Cross Cemetery, Franklin, 03235. Tel: 603-934-5013; Fax: 603-934-3469.

Mount Calvary Cemetery, (Gonic), Rochester, 03839. Tel: 603-332-1863; Fax: 603-330-0865.

Holy Family Cemetery, Gorham, 03581. Tel: 603-446-2335; Fax: 603-466-3490.

St. Francis Xavier Cemetery, Groveton, 03582. Tel: 603-636-1047; Fax: 603-636-2549.

St. Denis, Harrisville, 03450. Tel: 603-924-7647; Fax: 603-924-8365.

St. Joseph Cemetery, Hinsdale, 03451. Tel: 603-352-1311; 603-336-5804; Fax: 603-336-7314.

Holy Rosary Cemetery, Hooksett, 03106. Tel: 603-485-3523; Fax: 603-485-8435.

Holy Cross Cemetery, Hudson, 03051. Tel: 603-881-8131; Fax: 603-557-9817.

St. Patrick Cemetery, Hudson, 03051. Tel: 603-881-8131; Fax: 603-577-9817.

St. Patrick Cemetery, Jaffrey, 03452. Tel: 603-532-6634; 603-532-6484; Fax: 603-532-6633.

St. Joseph Cemetery, Keene, 03435. Tel: 603-357-3967; Fax: 603-352-7472.

Sacred Heart Cemetery, Laconia, 03247. Tel: 603-524-9609; Fax: 603-527-2612.

St. Lambert's Cemetery, Laconia, 03247. Tel: 603-524-1442; Fax: 603-527-3534.

All Saints Cemetery, Lancaster, 03584. Tel: 603-788-2083; Fax: 603-788-5553.

Calvary Cemetery, Lancaster, 03584. Tel: 603-788-2083; Fax: 603-788-5553.

St. Rose of Lima Cemetery, Littleton, 03561. Tel: 603-444-2593; Fax: 603-444-3126.

Holy Cross Cemetery, Londonderry, 03053. Tel: 603-622-3215; Fax: 603-624-8638.

St. Augustine Cemetery, 03111. Tel: 603-668-1355; Fax: 603-626-1517.

Mount Calvary Cemetery, 03111. Tel: 603-622-4615; Fax: 603-624-8638.

Mount Calvary Cemetery, Marlborough, 03455. Tel: 603-357-3967; Fax: 603-352-7472.

St. Louis Cemetery, Nashua, 03064. Tel: 603-886-1302; Fax: 603-886-5361.

St. Francis Xavier Cemetery, Nashua, 03064. Tel: 603-886-1302; Fax: 603-886-5361.

St. Stanislaus Cemetery, Nashua, 03064. Tel: 603-886-1302; Fax: 603-886-5361.

Sacred Heart of Jesus Cemetery, New Ipswich, 03071. Tel: 603-878-1121; Fax: 603-878-4657.

Calvary Cemetery, Newmarket, 03857. Tel: 603-659-3643; Fax: 603-659-8924.

St. Patrick Cemetery, Newport, 03773. Tel: 603-863-1422; Fax: 603-863-7898.

Our Lady of the Mountains Cemetery, North Conway, 03860. Tel: 603-356-2535; Fax: 603-356-2877.

Sacred Heart Cemetery, North Stratford, 03590. Tel: 603-636-1047; 802-962-3364; Fax: 603-636-2549.

Calvary Cemetery, Penacook, 03303. Tel: 603-753-4413; Fax: 603-753-4071.

St. Peter Cemetery (old), Peterborough, 03458. Tel: 603-924-7647; Fax: 603-924-8365.

St. Peter Cemetery (new), Peterborough, 03458. Tel: 603-924-7647; Fax: 603-924-8365.

Mount Calvary Cemetery, Pittsfield, 03263. Tel: 603-435-6242; Fax: 603-435-8840.

Holy Angels Cemetery, Plaistow, 03865. Tel: 603-382-8324; Fax: 603-382-1113.

Calvary Cemetery, Portsmouth, 03804. Tel: 603-436-9239; Fax: 603-436-3985.

St. Mary Cemetery, Portsmouth, 03804. Tel: 603-436-9239; Fax: 603-436-3985.

Holy Rosary Cemetery, Rochester, 03839. Tel: 603-332-1863; Fax: 603-330-0865.

St. Mary's Cemetery, Rochester, 03839. Tel: 603-332-1869; 603-332-7484; Fax: 603-332-2040.

St. Patrick Cemetery, Rollinsford, 03805. Tel: 603-692-4367; Fax: 603-692-4454.

Mount Calvary Cemetery, Sanbornville, 03872. Tel: 603-522-3304; Fax: 603-522-8273.

Holy Trinity Cemetery, Somersworth, 03878. Tel: 603-692-4367; 603-692-0524; Fax: 603-692-4454.

Mount Calvary Cemetery, Somersworth, 03878. Tel: 603-692-2172; 603-692-0524; Fax: 603-692-2499.

St. John the Baptist Cemetery, Suncook, 03275. Tel: 603-485-3113; Fax: 603-485-2113.

St. John the Baptist Old Cemetery, Suncook, 03275. Tel: 603-485-3113; Fax: 603-485-2113.

St. John's Cemetery, Tilton, 03299. Tel: 603-286-4445; 603-630-0673; Fax: 603-286-4663.

Mount Carmel Cemetery, Troy, 03465. Tel: 603-357-3967; Fax: 603-352-7472.

St. Margaret Cemetery, Twin Mountain, 03595. Tel: 603-837-2558; Fax: 603-837-2558 (Call first).

St. Peter Cemetery (Drewsville), Walpole, 03608. Tel: 603-826-3359; 603-445-5304; Fax: 603-826-5875.

St. Albert Cemetery, West Stewartstown, 03597. Tel: 603-237-4342; Fax: 603-237-8580.

St. Matthew Cemetery, Whitefield, 03598. Tel: 603-837-2558; Fax: 603-837-2558 (Call first).

Mount Calvary Cemetery, Wilton, 03086. Tel: 603-654-6554.

Friends of Saint Patrick School Trust Fund, P.O. Box 310, 03105-0310.

Friends of the St. Thomas Aquinas School Trust Fund c/o Roman Catholic Bishop of Manchester, a corporation sole., 153 Ash St., 03104. Tel: 603-669-3100. Email: gchapdelaine@rcbm.org. Web: catholicnh.org. Mr. Guy D. Chapdelaine, CPA, Finance Officer & Contact Person.

Infant Jesus School Trust Fund (c/o Roman Catholic Bishop of Manchester, a corporation sole), 153 Ash St., 03104. Tel: 603-669-3100. Email: gchapdelaine@rcbm.org. Web: www.catholicnh.org. Mr. Guy D. Chapdelaine, CPA, Finance Officer & Contact Person.

Saint Jude Parish Capital Campaign Trust c/o Roman Catholic Bishop of Manchester, a corporation sole., 153 Ash St., 03104. Tel: 603-669-3100. Email: gchapdelaine@rcbm.org.

Web: catholicnh.org. Mr. Guy D. Chapdelaine, CPA, Finance Officer & Contact Person.

Priests Retirement Trust Fund, P.O. Box 310, 03105-0310.

GILFORD. *The Missionary Servants of Pope John Paul I* (1978) 22 Boyd Hill Rd., 03249. Tel: 603-524-4740; Fax: 603-524-4740. The Missionary Servants of Pope John Paul I is a lay association founded in 1978 to aid established missionaries with help mainly given to Mother Teresa's missions in Haiti.

NASHUA. *Corpus Christi Food Pantry and Assistance, Inc.*, 43 Franklin St., 03064. Tel: 603-882-6372 (Pantry); 603-598-1641 (Assistance); Fax: 603-598-1641. Email: corpuschristifp@aol.com. Web: www.corpuschristifoodpantry.org. Kay Golden, Exec. Dir.

Marguerite's Place, 87 Palm St., 03060. Tel: 603-598-1582; Fax: 603-598-7574. Email: balves@margueritesplace.org. Web: www.margueritesplace.org. Barbara A. Alves, CEO. Total Assisted 26; Total Staff 17; Bed Capacity 30.

RELIGIOUS INSTITUTES OF MEN REPRESENTED IN THE DIOCESE

For further details refer to the corresponding bracketed number in the Religious Institutes of Men or Women section.

[]—*Apostles of Jesus* (Nairobi, Kenya)—A.J.

[0200]—*Benedictine Monks* (St. Anselm Abbey)—O.S.B.

[1100]—*Brothers of the Sacred Heart* (New England Prov.)—S.C.

[1330]—*Congregation of the Mission* (New England Prov.)—C.M.

[0520]—*Franciscan Friars* (Province of the Immaculate Conception)—O.F.M.

[0690]—*Jesuit Fathers and Brothers* (New England Prov.)—S.J.

[0730]—*Legionaries of Christ*—L.C.

[0770]—*Marist Brothers of the Schools* (Esopus Prov.)—F.M.S.

[0720]—*The Missionaries of Our Lady of La Salette* (Immaculate Heart of Mary & Our Lady of Seven Dolors Provinces)—M.S.

[0910]—*Oblates of Mary Immaculate*—O.M.I.

[0140]—*Order of St. Augustine*—O.S.A.

[0470]—*Order of Friars Minor Capuchin*—O.F.M.Cap.

[]—*Order of Preachers* (Prov. of St. Joseph-Eastern Dominican Prov.)—O.P.

[1250]—*Somascan Fathers*—C.R.S.

RELIGIOUS INSTITUTES OF WOMEN REPRESENTED IN THE DIOCESE

[0200]—*Benedictine Sisters*—O.S.B.

[1000]—*Congregation of Divine Providence of Kentucky*—C.D.P.

[]—*Congregation of the Sisters of St. Joseph Boston*—C.S.J.

[0750]—*Daughters of the Charity of the Sacred Heart of Jesus*—F.C.S.C.J.

[0420]—*Discalced Carmelites Nuns*—O.C.D.

[1070-16]—*Dominican Sisters of Hope*—O.P.

[1170]—*Felician Sisters*—C.S.S.F.

[2575]—*Institute of the Sisters of Mercy of the Americas* (Manchester, NH)—R.S.M.

[]—*Little Sisters of St. Francis*—O.S.F.

[2410]—*Marianites of Holy Cross*—M.S.C.

[2480]—*Medical Missionaries of Mary*—M.M.M.

[]—*Missionary Servants of the Word*—H.S.M.P.

[3450]—*Religious of Jesus and Mary*—R.J.M.

[2970]—*School Sisters of Notre Dame*—S.S.N.D.

[1680]—*School Sisters of St. Francis*—O.S.F.

[0110]—*The Sisters Adorers of the Precious Blood*—A.P.B.

[0490]—*Sisters of Charity of Montreal (Grey Nuns)*—S.G.M.

[0610]—*Sisters of Charity of St. Hyacinthe (Grey Nuns)*—S.C.S.H.

[0640]—*Sisters of Charity of St. Vincent De Paul, Halifax*—S.C.

[1930]—*Sisters of Holy Cross*—C.S.C.

[3000]—*Sisters of Notre Dame de Namur - Boston Province*—S.N.D.deN.

[3000]—*Sisters of Notre Dame de Namur - Ipswich Province*—S.N.D.deN.

[3360]—*Sisters of Providence of Saint Mary-of-the-Woods, IN*—S.P.

[]—*The Sisters of St. Francis of Philadelphia*—O.S.F.

[3718]—*Sisters of St. Ann*—S.S.A.

[3310]—*Sisters of the Presentation of Mary*—P.M.

[]—*Society of Sisters for the Church*—S.S.C.

NECROLOGY

† Clifford, Francis M., (Retired)—Died March 7, 2009

† Cote, Joseph A.—Died March 19, 2009

† Montplaisir, Roland A., (Retired)—Died June 21, 2009

† Robichaud, George H.—Died Aug. 30, 2009

† Ruzzo, Paul F., Pelham, NH St. Patrick—Died Nov. 23, 2009

An asterisk (*) denotes an organization that has established tax-exempt status directly with the IRS and is not covered by the USCCB Group Ruling.

Diocese of Marquette

(Dioecesis Marquettensis)

Most Reverend

ALEXANDER K. SAMPLE, J.C.L.

Bishop of Marquette; ordained June 1, 1990; appointed Bishop of Marquette December 13, 2005; installed January 25, 2006. *Office: 117 W. Washington St., Ste. 3A, P.O. Box 1000, Marquette, MI 49855*. Tel: 906-227-9115.

Chancery Office: 117 W. Washington St., Ste. 3A, P.O. Box 1000, Marquette, MI 49855. Tel: 906-225-1141; Fax: 906-225-0437.

Email: bparis@dioceseofmarquette.org

Web: www.dioceseofmarquette.org

Most Reverend

JAMES H. GARLAND, M.A., M.S.W., D.D.

Retired Bishop of Marquette; ordained 1959; appointed Titular Bishop of Garriana and Auxiliary Bishop of Cincinnati June 2, 1984; consecrated July 25, 1984; appointed Bishop of Marquette October 6, 1992; installed November 11, 1992; retired December 13, 2005. *Res.: 300 Rock St., Marquette, MI 49855*. Tel: 906-225-1141.

Most Reverend

MARK F. SCHMITT, D.D.

Retired Bishop of Marquette; ordained May 22, 1948; appointed Titular Bishop of Kells and Auxiliary of Green Bay May 5, 1970; consecrated June 24, 1970; appointed to Marquette March 21, 1978; installed May 8, 1978; retired November 11, 1992. *Res.: Grellinger Hall, Apt. 12, 224 Iroquois Ave., Green Bay, WI 54301.*

VICARIATE-APOSTOLIC JULY 29, 1853; DIOCESE 1857.

Square Miles 16,281.

Comprises the Upper Peninsula of the State of Michigan.

For legal titles of parishes and diocesan institutions, consult the Pastoral Office.

STATISTICAL OVERVIEW

Personnel	
Bishop	1
Retired Bishops	2
Priests: Diocesan Active in Diocese	48
Priests: Diocesan Active Outside Diocese	2
Priests: Retired, Sick or Absent	35
Number of Diocesan Priests	85
Religious Priests in Diocese	7
Total Priests in Diocese	92
Extern Priests in Diocese	6
Ordinations:	
Diocesan Priests	2
Permanent Deacons in Diocese	47
Total Sisters	49
Parishes	
Parishes	72
With Resident Pastor:	
Resident Diocesan Priests	40
Resident Religious Priests	7
Without Resident Pastor:	
Administered by Priests	19
Administered by Religious Women	3
Missions	22
Professional Ministry Personnel:	
Sisters	7
Lay Ministers	17
Welfare	
Catholic Hospitals	1
Total Assisted	196,495
Homes for the Aged	1
Total Assisted	109
Special Centers for Social Services	8
Total Assisted	2,100
Educational	
Diocesan Students in Other Seminaries	9
Total Seminarians	9
Elementary Schools, Diocesan and Parish	9
Total Students	1,260
Catechesis/Religious Education:	
High School Students	875
Elementary Students	2,587
Total Students under Catholic Instruction	4,731
Teachers in the Diocese:	
Sisters	1
Lay Teachers	96
Vital Statistics	
Receptions into the Church:	
Infant Baptism Totals	559
Minor Baptism Totals	39
Adult Baptism Totals	26
Received into Full Communion	90
First Communions	589
Confirmations	189
Marriages:	
Catholic	205
Interfaith	108
Total Marriages	313
Deaths	1,325
Total Catholic Population	48,630
Total Population	300,000

Former Bishops—Most Revs. FREDERIC BARAGA, D.D., first Bishop; cons. Nov. 1, 1853; died Jan. 19, 1868; IGNATIUS MRAK, D.D., cons. Feb. 7, 1869; resigned 1878; transferred to Antinoe 1879; died Jan. 2, 1901; JOHN VERTIN, D.D., cons. Sept. 14, 1879; died Feb. 26, 1899; FREDERICK EIS, D.D., cons. Aug. 24, 1899; made Asst. at the Pontifical Throne July 13, 1922; resigned July 8, 1922; appt. Titular Bishop of Bita; died May 5, 1926; PAUL JOSEPH NUSSBAUM, D.D., cons. Bishop of Corpus Christi May 20, 1913; resigned March 26, 1920; appt. Bishop of Marquette Nov. 14, 1922; died June 24, 1935; JOSEPH CASIMIR PLAGENS, D.D., LL.D., cons. Sept. 30, 1924, Auxiliary Bishop of Detroit; Titular Bishop of Rhodiopolis; appt. to See of Marquette Nov. 16, 1935; transferred to the See of Grand Rapids Dec. 16, 1940; died March 31, 1943; FRANCIS J. MAGNER, D.D., appt. Dec. 21, 1940; cons. Feb. 24, 1941; died June 13, 1947; THOMAS L. NOA, D.D., cons. March 19, 1946; Titular Bishop of Salona and Coadjutor Bishop of Sioux City; appt. Bishop of Marquette Aug. 20, 1947; retired March 25, 1968; died March 13, 1977; CHARLES A. SALATKA, D.D., appt. Titular Bishop of Cariana and Auxiliary of Grand Rapids Dec. 9, 1961; cons. March 6, 1962; appt. Bishop of Marquette Jan. 10, 1968; installed March 25, 1968; appt. Archbishop of Oklahoma City Oct. 11, 1977; installed Dec. 15, 1977; retired Nov. 24, 1992; died March 17, 2003.; MARK F. SCHMITT, D.D. (Retired), appt. Titular Bishop of Kells and Auxiliary of Green Bay May 5, 1970; cons. June 24, 1970; appt. Bishop of Marquette March 21, 1978; installed May 8, 1978; retired Nov. 11, 1992; JAMES H. GARLAND, M.A., M.S.W., D.D., ord. 1959; appt. Titular Bishop of Garriana and Auxiliary Bishop of Cincinnati June 2, 1984; cons. July 25, 1984; appt. Bishop of Marquette Oct. 6, 1992; installed Nov. 11, 1992; retired Dec. 13, 2005.

Chancery Office—117 W. Washington St., Ste. 3A, P.O. Box 1000, Marquette, 49855. Tel: 906-225-1141; Fax: 906-225-0437. Office Hours: Mon.-Fri. 8:30-4:30.

Vicars General—Revs. MICHAEL J. STEBER; RONALD T. BROWNE, Moderator of the Curia.

Chancellor—Rev. BENEDETTO J. PARIS, J.C.L.

Secretary to the Bishop—JUDY M. JASON. Tel: 906-227-9115.

Diocesan Tribunal—117 W. Washington St., Ste. 3A, P.O. Box 1000, Marquette, 49855. Tel: 906-227-9111.

Judicial Vicar—Rev. Msgr. PETER OBERTO, J.C.L.

Adjutant Judicial Vicar—VACANT.

Diocesan Judge—Rev. Msgr. PETER OBERTO, J.C.L.

Defensore Vinculi—Rev. JOHN J. SHIVERSKI (Retired).

Advocates—Revs. FRANCIS J. DEGROOT; JAMES M. ROETZER.

Administrator and Notary—Rev. BENEDETTO J. PARIS, J.C.L.

Promoter of Justice—Rev. BENEDETTO J. PARIS, J.C.L.

Priests' Council—

Executive Board—Revs. BENEDETTO J. PARIS, J.C.L., Chm.; ARNOLD J. GRAMBOW, Vice Chm.

Vicars Forane—Revs. THEODORE J. BRODEUR, Holy Name of Mary Vicariate; ROBB M. JURKOVICH, St. John Neumann Vicariate; JOY JOSEPH ADIMAKKEEL, St. Mary Rockland Vicariate; JOHN E. MARTIGNON, The Most Holy Name of Jesus Vicariate; FRANCIS J. DEGROOT, St. Joseph-St. Patrick Vicariate; BENEDETTO J. PARIS, J.C.L., St. Peter Cathedral Vicariate; MICHAEL A. WOEMPNER, St. Mary Norway Vicariate.

Consultors—Revs. RONALD T. BROWNE; COREY J. LITZNER; MICHAEL A. WOEMPNER; LARRY P. VAN DAMME; MICHAEL J. STEBER; FRANCIS G. DOBRZENSKI.

Diocesan Offices and Directors

Administration & Finance, Dept. of—TIMOTHY D. THOMAS, CPA, Dir.; CAROL J. PARKER, Accountant & Human Resource Coord., 117 W. Washington St., Ste. 3A, P.O. Box 1000, Marquette, 49855. Tel: 906-227-9105; Fax: 906-225-0437.

Archives—ELIZABETH DELENE, Archivist, 347 Rock St., Marquette, 49855. Tel: 906-227-9117; Fax: 906-228-2469.

Catholic Social Services, Dept. of—JUDY BOYLE, Interim Dir., 347 Rock St., Marquette, 49855. Tel: 906-227-9119; Fax: 906-228-2469 Branch Offices: Houghton, Escanaba, Iron Mountain, Sault Ste. Marie, Ironwood, Iron River.

Communication Services, Dept. of—LOREENE ZENO KOSKEY, Dir., 117 W. Washington St., Ste. 3A, P.O. Box 1000, Marquette, 49855. Tel: 906-227-9129; Fax: 906-225-0437.

Faith Formation & Education, Dept. of—MARK SALISBURY, Supt. Schools, Mailing Address: 117 W. Washington St., Ste. 3A, P.O. Box 1000, Marquette, 49855. Tel: 906-227-9127; Fax: 906-225-0437; ROBERT MAHANEY, School Bd.; GREG GOSTOMSKI, Dir. Youth Ministry. Tel: 906-227-9125; DENISE M. FOYE, Dir. Faith Formation Office. Tel: 906-227-9130.

Newspaper "The U.P. Catholic"—JOHN FEE, Editor, 117 W. Washington St., Ste. 3A, P.O. Box 1000, Marquette, 49855. Tel: 906-227-9131; Fax: 906-225-0437.

Ministry Personnel Services, Dept. of—Rev. RONALD T. BROWNE, Dir., 117 W. Washington St., Ste. 3A, P.O. Box 1000, Marquette, 49855. Tel: 906-227-9107; Fax: 906-225-0437.

Clergy Support Services—STEPHEN J. LYNOTT, M.S.W., M.P.S., Mgr., Mailing Address: 117 W. Washington St., Ste. 3A, P.O. Box 1000, Marquette, 49855. Tel: 906-227-9103; Fax: 906-225-0437.

Apostleship of the Sea—Rev. BENEDETTO J. PARIS, J.C.L., Port Chap. Marquette, MI. Tel: 906-227-9143.

Bishop Baraga Association Inc.— An international organization to promote the Cause of the Beatification of the Most Rev. Frederic Baraga. *347 Rock St., Marquette, 49855.* Tel: 906-227-9117; Fax: 906-228-2469. Most Rev. JAMES H. GARLAND, M.A., M.S.W., D.D., Exec. Dir.; Dr. ANDREA AMBROSI, Postulator; ELIZABETH J. DELENE, Archivist & Editor of the Baraga Bulletin.

Building Commission, Diocese of Marquette—TIMOTHY D. THOMAS, CPA, Sec., Mailing Address: P.O. Box 1000, Marquette, 49855. Tel: 906-227-9108.

Catholic Relief Services—Rev. LAWRENCE T. GAUTHIER, Dir. (Retired), Mailing Address: P.O. Box 1000, Marquette, 49855.

Cemeteries—TIMOTHY D. THOMAS, CPA, Bishop's Rep. for Catholic Cemeteries, 117 W. Washington St., Ste. 3A, P.O. Box 1000, Marquette, 49855. Tel: 906-227-9102.

Charismatic Prayer Groups—Rev. MICHAEL J. STEBER, Liaison, St. Peter Cathedral, 311 W. Baraga Ave., Marquette, 49855. Tel: 906-226-6548.

Ongoing Formation of Priests—Rev. JAMES C. ZIMINSKI, Dir., Mailing Address: Marygrove, P.O. Box 38, Garden, 49835. Tel: 906-644-2771.

Cursillo—Rev. JAMES C. ZIMINSKI, Diocesan Moderator, Marygrove, P.O. Box 38, Garden, 49835. Tel: 906-644-2771.

Ecumenical Officer—VACANT.

Family Life Office—COLIN JENKINS, Coord., 347 Rock St., Marquette, 49855. Tel: 906-227-9178.

Holy Childhood Association—Rev. LAWRENCE T. GAUTHIER, Dir. (Retired), Mailing Address: P.O. Box 1000, Marquette, 49855. Tel: 906-227-9109.

Knights of Columbus—Rev. BENEDETTO J. PARIS, J.C.L., Diocesan Chap., Mailing Address: P.O. Box 1000, Marquette, 49855. Tel: 906-227-9111.

Panama Mission Fund—Rev. PAUL G. MANDERFIELD, Mailing Address: P.O. Box 1000, Marquette, 49855. Tel: 906-225-1141.

Permanent Diaconate Formation Program—Deacon SCOTT JAMIESON, Dir., Mailing Address: P.O. Box 1000, Marquette, 49855. Tel: 906-227-9111; Fax: 906-225-0437.

Propagation of the Faith—Rev. LAWRENCE T. GAUTHIER, Diocesan Dir. (Retired), Mailing Address: P.O. Box 1000, Marquette, 49855. Tel: 906-227-9109.

Retreats—Rev. JAMES C. ZIMINSKI, Dir., Marygrove Retreat Center, Garden, 49835. Tel: 906-644-2771.

Victim Assistance Coordinator—ROSALYN GROVES, 8260 - 23.3 Lane, Rapid River, 49878. Tel: 866-857-6459 (Toll Free). Email: regroves@chartermi.net.

St. Joseph Association— An Association of the Priests of the Diocese to provide Retirement Benefits. Rev. LARRY P. VAN DAMME, Pres., St. Michael Parish, 401 W. Kaye Ave., Marquette, 49855. Tel: 906-228-8180.

U.P. Catholic Services Appeal—TIMOTHY D. THOMAS, CPA, Coord., 117 W. Washington St., Ste. 3A, P.O. Box 1000, Marquette, 49855. Tel: 906-227-9101.

Vocation Office—Rev. GREGORY R. HEIKKALA, Dir., 117 W. Washington St., Ste. 3A, P.O. Box 1000, Marquette, 49855. Tel: 906-227-9112; 866-375-2643; Fax: 906-225-0437.

Women Religious—Sr. MARCELYN GERVAIS, O.S.F., Mailing Address: P.O. Box 1000, Marquette, 49855. Tel: 906-226-2265.

CLERGY, PARISHES, MISSIONS AND PAROCHIAL SCHOOLS

CITY OF MARQUETTE

(MARQUETTE COUNTY)

1—ST. PETER CATHEDRAL Revs. Michael J. Steber; Timothy M. Ekaitis; Deacons Scott A. Jamieson; John S. Leadbetter; Lawrence H. Londo; Donald Thoren; Thomas E. Foye; Dean J. Jackson.
Res.: 311 Baraga Ave., 49855. Tel: 906-226-6548; Fax: 906-226-8683. Web: www.stpetercathedral.org.
See Fr. Marquette Catholic Central Schools System, Marquette under Elementary Interparochial Schools located in the Institution section.
Catechesis/Religious Program—Tel: 906-226-6548, Ext. 207. Students 60.
Mission—St. Mary Big Bay, Marquette Co.

2—ST. CHRISTOPHER Rev. Jeff G. Johnson, Canonical Pastor & Sacramental Min.; Sr. Colleen Sweeting, O.S.F., Pastoral Coord.; Deacon Steven M. Gualdoni.
Res.: 2372 Badger St., 49855. Tel: 906-226-2265; Fax: 906-226-8678.

3—ST. JOHN THE BAPTIST (1986) Closed. For inquiries for parish records, contact St. Peter's Cathedral, Marquette.

4—ST. LOUIS THE KING (HARVEY) (Harvey) Rev. Benedetto J. Paris; Senior Deacon David P. Adler; Deacons Gregg R. St. John; Warren K. Vonck.
Res.: 264 Silver Creek Rd., 49855. Tel: 906-249-1438; Fax: 906-249-3428.
See Fr. Marquette Catholic Central Schools System, Marquette under Elementary Interparochial Schools located in the Institution section.
Catechesis/Religious Program—Students 93.

5—ST. MICHAEL (1942) Revs. Larry P. Van Damme; Benjamin J. Hasse; Deacons Dennis R. Maki; Robert K. LaCosse.
Res.: 401 W. Kaye Ave., 49855. Tel: 906-228-8180; Fax: 906-228-5502. Email: stmichael@chartermi.net.
See Fr. Marquette Catholic Central Schools System, Marquette under Elementary Interparochial Schools located in the Institution section.
Catechesis/Religious Program—Students 75.

OUTSIDE THE CITY OF MARQUETTE

AHMEEK, KEWEENAW CO., OUR LADY OF PEACE, (Keweenaw Catholic Missions) Rev. Abraham J. Mupparathara, M.C.B.S. (India).
Mailing Address: 301 - 8th St., Calumet, 49913. Tel: 906-337-1966; Fax: 906-337-1966.
Catechesis/Religious Program—Jim Berryman, D.R.E. Students 4.
Mission—Holy Redeemer Eagle Harbor, Keweenaw Co.
Mission—Our Lady of the Pines Copper Harbor, Keweenaw Co.

ALPHA, IRON CO., ST. EDWARD, Closed. For inquiries for parish records contact the chancery.

ASSININS, BARAGA CO., THE MOST HOLY NAME OF JESUS-BLESSED KATERI TEKAKWITHA Revs. John L. Longbucco; Janusz Romanek; Deacon John M. Cadeau.
Mailing Address & Res.: 318 Lyons St., Baraga, 49908.
Res.: 14808 Assinins Rd., Atlantic Mine, 49905. Tel: 906-353-6565; Fax: 906-353-6568.
Catechesis/Religious Program—Christy Miron, D.R.E. Students 4.

BARAGA, BARAGA CO., ST. ANN Revs. John L. Longbucco; Janusz Romanek; Deacon Robert L. Wahmhoff.
Res.: 318 Lyons St., 49908. Tel: 906-353-6565; Fax: 906-353-7134.
Catechesis/Religious Program—Students 29.

BARBEAU, CHIPPEWA CO., HOLY FAMILY MISSION Rev. John S. Hascall, O.F.M.Cap.
Res.: 1529 Marquette Ave., Sault Sainte Marie, 49783. Tel: 906-632-3213; Fax: 906-632-8490.
Catechesis/Religious Program—Tel: 906-253-9896. Michelle LaJoie, D.R.E. Students 34.

BARK RIVER, DELTA CO., ST. ELIZABETH ANN SETON, [CEM], Formerly St. George, Bark River; Sacred Heart of Jesus, Schaffer; & St. Michael, Perronville. Rev. Mark A. McQuesten.
Res.: 1216 12th Rd., P.O. Box 187, 49807. Tel: 906-466-9938; Fax: 906-466-0194.
Catechesis/Religious Program—Arlene Anzalone, D.R.E. Students 92.
Mission—St. Joseph Foster City, Dickinson Co.

BESSEMER, GOGEBIC CO., ST. SEBASTIAN Rev. Joy Joseph Adimakkeel (India).
Res.: 210 E. Iron St., 49911. Tel: 906-667-0952; Fax: 906-667-0952. Email: stsebastian@charter.net.
Catechesis/Religious Program—Angie Mazurek, D.R.E. Students 61.

BRIMLEY, CHIPPEWA CO., ST. FRANCIS XAVIER Rev. Theodore J. Brodeur; Deacon Joseph A. LaPlante.
Mailing Address: P.O. Box 429, 49715. Tel: 906-248-3443.
Catechesis/Religious Program—Tel: 906-248-5386. Amy Perron, D.R.E. Students 30.
Mission—Blessed Kateri Tekakwitha Bay Mills, Chippewa Co. Fax: 906-248-3443. (Formerly St. Catherine).
Catechesis/Religious Program—Students 59.

CALUMET, HOUGHTON CO.

1—ST. PAUL THE APOSTLE (1908) Rev. Abraham J. Mupparathara, M.C.B.S. (India).
Res.: 301 Eighth St., 49913. Tel: 906-337-2044; Fax: 906-337-2058.
Catechesis/Religious Program—Students 73.

2—SACRED HEART (1868) Rev. Abraham J. Mupparathara, M.C.B.S. (India).
Res.: P.O. Box 546, 49913. Tel: 906-337-0810; Fax: 906-337-6424. Web: www.sacredheartcalumet.org.
Catechesis/Religious Program—Debbie Berryman, D.R.E. Students 57.

CASPIAN, IRON CO., ST. CECILIA Rev. Norman A. Clisch; Deacon Robert J. Kostka.
Mailing Address: P.O. Box 517, 49915. Tel: 906-265-3777.
Catechesis/Religious Program—Students 28.

CHAMPION, MARQUETTE CO., SACRED HEART, [CEM] Rev. Gregory R. Heikkala, Canonical Pastor; Sisters Margey Schmelzle, O.S.F., Pastoral Coord.; Lois Risch, O.S.F., Pastoral Coord.
Mailing Address: P.O. Box 99, 49814. Tel: 906-376-8475; Fax: 906-376-8475.
Catechesis/Religious Program—

CHANNING, DICKINSON CO., ST. ROSE Rev. Jeffrey A. Kurtz, Parochial Admin.
Mailing Address: P.O. Box 235, 49815. Tel: 906-542-3215; Fax: 906-542-3245.
Catechesis/Religious Program—Tel: 906-542-6341. Nancy Reese, D.R.E. Students 23.

CHASSELL, HOUGHTON CO., ST. ANNE (1887) Rev. Allen P. Mott; Sr. Ellen Enright, I.B.V.M., Pastoral Assoc.; Deacon Thomas F. Corrigan.
Mailing Address: P.O. Box 407, 49916. Tel: 906-523-4912; Fax: 906-523-4904.
Catechesis/Religious Program—Students 43.
Mission—Sacred Heart Painesdale, Houghton Co. Closed. For inquiries for parish records contact Holy Family, South Range.
Mission—Immaculate Heart of Mary Donken, Houghton Co. Closed. For inquiries for parish records contact Holy Family, South Range.

COOKS, SCHOOLCRAFT CO., ST. MARY MAGDALENE, [CEM] Revs. James C. Ziminski; Brian C. Gerber.
Mailing Address: P.O. Box 68, Garden, 49835. Tel: 906-644-2626; Fax: 906-644-2626.
Catechesis/Religious Program—Joanne Annelin, D.R.E. Students 9.

CRYSTAL FALLS, IRON CO., GUARDIAN ANGELS Rev. Jeffrey A. Kurtz; Deacon Bernard Kut.
Res.: 412 Crystal Ave., 49920. Tel: 906-875-3019; Fax: 906-875-1034. Email: guardang@up.net.
Catechesis/Religious Program—Jeanne Brown, D.R.E. Students 39.

DAGGETT, MENOMINEE CO., ST. FREDERICK, Closed. For inquiries for parish records contact Precious Blood Parish, Stephenson.

DETOUR, CHIPPEWA CO., SACRED HEART Rev. George Vaniyepurackal (India); Deacon Ronald P. Andrzejewski.
Mailing Address: P.O. Box 8, 49725. Tel: 906-297-5211; Fax: 906-297-5108. Email: sskols@lighthouse.net.
Catechesis/Religious Program—Kim Aubert, D.R.E. Students 23.
Mission—St. Florence Drummond Island, Chippewa Co. Tel: 906-297-5211.

ENGADINE, MACKINAC CO., OUR LADY OF LOURDES, Closed. For parish records, contact St. Gregory Parish, Newberry.

ESCANABA, DELTA CO.

1—ST. ANNE (1888) Rev. Francis J. DeGroot; Deacons Lewis Vailliencourt; Michael LeBeau.
Res.: 817 S. Lincoln Rd., 49829. Tel: 906-786-1421; Fax: 906-786-9346.
See Holy Name Central Grade School, Escanaba under Elementary Interparochial Schools located in the Institution section.
Catechesis/Religious Program—Sharon Mellinger, D.R.E. Students 120.

2—ST. JOSEPH & ST. PATRICK (1997), (Formerly St. Joseph, Escanaba; Formerly St. Patrick, Escanaba). Rev. Eric E. Olson; Deacon William D. Hemes.
Res.: 709 First Ave. S., 49829. Tel: 906-789-6244; Fax: 906-789-1213.

See Holy Name Central Grade School, Escanaba under Elementary Interparochial Schools located in the Institution section.
Catechesis/Religious Program—Hans Whitmer, D.R.E. Students 41.

3—ST. THOMAS THE APOSTLE Rev. Rick L. Courier.
Res.: 1820 Ninth Ave. N., 49829. Tel: 906-786-4627; Fax: 906-789-5558. Web: www.stanthonystthomas.org.
See Holy Name Central Grade School, Escanaba under Elementary Interparochial Schools located in the Institution section.
Catechesis/Religious Program—Tel: 906-233-9566. Hans Whitmer, D.R.E. Students 40.

EWEN, ONTONAGON CO., SACRED HEART (1892) Rev. Sebastian Ettolil, M.C.B.S. (India).
Mailing Address: P.O. Box 50, 49925. Tel: 906-988-2310; Fax: 906-988-2310. Email: shewen@charter.net.
Catechesis/Religious Program—Tracy Niemi, D.R.E. Tel: 906-827-3617. Students 21.
Mission—St. Ann Bergland, Ontonagon Co.

GARDEN, DELTA CO., ST. JOHN THE BAPTIST Revs. James C. Ziminski; Brian C. Gerber; Deacon Rodney Groleau.
Mailing Address: P.O. Box 68, 49835. Tel: 906-644-2626; Fax: 906-644-2626.
Catechesis/Religious Program—Students 10.

GLADSTONE, DELTA CO.

1—ALL SAINTS Rev. Arnold J. Grambow.
Res.: 715 Wisconsin Ave., P.O. Box 392, 49837. Tel: 906-428-3199; Fax: 906-428-2829.
Catechesis/Religious Program—Students 122.

2—HOLY FAMILY Rev. Jose J. Maramattam (India).
Res.: 4011 CO 416-20th Rd., 49837. Tel: 906-786-1209; Fax: 906-786-0846.
Catechesis/Religious Program—Cathy Flagstadt, D.R.E. Students 130.

GOETZVILLE, CHIPPEWA CO., ST. STANISLAUS KOSTKA (1897) [CEM] Rev. George Vaniyepurackal (India); Deacon Ronald P. Andrzejewski.
Mailing Address: 12841 E. Traynor Rd., 49736. Tel: 906-297-5211; Fax: 906-297-5108. Email: sskols@lighthouse.net.
Catechesis/Religious Program—Roxanne Eberts, D.R.E.; Darlene Krzycki, D.R.E. Students 36.
Mission—Our Lady of the Snows Hessel, Mackinac Co. Tel: 906-484-3825; 906-484-2773 (Parish House).

GRAND MARAIS, ALGER CO., HOLY ROSARY CHURCH (1895) [CEM] Rev. Timothy W. Hruska.
Mailing Address: P.O. Box 424, 49839. Tel: 906-494-2589; Fax: 906-494-2589. Email: holyrosary@gmail.com.
Catechesis/Religious Program—Jean Rochefort, Administrative Asst.
Mission—St. Therese Germfask, Schoolcraft Co.
Mission—St. Timothy Curtis, Mackinac Co.

GWINN, MARQUETTE CO., ST. ANTHONY Rev. Ronald K. Timock.
Res.: 280 N. Boulder, P.O. Box 1358, 49841. Tel: 906-346-5312; Fax: 906-346-3040. Email: stant@chartermi.net.
Catechesis/Religious Program—Tel: 906-346-9116. Bonnie Hurkmans, D.R.E. Students 44.
Mission—St. Joseph Northland, Marquette Co. Tel: 906-346-3040; Fax: 906-346-5312.

HANCOCK, HOUGHTON CO., RESURRECTION, [CEM] Rev. Augustin George (India).
Res.: 900 Quincy St., 49930. Tel: 906-482-0215; Fax: 906-482-5268. Email: resurrection@chartermi.net.
Catechesis/Religious Program—Tel: 906-482-1175. Kristine Davis, D.R.E. Students 79.
Mission—St. Francis of Assisi Dollar Bay, Houghton Co. Tel: 906-482-6489.

HERMANSVILLE, MENOMINEE CO., ST. JOHN NEUMANN (1995) [CEM] [JC], (Formerly St. Mary, Hermansville; St. Francis Xavier, Spalding). Rev. Michael T. Vichich.
Res.: P.O. Box 135, Spalding, 49886. Tel: 906-497-4578 (Rectory); 906-497-5800 (Office); Fax: 906-498-5800.
Catechesis/Religious Program—Lana Scott, D.R.E. Students 79.

HOUGHTON, HOUGHTON CO.

1—ST. ALBERT THE GREAT UNIVERSITY PARISH (1963), (Michigan Technological University) Rev. Allen P. Mott; Sr. Ellen Enright, I.B.V.M., Pastoral Assoc.
Res.: 411 MacInnes Dr., 49931. Tel: 906-482-5530; Fax: 906-482-4828.

2—ST. IGNATIUS LOYOLA Rev. John E. Martignon.
Res.: 305 Portage St., 49931. Tel: 906-482-0212; Fax: 906-482-8110. Email: stignatius@chartermi.net.
Catechesis/Religious Program—Students 119.
Mission—St. Mary Atlantic Mine, Houghton Co. Closed. For inquiries for parish records contact St. Ignatius Loyola, Houghton.

HUBBELL, HOUGHTON CO., ST. CECILIA, Closed. For parish records, contact St. Joseph, Lake Linden.

IRON MOUNTAIN, DICKINSON CO.

1—IMMACULATE CONCEPTION OF THE BLESSED VIRGIN MARY Rev. Msgr. James A. Kaczmarek.
Res.: 500 E. Blaine St., 49801-1840. Tel: 906-774-0511; Fax: 906-779-9953. Email: ironmtic@sbcglobal.net.
See Dickinson Area Catholic School System, Iron Mountain under Elementary Interparochial Schools located in the Institution section.
Catechesis/Religious Program—Students 41.

2—ST. MARY AND ST. JOSEPH Revs. Daniel S. Zaloga; Daniel Moll; Deacon Donald R. Christy.
Res.: 411 W. B St., 49801. Tel: 906-774-2046; Fax: 906-774-6015.
See Bishop Baraga Catholic School, Iron Mountain under Elementary Interparochial Schools located in the Institution section.
Catechesis/Religious Program—Mary Kay Cahill, D.R.E.; Karen Hackstock, D.R.E. Students 131.

IRON RIVER, IRON CO., ST. AGNES Rev. Norman A. Clisch; Deacon Robert J. Kostka.
Res.: 702 N. Fourth St., 49935. Tel: 906-265-4557; Fax: 906-265-7155. Email: stagnes@up.net. Web: www.stagnes-stcecilia.com.
Catechesis/Religious Program—Students 92.

IRONWOOD, GOGEBIC CO.

1—ST. AMBROSE, Consolidated with Holy Trinity & St. Michael to form Our Lady of Peace Parish, 1986.

2—ST. MICHAEL, Consolidated with St. Ambrose & Holy Trinity to form Our Lady of Peace Parish, 1986.

3—OUR LADY OF PEACE (1986), Consolidated from Holy Trinity, St. Ambrose & St. Michael. Rev. Darryl J. Pepin; Deacon Robert A. Hamen.
Res.: 108 S. Marquette St., 49938-2060. Tel: 906-932-0174; Fax: 906-932-1019.
Catechesis/Religious Program—Patricia Niksich, Dir. Faith Formation. Students 89.

ISHPEMING, MARQUETTE CO.

1—ST. JOHN THE EVANGELIST Rev. Gregory R. Heikkala.
Res.: 325 S. Pine, 49849. Tel: 906-486-6212. Email: stjohnschurch@charterinternet.com.
Religious Education Center—335 S. Pine St., 49849. Tel: 906-486-9361. Angela Johnson, Dir. Faith Formation. Students 91.

2—ST. JOSEPH Rev. James Challancin; Deacon Steven M. Schaffer.
Office (All Mail):—1889 Prairie Ave., 49849-1045. Tel: 906-485-4200.
Res.: 1890 Prairie Ave., 49849-1044. Tel: 906-485-4626; Fax: 906-485-4185. Email: stjoeoffice@sbcglobal.net.
Catechesis/Religious Program—Angela Johnson, D.R.E. Students 72.

3—ST. PIUS X, Closed. For inquiries for parish records contact St. Joseph Church, 1889 Prairie Ave., Ishpeming, MI 49849.

KINGSFORD, DICKINSON CO.

1—AMERICAN MARTYRS Rev. Joseph O. Gouin.
Res.: 908 W. Sagola Ave., 49802. Tel: 906-774-0630; Fax: 906-774-4417. Email: frjoe@att.net. Web: www.americanmartyrskg.org.
Catechesis/Religious Program—Carol Gayan, D.R.E. Students 206.

2—ST. MARY QUEEN OF PEACE (1945) Rev. Michael A. Woempner.
Church & Office: 600 Marquette Blvd., 49802. Tel: 906-774-6122; Fax: 906-774-2349. Web: www.stmaryqueenofpeace.org. Email: stmaryqueenofpeace@chartermi.net.
Catechesis/Religious Program—Mary Beth Casanova, C.R.E.; Jody Marek, C.R.E. Students 93.

L'ANSE, BARAGA CO., SACRED HEART (1894) Revs. John L. Longbucco; Janusz Romanek.
Res.: 16 S. Sixth St., 49946. Tel: 906-524-6424; Fax: 906-524-7585. Web: www.sacredheart-lanse.com. Email: sachartl@up.net.
School—433 E. Baraga Ave., 49946. Tel: 906-524-5157; Fax: 906-524-5154. Web: www.sacredheart-lanse.com/school. Lay Teachers 4; Students 34.
Catechesis/Religious Program—Tel: 906-524-6425. Christy Miron, D.R.E. Students 37.

LAKE LINDEN, HOUGHTON CO., ST. JOSEPH (1871) Rev. Francis G. Dobrzenski.
Res.: 701 Calumet St., 49945. Tel: 906-296-6851.
Catechesis/Religious Program—Students 58.

MACKINAC ISLAND, MACKINAC CO., STE. ANNE DE MICHILIMACKINAC (1695) Rev. Reynaldo A. Garcia, S.J.
Mailing Address: P.O. Box 537, 49757. Tel: 906-847-3507. Web: steanneschurch.org.

MANISTIQUE, SCHOOLCRAFT CO., ST. FRANCIS DE SALES Rev. Glenn J. Theoret; Deacons Gilbert G. Sablack; Robert M. Cross.
Res.: 330 Oak St., 49854. Tel: 906-341-5355; Fax: 906-341-3984.
School—Tel: 906-341-5512. Sr. Lauretta R. Koscielniac, S.S.N.D., Prin. Sisters 1; Lay Teachers 10; Students 188.
Catechesis/Religious Program—Tel: 906-341-8151. Mary Desjarden, D.R.E. Students 115.
Mission—Divine Infant of Prague Gulliver, Schoolcraft Co.

MENOMINEE, MENOMINEE CO.

1—HOLY REDEEMER (Birch Creek) Rev. Joseph Augustine Vandannoor, M.S.T. (India); Deacon Roland Chaltry.
Res.: W-5541 Birch Creek Rd. No. 6, 49858. Tel: 906-863-6920; Fax: 906-863-7303.
See Menominee Catholic Central, Menominee under Elementary Interparochial Schools located in the Institution section.
Catechesis/Religious Program—Students 56.

2—HOLY SPIRIT Rev. Ronald J. Skufca.
Res.: 1016 10th Ave., 49858. Tel: 906-863-5239; Fax: 906-863-2249. Web: holyspirit.cybrzn.com.
Catechesis/Religious Program—Tel: 906-863-2249. Marlene Varady, D.R.E. Students 48.

3—RESURRECTION Revs. Robb M. Jurkovich; Michael D. Chenier; Deacons Vincent W. Beckley; Gerald G. Roetzer.
Res.: 2607 18th St., 49858. Tel: 906-863-3405; Fax: 906-863-9090. Email: resparish@new.rr.com.
See Menominee Catholic Central, Menominee under Elementary Interparochial Schools located in the Institution section.
Catechesis/Religious Program—Students 51.

MORAN, MACKINAC CO., IMMACULATE CONCEPTION, [CEM] Rev. Pawel J. Mecwel.
Res.: 120 Church St., St. Ignace, 49781. Tel: 906-643-7671; Fax: 906-643-7755.
Catechesis/Religious Program—Students 5.

MUNISING, ALGER CO., SACRED HEART OF JESUS Rev. Christopher B. Gardiner; Deacons James E. Anderson; Thomas W. Moseley Jr.
Office: 110 W. Jewell St., P.O. Box 99, 49862. Tel: 906-387-4900; Fax: 906-387-4422.
Catechesis/Religious Program—Tel: 906-387-4901. Barbara Feldhusen, D.R.E. Students 60.
Mission—St. Therese Autrain, Alger Co. Tel: 906-892-8189.

NADEAU, MENOMINEE CO., ST. BRUNO Rev. Michael T. Vichich.
Res.: P.O. Box 95, 49863. Tel: 906-639-2388; Fax: 906-639-2301.
Catechesis/Religious Program—Nicola DuPont, D.R.E. Students 40.

NAHMA, DELTA CO., ST. ANDREW Revs. James C. Ziminski; Brian C. Gerber; Deacon Rodney Groleau.
Mailing Address: P.O. Box 68, Garden, 49835. Tel: 906-644-2626; Fax: 906-644-2626.
Catechesis/Religious Program—Students 22.

NEGAUNEE, MARQUETTE CO., ST. PAUL Rev. Msgr. Peter Oberto.
Res.: 202 W. Case St., 49866. Tel: 906-475-9969; Fax: 906-475-9987. Web: www.stpaulchurchnegaunee.com. Email: stpaul@chartermi.net.
Catechesis/Religious Program—Tel: 906-475-5245. Jodi Johnson, D.R.E. Students 88.
Mission—Our Lady Perpetual Help Palmer, Marquette Co. Tel: 906-475-4630.

NEWBERRY, LUCE CO., ST. GREGORY Rev. Francis Ricca.
Office: 212 W. Harrie St., 49868. Tel: 906-293-5511; Fax: 906-293-5560. Email: stgreg@sbcglobal.net.
Res.: 111 W. Harrie St., 49868. Tel: 906-293-5001.
Catechesis/Religious Program—Dawn Stephenson, D.R.E. Students 49.
Mission—Our Lady of Victory Paradise, Chippewa Co.
Mission—St. Stephen Naubinway, Mackinac Co.

NORWAY, DICKINSON CO., ST. MARY (1878) Rev. James M. Roetzer; Deacon Ronald J. LeMire Sr.
Res.: 401 Main St., 49870. Tel: 906-563-9845; Fax: 906-563-7623. Email: saintmary@norwaymi.com.
See Holy Spirit Central School, Norway under Elementary Interparochial Schools located in the Institution section.
Catechesis/Religious Program—Nancy Degnan, D.R.E. Students 74.

ONTONAGON, ONTONAGON CO., HOLY FAMILY, [CEM] Rev. Michael J. Jacobus.
Res.: 515 Pine St., 49953. Tel: 906-884-2569; Fax: 906-884-6030. Email: hfcc@up.net.
Catechesis/Religious Program—Students 69.

PERKINS, DELTA CO., ST. JOSEPH (1901) Rev. Jacek S. Wtyklo.
Mailing Address: 5803 Hwy. M-35, P.O. Box 99, 49872. Tel: 906-359-4701; Fax: 906-359-4701.
Catechesis/Religious Program—Students 72.

PERRONVILLE, MENOMINEE CO., ST. ELIZABETH ANN SETON, (See Bark River.)

QUINNESEC, DICKINSON CO., ST. MARY, Closed. For inquiries for parish records contact St. Joseph Church, 1889 Prairie Ave., Ishpeming, MI 49849.

RAMSAY, GOGEBIC CO., CHRIST THE KING, Closed. For inquiries for parish records contact St. Sebastian, Bessemer.

RAPID RIVER, DELTA CO., ST. CHARLES BORROMEO Rev. Jacek S. Wtyklo.

Res.: P.O. Box 247, 49878. Tel: 906-474-6606; Fax: 906-474-9087.
Catechesis/Religious Program—Julie Hayes-Moe, D.R.E. Students 40.

REPUBLIC, MARQUETTE CO., ST. AUGUSTINE, [CEM] Revs. Gregory R. Heikkala, Canonical Pastor; James Challancin, Sacramental Min.; Sisters Margey Schmelzle, O.S.F., Pastoral Coord.; Lois Risch, O.S.F., Pastoral Coord.
Mailing Address: 574 Kloman Ave., 49879. Tel: 906-376-8475; Fax: 906-376-8475.

ROCKLAND, ONTONAGON CO., ST. MARY Rev. Michael J. Jacobus; Deacon Karl L. Wadman.
Mailing Address: Holy Family Parish, 515 Pine St., Ontonagon, 49953. Tel: 906-884-2569; Fax: 906-884-6030.

RUDYARD, CHIPPEWA CO., ST. JOSEPH Rev. Cyriac Kottayarikil, M.C.B.S. (India); Deacon Roger A. Bygrave.
Mailing Address: 11509 W. H-40, 49780. Tel: 906-478-4331; Fax: 906-478-4333. Email: stjoseph@lighthouse.net.
Catechesis/Religious Program—Gerri Stelmaszek, D.R.E. Students 67.
Mission—St. Mary Trout Lake, Chippewa Co.
Station—Kinross Correctional Facility Kincheloe.
Station—Chippewa Correctional Facility Kincheloe.
Station—Chippewa Regional Facility Kincheloe.

ST. IGNACE, MACKINAC CO., ST. IGNATIUS LOYOLA, [CEM] Rev. Pawel J. Mecwel; Deacons Thomas McClelland; Donald F. Olmstead.
Res.: 120 Church St., 49781. Tel: 906-643-7671; Fax: 906-643-7755.
Catechesis/Religious Program—Tel: 906-643-8887. Students 52.

SAULT SAINTE MARIE, CHIPPEWA CO.

1—HOLY NAME OF MARY Rev. Sebastian Kavumkal, M.S.T. (India).
Res.: 377 Maple St., 49783. Tel: 906-632-3381; Fax: 906-632-0741.
Catechesis/Religious Program—Students 13.
Mission—Sacred Heart Sugar Island, Chippewa Co.

2—ST. ISAAC JOGUES MISSION Rev. John S. Hascall, O.F.M.Cap.
Res.: 1529 Marquette Ave., 49783. Tel: 906-632-3213; Fax: 906-632-8490. Email: jhascall@sbcglobal.net.
Catechesis/Religious Program—Tel: 906-632-2856. Students 21.

3—ST. JOSEPH Rev. Piotr Zaczynski; Deacon William J. Piche, (Retired).
Res.: 606 E. Fourth Ave., 49783. Tel: 906-632-9625; Fax: 906-632-5122.
Catechesis/Religious Program—Tel: 906-632-9625, Ext. 13. Danna Schmitter, D.R.E. Students 58.

4—NATIVITY OF OUR LORD, Closed. For inquiries for parish records contact St. Joseph, Sault Sainte Marie.

SCHAFFER, DELTA CO., ST. ELIZABETH ANN SETON, See separate listing. Formerly Sacred Heart of Jesus. See Bark River.

SOUTH RANGE, HOUGHTON CO., HOLY FAMILY Rev. John E. Martignon.
Res. & Mailing Address: 305 Portage St., Houghton, 49931. Tel: 906-482-0684; Fax: 906-482-8110.
Church: 107 Atlantic Ave., 49963.
Catechesis/Religious Program—Kim Harris, D.R.E. Students 41.

SPALDING, MENOMINEE CO., ST. FRANCIS XAVIER, See separate listing. St. John Neumann, P.O. Box 135, Spalding, MI 49886.

STEPHENSON, MENOMINEE CO., PRECIOUS BLOOD CHURCH (1880) [CEM] Rev. Corey J. Litzner; Deacon Thomas J. Rivard.
Res.: S. 304 Bluff St., 49887. Tel: 906-753-2562; Fax: 906-753-2811. Email: pbchurch@dreamscp.com. Web: www.preciousbloodchurch.net.
Catechesis/Religious Program—Tel: 906-753-4771. Mary Oczus, D.R.E. Students 103.

TRENARY, ALGER CO., ST. RITA (1947) Rev. Jacek S. Wtyklo.
Mailing Address: P.O. Box 207, 49891. Tel: 906-446-3350; Fax: 906-446-3523.
Catechesis/Religious Program—Tel: 906-439-5696. Jewell Hoy, D.R.E. Students 19.

VULCAN, DICKINSON CO., ST. BARBARA Rev. James M. Roetzer; Deacon Ronald J. LeMire Sr.
Mailing Address: P.O. Box 493, 49892. Tel: 906-563-9834; Fax: 906-563-7664.
See Holy Spirit Central School, Norway under Elementary Interparochial Schools located in the Institution section.
Catechesis/Religious Program—401 Main St., Norway, 49870. Students 41.

WAKEFIELD, GOGEBIC CO., IMMACULATE CONCEPTION OF THE BLESSED VIRGIN MARY Rev. Joy Joseph Adimakkeel (India).
Res.: 407 Ascherman St., 49968. Tel: 906-224-7851; Fax: 906-224-9118.
Rectory—210 E. Iron St., Bessemer, 49911. Tel: 906-667-0952.
Mission—St. Catherine Marenisco, Gogebic Co. Tel: 906-787-2258.
Catechesis/Religious Program—Lucretia Mayer, D.R.E. Students 27. In Res., Rev. Raymond F. Moncher (Retired).

WATERSMEET, GOGEBIC CO., IMMACULATE CONCEPTION Revs. Sebastian Ettolil, M.C.B.S. (India); George S. Maki.
Mailing Address: E23933 D Ave., P.O. Box 398, 49969. Tel: 906-358-4360.
Catechesis/Religious Program—Students 15.

WELLS, DELTA CO., ST. ANTHONY Rev. Rick L. Courier; Deacon David A. Talford.
Mailing Address: 1820 9th Ave. N., Escanaba, 49829. Tel: 906-786-4627; Fax: 906-789-5558.
Res.: 6596 N. 3rd St., Escanaba, 49829.
Catechesis/Religious Program—Hans Whitmer, D.R.E. Students 30.

WHITE PINE, ONTONAGON CO., ST. JUDE (1956) Rev. Michael J. Jacobus.
Mailing Address: 8 Cedar St., P.O. Box 427, 49971. Tel: 906-885-5763; Fax: 906-885-5763.
Catechesis/Religious Program—Students 3.

Indian Missions

ASSININS, BARAGA CO., THE MOST HOLY NAME OF JESUS-BLESSED KATERI TEKAKWITHA, Indian Mission. Revs. John L. Longbucco; Janusz Romanek.
Res.: 318 Lyons St., Baraga, 49908.

BAY MILLS, CHIPPEWA CO., BLESSED KATERI TEKAKWITHA Rev. Theodore J. Brodeur.
Mailing Address: P.O. Box 429, Brimley, 49715.
Catechesis/Religious Program—Amy Perron, D.R.E. Students 59.

SAULT SAINTE MARIE, CHIPPEWA CO., ST. ISAAC JOGUES Rev. John S. Hascall, O.F.M.Cap.
1529 Marquette Ave., 49783.

SUGAR ISLAND, CHIPPEWA CO., SACRED HEART, Indian Missionaries, East. Rev. Sebastian Kavumkal, M.S.T. (India).
377 Maple St., Sault Sainte Marie, 49783.

WATERSMEET, GOGEBIC CO., LAC VIEUX DESERT RESERVATION Rev. Sebastian Ettolil, M.C.B.S. (India).
Mailing Address: P.O. Box 398, 49969.

Chaplains of Public Institutions

MARQUETTE. *Marquette General Hospital*, Tel: 906-228-9440. Rev. Jeff G. Johnson.

IRON MOUNTAIN. *Veterans Administration Center*. Rev. Msgr. James A. Kaczmarek, Chap.

On Duty Outside the Diocese:
Revs.—
Murphy, Patrick E., 5500 Armstrong Rd., (118c), Battle Creek, 49016. Dept. of Veterans Affairs Medical Center.
Oniskiewicz, Mieczyslaw T., St. Mary Parish, P.O. Box 68, Kinde, 48455-0068.

Special Assignment:
Revs.—
Heikkala, Gregory R., Dir., Vocations
Ziminski, James C., Dir., Marygrove Retreat Center

Leave of Absence:
Revs.—
Schaeffer, Richard C.
Silvestrini, Dino F.

Retired:
Rev. Msgr.—
Desrochers, Timothy H., P.O. Box 693, Gwinn, 49841.
Revs.—
Borca, Dennis L., P.O. Box 436, Bardstown, KY 40004-9998.
Bracket, Louis P., 307 Eddy St., Wakefield, 49968.
Gauthier, Lawrence T., 300 Rock St., 49855.
Gondek, Joseph A., P.O. Box 624, Caspian, 49915.
Hasenberg, Aloysius J., E23933 "D" Ave., P.O. Box 398, Watersmeet, 49969.
Landreville, Norbert B., P.O. Box 345, St. Ignace, 49781.
Lehman, John J., Winter: 2425 Privateer Blvd, Barataria, LA 70036. Summer: P.O. Box 1, Sault Sainte Marie, 49783.
Lenz, Frank, 207Z Saux Head Rd., Co. Rd. 550, 49855.
Manderfield, R.P. Geraldo, Apartado 2810, Managua, Nicaragua.
Marcotte, Wayne E., 705 Calumet St., Lake Linden, 49945.
Mayotte, Allan J., 405 'C' St., Wakefield, 49968.
McArdle, John F., 4305 Sixth St., Menominee, 49858.
Menapace, James L., 703 N. Corbridge Rd., Gulliver, 49840.
Minelli, Peter A., 114 Provider, Gwinn, 49841.
Moncher, Raymond F., P.O. Box 175, Marenisco, 49947.
Neurohr, Gilbert N., 900 First Ave., S., Apt. 4, Escanaba, 49829.
Nomellini, Paul J., 3883 Town Rd. A.A., Florence, WI 54121.
Norden, Emmett M., P.O. Box 562, Escanaba, 49829.
Nowacki, Jerome A.
Olivier, John H., S.S., St. Charles Villa, 603 Maiden Choice Ln., Baltimore, MD 21228.
Poisson, Thomas L., 300 Rock St., 49855.
Rupp, Daniel N., P.O Box 771, 49855.
Sartorelli, Otto, P.O. Box 494, Caspian, 49915.
Schiska, Paul A., 1490 15.5 Rd., Bark River, 49807.
Sedlock, David W., P.O. Box 536, Gwinn, 49841.
Shiroda, Donald L., 605 W. Portage Ave., #9, Sault Sainte Marie, 49783.
Shiverski, John J., 415 Forestville Basin Trl., 49855.
Strelick, Charles J., 4420 Devonshire Ave., Spring Hill, FL 34609.
Valerio, Raymond A., 831 E. Grant, 49801.
Vanitvelt, Milton H., 1524 Seventh St., Menominee, 49858.
Wantland, Thomas A., 2628 Del Prado Blvd., Cape Coral, FL 33904.
Williams, James J., 1203 Wenniway, Mackinaw City, 49701.
Zeugner, Raymond L., 5096 Dunns Pt. Rd., Florence, WI 54121.

Permanent Deacons:
Adler, David, St. Louis the King, Marquette
Anderson, James, Sacred Heart of Jesus, Munising
Andrzejewski, Ronald P., St. Stanislaus Kostka, Goetzville; Our Lady of Snows Mission, Hessel; Sacred Heart, DeTour; St. Florence Mission, Drummond Island
Beckley, Vincent W., Resurrection, Menominee
Bygrave, Roger A., St. Joseph, Rudyard; St. Mary Mission, Trout Lake
Cadeau, John M., Holy Name of Jesus/Blessed Kateri Tekakwitha, Assinins
Chaltry, Roland, Holy Redeemer, Menominee
Christy, Donald R., St. Mary-St. Joseph, Iron Mountain
Corrigan, Thomas F., St. Anne, Chassell
Cross, Robert M., St. Francis de Sales, Manistique; (Incardinated in Diocese of Sioux Falls, South Dakota)
Foye, Thomas E., St. Peter Cathedral, Marquette
Green, William, St. Anne, Wausau, WI
Gretzinger, Stephen S., Holy Spirit, Menominee
Groleau, Rodney R., Garden Area Churches, Garden
Gualdoni, Steven J., St. Christopher, Marquette
Hamen, Robert, Our Lady of Peace, Ironwood
Hemes, Dr. Bill D., St. Joseph & St. Patrick, Escanaba
Hermann, Dean A., St. Anne, Mackinac Island (Incardinated in Archdiocese of Chicago, IL)
Jackson, Dean J., St. Peter Cathedral, Marquette
Jamieson, Scott A., St. Peter Cathedral, Marquette
Kostka, Robert J., St. Cecilia, Caspian; St. Agnes, Iron River
Kut, Bernard, Guardian Angels, Crystal Falls; (Incardinated in Archdiocese of Chicago, IL)
LaCosse, Robert K., Chancery Office & St. Michael, Marquette; (Incardinated in Archdiocese of Chicago, IL)
LaPlante, Joseph A., St. Francis Xavier, Brimley; Mission of Blessed Kateri Tekakwitha, Bay Mills-;(Incardinated in Diocese of Rockford, IL)
Leadbetter, John S., St. Peter Cathedral, Marquette
LeBeau, Michael, St. Anne, Escanaba
LeMire, Ronald J., Sr., St. Mary, Norway
Londo, Lawrence H., Diocese of Marquette
Maki, Dennis R., St. Michael, Marquette
McClelland, Thomas, St. Ignatius Loyola, St. Ignace
Moseley, Thomas W., Jr., Sacred Heart, Munising
Olmstead, Donald F., St. Ignatius Loyola, St. Ignace
Piche, William J., St. Joseph, Sault Ste. Marie
Rivard, Thomas J., Precious Blood, Menominee
Roetzer, Gerald G., Resurrection, Menominee
Sablack, Gilbert G., St. Francis de Sales & Divine Infant of Prague, Manistique
Sanders, Claire W., St. Mary, Norway; St. Barbara, Vulcan
Schaffer, Steven M., St. Joseph, Ishpeming
St. John, Gregg R., St. Louis the King, Marquette
Stancher, Arthur, St. Paul, Calumet

Talford, David A., St. Anthony of Padua, Wells
Thoren, Donald W., St. Peter Cathedral, Marquette
Vailliencourt, Lewis, St. Anne, Escanaba
Vonck, Warren K., St. Peter Cathedral, Marquette
Wadman, Karl L., St. Mary, Rockland
Wahmhoff, Robert L., St. Ann, Baraga
Wittak, Jay W., Union Grove, WI

INSTITUTIONS LOCATED IN THE DIOCESE

[A] ELEMENTARY INTERPAROCHIAL SCHOOLS

MARQUETTE. *Fr. Marquette Catholic Central Schools System*, 500 S. Fourth St., 49855. Tel: 906-225-1129; Fax: 906-225-1987. Web: fathermqt.org. Jackie Wright, Prin.; Karen Ogles, Prin. Serving the following parishes: St. Peter's Cathedral; St. Louis; St. Michael; St. Christopher. Lay Teachers 23; Students 300.

ESCANABA. *Holy Name Catholic School*, 409 S. 22nd St., 49829. Tel: 906-786-7550; Fax: 906-786-7582. Email: office@holynamecrusaders.com. Web: holynamecrusaders.com. Joseph L. Carlson, Prin. Lay Teachers 16; Students 259.

IRON MOUNTAIN. *Bishop Baraga Catholic School*, 406 W. B St., 49801. Tel: 906-774-2277; Fax: 906-774-8704. Email: kbal@baragaup.com. Web: www.baragaup.com. Adela Goniea, Prin. Lay Teachers 10; Students 143.

IRONWOOD. *All Saints Catholic Academy*, 106 S. Marquette St., 49938. Tel: 906-932-3200; Fax: 906-932-1019. Betty Perkis, Prin.; April Lynott, Librarian. Serving Our Lady of Peace, Ironwood. Lay Teachers 8; Students 54.

MENOMINEE. *Menominee Catholic Central*, 1406 10th Ave., 49858. Tel: 906-863-3190; Fax: 906-863-3990. Email: dpaul@mccspartans.org. Dan Paul, Prin. Lay Teachers 9; Students 104.

NORWAY. *Holy Spirit Central School*, 201 Saginaw St., 49870. Tel: 906-563-8817; Fax: 906-563-8854. Elizabeth A. Stack, Prin. Lay Teachers 9; Students 59.

SAULT SAINTE MARIE. *St. Mary School* Serves the parishes of St. Mary & St. Joseph, Sault Sainte Marie., 360 Maple St., 49783. Tel: 906-635-6141. Maria Farney, Prin. Lay Teachers 7; Students 121.

[B] ENDOWMENT FUNDS

MARQUETTE. *Endowment Foundation of the Diocese of Marquette*, 117 W. Washington St., Ste 3A, P.O. Box 1000, 49855. Tel: 906-227-9138; Fax: 906-225-0437. Email: lkoskey@dioceseofmarquette.org. Web: dioceseofmarquette.org. Loreen Zeno Koskey, Dir. Communications & Devel.

St. John's Memorial Scholarship Committee, 107 N. Lakeshore Blvd., Apt. 2E, 49855. Tel: 906-225-1936. Joylyn Wahla, Pres.

Marquette Area Catholic Education Fund, P.O. Box 1000, 49855. Tel: 906-227-9130.

BESSEMER. *St. Sebastian School Endowment Fund*, 210 E. Iron St., 49911. Tel: 906-667-0952; Fax: 906-667-0952. Rev. Joy Joseph Adimakkeel (India).

ESCANABA. *Holy Name Endowment Fund*, 409 S. 22nd St., 49829. Tel: 906-786-7550; Fax: 906-786-7582.

Holy Name Scholarship Foundation, 409 S. 22nd St., 49829. Tel: 906-786-7550; Fax: 906-786-7582.

IRON MOUNTAIN. *Bishop Baraga Catholic School Foundation*, 406 W. B St., 49801. Tel: 906-774-2277; Fax: 906-774-8704.

IRONWOOD. *Our Lady of Peace School Educational Fund*, 108 S. Marquette St., 49938-2060. Tel: 906-932-0174; Fax: 906-932-1019. Rev. Darryl J. Pepin.

L'ANSE. *Sacred Heart School Endowment Fund*, 16 S. 6th St., 49946. Tel: 906-524-6424; Fax: 906-524-6422. Web: sacredheartschoolanse.org. Rev. John L. Longbucco.

MANISTIQUE. *St. Francis de Sales Education Foundation*, 330 Oak St., 49854. Tel: 906-341-5355; Fax: 906-341-3984. Web: stfrancisofmanistique41pi.org.

MENOMINEE. *Menominee Catholic Education Fund*, 1406 Tenth Ave., 49858-2604. Tel: 906-863-2723; Fax: 906-863-3990. Elaine Blair-Klitzke, Office Mgr.

NEGAUNEE. *Negaunee St. Paul Endowment Fund*, 202 W. Case St., 49866. Tel: 906-475-9969. Rev. Msgr. Peter Oberto, J.C.L.

NORWAY. *Holy Spirit Central School Educational Fund*, 201 Saginaw, 49870. Tel: 906-563-8817; Fax: 908-563-8854. Email: holyspirit01@hotmail.com.

SAULT SAINTE MARIE. *Holy Family School Endowment Fund, Inc.*, 377 Maple St., 49783. Tel: 906-632-3381; Fax: 906-632-0741.

St. Mary School Endowment Fund, 377 Maple St., 49783. Tel: 906-632-3381; Fax: 906-632-0741.

[C] GENERAL HOSPITALS

ESCANABA. *O.S.F. St. Francis Hospital* O.S.F. Healthcare System., 3401 Ludington, 49829. Tel: 906-786-3311; Fax: 906-786-4004. Web: www.osfhealthcare.org. Peter G. Jennings, Pres. & CEO; Rev. Emmett M. Norden, Chap. (Retired). Staff 538; Bed Capacity 98; Patients Assisted Annually 196,495.

[D] HOMES FOR THE AGED

ESCANABA. *Bishop Noa Home for Senior Citizens*, 2900 3rd Ave. S., 49829. Tel: 906-786-5810; Fax: 906-786-5372. Web: bishopnoahome.com. Sisters of St. Paul de Chartres. Sisters 7; Residents 109.

[E] CONVENTS AND RESIDENCES OF SISTERS

MARQUETTE. *Provincialate of the Sisters of St. Paul de Chartres*, 1300 County Rd. 492, 49855. Tel: 906-226-3932; Fax: 906-226-2139. Web: sistersofstpaulusa.org. Sr. Gloria J. Schultz, S.P.C., Dist. Supr. Sisters 15.

IRON MOUNTAIN. *Monastery of the Holy Cross*, N4028 Hwy. U.S. 2, P.O. Box 397, 49801. Tel: 906-774-0561. Sr. Maria of Jesus, O.C.D., Prioress; Rev. Sean P. Kopczynski (Mar), Chap. Discalced Carmelite Nuns. Cloistered Nuns: Professed 16; Extern Professed Sisters 2; Temporary Professed Sisters 1; Postulants 2.

[F] RETREAT HOUSES

GARDEN. *Marygrove Retreat Center*, P.O. Box 38, 49835. Tel: 906-644-2771; Fax: 908-644-2463. Email: mgc@uplogon.com. Web: www.marygrove.org. Rev. James C. Ziminski, Dir. Retreats and workshops for priests, religious and laity.

[G] NEWMAN CLUBS

MARQUETTE. *Catholic Campus Ministry-Northern Michigan University* 401 W. Kaye Ave., 49855. Tel: 906-228-3302; Fax: 906-228-5502. Email: ccm@nmu.edu. Web: www.nmumqt.cem. Revs. Larry P. Van Damme; Benjamin J. Hasse; Catherine Hardenbergh, Campus Min.

HOUGHTON. *St. Albert the Great, University Parish* (1963) 411 MacInnes Dr., 49931. Tel: 906-482-5530; Fax: 906-482-4828. Email: fralmott@charterinternet.com. Web: stalbert.students.mtu.edu. Rev. Allen P. Mott, Contact Person.

SAULT SAINTE MARIE. *Lake Superior State University, Newman Center* 517 W. Easterday, 49783. Tel: 906-253-1285. Danna Schmitter, Contact Person.

[H] ASSOCIATIONS OF THE FAITHFUL

PARADISE. *Companions of Christ the Lamb*, P.O. Box 12, 49768. Tel: 906-492-3647; Fax: 906-492-3648. Rev. John Fabian, Moderator.

[I] MISCELLANEOUS

MARQUETTE. *St. Vincent De Paul Society*, 2119 Presque Isle Ave., Rm. 101, 49855. Tel: 906-226-2311; Fax: 906-226-4599. Email: stvin@charterinternet.com. Web: www.stvincentup.org.

RELIGIOUS INSTITUTES OF MEN REPRESENTED IN THE DIOCESE

For further details refer to the corresponding bracketed number in the Religious Institutes of Men or Women section.

[0470]—*The Capuchin Friars* (Detroit, MI)—O.F.M.Cap.
[0820]—*Congregation of the Fathers of Mercy* (Auburn, KY)—C.P.M
[0520]—*Franciscan Friars* (Cincinnati, OH)—O.F.M.
[0690]—*Jesuit Fathers & Brothers* New England Province—S.J.

RELIGIOUS INSTITUTES OF WOMEN REPRESENTED IN THE DIOCESE

[3710]—*Congregation of the Sisters of Saint Agnes*—C.S.A.
[0420]—*Discalced Carmelite Nuns*—O.C.D.
[1070-09]—*Dominican Sisters*—O.P.
[1070-13]—*Dominican Sisters*—O.P.
[1630]—*Franciscan Sisters of Christian Charity*—O.S.F.
[2380]—*Institute of the Blessed Virgin Mary (Sisters of Loretto)*—I.B.V.M.
[2970]—*School Sisters of Notre Dame*—S.S.N.D.
[3840]—*Sisters of St. Joseph of Carondelet*—C.S.J.
[3980]—*Sisters of St. Paul of Chartres*—S.P.C.
[2180]—*Sisters of the Immaculate Heart of Mary*—I.H.M.
[3260]—*Sisters of the Precious Blood*—C.PP.S.
[1770]—*Sisters of the Third Order of St. Francis* (Peoria, Illinois)—O.S.F.

DIOCESAN CEMETERIES

MARQUETTE. *Holy Cross*
ESCANABA. *Holy Cross Catholic Cemetery*

NECROLOGY

† Harris, David T., (Retired)—Died Feb. 24, 2009

An asterisk (*) denotes an organization that has established tax-exempt status directly with the IRS and is not covered by the USCCB Group Ruling.

Diocese of Memphis

(Memphitana in Tennesia)

Most Reverend

J. TERRY STEIB, S.V.D., D.D.

Bishop of Memphis; ordained January 6, 1967; appointed Titular Bishop of Fallaba and Auxiliary Bishop of St. Louis December 6, 1983; consecrated February 10, 1984; appointed Bishop of Memphis March 23, 1993; installed May 5, 1993.

Catholic Center: P.O. Box 341669, Memphis, TN 38184-1669. Tel: 901-373-1200; Fax: 901-373-1269.

Web: www.cdom.org

ESTABLISHED JANUARY 6, 1971.

Square Miles 10,682.

Comprises the Counties of Benton, Carroll, Chester, Crockett, Decatur, Dyer, Fayette, Gibson, Hardeman, Hardin, Haywood, Henderson, Henry, Lake, Lauderdale, McNairy, Madison, Obion, Shelby, Tipton and Weakley in the State of Tennessee.

For legal titles of parishes and diocesan institutions, consult the Chancery Office.

STATISTICAL OVERVIEW

Personnel	
Bishop	1
Priests: Diocesan Active in Diocese	48
Priests: Diocesan Active Outside Diocese	4
Priests: Retired, Sick or Absent	10
Number of Diocesan Priests	62
Religious Priests in Diocese	19
Total Priests in Diocese	81
Extern Priests in Diocese	7
Ordinations:	
Diocesan Priests	6
Permanent Deacons in Diocese	64
Total Brothers	30
Total Sisters	55
Parishes	
Parishes	42
With Resident Pastor:	
Resident Diocesan Priests	35
Resident Religious Priests	7
Missions	5
Pastoral Centers	1
Professional Ministry Personnel:	
Brothers	1
Sisters	3
Lay Ministers	46
Welfare	
Homes for the Aged	3
Total Assisted	1,102
Day Care Centers	5
Total Assisted	850
Specialized Homes	2
Total Assisted	350
Special Centers for Social Services	1
Total Assisted	12,000
Residential Care of Disabled	1
Total Assisted	250
Other Institutions	7
Total Assisted	800
Educational	
Diocesan Students in Other Seminaries	24
Total Seminarians	24
Colleges and Universities	1
Total Students	1,773
High Schools, Diocesan and Parish	4
Total Students	1,488
High Schools, Private	3
Total Students	1,229
Elementary Schools, Diocesan and Parish	22
Total Students	5,065
Elementary Schools, Private	1
Total Students	676
Non-residential Schools for the Disabled	1
Total Students	6
Catechesis/Religious Education:	
High School Students	795
Elementary Students	3,421
Total Students under Catholic Instruction	14,477
Teachers in the Diocese:	
Priests	1
Brothers	7
Sisters	14
Lay Teachers	657
Vital Statistics	
Receptions into the Church:	
Infant Baptism Totals	1,359
Minor Baptism Totals	168
Adult Baptism Totals	91
Received into Full Communion	252
First Communions	1,429
Confirmations	1,101
Marriages:	
Catholic	107
Interfaith	122
Total Marriages	229
Deaths	437
Total Catholic Population	74,254
Total Population	1,503,679

Former Bishops—Most Revs. CARROLL T. DOZIER, D.D., ord. March 19, 1937; appt. Nov. 17, 1970; cons. Jan. 6, 1971; retired July 27, 1982; died Dec. 7, 1985; J. FRANCIS STAFFORD, D.D., ord. Dec. 15, 1957; cons. Bishop Feb. 29, 1976; appt. Nov. 16, 1982; appt. to Archdiocese of Denver, June 3, 1986; DANIEL M. BUECHLEIN, O.S.B., D.D., ord. May 3, 1964; appt. Jan. 20, 1987; appt. to Archdiocese of Indianapolis, July 14, 1992.

Vicar General—Rev. Msgr. PETER P. BUCHIGNANI, P.A., J.C.L., V.G., St. Francis of Assisi, 8151 Chimney Rock, Cordova, 38018. Tel: 901-756-1213.

Catholic Center Offices—Mailing Address: P.O. Box 341669, Memphis, 38184-1669. Tel: 901-373-1200; Fax: 901-373-1269. *5825 Shelby Oaks Dr., Memphis, 38134.* Office Hours: Mon.-Fri. 7:45-4:45.

Diocesan Offices & Directors

All diocesan office addresses & phone numbers are the same as mentioned above under Catholic Center Offices unless otherwise noted.

Chancellor—Rev. MICHAEL P. JOYCE, C.M., J.C.D.

Archives—Rev. RICHARD L. MICKEY, M.Ed., Archivist.

Notaries—MARIANNA BEATY; NANCY HENNESSEY.

Dean of the Jackson Deanery—Rev. Msgr. THOMAS D. KIRK, St. Mary's Church, 1665 Hwy. 45 Bypass, Jackson, 38305-4414. Tel: 731-668-2596.

Catholic Public Policy Commission of Tennessee—Mailing Address: P.O. Box 341669, Memphis, 38184-1669.

College of Consultors—Rev. JOHN V. ATKINSON (Retired); Rev. Msgrs. PETER P. BUCHIGNANI, P.A., J.C.L., V.G.; VICTOR P. CIARAMITARO; Revs. RICHARD D. COY; ERNIE DEBLASIO; Rev. Msgr. JOHN B. MCARTHUR; Revs. ROBERT W. MARSHALL JR.; JAMES J. MARTELL; JOSEPH L. PAOLOZZI; KEITH STEWART.

Presbyteral Council—Rev. JOHN V. ATKINSON (Retired); Rev. Msgrs. PETER P. BUCHIGNANI, P.A., J.C.L., V.G.; VICTOR P. CIARAMITARO; Revs. RICHARD D. COY; ERNIE DEBLASIO; MICHAEL P. JOYCE, C.M., J.C.D.; Rev. Msgr. JOHN B. MCARTHUR; Revs. ROBERT W. MARSHALL JR.; JAMES J. MARTELL; JOSEPH L. PAOLOZZI; KEITH STEWART; MICHAEL E. WERKHOVEN.

Clergy Personnel Board—Rev. Msgr. VICTOR CIARAMITARO; Rev. ROBERT W. MARSHALL JR.; Rev. Msgr. JOHN B. MCARTHUR; Rev. MICHAEL P. JOYCE, C.M., J.C.D.; Rev. Msgr. PETER P. BUCHIGNANI, P.A., J.C.L., V.G.

Media Consultant—Rev. JOHN J. GEANEY, C.S.P.

Tribunal

Judicial Vicar—Rev. MICHAEL P. JOYCE, C.M., J.C.D.

Adjutant Judicial Vicar—Rev. Msgr. PETER P. BUCHIGNANI, P.A., J.C.L., V.G.

Defenders of the Bond—Rev. Msgr. J. EDWIN CREARY; Rev. JOSEPH L. TAGG III, J.D., J.C.L.

Promoter of Justice—Rev. JOSEPH L. TAGG III, J.D., J.C.L.

Judges—Rev. GREGORY LUYET, J.C.L.; Rev. Msgr. VICTOR P. CIARAMITARO; Rev. MICHAEL L. STEWART (Retired); Deacon J. GERARD QUINN, J.C.L.; ANNA M. DANKS, J.C.L.

Ecclesiastical Notaries—NANCY HENNESSEY; MARIANNA BEATY; LYNNE LOVELL.

Department For Administration

Secretary for Administration—Rev. MICHAEL P. JOYCE, C.M., J.C.D.

Facilities and Risk Management—Deacon WILLIAM F. HERBERS, Dir.

Catholic Cemeteries— Calvary, Memphis; All Saints, Memphis; Mount Calvary, Jackson, TN Mr. PATRICK POSEY, Dir., 1663 Elvis Presley Blvd., Memphis, 38106. Tel: 901-948-1529.

Engineering & Maintenance—Mr. ROBERT PELT, Dir., 1325 Jefferson Ave., Memphis, 38104. Tel: 901-722-4700; Fax: 901-722-4791. Mailing Address: P.O. Box 41705, Memphis, 38174-1705.

Human Resources—Mrs. SANDRA GOLDSTEIN, Dir.

Employee Benefits—Mrs. SHARON ICHNIOWSKI.

Office for Professional Responsibilities/Child and Youth Protection—Dr. JAMES B. LATTA, D.Min., Dir. Tel: 901-359-2027. Email: jb2latta@aol.com.

Technical Services—Ms. KATHY SABA, M.C.S.E., Dir.

Department for Social Ministries

Episcopal Vicar for Social Ministry—Rev. TIMOTHY F. SULLIVAN, C.S.P., Dir. & Episcopal Vicar. Tel: 901-722-4747; Fax: 901-722-4791; Mrs. ALIE LIFSEY, Campus Coord. & Exec. Asst. Tel: 901-722-4750.

Catholic Charities of West Tennessee—325 Jefferson Ave., Memphis, 38104. Tel: 901-722-4700. Web: www.ccwtn.org. Mrs. CAROLYN TISDALE, Dir. Agency. Tel: 901-722-4727; Fax: 901-722-4791; Mrs. LUCIE JOHNSON, Administrative Asst. Tel: 901-722-4741.

Finance—Mr. JOE CURTIS, Dir. Tel: 901-722-4763; Fax: 901-722-4766.

Marketing & Public Relations—Mr. DARRELL HARDEN, Dir. Tel: 901-722-4794; Fax: 901-722-4791.

Extended Child Care Services—Ms. VIRGINIA DAVENPORT, Div. Dir. & Training Coord. Tel: 901-722-4718; Fax: 901-722-4791.

Camp Love & Learn—EVELYN VELASCO, Camp Dir. Tel: 901-722-4716.

Immaculate Conception Extended Care— (After-School Care) Ms. ANGELA SURIANI, Prog. Dir. Tel: 901-725-2710.

St. Louis Extended Care— (after school care) Ms. LORI TUCKER, Prog. Dir. Tel: 901-626-1268.

St. Paul Extended Care— (after school care) Ms. ANGELA ATKINS, Prog. Dir. Tel: 901-346-1190.

St. Mary's Jackson— (after school care) Ms. JANICE BITONDO, Prog. Dir. Tel: 731-616-2341.

Community & Parish Social Services—Mrs. CAROLYN TISDALE, Dir. Tel: 901-722-4727.

Homeless Residential Treatment Services—Mrs. KIM JORDAN-FLUKER, Div. Dir. Tel: 901-722-4758; Fax: 901-722-4791.

Genesis House—Ms. MARY JORDON, Prog. Dir., 300 N. Bellevue, Memphis, 38104. Tel: 901-726-9786; Fax: 901-725-1649.

Dozier House—Ms. AMY JONES, Prog. Dir., 85 N. Cleveland, Memphis, 38104. Tel: 901-722-4719; Fax: 901-728-6171.

Sophia's House—Tel: 901-722-4700. AMANDA COOK MYERS, Prog. Dir. Tel: 901-722-4700; Fax: 901-722-4791.

Diocese of Memphis Housing Corporation—1325 Jefferson Ave., Memphis, 38104 Web: dmhcorp.org. Mr. DENNY CALLOWAY, Dir. Tel: 901-722-4772; Ms. CHERRY BROOKS, Exec. Asst. Tel: 901-722-4795.

Refugee and Immigration Services—Mrs. VINODINI JAYARAMAN, Div. Dir. Tel: 901-722-4714; Fax: 901-722-4791.

St. Peter Ministries— (Maternity Services, Emergency Assistance, Counseling Services & Adoption) Mrs. ANNE MCINNIS, Div. Dir. Tel: 901-722-4711; Fax: 901-722-4791.

St. Peter Villa Rehabilitation & Nursing Center—Mrs. KAE WERKHOVEN, Admin., 141 N. McLean, Memphis, 38104. Tel: 901-276-2021; Fax: 901-725-3564.

Public Relations—Ms. EMILY GARRETT, Dir. Tel: 901-725-3568.

Department for Catholic Education

Secretary for Catholic Education—Dr. MARY MCDONALD.

Catholic Schools—Dr. MARY MCDONALD, Sec. Educ. & Supt. Tel: 901-373-1205; Mrs. JANET M. DONATO, Assoc. Supt. Tel: 901-373-1221; Mrs. DENISE MASON, Dir. Curriculum & Instruction. Tel: 901-373-1250; Mrs. SONDRA MORRIS, Dir. Diocesan Athletics. Tel: 901-260-2874; CHARLOTTE PERRY, Dir. School Nutrition. Tel: 901-373-1219; Mrs. SHARON MASTERSON, Dir. School Communications. Tel: 901-260-2871; Dr. COLLEEN BUTTERICK, Dir. School Counseling Svcs. Tel: 901-373-1219; PATRICK MCCARROLL, Dir. School Progs. & Svcs. Tel: 901-373-1211; Sr. ROSE MARTIN GLENN, S.Sp.S., Dir. Health Svcs. Tel: 901-373-1265; Mrs. MARY HELEN MCCRAREY, Exec. Asst. to Supt./Community Rels. Tel: 901-373-1205; Mr. JOSE GARCIA, Jubilee Schools Technology Coord. Tel: 901-373-1219; Mrs. LAURIE COTROS, Dir. Fine & Performing Arts. Tel: 901-373-1219; Mrs. HARDIE MAE FITZGERALD, Diocesan Dir. School Housekeeping Svcs. Tel: 901-373-1219; Mrs. SHARON JONES, Educ. Initiatives Coord. Tel: 901-373-1254.

Department for Finance

Secretary for Finance—Mr. JAMES ABERNATHY.

Controller—KEVIN JONES, CPA.

Regional Controller—Ms. KATHY OWINGS.

Department for Ministry Services

Secretary for Ministry Services—Rev. MICHAEL P. JOYCE, C.M., J.C.D.

Continuing Education for Clergy—Rev. CARL J. HOOD, Dir.

Formation of Permanent Deacons—Deacon FRANK WILLIAMS, Contact.

Permanent Deacons—Deacon FRANK WILLIAMS, Dir. Tel: 901-388-3509.

Seminarians—Rev. KEITH STEWART, Dir. Tel: 901-323-3817.

Villa Vianney Priests Retirement Residence—Rev. RICHARD L. MICKEY, M.Ed., Dir., 10605 Bishop Dozier Dr., Cordova, 38016. Tel: 901-752-0766.

Vicar for Religious—Sr. CATHY GALASKIEWICZ, O.P.

Vocations—Rev. KEITH STEWART, Dir. Tel: 901-323-3817.

Department For Multicultural Ministries

Secretary for Multicultural Ministries—Rev. ANTHONY CLARK, S.V.D., 1325 Jefferson Ave., Memphis, 38104. Tel: 901-722-4760; Fax: 901-722-4766. Mailing Address: P.O. Box 41705, Memphis, 38174-1705.

African American Catholics—Rev. ANTHONY CLARK, S.V.D., Dir. Tel: 901-722-4760; Sr. VICKIE CHAMBERS, S.S.N.D., Chm. Tel: 901-726-1221.

Filipino Catholic Ministry—Dr. OLIVIA KABIGAO, Pres. Tel: 901-921-3719.

Hispanic Catholic Ministry—Rev. CARLOS PANIAGUA-MONROY, S.V.D., Dir. Tel: 901-722-4759; 901-605-3952.

Korean Catholic Ministry—Rev. KAZIMIERZ ABRAHAMCZYK, S.V.D., Dir. Tel: 901-828-6832.

Native American Catholic Ministry—Mrs. RUTH ALLEN, Chm. Tel: 901-685-8135.

Polish Catholic Ministry—Mrs. BARBARA WALKOWC, Pres. Tel: 901-754-1649; Rev. KAZIMIERZ ABRAHAMCZYK, S.V.D., Spiritual Advisor. Tel: 901-754-1649; 901-828-6832.

Vietnamese Catholic Ministry—Rev. JOSEPH DAO VU, S.V.D., Dir. Tel: 901-726-1891.

African Catholic Ministry—Rev. HERBERT ENE, Dir. Tel: 901-725-2700.

Department for Pastoral Services

Secretary for Pastoral Services—Ms. ALMA ABUELOUF.

Campus & Young Adult Ministry—Ms. ALMA ABUELOUF; MARGARETTA DALOMBA DOBBS, 3625 Mynders Ave., Memphis, 38111. Tel: 901-323-3051 See Section (J) Newman Centers for additional information.

Community Health Ministry— (Ministry to Sick, Ministry for People with Disability and Special Needs, Mid-South Area Assoc. of Catholic Nurses, Health Ministries Network of the Mid-South, Council for Mental Illness Ministry). Ms. ALMA ABUELOUFF, Dir.

Evangelization—Ms. ALMA ABUELOUF, Dir.

Family Ministries—Mrs. PATRICIA MITCHELL PERRY, Dir., 1325 Jefferson Ave., Memphis, 38104. Tel: 901-722-4735. Email: patricia.perry@acc.cdom.org; Mailing Address: 5825 Shelby Oaks Dr., Memphis, 38134.

Active Parenting Training—

Sponsor Couple Training— (Couples working with those preparing for marriage).

FOCCUS Training— (Training for priest and deacons to use this tool with couples preparing for marriage).

Grief Ministry—

Windows Training— (Loss of any kind).

Hispanic Marriage Preparation—

Hispanic Marriage Enrichment—

Individual, Couples & Family Counseling—

Marriage Encounter—

Marriage Enrichment—

Programs for the Engaged—

Project Rachel/Rachel's Vineyard—

Retrouvaille—

Singles 40 Years and Older—

Natural Family Planning & Chastity Education—MARY PAT VAN EPPS, Dir. Tel: 901-373-1285. Email: marypat.vanepps@cc.cdom.org.

Mother/Daughter and Father/Son Fertility Appreciation & Chastity Programs— (Chastity promotion materials).

Office of Catechesis—Sr. CATHY GALASKIEWICZ, O.P., Dir.

Parish Evangelization Team Training—Ms. ALMA ABUELOUF, Dir.

Parish Pastoral Councils—Ms. ALMA ABUELOUF, Dir.

Prison Ministries—Deacon WILLIAM DAVIS, Dir.

Resource Library—Mrs. MARY BETH BOLTON, Dir.

Youth Ministries—Mrs. DIANNE DOLAN, Dir.

Leadership Camp—Rev. JOEY KAUMP, Spiritual Dir.

Quest—Rev. JOEY KAUMP, Spiritual Dir.

Voyage—Rev. JOEY KAUMP, Spiritual Dir.

Search—Rev. MICHAEL E. WERKHOVEN, Spiritual Dir.

Scouting—Mr. CHUCK SCHRADRACK, Chm.; Rev. WAYNE H. ARNOLD, Chap.

Department for Strategic Planning & Development

Secretary for Strategic Planning & Development—Mr. CHRIS KOCH. Tel: 901-373-1208.

Diocesan Spokesperson—Rev. JOHN J. GEANEY, C.S.P. Tel: 901-289-0760.

Newspaper— "West Tennessee Catholic" Mrs. PAM FLYNN, Mng. Editor. Tel: 901-373-1213.

Planned Giving—Mr. DAVID CREMERIUS, Dir. Tel: 901-373-1273.

Department of Worship and Spiritual Life

Secretary for Worship & Spiritual Life—Mr. MICHAEL ZIEGLER, 1325 Jefferson Ave., Memphis, 38104. Tel: 901-722-4744; Fax: 901-722-4791. Mailing Address: P.O. Box 41705, Memphis, 38174-1705.

Institute for Liturgy and Spirituality—Mr. MICHAEL ZIEGLER, Dir. Tel: 901-722-4744.

Liturgical Music—Mrs. BARBARA GOLDSMITH, Dir., 1695 Central Ave., Memphis, 38104. Tel: 901-725-2703.

Ministry with Gay & Lesbian Persons—Co Directors: Mrs. JUDY GRAY. Tel: 901-725-2714; Sr. MAUREEN GRINER, O.S.U. Tel: 901-725-2707.

Our Lady Queen of Peace Retreat Center—Sr. EILEEN FUCITO, C.P., Dir., 3630 Dancyville Rd., Stanton, 38069-4711. Tel: 731-548-2500.

Rites and Sacraments—Mr. MICHAEL ZIEGLER, Dir. Tel: 901-722-4744.

Spiritual Formation—Sr. EILEEN FUCITO, C.P., Dir., 3630 Dancyville Rd., Stanton, 38069-4711. Tel: 731-548-2500.

Charismatic Renewal—Deacon WERNER ROSE, Diocesan Liaison.

Cursillo—Deacon MICHAEL HOVANEC, Diocesan Liaison.

CLERGY, PARISHES, MISSIONS AND PAROCHIAL SCHOOLS

CITY OF MEMPHIS

(SHELBY COUNTY)

1—CATHEDRAL OF THE IMMACULATE CONCEPTION (1921) Rev. Msgr. Valentine N. Handwerker, Rector; Rev. Herbert Ene (Nigeria); Deacons Frank Williams; Bill Lifsey.
Offices: 1695 Central Ave., 38104. Tel: 901-725-2700; Fax: 901-725-2709. Web: www.iccathedral.org.
School—(Grades PreK-12), 1665 Central Ave., 38104. Tel: 901-725-2710; Fax: 901-725-2715. Web: iccathedralschool.org. Elizabeth Buchignani, Prin. (Elementary); Sally Hermsdorfer, Prin. (High School); Kate Hanney, Librarian. Priests 2; Lay Teachers 42; Students 367.
Catechesis/Religious Program—Tel: 901-435-5281; 901-725-2700; Fax: 901-725-2709. Aileen G. Palmer, D.R.E. Students 40.

2—ST. ANN (Bartlett) (1950) Revs. Richard D. Coy; Elbert Callis; Jacek L. Kowal; Deacons Chip Jones; Bob Skinner.
Res.: 6529 Stage Rd., Bartlett, 38134. Tel: 901-373-6011; Fax: 901-373-9030.
School—Tel: 901-386-3328; Fax: 901-386-1030. Sisters 1; Lay Teachers 41; Students 574.
Catechesis/Religious Program—6529 Stage Rd., Bartlett, 38134. Tel: 901-373-6011; Fax: 901-373-9030. Students 322.

3—ST. ANNE'S (1933) Rev. J. David Graham; Deacons Jack Chitwood; Charles O'Bryant; David Woolley. In Res., Rev. Keith Stewart.
Res.: 706 S. Highland St., 38111. Tel: 901-323-3817; Fax: 901-323-3151.
School—670 S. Highland St., 38111. Tel: 901-323-1344; Fax: 901-458-5215. Lay Teachers 8; Students 95.
Catechesis/Religious Program—Tel: 901-379-9739. Karen Gibbs, D.R.E. Students 10.

4—ST. AUGUSTINE (1937), (African American), Rev. John J. Geaney, C.S.P.; Deacon Joseph Randolph Jr.
Church: 1169 Kerr Ave., 38106. Tel: 901-774-2297; Fax: 901-774-3067. Email: staugchurch@aol.com. Web: www.staugustinememphis.org.
Catechesis/Religious Program—Tel: 901-774-2298. Students 43.

5—BLESSED SACRAMENT (1912) Rev. Kevin W. Bravata.
Church: 2564 Hale Ave., 38112. Tel: 901-452-1543; Fax: 901-452-1592. Web: chblessedsacrament.com.
Catechesis/Religious Program—Mrs. Lorena Ramrez, D.R.E. Students 100.

6—ST. BRIGID (1992) Rev. R. Bruce Cinquegrani.
Church: 7801 Lowrance Rd., 38125-2825. Tel: 901-758-0128; Fax: 901-758-8862. Email: hprewitt@stbrigidcc-mem.org. Web: www.stbrigidmemphis.org.
Res.: 4200 Thunderstone Cir. W., 38125-3108. Tel: 901-759-9628.
Catechesis/Religious Program—Rose Anne Hembree, D.R.E. Students 50.

7—CHURCH OF THE ASCENSION (1974) Revs. Robert W. Marshall Jr.; Simon Thoi Hoang, S.V.D.; Deacons John T. Oates; Harvey Stewart; G. Richmond Quinton; Michael Richardson.
Res.: 3680 Ramill Rd., 38128. Tel: 901-372-1364; Fax: 901-372-9411. Email: ascensionmemphis@bellsouth.net.
Catechesis/Religious Program—Lois Wilber, D.R.E. Students 200.

8—CHURCH OF THE HOLY SPIRIT (1975) Rev. Msgr. Albert E. Kirk; Rev. Mathew Joseph Panackachira, M.C.B.S.; Deacons Ned Turner; Richard Griffith; Bill Nourse; Werner Rose.
Church: 2300 Hickory Crest Dr., 38119-6805. Tel: 901-754-7146; Fax: 901-754-0102. Web: www.hspirit.com.
Catechesis/Religious Program—Tel: 901-754-7146, Ext. 104. Students 199.

9—CHURCH OF THE INCARNATION (1978) Revs. William J. Parham; Kevin J. Stockbridge; Deacons Miles Merwin; David Lucchesi; Robert Walker.
Office & Res.: 360 Bray Station Rd., Collierville,

38017. Tel: 901-853-7468; Fax: 901-854-0536. Web: www.incarnationchurch.com.
School—(Grades PreK-8) Tel: 901-853-7804; Fax: 901-850-2699. Web: www.goics.org. Connie Berman, Prin.; Mrs. Kathy Rybczyk, Sec.; Nancy Allee, Librarian. Students 224.
Catechesis/Religious Program—Tel: 901-853-0135. Martha Drennan, D.R.E. Students 664.

10—CHURCH OF THE NATIVITY (1979) Rev. Michael A. Morgera; Deacon Franklin O. Larker. In Res., Rev. Adam M. Rust.
Res.: 5955 St. Elmo, Barlett, 38135-1516. Tel: 901-382-2504; Fax: 901-382-3644. Email: gay.brigance@nativity.cdom.org.
Catechesis/Religious Program—Theresa Krier, D.R.E. Students 119.

11—CHURCH OF THE RESURRECTION (1973) Revs. Ernie DeBlasio; Miguel Angel Espadas.
Res.: 5475 Newberry Ave., 38115-3629. Tel: 901-794-8970; Fax: 901-794-8806. Email: cresurre@comcast.net. Web: resurrectionmemphis.com/Home_Page.html.
Catechesis/Religious Program—Tel: 901-794-8971. Email: predirector@comcast.net. Jacky Becker, D.R.E. Students 215.

12—ST. FRANCIS OF ASSISI (1985) Rev. Msgr. Peter P. Buchignani; Revs. Martin M. Orjianioke (Nigeria); Robert J. Stellini; Deacons Chuck Lightcap; Mick Hovanec; William Davis; John Knight.
Res. & Church: 8151 Chimneyrock Blvd., Cordova, 38016. Tel: 901-753-1494 (Rectory); 901-756-1213 (Church); Fax: 901-755-2168.
School—2100 N. Germantown Pkwy., Cordova, 38016. Tel: 901-388-7321; Fax: 901-388-8201. Email: beth.york@sfaschool.cdom.org. Mrs. Beth York, Prin. Faculty 121; Students 890.
Catechesis/Religious Program—Email: peggy.holt@sfachurch.cdom.org. Web: www.cdom.org. Mrs. Terry Harvey, D.R.E. Students 365.

13—HOLY NAMES OF JESUS AND MARY (1939) Unassigned. Revs. Maurice J. Nutt, C.Ss.R.; Marcel Emeka Okwara, C.Ss.R; Bro. Eugene G. Patin, C.Ss.R.; Mr. Cleo Hayes, Dir. Parish Opers.
Res.: 697 Keel Ave., 38107-2599. Tel: 901-525-9870; Fax: 901-527-7436. Email: info@thenameschurch.org. Web: www.thenameschurch.org.
Catechesis/Religious Program—Students 30.

14—HOLY ROSARY (1955) Revs. James J. Martell; Charles A. Bauer; Deacons Kenneth McCarver; Fred Brunner; Daniel Brown; Jeffrey Drzycimski.
Church, Res. & Office: 4851 Park Ave., 38117. Tel: 901-767-6949; Fax: 901-767-8504.
School—4841 Park Ave., 38117. Tel: 901-685-1231; Fax: 901-818-0335. Sisters 1; Students 403.
Catechesis/Religious Program—Students 35.

15—ST. JAMES (1956) Rev. William R. Kantner.
Res.: 4180 LeRoy, 38108. Tel: 901-767-8672; Fax: 901-767-8576. Email: stjamescatholic@bellsouth.net.

16—ST. JOHN'S (1947) Rev. Kazimierz Abrahamczyk, S.V.D.; Deacon Walt Bolton.
Res.: 2742 Lamar Ave., 38114. Tel: 901-743-4551; Fax: 901-743-5944. Email: abrahamczyk@aol.com.
Catechesis/Religious Program—Walter Bolton, D.R.E. Students 4.

17—ST. JOSEPH'S (1878) Revs. Anthony Clark, S.V.D.; Carlos Pariogua-Monray, S.V.D.; Deacons James Calicott; Curtiss Talley.
Res.: 3825 Neely Rd., 38109. Tel: 901-396-9996; Fax: 901-332-8691. Email: hstjosephchurc@comcast.net.
Catechesis/Religious Program—Students 39.

18—ST. LOUIS (1957) Rev. Msgr. John B. McArthur; Rev. Dennis Schenkel; Deacons Ralph Donati, (Retired); Jack Conrad. In Res., Rev. Saji Ellickal, M.C.B.S.
Office:—203 S. White Station Rd., 38117. Tel: 901-682-6606; Fax: 901-680-0571. Web: www.stlouischurchmphs.org.
School—5192 Shady Grove Rd., 38117. Tel: 901-682-9692; Fax: 901-328-9798. Web: www.stlouismemphis.org. Lay Teachers 28; Aides 4; Students 482.
Catechesis/Religious Program—Libby Pretti, D.R.E. Students 178.

19—ST. MARY CHURCH (1860) Rev. Eric Peterson.
Church & Office: 155 Market St., 38105. Tel: 901-522-9420; Fax: 901-522-8314. Web: stmary-memphis.com.
Catechesis/Religious Program—Students 30.

20—ST. MICHAEL'S (1951) Rev. Msgr. Victor P. Ciaramitaro; Rev. Enrique Garcia Granados; Deacons Joseph Mensi; Norman Alexander.
Office: 3848 Forrest Ave., 38122. Tel: 901-323-0896; 901-324-6411; Fax: 901-323-3557.
Res.: 3867 Summer Ave., 38122. Tel: 901-452-5755.
School—3880 Forrest Ave., 38122. Tel: 901-323-2162; Fax: 901-323-0481. Web: www.stmichaelmemphis.org. Lay Teachers 15; Students 162.
Catechesis/Religious Program—Students 341.

21—OUR LADY OF PERPETUAL HELP (1952) Rev. Msgr. J. Edwin Creary; Revs. Krzysztof Rusin (Poland); Jolly Sebastian, M.C.B.S. (India); Deacons Paul Hamblen; William Herbers; John Moskal; Matt Hudson, Sr. High Youth Min.; Ed Zieseniss, Athletic Dir.; Carol Schaefgen, Office Mgr.; Ben Legett, Music Dir.
Res.: 8151 Poplar, Germantown, 38138. Tel: 901-754-1204; Fax: 901-754-0969. Web: www.olphgermantown.org.
School—(Grades PreK-8), 8151 Poplar, Germantown, 38138. Tel: 901-753-1181, Ext. 340; Fax: 901-754-1475. Mrs. Patricia Wyckoff, Prin.; Mrs. Lynn Lifsey, Asst. Prin.; Mrs. Angela Saba, Sec. Faculty 43; Students 247.
Catechesis/Religious Program—Mr. Craig DeMille, D.R.E. Students 272.

22—OUR LADY OF SORROWS (1926) Rev. Bryan P. Timby; Deacons Donald A. Bennis; Henry P. Littleton.
Res.: 3700 Thomas St., 38127. Tel: 901-353-1530; Fax: 901-353-1052. Email: olsmemphis@aol.com. Web: www.ourladyofsorrowschurch.org.
School—3690 Thomas St., 38127. Tel: 901-358-7431; Fax: 901-353-1153. Email: julia.willhite@ols.cdom.org. Web: olos.schoolfusion.us. Lay Teachers 12; Students 103.
Catechesis/Religious Program—Brenda Plessinger, D.R.E. Students 46.

23—ST. PATRICK'S (1866) Revs. Timothy F. Sullivan, C.S.P.; Bruce Nieli, C.S.P.; Deacon Eugene Champion.
Res.: 277 S. Fourth St., 38126. Tel: 901-527-2542; Fax: 901-525-1147. Web: www.stpatsmemphis.org.
Catechesis/Religious Program—Students 168.

24—ST. PAUL THE APOSTLE (1944) Revs. James L. Pugh; Benjamin P. Bradshaw.
Res.: 1425 E. Shelby Dr., 38116. Tel: 901-346-2380; Fax: 901-346-2385. Email: info@stpaulmemphis.org. Web: www.stpaulmemphis.org.
School—Tel: 901-346-0862; Fax: 901-396-2677. Sisters 2; Lay Teachers 16; Students 220.
Catechesis/Religious Program— Ellen Austin, D.R.E.; Maria Smith, D.R.E. Students 93.

25—ST. PETER CHURCH (1840) Revs. Thomas M. Condon, O.P.; John M. Pitzer, O.P.; William S. Daniels, O.P.; Paul D. Watkins, O.P.
Res.: 190 Adams Ave., 38103. Tel: 901-527-8282; Fax: 901-526-6882.
Catechesis/Religious Program—Christina Klyce, D.R.E. Students 196.

26—SACRED HEART CHURCH (1899) Rev. Joseph Dao Vu, S.V.D.
1324 Jefferson Ave., 38104.
Res.: 1254 S. Lauderdale, 38106. Tel: 901-726-1891; Fax: 901-726-9272. Email: sacredheartparish@hotmail.com. Web: www.parishesonline.com.
Catechesis/Religious Program—Students 66.

27—ST. THERESE THE LITTLE FLOWER (1930) Rev. Carl J. Hood; Deacon James P. Schmall.
Res.: 1644 Jackson Ave., 38107. Tel: 901-276-1412; Fax: 901-274-4476. Email: sttherese@stlfchurch.cdom.org.
Catechesis/Religious Program—Mrs. Burma Schmall, D.R.E. Students 43.

28—ST. WILLIAM (1951) Rev. William F. Burke.
Res.: 4932 Easley Ave., Millington, 38053. Tel: 901-872-4099 (Parish Office); 901-872-2279 (Religious Education); Fax: 901-872-8920. Web: www.cdom.org/web_sites/stwilliam/default.html.
Catechesis/Religious Program—Judy Longoria, D.R.E. Students 107.

OUTSIDE SHELBY COUNTY

BOLIVAR, HARDEMAN CO., ST. MARY CHURCH (1950) Rev. Wayne H. Arnold.
Res.: 223 Mecklenburg Dr., 38008-1736. Tel: 731-658-4627; Fax: 731-658-4627.
Catechesis/Religious Program—Students 10.

BROWNSVILLE, HAYWOOD CO., ST. JOHN CHURCH (1949) Rev. Msgr. Thomas D. Kirk; Rev. Robert D. Favazza.
Church: 910 N. Washington Ave., P.O. Box 872, 38012. Tel: 731-668-2596; 731-772-3514.
Catechesis/Religious Program—Tommy Sellari, D.R.E. Students 44.

CAMDEN, BENTON CO., ST. MARY CHURCH (1981) Rev. Richard J. Kaump Jr.
Res.: 220 W. Main St., 38320. Tel: 731-584-6459; Fax: 731-584-6446. Email: stmaryscatholic@bellsouth.net.
Catechesis/Religious Program—Sandra Simpson, D.R.E. Students 48.
Mission—Holy Family Church 265 Cotham Dr., Huntingdon, Carroll Co. 38344. Tel: 731-986-2817.

COVINGTON, TIPTON CO., ST. ALPHONSUS CHURCH (1952) Rev. John J. Hourican.
Res.: 1512 Evergreen, 38019. Tel: 901-476-0374; Fax: 901-476-9650. Email: stalphonsus27923@bellsouth.net. Web: www.saintalphonsuschurch.org.
Church: 1225 Hwy. 51 S., P.O. Box 430, 38019-3236. Tel: 901-476-8140.
Catechesis/Religious Program—Maureen Stephens, D.R.E. Students 34.
Mission—Ave Maria 664 S. Washington, Ripley, Lauderdale Co. 38063.

DYERSBURG, DYER CO., HOLY ANGELS CHURCH (1938) Rev. Russell D. Harbaugh.
Res.: 535 Tucker St., 38024. Tel: 731-287-8000; Fax: 731-287-7632. Email: hachurch@cableone.net. Web: www.holyangelscatholicchurch.net.
Catechesis/Religious Program—Ann Dedmon, D.R.E. (K-5). Tel: 731-285-9189; Deborah McCallen, D.R.E. (6-12). Tel: 731-286-6467. Students 82.

HUMBOLDT, GIBSON CO., SACRED HEART (1872) Rev. Michael E. Werkhoven; Deacon Ed Kutz.
Res.: 2881 E. Main St., P.O. Box 660, 38343. Tel: 731-784-3904; Fax: 731-784-5048. Email: sacredheart1@bellsouth.net.
Catechesis/Religious Program—Students 15.
Mission— 9060 Telecom, Milan, Northern Gibson Co. 38358. Tel: 731-686-8686.

JACKSON, MADISON CO., ST. MARY CHURCH (1867) Rev. Msgr. Thomas D. Kirk; Rev. Robert D. Favazza; Deacons Dr. William Lafont, (Retired); Jim Moss; Dale Brown.
Res.: 1665 Hwy. 45 Byp., 38305. Tel: 731-668-2596; Fax: 731-668-9809.
School—Tel: 731-668-2525; Fax: 731-668-1164. Web: www.stmarysschool.tn.org. Sisters 4; Lay Teachers 27; Students 347.
Catechesis/Religious Program—Email: kathleen.hicks@stmarys.tn.org. Kathleen Hicks, D.R.E. Students 175.
Mission—St. John Church P.O. Box 872, Brownsville, Haywood Co. 38012. Tel: 731-772-3514.

LEXINGTON, HENDERSON CO., ST. ANDREW THE APOSTLE (1981) Rev. Gary E. Lamb; Sr. Janet Delperdang, Pastoral Assoc.
Church: 895 N. Broad St., 38351. Tel: 731-968-6393; Fax: 731-968-2933. Email: standrewtheapostle@bellsouth.net.
Res.: 901 N. Broad St., 38351. Tel: 731-968-7944; Fax: 731-967-1228.
Catechesis/Religious Program—Tel: 731-847-2054; Fax: 731-847-2054. Students 29.
Mission—St. Regina 108 Skyline Ln., P.O. Box 92, Parsons, Decatur Co. 38363. Tel: 731-847-2054.
Catechesis/Religious Program—Students 34.

MARTIN, WEAKLEY CO., ST. JUDE'S (1962) Rev. Joseph L. Paolozzi; Deacon Rodney Freed.
Church & Res.: 110 Hannings Ln., 38237. Tel: 731-588-5675 (Res.); 731-587-9777 (Church); Fax: 731-587-9778.
Catechesis/Religious Program—Students 61.

MILAN, GIBSON CO., ST. MATTHEW MISSION (1977) Rev. Michael E. Werkhoven; Deacon Ed Kutz.
Mailing Address: *c/o Sacred Heart Church*, P.O. Box 660, Humboldt, 38343. Tel: 731-784-3904; Fax: 731-784-5048. Email: sacredheart1@bellsouth.net.
Catechesis/Religious Program—Students 12.

PARIS, HENRY CO., HOLY CROSS (1921) Rev. Edward K. Fisher; Deacons Michael Gore; Rodney Seyller.
Res.: 1210 E. Wood St., 38242. Tel: 731-642-4681; Fax: 731-644-9668. Email: leila.kackley@holycross.cdom.org. Web: www.holycrossparis.org.
School—(Grades PreK) Angie Taylor, Dir. Students 26.
Catechesis/Religious Program—Students 150.

SAVANNAH, HARDIN CO., ST. MARY CHURCH (1948) Rev. Anthony Azuwike (Nigeria).
Church & Res.: 2315 Pickwick St., 38372. Tel: 731-925-4852; Fax: 731-925-9612. Email: smccsavannah1@gmail.com. Web: www.stmary-savannah.org.
Catechesis/Religious Program—Patti Erisman, D.R.E. Students 55.
Mission—Our Lady of the Lake Pickwick Dam, Hardin Co.

SELMER, MCNAIRY CO., ST. JUDE THE APOSTLE CATHOLIC CHURCH (1982) Rev. Wayne H. Arnold; Deacon Jim Gray.
Res.: 1318 E. Poplar Ave., 38375. Tel: 731-645-4188; Fax: 731-645-4188. Email: stjude9@bellsouth.net.
Catechesis/Religious Program—Students 42.

SOMERVILLE, FAYETTE CO., ST. PHILIP THE APOSTLE (1981) Rev. Stephen K. Kenny; Deacon Michael Blome.
Church: 11710 Hwy. 64, 38068. Tel: 901-465-8685; Fax: 901-466-1645. Email: stphilipcc@bellsouth.net.
Catechesis/Religious Program—Ginny Modlin, D.R.E. Students 56.

UNION CITY, OBION CO., IMMACULATE CONCEPTION (1891) Rev. Robert D. Ponticello.
Res.: 1303 E. Reelfoot Ave., 38261. Tel: 731-885-0963; Fax: 731-885-9960. Email: secretary@icuctn.com. Web: www.icuctn.com.
School—Immaculate Conception School, (PreK) Dawn Black, Dir.
Catechesis/Religious Program—Teresa Vallee, D.R.E. Students 105.

Chaplains of Public Institutions

MEMPHIS. *Federal Correctional Institute at Memphis.* Rev. Faustino Maramot, Chap.

On Duty Outside the Diocese:
Rev.—
Barre, Michael L., S.S.

Graduate Studies:
Rev.—
Rust, Adam M., Pontifical North American College 00120 Vatican City State.

Military Chaplains:
Rev.—
Danner, James L., Navy, Sr. Chap., 5813 S. Gordon Ave., Tampa, FL 33611.

Absent on Leave:
Revs.—
Pecoraro, John C.
Schultz, Joel P.

Retired:
Rev. Msgr.—
Davis, William F., 745 Loeb St., 38111.
Revs.—
Atkinson, John V., Villa Vianney, 10599 Bishop Dozier Dr., Apt. 3, Cordova, 38016. Tel: 901-752-0766
Foley, David M., 995 Anglers Cove, #502, Marco Island, FL 34145.
Kelly, Edward E., 8740 Delmar, #2 E., St. Louis, MO 63124.
Knight, David B., c/o His Way Spiritual Growth Ctr., 1306 Dellwood Ave., 38127. Tel: 901-357-6662
Lattas, Joseph, Villa Vianney, 10611 Bishop Dozier Dr., Cordova, 38016.
Murphy, James W., Villa Vianney, 10599 Bishop Dozier Dr., Cordova, 38016. Tel: 901-752-0766
Nobile, Angelo
Stewart, Michael L., 1980 S. Bailey Woods, Apt. 103, Collierville, 38017.

Permanent Deacons:
Bennis, Donald
Bonaiuto, Nick
Brunner, Fred
Calicott, James
Champion, Eugene
Champion, James, (Retired)
Chitwood, Jack
Conrad, Jack
Cooley, Jim
Cranford, William R.
Davis, William
Donati, Ralph, (Retired)
Gore, Michael
Gray, Jim
Griffith, Richard
Hamblen, Paul
Herbers, Bill
Herbers, Jerome E., (Inactive)
Hicks, Joseph, (Inactive)
Hivner, John, (Retired)
Hovanec, Mick
Howell, Larry, (Retired)
Johnson, Eldon
Jones, Chip
Kang, John
Lafont, Bill
Larker, Frank
Lightcap, Charles
McCarver, Kenneth
Mensi, Joseph
Merwin, Miles
Miller, James, (Inactive)
Nourse, Bill
O'Bryant, Charles
Oates, John
Ramsey, Eddie
Rose, Werner
Schmall, James
Seyller, Rod
Steele, Mike
Stewart, Harvey
Talley, Curtiss
Terry, Andrew, Jr.
Tucker, Jim
Turner, Ned
Van Tassel, Everell E., (Inactive)
Wells, Charles, (Inactive)
Williams, Frank
Yarbrough, Harold

INSTITUTIONS LOCATED IN THE DIOCESE

[A] COLLEGES AND UNIVERSITIES

MEMPHIS. **Christian Brothers University* (1871) (Coed), 650 E. Parkway S., 38104. Tel: 901-321-3000; Fax: 901-321-3290. Web: www.cbu.edu. H. Lance Forsdick, Interim Pres.; Bro. Louis Althaus, F.S.C., Asst. to Pres.; Dr. Frank Buscher, Interim Academic Vice Pres.; Ms. Melissa Hanson, Dir. Grants & Research; Bro. Robert Veselsky, F.S.C., Dir. of Mission & Ministry; Mr. Dan Wortham, Vice Pres. Admin. & Finance; Dr. Michael Ryan, Vice Pres. Advancement; Ms. Betty McWillie, Dir. Career Devel. & Placement; Mr. Thomas Cochran, Controller; Mr. Chris Matz, Dir., Plough Library.
Christian Brothers Univ. (of Memphis, Tenn.), Four-Year University with Schools of Business, Engineering, Arts, and Sciences. Graduate programs in Business, Catholic Studies, Engineering, Education, and Executive Leadership. Brothers 18; Lay Teachers 172; Students 1,758.

[B] DIOCESAN SCHOOLS

MEMPHIS. *St. Augustine School*, 1169 Kerr Ave., 38106. Tel: 901-942-8002; Fax: 901-942-4564. Email: staugustinememphis@gmail.com. LaTonya Rayford, Prin.; Sara O'Dell, Librarian. Lay Teachers 14; Students 110.
Bishop Byrne Middle/High School (1965) 1475 E. Shelby Dr., 38116. Tel: 901-346-3060; Fax: 901-346-9488. Web: www.bishopbyrne.org. Dr. Donald Edwards, Pres. & Prin. Sisters 2; Lay Teachers 19; Students 242.
De La Salle Elementary at Blessed Sacrament (2000) 2540 Hale Ave., 38112. Tel: 901-866-9084; Fax: 901-866-9086. Email: brother.mark@delasalle.cdom.org. Web: www.cdom/schools/schools/delasalle.html. Bro. Mark Snodgrass, F.S.C., Prin. Brothers 1; Lay Teachers 12; Lay Staff 5; Students 160.
Holy Names of Jesus and Mary School, 709 Keel Ave., 38107. Tel: 901-507-1503; Fax: 901-507-1507. Email: donna.banfield@holynamesschool.cdom.org. Web: www.holynamesmemphis.org. Sr. Donna M. Banfield, S.B.S., Prin.; Mrs. Francine Washington, Sec. Lay Teachers 7; Students 80.
St. John Catholic School, 2718 Lamar Ave., 38114. Tel: 901-743-6700; Fax: 901-743-6720. Email: teddi.niedzwiedz@stjohn.cdom.org. Teddi Niedzwiedz, Prin.; Susan MacArthur, Librarian. (Reopened 2000) Lay Teachers 13; Students 178.
St. Joseph School, (Grades PreK-6), 3851 Neely Rd., 38109. Tel: 901-344-0021; Fax: 901-348-0787. Email: phil.amido@stjoseph.cdom.org. Mr. Dorian P. Amido, Prin.; Lynn Ward, Librarian. Lay Teachers 21; Students 183.
Little Flower School, 1666 Jackson Ave., 38107. Tel: 901-725-9900; Fax: 901-725-5779. Email: barbara.petit@stlfschool.cdom.org. Sr. Lynn Marie Ralph, S.B.S., Prin.; Mrs. Mary Neu, Librarian. Priests 1; Lay Teachers 9; Lay Staff 13; Students 74.
Memphis Catholic High School and Middle School, (Grades 7-12), 61 N. McLean Blvd., 38104. Tel: 901-276-1221; Fax: 901-725-1447. Email: jpohlman@memphiscatholic.org. Web: www.memphiscatholic.org. Mr. Jim Pohlman, Pres. & Prin.; Christopher Robbins, Dean, Academics; Sr. Vickie Chambers, S.S.N.D., Librarian. Sisters 1; Lay Teachers 17; Students 162.
See Education That Works, LLC in the Institution Section under Miscellaneous.
St. Patrick School (1867) (Grades PreK-6), 287 S. Fourth St., 38126. Tel: 901-521-3252; Fax: 901-521-8265. Email: kenneth.bernardini@stpat.cdom.org. Kenneth Bernardini, Prin.; Erin Van Epps, Librarian. (closed 1950; reopened 2003). Lay Teachers 12; Lay Staff 9; Students 168.
Resurrection Catholic School, (Grades PreK-3), 3572 Emerald St., 38115. Tel: 901-546-9926; Fax: 901-546-9928. Email: debbie.bell@resurrectionschool.cdom.org. Web: www.cdom.org. Mrs. Debbie Bell, Prin. Brothers 1; Lay Teachers 8.

CORDOVA. *St. Benedict at Auburndale High School*, 8250 Varnavas Dr., 38016. Tel: 901-260-2840; Fax: 901-260-2850. Email: valadieg@sbaeagles.org. Web: www.sbaeagles.org. Mr. George Valadie, Pres. of Campus & Prin. (Grades 9-12); Rebecca Hall, Librarian. Special programs for gifted and learning disabled. Lay Teachers 79; Students 974.

[C] HIGH SCHOOLS, PRIVATE AND PAROCHIAL

MEMPHIS. *St. Agnes Academy* (1851) 4830 Walnut Grove Rd., 38117. Tel: 901-767-1356; Fax: 901-435-5866. Email: jmaness@saa-sds.org. Web: www.saa-sds.org. Barbara Daush, Pres.; Mrs. Gretchen K. Kirk, D.R.E.; Mrs. Joy Maness, Dean of Upper School. Dominican Sisters of Peace., Title of Incorporation: St. Agnes Academy Lay Teachers 39; Students 319.
**Christian Brothers High School* (1871) 5900 Walnut Grove Rd., 38120-2174. Tel: 901-261-4900; Fax: 901-261-4909. Email: info@cbhs.org. Web: www.cbhs.org. Bros. Christopher Englert, F.S.C., Pres.; Michael Fugger, F.S.C., Dir. Brothers' Community; Chris Fay, Prin.; Ellen B. Davis, Librarian. Title of Incorporation: Christian Brothers (LaSalle) High School. Priests 1; Brothers 6; Lay Teachers 66; Students 882.
Immaculate Conception Cathedral School (1950) (Grades PreK-12), 1725 Central Ave., 38104. Tel: 901-725-2705 High School; Fax: 901-725-2701 High School. Email: cathy.mcdonald@ic.cdom.org. Web: www.myiccs.org. Elementary: 1669 Central Ave., 38104. Tel: 901-725-2710; Fax: 901-725-2715. Betty Buchignani, Prin. (Elementary); Diane Allen, Vice Prin. (Elementary); Sally Hermsdorfer, Prin. (High School); Rev. Msgr. Valentine N. Handwerker; Kate Hanney, Librarian. Sisters 1; Lay Teachers 38; Students 461.

JACKSON. *Sacred Heart of Jesus High School*, 185 Greenfield Dr., 38305. Tel: 731-660-4774; Fax: 731-984-7200. Email: frwheatley@aeneas.com. Web: www.shjhs.org. Rev. R. Carroll Wheatley, Ed.S., D.Min., Prin.

[D] ELEMENTARY SCHOOLS, PRIVATE

MEMPHIS. *St. Agnes Academy*, (Grades PreK-8), 4830 Walnut Grove Rd., 38117. Tel: 901-767-1377; Fax: 901-684-5316. Email: kboccia@saa-sds.org. Web: www.saa-sds.org. Barbara Daush, Pres.; Mrs. Gretchen K. Kirk, D.R.E.; Mrs. Kathleen Toes-Boccia, Dean of Lower School; Mrs. Joy Maness, Dean Upper School. Dominican Sisters of Peace. Lay Teachers 19; Students 304.
St. Dominic Boys School, (Grades PreK-8), 30 Avon Rd., 38117. Tel: 901-682-3011; Fax: 901-681-0047. Email: jmurphy@saa-sds.org. Web: www.saa.sds.org. Barbara Daush, Pres.; Mrs. Gretchen K. Kirk, D.R.E.; Mr. John Murphy, Dean. Dominican Sisters of Peace. Lay Teachers 22; Students 275.

[E] ADULT RESIDENCES & HOMES FOR AGED

MEMPHIS. *Diocese of Memphis Housing Corp.*, 1325 Jefferson Ave., 38104. Tel: 901-722-4772; 901-722-4795; Fax: 901-722-4732. Web: www.dmhcorp.org. Mr. Denny Calloway, Dir. Bed Capacity 654; Total Assisted Annually 800; Total Staff 41.
St. Peter Manor, LLC, 108 N. Auburndale, 38104. Tel: 901-278-8200; Fax: 901-278-8210. Mary Dowling, Mgr. Staff 15; Bed Capacity 283; Total Assisted Annually 318.
St. Peter Chapel & Activity Center Tel: 901-278-8200; Fax: 901-278-8210. Email: mkdowling14@msn.com.
St. Peter Villa, 141 N. McLean, 38104-2644. Tel: 901-276-2021; Fax: 901-725-3564. Email: kae.werkhoven@villa.cdom.org. Mrs. Kae Werkhoven, Admin. Diocesan Nursing Home. Bed Capacity 180; Days of Care 69,120; Total Staff 182.

DYERSBURG. *St. Joseph Village, Inc.*, 885 Hwy. 51 Byp. W., 38024. Tel: 901-285-8560; Fax: 901-285-8562. Email: beverlybates@bellsouth.net. Beverly Bates, Mgr. Total Assisted Annually 112; Total Staff 5.

HUMBOLDT. *St. Matthew Manor*, 2575 Viking Dr., 38343. Tel: 731-784-7229; 731-784-9309; Fax: 731-784-9309. Email: boazcarol@yahoo.com. Carol Boaz, Mgr. Total Staff 2; Bed Capacity 40; Total Assisted 41.
St. Matthew Manor - West, 2575 Viking Dr., 38343. Tel: 731-824-3793; Fax: 731-784-3793 303. Email: carolboaz@yahoo.com. Carol Boaz, Mgr. Total Staff 2; Bed Capacity 27; Total Assisted 27.

JACKSON. *St. Mary Manor, LLC*, 1771 Hwy. 45 Byp., 38305. Tel: 731-668-5633; Fax: 731-668-9252. Email: stmary1@aeneas.net. Anne M. Sain, Mgr. Total Staff 10; Independent Living Apartments 149.

MOSCOW. *St. Mark Village Apartments*, 85 St. Mark Cove, 38057. Tel: 901-877-3456; Fax: 901-877-3457. Email: saintmarkvillage@bellsouth.net. Mary Gordon, Mgr. Bed Capacity 24; Total Staff 5.

[F] RESIDENCES OF PRIESTS AND BROTHERS

MEMPHIS. *Brothers of the Christian Schools (Mid-West Prov.), F.S.C.*, Christian Brothers University, 650

E. Parkway S., 38104. Tel: 901-321-3251; Fax: 901-321-3290. Email: jsmarrel@cbu.edu. Web: www.cbu.edu. John Smarrelli Jr., Ph.D., Pres.

Christian Brothers High School, 5900 Walnut Grove Rd., 38119. Tel: 901-261-4900; Fax: 901-261-4909. Email: brchris@cbhs.org. Web: www.cbhs.org. Brothers 28.

The Dominican Friars of Memphis, Inc., 190 Adams Ave., 38103. Tel: 901-527-8282; Fax: 901-526-6882. Revs. Thomas M. Condon, O.P.; William S. Daniels, O.P.; John M. Pitzer, O.P.; Paul D. Watkins, O.P.

Redemptorists of Tennessee, Holy Names of Jesus and Mary Church, 697 Keel Ave., 38107. Tel: 901-525-9870; Fax: 901-527-7436. Revs. Maurice J. Nutt, C.Ss.R., D.Min.; Marcel Emeka Okwara, C.Ss.R; Bro. Eugene G. Patin, C.Ss.R.

Society of the Divine Word (Chicago Province), 1254 S. Lauderdale, 38106. Tel: 901-774-8191; Fax: 901-774-8192. Email: dominicnsvd@hotmail.com. Revs. Joseph Dao Vu, S.V.D.; Anthony Clark, S.V.D.; Carlos Paniagua-Monroy, S.V.D.; Kazimierz Abrahamczyk, S.V.D.; Simon Thoi Hoang, S.V.D.; Kieran Jianjun Sun, S.V.D.; Chako Parekatt. Priests 6.

Villa Vianney Senior Priests Residence, 10605 Bishop Dozier Dr., Cordova, 38016-5558. Tel: 901-752-0766; Fax: 901-752-0633. Rev. Richard L. Mickey, M.Ed., Dir. In Residence (Retired) 5; Total Staff 3.

[G] CONVENTS AND RESIDENCES FOR SISTERS

MEMPHIS. *Missionaries of Charity*, 700 N. 7th St., 38107. Tel: 901-527-4947. Sisters 4. *Shelter* Tel: 901-526-5456. Sr. M. Jonathan, M.C., Supr. Sisters 4; Total Assisted 464.

Missionary Sisters Of The Society Of Mary (Waltham, MA) S.M.S.M., 60 S. Auburndale, 38104. Tel: 901-272-2808. Email: smsm60au@aol.com. Sisters 2.

Missionary Sisters Servants of the Holy Spirit, S.Sp.S., 5280 Brenton, 38120. Tel: 901-685-3649. Sisters 3.

Monastery Of St. Clare O.S.C. (1932) 1310 Dellwood Ave., 38127. Tel: 901-357-6662. Email: memphisclares@gmail.com. Web: www.poorclare.org/memphis. Sr. Mary Marguerite, O.S.C., Abbess. Sisters 5; Huehuetenango, Guatemala 2.

Sisters of St. Charles Borromeo, C.B., 4778 Normandy Ave., 38117. Tel: 901-818-9180. Email: csusindr@hotmail.com. Web: www.cbsisters.org. Sisters 2.

[H] NEWMAN CENTERS

MEMPHIS. *Catholic Campus Ministry* 3625 Mynders Ave., 38111. Tel: 901-323-3051; Fax: 901-323-0925. Email: info@ccm.cdom.org. Margaretta daLomba Dobbs, Campus Min.; Deacon James Schmall, Admin. Asst.; Sr. Sharon Glumb, S.L.W., Dir., Campus Min.

JACKSON. *Lambuth University* 705 Lambuth Blvd., 38301. Sam Mauck, Campus Min. Tel: 731-425-3476.

MARTIN. *Interfaith Student Center* 312 Lovelace Ave., 38237. Tel: 901-587-2603. Email: interfaith@charterinternet.net. Web: www.utm.edu/organizations/ifaith. Rev. Joseph L. Paolozzi; Deacon Rodney Freed.

[I] MISCELLANEOUS

MEMPHIS. *St. Anne Lay Carmelite Community, c/o St. Anne Church*, 706 S. Highland, 38111. Tel: 901-937-1073 (Dir.). Email: carmemphis@gmail.com.

The Catholic Cafe, Inc., c/o 1700 One Commerce Sq., 38103. Tel: 901-576-1714; Fax: 901-525-2389. Web: www.thecatholiccafe.com. Robert Hutton, Pres.

Catholic Charities, Inc., 1325 Jefferson Ave., 38104-2097. Tel: 901-722-4700; Fax: 901-722-4791. Web: www.cewtn.org. P.O. Box 41705, 38174-1705. Tel: 901-722-4700; Fax: 901-722-4791. Mrs. Carolyn Tisdale, Dir.

Diocesan Council of Catholic Women, 5918 Cottage Hill Dr., Millington, 38053. Tel: 901-872-2132. Email: maryiredmond03@aol.com.

Education That Works, LLC, 61 N. McLean Blvd., 38104. Tel: 901-276-1221; Fax: 901-725-1447. Mr. Ted Schreck, Dir. Work Study Program.

House of the Good Shepherd of Memphis DeNeuville Learning Center (1825) 190 S. Cooper St., 38104. Tel: 901-726-5902; Fax: 901-726-1960. Email: deneuville@bellsouth.net. Web: www.deneuvillecenter.org. Sr. Lakshmie Napagoda, R.G.S., Dir.

Knights of St. Peter Claver (3rd Degree St. Benedict the Black Council No. 188) and Assembly 26 Bishop James P. Lyke 4th Degree), 2744 Gerald Ford Dr. W, Cordova, 38018. Tel: 901-377-1201; Fax: 901-396-8315. William Thompson, Grand Knight.

Ladies of Charity of Memphis (1937) P.O. Box 17699, 38187-0699. Tel: 901-854-5894. Email: memphislofc@yahoo.com. Web: www.famvin.org/lcusa. Rose LaVoice, Pres.

**Madonna Circle, Inc.* (Catholic Women's Service Organization), P.O. Box 172174, 38187-2174. Tel: 901-683-4991. Martha Montesi, Pres.

St. Martin de Porres Shrine & Institute, 190 Adams Ave., 38103. Tel: 901-578-2643; Fax: 901-578-3735. Email: institutest@bellsouth.net. Web: www.stmartinshrine.org.

St. Patrick's Center, 277 S. Fourth St., 38126. Tel: 901-543-9924; Fax: 901-529-8304. Email: tim.sullivan@stpat.cdom.org. Web: www.stpatsmemphis.org. Rev. Timothy F. Sullivan, C.S.P., Dir.; Deacon Eugene Champion, Exec. Dir.

Serra Club of Memphis, c/o The Catholic Center, 5825 Shelby Oaks Dr., 38134. Marianne Shadrack, Pres. Tel: 901-685-8914; Rev. Msgr. John B. McArthur, Chap.

CAMDEN. *Good Samaritan Village*, 192A Post Oak Ave., 38320. Tel: 731-584-1300; Fax: 731-584-1344. Email: gsvff@bellsouth.net. Mrs. Amber Kee, Mgr.

CORDOVA. *Society of St. Vincent DePaul*, 8277 Belgrade Pl., 38016. Tel: 901-382-8066; Fax: 901-388-7019. Email: ewilliams@frankwilliams.com. Web: www.svdpmemphis.org. Ms. Bambi Williams, Pres.; Rev. Michael A. Morgera, Spiritual Advisor.

Sr. Ruth Ann Center (Special Education), 8250 Varnavas Dr., 38016. Tel: 901-260-2840; Fax: 901-260-2850. Mr. George Valadie, Admin.; Mrs. Michele Cervetti, Dir. & Educator; Mrs. Nancy Valadie, Admin. Asst. Lay Teachers 2; Students 6.

STANTON. *Our Lady Queen of Peace Spiritual Center*, 3630 Dancyville Rd., 38069-4711. Tel: 731-548-2500; Fax: 731-548-2520. Email: debbie.voyles@olqp.cdom.org. Web: www.cdom.org (Our Lady Queen of Peace Retreat Center). Sisters Eileen Fucito, C.P., Dir.; Anna Maria Becker, C.P., Assoc. Dir.

RELIGIOUS INSTITUTES OF MEN REPRESENTED IN THE DIOCESE

For further details refer to the corresponding bracketed number in the Religious Institutes of Men or Women section.

[0330]—*Brothers of the Christian Schools* (Midwest Prov.)—F.S.C.
[1330]—*Congregation of the Mission-Midwest Province*—C.M.
[]—*Missionary Congregation of the Blessed Sacrament*—M.C.B.S.
[0430]—*Order of Preachers (Dominicans)*—O.P.
[1030]—*Paulist Fathers*—C.S.P.
[1070]—*Redemptorists*—C.Ss.R.
[0420]—*Society of Divine Word*—S.V.D.

RELIGIOUS INSTITUTES OF WOMEN REPRESENTED IN THE DIOCESE

[1070-03]—*Dominican Sisters*—O.P.
[1070-07]—*Dominican Sisters*—O.P.
[1115]—*Dominican Sisters of Peace*—O.P.
[2420]—*Marist Missionary Sisters*—S.M.S.M.
[2710]—*Missionaries of Charity*—M.C.
[3530]—*Missionary Sisters Servants of the Holy Spirit*—S.Sp.S.
[3760]—*Order of St. Clare* (Memphis, TN)—O.S.C.
[2970]—*School Sisters of Notre Dame* (Milwaukee Prov)—S.S.N.D.
[0440]—*Sisters of Charity of Cincinnati, Ohio*—S.C.
[0500]—*Sisters of Charity of Nazareth*—S.C.N.
[]—*Sisters of Charity of St. Charles Borromeo*—C.B.
[0430]—*Sisters of Charity of the Blessed Virgin Mary*—B.V.M.
[]—*Sisters of Mercy* (Ireland)—R.S.M.
[2575]—*Sisters of Mercy of the Americas*—R.S.M.
[3710]—*Sisters of St. Agnes*—C.S.A.
[0260]—*Sisters of the Blessed Sacrament*—S.B.S.
[3180]—*Sisters of the Cross and Passion*—C.P.
[1830]—*Sisters of the Good Shepherd* (St. Louis Prov.)—R.G.S.
[2350]—*Sisters of the Living Word*—S.L.W.
[4120-05]—*Ursuline Nuns of the Congregation of Paris* (Owensboro, KY)—O.S.U.

DIOCESAN CEMETERIES

MEMPHIS. *All Saints*, c/o Calvary Cemetery, 1663 Elvis Presley Blvd., 38106. Tel: 901-948-1529; Fax: 901-948-1511. Email: pat.posey@cemeteries.cdom.org. Web: www.cdom.org.

Calvary, 1663 Elvis Presley Blvd., 38106. Tel: 901-948-1529; Fax: 901-948-1511.

JACKSON. *Mount Calvary*, c/o 1663 Elvis Presley Blvd., 38106. Tel: 901-948-1592; Fax: 901-948-1511.

NECROLOGY

(No Deaths)

An asterisk (*) denotes an organization that has established tax-exempt status directly with the IRS and is not covered by the USCCB Group Ruling.

Diocese of Metuchen

Most Reverend

PAUL G. BOOTKOSKI, D.D.

Bishop of Metuchen; ordained May 28, 1966; appointed Titular Bishop of Zarna and Auxiliary Bishop of Newark July 8, 1997; ordained September 5, 1997; appointed Fourth Bishop of Metuchen January 4, 2002; installed March 19, 2002. *Res.: 10 Library Pl., Metuchen, NJ 08840.*

Most Reverend

EDWARD T. HUGHES, D.D.

Bishop Emeritus of Metuchen; ordained May 31, 1947; appointed Auxiliary to Archbishop of Philadelphia and Titular Bishop of Segia June 14, 1976; consecrated July 21, 1976; appointed Second Bishop of Metuchen December 16, 1986; installed February 5, 1987; retired September 8, 1997. *Res.: Bethany Ridge, 914 Milford-Warren Glen Rd., Milford, NJ 08848.*

ESTABLISHED NOVEMBER 19, 1981.

Square Miles 1,425.

Legal Corporate Title: The Diocese of Metuchen.

Comprises the Counties of Warren, Hunterdon, Somerset and Middlesex in the State of New Jersey.

146 Metlars Lane, Piscataway, NJ 08854. Tel: 732-562-1990; Fax: 732-562-1399. *Mailing Address: The Diocesan Center, P.O. Box 191, Metuchen, NJ 08840*

Web: www.diometuchen.org

STATISTICAL OVERVIEW

Personnel	
Bishop	1
Retired Bishops	1
Priests: Diocesan Active in Diocese	127
Priests: Diocesan Active Outside Diocese	18
Priests: Retired, Sick or Absent	43
Number of Diocesan Priests	188
Religious Priests in Diocese	42
Total Priests in Diocese	230
Extern Priests in Diocese	29
Ordinations:	
Diocesan Priests	3
Transitional Deacons	2
Permanent Deacons in Diocese	164
Total Brothers	20
Total Sisters	309
Parishes	
Parishes	103
With Resident Pastor:	
Resident Diocesan Priests	88
Resident Religious Priests	8
Without Resident Pastor:	
Administered by Priests	8
Missions	6
Pastoral Centers	3
Professional Ministry Personnel:	
Brothers	16
Sisters	149
Lay Ministers	109
Welfare	
Catholic Hospitals	1
Total Assisted	398,274
Health Care Centers	4
Total Assisted	37,702
Homes for the Aged	5
Total Assisted	1,870
Day Care Centers	2
Total Assisted	279
Specialized Homes	6
Total Assisted	141
Special Centers for Social Services	9
Total Assisted	20,772
Residential Care of Disabled	1
Total Assisted	5
Educational	
Diocesan Students in Other Seminaries	11
Total Seminarians	11
High Schools, Diocesan and Parish	3
Total Students	2,114
High Schools, Private	2
Total Students	1,149
Elementary Schools, Diocesan and Parish	32
Total Students	9,353
Non-residential Schools for the Disabled	1
Total Students	45
Catechesis/Religious Education:	
High School Students	1,135
Elementary Students	35,956
Total Students under Catholic Instruction	49,763
Teachers in the Diocese:	
Brothers	10
Sisters	49
Lay Teachers	935
Vital Statistics	
Receptions into the Church:	
Infant Baptism Totals	4,839
Minor Baptism Totals	162
Adult Baptism Totals	110
Received into Full Communion	293
First Communions	6,313
Confirmations	5,756
Marriages:	
Catholic	843
Interfaith	212
Total Marriages	1,055
Deaths	3,554
Total Catholic Population	566,087
Total Population	1,347,827

Former Bishops—Most Revs. THEODORE E. MCCARRICK, ord. May 31, 1958; appt. Titular Bishop of Rusibisir and Auxiliary to the Archbishop of New York, May 24, 1977; cons. June 29, 1977; appt. first Bishop of Metuchen, Nov. 19, 1981; installed Jan. 31, 1982; promoted to the Archdiocese of Newark, June 3, 1986; installed July 25, 1986; EDWARD T. HUGHES (Retired), ord. May 31, 1947; appt. Titular Bishop of Segia and Auxiliary to the Archbishop of Philadelphia, June 14, 1976; cons. July 21, 1976; appt. second Bishop of Metuchen, Dec. 16, 1986; installed Feb. 5, 1987; retired Sept. 8, 1997; VINCENT DEPAUL BREEN, D.D., ord. July 15, 1962; appt. Third Bishop of Metuchen July 8, 1997; cons. and installed Sept. 8, 1997; retired Jan. 4, 2002; died March 30, 2003.

The Diocesan Center—Mailing Address: P.O. Box 191, Metuchen, 08840. Tel: 732-562-1990; Fax: 732-562-1399.

Vicars General—Rev. Msgrs. WILLIAM BENWELL, J.C.L., V.G.; JOHN B. SZYMANSKI, P.A., V.G., Emeritus (Retired).

Episcopal Vicars—Rev. Msgrs. DANIEL J. HERLIHY; JOSEPH M. CURRY; Very Rev. RICHARD M. RUSK; Rev. Msgr. ROBERT J. ZAMORSKI.

The Diocesan Curia

Moderator—Rev. Msgr. WILLIAM BENWELL, J.C.L., V.G.

The Chancery

Office of the Chancellor—LORI ALBANESE, J.C.L.
Vice Chancellor—CAROL M. MACDERMOTT.

Office of Legal and Mediation Services— St. Thomas More Society.

Commission for Ecumenical and Interreligious Initiatives—

The Tribunal

The Diocesan Center—Mailing Address: P.O. Box 191, Metuchen, 08840. Tel: 732-562-1990; Fax: 732-562-1193.

Judicial Vicar—Very Rev. RICHARD J. LYONS, J.C.L.; SARA T. ACEVEDO, Admin.

Canonical Staff—Rev. Msgr. WILLIAM BENWELL, J.C.L., V.G.; LORI ALBANESE, J.C.L.; Revs. NEIL W. DAVIN, C.P., J.C.L.; ROBERT V. MEYERS, J.C.L.; ROBERT B. KOLAKOWSKI, J.C.L.

Auditors—SARA T. ACEVEDO; MARY E. HOPF; CAROL M. MACDERMOTT; Rev. MATTHEW R. PARATORE.

Psychological Consultants—Rev. RICHARD MUCOWSKI, O.F.M., Ed.D., Ph.D.; JEROME TRAVERS, Ph.D.; MARY BERTANI, Ed.S., L.M.F.T.

Notaries—SARA T. ACEVEDO; CAROL M. MACDERMOTT.

Office of Child and Youth Protection—LAWRENCE V. NAGLE, Dir.

Victim Assistance Coordinator—CARMEN DIAZ-PETTI, L.C.S.W. Tel: 908-722-1881. Email: cdiaz@ccdom.org.

Office of Communications and Public Relations—JOANNE WARD, Dir.

"The Catholic Spirit"—JOANNE WARD, Assoc. Publisher; KATHLEEN OGLE, Mng. Editor.

Department of Administrative Services

Department of Administrative Services—THOMAS G. TOOLAN, Exec. Dir.; LEONARDO G. CORTELEZZI, Assoc. Exec. Dir.

Office of Finance—THOMAS G. TOOLAN, Dir.; JENNIFER MAYO, Accounting Mgr.

Office of Cemeteries—899 Lincoln Ave., Piscataway, 08854. Tel: 732-463-1424; Fax: 732-463-8807. Deacon RUSSELL B. DEMKOVITZ, Dir.

Office of Information Systems—LEONARDO G. CORTELEZZI, Dir.; DAVID G. TORRES, Asst. Dir.

Office of Property and Facilities Management—

MONICA P. DEMKOVITZ, Dir.

Office of Human Resources—ERIC DILL, Dir.; MELISSA GARCIA, Asst. Dir.

Office of Data Processing—VACANT.

Department of Education

Department of Education—Rev. Msgr. MICHAEL J. CORONA, P.A., Exec. Dir.

Office of the Schools—ELLEN AYOUB, Supt. Assistant Superintendents: Sr. SHEILA CONLEY, SCH; Mrs. DONNA KANOWITZ; Mrs. IRENE D. SENA; JAMES MASUCCI, Technology Coord.; TAMARA HEMINGWAY, Coord. Institutional Advancement.

Office of Pontifical Mission Societies—Rev. Msgr. RICHARD A. BEHL, Dir.; MELISSA LEGACKI, Asst. Dir.

Catholic Scouting Apostolate—Rev. Msgr. MICHAEL J. CORONA, P.A., Moderator.

Diocesan Coordinating Committee for Home School Associations—ELLEN AYOUB, Moderator.

Department of Clergy and Religious Personnel

Department of Clergy and Religious Personnel—Very Rev. EDWARD C. PULEO, Exec. Dir.

Office of Ministry to Priests, Deacons and Their Families—VACANT.

Office for Priest Personnel—Very Rev. EDWARD C. PULEO, Dir.

Office of the Diaconate—Deacon SAMUEL J. COSTANTINO, Dir.

Office for Religious—Sr. ASCENZA TIZZANO, M.P.F., Dir.

Office of Vocations—Revs. RANDALL J. VASHON, Dir.; KEITH CERVINE, Assoc. Dir.; Very Rev. PETER CEBULKA, C.O.; Bro. ROBERT ZIOBRO, S.C.

Board for Seminary Education—Rev. RANDALL J. VASHON, Chm.

Office of Hospital Chaplaincy—Rev. SEAN G. WINTERS, Coord.

Office of Prison Ministry—Rev. MICHAEL P. SCOTT, Dir.

Department of Diocesan Planning—JEFFRY KORGEN, Exec. Dir.

Department of Stewardship and Development

Department of Stewardship and Development—Very Rev. SYLVESTER J. CRONIN, Exec. Dir.; SUE MANTARRO, Assoc. Dir., Office of Stewardship.

Department of Worship and Liturgical Formation

Department of Worship and Liturgical Formation—Very Rev. ROBERT W. MEDLEY, Exec. Dir.

Office of Liturgical Music—THOMAS A. DELESSIO, Diocesan Dir.

Office of Liturgical Formation—CLARE GIANGRECO, Dir.

Diocesan Eucharistic League—Rev. GUY W. SELVESTER, Dir.

Holy Name Society—Rev. CHESTER H. CARINA, J.C.L., Moderator.

Department of Pastoral Life

Pastoral Life—JUDITH A. PSOTA, Exec. Dir.

Office of Family Life Ministry—JUDITH A. PSOTA, Dir.

Office of Social Justice—VACANT, Dir.

Office for Multicultural Ministries—Rev. ARLINDO PAUL DASILVA, Dir.

Black Catholic Apostolate—JOSEPH L. POWELL, Coord.

Filipino Apostolate—VACANT.

Commission for Hispanic Ministry—VACANT.

Chinese Apostolate—Rev. VINCENT P. CHEN, Coord.

Portuguese Apostolate—Rev. LAURO COLEN SEDLMAYER, Coord.

Vietnamese Apostolate—VACANT.

Commission for Pro-Life Action—Rev. Msgr. RICHARD A. BEHL, Chm.

Office of Respect for Life—JENNIFER A. RUGGIERO, Dir.

Commission for Ministry for People with Disabilities—VACANT.

Office of Hispanic Ministry—Co Directors: RONALD BONNEAU, C.Ss.R.; Rev. JAMES GILMOUR, C.Ss.R.

Department of Formation and Leadership

Formation and Leadership—CECELIA REGAN, Exec. Dir.

Office for Catechesis—CECELIA REGAN, Dir.; MARY CLINTON, Asst. Dir.; PATRICIA MARTIN, Prog. Coord.

Office of Parish Leadership Formation—VACANT, Dir.

Office of Youth and Young Adult Ministry—MICHAEL J. WOJCIK, Dir.

Office of Evangelization—JODIE D'ANGIOLILLO, Dir.

Legion of Mary—Rev. A. PAUL DA SILVA, Moderator.

Charismatic Movement—DORIS BRENNAN, Moderator.

Diocesan Council of Catholic Women—Rev. Msgr. EDWARD M. O'NEILL, Moderator.

Office of RCIA—SARA SHARLOW, Dir.

Department of Catholic Social Services

Department of Catholic Social Services—MARIANNE MAJEWSKI, L.C.S.W., Exec. Dir., (See category for Catholic Charities under Institutions located in the Diocese for the full listing).

Catholic Relief Services—Rev. JOSEPH J. KERRIGAN, Dir.

Consultative Bodies

College of Consultors—Rev. Msgrs. ROBERT J. ZAMORSKI; WILLIAM BENWELL, J.C.L., V.G.; SEAMUS F. BRENNAN; MICHAEL J. CORONA, P.A.; Very Revs. CHARLES W. CICERALE; SYLVESTER J. CRONIN; RONALD L. JANDERNOA; EDWARD C. PULEO; Revs. DANIEL SLOAN; THOMAS J. WALSH. Liturgical Advisor: Very Rev. ROBERT W. MEDLEY.

Deans—Very Revs. CHARLES W. CICERALE, Cathedral Deanery; ROBERT G. LYNAM, Forsgate Deanery; RONALD L. JANDERNOA, Morris Canal Deanery; JONATHAN S. TOBOROWSKY, Raritan Bay Deanery; Rev. Msgr. SEAMUS F. BRENNAN, County Seat Deanery; Very Revs. BRIAN J. NOLAN, Somerset Hills Deanery; J. WILLIAM MICKIEWICZ, Round Valley Deanery; VACANT, New Brunswick Deanery; VACANT, Perth Amboy Deanery; Very Rev. PATRICK J. KUFFNER, Middlebrook Deanery.

Presbyteral Council—Most Rev. PAUL G. BOOTKOSKI, D.D., Pres.

Theological Commission—Rev. GLENN J. COMANDINI, S.T.D., Chm.

Diocesan Pastoral Council—Most Rev. PAUL G. BOOTKOSKI, D.D.

CLERGY, PARISHES, MISSIONS AND PAROCHIAL SCHOOLS

BOROUGH OF METUCHEN

(MIDDLESEX COUNTY), CATHEDRAL OF ST. FRANCIS OF ASSISI (1871) Rev. Msgr. Robert J. Zamorski, Rector; Revs. Matthew R. Paratore, Parochial Vicar; Bede Kim, Parochial Vicar; Deacons Frank J. Cammarano; Paul G. Licameli, Deacon Emeritus; Guido J. Brossoni; Kenneth Hamilton; Eduardo Olegario. In Res., Very Rev. Sylvester J. Cronin.
Res.: 32 Elm Ave., 08840. Tel: 732-548-0100; Fax: 732-549-1033. Web: www.stfranciscathedral.org.
School—(Grades PreSchool-8), 528 Main St., 08840. Tel: 732-548-3107; Fax: 732-548-5760. Web: www-.stfranciscathedralschool.org. Mrs. Barbara Stevens, Prin.; Mrs. Helen DeMarco, Librarian. Sisters of Christian Charity 3; Lay Teachers 31; Preschool 75; Students 445.

OUTSIDE THE BOROUGH OF METUCHEN

ALPHA, WARREN CO., ST. MARY (1902) [CEM] Rev. Msgr. Terrance M. Lawler; Rev. Gerardo Paderon, Parochial Vicar; Deacons Keith B. McCarthy; George L. Bolash; John B. Van Haute.
Res.: 830 Fifth Ave., P.O. Box 1133, 08865. Tel: 908-454-0444; Fax: 908-454-7745. Web: www.st-maryrc.org.

ANNANDALE, HUNTERDON CO., IMMACULATE CONCEPTION (1864) [CEM 2] Revs. Randall J. Vashon, Admin.; Keith Cervine, Parochial Vicar; Deacons William R. Bauer; Joseph P. Campbell.
Res.: 316 Old Allerton Rd., 08801. Tel: 908-735-7319; Fax: 908-735-4552. Web: www.icc-clintonnj.org.
School—*Immaculate Conception School*, (Grades PreK-8), 314 Old Allerton Rd., 08801. Tel: 908-735-6334; Fax: 908-238-0724. Web: www.icsclinton.org. Annamarie C. Reilly, Prin.; Kathryn Puleo, Librarian. Lay Teachers 34; Students 534.
Station—*Edna Mahan Correctional Facility for Women* Clinton. Tel: 908-735-7111; Fax: 908-735-5246.
Station—*Hunterdon Developmental Center* Clinton. Tel: 908-735-4031; Fax: 908-730-1311.

AVENEL, MIDDLESEX CO., ST. ANDREW (1920) Rev. David B. Kosmoski; Deacon Walter S. Maksimik.
Res.: 244 Avenel St., 07001. Tel: 732-634-4355; Fax: 732-750-5905. Email: our.church@standrewparish.com. Web: www.standrewparish.com.
Station—*Woodbridge State School*
Station—*Woodbridge Emergency Reception Center* 07001. Tel: 732-636-4261.

BAPTISTOWN, HUNTERDON CO., OUR LADY OF VICTORIES (1973) Rev. Msgr. David I. Fulton; Deacon John T. Monahan.
Res.: 1005 Rte. 519, P.O. Box 127, 08803. Tel: 908-996-2068; Fax: 908-996-3525.

BASKING RIDGE, SOMERSET CO., ST. JAMES (1864) Revs. Glenn J. Comandini, S.T.D.; Dario Endiape, Parochial Vicar; Deacon Luke J. Hally.
Res.: 184 S. Finley Ave., P.O. Box 310, 07920. Tel: 908-766-0888; Fax: 908-766-1815. Web: www.saintjamesbr.org.
School—(Grades PreSchool-8), 200 S. Finley Ave., P.O. Box 310, 07920. Tel: 908-766-4774; Fax: 908-766-4432. Web: www.sjsbr.org. Mr. Jeremiah Kenny, Prin.; Beth Albanese, Librarian. Lay Teachers 33; Students 379.

BELVIDERE, WARREN CO., ST. PATRICK (1892) Very Rev. Richard M. Rusk; Rev. Andrzej Wieliczko, Parochial Vicar; Deacons John F. Dumschat; William Kintis.
Res.: 327 Greenwich St., 07823. Tel: 908-475-2559; Fax: 908-475-1943. Web: www.stpatrickbelvidere-.parishesonline.com.

BERNARDSVILLE, SOMERSET CO., OUR LADY OF PERPETUAL HELP (1898) [CEM] Rev. John N. Fell, S.T.D.; Rev. Msgr. John R. Torney, Pastor Emeritus (Retired); Rev. Antonio M. Alvarez, Parochial Vicar; Deacons Joseph E. O'Keefe; Joel R. Livingston; Benigno Ruiz-Diaz.
Res.: 111 Claremont Rd., 07924. Tel: 908-766-0079; Fax: 908-766-1185. Email: olphemail@aol.com. Web: www.olphbernardsville.org.
School—*School of St. Elizabeth*, (Grades PreK-8), Seney Dr., 07924. Tel: 908-766-0244; Fax: 908-766-5372. Web: www.steschool.org. Mr. William Venezia, Prin. Sisters of Christian Charity 1; Lay Teachers 11; Students 165.
Chapel—*Bernardsville, Sacred Heart (Chapel of Convenience)*

BLAIRSTOWN, WARREN CO., ST. JUDE (1945) Very Rev. Ronald L. Jandernoa; Deacon Michael J. Sullivan Jr.
Res.: 7 Eisenhower Rd., P.O. Box N, 07825. Tel: 908-362-6444; Fax: 908-362-6862. Email: stjudech@ptd.net. Web: www.stjudeblairstown.parishesonline.com.

BLOOMSBURY, HUNTERDON CO., CHURCH OF THE ANNUNCIATION (1948) Rev. Roberto Coruna.
Res.: 80 Main St., P.O. Box 136, 08804-0136. Tel: 908-479-4905; Fax: 908-479-4453. Email: annunciationrcc@earthlink.net.

BOUND BROOK, SOMERSET CO.

1—ST. JOSEPH (1876) [CEM] Revs. Charles T. O'Connor; Jose M. Marcelo, Parochial Vicar; Deacons George D. Coleman; Gustavo Sandoval.
Office: 124 E. Second St., P.O. Box 72, 08805. Tel: 732-356-0027; Fax: 732-356-8092.
Res.: 304 John St., 08805. Tel: 732-356-8936.

2—ST. MARY OF CZESTOCHOWA (1914), (Polish), Rev. Leon S. Aniszczyk.
Res.: 193 W. High St., 08805. Tel: 732-868-6942. Email: stmarybb@verizon.net. Web: www.stmarys-boundbrook.org.
Church: 201 Vosseller Ave., 08805. Tel: 732-356-0358; Fax: 732-356-1338.

BRIDGEWATER, SOMERSET CO.

1—ST. BERNARD OF CLAIRVAUX (1843) [CEM] Revs. Joseph G. Celano; Timothy J. Lambert, Parochial Vicar; Deacons Patrick J. Cline; Paul L. Anderson; Gerard C. Sims.
Res.: 500 Rte. 22, 08807. Tel: 908-725-0552 (Office); Fax: 908-725-4524. Web: www.stbernardbridgewater.org.
School—*St. Bernard Pre-School & Kindergarten*, Tel: 908-725-0552, Ext. 813; Fax: 908-237-9789. Barbara Turse, Dir. Lay Teachers 20; Students 102.

2—HOLY TRINITY (1948) Revs. John R. Pringle; Thomas Myladil, O.C.D.; Deacon Michael A. Forrestall.
Res.: 60 Maple St., 08807. Tel: 908-526-2394; Fax: 908-526-5837. Email: htchurch08807@yahoo.com. Web: www.holytrinitynj.org.

CALIFON, HUNTERDON CO., ST. JOHN NEUMANN (1982) Very Rev. J. William Mickiewicz.
Res.: 398 County Rd. 513, P.O. Box 455, 07830. Tel: 908-832-2513; Fax: 908-832-7618. Email: sjn@ccsjn.org. Web: www.ccsjn.org.

CARTERET, MIDDLESEX CO.

1—ST. ELIZABETH OF HUNGARY (1914), (Hungarian), Rev. James W. McGuffey.
Mailing Address: 55 High St., 07008. Tel: 732-541-8946; Fax: 732-541-0500.
Res.: 119 Washington Ave., 07008.

2—HOLY FAMILY (1907), (Polish), Revs. Edmund J. Shallow; John Stec, Parochial Vicar.
Res.: 213 Pershing Ave., 07008. Tel: 732-541-5768; Fax: 732-541-5871.
Convent—140 Emerson St., 07008. Tel: 732-541-6243. Sisters 5.

3—ST. JOSEPH (1893) Rev. James W. McGuffey; Rev. Msgr. Donald M. Endebrock (Retired); Deacons Philip Fiore; Ramon L. Torres.
Res.: 55 High St., 07008. Tel: 732-541-8946; Fax: 732-541-0500. Web: www.stjosephparishfamily.com.
School—(Grades PreK-8), 865 Roosevelt Ave., 07008. Tel: 732-541-7111; Fax: 732-541-0676. Web: www.sjps.net. Mrs. Roseann Johnson, Prin. Lay Teachers 17; Students 182.

4—SACRED HEART (1910), (Slovak), Revs. Edmund J. Shallow; John Stec, Parochial Vicar.

Mailing Address: 213 Pershing Ave., 07008.
Res.: 67 Fitch St., 07008. Tel: 732-541-5871; Fax: 732-541-5678.

COLONIA, MIDDLESEX CO., ST. JOHN VIANNEY (1959) Rev. Msgr. Edward M. O'Neill; Revs. Joseph Kubiak, O.F.M.Cap.; John C. Gloss, Parochial Vicar; Deacons Joseph D. Ragucci; Thomas S. Michnewicz.
Res.: 420 Inman Ave., 07067. Tel: 732-574-0150; Fax: 732-574-0050. Web: www.sjvianney.com.
School—(Grades PreK-8), 420 Inman Ave., 07067. Tel: 732-388-1662. Web: www.sjv.net. Mrs. Carol Woodburn, Prin. Bernardine Sisters 2; Lay Teachers 29; Students 509.

DUNELLEN, MIDDLESEX CO., ST. JOHN THE EVANGELIST (1879) Rev. John C. Siceloff; Deacon Michael P. Gleason.
Res.: 317 First St., 08812. Tel: 732-968-2621; Fax: 732-968-3709.

EAST BRUNSWICK, MIDDLESEX CO., ST. BARTHOLOMEW (1959) Revs. Thomas J. Walsh; Krystian Burdzy, Parochial Vicar; Damian Breen, Parochial Vicar; Deacons John F. Kenny; Anthony J. Gostkowski; Filippo Tartara.
Res.: 470 Ryders Ln., 08816. Tel: 732-257-7722; Fax: 732-257-7723.
School—(Grades PreK-8) Ruth Mazzarella, Prin. Lay Teachers 18; Students 265.

EDISON, MIDDLESEX CO.

1—GUARDIAN ANGELS (1959) Rev. Msgr. James P. Moran.
Res.: 37 Plainfield Ave., P.O. Box 1216, 08818-1216. Tel: 732-985-7565; Fax: 732-985-0970. Email: guardian.angels@verizon.net.
Mission—St. Margaret Mary Alacoque Woodbridge Ave., Middlesex Co. 08817.

2—ST. HELENA (1965) Revs. Anthony M. Sirianni; Joseph Lukose, C.M., Parochial Vicar; Deacon Paul J. Sheptuck.
Res.: 950 Grove Ave., 08820. Tel: 732-494-3399; Fax: 732-494-2076.
School—(Grades PreK-8), 930 Grove Ave., 08820. Tel: 732-549-6234; Fax: 732-549-6205. Web: www.sthelenaedison.org. Sr. Mary Charles Wienckoski, C.S.S.F., Prin. Felician Sisters 1; Lay Teachers 19; Students 225.

3—ST. MATTHEW THE APOSTLE (1952) Rev. George Targonski, Admin.; Deacons Barry C. Demarest; Frank Yuhas. In Res., Rev. Joseph L. Desmond.
Res.: 81 Seymour Ave., 08817. Tel: 732-985-5063; Fax: 732-985-9104. Web: www.stmatthewtheapostle.com.
School—St. Matthew School, (Grades PreK-8), 100 Seymour Ave., 08817. Tel: 732-985-6633; Fax: 732-985-7748. Web: www.stmatthewtheapostle.com/school. Eileen Sullivan, Prin. Lay Teachers 13; Students 184.

FAR HILLS, SOMERSET CO., ST. ELIZABETH (1906) Very Rev. Edward C. Puleo; Deacon Lawrence Duffy.
Res.: 34 Peapack Rd., Box 37, 07931. Tel: 908-234-0079; Fax: 908-234-2923. Web: www.saintelizabeth-saintbrigid.org.
Mission—St. Brigid 129 Main St., P.O. Box 33, Peapack, 07977. Tel: 908-234-1265; Fax: 908-234-2923.

FLEMINGTON, HUNTERDON CO., ST. MAGDALEN DE PAZZI (1864) [CEM] Revs. Timothy Christy; John Primich; Joseph Kabali, Parochial Vicar; Deacons Thaddeus Wislinski; Roy Rabinowitz.
Res.: 105 Mine St., 08822. Tel: 908-782-2922; Fax: 908-782-0952. Web: www.stmagdalen.org.
School—(Grades PreSchool-PreK) Amy Weckesser, Dir. Lay Teachers 3; Students 33.

FORDS, MIDDLESEX CO., OUR LADY OF PEACE (1919) Rev. Msgr. Andrew L. Szaroleta; Rev. Frank W. Fellrath, Parochial Vicar; Deacon William B. McGann. In Res., Rev. Pauly Thekkan, C.M.I.
Res.: 26 Maple Ave., Edison, 08837. Tel: 732-738-7940; Fax: 732-738-3848. Web: www.olpfords.org.
School—(Grades PreK-8), Amboy Ave., 08863. Tel: 732-738-7464; Fax: 732-738-0026. John M. Donza, Prin. Lay Teachers 14; Students 220.

GREAT MEADOWS, WARREN CO., SS. PETER AND PAUL (1921) Revs. Pawel Dolinksi, S.D.S., Admin.; David Adamczak, S.D.S., Parochial Vicar; Deacon Stephen Gunther.
Res.: 360 Rte. 46, P.O. Box 156, 07838. Tel: 908-637-4269; Fax: 908-637-6896. Email: stpeterandpaul@comcast.net. Web: www.parishesonline.com/sspeterpaulgreatmeadows.

HACKETTSTOWN, WARREN CO., ASSUMPTION OF THE BLESSED VIRGIN MARY (1864) Rev. David J. Pekola; Deacon Walter H. Pidgeon.
Res.: 302 High St., P.O. Box 547, 07840-0547. Tel: 908-952-3320; Fax: 908-852-2361.
School—(Grades PreK-8), Cook & Liberty Sts., 07840. Tel: 908-852-4791; Fax: 908-852-4180. Marilyn Walsh, Prin.; Mrs. Kay Tynan, Librarian. Lay Teachers 11; Students 181.

HAMPTON, HUNTERDON CO., ST. ANN (1859) [CEM] Rev. Michael C. Saharic; Deacon Joseph J. Foldvary.
Res.: P.O. Box 405, 08827. Tel: 908-537-2221; Fax: 908-537-9465. Web: www.saintann1859.org.
Church: 6 Church St., 08827.
Station—NJ State Hospital for Geriatrics Glen Gardner.

HELMETTA, MIDDLESEX CO., HOLY TRINITY (1911), (Polish), [CEM] Rev. Stanley Jarosz; Deacon Gregory R. D'Angelo.
Res.: 100 Main St., 08828. Tel: 732-521-0172; Fax: 732-521-0824.

HIGH BRIDGE, HUNTERDON CO., ST. JOSEPH (1880) Rev. Maurice T. Carlton.
Res.: 59 Main St., 08829. Tel: 908-638-6211; Fax: 908-638-5802.

HIGHLAND PARK, MIDDLESEX CO., ST. PAUL THE APOSTLE (1912) Rev. Robert V. Meyers; Deacon Edward Krupa.
Parish Center: 23 S. Fifth Ave., 08904. Tel: 732-572-0977; Fax: 732-572-7497.
Res.: 502 Raritan Ave., 08904. Email: stpaulhpnj@verizon.net. Web: www.rc.net/metuchen/st.paul.

HILLSBOROUGH, SOMERSET CO.

1—ST. JOSEPH (Millstone Borough) (1883) Rev. Msgr. Raymond L. Cole; Deacons Joseph C. Moscinski; John Craig; Timothy A. Lawless.
Church: 34 Yorktown Rd., 08844. Tel: 908-874-3141; Fax: 908-874-7040.
Res.: 41 Yorktown Rd., 08844. Tel: 908-874-3141; Fax: 908-874-7040. Web: www.stjosephsparish.com.

2—MARY, MOTHER OF GOD (1948) Revs. Sean A. Broderick, C.S.Sp., Admin.; Lancelot McGrath, Parochial Vicar.
Res.: 157 S. Triangle Rd., 08844. Tel: 908-874-8220; Fax: 908-874-4183. Web: www.marymotherofgod.org.
School—(Grades PreSchool) Teachers 3; Preschool 80.

HOPELAWN, MIDDLESEX CO., OUR LADY OF THE MOST HOLY ROSARY (1904) [CEM] Rev. Michael G. Krull.
Res.: 625 Florida Grove Rd., 08861. Tel: 732-826-2771; Fax: 732-826-0320. Web: www.holyrosarychurchnj.org.

ISELIN, MIDDLESEX CO., ST. CECELIA (1923) Revs. Jerome A. Johnson; Alfonso R. DeCondorpusa; Deacon Richard Lutomski.
Res.: 45 Wilus Way, 08830. Tel: 732-283-2300; Fax: 732-283-3326. Web: www.stcecelia.com.
School—(Grades PreK-8) Tel: 732-283-2824; Fax: 732-283-5023. Web: www.stceceliaschool.org. Sr. Margaret Mary Hanlon, M.P.F., Prin. Religious Teachers Filippini 3; Lay Teachers 16; Students 224.
Station—NJ State Home for Disabled Veterans
Station—Roosevelt Care Center

JAMESBURG, MIDDLESEX CO., ST. JAMES THE LESS (1878) [CEM] Revs. Kevin P. Duggan, Admin.; Charles P. Scillieri, Parochial Vicar.
Res.: 36 Lincoln Ave., 08831. Tel: 732-521-0100; Fax: 732-521-8287. Email: jamestheless@comcast.net.
Station—State Home for Boys Monroe Township. Tel: 732-521-0030.

KENDALL PARK, MIDDLESEX CO., ST. AUGUSTINE OF CANTERBURY (1952) Very Rev. Robert G. Lynam; Deacons Richard McCarron; Denis Mayer.
Res.: 45 Henderson Rd., 08824. Tel: 732-297-3000; Fax: 732-940-1746. Web: www.staugustinenj.org.
School—(Grades PreSchool-8) Tel: 732-297-6042; Fax: 732-297-7062. Sisters Mary Louise Shulas, M.P.F., Prin.; Lucy Zanoni, Librarian. Brothers of Sacred Heart 1; Religious Teachers Filippini 4; Lay Teachers 31; Students 434; Preschool 106.

LAMBERTVILLE, HUNTERDON CO., ST. JOHN THE EVANGELIST (1843) [CEM] Rev. Robert B. Kolakowski, Admin.; Deacons Joseph J. Masterson; Michael Semko.
Res.: 44 Bridge St., 08530. Tel: 609-397-3350; Fax: 609-397-8713. Email: info_stjohnschurch@yahoo.com. Web: www.stjohnlambertville.parishesonline.com.
School—The Jesus School, (Grades PreK-K) Tel: 609-397-0593. Email: mconaughton@diometuchen.org. Sr. Marie Conaughton, Prin. Teachers 4; Students 52.
Mission—St. Agnes Main St., Stockton, 08559.

LAURENCE HARBOR, MIDDLESEX CO., ST. LAWRENCE (1943) Very Rev. Jonathan S. Toborowsky, Admin.; Deacons Stephen J. Gajewski; Gregory Ris.
Res.: 109 Laurence Pkwy., 08879. Tel: 732-566-1093; Fax: 732-765-9311.

MANVILLE, SOMERSET CO.

1—CHRIST THE KING (1948) Revs. Stanislaw Slaby, C.Ss.R., Admin.; Slawomir Romanowski, C.Ss.R., Parochial Vicar; Deacon Thomas J. Giacobbe.
Res.: 211 Louis St., 08835. Tel: 908-231-1330; Fax: 908-231-1645. Web: christtheking-manville.e-paluch.com.
School—(Grades PreSchool-8), 99 N. 13th Ave., 08835. Tel: 908-526-1339; Fax: 908-526-3541. Web: www.ctkmanville.com. Mrs. Christine N. Benson, Prin. Lay Teachers 14; Preschool 34; Students 117.

2—SACRED HEART OF JESUS (1919), (Polish), [CEM] Revs. Stanislaw Slaby, C.Ss.R., Admin.; Lukasz Drozak, C.Ss.R., Parochial Vicar; Deacon William G. Stefany. In Res., Rev. Eugeniusz Fasuga, C.Ss.R.
Res.: 136 S. Main St., P.O. Box 924, 08835. Tel: 908-725-0072; Fax: 908-685-3029. Web: www.sacredheart-church.org.

MARTINSVILLE, SOMERSET CO., BLESSED SACRAMENT (1968) Rev. Msgr. Eugene Prus; Rev. Rico Paril; Deacon Louis Pizzigoni III.
Res.: 852 Newmans Ln., P.O. Box 563, 08836. Tel: 732-356-4442; Fax: 732-356-5172.

MIDDLESEX, MIDDLESEX CO., OUR LADY OF MOUNT VIRGIN (1943) Very Rev. Patrick J. Kuffner; Rev. Virgilio T. Tolentino, Parochial Vicar; Deacon John R. Tietjen.
Res.: 650 Harris Ave., 08846. Tel: 732-356-2149; Fax: 732-356-1302. Web: www.olmv.net.
School—(Grades PreSchool-8), 450 Drake Ave., 08846. Tel: 732-356-6560; Fax: 732-356-7860. Web: www.olmv.net. Ms. Ann Major, Prin. Lay Teachers 15; Preschool 16; Students 197.

MILFORD, HUNTERDON CO., ST. EDWARD THE CONFESSOR (1944) Rev. Krzysztof Kaczynski, Admin.
Res.: 61 Mill St., P.O. Box 522, 08848. Tel: 908-995-4723; Fax: 908-995-9353. Web: www.stedwardmilford.parishesonline.com.

MILLTOWN, MIDDLESEX CO., OUR LADY OF LOURDES (1921) Rev. Edward A. Czarcinski; Deacon Robert Gerling.
Res.: 233 N. Main St., 08850. Tel: 732-828-0011; Fax: 732-828-3133. Email: olol678@aol.com. Web: www.ololchurchnj.org.
School—(Grades PreK-8), 43 Cleveland Ave., 08850. Tel: 732-828-1951; Fax: 732-828-7871. Web: www.ololschoolnj.org. Sr. Maria Gruszka, L.S.I.C., Prin. Little Servant Sisters of the Immaculate Conception 4; Lay Teachers 11; Students 175.

MONMOUTH JUNCTION, MIDDLESEX CO., ST. CECILIA (1914) Rev. Daniel Sloan; Deacon Michael P. Murtha.
Office: 10 Kingston Ln., 08852. Tel: 732-329-2893; Fax: 732-329-4693. Web: www.stceciliaparish.net.
Res.: 46 Kingston Ln., 08852.

MONROE TOWNSHIP, MIDDLESEX CO., NATIVITY OF OUR LORD (1992) Rev. Edward R. Flanagan.
Res.: 185 Applegarth Rd., 08831. Tel: 609-371-0499; Fax: 609-371-0677. Web: www.nativitymonroe.org.

NEW BRUNSWICK, MIDDLESEX CO.

1—ST. JOHN THE BAPTIST (1867), (German), [CEM] Rev. Marco A. Caceres; Deacon Luis F. Moral.
Res.: 29 Abeel St., 08901. Tel: 732-545-5267; Fax: 732-545-0446.
Church: Neilson and Carman Sts., 08901.

2—ST. JOSEPH (1924), (Polish), Rev. Joseph A. Krajewski.
Res.: 15 Maple St., 08901. Tel: 732-545-2195; Fax: 732-545-8778.

3—ST. LADISLAUS (1904), (Hungarian), Rev. Capistran L. Polgar, O.F.M.
Res.: 215 Somerset St., 08901. Tel: 732-545-1427; Fax: 732-545-8501. Email: stladislaus@optonline.net.

4—ST. MARY OF MOUNT VIRGIN (1904), (Italian), Rev. Robert L. Santa Barbara.
Res.: 190 Sandford St., 08901. Tel: 732-545-5090; Fax: 732-937-9290.
Mission—St. Theresa of the Infant Jesus 15 Fox Rd., Edison, 08817.

5—OUR LADY OF MT. CARMEL (1977), (Hispanic), Revs. Raymond L. Nacarino; Jose Lorente, Parochial Vicar; Manuel Lorente, Parochial Vicar.
Res. & Church: 75 Morris St., 08901. Tel: 732-846-5873; Fax: 732-846-5397.

6—ST. PETER THE APOSTLE (1829) [CEM] Revs. Thomas A. Odorizzi, C.O.; Kevin Kelly, C.O., Parochial Vicar; Deacon Helmut Wittreich. In Res., Very Rev. Peter R. Cebulka, C.O.; Deacon Jeffrey Calia, C.O.; Bro. Robert Peck, C.O.
Res.: 94 Somerset St., 08901. Tel: 732-545-6820; Fax: 732-545-4069. Web: www.stpetertheapostle.org.

7—SACRED HEART (1883) Rev. Joseph J. Kerrigan.
Res.: 56 Throop Ave., 08901. Tel: 732-545-1681; Fax: 732-545-5059. Web: www.hub4sacredheart.org.

NORTH BRUNSWICK, MIDDLESEX CO., OUR LADY OF PEACE (1969) Rev. John V. Polyak; Deacons Francis D'Mello; David A. DeFrange.
Res.: 277 Washington Pl., 08902. Tel: 732-297-9680; Fax: 732-297-1024.

NORTH PLAINFIELD, SOMERSET CO.

1—ST. JOSEPH (1882) Rev. George A. Farrell; Deacon Phillip Gonzalez. In Res., Very Rev. Richard J. Lyons.
Office: 99 Westervelt Ave., 07060.
Res.: 41 Manning Ave., 07060. Tel: 908-756-3383; Fax: 908-756-1155.

2—ST. LUKE (1965) Rev. A. Gregory Uhrig.
Res.: 300 Clinton Ave., 07063. Tel: 908-754-8811; Fax: 908-754-0120.

OLD BRIDGE, MIDDLESEX CO.

1—ST. AMBROSE (1961) Revs. Robert G. Gorman; John J. Werner, Parochial Vicar; Deacons Charles

J. Damian; Andrew J. Strus.
Res.: 96 Throckmorton Ln., 08857. Tel: 732-679-5666; Fax: 732-679-0853. Web: www.saintambroseparish.com.
School—(Grades K-8) Tel: 732-679-4700; Fax: 732-679-6062. Web: www.stambroseschool.net. Mr. Joseph W. Norris, Prin. Sisters of St. Joseph (Chestnut Hill) 1; Lay Teachers 32; Students 430.
Convent—94 Throckmorton Ln., 08857. Tel: 732-679-5509.

2—MOST HOLY REDEEMER (1983) Rev. Chester H. Carina; Deacons Robert T. McGovern; A. Keith Berg; Frank C. D'Auguste. In Res., Rev. Michael P. Scott.
Res.: 133 Amboy Rd., Matawan, 07747. Tel: 732-566-9334; Fax: 732-566-2245. Web: www.mostholyredeemerchurch.org.

3—ST. THOMAS THE APOSTLE (1921) Rev. Msgr. Richard A. Behl; Revs. A. David Chalackal, Parochial Vicar; Danilo A. Canceran; Deacons John J. Fitzsimmons; Robert Bonfante Sr.
Res.: One St. Thomas Plaza, 08857. Tel: 732-251-4000; Fax: 732-251-4946. Web: www.saintthomasob.com.
School—(Grades PreK-8), 333 Hwy. 18, 08857. Tel: 732-251-4812; Fax: 732-251-5315. Miss Thomasina Wyatt, Prin. Lay Teachers 28; Students 358.

OXFORD, WARREN CO., ST. ROSE OF LIMA (1864) [CEM] Very Rev. Richard M. Rusk.
Res.: Academy St., P.O. Box 88, 07863. Tel: 908-453-2034. Web: www.stroseoflimaoxford.parishesonline.com.

PARLIN, MIDDLESEX CO., ST. BERNADETTE (1956) Revs. James W. Hagerman; Arulraj S. Singarayer, Parochial Vicar; Deacons Samuel Rutch; Donald Zampella.
Res.: 20 Villanova Rd., 08859. Tel: 732-721-2772; Fax: 732-727-5188.

PERTH AMBOY, MIDDLESEX CO.

1—HOLY SPIRIT (1944) Rev. Michael G. Krull; Deacon Sam Costantino. In Res., Revs. Sean G. Winters; John J. Morley.
Res.: 580 Hazel Ave., 08861. Tel: 732-826-4859; Fax: 732-826-6078. Web: www.holyspiritrcc.com.

2—HOLY TRINITY (1899), (Slovak), [CEM] Rev. Wladyslaw Wiktorek, Admin.
Mailing Address: 474 Penn St., 08861. Tel: 732-826-0439; Fax: 732-442-3037.
Church: 315 Lawrie St., 08861.

3—LA ASUNCION (1981), (Hispanic), Revs. John B. Gordon; Nicholas Norena; Deacons Enrique Garcia; Corpus V. Perez; Noe Cortez.
Mailing Address: 777 Cortlandt St., P.O. Box 1335, 08862. Tel: 732-826-4991; Fax: 732-826-6951. Email: asuncionchurch@aol.com.

4—ST. MARY (1845) Rev. Waldemar Latkowski, C.Ss.R.; Deacon Basilio A. Perez.
Res.: 104 Center St., 08861. Tel: 732-442-0039; Fax: 732-324-4383. Web: www.stmaryperth.com.

5—OUR LADY OF FATIMA (1960), (Hispanic), Revs. Joshy T. Nirappel, C.M.F., Admin.; Edmundo Andres, C.M.F., Parochial Vicar; Deacons Angel P. Perez; Herminio Rivera; Pablo Bencosme. In Res., Rev. Richard Todd, C.M.F.; Bro. Richard Paquette, C.M.F.
Res.: 380 Smith St., 08861. Tel: 732-442-6634; Fax: 732-293-2544.

6—OUR LADY OF HUNGARY (1902), (Hungarian), [CEM] Rev. John B. Gordon; Deacon Cornelius S. Smoyak.
Res.: 697 Cortlandt St., 08861. Tel: 732-442-0512; Fax: 732-442-3037.

7—OUR LADY OF THE ROSARY OF FATIMA (1981), (Portuguese), Rev. Lauro Colen Sedlmayer, Admin.
Res.: 188 Wayne St., 08861. Tel: 732-826-4350; Fax: 732-826-5167.

8—ST. STEPHEN (1892), (Polish), [CEM] Revs. Waldemar Latkowski, C.Ss.R.; Marian Furca, C.Ss.R., Parochial Vicar; Wojciech Kusek, C.Ss.R., Parochial Vicar.
Res.: 490 State St., 08861. Tel: 732-826-1395; Fax: 732-826-4217. Web: www.st-stephens-church.com.

PHILLIPSBURG, WARREN CO.

1—SS. PETER AND PAUL (1913), (Slovak), Closed. Records at St. Philip & St. James, Phillipsburg.

2—ST. PHILIP & ST. JAMES (1860) [CEM] Revs. John J. Barbella; James A. Kyrpczak, Parochial Vicar; Alphonsus Mwariri Kariuki, I.M.C., Parochial Vicar; Deacons John T. Flynn; Enock Berluche Sr.; George Frank. In Res., Rev. Vincent P. Chen.
Res.: 430 S. Main St., 08865-3094. Tel: 908-454-0112; Fax: 908-454-0125. Web: www.spsj.org.
School—(Grades K-8), 137 Roseberry St., 08865. Tel: 908-859-1244; Fax: 908-859-1202. Mrs. Judith W. Francisco, Prin. Lay Teachers 18; Students 232.
Mission—St. Christopher New Village, Warren Co.

PISCATAWAY, MIDDLESEX CO.

1—ST. FRANCES CABRINI (1961) Rev. James F. Considine; Deacon Roger Ladao. In Res., Rev. Msgr. Reynaldo Nunez.
Res.: 208 Bound Brook Ave., 08854-4097. Tel: 732-885-5313; Fax: 732-885-9031. Email: sfc208@yahoo.com.

2—OUR LADY OF FATIMA (1948) Revs. Arlindo Paul DaSilva; Herbert J. Stab, Pastor Emeritus (Retired); Mark Kehoe, Parochial Vicar; Deacons Stanley J. Lorenc; Lawrence P. Reilly.
Res.: 501 New Market Rd., 08854. Tel: 732-968-5556. Web: www.olfparish.org.
Rectory, Parish Center & CCD Office: 50 Van Winkle Pl., 08854. Tel: 732-968-5555; Fax: 732-968-5959.
School—(Grades PreSchool-8), 499 New Market Rd., 08854. Tel: 732-968-5017; Fax: 732-968-9259. Web: www.olfatima.net. Mr. Nicholas A. Diaz, Prin.; Mrs. Deborah Chippendale, Librarian. Lay Teachers 14; Students 134; Preschool 26.

PITTSTOWN, HUNTERDON CO., ST. CATHERINE OF SIENA (1992) Rev. Peter Suhaka; Deacons Anthony Russo; Dennis K. Webster.
Res.: 2 Whitebridge Rd., P.O. Box 245, 08867-0245. Tel: 908-735-4024; Fax: 908-735-0355. Email: stcofs@embarqmail.com.

PLAINSBORO, MIDDLESEX CO., QUEENSHIP OF MARY (1982) Very Rev. Robert W. Medley.
Res.: 16 Dey Rd., 08536. Tel: 609-799-7511; Fax: 609-799-8904. Web: www.qomchurch.org.

PORT MURRAY, WARREN CO., ST. THEODORE (1983) Rev. Zenon Boczek, S.D.S.
Res.: 855 Route 57, P.O. Box 146, 07865. Tel: 908-689-8318; 908-689-8393 (Rel. Educ. Office); Fax: 908-689-9242. Email: sttheodorenj@comcast.net. Web: www.sttheodorenj.org.

PORT READING, MIDDLESEX CO., ST. ANTHONY OF PADUA (1906) Revs. William J. Smith; Michael Gromadzki, Parochial Vicar; Deacons Michael Brucato; Albert Coppola.
Res.: 436 Port Reading Ave., 07064. Tel: 732-634-1403; Fax: 732-602-0119. Email: info_stanthony@verizon.net. Web: www.saintanthonypadua.org.

RARITAN, SOMERSET CO.

1—THE CATHOLIC CHURCH OF ST. ANN (1903), (Italian), Rev. Msgr. Michael J. Corona; Rev. Edmund A. Luciano III, Parochial Vicar; Deacons John R. Pacifico; Conrad Paulus.
Res.: 45 Anderson St., 08869. Tel: 908-725-1008; Fax: 908-707-1915. Web: www.stannparish.com.
School—(Grades PreK-8), 29 Second Ave., 08869. Tel: 908-725-7787; Fax: 908-541-9335. Sr. Gloria Caglioti, M.P.F., Prin. Religious Teachers Filippini 1; Lay Teachers 9; Students 165.

2—ST. JOSEPH (1912), (Slovak), Rev. Kenneth R. Kolibas.
Res.: 16 E. Somerset St., 08869. Tel: 908-725-0163; Fax: 908-725-2333. Web: www.stjosephraritan.4LPI.com. Email: parishoffice@sjraritan.org.

SAYREVILLE, MIDDLESEX CO.

1—OUR LADY OF VICTORIES (1885) [CEM] Revs. Thomas F. Ryan; John C. Grimes, Parochial Vicar; John J. O'Kane, Parochial Vicar; Deacon Thomas C. Yondolino.
Mailing Address: 42 Main St., 08872.
Res.: 24 Main St., 08872. Tel: 732-257-0077; Fax: 732-651-1898. Web: olvsayrenj.com.
School—(Grades PreK-8), 36 Main St., 08872. Tel: 732-254-1676; Fax: 732-254-5066. Mrs. Rosalind M. Esemplare, Prin.; Ms. Mary Ann Jones, Librarian. Religious 1; Lay Teachers 12; Students 212.

2—ST. STANISLAUS KOSTKA (1914), (Polish), [CEM] Rev. Kenneth R. Murphy; Deacons David Mikolai; Andrew Ozga.
Res.: 225 MacArthur Ave., 08872. Tel: 732-254-0212; Fax: 732-390-2989.
School—(Grades K-8), 221 MacArthur Ave., 08872. Tel: 732-254-5819; Fax: 732-254-7220. Mrs. Harriet Samim, Prin. Lay Teachers 22; Students 230.

SKILLMAN, SOMERSET CO., ST. CHARLES BORROMEO (1982) Rev. Msgr. Gregory E. S. Malovetz.
Res.: 376 Burnt Hill Rd., 08558. Tel: 609-466-0300; Fax: 609-466-0602. Web: www.borromeo.org.

SOMERSET, SOMERSET CO., ST. MATTHIAS (1962) Rev. Douglas J. Haefner; Deacons Stephen J. Holzinger II; Ronald J. Caimi; John M. Radvanski; Russell B. Demkovitz.
Mailing Address: 168 J.F. Kennedy Blvd., 08873. Tel: 732-828-1400; Fax: 732-828-0866. Web: www.stmatthias.net.
Res.: 166 J.F. Kennedy Blvd., 08873.
School—(Grades PreK-8), 170 J.F. Kennedy Blvd., 08873. Tel: 732-828-1402; Fax: 732-946-3099. Web: www.stmatthias.info. Steven Rizzoli, Prin.; Stephanie Lanzalotto, Librarian; Marion Fischer, Librarian. Lay Teachers 27; Students 554.

SOMERVILLE, SOMERSET CO., IMMACULATE CONCEPTION (1882) [CEM] Rev. Msgr. Seamus F. Brennan; Revs. Alexander J. Carles, Parochial Vicar; Charles A. Sabella, Parochial Vicar; Deacons John B. Ivers; Arnold J. DeMarco; Anthony Hancock; Frank J. Quinn; Luis E. Vindas.
Res.: 35 Mountain Ave., 08876. Tel: 908-725-1112; Fax: 908-725-6269. Web: www.immaculateconception.org.
School—(Grades PreK-8), 41 Mountain Ave., 08876. Tel: 908-725-6516; Fax: 908-725-3172. Sr. Mary John Magdalen, I.H.M., Prin. Sisters 3; Lay Teachers 34; Preschool 15; Students 449.
High School—Immaculata High School, 240 Mountain Ave., 08876. Tel: 908-722-0200; Fax: 908-218-7765. Sr. Regina Havens, I.H.M., Prin. Sisters 8; Lay Teachers 68; Students 845.
Convent—Sisters, Servants of the Immaculate Heart of Mary, 230 Mountain Ave., 08876. Tel: 908-722-6894.

SOUTH AMBOY, MIDDLESEX CO.

1—ST. MARY (1864) [CEM 2] Rev. Dennis R. Wezorak; Deacons Stephen N. Laikowski; Richard O'Brien.
Res.: 256 Augusta St., 08879. Tel: 732-721-0179; Fax: 732-721-0360.

2—SACRED HEART (1895), (Polish), [CEM] Revs. Joseph V. Romanoski; Marian Drozd, Parochial Vicar; Deacon Serge Bernatchez.
Res.: 224 N. Feltus St., 08879. Tel: 732-721-0040. Web: www.sacred-heart-church.net.
School—Sacred Heart School, (Grades PreSchool-8), 229 Cedar St., 08879. Tel: 732-721-0834; Fax: 732-316-0326. Sr. Marie Connolly, O.F., Prin. Religious 2; Lay Teachers 15; Students 203.
School—Sacred Heart Creative Kids Center Pre School, (Grades PreSchool), 531 Washington St., 08879. Tel: 732-721-1446. Paula Ryan, Prin. & Dir. Students 89.
Convent—Sacred Heart Convent, 229 Walnut Ave., 08879. Sisters 2.

SOUTH BOUND BROOK, SOMERSET CO., OUR LADY OF MERCY (1949) Rev. Msgr. Daniel J. Herlihy; Deacon Donald J. DeLorenzo.
Res.: 122 High St., 08880. Tel: 732-356-1037; Fax: 732-356-1318. Web: www.olmsbb.org.

SOUTH PLAINFIELD, MIDDLESEX CO.

1—OUR LADY OF CZESTOCHOWA (1943), (Polish), Rev. J. Maciej Melaniuk; Deacon Richard Kenton.
Res.: 120 Kosciusko Ave., 07080. Tel: 908-756-1333; Fax: 908-756-8557. Email: olcchurch@verizon.net.

2—SACRED HEART (1906) [CEM 2] Rev. John Paul Alvarado; Deacons Gregory Caruso; Wayne Otlowski; Joseph J. Stanczak, (Retired).
Res.: 149 S. Plainfield Ave., 07080. Tel: 908-756-0633; Fax: 908-757-5655. Web: www.churchofthesacredheart.net.
School—(Grades K-8) Tel: 908-756-0632; Fax: 908-756-7062. Web: www.sacredheartsp.net. Terrance Golden, Prin. Sisters 1; Lay Teachers 14; Students 175.
Convent—200 Randolph Ave., 07080. Tel: 908-756-0631. Sisters 3.

SOUTH RIVER, MIDDLESEX CO.

1—CORPUS CHRISTI (1944) Rev. John L. Brundage.
Rectory—Res.: 100 James St., 08882. Tel: 732-254-1800; Fax: 732-254-8063. Web: www.corpuschristi-southriver.parishesonline.com.

2—ST. MARY OF OSTRABRAMA (1903), (Polish), [CEM] Revs. Stanley G. Gromadzki; Pafnuzio Wassef. In Res., Rev. Joseph Szulwach (Retired).
Res.: 30 Jackson St., 08882. Tel: 732-254-2220; Fax: 732-651-8182.

3—ST. STEPHEN PROTOMARTYR (1907), (Hungarian), Rev. John Szczepanik; Deacon John Bertrand.
Res.: 20 William St., 08882. Tel: 732-257-0100; Fax: 732-257-4646. Email: saintstephen1@verizon.net.

SPOTSWOOD, MIDDLESEX CO., IMMACULATE CONCEPTION (1946) Rev. Msgr. Joseph M. Curry; Rev. John M. Rozembajgier, Parochial Vicar; Deacon John H. McGuire. In Res., Revs. Robert L. Daly (Retired); Lazaro Perez.
Res.: 18 South St., 08884. Tel: 732-251-3110; Fax: 732-251-2407. Email: office@icspotswood.com. Web: www.chicspotswood.com.
School—(Grades PreK-8), 23 Manalapan Rd., 08884. Tel: 732-251-3090; Fax: 732-251-8270. Web: www.icsspotswood.org. Mrs. Mary Hamm, Prin.; Kathleen Gately, Librarian. Felician Sisters 2; Lay Teachers 27; Students 484.
Convent—21 Manalapan Rd., 08884. Tel: 732-251-3446; Fax: 732-251-4031.

THREE BRIDGES, HUNTERDON CO., ST. ELIZABETH ANN SETON (1984) Rev. Thomas J. Serafin; Deacon Paul Santella.
Res.: 105 Summer Rd., 08887. Tel: 908-782-1475; Fax: 908-782-6230. Email: parishoffice@easton.net. Web: www.parishesonline.com/seasthreebridges.

WARREN, SOMERSET CO., OUR LADY OF THE MOUNT (1911) Rev. Sean W. Kenney; Deacon Thomas Sicola.
Res.: 167 Mount Bethel Rd., 07059. Tel: 908-647-1075; Fax: 908-647-7885. Web: www.olmwarren.org.

WASHINGTON, WARREN CO., ST. JOSEPH (1872) [CEM] Rev. Blaise R. Baran; Deacons Edmund Hartmann Jr.; Sylvan Webb.

Res.: 200 Carlton Ave., 07882. Tel: 908-689-0058; Fax: 908-689-3436. Web: www.stjosephwashington-.parishesonline.com.

WATCHUNG, SOMERSET CO., ST. MARY-STONY HILL (1847) [CEM] Very Rev. Brian J. Nolan; Deacon Arthur J. Wise, Emeritus.
Res.: 225 Mountain Blvd., 07069. Tel: 908-756-6524; Fax: 908-756-2111. Email: stmarywatchung@aol.com. Web: www.stmarys-watchung.org.

WHITEHOUSE STATION, HUNTERDON CO., OUR LADY OF LOURDES (1923) Rev. Leonard E. Rusay; Deacon Charles Paolino.
Res.: 390 County Rd. 523, 08889. Tel: 908-534-2319; Fax: 908-534-5670. Email: ollparish@embarqmail.com. Web: www.ollwhs.org.

WOODBRIDGE, MIDDLESEX CO.
1—ST. JAMES (1860) [CEM 2] Very Rev. Charles W. Cicerale, Admin.; Rev. Peter Tran; Deacons Michael Choi; John DiJoseph; Carl E. Psota; William F. Lange. In Res., Rev. Msgr. George M. Brembos (Retired); Rev. Sebastian D. Kaithackal, C.M.I.
Rectory—Res.: 148 Grenville St., 07095. Tel: 732-634-0500; Fax: 732-602-1487. Web: www.stjamesinfo.org.
School—(Grades PreK-8), 341 Amboy Ave., 07095. Tel: 732-634-2090. Miss Mary Erath, Prin. Bernardine Franciscan Sisters 1; Lay Teachers 17; Students 290.
Convent—149 Grove St., 07095. Tel: 732-634-0176.
2—OUR LADY OF KOREA Rev. Hong-Tae Kim (Korea, South), Admin.; Deacon Ignatius Seock Ro Youn. 267 E. Smith St., 07095. Tel: 732-634-8787; Fax: 732-634-6759.
3—OUR LADY OF MOUNT CARMEL (1921) Revs. William J. Smith; Michael Gromadzki, Parochial Vicar. Res.: 267 E. Smith St., 07095. Tel: 732-634-1438; Fax: 732-634-5368. Web: www.geocities.com/olmcwnj.

Chaplains of Public Institutions

ANNANDALE. *Mountainview Youth Correctional Facility* 08801. Tel: 732-741-6208. Attended by Immaculate Conception, Annandale.

AVENEL. *Woodbridge Developmental Center*. Attended by St. Andrew.

BELLE MEAD. *Carrier Clinic*. Deacon Joseph Moscinski, Chap.

BELVIDERE. *Warren Correctional Center*. Attended by St. Patrick, Belvidere.

CLINTON. *Edna Mahan Correctional Facility for Women*, Tel: 908-735-7319. Attended by Immaculate Conception, Annandale.
Hunterdon Developmental Center. Vacant. Attended by Immaculate Conception, Annandale.

EDISON. *John F. Kennedy Medical Center*. Revs. John J. Morley, Chap., Pauly Thekkan, C.M.I.

FLEMINGTON. *Hunterdon Medical Center*. Rev. Joseph Kabali, Chap. Attended by St. Magdalen de Pazzi.

GLEN GARDNER. *N.J. State Hospital for Geriatrics*. Attended by St. Ann, Hampton.

HACKETTSTOWN. *Hackettstown Community Hospital*. Attended by Assumption of the Blessed Virgin Mary.

JAMESBURG. *N.J. State Training School for Boys*. Attended by St. James the Less.

LYONS. *U.S. Veterans Medical Center*. Revs. Joseph C. Chacko, William C. Warman (BAL).

MENLO PARK. *Roosevelt State Hospital*. Attended by St. Cecelia, Iselin.

NEW BRUNSWICK. *Robert Wood Johnson University Hospital*. Revs. Joseph L. Desmond, Chap., Thomas P. Ganley, Chap.

NORTH BRUNSWICK. *Middlesex County Adult Detention Center*. Attended by Our Lady of Peace.

OLD BRIDGE. *Raritan Bay Medical Center-Old Bridge*. Rev. A. David Chalackal, Chap. Attended by St. Ambrose.

PERTH AMBOY. *Raritan Bay Medical Center*, Tel: 732-826-2771. Revs. Sean G. Winters, Sebastian D. Kaithackal, C.M.I.

PHILLIPSBURG. *Warren Hospital*, Tel: 908-454-0112. Rev. Alphonsus Mwariri Kariuki, I.M.C., Chap.

RAHWAY. *East Jersey State Prison*, Tel: 732-634-4355. Attended from St. Andrew Church, Avenel.

SKILLMAN. *NJ State Neuropsychiatric Institute*. Attended by St. Charles Borromeo.

SOMERVILLE. *Somerset Medical Center*, Tel: 908-526-2394. Revs. Eugeniusz Fasuga, C.Ss.R., Chap., Waldemar Latkowski, C.Ss.R.

SOUTH AMBOY. *South Amboy Memorial Hospital*. Attended by St. Mary and Sacred Heart.

On Duty Outside the Diocese:
Revs.—
Albaladejo, Juan A., Society of Jesus Christ the Priest
Bochnak, Zenon A., Military
Brighenti, Kenneth D., Mount St. Mary Seminary, Emmitsburg, MD.
Haddad, Wayne M., Military
Leonard, Raymond J.
Marin, John L., Society of Jesus Christ the Priest, Guayaquil, Ecuador
Marincioni, Raniero A., Society of Jesus Christ the Priest, Ecuador
McCord, Kent G.
Pepel, Clement
Ruiz, Faustino C., Society of Jesus Christ the Priest, Chile
Venditti, J. Michael, Eparchy of Passaic, NJ

Retired:
Rev. Msgrs.—
Brembos, George M., Ed.D.
Capik, William J.
Endebrock, Donald M.
Haughney, William J.
Kasprzyk, Leon J.
Kennedy, J. Nevin
Perini, Armando J.
Szymanski, John B., P.A., V.G.
Torney, John R., P.A.
Revs.—
Attanasio, Raymond V.
Brown, Gerald
Cornejo, Vincent C.
Crowley, R. Kevin
Dandry, Anthony M.
Driscoll, Michael A.
Egierd, Henry A.
Giordano, John C.
Hemmerling, Henry L.
Hogan, Joseph F.
Kearns, Edward A..
Kelly, Charles F.
McLaughlin, James W.
Muccilli, Sebastian
Perunilam, Thomas V.
Roca, Albert L.
Schellberg, Eugene
Stab, Herbert J.
Stingel, Louis F.
Struzik, Edward J.
Szulwach, Joseph
Vadakkekara, J. Philip
Walega, Stanley J.

Permanent Deacons:
Abatemarco, Michael, (On Leave)
Albert, Henry F., (On Leave)
Alexander, Russell C., (Retired)
Anderson, Paul L.
Bauer, William R.
Bell, James S., (Retired)
Bencosme, Pablo
Berg, Albert K.
Berluche, Enock, Sr.
Bernatchez, Serge
Bertrand, John
Bolash, George L.
Bonfante, Robert, Sr.
Brossoni, Guido J.
Brucato, Michael
Caimi, Ronald J.
Cammarano, Frank J.
Campbell, Joseph P.
Caruso, Gregory
Choi, Michael
Cline, Patrick J.
Coleman, George D.
Coppola, Albert
Cortez, Noe
Costantino, Samuel J.
Craig, John
Czekaj, John R., (On Leave)
D'Angelo, Gregory R.
D'Auguste, Frank C.
D'Mello, Francis
Daley, James M., (Retired)
Damian, Charles J.
Damiano, Samuel J., (On Leave)
DeFrange, David A.
DeLorenzo, Donald J.
DeMarco, Arnold J.
Demarest, Barry C.
Demkovitz, Russell B.
Di Joseph, John
Dominiecki, Thomas F.
Duffy, Lawrence J.
Dumschat, John F.
Fiore, Philip
Fitzsimmons, John J.
Flynn, John T.
Foldvary, Joseph J.
Forrestall, Michael J.
Frank, George A.
Gagliano, Salvatore J., (On Leave)
Gajewski, Stephen J.
Garcia, Enrique
Gargiulo, Robert, (On Leave)
Gerling, Robert
Giacobbe, Thomas J.
Gilheany, Thomas J., (Retired)
Gimblett, John, (On Leave)
Gleason, Michael P.
Gonzalez, Phillip
Gostkowski, Anthony J.
Gunther, Stephen
Hally, Luke J.
Hamilton, Kenneth
Hancock, Anthony
Hartmann, Edmund, Jr.
Heissenbuttel, Thomas A., (Retired)
Hendrix, James W., (On Leave)
Holowienka, Edward, (On Leave)
Holzinger, Stephen J., II
Ibern, Jose, (On Leave)
Ivers, John B.
Kaseta, Richard R., (On Leave)
Kenny, John F.
Kenton, Richard
Kintis, William
Koy, Martin L., (Retired)
Krupa, Edward
La Police, George D., (Retired)
Ladao, Rogelio
Laikowski, Stephen N.
Lange, William F.
Lawless, Timothy A.
Licameli, Paul G., (Retired)
Livingston, Joel R.
Long, James A., (On Leave)
Lorenc, Stanley J.
Lupini, Belardino A., (Retired)
Lutomski, Richard
Maksimik, Walter S.
Marano, Francis J., (Retired)
Martinez, Jose M., (On Leave)
Massimei, Eric S., (Retired)
Maurer, Joseph S., (Retired)
Mayer, Denis
McCarron, Richard
McCarthy, Keith B.
McGann, William B.
McGovern, Robert T.
McGreevy, Robert A., (Retired)
McGuire, John H.
McShane, John P., (Retired)
Mendoza, Alexander, (On Leave)
Michnewicz, Thomas S.
Mikolai, David
Monahan, John T.
Moral, Luis S.
Morend, Michel G., (Retired)
Moscinski, Joseph C.
Mulroy, Martin B., (Retired)
Murtha, Michael P.
Nardi, Samuel, (Retired)
O'Brien, Richard
O'Keefe, Joseph E.
Olegario, Eduardo
Otlowski, Wayne
Ozga, Andrew
Pacifico, John R.
Paolino, Charles
Paulus, Conrad
Payne, Alfred C., Jr., (On Leave)
Perez, Angel P., (Retired)
Perez, Basilio A., (On Leave)
Perez, Corpus V.
Pidgeon, Walter H.
Pizzigoni, Louis, III
Psota, Carl E.
Quinn, Frank J.
Rabinowitz, Roy
Raczkowski, Thaddeus C., (On Leave)
Radvanski, John M.
Ragucci, Joseph D.
Reilly, Lawrence P.
Ris, Gregory
Rivera, Herminio
Ruiz-Diaz, Benigno I.
Russo, Anthony
Rutch, Samuel
Sandoval, Gustavo
Santella, Paul
Semko, Michael
Sheptuck, Paul J.
Sheridan, John T., (Retired)
Sicola, Thomas
Sims, Gerard C.
Smoyak, Cornelius S.
Stanczak, Joseph J., (Retired)
Stefany, William G.
Strus, Andrew J.
Sullivan, Michael J., Jr.
Tartara, Filippo
Tietjen, John R.

Torres, Ramon L.
Van Haute, John B.
Vanzino, William C., (On Leave)
Vindas, Luis E.
Webb, Sylvan
Webster, Dennis K.
Wise, Arthur J., (Retired)
Wislinski, Thaddeus
Wittreich, Helmut
Yondolino, Thomas C.
Youn, Seock Ro
Yuhas, Frank
Zampella, Donald

INSTITUTIONS LOCATED IN THE DIOCESE

[A] HIGH SCHOOLS, DIOCESAN

EDISON. *Bishop Ahr High School* (1969) One Tingley Ln., 08820. Tel: 732-549-1108; Fax: 732-494-2229. Email: dtrukowski@diometuchen.org. Web: www.bgahs.org. Sr. Donna Marie Trukowski, C.S.S.F., Prin.; Ms. Sharon Taub, Librarian. Felician Sisters 2; Lay Teachers 71; Students 944.

SOUTH AMBOY. *Cardinal McCarrick High School* (1885) 310 Augusta St., 08879. Tel: 732-721-0748; Fax: 732-727-7018. Web: www.cardinalmccarrick.com. Jean G. Kline, Prin.; Rev. John B. Gordon, Chap. Sisters 2; Lay Teachers 27; Students 325.

[B] HIGH SCHOOLS, PRIVATE

METUCHEN. *St. Joseph High School*, 145 Plainfield Ave., 08840-1099. Tel: 732-549-7600; Fax: 732-549-0664. Web: www.stjoes.org. Mr. Lawrence N. Walsh, Pres.; Bro. Matthew Scanlon, S.C., D.R.E.; Deacon Richard McCarron, Campus Ministry; Mr. John A. Anderson, Prin.; Mrs. Patricia Brennan, Librarian. Brothers of the Sacred Heart 10; Sisters of St. Joseph (Philadelphia) 2; Lay Teachers 46; Boys 800.

WATCHUNG. *Mount St. Mary Academy* (1908) 07069. Tel: 908-757-0108; Fax: 908-756-5751. Email: lgambacorto@mountsaintmary.org. Web: www.mountsaintmary.org. Sr. Lisa D. Gambacorto, R.S.M., E.D.S., Directress & Prin.; Rev. William T. Morris, Chap.; Jan Leavitt, B.A., M.L.S., Librarian. Day school for girls. College preparatory only. Sisters of Mercy 1; Lay Teachers 39; Girls 349.

[C] INTER-PAROCHIAL ELEMENTARY SCHOOLS

BOUND BROOK. *Holy Family Academy*, (Grades PreK-8), 120 E. Second St., 08805. Tel: 732-356-1151; Fax: 732-356-6844. Email: jclayton@diometuchen.org. Web: www.hfawildcats.com. Judith Clayton, Prin. Teachers 14; Students 150.

NEW BRUNSWICK. *St. Mary and St. Peter Catholic Academy*, (Grades K-8), 167 Somerset St., 08901. Tel: 732-545-1482; Fax: 732-545-2508. Frances Comiskey, Prin.; Sr. Maureen Cawley, S.C., Librarian. Religious 1; Lay Teachers 14; Students 106.

PERTH AMBOY. *Perth Amboy Catholic Primary School*, (Grades PreK-3), 613 Carlock Ave., 08861. Tel: 732-826-5747; Fax: 732-826-6096. Web: www.pacatholic.org. Sisters Beverly Policastro, S.C., Prin.; Dorothy Mary Sajczuk, Librarian. Lay Teachers 9; Students 154.

Perth Amboy Catholic School, (Grades 4-8), 500 State St., 08861. Tel: 732-826-1598; Fax: 732-826-7063. Email: rpiatek@diometuchen.org. Web: www.pacatholicschool.org. Sisters M. Rebecca Piatek, C.S.S.F., Prin.; Dorothy M. Sajczuk, C.S.S.F., Librarian. Lay Teachers 9; Students 131.

Perth Amboy Catholic School - Main Central Office, 500 State St., 08861. Tel: 732-442-9533; Fax: 732-442-2887. Web: www.pacatholicschools.org. Sr. Jeanette DeSena, M.P.F., Admin.

[D] PRE-SCHOOLS

MARTINSVILLE. *Little Friends of Jesus Nursery School*, 1881 Washington Valley Rd., 08836. Tel: 732-667-5275; Fax: 732-667-5277.

[E] SPECIAL SCHOOLS, PRIVATE

WATCHUNG. *McAuley School for Exceptional Children* (1966) 1633 U.S. Hwy. 22, 07069. Tel: 908-754-4114; Fax: 908-754-3312. Email: mcaschool@aol.com. Web: www.mcauleyschool.org. Sr. Lee Ann Amico, R.S.M., Dir.; Gina Donath, Prin. Sisters 3; Lay Teachers 21; Students 45.

[F] CATHOLIC CHARITIES

PERTH AMBOY. *Catholic Charities Central Office*, 319 Maple St., 08861. Tel: 732-324-8200; Fax: 732-826-3549. Web: www.ccdom.org. Marianne Majewski, L.C.S.W., Exec. Dir.; Julio Coto, Asst. Exec. Dir.; Joan Lorah, L.C.S.W., Asst. Exec. Dir.; Christine Benitez, M.B.A., CPA, CFO; Douglas J. Susan, J.D., Dir. Compliance; J. Patrick Byrne, B.S., Admin. Svcs. Dir.

Bridgewater Family Service Center, 540 U.S. Rte. 22 E., Bridgewater, 08807. Tel: 908-722-1881; Fax: 908-704-0215. Web: ccdom.org. Carmen Diaz, Asst. Div. Dir.

East Brunswick Family Service Center, 288 Rues Ln., East Brunswick, 08816. Tel: 732-257-6100; Fax: 732-651-9834. Web: www.ccdom.org. Ann Basil, L.C.S.W., Asst. Division Dir.

Catholic Charities, Edison Family Service Center, 26 Safran Ave., Edison, 08837. Tel: 732-738-1323; Fax: 732-738-3896. Web: www.ccdom.org. Wesley R. Moore, M.Div., B.S., C.S.W., Div. Dir. Housing & Social Concerns.

Flemington Family Service Center, 6 Park Ave., Flemington, 08822. Tel: 908-782-7905; Fax: 908-782-5934. Web: www.ccdom.org. Martha Rezeli, M.A., C.S.W., Site Supvr.

Trinity Family Services of Catholic Charities, 271 Smith St., 08861. Tel: 732-826-9160; Fax: 732-826-8342. Web: www.ccdom.org. Sharon Oshatz, M.P.H., M.T. (A.S.C.P.), Div. Dir.

Phillipsburg Family Service Center, 700 Sayre Ave., Phillipsburg, 08865. Tel: 908-454-2074; Fax: 908-454-9871. Web: www.ccdom.org. Marci Booth, Div. Dir. & Residential.

Social Service Center (1982) 372 S. Main St., Phillipsburg, 08865. Tel: 908-859-5447; Fax: 908-859-6375. Email: mpopovice@ccdom.org. Sr. M. Michaelita Popovice, R.S.M., Prog. Dir.

The Ozanam Shelter for Families and Single Women, 89 Truman Dr., Edison, 08817. Tel: 732-985-0327; Fax: 732-985-2449. Web: www.ccdom.org. Wesley R. Moore, M.Div., B.S., C.S.W., Div. Dir. Housing & Social Concerns.

Nicholas House, 384 Vath St., Jackson, 08527. Tel: 732-408-0298; Fax: 732-408-1821. Web: www.ccdom.org. Marci Booth, Div. Dir. Residential. Residential Services.

Catholic Charities Ozanam Inn, 20-22 Abeel St., New Brunswick, 08901. Tel: 732-729-0850; Fax: 732-729-0794. Web: www.ccdom.org. Wesley R. Moore, M.Div., B.S., C.S.W., Div. Dir. Housing & Social Concerns.

St. John's Health & Family Service Center, 24 Abeel St., New Brunswick, 08901. Tel: 732-745-9800; Fax: 732-745-9107. Web: www.ccdom.org. Sharon Oshatz, M.P.H., M.T. (A.S.C.P.), Div. Dir.

Community House at St. Thomas, 124 Bentley Ave., Old Bridge, 08857. Tel: 732-251-0022; Fax: 732-251-3482. Web: www.ccdom.org. Susan Kuzma, Case Mgr.; Sharon Oshatz, M.P.H., M.T. (A.S.C.P.), Exec. Dir.

Metuchen Community Services Corporation, 319 Maple St., 08861. Tel: 732-324-8200; Fax: 732-826-3549. Email: jlorah@ccdom.org. Joan Lorah, Exec. Dir.

Nazareth House, 156 Wayne St., 08861. Tel: 732-324-0331; Fax: 732-442-7930. Web: www.ccdom.org. Marci Booth, Div. Dir.

St. Peter and Paul House, 702 Sayre Ave., Phillipsburg, 08865. Tel: 908-454-0912; Fax: 908-454-3085. Web: www.ccdom.org. Marci Booth, Div. Dir. Residential.

Community Child Care Solutions, 103 Center St., 08861.

[G] GENERAL HOSPITALS

NEW BRUNSWICK. *Saint Peter's Healthcare System, Inc.*, 254 Easton Ave., 08901. Tel: 732-745-8588; Fax: 732-745-9099.

Saint Peter's Foundation, 254 Easton Ave., 08901. Tel: 732-745-8542; Fax: 732-745-7573.

Saint Peter's Health & Management Services Corporation, 254 Easton Ave., 08901. Tel: 732-745-8556; Fax: 732-745-9099.

Saint Peter's Properties Corporation, Inc., 254 Easton Ave., 08901. Tel: 732-745-8588; Fax: 732-745-9099.

Saint Peter's University Hospital (1907) 254 Easton Ave., P.O. Box 591, 08903-0591. Tel: 732-745-8600; Fax: 732-745-9099. Email: kkillion@saintpetersuh.com. Web: www.saintpetersuh.com. Revs. Cecilio E. Sipaco, Chap.; Lazaro Perez, Chap.; Sisters Breda Boyle, C.S.J.P., Chap.; Barbara Ortmann, O.P., Chap.; Mary Jane Bransfield, I.H.M., Chap.; James Jones, Chap.; Jerome Herauf, M.A., Dir. Pastoral Care. Bed Capacity 478; Bassinets 66; Neonatal Intensive Care Bassinets 35; Intermediate Care Bassinetts 19; Patients Assisted Annually 398,274.

[H] HOMES FOR AGED

SOMERSET. *McCarrick Care Center*, 15 Dellwood Ln., 08873. Tel: 732-545-4200; Fax: 732-846-1089. James F. Caron, Admin.; Rev. Thomas P. Ganley, Chap.; Peg Bradley, Dir. Admissions. Patients Assisted Annually 1,697.

WOODBRIDGE. *St. Joseph Assisted Living*, One St. Joseph Terr., 07095. Tel: 732-634-0004; Fax: 732-634-4586. Sr. Jadwiga Zaremba, L.S.I.C., Admin.

St. Joseph Home, Assisted Living and Nursing Center Little Servant Sisters 8; Residents 60; Staff 35.

St. Joseph Nursing Home, 3 St. Joseph Ter., 07095. Little Servant Sisters 4; Bed Capacity 51; Staff 49.

[I] MONASTERIES AND RESIDENCES FOR PRIESTS AND BROTHERS

METUCHEN. *Brothers of the Sacred Heart* (1901) 145 Plainfield Ave., 08840. Tel: 732-548-2292; Fax: 732-548-3101. Bro. Ron Travers, S.C., Supr. Brothers 10.

NEW BRUNSWICK. *The New Brunswick Congregation of the Oratory of St. Philip Neri*, 94 Somerset St., 08901. Tel: 732-545-6820; Fax: 732-545-4069. Email: oratorians@nboratory.org. Web: www.nboratory.org. Very Rev. Peter R. Cebulka, C.O., Provost; Revs. Thomas A. Odorizzi, C.O., Vicar & Treas.; Kevin Kelly, C.O., Sec.; Deacon Jeffrey Calia, C.O.; Bro. Robert Peck, C.O. Priests 3; Novices 1.

PRINCETON. *Vincentian Residence*, 65 Mapleton Rd., 08540-9614. Tel: 609-520-9626; Fax: 609-452-7242. Web: www.sjseminary.org. Revs. Peter J. Albano, C.M.; Jean R. Bonenge, C.M.; Thomas S. Krafinski, C.M.; Charles F. Krieg, C.M.; Richard J. Kehoe, C.M.; Francis W. Sacks, C.M.; Bro. Carmen V. Ciardullo, C.M.

RARITAN. *Clairvaux House*, 52 W. Somerset St., 08869. Tel: 908-722-1489; Fax: 908-393-4978. Web: www.shrine.cnjnet.com. Rev. Guy W. Selvester.

SAYREVILLE. *Federation of the Brothers of the Sacred Heart*, 219 MacArthur Ave., 08872. Tel: 718-522-3309.

SOMERSET. *Consolata Society for Foreign Missions* (1901) *Provincial Headquarters*, 2301 Rt. 27, P.O. Box 5550, 08875-5550. Tel: 732-297-9191; Fax: 732-940-3121. Email: supreus@consolata.net. Web: www.consolata.org. Revs. Charles Bonelli, I.M.C., Prov. Supr.; David Kamau Gikonyo, I.M.C.; Van Allen Hager, I.M.C.; John Saffirio, I.M.C.; Giuseppe Sesana, I.M.C., Prov. Admin.; Paul Stefanowich, I.M.C.; Marco S. Bagnarol, I.M.C.

Maria Regina Residence, 5 Dellwood Ln., 08873. Tel: 732-828-6800; Fax: 732-828-7206. Rev. Msgrs. John B. Szymanski, P.A., V.G., Dir. (Retired); William J. Haughney (Retired); Leon J. Kasprzyk (Retired); John R. Torney, P.A. (Retired); Revs. Gerald Browne (Retired); Neil W. Davin, C.P., J.C.L.; Thomas P. Ganley; Charles F. Kelly (Retired); Rev. Msgr. J. Nevin Kennedy (Retired); Revs. Louis A. Mattina; Laurence Murphy, M.M. (Retired); Herbert J. Stab (Retired); Louis F. Stingel (Retired); Edward J. Struzik (Retired); Sr. Marianne Troendle, F.S.G.M., Mgr. Retirement home for Diocesan priests.

SOUTH RIVER. *Passionist Provincial Office*, 80 David St., 08882. Tel: 732-257-7177; Fax: 732-257-0042. Email: jdougcp@aol.com. Web: www.thepassionists.org. Rev. John Douglas, Province Sec.

St. Paul's Benevolent, Educational and Missionary Institute, Inc. Priests 3.

Consultors: Very Revs. Joseph R. Jones, C.P., Provincial; James O'Shea, C.P.; James Price, C.P.

Religious of the Province in Residences Not Listed Elsewhere: Very Rev. James O'Shea, C.P., Our Lady of Monseratte, 134 Vernon Ave., Brooklyn, NY 11206; Revs. James Barry, C.P., 8433-A Dempster St., Niles, IL 60714. Tel: 845-384-0134; Thomas Bonacci, C.P. (Retired), 640 Bailey Rd., #301, Pittsburg, CA 94565; Kevin Casey, C.P., Corpus Christi, 100 James St., 08882. Tel: 732-254-1800; Fax: 732-254-8063; John Cashman, C.P., 4 Chateau Way, Naples, FL 34112. Tel: 239-732-6471; Paul Cusack, C.P., 84 Clarinda Dr., Toronto ON M2K 1V3 Canada. Tel: 416-229-9690; Fax: 416-225-5445; Neil W. Davin, C.P., J.C.L., Maria Regina Residence, 5 Dellwood Ln., Somerset, 08873; Edward Deviny, C.P.; Charles Dougherty, C.P. (Retired), 4777 Tramway Blvd. N.E., Apt. 517, Albuquerque, NM 87111; Stephen Dunn, C.P., St. Gabriel's Monastery, 650 Sheppard Ave. E., Willowdale ON M2K 1B7 Canada. Tel: 416-221-8866; Fax: 412-221-8893; Francis Finnigan, C.P., 50 Ave. Hoche, Paris 75008 France; Gerald Hynes, C.P., St. Ursula Rectory, 8801 Harford Rd., Baltimore, MD 21234. Tel: 410-665-2111; Fax: 410-665-0758; Bernard McEachern, C.P., 84 Clarinda Dr., Toronto ON M2K 1V3 Canada. Tel: 416-229-9690; Fax: 416-225-5445; David Monaco, C.P., 5110 S. Kenwood Ave., Apt. 706, Chicago, IL 60615. Tel: 773-575-1380; Peter O'Rourke, C.P., Assumption of the BVM, 200

Chestnut St., Centereach, NY 11720. Tel: 631-585-8760; Fax: 631-585-3601; Robin Ryan, C.P., CTU Student Residence, 5417 S. Cornell Ave., Chicago, IL 60615; Lawrence Rywalt, C.P., Curia Generalizia Dei Passionisti, Piazza SS Giovanni E Paolo 13, Rome 00184 Italy. Tel: 39-060-772-711; Fax: 39-06-700-8454; Carrol W. Thorne, C.P, 316 N. 6th St., Apt. 101, Leavenworth, KS 66048. Tel: 913-651-2647; Theodore Vitali, C.P., 5859 Nottingham St., Saint Louis, MO 63109. Tel: 314-977-3149; Fax: 314-377-3696; Paul Zilonka, C.P., CTU Student Residence, 5417 S. Cornell Ave., Chicago, IL 60615; Bro. Augustine Paul Lowe, C.P., P.O. Box 1800, Orlando, FL 32802-1800. Tel: 407-246-4800; Fax: 407-246-4941.

Retired Members: Revs. Brendan Breen, C.P. (Retired), 30 Julio Drive, Apt. 467, Shrewsbury, MA 01545; Fidelis Connolly, C.P. (Retired), 30 Julio Drive, Apt. 468, Shrewsbury, MA 01545; James Kiernan Earley, C.P. (Retired), 30 Julio Drive, Apt. 472, Shrewsbury, MA 01545; Brice Edwards, C.P. (Retired), 30 Julio Drive, Apt. 480, Shrewsbury, MA 01545; Sebastian Kolinovsky, C.P. (Retired), 1 Pioneer Pl., Moscow, PA 18444; Bonaventure Moccia, C.P. (Retired), 30 Julio Drive, Apt. 469, Shrewsbury, MA 01545; Columkille O'Grady, C.P.; Bro. Terrence Skorka, C.P., 110 Monastery Pl., West Springfield, MA 01089.

Foreign Missions: Revs. Award, C.P.; Thomas Brislin, C.P.; Richard Frechette, C.P.; Aelred Lacomara, C.P.; Gaston Nsongolo, C.P., Immaculate Conception Church of Stony Hill, P.O. Box 6, Kingston 9, Jamaica; Claudio Piccinini, C.P., 1458 Housey's Rapid Rd. RR 3, Gravehurst ON P1P-1R3 Canada; Paul Ruttle, C.P.; Richard Scheiner, C.P.; Bro. Michael Stomber, C.P.

[J] CONVENTS AND RESIDENCES FOR SISTERS

METUCHEN. *St. Clare Convent*, 52 Elm Ave., 08840. Tel: 732-549-7598. Felician Sisters 2.

St. Francis Convent, 44 Elm Ave., 08840. Tel: 732-549-3050. Sisters of Christian Charity 4.

EAST BRUNSWICK. *DePaul House - Daughters of Charity of St. Vincent de Paul*, 528 Ryders Ln., 08816. Tel: 732-238-3638. Email: dcebnj@comcast.net. Web: www.dc-northeast.org. Sisters 2.

EDISON. *St. Thomas Aquinas Convent* (1969) 15 Wren Ct., 08820. Tel: 732-321-0137; Fax: 732-549-9050. Email: srcynthia@bgahs.org. Sisters Cynthia Marie Babyak, C.S.S.F., Local Min.; Donna Marie Trukowski, C.S.S.F. Sisters 3.

FLEMINGTON. *The Carmel of Mary Immaculate and St. Mary Magdalen*, 26 Harmony School Rd., 08822. Tel: 908-782-4802. Web: www.flemingtoncarmel.org. Rev. Dominic Nattunilam, C.M.I., Chap. Nuns Professed with Solemn Vows 16; Novices 2.

MARTINSVILLE. *Blessed Sacrament Convent*, 1881 Washington Valley Rd., 08836. Tel: 732-667-5275; Fax: 732-667-5277. Sr. Romilda Borges, S.D.V., Local Supr. Vocationist Sisters 5.

NEW BRUNSWICK. *Sisters of St. Joseph of Peace* (1884) 61 Jefferson Ave., 08901. Tel: 732-249-5644. Email: jrusch@saintpetersuh.com. Sisters 2.

PISCATAWAY. *St. Joseph of Chestnut Hill*, 137 Metlars Ln., 08854. Tel: 732-393-9640. Email: metlarslane@yahoo.com. Sisters 3.

SOMERSET. *St. Elizabeth Convent*, 13 Renfro Rd., 08873. Tel: 732-247-3697. Email: vocations@altonfranciscans.org. Sr. Marianna Troendle, F.S.G.M., Supr. Sisters 4.

WATCHUNG. *McAuley Hall Inc.*, Health Care Center, 1633 U.S. Hwy 22, 07069-6505. Tel: 908-754-3663; Fax: 908-754-3502. Retired Sisters 50.

Mount St. Mary, 1645 U.S. Hwy. 22 W., 07069-6587. Tel: 908-756-0994; Fax: 908-754-0164. Web: www.mercymidatlantic.org. Sr. Christine McCann, R.S.M., Pres. Mid-Atlantic Community. Sisters of Mercy of the Americas, Mid-Atlantic Community. Professed Sisters in Residence 48.

WOODBRIDGE. *St. Joseph Convent*, 184 Amboy Ave., 07095. Tel: 732-634-0807; Fax: 732-634-7888. Email: lsicmaria@aol.com. Sr. Maria Pietrzyk, L.S.I.C., Supr. Sisters 8.

St. Joseph Home Convent, 3 Woodbridge Ter., 07095. Tel: 732-634-0004; Fax: 732-634-4586. Sr. Anatolia Kopec, L.S.I.C., Supr. Little Servant Sisters 15.

[K] RETREAT HOUSES

FLEMINGTON. *Our Lady of Providence*, 31 Britton Dr., 08822. Tel: 908-782-4495. Sr. Jean, L.S.P., Dir. Little Sisters of the Poor.

MILFORD. *Bethany Ridge*, 914 Milford-Warren Glen Rd., 08848. Tel: 908-995-9758; Fax: 908-995-7299. Rev. Peter Suhaka, Dir. Spirituality Center for Priests.

WATCHUNG. *Mt. St. Mary House of Prayer* (1976) 1651 U.S. Hwy. 22, 07069-6587. Tel: 908-753-2091; Fax: 908-757-0792. Email: msmhope@msmhope.org. Web: www.msmhope.org. Sisters Theresina Flannery, R.S.M., Co-Dir.; Eileen P. Smith, R.S.M., Co-Dir.; Mary Jo Kearns, R.S.M., Co-Dir. Sisters 3.

[L] SHRINES AND PUBLIC ORATORIES

BERNARDSVILLE. *Sacred Heart Chapel* , (Chapel of Convenience), Bernards Ave., 07924. Tel: 908-766-0079; Fax: 908-766-1185. Rev. John N. Fell, S.T.D., Pastor.

RARITAN. *Shrine Chapel of the Blessed Sacrament* 50 W. Somerset St., 08869. Tel: 908-722-1489; Fax: 908-526-6232. Email: blessedsacrament.shrine@verizon.net. Web: www.shrine.cnjnet.com. Rev. Guy W. Selvester, Rector.

WASHINGTON. *National World Apostolate of Fatima, USA, Inc. Blue Army Shrine of the Immaculate Heart of Mary* 674 Mountainview Rd., P.O. Box 976, 07882. Tel: 908-689-1700; Fax: 908-689-0721. Email: service@bluearmy.com. Web: www.wafusa.org.

[M] PUBLIC ASSOCIATIONS OF THE FAITHFUL

BLOOMSBURY. *Sisters of Jesus Our Hope* (1992) 376 Bellis Rd., 08804. Tel: 908-995-7261; Fax: 908-995-7262. Web: www.sistersofjesusourhope.org. Sr. Claire Marie Lessard, S.J.H., Community Sister Servant. Sisters 6.

BOUND BROOK. *Sisters of Jesus Our Hope* (1992) 514 Church St., 08805. Tel: 732-271-5777. Web: www.sistersofjesusourhope.org. Sisters 5.

FLEMINGTON. *Dominican Sisters of Divine Providence* (1982) 25 Harmony School Rd., 08822. Tel: 908-782-1504; Fax: 908-788-7394. Email: smtolp@yahoo.com. Sr. M. Trinitas Sullivan, O.P., Supr. Sisters 2; Postulants 2.

Sisters of Jesus Our Hope, 83 Bonnell St., 08822. Tel: 908-806-3332. Web: www.sistersofjesusourhope.org. Sr. Barbara Haworth, S.J.H., Sister Servant. Sisters 3.

OXFORD. *The Anawim Community* (1975) 85 Academy St., P.O. Box 207, 07863. Tel: 908-453-3886; 908-916-5202; Fax: 908-453-3786. Email: oxford@anawim.com. Web: www.anawim.com. Rev. Daniel H. Healy, Dir.; Very Rev. Richard M. Rusk, Missions Dir. & Vocations Dir. Priests 2; Staff 15.

STEWARTSVILLE. *Society of Jesus Christ the Priest*, P.O. Box 157, 08886. Tel: 908-213-1447; Fax: 908-859-5210. Email: meadwater@verizon.net. 70 Edison Rd., 08886. Revs. Jose Lorente; Manuel Lorente; Raymond L. Nacarino, Treas.; Lope D. Pascual, Dir.

[N] CAMPUS MINISTRY

NEW BRUNSWICK. *Catholic Center at Rutgers University* 84 Somerset St., 08901. Tel: 732-545-6663; Fax: 732-545-3495. Email: coldon@rci.rutgers.edu. Web: www.catholic-center.rutgers.edu. Very Rev. Peter Cebulka, C.O., Dir. & Chap.; Bros. Ken Apuzzo, B.H., Chap.; Adam Neri, B.H., Chap.; Sr. Ellen Kraft, S.J.H., Chap.

[O] MISCELLANEOUS LISTINGS

METUCHEN. *The Foundation for Catholic Education*, P.O. Box 191, 08840. Most Rev. Paul G. Bootkoski, D.D.

The Fund for the Future, Inc., P.O. Box 191, 08840. Most Rev. Paul G. Bootkoski, D.D.

The Priestly Education Fund, Inc., P.O. Box 191, 08840. Most Rev. Paul G. Bootkoski, D.D.

SOMERSET. *The Center for Great Expectations, Inc.*, 19 B Dellwood Ln., 08873. Tel: 732-247-7003, Ext. 27; Fax: 732-247-7043. Web: www.thecenterforgreatexpectations.org. Mrs. Peg Wright, Pres.

WOODBRIDGE. *Mt. Carmel Home Nursing Service*, 184 Amboy Ave., 07095. Tel: 732-634-0807; Fax: 732-634-7888. Sr. Maria Wojcik, L.S.I.C., Dir.

RELIGIOUS INSTITUTES OF MEN REPRESENTED IN THE DIOCESE

For further details refer to the corresponding bracketed number in the Religious Institutes of Men or Women section.

[]—*Brotherhood of Hope*—B.H.
[1100]—*Brothers of the Sacred Heart*—S.C.
[0470]—*The Capuchin Friars*—O.F.M.Cap.
[0275]—*Carmelites of Mary Immaculate*—C.M.I.
[0360]—*Claretian Missionaries* (Eastern Prov.)—C.M.F.
[1330]—*Congregation of the Mission*—C.M.
[1000]—*Congregation of the Passion*—C.P.
[0390]—*Consolata Missionaries*—I.M.C.
[0520]—*Franciscan Friars* (Custody of St. John Capistran)—O.F.M.
[0650]—*Holy Ghost Fathers*—C.S.Sp.
[0950]—*Oratorians*—C.O.
[]—*Order of Discaleed Carmelites*—O.C.D.
[]—*Order of Friars Minor Capachin*—O.F.M.Cap.
[]—*Order of St. Benedict*—O.S.B.
[1070]—*Redemptorist Fathers*—C.Ss.R.
[1190]—*Salesians of Don Bosco*—S.D.B.
[1200]—*Society of the Divine Savior*—S.D.S.
[1335]—*Vincentian Retreat Master*—V.C.

RELIGIOUS INSTITUTES OF WOMEN REPRESENTED IN THE DIOCESE

[1810]—*Bernardine Sisters of the Third Order of St. Francis*—O.S.F.
[3820]—*Congregation of St. John the Baptist*—C.S.J.B.
[0760]—*Daughters of Charity of St. Vincent De Paul* (Albany Prov.)—D.C.
[0420]—*Discalced Carmelite Nuns*—O.C.D.
[1070-18]—*Dominican Sisters* (Caldwell)—O.P.
[]—*Dominican Sisters of Divine Providence*—O.P.
[1070-06]—*Dominican Sisters of Hope* (Ossining, N.Y.)—O.P.
[1170]—*Felician Sisters* (Immaculate Conception Prov.)—C.S.S.F.
[1180]—*Franciscan Sisters of Allegany* (St. Bonaventure, NY)—O.S.F.
[2575]—*Institute of the Sisters of Mercy of the Americas*—R.S.M.
[2300]—*Little Servant Sisters of the Immaculate Conception*—L.S.I.C.
[2340]—*Little Sisters of the Poor* (Brooklyn Prov.)—L.S.P.
[2700]—*Missionary Catechists of the Sacred Hearts of Jesus and Mary*—M.C.S.H.
[2810]—*Missionary Sisters of the Mother of God* (Byzantine-Ukrainian)—M.S.M.G.
[0950]—*Pious Society Daughters of St. Paul*—F.S.P.
[3320]—*Presentation of the Blessed Virgin Mary* (New Windsor, NY)—P.B.V.M.
[3430]—*Religious Teachers Filippini* (St. Lucy Prov.)—M.P.F.
[1700]—*School Sisters of the Third Order of St. Francis*—O.S.F.
[0590]—*Sisters of Charity of Saint Elizabeth, Convent Station*—S.C.
[0640]—*Sisters of Charity, Halifax*—S.C.
[0660]—*Sisters of Christian Charity* (North American Eastern Prov.)—S.C.C.
[]—*Sisters of Jesus Our Hope*—S.J.H.
[3893]—*Sisters of Saint Joseph of Chestnut Hill, Philadelphia*—S.S.J.
[1600]—*Sisters of St. Francis of the Martyr St. George*—F.S.G.M.
[3890]—*Sisters of St. Joseph of Peace*—C.S.J.P.
[2170]—*Sisters Servants of the Immaculate Heart of Mary*—I.H.M.
[]—*Trinitarium Sisters of Redemptor Homini*—T.R.H.
[4210]—*Vocationist Sisters*—S.V.D.

DIOCESAN CEMETERIES

EAST BRUNSWICK. *The Crematory at Holy Cross Burial Park*, 840 Cranbury Rd., 08816.

JAMESBURG. *Holy Cross Burial Park, Diocese of Metuchen Office of Cemeteries Resurrection Cemetery & Mausoleum*, 899 Lincoln Ave., Piscataway, 08854. Tel: 732-463-1424; Fax: 732-463-8807. Deacon Russell B. Demkovitz, Dir.

PISCATAWAY. *Resurrection Burial Park, Diocese of Metuchen Office of Cemeteries Resurrection Cemetery & Mausoleum*, 899 Lincoln Ave., 08854. Tel: 732-463-1424; Fax: 732-463-8807. Deacon Russell B. Demkovitz, Dir.

NECROLOGY

† Alliegro, Rev. Msgr. Michael J., Metuchen, NJ Cathedral of St. Francis of Assisi—Died Aug. 17, 2009
† Ewing, Richard A., (Retired)—Died April 23, 2009
† Nebus, Vincent J., (Retired)—Died June 5, 2009

Archdiocese of Miami

(Archidioecesis Miamiensis)

Most Reverend

JOHN C. FAVALORA, D.D.

Archbishop of Miami; ordained December 20, 1961; appointed Bishop of Alexandria June 16, 1986; ordained and installed July 29, 1986; appointed Third Bishop of St. Petersburg March 7, 1989; installed May 16, 1989; appointed Third Bishop of Miami November 3, 1994; installed December 20, 1994. *Office: 9401 Biscayne Blvd., Miami Shores, FL 33138.*

Most Reverend

AGUSTIN A. ROMAN, D.D.

Retired Auxiliary Bishop of Miami; ordained July 5, 1959; appointed Titular Bishop of Sertei and Auxiliary of Miami February 6, 1979; consecrated March 24, 1979; retired June 7, 2003.

Most Reverend

GILBERTO FERNANDEZ, D.D.

Retired Auxiliary Bishop of Miami; ordained May 17, 1959; appointed Titular Bishop of Irina and Auxiliary of Miami June 24, 1997; consecrated September 3, 1997; retired December 10, 2002.

Pastoral Center: 9401 Biscayne Blvd., Miami Shores, FL 33138. Tel: 305-757-6241; Fax: 305-754-1897.

Web: www.archdioceseofmiami.org

Email: information@theadom.org

Most Reverend

FELIPE DE JESUS ESTEVEZ, D.D., V.G.

Auxiliary Bishop of Miami; ordained May 30, 1970; appointed Titular Bishop of Kearney and Auxiliary Bishop of Miami November 21, 2003; consecrated January 7, 2004. *Office: 9401 Biscayne Blvd., Miami Shores, FL 33138.*

Most Reverend

JOHN G. NOONAN, D.D., V.G.

Auxiliary Bishop of Miami; ordained September 23, 1983; appointed Titular Bishop of Bonusta and Auxiliary Bishop of Miami June 21, 2005; ordained August 24, 2005. *Office: 9401 Biscayne Blvd., Miami Shores, FL 33138.*

ESTABLISHED AUGUST 13, 1958.

Square Miles 4,958.

Created an Archbishopric, June 13, 1968.

Comprises the Counties in the southern part of the State of Florida, namely, Broward, Miami-Dade and Monroe.

For legal titles of Parishes and Archdiocesan institutions, consult the Pastoral Center.

STATISTICAL OVERVIEW

Personnel	
Archbishops	1
Auxiliary Bishops	2
Retired Bishops	2
Priests: Diocesan Active in Diocese	171
Priests: Diocesan Active Outside Diocese	7
Priests: Diocesan in Foreign Missions	1
Priests: Retired, Sick or Absent	82
Number of Diocesan Priests	261
Religious Priests in Diocese	76
Total Priests in Diocese	337
Extern Priests in Diocese	70
Ordinations:	
Diocesan Priests	3
Religious Priests	1
Transitional Deacons	1
Permanent Deacons in Diocese	128
Total Brothers	48
Total Sisters	277
Parishes	
Parishes	101
With Resident Pastor:	
Resident Diocesan Priests	93
Resident Religious Priests	8
Missions	4
Pastoral Centers	2
Closed Parishes	13
Professional Ministry Personnel:	
Brothers	4
Sisters	34
Lay Ministers	107
Welfare	
Catholic Hospitals	2
Total Assisted	837,923
Health Care Centers	10
Total Assisted	10,938
Homes for the Aged	5
Total Assisted	5,096
Residential Care of Children	2
Total Assisted	255
Day Care Centers	7
Total Assisted	3,211
Specialized Homes	2
Total Assisted	310
Special Centers for Social Services	16
Total Assisted	28,695
Residential Care of Disabled	2
Total Assisted	153
Other Institutions	9
Total Assisted	5,431
Educational	
Seminaries, Diocesan	1
Students from This Diocese	19
Students from Other Diocese	55
Diocesan Students in Other Seminaries	13
Total Seminarians	32
Colleges and Universities	2
Total Students	11,000
High Schools, Diocesan and Parish	9
Total Students	9,197
High Schools, Private	4
Total Students	3,270
Elementary Schools, Diocesan and Parish	50
Total Students	20,331
Elementary Schools, Private	2
Total Students	1,120
Non-residential Schools for the Disabled	2
Total Students	1,143
Catechesis/Religious Education:	
High School Students	3,647
Elementary Students	36,340
Total Students under Catholic Instruction	86,080
Teachers in the Diocese:	
Priests	32
Brothers	25
Sisters	66
Lay Teachers	4,086
Vital Statistics	
Receptions into the Church:	
Infant Baptism Totals	13,692
Minor Baptism Totals	871
Adult Baptism Totals	640
Received into Full Communion	785
First Communions	11,269
Confirmations	8,246
Marriages:	
Catholic	1,852
Interfaith	241
Total Marriages	2,093
Deaths	4,129
Total Catholic Population	703,950
Total Population	4,221,722

Former Archbishops—Most Revs. COLEMAN F. CARROLL, D.D., ord. June 15, 1930; appt. Titular Bishop of Pitanae and Auxiliary Bishop of Pittsburgh, Aug. 25, 1953; cons. Nov. 10, 1953; appt. first Bishop of Miami, Aug. 13, 1958; installed Oct. 7, 1958; appt. Archbishop of Miami, March 13, 1968; died July 26, 1977; EDWARD A. MCCARTHY, D.D., S.T.D., J.C.D., ord. May 29, 1943; appt. Coadjutor Archbishop of Miami "cum jure successionis," Sept. 17, 1976; appt. Archbishop of Miami, July 26, 1977; retired Nov. 3, 1994; died June 7, 2005.

Pastoral Center—9401 Biscayne Blvd., Miami Shores, 33138. Tel: 305-757-6241; Fax: 305-754-1897.

Vicars General—Most Revs. FELIPE DE JESUS ESTEVEZ, D.D., S.T.D., V.G.; JOHN G. NOONAN, D.D., V.G.; Rev. Msgr. WILLIAM J. HENNESSEY, S.T.L., M.S., V.G., P.A.

Chancellor—Rev. Msgr. MICHAEL A. SOUCKAR. Email: msouckar@theadom.org.

Moderator of the Curia—Rev. Msgr. WILLIAM J. HENNESSEY, S.T.L., M.S., V.G., P.A.

Secretary to the Archbishop—Rev. Msgr. MICHAEL A. SOUCKAR. Email: msouckar@theadom.org.

Metropolitan Tribunal— Address all Rogatory commissions and matrimonial matters to the Tribunal, *9401 Biscayne Blvd., Miami Shores, 33138.* Tel: 305-762-1161; Fax: 305-762-1178. Email: tribunal@theadom.org.

Judicial Vicar—Rev. Msgr. ANDREW L. ANDERSON.

Adjutant Judicial Vicar—Rev. Msgr. KENNETH K. SCHWANGER, J.C.D.

Judges—Rev. Msgrs. MICHAEL A. SOUCKAR; TOMAS M. MARIN, V.F.; Revs. JOSE BIAIN, O.F.M.; CHARNEL JEANTY, J.C.L.; FERNANDO HERIA, J.C.L.; ERNESTO MOLANO, J.C.L. (Retired); ALVARO PINZON, J.C.D.; MARK THOMAS REEVES, J.C.L.; EDWARD SANTANA, J.C.D.

Promoters of Justice—Rev. CARL T. MORRISON, J.C.L.; Rev. Msgr. KENNETH K. SCHWANGER, J.C.D., (non-matrimonial cases).

Defenders of the Bond—Revs. CARL T. MORRISON, J.C.L.; RONALD PUSAK, J.C.L. (Retired).

Notaries—Ms. GORETTI ANTHONY; Ms. KATIA ARRIAZA; Ms. MAITE LENOZ.

Assessors—DEE DUGGAN; ROBERTO AGUIRRE.

Advocates—Deacon ANTONIO MACEO; ROSARIO BERGOUIGNAN.

Counsel-Assistant to the Tribunal—Mr. J. PATRICK FITZGERALD, Esq.

Consultors—Most Revs. FELIPE DE JESUS ESTEVEZ, D.D., S.T.D., V.G.; JOHN G. NOONAN, D.D., V.G.; Rev. Msgrs. WILLIAM J. HENNESSEY, S.T.L., M.S., V.G., P.A.; VINCENT T. KELLY; PABLO A. NAVARRO;

MICHAEL A. SOUCKAR; JEAN PIERRE.

Deans and Deaneries—Very Revs. JEREMIAH SINGLETON, (Northeast Broward); GEORGE PUTHUSSERIL, V.F., (Northwest Broward); THOMAS O'DWYER, V.F., (South Broward); JOSE L. HERNANDO, V.F., (East Dade); Rev. Msgrs. SEAMUS DOYLE, V.F., (Northeast Dade); TOMAS M. MARIN, V.F., (Northwest Dade); Very Revs. JAMES FETSCHER, V.F., (South Dade); BERNARD G. KIRLIN, V.F., (West Dade); GERALD R. MORRIS, V.F., (Monroe).

Incardination Committee—Most Revs. JOHN CLEMENT FAVALORA, D.D., S.T.L.; FELIPE DE JESUS ESTEVEZ, D.D., S.T.D., V.G.; JOHN G. NOONAN, D.D., V.G.; Rev. Msgrs. WILLIAM J. HENNESSEY, S.T.L., M.S., V.G., P.A.; PABLO A. NAVARRO; VINCENT T. KELLY; MICHAEL A. SOUCKAR; Rev. JAMES MURPHY.

Presbyteral Council—Most Rev. JOHN CLEMENT FAVALORA, D.D., S.T.L.; Rev. Msgr. TERENCE HOGAN, S.L.D., Pres.; Rev. MICHAEL HOYER, Sec.

Priests' Personnel Board—Rev. Msgr. PABLO A. NAVARRO, Chm.; Most Revs. FELIPE DE JESUS ESTEVEZ, D.D., S.T.D., V.G.; JOHN G. NOONAN, D.D., V.G.; Rev. Msgrs. WILLIAM J. HENNESSEY, S.T.L., M.S., V.G., P.A.; MICHAEL A. SOUCKAR; Very Rev. GEORGE PUTHUSSERIL, V.F.; Rev. Msgr. JEAN PIERRE; Rev. ENRIQUE J. ESTRADA.

Ministry of General Services

Executive Director—Rev. Msgr. WILLIAM J. HENNESSEY, S.T.L., M.S., V.G., P.A. Tel: 305-762-1222.

Catholic Legal Services, Archdiocese of Miami, Inc.—RANDOLPH P. MCGRORTY, CEO; MYRIAM MEZADIEU, Chief Admin., Main Office: 150 S.E. Second Ave., Ste. 200, Miami, 33131. Tel: 305-373-1073; Fax: 305-373-1173. Web: cclsmiami.org; Miami Springs Office: 700 S. Royal Poinciana Blvd., Ste. 800, Miami Springs, 33166. Tel: 305-887-8333; Fax: 305-883-4498. Broward Office: 1061 W. Oakland Park Blvd., Ste. 101-106, Fort Lauderdale, 33311. Tel: 800-691-7530; Fax: 888-691-5203.

Chancellor's Office—Rev. Msgr. MICHAEL A. SOUCKAR, Chancellor. Tel: 305-762-1220.

Coordinator of Special Projects—Rev. PATRICK O'NEILL.

Legal Services—Mr. PATRICK FITZGERALD, 110 Merrick Way, Ste. 3-B, Coral Gables, 33134. Tel: 305-443-9162; Fax: 305-443-6613.

Archdiocesan Safe Environment Program—MARY ROSS AGOSTA, Coord. Tel: 305-762-1043; Deacon RICHARD A. TURCOTTE, Victim Asst. Coord. Tel: 866-802-2873.

Communications Department—MARY ROSS AGOSTA, Dir.; TERESA MARTINEZ, Media Coord. & Digital Specialist; SARA MONTES, Admin. Asst.

Public and Media Relations—MARY ROSS AGOSTA, Dir.

Community Information—MARY ROSS AGOSTA, Dir., Mailing Address (for Communications, Public and Media Relations and Community Information), 9401 Biscayne Blvd., Miami, 33138. Tel: 305-762-1043; 305-762-1045; Fax: 305-751-6227.

Newspapers—MARY ROSS AGOSTA, Dir., Mailing Address for Newspapers, 9401 Biscayne Blvd., Miami, 33138.

"The Florida Catholic"—ANA RODRIGUEZ-SOTO, Editor (English). Tel: 305-762-1131; Fax: 305-762-1132.

"La Voz Catolica" Digital—

Pax Catholic Communications—1779 N.W. 28th St., Miami, 33142. Rev. Msgr. PABLO NAVARRO, Pres. Tel: 305-253-3101. Web: www.paxcc.org.

Spirit Online Radio - English Language Internet Radio—Rev. Msgr. PABLO NAVARRO. Tel: 305-253-3101.

Radio Paz - WACC, 830 AM. Spanish Language Radio Ministry—Rev. Msgr. PABLO NAVARRO; ISAUL GONZALEZ, Station Mgr.; IVETTE ACOSTA, Admin. & Office Mgr., 1779 N.W. 28 St., North Miami, 33142. Tel: 305-638-9729; Fax: 305-636-3976; MARITE ALFONSO, Programming Dir.

Radio Ke Poze - WLQY, 1320 AM. Haitian Radio Ministry—Rev. Msgr. PABLO NAVARRO. Tel: 305-638-9729.

PaxNet/Radio Paz Satelital—1779 N.W. 28 St., Miami, 33142. Tel: 305-638-9729; Fax: 305-638-9944. Rev. Msgr. PABLO NAVARRO; Mr. GONZALO PENAGOS, Dir. Oper.

Catholic Office for Inter-Faith Activities and Catholic-Jewish Relations Commission—Rev. PATRICK H. O'NEILL, Exec. Dir., 9401 Biscayne Blvd., Miami Shores, 33138. Tel: 305-762-1254; Fax: 305-754-1897.

Christian Unity Commission—Rev. PATRICK H. O'NEILL, Ecumenical Officer, 9401 Biscayne Blvd., Miami Shores, 33138. Tel: 305-762-1254; Fax: 305-754-1897.

Ministry of Christian Formation

Vicar for Christian Formation—Rev. Msgr. VINCENT T. KELLY.

Executive Director of Christian Formation and Superintendent of Schools—Bro. RICHARD J. DEMARIA, C.F.C.

Department of Schools—Bro. ANGELO PALMIERI, F.M.S., Assoc. Supt. Secondary Schools; KRISTEN HUGHES, Assoc. Supt. Elementary Schools; JOSEPHINE KENNA, Asst. Supt. Elementary Schools.

Department of Religious Education—MARIA JOSE MITSOULIS, D.R.E.; ANYELY GARCIA, Administrative Asst.

Archdiocesan Resource Center—Tel: 305-762-1107.

Department of Lay Ministry and Adult Faith Formation—CHERYL J. ORWIG WHAPHAM, Dir.; Mr. ROGELIO ZELADA, Assoc. Dir.

Archdiocese of Miami Endowment Fund, Inc.—EMILIO ALONSO-MENDOZA, Pres. Tel: 305-762-1053. Email: eamendoza@theccf.org.

Ministry of Catholic Charities—

Catholic Charities of the Archdiocese of Miami, Inc.—Rev. Msgr. WILLIAM J. HENNESSEY, S.T.L., M.S., V.G., P.A., Pres.; Deacon RICHARD A. TURCOTTE, CEO; Rev. ROBERTO GARZA, Dir. Mission Effectiveness; LIZETH CAMARENA, CAO; Dr. JULIAN SERRANO, COO; JULES JONES, CFO, 1505 N.E. 26th St., Wilton Manors, 33305. Tel: 305-762-1330; Fax: 305-754-6649. Web: ccadm.org.

Social Advocacy—VACANT.

Catholic Campaign for Human Development—1505 N.E. 26th St., Wilton Manors, 33305. Tel: 305-754-2444; Fax: 305-754-6649.

Miami-Dade Region—

Elderly Services Congregate Meals—9900 N.E. 2nd Ave., Miami, 33138. Tel: 305-751-5203. Email: congregatemeals@ccadm.org.

Refugee Resettlement and Employment Services—700 S. Royal Poinciana, Ste. 800, Miami Springs, 33166 Email: refugee@ccadm.org.

Pierre Toussaint Haitian Center—9920 N.E. 2nd Ave., Miami, 33138. Tel: 305-759-3050; Fax: 305-754-7423. Email: pierretoussaint@ccadm.org.

Unaccompanied Refugee Minors Program—700 S. Royal Poinciana Bldg. #806, Miami, 33166. Tel: 305-883-3383. Email: urmp@ccadm.org.

Unaccompanied Minors—Mailing Address: P.O. Box 971580, Miami, 33157. Tel: 305-380-0141. Email: ump@ccadm.org.

Emergency Services—3620 N.W. First Ave., Miami, 33127. Tel: 305-573-3333; Fax: 305-576-5111.

Family and Individual Counseling—7707 N.W. 2nd Ave., Miami, 33150. Tel: 866-758-0025.

New Life Family Center—Tel: 305-573-3333; Fax: 305-576-5111. Email: newlifeadm@ccadm.org.

Substance Abuse—

St. Luke's Prevention—7707 N.W. 2nd Ave., Miami, 33150. Tel: 305-795-0077; Fax: 305-795-0030.

Monroe Region—RICHARD MCGILL. Tel: 305-292-9790; Fax: 305-292-5257. Email: stbedes@ccadm.org.

Theresa House—1621 Spaulding Ct., Key West, 33040. Tel: 305-292-9790.

Homeless Drop-In Center—2700 Flagler Ave., Key West, 33040. Tel: 305-292-9790.

St. Bede Permanent Housing—2700 Flagler Ave., Key West, 33040. Tel: 305-292-9790.

Child Care—

Centro Hispano Catolico Child Care Center—125 N.W. 25th St., Miami, 33127. Tel: 305-573-9093; Fax: 305-576-6446. Email: centrohispano@ccadm.org.

Good Shepherd Child Care Center—18601 S.W. 97th Ave., Perrine, 33157. Tel: 305-235-1756; Fax: 305-255-2788. Email: goodshepherd@ccadm.org.

Notre Dame Child Care Center—130 N.E. 62nd St., Miami, 33138. Tel: 305-751-6778; Fax: 305-751-6959. Email: notredame@ccadm.org.

Sagrada Familia Child Care Center—970 S.W. 1st St., Miami, 33130. Tel: 305-324-5424; Fax: 305-325-0642. Email: sagradafam@ccadm.org.

South Dade Child Care Center—28520 S.W. 148th Ave., Leisure City, 33033. Tel: 305-245-0979; Fax: 305-242-8796. Email: southdade@ccadm.org.

Broward Region—

Counseling—1503 N.E. 26th St., Wilton Manors, 33305. Tel: 866-758-0025.

Providence Place—1079 S.E. 22nd Ave., Pompano Beach, 33062. Tel: 954-568-6610. Email: providenceplace@ccadm.org.

Adult Day Care Programs—

Central West—6915 Stirling Rd., Davie, 33314. Tel: 954-583-6446. Email: centralwest@ccadm.org.

Centro Oeste—6915 Stirling Rd., Davie, 33314. Tel: 954-581-9719. Email: centrooeste@ccadm.org.

St. Elizabeth—801 N.E. 33rd St., Pompano Beach, 33064. Tel: 954-781-0461. Email: stelizabeth@ccadm.org.

Wilton Manors—1503 N.E. 26th St., Wilton Manors, 33305. Tel: 954-630-9501; Fax: 954-566-6026. Email: browardelderly@ccadm.org.

Ministry of Catholic Health Services

Catholic Health Services, Inc.—Mr. JOSEPH M. CATANIA, Pres. & CEO; JAMES A. BALL, C.O.O., 4790 N. State Rd. 7, Lauderdale Lakes, 33319. Tel: 954-484-1515.

Catholic Housing for the Elderly and Handicapped, Inc.—

Catholic Housing Management—TERE SPRING, Vice Pres. Elderly Housing Svcs., 11410 N. Kendall Dr., Ste. 201, Miami, 33176. Tel: 305-757-2824.

Archbishop Carroll Manor—MARIO YANES, Mgr., 3667 S. Miami Ave., Miami, 33133. Tel: 305-854-8953.

Archbishop Hurley Hall—MARIA AMARO, Mgr., 632 N.W. 1st St., Hallandale, 33009. Tel: 954-454-0855.

Marian Towers—ADA G. HERNANDEZ, Mgr., 17505 N. Bay Rd., Miami Beach, 33160. Tel: 305-932-1300.

Archbishop McCarthy Residence—ROSLYN WILLIAMS, Mgr., 13201 N.W. 28th Ave., Opa Locka, 33054. Tel: 305-688-2700.

Palmer House—MERCEDES PUJALS, Mgr., 1225 S.W. 107th Ave., Miami, 33174. Tel: 305-221-9566.

St. Andrew Towers—CAROL NICHOLS, Mgr., 2700 N.W. 99th Ave., Coral Springs, 33065. Tel: 954-752-3960.

St. Dominic Gardens—MARIO YANES, Mgr., 5849 N.W. 7th St., Miami, 33126. Tel: 305-262-0962.

St. Elizabeth Gardens—JOHN CAMERON, Mgr., 801 N.E. 33rd St., Pompano Beach, 33064. Tel: 954-941-4597.

St. Joseph Towers—DEBRA HAMELRATH, Mgr., 3475 N.W. 30th St., Lauderdale Lakes, 33311. Tel: 954-485-5150.

St. Mary Towers—ARIESKY VAZQUEZ, Mgr., 7615 N.W. 2nd Ave., Miami, 33150. Tel: 305-757-3190.

Stella Maris House—SELMA CUNNINGHAM, Mgr., 8638 Harding Ave., Miami Beach, 33141. Tel: 305-865-6841.

St. Anne's Gardens—MERCEDES PUJALS, Mgr., 11800 Quail Roost Dr., Miami, 33177. Tel: 305-234-1994.

St. Boniface Gardens—8200 Johnson St., Pembroke Pines, 33024. Tel: 305-433-3899. ALEJA PAGAN, Mgr.

St. Vincent de Paul Gardens—BLANCA AIBELO, 10160 N.W. 19th Ave., Miami, 33147. Tel: 305-757-2824.

St. Mary Star of the Sea Affordable Housing—c/o 4790 N. State Rd. 7, Lauderdale Lakes, 33319. Tel: 954-484-1515.

St. Monica Gardens, Inc.—3425 N.W. 189th St., Miami Gardens, 33056. ISABEL SOTO NORIEGA, Mgr.

Nursing and Retirement Centers—

BROWARD:

St. Joseph Residence, Inc., RON BONAVITA, Admin., 3485 N.W. 30th St., Lauderdale Lakes, 33311. Tel: 954-739-1483. *St. John's Rehabilitation Hospital and Nursing Center, Inc.*, dba St. John's Nursing Center DIANE STONE, Exec. Dir., 3075 N.W. 35th Ave., Lauderdale Lakes, 33311. Tel: 954-739-6233. *St. John's Rehabilitation Hospital and Nursing Center, Inc.*, dba St. Anthony's Rehabilitation Hospital LINDA MOTTE, Admin., 3487 N.W. 30th St., Lauderdale Lakes, 33319. Tel: 954-739-6233. *Catholic Hospice of Broward, Inc., 4790 N. State Rd. 7, Lauderdale Lakes, 33319.* Tel: 954-484-1515. *Catholic Home Health Medicare Services, Inc., 4790 N. State Rd. 7, Lauderdale Lakes, 33319.* Tel: 954-484-1515. *Catholic Home Health Services, Inc., 4790 N. State Rd. 7, Lauderdale Lakes, 33319.* Tel: 954-484-1515. *Catholic Home Health Services of Broward, Inc.*, CAROL HYLTON, Admin., 3075 N.W. 35th Ave., Lauderdale Lakes, 33311. Tel: 954-486-3660.

DADE:

**St. Anne's Nursing Center, St. Anne's Residence, Inc.*, TONY FARINELLA, Exec. Dir., 11855 Quail Roost Dr., Miami, 33177. Tel: 305-252-4000. *Miami-Dade Nursing Center, Inc., c/o 4790 N. State Rd. 7, Lauderdale Lakes, 33319.* Tel: 954-484-1515. *Villa Maria Nursing and Rehabilitation Center, Inc.*, dba Villa Maria Nursing Center Mr. JAMES REISS, Exec. Dir., 1050 N.E. 125 St., North Miami, 33161. Tel: 305-891-8850. *Villa Maria Nursing and Rehabilitation Center, Inc.*, dba Villa Maria West Skilled Nursing Facility Mr. NATHANIEL JOHNSON, Admin., 8850 N.W. 122nd St., Hialeah Gardens, 33018. Tel: 305-351-7181. *Villa Maria Nursing and Rehabilitation Center, Inc.*, dba St. Catherine's Rehabilitation Hospital Mr. JAIME GONZALEZ, Admin., 1050 N.E. 125th St., North Miami, 33161. Tel: 305-357-1735. *Villa Maria Nursing and Rehabilitation Center, Inc.*, dba St. Catherine's West Rehabilitation Hospital Mr. JAIME GONZALEZ, Admin., 8850 N.W. 122nd St.,

Hialeah Gardens, 33018. Tel: 305-351-7181. *Villa Maria Health Care Services, Inc.*, dba Catholic Home Health Services of Miami Dade CAROL HYLTON, Admin., 1050 N.E. 125th St., North Miami, 33161. Tel: 305-899-0400. *Villa Maria Foundation, Inc., 1050 N.E. 125th St., North Miami, 33161.* Tel: 305-891-8850. *Special Education*, THOMAS HORAN, Ed.D., Exec. Dir., 15701 N.W. 37th Ave., Miami Gardens, 33054. Tel: 305-625-8354 (School); 305-200-8927 (Admin.); Fax: 305-200-8926. (Developmentally handicapped and mentally retarded) Marian Center School and Services, Inc. *Marian Center Charitable Trust, 15701 N.W. 37th Ave., Miami Gardens, 33054.* Tel: 305-200-8927.

Catholic Cemeteries of the Archdiocese of Miami, Inc.—PAUL JOHNSON, Vice Pres. Cemetery Svcs.; FERNANDO PIMENTEL, Exec. Dir., 11411 N.W. 25th St., Miami, 33172. Tel: 305-592-0521.

Archdiocesan Cemeteries—Our Lady of Mercy Cemetery, 11411 N.W. 25th St., Miami, 33172. Tel: 305-592-0521. *Our Lady Queen of Heaven Cemetery, 1500 S. State Rd. 7, North Lauderdale, 33068.* Tel: 954-972-1234.

Catholic Elderly Services, Inc.— dba Catholic Health Services Foundation *4790 N. State Rd. 7, Lauderdale Lakes, 33319.* Tel: 954-484-1515.

Centro Mater Child Care Services, Inc.—Mr. JOSEPH M. CATANIA, Pres. & CEO; MIRIAM ROMAN, Exec. Dir., 4790 N. State Rd. 7, Lauderdale Lakes, 33319. Tel: 954-484-1515; Fax: 954-484-5416.

Centro Mater Child Care Center—418 S.W. 4th Ave., Miami, 33130. Tel: 305-545-0760; Fax: 305-324-6162.

Centro Mater Child Care Center II—421 S.W. 4th St., Miami, 33130. Tel: 305-545-0760; Fax: 305-324-6162.

Centro Mater West Child Care Center—8298 N.W. 103rd St., Hialeah Gardens, 33016. Tel: 305-357-4395; Fax: 305-357-4395.

Centro Mater West II Child Care Center—7700 N.W. 98th St., Hialeah Gardens, 33016. Tel: 305-827-4050.

Centro Mater Walker Park—800 W. 29th St., Hialeah, 33010. Tel: 305-881-1140.

Ministry of Pastoral Services

Ministry of Pastoral Services—Most Rev. FELIPE DE JESUS ESTEVEZ, D.D., S.T.D., V.G., Exec. Dir., 9401 Biscayne Blvd., Miami, 33138. Tel: 305-762-1091. Email: festevez@theadom.org.

Campus Ministry—Rev. HARRY LOUBRIEL, St. Thomas University, 16401 N.W. 37th Ave., Miami Gardens, 33054. Tel: 305-628-6525. Email: hloubriel@stu.edu.

Campus Minister—EBY KURIAN, Campus Ministry Asst., Archdiocese of Miami. Email: ekurian@stu.edu. Graduate Assistant - Migrant Workers: CLAUDIA HERRERA. Email: cherrera7@stu.edu.

Barry University—Rev. SCOTT O'BRIEN, O.P., D.Min., Chap. Tel: 305-899-3681. Email: sobrien@mail.barry.edu; Bro. FERNANDO SOROLLA-DELGADO, O.P., Campus Min. Email: fsorolla-delgado@mail.barry.edu; MICHELLE BROWN, Admin. Asst., 11300 N.E. 2nd Ave., Miami Shores, 33161. Tel: 305-899-3650. Email: mbrown@mail.barry.edu; Sr. MARY FLEISCHAKER, O.P., Liturgy & Music. Tel: 305-899-3650. Email: mfleischaker@mail.barry.edu; ALEX SCHLICH, Svc. Learning. Tel: 305-899-3650. Email: hschlich@mail.barry.edu.

FIU-University Park—Revs. ROLANDO G. GARCIA, Dir. Email: frgarcia@stagathaonline.org; ALEXANDER EKECHUKWU, C.S.Sp., Chap. Email: fralex@stagathaonline.org; BILL HARVELLE, Campus Min., St. Agatha Church, 1111 S.W. 107th Ave., Miami, 33174. Tel: 305-807-1375. Email: bibalive2000@yahoo.com.

St. Thomas University—Rev. HARRY LOUBRIEL, Dir. Campus Ministry. Tel: 305-628-6525. Email: hloubriel@stu.edu; ERIK ARELLANO, Graduate Asst., The Gathering Place. Tel: 305-628-6748. Email: earellano@stu.edu; MARIA THOMPSON, Administrative Asst., 16400 N.W. 32nd Ave., Miami, 33054. Tel: 305-628-6525. Email: msthompson@stu.edu.

University of Miami—Very Rev. BERNARD G. KIRLIN, V.F., University Chap. Email: kirlin@saintaugustinechurch.org; RIGOBERTO VEGA, Dir. & Campus Min., St. Augustine Church, 1400 Miller Rd., Coral Gables, 33146. Tel: 305-661-1648. Email: campus@saintaugustinechurch.org.

Miami Dade College-Kendall Campus—Rev. MICHAEL A. KISH, Chap., 7270 S.W. 120th St., Miami, 33156. Tel: 305-238-7562. Email: frkish@catholic.org; ELIZABETH DE ARAZOZA, Faculty Advisor. Tel: 305-237-2976. Email: edearazo@mdc.edu.

Miami Dade College-Wolfson Campus—Rev. EDUARDO ALVAREZ, S.J., Chap., Gesu Church, 118 N.E. 2nd St., Miami, 33132. Tel: 305-379-1424. Email: gesumiami@yahoo.com.

Miami Dade College - North Campus—Prof. JULIO BORGES, Faculty Advisor. Tel: 305-237-1236. Email: jborges@mdc.edu; ANA CAROLINA CORRALES, Faculty Advisor. Tel: 305-237-1239. Email: acorrale@mdc.edu.

Catholic Daughters of America—Court 634, Regent: IRIS BERNREUTER, St. Mary Star of the Sea Parish, 1010 Windsor Ln., Key West, 33040. Tel: 305-294-9233. Vice-Regent: JEAN MAUM. Local Chaplain: Rev. JOHN C. BAKER.

Family Life Ministry—Rev. EDUARDO JIMENEZ, Dir. & Coord. Hispanic Ministry. Tel: 305-762-1157; 305-762-1140. Web: www.miamicatholicfamily.org; JEAN VALDES-FAULI DUDA, Separated, Divorce & Bereavement Ministries. Tel: 305-762-1142; MIMI LEON, Ministry to Engaged & Married Couples. Tel: 305-762-1140; 305-762-1148.

Camino Al Matrimonio (Spanish)—Deacon JORGE GONZALEZ, Spiritual Dir., Mailing Address: P.O. Box 524160, Miami, 33152-4160. Tel: 305-226-4664.

Lay Apostolic Movements and Associations—

Agrupacion Catolica Universitaria (ACU)—Rev. AMANDO LLORENTE, S.J., Spiritual Dir., 720 N.E. 27th St., Miami, 33137. Tel: 305-573-1418; 305-576-2748. Web: acu-adsum.org; estovir.org.

St. Martin de Porres Assoc.—LEONA H. COOPER, Pres., Mailing Address: P.O. Box 330102, Miami, 33133. Tel: 305-443-9466; Fax: 305-461-8669.

Archdiocesan Council of Catholic Women—Rev. Msgr. ANDREW L. ANDERSON, Moderator, 9401 Biscayne Blvd., Miami Shores, 33138. Tel: 305-762-1158; Mrs. THERESA SPIRITO, Pres., Miami Archdiocesan Council of Catholic Women (MACCW). Email: tmsmaccw1941@aol.com. Spiritual Moderators: Revs. JOHN P. PELOSO, (Monroe District); ERIC D. ZEGEER, (Broward District); MICHAEL GREER, (South Dade District); WILLIAM ELBERT, (North Dade District).

Catholic Charismatic Services--Archdiocese of Miami—Revs. DANIEL DOYLE, S.M., Spiritual Dir. (English) & Archdiocesan Liaison, Charismatic Services: P.O. Box 816128, Hollywood, 33081-0128. Tel: 954-961-1856; Fax: 954-961-3662; JOHN FINK, Asst. Spiritual Dir. (English) & Archdiocesan Liaison. Spanish: Deacon RAFAEL DE LOS REYES, Spiritual Dir.; CONCEPCION GONZALEZ, Coord.; EDUARDO GONZALEZ, Coord., Centro Carismatico Catolico: 500 N.W. 22 Ave., Miami, 33125. Tel: 305-631-1007; Fax: 305-642-0006. Email: rcch@bellsouth.net.

Ministry to Cultural Groups (Non-Hispanic Ethnicities)—Rev. Msgr. JEAN PIERRE, Dir. Tel: 305-762-1236; Fax: 305-762-1348.

Nigerian Apostolate—Rev. ALEXANDER EKECHUKWU, C.S.Sp., Asst., St. Agatha, 1111 S.W. 107th Ave., Miami, 33174. Tel: 305-222-1500; Fax: 305-222-1505.

Brazilian and Portuguese Apostolate—Revs. VOLMAR SCARAVELLI, C.S., Dir., St. Vincent, 6350 N.W. 18th St., Margate, 33063-2320. Tel: 954-972-0434; Fax: 954-971-9411; GERMAN VARGAS, C.S., Assoc. Dir.; Sr. JUDITH CLEMENS, S.N.D., Pastoral Asst.

Chinese Apostolate—Deacon ALEX LAM, St. Louis Catholic Church, 7270 S.W. 120 St., Miami, 33156. Tel: 350-238-7562, Ext. 105; BERNADETTE CHIK. Tel: 954-704-1595.

Filipino Apostolate—Ms. JANET MACASERO, Asst., 6320 Plunkett St., Hollywood, 33023. Tel: 954-981-7843.

Haitians—Rev. Msgr. JEAN PIERRE, Apostolate Dir., Haitian Apostolate, 9401 Biscayne Blvd., Miami, 33138. Tel: 305-762-1236; Fax: 305-762-1348; Revs. REGINALD JEAN-MARY, 110 N.E. 62 St., Miami, 33138. Tel: 305-751-6289 Notre Dame D'Haiti Mission; JEAN JADOTTE, Notre Dame D'Haiti Mission. Tel: 305-751-6289.

Hungarians—Deacon MIKLOS A. BEREGSZASZI, St. Catherine of Siena Parish, 9200 S.W. 107th Ave., Miami, 33176. Tel: 305-274-6333; Fax: 305-274-6337.

Indians—Rev. ZACHARIAS THOTTUVELIL, Our Lady of Health (Syro-Malabar Church), 201 N. University Dr., Coral Springs, 33071. Tel: 954-227-6985.

Italian—Rev. CHRISTOPHER MARINO, St. Michael the Archangel, 2987 W. Flagler St., Miami, 33135. Tel: 305-649-1811.

Caribbean Apostolate—Dr. PRINCE SMITH, 755 N.W. 184th Dr., Miami Gardens, 33169. Tel: 305-653-8492.

Native Americans—Rev. Msgr. JEAN PIERRE, Dir. Tel: 305-762-1236.

Korean—Rev. JAE JIN CHO, 14344 S. Royal Cove Cir., Davie, 33325. Tel: 954-474-9091.

Polish - (Our Lady of Czestochowa Polish Mission)—Rev. KLEMENS DABROWSKI, S.Ch., Dir., 2400 N.E. 12th St., Pompano Beach, 33062. Tel: 954-946-6347; Fax: 954-946-0512.

Vietnamese—Rev. ISIDORE BAKY, Coord., St. Helen Church, 3033 N.W. 33rd Ave., Lauderdale Lakes, 33311. Tel: 954-714-9860; Fax: 954-739-9632.

Christian Family Movement— Spanish: Deacon JORGE PRIETO, Spiritual Dir., Casa Cana, 480 E. 8th St., Hialeah, 33010. Tel: 305-888-4819. Web: www.casacana.org.

Archicofradia Nuestra Senora de la Caridad (Spanish)—Rev. Msgr. OSCAR F. CASTANEDA, Rector. Email: padreoscar@ermitadelacaridad.org. Web: ermitadelacaridad.org; Most Rev. AGUSTIN A. ROMAN, D.D., Rector Emeritus (Retired), 3609 S. Miami Ave., Miami, 33133. Tel: 305-854-2404; Fax: 305-854-8022.

Ministry to the Deaf or Disabled—Mr. FRANK CASALE, Exec. Dir.; DENNIS ROHAN, Dir. Rel. Formation; NANCY VIDAURRE, Dir. Grants & Planning; MARY ROUKAS, Dir. Residences & Counselor; GLORIA NEIL, Dir. Devel.; LIZ DISNEY, Dir. Progs.; AUDREY BROWN, Dir. Human Resources, Schott Memorial Center, Inc., 6591 S. Flamingo Rd., Cooper City, 33330. Tel: 954-434-3306; Fax: 954-434-3307.

Comunidad de Vida Cristiana, Regina Mundi, South Florida Region—Rev. PEDRO A. SUAREZ, S.J., Spiritual Dir., Villa Javier, 12725 S.W. 6th St., Miami, 33184. Tel: 786-621-4609.

Cursillo Movement—

Cursillos de Cristiandad (Spanish)—Rev. SANTIAGO MATHEU, Spiritual Dir. Email: jmatheu41@aol.com; ALFREDO JACOMINO, Lay Coord., Casa Emaus, 16250 S.W. 112th Ave., Miami, 33157. Tel: 305-235-7160; 305-235-4215; Fax: 305-235-7392.

Cursillo (English)—Deacon ROBERT BINDER, Spiritual Dir., St. John Neumann. Tel: 305-255-6642. Email: margedun@bellsouth.net.

Emmaus Experience Parish Retreats—MYRNA GALLAGHER, Contact. Tel: 305-273-7650; JUDITH PASOS, Spanish Contact. Tel: 305-279-7759. Email: pasos_bravo@bellsouth.net.

Encuentros Familiares y Casa Manresa (Spanish)—Casa Manres, P.O. Box 651512, Miami, 33265. Tel: 305-596-0001; Fax: 305-596-9655. Email: manresamiami@yahoo.com. Web: www.efyc.com. Rev. FLORENTINO AZCOITIA, S.J., Dir.

Encuentros Juveniles (Spanish and English)—Sr. CLAUDIA ORTEGA, R.M.I., Spiritual Dir., Miami Youth Center, 3333 S. Miami Ave., Miami, 33133. Tel: 305-856-3404; Fax: 305-854-8888.

Impactos de Cristiandad (Spanish)—Deacon JOSE MANUEL GORDILLO, Spiritual Dir., Mailing Address: P.O. Box 440967, Miami, 33144. Tel: 305-571-7111; Fax: 305-222-8769. Email: impactos@impactos.org. Web: www.impactos.org.

Knights of Columbus (English and Spanish)—Rev. LUIS R. RIVERA, Archdiocesan Chap., Our Lady of Divine Providence, 10205 W. Flagler St., Miami, 33174. Tel: 305-551-8113. Web: www.floridastatecouncil.com; Mr. OSCAR LAY, Contact. Tel: 305-362-8612.

La Nueva Jerusalen Community - Comunidad de Alianza—WILLIAM F. BROWN JR., Regl. Coord. Email: wfbrownjr@gmail.com.

Legion of Mary— (English Speaking) Rev. RICHARD SOULLIERE, Spiritual Dir. (Retired). Lay Contacts: JUDITH PADRON (Spanish)Tel: 305-821-3673. Email: jtp1227@aol.com; MARGARET ANNIS (English)Tel: 305-895-0003. Email: mzannis@mac.com.

Marian Movements & Devotions—Rev. RICHARD SOULLIERE, Coord. (Retired), Mailing Address: P.O. Box 221937, Hollywood, 33022. Tel: 954-961-6740.

Apostleship of the Sea— (Serving Port Everglades, the Port of Miami, and Miami River) *Mailing Address: 4000 Island Blvd., Ste. 1902, Miami, 33160.* Tel: 786-514-4502. Rev. THOMAS W. FALKENTHAL, Archdiocesan Dir. Email: tfalkenthal@theadom.org; RAFAEL D. BAPTISTA, Asst. to Dir. Email: rbaptista@theadom.org.

Prison Ministry—Deacon EDGARDO FARIAS, Dir. Tel: 305-762-1093. Email: efarias@theadom.org. Associates: Deacons LORN A. GREEN; RAFAEL CRUZ. Tel: 305-762-1176.

Respect Life Ministry—Mrs. JOAN CROWN, Dir., 3600 S.W. 32nd Blvd., West Park, 33023. Tel: 954-981-2922; Fax: 954-981-2901. Email: ilovelife@bellsouth.net; Rev. JORDI RIVERO, Spiritual Dir.

Project Rachel—Tel: 877-908-1212.

Respect Life Branch Offices-Emergency Pregnancy Services—

North Dade Central Office, 3268 S. University Dr., Miramar, 33025. Tel: 305-653-2921.

North Broward Office, 5115 Coconut Creek Pkwy., Margate, 33063. Tel: 954-977-7769.

Hollywood Office (S. Broward), 5600 Hollywood Blvd., Hollywood, 33021. Tel: 954-963-2229.

Ft. Lauderdale Office, 2909 N. Andrews Ave.,

Wilton Manors, 33311. Tel: 954-565-8506.
South Miami Office, 9360 S.W. 72nd St., Ste. 238, Miami, 33173. Tel: 305-273-8507.

Rural Life Ministry—Rev. Msgr. PEDRO GARCIA, Dir.
Chapels—Everglades Villages, 19200 S.W. 380th St., Florida City, 33030. South Dade Ctr., 31248 S.W. 134th Ave., Homestead, 33033. Redlands Camp, 29200 S.W. 158th Ave., Homestead, 33033.

St. Ann Mission—
Naranja and Migrant Ministry—13875 SW 264th St., Naranja, 33032. Mailing Address: P.O. Box 924884, Princeton, 33092. Tel: 305-258-3968; 305-258-9682; Fax: 305-258-3591.

Youth and Young Adult Ministry—Most Rev. FELIPE J. ESTEVEZ, Pastoral Center, 9401 Biscayne Blvd., Miami Shores, 33138. Tel: 305-762-1101.
Scouting—HILDA MENDEZ, Coord. Tel: 305-762-1245. Email: hmendez@theadom.org; Deacon THOMAS FRANKLIN, Chap., 9401 Biscayne Blvd., Miami, 33138.

The St. Vincent De Paul Society, Archdiocesan Council of Miami, Inc.—Mailing Address: P.O. Box 431232, Miami, 33243. Tel: 305-378-1799; 305-474-9010. VICTOR MARTELL, Pres. & Trustee.

Ministry of Temporalities

Finance Office—MICHAEL A. CASCIATO, CPA, CFO; Mr. JOSEPH M. CATANIA, Treas.
Finance Council—MICHAEL A. CASCIATO, CPA, CFO. Members: Most Rev. JOHN CLEMENT FAVALORA, D.D., S.T.L.; Mr. THOMAS BEIER, Chm.; Most Revs. FELIPE DE JESUS ESTEVEZ, D.D., S.T.D., V.G.; JOHN G. NOONAN, D.D., V.G.; Rev. Msgrs. WILLIAM J. HENNESSEY, S.T.L., M.S., V.G., P.A.; NOEL FOGARTY, P.A., V.F.; MICHAEL A. SOUCKAR; TOMAS MARIN, J.C.L.; JUDE O'DOHERTY; Revs. GABRIEL O'REILLY; PAUL VUTURO; Mr. ALBERT DEL CASTILLO; Mr. PEDRO GARCIA; Mr. SEAN CLANCY; Mr. THOMAS CORNISH; Mr. THOMAS G. BENSON; Mrs. CHRISTINA BROCHIN.
Building Commission and Property Office—ERIC M. WEINER, Dir.; Mr. JAMES DETRICK, Asst. Dir.
Legal Council—Mr. J. PATRICK FITZGERALD, Esq.
Plant Operations—ERIC M. WEINER, Dir.
Archdiocese of Miami Health Plan Trust—Rev. Msgr. TOMAS M. MARIN, V.F., Chm.; Ms. SUSAN WADDELL, Acting Admin.
Pension—Most Rev. JOHN CLEMENT FAVALORA, D.D., S.T.L.; Rev. Msgrs. JUDE O'DOHERTY, Chm.; TOMAS M. MARIN, V.F., Vice Chm.

Ministry of Worship and Spiritual Life

Executive Director—Rev. Msgr. TERENCE HOGAN, S.L.D.; D. RYAN SAUNDERS, Asst. Dir.; Sr. CARMEN ORS, S.P.H.J.M., Admin. Asst.
Worship & Spiritual Life Commission—Rev. MICHAEL GREER, Chm.
Celebration and Rite Committee—Rev. Msgr. TERENCE HOGAN, S.L.D., Chm.
Spiritual Life Committee—SUSAN LORETTA.
Sacred Art & Architecture—Rev. PAUL V. VUTURO.
Liturgical Music—SUZANNE ARSENAULT.
Committee on Popular Piety—Rev. JUAN J. SOSA.

Ministry of Persons

Ministry of Persons—Most Rev. JOHN G. NOONAN, D.D., V.G., Exec. Dir.
Vocations—Rev. ROBERTO GARZA, Dir., 9401 Biscayne Blvd., Miami, 33138. Tel: 305-762-1137; ILEANA ROQUE, Sec. Tel: 305-762-1152.
Archdiocesan Vocations Review Board—Most Rev. JOHN G. NOONAN, D.D., V.G.; Very Rev. THOMAS O'DWYER, V.F.; Revs. JUAN CARLOS PAGUAGA; JUAN J. SOSA; Rev. Msgrs. KENNETH K. SCHWANGER, J.C.D.; JEAN PIERRE; Deacon EDUARDO BLANCO; Sisters CARMEN ORS, S.P.H.J.M.; YAMILE SAIEH, F.M.A.
Office for Religious—Most Rev. JOHN G. NOONAN, D.D., V.G. Tel: 305-762-1197.
Priestly Life and Ministry—Most Rev. JOHN G. NOONAN, D.D., V.G., Dir. Tel: 305-762-1197.
Permanent Diaconate—Most Rev. JOHN CLEMENT FAVALORA, D.D., S.T.L.; Rev. Msgr. KENNETH K. SCHWANGER, J.C.D., Chm. Advisory Board; Deacons VICTOR M. PIMENTEL, Exec. Dir.; LOUIS PHANG SANG, Asst. Dir.
Continuing Education for the Clergy—Most Rev. JOHN G. NOONAN, D.D., V.G., Dir. Tel: 305-762-1197.
Priests' Sabbaticals—Most Rev. JOHN G. NOONAN, D.D., V.G., Chm.
Retired Priests' Committee—Most Rev. JOHN G. NOONAN, D.D., V.G., Dir.; Rev. JOHN McLAUGHLIN (Retired); Rev. Msgr. XAVIER MORRAS (Retired); Mr. PATRICK FITZGERALD, (Legal).
Ministry to Professional Groups—
Catholic Educators' Guild—Rev. CHRISTOPHER MARINO, Chap.
Catholic Funeral Directors' Guild—Rev. Msgr. ANDREW L. ANDERSON, Chap.
Catholic Lawyers' Guild—Rev. Msgr. ANDREW L. ANDERSON, Chap.
Catholic Physicians' and Dentists' Guild—Rev. Msgr. TOMAS M. MARIN, V.F., Chap., Dade & Broward.
Catholic Law Enforcement Ministry—Rev. DANIEL DOYLE, S.M., Voluntary Chap., Hollywood Police Dept. Police Chaplains: Revs. MANUEL A. SOLER, (Miami Beach & Key Biscayne Police); MICHAEL A. KISH, (City of Miami Police); VACANT, (Florida Highway Patrol, Troop K).
Catholic Fire Service Ministry—Rev. Msgr. TOMAS M. MARIN, V.F., Chap., Miami-Dade Fire Rescue; Revs. MICHAEL LYNCH, Fire Chap., City of Coral Gables; JAMES A. QUINN, Chap. Miami Office of the Federal Bureau of Investigations & Hallandale Beach Police Dept.

Special Apostolates

Amor en Accion (Love in Action)—Mailing Address: P.O. Box 141523, Coral Gables, 33114. Tel: 305-762-1226. ALICIA MARRILL, Pres.; TERESITA GONZALEZ, Dir. & Contact.
Archbishop Hurley Scholarship Fund—Rev. Msgr. VINCENT T. KELLY, Vicar, Christian Formation, 9401 Biscayne Blvd., Miami, 33138. Tel: 305-762-1076.
Downtown Senior Citizens' Community Center at Gesu Church—Sisters MARIA ISABEL RINCON, O.P.; CECILIA ALONSO, O.P.; JULIA BARRETO, O.P., 118 N.E. 2nd St., Miami, 33132. Tel: 305-374-6099.
Pontifical Mission Societies—Rev. Msgr. JEAN PIERRE, Dir.
Society for the Propagation of the Faith—
Holy Childhood Association—
The Society of St. Peter Apostle—
Missionary Union of Priests and Religious—
Priests Purgatorial Society—
Serra Club—
Miami—SALLYE JUDE, Pres., 200 Edgewater Dr., Coral Gables, 33133. Tel: 305-325-0045; 305-667-3233.
Broward—Mr. THOMAS J. METZGER SR., Vice Pres., 2811 N.E. 53rd Ct., Lighthouse Point, 33064. Tel: 954-803-1001.
Chaplain--Dade County - Serra Club—Rev. MANUEL FRANCISCO ALVAREZ.
Chaplain--Broward County - Serra Club—Rev. ANTHONY MULDERRY.

CLERGY, PARISHES, MISSIONS AND PAROCHIAL SCHOOLS

CITY OF MIAMI

(DADE COUNTY)

1—ST. MARY'S CATHEDRAL (1930) Rev. Msgr. Terence Hogan, Rector; Rev. Esteker Elyse, S.M.M. (Haiti). In Res., Revs. Alvaro Pinzon (Colombia); James A. Suchocki (GAY) (Retired); Roberto Garza; Deacon Ian Taylor.
Res.: 7525 N.W. Second Ave., Miami, 33150. Tel: 305-759-4531; 305-759-4532; Fax: 305-757-7456. Web: www.cathedralofsaintmary.com.
School—7485 N.W. Second Ave., Miami, 33150. Tel: 305-795-2000; Fax: 305-795-2013. Sr. Jane Stoecker, S.S.J., Prin. Sisters of St. Joseph of St. Augustine 1; Servants of the Pierced Heart of Jesus & Mary 5; Lay Teachers 14; Students 321.
Catechesis/Religious Program—Tel: 305-795-2016; Fax: 305-757-6870. Students 430.
St. Mary's Cathedral Foundation Trust—9401 Biscayne Blvd., 33138. Mike Casciato, Contact Person.

2—ST. AGATHA (1971) Revs. Rolando G. Garcia; Raul S. Soutuyo; Alexander Ekechukwu, C.S.Sp.; Deacon Angel Pintado.
Res.: 1111 S.W. 107th Ave., Miami, 33174. Tel: 305-222-1500; Fax: 305-222-1505. Email: rectory@stagathaonline.org. Web: www.stagathaonline.org.
School—1125 S.W. 107th Ave., Miami, 33174. Tel: 305-222-8751; Fax: 305-222-1517. Email: office@stagathaonline.com. Mrs. Maria P. Glass, Prin.; Patricia Hernandez, Asst. Prin. Lay Teachers 30; Students 521.
Catechesis/Religious Program—Tel: 305-222-8067; Fax: 305-222-8078. Email: reledu@stagathaonline.org. Sisters Martha Maria Gomez-Chow, S.C.T.J.M., D.R.E.; Laura Garcia, S.C.T.J.M., Asst. D.R.E. Students 436.

3—ST. BRENDAN (1954) Revs. Fernando Heria; Andrzej Pietraszko; Flavio Montes-Colon; Isidro Perez (Cuba); Sergio Cabrera (Retired); Francisco Calderon, O.P.; Deacons Billy Lannon Jr.; Edward Blanco; Rafael Calvo-Forte.
Res.: 8725 S.W. 32nd St., Miami, 33165. Tel: 305-221-0881; Fax: 305-226-6249.
School—8755 S.W. 32 St., Miami, 33165. Tel: 305-221-2722; Fax: 305-554-6726. Elizabeth Furmanick, Prin. Lay Teachers 51; Students 638.
Catechesis/Religious Program—Tel: 305-226-2628; 305-221-2861. Students 316.

4—ST. CATHERINE OF SIENA (1968) Revs. Juan J. Sosa; Damian Flanagan; Deacons Miklos A. Beregszaszi; Vicente Moreno.
Res.: 9200 S.W. 107th Ave., Miami, 33176. Tel: 305-274-6333; Fax: 305-274-6337. Web: www.saintcatherineofsiena.us.
Catechesis/Religious Program—Tel: 305-274-6333, Ext. 26. Lydia Mayorga, D.R.E. Students 317.

5—CHRIST THE KING (1961) Rev. William Mason, O.M.I.; Deacon George Gibson. In Res., Revs. Lucien Bouchard, O.M.I.; Antonyra Arumainathan, O.M.I. (India).
Res.: 16000 S.W. 112th Ave., Miami, 33157. Tel: 305-238-2485; Fax: 305-254-0330.
Catechesis/Religious Program—Tel: 305-235-0293. Students 124.

6—CORPUS CHRISTI (1941) Revs. Jose L. Menendez; Manuel A. Soler; Deacon Luis Benavides, Pastoral Assoc.
Res.: 3220 N.W. 7th Ave., Miami, 33127. Tel: 305-635-1331; Fax: 305-635-2031.
Catechesis/Religious Program—Sr. Carmen Alvarez, R.M.I. Tel: 305-633-5824. Students 511.
Mission—San Francisco y Santa Clara 402 N.E. 29th St., Miami, 33137.
Mission—San Juan Bautista 3116 N.W. 2nd Ave., Miami, 33127.
Mission—Nuestra Senora de Altagracia 1779 N.W. 28th St., Miami, 33142.
Mission—La Milagrosa 1860 N.W. 18th Ter., Miami, 33125.

7—ST. DOMINIC (1962) Revs. Alberto Rodriguez, O.P.; Restituto Perez, O.P.; Desiderio Eguino, O.P. In Res., Revs. Mark Wedig, O.P.; Scott O'Brien, O.P.; Jorge L. Presmanes, O.P.; Eduardo Gabriel, O.P.; Bro. Fernando Sorolla-Delgado, O.P.
Res.: 5909 N.W. 7th St., Miami, 33126. Tel: 305-264-0181; Fax: 305-262-4685.
Catechesis/Religious Program—Tel: 305-264-3372. Students 204.

8—EPIPHANY (1951) Rev. Msgr. Jude O'Doherty; Rev. Rolando Cabrera (Cuba); Deacons Jose Carrion; Donald Livingstone; Paul H. Munter; Norman Ruiz-Castaneda; Thomas V. Eagan.
Res.: 8081 S.W. 54 Ct., Miami, 33143. Tel: 305-667-4911; Fax: 305-667-8067.
School—5557 S.W. 84th St., Miami, 33143. Tel: 305-667-5251; Fax: 305-667-6828. Sr. Margaret Fagan, I.H.M., Prin. Sisters Servants of the Immaculate Heart of Mary 3; Lay Teachers 71; Students 952.
Catechesis/Religious Program—Tel: 305-665-0037. Students 261.
Church of the Epiphany Parish Endowment Trust—9401 Biscayne Blvd., 33138. Mike Casciato, Contact Person.

9—ST. FRANCIS XAVIER (1927) Merged with and sacramental records at Gesu Parish, Miami.

10—GESU (1896) Revs. Eduardo Alvarez, S.J.; Sergio Figueredo, S.J. In Res., Rev. Thomas A. Griffin, S.J.
Res.: 118 N.E. 2nd St., Miami, 33132. Tel: 305-379-1424; Fax: 305-372-9544. Email: gesumiami@yahoo.com. Web: www.gesumiami.org.
Catechesis/Religious Program—Tel: 305-374-6099. Students 70.

11—GOOD SHEPHERD (1977) Revs. Michael Greer; Jorge Rodriguez De La Vuda; Emmanuel Bastien; Deacons Jorge Prieto; Santos Rodriguez; Julio Zayas; Arthur Merkel. In Res., Rev. Sammy Alvero (Philippines).
Res. & Church: 14187 S.W. 72nd St., Miami, 33183. Tel: 305-385-4320; Fax: 305-386-2407. Email: info@gscatholic.org. Web: www.gscatholic.org.
School—(Grades PreK-8) Tel: 305-385-7002; Fax: 305-385-7026. Email: office@good-shepherd-school.org. Web: www.good-shepherd-school.org. Mrs. Susana Del Riego, Prin.; Eileen Beregszaszi, Librarian. Lay Teachers 18; Students 222.
Catechesis/Religious Program—Tel: 305-385-4320, Ext. 202. Mr. Juan Pablo Pages, D.R.E. Students 679.

12—HOLY REDEEMER (1950), (African American), Rev. John T. Cox, O.M.I. In Res., Rev. Fidelis Nwankwo, C.S.Sp.
Church: 1301 N.W. 71st St., Miami, 33147. Tel: 305-691-1701; Fax: 305-691-7074. Email: hredeemr@bellsouth.net.
Catechesis/Religious Program—Students 38.

13—ST. JAMES (1952) Rev. Msgrs. Jean Pierre; Augustin Almy (Haiti); Rev. Sterling Laurent (Haiti), Parochial Vicar. In Res., Rev. Martin K. Adu.
Res.: 540 N.W. 132nd St., Miami, 33168. Tel: 305-681-7428; Fax: 305-685-0631.
School—601 N.W. 131st St., North Miami, 33168. Tel: 305-681-3822; Fax: 305-681-6435. Religious 2; Lay Teachers 17; Students 355.

St. James Early Learning Center—565 N.W. 131st St., Miami, 33168. Tel: 305-403-0626. Mrs. Doreen Roberts, Dir. & Contact.
Catechesis/Religious Program—Tel: 305-681-2676. Students 135.

14—ST. JOACHIM (1972) Revs. Jesus J. Arias; Alejandro Flores (Nicaragua). In Res., Rev. Paul Suffrin (Haiti).
Rectory—11740 S.W. 192nd St., Miami, 33177. Tel: 305-233-1278; Fax: 305-233-2573.
Church: 19150 S.W. 117th Ave., Miami, 33177.
Catechesis/Religious Program—Students 473.

15—ST. JOHN BOSCO (1962) Revs. Juan Carlos Paguaga; Robert M. Ayala; Deacon Diego Chavez.
Res. & Rectory: 1358 N.W. First St., Miami, 33125. Tel: 305-649-5464; 305-649-5465; Fax: 305-541-0988. Email: stjohnboscochurch@sjbmiami.org.
Catechesis/Religious Program—Elisa P. de Gomez, D.R.E. Students 490.

16—ST. JOHN NEUMANN (1980) Rev. Msgr. Pablo A. Navarro; Revs. Craig S. Malzacher, Parochial Vicar; Juan R. Rumin-Dominguez, O.F.M., Parochial Vicar; Deacons Thomas Aguilu; Robert Binder; Ralph Gazitua; Louis Phang Sang.
Res.: 12125 S.W. 107th Ave., Miami, 33176. Tel: 305-255-6642; Fax: 305-233-3742. Email: rejoiceinthelordsjn@yahoo.com. Web: www.sjn-miami.org.
School—12115 S.W. 107th Ave., Miami, 33176. Tel: 305-255-7315; 786-242-1514; Fax: 305-255-7316. Mrs. Maria Elena Vilas, Prin. Lay Teachers 25; Aides 9; Students 347.
Catechesis/Religious Program—Tel: 305-253-3081. John Fernandez, D.R.E. Students 829.

17—ST. KEVIN (1963) Revs. Jesus Saldana; Jorge Perales; Jorge Luis Bello; Deacons Robert B. Dinsmore; Michael Fresneda; Esteban Ortiz.
Res.: 12525 S.W. 42nd St., Miami, 33175. Tel: 305-223-0633; Fax: 305-554-9950. Email: stkev@bellsouth.net.
School—4001 S.W. 127 Ave., Miami, 33175. Tel: 305-227-7571; Fax: 305-227-7574. Web: www.stk-s.org. Email: kevsch@miamiarch.org. Dr. Mayra R. Constantino, Prin.; Dr. Sharyn D. Henderson, Asst. Prin. Lay Teachers 42; Students 685.
Catechesis/Religious Program—Tel: 305-223-2469. Mrs. Amparo Martinez, D.R.E. Students 583.

18—ST. KIERAN (1967) Rev. Marcos A. Somarriba.
Res.: 3605 S. Miami Ave., Miami, 33133. Tel: 305-854-1521. Email: stkieranchurch@aol.com.
Catechesis/Religious Program—Tel: 305-854-7166. Students 71.

19—ST. LOUIS (1963) Revs. James F. Fetscher; Michael A. Kish; David A. Zirilli, Parochial Vicar; Deacons John Green; Thomas Hanlon; Alex Lam; Vincent McInerney; John Peremenis; Jeffrey J. Reyes; Robert Yglesias.
Res.: 7270 S.W. 120th St., Pinecrest, 33156. Tel: 305-238-7562; Fax: 305-238-6844.
School—Tel: 305-238-7562, Ext. 200; Fax: 305-238-4296. Christine Mathisen, Prin. Lay Teachers 33; Students 465.
Catechesis/Religious Program—Tel: 305-238-7562. Maria Teresa Lopez, D.R.E. Students 812.

20—ST. MICHAEL THE ARCHANGEL (1947) Revs. Christopher Marino; Richard J. Vigoa, Parochial Vicar; Deacon Ernesto Rodriguez.
Res.: 2987 W. Flagler St., Miami, 33135. Tel: 305-649-1811; Fax: 305-642-6815. Web: www.stmichaelmiami.org.
School—300 N.W. 28th Ave., Miami, 33125. Tel: 305-642-6732; Fax: 305-649-5867. Web: stmichaelmiami.com. Carmen Alfonso, Prin. Sisters 1; Lay Teachers 35; Students 376.
Catechesis/Religious Program—Tel: 305-643-4661; Fax: 305-642-8574. Yolanda Del Rivero, D.R.E. Students 181.

21—MOTHER OF CHRIST (1983) Revs. Raul Angulo; Julio R. Solano; Deacons Jose Leroy Martinez; Manuel Saavedra; Lazaro Ulloa; Jose F. Rosado.
Rectory—2390 S.W. 139th Pl., Miami, 33175. Tel: 305-551-7046.
Church: 14141 S.W. 26th St., Miami, 33175. Tel: 305-559-6111; Fax: 305-551-7047.
School—(Grades PreK-8) Tel: 786-497-6111; Fax: 786-497-6113. Web: www.motherofchristcatholicschool.net. Sisters 1; Lay Teachers 17; Students 318.
Catechesis/Religious Program—Tel: 305-559-0163. Students 715.

22—MOTHER OF OUR REDEEMER (1988) Rev. Jaime H. Acevedo.
Church: 8445 N.W. 186th St., Miami, 33015. Tel: 305-829-6141; Fax: 305-829-3059. Email: info@motherofourredeemer.org.
School—Tel: 306-829-3088. Mrs. Evelyn Salinas, Prin. Lay Teachers 13; Students 201.
Catechesis/Religious Program—Tel: 305-829-3988; Fax: 305-829-3019. Students 500.

23—NOTRE DAME D'HAITI (1981) Revs. Reginald Jean-Mary; Jean Jadotte, Parochial Vicar.
Mailing Address: 110 N.E. 62nd St., Miami, 33138. Tel: 305-751-6289.
Catechesis/Religious Program—Tel: 305-758-5560; Fax: 305-895-1851; 305-751-6234. Rosel Lebreton, D.R.E. Students 232.

24—OUR LADY OF DIVINE PROVIDENCE (1973) Revs. Luis R. Rivera; Fermin Solana (Cuba); Deacon Eduardo Panellas.
Church & Mailing Address: 10205 W. Flagler St., Miami, 33174. Tel: 305-551-8113; 305-551-8114; Fax: 305-220-3164. Web: www.oldpcatholicchurch.com.
Res.: 10420 S.W. 4th St., Miami, 33174. Tel: 305-226-5058.
Catechesis/Religious Program—Tel: 305-551-8113, Ext. 18. Students 160.

25—OUR LADY OF GUADALUPE (2001) Rev. Msgr. Tomas M. Marin.
Mailing Address: 3900 N.W. 79th Ave., Ste. 731, Doral, 33166. Tel: 305-593-6123; Fax: 305-593-6130.
Catechesis/Religious Program—Students 420.

26—OUR LADY OF LOURDES (1985) Rev. Msgr. Kenneth K. Schwanger; Revs. Alejandro J. Rodriguez, Parochial Vicar; Luis Roger Largaespada; Deacon Michael Plummer. In Res., Rev. Matthew Ibok (Nigeria).
Res.: 10452 S.W. 134th Pl., Miami, 33186. Tel: 305-380-7673.
Church: 11291 S.W. 142nd Ave., Miami, 33186. Tel: 305-386-4121; Fax: 305-386-6881. Web: www.ololourdes.org.
School—Tel: 305-386-8446; Fax: 305-386-6694. Web: www.ololjaguars.org. Thomas Halfaker, Prin.; Laura G. Sanchez, Asst. Prin. Lay Teachers 28; Students 637.
Catechesis/Religious Program—Tel: 305-386-4894; Fax: 305-386-6670. Students 643.

27—OUR LADY OF THE HOLY ROSARY (1959) Revs. Luis A. Perez; Lucien E. Pierre.
Res.: 9500 S.W. 184th St., Cutler Bay, 33157. Tel: 305-235-5135; Fax: 305-254-9045. Email: info@holyrosarymiami.org. Web: www.holyrosarymiami.org.
School—18455 Franjo Rd., Cutler Bay, 33157. Tel: 305-235-5442; Fax: 305-235-5670. Dr. Emma Ventura, Prin. Lay Teachers 26; Students 418.
Catechesis/Religious Program—Tel: 305-235-5442, Ext. 110. Students 246.

28—SS. PETER AND PAUL (1938) Revs. Juan M. Lopez; Juan Luis Sanchez.
Res.: 900 S.W. 26th Rd., Miami, 33129. Tel: 305-858-2621; Fax: 305-858-8073.
School—1435 S.W. 12th Ave., Miami, 33129. Tel: 305-858-3722; Fax: 305-856-4322. Lay Teachers 26; Students 512.
Catechesis/Religious Program—Students 192.

29—PRINCE OF PEACE (1987) Rev. Francisco G. Diaz; Deacon Manuel Castellanos.
Church & Res.: 12800 N.W. 6th St., Miami, 33182. Tel: 305-559-3171; Fax: 305-559-3172.
Catechesis/Religious Program—Vivian Lorenzo, D.R.E. Students 427.

30—ST. RAYMOND (1969) Revs. Omar A. Huesca (Retired); David Smith.
Res.: 3475 S.W. 17th St., Miami, 33145. Tel: 305-446-2427; Fax: 305-445-7448. Web: www.straymond.info.
Catechesis/Religious Program—Students 140.

31—ST. RICHARD (1969) Rev. Stephen J. Hilley. In Res., Revs. Charles Clements (Retired); Henrick Jose (India); Deacon Robert F. O'Malley Jr.
Res.: 7500 S.W. 152nd St., Village of Palmetto Bay, Miami, 33157-2434. Tel: 305-233-8711; Fax: 305-254-2756.
Catechesis/Religious Program—Tel: 305-233-8755. Students 360.

32—ST. ROBERT BELLARMINE (1968) Merged with and sacramental records at Corpus Christi Parish, Miami.

33—ST. THOMAS THE APOSTLE (1959) Revs. Daniel I. Kubala; Joaquin Rodriguez; Alvaro Huertas (Colombia); Deacon Carlos Pulido.
Res.: 7377 S.W. 64th St., Miami, 33143. Tel: 305-665-5600; Fax: 305-662-9034. Email: info@stamiami.org. Web: www.stamiami.org.
School—Tel: 305-661-8591; Fax: 305-661-2181. Email: school@stamiami.org. Lisa Figueredo, Prin. Lay Teachers 52; Students 640.
Catechesis/Religious Program—Tel: 305-665-6862. Email: religioused@stamiami.org. Students 232.

34—ST. TIMOTHY (1960) Revs. Jordi Rivero; Miguel A. Sepulveda; Yader F. Centeno, Sch.P. (Nicaragua); Jose I. Somoza, O.F.M.; Deacons Fernando Bestard; Manuel Buigas; Manuel Canovaca; Henri Gonzalez; Benito Loyola; Roberto Ochoa.
Office: 5400 S.W. 102nd Ave., Miami, 33165. Tel: 305-274-8224; Fax: 305-598-1159. Web: www.sainttimothycatholic.org.
School—Tel: 305-274-8229; Fax: 305-598-7107. Richard Jean, Prin. Lay Teachers 40; Students 662.
Sister Carolyn Learning Center—Tel: 305-598-3184; Fax: 305-412-6650. Mrs. Rosa I. Gonzalez, D.R.E. (PreK & 2-3) Lay Teachers 10; Students 90.
Catechesis/Religious Program—Tel: 305-274-8225; Fax: 305-412-6608. Gerardo Gonzalez, D.R.E. Students 456.

35—ST. VINCENT DE PAUL (1962) Merged with and sacramental records at Saint Rose of Lima Parish, Miami Shores.

36—VISITATION (1956) Rev. Curtis A. Kiddy. In Res., Rev. Harry Loubriel.
Res.: 19100 N. Miami Ave., Miami Gardens, FL 33169. Tel: 305-652-3624; Fax: 305-652-5207. Email: visitationparish@bellsouth.net. Web: www.visitationmiami.parishesonline.com.
Catechesis/Religious Program—100 N.E. 191st St., Miami, 33169. Tel: 305-651-7044. Email: ccddre@bellsouth.net. Students 124.

METROPOLITAN DADE COUNTY

COCONUT GROVE, ST. HUGH (1959), (Hispanic), Revs. George A. Garcia; Juan R. Torres.
Res.: 3455 Royal Rd., 33133. Email: sthugh@bellsouth.net. Web: www.st-hugh.org.
Office: 3460 Royal Rd., 33133. Tel: 305-444-8363; Fax: 305-444-4312.
School—Tel: 305-448-5602; Fax: 305-444-4299. Email: principal@st-hugh.org. Mr. Antonio Cejas, Prin. Sisters 1; Lay Teachers 26; Students 280.
Catechesis/Religious Program—Students 240.

CORAL GABLES

1—ST. AUGUSTINE (1969) Very Rev. Bernard G. Kirlin; Rev. Carmelo Romanello.
Office & Church: 1400 Miller Rd., 33146. Tel: 305-661-1648; Fax: 305-661-6392. Web: www.saintaugustinechurch.org.
Catechesis/Religious Program—Students 281.

2—LITTLE FLOWER (1926) Revs. Arthur Dennison; Alfredo Rolon; Deacon Miguel Parlade. In Res., Rev. Sean O'Sullivan (Retired).
Office: 2711 Indian Mound Tr., 33134. Tel: 305-446-9950; Fax: 305-446-7624. Web: www.churchofthelittleflower.com.
Res.: 1270 Anastasia Ave., 33134. Tel: 305-529-5475.
School—2701 Indian Mound Tr., 33134. Tel: 305-446-1738; Fax: 305-446-2877. Email: srrosalie@stscg.org. Sisters 4; Lay Teachers 44; Students 914.
Catechesis/Religious Program—Tel: 305-446-5540; Fax: 305-446-3784. Students 306.

HIALEAH

1—ST. BENEDICT (1973) Rev. Jose L. Paniagua (Spain).
Res.: 650 W. 80th St., 33014-4125. Tel: 305-558-2150.
Church: 701 W. 77th St., 33014-4125. Tel: 305-558-2150; Fax: 305-558-3705. Email: stbenedictcathol@bellsouth.net.
Catechesis/Religious Program—Tel: 305-557-2511. Maria de la Fe, D.R.E. Students 164.

2—ST. CECILIA (1971) Merged with and sacramental records at Saint John the Apostle Parish, Hialeah.

3—IMMACULATE CONCEPTION (1954) Revs. Francisco J. Hernandez; Joaquin Perez-Pupo (Cuba); Alfred Cioffi; Deacons Abelardo DeGuzman; Manuel Alfonso. In Res., Rev. Ronald Noguera (Retired).
Res.: 4497 W. First Ave., 33012. Tel: 305-822-2011; Fax: 305-821-3481. Web: www.icsmiami.org.
School—125 W. 45th St., 33012. Tel: 305-822-6461; Fax: 305-822-0289. Email: icschool@miamiarch.org. Mr. Eddy Garcia, Prin. Lay Teachers 47; Students 812.
Catechesis/Religious Program—Tel: 305-823-9563; Fax: 305-822-7868. Nubia Stanley, D.R.E. Students 400.

4—ST. JOHN THE APOSTLE (1945) Rev. Msgr. Emilio Martin; Rev. Jorge Noda. In Res., Revs. George Cardona (Retired); Ignacio Morras (Retired); Deacon Julke Llorens.
Res.: 475 E. 4th St., 33010. Tel: 305-888-9769; Fax: 305-888-9341.
School—Tel: 305-888-6819; Fax: 305-887-1256. Web: www.stjohntheapostleschool.com. Mrs. Marilyn S. Bimonte, Prin. Lay Teachers 13; Students 280.
Catechesis/Religious Program—Angelica Millan, D.R.E. Students 400.

5—SAN LAZARO (1982) Rev. Jose Espino.
Res.: 4400 W. 18th Ave., 33012. Tel: 305-556-1717; Fax: 305-556-8918.
Catechesis/Religious Program—Tel: 305-558-4078. Sr. Blanca Hernandez, D.R.E. Students 315.

6—SANTA BARBARA (1987) Rev. Miguel Gomez.
Mailing Address: 6801 W. 30th Ave., 33018. Tel: 305-556-4442; Fax: 305-558-7256.
Res.: 3004 W. 68th Pl., 33018. Tel: 305-827-1110.
Catechesis/Religious Program—Tel: 305-556-4442, Ext. 106. Students 614.

HOMESTEAD, SACRED HEART (1929) Revs. James McCreanor; Ferry Brutus (Haiti).
Church & Res.: 106 S.E. First Dr., 33030-7322. Tel: 305-247-4405; Fax: 305-245-3002. Web: sacredhearthomestead.com.
Catechesis/Religious Program—Tel: 305-247-0760. Students 443.

KEY BISCAYNE, ST. AGNES (1954) Very Rev. Jose L. Hernando; Rev. Israel E. Mago.
Res.: 100 Harbor Dr., 33149. Tel: 305-361-2351; 305-361-2451; Fax: 305-361-8514. Email: stagneschurch@bellsouth.net. Web: www.stagneschurchkb.org.
School—122 Harbor Dr., 33149. Tel: 305-361-3245; Fax: 305-361-6329. Mrs. Sheila Cruse, Prin. Lay Teachers 32; Students 462.
Catechesis/Religious Program—Tel: 305-361-1378. Nery Quintela, D.R.E. Students 522.

LEISURE CITY, ST. MARTIN DE PORRES CATHOLIC CHURCH (1990), (Hispanic), Rev. Carlos Vega.
Mailing Address: 14881 S.W. 288th St., 33033. Tel: 305-248-5355; Fax: 305-245-3047. Email: stmdp@bellsouth.net.
Catechesis/Religious Program—Students 303.

MIAMI BEACH

1—ST. FRANCIS DE SALES (1964) Rev. Gabriel Vigues; Deacon Jose Irizarry.
Res.: 621 Alton Rd., 33139. Tel: 305-672-0093; Fax: 305-673-8559. Web: www.saintfrancisonthebeach.com.
Catechesis/Religious Program—Students 75.

2—ST. JOSEPH (1942) Revs. Enrique J. Estrada; George Packuvettithara (India).
Res.: 8670 Byron Ave., 33141. Tel: 305-866-6567; Fax: 305-864-1069. Web: wwww.stjosephmiamibeach.com.
School—8625 Byron Ave., 33141. Tel: 305-866-1471; Fax: 305-866-3175. Dr. Maria Elena Chelala, Prin. Lay Teachers 21; Students 138.
Catechesis/Religious Program—Fax: 305-864-1049. Students 140.

3—ST. PATRICK (1926) Rev. Msgr. John J. Vaughan; Revs. Jesus Alberto Bohorquez; Joel Mathew, O.I.C. (India).
Office: 3716 Garden Ave., 33140. Tel: 305-531-1124; Fax: 305-538-3203.
Res.: 3700 Meridian Ave., 33140.
School—Tel: 305-534-4616; Fax: 305-538-5463. Bertha Moro, Prin. Lay Teachers 19; Students 230.
Catechesis/Religious Program—Students 194.

MIAMI GARDENS, ST. MONICA (1959) Rev. Samuel Muodiaju, C.S.Sp. (Nigeria); Deacon Marco Rosales.
Res.: 3490 N.W. 191st St., 33056. Tel: 305-621-9846; Fax: 305-621-5608. Email: pastor@saintmonica.org. Web: www.saintmonica.org.
Catechesis/Religious Program—Students 135.

MIAMI LAKES, OUR LADY OF THE LAKES (1967) Revs. James Murphy; Carlos Miyares; Deacons Pablo A. Fernandez; Carlos Ramirez.
Res.: 15801 N.W. 67 Ave., 33014. Tel: 305-558-2202; Fax: 305-558-2631. Email: jpmurphy@ollnet.com.
School—6600 Miami Lakeway N., 33014. Tel: 305-362-5315. Ricardo Bris, Prin. Lay Teachers 34; Students 520.
Catechesis/Religious Program—Anita Brown, D.R.E.; Rosa Diaz, D.R.E. Students 967.

MIAMI SHORES

1—ST. MARTHA (1970) Rev. Federico Capdepon. In Res., Rev. Carl T. Morrison.
Res.: 9221 Biscayne Blvd., 33138. Tel: 305-751-0005; Fax: 305-754-6930. Web: www.saintmartha.com.
Catechesis/Religious Program—Tel: 305-751-8759. Students 180.

2—ST. ROSE OF LIMA (1946) Rev. Msgr. Seamus Doyle; Revs. Henryk Pawelec; Charnel Jeanty.
Res.: 415 N.E. 105th St., 33138. Tel: 305-758-0539; Fax: 305-751-8398. Web: www.stroseoflimamiamishores.org.
School—425 N.E. 105th St., 33138. Tel: 305-751-4257; Fax: 305-751-5034. Sr. Bernadette Keane, I.H.M., Prin. Sisters 3; Lay Teachers 40; Students 542.
Catechesis/Religious Program—Tel: 305-757-6434. Students 173.

MIAMI SPRINGS, BLESSED TRINITY (1952) Revs. Joseph T. Carney; Cristobal De Paula; Deacon Dennis E. Jordan.
Res.: 4020 Curtiss Pkwy., 33166. Tel: 305-871-5780; Fax: 305-871-5781. Web: www.blessed-trinity.org.
School—Tel: 305-871-5766; Fax: 305-876-1755. Mrs. Maria Teresa Perez, Prin. Lay Teachers 22; Students 273.
Catechesis/Religious Program—Tel: 305-876-1749. Students 200.

NORTH MIAMI, HOLY FAMILY (1950) Rev. Franky Jean. In Res., Rev. Daniel Asue (Nigeria).
Res.: 14500 N.E. 11 Ave., 33161. Tel: 305-947-5043; 305-947-1471; Fax: 305-949-5591.
School—14650 N.E. 12th Ave., 33161. Tel: 305-947-6535; Fax: 305-947-1826. Ms. Mary Ellen McKinney, Prin. Lay Teachers 15; Students 325.
Catechesis/Religious Program—Tel: 305-947-7739; Fax: 305-947-1417. Students 160.

NORTH MIAMI BEACH, ST. LAWRENCE (1956) Rev. William Elbert.
Res.: 2200 N.E. 191st St., 33180. Tel: 305-932-3560; Fax: 305-936-8050.
School—Tel: 305-932-4912; Fax: 305-932-7898. Web: www.stlaw.org. Mrs. Dian Hyatt, Prin. Lay Teachers 11; Students 147.
Child Care Center—Tel: 305-932-5366. Email: stlawrenceccc@aol.com. Lay Teachers 10; Students 90.
Catechesis/Religious Program—Tel: 305-931-6650. Kelly Lee, D.R.E.; Joanne Lambert, D.R.E. Students 240.

OPA LOCKA

1—OUR LADY OF PERPETUAL HELP CHURCH (1954) Merged with and sacramental records at Saint James Parish, North Miami.

2—ST. PHILIP (1953) Merged with and sacramental records at Saint Monica Parish, Miami Gardens.

PRINCETON, ST. ANN MISSION (1960) Rev. Msgr. Pedro Garcia.
Mailing Address: P.O. Box 924884, 33092-4884. Tel: 305-258-3968; 305-258-9682; Fax: 305-258-3591. Email: stannsmission@bellsouth.net. 13875 S.W. 264 St., Naranja, 33032.
Catechesis/Religious Program—Tel: 305-248-3735. Students 800.

SUNNY ISLES BEACH, ST. MARY MAGDALEN (1955) Rev. Thomas G. Honold. In Res., Rev. Andrzej Pietraszko.
Res.: 17775 N. Bay Rd., 33160. Tel: 305-931-0600; Fax: 305-931-0601. Email: parishoffice@stmmsib.org. Web: www.stmmsib.org.
Catechesis/Religious Program—Students 149.

OUTSIDE METROPOLITAN DADE COUNTY

BIG PINE KEY, MONROE CO., ST. PETER (1962) Rev. Thomas Mullane.
Res.: 31300 Overseas Hwy., P.O. Box 430657, 33043. Tel: 305-872-2537; Fax: 305-872-0122. Email: info@stpeterbpk.com. Web: www.stpeterbpk.com.
Catechesis/Religious Program—Students 70.
Mission—Sugarloaf Firehouse Sugarloaf Shores, 33042.

COCONUT CREEK, BROWARD CO., ST. LUKE (1985) Merged with and sacramental records at Saint Vincent Parish, Margate.

CORAL SPRINGS, BROWARD CO.

1—ST. ANDREW (1969) Very Rev. George Puthusseril; Revs. Andrew Chan-A-Sue; Lazarus J. Govin, Parochial Vicar; Mathew Thundathil (India); Deacon Denis Mieyal.
Res.: 9950 N.W. 29th St., 33065-6103. Tel: 954-752-3950; Fax: 954-752-3986. Email: parish@sacccs.org. Web: www.standrewparish.org.
School—9990 N.W. 29th St., 33065. Tel: 954-753-1280; Fax: 954-753-1933. Email: andsch@miamiarch.org. Mrs. Lois Lawlor, Prin. Lay Teachers 21; Students 290.
Catechesis/Religious Program—Tel: 954-905-6323. Mary Dorris, D.R.E. Students 762.

2—ST. ELIZABETH ANN SETON (1985) Revs. Edward M. Kelly; Patrick J. Naughton (SCR); Deacons John Friel; Frank Gonzalez.
Res.: 1401 Coral Ridge Dr., 33071. Tel: 954-753-3330; Fax: 954-753-8442. Email: setonoffice@aol.com. Web: www.steascc.org.
Catechesis/Religious Program—Tel: 954-345-7071. Students 965.

DANIA BEACH, BROWARD CO., CHURCH OF THE RESURRECTION (1958) Merged with and sacramental records at Saint Maurice Parish, Dania Beach.

DAVIE, BROWARD CO., ST. DAVID (1974) Revs. Gabriel O'Reilly; Randall Musselman.
Res.: 3900 S. University Dr., 33328. Tel: 954-475-8046; Fax: 954-370-0819.
School—Tel: 954-472-7086; Fax: 954-452-8243. Mrs. Mariann Kiar, Prin. Lay Teachers 45; Students 550.
Catechesis/Religious Program—Tel: 954-475-1521. Pam McMillan, D.R.E. Students 504.

DEERFIELD BEACH, BROWARD CO.

1—ST. AMBROSE (1962) Revs. John Bryan Dalton; James Connaughton, Pastor Emeritus (Retired); Michael Lynch.
Res. & Office: 380 S. Federal Hwy., 33441. Tel: 954-427-2225; Fax: 954-421-1638. Email: stambrosedeerfield@yahoo.com. Web: www.stambrosechurch.catholicweb.com.
School—Tel: 954-427-2226; Fax: 954-427-4293. Email: ambsch@miamiarch.org. Web: www.stambroseschooldeerfield.catholicweb.com. Ms. Anita Gentile, Prin. Lay Teachers 20; Students 200.
Catechesis/Religious Program—Students 131.

2—OUR LADY OF MERCY (1974) Rev. Msgr. James Parappally (India).
Parish Center & Office—5201 N. Military Tr., 33064. Tel: 954-421-3246; Fax: 954-421-1973.
Catechesis/Religious Program—Students 50.

FORT LAUDERDALE, BROWARD CO.

1—ST. ANTHONY (1921) Very Rev. Jeremiah Singleton; Rev. Linus Nangwele (Ghana).
Res.: 901 N.E. 2nd St., 33301. Tel: 954-463-4614; Fax: 954-527-5411. Email: stanthony@bellsouth.net. Web: www.saintanthonyfl.org.
School—820 N.E. Third St., 33301. Tel: 954-467-7747; Fax: 954-467-9908. Mrs. Norma Kramer, Prin. Lay Teachers 30; Students 399.
Catechesis/Religious Program—Tel: 954-467-7749. Email: sasreligioused@yahoo.com. Students 226.

2—ST. BONAVENTURE (1985) Rev. Edmond Prendergast; Deacons Arthur DeNunzio; Joseph M. Pearce; Thomas Malinoski; Domingo Vasquez; Peter Trahan.
Res.: 1301 S.W. 136th Ave., Davie, 33325-4300. Tel: 954-424-9504; 954-424-9505; Fax: 954-424-9505. Email: info@stbonaventurechurch.com. Web: www.stbonaventurechurch.com.
Catechesis/Religious Program—Tel: 954-476-5204; Fax: 954-236-7983. Susan McCrea, D.R.E. Students 1,315.

3—ST. CLEMENT (1954) Revs. Robes C. Charles; Wilfredo Contreras. In Res., Revs. Henry Mullin, C.S.Sp.; Armando Alonso.
Res.: 2975 N. Andrews Ave., 33311. Tel: 954-563-1183; Fax: 954-564-6628.
Catechesis/Religious Program—Tel: 954-561-4641. Bridget Gilligan, D.R.E.; Sr. Anne Stinfil, D.R.E. Students 161.

4—DIVINE MERCY MISSION (1980) Merged with and sacramental records at Saint Clement Parish, Fort Lauderdale.

5—ST. HELEN (1968) Rev. Msgr. William Dever; Revs. Isidore Baky; Yves Jocelyn (Haiti). In Res., Rev. Msgr. John W. Delaney (Retired).
Res.: 3033 N.W. 33rd Ave., 33311. Tel: 954-731-7314; Fax: 954-739-9632.
School—3340 W. Oakland Park Blvd., 33311. Tel: 954-739-7094; Fax: 954-739-0797. Terry Mavis, Prin. Lay Teachers 17; Students 176.
Catechesis/Religious Program—Tel: 954-484-3036. Students 160.

6—ST. JEROME (1960) Rev. Michael W. Davis; Deacon Frank B. O'Gorman.
Res.: 2533 S.W. 9th Ave., 33315. Tel: 954-525-4133; Fax: 954-525-0964. Web: stjeromechurch.org.
School—Tel: 954-524-1990; Fax: 954-524-7439. Sr. Vivian Gomez, R.F., Prin. Sisters of St. Philip Neri 4; Lay Teachers 19; Students 280.
Catechesis/Religious Program—2601 S.W. 9th Ave., 33315. Students 52.

7—ST. JOHN THE BAPTIST (1969) Rev. Msgr. Vincent T. Kelly; Revs. William H. Bowles (NU); Paul Frank, O.M.I. In Res., Rev. William J. Sullivan, O.S.S.T.
Res.: 4595 Bayview Dr., 33308. Tel: 954-771-8950; Fax: 954-771-4178. Email: church@stjohncc.org.
Catechesis/Religious Program—Students 220.

8—ST. MARK (1985) Revs. Edmond F. Whyte; Cesar E. Pena, Parochial Vicar; Thomas Mannix Stack; Deacons Vincent Farinato; John Lorenzo.
Office: 5601 S. Flamingo Rd., Southwest Ranches, 33330. Tel: 954-434-3777; Fax: 954-434-3125. Email: stmark5601@aol.com.
Res.: 5551 S.W. 127th Ave., Southwest Ranches, 33330.
School—Tel: 954-434-3887; Fax: 954-434-3595. Shirley Sandusky, Prin. Students 670.
Catechesis/Religious Program—Tel: 954-252-9899. Susan Mikluscak, D.R.E. Students 1,080.

9—ST. MAURICE (1970) Rev. Roger Holoubek; Deacon Norman Carroll.
Res.: 2851 Stirling Rd., Dania Beach, 33312. Tel: 954-961-7777; Fax: 954-961-4358. Web: www.stmaurice.org.
Day Care Center: Tel: 954-961-5585; Fax: 954-961-5510.
Catechesis/Religious Program—Students 124.

10—OUR LADY QUEEN OF MARTYRS (1956) Revs. Michael Hoyer; Armando Perez; Jude Ezeanokwasa (Nigeria).
Res.: 2731 S.W. 11 Ct. (Happy Hoyer Street), 33312. Tel: 954-583-8725; Fax: 954-583-9315.
School—2785 Happy Hoyer St., 33312. Tel: 954-583-8112; Fax: 954-797-4984. Web: bestcatholicschool-.com. Mrs. Althea Mossop, Prin. Lay Teachers 16; Students 190.
Catechesis/Religious Program—Students 185.

11—ST. PIUS X (1959) Revs. Patrick C. Slevin; Harry Ringenberger; Deacon George P. Sutcavage.
Res.: 2500 N.E. 33rd Ave., 33305. Tel: 954-564-1763; Fax: 954-568-2212. Web: www.saintpiusthetenth.org.
Church: 2511 N. Ocean Blvd. (A1A), 33308.
Catechesis/Religious Program—Students 27.

12—ST. SEBASTIAN (1959) Rev. Liam Quinn.
Parish Office: 2000 S.E. 25th Ave., 33316. Tel: 954-524-9344; Fax: 954-524-9347. Email: stsebastia@aol.com.
Rectory—2518 Barbara Dr., 33316.
Catechesis/Religious Program—Students 45.

HALLANDALE, BROWARD CO.

1—ST. CHARLES BORROMEO (1968) Merged with and sacramental records at Saint Matthew Parish, Hallandale Beach.

2—ST. MATTHEW (1959) Rev. James A. Quinn.
Res.: 542 Blue Heron Dr., Hallandale Beach, 33009. Tel: 954-458-1590; Fax: 954-458-0612. Web: www.saintmatthew.com.

Catechesis / Religious Program—Tel: 954-458-3600. Students 35.

HOLLYWOOD, BROWARD CO.

1—ST. BERNADETTE (1959) Rev. Brendan Dalton.
Res.: 7450 Stirling Rd., 33024. Tel: 954-432-5313; Fax: 954-432-5344. Web: www.stbernadette-fl.com.
School—Tel: 954-432-7022; Fax: 954-443-8030. Mrs. Michele Sanders, Prin. Lay Teachers 18; Students 278.
Catechesis / Religious Program—Tel: 954-432-6300; Fax: 954-432-0661. Students 130.

2—LITTLE FLOWER (1924) Very Rev. Thomas O'Dwyer; Revs. Richard Mullen, O.S.A.; Patrick O'Shea; Deacons Walter Keough; William A. Watkins.
Res.: 1805 Pierce St., 33020. Tel: 954-922-3517; Fax: 954-922-6634. Email: littleflower_hwd@hotmail.com. Web: www.littleflowerhwd.org.
School—1843 Pierce St., 33020. Tel: 954-922-1217; Fax: 954-927-8962. Web: www.littleflowerhollywood-fl.org. Mrs. Maureen McNulty, Prin. Lay Teachers 19; Students 288.
Catechesis / Religious Program—Tel: 954-923-7634. Students 91.

3—NATIVITY (1960) Revs. Patrick J. Murnane; Michael Grady; Victor Babin; Deacons Chandy Luka; Richard A. Turcotte.
Res.: 5220 Johnson St., 33021. Tel: 954-987-3300; Fax: 954-987-3044.
School—Tel: 954-987-3300, Ext. 221; Fax: 954-987-6368. Mrs. Elena Ortiz, Prin.; Ms. Judy Skehan, Vice Prin. Lay Teachers 44; Students 870.
Catechesis / Religious Program—Tel: 954-987-3300, Ext. 214. Students 400.

4—OUR LADY APARECIDA MISSION (1996) Merged with and sacramental records at Saint Vincent Parish, Margate.

KEY LARGO, MONROE CO., ST. JUSTIN MARTYR (1973) [CEM] Rev. Enrique Delgado.
Res.: 105500 Overseas Hwy., 33037. Tel: 305-451-1316; Fax: 305-451-4633. Web: www.st-justinthemartyr.org.
Catechesis / Religious Program—Tel: 305-451-6414. Donna Roberts, D.R.E. Students 90.

KEY WEST, MONROE CO., ST. MARY, STAR OF THE SEA (1846) Revs. John C. Baker; Lesly Jean (Haiti); Deacon Peter Batty.
Res.: 1010 Windsor Ln., 33040. Tel: 305-294-1018; Fax: 305-292-8096. Email: stmarystar@bellsouth.net. Web: www.keywestcatholicparish.org.
School—700 Truman Ave., 33040. Tel: 305-294-1031; Fax: 305-294-2095. Brothers 1; Lay Teachers 10; Students 178.
Catechesis / Religious Program—Tel: 305-295-0306. Students 186.
Mission—St. Mary, Star of the Sea Outreach Mission 5640 Mac Donald Ave., Monroe Co. 33040. Tel: 305-292-3013; Fax: 305-292-3014.

LAUDERDALE BY-THE-SEA, BROWARD CO., ASSUMPTION (1959) Rev. Msgr. Martin J. Cassidy.
Res.: 2001 S. Ocean Blvd., Lauderdale-by-the-Sea, 33062. Tel: 954-941-7647; Fax: 954-941-9620.
Catechesis / Religious Program—

LAUDERHILL, BROWARD CO., ST. GEORGE (1964) Merged with and sacramental records at Our Lady Queen of Martyrs Parish, Fort Lauderdale.

LIGHTHOUSE POINT, BROWARD CO., ST. PAUL THE APOSTLE (1968) Rev. Msgr. Frederick J. Brice; Rev. Joseph Maroor (India).
Res.: 2700 N.E. 36th St., 33064. Tel: 954-943-9154; 954-943-9155; Fax: 954-943-1954.
Catechesis / Religious Program—Students 105.

MARATHON, MONROE CO., SAN PABLO (1958) Very Rev. Gerald R. Morris.
Res.: 550 122nd St. Ocean, 33050. Tel: 305-289-0636; Fax: 305-743-8192. Email: sanpablo1@aol.com. Web: www.sanpablochurch.com.
Catechesis / Religious Program—Students 50.

MARGATE, BROWARD CO., ST. VINCENT (1960) Revs. Joseph F. Pranzo, C.S.; Volmar Scaravelli, C.S.; German Vargas, C.S.; Deacon Allen Asselin.
Parish Office: 6350 N.W. 18th St., 33063-2320. Tel: 954-972-0434; Fax: 954-971-9411. Email: stvincent7@aol.com.
Res.: 6280 N.W. 18th St., 33063-2320. Tel: 954-971-0501.
Catechesis / Religious Program—Tel: 954-972-9907. Students 440.

MIRAMAR, BROWARD CO.

1—ST. BARTHOLOMEW (1962) Revs. Paul V. Vuturo; Patrick Charles; Deacons David Smith; Michel du Chaussee.
Res.: 8005 Miramar Pkwy., 33025. Tel: 954-431-3600; Fax: 954-435-9591.
School—8003 Miramar Pkwy., 33025. Tel: 954-431-5253; Fax: 954-431-3385. Christine M. Gonzalez, Prin. Lay Teachers 18; Students 253.
Catechesis / Religious Program—Students 515.

2—BLESSED JOHN XXIII CHURCH (2002) Rev. Ernest Biriruka (Burundi).
Office: 16800 Miramar Pkwy., 33027. Tel: 954-392-5062; Fax: 954-392-5063. Email: blessedjohn23@hotmail.com.
Res.: 3638 S.W. 166th Ave., 33027.
Catechesis / Religious Program—Students 464.

3—ST. STEPHEN (1956) Revs. Alejandro Roque, O.M.I.; Jonathan Closner-Benavidez, O.M.I.; Quilin Bouzi, O.M.I.
Mailing Address: 6044 S.W. 19th St., 33023. Tel: 954-987-1100; Fax: 954-966-9881.
Church: 2000 S. State Rd. 7, 33023.
Catechesis / Religious Program—Tel: 954-962-8801. Students 345.

NORTH LAUDERDALE, BROWARD CO., OUR LADY QUEEN OF HEAVEN (1974) Rev. Kidney M. Saint Jean.
Res. & Church: 1400 S. State Rd. 7, 33068. Tel: 954-971-5400; Fax: 954-972-4008.
Catechesis / Religious Program—Students 212.

OAKLAND PARK, BROWARD CO., BLESSED SACRAMENT (1961) Rev. Robert F. Tywoniak; Deacon Michael Leon.
Res.: 1701 E. Oakland Park Blvd., 33334. Tel: 954-564-1010; Fax: 954-566-0301. Email: bscc1701@aol.com.
Catechesis / Religious Program—Students 20.

PARKLAND, BROWARD CO., MARY HELP OF CHRISTIANS CHURCH (1989) Revs. Thomas Wisniewski; Manuel Francisco Alvarez; Deacon Vincent Eberling Jr.
Church: 5980 University Dr., 33067. Tel: 954-323-8012; Fax: 954-323-8011. Email: parish@mhoc.org. Web: www.mhocrc.org.
School—6000 University Dr., 33067. Tel: 954-323-8006; Fax: 954-323-8010. Web: mhocschool.org. Robert J. Messina, Prin. Lay Teachers 26; Students 420.
Catechesis / Religious Program—Tel: 954-323-8025. Students 724.

PEMBROKE PINES, BROWARD CO.

1—ST. BONIFACE (1971) Revs. Antonio R. Silio; Guy Fenger. In Res., Rev. Kris Bartos.
Res.: 8330 Johnson St., 33024. Tel: 954-432-2750; Fax: 954-432-2756.
Catechesis / Religious Program—Students 210.

2—ST. EDWARD (1995) Rev. Msgr. Michael J. Eivers; Rev. Christian Plancher, S.M.M.; Deacons Arnold J. DeLuca; Carl R. Cramer; Mario Ganuza.
Res. & Church Address: 19000 Pines Blvd., 33029. Tel: 954-436-7944; Fax: 954-436-7506.
Catechesis / Religious Program—Tel: 954-430-4107. Students 2,000.

3—ST. MAXIMILIAN KOLBE (1983) Revs. Jeffrey McCormick; Anthony O'Brien; Hector A. Perez; Deacons Carl Carieri; Jose Bermudez; Scott Joiner; Pierre Douyon.
Res.: 11051 N.W. 16th St., 33026-4034. Tel: 954-432-8289. Email: office@stmax.cc. Web: www.stmax.cc.
Church: 701 N. Hiatus Rd., 33026. Tel: 954-432-0206; Fax: 954-432-0775.
School—St. Maximilian Kolbe Education Center, Pre School (2.5 - 4 years old), 601 N. Hiatus Rd., 33026. Tel: 954-885-7250; Fax: 954-885-7252. Email: pre-school@stmax.cc. Mrs. Bernadette Viscome, Dir. Students 73.
Catechesis / Religious Program—Tel: 954-885-7260; Fax: 954-885-7261. Students 792.

PLANTATION, BROWARD CO., ST. GREGORY (1959) Rev. Msgr. Noel Fogarty; Rev. Roberto Cid. In Res., Rev. Vivian Loughrey (Ireland).
Res.: 200 N. University Dr., 33324. Tel: 954-473-6261; Fax: 954-473-4599. Web: www.cherubim.org.
School—Tel: 954-473-8169; Fax: 954-472-1638. Mrs. Cari Canino, Prin.; Mrs. Alexandra Fernandez, Asst. Prin. Lay Teachers 43; Students 810.
Catechesis / Religious Program—Tel: 954-473-8321. Students 301.

POMPANO BEACH, BROWARD CO.

1—ST. COLEMAN (1959) Revs. Thomas F. Foudy; Pedro Lleo; Luis Garcia.
Res.: 1200 S. Federal Hwy., 33062. Tel: 954-942-3533; Fax: 954-942-7869.
School—Tel: 954-942-3500; Fax: 954-785-0603. Lay Teachers 36; Aides 7; Students 636.
Catechesis / Religious Program—1285 S.E. 22nd Ave., 33062. Tel: 954-782-1461. Students 202.

2—ST. ELIZABETH OF HUNGARY CATHOLIC CHURCH (1959) Revs. Paul Kane; Fritzner Bellonce; Deacons Willie Harris Sr.; Daniel Moretti; Vidal Camacho.
Res.: 3331 N.E. 10th Ter., 33064-5298. Tel: 954-941-8117; Fax: 954-941-0999.
School—901 N.E. 33rd. St., 33064. Tel: 954-942-2161; Fax: 954-942-7551. Mr. Craig Mousseau, Prin. Sisters 1; Lay Teachers 17; Students 158.
Catechesis / Religious Program—Tel: 954-943-6801; Fax: 954-941-0999. Mrs. Deborah Andra, D.R.E. Students 500.

3—ST. GABRIEL (1967) Rev. Anthony Mulderry; Deacon Joseph O. Soucy.
Res.: 731 N. Ocean Blvd., 33062. Tel: 954-943-3684; Fax: 954-943-3656.
Catechesis / Religious Program—Students 11.

4—ST. HENRY (1969) Rev. Francis Akwue, C.S.Sp.
Res.: 1500 S. Andrews Ave., 33069. Tel: 954-785-2450; Fax: 954-785-6958. Email: pastor@sainthenrys.org. Web: www.sainthenrys.org.
Catechesis / Religious Program—Students 40.

5—ST. JOSEPH MISSION (1981) Merged with and sacramental records at Saint Elizabeth of Hungary Parish, Pompano Beach.

6—OUR LADY OF CZESTOCHOWA MISSION (1997), (Polish), Rev. Klemens Dabrowski, S.Ch.
2400 N.E. 12th St., 33062. Tel: 954-545-3861; Fax: 954-946-0512. Web: www.polishchurch.com.
Catechesis / Religious Program—Students 45.

7—SAN ISIDRO (1970) Revs. Abel Barajas; Albert Lahens.
Res.: 2310 Martin Luther King Blvd., 33069-1591. Tel: 954-971-8780; Fax: 954-972-3607. Email: myhome@sanisidro.org. Web: www.sanisidro.org.
Catechesis / Religious Program—Students 181.

SUNRISE, BROWARD CO.

1—ALL SAINTS (1982) Revs. Anibal Morales; Eric D. Zegeer; Deacons Vincent Tola; Giuseppe Tollis.
Office: 10900 W. Oakland Park Blvd., 33351. Tel: 954-742-2666; Fax: 954-741-7238. Web: www.allsaintsvillage.com.
School—Tel: 954-742-4842; Fax: 954-742-4870. Mrs. Antoinette McNamara, Prin. Students 278.
Catechesis / Religious Program—Tel: 954-742-7742. Students 431.

2—ST. BERNARD (1971) Rev. Michael Hourigan.
Res.: 8279 Sunset Strip, 33322. Tel: 954-741-7800; Fax: 954-742-4558.
Catechesis / Religious Program—Tel: 954-741-0275. Students 135.

TAMARAC, BROWARD CO., ST. MALACHY (1973) Revs. Dominick O'Dwyer; Rafael Cos (Cuba); Deacons Nicholas Costea; Joseph Sommovigo; Bernard Bonnick (Jamaica).
Res.: 6200 John Horan Terr., 33321. Tel: 954-726-1237; Fax: 954-726-0822. Email: stmalachy@comcast.net.
Catechesis / Religious Program—Tel: 954-721-5337. Concetta Sobkowski, D.R.E. Students 134.

TAVERNIER, MONROE CO., SAN PEDRO (1954) Rev. John P. Peloso.
Res.: 89500 Overseas Hwy., Plantation Key, 33070. Tel: 305-852-5372; Fax: 305-852-3315. Web: www.sanpedroparish.org.
Catechesis / Religious Program—Students 123.

WEST HOLLYWOOD, BROWARD CO., ANNUNCIATION (1959) Rev. Michael Quilligan; Deacon Mitchell C. Abdallah.
Res.: 3781 S.W. 39th St., 33023. Tel: 954-989-0606; Fax: 954-989-0660.
School—3751 SW 39th St., 33023. Tel: 954-989-8287. Web: www.annum.org. Mr. Nestor Periera Jr., Prin. Sisters 1; Lay Teachers 18; Students 302.
Catechesis / Religious Program—Students 50.

WESTON, BROWARD CO., ST. KATHARINE DREXEL (2001) Rev. Pedro M. Corces; Deacon Paul Brancheau.
Office: 2700 Glades Cir., Ste. 200, 33327. Tel: 954-389-5003; Fax: 954-389-1228. Email: stkatdrx@bellsouth.net. Web: www.st-katharinedrexel.org.
Catechesis / Religious Program—Tel: 954-389-1219. Students 680.

Special Assignment:
Rev. Msgrs.—
Anderson, Andrew L., Judicial Vicar
Hennessey, William J., S.T.L., M.S., V.G., P.A.
Souckar, Michael A., Chancellor
Revs.—
Adu, Martin K., Chap., Jackson Memorial Hospital
Fink, John, Chap., Broward General Hospital
Fishwick, Joseph, Chap. (Retired), Baptist Hospital & South Miami Hospital, Miami
Jimenez, Eduardo, Family Life Ministry
O'Neill, Patrick H., Coord. Special Projects, Ministry of General Services

---

On Duty Outside the Archdiocese:
Revs.—
O'Hala, Stephen, Boynton Beach (St. Vincent de Paul Seminary) (West Palm Beach)
O'Leary, John, Peru
Quijano, Jose Juan, (St. Vincent de Paul Seminary, Palm Beach)
Saenz, Jorge L., (Archdiocese of San Juan, Puerto Rico)
Scheiding, Philip, Mexico

Military Chaplains:
Rev.—
Gubbins, John

Absent on Sick Leave:
Revs.—
Montoya, Juan
Puerta, Jorge

Absent on Leave:
Revs.—
Castillo, Rolando
Christman, Robert
Colominas, Octavio
Dueppen, David
Garcia, Michel
Grogan, Brendan
Guichard, Alvaro
Healy, George
Hyland, Sean
Keener, Michael
Kudlo, Frank
Malicki, Jan
Piano, Timothy
Powers, Charles

Retired:
Most Revs.—
Fernandez, Gilberto, D.D.
Roman, Agustin A., D.D.
Rev. Msgrs.—
Balado, Armando
Delaney, John W.
Glorie, John W.
Morras, Xavier
Ordax, Emiliano
Perez, Pedro Luis
Reynolds, James B.
Vallina, Emilio
Revs.—
Acevedo, Antonio
Angelini, Joseph
Bennett, Noel I.
Blasco, Ignacio
Boned, Enrique
Brohammer, Ronald
Cabrera, Sergio
Cahill, Frank
Carbajales, Ignacio
Cardona, George
Carrillo, Sergio
Casabon, Luis
Castellanos, Ricardo C.
Clements, Charles
Connaughton, James
Conway, Laurence
Coucelo, Andres
Doherty, Neil
Duffy, George
Engbers, Thomas
Fernandez, Nelson
Fishwick, Joseph
Garcia, Jose
Garcia-Miro, Sergio
Gonzalez-Abreu, Hector
Huck, Joseph
Huesca, Omar A.
Kent, Daniel
Lyons, Lawrence
Massi, Anthony
McGrath, Gerald
McGrath, John
McLaughlin, John
Medina, Rolando
Melley, James J.
Mercieca, Anthony
Mitchell, Walter
Miyares, Gustavo
Molano, Ernesto, J.C.L.
Morras, Ignacio
Mulcahy, Sean
Noguera, Ronald
O'Sullivan, Sean
Olszewski, Edward T.
Pedroso, Rafael
Planas, Salvador
Puisis, Leonard
Pusak, Ronald, J.C.L.
Quinn, James E.
Rausch, Dennis
Rivas, Romeo
Russell, David
Shannon, Brendan
Smith, Trevor
Soulliere, Richard
Sullivan, Michael P.
Valoret, Joseph
Villegas, Hernando
Whittaker, Kenneth

Permanent Deacons:
Abdallah, Mitchell C.
Aceto, Igino, Rockville Center, NY
Aguayo, Orlando
Aguilu, Thomas
Alfonso, Manuel
Apodaca, Steve W., (Outside the Archdiocese)
Asselin, Allen
Avery, John, (Outside the Archdiocese)
Baez, Rodolfo
Batty, Peter
Benavides, Luis
Beregszaszi, Miklos A.
Bermudez, Jose, San Juan, Puerto Rico
Bestard, Fernando
Binder, Robert
Blaha, Daniel C.
Blanco, Eduardo
Bloom, David, (Outside the Archdiocese)
Bonnick, Bernard (Jamaica), Jamaica
Brancheau, Paul
Breitfelder, Edward J., (Outside the Archdiocese)
Buigas, Manuel
Calvo-Forte, Rafael, Venezuela
Camacho, Vidal, New York
Canovaca, Manuel
Carieri, Carl
Carrion, Jose
Carroll, Norman
Castellanos, Manuel, Santo Domingo
Coburn, Wilfred, Tulsa
Coniglio, Philip, (Outside the Archdiocese)
Costea, Nicholas
Cramer, Carl R.
Crawford, Jr. Frederick, (Outside the Archdiocese)
Cresswell, William H., (Outside the Archdiocese)
Cruz, Rafael, Brooklyn, NY
Cuesta, Angel L., (Outside the Archdiocese)
Currier, Roger
Dawson, Thomas
DeGuzman, Abelardo
DeLuca, Arnold J.
DeNunzio, Arthur
Desmornes, Jean E.
Dietsch, Charles, (Outside the Archdiocese)
Dinsmore, Robert B.
Draughon, Woodworth R., Jr., (Outside the Archdiocese)
Dugan, Richard, (Outside the Archdiocese)
Eberling, Vincent, Jr.
Estrada, Francisco, (Outside the Archdiocese)
Farias, Edgardo
Farinato, Vincent
Fathauer, Ronald, (Outside the Archdiocese)
Fernandez, Pablo A.
Fiore, Charlie, (Outside the Archdiocese)
Franklin, Thomas
Friel, John
Fugere, Joseph, St. Louis, Missouri
Galard, John, (Outside the Archdiocese)
Galvez, Rene, Arlington, VA
Gazitua, Ralph
Gervasi, Angelo
Gibson, George
Gonzalez, Henri
Gonzalez, Jorge G.
Gordillo, Jose Manuel
Green, John F.
Green, Lorn A.
Gutierrez, Albert D., (Outside the Archdiocese)
Gutierrez, Roberto F.
Hanlon, Thomas F.
Harris, Willie, Sr.
Hubbell, Carl, (Outside the Archdiocese)
Irizarry, Jose
Jordan, Dennis E., C.A.C.
Karrenberg, William H., (Outside the Archdiocese)
Keough, Walter
Kirk, John, Camden, NJ
Knox, Terrence, (Outside the Archdiocese)
Lam, Alex S.
Lannon, Billy, Jr.
Leon, Michael
Livingstone, Donald
Llorens, Julke
Lopez, Mario
Lopez, Pedro, (Outside the Archdiocese)
Lorenzo, John
Loyola, Benito
Luka, Chandy
Malinoski, Thomas, B.A., Baton Rouge, LA
Martinez, Jose
McInerney, Vincent
Merkel, Arthur, Panama
Mickwee, George, (Outside the Archdiocese)
Mieyal, Denis
Mindel, Albert
Moreno, Vicente
Moretti, Daniel
Munter, Paul H.
O'Gorman, Frank B.
O'Malley, Robert F., Jr.
Ochoa, Roberto
Onelien, Montas, (Outside the Archdiocese)
Ortega, Ray, (Outside the Archdiocese)
Ortiz, Esteban
Panellas, Eduardo
Parlade, Miguel
Pearce, Joseph M.
Peremenis, John
Perez, Manuel
Phang Sang, Louis
Pierce, John, Palm Beach, FL
Pimentel, Victor M.
Pineda, Roberto, Washington, D.C.
Pintado, Angel
Plummer, Joseph, (Outside the Archdiocese)
Plummer, Michael
Prieto, Jorge
Pulido, Carlos, (Cienfuegos)
Raymond, Donald, (Outside the Archdiocese)
Reyes, Jeffrey J.
Reyes, Rafael de los
Rodriguez, Ernesto
Rodriguez, Jorge, (Outside the Archdiocese)
Rodriguez, Santos
Rosado, Jose, Newark, NJ
Rosalez, Marco V.
Ruiz-Castaneda, Norman
Saavedra, Manuel
Sierra, Feliciano, (Outside the Archdiocese)
Smith, David
Solorzano, Jose, (Outside the Archdiocese)
Sommovigo, Joseph
Soucy, Joseph O.
Starzinski, Louis
Sutcavage, George P.
Taylor, Ian
Taylor, Timm, (Outside the Archdiocese)
Thesing, John
Tola, Vincent
Tollis, Giuseppe
Tosco, Jesus
Turcotte, Richard A.
Ulloa, Lazaro
Valdes, Melanio, (Ciego De Avila)
Vasquez, Domingo, New York
Venezia, Richard, Palm Beach, FL
Vitale, Perry, (Outside the Archdiocese)
Watkins, William A.
Yglesias, Robert
Zayas, Julio, (Outside the Archdiocese)
Zayas, Luis, (Outside the Archdiocese)

INSTITUTIONS LOCATED IN THE ARCHDIOCESE

[A] SEMINARIES, ARCHDIOCESAN

MIAMI. *St. John Vianney College Seminary*, 2900 S.W. 87th Ave., 33165. Tel: 305-223-4561; 305-223-4562; Fax: 305-223-0650. Email: carruthers@sjvcs.edu. Web: www.sjvcs.edu. Rev. Msgr. Michael Carruthers, Rector; Dr. Ramon J. Santos, Academic Dean; Maria Rodriguez, Librarian; Revs. Robert Vallee, Assoc. Prof. Philosophy & Liturgy Dir.; Jose Alvarez, Dean of Students; Juan Carlos Rios, Spiritual Dir.; Joseph Kottayil, Spiritual Dir.; Ferdinand Santos (Philippines), Philosophy Prof. Priests 6; Lay Teachers 5; Total Staff 20; Students 74.

[B] COLLEGES AND UNIVERSITIES

MIAMI. *Barry University* (1940) President's Office, 11300 N.E. 2nd Ave., 33161. Tel: 305-899-3010; Fax: 305-899-3018. Email: lbevilacqua@mail.barry.edu. Web: www.barry.edu. Sisters Linda Bevilacqua, O.P., Ph.D., Pres.; Jeanne O'Laughlin, O.P., Ph.D., Chancellor; Mr. Bruce Edwards, Vice Pres. Business & Finance; Dr. Michael Griffin, Ed.D., Vice Pres. Student Affairs; Dr. Linda Peterson, Provost; Dr. Carol-Rae Sodano, Dean School of Adult & Continuing Education; Angela M. Scott, Asst. Vice Provost Enrollment; Dr. Eileen McDonough, Assoc. Vice Pres. Student Affairs; Dr. Maria Luisa Alvarez, Assoc. Vice Pres. Student Affairs & Dean of Students; Revs. Mark Wedig, O.P., Ph.D.; Pedro A. Suarez, S.J.; Scott O'Brien, O.P., D.Min.; Jorge L. Presmanes, O.P., D.Min.; Yvette Brown, Chief Information Officer; Dr. Terry Piper, Dean School of Education; John P. Nelson, D.P.M., Interim Dean School of Pediatric Medicine; Dr. Tomislav Mandakovic, Dean School of Business; Mr. Kenneth S. Venet, Interim Dir. Library; Dr. Pegge Bell, Ph.D., Dean College of Health Sciences; Dr. Debra McPhee, Dean School of Social Work; Dr. Karen A. Callaghan, Dean, College of Arts & Sciences; Ann Paton, Vice Pres., Institutional Advancement; Dr. Christopher Starrat, Dean School of Human Performance (Acting); Ms. Leticia M. Diaz, Dean, School of Law. Sisters of St. Dominic (Adrian, MI). Priests 5; Brothers 1; Sisters 19; Lay Teachers 636; Students 8,581.

MIAMI GARDENS. *St. Thomas University* (1961) (Coed), 16401 N.W. 37th Ave., 33054. Tel: 305-628-6000; Fax: 305-628-6703. Email: signup@stu.edu. Web: www.stu.edu. Susan Angulo, Librarian. Priests 1;

Lay Teachers 100; Students 2,419.
Board of Trustees: Rev. Msgr. William J. Hennessey, S.T.L., M.S., V.G., P.A.; Rudy Cecchi; Bob Dickinson; Paul Garcia; Gary Goldbloom; Ervin Gonzalez; Ray Gonzalez; Cyrus M. Jollivette; Joseph P. Lacher; Victor H. Mendelson; Dominick Miniaci; Mario Murgado; Jose Navarro; Peter Prieto; Frances Sevilla-Sacasa; Rodger Shay; Dr. P. Alan Smurfit, Trustee Emeritus; Gregory T. Swienton.
The Member: Most Rev. John Clement Favalora, D.D., S.T.L.; Stanley G. Tate; Mario Trueba; Wini Amaturo; John J. Dooner.
Of Counsel: Mr. J. Patrick Fitzgerald, Esq.
Administration: Rev. Msgr. Franklyn M. Casale, Pres.; Rev. Edward A. Blackwell, Dir. of Campus Ministry; Beverly Bachrach, Vice Pres. Univ. Advancement; Terry O'Connor, Vice Pres. for Admin. & Treas. & CFO; Alfredo Garcia, Dean of the School of Law; Gregory Chan, Provost of the Univeristy, Chief Academic Officer; Dr. Joseph Iannone, Dean of the School of Graduate Studies; Dr. Breatriz Robinson, Vice Pres. Planning & Enrollment; Marivi Prado, Dir. of Mktg. & Communications, 16401 N.W. 37th Ave., 33054. Tel: 305-474-6880.
Clergy and Religious Full-Time Faculty: Revs. Harry Loubriel; James L. MacDougall, O.S.A.

[C] HIGH SCHOOLS, ARCHDIOCESAN

MIAMI. *Archbishop Coleman Carroll High School*, 10300 S.W. 167th Ave., 33196. Tel: 305-388-6700; Fax: 305-388-4371. Email: mail@colemancarroll.org. Web: www.colemancarroll.org. Sr. Marisa Ducote, O.C.D., Prin.; Rev. Msgr. Kenneth K. Schwanger, J.C.D., Pres. Priests 2; Carmelite Sisters of the Most Sacred Heart 4; Deacons 2; Lay Teachers 39; Total Staff 70; Students 600.

Archbishop Curley-Notre Dame High School (1953) 4949 N.E. 2nd Ave., 33137-3199. Tel: 305-751-8367; Fax: 305-751-3517. Email: officeoftheprincipal@acnd.net. Web: www.acnd.net. Bro. Patrick Sean Moffett, C.F.C., Prin.; Mrs. Maria Diaz, Vice Prin. for Academics; Mr. Douglas Romanik, Vice Prin. Student Svcs. Priests 1; Deacons 1; Brothers 5; Sisters 2; Lay Teachers 25; Students 324.

St. Brendan High School (1975) 2950 S.W. 87th Ave., 33165. Tel: 305-223-5181; Fax: 305-220-7434. Email: sabres@stbhs.org. Web: www.stbhs.org. Bro. Felix A. Elardo, F.M.S., Prin.; Rev. Jose Alvarez, Supervising Prin.; Dr. Carmen Castello, Asst. Prin.; Mrs. Isabel Lopez-Healy, Asst. Prin.; Ms. Barbara Behnke, Dean of Students; Mildred A. Copeland, Librarian; Alicia A. Rivero, Librarian. Brothers 4; Lay Teachers 72; Counselors 5; Students 1,148.

Immaculata La Salle High School (1958) 3601 S. Miami Ave., 33133. Tel: 305-854-2334; Fax: 305-858-5971. Email: principal@lasallehighschool.com. Web: www.lasallehighschool.com. Sr. Patricia Roche, F.M.A., Prin.; Dr. Erik Shane, Asst. Prin. for Student Affairs; Mrs. Luisa Serratore, Asst. Prin. for Curriculum; Mrs. Maria Haugland, Financial Admin.; Mr. Christopher Crotty, Athletic Dir.; Ms. Carmen Hoyos, Activities Dir.; Mr. Jose Naranjo, Librarian. Sisters 3; Lay Teachers 60; Students 739.

Msgr. Edward Pace High School (1961) 15600 Spartan Blvd., N.W. 32nd Ave., 33054. Tel: 305-624-8534; Fax: 305-521-0185. Email: agarcia@pacehs.com. Web: www.pacehs.com. Mrs. Ana Garcia, Prin.; Teresita Wardlow, Asst. Prin. Curriculum Instruction; Rebeca Bautista, Dean of Academics; Mr. Samuel Lilly, Dean of Students (Grades 10-11); Valarie Lloyd, Dean of Students (Grades 9-12); Les Brown, Dean of Students; Theresa Gula, Librarian. Email: tgula@pacehs.com. Priests 1; Lay Teachers 53; Students 970.

Our Lady of Lourdes Academy (1963) 5525 S.W. 84th St., 33143. Tel: 305-667-1623; Fax: 305-663-3121. Email: sfoy@olla.org. Web: www.olla.org. Sr. M. Sheila Foy, I.H.M., Prin.; Ileana Armengol, Librarian. Sisters (Servants of the Immaculate Heart of Mary) 4; Lay Teachers 67; Students 833.

FORT LAUDERDALE. *Archbishop Edward A. McCarthy High School* (1998) 5451 S. Flamingo Rd., 33330. Tel: 954-434-8820; Fax: 954-680-4835. Email: maverick@mccarthyhigh.org. Web: www.mccarthyhigh.org. Rev. Brendan Dalton, Supervising Prin.; Dr. Richard Perhla, Prin.; Mrs. Camille Henderson, Librarian. Priests 2; Lay Teachers 69; Students 1,403.

Cardinal Gibbons High School (1961) 2900 N.E. 47th St., 33308. Tel: 954-491-2900; Fax: 954-772-1025. Email: cghs@cghsfl.org. Web: www.cghsfl.org. Sr. Marie Schramko, O.S.F., Asst. Prin.; Mr. Paul D. Ott, Prin.; Revs. Oscar Alonso, Sch.P.; Charles Newburn, Sch.P.; John Callan, Sch.P.; Bros. Grant R. Ferris, O.S.F.S.; Michael Brickmann, C.S.C., Guidance Counselor; Kathleen Tavernia, Librarian. Priests 3; Brothers 2; Sisters of St. Francis 2; Lay Teachers 66; Students 1,172.

St. Thomas Aquinas High School (1936) 2801 S.W. 12th St., 33312. Tel: 954-581-2127; 954-581-0700; Fax: 954-581-8263. Email: tjones@aquinas-sta.org. Web: www.aquinas-sta.org. Rev. Msgr. Vincent T. Kelly, Supervising Prin.; Mrs. Tina Jones, Prin.; Rev. William J. Sullivan, O.S.S.T., Asst. Supervising Prin.; Dr. Robert Mulder, Asst. Prin.; Dr. Denise Aloma, Asst. Prin.; Dr. Ian Robertson, Dept. Chair, Theology; Mrs. Kathy Myrick, Campus Min.; Mr. Rob Biasotti, Dean of Students; Mr. George Smith, Dir. of Athletics; Mrs. Alane Klink, Guidance Dir.; Mrs. Mary Lynn McAloon, Librarian. Priests 2; Sisters 1; Lay Teachers 116; Students 2,154.

[D] HIGH SCHOOLS, PRIVATE

MIAMI. *Belen Jesuit Preparatory School* (1854) 500 S.W. 127th Ave., 33184. Tel: 305-223-8600; Fax: 305-227-2565. Email: webmaster@belenjesuit.org. Web: www.belenjesuit.org. Revs. Pedro A. Suarez, S.J., Pres & Contact; Guillermo Garcia-Tunon, S.J., Prin.; Juan Manuel Dorta, S.J.; Francisco Perez-Lerena, S.J.; Francisco Permuy, S.J.; Pedro Cartaya, S.J.; Nelson Garcia, S.J.; Lionel Lopez; Ernesto Fernandez Travieso, S.J.; Eduardo Barrios, S.J.; Marta Cosculluela, Librarian. Priests 9; Sisters 1; Lay Teachers 120; Students 1,498.

Our Lady of Belen Jesuit Foundation, Inc., 12725 S.W. 6th St. #204, 33184. Tel: 786-621-4043; Fax: 786-621-4044.

Carrollton School of the Sacred Heart (1962) 3747 Main Hwy., 33133. Tel: 305-446-5673; Fax: 305-529-6533. Email: scooke@carrollton.org. Web: www.carrollton.org. Sr. Suzanne Cooke, R.S.C.J., Headmistress; Mr. Adolfo Danguillecourt, Prin.; Roberta Rand, Librarian. Religious of the Sacred Heart 3; Lay Teachers 130; Students 790.

Christopher Columbus High School, 3000 S.W. 87 Ave., 33165. Tel: 305-223-5650; Fax: 305-559-4306. Web: www.columbushs.com. Bros. Michael Brady, F.M.S., Prin.; Edmund Sheehan, F.M.S., Librarian; Kenneth Curtin, F.M.S., Admissions Dir.; Kevin Handibode, F.M.S., Pres.; Mrs. Patricia Call, Asst. Prin. (Academic Dean); Mr. Pedro Garcia-Casals, Asst. Prin. & Academic Dean; Dr. James Dugard, Campus Min. Dept. Leader of Rel.; Mr. David Pugh, Dean of Students; Mr. Christopher McKeon, Dean of Students. Christopher Columbus High School Endowment Trust. Priests 2; Marist Brothers 14; Lay Teachers 74; Students 1,380.

HOLLYWOOD. *Chaminade-Madonna College Preparatory* (1960) 500 Chaminade Dr., 33021-5800. Tel: 954-989-5150; Fax: 954-983-4663. Email: info@chaminade-madonna.org. Web: www.chaminade-madonna.org. Rev. Lawrence Doersching, S.M., Pres.; M. Gloria Ramos, Prin.; Ron Belanger, Librarian. Marianist Priests 1; Marianist Brothers 2; Lay Teachers 56; Students 675.

[E] ELEMENTARY SCHOOLS, PRIVATE

KEY WEST. *Mary Immaculate Star of the Sea* (1868) 700 Truman Ave., 33040. Tel: 305-294-1031; Fax: 305-294-2095. Web: maryimmaculatestarofthesea.com. Beth Harris, Prin. Brothers 1; Sisters 3; Lay Teachers 18; Students 170.

[F] SHELTERS

MIAMI. *Camillus House, Inc.* (1960) 336 N.W. 5th St., 33128. Tel: 305-374-1065, Ext. 308; Fax: 305-372-1402. Email: dr.paul@camillus.org. Web: www.camillus.org. Dr. Paul R. Ahr, Ph.D., Pres. & CEO. Provides services to the homeless: emergency services, substance abuse rehabilitation, transitional and permanent housing. Bed Capacity 800; Total Assisted Annually 11,384; Total Staff 160.

Camillus Health Concern, Inc. (1984) P.O. Box 012408, 33101-2408. Tel: 305-374-1065; Fax: 305-373-7431. Web: www.camillus.org. Provides medical, dental, mental health and social services to the homeless and indigent. Total Assisted Annually 4,498; Total Staff 48.

Charity Unlimited of Florida, Inc. (1995) Tel: 305-758-7439; Fax: 305-372-1402. Provides buildings and grounds for charitable works.

Brothers of the Good Shepherd, Inc. (1960) Tel: 305-759-8206; Fax: 305-756-9014. Web: www.lbgs.org. Rev. Raphael Mieszala, B.G.S., Mission Integration Dir. A Religious Congregation. Brothers 5.

Brothers of the Good Shepherd of Haiti, Inc. (1996) Tel: 305-759-8206; Fax: 305-756-9014. Email: raphaelbgs@yahoo.com. Provides aid and assistance to orphanages and schools operated in Haiti by the Brothers of Good Shepherd.

Gift of Hope, Missionaries of Charity (1981) 724 N.W. 17th St., 33136. Tel: 305-326-0032. Sr. M. Prema, M.C., Supr. Gen.

Women's and Children's Shelter Tel: 305-326-0032. Bed Capacity 24; Total Women Assisted 290; Total Children Assisted 64.

Soup Kitchen (1981) Tel: 305-326-0032. Total Assisted 78,837; Total Staff 6.

[G] MINISTRY OF CATHOLIC CHARITIES

WILTON MANORS. *Boystown of Florida, Inc.*, 1505 N.E. 26 St., 33305. Tel: 305-762-1332; Fax: 305-754-6649.

[H] CATHOLIC CHARITIES OF THE ARCHDIOCESE OF MIAMI, INC.

WILTON MANORS. *Catholic Network of Florida, Inc.*, 1505 N.E. 26 St., 33305. Tel: 305-762-1332; Fax: 305-754-6649.

[I] MINISTRY OF CATHOLIC HEALTH SERVICES

LAUDERDALE LAKES. *Centro Mater Child Care Services, Inc.*, 4790 N. State Rd. 7, 33319. Tel: 954-484-1515; Fax: 954-484-5416.

St. Mary Star of the Sea Affordable Housing, Inc., 4790 N. State Rd. 7, 33319. Tel: 954-484-1515; Fax: 954-484-5416.

St. Monica Gardens, Inc., Mailing Address: 4790 N. State Rd. 7, 33319. Tel: 954-484-1515; Fax: 954-484-5416. 3425 N.W. 189th St., Miami Gardens, 33056.

[J] GENERAL HOSPITALS

MIAMI. *Mercy Hospital* (1950) 3663 S. Miami Ave., 33133. Tel: 305-854-4400; Fax: 305-285-2114. Web: www.mercymiami.org. Sisters Barbara Cekosh, S.S.J., Chm. of the Bd. of Trustees; Edith Gonzalez, S.S.J., Vice Pres., Mission Integration & Contact; Revs. Joseph Fishwick, Chap. (Retired); Fabio Arango (Colombia), Chap.; Julio Estada, Chap.; Jairo Tellez, Chap. Sponsored by the Sisters of St. Joseph of St. Augustine, FL. Sisters 5; Bed Capacity 473; Patients Assisted Annually 353,191; Total Staff 1,776.

Mercy Mission Services, Inc.

Mercy Outpatient Services, Inc. dba Sister Emmanuel Hospital for Continuing Care Tel: 305-285-2939; Fax: 305-285-5042. Raul Lopez, M.D., Chm., Bd. of Directors; Efrain Garcia M.D., Pres., Medical Staff; Shed Boren, CEO & Contact. Bed Capacity 29; Patients Assisted Annually 325; Total Staff 109.

FORT LAUDERDALE. *Holy Cross Hospital* (1955) 4725 N. Federal Hwy., 33308. Tel: 954-771-8000; Fax: 954-351-5947. Email: john.johnson@holy-cross.com. Web: www.holy-cross.com. John C. Johnson, Pres. & CEO; Sr. Rita Levasseur, R.S.M., Vice Pres. of Mission; Ms. Barbara Ouellette, Dir. of Spiritual Care; Revs. William Muniz, Chap.; Robert Monti, Chap.; James Nero, O.F.M., Chap.; Gary Wiesmann, (Jamaica); Sr. Claudia Steger, O.S.F., Mgr., Spiritual Care; Rev. Joanne M. Afshar, Chap.; Rev. Tabatha Lennon, Chap.; Mr. Alex Garvey, Assoc. Chap. Sisters of Mercy 6; Sisters of St. Francis 1; Total Staff 2,846; Bed Capacity 563; Patients Assisted Annually 484,732.

Holy Cross Hospital, Inc. Tel: 954-492-5796; Fax: 954-351-5947.

Holy Cross Long Term Care, Inc. Tel: 954-492-5796; Fax: 954-351-5947.

[K] MONASTERIES AND RESIDENCES OF PRIESTS AND BROTHERS

MIAMI. *Casa San Lorenzo*, 16401 N.W. 37th Ave., Miami Gardens, 33054. Tel: 305-624-0775; Fax: 305-625-4529. Revs. James L. MacDougall, O.S.A., Prior, Contact; Richard Mullen, O.S.A.; Luis M. Madera, O.S.A.; Arthur Johnson, O.S.A. Augustinian Fathers. Total in Residence 4.

Dominican Fathers of Miami, Inc., 5909 N.W. 7th St., 33126. Tel: 305-264-0181, Ext. 25; Fax: 305-262-4685. Email: sobrien@mail.barry.edu. Web: www.opsouth.org. Revs. Restituto Perez, O.P.; Desiderio Eguino, O.P.; Mark Wedig, O.P., Ph.D.; Scott O'Brien, O.P., D.Min.; Jorge L. Presmanes, O.P., D.Min.; Alberto Rodriguez, O.P.; Eduardo Gabriel, O.P.; Marcelo Solorzano, O.P.; Bro. Fernando Sorolla-Delgado, O.P. House of Religious Men 1; Total in Residence 8.

Marist Brothers of the Schools, Inc., 3000 S.W. 87th Ave., 33165. Tel: 305-221-0824, Ext. 22.

Marist Residences Community #1: 3000 S.W. 87th Ave., 33165. Tel: 305-221-0834. Bros. Herbert Baker, F.M.S., Dir.; Felix Anthony, F.M.S.; Edward Breslin, F.M.S.; Eladio Gonzalez, F.M.S.; Peter Guadalupe, F.M.S.; John Healy, F.M.S.; Stephen Kappes, F.M.S.; Marcos Longoria, F.M.S.; Rafael Martin, F.M.S.; Joseph Maura, F.M.S.; Vincent

Moriarty, F.M.S.; Patrick McNulty, F.M.S.; Angelo Palmieri, F.M.S.; Edmund Sheehan, F.M.S.; Eugene Trzecieski, F.M.S.; Julio Vitores, F.M.S. Community #2: 8230 S.W. 136th St., Palmetto Bay, 33158. Tel: 305-251-6484; Fax: 305-378-2081. Bros. William Lavigne, F.M.S., Dir.; Daniel J. Grogan, F.M.S.; Chanel Lambert, F.M.S. Community #3: 2790 S.W. 89th Ave., 33165. Tel: 305-223-5570. Bros. Charles Filiatrault, F.M.S., Dir.; Ronald D. Barabino, F.M.S.; Fabian Mayor, F.M.S.; Bernard Nolan, F.M.S.; Joseph Teston, F.M.S.; Vincent J. Dougherty, F.M.S. Community #4: 8415 S.W. 81st Ter., 33143. Tel: 305-274-5946. Bros. Kenneth Curtin, F.M.S., Dir.; Michael Brady, F.M.S.; Albert Rivera, F.M.S.; Kevin Handibode, F.M.S.

Villa Javier Belen Jesuit Fathers, Inc., 12725 S.W. 6th St., 33184-1305. Tel: 786-621-4593; Fax: 305-222-1256. Email: belensj@aol.com. Web: www.belenjesuit.org. Revs. Guillermo Arias, S.J., Counselor & Prof.; Florentino Azcoitia, S.J., Dir. of Retreats; Marcelino Garcia, S.J., Pres. of Belen Jesuit Prep School; Guillermo Garcia-Tunon, S.J., Prin.; Francisco Perez-Lerena, S.J., Supr.; Juan Manuel Dorta, S.J., Dir. of Alumni Assoc.; Eduardo Barrios, S.J., Admin., Treas., & Chap.; Pedro Cartaya, S.J., Theology, Spanish Prof.; Pedro A. Suarez, S.J., Pres. Belen Jesuit Preparatory School; Oscar Mendez, S.J. (Retired); Nelson Garcia, S.J., Counselor, Retreats; Jose F. Permuy, S.J.; Ernesto Fernandez Travieso, S.J.; Michael Chesney, S.J., Theology Teacher & Counselor. *Belen Jesuit Alumni Association* Tel: 305-661-6180; Fax: 305-661-9639. Rev. Juan Manuel Dorta, S.J., Moderator of Alumni Assoc.

[L] CONVENTS AND RESIDENCES FOR SISTERS

MIAMI. *Claretian Missionary Sisters of Florida, Inc.*, 7080 S.W. 99th Ave., 33173. Tel: 305-274-6148; Fax: 305-274-6148. Email: usdelegation@claretiansisters.org. Web: www.claretiansisters.org. Sr. Ondina Cortes, R.M.I., Pres. Sisters 13.

Daughters of Charity of St. Vincent de Paul (1971) (Santurce, P.R.), Mision San Vicente de Paul., 500 N.W. 63rd Ave., 33126. Tel: 305-266-6485; Fax: 305-265-9671. Email: caridad@gate.net; eperezpuella@yahoo.com. Web: www.gate.net/~caridad. Asociacion Hijas de la Caridad de San Vicente de Paul del Estado de la Florida, Inc.

Ermita Nacional de Nuestra Senora de la Caridad (1973) 3609 S. Miami Ave., P.O. Box 330555, 33133. Tel: 305-854-2404; Fax: 305-854-8022. Sr. Eva Perez-Puelles, Contact.

Daughters of St. Paul Convent (1959) 11117 S.W. 2nd St., 33174. Tel: 305-554-0175; Fax: 305-220-1639. Email: miami@pauline.org. Web: www.pauline.org. Sr. Maria Teresa Meza, F.S.P., Supr., Contact. Houses of Religious Women 1; Total in Residence 7.

Pauline Books & Media, Office: 145 S.W. 107th Ave., 33174. Tel: 305-559-6715; Fax: 305-559-6717. Web: www.pauline.org.

Guadalupan Missionaries of the Holy Spirit (1930) 2483 S.W. 4th St., 33135-2907. Tel: 305-642-9544; Fax: 305-649-2422. Email: mgspsusa@bellsouth.net. Sr. Oliva Olivares, Treas.

Missionary Guadalupanas of the Holy Spirit, Inc. In Residence 4.

Handmaids of the Sacred Heart of Jesus A.C.J. (1975) St. Rafaela's Faith Community, 1615 N.E. 108th St., 33161. Tel: 305-891-9161; Fax: 305-891-8791. Email: mjsagaseta@gmail.com. Web: www.acjusa.org. Sisters 4.

Missionaries of Charity (1980) 727 N.W. 17th St., 33136. Tel: 305-545-5699. Sr. M. Ajaya, Supr. Houses of Religious Women 1; Total in Residence 6; Total Assisted 2,612.

Monastery of the Most Holy Trinity, (Discalced Carmelite Nuns) (2001) 4525 W. Second Ave., Hialeah, 33012. Tel: 305-558-7122; Fax: 305-558-1190. Sr. M. Teresa Lopez, O.C.D., Prioress.

Religious of the Apostolate of Florida, Inc., 2160 S.W. 16th Ave. Apt. #320, 33145-2871. Tel: 305-285-1585. Email: apostolatesister@bellsouth.net. Sisters Alicia Velazquez, R.A., Contact Person; Maria del Rosario Delgado, R.A., Admin.

**Siervas de los Corazones Traspasados de Jesus y Maria, Inc. (Servants of the Pierced Hearts of Jesus and Mary), Two Hearts Convent (Mother House)*, 3098 S.W. 14th St., 33145. Tel: 305-444-7437. Email: sisterana@piercedhearts.org. Sr. Ana M. Lanzas, S.P.H.J.M., Contact Person. Professed Sisters 25.

St. Therese Convent, 2996 S.W. 14th St., 33145.

Saint Pio's Convent, 3046 S.W. 14th St., 33145.

Immaculate Convent, 1420 S.W. 31st Ave., 33145.

HIALEAH. *Discalced Carmelite Nuns, Inc.*, 4525 W. 2nd Ave., 33012. Tel: 305-558-7122; Fax: 305-558-1190. Sr. M. Teresa Lopez, O.C.D., Pres.

Servants of Jesus of Charity, Inc., 126 W. 45th St., 33012. Tel: 305-231-2063; Fax: 305-231-2063.

HOMESTEAD. *Daughters of Mary, Mothers of Mercy (Nigeria), Inc.*, 18444 S.W. 293rd Ter., 33030. Tel: 863-824-7576.

MIAMI SHORES. *Franciscan Sisters of Allegany* 124 N.E. 111 St., 33161. Tel: 305-751-3093; Fax: 305-751-3093. Total in Residence 2.

St. Francis Hospital, Inc. dba Franciscan Sisters of Allegany Ministries (1966) Tel: 305-751-3093; Fax: 305-751-3093.

WESTCHESTER. *Congregation of the French-Cuban Dominican Sisters of Holy Rosary, Inc.*, 7920 S.W. 23rd St., Miami, 33155. Tel: 305-265-9759. Sr. Mary Cecilia Alonso, O.P., Pres., Treas. & Contact. Houses of Religious Women 1; Total in Residence 4.

[M] RETREAT HOUSES

MIAMI. *John Paul II Retreat House*, 720 N.E. 27th St., 33137-4697. Tel: 305-576-2748; 305-573-1418; Fax: 305-576-2748. Email: webmaster@acu-adsum.org. Web: www.acu-adsum.org. Rev. Amando Llorente, S.J., Spiritual Dir., Contact. Total in Residence 2; Total Staff 8.

Agrupacion Catolica Universitaria, Inc Tel: 305-573-1418; Fax: 305-576-2748.

ACU Holdings, Inc., Jesus Maestro Inc., 717 N.E. 27th St., 33137.

Jesuit Fathers of the Province of the Antilles, Inc.

PINECREST. *MorningStar Renewal Center, Inc.*, 7275 S.W. 124th St., 33156-4649. Tel: 305-238-4367; Fax: 305-238-4766. Email: info@morningstarrenewal.org. Web: www.morningstarrenewal.org. Very Rev. James Fetscher, V.F., Spiritual Dir.; Sue S. DeFerrari, Dir.

[N] MINISTRY OF CHRISTIAN FORMATION

MIAMI . *Hispania International Institute, Inc.*, 8670 S.W. 27th Ln., 33155. Tel: 786-390-3047. Email: clflorida1@gmail.com.

[O] CENTERS

MIAMI. *National Shrine of Our Lady of Charity* 3609 S. Miami Ave., 33133. Tel: 305-854-2404; Fax: 305-854-8022. Email: padreoscar@ermitadelacaridad.org. Web: www.ermitadelacaridad.org. Most Rev. Agustin A. Roman, D.D., Rector Emeritus (Retired); Rev. Msgr. Oscar F. Castaneda, Rector; Rev. Carlos J. Cespedes (Cuba); Deacon Manuel Perez. Sisters 3; Houses of Religious Women 1; Total in Residence 3.

Pauline Book & Media Center (1959) 145 S.W. 107th Ave., 33174. Tel: 305-559-6715; Fax: 305-559-6717. Email: miami@pauline.org. Web: www.pauline.org. Sr. Maria Teresa Meza, F.S.P., Supr. Daughters of St. Paul 7; Houses of Religious Women 1; Total in Residence 7; Pauline Book & Media Center 3; Total Staff 5.

Paulinas Spanish Distribution Center (1996) Tel: 305-225-2513; 800-872-5852; Fax: 305-225-4189. Web: www.pauline.org (Spanish). Sr. Majorina Zanatta, F.S.P., Manager. Religious 2; Lay Staff 2.

Respect Life Ministry, 3600 S.W. 32 Blvd., West Park, 33023. Tel: 954-981-2922; Fax: 954-981-2901. Email: ilovelife@bellsouth.net. Web: www.respectlifemiami.com. Rev. Jordi Rivero, Spiritual Dir.; Mrs. Joan Crown, Dir. Special Centers for Social Services 5; Total Assisted 10,707; Total Staff 3.

Southeast Pastoral Institute, 7700 S.W. 56th St., 33155. Tel: 305-279-2333; Fax: 305-279-0925. Email: sepimiami@aol.com. Web: www.sepimiami.org. Revs. Mario B. Vizcaino, Sch.P., Assoc. Dir. Devel.; Jose P. Burgues, Sch.P., Dir.; Zulima Marin, Admin. Asst. & Office Mgr.

Southeast Regional Office for Hispanic Ministry, Inc., 7700 S.W. 56th St., 33155. Tel: 305-279-2333; Fax: 305-279-0925. Email: sepimiami@aol.com. Web: www.sepimiami.org. Revs. Mario B. Vizcaino, Sch.P., Asst. Dir, Devel. & Prov., Piarist Fathers USA Prov.; Jose P. Burgues, Sch.P., Dir.; Zulima Marin, Admin. Asst. & Office Mgr.

MIAMI SHORES. *Family Life Ministry*, 9401 Biscayne Blvd., 33138. Tel: 305-762-1157; Fax: 305-762-1144. Email: ejimenez@theadom.org. Web: www.miamicatholicfamily.org. Rev. Eduardo Jimenez, Dir.; Jean Valdes-Fauli Duda. Tel: 305-762-1140 Separated, Divorced and Bereavement Ministries; Herminia Leon, Sec. Tel: 305-762-1140; Deacon Jorge Gonzalez, Spiritual Dir., P.O. Box 524160, 33152-4160. Tel: 305-226-4664. Web: www.caminante.com. Camino Al Matrimonio (Spanish).

[P] PERSONAL PRELATURE

MIAMI. *Prelature of the Holy Cross and Opus Dei*, 4415 S.W. 88th Ave., 33165. Tel: 305-551-7956; Fax: 305-551-7957. Email: vacortes@earthlink.net. Revs. Victor Cortes, Contact Person; Francisco Vera; Christopher Schmitt.

[Q] MISCELLANEOUS LISTINGS

MIAMI. *Alumni Association of the Apostolate of Cuba (in Exile), Inc.*, P.O. Box 650721, 33265-0721. Tel: 305-267-0352. Web: www.geocities.com/aaapostolado. Cira Hernandez Borges, Pres.; Marina Alvarez Rodriguez, Sec.

Alumni of Apostolate Charity Foundation, Inc. (1985) 10990 S.W. 59th Ter., 33173-1148. Tel: 305-271-4151; Fax: 305-271-4341. Web: www.geocities.com/aaapostolado. Berta San Pedro, Pres. Tel: 305-445-8900; Maria Antonia D. Pena, Treas., Contact. Tel: 305-271-4151.

Brother Keily Place, Inc., 336 N.W. 5th St., 33128.

Brownsville Housing, Inc., 336 N.W. 5th St., 33128.

Charity Unlimited Foundation, Inc., 336 N.W. 5th St., 33128.

Charity Unlimited Holding, Inc., 336 N.W. 5th St., 33128.

Charity Unlimited Leasing, Inc., 336 N.W. 5th St., 33128.

Claretian Missions, Inc., 7080 S.W. 99th Ave., 33173. Tel: 305-274-6148; Fax: 305-274-5695. Email: ondina@claretiansisters.org. Web: www.claretiansisters.org. Sr. Ondina Cortes, R.M.I., Pres.

Emmaus Place, Inc., 336 N.W. 5th St., 33128.

Federacion de Institutos Pastorales, Inc., 7700 S.W. 56th St., 33155. Tel: 305-279-2333; Fax: 305-279-0925. Sr. Ruth Bolarte, I.H.M., Pres. Email: srruthbolarte@aol.com.

Foundation of the Cuban Association of the S.M.O. of Malta, Inc. (1993) 2950 S.W. 27th Ave., #300, 33133. Tel: 305-285-0800; Fax: 305-285-0837. Email: juan.t.onaghten@ondlaw.com. Fernando Garcia-Chacon, Pres.; Juan T. O'Naghten, Vice Pres.; Luis F. Parajon, Treas.; Jose Joaquin Centurion, Dir.; Luis Miguel O'Naghten, Sec.

Good Shepherd Villas, Inc., 336 N.W. 5th St., 33128.

Labre Place, Inc., 336 N.W. 5th St., 33128.

Leadership Learning Center at St. John Bosco, Inc., 1366 N.W. First St., 33125.

St. Luke's Center, Inc., 7707 N.W. 2nd Ave., 33150. Tel: 305-795-0077; Fax: 305-795-2022. Email: stlukes@catholiccharitiesadm.org. Web: www.catholiccharitiesadm.org/stluke. Dr. Mark L. Szurek, Ph.D., Dir. Total in Residence 50; Total Staff 25.

Addiction Recovery Center

Magnificat, Inc., 14130 S.W. 151 Ct., 33196. Tel: 305-253-8764; Fax: 305-205-5599. Floredenis Brown, Coord.; Valli Leoni, Historian; Virginia Vega, Asst Coord.; Cecilia Quevedo, Treas.

Matt Talbot House, Inc., 336 N.W. 5th St., 33128.

**Opus Caritatis Corp.*, 3609 S. Miami Ave., 33133. Tel: 305-854-2404; Fax: 305-854-8022. Rev. Msgr. Oscar F. Castaneda, Dir.

Peruvian Mission, Inc. (1994) (A Florida Not-for-Profit Corporation), P.O. Box 472745, 33143. Tel: 305-542-1589; Fax: 305-596-6738. Email: perumision@aol.com. Most Revs. Miguel Irizar, C.P., Bishop of Callao, Pres.; Luis Bambaren, S.J., Bishop of Chimbote (Retired); Very Rev. Mario Busquets Jorda, Bishop Prelature of Chuquibamba; Maria Delia Salazar, Dir., Sec. & Contact Person Board Members Most Revs. Luis Abilio Sebastiani Aguirre, S.M., Archbishop of Ayacucho; Pedro Barreto, S.J., Archbishop of Huancayo; Jose L. Astigarraga, C.P., Bishop of the Vicariate of Yurimaguas; Jorge Carrion, Bishop of Puno; Isidro Sala, Bishop of Abancay (Retired).

SEPI Evangelization and Education Foundation, Inc., 7700 S.W. 56th St., 33155. Tel: 305-279-2333; Fax: 305-279-0925. Email: sepimiami@aol.com. Rev. Jose P. Burgues, Sch.P., Exec. Dir., Sec., Contact.

Somerville Residence, Inc., 336 N.W. 5th St., 33128.

**St. Anne's Nursing Center St. Anne's Residence, Inc.*, 11855 Quail Roost Dr., 33177-3956. Karen Batey, Contact Person.

Teresian Institute, (Rome, Italy), Teresian Institute of Florida, Inc. (1911) An International Association of the Faithful., 3400 S.W. 99 Ave., 33165. Tel: 305-554-0035; Fax: 305-764-8222. Email: garmendia@bellsouth.net. Web: www.institucionteresiana.org. Ela Alvarado, Contact; Maria J. Garmendia, U.S. Delegate. Total in Residence 2; Total Staff 4.

Center of Activities, National Headquarters Web: www.institucionteresiana.org.

Theatine Sisters of the Immaculate Conception, Co. aka Religiosas Teatinas de la Immaculada Concepcion 12261 S.W. 6th St., 33184. Tel: 305-223-2512; Fax: 305-227-6951. Email: teatinas@bellsouth.net. Sr. Nilsa Castillo, R.T., Supr.

Vida Humana Internacional, 45 S.W. 71st Ave., 33144. Tel: 305-260-0525; Fax: 305-260-0595. Email: vhi@vidahumana.org. Web: www.vidahumana.org. Rev. Thomas J. Euteneuer, Pres.

COOPER CITY. *Discalced Carmelite Friars of Miami, Inc.*, 6525 Schott Cir., 33330-3902. Tel: 954-533-2640. Web: carmelitesmiami.com. Bro. Jorge Llorentes, O.C.D., Supr. Total in Residence 1.

Schott Memorial Center Foundation, Inc. (A Florida Not-for-Profit Corporation), 6591 S. Flamingo Rd., 33330. Tel: 954-434-3306; Fax: 954-434-3307. Mr. Frank Casale, Exec. Dir., Contact.

Schott Memorial Center, Inc. dba Schott Communities Tel: 954-434-3306; Fax: 954-434-3307. Email: fcasale@schottcomunities.org. Web: schottcommunities.org. Programs, residences and services for persons who are deaf or disabled Total Assisted 1,000; Total Staff 22.

CORAL GABLES. *House of the Divine Will, Inc. dba Casa de la Divina Voluntad* (1996) 5900 Leonardo St., 33146-3332. Tel: 305-667-5714; Fax: 305-667-7173. Email: casadivinavoluntad@msn.com. Web: www.casadeladivinavoluntad.org. Rev. Carlos Antonio Massieu Avila, Pres. & Chm.; Marianela Perez, Treas. & Contact Person.

HIALEAH. *Dominicas de la Inmaculada Concepcion*, 571 W. 33rd Pl., 33012. Tel: 305-823-3282. Email: domecu@bellsouth.net. Sisters Maria Ines Siguenza, O.P., Supr.; Enith Montero, O.P.; Carmen Aguilar, O.P.; Blanca Hernandez, O.P. Houses of Religous Women 1; Total in Residence 4.

HOLLYWOOD. *Catholic Charismatic Services of the Archdiocese of Miami, Inc.* (1980) P.O. Box 816128, 33081-0128. Tel: 954-961-1856; Fax: 954-961-3662. Email: ccs112@bellsouth.net. Emery Horvath, Dir.; Mary Horvath, Co-Dir.

HOMESTEAD. **Centro de Artes y Oficios De La Salle, Inc., Vocational Center*, 31250 S.W. 134th Ave., 33033-5617. Tel: 305-245-5810; Fax: 305-553-3032. Web: www.cesalleh.org. Mailing Address: P.O. Box 653836, Miami, 33265-3836. Jose M. Dorado, Pres.; Julio Gonzalez-Portuondo, Sec. Vocational Center for adults. Classes are free of charge. Also after school for children K-9. Staff 9; Total Assisted 129.

Lauderdale Lakes

Miramar Senior Housing Project, Inc., 4790 N. State Rd. 7, Lauderdale Lakes, 33319.

MIAMI LAKES. *Catholic Hospice, Inc.*, 14875 N.W. 77th Ave., Ste. 100, 33014. Tel: 305-822-2380; Fax: 305-824-0665. Web: www.catholichospice.org. Brian Payne, Pres. & CEO. Sponsored by the Archdiocese of Miami and Mercy Hospital.

MIAMI SHORES. *Apostleship of the Sea (Archdiocese of Miami)* (1978)Mailing Address: 4000 Island Blvd., Ste. 1902, Aventura, 33160. Tel: 786-514-4502. Rev. Thomas W. Falkenthal, Archdiocesan Dir. Email: tfalkenthal@theadom.org; Mrs. Angela Gregorio, Miami Center Coord. (Port of Miami); Rafael D. Baptista, Asst. to Dir. Serving Port of Miami, Port Everglades & Miami River

Archdiocese of Miami Development Corporation, 9401 Biscayne Blvd., 33138. Tel: 305-762-1243. Emilio Alonso-Mendoza, Pres.

Archdiocese of Miami Millennium Appeal, Inc., 9401 Biscayne Blvd., 33138. Tel: 305-757-6241; Fax: 305-758-5261. Most Rev. John Clement Favalora, D.D., S.T.L., Pres.; Rev. Msgrs. William J. Hennessey, S.T.L., M.S., V.G., P.A., Vice Pres.; Michael A. Souckar, Sec.

Archdiocese of Miami, Inc. (1958) 9401 Biscayne Blvd., 33138. Tel: 305-757-6241; Fax: 305-758-5261. Most Rev. John Clement Favalora, D.D., S.T.L., Pres.; Rev. Msgr. William J. Hennessey, S.T.L., M.S., V.G., P.A., Vice. Pres.; Mr. Joseph M. Catania, Treas.; Rev. Msgr. Michael A. Souckar, Sec.

Asociacion Nacional de Diaconos Hispanos, Inc., 9401 Biscayne Blvd., 33138. Tel: 305-223-2065. Deacons George Benavente, Pres.; Fernando Bestard, Vice Pres. Tel: 305-762-6510; 305-271-9586.

Bahamas Mission of Florida, Inc., Archdiocese of Miami, 9401 Biscayne Blvd., 33138. Tel: 305-762-1220. Email: tmarin@adom.us. Rev. Msgr. Tomas M. Marin, V.F., Vice Pres.

Catholic Community Foundation in the Archdiocese of Miami, Inc. (1999) 9401 Biscayne Blvd., 33138-2998. Tel: 305-762-1080; Fax: 305-762-1020. Email: info@the-ccf.org. Web: www.the-ccf.org. Mr. Thomas Beier, Chm.; Emilio Alonso-Mendoza, Pres.; L.J. Rodriguez, Vice Pres.; Mr. Sean Clancy, Sec.

DOM, Inc., 9401 Biscayne Blvd., 33138. Tel: 305-762-1098; Fax: 305-758-5261.

Ecclesiastical Province of Miami, Inc., 9401 Biscayne Blvd., 33138. Tel: 305-762-1098.

Francis Realty Corporation, 9401 Biscayne Blvd., 33138. Tel: 305-762-1098; Fax: 305-758-5261.

P.O.M., Inc., 9401 Biscayne Blvd., 33138. Tel: 305-762-1098; Fax: 305-758-5261.

Provincial Realty Associates, Inc. (A Florida Not-for-Profit Corporation), 9401 Biscayne Blvd., 33138. Tel: 305-762-1098; Fax: 305-758-5261. Land Holding Corporation.

South Dade Catholic Residential Center, Inc., 9401 Biscayne Blvd., 33138. Tel: 305-762-1098.

Stella Maris Seamen Center, Inc., Mailing Address: 9401 Biscayne Blvd., 33138. Tel: 954-734-1580; Fax: 954-766-2699. Rev. Thomas W. Falkenthal, Archdiocesan Dir.

POMPANO BEACH. *Ministerio Catolico Verbo y Vida, Inc.*, 2310 Martin Luther King Blvd., 33069. Tel: 954-791-8780; Fax: 954-972-3607. Email: verboyvida@sanisidro.org. Web: www.verboyvida.org. Rev. Abel Barajas, Pres.

Word & Life Catholic Ministry, Inc. (1986) 2310 Martin Luther King Blvd., 33069. Tel: 954-970-7766; Fax: 954-970-7277. Email: wordandlife@sanisidro.org. Rev. Abel Barajas, Pres.

RELIGIOUS INSTITUTES OF MEN REPRESENTED IN THE ARCHDIOCESE

For further details refer to the corresponding bracketed number in the Religious Institutes of Men or Women section.

[0140]—*The Augustinians* (St. Thomas of Villanova Prov.)—O.S.A.

[0580]—*Brothers of the Good Shepherd*—B.G.S.

[0470]—*Capuchin Friars* (Detroit, MI)—O.F.M.Cap.

[0310]—*Congregation of Christian Brothers* (Eastern Prov.)—C.F.C.

[0260]—*Discalced Carmelite Friars*—O.C.D.

[0650]—*Holy Ghost Fathers*—C.S.Sp.

[0690]—*Jesuit Fathers and Brothers* (Antilles)—S.J.

[0770]—*The Marist Brothers* (Bayonne, N.J. & Poughkeepsie Provs.)—F.M.S.

[1210]—*Missionaries of St. Charles-Scalabrinians*—C.S.

[]—*Missionaries of the Company of Mary* (U.S. Prov.)—S.M.M.

[0910]—*Oblates of Mary Immaculate*—O.M.I.

[0920]—*Oblates of St. Francis de Sales*—O.S.F.S.

[]—*Order of Carmelites* (North American Prov. of St. Elias)

[0430]—*Order of Preachers (Dominican)* (St. Joseph & Southern Provs.)—O.P.

[1310]—*Order of the Holy Trinity*—O.SS.T.

[]—*Order of the Imitation of Christ*—O.I.C.

[1020]—*Pauline Fathers & Brothers*—S.S.P.

[1040]—*Piarist Fathers*—Sch.P.

[1260]—*Society of Christ*—S.Ch.R.

[0760]—*Society of Mary (Marianists)*—S.M.

[0370]—*Society of St. Columban*—S.S.C.

RELIGIOUS INSTITUTES OF WOMEN REPRESENTED IN THE ARCHDIOCESE

[]—*Assumption Sisters of Eldoret* (Kenya, Africa)—A.S.E.

[0370]—*Carmelite Sisters of the Most Sacred Heart of Los Angeles*—O.C.D.

[0685]—*Claretian Missionary Sisters*—R.M.I.

[0270]—*Congregation of Bon Secours*—C.B.S.

[1710]—*Congregation of the Third Order of St. Francis of Mary Immaculate, Joliet, IL*—O.S.F.

[0760]—*Daughters of Charity of St. Vincent de Paul*—D.C.

[0850]—*Daughters of Mary Help of Christians*—F.M.A.

[]—*Daughters of Mary, Mother of Mercy (Nigeria)*—D.M.M.M.

[0420]—*Discalced Carmelite Nuns*—O.C.D.

[1070-13]—*Dominican Sisters (Adrian)*—O.P.

[1070-06]—*Dominican Sisters (Newburgh)*—O.P.

[]—*Dominican Sisters of Our Lady of the Most Holy Rosary (Colombia)*—O.P.

[]—*Dominicas de la Inmaculada Concepcion (Ecuador)*

[1180]—*Franciscan Sisters of Allegany, New York*—O.S.F.

[1845]—*Guadalupan Missionaries of the Holy Spirit* (Mexico)—M.G.Sp.S.

[1870]—*Handmaids of the Sacred Heart of Jesus*—A.C.J.

[2575]—*Institute of the Sisters of Mercy of the Americas* (Pittsburgh, PA; Rochester, NY; Clogher, Ireland; Newfoundland, Canada)—R.S.M.

[]—*Marianitas* (Santa Mariana de Jesus Institute, Inc.)—R.M.

[2710]—*Missionaries of Charity*—M.C.

[3040]—*Oblate Sisters of Providence*—O.S.P.

[]—*Our Lady of Good Counsel* (Canada), S.B.C.

[3130]—*Our Lady of Victory Missionary Sisters*—O.L.V.M.

[0950]—*Pious Society Daughters of St. Paul*—F.S.P.

[3380]—*Religious of the Apostolate of the Sacred Heart*—R.A.

[3390]—*Religious of the Assumption*—R.A.

[2970]—*School Sisters of Notre Dame* (Baltimore, MD; Chicago, IL)—S.S.N.D.

[]—*Servants of Jesus of Charity*—S.de.J.

[]—*Servants of the Pierced Hearts of Jesus and Mary*—S.P.H.J.M.

[]—*Sisters of Charity* Cincinnati, Ohio—S.C.

[]—*Sisters of Jesus the Saviour* (Nigeria)—S.J.S.

[]—*Sisters of Notre Dame* Chardon, Ohio—S.N.D.

[3000]—*Sisters of Notre Dame de Namur (Baltimore, MA)*—S.N.D.deN.

[]—*Sisters of Our Lady of LaSalette*—S.N.D.S.

[3350]—*Sisters of Providence*—S.P.

[4090]—*Sisters of Social Service*—S.S.S.

[1620]—*Sisters of St. Francis of Millvale, Pennsylvania*—O.S.F.

[1630]—*Sisters of St. Francis of Penance and Christian Charity*—O.S.F.

[3830-13]—*Sisters of St. Joseph (Baden, PA)*—C.S.J.

[]—*Sisters of St. Joseph Benedict Cottolengo*—S.S.J.C.

[3830-09]—*Sisters of St. Joseph (Erie, PA)*—S.S.J.

[3850]—*Sisters of St. Joseph of Chambery* (Hartford, CT)—C.S.J.

[3900]—*Sisters of St. Joseph of St. Augustine, Florida*—S.S.J.

[]—*Sisters of St. Philip Neri Missionary Teachers*—R.F.

[2180]—*Sisters of the Immaculate Heart of Mary*—I.H.M.

[1490]—*Sisters of the Third Franciscan Order*—O.S.F.

[2160]—*Sisters, Servants of the Immaculate Heart of Mary* (Spain)—I.H.M.

[2180]—*Sisters, Servants of the Immaculate Heart of Mary* (Miami, FL)—I.H.M.

[2170]—*Sisters, Servants of the Immaculate Heart of Mary* (Immaculata, PA)—I.H.M.

[4020]—*Society of St. Teresa of Jesus*—S.T.J.

[4070]—*Society of the Sacred Heart*—R.S.C.J.

[]—*Theatine Sisters of the Immaculate Conception (Religiosas Teatinas de la Inmaculada Concepcion)*—R.T.

NECROLOGY

† Darbouze, Rev. Msgr. Gerard, North Miami, FL Saint James—Died March 21, 2009

† Brantome, Oscar, (Retired)—Died Feb. 11, 2009

† Escala, Rafael, (Retired)—Died Jan. 27, 2009

† Ireland, Donald J., (Retired)—Died April 15, 2009

† Lucking, Aloysius, (Retired)—Died Sept. 16, 2009

† Lyons, Francis, (Retired)—Died Oct. 17, 2009

† Mylchreest, William F., Fort Lauderdale, FL Saint Sebastian—Died July 29, 2009

† Peterman, Charles O., Deerfield Beach, FL Saint Ambrose—Died Dec. 11, 2009

Archdiocese for the Military Services, U.S.A.

Ordinariatus Castrensis

Most Reverend

JOSEPH T. DIMINO, D.D.

Former Archbishop for the Military Services; ordained June 4, 1949; appointed Titular Bishop of Carini and Auxiliary Bishop to the Military Ordinariate March 29, 1983; consecrated May 10, 1983; appointed Ordinary for the Military Services May 13, 1991; retired August 12, 1997.

Most Reverend

FRANCIS X. ROQUE, D.D.

Retired Auxiliary Bishop for the Military Services; ordained September 19, 1953; appointed Titular Bishop of Bagai and Auxiliary Bishop to the Military Ordinariate March 29, 1983; consecrated May 10, 1983; retired August 15, 2004.

Most Reverend

JOSEPH J. MADERA, M.SP.S., D.D.

Retired Auxiliary Bishop for the Military Services; ordained June 15, 1957; appointed Coadjutor Bishop of Fresno with the right of succession December 18, 1979; consecrated March 4, 1980; succeeded to See July 1, 1980; appointed Titular Bishop of Orte and Auxiliary Bishop of the Archdiocese for the Military Services May 28, 1991; retired August 15, 2004.

Most Reverend

TIMOTHY P. BROGLIO, J.C.D., S.T.B., M.A.

Archbishop for the Military Services; ordained May 19, 1977; appointed Titular Archbishop of Amiternum & Apostolic Nuncio to the Dominican Republic February 27, 2001; ordained a bishop March 19, 2001; appointed Archbishop for the Military Services November 17, 2007; installed January 25, 2008.

Chancery: 1025 Michigan Ave., N.E., P.O. Box 4469, Washington, DC 20017-0469. Tel: 202-719-3600; Fax: 202-269-9022.

Web: www.milarch.org

Email: info@milarch.org

Most Reverend

RICHARD B. HIGGINS, S.T.L., D.D.

Auxiliary Bishop for the Military Services; ordained March 9, 1968; appointed Titular Bishop of Casae Calanae and Auxiliary Bishop of the Archdiocese for the Military Services May 7, 2004; ordained July 3, 2004.

Most Reverend

JOSEPH W. ESTABROOK, D.D.

Auxiliary Bishop for the Military Services; ordained May 30, 1969; appointed Titular Bishop of Flenucleta and Auxiliary Bishop of the Archdiocese for the Military Services May 7, 2004; ordained July 3, 2004.

Established as the Archdiocese For The Military Services, U.S.A. (Ordinariatus Castrensis) March 25, 1985.

Serving U.S. Catholics of the Army, Navy, Air Force, Marine Corps, Coast Guard, Department of Veterans Affairs and those in Government Service overseas.

STATISTICAL OVERVIEW

Personnel

Archbishops	1
Retired Archbishops	1
Auxiliary Bishops	2
Retired Bishops	2

Vital Statistics

Receptions into the Church:	
Infant Baptism Totals	4,926
Adult Baptism Totals	825
Received into Full Communion	358
First Communions	2,771
Confirmations	2,165
Marriages:	
Catholic	414
Interfaith	287
Total Marriages	701

Former Military Vicars—His Eminence PATRICK CARDINAL HAYES, cons. Titular Bishop of Tagaste, Oct. 28, 1914; appt. "Bishop Ordinary of U.S. Army and Navy Chaplains," Nov. 24, 1917; appt. Archbishop of New York, March 10, 1919; created Cardinal, March 24, 1924; died Sept. 4, 1938; FRANCIS CARDINAL SPELLMAN, cons. Auxiliary Bishop of Boston, Sept. 8, 1932; appt. Archbishop of New York, April 15, 1939; appt. "Military Vicar for the Armed Forces of U.S.," Dec. 11, 1939; created Cardinal, Feb. 18, 1946; died Dec. 2, 1967; TERENCE CARDINAL COOKE, cons. Auxiliary Bishop of New York, Dec. 13, 1965; appt. Archbishop of New York, March 2, 1968; appt. "Military Vicar of U.S. Armed Forces," April 4, 1968; created Cardinal, April 28, 1969; died Oct. 6, 1983; Most Revs. JOSEPH T. RYAN, appt. first Archbishop of Anchorage, Feb. 7, 1966; cons. March 25, 1966; appt. Titular Archbishop of Gabi and Coadjutor (Archbishop) of the Military Ordinariate, Oct. 24, 1975; installed first Ordinary of the Archdiocese for the Military Services March, 25, 1985; retired May 13, 1991; died Oct. 9, 2000; JOSEPH T. DIMINO, D.D. (Retired), appt. Auxiliary Bishop of Military Odinariate and Titular Bishop of Carini, March 29, 1983; cons. May 10, 1983; appt. second Ordinary for the Military Services, May 13, 1991; retired Aug. 12, 1997; EDWIN F. O'BRIEN, ord. May 29, 1965; appt. Titular Bishop of Tizica and Auxiliary Bishop of New York Feb. 6, 1996; cons. March 25, 1996; appt. Coadjutor April 8, 1997; succeeded as Ordinary to the Military Services Aug. 12, 1997; appt. Archbishop of Baltimore July 12, 2007.

Vicar General & Moderator of the Curia—Rev. Msgr. FRANK A. PUGLIESE, M.Div., M.A., M.S. (Ed).

Archdiocese Offices

Chancery—Mailing Address: P.O. Box 4469, Washington, 20017. Tel: 202-719-3600; Fax: 202-269-9022. Email: info@milarch.org. Web: www.milarch.org.

Chancellor—Deacon MICHAEL D. YAKIR, M.B.A.

Vice Chancellor—Sr. HELEN SUMANDER, M.C.S.T.

Office of Evangelization—

Vice Chancellor for Evangelization—Dr. MARK MOITOZA.

Vicar for Evangelization—Most Rev. JOSEPH W. ESTABROOK, D.D.

Office of Veterans Concerns—

Vicar for Veteran Concerns—Most Rev. RICHARD B. HIGGINS, S.T.L., D.D.

Office of Vocations—

Director of Vocations—Rev. JOHN R. MCLAUGHLIN JR., M.Div.

Assistant to the Archbishop—Sr. MARY HANAH DOAK, R.S.M.

Chief Financial Officer—VACANT.

Controller—Mr. WILLIAM BIGGS.

Director of Development—Mr. WILLIAM KIRST.

Archivist—Sr. HELEN SUMANDER, M.C.S.T.

Tribunal—

Judicial Vicar—Rev. Msgr. THOMAS P. OLSZYK, J.C.L., Th.M.

Judges—Revs. JAMES E. BAKER, J.C.L.; G. PAUL HERBERT, J.C.L.; JOHN B. WARD, J.C.L.; Ms. LINDA E. PRICE, J.C.L.; Ms. DEBORAH BARTON, J.C.L.

Defenders of the Bond—Revs. JORDAN F. HITE, T.O.R., J.C.L.; RICHARD H. HUGLI; JOSEPH A. GRIMALDI, J.C.L.; Ms. ZABRINA DECKER, J.C.L.

Procurator-Advocate—VACANT.

Assessor—JOHN L. SCHLAGETER, Esq., J.D.

Notary—Miss PATRICIA HUTCHISON.

General Counsel—JOHN L. SCHLAGETER, Esq., J.D.

Presbyteral Council—Most Revs. JOSEPH W. ESTABROOK, D.D.; RICHARD B. HIGGINS, S.T.L., D.D.; Rev. Msgr. FRANK A. PUGLIESE, M.Div., M.A., M.S. (Ed); Deacon MICHAEL D. YAKIR, M.B.A.; Rev. Msgrs. DONALD L. RUTHERFORD; GERALD D. MCMANUS; Revs. JOHN R. MCLAUGHLIN JR., M.Div.; ROBERT A. BRUNO, O.F.M.; WILLIAM F. CUDDY; GREGORY G. CAIAZZO; JAMES E. BURNETT; PAUL STEPHEN HOLT.

Military Council of Catholic Women—Most Rev. RICHARD B. HIGGINS, S.T.L., D.D., Episcopal Moderator.

Areas of Service

Armed Forces, Active Duty: The Archdiocese for the Military Services is responsible for the pastoral care of the Catholic men and women who serve on active duty in the U.S. Armed Forces. It is also responsible for the dependents of these persons. Included also are the cadets and resident personnel of the three military academies (West Point--the U.S. Military Academy, the U.S. Air Force Academy at Colorado Springs, the U.S. Naval Academy at Annapolis) and the U.S. Coast Guard Academy at New London. Pastoral care is provided by priest-chaplains on loan from their dioceses or religious communities to serve as chaplains for the Military and Department of Veterans Affairs. Members of the Marines and Coast Guard are served by Navy Chaplains; Armed Forces, Reserves, National Guard: In addition to the personnel on active duty in the Armed Forces, there is a considerable reserve component. Some of these personnel serve a number of days each year on active duty with a branch of the service; some serve on extended tours of active duty; all are subject to recall to active duty in a national emergency. In addition to the reserve components of the Army, Air Force, Navy and Coast Guard, there are also the Air National Guard and the Army National Guard, which are organized on a state-by-state basis; Department of Veterans Affairs: The Archdiocese for the Military Services is responsible for the spiritual care of Catholics at V.A. medical facilities. Chaplaincy services are provided by full- and part-time priests, many of whom are retired military chaplains; U.S. Government Civilian Employees Abroad: U.S. citizens in government service abroad (and their family members living with them) are subjects of the Archdiocese for the Military Services; Civil Air Patrol: The Civil

Air Patrol, as an auxiliary of the Air Force, is under the jurisdiction of the Archdiocese for the Military Services. The jurisdiction applies to its chaplains and members only when participating in exercises on a military installation.

UNITED STATES ARMY CHAPLAINS

Army Chaplains:
Rev. Msgrs.—
Hill, Philip W. (NY)
Rutherford, Donald L.
Revs.—
Albano, Alwyn M. (Philippines)
Albertson, Eric J. (ARL)
Barkemeyer, John F. (CHI)
Bendorf, Richard, O.F.M.
Besinga, Dino J. (Philippines)
Betz, James F. (CAM)
Blick, Ned (WCH)
Brocato, John K. (ALX)
Buckon, Neal J. (CLV)
Carlson, Kenneth F., M.Div. (CHI)
Congdon, John (FRS), Chap.
D'Emma, Gregory J. (NEW)
Dormer, David J. (SCR)
Dynek, Wieslaw A. (Poland)
Eke, Rafael E. (Nigeria) (SAT)
Fleury, Joseph M., S.M.
Foley, Matthew E. (CHI)
Fukes, Gary M. (SY)
Fuller, Orlando R. (Philippines)
Gabriel, John B. (India)
Glasgow, Robert K. (WIL)
Gonzalez, George G. (SAT)
Greschel, Mark (CHI), Chap.
Gross, Gary L. (LIN)
Ha, Hieu Minh (ATL)
Halka, Frantisek A. (ALT)
Halladay, Paul A. (MOB)
Hannon, Joseph F., S.D.B.
Hernandez, Anselmo, L.C.
Herrera, Jose G. (STV)
Herron, John B. (FAR)
Hesseling, Jason E. (MAD)
Honor, Michael P. (Philippines)
Hubbs, Timothy L. (CAM)
Hurley, Paul K. (BO)
Iheke, Uche G., S.M.M.M.
Ijeoma, John Vianney (Nigeria) (LKC)
Ilokaba, Damian O. (Nigeria)
Inghilterra, Vincent J. (TR)
Irizarry, Alan M. (ARE)
Jong, Lyndon A. (Philippines)
Kalinowski, Joseph J. (E)
Kaverenge, Fausto K. (Kenya)
Kazarnowicz, Anthony S. (WOR)
Kelley, Edward J. (PRO)
Kenehan, David A., O.S.F.S.
Kilumbu, Claudes (Congo)
Kirchhoefer, Thomas A. (STL)
Kirk, David R. (TOL)
Kokeram, Sudash J. (NEW)
Kopec, Krzysztof A. (WIL)
Kopec, Rajmund (NEW)
Kumai, Felix K. (Nigeria) (NY)
Lanuevo, Victor (HON)
Lawrence, Andrew F. (DUB)
Lorenc, Henryk (Poland)
LosBanes, Hermes (Philippines)
Madej, Paul D. (SY)
Madu, Ferdinand E. (Nigeria)
Magnuson, Sean R. (STP)
Manuel, Vincent (Nigeria) (ALX)
Martin, Edward (VEN)
Moras, Leo (India) (LUB)
Napieralski, Maciej (FBK)
Nielson, Kenneth W. (AUS)
O'Grady, J. Frank (PAT)
O'Neal, James E. (STA)
Obeng-Kyeremeh, Simon (STV)
Ohm, Edward U. (PEO)
Okoth, George (Kenya)
Opara, Christopher (Nigeria) (NY)
Opara, Isaac (Nigeria) (LAF)
Panzer, Joel (LIN)
Passamonti, Paul G. (WDC)
Pawlikowski, Matthew (NEW)
Peek, Kevin T., B.A., M.Div. (ATL)
Perez, John C. (SJN)
Reyes, Armando I. (Philippines)
Roetzel, Robert E., C.S.C.
Rzasowski, Jerzy (Poland)
Sheil, James (CLV)
Spencer, F. Richard (BAL)
Studniewski, Gary R. (WDC)
Subler, Carl A. (COL)
Tadeo, Victor C. (Philippines)
Travaglione, Michael, O.F.M.
Ugwuanya, Valentine C. (NEW)
Uhde, Peter M. (NEW)
Valentine, Timothy S., S.J.
Van Alstyne, Donald J., M.I.C.
Van Durme, Patrick, S.T.L. (ROC)
Villanueva, Edgar (HON)
Wendel, Alfred W. (ATL)
Wood, Tyson J. (BAL)
Yoakam, Lee R., O.S.B.

Army National Guard Chaplains:
Rev. Msgrs.—
Coyle, Edward J., M.A., Th.M. (ALN)
Thomas, Royce R., J.C.L., J.V. (LR)
Revs.—
Allen, Richard J. (E)
Alvardo de Jesus, Jose (PCE)
Austin, Walter J. (NO)
Brownell, Patrick P. (KNX)
Cavanaugh, Kevin P. (HRT)
Constant, Van (HT)
Converse, Brian J. (NOR)
Corneille, Cecil C. (STV)
Dolan, Patrick J., Ph.D., S.T.D. (L)
Farley, Daniel H. (LC)
Fehn, Jerome W. (STP)
Feltz, John G. (BUR)
Figueroa, Honecimo (BWN)
Giese, Samuel C. (WDC)
Gonzalez, Julio Angel (MGZ)
Holzhauser, John J. (SFS)
Jaramillo, Peter (AMA)
Kaminski, Louis T. (SCR)
Kane, Brian P. (LIN)
Kilmurray, Fintan J. (BLX)
Kozen, Bert S. (SCR)
Lemoi, Paul R. (PRO)
Lindsay, Michael P. (LSC)
Lippstock, Paul Eldon (DUB)
Meier, Timothy, S.J.
Murphy, David F. (WIL)
Russo, Ricardo, O.F.M.
Sanchez-Munoz, Alejandro (STV)
Skufca, Ronald J. (MAR)
Stang, William J., C.PP.S., M.D.
Stodola, Francis (LAR)
Weberg, Paul, O.S.B.
Whorton, Jeffrey T. (SFE)
Worster, John R. (B)

Army Reserve Chaplains:
Revs.—
Augustyn, Boguslaw Adam, C.Ss.R.
Bleboo, Lawrence T. (Ghana)
Bucon, Raymond H. (DET)
Caballejo, Romeo J. (Philippines)
Caballejo, Yuen (ATL)
Coe, Austin J. (Korea, South)
Denemark, Emil J., S.J.
Dinello, John E. (PIT)
Dominic, Michael M. (Kenya)
Donahue, Brian G. (FAR)
Fitzgibbons, Peter L. (CHL)
Grice, Edward M. (NO)
Kanai, Charles (Kenya)
Kneemiller, William C. (DAV)
Krische, James J. (BRK)
Mahalic, Philip A. (LFT)
McCabe, Edward D. (BO)
McDermott, Stephen C. (PH)
Morse, Jonathan K. (STF)
Munoz-Lasalle, Jesus M. (ARE)
Nolan, Kevin L., V.F. (LA)
Ochalek, Arkadiusz (BAL)
Pamula, Robert (Poland)
Piekarczyk, Marian A., S.D.S.
Piontkowski, Richard L., Jr., S.T.L., J.C.L. (GI)
Plaushin, Mark, O.S.F.S.
Rosario, Mario S. (Philippines)
Sousa, Peter E., C.Ss.R.
Tyhovych, Ivan (STF)
Vigilanti, John A., J.C.L., Ph.D. (NY)
Yebra, Bernardino S. (Philippines) (CHR)

UNITED STATES AIR FORCE CHAPLAINS

Air Force Chaplains:
Rev. Msgrs.—
Butler, Michael T. (STL)
Charbonneau, William R. (HRT)
McManus, Gerald D. (PH)
Very Rev.—
Cannon, Col. Robert R., J.C.L. (VEN)
Revs.—
Abbot, Kerry M., O.F.M.Conv.
Adversario, Efran F. (AGN)
Angelo, Thomas M. (NOR)
Bailey, J. Lawrence (SEA)
Bartoul, William (SAM)
Beale, Kenneth R. (NEW)
Beck, R. Patrick (BEA)
Breig, Gary R. (STL)
Bruno, Robert A., O.F.M.
Butler, Timothy A. (BO)
Catungal, Mario T., O.C.D.
Clemens, Neal C. (OAK)
Cody, Kevin W. (MAN)
De Guzman, Dennis (OM)
Deichert, Joseph (BIS)
Del Toro, Jose L., T.O.R.
Dunn, Richard B. (SY)
Fadallan, Elbert A. (LUB)
Fitz-Patrick, David M. (WDC)
Fitzgerald, R. Martin (R)
Fletcher, Patrick (PCE)
Gajda, Piotr J. (CC)
Garcia, Gildardo (Colombia)
Gills, Thomas (BAL)
Glaros, Matthew J. (CLV)
Hall, Douglas C. (OM)
Hamel, James A. (NEW)
Harbour, Linn S. (MOB)
Hirten, Timothy J. (BRK)
Horgan, Daniel B. (PMB)
Juszczak, John W., C.Ss.R.
Kaim, Phillip (RCK)
King, Martin (P)
Kinney, John M. (LFT)
Kruse, David B. (BAL)
Licanda, Samuel (SFR)
Lim, Joseph D. (Philippines)
Linsky, Gary S. (CHR)
Llanos, Phillip S. (LA)
Lowe, Francis E. (SB)
McGuire, David V. (RIC)
Monagle, Robert J. (BO)
Moreno, Antonio O., O.F.M.Conv.
Navarrete, Jesus (Spain)
Nguyen, Hoang Peter (CHI)
Nguyen, Son, S.V.D.
Novotny, Richard (RC)
Nwoga, Laserian (CAM)
Okorie, Onyema (FRS)
Omana, Max B. (Philippines)
Pieczara, Stanislaw (Poland)
Poole, Richard (SPK)
Raux, Redmond P. (BO)
Rigonan, Antonio R. (Philippines)
Romero, Donald (DEN)
Rowan, Mark P. (RVC)
Salditos, Ricardito P. (Philippines)
Sanchez, Albert N. (Philippines)
Srode, John S., C.PP.S.
Tenorio, Michael C., O.F.M.Cap.
Theisen, Eugene J. (STP)
Vitaliano, Dominic J. (PEO)
Voelker, David A. (BEL)
Voyt, Stephen A. (PT)
Weber, Michael J., O.Praem.
Zielinski, Chad W. (GAY)
Zygadlo, Mitchell (ROC)

Air National Guard Chaplains:
Revs.—
Barnhill, Robert K. (LIN)
Barry, Robert L., O.P.
Bergbower, Daniel J. (SFD)
Bohorquez, Carlos M. (SFD)
Cooney, Patrick, O.S.B.
Crowley, Edmund G. (MAN)
Cunningham, Douglas D. (SY)
Decker, Douglas A. (OG)
Donovan, Bernard Thomas (SFD)
Echert, John P., S.S.L. (STP)
Fitzgerald, John P., C.A.C. (PIT)
Fuller, Timothy M. (OKL)
Giamello, Anthony (WIL)
Gomez, Walter (SJN)
Humenay, Robert L. (E)
Jaeger, James P. (ROC)
Jeselnick, Stephen E. (E)
Laible, Jeffrey G. (PEO)
LaMorte, Joseph P. (NY)
Love, John W. (LA)
Ludwig, Thomas (KC)
Marciano, Robert L. (PRO)
Martinez, Michael (TUC)
McKenna, Timothy J. (SEA)
Mink, John J. (WIL)
Mizeur, Thomas R. (PEO)
Moenkedick, Leo (SCL)
Myers, Christopher P., S.O.L.T.
Ramatowski, Edward F. (STL)
Rogers, Patrick W. (COL)
Santana, Edward, J.C.L. (ARE)
Silva, Caesar (HT)
Sirianni, Richard D. (P)
Stephenson, Alfonse J. (PAT)
Stevens, David E. (SFS)
Tirado, Ramon Orlando, C.M.
Vit, William J., Jr. (SC)
Weber, Joseph A. (STL)
Winters, Darvin E. (IND)

Air Force Reserve Chaplains:
Rev. Msgrs.—

Moore, William C. (STO)
Randall, Kevin S. (NOR)
Very Revs.—
Cuevas, Randy M., S.T.L., V.F. (BR)
Erickson, Richard M. (BO)
Fischer, Richard O. (BAK)
Hoffmann, Christopher (ORL)
Johnson, James B., V.F. (SP)
Kayatta, Francis P. (PRO)
Osinski, Ronald V., V.F. (ALT)
Zalewski, Peter Lawrence, V.F. (PT)
Revs.—
Amaliri, Paul Obi (TLS)
Ballou, Jeffrey A. (SPR)
Baratelli, David J., Ed.D. (NEW)
Bastian, James R. (BUF)
Beers, John Michael, Ph.D. (ALN)
Blake, Lawrence R. (STP)
Brosk, Steven J. (NEW)
Caggianelli, Gregg (VEN)
Coogan, Roch A., O.F.M.
Cordery, Robert J.
Densmore, Anthony M. (DAL)
Dinh, Van (OAK)
Dowling, Joseph K. (NSH)
Drabek, Howard E. (GAL)
Fonseca, Oscar D. (NEW)
Fredericks, Michael (SB)
Freihofer, Michael A. (DEN)
Gaglione, John R. (BUF)
Herbert, G. Paul, J.C.L. (WDC)
Hewes, Robert S. (RVC)
Jones, Michael T. (WDC)
Kadera, Thomas R., J.C.L. (CHY)
Kelleher, Mark A. (WIL)
Keller, Robert J. (DET)
Kelly, Thomas D. (DEN)
Kowalik, Jacek (VEN)
LaBranch, Derek R. P., M.Ed., M.A., M.Div. (SAC)
Laroche, Christopher J. (PRT)
Lillpopp, Michael (SPR)
Lilly, Thomas C. (ANC)
Loseke, Jeffrey S. (OM)
Mack, John P. (BUF)
Maikowski, Thomas R., Ph.D., Ed.D. (GLP)
Malloy, Francis X. (MIL)
Mattina, Louis A. (MET)
McDowell, Leo G. (GF)
McGrade, Kevin M. (BO)
McGuill, Martin F. (ARL)
McGuine, Peter M. (SD)
McNamara, Brian J. (RVC)
Medas, Michael B., M.S.W. (BO)
Mockler, Patrick J. (BLX)
Morris, Michael J. (SP)
Morrow, Michael J. (NY)
Nguyen, Hung Van, S.O.L.T.
O'Hara, Daniel J. (SY)
Padazinski, Michael C., J.C.D. (SFR)
Reeson, David G. (OM)
Richtsteig, Erik J. (SLC)
Robbins, Thomas P. (COV)
Safraniec, Joseph N. (STU)
Schuetze, John W. (GB)
Sewell, Jack, J.C.L. (ORG)
Stakem, Ward G., O.F.M.Cap.
Stewart, Paul (PT)
Sweeney, Daniel, S.J.
Tero, Richard D. (ANC)
Tomasiewicz, Mark A. (OM)
Tran, Luan Quach (P)
Travers, Patrick J., J.C.L., J.D. (JUN)
Vaverek, Hayden J. (CHR)
Vu, Joseph Dang-Hai, S.D.D.
Wedeking, Patrick (GLP)
Willette, Donald C. (DEN)
Wulinski, Stanley F. (BRK)
Yanju, Henry M. (BO)
Zimmer, Eric A., S.J.
Very Rev. Archpriest—
Kaszczak, Ivan, Ph.D., M.A., B.A. (STF)

UNITED STATES NAVY CHAPLAINS

Navy Chaplains:
Revs.—
Aguilera, Salvador (ELP)
Bargola, Cerino O. (Philippines)
Barrett, Miles J. (SC)
Bautista, Antonio (LA)
Berchmanz, Anthony (NEW)
Borzych, Alexander J. (GI)
Brown, Shaun S. (NTN)
Brzek, Jon J. (PIT)
Caiazzo, Gregory G. (RIC)
Coffey, Joseph L. (PH)
Colvin, Andrew (BAK)
Concha, Alfonso J. (PH)
Creider, Philip B. (OKL)
Cuddy, William F. (BO)
Daigle, David A. (BGP)
Dang, Chin Van (RIC)
Danner, James L. (MEM)
Deeley, Kevin J. (BO)
Delis, Robert, S.D.B.
Dermott, William R. (ALN)
Devine, William D. (BO)
Dillon, Jerome V. (OM)
Dorwart, William D., C.S.C.
Dory, Michael (GB)
Enriquez, Rean F. (Philippines)
Finley, James F. (BRK)
Fix, Donald P. (PIT)
Foley, Francis P. (PH)
Fullerton, Daniel J. (SCR)
Gegotek, Tadeusz (BEL)
Haddad, Wayne M. (MET)
Hall, Thomas P., C.S.P.
Hannigan, John T. (CHI)
Hellwig, Lee W. (HRT)
Hicks, Steven (SAN)
Hoke, John R. (HBG)
House, Richard M. (YAK)
Ianucci, Thomas (RIC)
Johnson, Charles W. (AUS)
Johnson, Lawrence P. (DUL)
Joslyn, James W. (CHI)
Kanicki, Philip A. (RIC)
Karava, Norbert, O.F.M.Cap.
Kawcznski, Ronald L. (FAR)
Keane, Robert L., S.J.
Keener, Robert J. (CHI)
Kelly, John E. (BUF)
Kennedy, William M. (BO)
Kersten, Jay J. (LAN)
Klepacki, Michael S. (CHL)
Kloak, David G. (CHI)
Koch, Joseph A., C.V.
Koester, Timothy J. (BUF)
Kuss, Allen R. (BIS)
Le, Peter Tai Thanh (HT)
Lindblad, Karl-Albert (NY)
Logan, Aidan Arthur H., O.C.S.O.
Lyle, John W., O.S.F.S.
Mandato, Kieran (NY)
McClanahan, Robert P., Jr. (PT)
McCormick, Patrick J. (ATL)
Mensah, Gabriel (VIC)
Merris, Christopher (SD)
Mikstay, Michael (Y)
Mode, Daniel L. (ARL)
Monahan, John C., S.J.
Moss, Donald G. (SP)
Mudd, David A. (WDC)
Mueller, Michael (ORL)
Muhm, William M. (NY)
O'Flanagan, Thomas P. (PMB)
Parisi, Michael (PAT)
Reardon, Joseph D. (KC)
Rodes, Kenneth J.
Salamoni, Vincent, M.S.A.
Shaughnessy, Paul J., S.J.
Shimotsu, John M. (ORG)
Shuley, Keith J. (CC)
Sikorski, Leszek (NY)
Simpson, Brian L. (CHI)
Spencer, Robert A. (CHR)
Stake, Ronald P. (CHI)
Sweeney, Kevin (ORG)
Targonski, Conrad A., O.F.M.
Tiongson, Joselito S. (Philippines)
Ubalde, Ulysses L. (NEW)
Vanden Boogard, Richard J., O.Praem.
Welch, Bernard J. (PRT)

Navy Reserve Chaplains:
Very Rev.—
Donohue, Michael T. (NOR)
Revs.—
Arnone, Leo (ALT)
Barber, Michael C., S.J.
Barch, Howard C. (PEO)
Bergner, David J., S.D.S.
Bishop, Marc J. (BO)
Bower, Lawrence C. (BAK) (Retired)
Brighenti, Kenneth D. (MET)
Cain, Robert K.C. (TLS)
Calderone, Joseph D., O.S.A.
Cannon, Richard E. (BO)
Cheney, James (FAR)
Cienik, Kenneth, S.A.
Clark, Robert J., O.S.B.
Close, John L. (ALB)
Clovis, Stephen M. (P)
Condon, William G., C.S.C.
Connolly, James M.T. (ALN)
Coyle, Robert (RVC)
Cricchio, Santo, O.F.M.Conv.
Cunha, Egionor (NEW)
Cusick, Kevin M. (WDC)
D'Aurora, Joseph A. (RIC)
Davantes, Carlo B.
DeSocio, John A. (ROC)
Dhein, William A. (LC)
Donohoe, Stephen S., M.Div. (BO)
Doyle, Michael J. (BO)
Duesterhaus, Michael R. (ARL)
Emechete, Innocent (Nigeria) (SAC)
Ethen, Jeffrey D. (SCL)
Foote, Job, O.S.B.
Fronk, Christopher S., S.J.
Gardocki, Patrick M., O.F.M.
Gayton, John J., M.I.C.
Glassmire, David R. (BUF)
Gorman, Edward M., O.P.
Griffin, Thomas, O.S.A.
Hamaday, Ronald A., O.S.A.
Hendrickson, Michael D. (SJ)
Hoak, Jack W., O.F.M.
Johnson, Patrick D., C.S.P.
Judge, Timothy M., M.Div. (PH)
Kantor, Robert Joseph (VEN)
Kehoe, James P. (CHI)
Kilian, Waldemar Aleksander (CHI)
Klarer, Michael E. (MAD)
Kucharczyk, Dennis H. (SAG)
Langan, William J.P., V.F. (SCR)
Legaspi, Alex L. (SFR)
Legaspi, Fulgencio Paul (Philippines)
Madey, Louis (LAN)
McCandless, William T., O.S.F.S.
Neitzke, Ron P. (JOL)
Nguyen, Van T. (NO)
O'Brien, Sean Patrick (SY)
O'Connell, Terry J. (P)
O'Neill, John J. (SFR)
Parenti, Thomas M. (SFR)
Pimentel, Joseph W., O.P.
Porpiglia, Joseph D. (BUF)
Reamer, Mark G., O.F.M.
Reilly, Mark R. (OG)
Robichaud, Paul G., C.S.P.
Sera, Enrique J. (ORG)
Slowinski, Thomas F. (DET)
Stavoy, Stephen J. (SCR)
Sullivan, Robert J. (BIR)
Thorne, Thomas P. (BGP)
Thottankara, Raju (CC)
Wallace, Richard (P)

DEPARTMENT OF VETERANS AFFAIRS HOSPITALS AND CHAPLAINS:

Rev. Msgrs.—
Callahan, Kevin G. (STL)
Chacko, Joseph C. (Philippines)
Wolbach, Richard A. (OM) (Retired)
Very Revs.—
Christopher, Patrick J., V.F. (STL)
Clements, Thomas P.
Kachel, Steven J. (LC)
Revs.—
Aban, Adolfo Aristotle (Philippines)
Adejoh, Patrick O. (Nigeria)
Anthony, Joseph (RNO)
Axtmann, Mark A. (SFS)
Bain, Richard C. (SFR) (Retired)
Barber, Bradley A. (CC)
Bartsch, Kenneth W., O.F.M.Conv.
Beyer, Richard J. (DAV)
Blas, Mario W. (Philippines)
Boateng-Mensah, Samanhyia (Ghana)
Bonneville, Lionel E. (SPR) (Retired)
Brandow, Stephen J. (ALX)
Brennan, George P. (STL) (Retired)
Brioso-Texidor, Luis (SJN)
Burnett, James E. (DAV)
Butler, John J. (HON)
Caffrey, Gerald, C.M.F.
Cavey, Donald J. (RIC)
Chinnappan, Benjamin (India)
Clapham, Bruce (SYM)
Coleman, John Kenneth (SFR)
Connery, Sean P., O.S.F.S.
Craig, Robert N., O.F.M.Cap.
Craig, Robert G. (E)
Crehan, Matthias J., O.F.M.
Czartoryński, David F. (ALN)
D'Silva, Joseph R. (India)
D'Sousa, Maurice, C.S.C.
Dagle, Harold F., M.A. (ALN) (Retired)
Dahms, Paul G. (RC)
Damian, Rinaldo (WOR)
David, Craig (ATL)
De la Pena, Uldarico (Philippines)
De La Riva, John, O.F.M.Cap.
DeWane, E. Thomas, O.Praem.
Diaz, Hector (SJN)
Dieter, Thomas M. (JOL)
Eis, Charles R. (SPK) (Retired)
Eraly, Mathew (India)
Erestain, Alfonso E. (Philippines)
Everett, Willis E. (COL)
Florido, Robert (CHI)
Francis, R. Peter (RVC)

Franco, Joseph E. (NY)
Gallagher, Daniel N. (JKS)
Gardocki, Patrick M., O.F.M.
Gebhard, Robert L. (BUF)
George, George C. (AUS)
Gollob, Timothy A. (DAL)
Gould, Lawrence, S.A.C.
Grace, Joseph W. (LFT) (Retired)
Grasso, Joseph A., C.PP.S.
Hamilton, William J., S.J.
Hamperzonian, Jerry (PSC)
Henry, Paul J. (BAL)
Hickey, Joseph W. (NY) (Retired)
Holt, Paul Stephen (WDC), Assoc. Dir., VA National Chap. Center
Hyde, Robert P., Jr., J.C.L. (SY)
Iheaka, Emmanuel K. (Nigeria)
James, David John (SY)
Jones, Rick L. (SPC)
Joseph, Vio O., S.A.C.
Kakkuzhiyil, John, S.D.B.
Kauffman, William B. (WIL)
Kiene, Joseph, O.F.M.Conv.
Kleiber, Kenneth R. (CHI)
Klein, David O., C.S.B.
Koilparampil, Augustine
Lacroix, Maurice R. (MAN) (Retired)
Lagacé, Raymond R., O.F.M.
Laghezza, Pasquale V., SS.CC.
Lamp, Edward (SP)
Langford, Terry L. (L)
Lankford, Michael G. (TR)
Legarski, Joseph (ALT)
Leonhardt, Louis J. (DAV)
Lipareli, Michael A. (NY)
Lisowski, Edward E. (MIL) (Retired)
Malone, H. Patrick (WCH) (Retired)
Malone, John S., C.S.Sp.
Mani, L. David (India)
McCord, Kent G. (MET)
McNally, Michael R. (SB) (Retired)
McNulty, Gerard J. (LA)
Meier, Denis E. (SFS)
Menz, Anthony E., O.C.S.O.
Mestas, Leonard J. (BWN)
Michiels, Philip F. (SHP)
Milewski, John A. (KNX)
Miller, James Norman (NSH)
Mohr, Richard G. (BEL)
Moster, James, O.F.M.Cap.
Mullin, Thomas J. (NY)
Murphy, Patrick E. (MAR)
Myers, Christopher P., S.O.L.T.
Neuizil, Lowell Greg (KNX)
Nichols, Henry P. (BO)
Ntsiful-Amissah, Dominic Kofi (ALB)
O'Connor, Paul F., C.S.B. (Canada)
O'Keeffe, Joseph (ALB)
Ochu, Austin Charles, S.M.A.
Odemokpa, Paschal (Nigeria)
Odor, Luke U. (Nigeria)
Oguamanam, Mark (Nigeria)
Okoro, Alexander A. (Nigeria)
Onuwmere, Leonard, J.P. (Nigeria)
Oswald, Norman R. (MIL)
Palatucci, John F. (NY)
Paulish, W. Jeffrey (SCR)
Pavlick, Raymond A. (PAT)
Pesaresi, Thomas, M.M.
Phelan, Walter M. (GI) (Retired)
Piekarczyk, Marian A., S.D.S.
Putich, Michael J., O.F.M.
Rara, Clarito Z. (Philippines)
Reardon, James A. (E)
Reinders, David H. (TUC)
Rimmele, Leo R., O.S.B.
Ritzert, William J. (PIT) (Retired)
Robert, Darin T. (LAN) (Retired)
Roesch, David H. (ALT)
Rowgh, Matthew T. (WH)
Saavedra, Ramon (Philippines)
Saldua, Max Ernesto M. (Philippines)
Salois, Philip G., M.S.
Santiago, Leoncio S. (CHI)
Sarnecki, Thomas G. (SCR)
Schill, Gerald F. (Damien) (FAR)
Schneider, John H. (STL)
Schuler, Emett J., O.F.M.Cap.
Scott, Daniel J., M.S.
Shepley, Brian J. (DAV)
Sioleti, Andrew, i.v.dei.
Smith, Charles F., S.V.D.
Smith-Soucier, Martin D. (STU)
Soto, Charles, O.F.M. (Retired)
Stavoy, Stephen J. (SCR)
Steinmetz, Thomas P. (NTN)
Striegel, Robert M. (DAV)
Stump, James M., O.F.M.Cap.
Timoney, Conan H., C.P.
Torres, Ivan J. (SJN)
Torres, Ivan J. (SJN)
Tran, Quang Mihn
Ubanii, Angelo B., S.M.M.M.
Ugochukwu, Sebastian A. (Nigeria)
Uralikunnel, George V. (India)
Vander Heyden, William F. (GB)
VanDoan, Vincent (LAN)
Vennetti, Robert C., M.I.C.
Vistal, Felix (DAL)
Vu, Joseph Duc (Vietnam)
Warman, William C. (BAL)
Westfall, Joseph B. (LFT)
Wickham, William E., C.S.C.
Wydeven, John L. (OAK)
Young, Dennis M. (STA)

CIVIL AIR PATROL:
Rev. Msgr.—
McGuire, Richard J. (E) (Retired)
Revs.—
Birk, John G. (SPK) (Retired)
Juroszek, Robert S. (TOR)
O'Connor, Michael S. (BLX)
Parker, James (CHR) (Retired)
Reiter, James (E)
Shortt, David J. (PBR)
Sommer, Allan J. (MIL)
Van Sickler, Robert (BAK) (Retired)

DIOCESES WITH PRIESTS SERVING IN UNIFORM IN THE ARCHDIOCESE FOR THE MILITARY SERVICES

Agana, Guam.
Albany.
Alexandria.
Allentown.
Altoona-Johnstown.
Arecibo, Puerto Rico.
Arlington.
Atlanta.
Austin.
Baker.
Baltimore.
Beaumont.
Belleville.
Bismarck.
Boston.
Bridgeport.
Brooklyn.
Buffalo.
Camden.
Charleston.
Charlotte.
Chicago.
Cleveland.
Columbus.
Corpus Christi.
Denver.
Detroit.
Dubuque.
Duluth.
El Paso.
Erie.
Fargo.
Fresno.
Gaylord.
Grand Island.
Green Bay.
Harrisburg.
Hartford.
Honolulu.
Houma-Thibodaux.
Kansas City-St. Joseph.
LaCrosse.
Lafayette, IN.
Lansing.
Lincoln.
Los Angeles.
Louisville.
Lubbock.
Madison.
Manchester.
Marquette.
Memphis.
Metuchen.
Mobile.
Newark.
Newton (Melkite Rite).
New York.
Norwich.
Oakland.
Oklahoma City.
Omaha.
Orange.
Orlando.
Palm Beach.
Paterson.
Pensacola-Tallahassee.
Peoria.
Philadelphia.
Pittsburgh.
Ponce, Puerto Rico.
Portland, ME.
Portland, OR.
Providence.
Raleigh.
Rapid City.
Richmond.
Rochester.
Rockford.
Rockville Centre.
St. Augustine.
St. Louis.
St. Maron.
St. Nicholas.
St. Paul-Minneapolis.
St. Petersburg.
St. Thomas, Virgin Islands.
San Angelo.
San Antonio.
San Bernardino.
San Diego.
San Juan, Puerto Rico.
Santa Fe.
Scranton.
Seattle.
Sioux City.
Spokane.
Syracuse.
Toledo.
Trenton.
Tulsa.
Venice.
Victoria.
Washington, D.C.
Wichita.
Wilmington.
Worcester.
Yakima.
Youngstown.

RELIGIOUS INSTITUTES WITH PRIESTS SERVING IN UNIFORM IN THE ARCHDIOCESE FOR THE MILITARY SERVICES

[]—*Vincentian Fathers*—C.M.
[]—*Society of the Precious Blood*—C.PP.S.
[]—*Congregation of the Holy Cross*—C.S.C.
[]—*Paulist Fathers*—C.S.P.
[]—*Redemptorist Fathers*—C.SS.R.
[]—*Congregation of Marians of the Immaculate Conception*—M.I.C.
[]—*Missionaries of the Holy Apostles*—M.S.A.
[]—*Carmelite Fathers*—O.Carm.
[]—*Cistercians of the Strict Observance*—O.C.S.O.
[]—*Franciscan Fathers*—O.F.M.
[]—*Cap. Capuchins*—O.F.M.
[]—*Conv. Conventual Franciscans*—O.F.M.
[]—*Dominican Fathers*—O.P.
[]—*Norbertines*
[]—*Order of St. Benedict*—O.S.B.
[]—*Oblates of St. Francis de Sales*—O.S.F.S.
[]—*Salesian Fathers*—S.D.B.
[]—*Jesuit Fathers*—S.J.
[]—*Society of Mary*—S.M.
[]—*Society of Our Lady of the Most Holy Trinity*—S.O.L.T.
[]—*Society of the Divine World*
[]—*Third Order Regular of St. Francis*—T.O.R.

ASSOCIATIONS SUPPORTING THE MISSION OF THE ARCHDIOCESE

21st Century Centurions.
The Chaplains Aid Association.
National Conference of Veterans Affairs Catholic Chaplains, Inc. Most Rev. Richard B. Higgins, (Episcopal Advisor), Rev. William F. Vander Heyden (GB). Tel: 847-688-1900, Ext. 83163 President 2004.
Catholic War Veterans, USA, Inc., 441 N. Lee St., Alexandria, VA 22314-2301. Tel: 703-549-3622.

Archdiocese of Milwaukee

(Archidioecesis Milvauchiensis)

Most Reverend

JEROME E. LISTECKI

Archbishop of Milwaukee; ordained May 14, 1975; appointed Auxiliary Bishop of Chicago and Titular Bishop of Nara November 7, 2000; consecrated January 8, 2001; appointed Bishop of La Crosse December 29, 2004; installed March 1, 2005; appointed Archbishop of Milwaukee November 14, 2009; installed January 4, 2010. *Chancery Office: Archbishop Cousins Catholic Center, 3501 S. Lake Dr., P.O. Box 070912, Milwaukee, WI 53207-0912.*

Chancery Office: Archbishop Cousins Catholic Center, 3501 S. Lake Dr., P.O. Box 070912, Milwaukee, WI 53207-0912. Tel: 414-769-3340; Fax: 414-769-3408.

Web: www.archmil.org

Email: information@archmil.org

Most Reverend

REMBERT G. WEAKLAND, O.S.B., D.D.

Archbishop Emeritus of Milwaukee; ordained June 24, 1951; appointed Archbishop of Milwaukee September 20, 1977; consecrated and installed as Ninth Archbishop November 8, 1977; retired May 24, 2002. *Res.: Wilson Commons, 1400 W. Sonata Dr., #218, Milwaukee, WI 53221.*

Most Reverend

RICHARD J. SKLBA, D.D.

Auxiliary Bishop of Milwaukee; ordained December 20, 1959; appointed Auxiliary Bishop of Milwaukee and Titular Bishop of Castro November 6, 1979; consecrated December 19, 1979. *Res.: 836 N. Broadway, Milwaukee, WI 53202-3608.* Tel: 414-962-3941. *All official communications should be addressed to: Archbishop Cousins Catholic Center, 3501 S. Lake Dr., P.O. Box 070912, Milwaukee, WI 53207-0912.* Tel: 414-769-3486.

Most Reverend

WILLIAM P. CALLAHAN, O.F.M.CONV.

Auxiliary Bishop of Milwaukee; ordained April 30, 1977; appointed Auxiliary Bishop of Milwaukee and Titular Bishop of Lares October 30, 2007; ordained December 21, 2007. *Res.: Saint Francis Seminary, 3257 S. Lake Dr., St. Francis, WI 53235. All official communications should be addressed to: Archbishop Cousins Catholic Center, 3501 S. Lake Dr., P.O. Box 070912, Milwaukee, WI 53207-0912.* Tel: 414-769-3300.

Square Miles 4,758.

Established November 28, 1843; Created Archbishopric February 12, 1875.

Corporate Title: Archdiocese of Milwaukee.

Comprises the Counties of Dodge, Fond du Lac, Kenosha, Milwaukee, Ozaukee, Racine, Sheboygan, Walworth, Washington and Waukesha in the State of Wisconsin.

For legal titles of parishes and archdiocesan institutions, consult the Chancery Office.

STATISTICAL OVERVIEW

Personnel	
Archbishops	1
Retired Archbishops	1
Auxiliary Bishops	2
Retired Bishops	1
Abbots	1
Retired Abbots	2
Priests: Diocesan Active in Diocese	179
Priests: Diocesan Active Outside Diocese	15
Priests: Diocesan in Foreign Missions	2
Priests: Retired, Sick or Absent	146
Number of Diocesan Priests	342
Religious Priests in Diocese	321
Total Priests in Diocese	663
Extern Priests in Diocese	39
Ordinations:	
Diocesan Priests	6
Religious Priests	2
Transitional Deacons	2
Permanent Deacons	10
Permanent Deacons in Diocese	171
Total Brothers	61
Total Sisters	1,402
Parishes	
Parishes	210
With Resident Pastor:	
Resident Diocesan Priests	138
Resident Religious Priests	37
Without Resident Pastor:	
Administered by Priests	28
Administered by Deacons	1
Administered by Lay People	6
Professional Ministry Personnel:	
Brothers	5
Sisters	34
Lay Ministers	372
Welfare	
Catholic Hospitals	10
Total Assisted	1,212,268
Health Care Centers	1
Total Assisted	10,250
Homes for the Aged	16
Total Assisted	3,042
Day Care Centers	4
Total Assisted	580
Specialized Homes	5
Total Assisted	2,213
Special Centers for Social Services	12
Total Assisted	160,627
Residential Care of Disabled	3
Total Assisted	164
Other Institutions	17
Total Assisted	26,089
Educational	
Seminaries, Diocesan	1
Students from This Diocese	21
Diocesan Students in Other Seminaries	6
Seminaries, Religious	2
Students Religious	149
Total Seminarians	176
Colleges and Universities	5
Total Students	25,418
High Schools, Diocesan and Parish	7
Total Students	3,541
High Schools, Private	6
Total Students	2,960
Elementary Schools, Diocesan and Parish	104
Total Students	27,407
Elementary Schools, Private	2
Total Students	203
Non-residential Schools for the Disabled	1
Total Students	11
Catechesis/Religious Education:	
High School Students	6,501
Elementary Students	29,545
Total Students under Catholic Instruction	95,762
Teachers in the Diocese:	
Priests	53
Brothers	12
Sisters	110
Lay Teachers	4,124
Vital Statistics	
Receptions into the Church:	
Infant Baptism Totals	7,298
Minor Baptism Totals	383
Adult Baptism Totals	192
Received into Full Communion	442
First Communions	7,776
Confirmations	5,664
Marriages:	
Catholic	1,314
Interfaith	628
Total Marriages	1,942
Deaths	4,969
Total Catholic Population	657,519
Total Population	2,315,958

Former Bishops—Most Revs. JOHN MARTIN HENNI, D.D., cons. March 19, 1844; created Archbishop, Feb. 11, 1875; died Sept. 7, 1881; MICHAEL HEISS, D.D., cons. Bishop of La Crosse, Sept. 6, 1868; appt. Coadjutor of Milwaukee and Titular Archbishop of Adrianople, March 14, 1880; succeeded to Archbishop Henni in 1881; died March 26, 1890; FREDERICK XAVIER KATZER, D.D., cons. Sept. 21, 1886; Bishop of Green Bay; transferred to Milwaukee and raised to the Archiepiscopal Dignity, Jan. 30, 1891; died July 20, 1903; SEBASTIAN GEBHARD MESSMER, D.D., D.C.L., ord. July 23, 1871; cons. March 27, 1892; Bishop of Green Bay; transferred to Milwaukee and raised to the Archiepiscopal dignity Dec. 10, 1903; made assistant at the Pontifical Throne, Nov. 16, 1906; died Aug. 4, 1930; His Eminence SAMUEL ALPHONSUS STRITCH, D.D., ord. May 21, 1910; cons. Nov. 30, 1921; Bishop of Toledo; transferred to Milwaukee and raised to the Archiepiscopal dignity, Aug. 26, 1930; transferred to Chicago, Dec. 27, 1939; created Cardinal, Feb. 18, 1946; died May 27, 1958; Most Rev. MOSES E. KILEY, S.T.D., appt. Bishop of Trenton, Feb. 10, 1934; cons. March 17, 1934; appt. Archbishop of Milwaukee, Jan. 1, 1940; died April 15, 1953; His Eminence ALBERT G. MEYER, S.T.D., S.S.L., ord. July 11, 1926; cons. Bishop of Superior, April 11, 1946; appt. Archbishop of Milwaukee, July 21, 1953; transferred to Chicago, Sept. 24, 1958; created Cardinal, Dec. 14, 1959; died April 9, 1965; Most Revs. WILLIAM E. COUSINS, D.D., ord. April 23, 1927; appt. Titular Bishop of Forma and Auxiliary Bishop of Chicago Dec. 17, 1948; cons. March 7, 1949; appt. Bishop of Peoria, May 19, 1952; installed July 2, 1952; appt. Archbishop of Milwaukee, Dec. 18, 1958; installed Jan. 27, 1959; retired Sept. 20, 1977; died Sept. 14, 1988; REMBERT G. WEAKLAND, O.S.B. (Retired), ord. June 24, 1951; appt. Archbishop of Milwaukee,

Sept. 20, 1977; cons. and installed as Ninth Archbishop, Nov. 8, 1977; retired May 24, 2002; TIMOTHY M. DOLAN, ord. June 19, 1976; appt. Auxiliary Bishop of St. Louis June 19, 2001; installed Aug. 15, 2001; appt. Archbishop of Milwaukee June 25, 2002; installed as Tenth Archbishop Aug. 28, 2002; appt. Archbishop of New York Feb. 23, 2009.

Archbishop Cousins Catholic Center—3501 S. Lake Dr., P.O. Box 070912, Milwaukee, 53207-0912. Tel: 414-769-3300; Fax: 414-769-3408.

St. Joseph Center—1501 S. Layton Blvd., Milwaukee, 53215. Tel: 414-758-2200.

Archbishop Cousins Catholic Center—3501 S. Lake Dr., P.O. Box 070912, Milwaukee, 53207-0912.

Moderator of the Curia—Most Rev. WILLIAM P. CALLAHAN, O.F.M.Conv.

Vicars General—Most Revs. RICHARD J. SKLBA, S.S.L., S.T.D.; WILLIAM P. CALLAHAN, O.F.M.Conv.; Very Rev. PATRICK E. HEPPE.

Chief of Staff—JEROME T. TOPCZEWSKI. Tel: 414-769-3590; Fax: 414-769-3430. Email: topczewskij@archmil.org.

Archdiocesan Consultors—Most Revs. RICHARD J. SKLBA, S.S.L., S.T.D.; WILLIAM P. CALLAHAN, O.F.M.Conv.; Revs. DENNIS ACKERET; CURT J. FREDERICK, J.C.L., M.Div.; Rev. Msgr. T. GEORGE GAJDOS; Rev. RALPH C. GROSS; Very Rev. JEFFREY R. HAINES; Revs. JOHN D. HEMSING; JOSEPH F. HORNACEK; JEROME M. HUDZIAK, Ph.D. (Retired); JOSEPH G. STOBBA, O.S.A.

Archdiocesan Council of Priests— (Pending)

Archdiocesan Pastoral Council— (Pending)

Archbishop's Executive Council—Most Revs. RICHARD J. SKLBA, S.S.L., S.T.D.; WILLIAM P. CALLAHAN, O.F.M.Conv.; Very Rev. PATRICK E. HEPPE; Dr. BARBARA ANNE CUSACK, J.C.D.; JOHN J. MAREK; JEROME T. TOPCZEWSKI.

Archives—3501 S. Lake Dr., P.O. Box 070912, Milwaukee, 53207-0912.

Archivist—SHELLY SOLBERG. Tel: 414-769-3407. Email: solbergs@archmil.org.

Building Services—Mailing Address: 3501 S. Lake Dr., P.O. Box 070912, Milwaukee, 53207-0912.

Maintenance Coordinator—STEVE JUPP. Tel: 414-769-3566. Email: jupps@archmil.org.

Campus Ministry—St. Joseph Center, 1501 S. Layton Blvd., Milwaukee, 53215.

Coordinator—RANDY NOHL. Tel: 414-758-2216. Email: nohlr@archmil.org.

Directors—Rev. MICHAEL LIGHTNER, UW-Milwaukee Newman Center, 3001 N. Downer Ave., Milwaukee, 53211. Tel: 414-964-6640. Email: lightnerm@archmil.org; BRIAN ZANIN, UW-Whitewater Campus Ministry, 344 N. Prairie St., Whitewater, 53190. Tel: 262-473-5555. Email: zaninb@uww.edu.

Catechesis and Youth Ministry Office—St. Joseph Center, 1501 S. Layton Blvd., Milwaukee, 53215.

Director—GARY POKORNY, M.Div., D.Min. (Cand.). Tel: 414-758-2242. Email: pokornyg@archmil.org.

Catholic Charities—3501 S. Lake Dr., P.O. Box 070912, Milwaukee, 53207-0912.

Acting Director—JAMES M. BRENNAN. Tel: 414-769-3330. Email: jbrennan@ccmke.org.

Executive and Administrative Support Coordinator—KELLY JASPER. Tel: 414-769-3401. Email: kjasper@ccmke.org.

Human Resource Director—ANTHONY KIESLER. Tel: 414-769-3351. Email: akiesler@ccmke.org.

Controller—VACANT. Tel: 414-769-3413.

Advancement Director—NANCY SEIDL NELSON. Tel: 414-769-3524. Email: nnelson@ccmke.org.

Communications Director—SHARON BRUMER. Tel: 414-769-3543. Email: sbrumer@ccmke.org.

Information/Telecommunications Systems Director—RICK BERG. Tel: 414-769-3543. Email: rberg@ccmke.org.

Adult Care Ministries Director—VACANT.

Family and Children's Ministries Director—RICARDO CISNEROS. Tel: 414-769-3330. Email: rcisneros@ccmke.org.

Social Justice Ministries Director—VACANT.

Legal Services for Immigrants Services Director—BARBARA GRAHAM. Tel: 414-643-8570. Email: bgraham@ccmke.org.

"Catholic Herald"—Mailing Address: 3501 S. Lake Dr., P.O. Box 070912, Milwaukee, 53207-0912.

Publisher—Most Rev. JEROME E. LISTECKI. Tel: 414-769-3497. Email: archbishoplistecki@archmil.org.

Executive Editor and General Manager—BRIAN T. OLSZEWSKI. Tel: 414-769-3466. Email: olszewskib@archmil.org.

Managing Editor—MARYANGELA LAYMAN ROMAN. Tel: 414-769-3476. Email: laymanromanm@archmil.org.

Cemeteries and Mausoleums—7301 W. Nash St., Milwaukee, 53216.

Director—THOMAS G. CHAMPA. Tel: 414-438-4420. Email: champat@archmil.org.

Spiritual Director—Rev. MARVIN I. LAZARSKI, 3801 W. Morgan Ave., Milwaukee, 53221. Tel: 414-645-0611.

Chancery Office—

Chancellor—Dr. BARBARA ANNE CUSACK, J.C.D. Tel: 414-769-3341. Email: cusackb@archmil.org.

Vice Chancellor—Rev. JAMES E. CONNELL, J.C.D.

*Communications Office—Mailing Address: 3501 S. Lake Dr., P.O. Box 070912, Milwaukee, 53207-0912*Email: communication@archmil.org.

Director—JULIE WOLF. Tel: 414-769-3494. Email: wolfj@archmil.org.

Assistant Director—GILLIAN LESTER-GEORGE. Tel: 414-769-3461. Email: lestergeorgeg@archmil.org.

Communications Coordinator—ERIN DOLAN. Tel: 414-769-3453. Email: dolane@archmil.org.

Ecumenical and Interfaith Concerns—3501 S. Lake Dr., P.O. Box 070912, Milwaukee, 53207-0912.

Director—JUDITH A. LONGDIN. Tel: 414-769-3483. Email: longdinj@archmil.org.

Financial Services—3501 S. Lake Dr., P.O. Box 070912, Milwaukee, 53207-0912.

Archdiocesan Treasurer and Finance Officer—JOHN J. MAREK. Tel: 414-769-3334. Email: marekj@archmil.org.

Diocesan Fiscal Services Director—MICHAEL FRIES. Tel: 414-769-3347. Email: friesm@archmil.org.

Parish and School Financial Services Director—JAY FRYMARK. Tel: 414-769-3336. Email: frymarkj@archmil.org.

Parish and School Financial Services Associate Director—DOUG MILLER. Tel: 414-769-3377. Email: millerdb@archmil.org.

Staff Accountants—CHRISTINE HAUCK. Tel: 414-769-3314. Email: hauckc@archmil.org; JANICE O'CONNOR. Tel: 414-769-3315. Email: oconnorj@archmil.org.

Archdiocesan Marian Shrine—Tel: 414-257-0155.

Human Resource Services—3501 S. Lake Dr., P.O. Box 070912, Milwaukee, 53207-0912.

Director Personnel Services—RICHARD J. TANK. Tel: 414-769-3458. Email: tankr@archmil.org.

Central Offices and Agencies Director—SUSAN GORSKI. Tel: 414-769-3328. Email: gorskis@archmil.org.

Parish and School Personnel Director—JANE BUDNEY. Tel: 414-769-3370. Email: budneyj@archmil.org.

Coordinator of Catholic AIDS Ministry—Rev. MICHAEL J. HAMMER. Tel: 414-223-5101.

Information Services—3501 S. Lake Dr., P.O. Box 070912, Milwaukee, 53207-0912.

Director and System Administrator—ALLAN RIES. Tel: 414-769-3332. Email: riesa@archmil.org.

Webmaster and Coordinator of Electronic Communications—MARK BARTHEL. Tel: 414-769-3454. Email: barthelm@archmil.org.

Computer Systems Trainer and Help Desk—MARGARET ERHART. Tel: 414-769-3335. Email: erhartm@archmil.org.

Intercultural Ministry—3501 S. Lake Dr., P.O. Box 070912, Milwaukee, 53207-0912.

Coordinator—EVA J. DIAZ, M.A.P.S. Tel: 414-769-3397. Email: diaze@archmil.org.

Associate for Hispanic Ministry—JORGE BENAVENTE. Tel: 414-769-3393. Email: benaventej@archmil.org.

John Paul II Center—St. Joseph Center, 1501 S. Layton Blvd., Milwaukee, 53215.

John Paul II Center Coordinator—RANDY NOHL. Tel: 414-758-2215. Email: nohlr@archmil.org.

Ministry Formation Institute Director—Deacon JOHN A. EBEL. Tel: 414-758-2212. Email: ebelj@archmil.org.

Ministry Formation Institute Associate Director—MANUEL MALDONADO. Tel: 414-758-2207. Email: maldonadom@archmil.org.

Nazareth Project Director—LYDIA LOCOCO. Tel: 414-758-2213. Email: lococol@archmil.org.

Nazareth Project Associate Director—JENNIFER OLIVA. Tel: 414-758-2211. Email: olivaj@archmil.org.

Liturgy—Mailing Address: 3501 S. Lake Dr., P.O. Box 070912, Milwaukee, 53207-0912.

Coordinator—DEAN DANIELS. Tel: 414-769-3359. Email: danielsd@archmil.org.

Metropolitan Tribunal—

Judicial Vicar—Very Rev. PAUL B.R. HARTMANN, M.Div., J.C.L. Tel: 414-769-3304. Email: hartmannp@archmil.org.

Tribunal Chancellor—Ms. ZABRINA R. DECKER, J.C.L. Tel: 414-769-3302. Email: deckerz@archmil.org.

Office Manager—Mr. MAURICE C. THOMPSON, B.S. Tel: 414-769-3301. Email: thompsonm@archmil.org.

Judges for First Instance—Very Rev. PAUL B.R. HARTMANN, M.Div., J.C.L.; JESUS CABRERA, J.C.L.; Rev. BERNARD S. SIPPEL, M.Div. (Retired).

Judges for Second Instance—Revs. JOHN CELLA, O.F.M., J.C.D., M.Div., M.B.A.; JAMES E. CONNELL, J.C.D.; Dr. BARBARA ANNE CUSACK, J.C.D.; JESUS CABRERA, J.C.L.; Rev. CURT J. FREDERICK, J.C.L., M.Div.; Very Rev. PAUL B.R. HARTMANN, M.Div., J.C.L.; Rev. DENNIS C. KLEMME, J.C.D. (Retired); Very Rev. MICHAEL T. NEWMAN, J.C.L.; Revs. PHILIP D. REIFENBERG, J.C.L.; BERNARD S. SIPPEL, M.Div. (Retired).

Defenders of the Bond—Rev. JOHN D. AIELLO, M.Div.; Ms. ZABRINA R. DECKER, J.C.L.; Sr. AUDREY STRAUB, S.S.N.D., J.C.L.

Procurators and Advocates—STEPHEN J. HARVEY, M.Div.; Mr. MAURICE C. THOMPSON, B.S.; ANDREW R.J. VAUGHN, M.A.

Promoter of Justice—Rev. PHILIP D. REIFENBERG, J.C.L.

Office for Marital Reconciliation-Separation—Very Rev. PAUL B.R. HARTMANN, M.Div., J.C.L.

Archdiocesan Court of Equity—Very Rev. PAUL B.R. HARTMANN, M.Div., J.C.L.; Ms. ZABRINA R. DECKER, J.C.L.

Notaries—MARY CHRISTINE ELLISON; KAREY GAWRYCH; Mr. MAURICE C. THOMPSON, B.S.

Ordained and Lay Ecclesial Ministry—Archbishop Cousins Catholic Center, 3501 S. Lake Dr., P.O. Box 070912, Milwaukee, 53207-0912.

Vicar for Ordained and Lay Ecclesial Ministry—Very Rev. PATRICK E. HEPPE. Tel: 414-769-3490. Email: heppep@archmil.org.

Director of Priest and Lay Ecclesial Personnel, Placement—RICHARD J. TANK. Tel: 414-769-3458. Email: tankr@archmil.org.

Minister to Priests—VACANT.

Services for Senior Priests Coordinator—Rev. THOMAS J. WALKER. Tel: 414-769-3345. Email: walkert@archmil.org.

Deacon Services Coordinator—Deacon DAVID L. ZIMPRICH. Tel: 414-769-3409. Email: zimprichd@archmil.org.

Parish Mission—3501 S. Lake Dr., P.O. Box 070912, Milwaukee, 53207-0912.

Coordinator—MARK KEMMETER. Tel: 414-769-3352. Email: kemmeterm@archmil.org.

Schools Office—St. Joseph Center, 1501 S. Layton Blvd., Milwaukee, 53215.

Superintendent—VACANT.

Associate Superintendents—SUSAN NELSON. Tel: 414-758-2263. Email: nelsons@archmil.org; CAROL WARD. Tel: 414-758-2262. Email: wardc@archmil.org; BRENDA WHITE. Tel: 414-758-2252. Email: whiteb@archmil.org.

Special Assistant—Bro. NIVARD SCHEEL, C.F.X. Tel: 414-758-2257. Email: scheeln@archmil.org.

Sexual Abuse Prevention and Response Services—St. Joseph Center, 1501 S. Layton Blvd., Milwaukee, 53215.

Victim Assistance Coordinator—AMY PETERSON. Tel: 414-758-2232. Email: petersona@archmil.org.

Safe Environment Coordinator—PATTI LOEHRER. Tel: 414-769-3449. Email: loehrerp@archmil.org.

Social Justice Ministry—St. Joseph Center, 1501 S. Layton Blvd., Milwaukee, 53215.

Coordinator—ROBERT SHELLEDY. Tel: 414-758-2286. Email: shelledyr@archmil.org.

Stewardship and Development—3501 S. Lake Dr., P.O. Box 070912, Milwaukee, 53207-0912.

Development Director—DEBRA LETHLEAN. Tel: 414-769-3322. Email: lethleand@archmil.org.

Catholic Stewardship Appeal Director—ROBERT BOHLMANN. Tel: 414-769-3320. Email: bohlmannr@archmil.org.

Major and Planned Giving Director—MICHELE WEINSCHROTT. Tel: 414-769-3583. Email: weinschrottm@archmil.org.

Parish Stewardship Director—BARBARA VITE. Tel: 414-769-3485. Email: viteb@archmil.org.

Systems and Operations Director—LORETTA O'KELLY. Tel: 414-769-3323. Email: okellyl@archmil.org.

World Mission Ministries—St. Joseph Center, 1501 S. Layton Blvd., Milwaukee, 53215.

Director—FRAN CUNNINGHAM, O.S.F. Tel: 414-758-2282. Email: cunninghamf@archmil.org.

International Mission Coordinator—ROSEMARY HUDDLESTON, O.P. Tel: 414-758-2283. Email: huddlestonr@archmil.org.

CLERGY, PARISHES, MISSIONS AND PAROCHIAL SCHOOLS

CITY OF MILWAUKEE

(MILWAUKEE COUNTY)

1—CATHEDRAL OF ST. JOHN THE EVANGELIST (1847) Very Rev. Carl A. Last, Rector; Deacon Thomas N. Hunt.
Mailing Address: 831 N. Van Buren St., 53202. In Res., Rev. R. Thomas Venne (Retired).
Res.: 802 N. Jackson St., 53202. Tel: 414-276-9814; Fax: 414-276-8285. Email: cathedral@stjohncathedral.org. Web: stjohncathedral.org.
Catechesis/Religious Program—East Side Child & Youth Ministry, 2480 N. Cramer St., 53211. Tel: 414-263-8230; Fax: 414-962-3829. Students 17.

2—ST. ADALBERT (1908), (Polish—Hispanic), Very Rev. Luis Pacheco-Sanchez.
Office: 1923 W. Becher St., 53215. Tel: 414-645-0413; Fax: 414-645-0166. Email: stadalberto@hotmail.com.
School—1913 W. Becher St., 53215-2688. Tel: 414-645-5450; Fax: 414-645-5510. Ms. Julia Hutchinson, Prin. Lay Teachers 25; Students 477.
Catechesis/Religious Program—Students 445.

3—ST. AGNES, Closed. For sacramental records, contact Archdiocese of Milwaukee Archives Office, Tel: 414-769-3407.

4—ST. ALBERT, Closed. For sacramental records, contact Archdiocese of Milwaukee Archives Office, Tel: 414-769-3407.

5—ST. ALEXANDER (1926), (Polish), Revs. Michael A. Ignaszak; Norberto Sandoval.
Res.: 3373 S. 15th Pl., 53215. Tel: 414-744-3695; Fax: 414-744-2874.
See Holy Wisdom Academy, Milwaukee under Consolidated Elementary Schools located in the Institution section.
Catechesis/Religious Program—Twinned with St. Helen, Milwaukee, 3307 S. 10th St., 53215. Tel: 414-744-3695; Fax: 414-744-2874. Students 72.

6—ALL SAINTS (1994) Rev. Carl E. Diederichs; Deacon Edward Blaze.
Office: 4060 N. 26th St., 53209-6695. Tel: 414-444-5610; Fax: 414-444-5709.
Catechesis/Religious Program—Students 55.
Mission—St. John's Chapel 3717 W. Keefe, Milwaukee Co. 53216.

7—ST. ANNE, Closed. For sacramental records, contact Archdiocese of Milwaukee Archives Office, Tel: 414-769-3407.

8—ST. ANTHONY OF PADUA (1872) Rev. Hilary Brzezinski, O.F.M. In Res., Revs. James Gannon, O.F.M.; Stephen E. Malkiewicz, O.F.M.; Albert Lis, O.F.M.
Church & Res.: 1711 S. 9th St., 53204. Tel: 414-645-1455; Fax: 414-645-1456. Email: antonius@archmil.org. Web: stanthonyofpaduaparish.org.
School—1727 S. 9th St., 53204. Tel: 414-384-6612; Fax: 414-384-6613. Email: brownt@archmil.org. Web: www.stanthonysschool.org. Terry Brown, Pres.; Ramon Cruz, Prin.; Mrs. Holly Cerveny, Vice Prin. Lay Teachers 57; Students 1,296.
Catechesis/Religious Program—Tel: 414-235-6250. Email: melendeze@archmil.org. Students 281.

9—ST. ANTHONY OF PADUA (1923) Closed. For sacramental records, contact St. Vincent Pallotti Parish, Milwaukee, 53223, Tel: 414-453-4225.

10—ST. AUGUSTINE OF HIPPO (1888) Rev. Jan M. Kieliszewski; Ms. Chiara Sainer, Pastoral Assoc.; Paul Weisenberger, Dir. Worship; Heather Warner, Youth Min.
Res.: 2530 S. Howell Ave., 53207. Tel: 414-744-0808; Fax: 414-744-1231. Email: staugy1@wi.rr.com. Web: www.staugustine.4lpi.com.
See St. Thomas Aquinas Academy located in the institution section under Consolidated Elementary Schools.
Catechesis/Religious Program—Students 98.

11—ST. BARBARA, Closed. For sacramental records, contact Archdiocese of Milwaukee Archives Office, Tel: 414-769-3407.

12—BASILICA OF ST. JOSAPHAT (1888), (Polish), Very Rev. James M. Jankowski, O.F.M.Conv., Pastor & Rector; Rev. James M. Ciaramitaro, O.F.M.Conv., Parochial Vicar; Bro. James Dufresne, O.F.M.Conv., Pastoral Assoc. In Res., Bro. Robert Cook, O.F.M.Conv.
Res.: 2333 S. 6th St., 53215. Tel: 414-645-5623; Fax: 414-645-2216. Email: sjbdome@archmil.org. Web: www.thebasilica.org.
School—801 W. Lincoln Ave., 53215. Tel: 414-645-4378; Fax: 414-645-1978. Mrs. Carolyn Trawitzki. Lay Teachers 16; Students 213; School Sisters of St. Francis 2; School Sisters of Notre Dame 2.
Basilica of Saint Josaphat Endowment Fund—Mailing Address: 2333 S. 6th St., 53215. Tel: 414-645-5623. Email: sjbdome@archmil.org.
Saint Josaphat Parish School Endowment Fund—Mailing Address: 2333 S. 6th St., 53215. Tel: 414-645-5623. Email: sjbdome@archmil.org.
Catechesis/Religious Program—Parish Center, 2322 S. 7th St., 53215. Tel: 414-671-3938. Students 108.

13—ST. BENEDICT THE MOOR (1908) Rev. Jerome Schroeder, O.F.M.Cap.; Deacon John I. Champagne. In Res., Revs. Michael Crosby, O.F.M.Cap.; James Zelinski, O.F.M.Cap.; Bro. David Schwab, O.F.M.Cap.
Res.: 1015 N. 9th St., 53233. Tel: 414-271-0135; Fax: 414-271-0637. Email: stbens@sbcglobal.net. Web: www.stbensmilwaukee.org.
Catechesis/Religious Program—Students 17.

14—ST. BERNADETTE (1958) Rev. Allan J. Sommer.
Res.: 8200 W. Denver Ave., 53223. Tel: 414-358-4600; Fax: 414-358-1478. Email: stbernadette@archmil.org. Web: www.stbweb.com.
School—Northwest Catholic School - West Campus formerly St. Bernadette School, 8202 W. Denver Ave., 53223. Tel: 414-358-4603; Fax: 414-760-1037. Mary Lorusso, Prin. Lay Teachers 14; Students 170.
Catechesis/Religious Program—Tel: 414-365-2020. Twinned with St. Catherine of Alexandria. Students 14.

15—BLESSED SACRAMENT (1927), (Polish), Rev. Robert D. Turner; Deacon Paul Klingseisen.
Res.: 3100 S. 41st St., 53215. Tel: 414-649-4720; Fax: 414-649-4727. Email: blsacrament@voyager.net. Church: S. 41st St. and W. Oklahoma Ave., 53215.
School—3126 S. 41st St., 53215. Tel: 414-649-4730; Fax: 414-649-4726. Email: blschool@archmil.org. Web: www.blsacrament.com. Janet Orlowski, Prin. Lay Teachers 14; Students 123.
Catechesis/Religious Program—Students 104.

16—BLESSED SAVIOR PARISH (2007) Rev. Gregory A. Chycinski; Judy Adrian, Pastoral Assoc.
8607 W. Villard Ave., 53225. Tel: 414-464-5033. Email: blessedsavior@archmil.org. (A merger of the following parishes: Corpus Christi, Mary Queen of Martyrs, Our Lady of Sorrows and St. Philip Neri).
School—Blessed Savior Catholic School Lay Teachers 53; Students 673.
School—West Campus, 8545 W. Villard Ave., 53225. Tel: 414-464-5775; Fax: 414-464-5737. Roger A. Baehr, Prin.
School—East Campus, 5135 N. 54th St., 53218. Tel: 414-438-2745; Fax: 414-438-9330. Barbara O'Donnell, Prin.
School—North Campus, 5501 N. 68th St., 53218. Tel: 414-466-0470; Fax: 414-466-3740. Thomas Hage, Prin.
School—South Campus, 4059 N. 64th St., 53216. Tel: 414-463-3878; Fax: 414-535-9265. Patricia Wilkum, Prin.
Catechesis/Religious Program—Sr. Judene Studer, S.S.N.D., Dir. Faith Formation. Students 60.

17—BLESSED VIRGIN OF POMPEI, Closed. For sacramental records, contact Archdiocese of Milkwaukee Archives Office, Tel: 414-769-3407.

18—ST. BONIFACE, Closed. For sacramental records, contact Archdiocese of Milwaukee Archives Office, Tel: 414-769-3407.

19—ST. CASIMIR (1894), (Polish—Spanish), Closed. For sacramental records, contact Our Lady of Divine Providence, Milwaukee, Tel: 414-264-0049.

20—ST. CATHERINE (1922) Rev. John R. Kern; Deacon Ralph W. Kornburger Jr. In Res., Rev. Thomas Suriano (Retired).
Res.: 5101 W. Center St., 53210. Tel: 414-445-5115; Fax: 414-445-5198.
School—2647 N. 51st St., 53210. Tel: 414-445-2846; Fax: 414-445-0448. Deborah Zabinski, Prin. Lay Teachers 20; Students 209.
Catechesis/Religious Program—Cindy Lieb, D.R.E. Students 55.

21—ST. CATHERINE (Granville) (1855) [CEM] Debra A. Hintz, Parish Dir.; Deacon Daniel T. Zozakiewicz.
Res.: 8661 N. 76th Pl., 53223. Tel: 414-365-2020; Fax: 414-365-2021 (Office). Email: stc_alex@execpc.com. Web: www.saintcatherinealexandria.org.
See Northwest Catholic School Association, Milwaukee in the Institution Section under Consolidated Elementary Schools.
Catechesis/Religious Program—Nicole Fastabend, Dir. Christian Formation. Students 49.

22—ST. CHARLES BORROMEO (1960) Rev. Anthony J. Zimmer.
Res.: 5571 S. Marilyn Ave., 53221. Tel: 414-281-8115; Fax: 414-281-8150. Email: info@scbmil.org. Web: www.scbmil.org.
School—3100 W. Parnell Ave., 53221. Tel: 414-282-0767; Fax: 414-817-9605. Email: school@scbmil.org. Lay Teachers 18; Students 181.
Catechesis/Religious Program—Tel: 414-281-8115, Ext. 24. Email: ckrol@scbmil.org. Web: www.scbmil.org. Students 224.

23—CONGREGATION OF THE BLESSED TRINITY (1991) Rev. Michael Barrett.
Pastoral Offices—4717 N. 38th St., 53209. Tel: 414-463-6921; Fax: 414-463-0349. Email: btrinity@archmil.org.
Catechesis/Religious Program—Students 8.

24—CONGREGATION OF THE GREAT SPIRIT (1989), (Native American), Rev. Edward J. Cook.
Res. & Mailing Address: 1050 W. Lapham Blvd., 53204. Tel: 414-672-6989; Fax: 414-643-5688. Email: siggenauk@sbcglobal.net. Web: www.congregationofthegreatspirit.org.
Catechesis/Religious Program—Students 37.

25—CORPUS CHRISTI (1958) Closed. For sacramental records, contact Blessed Savior, Milwaukee, Tel: 414-464-5033

26—SS. CYRIL AND METHODIUS (1893) Rev. Andrzej Galant, S.Ch.
Office: 2427 S. 15th St., 53215. Tel: 414-383-3973; Fax: 414-383-3974.

27—ST. ELIZABETH, Closed. For sacramental records, contact Archdiocese of Milwaukee Archives Office, Tel: 414-769-3407.

28—ST. EMERIC (1919) Closed. For sacramental records, contact Sacred Heart, Milwaukee, Tel: 414-774-9418.

29—ST. FLORIAN (1911), (German—Austrian), Revs. Leonard R. Copeland, O.C.D.; Timothy McGough, O.C.D.; Elijah Martin, O.C.D.; Michael Berry, O.C.D. In Res., Revs. William Healy, O.C.D.; Ralph Elias-Haddix, O.C.D.; Bro. Bonaventure Potter, O.C.D.
Res.: 1233 S. 45th St., 53214. Tel: 414-383-3565; Fax: 414-383-2708. Email: stflorian@archmil.org. Web: www.stflorian.org.
See Mary Queen of Saints Catholic Academy located in Institution Section listed under Consolidated Elementary Schools section.
Catechesis/Religious Program—Students 58.

30—ST. FRANCIS OF ASSISI (1871), (Hispanic—African American), Friar Michael Bertram, O.F.M.Cap.
Mailing Address: 1927 N. 4th St., 53212. In Res., Bro. Isidore Herriges, O.F.M.Cap.
Res.: 327 W. Brown St., 53212. Tel: 414-374-5752.
St. Francis Institute Milwaukee—1927 N. 4th St., 53212. Tel: 414-374-8841, Ext. 438. Rev. Jerome Schroeder, O.F.M.Cap., Dir. & Contact Person.
Catechesis/Religious Program—1927 N. 4th St., 53212. Tel: 414-374-5750; Fax: 414-374-5553. Students 54.

31—ST. GABRIEL (1913), (Lithuanian), Closed. For sacramental records, contact Archdiocese of Milwaukee Archives Office, Tel: 414-769-3407.

32—ST. GALL, Closed. For sacramental records, contact Archdiocese of Milwaukee Archives Office, Tel: 414-769-3407.

33—ST. GERARD (1925) Closed. For sacramental records, contact Archdiocese of Milwaukee Archives Office, Tel: 414-769-3407.

34—GESU PARISH (1893) Revs. Karl D. Voelker, S.J.; Kenneth J. Herian, S.J.; Patrick E. Walsh, S.J.; Lawrence A. Jonas, S.J.; Matthew S. Walsh, S.J.
Res.: 1210 W. Michigan St., P.O. Box 495, 53201-0495. Tel: 414-288-7101; Fax: 414-288-5339. Email: gesuparish@gmail.com. Web: www.gesuparish.org.
Catechesis/Religious Program—Students 135.

35—ST. GREGORY THE GREAT (1955) Rev. Thomas P. Demse.
Office: 3160 S. 63rd St., 53219. Tel: 414-543-8292; Fax: 414-328-3881.
Res.: 3129 S. 63rd St., 53219.
School—3132 S. 63rd St., 53219. Tel: 414-321-1350. Lay Teachers 22; Students 316.
Catechesis/Religious Program—Tel: 414-543-8292. Students 243.

36—ST. HEDWIG (1871), (Polish), Closed. For sacramental records, contact Archdiocese of Milwaukee Archives Office, Tel: 414-769-3407.

37—ST. HELEN (1925), (Polish), Revs. Michael A. Ignaszak; Norberto Sandoval.
Res.: 3307 S. 10th St., 53215. Tel: 414-744-3695; 414-744-8292; Fax: 414-744-2874.
See Holy Wisdom Academy, Milwaukee under Consolidated Elementary Schools located in the Institution section.
Catechesis/Religious Program—Fax: 414-744-2874. Students 40.

38—HOLY ANGELS, Closed. For sacramental records, contact Archdiocese of Milwaukee Archives Office, Tel: 414-769-3407.

39—HOLY CROSS (1879) Closed. For sacramental records, contact St. Vincent Pallotti, Milwaukee, Tel: 414-453-4225.

40—HOLY REDEEMER, Closed. For sacramental records, contact Archdiocese of Milwaukee Archives Office, Tel: 414-769-3407.

41—HOLY ROSARY (1885), (Irish), Closed. For sacramental records, contact Archdiocese of Milwaukee

Archives Office, Tel: 414-769-3407.

42—HOLY SPIRIT (1902), (German), Closed. For sacramental records, contact Archdiocese of Milwaukee Archives Office, Tel: 414-769-3407.

43—HOLY TRINITY-OUR LADY OF GUADALUPE (1849), (Hispanic), Closed. For sacramental records, contact Our Lady of Guadalupe, Milwaukee, Tel: 414-271-6181.

44—ST. HYACINTH (1883), (Polish—Hispanic), Revs. Carlos Florez-Ardilla; Jose German Zapata; William E. Doepke, Dir. Admin. Svcs.
Mailing Address: 1138 S. 25th St., 53204-1940.
Church: 1414 W. Becher St., 53215. Tel: 414-645-8786; Fax: 414-645-8918. Email: sthy@archmil.org.
Catechesis/Religious Program—Students 128.

45—ST. IGNATIUS LOYOLA, Closed. For sacramental records, contact Archdiocese of Milwaukee Archives Office, Tel: 414-769-3407.

46—IMMACULATE CONCEPTION (1870) Rev. Ronald E. Kotecki; Deacon Rob Chalhoub.
Res.: 1023 E. Russell Ave., 53207. Tel: 414-769-2480; Fax: 414-769-2492. Email: icbayview@voyager.net.
See St. Thomas Aquinas Academy located in the Institution Section under Consolidated Elementary Schools
Catechesis/Religious Program—Fax: 414-769-2492. Students 68.

47—ST. JOHN DE NEPOMUC, Closed. For sacramental records, contact Archdiocese of Milwaukee Archives Office, Tel: 414-769-3407.

48—ST. JOHN KANTY (1907), (Polish), Revs. Michael A. Ignaszak; Norberto Sandoval.
Res.: 3307 S. 10th St., 53215. Tel: 414-744-3695; Fax: 414-744-2874.
School—2840 S. 10th St., 53215. Tel: 414-483-8780; 414-744-1846; Fax: 414-744-1846. Beth Eichman, Prin. Students 187.
Catechesis/Religious Program— Program is in collaboration with St. Helen & St. Alexander. Students 10.

49—ST. JOSEPH, Closed. For sacramental records, contact St. Joseph, Wauwatosa, Tel: 414-771-4626.

50—ST. LAWRENCE (1888) Closed. For sacramental records, contact Archdiocese of Milwaukee Archives Office, Tel: 414-769-3407.

51—ST. LEO, Closed. For sacramental records, contact Archdiocese of Milwaukee Archives Office, Tel: 414-769-3407.

52—ST. MARGARET MARY (1955) Rev. Vincent F. Kobida. Tel: 414-502-0280.
Rectory, Office & Parish Ctr.: 3970 N. 92nd St., 53222-2588. Tel: 414-461-6073; Fax: 414-462-8449. Email: ladams@stmmp.org. Web: www.stmmp.org.
School—3950 N. 92nd St., 53222-2587. Tel: 414-463-8760; Fax: 414-463-2373. Richard Goeden, Prin. Lay Teachers 20; Students 179.
Catechesis/Religious Program—3970 N. 92nd St., 53222. Fax: 414-462-8419. Students 76.

53—ST. MARTIN DE PORRES (1994), (African American), Rev. David Preuss, O.F.M.Cap.
Office: 128 W. Burleigh St., 53212-2046. Tel: 414-372-3090; Fax: 414-372-0356. Email: smdp@smdpmilw.com. Web: stmdpmw.tripod.com.
Catechesis/Religious Program—Margaret A. Lee, D.R.E. Students 60.

54—ST. MARY MAGDALEN (1925), (Polish—Korean), Rev. Paul A. Stanosz.
Res.: 1854 W. Windlake Ave., 53215. Tel: 414-645-4773; Fax: 414-645-5622. Email: stmarymagd@yahoo.com.
Catechesis/Religious Program—Students 6.

55—ST. MARY OF CZESTOCHOWA (1907), (Polish), Closed. For sacramental records, contact Our Lady of Divine Providence, Milwaukee, Tel: 414-264-0049.

56—MARY, QUEEN OF MARTYRS (2001) Closed. For sacramental records, contact Blessed Savior, Milwaukee, Tel: 414-464-5033.

57—ST. MATTHEW (1892) Closed. For sacramental records, contact Archdiocese of Milwaukee Archives Office, Tel: 414-769-3407.

58—ST. MATTHIAS (1850) [CEM] Revs. David E. Cooper; Dennis M. Witz; Deacon David W. Sommers.
9306 W. Beloit Rd., 53227. Tel: 414-321-0893; Fax: 414-321-1330. Email: info@stmatthias-milw.org. Web: www.stmatthias-milw.org.
School—9300 W. Beloit Rd., 53227. Tel: 414-321-0894; Fax: 414-321-9228. Sisters 1; Lay Teachers 30; Students 510.
Catechesis/Religious Program—Students 458.

59—ST. MAXIMILIAN KOLBE, (Polish), Rev. Andrzej Galant, S.Ch.
Res.: 2427 S. 15th St., 53215. Tel: 414-383-3973; Fax: 414-383-3974. Email: pastor@sscmmkparish.org. Web: www.sscmmkparish.org.

60—ST. MICHAEL (1883) Rev. Dennis J. Lewis, Admin.; Sr. Alice Thepouthay, Laotian Pastoral Ministry & Pastoral Assoc.; Shanedra Johnson, Youth Dir. & Pastoral Assoc.
Res.: 1445 N. 24th St., 53205. Tel: 414-933-3143; Fax: 414-933-1915. Email: st.michaelsrectory@sbcglobal.net.
Catechesis/Religious Program— Patricia Roehrig, D.R.E. Students 94.

61—MOTHER OF GOOD COUNSEL (1925) Rev. Robert Marsicek, S.D.S.; Deacons Dean J. Collins; Andrew Meuler.
Church: 6924 W. Lisbon Ave., 53210-1259. Tel: 414-442-7600; Fax: 414-444-0408. Email: mgc@mgcparish.org. Web: www.mgcparish.org.
School—3001 N. 68th St., 53210-1299. Tel: 414-442-7600, Ext. 118. Regina Shaw, Prin. Lay Teachers 21; Students 253.
Catechesis/Religious Program—Tel: 414-442-7600, Ext. 126. Email: mortell@mgcparish.org. Students 95.

62—MOTHER OF PERPETUAL HELP (1941) Closed. For sacramental records, contact Archdiocese of Milwaukee Archives Office, Tel: 414-769-3407.

63—ST. NICHOLAS, Closed. For sacramental records, contact Archdiocese of Milwaukee Archives Office, Tel: 414-769-3407.

64—OLD ST. MARY (1846), (Bavarian—German), Very Rev. Timothy L. Kitzke; Rev. Brian G. Mason. In Res., Most Rev. Richard J. Sklba.
Res.: 836 N. Broadway, 53202. Tel: 414-271-6180; Fax: 414-271-7782. Email: info@oldsaintmary.org.
Catechesis/Religious Program—Students 47.

65—OUR LADY OF DIVINE PROVIDENCE (2003) Rev. Gerald Hessel.
Res.: 3055 N. Fratney St., 53212. Tel: 414-264-0049; Fax: 414-264-7177. Email: oldp3055@tds.net. Web: www.oldp.4lpi.com.
Catechesis/Religious Program—2480 N. Cramer St., 53211. Tel: 414-962-3776; Fax: 414-962-3829. Email: escym@sbcglobal.net. Students 8.

66—OUR LADY OF GOOD HOPE (1952) Rev. Charles G. Zabler, Admin.; Deacons Michael E. Cesarec, (Retired); Joseph H. Kastenholz, (Retired); Barbara Krieger, Pastoral Assoc.; Addy Stoiber, Pastoral Musician.
Office: 7152 N. 41st St., 53209. Tel: 414-352-1148; Fax: 414-352-3042. Email: parish.office@olghparish.org. Web: www.olghparish.org.
School—Northwest Catholic - East Campus, 7140 N. 41st St., 53209. Tel: 414-352-7980; Fax: 414-352-7358. Jodeen Casetta, Prin. Lay Teachers 18; Students 175.
Catechesis/Religious Program—Tel: 414-352-8140. Pam Williams, Youth Coord. Students 79.

67—OUR LADY OF GUADALUPE PARISH (2000), (Hispanic), Rev. Jose Luis Moreno, S.J.; Deacon Juan A. Molina Sr., (Retired).
Mailing Address: 723 W. Washington St., 53204.
Res.: 613 S. 4th St., 53204. Tel: 414-645-7624; Fax: 414-645-3733. Email: guadalupe@archmil.org.
Catechesis/Religious Program—Total combined with St. Patrick, Milwaukee 91.

68—OUR LADY OF LOURDES (1958) Rev. William C. Burkert; Deacon John P. Monday; Mrs. Judith Bialk, Pastoral Assoc.
3722 S. 58th St., 53220. Tel: 414-545-4316; Fax: 414-541-2251. Email: olol@archmil.org. Web: www.olol.4lpi.com.
Catechesis/Religious Program—Tel: 414-541-9470. Students 245.

69—OUR LADY OF SORROWS (1955) Closed. For Sacramental records, contact Blessed Savior, Milwaukee, Tel: 414-464-5033.

70—OUR LADY QUEEN OF PEACE (1948) Rev. Gregory M. Spitz.
Res.: 3222 S. 29th St., 53215. Tel: 414-672-0313; Fax: 414-672-0441. Email: parish@olqpmke.org. Web: www.olqpmke.org.
School—2733 W. Euclid Ave., 53215. Tel: 414-672-6660; Fax: 414-672-2739. Email: school@olqpmke.org. Janet Orlowski, Prin. Lay Teachers 17; Students 161.
Catechesis/Religious Program—Students 7; Twinned with Blessed Sacrament 150.

71—ST. PATRICK (1876) [CEM] Rev. Jose Luis Moreno, S.J.
Res.: 723 W. Washington St., 53204. Tel: 414-645-7624; Fax: 414-645-3733. Email: stpats@archmil.org.
Catechesis/Religious Program—Total combined with Our Lady of Guadalupe, Milwaukee 91.

72—ST. PAUL (1920) Rev. Romanus N. Nwaru.
Res.: 1720 E. Norwich Ave., 53207. Tel: 414-482-3510; Fax: 414-482-1031.
See St. Thomas Aquinas Academy located in the Institution Section under Consolidated Elementary Schools.
Catechesis/Religious Program—Tel: 414-481-0777; Fax: 414-482-3025. Students 54.

73—SS. PETER AND PAUL (1889), (German), Rev. Michael F. Michalski.
Res.: 2491 N. Murray Ave., 53211. Tel: 414-962-2443; Fax: 414-962-8183. Email: sspp@execpc.com. Web: www.ssppmilw.org.
See Catholic East Elementary, Milwaukee under Consolidated Elementary Schools located in the Institution section.
Catechesis/Religious Program—East Side Child & Youth Ministry, Consolidated from the following parishes: SS. Peter & Paul, Our Lady of Divine Providence, Cathedral of St. John the Evangelist, and Three Holy Women., 2480 N. Cramer St., 53211. Tel: 414-962-3776; Fax: 414-962-3839. Email: escym@sbcglobal.net. Students 89.

74—ST. PHILIP NERI (1956) Closed. For sacramental records, contact Blessed Savior, Milwaukee, Tel: 414-464-5033.

75—PRINCE OF PEACE/PRINCIPE DE PAZ (1999) Revs. Carlos Florez-Ardilla; Jose German Zapata; William E. Doepke, Dir. Admin. Svcs.
Office: 1138 S. 25th St., 53204-1940. Tel: 414-645-8786; Fax: 414-645-8918. Email: doepkew@archmil.org.
School—(25th St. Campus), 1114 S. 25th St., 53204. Tel: 414-383-2157; Fax: 414-383-7645.
School—(22nd St. Campus), 1646 S. 22nd St., 53204. Tel: 414-645-4922; Fax: 414-645-4940. Ms. Judith Birlem, Prin. Religious 2; Lay Teachers 28; Students 449.
Catechesis/Religious Program—Sr. Carmelita De Anda, D.R.E.; José Antonio Martin, Dir. Liturgy & Music. Students 238.

76—ST. RAFAEL THE ARCHANGEL (1999), (Hispanic), Rev. Luis Pacecho-Sanchez; Mary Louise Stenger, Business Mgr.
Res.: 2059 S. 33rd St., 53215. Tel: 414-645-9172; Fax: 414-645-4732.
School—Tel: 414-645-1300; Fax: 414-645-1415. Mrs. Carolyn Ettlie, Prin. Lay Teachers 14; Students 320.
Catechesis/Religious Program—Students 179.

77—ST. RITA (1936), (Italian), Closed. For sacramental records, contact Archdiocese of Milwaukee Archives Office, Tel: 414-769-3407.

78—ST. ROMAN (1956), (Polish), Revs. Brian T. Holbus; John J. Pulice (Retired).
Res.: 1710 W. Bolivar Ave., 53221. Tel: 414-282-9063; Fax: 414-282-6464. Email: stroman@stromans.com. Web: www.stromans.com.
School—1810 W. Bolivar Ave., 53221. Tel: 414-282-7970; Fax: 414-282-5140. Email: stromanschool@stromans.com. Lay Teachers 19; Students 283.
Catechesis/Religious Program—Students 227.

79—ST. ROSE (1888) Rev. Dennis J. Lewis; Deacon Julio Lopez.
Res.: 528 N. 31st St., 53208. Tel: 414-342-1778; Fax: 414-342-7510. Email: stroseco@sbcglobal.net.
See St. Rose Catholic Urban Academy, Milwaukee under Elementary Schools, Archdiocesan located in the Institution section.
Catechesis/Religious Program—Students 30.

80—SACRED HEART (1917), (Croatian), Rev. Paul Maslach, O.F.M. (Croatia).
Res.: 917 N. 49th St., 53208. Tel: 414-774-9418; Fax: 414-774-7406. Email: sh.croatian@yahoo.com.
Catechesis/Religious Program—Students 38.

81—ST. SEBASTIAN (1911) Rev. Richard J. Aiken; Deacons Warren D. Braun, (Retired); James J. Peterson.
Res.: 5400 W. Washington Blvd., 53208. Tel: 414-453-1061; Fax: 414-453-9449. Email: saintsebs@saintsebs.org. Web: www.saintsebsonline.net.
School—1747 N. 54th St., 53208. Tel: 414-453-5830. Web: www.saintsebastianonline.net/school/. Lay Teachers 24; Students 317.
St. Sebastian School Foundation, Inc.—
Catechesis/Religious Program—Tel: 414-453-7150. Students 195.

82—ST. STANISLAUS (1866) Rev. Canon Olivier Meney.
Church & Bus. Office: 524 W. Historic Mitchell St., 53204. Tel: 414-226-5490; Fax: 414-226-5534. Email: ststanislaus@institute-christ-king.org.

83—ST. STEPHEN, MARTYR (1907), (Slovak), Closed. For sacramental records, contact Archdiocese of Milwaukee Archives Office, Tel: 414-769-3407.

84—ST. THERESE (1956) Dr. Alexandra Guliano, Parish Dir.; Elterine Jankowski-Biggers, Pastoral Musician.
Mailing Address: 9525 W. Bluemound Rd., 53226.
Res.: 9427 W. Bluemound Rd., 53226. Tel: 414-771-2500; Fax: 414-771-2410. Email: info@sainttheresemilwaukee.org. Web: www.sainttheresemilwaukee.org.
Catechesis/Religious Program—Cathy Smith, C.R.E. Students 35.

85—ST. THOMAS AQUINAS, Closed. For sacramental records, contact Archdiocese of Milwaukee Archives Office, Tel: 414-769-3407.

86—THREE HOLY WOMEN CATHOLIC PARISH (2000) Very Rev. Timothy L. Kitzke; Rev. Brian G. Mason.
Res.: 2003 N. Oakland Ave., 53202. Email: tkitzke@threeholywomen.org.
Church Office: 1716 N. Humboldt Ave., 53202. Tel:

414-271-6577; Fax: 414-271-7988. Email: mbergemann@threeholywomen.org. Web: www.threeholywomen.org.
Catechesis/Religious Program—(Collaborative), 2480 N. Cramer St., 53211. Tel: 414-962-3776; Fax: 414-962-3829. Email: escym@sbcglobal.net. Students 36.

87—St. Veronica (1925) Very Rev. Mark Payne.
Mailing Address: 353 E. Norwich St., 53207. Tel: 414-482-2920. Email: parishoffice@saintveronica.org. Web: saintveronica.org.
See St. Thomas Aquinas Academy located in the Instutition Section under Consolidated Elementary Schools.
Catechesis/Religious Program—Tel: 414-481-0777; Fax: 414-482-3025. Karen Bushman, D.R.E.; Michael Sharkey, Youth Min. Students 305.

88—St. Vincent de Paul (1888), (Polish), [CEM] Revs. Carlos Florez-Ardilla; Jose German Zapata; William E. Doepke, Dir. Admin. Svcs.
Mailing Address: 1138 S. 25th St., 53204-1940.
Church: 2114 W. Michell St., 53204. Tel: 414-645-8786; Fax: 414-645-8918. Email: stvincent@archmil.org.
Catechesis/Religious Program—Students 35.

89—St. Vincent Pallotti (1998) Rev. Sergio Lizama, S.A.C.
Res.: 5424 W. Bluemound Rd., 53208. Tel: 414-453-5344, Ext. 102; Fax: 414-453-4225. Web: www.stvincentpallotti.org.
School—St. Vincent Pallotti Catholic School, 201 N. 76th St., 53213. Tel: 414-258-4165; Fax: 414-258-9844. Mr. Jeffrey Johnson, Prin. Lay Teachers 18; Students 163.
Catechesis/Religious Program—Tel: 414-453-5344, Ext. 116. Students 25.

90—St. Wenceslaus (1883), (Hispanic), Closed. For sacramental records, contact Archdiocese of Milwaukee Archives Office, Tel: 414-769-3407.

OUTSIDE THE CITY OF MILWAUKEE

Adell, Sheboygan Co., St. Patrick (1853), (Irish), Closed. For sacramental records, contact Archdiocese of Milwaukee Archives Office, Tel: 414-769-3407, Fax: 414-769-3408.

Allenton, Washington Co.

1—St. Anthony (1851) Closed. For sacramental records, contact Resurrection, Allenton, Tel: 262-629-5240.

2—Resurrection (1997) [CEM 3], Consolidation of Sacred Heart, Allenton; St. Anthony, Allenton and Ss. Peter and Paul, Nenno. Revs. Richard J. Stoffel, Team Mod.; Joseph Dominic, S.A.C. (India), Team Member.
Parish Office—215 Main St., P.O. Box 96, 53002. Tel: 262-629-5240. Email: alleluia@nconnect.net.
Church: 215 Main St., 53002.
Catechesis/Religious Program—Tel: 262-629-1500. Email: reled@nconnect.net. Students 113.

3—Sacred Heart (1917) Closed. For sacramental records, contact Resurrection, Allenton, Tel: 262-629-5240.

Armstrong, Fond du Lac Co., Our Lady of Angels (1856), (Irish), Closed. For sacramental records, contact Shepherd of the Hills (Good Shepherd), Eden, Tel: 920-477-3201.

Ashford, Fond du Lac Co., St. Martin (1847) [CEM] Rev. Neil G. Zinthefer; Deacon Robert J. Fazen; Jane M. Osypowski, Business Mgr.
Mailing Address: P.O. Box 740, Campbellsport, 53010. Tel: 920-533-4441; Fax: 920-533-5280. Email: stmatts@archmil.org. N1271 Minnie Ln., Campbellsport, 53010.
Catechesis/Religious Program—Included with St. Matthew, Campbellsport., 419 Mill St., P.O. Box 740, Campbellsport, 53010. Email: stmatts@archmil.org. Beth Schmidt, D.R.E. Students 23.

Auburn, Fond du Lac Co., St. Matthias (1863), (German), Closed. For sacramental records, contact Holy Trinity, Kewaskum, Tel: 262-626-2860.

Beaver Dam, Dodge Co.

1—St. Katharine Drexel (2003) [CEM] Revs. John P. Schreiter; Jose Marcos Gonzalez, O.F.M.
Mailing Address: 131 W. Maple Ave., 53916.
Church: 511 S. Spring St., 53916. Tel: 920-881-2082; Fax: 920-885-7602. Email: singsheimp@stkatharinedrexelbd.org. Web: stkatharinedrexelbd.org.
School—(Grades PreSchool-8), 503 S. Spring St., 53916. Tel: 920-885-5558; Fax: 920-885-7610. Web: www.skds.org. Barbara M. Haase, Prin.; Ruth Kaiser, Librarian. Lay Teachers 19; Students 305.
Catechesis/Religious Program—Combined program (PreK - 11). Students 280.

2—St. Michael (1893) Closed. For sacramental records, contact St. Katharine Drexel, Beaver Dam, Tel: 920-887-2082.

3—St. Patrick (1860) Closed. For sacramental records, contact St. Katharine Drexel, Beaver Dam, Tel: 920-887-2082.

4—St. Peter (1855) Closed. For sacrament records, contact St. Katharine Drexel, Beaver Dam, Tel: 920-887-2082.

Belgium, Ozaukee Co., St. Mary (1848), (German—Luxembourg), [CEM] Revs. Richard J. Fleischman, Team Moderator; Guy Gurath, Team Mem.
Res.: 6092 Lake Church Rd., 53004-9721. Tel: 262-285-3040; Fax: 262-285-4104. Email: smplcb@archmil.org.
Church: 675 Co. Rd. D, 53004-9799.
Catechesis/Religious Program—Tel: 262-285-4361. Jane Helminiak, D.R.E. Students 198.

Big Bend, Waukesha Co., St. Joseph (1920) Rev. Richard J. Robinson.
Res.: S89 W22650 Milwaukee Ave., 53103. Tel: 262-662-2832; Fax: 262-662-0783. Email: parish@stjoesbb.com. Web: www.stjoesbb.com.
School—Tel: 262-662-2737; Fax: 262-662-2684. Email: school@stjoesbb.com. Susan Shawver, Prin. Lay Teachers 15; Students 120.
Catechesis/Religious Program—Tel: 262-662-3317. Email: cfm@stjoesbb.com. Mary L. Kozlik, D.R.E.; Lorraine Labadie, D.R.E. Students 574.

Brandon, Fond Du Lac Co., St. Brendan (1921), (German), [CEM], Also serves St. Joseph, Waupun and St. Mary, Springvale. Rev. Michael O. Sturm.
Mailing Address: 118 W. Main St., Waupun, 53963. Tel: 920-324-5400; Fax: 920-324-1040. Email: pastor@saintjoes.com.
Catechesis/Religious Program—Tel: 920-346-5110. Students 16.

Brighton, Kenosha Co., St. Francis Xavier (1838), (German), [CEM] Rev. Gary D. Nowicki; Lynn C. Schultz, Dir. Music.
Res. & Mailing Address: 1704 240th Ave., Kansasville, 53139. Tel: 262-878-2267; Fax: 262-878-3683. Email: sfxsjb@archmil.org.
School—Providence Catholic School, Consolidated with St. John the Baptist, 1481-172 N. Ave., Paris, Union Grove, WI 53182., 1714 240th Ave., Kansasville, 53139. Tel: 262-878-2713; Fax: 262-878-3299. Email: westcampus@providencecatholicschool.org. Web: www.providencecatholicschool.org. Mrs. Donna Stevens, Prin. Lay Teachers 8; Students 99.
Catechesis/Religious Program—Combined with St. John the Baptist, Paris. Sr. Kathryn Dean Strandell, O.S.F., D.R.E. (Gr. K-8). Students 110.

Bristol, Kenosha Co.

1—Holy Cross (2009) Rev. Roger A. Savage.
Res.: 18700 116th St., 53104. Tel: 262-857-2068.
Catechesis/Religious Program—Tel: 262-857-9032. Students 186.

2—St. Scholastica (1945) [CEM] Closed. For sacramental records, contact Holy Cross, Bristol, Tel: 262-857-2068.

Brookfield, Waukesha Co.

1—St. Dominic (1866) Revs. David H. Reith; Sean T. O'Connell; Deacons Gregory H. Diciaula; Larry LaFond; Rich Harter, Pastoral Assoc. for Admin Svcs & Adult & Family Min.; Susan Petersen McNeil, Pastoral Assoc. for Human Concerns; Julie Cucuwato, Liturgy & Music Dir.; Karen Chaffee, Dir. Finance Admin. & Technology; Meg Picciolo, Dir. Mktg. & Communication.
18255 W. Capitol Dr., 53045-1422. Tel: 262-781-3480; Fax: 262-781-3283. Email: parish@stdominic.net. Web: www.stdominic.net.
Rectory—3760 Arroyo Rd., 53045-1422. Tel: 262-781-2002.
School—18105 W. Capitol Dr., 53045-1425. Tel: 262-783-7565; Fax: 262-783-5947. Email: john.chovanec@stdominic.net. Mr. John Chovanec, Prin. Lay Teachers 29; Students 453.
Catechesis/Religious Program—Kathleen Beuscher, Dir. Child Ministry; Debbie Olla, Dir. Youth & Young Adult Ministry. Students 603.

2—St. John Vianney (1956) Revs. Kenneth P. Knippel; Phillip A. Bogacki; Deacon John A. Ebel; David Sanders, Dir. Liturgy & Music; Mary Janowak, Dir. Adult & Family Ministry & Human Concerns; James R. Hessling, Dir. Parish Svcs.
1755 N. Calhoun Rd., 53005-5036. Tel: 262-796-3940; Fax: 262-796-3958. Email: sjv@stjohnv.org. Web: www.stjohnv.org.
School—17500 W. Gebhardt Rd., 53045-5096. Tel: 262-796-3942; Fax: 262-796-3953. Jayme Hartmann, Prin. Lay Teachers 26; Students 512.
Catechesis/Religious Program—Tel: 262-796-3944. Email: dawnv@stjohnv.org. Erik Anderson, Youth Min.; Claire Hoffmeyer, Assoc. Dir., Youth Min.; Dawn Van Dorf, Dir. Child Ministry. Students 813.

3—St. Luke (1956) Rev. Kenneth J. Augustine.
Res.: 18000 W. Greenfield Ave., 53045. Tel: 262-782-0032; Fax: 262-782-6057. Email: stluke@stlukebrookfield.org. Web: www.stlukebrookfield.org.
Catechesis/Religious Program—Marian Lamoureux, D.R.E. Students 142.
Convent—

Burlington, Racine Co.

1—St. Charles (1908) [CEM] Revs. Steven J. Amann; Omar Antillon.
Res.: 440 Kendall St., 53105. Tel: 262-763-2260; Fax: 262-763-9171. Email: jmorrow@mystcharles.org. Web: www.mystcharles.org.
School—449 Conkey St., 53105. Tel: 262-763-2848; 262-762-2637 (Grade School); Fax: 262-763-3818. Email: principalstcharles@wi.rr.com. Sr. Margaret Pietsch, Prin. Lay Teachers 16; Students 207.
Catechesis/Religious Program—Tel: 262-763-1505; Fax: 262-763-4229. Email: parishoffice@stmarysburlingtonwi.org. Students 447.

2—Immaculate Conception (1838), (German), [CEM] Rev. Robert D. Gosma, Temporary Admin. (Retired).
Res.: 108 McHenry St., 53105. Tel: 262-763-1500; Fax: 262-763-1680. Email: parishoffice@stmb.org.
School—225 W. State St., 53105. Tel: 262-763-1515; Fax: 262-763-1508. Web: www.stmb.org. Priests 1; Lay Teachers 18; Students 340.
Catechesis/Religious Program—Students 130.
Chapel—

Butler, Waukesha Co., St. Agnes (1915) Rev. Timothy C. Bickel; Deacon Raymond Waitrovich.
Office: 12801 W. Fairmount Ave., 53007. Tel: 262-781-9521; Fax: 262-781-3512. Email: stagnes007@archmil.org.
School—Tel: 262-781-4996. Susan Booth, Prin. Sisters 1; Lay Teachers 14; Students 163.
Catechesis/Religious Program—Tel: 262-781-6998. Gerry Wolf, D.R.E. Students 155.

Byron, Fond du Lac Co.

1—St. John (1847) Closed. For sacramental records, contact Sons of Zebedee: Saints James and John, Byron, Tel: 920-922-1167.

2—Sons of Zebedee: Saints James and John (2000) [CEM] Rev. Michael C. Petersen.
Mailing Address: W5882 Church Rd., Fond du Lac, 54937-8602. Tel: 920-922-1167; Fax: 920-922-1924.
Catechesis/Religious Program—Students 110.

Caledonia, Racine Co., St. Louis (1846) [CEM] Rev. Mark J. Danczyk; Deacon Jim Zdeb.
Parish Office—13207 Hwy. G, 53108-9533. Tel: 262-835-4533; Fax: 262-835-0421. Email: stlouis@wi.rr.com. Web: stlouis4lpi.com.
Catechesis/Religious Program— Michael Riedl, D.R.E. Students 161.
Mission—Tel: 262-835-4533.

Campbellsport, Fond du Lac Co., St. Matthew (1864) [CEM] Rev. Neil G. Zinthefer; Deacon Robert J. Fazen; Jane M. Osypowski, Business Mgr.
Parish Center—419 Mill St., P.O. Box 740, 53010. Tel: 920-533-4441; Fax: 920-533-5280. Email: stmatts@archmil.org.
School—P.O. Box 639, 53010. Tel: 920-533-4103; Fax: 920-533-8078. Email: smslions@charter.net. Joan Schlaefer, Prin. Lay Teachers 11; Students 131.
Catechesis/Religious Program—Tel: 920-533-5776. Beth Schmidt, D.R.E. Students 192.

Cascade, Sheboygan Co., St. Mary-Cascade (1852) Closed. For sacramental records, contact Archdiocese of Milwaukee Archives Office, Tel: 414-769-3407.

Cedarburg, Ozaukee Co.

1—Divine Word (1970) Closed. For sacramental records, contact St. Francis Borgia, Cedarburg, Tel: 262-377-1070.

2—St. Francis Borgia (1844) [CEM] Very Rev. Thomas P. Eichenberger; Rev. Daniel R. Janasik.
Cemetery: Pioneer Rd., Mequon, 53092.
Res.: 1375 Covered Bridge Rd., 53012. Email: office@saintfrancisborgia.org. Web: www.saintfrancisborgia.org.
School—N43 W6005 Hamilton Rd., 53012. Tel: 262-377-2050; Fax: 262-377-4099. Email: office@sfbschool.org. Sue Brandley, Co-Prin.; Kelly Swietlik, Co-Prin. Lay Teachers 34; Students 380.
Catechesis/Religious Program—Students 613.

Clyman, Dodge Co., St. John (1900), (German—Irish), [CEM 2], Also serves Holy Family, Reeseville & St. Columbkille, Elba. Rev. Richard Wendell.
Mailing Address: 302 Prairie St., P.O. Box 277, Reeseville, 53579-0277. Tel: 920-927-3102.
Catechesis/Religious Program—Debbie Caine, D.R.E. Tel: 920-927-3885. Students 4.

Cudahy, Milwaukee Co.

1—St. Frederick (1896) Closed. For sacramental records, contact Nativity of the Lord, Cudahy, Tel: 414-744-6622.

2—Holy Family (1900) Closed. For sacramental records, contact Nativity of the Lord, Cudahy, Tel: 414-744-6622.

3—St. Joseph (1909), (Slovak—Moravian), Closed. For sacramental records, contact Nativity of the Lord, Cudahy, Tel: 414-744-6622.

4—NATIVITY OF THE LORD PARISH (2000) [JC] Rev. Philip D. Reifenberg; Bryan Martin, Dir. Admin. Svcs.
Res. & Office: 4611 S. Kirkwood Ave., 53110. Tel: 414-744-6622; Fax: 414-483-4599. Email: nativityparish@voyager.net.
Church: 3672 E. Plankinton Ave., 53110.
See St. Thomas Aquinas Academy located in the Institution Section under Consolidated Elementary Schools.
Catechesis/Religious Program—3658 E. Plankinton Ave., 53110. Tel: 414-481-6880. Email: robertjboehm@live.com. Students 120.

DACADA, SHEBOYGAN CO., ST. NICHOLAS (1848), (Luxembourgian), Closed. For sacramental records, contact Archdiocese of Milwaukee Archives Office, Tel: 414-769-3407.

DELAFIELD, WAUKESHA CO., ST. JOAN OF ARC (1923) [CEM] Rev. Michael D. Strachota.
Res.: 120 Nashotah Rd., Nashotah, 53058. Tel: 262-646-8078; Fax: 262-646-8079. Email: parish@sjarc.org. Web: www.sjarc.org.
School—Tel: 262-646-5821; Fax: 262-646-5861. Email: school@sjarc.org. Mary Ann Rudella, Prin. Lay Teachers 10; Students 91.
Catechesis/Religious Program—Tel: 262-646-5979. Email: re@sjarc.org. Students 341.

DELAVAN, WALWORTH CO., ST. ANDREW (1848) [CEM] Rev. James T. Schuerman; Deacon Philip O. Kilkenny.
Res.: 714 E. Walworth Ave., 53115. Tel: 262-728-5922; Fax: 262-728-5878. Email: standrewsdelavan@sbcglobal.net.
School—115 S. 17th St., 53115. Tel: 262-728-6211; Fax: 262-728-3683. Web: standrews-delavan.org. Julie Kadrich, Prin. Lay Teachers 13; Students 118.
Catechesis/Religious Program—Tel: 262-728-2792. Joan Zomer, C.R.E. (English Students); Sr. Graciela Peredes, C.R.E. (Hispanic Students); Patty Kostechka, C.R.E. (Deaf Students). Students 275.

DOTYVILLE, FOND DU LAC CO., ST. MICHAEL (1853), (German), Closed. For sacramental records, contact Good Shepherd, Eden, Tel: 920-477-3201.

DOUSMAN, WAUKESHA CO., ST. BRUNO (1852) [CEM] Rev. Ralph C. Gross; Deacons Tom Filipiak; Gordon J. Snyder; Karen Warnes, Pastoral Assoc.
Office: 226 W. Ottawa Ave., 53118. Tel: 262-965-2332; Fax: 262-965-4749. Email: stbruno@wi.rr.com. Web: www.stbrunoparish.com.
Res.: 266 W. Ottawa Ave., 53118.
School—246 W. Ottawa Ave., 53118. Tel: 262-965-2291; Fax: 262-965-2249. Email: rlynch@wi.rr.com. Mr. Ralph Lynch, Prin. Lay Teachers 13; Students 109.
Catechesis/Religious Program—Tel: 262-965-4200. Students 254.

EAGLE, WAUKESHA CO., ST. THERESA (1852) [CEM 2] Rev. Dennis Ackeret.
Office: 136 W. Waukesha Rd., 53119-2026. Tel: 262-594-5200; Fax: 262-594-5201. Email: parishoffice@sttheresaeagle.com. Web: www.sttheresaeagle.com.
Catechesis/Religious Program—Tel: 262-594-5201. Students 233.

EAST TROY, WALWORTH CO., ST. PETER (1854), (Irish—German), [CEM] Rev. Lawrence J. Chapman; Deacon Donald Kuban.
Res. & Mailing Address: 1975 Beulah Ave., 53120. Tel: 262-642-7225, Ext. 3; Fax: 262-642-7228. Email: stpeterset@centurytel.net. Web: steepleconnection.com.
School—3001 Elm St., 53120. Tel: 262-642-5533; Fax: 262-642-5897. Sarah Halbesma, Prin. Lay Teachers 13; Students 119.
Catechesis/Religious Program—Tel: 262-642-7225, Ext. 5. Students 290.

EDEN, FOND DU LAC CO.
1—ST. MARY (1888), (Irish), Closed. For sacramental records, contact Good Shepherd, Eden, Tel: 920-477-3201.
2—SHEPHERD OF THE HILLS (GOOD SHEPHERD) (2001) [JC 6] Very Rev. Joseph J. Juknialis. In Res., Rev. Charles H. Wester (Retired).
Res.: N4348 Mercury Ln., 53019. Tel: 920-477-2079; Fax: 920-477-3030. Email: jjj@sothparish.org. Web: www.sothparish.org.
School—W1562 Cty. Rd. B, 53019. Tel: 920-477-3551. Email: jhively@sothparish.org. Thomas Wegner, Prin. Lay Teachers 12; Students 93.
Catechesis/Religious Program—Mary Borgen, D.R.E. Students 207.
Mission—St. Michael Chapel N3604 Scenic Dr., Cascade, Sheboygan Co. 53011. Tel: 920-477-3201; Fax: 920-477-3030.

ELBA, DODGE CO., ST. COLUMBKILLE (1856), (Irish), [CEM], Also serves Holy Family, Reeseville and St. John the Baptist, Clyman. Rev. Richard Wendell.
Mailing Address: 302 Prairie St., P.O. Box 277, Reeseville, 53579-0277. Tel: 920-623-3989; 920-927-3102.
Catechesis/Religious Program—Fax: 920-927-1970. Students 12.

ELDORADO, FOND DU LAC CO.
1—ST. MARY, Closed. For sacramental records, contact Our Risen Savior, Eldorado, Tel: 920-922-2412.
2—OUR RISEN SAVIOR (1998), (Irish—German), [CEM 2] Rev. John L. Simon.
Church: W8272 Forest Avenue Rd., 54932. Tel: 920-922-2412; Fax: 920-921-1309. Email: motherandson@charter.net.
Catechesis/Religious Program—Students 54.

ELKHART LAKE, SHEBOYGAN CO.
1—ST. GEORGE (1896) Closed. For sacramental records, contact St. Thomas Aquinas, Elkhart Lake, Tel: 920-876-2457.
2—ST. THOMAS AQUINAS (2001) [CEM 2], (Merger of St. George, Elkhart Lake and St. Fridolin, Glenbeulah.) Very Rev. Dennis E. Van Beek.
Res.: 94 N. Lincoln St., P.O. Box T, 53020-0396. Tel: 920-876-2457; Fax: 920-876-2036. Email: st.thomas.aquinas@verizon.net.
Catechesis/Religious Program—Students 163.

ELKHORN, WALWORTH CO., ST. PATRICK (1878), (Irish—German), [CEM] Rev. James A. Jaeger.
Res.: 107 W. Walworth St., 53121. Tel: 262-723-5565; Fax: 262-723-7856. Email: stpatelkhorn@charter.net. Web: www.stpatrickselkhorn.org.
School—534 Sunset Dr., 53121. Tel: 262-723-4258; Fax: 262-723-1577. Email: stpatricksschool@charter.net. Miss Julie Muellenbach, Prin. Lay Teachers 9; Students 78.
Catechesis/Religious Program—Tel: 262-723-5565. Students 281.

ELM GROVE, WAUKESHA CO., ST. MARY'S VISITATION (1848) [CEM] Rev. Laurin J. Wenig; Deacons Charles J. Kustner; Richard T. Piontek.
Res.: 1260 Church St., 53122. Tel: 262-782-4575; Fax: 262-782-0677. Email: stmary@stmaryeg.org. Web: www.stmaryeg.org.
School—13000 Juneau Blvd., 53122. Tel: 262-782-7057; Fax: 262-782-3035. Lynn Ann Reesman, Prin. Lay Teachers 24; Students 328.
Catechesis/Religious Program—Tel: 414-771-4626; Fax: 262-782-0677. Email: stmaryeg@stmaryeg.org. Students 215.

FARMINGTON, WASHINGTON CO., ST. JOHN OF GOD (1859), (Irish), Closed. For sacramental records, contact St. Michael, St. Michael, 53040, Tel: 262-334-5270.

FOND DU LAC, FOND DU LAC CO.
1—HOLY FAMILY (2000) Revs. Victor R. Capriolo; Carmelo Giuffre, Team; Very Rev. Robert X. Stiefvater, Team; Rev. Luke N. Strand, Team.
Church: 271 Fourth Street Way, 54937. Tel: 920-921-0580; Fax: 920-922-4866. Email: holyfam@hffdl.org. Web: www.hffdl.org.
Catechesis/Religious Program—Fax: 920-922-4866. Students 937.
2—ST. JOSEPH (1871) Closed. For sacramental records through June 12, 1967, contact Archdiocese of Milwaukee Archives Office, Tel: 414-769-3407. For records after June 12, 1967, contact Holy Family, Fond du Lac, Tel: 920-921-0580.
3—ST. LOUIS (1847), (French), Closed. For sacramental records through September 19, 1959, contact Archdiocese of Milwaukee Archives Office, Tel: 414-769-3407. For records after September 19, 1959, contact Holy Family, Fond du Lac, Tel: 920-921-0580.
4—ST. MARY (1866), (German), Closed. For sacramental records through 1975, contact Archdiocese of Milwaukee Archives Office, Tel: 414-769-3407. For records after 1975, contact Holy Family, Fond du Lac, Tel: 920-921-0580.
5—ST. PATRICK (1855) Closed. For sacramental records through September 18, 1960, contact Archdiocese of Milwaukee Archives Office, Tel: 414-769-3407. For records after September 18, 1960, contact Holy Family, Fond du Lac, Tel: 920-921-0580.
6—SACRED HEART (1957), (German), Closed. For sacramental records through November 1970, contact Archdiocese of Milwaukee Archives Office, Tel: 414-769-3407. For records after November 1970, contact Holy Family, Fond du Lac, Tel: 920-921-0580.

FONTANA, WALWORTH CO., ST. BENEDICT (1912) [JC] Rev. Daniel J. Sanders.
Res.: 137 Dewey Ave., 53125-1239. Tel: 262-275-2480; Fax: 262-275-6426. Email: stbenedict@charter.net. Web: www.stbensparish.org.
Catechesis/Religious Program—Tel: 262-275-2993. Michael Dowling, Dir. Faith Formation; Beth Peyer, C.R.E. (Gr. K-11). Students 188.

FOX LAKE, DODGE CO.
1—ANNUNCIATION (1998) [CEM 3] Rev. Michael L. Wild.
Res.: 305 W. Green St., 53933-9472. Tel: 920-928-3513; Fax: 920-928-6334.
Catechesis/Religious Program—Tel: 920-928-6022. Marion Moeller, D.R.E. Students 73.
2—ST. MARY (1850), (Irish), Closed. For sacramental records, contact Annunciation, Fox Lake, Tel: 920-928-3513.

FOX POINT, MILWAUKEE CO., ST. EUGENE (1957) Revs. Jerome Herda; Charles Mbuyi Banduku (Congo); Paul J. Fliss; Sr. Kathy Slesar, O.P., Pastoral Assoc.; William Lieven, Dir. Music & Liturgy; Douglas Byers, Dir. Admin. Svcs.; Kathleen Neidert, Dir. Parish Stewardship Devel. & Office Mgr.
Res.: 7600 N. Port Washington Rd., 53217. Tel: 414-918-1100; Fax: 414-918-1111. Email: sainteugene@archmil.org. Web: www.steugenecongregation.org.
School—Tel: 414-918-1120; Fax: 414-918-1122. Mr. Michael Taylor, Prin. Lay Teachers 20; Students 199.
Catechesis/Religious Program—Tel: 414-918-1130. Ms. Jeanette Lambrecht, D.R.E. (Child Ministry); Rita Capriolo, D.R.E. (Youth Ministry). Students 199.

FRANKLIN, MILWAUKEE CO.
1—ST. JAMES (1857) [CEM] Daniel L. Hull, Parish Dir.; Rev. Bernard S. Sippel (Retired).
Office: 7219 S. 27th St., 53132. Tel: 414-761-0480; Fax: 414-761-2208. Web: www.stjames-franklin.4lpi.com.
Catechesis/Religious Program—Tel: 414-761-2208. Students 15.
2—ST. MARTIN OF TOURS (1998) [CEM] Revs. Yvon Sheehy, S.C.J.; Francis Vu Tran, S.C.J.; Robert Naglich, S.C.J.; Bro. Long Nguyen, S.C.J.
Res.: 7963 S. 116th St., 53132. Tel: 414-425-1114; Fax: 414-425-2527. Email: parish@stmoftours.org. Web: www.stmoftours.org.
School—7933 S. 116th St., 53132. Tel: 414-425-9200. Jeanne Johnson, Prin. Lay Teachers 15; Students 153.
Catechesis/Religious Program—Students 252.
3—SACRED HEARTS OF JESUS AND MARY (1858) Closed. For sacramental records, contact St. Martin of Tours, Franklin, Tel: 414-425-1114.

FREDONIA, OZAUKEE CO.
1—HOLY ROSARY (2001) [CEM 4], (Merger of St. Rose of Lima, Fredonia; Mother of Sorrows, Little Kohler and Holy Cross, Holy Cross.) Revs. Richard J. Fleischman, Team Mod.; Guy Gurath, Team Mem.
Res.: 305 Fredonia Ave., P.O. Box 250, 53021-0250. Tel: 262-692-9994; Fax: 262-692-3085.
School—Rosemary Catholic 53021. Tel: 262-692-2141. Lay Teachers 8; Students 91.
Catechesis/Religious Program—Tel: 262-692-9994, Ext. 315. Students 190.
2—ST. ROSE OF LIMA (1909) Closed. For sacramental records, contact Holy Rosary, Fredonia, Tel: 262-692-9994.

GENESEE DEPOT, WAUKESHA CO., ST. PAUL (1863) [CEM] Rev. Mark Molling; Deacon Larry E. Normann, Liturgy Dir. & Biblical Stewardship; Len Grassmann, Pastoral Assoc.; Rosemarie Etzel, Dir. Admin. Svcs.; Peggy Kolonko, Music Dir.
Mailing Address: S38 W31602 Hwy. D, P.O. Box 95, 53127. Tel: 262-968-3865; Fax: 262-968-5546. Email: office@stpaulgenesee.net. Web: www.stpaulgenesee.net.
School—Tel: 262-968-3175; Fax: 262-968-3867. Cheryl Sandford, Prin. Lay Teachers 15; Students 122.
Catechesis/Religious Program—Tel: 262-968-2276. Janet Shanahan, D.R.E. (Grades K-12); Amy Golden, Youth Min. (Grades 9-12); Mariangela Pledl, D.R.E. (Adult). Students 613.

GERMANTOWN, WASHINGTON CO., ST. BONIFACE (1845) [CEM] Rev. Todd Budde.
Res.: W204 N11940 Goldendale Rd., 53022. Tel: 262-628-2040; Fax: 262-628-2076. Email: jjaeger@stbonifacewi.org. Web: stbonifacewi.org.
School—W204 N11968 Goldendale Rd., 53022. Tel: 262-628-1955; Fax: 262-628-1689. Lay Teachers 11; Students 241.
Catechesis/Religious Program—Tel: 262-628-8143. Students 568.

GLENBEULAH, SHEBOYGAN CO., ST. FRIDOLIN (1878) Closed. For sacramental records, contact St. Thomas Aquinas, Elkhart Lake, Tel: 920-876-2457.

GRAFTON, OZAUKEE CO., ST. JOSEPH (1849) [CEM] Dr. Mary M. Foley, Parish Dir.
Pastoral Center—1619 Washington St., 53024. Tel: 262-375-6500; Fax: 262-375-6509. Email: stjosephs@wi.rr.com. Web: www.stjosephgrafton.org.
School—Tel: 262-375-6505. Lay Teachers 17; Students 210.
Catechesis/Religious Program—Students 496.

GREENDALE, MILWAUKEE CO., ST. ALPHONSUS (1938) Revs. Alan F. Jurkus; Mark J. Brandl; Deacons Theodore A. Gurzynski; James Leggett.
Parish Ministry Center: 5960 W. Loomis Rd., 53129. Tel: 414-421-2442; Fax: 414-421-8744. Email: stals@st-alphonsus.org. Web: www.st-alphonsus.org.
School—6000 W. Loomis Rd., 53129. Tel: 414-421-1760. Patrice Wadzinski, Prin. Lay Teachers 25;

Students 343.
Catechesis/Religious Program—Tel: 414-421-0690. Students 720.

GREENFIELD, MILWAUKEE CO., ST. JOHN THE EVANGELIST (1916) Rev. Daniel P. Volkert.
Res.: 8500 W. Cold Spring Rd., 53228. Tel: 414-321-1965; Fax: 414-321-4407. Email: rectory@stjohns-grfd.org. Web: www.stjohns-grfd.org.
School— 53228. Tel: 414-321-8540; Fax: 414-321-4450. Email: principal@stjohns-grfd.org. Mary Laidlaw Otto, Prin. Lay Teachers 16; Students 184.
Catechesis/Religious Program—Tel: 414-321-8922; Fax: 414-321-8922. Debbie Melian, D.R.E. Tel: 414-321-4450. Students 141.

HALES CORNERS, MILWAUKEE CO., ST. MARY (1842) [CEM] Rev. Charles H. Schramm; Deacons John R. Burns; William Goulding; Mary Matestic, Pastoral Assoc.
9520 W. Forest Home Ave., 53130.
School—9553 W. Edgerton Ave., 53130. Tel: 414-425-3100; Fax: 414-425-6270. Email: school@stmaryhc.org. Gina Brown, Prin. Lay Teachers 31; Students 472.
Catechesis/Religious Program—Tel: 414-425-3101; Fax: 414-425-9432. Jim Beuscher, D.R.E. (Children); Wendy Rappe, Dir. Adult & Family Min. Students 559.

HARTFORD, WASHINGTON CO., ST. KILIAN (1863) [CEM 4] Rev. David W. La Plante; Sr. Eileen Brynda, O.P., Pastoral Assoc.
Office & Mailing Address: 428 Forest St., 53027. Tel: 262-673-4831; Fax: 262-673-4872. Web: stkiliancong.org.
School—245 High St., 53027. Tel: 262-673-3081; Fax: 262-673-0412. Mort Zaydel, Prin. Tel: 262-673-3081, Ext. 116. Lay Teachers 15; Students 199.
Catechesis/Religious Program—Tel: 262-673-4831, Ext. 307. June Strobel, D.R.E. Tel: 262-673-4831, Ext. 406. Students 309.

HARTLAND, WAUKESHA CO., ST. CHARLES (1906) [CEM] Very Rev. Kenneth E. Omernick.
Office: 313 Circle Dr., 53029-1824. Tel: 262-367-0800; Fax: 262-367-6960. Email: stcharlesparish@sbcglobal.net. Web: www.stcharleshartland.com.
Res.: 521 Renson Rd., 53029. Tel: 262-367-9936.
School—526 Renson Rd., 53029. Tel: 262-367-2040. Web: www.stcharleshartland.com. Michael Halstead, Prin. Lay Teachers 14; Students 161.
Catechesis/Religious Program—Tel: 262-367-3277. Students 857.

HOLY CROSS, OZAUKEE CO., HOLY CROSS (1845), (Luxembourgian), Closed. For sacramental records, contact Holy Rosary, Fredonia, Tel: 262-692-9994.

HORICON, DODGE CO.
1—ST. MALACHY (1856) Closed. For sacramental records, contact Sacred Heart, Horicon, Tel: 920-485-0694.
2—SACRED HEART (2001) [CEM 2], (Merger of St. Malachy, Horicon and Immaculate Conception, Juneau.) Rev. Michael J. Petrie.
Mailing Address: 950 Washington St., P.O. Box 27, 53032. Email: sheartchurch@sbcglobal.net. Web: www.sheart.org.
Catechesis/Religious Program—Tel: 920-485-0694; Fax: 920-485-0906. Students 253.

HUBERTUS, WASHINGTON CO.
1—ST. GABRIEL (2002) [CEM] [JC 3] Rev. Charles T. Hanel.
Res.: 1200 St. Gabriel Way, 53033. Tel: 262-628-1141; Fax: 262-628-1911. Email: sgabriel@sgabrielp.org. Web: www.stgabrielparish.4lpi.com.
School—3733 Hubertus Rd., 53033. Tel: 262-628-1711; Fax: 262-628-0280. Web: www.sgabriel.org. Lay Teachers 10; Students 128.
Catechesis/Religious Program—Students 348.
2—ST. HUBERT (1846) Closed. For sacramental records after 1960, contact St. Gabriel Parish, Hubertus, Tel: 262-628-1141. For sacramental records prior to 1961, contact the Archdiocese of Milwaukee Archives, Tel: 414-769-3407.
3—ST. MARY OF THE HILL (1924), (German—Irish), [CEM] [JC] Rev. Fred Alexander, O.C.D.
Mailing Address: 1515 Carmel Rd, 53033-9770. Tel: 262-628-3606; Fax: 262-673-7505. Email: secretary@stmaryhh.org. Web: www.stmaryhh.org.
Res.: 1525 Carmel Rd., 53033. Tel: 262-628-1838; Fax: 262-673-7568.
Catechesis/Religious Program—Tel: 262-628-3606, Ext. 4. Email: dre@stmaryhh.org. Tammy Streitmatter, D.R.E. Students 115.

JOHNSBURG, FOND DU LAC CO., ST. JOHN THE BAPTIST (1840) [CEM] Rev. Joseph H. Coerber.
Res.: N9288 County W, Fond Du Lac, 54937. Tel: 920-795-4316; Fax: 920-898-9002.
School— Consolidated Parochial Elementary School (CPES): St. John the Baptist, Johnsburg; St. Mary, Marytown; Holy Cross, Mount Calvary; St. Cloud, St. Cloud. Lay Teachers 13; Students 103.
Catechesis/Religious Program—Tel: 920-898-4040. Students 70.

JUNEAU, DODGE CO., IMMACULATE CONCEPTION (1875) Closed. For sacramental records, contact Sacred Heart, Horicon, Tel: 920-485-0694.

KANSASVILLE, RACINE CO., ST. MARY-DOVER (1869) [CEM] Rev. Howard G. Haase.
23211 Church Rd., 53139.
Res.: 3320 S. Colony, Union Grove, 53182. Tel: 262-878-1762; Fax: 262-534-2596. Email: stmdover@bizwi.rr.com. Web: www.foursaints.org.
Catechesis/Religious Program—Tel: 262-878-3476; Fax: 262-878-0194. Email: dillonc@foursaints.org. Students 75.

KENOSHA, KENOSHA CO.
1—ST. ANTHONY (1910), (Slovak), [JC] Revs. Roman Stikel; Stephen E. Lattner, O.S.B.
Mailing Address: 2223 51st St., 53140. Tel: 262-652-1844; Fax: 262-605-8262.
Catechesis/Religious Program—Students 21.
2—ST. CASIMIR (1901) Closed. For sacramental records, contact Archdiocese of Milwaukee Archives Office, Tel: 414-769-3407.
3—ST. ELIZABETH (2000), (Polish—German), [CEM 2] Revs. Roman Stikel; Stephen E. Lattner, O.S.B.
Mailing Address: 4816 7th Ave., 53140.
Res.: 4804 7th Ave., 53140. Tel: 262-657-6875.
Catechesis/Religious Program—Students 70.
4—ST. GEORGE (1851), (German), Closed. For sacramental records, contact Archdiocese of Milwaukee Archives Office, Tel: 414-769-3407.
5—ST. JAMES (1845), (Irish), [CEM] Rev. Dominic Thomas, M.C.B.S.
Res.: 5804 Sheridan Rd., 53140. Tel: 262-658-8071; Fax: 262-658-2490. Email: stjames@wi.rr.com.
Catechesis/Religious Program—Students 30.
6—ST. MARK (1924) Rev. Stephen Forrest; Deacon Alvaro Dominguez; Karen Metallo, Pastoral Assoc.
Res.: 7117 14th Ave., 53143. Tel: 262-656-7373; Fax: 262-656-7375. Email: stmark@archmil.org. Web: www.stmark-kenosha.org.
School—7207 14th Ave., 53143. Tel: 262-656-7360. Frank Germinaro, Prin. School Sisters of St. Francis 1; Lay Teachers 9; Students 103.
Catechesis/Religious Program—Tel: 262-656-7362. Colleen A. Reddy, D.R.E. Students 456.
Latin American Center—7101 13th Ave., 53143-5459. Tel: 262-656-7370.
7—ST. MARY (1929) Very Rev. Michael T. Newman; Rev. Joseph J. Shimek; Deacons Ronald F. Lesjak; James S. Francois; Wilson A. Shierk.
Res.: 7307 40th Ave., 53142. Tel: 262-694-6018; Fax: 262-694-6048.
School—7400 39th Ave., 53142. Tel: 262-694-6018, Ext. 130; Fax: 262-694-6740. Sandra Wiercinski, Prin. Lay Teachers 22; Students 304.
Catechesis/Religious Program—7401-40th Ave., 53142. Jane Delfield, Dir. Adult & Family Min.; Sandy Slivon, Dir. Child Min.; Brian Magliocco, Youth Min. Students 531.
8—OUR LADY OF MOUNT CARMEL (1904), (Italian), Rev. Donald J. Gibbs, O.S.B. In Res., Rev. Stephen E. Lattner, O.S.B.
Res.: 1919 54th St., 53140. Tel: 262-652-7660; 262-652-7683; Fax: 262-652-2542. Email: mtcarmelparish@wi.rr.com.
School—5400 19th Ave., 53140. Lay Teachers 5.
Catechesis/Religious Program—Tel: 262-652-5057. Twinned with Our Lady of the Holy Rosary, Kenosha. Students 95.
9—OUR LADY OF THE HOLY ROSARY (1904) Rev. Alan D. Veik, O.F.M.Cap.
Res.: 2224 45th St., 53140. Tel: 262-652-2771; Fax: 262-652-0183. Email: rectory@hrosary.org. Web: www.hrosary.org.
School—4400 22nd Ave., 53140. Tel: 262-652-5950; Fax: 262-652-6179. Sr. Lucillann, Prin. Franciscan Sisters of St. Joseph (Hamburg, NY) 6; Lay Teachers 12; Students 189.
Catechesis/Religious Program—Delia Chiappetta, Coord. Christian Formation. Twinned with Our Lady of Mount Carmel, Kenosha. Students 195.
10—ST. PETER (1903) Revs. William Hayward, M.I.C.; Iraneusz Chodakowski, M.I.C.; Deacon Terrance A. Maack.
Res.: 2224 30th Ave., 53144. Tel: 262-551-9004; Fax: 262-552-7004. Web: www.stpeterskenosha.com.
School—Tel: 262-551-8383; Fax: 262-551-9833. Jacqueline Grajera, Prin. Lay Teachers 7; Students 76.
Catechesis/Religious Program—Students 210.
11—ST. THERESE (1953) Rev. Michael E. Nowak.
Res.: 9005 22nd Ave., 53143-6699. Tel: 262-694-4695; Fax: 262-694-7284. Email: valang@tds.net. Web: www.st-therese-kenosha.org.
School—2020 91st St., 53143. Tel: 262-694-8080. Mrs. Carol Degen, Prin. Lay Teachers 10; Students 75.
Catechesis/Religious Program—Tel: 262-694-0118. Students 145.
12—ST. THOMAS AQUINAS (1911) Closed. For sacramental records, contact Archdiocese of Milwaukee Archives Office, Tel: 414-769-3407.

KEWASKUM, WASHINGTON CO., HOLY TRINITY (1861) [CEM 2] [JC 3] Rev. Edwin M. Kornath; Deacon Ralph E. Horner.
Res.: 331 Main St., P.O. Box 461, 53040. Tel: 262-626-2860; Fax: 262-626-2301. Email: htkewaskum@alexssa.net.
School—305 Main St., 53040. Tel: 262-626-2603; Fax: 262-626-8863. Web: htschool.alexssu.net. Ms. JoAnn Karpin, Prin. Lay Teachers 15; Students 154.
Catechesis/Religious Program—Combined program with St. Michaels, St. Michael., Tel: 262-626-2650. Ms. Bonnie Rapkin, D.R.E. Students 214.

KOHLER, SHEBOYGAN CO., ST. JOHN EVANGELIST (1927) Rev. Robert J. Lotz.
Res.: 600 Green Tree Rd., 53044. Tel: 920-452-9623; Fax: 920-452-9633.
Catechesis/Religious Program—Tel: 920-458-9931. Students 150.

LAKE FIVE, WASHINGTON CO., ST. COLUMBA (1843) Closed. For sacramental records, contact St. Gabriel, Hubertus, Tel: 262-628-1141.

LAKE GENEVA, WALWORTH CO., ST. FRANCIS DE SALES (1842) [CEM] Very Rev. Terrance J. Huebner; Rev. Jose-Angel Anaya-Estrada (Colombia).
Res.: 148 W. Main St., 53147. Tel: 262-248-8524; Fax: 262-248-5302. Email: office@stfrancislg.com. Web: www.stfrancislg.com.
School—130 W. Main St., 53147. Tel: 262-248-2778; Fax: 262-248-7860. Lay Teachers 10; Students 159.
Catechesis/Religious Program—Tel: 262-248-8526. Email: rep@stfrancislg.com. Mrs. Anne Trautner, D.R.E. Students 365.

LE ROY, DODGE CO., ST. ANDREW (1849) [CEM], Also serves St. Mary, Mayville. Rev. Thomas E. Biersack.
Res.: W3081 County Tr. Y, Lomira, 53048. Tel: 920-583-4125; 920-387-3130, Ext. 335; Fax: 920-387-1121.
Catechesis/Religious Program—Students 53.

LIMA, SHEBOYGAN CO., ST. ROSE (1860) Closed. For sacramental records, contact Blessed Trinity, Sheboygan Falls, Tel: 920-467-4616.

LITTLE KOHLER, OZAUKEE CO., MOTHER OF SORROWS, Closed. For sacramental records, contact Holy Rosary, Fredonia, Tel: 262-692-9994.

LOMIRA, DODGE CO., ST. MARY (1870), (German), [CEM] Rev. Dennis G. Budka.
Res.: 699 Milwaukee St., 53048. Tel: 920-269-4429; Fax: 920-269-7359. Email: natheres@charter.net.
School—(Grades K-8), Consolidated with St. Theresa to form Consolidated Catholic School of Lomira-Theresa., 705 Milwaukee St., 53048. Tel: 920-269-4326. Dorothy Zitlow, Prin. Lay Teachers 4; Students 30.
Catechesis/Religious Program—Tel: 920-269-7273. Mary Straub, D.R.E. Students 125.

LOST LAKE, DODGE CO., ST. MARY (1893) Closed. For sacramental records, contact Annunciation, Fox Lake, Tel: 920-928-3513.

LYONS, WALWORTH CO.
1—ST. JOSEPH (1870), (German), [CEM 2] Rev. John H. Baumgartner.
Res.: 1540 Mill St., Box 60, 53148-0060. Tel: 262-763-2050; Fax: 262-763-9377. Email: saintjoe@bizwi.rr.com.
Catechesis/Religious Program—Students 82.
2—ST. KILIAN, Closed. For sacramental records, contact St. Joseph, Lyons, Tel: 262-763-2050.

MAPLETON, WAUKESHA CO., ST. CATHERINE (1847), (Irish), [CEM] Rev. David A. Verhasselt.
Res.: W359 N8512 Brown St., Oconomowoc, 53066. Tel: 920-474-7000; 877-871-8489 (Toll Free); Fax: 920-474-4661.
Catechesis/Religious Program—Fax: 920-474-4461. Students 303.

MARYTOWN, FOND DU LAC CO., ST. MARY (1849) [CEM] Rev. Joseph H. Coerber.
Res.: N10232 Hwy. G, New Holstein, 53061. Tel: 920-898-4040; Fax: 920-898-9002. Email: vsitbvm@tcei.com.
Catechesis/Religious Program—Students 34.

MAYVILLE, DODGE CO., ST. MARY (1856) [CEM], Also serves St. Andrew, LeRoy. Rev. Thomas E. Biersack; Deacon Willis Heideman.
Res.: W3081 Hwy. Y, Lomira, 53048.
Church: 302 S. German St., P.O. Box 22, 53050-0022. Tel: 920-387-2470; 920-387-3130 (Parish Center); Fax: 920-387-1121. Web: www.stmary-standrew.org.
School—(Grades K-8), 28 Naber St., 53050. Tel: 920-387-2920. Lay Teachers 5; Students 67.
Catechesis/Religious Program—Fax: 920-387-0362. Students 168.

MENOMONEE FALLS, WAUKESHA CO.
1—ST. ANTHONY (1846) [CEM] Rev. Dennis J. Wieland.
Res.: N74 W13604 Appleton Ave., 53051. Tel: 262-251-5910; Fax: 262-251-6564. Web: www.stanthony-parish.org.
School—N74 W13646 Appleton Ave., 53051. Tel: 262-251-4390; Fax: 262-251-2412. Anne Schramka, Prin. Lay Teachers 17; Students 194.

Catechesis/Religious Program—Tel: 262-251-8868. Drew Dederich, Dir. Youth and Adult & Family Min.; John Hying, Dir. Child Min. Students 446.

2—GOOD SHEPHERD (1957) Rev. Kenneth A. Mich; Deacons Eugene M. Christensen; Sanford Sites; Mark Steimle, Dir. of Admin. Svcs.; Jane Clare Ishiguro, Pastoral Assoc.
Church & Office: N88 W17658 Christman Rd., 53051-2630. Tel: 262-255-2035; Fax: 262-255-2020. Email: goodshepherd@gdinet.com. Web: www.mygoodshepherd.org.
Catechesis/Religious Program—Suzanne Foster, Dir. Youth Ministry; Lorrie Maples, Dir. Child Ministry. Students 324.

3—ST. JAMES (1847) [CEM] Rev. Arthur G. Heinze; Daryl Olszewski, Pastoral Assoc.
Res.: W 220-N 6588 Town Line Rd., 53051. Tel: 262-251-3944; Fax: 262-250-2679. Web: www.stjames-parish.com.
Catechesis/Religious Program—Tel: 262-251-0897. Tracy Derezynski, D.R.E. (Youth Min.); Sue Devine-Simon, D.R.E. (Child Min.). Students 922.

4—ST. MARY (1905) [CEM] Rev. Gregory J. Greiten; Sr. Jane Mary Lorbiecki, S.S.N.D., Pastoral Assoc.; Deacons Robert H. Buth, (Retired); Thomas H. Wuchterl; Thomas C. Monday.
Church: N89 W16297 Cleveland Ave., 53051. Tel: 262-251-0220; Fax: 262-251-6948. Email: stmarymf@archmil.org. Web: stmarymf.org.
School—N89 W16215 Cleveland Ave., 53051. Tel: 262-251-1050; Fax: 262-502-1671. Mrs. Linda Joyner, Prin. Lay Teachers 24; Students 349.
Catechesis/Religious Program—Tel: 262-251-1154. Students 226.

MEQUON, OZAUKEE CO.

1—ST. JAMES (1851), (German), Closed. For sacramental records, contact Lumen Christi, Mequon, Tel: 262-242-7967.

2—LUMEN CHRISTI (2005) Revs. John D. Hemsing; Peter Berger; Deacons Anthony Monfre; Joseph P. Wenzler.
11300 N. St. James Ln., 28W, 53092. Tel: 262-242-7967; Fax: 262-242-7970. Email: lcmail@lumenchristiparish.org. Web: www.lumenchristiparish.org.
School—(1984) Tel: 262-242-7960; Fax: 262-512-8986. Email: markowskig@lumenchristiparish.org. Web: www.lumenchristiparish.org/school/. Miss Gloria Markowski, Prin. Lay Teachers 37; Students 465.
Catechesis/Religious Program—Web: www.lumenchristiparish.org/cf/. Terri Schiller, Dir. Formation. Students 554.

MITCHELL, SHEBOYGAN CO., ST. MICHAEL (1852) Closed. For sacramental records, contact Archdiocese of Milwaukee Archives Office, Tel: 414-769-3407.

MONCHES, WAUKESHA CO., ST. JOHN (1843) [CEM] Closed. For sacramental records, contact Blessed Teresa of Calcutta, North Lake, Tel: 262-966-3191.

MOUNT CALVARY, FOND DU LAC CO., HOLY CROSS (1849) [CEM] Rev. Steven Kropp, O.F.M.Cap.
Res.: P.O. Box 176, 53057. Tel: 920-753-3311.
Catechesis/Religious Program—Students 98.

MUKWONAGO, WAUKESHA CO., ST. JAMES (1896) Rev. Michael G. Savio.
Res.: 830 Cty. Rd. NN East, 53149. Tel: 262-363-7615; Fax: 262-363-2416. Email: parish@stjmuk.org. Web: www.stjamesmukwonago.org.
School—Tel: 262-363-7615, Ext. 128. Martha Meyer, S.S.N.D., Prin. Lay Teachers 11; Students 89.
Catechesis/Religious Program—Tel: 262-363-7615, Ext. 124. David Zampino, D.R.E. Students 503.

MUSKEGO, WAUKESHA CO., ST. LEONARD CONGREGATION (1957) Rev. William E. Kohler; Deacons Rick J. Wirch; Ralph Wisniewski; Carlene S. Larson, Pastoral Assoc.
Res.: W173 S7743 Westwood Dr., 53150. Tel: 262-679-1773; Fax: 262-679-4210. Email: parish@stleonards.org. Web: www.stleonards.org.
School—Sue Watkinson, Prin. Lay Teachers 18; Students 211.
Catechesis/Religious Program—Tel: 262-679-0880; Fax: 262-679-8502. Web: www.stleonard-reled.com. Lisa Jachimiec, D.R.E. Students 854.

NABOB, WASHINGTON CO., ST. MATTHIAS (1848) Closed. For sacramental records, contact St. Lawrence, St. Lawrence, Tel: 262-644-5701.

NENNO, WASHINGTON CO.

1—ST. ANTHONY, Closed. For sacramental records, contact Resurrection, Allenton, Tel: 262-629-5240.

2—SS. PETER AND PAUL (1848) Closed. For sacramental records, contact Resurrection, Allenton, Tel: 262-629-5240.

NEOSHO, DODGE CO., ST. MATTHEW (1857), (German), [CEM], Also serves St. Mary, Woodland & St. John, Rubicon. Rev. Alois Van Beek.
Res.: 148 W. Lehman St., P.O. Box 45, 53059. Tel: 920-625-3144. Email: mattneo3@nconnect.net. Web: mjmtriparish.org.
Catechesis/Religious Program—Tel: 920-625-3092. Combined with St. Mary, Woodland. Students 110.
Mission—St. Mary Woodland, Dodge Co. 53099.

NEW BERLIN, WAUKESHA CO.

1—ST. ELIZABETH ANN SETON (1981) Rev. Joseph A. Aufdermauer; Deacon Jeffrey J. Copson; Liz Hanna, Pastoral Assoc.; Dennis Wisialowski, Dir. Admin. Svcs.; Linda Noel Halverson, Dir. Music & Worship; Mickey Holtz, Dir. Youth Ministry.
Church & Office: 12700 W. Howard Ave., 53151. Tel: 262-782-6760; Fax: 262-782-4763. Email: seaseton@tds.net. Web: mystelizabeth.com.
Catechesis/Religious Program—Tel: 262-782-8982. Marilyn Zwick, Dir. Christian Formation; Ann Hepp, Coord. Christian Formation. Students 472.

2—HOLY APOSTLES (1855) [CEM] Revs. David C. Filut; Joseph G. Anderson (Retired).
Res.: 16000 W. National Ave., 53151. Tel: 262-786-7330; Fax: 262-786-0425. Email: rmueller@hanb.org. Web: www.hanb.org.
School—3875 S. 159 St., 53151. Tel: 262-786-7331. Gregory Young, Prin. Sisters 1; Lay Teachers 26; Students 459.
Catechesis/Religious Program—Tel: 262-786-2035. Students 493.

NEW MUNSTER, KENOSHA CO., ST. ALPHONSUS (1849), (German), [CEM] Rev. Michael J. Erwin.
Res.: 6301 344th Ave., P.O. Box 767, 53152. Tel: 262-537-4370; Fax: 262-537-3527. Email: rectory@st-alphonsus.com.
School—6211 344th Ave., P.O. Box 922, 53152. Tel: 262-537-4379. Lay Teachers 13; Students 110.
Catechesis/Religious Program—Tel: 262-537-4359. Students 162.

NEWBURG, WASHINGTON CO., HOLY TRINITY (1859), (German), [CEM 3] Rev. Kevin J. Kowalske; Deacon Steven J. Przedpelski.
521 Congress St., Box 16, 53060-0016.
Res.: Box 16, 53060-0016. Tel: 262-675-6256. Email: htrinity@execpc.com.
Catechesis/Religious Program—Tel: 262-675-6933. Students 51.
Station—St. Augustine (1857) Trenton.
Station—St. Peter (1855) Farmington.

NORTH FOND DU LAC, FOND DU LAC CO., PRESENTATION OF THE BLESSED VIRGIN MARY (1902), (Irish—German), [JC] Rev. John L. Simon; Deacon Paul S. Monzel.
Rectory—705 Michigan Ave., 54937. Tel: 920-921-9383; Fax: 920-921-1309. Email: motherandson@charter.net.
Catechesis/Religious Program—Tel: 920-921-5873. Email: motherandsonre@charterinternet.com. Students 167.

NORTH LAKE, WAUKESHA CO.

1—BLESSED TERESA OF CALCUTTA (2006) [JC 2] Rev. Anthony T. McCarthy.
P.O. Box 68, 53064-0068. Tel: 262-966-2191. Email: office@blteresaparish.org. Web: www.blteresaparish.org.
Catechesis/Religious Program—Karin Frederickson, D.R.E. Students 318.

2—ST. CLARE (1916) [CEM] Closed. For sacramental records, contact Blessed Teresa of Calcutta, North Lake, Tel: 262-966-2191.

OAK CREEK, MILWAUKEE CO.

1—ST. MATTHEW (1841) [CEM] Rev. Patrick J. O'Loughlin.
Res.: 9303 S. Chicago Rd., 53154. Tel: 414-762-4200. Email: parish@stmattoc.org. Web: www.stmattoc.org.
School—9329 S. Chicago Rd., 53154. Tel: 414-762-6820; Fax: 414-762-3686. Email: school@stmattoc.org. Lay Teachers 12; Students 203.
Catechesis/Religious Program— Shelly Madden, Dir. Youth Ministry; Carol Daun, Dir. Family & Child. Students 379.

2—ST. STEPHEN (Airport) (1847), (German), [CEM 2] Rev. Richard A. Liska; Deacon Leon J. Zalewski.
Mailing Address: 1441 W. Oakland Rd., 53154. Tel: 414-483-2685; Fax: 414-483-3160.
Catechesis/Religious Program—Tel: 414-483-2658. Sr. Therese MacKinnon, D.C., D.R.E. Religious 1; Lay Teachers 9; Students 212.

OAKFIELD, FOND DU LAC CO., ST. JAMES (1909) Closed. For sacramental records, contact Sons of Zebedee: Saints James and John, Byron, Tel: 920-583-4376.

OCONOMOWOC, WAUKESHA CO., ST. JEROME (1860) [CEM] Very Rev. John G. Yockey.
Res.: 995 S. Silver Lake St., 53066. Tel: 262-569-3020; Fax: 262-569-3022. Email: parish@stjerome.org. Web: www.stjerome.org.
School—1001 S. Silver Lake St., 53066. Tel: 262-569-3030; Fax: 262-569-3023. Email: school@stjerome.org. Third Order Schoenstatt 1; Lay Teachers 25; Students 329.
Catechesis/Religious Program—Tel: 262-569-3025. Email: prep@stjerome.org. Students 332.

PARIS, KENOSHA CO., ST. JOHN THE BAPTIST (1859) [CEM] Rev. Gary D. Nowicki; Lynn C. Schultz, Dir. Liturgy & Music.
Parish Office—1704 240th Ave., Kansasville, 53139. Tel: 262-859-2484; Fax: 262-859-2684. Email: sfxsjb@archmil.org.
School—Providence Catholic School, Consolidated with St. Francis Xavier, Brighton, 1481 172nd Ave., Union Grove, 53182. Tel: 262-859-2007; 262-878-2713; Fax: 262-859-2604. Email: eastcampus@providencecatholicschool.org. Web: www.providencecatholicschool.org. Mrs. Donna Stevens, Prin. Lay Teachers 8; Students 99.
Catechesis/Religious Program—Tel: 262-878-2267; Fax: 262-878-3683. Sr. Kathryn Dean Strandell, O.S.F., D.R.E. (Grades K-8). Students 110.

PELL LAKE, WALWORTH CO., ST. MARY (1928) [JC] Closed. For sacramental records, contact St. Francis de Sales, Lake Geneva, Tel: 262-248-8524/8525.

PEWAUKEE, WAUKESHA CO.

1—ST. ANTHONY ON THE LAKE (1918) Rev. Joseph F. Hornacek; Kathie Amidei, Pastoral Assoc.
Res.: W 280 N. 2101 Hwy. SS., 53072. Tel: 262-691-2326; Fax: 262-691-2063. Email: parish@stanthony.cc. Web: www.stanthony.cc.
School—Tel: 262-691-0460; 262-691-1173 (Parish Center); Fax: 262-691-7376. Email: principal@stanthony.cc. Lay Teachers 15; Students 207.
Catechesis/Religious Program—Tel: 262-691-9170. Email: parish@stanthony.cc. Ann Fons, D.R.E.; Debbie Kusch, D.R.E.; Cindi Petre, D.R.E. Students 869.

2—ST. MARY (1858) Closed. For sacramental records, contact Queen of Apostles, Pewaukee, Tel: 262-691-1535.

3—SS. PETER AND PAUL (1848) Closed. For sacramental records, contact Queen of Apostles, Pewaukee, Tel: 262-691-1535.

4—QUEEN OF APOSTLES (1997) [CEM 2], Consolidation of St. Mary's, Pewaukee and Ss. Peter and Paul, Pewaukee. Rev. Robert J. Drutowski; Deacons Eugene A. Kempka; Gregory R. Price.
Mailing Address: P.O. Box 220, 53072-0220. N35 W23360 Capitol Dr., 53072. Tel: 262-691-1535; Fax: 262-691-9219. Email: qoapar@execpc.com. Web: www.queenofapostles.net.
School—449 W. Wisconsin Ave. Tel: 262-691-2120; Fax: 262-691-8606. Email: qoaschool@wi.rr.com. Web: queenofapostlesschool.net. Mr. Laurence Patterson, Prin. Tel: 262-691-2120. Lay Teachers 15; Students 146.
Catechesis/Religious Program—Tel: 262-691-2878. Lynn Famularo, D.R.E.; Bill Eder, Youth Min. Students 265.

PLEASANT PRAIRIE, KENOSHA CO., ST. ANNE (1998) Rev. Donald H. Thimm.
Church: 9091 Prairie Ridge Blvd., 53158. Tel: 262-942-8300; Fax: 262-942-8472. Email: info@saint-anne.org. Web: www.saint-anne.org.
Catechesis/Religious Program—Tel: 262-694-0026; Fax: 262-942-8472. Email: info@saint-anne.org. Students 298.

PLYMOUTH, SHEBOYGAN CO., ST. JOHN THE BAPTIST (1861) [CEM] Very Rev. Dennis E. Van Beek.
Res.: 115 Plymouth St., 53073. Tel: 920-892-4006; Fax: 920-893-8444. Email: sjparish@sjbplymouth.org. Web: www.sjbplymouth.org.
School—116 Pleasant St., 53073. Tel: 920-893-5961; Fax: 920-893-3160. Email: tstjohnthebap@wi.rr.com. Jeanne Bitkers, Prin. Lay Teachers 22; Students 270.
Catechesis/Religious Program—Tel: 920-892-6015. Email: sjbreled@hotmail.com. Students 377.

PORT WASHINGTON, OZAUKEE CO.

1—ST. MARY (1853) [CEM] Revs. Patrick Wendt, In Solidum Team Mod.; Thomas F. Lijewski, In Solidum Team Mem.
Office: 430 N. Johnson St., 53074. Tel: 262-284-5771; Fax: 262-284-4112. Email: maryport@archmil.org. Web: stmaryport.org.
School—Consolidated with St. Peter of Alcantara to form Port Washington Catholic School, Inc., 1802 N. Wisconsin St., 53074. Tel: 262-284-2441 (PreK-4); 262-284-2682 (Grades 5-8); Fax: 262-284-4216. Email: ptcath2@execpc.com. Web: www.portcatholic.org. School Sisters of Notre Dame 1; Lay Teachers 19; Students 254.
Catechesis/Religious Program—Consolidated with St. Peter of Alcantara, Port Washington., Tel: 262-284-6472. Email: portchild@archmil.org. Denise Murre, D.R.E. (Grades K-6); Maureen Kavanaugh, D.R.E. (Grades 7-11). Tel: 262-284-2102. Students 230.

2—ST. PETER OF ALCANTARA (1966) Revs. Patrick Wendt, In Solidum Team Mod.; Thomas F. Lijewski, In Solidum Team Mem.; Deacon Thomas J. Surges; Mary McHugh, Pastoral Assoc.; Mr. Timothy Charek, Dir. Admin. Svcs.
Res.: 1800 N. Wisconsin St., 53074. Tel: 262-284-4266; Fax: 262-284-4216. Email:

stpeterport@archmil.org. Web: www.stpeterport.org.
See school listing under St. Mary, Port Washington for details.
Catechesis/Religious Program—Clustered with St. Mary, Port Washington., Tel: 262-284-6472 (Child Ministry); 262-284-2102 (Youth Ministry). Web: www.portyouth.org (Youth Ministry); www.stmary-stpeter-kids.com (Child Ministry). Denise Murre, D.R.E. (Grades K-6); Maureen Rotramel, D.R.E. (Grades 7-12). Students 200.

RACINE, RACINE CO.

1—ST. CASIMIR (1913), (Lithuanian), Closed. For sacramental records, contact Archdiocese of Milwaukee Archives Office, Tel: 414-769-3407.

2—CRISTO REY (1980), (Hispanic), Rev. Esteban Redolad.
Res.: 800 Wisconsin Ave., 53403. Tel: 262-632-3151. Email: cristorey@archmil.org.
Catechesis/Religious Program—Students 125.

3—ST. EDWARD (1919) Rev. Allen J. Bratkowski.
Office and Res.: 1401 Grove Ave., 53405. Tel: 262-636-8040; Fax: 262-636-8052. Email: stedwards@wi.rr.com. Web: www.stedwardracine.org.
School—1435 Grove Ave., 53405. Fax: 262-636-8045. Email: steds@wi.rr.com. Ms. Jessica Knierim, Prin. Dominican Sisters (Racine) 1; Lay Teachers 19; Students 270.
Catechesis/Religious Program—Tel: 262-636-8040, Ext. 4. Students 77.

4—HOLY NAME (1884), (German), Closed. For sacramental records, contact Archdiocese of Milwaukee Archives Office, Tel: 414-769-3407.

5—HOLY TRINITY (1914) Closed. For sacramental records, contact Archdiocese of Milwaukee Archives Office, Tel: 414-769-3407.

6—ST. JOHN NEPOMUK (1896) [JC] Janet M. Ruidl, Parish Dir.; Rev. Donald F. Zerkel (Retired).
Res.: 700 English St., 53402. Tel: 262-634-5647; Fax: 262-637-1436. Email: stjohnnepomuk@wi.rr.com.
See John Paul II Academy at Sacred Heart Congregation, Racine.
Catechesis/Religious Program—1911 Green St., 53402. Tel: 262-634-5647; Fax: 262-634-1436. Students 22.

7—ST. JOSEPH (1875) [JC 4] Rev. John D. Aiello.
Office: 1532 N. Wisconsin St., 53402. Tel: 262-633-8284; Fax: 262-633-8285. Email: info@st-joes.org. Web: st-joes.org.
Res.: 1526 Erie St., 53402. Tel: 262-632-6487.
School—1525 Erie St., 53402. Tel: 262-633-2403. Joseph Majowski, Prin. Lay Teachers 18; Students 172.
Catechesis/Religious Program—Tel: 262-633-9005. Susan Gehrig, D.R.E. Students 154.

8—ST. LUCY (1958) Rev. Mark R. Jones; Deacon Dan Burmeister.
Res.: 3101 Drexel Ave., 53403. Tel: 262-554-1801; Fax: 262-554-2009. Email: stlucy@archmil.org. Web: www.stlucychurch.org.
Rectory—2337 Mitchell, 53403.
School—3035 Drexel Ave., 53403. Fax: 262-554-7618. Email: stlucyschool@archmil.org. Web: www-.stlucysschool.com. Lay Teachers 15; Students 222.
School—Little Lucy's Academy, (preschool), 2516 Winthrop Ave., 53403. Tel: 262-554-9633. Email: dieterichm@archmil.org. Lay Teachers 1; Students 9.
Catechesis/Religious Program—Tel: 262-554-1801, Ext. 208; Fax: 262-554-2009. Sandra Gottfredsen, D.R.E. Students 262.

9—ST. MARY BY THE LAKE (1852) [JC] Rev. Stephen J. Stradinger.
Mailing Address: P.O. Box 044200, 53404-7004. Tel: 262-639-3616; Fax: 262-639-1999. Email: stmarybl@wi.twcbc.com. Web: http://stmarybythelake.raydoshack.com.
Church: 7605 Lakeshore Dr., 53402. Tel: 262-321-0989.
Catechesis/Religious Program—Tel: 262-639-4493; Fax: 262-639-1999. Students 89.

10—ST. PATRICK (1856) [JC 4] Rev. Esteban Redolad; Deacons Emilio Coca; Leonides Rocha.
Res.: 1100 Erie St., 53402. Tel: 262-632-8808; Fax: 262-637-1536. Email: church@stpatrickracine.com. Web: stpatrickracine.com.
Catechesis/Religious Program—Email: church@stpatrick.com. Laura Gabriela Cabrera, D.R.E. Students 205.

11—ST. PAUL THE APOSTLE (1965) [JC] Rev. William J. Dietzler; Deacons Patrick H. Frye; Keith A. Hansen; Dale T. Nees; Willard M. Widmar; Ronnie Quella, Music Dir.
Res.: 6400 Spring St., 53406. Tel: 262-886-0530; Fax: 262-886-0737. Email: stpaulracine@tds.net. Web: www.stpaulracine.org.
Catechesis/Religious Program—Tel: 262-886-0531. Leticia Gutierrez-Kenny, Dir. Child Ministry; Colleen Kechter, Dir. Admin. Svcs.; David Kenny, Dir. Youth & Young Adult Ministry; Dorothy Morse, Dir. Adult Formation. Students 228.

12—ST. RICHARD OF CHICHESTER (1998) [JC] Rev. Ronald J. Gramza; Deacon Howard J. Wirtz.
Res.: 1509 Grand Ave., 53403. Tel: 262-637-8374; Fax: 262-635-2426. Email: strichard@archmil.org. Web: www.strichardparish.org.
Catechesis/Religious Program—Students 57.

13—ST. RITA (1926) [CEM] Revs. Joseph G. Stobba, O.S.A.; Ray Elam, O.S.A. In Res., Revs. Gerald A. Nicholas, O.S.A.; Henry Maibusch, O.S.A.; Bro. Robert J. Schurman, O.S.A.; Rev. Edward J. Kersten, O.S.A.
Res.: 4339 Douglas Ave., 53402. Tel: 262-639-3223; Fax: 262-639-3602. Email: sritarac@archmil.org. Web: www.st-ritas.org.
School—4433 Douglas Ave., 53402. Tel: 262-639-3333. Email: principal@st-ritas.org. Lay Teachers 18; Students 257.
Catechesis/Religious Program—Tel: 262-639-6280; Fax: 262-639-3370. Leticia Gutierrez-Kenny, D.R.E. Students 252.

14—ST. ROSE (1886) Closed. For sacramental records, contact Archdiocese of Milwaukee Archives Office, Tel: 414-769-3407.

15—SACRED HEART CONGREGATION (1916) [CEM 4] [JC 12] Very Rev. Ronald O. Crewe.
Res.: 2201 Northwestern Ave., 53404. Tel: 262-634-5526; Fax: 262-634-5767. Email: shracine@archmil.org. Web: www.sacredheartracine.com.
School—John Paul II Academy, 2023 Northwestern Ave., 53404. Tel: 262-637-2012; Fax: 262-637-5130. Robert Hesse, Prin.; Thomas Siefert, Prin. Sacred Heart & St. John Nepomuk schools merged. Lay Teachers 15; Students 219.
Catechesis/Religious Program—Tel: 262-634-3607. Mrs. Donna Joas, D.R.E. Students 102.

16—ST. STANISLAUS (1904), (Polish), Closed. For sacramental records, contact Archdiocese of Milwaukee Archives Office, Tel: 414-769-3407.

RANDOLPH, COLUMBIA CO., ST. GABRIEL, Closed. For sacramental records, contact Annunciation, Fox Lake, Tel: 920-928-3513.

RANDOM LAKE, SHEBOYGAN CO.

1—ST. MARY (1855) Closed. For sacramental records, contact Archdiocese of Milwaukee Archives Office, Tel: 414-769-3407.

2—OUR LADY OF THE LAKES (1998) [CEM 4] Revs. Guy Gurath, Co-Pastor; Richard J. Fleischman, Co-Pastor; Debbie Hamm, Pastoral Assoc.
Mailing Address: 230 Butler St., 53075-1710. Tel: 920-994-4380; Fax: 920-994-2605. Email: ourladyrlp@archmil.org. Web: www.ourladylakes.org.
School—(Grades 3-6), 306 Butler St., 53075-1712. Tel: 920-994-9962; Fax: 920-994-2499. Email: ourladyrls@archmil.org. Catherine Pohl, Prin. Lay Teachers 8; Students 71.
Child Care Center—Tel: 920-994-2273.
Catechesis/Religious Program—Tel: 920-994-8033. Teresa Mahler, D.R.E. Students 126.
Chapel—St. Mary 300 Butler St., 53075.
Chapel—St. Nicholas W4274 Hwy. K, 53075.
Chapel—St. Patrick W4690 Hwy. A, Adell, 53001.

REESEVILLE, DODGE CO., HOLY FAMILY (1901), (German—Irish), [CEM], Also serves St. Columbkille, Elba and St. John the Baptist, Clyman. Rev. Richard Wendell.
302 Prairie St., P.O. Box 277, 53579-0277. Tel: 920-927-3102; Fax: 920-927-1970.
Res.: 714 Church St., Box 190, Clyman, 53016. Tel: 920-386-8039; Fax: 920-927-1970. Email: triparish@charter.net.
Catechesis/Religious Program—Students 27.

RICHFIELD, WASHINGTON CO., ST. MARY (1854), (German), Closed. For sacramental records after 1966, contact St. Gabriel, Hubertus, Tel: 262-628-1141. For sacramental records before 1967, contact Archdiocese of Milwaukee Archives Office, Tel: 414-769-3407.

RIPON, FOND DU LAC CO.

1—ST. CATHERINE OF SIENA (2005) [CEM] Rev. Robert A. Fictum.
218 Blossom St., 54971-1526. Tel: 920-748-2345. Email: ccofripon@centurytel.net. Web: www.stcatofsiena.org.
Catechesis/Religious Program—Fax: 920-748-3760. Email: karenmiller@centurytel.net. Students 232.

2—ST. PATRICK (1858) Closed. For sacramental records, contact St. Catherine of Siena, Ripon, Tel: 920-748-2345.

3—ST. WENCESLAUS (1896), (Polish), Closed. For sacramental records, contact St. Catherine of Siena, Ripon, Tel: 920-748-2345.

RUBICON, DODGE CO., ST. JOHN (1870), (German), [CEM] [JC], Also serves St. Matthew, Neosho and St. Mary, Woodland. Rev. Alois VanBeek.
Mailing Address: W1170 Rome Rd., 53078. Tel: 262-673-3380.
Res.: 148 W. Lehman, Neosho, 53059. Tel: 920-625-3144.
Church: W1170 Rome Rd., P.O. Box 17, 53078. Tel: 262-673-3380.
Catechesis/Religious Program—Tel: 262-673-4397. Students 137.

ST. CLOUD, FOND DU LAC CO., ST. CLOUD (1870), (German), [CEM] Rev. Steven Kropp, O.F.M.Cap.
Res.: 924 Main St., P.O. Box 138, 53079. Tel: 920-753-3311.
School—(Grades 4-8), 920 Main St., Box 89, 53079-0138. Tel: 920-999-2411; Fax: 920-753-2411. Christine Morluck, Bldg. Coord. Consolidated Parochial Elementary School. See St.John the Baptist, Johnsburg.
Catechesis/Religious Program—Tel: 920-753-3311. Students 18.

ST. FRANCIS, MILWAUKEE CO., SACRED HEART OF JESUS (1868) [CEM] Rev. Robert F. Surges.
Office: 3635 S. Kinnickinnic Ave., 53235-3741. Tel: 414-481-2330; Fax: 414-744-7222. Email: shjsf@execpc.com. Web: sacredheartofjesus.4lpi.com.
See St. Thomas Aquinas Academy located in the Institution Section under Consolidated Elementary Schools.
Catechesis/Religious Program—Combined program with Immaculate Conception, Milwaukee and Nativity of the Lord, Cudahy., Tel: 414-481-6880. Email: bobboehm@archmil.org. Students 155.

ST. GEORGE, SHEBOYGAN CO., ST. GEORGE (1860) Closed. For sacramental records, contact Blessed Trinity, Sheboygan Falls, Tel: 920-467-4616.

ST. JOE, FOND DU LAC CO., ST. JOSEPH (1858), (German), [CEM] Rev. Steven Kropp, O.F.M.Cap.
Res.: W620 County G, P.O. Box 138, St. Cloud, 53079-0138. Tel: 920-753-3311.
Catechesis/Religious Program—Tel: 920-753-3311. Students 23.

ST. KILIAN, FOND DU LAC CO., ST. KILIAN (1848) [CEM] Rev. Neil G. Zinthefer; Deacon Robert J. Fazen; Jane M. Osypowski, Business Mgr.
N189 County Rd. W., P.O. Box 740, Campbellsport, 53010. Tel: 920-533-4441; Fax: 920-533-5280. Email: stmatts@archmil.org.
Catechesis/Religious Program—419 Mill St., P.O. Box 740, Campbellsport, 53010. Tel: 920-533-4441; Fax: 920-533-5280. Beth Schmidt, D.R.E. (Twinned with St. Matthew)

ST. LAWRENCE, WASHINGTON CO., ST. LAWRENCE (1846), (German), [CEM] Rev. Joseph Dominic, S.A.C. (India).
Res.: 4886 Hwy. 175, Hartford, 53027. Tel: 262-644-5701; Fax: 262-644-5701. Email: stlaw@netwurx.net.
Catechesis/Religious Program—Tel: 262-644-0011. Email: stlawreled@netwurx.net. Students 163.

ST. MARTIN, MILWAUKEE CO., HOLY ASSUMPTION, Closed. For sacramental records through 1990, contact St. Mary, Hales Corners, Tel: 414-425-2174. For sacramental records after 1990, contact St. Martin of Tours, Franklin, Tel: 414-425-1114.

ST. MICHAEL, WASHINGTON CO., ST. MICHAEL (1846), (German—Irish), [CEM] [JC 2] Rev. Edwin M. Kornath; Deacon Ralph E. Horner.
8883 Forestview Rd., Kewaskum, 53040. Email: stmickew@hnet.net.
Res.: 331 Main St., Kewaskum, 53040. Tel: 262-334-5270; Fax: 262-334-5233. Email: htkewaskum@alexssa.net.
Catechesis/Religious Program—Tel: 262-626-2650. Email: brapkin@holytrinity.wi.k12us.com. Ms. Bonnie Rapkin, D.R.E. Twinned with Holy Trinity. Students 814.

ST. PETER, FOND DU LAC CO., ST. PETER (1867), (German), Closed. For sacramental records through 1952, contact Archdiocese of Milwaukee Archives Office, Tel: 414-769-3407. For records after 1952, contact Holy Family, Fond du Lac, Tel: 920-921-0580.

SAUKVILLE, OZAUKEE CO., IMMACULATE CONCEPTION (1858) [CEM] Revs. Patrick Wendt, In Solidum Team Mod.; Thomas F. Lijewski, In Solidum Team Mem.; Mr. Timothy Charek, Dir. Admin. Svcs.
Res.: 145 W. Church St., 53080. Tel: 262-284-0276; Fax: 262-284-3090.
Catechesis/Religious Program—Tel: 262-284-0277. Students 118.

SHARON, WALWORTH CO., ST. CATHERINE (1854) [CEM] Mr. Thomas McKenna, Parish Dir.
Mailing Address: P.O. Box 502, 53585. Tel: 262-736-4615.
Res.: Tel: 815-569-2530.
Catechesis/Religious Program—Students 26.

SHEBOYGAN, SHEBOYGAN CO.

1—ST. CLEMENT (1914) [JC] Revs. James E. Connell; Sergio Balderrama (Mexico); Deacon Baleriano O. Gonzalez.
Res.: 522 New York Ave., 53081. Tel: 920-457-4629; Fax: 920-452-2417. Email: scparish@charterinternet.com.
Catechesis/Religious Program—Tel: 920-452-0129. Collaborated with Holy Name of Jesus. Students 83.

2—SS. CYRIL AND METHODIUS (1910), (Slovenian), [CEM] Rev. Glenn E. Powers.
Office & Mailing Address: 2705 S. 14th St., 53081-6707. Tel: 920-457-7110; Fax: 920-457-5885. Email: sscm@charter.net.
Church: 822 New Jersey Ave., 53081.
Catechesis/Religious Program—Tel: 920-457-8422; Fax: 920-457-4001. Students 62.

3—ST. DOMINIC (1927), (German—Dutch), [JC] Rev. John J. Radetski; Deacon Donald J. Lydolph.
Res.: 2133 N. 22nd St., 53081. Tel: 920-458-7070. Email: dominic@stdominic.us. Web: www.stdominic.us.
School—2108 N. 21st St., 53081. Tel: 920-452-8747; Fax: 920-458-4809. Peggy Henseler, Prin. Lay Teachers 13; Students 127.
Catechesis/Religious Program—Tel: 920-458-5390. Students 332.

4—HOLY NAME (1845), (German), [JC] Rev. James E. Connell.
Res.: 807 Superior Ave., 53081-3442. Tel: 920-458-7721; Fax: 920-459-9108. Email: holyname1@charter.net. Web: www.holynamesheboygan.org.
School—814 Superior Ave., 53081. Tel: 920-452-1571; Fax: 920-208-4371. Web: webpages.charter.net/hfs_school. Kay Miller, Prin. Lay Teachers 15; Students 187.
Catechesis/Religious Program—824 Superior Ave., 53081. Tel: 920-452-0129. Betty Macknick, C.R.E. (Gr. K-8); Jennifer Lowery, Youth Min. (Gr. 9-12). Students 184.

5—IMMACULATE CONCEPTION (1903), (Lithuanian), [CEM] Rev. Glenn E. Powers.
Res.: 2705 S. 14 St., 53081. Tel: 920-457-3967; Fax: 920-457-5885. Email: icparish@charter.net.
Christ Child Academy—2722 Henry St., 53081. Tel: 920-459-2660. Tom Edson, Prin. Lay Teachers 14; Students 162.
Catechesis/Religious Program—834 New Jersey Ave., 53081. Tel: 920-208-7922. Email: icdre@charterinternet.com. Sally Schenk, D.R.E. Students 123.

6—ST. PETER CLAVER (1888), (German), [CEM] Rev. Richard J. Cerpich (Retired); Deacon Michael F. Burch, Dir.; Sr. Marilyn Brodd, O.S.F., Pastoral Assoc.
Res.: 1444 S. Eleventh St., 53081. Tel: 920-457-9408; Fax: 920-803-2470. Email: spcparish@archmil.org. Web: www.spcparish.com.
Christ Child Academy—(Grades PreK-5), See Immaculate Conception for Details., Tel: 920-459-2663; Fax: 920-457-5885. Email: christ-child-academy@archmil.org.
Catechesis/Religious Program—Tel: 920-452-2759. Barbara Leonhardt, D.R.E. Students 123.

SHEBOYGAN FALLS, SHEBOYGAN CO.

1—BLESSED TRINITY (2001), (German), [CEM] [JC 3], (Merger of St. Mary, Sheboygan Falls; St. Rose, Lima; and St. George, St. George.) Rev. Robert J. Lotz.
Rectory—327 Giddings Ave., 53085-1598. Tel: 920-467-4616; Fax: 920-467-4290. Email: sandy@blessedtrinityparish.org. Web: www.blessedtrinityparish.org.
Catechesis/Religious Program—Tel: 920-467-6282. Students 243.

2—ST. MARY (1896), (German), Closed. For sacramental records, contact Blessed Trinity, Sheboygan Falls, Tel: 920-467-4616.

SHOREWOOD, MILWAUKEE CO., ST. ROBERT (1912) Rev. Dennis A. Dirkx; Elizabeth Cleveland, Business Mgr.; Lisa Lesjak, Dir. School Advancement; Claire Anderson, Pastoral Assoc.; Cathy Presti, Pastoral Care Min. In Res., Revs. John Mary Ssozi (Uganda); Augustine Kalemeera (Uganda).
Res.: 4019 N. Farwell Ave., 53211. Tel: 414-332-1164; Fax: 414-332-2599. Web: www.strobert.org.
School—2200 E. Capitol Dr., 53211. Tel: 414-332-1164, Ext. 3018; Fax: 414-332-7355. Lauren Beckmann, Prin. Lay Teachers 26; Students 316.
Catechesis/Religious Program—Tel: 414-332-1164, Ext. 3012. Gail DeFrancisco, D.R.E.; Ben Wolf, Youth Min. Students 230.

SLINGER, WASHINGTON CO., ST. PETER (1856), (German), [CEM 2] Rev. Richard J. Stoffel; Deacon Bernard J. Wendt.
Mailing Address: 208 E. Washington St., 53086.
Res.: 214 E. Washington St., 53086. Tel: 262-644-8083; Fax: 262-644-7951. Email: stpeter@nconnect.net. Web: www.stpeterslinger.com.
School—206 E. Washington St., 53086. Web: www-.stpeterslinger.com. Ms. Virginia Miller, Prin. Lay Teachers 8; Students 51.
Catechesis/Religious Program—Judith Dillman, D.R.E. Students 456.

SOUTH MILWAUKEE, MILWAUKEE CO.

1—ST. ADALBERT (1898) Closed. For sacramental records, contact Divine Mercy, South Milwaukee, Tel: 414-762-6810.

2—DIVINE MERCY (2003) [JC] Revs. Robert Betz, Team Mod.; Steve Verghase, S.A.C. (India), Team Mem.; Deacon Dave Backes.
Office and Church: 1304 Manitoba Ave., 53172. Tel: 414-762-6810; Fax: 414-762-8326. Email: dmparish@archmil.org. Web: www.divinemercysm.org.
School—College Ave., 695 College Ave., 53172. Tel: 414-764-4360; Fax: 414-764-6740. Email: divinemercy@archmil.org. Judy Kalinowski, Prin. Tutors 1; Lay Teachers 18; Students 224.
Catechesis/Religious Program—Students 400.

3—ST. JOHN (1893), (Irish), Closed. For sacramental records, contact Divine Mercy, South Milwaukee, Tel: 414-762-6810.

4—ST. MARY (1893) Closed. For sacramental records, contact Divine Mercy, South Milwaukee, Tel: 414-762-6810.

5—ST. SYLVESTER (1962), (Polish—Irish), Closed. For sacramental records, contact Divine Mercy, South Milwaukee, Tel: 414-762-6810.

SPRINGVALE, COLUMBIA CO., ST. MARY (1858), (Irish), [CEM], See Immaculate Conception for Details. Rev. Michael O. Sturm.
Mailing Address: 118 W. Main St., Waupun, 53963-1453. Tel: 920-324-5400; Fax: 920-324-1040.
Catechesis/Religious Program—Tel: 920-346-5110. Students 7.

STURTEVANT, RACINE CO., ST. SEBASTIAN (1905) Rev. Paul L. Raczynski.
Res.: 3126 95th St., 53177. Tel: 262-886-4398; Fax: 262-886-2055.
School—3030 95th St., 53177. Tel: 262-886-2806. Ray Henderson, Prin. Religious 1; Lay Teachers 8; Students 125.
Catechesis/Religious Program—Tel: 262-886-4420. Students 32.

THERESA, DODGE CO., ST. THERESA (1849) [CEM] Rev. Dennis G. Budka.
102 Church St., St. Theresa, 53091. Tel: 920-269-4429. Mailing Address: 699 Milwaukee St., Lomira, 53048. Email: natheres@charter.net.
School—Consolidated Catholic School of Lomira-Theresa, Day care, before and after school care and pre-school., 105 W. Rock River St., 53091. Tel: 920-488-4543. Dorothy Zitlow, Prin.
Catechesis/Religious Program—Tel: 920-269-7273; Fax: 920-269-7359. Mary Straub, D.R.E. Students 46.

THIENSVILLE, OZAUKEE CO., ST. CECILIA (1919) Closed. For sacramental records, contact Lumen Christi, Mequon, Tel: 262-242-7967.

THOMPSON, WASHINGTON CO., ST. PATRICK (Tn. Erin) (1855), (Irish), Closed. For sacramental records, contact St. Kilian, Hartford, Tel: 262-673-4831.

TWIN LAKES, KENOSHA CO., ST. JOHN THE EVANGELIST (1932) [CEM] Rev. Michael J. Erwin; Deacon Stanley Cebrzynski.
Res.: 701 N. Lake Ave., 53181. Tel: 262-877-2557; Fax: 262-877-2431.
Catechesis/Religious Program—Tel: 262-877-3033, Ext. 222. Email: stjohnevfaith@archmil.org. Students 206.

UNION GROVE, RACINE CO., ST. ROBERT BELLARMINE (1965) Rev. Howard G. Haase.
Res.: 3320 S. Colony Ave., 53182. Tel: 262-878-3476; Fax: 262-878-0194. Email: rstrobertbella@wi.rr.com. Web: www.foursaints.org.
Catechesis/Religious Program—Corinne Dillon, Dir. Christian Formation. Students 327.

WATERFORD, RACINE CO., ST. THOMAS AQUINAS (1851) [CEM] Rev. Eugene J. Doda Jr.; Deacons Carl A. Mahnke, (Retired); Jim Nickel; Joseph H. Hying, (Retired).
Res.: 305 S. First St., 53185. Tel: 262-534-2255; Fax: 262-534-2929. Email: rectory@stthomas.pvt.k12.wi.us.
School—262-534-2265; Fax: 262-534-5549. Web: www.stthomaswaterford.org. Lay Teachers 17; Students 195.
Catechesis/Religious Program—Students 495.

WAUKESHA, WAUKESHA CO.

1—ST. JOHN NEUMANN (1981) Rev. James P. Loehr; June Wessa, Pastoral Assoc.; Cheryl Marotta, Business Mgr.
Mailing Address: 2400 W. State Hwy. 59, 53189-6323. Tel: 262-549-0223; 262-549-0898; Fax: 262-549-0444.
School—Waukesha Catholic School System, (Grades PreK-8) Tel: 262-896-2920 (St. William); 262-896-2930 (St. Joseph); 262-896-2932 (St. Mary); Fax: 262-896-2925.
Catechesis/Religious Program—Students 94.

2—ST. JOSEPH (1844), (Hispanic), Rev. William W. Key; Deacons Aristeo Ortiz; Antonio Palacios.
Parish Office—818 N. East Ave., 53186. Tel: 262-542-2589; Fax: 262-542-2570.
Res.: 822 N. East Ave., 53186. Tel: 262-542-5487.
School—Waukesha Catholic School System, (Grades 6-8), 841 Martin St., 53186. Tel: 262-896-2930; Fax: 262-896-2935. Mrs. Kathleen Rempe, Prin.
Catechesis/Religious Program—Tel: 262-542-2589, Ext. 211. Ruth Weiss, D.R.E. Students 265.

3—ST. MARY (1950) Very Rev. James T. Volkert.
Res.: 225 S. Hartwell Ave., 53186-6400. Tel: 262-547-6555; Fax: 262-547-6714. Email: office@stmarywk.org. Web: stmarywaukesha.4lpi.com.
School—School is a campus of the Waukesha Catholic School System., 520 E. Newhall Ave., 53186. Tel: 262-896-2932; Fax: 262-896-2931. Web: www.waukeshacatholicschoolsystem.org. Mrs. Lisa Kovaleski, Prin. Lay Teachers 17; Students 322.
Catechesis/Religious Program—Mr. Jim Gill, D.R.E. Students 345.

4—ST. WILLIAM (1957) [JC] Revs. Curt J. Frederick; Jason Lavann; Charlotte Villwock, Liturgy/Music Min.
Res.: 440 N. Moreland Blvd., 53188. Tel: 262-349-9585; Fax: 262-547-3616. Email: frederick@archmil.org. Web: swparish.org.
School—Waukesha Catholic, (Grades PreK-5), 444 N. Moreland Blvd., 53188. Tel: 262-896-2920; Fax: 262-896-2925. Robert Radomski, Campus Prin. Students 293.
Catechesis/Religious Program—Tel: 262-547-2763, Ext. 206. Kay Hokans, D.R.E. (Child Min.); Barb Gawlik, D.R.E. (Youth Min.); Cindy Bergland, D.R.E. (Adult & Family Min.). Students 704.

WAUPUN, FOND DU LAC CO., ST. JOSEPH (1866), (Irish), [CEM], Also serves St. Brendan, Brandon & St. Mary, Springvale. Rev. Michael O. Sturm.
Office: 118 W. Main St., 53963. Tel: 920-324-5400; Fax: 920-324-1040. Email: office@stjoeschurch.org. Web: www.stjoeschurch.org.
Catechesis/Religious Program—Tel: 920-324-3891. Terese Markl, D.R.E. Students 136.

WAUWATOSA, MILWAUKEE CO.

1—ST. BERNARD (1911), (Irish), Rev. Peter C. Drenzek.
Res.: 7474 Harwood Ave., 53213. Tel: 414-258-4320; Fax: 414-258-9972. Email: admin@stbernardparish.org. Web: www.stbernardparish.org.
School—1500 Wauwatosa Ave., 53213. Tel: 414-258-9977. William Strube, Prin. Religious 1; Lay Teachers 11; Students 120.
Catechesis/Religious Program—Students 170.

2—CHRIST KING (1939) Rev. Msgr. T. George Gajdos; Rev. Thomas D. DeVries; Deacon Arthur C. Dallman.
Res.: 2604 N. Swan Blvd., 53226. Tel: 414-258-2604; Fax: 414-258-1993. Email: parish@christkingparish.org. Web: www.christkingparish.
School—2646 N. Swan Blvd., 53226. Tel: 414-258-4160. Sr. Janet Neureuther, Prin. Lay Teachers 28; Students 405.
Catechesis/Religious Program—Liz Kuhn, D.R.E. Students 233.

3—ST. JOSEPH CONGREGATION (1855) Rev. James Kimla.
Mailing Address: 12130 W. Center St., 53222-4096. Email: brenda@stjoetosa.archmil.org. Web: www.stjoetosa.com.
School—2750 N. 122nd St., 53222. Fax: 414-771-9826. Linda Cooney, Prin. Lay Teachers 16; Students 218.
Catechesis/Religious Program—Students 345.

4—ST. JUDE THE APOSTLE (1928) Rev. Charles Conley; Deacon Donald A. Borkowski; James Pluer, Liturgy/Music Dir.; Lynn Musolf, Dir. Admin. Svcs. In Res., Revs. Juvenalis Asantemungu (Tanzania); Jean Pierre Kabongo-Mukuna.
Res.: 734 Glenview Ave., 53213. Tel: 414-258-8821; Fax: 414-258-7371. Web: www.stjudewauwatosa.org.
School—800 Glenview Ave., 53213. Tel: 414-771-1520; Fax: 414-771-3748. Catherine LaDien, Prin. Sisters 1; Lay Teachers 35; Students 470.
Catechesis/Religious Program—Tel: 414-259-0950. Gary Heun, D.R.E. Students 171.

5—ST. PIUS X (1952) Rev. Robert Marsicek, S.D.S.
Res.: 2506 Wauwatosa Ave., 53213. Tel: 414-453-3875; Fax: 414-453-7570. Email: stpiusx@mcleodusa.net. Web: st.piusparish.org.
School—2520 Wauwatosa Ave., 53213. Tel: 414-778-0880. Lay Teachers 12; Students 120.
Catechesis/Religious Program—Tel: 414-453-1153. Students 194.

WAYNE, WASHINGTON CO., ST. BRIDGET, Closed. For sacramental records, contact Holy Trinity, Kewaskum, Tel: 262-626-2860.

WEST ALLIS, MILWAUKEE CO.

1—ST. ALOYSIUS GONZAGA (1920) Revs. Jeffery A. Prasser; Thomas Vathappallil, M.C.B.S.
Rectory—1414 S. 93rd St., 53214. Tel: 414-476-3803; Fax: 414-774-7727. Email: staloysius@archmil.org. Web: www.staloysius.41pi.com.
Catechesis/Religious Program—Tel: 414-727-4451. Anita Hallman Kowalski, D.R.E. Students 177.

2—ST. AUGUSTINE (1928), (Croatian), [CEM] Rev. Lawrence Frankovich, O.F.M.
Res.: 6762 W. Rogers St., 53219. Tel: 414-541-5207; Fax: 414-541-0273. Email: staugwa@execpc.com.

See Mary Queen of Saints Catholic Academy under Consolidated Elementary Schools located in the Institution section.
Catechesis/Religious Program—6753 W. Rogers St., 53219. Students 32.

3—HOLY ASSUMPTION (1902) Revs. Robert E. Massey; Leonard R. Copeland, O.C.D., Admin.; Deacon George P. Sherman.
Res.: 1525 S. 71st St., 53214. Tel: 414-774-3010; Fax: 414-774-3735. Email: haparish@execpc.com. Web: www.haparish.org.
Catechesis/Religious Program—Students 41.

4—IMMACULATE HEART OF MARY (1948) Rev. Karl J. Schneider; Deacons Dennis E. Fietz; Walter Henry; Keith R. Marx.
Res.: 1121 S. 116th St., 53214. Tel: 414-453-5192; Fax: 414-453-0137. Email: info@ihmwestallis.com. Web: ihmwestallis.com.
Catechesis/Religious Program—Tel: 414-453-0300. Web: ihmwestallis.com. Students 58.

5—ST. JOSEPH (1909), (Polish), Closed. For sacramental records, contact Archdiocese of Milwaukee Archives Office, Tel: 414-769-3407.

6—ST. MARY, HELP OF CHRISTIANS (1907), (Slovenian), [CEM] Closed. For sacramental records, contact Archdiocese of Milwaukee Archives Office, 414-769-3407.

7—MARY, QUEEN OF HEAVEN (1958) Rev. Michael F. Merkt.
Office: 2322 S. 106th St., 53227. Tel: 414-328-5566; Fax: 414-328-5561.
See Mary Queen of Saints Academy in the Institution Section listed under Consolidated Elementary schools.
Catechesis/Religious Program—Tel: 414-328-5570. Nicholas Balducci, D.R.E. Students 121.

8—OUR LADY OF MT. CARMEL (1938), (Italian), Closed. For sacramental records, contact Archdiocese of Milwaukee Archives Office, Tel: 414-769-3407.

9—ST. RITA (1924) Revs. Jeffery A. Prasser; Thomas Vathappallil, M.C.B.S.
Res.: 2318 S. 61st St., 53219. Tel: 414-541-7515; Fax: 414-541-7568. Email: stritaparishwa@wi.rr.com. Web: stritaparish-westallis.4lpi.com.
See Mary Queen of Saints Catholic Academy Association under Consolidated Elementary Schools located in the Institution section.
Catechesis/Religious Program—Tel: 414-541-7515. Karen Barczak, D.R.E. Students 109.

WEST BEND, WASHINGTON CO.

1—ST. FRANCES CABRINI (1955) Very Rev. Jeffrey R. Haines; Rev. Nathan D. Reesman; Deacons Michael S. Koebel; Ronald Schneider.
Parish Office—1025 S. 7th Ave., 53095. Tel: 262-338-2366, Ext. 13; Fax: 262-338-2348. Web: www.saintfrancescabrini.com.
School—529 Hawthorn Dr., 53095. Tel: 262-334-7142; Fax: 262-334-8168. Web: stfcabrini.com. Mark Quinn, Prin. Lay Teachers 30; Students 418.
Catechesis/Religious Program—Tel: 262-334-9511. Judy Schroeder, D.R.E. Students 493.

2—HOLY ANGELS (1852) [CEM] Revs. Gerald W. Brittain; Nathan D. Reesman; Deacon Mark Jansen.
Res.: 138 N. 8th Ave., 53095. Tel: 262-334-3038; Fax: 262-334-3088. Email: parish@hawb.org. Web: hawb.org.
School—230 N. 8th Ave., 53095. Tel: 262-338-1148. Email: has@has.pvt.k12.wi.us. Web: www.has.pvt.k12.wi.us. Mike Sternig, Prin. Lay Teachers 21; Students 390.
Catechesis/Religious Program—Tel: 414-334-9393. Email: dre@hawb.org. Joseph Heit, D.R.E. Students 354.

3—IMMACULATE CONCEPTION (1857) [CEM 2] Rev. Michael F. Moran; Dan Schroeder, Pastoral Assoc.; Marilyn Muraski, Music Coord.
Res.: 406 Jefferson St., 53090. Tel: 262-338-5600; Fax: 262-335-2475. Email: stmy@charterinternet.com. Web: www.stmaryswb.org.
School—415 Roosevelt St., 53090. Tel: 262-338-5602. Gail Kraig, Prin. Lay Teachers 8; Students 105.
Catechesis/Religious Program—Tel: 262-338-5605. Mary Abel, D.R.E.; Marge Schinker, D.R.E. Students 183.

WHITEFISH BAY, MILWAUKEE CO.

1—HOLY FAMILY (1949) Revs. Dennis A. Dirkx; Robert C. Kacalo.
Office: 4825 N. Wildwood Ave., 53217. Tel: 414-332-9220; Fax: 414-961-7396. Email: holyfam@archmil.org. Web: www.hfparish.org.
School—4849 N. Wildwood Ave., 53217. Tel: 414-332-8175; Fax: 414-961-7196. Email: hfpschool@archmil.org. Angela Little, Prin. Lay Teachers 20; Students 200.
Catechesis/Religious Program—Tel: 414-332-8156; Fax: 414-961-7396. Email: hfreled@archmil.org. Gail DeFrancisco, D.R.E. Students 285.

2—ST. MONICA (1923) Revs. Jerome Herda; Paul J. Fliss; Deacon Eugene E. Van Garsse. In Res., Rev. John R. Paczesny (Retired).
Res.: 160 E. Silver Spring Dr., 53217. Tel: 414-332-1576; 414-332-1577; Fax: 414-332-2462. Email: office@st-monica.org. Web: www.st-monica.org.
School—5635 N. Santa Monica Blvd., 53217. Tel: 414-332-3660; Fax: 414-332-8649. Web: www.st-monicaschool.org. Maria Schram, Prin. Lay Teachers 32; Students 439.
Catechesis/Religious Program—Tel: 414-964-8780; Fax: 414-964-2493. Andre Lesperance, D.R.E. Students 412.

WHITEWATER, WALWORTH CO., ST. PATRICK (1853) [CEM] Rev. Rafael Rodriguez.
Office: 1225 W. Main St., 53190-1620. Tel: 262-473-3143; Fax: 262-473-3052.
Catechesis/Religious Program—Tel: 262-473-8834. Katie DeBruin, Dir Faith Formation. Students 198.

WILMOT, KENOSHA CO., HOLY NAME OF JESUS (1856) [CEM] Closed. For sacramental records, contact Holy Cross, Bristol, Tel: 262-857-2068.

WIND LAKE, RACINE CO., ST. CLARE (1965) Rev. Aurelio H. Perez.
Res. & Mailing Address: Parish Office, 7616 Fritz St., 53185. Tel: 262-895-2729; Fax: 262-895-3601. Email: clarewl@tds.net.
Catechesis/Religious Program—Tel: 262-895-2797. Ms. Peggy Liginski, D.R.E. Students 333.

WOODHULL, FOND DU LAC CO., ST. JOHN THE BAPTIST, Closed. For sacramental records, contact Our Risen Savior, Eldorado, Tel: 920-922-2412.

WOODLAND, DODGE N CO., ST. MARY, (German), [CEM], Also serves St. Matthew, Neosho & St. John, Rubicon. Rev. Alois VanBeek.
Mailing Address: 148 W. Lehman St, P.O. Box 45, Neosho, 53059. Tel: 920-625-3144; Fax: 920-625-2143. Email: mattneo3@nconnect.net. Web: mjmtriparish.org.
Catechesis/Religious Program—Combined with St. Matthew, Neosho., Tel: 920-625-3092. Students 37.

Chaplains of Public Institutions

MILWAUKEE. *St. Luke's Medical Center*, 2900 W. Oklahoma Ave., 53215.
Milwaukee County House of Correction. Attended by St. James, Franklin.
Milwaukee County Jail. Bro. Jerome Smith, O.F.M.Cap., Chap.

JUNEAU. *Dodge County Center*. Attended by Sacred Heart, Horicon.

KENOSHA. *Kenosha Hospital and Medical Center*, 6308 8th Ave., 53143-5082. Vacant.

WALES. *Ethan Allen School for Boys*, P.O. Box 900, 53183-0900. Tel: 414-646-3341. Vacant.

WAUWATOSA. *Froedtert Memorial Lutheran Hospital*, 9200 W. Wisconsin Ave., 53226. Rev. Jean Pierre Kabongo-Mukuna, Chap.

WEST ALLIS. *West Allis Memorial Hospital*, 8901 W. Lincoln Ave., 53227. Tel: 414-328-6000.

WOOD. *Veterans Administration Medical Center* 53193. Tel: 414-384-2000. Rev. Norman R. Oswald, Chief, Chap. Svc.

Special Assignment:
Most Rev.—
Sklba, Richard J., S.S.L., S.T.D., Auxiliary Bishop, 3501 S. Lake Dr., P.O. Box 070912, 53207-0912.
Very Revs.—
Hartmann, Paul B.R., M.Div., J.C.L., Metropolitan Tribunal, 3501 S. Lake Dr., P.O. Box 070912, 53207-0912. President Catholic Memorial High School, 601 E. College Ave., Waukesha, 53186-5538.
Heppe, Patrick E., Dir. Ordained & Lay Ecclesiastical Min., 3501 S. Lake Dr., P.O. Box 070912, 53207-0912. Tel: 414-769-3490
Hying, Donald J., Rector, Saint Francis Seminary, 3257 S. Lake Dr., St. Francis, 53235.
Revs.—
Avella, Steven M., Faculty, Marquette University, 3222 S. 29th St., 53215.
Bustos, Javier, S.T.D., Dir., Sacred Heart School of Theology Faculty, P.O. Box 429, Hales Corners, 53130-0429.
Cane-Gombau, Pere, Missionary Community of St. Paul, 2512 Westwood Dr., Racine, 53404.
Connell, James E., J.C.D., Vice Chancellor, Archdiocese of Milwaukee, 3501 S. Lake Dr., P.O. Box 07912, 53207-0912. Tel: 414-769-3338
Duffy, James H., Madonna House, Combermere ON KOJ 1LO Canada.
Gaberle, Jiri, Ministry to Healthcare Facilities, 4800 Coldspring Rd. #28, Greenfield, 53220.
Hammer, Michael J., Coord. Catholic AIDS Ministry, 802 N. Jackson St., 53202-3879.
Keefe, Charles R., Pastoral Care Dir., Milwaukee Catholic Home, 2462 N. Prospect Ave., 53211-4462.
Knoebel, Thomas L., Ph.D., M.Div., Sacred Heart School of Theology Faculty & Acting Rector, P.O. Box 429, Hales Corner, 53130-0429.
Lazarski, Marvin I., Arch. Cemetery System, 3801 W. Morgan Ave., 53321. Tel: 414-645-0611
Lightner, Michael, Chap., Newman Center-UW Milwaukee, 3001 N. Downer Ave., 53211.
Lobacz, James E., Dir., Vocations Office, Archdiocese of Milwaukee, 3257 S. Lake Dr., St. Francis, 53235.
Massingale, Bryan N., Marquette University, P.O.Box 1881, 53202-1881. (Faculty)
Michalski, Melvin E., Ph.L., Th.D., Sacred Heart School of Theology Faculty, Saint Francis Seminary, 3257 S. Lake Dr., St. Francis, 53235.
O'Brien, Timothy J., Faculty, Marquette University, 8521 Kenyon Ave., Wauwatosa, 53226.
Oswald, Norman R., Chief Chap., Veterans Administrative Medical Center, 5000 W. National Ave., 53295.
Pocernich, Eugene, Chap., Columbia-St. Mary Hospital, 2323 N. Lake Dr., 53211.
Stanfield, William L., Dir., Vice Rector & Dean Formation, St. Francis Seminary, Continuing Formation of Clergy, 3257 S. Lake Dr., St. Francis, 53235. Tel: 414-747-6410
Walker, Thomas J., Coord. Services for Senior Priests, 3501 S. Lake Dr., P.O. Box 070912, 53207-0912. Tel: 414-769-3345

On Duty Outside the Archdiocese:
Rev. Msgrs.—
Malloy, David J., USCCB, 3211 4th St., N.E., Washington, DC 20017-1194.
Shecterle, Ross A., Rector, American College of Louvain, Naamsestraat 100, Leuven B-3000 Belgium.
Revs.—
Brophy, John L., St. John DeBritto, P.O. Box 108, Britton, SD 57430.
Brundage, Thomas T., M.Div., J.C.L., Tribunal, Archdiocese Anchorage, Pastoral Center, 225 Cordova St., Anchorage, AK 99501.
Colom, Marti, La Sagrada Familia, Apartado 53, Azua, Dominican Republic.
Heck, Quintin T., Scripps Medical Center, 435 H St., Chula Vista, CA 91910.
Kinney, M. Eugene, St. Anthony of Padua, 5081 N. Rainbow Blvd., #107, Las Vegas, NV 89130.
Konkel, Eugene J., S.S., Vatican II Institute, 320 Middlefield Rd., Menlo Park, CA 94025.
Lamb, Matthew L., Faculty, Ave Maria University, 5050 Ave Maria Blvd., Immokalee, FL 34142-9505.
Marek, Dean V., Chap., Box 1332, Rochester, MN 55903-1332. Rochester Methodist Hospital
McDermott, Robert T., St. Roch Parish, 6052 Waterman Blvd., St. Louis, MO 63112.
Mikalofsky, Hilarion A., Ch. Lt. Col. (Retired), 82 Edgewater Dr., Lakeside City, TX 76308.
Olszyk, Thomas P., J.C.L., Tribunal, Military Archdiocese, P.O. Box 4469, Washington, DC 20017-0469.
Regales, Oriol, La Sagrada Familia, Apartado 53, Azua, Dominican Republic.
Schwartz, Norman R., Chap., Georgetown University Medical Center, Washington, DC 20007.
Tino, Robert F., Western State Hospital, 9601 Steilacoom Blvd., S.W., Tacoma, WA 98498-7213.
Witczak, Michael G., M.Div., S.L.D., Faculty, Catholic University of America, 620 Michigan Ave, NE, Washington, DC 20064.

On Leave:
Rev.—
Dulek, Lawrence V.

Study Leave:
Revs.—
Esch, Aaron J., Pontifical North American College, Vatican City State, Europe 00120.
Martin Pinillos, Ricardo, Catholic University of America, Washington, DC 20064.

Personal Leave:
Revs.—
Fait, Thomas G.
Lee, Roy
Richter, Robert J.

Sick Leave:
Rev.—
Kienzle, Jerome C.

Awaiting Assignment:
Revs.—
Malloy, Francis X.
Thielen, Jeffrey M.

Not Assigned:
Rev.—
Slodowski, Bruno

Retired:
Most Rev.—
Weakland, Rembert G., O.S.B.
Rev. Msgrs.—
Donovan, John T., c/o J. Patrick Ronan, 7020 N. Port Washington Rd., #202, 53217.
Schmit, Ralph R., Alexian Village, 9301 N. 76th St. #412, 53223.
Very Rev.—
Rinzel, Jerome A., 121 River Ct., Theresa, 53091-9548.
Revs.—
Acker, Karl H., Wilson Commons, 1400 W. Sonata Dr., #140, 53221.
Anderson, Joseph G., 17452 W. Lincoln Ave., New Berlin, 53146.
Andre, Leonard J., Alexian Village, 7979 Glenbrook Rd., #4021, 53223.
Arciszewski, Gilbert, 9151 S. Aspen Dr., #9, Oak Creek, 53154.
Artmann, Robert J., W 169 N 8775 Sheridan Dr., Menomonee Falls, 53051.
Bales, Robert, St. Albert the Great, 2420 St. Albert Dr., Sun Prairie, 53590-9336.
Baran, Joseph L., 2022 N. 86th St., Wauwatosa, 53226-2745.
Baranowski, Stanley A., W782 County Rd. A, Randolph, 53956.
Barbian, Leonard M., 6750 Parkedge Cir., Franklin, 53132.
Beck, Richard P., 5606 Cynthia Ln., Sarasota, FL 34235.
Berghammer, Robert J., 201 A-J Ct., Theresa, 53091.
Bittner, Wayne W., 306 N. Highland Ave., #327, Plymouth, 53073.
Brady, James J., Wilson Commons #433, 1400 W. Sonata Dr., 53221.
Brahm, Harvey, San Camillo #725, 10200 W. Bluemound Rd., Wauwatosa, 53226.
Breit, Melvin P., 6921 W. Orchard, #104, West Allis, 53214.
Breitbach, Richard C., 14140 Regis St., Brookfield, 53005.
Bryl, Thaddeus J., c/o Arlene Szmurlo, 3939 Lakewood Rd., Harshaw, 54529.
Carek, Peter P., St. Anne Salvatorian Campus, 3800 N. 92nd St., #123A, 53222.
Carroll, Edward E., 3524 7th Ave. Apt. 127, Kenosha, 53140.
Cera, James B., Alexian Village #116, 9301 N. 76th St., 53223.
Cerpich, Richard J., 2532 S. 7th St., Sheboygan, 53081.
Cunningham, Joseph L., W 369 S10450 Shearer Rd., Eagle, 53119.
Dammeir, James L., 4208 N. 16th St., 53209-6923.
Daniels, Paul A., 1216 N. Sunnyslope Dr., #103, Racine, 53406.
Debski, Joseph E., 2209 Browns Lake Dr. #105, Burlington, 53105.
DeLeers, Stephen V., 1742 N. Prospect Ave., #313, 53202.
Derfus, Kenneth J., Camillus Court East #205, 10100 W. Bluemound Rd., Wauwatosa, 53226.
Dineen, Michael P., 2518 N. 7th St., Sheboygan, 53083.
Dolezal, Richard R., 5053 N. Ridgeway, Chicago, IL 60625-6021.
Endejan, John, 9410 W. Loomis Rd., #5, Franklin, 53132.
Ernster, James M., 570 Hwy. D, Belgium, 53004.
Eschweiler, Edward R., Clement Manor, 9405 W. Howard Ave., #369, Greenfield, 53228.
Esser, Paul M., P.O. Box 148, Nashotah, 53058.
Fleischmann, George R., High Grove, 3940 S. Prairie Hill Ln., #215, Greenfield, 53228.
Frederick, Joseph B., 237 Southtowne Pl., #BB212, South Milwaukee, 53172.
Gloudeman, Robert J., 10020 Whitnall Edge Dr. # D, Franklin, 53132.
Gosma, Robert D., W379 S4988 W. Pretty Lake Rd., Dousman, 53118.
Grellinger, R. Michael, 250 Meadow Ln., Hartland, 53029-1832.
Haas, Joseph H., P.O. Box 14363, West Allis, 53214-0363.
Hauser, Gerald B., 21025 George Hunt Circle, #1203, Waukesha, 53186.
Hentzner, John T., San Camillo, 10200 W. Bluemound Rd., #1021, Wauwatosa, 53226.
Hmircik, Donald A., 237 Winnebago St., #214, North Fond Du Lac, 54937.
Hudziak, Jerome M., Ph.D., 10020 Whitnall Edge Dr., Unit C, Franklin, 53132.
Hussli, Edward J., HCR1, Box 81, Clam Lake, 54517.
Janette, Paul, San Camillo, 10200 W. Bluemound Rd., #402, Wauwatosa, 53226.
Johnson, Howard J., W6332 Lake Ellen Dr., Cascade, 53011.
Kasten, Edward F., Alexian Village, 7979 W. Glenbrook Rd., #6002, 53223.
Katorski, Robert, 8367 S. 76th St., Franklin, 53132.
Kazmierczak, Carl M., 8051 W. Leroy Ave., 53220.
Klauck, Stanley B., Alexian Village, 9301 N. 76th St. #343, 53223.
Klemme, Dennis C., J.C.D., W267 N2517 Meadowbrook Rd., Pewaukee, 53072.
Klink, Anthony G., P.O. Box 93, Berlin, 54923.
Lasecki, Daniel J., 1601 Division Ave., Sheboygan, 53083.
Le Mieux, Thomas A., P.O. Box 210048, 53221-8001.
Lippert, Paul R., Box 238, Plainfield, 54966-0238.
Lisowski, Edward E., P.O. Box 210182, 53221.
Loehr, Charles D., W1452 Hwy. T, Mount Calvary, 53057.
Luljak, Louis P., 138 N. 8th Ave., West Bend, 53095.
Macoskie, Melvin H., 280 Birch Rock Way, C-9, Mukwonago, 53149.
Maney, Robert L., 3301 S. 93rd St., #107, 53227.
Mateljan, Roy A., 868 Americana Dr., Fond Du Lac, 54935-2954.
Matt, Erwin H., Juniper Court #103, 3209 S. Lake Dr., St. Francis, 53235.
Metz, Kenneth J., All Souls Catholic Church, 301 W. 8th St., Sanford, FL 32771.
Miralbes-Drago, Julio E., P.O. Box 070912, 53207-0912.
Mirsberger, Richard E., 9995 W. North Ave. #353, Wauwatosa, 53226.
Molter, Richard J., 6545 Mariner Dr., #6, Racine, 53406.
Mueller, Robert F., Camillus Court E. #301, 10100 W. Bluemond Rd., Wauwatosa, 53226.
Murphy, Daniel T., 4260 S. 94th St., Greenfield, 53228.
Murray, William F., Marquette Manor #219, 2409 10th Ave., South Milwaukee, 53172.
Myszel, George G., Camillus Court East #212, 10100 W. Bluemound Rd., Wauwatosa, 53226.
Nawrocki, Robert W., 3589A S. 14th St., 53221.
Nelson, Andrew L., 2525 S. Shore Dr., #21F, 53207.
Neuman, Eugene C., 1061 Lowell, Apt. 2, Oconomowoc, 53066.
Novotny, Robert J., Wilson Commons, 1400 Sonata Dr., #223, 53221.
Orzechowski, Walter B., N8180 Lakeview Rd., Fond du Lac, 54935.
Paczesny, John R., 160 E. Silver Spring Dr., Whitefish Bay, 53217.
Pulice, John J., 2325 W. Jonathan Dr., Oak Creek, 53154.
Quartana, Donald F., 9405 W. Howard Ave., #263, 53228.
Rausch, John W., Box 475, Eagle, 53119.
Rebatzki, George M., 17330 W. Birch Dr. #102, Brookfield, 53045.
Repenshek, Jerome V., 2060 Rainbow Lakes, Unit 216, West Bend, 53090.
Richetta, John J., 4014 81st St., Kenosha, 53142.
Rodriguez, Robert, 502 Amber Horizon St., Henderson, NV 89015.
Roensch, Frederick J., P.O. Box 210, Nashotah, 53058.
Roetzer, Russell G., c/o Bob Miller, 1438 Woodchuck Ct. #102, Racine, 53406.
Roscioli, Dominic J., 5412 23rd Ave., Kenosha, 53140-3505.
Safiejko, Edward M., 10420 Plum Tree Cir., #102, Hales Corners, 53130.
Sanfelippo, Frank J., Alexian Village, 7979 W. Glenbrook Rd., #6017, 53223.
Scheuerell, Charles A., P.O. Box 211, Nashotah, 53058.
Schlenker, Richard J., Wilson Commons #223, 1400 Sonata Dr., 53221.
Schmidt, Donald, Marquette Manor, 2409 10th Ave., Unit 10, South Milwaukee, 53172.
Schmitz, John A., 1011 Berlin Rd., Ripon, 54971.
Schubert, Herbert, 5104 S. Hidden Dr., # 21, Greenfield, 53221.
Sepich, Lawrence, 8638 Westlake Dr., Greendale, 53129.
Sippel, Bernard S., M.Div., 10300 W. Bluemound Rd., #220, Wauwatosa, 53226.
Sippel, Edward F., 519 W. 11th St., Fond du Lac, 54935.
Skeris, Robert A., 722 Dillingham Ave., Sheboygan, 53081.
Stangel, Mark J., Clement Manor, 9405 W. Howard Ave., #358, Greenfield, 53228.
Stommel, Russel J., 1400 G West St., #4, Union Grove, 53182.
Strupp, James A., 580 S. 18th Ave., West Bend, 53095-3755.
Suriano, Thomas, 5101 W. Center St., 53210-2361.
Talaska, Richard J., 8891 Woodbridge Dr., Greendale, 53129.
Theisen, John J., 536 Lake Dr., Random Lake, 53075.
Tikalsky, Russell F., 3055 N. Fratnet St., 53212.
Twomey, John E., The Heritage #318, 3223 North St., East Troy, 53120.
Uhen, Cletus V., 1100 Fountain Dr., #208A, Racine, 53406-3767.
Van Abel, John W., 235 Tamarack Dr., #8, Lake Mills, 53551.
Van Vlaenderen, Leonard S., P.O. Box 100522, Cudahy, 53110.
Venne, R. Thomas, 802 N. Jackson Ave., 53202.
Verberg, Richard R., 8565 W. Waterford Ave., #4, Greenfield, 53228.
Verhalen, Charles J., Camillus Health Center, 10101 W. Wisconsin Ave., #1124, Wauwatosa, 53226.
Vogel, Walter J., 6845 S. 68th St., #104, Franklin, 53132-8239.
Vojtik, James P., W228 S2376 Oriole Dr., Waukesha, 53186.
Wawiorka, Ray W., P.O. Box 578, Kenosha, 53141.
Wawrzyniakowski, Edward J., N7594 Sandy Beach Rd., Fond du Lac, 54937.
Weis, Denis P., 322 N. 90th St., 53226.
Weishar, Paul M., The Gables at Germantown, N109 W17110 Ava Cir. #315, Germantown, 53022.
Wester, Charles H., N4346 Mercury Ln., Eden, 53019.
Whalen, William, W3327 Orchard Ave., Green Lake, 54941.
Wheatley, Charles, 210 Glen Este Blvd., Haines City, FL 33844.
Wilimek, Louis, 1833 Northwood Ct., Sheboygan, 53081.
Winkler, Eugene, Clement Manor, 3939 S. 92nd St., #120, Greenfield, 53228.
Witon, Russell F., 11515 W. Cleveland Ave., # 303A, West Allis, 53227.
Wittliff, Thomas F., 2260 S. 4th St., 53207.
Wolf, Joseph A., N84 W13920 Fond du Lac Ave., Menomonee Falls, 53051.
Zerkel, Donald F., P.O. Box 74, Newburg, 53060.
Zwaska, Victor L., Westwood, 925 Kenwood Dr., #3172, Duluth, MN 55811.

Permanent Deacons:
Acosta, Carlos R., (Retired)
Aird, Gordon R., St. Francis Borgia, Cedarburg; (Diocese of Phoenix)
Alexander, Jack, St. Alphonsus, Greendale
Aschenbrener, James L., (Retired)
Backes, David, Divine Mercy, South Milwaukee
Banach, James D., St. Gregory the Great, Milwaukee
Banach, William A., Basilica of St. Josaphat, Milwaukee
Benavente, Jorge, St. Joseph, Waukesha
Blas, Franciso, Cristo Rey, Racine
Blaze, Edward, All Saints, Milwaukee
Borkowski, Donald A., St. Jude the Apostle, Wauwatosa
Brah, Eugene D., Mary Queen of Heaven, West Allis
Braun, Warren D., (Retired)
Brousseau, Gerald A., (Retired)
Brown, Richard J., St. Joseph, Big Bend
Burch, Michael F., St. Peter Claver, Sheboygan
Burmeister, Dan, St. Lucy, Racine
Burns, John R., St. Mary, Hales Corners
Buth, Robert H., St. Mary's, Menomonee Falls
Buyck, Gerald W., (Out of Archdiocese)
Byrnes, Timothy J., St. Katherine Drexel, Beaver Dam; (Archdiocese of Chicago)
Campbell, Scott, St. William, Waukesha
Cebrzynski, Stanley, (Retired)
Cesarec, Michael E., (Retired)
Chalhoub, Robert, Immaculate Conception, Milwaukee
Champagne, John I., St. Benedict the Moor, Milwaukee
Chmielewski, Michael J., Holy Apostles, New Berlin
Chrisien, James, (Personal Leave)
Christensen, Eugene M., Good Shepherd, Menomonee Falls
Clark, William, St. Anne, Pleasant Prairie; (Archdiocese of Chicago)
Coca, Emilio, St. Patrick, Racine
Cody, Edward F., St. Katharine Drexel, Beaver Dam
Collins, Dean J., Mother of Good Counsel, Milwaukee
Connors, Joseph, (Retired)
Copson, Jeffrey J., St. Elizabeth Ann Seton, New Berlin
Cornejo, Carlos, St. Anthony, Milwaukee
D'Alessio, John, St. Elizabeth Ann Seton, New Berlin
Dahlen, Clarence J., (Retired)
Dallman, Arthur C., (Retired)

Diciaula, Gregory H., St. Dominic, Brookfield
Dominguez, Alvaro, St. Mark, Kenosha
Doyle, James B., St. Mary, Waukesha
Dunn, William, (Archdiocese of Chicago) St. Patrick, Elkhorn
Ebel, John A., St. John Vianney, Brookfield
Fazen, Robert J., St. Matthew, Campbellsport
Ference, Dennis H., (Retired)
Fietz, Dennis E., Immaculate Heart of Mary, West Allis
Filipiak, Thomas P., St. Bruno, Dousman
Finley, Michael J., St. John Neumann, Waukesha
Foeckler, Allan J., St. Charles Borromeo, Milwaukee
Fogarty, Thomas
Francois, James S., St. Mary, Kenosha
Frye, Patrick H., Paul the Apostle, Racine
Fuentes, Roberto, Cristo Rey, Racine
Gaudioso, Carmelo, Holy Family, Whitefish Bay
Gavin, John R., Immaculate Conception, Sheboygan
Gonzales, Jose U., St. Joseph, Wauwatosa
Gonzalez, Baleriano O., St. Clement, Sheboygan
Goodman, Robert E., Three Holy Women, Milwaukee
Goulding, William, St. Mary, Hales Corners
Govek, Richard J., (Retired)
Griffiths, Joseph J., (Out of Archdiocese)
Gulig, Richard P., St. Peter Claver, Sheboygan
Gurzynski, Theodore A., St. Alphonsus, Greendale
Guzman, Armindo, (Out of Archdiocese)
Hansen, Keith A., St. Paul the Apostle, Racine
Heideman, Willis, St. Mary, Mayville; St. Andrew, LeRoy
Henry, Walter, Immaculate Heart of Mary, West Allis
Hiller, Richard D., (Retired)
Horner, Ralph E., Holy Trinity, Kewaskm, St. Michael, St. Michaels
Huber, Paul, (Personal Leave)
Hughes, Larry L., Holy Family, Fond du Lac
Hunt, Thomas N., Cathedral of St. John the Evangelist, Milwaukee
Hying, Joseph H., St. Thomas Aquinas, Waterford
Iwan, Henry, (Archdiocese of Chicago); St. Benedict, Fontana
Jansen, Mark, Holy Angels, West Bend
Jens, William T., Blessed Trinity, Sheboygan Falls
Kabara, Donald F., (Retired)
Kaczmarek, Raymond J., (Retired)
Kastenholz, Joseph H., (Retired)
Kehrer, Daniel F., St. Elizabeth, Kenosha
Kempka, Eugene A., St. Joseph, Waukesha
Kennedy, Claude V., St. James, Franklin
Kennedy, David L., (Out of Archdiocese)
Kilkenny, Philip O., St. Andrew, Delavan
Klingseisen, Paul, Blessed Sacrament, Milwaukee
Klinkhammer, Phillip H., (Retired)
Koebel, Michael S., St. Frances Cabrini, West Bend
Kornburger, Ralph W., Jr., St. Catherine, Milwaukee
Kuban, Donald J., St. Peter, East Troy, (Diocese of Phoenix)
Kustner, Charles J., St. Mary, Elm Grove
La Fond, M. Larry, Jr., St. Dominic, Brookfield
Lauer, David A., (Personal Leave)
Lazaga, Alfred C., (Out of Archdiocese)
Lebron, Gregorio M., (Retired)
Leggett, A. James, Divine Mercy, South Milwaukee
Lesjak, Ronald F., St. Mary, Kenosha
Libecki, John K., (Retired)
Lopez, Julio, Sts. Rose and Michael, Milwaukee
Losiniecki, Thomas, (Retired)
Lowe, Stanley, St. Charles Borromeo, Milwaukee
Lydolph, Donald J., St. Dominic, Sheboygan
Maack, Terrance A., St. Peter, Kenosha
Macias, Rogelio, St. Patrick and St. Rafael the Archangel, Milwaukee
Mahnke, Carl A., (Retired), St. Thomas Aquinas, Waterford; St. Clare, Wind Lake
Majewski, Edward H., (Retired)
Major, Troy, St. Francis of Assisi, Milwaukee
Malueg, Gerald D., Holy Rosary, Fredonia
Martino, Anthony, (On Duty Outside of the Archdiocese)
Marx, Keith R., Immaculate Heart of Mary, West Allis
McGuine, Thomas W., (On Duty Outside of the Archdiocese)
Mensah, Anthony J., (Retired)
Meuler, Andrew, Mother of Good Counsel, Milwaukee
Miller, Kenneth J., (Retired)
Missureli, Russell A., St. Edward, Racine
Moczydlowski, Chester A., (Retired)
Molina, Juan A., Sr., (Retired)
Monday, John P., Our Lady of Lourdes, Milwaukee
Monday, Thomas C., St. Mary, Menomonee Falls
Monfre, Anthony, Lumen Christi, Mequon
Monzel, Paul S., Presentation, North Fond du Lac; Our Risen Savior, Eldorado
Munoz, Ricardo, Holy Family, Fond du Lac
Nawrocik, Zenon L., (Out of Archdiocese)
Nees, Dale T., St. Paul the Apostle, Racine
Nguyen, Bruno Long H., St. Martin of Tours, Franklin
Nickel, James, St. Thomas Aquinas, Waterford
Niggemann, Richard D., Waukesha County Jail, Waukesha
Normann, Larry E., St. Paul, Genesee Depot
Nowicki, Edward J., (Retired)
Ode, LeRoy, Sacred Heart of Jesus, St. Francis
Ortiz, Aristeo, St. Joseph, Waukesha
Palacios, Antonio, St. Joseph, Waukesha
Pemper, Frank, (Out of Archdiocese)
Pena, Luis, Sts. Hyacinth and Vincent de Paul, Milwaukee
Peterson, James J., St. Sebastian, Milwaukee
Pettey, Lawrence C., (Retired)
Piontek, Richard T., St. Mary, Elm Grove; (Archdiocese of Chicago)
Pollak, David R., St. Charles Borromeo, Milwaukee
Ponec, Gerald R., Nativity of the Lord, Cudahy
Price, Gregory R., Queen of Apostles, Pewaukee; (Archdiocese of Chicago)
Przedpelski, Steven J., Holy Trinity, Newburg
Ramirez-Murphy, Eugenio, Our Lady of Divine Providence, Milwaukee
Regan, Sylvester R., (Retired)
Reyes, Edwin, St. Alexander, Helen; St. John Kanty, Milwaukee
Rocha, Leonides, St. Patrick, Racine
Rodriguez, Virgilio, (Out of Archdiocese)
Rooney, Michael R., St. James, Menomonee Falls
Rosado, Salvador, St. Francis of Assisi, Milwaukee
Salazar, Roberto, (On Duty Outside of the Archdiocese)
Schieffer, Robert M., (Retired)
Schimmels, Thomas J., (Retired)
Schneider, Ronald W., St. Francis Cabrini, West Bend; (Archdiocese of Washington, D.C.)
Schopper, Eugene E., (Retired)
Sherman, George P., (Retired)
Shierk, Wilson A., St. Mary, Kenosha
Sites, Sanford, Good Shepherd, Menomonee Falls
Snyder, Gordon J., St. Bruno, Dousman
Sommers, David W., St. Matthias, Milwaukee
Starns, Terry, St. Mary, Waukesha
Starr, Robert G., St. Mary of the Lake, Racine; (Archdiocese of Chicago)
Stodola, John, St. Matthew, Oak Creek
Surges, Thomas J., St. Peter of Alcantara, Port Washington
Treichel, Robert B., (Out of Archdiocese)
Van Garsse, Eugene E., St. Monica, Whitefish Bay
Villarreal, Hector, St. Patrick, Whitewater
Waitrovich, Raymond, (Retired)
Weber, C. Edward, (Retired)
Wells, Randal S., St. Katharine Drexel, Beaver Dam
Wendt, Bernard J., St. Peter, Slinger
Wenzler, Joseph P., Lumen Christi, Mequon
Widmar, Willard M., St. Paul the Apostle, Racine
Winkowski, Richard, (Personal Leave)
Wirch, Rick J., St. Leonard, Muskego
Wirtz, Howard J., St. Richard, Racine
Wisniewski, DeSales, O.F.M., (On Duty Outside the Archdiocese)
Wisniewski, Ralph, St. Leonard, Muskego
Wittak, Jay W., St. Robert Bellarmine, Union Grove; (Diocese of Marquette)
Wodushek, Robert A., (Retired)
Wolf, Kenneth W., (Retired)
Wuchterl, Thomas H., St. Mary, Menomonee Falls
Yang, Blong P., (Personal Leave)
Zalewski, Leon J., St. Stephen, Milwaukee
Zdeb, James, St. Louis, Caledonia; (Archdiocese of Chicago)
Zimprich, David L., St. William, Waukesha
Zozakiewicz, Daniel T., St. Catherine of Alexandria, Milwaukee
Zuniga, Jorge, Prince of Peace-Principe de Paz, Milwaukee

INSTITUTIONS LOCATED IN THE DIOCESE

[A] SEMINARIES, ARCHDIOCESAN

ST. FRANCIS. *Saint Francis de Sales Seminary*, 3257 S. Lake Dr., 53235. Tel: 414-747-6400; Fax: 414-747-6442. Email: dbrotz@sfs.edu. Web: www.sfs.edu. Very Rev. Donald J. Hying, Pres. & Rector; Revs. William L. Stanfield, Vice Rector; Robert Joseph Switanowski, O.F.M.Conv., Spiritual Dir.; Dr. Barbara V. Schauer, D.Min., Dir. Pastoral Formation; Rev. Stephen E. Malkiewicz, O.F.M., M.A., Dir. Worship; Sr. Roseann Wagner, S.S.S.F., B.M., M.T.S., Liturgical Music Dir.; Kathleen Frymark, Co-Dir. Salzmann Library; Rev. David E. Windsor, C.M., Psy.D., Dir. Admissions. Priests 5; Sisters 2; Administration & Faculty 9; Lay Staff 1; Seminarians 36.

[B] SEMINARIES, RELIGIOUS OR SCHOLASTICATES

FRANKLIN. *Xaverian Missionary Fathers College Seminary*, 4500 Xavier Dr., 53132. Tel: 414-421-0831; Fax: 414-421-9108. Email: xavmissionswi@hotmail.com. Web: www.xaviermissionaries.org. Rev. Adolph Menendez, S.X., Formator; Very Rev. Alfredo Turco, S.X. (Italy), Supr./Rector; Revs. Lawrence Crosara, S.X.; Victor Mosele, S.X. (Italy); Dominic Caldognetto, S.X. (Italy). Priests 5; Theology Seminarians 3; Philosophy Seminarians 2.

HALES CORNERS. *Sacred Heart School of Theology*, 7335 S. Hwy. 100, P.O. Box 429, 53130-0429. Tel: 414-425-8300; Fax: 414-529-6999. Email: tknoebel@shst.edu. Web: www.shst.edu. Revs. Jan de Jong, S.C.J., S.T.D., S.T.L., Pres. Rector; Thomas L. Knoebel, Ph.D., M.Div., Vice Rector; Vice Pres. External Affairs; Dir., Recruitment & Admissions; Raul Gomez Ruiz, S.D.S., Vice Pres. Academic Affairs; Dir. Intellectual Formation; James Walters, S.C.J., M.S., M.Div., Dir. Hispanic Studies; Robert W. Schiavone, M.A., Vice Pres. Pastoral Formation; Peter Schuessler, S.D.S., M.A., Vice Pres. Human & Spiritual Formation; C. Michael Weldon, O.F.M., M.Div., Dir. Spiritual Formation; Mr. Jonathan Drayna, Dir. Public Rels.; Mr. Michael Erato, Dir. Plant Opers.; Ms. Kathleen M. Harty, M.R., M.A.L.S., Dir. Library; Ms. Rose Kopenec, M.A., Registrar & Asst. to Vice Pres. Academic Affairs; Dir. Pre-Theology Academics; Ms. Sally Smits, M.B.A., Vice Pres. Finance & Personnel; Revs. Otto N. Bucher, O.F.M.Cap., S.S.L., S.T.L., Prof. Emeritus; Joseph Gole, S.T.D. (Slovenia), Prof. Emeritus; Sisters Martine Hundelt, S.S.S.F., Ph.D., Prof. Emerita; Joan Koehler, S.S.S.F., M.Ed., M.A., Prof. Emerita; Dr. Bruce Malchow, Ph.D., Prof. Emeritus. Priests 21; Sisters 6; Lay Teachers 13; Non-Catholic Clergy 1; Bishops 1; Lay Staff 21; Total Enrollment 149.

Full-Time Faculty: Revs. Hugh G. Birdsall, S.D.S., M.A., M.S.; Charles Brown, S.C.J., Ph.D.; Javier Bustos, S.T.D.; Jerome M. Hudziak, Ph.D. (Retired); Thomas M. McLernon, M.Ed.; Melvin E. Michalski, Ph.L., Th.D.; Andre Papineau, S.D.S., M.A.; Bro. Raymond Kozuch, S.C.J.; Sisters Mary C. Carroll, S.S.S.F., M.A., D.Min.; Marilyn Cowser, O.S.F., M.A.; Lucille Flores, S.S.M., M.P.S., M.A.; Susan Klein, O.P.; Dr. John Gallam, Ph.D.; Dr. Richard Lux, Ph.D.; Dr. Patrick J. Russell, Ph.D.; Dr. Steven Shippee, Ph.D., Dir. MA Prog.; Mr. C. Christian Rich, B.A., M.M.; Ms. Ruth MacKechnie, M.Ed., Ph.D. (Cand.).

Part-Time Faculty: Most Rev. Richard J. Sklba, S.S.L., S.T.D.; Revs. Steven M. Avella; John Cella, O.F.M., J.C.D., M.Div., M.B.A.; James E. Lobacz; Stephen E. Malkiewicz, O.F.M., M.A.; Daniel Pekarske, S.D.S., Ph.D.; Michael van der Peet, S.C.J., M.A., M.Div.; Dr. Sherry Blumberg, Ph.D.; Dr. Barbara Anne Cusack, J.C.D.; Dr. Lance Richey, Ph.D.; Dr. Barbara V. Schauer, D.Min.; Ms. Zabrina R. Decker, J.C.L.; Ms. Brigid O'Donnell, M.A.; Ms. Barbara Scherrer, B.A., M.S.T.; Eva J. Diaz, M.A.P.S.

MOUNT CALVARY. *St. Lawrence Seminary* 53057. Tel: 920-753-7500; Fax: 920-753-7507. Web: stlawrence.edu. Revs. Dennis Druggan, O.F.M.Cap., Rector & Pres.; Campion Baer, O.F.M.Cap.; Oliver Bambenek, O.F.M.Cap., Librarian; Jerome Higgins, O.F.M.Cap., M.Ed., M.A.S., D.Min. (Retired); Gary Wegner, O.F.M.Cap., Dean Students; Werner Wolf, O.F.M.Cap., Local Min.; Bros. Douglas Bode, O.F.M.Cap.; Jerome Campbell, O.F.M.Cap.; Lawrence Groeschel, O.F.M.Cap; Neal Plale, O.F.M.Cap.; Carl Schaefer, O.F.M.Cap.; John Scherer, O.F.M.Cap.; Ron Smith, O.F.M.Cap.; John Willger, O.F.M.Cap.; Mr. David Bartel, Academic Dean; Mr. Timothy Schroeder, Business Mgr. High School Seminary and Ministry Program Priests 6; Brothers 8; Sisters 2; Lay Teachers 18; Non-Teaching Lay Staff 45; Students 200; Total Staff 79.

[C] COLLEGES AND UNIVERSITIES

MILWAUKEE. *Alverno College*, 3400 S. 43rd St., P.O. Box 343922, 53234-3922. Tel: 414-382-6000; Fax: 414-362-6354. Web: www.alverno.edu. Marc McSweeney, Chm., Bd. of Trustees; Mary J. Meehan, Pres.; Sr. Kathleen O'Brien, O.S.F., Sr. Vice Pres. Academic Affairs; Mr. James Oppermann, Sr. Vice Pres. Finance & Mgmt. Svcs.; Carol Brill, Library Dir. Sisters 16; Faculty 119; Students 2,815; Total Staff 268.

Cardinal Stritch University (1937) 6801 N. Yates Rd., 53217. Tel: 414-410-4000; Fax: 414-410-4239. Email: admityou@stritch.edu. Web: www.stritch.edu. Dr. Helen C. Sobehart, Ph.D.,

Pres.; Dr. Daniel Blankenship, Provost; Revs. James Gannon, O.F.M., Office of Campus Ministry; Trinette McCray, Office of Campus Ministry. Conducted by Sisters of St. Francis of Assisi. Priests 1; Sisters 16; Lay Teachers 124; Students 6,242; Total Staff 319.

**Marquette University* (1881) *Office of Institutional Research*, P.O. Box 1881, 53201-1881. Tel: 414-288-1906; Fax: 414-288-6318. Email: webquestions@marquette.edu; ir.surveys@marquette.edu. Web: www.marquette.edu.

Marquette University, Conducted under the auspices of the Society of Jesus. Jesuit Priests 21; Women Religious 5; Lay Teachers 1,096; Students 11,689.

Major University Officers: Rev. Robert A. Wild, S.J., Pres.; Mr. John C. Lamb, Vice Pres. Finance; Ms. Cynthia M. Bauer, Vice Pres. & Gen. Counsel; Ms. Rana Altenburg, Vice Pres. Public Affairs; Mr. Gregory J. Kliebhan, Senior Vice Pres.; Dr. L. Christopher Miller, Vice Pres. Student Affairs; Ms. Julie Tolan, Vice Pres. Univ. Advancement; Dr. John Pauly, Provost; Dr. Margaret Bloom, Vice Provost Undergraduate Programs & Teaching; Dr. Gary Levy, Assoc. Vice Provost for Inst. Research & Assessment; Dr. William R. Wiener, Vice Provost Research & Dean Graduate School; Ms. Stephanie Russell, Exec. Dir. Univ. Mission & Identity; Mr. Arthur F. Scheuber, Vice Pres. Admin.; Ms. Patricia L. Geraghty, Vice Pres. Office of Mktg.

Deans: Dr. Jeanne Hossenlopp, Interim Dean Helen Way Klinger College of Arts & Sciences; Dr. Linda Salchenberger, Dean College of Business Admin.; Dr. Lynn Turner, Interim Dean J. William and Mary Diederich College of Communication; Dr. William K. Lobb, Dean School of Dentistry; Dr. William Henk, Dean College of Educ.; Dr. Stanley V. Jaskolski, Dean College of Engineering; Dr. William Cullinan, Dean College of Health Sciences; Dr. Janice Simmons-Welburn, Dean Libraries; Dr. Margaret Callahan, Dean College of Nursing; Dr. Robert J. Deahl, Dean College of Professional Studies; Mr. Joseph D. Kearney, Dean Law School.

Additional Department Heads: Rev. John Mathie, S.J., Dir. Univ. Ministry; Dr. Susan Wood, Chair Dept. of Theology.

Mount Mary College (1913) 2900 N. Menomonee River Pkwy., 53222-4545. Tel: 414-258-4810; Fax: 414-256-1224. Web: www.mtmary.edu. Eileen Schwalbach, Pres.; Julie Kamikawa, Acting Dir. Library. School Sisters of Notre Dame. Sisters 14; Lay Teachers 69; Students 1,781; Total Staff 368.

FOND DU LAC. *Marian University, Inc.* (1936) 45 S. National Ave., 54935. Tel: 920-923-7617; Fax: 920-923-8087. Email: admissions@marianuniversity.edu. Web: www.marianuniversity.edu. Sisters Mary Mollison, C.S.A., Acting Pres.; Deborah Golias, C.S.A., Interim Vice Pres. Academic Affairs; Marie Scott, C.S.A., Campus Min.; Mary Ellen Gormican, Librarian. Sisters of the Congregation of St. Agnes 5; Lay Teachers 88; Students 2,891; (incl. all part-time & adjunct) 304.

[D] HIGH SCHOOLS, ARCHDIOCESAN AND PAROCHIAL

MILWAUKEE. *Pius XI High School* (1929) 135 N. 76th St., 53213. Tel: 414-290-7000; Fax: 414-290-7001. Email: piusxi@piusxi.org. Web: www.piusxi.org. Dr. Melinda Skrade, Chief Admin.; Betty Hunt, Dir. Academic Operations. School Sisters of St. Francis 4; Lay Teachers 88; Students 1,000.

Thomas More High School, 2601 E. Morgan Ave., 53207. Tel: 414-481-8370; Fax: 414-481-3382. Email: ljanick@tmore.org. Web: www.tmore.org. Mr. Terry Benter, Prin. (Coed) Sisters 1; Lay Teachers 31; Students 436; Total Staff 52.

BURLINGTON. *Catholic Central High School* (1925) 148 McHenry St., 53105. Tel: 262-763-1510; Fax: 262-763-1509. Email: ggroth@cchsnet.org. Web: www.cchsnet.org. Gregory Groth, Prin.; Jean Pyzyk, Asst. Prin. Lay Teachers 18; Students 149.

KENOSHA. *St. Joseph High School*, 2401 69th St., 53143. Tel: 262-654-8651; Fax: 262-654-1615. Email: rfreund@kenoshastjoseph.com. Web: www.kenoshastjoseph.com. Mr. Robert Freund, Pres.; Edward G. Kovochich, Prin. Sisters 1; Lay Teachers 33; Students 295; Total Staff 42.

WAUKESHA. *Catholic Memorial High School* (1949) 601 E. College Ave., 53186-5538. Tel: 262-542-7101; Fax: 262-542-1633. Email: fr.hartmann@catholicmemorial.net. Web: www.catholicmemorial.net. Very Rev. Paul B.R. Hartmann, M.Div., J.C.L., Pres. Tel: 262-542-7101, Ext. 243; Fax: 262-521-4444; Mr. Bob Hall, Prin. Clergy 1; Lay Teachers 61; Students 753; Total Staff 80.

[E] HIGH SCHOOLS, PRIVATE

MILWAUKEE. *Divine Savior Holy Angels High School, Inc.* (Girls), 4257 N. 100th St., 53222. Tel: 414-462-3742; Fax: 414-466-0590. Email: dsha@dsha.k12.wi.us. Web: www.dsha.info. Ellen Bartel, Pres.; Dan Quesnell, Prin.; Mary Wyn Bjorkquist, Librarian. Sponsored by the Sisters of the Divine Savior. Sisters 2; Lay Teachers 63; Students 656; Total Staff 93.

St. Joan Antida High School, Inc. (Girls), 1341 N. Cass St., 53202. Tel: 414-272-8423; Fax: 414-272-3135. Email: mkurhajetz@saintjoanantida.org. Web: www.saintjoanantida.org. Cynthia A. Marino, Pres.; Mary Kurhajetz, Prin. Sisters of Charity of St. Joan Antida 3; Lay Teachers 27; Students 337; Total Staff 45.

Marquette University High School (Boys)., 3401 W. Wisconsin Ave., 53208. Tel: 414-933-7220; Fax: 414-937-8588. Web: www.muhs.edu. Revs. John M. Belmonte, S.J., Prin.; Terrence M. Brennan, S.J.; Mark A. Carr, S.J.; Thomas C. Manahan, S.J.; Warren J. Sazama, S.J., Pres.; Charles L. Stang, S.J.; Ms. Ann O'Hara, Librarian. (See separate listing for resident information). Priests 6; Religious 2; Lay Teachers 75; Students 1,054; Total Staff 133.

**Messmer High School* (1926) 742 W. Capitol Dr., 53206. Tel: 414-264-5440; Fax: 414-264-0672. Email: generalinfo@messmerschools.org. Web: www.messmerschools.org. Bro. Bob Smith, Pres.; Jeff Monday, Vice Pres. & Prin.; Polly Partain, Librarian. Brothers 1; Teachers 53; Part-Time Teachers 5; Students 656; Lay Staff 29.

Messmer Preparatory School (1999) 3027 N. Fratney St., 53212. Tel: 414-264-6070; Fax: 414-264-6430. Email: generalinfo@messmerschools.org. Web: www.messmerschools.org. Jeff Monday, Vice Pres.; Michelle Paris, Prin.; Darlene Packard, Librarian. Brothers 1; Lay Teachers 32; Students 451.

RACINE. *St. Catherine's High School* (1864) 1200 Park Ave., 53403. Tel: 262-632-2785; Fax: 262-632-5144. Web: www.saintcats.org. Mr. Christopher Olley, Pres.; Mr. Andrew Meuler, Prin.; Sr. Jane Weiss, Asst. Prin. Dominican Sisters (Racine) 3; Lay Teachers 26; Students 363.

WHITEFISH BAY. *Dominican High School* (1956) 120 E. Silver Spring Dr., 53217. Tel: 414-332-1170; Fax: 414-332-4101. Email: dhs@dominicanhighschool.com. Web: dominicanhighschool.com. Edward Foy, Dean Academics; Brian Geittmann, Dean Students; Amy Krzykowski, Librarian; Henry Reyes, Campus Min. Sponsored by Sinsinawa Dominicans. Dominican Sisters of the Congregation of the Most Holy Rosary, Sinsinawa, WI 1; Administrators 3; Lay Teachers 32; Students 350.

[F] ELEMENTARY SCHOOLS, ARCHDIOCESAN

MILWAUKEE. *St. Rose and St. Leo Catholic School*, 514 N. 31st St., 53208. Tel: 414-933-6070; Fax: 414-933-3071. Email: generalinfo@messmerschools.org. Web: www.messmerschools.org. Bro. Bob Smith, Pres.; Jeff Monday, Vice Pres.; Lewis Lea, Prin. In partnership with Messmer Catholic Schools. Brothers 1; Lay Teachers 19; Staff 8; Students 203.

[G] ELEMENTARY SCHOOLS, PRIVATE

MILWAUKEE. *St. Coletta Day School of Milwaukee* (1956) 1740 N. 55th St., 53208. Tel: 414-453-1850; Fax: 414-453-9449. Email: info@scdsmke.org. Web: www.scdsmke.org. William A. Koehn, Prin. & Admin. For Exceptional Children. Lay Teachers 2; Students 11.

Nativity Jesuit Middle School, Inc. (Boys), 1515 S. 29th St., 53215-1912. Tel: 414-645-1060. Email: nativity@njms.org. Web: www.njms.org. Gregory Meuler, Pres.; Ms. Melodie Hessling, Prin. Wisconsin Province of the Society of Jesus. Priests 1; Religious 1; Lay Teachers 9; Students 82; Total Staff 17.

Notre Dame Middle School, Inc. (1996) 1420 W. Scott St., 53204. Tel: 414-671-3000; Fax: 414-671-6138. Email: info@ndmswi.org. Web: ndmswi.org. Mary McIntosh, Pres.; Sisters Jean Ellman, S.S.N.D., Prin.; Doris Jean LaBrun, S.S.N.D., Librarian. Sponsored by: School Sisters of Notre Dame. Sisters 3; Lay Teachers 12; Volunteers 2; Students 121.

[H] CONSOLIDATED ELEMENTARY SCHOOLS

MILWAUKEE. *All Saints Catholic East School System, Inc.*, 2461 N. Murray Ave., 53211. Tel: 414-964-1770; Fax: 414-964-6578. Email: robinsonj@archmil.org. Rev. Michael F. Michalski, Bd. Chm.; Mrs. Julie Ann Robinson, Prin. Sponsored by the following Milwaukee parishes: Cathedral of St. John the Evangelist; Our Lady of Divine Providence; Old St. Mary's; Ss. Peter and Paul; Three Holy Women Catholic Parish. Lay Teachers 17; Students 146.

Holy Wisdom Academy (2002) c/o *St. Alexander Congregation*, 3307 S. 10th, 53215-5039. Tel: 414-744-3695; Fax: 414-744-2874. Revs. Michael A. Ignaszak, Contact; Norberto Sandoval; Mr. Richard Mason, Prin. Sponsored by St. Alexander and St. Helen Parishes, Milwaukee. Sisters 5; Lay Teachers 16; Total Enrollment 266.

Northwest Catholic School Association Formerly St. Bernadette, St. Catherine of Alexandria, and Our Lady of Good Hope Schools., 8202 W. Denver Ave., 53223. Tel: 414-358-4603. Debra A. Hintz, Contact Person.

St. Thomas Aquinas Academy Association, 341 E. Norwich St., 53207. Tel: 414-744-1214; Fax: 414-744-8340. Web: thomasaquinasacademy.com. Rev. Romanus N. Nwaru, Contact Person; Rhonda Friday, Prin.; Mrs. Diane Karabon, Librarian. Sponsored by St. Augustine, St. Paul, St. Veronica & Immaculate Conception, Milwaukee; Nativity of the Lord, Cudahy, and Sacred Heart of Jesus, St. Francis. Lay Teachers 23; Students 225.

JOHNSBURG. *Consolidated Parochial Elementary School* (1969) N9290 County Rd. W, Fond Du Lac, 54937. Tel: 920-795-4222; Fax: 920-795-4126. Email: cpes@ppcws.net. Web: cpesonline.com. Mary Beth Leonard, Prin. & Admin. Members: St. John the Baptist, Johnsburg; St. Mary, Marytown; Holy Cross, Mount Calvary; St. Cloud, St. Cloud. Priests 2; Lay Teachers 13; Students 102.

LOMIRA. *Consolidated Catholic School, Lomira-Theresa*, 705 Milwaukee St., 53048-9520. Tel: 920-269-4326; Fax: 920-269-7342. Email: cclt@charter.net. Dorothy Zitlow, Prin.; Jackie Hettenhaus, Librarian. Members: St. Mary, Lomira; St. Theresa, Theresa. Lay Teachers 4; Students 30.

WAUKESHA. *Waukesha Catholic School System, Inc.* (1990) 221 S. Hartwell Ave., 53186. Tel: 262-896-2929; Fax: 262-896-2934. Email: business@waukeshacatholicschoolsystem.org. Rev. Jason Lavann, Pastor Liaison. Tel: 262-542-2589. Members: St. Joseph, St. Mary, St. John Neumann, St. William.

St. Joseph Campus, 818 N. East Ave., 53186. Tel: 262-896-2930; Fax: 262-896-2935. Email: stjoe@wcssonline.org. Mrs. Kathleen Rempe, Prin. Lay Teachers 18; Students 221.

St. Mary Campus, 520 N. Newhall Ave., 53186. Tel: 262-896-2932; Fax: 262-896-2931. Email: stmary@wcssonline.org. Ms. Lisa Kovaleski, Prin. Lay Teachers 18; Students 316.

St. William Campus, 444 N. Moreland Blvd., 53188. Tel: 262-896-2920; Fax: 262-896-2925. Email: stwm@wcssonline.org. Robert Radomski, Prin. Lay Teachers 11; Students 163.

WEST ALLIS. *Mary Queen of Saints Catholic Academy* (2004) Greenfield Avenue Campus, 1435 S. 92nd St., 53214. Tel: 414-476-0751; Fax: 414-259-9285. Web: mqsca.org. Rev. Leonard R. Copeland, O.C.D., Priest Designate; Beverley Walloch, Librarian. Sponsored by St. Florian, West Milwaukee; Holy Assumption, Immaculate Heart of Mary, Mary Queen of Heaven, St. Aloysius, St. Augustine & St. Rita, West Allis. Lay Teachers (Full-Time) 8; Lay Teachers (Part-Time) 7; Students 99.

[I] SCHOOL SYSTEMS

FOND DU LAC. *St. Mary's Springs Academy aka FACES-Springs Catholic Education System aka St. Mary's Springs High School, Inc.* (Grades K-12), Admin. Office: 114 Armory St., 54935. Tel: 920-924-0993; 920-921-4870, Ext. 8009 (Business Office); Fax: 920-922-7849. Web: www.faces.k12.wi.us. Sr. Judith Schmidt, Pres. Tel: 920-924-0993; Joanne Michaels, Librarian. Lay Teachers 34; Students 482; Total Staff 62.

Pre-School & Elementary (Grades PreK-2), 95 E. 2nd St., 54935. Tel: 920-921-5300; Fax: 920-921-5908. Email: cjaeger@faces.k12.wi.us. Cheryl Jaeger, Prin.

Elementary & Middle School (Grades 3-8), 63 E. Merrill Ave., 54935. Tel: 920-921-9610; Fax: 920-921-0457. Email: cjaeger@faces.k12.wi.us. Cheryl Jaeger, Prin.

High School, 255 County Rd. K, 54937. Tel: 920-921-4870; Fax: 920-921-2786. Email: tborek@springs.k12.wi.us. Web: www.springs.k12.wi.us. Tom Borek, Prin. Sisters 2; Lay Teachers 22; Students 252; Faculty 24.

[J] CHILD CARE CENTERS

MILWAUKEE. *Child Development Center of St. Joseph* (1999) 1600 W. Oklahoma Ave., 53215. Tel: 414-645-5337; Fax: 414-645-5329. Email: jvasquez@cdcsj.org. Web: www.cdcsj.org. Jose Vasquez, CEO. Felician Sisters 3; Lay Teachers 37; Children 213; Total Staff 54; Other Staff 14.

Guardian Angel Learning Center, Inc., 1540 N. Jefferson, 53202. Tel: 414-277-9474; Fax: 414-277-9482. Email: gschool1@wi.rr.com. Web: www.scsja.org. Sr. Marie Louise Balistrieri, S.C.S.J.A., Admin. Sisters of Charity of St. Joan Antida, The center is licensed for ages 6 weeks to 12 years. Sisters of Charity of St. Joan Antida 1; Sisters of Charity B.V.M. 1; Lay Teachers 22; Students 85.

Seton Children's School, Inc. (1981) 8647 N. Port Washington Rd., Fox Point, 53217. Tel: 414-352-6115; Fax: 414-540-9374. Email: amarquar@columbia_stmarys.org. Operated by the Ascension Health System. A licensed center for comprehensive early childhood educational programs and day care. Lay Teachers 12; Children 112.

Other Location:

2330 N. Prospect Ave., 53211. Tel: 414-220-8494. Lay Teachers 7; Children 120.

SOUTH MILWAUKEE. *Franciscan Villa Child Day Care Center*, 3601 S. Chicago Ave., 53172. Tel: 414-570-5410; Fax: 414-764-0706. Email: stacysuehring@catholichealth.net. Web: www.franciscanvilla.com. Affiliate of Catholic Health Initiatives. Lay Teachers 10; Children 50.

[K] GENERAL HOSPITALS

MILWAUKEE. *Columbia St. Mary's Hospital Milwaukee, Inc.* (1859) 2323 N. Lake Dr., P.O. Box 503, 53201-0503. Tel: 414-326-1734; Fax: 414-326-1739. Email: amarquar@columbia-stmarys.org. Web: www.columbia-stmarys.org. William Haft, Vice Pres. Hospital Opers.; Rev. Eugene Pocernich, Chap.; Sr. Rosalynn Dzikonski, O.S.F., Chap.; Pedro Acosta Zapata, Chap. Corporate Title: Columbia St. Mary's Hospital Milwaukee, Inc.; Ascension Health System. Bed Capacity 664; Patients Assisted Annually 285,170; Total Staff 3,816.

Ministry Health Care, Inc. (1984) 11925 W. Lake Park Dr., 53224. Tel: 414-359-1060; Fax: 414-359-1033. Email: info@ministryhealth.org. Web: www.ministryhealth.org. Nicholas Desien, Pres. & CEO.

Subsidiaries and Affiliated Hospitals located throughout Wisconsin:

Door County Memorial Hospital (1942) Sturgeon Bay. Tel: 920-743-5566; Fax: 920-743-8165.

Mercy Medical Center of Oshkosh, Inc. (1891) Oshkosh. Tel: 920-223-2000; Fax: 920-223-0508.

Ministry Behavioral Health of St. Michael's Hospital, Inc. (1970) Stevens Point. Tel: 715-344-4611; Fax: 715-344-8127.

Ministry Home Care, Inc. (1998) Marshfield. Tel: 715-389-3802; Fax: 715-387-9950.

Ministry Weight Management, Inc. (1995) Rhinelander. Tel: 715-361-2000; Fax: 715-361-2011.

Sacred Heart-Saint Mary's Hospitals, Inc. (1981) Tomahawk and Rhinelander, WI, Tel: 715-369-6600; Fax: 715-369-6441.

Saint Elizabeth's Hospital's of Wabasha, Inc. (1898) Wabasha, MN. Tel: 651-565-4531; Fax: 651-565-2482.

Saint Joseph's Hospital of Marshfield, Inc. (1955) Marshfield. Tel: 715-387-1713; Fax: 715-387-8601.

Saint Clare's Hospital of Weston, Inc. (2002) Wausau. Tel: 715-393-3000; Fax: 715-359-1087.

St. Michael's Hospital of Stevens Point, Inc. (1913) Stevens Point. Tel: 715-346-5000; Fax: 715-346-5088.

Our Lady of Victory Hospital, Inc., Stanley. Tel: 715-644-5571; Fax: 715-644-6221.

Dr. Kate Newcomb Convalescent Center, Inc. (1980) Woodruff. Tel: 715-356-8888; Fax: 715-356-8861.

Eagle River Memorial Hospital, Incorporated (1941) Eagle River. Tel: 715-479-7411; Fax: 715-479-2748.

The Howard Young Medical Center, Inc. (1954) Woodruff. Tel: 715-356-8000; Fax: 715-356-6097.

Howard Young Health Care, Inc. (1984) Woodruff. Tel: 715-356-8000; Fax: 715-356-6097.

Affinity Health System (1999) Menasha, 54952. Tel: 920-720-1700; Fax: 920-720-1907.

Agape Community Center of Milwaukee, Inc. (1989) Tel: 414-464-4440; Fax: 414-464-9420.

Ministry Medical Group, Inc. Tel: 414-359-1060; Fax: 414-359-1656.

Wheaton Franciscan Healthcare - St. Francis, Inc. (1946) 3237 S. 16th St., 53215. Tel: 414-647-5000; Fax: 414-647-5565. Web: www.mywheaton.org. Daniel Mattes, Pres.; Rev. Kevin Ori, Chap. Sponsored by the Congregation of the Sisters of St. Felix of Cantalice of the United States of America, Chicago Province (Felician Sisters). Sisters 9; Bed Capacity 260; Patients Assisted Annually 152,509; Total Staff 1,155.

Wheaton Franciscan, Inc. (1927) St. Joseph Campus: 5000 W. Chambers St., 53210. Tel: 414-447-2000; Fax: 414-874-4393. Web: www.mywheaton.org. Wisconsin Heart Hospital Campus: 10000 W. Bluemound Rd., Wauwatosa, 53226. Debra K. Standridge, Pres.; Trisha Crissman, Interim Regl. Dir. Franciscan Sisters, Daughters of the Sacred Hearts of Jesus and Mary (Wheaton, IL) 8; Bed Capacity 947; Patients Assisted Annually 122,664; Total Staff 2,016.

BROOKFIELD. *Wheaton Franciscan Healthcare - Elmbrook Memorial, Inc.* (1915) 19333 W. North Ave., 53045. Tel: 262-785-2000; Fax: 262-785-2444. Web: www.mywheaton.org. Debra K. Standridge, Pres.; Trisha Crissman, Interim Regl. Dir. Franciscan Sisters, Daughters of the Sacred Hearts of Jesus and Mary (Wheaton, IL). Bed Capacity 166; Patients Assisted Annually 47,215; Total Staff 613.

FOND DU LAC. *Agnesian Health Care, Inc. dba St. Agnes Hospital* 430 E. Division St., 54935. Tel: 920-929-2300; Fax: 920-926-4866. Email: fale@agnesian.com. Web: www.agnesian.com. Mr. Robert A. Fale, Pres. & CEO. Sisters 5; Bed Capacity 184; (TCU) 8; Patients Assisted Annually 201,777; Total Staff 1,451.

KENOSHA. *St. Catherine's Hospital Inc.* (1917) 6308 Eighth Ave., 53143. Tel: 262-656-2112; Fax: 262-654-2624. Richard O. Schmidt Jr., Pres. & CEO. Sponsored by Wheaton Franciscan Healthcare

MEQUON. *St. Mary's Hospital Ozaukee, Inc.* (1995) 13111 N. Port Washington Rd., 53097. Tel: 414-243-7300; Fax: 414-243-7416. Email: gstaffil@columbia-stmarys.org. Web: www.columbia-stmarys.org. Gerri Staffileno, Vice Pres. Hospital Opers. & Nurse Exec.; Rev. Paul Schwan, Chap.; Sr. Angela Spence, Chap. Ascension Health System Bed Capacity 182; Patients Assisted Annually 133,685; Total Staff 1,217.

RACINE. *Wheaton Franciscan Healthcare - All Saints, Inc.* (1974) 3801 Spring St., 53405. Tel: 262-687-4011; Fax: 262-687-8039. Web: www.mywheaton.org. Kenneth R. Buser, Pres. Bed Capacity 413; Total Patients Assisted 115,484; Total Staff 2,056.

SHEBOYGAN. *St. Nicholas Hospital* (1890) 3100 Superior Ave., 53081. Tel: 920-459-8300; Fax: 920-452-8336. Email: mbrasseaux@sns.hshs.org. Web: www.stnicholashospital.org. Mary T. Brasseaux, CEO; Sr. Christa Strewing, O.S.F., Rel. Coord.; Martin Folan, Dir. Spiritual & Pastoral Support Svcs. Hospital Sisters of the Third Order of St. Francis 2; Bed Capacity 185; Total Assisted Annually 98,182; Total Staff 578.

WAUPUN. *Waupun Memorial Hospital, Inc.*, 620 W. Brown St., 53963. Tel: 920-324-5581; Fax: 920-324-2085. Web: www.agnesian.com. Deann Thurmer, COO. Corporate Title: Waupun Memorial Hospital, Inc. Bed Capacity 25; Patients Assisted Annually 46,567; Total Staff 178.

[L] SPECIAL HOSPITALS AND SANATORIA

MILWAUKEE. *Sacred Heart Rehabilitation Institute, Inc.* (1955) 2025 E. Newport Ave., 53211. Tel: 414-326-1740; Fax: 414-326-1739. Connie Bradley, Vice Pres. Nursing; Anne Jurenec, Dir. of Oper.; Sr. Margaret Ann Arnold, Chap. Office; Rev. Vicki Watkins, Chap. Ascension Health System. Bed Capacity 67; Patients Assisted Annually 10,250; Total Staff 124.

[M] PROTECTIVE INSTITUTIONS

MILWAUKEE. *St. Charles Youth and Family Services, Inc.* (1920) 151 S. 84th St., 53214. Tel: 414-476-3710; Fax: 414-778-5985. Email: scarpenter@stcharlesinc.org. Web: www.stcharlesinc.org. Ms. Cathy Connolly, Pres. Bed Capacity 118; Residents 136; Total Assisted Annually 3,000; Total Staff 275.

Daystar, Inc., P.O. Box 2130, 53201-2130. Tel: 414-385-0334; Fax: 414-385-0336. Email: daystar@daystarinc.org. Web: www.daystarinc.org. Transitional living program for formerly battered women without children, for up to two years. Bed Capacity 10; Residents 10; Total Assisted Annually 25; Total Staff 5.

Rosalie Manor Community & Family Services, Inc., 4803 W. Burleigh St., 53210. Tel: 414-449-2868; Fax: 414-449-2870. Email: d.groshek@rmcfs.org. Web: www.rosaliemanor.org. Don Shane, Exec. Dir. Sponsored by the Archdiocese of Milwaukee, Community Programs that strengthen Milwaukee families by empowering parents to be nurturing & by guiding youth toward positive futures. Total Assisted 1,000; Total Staff 24.

MOUNT CALVARY. *Cristo Rey Ranch, Inc.*, N8102 Calvary St., 53057. Tel: 920-753-2026; 920-753-3211; Fax: 920-753-3100. Email: wbodden@villalorettonh.org; nunbetterfarm@hotmail.com. Sister Servants of Christ the King, Provides weekend respite services to families caring for emotionally/behaviorally challenged children and adolescents. Program emphasis on pet therapy. Some day and evening programs thru County Social Services Department. Bed Capacity 4; Total Assisted Annually 8; Total Staff 3.

WAUWATOSA. *Carmelite Home, Inc.* (1917) 1214 Kavanaugh Pl., 53213. Tel: 414-258-4791; Fax: 414-258-8464. Email: carmelitedcl@sbcglobal.net. Sr. Maria Goretti, D.C.J., Admin.; James E. Lewis, M.S.W., Treatment Dir. MSW & ICSW. Residential Treatment Center for Adolescent Boys. Carmelite Sisters D.C.J. 3; Residents 30; Lay Teachers 2; Total Staff 21.

[N] HOMES FOR AGED AND NURSING HOMES

MILWAUKEE. *Alexian Village of Milwaukee, Inc.* (1980) 9301 N. 76th St., 53223. Tel: 414-355-9300; Fax: 414-357-5106. Email: gmohn@alexianbrothers.net. Web: www.alexianvillage.net. Gary Mohn, CEO; Rev. Joe Jagodensky, S.D.S., Chap. Congregation of Alexian Brothers, Immaculate Conception Province, Continuing Care Retirement Community. Units 457; Residents 491; Brothers 3; Total Assisted Annually 79; Total Staff 302.

St. Ann Rest Home, 2020 S. Muskego Ave., 53204-3522. Tel: 414-383-2642; Fax: 414-383-0305. Web: www.stannresthome.org. Rev. Linus E. Kopczewski, O.F.M., Pastoral Care Min.; Sr. Andrea K. Andrzejewska, Admin. Conducted by the Dominican Sisters (Congregation of the Immaculate Conception). Sisters 7; Bed Capacity 50; Residents 50; Total Staff 47.

St. Anne's Salvatorian Campus, 3800 N. 92nd St., 53222. Tel: 414-463-7570; Fax: 414-463-2311. Email: lvogt@wi.rr.com. Web: www.stannessc.org. Ms. Lynn Vogt, Admin.; Rev. Michael Burns, S.D.S., Chap. Sisters of the Divine Savior. Assisted Living Apartments 43; Residents 106; Total Staff 247.

**Milwaukee Catholic Home*, 2462 N. Prospect Ave., 53211-4462. Tel: 414-224-9700; Fax: 414-224-1666. Email: info@milwaukeecatholichome.org. Web: milwaukeecatholichome.org. Mr. Paul J. Connolly, N.H.A., Exec. Dir.; Rev. Charles R. Keefe, Dir. Pastoral Care. Corporate Title: Milwaukee Catholic Home, Inc. Retirement Home Residents 120; Retirement Home Total Staff 67; Nursing Home Residents 122; Nursing Home Total Staff 200; Day Care (Adult) 20; Assisted Living 29.

Villa St. Francis, Inc. (1990) 1910 W. Ohio Ave., 53215. Tel: 414-649-2888; Fax: 414-649-2880. Email: jvasquez@villastfrancis.org. Web: www.villastfrancis.org. Jose Vasquez, CEO. Sponsored by the Congregation of the Sisters of St. Felix of Cantalice of the United States of America, Inc. Chicago Province (Felician Sisters), Assisted Living Facility for the Elderly Resident Apartments 128; Total Assisted Annually 190; Total Staff 78.

Wheaton Franciscan Healthcare-Terrace at St. Francis, Inc. (1994) 3200 S. 20th St., 53215. Tel: 414-389-3200; Fax: 414-389-3300. James D. Gresham, Pres. Member of Wheaton Franciscan Healthcare. Sponsored by the Felician Sisters and the Wheaton Franciscan Sisters., Skilled Nursing Facility for Transitional & Extended Subacute Care. Bed Capacity 81; Patients Assisted Annually 562; Total Staff 80.

BROOKFIELD. **Wheaton Franciscan Healthcare - Marian Franciscan Center, Inc. dba Wheaton Franciscan Healthcare - Franciscan Woods* (1987) 19525 W. North Ave., 53045. Tel: 262-780-3100. Web: www.mywheaton.org. James D. Gresham, Pres. Franciscan Sisters, Daughters of the Sacred Hearts of Jesus and Mary, Wheaton, IL. Bed Capacity 120; Total Assisted Annually 748; Total Staff 116.

FOND DU LAC. *St. Francis Home* (1978) 33 Everett St., 54935. Tel: 920-923-7980; Fax: 920-923-7995. Douglas Trost, CEO. Sisters of St. Agnes, C.S.A. Sisters 2; Residents 107; Total Staff 204.

St. Clare Terrace (1991) Tel: 920-923-7996; Fax: 920-923-7995. Residents 29; Independent Elderly Apartments 30; Total Staff 2.

St. Francis Terrace (1998) Tel: 920-923-7980; Fax: 920-923-7995. Residents 54; Assisted Living Units 55; Total Staff 15.

GREENFIELD. *Clement Manor Health Center*, 3939 S. 92nd St., 53228. Tel: 414-321-1800; Fax: 414-546-7357. Web: www.clementmanor.com. Richard Rau, Pres. & CEO; Mr. Dennis Ferger, Admin.; Rev. Albert Lis, O.F.M., Chap. Sponsored by School Sisters of St. Francis., Corporate Title: Clement Manor, Inc. Residents 166; Adult Day Care 35; Child Day Care 30.

KENOSHA. *St. Joseph's Home for the Aged*, 9244 29th Ave., 53143. Tel: 262-694-0080; Fax: 262-694-7325. Email: asi@tds.net. Web: stjosephshome.com. Sisters Mary Emmanuel Apanites, D.C.J., Admin. Supr.; M. Jacinta Cusumano, D.C.J.; Rev. Anthony Jelinek. Corporate Title: Carmelite Sisters of the Divine Heart of Jesus; St. Joseph's Villa, Independent living units. Sisters 7; Bed

Capacity 93; Residents 93; Apartments 44; Adult Day Care 45; Total Assisted Annually 40; Total Staff 150.

MOUNT CALVARY. *Villa Loretto Nursing Home*, N8114 County WW, 53057. Tel: 920-753-3211; Fax: 920-753-3100. Email: sistertheresa@villalorettonh.org. Web: villalorettonh.org. Sr. Stephen Bloesl, Supr. Corporate Title: Sister Servants of Christ the King, Inc. dba Villa Loretto. Sisters 5; Bed Capacity 52; Total Assisted Annually 89; Total Staff 125.

Villa Rosa, Inc., N8120 County WW, 53057. Tel: 920-753-3015; Fax: 920-753-2508. Email: ckramer@villalorettonh.org; nunbetterfarm@villalorettonh.org. Web: villalorettonh.org. Sr. Stephen Bloesl, Pres.; Colleen Kramer, Dir. Bed Capacity 20; Total Assisted Annually 28; Total Staff 12.

RACINE. *Marian Housing Center, Inc.* (1985) 4105 Spring St., 53405. Tel: 262-633-5807; Fax: 262-633-9780. Web: www.wfhealthcare.org. Units 40; Total Staff 3; Residents 43.

St. Monica's Senior Citizens Home, Inc., 3920 N. Green Bay Rd., 53404. Tel: 262-639-5050; Fax: 262-639-5673. Email: sr.irene@sbcglobal.net. Sr. Irene Hanika, O.S.A., Supr. & Admin. Nonprofit Corp. Sisters of St. Rita 6; Bed Capacity 110; Residents 110; Total Assisted Annually 29,200; Total Staff 49.

SOUTH MILWAUKEE. *Franciscan Villa of South Milwaukee, Inc.* (1966) Residential Care Apartment Complex., 3601 S. Chicago Ave., 53172. Tel: 414-764-4100; Fax: 414-764-0706. Email: daninecasper@catholichealth.net. Web: www.franciscanvilla.org. Jamie Weibeler, Admin. & CEO. Catholic Health Initiatives Residents 150; Alzheimer's Assisted Living 64; Child Day Care 36; Franciscan Courts (Apartments) 39; Franciscan Garden (Apartments) 48; Total Staff 360.

WAUWATOSA. *St. Camillus Health Center, Inc.*, 10101 W. Wisconsin Ave., 53226. Tel: 414-258-1814; Fax: 414-259-4987. Email: rljohnson@stcam.com. Web: www.stcam.com. Very Rev. Richard O'Donnell, M.I., Prov.; Rev. Augustin Orosa, M.I., Chap.; Bro. Mario Crivello, M.I., Chap.; Rick Johnson, Pres. & CEO; Chris Winkowski, Chap. Order of the Servants of the Sick (Order of St. Camillus), Skilled Nursing Home and Assisted Living. Bed Capacity 217; Patients Assisted Annually 250; Total Staff 500.

[O] PERSONAL PRELATURES

BROOKFIELD. *Prelature of the Holy Cross and Opus Dei Layton Study Center*, 12900 W. North Ave., 53005. Tel: 262-784-1523; Fax: 262-782-5183. Email: info@opusdei.org. Revs. Timothy J. Uhen; John C. Kubeck.

[P] MONASTERIES AND RESIDENCES FOR PRIESTS AND BROTHERS

MILWAUKEE. *Alexian Brothers Community* (1980) Immaculate Conception Province, 8000 Limerick Rd., 53223-1072. Tel: 414-507-9157; Fax: 414-357-5290. Email: dmccormick@alexianbrothers.net. Web: www.alexianbrothers.net. Bros. John Grider, C.F.A.; Daniel McCormick, C.F.A.; Robert Petersen, C.F.A. Brothers 3.

Arrupe House Jesuit Community, 831 N. 13th St., 53233-1706. Tel: 414-288-5855; Fax: 414-288-5852. Revs. Peter J. Etzel, S.J.; Walter E. Boehme, S.J.; Patrick J. Burns, S.J.; D. Thomas Hughson, S.J.; Michael R. Kolb, S.J.; Very Rev. G. Thomas Krettek, S.J.; Revs. Thomas A. Lawler, S.J.; Eugene F. Merz, S.J.; John M. Paul, S.J., Min.; Cletus H. Pfab, S.J.; Philip J. Rossi, S.J.; Warren J. Sazama, S.J.; Thomas P. Sweetser, S.J.; John L. Treloar, S.J., Supr.; Matthew S. Walsh, S.J. Society of Jesus, Wisconsin Prov. Priests 15.

St. Camillus Provincialate, 3345 S. 10th St., 53215. Tel: 414-481-3696; Fax: 414-481-8044. Very Rev. Richard O'Donnell, M.I., Prov.; Revs. Bernard Blasich; Scott Binet, M.I., M.D.; Joseph L. Bisoffi, M.I., Prov. Counselor; Stephen Braddock; William Cronin, M.I.; Louis Lussier, M.I.; Carlo Notaro, M.I.; Augustin Orosa, M.I., Chap.; Albert Schempp, M.I., Chap. & Prov. Counselor. Provincial offices for the North American Province of the Order of the Servants of the Sick (Order of Saint Camillus) Priests 9.

St. Conrad Friary, 3138 N. 2nd St., 53212. Tel: 414-372-3620. Revs. Brian Braun, O.F.M.Cap.; Richard Hart, O.F.M.Cap.; William Hugo, O.F.M.Cap.; Niles J. Kauffman, O.F.M.Cap., M.A.; Randall Knauf, O.F.M.Cap; Martin Pable, O.F.M.Cap.; David Preuss, O.F.M.Cap.; Bros. Phillip Gardner, Postulant; Stephen Greco, Postulant; Michael Joseph Groark, Postulant; Craig McWade, Postulant. Capuchin Friars, Province of St. Joseph. Priests 7; Brothers 4; Total in Residence 11.

Jesuit Community at Marquette University, 1404 W. Wisconsin Ave., 53233. Tel: 414-288-5000; Fax: 414-288-1758. Revs. James P. Flaherty, S.J., Rector; Thomas S. Anderson, S.J.; John M. Belmonte, S.J.; Ronald Bieganowski, S.J.; Thaddeus J. Burch, S.J.; Thomas A. Caldwell, S.J.; Michael D. Class, S.J.; Martin-Claude Domfang, S.J.; J. Patrick Donnelly, S.J.; Robert M. Doran, S.J.; Eugene M. Dutkiewicz, S.J.; Robert L. Faricy, S.J.; John P. Fitzgibbons, S.J.; Gerald E. Goetz, S.J., Min.; G. Simon Harak, S.J.; Phillip R. Hurley, S.J.; Robert J. Joda, S.J.; William J. Kelly, S.J.; William J. Kidd, S.J.; James M. Kubicki, S.J.; William S. Kurz, S.J.; Jeffrey T. LaBelle, S.J.; John D. Laurance, S.J.; Douglas J. Leonhardt, S.J.; Robert W. Leiweke, S.J.; Frank A. Majka, S.J.; Thomas C. Manahan, S.J.; D. Edward Mathie, S.J.; Donald R. Matthys, S.J.; James E. Mauel, S.J.; Richard A. McGarrity, S.J.; Jose Moreno, S.J.; Joseph G. Mueller, S.J.; Patrick Mulemi, S.J.; James J. O'Leary, S.J.; Gregory J. O'Meara, S.J.; Nicholas F. Pope, S.J.; Francis Paul Prucha, S.J.; Luis Rodriguez, S.J.; Thomas N. Schloemer, S.J.; David G. Schultenover, S.J.; David M. Shields, S.J.; Walter J. Stohrer, S.J.; Roland J. Teske, S.J.; Andrew J. Thon, S.J.; Richard A. Tomasek, S.J.; Karl D. Voelker, S.J.; James B. Warosh, S.J.; Robert A. Wild, S.J.; Frederick P. Zagone, S.J.; Michael J. Zeps, S.J.; Mr. Charles T. Olsen, SJ. Marquette Jesuit Associates, Inc. Priests 51; Scholastics 1.

Jesuit Provincial Office, Wisconsin Province, P.O. Box 080288, 53208-0288. Tel: 414-937-6949; Fax: 414-937-6950. Email: wisprov@jesuitswisprov.org. Web: www.jesuitswisprov.org. Very Rev. G. Thomas Krettek, S.J., Prov.; Revs. Patrick J. Burns, S.J., Dir. Planning & Implementation for Prov. Reconfiguration; Eugene M. Dutkiewicz, S.J., Asst. for Finance & Treas.; James J. Gladstone, S.J., Asst. for Personnel; Thomas A. Lawler, S.J., Vocation Dir.; Frank A. Majka, S.J., Asst. for Secondary Educ.; Richard A. McGarrity, S.J., Special Asst. Devel.; John M. Paul, S.J., Dir. Formation; Luis Rodriguez, S.J., Asst. Prov. & Asst. for Pastoral Ministries; John L. Treloar, S.J., Asst. for Higher Educ. & Prov. Delegate for Conduct in Ministry. Corporate Title: Wisconsin Province of the Society of Jesus. Priests 10.

Priests of the Province Serving Abroad: Revs. Frederick E. Brenk, S.J., Rome, Italy; James E. Grummer, S.J., Rome, Italy; Jonathan Haschka, S.J., Mwanza, Tanzania; John D. Mace, S.J., Dili, Timor-Leste; Daniel C. McDonald, S.J., Rome, Italy; John R. Schak, S.J., Salta, Argentina; Nicholas E. Schiel, S.J., Olancho, Honduras; James J. Strzok, S.J., Karen, Kenya; Anthony J. Wach, S.J., Kampala, Uganda; Christopher J. Krall, S.J., Toronto, Ontario.

Members of the Province Not Otherwise Listed: Revs. Joseph A. Brown, S.J.; Charles F. Burns, S.J., San Diego, CA; William J. Ellos, S.J., San Antonio, TX; Jeffrey R. Loebl, S.J., Milwaukee, WI; Patrick L. Murphy, S.J., Cape Canaveral, FL; James M. Radde, S.J., St. Paul, MN; Gregory A. Schissel, S.J., Dittmer, MO; Bro. Gerald E. Peltz, S.J.; Mr. Andrew M. Jaspers, S.J.

La Salette Fathers Missionaries of Our Lady of La Salette, 1607 E. Howard Ave., 53207. Tel: 414-769-7113; Fax: 414-769-1057. Bro. Gerald Buraczewski, M.S. Brothers 1; Total in Residence 1.

Pallotti House, 5424 W. Bluemound Rd., 53208. Tel: 414-258-0653; Fax: 414-258-9314. Email: pallotti_milw@yahoo.com. Web: www.pallottines.org. Revs. Joseph Dominic, S.A.C. (India); Davis Edassery, S.A.C. (India); Joseph Dominic Elukunnel, S.A.C. (India); Jose Eluvathingal, S.A.C. (India); Jerome A. Hapka, S.A.C.; Stephen Kaichiramattathil, S.A.C. (India); Joseph Koyickal, S.A.C. (India); Thomas Kuttiyanickal, S.A.C. (India); Sergio Lizama, S.A.C.; Very Rev. Leon J. Martin, S.A.C., Prov. Supr.; Revs. James Palakudy, S.A.C. (India); John R. Scheer, S.A.C.; Bruce J. Schute, S.A.C.; Gregory P. Serwa, S.A.C.; Thunkuchan Steve Varghese, S.A.C. (India); Bro. James Scarpace, S.A.C., Coord. Residence of Fathers and Brothers and Offices of Mother of God Province of the Society of the Catholic Apostolate also, Formation House: Novitiate. Priests 12; Brothers 1.

Pere Marquette Jesuit Community, 726 N. 34th. St., 53208-3301. Tel: 414-342-7503; Fax: 414-937-8588. Revs. Mark A. Carr, S.J., Supr.; Terrence M. Brennan, S.J.; Charles L. Stang, S.J.; Mr. Paul J. Shelton, S.J. Society of Jesus, Wisconsin Province. Priests 3; Scholastics 1.

Provincial Offices - Discalced Carmelites (1947) 1233 S. 45th St., 53214-3693. Tel: 414-672-7212; Fax: 414-672-3138. Email: projjs@gmail.com. Web: www.ocdwashprov.com. Very Rev. John Sullivan, O.C.D., Prov.; Sr. Beth Lyman, S.S.S.F., Prov. Admin. Asst. Priests 19; Brothers 3.

Serving Abroad: Revs. Arnold Boehme, O.C.D. (Philippines), Parish Priest; Reginald Foster, O.C.D., Chief Latinist for Vatican, Rome; Dennis Geng, O.C.D. (Kenya), Treas., Formation Team; Thomas Martin, O.C.D., Formation Team, Retreats, Philippines; Ignacio Read, O.C.D., Novice Formation Team, Philippines; Alan J. Rieger, O.C.D., Local Supr. & Spirituality Ctr., Philippines; Eugene C. Wehner, O.C.D. (Kenya), Community Svc. Librarian.

Priests of the Province Not Otherwise Listed: Most Rev. Julio Labayen, O.C.D. (Philippines) (Retired); Revs. Joseph Okanda Abwanda, O.C.D. (Kenya), Local Supr., Tindinyo; Nicholas Olonde Adongo, O.C.D. (Kenya), Community Svc. Chaplain Kisii nuns & priest at outstation.; Joseph Uri Baru, O.C.D. (Kenya), Graduate Studies, Rome, Italy.; Lawrence Daniels, O.C.D. (Uganda); Michael Dodd, O.C.D.; Santulino Ekada, O.C.D. (Kenya), Parish Priest, Tindinyo; Fred Hickey, O.C.D.; Jose Maria Lopez, O.C.D. (Philippines); Jacob Mugo Mbiti, O.C.D. (Kenya), Dir. Retreat House; Raymond Achuka Onsongo, O.C.D. (Kenya), (Kisii); Richard Opendi, O.C.D. (Kenya), Vocation Dir.; Steven Payne, O.C.D. (Kenya), Formation Team & Dir. ISRF; Abednecco Wambua Peter, O.C.D. (Kenya), Asst. Parish Priest, Tindinyo; Very Rev. Phillip Thomas, O.C.D., Rector & Supr.; Rev. Bernard Ybiernas, O.C.D. (Philippines); Bros. Daniel Mutuku Ngwili, O.C.D. (Kenya); Sebastian Reale, O.C.D.

Salvatorian Provincial Offices, 1735 N. Hi-Mount Blvd., 53208-1720. Tel: 414-258-1735; Fax: 414-258-1934. Email: sds@salvatorians.com. Web: salvatorians.com. Society of the Divine Savior.

Provincial Council: Revs. David Bergner, S.D.S., Prov.; Jeffrey Wocken, S.D.S., Vicar Prov.; Robert Marsicek, S.D.S., Consultor; Michael Newman, Consultor (Retired); Scott Wallenfelsz, S.D.S., International Dir. Finance; Bro. Sean McLaughlin, S.D.S., Consultor.

Priests in Residence: Rev. Daniel Pekarske, S.D.S., Ph.D.

Priests at Residences Not Listed Elsewhere: Revs. Keith Brennan, S.D.S. (Retired); Bruce Brentrup, S.D.S.; James Bretl, S.D.S. (Retired), 503 Mullican St., Mc Minnville, TN 37110. Tel: 931-507-3223; Paul Brick, S.D.S. (Retired), 727 Third Ave., Columbus, GA 31901-2957. Tel: 706-494-2675; Bruce Clanton, S.D.S., P.O. Box 574, Racine, 53401-0574. Tel: 262-880-5047; Peter Coffey, S.D.S. (Retired), 14832 60th Ave., Flushing, NY 11355. Tel: 718-463-2416; Cyril Dickrell, S.D.S. (Retired), W2754 St. Charles Rd., Chilton, 53014-9625. Tel: 920-849-4175; John E. Gorman, S.D.S., 10900 Coastal Hwy., Apt. 904, Ocean City, MD 21842. Tel: 410-524-1701; Julian Guzman, S.D.S.; Michael Henseler, S.D.S.; Michael Hoffman, S.D.S., Asst. Archivist, 7811 W. Center St., 53222-4920; Lloyd Kramlich, S.D.S.; Karl LeClaire, S.D.S.; Richard Maloney, S.D.S., P.O. Box 191, Fort Ashby, WV 26719; Roman Stadtmueller, S.D.S.; Joseph Wambach, S.D.S., 995 E. Baseline Rd. #1086, Tempe, AZ 85283-1333. Tel: 480-777-7686; Jude Weisenbeck, S.D.S. (Retired), 4325 Fireclay Ct., Apt. 3, La Crosse, 54601-2325. Tel: 608-788-2621.

7100 W. Old Loomis Rd., Greendale, 53129-2761. Tel: 414-427-8352. Revs. Hugh G. Birdsall, S.D.S., M.A., M.S., 7100 W. Old Loomis Rd., Greendale, 53129-2761. Tel: 414-427-8352; Scott Jones, S.D.S., Dir. Vocations, 2255 W. Orange Grove, Apt. 9201, Tucson, AZ 85741-3156. Tel: 520-623-2563; Andre Papineau, S.D.S., M.A.; Thomas Tureman, S.D.S., Dir. Missions. Society of the Divine Savior. Priests 4.

Priests of the USA Province serving at the Generalate in Rome, Italy: Very Rev. Paul Portland, S.D.S., Generalate. *St. Joseph's Salvatorian Community (Novitiate)*, 3221-C S. Lake Dr., St. Francis, 53235-3702. Tel: 414-744-2402. Revs. Joseph Lubrano, S.D.S., Dir. Novices; Thomas Perrin, S.D.S. *Salvatorian Formation House*, 9077 S. 49 St., Franklin, 53132-7606. Tel: 414-235-4395. Revs. John Vianney Muweesi, S.D.S.; Raul Gomez Ruiz, S.D.S.

Salvatorians - Jordan Hall, 7979 W. Glenbrook Rd., 53223-1055. Bro. John Hauenstein, S.D.S., Coord.; Revs. David Brusky, S.D.S. (Retired); Neil Durham, S.D.S. (Retired); Cletus LaMere, S.D.S. (Retired); Thomas Novak, S.D.S.; Eric Middlecamp, S.D.S. (Retired); Patrick Ritter, S.D.S. (Retired); Robert Wagner, S.D.S. (Retired); Bros. George Armstrong, S.D.S., (Retired); Paul Bauer, S.D.S., (Retired); Nicholas Crosby, S.D.S., (Retired); Andre Duhaime, S.D.S., (Retired); Bertrand Hanf, S.D.S., (Retired); John Rice, S.D.S. Fathers & Brothers of the Society of the Divine Savior. Priests 7; Brothers 7.

SCJ Community (1979) 937 N. 37th St., 53208. Tel: 414-344-0710; Fax: 414-937-6665. Revs. Charles

Brown, S.C.J., Ph.D.; Thomas Cassidy, S.C.J.; Paul Kelly, S.C.J.; John Klingler, S.C.J.; Robert Naglich, S.C.J.; Thi Pham, S.C.J.; Yvon Sheehy, S.C.J.; Francis Vu Tran, S.C.J.; Mark Mastin, S.C.J.; Bro. Frank Presto, S.C.J.; Deacon David Nagel, Treas. Priests of the Sacred Heart. Priests 9; Brothers 1; Deacons 1.

St. Vincent Community, 145 S. 76th St., 53214. Tel: 414-476-2447. Email: pallotti_milw@yahoo.com. Web: www.pallottines.org. Revs. John R. Scheer, S.A.C., Rector; Eugene H. Jarosch, S.A.C.; Richard J. Lorenz, S.A.C. Priests 3.

BENET LAKE. *St. Benedict's Abbey* (1945) 12605 224th Ave., 53102. Tel: 262-396-4311; Fax: 262-396-4365. Email: benedictines@msn.com. Web: www.BenetLake.org. Rt. Revs. Edmund J. Boyce, O.S.B., Abbot; Andrew V. Garber, O.S.B., Resigned Abbot, Prior; Robert C. Schoofs, O.S.B., Resigned Abbot; Leo M. Ryska, O.S.B., Resigned Abbot; Very Rev. Henry V. Nurre, O.S.B., Sub-Prior; Revs. Lawrence L. Fedor, O.S.B.; Donald J. Gibbs, O.S.B.; Kevin J. Murphy, O.S.B.; Stephen E. Lattner, O.S.B. Priests 9; Brothers 11.

BURLINGTON. *St. Francis Friary, St. Francis Center*, 2457 Browns Lake Dr., 53105. Tel: 262-763-3600. In Res. Bro. Michael Kulan, O.F.M.

Queen of Peace Friary, 2281 Browns Lake Dr., 53105. Tel: 262-763-3241; Fax: 262-763-3326. Revs. Thomas Kamenski, O.F.M.; Felix Reczek, O.F.M.; Vianney Sipulski, O.F.M.; DePaul Sobotka, O.F.M.; Louis Stislow, O.F.M.; Howard Stunek, O.F.M.; Richard Tulko, O.F.M.; Rudolph Wieszczek, O.F.M.; Raymond Zsolczai; Bros. David Dodge, O.F.M.; Gregory Havel, O.F.M.; Joseph Krymkowski, O.F.M.; Michael Kulan, O.F.M.; Edward Makowiecki, O.F.M.; Andrew Martino, O.F.M.; Michael May, O.F.M., Guardian. Franciscan Friars of the Assumption B.V.M. Province., Retirement Home for Franciscan Friars Priests 10; Brothers 7.

EAST TROY. *Divine Word Missionaries* (1875) Box 107, 53120-0107. Tel: 262-642-3300; Fax: 262-642-7754. Email: edpekco@aol.com. Revs. Andrew Biller, S.V.D. (Retired); John F. Fincutter, S.V.D. (Retired); Patrick Fincutter, S.V.D. (Retired); Lucien Gaudreault, S.V.D.; Charles Heskamp, S.V.D. (Retired); Vincent Ohlinger, S.V.D.; Edward Peklo, S.V.D., Rector; Bro. Bernard Scherger, S.V.D. Society of the Divine Word. Priests 7; Brothers 1; Total in Residence 8.

FRANKLIN. *Dehon Study Center* (1993) 10731 W. Rawson Ave., 53132. Tel: 414-425-3768; Fax: 414-425-8768. Email: mcguirescj@aol.com. Web: www.scj.org. Rev. Paul J. McGuire, S.C.J. Priests of the Sacred Heart.

Francis and Clare Friary (2002) 9230 W. Highland Park Ave., 53132. Tel: 414-525-9253; Fax: 414-525-9289. Email: province@ofm-abvm.org. Web: www.franciscan-friars.org. *Provincial Offices of the Franciscan Friars, Assumption BVM Province, Inc.* (2002) Tel: 414-525-9253; Fax: 414-525-9289. Email: province@ofm-abvm.org. Revs. John Cella, O.F.M., J.C.D., M.Div., M.B.A., Dir., Franciscan Pilgrimage Programs, Inc.; Leslie Hoppe, O.F.M., Prov. Min.; Roch Niemier, O.F.M., Prov. Spiritual Asst. of SFO; John Puodziunas, O.F.M., Prov. Vicar; Paul Reczek, O.F.M., Communications Dir.; Michael Weldon, O.F.M., Faculty, Sacred Heart Seminary, Hales Corners; Bros. Regis Howitz, O.F.M.; Patrick McCormack, O.F.M., Devel. Office. Priests 7; Brothers 3.

St. Francis Residence (1985) 12001 W. Woods Rd., 53132. Tel: 414-529-0332; Fax: 414-529-8777. Revs. Byron Haaland, S.C.J.; Paul J. McGuire, S.C.J.; Anthony P. Russo, S.C.J.; Bros. Andrew Lewandowski, S.C.J.; John Monek, S.C.J. Priests 3; Brothers 2.

Villa Maria (1989) 7330 S. Lovers Lane Rd., 53132. Tel: 414-425-5968; 414-425-5981; Fax: 414-425-0268. Web: www.scj.org. Most Rev. Joseph James Potocnak, S.C.I. (Retired); Revs. Donald Barnd, S.C.J.; James D. Brackin, S.C.J., M.Div., J.D., Local Coord. & Dir. Elder Svcs.; Michael Burke, S.C.J.; Paul Casper, S.C.J.; Edward Griesemer, S.C.J.; Patrick Lloyd, S.C.J.; Lawrence Rucker, S.C.J.; Michael van der Peet, S.C.J., M.A., M.Div.; Thomas Westhoven, S.C.J.; Stephen Wiese, S.C.J.; Bros. Matthew Miles, S.C.J.; Lawrence Gauthier, S.C.J. Bishops 1; Priests 13; Brothers 2.
Attached to the Community But Living Elsewhere: Revs. Joseph Gole, S.T.D. (Slovenia); Vincent MacDonald, S.C.J., The Congregational Home, 3150 Lilly Rd., Brookfield, 53005; Richard Zelonis, S.C.J., The Congregational Home, 3150 Lilly Rd., Brookfield, 53005.

HALES CORNERS. *Priests of the Sacred Heart* (1933) 7373 S. Lovers Lane Rd., P.O. Box 289, 53130-0289. Tel: 414-425-6910; Fax: 414-425-2938. Email: provsec@poshusa.org. Web: www.scjusa.net. Revs. Thomas Cassidy, S.C.J., Prov. Supr.; James D. Brackin, S.C.J., M.Div., J.D., Dir. Senior Life; Joseph Dean, S.C.J., Dir. Admissions; Mark Mastin, S.C.J., Dir. Justice & Peace; Thi Pham, S.C.J., Dir. Vocations; Yvon Sheehy, S.C.J., Dir. Formation; Francis Vu Tran, S.C.J., Dir. Missions; Bro. Frank Presto, S.C.J., Prov. Sec.
Priests of the Province Serving Abroad: Most Rev. Evert Baaij, S.C.J., Upper Dickens Nazareth, N. Mandela Metlo 6001 South Africa. Tel: 27-41-373-4734; Fax: 27-41-373-6141.
Attached to the Province but Living Elsewhere: Revs. Jerome Clifford, S.C.J., 5463 Dempsey, Saint Louis, MO 63110. Tel: 314-771-5867; Bryan Benoit, S.C.J., P.O. Box 220, Dittmer, MO 63023. Tel: 636-285-1733; Michael McMillen, S.C.J., 5728 N. Talman, Chicago, IL 60659. Tel: 773-944-5448; James Schroeder, S.C.J., 5375 Kenrick Parke Dr. N. #305, St. Louis, MO 63119. Tel: 314-968-3765; Fax: 314-647-3688; Bro. Bernard Taube, S.C.J., 2833 Moland St., #3, Madison, 53704; Rev. David Szatkowski, S.C.J., Via Casale S. Pio V 20, Rome 00165 Italy. Tel: 011-39-06-660-560.

Sacred Heart Monastery (1929) 7335 S. Lovers Ln. Rd., P.O. Box 566, 53130. Tel: 414-425-8300; Fax: 414-529-6988. Email: preid@shst.edu. Web: www.scj.org. *Priests of the Sacred Heart*, 7335 S. Lovers Ln. Rd., P.O. Box 566, 53130-0566. Tel: 414-425-5323; Fax: 414-529-6988. Revs. Charles Bisgrove, S.C.J.; Jan de Jong, S.C.J., S.T.D., S.T.L.; Paul Grizzelle-Reid, S.C.J., M.S., M.Div.; Wayne Jenkins, S.C.J.; James Schifano, S.C.J; James Walters, S.C.J., M.S., M.Div.; Charles Wonch, S.C.J.; Bros. Raymond Kozuch, S.C.J.; Long Nguyen, S.C.J. Priests 7; Brothers 2.

HOLY HILL. *Discalced Carmelite Monastery - Holy Hill Basilica of the National Shrine of Mary, Help of Christians, Holy Hill* (Shrine 1863) (Carmelite Friars 1906) Mailing Address: 1525 Carmel Rd., Holy Hill, Hubertus, 53033. Tel: 262-628-1838; Fax: 262-628-0170. Email: juderj@juno.com. Web: www.holyhill.com. Revs. Fred Alexander, O.C.D., Pastor, St. Mary of the Hill; Emmanuel Bettaso, O.C.D., Mission Procurator; Donald Brick, O.C.D., Rector, First Councilor; Patrick J. Farrell, O.C.D.; Michael Griffin, O.C.D.; Cyril Guise, O.C.D., Dir. Devel.; Jude Peters, O.C.D., Prior; Redemptus Short, O.C.D. (Retired); Ernest Unverdorben, O.C.D., Prov. Treas.; Bros. Martin Murphy, O.C.D.; Frank Salamone, O.C.D. Priests 12; Brothers 2. *Retreat Center*, 1525 Carmel Rd., Hubertus, 53033. Tel: 262-628-1838, Ext. 127; Fax: 262-628-4294. Email: karengirard@holyhill.com. Web: www.holyhill.com. Revs. John Grennon, O.C.D., Provincial Delegate to O.C.D's; Daniel Thomas McCauley, O.C.D. (Retired); Matthias Montgomery, O.C.D., Novice Master.

KENOSHA. *Missionary Congregation of the Blessed Sacrament, Inc., Zion Province*, 5804 Sheridan Rd., 53140. Tel: 262-658-8071; Fax: 262-658-2490. Email: thomasd@archmil.org. Revs. Abraham Karott, M.C.B.S., Member; Joseph Mulangattil, M.C.B.S., Member; Joseph Pottenparambil, Member; Dominic Thomas, M.C.B.S., Contact Person; Thomas Vathappallil, M.C.B.S., Member.

MOUNT CALVARY. *St. Felix Friary*, N8477 County Rd. WW, 53057. Tel: 920-753-3111; Fax: 920-753-2306. Email: froliver@stlawrence.edu. Revs. Oliver Bambenek, O.F.M.Cap.; Garret Keegstra, O.F.M.Cap. Priests 2.

St. Lawrence Friary (1856) 301 Church St., 53057. Tel: 920-753-7500; Fax: 920-753-7507. Email: frwerner@stlawrence.edu. Web: stlawrence.edu. Revs. Campion Baer, O.F.M.Cap., Teacher; Dennis Druggan, O.F.M.Cap., Rector & Teacher; Jerome Higgins, O.F.M.Cap., M.Ed., M.A.S., D.Min., Sisters Chap. & Spiritual Dir. (Retired); Ronald Jansch, O.F.M.Cap. (Retired); Elroy Pesch, O.F.M.Cap. (Retired); Kenan Siegel, O.F.M.Cap. (Retired); Ken Smits, O.F.M.Cap., Chap.; Joachim Strupp, O.F.M.Cap., Sisters' Chap. (Retired); Vernon Wagner, O.F.M.Cap. (Retired); Gary Wegner, O.F.M.Cap., Teacher & Dean of Students; Eugene Wolf, O.F.M.Cap. (Retired); Joseph Wolf, O.F.M.Cap., Chap. St. Francis Home (Retired); Werner Wolf, O.F.M.Cap., Local Minister; Paul Yaroch, O.F.M.Cap., Chap. St. Joseph Convent, Campbellsport (Retired); Michael Zuelke, O.F.M.Cap.; Bros. Douglas Bode, O.F.M.Cap., Prof. of Theology; Jerome Campbell, O.F.M.Cap., Maintenance Personnel; Lawrence Groeschel, O.F.M.Cap; Ron Smith, O.F.M.Cap. Priests 13; Brothers 7. Supervisory Seminary Staff: Bros. Neal Plale, O.F.M.Cap., Prof. of Theology; Carl Schaefer, O.F.M.Cap., Spiritual Dir.; John Scherer, O.F.M.Cap., Vicar, Teacher; John Willger, O.F.M.Cap., Teacher.

RACINE. *Augustinian Novitiate*, 4335 Douglas Ave., 53402-2956. Tel: 262-681-3221; Fax: 262-681-0628. Revs. Edward J. Kersten, O.S.A., Prior; Gerald A. Nicholas, O.S.A., Novice Dir. Priests 2; Novices 4.

TWIN LAKES. *La Salette Missionaries* (1967) 10330-336th Ave., Box 777, 53181. Tel: 262-877-3111. Web: www.lasaletteshrine.org. Revs. Gerald Lebanowski, M.S., Dir.; James Stajkowski, M.S.; Bros. Adam Mateja, M.S.; Anthony Sepanik, M.S. Priests 2; Brothers 2.

WAUWATOSA. *Jesuit Community at St. Camillus*, 10100 W. Bluemound Rd., 53226-4377. Tel: 414-259-3731 (nurse manager); Fax: 414-259-4950. Revs. James J. Gladstone, S.J., Supr.; Anthony L. Dagelen, S.J., Asst. Supr.; Richard H. Ahler, S.J.; William J. Brennan, S.J.; Robert E. Brodzeller, S.J.; Joseph F. Eagan, S.J.; Harry S. Eglsaer, S.J.; Robert H. Fitzgerald, S.J.; James E. Fitzgerald, S.J.; Joseph C. Gill, S.J.; J. Cletus Healy, S.J.; John A. Hennessy, S.J.; Robert E. Hoene, S.J.; William M. Kegel, S.J.; Daniel J. Kenney, S.J.; William T. Kolarec, S.J.; Michael D. Kurimay, S.J.; Robert W. Lambeck, S.J.; John J. Lynch, S.J.; William L. Mugan, S.J.; John E. Naus, S.J.; Joseph N. Pershe, S.J.; John H. Rainaldo, S.J.; Leon S. Rausch, S.J., Min.; Gerald T. Regan, S.J.; Aloysius F. Schmitz, S.J.; Richard F. Sherburne, S.J.; Paul B. Steinmetz, S.J.; William J. Sullivan, S.J.; Kenneth T. Walleman, S.J.; John W. Wambach, S.J.; Bros. James F. Becwar, S.J.; William E. Biernatzki, S.J. Society of Jesus, Wisconsin Province. Priests 31; Brothers 2.

[Q] CONVENTS AND RESIDENCES FOR SISTERS

MILWAUKEE. *Ancilla Convent* Inter-Community living for religious women.
3601 S. 41st St., 53221. Tel: 414-384-6535. Sr. Barbarina Jantsch, S.S.S.F., Dir. Sisters 20.

St. Clare Convent, 3276 S. 16th St., 53215. Tel: 414-647-2437. Email: stclaremil@wi.rr.com. Sr. M. Samuel Holowacz, Local Min. Felician Sisters. Sisters 4.

Dominican Sisters of the Perpetual Rosary (1897) 217 N. 68th St., 53213. Tel: 414-258-0579; Fax: 414-258-8831. Email: frannl@wi.rr.com; domsisters@wi.rr.com. Web: www.op-milwaukee.org. Sr. Miriam Leonard, O.P., Prioress. Cloistered Dominican Sisters of the Perpetual Rosary. Professed Sisters 9.

St. Felix Convent, 3159 S. 17th St., 53215. Tel: 414-389-9803. Sr. Michelle Marie Konieczny, Local Min. Felician Sisters. Sisters 3.

St. Francis Convent, 3170 S. 17th St., 53215. Tel: 414-643-6387; Fax: 414-647-5372. Email: beatricecssf@hotmail.com. Sr. M. Beatrice Knipple, Local Min. Felician Sisters. Sisters 5.

St. Joseph Convent, General Motherhouse of the School Sisters of St. Francis (1874) 1501 S. Layton Blvd., 53215. Tel: 414-384-4105; Fax: 414-944-6060. Email: generalate@sssf.org. Web: www.sssf.org. Sisters Kathleen Kluthe, O.S.F., Pres.; Patricia Baier, 1st Vice Pres.; Arlene Woelfel, O.S.F., Vice Pres.; Rita Eble, O.S.F, Vice Pres.; Barbara Kraemer, O.S.F., Prov.
School Sisters of St. Francis, Inc. Sisters 56; Total in Congregation 1,036.

Mercedes Molina - Instituto Santa Mariana de Jesus, 1234 N. 24th Pl., 53205. Tel: 414-931-7163. Email: cardeanda@hotmail.com. Sr. Maria del Carmen de Anda, R.M., Supr. Corporate Title: Mercedes Molina, Inc. Sisters 4.

Sacred Heart Center, 1545 S. Layton Blvd., 53215. Tel: 414-383-9038; Fax: 414-647-4889. S. Joann Riesterer, O.S.F., Coord. of Health & Housing Svcs.; Sisters Therese Thoenen, O.S.F., Coord. Sisters Living Group; Marcian Swanson, Facility Dir. Home for retired and infirm School Sisters of St. Francis Sisters 50.

San Damiano Convent (2000) 2008 E. Euclid Ave., 53207. Tel: 414-489-9195; Fax: 414-483-5861. Email: smramona@fs-inc.net. Sr. Mary Ramona Dombrowski, C.S.S.F., Local Min. Felician Sisters 3.

Sisters of Charity of St. Joan Antida Convent (Presentation), 1329 N. Cass St., 53202. Tel: 414-276-4173. Email: present@scsja.org. Sr. Elizabeth A. Weber, S.C.S.J.A., Supr. Sisters 7.

Sisters of Charity of St. Joan Antida Convent (St. Charles Community), 3214 W. Parnell Ave., 53221. Tel: 414-282-9627. Email: stchas@scsja.org. Sr. Monica Fumo, S.C.S.J.A., Supr. Sisters 8.

Sisters of Charity of St. Joan Antida Regina Mundi Provincial House and Novitiate, 8560 N. 76th Pl., 53223. Tel: 414-354-9233; Fax: 414-355-6463. Email: sisters@scsja.org. Web: www.scsja.org. Sr. Anne Marie Baemmert, S.C.S.J.A., Prov. Sisters 5; Total in Community 35.

Sisters of the Divine Savior (1888) 4311 N. 100th St., 53222-1393. Tel: 414-466-0810; Fax: 414-466-4335. Email: smithb@salvatoriansisters.org. Web: www.sdssisters.org. Provincial Administration
Provincial Team: Corporate Title: Sisters of the Divine Savior, Inc. Sisters Carol Thresher, S.D.S., Prov. Leader; Patricia Colletti, S.D.S., Vicaress; Ellen Sinclair, S.D.S., Treas.

Salvatorian Sisters Residence (2001) 3810 N. 92nd St., 53222. Tel: 414-760-7900; Fax: 414-358-9906. Sr. Virginia Honish, S.D.S., Coord. Sisters 24.

United States Province, 1515 S. Layton Blvd., 53215. Tel: 414-384-1515; Fax: 414-384-1950. Email: info@sssf.org. Web: www.sssf.org. Sisters Barbara Kraemer, O.S.F., Prov. Team; Elizabeth Heese, O.S.F., Prov. Team; Maureen McCarthy, O.S.F., Prov. Team. School Sisters of St. Francis, Corporate Title: The School Sisters of St. Francis of St. Joseph's Convent, Milwaukee, Wisconsin, Inc.; Corporate Title: Congregational Support Charitable Trust. Total in U.S. Province 619.

BROWN DEER. *Sisters of the Sorrowful Mother-Generalate, Inc.* (1980) 9056 N. Deerbrook Tr., 53223-2474. Tel: 414-357-8940; Fax: 414-357-8950. Web: www.ave-mater-dolorosa.org. Sr. M. Teresina Marra, Gen. Supr.

BURLINGTON. *Misioneras Franciscanas de la Juventud, Inc.*, 456 Kendall St., 53105. Tel: 262-767-0796. Email: emtenu@yahoo.com. Sr. Emma Teresa, M.F.J., Contact Person.

Missionary Sisters of the Holy Family, 31144 Hunters Tr., 53105. Tel: 262-514-2076. Email: misifab@wi.rr.com. Sr. Joanna Barbara Kacka, M.S.F., Supr. Total in Community 7.

CAMPBELLSPORT. *St. Joseph Convent*, 526 Mill St., 53010. Tel: 920-533-1100; Fax: 920-533-1145. Michael Kurtz, Facility Dir.; Sisters Marilita Lorenz, Living Group Coord.; Charlotte Schuele, O.S.F., Dir. Pastoral Svcs. School Sisters of St. Francis, Retirement Home/Health Care Center. Sisters 149.

CEDAR GROVE. *Sacred Heart of the Lake Chalet*, Box 46A, 53013. Tel: 262-285-3084. *St. Mary's Home*, 2005 Division St., Manitowoc, 54220. Sr. Mary Odelle Sisoski, Contact Person. Recreation Home for Felician Sisters of the Mother of Good Counsel Province.

DELAVAN. *Villa Celine*, 3127 S. Shore Dr., 53115. Tel: 773-792-6363; Fax: 773-792-9590. Sr. Virginia Ann Wanzer, C.R., Prov. Supr. & Contact Person. Summer Rest Home for Sisters of the Resurrection.

ELM GROVE. *Notre Dame of Elm Grove*, 13105 Watertown Plank Rd., 53122-2291. Tel: 262-782-1450; Fax: 262-782-2349. Email: mkuczynski@ssnd-milw.org. Web: www.ssnd-milw.org. Sr. Marie Estelle Kuczynski, S.S.N.D., Admin. Leader. The School Sisters of Notre Dame, Milwaukee Province, Inc., S.S.N.D. Assisted Care, Independent Living. Total in Residence 147; Total Staff 120.

School Sisters of Notre Dame, Provincial Offices, 13105 Watertown Plank Rd., 53122-2291. Tel: 262-782-9850; Fax: 262-782-5725. Email: dsciano@ssnd-milw.org. Web: www.ssnd-milw.org. Sr. Debra Marie Sciano, S.S.N.D., Prov. Leader.

School Sisters of Notre Dame, Milwaukee Province, Inc.

School Sisters of Notre Dame at Milwaukee, Wisconsin, Inc. Charitable Trust Total in Milwaukee Province 387; Total Staff 34.

School Sisters of Notre Dame of North America, Inc., c/o NAMA Coordinating Center, 13105 Watertown Plank Rd., 53122-2291. Tel: 262-207-0047; Fax: 262-754-4878. Email: pmurphy@ssnd.org. Sr. Patricia Murphy, S.S.N.D., Dir.

FOND DU LAC. *Nazareth Center-Nazareth Court* (1998) 375 Gillett St., 54935. Tel: 920-923-7993; Fax: 920-926-6200. Email: jmeyercsa@gmail.com. Douglas Trost, Admin. Retirement Home of the Congregation of Sisters of St. Agnes., Retirement Home of the Congregation of Sisters of St. Agnes Sisters 51.

St. Agnes Convent (1858) Motherhouse, 320 County Rd. K, 54937-8158. Tel: 920-907-2300; Fax: 920-923-3194. Web: www.csasisters.org. Sr. Joann Sambs, C.S.A., Gen. Supr.

Congregation of Sisters of St. Agnes of Fond du Lac, Wisconsin, Inc. Sisters 26; Total in Community 27.

KENOSHA. *Dominican Sisters of St. Catherine of Siena, Inc.* (1952) P.O. Box 1288, 53141-1288. Tel: 262-694-2067; Fax: 262-694-6542. Email: kenoshaop@aol.com. Sr. Susan Anne Snyder, O.P., Prioress. Dominican Sisters of St. Catherine of Siena of Kenosha, WI. Total Religious in Community 8.

MEQUON. *Sisters of the Sorrowful Mother, Novitiate House*, 4823 W. Bonniwell Rd., 53097-2202. Tel: 262-242-5770; Fax: 262-236-0174. Email: ssmfarm@aol.com. Web: ssmfranciscans.org. Sisters 3.

MOUNT CALVARY. *Loretto Convent*, N8114 County WW, 53057. Tel: 920-753-3211; Fax: 920-753-3100. Email: sistertheresa@villalorettonh.org. Web: villalorettonh.org. General Motherhouse of Sister-Servants of Christ the King; Corporate Title: Congregation of Sister Servants of Christ the King, Inc. Sisters 7.

Our Lady of Mt. Carmel Convent 53057. Tel: 920-753-2131; 920-753-2036; Fax: 920-753-2116. Email: mbauer@ssnd-milw.org. Sr. Maxine Bauer, S.S.N.D., Leadership. Home for Retired Sisters. School Sisters of Notre Dame 27.

OCONOMOWOC. *St. Joseph Convent*, 2653 Mill Rd., 53066. Tel: 414-646-2707. Sr. M. Margaret Narloch, C.S.S.F., Local Min. Sponsored by the Congregation of the Sisters of St. Felix of Cantalice of the United States of America, Inc. Chicago Province. Sisters 2.

PEWAUKEE. *Carmel of the Mother of God* (1940) W267 N2517 Meadowbrook Rd., 53072-4528. Tel: 262-691-0336; Fax: 262-695-0143. Email: pewaukeecarmel@aol.com. Web: www.pewaukeecarmel.com. Sr. Mary Agnes Kramer, O.C.D., Prioress; Rev. Dennis C. Klemme, J.C.D., Chap. (Retired). Discalced Carmelite Nuns. Professed Sisters 9.

RACINE. *Convent of St. Catherine of Siena* (1862) Tel: 262-639-4100; Fax: 262-639-9702. Email: sienactr3@racinedominicans.org. Web: www.racinedominicans.org. Motherhouse of the Sisters of St. Dominic (Congregation of St. Catherine of Siena)., Corporate Title: Sisters of St. Dominic.; Corporation Founded 1903.

Siena Center, 5635 Erie St., 53402-1900. Tel: 262-639-4100; Fax: 262-639-9702. Web: www.racinedominicans.org. Sr. Sharon Simon, O.P., Pres. Sisters in Archdiocese 141; Total Religious in Community 164.

St. Rita's Convent, 4014 N. Green Bay Rd., 53404. Tel: 262-639-1766; Fax: 262-639-5673. Email: sr.irene@sbcglobal.net. Web: sistersofstrita.org. Sr. Irene Hanika, O.S.A., Supr. & Contact Person. Sisters 6.

ST. FRANCIS. *St. Francis Convent, Motherhouse of the Sisters of St. Francis of Assisi* (1849) 3221 S. Lake Dr., 53235-3799. Tel: 414-744-1160; Fax: 414-744-7193. Email: lakeosfs@lakeosfs.org. Web: www.lakeosfs.org. Sisters Florence Deacon, O.S.F., Dir. of the Congregation; Diana De Bruin, O.S.F., Assoc. Dir.; Margaret Kruse, O.S.F., Assoc. Dir.

The Sisters of St. Francis of Assisi, Inc.

The Ongoing Community Support Trust of the Sisters of St. Francis of Assisi, Corporate Title: The Sisters of St. Francis of Assisi, Milwaukee, Wis. Total in Community 254; Sisters in Archdiocese 171.

WAUWATOSA. *Provincial Motherhouse of the Carmelite Sisters of the Divine Heart of Jesus* (1891) 1230 Kavanaugh Pl., 53213. Tel: 414-453-4040; Fax: 414-453-5603. Email: simmaculatao@gmail.com. Web: carmelitedejnorth.org. Sr. Maria Giuseppe, Prov. Supr. Corporate Title: Carmelite Sisters of the Divine Heart of Jesus, Milwaukee, Wisconsin. Sisters 2; Novices 3; Total Religious in Province 28; Total Assisted 185; Total Staff 93.

WEST ALLIS. *Missionary Sisters of the Holy Family* (1905) 1665 S. 64th St., 53214. Tel: 414-327-4068; Fax: 414-327-4068. Email: misifa@wi.rr.com. Sr. Danuta Kujalowicz, M.S.F., Supr. Total in Community 16.

Sisters of Charity of St. Joan Antida Convent (Regina Coeli), 2716 Root River Pkwy., 53227. Tel: 414-545-2917. Email: rcoeli@scsja.org. Sr. Kathleen M. Lundwall, S.C.S.J.A., Supr. Sisters 2.

[R] HERMITAGES

SLINGER. *Carmelite Hermit of the Trinity - CHT* (1982) Mount Carmel Hermitage, 4270 Cedar Creek Rd., 53086-9372. Tel: 262-388-2234. Email: jmjose@catholic.org. Web: carmelitehermit.homestead.com. Rev. James M. Tambornino, S.O.L.T.; Sr. Joseph Marie, C.H.T., Foundress, Vocation & Formation Dir. Priests 1; Hermit Sisters (Professed) 1; Aspirants 1.

[S] RETREAT HOUSES

MILWAUKEE. *The Dwelling Place* (1986) 1611 Manitoba, South Milwaukee, 53172. Tel: 414-571-1027. Email: jschroeder23@wi.rr.com. Revs. Francis Dombrowski, O.F.M.Cap.; Jerome Schroeder, O.F.M.Cap.; Mary Klotz, Team Member. Priests 2; Total in Residence 3; Total Staff 3.

BENET LAKE. *St. Benedict's Abbey Retreat Center* (1945) 12605 224th Ave., 53102. Tel: 262-396-4311; Fax: 262-396-4365. Email: benetlakeretreatcenter@msn.com. Web: www.benetlake.org. Rt. Rev. Leo M. Ryska, O.S.B., Dir.; Denise R. Moczulewski, Co-Dir.

BRISTOL. *Mercy Retreat Center*, 12009 221st Ave., 53104. Tel: 262-862-6648. Sr. Timothy Matthews, R.S.M., Contact Person. Tel: 630-365-0828. Sisters of Mercy of the Americas West Midwest Community.

ELKHORN. *St. Vincent Pallotti Center* Pallottine Fathers, N. 6409 Bowers Rd., 53121. Tel: 262-723-2108; Fax: 262-723-8608. Email: vpallelk@elknet.net; pallotti_milw@yahoo.com. Web: www.elknet.net/vpallelk. Retreat and Christian Formation Center Lay Staff 3.

OCONOMOWOC. *The Redemptorist Retreat Center*, 1800 N. Timber Trail Ln., 53066-4897. Tel: 262-567-6900; Fax: 262-567-0134. Email: rrc@redemptoristretreat.org. Web: www.redemptoristretreat.org. Revs. Charles Beierwaltes, C.Ss.R.; Richard Boever, C.Ss.R., Dir.; Edward F. Monroe, C.Ss.R.; Lawrence Sanders, C.Ss.R.; James White, C.Ss.R.; Bro. Gerard Patin, C.Ss.R. Priests 3; Total in Residence 5; Brothers 1.

RACINE. *Racine Dominican Ministries, Inc. - Racine Dominican Retreat Program* (1966) 5635 Erie St., 53402-1900. Tel: 262-639-4100; Fax: 262-898-7332. Email: retreats@racinedominicans.org. Web: www.racinedominicans.org. Sr. Rita Lui, O.P., Dir.

WAUKESHA. *Schoenstatt Retreat Center*, W284 N698 Cherry Ln., 53188-9402. Tel: 262-522-4300; Fax: 262-522-4301. Email: intlcenter@schsrsmary.org. Web: www.schoenstattwisconsin.org. Sisters M. Taqui Perez, Supr.; M. Jacinta Brunner, Dir. Sisters 12; Total Staff 2.

[T] SECULAR INSTITUTES

MILWAUKEE. *Secular Institute of the Schoenstatt Sisters of Mary* (1926) 5310 W. Wisconsin Ave., 53208-3061. Tel: 414-774-3536; Fax: 414-774-0520. Sr. Janice Heyl, Supr. Sisters 4.

Secular Institute of the Schoenstatt Sisters of Mary - Adoration House, 5522 Bluemound Rd., 53208-3012. Tel: 414-453-5492. Sr. M. Gloriana Rivera, Supr. Sisters 4.

WAUKESHA. *Secular Institute of Schoenstatt Fathers* (1965) Tel: 262-548-9061; Fax: 262-548-9593. Email: frgerold@hotmail.com. Web: www.schoenstatt-wisconsin.org.

Schoenstatt Fathers (1965) W284 N746 Cherry Ln., 53188. Tel: 262-548-9061; Fax: 262-548-9593. Revs. Dietrich A. Haas; Gerold M. Langsch; Jonathan J. Niehaus; Mark J. Niehaus; Francisco Rojas. Priests 8; Total in Residence 5.

Attached to the house but living elsewhere: Revs. Christian Christensen, I.S.S.S., Supr. (Austin, TX); Jesus Ferras (Austin, TX); Hector R. Vega, C.C., (Corpus Christi, TX).

Secular Institute of the Schoenstatt Sisters of Mary (1926) W284 N404 Cherry Ln., 53188-9416. Tel: 262-522-4200; Fax: 262-522-4201. Email: schoenstattsisters@schsrsmary.org. Web: www.schsrsmary.org. Sisters M. Virginia Riedl, Prov. Supr.; M. Cynthia Day, Supr. Sisters 30.

[U] ASSOCIATIONS OF THE FAITHFUL

BELOIT. *Franciscan Sisters of Our Lady* (1981) 2110 Bootmaker Dr., 53511-2318. Tel: 608-365-7257. Sr. Mary James Geenen, F.S.O.L., Supr. Sisters 3.

FRANKLIN. *Franciscan Sisters of Saint Clare, Inc.* (1977) 7732 S. 51st St., 53132. Tel: 414-423-5277; Fax: 414-421-7869. Email: smcs@wi.rr.com. Web: fssclare.org. Sr. Mary Celine Stein, F.S.S.C., Supr. Gen. Non-Cloistered Contemplative Community. Professed Sisters 2; Assoc. Sisters 1; Lay Affiliates 27.

[V] MISSIONARY ACTIVITIES

MILWAUKEE. *Milwaukee Archdiocesan Office for World Mission* (1966) (Formerly Latin American Office), 1501 S. Layton Blvd., P.O. Box 3087, 53201-3087. Tel: 414-758-2281; Fax: 414-769-3408. Email: wmo@archmil.org. Web: www.archmil.org/dept/wmo. Sr. Frances P. Cunningham, O.S.F., Dir.; Rosemary Huddleston, O.P., Intl. Mission Coord. Sends priests and supports laity in overseas mission. Educates and raises funds for worldwide mission. Promotes parish twinning between archdiocese and other countries.

Milwaukee Archdiocesan Office for World Mission-Family Unity International, Inc., 1501 S. Layton Blvd., P.O. Box 3087, 53201-3087. Tel: 414-768-2281; Fax: 414-769-3408. Email: jparks@wi.rr.com. Web: www.workingboyscenter.org. Sr. Frances P. Cunningham, O.S.F., Contact Person; Rosemary Huddleston, O.P., Intl. Mission Coord.

Our Blessed Lady of Victory Mission, Inc. (1933) 5422 W. Vliet St., 53208. Tel: 414-774-3128. Email: oblvmission@yahoo.com. Lisa Hutchinson, Pres.

Society for the Propagation of the Faith, Archdiocese of Milwaukee (1822) (Pontifical Mission Aid Societies), 1501 S. Layton Blvd., P.O. Box 3087, 53201-3087. Tel: 414-758-2281; Fax: 414-769-3408. Email: wmo@archmil.org. Web: www.archmil.org/dept/wmo. Sr. Frances P. Cunningham, O.S.F., Dir.; Rosemary Huddleston, O.P., Intl. Mission Coord.

Society for the Propagation of the Faith, Holy Childhood Association dba Society for the Propagation of the Faith, Archdiocese of Milwaukee (1822) (Pontifical Mission Aid Societies), 1501 S. Layton Blvd., P.O. Box 3087, 53201-3087. Tel: 414-758-2281; Fax: 414-769-3408. Email: wmo@archmil.org. Web: www.archmil.org/dept/wmo. Sr. Frances P. Cunningham, O.S.F., Dir.; Rosemary Huddleston, O.P., Intl. Mission Coord.

GREENDALE. *Volunteer Missionary Movement (VMM)*, 5980 W. Loomis Rd., 53129. Tel: 414-423-8660; Fax: 414-423-8964. Email: vmm@vmmusa.org. Web: www.vmmusa.org. Julia M. Pagenkopf, Exec. Dir. Recruits, trains, and sends Christian men and women to serve for two years in areas of need in the world.

RACINE. *Community of St. Paul, Inc.* (1994) 1505 Howard St., 53404. Tel: 262-634-2666; Fax: 262-635-1910. Email: racine@comsp.org. Revs. Pere Cane-Gombau, Pres.; Marti Colom, Sec.; Stephen Forrest, Bd. Member; Ricardo Martin, Treas.; Oriol Regales, Bd. Member. Public Association of Christian Faithful, comprised of clergy and laity. It is present in North and South America. It fosters pastoral activities and human development initiatives, while promoting mission awareness internationally.

[W] SOCIETIES

MILWAUKEE. **Christ Child Society, Inc. - Milwaukee Chapter*, 4033 W. Good Hope Rd., 53209-2268. Tel: 414-540-0489; Fax: 414-540-0549. Email: mkeccs@sbcglobal.net. Web: www.christchildsociety.com. Bernadean Rice, Pres.

Priests' Purgatorial Society, 3501 S. Lake Dr., P.O. Box 070912, 53207-0912. Tel: 414-769-3340; Fax: 414-769-3908. Email: cusackb@archmil.org. Web: archmil.org. Dr. Barbara Anne Cusack, J.C.D., Sec.

**St. Vincent de Paul Society of Milwaukee*, 9601 W. Silver Spring Dr., 53225-3301. Tel: 414-462-7837; Fax: 414-462-5458. Mr. Gerald H. Felsecker, Contact Person.

FOND DU LAC. **Christ Child Society - Fond du Lac Chapter*, 739 Meadowbrook Ct., 54935. Tel: 920-921-6112. Joyce Ludovic, Pres.
739 Meadowbrook Ct., 54935. Tel: 920-921-6112.

WAUWATOSA. *Legion of Mary*, 10101 W. Wisconsin Ave., 53226. Tel: 414-259-4628. Rev. Charles J. Verhalen, Spiritual Dir. (Retired), 10100 W. Blue Mound Rd., #216, 53226; Floyd Mehrwerth, Pres.

Milwaukee Archdiocesan Holy Name Union, 2431 N. 63rd St., 53213. Tel: 414-258-1310. Email: floydm@milwpc.com. Floyd Mehrwerth, Communication Vice Pres.; Rev. Edward Griesemer, S.C.J.

WHITEWATER. *Cursillos in Christianity*, 236 S. Elizabeth St., 53190. Tel: 262-473-3130. Email: james.carlson@wicourts.gov. Web: www.cursillo.org/milwaukee. Rev. William W. Key, Spiritual Dir., English Speaking Secretariat; James Carlson, Lay Dir. Tel: 262-639-6576. Total Staff 7.

[X] NEWMAN CENTERS

MILWAUKEE. *Marquette University/Campus Ministry* P.O. Box 1881 - AMU236, 53201-1881. Tel: 414-288-6873; Fax: 414-288-3696. Email: susan.niemi@marquette.edu. Web: www.mu.edu/cm. Rev. D. Edward Mathie, S.J., Dir.; Gerald Fischer, Assoc. Dir.

Milwaukee Archdiocesan Campus Ministry P.O. Box 3087, 53201-3087. Tel: 414-758-2216; Fax: 414-769-3408. Email: nohlr@archmil.org. Web: www.archmil.org.

Campus Ministry of the Archdiocese of Milwaukee University of Wisconsin - Milwaukee, Newman Center 3001 N. Downer Ave., 53211. Tel: 414-964-6640; Fax: 414-964-3608. Email: newmancenter@gmail.com. Rev. Michael Lightner, Dir. Campus Ministry; Reanna Shellman, Outreach Coord.

Whitewater Campus Ministry (Whitewater) 344 N. Prairie St., Whitewater, 53190. Tel: 262-473-5555; Fax: 262-473-5855. Email: zaninb@uww.edu. Brian Zanin, Dir. Campus Ministry.

[Y] MISCELLANEOUS

MILWAUKEE. *Adult Learning Center, Inc.*, 1916 N. 4th St., 53212. Tel: 414-431-2031; Fax: 414-431-2031. Email: herb@mlkalc.org. Herb Hayden, Exec. Dir.; Sr. Callista Robinson, Asst. Admin.; Kate Tarpey, Fin. Mgr.

Agape Community Center of Milwaukee, Inc. (1989) 6100 N. 42nd St., 53209. Tel: 414-464-4440; Fax: 414-464-9420. Email: abachrach@agape-center.org. Web: www.ministryhealth.org. Ann Bachrach, Exec. Dir. Corporate Sponsor: Ministry Health Care, Inc. (Milwaukee, WI); Sponsored by Sisters of the Sorrowful Mother. Total Staff 13; Total Assisted 1,500.

Alexian Elderly Services, Inc., 9301 N. 76th St., 53223. Tel: 414-355-9300; Fax: 414-357-5106. Email: gmohn@alexianbrothers.net. Gary Mohn, Contact Person.

Alternative Residential Arrangements, Inc., 6609 N. 53rd St., 53223. Tel: 414-358-0852; Fax: 414-358-0669. Group Homes for Developmentally disabled adults.
Other Locations:
6609 N. 53rd St., 53223. Tel: 414-358-0852; Fax: 414-358-0669.
5255 S. 18th St., 53221. Tel: 414-282-6366; Fax: 414-282-3205.

St. Ann Center for Intergenerational Care, Inc., 2801 E. Morgan Ave., 53207. Tel: 414-977-5000; Fax: 414-977-5050. Email: jpglaser@stanncenter.org. Web: www.stanncenter.org. John P. Glaser, CFO.

Apostleship of Prayer, 3211 S. Lake Dr., Ste. 216, 53235. Tel: 414-486-1152; Fax: 414-486-1159. Email: info@apostleshipofprayer.org. Web: www.apostleshipofprayer.org. Revs. Phillip R. Hurley, S.J., Dir. Youth & Young Adults; James M. Kubicki, S.J., Dir.

Archdiocesan Marian Shrine, P.O. Box 070912, 53207-0912.

**Archdiocese of Milwaukee Catholic Community Foundation, Inc.*, 637 E. Erie St., 53202. Tel: 414-431-6402; Fax: 414-431-6407. Email: info@legaciesoffaith.org. Web: legaciesoffaith.org. Ms. Mary Ellen Markowski, Pres.

**Archdiocese of Milwaukee Supporting Fund, Inc.*, 125 S. 84th St., Ste. 110, 53214. Tel: 414-607-6040; Fax: 414-607-6045. Paula N. John, Pres.

Assisi Homes - Jefferson Court, Inc. (1993) 415 E. Knapp St., 53202. Tel: 414-271-5370; Fax: 414-271-5988. Web: www.wfhealthcare.org. Housing Units 222; Residents 224; Total Staff 11.

Association of Franciscan Colleges and Universities, Inc. (1998) 6801 N. Yates Rd., P.O. Box 334, 53217. Tel: 414-410-4109; Fax: 414-410-4120. Email: gkowalski@stritch.edu. Web: www.franciscancollegesuniversities.org. Sr. Gabrielle Kowalski, Exec. Dir.

St. Benedict Community Meal (1970) (Province of St. Joseph of the Capuchin Order, Inc.)., 1015 N. 9th St., 53233. Tel: 414-271-0135; Fax: 414-271-0637. Email: stbens@sbcglobal.net. Web: stbensmilwaukee.org. Bro. David Schwab, O.F.M.Cap., Meal Dir. Provides a free evening meal Sunday through Friday to those in need. Total Assisted 100,000; Total Staff 8.

St. Camillus Communities, Inc., 3345 S. 10th St., 53215. Tel: 414-481-3696. Very Rev. Richard O'Donnell, M.I., Prov.; Revs. Louis Lussier, M.I.; Albert Schempp, M.I. Total in Residence 7.

Capuchin Franciscan Volunteer Corps, Inc., 1927 N. 4th St., 53212. Tel: 414-374-8841, Ext. 29; Fax: 414-374-8843. Email: capcorps@thecapuchins.org. Web: www.capcorps.org. Shelly Roder, Dir. Purpose: In the spirit of Jesus Christ and Francis and Clare of Assisi, the Capuchin Franciscan Volunteer Corps is a community of women and men who serve among people in need as full-time volunteers, sharing common prayer and simple living. Total Assisted 10,000; Total Staff 1.

Casa Romero Renewal Center, Inc. (2001) 423 W. Bruce St., 53204. Tel: 414-224-7564; Fax: 414-270-9817. Email: casaromero@wi.rr.com. Web: www.casaromerocenter.org. Rev. David M. Shields, S.J., Founder & Pres.

St. Catherine Residence, Inc. (1913) 1032 E. Knapp St., 53202. Tel: 414-272-8470; Fax: 414-272-7579. Web: www.stcatherineresidence.org. Lynne J. Oehlke, Pres.

St. Catherine Residence, Inc., Affordable housing serving women in transition, and those who will benefit from an environment where women support, encourage, and network with each other. Includes a Right Start Program for first-time, single, pregnant women over the age of 17. Residents 150.

The Catholic Charismatic Renewal Office of Southeastern Wisconsin, Inc. (1980) P.O. Box 70637, 53207-0637. Tel: 414-482-1727; Fax: 414-482-3616. Email: ccr@archmil.org. Web: www.ccrmilwaukee.catholicweb.com. Deacon Patrick H. Frye, Liaison; Rosalita Villa, Office Mgr.

Magnificat-West Bend Chapter: Mary Mother of All Hearts, 3351 Town Line Rd., West Bend, 53095. Tel: 262-677-1192. Terri Biertzer, Pres. & Coord.

Catholic Charities Foundation, Inc., 3501 S. Lake Dr., P.O. Box 070912, 53207-0912. Tel: 414-769-3400; Fax: 414-769-3428. Email: Catholiccharities@ccmke.org. Web: www.ccmke.org. Hannah C. Dugan, Exec. Dir.; James M. Brennan, Deputy Dir.

Catholic Charities of the Archdiocese of Milwaukee, Inc. (1920) 3501 S. Lake Dr., P.O. Box 070912, 53207-0912. Tel: 414-769-3400; Fax: 414-769-3428. Email: catholiccharities@ccmke.org. Web: www.ccmke.org. Hannah C. Dugan, Exec. Dir.; James M. Brennan, Deputy Dir.
Area Offices:
2021 N. 60th St., 53208. Tel: 414-771-2881; Fax: 414-771-1674. Tracy Nickels, Site Supervisor.
1111 Douglas Ave., Racine, 53402. Tel: 262-637-8888; Fax: 262-637-0695. Delia Cooper, Site Supvr.
503 Wisconsin Ave., Sheboygan, 53081. Tel: 920-458-5726; Fax: 920-458-5826. Ruth Hansen, Site Supvr.
741 N. Grand Ave., Ste. 210, Waukesha, 53186. Tel: 262-547-2463; Fax: 262-547-8002. Mary Taylor, Site Supervisor.
731 W. Washington St., 53204. Tel: 414-643-8570; Fax: 414-643-6726. Victor Paredes, Site Supervisor; Annette Jankowski, Contact.

Adult Day Services & Resource Center, 1919 N. 60th St., 53208. Tel: 414-771-2881; Fax: 414-771-9115. Susan Yee, Contact Person.

Adult Day Services & Resource Center, 13700 W. National Ave., New Berlin, 53151. Tel: 262-782-0740; Fax: 262-782-0024. Other Offices: Beaver Dam, Brookfield, Burlington, Fond du Lac, Fontana, Kenosha, Menomonee Falls, Port Washington, West Bend. Total Assisted Annually 13,000.

St. Clare Management, Inc., 1545 S. Layton Blvd., 53215. Tel: 414-385-5330; Fax: 414-385-5333. Web: www.stclaremgmtorg. Margaret E. Kidder, Exec. Dir. Sponsored by the School Sisters of St. Francis, Housing Management organization committed to providing quality residential services to low income elderly and/or persons with disabilities.

Clare Towers, Inc. dba Clare Towers, Clare Woods, Clare Heights, Clare Meadows, Clare Court, & Clare Lakes 1545 S. Layton Blvd., 53215. Tel: 414-385-5330; Fax: 414-385-5333. Web: www.stclaremgmt.org. Sponsored by School Sisters of St. Francis, Housing facilities for physically disabled to live independently. Apartments 140.

Dismas Ministry (2000) P.O. Box 070363, 53207. Tel: 414-977-5064; Fax: 414-481-6764. Email: dismas@dismasministry.org. Web: www.dismasministry.org. Ronald Zeilinger, Exec. Dir. A national Catholic outreach to inmates, victims, their families, those released from prison, and the community.

Dominican Center for Women, Inc., 2470 W. Locust St., 53206-1134. Tel: 414-444-9930; Fax: 414-444-4041. Email: amhalloran@aol.com. Sr. Ann Halloran, O.P., Dir. & Contact Person.

Eastside Senior Services (1974) 2618 N. Hackett Ave., 53211. Tel: 414-961-0661; Fax: 414-961-0661. Email: eastside@interfaithmilw.org. Jane Raymer, Dir. Corporate Title: Eastside Senior Services, Inc. - an Interfaith Outreach Program; Sponsored by SS. Peter and Paul, Lake Park Lutheran Church, ELCA, St. Mark's Episcopal Church, Plymouth Church, United Church of Christ, Our Lady of Divine Providence, Three Holy Women, Epikos Church, Immanuel Presbyterian, Cathedral of St. John the Evangelist, Old St. Mary's and Summerfield United Methodist, Milwaukee. Total Assisted 700; Total Staff 2.

Faith in Our Future Trust, P.O. Box 070504, 53207-0504. Tel: 414-769-3300. Most Revs. Timothy Michael Dolan, Trustee. Tel: 414-769-3497; William P. Callahan, O.F.M.Conv.

**St. Francis Foundation of Milwaukee, Inc.* (1968) 1600 W. Oklahoma Ave., 53215. Tel: 414-645-5337, Ext. 270; Fax: 414-645-9002. Email: dmccauley@cdcsj.org. Web: www.touchingliveseveryday.org. Sponsored by the Felician Sisters., Fund development for Villa St. Francis, Child Development Center of St. Joseph and other ministries of the Felician Sisters.

Franciscan Peacemakers, Inc., Milwaukee (1995) 128 W. Burleigh St., 53212. Tel: 414-559-5761; 414-562-4780. Email: przedpel@yahoo.com. Web: www.franpax.com. Deacon Steven J. Przedpelski, Exec. Dir.; Carmen Rojica, Assoc. Dir. Total Assisted Annually 37,000; Total Staff 2.

House of Peace (1968) 1702 W. Walnut St., 53205-1616. Tel: 414-933-1300; Fax: 414-933-0395. Email: markdcarrico@juno.com. Web: www.houseofpeacemilwaukee.org. Bro. Mark Carrico, O.F.M.Cap., Dir.; Rev. Matthew Gottschalk, O.F.M.Cap., Spiritual Dir. In Res. Rev. Alan D. Veik, O.F.M.Cap.
Affiliates: Rev. Michael Fountain, O.F.M.Cap.; Bros. T.L. Michael Auman, O.F.M.Cap.; Isidore Herriges, O.F.M.Cap.

The Jesuit Partnership, 3400 W. Wisconsin Ave., 53208-3841. Tel: 414-937-6955; Fax: 414-937-6950. Very Rev. G. Thomas Krettek, S.J., Pres.; Revs. Luis Rodriguez, S.J., Vice Pres.; Eugene M. Dutkiewicz, S.J., Treas.

**St. Joan Antida High School Foundation, Ltd.*, 1341 N. Cass St., 53202. Tel: 414-354-9233; Fax:

414-355-6463. 8560 N. 76th Pl., 53223. Sr. Kathleen M. Lundwall, S.C.S.J.A., Contact Person.

**St. Josaphat Basilica Foundation, Inc.*, 620 W. Lincoln Ave., 53215. Tel: 414-902-3524; Fax: 414-643-8376. Email: sjbfoundation@archmil.org. Web: www.thebasilica.org. Mr. Michael J. Murry, Chm.; Susan A. Rabe, Exec. Dir.

The Korean Catholic Community of Milwaukee, 1854 W. Windlake Ave., 53215. Tel: 414-645-4773; Fax: 414-645-5622. Email: st.marymagd@aol.com. Revs. Paul A. Stanosz; Benedict Ko, M.S.C.

**LaFarge Lifelong Learning Institute, Inc.* (1969) 1501 S. Layton Blvd., 53215. Tel: 414-944-6023; Fax: 414-944-6060. Email: cfoxho@sssf.org. Sr. Charlita Foxhoven, Corp. Sec. Continuing Education Program for older adults.

Lay Salvatorians, Inc. (2003) 1735 N. Hi-Mount Blvd., 53208-1720. Tel: 414-744-1160. Rev. Scott Wallenfelsz, S.D.S., Dir. Finance & Contact Person.

Layton Blvd. West Neighbors, Inc., 1545 S. Layton Blvd., 53215. Tel: 414-383-9038; Fax: 414-647-4886. Email: lbwn@execpc.com. Web: www.lbwn.org. Charlotte John-Gomez, Exec. Dir. Sponsored by School Sisters of St. Francis, Purpose: To stabilize and revitalize the area of the city known as Layton Blvd. West Neighbors by building partnerships which achieve shared responsibility for the Neighborhood.

MAREDA, 1501 S. Layton Blvd., P.O. Box 3087, 53201-3087. Tel: 414-758-2242; Fax: 414-769-3408. Email: pokornyg@archmil.org. Web: www.archmil.org. Dave Baudry, Chm. Archdiocese of Milwaukee, Office of Catechesis and Youth Ministry

Milwaukee Achiever Literacy Services, Inc. (1983) 1512 W. Pierce St., 53204. Tel: 414-463-8820; Fax: 414-643-8804. Email: ppalmer@milwaukeeachiever.org. Web: www.milwaukeeachiever.org. Dennis J. Purtell, Esq., Legal Counsel. Founded by the School Sisters of St. Francis; Sisters of St. Francis of Assisi; School Sisters of Notre Dame, Purpose: To provide adult literacy education and workforce development to economically and educationally disadvantaged adults in the Greater Milwaukee area. Total Assisted Annually 850; Total Staff 33.

Milwaukee Archdiocesan Council of Deacons (1975)Tel: 414-769-3409; Fax: 414-769-3408. Email: zimprichd@archmil.org. Advisory/Governing Board of Deacons.

P.O. Box 070912, 53207-0912. Tel: 414-769-3409; Fax: 414-769-3408. Deacon Michael J. Finley.

Milwaukee Archdiocesan Principals' Association (MAPA), P.O. Box 3087, 53201-3087. Tel: 414-758-2251; Fax: 414-769-3408. Email: lodesd@archmil.org. Dr. David Lodes, Supt. Archdiocese of Milwaukee, Office for Schools.

Milwaukee Archdiocesan Secondary Principals' Association (MASPA), P.O. Box 3087, 53201-3087. Tel: 414-758-2251; Fax: 414-769-3408. Email: lodesd@archmil.org. Mary Kurhajetz, Prin.; Dr. David Lodes, Supt.

Milwaukee Catholic Press Apostolate (1869) 3501 S. Lake Dr., P.O. Box 070913, 53207-0913. Tel: 414-769-3500; Fax: 414-769-3468. Email: chnonline@archmil.org. Web: www.chnonline.org. Brian T. Olszewski, Exec. Editor & Gen. Mgr.

**Ministry Medical Group, Inc.* (1999) 11925 W. Lake Park Dr., 53224. Tel: 414-359-1060; Fax: 414-359-1656. Email: info@ministryhealth.org. Web: www.ministrymedicalgroup.org. Stewart Watson, M.D., Pres. & CEO.

National Association of Catholic Chaplains, 5007 S. Howell Ave., Ste. 120, 53207-6159. Tel: 414-483-4898; Fax: 414-483-6712. Mr. David A. Lichter, Exec. Dir.

National Office of Post-Abortion Reconciliation and Healing, Inc. (1991) 3501 S. Lake Dr., P.O. Box 070477, 53207-0477. Tel: 414-483-4141; 800-593-2273; Fax: 414-483-7376. Email: noparh@juno.com. Web: www.noparh.org. Victoria M. Thorn, Pres. Total Assisted 4,500; Total Staff 3.

O.S.F. Services, Inc. (1983) 400 W. River Woods Pkwy., 53212. Tel: 414-465-3111; Fax: 414-465-3001. John D. Oliverio, Pres. Sponsored by Franciscan Sisters, Daughters of the Sacred Hearts of Jesus and Mary, Wheaton, IL.

Pallottine Fathers and Brothers, Inc., Disability Trust, 5424 W. Bluemound Rd., 53208. Tel: 414-259-0688; Fax: 414-258-9314. Email: pallotti_milw@yahoo.com. Web: www.pallottines.org. Very Rev. Leon J. Martin, S.A.C., Pres. & Treas.

Pallottine Fathers and Brothers, Inc., Educational and Apostolic Ministry Trust, 5424 W. Bluemound Rd., 53208. Tel: 414-259-0688; Fax: 414-258-9314. Email: pallotti_milw@yahoo.com. Web: www.pallottines.org. Very Rev. Leon J. Martin, S.A.C., Prov. & Treas.

Priests of the Sacred Heart Christ the King Parish Building Trust, Priests of the Sacred Heart, P.O. Box 289, Hales Corners, 53130. Tel: 414-425-6910; Fax: 414-425-2938. Deacon David Nagel, Contact Person.

S.E.T. Ministry, Inc., 2977 N. 50th St., 53210. Tel: 414-449-2680; Fax: 414-442-1770. Laurene Gramling Laehn, Pres. & CEO. Wheaton Franciscan Services, Inc., Corporate Sponsor, Joint Sponsored by 18 Religious Congregations, Health and Human Services Outreach Programs. Total Assisted 5,100.

Salvatorian Institute of Philosophy and Theology, Inc. (1993) 1735 N. Hi-Mount Blvd., 53208-1720. Tel: 414-258-1735. Rev. Scott Wallenfelsz, S.D.S., Dir. Finance.

**Santa Fe Communications, Inc.*, 1126 S. 70th St., 53214-3155. Tel: 414-475-4444. Bruno John, Pres./Contact Person.

SASC, Inc., 3800 N. 92nd St., 53222-2589. Tel: 414-463-7570; Fax: 414-463-2311. Ms. Lynn Vogt, Admin. & Contact Person.

SDS Hope House, Inc., 4311 N. 100th St., 53222. Tel: 414-466-0810. Sr. Carol Thresher, S.D.S., Contact Person.

Servants of Saint Camillus Disaster Relief Services, Inc., 1039 E. Russell Ave., 53207. Tel: 414-731-7318. Rev. Scott Binet, M.I., M.D., Contact Person.

Society of the Divine Savior Ongoing Community Support Trust, 1735 N. Hi Mount Blvd., 53208-1720. Tel: 414-258-1735; Fax: 414-258-1934. Email: sds@salvatorians.com. Web: salvatorians.com.

Ongoing Community Support Trust

St. Stephen's League (of the Archdiocesan Council of Deacons), P.O. Box 070912, 53207-0912. Tel: 414-769-3409; Fax: 414-769-3408. Email: zimprichd@archmil.org. Deacon David L. Zimprich.

Telos, Inc. Clare Place and Clare Central., 1545 S. Layton Blvd., 53215. Tel: 414-385-5330; Fax: 414-385-5333. Web: www.stclaremgmt.org. Sponsored by the School Sisters of St. Francis., Housing for physically disabled to live independently.

1545 S. Layton Blvd., 53215. Tel: 414-643-6501; Fax: 414-643-4474. Apartments 24.

Theological Studies, Inc., Marquette University, 100 Coughlin Hall, P.O. Box 1881, 53201-1881. Tel: 414-288-3165; Fax: 414-288-1413. Email: tseditor@marquette.edu. Web: www.ts.mu.edu. Revs. David G. Schultenover, S.J., Editor; J. Leon Hooper, S.J., Book Review Editor. Tel: 202-687-4250; Fax: 202-687-5835; John L. Treloar, S.J., Business Mgr. Publisher of the quarterly Theological Studies.

**Wheaton Franciscan Healthcare-Foundation for St. Francis, Inc.*, 3237 S. 16th St., 53215. Tel: 414-647-5000. Eloise Samano Williamson, Exec. Dir. & Contact Person.

**Wheaton Franciscan Healthcare-Southeast Wisconsin, Inc.* (1986) 400 W. River Woods Pkwy., 53212. Tel: 414-465-3111; Fax: 414-465-3001. Web: www.mywheaton.org. John D. Oliverio, Pres. & CEO. Franciscan Sisters, Daughters of the Sacred Hearts of Jesus and Mary, Wheaton, IL.

**Wheaton Franciscan Medical Group, Inc.* (1933) 400 W. River Woods Pkwy., 53212. Tel: 414-465-3000; Fax: 414-465-3001. Web: www.mywheaton.org. Loren Meyer, M.D., Pres. & C.E.O.

Wheaton Franciscan St. Joseph Foundation, Inc. (1984) 5000 W. Chambers St., 53210. Tel: 414-447-2844; Fax: 414-874-4399. Web: www.mywheaton.org. Rachelle Marquardt, Exec. Dir. Sponsored by Franciscan Sisters, Daughters of the Sacred Hearts of Jesus and Mary, Wheaton, IL.

Wisconsin Association of Principals of Catholic Secondary Schools, P.O. Box 3087, 53203-3087. Tel: 414-758-2251; Fax: 414-769-3408. Email: lodesd@archmil.org. Dr. David Lodes, Supt. Archdiocese of Milwaukee, Office for Schools.

BROOKFIELD. **Wheaton Franciscan Healthcare-Circle of Life Foundation, Inc.*, 13950 W. Capitol Dr., 53005. Tel: 414-535-6829. Web: www.mywheaton.org. James D. Gresham, Exec. Dir.

**Wheaton Franciscan Healthcare-Elmbrook Memorial Foundation, Inc.* (2001) 19333 W. North Ave., 53045-4198. Tel: 262-785-2000. Email: shelli.marquardt@wfhc.org. Web: www.mywheaton.org. Rachelle Marquardt, Exec. Dir.

Wheaton Franciscan Home Health and Hospice, Inc. (1986) 13950 W. Capitol Dr., 53005. Tel: 414-874-6161. Web: www.mywheaton.org. James D. Gresham, Pres. Franciscan Sisters, Daughters of the Sacred Hearts of Jesus and Mary, Wheaton, IL. Total Assisted Annually 6,277; Total Staff 158.

BROWN DEER. *Sisters of the Sorrowful Mother Charitable Trust* (1990) 9056 N. Deerbrook Tr., 53223-2474. Tel: 414-357-8940; Fax: 414-357-8950. Web: ssmfranciscans.org. Sr. M. Teresina Marra, Trustee. To help provide for the needs of the aged and infirm members of the Sisters of the Sorrowful Mother.

Sisters of the Sorrowful Mother International Finance, Inc. (1976) 9056 N. Deerbrook Tr., 53223-2474. Tel: 414-357-8940; Fax: 414-357-8950. Web: ssmfranciscans.org. Sr. M. Teresina Marra, Chairperson.

BURLINGTON. *General Secretariat of the Franciscan Missions, Inc.*, P.O. Box 130, Waterford, 53185. Tel: 262-534-5470; Fax: 262-534-4342. Email: framis@wi.net. Web: franciscanmissions.org. Revs. Sereno Baiardi, O.F.M., Dir.; Sante De Angelis, O.F.M., Assoc. Dir.; Ponciano Macabalo, O.F.M. General Secretariat of the Franciscan Missions, Inc. Missionaries 5,400.

**The National Communicators Network for Women Religious (NCNWR)*, 525 Madison St., 53105. Tel: 262-767-9986. Email: coordinator@ncnwr.org. Web: www.ncnwr.org. Susan Oxley, Coord.

FOND DU LAC. **Agnesian HealthCare Foundation, Inc.*, 430 E. Division St., 54936. Tel: 920-926-4964. Jane Hyde, Contact Person.

Hazotte Ministries, Inc., 320 County Rd. K, 54937-8158. Tel: 920-907-2300; Fax: 920-923-3194. Sr. Hertha Longo, C.S.A., Pres. Sponsored by the Congregation of Sisters of St. Agnes.

FRANKLIN. *Franciscan Pilgrimage Programs, Inc.* (1974) P.O. Box 321490, 53132-6231. Tel: 414-427-0570; Fax: 414-427-0590. Email: linda@franciscanpilgrimages.com. Web: www.franciscanpilgrimages.com. Rev. John Cella, O.F.M., J.C.D., M.Div., M.B.A., Dir. & CEO. Catholic Franciscan Pilgrimages for religious men and women, leaders in Franciscan based institutions, members of the Secular Franciscan Order and any others who desire to deepen or discover Franciscan values and spirituality.

GLENDALE. **Columbia St. Mary's Foundation*, 4425 N. Port Washington Rd., 53212. Tel: 414-326-2077; Fax: 414-326-2074. Micael M. Grebe, Chm. Bd. Dirs.

Seton Health Corporation of Wisconsin (1984) 4425 N. Port Washington Rd., 53212. Tel: 414-326-1740; Fax: 414-326-1739. Email: amarquar@columbia-stmarys.org. Christopher Doerr, Bd. Chm. Operated by Ascension Health System.

**Wheaton Franciscan Healthcare-The Wisconsin Heart Hospital, Inc.* (1975) 400 W. River Woods Pkwy., 53212. Tel: 414-465-3000; Fax: 414-465-3582. John D. Oliverio, Pres.; Elizabeth Cliffe Kucharski, Contact Person. Franciscan Sisters, Daughters of the Sacred Hearts of Jesus and Mary, Wheaton, IL.

GREENFIELD. *Clement Manor Retirement Community*, 9339 W. Howard, 53228. Tel: 414-546-7374; Fax: 414-546-7357. Web: www.clementmanor.com. Mr. Greg Szpak, Dir. Res. Svcs.; Rev. Albert Lis, O.F.M., Chap. Sponsored by the School Sisters of St. Francis, Corporate Title: Clement Manor, Inc. Residents 235; Apartments 129; Assisted Living Apartments 85.

HALES CORNERS. *Congregation of the Priests of the Sacred Heart Support and Maintenance Trust* (1991) 7373 S. Lovers Lane Rd., P.O. Box 289, 53130. Tel: 414-425-6910; Fax: 414-425-2938. Email: provsec@poshusa.org. Web: www.scj.org. Revs. Paul J. McGuire, S.C.J., Trustee; James Walters, S.C.J., M.S., M.Div., Trustee; Bro. Raymond Kozuch, S.C.J., Trustee.

Development Office (1929) Sacred Heart Monastery-Priests of the Sacred Heart-Reign of the Sacred Heart, Inc., 6889 S. Lovers Lane Rd., P.O. Box 900, 53130. Tel: 414-425-3383; Fax: 414-425-5719. Web: www.scj.org. Mr. William Rondeau, Pres. U.S. Province of the Priests of the Sacred Heart.

KENOSHA. *Assisi Homes - Kenosha, Inc.* (1994) Independent Housing for Low Income Elderly, 1860 27th Ave., 53140. Tel: 262-551-9821; Fax: 262-551-9843. Web: www.wfhealthcare.org. Units 60; Residents 60; Staff 3.

Assisi Homes - Saxony, Inc. (1994) Independent Housing for Low Income Elderly, 1876 22nd Ave., 53140. Tel: 262-551-9005; Fax: 262-551-7586. Web: www.wfhealthcare.org. Housing Units 224; Residents 218; Total Staff 8.

Catholic Woman's Club, c/o PPG Management Consultants, LLC, 5525 Green Bay Rd., 53144. Tel: 262-657-2060; Fax: 262-657-2080. Email: osterj@ppgmanagement.net. Lillian DeFazio, Pres. & Contact Person.

Franciscan Seniors, Kenosha, Inc. (1994) 1920 27th Ave., 53140. Tel: 630-462-9271; 262-551-0989; Fax: 262-551-8683. Web: www.wfhealthcare.org. Housing Units 60; Residents 55; Total Staff 3.

St. Joseph's Adult Day Care Center, Inc. (1982) 9244 29th Ave., 53143. Tel: 262-694-6000; Fax: 262-925-8122. Email: joycem@tds.net. Web: www.stjoseph.com. Ms. Joyce Mitchell, Dir. Sponsored by: Carmelite Sisters of the Divine Heart of Jesus. Total Assisted Annually 120; Total Staff 15.

St. Mark Latin American Center, 7101 13th Ave., 53143. Tel: 262-656-7370; Fax: 262-656-7375. Email: stmark@archmil.org. Web: www.stmark-kenosha.org. Rev. Stephen Forrest; Deacon Alvaro Dominquez; Betty Regalado, Coord. of Human Resources; Martha Sanchez, Sec. Total Assisted 2,500; Total Staff 3.

RACINE. *Catherine Marian Housing, Inc.* (1989) 5635 Erie St., 53402. Tel: 262-639-4100; Fax: 262-639-9702. Web: www.racinedominicans.org. Congregation of St. Catherine of Siena.

St. Catherine's High School Corporation (1972) 1200 Park Ave., 53403. Fax: 262-632-5144. Tom Leuenberger, Chm.

St. Catherine's High School of Racine, Inc. (1957) 5635 Erie St., 53402-1900. Tel: 262-639-4100; Fax: 262-639-9702. Sr. Sharon Simon, O.P., Pres.

St. Catherine's Infirmary, Inc. (1966) 5635 Erie St., 53402-1900. Tel: 262-639-4100; Fax: 262-639-9702. Sr. Sharon Simon, O.P., Pres.

Dominican College of Racine, Inc. (1957) 5635 Erie St., 53402-1900. Tel: 262-639-4100; Fax: 262-639-9702. Sr. Sharon Simon, O.P., Pres.

HOPES Center of Racine, Inc., 506 7th St., 53403. Tel: 262-898-2940; Fax: 262-898-1772. Email: apratt@hopescenter.org. Sr. Ann Pratt, Exec. Dir.

Racine Area Catholic Formation/Education Association (2003) 700 English, P.O. Box 085293, 53408-5293. Tel: 262-633-3822; Fax: 262-633-3822. Email: car-amc@sbcglobal.net. Web: www.catholicassociationofracine.org. Anna Marie Clausen, Dir. of Cooperative Svcs.

Racine Dominican Ministries, Inc. (1989) 5635 Erie St., 53402-1900. Tel: 262-639-4100; Fax: 262-639-9702. Web: www.racinedominicans.org. Sr. Sharon Simon, O.P., Pres.

Racine Dominican Ministries, Inc.-Eco-Justice Center, 7133 Michna Rd., 53402. Tel: 262-681-8527. Email: jaweyk@miliserv.net. Web: www.racinedominicans.org. Sr. Janet Weyker, O.P., Dir. & Contact Person.

Racine Dominican Ministries, Inc.-Senior Companion Program (1978) 5635 Erie St., 53402. Tel: 262-639-4100; Fax: 262-639-9702. Email: scp@racinedominicans.org. Web: www.racinedominicans.org. Gloria Stedman Brown, Dir.

Wheaton Franciscan Healthcare-All Saints Foundation, Inc. (1986) 1320 Wisconsin Ave., 53403. Tel: 262-687-2239; Fax: 262-687-2674. Web: www.mywheaton.org. Christopher Krizek, Exec. Dir. Franciscan Sisters, Daughters of the Sacred Hearts of Jesus and Mary, Wheaton, IL.

ST. FRANCIS. *Archdiocese of Milwaukee Cemeteries Perpetual Care Trust*, 3501 S. Lake Dr., 53235. Tel: 414-769-3497. Most Revs. Timothy Michael Dolan, Contact Person; William P. Callahan, O.F.M.Conv.

Canticle Court, Inc. (1987) 3201 S. Lake Dr., 53235. Tel: 414-744-5878; Fax: 414-744-7636. Email: jschmitt@lakeosfs.org. Mr. John Schmitt, Pres. & CEO. An Apartment building sponsored by the Sisters of St. Francis of Assisi funded by HUD for low income elderly persons who can live independently. Units 48; Total in Residence 49; Total Assisted Annually 43; Total Staff 3.

Foundation for Religious Retirement, Inc. (1987) 3221 S. Lake Dr., 53235. Tel: 414-294-7324; Fax: 414-744-7193. Email: jparrott@lakeosfs.org. Web: www.thefrr.org. Jan Parrott, Exec. Dir. To raise funds to assist in supporting retired women religious in the Milwaukee Archdiocese.

Juniper Court, Inc. (1993) 3209 S. Lake Dr., 53235-3702. Tel: 414-744-5878; Fax: 414-744-7636. Email: jschmitt@lakeosfs.org. Mr. John Schmitt, Pres. & CEO. Sponsored by the Sisters of St. Francis of Assisi, St. Francis, WI., An apartment building for persons of low to moderate income who can live independently. Total in Residence 55; Total Units 52; Total Assisted Annually 49; Total Staff 3.

Southeastern Wisconsin Catholic Parish Investment Management Trust, 3501 S. Lake Dr., 53235. Tel: 414-769-3334. Most Revs. Timothy M. Dolan, Trustee; William P. Callahan, O.F.M.Conv.; John J. Marek, Treas. & Contact Person.

SHEBOYGAN. *The Sheboygan County Catholic Fund, Inc.*, 522 New York Ave., 53081. Tel: 920-457-4629. A fund to provide youth and adult religious education programs within the county.

STONE BANK. **Tyme Out Youth Ministry Center, Inc.* (1980) W332 N6786 County Rd. C, Nashotah, 53058-9737. Tel: 262-966-1800; Fax: 262-966-1815. Email: youth@tymeout.org. Web: www.tymeout.org. Ben Brzeski, Exec. Dir. Total Staff 10.

WAUKESHA. *St. Thomas More Lawyers Society*, 610 E. College Ave., 53186. Tel: 262-542-7101; Fax: 262-521-4444. Email: webmaster@stthomasmorewi.org. Web: www.stthomasmorewi.org. Very Rev. Paul B.R. Hartmann, M.Div., J.C.L., Chap.

WAUWATOSA. *St. Camillus Health System, Inc.*, 10101 W. Wisconsin Ave., 53226. Tel: 414-258-1814. Very Rev. Richard O'Donnell, M.I., Pres. & Prov.; Revs. Louis Lussier, M.I., Counselor; Albert Schempp, M.I., Treas. Management Corporation. Order of the Servants of the Sick (Order of St. Camillus). Total Assisted 596.

St. Camillus Ministries, Inc., 10101 W. Wisconsin Ave., 53226. Tel: 414-258-1814. Very Rev. Richard O'Donnell, M.I., Prov. & Pres.; Revs. Louis Lussier, M.I., Counselor; Albert Schempp, M.I., Treas. St. Camillus Ministries, Inc. operates under the auspices of the Order of St. Camillus and sponsors all social concerns ministry of the Order. Total Served 596; Total Staff 6.

Friends of Calvary Cemetery, Inc., 2515 N. 66th St., 53213. Tel: 414-778-1187; Fax: 414-778-1187. Email: swerk@juno.com. Mr. Keith Schultz, Pres. Purpose: To raise funds in connection with the restoration of Calvary Chapel located at Calvary Cemetery, 5503 West Bluemound Rd., Milwaukee, WI and overseeing such restoration.

The Milwaukee Guild of the Catholic Medical Association, 737 N. Robertson St., 53213-3337. Tel: 414-771-7962; Fax: 414-771-7962. Email: milwaukee@wisconsincma.org. Web: www.wisconsincma.org. Franklin Smith, Pres.

Order of St. Camillus Foundation, Inc., 10200 W. Bluemound Rd., 53226. Tel: 414-259-8335; Fax: 414-259-4590. David Kremer, Exec. Dir. & Contact Person; Very Rev. Richard O'Donnell, M.I., Provincial; Revs. Louis Lussier, M.I.; Albert Schempp, M.I.

San Camillo, Inc., 10200 W. Blue Mound Rd., 53226. Tel: 414-259-6300. Rev. Louis Lussier, M.I.; Very Rev. Richard O'Donnell, M.I., Prov.; Rev. Albert Schempp, M.I., Chap. & Treas.; Marie D'Amico, Vice Pres. Housing. Order of the Servants of the Sick (Order of St. Camillus), Independent living facilities for older adults. Residents 340; Total Assisted 200; Total Staff 500.

WEST ALLIS. **Catholic Schools Staff Development Association* (1961) 6021 W. Lincoln Ave., 53219. Tel: 414-327-5020; Fax: 414-327-7308. Email: larsond@archmil.org. Donna Larson, Prin. Purpose: To build a community of educators in Catholic education, emphasizing the critical importance of on-going professional development.

WEST BEND. *Casa Guadalupe Education Center, Inc.*, 479 N. Main St., 53090. Tel: 262-306-2900; Fax: 262-306-2901. Email: mlbcasaguadalupe@sbcglobal.net. Web: www.casaguadalupeonline.com. Mary Lynn Bennett, Pres. & Contact Person.

[Z] CLOSED PARISHES

MILWAUKEE. *St. Agnes* For sacramental records, contact Archives, Archdiocese of Milwaukee, P.O. Box 070912, Milwaukee, 53207-0912. Tel: 414-769-3407; Fax: 414-769-3408

St. Albert For sacramental records, contact Archives, Archdiocese of Milwaukee, P.O. Box 070912, Milwaukee, 53207-0912. Tel: 414-769-3407; Fax: 414-769-3408

St. Anne For sacramental records, contact Archives, Archdiocese of Milwaukee, P.O. Box 070912, Milwaukee, 53207-0912. Tel: 414-769-3407; Fax: 414-769-3408

St. Anthony of Padua For sacramental records, contact St. Vincent Pallotti, 7622 W. Stevenson St., Milwaukee, 53223. Tel: 414-453-5344; Fax: 414-453-4225

St. Barbara For sacramental records, contact Archives, Archdiocese of Milwaukee, P.O. Box 070912, Milwaukee, 53207-0912. Tel: 414-769-3407; Fax: 414-769-3408

Blessed Virgin of Pompei For sacramental records, contact Archives, Archdiocese of Milwaukee, P.O. Box 070912, Milwaukee, 53207-0912 Tel: 414-769-3407; Fax: 414-769-3408.

St. Boniface For sacramental records, contact Archives, Archdiocese of Milwaukee, P.O. Box 070912, Milwaukee, 53207-0912. Tel: 414-769-3407; Fax: 414-769-3408

St. Casimir For sacramental records, contact Our Lady of Divine Providence, 3055 N. Fratney St., Milwaukee, 53212, Tel: 414-264-0049, Fax: 414-264-7177.

Corpus Christi For sacramental records, contact Blessed Savior, 8607 W. Villard Ave., Milwaukee, 53225, Tel: 414-464-5033; Fax: 414-464-0079

St. Elizabeth For sacramental records, contact Archives, Archdiocese of Milwaukee, P.O. Box 070912, Milwaukee, 53207-0912. Tel: 414-769-3407; Fax: 414-769-3408

St. Emeric For sacramental records, contact Sacred Heart, 917 N. 49th St., Milwaukee, 53208. Tel: 414-774-9418; Fax: 414-774-7406

St. Gabriel For sacramental records, contact Archives, Archdiocese of Milwaukee, P.O. Box 070912, Milwaukee, 53207-0912. Tel: 414-769-3407; Fax: 414-769-3408

St. Gall For sacramental records, contact Archives, Archdiocese of Milwaukee, P.O. Box 070912, Milwaukee, 53207-0912. Tel: 414-769-3407; Fax: 414-769-3408

St. Gerard For sacramental records, contact Archives, Archdiocese of Milwaukee, P.O. Box 070912, Milwaukee, 53207-0912. Tel: 414-769-3407; Fax: 414-769-3408

St. Hedwig For sacramental records, contact Archives, Archdiocese of Milwaukee, P.O. Box 070912, Milwaukee, 53207-0912. Tel: 414-769-3407, Fax: 414-769-3408

Holy Angels For sacramental records, contact Archives, Archdiocese of Milwaukee, P.O. Box 070912, Milwaukee, 53207-0912. Tel: 414-769-3407; Fax: 414-769-3408

Holy Cross For sacramental records, contact St. Vincent Pallotti, 7622 W. Stevenson St., Milwaukee. Tel: 414-453-5344; Fax: 414-453-4225

Holy Redeemer For sacramental records, contact Archives, Archdiocese of Milwaukee, P.O. Box 070912, Milwaukee, 53207-0912. Tel: 414-769-3407; Fax: 414-769-3408

Holy Rosary For sacramental records, contact Archives, Archdiocese of Milwaukee, P.O. Box 070912, Milwaukee, 5307-0912. Tel: 414-769-3407, Fax: 414-769-3408

Holy Spirit For sacramental records, contact Archives, Archdiocese of Milwaukee, P.O. Box 070912, Milwaukee, 53207-0912. Tel: 414-769-3407; Fax: 414-769-3408

Holy Trinity-Our Lady of Guadalupe For sacramental records, contact Our Lady of Guadalupe, 613 S. 4th St., Milwaukee, 53204. Tel: 414-271-6181; Fax: 414-278-6090

St. Ignatius For sacramental records, contact Archives, Archdiocese of Milwaukee, P.O. Box 070912, Milwaukee, 53207-0912. Tel: 414-769-3407; Fax: 414-769-3408

St. John de Nepomuc For sacramental records, contact Archives, Archdiocese of Milwaukee, P.O. Box 070912, Milwaukee, 53207-0912. Tel: 414-769-3407; Fax: 414-769-3408

St. Joseph For sacramental records, contact St. Joseph, 12130 Center St., Wauwatosa, 53222-4096. Tel: 414-771-4626; Fax: 414-771-4311

St. Lawrence For sacramental records, contact Archives, Archdiocese of Milwaukee, P.O. Box 070912, Milwaukee, 53207-0912. Tel: 414-769-3407; Fax: 414-769-3408

St. Leo For sacramental records, contact Archives, Archdiocese of Milwaukee, P.O. Box 070912, Milwaukee, 53207-0912. Tel: 414-769-3407; Fax: 414-769-3408

St. Mary of Czestochowa For sacramental records, contact Our Lady of Divine Providence, 3055 N. Fratney St., Milwaukee, 53212. Tel: 414-264-0049, Fax: 414-264-7177

Mary Queen of Martyrs For sacramental records, contact Blessed Savior, 8607 W. Villard Ave., Milwaukee, 53225. Tel: 414-464-5033; Fax: 414-464-0079

St. Matthew For sacramental records, contact Archives, Archdiocese of Milwaukee, P.O. Box 070912, Milwaukee, 53207-0912. Tel: 414-769-3407; Fax: 414-769-3408

St. Michael For sacramental records, contact Good Shepherd, W762 Armstrong Rd., Campbellsport, 53010-1400. Tel: 920-477-3201 Fax: 920-477-3030

Mother of Perpetual Help For sacramental records, contact Archives, Archdiocese of Milwaukee, P.O. Box 070912, Milwaukee, 53207-0912. Tel: 414-769-3407; Fax: 414-769-3408

St. Nicholas For sacramental records, contact Archives, Archdiocese of Milwaukee, P.O. Box 070912, Milwaukee, 53207-0912. Tel: 414-769-3407; Fax: 414-769-3408

Our Lady of Sorrows For sacramental records, contact Blessed Savior, 8607 W. Villard Ave., Milwaukee, 53225. Tel: 414-464-5033, Fax: 414-464-0079

St. Philip Neri For sacramental records, contact Blessed Savior, 8607 W. Villard Ave., Milwaukee, 53225. Tel: 414-464-5033; Fax: 414-464-0079

St. Rita For sacramental records, contact Archives, Archdiocese of Milwaukee, P.O. Box 070912, Milwaukee, 53207-0912. Tel: 414-769-3407, Fax: 414-769-3408

St. Stephen Martyr For sacramental records, contact Archives, Archdiocese of Milwaukee, P.O. Box 070912, Milwaukee, 53207-0912. Tel: 414-769-3407; Fax: 414-769-3408

St. Thomas Aquinas For sacramental records, contact Archives, Archdiocese of Milwaukee, P.O. Box 070912, Milwaukee, 53207-0912. Tel: 414-769-3407; Fax: 414-769-3408

St. Wenceslaus For sacramental records, contact Archives, Archdiocese of Milwaukee, P.O. Box 070912, Milwaukee, 53207-0912. Tel: 414-769-3407, Fax: 414-769-3408

ADELL. *St. Patrick* For sacramental records, contact Archives, Archdiocese of Milwaukee, P.O. Box 070912, Milwaukee, 53207-0912. Tel: 414-769-3407; Fax: 414-769-3408

ALLENTON. *Sacred Heart* For sacramental records, contact Resurrection, P.O. Box 96, Allenton, 53002-0096. Tel: 262-629-5240

ARMSTRONG. *Our Lady of Angels* For sacramental records, contact Good Shepherd, 303 E. Main St., P.O. Box 128, Eden. Tel: 920-477-3201; Fax: 920-477-3030

AUBURN. *St. Matthias* For sacramental records, contact Holy Trinity, 331 Main St., P.O. Box 461, Kewaskum, 53040. Tel: 262-626-2860, Fax: 262-626-2301

BEAVER DAM. *St Michael* For sacramental records, contact St. Katharine Drexel, 131 W. Maple Ave., Beaver Dam, 53916. Tel: 920-887-2082, Fax: 920-885-7602

St. Patrick For sacramental records, contact St. Katharine Drexel, 131 W. Maple Ave., Beaver Dam, 53916. Tel: 920-887-2082, Fax: 920-885-7602

St. Peter For sacramental records, contact St. Katharine Drexel, 131 W. Maple Ave., Beaver Dam, 53916. Tel: 920-887-2082, Fax: 920-885-7602

BRISTOL. *St. Scholastica* For sacramental records, contact Holy Cross, Bristol.

BYRON. *St. John* For sacramental records, contact Sons of Zebedee: Saints James and John, W5882 Church Rd., Fond du Lac, 54937-8602. Tel: 920-922-1167

CASCADE. *St. Mary* For sacramental records, contact Archives, Archdiocese of Milwaukee, P.O. Box 070912, Milwaukee, 53207-0912. Tel: 414-769-3707, Fax: 414-769-3408

CEDARBURG. *Divine Word* For sacramental records, contact St. Francis Borgia, 1375 Covered Bridge Rd., Cedarburg, 53012. Tel: 262-377-1070; Fax: 262-377-6898

COLGATE. *St. Columba* For sacramental records, contact St. Francis Borgia Parish, 1375 Covered Bridge Rd., Cedarburg, 53012. Tel: 262-377-1070; Fax: 262-377-6898

CUDAHY. *St. Frederick* For sacramental records, contact Nativity of the Lord, 4611 S. Kirkwood Ave., Cudahy, 53110. Tel: 414-744-6622

Holy Family For sacramental records, contact Nativity of the Lord, 4611 S. Kirkwood Ave., Cudahy, 53110. Tel: 414-744-6622

St. Joseph For sacramental records, contact Nativity of the Lord, 4611 S. Kirkwood Ave., Cudahy, 53110. Tel: 414-744-6622

DACADA. *St. Nicholas* For sacramental records, contact Archives, Archdiocese of Milwaukee, P.O. Box 070912, Milwaukee, 53207-0912. Tel: 414-769-34074, Fax: 414-769-3408

DOTYVILLE. *St. Michael* For sacramental records, contact Good Shepherd, 303 E. Main St., P.O. Box 128, Eden. Tel: 920-477-3201; Fax: 920-477-3030

EDEN. *St. Mary* For sacramental records, contact Good Shepherd, 303 E. Main St., P.O. Box 128, Eden. Tel: 920-477-3201; Fax: 920-477-3030

ELDORADO. *St. Mary* For sacramental records, contact Our Risen Savior, W8272 Forest Avenue Rd., Eldorado, 54932-9801. Tel: 920-922-2412

ELKHART LAKE. *St. George* For sacramental records, contact St. Thomas Aquinas, P.O. Box T, Elkhart Lake, 53020-0396. Tel: 920-876-2457

FARMINGTON. *St. John of God* For sacramental records, contact St. Michael, 8877 Forestview Rd., Kewaskum, 53040. Tel: 262-334-5270; Fax: 262-334-5233

FOND DU LAC. *St. Joseph* Closed. For sacramental records prior to June 12, 1967, contact Archdiocese of Milwaukee Archives. Tel: 414-769-3407; For records after June 12, 1967, contact Holy Family, 271 Fourth St. Way, Fond du Lac, 54935. Tel: 920-921-0580

St. Louis Closed. For sacramental records prior to Sept. 20, 1959, contact Archdiocese of Milwaukee Archives. Tel: 414-769-3407; For records after Sept. 20, 1959, contact Holy Family, 271 Fourth St. Way, Fond du Lac, 54935. Tel: 920-921-0580

St. Mary Closed. For sacramental records through 1975, contact Archdiocese of Milwaukee Archives. Tel: 414-769-3407; For records after 1975, contact Holy Family, 271 Fourth St. Way, Fond du Lac, 54935. Tel: 920-921-0580.

St. Patrick For sacramental records prior to September 19, 1960, contact Archdiocese of Milwaukee Archives. Tel: 414-769-3407; For records after September 19, 1960, contact Holy Family, 678 Western Ave., Fond du Lac, 54935. Tel: 920-921-0580

Sacred Heart Closed. For sacramental records prior to December, 1970, contact Archdiocese of Milwaukee Archives. Tel: 414-769-3407; For records after November, 1970, contact Holy Family, 271 Fourth St. Way, Fond du Lac, 54935. Tel: 920-921-0580

FOX LAKE. *St. Mary* For sacramental records, contact Annunciation, 305 Green St., P.O. Box 85, Fox Lake, 53933-0085. Tel: 920-928-3513; Fax: 920-928-6334

FRANKLIN. *Sacred Hearts of Jesus and Mary* For sacramental records, contact St. Martin of Tours, 7963 S. 116th St., Franklin, 53132. Tel: 414-425-1114; Fax: 414-425-2527

FREDONIA. *St. Rose of Lima* For sacramental records, contact Holy Rosary, 305 Fredonia Ave., P.O. Box 250, Fredonia, 53021-0250. Tel: 262-692-9994; Fax: 262-692-3085

GLENBEULAH. *St. Fridolin* For sacramental records, contact St. Thomas Aquinas, P.O. Box T, Elkhart Lake, 53020-0396. Tel: 920-876-2457

HOLY CROSS. *Holy Cross* For sacramental records, contact Holy Rosary, 305 Fredonia Ave., P.O. Box 250, Fredonia, 53021-0250. Tel: 262-692-9994; Fax: 262-692-3085

HORICON. *St. Malachy* For sacramental records, contact Sacred Heart, 113 Valley St., Horicon, 53032. Tel: 920-485-0694

HUBERTUS. *St. Hubert* For sacramental records prior to 1961, contact the Archdiocese of Milwaukee Archives, Tel: 414-769-3407. For sacramental records after 1960, contact St. Gabriel, 1200 St. Gabriel Way, Hubertus, 53033-9794, Tel: 262-628-1141, Fax: 262-628-1911.

JUNEAU. *Immaculate Conception* For sacramental records, contact Sacred Heart, 113 Valley St., Horicon, 53032. Tel: 920-485-0694

KENOSHA. *St. Casmir* For sacramental records, contact the Archdiocese of Milwaukee Archives. Tel: 414-769-3407

St. George For sacramental records, contact the Archdiocese of Milwaukee Archives. Tel: 414-769-3407

St. Thomas Aquinas For sacramental records, contact Archdiocese of Milwaukee Archives, Tel: 414-769-3407.

LAKE FIVE. *St. Columba* For sacramental records, contact St. Gabriel, 1200 St. Gabriel Way, Hubertus 53033-9794. Tel: 262-628-1141, Fax: 262-628-1911

LIMA. *St. Rose of Lima* For sacramental records, contact Blessed Trinity, 327 Giddings Ave., Sheboygan Falls, 53085. Tel: 920-467-4616; Fax: 920-467-4290

LITTLE KOHLER. *Mother of Sorrows* For sacramental records, contact Holy Rosary, 305 Fredonia Ave., P.O. Box 250, Fredonia, 53021-0250. Tel: 262-692-9994; Fax: 262-692-3085

LOST LAKE. *St. Mary* For sacramental records, contact Annunciation, 305 Green St., P.O. Box 85, Fox Lake, 53933-0085. Tel: 920-928-3513; Fax: 920-928-6334

LYONS. *St. Kilian* For sacramental records, contact St. Joseph, 1540 Mill St., P.O. Box 60, Lyons, 53148-0060. Tel: 262-763-2050; Fax: 262-763-9377

MEQUON. *St. James* For sacramental records, contact Lumen Christi, 11300 N. St. James Ln., 28W. Mequon, 53092, Tel: 262-242-7967; Fax: 262-242-7970.

MITCHELL. *St. Michael* For sacramental records, contact Archives, Archdiocese of Milwaukee, P.O. Box 070912, Milwaukee, 53207-0912. Tel: 414-769-3407, Fax: 414-769-3408

MONCHES. *St. John* (1843) For sacramental records, contact Blessed Teresa of Calcutta, P.O. Box 68, North Lake, 53064-0068, Tel: 262-966-2191, Fax: 262-966-1829.

NABOB. *St. Matthias* For sacramental records, contact St. Lawrence, St. Lawrence.

NENNO. *St. Anthony* For sacramental records, contact Resurrection, P.O. Box 96, Allenton, 53002-0096. Tel: 262-629-5240

SS. Peter and Paul For sacramental records, contact Resurrection, P.O. Box 96, Allenton, 53002-0096. Tel: 262-629-5240

NORTH LAKE. *St. Clare* Closed. For sacramental records, contact Blessed Teresa of Calcutta, P.O. Box 68, North Lake, 53064-0068, Tel: 262-966-2191, Fax: 262-966-1829.

OAKFIELD. *St. James* For sacramental records, contact Sons of Zebedee: Saints James and John, Byron.

PELL LAKE. *St. Mary* Closed. For sacramental records, contact St. Francis de Sales, 148 W. Main St., Lake Geneva, 53147, Tel: 262-258-8524/8525; Fax: 262-691-7376

PEWAUKEE. *St. Mary* For sacramental records, contact Queen of Apostles, W280 N2101 Hwy. SS, Pewaukee, 53072. Tel: 262-691-1535; Fax: 262-691-7376

SS. Peter and Paul For sacramental records, contact Queen of Apostles, W280 N2101 Hwy. SS, Pewaukee, 53072. Tel: 262-691-1535; Fax: 262-691-7376

RACINE. *St. Casimir* For sacramental records, contact Archives, Archdiocese of Milwaukee, P.O. Box 070912, Milwaukee, 53207-0912. Tel: 262-769-3407; Fax: 262-769-3408

Holy Name For sacramental records, contact Archives, Archdiocese of Milwaukee, P.O. Box 070912, Milwaukee, 53207-0912. Tel: 262-769-3407; Fax: 262-769-3408

Holy Trinity For sacramental records, contact Archives, Archdiocese of Milwaukee, P.O. Box 070912, Milwaukee, 53207-0912. Tel: 262-769-3407; Fax: 262-769-3408

St. Rose For sacramental records, contact Archives, Archdiocese of Milwaukee, P.O. Box 070912, Milwaukee, 53207-0912. Tel: 262-769-3407; Fax: 262-769-3408

St. Stanislaus For sacramental records, contact Archives, Archdiocese of Milwaukee, P.O. Box 070912, Milwaukee, 53207-0912. Tel: 262-769-3407; Fax: 262-769-3408

RANDOLPH. *St. Gabriel* For sacramental records, contact Annunciation, 305 Green St., P.O. Box 85, Fox Lake, 53933-0085. Tel: 920-928-3513; Fax: 920-928-6334

St. Mary For sacramental records, contact Annunciation, 305 Green St., P.O. Box 85, Fox Lake, 53933-0085. Tel: 920-928-3513, Fax: 920-928-6334

RANDOM LAKE. *St. Mary* For sacramental records, contact Archdiocese of Milwaukee Archives.

RICHFIELD. *St. Mary* For sacramental records before 1967, contact Archives, Archdiocese of Milwaukee, P.O. Box 070912, Milwaukee, 53207-0912, Tel: 414-769-3707; Fax: 414-769-3408. For sacramental records after 1966, contact St. Gabriel, Hubertus.

RIPON. *St. Patrick* For sacramental records, contact St. Catherine of Siena, 218 Blossom St., Ripon, 54971-1560. Tel: 920-748-2345.

St. Wenceslaus For sacramental records, contact St. Catherine of Siena, 218 Blossom St., Ripon, 54971-1560, Tel: 920-748-2345.

ST. GEORGE. *St. George* For sacramental records, contact Blessed Trinity, 327 Giddings Ave., Sheboygan Falls, 53085. Tel: 920-467-4616; Fax: 920-467-4290

ST. MARTIN. *Holy Assumption* For sacramental records through 1990, contact St. Mary, 9520 W. Forest Home Ave., Hales Corners, 53130. Tel: 414-425-2174; Fax: 414-425-9432. For records after 1990, contact St. Martin of Tours, 7963 S. 116th St., Franklin, 53132. Tel: 414-425-1114; Fax: 414-425-1114

ST. PETER. *St. Peter* For sacramental records prior to 1953, contact Archdiocese of Milwaukee Archives; Tel: 414-769-3407. For records after 1952, contact Holy Family, 271 Fourth St. Way, Fond du Lac, 54935, Tel: 920-921-0580.

SOUTH MILWAUKEE. *St. Adalbert* For sacramental records, contact Divine Mercy, 1304 Manitoba Ave., South Milwaukee, 53172. Tel: 414-762-6810

St. John For sacramental records, contact Divine Mercy, 1304 Manitoba Ave., South Milwaukee, 53172. Tel: 414-762-6810

St. Mary For sacramental records, contact Divine Mercy, 1304 Manitoba Ave., South Milwaukee, 53172. Tel: 414-762-6810

St. Sylvester For sacramental records, contact Divine Mercy, 1304 Manitoba Ave., South Milwaukee, 53172. Tel: 414-762-6810

THIENSVILLE. *St. Cecilia* For sacramental records, contact Lumen Christi, 11300 N. St. James Ln., 28W, Mequon, 53092, Tel: 262-242-7967, Fax: 262-242-7970.

THOMPSON. *St. Patrick* For sacramental records, contact St. Kilian, 264 W. State St., Hartford, 53027. Tel: 262-673-4831

WAYNE. *St. Bridget* For sacramental records, contact Holy Trinity, 331 Main St., P.O. Box 461, Kewaskum, 53040. Tel: 262-626-2860; Fax: 262-626-2301

WEST ALLIS. *St. Joseph* For sacramental records, contact Archives, Archdiocese of Milwaukee, P.O. Box 070912, Milwaukee, 53207-0912. Tel: 414-769-3407; Fax: 414-769-3408

Our Lady of Mount Carmel For sacramental records, contact Archives, Archdiocese of Milwaukee, P.O. Box 070912, Milwaukee, 53207-0912. Tel: 414-769-3407; Fax: 414-769-3408

St. Mary Help of Christians For sacramental records, contact Archives, Archdiocese of

Milwaukee, P.O. Box 070912, Milwaukee, 53207-0912. Tel: 414-769-3407; Fax: 414-769-3408

WILMOT. *Holy Name of Jesus* For sacramental records, contact Holy Cross, Bristol.

WOODHULL. *St. John the Baptist* For sacramental records, contact Our Risen Savior, W8272 Forest Avenue Rd., Eldorado, 54932-9801. Tel: 920-922-2412

RELIGIOUS INSTITUTES OF MEN REPRESENTED IN THE ARCHDIOCESE

For further details refer to the corresponding bracketed number in the Religious Institutes of Men or Women section.

[0120]—*Alexian Brothers* (Immaculate Conception Prov.)—C.F.A.

[0140]—*The Augustinians* (Mother of Good Counsel Prov.)—O.S.A.

[0200]—*Benedictine Monks*—O.S.B.

[0600]—*Brothers of the Congregation of Holy Cross* (Midwest Prov.)—C.S.C.

[0470]—*The Capuchin Friars* (Prov. of St. Joseph)—O.F.M.Cap.

[0740]—*Congregation of Marians of the Immaculate Conception*—M.I.C.

[1130]—*Congregation of the Priests of the Sacred Heart*—S.C.J.

[0480]—*Conventual Franciscans* (St. Bonaventure, Prov. of Our Lady of Consolation)—O.F.M.Conv

[0260]—*Discalced Carmelite Friars* (Prov. of the Immaculate Heart of Mary)—O.C.D.

[0520]—*Franciscan Friars*—O.F.M.

[0690]—*Jesuit Fathers and Brothers*—S.J.

[0720]—*The Missionaries of Our Lady of La Salette* (Prov. of Mary, Queen of Peace)—M.S.

[0430]—*Order of Preachers* (Province of St. Albert the Great)—O.P.

[0240]—*Order of St. Camillus-Camillian Fathers and Brothers*—O.S.Cam.

[1070]—*Redemptorist Fathers* (St. Louis Prov.)—C.SS.R.

[0990]—*Society of the Catholic Apostolate* (Mater Dei Prov.)—S.A.C.

[1200]—*Society of the Divine Savior* (American Prov.)—S.D.S.

[0420]—*Society of the Divine Word* (Northern Prov.)—S.V.D.

[1360]—*Xaverian Missionary Fathers*—S.X.

RELIGIOUS INSTITUTES OF WOMEN REPRESENTED IN THE ARCHDIOCESE

[0230]—*Benedictine Sisters of Pontifical Jurisdiction* (Erie, PA)—O.S.B.

[0360]—*Carmelite Sisters of the Divine Heart of Jesus*—Carmel.D.C.J.

[]—*The Christian Sisters (Pious Union)*—C.S.

[]—*Congregation of Institutio Santa Mariana de Jesus*

[3710]—*Congregation of the Sisters of Saint Agnes*—C.S.A.

[1780]—*Congregation of the Sisters of the Third Order of St. Francis of Perpetual Adoration* (Eastern Region)—F.S.P.A.

[0760]—*Daughters of Charity of St. Vincent De Paul*—D.C.

[0790]—*Daughters of Divine Charity*—F.D.C.

[0420]—*Discalced Carmelite Nuns*—O.C.D.

[1060]—*Dominican Contemplative Sisters*—O.P.

[1070-03]—*Dominican Sisters*—O.P.

[]—*Dominican Sisters* (Vietnam)

[1070-09]—*Dominican Sisters*—O.P.

[1070-27]—*Dominican Sisters*—O.P.

[1070-25]—*Dominican Sisters*—O.P.

[1115]—*Dominican Sisters of Peace*—O.P.

[1170]—*Felician Sisters*—C.S.S.F.

[1230]—*Franciscan Sisters of Christian Charity*—O.S.F.

[1310]—*Franciscan Sisters of Little Falls, MN*—O.S.F.

[1415]—*Franciscan Sisters of Mary*—F.S.M.

[1430]—*Franciscan Sisters of Our Lady of Perpetual Help*—O.S.F.

[]—*Franciscan Sisters of Our Lady (Pious Union)*—F.S.O.L.

[]—*Franciscan Sisters of St. Clare (Pious Union)*—F.S.S.C.

[1470]—*Franciscan Sisters of St. Joseph*—F.S.S.J.

[1240]—*Franciscan Sisters, Daughters of the Sacred Hearts of Jesus and Mary*—O.S.F.

[]—*Hermitage of the Trinity*

[1820]—*Hospital Sisters of the Third Order of St. Francis*—O.S.F.

[]—*Missionary Sisters of the Holy Family*—M.S.F.

[3230]—*Poor Handmaids of Jesus Christ*—P.H.J.C.

[2970]—*School Sisters of Notre Dame*—S.S.N.D.

[1680]—*School Sisters of St. Francis*—O.S.F.

[]—*Secular Institute of Schoenstatt Sisters of Mary*—I.S.S.M.

[0600]—*Sisters of Charity of St. Joan Antida*—S.C.S.J.A.

[0430]—*Sisters of Charity of the Blessed Virgin Mary*—B.V.M.

[2575]—*Sisters of Mercy of the Americas*—R.S.M.

[3800]—*Sisters of St. Elizabeth*—S.S.E.

[1705]—*The Sisters of St. Francis of Assisi*—O.S.F.

[1520]—*Sisters of St. Francis of Christ the King*—O.S.F.

[3930]—*Sisters of St. Joseph of the Third Order of St. Francis*—S.S.J.-T.O.S.F.

[4020]—*Sisters of St. Rita*—O.S.A.

[1030]—*Sisters of the Divine Savior*—S.D.S.

[4100]—*Sisters of the Sorrowful Mother (Third Order of St. Francis)*—S.S.M.

[3510]—*Sisters Servants of Christ the King*—S.S.C.K.

ARCHDIOCESAN CEMETERIES

MILWAUKEE. *St. Adalbert*
Calvary
Holy Cross
Holy Trinity
Mount Olivet

FRANKLIN. *All Souls*

KENOSHA. *All Saints*

MEQUON. *Resurrection*

SOUTH MILWAUKEE. *Holy Sepulcher*, 675 College Ave., 53172-1252. Tel: 414-762-6800. Gregg F. Apostoloff, Archdiocesan Dir.

TAYCHEEDAH. *St. Charles Cemetery* 54935. Tel: 920-921-0347. (See St. Patrick Parish, Fond du Lac)

WAUKESHA. *St. Joseph*

NECROLOGY

† Beitzinger, George J., (Retired)—Died March 17, 2009

† Braun, Donald B., (Retired)—Died Nov. 3, 2009

† Pakenham, Daniel J., Elm Grove, WI St. Mary's Visitation—Died Jan. 15, 2009

† Rykowski, Valerian J., (Retired)—Died March 1, 2009

† Shmauz, Donald A., (On Duty Outside the Archdiocese)—Died Oct. 10, 2009

† Thanh-Hung, John B., (Retired)—Died July 1, 2009

† Walter, John F., (Retired)—Died June 14, 2009

† Weber, Gordon A., (Retired)—Died July 4, 2009

An asterisk (*) denotes an organization that has established tax-exempt status directly with the IRS and is not covered by the USCCB Group Ruling.

Archdiocese of Mobile

(Archidioecesis Mobiliensis)

Most Reverend

THOMAS J. RODI

Archbishop of Mobile; ordained May 20, 1978; appointed Bishop of Biloxi May 15, 2001; ordained and installed July 2, 2001; appointed Archbishop of Mobile April 2, 2008; installed June 6, 2008. *400 Government St., P.O. Box 1966, Mobile, AL 36633.* Tel: 251-434-1585.

Most Reverend

OSCAR H. LIPSCOMB, D.D., PH.D.

Archbishop Emeritus of Mobile; ordained July 15, 1956; appointed July 29, 1980; consecrated November 16, 1980; retired April 2, 2008. *Res.: 400 Government St., P.O. Box 1966, Mobile, AL 36633.* Tel: 251-434-1585.

CARITAS CHRISTI URGET NOS

Chancery Office: 400 Government St., P.O. Box 1966, Mobile, AL 36633. Tel: 251-434-1585; Fax: 251-434-1588.

Email: aom_chan@bellsouth.net

Square Miles 22,969.

Established as Vicariate-Apostolic of Alabama and the Floridas, 1825; Diocese of Mobile, May 15, 1829; Name changed to Diocese of Mobile-Birmingham, July 9, 1954; Redesignated, June 28, 1969. Raised to rank of Archdiocese November 16, 1980.

Comprises the lower 28 Counties of the State of Alabama, namely: Choctaw, Clarke, Wilcox, Dallas, Autauga, Elmore, Lee, Russell, Macon, Montgomery, Lowndes, Barbour, Bullock, Pike, Crenshaw, Butler, Monroe, Conecuh, Escambia, Covington, Coffee, Geneva, Dale, Henry, Houston, Washington, Baldwin and Mobile.

For legal titles of parishes and archdiocesan institutions consult the Chancery Office.

STATISTICAL OVERVIEW

Personnel	
Archbishops	1
Retired Archbishops	1
Priests: Diocesan Active in Diocese	61
Priests: Diocesan Active Outside Diocese	7
Priests: Retired, Sick or Absent	29
Number of Diocesan Priests	97
Religious Priests in Diocese	36
Total Priests in Diocese	133
Extern Priests in Diocese	5
Ordinations:	
Transitional Deacons	3
Permanent Deacons	1
Permanent Deacons in Diocese	55
Total Brothers	10
Total Sisters	112
Parishes	
Parishes	76
With Resident Pastor:	
Resident Diocesan Priests	52
Resident Religious Priests	14
Without Resident Pastor:	
Administered by Priests	10
Missions	10
Pastoral Centers	3
Professional Ministry Personnel:	
Brothers	2
Sisters	5
Lay Ministers	33
Welfare	
Catholic Hospitals	1
Total Assisted	170,433
Health Care Centers	3
Total Assisted	6,119
Homes for the Aged	4
Total Assisted	1,613
Residential Care of Children	1
Total Assisted	65
Day Care Centers	4
Total Assisted	365
Specialized Homes	1
Total Assisted	10
Special Centers for Social Services	11
Total Assisted	58,653
Residential Care of Disabled	3
Total Assisted	134
Other Institutions	2
Total Assisted	256
Educational	
Diocesan Students in Other Seminaries	18
Total Seminarians	18
Colleges and Universities	1
Total Students	1,867
High Schools, Diocesan and Parish	3
Total Students	1,526
Elementary Schools, Diocesan and Parish	15
Total Students	4,523
Catechesis/Religious Education:	
High School Students	709
Elementary Students	3,442
Total Students under Catholic Instruction	12,085
Teachers in the Diocese:	
Priests	2
Brothers	5
Sisters	5
Lay Teachers	504
Vital Statistics	
Receptions into the Church:	
Infant Baptism Totals	1,060
Minor Baptism Totals	55
Adult Baptism Totals	216
Received into Full Communion	302
First Communions	857
Confirmations	1,127
Marriages:	
Catholic	151
Interfaith	176
Total Marriages	327
Deaths	566
Total Catholic Population	69,317
Total Population	1,717,010

Former Prelates—Rt. Revs. MICHAEL PORTIER, D.D., ord. May 16, 1818; First Bishop; cons. Nov. 5, 1826; died May 14, 1859; JOHN QUINLAN, D.D., ord. Aug. 30, 1852; cons. Dec. 4, 1859; died March 9, 1883; DOMINIC MANUCY, D.D., ord. Aug. 15, 1850; appt. Vicar Apostolic of Brownsville and cons. Bishop of Dulma Dec. 8, 1874; transferred to Mobile March 9, 1884, but resigned in the same year; died at Mobile, Dec. 4, 1885; JEREMIAH O'SULLIVAN, D.D., ord. June 30, 1868; cons. Sept. 20, 1885; died Aug. 10, 1896; E. P. ALLEN, ord. Dec. 17, 1881; cons. May 16, 1897; died Oct. 21, 1926; Most Revs. THOMAS J. TOOLEN, D.D., ord. Sept. 27, 1910; cons. May 4, 1927; appt. Archbishop "ad personam," May 27, 1954; resigned Oct. 8, 1969; died Dec. 4, 1976; JOHN L. MAY, D.D., ord. May 3, 1947; appt. Titular Bishop of Tagarbala and Auxiliary Bishop of Chicago, June 21, 1967; cons. Aug. 24, 1967; transferred to Mobile, Oct. 8, 1969; installed Dec. 10, 1969; appt. to Saint Louis, Jan. 29, 1980; died March 24, 1994; OSCAR H. LIPSCOMB, D.D., Ph.D. (Retired), ord. July 15, 1956; appt. July 29, 1980; cons. Nov. 16, 1980; retired April 2, 2008.

Vicar General—Rev. Msgrs. FRANCIS V. CUSACK, V.G., Vicar Gen. & Vicar for Priests, 1621 Boykin Blvd., Mobile, 36605. Tel: 251-479-9885; Fax: 251-479-9892; MICHAEL L. FARMER, V.G., S.T.L., Vicar Gen. & Moderator of the Curia, Mailing Address: P.O. Box 1966, Mobile, 36633. Tel: 251-434-1585; Fax: 251-434-1588.

Vicars Forane—Very Rev. JAMES F. ZOGHBY, Mobile Deanery, 6300 McKenna Dr., Mobile, 36608. Tel: 251-342-1852; Fax: 251-342-6313; Rev. Msgrs. F. CHARLES TRONCALE, Montgomery Deanery, 8570 Vaughn Rd., Montgomery, 36117. Tel: 334-277-5631; Fax: 334-272-1008; PATRICK J. GALLAGHER, Dothan Deanery, 2700 W. Main St., Dothan, 36301. Tel: 334-793-5802; Fax: 334-792-2816; Very Rev. PAUL G. ZOGHBY, Baldwin/Escambia Deanery, 601 W. Laurel, Foley, 36535. Tel: 251-943-4009; Fax: 251-943-4010.

Chancellor—Rev. Msgr. MICHAEL L. FARMER, V.G., S.T.L.

Archivist—Mr. RICHARD CHASTANG.

Archives Office—14 S. Franklin St., P.O. Box 1966, Mobile, 36633. Tel: 251-415-3850; Fax: 251-434-1588.

Metropolitan Tribunal—14 S. Franklin St., P.O. Box 2405, Mobile, 36652-2405. Tel: 251-432-4609; Fax: 251-432-4647. Please address all rogatory commissions and matrimonial matters to the Office of the Tribunal.

Judicial Vicar—Rev. Msgr. JAMES S. KEE, S.T.L., J.C.L., J.V.

Associate Judges—Rev. Msgr. KENNETH J. KLEPAC, J.C.L.; Mrs. KATHERINE S. WEBER, M.S. (Th), J.C.L.; Mr. VICTOR WHELAN, S.T.M.; Rev. JAMES MONTINI-COLEMAN, M.Div., J.C.L.

Judicial Consultant—Rev. Msgr. ANTHONY MCDEVITT, J.C.D., S.T.L. (Retired).

Defender of the Bond—Deacon J. DOUGLAS SINCHAK.

Advocate—Mr. VICTOR WHELAN, S.T.M.

Court Clerk and Notary—Mrs. DANICE ENTREKIN, M.Ed.

Notaries and Secretaries—Mrs. SHARON B. CUSIMANO; Mrs. PATRICIA K. CONNER.

Archdiocesan Consultors—Rev. Msgrs. PETER J. CUNNINGHAM; FRANCIS V. CUSACK, V.G.; MICHAEL L. FARMER, V.G., S.T.L.; JAMES S. KEE, S.T.L., J.C.L., J.V.; Rev. JAMES J. CINK; Rev. Msgr. WILLIAM J. SKONEKI.

Vicars for Religious—Rev. ROBERT B. RIMES, S.J., Spring Hill College, 4000 Dauphin St., Mobile, 36608. Tel: 251-460-2175; Sr. PAUL MARY OF JESUS, L.S.P., Liaison with Religious Sisters, Nuns & Brothers, 1655 McGill Ave., Mobile,

36604. Tel: 251-476-6335.

Archdiocesan Finance Council— c/o Mr. Walter C. Puckett, Exec. Dir. for Financial Svcs. *356 Government St., P.O. Box 230, Mobile, 36601.* Tel: 251-432-2737; Fax: 251-434-1547. Email: wpuckett@mobilearchdiocese.org.

Presbyteral Council—Most Rev. Thomas J. Rodi, Pres. Officers: Very Rev. James F. Zoghby, Chm.; Rev. James J. Cink, Vice Chm.; Rev. Msgr. Michael L. Farmer, V.G., S.T.L., Sec.

Elected Members—Group I: Rev. Msgr. F. Charles Troncale. Group II: Rev. Steven T. Williams. Group III: Very Rev. Stephen E. Martin.

Religious—Vacant.

Jesuit—Rev. Marvin Kitten, S.J.

Priests' Personnel Committee—Very Rev. James F. Zoghby, Chm., Corpus Christi Parish, 6300 McKenna Dr., Mobile, 36608. Tel: 251-342-1852.

Priests' Retirement Board/Clergy Retirement Association—Mr. Walter C. Puckett, Mailing Address: P.O. Box 230, Mobile, 36601. Tel: 251-432-2737.

Archdiocesan Offices and Directors

Catholic Education—Mailing Address: P.O. Box 129, Mobile, 36601. Tel: 251-438-4611.

Executive Director—Miss Gwendolyn P. Byrd. Email: gbyrd@mobilearchdiocese.org.

Schools Office—Miss Gwendolyn P. Byrd, Supt., Mailing Address: P.O. Box 129, Mobile, 36601. Tel: 251-438-4611.

Catholic Youth Organization—Mr. Paul Crane, Exec. Dir., Mailing Address: P.O. Box 6955, Mobile, 36660. Tel: 251-471-0062.

Catholic Youth Ministry—Mrs. Janet Masline, Dir., Mailing Address: P.O. Box 129, Mobile, 36601. Tel: 251-433-4138. Email: jmasline@mobilearchdiocese.org.

Office of Religious Education—Mrs. Rebecca Titford, Dir., 352 Government St., P.O. Box 2405, Mobile, 36652. Tel: 251-433-6991. Email: rtitford@mobilearchdiocese.org. Associate Directors: Ms. Jeanne C. Howard, Cathechesis & Evangelization; Mr. David M. O'Brien, Lay Ministry; Sisters Theresa R. Bretthauer, M.S.B.T., Montgomery Office: 2815 Forbes Rd., Montgomery, 36110. Tel: 334-269-2389; Mary M. "Penny" Smith, O.P., Mailing Address: 375 County Rd. 404, Ozark, 36360. Tel: 334-299-6671.

Catholic Publishing Co., Inc.— Publisher of the Archdiocesan Newspaper "The Catholic Week" Larry Wahl, Editor, Mailing Address: P.O. Box 349, Mobile, 36601. Tel: 251-432-3529.

Catholic Social Services—400 Government St., Mobile, 36602. Mailing Address: P.O. Box 759, Mobile, 36601. Tel: 251-434-1550; Fax: 251-431-1549. Mrs. Marilyn D. King, Exec. Dir. Email: mdking@cssmobile.org. Total Assisted Annually 42,051.

Apostolate for Persons with Disabilities—Mrs. Ruth P. Breland, Dir., 400 Government St., Mobile, 36602. Tel: 251-342-6449. Email: rbreland@cssmobile.org.

Catholic Deaf Ministry—Mr. William F. Jones. Tel: 251-340-0990.

Mass for Shut-Ins—Mr. Tom Stout. Tel: 251-433-0013.

Pregnancy Services—

2-B Choices for Women—100 S. University Blvd., Mobile, 36608. Tel: 251-343-4636; Fax: 251-343-6176. Jerry Bodden, Dir. Total Assisted 1,215.

To Be Help for Pregnant Women—399 S. Section St., P.O. Box 783, Fairhope, 36532. Tel: 251-928-8661; Fax: 251-928-8871. Sonja Brueck, Dir. Total Assisted 168.

Refugee Resettlement—406 Government St., Mobile, 36602. Tel: 251-432-2727; Fax: 251-432-2927. Jana Curran, Dir. Total Assisted 484.

Respect Life Office—400 Government St., Mobile, 36602. Tel: 251-434-1550; Fax: 251-434-1549. Miss Elizabeth C. Burgess, Dir. Email: bburgess@cssmobile.org.

Service Center of Catholic Social Services—555 Dauphin St., Mobile, 36602. Tel: 251-434-1500; Fax: 251-434-1509. Email: cscadmin@mobilecss.org. Web: www.mobilecss.org. Sr. Judith Smiths, C.S.A., M.A., Dir. Total Assisted 34,423. Total Staff 18.

Bay Minette Office—610 Railroad Ave., Bay Minette, 36507. Tel: 251-937-7858. Mrs. Buffy L. Marston, Dir. Email: fscbm@aol.com. Total Assisted 956.

Robertsdale Baldwin Office—23010 Hwy. 59 N., P.O. Box 870, Robertsdale, 36567. Tel: 251-947-2293; Fax: 251-947-4058. Ms. Michele J. Prockup, Dir. Email: michelecssbald@gulftel.com. Total Assisted Annually 4,341.

Clarke County Office—3309 College Ave., P.O. Box 85, Jackson, 36545. Tel: 251-246-0131; Fax: 251-246-4414. Mrs. Shiela L. Smith, Dir. Email: cssclarke@mindspring.com. Total Assisted 1,845.

Dothan Office—557 W. Main St., Dothan, 36302. Tel: 334-793-3601; Fax: 334-702-0825. Ms. Vickie A. Alleman, Dir. Email: vaua@aol.com. Total Assisted Annually 3,118.

Montgomery Office—4455 Narrow Lane Rd., Montgomery, 36116. Tel: 334-288-8890; Fax: 334-288-9322. Mr. Barry F. Cavan, Dir. Email: cavan@cssalabama.org. Total Assisted 3,000.

St. Margaret's Services—Mrs. Carol B. Herron, Supvr. Email: herron@cssalabama.org.

Other Social Service Ministries—

Allen Memorial Home—Ms. Cheryl Robinson, Admin. Bed Capacity 119; Patients Assisted Annually 1,154; Total Staff 160. 735 S. Washington Ave., Mobile, 36603. Tel: 251-433-2642; Fax: 251-433-5502. Email: allenmhome@aol.com.

Campaign for Human Development—Mrs. Marilyn D. King, Dir. Funding Office for charitable and other works of Archdiocese. 400 Government St., Mobile, 36602. Tel: 251-434-1550; Fax: 251-431-1549. Mailing Address: P.O. Box 759, Mobile, 36601.

Ladies of Charity—Baldwin-Escambia Deanery, 22524 Hightower Dr., Foley, 36535. Mailing Address: Mobile Deanery, P.O. Box 6987, Mobile, 36660. Tel: 251-661-9448. *St. Jude, 3300 S. Boone St., Montgomery, 36108.*

St. Mary's Home—4350 Moffat Rd., Mobile, 36618. Tel: 251-344-7733; Fax: 251-344-9753. Mr. Phillip A. Wynne, Admin. Dependent Children 65.

Censor Librorum—Rev. Msgr. Michael L. Farmer, V.G., S.T.L., Mailing Address: P.O. Box 1966, Mobile, 36633. Tel: 251-434-1585; Fax: 251-434-1588. Email: mfarmer@mobilearchdiocese.org.

Development Office—356 Government St., P.O. Box 230, Mobile, 36601. Tel: 251-438-9668; Fax: 251-434-1547. Deacon Robert E. Kirby, Dir. Funding Office for charitable and other works of Archdiocese. Encompasses: Catholic Charities Appeal Office and Planned Giving.

Financial Services—356 Government St., P.O. Box 230, Mobile, 36601. Tel: 251-432-2737; Fax: 251-434-1547.

Executive Director—Mr. Walter C. Puckett. Email: wpuckett@mobilearchdiocese.org.

Accounting Department—Mrs. Cindy S. Larry, CPA, Comptroller.

Administration—Mr. David V. Wilton, Dir.

Human Resources and Payroll—Mrs. Vicki A. Stricklin, Dir.

Information Systems—Mr. William K. Ellis, Dir.

Information Technology—Mr. Joseph E. Robertson, Dir.

Real Estate, Property/Liability Insurance & Risk Management—Mr. James D. Weisser.

Catholic Cemetery—1700 Dr. Martin Luther King, Jr. Ave., Mobile, 36601. Tel: 251-479-5305. *Mailing Address: P.O. Box 230, Mobile, 36601.* Mr. Robert Overmeyer, Mgr.

Friends of Catholic Cemetery—Mailing Address: 1400 Joyce Rd., Mobile, 36618. Mrs. Perilla A. Wilson, Pres. Tel: 251-509-6330. Email: perilla.w@juno.com.

Catholic Housing of Mobile, Inc.—Most Rev. Thomas J. Rodi, Pres.; Rev. Msgr. Michael L. Farmer, V.G., S.T.L., Vice Pres., Mailing Address: P.O. Box 230, Mobile, 36601. Nonprofit Corp. of the State of Alabama; Encompasses Cathedral Place Apartments.

Catholic Housing Authority of Montgomery, Inc.—Most Rev. Thomas J. Rodi, Pres., 3721 Wares Ferry Rd., Montgomery, 36109. Nonprofit Corp. of the State of Alabama; Encompasses Seton Haven Apartments.

Holy Childhood Association—Rev. Leo Blanchet, Dir., Mailing Address: St. Bridget, P.O. Box 13357, Eight Mile, 36613. Tel: 251-457-6847.

McGill Institute, A Corporation—Mailing Address: P.O. Box 230, Mobile, 36601.

McGill-Toolen Foundation—Mrs. Kathleen M. Killion, Dir., Mailing Address: 1501 Old Shell Rd., Mobile, 36604. Tel: 251-445-2939; Fax: 251-433-8356.

Pontifical Mission Societies of the United States—Rev. Leo Blanchet, Dir., Mailing Address: St. Bridget, P.O. Box 13357, Eight Mile, 36613. Tel: 251-457-6847 Encompasses: Propagation of the Faith, Holy Childhood Assoc., Missionary Co-op.

Liturgical Commission—Rev. Msgr. Michael L. Farmer, V.G., S.T.L., Chm., Mailing Address: P.O. Box 1966, Mobile, 36633. Tel: 251-434-1585; Fax: 251-434-1588. Email: mfarmer@mobilearchdiocese.org.

Pastoral Services—Mailing Address: P.O. Box 1966, Mobile, 36633. Tel: 251-434-2606; Fax: 251-434-1588. Very Rev. Stephen E. Martin, Exec. Dir. Email: pastoralservices@mobilearchdiocese.org.

Apostleship of Prayer—Rev. Msgr. Michael L. Farmer, V.G., S.T.L., Mailing Address: P.O. Box 1966, Mobile, 36633. Tel: 251-434-1585. Email: mfarmer@mobilearchdiocese.org.

Apostleship of the Sea—Rev. Lito J. Capeding, Chap. Email: lcapeding@mobilearchdiocese.org; Deacon Joseph V. Connick, Dir., Catholic Maritime Club, 354 Government St., Mobile, 36601. Tel: 251-432-7339; Fax: 251-433-4618. Email: jconnick@mobilearchdiocese.org.

Apostolate for Aging—Deacon Stephen R. Seymour, 5305 Woodline Dr. S., Mobile, 36693. Tel: 251-666-9916.

Archdiocesan Council of Catholic Women (ACCW)—Mrs. Gail Johnson, Pres.; Mrs. Margaret Bolton, Pres., Priests' Burse Club, 400 Government St., Mobile, 36602.

Charismatic Movement—Deacon James Labadie, Our Lady Queen of Mercy, 4421 Narrow Lane Rd., Montgomery, 36116. Tel: 334-284-3463; Fax: 334-281-7884.

Ecumenical Commission—Rev. David J. Tokarz, Dir., 1801 Cody Rd. S., Mobile, 36695. Tel: 251-633-6762; Fax: 251-633-7790. Email: dtokarz@mobilearchdiocese.org.

Family Life Office—Mr. Tom McDonald; Mrs. Caroline McDonald, Mailing Address: 1413 Old Shell Rd., Mobile, 36604. Tel: 251-490-1027.

Hispanic Apostolate—Rev. John E. Kane, C.M., Archdiocesan Dir., 1000 Fourth Ave., Opelika, 36801. Tel: 334-749-8359; Fax: 334-749-6312.

Mobile & Baldwin/Escambia Deaneries—Mrs. Floria Salazar, Dir., 712 Dauphin Island Pkwy., Mobile, 36606. Tel: 251-478-3737; Fax: 251-478-9990. Email: hispanicaom@bellsouth.net. Sacramental Ministers: Revs. Christopher J. Viscardi, S.J.; Francisco J. San Martin, S.J.

Montgomery Deanery—Co Directors: Sisters Veronica Ryan, O.S.B., 1000 Fourth Ave., Opelika, 36801. Tel: 334-749-8359; Fax: 334-749-6312; Janet Santibanez, M.S.B.T., St. Peter, 219 Adams Ave., Montgomery, 36101. Tel: 334-202-7626. Email: vryan@mobilearchdiocese.org. Sacramental Ministers: Revs. Jose J. Paillacho; Philip A. McKenna.

Dothan Deanery—Sr. Grace Raymond Tighe, M.S.B.T., Dir., 2700 W. Main St., Dothan, 36301. Tel: 334-618-2029; Fax: 334-792-2816. Sacramental Ministers: Rev. Marco Antonio Sanchez Mendoza, S.T.; Deacon Alfonso Diaz-Rivera.

Holy Name Society—Deacon Joseph V. Connick, 354 Government St., Mobile, 36601. Tel: 251-432-7339.

Prison Ministry—Rev. Michael J. Sreboth, Archdiocesan Dir., Our Lady Queen of Mercy, 4421 Narrow Lane Rd., Montgomery, 36116. Tel: 334-288-2850. Email: msreboth@mobilearchdiocese.org.

Vicar for Vietnamese Affairs—Rev. Cu Minh Duong, Archdiocesan Dir., St. Monica, 1131 Dauphin Island Pkwy., Mobile, 36605. Tel: 251-479-7360.

Permanent Diaconate Program—Deacon Stephen R. Seymour, Dir., 1801 Cody Rd. S., Mobile, 36695. Tel: 251-633-6762, Ext. 202. Email: sseymour@mobilearchdiocese.org.

Priests' Eucharistic League—Rev. Michael Den Irwin Jr., Chm., 5023 Camelot Dr., Mobile, 36619. Tel: 251-661-3908; Fax: 251-665-4956. Email: dirwin@mobilearchdiocese.org.

Victim Assistance Coordinator—Rev. James J. Cink, Dir., P.O. Box 230, Mobile, 36601. Tel: 251-434-1559 (Office). Email: childprotection@bellsouth.net.

Vocations—Revs. Alejandro E. Valladares, S.T.L., Dir., 6051 Old Shell Rd., Mobile, 36608. Tel: 251-343-3662. Email: avalladares@mobilearchdiocese.org; David M. Shoemaker, Asst. Dir., Holy Redeemer, 515 W. Broad St., Eufaula, 36027. Tel: 334-687-3716. Email: dshoemaker@mobilearchdiocese.org.

CLERGY, PARISHES, MISSIONS AND PAROCHIAL SCHOOLS

CITY OF MOBILE

(Mobile County)

1—Cathedral of the Immaculate Conception (1704) Most Rev. Thomas J. Rodi; Rev. Msgr. Michael L. Farmer, Rector; Rev. Michael Okodua (Nigeria); Deacons John T. Cretaro; Joseph V. Connick. In Res., Most Rev. Oscar H. Lipscomb (Retired).

Cathedral & Rectory—400 Government St., P.O. Box 1966, 36633. Tel: 251-434-1565; Fax: 251-434-1588.

2—St. Catherine of Siena (1913) Rev. Msgr. James S. Kee.

Res.: 2605 Springhill Ave., 36607. Tel: 251-473-1415; 251-473-1427; Fax: 251-473-6307.

Catechesis/Religious Program—Students 13.

3—CORPUS CHRISTI (1958) Very Rev. James F. Zoghby; Rev. John S. Boudreaux; Deacon Arthur W. Robbins.
Res.: 6300 McKenna Dr., 36608. Tel: 251-342-1852; Fax: 251-342-6313. Email: church@corpuschristiparish.com. Web: corpuschristiparish.com.
School—(Grades K-8) Tel: 251-342-5474; Fax: 251-380-0325. Mrs. Joan T. McMullen, Prin.; Barbara Lenaghan, Librarian. Lay Teachers 27; Students 560; Aides 14.
Catechesis/Religious Program—Tel: 251-342-5474, Ext. 2; Fax: 251-380-0325. Students 155.

4—ST. DOMINIC (1958) Revs. James J. Cink; James A. Havens, Parochial Vicar; Deacons Edward Connick; Robert Kirby. In Res., Rev. Msgr. Francis C. Murphy (Ireland) (Retired).
Res.: 4156 Burma Rd., 36693. Tel: 251-661-5130; Fax: 251-661-0469. Web: www.stdominicmobile.org.
School—(Grades K-8), 4160 Burma Rd., 36693. Tel: 251-661-5226; Fax: 251-660-2242. Mrs. Martha Mundine, Prin. Lay Teachers 32; Students 520.
Catechesis/Religious Program—Students 100.
Convent—Tel: 251-661-3229.

5—ST. FRANCIS XAVIER (1867), (African American), Rev. Akama Ukanide, M.S.P.; Deacon Alexander Moore, Pastoral Assoc.
Res.: 2034 St. Stephens Rd., 36617. Tel: 251-473-4975; Fax: 251-473-4940.
Catechesis/Religious Program—Students 34.

6—HOLY FAMILY (1959) Rev. Mark I. Neske.
Res.: 1400 Joyce Rd., 36618. Tel: 251-344-0271; Fax: 251-344-0296.

7—ST. IGNATIUS (Spring Hill) (1947) Very Rev. Stephen E. Martin; Rev. Vincent Huo Phan; Deacons Charles J. Fontana; Marvin C. Johns.
Res.: 3704 Springhill Ave., 36608. Tel: 251-342-9221; Fax: 251-341-1481.
School—(Grades PreK-8), 3650 Springhill Ave., 36608. Tel: 251-342-5442; Fax: 251-344-0944. Miss Janet Murray, Prin.; Mr. Ralph McLaney, Vice Prin.; Mrs. Dorothy Beattie, Librarian. Lay Teachers 32; Students 506.
Mother's Day Out—Tel: 251-445-6750; Fax: 251-345-1064. Lay Teachers 5; Students 31.
Catechesis/Religious Program—Students 193.

8—ST. JOAN OF ARC (1920) Rev. Msgr. Kenneth J. Klepac.
Res.: 1260 Elmira St., 36604. Tel: 251-432-3505.

9—ST. JOSEPH (1857) Rev. Msgr. Michael L. Farmer.
Res.: 808 Springhill Ave., 36602. Tel: 251-432-4218.

10—ST. JOSEPH (Maysville) (1944), (African American), Rev. Jeremiah A. Brady, S.S.J.; Deacon Ronnie A. Hathorne.
Res.: 1703 Dublin St., 36605. Tel: 251-473-3761.
Convent—1701 Dublin St., 36605. Tel: 251-478-3292.

11—LITTLE FLOWER (1928) Rev. John G. Lynes. In Res., Rev. J. Francis Sofie Jr.
Res.: 2053 Government St., 36606. Tel: 251-478-3381; Fax: 251-473-3340.
School—(Grades K-8), 2103 Government St., 36606. Tel: 251-479-5761; Fax: 251-450-3696. Clara Brunk, Prin. Lay Teachers 10; Students 161.
Catechesis/Religious Program—Students 38.
Convent—359 Pinehill Dr., 36606. Tel: 251-479-9116.

12—ST. MARY (1867) Rev. Msgr. Peter J. Cunningham; Rev. Antony Kadavil; Sr. M. Magdalena Langlois, C.S.A., Pastoral Assoc.; Deacons Ernest J. Johnson Jr.; Holcombe Pryor.
Mailing Address: 106 Providence St., 36604.
Res.: 1453 Old Shell Rd., 36604. Tel: 251-432-8679; Fax: 251-432-1009.
School—(Grades PreK-8) Tel: 251-433-9904; Fax: 251-438-9069. Mrs. Debbie Ollis, Prin.; Sue Lyon, Librarian. Lay Teachers 34; Students 461.
Catechesis/Religious Program—Students 23.

13—ST. MATTHEW (1904) Rev. Joseph M. Bolling.
Res.: 906 Garrity St., 36605-4699. Tel: 251-432-4784.

14—ST. MONICA (1950) Rev. Cu Minh Duong; Deacon Truat Van Nguyen.
Res.: 1131 Dauphin Island Pkwy., 36605. Tel: 251-479-7360.

15—MOST PURE HEART OF MARY (1899), (African American), Revs. Patrick Healy, S.S.J.; Godwin Ani, S.S.J., Parochial Vicar; Deacon James D. Bryant.
Res. & Mailing Address: 304 Sengstak St., 36603. Tel: 251-432-3344; Fax: 251-432-1192. Email: mphm@catholic.org. Web: www.josephite.com/parish/al/mphm.
School—*Most Pure Heart of Mary*, (Grades K-8) Tel: 251-432-5270; Fax: 251-432-5271. Sr. Nancy Crossen, O.S.F., Prin.; Sheila Mahoney, Librarian. Students 240.
Catechesis/Religious Program—Students 28.
Convent—310 Sengstak St., 36603. Tel: 251-433-6519.

16—OUR LADY OF LOURDES (1941) Rev. Msgr. Francis V. Cusack; Deacon Gordon Kenny.
Res.: 1621 Boykin Blvd., 36605. Tel: 251-479-9885; Fax: 251-479-9892.
Catechesis/Religious Program—Students 32.

17—OUR SAVIOR (1977) Rev. David J. Tokarz; Deacons Stephen R. Seymour; Charles H. Kenny.
Office:—1801 Cody Rd. S., 36695. Tel: 251-633-6762; Fax: 251-633-7790.
Catechesis/Religious Program—Students 148

18—ST. PIUS X (1954) Revs. W. Bry Shields, Admin.; James F. Carlsen, Parochial Vicar; Deacon William L. Tew.
Res.: 217 S. Sage Ave., 36606. Tel: 251-471-2449; Fax: 251-471-2441.
School—(Grades K-8) Tel: 251-473-5004; Fax: 251-473-5008. Mrs. Lauren Alvarez, Prin. Sisters 1; Lay Teachers 27; Students 398.
Catechesis/Religious Program—Tel: 251-473-4381. Students 31.

19—PRINCE OF PEACE (1970), (African American), Rev. George W. Burden, S.S.J.
Res.: 454 Charleston St., 36603. Tel: 251-432-2364; Fax: 251-432-2372.
Catechesis/Religious Program—Tel: 251-433-1494. Students 30.

OUTSIDE THE CITY OF MOBILE

ANDALUSIA, COVINGTON CO., CHRIST THE KING (1933) Rev. Antony Pullukattu Xavier, Admin.
Res.: 504 Sanford Rd., P.O. Drawer 1546, 36420. Tel: 334-222-4808. Email: ctk@centurytel.net.
Catechesis/Religious Program—Students 36.

ATMORE, ESCAMBIA CO., ST. ROBERT BELLARMINE (1943) Rev. Gordon Milsted.
Res.: 600 S. Main St., 36502-2825. Tel: 251-368-3615; Fax: 251-368-1801.
Catechesis/Religious Program—Students 28.

AUBURN, LEE CO., ST. MICHAEL (1912) Rev. Msgr. William J. Skoneki; Deacon John Read Haughery.
Res.: 1100 N. College St., 36830. Tel: 334-887-5540; 334-887-5573; Fax: 334-887-5572. Email: stmichaels@charter.net. Web: www.stmichaelsauburn.com.
Catechesis/Religious Program—Students 350.
Joyland Child Development Center—Tel: 334-821-7624; Fax: 334-821-5583.
Chaplaincy—Email: cdmimiller@gmail.com. Web: www.aucatholic.org. Auburn University, Catholic Students Organization.

BAY MINETTE, BALDWIN CO., ST. AGATHA CHURCH (1951) Rev. Ernest R. Hyndman Jr.
Church: 1001 Hand Ave., 36507. Tel: 251-937-2026. Web: stagathaparish.org.

BAYOU LABATRE, MOBILE CO., ST. MARGARET (1880) [CEM] Rev. Bieu Van Nguyen.
Res.: P.O. Box 365, Bayou La Batre, 36509. Tel: 251-824-2415; Fax: 251-824-2415.

BELLE FONTAINE, MOBILE CO., ST. PHILIP NERI (1908) Rev. James Montini Coleman; Deacon James L. Scott.
Res.: 9101 Dauphin Island Pkwy., 36582. Tel: 251-973-2096.
Catechesis/Religious Program—Students 41.

BREWTON, ESCAMBIA CO., ST. MAURICE (1948) Rev. Adrian L. Cook.
Res.: 202 E. Jackson St., P.O. Box 206, 36427-0206. Tel: 251-867-5189.

BUTLER, CHOCTAW CO., ST. JOHN THE EVANGELIST (1958) Rev. Patrick Madden.
Res.: 401 E. Pushmataha St., P.O. Box 456, 36904. Tel: 205-459-3129.
Mission—*St. Paul* Chatom, 36518. P.O. Box 456, Washington Co. 36904.

CAMDEN, WILCOX CO., ST. JOSEPH Rev. Johnny Savoie.
Res.: 490 Whiskey Run Rd., 36767.
Mission—*Mission of Annunciation Parish* P.O. Box 883, Monroeville, Wilcox Co. 36461. Tel: 251-575-2644.

CHASTANG, MOBILE CO., ST. PETER THE APOSTLE (1860) [CEM] Rev. Andrew Toyinbo, M.S.P.
Mailing Address: P.O. Box 456, Mount Vernon, 36560. Tel: 251-829-5134; Fax: 251-829-6874.
Catechesis/Religious Program—Students 16.
Mission—*Our Lady of Sorrows* Fairford, Washington Co.

CHICKASAW, MOBILE CO., ST. THOMAS THE APOSTLE (1947) Rev. William Patrick Saucier; Deacon Tony LePiane.
Res.: 251 N. Craft Hwy., 36611. Tel: 251-456-7931; Fax: 251-452-9837.
Parish Center—253 N. Craft Hwy., 36611. Tel: 251-452-9837.

CITRONELLE, MOBILE CO., ST. THOMAS (1913) [CEM] Rev. John Coghlan.
Res.: 8025 State St., P.O. Box 61, 36522. Tel: 251-866-7505.
Mission—*St. Theresa* Mount Vernon, Mobile Co. 36560. Tel: 251-829-6900.

DAPHNE, BALDWIN CO.

1—CHRIST THE KING (1896) [CEM] Revs. Matthew O'Connor; William Fields, O.P.; Deacons Malcolm Zellner; Walter Crimmins; William Pearson; Henry F. O'Brien, (Retired). In Res., Rev. Msgr. Timothy J. Deasy (Retired).
Res.: 711 College Ave., 36526. Tel: 251-626-2343; 251-626-3740; Fax: 251-621-1640. Email: ctk@zebra.net. Web: ctk-daphne.org.
School—(Grades K-8), 1503 Main St., P.O. Box 1890, 36526. Tel: 251-626-1692; Fax: 251-626-9976. Email: cksdaphne@aol.com. Mr. Maxwell Crain, Prin. Lay Teachers 30; Students 500.
Catechesis/Religious Program—Tel: 251-626-5963. Terry Abeln, D.R.E. Students 430.

2—SHRINE OF THE HOLY CROSS (1948) Rev. Lito J. Capeding (Philippines); Deacon Joseph G. Gottstine.
Res.: 612 Main St., 36526. Tel: 251-621-9793; Fax: 251-621-9315.

DAUPHIN ISLAND, MOBILE CO., ST. EDMUND-BY-THE-SEA, [CEM] Rev. William N. Gorman.
Res.: P.O. Box 6, 36528. Tel: 251-861-2352.
Church: Cadillac Ave., 36528.

DOTHAN, HOUSTON CO., ST. COLUMBA (1943) Rev. Msgr. Patrick J. Gallagher; Deacon Rick Risher.
Res.: 2700 W. Main St., 36301. Tel: 334-793-5802; Fax: 334-792-2816. Web: stcolumbacatholic.com.
Rectory—109 Pinetree Dr., 36301.
Catechesis/Religious Program—Tel: 334-792-3065. Students 229.

ELBERTA, BALDWIN CO., ST. BARTHOLOMEW (1911), (German), [CEM] Rev. Howard R. Moussier, O.S.B.; Deacon Kenneth J. Kaiser.
Res.: P.O. Drawer 280, 36530. Tel: 251-986-8142; Fax: 251-987-5251.
School—*St. Benedict's*, (Grades K-8), P.O. Box 819, 36530. Tel: 251-986-8143; Fax: 251-986-8144. Ms. Kendall F. McKee, Prin. Lay Teachers 15; Students 230; Aides 4.
Catechesis/Religious Program—Students 40.

ENTERPRISE, COFFEE CO., ST. JOHN (1959) Rev. Gregory Okorobia; Deacon Karl Lukas.
Res.: 614 Alberta, 36330. Tel: 334-347-7345.
Church: 123 Heath St., 36330-1915. Tel: 334-347-6751; Fax: 334-347-0849. Email: stjohn007@centurytel.net. Web: www.stjohnenterprise.org.
Mission—*St. Mary* 100 S. Commerce, Geneva, Geneva Co. 36340.

EUFAULA, BARBOUR CO., HOLY REDEEMER (1859) Rev. David M. Shoemaker.
Res.: 515 W. Broad St., 36027. Tel: 334-687-3716; Fax: 334-687-3766. Email: holyredeemer@eufaula.rr.com. Web: www.holyredeemeronline.com.
Catechesis/Religious Program—Students 27.
Mission—*St. Pius X* 308 Kennon St., Union Springs, Bullock Co. 36089.
Mission—*Bullock County Correctional Facility* P.O. Box 5107, Union Springs, Bullock Co. 36089. Tel: 334-738-5625.
Mission—*Ventress Correctional Facility* P.O. Box 769, Clayton, Barbour Co. 36016. Tel: 334-775-3331.

FAIRHOPE, BALDWIN CO., ST. LAWRENCE (1961) Revs. Steven T. Williams; Austin Conry; Deacon George W. Yeend Jr.
Res.: 370 S. Section St., 36532. Tel: 251-928-5931; Fax: 251-928-5938.
Catechesis/Religious Program—Students 281.
Chapel—*Battles Wharf, Baldwin Co., Sacred Heart*

FOLEY, BALDWIN CO., ST. MARGARET QUEEN OF SCOTLAND (1951) [CEM] Very Rev. Paul G. Zoghby; Deacon William Scarboro Jr.
Res.: 601 W. Laurel Ave., 36535. Tel: 251-943-4009; 251-943-3528 (Rectory); Fax: 251-943-4010.

GRAND BAY, MOBILE CO., ST. JOHN BAPTIST (1924) Rev. Msgr. G. Warren Wall.
Res.: P.O. Box 417, 36541. Tel: 251-865-6902; Fax: 251-865-1412.
Church: 12450 Hwy. 188, Shell Rd., 36541.

GREENVILLE, BUTLER CO., ST. ELIZABETH (1894) Rev. Antony Pullukattu Xavier, Admin.
Res.: 407 E. Walnut St., 36037. Tel: 334-382-6203.

GROVE HILL, CLARKE CO., SACRED HEART (1944) Rev. Patrick J. Madden.
Res.: Hwy. 43 N., P.O. Box 70, 36451. Tel: 251-275-3665.
Mission—*Visitation* 135 W. Clinton St., Jackson, Clarke Co. 36545.
Mission—*St. Joseph* W. Front St., Thomasville, Clarke Co. 36784.

GULF SHORES, BALDWIN CO., OUR LADY OF THE GULF (1952) Rev. Msgr. Robert W. Fulton.
Res.: 308 E. 22nd Ave., P.O. Box 515, 36547-0515. Tel: 251-968-7062.
Catechesis/Religious Program—Tel: 251-967-2537. Suzette Taylor, D.R.E. Students 37.

HERON BAY, MOBILE CO., ST. MICHAEL THE ARCHANGEL (1880) Rev. Bieu Van Nguyen.
Mailing Address: 15872 Heron Bay Loop Rd. E., Coden, 36523. Tel: 251-873-4719.

HOLY TRINITY, RUSSELL CO., ST. JOSEPH (1925) Revs. Guy Wilson, S.T.; Marco Antonio Sanchez Mendoza, S.T., Parochial Vicar. In Res., Bros. David Sommer, S.T.; Crucito Concepcion, S.T.

Church: 1444 Hwy. 165, Fort Mitchell, 36856. Tel: 334-855-3148; Fax: 334-855-3115. Email: stjosephcathch@yahoo.com. Web: www.way.to/stjoseph.
St. Joseph Child Development Center—Tel: 334-855-4675. Teachers 5; Students 45.
Mission—John XXIII Center 16 Sussex St., Hurtsboro, Russell Co. 36860. Tel: 334-667-7770; Fax: 334-667-0708.

LILLIAN, BALDWIN CO., ST. JOSEPH (1941) [JC] Rev. Joseph Mudavankunnell, M.S.F.S.; Deacons Richard M. Sullivan; Eugene Geri.
Res.: 34290 U.S. Hwy. 98, 36549. Tel: 251-962-2049; Fax: 251-962-3649.

MAGNOLIA SPRINGS, BALDWIN CO., ST. JOHN THE BAPTIST (1881) [CEM] [JC 2] Rev. Msgr. Guido Calleja.
Res.: 10800 St. John's Ln., P.O. Box 206, 36555. Tel: 251-965-7719.
Mission—Our Lady of Bon Secour Bon Secour, Baldwin Co.

MILLBROOK, ELMORE CO., ST. ELIZABETH ANN SETON (1978) Merged with St. Mark's Mission, Wetumpka to form Our lady of Guadalupe, Wetumpka.

MON LUIS ISLAND, MOBILE CO., ST. ROSE OF LIMA (1853) [CEM] Rev. Patrick Maher.
Res.: 2951 Durette Ave. (Mon Luis Island), Coden, 36523. Tel: 251-973-2592.

MONROEVILLE, MONROE CO., ANNUNCIATION (1982) Rev. Johnny Savoie.
Res.: 565 Whetstone St., 36460. Tel: 251-575-2644.
Catechesis/Religious Program—Students 18.
Mission—St. Joseph 490 Whiskey Run Rd., Camden, Wilcox Co. 36767.

MONTGOMERY, MONTGOMERY CO.

1—ST. ANDREW (1910) Rev. Wilbur T. Kissell.
Mailing Address: P.O. Box 241303, 36124.
Res.: 433 Clayton St., 36124. Tel: 334-262-3241.

2—ST. BEDE THE VENERABLE CATHOLIC CHURCH (1925) Revs. David P. Carucci; Jose J. Paillacho; Deacons Charles Gulley; Arnold Brewer; Joseph Phung.
Office: 3870 Atlanta Hwy., 36109. Tel: 334-272-3463. Web: www.stbede.org.
School—Montgomery Catholic Preparatory School - St. Bede Campus, (Grades K-6), 3850 Atlanta Hwy., 36109. Tel: 334-272-3033; Fax: 334-272-9394. Web: montgomerycatholic.org. Mrs. Susan Duke, Prin. Lay Teachers 23; Students 381.
Catechesis/Religious Program—Generations of Faith Program Students 138.
St. Bede Child Development Center—3840 Atlanta Hwy., 36109. Tel: 334-277-8551; Fax: 334-213-2347.

3—CHURCH OF THE HOLY SPIRIT (1977) Rev. Msgr. F. Charles Troncale; Rev. Philip A. McKenna; Deacon Eugene Wadas.
Res.: 8570 Vaughn Rd., 36117. Tel: 334-277-5631; Fax: 334-272-1008. Email: office@holy-spirit-church.com. Web: www.holy-spirit-church.com.
Catechesis/Religious Program—Tel: 334-277-3428. Email: ktryan@holy-spirit-church.com. Students 273.

4—ST. JOHN THE BAPTIST (1908) Rev. Patrick Remmers Driscoll, Admin.
Res.: 543 S. Union St., 36104. Tel: 334-264-6274; Fax: 334-262-3012.

5—ST. JUDE PARISH (1934), (African American), Rev. Paul McQuillen, S.S.E.; Deacon Fred J. Briers. In Res., Rev. Matthew A. Sindik (Retired).
Res.: 2048 W. Fairview Ave., 36108. Tel: 334-265-1390; Fax: 334-265-1399. Web: www.csjchurch.blogspot.com.
High School—(Grades 7-12) Tel: 334-264-5376; Fax: 334-264-6669. Web: www.stjudeee.org. Mrs. Wanda Twitty, Prin. Lay Teachers 20; Students 163.
Catechesis/Religious Program—Students 30.

6—OUR LADY QUEEN OF MERCY (1954) Rev. Michael R. Sreboth.
Res.: 4421 Narrow Lane Rd., 36116. Tel: 334-288-2850; Fax: 334-281-7884.
Catechesis/Religious Program—Students 24.
Child Development Center—Tel: 334-613-0340.

7—ST. PETER (1834) [CEM] Rev. Patrick Remmers Driscoll.
Res.: 219 Adams Ave., P.O. Box 114, 36101. Tel: 334-262-7304; Fax: 334-262-9735. Web: stpetersof-montgomery.com.

8—RESURRECTION CATHOLIC CHURCH (1943) Revs. Manuel Williams, C.R.; Fred Briers, C.R.
Res.: 2815 Forbes Rd., 36110. Tel: 334-269-1770; Fax: 334-265-8081. Email: parish@rcmsouth.org. Web: www.rcmsouth.org.
School—Resurrection Catholic School, (Grades K-8) Tel: 334-265-4615; Fax: 334-265-4568. Sr. Gail Trippett, C.S.J., Prin.; Laura Guilford, Librarian. Lay Teachers 16; Students 125.
Mission—Resurrection Catholic Mission 2815 Forbes Rd., Montgomery Co. 36110. Tel: 334-263-4221; Fax: 334-263-4999. Rev. Manuel Williams, C.R., Dir.

MOUNT VERNON, MOBILE CO., ST. CECILIA (1929) [CEM] Rev. John Coghlan.
Res.: 1305 Military Rd., P.O. Box 847, 36560. Tel: 251-866-7505.

OPELIKA, LEE CO., ST. MARY OF THE MISSION (1910) Rev. John E. Kane, C.M.; Deacon Donald Canonica.
Res.: 1000 4th Ave., 36801. Tel: 334-749-8359; Fax: 334-749-6312.
Catechesis/Religious Program—Tel: 334-745-3432. Students 34.

ORANGE BEACH, BALDWIN CO., ST. THOMAS BY THE SEA (1991) Rev. James E. Dane; Deacons Henry Pouliot; Patrick J. Clemens.
Mailing Address: 26547 Perdido Beach Blvd., P.O. Box 1190, 36561. Tel: 251-981-8132; Fax: 251-981-1981. Email: stthomas@gulftel.com. Web: www.st-thomasbythesea.com.

ORRVILLE, DALLAS CO., IMMACULATE CONCEPTION Rev. Carroll W. Plourde, S.S.E.
Church: 13663 Alabama Hwy. 22 W., 36767.
Res.: 309 Washington St., Selma, 36703. Tel: 334-874-8931; Fax: 334-874-8976.

OZARK, DALE CO., ST. JOHN (1958) [JC] Rev. Paul Egbe, Admin.; Deacon John Ross Jr.
Res.: 475 Camilla Ave., P.O. Box 1008, 36361-1008. Tel: 334-774-6826; Fax: 334-774-8675.
Catechesis/Religious Program—Students 23.

PHENIX CITY, RUSSELL CO.

1—MOTHER MARY PARISH (1940) Rev. Thomas D. Weise, Admin.
Res.: 1502 Broad St., 36867. Tel: 334-298-9025; Fax: 334-298-9233.
School—(Grades K-8) Tel: 334-298-6371; Fax: 334-298-7934. Sr. M. Cecelia Harrison, F.M.S., Prin. Sisters 2; Lay Teachers 12; Students 88.
Catechesis/Religious Program—Students 21.
Convent—Franciscan Missionary Sisters of Our Lady of Perpetual Help of Jamaica, Tel: 334-291-0122.

2—ST. PATRICK (1911) Rev. Thomas D. Weise.
Res.: 1502 Broad St., P.O. Box 147, 36868-0147. Tel: 334-298-9025; Fax: 334-298-9233. Email: stpats123@gmail.com. Web: home.etvea.net/~stpats/index.
School—(Grades K-8), 3910 Lakewood Dr., P.O. Box 1614, 36868. Tel: 334-298-3408; Fax: 334-298-3352. Mr. Dom Manio, Prin. Lay Teachers 12; Students 76; Aides 3.
Catechesis/Religious Program—Students 82.

PLATEAU, MOBILE CO., OUR MOTHER OF MERCY (1926), (African American), Rev. Akama Ukanide, M.S.P.
Mailing Address: P.O. Box 10306, Prichard, 36610. Tel: 251-473-4975; Fax: 251-473-4940.
Res.: 805 East St., 36610.

PRATTVILLE, AUTAUGA CO., ST. JOSEPH CHURCH (1963) Rev. Jan Zagorski; Sr. Jane O'Conner, M.S.B.T., Pastoral Assoc.
Res.: 511 N. Memorial Dr., 36067-2133. Tel: 334-365-8680; Fax: 334-365-2267.
Catechesis/Religious Program—Tel: 334-365-3283. Students 281.

PRICHARD, MOBILE CO.

1—ST. JAMES MAJOR (1925), (African American), Revs. Patrick Healy, S.S.J.; Godwin Ani, S.S.J., Parochial Vicar.
Res.: 714 S. College St., 36610. Tel: 251-456-6842; Fax: 251-456-6843.
Catechesis/Religious Program—Students 69.
Convent—927 W. Prichard Ave., 36610. Tel: 251-457-9396.

2—OUR LADY OF FATIMA (1949) Closed. For inquiries for parish records contact the chancery.

ROBERTSDALE, BALDWIN CO., ST. PATRICK (1974) Rev. Msgr. William R. James.
Res.: P.O. Box 1367, 36567. Tel: 251-947-5054; Fax: 251-947-3860.
School—(Grades K-8), P.O. Drawer 609, 36567. Tel: 251-947-7395. Sr. Margaret Harte, P.B.V.M., Prin. Presentation Sisters 1; Lay Teachers 13; Students 210.
Catechesis/Religious Program—Students 57.
Convent—P.O. Box 609, 36567. Tel: 251-947-7396.

SELMA, DALLAS CO., OUR LADY QUEEN OF PEACE (1850) Rev. Carroll W. Plourde, S.S.E.
Res.: 2511 Summerfield Rd., 36701. Tel: 334-874-8475. Email: queenofpeace@bellsouth.net.
Office: 309 Washington St., 36703. Tel: 334-874-8931 (Office & Res.); Fax: 334-874-8976.
Catechesis/Religious Program—Students 32.

SEMMES, MOBILE CO., HOLY NAME OF JESUS (1977) Rev. John L. Holleman, Admin.; Deacons Frank Lee; Joseph Gottstine.
Res.: 2275 Snow Rd. N., P.O. Box 557, 36575. Tel: 251-649-4794; Fax: 251-649-7660.
Catechesis/Religious Program—Students 73.

TALLASSEE, ELMORE CO., ST. VINCENT DE PAUL (1955) [JC] Rev. Francis A. Lynch, C.M.; Deacon Frank May.
Res.: 620 Gilmer Ave., P.O. Box 780487, 36078-0487. Tel: 334-283-2169; Fax: 334-283-8500.

TILLMAN'S CORNER, MOBILE CO., ST. VINCENT DE PAUL (1971) Rev. Michael Den Irwin Jr.; Deacon Robert Nouwen, (Retired).
Res.: 5023 Camelot Dr., 36619. Tel: 251-661-3908; Fax: 251-665-4956. Web: svsparish.com.
School—6571 Larkspur Dr., 36619. Tel: 251-666-8022; Fax: 251-666-1296. Mary McLendon, Prin. Lay Teachers 10; Students 181.
Catechesis/Religious Program—Tel: 251-661-3908. Students 50.

TROY, PIKE CO., ST. MARTIN OF TOURS (1915) Rev. Eamon Miley, Admin.
Res.: 725 Elba Hwy., 36079. Tel: 334-566-2630.
Catechesis/Religious Program—Students 22.

TUSKEGEE INSTITUTE, MACON CO., ST. JOSEPH (1940) Rev. Romanus Ezeugwa, M.S.P.; Deacon Stanley B. Maxwell.
Res.: 2007 Montgomery Rd., 36088. Tel: 334-727-2710.
School—(Grades K-8), 2009 Montgomery Rd., 36088. Tel: 334-727-0620; 334-727-0642. Mr. Clima White, Interim Prin. Lay Teachers 8; Students 100.

WETUMPKA, ELMORE CO., OUR LADY OF GUADALUPE (2006) Rev. Albert P. Kelly.
Mailing Address: P.O. Box 479, Elmore, 36025.
Res. & Church: 545 White Rd., 36092. Tel: 334-285-9988; Fax: 334-567-0311.

WHISTLER, MOBILE CO., ST. BRIDGET (1864) Rev. Leo Blanchet.
Res.: 3625 W. Main St., P.O. Box 13357, 36613. Tel: 251-457-6847.

Chaplains of Public Institutions

CLAYTON. *Ventress Correctional Institution.* Rev. David M. Shoemaker.
515 W. Broad St., Eufaula, 36027. Tel: 334-687-3716; Fax: 334-687-3766.

UNION SPRINGS. *Bullock County Correctional Facility.* Rev. David M. Shoemaker.
515 W. Broad St., Eufaula, 36027. Tel: 334-687-3716; Fax: 334-687-3766.

On Leave from the Archdiocese:
Rev. Msgr.—
Amos, John R.
Revs.—
Dalton, Peadar
Kreitinger, Todd
Lemming, Patrick W.
McGuiness, David
McManus, Dennis Douglas, Prof., Conception Seminary College, P.O. Box 502, Conception, MO 64433.
Nicholson, Patrick
Prendergast, Fergus J.
Reskey, George A.
Robinson, Jerome
Smith, Edward E.
Staff, Stephen M.
Trosch, David
Wadas, Joseph S.
Walters, Erik T.A.

On Leave for Military:
Revs.—
Halladay, Paul A.
Harbour, Linn S.

On Administrative Leave:
Revs.—
Evans, Timothy W.
Schrenger, Arthur C.

Retired:
Rev. Msgrs.—
Jennings, Joseph
McDevitt, Anthony, J.C.D., S.T.L.
Murphy, Francis
Shields, Maurice L.
Revs.—
Becherer, David A.
Biven, Louis Russell
Bolling, Francis Joseph
Dorrill, James F., Ph.D.
Folsom, William P., Jr.
Hay, Theodore H., S.T.L.
Keller, Brendan
Kieltyka, Robert
Messing, Francis
Robinson, John C.
Sindik, Matthew A.
Stauter, Andrew

Permanent Deacons:
Bosarge, Vincent
Brewer, Arnold L., (Retired)
Briers, Fred J.
Bryant, James D.
Canonica, Donald A., (Retired)

Clemens, Patrick J.
Connick, Edward G.
Connick, Joseph V.
Cretaro, John T.
Crimmins, Walter J.
Diaz-Rivera, Alfonso
Dolan, William R., (Retired)
Fontana, Charles J., (Retired)
Geri, Eugene
Gottstine, Joseph G.
Grant, Harold
Gulley, Charles, (Retired)
Hamilton, John B., (On Leave)
Hathorne, Ronnie A.
Haughery, John Read
Johns, Marvin C., (Retired)
Johnson, Ernest
Kaiser, Kenneth J.
Kenny, Charles H.
Kenny, Gordon
King, A. B., (On Leave)
Kirby, Robert E.
Labadie, James
Lee, Frank A., (Retired)
LePiane, Tony
Lopez, Abraham, (Retired)
Lukas, Karl L.
Maxwell, Stanley B.
May, Frank J.
McGonagle, Joseph P., (Retired)
Mears, Clarence L.
Moore, Alexander
Nguyen, Truat Van
Nouwen, Robert, (Retired)
O'Brien, Henry F., (Retired)
Pearson, William
Phung, Joseph H.
Pouliot, Henry, (Retired)
Pryor, William Holcombe
Quintero, Mario
Risher, Rick
Robbins, Arthur
Ross, John
Scarboro, William, Jr.
Scott, James L.
Seymour, Stephen R.
Sheldon, Paul
Shippen, Samuel, (Retired)
Sinchak, J. Douglas
Sullivan, Richard M., (Retired)
Surek, Christopher, (On Leave)
Tew, William L.
Wadas, Eugene
Yeend, George W., Jr.
Zellner, Malcolm

INSTITUTIONS LOCATED IN THE ARCHDIOCESE

[A] COLLEGES AND UNIVERSITIES

MOBILE. *Spring Hill College* (1830) 4000 Dauphin St., 36608. Tel: 251-380-4000; Fax: 251-460-2195. Web: www.shc.edu. Revs. Richard P. Salmi, S.J., Pres.; Edward B. Arroyo, S.J., Rector; David Borbridge, S.J.; Stephen Campbell, S.J.; Marvin Kitten, S.J.; Gregory Lucey, S.J.; Jesus Rodriguez, S.J.; Robert B. Rimes, S.J.; Javier San Martin, S.J.; Michael A. Williams, S.J.; Christopher J. Viscardi, S.J.; Bro. Ferrell Blank. Priests 11; Brothers 3; Lay Teachers 61; Students 1,867.

[B] HIGH SCHOOLS, ARCHDIOCESAN

MOBILE. *McGill-Toolen Catholic High School*, 1501 Old Shell Rd., 36604. Tel: 251-432-0784; Fax: 251-433-8356. Email: shieldsb@mcgill.pvt.k12.al.us. Web: www.mcgill-toolen.org. Revs. W. Bry Shields, Pres.; J. Francis Sofie Jr., Chap.; Deacon Holcombe Pryor; Mrs. Michelle Haas, Prin. Priests 2; Brothers of the Sacred Heart 3; Sisters of Loretto 1; Lay Teachers 91; Students 1,077.

MONTGOMERY. *St. Jude Educational Institute*, 2048 W. Fairview Ave., 36108. Tel: 334-263-6121; Fax: 334-264-6669. Web: www.stjudeei.org. Mrs. Wanda Twitty, Interim Prin.; Marilyn Bibbins, Librarian. Lay Teachers 20; Students 206.

Montgomery Catholic Preparatory School (1873) (Grades K-12), 5350 Vaughn Rd., 36116. Tel: 334-272-7220; Fax: 334-272-2440. Email: aceasar@montgomerycatholic.org. Web: montgomerycatholic.org. Mrs. Anne O. Ceasar, Pres. Lay Teachers 57; Total Enrollment 798.

St. Bede Campus (1958) (Grades K-6), 3850 Atlanta Hwy., 36109. Tel: 334-272-3033; Fax: 334-272-9394. Email: sduke@montgomerycatholic.org. Mrs. Susan Duke, Prin. Teachers 26; Students 351.

High School Campus (1873) Mrs. Fran Taylor, Prin. Teachers 26; Students 286.

Middle School Campus (2004) (Grades 7-8), 5350 Vaughn Rd., 36116. Tel: 334-272-2465; Fax: 334-272-2330. Email: mnolen@montgomerycatholic.org. Ms. Maria Nolen, Prin.; Lee Barranco, Librarian (K-6); Amy Johnson, Librarian (7-12). Teachers 11; Students 161.

[C] CHILDREN'S HOMES

MOBILE. *St. Mary's Home*, 4350 Moffat Rd., 36618. Tel: 251-344-7733; Fax: 251-344-9753. Mr. Phillip A. Wynne, Admin. Dependent Children 65.

[D] GENERAL HOSPITALS

MOBILE. *Providence Foundation* (1985) 6701 Airport Blvd. B 227, P.O. Box 850429, 36608. Tel: 251-639-2050; Fax: 251-639-2052. Russell Allman, Chm. of the Bd.; Jean Wilkins, Sec.; Tim Gaston, Treas.

Providence Healthcare Services (1986) 6801 Airport Blvd., P.O. Box 850429, 36685. Tel: 251-633-1600; Fax: 251-633-1679. Mr. Thomas A. Gangle, Chm.; Mr. David M. Phillips, M.D., Vice Chm.; Mr. Clark P. Christianson, Pres. Total Staff 48.

Providence Hospital (1854) 6801 Airport Blvd., P.O. Box 850429, 36685. Tel: 251-633-1600; Fax: 251-633-1679. Web: www.providencehospital.org. Mr. Clark P. Christianson, Pres. & CEO; Ms. Beth McFadden Rouse, Chm.; Rev. Leo Weishaar, Chap. Daughters of Charity of St. Vincent de Paul 9; Bed Capacity 349; Patients Assisted Annually 170,433; Nurses 576; Total Staff 1,980.

Seton Health Corp. of South Alabama (1986) 6801 Airport Blvd., P.O. Box 850429, 36608. Tel: 251-633-1660; Fax: 251-633-1679. Web: providencehospital.org. Mr. Clark P. Christianson, Pres.; Sr. Marilyn Moore, D.C., Sec. & Treas.; Ms. Beth McFadden Rouse, Chm.

Seton Medical Management, Inc. (1986) 6701 Airport Blvd., Ste. D-241, 36608. Tel: 251-639-2661; Fax: 251-639-2664. Mr. Thomas A. Gangle, Chm.; Dr. James L. Walker, Pres. & Vice Chair; Vince N. Formica, Sec. & Treas. Patients Assisted Annually 218,586; Nurses 45; Total Staff 285.

[E] SPECIAL HOSPITALS, SCHOOLS AND HOMES FOR THE AGED

MOBILE. *Allen Memorial Home Skilled Nursing Facility*, 735 S. Washington Ave., 36603. Tel: 251-433-2642; Fax: 251-433-5502. Email: allenmhome@aol.com. Ms. Cheryl Robinson, Admin. Bed Capacity 119; Patients Assisted Annually 1,154; Total Staff 175.

Corpus Christi Preschool (Full Day Infant-PK4), 6300 McKenna Dr., 36608. Tel: 251-342-2424; Fax: 251-343-3119. Mrs. Linda M. Hawkins, Dir.

Little Sisters of the Poor, Home For the Aged, Inc. (1901) Sacred Heart Residence, 1655 McGill Ave., 36604. Tel: 251-476-6335; Fax: 251-478-6519. Email: msmobile@littlesistersofthepoor.org. Web: www.littlesistersofthepoor.org. Sr. Paul M. Wilson, L.S.P., Supr. Sisters 9; Residents 90. In Res. Revs. David A. Becherer (Retired); L. Russell Biven (Retired); Francis Joseph Bolling (Retired); F. Thomas Moore (STA) (Retired); Andrew Stauter (Retired).

DAPHNE. *Mercy Medical* (1949) P.O. Box 1090, 36526. Tel: 251-621-4200; Fax: 251-621-4845. Email: donnaw@mercymedical.com. Web: www.mercymedical.com. Mr. Jack Bell, Pres. & CEO; Rev. Msgr. Maurice L. Shields, Chap. (Retired). Acute Rehabilitation Hospital, Hospice, Home Health, Long Term Care, Skilled Nursing Facility, Alzheimer's Care, Assisted Living, Lifecare Retirement. Sisters of Mercy 4; Professional Nurses 196; Bed Capacity 142; Patients/Residents Assisted Annually 4,875; Residential Care Units 308; Total Staff 419.

Carroll Place, Fairhope, 36532. Tel: 251-928-5555; Fax: 251-990-2620. (Assisted living community.)

Catherine Place, 36526. Tel: 251-626-9000; Fax: 251-626-7981. (Assisted living community.)

The Hamlet, Fairhope, 36532. Tel: 251-928-5413; Fax: 251-990-3035. (Retirement community.)

McAuley Place, 36608. Tel: 251-344-3866; Fax: 251-304-3035. (Assisted living community.)

Portier Place, 36608. Tel: 251-343-4449; Fax: 251-304-3143. (Retirement community.)

John McClure Snook Regional Center, 27296 County Rd. 13, 36526. Tel: 251-625-2555; Fax: 251-625-2556. (Assisted living Alzheimer community.)

DOTHAN. *St. Columba Preschool*, 2700 W. Main St., 36301. Tel: 334-793-6742; Fax: 334-792-2816. Email: cdstc@alanet.com. Mrs. Cathy Dedmon, Dir.

MONTGOMERY. *St. Bede Child Development Center*, 3870 Atlanta Hwy., 36109. Tel: 334-277-8551. Email: cjones@school.stbede.org. Cathy Jones, Dir. Students 125; Total Staff 28.

[F] HOUSING FOR THE ELDERLY

MOBILE. *Cathedral Place*, 351 Conti St., 36602. Tel: 251-434-1590; Fax: 251-434-1592. Email: marie.dismukes@royalmgmt.com. Web: www.royalmgmt.com. Marie Dismukes, Managing Agent; Angela Washington, Mgr. Residents 156; Total Staff 5.

Rendu Terrace West, Inc., c/o 6801 Airport Blvd., P.O. Box 850429, 36685. Porter Sue Simpson, Mgr.

MONTGOMERY. *Seton Haven*, 3721 Wares Ferry Rd., 36109. Tel: 334-272-4000; Fax: 334-272-1788. Email: setonhaven@bellsouth.net. Ms. A. Ann Alosi, Admin. Residents 100; Total Staff 12.

[G] MONASTERIES AND RESIDENCES OF PRIESTS AND BROTHERS

MOBILE. *Brothers of the Sacred Heart* (1821) 2609 Springhill Ave., 36607. Tel: 251-438-3812. Bros. Francis Fleming, S.C.; Joseph Donovan, S.C.; Matthias Amos, S.C.; Lee Barker, S.C., M.Ed.; Celestine Algero, S.C., Ph.D.; Paul Mulligan, S.C., M.R.E.; Virgil Harris, S.C. Brothers 7.

SELMA. *Edmundite Fathers*, Edmundite Missions House, 1401 Broad St., 36701. Tel: 334-872-6221; Fax: 334-872-8123. Email: myhalyk@aol.com. Web: www.edmunditemissions.com. Revs. Carroll W. Plourde, S.S.E., Supr. & Pres.; Paul McQuillen, S.S.E.; Richard Myhalyk, S.S.E., Mission Dir. & CEO; Stephen Hornat, S.S.E.; Roger J. LaCharite, S.S.E.; Maurice F. Ouellet, S.S.E.; Bro. Peter J. Stanfield, S.S.E., Pastoral Assoc.

Fathers of St. Edmund Southern Missions, Inc. Priests 6; Brothers 1; Total Assisted 155,520; Total Staff 52.

[H] CONVENTS AND RESIDENCES OF SISTERS

MOBILE. *Blessed Trinity Missionary Cenacle*, 604 Barksdale Dr. W., 36606. Tel: 251-476-4803. Missionary Servants 4.

Convent of the Sisters of Mercy of the Americas South Central Community, 101 Wimbledon Dr. W., 36608. Tel: 251-344-1377; Fax: 251-344-1617. Email: scoberkirch@bellsouth.net. Web: www.mercysistersbalt.com. Sr. Carolyn Oberkirch, R.S.M., Admin. Sisters 14; Total Staff 15.

Other Residences: *Convent of the Sisters of Mercy of the Americas South Central Community*, 4301 Bit & Spur Rd., 36608. Tel: 251-343-3674. *Convent of the Sisters of Mercy of the Americas South Central Community*, 2902 Brierwood Dr., 36606. Tel: 251-476-4605. *Convent of the Sisters of Mercy of the Americas South Central Community*, 172 N. Lafayette St., 36604. Tel: 251-432-3178. *Convent of the Sisters of Mercy of the Americas South Central Community*, 3700 Whispering Pines, Apt. 47C, 36608-1149. Tel: 251-343-4435.

Convent of the Sisters of St. Agnes, 1701 Dublin St., 36605. Tel: 251-478-3292. Email: smitscsa@bellsouth.net. Web: www.csasisters.org. Sisters 4.

Monastery of Discalced Carmelite Nuns (1943) 716 Dauphin Island Pkwy., 36606. Sr. Marie Therese, O.C.D., Prioress. Solemnly Professed 4.

Sisters of Loretto (1926) 1408 Old Shell Rd., 36604-2244. Tel: 251-454-9898. Email: sistersofloretto@bellsouth.net. Sr. Sandra Ardoyno, S.L.

Visitation Monastery and Retreat House (1833) 2300 Spring Hill Ave., 36607. Tel: 251-473-2321; Fax: 251-476-9761. Web: www.VisitationMonasteryMobile.org. Sr. Rose Marie Kinsella, Supr. Sisters 7; Total Staff 3.

CAMDEN. *Sisters of St. Joseph*, 112 Bridgeport Rd., 36726. Tel: 334-682-4144; Fax: 251-746-2467. Email: roseannecook@yahoo.com.

HOLY TRINITY. *Blessed Trinity Shrine Retreat and Cenacle*, 107 Holy Trinity Rd., Fort Mitchell, 36856. Tel: 334-855-4474; Fax: 334-855-4525. Web: www.msbt.org/mis_btsr.htm. Sisters Theresa Mary Finan, M.S.B.T., Co-Dir.; Barbara De Moranville, M.S.B.T., Co-Dir. Missionary Servants of the Most Blessed Trinity 6; Retreat House Capacity 40.

MARBURY. *Dominican Monastery of St. Jude (St. Jude Monastery)*, P.O. Box 170, 36051. Tel: 205-755-1322; Fax: 205-755-9847. Email: stjudemonastery@aol.com. Web: www.stjudemonastery.org. Sr. Mary Aimee, O.P., Prioress. Cloistered Dominican Nuns of Perpetual Adoration and Rosary. Professed Sisters 6; Novices 1; Postulants 1.

MONTGOMERY. *Mater Dei Missionary Cenacle*, 784 Spring Valley Rd., 36116. Tel: 334-288-4544; Fax: 334-288-9322. Email: nagle@cssalabama.org. Web: cssalabama.org. Missionary Servants of the Most Blessed Trinity 4.

OZARK. *Sinsinawa Dominican Sisters*, 375 County Rd. 404, 36360. Tel: 334-299-6671. Email: psmithop@charter.net. Sr. Penny Smith, O.P.

PINE APPLE. *Sisters of St. Joseph of Rochester*, 702 County Rd. 59, 36768. Tel: 251-746-2584; Fax: 251-746-2584. Email: ssjpineapple59@hotmail.com. Web: www.ssjrochester.org. Sisters 2.

SELMA. *Sisters Residence*, 911 Mabry St., 36701. Tel: 334-874-6536. Email: ellennp@aol.com. Sisters 3.

[I] NEWMAN CENTERS

MOBILE. *Sacred Heart of Jesus Catholic Student Center at University of South Alabama* (2003) Catholic Student Center, 6051 Old Shell Rd., 36608. Tel: 251-343-3662; Fax: 251-460-4687. Email: sacredhrtfralex@mindspring.com. Rev. Alejandro E. Valladares, S.T.L., Campus Min. & Vocations Dir.

Spring Hill College Campus Ministry 4000 Dauphin St., 36608-1791. Tel: 251-380-3495; Fax: 251-460-2174. Web: www.shc.edu. Rev. Edward B. Arroyo, S.J., Rector.

AUBURN. *Auburn University Newman Center* 115 Mitcham Ave., 36830. Tel: 334-887-5380; Fax: 334-887-5572. Web: www.aucatholic.org. Rev. Msgr. William J. Skoneki.

DOTHAN. *George C. Wallace Jr. Community College Newman Center* 2700 W. Main St., 36301. Tel: 334-793-5802; Fax: 334-792-2816. Email: saintcolumba@ala.net. Rev. Msgr. Patrick J. Gallagher.

MONROEVILLE. *Alabama Southern Community College Newman Center* 565 Whetstone St., 36460. Tel: 251-575-2644. Email: annuneat@frontiernet.net. Rev. Johnny Savoie.

MONTGOMERY. *Alabama State University Newman Center* 553 S. Union St., 36104. Tel: 334-264-6274. Rev. Wilbur T. Kissell.

Huntington College Newman Center 4421 Narrow Lane Rd., 36116. Tel: 334-288-2850. Email: frsreboth@olam.org. Web: www.olqm.org. Rev. Michael R. Sreboth.

SELMA. *Marion Institute Newman Center* 309 Washington St., 36703. Tel: 334-874-8931; Fax: 334-874-8976. Rev. Carroll W. Plourde, S.S.E. Students 67.

TROY. *University Newman Center* 725 Elba Hwy., 36079. Tel: 334-566-2630; Fax: 334-566-2630. Rev. Eamon Miley.

TUSKEGEE INSTITUTE. *Tuskegee University Newman Center* 2007 Montgomery Rd., 36088. Tel: 334-727-2710; Fax: 334-727-5767. Rev. Romanus Ezeugwa, M.S.P. Total Staff 1.

[J] MISCELLANEOUS LISTINGS

MOBILE. *Apostleship of Prayer*, P.O. Box 1966, 36633. Tel: 251-434-1585. Rev. Msgr. Michael L. Farmer, V.G., S.T.L.

Catholic High Schools Alumni Association of Mobile (1979) 1501 Old Shell Rd., 36604. Tel: 251-441-0809; Fax: 251-433-8356. Email: wattsm@mcgill.pvt.k12.al.us. Web: www.mcgill-toolen.org. Marian Watts, Alumni Dir.

Catholic University, Friends of, Sacred Heart Residence, 1655 McGill Ave., 36604. Tel: 251-476-6335. Rev. Louis Russell Biven (Retired).

Cursillo, Our Savior Parish, 1801 Cody Rd. S., 36695. Tel: 251-633-6762; Fax: 251-633-7790. Rev. David J. Tokarz, Spiritual Dir.; Sr. Margaret Cosgrove, M.S.B.T., Asst. Dir. Tel: 251-471-3449; Mr. Woody H. Perkins, Lay Dir. Tel: 251-343-7088.

L'Arche, 151 S. Ann St., 36604. Tel: 251-438-2094; Fax: 251-438-2094. Email: larchmob@hotmail.com. Web: larchemobile.org. Christian nonprofit organization-community where persons with intellectual disabilities share their lives together in a home. Disabled People 22; Team Members 40.

Ladies of Charity, P.O. Box 6987, 36660-0987. Tel: 251-661-9448.

Mobile Provincial Conference of Bishops and Priests' Councils, Mailing Address: P.O. Box 1966, 36633. Tel: 251-434-1585.

**Providence Building Corporation* (1985) P.O. Box 850429, 36685. Tel: 251-633-1600; Fax: 251-633-1679. Web: providencehospital.org. 6801 Airport Blvd., 36608. Tel: 251-633-1600; Fax: 251-633-1679. Sr. Patricia Huffman, D.C., Chm.; James Hirs, Sec. & Treas.

Serra Club of Mobile, P.O. Box 1966, 36633. Mr. Jon Green, Pres.

DAPHNE. *Serra Club of Daphne*, P.O. Box 1966, 36633.

DOTHAN. *Serra Club of Dothan*, P.O. Box 1966, 36633. Dr. Nicholas E. Barreca, Pres.

ELBERTA. *Mary's Shelter*, 14001 Boros Rd., P.O. Box 18, 36530. Tel: 251-986-6200; Fax: 251-986-6357. Email: maryssheIter@gulftel.com. Web: maryshelter.org. Ms. Donna McCarley, M.S.W., Exec. Dir.

FAIRHOPE. **Archangel Communications*, 399 S. Section St., P.O. Box 1526, 36533. Tel: 251-928-2111; Fax: 251-929-2660. Joseph Roszkowski, Pres.; Daniel Di Silva, Station Mgr.; Daniel F. Lord, Opers. Coord.

Boy Scouts, 370 S. Section St., 36532. Tel: 251-928-5931. Rev. Steven T. Williams, Chap.

HURTSBORO. *Blessed John XXIII Center* (1964) P.O. Box 117, 36860. Tel: 334-667-7770; Fax: 334-667-0708. Email: blessedjohnXXIIIcenter@earthlink.net. Rev. Dennis M. Berry, S.T., Admin.; Mr. Lewis H. Smith, Dir.

MONTGOMERY. *Central Alabama Laubach Literacy (CALL) Center* (1985) 2048 W. Fairview Ave., 36108. Tel: 334-264-1239; Fax: 334-264-1239 (call before faxing). Email: callmgm@juno.com. Sr. Leanne M. Sitter, C.S.A., Dir.

City of St. Jude, Inc., The (1934) Mailing Address: 2048 W. Fairview Ave., 36108. Tel: 334-265-6791; Fax: 334-269-6750. Email: csjdirector@cityofstjude.org. Web: www.cityofstjude.org. Rev. Paul McQuillen, S.S.E., Dir.; Mr. Douglas H. Watson, Exec. Dir.

St. Jude Church & Rectory Tel: 334-265-1390; Fax: 334-265-1399.

City of St. Jude Apartments (1992) Tel: 334-265-8356; Fax: 334-265-1908. Barbara J. Peters, Mgr. Units 96; Total Staff 2.

Father Purcell Memorial Exceptional Children's Center (1958) Tel: 334-269-1983; Fax: 334-269-1988. Ms. Brenda Withers, Admin. Patients Assisted Annually 58; Total Staff 103.

St. Jude Social Services Center Tel: 334-269-1983; Fax: 334-269-1988. Sr. Barbara Ann Lengvarsky, V.S.C., Dir. Total Assisted Annually 1,475; Total Staff 3.

St. Jude Educational Institute (1938) Tel: 334-264-5376 (H.S.); Fax: 334-264-6669 (H.S.). Students 214; Total Staff 25.

St. Jude Head Start (1966) Tel: 334-262-6197. Students 80; Total Staff 8.

Montgomery Deanery Respect Life Committee, 2130 Cottingham Dr., 36106. Tel: 334-279-6998. Mrs. Mary Stojak, Dir.

Resurrection Catholic Missions, 2815 Forbes Rd., 36110. Tel: 334-263-4221; Fax: 334-263-4999. Rev. Manuel Williams, C.R., Missions Dir.

Resurrection Catholic Nursing Home, 2815 Forbes Rd., 36110. Tel: 334-269-1770; Fax: 334-265-8081. Kenneth Owens, Admin. Skilled Nursing Facility and Assisted Living Facility. Registered Nurses 4; Licensed Practical Nurses 10; Bed Capacity 65; Inpatients 61.

Father Walter Memorial Center for Handicapped Children Tel: 334-262-6421; Fax: 334-262-2265. Kim K. Johnson, Admin. A skilled nursing facility for the mentally and physically handicapped child. Operated by The Resurrection Catholic Missions. RN's 8; LPN's 13; Bed Capacity 54; Patients Assisted Annually 54; Total Staff 82.

Resurrection Early Childhood Center Tel: 334-265-4615; Fax: 334-265-4568. Sr. Gail Trippett, C.S.J., Prin. Licensed by Alabama State Dept. of Human Resources for 45 Students, Ages 2 1/2 to 5.

Serra Club of Montgomery, P.O. Box 1966, 36633. Mr. Lawrence Russo.

Seton Haven Management Corporation, 3721 Wares Ferry Rd., 36109. Tel: 334-272-4000. Mr. Gary Tomlin, Pres.

SELMA. *Edmundite Guild* Society of St. Edmund, Inc., P.O. Drawer 490, 36701. Tel: 888-540-7722; Fax: 334-875-8189. Email: myhalyk@aol.com. Rev. Richard Myhalyk, S.S.E., Mission Dir. & CEO. Priests 5; Brothers 1.

RELIGIOUS INSTITUTES OF MEN REPRESENTED IN THE ARCHDIOCESE

For further details refer to the corresponding bracketed number in the Religious Institutes of Men or Women section.

[0200]—*Benedictine Monks*—O.S.B.
[1100]—*Brothers of the Sacred Heart* (New Orleans Prov.)—S.C.
[1330]—*Congregation of the Mission* (Eastern Prov.)—C.M.
[1080]—*Congregation of the Resurrection* (Chicago Prov.)—C.R.
[0690]—*Jesuit Fathers and Brothers* (New Orleans Prov.)—S.J.
[]—*Missionaries of St. Francis de Sales*—M.S.F.S.
[0840]—*Missionary Servants of the Most Holy Trinity*—S.T.
[0854]—*Missionary Society of St. Paul of Nigeria*—M.S.P.
[0440]—*Society of Saint Edmund* (Selma, AL)—S.S.E.
[0700]—*St. Joseph's Society of the Sacred Heart* (Baltimore, MD)—S.S.J.

RELIGIOUS INSTITUTES OF WOMEN REPRESENTED IN THE ARCHDIOCESE

[3710]—*Congregation of the Sisters of Saint Agnes*—C.S.A.
[1780]—*Congregation of the Sisters of the Third Order of St. Francis of Perpetual Adoration*—F.S.P.A.
[0760]—*Daughters of Charity of St. Vincent de Paul*—D.C.
[]—*Daughters of Mary Mother of Mercy*—D.M.M.M.
[0820]—*Daughters of the Holy Spirit*—D.H.S.
[0960]—*Daughters of Wisdom*—D.W.
[0420]—*Discalced Carmelite Nuns*—O.C.D.
[1050]—*Dominican Contemplative Nuns*—O.P.
[1070-03]—*Dominican Sisters*—O.P.
[1070-13]—*Dominican Sisters*—O.P.
[1070-18]—*Dominican Sisters*—O.P.
[]—*Franciscan Missionary Sisters* (Jamaica)—F.M.S.
[2575]—*Institute of the Sisters of Mercy of the Americas*—R.S.M.
[2340]—*Little Sisters of the Poor*—L.S.P.
[2790]—*Missionary Servants of the Most Blessed Trinity*—M.S.B.T.
[3040]—*Oblate Sisters of Providence*—O.S.P.
[]—*Order of St. Benedict*—O.S.B.
[]—*Sisters for Christian Community*—S.F.C.C
[0430]—*Sisters of Charity of the Blessed Virgin Mary*—B.V.M.
[2360]—*Sisters of Loretto At the Foot of the Cross*—S.L.
[2550]—*Sisters of Mercy*—R.S.M.
[3360]—*Sisters of Providence of Saint Mary-of-the-Woods, Indiana*—S.P.
[1650]—*Sisters of St. Francis of Philadelphia*—O.S.F.
[3830-14]—*Sisters of St. Joseph*—S.S.J.
[3830-15]—*Sisters of St. Joseph*—C.S.J.
[3840]—*Sisters of St. Joseph of Carondelet*—C.S.J.
[3850]—*Sisters of St. Joseph of Chambery*—C.S.J.
[3480]—*Sisters of the Resurrection*—C.R.
[2150]—*Sisters, Servants of the Immaculate Heart of Mary*—I.H.M.
[3330]—*Union of the Sisters of the Presentation of the Blessed Virgin Mary*—P.B.V.M.
[4170]—*Vincentian Sisters of Charity* (Perryville, PA)—V.S.C.
[4190]—*Visitation Nuns*—V.H.M.

NECROLOGY

† Aherne, Rev. Msgr. John P., (Retired)—Died April 27, 2009
† Maguire, Rev. Msgr. Hugh, Grand Bay, AL St. John the Baptist—Died Feb. 21, 2009

An asterisk (*) denotes an organization that has established tax-exempt status directly with the IRS and is not covered by the USCCB Group Ruling.

Diocese of Monterey in California

(Montereyensis in California)

Most Reverend

RICHARD J. GARCIA, D.D.

Bishop of Monterey; ordained June 15, 1973; appointed Titular Bishop of Bapara and Auxiliary Bishop of Sacramento November 25, 1997; ordained January 28, 1998; appointed Fourth Bishop of Monterey December 19, 2006; installed January 30, 2007. Email: rjgb@dioceseofmonterey.org.

Pastoral Office: 425 Church St., Monterey, CA 93940. Tel: 831-373-4345; Fax: 831-373-1175. *Mailing Address: P.O. Box 2048, Monterey, CA 93942-2048*

Web: www.dioceseofmonterey.org

Email: diocese@dioceseofmonterey.org

ESTABLISHED DECEMBER 14, 1967.

Square Miles 21,916.

Comprises the Counties of Monterey, San Benito, San Luis Obispo and Santa Cruz in the State of California.

Legal Titles:
Diocese of Monterey in California.
The Roman Catholic Bishop of Monterey, California, a Corporation Sole.
The Diocese of Monterey Education & Welfare Corporation.
The Bishop Harry A. Clinch Endowment Fund of the Diocese of Monterey.
Catholic Charities of the Diocese of Monterey (Corporation).
Villa Serra Corporation.
Ave Maria Convalescent Hospital, Inc.
St. Francis Central Coast Catholic High School, Inc.
Bishop Harry A. Clinch Trust Fund.
For legal titles of parishes and diocesan institutions, consult the Pastoral Office.

STATISTICAL OVERVIEW

Personnel	
Bishop	1
Retired Bishops	1
Priests: Diocesan Active in Diocese	57
Priests: Diocesan Active Outside Diocese	1
Priests: Retired, Sick or Absent	23
Number of Diocesan Priests	81
Religious Priests in Diocese	27
Total Priests in Diocese	108
Extern Priests in Diocese	18
Ordinations:	
Diocesan Priests	2
Transitional Deacons	1
Permanent Deacons	4
Permanent Deacons in Diocese	19
Total Brothers	30
Total Sisters	87
Parishes	
Parishes	46
With Resident Pastor:	
Resident Diocesan Priests	42
Resident Religious Priests	3
Without Resident Pastor:	
Administered by Deacons	1
Missions	7
Welfare	
Catholic Hospitals	1
Special Centers for Social Services	4
Total Assisted	12,557
Educational	
Diocesan Students in Other Seminaries	10
Total Seminarians	10
High Schools, Diocesan and Parish	2
Total Students	566
High Schools, Private	3
Total Students	1,034
Elementary Schools, Diocesan and Parish	11
Total Students	2,588
Elementary Schools, Private	3
Total Students	664
Catechesis/Religious Education:	
High School Students	753
Elementary Students	3,069
Total Students under Catholic Instruction	8,684
Teachers in the Diocese:	
Priests	1
Sisters	8
Lay Teachers	282
Vital Statistics	
Receptions into the Church:	
Infant Baptism Totals	6,917
Minor Baptism Totals	261
Adult Baptism Totals	139
Received into Full Communion	233
First Communions	4,715
Confirmations	1,408
Marriages:	
Catholic	882
Interfaith	122
Total Marriages	1,004
Deaths	1,182
Total Catholic Population	196,274
Total Population	981,371

Former Prelates of the Diocese of Monterey—Most Revs. HARRY ANSELM CLINCH, D.D., ord. June 6, 1936; appt. Titular Bishop of Badiae and Auxiliary to the Bishop of Monterey-Fresno, Dec. 5, 1956; cons. Feb. 27, 1957; installed as first Bishop of Monterey in California, Dec. 14, 1967; retired Jan. 19, 1982; died March 8, 2003; THADDEUS SHUBSDA, D.D., ord. April 26, 1950; Titular Bishop of Trau and Auxiliary Bishop of Los Angeles; Episcopal Ordination; appt. Feb. 19, 1977; named Bishop of Monterey in California, June 1, 1982; installed as second Bishop of Monterey, July 1, 1982; died April 26, 1991; SYLVESTER D. RYAN, D.D. (Retired), ord. May 3, 1957; appt. Auxiliary Bishop of Los Angeles and Titular Bishop of Remesiana Feb. 17, 1990; ord. Bishop on May 31, 1990; appt. Third Bishop of Monterey Jan. 28, 1992; installed March 19, 1992; retired Dec. 19, 2006.

Vicar General—Very Rev. PETER A. CRIVELLO, V.G., 425 Church St., Monterey, 93940. Mailing Address: P.O. Box 2048, Monterey, 93942-2048. Tel: 831-373-4345; Fax: 831-373-1175. Email: frpeter@sancarloscathedral.org.

Chancellor—Sr. PATRICIA M. MURTAGH, I.M., Chancellor & Dir. Protection of Children & Young People, 425 Church St., Monterey, 93940. Mailing Address: P.O. Box 2048, Monterey, 93942-2048. Tel: 831-373-4345; Fax: 831-373-1175. Email: srpmurtagh@dioceseofmonterey.org.

Vicar for Clergy—Rev. PAUL P. MURPHY, St. Angela Merici, 146 8th St., Pacific Grove, 93950. Tel: 831-372-0338; Fax: 831-372-0338; Cell: 831-254-9294. Email: montereypriest@yahoo.com.

Vicar for Hispanic Clergy—Rev. EUGENIO ARAMBURO, Christ Child, 213230 Summit Rd., Los Gatos, 95033. Tel: 408-353-2210; Fax: 408-353-8680. Email: freugenio@christchild.org.

Vicar for Religious—VACANT.

Vicar for Retired Priests—Rev. PAUL R. VALDEZ, K.C.H.S., J.C.L., St. Jude, 303 Hillcrest Ave., Marina, 93933. Tel: 831-384-7011.

Vicar for Temporalities & Administration—THOMAS H. RIORDAN, 425 Church St., Monterey, 93940. Tel: 831-373-4345; Fax: 831-373-1175. Mailing Address: P.O. Box 2048, Monterey, 93942-2048. Email: triordan@dioceseofmonterey.org.

Moderator of the Curia—Rev. ROY SHELLY, 425 Church St., Monterey, 93940. Tel: 831-373-4345; Fax: 831-373-1175. Mailing Address: P.O. Box 2048, Monterey, 93942-2048. Email: frrshelly@dioceseofmonterey.org.

Pastoral Office—Administrative Assistants: DONA LOGEMAN ACUFF. Email: dacuff@dioceseofmonterey.org; LETICIA FLORES-MCPHERSON. Email: lmcpherson@dioceseofmonterey.org; ANALUISA GONZALEZ. Email: agonzalez@dioceseofmonterey.org; AIKO SOKOLOWSKI. Email: asokolowski@dioceseofmonterey.org; 425 Church St., Monterey, 93940. Mailing Address: P.O. Box 2048, Monterey, 93942-2048. Tel: 831-373-4345; Fax: 831-373-1175. Email: diocese@dioceseofmonterey.org.

Pastoral Office, Ecclesiastical Notaries—DONA LOGEMAN ACUFF; ANALUISA GONZALEZ. Email: agonzalez@dioceseofmonterey.org.

Vicars Forane—Very Revs. JAMES HENRY, V.F., Salinas and Monterey; MATTHEW PENNINGTON, V.F., Santa Cruz; RUDY RUIZ, V.F., San Benito; IGNACIO MARTINEZ, V.F., Salinas Valley; KENNETH J. BROWN, V.F., San Luis Obispo.

Diocesan Consultors—Very Revs. KENNETH J. BROWN, V.F.; PETER A. CRIVELLO, V.G.; Revs. PAUL P. MURPHY; ROBERTO VERA; Very Revs. JAMES R. HENRY, V.F.; MATTHEW PENNINGTON, V.F.; Rev. ROY SHELLY, M.A., Ph.D.

Diocesan Departments, Directors and Offices

Archives—Rev. CARL M.D. FARIA, 580 Fremont St., Monterey, 93940. Tel: 831-373-2127; Fax: 831-655-4809. Email: archives@dioceseofmonterey.org; Mailing Address: P.O. Box 2048, Monterey, 93942-2048.

Office of Legal Counsel—SUSAN A. MAYER, Esq., 425 Church St., Monterey, 93940. Email: smayer@dioceseofmonterey.org; Mailing Address: P.O. Box 2048, Monterey, 93942-2048. Tel: 831-373-4345; Fax: 831-373-5765.

Finance Officer—THOMAS H. RIORDAN, 425 Church St., Monterey, 93940. Tel: 831-373-4345; Fax: 831-373-1175. Email: triordan@dioceseofmonterey.org; Mailing Address: P.O. Box 2048, Monterey, 93942-2048.

Communication— "Vistas" Monterey Office - Spokesperson: Deacon WARREN HOY, Mailing Address: P.O. Box 2048, Monterey, 93942. Tel: 831-373-4345; Fax: 831-373-1175. Email: observer@dioceseofmonterey.org.

Accounting Office—STEPHANIE MAYER, Controller The Roman Catholic Bishop of Monterey. Email: stephanie.mayer@dioceseofmonterey.org; ANNE M. MCGUIRE, Dir. Business Support. Email: amcguire@dioceseofmonterey.org; STEVE HAWTHORNE, Information Systems Mgr. Email: shawthorne@dioceseofmonterey.org; KATHY SINGH, Controller, Bishop Clinch Endowment & Catholic Charities. Email: ksingh@dioceseofmonterey.org;

NANCY SOTO, Payroll Specialist. Email: nsoto@dioceseofmonterey.org; CAROLYN HISERMAN, Accounts Receivable. Email: chiserman@dioceseofmonterey.org; KAREN PRESTIGIACOMO, Accounts Payable. Email: kprestigiacomo@dioceseofmonterey.org; ROSE GRAHAM, Annual Ministries Appeal. Email: rgraham@dioceseofmonterey.org; 425 Church St., Monterey, 93940. Tel: 831-373-4346; Fax: 831-373-2831. Mailing Address: P.O. Box 2048, Monterey, 93942-2048.

Human Resources—SUSAN A. MAYER, Esq., Dir.; STEFANIE OLSEN, Human Resources Assoc. Dir., 425 Church St., Monterey, 93940. Tel: 831-373-4345; Fax: 831-373-5765. Email: humanres@dioceseofmonterey.org; Mailing Address: P.O. Box 2048, Monterey, 93942-2048.

Catholic Schools Department—485 Church St., Monterey, 93940. Mailing Address: P.O. Box 350, Monterey, 93942-0350. Tel: 831-373-1608; Fax: 831-373-0173. KIM PRYZBYLSKI, Ph.D., Supt. Email: kpryzbylski@dioceseofmonterey.org; MIRIAM "MIMI" SCHWERTFEGER, Asst. Dir. Email: mschwertfeger@dioceseofmonterey.org.

Cemeteries—TIM BENNETT, Dir., Administrative Office, 725 Fremont Blvd., Monterey, 93940. Mailing Address: P.O. Box 2048, Monterey, 93942-2048. Tel: 831-372-0327; Fax: 831-372-8726. Email: tbennett@dioceseofmonterey.org.

Diocesan Tribunal—435 Church St., Monterey, 93940. Mailing Address: P.O. Box 350, Monterey, 93942-0350. Tel: 831-373-1833; Fax: 831-373-6761. Email: fsanfilippo@dioceseofmonterey.org.

Judicial Vicar—Rev. KENNETH J. LAVERONE, O.F.M., M.A., J.C.L.; FRAYLNE SAN FILIPPO, Dir.

Judges—Revs. KENNETH J. LAVERONE, O.F.M., M.A., J.C.L.; DAVID SCHUYLER, S.M., J.C.D.; Sr. ELIZABETH MCDONOUGH, O.P., J.C.D., S.T.L.

Defenders of the Bond—Sr. LILIANA BONELLO, I.M., J.C.L.; Revs. ROBERT HAYES, J.C.L.; EMIL ROBU; PAUL R. VALDEZ, K.C.H.S., J.C.L.

Advocates—Very Rev. JOHN C. GRIFFIN, V.U.; Rev. MICHAEL MARINI (Retired).

Promoter of Justice—Rev. EMIL ROBU.

Notary—FRAYLNE SAN FILIPPO.

Divine Worship Department—Sr. BARBARA ANN LONG, O.P., Dir.; KAREN BENNETT, Administrative Asst., 126 High St., Santa Cruz, 95060. Tel: 831-423-4973; Fax: 831-423-4973. Email: worship@dioceseofmonterey.org.

Pastoral Response Coordinator—CAROL KAPLAN, Dir. MFT, 425 Church St., Monterey, 93940. Tel: 800-321-5220; Fax: 831-373-5765. Mailing Address: P.O. Box 2048, Monterey, 93942-2048.

Pastoral Support—Rev. ROY SHELLY, Dir., 425 Church St., Monterey, 93940. Tel: 831-373-4345, Ext. 266; Fax: 831-373-1175. Email: frrshelly@dioceseofmonterey.org; Mailing Address: P.O. Box 2048, Monterey, 93942-2048.

Protection of Children and Young People—Sr. PATRICIA M. MURTAGH, I.M., Dir., 425 Church St., Monterey, 93940. Tel: 831-373-4345, Ext. 221; Fax: 831-373-1175. Email: srpmurtagh@dioceseofmonterey.org; Mailing Address: P.O. Box 2048, Monterey, 93942-2048.

Clergy Life & Ministry—Rev. PAUL P. MURPHY, St. Angela Merici, 146 8th St., Pacific Grove, 93950. Tel: 831-372-0338; Cell: 831-254-9294; Fax: 831-372-0338. Email: montereypriest@yahoo.com.

Evangelization and Stewardship—Mailing Address: P.O. Box 2048, Monterey, 93942-2048. 485 Church St., Monterey, 93940. Tel: 831-373-1834; Fax: 831-373-3534. Email: stewardship@dioceseofmonterey.org. THERESA ALLION, Administrative Asst. Tel: 831-645-2812. Email: tallion@dioceseofmonterey.org.

Office of Faith Formation—Rev. ROY SHELLY, Dir., 485 Church St., Monterey, 93940. Tel: 831-373-1335; Fax: 831-373-3351. Email: frrshelly@dioceseofmonterey.org.

Campus Ministry Department—Revs. ROY SHELLY, Dir., 485 Church St., Monterey, 93940. Tel: 831-373-1335; Fax: 831-373-3351. Email: frrshelly@dioceseofmonterey.org; RODOLFO CONTRERAS, University of California - Santa Cruz, 285 Meder St., Santa Cruz, 95060. Tel: 831-423-9400; Fax: 831-423-8163. Email: rcontreras@dioceseofmonterey.org. Web: www.newmanite.org; VACANT, Dir. Campus Ministry, California State University at Monterey Bay (CSUMB), 485 Church St., Monterey, 93940. Tel: 831-373-1335, Ext. 248; Fax: 831-373-3351; Revs. JOHN ULRICH, S.M, M.A., Dir. Campus Ministry, California State Polytechnic University, San Luis Obispo. Email: frjohn@slonewman.org; KEVIN DUGGAN, S.M., M.Div., Assoc. Dir. Campus Ministry, California State Polytechnic University, San Luis Obispo, 1472 Foothill Blvd., San Luis Obispo, 93401. Tel: 805-543-4105; Fax: 831-543-5671.

Catechetical Ministries Department—485 Church St., Monterey, 93940. Tel: 831-373-1335; Fax: 831-373-3351. TISH SCARGILL, Dir. Email: tscargill@dioceseofmonterey.org; OLGA FLORES, Administrative Asst. Tel: 831-373-1335; Fax: 831-373-3351. Email: oflores@dioceseofmonterey.org; TERRY BURROWS, Consultant, San Luis Obispo Deanery, 221 Daly Ave., San Luis Obispo, 93405. Tel: 805-458-2006; Fax: 805-544-6756. Email: tburrows@dioceseofmonterey.org.

Hispanic Ministry Department—Sr. LYDIA SCHNEIDER, I.M., Dir., 485 Church St., Monterey, 93940. Tel: 831-373-1335; Fax: 831-373-3351. Email: hispanic@dioceseofmonterey.org.

Migrant Ministry Coordinator—MARINA OCAMPO, 405 Palma Dr., Salinas, 93901-1822. Tel: 831-796-0136; Fax: 831-796-0138.

Permanent Diaconate—Rev. ROY SHELLY, Dir. Deacon Formation; Deacon NICHOLAS PASCULLI, Dir. Deacon Life & Community. Tel: 831-373-1335, Ext. 248; Fax: 831-373-3351. Email: npasculli@dioceseofmonterey.org; Mrs. CLAUDIA LARRAZA, Administrative Asst., 485 Church St., Monterey, 93940. Tel: 831-373-1335; Fax: 831-373-3351. Email: formation@dioceseofmonterey.org.

Family Life/Respect Life and Social Justice Ministry—Ms. SHEILAH LYNCH, Dir., 485 Church St., Monterey, 93940. Tel: 831-373-1335; Fax: 831-373-3351. Email: slynch@dioceseofmonterey.org.

Spiritual Direction Ministry—Mrs. BARBARA WINSTON, Coord., 485 Church St., Monterey, 93940. Tel: 831-373-1335; Fax: 831-373-3351. Email: bwinston@dioceseofmonterey.org.

Youth and Young Adult Ministry—VACANT, Dir.; MARIA OROZCO, Administrative Asst., 485 Church St., Monterey, 93940. Tel: 831-373-1335; Fax: 831-373-3351. Email: youth@dioceseofmonterey.org.

Scouting—VACANT, Chap., 485 Church St., Monterey, 93940. Tel: 831-373-4335; Fax: 831-373-3351. Email: youth@dioceseofmonterey.org.

Vocations Director—Rev. ROY SHELLY, M.A., Ph.D., Dir.; MARIA OROZCO, Administrative Asst., 435 Church St., Monterey, 93940. Tel: 831-645-2813; Fax: 831-373-6761. Email: vocations@dioceseofmonterey.org; Mailing Address: P.O. Box 2048, Monterey, 93942-2048.

Holy Childhood Association—VACANT, Diocese of Monterey, 425 Church St., Monterey, 93940. Tel: 831-373-2628; Fax: 831-373-1175. Mailing Address: P.O. Box 2048, Monterey, 93942-2048.

Pontifical Mission Societies—Sr. PATRICIA M. MURTAGH, I.M., Coord., Diocese of Monterey, 425 Church St., Monterey, 93940. Tel: 831-373-2628; Fax: 831-373-1175. Email: srpmurtagh@dioceseofmonterey.org; Mailing Address: P.O. Box 2048, Monterey, 93942-2048.

St. Joseph's Conference Center—485 Church St., Monterey, 93940.

Catholic Charities of the Diocese of Monterey—

Administrative Office—CORY JO ALLEN, Interim Exec. Dir. Email: callen@dioceseofmonterey.org; GABRIELA ANDERSON, Administrative Accounting Assoc. Email: ganderson@dioceseofmonterey.org.

Catholic Charities - Salinas Office—Buckley Hall, St. Mary of the Nativity, 1705 2nd Ave., Salinas, 93905. Immigration & Citizenship. Tel: 831-422-0602; Fax: 831-422-0759. *Family Supportive Services.* Tel: 831-753-5314; Fax: 831-422-0759.

Catholic Charities - San Luis Obispo Office—Mission San Luis Obispo, 751 Palm Ave., San Luis Obispo, 93401. Tel: 805-541-9110; Fax: 805-541-9121. (Immigration & Citizenship Svcs.; Family Supportive Svcs.)

Catholic Charities - Watsonville Office—217 E. Lake St., Watsonville, 95076. Tel: 831-722-2675; Fax: 831-722-9921. (Family Supportive Svcs.; Immigration & Citizenship Svcs. & Mental Health Counseling)

Campaign for Human Development—Ms. SHEILAH LYNCH, Dir., 485 Church St., Monterey, 93940. Tel: 831-373-1335; Fax: 831-373-3351. Email: slynch@dioceseofmonterey.org.

Catholic Relief Service—Ms. SHEILAH LYNCH, Dir., 485 Church St., Monterey, 93940. Tel: 831-373-1335; Fax: 831-373-3351. Email: slynch@dioceseofmonterey.org.

Committees and Councils

Administrative Committee Priests' Pension Plan—Most Rev. RICHARD J. GARCIA, D.D.; Revs. EUGENIO ARAMBURO; JOSEPH L. OCCHIUTO; GREGORY SANDMAN; EDWARD FITZ-HENRY; PAUL R. VALDEZ, K.C.H.S., J.C.L., Chm.

Ave Maria Board—Most Rev. RICHARD J. GARCIA, D.D., Pres.; CLANCY D'ANGELO, Sec.; THOMAS H. RIORDAN, Finance Officer; DONA LOGEMAN ACUFF, Recording Sec.

Bishop Harry A. Clinch Endowment Fund, The Bishop Sylvester D. Ryan Continuing Education Fund— The Bishop Shubsda Memorial Seminary Endowment Burse and The Cemetery Endowment Burse Most Rev. RICHARD J. GARCIA, D.D.; J. D. CHILDS; LEAH DUNCAN; JAMES HARRISON; ELIZABETH HELFRICH; SUSAN A. MAYER, Esq., Ex Official; MICHAEL MORRIS; RONALD PASQUINELLI; JOSEPH PEZZINI; THOMAS H. RIORDAN, Finance Officer, (Staff); LARRY SAGE; ROBERT SEMAS; KATHY SINGH, Controller, (Staff).

Building Commission—Contact Persons: Very Rev. JOHN C. GRIFFIN, V.U., Carmel Mission, P.O. Box 2235, Carmel, 93921-2235. Tel: 831-624-1271; Fax: 831-624-8050; THOMAS H. RIORDAN, Diocese of Monterey, 425 Church St., P.O. Box 2048, Monterey, 93942-2048. Tel: 831-373-4345; Fax: 831-373-1175. Email: triordan@dioceseofmonterey.org.

Catholic Charities Board—Most Rev. RICHARD J. GARCIA, D.D., Chm.; ALBERT NICORA, Pres.; Rev. JERRY MCCORMICK, Sec. (Retired); LARRY SAGE, Treas.; MARIA ANDERSON; JIM COOK; GEORGETTE DUFRESNE; RON FREDERICKSON; CHRIS HAUPT; Very Rev. IGNATIUS MARTINEZ; MARTINA O'SULLIVAN, M.S.W.; CHRISTOPHER PANETTA; CAMERINO PDILLA; ANA VENTURA-PHARAS; CYNTHIA ZOLLER-SILVER. Staff: SUSAN A. MAYER, Esq., Gen. Counsel & Bd. Member; THOMAS H. RIORDAN, Finance Officer; CORY JO ALLEN, Interim Exec. Dir.

Diocesan Consultors—Very Revs. KENNETH J. BROWN, V.F.; PETER A. CRIVELLO, V.G.; JAMES R. HENRY, V.F.; Rev. PAUL P. MURPHY; Very Rev. MATTHEW PENNINGTON, V.F.; Revs. ROY SHELLY; ROBERTO VERA.

Finance Council—ROSEMARY ANDERSON; Very Rev. PETER A. CRIVELLO, V.G.; RICHARD FALGE; HARRY HOW; RONALD PASQUINELLI; JIM ROTTER; Most Rev. RICHARD J. GARCIA, D.D.; TOD SANCHEZ; Rev. PAUL R. VALDEZ, K.C.H.S., J.C.L. Ex Officio: THOMAS H. RIORDAN, Finance Officer; SUSAN A. MAYER, Esq., Gen. Counsel; DONA LOGEMAN ACUFF, Recording Sec.

Insurance Committee—SUSAN A. MAYER, Esq.; THOMAS H. RIORDAN; Rev. PAUL R. VALDEZ, K.C.H.S., J.C.L.

Lay Employees Non-Qualified Pension Committee—THOMAS H. RIORDAN, Chm.; TONY KARACHALE, Consultant.

Lay Employee Pension Plan Committee—CLANCY D'ANGELO; TONY KARACHALE, Consultant; SUSAN A. MAYER, Esq.; RONALD PASQUINELLI; THOMAS H. RIORDAN, Ex Officio; TOD D. SANCHEZ; DAVID J. SULLIVAN.

Permanent Diaconate Advisory Board—Deacons NICHOLAS PASCULLI, Dir.; ANDRES LARRAZA; Mrs. CLAUDIA LARRAZA; Deacon MANUEL ESPINOZA; Mrs. FRANCISCA ESPINOZA; Deacon DOUGLAS WINSTON; Mrs. BARBARA WINSTON; Rev. ROY SHELLY, Moderator of the Curia.

Presbyteral Council—Very Rev. PETER A. CRIVELLO, V.G.; Rev. ROY SHELLY, Moderator of the Curia; Very Revs. JAMES R. HENRY, V.F.; KENNETH J. BROWN, V.F.; Revs. MICHAEL MILLER; ROBERTO VERA; MICHAEL MARINI (Retired); RAYMOND TINTLE, O.F.M.; Very Rev. MATTHEW PENNINGTON, V.F.; Revs. PAUL P. MURPHY, Vicar for Clergy; EDWIN LIMPIADO; Most Rev. RICHARD J. GARCIA, D.D.; DONA LOGEMAN ACUFF, Recording Sec.

Clergy Life and Ministry Board—Most Rev. RICHARD J. GARCIA, D.D.; Revs. PAUL P. MURPHY, Dir.; PATRICK DOOLING; ANALUISA GONZALEZ, Recording Sec.; Deacon ANDRES LARRAZA; Revs. JERRY MAHER; EFRAIN MEDINA; LUCAS PANTOJA; JOSE ALBERTO VASQUEZ-MARTINEZ; JONDELL DEVEAUX WRIGHT.

Clergy Personnel Board—Revs. ROY SHELLY, Moderator of the Curia; MIGUEL ANGEL GRAJEDA; Very Revs. IGNACIO MARTINEZ, V.F.; PETER A. CRIVELLO, V.G.; Revs. EUGENIO ARAMBURO, Vicar for Hispanic Clergy; PAUL P. MURPHY, Vicar for Clergy; Deacon ANDRES LARRAZA; Most Rev. RICHARD J. GARCIA, D.D.; Rev. GREGORY SANDMAN; Sr. PATRICIA M. MURTAGH, I.M., Chancellor; Mrs. NICKI PASCULLI.

Safety Committee—TIM BENNETT; SUSAN A. MAYER, Esq.; ANNE MCGUIRE; THOMAS H. RIORDAN; KIM PRYZBYLSKI, Ph.D.; KAREN VICTORINO; MIRIAM "MIMI" SCHWERTFEGER, Recording Sec.; Sr. PATRICIA M. MURTAGH, I.M.; TISH SCARGILL; SUZY BROWN.

St. Francis Central Coast Catholic High School, Inc.—Most Rev. RICHARD J. GARCIA, D.D.; Very Rev. TIMOTHY PLOCH, S.D.B.; Most Rev. SYLVESTER D. RYAN, D.D., Retired Bishop of Monterey (Retired); Rev. THOMAS PRENDEVILLE, S.D.B.; THOMAS H. RIORDAN; Bro. MICHAEL TOUCHSTONE, S.D.B., M.A.; DONA LOGEMAN ACUFF, Recording Sec.

Vocations Board—Sr. CARMEN BOTELLO, F.M.A.; Mrs. SALLY GRIEG; Revs. LUCAS PANTOJA; ROY SHELLY, M.A., Ph.D.; ROBERTO VERA.

Web Site Development Committee—GARY KREEGER.

CLERGY, PARISHES, MISSIONS AND PAROCHIAL SCHOOLS

CITY OF MONTEREY

(MONTEREY COUNTY), CATHEDRAL OF SAN CARLOS BORROMEO (1770) Very Rev. Peter A. Crivello, Rector; Rev. Patrick Dooling, Parochial Vicar; Deacon Andres Larraza; Sr. Maria Romero, Pastoral Assoc.
Mailing Address: 500 Church St., 93940. Tel: 831-373-2628; Fax: 831-373-0518. Web: www.sancarloscathedral.net.
Res.: 550 Church St., 93940.
School—(1898), (Grades K-8), 450 Church St., 93940. Tel: 831-375-1324; Fax: 831-375-9736. Email: principal@sancarlosschool.org. Web: www.sancarlosschool.org. Teresa Bennett, Prin.; Jack Marchi, Prin.; Mrs. Carole Olsen, Vice Prin.; Mr. Timothy Krislyn, Asst. Prin. Lay Teachers 15; Total Staff 29; Students 268.
Catechesis/Religious Program—Tel: 831-373-2628; Fax: 831-373-0516. Cynthia Friesen, C.R.E. Students 160.

OUTSIDE THE CITY OF MONTEREY

APTOS, SANTA CRUZ CO., RESURRECTION (1968) Rev. Ronald Shirley; Deacon Patrick Conway.
Res.: 7600 Soquel Dr., P.O. Box 87, 95001. Tel: 831-688-4300; Fax: 831-688-6921. Email: resurrectionparish@sbcglobal.net. Web: www.resurrection-aptos.org.
School—Good Shepherd School (Inter-Parish), (Grades PreK-8), 2727 Mattison Ln., Santa Cruz, 95065. Tel: 831-476-4000; Fax: 831-476-0948. Email: snelson@gsschool.org. Web: www.gsschool.org. Daniel Anderson, Prin. Lay Teachers 18; Students 214.
Catechesis/Religious Program—Tel: 831-688-4300; Fax: 831-688-6921. Students 176.

ARROYO GRANDE, SAN LUIS OBISPO CO., ST. PATRICK (1886) Very Rev. Kenneth J. Brown; Rev. Francisco X. Montes, Parochial Vicar.
Res.: 501 Fair Oaks Ave., P.O. Box 860, 93421. Tel: 805-489-2680; Fax: 805-489-1316. Email: info@stpatsag.org. Web: www.stpatsag.org.
School—(1963), (Grades PreSchool-8), 900 W. Branch St., 93420. Tel: 805-489-1210; Fax: 805-489-7662. Email: mhalderman@stpatricksschool.net. Web: www.stpatricksschool.net. Maureen Halderman, Prin. Sisters of Mercy 1; Lay Teachers 9; Total Staff 38; Students 268.
Catechesis/Religious Program—Tel: 805-481-2990. Students 315.
Mission—St. Francis of Assisi 17th & Beach, Oceano, San Luis Obispo Co. 93445.
Shamrock Thrift Shop—924 Grand Ave., Grover City, 93433. Tel: 805-481-0612. Alanna Owen, Mgr.

ATASCADERO, SAN LUIS OBISPO CO., ST. WILLIAM'S (1948) [JC] Rev. George Batchelder.
Res.: 6410 Santa Lucia Rd., 93422. Tel: 805-466-0849; Fax: 805-461-0743. Email: office@st-williams.org. Web: www.st-williams.org.
Catechesis/Religious Program—Troylyn Lindsay, Parish Catechetical Leader. Students 282.

BOULDER CREEK, SANTA CRUZ CO., ST. MICHAEL (1921) Rev. Robert Murrin, Parochial Admin.
Res.: 13005 Pine St., 95006. Tel: 831-338-6112; Fax: 831-338-7522. Email: st.michaelschurch@sbcglobal.net.
Catechesis/Religious Program—Debbie Esteban-Moyer, C.R.E. Students 33.

CAMBRIA, SAN LUIS OBISPO CO., SANTA ROSA (1961) [CEM] Rev. Mark Stetz; Deacon Daniel Weber.
Res.: 1174 Main St., 93428. Tel: 805-927-4816; Fax: 805-927-2880. Email: admin@santarosaparish.org. Web: www.santarosaparish.org.
Catechesis/Religious Program—Tel: 805-924-1728. Students 136.

CAPITOLA, SANTA CRUZ CO., ST. JOSEPH (1904) [JC] Very Rev. Matthew Pennington.
Res.: 435 Monterey Ave., 95010. Tel: 831-475-8211; Fax: 831-475-2601. Email: stjosephs@stjoscap.org. Web: www.stjoscap.org.
School—Good Shepherd School (Inter-Parish), (Grades K-8), 2727 Mattison Ln., Santa Cruz, 95065. Tel: 831-476-4000; Fax: 831-476-0948. Email: snelson@gsschool.org. Web: www.gsschool.org. Daniel Anderson, Prin. Lay Teachers 18; Students 202.
Catechesis/Religious Program—Tel: 831-475-9510; Fax: 831-475-2601. Cathy Gabrio, D.R.E. Students 143.

CARMEL VALLEY, MONTEREY CO., OUR LADY OF MT. CARMEL (1953) Rev. Emil Robu. In Res., Rev. Derek Hughes (Ireland).
Res.: 9 El Caminito Rd., 93924. Tel: 831-659-2224; Fax: 831-659-9186. Email: olmc@ourladycarmelvalley.org. Web: www.ourladycarmelvalley.org.
Catechesis/Religious Program—Students 37.

CARMEL, MONTEREY CO., SAN CARLOS BORROMEO BASILICA (1771) [CEM], (Carmel Mission) Very Rev. John C. Griffin. In Res., Rev. Roy Shelly.
Res.: 3080 Rio Rd., 93923. Tel: 831-624-1271; Fax: 831-624-8050. Email: info@carmelmission.org. Web: www.carmelmission.org.
School—Junipero Serra School, (Grades K-8), 2992 Lasuen Dr., 93923. Tel: 831-624-8322; Fax: 831-624-8311. Margaret A. Burger, Prin. Lay Teachers 16; Students 174.
Catechesis/Religious Program—Tel: 831-624-1271, Ext. 216; Fax: 831-624-6840. Students 165.
Mission—St. Francis of the Redwoods Hwy. 1, Big Sur, Monterey Co. 93920.
Chapel—Blessed Sacrament

CASTROVILLE, MONTEREY CO., OUR LADY OF REFUGE (1869) [JC] Rev. Roberto Vera Vasquez.
11140 Preston St., 95012. Tel: 831-633-4015; Fax: 831-633-4653.
Res.: 14931 Charter Oak Blvd., Salinas, 93907.
Catechesis/Religious Program—Tel: 831-633-4016. Sr. Christina Bortolotti, D.R.E. Students 470.

CAYUCOS , SAN LUIS OBISPO CO., ST. JOSEPH (1905) Rev. Edward J. Holterhoff, Admin.; Rev. Msgr. Charles G. Fatooh, Sacramental Min.
Res.: 360 Park Ave., P.O. Box 437, 93430. Tel: 805-995-3243; Fax: 805-995-2838. Email: stjosephcayucos@charter.net.
Catechesis/Religious Program—

CORRALITOS, SANTA CRUZ CO., HOLY EUCHARIST (1969) Rev. Joseph A. Grimaldi (HON), Admin.
Res.: 527 Corralitos Rd., 95076. Tel: 831-722-5490; Fax: 831-722-5421. Email: office.holyeucharistca@yahoo.com. Web: www.holyeucharistca.com.
Catechesis/Religious Program—Email: susan@holyeucharistca.com. Students 56.

DAVENPORT, SANTA CRUZ CO., ST. VINCENT DE PAUL (1915) Rev. James Catalano, O.S.J., Parochial Admin.
123 Marine View Ave., 95017. Tel: 831-471-1702.
Res.: 544 W. Cliff Dr., Santa Cruz, 95060. Tel: 831-457-1868; Fax: 831-457-1317.
Catechesis/Religious Program—123 Marine View Ave., 95017. Tel: 831-423-5373. Students 8.

FELTON, SANTA CRUZ CO., ST. JOHN'S (1952) Rev. Michael L. Cross.
Res.: 120 Russell Ave., P.O. Box M-1, 95018. Tel: 831-335-4657; Fax: 831-335-4648. Email: st.johns.ch@sbcglobal.net.
Catechesis/Religious Program—Noli Farwell, D.R.E. Students 55.

GONZALES, MONTEREY CO., ST. THEODORE (1892) [JC] Rev. Efrain Medina, Admin.
Office:—125 S. Center St., P.O. Box B, 93926.
Res.: 120 First St., P.O. Drawer B, 93926. Tel: 831-675-3648; Fax: 831-675-8360.
Catechesis/Religious Program—Tel: 831-675-3668, Ext. 7; Fax: 831-675-2974. Students 180.
Mission—Chualar Mission Scott & Grant Sts., Chualar, Monterey Co. 93925. Tel: 831-679-2981.

GREENFIELD, MONTEREY CO., HOLY TRINITY (1951), (Mexican—Italian), Rev. Enrique Herrera.
Res.: 27 S. El Camino Real, Box 276, 93927. Tel: 831-674-5428; Fax: 831-674-5285. Web: holytrinitygreenfield.org.
Catechesis/Religious Program—Tel: 831-674-3695. Gloria Aguilar, D.R.E. Students 300.

HOLLISTER, SAN BENITO CO
1—ST. BENEDICT, Merged with Sacred Heart, Hollister to form Sacred Heart/St. Benedict Catholic Community, Hollister.
2—SACRED HEART (1877) Merged with St. Benedict, Hollister to form Sacred Heart/St. Benedict Catholic Community, Hollister.
3—SACRED HEART/ST. BENEDICT CATHOLIC COMMUNITY (1877) [CEM] Very Rev. Rudy Ruiz; Revs. Heibar Castanada, Parochial Vicar Pro Tem; Fabian Vela (Retired).
Res.: 540 College St., 95023. Tel: 831-637-9212; Fax: 831-637-7299. Email: shparish@sacredheart-stbenedict.org.
St. Benedict: 1200 Fairview Rd., 95023.
Pastoral Center—680 College St., 95023. Fax: 831-637-7299.
School—(Grades PreSchool-8), 670 College St., 95023. Tel: 831-637-4157; Fax: 831-637-4164. Email: gjurevich@sacredheartschool.org. Web: sacredheartschool.org. Gayla Jurevich, Prin. Lay Teachers 17; Students 263.
Catechesis/Religious Program—Tel: 831-637-8291. Jeanmarie Centeno, D.R.E.; Dolores Fenzel, S.A., D.R.E. Students 816.

JOLON, MONTEREY CO., SAN ANTONIO MISSION (1771) Rev. Dennis M. Peterson, Parochial Admin.; Deacon Dustin Miller.
Res.: Box 803, 93928. Tel: 831-385-4478; Fax: 831-386-9332. Email: office@missionsanantonio.net. Web: missionsanantonio.net.
Catechesis/Religious Program—Joan Steele, D.R.E./ Mgr. Mission; Victoria Villegas, Catechist. Students 13.

KING CITY, MONTEREY CO., ST. JOHN THE BAPTIST (1891), (Hispanic), Rev. Claudio Cabrera Carranza.
Res.: 504 N. Third St., 93930. Tel: 831-385-3377; Fax: 831-385-3317. Email: stjohnscc@att.net.
Catechesis/Religious Program—Tel: 831-385-3464. Students 374.
Mission—St. Luke Main St., San Lucas, Monterey Co. 93954.

LOS GATOS, SANTA CRUZ CO., CHRIST CHILD (1983) Rev. Eugenio Aramburo.
Res.: 23230 Summit Rd., 95033. Tel: 408-353-2210; Fax: 408-353-8680.
Catechesis/Religious Program—Kim Avoy, D.R.E. Students 51.

LOS OSOS, SAN LUIS OBISPO CO., ST. ELIZABETH ANN SETON (1984) Rev. Lucas Pantoja, Parochial Admin.
Res. & Mailing Address: 2050 Palisades Ave., 93402. Tel: 805-528-5319; Fax: 805-528-8893.
Catechesis/Religious Program—Students 80.

MARINA, MONTEREY CO., ST. JUDE PARISH COMMUNITY (1963), (Filipino—Korean), Rev. Paul R. Valdez, K.C.H.S.
Res.: 303 Hillcrest Ave., 93933. Tel: 831-384-5434; Fax: 831-384-7011. Email: st_jude_marina_amy@sbcglobal.net.
Catechesis/Religious Program—Tel: 831-384-8268. Annie F. Punzalan, D.R.E. Students 187.

MORRO BAY, SAN LUIS OBISPO CO., ST. TIMOTHY (1950) Rev. Edward J. Holterhoff, Parochial Admin.
Mailing Address: 962 Piney Way, 93442. Tel: 805-772-2840; Fax: 805-772-3184. Email: osainttims@sbcglobal.net. Web: www.sttimothymorrobay.org.
Catechesis/Religious Program—Students 65.

NIPOMO, SAN LUIS OBISPO CO., ST. JOSEPH (1968) Rev. Ronald L. Green, Parochial Admin.; Most Rev. Sylvester D. Ryan, Retired Bishop of Monterey (Retired); Deacon Gregory Dutra.
Res.: 298 S. Thompson, 93444. Tel: 805-929-1922; Fax: 805-929-2662.
Catechesis/Religious Program—Tel: 805-929-3730. Students 205.

PACIFIC GROVE, MONTEREY CO., ST. ANGELA MERICI CHURCH (1928) [CEM] Revs. Paul P. Murphy; Joey R. Buena, C.S.S.
Res.: 161 9th St., 93950. Tel: 831-655-4160; Fax: 831-372-5026. Email: stangelachurch@gmail.com. Web: www.stangelapacificgrove.org.
Church: 362 Lighthouse Ave., 93950.
Office:—146 Eighth St., 93950.
Preschool - Children's Center—136 Eighth St., 93950. Tel: 831-372-3555; Fax: 831-372-1965. Email: stangelas@redshift.com. Virginia Ziomek, Prin. Lay Teachers 8; Students 62.
Catechesis/Religious Program—Students 80.

PAJARO, MONTEREY CO., OUR LADY OF THE ASSUMPTION (1953), (Hispanic), [CEM] Revs. Walter Espinoza Rivera; Gregory Sandman.
Res.: 100 Salinas Rd., Watsonville, 95076. Tel: 831-722-1104; Fax: 831-722-1931.
Catechesis/Religious Program—Tel: 831-722-9938. Marielena Curiel, D.R.E. Students 483.

PASO ROBLES, SAN LUIS OBISPO CO., ST. ROSE (1922) [CEM] [JC] Rev. Wayne Dawson, Admin. Pro Tem.
Office: 642 Trigo Ln., P.O. Box 790, 93447. Tel: 805-238-2218; Fax: 805-238-2762. Email: info@saintrosechurch.org. Web: www.saintrosechurch.org.
Res.: 820 Creston Rd., P.O. Box 790, 93447. Tel: 805-238-2218; Fax: 805-238-2762.
School—(Grades PreK-8), 900 Tucker Ave., 93446. Tel: 805-238-0304; Fax: 805-238-7393. Email: strose4@arrival.net. Web: www.strose.info. Sr. Rebecca Munoz, S.J.S., Prin. Lay Teachers 14; Students 241.
Catechesis/Religious Program—Students 461.

PISMO BEACH, SAN LUIS OBISPO CO., ST. PAUL THE APOSTLE (1929) [JC] Revs. Victor P. Abegg, O.F.M.-Conv.; Alphonse Van Guilder, O.F.M.Conv., Parochial Vicar; Bro. Robert Ouellette, O.F.M.Conv., Pastoral Assoc. In Res., Revs. Peter Parchem, O.F.M.Conv., Pastor Emeritus; John Farao, O.F.M.Conv., Prison Chap. (CA Men's Colony).
Res.: 800 Bello St., 93449. Tel: 805-773-2219; Fax: 805-773-8617. Email: stpaulspismobeach@charter.net. Web: www.stpaulspismobeach.com.
Catechesis/Religious Program—Tel: 805-773-3185. Students 50.

SALINAS
1—CHRIST THE KING (1995), (Hispanic), Rev. Antonio Sanchez.
Res.: 240 Calle Cebu, 93901. Tel: 831-422-6543; Fax: 831-422-7218.
Religious Education Office—Tel: 831-422-6722.
Catechesis/Religious Program—Students 440.
2—MADONNA DEL SASSO (1960) Very Rev. James R. Henry; Rev. Edwin Limpiado, Parochial Vicar.
Res.: 320 E. Laurel Dr., 93906. Tel: 831-422-5323; Fax: 831-422-0536.
School—(Grades PreK-8), 20 Santa Teresa Way,

93906. Tel: 831-424-7813; Fax: 831-424-3359. Web: madonnadelsasso.com. Dr. Charles E. White, Prin. Sisters of Notre Dame 1; Lay Teachers 14; Students 307.
Catechesis/Religious Program—Students 748.
3—ST. MARY OF THE NATIVITY (1947), (Hispanic), Rev. Jose Alberto Vasquez-Martinez.
Res.: 1702 Second Ave., 93905. Tel: 831-758-1669; Fax: 831-758-4715. Web: www.stmarysalinas.org.
Catechesis/Religious Program—Tel: 831-422-9964; Fax: 831-422-1217. Web: www.stmarysalinas.org/ingles/religiouseducation.html. Ms. Edith Sanchez, D.R.E. Students 800.
4—SACRED HEART (1877) [JC] Revs. Michael J. Miller; Louis Fernando Orozco Flores, Parochial Vicar; Ronald Wiecek, C.P.P.S., Parochial Vicar; Deacons Rick Gutierrez; Douglas Winston.
Res.: 22 Stone St., 93901-2643. Tel: 831-424-1959; Fax: 831-424-0788. Email: scrhrtchurch@sbcglobal.net. Web: www.shsalinas.org.
School—(Grades K-8), 123 W. Market St., 93901. Tel: 831-771-1310; Fax: 831-771-1314. Email: shs1906@yahoo.com. Ms. Jennifer Dean, Prin. Sisters 1; Lay Teachers 11; Total Staff 12; Students 251.
Catechesis/Religious Program—Tel: 831-772-8223. Mary Scattini, D.R.E. Students 410.
SAN JUAN BAUTISTA, SAN BENITO CO., SAN JUAN BAUTISTA (1797), (Hispanic), [CEM], (Old Mission) Rev. Edward Fitz-Henry.
Res.: 406 Second St., P.O. Box 400, 95045. Tel: 831-623-2127; Fax: 831-623-2433. Web: www.oldmissionsjb.org.
Catechesis/Religious Program—Tel: 831-623-4178. Email: faithformation@oldmissionsjb.org. Students 159.
SAN LUIS OBISPO, SAN LUIS OBISPO CO.
1—NATIVITY OF OUR LADY (1964) Rev. Michael Cicinato; Deacon Greg Wilhelm.
Res.: 221 Daly Ave., 93405-1099. Tel: 805-544-2357; Fax: 805-544-6756. Email: parish@nativityslo.org. Web: www.nativityslo.org.
Catechesis/Religious Program—Patty L. Miller, D.R.E. Students 90.
2—SAN LUIS OBISPO (1772), (Old Mission) Revs. Russell D. Brown; Dennis Gallo, Parochial Vicar; Deacon Charles M. Roeder.
Res.: 751 Palm St., 93401. Tel: 805-781-8220; Fax: 805-781-8214. Email: office@oldmissionslo.org. Web: www.missionsanluisobispo.org.
Preschool—221 Daly St., 93401. Tel: 805-549-8819. Teri Stegman, Prin.
School—(Grades PreK-8), 761 Broad St., 93401. Tel: 805-543-6019; Fax: 805-543-6246. Teri Stegman, Prin. Lay Teachers 18; Students 328.
Catechesis/Religious Program—Tel: 805-781-8220, Ext. 18. Students 235.
SAN MIGUEL, SAN LUIS OBISPO CO., SAN MIGUEL (1797), (Hispanic—Filipino), [CEM], (Old Mission) Rev. Raymond Tintle, O.F.M. In Res., Revs. Thomas Frost, O.F.M.; John E. Gini, O.F.M.; Larry Gosselin, O.F.M.; Joseph Zermeno, O.F.M.
Res.: 775 Mission St., P.O. Box 69, 93451. Tel: 805-467-2131; Fax: 805-467-2141. Email: friars@tcsn.net. Web: www.missionsanmiguel.org.
Catechesis/Religious Program—Tel: 805-467-2325. Students 82.
Mission—Our Lady of Ransom San Ardo, Monterey Co.
Mission—Our Lady of Guadalupe Bradley, Monterey Co.
Station—Heritage Ranch Paso Robles.
SANTA CRUZ, SANTA CRUZ CO.
1—HOLY CROSS (1791) [CEM 3] [JC 2] Rev. Joseph L. Occhiuto.
Res.: 126 High St., 95060. Tel: 831-423-4182; Fax: 831-423-1043. Email: office@holycrosssantacruz.com. Web: www.holycrosssantacruz.com.
School—Holy Cross School (1862), (Grades PreSchool-8), 150 Emmet St., 95060. Tel: 831-423-4447; Fax: 831-423-0752. Email: admin@holycsc.org. Web: www.holycsc.org. Kathleen Ryan, Prin. Adrian Dominican Sisters 2; Lay Teachers 22; Total Staff 24; Students 209.
Catechesis/Religious Program—Tel: 831-458-3041; Fax: 831-458-1043. Email: faith@holycrosssantacruz.com. Students 155.
Mission—Mision Galeria 130 Emmet St., Santa Cruz Co. 95060. Tel: 831-426-5686. Web: www.geocities.com/missionbell.
2—STAR OF THE SEA (1947) [CEM] Rev. Alberto Cabrera.
Res.: 515 Frederick St., 95062. Tel: 831-429-1018; Fax: 831-429-5832. Web: www.ourladystar.org.
School—Good Shepherd School, 2727 Mattison Ln., 95062. Tel: 831-476-4000; Fax: 831-476-0948. Web: www.gsschool.org. Daniel Anderson, Prin. (Inter-Parish) Lay Teachers 18; Students 209.
Catechesis/Religious Program—Students 470.
Chapel—Villa Maria del Mar, Tel: 831-475-1236; Fax: 831-475-8867.
SANTA MARGARITA, SAN LUIS OBISPO CO., SANTA MARGARITA DE CORTONA (1934) [JC] Rev. Robert Travis.
Res.: 22515 "H" St., P.O. Box 350, 93453. Tel: 805-438-5383; Fax: 805-438-4313. Email: decortona@aol.com.
Catechesis/Religious Program—Tel: 805-239-1597. Lynn Stroble, D.R.E. Students 35.
Mission—St. James Mission P.O. Box 3055, Carrissa Plains, San Luis Obispo Co. 93453. Tel: 805-475-2222.
SCOTTS VALLEY, SANTA CRUZ CO., SAN AGUSTIN (1969) Rev. Jerry Maher.
Res.: 257 Glenwood Dr., 95066. Tel: 831-438-3633; Fax: 831-438-0973. Email: sanagustin@sbcglobal.net.
Catechesis/Religious Program—Students 280.
SEASIDE, MONTEREY CO., ST. FRANCIS XAVIER (1950) Revs. Michael Volk; Dominic Joseph Castro, Parochial Vicar.
Res.: 1475 LaSalle Ave., 93955. Tel: 831-394-8546; Fax: 831-394-5414.
Catechesis/Religious Program—Sr. Carmelita Heredia, S.A., D.R.E. Students 414.
Mission—, Seaside, Monterey Co. 93955. Tel: 831-394-3759. Email: gsfrparish@aol.com.
SOLEDAD, MONTEREY CO., OUR LADY OF SOLITUDE (1933), (Spanish), [CEM] [JC] Very Rev. Ignacio Martinez.
235 Main St., 93960. Tel: 831-678-2731; Fax: 831-678-2968.
Catechesis/Religious Program—Tel: 831-678-1277; Fax: 831-678-0111. Sr. Mary Liza Raphael, I.M., D.R.E. Students 977.
Mission—Nuestra Senora de la Soledad Rte. 1, Box 72, Monterey Co. 93960. Tel: 408-678-2586.
SPRECKELS, MONTEREY CO., ST. JOSEPH (1969) Rev. James Nisbet.
Mailing Address: Spreckels Blvd. & Railroad Ave., P.O. Box 7158, 93962. Email: office@stjchurch.org. Web: stjchurch.org.
Catechesis/Religious Program—St. Joseph's Religion Center, 15 First St., P.O. Box 7158, 93962. Tel: 831-455-8720; Fax: 831-455-9357. Carrie Aragon, D.R.E. Students 284.
TRES PINOS, SAN BENITO CO., IMMACULATE CONCEPTION (1892) Very Rev. Larry Kambitsch.
Mailing Address: P.O. Box 247, 95075.
Res.: 7290 Airline Hwy., 95075. Tel: 831-628-3216; Fax: 831-628-3602. Email: secretary@icctp.org.
Catechesis/Religious Program—Email: religioused@icctp.org. Ann Ventura, D.R.E. Students 85.
WATSONVILLE, SANTA CRUZ CO.
1—OUR LADY HELP OF CHRISTIANS (1854), (Portuguese—Spanish), Revs. Harry W. Rasmussen, S.D.B.; Tho Bui, S.D.B.; Albert Mengon, S.D.B.; Jesse Montes, S.D.B.; Marc Rougeau, S.D.B. In Res., Bro. Abel Zanella, S.D.B., (Retired).
Res.: 2401 E. Lake Ave., 95076. Tel: 831-722-2665; Fax: 831-722-8305. Email: olhcchurch@yahoo.com.
Catechesis/Religious Program—Tel: 831-722-2392. Sr. Silva Castillo, F.M.A., D.R.E. Students 335.
2—ST. PATRICK (1861) Revs. Miguel Angel Grajeda; Marc Rene Dauphine; Roy Margallo, Parochial Vicar.
Res.: 721 Main St., 95076. Tel: 831-724-1317; Fax: 831-724-1627. Email: saintpatricks@sbcglobal.net.
Catechesis/Religious Program—Tel: 831-724-2141. Sylvia Pineda, D.R.E. (English & Spanish); Mariana Arreola-Flores, D.R.E. Students 423.

Shrines

SANTA CRUZ, SANTA CRUZ CO., SHRINE OF ST. JOSEPH GUARDIAN OF THE REDEEMER (1952) Rev. John Warburton, O.S.J.
Res.: 544 W. Cliff Dr., 95060-6147. Tel: 831-471-0442; Fax: 831-457-1317. Email: guardian@osjoseph.org. Web: www.osjoseph.org.
Guardian of the Redeemer Bookstore—Tel: 831-471-1700.

Chaplains of Public Institutions

ATASCADERO. *Atascadero State Hospital*. Deacon Daniel Weber.
PASO ROBLES. *El Paso de Robles School*. Mr. Jose Domingo Ojeyda. Dept. of the Youth Authority.
SAN LUIS OBISPO. *California Men's Colony East*. Rev. John Farao, O.F.M.Conv., Chap.
California Men's Colony West. Rev. John Farao, O.F.M.Conv.
SOLEDAD. *Correctional Training Facility*. Christina McNamara, Chap. , Christina McNamara, Chaplain
Salinas Valley State Prison. Rev. Joel J. Almendras, Chap.

Special Assignment:
Very Rev.—
Crivello, Peter A., V.G., Pastoral Office, 631 Abrego St., P.O. Box 2048, 93942-2048. Tel: 831-373-4345; Fax: 831-373-1175
Revs.—
Laverone, Kenneth J., O.F.M., M.A., J.C.L., Judicial Vicar, Diocesan Tribunal, 435 Church St., 93940. Tel: 831-373-1833; Fax: 831-373-6761
McCarthy, Scott, Catholic Chap., Ave Maria Convalescent Hospital, 1249 Josselyn Canyon Rd., 93940. Tel: 831-601-4679; Fax: 831-373-2238
O'Brien, Seamus, Catholic Chap., Dominican Santa Cruz Hospital, 1555 Soquel Ave., Santa Cruz, 95065. Tel: 831-462-7707; Fax: 831-462-7558
Shelly, Roy, Dir. Vocations, 435 Church St., 93940. Tel: 831-645-2813; Fax: 831-373-6761
Wiecek, Ronald, C.P.P.S., Asst. Dir. Vocations, Sacred Heart Church, 22 Stone St., Salinas, 93901. Tel: 831-424-1959; Fax: 831-424-0788

On Leave:
Revs.—
Chavez, Jose
Cortes, Antonio
Cuevas, Geronimo, 6790 Caporetto Ln., Unit 202, North Las Vegas, NV 89084. Email: Gerencuem8@aol.com
Gilbert, Dennis M., Church of the Resurrection, 725 Cascade Dr., Sunnyvale, 94087.
Gomez, Miguel

Educational Leave:
Rev.—
Espinoza-Espinoza, Pedro, Pontifical North American College (CSM), Ufficio Merci 00120 Vatican City State. Email: pespinoza005@aol.com

Retired:
Rev. Msgrs.—
MacMahon, Eamon, 24631 Guadalupe St., Carmel, 93923. Tel: 831-624-2275
Murphy, D. Declan, P.A., Ceann Mhara, Myrtleville, County Cork, Ireland. Tel: 011-353-4831-566
Stieger, Joseph, c/o 161 Broad St., San Luis Obispo, 93405. Tel: 805-543-3284
Revs.—
Adams, Michael T., Mary Star of the Sea Church, 870 8th St., San Pedro, 90731. Tel: 310-833-3541
Arul, John
Betrozoff, Larry, 528-B Sixth St., Hollister, 95023-3818. Tel: 831-636-7844. P.O. Box 1136, Tres Pinos, 95075-1136.
Canal, Manuel, 670 Edwards Ave., Salinas, 93901. Tel: 831-754-6304
Carvajal, Raul H.
Clark, Richard, 155 Boulder St., Boulder Creek, 95006.
Freiermuth, Harry, 41 Tharp Ave., Watsonville, 95076. Tel: 831-724-4460
Frerkes, James, 5073 Meadowlark Ln., Paso Robles, 93446. Tel: 805-239-2720
Hercek, Joseph R., V.F., P.O. Box 2230, Atascadero, 93423.
Marini, Michael, 518 King St., Santa Cruz, 95060. Tel: 831-457-8628
Matz, Leo, 2609 San Martin Ct., Mission Viejo, 92692.
McCormick, Jerry, P.O. Box 51338, Pacific Grove, 93950. Tel: 831-372-8644
McDonald, Martin, 2 Huband Meys, Stephens Ln., Dublin 2, Ireland. Cell: 011-35-387-969-0117. Email: martinjmcdonald@hotmail.com
McSweeney, John, Girramreigh East, Lissarda, Co. Cork Ireland.
O'Halloran, Richard, New Bethany, 1441 Berkeley Dr., Los Banos, 93635. Tel: 209-828-6077
Plastino, James L., Ave Maria Convalescent Hospital, 1249 Josselyn Canyon Rd., 93940. Tel: 916-791-4907
Santamaria, Max, Ctra. De Arizala #5, Abarzuza, Navarra 31178 Spain. Tel: 011-344-452-0021
Schwarz, Robert, 4103 Golden Oaks Ln., 93940. Tel: 831-372-8848
Vela, Fabian, Sacred Heart Church, 680 College St., Hollister, 95023. Tel: 831-637-9212

Permanent Deacons:
Conway, Patrick, 88 Mar Monte Ave., La Selva Beach, 95076. Tel: 831-840-3750 (Home) (Resurrection, Aptos)
Cooper, Jim, (Retired), 1625 Morro Bay, P.O. Box 1625, Morro Bay, 93443. Tel: 805-225-1212
Dutra, Greg, 210 LaJoya Dr., Nipomo, 93444. Tel: 805-929-1235 (Home) (St. Joseph's, Nipomo)
Espinoza, Manuel, 1813 Driftwood Dr., Paso Robles, 93447. Tel: 805-238-5588 (St. Rose of Lima, Paso Robles)
Figenshow, Carl, 22551 Murietta Rd., Salinas, 93908. Tel: 831-455-0377 (Home); Cell: 831-676-8169 (Madonna del Sasso, Salinas)
Gerich, Donald, (Retired), 731 Palmer St., Nipomo, 93444. Tel: 805-929-2412 (St. Joseph's, Nipomo)
Gutierrez, Richard, 59 First St., P.O. Box 7254,

Spreckels, 93962. Tel: 831-455-1640 (Home); Cell: 831-594-1836 (Sacred Heart & Prison Youth Ministry, Salinas)

Hoy, Warren, 1168 Roosevelt St., 93940. Tel: 831-642-9821 (Carmel Mission, Carmel)

Larraza, Andres, P.O. Box 7392, Carmel, 93921. Tel: 831-402-0472 (San Carlos Cathedral, Monterey)

Michaelson, Steve D., (Retired), P.O. Box 172, Templeton, 93465. Tel: 805-237-0460

Miller, Dustin, 49397 Sapaque Rd., Bradley, 93426. Tel: 805-472-2749 (Mission San Antonio, Jolon)

Miller, Harold, (Retired), 121 Robin Dr., Marina, 93933. Tel: 831-883-2601

Pasculli, Nick, 25385 Markham Ln., Salinas, 93908. Tel: 831-758-6425 (Home); Cell: 831-905-9632 (Carmel Mission Basilica, Carmel)

Reichmuth, William (Bill), 1135 Mestres Dr., Pebble Beach, 93953. Tel: 831-646-0358 (Home); Cell: 831-233-9551 (Carmel Mission, Carmel)

Roeder, Chuck, 6082 Pebble Beach Way, San Luis Obispo, 93401. Tel: 805-544-2707 (Home); Cell: 805-745-1718 (Old Mission, San Luis Obispo)

Rutledge, Clark, P.O. Box 1232, Morro Bay, 93443. Tel: 805-772-2993 (Home) (St. Timothy's, Morro Bay)

Weber, Dan, Office of the Catholic Chaplain, P.O. Box 7001, Atascadero, 93423-7001. Tel: 805-468-2489 (Santa Rosa Church & Atascadero State Hospital, Cambria)

Wilhelm, Greg, 779 Mutsuhito Ave., San Luis Obispo, 93401. Tel: 805-544-0431 (Home Office); Cell: 805-550-0739 (Nativity of Our Lady, San Luis Obispo)

Winston, Douglas, 235 Montclair Ln., Salinas, 93906. Tel: 831-449-5636 (Home); Cell: 831-595-1939 (Sacred Heart, Salinas)

INSTITUTIONS LOCATED IN THE DIOCESE

[A] HIGH SCHOOLS, PRIVATE

MONTEREY. *Santa Catalina Upper School* (1950) (Girls), 1500 Mark Thomas Dr., 93940-5291. Tel: 831-655-9300; Fax: 831-649-3056. Email: sister_claire@santacatalina.org. Web: www.santacatalina.org. Sr. Claire Barone, Head of School; Dr. John Murphy, Head of Upper School; Diane Kabat, Librarian. Lay Teachers 41; Total Enrollment 240.

SALINAS. *Christian Brothers Institute of California, Inc. dba Palma High School* (1951) (Boys), 919 Iverson St., 93901-1816. Tel: 831-422-6391; Fax: 831-422-5065. Email: dunne@palmahs.org. Web: www.palmahs.org. Bro. Patrick D. Dunne, C.F.C., Pres.; Rev. Greg Sandman, Chap. at Palma H.S.; David J. Sullivan, Prin.; Mrs. Anne Gosch, Librarian. Congregation of Christian Brothers. Priests 1; Brothers 2; Lay Teachers 36; Boys (Jr. High) 142; Boys (Total) 577; Total Staff 46.

Congregation of Christian Brothers Residence, 919 Iverson St., 93901. Tel: 831-422-6391; Fax: 831-422-5065. Bro. Bernard S. Samp, C.F.C., Community Leader. Brothers 2.

[B] HIGH SCHOOLS, DIOCESAN

SALINAS. *Notre Dame High School*, 455 Palma Dr., 93901. Tel: 831-751-1850; Fax: 831-757-5749. Email: info@notredamesalinas.org. Web: www.notredamesalinas.org. Andrew Bedell, Prin.; Cheryl Duren, Librarian. Lay Teachers 29; Girls 271.

SAN LUIS OBISPO. *Mission College Preparatory Catholic High School*, 682 Palm St., 93401. Tel: 805-543-2131; Fax: 805-543-4359. Email: info@missionprep.org. Web: www.missionprep.org. James D. Childs, Prin. Lay Teachers 26; Students 288; Total Staff 36.

WATSONVILLE. *St. Francis Central Coast Catholic High School* (2001) 2400 E. Lake Ave., 95076. Tel: 831-724-5933; Fax: 831-724-5995. Email: principal@stfrancishigh.net. Web: www.stfrancishigh.net. Mr. Keith B. Mathews, Prin. & Pres.; Rev. Tho Bui, S.D.B., Coord. Youth Ministry. Joint High School between Diocese of Monterey and Salesians of St. John Bosco. Priests 1; Lay Teachers 20; Total Enrollment 218; Total Staff 21.

Moreland Notre Dame School (1899) 133 Brennan St., 95076. Tel: 831-728-2051; Fax: 831-728-2052. Email: cgrul@mndschool.org. Web: www.mndschool.org.

Sisters of Notre Dame de Namur (1899) Tel: 831-728-2051; Fax: 831-728-2052. Email: leahy@sndden.org. Web: sndden.org. Christine Grul, Prin. Sisters 4; Lay Teachers 9; Students 240.

[C] ELEMENTARY SCHOOLS, PRIVATE

MONTEREY. *Santa Catalina Lower School* (1950) (Grades PreK-8), (Coed), 1500 Mark Thomas Dr., 93940-5291. Tel: 831-655-9324; Fax: 831-655-9303. Email: christy_pollacci@santacatalina.org. Web: www.santacatalina.org. Sr. Claire Barone, Head of School; Mrs. Linda Mutty, Div. Head, Grades 6-8/ Dir. Admission; Christy Pollacci, Div. Head, PreK-5; Linda Hughes, Admin. Assist.; Diane Kabat, Librarian. Lay Teachers 30; Total Enrollment 270.

CORRALITOS. *Salesian Elementary & Jr. High School: Mary Help of Christians Youth Center* (1978) (Grades K-8), 605 Enos Ln., 95076. Tel: 831-728-5518; Fax: 831-728-0273. Web: salesian-sisters.org. Sr. Carmen Botello, F.M.A., Prin.; Mrs. Danica Salazar, Librarian. Sisters 6; Lay Teachers 8; Students 171.

WATSONVILLE. *St. Francis Youth Center*, 2401 E. Lake Ave., 95076. Tel: 831-722-2665; Fax: 831-722-8305. Rev. Albert Mengon, S.D.B., Dir. St. Francis Youth Center supports youth activities at parish summer camp and school level. Priests 2; Brothers 3; Total Staff 5.

[D] GENERAL HOSPITALS

SANTA CRUZ. *Dominican Hospital dba Catholic Healthcare West* 1555 Soquel Dr., 95065. Tel: 831-462-7700; Fax: 831-462-7555. Web: www.dominicanhospital.org. Dr. Nanette Mickiewicz, M.D., Pres. Sponsored by Sisters of St. Dominic, Congregation of the Most Holy Rosary, Adrian, MI. Sisters 11; Bed Capacity 379; Total Assisted 189,551; Total Staff 1,705.

[E] SPECIAL HOSPITALS AND SANATORIA ACUTE CARE HOSPITAL

MONTEREY. *Ave Maria Convalescent Hospital* (1954) 1249 Josselyn Canyon Rd., 93940. Tel: 831-373-1216; Fax: 831-373-2238. Email: gjamch@comcast.net. Franciscan Sisters of the Immaculate Conception 1; Bed Capacity 31; Patients Assisted Annually 31; Total Staff 56.

[F] MONASTERIES AND RESIDENCES OF PRIESTS AND BROTHERS

MONTEREY. *Oratorian Community-Congregation of the Oratory of Pontifical Right*, 302 High St., P.O. Box 1688, 93942-1688. Tel: 831-373-0476; Fax: 831-373-1718. Very Rev. Peter C. Sanders, Provost. Tel: 831-375-9769; Rev. Thomas A. Kieffer, Orat., Vicar & Sec. Tel: 831-372-1325. Priests 2.

ARROYO GRANDE. *St. Joseph Cupertino Friary*, 1352 Dale Ave., P.O. Box 820, 93421-0820. Tel: 805-473-2256; Fax: 805-489-8303. Revs. Christopher Deitz, O.F.M.Conv., Guardian; Charles Shelton, O.F.M.Conv.; Bro. Michael Paul, O.F.M.Conv. Priests 2; Brothers 1.

St. Joseph Cupertino Province, Provincial Center, P.O. Box 820, 93421. Tel: 805-489-1012; Fax: 805-489-8303. Email: cldeitz@earthlink.net. Very Revs. Christopher L. Deitz, Min. Prov.; Gary Klauer, O.F.M.Conv., Vicar Prov.; Rev. Stephen Gross, O.F.M.Conv.; Bro. George Cherrie, O.F.M.Conv., Prov. Econom. Priests 4; Brothers 1.

Attached to the Province but outside friaries: Rev. Kerry Abbott, O.F.M.Conv., Chap., (U.S.A.F., Major).

BIG SUR. *New Camaldoli Hermitage* (1958) 62475 Coast Hwy. # 1, 93920-9533. Tel: 831-667-2456; Fax: 831-667-0209. Email: monks@contemplation.com. Web: www.contemplation.com. Very Rev. Raniero Hoffman, O.S.B.Cam., Prior; Revs. Bruno Barnhardt, O.S.B.Cam.; Cyprian Consiglio, O.S.B.Cam.; Michael Fish, O.S.B.Cam.; Daniel Manger, O.S.B.Cam.; Bernard Massicotte, O.S.B.Cam.; Zacchaeus Maria Naegele, O.S.B.Cam.; Isaiah Teichert, O.S.B.Cam.; Robert Hale, O.S.B.Cam., Incarnation Monastery, 1369 La Loma Ave., Berkeley, 94708. Tel: 510-845-0601; Fax: 510-548-6439. Professed Monks (including 13 Priests) 20; Brothers 7.

On Special Assignment: Revs. Andrew Colnaghi, O.S.B.Cam., Supr., Incarnation, Incarnation Monastery, 1369 La Loma Ave., Berkeley, 94708. Tel: 510-845-0601; Fax: 510-548-6439; Thomas Matus, O.S.B.Conv.; Arthur Poulin, O.S.B.Cam., Incarnation Monastery, 1369 La Loma Ave., Berkeley, 94708. Tel: 510-845-0601; Fax: 510-548-6439; Joseph Wong, O.S.B.Cam.

SALINAS. *Palma Community* (1951) 263 W. Acacia St., 93901. Tel: 831-758-2127; Fax: 831-422-5065. Email: brosamp@palmahs.org. Web: palmahs.org. Bros. B. Sebastian, C.F.C.; Patrick D. Dunne, C.F.C., Prin.; Gerard F. Murray, C.F.C. Congregation of Christian Brothers. Brothers 3.

SAN JUAN BAUTISTA. *Franciscan Friars*, P.O. Box 970, 95045-0970. Tel: 831-623-4234; Fax: 831-623-9046. Email: info@stfrancisretreat.com. Web: www.stfrancisretreat.com. Revs. Barry Brunsman, O.F.M., D.Min., Guardian; William Haney, O.F.M., S.T.D., S.T.L., Assoc. Dir.; Bros. Bill Short, O.F.M., Dir.; Keith Warner, O.F.M., Ph.D. Priests 2; Brothers 2; Total Staff 24.

SAN LUIS OBISPO. *Monastery of the Risen Christ*, P.O. Box 3931, 93403. Tel: 805-544-1810; Fax: 805-544-1810. Email: monrc87@aol.com. Web: www.daily-word-of-life.com/monastery.htm. Priests 5; Brothers 2. *Men's Residence*, 2308 O'Connor Way, 93405. Tel: 805-544-1810; Fax: 805-544-1810. Email: monrc87@aol.com. Web: www.daily-word-of-life.com/monastery.htm. Rt. Rev. David Geraets, O.S.B., Prior; Revs. Raymond V. Roh, O.S.B., Subprior; Stephen Odenbrett, O.S.B.; Albert Meyer, O.S.B.; Raymond Greco, O.S.B. (Retired); Bros. Alfonso Daniel, O.S.B.; Michael Rodgers, O.S.B., Novice. Junior Monk (Simple Profession) 1; Total Staff 7; (Novices & Oblates in Residence) 7.

Society of Mary (Marists)-S.M. (1816) 695 Cerro Romauldo Ave., 93405. Tel: 805-541-4954. Revs. John Ulrich, S.M, M.A., Contact; Kevin Duggan, S.M., M.Div., Supr. Community. Priests 2.

SAN MIGUEL. *Franciscan Friars, O.F.M.* (Province of St. Barbara, Old Mission), P.O. Box 69, 93451. Tel: 805-467-3256; Fax: 805-467-2448. Revs. Thomas Frost, O.F.M., Asst. Novicemaster; Larry Gosselin, O.F.M., Guardian; Raymond Tintle, O.F.M.; Joseph Zermeno, O.F.M.; Bros. Regan Chapman, O.F.M, Novicemaster; Victor Hunter, O.F.M.; Anthony Lavorin, O.F.M.; Arturo Noyes, O.F.M.; Rev. John E. Gini, O.F.M.; Bros. Michael Minton, O.F.M.; Bonaventure Pearsall, O.F.M., Vicar; Phillip Polk, O.F.M.; Ryan Thorton, O.F.M. Brothers 8; Total in Residence 8; Total Staff 6.

Novitiate House for the Franciscan Friars, O.F.M. (Province of St. Barbara), P.O. Box 69, 93451. Tel: 805-467-2801; Fax: 805-467-2448. Bro. Regan Chapman, O.F.M, Master of Novices; Revs. Thomas Frost, O.F.M., Asst.; Larry Gosselin, O.F.M., Guardian. Novices 3; Total in Residence 5.

SANTA CRUZ. *Oblates of St. Joseph Provincial House and Shrine*, 544 W. Cliff Dr., 95060. Tel: 831-457-1868; Fax: 831-457-1317. Email: provincial@osjoseph.org. Web: www.osjoseph.org.

Oblates of St. Joseph, Provincial House and Shrine of St. Joseph, Guardian of the Redeemer Religious Community Tel: 831-471-1702; Fax: 831-457-1317. Email: guardian@osjoseph.org. Web: www.osjoseph.org. Brothers 1. *Provincial* Tel: 831-457-1868; Fax: 831-457-1317. Email: provincial@osjoseph.org. Web: www.osjoseph.org. *Shrine of St. Joseph* Tel: 831-471-0442; Fax: 831-457-1317. Email: guardian@osjoseph.org. Web: www.osjoseph.org. Revs. John Warburton, O.S.J., Prov. Supr. & Rector; James Catalano, O.S.J.; Bro. Duain O'Mara, O.S.J. Priests 3; Brothers 1; Total in Residence 4. In Res. Rev. Aldo Grasso, O.S.J. (Italy). *Religious Community* Tel: 831-471-1702; Fax: 831-457-1317. Web: www.osjoseph.org.

WATSONVILLE. *Salesians of St. John Bosco Saint Francis Salesian Community*, 2401 East Lake Ave., 95076-2670. Tel: 831-722-2665; Fax: 831-722-8305. Web: www.donboscowest.org. Revs. Tho Bui, S.D.B., Coord. Youth Ministry; Albert Mengon, S.D.B., Dir.; Jesse Montes, S.D.B.; Harry W. Rasmussen, S.D.B.; Marc Rougeau, S.D.B.; Bro. Michael Herbers, S.D.B., Camp Dir. Brothers 2. In Res. Bro. Abel Zanella, S.D.B., (Retired).

[G] CONVENTS AND RESIDENCES FOR SISTERS

MONTEREY. *Ave Maria Convent*, 1249 Josselyn Canyon Rd., P.O. Box 1977, 93942-1977. Tel: 831-373-1216; 831-375-8680; Fax: 831-373-2238. Motherhouse of the Franciscan Sisters of the Immaculate Conception and St. Joseph for the Dying.

APTOS. *St. Joseph's Monastery of the Poor Clares (Colettines)* (1921) 1671 Pleasant Valley Rd., P.O. Box 160, 95001-0160. Tel: 831-761-9659; 831-761-9481; Fax: 831-761-9481. Sr. Francis Maria, P.C.C., Abbess. Poor Clares of California, Inc. Professed Sisters Cloistered 9; Extern Sisters 2.

ARROYO GRANDE. *Sisters of Mercy*, 451 Woodland, 93420. Tel: 805-489-8788; Fax: 805-489-4367.

CARMEL. *Carmelite Monastery of Our Lady and St. Therese* (1925) 27601 Hwy. 1, 93923-9612. Tel: 831-624-3043; Fax: 831-624-5495. Email: carmelitesofcarmelca@catholic.org. Web: www.carmelitesistersbythesea.net. Sr. Teresita Flynn, O.C.D., Prioress. Professed Nuns 10.

Sisters of Notre Dame de Namur (1930) 27951 Hwy. 1, 93923. Tel: 831-624-9416; Fax: 831-624-4865. Email: carmelhop@sndden.org.

CORRALITOS. *Daughters of Mary Help of Christians* (1872) 605 Enos Ln., 95076. Tel: 831-728-4700; Fax: 831-728-5802. Email: fmasuocor@gmail.com. Sr. Carmen Botello, F.M.A., Supr. & Prin. Sisters 6.

GONZALES. *Sisters of Charity of the Infant Mary Capitanio Convent*, 512 Fairview Dr., P.O. Box 178, 93926. Tel: 831-675-2975; Fax: 831-675-2974. Email: sistersmb@aol.com. Sr. Rosangela Filippini, I.M., Supr. Residents 7.

MORRO BAY. *Immaculate Heart of Mary*, P.O. Box 695, 93443-0695. Tel: 805-772-8146.

PISMO BEACH. *Franciscan Sisters of the Atonement (Graymoor)*, 344 Pomeroy Ave., 93449. Tel: 805-773-3427.

SALINAS. *Sisters of Charity of the Infant Mary*, 15785 Alto Way, 93907-9148. Tel: 831-663-3675; Fax: 831-663-3749. Email: virgennina@aol.com. Sr. Patricia M. Murtagh, I.M., Supr. Sisters of Charity of the Infant Mary. Residents 5.

Sisters of Notre Dame, 56 Talbot St., 93901. Tel: 831-424-4370. Email: bmatasci@aol.com. Residents 2.

Sisters of St. Joseph of Carondolet (1950) 1335 Byron Dr., 93901. Tel: 831-758-0931; Fax: 831-758-1318. Email: srroberta@catholic.org. Web: www.csjla.org. Madonna Manor.

SAN JUAN BAUTISTA. *Franciscan Sisters of the Atonement*, 408 Second St., P.O. Box 1094, 95045. Tel: 831-623-4267; Fax: 831-623-4359. Franciscan Sisters of the Atonement 4.

SAN LUIS OBISPO. *Monastery of the Risen Christ* (Women's Residence), P.O. Box 3931, 93403-3931. Tel: 805-544-7808; Fax: 805-544-1810. Email: monrc87@aol.com. Web: www.daily-word-of-life.com/monastery.htm. 2304 O'Connor Way, 93405. Tel: 805-544-7808; Fax: 805-554-1810. Connie Mayrhofer, O.B.L., O.S.B.

SAN MIGUEL. *Franciscan Sisters of the Atonement (Graymoor)* (1909) 1075 Mission St., P.O. Box 238, 93451. Tel: 805-467-0022.

SANTA CRUZ. *Franciscan Hospitaller Sisters of the Immaculate Conception* (1871) 907 Columbia St., 95060. Tel: 831-426-5035. Sr. Elisa Santos, F.H.I.C., Local Supr. Total in Residence 3.

SOQUEL. *St. Clare's Retreat* (1950) 2381 Laurel Glen Rd., 95073. Tel: 831-423-8093. Email: stclares@sbcglobal.net. Web: www.nonprofitpages.com/stclaresretreat/. Sr. Maureen Theresa, O.S.F., Supr. Total in Residence 6.

WATSONVILLE. *Moreland Notre Dame Convent*, 656 Main St., 95076. Tel: 831-724-7696; Fax: 831-768-9828. Email: taleahysnd@aol.com. Web: sndden-ca.org. Sr. Teresa Ann Leahy, Coord. Sisters of Notre Dame de Namur. Residents 5.

Sisters of the Holy Names of Jesus and Mary, Watsonville Community (1990) 26 Kilburn St., 95076. Tel: 831-728-4063. Sisters 2.

[H] RETREAT HOUSES

APTOS. *Camp St. Francis*, 2320 Sumner Ave., 95003. Tel: 831-684-1439; Fax: 831-662-2454. Bro. Michael Herbers, S.D.B., Dir. Conducted by Salesians of St. John Bosco.; Summer Camp for Boys 8-13, Meeting Center for large groups and Retreat Center for large groups of youth and adults.

SAN JUAN BAUTISTA. *St. Francis Retreat Center* Conducted by Franciscan Friars. Province of St. Barbara., P.O. Box 970, 95045. Tel: 831-623-4234; Fax: 831-623-9046. Email: info@stfrancisretreat.com. Web: www.stfrancisretreat.com. Revs. Barry Brunsman, O.F.M., D.Min., Coord.; William Haney, O.F.M., S.T.D., S.T.L., Asst. Retreat Dir.; Bros. William Short, O.F.M., S.T.L., S.T.D., Dir.; Keith Warner, O.F.M., Ph.D. Retreats for men, women, singles, married couples, A.A. and 12-step. Programs include Spiritual Growth, Ecumenical, Spanish. Priests 2; Brothers 2; Total in Residence 4; Total Staff 20.

SAN MIGUEL. *San Miguel Retreat House*, P.O. Box 69, 93451. Tel: 805-467-3256; Fax: 805-467-2448. Rev. Larry Gosselin, O.F.M., Guardian. Staff 2.

SANTA CRUZ. *Villa Maria del Mar*, 21918 E. Cliff Dr., 95062. Tel: 831-475-1236; Fax: 831-475-8867. Email: villamariadelmar@earthlink.net. Web: www.villamariadelmar.org. Sr. Patricia Doyle, S.N.J.M., Admin. Sisters of the Holy Names of Jesus and Mary, U.S.-Ontario Province Corp. Sisters 6; Lay Staff 17; Total Staff 24.

SOQUEL. *St. Clare's Retreat House* (1950) 2381 Laurel Glen Rd., 95073. Tel: 831-423-8093. Email: stclares@sbcglobal.net. Web: www.nonprofitpages.com/stclaresretreat. Sr. Maureen Theresa, O.S.F, Retreat Dir. Franciscan Missionary Sisters of Our Lady of Sorrows 6; Total Staff 8.

[I] NEWMAN CHAPLAINS AND CENTERS

MONTEREY. *Department of Campus Ministry* (1970) 485 Church St., 93940. Tel: 831-373-1335; Fax: 831-373-3351. Email: frrshelly@dioceseofmonterey.org. Web: www.dioceseofmonterey.org. Rev. Roy Shelly, Dir. Total Staff 9.

California State Polytechnic Institute / Cuesta College Newman Catholic Center, 1472 Foothill Blvd., San Luis Obispo, 93405-1416. Tel: 805-543-4105; Fax: 805-543-5671. Email: ncc@slonewman.org. Web: www.slonewman.org. Revs. John Ulrich, S.M, M.A., Dir.; Kevin Duggan, S.M., M.Div., Assoc. Dir.; Linda Garcia-Inchausti, Dir. of Admin.

Cabrillo College Santa Cruz, 95064. Tel: 831-479-6100; Fax: 831-423-8163. Sr. Maryann Cantlon, C.S.J., Dir.

University of California at Santa Cruz 285 Meder St., Santa Cruz, 95060. Tel: 831-423-9400; Fax: 831-423-8163. Email: newmanslug@aol.com. Web: www.newmanite.org. Sr. Maryann Cantlon, C.S.J., Dir.

California State University of Monterey Bay 485 Church St., 93940. Tel: 831-373-1335; Fax: 831-373-3315.

485 Church St., 93940. Tel: 831-373-1335; Fax: 831-373-3315. Mr. James Micheletti, Dir.

[J] SENIOR RESIDENCES

SANTA CRUZ. *Dominican Oaks Corporation* (1988) 3400 Paul Sweet Rd., 95065. Tel: 831-462-6257; Fax: 831-462-6742. Web: www.dominicanoaks.com. Sponsored by Dominican Hospital, a dba of Catholic Healthcare West. Total in Residence 230; Total Staff 90.

[K] MISCELLANEOUS

MONTEREY. *Newman Institute for Historical and Religious Studies, Domus Patris Foundation*, P.O. Box 748, 93942. Tel: 831-373-0477. Rev. Thomas A. Kieffer, Orat., Admin.

SALINAS. *Magnificat the Monterey Bay Chapter*, 302 San Juan Grade Rd., 93906. Tel: 831-449-1069; Fax: 831-449-1069. Email: dlraras@pacbell.net. Dora Lee Raras, Coord.; Stella Marquez, Treas.; Rev. Roberto Vera, Spiritual Advisor; Josee Henrard, Asst. Coord. A Ministry to Catholic Women

WATSONVILLE. *St. Thomas More Society*, c/o 262 E. Lake Ave., 95076. Tel: 831-722-2456; Fax: 831-722-0414.

RELIGIOUS INSTITUTES OF MEN REPRESENTED IN THE DIOCESE

For further details refer to the corresponding bracketed number in the Religious Institutes of Men or Women section.

[]—*Camaldolese Hermits*—O.S.B.Cam.

[0310]—*Congregation of Christian Brothers* (Western U.S. Prov., Joliet, IL)—C.F.C.

[0480]—*Conventual Franciscans*—O.F.M.Conv.

[0520]—*Franciscan Friars* (Santa Barbara Prov.)—O.F.M.

[0930]—*Oblates of St. Joseph* (Asti, Italy)—O.S.J.

[0950]—*Oratorians*—Orat.

[0200]—*Order of St. Benedict* (Monastery of the Risen Christ)—O.S.B.

[1070]—*Redemptorist Fathers*—C.SS.R.

[1190]—*Salesians of Don Bosco (Turin, Italy)*—S.D.B.

[0780]—*Society of Mary - Marists Fathers*—S.M.

RELIGIOUS INSTITUTES OF WOMEN REPRESENTED IN THE DIOCESE

[1070-13]—*Congregation of the Most Holy Rosary - Adrian Dominican Sisters*—O.P.

[0880]—*Daughters of Mary & Joseph*—D.M.J.

[0850]—*Daughters of Mary of Help of Christians - Salesian Sisters*—F.M.A.

[0420]—*Discalced Carmelite Nuns*—O.C.D.

[1270]—*Franciscan Hospitaller Sisters of the Immaculate Conception*—F.H.I.C.

[1390]—*Franciscan Missionary Sisters of Our Lady of Sorrows*—O.S.F.

[1190]—*Franciscan Sisters of the Atonement*—S.A.

[1300]—*Franciscan Sisters of the Immaculate Conception and St. Joseph for the Dying*—O.S.F.

[]—*Immaculate Heart of Mary*—I.H.M.

[]—*Immaculate Heart Sisters of Africa*

[3760]—*Order of St. Clare* (Poor Clares Colettines P.C.C.)—P.C.C.

[]—*Redwood Franciscans*—O.S.F.

[]—*Schools Sisters of Notre Dame*—S.S.N.D.

[]—*Sister Servants of the Blessed Sacrament*

[]—*Sisters of Charity of the Infant Mary*—I.M.

[2549]—*Sisters of Mercy* (Irish American Prov.)—R.S.M.

[]—*Sisters of Mercy Burlingame Region*—R.S.M.

[3000]—*Sisters of Notre Dame de Namur*—S.N.D.deN.

[3840]—*Sisters of St. Joseph of Carondelet*—C.S.J.

[1030]—*Sisters of the Divine Savior* (Salvatorians)—S.D.S.

[]—*Sisters of the Holy Family*—S.H.F.

[1990]—*Sisters of the Holy Name of Jesus and Mary*—S.N.J.M.

DIOCESAN CEMETERIES

MONTEREY. *Diocesan Cemeteries Office*, Mailing Address: P.O. Box 2048, 93942-2048. 792 Freemont Blvd., 93940. Tel: 831-372-0327; Fax: 831-372-8726. Email: cemeteries@dioceseofmonterey.org. Tim Bennett, Dir.

San Carlos (Monterey), 792 Freemont Blvd., 93940. Tel: 831-372-0327; Fax: 831-372-8726.

CAMBRIA. *Old Santa Rosa (Cambria)*, c/o 9 S. Higuera, San Luis Obispo, 93401. Tel: 805-541-0584; Fax: 805-541-2127.

HOLLISTER. *Sacred Heart / Calvary Hollister*, 1100 Hillcrest Rd., 95023. Tel: 831-637-0131; Fax: 831-637-2980.

SALINAS. *Queen of Heaven Salinas*, 18200 Damian Way, 93907. Tel: 831-449-5890; Fax: 831-449-6928.

SAN LUIS OBISPO. *Old Mission San Luis Obispo*, c/o 9 S. Higuera, 93401. Tel: 805-541-0584; Fax: 805-541-2127.

SANTA CRUZ. *Holy Cross Santa Cruz*, 2271 7th Ave., 95062. Tel: 831-475-3222; Fax: 831-475-6132.

NECROLOGY

† Morgan, Rev. Msgr. Thomas, (Retired)—Died April 19, 2009

† Agar, Tom, Monterey, CA Cathedral of San Carlos Borromeo—Died May 1, 2009

† Bonjean, Richard, (Retired)—Died Dec. 9, 2009

† Soares, Manuel Bernardo, (Retired)—Died May 19, 2009

An asterisk (*) denotes an organization that has established tax-exempt status directly with the IRS and is not covered by the USCCB Group Ruling.

Diocese of Nashville

(Dioecesis Nashvillensis)

Most Reverend

DAVID R. CHOBY

Bishop of Nashville; ordained September 6, 1974; appointed Bishop of Nashville December 20, 2005; ordained February 27, 2006. *Office: 2400 21st Ave., S., Nashville, TN 37212.*

Chancery Office: 2400 21st Ave., S., Nashville, TN 37212. Tel: 615-383-6393; Fax: 615-292-8411.

Web: www.dioceseofnashville.com

ESTABLISHED JULY 28, 1837.

Square Miles 16,302.

Comprises the Counties of Bedford, Cannon, Cheatham, Clay, Coffee, Davidson, DeKalb, Dickson, Franklin, Giles, Grundy, Hickman, Houston, Humphreys, Jackson, Lawrence, Lewis, Lincoln, Macon, Marshall, Maury, Montgomery, Moore, Overton, Perry, Putnam, Robertson, Rutherford, Smith, Stewart, Sumner, Trousdale, VanBuren, Warren, Wayne, White, Williamson and Wilson in the State of Tennessee.

For legal titles of parishes and diocesan institutions, consult the Chancery Office.

STATISTICAL OVERVIEW

Personnel	
Bishop	1
Priests: Diocesan Active in Diocese	29
Priests: Diocesan Active Outside Diocese	1
Priests: Retired, Sick or Absent	12
Number of Diocesan Priests	42
Religious Priests in Diocese	26
Total Priests in Diocese	68
Extern Priests in Diocese	19
Ordinations:	
Diocesan Priests	1
Transitional Deacons	2
Permanent Deacons in Diocese	73
Total Brothers	2
Total Sisters	231
Parishes	
Parishes	53
With Resident Pastor:	
Resident Diocesan Priests	29
Resident Religious Priests	14
Without Resident Pastor:	
Administered by Priests	9
Administered by Deacons	1
Missions	3
Pastoral Centers	2
New Parishes Created	2
Professional Ministry Personnel:	
Brothers	1
Sisters	2
Lay Ministers	32
Welfare	
Catholic Hospitals	4
Total Assisted	615,143
Homes for the Aged	2
Total Assisted	338
Day Care Centers	3
Total Assisted	783
Special Centers for Social Services	8
Total Assisted	55,858
Educational	
Diocesan Students in Other Seminaries	17
Total Seminarians	17
Colleges and Universities	1
Total Students	1,983
High Schools, Diocesan and Parish	2
Total Students	1,508
High Schools, Private	1
Total Students	265
Elementary Schools, Diocesan and Parish	16
Total Students	3,862
Elementary Schools, Private	2
Total Students	633
Catechesis/Religious Education:	
High School Students	1,454
Elementary Students	6,416
Total Students under Catholic Instruction	16,138
Teachers in the Diocese:	
Sisters	44
Lay Teachers	640
Vital Statistics	
Receptions into the Church:	
Infant Baptism Totals	1,669
Minor Baptism Totals	141
Adult Baptism Totals	172
Received into Full Communion	427
First Communions	1,677
Confirmations	1,321
Marriages:	
Catholic	222
Interfaith	202
Total Marriages	424
Deaths	497
Total Catholic Population	75,593
Total Population	2,248,497

Former Bishops—Rt. Revs. RICHARD PIUS MILES, O.P., D.D., cons. Sept. 16, 1838; died Feb. 21, 1860; JAMES WHELAN, O.P., D.D., cons. May 8, 1859; resigned May, 1863; died Feb. 18, 1878; P. A. FEEHAN, cons. Nov. 1, 1865; created first Archbishop of Chicago, Sept. 10, 1880; died July 12, 1902; JOSEPH RADEMACHER, D.D., cons. June 24, 1883; transferred to Ft. Wayne, July 13, 1893; died Jan. 12, 1900; THOMAS S. BYRNE, D.D., cons. July 25, 1894; died Sept. 4, 1923; Most Revs. ALPHONSE J. SMITH, D.D., cons. March 25, 1924; died Dec. 16, 1935; WILLIAM L. ADRIAN, D.D., cons. April 16, 1936; died Feb. 13, 1972; JOSEPH A. DURICK, D.D., cons. March 24, 1955; retired April 8, 1975; died June 26, 1994; JAMES D. NIEDERGESES, D.D., cons. May 20, 1975; retired Oct. 13, 1992; died Nov. 16, 2007; EDWARD U. KMIEC, D.D., S.T.L. ord. Dec. 20, 1961; appt. Titular Bishop of Simidicca and Auxiliary Bishop of Trenton Aug. 26, 1982; cons. Nov. 3, 1982; appt. Bishop of Nashville Oct. 13, 1992; installed Dec. 3, 1992; appt. Bishop of Buffalo Aug. 12, 2004.

Vicar General—Very Rev. DAVID R. PERKIN, J.C.L., V.G., 2400 21st Ave., S., Nashville, 37212.

Moderator of the Curia and Vicar General—Very Rev. DAVID R. PERKIN, J.C.L., V.G., The Catholic Center, 2400 21st Ave., S., Nashville, 37212.

Deans—Revs. PHILLIP BREEN, Central Deanery; JOSEPH MCMAHON, Northeast Deanery; DAVID GAFFNY, Northwest Deanery; JOSE KARIAMADAM, C.M.I., Southeast Deanery; EDWARD T. ALBERTS, Southwest Deanery.

Vicar for Catholic Charities—Rev. PHILIP M. BREEN, 5101 Charlotte Ave., Nashville, 37209.

Chancery Office—2400 21st Ave. S., Nashville, 37212. Tel: 615-383-6393; Fax: 615-292-8411. Office Hours: Mon.-Fri. 8-4:30; All Official business should be directed to this office.

Chancellor—Deacon HANS M. TOECKER.

Executive Assistant & Vice Chancellor—MARY MARGARET LAMBERT.

Vice Chancellor and Catholic Center Manager—Deacon PRENTICE C. DEAN.

Accounting Systems—Mr. FRANK KRUEGER, CFO; Mr. DOUG ANDERSON, Controller; TERESA OSBORNE, Asst. Controller, Central Accounting.

General Counsel—Rev. JAMES K. MALLETT (Retired).

Diocesan Tribunal—2400 21st Ave. S., Nashville, 37212. Tel: 615-783-0273; Fax: 615-783-0779.

Judicial Vicar—Very Rev. DEXTER S. BREWER, J.C.L., J.V.

Adjutant Judicial Vicar—Very Rev. DAVID R. PERKIN, J.C.L., V.G.

Coordinator of Tribunal Affairs and Promoter of Justice—Ms. JANETTE BUCHANAN, J.C.L.

Defenders of the Bond—Revs. JOHN C. HENRICK; JOHN SIMS BAKER; Ms. JANETTE BUCHANAN, J.C.L.

Advocates—Mrs. PATRICIA STORY; Mrs. JULIE CONNOLLY; Mrs. LINDA NELSON.

Judges—Most Rev. DAVID R. CHOBY, D.D., J.C.L.; Very Rev. DEXTER S. BREWER, J.C.L., J.V.; Revs. RICHARD G. BUCHIGNANI, J.C.L. (Retired); WILLIAM S. BEVINGTON (Retired); JAMES K. MALLETT (Retired); Very Rev. DAVID R. PERKIN, J.C.L., V.G.

Assessors—Mrs. LINDA NELSON; Mrs. PATRICIA STORY.

Formal Case Instructor—Mrs. JULIE CONNOLLY.

Documentary Case Instructor—Mrs. LINDA NELSON.

Auditors— All priests and deacons assigned in the Nashville and Knoxville dioceses.

Secretary-Notaries—Mrs. PATRICIA STORY; Mrs. JULIE CONNOLLY; Mrs. LINDA NELSON; Mrs. ANN H. KANENGIETER.

Presbyteral Council—Very Rev. DEXTER S. BREWER, J.C.L., J.V.; Revs. JOHN SIMS BAKER; JOHN C. HENRICK; ZACHARIAS PAYIKAT, C.M.I.; MARK BECKMAN; PHILLIP BREEN; EDWARD F. STEINER III; J. PATRICK CONNOR, V.G.; JOHN EATON, O.F.M.; Very Rev. DAVID R. PERKIN, J.C.L., V.G.; Revs. JOSEPH MCMAHON; DAVID RAMIREZ.

Diocesan Finance Board—Most Rev. DAVID R. CHOBY, D.D., J.C.L.; Rev. STEPHEN A. KLASEK; Very Rev. DAVID R. PERKIN, J.C.L., V.G.; Mr. FRANK KRUEGER; Mr. DENNIS DONOVAN; Mr. MICHAEL J. KANE; Mr. JOHN SCHNEIDER; Mr. WILLIAM HILL; Ms. SHEILA JACKSON PRIEBEL; Mr. KEVIN MARCHETTI; Mr. EDWARD STACK; Mr. WILLIAM P. VARLEY; Mr. GEORGE SMITH; Mr. MICHAEL F. WALSH; SANDRA MCCAFFREY; Mr. PAT WATSON; DON WILLIAMSON.

DIONASH— A Partnership acting as Nominee for marketable securities for the Diocese of Nashville.

Diocesan Offices and Directors

The following offices and agencies are located at the Chancery unless otherwise indicated.

Archives and Records—Deacon HANS M. TOECKER.

Campaign for Human Development—Mr. WILLIAM P. SINCLAIR, A.C.S.W., Dir., St. Mary Villa, 30 White Bridge Rd., Nashville, 37205.

Campus Ministries—VACANT.

Vanderbilt—Rev. JOHN SIMS BAKER, 2417 W. End Ave., Nashville, 37240. Tel: 615-322-0104.

MTSU-Murfreesboro—Rev. MARK SAPPENFIELD, St. Rose of Lima Church, 1601 N. Tennessee Blvd., Murfreesboro, 37130. Tel: 615-893-1843.

Austin Peay-Clarksville—Deacon TIMOTHY F. WINTERS, Immaculate Conception, 709 Franklin St., Clarksville, 37040. Tel: 931-645-6275.

Tenn. Tech-Cookeville—Rev. DONALD LOSKOT, S.D.S., St. Thomas Aquinas Church, 401 N. Washington Ave., Cookeville, 38501. Tel: 931-372-3217.

Fisk-Meharry-Tennessee State University Campus Ministries—Deacon HENRY HARRINGTON JR., St. Vincent de Paul Church, 1700 Heiman St., Nashville, 37208. Tel: 615-320-0695.

Univ. of South-Sewanee—Rev. JEAN BAPTISTE KYABUTA, Good Shepherd Church, 2021 Decherd Blvd., Decherd, 37324. Tel: 931-967-0961.

Catholic Charismatic Renewal—Rev. JOHN L. KIRK, Bishop's Liaison; Mrs. TERESA SEIBERT, Assoc. Liaison.

Catholic Charities of Tennessee, Inc.—Mr. WILLIAM P. SINCLAIR, A.C.S.W., Dir., St. Mary Villa, 30 White Bridge Rd., Nashville, 37205. Tel: 615-352-3087; Fax: 615-352-8591.

Catholic Medical Association, Nashville Chapter—RACHEL KAISER, M.D., Pres. Email: rtkaiser@bellsouth.net. Web: www.cathmed.org.

Catholic Public Policy Commission of TN—JENNFIER MURPHY, Exec. Sec.

Catholic Relief Services—Deacon HANS M. TOECKER, Dir.

Catholic Social Services of Nashville—Ms. EILEEN BEEHAN, Dept. Dir., St. Mary Villa, 30 White Bridge Rd., Nashville, 37205. Tel: 615-352-3087.

Catholic Youth Office and Search Program—Rev. NICHOLAS ALLEN, 2011 West End Ave., Nashville, 37203. Tel: 615-327-0674.

Cemeteries—VACANT.

Censor Librorum—Rev. JAMES K. MALLETT (Retired).

Priest Benefit Foundation—Revs. EDWARD F. STEINER III, Chm.; J. PATRICK CONNOR, V.G.; Very Rev. DEXTER S. BREWER, J.C.L., J.V.; Rev. STEPHEN A. KLASEK; Most Rev. DAVID R. CHOBY, D.D., J.C.L.; Revs. JOHN SIMS BAKER; PHILLIP BREEN; Mr. FRANK KRUEGER; TERRY ROBINSON, P.H.R.

Clergy Personnel Board—Revs. STEPHEN A. KLASEK; MARK BECKMAN; Very Rev. DAVID R. PERKIN, J.C.L., V.G.; Revs. PHILIP M. BREEN; ZACHARIAS PAYIKAT, C.M.I.

Continuing Education of Clergy—Rev. EDWARD STEINER, Dir.

Cursillo—Ms. MARGIE HEIAR, Lay Dir.; Deacon MARTIN DESCHENES, Assoc. Spiritual Advisor.

Permanent Diaconate Office—Deacon RONALD B. DEAL JR., Dir.

Diocesan Communications Director—RICK MUSSACHIO.

Diocesan Planning—Rev. STEPHEN A. KLASEK, Dir.

Ecumenical and Interreligious Relations—Deacon WILLIAM J. DICKSON, Dir.

Hispanic Ministry—Rev. RICHARD GAGNON, S.D.S., Dir.; Mrs. ANABELL C. TREVINO, Asst. Dir.; Rev. ANTHONY LOPEZ, Coord. Maury & Lawrence Counties.

Korean Catholic Community of St. Joseph—Rev. JEONGSEOB SEO, Dir., 5565 Pettus Rd., Antioch, 37013. Tel: 615-727-1225. Email: koreancc@comcast.net.

Holy Childhood Association—Deacon HANS M. TOECKER, Dir.

Human Resources—TERRY ROBINSON, P.H.R., Dir.

Lay Retirement Administrative Board—Mr. FRANK KRUEGER; Mr. GERRY ARMBRUSTER, Chm.; ROBERT TRUE; Mr. JOHN SCHNEIDER; TERRY ROBINSON, P.H.R.

Liturgical Life—VACANT.

Ministry Formation—SHERI ISHAM, Office of Catechetical Formation, Catechetical Coord.; TOM SAMORAY, Engaged Couple Formation, Prog. Coord.

Newspaper— "The Tennessee Register" RICK MUSACCHIO, Editor in Chief.

Prison Ministry—TERRANCE HORGAN, Ph.D., Criminal Justice Advocacy.

Pontifical Mission Societies—Deacon HANS M. TOECKER, Dir.

Catholic Charities Refugee Services—KELLYE BRANSON, Dir., 10 S. 6th St., Nashville, 37206. Tel: 615-259-3567; Fax: 615-259-2851.

Schools Office—THERESE WILLIAMS, Supt., 30 White Bridge Rd., Nashville, 37205. Tel: 615-352-3087.

Stewardship and Development—VACANT.

Victim Assistance Coordinator—Deacon HANS M. TOECKER, 2400 21st Ave., S., Nashville, 37212. Tel: 615-783-0765; Fax: 615-292-8411. Email: hans.toecker@dioceseofnashville.com.

Vietnamese Ministry—Rev. PETER DO QUANG CHAU, P.O. Box 55, Ashland City, 37015. Tel: 615-792-4255.

Vocations—Most Rev. DAVID R. CHOBY, D.D., J.C.L., 2400 21st Ave. S., Nashville, 37212.

CLERGY, PARISHES, MISSIONS AND PAROCHIAL SCHOOLS

CITY OF NASHVILLE

(DAVIDSON COUNTY)

1—CATHEDRAL OF THE INCARNATION (1909) Revs. Edward F. Steiner III; Zacharias Payikat, C.M.I.; Deacons Mark Faulkner; Thales Finchum; John G. Krenson; James W. McKenzie.
Church: 2015 W. End Ave., 37203. Tel: 615-327-2330; Fax: 615-320-5650.
Catechesis/Religious Program—Suzanne Southworth, D.R.E. Students 310.

2—ST. ANN (1921) Rev. Philip M. Breen; Deacons John P. Casey; William J. Dickson; James Walsh; Martin Mulloy, Pastoral Assoc.
Church: 5101 Charlotte Ave., 37209. Tel: 615-298-1782; Fax: 615-297-4326.
School—(Grades K-8) Tel: 615-269-0568; Fax: 615-297-1383. Mr. John Foreman, Prin.; Judy Graham, Librarian. Lay Teachers 14; Students 191.
Catechesis/Religious Program—Students 70.

3—ASSUMPTION (1859) Attended by St. Pius X Church, Nashville. Rev. Michael D'Souza; Deacon Prentice C. Dean. In Res., Rev. Athanasius Abanulo.
Church: 1227 Seventh Ave. N., 37208. Tel: 615-256-2729; Fax: 615-256-0987.
Catechesis/Religious Program—Students 76.

4—CHRIST THE KING (1937) Very Rev. Dexter S. Brewer; Deacons Andrew D. McKenzie; James E. Stanford; Robert H. True; David Lybarger. In Res., Rev. Bashir Eldaw Abdelsamad.
Church: 3001 Belmont Blvd., 37212. Tel: 615-292-2884; Fax: 615-383-0026.
School—(Grades K-8) Tel: 615-292-9465; Fax: 615-292-2477. Dr. Christine Caron Gebhardt, Prin.; Nelda McCain, Librarian. Lay Teachers 25; Students 240.
Catechesis/Religious Program—Students 94.

5—CHURCH OF THE MOST HOLY NAME (1857) Rev. Joseph P. Edwidge Carre; Deacon Robert L. Mahoney.
Church: 521 Woodland St., 37206. Tel: 615-254-8847; Fax: 615-254-1106.
Catechesis/Religious Program—Tel: 615-227-0705. Mary Catherine Dean, D.R.E. Students 20.

6—ST. EDWARD (1952) Revs. Joseph P. Breen; Anthony Lopez; Deacons Brian Edwards; Milton Von Mann; John Calzavara; Edgardo Jayme.
Church: 188 Thompson Ln., 37211. Tel: 615-833-5520; Fax: 615-833-3738.
School—(Grades K-8), 190 Thompson Ln., 37211. Tel: 615-833-5770; Fax: 615-833-9739. Dr. Sue Baumgartner, Prin. Lay Teachers 26; Students 465.
Catechesis/Religious Program—Students 90.

7—ST. HENRY (1955) Revs. Michael O. Johnston; Stephen J. Wolf; Deacons Jack Srouji; Martin Deschenes; Gregory Meinhart.
Church: 6401 Harding Rd., 37205. Tel: 615-352-2259; Fax: 615-356-6321.
School—(Grades K-8) Tel: 615-352-1328; Fax: 615-356-9293. Sr. Ann Hyacinth Genow, O.P., Prin.; Mrs. Patricia McCulloch, Librarian. Dominican Sisters of St. Cecilia Congregation 4; Lay Teachers 43; Students 644.
Catechesis/Religious Program—Tel: 615-353-0668. Betsy Gromos, D.R.E.; Kristin Hoback, D.R.E. Students 144.

8—HOLY ROSARY (1954) Rev. Mark Hunt; Deacons Gilbert P. Huhlein; Kenneth Steinbrecher; Wayne Gregory.
Church: 192 Graylynn Dr., 37214. Tel: 615-889-4065; Fax: 615-889-3421.
School—(Grades K-8) Tel: 615-883-1108; Fax: 615-885-5100. Mrs. Mary Hart, Prin. Lay Teachers 33; Students 427.
Catechesis/Religious Program—Students 56.

9—ST. MARY OF THE SEVEN SORROWS (1847) Rev. James Norman Miller.
Mailing Address: P.O. Box 190606, 37219.
Res.: Harrison Sq., #401, 3701 Criddle St., 37219. Tel: 615-252-6414.
Church: 330 Fifth Ave. N., 37219. Tel: 615-256-1704; Fax: 615-256-7307.

10—ST. MARY VILLA PARISH COMMUNITY (1982) Rev. Msgr. George W. Rohling; Deacon Harold McBrayer.
Church: 34 White Bridge Rd., 37205. Tel: 615-352-3087; Fax: 615-352-8591.

11—ST. PATRICK (1890) Very Rev. David R. Perkin; Deacon Thomas H. Cook.
Church: 1219 2nd Ave. S., 37210. Tel: 615-256-6498; Fax: 615-256-6476.
Catechesis/Religious Program—Students 20.

12—ST. PIUS X (1958) Rev. Michael D'Souza.
Church: 2800 Tucker Rd., 37218. Tel: 615-244-4093; Fax: 615-244-4093.
School—(Grades K-8) Tel: 615-255-2049; Fax: 615-255-2049. Katherine Kendall, Prin. Dominican Sisters of St. Cecilia Congregation 2; Lay Teachers 10; Students 120.
Catechesis/Religious Program—Allison Bernhardt-Gafford, D.R.E.

13—ST. VINCENT DE PAUL (1932) Rev. John Eaton, O.F.M.; Deacons Henry Harrington Jr.; William Hill.
Church: 1700 Heiman St., 37208. Tel: 615-320-0695; Fax: 615-320-0698.
Catechesis/Religious Program—Marian Smith, D.R.E. Students 50.

OUTSIDE THE CITY OF NASHVILLE

ANTIOCH, DAVIDSON CO.

1—ST. IGNATIUS OF ANTIOCH (1976) Rev. John C. Henrick; Deacons P. J. Hoefler; Doug Shafer.
Church: 601 Bell Rd., 37013. Tel: 615-367-0085; Fax: 615-367-1712.
Catechesis/Religious Program—Jan Trahan, D.R.E. Students 212.

2—OUR LADY OF GUADALUPE Revs. Fernando Garcia; Anthony Lopez.
3112 Nolensville Rd., 37211. Tel: 615-333-8660.

ASHLAND CITY, CHEATHAM CO., ST. MARTHA (1975) Rev. Peter Do Quang Chau.
Mailing Address: P.O. Box 55, 37015.
Church: 3331 Bell St., 37015. Tel: 615-792-4255; Fax: 615-792-4255.
Catechesis/Religious Program—Teresa Fraim, D.R.E. Students 90.

BRENTWOOD, WILLIAMSON CO., HOLY FAMILY (1989) Rev. Edward T. Alberts; Deacons Jack Nulty; Richard Weller.
Church & Mailing Address: 9100 Crockett Rd., 37027. Tel: 615-373-4696; Fax: 615-377-3823.
Catechesis/Religious Program—Tel: 615-373-4351. Catherine Birdwell, D.R.E. Students 1,231.

CENTERVILLE, HICKMAN CO., CHRIST THE REDEEMER (1983) Attended by Holy Trinity, Hohenwald. Rev. Joseph K. Dowling.
Mailing Address: P.O. Box 323, 37033. Tel: 931-796-3738.
Church: 1515 Woodland Dr., 37033. Tel: 931-729-4669.
Catechesis/Religious Program—Elise Walls, D.R.E. Students 14.

CLARKSVILLE, MONTGOMERY CO., IMMACULATE CONCEPTION (1845) Revs. David J. Gaffny; Theophilus Ebulueme; Charles Mathew, O.F.M.; Deacons Dominick Azzara; Robert Berberich; Timothy Winters.
Res.: 709 Franklin St., 37040. Tel: 931-645-6275; Fax: 931-552-0331.
School—St. Mary's School, (Grades K-8), 1901 Madison St., 37043. Tel: 931-645-1865; Fax: 931-645-1160. Denise Tucker, Prin. Lay Teachers 14; Students 116.
Catechesis/Religious Program—Students 424.

COLUMBIA, MAURY CO., ST. CATHERINE (1843) Rev. Davis Chackaleckel, M.S.F.S.; Deacon Price Keller.
Church & Mailing Address: 3019 Cayce Ln., 38401. Tel: 931-388-3803; Fax: 931-381-8837.
Catechesis/Religious Program—Tel: 931-381-6784. Jeanette Sparkman, D.R.E. Students 190.

COOKEVILLE, PUTNAM CO., ST. THOMAS AQUINAS (1951) Revs. Chad Puthoff, S.D.S.; Reed Mungovan, S.D.S.; Deacon James Keany. In Res., Rev. Donald Loskot, S.D.S.
Church: 421 N. Washington Ave., 38501. Tel: 931-526-2575; Fax: 931-526-5869.
Catechesis/Religious Program—Tel: 931-526-4411. Valerie Richardson, D.R.E. Students 221.
Mission—Divine Savior Celina, Clay Co.

DECHERD, FRANKLIN CO., GOOD SHEPHERD (1900) Rev. Jean Baptiste Kyabuta.
Church: 2021 Decherd Blvd., 37324. Tel: 931-967-0961; Fax: 931-967-3569.
School—(Grades PreK-8), 2037 Decherd Blvd., 37324. Tel: 931-967-5673. Diane Jernigan, Prin. Lay Teachers 12; Students 103.
Catechesis/Religious Program—Brigid Stewart, D.R.E. Students 32.
Mission—St. Margaret Mary 9458 Old Alto Hwy., Alto, Franklin Co. 37324.

DICKSON, DICKSON CO., ST. CHRISTOPHER (1951) Rev. Mathew Perumpally.
Church: 713 W. College St., 37055. Tel: 615-446-3927; Fax: 615-446-7339.
Catechesis/Religious Program—Michelle Brenner, D.R.E.; Amber Gonzales, D.R.E. Students 158.

DOVER, STEWART CO., ST. FRANCIS OF ASSISI (1982) Rev. David J. Gaffny.
Mailing Address: P.O. Box 307, 37058-0307.
Church: 1489 Donelson Pkwy. Tel: 931-232-9422.
Catechesis/Religious Program—Tel: 931-232-1924. Linda Allen, D.R.E. Students 26.

FAYETTEVILLE, LINCOLN CO., ST. ANTHONY (1983) Rev. Jose Kariamadam, C.M.I.
Church: 1900 Huntsville Hwy., 37334. Tel: 931-433-6525; Fax: 931-433-6283.
Catechesis/Religious Program—Students 37.

FRANKLIN, WILLIAMSON CO.
1—ST. MATTHEW (1979) Revs. Mark Beckman; Nicholas Allen; Deacon John W. Myers.
Church: 535 Sneed Rd. W., 37069. Tel: 615-646-0378; Fax: 615-646-5230.
School—(Grades K-8), 533 Sneed Rd. W., 37069. Tel: 615-662-4044; Fax: 615-662-6822. Barby Magness, Prin. Lay Teachers 25; Students 387.
Catechesis/Religious Program—Sr. Lauren Cole, R.S.M., D.R.E. Students 245.
2—ST. PHILIP (1843) Rev. Marneni Showraiah, O.F.M., Admin.
Church: 113 2nd Ave. S., 37064. Tel: 615-794-4236; Fax: 615-794-3083.
Catechesis/Religious Program—Tel: 615-794-8588. Kimberlie Leisinger, D.R.E. Students 699.

GALLATIN, SUMNER CO., ST. JOHN VIANNEY (1929) Rev. Stephen G. Gideon; Deacon Jayd Neely.
Church: 449 N. Water St., 37066. Tel: 615-452-2977; Fax: 615-452-0323.
School—(Grades PreK-8) Tel: 615-230-7048; Fax: 615-206-9839. Sr. Peter Marie, O.P., Prin. Lay Teachers 11; Students 160; Dominican Sisters of St. Cecilia 3.
Catechesis/Religious Program—Students 122.

HENDERSONVILLE, SUMNER CO., OUR LADY OF THE LAKE (1969) Revs. Eric L. Fowlkes; Luckas Arulappa, M.S.F.S.; Sr. Maria Edwards, R.S.M., Pastoral Assoc.; Deacon James F. Carr.
Mailing Address: 1729 Stop Thirty Rd., 37075.
Church: 1739 Stop Thirty Road, 37075. Tel: 615-824-3276; Fax: 615-824-7989.
Catechesis/Religious Program—Cyndi Sabatino, D.R.E. Students 418.

HOHENWALD, LEWIS CO., HOLY TRINITY (1983) Rev. Joseph K. Dowling.
Church: 610 Kimmins St., 38462. Tel: 931-796-3738; Fax: 931-796-3738.
Catechesis/Religious Program—Darie McCarthy, D.R.E. Students 20.

JOELTON, DAVIDSON CO., ST. LAWRENCE (1885) [CEM] Rev. Abraham M. Panthalanickal; Deacon Thomas Miller.
Church: 5655 Clarksville Hwy., 37080. Tel: 615-876-2127; Fax: 615-876-7923.
Catechesis/Religious Program—Students 30.

LAFAYETTE, MACON CO., HOLY FAMILY (1982) Rev. Dennis Holly, G.H.M.
Church: 901 Vinson Rd., 37083. Tel: 615-666-6466.
Catechesis/Religious Program—Mrs. Jennifer McPherson, D.R.E. Students 19.

LAWRENCEBURG, LAWRENCE CO., SACRED HEART (1870) [CEM] Rev. Joseph Mundakal, C.M.I.
Mailing Address: P.O. Box 708, 38464.
Church: 222 Berger St., 38464. Tel: 931-762-3183; Fax: 931-762-5128.
School—(Grades K-8), 220 Berger St., 38464. Tel: 931-762-6125; Fax: 931-762-6125. Rosemary Harris, Prin. Lay Teachers 6; Students 83.
Catechesis/Religious Program—Students 58.

LEBANON, WILSON CO., ST. FRANCES CABRINI (1953) Rev. Michael O'Bryan; Deacon James A. Dixon.
Church: 300 S. Tarver Ave., 37087. Tel: 615-444-0524; Fax: 615-444-3704.
Catechesis/Religious Program—Students 175.
Station—Smith & Trousdale counties

LEWISBURG, MARSHALL CO., ST. JOHN THE EVANGELIST (1982) Rev. William Kelly, S.D.S.
Church: 1061 S. Ellington, 37091. Tel: 931-359-5017; Fax: 931-359-5281.
Catechesis/Religious Program—Students 84.

LORETTO, LAWRENCE CO., SACRED HEART (1872) [CEM] Rev. Tomy P. Joseph, M.S.F.S.; Deacon Samuel Beckman.
Mailing Address: P.O. Box 86, 38469.
Church: 305 Church St., 38469. Tel: 931-853-4370; Fax: 931-853-4373.
School—307 Church St., 38469. Tel: 931-853-4388. Mrs. Catherine N. Bradley, Prin. Lay Teachers 9; Students 63.
Catechesis/Religious Program—Kathryn Thomas, D.R.E. Students 35.

MADISON, DAVIDSON CO., ST. JOSEPH (1953) Rev. Joseph V. McMahon; Deacons Gordon W. McBride Sr.; Theodore B. Welsh; Don Craighead.
Church: 1225 Gallatin Pike S., 37115-4698. Tel: 615-865-1071; Fax: 615-868-4900.
School—(Grades K-8) Tel: 615-865-1491; Fax: 615-612-0228. Sr. Martha Ann Titus, O.P., Prin.; Susan Guyton, Librarian. Dominican Sisters of St. Cecilia Congregation 4; Lay Teachers 25; Students 400.
Catechesis/Religious Program—Jacqueline Beals, D.R.E. Students 90.

MANCHESTER, COFFEE CO., ST. MARK (2000) Rev. Stephen A. Klasek; Deacon Ronald F. Munn.
Mailing Address: P.O. Box 1095, 37355. Tel: 931-723-4107; Fax: 931-723-4123.
Res.: 304 W. Gizzard St., Tullahoma, 37388. Tel: 931-455-3060; Fax: 931-461-9652.
Church: 2941 McMinnville Hwy., 37349.
Catechesis/Religious Program—Students 37.

MCEWEN, HUMPHREYS CO., ST. PATRICK'S (1855) [CEM] Rev. Michael Baltrus.
Mailing Address: 175 St. Patrick's St., 37101.
Church: 175 St. Patrick's St., 37101. Tel: 931-582-3493; Fax: 931-582-6386.
School—(Grades PreK-8) Tel: 931-582-3493. Sr. Mary Raymond Thye, O.P., Prin. Dominican Sisters of St. Cecilia Congregation 4; Lay Teachers 5; Students 82.
Catechesis/Religious Program—Alyssa Ginter, D.R.E. Students 35.

MCMINNVILLE, WARREN CO., ST. CATHERINE (1958) Rev. David Cooney, S.D.S. In Res., Rev. James J. Bretl, S.D.S. (Retired).
Church: 1024 Faulkner Spring Rd., 37110. Tel: 931-473-4932; Fax: 931-473-0799.
Catechesis/Religious Program—Judy Davis, D.R.E.; Janice Saylors, D.R.E. Students 83.

MURFREESBORO, RUTHERFORD CO., ST. ROSE OF LIMA (1929) Revs. Mark Sappenfield, Admin.; Jacob Dio, M.S.F.S.; Deacons Thomas McGrane; Roger F. Huber; Peter Semich.
Church & Res.: 1601 N. Tennessee Blvd., 37130. Tel: 615-893-1843; Fax: 615-895-1150.
School—(Grades K-8) Tel: 615-898-0555; Fax: 615-898-0497. Sr. Mary Cecilia Goodrum, O.P., Prin.; Holly Bruser, Librarian. Sisters 4; Teachers 26; Students 316.
Catechesis/Religious Program—Mary Parod, D.R.E. Students 525.

OLD HICKORY, WILSON CO., ST. STEPHEN (1942) Rev. Patrick J. Kibby; Deacons Gordon S. Rose; Hans Toecker; Fred Bourland.
Church: 14544 Lebanon Rd., 37138. Tel: 615-758-2424; Fax: 615-754-0043.
Catechesis/Religious Program—Scott Goudeau, D.R.E.; Greg Karn, D.R.E. Students 383.

PULASKI, GILES CO., IMMACULATE CONCEPTION (1941) Rev. Jose Karimadam, C.M.I.; Deacon W. Michael Hume, Parish Coord.
Mailing Address: 100 Chapel Rd., 38478. Tel: 931-363-5776; Fax: 931-363-6953.
Catechesis/Religious Program—Jewel Dobry, D.R.E. Students 18.

SAINT JOSEPH, LAWRENCE CO., ST. JOSEPH (1872) Attended by Sacred Heart, Loretto. Rev. Tomy P. Joseph, M.S.F.S.
Mailing Address: P.O. Box 86, Loretto, 38469. Tel: 931-853-4370; Fax: 931-853-4373.
Church: American Blvd., St. Joseph, 38481.

SHELBYVILLE, BEDFORD CO., ST. WILLIAM (1941) Rev. Richard Driscoll, S.D.S.
Church: 719 N. Main St., 37160. Tel: 931-684-8745; Fax: 931-684-6154.
Catechesis/Religious Program—Mr. Dan Strasser, D.R.E.; Mrs. Dan Strasser, D.R.E. Students 54.

SMITHVILLE, DEKALB CO., ST. GREGORY (1982) Attended by St. Catherine, McMinnville. Rev. David Cooney, S.D.S.
Mailing Address: P.O. Box 712, 37166.
Church: 712 Main St. Tel: 931-473-4932; Fax: 931-473-0799.
Catechesis/Religious Program—Maureen Nokes, D.R.E. Students 22.

SMYRNA, RUTHERFORD CO., ST. LUKE (1982) Rev. Richard Gagnon, S.D.S.; Deacons Ken Levinson; Simeon Panagatos; Jose G. Pineda.
Mailing Address: P.O. Box 907, 37167-0907.
Church: 10682 Old Nashville Hwy., 37167. Tel: 615-459-9672; Fax: 615-459-3989.
Catechesis/Religious Program—Denise M. Leaver, D.R.E. Students 220.

SPARTA, WHITE CO., ST. ANDREW (1982) Rev. John Pantuso, S.D.S.
Church: 829 Valley View Dr., 38583. Tel: 931-738-2140; Fax: 931-738-2592.
Catechesis/Religious Program—Students 36.

SPRING HILL, MAURY CO., CHURCH OF THE NATIVITY Rev. John L. Kirk; Deacon Ronald B. Deal Jr.
2001 Campbell Station Pkwy., Ste. C-7, 37174. Tel: 615-302-4004. Web: www.nativitycatholic.net.
Catechesis/Religious Program—Students 427.

SPRINGFIELD, ROBERTSON CO., OUR LADY OF LOURDES (1946) [CEM] Rev. George Chennapallil.
Church: 103 Golf Club Ln., 37172. Tel: 615-384-6200; Fax: 615-384-5837.
Catechesis/Religious Program—Carol Twork, D.R.E. Students 112.
Mission—St. Michael [CEM] Cedar Hill, Robertson Co.

TENNESSEE RIDGE, HOUSTON CO., ST. ELIZABETH ANN SETON (1977) Attended by St. Patrick, McEwen.
Church & Mailing Address: 755 State Rte. 49, 37178. Tel: 931-721-3769.
Catechesis/Religious Program— Michael Lewis, D.R.E. Students 22.

TULLAHOMA, COFFEE CO., ST. PAUL THE APOSTLE (1954) Rev. Stephen A. Klasek; Deacon Ronald F. Munn.
Church: 304 W. Grizzard St., 37388. Tel: 931-455-3050; Fax: 931-461-9652.
School—(Grades K-8) Tel: 931-455-4221. Susan Molvik, Prin. Lay Teachers 14; Students 92.
Catechesis/Religious Program—Students 73.

WAYNESBORO, WAYNE CO., ST. CECILIA (1982) Attended by Holy Trinity, Hohenwald. Rev. Joseph K. Dowling.
Mailing Address: *Holy Trinity Church*, 610 Kimmins St., Hohenwald, 38462.
Church: 526 Hwy. 64 E., 38485. Tel: 931-796-3738; Fax: 931-796-3738.
Catechesis/Religious Program—Jennifer Ostrowski, D.R.E.

On Special Assignment:
Very Rev.—
Perkin, David R., J.C.L., V.G., Moderator of the Curia & Vicar Gen.

On Duty Outside the Diocese:
Rev.—
Campion, Owen F., Our Sunday Visitor, 200 Noll Plaza, Huntington, IN 46750.

Unassigned:
Revs.—
Sappenfield, John P.
Tran, Tien

Retired:
Revs.—
Bevington, William S.
Bielawa, Thomas, S.D.S.
Bretl, James J., S.D.S., 503 Mullican St., Mc Minnville, 37110.
Buchignani, Richard G., J.C.L.
Burakowski, Wieslaw
Clements, Daniel A., P.O. Box 26122, Knoxville, 37912.
Connor, J. Patrick, V.G., 9126 Sawyer Brown Rd., 37221.
Mallett, James K., 728 Bacon Tr., #61, Chattanooga, 37412.
McMurry, John E., S.S.
McMurry, Vincent deP., S.S.
Murray, James B., 10605 Bishop Dozier Dr., Cordova, 38016.
Niedergeses, Bernard
Schmit, Fred J., S.D.S.

Permanent Deacons:
Azzara, Dominic D., Immaculate Conception, Clarksville
Bainbridge, Frank, Prison Ministry, Nashville
Batcheldor, James M., Jr., (Retired)
Beckman, Samuel C., Sacred Heart, Loretto
Berberich, Robert R., Immaculate Conception, Clarksville
Bourland, Fred, St. Stephen, Old Hickory
Calzavara, John, St. Edward, Nashville
Carr, James F., Our Lady of the Lake, Hendersonville
Carroll, John B., (Retired)
Casey, Bernard J., St. Rose of Lima, Murfreesboro
Casey, John P., St. Ann, Nashville
Cheasty, John C., (On Duty Outside the Diocese)
Coen, Joseph, Sr., (Retired)
Cook, Thomas H., St. Patrick, Nashville
Craighead, Don, St. Joseph, Madison
Deal, Ronald B., Jr., Church of the Nativity
Deschenes, Martin, St. Henry, Cursillo, Nashville
Dickson, William J., St. Ann, Nashville; Diocesan Ecumenical Dir.
Dixon, James A., St. Francis Cabrini, Lebanon
Edwards, Brian, John Paul II High School, Hendersonville
Faulkner, Mark C., Cathedral of the Incarnation, Nashville
Finchum, Thales, Cathedral of the Incarnation, Nashville
Francescon, Samuel A., (Retired)
Graham, Robert L., (Retired)
Gregory, L. Wayne, Holy Rosary, Nashville
Harrington, Henry, Jr., St. Vincent de Paul, Nashville
Henry, James R., (Retired)
Hill, William, St. Vincent de Paul, Nashville
Hoefler, Paul J., St. Ignatius, Antioch
Huber, Roger F., St. Rose of Lima, Murfreesboro
Huhlein, Gilbert P., Holy Rosary, Nashville
Hume, W. Michael, Immaculate Conception, Springfield
Jayme, Edgardo, St. Edward, Nashville
Keany, James, St. Thomas Aquinas, Cookeville
Keller, I. Price, St. Catherine, Columbia
Kopczynski, Michael R., St. John Vianney, Gallatin
Krenson, John G., Cathedral of the Incarnation, Nashville
Levinson, Ken, St. Luke, Smyrna
Lovell, David, (Unassigned)

Lybarger, David, Christ the King, Nashville
Mahoney, Robert L., Holy Name, Nashville
McBrayer, J. Harold, Jr., St. Mary Villa Parish Community, Nashville
McBride, Gordon W., Sr., St. Joseph, Madison
McGinn, George P., (Retired)
McGrane, Thomas J., St. Rose Lima, Murfreesboro
McKenzie, Andrew D., Christ the King, Nashville
McKenzie, James W., Cathedral of the Incarnation, Nashville
Meinhart, Gregory, St. Henry, Nashville
Melchior, Daniel, St. Anthony, Fayetteville
Miller, Thomas, St. Lawrence, Joelton
Montini, Robert A., (On duty outside of Diocese)
Mulloy, Martin, St. Ann, Nashville
Munn, Ronald F., St. Mark, Manchester; St. Paul the Apostle, Tullahoma
Myers, John W., St. Matthew, Franklin
Nulty, Jack, Holy Family, Brentwood
Panagatos, Simeon W., St. Luke, Smyrna
Pineda, Jose G., St. Luke, Smyrna
Randall, Ralph, (Retired)
Rose, Gordon, St. Stephen, Old Hickory
Semich, Peter, St. Rose of Lima, Murfreesboro
Shafer, L. Douglas, St. Ignatius of Antioch, Antioch
Srouji, Jack, St. Henry, Nashville
Stanford, James E., Christ the King, Nashville
Steinbrecher, Kenneth, Holy Rosary, Nashville
Toecker, Hans M., St. Stephen, Old Hickory; Chancellor
True, Robert H., Christ the King, Nashville
Von Mann, Milton, (Retired)
Walsh, James, St. Ann, Nashville
Walter, James, (On Duty Outside of Diocese)
Weaver, Matthew, (On Duty Outside of Diocese)
Weller, Richard, Holy Family, Brentwood
Welsh, Theodore B., St. Joseph, Madison
Winters, Timothy F., Immaculate Conception, Clarksville

INSTITUTIONS LOCATED IN THE DIOCESE

[A] COLLEGES

NASHVILLE. *Aquinas College*, 4210 Harding Rd., 37205. Tel: 615-297-7545; Fax: 615-279-3893. Email: admissions@aquinascollege.edu. Web: www.aquinascollege.edu. Sisters Ann Marie Karlovic, O.P., Chm., Bd Directors; Mary Peter Muehlenkamp, O.P., Pres.; Thomas More Stepnowski, O.P., Vice Pres., Academic Affairs; Rev. Thomas Kalam, C.M.I.; Mark Hall, Librarian. Dominican Sisters of St. Cecilia Congregation. Priests 1; Sisters 14; Lay Teachers 150; Students 1,983.

[B] HIGH SCHOOLS, DIOCESAN

NASHVILLE. *Father Ryan High School* (1925) Corporate Title: Father Ryan High School, Inc., 700 Norwood Dr., 37204. Tel: 615-383-4200; Fax: 615-383-9056. Email: mcintyrej@fatherryan.org. Web: www.FATHERRYAN.org. Mr. James McIntyre, Pres.; Rev. Nicholas Allen, Part-Time Chap. Priests 1; Lay Teachers 85; Students 894.

Father Ryan Board of Trust, Devel. & Alumni Office, 770 Norwood Dr., 37204. Tel: 615-269-7926.

HENDERSONVILLE. *Pope John Paul II High School, Inc.* (2002) 117 Caldwell Ln., 37075. Tel: 615-822-2375; Fax: 615-822-6226. Email: info@jp2hs.org. Web: www.jp2hs.org. Faustin N. Weber, Headmaster. Lay Teachers 67; Students 614.

[C] HIGH SCHOOLS, PRIVATE

NASHVILLE. *St. Cecilia Academy* (1860) The Dominican Campus, 4210 Harding Rd., 37205. Tel: 615-298-4525; Fax: 615-783-0561. Email: hayesd1@stcecilia.edu. Web: www.stcecilia.edu. Sr. Mary Thomas Huffman, O.P., Prin.; Linda Braddock, Librarian.

St. Cecilia Academy. Conducted by the St. Cecilia Congregation of Dominican Sisters. Sisters 7; Lay Teachers 25; Students 265.

[D] ELEMENTARY SCHOOLS, PRIVATE

NASHVILLE. **St. Bernard Academy*, (Grades PreK-8), 2020 24th Ave. S., 37212-4202. Tel: 615-385-0440; Fax: 615-783-0241. Web: www.stbernardacademy.org. Carl Sabo, Head of School; Jennifer Kitchell, Librarian.

Saint Bernard Academy Corporation. Sisters 1; Lay Teachers 26; Students 299.

Overbrook School (1936) (Grades PreK-8), 4210 Harding Rd., 37205. Tel: 615-292-5134; Fax: 615-783-0560. Web: www.overbrook.edu. Sr. Marie Blanchette, O.P., Prin.; Margaret Lang, Office Mgr. The St. Cecilia Congregation of Dominican Sisters. Sisters 5; Lay Teachers 30; Students 334.

[E] CHILD-CARING INSTITUTIONS

NASHVILLE. **St. Bernard After School Program*, 2020 24th Ave. S., 37212. Tel: 615-298-1298; Fax: 615-783-0241. Doug Frame, Dir. Lay Staff 10; Students 155.

St. Mary Villa Child Development Center, 30 White Bridge Rd., 37205. Tel: 615-356-6336; Fax: 615-356-6421. Email: mmiller@stmaryvilla.org. Michael Miller, Exec. Dir. Total Staff 52; Children 210.

St. Mary Villa, Inc., 30 White Bridge Rd., 37205. Tel: 615-356-6336; Fax: 615-356-6421.

[F] GENERAL HOSPITALS

NASHVILLE. *Baptist Hospital*, 2000 Church St., 37236. Tel: 615-284-5555; Fax: 615-284-1592. Web: www.baptisthospital.com. Bernard J. Sherry, Pres. & CEO.

Seton Corporation dba Baptist Hospital Chaplains 3; Bed Capacity 683; Patients Assisted Annually 96,327; Lay Staff 3,144.

Baptist Hospital Foundation (1978) 4220 Harding Rd., 37205. Tel: 615-222-6800; Fax: 615-222-6159. Web: sths.com/foundation.php.

Saint Thomas Health Services Fund dba Baptist Hospital Foundation (fka Saint Thomas Foundation)

St. Thomas Hospital (1898) 4220 Harding Rd., 37205. Tel: 615-222-2111; Fax: 615-222-6502. Email: nshlsthl@stthomas.org. Web: www.saintthomas.org. Les Donahue, Pres. & CEO; Rev. Bashir Eldaw Abdelsamad, Chap.; Jerry Kearney, Vice Pres. Mission.

St. Thomas Hospital. Daughters of Charity of St. Vincent de Paul, (East Central Prov., Evansville, IN). Sisters 2; Chaplains 12; Bed Capacity 541; Lay Staff 2,000.

Saint Thomas Foundation Tel: 615-222-6800; Fax: 615-222-6159.

St. Thomas Network aka St. Thomas Health Services (1986) 4220 Harding Rd., 37205. Tel: 615-222-2111; Fax: 615-222-6502.

Saint Thomas Network (fka Saint Thomas Health Services

Covenant Care, Inc. Tel: 615-222-2111; Fax: 615-222-6502.

Seton Corporation (2001) 4220 Harding Rd., 37205. Tel: 615-252-3286; Fax: 615-252-6386. Email: jhardcastle@boultcummings.com. Web: www.stthomas.org. Jay Hardcastle, Attorney.

CENTERVILLE. *Hickman Community Hospital aka Baptist Hickman Community Hospital* 135 E. Swan St., 37033-1466. Tel: 931-729-4271; Fax: 931-729-4612. Email: jack.keller@baptisthospital.com. Web: www.hickmanhospital.com. Jack Keller, CEO/Admin.

Hickman Community Health Care Services, Inc. dba Hickman Community Hospital (fka Baptist Hickman Community Health Care Services, Inc. dba Baptist Hickman Community Hospital) Bed Capacity 25; Patients Assisted Annually 36,759; Lay Staff 156.

MURFREESBORO. *Middle Tennessee Medical Center*, 400 N. Highland Ave., 37130. Tel: 615-396-4101; Fax: 615-396-4659. Web: www.mtmc.net. Gordon Ferguson, Pres. & CEO.

Middle Tennessee Medical Center, Inc. Chaplains 2; Bed Capacity 286; Patients Assisted Annually 155,200; Lay Staff 1,300.

Middle Tennessee Medical Center Foundation, 400 N. Highland Ave., 37130. Tel: 615-396-4693; Fax: 615-396-4997. Web: www.mtmc.org.

Middle Tennessee Medical Center Foundation

[G] HOMES FOR THE AGED

NASHVILLE. *Villa Maria Manor, Inc. dba Villa Maria Manor* 32 White Bridge Rd., 37205. Tel: 615-352-3084; Fax: 615-352-0553. Email: sclinton@VillaMariaManor.org. Mr. David Glascoe, Mng. Agent. Residents 230.

[H] MONASTERIES AND RESIDENCES OF PRIESTS AND BROTHERS

NASHVILLE. *Franciscan Friars*, 1608 Tynewood Dr., 37215-4214. Tel: 615-665-7313; Fax: 615-320-0698. Email: shadeaura@aol.com. Revs. John Eaton, O.F.M.; Albert Merz, O.F.M.

[I] CONVENTS AND RESIDENCES FOR SISTERS

NASHVILLE. *St. Cecilia Convent* Motherhouse and Novitiate of St. Cecilia Congregation of Dominican Sisters., 801 Dominican Dr., 37228-1909. Tel: 615-256-5486; Fax: 615-687-3512. Web: www.nashvilledominican.org. Sisters Ann Marie Karlovic, O.P., Prioress Gen.; Mary Aquinas Halbmaier, O.P., Prioress. Sisters in Residence 143; Novices 13; Postulants 23.

Mercy Convent, 2629 Pennington Bend Rd., 37214. Tel: 615-885-1863; Fax: 615-885-4304. Sr. Mary Judith Coode, R.S.M., Coord.; Rev. Abraham M. Panthalanickal.

Sisters of Mercy of Nashville, TN, Inc. Sisters 19.

[J] CAMPS AND COMMUNITY CENTERS

FAIRVIEW. *Camp Marymount* Catholic summer camp for boys and girls., 1318 Fairview Blvd., 37062. Tel: 615-799-0410; Fax: 615-799-2261. Email: Thagey@campmarymount.com. Web: www.campmarymount.com. Tommy Hagey, Dir.

[K] RENEWAL CENTERS

LIBERTY. *Carmel Center of Spirituality*, P.O. Box 117, 37095. Tel: 615-536-5177. Email: carmliberty@yahoo.com. Web: www.saintfrancescabrinichurch.org/gallery2.htm. P.O. Box 117, 37095. Revs. Zachary Payikat, C.M.I., Assoc. Dir.; Thomas Kalam, C.M.I.; Jose Kariamadam, C.M.I.

[L] MISCELLANEOUS

NASHVILLE. *Catholic Community Investment and Loan, Inc.*, 2400 21st Ave. S., 37212.

Catholic Foundation of Tennessee, Inc., 2400 21st Ave. S., 37212. Tel: 615-783-0774; Fax: 615-292-8411.

**Catholic Media Productions*, 700 Harpeth Knoll Ct., 37221. Tel: 615-646-4041; Fax: 615-662-7454. Email: JimWalsh@webelieveshow.org. Web: www.webelieveshow.org. James F. Walsh Jr., Chm. & CEO.

Diocesan Council of Catholic Women, 2400 21st Ave. S., 37212. Tel: 615-889-4065; Fax: 615-889-3421. Email: merve8371@aol.com. Rev. Kevin Dowling, Dir.

Diocesan Properties, Inc. dba Marina Manor East Apartments 2400 21st Ave. S., 37212. Tel: 615-383-6393; Fax: 615-292-8411. Mr. Frank Krueger, Sec. & Treas.

Dominican Campus, 4210 Harding Rd., 37205. Tel: 615-383-3230; Fax: 615-383-3196. Email: sparks@dominicancampus.org. Roger Muehe, CFO; Rev. Thomas Kalam, C.M.I.

Endowment for the Advancement of Catholic Schools, Trust, 2400 21st Ave. S., 37212. Tel: 615-383-6393; Fax: 615-292-8411. Most Rev. David R. Choby, D.D., J.C.L.

FrassatiUSA Inc., P.O. Box 50571, 37205.

Growing in Faith for Tomorrow Capital Campaign Trust, Inc., 2400 21st Ave., S., 37212. Tel: 615-783-0253; Fax: 615-292-8411. Mr. Edward Stack, Pres.

**St. Henry Property Development, Inc. dba The Cloister* 30 White Bridge Rd., 37205. Tel: 615-760-4424; Fax: 615-352-8591. Email: david@maryqueenofangels.com. David Glacoe, Admin.

Ladies of Charity of Nashville, Inc., 2216 State St., 37203. Tel: 615-327-3453; 615-327-3430; Fax: 615-321-3312. Affiliated with the Ladies of Charity of the United States of America, LCUSA, and the Association of International Charities, AIC.

Ladies of Charity Welfare Agency, Inc. (1617) 2212 State St., 37203. Tel: 615-327-3430; Fax: 615-321-3312. Email: locwelfare@bellsouth.net. Mrs. Terri Puma, Exec. Dir.; Rev. Philip M. Breen, Moderator; Rev. Msgr. George W. Rohling, Moderator, Emeritus.

Mary, Queen of Angels. Inc. (1999) 30 White Bridge Rd., 37205. Tel: 615-760-4424; Fax: 615-352-8591. Email: david@maryqueenofangels.com. Web: www.maryqueenofangels.com. Mr. David Glascoe, CEO.

Mid-Tennessee Rural Outreach Association, 30 White Bridge Rd., 37205. Tel: 615-352-3087.

Mid-Tennessee Rural Outreach Association; Assumption-St. Vincent North Nashville Outreach Association.

Parish Twinning Program of the Americas, 309 Windemere Woods Dr., 37215. Tel: 615-356-5999; Fax: 615-352-5114. Email: parishprogram@aol.com. Web: www.parishprogram.org. Theresa Patterson, Exec. Dir.

**Visitation Hospital Foundation*, 237 Old Hickory Blvd., Ste. 201, 37221. Tel: 615-673-3501; Fax: 615-673-3503. Email: visitationHF@aol.com. Theresa Patterson, Exec. Dir.; Jeff Patterson, Assoc. Dir.; Fran Rajotte, Dir. Devel. & Communications.

HENDERSONVILLE. *Legion of Mary*, 200 Sanders Ferry Rd., Apt. 2412, 37075. Tel: 615-431-0472. Email: wsbev@aol.com. Rev. William S. Bevington, Dir. (Retired).

Priests Eucharistic League, 200 Sanders Ferry Rd., Apt. 2412, 37075. Tel: 615-431-0472. Email: wsbev@aol.com. Rev. William S. Bevington, Dir. (Retired).

RELIGIOUS INSTITUTES OF MEN REPRESENTED IN THE DIOCESE

For further details refer to the corresponding bracketed number in the Religious Institutes of Men or Women section.

[0275]—*Carmelites of Mary Immaculate*—C.M.I.

[0520]—*Franciscan Friars* (Prov. of Sacred Heart)—O.F.M.

[0570]—*Glenmary Home Missioners*—G.H.M.

[0690]—*Jesuit Fathers and Brothers*—S.J.

[]—*Missionaries of St. Francis de Sales* (Annecy, France)—M.S.F.S.

[1200]—*Society of the Divine Savior* (Milwaukee, WI)—S.D.S.

RELIGIOUS INSTITUTES OF WOMEN REPRESENTED IN THE DIOCESE

[0760]—*Daughters of Charity of St. Vincent de Paul* (East Central Prov., Evansville, IN)—D.C.

[1070-03]—*Dominican Sisters*—O.P.

[1070-07]—*Dominican Sisters*—O.P.

[1070-09]—*Dominican Sisters*—O.P.

[2575]—*Institute of the Sisters of Mercy of the Americas* (Baltimore, MD; Cincinnati, OH)—R.S.M.

[]—*Sacred Heart Congregation* (Mexico)

[]—*Sacred Heart Congregation (India)*—S.H.

[1680]—*School Sisters of St. Francis*—O.S.F.

[]—*Sisters for Christian Community* (St. Louis)—S.F.C.C.

[0990]—*Sisters of Divine Providence* (St. Louis Prov.)—C.D.P.

[1705]—*Sisters of St. Francis of Assisi*—O.S.F.

[3270]—*Sisters of the Most Precious Blood*—C.PP.S.

DIOCESAN CEMETERIES

NASHVILLE. *Calvary Cemetery*, 1001 Lebanon Rd., 37210.

NECROLOGY

† Hitchcock, Rev. Msgr. James R., (Retired)—Died Dec. 9, 2008

An asterisk (*) denotes an organization that has established tax-exempt status directly with the IRS and is not covered by the USCCB Group Ruling.

Archdiocese of Newark

(Archidioecesis Novarcensis)

Most Reverend

PETER LEO GERETY, D.D.

Archbishop Emeritus of Newark; ordained June 29, 1939; appointed Coadjutor Bishop of Portland March 4, 1966; Episcopal ordination June 1, 1966; appointed Apostolic Administrator February 18, 1967; succeeded to See September 15, 1969; appointed Archbishop of Newark April 2, 1974; installed June 28, 1974; Pallium conferred December 12, 1974; retired June 1, 1986. *Res.: 60 Home Ave., Rutherford, NJ 07070.* Tel: 201-460-1369; Fax: 201-842-0724.

Most Reverend

DOMINIC A. MARCONI, D.D.

Retired Auxiliary Bishop of Newark; ordained May 30, 1953; appointed Titular Bishop of Bure and Auxiliary Bishop of Newark May 3, 1976; Episcopal ordination June 25, 1976; retired July 1, 2002. *Res.: 71 Washington Ave., Chatham, NJ 07928-2014.* Tel: 973-635-8777; Fax: 973-635-8647.

Most Reverend

DAVID ARIAS, O.A.R.

Retired Auxiliary Bishop of Newark; ordained May 31, 1952; appointed Titular Bishop of Badie and Auxiliary Bishop of Newark January 25, 1983; Episcopal ordination April 7, 1983; retired May 21, 2004. *Res.: St. Joseph of the Palisades Rectory, 6401 Palisade Ave., West New York, NJ 07093.* Tel: 201-854-7006. *Office:* . Tel: 201-861-6644; Fax: 201-861-7744.

Most Reverend

CHARLES J. McDONNELL

Retired Auxiliary Bishop of Newark; ordained May 29, 1954; appointed Titular Bishop of Pocofelto and Auxiliary Bishop of Newark March 15, 1994; Episcopal ordination May 12, 1994; retired May 21, 2004. *Res.: Holy Trinity Rectory, 34 Maple Ave., Hackensack, NJ 07601.* Tel: 201-343-5170; Fax: 201-343-5067.

Most Reverend

JOHN J. MYERS, J.C.D., D.D.

Archbishop of Newark; ordained December 17, 1966; appointed Coadjutor Bishop of Peoria July 14, 1987; Episcopal ordination September 3, 1987; succeeded to See of Peoria January 23, 1990; appointed Fifth Archbishop of Newark July 24, 2001; installed October 9, 2001; Pallium conferred June 29, 2002. *Res.: Cathedral Basilica of the Sacred Heart, 89 Ridge St., Newark, NJ 07104.* Tel: 973-484-4600; Fax: 973-497-4018.

Archdiocesan Center: 171 Clifton Ave., P.O. Box 9500, Newark, NJ 07104-9500. Tel: 973-497-4000; Fax: 973-497-4033.

Web: www.rcan.org

Email: webmaster@rcan.org

Most Reverend

EDGAR M. DA CUNHA, S.D.V.

Auxiliary Bishop of Newark; ordained March 27, 1982; appointed Titular See of Ucres and Auxiliary Bishop of Newark June 27, 2003; Episcopal ordination September 3, 2003. *Res.: 170 Broad St., Newark, NJ 07104.* Tel: 973-482-8619; Fax: 973-497-4555.

Most Reverend

THOMAS A. DONATO, D.D.

Auxiliary Bishop of Newark; ordained May 29, 1965; appointed Titular Bishop of Jamestown and Auxiliary Bishop of Newark May 21, 2004; Episcopal ordination August 4, 2004. *Res.: St. Henry's Parish, 82 W. 29th St., Bayonne, NJ 07002.* Tel: 201-436-0857; Fax: 201-823-4611.

Most Reverend

JOHN W. FLESEY, S.T.D., D.D.

Auxiliary Bishop of Newark; ordained May 31, 1969; appointed Titular Bishop of Allegheny and Auxiliary Bishop of Newark May 21, 2004; Episcopal ordination August 4, 2004. *Res.: Most Blessed Sacrament, 787 Franklin Lake Rd., Franklin Lakes, NJ 07417.* Tel: 201-891-4200; Fax: 201-891-4243.

Most Reverend

MANUEL A. CRUZ

Auxiliary Bishop of Newark; ordained May 31, 1980; appointed Titular Bishop of Gaguari and Auxiliary Bishop of Newark May 19, 2008; Episcopal ordination September 8, 2008; installed September 8, 2008. *Res.: 306 Martin Luther King Blvd., Newark, NJ 07102.* Tel: 973-497-4009; Fax: 973-497-4525.

Square Miles 513.

Diocese Established, 1853; Erected an Archdiocese, December 10, 1937.

Comprises Four Counties in the State of New Jersey, viz.: Bergen, Hudson, Essex and Union.

For legal titles of parishes and archdiocesan institutions, consult the Chancery Office.

STATISTICAL OVERVIEW

Personnel	
Archbishops	1
Retired Archbishops	1
Auxiliary Bishops	4
Retired Bishops	3
Abbots	1
Priests: Diocesan Active in Diocese	436
Priests: Diocesan Active Outside Diocese	56
Priests: Diocesan in Foreign Missions	14
Priests: Retired, Sick or Absent	223
Number of Diocesan Priests	729
Religious Priests in Diocese	165
Total Priests in Diocese	894
Extern Priests in Diocese	82
Ordinations:	
Diocesan Priests	13
Transitional Deacons	13
Permanent Deacons in Diocese	167
Total Brothers	74
Total Sisters	1,003
Parishes	
Parishes	222
With Resident Pastor:	
Resident Diocesan Priests	182
Resident Religious Priests	24
Without Resident Pastor:	
Administered by Priests	16
Closed Parishes	2
Professional Ministry Personnel:	
Brothers	4
Sisters	64
Lay Ministers	502
Welfare	
Catholic Hospitals	5
Total Assisted	621,226
Health Care Centers	1
Total Assisted	8,000
Homes for the Aged	4
Total Assisted	568
Day Care Centers	4
Total Assisted	575
Specialized Homes	6
Total Assisted	893
Special Centers for Social Services	23
Total Assisted	71,803
Educational	
Seminaries, Diocesan	3
Students from This Diocese	100
Students from Other Diocese	64
Diocesan Students in Other Seminaries	7
Students Religious	35
Total Seminarians	142
Colleges and Universities	4
Total Students	17,544
High Schools, Diocesan and Parish	11
Total Students	6,244
High Schools, Private	21
Total Students	8,134
Elementary Schools, Diocesan and Parish	84
Total Students	18,406
Elementary Schools, Private	5
Total Students	1,170
Catechesis/Religious Education:	
High School Students	4,042
Elementary Students	70,021
Total Students under Catholic Instruction	125,703
Teachers in the Diocese:	
Priests	30
Brothers	16
Sisters	16
Lay Teachers	2,482
Vital Statistics	
Receptions into the Church:	
Infant Baptism Totals	13,936
Minor Baptism Totals	313
Adult Baptism Totals	301
Received into Full Communion	216
First Communions	12,224
Confirmations	9,576
Marriages:	
Catholic	2,468
Interfaith	363
Total Marriages	2,831
Deaths	9,883
Total Catholic Population	1,318,557
Total Population	2,784,183

Former Bishops—Most Revs. JAMES ROOSEVELT BAYLEY, D.D., cons. Oct. 30, 1853; promoted to the Archiepiscopal See of Baltimore, July 30, 1872; died Oct. 3, 1877; MICHAEL AUGUSTINE CORRIGAN, D.D., cons. May 4, 1873; promoted to the Archiepiscopal See of Petra, Oct. 1, 1880; succeeded to the Archiepiscopal See of New York, Oct. 10, 1885; died May 5, 1902; WINAND MICHAEL WIGGER, D.D., cons. Oct. 18, 1881; died Jan. 5, 1901; JOHN JOSEPH O'CONNOR, D.D., ord. Dec. 22, 1877; cons. July 25, 1901; died May 20, 1927; THOMAS J. WALSH, S.T.D., J.C.D., ord. Jan. 27, 1900; appt. Bishop of Trenton, May 10, 1918; cons. July 25, 1918; made Assistant at the Pontifical Throne March 13, 1922; transferred to the See of Newark, March 2, 1928; appt. First Archbishop of Newark, Dec. 10, 1937; Pallium conferred, Dec. 18, 1937; installed April 27, 1938; died June 6, 1952; THOMAS A. BOLAND, S.T.D., LL.D., ord. Dec. 23, 1922; appt. Titular Bishop of Hirina and Auxiliary to the Archbishop of Newark, May 21, 1940; cons. July 25, 1940; transferred to Paterson, June 21, 1947; appt. Second Archbishop of Newark, Nov. 15, 1952;

installed Jan. 14, 1953; Assistant at the Pontifical Throne, May 6, 1965; retired April 2, 1974; died March 16, 1979; PETER LEO GERETY, D.D. (Retired), ord. June 29, 1939; appt. Coadjutor Bishop of Portland, March 4, 1966; cons. June 1, 1966; succeeded to See, Sept. 15, 1969; appt. Third Archbishop of Newark, April 2, 1974; installed June 28, 1974; retired June 1, 1986; THEODORE E. MCCARRICK, Ph.D., ord. May 31, 1958; appt. Auxiliary Bishop of New York and Titular Bishop of Rusibisir, May 24, 1977; Episcopal ordination June 29, 1977; appt. First Bishop of Metuchen, Nov. 19, 1981; appt. Fourth Archbishop of Newark, May 30, 1986; Pallium conferred June 29, 1986; installed July 25, 1986; appt. to See of Washington, D.C., Nov. 21, 2000; installed Jan. 3, 2001.

Archdiocesan Officials

Vicar General, Moderator of the Curia and Acting Chancellor—Rev. Msgr. JOHN E. DORAN, V.G. Tel: 973-497-4002.

Episcopal Regional Vicar for Union County—Most Rev. MANUEL A. CRUZ, D.D. Tel: 908-464-7600.

Judicial Vicar—Rev. Msgr. JAMES M. SHEEHAN, J.C.D. Tel: 973-497-4149.

Vicar for Education and Superintendent of Schools—Rev. Msgr. KEVIN M. HANBURY, Ed.D. Tel: 973-497-4260.

Vicar for Pastoral Life—Rev. Msgr. RICHARD J. ARNHOLS, M.Div. Tel: 973-497-4321.

Minister for Priests—Rev. Msgr. KENNETH J. HERBSTER, V.F. Tel: 973-226-0979.

Delegate for Religious—Sr. MARGARET THOMAS MCGOVERN, O.P. Tel: 973-497-4582.

Vice Chancellor and Secretary to the Archbishop—Rev. Msgr. MICHAEL A. ANDREANO, M.B.A. Tel: 973-497-4005.

Vice Chancellor for Administration—Deacon JOSEPH A. DWYER JR. Tel: 973-497-4128.

Director of Vocations—Rev. JOHN D. GABRIEL. Tel: 973-497-4365.

Director of Communications and Public Relations—JAMES GOODNESS. Tel: 973-497-4186.

Fiscal Officer—GEORGE R. PERALTA. Tel: 973-497-4560.

Regional Bishops, Regional Vicars & Deans

Regional Bishops, Regional Vicars & Deans—Most Revs. JOHN W. FLESEY, S.T.D., D.D., Regl. Bishop for Bergen County; EDGAR M. DA CUNHA, S.D.V., D.D., Regl. Bishop for Essex County; THOMAS A. DONATO, D.D., Regl. Bishop for Hudson County; MANUEL A. CRUZ, D.D., Regl. Vicar for Union County.

BERGEN COUNTY

Northwest Bergen Region Deanery 1: Rev. THOMAS P. LIPNICKI, Our Lady of Perpetual Help, 25 Purdue Ave., Oakland, 07436. Tel: 201-337-7596; Fax: 201-337-7810. Northern Valley Bergen Deanery 2N: Very Rev. GERALD T. HAHN, V.F., St. Anthony, 199 Walnut St., Northvale, 07647-2122. Tel: 201-768-1177; Fax: 201-768-2522. Bergen Pascack Valley Deanery 2P: Very Revs. CHARLES P. GRANDSTRAND, V.F., Our Lady of Mercy, 2 Fremont Ave., Park Ridge, 07656. Tel: 201-391-5315; Fax: 201-391-5614; CHARLES P. GRANSTRAND, V.F., Our Lady of Mercy Parish, 2 Fremount Ave., Park Ridge, 07656. Tel: 201-391-5315; Fax: 201-391-5614. Central Bergen Region Deanery 3: Rev. DAVID W. MILLIKEN, Ascension, 256 Azalea Dr., New Milford, 07646. Tel: 201-836-8961; Fax: 201-836-5896. Southwest Bergen Region Deanery 4: Rev. Msgr. WILLIAM J. REILLY, V.F., Most Holy Name Parish, 99 Marsellus Pl., Garfield, 07026. Tel: 973-340-0032; Fax: 973-340-1618. South Central Bergen Deanery 5: Rev. ARTHUR F. HUMPHREY, St. Margaret of Cortona, 31 Chamberlain Ave., Little Ferry, 07643. Tel: 201-641-2988; Fax: 201-641-0664. Southeast Bergen Region Deanery 6: Very Rev. STEVEN CONNER, V.F., Holy Trinity, 2367 Lemoine Ave., Fort Lee, 07024. Tel: 201-947-1216. South Bergen Region Deanery 7: Rev. Msgr. LEWIS V. PAPERA, V.F., Corpus Christi Parish, 218 Washington Pl., Hasbrouck Heights, 07604. Tel: 201-288-4844; Fax: 201-288-0237.

HUDSON COUNTY

North Hudson Deanery 8: Very Rev. CARLO FORTUNIO, O.P., V.F., Holy Redeemer Parish, 6502 Jackson Ave., West New York, 07093. Tel: 201-868-9444; Fax: 201-868-5944. Central Hudson Region Deanery 9: Very Rev. JAMES P. WHELAN, V.F., St. Lawrence Parish, 22 Hackensack Ave., Weehawken, 07086. Tel: 201-863-6464; Fax: 201-863-6656. Jersey City North Region Deanery 10: Rev. ANDRES J. REYES, St. Paul of the Cross, 156 Hancock Ave., Jersey City, 07307. Tel: 201-798-7900. Jersey City Downtown Deanery 11: Very Rev. VICTOR P. KENNEDY, V.F., Parish of the Resurrection, 209 Third St., Jersey City, 07302-0407. Tel: 201-434-8500; Fax: 201-333-1816. Jersey City South Deanery 12: Rev. JOHN J. CRYAN, V.F., M.Div., Our Lady of Mercy & Our Lady of Sorrows, 40 Sullivan Dr., Jersey City, 07302. Tel: 201-434-0798; Fax: 201-432-2885. Bayonne Deanery 13: Rev. Msgr. PAUL D. SCHETELICK, V.E., V.F., St. Andrew Parish, 125 Broadway, Bayonne, 07002. Tel: 201-437-0833; Fax: 201-858-3477. West Hudson Region Deanery 14: Very Rev. MICHAEL G. WARD, V.F., St. Cecilia Parish, 120 Kearny Ave., Kearny, 07032-2316. Tel: 201-991-1116; Fax: 201-998-4437.

ESSEX COUNTY

West Essex Deanery 15: Rev. ANTHONY J. RANDAZZO, Notre Dame, 359 Central Ave., North Caldwell, 07006. Tel: 973-226-0979; Fax: 973-226-4118. North Essex Deanery 16: Rev. Msgr. DAVID C. HUBA, St. Mary Church, 17 Msgr. Owens Place, Nutley, 07110. Tel: 973-235-1100. Central Essex Deanery 17: Rev. GEORGE FAOUR, St. John, 94 Ridge St., Orange, 07050. Tel: 973-674-0110; Fax: 973-674-3965. South Essex Deanery 18: Rev. MICHAEL A. SAPORITO, St. Joseph, 767 Prospect St., Maplewood, 07040. Tel: 973-761-5933. North Newark Essex Deanery 19: Rev. JAN SASIN, St. Francis Xavier, 243 Abington Ave., W., Newark, 07107. Tel: 973-482-8410; Fax: 973-485-7471. Central Newark Deanery 20: Very Rev. PHILIP J. WATERS, O.S.B., St. Mary of the Immaculate Conception, 528 Martin Luther King Blvd., Newark, 07102-1314. Tel: 973-792-5793; Fax: 973-643-6922. Ironbound Deanery 21: Rev. Msgr. JOSEPH F. AMBROSIO, V.F., Our Lady of Mt. Carmel, 259 Oliver St., Newark, 07105. Tel: 973-589-2090; Fax: 973-589-2662.

UNION COUNTY

Union Northwest Deanery 22: Rev. JOHN M. MCCRONE, Our Lady of Lourdes, 300 Central Ave., Mountainside, 07092. Tel: 908-232-1162; Fax: 908-232-0776. Union North Deanery 23: Rev. JOSEPH S. BEJGROWICZ, V.F., St. Theresa, 541 Washington Ave., Kenilworth, 07033. Tel: 908-272-4444; Fax: 908-272-4424. Union County Southeast Deanery 24: Rev. ROBERT G. MCBRIDE, J.C.L., Saint John the Apostle, 1805 Penbrook Ter., Linden, 07036. Tel: 908-486-6363; Fax: 908-486-5345. Elizabeth Deanery 25: Very Rev. JOHN E. WASSELL, V.F., Holy Rosary/St. Michael, 52 Smith St., Elizabeth, 07201. Tel: 908-354-2454; Fax: 908-354-3207. Union County Southwest Deanery 26: Rev. JOHN J. PALADINO, St. Bartholomew, 2032 Westfield Ave., Scotch Plains, 07076.

Advisory Bodies

College of Consultors—Members: Most Revs. EDGAR M. DA CUNHA, S.D.V., D.D.; THOMAS A. DONATO, D.D.; JOHN W. FLESEY, S.T.D., D.D.; MANUEL A. CRUZ, D.D.; Rev. Msgrs. JOHN E. DORAN, V.G.; RONALD J. ROZNIAK, V.G., P.A., Sec.; RICHARD J. ARNHOLS, M.Div.; Revs. JOSEPH S. BEJGROWICZ, V.F.; JOSEPH A. FERRARO; JOHN D. GABRIEL; Rev. Msgrs. RENATO GRASSELLI; ANTHONY J. KULIG, M.A., K.H.S.

Presbyteral Council—Members: Most Revs. EDGAR M. DA CUNHA, S.D.V., D.D.; THOMAS A. DONATO, D.D.; MANUEL A. CRUZ, D.D., (Ex Officio); JOHN W. FLESEY, S.T.D., D.D.; Rev. Msgrs. JOHN E. DORAN, V.G.; JOSEPH F. AMBROSIO, V.F.; RICHARD J. ARNHOLS, M.Div.; PAUL L. BOCHICCHIO, V.F.; EDWARD G. BRADLEY, S.T.L., M.A.; Rev. EDWARD M. DONOVAN; Very Rev. CARLO FORTUNIO, O.P., V.F.; Rev. GEORGE D. GILLEN; Rev. Msgr. THOMAS P. NYDEGGER, Ed.D., M.Div.; Rev. JOHN J. PALADINO; Rev. Msgrs. RONALD J. ROZNIAK, V.G., P.A.; MICHAEL A. ANDREANO, M.B.A.; Very Rev. ROBERT A. ANTCZAK, V.F.; Revs. JOSEPH S. BEJGROWICZ, V.F.; JOSEPH A. FERRARO; JOHN D. GABRIEL; Rev. Msgr. KEVIN M. HANBURY, Ed.D.; Revs. RICHARD J. KELLY; MARIUSZ KOCH, C.F.R.; Rev. Msgr. JOHN J. LAFERRERA; Rev. JAMES M. MANOS; Rev. Msgrs. LEWIS V. PAPERA; JAMES M. SHEEHAN, J.C.D.; Rev. MARC A. VICARI; Very Rev. MICHAEL G. WARD, V.F.

Archdiocesan Finance Council—LESLIE A. HYNES, Esq., Chm.; GARRY J. SCHEURING, Vice Chm. Members: HENRY J. AMOROSO, Esq.; ROBERT C. BUTLER; CHARLES C. CARELLA, Esq.; Rev. Msgr. JOHN E. DORAN, V.G.; GEORGE FIORE; ADRIAN M. FOLEY JR., Esq.; WILLIAM C. FREDA; JAMES H. FREIS, Esq.; ALBERT R. GAMPER JR.; BRIAN D. MCAULEY; W. PETER MCBRIDE; JOSEPH L. MUSCARELLE JR.; Rev. Msgr. RONALD J. ROZNIAK, V.G., P.A.; Ms. DENISE ROVER; Ms. LIZA M. WALSH, Esq. Consultant: RICHARD MANDELBAUM.

Priest Personnel Policy Board—Rev. Msgrs. JOSEPH A. PETRILLO, Archbishop's Liaison; WILLIAM J. FADROWSKI, Archbishop's Delegate. Ex Officio Members: Rev. Msgr. EDWARD G. BRADLEY, S.T.L., M.A.; Rev. STANLEY GOMES. Elected Members: Rev. Msgr. MICHAEL J. DESMOND; Revs. LAWRENCE J. FAMA; GEORGE D. GILLEN; Rev. Msgrs. DONALD E. GUENTHER (Retired); CHARLES W. GUSMER, S.T.D., V.E.; Rev. MICHAEL A. SAPORITO.

Diaconate Executive Committee—Deacons JOHN J. MCKENNA, Dir.; JOSEPH YANDOLI, Chm.

Archdiocesan Stewardship Advisory Committee—KENNETH DIPAOLA, Chm. Tel: 973-497-4332; Rev. Msgr. PAUL L. BOCHICCHIO, V.F. Tel: 973-667-0026; Revs. LARRY EVANS; MICHAEL J. KREDER; Deacon NICHOLAS J. DELUCCA; Ms. EVEY JOHNSON.

Archdiocesan Implementation Team—Rev. Msgrs. JOHN E. DORAN, V.G.; WILLIAM C. HARMS. Tel: 973-497-4047; Fax: 973-497-4555. Members: Rev. KEVIN E. CARTER; Very Rev. JOHN E. WASSELL, V.F.; Deacon JOSEPH A. DWYER JR.; Mrs. LINDA ENGLISH; Rev. JOHN R. O'CONNELL, V.F.; Sr. LINDA KLAISS, S.S.J.; Mrs. JENNIFER LEITNER; Mrs. GLADYS POZZA; Mr. MARK HOWARD.

Archdiocesan Offices and Agencies

Office of the Archbishop—Fax: 973-497-4018.

Vice Chancellor and Secretary to the Archbishop—Rev. Msgr. MICHAEL A. ANDREANO, M.B.A. Tel: 973-497-4005.

Executive Assistant to the Archbishop—ROSEANN BIASI-VAZQUEZ. Tel: 973-497-4006.

Assistant to the Archbishop for Public Affairs—Rev. Msgr. CHRISTOPHER J. HYNES, Ed.S. Tel: 973-497-4107.

Office of the Vicar General and Moderator of the Curia—Fax: 973-497-4525.

Executive Assistant to the Vicar General—LEOCADIA MATUSZCZAK, M.B.A. Tel: 973-497-4003.

Secretary and Receptionist—MARGARET DEAN. Tel: 973-497-4020.

Office of the Chancellor—Fax: 973-497-4525.

Director of Child and Youth Protection—ROSEMARIE PAPALEO, M.A. Tel: 973-497-4011.

Victims Assistance Coordinator—JULIE WILLIS, M.S.W. Tel: 201-407-3256.

Administrative Assistant—AMY BARR. Tel: 201-497-4008.

Advocate Publishing Corporation— Publisher of "The Catholic Advocate" (the Archdiocesan newspaper), "New Jersey Catolico" (Spanish language monthly), and Directory & Almanac Tel: 974-497-4200 Main Office; Fax: 973-497-4192. MICHAEL GABRIELE, Editor & Assoc. Publisher. Tel: 973-497-4193. Email: gabrielma@rcan.org; WARD MIELE, Mng. Editor. Tel: 973-497-4199. Email: mielejos@rcan.org; MARGE PEARSON-MCCUE, Dir. Advertising & Oper. Tel: 973-497-4201. Email: pearsoma@rcan.org.

Office of Banking and Investments—MATTHEW PHELAN, Dir. Tel: 973-497-4069; Fax: 973-497-4320. Email: phelanma@rcan.org.

Office of Black Catholic Affairs—Sr. PATRICIA LUCAS, D.H.M., Dir.

Campus Ministry—MAUREEN MADIGAN, M.T.S., Dir. Tel: 973-497-4305; Fax: 973-497-4317.

Catechetical Office—Mr. RONALD L. PIHOKKER, M.A., Dir. Tel: 973-497-4285.

Office of Catholic Cemeteries—Tel: 973-497-7981; Fax: 973-497-7984.

Cemeteries Office—Tel: 973-497-7981.

Mausoleum Office—Tel: 973-497-7988. Rev. Msgr. WILLIAM B. NAEDELE, Dir.; ANDREW P. SCHAEFER, Exec. Dir. Tel: 973-497-7975. Email: schafean@rcan.org.

Centro Guadalupe—547 35th St., Union City, 07087. Tel: 201-348-8400; Fax: 201-348-1809. Revs. ANGEL SAN EUFRASIO, O.A.R., Dir.; JUAN LUIS CALDERON, O.A.R., Asst. Dir. Email: njcentroguadalupe@hotmail.com.

Office of Clergy Personnel—Fax: 973-497-4219. Rev. Msgr. JOSEPH A. PETRILLO, Exec. Dir. Tel: 973-497-4222; CRISTINA PARDO, Administrative Asst. Tel: 973-497-4220.

Archdiocesan Priest Personnel—Fax: 973-497-4219. Rev. Msgr. JOSEPH A. PETRILLO, Dir. Tel: 973-497-4222; CRISTINA PARDO, Administrative Asst. Tel: 973-497-4220.

Adjunct Clergy Personnel—Fax: 973-497-4180. Rev. STANLEY GOMES, Dir. Tel: 973-497-4374; ANNETTE CHIRICHELLA, Administrative Asst. Tel: 973-497-4220.

Continuing Education and Formation of Priests—Fax: 973-497-4180. Rev. DONALD K. HUMMEL, D.Min., Dir. Tel: 973-497-4218; ANNETTE CHIRICHELLA, Administrative Asst. Tel: 973-497-4225.

Office of the Permanent Diaconate—Revs. JAMES V. TETI, J.C.L., Dir. Selection & Deacon Formation, Annunciation, 50 W. Midland Ave., Paramus, 07652-2140. Tel: 201-261-6322; DONALD K. HUMMEL, D.Min., Assoc. Dir. Formation for the Permanent Diaconate. Tel: 973-497-4218; Deacon JOHN J. MCKENNA, Dir. Deacon Personnel. Tel: 973-497-4195; ANNETTE CHIRICHELLA, Administrative Asst. Tel: 973-497-4225.

Ministry to Retired Priests—Rev. Msgr. EDWARD G. BRADLEY, S.T.L., M.A., Dir., Seton Hall Preparatory, 11 Beverly Rd., West Orange,

07052. Tel: 973-669-9561.

Office of Communications and Public Relations—JAMES GOODNESS, Dir. Tel: 973-497-4186; Fax: 973-497-4185. Email: goodneja@rcan.org.

Office of Information Technology Services—ROBERT J. KENNELLY, Dir. Tel: 973-497-4161; Fax: 973-497-4277. Email: kennelro@rcan.org.

Office of Archdiocesan Counsel— Carella, Byrne, Bain, Gilfillan, Ceechi, Stewart & Olstein, Archdiocesan Counsel *5 Becker Farm Rd., Roseland, 07068-1739*. Tel: 973-994-1700; Fax: 973-994-1744. CHARLES M. CARELLA, Esq., Counsellor-at-Law.

Delegate for Religious—Sr. MARGARET THOMAS MCGOVERN, O.P. Tel: 973-497-4582; Fax: 973-497-4219.

Office of Development—CARLA REPOLLET, Exec. Dir. Tel: 973-497-4127; Fax: 973-497-4031. Email: gonzalca@rcan.org; WILLIAM T. EVANS, Exec. Dir. Major Gifts. Tel: 973-497-4584; Fax: 973-497-4049. Email: evaanswil@rcan.org.

Archbishop's Annual Appeal—CARLA REPOLLET, Dir. Tel: 973-497-4042 Gen. Inquiries; 973-497-4127 Archbishop's Annual Appeal Inquiries.

Office of Major Gifts and Planned Giving—WILLIAM T. EVANS, Exec. Dir. Major Gifts. Tel: 973-497-4584. Email: evanswil@rcan.org; ANNE DEVIVO DEMESA, Dir. Planned Giving. Tel: 973-497-4048. Email: demesaan@rcan.org; THERESA LYNCH, Coord. Devel. Tel: 973-497-4042. Email: lynchthe@rcan.org.

Parish Capital Campaigns—KENNETH DIPAOLA, Assoc. Dir. Tel: 973-497-4332. Email: dipaolke@rcan.org.

Capital Campaigns and Architectural Historian—TROY JOSEPH SIMMONS, M.A., C.C., Assoc. Dir. Tel: 973-497-4116; Fax: 973-497-4031.

Stewardship and Special Projects—LYNN GULLY, Assoc. Dir. Tel: 973-497-4589. Email: gullylyn@rcan.org.

Office of Evangelization—Fax: 973-497-4317. Most Rev. EDGAR M. DA CUNHA, S.D.V., D.D., Vicar for Evangelization. Tel: 973-497-4318. Email: dacunhed@rcan.org; LILIANA SOTO, Coord. Evangelization. Tel: 973-497-4353. Email: sotolili@rcan.org.

Family Life Ministries—Fax: 973-497-4317. Rev. MARC A. VICARI, Vicar for Family Life. Tel: 973-497-4324; NANCY DELLI SANTI, Pre-Cana Reservations. Tel: 973-497-4328. Web: www.rcan.org/famlife/precana.htm (Pre-Cana registration online).

Ministry to the Bereaved, Separated, Divorced, Retrouvaille—JANET MCCORMICK, M.A., Assoc. Dir.; Rev. THOMAS G. ARMINIO, Chap., Widows & Widowers (Retired). Tel: 973-497-4327.

Hispanic Family Life Ministries—REINA BASUALDO, Assoc. Dir. Tel: 973-497-4326.

Couples for Christ—Rev. PAUL J. LEHMAN, Spiritual Dir. (Retired). Tel: 973-948-4546; SONNY AGUILING, Area Dir., CFC, NJ. Tel: 908-272-3867. Email: saguiling@comcast.net; JOE DE LEON, Cluster Head, CFC Central Cluster. Tel: 973-403-2650.

Families for Nazareth—Fax: 908-486-0398. WALTER BOROWSKI, Regl. Animator for the Northeast Region Movement. Tel: 908-486-3366; Rev. JAROSLAW ZANIEWSKI, Spiritual Dir. Founder of Families of Nazareth in the United States. Tel: 973-743-0220. Web: www.inthearmsofmary.org.

Focolare Movement (East Coast Regional Directors)—MARIGEN LOHLA; TERRY GUNN; MARIAPOLIS LUMINOSA, 200 Cardinal Rd., Hyde Park, NY 12538. Tel: 845-229-0230. Local Coordinators: JIM MILWAY; MARY JANE MILWAY. Tel: 973-726-6224. Web: www.rc.net/focolare.

Engaged Encounter—Rev. JAMES M. MORAN, Chap., St. Leo, 324 Market St., Elmwood Park, 07407. Tel: 201-796-3521. Coordinators: PAUL GERBINO; SANDY GERBINO. Tel: 973-497-4323 (Engaged Encounter Registration).

Worldwide Marriage Encounter—Tel: 800-823-5683. Newark Ecclesial Team: Rev. Msgr. FRANCIS J. HOUGHTON, Chap. (Retired); JAN ZIOBRO; ELA ZIOBRO. Tel: 973-746-3421. Section III Coordinator: Rev. MICHAEL M. WALTERS, J.C.L.

Registration Couple—Tel: 800-823-LOVE. SYLVIA VASSALO; SAL VASSALO. Tel: 800-823-5683. Web: www.wwme.org.

Natural Family Planning—Chaircouple: DAMON OWENS; MELANIE OWENS. Tel: 973-497-4325. Email: nfp@rcan.org; Rev. Msgr. THOMAS P. NYDEGGER, Ed.D., M.Div., Chap. & Coord.

Office of Divine Worship—Fax: 973-497-4314. Revs. THOMAS A. DENTE, Dir. Tel: 973-497-4347; THOMAS B. IWANOWSKI, Assoc Dir. Parish Life. Tel: 973-497-4344; MICHAEL J. SHEEHAN, Dir. R.C.I.A. Tel: 973-497-4346; JOAN M. CONROY, Coord. Tel: 973-497-4343; 973-497-4361 Book Orders; Rev. Msgrs. RICHARD F. GRONCKI, Archdiocesan Ceremonies. Tel: 973-484-4600; CHARLES W. GUSMER, S.T.D., V.E., Liturgical Consultant. Tel: 973-239-7960; JOHN J. MILLER, Music Ministry. Tel: 973-497-4346; REGINA CHAMBERLAIN, Administrative Asst. Tel: 973-497-4345.

Office of Finance—Fax: 973-497-4033. JOSEPH PESCATORE, Fiscal Officer. Tel: 973-497-4560. Email: pescatjo@rcan.org; BEN CARADANG, Dir. Tel: 973-497-4054.

Hispanic Apostolate—Most Rev. MANUEL A. CRUZ, D.D., Episcopal Vicar. Tel: 973-497-4009; Fax: 973-497-4525; Rev. JOSE I. GAMBA, Coord. Tel: 973-497-4335. Email: hisp_apost@rcan.org. Web: www.rcan.org/hispanic/.

Department of Human Concerns—KAY FURLANI, Dir. Tel: 973-497-4341; Fax: 973-497-4317. Email: furlanca@rcan.org.

Office of Human Resources—Fax: 973-497-4103. Deacon JOHN J. MCKENNA, Exec. Dir. Tel: 973-497-4125. Email: mckennjo@rcan.org; DOUG MCGUIRK, Assoc. Dir. Tel: 973-497-4095. Email: mcguirdo@rcan.org; RAMONA FLORES, Assoc. Dir. Tel: 973-497-4026. Email: floresra@rcan.org; SERENA JOHNSON, Benefits Admin. Tel: 973-497-4092. Email: johnsosr@rcan.org; MARIA DEPAULA, Admin. & Technical Supvr. Tel: 973-497-4089. Email: depaulma@rcan.org.

Office Services/Mailroom—Tel: 973-497-4035 Mailroom. LUCIA LOPEZ, Oper. Supvr. Tel: 973-497-4045. Email: lopezluc@rcan.org; ELIZABETH MATOS, Supvr. Mailroom. Tel: 973-497-4035. Email: matoseli@rcan.org.

Metropolitan Tribunal— N.B. Dispensation requests or questions regarding canonical matters can be directed to Rev. Msgr. James M. Sheehan at 973-497-4148 or 171 Clifton Ave., Newark, NJ 07104. Rev. Msgr. JAMES M. SHEEHAN, J.C.D., Judicial Vicar; Rev. EMMETT GAVIN, O.Carm., J.C.L., Adjutant Judicial Vicar. Tel: 973-497-4145.

Full-time Staff—Sr. CATHERINE MARY RAYMOND, J.C.L.

Archdiocesan Judges—Revs. JOHN J. CRYAN, V.F., M.Div.; JOSEPH A. D'AMICO; Rev. Msgrs. FRANK G. DEL PRETE, J.C.D.; ROBERT J. HARRINGTON, M.Div.; Revs. NORBERT F. LASKOWSKI, B.A.; ROBERT G. MCBRIDE, J.C.L.; BERNARD N. MOHAN, B.S. (Retired); MICHAEL M. WALTERS, J.C.L.; FRANK ROSE, M.Div.; Rev. Msgr. JAMES P. MCMENEMIE, S.T.L. (Retired).

Promoter of Justice—Rev. ROBERT G. MCBRIDE, J.C.L.

Defenders of the Bond—Rev. Msgr. VINCENT J. DOYLE, J.C.D. (Retired); Rev. ROBERT S. MEYER, S.T.L., J.D., J.C.L.

Part-time Staff—Revs. YUNIOR ALMONTE; PIUS CACCAVELLE, O.F.M.Cap.; PAUL A. CANNARIATO; ESTERMINIO CHICA; Deacon EDWARD CAMPANELLA; Revs. A. BENITO PRADO; ROBERT WOLFEE.

Notaries—SANDRA PERRINI; JOHN WALSH. Fax: 973-497-4138.

N.B. Dispensation requests or questions regarding canonical matters can be directed to Rev. Msgr. James M. Sheehan at the above number or address.

Ministerial Development Center—Rev. MITCH WALTERS, Dir. Tel: 973-497-4350; Fax: 973-497-4317. Email: waltermi@rcan.org.

Multicultural Affairs—Fax: 973-497-4555. Rev. Msgr. WILLIAM J. REILLY, V.F., Coord.

Brazilian Apostolate—Saint James, 143 Madison St., Newark, 07105. Tel: 973-344-8322. Rev. CLEMENT M. KRUG, C.Ss.R., Coord.

Chinese Apostolate—Holy Trinity, 34 Maple Ave., Hackensack, 07601. Tel: 201-343-5170. Rev. JOSEPH CHENG, Acting Coord.

Filipino Apostolate—St. John the Evangelist, 29 N. Washington Ave., Bergenfield, 07621. Tel: 201-384-0101. Rev. ERNESTO C. TIBAY, Coord.

Haitian Apostolate—Saint Leo, 103 Myrtle Ave., Irvington, 07111. Tel: 973-372-1272. Rev. Msgr. BEAUBRUN ARDOUIN, Coord.

Asian-Indian Apostolate—Saint Aloysius, 691 West Side Ave., Jersey City, 07304. Tel: 201-433-6365. Rev. THOMAS THOTTUNGAL, Coord.

Chaplain to the India Catholic Association (Syro-Malabar Rite)—Our Lady of Sorrows, 30 Madonna Pl., Garfield, 07026. Tel: 973-772-7889. Rev. JOY ALAPPAT, Coord.

Liaison to the Irish Community—Seton Hall Prep, 120 Northfield Ave., West Orange, 07052. Tel: 973-325-6624. Rev. Msgr. MICHAEL E. KELLY, M.A.

Italian Apostolate—Our Lady of Mount Carmel Rectory, 259 Oliver St., Newark, 07105. Tel: 973-589-2090. Rev. Msgr. JOSEPH F. AMBROSIO, V.F., Coord.

Korean Apostolate—St. Andrew Kim (Korean), 280 Parker Ave., Maplewood, 07040. Tel: 973-763-1170. Rev. MINHYUN CHO, Coord.

Nigerian IBO Catholic Community—Blessed Sacrament/Saint Charles Borromeo, 15 Van Ness Pl., Newark, 07108. Tel: 973-824-6548. Rev. Msgr. ANSELM I. NWAORGU, Ph.D., Coord.

Polish Apostolate—Rev. ANDRZEJ OSTASZEWSKI, Coord., St. Casimir, 164 Nichols St., Newark, 07105-2596. Tel: 973-344-2743.

Portugese Apostolate—Our Lady of Fatima, 403 Spring St., Elizabeth, 07201. Tel: 908-355-3810. Rev. Msgr. JOHN S. ANTAO, Coord.

Vietnamese Apostolate—Saint Michael Rectory, 252 Ninth St., Jersey City, 07302. Tel: 201-434-8500. Rev. JOSEPH MINH TRI NGUYEN, Coord.

Office of Parish Internal Audit—Fax: 973-497-4320. NANCY F. LYSTASH, Dir. Tel: 973-497-4074. Email: lystasna@rcan.org; THERESE A. KROPP, Asst. Dir. Tel: 973-497-4073. Email: kroppter@rcan.org.

Pastoral Ministry with the Deaf—Fax: 973-497-4317. Deacon THOMAS SMITH, B.A., C.S.W., Dir. Tel: 973-497-4312; Teletype: 973-497-4311.

Pastoral Ministry with Persons with Disabilities—ANNE MASTERS, M.A., Dir. Tel: 973-497-4309; Fax: 973-497-4317.

Ministry to People on the Move—

Apostleship of the Air—Newark International Airport Chaplaincy, P.O. Box 2220, Newark, 07114. Tel: 973-961-0260. Rev. DAVID J. BARATELLI, Ed.D., Chap.

Apostleship of the Sea—Newark International Airport Chaplaincy, Stella Maris Chapel, 114 Corbin St., Port Newark, 07101. Tel: 973-589-7946. Rev. JOHN F. CORBETT, Dir.

Office of Property Management Administration—Fax: 973-497-4362. Mr. STEVEN BELLOISE, Exec. Dir. Tel: 973-497-4118.

The Heritage Tour—TROY JOSEPH SIMMONS, M.A., C.C., Assoc. Dir. Capital Campaigns & Architectural Historian. Tel: 973-497-4116.

Office of Research and Planning—Mr. MARK HOWARD, Dir. Tel: 973-497-4024. Email: howardma@rcan; PATRICIA RUSSILLO, Coord. Tel: 973-497-4027. Email: russilpa@rcan.org.

Respect Life Office—1805 Penbrook Terr., Linden, 07036. Tel: 732-388-8211; Fax: 908-486-5345. Email: arnewrespect@sjanj.net. Rev. JOSEPH A. MEAGHER, Dir.; MICHELLE KRYSTOFIK, Assoc. Dir.

Risk Management, Insurance Services and Business Administration—Fax: 973-497-4313. JOSEPH A. FRANK, Exec. Dir. Tel: 973-497-4041. Email: frankjoe@rcan.org; DONNA M. WROBEL, Asst. Dir. Tel: 973-497-4044. Email: wrobeldo@rcan.org.

Office of the Superintendent of Schools/Vicariate for Education—Tel: 973-497-4260; Fax: 973-497-4249. Rev. Msgr. KEVIN M. HANBURY, Ed.D., Vicar for Educ. & Supt. Schools; Bro. RALPH DARMENTO, F.S.C., Deputy Supt. Schools; Sr. PATRICIA BUTLER, S.C., M.A., Assoc. Supt. Elementary School Admin. Assistant Superintendents for Elementary Schools: Sisters PATRICIA BUTLER, S.C., M.A., Assoc. Supt. Elementary Admin. (Essex and Union Counties); MARIE GAGLIANO, M.P.F., M.A., Asst. Supt. (Hudson and Bergen).

Assistant Superintendent of Curriculum, Instruction and Assessment—Ms. BARBARA DOLAN. Directors: GLORIA CASTUCCI, M.A., Early Childhood; THOMAS HART, Ph.D., Educational Technology; Sr. LORETTA HOGAN, S.S.J., M.A., Elementary School Finance; Mrs. GRACE PIETROPINTO, B.S., Regl. High School Finance; MARY MCELROY, Esq., NJ Network of Catholic School Families; LAURA CRISTIANO, School Mktg.; Sr. ANNE KAVANAGH, R.D.C., Govt. Programs, Personnel & Events.

Child Nutrition Program—Fax: 973-497-4174. EVERETTE GEORGE, Child Nutrition Coord. Tel: 973-497-4164.

Vicar for Pastoral Life—Fax: 973-497-4317. Rev. Msgr. RICHARD J. ARNHOLS, M.Div. Tel: 973-497-4321; MARISA ACOSTA, Administrative Asst. Tel: 973-497-4013.

Vice Chancellor for Administration—Fax: 973-497-4552. Deacon JOSEPH A. DWYER JR. Tel: 973-497-4128. Email: dwyerjos@rcan.org; FRED BAUER, Dir. Strategic Planning. Tel: 973-497-4207. Email: bauerfre@rcan.org; VERONICA ROCCISANO, Exec. Asst. Tel: 973-497-4559. Email: roccisve@rcan.org.

Vocations Office—Rev. JOHN D. GABRIEL, Dir.; BARBARA KELLY, Exec. Sec. Tel: 973-497-4365; Fax: 973-497-4369.

Emmaus House of Discernment—91 Washington St., Newark, 07102. Tel: 973-624-1301. Rev. JOHN D. GABRIEL, Dir.

Youth and Young Adult Ministries—499 Belgrove Ave., Kearny, 07032. Tel: 201-998-0088; Fax: 201-998-9606. Rev. JOSEPH A. MANCINI, Exec. Dir. Tel: 201-998-0088, Ext. 4142. Email: mancinjo@rcan.org; JAMES GOODNESS, Acting Dir. Youth & Young Adult Svcs. Tel: 973-497-4000 Communications Office; TRACEY VIEIRA, Assoc. Dir. AYRC Retreats & Spirituality. Tel: 201-998-0088, Ext. 4153.

CYO Retreat Center—499 Belgrove Dr., Kearny, 07032. Tel: 201-998-0088; Fax: 201-299-0801. JUDY FURKA, Facility Coord. Tel: 201-998-0088,

Ext. 4148. Email: furkajud@rcan.org; LEANNE CHRISTMANN, Reservation Coord. Tel: 201-998-0088, Ext. 4145. Email: christle@rcan.org; RICH DONOVAN, Coord. Special Events & Summer Camp Prog. (June-Aug.). Tel: 201-998-0088, Ext. 4155 (Special Events); 201-998-0088, Ext. 4150 (Summer Camp Prog.). Email: donovari@rcan.org.

Boy Scouts of America/Catholic Committee on Scouting—499 Belgrove Dr., Kearny, 07032. Tel: 201-998-0088. GABRIEL D. FELTZ, Dir. Tel: 201-998-0088, Ext. 4143. Email: feltzgab@rcan.org; Very Rev. VICTOR P. KENNEDY, V.F., Archdiocesan Chap. Tel: 201-434-8500; Rev. MICHAEL M. WALTERS, J.C.L., Asst. Chap. Tel: 973-673-1077; JOSEPH WAGNER, Committee Chm. Tel: 908-580-0181; Revs. EUGENE J. FIELD, Area Chap. Tel: 201-641-6464; DONALD K. HUMMEL, D.Min., Chm. Tel: 973-497-4218; KEVIN O'BOYLE, Bergen County. Tel: 201-385-2261; GREGORY NITKOWSKI, Essex County. Tel: 973-338-1974; LOUIS CAPPELLUTI, Hudson County. Tel: 201-798-6880; HENRY PETERS, Hudson County. Tel: 201-965-5881; JOSE JEREZE, Hudson County. Tel: 201-798-7294; JOSEPH WAGNER, Union County. Tel: 908-580-0181; Revs. JOSEPH A. MANCINI, Watchung Council, CYO/Youth and Young Adult Ministries, 499 Belgrove Dr., Kearny, 07032. Tel: 201-998-0088; MANUEL D. RIOS, Chap. Tel: 973-763-5204.

Archdiocesan Girl Scouts—Rev. DONALD K. HUMMEL, D.Min., Chap. Tel: 973-497-4512.

Catholic Health and Human Services

Catholic Health and Human Services Corporation—1160 Raymond Blvd., Newark, 07102. Tel: 973-854-2447.

Administration—Rev. Msgr. RONALD J. ROZNIAK, V.G., P.A., Chm. & CEO.

Catholic Charities of the Archdiocese of Newark—

Administration—37 Evergreen Pl., East Orange, 07018. Tel: 973-266-7960; Fax: 973-596-4056. HENRY J. AMOROSO, Esq., Chairperson, 170 W. 7th St., New York, NY 10011. Tel: 212-604-2300; PHILLIP FRESE, Ph.D., CPA, Pres. & CEO, 590 N. 7th St., Newark, 07107. Tel: 973-596-4052; ALLAN J. DAUL, M.S.W., Exec. Dir., 37 Evergreen Pl., East Orange, 07018. Tel: 973-596-4050; Fax: 973-596-4056.

Education Division—Superintendent's Office: 100 Valley Way, West Orange, 07052. Tel: 973-325-4400; Fax: 973-669-8450. JOSEPH A. MARINO, Supt.

Child Study Team—100 Valley Way, West Orange, 07052. Tel: 973-325-4400, Ext. 227; Fax: 973-669-1246. ADRIA GOLDENKRANTZ, Case Mgr.; LIZ DRISCOLL, Prog. Dir.

Social Services Division—ELIZABETH MCCLENDON, L.C.S.W., Assoc. Exec. Dir., 37 Evergreen Pl., East Orange, 07018. Tel: 973-266-7989; Fax: 973-266-7950.

Children and Family Services, Hudson County Homeless Shelters, Transitional Housing and Aids Permanent Housing—3040 Kennedy Blvd., Jersey City, 07306. Tel: 201-798-9957; Fax: 201-659-6216. LESLEY MOORE, L.C.S.W., Div. Dir.

Housing Division—619 Grove St., Jersey City, 07310. Tel: 201-653-3366, Ext. 30; Fax: 201-656-0412. BRENDA PULASKI, Prog. Dir.

Family and Adoption Services—499 Belgrove Dr., Kearny, 07032. Tel: 201-246-7378; Fax: 201-991-3771. PATRICIA CHIARELLO, M.S.W., Prog. Mgr.

Workforce Development Division—321 Central Ave., Newark, 07103. Tel: 973-268-3162; Fax: 973-350-0792. KRISTIN RETLIN, Dir.

Adult Services, Refugee Resettlement & Immigration Assistance, Adult Restorative Justice, Older Adult Services, Human Trafficking, and Project Home—505 South Ave. E., Cranford, 07016. Tel: 908-497-3938; Fax: 908-709-9580. CLARE ELTON, L.S.W., Div. Dir.

Bishop Francis Center for Immigration Services—976 Broad St., Newark, 07102. Tel: 973-733-3516; 866-999-9007 (Human Trafficking Hotline). Sr. JOANN MARIE AUMAND, S.C.C., Prog. Mgr. Tel: 973-733-3516, Ext. 225; Fax: 973-733-9631; GEOFFREY SCOWCROFT ESQ., Mng. Attorney.

Pastoral & Social Ministry, Catholic Campaign for Human Development, Volunteers, Parish Access Centers, 800-HELP LINE—37 Evergreen Pl., East Orange, 07018. Tel: 973-266-7978; Fax: 973-676-0172. CATHERINE L'INSALATA, M.S., C.S.W., Div. Dir. Catholic Campaign for Human Development Volunteers.

Parish Access Centers— Information and Referral *37 Evergreen Pl., East Orange, 07018.* Tel: 800-227-7413 (Information & Referrals).

Essex/Union—37 Evergreen Pl., East Orange, 07018. Fax: 973-266-7949. SCOTT DAVIS. Tel: 973-226-7991; Fax: 973-266-7949; GLORIA WIERZALIS. Tel: 908-497-3966; Fax: 908-276-7185.

Hudson/Bergen—3040 Kennedy Blvd., Jersey City, 07306. Tel: 201-798-9958; Fax: 201-659-6216. CHAQUIRA VASQUEZ. Tel: 201-798-9960; Fax: 201-659-6216.

Emergency Food and Nutrition Network—37 Evergreen Pl., East Orange, 07018. Tel: 973-266-7966; Fax: 973-675-6935. SHARON REILLY-TOBIN, B.A., C.S.W.

New Day Community—36 Evergreen Pl., East Orange, 07018. Tel: 973-763-6430. VINCENT MCMAHON, Ed.D., Dir.

Social Service Helpline—37 Evergreen Pl., East Orange, 07018. Tel: 800-227-7413.

School Social Work Services—37 Evergreen Pl., East Orange, 07018. Tel: 973-266-7983. SHELLEY STEINBERG, Prog. Dir.

Mount Carmel Guild Behavioral Health System—590 N. 7th St., Newark, 07107. Tel: 973-596-4052; Fax: 973-596-4057. PHILLIP FRESE, Ph.D., CPA, Pres. & CEO. Tel: 973-596-4052; Fax: 973-596-4057; ARTURO ACHILIA, Medical Dir. Tel: 973-596-3857; Fax: 973-596-3701; JOHN WESTERVELT, B.A., CFO & Vice Pres. Support Svcs. Tel: 973-596-3984; Fax: 973-412-7710; MICHAEL ZAVADA, L.C.S.W., Dir. Outpatient Adult Svcs., 58 Freeman St., Newark, 07105. Tel: 973-596-3998; JENNIFER WEBERMAN, Ph.D., Dir. Partial Care Progs., 58 Freeman St., Newark, 07105. Tel: 973-596-4115.

PACT (Program for Assertive Community Treatment)—THOMAS RITTER, Mgr. Tel: 973-466-1348.

ICMS-Essex (Integrated Case Management Services-Essex County)—DORIS BOYD, Mgr. Tel: 973-522-2125.

ICMS-Union (Integrated Case Management Services-Union County)—ANGELA ROMANO-LUCKY, L.C.S.W., Mgr. Tel: 908-497-3923.

Cathedral Healthcare Systems—1160 Raymond Blvd., Newark, 07102. Tel: 973-690-3500; Fax: 973-690-3601. Rev. Msgrs. RONALD J. ROZNIAK, V.G., P.A., Chm. & Pres.; JOSEPH T. SLINGER, Ph.D., Vice Chm. & Archbishop's Liaison.

Affiliated Facilities—

Cathedral Health Services, Inc.—Tel: 973-690-3606; Fax: 973-690-3601. Rev. Msgr. JOSEPH T. SLINGER, Ph.D., Chm.

St. Michael's Medical Center—Newark, 07102. Tel: 973-877-5000; Fax: 973-877-5672.

St. James Campus of Saint Michael's Medical Center—Newark, 07105. Tel: 973-589-1300; Fax: 973-465-2861.

Cathedral Foundation, Inc.—Tel: 973-690-3606; Fax: 973-690-3601. Rev. Msgr. RONALD J. ROZNIAK, V.G., P.A., Chm. & Pres.

University Heights Property Co., Inc.—Tel: 973-690-3606; Fax: 973-690-3601. Rev. Msgr. JOSEPH T. SLINGER, Ph.D., Chm.

Cathedral Affiliated Group at Orange, Inc.—Tel: 973-690-3606; Fax: 973-690-3601. Rev. Msgr. JOSEPH T. SLINGER, Ph.D., Chm.

Orange Mountain Healthcare, Inc.—Tel: 973-690-3606; Fax: 973-690-3601. HAROLD G. STERLING, Esq., Chm.

The Hospital Center at Orange—Tel: 973-690-3606; Fax: 973-690-3601. HAROLD G. STERLING, Esq., Chm.

Cathedral/Columbus Group, Inc.—Tel: 973-690-3606; Fax: 973-690-3601. Rev. Msgr. RONALD J. ROZNIAK, V.G., P.A., Chm.

Cathedral Affiliated Group at Montclair, Inc.—Tel: 973-690-3606; Fax: 973-690-3601. Rev. Msgr. JOSEPH T. SLINGER, Ph.D., Chm.

Montclair Community Hospital—Tel: 973-690-3606; Fax: 973-690-3601. Rev. Msgr. JOSEPH T. SLINGER, Ph.D., Chm.

Commissions and Organizations

Bukas-Loob Sa Diyos Community (BLD) (Open to the Spirit of God)—321 Millburn Ave., Ste. 2, Millburn, 07041. Tel: 732-367-3848. Secretaries: FRANK BELLARMINO; SALLY BELLARMINO; Rev. PAUL J. LEHMAN, Spiritual Dir. (Retired). District Council of Stewards: NESTOR LAXINA; BECBEC LAXINA; GEORGE DEL FIERRO; CATHY DEL FIERRO; LITO VIBAR; GIGI VIBAR.

Charismatic Renewal—5808 Kennedy Blvd., West New York, 07093. Tel: 201-867-5535. Rev. PHILIP J. ROTUNNO, Coord. English & Multicultural Prayer Groups.

Archdiocesan Commission of Christain Unity—Revs. LUKE A. EDELEN, O.S.B., Chm. Tel: 973-643-4800; PHILIP F. LATRONICO, M.A., M.Div., Exec. Sec. Tel: 201-935-6492.

The Community of God's Love—70 W. Passaic Ave., Rutherford, 07070. ROBERT ROLLER, Dir. Tel: 201-935-0344; Rev. PHILIP F. LATRONICO, M.A., M.Div., Chap. Tel: 201-935-6492.

Cursillo Movement—25 Perdue Ave., Oakland, 07436. Rev. THOMAS P. LIPNICKI, Spiritual Dir. Tel: 201-337-7596; KATHY GLOWSKI, Lay Dir. Tel: 201-836-2783; LINDA ARMONAITIS, Cursillo Sec., 504 River Renaissance, East Rutherford, 07073. Tel: 973-249-0049.

Archdiocesan Commission for Interreligious Affairs—Rev. Msgr. JOHN J. GILCHRIST, Chm. (Retired). Tel: 973-941-3593; Rev. PHILIP F. LATRONICO, M.A., M.Div., Exec. Sec. Tel: 201-935-6492.

Archdiocesan Commission on Justice and Peace—Deacon WILLIAM TOTH, Ph.D., Chm.; KAY FURLANI, Exec. Sec. Tel: 973-497-4341.

Archdiocesan Liturgical Commission—Rev. Msgr. GERARD H. MCCARREN, S.T.D., Chm. Tel: 973-497-4345. Members: Rev. Msgr. BEAUBRUN ARDOUIN; Rev. ANTONIO I. BICO, S.T.D.; MARY CLINTON; Rev. THOMAS A. DENTE; ANITA FOLEY; Rev. Msgrs. RICHARD F. GRONCKI; CHARLES W. GUSMER, S.T.D., V.E.; HOLLY LAWMASTER; Rev. Msgr. JOSEPH P. MASIELLO, V.F.; Rev. CHARLES MILLER; JOHN J. MILLER; Revs. CHARLES PINYAN; NEIL XAVIER O'DONOGHUE, Ph.D.; NIVEDDITA SRINIVASA.

Magnificat, A Ministry to Catholic Women—160 Jefferson Ave., Emerson, 07630. Tel: 201-262-1122. Email: grand174@aol.com. Rev. PAUL A. CANNARIATO, Spiritual Advisor; ELIZABETH TOBIN, Coord.; MELANIE SUTER, Asst. Coord.; PATRICIA PATTERMAN, Treas.; GAIL ARTOLA, Sec.

Commission for the Men's Apostolate—45 S. Springfield Ave., Springfield, 07081. Tel: 973-376-3044. Rev. Msgr. WILLIAM C. HATCHER, Chm.

Pontifical Mission Societies—

Propagation of the Faith; Society of St. Peter the Apostle; Holy Childhood Association; Missionary Union of Priests & Religious—Fax: 973-497-4371. Rev. Msgr. ROBERT J. FUHRMAN, Dir. Tel: 973-497-4375; Sr. ARLINE ZURICH, O.S.B., Mission Moderator for Holy Childhood Assoc. Tel: 973-497-4376.

Archdiocesan Pro-Life Commission—1805 Penbrook Terr., Linden, 07036. Tel: 732-388-8211. JAMES SONDEY, Chm.

Renew International—1232 George St., Plainfield, 07062-1717. Tel: 908-769-5400; Fax: 908-769-5660. Email: renew@renewintl.org. Web: www.renewintl.org; www.parishlife.com; www.whycatholic.org; www.campusrenew.org; www.renewtot.org. Rev. Msgr. THOMAS A. KLEISSLER, Pres.; Sisters THERESA RICKARD, O.P., D.Min., Dir.; KATHLEEN (KASS) COLLINS, S.F.C.C., Asst. Dir.; HONORA NOLTY, O.P., Co Leader, Pastoral Svcs.; EILEEN CARMODY, P.B.V.M., Human Resources Admin.; KATHLEEN PHELAN, O.P., C.F.R.E., Dir. Devel.; MARY BETH ORIA, Business Mgr.; Sr. MARIE COOPER, S.J.C., Co Leader Pastoral Svcs.; ROBERT KELLY, Coord. Publications & Resources; DEIRDRE TRABERT MALACREA, Dir. Mktg. & Communications; Sr. MARY MCGUINNESS, O.P., Special Projects Coord.; RICHARD MICHALOWSKI, Finance Controller.

Archdiocesan Council of Catholic Women (N.C.C.W.)—Tel: 973-497-4356; Fax: 973-497-4317. MARY R. LOFTUS, Pres., 263 Concord Dr., Paramus, 07652. Tel: 201-265-2048. Email: loftusma@rcan.org; Rev. DENNIS E. REIFF, Moderator; MARGARET HENDERSON, First Vice Pres.; FRANCES DONNELLY, Second Vice Pres.; MARY ROEFARO, Recording Sec.; ETTA MARIE RIZZUTO, Corresponding Sec.; ADELE CICCONE, Treas.

District Moderators and Officers—Deacon NICHOLAS SIMONELLI, Bergen-Hackensack; CLARINDA BRUECK, Pres. Tel: 201-939-3855; Rev. DENNIS E. REIFF, Bergen-Paramus; FLORENCE HORGAN, Pres. Tel: 201-967-7614; VACANT, Essex-Suburban; ETTA MARIE RIZZUTO, Pres. Tel: 973-676-4725; AUDREY CALLIGY, Contact-Hudson County. Tel: 201-659-5723; FRANCES DONNELLY, Contact-Essex County. Tel: 908-688-1032.

Archdiocesan Women's Commission—PAMELA MUELLER-SWARTZEBERG, Chm.; LORETTA LOVELL, Administrative Asst. Tel: 973-497-4010. Members: ANN BURGMEYER; MARTA CABRERA; MARY ELAINE CONNELL; ANNA GROVES; CATHERINE L'INSALATA, M.S., C.S.W.; Sr. MARGARET T. MCGOVERN, O.P.; CHRISTINE FLAHERTY; HOLLY LAWMASTER; LILIANA SOTO; NIVEDITA SRINIVAS.

Miscellaneous Organizations in the Archdiocese

Affirmative Action—5 Becker Farm Rd., Roseland, 07068. Tel: 973-994-1700. CHARLES M. CARELLA, Esq., Counselor at Law, Officer.

Archdiocesan/University Archives—Seton Hall University, Walsh Library, 400 S. Orange Ave., South Orange, 07079. Tel: 973-761-9476; Fax: 973-761-9550. Rev. Msgr. FRANCIS R. SEYMOUR, Archdiocesan Archivist. Tel: 973-761-9126. Email: seymoufr@shu.edu; ALAN DELOZIER, University Archivist. Tel: 973-275-2378. Email: delozial@shu.edu; Dr. KATHLEEN DODDS, Archival Asst. Tel: 973-761-9476. Email: doddskat@shu.edu.

Censores Librorum—Rev. Msgr. CHARLES W. GUSMER, S.T.D., V.E.; Rev. DONALD E. BLUMENFELD, Ph.D.;

Rev. Msgr. JAMES M. CAFONE, S.T.D.; Rev. THOMAS G. GUARINO, S.T.D.; Rev. Msgr. GERARD H. MCCARREN, S.T.D.; Rev. LAWRENCE B. PORTER, Ph.D.; Rev. Msgrs. JOSEPH R. REILLY, S.T.L., Ph.D.; C. ANTHONY ZICCARDI, S.T.L., S.S.L.

Holy Name Federation—1805 Penbrook Terr., Linden, 07036. Tel: 908-486-6363. Rev. Msgr. JOHN J. LAFERRERA, Essex-West Hudson County Dir.; Revs. RICHARD J. CARRINGTON, Hudson County Dir.; JOSEPH G. SHEEHAN, Union County Dir. (Retired).

Legion of Mary—

Archdiocese of Newark Commitium—St. Michael's Church, 172 Broadway, Newark, 07104. Tel: 973-484-7100. Rev. ENZIO ANTUNES, S.D.V., Spiritual Dir.

Bergen County Curia—Our Lady of the Most Holy Eucharist Curia of Bergen County. VACANT, Spiritual Dir.

Hispanic Curia of Essex and Union Counties—Saint Lucy, 118 Seventh Ave., Newark, 07104. Tel: 973-482-6663. Rev. CARLOS VIEGO, Spiritual Dir.

Hispanic Curia of Hudson County—Rev. FELIPE LOPEZ, Dir., 3900 New York Ave., Union City, 07087.

Maria Immaculata Curia of Hudson County—St. John Vianney Residence, 60 Home Ave., Rutherford, 07070. Tel: 201-933-5155. Rev. JAMES W. MCFARLAND, Spiritual Dir. (Retired).

Our Lady, Gate of Heaven Curia (Korean)—257 Central Ave., Orange, 07050. Tel: 973-672-6650. Rev. Msgr. AUGUSTIN PARK, Spiritual Dir. (Retired).

Mary Most Humble Curia (Korean)—VACANT, Spiritual Dir.

Our Lady Mother of God Curia (Korean)—Church of Korean Martyrs, 595 Saddle River Rd., Saddle Brook, 07663. Tel: 201-703-0080. Rev. Msgr. AUGUSTIN PARK, Spiritual Dir. (Retired).

New Jersey Historical Records Commission—Most Rev. DOMINIC A. MARCONI, D.D., Chm. (Retired); JOSEPH F. MAHONEY, Ph.D., Dir., Seton Hall University, Fahy Hall, 400 South Orange Ave., South Orange, 07079. Tel: 973-275-2773.

Our Lady of Fatima First Saturday Family—(Ministry to the Disabled) Revs. PETER J. PALMISANO, Chap., Our Lady of Mount Virgin Rectory, 188 MacArthur Ave., Garfield, 07026. Tel: 973-772-2295; KEVIN E. CARTER, Chap., Saint Nicholas Rectory, 122 Ferry St., Jersey City, 07307. Tel: 201-659-5354.

Pastoral Association for Music & Liturgy—Mr. ANDREW CYR.

Serra Clubs—GEORGE KINGSTON, Regl. Representative, 12 Stonegate Dr., Mount Holly, 08060; ANTHONY ORTWEIN, Deputy Regl. Representative, 755 Johnston Dr., Bethlehem, PA 18017; JOSEPH PAGANO, Governor, District 22, 469 Teal Pl., Secaucus, 07094.

Serra Club of Bergen County—Dr. MARY NORTON, 116 Boston Ave., North Arlington, 07031; Rev. JOSEPH M. QUINLAN, Chap. (Retired).

Serra Club of the Oranges—ROSE MARIE DEEHAN, 331 S. Ridgewood Rd., South Orange, 07079; Rev. Msgr. THOMAS P. NYDEGGER, Ed.D., M.Div., Chap.

Serra Club of Union County West—JOSEPH DUNA; JOHN SALVO, 139 Stoneridge Rd., New Providence, 07974. Tel: 908-289-7979; Rev. ALEX PINTO, Chap.

Serra Club of West Essex—DAVID O'BOYLE, 45 Musano Ct., West Orange, 07052; Rev. DANIEL A. DANIK, Chap. (Retired).

Serra Club of North Essex—Rev. WARD P. MOORE, St. Thomas More Parish, Fairfield, 07004.

Serra Club of Hudson County—VICTOR DONOFRIO, 121 W. 8th St., Bayonne, 07002. Tel: 201-858-8537; Rev. Msgr. LAWRENCE J. MILLER, Chap.

The Scholarship Fund for Inner City Children—Fax: 973-497-4282. GERARD O'CONNOR, Exec. Dir. Tel: 973-497-4579; HOPE LARSON, Dir. Donor Rels.; NANCY LOZANO, Database Mgr.; MARY FLANNERY, Exec. Asst.; VACANT, Finance Mgr. Tel: 973-497-4581.

Archdiocesan School Council Membership Roster 2008-2009—Mrs. DONNA J. BABOULIS, Esq., Pres.; Mrs. ELLEN SHORT, Vice Pres.; Bro. RALPH DARMENTO, F.S.C., Deputy Supt. of Schools Liaison to Council; Mrs. KAY GRUSENSKI, Sec. Members: Mrs. ROSE BRIZAN; Ms. CATHERINE M. COWLEY; Mrs. PATRICIA DRIMONES; Mrs. PATRICIA GAGLIARDI ESQ.; Dr. MADELYN M. HEALY; Mr. JAMES MCKENNA; Mr. KEVIN LYONS; Ms. AGATHA NIEMIEC; Mr. LOUIS PANICO; Mr. BRIAN MURPHY; Ms. PAULA FRANZESE ROSELLA ESQ.; Mr. MARK SWARTZBERG.

CLERGY, PARISHES, MISSIONS AND PAROCHIAL SCHOOLS

CITY OF NEWARK

1—CATHEDRAL BASILICA OF THE SACRED HEART (1898) Rev. Msgrs. Richard F. Groncki, Rector; James M. Sheehan; Rev. Giuseppe Fedele, Parochial Vicar; Deacons Thomas DeBenedictis; Guy W. Mier; Michael J. Keary; Eduardo Pons; Francisco Rodriquez. In Res., Most Rev. John J. Myers; Rev. Msgrs. John E. Doran; Michael A. Andreano.
Res.: 89 Ridge St., 07104. Tel: 973-484-4600; Fax: 973-483-8253. Web: www.cathedralbasilica.org.

2—ST. ALOYSIUS (1877) Revs. Paulo Frade; Elky Reyes Pichardo.
Res.: 66 Fleming Ave., 07105. Tel: 973-344-4736; Fax: 973-522-1169.
Catechesis/Religious Program—Students 160.

3—ST. ANN (1886) Merged with St. Rocco's, Newark to form The Parish of the Transfiguration, Newark.

4—ST. ANTONINUS (1875) Rev. William J. Halbing; Deacon Rajgopal K. Srinivasa; Gerard Cleffi, Pastoral Assoc. In Res., Revs. Paul J. Lehman, Pastor Emeritus (Retired); Michael Fugee.
Res.: 337 South Orange Ave., 07103. Tel: 973-623-0258; Fax: 973-623-0694. Email: st_antoninus@msn.com.
Catechesis/Religious Program—Students 16.

5—ST. AUGUSTINE'S (1874), (German), Rev. Manoel J. Oliveira, Admin.
Church Office: P.O. Box 7126, 07107. Tel: 973-482-1817; Fax: 973-482-1817.
Convent—Sisters Missionaries of Charity, 168 Sussex Ave., 07103. Tel: 973-483-0165.
Soup Kitchen and Women's Shelter Queen of Peace—170 Sussex Ave., 07103. Tel: 973-481-9056.
Catechesis/Religious Program—Students 60.

6—ST. BENEDICT'S (1854) Revs. Manoel J. Oliveira; Mate Skublics; Sr. Ann Jerome Kociolek, O.P., Pastoral Assoc. In Res., Rev. Javier Losarcos.
Res.: 65 Barbara St., 07105. Tel: 973-589-7930; Fax: 973-589-3665.
See Ironbound Catholic Academy, Newark under St. Casimir's, Newark for details.
Catechesis/Religious Program—Students 125.

7—BLESSED SACRAMENT-ST. CHARLES BORROMEO (1905), (African American), Rev. Msgr. Anselm I. Nwaorgu; Rev. Longinus N. Ugwuegbulem.
Res.: 15 Van Ness Pl., 07108. Tel: 973-824-6548; Fax: 973-624-6030. Web: www.bssc.fatcow.com.
Catechesis/Religious Program—Email: bsscbchurch@yahoo.com. Web: www.bsscbchurch-.com. Students 25.

8—ST. BRIDGET'S (1887) Merged with St. Patrick's Pro-Cathedral. Records located at St. Patrick's, Newark. Tel: 973-623-0497.

9—ST. CASIMIR'S (1908), (Polish), Rev. Andrew Ostaszewski.
Res.: 164 Nichols St., 07105-2596. Tel: 973-344-2743; Fax: 973-344-8182. Email: stcrectory@stcasimirrcc.com.
School—Ironbound Catholic Academy (1910), Serves St. Benedict's, St. Casimir's, Immaculate Heart of Mary, St. James, and Our Lady of Mt. Carmel, Newark., 380 E. Kinney St., 07105. Tel: 973-589-0108; Fax: 973-589-0239. Mrs. Lorraine Novak, Prin. Lay Teachers 13; Students 209.
Catechesis/Religious Program—Tel: 973-849-1727. Maria Murano, D.R.E. Students 15.

10—ST. CHARLES BORROMEO'S (1910) Merged with Blessed Sacrament. Records located at Blessed Sacrament, Newark. Tel: 973-824-6548.

11—ST. COLUMBA'S (1869), (Hispanic), Revs. Luis O. Gonzalez; Andres Codoner Contell.
Res.: 25 Thomas St., 07114. Tel: 973-622-7712; Fax: 973-504-8075. Email: scolumba@verizon.net.
Catechesis/Religious Program—Dr. Mercedes Valle, D.R.E. Students 130.
Convent—Sisters of Charity, 7 South St., 07102. Tel: 973-622-7325.

12—ST. FRANCIS XAVIER (1914) [JC] Revs. Jan Sasin; Romeo Panes, O.S.J.
Res.: 243 Abington Ave., 07107-2598. Tel: 973-482-8410; Fax: 973-485-7471. Email: xavier@familink.net.
School—(1924), (Grades PreK-8), 594 N. Seventh St., 07107. Tel: 973-482-9410; Fax: 973-482-2466. Maestre Pie Filippini (Religious Teachers Filippini) 2; Lay Teachers 12; Students 254.
Catechesis/Religious Program—Sr. Clare Ricciardelli, M.P.F., D.R.E. Students 306.
Convent—Tel: 973-484-5200.

13—HOLY TRINITY (1901), (Lithuanian), Merged with Epiphany, Newark. Sacramental records located at Holy Trinity - Epiphany, Newark.

14—HOLY TRINITY - EPIPHANY (1992), (Portuguese), Rev. J. Bosco Lima, Admin.
Rectory—Holy Trinity - Epiphany, 207 Adams St., 07105. Tel: 973-491-9761; Fax: 973-344-5641.
Catechesis/Religious Program—Students 94.

15—IMMACULATE CONCEPTION (1925), (Italian), Rev. Luis P. Gonzalez. In Res., Rev. Owen F. Ince; Very Rev. John F. Connor (Retired).
Office & Res.: 654 Summer Ave., 07104. Tel: 973-482-1274; Fax: 973-482-8257. Web: olgc-ic.org.
Catechesis/Religious Program—Mariana Villegas, D.R.E. Students 68.

16—IMMACULATE HEART OF MARY (1926), (Spanish), Revs. Luis A. Vargas, T.O.R. (Peru); Lucio Nontol, T.O.R. (Peru), Parochial Vicar; Deacon Miguel Loperena.
Res.: 114 Prospect St., 07105. Tel: 973-589-8249; Fax: 973-589-1858. Email: heart.of.mary@verizon.net.
See Ironbound Catholic Academy, Newark under St. Casimir's, Newark for details.
Catechesis/Religious Program—121 Congress St., 07105. Tel: 973-589-5794; Fax: 973-589-0154. Mrs. Lupe Rivera, D.R.E. Students 360.

17—ST. JAMES (1854), (Brazilian—Portuguese), Revs. Clement M. Krug, C.Ss.R.; Marcos Vinicius T. Borges, C.Ss.R. (Brazil); Gerard Oberle, C.Ss.R.; Celso Martins Jr., C.Ss.R.
Parish Center & Mailing Address: 142 Jefferson St., 07105. Tel: 973-344-8322; Fax: 973-344-6158.
See Ironbound Catholic Academy, Newark under St. Casimir's, Newark for details.
Rectory—143 Madison St., 07105.
Catechesis/Religious Program—Sr. Hilaria de Oliveira, O.S.F., D.R.E. Students 53.

18—ST. JOHN'S (1826) Rev. Msgr. Neil J. Mahoney; Barbara Moran, Pastoral Assoc.; Vincent Smith, Pastoral Assoc.; Andrew Burt, Pastoral Assoc. In Res., Rev. David S. McLaughlin.
Res.: 22 Mulberry St., P.O. Box 200147, 07102. Tel: 973-623-0822; Fax: 973-623-6804. Email: saint.johns@worldnet.att.net. Web: www.saintjohnsnewark.org.
Chapel—St. John's Chapel Gateway I, 07102.

19—ST. JOSEPH'S (1850) Closed. Records located at Seton Hall University Archives, South Orange. Tel: 973-761-9476; Fax: 973-761-9550.

20—ST. LUCY'S (1891), (Italian), Rev. Luigi Zanotto, M.C.C.J.; Rev. Msgr. Joseph J. Granato, Pastor Emeritus; Revs. Carlos M. Viego; Stephen Aribe; Deacon Louis Loffredo Jr.
Res.: 118 Seventh Ave., 07104. Tel: 973-482-6663; Fax: 973-482-6575. Email: stlucysnwk@verizon.net. Web: www.saintlucy.net.
Catechesis/Religious Program—Tel: 973-482-6663; Fax: 973-482-6575. Alba Rose Colucci, D.R.E. Students 350.

21—ST. MARY MAGDALENE (1893) Closed. Records located at Seton Hall University Archives, South Orange. Tel: 973-761-9476; Fax: 973-761-9550.

22—ST. MARY'S (1842), (Newark Abbey Church) Very Rev. Philip J. Waters, O.S.B.; Rev. Linus V. Edogwo (Nigeria); Sr. Linda Klaiss, S.S.J., Pastoral Assoc.
Res.: 528 Martin Luther King, Jr. Blvd., 07102. Tel: 973-792-5793; Fax: 973-643-6922. Email: pwaters@sbp.org. Web: www.smpnewark.org.
School—Tel: 973-792-5749; Fax: 973-286-3873. Sr. Teresa Shaw, S.S.J., Prin. Sisters of St. Joseph of Chestnut Hill 3; Lay Teachers 16; Students 260.
Catechesis/Religious Program— Sr. Linda Klaiss, S.S.J., D.R.E. Students 36.

23—ST. MICHAEL'S (1878) Revs. Antonio L. da Silva, S.D.V. (Brazil); Rijo Johnson, S.D.V. (India); Javier Flores, S.D.V. (Venezuela); Deacons Daniel Ravelo; Restituto Quintana; Cecilio S. Polanco; Miguel Figueroa; Jose A. Negron.
Res.: 25 Crittenden St., 07104. Tel: 973-484-7100; Fax: 973-482-7209. Email: smc172broadway@yahoo.com. Web: www.saintmichaelparish.com.
School—(1881) 27 Crittenden St., 07104. Tel: 973-482-7400; Fax: 973-482-1833. Web: www.stmichael-nwkpenguins.com. Linda C. Cerino, Prin. Sisters of St. Martha 3; Lay Teachers 24; Students 515.
Perpetual Help Day Nursery—170 Broad St., 07104. Tel: 973-484-3535; Fax: 973-484-2526. Vocationist Sisters 7; Lay Teachers 13; Children 140.
Catechesis/Religious Program—Tel: 973-482-1109; Fax: 973-482-7209. Sr. Joy Sabesaje, S.D.V., D.R.E. Students 375.
Convent—Tel: 973-484-5261 (Sisters of St. Martha); 973-484-3535 (Vocationist Sisters).

24—OUR LADY OF FATIMA (1956), (Portuguese), Revs. Antonio F. DaSilva; Jorge Amaro; Antonio Nuno Rocha; Deacon Albino P. Marques.
Res.: 82 Congress St., 07105. Tel: 973-589-8433; Fax: 973-589-2611.
See Ironbound Catholic Academy, Newark under St. Casimir's, Newark for details.
Day Nursery—79 Jefferson St., 07105. Tel: 973-589-1639.
Catechesis/Religious Program—Mary Jo Branco, D.R.E. Students 4.

25—OUR LADY OF GOOD COUNSEL (1902) Rev. Luis P. Gonzalez; Deacons Oscar Rivera; Jose Rodriguez. In Res., Rev. Msgr. Joseph P. Plunkett (Retired); Very Rev. John F. Connor (Retired).
Res.: 654 Summer Ave., 07104. Tel: 973-482-1274; Fax: 973-482-8257. Web: olgc-ic.org.
See Christ the King Preparatory School of Newark, N.J., Corp. in the Institution Section under High Schools, Private for details.
Catechesis/Religious Program—Mariana Villegas, D.R.E. Students 195.

26—OUR LADY OF MT. CARMEL (1889), (Italian), Rev. Msgr. Joseph F. Ambrosio; Rev. Anthony Forte, Parochial Vicar. In Res., Rev. Nicholas G. Figurelli.
Res.: 259 Oliver St., 07105. Tel: 973-589-2090; Fax: 973-589-2662. Email: mtcarmel259@optonline.net. Web: www.ourladyofmtcarmelnewark.e-paluch.com.
See Ironbound Catholic Academy, Newark under St. Casimir's, Newark for details.
Catechesis/Religious Program—Regina Oliveira, D.R.E. Students 27.

27—OUR LADY OF THE ROSARY (1918), (Italian), Closed. For inquiries for parish records contact Our Lady of Mt. Carmel, Newark. Tel: 973-589-2090.

28—THE PARISH OF THE TRANSFIGURATION Rev. Josephat Kato Kalema, O.C.S.O. (Uganda), Admin.; Deacons Justo Rodriguez; Cesar A. Ortega-Escobar. 103 16th Ave., 07103. Tel: 973-642-4217. In Res., Rev. Eustace Edomobi (Nigeria).

29—ST. PATRICK'S PRO-CATHEDRAL (1848) Rev. Msgr. Neil J. Mahoney; Deacon Leonides Aponte; Evelyn De Jesus, Admin. Asst.
Mailing Address: 91 Washington St., 07102.
Res.: 39 Bleeker St., 07102. Tel: 973-623-0497; Fax: 973-623-2030. Email: evelydjss@aol.com.
Catechesis/Religious Program—Students 28.

30—ST. PETER'S (1864) Closed. For inquiries for parish records contact Seton Hall University Archives, South Orange. Tel: 973-761-9476; Fax 973-761-9550.

31—ST. PHILIP NERI (1887) Closed. For inquiries for parish records contact Seton Hall University Archives, South Orange. Tel: 973-761-9476; Fax 973-761-9550.

32—QUEEN OF ANGELS (1930), (African American), Rev. James J. McConnell, S.M.A.; Deacon Willie E. Moore Jr., (Retired); Tracey G. Battles, Pastoral Assoc.
Res.: 44 Irvine Turner Blvd., 07103. Tel: 973-642-1610; Fax: 973-642-0755. Email: queenofangelsrc@msn.com.
School—40 Irvine Turner Blvd., 07103. Tel: 973-642-1531; Fax: 973-622-0472. Everlyn V. Hay, Prin. Lay Teachers 11; Students 201.
Catechesis/Religious Program—Tel: 973-372-4992; Fax: 973-642-1610. Students 30.

33—ST. ROCCO'S (1899) Merged with St. Ann, Newark to form The Parish of the Transfiguration, Newark.

34—ST. ROSE OF LIMA (1888) Rev. Msgr. William J. Linder; Rev. Robert J. Cormier, Parochial Vicar; Deacon Alejandro Estremera; Sisters Monica Alvarado, Pastoral Assoc.; Pauline Echebiri, Pastoral Assoc.; Ms. Madge Wilson, Pastoral Assoc.
Res.: 11 Gray St., 07107. Tel: 973-482-0682; Fax: 973-482-2137. Email: linder@newcommunity.org.
Catechesis/Religious Program—Sr. Madestus Obasi, D.R.E. Students 217.
Convent—Tel: 973-481-5582; 973-481-6717.

35—SACRED HEART (Vailsburg) (1892) Revs. Frederick A. Pfeifer, Admin.; William C. Reed; Deacon Carlos Valentin; Cynthia Williams, Business Admin.
481 Sanford Ave., 07106. Tel: 973-373-9790; Fax: 973-373-3837. Email: shvailsburg@verizon.net. Web: www.sacredheart-vailsburg.org.
School—Saint Joseph School, 115 Telford St., East Orange, 07018. Tel: 973-674-2326. Mrs. Marion Alexander, Prin.
Catechesis/Religious Program—Dolores A. Thompson, Dir. Faith Formation.

36—ST. STANISLAUS (1889), (Polish), Rev. Bogumil Chrusciel.
Res.: 146 Irvine Turner Blvd., 07103. Tel: 973-642-7961; Fax: 973-642-2295. Email: ststannk@optonline.net.

37—ST. STEPHEN'S (1902) Closed. For inquiries for parish records contact Seton Hall University Archives, South Orange. Tel: 973-761-9476; Fax: 973-761-9550.

38—ST. THOMAS AQUINAS (1957), (Hispanic), Rev. Raul E.L. Comesanas; Deacon Mario Eschavarria.
Res.: 40 Ludlow St., 07114. Tel: 973-242-6703; Fax: 973-242-7143.
Catechesis/Religious Program—Ms. Madeline Santiago, D.R.E. Students 65.

OUTSIDE THE CITY OF NEWARK

ALLENDALE, BERGEN CO., GUARDIAN ANGEL (1954) Rev. Charles Pinyan.
Res.: 320 Franklin Turnpike, 07401. Tel: 201-327-4359; Fax: 201-327-6478. Email: gachurch@guardianangelchurch.org. Web: www.guardianangelallendale.parishesonline.com.
Catechesis/Religious Program—Tel: 201-327-0352. Email: inayden@guardianangelchurch.org. Irene Nayden, D.R.E. Students 399.

BAYONNE, HUDSON CO.

1—ST. ANDREW'S (1914) Rev. Msgr. Paul D. Schetelick; Rev. John R. Doherty, Pastor Emeritus (Retired). In Res., Revs. Thomas M. Foye (Retired); John R. Barno.
Res.: 125 Broadway, 07002. Tel: 201-437-0833; Fax: 201-858-3477. Email: andrew3513@aol.com. Web: www.saintandrewsparish.com.
See All Saints Catholic Academy, Bayonne under St. Mary Star of the Sea
Catechesis/Religious Program—Students 240.

2—ST. HENRY'S (1889) Most Rev. Thomas A. Donato; Revs. Robert James Gelinas; Richard J. Berbary.
Res.: 82 W. 29th St., 07002. Tel: 201-436-0857; Fax: 201-823-4611. Email: sthenryrc@verizon.net. Web: www.sthenry.net.
See All Saints Catholic Academy, Bayonne under St. Mary Star of the Sea
Catechesis/Religious Program—Avenue C & 28 St., 07002. Tel: 201-339-0319. Marie Pope, C.R.E. Students 440.

3—ST. JOSEPH'S (1888), (Slovak), Merged with St. Michael's, Bayonne to form Saint Michael/Saint Joseph Parish, Bayonne.

4—ST. MARY STAR OF THE SEA (1861) Rev. Msgr. Lawrence J. Miller; Revs. Thomas P. Conheeney; Jose Manuel De la Pena.
Res.: 326 Avenue C, 07002. Tel: 201-437-4090; Fax: 201-437-0388. Email: stmaryss@optonline.net.
School—All Saints Catholic Academy (2008), (Grades PreK-8), 19 W. 13th St., 07002. Tel: 201-443-8384; Fax: 201-437-6084. Sr. Eileen Jude Wust, S.S.J., Prin. Lay Teachers 23; Students 498.
Catechesis/Religious Program—Tel: 201-437-0010. Ms. Philomena Coco, D.R.E. Students 90.

5—ST. MICHAEL'S (1907), (Lithuanian), Merged with St. Joseph, Bayonne to form Saint Michael/Saint Joseph Parish, Bayonne.

6—SAINT MICHAEL AND SAINT JOSEPH Revs. Gerard Michael Lombardo; John J. Gibbons, Pastor Emeritus (Retired); Rev. Msgr. Edward M. Matash, Pastor Emeritus (Retired), St. John Vianney Residence, 60 Home Ave., Rutherford, 07070. Tel: 201-438-2984; Rev. Czeslaw Zalubski.
Res.: 15-21 E. 23rd St., 07002-3737. Tel: 201-436-1412; Fax: 201-436-5979.
Rectory—42 E. 25th St., 07002. Tel: 201-436-5981 (Office); Fax: 201-436-5983. In Res., Rev. J. M. Patricius, Hospital Chap. (Retired).
See All Saints Catholic Academy, Bayonne under St. Mary Star of the Sea
Catechesis/Religious Program—Barbara Godfrey, D.R.E.; Ms. Kathryn Sullivan, Youth Min. Students 50.

7—MT. CARMEL (1898), (Polish), [CEM] Rev. Msgr. Ronald J. Marczewski; Revs. Robert A. Pachana; Gregorz Poliadlo; Ernest G. Rush.
Res.: 39 E. 22nd St., 07002. Tel: 201-339-2070; Fax: 201-339-3676. Web: www.olmc.bayonne.net.
See All Saints Catholic Academy, Bayonne under St. Mary Star of the Sea
Catechesis/Religious Program—Students 92.

8—OUR LADY OF THE ASSUMPTION (1902), (Italian), Revs. Joseph F. Barbone; Thomas D. Nicastro Jr., Parochial Vicar; Deacon William Giordano. In Res., Rev. Thomas C. Roberts.
Res.: 93 W. 23rd St., 07002-2621. Tel: 201-436-8160; Fax: 201-436-4135. Email: olassumption@hotmail.com. Web: www.olassumption.org.
Church: 91 W. 23rd St., 07002-2621. Fax: 201-436-3145.
See All Saints Catholic Academy, Bayonne under St. Mary Star of the Sea
Catechesis/Religious Program—Tel: 201-437-1867; Fax: 201-436-4897. Marco Guerrero, D.R.E. Students 375.

9—ST. VINCENT DE PAUL (1894) Revs. James M. Manos; Marvin S. Mejia, Parochial Vicar; Robert E. Tooman, Parochial Vicar; Deacon Michael P. Missaggia; Sr. Angelita Vazzano, C.S.J.B., Pastoral Assoc. In Res., Rev. Carl J. Arico (Retired).
Res.: 979 Ave. C, 07002. Tel: 201-436-2222; Fax: 201-437-5235.
See All Saints Catholic Academy, Bayonne under St. Mary Star of the Sea
Catechesis/Religious Program—Tel: 201-823-0184. Sr. Claudette Marie Jaszczynski, C.S.J.B., D.R.E. Students 335.

BELLEVILLE, ESSEX CO.

1—ST. ANTHONY'S (1901), (Italian), Revs. Joseph A. Ferraro; Edito Gamallo; Dave Thomas N. Sison; Deacon Louis Acocella.
Res.: 750 N. Seventh St., 07107. Tel: 973-481-1991; Fax: 973-481-1993.
Church: 63 Franklin St., 07109.
Catechesis/Religious Program—25 N. 7th St., 07109. Tel: 973-751-0549. Students 179.

2—ST. PETER'S (1837) [CEM] Revs. Ivan Sciberras; Mark A. O'Connell; Deacons William Valladares; Julio Roig, (Retired).
Res.: 155 William St., 07109. Tel: 973-751-2002; Fax: 973-751-6201.
School—(1854), (Grades PreK-8), 152 William St., 07109. Tel: 973-759-3143; Fax: 973-759-4160. Marilyn Castellano, Prin. Lay Teachers 11; Students 195.
Catechesis/Religious Program—Tel: 973-751-4290. Students 406.
Retreat Center—149 Williams St., 07109.

BERGENFIELD, BERGEN CO., ST. JOHN THE EVANGELIST (1905) Rev. Msgr. Richard J. Arnhols; Revs. Ernesto C. Tibay; Raymond R. Filipski; Manuel Dueñas; Francesco Carraro.
Res.: 29 N. Washington Ave., 07621. Tel: 201-384-0101; Fax: 201-384-2055. Email: pastor@sjrc.org. Web: www.sjrc.org.
School—Transfiguration Academy - Lower Campus (2006), (Grades PreK-4), 10 Bradley Ave., 07621. Tel: 201-384-3627; Fax: 201-384-0293. Email: principal@transfigurationacademy.org. Web: www.transfigurationacademy.org. Sr. Madeline Hanson, S.S.N.D., Dir. Sisters of Notre Dame 1; Lay Teachers 15; Students 208.
Catechesis/Religious Program—15 N. Washington Ave., 07621. Tel: 201-384-3601; Fax: 201-384-9306. Web: www.sjrc.org. Rosemarie Flood, D.R.E. Students 760.

BERKELEY HEIGHTS, UNION CO., CHURCH OF THE LITTLE FLOWER (1955) Revs. Andrew M. Prachar; Marek Chachlowski (Poland); Michael A. Patete, (Asst. Weekends) (Retired); Deacons James P. Stumbar; Michael V. Montemurro.
Res. & Church: 110 Roosevelt Ave., 07922. Tel: 908-464-1585; Fax: 908-464-6342. Email: ebonacci@lfbhnj.org. Web: www.lfbhnj.org.
Catechesis/Religious Program—Tel: 908-464-7444. Students 761.

BLOOMFIELD, ESSEX CO.

1—CHURCH OF ST. THOMAS THE APOSTLE (1939) Revs. Charles J. Miller, O.F.M.; Philip A. Sanders, Parochial Vicar; Nnaemeka A. Onyemaobi; Mr. Robert Miller, Pastoral Assoc.; Timothy Dennin, Youth Min. In Res., Rev. Thomas F. Blind.
Res.: 60 Byrd Ave., 07003. Tel: 973-338-9190; Fax: 973-338-4224.
School—(1939), (Grades PreK-8), 50 Byrd Ave., 07003. Tel: 973-338-8505; Fax: 973-338-9565. Joan Ferraer, Prin.; Ann Bialkowski, Librarian. Sisters 1; Lay Teachers 20; Students 294.
Catechesis/Religious Program—Tel: 973-338-7400. Students 645.
Convent—55 Day St., 07003. Tel: 973-338-9118; Fax: 973-338-6495.

2—SACRED HEART (1878) [CEM] Revs. James T. Brown; Daniel A. Danik, Pastor Emeritus (Retired); Andrew J. Park; Deacon Jerry S. Rossi; Dr. Ryan Malone, Music Dir.
Res.: 76 Broad St., 07003. Tel: 973-748-1800; Fax: 973-748-2028. Email: sacredheart10@comcast.net. Web: sacredheartbloomfield.4lpi.com.
Catechesis/Religious Program—Tel: 973-743-4061. Nancy Plate, D.R.E. Students 170.

3—ST. VALENTINE (1899), (Polish), Rev. Juancho G. DeLeon; Deacon Joseph J. Malanga. In Res., Rev. John J. Donohue.
Res.: 125 N. Spring St., 07003. Tel: 973-743-0220; Fax: 973-743-2041.
Catechesis/Religious Program—Tel: 973-743-6122. Josephine Sarno, D.R.E. Students 215.

BOGOTA, BERGEN CO., ST. JOSEPH'S (1929) Revs. Richard Supple, O.Carm.; Paul Schweizer, O.Carm.; Ms. Mary Sause, Pastoral Assoc.; Deacons Walter Lynn; Michael Fitzgerald. In Res., Rev. Gregory Battafarano, O.Carm.
Res.: 115 E. Fort Lee Rd., 07603-1301. Tel: 201-342-6300; Fax: 201-883-9392.
School—(1925) 131 E. Fort Lee Rd., 07603-1301. Tel: 201-487-8641; Fax: 201-487-7405. James Newman, Prin. Lay Teachers 10; Students 241.
Catechesis/Religious Program—Tel: 201-343-4316; Fax: 201-883-9302. Patricia Rodriguez, D.R.E. Students 286.
Convent—Tel: 201-342-4684.

CALDWELL, ESSEX CO., ST. ALOYSIUS (1892) Rev. Msgr. Michael J. Desmond; Revs. Jacek J. Napora; Patrick R. Flannery; Deacon William J. McDermott; Joseph T. Wozniak, Music Min. In Res., Rev. Msgr. Benjamin A. Piazza (Retired).
Res.: 219 Bloomfield Ave., 07006. Tel: 973-226-0221; Fax: 973-226-2204. Email: stalscaldwell@verizon.net. Web: www.rc.net/newark/st_aloysius.
School—Trinity Academy (1991), (Grades PreK-8), 235 Bloomfield Ave., 07006. Tel: 973-226-3386; Fax:

973-226-6548. Mrs. Dorothy McMahon, Prin. (Co-Sponsored) Trinity Academy. Inter-Parochial Lay Teachers 32.
Catechesis/Religious Program—Tel: 973-226-0209; Fax: 973-226-0923. Edward Karpinski, D.R.E.; Sisters Agnes Egan, D.R.E. (Jr. High); Justine Pinto, O.P., Adult Educ. & Social Concerns. Students 880.

CEDAR GROVE, ESSEX CO., ST. CATHERINE OF SIENA (1949) Rev. Msgrs. Robert H. Slipe; Charles W. Gusmer, Pastor Emeritus; Revs. Piotr Koziolkiewicz, Parochial Vicar; Robert K. Suszko; Mrs. Carol Orlando, Pastoral Assoc.
Res.: 339 Pompton Ave., 07009. Tel: 973-239-7960; Fax: 973-239-1008. Email: stcatherine@scscedargrove.org.
School—(1958) 39 E. Bradford Ave., 07009. Tel: 973-239-6968. Celine Kerwin, Prin. Sisters of St. Dominic 1; Lay Teachers 20; Students 270.
Catechesis/Religious Program—Tel: 973-239-3332. Rosemary Couillou, D.R.E. Students 270.
Convent—Tel: 973-239-3362.

CLARK, UNION CO., ST. AGNES (1961) Revs. Dennis J. Cohan; Denis S. Surban. In Res., Rev. Donald K. Hummel.
Res.: 332 Madison Hill Rd., 07066. Tel: 732-388-7852; Fax: 732-388-7064. Email: stagneschurch@comcast.net. Web: www.stagnesparish.com.
School—(1963), (Grades PreK-8), 342 Madison Hill Rd., 07066. Tel: 732-381-0850; Fax: 732-381-1745. Web: stagnesschool.com. Sr. Claire Ouimet, M.P.F., Prin. Lay Teachers 16; Students 135.
Catechesis/Religious Program—Tel: 732-388-2560. Email: cff@stagnesparish.com. Sr. Margaret McDermott, S.S.J., D.R.E. Students 676.

CLIFFSIDE PARK, BERGEN CO., EPIPHANY (1916) Very Rev. Donald DiPasquale; Revs. James G. Tucker; Miroslaw Kusibab, C.S.M.A. (Poland).
Res.: 247 Knox Ave., 07010. Tel: 201-943-7320; Fax: 201-943-1779. Email: epiphanycp@juno.com.
Catechesis/Religious Program—263 Lafayette Ave., 07010. Students 110.

CLOSTER, BERGEN CO., ST. MARY (1911) Revs. Paul A. Cannaziato; John Z. Radwan.
Res.: 20 Legion Pl., 07624. Tel: 201-768-7565; Fax: 201-784-5814.
See Holy Family Catholic Academy, Norwood under Immaculate Conception, Norwood for details.
Catechesis/Religious Program—Tel: 201-767-8247. Mary Lowe, D.R.E. Students 170.

CRANFORD, UNION CO., ST. MICHAEL'S (1872) Rev. John P. McGovern; Rev. Msgr. Timothy J. Shugrue, Parochial Vicar; Rev. Edgardo P. Jocson; Rev. Msgr. Louis F. Fimiani (Retired); Deacon Daniel Wilverding; Joan F. Genova, Bus. Admin.
Res.: 40 Alden St., 07016. Tel: 908-276-0360; Fax: 908-272-0273.
School—(1929), (Grades PreK-8), Alden & Miln Sts., 07016. Tel: 908-276-9425; Fax: 908-276-4391. Allesandra Miragliotta, Prin.; Maria Singer, Librarian. Lay Teachers 24; Students 322.
Catechesis/Religious Program—100 Alden St., 07016. Tel: 908-276-2050. Lynda Furey, D.R.E. Students 1,603.

CRESSKILL, BERGEN CO., ST. THERESE OF LISIEUX (1925) Rev. Joseph O'Brien, O.Carm.; Deacon James Looby, Pastoral Assoc. In Res., Rev. Joseph McGowan, O.Carm.
Res.: 120 Monroe Ave., 07626. Tel: 201-567-2528; Fax: 201-567-6759. Email: therese1@optonline.net. Web: www.4sttherese.org.
School—(Grades PreK-8), 220 Jefferson Ave., 07626. Tel: 201-568-4296; Fax: 201-568-3179. Sr. Helene Byrne, M.F.I.C., Prin. Lay Teachers 15; Students 228.
Catechesis/Religious Program—200 Jefferson Ave., 07626. Tel: 201-567-4781; Fax: 201-541-1269. Lois Pagnozzi, D.R.E. Students 575.
Convent—Tel: 201-568-0100.

DEMAREST, BERGEN CO.
1—ST. JOSEPH (1989), (Korean), Merged with St. Joseph's, Demarest to form the Parish of St. Joseph, Demarest.
2—ST. JOSEPH'S (1931) Merged with St. Joseph, Demarest to form the Parish of St. Joseph, Demarest.
3—PARISH OF ST. JOSEPH (2008) Revs. Jungsoo Kim; Dong Kyum Kim; Donato Cabardo; Deacon James J. Puliatte.
Res. & Mailing Address: 573 Piermont Rd., 07627. Tel: 201-768-2371; Fax: 201-767-8874. Email: stjosephdemarest@gmail.com. Web: www.stjosephdemarest.com.
Catechesis/Religious Program—Students 360.
See Holy Family Catholic Academy, Norwood under Immaculate Conception, Norwood for details.

DUMONT, BERGEN CO., ST. MARY'S (1914) Revs. Robert G. Laferrera; Raul R. Gaviola. In Res., Rev. Onyedika Michael Otuwurunne.
Res.: 280 Washington Ave., 07628. Tel: 201-384-0557; Fax: 201-384-4986.
Catechesis/Religious Program—Tel: 201-384-3062. William J. Mascitello, D.R.E. Students 538.

EAST NEWARK, HUDSON CO., ST. ANTHONY'S (1901), (Italian), Very Rev. Michael G. Ward.
Res.: 409 N. Second St., 07029. Tel: 973-483-4680; Fax: 973-483-2396. Email: stanthony4@verizon.net.
Catechesis/Religious Program—Margaret A. Sanzo, D.R.E. Students 150.

EAST ORANGE, ESSEX CO.
1—HOLY NAME OF JESUS (1910) Revs. William G. Cook; Jude Caliba; Deacon Leo Woodruff.
Res.: 184 Midland Ave., 07017. Tel: 973-675-5901; Fax: 973-674-1767. Email: holynameeo@verizon.net.
Parish Center—200 Midland Ave., 07017-1855. Tel: 973-675-4444; Fax: 973-674-1767.
2—HOLY SPIRIT-OUR LADY HELP OF CHRISTIANS (1882), (African American—Haitian), Rev. Jean Max Osias, Admin.; Deacon Pierre J. Merceus.
Res.: 17 N. Clinton St., 07017. Tel: 973-673-1077; Fax: 973-676-6494.
School—(1883), (Grades PreK-8), 23 N. Clinton St., 07017. Tel: 973-677-1546; Fax: 973-677-3939. Sr. Patricia Hogan, O.P., Prin. Lay Teachers 14; Students 246.
Catechesis/Religious Program—Anita Hernandez, D.R.E. Students 75.
3—SAINT JOSEPH PARISH Rev. Frederick A. Pfeifer, Admin.; Deacons Alonzo C. Jackson; Carlos Valentin; Madeline Fuccille, Pastoral Assoc.
110 Telford St., 07018. Tel: 973-678-4030; Fax: 973-677-7875. Email: stjosepheo@intac.ocm.
School—Saint Joseph School, 115 Telford St., 07018. Tel: 973-674-2326. Mrs. Marion Alexander, Prin. Religious Teachers Filippini 2; Lay Teachers 22; Students 381.
4—OUR LADY OF ALL SOULS (1914) Closed. For inquiries for parish records contact Seton Hall University Archives, South Orange, Tel: 973-761-9476; Fax: 973-761-9550.
5—OUR LADY OF THE MOST BLESSED SACRAMENT (1916) Closed. For inquiries for parish records contact Seton Hall University Archives, South Orange. Tel: 973-761-9476; Fax: 973-761-9550.

EAST RUTHERFORD, BERGEN CO., ST. JOSEPH'S (1872) [CEM] Revs. Kevin Daly, O.F.M.; Zachary Elliott, O.F.M.; Sr. Marigene Kennedy, O.S.F., Pastoral Min. Tel: 201-939-0457.
Res.: 120 Hoboken Rd., 07073. Tel: 201-939-0457; Fax: 201-939-4196.
School—(1879), (Grades PreK-8), 20 Hackensack St., 07073. Tel: 201-939-3193; Fax: 201-939-1913. Mrs. Frances Alberta, Prin. Lay Teachers 13; Students 194.
Catechesis/Religious Program—Tel: 201-939-3441. Verna Paiotti, D.R.E. Students 424.

EDGEWATER, BERGEN CO., HOLY ROSARY (1906) Rev. George Ruane; Deacons Robert E. Thomson; Michael A. Lydon.
Res.: 365 Undercliff Ave., 07020. Tel: 201-945-6329 (Parish Center); Fax: 201-945-6599. Email: holyrosary@aol.com. Web: www.edgewateronlin.com/holyrosarychurch.
See Christ the Teacher Interparochial School, under Madonna, Fort Lee.
Catechesis/Religious Program—Linda Corona, D.R.E. Students 88.

ELIZABETH, UNION CO.
1—ST. ADALBERT'S (1905), (Polish), Merged with SS. Peter & Paul, Elizabeth to form Saint Adalbert/Saints Peter & Paul Parish, Elizabeth.
2—SAINT ADALBERT AND SAINTS PETER & PAUL, [CEM] Revs. Krzysztof Szczotka, S.D.S. (Poland); John Thottukulappananiyil, O.F.M.Cap.; Deacon Philip Rejrat.
Res.: 250 E. Jersey St., 07206. Tel: 908-352-2791; Fax: 908-354-2828. Email: office@stadalbert.us; pastor@stadalbert.us.
Catechesis/Religious Program—Ms. Agatha Niemiec, D.R.E. Students 40.
3—ST. ANTHONY'S (1895), (Italian), Revs. Patrick Diver, S.D.B.; Gennaro J. Sesto, S.D.B.; Richard Crager; Javier Aracil; Deacon Joseph Caporaso.
Res.: 853 Third Ave., 07202. Tel: 908-351-3300; Fax: 908-351-3609. Email: elizsdb@aol.com.
School—Our Lady of Guadalupe Academy, (Grades PreK-8), 227 Centre St., 07202. Tel: 908-352-7419; Fax: 908-352-7062. Sisters of Charity of Convent Station 1; Benedictine Sisters 4; Lay Teachers 18; Students 220.
Catechesis/Religious Program—Sr. M. Charitina Frabizio, S.C., D.R.E. Students 350.
Convent—Tel: 908-354-0825; Fax: 908-354-4451.
4—BLESSED SACRAMENT (1922) Rev. Fernando E. Guillen; Deacon Jose R. Fernandez; Cristina Pardo, Pastoral Assoc. In Res., Revs. Alejandro Lopez-Cardinale; Thomas R. McLaughlin.
Res.: 1096 North Ave., 07201. Tel: 908-352-0338; Fax: 908-352-4553.
See Our Lady of Guadalupe Academy under St. Anthony, Elizabeth.
Catechesis/Religious Program—Ms. Marylou Podolski, D.R.E. (English); Cristina Pardo, D.R.E. (Spanish). Students 211.
5—ST. GENEVIEVE'S (1920) Revs. George D. Gillen; Roy James DeLeo, Pastoral Assoc.; Ronnie Nombre (Philippines), Pastoral Assoc.; Joseph Khai Vu (Vietnam), Pastoral Assoc.
Res.: 200 Monmouth Rd., 07208. Tel: 908-351-4444; Fax: 908-351-5454. Email: stgens@optonline.net.
School—(1929), (Grades PreK-8), 209 Princeton Rd., 07208. Tel: 908-355-3355; Fax: 908-355-1460. Catherine Coyle, Prin. Lay Teachers 18; Students 339.
Catechesis/Religious Program—Tel: 908-355-1584. Students 177.
Convent—
6—ST. HEDWIG'S (1925), (Polish), Revs. Andrzej Zmarlicki; Piotr J. Maslanka.
Parish Office: 717 Polonia Ave., 07202. Tel: 908-352-1448; Fax: 908-352-8389.
Res.: 716 Clarkson Ave., 07202.
Church: 600 Myrtle St., 07202.
Religious Education Center—717 Polonia Ave., 07202. Michele Yamakaitis, D.R.E. Students 45.
7—HOLY ROSARY (1886) Merged Records at Our Lady of Most Holy Rosary/St. Michael, Elizabeth. Tel: 908-354-2454; Fax: 908-354-3207.
8—IMMACULATE CONCEPTION (1907) Revs. Jorge Chacon; Wilson Bello. In Res., Rev. Brendan Quinn.
Pastoral Center: 417 Union Ave., 07208. Tel: 908-352-6662; Fax: 908-352-8484. Web: iconceptionparish.org.
Res.: 425 Union Ave., 07208. Tel: 908-352-6662.
Catechesis/Religious Program—417 Union Ave., 07208. Tel: 908-351-4242. Students 161.
9—IMMACULATE HEART OF MARY (1947), (Hispanic), Merged with St. Patrick's, Elizabeth to form Immaculate Heart of Mary and Saint Patrick, Elizabeth.
10—IMMACULATE HEART OF MARY AND SAINT PATRICK (1858), (Hispanic), [CEM] Revs. Fabio De Jesus Brenes-Chaves; Justino Cornejo-Castillero; Deacon Nestor Charriez.
Res.: 215 Court St., 07206. Tel: 908-354-0023; Fax: 908-355-0526.
Raphael's Life House—231 Court St., 07206. Tel: 908-354-4750.
School—St. Patrick Academy, (Grades 5-8), 227 Court St., 07206. Tel: 908-351-2188; Fax: 908-351-6086. Joseph Picaro, Prin.; Ms. Kathleen Collura, Dir.
High School—(1863) 221 Court St., 07206. Tel: 908-353-5220; Fax: 908-629-1123. Joseph Picaro, Prin.; Rev. Dennis J. Kaelin, Campus Min. Brothers 1; Sisters 1; Lay Teachers 15; Students 233.
Catechesis/Religious Program—Students 241.
11—ST. JOSEPH'S (1911), (Slovak), Closed. Records at Holy Family, Linden. Tel: 908-862-1060.
12—ST. MARY OF THE ASSUMPTION (1844) [CEM] Rev. Msgr. Robert J. Harrington; Revs. John Martin; Esterminio Chica; Deacon Luis Carlos Lorza; Sr. Elaine Maguire, F.S.P., Pastoral Assoc.; Maria Castillo-Lorza, Pastoral Assoc. In Res., Rev. Msgr. Jeremias R. Rebanal (Retired).
Res.: 155 Washington Ave., 07202. Tel: 908-352-5154; Fax: 908-352-0350.
See Our Lady of Guadalupe Academy, Elizabeth under St. Anthony
High School—237 S. Broad St., 07202. Tel: 908-352-4350; Fax: 908-352-2359. Janet Malko, Prin.; Anna Rojas, Dir. Lay Teachers 18; Students 235.
Child Care Center—Tel: 908-355-8723. Students 35.
Catechesis/Religious Program—Tel: 908-352-0926. Ann Borden, D.R.E. Students 300.
Convent—Tel: 908-352-1455.
13—OUR LADY OF FATIMA (1973), (Portuguese), Rev. Msgr. John S. Antao; Rev. Jose Manuel Fernandes (Portugal). In Res., Rev. John F. Corbett.
Res.: 403 Spring St., 07201. Tel: 908-355-3810; Fax: 908-355-4791.
Catechesis/Religious Program—Tel: 908-477-0190. Students 701.
14—OUR LADY OF MOST HOLY ROSARY/ST. MICHAEL (1886/1852) [JC] Very Rev. John E. Wassell; Revs. Dieuseul Adain (Haiti); Zephyrin K. Katompa; Deacon Orlando Sanchez.
Res.: 52 Smith St., 07201. Tel: 908-354-2454; Fax: 908-354-3207. Email: secretary@holyrosarystmichael.com. Web: www.holyrosarystmichael.com.
Catechesis/Religious Program—Students 165.
15—ST. PATRICK, Merged with Immaculate Heart of Mary, Elizabeth to form Immaculate Heart of Mary and Saint Patrick, Elizabeth.
16—SS. PETER AND PAUL'S (1895), (Lithuanian), Merged with St. Adalbert, Elizabeth to form Saint Adalbert/Saints Peter & Paul Parish, Elizabeth.
17—SACRED HEART (1871) Merged Records at Our Lady of Fatima Parish, Elizabeth. Tel: 908-355-3810.

ELMWOOD PARK, BERGEN CO., ST. LEO'S (1931) Revs. Bartley Baker; James M. Moran, Parochial Vicar.
Res.: 324 Market St., 07407. Tel: 201-796-3521; Fax: 201-703-8408. Email: stleoschurch2001@yahoo.com. Web: www.stleosep.net.
School—(1912), (Grades PreK-8), 300 Market St., 07407. Tel: 201-796-5156; Fax: 201-796-2092. Web: www.stleonj.org. Elizabeth Pinto, Prin. Franciscan Sisters of Peace 1; Lay Teachers 15; Students 297.
Catechesis/Religious Program—William Schulenburg, Pastoral Assoc./Faith Formation. Students 188.
Convent—Tel: 201-797-6993.

EMERSON, BERGEN CO., CHURCH OF THE ASSUMPTION (1947) Revs. Dominick J. Lenoci; Camilo Lopez; Deacon John E. Hogan.
Res.: 29 Jefferson Ave., 07630. Tel: 201-262-1122; Fax: 201-262-7855. Email: church@assumptionacad.org. Web: www.geocities.com/assumption07630/church.
School—(Grades PreK-8), 35 Jefferson Ave., 07630. Tel: 201-262-0300; Fax: 201-262-5910. Dr. Maria Cleary, Prin. Sisters 1; Lay Teachers 19; Students 260.
Catechesis/Religious Program—Tel: 201-986-0970. Sr. Dominic Marie McDonnell, O.P., D.R.E. Students 500.

ENGLEWOOD, BERGEN CO., ST. CECILIA'S (1866) [JC] Revs. Hilary Milton, O.Carm.; Herman Kinzler, O.Carm., Parochial Vicar. In Res., Revs. Ashley J. Harrington, O.Carm.; Anthony Palo, O.Carm.; Robert A. Wolfe, O.Carm.
Res.: 55 W. Demarest Ave., 07631. Tel: 201-568-0364; Fax: 201-568-0654.
School—*St. Cecilia Interparochial School* (1874), (Grades PreK-8), 85 W. Demarest Ave., 07631. Tel: 201-568-2615; Fax: 201-568-7071. Ann Walsh, Prin. Lay Teachers 12; Students 140.
Catechesis/Religious Program—Tel: 201-568-7882. Esther Lara, D.R.E. Students 160.

FAIR LAWN, BERGEN CO., ST. ANNE'S (1909) Revs. Joseph C. Doyle; Colin Adrian Kay; Deacons Walter J. Maher; Richard M. McGarry.
Res.: 15-05 Saint Anne St., 07410. Tel: 201-791-1616; Fax: 201-791-1871.
School—(1949) 1-30 Summit Ave., 07410. Tel: 201-796-3353; Fax: 201-796-9058. Loretta Stachiotti, Prin. Lay Teachers 25; Students 316.
Catechesis/Religious Program—Donna Stickna, D.R.E. Students 783.

FAIRFIELD, ESSEX CO., ST. THOMAS MORE (1962) Revs. Ward P. Moore; Eugene Gniewyk; Deacons P. Aidan King; Dominick Messina; Gregory C. Quinn.
Res.: 210 Horseneck Rd., 07004. Tel: 973-227-0055; Fax: 973-227-2495. Email: stmparish@verizon.net. Web: www.stmchurch.net.
Catechesis/Religious Program—12 Hollywood Ave., 07004. Tel: 973-227-3607; Fax: 973-808-9032. Cabrina Kinslow, D.R.E. Students 712.

FAIRVIEW, BERGEN CO.

1—ST. JOHN THE BAPTIST (1873) Revs. Jose I. Gamba; Giordano Belanich; Gerardo Gallo; Deacons Anton Tarabokija; John C. Holoduek.
Res.: 239 Anderson Ave., 07022. Tel: 201-945-4865; Fax: 201-945-8171. Email: sjbhope@verizon.net.
Catechesis/Religious Program—Students 173.

2—OUR LADY OF GRACE (1913), (Italian), Very Rev. Peter T. Sticco, S.A.C.; Rev. Francis M. Gaetano, S.A.C.
Res.: 395 Delano Pl., 07022. Tel: 201-943-0904; Fax: 201-313-5616. Email: frpeter@nj.rr.com. Web: www.olgrc.org.
School—(Grades PreK-8), 400 Kamena St., 07022. Tel: 201-945-8300; Fax: 201-945-4580. Email: olgschool@olgfairview.org. Web: www.olgfairview.org. Sr. Alice Marie D'Onofrio, C.S.A.C., Prin. Lay Teachers 16; Students 260.
Catechesis/Religious Program—Tel: 201-945-1201. Students 150.
Convent—*St. Vincent Pallotti*, 545 Victory Ave., Ridgefield, 07657.

FORT LEE, BERGEN CO.

1—HOLY TRINITY (1906) Very Rev. Steven Conner; Revs. Edmundo Sombilon; Vinh Quang Nguyen; Peter Baratta Jr., Music Min.
Res.: 2367 Lemoine Ave., 07024-6269. Tel: 201-947-1216; Fax: 201-947-1217.
School—*Christ the Teacher Interparochial School*, (Grades PreK-8) Tel: 201-944-0421; Fax: 201-994-6293. Sr. Rosemarie Bartnicki, O.S.F., Prin. Co-Sponsored. (See Madonna Parish, Fort Lee).
Catechesis/Religious Program—Tel: 201-947-1216. Sr. Rose O'Brien, C.B.S., D.R.E. Students 181.
Convent—Tel: 201-944-2911.

2—MADONNA (1858) [CEM] Revs. Stephen A. Carey; Paul Kyung Lee.
Res.: 340 Main St., 07024. Tel: 201-944-2727; Fax: 201-944-5986. Email: madonnachurch@verizon.net.
School—*Christ the Teacher Interparochial School*, (Grades PreK-8), 359 Whiteman St., 07024. Tel: 201-944-0421; Fax: 201-944-6293. Sr. Rosemarie Bartnicki, O.S.F., Prin. Students 294.
Catechesis/Religious Program—*Madonna Religious Education Center*, Tel: 201-944-4266. Students 145.

FRANKLIN LAKES, BERGEN CO., MOST BLESSED SACRAMENT (1961) Most Rev. John W. Flesey; Rev. Renato J. Bautista.
Parish Center: 787 Franklin Lake Rd., 07417. Tel: 201-891-4200; Fax: 201-891-4243. Web: mostblessedsacrament.ws. In Res., Rev. Michael Donovan.
Res.: 835 High Mountain Rd., 07417. Tel: 201-848-9717.
School—(1963), (Grades PreK-8), 785 Franklin Lake Rd., 07417. Tel: 201-891-4250; Fax: 201-847-9227. Email: jmathews@rcmbs.org. Web: www.mbs4u.us. Ms. JoAnn Mathews, Prin. Lay Teachers 27; Students 248.
Catechesis/Religious Program—Tel: 201-891-8390. Marcia Klink, D.R.E. Students 672.
Convent—Fax: 201-891-4292.

GARFIELD, BERGEN CO.

1—CHURCH OF OUR LADY OF SORROWS (1917) Revs. Joy Alappat, Admin.; Michael Guba.
Res.: 69 Market St., 07026. Tel: 973-772-7889; Fax: 973-772-7806. Email: olosc@optonline.net.
Church: 30 Madonna Pl., 07026.
Catechesis/Religious Program—Tel: 973-478-4929. Kathleen Skrupskis, D.R.E. Students 175.

2—HOLY NAME (1911), (Hispanic), Rev. Msgr. William J. Reilly; Deacon Cesar Torres.
Res.: 99 Marsellus Pl., 07026. Tel: 973-340-0032; Fax: 973-340-1618.
Catechesis/Religious Program—Students 162.

3—OUR LADY OF MT. VIRGIN (1901), (Italian), Revs. Peter J. Palmisano; Pedro Bismarck Chau; Bro. James Konchalski, O.S.B.
Res.: 188 MacArthur Ave., 07026. Tel: 973-772-2295; Fax: 973-478-4389.
Catechesis/Religious Program— Sr. Jo Ann Jankowski, M.P.F., D.R.E. Students 124.
Convent—410 Maywood Ave., Maywood, 07607. Tel: 201-845-9568.

4—ST. STANISLAUS KOSTKA (1917), (Polish), Revs. Edward P. Szpiech; Marek Wiorkiewicz, S.D.S.; Mariusz G. Luksza; Piotr Haldas, S.D.S.
Res.: 184 Ray St., 07026. Tel: 973-772-7922; Fax: 973-772-4178. Email: ststankostka@optonline.net.
Catechesis/Religious Program—Tel: 973-772-7222. Ethel Kordosky, D.R.E. Students 265.
Convent—Tel: 973-772-4644.

GARWOOD, UNION CO., CHURCH OF ST. ANNE (1925) Rev. Richard A. Villanova.
Res.: 325 Second Ave., 07027. Tel: 908-789-0280; Fax: 908-789-3099. Email: saintanne@comcast.net. Web: www.churchofsaintanne.org.
Catechesis/Religious Program—Tel: 908-789-4745. Email: stannereled@comcast.net. Students 101.

GLEN ROCK, BERGEN CO., ST. CATHARINE (1953) Revs. Thomas S. Wisniewski; William F. Benedetto; Annette Gallagher, Pastoral Assoc.; Sally Trahan, Pastoral Assoc.; Rosemary Miller, Pastoral Assoc.; Deacons Leonard A. Minichino, Pastoral Assoc.; James A. Mueller, Pastoral Assoc.; John A. Sarno, Pastoral Assoc. In Res., Rev. Sebastian M. Fernando.
Res.: 905 S. Maple Ave., 07452. Tel: 201-445-3703; Fax: 201-670-7149. Email: parishoffice@stcatharinechurch.org. Web: www.stcatharinechurch.org.
School—*Academy of Our Lady*, (Grades PreK-8), 180 Rodney St., 07452. Tel: 201-445-0622; Fax: 201-445-8345. Email: principal@academyofourlady.org. Web: www.academyofourlady.org. Patricia Keenaghan, Prin. Lay Teachers 36; Students 445.
Catechesis/Religious Program—Tel: 201-444-5690; Fax: 201-445-8345. Email: religiouseducation@stcatharinechurch.org. Roberta Maguire, D.R.E. Students 820.

GUTTENBERG, HUDSON CO., ST. JOHN NEPOMUCENE (1910), (Slovak), Merged with Our Lady Help of Christians, West New York to form Holy Redeemer, West New York.

HACKENSACK, BERGEN CO.

1—CHURCH OF ST. FRANCIS OF ASSISI (1917), (Italian—Hispanic), Revs. Brian Tomlinson, O.F.M-.Cap.; Anthony Giudice, O.F.M.Cap.; Sam Frapaul, O.F.M.Cap.; Nancy Carucci, Pastoral Assoc.; Deacons Alejandro Polanco; Joseph G. Vrindten.
Res.: 50 Lodi St., 07601. Tel: 201-343-6243; Fax: 201-343-0854.
School—*Padre Pio Academy*, (Grades PreK-8), 100 S. Main St., 07601. Tel: 201-488-8862; Fax: 201-525-0498. Patricia Vrindten, Prin. Lay Teachers 25; Students 230.
Catechesis/Religious Program—Tel: 201-488-2614. Mr. Alex Collantes, D.R.E. Students 250.

2—HOLY TRINITY (1861) [CEM] Revs. Paul Prevosto; Patrick W. Donohue, Parochial Vicar; Jorge E. Acosta; Joseph Cheng; Sr. Emily Marie Walsh, S.C., Parish Min. In Res., Rev. David S. McLaughlin.
Res.: 34 Maple Ave., 07601. Tel: 201-343-5170; Fax: 201-343-5067. Email: churchholytrinity@yahoo.com. Web: www.holytrinitysite.org.
See Padre Pio Academy, Hackensack under Church of St. Francis of Assisi
Catechesis/Religious Program—Mrs. Carol Thee, D.R.E. Students 395.
Convent—Tel: 201-342-1996; Fax: 201-968-0035.

3—IMMACULATE CONCEPTION (1891) Rev. Gerard J. Graziano.
Res.: 49 Vreeland Ave., 07601. Tel: 201-440-2798; Fax: 201-440-6756. Email: immcon@verizon.net. Web: www.icchackensack.org.
See Padre Pio Academy under Church of St. Francis of Assisi, Hackensack.
Catechesis/Religious Program—Students 81.

4—ST. JOSEPH'S (1909), (Polish), Rev. Wieslaw P. Strzadala, S.D.S.
Res.: 460 Hudson St., 07601. Tel: 201-440-3224; Fax: 201-641-8685.
Catechesis/Religious Program—Agnieszka Barowicz, D.R.E. (Polish).

HARRINGTON PARK, BERGEN CO., OUR LADY OF VICTORIES (1910) Rev. Bryan F.J. Adamcik; Deacon Al McLaughlin.
Res.: 81 Lynn St., 07640-1831. Tel: 201-768-1706; Fax: 201-768-3962. Email: olvch@juno.com. Web: www.ourchurch.com/member/o/olvparish.
See Holy Family Catholic Academy, Norwood under Immaculate Conception, Norwood for details.
Catechesis/Religious Program—155 The Parkway, 07640-1820. Tel: 201-768-1400. Katherine Mazzacano, D.R.E. Students 330.
Convent—145 The Parkway, 07640-1820. Tel: 201-768-1705.

HARRISON, HUDSON CO.

1—HOLY CROSS (1865) Rev. Thomas Thottungal, Admin.; Rev. Msgr. John J. Gilchrist, Pastor Emeritus (Retired); Rev. Felix I. Filho (Brazil). In Res., Rev. Robert J. Cio.
Res.: 16 Church Sq., 07029. Tel: 973-484-5678; Fax: 973-484-0906. Email: hcsecretary@verizon.net.
See Mater Dei Academy, Kearny under St. Stephen
Catechesis/Religious Program—Frederick Osterkorn Jr., D.R.E. Students 160.
Convent—*Carmelite Friars*, 324 Jersey St., 07029. Tel: 973-485-7233.

2—OUR LADY OF CZESTOCHOWA (1908), (Polish), Revs. Rudolf Zubik; Marian Spanier, S.T.L.
Res.: 115 S. Third St., 07029. Tel: 973-483-2255; Fax: 973-483-4688. Email: rectory@olczestochowa.com. Web: www.olczestochowa.com.
Catechesis/Religious Program—Marzena Zmuda, D.R.E. Students 75.

HASBROUCK HEIGHTS, BERGEN CO., CORPUS CHRISTI (1897) Rev. Msgr. Lewis V. Papera; Revs. Raymond M. Holmes; Jerzy R. Zaslona; Deacon Vincent J. DeFedele; Joanna Kowalska, Music Min.
Parish Offices & Center—218 Washington Pl., 07604. Tel: 201-288-4844; Fax: 201-288-0237.
School—(1928), (Grades PreK-8), 215 Kipp Ave., 07604. Tel: 201-288-0614; Fax: 201-288-5956. Michelle Murillo, Prin. Lay Teachers 29; Students 415.
Catechesis/Religious Program—Tel: 201-288-5133; Fax: 201-288-0137. Josephine Nese, D.R.E. Students 461.

HAWORTH, BERGEN CO., SACRED HEART (1914) Rev. Stephen J. Fichter; Rev. Msgr. Martin F. O'Brien (Retired).
Res.: 123 Maple St., P.O. Box S, 07641. Tel: 201-387-0080; Fax: 201-439-1395.
See Holy Family Catholic Academy, Norwood under Immaculate Conception, Norwood for details.
Catechesis/Religious Program—102 Park St., 07641. Students 200.

HILLSDALE, BERGEN CO., ST. JOHN THE BAPTIST (1925) Rev. John J. Korbelak; Rev. Msgr. Philip D. Morris, Pastor Emeritus (Retired); Rev. Bruce E. Harger; Sr. Mary McFarland, O.P., Pastoral Assoc.; Catherine Wollyung, Pastoral Assoc. for Catechetics; Deacons Albert J. Ganter; John A. Gray. In Res., Rev. Msgr. Thomas M. O'Leary (Retired).
Res.: 69 Valley St., 07642. Tel: 201-664-3131; Fax: 201-664-0772.
School—*St. John's Academy Interparochial* (1955), (Grades PreK-8), 460 Hillsdale Ave., 07642. Tel: 201-664-6364; Fax: 201-664-8096. Elizabeth Viola, Prin.; Sharon Gallagher, Asst. Prin. Sisters 1; Lay Teachers 27; Students 427.
Catechesis/Religious Program—*Faith Formation Center*, 1 Valley St., 07642. Tel: 201-666-2707. Students 1,240.

HILLSIDE, UNION CO.

1—ST. CATHERINE OF SIENA (1912) Revs. Aurelio Yanez Gomez (Colombia); Guillermo Mora (Colombia).
Res.: 19 King St., 07205. Tel: 908-351-1515; Fax: 908-351-2139. Email: scatherineparish@aim.com.

Web: stcathshillside.rcan.org.
Catechesis/Religious Program—Elizabeth. Lucero A. Munoz, D.R.E. Students 224.

2—CHRIST THE KING (1948) Rev. Msgr. Venantius M. Fernando; Rev. Sergio D. Nadres (Philippines).
Res.: 411 Rutgers Ave., 07205. Tel: 908-686-0722; Fax: 908-686-2504. Email: christthekinghillside@yahoo.com. Web: www.christtheking-hillsidenj.com.
School—Hillside Catholic Academy, Hillside (2004) 397 Columbia Ave., 07205. Tel: 908-686-6740; Fax: 908-686-3819. Web: hillsidecatholicacademy.org. Michael Butchko, Prin. Sisters 1; Lay Teachers 17; Students 223.
Catechesis/Religious Program—Tel: 908-686-0234. Gloria Ferro, D.R.E. Students 65.

HOBOKEN, HUDSON CO.

1—ST. ANN'S (1900), (Italian), Very Rev. Vincent Fortunato, O.F.M.Cap.; Rev. Edmund Walker, O.F.M.Cap.
Res.: 704 Jefferson St., 07030. Tel: 201-659-1114; Fax: 201-659-1416.
School—Hoboken Catholic Academy, (Grades PreK-8), 555 Seventh St., 07030. Tel: 201-963-9535; Fax: 201-963-1256. Mrs. Rose Perry, Prin.
Catechesis/Religious Program—Students 43.

2—ST. FRANCIS (1888), (Italian), Revs. Michael V. Guglielmelli; Dominick M. Dellaporte (MET), Parochial Vicar.
Res.: 308 Jefferson St., 07030. Tel: 201-659-1772; Fax: 201-222-7975. Email: 3rdjeff@att.net. Web: stfrancishoboken.com.
See Hoboken Catholic Academy, Hoboken under St. Ann's, Hoboken for details.
Catechesis/Religious Program—Email: dre@stfrancishoboken.com. Ms. Frances Fitzgerald, D.R.E. Students 125.

3—ST. JOSEPH'S (1871) Merged with Our Lady of Grace, Hoboken to form Our Lady of Grace and Saint Joseph Parish, Hoboken. For inquiries for parish records, contact Our Lady of Grace and Saint Joseph Parish.

4—OUR LADY OF GRACE (1851) Merged with St. Joseph's, Hoboken to form Our Lady of Grace and Saint Joseph Parish, Hoboken.

5—OUR LADY OF GRACE AND SAINT JOSEPH PARISH (1851) Revs. Alexander M. Santora; Ordanico De La Pena, Parochial Vicar; Megan Moffit, Pastoral Assoc. In Res., Rev. Martin Okoro, C.M.F.
Rectory—400 Willow Ave., 07030. Tel: 201-659-0369; Fax: 201-659-5833. Email: olgrace@optonline.com. Web: www.olghoboken.com.
See Hoboken Catholic Academy, Hoboken under St. Ann's, Hoboken for details.
Catechesis/Religious Program—Students 52.

6—SS. PETER AND PAUL'S (1889) Rev. Msgr. Frank G. Del Prete; Rev. A. Benito Prado; Sisters Felice Donelin, S.C.C., Pastoral Assoc.; Patricia Wormann, O.P., Pastoral Assoc. & Faith Formation Dir.
Res.: 404 Hudson St., 07030. Tel: 201-659-2276; Fax: 201-659-5062. Email: fdpiii@aol.com. Web: www.spphoboken.com.
See Hoboken Catholic Academy, Hoboken under St. Ann's, Hoboken for details.
Catechesis/Religious Program—Students 52.

HO HO KUS, BERGEN CO., ST. LUKE'S (1864) [CEM] Revs. James J. Weiner; James R. White; Deacon John McKeon. In Res., Revs. Paschal B. Tsiquaye; Dominic G. Ciriaco.
Res.: 340 N. Franklin Tpke., 07423. Tel: 201-444-0272; Fax: 201-652-7044. Web: www.churchofstluke-.org. Email: admin@churchofstluke.org.
Catechesis/Religious Program—Tel: 201-447-2779. Email: ccd@churchofstluke.org. Miss Bridget Sarkowicz, D.R.E. Students 717.

IRVINGTON, ESSEX CO.

1—ASSUMPTION OF THE BLESSED VIRGIN MARY (1907), (Hungarian), Closed. For inquiries for parish records contact Seton Hall University Archives, South Orange. Tel: 973-596-9476.

2—GOOD SHEPHERD (2005) Rev. Frank J. Rocchi; Deacon Gerald Freeman.
Res.: 954 Stuyvesant Ave., 07111. Tel: 973-375-8568; Fax: 973-375-7040. Email: gsirvington@comcast.net. Web: goodshepherd.150m.com.
School—Good Shepherd Academy (2005) 285 Nesbit Ter., 07111. Tel: 973-375-0659; Fax: 973-375-0766. Thomas Scalea, Prin. Students 201.
Catechesis/Religious Program—Tel: 973-375-2688. Students 35.

3—ST. LEO'S (1878) Rev. Msgr. Beaubrun Ardouin; Revs. Louis Aumaitre; Jose Helbert Victor; Richard J. Mroz; Deacon Nelson Ramirez.
Res.: 103 Myrtle Ave., 07111. Tel: 973-372-1272; Fax: 973-416-8819. Email: saintleochurch@comcast.net.
See St. Leo's/Sacred Heart School, Irvington for details.
Catechesis/Religious Program—Students 140.
Convent—Tel: 973-757-2432.

4—ST. PAUL THE APOSTLE (1948) Merged with Immaculate Heart of Mary, Maplewood to form Good Shepherd, Irvington.

5—SACRED HEART OF JESUS (1925), (Polish), Rev. Tadeusz Trela.
Res.: 537 Grove St., 07111. Tel: 973-373-2232; Fax: 973-373-5935. Email: sacredheart07111@gmail.com.
School—St. Leo's/Sacred Heart School, (Grades PreK-8), 123 Myrtle Ave., 07111. Tel: 973-372-7555; Fax: 973-416-8819. Sr. Carina Okeke, D.M.M.M., Prin.
Catechesis/Religious Program—Students 62.

JERSEY CITY, HUDSON CO.

1—ST. AEDAN'S (1912) Revs. Joseph J. Astarita, Admin.; Sebastian J. Garcia; Oliver Yalong.
Res.: 800 Bergen Ave., 07306. Tel: 201-433-6800; Fax: 201-433-1222. Web: www.staedanparish.com.
Catechesis/Religious Program—Reina Osi, D.R.E. Students 40.
Convent—

2—ST. ALOYSIUS (1897) Revs. Joseph A. D'Amico; Juan Carlos Zapata; Jose Monte De Oca; Sr. Georgette A. Gavioli, S.S.J., Pastoral Assoc.; Deacon Alfredo Zapata. In Res., Rev. Msgr. Charles G. Stengel (Retired); Revs. Edward S. Malkiewicz (Retired); James Delaney, C.S.Sp.; George Joseph; Warren R. Hall.
Res.: 691 West Side Ave., 07304. Tel: 201-433-6365; Fax: 201-451-6438. Email: staloy@verizon.net.
School—(1897), (Grades PreK-8), 721 West Side Ave., 07306. Tel: 201-433-4270; Fax: 201-433-6916. Helen O'Connell, Prin. Lay Teachers 15; Students 333.
Convent—Tel: 201-433-5759.

3—ST. ANN'S (1910), (Lithuanian), Closed. For inquiries for parish records contact Seton Hall University Archives, South Orange. Tel: 201-761-9476, Fax: 201-761-9550.

4—ST. ANN'S (1911), (Polish), Rev. Kazimierz Kuczynski.
Res.: 291 St. Paul's Ave., 07306-5008. Tel: 201-656-4018; Fax: 201-656-0741.
Catechesis/Religious Program—Myra Wladyslawska, D.R.E. Students 35.
Mission—, Hudson Co. Tel: 201-656-0405.

5—ST. ANNE'S (1903) Revs. Jose Saltarin; Titus C. Njoku, Parochial Vicar; Edward T. Veluz, Parochial Vicar.
Res.: 3545 John F. Kennedy Blvd., 07307. Tel: 201-656-2490; Fax: 201-795-3817. Email: sarc2000@verizon.net. Web: stannesjc.com.
School—(1904), (Grades PreK-8), 255 Congress St., 07307. Tel: 201-659-0450. Web: mysite.verizon.net/gerrity/. Ms. Gina Marie Iacona, Prin. Lay Teachers 11; Students 220.
Catechesis/Religious Program—Tel: 201-659-1794. Sr. Alberta Manzo, O.S.F., D.R.E. Students 110.
Convent—Tel: 201-963-0998.

6—ST. ANTHONY OF PADUA (1884), (Polish), Rev. Joseph Urban.
Res.: 330 Sixth St., 07302. Tel: 201-653-0343; Fax: 201-653-0005. Email: saopjcnj@comcast.net. Web: www.stanthonyjc.com.
Catechesis/Religious Program—Students 54.

7—ASSUMPTION/ALL SAINTS (1896) Merged with St. Patrick's, Jersey City to form St. Patrick and Assumption/All Saints Church, Jersey City.

8—ST. BONIFACE'S (1863) Merged with St. Bridget, St. Mary, St. Michael and St. Peter to form Parish of the Resurrection, June 1997. For inquiries for parish records call Tel: 201-434-8500.

9—ST. BRIDGET'S (1869) Merged with St. Boniface, St. Mary, St. Michael and St. Peter to form Parish of the Resurrection, June 1997. For inquiries for parish records call Tel: 201-434-8500.

10—CHRIST, THE KING (1930), (African American), Rev. Stephen J. Giorno, S.T.; Deacon Keith McKnight.
Res.: 768 Ocean Ave., 07304. Tel: 201-333-4862; Fax: 201-433-6352.
Catechesis/Religious Program—Students 25.

11—CHURCH OF OUR LADY OF SORROWS (1914) Rev. John J. Cryan; Sisters Alice McCoy, O.P., Pastoral Assoc.; Elise Redmerski, O.P., Pastoral Assoc.
93-95 Clerk St., 07305. Tel: 201-433-0626; Fax: 201-433-2928. Email: ols9395@comcast.net. Web: olsjc.com.
Res.: *Our Lady of Mercy*, 340 Winfield Ave., 07305.
Catechesis/Religious Program—Students 49.

12—HOLY ROSARY (1885), (Italian), Rev. Rino Lavaroni. In Res., Rev. Jaroslaw Zaniewski.
Res.: 344 Sixth St., 07302. Tel: 201-795-0120; Fax: 201-610-1389.
Catechesis/Religious Program—Sr. Paula Rodrigo.

13—ST. JOHN THE BAPTIST (1884) Revs. Michael C. Santoro; Joseph A. Meagher. In Res., Revs. Robert J. Sandoz, O.F.M.; Gregory V. Gebbia, O.F.M.
Res.: 3026 John F. Kennedy Blvd., 07306. Tel: 201-653-8814; Fax: 201-653-3771. Email: johns3026@comcast.net.
Catechesis/Religious Program—Twinned with Our Lady of Mt. Carmel, Jersey City. Students 10.

14—ST. JOSEPH (1856) Revs. James V. Pagnotta; Francisco Ponce.
Res.: 511 Pavonia Ave., 07306-1303. Tel: 201-653-0392; Fax: 201-222-6481. Email: stjosephjc@yahoo.com. Web: www.stjosephjc.com.
Church: Baldwin Ave., 07306.
School—(1876), (Grades PreK-8), 509 Pavonia Ave., 07306. Tel: 201-653-0128; Fax: 201-222-5324. John Richards, Prin. Lay Teachers 11; Students 200.
Catechesis/Religious Program—Tel: 201-659-5929. Ms. Maria C. Pellecchia, D.R.E. Students 141.

15—ST. LUCY'S (1884) Closed. For inquiries for parish records contact Parish of the Resurrection. Tel: 201-434-8500.

16—ST. MARY'S (1854), (Hispanic—Filipino), Merged with St. Boniface, St. Bridget, St. Michael, and St. Peter, to form Parish of the Resurrection, June 1997. For inquiries for parish records call Tel: 201-434-8500.

17—ST. MICHAEL'S (1867) Merged with St. Boniface, St. Bridget, St. Mary and St. Peter to form Parish of the Resurrection, June 1997. For inquiries for parish records call Tel: 201-434-8500.

18—ST. NICHOLAS (1886), (German), Revs. Kevin E. Carter; Alex Ver (Philippines); Deacons Robert A. Baker Sr.; Wilson Cordero; Clodualdo M. Leonida.
Res.: 122 Ferry St., 07307. Tel: 201-659-5354; Fax: 201-798-6868. Web: www.saintnicholasparishjcnj.org.
School—(1886), (Grades PreK-8), 118 Ferry St., 07307. Tel: 201-659-5948. Sr. Ellen Fischer, S.C.C., Prin. Sisters of Christian Charity 3; Lay Teachers 11; Students 230.
Catechesis/Religious Program—Tel: 201-659-5354. Lorraine Glasser, D.R.E.; Julia Cordero, D.R.E. (Spanish). Students 160.
Convent—Tel: 201-659-5644.

19—OUR LADY OF CZESTOCHOWA (1911) Rev. Thomas J. Ciba; Sr. Sandra Demasi, Pastoral Assoc. In Res., Rev. Thomas A. Dente.
Res.: 120 Sussex St., 07302. Tel: 201-434-0798; Fax: 201-985-0918. Email: olcjc@olcjc.org. Web: www.olcjc.org.
School—(1911), (Grades PreK-8), 248 Marin Blvd., 07302. Tel: 201-434-2405; Fax: 201-434-6068. Email: stefanellia@olcschool.org. Web: www.olcschool.org. Mrs. Anne Stefanellli, Prin. Lay Teachers 40; Students 358.
Catechesis/Religious Program—Students 15.

20—OUR LADY OF MERCY (1963), (Filipino), Revs. John J. Cryan; Martin Borbon Jacinto; Manuel R. Romerde; Ralph C. Siendo; Deacon Nicholas Fargo.
Res.: 40 Sullivan Dr., 07305. Tel: 201-434-7500; Fax: 201-432-2885. Email: olmjcnj@aol.com. Web: www.olmnj.org.
School—(Grades PreK-8), 254 Bartholdi Ave., 07305. Tel: 201-434-4091; Fax: 201-434-8405. Email: principalolm@aol.com. Victoria Hayes, Prin. Lay Teachers 30; Students 290.
Catechesis/Religious Program—Email: religioused@aol.com. Students 198.

21—OUR LADY OF MT. CARMEL (1905), (Italian), Revs. Michael C. Santoro; Hector F. Galvis Rios.
Res.: 99 Broadway, 07306. Tel: 201-435-7080; Fax: 201-432-4476. Email: mtcarmelschool@comcast.net.
Catechesis/Religious Program—JoAnne Oziemblo, D.R.E. Students 88.

22—OUR LADY OF VICTORIES (1917) Revs. Victor E. Paloma; Christopher Panlilio. In Res., Rev. James Tortora.
Res.: 2217 John F. Kennedy Blvd., 07304-1416. Tel: 201-433-4152; Fax: 201-433-0705. Email: olvictories1@aol.com.
Catechesis/Religious Program—Students 56.

23—PARISH OF THE RESURRECTION (1997), (Formerly Parishes of St. Boniface, St. Bridget, St. Mary, St. Michael and St. Peter) Very Rev. Victor P. Kennedy; Rev. Marcos Sequiera-Ruiz; Bro. Louis N. Mauro, S.J., Business Mgr.; Deacons Marcelo David; Pedro Gonzalez; Cesar C. Sarmiento; Leopoldo Polanco; Ralph M. Savo; Ms. Roxanne Clark, Pastoral Assoc.; Ms. Elizabeth Hopf, Pastoral Assoc. In Res., Rev. Joseph Minh Tri Nguyen.
Mailing Address & Parish Office: 209 Third St., 07302. Tel: 201-434-8500; Fax: 201-333-1816. Email: resjc@aol.com.
School—Resurrection, Brunswick Campus (1873), (Grades PreK-8), 189 Brunswick St., 07302. Tel: 201-653-1699; Fax: 201-418-9019. Email: rs.office@yahoo.com. Sisters Eleanor Uhl, Co-Prin. (Grades 4-8); Barbara Nesbihal, S.C., Co-Prin.
High School—St. Mary, 209 Third St., 07302. Tel: 201-656-8008; Fax: 201-653-4518. Mrs. Beatriz Esteban-Messina, Prin.
Catechesis/Religious Program—Tel: 201-795-3426; Fax: 201-333-1816. Sr. Mary Lynch, S.S.N.D., D.R.E. Students 285.
St. Boniface—, Merged with St. Bridget, St. Michael, St. Mary, & St. Peter, Jersey City to form Parish of

the Resurrection, Jersey City.
St. Bridget—, Merged with St. Boniface, St. Michael, St. Mary & St. Peter, Jersey City to form Parish of the Resurrection, Jersey City.
St. Michael—, Merged with St. Boniface, St. Bridget, St. Mary & St. Peter, Jersey City to form Parish of the Resurrection, Jersey City. (Shrine of St. Jude Perpetual Novena)
St. Mary—, Merged with St. Boniface, St. Bridget, St. Michael & St. Peter, Jersey City to form Parish of the Resurrection, Jersey City.
St. Peter—, Merged with St. Boniface, St. Bridget, St. Michael & St. Mary, Jersey City to form Parish of the Resurrection, Jersey City., 144 Grand St., 07302.

24—St. Patrick and Assumption/All Saints Church Revs. Eugene P. Squeo; Marc Arthur Francois (Haiti); Francis E. Schiller; Deacon Jesus Reyes.
Res.: 492 Bramhall Ave., 07304. Tel: 201-332-8600; Fax: 201-324-3919.
School—(1909), (Grades PreK-8), 509 Bramhall St., 07304. Tel: 201-433-4664; Fax: 201-433-0935. Sr. Maeve McDermott, S.C., Co-Prin.; Michele Link, Co-Prin. Sisters of Charity of St. Elizabeth 5; Lay Teachers 40; Students 495.
Convent—345 Pacific Ave., 07304. Tel: 201-451-2765.
Catechesis/Religious Program—Ann Marie Padilla, D.R.E. Students 123.

25—St. Patrick's (1869) Merged with Assumption/All Saints, Jersey City to form St. Patrick and Assumption/All Saints Church, Jersey City.

26—St. Paul of the Cross (1868) Revs. Andres J. Reyes; Melvin Oseguera.
Res.: 156 Hancock Ave., 07307. Tel: 201-798-7900; Fax: 201-798-7902. Email: stpaulcros@aol.com. Web: www.stpaulcrossjc.com.
Catechesis/Religious Program—Students 189.
Convent—Tel: 201-659-1414.

27—St. Paul's (1861) Very Rev. Robert A. Antczak; Revs. Felipe Lopez; Joseph Udeze; Deacon Frank Gonzalez; Sr. Mary Ann Ronneburger, O.P., Pastoral Assoc. In Res., Rev. Raymond T. McKeon (Retired); Rev. Msgr. James J. Finnerty (Retired).
Res.: 14 Greenville Ave., 07305. Tel: 201-433-8500; Fax: 201-433-9886. Email: stpauljc@aol.com.
Catechesis/Religious Program—Students 200.
Convent—Tel: 201-434-2962.

28—St. Peter's (1831), (Hispanic), Merged with St. Boniface, St. Bridget, St. Mary and St. Michael to form Parish of the Resurrection, June 1997. For parish inquiries call Tel: 201-434-8500.

29—Sacred Heart (1905) Closed. For inquiries for parish records contact Seton Hall University Archives, South Orange. Tel: 973-761-9476; Fax: 973-761-9550.
School—Sacred Heart, (Grades K-8), 183 Bayview Ave., 07307. Tel: 201-332-7111; Fax: 201-332-7160. Sr. Frances Salemi, S.C., Prin. Lay Teachers 14; Students 247.

Kearny, Hudson Co.

1—St. Cecilia's (1893) Very Rev. Michael G. Ward; Rev. Yuvan Arbey Alvarez.
Res.: 120 Kearny Ave., 07032. Tel: 201-991-1116; Fax: 201-998-4437. Email: stcecilia@stceciliakearny.org. Web: www.stceciliakearny.org.
Catechesis/Religious Program—Holly Lawmaster, D.R.E. Students 305.

2—Our Lady of Sorrows (1915), (Lithuanian), Revs. James J. Reilly; Salvatore DiStefano; Deacons Leonard J. Mackesy; John P. Sarnas. In Res., Rev. Patrick R.C. Wilhelm (Retired).
Res.: 136 Davis Ave., 07032. Tel: 201-998-4616; Fax: 201-997-8659. Email: olskrny@verizon.net.
Catechesis/Religious Program—Madeline Leger, D.R.E. Students 38.

3—St. Stephen (1904) Revs. Richard E. Cabezas; Paciano A. Barbieto; Joseph A. Mancini; Deacons Herbert R. Gimbel; Earl W. White; Robert Maidhof, Music Min.
Res.: 141 Washington Ave., 07032. Tel: 201-998-3314; Fax: 201-998-4924.
School—Mater Dei Academy (1904) 131 Midland Ave., 07032. Tel: 201-991-3217; Fax: 201-991-7829. Mrs. Deborah DeMattia, Prin. Lay Teachers 12; Students 256.
Catechesis/Religious Program—Tel: 201-991-0236. Sr. Rita Kearney, S.S.J., D.R.E. Students 200.

Kenilworth, Union Co., St. Theresa's (1949) Revs. Joseph S. Bejgrowicz; Jose Erlito Ebron (Philippines); Richard Donovan, Youth Min. Tel: 908-709-1930. In Res., Revs. George M. Keating (Retired); Al Kowalski (Retired).
Res.: 541 Washington Ave., 07033. Tel: 908-272-4444; Fax: 908-272-4424. Email: sainttheresa@icatholiczone.com.
School—(Grades PreK-8), 540 Washington Ave., 07033. Tel: 908-276-7220; Fax: 908-709-1103. Sr. Emy DeFilippi, F.M.A., Prin. Salesian Sisters 4; Lay Teachers 17; Students 310.
Catechesis/Religious Program—Tel: 908-276-4881. Sr. Monique Huarte, F.M.A., Pastoral Min. Catechesis. Students 675.
Convent—Tel: 908-276-5028.

Leonia, Bergen Co., St. John the Evangelist's (1912) Revs. Richard P. Kwiatkowski; Arlou Buslon (Philippines); Sr. Patricia McDermott, F.S.P., Pastoral Assoc.; Deacon Joseph Yandoli, Business Mgr.
Res.: 235 Harrison St., 07605. Tel: 201-947-4545; Fax: 201-947-3891.
School—260 Harrison St., 07605. Tel: 201-944-4361; Fax: 201-944-2195. Sr. Mary Kelly, S.S.N.D., Prin. School Sisters of Notre Dame 1; Lay Teachers 15; Students 167.
Catechesis/Religious Program—Tel: 201-944-4346. Gerri Bianchi, D.R.E. Students 250.
Convent—Tel: 201-944-4362.

Linden, Union Co.

1—St. Elizabeth of Hungary (1909) Very Rev. Benedict Michael Worry, O.S.B.; Revs. Andres F. Querijero, O.C.D.; Alexander Cruz; Anthony Sargent, O.S.B.; Deacon John P. Bejgrowicz.
Res.: 179 Hussa St., 07036. Tel: 908-486-2514; Fax: 908-486-1757. Web: www.sainteonline.org.
School—Saints Mary and Elizabeth Academy, (Grades PreK-8), 170 Hussa St., 07036. Tel: 908-486-2507; Fax: 908-486-4032. Web: www.s-meacademy.org. Mrs. Maritess Kaminski, Prin.; Fides O'Donnell, Librarian. Students 260.
Catechesis/Religious Program—170 Hussa St., 07036. Tel: 908-486-2509; Fax: 908-487-1757. Students 145.

2—Holy Family (Tremley Point) (1955), (Slovak), [CEM] Rev. Eugene Diurczak.
Res.: 210 Monroe St., 07036. Tel: 908-862-1060; Fax: 908-862-7331.
Church: 2709 Parkway Ave., 07036. Fax: 908-862-1060.
Catechesis/Religious Program—Students 24.

3—St. John the Apostle (1948) Revs. Robert G. McBride; Luke Tran; Paolo Tanzini; Deacons Michael D. York; Edward A. Campanella; Guy Paredes, (Retired).
Res.: 1805 Penbrook Ter., 07036. Tel: 908-486-6363; Fax: 908-486-5345. Email: parish@sjanj.net. Web: www.sjanj.net.
School—(1950), (Grades PreK-8), Valley Rd., Clark, 07066. Tel: 732-388-1360; Fax: 732-388-0775. Web: www.sjanj.org. Sr. Donna Marie O'Brien, O.P., Prin. Sisters of St. Dominic 1; Lay Teachers 23; Students 391.
Catechesis/Religious Program—Tel: 732-388-1253. Michelle Angelo, D.R.E. Students 626.
Convent—1731 Valley Rd., 07036. Tel: 908-486-3701.

4—St. Theresa of the Child Jesus (1925), (Polish), Rev. Msgr. Bronislaw Wielgus; Rev. Tadeusz Jank.
Res.: 122 Liberty St., 07036. Tel: 908-862-1116; Fax: 908-862-2930.
Church: 131 E. Edgar Rd., 07036.
Catechesis/Religious Program—Tel: 908-862-1388. Students 460.

Little Ferry, Bergen Co., St. Margaret of Cortona (1912) Rev. Arthur Frank Humphrey; Sr. Dorothy A. Donovan, S.S.J., Pastoral Assoc.
Res.: 31 Chamberlain Ave., 07643-1898. Tel: 201-641-2988; Fax: 201-641-0664. Email: smcortona1912@aol.com.
Catechesis/Religious Program—Tel: 201-641-3937. Students 210.

Livingston, Essex Co.

1—St. Philomena (1927) Rev. Msgrs. John J. Laferrera; Kevin M. Hanbury, Weekend/Part-Time Ministry; Revs. Brian X. Needles; Gerald Buonopane; Deacon Fred Smith. In Res., Rev. Matthew Eraly (India).
Res.: 386 S. Livingston Ave., 07039. Tel: 973-992-0994; Fax: 973-992-0970. Email: staff@stphilomena.org. Web: www.stphilomena.org.
School—Aquinas Academy (1952), (Grades PreK-8), 388 S. Livingston Ave., 07039. Tel: 973-992-1587; Fax: 973-992-1742. Sr. Lena Picillo, O.P., Prin. Dominican Sisters of Caldwell 1; Lay Teachers 19; Students 170.
Early Childhood Center—Tel: 973-992-5181; Fax: 973-992-2652. Gloria Castucci, Dir. Lay Teachers 3; Aides 6; Students 98.
Catechesis/Religious Program—Tel: 973-992-4466. Email: hdiskin@aol.com. Students 736.
Convent—Tel: 973-992-1581.

2—St. Raphael (1961) Revs. Gerald F. Greaves; Peter M. Aquino; Yolanda Cifarelli, Pastoral Assoc.; Ann Marie Gesualdo, Youth Min.; Casey Fabyanski, Music Min.
Res.: 346 E. Mt. Pleasant Ave., 07039. Tel: 973-992-9490; Fax: 973-740-0236. Email: straphaelrcc@comcast.net.
Catechesis/Religious Program—Students 450.

Lodi, Bergen Co.

1—St. Francis de Sales (1854) [CEM] Rev. John J. Galeano; Sisters Martine M. Pijanowski, C.S.S.F.; Josephina Morales, L.C.S.W. In Res., Rev. Stephen J. Toth.
Res.: 125 Union St., 07644. Tel: 973-779-4330; Fax: 973-779-8842. Email: francisdesales@optonline.net.
Catechesis/Religious Program—Tel: 973-779-3949. Students 159.
Convent—Tel: 973-773-4366.

2—St. Joseph's (1917) Revs. Michael Marotta, C.R.M.; Americo Salvi, C.R.M.; Anastacio Villaluz, C.R.M., Parochial Vicar.
Res.: 40 Spring St., 07644. Tel: 973-779-0643; Fax: 973-471-1442. Email: stjoelodi@aol.com.
Catechesis/Religious Program—Tel: 973-779-8275; Fax: 973-779-0490. Email: sjreolodi@aol.com. Virginia Interdamato, D.R.E. Students 260.

Lyndhurst, Bergen Co.

1—St. Michael's (1912), (Polish), Revs. Stanley Kostrzomb; Joseph Szklarski; Deacon Vincent Serzan. In Res., Rev. Msgr. James P. McMenemie (Retired).
Res.: 624 Page Ave., 07071. Tel: 201-939-1161; Fax: 201-939-7571. Email: stmichaelparish@comcast.net. Web: www.st-michael.org.
Catechesis/Religious Program—Mr. Gene DeHaven, D.R.E. Students 102.
Convent—Tel: 201-438-1882.

2—Our Lady of Mount Carmel (1966), (Italian), Rev. Nazareno Orandi.
Res.: 197 Kingsland Ave., 07071. Tel: 201-935-1177; Fax: 201-935-5675. Email: olmc1177@verizon.net.
Catechesis/Religious Program—146 Copeland Ave., 07071. Tel: 201-935-5467. Patricia Hirsch, D.R.E. Students 298.

3—Sacred Heart (1905) [CEM] Revs. James E. Starasinich; Marek B. Wysocki; Deacon Stephen Rodack, (Retired).
Res.: 324 Ridge Rd., 07071. Tel: 201-438-1147; Fax: 201-507-5861. Email: sacredheart@comcast.net.
School—(Grades PreK-8), 620 Valley Brook Ave., 07071. Tel: 201-939-4277; Fax: 201-939-0534. Email: sacredheartlynd@hotmail.com. Web: sacredheartlynd.org. Margaret Smiriga, Prin. Sisters 2; Lay Teachers 10; Students 245.
Catechesis/Religious Program—Email: sacredheartchurch@comcast.net. Mrs. Margaret Dacchille, D.R.E. Students 217.

Mahwah, Bergen Co.

1—Immaculate Conception (1930) Rev. William P. Sheridan; Deacon Fritz Kautz.
Res.: 900 Darlington Ave., 07430. Tel: 201-327-1276; Fax: 201-327-0185. Email: churchimmaculateconception@yahoo.com. Web: www.immaculateconceptionmahwah.org.
See St. Paul's Interparochial School, Ramsey under St. Paul's, Ramsey for details.
Catechesis/Religious Program—Tel: 201-825-0333. Michael Hans, Catechetical Associate. Students 396.

2—Immaculate Heart of Mary (1915), (Polish), Revs. Floyd Rotunno; Marek Bokota.
Res.: 47 Island Rd., 07430. Tel: 201-529-3517; Fax: 201-529-4401. Email: ihmpastor@optonline.net.
See St. Paul's Interparochial School, Ramsey under St. Paul's, Ramsey for details.
Catechesis/Religious Program—Tel: 201-529-2294. Barbara A. Dillon, D.R.E. Students 255.

Maplewood, Essex Co.

1—St. Andrew Kim (1972), (Korean), Revs. Minhyun Cho; Hooyeon Cho, Parochial Vicar; Deacon Thomas Bulgia. In Res., Rev. Msgr. Augustin C. Park, Pastor Emeritus, Coord. Korean Apostolate.
Res.: 280 Parker Ave., 07040. Tel: 973-763-5019; Fax: 973-763-9010. Email: catholicmaplewood@yahoo.com. Web: www.alovesak.org.
Catechesis/Religious Program—Students 245.
Convent—Tel: 973-762-1297; Fax: 973-763-1169. Email: orangsr@hanmail.net.

2—Immaculate Heart of Mary (1954) Merged with St. Paul the Apostle, Irvington to form Good Shepherd, Irvington.

3—St. Joseph's (1914) Revs. Michael A. Saporito; Manolo Punzalan; Mrs. Jennifer Leitner, Pastoral Assoc.; Ms. Diane Pew, Pastoral Assoc.; Ms. Mary Beth Walsh, Pastoral Assoc.; Ms. Dugan McGinley, Dir. Music & Liturgy. In Res., Rev. Msgr. William B. Naedele.
Res.: 767 Prospect St., 07040. Tel: 973-761-5933; Fax: 973-761-6705. Email: info@stjosephmaplewood.org. Web: www.stjosephmaplewood.org.
School—(1930), (Grades PreK-8), 240 Franklin Ave., 07040. Tel: 973-761-4033. Email: admin@stjosephmaplewood.org. Susan Jurevich, Prin. Lay Teachers 10; Students 209.
Catechesis/Religious Program—Students 184.

Maywood, Bergen Co., Our Lady Queen of Peace (1950) Revs. Lawrence J. Fama; Kevin J. Schott; Deacons Anthony Balistieri; Joseph L. Mantineo; Steven Taylor, Music Min.; Thomas Viola, Youth Min.
Res.: 400 Maywood Ave., 07607. Tel: 201-845-9566;

Fax: 201-845-3742. Web: www.olqp.org.
Catechesis/Religious Program—Tel: 201-845-9545. Sr. Louise DelCarpine, M.P.F., D.R.E. Students 225.
Convent—Tel: 201-845-9568.

MIDLAND PARK, BERGEN CO., NATIVITY (1955) Revs. Peter K. Funesti; Raymond E. Rodrigue. In Res., Rev. Msgr. James A. Burke (Retired); Rev. Ron Stanley.
Res.: 315 Prospect St., 07432. Tel: 201-444-6362; Fax: 201-444-5056.
Catechesis/Religious Program—Tel: 201-447-1776. Ms. Olivia Harrington, D.R.E. Students 478.

MONTCLAIR, ESSEX CO.

1—IMMACULATE CONCEPTION (1864) [CEM] Revs. Joseph A. Scarangella; Frank J. Burla; Arokiasamy Irudayanathan; Sr. Cora Marie McGuire, M.S.B.T., Pastoral Assoc.; Jon W. Bonesteel, Pastoral Assoc.; Preston L. Dibble, Music Min. In Res., Rev. Louis M. Pambello.
Res.: 30 N. Fullerton Ave., 07042. Tel: 973-744-1005; Fax: 973-744-7936.
Parish Center—1 Munn St., 07042. Tel: 973-744-5650; Fax: 973-744-7936. Email: parishoffice@mtcimmaculate.org. Web: www.mtcimmaculate.org.
Preschool— (1997) Tegakwita Academy, 1 Munn St., 07042. Tel: 973-744-5650. Lay Teachers 2; Students 15.
See Immaculate Conception High School (Coed), Montclair in the Institution Section under High Schools, Private for details.
Catechesis/Religious Program—Students 365.

2—OUR LADY OF MT. CARMEL (1907), (Italian), Rev. Anthony J. Lionelli. In Res., Rev. Thomas M. Cembor.
Res.: 94 Pine St., 07042. Tel: 973-744-1074; Fax: 973-744-0205. Email: olmc_mont@verizon.net.
Catechesis/Religious Program—Bruno Suria, D.R.E. Students 70.

3—ST. PETER CLAVER (1931), (African American), Rev. Richard D. Carlson; Deacon Wilfrid Leconte.
Res.: 56 Elmwood Ave., 07042. Tel: 973-783-4852; Fax: 973-783-3261. Email: peterclave@aol.com. Web: www.saintpeterclaverchurch.org.
Catechesis/Religious Program—Sharon Huebner, D.R.E. Students 105.

MOONACHIE, BERGEN CO., ST. ANTHONY (1931) Closed. For inquiries for parish records contact Seton Hall University Archives: South Orange. Tel: 973-761-9476; Fax: 973-761-9550.

MOUNTAINSIDE, UNION CO., CHURCH OF OUR LADY OF LOURDES (1958) Revs. John M. McCrone; Grace G. Arachi. In Res., Rev. Msgr. Thomas J. McDade.
Res.: 300 Central Ave., 07092. Tel: 908-232-1162; Fax: 908-232-0776. Web: www.ollmountainside.org.
School—Holy Trinity Interparochial School (Westfield Campus) (1991), (Grades PreK-8), 336 First St., Westfield, 07090. Tel: 908-233-0484; Fax: 908-233-6204. Email: htismc@comcast.net. Web: www.htisnj.com. Sr. Maureen Fichner, S.S.J., Prin. Lay Teachers 15; Students 128.
Catechesis/Religious Program—Tel: 908-233-1777. Christina Nixon, D.R.E. Students 384.

NEW MILFORD, BERGEN CO., ASCENSION (1953) Revs. David W. Milliken; Arcadio Munoz (Philippines); Deacons Harold Bates; Paul Kliauga.
Res.: 256 Azalea Dr., 07646. Tel: 201-836-8961; Fax: 201-836-5896.
School—Transfiguration Academy, (Grades 5-8), 1092 Carnation Dr., 07646. Tel: 201-836-7074; Fax: 201-836-4475. Salvatore Tralongo, Prin. Students 115.
Catechesis/Religious Program—Tel: 201-836-3085. Theresa Carbone, C.R.E. Students 303.

NEW PROVIDENCE, UNION CO., OUR LADY OF PEACE (1942) Rev. William A. Mahon; Rev. Msgr. Paul J. Hayes, Pastor Emeritus (Retired); Revs. Eugene Newman Joseph; Peter O. Iwuala.
Res.: 111 South St., 07974. Tel: 908-464-7600; Fax: 908-508-1845. Email: olpnp@aol.com. Web: www.ourladyofpeaceparish.org.
School—The Academy of Our Lady of Peace, (Grades PreK-8), 99 South St., 07974. Tel: 908-464-8657; Fax: 908-464-3377. Thomas C. Berrios, Prin. Lay Teachers 18; Students 153.
Catechesis/Religious Program—Tel: 908-464-8156. Email: olpcatoff@aol.com. Students 475.
Convent—Tel: 908-464-8223.

NORTH ARLINGTON, BERGEN CO., QUEEN OF PEACE (1922) Rev. Msgrs. William J. Fadrowski; Thomas G. Madden, Pastor Emeritus (Retired); Revs. Scott Attanasio; Charles M. Kelly; Stephen A. Kopacz; Sr. Anita Maria O'Dwyer, S.S.J., Pastoral Assoc.; Deacons William R. Benedetto; William H. Myers.
Res.: 10 Franklin Pl., 07031. Tel: 201-997-0700; Fax: 201-997-6214. Email: qpchurch@comcast.net. Web: www.qpgs.org/church.htm.
School—(1925), (Grades PreK-8), 21 Church Pl., 07031. Tel: 201-998-8222; Fax: 201-997-7930. Email: info@qpgs.org. Web: www.qpgs.org. Ms. Terri Suchocki, Prin. Sisters of St. Joseph of Chestnut Hill 1; Lay Teachers 18; Students 400.
High School—(1930) 191 Rutherford Pl., 07031. Tel: 201-998-8227; Fax: 201-998-3040. Email: qphs@qphs.org. Web: www.qphs.org. Bro. Lawrence Lavallee, F.M.S., Prin.; George Linke, Asst. Prin. Sisters 3; Brothers 1; Lay Teachers 40; Students 525.
Catechesis/Religious Program— Mary Fleischbein, D.R.E. Students 550.
Convent—Tel: 201-997-2141; 201-991-0235 (Parish Center).

NORTH BERGEN, HUDSON CO.

1—ST. BRIGID (1900) Merged with St. Rocco's, Union City to form Saint Rocco/Saint Brigid, Union City. For inquiries see Saint Rocco/Saint Bridgid, Union City listing.

2—OUR LADY OF FATIMA (1963) Rev. Peter G. Wehrle.
Res.: 8016 Kennedy Blvd., 07047. Tel: 201-869-7244; Fax: 201-869-0940. Email: olfnb@optonline.net.
Catechesis/Religious Program—Tel: 201-869-0506. Robert Burkot, D.R.E. Students 168.

3—SACRED HEART (1917), (Polish), Rev. Anthony G. Robak.
Mailing Address: Box 9007, 07047. Email: att33940@attglobal.net.
Res.: 246 Hudson Pl., Cliffside Park, 07010. Tel: 201-943-0305; Fax: 201-943-2676. Email: att33940@attglobal.net.
Catechesis/Religious Program—Mr. Robert Francin Jr., D.R.E. Students 67.

NORTH CALDWELL, ESSEX CO., NOTRE DAME (1962) Rev. Anthony J. Randazzo; Sr. Carol Jaruszewski, R.S.M., Pastoral Assoc. In Res., Rev. Msgr. Kenneth J. Herbster.
Res.: 359 Central Ave., 07006. Tel: 973-226-0979; Fax: 973-226-4118. Email: ndparish@aol.com. Web: www.notredameparish.com.
See Trinity Academy under St. Aloysius, Caldwell for details.
Catechesis/Religious Program—Tel: 973-228-3338. Students 810.

NORTHVALE, BERGEN CO., ST. ANTHONY'S (1890) Very Rev. Gerald T. Hahn. In Res., Rev. Benedict P. Militello (Retired).
Res.: 199 Walnut St., 07647. Tel: 201-768-1177; Fax: 201-768-2522. Email: stanthonychurch@optonline.net.
See Holy Family Catholic Academy, Norwood under Immaculate Conception, Norwood for details.
Catechesis/Religious Program—Tel: 201-768-5945. Students 285.

NORWOOD, BERGEN CO., IMMACULATE CONCEPTION (1921) Rev. Leo J. Butler; Sr. Elizabeth Holler, S.C., Pastoral Assoc.
Res.: 211 Summit St., 07648. Tel: 201-768-1600; Fax: 201-768-8006. Email: immaculateconception@verizonmail.com. Web: www.iccnorwood.org.
School—Holy Family Catholic Academy (1991), (Grades PreK-8), 200 Summit St., 07648. Tel: 201-768-1605; Fax: 201-768-0796. Ms. Sharon Goodman, Prin. Sisters 1; Lay Teachers 26; Students 175.
Catechesis/Religious Program—Tel: 201-768-1771. Sr. Susanne Reynolds, S.S.J., D.R.E. Students 257.

NUTLEY, ESSEX CO.

1—HOLY FAMILY (1909), (Italian), Rev. Msgr. Paul L. Bochicchio; Revs. John F. Gordon; Mauro Primavera; Sr. Eileen Hubbert, S.S.J., Pastoral Assoc.; Deacon Joseph A. Dwyer Jr.
Res.: 28 Brookline Ave., 07110. Tel: 973-667-0026; Fax: 973-661-1714.
School—Good Shepherd Academy, Elementary, 24 Brookline Ave., 07110. Tel: 973-667-2049; Fax: 973-661-9259. Sr. Domenica Troina, M.P.F., Prin.
Catechesis/Religious Program—Tel: 973-667-6018. Sr. Angelina DelVecchio, M.P.F., D.R.E. Students 353.
Convent—

2—ST. MARY'S (1876) Rev. Msgr. David C. Hubba; Revs. Matthew Kunnath; George F. Sharp. In Res., Most Rev. Charles J. McDonnell (Retired); Rev. Henry Schreitmueller (Retired); Deacon Reynaldo M. Trinidad.
Res.: 17 Msgr. Owens Pl., 07110. Tel: 973-235-1100; Fax: 973-661-0233.
See Good Shepherd Academy, Nutley under Holy Family, Nutley for details.
Catechesis/Religious Program—Tel: 973-667-8239; Fax: 973-661-0233. Brian Lynch, D.R.E. Students 525.

3—OUR LADY OF MOUNT CARMEL (1925), (Polish), Revs. Dennis E. Reiff; Rodrigo S. Samson; Deacon Aldo P. Antola.
Res.: 120 Prospect St., 07110. Tel: 973-667-2580; Fax: 973-667-0648. Email: olmc.nutley@optimum.net. Web: www.olmc-nutley.org.
See Good Shepherd Academy, Nutley under Holy Family, Nutley for details.
Catechesis/Religious Program—Email: olmc.religion@optimum.net. Sr. Arlene Oswald, O.P., D.R.E. Students 110.

OAKLAND, BERGEN CO., OUR LADY OF PERPETUAL HELP (1960) Rev. Thomas P. Lipnicki; Carol Willis, Pastoral Assoc.
25 Purdue Ave., 07436. Tel: 201-337-7596; Fax: 201-337-7810. Email: olph.parish@verizon.net. Web: olphchurch-oaklandnj.org.
Catechesis/Religious Program—Tel: 201-337-5537. Email: ccd@olphchurch-oaklandnj.org. Ms. Sydney Kucan, D.R.E. Students 540.

OLD TAPPAN, BERGEN CO., ST. PIUS X (1954) Rev. Patrick M. Mulewski; Deacon John J. McKenna; Ron Binaghi, Youth Min.; Jeanine Binaghi, Youth Min.; Fred Golz, Music Min.
Res.: 268 Old Tappan Rd., 07675. Tel: 201-664-0913; Fax: 201-664-1013. Email: stpiusot@optonline.net. Web: www.saintpiuschurch-.com.
See Holy Family Catholic Academy, Norwood under Immaculate Conception, Norwood for details.
Catechesis/Religious Program—Tel: 201-664-0927. Students 309.

ORADELL, BERGEN CO., ST. JOSEPH'S (1903) Revs. George M. Reilly; Robert S. Gajewski; Raul Silva; Deacon Michael J. Cechony.
Res.: 105 Harrison St., New Milford, 07646. Tel: 201-261-0148; Fax: 201-261-0369. Email: churchinfo@sjcnm.org. Web: www.sjc-oranm.4lpi.com.
School—(1939), (Grades PreK-8), 305 Elm St., 07649. Tel: 201-261-2388; Fax: 201-261-0830. Colette Vail, Prin. Lay Teachers 26; Students 405.
Catechesis/Religious Program—300 Elm St., 07649. Tel: 201-261-1144; Fax: 201-634-0640. Anthony Armando, C.R.E. Students 915.

ORANGE, ESSEX CO.

1—HOLY SPIRIT (1931) Merged For inquiries for parish records contact Holy Spirit-Our Lady Help of Christians, East Orange. Tel: 201-673-1077.

2—ST. JOHN'S (1851), (Hispanic), [CEM] Revs. George Faour; Cristobal de Jesus Puertas; Rev. Msgr. Ricardo Gonzalez, Pastor Emeritus (Retired); Deacon Jerry Romero.
Res.: 94 Ridge St., 07050. Tel: 973-674-0110; Fax: 973-674-3965. Email: stjohnora@comcast.net.
School—(1855), (Grades PreK-8), 455 White St., 07050. Tel: 973-674-8951; Fax: 973-674-6126. Sr. Kieran Chidi Nduagbo, D.D.L., Prin. Sisters of Charity 2; Daughters of Love 2; Lay Teachers 11; Students 205.
Catechesis/Religious Program—Students 250.
Convent—Tel: 973-673-1263; Fax: 973-731-9604.

3—MT. CARMEL (1896), (Italian), Revs. Sean Britto, C.S.J.; Victor Shoemaker, C.S.J.; Marianus Hough, C.S.J.
Res.: 103 S. Center St., 07050. Tel: 973-674-2052; Fax: 973-675-1342. Email: mtcarmel@ourladyofmtcarmel.info. Web: www.ourladyofmtcarmel.info.
Catechesis/Religious Program—Mr. Michael Reiser, D.R.E. Students 32.

4—OUR LADY OF THE VALLEY (1873) Revs. John Grinsell, S.D.B.; Armand Quinto, S.D.B.
Res.: 510 Valley St., 07050. Tel: 973-674-7500; Fax: 973-672-8341. Email: olvgeneral@comcast.net. Web: www.olvalley.org.
Catechesis/Religious Program—Tel: 973-674-4272. Email: margaretnovak@comcast.net. Margaret Novak, D.R.E. Students 100.

5—ST. VENANTIUS (1886) Merged For inquiries for parish records contact Seton Hall University Archives at 973-761-9126.

PALISADES PARK, BERGEN CO.

1—ST. MICHAEL'S (1912) Revs. James F. Reilly; Ethiege Silva, O.M.I.; Deacon Joseph Kim; John Portscher, Music Dir. In Res., Rev. Stanley M. Lobo (Retired).
Res.: 19 E. Central Blvd., 07650-1799. Tel: 201-944-1061; Fax: 201-947-1798. Email: saintmichaelpp@aol.com.
School—Notre Dame Interparochial, Elementary Division (1991), (Grades PreK-8), 312 First St., 07650. Tel: 201-947-5262; Fax: 201-947-8319. Rita Miragliotta, Prin.
Catechesis/Religious Program—Margaret M. Manley, D.R.E. Students 50.

2—ST. NICHOLAS (1923), (Italian—Brazilian), Revs. Armando M. Palmieri, S.D.V. (Italy); Babu Thelappilly, S.D.V. (India), Parochial Vicar; James Butts, S.D.V.
Res.: 442 E. Brinkerhoff Ave., 07650. Tel: 201-944-1154; Fax: 201-944-9510. Email: stnicholas07650@nj.rr.com. Web: www.saintnicholasparish.info.
See Notre Dame Interparochial, Elementary Division under St. Michael's, Palisades Park for details.
Catechesis/Religious Program—Tel: 201-944-1138. Rev. Armando M. Palmieri, S.D.V. (Italy). Students 65.

PARAMUS, BERGEN CO.
1—CARMELITE CHAPEL OF ST. THERESE (1970) Revs. Eugene Joseph Bettinger, O.Carm.; Daniel Smith, O.Carm., Dir.; Guy McPartland, O.Carm.
Res.: 135 Gertrude Ave., 07652-2515. Tel: 201-845-6392.
Church: Bergen Mall, 07652. Tel: 201-845-6115.
2—CHURCH OF THE ANNUNCIATION (1953) Revs. James V. Teti; Joseph Kwiatkowski, Parochial Vicar; Deacons Joseph Niland; William D. Joyce; Edmund McKeown, Pastoral Assoc.; Sr. Clare DeGregorio, C.S.J., Pastoral Assoc.
Res.: 50 W. Midland Ave., 07652-2140. Tel: 201-261-6322; Fax: 201-261-6227. Email: info@annunciationchurch.org. Web: annunciationchurch.org.
Parish Center & Mailing Address: 49 Demarest Rd., 07652-2109.
See Visitation Academy, Paramus under Our Lady of Visitation, Paramus for details.
Catechesis/Religious Program—Tel: 201-261-4119. Edmund McKeown, D.R.E. Students 503.
3—OUR LADY OF THE VISITATION (1952) Rev. Msgr. Joseph T. Slinger; Revs. Michael E. Gubernat; Sebastian Kunnath. In Res., Very Rev. Mathias T. Conva (Retired).
Res.: 234 Farview Ave., 07652. Tel: 201-261-6080; Fax: 201-261-2995. Email: rectory@olvcommunity.org. Web: www.olvcommunity.org.
School—Visitation Academy (1991), (Grades PreK-8), 222 Farview Ave., 07652. Tel: 201-262-6067; Fax: 201-261-4613. Sr. Philomena Marie McCartney, O.P., Prin.; Carolyn O'Leary, Asst. Prin. Co-Sponsored. Sisters 1; Lay Teachers 20; Students 315.
Catechesis/Religious Program—Tel: 201-265-3812. Mrs. Barbara D'Arrigo, D.R.E. Students 587.

PARK RIDGE, BERGEN CO., OUR LADY OF MERCY (1902) Very Rev. Charles P. Granstrand; Rev. Robert T. Ulak; Rev. Msgr. James C. Turro, Weekend Asst. (Retired). In Res., Rev. Msgr. Carl D. Hinrichsen (Retired).
Res.: 2 Fremont Ave., 07656. Tel: 201-391-5315; Fax: 201-391-5614. Email: olm.church@gmail.com. Web: www.urolm.org.
School—Our Lady of Mercy School (1950), (Grades PreK-8), 25 Fremont Ave., 07656. Tel: 201-391-3838; Fax: 201-391-3080. Laraine Meehan, Prin. Lay Teachers 33; Students 410.
Catechesis/Religious Program—50 Pascack Rd., 07656. Tel: 201-391-3590; Fax: 201-802-1771. Amy Ballanco, D.R.E. Students 1,051.

PLAINFIELD, UNION CO.
1—ST. BERNARD'S (1921) Merged with St. Stanislaus Kostka to form The Parish of St. Bernard and St. Stanislaus, Plainfield.
2—ST. MARY (1851) [CEM] Revs. Kenneth Jones; Rafael Velazquez; Ivan Sant; Pablo A. Martinez; Deacon Pedro Nieves. In Res., Rev. Michael J. Feketie (Retired).
Res.: 516 W. Sixth St., 07060. Tel: 908-756-0085; Fax: 908-756-1658. Email: stmarysplainfield@msn.com. Web: www.stmarysnj.com.
Catechesis/Religious Program—Students 650.
Convent—Missionaries of Charity, (Contemplative), 513 Liberty St., 07060. Tel: 908-754-1978. Sisters 14.
3—THE PARISH OF ST. BERNARD AND ST. STANISLAUS (2005) Revs. Frank Rose; Jan Krzystof Lebdowicz (Poland).
Office & Rectory: 368 Sumner Ave., 07062. Tel: 908-756-3393; Fax: 908-756-3059. Email: office@bestchurch.net. Web: www.bestchurch.net.
Catechesis/Religious Program—Ms. Patricia Cook, D.R.E. Students 125.
4—ST. STANISLAUS KOSTKA (1919) Merged with St. Bernard's to form The Parish of St. Bernard and St. Stanislaus, Plainfield.

RAHWAY, UNION CO.
1—ST. MARK'S (1871), (German), Revs. Dennis J. Kaelin; Michael C. Barone; Joseph A. Klenner, Pastoral Assoc.; Bro. William Lavigne, F.M.S., Pastoral Assoc.
Res.: 287 Hamilton St., 07065. Tel: 732-499-9230; Fax: 732-388-7036. Web: www.rc.net/newark/stmark.
Catechesis/Religious Program—Tel: 732-388-7036. Mary Anne Conroy, D.R.E. Students 199.
2—ST. MARY'S (1854) [CEM] Revs. Dennis J. Kaelin; Peter Vo; Reinerio Agaloos; Oscar Ramirez Ruiz; Deacon Robert Fencik.
Res. & Office: 232 Central Ave., 07065. Tel: 732-388-0082; Fax: 732-388-0020. Email: stmaryschurchnj@comcast.net. Web: www.rc.net/newark/stmary.
See Sts. Mary & Elizabeth Academy, Linden under St. Elizabeth's, Linden for details.
Catechesis/Religious Program—Tel: 732-382-0004; Fax: 732-382-4784. Email: smrec@verizon.net. Students 243.

RAMSEY, BERGEN CO., ST. PAUL (1939) Rev. Msgr. Lawrence W. Cull; Rev. Nigel R. Mohammed, Parochial Vicar; Deacons Jeremiah K. Rehse; Fritz Kautz.
Res.: 200 Wyckoff Ave., 07446. Tel: 201-327-0976; Fax: 201-327-6197.
School—St. Paul's Interparochial School, 187 Wyckoff Ave., 07446. Tel: 201-327-1108; Fax: 201-236-1318. Gail Ritchie, Prin. Lay Teachers 30; Students 300.
Catechesis/Religious Program—Tel: 201-327-8010. Ms. Diane Campbell, D.R.E. Students 1,750.

RIDGEFIELD PARK, BERGEN CO., ST. FRANCIS OF ASSISI (1890) Revs. Eugene J. Field; Yunior Almonte.
Res.: 114 Mt. Vernon St., 07660. Tel: 201-641-6464; Fax: 201-641-2282. Email: stfranrpmission@aol.com. Web: www.stfrancisrp.org.
School—(1915), (Grades PreK-8), 110 Mt. Vernon St., 07660. Tel: 201-641-9159; Fax: 201-641-4091. Sr. Patricia Meidhof, S.C., Prin. Sisters 1; Lay Teachers 18; Students 273.
Catechesis/Religious Program—Celeste Farrell, D.R.E. Students 300.

RIDGEFIELD, BERGEN CO., ST. MATTHEW'S (1899) Revs. Donald P. Sheehan; Jose Manuel; Deacon Joseph A. Dickson. In Res., Rev. Msgr. William J. Koplik (Retired).
Res.: 555 Prospect Ave., 07657. Tel: 201-945-3500; Fax: 201-945-3796. Email: stmatthews@nj.rr.org. Web: stmatthewridgefield.org.
School—Notre Dame Interparochial Primary Division (1991), (Grades PreK-8), 312 First St., Palisades Park, 07650. Tel: 201-947-5262; Fax: 201-947-8319. Web: www.notredameint.org. Rita Miragliotta, Prin.; Jeanne Loukas, Librarian. Lay Teachers 16; Students 242.
Catechesis/Religious Program—Margaret M. Manley, D.R.E. Students 292.

RIDGEWOOD, BERGEN CO., OUR LADY OF MOUNT CARMEL (1889) Rev. Msgr. Ronald J. Rozniak; Revs. Sean Manson; Thomas Patrick Quinn; Deacons Robert V. Thomann; Nicholas De Lucca; Mrs. Linda English, Pastoral Assoc.; Mr. Peter Sicko, Music Min.; Glenn McCall, Youth Min. In Res., Revs. Mert Cordero; Thomas E. Pendrick.
Res.: 1 Passaic St., 07450-4309. Tel: 201-444-2000, Ext. 205; Fax: 201-444-2002. Web: www.olmcridgewood.com. Email: pfrazza@olmcridgewood.com.
School—Academy of Our Lady, (Grades PreK-8) Tel: 201-445-0622; Fax: 201-445-8345. Patricia Keenaghan, Prin.
Catechesis/Religious Program—Tel: 201-444-0211; Fax: 201-444-4421. Ms. Cathy Hunt, D.R.E.; Marie Cummings, D.R.E. Students 1,760.

RIVER EDGE, BERGEN CO., ST. PETER THE APOSTLE (1948) Rev. Michael J. Sheehan; Rev. Msgr. David J. Casazza, Pastor Emeritus (Retired); Revs. Michael J. German; Matthew R. Dooley; Deacons Edward Bowen; Andrew J. Golden.
Res.: 445 Fifth Ave., 07661. Tel: 201-261-3366; Fax: 201-261-0117. Email: spc445@aol.com. Web: www.saint-peter.org.
School—St. Peter Academy (1952) 431 Fifth Ave., 07661. Tel: 201-261-3468; Fax: 201-261-4316. Web: www.spare.org. Sr. Barbara Takacs, M.P.F., Prin. Sisters 2; Lay Teachers 17; Students 224.
Catechesis/Religious Program—Tel: 201-265-6019. Email: religed@optonline.net. Eileen Hanrahan, D.R.E.; Chris Black, D.R.E. Students 715.
Convent—Tel: 201-845-9568.

ROCHELLE PARK, BERGEN CO., SACRED HEART (1917) Rev. Norbert F. Laskowski.
Res.: 12 Terrace Ave., 07662. Tel: 201-843-1722; Fax: 201-843-3542.
See Visitation Academy, Paramus under Our Lady of the Visitation for details.
Catechesis/Religious Program—Tel: 201-843-1077. Karl Patterman, D.R.E. Students 245.

ROSELAND, ESSEX CO., OUR LADY OF THE BLESSED SACRAMENT (1955) Revs. Theodore W. Osbahr; Christopher D. Isinta; Deacon Pat Quagliana; Sr. Rie Crowley, S.S.J., Pastoral Assoc. (Sick and Homebound Parish Outreach); Donald Pennell, Pastoral Assoc. (Liturgical Music). In Res., Rev. James B. Sullivan (Retired).
Res.: 28 Livingston Ave., 07068. Tel: 973-226-7288; Fax: 973-226-4893. Email: olbsre@verizon.net. Web: www.olbs.org.
School—Trinity Academy - PreK Mrs. Dorothy McMahon, Prin.
See Trinity Academy under St. Aloysius in Caldwell for details (Grade K-8).
Catechesis/Religious Program—Tel: 973-226-5251; Fax: 973-403-8871. Catherine Gibbons, D.R.E. Students 669.

ROSELLE PARK, UNION CO., THE ASSUMPTION (1907) Rev. Ken Evans. In Res., Rev. Eugene Marcone.
Res.: 113 Chiego Pl., 07204. Tel: 908-245-1107; Fax: 908-245-2789. Email: assumption59@hotmail.com.
Catechesis/Religious Program—110 Chiego Pl., 07204. Rae Anello, D.R.E. Students 330.

ROSELLE, UNION CO., CHURCH OF ST. JOSEPH THE CARPENTER (1895) Revs. Krzysztof Maslowski; Marco Hurtado Olazo; John A. Quill; Deacon Vincent Belluscio. Sisters of St. Joseph, Chestnut Hill.
Res.: 157 E. Fourth Ave., 07203. Tel: 908-241-1250; Fax: 908-241-6311. Web: www.stjosephsroselle.org.
School—(1913), (Grades PreK-8), 150 E. Third Ave., 07203. Tel: 908-245-6560; Fax: 908-245-3342. Web: www.stjosephsroselle.org. Mary Ellen Woodstock, Prin. Sisters 1; Lay Teachers 20; Students 185.
Catechesis/Religious Program—Tel: 908-245-2119. Students 88.
Convent—135 E. Fourth Ave., 07203. Tel: 908-245-1594.

RUTHERFORD, BERGEN CO., CHURCH OF ST. MARY (1908) Revs. Michael J. Kreder; Charles W. Hartling; Deacons John Di Meo; James J. Guida; Michael Matthews.
91 Home Ave., 07070. Email: rcansmr@aol.com. Web: www.stmaryrutherford.org.
Res.: 98 Home Ave., 07070. Tel: 201-438-2200; Fax: 201-438-1098. Email: rcansmr@aol.com. Web: www.stmaryrutherford.org.
School—(1916), (Grades PreK-8), 72 Chestnut St., 07070. Tel: 201-933-8410; Fax: 201-531-9020. Email: principal.smes@gmail.com. Web: www.saintmaryelementary.org. Elena Simmons, Prin. Lay Teachers 18; Students 243.
High School—(1928) 64 Chestnut St., 07070. Tel: 201-933-5220; Fax: 201-933-0834. Web: www.stmaryhs.org. Roy Corso, Prin. Lay Teachers 30; Students 304.
Catechesis/Religious Program—Tel: 201-438-2476. Betty Hatler, D.R.E. Students 480.

SADDLE BROOK, BERGEN CO.
1—KOREAN MARTYRS (1998), (Korean), Revs. Hongshik Don Bosco Park, Admin.; Borromeo Bongchoon Lee.
Res.: 585 Saddle River Rd., 07663. Tel: 201-703-0002; Fax: 201-703-7111.
Catechesis/Religious Program—Sangkya Thomas Lee, D.R.E. Students 300.
2—ST. PHILIP THE APOSTLE (1953) Revs. Theesmas Pankiraj; Matthew Fonseka; Ireneusz Pierzchala.
Res.: 488 Saddle River Rd., 07663. Tel: 201-843-1888; Fax: 201-368-9161. Email: ourparish@stphilipsb.org. Web: www.stphilipsb.org.
Catechesis/Religious Program—Tel: 201-843-2240; Fax: 201-843-3150. Email: reled@stphilipsb.org. Web: reled-stphilipsb.org. Pat Schauble, D.R.E. Students 460.

SADDLE RIVER BOROUGH, BERGEN CO., ST. GABRIEL THE ARCHANGEL (1952) Rev. Msgr. Robert J. Fuhrman; Rev. Raphael Lee.
Res.: 3 W. Church Rd., 07458. Tel: 201-327-5663; Fax: 201-327-7063. Email: info@stgabrielchurch.com. Web: www.stgabrielchurch.com.
See St. John's Academy, Hillsdale under St. John the Baptist, Hillsdale for details.
Catechesis/Religious Program—Tel: 201-825-0275; Fax: 201-327-7063. Patricia Pula, D.R.E. Students 525.

SCOTCH PLAINS, UNION CO.
1—ST. BARTHOLOMEW (1948) Revs. John J. Paladino; Kevin A. Gugliotta; Deacon Robert Gurske; Paul Milan, Music Min.; Angela Kobliska, Youth Min.; Paul Kobliska, Youth Min. In Res., Revs. John J. Lester (Retired); Kevin F. Murphy; Rev. Msgr. John Philip O'Connor (Retired).
Res.: 2032 Westfield Ave., 07076. Tel: 908-322-5192; Fax: 908-322-2598.
School—St. Bartholomew Academy (1950), (Grades PreK-8) Tel: 908-322-4265; Fax: 908-322-7065. Sr. Elizabeth Calello, M.P.F., Prin.; Marianne Luongo, Librarian. Religious Teachers Filippini 1; Lay Teachers 16; Students 196.
Catechesis/Religious Program—Tel: 908-322-2359. Sr. Phyllis Vella, M.P.F., D.R.E.; Patricia Krema, D.R.E. Students 630.
Convent—Tel: 908-322-5619.
2—IMMACULATE HEART OF MARY (1964) Rev. Msgr. Sean R. Cunneen; Rev. Antonio Kuizon (Philippines); Felicia S. Levine, Pastoral Assoc.
Res.: 1571 S. Martine Ave., 07076. Tel: 908-889-2100; Fax: 908-889-9477. Email: ihm123@aol.com. Web: www.ihmparish.net.
Catechesis/Religious Program—Jeanne Fox, D.R.E.; Ms. Katie Wills, Music Min.; Ms. Pamela Streisel, 7th & 8th Grade Youth Min.; Mr. Matthew Butler, High School Youth Min. Students 708.

SECAUCUS, HUDSON CO., IMMACULATE CONCEPTION (1908) Revs. Joseph P. Pietropinto; John J. Prada; Deacon Earle S. Connelly Jr. In Res., Rev. Alan F. Guglielmo (Retired).
Res.: 1219 Paterson Plank Rd., 07094. Tel: 201-863-4840; Fax: 201-863-3537.
Catechesis/Religious Program—Tel: 201-863-4840, Ext. 28. Linda Meyer, D.R.E. Students 459.

SHORT HILLS, ESSEX CO., ST. ROSE OF LIMA (1852) [CEM] Rev. Msgr. George R. Trabold; Revs. M.

Christen Beirne, Parochial Vicar; Michael S.P. Trainor; Deacons Anthony Scalzo; Joseph M. Persinger; David J. Hughes.
Res.: 50 Short Hills Ave., 07078. Tel: 973-379-3912; Fax: 973-379-6157. Email: jschultz@stroseshorthills.org. Web: www.stroseshorthills.org.
School—(1869), (Grades PreK-8), 52 Short Hills Ave., 07078. Tel: 973-379-3973; Fax: 973-379-3722. Diane L. Pollak, Prin. Lay Teachers 23; Students 256.
Catechesis/Religious Program—Tel: 973-376-1960; Fax: 973-376-3818. Julia F. Persinger, D.R.E. Students 700.

SOUTH ORANGE, ESSEX CO., OUR LADY OF SORROWS (1887) Rev. Msgr. Robert E. Emery; Rev. Richard Pfannenstiel.
Res.: 217 Prospect St., 07079. Tel: 973-763-5454; Fax: 973-763-9506. Email: ols217so@msn.com. Web: www.olschurch.com.
School—(1890), (Grades PreK-8), 172 Academy St., 07079. Tel: 973-763-5169; Fax: 973-378-9781. Web: www.ourladyofsorrowsschool.org. Sr. Judith Blair, S.C.C., Prin. Religious 2; Lay Teachers 24; Students 192.
Day Care Nursery—Tel: 973-763-4040; Fax: 973-763-5151. Email: thenurseryols@verizon.net. Bonnie Hughes, Dir. Total Staff 5; Toddler 3; Infant 2.
Catechesis/Religious Program—Tel: 973-763-5454, Ext. 235. Email: reled@olschurch.com. Joan Csedrik, D.R.E. Students 418.

SPRINGFIELD, UNION CO., ST. JAMES THE APOSTLE (1923) Rev. Msgr. William C. Hatcher; Rev. James Worth; Sr. Roseann M. Treston, S.S.J., Pastoral Assoc.; Deacons Jerry Bongiovanni; Daniel O'Neill.
Res.: 45 S. Springfield Ave., 07081. Tel: 973-376-3044; Fax: 973-376-0560. Web: www.saintjamesparish.org.
School—41 S. Springfield Ave., 07081. Tel: 973-376-5194; Fax: 973-376-5228. Email: sjschool@saintjamesparish.org. Ms. Patricia Dolansky. Lay Teachers 16; Students 215.
Catechesis/Religious Program—Tel: 973-376-2061. Nancy Caputo, D.R.E. Students 460.

SUMMIT, UNION CO., ST. TERESA'S (1863) [CEM] Revs. Brian G. Plate; Maciej J. Zajac; Marco A. Celis Quintero; Angela Intili Stokes, Pastoral Assoc.; Michael Fusco, Pastoral Assoc.; Deacon Alcides Vega. In Res., Rev. Msgr. Donald E. Guenther (Retired).
Res.: 306 Morris Ave., 07901. Tel: 908-277-3700; Fax: 908-273-5909. Web: www.stteresachurch.org.
School—Tel: 908-273-6975; Fax: 908-273-1770. Leann Durner, Prin.
Catechesis/Religious Program—Tel: 908-273-6975; Fax: 908-273-1770. Students 1,550.

TEANECK, BERGEN CO., ST. ANASTASIA'S (1908) Revs. Daniel O'Neill, O.Carm.; William O'Malley, O.Carm.; Deacon Kevin J. Regan. In Res., Revs. Emmett Gavin, O.Carm.; Eugene Joseph Bettinger, O.Carm.
Res.: 1095 Teaneck Rd., 07666. Tel: 201-837-3354; Fax: 201-837-3360. Web: www.saintanastasia.org.
See St. Cecilia's Interparochial School, Englewood under St. Cecilia, Englewood for details.
Catechesis/Religious Program—Tel: 201-837-3356. Sr. Adrienne Bradley, S.S.J., D.R.E. Students 225.
Convent—Tel: 201-837-3153.

TENAFLY, BERGEN CO., OUR LADY OF MOUNT CARMEL (1873) Revs. Leonard Gilman, O.Carm.; Peter Byrth, O.Carm.; Deacons Lex Ferrauiola; David B. Loman. In Res., Rev. James Boyce, O.Carm.
Res.: 10 County Rd., 07670. Tel: 201-568-0545; Fax: 201-568-3215.
School—(1879), (Grades PreK-8) Tel: 201-567-6491; Fax: 201-568-1402. Sylvia Costino, Prin. Lay Teachers 17; Students 205.
Catechesis/Religious Program—Tel: 201-871-4662. Students 415.

UNION CITY, HUDSON CO.

1—ST. ANTHONY OF PADUA (1899), (Italian), Revs. Jose E. Marquez; Zeljko J. Guberovic, Parochial Vicar.
Res.: 615 Eighth St., 07087. Tel: 201-867-3818; Fax: 201-867-8859.
See Mother Seton Interparochial under Sts. Joseph and Michael, Union City.
Catechesis/Religious Program—Luis Tobar, D.R.E. Students 275.

2—ST. AUGUSTINE'S (1886) Revs. Thomas J. Devine, O.A.R.; Jose Antonio Ciordia; Julio Espinosa, O.A.R.; Blas Montenegro, O.A.R.; Deacon Edward Donosso.
Res.: 3900 New York Ave., 07087. Tel: 201-863-0233; Fax: 201-863-1841.
School—(1891), (Grades PreK-8), 3920 New York Ave., 07087. Tel: 201-865-5319; Fax: 201-865-2567. Sr. Lillian Sharrock, S.C., Prin. Sisters of Charity 4; Lay Teachers 18; Students 370.
Catechesis/Religious Program—Tel: 201-863-0233; Fax: 201-863-1341. Students 600.
Convent—342 39th St., 07087. Tel: 201-348-0527.

3—HOLY FAMILY (1857) Revs. Francisco J. Legarra, O.A.R.; Alberto Fuente, O.A.R. (Spain), Vicar.
Res.: 530 35th St., 07087. Tel: 201-867-6535; Fax: 201-867-1357.
Catechesis/Religious Program—Carol Stronach, D.R.E. (English); Juana Alvarado, D.R.E. (Spanish). Students 120.

4—STS. JOSEPH AND MICHAEL (1887; 1851) Revs. Richard J. Carrington; Christian Jaramillo Basquerizo; Deacons Thomas Barrett; Asterio Velasco; Ricardo L. Flores. In Res., Rev. Hector Larrea.
Res.: 1314 Central Ave., 07087. Tel: 201-865-2325; Fax: 201-348-4412.
School—Mother Seton Interparochial, (Grades PreK-8), 1501 New York Ave., 07087. Tel: 201-863-8433; Fax: 201-863-8145. Mary P. McErlaine, Prin. Lay Teachers 9; Students 192.
Catechesis/Religious Program—Tel: 201-863-8145. Students 383.

5—SAINT ROCCO/SAINT BRIGID (1912) Rev. Manuel D. Rios.
Res.: 4206 Kennedy Blvd., 07087. Tel: 201-863-1427; Fax: 201-863-3877. Email: strocco@verizon.net.
Catechesis/Religious Program—Sr. Catherine Santorsa, M.P.F., C.R.E. Students 137.
Mission House—4214 Kennedy Blvd., 07087. Tel: 201-863-5727.

UNION, UNION CO.

1—HOLY SPIRIT (1963) Revs. Armand Mantia; Alfred Burke; Deacons Joseph J. Carlo; Stanley W. Kwiatek.
Res.: 984 Suburban Rd., 07083. Tel: 908-687-3327; Fax: 908-687-1312.
School—(Grades PreK-8), 970 Suburban Rd., 07083. Tel: 908-687-8415; Fax: 908-687-3996. Barbara Prescott, Prin. Lay Teachers 14; Students 240.
Catechesis/Religious Program—984 Suburban Rd., 07083. Tel: 908-964-7533. Catherine Drake, D.R.E. Students 500.

2—ST. MICHAEL'S (1928) Revs. Charles B. McDermott; Robert Wolfee; Wilson A. Paculan; Sr. Ann Dominic, O.P., Pastoral Assoc. for Social Concerns; Jean O'Dowd, Business Mgr.
Res.: 1212 Kelly St., 07083. Tel: 908-688-1232; Fax: 908-810-1076.
School—(1931), (Grades PreK-8) Tel: 908-688-1063; Fax: 908-687-7927. Antoinette Telle, Prin. Sisters of St. Dominic 2; Lay Teachers 19; Students 371.
Catechesis/Religious Program—Tel: 908-964-0965. Sr. Virginia Wilkinson, P.V.B.M., D.R.E.; Philip Matrale, Youth Min. Students 678.
Convent—Tel: 908-686-3839.

UPPER MONTCLAIR, ESSEX CO., ST. CASSIAN (1895) Rev. Msgr. John G. Judge.
Res.: 187 Bellevue Ave., 07043. Tel: 973-744-2850; Fax: 973-744-6187. Email: stcassianchurch@algxmail.com.
School—(Grades PreK-8), 190 Lorraine Ave., 07043. Tel: 973-746-1636; Fax: 973-746-3271. Mary Cassels, Prin. Lay Teachers 15; Students 210.
Catechesis/Religious Program—Students 560.

UPPER SADDLE RIVER, BERGEN CO., CHURCH OF THE PRESENTATION (1961) Revs. Robert B. Stagg; Lope Lesigues; Jacek Marchewka. In Res., Rev. Msgr. Edward J. Ciuba (Retired).
Office: 271 W. Saddle River Rd., 07458. Tel: 201-327-1313; Fax: 201-760-2570. Web: www.churchofpresentation.org.
Res.: 41 Riverview Ter., 07458.
See St. Paul's Interparochial School, Ramsey under St. Paul's, Ramsey for details.
Catechesis/Religious Program—Fax: 201-327-8430. Students 1,424.

VERONA, ESSEX CO., OUR LADY OF THE LAKE (1923) Revs. Michael A. Hanly; Bryan Page; Jerome S. Arthasseril (India). In Res., Very Rev. Albert J. Berner.
Res.: 32 Lakeside Ave., 07044. Tel: 973-239-5696; Fax: 973-239-7190. Email: vita_moss@comcast.net. Web: www.ollverona.org.
School—(1924), (Grades PreK-8), 22 Lakeside Ave., 07044. Tel: 973-239-1160; Fax: 973-239-6496. Sr. Mary Agnes Sullivan, O.P., Prin. Sisters 1; Lay Teachers 10; Students 222.
Catechesis/Religious Program—Tel: 973-239-7643; Fax: 973-239-8283. Students 881.

WALLINGTON, BERGEN CO., MOST SACRED HEART OF JESUS (1942), (Polish), [CEM] Very Rev. Canon Felix R. Marciniak; Rev. Steven D. D'Andrea; Deacon Victor J. Puzio.
Res.: 127 Paterson Ave., 07057. Tel: 973-778-7405; Fax: 973-778-7750. Email: mostsacredheart@comcast.net. Web: www.mostsacredheart.org.
School—(1943), (Grades PreK-8), 6 Bond St., 07057. Tel: 973-777-4817. Email: mostsacredheartschool@comcast.net. Sr. Lisa Marie DiSabatino, C.S.S.F., Prin. Sisters 2; Lay Teachers 18; Students 217.
Catechesis/Religious Program—Tel: 973-777-9505; Fax: 973-778-7750; 973-777-4982. Sr. Marie Victoria Bartkowski, D.R.E. Students 297.

WASHINGTON TOWNSHIP, BERGEN CO., OUR LADY OF GOOD COUNSEL (1959) Revs. Stephen J. Cinque; Stephen J. Duffe; Sr. Joseph Miriam Blackwell, M.S.B.T., Pastoral Assoc.; Deacon Robert Glasner.
Res.: 668 Ridgewood Rd., 07676. Tel: 201-664-6624; Fax: 201-664-0095. Email: olgcwt@aol.com. Web: www.olgcwt.org.
See Our Lady of Mercy Interparochial School, Park Ridge under Our Lady of Mercy, Park Ridge for details.
See St. John's Academy Interparochial, Hillsdale under St. John The Baptist, Hillsdale for details.
Catechesis/Religious Program—Tel: 201-664-1679. Joyce Magras, D.R.E. Students 177.

WEEHAWKEN, HUDSON CO., ST. LAWRENCE'S (1887) Very Rev. James P. Whelan.
Res.: 22 Hackensack Ave., 07086. Tel: 201-863-6464; Fax: 201-863-6656. Email: stlawrencec@optonline.net. Web: www.stlawrence-church.net.
See Hoboken Catholic Academy, Hoboken under St. Ann's, Hoboken for details.
Catechesis/Religious Program—Students 95.

WEST NEW YORK, HUDSON CO.

1—HOLY REDEEMER Very Rev. Carlo Fortunio, O.P. (Italy); Rev. Mariano N. Dellagiovanna.
Res.: 6502 Jackson St., 07093. Tel: 201-868-9444; Fax: 201-868-6451.
Catechesis/Religious Program—Students 200.

2—ST. JOSEPH OF THE PALISADES (1875), (Hispanic), Rev. Msgr. Gregory J. Studerus; Revs. Armando Crisostomo, Parochial Vicar; Jozef Krajnak, S.D.B., Parochial Vicar; Jesus Orlando Rengifo, Parochial Vicar; Oscar D. Fonseca, Parochial Vicar. In Res., Most Rev. David Arias, O.A.R., Pastor Emeritus.
Res.: 6401 Palisade Ave., 07093. Tel: 201-854-7006; Fax: 201-861-7799. Email: st.joseph.wny@verizon.net. Web: www.sjpl.org.
School—(1872), (Grades PreK-8), 6408 Palisade Ave., 07093. Tel: 201-861-3227; Fax: 201-861-5744. Web: www.stjosephpalisadeselem.com. Eileen Donovan-Ferrando, Prin.; Lauren Lytle, Asst. Prin. Franciscan Missionary Sisters of the Sacred Heart 4; Lay Teachers 10; Students 180.
Catechesis/Religious Program—Andres Melendez, C.R.E.; Janet Melendez, C.R.E. Students 600.
Chapel—Immaculate Heart of Mary 7615 Broadway, North Bergen, 07047.
Chapel—Cor Jesu 5400 Broadway, 07093.
Convent—6414 Palisade Ave., 07093. Tel: 201-861-3337.

3—ST. MARY HELP OF CHRISTIANS (1895) Merged with St. John Nepomucene, Guttenberg to form Holy Redeemer, West New York.

4—OUR LADY OF LIBERA (1902), (Italian), Rev. Philip J. Rotunno; Deacon Jesus D. Aristy.
Res.: 5808 John F. Kennedy Memorial Blvd., 07093. Tel: 201-867-2642.
School—(Grades PreK-8), 5800 John F. Kennedy Memorial Blvd., 07093. Tel: 201-864-5557; Fax: 201-601-3156. Ana M. Castaneda, Prin. Lay Teachers 16; Students 175.
Catechesis/Religious Program—Students 150.

WEST ORANGE, ESSEX CO.

1—ST. JOSEPH'S (1931) Revs. Richard G. Francesco; Salvatore DiStefano; Deacon Luis Velo. In Res., Rev. Msgr. Thomas P. Ivory (Retired).
Res.: 44 Benvenue Ave., 07052. Tel: 973-669-3221; Fax: 973-669-0385. Email: stjosephwestorange@hotmail.com. Web: stjosephwestorange.com.
School—Blessed Pope John XXIII Academy (2006), (Grades PreK-8), (Co-Sponsored with Our Lady of Lourdes, West Orange), 8 St. Cloud Pl., 07052. Tel: 973-731-3503. Web: www.bpjxxiii.org. Lynda Wright, Prin. Lay Teachers 11; Students 176.
Catechesis/Religious Program—Pauline Alger, Pastoral Assoc. & D.R.E. Students 242.

2—OUR LADY OF LOURDES (1914) Rev. Msgr. Joseph A. Petrillo; Rev. James P. Ferry; Deacon Ernesto Abad. In Res., Rev. Hippolytus Duru (Nigeria) (NY).
Res.: 1 Eagle Rock Ave., 07052. Tel: 973-325-0110; Fax: 973-325-9105. Email: ollwo@comcast.net. Web: www.lourdeswestorgange.com.
See Blessed Pope John XIII Academy, West Orange under St. Joseph's, West Orange for details.
Catechesis/Religious Program—Tel: 973-325-0029. Eileen Morgan, D.R.E. Students 123.
Convent—Tel: 973-325-0318; Fax: 973-325-0691.

WESTFIELD, UNION CO.

1—ST. HELEN (1968) Rev. Msgrs. William C. Harms; James F. Bouffard; Rev. Tadeusz Pieniazek, S.D.S.; Deacon John W. Lynch.
Res.: 1600 Rahway Ave., 07090. Tel: 908-232-1214; Fax: 908-317-5459. Email: wharms@sainthelen.org. Web: www.westfieldnj.com/sthelens.
See Holy Trinity Interparochial school, Westfield under Holy Trinity, Westfield for details.

Catechesis/Religious Program—Tel: 908-233-8757. Students 1,807.

2—HOLY TRINITY (1872) Rev. Msgr. Joseph P. Masiello; Rev. Donald F. Cialone; Sr. Joan Connelly, S.S.N.D., Pastoral Assoc.; Deacons Thomas A. Pluta; Keith Gibbons.
Church & Office: 315 First St., 07090. Tel: 908-232-8137; Fax: 908-654-8780. Email: donna.campa@verizon.net. Web: www.htrcc.org.
School—Holy Trinity Interparochial, (Grades PreK-8), Interparochial (co-sponsored), 336 First St., 07090. Tel: 908-233-0484; Fax: 908-233-6204. Email: office-wc@htisnj.com. Web: www.htisnj.com. Sr. Maureen Fichner, S.S.J., Prin.; Renee Rauch, Librarian.
Catechesis/Religious Program—Tel: 908-233-7455; Fax: 908-233-0837. Email: dphillips@parishmail.com. Web: www.htrcc.com. Dianne Phillips, D.R.E. Students 816.

WESTWOOD, BERGEN CO., ST. ANDREW'S (1889) [CEM] Revs. John R. O'Connell; Rafael I. Galvez-Pineda; Deacons Joseph J. Paulillo; Robert S. Pontillo; Mary Jean Conroy, Pastoral Assoc., Child Catechesis; Barbara Stewart, Pastoral Assoc., Parish Ministries; Alan Pitman, Youth Min.
Res.: 120 Washington Ave., 07675. Tel: 201-666-1100; Fax: 201-722-1432. Email: info@standrewww.org. Web: www.saintandrewswestwood.com.
See St. John's Academy, Hillsdale under St. John the Baptist, Hillsdale for details.
Catechesis/Religious Program—Tel: 201-664-6777. Email: reled@standrewww.org. Students 1,625.

WOOD RIDGE, BERGEN CO., OUR LADY OF THE ASSUMPTION (1926) Revs. Brian Cullinane, O.F.M.; Paul Sinnema, O.F.M.; Thomas Kelly, O.F.M.; Deacon Nicholas Valdez.
Res.: 143 First St., 07075. Tel: 201-438-5555; Fax: 201-438-6747. Email: assumption143@yahoo.com. Web: www.assumption-parish.org.
School—(Grades PreK-8), 151 First St., 07075. Tel: 201-933-0239; Fax: 201-438-6408. Email: aswrnj@yahoo.com. Web: www.assumptionschoolwr.org. Heather Muller, Prin. Lay Teachers 16; Students 212.
Catechesis/Religious Program—Hayes Center, 142 Second St. Tel: 201-933-6118; Fax: 201-438-6747. Email: arewrnj@yahoo.com. Students 445.

WOODCLIFF LAKE, BERGEN CO., OUR LADY MOTHER OF THE CHURCH (1967) Rev. Richard J. Kelly; Rev. Msgr. Cajetan P. Salemi, Pastor Emeritus (Retired); Rev. Thomas G. Arminio, Pastor Emeritus (Retired); Deacon Stanley F. Fedison.
Church: 209 Woodcliff Ave., 07677. Tel: 201-391-2826; Fax: 201-391-7101. Email: judiolmc@yahoo.com. Web: www.motherofthechurch.com.
Rectory—130 Apple Ridge, 07677.
See St. John's Academy, Hillsdale under St. John the Baptist, Hillsdale for details.
Catechesis/Religious Program—Tel: 201-391-7400. Susan Furey, D.R.E. Students 305.

WYCKOFF, BERGEN CO., ST. ELIZABETH (1902) Rev. Msgr. Robert E. Harahan; Revs. Jerzy Pikulinski, O.F.M.; Jose Helber Victoria-Tovar; Gina Marie Alala, Youth Min.
Res.: 700 Wyckoff Ave., 07481. Tel: 201-891-1122; Fax: 201-847-8518. Web: www.saintelizabeths.org.
School—(Grades PreK-8), Greenwood Ave., 07481. Tel: 201-891-1481; Fax: 201-891-8669. Dr. Constance McCue, Prin.; Carol Ryan, Asst. Prin. Lay Teachers 30; Students 269.
Catechesis/Religious Program—Tel: 201-891-3262; Fax: 201-891-3708. Jonathan Camiolo, D.R.E. Students 1,135.

Hospital Chaplaincy

NEWARK. *Office of Health Care Personnel*. Most Rev. Manuel A. Cruz, D.D., Archdiocesan Dir., St. Michael's Medical Center, 306 Martin Luther King Blvd., 07104. Tel: 973-877-2572, Rev. Alan F. Guglielmo, Coord. Health Care Apostolate Cont. Ed. (Retired), 306 Martin Luther King Blvd., 07104. Tel: 973-743-0220.
Coordinator for Health Care Apostolate Continuing Education, Tel: 973-743-0220. Rev. Alan F. Guglielmo (Retired).

Bergen County

ENGLEWOOD. *Englewood Hospital & Medical Center*, 350 Engle St., 07631. Tel: 201-894-3000. Rev. Charles I. Anemelu, Chap.

HACKENSACK. *Hackensack University Medical Center*, 30 Prospect St., 07601. Tel: 201-996-2000; 201-996-2345. Revs. Bernard Duga, Chap. (Adjunct), Alex C. Nnaukwu, Chap. (Adjunct), Charles Okoye, Chap., Anthony Udogu, Chap. (Adjunct).

PARAMUS. *Bergen Regional Medical Center*, 230 E. Ridgewood Ave., 07652. Tel: 201-967-4177; Fax: 201-967-4277. Revs. Sebastian M. Fernando, Chap. (Adjunct), Michael Otuwurenne, Chap.

RIDGEWOOD. *Valley Hospital*, 223 N. Van Dien Ave., 07450. Tel: 201-447-8150. Revs. Mert Cordero, Chap., Stephen J. Toth, Chap.

TEANECK. *Holy Name Hospital*, 718 Teaneck Rd., 07666. Tel: 201-833-3000; 201-833-3243 (Pastoral Care). Sr. Lois Jablonski, S.S.J., M.Div., Pastoral Staff, Revs. Paterno Gorospe, Chap., John T. Michalczak, Chap., Deacon Willy Malarcher, Chap.

Essex County

NEWARK. *Beth Israel Medical Center*, 201 Lyons Ave., 07112. Tel: 973-926-7000; 973-926-7178 (Pastoral Care). Vacant.
Columbus Campus of St. Michael Medical Center, 495 N. 13th St., 07107. Tel: 201-268-1400. Vacant.
St. James Campus of St. Michael Medical Center, 155 Jefferson St., 07105. Tel: 973-465-2707; Fax: 973-465-2861. Vacant, Pastoral Staff. Tel: 973-465-2671.
St. Michael Medical Center, 111 Central Ave., 07102. Tel: 973-877-5467. Rev. Msgr. Robert E. Templeton, Chap., Revs. Eustace Edomobi (Nigeria), Chap., Clement Kagoma, Chap., Deacons Jose M. Class, Chap., Dennis F. La Scala, Chap., Edward McFadden, Chap.
University of Medicine & Dentistry (UMDNJ), 100 Bergen St., 07103. Tel: 973-972-4300. Deacon Sixto Lopez, Hospital Min.

BELLEVILLE. *Clara Maass Medical Center*, One Clara Maass Dr., 07109. Tel: 973-450-2000. Rev. John Donohue, Chap. (Adjunct).

CEDAR GROVE. *Essex County Hospital Center*, 125 Fairview Ave., 07009. Tel: 973-228-8000. Vacant.
St. Vincent Nursing Home, 315 E. Lindsley Rd., 07009. Tel: 973-754-4800. Sr. Elizabeth Ann Noonan, S.C., Chap., Deborah Quinn Martone, Admin.

EAST ORANGE. *Veterans Administration Hospital*, Tremont Ave. & Center St., 07019. Tel: 973-676-1000; 973-972-5688 (Pastoral Care). Rev. Mathew Eraly.

LIVINGSTON. *St. Barnabas Medical Center*, 94 Old Short Hills Rd., 07039. Tel: 973-533-5015. Rev. Hippolytus Duru (Nigeria) (NY), Chap. (Adjunct), Sr. MaryAnn Boyle, S.S.J., Chap.

MONTCLAIR. *Mountainside Hospital*, One Bay Ave., 07042. Tel: 973-429-6000; 973-429-6047 (Pastoral Care). Rev. Thomas M. Cembor, Chap.

ORANGE. *Hospital Center at Orange*, 188 S. Essex St., 07051. Vacant, Chap.
Pope John Paul II Pavilion, 135 S. Centre St., 07050. Tel: 973-266-3000. Vacant.

WEST ORANGE. *Kessler Institute for Rehabilitation*, 1199 Pleasant Valley Way, 07052. Tel: 973-731-3600. Rev. Louis M. Pambello, Chap.

Hudson County

BAYONNE. *Bayonne Medical Center*, 29 E. 29th St., 07002. Tel: 201-858-5000. Vacant.

JERSEY CITY. *Christ Hospital*, 176 Palisades Ave., 07304. Tel: 201-795-8200. Sr. Nancy Craig.
Jersey City Medical Center, 50 Baldwin Ave., 07304. Tel: 201-915-2000. Rev. George Joseph.

KEARNY. *West Hudson Hospital*, 206 Bergen Ave., 07032. Tel: 201-955-7000. Vacant.

NORTH BERGEN. *Palisades Medical Center*, 7600 River Rd., 07047. Tel: 201-854-5000. Vacant.

Union County

BERKELEY HEIGHTS. *Runnells Specialized Hospital*, 40 Watchung Ave., 07922. Tel: 908-771-5700. Vacant.

ELIZABETH. *Trinitas Regional Medical Center*, 225 Williamson St., 07202. Tel: 201-418-1000. Revs. John Quill, Brendan Quinn, Sisters Mary Corrigan, S.C., Pastoral Staff, Maria Kratz, I.H.M., Pastoral Staff, Prudentia Osuji, S.C., Pastoral Staff, Marie Tansey, S.C., Pastoral Staff.

RAHWAY. *Rahway Hospital*, 865 Stone St., 07065. Tel: 732-381-4200. Deacon William R. Benedetto.

SUMMIT. *Overlook Hospital*, 99 Beauvoir Ave., 07902. Tel: 908-522-2000. Rev. Anthony Onyekwelu, Chap., Sr. Patricia Murphy, S.S.J., Dir., Pastoral Staff.

Prison Ministry

NEWARK. *Office of Prison Ministry*, 8 Boxwood Dr., Fairfield, 07004. Cell: 973-650-2098. Email: GCQuinn57@aol.com. Deacons David B. Loman, Co-Dir., Gregory C. Quinn, Co-Dir. Tel: 973-618-3302.

Bergen County

HACKENSACK. *Bergen County Correctional Facility*, 160 S. River Rd., 07601. Tel: 201-527-3018. Rev. David S. McLaughlin, Chap.

PARAMUS. *Bergen County Juvenile Detention Center*, 296 E. Ridgewood Ave., 07652. Tel: 201-599-6185. Deacon Michael J. Cechony, Prison Minister.

Essex County

NEWARK. *Essex County Correctional Facility*, 354 Doremus Ave., 07105. Tel: 973-274-7826. Deacon Gregory Quinn, Chap.
Essex County Juvenile Detention Center, 80 Duryea St., 07103. Tel: 973-497-4720. Deacon Gregory Quinn, Chap.
Northern State Prison, 168 Frontage Rd., 07114. Tel: 973-465-0068, Ext. 4505. Revs. Thomas C. Roberts, Chap., Robert Cormier, Chap., Francisco Javier Cabezas, Deacon David Loman, Prison Min., Mr. Bob Donfield, Prison Min.

Hudson County

SECAUCUS. *Hudson County Juvenile Correctional Center*, 635 County Ave., 07094. Tel: 201-319-3750 (Promise/Outreach Ministry). Rev. Giordano Belanich, Sr. Antonelle Chunka, C.S.S.F., Pastoral Staff, Bro. Thomas Corey, B.S.C.D., Pastoral Staff.

SOUTH KEARNY. *Hudson County Correctional Center*, 35 Hackensack Ave., 07032. Tel: 973-491-5500. Revs. Paul Nolan, Prison Min., Oscar D. Fonseca, Prison Min., Mr. John Geelan, Pastoral Staff, Francis Koomson, Prison Min.
Talbot Hall Assessment Center, 100-140 Lincoln Highway. Tel: 973-589-1114. John Rennie, Prison Min.

Union County

NEWARK. *Delaney Hall Assessment Center*, 451 Doremus Ave., 07105. Tel: 908-289-6768. Rev. Paul Nolan, Deacon Michael York, Prison Min., Catherine Fink, Prison Min., Thomas More Fink, Prison Min.

ELIZABETH. *Elizabeth Federal Detention Center*, 625 Evans St., 07201. Tel: 908-352-3776. Revs. George F. Sharp, Thomas L. Sheridan, S.J.
Union County Jail, 15 Elizabethtown Plaza, 07207. Tel: 908-558-2636. Deacon Michael DeRoberts, Chap., Rev. Carlos Viejo, Prison Min.

Special Assignment in the Archdiocese:
Rev. Msgr.—
Kleissler, Thomas A., Pres.
Revs.—
Dowd, William J., Chap., 724 Drum Point Rd., Brick, 08723-7548.
Ortiz, Roberto

On Duty Outside the Archdiocese:
Rev. Msgrs.—
Baldacchino, Peter, Chancellor, Mission Sui Juris, Holy Cross Parish, Grand Turks Islands, Turks and Caicos Islands.
Casale, Franklyn M., 16500 Collins Ave., North Miami Beach, FL 33160.
Figueiredo, Anthony J., S.T.D., Pontifical Council Cor Unum Villa Stritch Via Della Nocetta 63, Rome, Vatican City State 00164 Italy.
Tiboni, Vito, Veterans' Hospital, 800 Poly Pl., Apt. 15W, Brooklyn, NY 11209.
Revs.—
Abalon, Jose Amante M., Holy Cross Mission, Gran Turks & Caicos Islands, British West Indies
Abalon, Jose Manuel M., St. Patrick Parish, 335 Main St., Brockton, MA 02301.
Alfaro, Gustavo A., SS. Peter & Paul Rooma Katoliku Kirik, Vene tn 18, Tallinn 10123 Estonia.
Arata, Miguel A., Rooma Katoliku Kirik Kogudus, Veski TN 1-1A, EE2400, Tartu, Estonia.
Barrow, Joseph A., Our Lady of the Assumption, 404 Sumner St., East Boston, MA 02128-2218.
Basile, Gioacchino, St. Gabriel Parish, 26-26 98th St., East Elmhurst, NY 11369.
Becerra, Robert L., Santa Clara Parish, P.O. Box 215, Santa Clara, NM 88026-0215.
Bornhauser, Emmanuel, 334 Avenue Alphonse Alphand, Montpelier 34080 France.
Busichio, Salvatore, 926 Woodway Bluff Cir., Cary, NC 27513-2029.
Caceres, Leonardo M., Notre Dame le Rouet, 60 Boulevard do Louvain, 13008 Marseille, France.
Carranza, Fernando, Immaculate Conception Church, 610 N.E. 17th St., Grand Prairie, TX 75050.
De Condorpusa, Alfonso R., St. Cecilia Parish, 45 Wilus Way, Iselin, 08830.
DiGiovanni, Alfonso, SS. Peter & Paul R.K. Kirik, Vene TN 18, 10123, Tallin, Estonia.
Donini, Leone, Paroisse Notre Dame de Routes, 648 Chemin de Rigoumel, Toulon 83200 France.
Flor, Carlos, Immaculate Conception, 22 Lowe St., Revere, MA 02151.
Gonzalez, Octavio, Parroquia San Jose, Apartado 25, Penuelas, PR 00624.
Guillen, Randy, 334 E. Pomona St., Santa Ana, CA 92707.
Ince, Owen F., Redemptoris Mater House of Formation, 672 Passaic Ave., Kearny, 07032.
Jaskowiak, Wojciech B., Redemptoris Mater Seminary, 130 Chalan Seminariu, Yona, GU 96915.
Klybus, Edward George, Our Lady of Divine Providence RC Mission, P.O. Box 340 Leeward Hwy., BWI Turks and Caicos Islands. Tel: 649-941-5136
Krol, Miroslaw K., Ss. Cyril and Methodius Seminary, 3535 Indian Tr., Orchard Lake, MI 48324.

Kukura, Joseph W., Cathedral Healthcare Partnership of NJ, 760 Alexander Rd., Princeton, 08543. Tel: 609-936-2213
Lek, Basil L., Holy Cross Mission, P.O. Box 70, Grand Turks & Caicos Islands, British West Indies
Lintz, Christoph, Redemptoris Mater Seminary, 672 Passaic Ave., Kearny, 07032. Tel: 495-416-3535. Holy Family Parish A.M. Bienenkorb 2, 81545 Muenchen, Germany.
Miller, Frederick L., Mt. St. Mary Seminary, 16300 Old Emmitsburg Rd., Emmitsburg, MD 21727.
Morelli, Attilio, Sacre Coeur Church, 301 Roosevelt, Creve Coeur, IL 61610.
Oddo, Peter A., P.O. Box 11, Swartswood, 07877.
Passant, Paul A., Redemptoris Mater House of Formation, 672 Passaic Ave., Kearny, 07032.
Perricone, John A., Sacred Heart Parish, 145 Randolph Ave., Clifton, 07011.
Picone, Alfonso (Italy), St. Raphael Parish, 162 Oak St., Bridgeport, CT 06604.
Prindiville, Gerald T., Pastor, St. Vincent de Paul Parish, P.O.Box 1067, Strawberry Hills NSW2012 Australia.
Randl, Ewald, Bei Alexander Fuchs, Ruthnerg 91/15/3, Vienna A-1210 Austria.
Roman, Julio I., Archdiocese of Asuncion C.C., 654 Mariscal Lopez, 130, Asuncion, Paraguay.
Russo, Michael A. (OAK), St. Mary College, Box 5166, Moraga, CA 94575.
Rwechungura, Siffredus B., Archbishop's House, P.O. Box 167, Dar es Salaam, Tanzania East Africa.
Sammarco, Bruno S., Our Lady of Divine Providence, Turks & Caicos Islands, British West Indies.
Schute, Arthur B. (Retired), 276 Orlando Blvd., Port Charlotte, FL 33954.
Smutelovic, Peter, Villa Stritch, Via della Nocetta 63, Rome 00164 Italy.
Tran, Joseph M. Duykim N., Toa Giam Muc, Kim Son, Ninh Binh Vietnam.
Trujillo-Gonzalez, Francisco de Asis, Diocese of Peoria, 607 N.E. Madison Ave., Peoria, IL 61603. Sacre Coeur Church, 301 Roosevelt, Creve Coeur, IL 61610.
Venturini, Fabio, Redemptoris Mater House of Formation, 672 Passaic Ave., Kearny, 07032.
West, Peter, Priests for Life, 128 Targee St., Staten Island, NY 10304.
Wilson, William P. (Retired), RR1 - Box 59, Falls, PA 18615-9726.

Military Chaplains:
Rev. Msgr.—
Newland, Ronald A. (Retired), 21 Park End Ter., P.O. Box 61, Fort Tilden, NY 11695-0061.
Revs.—
Beale, Kenneth R., Capt., 96 ABW/HC, 202 N. 8th St. Ste. 1, Eglin Afb, FL 32542-5651.
Berchmanz, Anthony, Chap., Naval Base-KITSAP, 2900 Ohio St., Silverdale, WA 98315.
Brosk, Steven J., 4 Liberty Place, P.O. Box 871, Sugarloaf, PA 18249.
D'Emma, Gregory J., P.O. Box 4781, Fort Eustis, VA 23604-0781.
Hamel, James A., Catholic Chaplain, 316 WG/HC, Andrews Afb, MD 20762.
Hanrahan, William P., Chap., P.O. Box 273, Seward, AK 99664-0273.
Kokeram, Sudash J., 9462 Gooden Dr., Fayetteville, NC 28314.
Kopec, Rajmund, Capt., 426 Hughes Rd., Huntsville, AL 35808.
Lesak, William P., 3519 Cranberry Ln., New Bern, NC 28562.
Pawlikowski, Matthew, Capt., 151 Lofton Dr., Fayetteville, NC 28311.
Ubalde, Ulysses, Brigade Chaplain Office, 20 Marine Expeditionary Brigade, Unit 73010, Fpo, AE 09510-3010.
Ugwuanya, Valentine C., Religious Activity Center, 2336 Hamilton Ave., Bldg. 1, Fort Bragg, NC 28310.
Uhde, Peter (OG), CMR 415, P.O. Box 4185, Apo, AE 09114-4100.

Retired:
Most Revs.—
Gerety, Peter Leo, D.D.
Marconi, Dominic A., D.D.
McDonnell, Charles J., D.D., St. Mary, 17 Monsignor Owens Pl., Nutley, 07110.
Arias, David, O.A.R., D.D.
McDonnell, Charles J., D.D.
Rev. Msgrs.—
Agan, Jose, c/o Maria Bocanegra, 332 Belgrove Dr., Kearny, 07032.
Burke, James A., Nativity Church, 315 Prospect St., Midland Park, 07432.
Burns, G. Thomas, 4264 Central Sarasota Pkwy., Sarasota, FL 34238.
Capozzelli, Emmanuel M., Rev. Msgr. James F. Kelley Residence, 247 Bloomfield Ave., Caldwell, 07006.
Casazza, David J., 426 Jefferson Ave., Avon-by-the-Sea, 07717.
Chabak, Robert M., V.F., 302 6th Ave., Normandy Beach, 08739.
Cheplic, Peter A., St. John Vianney Residence., 60 Home Ave., Rutherford, 07070.
Chiang, Joseph, St. John Vianney Residence, 60 Home Ave., Rutherford, 07070.
Ciuba, Edward J., Church of the Presentation, 271 W. Saddle River Rd., Saddle River, 07458.
Doyle, Vincent J., J.C.D., 134 Valencia Dr., Brick, 08723.
Eid, Frederick M., Our Lady of Grace, 75 Bloomfield Ave., Apt. 2E, Hoboken, 07030.
Fimiani, Louis F., St. Michael Parish, 40 Alden St., Cranford, 07016.
Finnerty, James J., St. Paul the Apostle Parish, 14 Greenville Ave., Jersey City, 07305.
Flusk, Joseph F., P.O. Box 66, Beachwood, 08722.
Gilchrist, John J., 499 Belgrove Dr., Kearny, 07032.
Gonzalez, Ricardo, 78 Meridian Dr., Brick, 08724.
Granato, Joseph J., 201 Clifton Ave., 07104.
Guenther, Donald E., St. Theresa of Avila, 306 Morris Ave., Summit, 07901.
Hajduk, Edward J., S.T.L., M.S.S., St. John Vianney Residence, 60 Home Ave., Rutherford, 07070.
Hayes, Paul J., St. Joseph for the Elderly, 140 Shepherd Ln., Totowa, 07512.
Hendry, Owen J., 7 Dogwood Dr., Ocean, 07712.
Hinrichsen, Carl D., Our Lady of Mercy Rectory, 2 Fremont Ave., Park Ridge, 07656.
Houghton, Francis J., 2316 Blue Jay Tr., Point Pleasant, 08742.
Ivory, Thomas P., S.T.D., St. Joseph Church, 44 Benvenue Ave., West Orange, 07052.
Kelly, Martin (Ireland), St. Joseph for the Elderly, 140 Shepherd, Totowa, 07512-2170.
Koplik, William J., St. Matthew, 555 Prospect Ave., Ridgefield, 07657.
Lennon, Peter F., Seton Hall University, South Orange, 07079.
LoBianco, Francis R., 32 Woodland Ave., Jamaica Plain, MA 02130.
Lutz, George C., 159 Franklin St., Apt. 6, Bloomfield, 07003.
Madden, Thomas G., St. John Vianney Residence, 60 Home Ave., Rutherford, 07070.
Matash, Edward M., St. John Vianney Res., 60 Home Ave., Rutherford, 07070.
McMenemie, James P., S.T.L., St. Michael the Archangel, 624 Page Ave., Lyndhurst, 07071.
Morris, Philip D., S.T.D., St. Rose of Lima, 50 Short Hills Ave., Short Hills, 07078.
Newland, Ronald A., 21 Park End Ter., P.O. Box 61, Fort Tilden, NY 11695-0061.
O'Brien, Martin F., 13 Hedden Ter., North Arlington, 07031.
O'Connor, John Philip, St. Bartholomew, 2032 Westfield Ave., Scotch Plains, 07076.
O'Donnell, Hugh A., 503 Gallows Hill Rd., Cranford, 07016.
O'Leary, Thomas M., St. John the Baptist, 69 Valley St., Hillsdale, 07642.
Park, Augustin, St. Venantius/St. Andrew Kim, 257 Central Ave., Orange, 07050.
Piazza, Benjamin A., St. Aloysius, 219 Bloomfield Ave., Caldwell, 07006.
Plunkett, Joseph P., Our Lady of Good Counsel Parish, 654 Summer Ave., 07104.
Pollard, Raymond J., 2316 Blue Jay Tr., Point Pleasant, 08742.
Rebanal, Jeremias R., J.C.D., Ph.D., St. Mary of Assumption, 155 Washington Ave., 07202.
Reynolds, Roger A., St. John Vianney Residence, 60 Home Ave., Rutherford, 07070.
Salemi, Cajetan P., 1600 16th Ave., Belmar, 07719.
Sheerin, James O., St. John Vianney Residence, 60 Home Ave., Rutherford, 07070.
Stengel, Charles G., St. Paul the Apostle, 14 Greenville Ave., Jersey City, 07305.
Turro, James C., Ph.D., Immaculate Conception Seminary, Seton Hall University, South Orange, 07079.
Zaccardo, Peter J., 53 Seaview Ave., Brick, 08723.
Very Revs.—
Connor, John F., S.T.B., Our Lady of Good Counsel, 654 Summer Ave., 07104-3418.
Conva, Mathias T., V.F., Our Lady of Visitation, 234 Farview Ave., Paramus, 07652.
Conva, Matthias T., Our Lady of the Visitation, 234 Fairview Ave., Paramus, 07652.
Revs.—
Arico, Carl J., St. Vincent de Paul Parish, 979 Avenue C, Bayonne, 07002.
Arminio, Thomas G., 1057 Trent Pl., Union, 07083.
Arvay, Alfred S., St. Joan of Arc Parish, 13485 Spring Hill Dr., Spring Hill, FL 34609.
Ashe, Kevin P., 446 Adamston Rd., Brick, 08723.
Ballance, Harvey, 92 Edgemont Rd., Montclair, 07043.
Ballweg, John M., P.O. Box 202, Monmouth Beach, 07750.
Basil, John E., 295 N. 7th St., Surf City, 08008-5206.
Bernas, Eugene (Philippines), c/o Florecita F. Bernas, 5523 W. Eddy St., Chicago, IL 60641.
Bernauer, Edmund G., B.A., M.A., Glenside Nursing Home, 144 Gales Dr., New Providence, 07974-2900.
Brennan, Robert M., St. John Viannex Annex, 64 Home Ave., Rutherford, 07070.
Buzzerio, Joseph E., 74 Third Place, Bogota, 07603.
Carroll, James J., 40010 Old Smalleytown Rd., Warren, 07059.
Celiano, Alfred V., Ph.D., Seton Hall University, 400 South Orange Ave., South Orange, 07079.
Coda, Joseph F., St. John Vianney Residence, 60 Home Ave., Rutherford, 07070.
Collins, Neil J., 135 Montgomery St., Jersey City, 07302.
Cooper, Donald A., 1674 Ferro Ln., P.O. Box 3, Toms River, 08755.
Cozzini, Robert P., Msgr. James F. Kelley Residence, 247 Bloomfield Ave., Caldwell, 07006.
Cron, Walter D., 347 Cupsaw Dr., Ringwood, 07456.
Daly, Robert L. (MET), Immaculate Conception Rectory, 18 South St., Spotswood, 08884.
Danik, Daniel A., 2046 Ingalls Ave., Linden, 07036.
DiGirolamo, Dante, Eucharistic Shrine of the Adorable Face of Jesus, P.O. Box 455, Kearny, 07032.
Doherty, John R., 362 Orient Way, Rutherford, 07070.
Dowling, John C., P.O. Box 641, Kenilworth, 07033.
Driscoll, William D., 51 Monterey Ave., Teaneck, 07666.
Farley, Leo O., Rev. Msgr. James F. Kelley Residence, 247 Bloomfield Ave., Caldwell, 07006.
Feehan, Stephen S., Ph.D., 49 Timerline Dr., Little Egg Harbor Twp, 08087-3060.
Feketie, Michael J., St. Mary Parish, 516 W. 6th St., Plainfield, 07060.
Fernando, Bernard, 2808 Theresa Dr., Kissimmee, FL 34744.
Ferrazoli, Henry R., 145 S. Ocean Ave., Apt 309, West Palm Beach, FL 33404-5755.
Fiorino, Dominic J., Msgr. James F. Kelley Residence, 247 Bloomfield Ave., Caldwell, 07006.
Foye, Thomas M., St. Andrew, 125 Broadway, Bayonne, 07002.
French, Walter V., 26 Rogerene Way, Landing, 07850.
Fu, Joseph, Resurrection Catholic Church, 100 Tsuipling Rd., Kwun Tong Kowloon, Hong Kong.
Fuccile, Dominic G., 7 Lance Dr., Brick, 08723.
Furrevig, Edward G., 1694 Tilford Boulevard, Brick, 08724.
Galdon, Peter P., 156 W. 33rd St., Bayonne, 07002.
Garoffolo, Vincent, Ashbrook Nursing Home, 1610 Raritan Rd., Scotch Plains, 07076.
Gibbons, John J., M.Div., 626 Aviary Way, Toms River, 08755.
Giblin, William M., Msgr. James F. Kelley Residence, 247 Bloomfield Ave., Caldwell, 07006.
Gibney, Robert G., Msgr. James F. Kelley Residence, 247 Bloomfield Ave., Caldwell, 07006.
Guglielmo, Alan F., Immaculate Conception, 1219 Paterson Plank Rd., Secaucus, 07094.
Gusmer, Charles, Our Lady of Peace, 111 South St., New Providence, 07974.
Hansen, Michael H., St. John Vianney Residence, 60 Home Ave., Rutherford, 07070.
Hazewski, Eugene J., 28 Oranjestad St., Toms River, 08757.
Heinen, Francis A., 247 Bloomfield Ave., Caldwell, 07006.
Holian, John P., 32 Lower Overlook Rd., Summit, 07901.
Horgan, Timothy J., St. Matthew, 102 Barbuda St., P.O. Box 3453, Toms River, 08756-3453.
Iaquinto, Robert, 47 Vendor Ln., Mays Landing, 08330.
Idzik, George, P.O. Box 1035, Clifton, 07014.
Jacunski, Robert D., Msgr. James F. Kelley Residence, 247 Bloomfield Ave., Caldwell, 07006.
Keating, George M., St. Theresa, 541 Washington Ave., Kenilworth, 07033.
Kennedy, John F., V.F., 25 Portsmouth St., Apt. B, Whiting, 08759-2051.
Kenny, Thomas A., 24 Chesapeake Ct., Barnegat, 08005.
Kilcarr, Stephen M., B.A., Seton House, 11 Beverly Rd., West Orange, 07052.
Kirchner, James A., P.O. Box 10522, Prescott, AZ 86304.
Kowalski, Alfred J., St. Theresa, 541 Washington Ave., Kenilworth, 07033.
Krozser, John J., 1616 Georgetowne Blvd., Sarasota, FL 34232.
Kunze, Robert W., St. Joseph Parish, 34 Yorktown

Rd., Millstone Borough, Hillsborough, 08844.
Langdon, Robert H., John Vianney Annex, 64 Home Ave., Rutherford, 07070.
Lehman, Paul J., P.O. Box 499, Branchville, 07826.
Lennon, Peter F., Seton Hall University, 400 South Orange Ave., South Orange, 07079.
Leonard, Patrick J., P.O. Box 3002, Fort Lee, 07024.
Lester, John J., St. Bartholomew, 2032 Westfield Ave., Scotch Plains, 07076.
Lobo, Stanley M., St. Michael Parish, 19E Central Blvd., Palisades Park, 07650.
Looney, Mathew D., 15 Nelson Ct., Toms River, 08757.
Losarcos, Javier, St. Benedict Parish, 65 Barbara St., 07105.
Lukenda, Raymond T., 133 Liberty Ave., Linden, 07036.
Macho, George S., 1825 Buttonwood Ave., Toms River, 08755.
Mader, George L., Msgr. James F. Kelley Residence, 247 Bloomfield Ave., Caldwell, 07006.
Maione, Francis T., 91 Clarken Dr., West Orange, 07052.
Malkiewicz, Edward S., St. Aloysius, 691 Westside Ave., Jersey City, 07304.
Manning, Paul R., McKeen Towers, 311 S. Flagler Dr., Apt. 1109, West Palm Beach, FL 33401.
Marchand, Gerald A., P.O. Box 3102, Point Pleasant, 08742.
Marcone, Eugene F., Assumption, 113 Chiego Pl., Roselle Park, 07204.
Marotta, Robert G., Farthingville, Dromina Charleville County Cork, Ireland.
McCarthy, Thomas A., 521 Piermont Ave., Apt. 209, Rivervale, 07675.
McFarland, James W., St. John Vianney Residence, 60 Home Ave., Rutherford, 07070.
McKeon, Raymond T., St. Paul the Apostle, 14 Greenville Ave., Jersey City, 07305.
McLaughlin, Donald E., 429 Compass Ave., Beachwood, 08722.
McNulty, Francis J., Msgr. James F. Kelley Residence, 274 Bloomfield Ave., Caldwell, 07006.
Melillo, William J., M.A., M.Div., Seton House, 11 Beverly Rd., West Orange, 07052.
Militello, Benedict P., St. Anthony, 199 Walnut St., Northvale, 07647.
Miodowski, Leonard A., Allendale Nursing Home, 85 Harreton Rd., Allendale, 07401.
Mohan, Bernard N., B.S., 409 Earl Dr., Brick, 08723.
Moran, Michael J., M.Div., 246 Larch Lane, Mahwah, 07430.
Morel, John J., 381 Park Ave., Apt. 2L, Scotch Plains, 07076.
Morley, John M., 1819 Boat Point Dr., Point Pleasant, 08742.
Morley, John F., Ph.D., 400 Seton Hall University, South Orange, 07079.
Morris, John J., 5424 Keystone Pl., Virginia Beach, VA 23464.
Mukalel, Joseph V., 2 Amherst Ct., Maplewood, 07040.
Mulvey, John J., 3907 San Rocco Dr., Unit 211, Punta Gorda, FL 33950.
Murphy, Joseph H., 175 Mount Nebo Rd., Milford, 08848.
Myers, J. Edward, 432 Bethel Village Cir., Lehigh Acres, FL 33936.
Naddeo, Henry M., c/o Carmine Naddeo, 97 Bryant Ave., Bloomfield, 07003.
Nardone, Richard M., Seton Hall University, 400 South Orange Ave., South Orange, 07079.
Navarro, Pedro, 1814 West St., Union City, 07087.
Nestor, Robert P., Ed.D., 400 Seton Hall University, South Orange, 07079.
Netta, John G., P.O. Box 144, West Creek, 08092.
Nolan, Paul J., 77 Lee Ct., Jersey City, 07305.
Norton, Thomas, 521 Piermont Ave., #424, River Vale, 07675.
O'Brien, William, 3436 Vicari Ave., Toms River, 08755.
O'Leary, Robert A., 252 Genes Dr., Toms River, 08753.
Olsen, Thomas F., 1800 Shore Blvd., Point Pleasant, 08742.
Olszewski, John S., S.T.L., 28 Orangestad St., Toms River, 08757.
Osorio, Rudolfo B., 664 Paulison Ave., Clifton, 07011.
Palasits, John A., 72B Bellhaven Ct., Whiting, 08759.
Patete, Michael A., 6 Merion Ln., Jackson, 08527.
Patricius, J. M., St. Michael Parish, 15 E. 23rd St., Bayonne, 07002.
Petrillo, Thomas J., 567 Garfield Ave., Toms River, 08753.
Pikula, Zygmunt, St. Mary Parish, 20 Legion Pl., Closter, 07624.
Provinzano, Rocco, 6 Bangiola Ct., Morris Plains, 07950-2202.
Quinlan, Joseph M. (TR), 18 Ellsworth Ct., Red Bank, 07701.
Ransom, Donald B., 6600 Boulevard East, Apt. 21G, West New York, 07093.
Redstone, James, 161 Briar Mills Dr., Brick, 08724.
Regula, Ronald R., P.O. Box 2281, Bloomfield, 07003.
Reinbold, Charles, Mt. St. Francis, 250 South St., Peekskill, NY 10566.
Revuelto, Manuel, Calle Julio Romero de Torres, 5 Urbanizacion Casablanca Marbella, Malaga 29600 Spain.
Rice, Joseph P., St. John Vianney Residence, 60 Home Ave., Rutherford, 07070.
Rischmann, Edward, 3003 Alicia Dr., Wall, 07719-4401.
Ruane, Gerald P., Ph.D., 11 Rushmore Dr., Brick, 08724.
Ryan, John P., P.O. Box 3621 Hemlock Farms, Lords Valley, PA 18428.
Sapeta, Joseph S., St. Hedwig, 1062 Dewey Pl., 07202.
Scherer, Donald R., P.O. Box 764, Robert, LA 70455.
Schreitmueller, Henry, 8 Poinsettia Ct., Kinnelon, 07405.
Schulte, William P., Brewster's Guest House, 477 Mt. Prospect Ave., 07104.
Schute, Arthur B., 276 Orlando Blvd., Port Charlotte, FL 33954.
Sheehan, Joseph G., P.O. Box 438, Island Heights, 08732-0273.
Spino, John J., 116 New Jersey Ave., Point Pleasant Beach, 08742.
St. Amand, Kenneth J., Allendale Nursing Home, 85 Harreton Rd., Allendale, 07401.
Stasik, Thaddeus, St. John Vianney Residence, 60 Home Ave., Rutherford, 07070.
Stulb, Joseph A., 100 Clinton St., #2C, Hoboken, 07030-2574.
Sullivan, James B., O.L. of the Blessed Sacrament, 28 Livingston Ave., Roseland, 07068.
Theobald, Charles, 602 Bloomfield Ave., Montclair, 07042.
Thompson, Edward C., 343 Manor Dr., Nazareth, PA 18064.
Waldron, John R., Allendale Nursing Home, 85 Harreton Rd., Allendale, 07401.
Wilhelm, Patrick R.C., Our Lady of Sorrows, 136 Davis Ave., Kearny, 07032.
Wilson, William P., RR1, Box 59, Falls, PA 18615-9726.
Wortmann, Joseph F., M.A., Seton Hall University, 400 South Orange Ave., South Orange, 07079.
Yeo, Wilfred, 4 Sumutka Ct., Carteret, 07008.
Zuber, Thaddeus F., St. John Vianney Residence, 60 Home Ave., Rutherford, 07070.

Permanent Deacons:
Abad, Ernesto, Our Lady of Lourdes, West Orange
Acocella, Louis, Ed.D., St. Anthony, Newark
Antola, Aldo P., Our Lady of Mt. Carmel, Nutley
Aponte, Leonides, St. Patrick's Pro-Cathedral, Newark
Aristy, Jesus D., Our Lady of Libera, West New York
Baker, Robert A., Sr., M.B.A., C.F.E., St. Nicholas, Jersey City
Balestrieri, Anthony A., Our Lady Queen of Peace, Maywood; B.S. Pollack Hospital, Jersey City
Baltus, John M., St. Theresa, Kenilworth
Barrett, Thomas J., St. Joseph's and St. Michael's, Union City
Bates, Harold L., Ascension, New Milford
Bejgrowicz, John P., St. Elizabeth, Linden
Bellascio, Vincent, St. Joseph the Carpenter, Roselle
Benedetto, William R., Queen of Peace, North Arlington; Rahway Hospital, Rahway
Besida, Dennis J., St. Thomas, Bloomfield
Bongiovanni, Jerome C., St. James, Springfield
Bowen, Edward J., St. Peter the Apostle, River Edge
Bulgia, Thomas, St. Andrew Kim, Maplewood
Campanella, Edward, St. John the Apostle, Linden
Caporaso, Joseph, St. Anthony of Padua, Elizabeth
Carlo, Joseph J., Holy Spirit, Union
Casanova, Eliot, Blessed Sacrament, Elizabeth
Cechony, Michael J., St. Joseph, Oradell/New Milford
Charriez, Nestor, St. Patrick/Immaculate Heart of Mary, Elizabeth
Class, Jose M., St. Michael Medical Center, Newark
Connelly, Earle S., Jr., Immaculate Conception, Secaucus
Cordero, Juan A., St. Nicholas, Jersey City
Coyle, Thomas J., St. Thomas, Bloomfield
David, Marcelo, Parish of the Resurrection, Jersey City
DeBenedictis, Thomas, Cathedral Basilica of the Sacred Heart, Newark
DeFedele, Vincent J., Corpus Christi, Hasbrouck Heights
DeLucca, Nicholas J., Our Lady of Mt. Carmel, Ridgewood
DeMaria, Joseph, Jr., (On Duty Outside the Diocese)
DeRoberts, Michael, Our Lady of Lourdes, Mountainside
Di Meo, John J., St. Mary, Rutherford
Dickson, Joseph A., St. Matthew, Ridgefield
Donosso, Edward G., St. Augustine, Union City
Dwyer, Joseph A., Jr., Holy Family Parish, Nutley
Echevarria, Mario, St. Thomas Aquinas, Newark
Emr, Peter R., Our Lady of the Visitation, Paramus
Estremera, Alejandro, St. Rose of Lima, Newark
Fargo, Nicholas C., Our Lady of Mercy, Jersey City
Fedison, Stanley F., Our Lady Mother of the Church, Woodcliff Lake
Fencik, Robert, St. Mary, Rahway
Fernandez, Jose R., Blessed Sacrament, Elizabeth
Ferraiuola, Lex, Our Lady of Mt. Carmel, Tenafly
Figueroa, Miguel, St. Michael, Newark
Fitzgerald, Michael J., St. Joseph, Bogota
Flores, Ricardo L., SS. Joseph & Michael, Union City
Freeman, Gerald, Good Shepard, Irvington
Ganter, Albert J., St. John the Baptist, Hillsdale
Gibbons, Keith, Holy Trinity, Westfield
Gimbel, Herbert, St. Stephen, Kearny
Giordano, William J., Our Lady of Assumption, Bayonne
Glasner, Robert, Our Lady of Good Counsel, Washington Township
Golden, Andrew J., St. Peter the Apostle, River Edge
Gonzalez, Frank, St. Paul the Apostle, Jersey City
Gonzalez, Pedro, Parish of the Resurrection, Jersey City
Gray, John A., St. John the Baptist, Hillsdale
Guida, James J., St. Mary, Rutherford
Gurske, Robert, St. Bartholomew, Scotch Plains
Haas, Henry W., (Retired)
Hodges, Richard G., (Retired)
Hogan, John E., Church of the Assumption, Emerson
Holoduek, John C., St. John the Baptist, Fairview
Hughes, David J., St. Rose of Lima, Short Hills
Inguaggiato, John M., Our Lady of Sorrows, South Orange
Jackson, Alonzo, St. Joseph, East Orange
Kautz, Frederick, Immaculate Conception, Mahwah
Keary, Michael J., Cathedral Basilica of the Sacred Heart, Newark
Kim, Joseph, St. Michael, Palisades Park
King, Patrick A., St. Thomas More, Fairfield
Kliauga, Paul, Ascension, New Milford
Kwiatek, Stanley W., Holy Spirit, Union
La Scala, Dennis F., St. Michael Med. Ctr., Newark; St. Lucy, Newark
Leary, Gerald, (Retired)
LeConte, Wilfrid, St. Peter Claver, Montclair
Leonida, Clodualdo M., St. Nicholas, Jersey City
Liptak, Stephen J., (Retired)
Loffredo, Louis, Jr., St. Lucy, Newark
Loman, David B., Our Lady of Mt. Carmel, Tenafly
Looby, James, St. Therese of Lisieux, Cresskill
Loperena, Miguel A., Immaculate Heart of Mary, Newark
Lopez, Sixto, University Hospital, Newark
Lorza, Louis C., St. Mary of the Assumption, Elizabeth
Lydon, Michael A., Holy Rosary, Edgewater
Lynch, John W., St. Helen, Westfield
Lynn, Walter, St. Joseph, Bogota
Mackesy, Leonard J., Our Lady of Sorrows, Kearny
Maione, Michael, (On Duty Outside the Diocese)
Malanga, Joseph J., St. Valentine, Bloomfield
Malarcher, Willy J., Holy Name Hospital, Teaneck
Mantineo, Joseph L., Our Lady Queen of Peace, Maywood
Marchese, Stephen, St. Joseph, Lodi
Marques, Albino P., Our Lady of Fatima, Newark
Matthews, Michael, St. Mary, Rutherford
McDermott, William, St. Aloysius, Caldwell
McFadden, Edward, St. Michael's Hospital, Newark
McGarry, Richard M., (Retired)
McKenna, John J., St. Pius X, Old Tappan
McKeon, John W., St. Luke, Hohokus
McKnight, Keith, Christ the King, Jersey City
McLaughlin, Albert, Our Lady of Victory, Harrington Park
McQuade, Francis, Our Lady of Sorrows, South Orange
Merceus, Pierre J., Holy Spirit/OLHC, East Orange
Messina, Dominic S., St. Thomas More, Fairfield
Meyers, Patrick, (Retired)
Mier, Guy W., Cathedral Basilica of the Sacred

Heart, Newark
Minichino, Leonard A., St. Catharine's, Glen Rock
Missaggia, Michael P., St. Vincent de Paul, Bayonne
Montemurro, Michael V., Little Flower, Berkeley Heights
Moore, Brett O., (Retired)
Moore, Willie, Queen of Angels, Newark
Mueller, James A., St. Catherine, Glen Rock
Myers, William, Queen of Peace, North Arlington
Negron, Jose A., St. Michael, Newark
Nieves, Pedro, St. Mary, Plainfield
Niland, Joseph, Annunciation, Paramus
O'Connell, Brian, (On Duty Outside the Archdiocese)
O'Hara, Richard, Seton Hall Prep
O'Neill, Daniel, St. James, Springfield
Ortega-Escobar, Cesar, Parish of the Transfiguration, Newark
Ortiz, Jaime, (On Duty Outside the Diocese)
Osborne, Charles E., (Retired)
Paredes, Guy, (Retired)
Paulillo, Joseph J., St. Andrew's, Westwood
Persinger, Joseph M., St. Rose of Lima, Short Hills
Pluta, Thomas A., Holy Trinity, Westfield
Polanco, Alejandro, St. Francis, Hackensack
Polanco, Cecilio S., St. Michael, Newark
Polanco, Leopoldo, Resurrection, Jersey City
Pons, Eduardo, Cathedral Basilica of the Sacred Heart, Newark
Pontillo, Robert, St. Andrew, Westwood
Porter, Edward W., (Retired)
Puliatte, James J., St. Joseph, Demarest
Puzio, Victor J., Sacred Heart, Wallington
Quagliana, Pat, Our Lady of the Blessed Sacrament, Roseland
Quinn, Gregory C., St. Thomas More, Fairfield
Quintana, Restituto, St. Michael's, Newark
Ramirez, Nelson, St. Leo, Irvington
Ravelo, Daniel, St. Michael's, Newark
Raymundo, Ranulfo, (On Duty Outside the Diocese)
Regan, Kevin J., St. Anastasia, Teaneck
Rehse, Jeremiah K., St. Paul, Ramsey
Rejrat, Philip J., St. Adalbert, Elizabeth
Reyes, Jesus, St. Patrick and Assumption/All Saints, Jersey City
Riccio, Dominick, (On Duty Outside the Diocese)
Rivera, Oscar, Our Lady of Good Counsel, Newark
Rodack, Stephen, (Retired)
Rodriguez, Jose A., Our Lady of Good Counsel, Newark
Rodriguez, Justo, The Parish of the Transfiguration, Newark
Rodriguez, Vicente, St. Francis Xavier, Newark
Roig, Julio, (Retired)
Romero, Jerry, St. John, Orange
Rosado, Jose F., (On Duty Outside the Diocese)
Rossi, Jerry S., Sacred Heart, Bloomfield
Sanchez, Orlando, Holy Rosary St. Michael, Elizabeth
Sarmiento, Cesar C., Parish of the Resurrection, Jersey City
Sarnas, John P., Our Lady of Sorrows, Kearny
Sarno, John A., St. Catherine, Glen Rock
Sav, Ralph M., Parish of the Resurrection, Jersey City
Scalzo, Anthony, St. Rose of Lima, Short Hills
Schneider, Paul, (Retired)
Serzan, Vincent C., St. Michael's, Lyndhurst
Smith, John F., St. Philomena, Livingston
Smith, Thomas M., Archdiocese of Newark; St. John, Newark
Soto, Anibal, (On Duty Outside the Diocese)
Srinivasa, Rajgopal K., St. Antoninus, Newark
Stumbar, James P., Little Flower, Berkeley Heights
Tarabokija, Anton, St. John the Baptist, Fairview
Thomann, Robert V., Mt. Carmel, Ridgewood
Thomson, Robert E., Holy Rosary, Edgewater
Tizzano, Albert H., St. Thomas, Bloomfield
Tobin, James, St. Mary, Closter
Torres, Cesar Augusto, Most Holy Name, Garfield
Trinidad, Reynaldo M., St. Mary, Nutley
Valdez, Nicholas, Assumption, Woodridge
Valentin, Carlos, Our Lady of Good Counsel, Newark
Valladares, Guillermo, St. Peter's, Belleville
Vega, Alcides, St. Teresa, Summit
Velasco, Asterio, SS. Joseph & Michael, Union City
Velo, Luis, St. Joseph, West Orange
Vrindten, Joseph G., St. Francis, Hackensack
Vuolo, Pasquale, (Retired)
Wedemeyer, John J., Our Lady of Lourdes, Mountainside
White, Earl, St. Stephen, Kearny
Yandoli, Joseph, St. John, Leonia
York, Michael D., St. John the Apostle, Linden
Zapata, Alfredo, St. Aloysius, Jersey City

INSTITUTIONS LOCATED IN THE ARCHDIOCESE

[A] SEMINARIES, ARCHDIOCESAN

KEARNY. *Redemptoris Mater Archdiocesan Missionary Seminary* (1990) 672 Passaic Ave., 07032. Tel: 201-997-3220; Fax: 201-997-5552. Email: secretary@rmnewark.org. Rev. Msgr. Renato Grasselli, Rector; Revs. Tobias Rodriguez, Vice Rector; Neil Xavier O'Donoghue, Ph.D., Prefect of Studies & Librarian; Roberto Santamaria, Spiritual Dir. Priests 4; Students 53.

SOUTH ORANGE. *Immaculate Conception Seminary*, 400 South Orange Ave., 07079. Tel: 973-761-9575; Fax: 973-761-9577. Email: theology@shu.edu. Web: www.shu.edu.

Administration Officers: Rev. Msgrs. Robert T. Sheeran, S.T.D., Pres.; Robert F. Coleman, J.C.D., Rector & Dean; Joseph R. Chapel, S.T.D., Assoc. Dean; Thomas P. Nydegger, Ed.D., M.Div., Vice Rector & Business Mgr.; Dianne M. Traflet, S.T.D., J.D., Assoc. Dean; Rev. Douglas J. Milewski, S.T.D., Asst. Dean Undergraduate Programs; Rev. Msgr. Gerard H. McCarren, S.T.D., Spiritual Dir.; Revs. John F. Russell, O.Carm., S.T.D., Asst. Spiritual Dir.; Lawrence B. Porter, Ph.D., Dir. Seminary Library; Donald E. Blumenfeld, Ph.D., Dir. Pastoral Formation; Rev. Msgr. Anthony J. Kulig, M.A., K.H.S., Formation Faculty & Dir. Liturgy; Diane M. Carr, M.A., Academic Svcs. & Admissions Coord.; Rev. Walter D. Lucey, Formation Faculty; Catherine A. Cunning, M.A., Dir. Seminary Devel.; Eilish R. Harrington, Institutional Research Specialist; Ewa Bracko, Asst. Business Mgr.; Stella Wilkins, M.A., M.L.S., Librarian.

Full-Time Faculty: Revs. Antonio I. Bico, S.T.D., Asst. Prof. Systematic Theology; W. Jerome Bracken, C.P., Ph.D., Assoc. Prof. Pastoral Theology; Rev. Msgr. Joseph R. Chapel, S.T.D., Assoc. Prof. & Dean; Rev. Christopher M. Ciccarino, S.S.L., S.T.D., Asst. Prof. Biblical Studies; Timothy P. Fortin, Ph.D, Asst. Prof. Philosophy; Revs. Pablo T. Gadenz, S.T.D., S.S.L., Asst. Prof. Biblical Studies; John S. Grimm, S.T.L., J.D., Asst. Prof. Pastoral Theology; Thomas G. Guarino, S.T.D., Prof. Systematic Theology; Eric M. Johnston, Ph.D., Asst. Prof. Undergraduate Theology; Rev. Msgr. Gerard H. McCarren, S.T.D., Spiritual Dir. & Assoc. Prof. Systematic Theology; Rev. Douglas J. Milewski, S.T.D., Asst. Dean; Jeffrey L. Morrow, Ph.D., Asst. Prof. Undergraduate Theology; Rev. Msgr. Robert J. Wister, Assoc. Prof. Church History, D.Eccl.Hist.; Revs. Mark O'Malley, Asst. Prof. Church History; Lawrence B. Porter, Ph.D., Prof. Systematic Theology, Ph.D.; John F. Russell, O.Carm., S.T.D., Prof. Systematic Theology; Zeni V. Fox, Ph.D., Prof. Pastoral Theology; Gregory Y. Glazov, D.Phil., Assoc. Prof. Biblical Studies; Joseph P. Rice, Ph.D., Asst. Prof. Philosophy; Dianne M. Traflet, S.T.D., J.D., Asst. Prof. Pastoral Theology & Assoc. Dean; Victor Velarde-Mayol, Ph.D., Asst. Prof., Philosophy.

Darlington Fund Tel: 973-761-9552; Fax: 973-761-9577. Development Agency for Immaculate Conception Seminary. Priests 18; Lay Teachers 8; Total Staff 23; Total Enrollment 129.

Seton Hall University College Seminary (1856) Saint Andrew's Hall, 07079. Tel: 973-761-9420; Fax: 973-761-9421. Email: reillyjr@shu.edu. Web: collegeseminary.shu.edu. Rev. Msgrs. Robert T. Sheeran, S.T.D., Pres.; Joseph R. Reilly, S.T.L., Ph.D., Rector; Revs. James F. Spera, M.Div., Vice Rector; Stanley Gomes, Spiritual Dir. Priests 3; Total Enrollment 27.

[B] COLLEGES AND UNIVERSITIES

CALDWELL. *Caldwell College, Inst. Research & Assessment Office*, 120 Bloomfield Ave., 07006. Tel: 973-618-3000; Fax: 973-618-3847. Email: admissions@caldwell.edu. Web: www.caldwell.edu. Incorporated under the laws of the State of New Jersey with full power to confer degrees. Priests 1; Sisters 2; Sisters of St. Dominic of Caldwell 14; Lay Teachers 201; Students 2,286.

College Faculty: Nancy H. Blattner, Ph.D., Pres.; Dr. Paul R. Douillard, Ph.D., Vice Pres., Dean for Academic Affairs; Dr. Peter Panos, Dir. Jennings Library.

JERSEY CITY. *Saint Peter's College*, 2641 Kennedy Blvd., 07306-5997. Tel: 201-761-6000; Fax: 201-761-6011. Email: lnieves@spc.edu. Web: www.spc.edu. Dr. Eugene Cornacchia, Ph.D., Pres.; Eileen L. Poiani, Vice Pres. Student Affairs; Mr. Kenneth Payne, Vice Pres. Office of Finance & Business; Dr. Marylou Yam, Vice Pres. Academic Affairs; Dr. Anna Cicirelli, Dean of Upper Classmen; Mr. Joe Giglio, Dir. Admissions & Enrollment Mktg.; Mr. Richard Petriello, Academic Dean; Mr. Ben Scholz, Dir. Enrollment, Research, & Technology; Mr. Steven Smith, Registrar & Exec. Dir. Enrollment Svcs.; Mary Sue Callan-Farley, Dir. Campus Ministry. Priests 22.

St. Peter's College Jesuit Community, Gothic Towers, 50 Glenwood Ave., 07306-4606. Fax: 201-432-7397. Priests 8; Lay Teachers 108; Students 3,800.

Jesuit Center, St. Peter Hall, 2652 Kennedy Blvd., 07306. Tel: 201-433-2527; 201-433-2528 (Rector's Office). Revs. Anthony Aracich, S.J.; Michael Braden, S.J.; John M. Buckley, S.J.; Mark T. DeStephano, S.J.; Juan Diaz Vilar; Charles A. Gallagher, S.J.; Robert E. Kennedy, S.J.; T. Patrick Lynch, S.J.; Donal T. MacVeigh, S.J.; Oscar G. Magnan; Edmund W. Majewski, S.J.; Michael Marcil, S.J.; Robert E. McCarty, S.J.; William A. McKenna, S.J.; Peter O'Brien, S.J.; Joseph J. Papaj, S.J.; John P. Ruane, S.J.; Jose Luis S. Salazar, S.J.; Raymond A. Schroth, S.J.; Thomas L. Sheridan, S.J.; David X. Stump, S.J.; John P. Wrynn.

LODI. *Felician College* 07644. Tel: 201-559-6000; Fax: 201-559-6188. Email: martink@felician.edu. Web: www.felician.edu. Priests 2; Brothers 1; Sisters 1; Religious 4; Faculty 115; Total Enrollment 2,436.

Lodi Campus, 262 Main St., 07644. Tel: 201-559-6000; Fax: 201-559-6188. Sr. Theresa Mary Martin, C.S.S.F., Pres.; Dr. Charles J. Rooney, Sr. Vice Pres. for Admin. & Finance; Susan M. Chalfin, Vice Pres. Student Svcs. & Admin., Rutherford Campus; Sisters Mary Rosita Brennan, C.S.S.F., Provost & Vice. Pres. for Academic Affairs; Mary Tarcilia Juchniewicz, C.S.S.F., Vice Pres. for Student Affairs; Marc J. Chalfin, Exec. Vice Pres. for Admin. & Finance; Alyssa McCloud, Vice Pres. Enrollment Mgmt.; Jerry Trombella, Coord. Planning; Dr. Beth M. Castiglia, Dean Dept. of Business; Dr. Donna M. Barron-Baker, Dean Div. of Teacher Education; Dr. Muriel M. Shore, Dean Div. of Health Sciences; Dr. William B. Morgan, Vice Pres. Office Campus Svcs.; Rev. Damian Colicchio, Dir. Campus Ministry; Celeste A. Oranchak, Vice Pres. Inst. Advancement; Dr. Edward S. Kubersky, Dean, Dept. Arts & Sciences; Paul Glassman, Dir. Library; Robert W. Decker, Assoc. Vice Pres. Business & Finance.

SOUTH ORANGE. *Seton Hall University* (1856) 400 South Orange Ave., 07079. Tel: 973-761-9000; Fax: 973-275-2361. Web: shu.edu. Rev. Msgr. Robert T. Sheeran, S.T.D., Pres. Priests 47; Lay Teachers 450; Students 9,700.

Officers of University: Rev. Paul Holmes, S.T.D., Exec. Vice Pres. Admin.; Dr. Amado Gabriel Esteban, Provost & Exec. Vice Pres. Academic Affairs; Laura A. Wankel, Ed.D., Vice Pres. Student Affairs; Dennis Garbini, M.B.A., Vice Pres. Finance & Technology; Catherine Kiernan, J.D., Vice Pres. & Univ. Counsel; Susan Basso, Vice Pres. Human Resources; Joseph Sandman, Vice Pres. for Univ. Advancement.

Administrators: Agnes Gottlieb, Interim Assoc. Provost, Enrollment Svcs.; Chrysanthy Grieco, Dean Univ. Libraries; Robert DeMartino, Ph.D., Dir. Grants & Contracts; Joseph Quinlan Jr., Dir. University Athletics; Rev. Msgr. James M. Cafone, S.T.D., Acting Min. to Priest Community; Rev. James F. Spera, M.Div., Dir. Campus Ministry; Rev. Msgr. James S. Choma, Dir. Priest Institute.

College of Arts and Sciences Joseph Marback, Dean. Tel: 973-761-9022.

School of Business Karen E. Boroff, Ph.D., Dean. Tel: 973-761-9013.

College of Education and Human Services Joseph De Pierro, Dean. Tel: 973-761-9025.

College of Nursing Phyllis Hansell, Ed.D., Dean. Tel: 973-761-9014.

School of Law Patrick E. Hobbs, J.D., L.L.M., Dean. One Newark Center, 07102. Tel: 973-642-8750.

School of Theology Rev. Msgr. Robert F. Coleman, J.C.D., Rector & Dean. Tel: 973-761-9016.

School of Health and Medical Science Brian B. Shulman, Ph.D., Dean.

School of Diplomacy and Intl. Rels. Ambassador John K. Menzies, Ph.D., Dean.

Priest Community: Rev. John F. Morley, Ph.D. (Retired); Rev. Msgrs. Robert F. Coleman, J.C.D.; Richard M. Liddy, Ph.D.; Dennis Mahon; Robert T. Sheeran, S.T.D.; James C. Turro, Ph.D. (Retired); Robert J. Wister; Revs. Anthony Bico; Donald E. Blumenfeld, Ph.D.; Ian Boyd; W. Jerome Bracken, C.P., Ph.D.; Alfred V. Celiano, Ph.D. (Retired); Christopher M. Ciccarino, S.S.L., S.T.D.; Rev. Msgr. James M. Cafone, S.T.D.; Revs. Gabriel B. Costa, Ph.D.; John D. Dennehy; Nicholas G. Figurelli, B.S., M.A.; Lawrence E. Frizzell, D.Phil.; Pablo T. Gadenz, S.T.D., S.S.L.; Nicholas S. Gengaro, S.T.D.; Stanley Gomes; John S. Grimm, S.T.L., J.D.; Thomas G. Guarino, S.T.D.; Rev. Msgr. Kevin M. Hanbury, Ed.D.; Rev. Paul A. Holmes, S.T.D., Vice Pres. & Interim Dean; Rev. Msgrs. Christopher J. Hynes, Ed.S., Adjunct Prof.; Anthony J.

Kulig, M.A., K.H.S.; Peter F. Lennon (Retired); Rev. Walter D. Lucey; Rev. Msgr. Gerard H. McCarren, S.T.D.; Revs. Robert S. Meyer, S.T.L., J.D., J.C.L.; John F. Morley, Ph.D. (Retired); Brian Keenan Muzas; Richard M. Nardone (Retired); Robert P. Nestor, Ed.D. (Retired); Mark O'Malley; John F. Russell, O.Carm., S.T.D.; Lawrence B. Porter, Ph.D.; Rev. Msgr. John A. Radano; Revs. John J. Ranieri, Ph.D.; Joseph Reilly; James F. Spera, M.Div.; Rev. Msgrs. Francis R. Seymour; James S. Choma; C. Anthony Ziccardi, S.T.L., S.S.L. In Res. Rev. Msgr. Joseph R. Chapel, S.T.D.; Rev. Douglas J. Milewski, S.T.D.; Rev. Msgr. Thomas P. Nydegger, Ed.D., M.Div.; Rev. Joseph F. Wortmann, M.A. (Retired).

[C] HIGH SCHOOLS, PRIVATE

NEWARK. *Saint Benedict's Preparatory School* (1868) (Grades 7-12), 520 Dr. Martin Luther King Blvd., 07102-1314. Tel: 973-792-5800; Fax: 973-643-6922. Email: graybee@sbp.org. Web: www.sbp.org. Rev. Edwin D. Leahy, O.S.B., Headmaster; Paul E. Thornton, Vice Pres. Devel.; Revs. Michael R. Scanlan, Asst. Headmaster; Edwin D. Leahy, O.S.B., Prin. Benedictine Monks of Newark Abbey 15; Priests 10; Brothers 5; Lay Teachers 52; Total Enrollment 550.

Christ the King Preparatory School of Newark, N.J., Corp., 239 Woodside Ave., 07104. Tel: 973-483-0033; Fax: 973-481-0693. Email: smsullivan@ctleprep.org. Web: www.ctkprep.org. Revs. Robert J. Sandoz, O.F.M., Pres.; Gregory V. Gebbia, O.F.M., Vice Pres. Student Life; Mr. Kevin P. Cuddihy, Prin. Priests 2; Sisters 2; Lay Teachers 18.

Christ the King Work Study Program, 239 Woodside Ave., 07104. Tel: 973-483-0033. Email: smsullivan@ctkprep.org. Web: www.ctkprep.org. Rev. Robert J. Sandoz, O.F.M., Pres.; Mr. Kevin P. Cuddihy, Prin. Priests 2; Sisters 2; Lay Teachers 18.

St. Vincent Academy (1869) (Girls), 228 W. Market St., 07103. Tel: 973-622-1613; Fax: 973-622-1128. Email: jfavata@svanj.org. Web: www.svanewark.org. Sisters June Favata, Admin. Dir.; Margaret Killough, Fin. Dir.; Mary F. Nolan, Student Svcs. Dir.; Sr. Monica Donohoe, Librarian. Sisters 7; Lay Teachers 27; Students 310.

BAYONNE. *Holy Family Academy* (1925) 239 Ave. A, 07002. Tel: 201-339-7341; Fax: 201-339-9295. Email: hfa@bayonne.net. Web: www.hfa.bayonne.net. Dr. Karen Fasanella, Pres.; Mrs. Dianne Osaben, Librarian & PR Dir.; Mrs. Susan Ward, Prin.; Mrs. Jean Stroud, Dean of Studies. Sisters of St. Joseph of Chestnut Hill, Philadelphia, PA. Sisters 5; Lay Teachers 22; Girls 175.

Marist High School (1954) (Coed), 1241 Kennedy Blvd., 07002. Tel: 201-437-4545; Fax: 201-437-6013. Email: rslaski@marist.org. Web: www.marist.org. Mr. Robert M. Slaski, Pres.; Bros. Steve Schlitte, F.M.S., Prin.; Luke Reddington, F.M.S., Guidance; James Devine, Teacher; Robert Warren, F.M.S., Teacher; William Maske, F.M.S., Teacher; Sisters Mary Fallon, S.C., Guidance Dir.; Rita Walsh, S.C., Substitute; Helen Moores, S.C., Focus Educ. Teacher; Mary Agnes Gore, O.P., Guidance Office Asst.; Ms. Diane DeVeaux, Librarian & Media Specialist. Marist Brothers. Brothers 5; Sisters 4; Lay Teachers 40; Students 512.

CALDWELL. *Mount St. Dominic Academy* (Girls), 3 Ryerson Ave., 07006-6196. Tel: 973-226-0660; Fax: 973-226-2693. Email: mainoffice@msdacademy.org. Web: www.msdacademy.org. Sr. Francis Sullivan, O.P., Head of School; Irena Telyan, Librarian. Sisters of St. Dominic of Caldwell. Sisters 3; Lay Teachers 36; Girls 326.

DEMAREST. *Academy of the Holy Angels* (Girls), 315 Hillside Ave., 07627. Tel: 201-768-7822; Fax: 201-768-6933. Web: www.holyangels.org. Sr. Virginia Bobrowski, Pres.; Jennifer Moran, Prin.; Catherine Korvin, Librarian. Conducted by School Sisters of Notre Dame. Sisters 9; Lay Teachers 60; (Girls) 568.

ELIZABETH. *Benedictine Academy*, 840 N. Broad St., 07208-2508. Tel: 908-352-0670; Fax: 908-352-0698; 908-352-9424. Web: www.benedictineacad.org. Email: principal@benedictineacad.org. Sr. Germaine Fritz, O.S.B., Pres.; Kenneth Jennings, Prin.; Sr. Martin Elizabeth Duffy, O.S.B., Librarian. Benedictine Sisters of Elizabeth, NJ., College Preparatory High School (Girls) Sisters 5; Lay Teachers 18; Total Staff 35; Girls 175.

St. Patrick High School (Coed), 221 Court St., 07206. Tel: 908-353-5220; Fax: 908-629-1123. Joseph L. Picaro, Prin.; Barbara McElroy, Librarian. Students 239.

JERSEY CITY. *St. Anthony High School*, 175 Eighth St., 07302. Tel: 201-653-5143; Fax: 201-653-8120. Email: friars@stanthonyhighschool.org. Web: www.stanthonyhighschool.org. Sr. Mary Alan, C.S.S.F., Pres.; Mathew Glowski, Prin. Conducted by Felician Sisters. Sisters 2; Lay Teachers 26; Total Staff 6; Students 260.

St. Dominic Academy (Girls), 2572 John F. Kennedy Memorial Blvd., 07304. Tel: 201-434-5938; Fax: 201-434-2603. Email: stdominicacad@hotmail.com. Web: www.stdominicacad.com. Deborah Egan, Prin.; Sharon Buge, Dir. Fin. Dominican Sisters of Caldwell. Sisters 9; Lay Teachers 36; Total Staff 49; Students 453.

St. Peter's Preparatory School (1872) 144 Grand St., 07302. Tel: 201-547-6400; Fax: 201-547-2341. Web: www.spprep.org. Revs. John A. Mullin, S.J., Supr. & Guidance Counselor; Robert E. Reiser, S.J., Pres.; Mr. James C. DeAngelo, Prin.; Ms. Mary Durante, Vice Prin.; Mr. James Horan, Vice Pres. Planning & Principal Giving; Mr. John Morris, Dean of Students; Mr. Daniel J. Healy, Asst. Dean of Students; Robert Nodine, Vice Pres. Fin.; John Irvine, Dir. Admissions; Francesca Lanning, Vice Pres. Inst. Advancement; Rev. Enrico Raulli, S.J., Teacher. Priests 6; Lay Teachers 72; Students 895. In Res. Revs. Thomas O'Connor, S.J., Pastoral Ministry; Harold J. Oppido, S.J., Pastoral Ministry; Bros. Louis N. Mauro, S.J., Deacon & Business Mgr. at Resurrection Parish; Edward P. Sheehy, S.J., Pastoral Ministry.

Jesuit Community, 180 Grand St., 07302. Revs. John A. Mullin, S.J., Supr. & Guidance Counselor; Anthony J. Azzarto, S.J., Preparator; James J. Dinneen, S.J., Faculty Chap.; Thomas F. McManus, S.J., Devel. Officer; Robert V. O'Hare, S.J., Student.

LODI. *Immaculate Conception High School* (1915) 258 S. Main St., 07644. Tel: 973-773-2400; Fax: 973-614-0893. Email: aadametz@ichslodi.org. Web: www.ichslodi.org. Sr. Mary Alicia Adametz, C.S.S.F., Prin.; Deborah Ebbinghousen, Librarian; Maria Grieco, Librarian. Sisters 1; Lay Teachers 17; Lay Staff 12; Girls 168.

MONTCLAIR. *Immaculate Conception High School* (Coed), 33 Cottage Pl., 07042. Tel: 973-744-7445; Fax: 973-744-3926. Email: ichsmont@yahoo.com. Web: www.ichspride.org. Sr. Maureen Crowley, S.C., Pres.; Jo Ann Degnan, Prin.; Sr. Ann Fay, S.C., Librarian. Sisters 4; Lay Teachers 22; Students 200.

ORADELL. *Bergen Catholic* (1955) (Boys), 1040 Oradell Ave., 07649. Tel: 201-261-1844; Fax: 201-599-9507. Email: president@bergencatholic.org. Web: www.bergencatholic.org. Rev. Thomas E. Pendrick, Chap.; Bro. Brian M. Walsh, C.F.C., Pres.; John Puzio, Librarian. Congregation of Christian Brothers. Priests 1; Brothers 4; Lay Teachers 51; Total Staff 57; Boys 738.

RAMSEY. *Don Bosco Preparatory High School* (1915) 492 N. Franklin Tpke., 07446. Tel: 201-327-8003; Fax: 201-327-3397. Web: donboscoprep.com. Rev. Louis J. Molinelli, S.D.B., Dir./Pres.; John F. Stanczak, Prin.; Rev. Brendan K. Kilroy, S.P.S., Senior Guidance Counselor; Albert Del Principio, Asst. Prin.; Revs. James Horan, S.D.B., Coord. Youth Min.; Richard Rosin, S.D.B., Guidance Dir.; John Janko, S.D.B., School Psychologist; James Marra, S.D.B., Dir. of Advancement; Joseph Bajorek, S.D.B. (Retired); Eugene Palumbo, S.D.B.; Jerzy Schneider, S.D.B. (Retired); Thomas Brennan, S.D.B., Chap.; Bro. James Wiegand, S.D.B., Asst. Athletic Dir.; Christine Green, Librarian; Revs. James Cerbone, S.D.B.; Armindo Laranjinha, S.D.B. Salesians of St. John Bosco. Priests 9; Brothers 1; Sisters 2; Lay Teachers 70; Students 875.

SOUTH ORANGE. *Marylawn of the Oranges*, 445 Scotland Rd., 07079. Tel: 973-762-9222; Fax: 973-378-7975. Email: schoolsecretary@marylawn.us. Web: www.marylawn.net. Christine Lopez, Prin.; Sr. Joan Digan, S.C., Librarian. Sisters 3; Lay Teachers 20; Girls 200.

SUMMIT. *Oak Knoll School of the Holy Child Upper School* (1924) (Grades 7-12), (Girls), 44 Blackburn Rd., 07901. Tel: 908-522-8100 (Main); 908-522-8130; Fax: 908-522-8191. Email: timothy.saburn@oakknoll.org. Web: www.oakknoll.org. Mr. Timothy J. Saburn, Head of School; Mrs. Mary Sciarrillo, Prin.; Joan Turk, Librarian; Mary Hoskins-Clark, Asst. Librarian. Conducted by the Sisters of the Holy Child Jesus. Lay Teachers 53; Total Staff 55; Students 339.

UPPER MONTCLAIR. *Lacordaire Academy, Secondary Division*, 155 Lorraine Ave., 07043. Tel: 973-744-1156; Fax: 973-783-9521. Web: www.lacordaire.net. Brian F. Morgan, Head of School. Sisters of St. Dominic. Sisters 1; Lay Teachers 19; Total Staff 26; Girls 130.

WEST ORANGE. *Seton Hall Preparatory School*, 120 Northfield Ave., 07052. Tel: 973-325-6624; Fax: 973-736-2930. Email: mkelly@shp.org. Web: www.shp.org. Rev. Msgr. Michael E. Kelly, M.A., Headmaster; Michael Gallo, Asst. Headmaster; Carole Marazzi, Librarian. Priests 5; Lay Instructors 90; Students 970.

Resident Faculty: Rev. Msgr. Edward G. Bradley, S.T.L., M.A.; Revs. Bruce G. Janiga, M.A.; Stephen M. Kilcarr, B.A. (Retired); William J. Melillo, M.A., M.Div. (Retired).

[D] HIGH SCHOOLS, ARCHDIOCESAN

CLARK. *Mother Seton (Girls) Regional High School*, One Valley Rd., 07066. Tel: 732-382-1952; Fax: 732-382-4725. Email: sreginamartin@motherseton.org. Web: www.motherseton.org. Sr. Regina Martin, S.C., Prin.; Joan Barron, Asst. Prin.; Sr. Jacquelyn Balasia, S.C., Asst. Prin.; Maureen Connell, Dir. Administrative Services; Sr. Mary Anne Katlack, S.C., Campus Minister; Marge Barkan, Librarian. Sisters of Charity of St. Elizabeth. Sisters 6; Lay Teachers 35; Girls 425.

JERSEY CITY. *Hudson Catholic Regional High School*, 790 Bergen Ave., 07306. Tel: 201-332-5970; Fax: 201-332-6373. Email: contact@hudsoncatholic.org. Web: www.hudsoncatholic.org. Rev. Warren R. Hall, Pres.; Sr. Joann Marie Aumand, S.C.C., Prin. Brothers of the Christian Schools. Brothers 4; Lay Teachers 21; Total Staff 32; Boys 320; Girls 72; Sisters 1.

MONTVALE. *St. Joseph Regional High School* (1962) (Boys), 40 Chestnut Ridge Rd., 07645. Tel: 201-391-3300; Fax: 201-391-8073. Web: www.saintjosephregional.org. Barry Donnelly, Prin. Brothers 11; Lay Teachers 37; Boys 500.

PARAMUS. *Paramus Catholic High School* (Coed), 425 Paramus Rd., 07652. Tel: 201-445-4466; Fax: 201-445-6440. Email: jvail@paramus-catholic.org. Web: www.paramuscatholic.org. James P. Vail, Pres.; Declan Lynch, Vice Pres., Finance; Ryan Casey, Vice Pres., Advancement; Joseph P. Agostino, Prin.; Leonard Lewandoski, Vice Prin.; Stephanie Macaluso, Vice Prin.; Vincent Sausto, Vice Prin., Academics; Rev. Larry Evans, Chap.; Oksana Korduba, Librarian; Rev. Dominic G. Ciriaco, Chap.; Mary Ann Lemieux, Dean of Student Svcs.; Stella Scarano, Dean of Students; Joseph F. Wilson, Dean of Campus Ministry; Ralph M. Manno, Dean of Students. Priests 2; Sisters 1; Lay Teachers 104; Total Staff 107; Students 1,552.

ROSELLE. *Roselle Catholic High School* (Coed), 350 Raritan Rd., 07203. Tel: 908-245-2350; Fax: 908-241-3869. Email: info@rosellecatholic.org. Web: www.rosellecatholic.org. Bro. Owen Ormsby, F.M.S., Pres.; Mr. Anthony LaPolla, Prin.; Sally Hanford, Librarian. Marist Brothers. Brothers 4; Sisters 1; Lay Teachers 45; Total Staff 50; Students 560.

SCOTCH PLAINS. *Union Catholic Regional High School* (Coed), 1600 Martine Ave., 07076. Tel: 908-889-1600; Fax: 908-889-7867. Email: mainoffice@unioncatholic.org. Web: www.unioncatholic.org. Sr. Percylee Hart, R.S.M., Prin.; James Reagan Sr., Librarian. Lay Teachers 49; Total Staff 86; Students 767.

SUMMIT. *The Oratory Catholic Preparatory School* (1907) (Grades 7-12), 1 Beverly Rd., 07901. Tel: 908-273-1084; Fax: 908-273-5505. Email: mainoffice@oratoryprep.org. Web: oratoryprep.org. Mr. Robert Costello, Headmaster; Sherry Mahan, Admin. Asst. to Headmaster, 1 Beverly Rd., 07901. Lay Teachers 27; Total Staff 14; Students 258.

WASHINGTON TOWNSHIP. *Immaculate Heart Academy* (Girls), 500 Van Emburgh Ave., 07676. Tel: 201-445-6800; Fax: 201-445-7416. Email: pmolloy@ihahs.com. Web: www.ihahs.com. Ms. Patricia Molloy, Prin. Sisters 1; Lay Teachers 66; Total Staff 82; Girls 838.

[E] ELEMENTARY SCHOOLS, PRIVATE

NEWARK. *Link Community School, Inc.*, 120 Livingston St., 07103. Tel: 973-642-0529; 973-642-8510; Fax: 973-642-1978. Email: leslie.mitchell@linkschool.org. Web: www.linkschool.org. Marnie G. McKoy, Prin. Dominican Sisters of Caldwell. Lay Teachers 15; Jesuit Volunteer 1; Students 135.

ELIZABETH. *St. Patrick Academy*, (Grades 5-8), 227 Court St., 07206. Tel: 908-351-2188; Fax: 908-629-1123. Web: www.stpatrickhs.org. Bro. Daniel McCulloch, C.F.C., Dir.; Joseph Picaro, Prin. Brothers 1; Lay Teachers 3; Total Staff 4; Total Enrollment 55.

JERSEY CITY. *Concordia Learning Center at St. Joseph's School for the Blind*, 761 Summit Ave., 07307. Tel: 201-876-5432; Fax: 201-876-5431. Email: info@sjsnj.org. Web: www.sjsnj.org. Judy Ortman, Exec. Dir. Non-graded and graded school for visually impaired, multi-disabled children; early intervention program, 5-day residential program, outreach services. Lay Teachers 23; Students 130; Total Staff 99.

St. Joseph's School for the Blind, 761 Summit Ave., 07307. Tel: 201-876-5432; Fax: 201-876-5431. Email: info@sjsnj.org. Web: www.sjsnj.org. Judy Ortman, Exec. Dir. Non-graded and graded school for visually impaired, multi-disabled children; early intervention program, 5-day residential program, outreach services. Lay Teachers 23; Students 130; Total Staff 99.

LODI. *The Felician School for Exceptional Children* (1971) 260 S. Main St., 07644. Tel: 973-777-5355; Fax: 973-777-0725. Email: fsecinlodi@aol.com. Web: www.fsec.org. Sisters Mary Ramona, C.S.S.F., Dir.; Mary Loretta, C.S.S.F., Prin. Sisters 6; Lay Teachers 18; Total Staff 49; Children 90.

Day Program Tel: 973-777-5355, Ext. 12; Fax: 973-777-0725. Capacity 150.

SUMMIT. *Oak Knoll School of The Holy Child, Lower School* (1924) (Grades K-6), (Coed), 44 Blackburn Rd., 07901. Tel: 908-522-8120; 908-522-8100 (Main); Fax: 908-598-9757. Email: timothy.saburn@oakknoll.org. Web: www.oakknoll.org. Mr. Timothy J. Saburn, Head of School; Mrs. Joanne L. Ainsworth, Prin.; Caitlan Starrs, Dir. Student Svcs.; Cheryl Werner, Librarian. Conducted by the Sisters of the Holy Child of Jesus. Lay Teachers 29; Total Staff 31; Students 235.

UNION CITY. *St. Francis Academy*, 1601 Central Ave., 07087. Tel: 201-863-4112; Fax: 201-601-5905. Email: lucy@stfrancisacademy.com. Web: www.stfrancisacademy.com. Sr. Mary Dora Sartino, O.S.F., Pres.; Ms. Deborah Savage, Prin.; Louise Levendusky, Librarian. Missionary Franciscan Sisters of the Immaculate Conception. Sisters 13; Lay Teachers 29; Students 261.

UPPER MONTCLAIR. *Lacordaire Academy-Elementary Division*, (Grades PreK-8), 153 Lorraine Ave., 07043. Tel: 973-746-2660; Fax: 973-783-6804. Email: lmazzari@lcordaire.net. Web: www.lacordaire.net. Lauren Mazzari, Head of Elementary Div.; Susan Sturgis, Admissions Dir.; Alexandria Kaousias, Media Resource Contact. Dominican Sisters of Caldwell. Lay Teachers 12; Students 155; Total Staff 2; Sisters 1.

[F] CATHEDRAL HEALTHCARE SYSTEM OF ARCHDIOCESE OF NEWARK

NEWARK. *Cathedral Healthcare System, Inc.*, 219 Chestnut St., 07105. Tel: 973-690-3600; Fax: 973-690-3601. Web: www.cathedral-health.org. Mailing Address: 1160 Raymond Blvd., 12th Fl., 07102. Rev. Msgr. Ronald J. Rozniak, V.G., P.A., Chm. & Pres.

Catholic Health New Jersey, Inc. Catholic Health New Jersey is the sole corporate member of Cathedral Healthcare System.

Cathedral/Columbus Group, Newark

Cathedral Foundation, Inc.

[G] GENERAL HOSPITALS

NEWARK. *Columbus Campus of Saint Michael's Medical Center, Newark* A member of Catholic Health East., 495 N. 13th St., 07107. Tel: 973-268-1475; Fax: 973-268-1523. Parent Institution: Catholic Health East. Bed Capacity 210; Total Staff 900; Admissions 9,575.

St. James Campus of Saint Michael's Medical Center, Newark A member of Catholic Health East., 155 Jefferson St., 07105. Tel: 973-589-1300; Fax: 973-465-2861. Web: www.cathedralhealth.org. Parent Corporation: Catholic Health East. Bed Capacity 186; Bassinets 12; Total Staff 470; Patients Assisted Annually 48,000.

Saint Michael's Medical Center A member of Catholic Health East., 111 Central Ave., 07102-9880. Tel: 973-877-5411; Fax: 973-877-5672. Rev. Eustace Edomobi (Nigeria), Chap.; Dr. Robert S. Spira, Pres. Medical Staff. Parent Corporation: Catholic Health East. Sisters 3; Bed Capacity 357; Admissions 8,565; Outpatient Visits 22,034; Total Staff 1,698.

Mount Carmel Guild Behavioral Health System, Inc., 590 N. 7th St., 07102. Tel: 973-266-7992; Fax: 973-596-4057. Web: www.ccnewark.org. Elizabeth McClendon, L.C.S.W., Assoc Exec. Dir.; Phillip Frese, Ph.D., CPA, Pres.& C.E.O. Behavioral Health Services in 3 counties. Total Staff 250; Patients Assisted Annually 8,000.

ELIZABETH. *Trinitas Regional Medical Center*, 225 Williamson St., 07207. Tel: 908-994-5000; Fax: 908-994-5756. Web: www.trinitasrmc.com. Gary S. Horan, Pres. & CEO; Sr. Mary Corrigan, S.C., Vice Pres. Mission Effectiveness. Sisters of Charity of Saint Elizabeth. Sisters 9; Total Staff 2,727; Bed Capacity 546; Bassinets 11; Patients Assisted Annually 350,338.

Trinitas Regional Medical Center, Williamson Street Campus, 225 Williamson St., 07207.

Trinitas Regional Medical Center, New Point Campus, 655 E. Jersey St., 07206.

**Marillac Corp.*, 240 Williamson St., 07207. Tel: 908-994-5756; Fax: 908-994-5520. Gary S. Horan, Pres. & CEO.

TEANECK. *Holy Name Hospital*, 718 Teaneck Rd., 07666. Tel: 201-833-3000; Fax: 201-833-3230. Web: www.holyname.org. Michael Maron, Pres. & CEO; Maureen Morosco, Chap.; Sr. Beatriz Duque, P.B.V.M., Chap. Sisters of St. Joseph of Peace. Bed Capacity 361; Bassinets 11; Total Staff 2,504; Total Assisted 44,000.

Holy Name EMS, 718 Teaneck Rd., 07666. Tel: 201-833-3248; Fax: 201-833-7213. Margaret Galvin, Vice Pres. Legal Affairs.

School of Nursing Tel: 201-833-3002. Sisters 4. Pastoral Care: Sisters Lois Jablonski, S.S.J., M.Div., Dir. Pastoral Care; Beatriz Duque, P.B.V.M., Chap.; Nora Molyneux, C.S.J.P., Vice Pres. Mission; Revs. Paterno Gorospe, Chap.; John T. Michalczak, Chap.; Deacon Willy Malarcher, Chap.; Maureen Morosco, Chap.

[H] HOMES FOR AGED

CALDWELL. *St. Catherine of Siena, Inc.*, 7 Ryerson Ave., 07006. Tel: 973-226-1577; Fax: 973-226-5058. Email: lramm@caldwellop.org. Web: www.caldwellop.org. Sisters Arlene Antczak, O.P., Prioress; Alice Uhl, O.P., Vicaress; Honora Werner, O.P., Sec.; Luella Ramm, O.P., Treas.; Ms. Deirdre Radtke, Admin. Bed Capacity 30; Total Assisted Annually 35; Total Staff 50.

CEDAR GROVE. *St. Vincent's Nursing Home* (Div. of St. Joseph's Regional Medical Center), 315 E. Lindsley Rd., 07009. Tel: 973-754-4800; Fax: 973-812-4491. Deborah Quinn Martone, Admin.; Sr. Elizabeth Noonan, Chap. Conducted by Sisters of Charity of St. Elizabeth. Sisters 2; Capacity: Long term care beds 151; Patients Assisted Annually 220; Total Staff 175.

JERSEY CITY. *St. Ann's Home for the Aged*, 198 Old Bergen Rd., 07305. Tel: 201-433-0950; Fax: 201-433-6554. Email: first_choice_home@yahoo.com. Web: www.saintannshome.com. Sr. Norah Clarke, C.S.J.P., LNHA CEO; Janet Merly-Liranzo, LNA Admin.; Sr. Josephine Pate, C.S.J.P., Admissions Coord.; James Barry, Pastoral Care. Sisters of St. Joseph of Peace 6; Total Staff 220; Under Care (Male & Female) 120; Adult Medical Day Care Clients 50.

Margaret Anna Cusack Care Center, Inc., 537 Pavonia Ave., 07306. Tel: 201-653-8300, Ext. 2152; Fax: 201-653-7705. Email: info@cusackcarecenter.org. Web: www.cusackcarecenter.org. Thomas P. Sheehy, Admin. Sponsored by the Sisters of St. Joseph of Peace., Skilled Nursing Facility for Men & Women. Sisters 2; Bed Capacity 139; Total Assisted Annually 193; Total Staff 200.

[I] HOMES FOR THE BLIND

JERSEY CITY. *St. Joseph's Home for the Blind* (1886) (Skilled nursing facility for men and women), 537 Pavonia Ave., 07306. Tel: 201-653-8300; Fax: 201-653-7705. Email: info@cusackcarecenter.org. Web: www.cusackcarecenter.org. Thomas P. Sheehy, Admin. Sisters of St. Joseph of Peace. Sisters 2; Total Staff 200; Nursing Home Patients 139; Total Assisted Annually 193.

[J] DAY NURSERIES

NEWARK. *Perpetual Help Day Nursery* (1967) 170 Broad St., 07104. Tel: 973-484-3535; Fax: 973-497-2526. Email: perhelp@yahoo.com. Sr. Romilda Borges, Prin. Vocationist Sisters. Sisters 7; Lay Teachers 15; Total Staff 22; Children 145.

JERSEY CITY. *St. Elizabeth's Child Care Center*, 129 Garrison Ave., 07306. Tel: 201-795-1443; Fax: 201-795-4121. Email: st.stelizabethfsse@yahoo.com. Sisters Rosita Chirayath, Supr.; Shelcy Catherine Kulangara, Prin. Franciscan Sisters of St. Elizabeth. Sisters 10; Total Staff 34; Children 300.

NUTLEY. *Holy Family Day Nursery and Convent*, 174 Franklin Ave., 07110. Tel: 973-235-1170; Fax: 973-235-1940. Sr. Romilda Chiga, F.S.S.E., Supr. Franciscan Sisters of St. Elizabeth. Sisters 9; Children 70.

RAMSEY. *St. Joseph Pre-School*, 372 Wyckoff Ave., 07446. Tel: 201-825-8386. Sr. Marie Elise Kurikombil, Prin. Franciscan Sisters of St. Elizabeth. Sisters 4; Children 60.

[K] PROTECTIVE INSTITUTIONS

NEWARK. *Missionaries of Charity, Queen of Peace Women's Shelter & Soup Kitchen* (1982) 60 Jay St., 07103. Tel: 973-481-9056; 973-483-0165. Missionaries of Charity. Total Staff 7; Total Assisted (Shelter) 300; Total Assisted (Soup Kitchen) 34,200.

HOBOKEN. *Good Counsel, Inc. (St. Francis Home)*, 411 Clinton St., 07030. Tel: 201-798-9059; 201-795-0637; 800-723-8331 (Hotline); Fax: 201-795-0809. Email: cbell@goodcounselhomes.org. Web: www.goodcounselhomes.org; www.postabortionhelp.org. Rev. Benedict J. Groeschel, C.F.R., Chm.; Christopher R. Bell, Pres. & Exec. Dir. Housing, counseling and referrals for single women who are pregnant or single mothers with children. Counseling for men and women experiencing post abortion stress.

Good Counsel, Inc., P.O. Box 6068, 07030. Rev. Benedict J. Groeschel, C.F.R., Chm.; Christopher R. Bell, Exec. Dir. Residences for single mothers and children. Post abortion counseling and referrals. Women & Children Assisted Annually 315; Total Staff 50; Total Assisted Annually 3,500; Total Hotline Assistance 2,800.

JERSEY CITY. *St. Joseph's Home*, 81 York St., 07302. Tel: 201-413-9280; Fax: 201-451-0952. Sr. Rosemary Coffey, Dir. Transitional housing for homeless women and children. Total Staff 13; Total Assisted 98; Bed Capacity 60.

The Nurturing Place Tel: 201-413-1982; Fax: 201-413-1223. Sr. Barbara Moran, C.S.J.P., Dir. Tel: 201-413-1982. A developmental child care center for disadvantaged youngsters. Total Staff 13; Total Assisted 130.

KEARNY. *New Jersey Boystown* Family Counseling Services., 499 Belgrove Dr., 07032. Tel: 201-991-3770. Janis Orlafsky, Dir.; Rev. Francis T. Maione, Clients Rights Advocate & Pastoral Care Coord. (Retired). Tel: 973-297-4749.

[L] HOMES FOR WOMEN

JERSEY CITY. *St. Mary's Residence*, 240 Washington St., 07302-3806. Tel: 201-432-6289; Fax: 201-451-0952. Sr. Harriet Hamilton, O.S.F., Admin. Sisters of St. Joseph of Peace., (Single working women of low income assisted; no children). Total Staff 6; Total Assisted 50.

[M] MONASTERIES AND RESIDENCES OF PRIESTS AND BROTHERS

NEWARK. *Franciscan Friars of the Renewal, Most Blessed Sacrament Friary*, 375 13th Ave., 07103. Tel: 973-622-6622; Fax: 973-624-8998. Revs. Glenn Sudano, C.F.R., Local Servant; Mariusz Koch, C.F.R.; Christopher Metzger, Local Vicar; Bros. Francis Edkins; Bernardine Sharpe; Peter Westall; Tazsi Ibizi. Novices 9.

Newark Abbey (1857) 528 Dr. Martin Luther King, Jr. Blvd., 07102. Tel: 973-792-5800; Fax: 973-643-6922. Email: newarkabbey@sbp.org. Web: www.newarkabbey.org. Rt. Rev. Melvin J. Valvano, O.S.B., Abbot; Very Revs. Mark M. Payne, O.S.B., Prior; Matthew S. Wotelko, O.S.B., Subprior; Rev. Albert T. Holtz, O.S.B., Novice Master; Bro. Maximillian Buonocore, O.S.B.; Revs. Augustine J. Curley, O.S.B.; Luke A. Edelen, O.S.B.; Francis Flood, O.S.B.; Bro. Mark Hayden, O.S.B.; Revs. Charles W. Henry, O.S.B.; Edwin D. Leahy, O.S.B.; Maynard G. Nagengast, O.S.B.; Bros. Gereon J. Reuter, O.S.B.; Anthony Streit, O.S.B.; Rev. Boniface J. Treanor, O.S.B.; Very Rev. Philip J. Waters, O.S.B.; Bro. Patrick Winbush, O.S.B.

BAYONNE. *Marist Brothers*, Champagnat Residence, 1241 Kennedy Blvd., 07002. Tel: 201-437-4115. Web: www.maristbr.com. Bro. William Maske, F.M.S., Dir. Brothers 8.

Marist Brothers of the Schools, Inc. The Marist Brothers, The Marist Brothers, Provincial Office, 1241 Kennedy Blvd., 07002. Tel: 201-823-1115; Fax: 201-823-2232. Email: maristbrothersus@aol.com. Web: www.maristbr.com. Bro. John Klein, F.M.S., Provincial.

CALDWELL. *The Rev. Msgr. James F. Kelley Residence for Retired Priests*, 247 Bloomfield Ave., 07006. Tel: 973-364-1121; Fax: 973-364-9873. Mrs. Joan Stevens, Admin.; Rev. Msgr. Emmanuel M. Capozzelli (Retired); Revs. Mathew Ayamanthil (Retired); James F. Benedetto, Dir. (Retired); Robert P. Cozzini (Retired); Leo O. Farley (Retired); Dominic J. Fiorino (Retired); William M. Giblin (Retired); Robert G. Gibney (Retired); Francis A. Heinen (Retired); Robert D. Jacunski (Retired); George L. Mader, Dir. (Retired); Francis J. McNulty (Retired).

CLIFFSIDE PARK. *St. Patrick's Missionary Society*, 70 Edgewater Rd., P.O. Box 3080, 07010-4080. Tel: 201-943-6575; Fax: 201-943-2946. Email: spsnj@spms.org. Web: www.spms.org. Revs. Patrick Cullen, S.P.S. (Retired); Brendan K. Kilroy, S.P.S.; Michael E. Morris, S.P.S.; William Mauric, S.P.S.

EAST RUTHERFORD. *Sacred Heart Friary*, 4 Jersey St., 07073. Tel: 973-778-1915; Fax: 973-777-5687. Web: hnp.org (Link to St. Anthony Guild). Rev. Joseph M. Hertel, O.F.M., Dir. St. Anthony Guild; Bro. Thomas J. Cole, O.F.M., Asst. Dir. & Guardian; Revs. Kevin Daly, O.F.M.; Zachary Elliott, O.F.M.; Richard Trezza, O.F.M.; Russell Becker, O.F.M.; Daniel Lanahan, O.F.M.; Joseph M. Hertel, O.F.M.; Bro. Octavio Duran, O.F.M.

JERSEY CITY. *Brothers of the Christian Schools* Hudson Catholic Brothers' Residence, 790 Bergen Ave., 07306-4535. Tel: 201-332-5970; 201-332-0971 (House); Fax: 201-332-6373. Bro. Patrick King, F.S.C., Dir. Brothers 6.

Jesuit Community of St. Peter's Prep, Inc., 180 Grand St., 07302-4433. Tel: 201-451-0149; Fax: 201-451-0390. Revs. Anthony J. Azzarto, S.J., Alumni Chap. & Guidance Counselor; Robert E. Reiser, S.J., Pres., St. Peter's Prep.; James J. Dinneen, S.J., Faculty Chap.; Thomas F. McManus, S.J., Chap. (St. Joseph's Home); John A. Mullin, S.J., Supr., Guidance Counselor; Thomas O'Connor, S.J., (Parish Ministry); Robert V. O'Hare, S.J., On Sabbatical for Studies.; Bros. Louis N. Mauro, S.J., Business Mgr. (Resurrection Parish); Edward P. Sheehy, S.J. Total in Residence 9; Priests 7; Brothers 2.

Jesuits of Saint Peter's College, Inc., 50 Glenwood Ave., 07306-4606. Tel: 201-761-6123; Fax: 201-432-7397. Email: eheavey@spc.edu. Revs. Anthony Aracich, S.J.; Michael Braden, S.J.; John M. Buckley, S.J.; Mark T. DeStephano, S.J.; J. Juan Diaz Vilar, S.J. (Spain); Charles A. Gallagher, S.J.; Robert E. Kennedy, S.J.; T. Patrick Lynch, S.J.; Donal T. MacVeigh, S.J.; Oscar G. Magnan; Edmund W. Majewski, S.J.; Michel Marcil, S.J., Exec. Dir. U.S. Catholic China Bureau; Robert E. McCarty, S.J.; William A. McKenna, S.J.; Peter O'Brien, S.J.; Joseph J. Papaj, S.J.; John P. Ruane, S.J.; Jose Luis S. Salazar, S.J., Prof. Theology; Raymond A. Schroth, S.J.; Thomas L. Sheridan, S.J.; David X. Stump, S.J.; John F. Wrynn, S.J. Total Staff 22; Total in Residence 22.

MAHWAH. *Paulist Fathers - Paulist Press*, 997 MacArthur Blvd., 07430. Tel: 201-825-7300; Fax: 201-825-8345. Email: info@paulistpress.com. Web: www.paulistpress.com. Revs. Lawrence Boadt, C.S.P., Pres. & Publisher; Michael Kerrigan, C.S.P., Editor; Kevin A. Lynch, C.S.P., Publisher Emeritus & Senior Editor.

MONTCLAIR. *Comboni Missionaries of the Heart of Jesus (Verona Fathers)*, 88 High St., P.O. Box 138, 07042-0138. Tel: 973-744-8080; Fax: 973-744-8919. Email: luigizb@yahoo.com. Revs. Luigi Zanotto, M.C.C.J., Supr.; Provvido Crozzoletto, M.C.C.J. Total Staff 2; Total in Residence 2.

MONTVALE. *Xaverian Brothers*, Xaverian Brothers' Residence, 40 Chestnut Ridge Rd., 07645. Tel: 201-391-8071; Fax: 201-391-8073. Brothers 1.

ORADELL. *Congregation of Christian Brothers*, Bergen Catholic Brothers' Residence, 1040 Oradell Ave., 07649. Tel: 201-634-4100; Fax: 201-599-9507. Brothers 6.

ORANGE. *The Salesian Community* (1998) Don Bosco Residence, 518-B Valley St., 07050. Tel: 973-674-2400; Fax: 973-674-7051. Revs. Stephen Leake, S.D.B., M.A., Dir.; Dominic Tran, S.D.B., M.A., Vice Dir. & Youth Minister; David Moreno, S.D.B.; Bros. Paul Chu, S.D.B., Ordinary; Minh Dang, S.D.B., Ordinary; Sean Hogan, S.D.B., Ordinary; Michael Leschinsky, S.D.B., M.A.; Gustavo Ramirez, S.D.B.; Dieunel Victor, S.D.B.; Wilgintz Polynice, S.D.B. Total Staff 3; Total in Residence 25; Candidates 21.

Don Bosco Vocation Office, Self Pl., South Orange, 07079. Tel: 973-761-0201. Revs. Steve Ryan, S.D.B., Vocation Dir. & Prov. Youth Min.; Franco Pinto, S.D.B., Asst. Vocation Dir.

RAMSEY. *Don Bosco Prep Salesian Residence* (1915) 492 N. Franklin Tpke., 07446-2811. Tel: 201-327-8100; Fax: 201-327-3397. Revs. Louis J. Molinelli, S.D.B., Director & Pres.; Joseph Bajorek, S.D.B. (Retired); James Horan, S.D.B., Coord. Youth Ministry; Eugene Palumbo, S.D.B.; Richard Rosin, S.D.B., Dir. Guidance; Jerzy Schneider, S.D.B. (Retired); John Janko, S.D.B., School Psychologist; James Marra, S.D.B., Dir. of Advancement; Bro. James Wiegand, S.D.B., Asst. Athletic Dir.; Revs. James Cerbone, S.D.B.; Armindo Laranjinha, S.D.B. Total in Residence 12. In Res. Rev. Thomas Brennan, S.D.B.

ROSELLE. *Marist Brothers Residence*, Roselle Catholic High School, 350 Raritan Rd., 07203. Tel: 908-245-3574; Fax: 908-620-9507. Brothers 10.

RUTHERFORD. *St. John Vianney Residence for Priests*, 60 Home Ave., 07070. Tel: 201-933-5155. Carol Hubba, Admin.; Rev. Msgr. Edward J. Hajduk, S.T.L., M.S.S., Dir. (Retired). Tel: 201-933-5155. Total in Residence 23; Total Staff 15. In Res. Most Rev. Peter L. Gerety, Archbishop Emeritus (Retired); Rev. Msgrs. Peter A. Cheplic (Retired); Roger A. Reynolds (Retired); Joseph Chiang (Retired); Thomas G. Madden (Retired); Edward M. Matash (Retired); Rev. Joseph F. Coda (Retired); Rev. Msgr. Edward J. Eilert (Retired); Revs. Eugene J. Hazewski (Retired); John E. Komar (Retired); Robert H. Langdon (Retired); James W. McFarland (Retired); Joseph P. Rice (Retired); Rev. Msgrs. James O. Sheerin (Retired); Richard T. Strelecki (Retired); Revs. Thaddeus Stasik (Retired); Thaddeus F. Zuber (Retired); Gerald A. Bajek; Robert M. Brennan (Retired); Michael Hansen; John J. Morel (Retired); Joseph A. Stulb (Retired).

SOUTH ORANGE. *Pallottine Fathers & Brothers*, 204 Raymond Ave., P.O. Box 979, 07079-0979. Tel: 973-762-2926; Fax: 973-762-2939. Very Rev. Peter T. Sticco, S.A.C., Prov.; Bro. Francis Meo, S.A.C., Admin.

Salesian Office of Youth Ministry & Vocations, 315 Self Pl., 07079. Tel: 973-761-0201; Fax: 973-763-9330. Email: salvoc@aol.com. Web: www.salesianym.com. Revs. Steve Ryan, S.D.B.; Franco Pinto, S.D.B.

TENAFLY. *Society of African Missions, Provincialate, S.M.A. Fathers*, 23 Bliss Ave., 07670. Tel: 201-567-0450; 201-567-9085; Fax: 201-541-1280; 800-670-8328. Email: smausa-c@smafathers.org. Web: www.smafathers.org. Very Rev. Michael P. Moran, S.M.A., Prov. Supr.; Revs. Frank Wright, S.M.A.; Brendan Darcy, S.M.A., Local Supr. & Vice Prov.; Thomas E. Hayden, S.M.A., Serving Outside Archdiocese.; Edward J. Biggane, S.M.A.; Daniel Cullen, S.M.A.; Terrance Doherty, S.M.A. (Retired), Serving Outside Archdiocese.; Joseph Foley, S.M.A. (Retired); Edward Galvin, S.M.A. (Retired); John Guiney, S.M.A. (Retired); James C. Hickey, S.M.A. (Retired); John Francis Murray, S.M.A.; James J. McConnell, S.M.A., Queen of Angels.; James Perrone, S.M.A. (Retired); Eugene Riordan, S.M.A. (Retired), Serving Outside of Archdiocese.

UNION CITY. *Augustinian Recollects, St. Nicholas of Tolentine Monastery* Prov. of St. Nicholas of Tolentine. , 3201 Central Ave., 07087. Tel: 201-433-7550; Fax: 201-422-7570. Email: nicholas@agustinosrecoletos.org. Rev. Francisco J. Legarra, O.A.R., Supr.

Capuchin Friars - Province of the Sacred Stigmata of St. Francis, P.O. Box 809, 07087. Tel: 201-865-0611; Fax: 201-866-7035. Email: stigmatanj@aol.com. Revs. Brian Tomlinson, O.F.M.Cap., Provincial Min.; Nicholas A. Mormando, O.F.M.Cap., Vicar Provincial; Ronald Giannone, O.F.M.Cap., Councillor; John LoSasso, O.F.M.Cap., Councillor; Provincial Sec.; Margaret Milizzo, Sec.; Rev. Ronald Giannone, O.F.M.Cap., Councillor; Bro. John Russo, O.F.M.Cap., Provincial Sec., Definitors. Priests 30; Brothers 15.

Congregation of the Passion (Passionists)-St. Michael's Residence, 526 Monastery Pl., 07087. Tel: 201-864-0018; Fax: 201-867-8651. Email: thepassionists@cpprov.org. Web: www.thepassionists.org. Rev. Victor Hoagland, C.P., Dir. *The Passionist Missionaries* Tel: 201-867-6400; Fax: 201-867-7596. John DeGraaf, Dir. *Passionist Press, Inc.* Tel: 201-867-6400; Fax: 201-867-8651. Email: crossplace@cpprov.org. Rev. Victor Hoagland, C.P. *"Compassion" Magazine* Tel: 201-867-6400; Fax: 201-864-1337. Revs. Victor Hoagland, C.P., Dir., Editor & Supr. Dir. Tel: 201-864-0018; Xavier Vitacolonna, C.P. Tel: 201-864-0018; Bro. James Fitzgerald, Editor. Tel: 201-864-0018. *Passionist Archives* Tel: 201-867-6400; Fax: 201-617-7011. Rev. Robert Carbonneau, C.P., Dir. Archives & Province Historian; Mr. Sean Pelagrine, Archivist. Tel: 201-867-6400.

VERONA. *The Salvatorian Fathers* (1881) (Polish Mission House), 23 Crestmont Rd., 07044. Tel: 973-746-8770; Fax: 973-857-7789. Email: salwatorianie@salvator.org. Web: www.salvator.org. Revs. Wieslaw P. Strzadala, S.D.S., Supr.; Palka Bogdan, S.D.S.; Andrzej Kielkowski, S.D.S.; Jan J. Mysliwiec, S.D.S.; Strzadala Wieslaw, S.D.S.; Marek Wiorkiewicz, S.D.S., Supr.; Bro. Piotr Bogawski, S.D.S.; Revs. Damian Tomiczek, S.D.S.; Pawel Dolinski, S.D.S.; Zenon Boczek, S.D.S., Vice Supr.; Ludwik Kolodziej, S.D.S.

WEST ORANGE. *Augustinian Recollects* Prov. Res., Monastery of St. Cloud, 29 Ridgeway Ave., 07052. Tel: 973-731-0616; Fax: 973-731-1033. Email: SAprovince@yahoo.com. Web: www.augustinianrecollects.org. Very Revs. Joseph Gallardo, O.A.R., Prior Prov.; Charles F. Huse, O.A.R., Prov. Sec.; Rev. Eliseo Gonzalez, O.A.R., Asst. Prov. Sec. & Procurator; Bro. Anthony Torretti, O.A.R., Prov. Procurator. Priests 3; Brothers 1.

[N] CONVENTS AND RESIDENCES FOR SISTERS

NEWARK. *Hermanas Misioneras del Corazon de Jesus (HMCJ)*, Sacred Heart Convent, 109 Parker St., 07104. Tel: 973-484-1516; Fax: 973-484-9701. Email: misionerascj@aol.com. Sr. Ana Josefa Fa jardo, Supr. Parish Ministry. Sisters 4.

Holy Family Sisters of the Needy, St. Rose of Lima Convent, 11 Gray St., 07103. Tel: 973-481-6717. Email: srmavit@yahoo.com. Sr. Mary Vitalis Iwuoha, Local Supr. Sisters 9.

Missionaries of Charity - St. Augustine Convent (1981) 168 Sussex Ave., 07103. Tel: 973-483-0165. Sisters 7.

Missionary Sisters of the Most Blessed Sacrament and Mary Immaculate Day Care Center., 121 Congress St., 07105. Tel: 973-589-5794; Fax: 973-589-2474. Email: grande815@msn.com; nepo867@msn.com. Sr. Milagros Delgado, M.SS.M.I., Supr.

Sisters of Charity of Ottawa, 182 Broadway, 07104. Tel: 973-497-0614. Sisters of St. Martha 4; Vocationist Sisters (172 Broad St., Nwk, NJ) 7; Total in Residence 11.

Sisters of St. Joseph of Chestnut Hill, Thea House (1992) 39 Bleeker St., 07102. Tel: 973-622-7056. Email: ssjthea@gmail.net. Total in Residence 5.

Vocationist Sisters (1921) (Our Lady of Perpetual Help Center). Perpetual Help Day Nursery., 170 Broad St., 07104. Tel: 973-484-3535; Fax: 973-484-2526. Email: perhelp@yahoo.com. Sisters 7; Total Assisted 145; Total Staff 22.

BLOOMFIELD. *Sisters of the Divine Compassion (RDC)*, 21 Spring St., Apt. 2, 07003. Tel: 973-748-6559. Email: skavan6578@msn.com. Sisters 2.

CALDWELL. *Motherhouse of Sisters of St. Dominic*, 1 Ryerson Ave., 07006. Tel: 973-403-3331; Fax: 973-228-9611. Email: hwerner@caldwellop.org. Web: www.caldwellop.org. Sr. Arlene Antczak, O.P., Prioress. Sisters in Community 163; Sisters in Diocese 161.

DEMAREST. *Missionary Benedictine Sisters of Tutzing* (1997) 274 County Rd., 07627. Tel: 201-767-3114; Fax: 201-767-8874. Sr. Asella Kim, O.S.B., Supr. Sisters 4.

ELIZABETH. *St. Walburga Monastery*, 851 N. Broad St., 07208-2593. Tel: 908-352-4278; Fax: 908-352-6331. Email: Bensisnj@aol.com. Web: www.catholic-forum.com/bensisnj. Benedictine Sisters of Elizabeth, NJ. Sisters in Archdiocese 38; Professed Sisters 44.

ENGLEWOOD CLIFFS. *St. Michael Villa*, 399 Hudson Ter., 07632. Tel: 201-871-1620; Fax: 201-871-7313. Sr. Ann Rutan, C.S.J.P., Admin.; Rev. William T. Morris, Chap. Sisters of St. Joseph of Peace., Senior Sisters Residence and Infirmary for St. Joseph Province. Sisters 37; Total Staff 52; Total in Residence 37.

Sisters of St. Joseph of Peace, 399 Hudson Ter., 07632. Tel: 201-568-6348; Fax: 201-568-9880. Web: www.csjp.org/sjp. Sisters Margaret Byrne, C.S.J.P., Congregation Leader; Theresa Donohue, C.S.J.P., Asst. Congregation Leader; Theresette Hunting, C.S.J.P., Archivist; Kristin Funari, C.S.J.P; Anne Hayes, C.S.J.P.; Coralie Muzzy, C.S.J.P.; Ann Taylor, C.S.J.P., Community Archivist. Congregation of Sisters of St. Joseph of Peace., Eastern U.S. Offices for Sisters of St. Joesph of Peace. Sisters in Community 101. Congregation Leadership Team:

St. Ann's Home for the Aged Tel: 201-433-0950; Fax: 201-433-6554. Total Staff 215; Total in Residence 120.

St. Ann Day Care Tel: 201-433-0950; Fax: 201-985-9638. Staff 10; Adults 50.

Cusack Care Center at St. Joseph Home for the Blind Tel: 201-653-8300; Fax: 201-963-4346. Total Staff 200; Total in Residence 193; Bed Capacity 139.

Concordia Learning Center at St. Joseph School for the Blind: A New Jersey Non-profit Corp. Tel: 201-876-5432; Fax: 201-876-5431. Total Staff 99; Students 130.

St. Joseph Home Tel: 201-413-9280. Bed Capacity 60; Total Staff 13; Total Assisted 105.

St. Mary's Residence Tel: 201-432-6289. Total Staff 11; Total Assisted 50.

Nurturing Place Day Care Tel: 201-413-1982. Child Development Center Total Staff 17; Total Assisted 62.

The York Street Project Tel: 201-451-9838; Fax: 201-451-0952. Total Staff 11.

Stella Maris Retreat Center Tel: 732-229-0216; Fax: 732-229-8960. Total Staff 11; Total in Residence 3.

Waterspirit Ministry Tel: 732-923-9788; Fax: 732-229-8960. Total Staff 3.

St. Joseph Messenger Office Tel: 201-798-4141. Total Staff 3.

FORT LEE. *Holy Trinity Convent (Inter Community)*, 199 Myrtle Ave., 07024. Tel: 201-944-2911. Dominican Sisters of Hope 1; Franciscan Sisters of St. Francis 2; Sisters of Charity 1.

IRVINGTON. *Immaculate Conception Convent*, 121 Myrtie Ave., 07111. Tel: 201-374-6397. Augustinian Recollect Sisters (Cloistered) 11.

JERSEY CITY. *St. Nicholas Convent*, 115 Ferry St., 07307. Tel: 201-659-5644; Fax: 201-798-6868. Email: sjmaumand@yahoo.com. Sr. Joann Marie Aumand, S.C.C., Supr.

LODI. *Immaculate Conception Convent* (1913) 260 S. Main St., 07644-2196. Tel: 973-473-7447; Fax: 973-473-7126. Email: fjeanryder@felicianslodi.org.

Web: www.feliciansisters.org. Revs. Damian Colicchio, Chap.; Placid Stroik, O.F.M., Chap. Provincial House, Novitiate and Infirmary of the Felician Sisters. Sisters in Community 151.

PLAINFIELD. *Contemplative Convent of the Missionaries of Charity*, 513 Liberty St., 07060. Tel: 908-754-1978. Sr. Viktorija, M.C., Supr. Total in Residence 20.

RIDGEFIELD. *Pallottine Sisters - St. Vincent Pallotti Convent*, 545 Victory Ave., 07567. Tel: 201-941-4552. Email: sralicemarie@gmail.com. Sisters 3.

SADDLE BROOK. *Miyazaki Caritas Sisters (Korea) - Caritas Sisters Convent*, 585 Saddle River Rd., 07663. Tel: 201-398-0199; Fax: 201-703-7111.

SCOTCH PLAINS. *Union Catholic Convent* (1962) 1600 Martine Ave., 07076. Tel: 908-889-1600. Sisters of Mercy of New Jersey (R.S.M.) and Sisters of St. Joseph (S.S.J.). Total in Residence 5.

SOUTH ORANGE. *Marylawn of the Oranges Convent* (1935) 425 Scotland Rd., 07079. Tel: 973-762-7218. Email: mloconvent@yahoo.com. Sisters 6.

SPRINGFIELD. *St. James Convent*, 35 S. Springfield Ave., 07081. Tel: 973-376-8753. Sisters of St. Joseph, Chestnut Hill, Philadelphia. Total in Residence 3.

SUMMIT. *Monastery of Our Lady of the Rosary* (1919) 543 Springfield Ave., 07901. Tel: 908-273-1228; Fax: 908-273-6511. Email: nunsopsummit@op.org. Web: www.nunsopsummit.org. Sr. Mary Martin Jacobs, O.P., Prioress.

Monastery of Our Lady of the Rosary, Dominican Nuns of the Perpetual Rosary Professed Sisters 15; Novices 5.

TENAFLY. *Convent of Our Lady of the Angels*, 253 Knickerbocker Rd., 07670. Tel: 201-568-2171; Fax: 201-568-2352. Email: franciscans253@yahoo.com. Web: www.mficusa.org. Sr. Catherine Finnerty, M.F.I.C., Supr. Missionary Franciscan Sisters of the Immaculate Conception. Sisters 46.

UNION. *Sisters of St. Francis of the Providence of God*, 1137 Burnet Ave., 07083. Tel: 908-206-1136. Sisters 2.

UNION CITY. *Holy Rosary Convent* (1904) 1514 Central Ave., 07087. Tel: 201-617-4638; Fax: 201-617-4638. Email: holyrosaryconvent@verizon.net. Sisters of the Catholic Apostolate (Pallottines). Sisters 3.

Monastery of the Dominican Nuns of the Perpetual Rosary (Cloistered), 605 14th St. & West St., 07087-3199. Tel: 201-866-7004. Sr. Mary Jordan, O.P., Prioress. Professed Sisters 3; Total Staff 1; Total in Residence 2.

[O] RETREAT HOUSES

KEARNY. *Archdiocesan Youth Retreat Center* Archdiocesan Youth Center and Retreat House. Retreats for groups, parishes, days of prayer recollection, workshops, seminars for laity, priests, and religious. Rooms for overnight and food service. High and Low ropes challenge course available., 499 Belgrove Dr., 07032. Tel: 201-998-0088; Fax: 201-299-0801. Web: www.newarkoym.org. Rev. Joseph A. Mancini, Exec. Dir.

MAHWAH. *Carmel Retreat* Carmelite Community and House of Prayer. Retreats (groups, directed, private), Days of prayer, rentals, meetings, seminars. , 1071 Ramapo Valley Rd., 07430. Tel: 201-327-7090; Fax: 201-327-9133. Email: mail@carmelretreat.com. Web: www.carmelretreat.com. Sr. Eileen T. McGovern, S.S.J., Dir. Priests 1; Sisters 1; Total in Residence 2. In Res. Rev. Michael J. Wastog, O.Carm.

[P] CAMPUS MINISTRY

NEWARK. *The Newman Catholic Center at University Heights (Rutgers/Newark/NJIT)* 91 Washington St., 07102. Tel: 973-624-1301; Fax: 973-623-1728. Email: NewmanCenter@optonline.net. Web: www.catholiccampusministry.org. Rev. Marc A. Vicari, Dir. & Chap.; Sisters Faustine of Jesus, Campus Min.; Jeanne Marie, Campus Min.; Jesse Mazzola, Campus Min.; Beatriz M. Capella, Office Mgr. & Budget Coord. Serving Essex County College, Rutgers University/Newark Campus, New Jersey Institute of Technology & UMDNJ Total Staff 5.

HOBOKEN. *Catholic Campus Ministry at Stevens Institute of Technology* Mailing Address: *Ss. Peter and Paul Parish Center*, 408 Hudson St., 07030. Web: www.ccm-nj.com. Maureen Madigan, M.T.S., Campus Min.; Rev. Amilcar B. Prado, Chap. (Part-Time). Total Staff 1.

JERSEY CITY. *New Jersey City University, Gilligan Student Union* 319 Kennedy Blvd., Grossnickle Hall Rm. 133, 07305-1597. Tel: 201-200-2565; 973-792-5710 (Residence); Fax: 201-200-2329. Web: www.catholiccampusministry.org. Rev. Luke A. Edelen, O.S.B., Chap. & Campus Min. Total Staff 1.

MAHWAH. *Ramapo College* (1969) 505 Ramapo Valley Rd., Room SC207, 07430. Tel: 201-684-7251; Fax: 201-825-0276. Email: wsherida@ramapo.edu. Web: www.ramapo.edu/studentlife/ministry/catholic_Ministry/CM_index.htm. Rev. William P. Sheridan, Chap. Total Staff 1; Students 5,500.

TEANECK. *Fairleigh Dickinson Univ.-Teaneck Campus* 1000 River Rd., 07666. Tel: 201-692-2570; Fax: 201-692-2769. Email: mmadigan@fdu.edu. Rev. Kevin F. Murphy, Chap. Total Staff 2.

UNION. *Kean University* Catholic Campus Ministry, 1000 Morris Ave., 07083-7131. Tel: 908-737-4835; Fax: 201-985-0918. Email: tblind@kean.edu. Rev. Thomas F. Blind, Chap.

UPPER MONTCLAIR. *Newman Catholic Center at Montclair State University* 894 Valley Rd., 07043-2116. Tel: 973-746-2323; Fax: 973-783-3313. Email: chernj@mail.montclair.edu. Web: www.msunewman.com. Rev. James N. Chern, Dir., Newman Catholic Ctr. & Chap. at Montclair State Univ.; Mary Kominsky, Office Mgr. & Pastoral Assoc. Total Staff 2.

[Q] SHRINES

KEARNY. *Eucharistic Shrine of the Adorable Face of Jesus* 672 Passaic Ave., 07032-1305. Tel: 201-997-1270; Fax: 201-997-5552. Email: eushrine@juno.com. Rev. Msgr. Renato Grasselli, Shrine Dir.

[R] MISCELLANEOUS LISTINGS

NEWARK. *Catholic Health and Human Services Corporation*, 1160 Raymond Blvd., 07102. Tel: 973-854-2447. Rev. Msgr. Ronald J. Rozniak, V.G., P.A., Chm.; Terence French, Exec. Vice Pres., Planning & Gov't Relations; Phillip Frese, Ph.D., CPA, Exec. V. P. Operations; John S. Grywalski Jr., Exec. Vice Pres. Finance & CFO.

CatholiCare, Inc., 171 Clifton Ave., P.O. Box 9500, 07104-0500. Tel: 973-497-4002; Fax: 973-497-4018. Rev. Msgr. John E. Doran, V.G., Vicar Gen. & Moderator of Curia.

Columbus Acquisition Corp. A member of Catholic Health East., 495 N. 13th St., 07107. Email: hatalaa@lourdesnet.org. Alexander J. Hatala, Pres.

Deacon St. Lawrence Welfare Fund, Office of Permanent Diaconate, 171 Clifton Ave., P.O. Box 9500, 07104-9500. Tel: 973-497-4223; Fax: 973-497-4219. Email: mckennajo@rcan.org. Deacon John J. McKenna.

Diaconate Executive Committee, Archdiocesan Center, 171 Clifton Ave., P.O. Box 9500, 07104-9500. Tel: 973-497-4223; Fax: 973-497-4219. Email: mckennajo@rcan.org. Deacon John J. McKenna.

New Jersey Caritas Corporation, Inc., 171 Clifton Ave., 07104. Tel: 973-497-4002; Fax: 973-497-4018. Rev. Msgr. John E. Doran, V.G.

Domus Corporation, Inc., 494 Broad St., 07102. Tel: 973-596-5118; Fax: 973-424-9596.

Canaan House, Inc., 494 Broad St., 07102. Tel: 973-596-5115; Fax: 973-424-9596.

Sunrise House, 185 Parkhurst St., 07114. Tel: 973-624-9478; Fax: 973-424-9596.

Carmel House of Jersey City, Inc., 494 Broad St., 07102. Tel: 973-596-5115; Fax: 973-424-9596.

Trinity Management & Technology Corp., 1160 Raymond Blvd., 07102. Tel: 973-596-3602; Fax: 973-690-3601. Rev. Msgr. Ronald J. Rozniak, V.G., P.A., Chm.; Bro. Benedict Lo Balbo, F.M.S., Sec. & Contact Person.

University Heights Property Company, Inc., 1160 Raymond Blvd., 07102. Tel: 973-690-3606; Fax: 973-690-3601. Rev. Msgrs. Joseph T. Slinger, Ph.D., Chm.; Ronald J. Rozniak, V.G., P.A., Pres.; Anita C. Holland, Sec.; John S. Grywalski Jr., Treas.

BAYONNE. *The Gregoire Trust*, 1241 Kennedy Blvd., 07002. Tel: 201-823-1115; Fax: 201-823-2232. Email: maristpto@aol.com. Bros. Benedict LoBalbo, F.M.S., Trustee; Edward Breslin, Trustee; Lawrence Lavallee, F.M.S., Trustee; Ken Hogan, F.M.S., Trustee; Richard Carey, F.M.S., Trustee.

Lewiston Mission Trust, 1241 Kennedy Blvd., 07002. Tel: 201-823-1115; Fax: 201-823-2232. Bros. Edward J. O'Neill, F.M.S., Trustee; Benedict Lo Balbo, F.M.S., Trustee & Contact Person.

Marist Brothers Support Trust, 1241 Kennedy Blvd., 07002. Tel: 201-823-1115; Fax: 201-823-2232. Email: maristpto@aol.com. Bros. Richard Carey, F.M.S., Trustee; Benedict Lo Balbo, F.M.S., Trustee. Congregation of the Marist Brothers.

ELIZABETH. *St. Joseph's Social Service Center* (1986) 118 Division St., 07201. Tel: 908-352-2989; 908-354-5456; Fax: 908-354-1433. Sr. Jacinta Fernandes, O.S.B., Dir. Total Staff 12; Total Assisted 7,800.

EMERSON. *Magnificat: A Ministry to Catholic Women* (2002) 160 Jefferson Ave., 07630. Tel: 201-265-2738; Fax: 201-265-3904. Email: grand174@aol.com.

Glen Rock NJ-Handmaid of the Lord Chapter Service Team Elizabeth Tobin, Coord., 160 Jefferson Ave., 07630. Tel: 201-265-2738; Fax: 201-265-3904. Email: grand174@aol.com; Melanie Suter, Asst. Coord.; Ann Marie Funk, Treas.; Gail Artola, Sec.

FAIRVIEW. *Pallottine Intra-Community Operating Corporation*, Mailing Address: P.O. Box 979, South Orange, 07079. Tel: 973-762-2926; Fax: 973-762-2939. 395 Delano Pl., 07022. Tel: 201-943-0972; Fax: 201-313-5616. Very Rev. Peter T. Sticco, S.A.C.

JERSEY CITY. *St. Patrick and Assumption All Saints Foundation*, 492 Bramhall Ave., 07304. Tel: 201-332-8600; Fax: 201-324-3919. Email: jcfran@bellatlantic.net. Rev. Francis E. Schiller, B.A., J.D., Contact Person.

St. Patrick's Housing Corp., 492 Bramhall Ave., 07304. Tel: 201-332-8600; Fax: 201-324-3919. Rev. Eugene P. Squeo, J.D., Pres.

Trinity Child Care Center, 492 Bramhall Ave., 07304. Tel: 201-332-8600. Sr. Maeve McDermott, S.C., Prin.; Rev. Francis E. Schiller, B.A., J.D., Contact Person.

KEARNY. *Family of Nazareth, Inc.* (1991) 672 Passaic Ave., 07032. Tel: 201-997-3220; Fax: 201-997-5552. Email: fnazareth@rmnewark.org. Fred Canlas, Pres.; Luis Abarca, Trustee. A foundation to support the work of the Redemptoris Mater Missionary Seminary and for the new evangelization.

New Jersey Boystown, 499 Belgrove Dr., 07032.

LODI. **The Promise Outreach, Inc.* (1982) Volunteers visit, correspond with, and provide opportunity for spirituality and other basic needs to teens in programs, correctional institutions and centers of rehabilitation., 260 S. Main St., 07644. Tel: 973-460-3229; Fax: 973-473-7126. Email: vimsters@aol.com. Web: home.catholicweb.com/thepromiseoutreachinc. Sr. Antonelle Chunka, C.S.S.F., Dir.; Bro. Thomas Corey, B.S.C.D., Co-Dir.; Sr. Lois Marie Parenti, C.S.S.F., Treas. Total Staff 20; Total Assisted Annually 1,000.

MAHWAH. *Paulist Press*, 997 MacArthur Blvd., 07430. Tel: 201-825-7300; Fax: 201-825-8345. Email: info@paulistpress.com. Web: www.paulistpress.com. Revs. Kevin A. Lynch, C.S.P., Senior Editor; Lawrence Boadt, C.S.P., Publisher; Michael Kerrigan, C.S.P., Editor. Priests 3; Total Staff 50.

MONTCLAIR. *Tri-State Coalition for Responsible Investment*, 40 S. Fullerton Ave., 07042. Tel: 973-509-8800; Fax: 973-509-8808. Email: Pdaly@tricri.org. Web: www.tricri.org. Sr. Patricia A. Daly, O.P., Exec. Dir.

ORANGE. *Mee Joo Catholic Inc.*, 18 Cleveland St., 07050. Tel: 973-672-6335; Fax: 973-672-0509. Email: augpark@yahoo.com. Web: www.koreancatholic.org. Rev. Msgr. Augustin C. Park, Coord.

PLAINFIELD. **The People of Hope* (1977) 1040 Plainfield Ave., St. Francis Bldg., 07060. Tel: 908-222-9722; Fax: 908-222-9755. Email: davetouhill@peopleofhope.net. David Touhill, Senior Coord. The People of Hope is a Catholic Family Charismatic Covenant community of prayer, family life, and evangelization. Officially recognized as a private association of the faithful in 2006 by Archbishop Myers, the People of Hope sponsors marriage and family retreats, youth, university, and young adult programs, Christian business seminars, and other evangelistic events. Its largest outreach is Koinonia Academy, a K-12 school, founded in 1984. The Community is organized to encourage individuals and families to dedicate their lives to God under the Lordship of Jesus Christ, to help in the renewal of the Catholic Church and to assist the spreading of the Gospel message of Jesus Christ locally and throughout the world. To be "a witness of an authentically Christian life, given over to God." (Pope Paul VI, Evangelii Nuntiandi, 1975).

RENEW International, 1232 George St., 07062-1717. Tel: 908-769-5400; Fax: 908-769-5660. Email: renew@renewintl.org. Web: www.renewintl.org. Rev. Msgr. Thomas A. Kleissler, Pres.; Sisters Theresa Rickard, O.P., D.Min., Exec. Dir.; Kathleen (Kass) Collins, S.F.C.C., Asst. Dir.; Kathleen Phelan, O.P., C.F.R.E., Dir. Devel.; Mary Beth Oria, Dir.; Richard Michalowski, Fin. Controller; Sr. Eileen Carmody, P.B.V.M., Human Resources Admin.

Team Leaders: Robert Kelly, Publications & Resources; Rev. Alejandro Lopez-Cardinale, Co-Dir. Pastoral Svcs.; Sr. Honora Nolty, O.P., Pastoral Svcs. Co-Dir.; Deirdre Trabert Malacrea, Mktg. & Communications Dir.

Pastoral Services Team: Dr. Irma Chavez; Sisters Maureen Colleary, F.S.P.; Marie Cooper, S.J.C.;

Marenid Fabre, O.P.; Alma Garcia; Manuel Hernandez; Greg Kremer; Theresa Leonetti; Leslie Maiman, M.B.A., M.T.S.; Sr. Veronica Mendez, R.C.D.; Mary Regina Morrell; Kathy Motyka; Rev. Abraham Orapankal; Sisters Eileen Rush, S.S.J.; Pat Thomas, O.P.; Gregory Welch.

Operations, Resources and Administrative Staff: Christopher Burns; Susan Capurso; Regina Crowley; Marty Hagedorn; Lynn Hull; Yvette Hutchins; Eartha Johnson; Sr. Mary McGuinness, O.P.; Alexandra Laguna; Margarita Morales; Carolyn Newkirk.

RUTHERFORD. *The Community of God's Love* Catholic Charismatic Community, 70 W. Passaic Ave., 07070. Tel: 201-935-0344; Fax: 201-935-0111. Email: theCGL@aol.com. Web: thecgl.org. Rev. Philip F. Latronico, M.A., M.Div., Chap.; Andrew Cevasco, Community Dir.

SHORT HILLS. *Friends of the Newark Monastery, Inc.*, 9 Grosvenor Rd., 07078. Email: aluzarraga@shearman.com. Alberto Luzarraga, Pres. & Contact Person.

SOUTH ORANGE. *The Pallottines of South Orange, Inc.*, 204 Raymond Ave., 07079-2305. Tel: 973-763-5591; Fax: 973-762-2939. Bro. Francis Meo, S.A.C., Supr.

Salesians of Don Bosco, Salesians House, 315 Self Pl., 07079. Tel: 973-761-0201; Fax: 973-763-9330. Email: salvoc@aol.com. Web: www.salesianym.org.

Offices of Vocation and Youth Ministry Tel: 973-761-0102; Fax: 973-763-9330. Email: salvoc@aol.com. Web: www.salesianvocation.com. Revs. Steve Ryan, S.D.B., Vocation Dir. & Prov. Councillor for Youth Ministry; P. Francis Pinto, S.D.B. Total in Residence 2.

U.S. Catholic China Bureau (1989) Seton Hall University, 07079-2689. Tel: 973-763-1131; Fax: 973-774-7084. Email: chinabur@shu.edu. Web: www.usccb.net. Dr. Regina Wentzel Wolfe, Chair, Bd. of Directors; Rev. Michel Marcil, S.J., Exec. Dir.; Sr. Janet Carroll, M.M., USCCB Scholar; Mengpin Hsiao, Admin. Asst. Exists to foster communication and friendship with the people of China through sharing the values of the Gospel of Jesus Christ. It promotes understanding among American Catholics about the Catholic Church and the situation of Catholic communities in China. It fosters re-engagement of the U.S. Catholic Church in a new missionary partnership with the Catholic Church in China. USCCB publishes the "China Church Quarterly", sponsors National Catholic China Conference, religious study tours to China and other activities to sustain a shared commitment to mission with the Catholic Church in China. Total Staff 3.

SUMMIT. *Association of the Monasteries of Nuns of the Order of Preachers in the United States of America*, 543 Springfield Ave., 07901-4400. Tel: 650-322-1801, Ext. 25; Fax: 650-322-6816. Sisters Mary John Molesworth, O.P., Pres.; Miriam Scheel, O.P., Vice Pres.; Mary Desmond, O.P., Sec. & First Counselor; Maria Christine Behlow, O.P., Treas.

Christ Child Society of Summit, N.J., P.O. Box 125, 07902-0125. Tel: 908-598-1377. Email: lambinewsham@msn.com. Lambi Newsham, Pres.

TEANECK. *Holy Name Health Care Foundation*, 718 Teaneck Rd., 07666. Tel: 201-833-7143; Fax: 201-833-7213. Email: foundation@mail.holyname.org. Web: www.holyname.org. Michael Maron, Pres. & CEO. Sisters of St. Joseph of Peace.

UNION. *Association of St. Philomena's Helpers and Servants to the Suffering & the Poor* (1996) P.O. Box 393, 07083-0393. Tel: 908-964-7653; Fax: 908-687-4209. Rev. George M. Keating, Spiritual Moderator (Retired).

UNION CITY. *Cofradia Arquidiocesana de la Virgen de la Caridad del Cobre, Inc.*, 3333 Hudson Ave., 07087. Tel: 201-941-0530. Manuel Sanchez, Treas.

RELIGIOUS INSTITUTES OF MEN REPRESENTED IN THE ARCHDIOCESE

For further details refer to the corresponding bracketed number in the Religious Institutes of Men or Women section.

[0100]—*Adorno Fathers*—C.R.M.
[0200]—*Benedictine Monks* (Newark Abbey; St. Mary Abbey)—O.S.B.
[0330]—*Brothers of Christian Schools* (Baltimore Prov.; Long Island/New England Prov.; New York Prov.)—F.S.C.
[0470]—*The Capuchin Friars* (Prov. of the Stigmata)—O.F.M.Cap.
[0270]—*Carmelite Fathers & Brothers* (American Prov.)—O.Carm.
[0380]—*Comboni Missionaries of the Heart of Jesus (Verona)*—M.C.C.J.
[]—*Community of Saint John*—C.F.J.
[0310]—*Congregation of Christian Brothers*—C.F.C.
[1000]—*Congregation of the Passion* (Eastern Prov.)—C.P.
[]—*Dominican Friars* (Order of Preachers)—O.P.
[0520]—*Franciscan Friars* (Prov. of Most Holy Name; Prov. of the Assumption)—O.F.M.
[0530]—*Franciscan Friars of the Atonement*—S.A.
[0535]—*Franciscan Friars of the Renewal*—C.F.R.
[0690]—*Jesuit Fathers and Brothers* (Prov. of New York)—S.J.
[0770]—*The Marist Brothers*—F.M.S.
[0840]—*Missionary Servants of the Most Holy Trinity*—S.T.
[0150]—*Order of the Augustinian Recollects* (Prov. of St. Augustine)—O.A.R.
[0150]—*Order of the Augustinian Recollects* (Prov. of St. Nicholas of Tolentine)—O.A.R.
[1030]—*Paulist Fathers*—C.S.P.
[]—*Province of the Immaculate Conception*
[1070]—*Redemptorist Fathers* (Byzantine Ukrainians)—C.Ss.R.
[1070]—*Redemptorist Fathers* (Prov. of Campo Grande, Brazil)—C.Ss.R.
[1190]—*Salesians of Don Bosco*—S.D.B.
[0110]—*Society of African Missions*—S.M.A.
[0990]—*Society of the Catholic Apostolate* (Prov. of the Immaculate Conception)—S.A.C.
[1200]—*Society of the Divine Savior*—S.D.S.
[1170]—*St. Patrick Missionary Society*—S.P.S.
[0560]—*Third Order Regular of Saint Francis* (U.S.A. Commissarate of the Spanish Prov.)—T.O.R.
[]—*Union Lumen Dei*—L.D.
[1340]—*Vocationist Fathers*—S.D.V.
[]—*Xaverian Brothers*—C.F.X.

RELIGIOUS INSTITUTES OF WOMEN REPRESENTED IN THE ARCHDIOCESE

[]—*Augustinian Recollect Sisters* (Mexico)—O.A.R.
[0230]—*Benedictine Sisters of Pontifical Jurisdiction-Newark* (Benedictine Sisters of Baltimore; Benedictine Sisters of Elizabeth)—O.S.B.
[1810]—*Bernardine Franciscan Sisters*—O.S.F.
[]—*Congregation of Caritas Sisters of Miyazaki* Korean Province
[]—*Congregation of Kkottongnae Sisters of Jesus*—C.S.K.J.
[]—*Congregation of the Immaculate Heart of Mary*
[]—*Daughters of Divine Love*—D.D.L.
[]—*Daughters of Mary*—D.M.
[0850]—*Daughters of Mary Help of Christians*—F.M.A.
[]—*Daughters of Mary, Mothers of Mercy* (Nigeria)—D.M.M.M.
[1050]—*Dominican Contemplative Nuns (Cloistered)*—O.P.
[1070-11]—*Dominican Sisters* (Sparkill, NY)—O.P.
[1070-18]—*Dominican Sisters* (Caldwell, NJ)—O.P.
[1070-15]—*Dominican Sisters* (Blauvelt, NY)—O.P.
[1070-06]—*Dominican Sisters of Hope* (Newburgh, NY)—O.P.
[1170]—*Felician Sisters*—C.S.S.F.
[1400]—*Franciscan Missionary Sister of the Sacred Heart*—F.M.S.C.
[1180]—*Franciscan Sisters of Allegany, New York*—O.S.F.
[1425]—*Franciscan Sisters of Peace*—F.S.P.
[1460]—*Franciscan Sisters of St. Elizabeth*—F.S.S.E.
[1190]—*Franciscan Sisters of the Atonement*—S.A.
[1440]—*Franciscan Sisters of the Poor*—S.F.P.
[]—*Hermanas Missionaras del Corazon de Jesus* (Dominican Republic)—H.M.C.J.
[]—*Holy Family Sisters of the Needy*—H.F.S.N.
[3790]—*Institute of the Sisters of St. Dorothy*—S.S.D.
[2300]—*Little Servant Sisters of the Immaculate Conception*—L.S.I.C.
[]—*Maryknoll Sisters of St. Dominic*—M.M.
[2710]—*Missionaries of Charity* (Active and Contemplative)—M.C.
[0210]—*Missionary Benedictine Sisters of Tutzing* (Korean Mission)—O.S.B.
[1360]—*Missionary Franciscan Sisters of the Immaculate Conception*—M.F.I.C.
[2790]—*Missionary Servants of the Most Blessed Trinity*—M.S.B.T.
[2760]—*Missionary Sisters of the Immaculate Conception of the Mother of God*—S.M.I.C.
[2780]—*Missionary Sisters of the Most Blessed Sacrament and Mary Immaculate*—M.SS.M.I.
[]—*Miyazaki Caritas Sisters* (Japan/Korea)—C.S.M.
[3430]—*Religious Teachers Filippini*—M.P.F.
[2970]—*School Sisters of Notre Dame*—S.S.N.D.
[1700]—*School Sisters of the Third Order of St. Francis* (Bethlehem, PA)—O.S.F.
[]—*Sisters of Charity (Halifax)*
[0590]—*Sisters of Charity of Saint Elizabeth, Convent Station*—S.C.
[0650]—*Sisters of Charity of St. Vincent de Paul of New York*—S.C.
[0660]—*Sisters of Christian Charity*—S.C.C.
[2575]—*Sisters of Mercy of the Americas* (New Jersey)—R.S.M.
[3893]—*Sisters of Saint Joseph of Chestnut Hill, Philadelphia*—S.S.J.
[1650]—*Sisters of St. Francis of Philadelphia*—O.S.F.
[1660]—*Sisters of St. Francis of Providence of God*—O.S.F.
[3820]—*Sisters of St. John the Baptist*—C.S.J.B.
[3890]—*Sisters of St. Joseph of Peace*—C.S.J.P.
[3937]—*Sisters of St. Martha of Antigonish, N.S.*—C.S.M.
[3140]—*Sisters of the Catholic Apostolate (Pallottine)*—C.S.A.C.
[0970]—*Sisters of the Divine Compassion*—R.D.C.
[]—*Sisters of the Holy Name of Jesus and Mary*—S.N.J.M.
[]—*Sisters of the Immaculate Heart of Mary of Mirinae*—I.H.M.M.
[3610]—*Sisters Servants of Mary Immaculate*—S.S.M.I.
[2160]—*Sisters, Servants of the Immaculate Heart of Mary (Scranton)*—I.H.M.
[4060]—*Society of the Holy Child Jesus*—S.H.C.J.
[]—*Union Lumen Dei*—L.D.
[4210]—*Vocationist Sisters*—S.D.V.

ARCHDIOCESAN CEMETERIES

COLONIA. *St. Gertrude*
DARLINGTON. *Maryrest*
EAST HANOVER. *Gate of Heaven*
EAST ORANGE. *Holy Sepulchre*
St. Mary
FRANKLIN LAKES. *Christ the King*
JERSEY CITY. *Holy Name*
Saint Peter
NORTH ARLINGTON. *Holy Cross*
RIVER VALE. *St. Andrew*

PAROCHIAL CEMETERIES

NEWARK. *Mount Olivet*
BELLEVILLE. *St. Peter's*
BLOOMFIELD. *Mount Olivet*
CLARK. *St. Mary's*
FORT LEE. *Madonna*
HACKENSACK. *St. Joseph's*
HOHOKUS. *St. Luke's*
LINDEN. *Mount Calvary*
LYNDHURST. *St. Joseph's*
ORANGE. *St. John's*
PLAINFIELD. *St. Mary's*
SHORT HILLS. *St. Rose of Lima*
SUMMIT. *St. Teresa's*
TENAFLY. *Mount Carmel*
UPPER MONTCLAIR. *Immaculate Conception*

NECROLOGY

† Fleming, Rev. Msgr. Edward J., (Retired)—Died Dec. 25, 2008
† Lennon, Rev. Msgr. Robert T., (Retired)—Died Dec. 1, 2008
† Sullivan, Rev. Msgr. Edwin V., (Retired)—Died Feb. 4, 2009
† Surban, Rev. Msgr. Edmundo A., (Retired)—Died Dec. 29, 2008
† Wojtycha, Rev. Msgr. Edward F., (Retired)—Died June 8, 2009
† Cestaro, Joseph J., (Retired)—Died July 19, 2009
† Gurski, John K., (Retired)—Died April 10, 2009
† Halliwell, Robert J., (Retired)—Died May 11, 2009
† Hermanns, Harold T., (Retired)—Died Oct. 7, 2009
† Laudati, Joseph J., (Retired)—Died Jan. 15, 2009
† Malanga, Salvatore T., (Retired)—Died Aug. 13, 2009
† Nealon, Joseph W., (Retired)—Died May 25, 2009

Archdiocese of New Orleans

(Archidioecesis Novae Aureliae)

Most Reverend

ALFRED C. HUGHES, S.T.D.

Former Archbishop of New Orleans; ordained December 15, 1957; appointed Auxiliary Bishop of Boston July 21, 1981; ordained Auxiliary Bishop of Boston September 14, 1981; appointed Bishop of Baton Rouge September 7, 1993; installed Bishop of Baton Rouge November 4, 1993; appointed Coadjutor Archbishop of New Orleans February 16, 2001; appointed Archbishop of New Orleans January 3, 2002; retired August 20, 2009. *Office: 7887 Walmsley Ave., New Orleans, LA 70125.* Tel: 504-861-9521.

Most Reverend

FRANCIS B. SCHULTE, D.D.

Former Archbishop of New Orleans; ordained May 10, 1952; appointed Titular Bishop of Afufenia and Auxiliary Bishop of Philadelphia June 27, 1981; ordained to the episcopacy August 12, 1981; appointed Sixth Bishop of Wheeling-Charleston June 4, 1985; promoted to Metropolitan See of New Orleans December 13, 1988; installed February 14, 1989; retired January 3, 2002. *Office: 7887 Walmsley Ave., New Orleans, LA 70125.*

Most Reverend

PHILIP M. HANNAN, D.D., J.C.D., S.T.L.

Former Archbishop of New Orleans; ordained December 8, 1939; appointed Titular Bishop of Hieropolis and Auxiliary Bishop of Washington June 16, 1956; consecrated August 28, 1956; promoted to Archbishop of New Orleans September 29, 1965; installed October 13, 1965; retired February 14, 1989. *106 Metairie Lawn Dr., Metairie, LA 70001.* Tel: 504-840-9898.

Most Reverend

GREGORY M. AYMOND, D.D.

Archbishop of New Orleans; ordained May 10, 1975; ordained Auxiliary Bishop of New Orleans January 10, 1997; appointed Coadjutor Bishop of Austin June 2, 2000; installed Bishop of Austin August 3, 2000; appointed Archbishop of New Orleans June 12, 2009; Pallium conferred by Pope Benedict XVI at the Vatican June 29, 2009; installed Archbishop of New Orleans August 20, 2009. *Archdiocesan Administration Building: 7887 Walmsley Ave., New Orleans, LA 70125-3496.* Tel: 504-861-9521.

Archdiocesan Administration Building: 7887 Walmsley Ave., New Orleans, LA 70125-3496. Tel: 504-861-9521; Fax: 504-866-2906.

Web: www.archdiocese-no.org

Most Reverend

SHELTON J. FABRE, V.G.

Auxiliary Bishop of New Orleans; ordained August 5, 1989; appointed Auxiliary Bishop of New Orleans and Titular Bishop of Prudenziana December 13, 2006; ordained February 26, 2007. *Office: 7887 Walmsley Ave., New Orleans, LA 70125-3496.*

Most Reverend

DOMINIC CARMON, S.V.D., D.D.

Retired Auxiliary Bishop of New Orleans; ordained February 2, 1960; appointed Auxiliary Bishop of New Orleans and Titular Bishop of Rusicade December 16, 1992; consecrated February 11, 1993; retired December 13, 2006. *Res.: 3270 Continental Dr., Kenner, LA 70065-2663.* Tel: 504-273-5863; Fax: 504-273-5747.

Square Miles 4,208.

Established April 25, 1793; Archdiocese July 19, 1850.

Comprises the following Parishes of Louisiana: Orleans, St. Bernard, Plaquemines, Jefferson, St. Charles, St. John the Baptist, St. Tammany and Washington.

For legal titles of parishes and archdiocesan institutions, consult the Chancery Office.

STATISTICAL OVERVIEW

Personnel	
Archbishops	1
Retired Archbishops	3
Auxiliary Bishops	1
Retired Bishops	1
Abbots	1
Priests: Diocesan Active in Diocese	130
Priests: Diocesan Active Outside Diocese	12
Priests: Retired, Sick or Absent	66
Number of Diocesan Priests	208
Religious Priests in Diocese	153
Total Priests in Diocese	361
Ordinations:	
Diocesan Priests	3
Transitional Deacons	1
Permanent Deacons	23
Permanent Deacons in Diocese	189
Total Brothers	59
Total Sisters	449
Parishes	
Parishes	108
With Resident Pastor:	
Resident Diocesan Priests	82
Resident Religious Priests	22
Without Resident Pastor:	
Administered by Priests	4
Missions	10
Pastoral Centers	2
Welfare	
Health Care Centers	12

Total Assisted	120,980
Homes for the Aged	26
Total Assisted	2,143
Residential Care of Children	1
Total Assisted	16
Day Care Centers	8
Total Assisted	952
Specialized Homes	3
Total Assisted	4,582
Special Centers for Social Services	72
Total Assisted	106,500
Residential Care of Disabled	12
Total Assisted	194
Other Institutions	5
Total Assisted	693
Educational	
Seminaries, Diocesan	2
Students from This Diocese	19
Students from Other Diocese	122
Diocesan Students in Other Seminaries	1
Seminaries, Religious	3
Students Religious	14
Total Seminarians	34
Colleges and Universities	3
Total Students	9,666
High Schools, Diocesan and Parish	10
Total Students	5,004
High Schools, Private	13
Total Students	9,438
Elementary Schools, Diocesan and Parish	56

Total Students	23,074
Elementary Schools, Private	5
Total Students	1,617
Non-residential Schools for the Disabled	1
Total Students	191
Catechesis/Religious Education:	
High School Students	3,623
Elementary Students	9,938
Total Students under Catholic Instruction	62,585
Teachers in the Diocese:	
Priests	26
Scholastics	4
Brothers	16
Sisters	79
Lay Teachers	3,199
Vital Statistics	
Receptions into the Church:	
Infant Baptism Totals	4,470
Minor Baptism Totals	183
Adult Baptism Totals	163
Received into Full Communion	140
First Communions	4,281
Confirmations	3,183
Marriages:	
Catholic	1,165
Interfaith	360
Total Marriages	1,525
Deaths	3,491
Total Catholic Population	471,783
Total Population	1,179,459

Former Bishops and Archbishops—Rt. Revs. LUIS PENALVER Y CARDENAS, D.D., cons. in 1793; transferred to Guatemala, in 1801; resigned in 1806; retired to Havana, Cuba; died in Havana, July 17, 1810; Under the administration of the Archbishop of Baltimore from 1805-1815.; FRANCIS PORRO Bishop-elect; LOUIS WILLIAM DUBOURG, S.S., D.D., cons. Sept. 24, 1815; died Archbishop of Besancon, Dec. 1833; JOSEPH ROSATI, C.M., D.D., cons. March 25, 1824; Bishop of Tanagre and coadjutor; transferred to St. Louis, March 20, 1827; died Sept. 25, 1843; LEO DE NECKERE, C.M., D.D., cons. Aug. 4, 1829; died Sept. 4, 1833; Most Revs. ANTOINE BLANC, first Archbishop; cons. Nov. 22, 1835; Archbishop, July 19, 1850; died June 20, 1860; JEAN MARIE ODIN, C.M., D.D., cons. Bishop of Claudiopolis and Vicar-Apostolic of Texas, March 6, 1842; transferred to Galveston, 1847; promoted to New Orleans in 1861; died at Ambierle, France, May 25, 1870; NAPOLEON J. PERCHE, cons. Bishop of Abdera and coadjutor, March 21, 1870; promoted to the See of New Orleans, May 25, 1870; died Dec. 1883; F. X. LERAY, D.D., cons. Bishop of Natchitoches, April 22, 1877; appt. coadjutor of New Orleans, and Bishop of Janopolis, Oct. 23, 1879; promoted to the See of New Orleans, Dec., 1883; died at Chateaugiron, France, Sept. 23, 1887; FRANCIS JANSSENS, D.D., cons. Bishop of Natchez, MS, May 1, 1881; promoted to the Archiepiscopal See of New Orleans, Aug. 7, 1888; died June 9, 1897; PLACIDE LOUIS CHAPELLE, D.D., Apostolic Delegate Extraordinary for Cuba and Puerto Rico; Archbishop of New Orleans; appt. Bishop of Arabissus and Coadjutor of Santa Fe cum jure successionis, Aug. 21, 1891; cons. Nov. 1, 1891; promoted to the Titular Archiepiscopal See of Sebaste May 10, 1893; Archbishop of Santa Fe, Jan. 9, 1894; appt. to New Orleans, Dec. 1, 1897; died Aug. 9, 1905; JAMES H. BLENK, S.M., D.D., appt. Bishop of Puerto Rico, June 12, 1899; cons. July 2, 1899; promoted to the See of New Orleans, April 20, 1906; died April 20, 1917; JOHN W. SHAW, D.D., appt. Coadjutor Bishop of San Antonio, Feb. 7, 1910; cons. Titular Bishop of Castabala, April 14, 1910; succeeded to the See of San Antonio, March 11, 1911; made assistant at the Pontifical Throne, Sept., 1916; promoted to the See of New Orleans, Jan. 25, 1918; died Nov. 2, 1934; JOSEPH FRANCIS RUMMEL, D.D., ord. May 24, 1902; appt. Bishop of Omaha, March 30, 1928; cons. May 29, 1928; appt. Archbishop of New Orleans, March 9, 1935; died Nov. 8, 1964; His Eminence JOHN CARDINAL CODY, D.D., S.T.D., cons. July 2, 1947; promoted to Coadjutor cum jure successionis of New Orleans, Aug. 10, 1961; acceded to the See, Nov. 8, 1964; transferred to Chicago, June 16, 1965; created Cardinal, June 26, 1967; died April 25, 1982; Most Revs. PHILIP M. HANNAN, D.D., J.C.D., S.T.L. (Retired), Archbishop of New Orleans; ord. Dec. 8, 1939; appt. Titular Bishop of Hieropolis and Auxiliary Bishop of Washington, June 16, 1956; cons. Aug. 28, 1956; promoted to Archbishop of New Orleans, Sept. 29, 1965; retired Feb. 14, 1989; FRANCIS B. SCHULTE, D.D. (Retired), Archbishop of New Orleans; ord. May 10, 1952; appt. Titular Bishop of Afufenia and Auxiliary Bishop of Philadelphia, June 27, 1981; appt. Sixth Bishop of Wheeling-Charleston, June 4, 1985; appt. Archbishop of New Orleans, Dec. 13, 1988; installed Feb. 14, 1989; Pallium conferred by Pope John Paul II at the Vatican, June 29, 1989; retired Jan. 3, 2002; ALFRED C. HUGHES, S.T.D. (Retired), ord. Dec. 15, 1957; appt. Auxiliary Bishop of Boston July 21, 1981; ord. Auxiliary Bishop of Boston Sept. 14, 1981; appt. Bishop of Baton Rouge Sept. 7, 1993; installed Bishop of Baton Rouge Nov. 4, 1993; appt. Coadjutor Archbishop of New Orleans Feb. 16, 2001; appt. Archbishop of New Orleans Jan. 3, 2002; retired June 12, 2009.

Vicar General—Most Rev. SHELTON J. FABRE, V.G.

Moderator of the Curia—Most Rev. SHELTON J. FABRE, V.G.

Chancellor—Very Rev. GERALD L. SEILER JR., M.Div., J.C.L., 7887 Walmsley Ave., New Orleans, 70125-3496. Tel: 504-861-6256; 504-861-9521; Fax: 504-866-2906.

Vice Chancellor and Special Delegate for Dispensations and Permissions—Deacon A. DAVID WARRINER JR.

Financial and Administrative Services—Mr. JOHN L. ECKHOLDT.

Archdiocesan Administration Building—7887 Walmsley Ave., New Orleans, 70125-3496. Tel: 504-861-9521; Fax: 504-866-2906. Office Hours: Mon.-Fri. 9-5.

Metropolitan Tribunal—Rev. RAYMOND C. FINN, O.P., Judicial Vicar All rogatorial commissions should be sent to this address c/o: 7887 Walmsley Ave., New Orleans, 70125-3496. Tel: 504-861-6291; Fax: 504-866-2906. Email: tribunal@archdiocese-no.org.

Court of First Instance—

Adjutant Judicial Vicar—Rev. Msgr. CLINTON J. DOSKEY, J.C.L. (Retired).

Court of Second Instance— Reviews all marriage cases from the six dioceses of Louisiana.

Adjutant Judicial Vicar—Very Rev. GERALD L. SEILER JR., M.Div., J.C.L., 7887 Walmsley Ave., New Orleans, 70125-3496. Tel: 504-861-6256; Fax: 504-866-2906.

Coordinator (Court of Second Instance)—Deacon A. DAVID WARRINER JR.

Judges—Rev. Msgr. L. EARL GAUTHREAUX, J.C.L.; Rev. VIEN THE NGUYEN, J.C.L., M.Div.; Rev. Msgr. ANDREW C. TAORMINA, J.D., V.F.

Associate Judges—Deacon FRANS LABRANCHE JR., J.D.; Sr. MARY JUDENE LILLIE, O.P.

Defenders of the Bond—Revs. JOHN J. PAYNE JR., J.C.L.; NICHOLAS P. PERICONE; LEE JOHN SALOY; Deacon A. DAVID WARRINER JR.

Approved Advocates— Priests and Deacons of the Archdiocese.

Appointed Special Advocates—Deacons ANDREA CAPACI; GERARD FASULLO SR.; ARTHUR KINGSMILL, J.D.; ROBERT D. NORMAND; NATHAN F. SIMONEAUX JR.; KEVIN M. STEEL; MICHAEL G. ZAIONTZ.

Secretaries/Ecclesiastical Notaries (Court of First Instance)—Ms. LOUANN HOOD; Ms. GERI WOODWARD.

Secretary/Ecclesiastical Notary (Court of Second Instance)—Ms. JANET URRUTIA.

Archdiocesan Consultors—Most Rev. SHELTON J. FABRE, V.G.; Rev. Msgr. CLINTON J. DOSKEY, J.C.L. (Retired); Very Revs. NEAL W. MCDERMOTT, O.P.; MICHAEL P. JACQUES, S.S.E., V.F.; Rev. JOSEPH S. PALERMO JR., J.D.

Deans—Very Revs. MICHAEL P. JACQUES, S.S.E., V.F., Cathedral Deanery I; DAVID J. ROBICHEAUX, V.F., City Park-Gentilly Deanery II; PHILIP G. LANDRY, V.F., Uptown Deanery III; Rev. Msgr. ANDREW C. TAORMINA, J.D., V.F., East Jefferson Deanery IV; Very Revs. JOHN-NHAN TRAN, V.F., St. John-St. Charles Deanery V; WARREN L. COOPER, V.F., West Bank Deanery VI; PAUL S. HART, V.F., Algiers-Plaquemines Deanery VII; DANILO C. DIGAL, V.F., St. Bernard Deanery VIII; RONALD L. CALKINS, V.F., West St. Tammany-Washington Deanery IX; MARK LOMAX, V.F., East St. Tammany-Washington Deanery X.

Archdiocesan Administrative Council—Most Revs. GREGORY M. AYMOND, Chm.; SHELTON J. FABRE, V.G., Vice Chm.; Deacon JESSE A. WATLEY, Sec. Members of the Board: Very Revs. NEAL W. MCDERMOTT, O.P.; GERALD L. SEILER JR., M.Div., J.C.L.; PATRICK J. WILLIAMS, M.Div., M.S.; Deacon A. DAVID WARRINER JR.; Sisters ANTHONY BARCZYKOWSKI, D.C.; SYLVIA THIBODEAUX, S.S.F.; Mrs. SARAH COMISKEY MCDONALD; Mr. JOHN L. ECKHOLDT.

Presbyteral Council of the Archdiocese of New Orleans—Most Rev. GREGORY M. AYMOND, Pres.

Archdiocesan Finance Council—Most Revs. GREGORY M. AYMOND, Chm.; SHELTON J. FABRE, V.G., Vice Chm.

Censores Librorum—Very Rev. GERALD L. SEILER JR., M.Div., J.C.L., Coord.

Louisiana Conference of Catholic Bishops—Mr. DANIEL J. LOAR, Dir., 3423 Hundred Oaks Ave., Baton Rouge, 70808-1548. Tel: 225-344-7120; Fax: 225-383-9591. Email: lccb@cox.net. Web: www.laccb.org.

Office of the Vicar General and Moderator of the Curia

Moderator of the Curia—Most Rev. SHELTON J. FABRE, V.G., 7887 Walmsley Ave., New Orleans, 70125-3496. Tel: 504-861-6262; Fax: 504-861-6312; 504-866-2906.

Vicar General—Most Rev. SHELTON J. FABRE, V.G., 7887 Walmsley Ave., New Orleans, 70125. Tel: 504-861-6262; Fax: 504-861-6254.

Archives and Records (Archdiocesan)—Mrs. EMILIE G. LEUMAS, C.A., 7887 Walmsley Ave., New Orleans, 70125-3496. Tel: 504-861-6241; Fax: 504-866-2906. Email: archives@archdiocese-no.org.

Canonical Permissions and Dispensations—Very Rev. GERALD L. SEILER JR., M.Div., J.C.L., 7887 Walmsley Ave., New Orleans, 70125-3496. Tel: 504-861-6256; 504-861-9521; Fax: 504-866-2906. Email: chancellor@archdiocese-no.org.

Catholic Foundation for the Archdiocese of New Orleans, Inc.—Mr. PETER R. QUIRK, Exec. Dir., 1000 Howard Ave., Ste. 700, New Orleans, 70113-1903. Tel: 504-596-3045; Fax: 504-596-3068. Email: catholicfoundation@archdiocese-no.org.

Communications, Office of—Mrs. SARAH COMISKEY MCDONALD, Dir., 1000 Howard Ave., Ste. 400, New Orleans, 70113. Tel: 504-596-3023; Fax: 504-596-3020. Email: communications@archdiocese-no.org.

Cultural Heritage Office—Mrs. EMILIE G. LEUMAS, C.A., Dir., 7887 Walmsley Ave., New Orleans, 70125-3496. Tel: 504-527-5781; Fax: 504-527-5797. Email: archives@archdiocese-no.org.

Stewardship & Development Office—Mr. PETER R. QUIRK, Exec. Dir., 1000 Howard Ave., Ste. 700, New Orleans, 70113-1903. Tel: 504-596-3045; Fax: 504-596-3068. Email: development@archdiocese-no.org.

Legal Services—CHARLES I. DENECHAUD III; OTTO SCHOENFELD; EDWARD DENECHAUD; RICHARD BORDELON; F. EVANS SCHMIDT; RALPH J. AUCOIN, 1010 Common St., Ste. 3010, New Orleans, 70112. Tel: 504-522-4756; Fax: 504-568-0783.

Newspaper— Newspaper of the Archdiocese of New Orleans. Published by Clarion Herald Publishing Co., Inc., "Clarion Herald" Rev. Msgr. CROSBY W. KERN, Moderator; PETER P. FINNEY JR., Gen. Mgr. & Exec. Editor, 1000 Howard Ave., Ste. 400, New Orleans, 70113-1903. Tel: 504-596-3035; Fax: 504-596-3020. Email: clarionherald@clarionherald.org.

Old Ursuline Convent—Rev. Msgr. CROSBY W. KERN, Admin., 1100 Chartres St., New Orleans, 70116. Mailing Address: 615 Pere Antoine Alley, New Orleans, 70116. Tel: 504-525-9585, Ext. 35.

Safe Environment Coordinator—Sr. MARY ELLEN WHEELAHAN, O.Carm., Coord., 7887 Walmsley Ave., New Orleans, 70125. Tel: 504-861-6278; Fax: 504-866-2906. Email: srmwheelahan@archdiocese-no.org.

Strategic Planning Office—Sr. ANTHONY BARCZYKOWSKI, D.C., Coord., 1000 Howard Ave., Ste. 100, New Orleans, 70113. Tel: 504-596-3092; Fax: 504-596-3466. Email: sranthony@archdiocese-no.org.

Strategic Planning Coordinating Committee—Mr. MICHAEL A. FLICK, Co Chm.; Rev. Msgr. ANDREW C. TAORMINA, J.D., V.F., Co Chm.; Sr. ANTHONY BARCZYKOWSKI, D.C., Coord., 1000 Howard Ave., Ste. 100, New Orleans, 70113. Tel: 504-596-3092; Fax: 504-596-3466.

Victims Assistance Coordinator—Sr. CARMELITA CENTANNI, M.S.C., Ph.D., 7887 Walmsley Ave., New Orleans, 70125-3496. Tel: 504-861-6253; 866-792-2873 (Toll Free); Fax: 504-866-2906. Email: srcarmelita@archdiocese-no.org.

Department of Christian Formation

Executive Director—Very Rev. NEAL W. MCDERMOTT, O.P., 7887 Walmsley Ave., New Orleans, 70125-3496. Tel: 504-861-6228; Fax: 504-861-6260. Email: cformation@archdiocese-no.org.

Campus Ministry—Very Rev. NEAL W. MCDERMOTT, O.P., 7887 Walmsley Ave., New Orleans, 70125-3496. Tel: 504-861-6228; Fax: 504-861-6260.

Catholic Schools Office—Sr. KATHLEEN FINNERTY, O.S.U., Supt., 7887 Walmsley Ave., New Orleans, 70125-3496. Tel: 504-866-7916; Fax: 504-861-6260. Email: superintendent@archdiocese.no.org; JUDY MULLA, Ed.D., Deputy Supt. Assoc. Superintendents, Elementary Schools: NANCY BAIRD, Ph.D., Govt. Programs; Sr. LEONA BRUNER, S.S.F., Early Childhood; Ms. CAROLE ELLIOT, Public Rels.; Mrs. CAROLYN MORVANT, Special Needs; Mr. WILLIS REY, Finance; Mr. JOSEPH R. ROSOLINO, Personnel/Curriculum/Instruction; Mr. VINCENT SCOZZARI, Counselors & Crisis; Dr. LISA TAYLOR, Assoc. Supt. Secondary Schools; Sr. MARY HILARY SIMPSON, O.P., Dir. Instrumental Music, 7887 Walmsley Ave., New Orleans, 70125-3496. Tel: 504-861-9521; Fax: 504-861-6260.

Office of Eucharistic Renewal—Mr. TODD AMICK, Dir., One Galleria Blvd., Ste. 744, Metairie, 70001. Tel: 504-482-8010; Fax: 504-849-2574.

Catholic Youth Organization - Youth and Young Adult Ministry Office—Mr. JOHN SMESTAD JR., Dir., 105 Bonnabel Blvd., Metairie, 70005-3736. Tel: 504-836-0551; Fax: 504-836-0552.

Youth Retreats— Youth Retreats: Contact CYO-Youth and Adult Ministry Office. *105 Bonnabel Blvd., Metairie, 70005-3736.* Tel: 504-836-0551.

Ministry of Evangelization & Spiritual Renewal—Rev. Msgr. ROBERT I. GUSTE, 1908 Short St., Kenner, 70062-7599. Tel: 504-464-0413; Fax: 504-465-0930.

Religious Education—Ms. CAROLE OBROKTA, Dir., 7887 Walmsley Ave., New Orleans, 70125. Tel: 504-861-6270; Fax: 504-861-6276.

Pontifical Mission Societies—

Pontifical Mission Societies/Holy Childhood Association/Propagation of the Faith—Propagation of the Faith, St. Peter the Apostle, Missionary Union, Mission Outreach Programs; Acompano, Sotuta Mission, Bridge Builders, Christ the Healer and Christ the Builder. Rev. JAMES J. JEANFREAU JR., Dir., 7887 Walmsley Dr., New Orleans, 70125. Tel: 504-527-5771; Fax: 504-527-5798. Email: pof@archdiocese-no.org.

Department of Clergy

Executive Director—Very Rev. PATRICK J. WILLIAMS, M.Div., M.S., 7887 Walmsley Ave., New Orleans, 70125-3496. Tel: 504-861-6268; Fax: 504-866-2906. Email: frpatwilliams@archdiocese-no.org.

Continuing Formation for Priests—Rev. Msgr. DOUGLAS A. DOUSSAN, Dir. Tel: 504-861-6269; Fax: 504-866-2906.

Permanent Diaconate—Deacon JAMES W. SWILER, Dir., 7887 Walmsley Ave., New Orleans, 70125-3496. Tel: 504-861-6329; 504-861-9521; Fax: 504-866-2906.

Priest Personnel Office—Rev. Msgr. DOUGLAS A. DOUSSAN, Dir.

Ministry to Retired Priests—Liaisons: Rev. LEO A. MEYER (Retired). Tel: 504-835-9605; Rev. Msgrs. MILTON L. REISCH (Retired). Tel: 504-341-2321; LANAUX J. RARESHIDE, V.F. Tel: 985-643-6124.

Ministry to Sick Priests—Rev. DOUGLAS C. BROUGHER, Coord. Tel: 504-899-1378.

Psychological Services—Mr. GLENN LEBOEUF, L.C.S.W., B.C.D., Coord. Tel: 504-861-6222; 504-885-4611.

Vocation Office—Revs. LUIS F. RODRIGUEZ, Dir.; STEVEN V. BRUNO, Assoc. Dir., 7887 Walmsley Ave., New Orleans, 70125-3496. Tel: 504-861-6298; 504-861-9521; Fax: 504-866-2906.

Department of Community Services

Executive Director—Sr. ANTHONY BARCZYKOWSKI, D.C., 1000 Howard Ave., Ste. 100, New Orleans, 70113-1900. Tel: 504-596-3092; Fax: 504-596-3466. Email: sranthony@archdiocese-no.org.

Apostleship of the Sea—Deacon PATRICK L. DEMPSEY, Dir. & Port Min., Stella Maris Maritime Center, 14538 River Rd., Destrehan, 70047. Tel: 985-307-0601.

Christopher Homes, Inc.—Mr. DENNIS F. ADAMS, Dir., 1000 Howard Ave., Ste. 100, New Orleans, 70113-1903. Tel: 504-596-3460; Fax: 504-596-3466. Web: www.christopherhomes.org. Email: dfadams@christopherhomesinc.org.

Disaster Relief—Sr. ANTHONY BARCZYKOWSKI, D.C., Dir., 1000 Howard Ave., Ste. 100, New Orleans, 70113-1900. Tel: 504-596-3092; Fax: 504-596-3466.

Catholic Charities

Catholic Charities Archdiocese of New Orleans—1000 Howard Ave., Ste. 1000, New Orleans, 70113. Tel: 504-523-3755; Fax: 504-523-2789; Tel: 866-891-2210 Care Line. Email: ccano@archdiocese-no.org. Web: www.ccano.org. If any additional information is needed, please contact the main office at 504-523-3755. Co Pres. & CEOs: Mr. GORDON R. WADGE; Mr. JAMES R. KELLY; Mrs. CHERYL D. LABORDE, CFO; Mr. ORVILLE DUGGAN, Chief Admin. Officer.

Adult Day Health Care Centers—Ms. PASHENA CASIMIRE, Div. Dir., 200 Beta St., Belle Chasse, 70037. Tel: 504-392-0502 Alpha House, Greenwalt, New Directions.

Cafe Hope— (An Affiliated Corporation planning to open a fully functioning restaurant which will train at-risk youth in job skills and life skills. The program, located on the historic Hope Haven campus in Jefferson, will facilitate a path to self-sufficiency by offering job-readiness and job placement) Mr. DON BOYD, Dir., 1101 Barataria Blvd., Marrero, 70072. Tel: 504-756-4673.

Communications Department—Mrs. MARGARET DUBUISSON, Dir.

Deaf Action Center of Greater New Orleans—

Development Department—Ms. HELEN READ SMITH, Dir.

Archbishop's Community Appeal (ACA)—1000 Howard Ave., Ste. 1000, New Orleans, 70113-1903. Tel: 504-592-5688; Fax: 504-581-2255.

Education Services—Ms. ARLEEN LANDRY, Dir., 8326 Apricot St., 2nd Fl., New Orleans, 70118. Tel: 504-861-6358; Fax: 504-861-6361.

After School Assembly—

Head Start Centers— El Yo Yo Head Start/Early Head Start, Incarnate Word Head Start/Early Head Start, Leslie Early Head Start, Louise Head Start, St. John the Baptist Head Start.

Summer Witness Program—

Food Programs—

Food for Families/Food for Seniors—Mr. TIMOTHY ROBERTSON, Exec. Dir. Tel: 504-245-7207; Fax: 504-248-2664.

**Second Harvest Food Bank of Greater New Orleans and Acadiana*Mrs. NATALIE JAYROE, Pres. & CEO, 1201 Sams Ave., Harahan, 70123-2236. Tel: 504-734-1322; Fax: 504-733-8336.

Foster Grandparents—

Health/Mental Health Programs—Dr. ELMORE RIGAMER, Medical Dir. Tel: 504-941-6044; 504-861-6344.

Counseling Solutions—Mrs. LORI BIRD, Dir. Tel: 504-835-5007 New Orleans/Metairie Office, St. Charles Office, St. John Office.

Family Behavioral Health & Supportive Housing—Ms. MARGARET CRUZ, Dir. Tel: 504-310-6940.

Catholic Charities School-Based Counseling (CCSBC)—

Ciara Community Services— Ciara Collaborative Housing, Ciara House Hospital Diversionary Program, Ciara House Transitional Living, Ciara Independent Living, Ciara Permanent Housing

Independent Living Skills Program—

Therapeutic Family Services—

Voyage House—

Neighborhood & Community Services—Mr. MARTIN GUTIERREZ, Exec. Dir. Tel: 504-310-6914; Fax: 504-596-3098.

Community Centers—Ms. SHIRLEY LACHMANN, Dir., 8326 Apricot St., New Orleans, 70118. Tel: 504-861-6345.

Annunciation— (serving Washington Parish)

Hope Haven— (serving West Bank of Jefferson Parish & Algiers)

Gert Town, Incarnate Word, St. Gabriel the Archangel, St. John the Baptist— (serving Orleans Parish)

Holy Family— (serving Washington & Tangipahoa Parishes)

St. Bernard— (serving St. Bernard Parish)

St. Luke the Evangelist— (serving St. Tammany Parish)

Domestic Violence Services—Ms. MARY CLAIRE LANDRY, Dir. Tel: 504-866-7481; 504-866-9554 Crisis Line; Fax: 504-866-7931.

Crescent House—

Harmony House Supervised Visitation Program—

New Orleans Family Justice Center—

Project SAVE (Stopping Abuse through Victim Empowerment—

Sexual Assault Program—

Hispanic Apostolate Community Services—Ms. MARIA CARCACHE, Dir. Tel: 504-457-3462; 504-457-3467.

Homeless & Transitional Housing Services—Mrs. CONNIE ANDRY, Dir. Tel: 504-310-8738.

Baronne Street Transitional Housing—

Beyond Shelter—

Bridges to Self-Sufficiency—

CARE Center—

Jefferson CARE Center—

Immigration and Refugee Services—Ms. MARIA CARCACHE, Dir. Tel: 504-457-3462; 504-457-3467.

Office of Justice and Peace—Mr. THOMAS M. COSTANZA, Dir. Tel: 504-596-3097; Fax: 504-596-3098.

Catholic Campaign for Human Development (CCHD)—

Catholic Relief Services (CRS)—

Cornerstone Builders—Mr. RONNIE MOORE, Dir. Tel: 504-310-8769.

Operation Helping Hands—Ms. JOAN DIAZ, Prog. Dir., 3738 Paris Ave., New Orleans, 70122. Tel: 504-324-4318; Fax: 504-286-1751.

PACE Greater New Orleans— (Program of All-inclusive Care for the Elderly) Ms. STEPHANIE SMITH, Exec. Dir., 4201 N. Rampart St., New Orleans, 70117. Tel: 504-945-1531; Fax: 504-945-1537.

Padua Community Services—Ms. PASHENA CASIMIRE, Div. Dir., 200 Beta St., Belle Chasse, 70037-1499. Tel: 504-392-0502; Fax: 504-367-6952.

Padua Community Homes— Ocean Avenue (Harvey), St. Jude the Apostle (Claire Ave., Gretna), Sts. Mary & Elizabeth (Elm St., Metairie), St. Peter the Fisherman (Airport Rd., Slidell), St. Rosalie (Kass St., Gretna)

Padua Home & Community-Based Waiver Program—

Padua Pediatric Program—

PHILMAT, Inc.—Co Presidents: Mr. GORDON R. WADGE; Mr. JAMES R. KELLY, 1000 Howard Ave., Ste. 800, New Orleans, 70113-1900. Tel: 504-596-3099; Fax: 504-596-3098.

Pro-Life Services—Ms. MICHELLE BLACK, Dir., 3019 N. Arnoult Rd., Metairie, 70002-4714. Tel: 504-885-1141; 866-566-1399 (Toll Free); Fax: 504-885-1519.

ACCESS Pregnancy & Referral Centers— 24-Hour Hotline: 504-581-LIFE. Toll Free: 866-566-1399. Metairie Office, Westbank Office, Kenner Office.

Adoption Services—

Project Rachel—

St. Vincent Maternity Clinic—

Sourner Truth Neighborhood Center—Ms. CAROL CARTER, Project Mgr., 2200 Lafitte St., New Orleans, 70119. Tel: 504-827-9963.

Volunteer Department—Ms. SHANNON MURPHY, Dir. Tel: 504-310-6962.

Department of Financial and Administrative Services

Officers—Mr. JOHN L. ECKHOLDT, CFO; Mr. JEFFREY J. ENTWISLE, COO, 7887 Walmsley Ave., New Orleans, 70125-3496. Tel: 504-861-6252; 504-861-9521; Fax: 504-866-2906. Email: amyers@archdiocese-no.org.

Accounting Office—Mr. KENNETH JAYROE, Chief Accounting & Budget Officer, 7887 Walmsley Ave., New Orleans, 70125-3496. Tel: 504-861-6236; 504-861-9521; Fax: 504-866-2906. Email: kjayroe@archdiocese-no.org.

Building Office—Mr. ANDRE L. VILLERE JR., Dir., 7887 Walmsley Ave., New Orleans, 70125-3496. Tel: 504-861-6210; 504-861-9521; Fax: 504-861-7652. Email: avillere@archdiocese-no.org.

Human Resources—Ms. BETH TINTO, Dir., 1000 Howard Ave., Ste. 1200, New Orleans, 70113. Tel: 504-310-8792; Fax: 504-568-1699. Email: etinto@archdiocese-no.org.

Insurance Office—Ms. CHERYL HARPER, Oper. Mgr., 1000 Howard Ave., Ste. 1202, New Orleans, 70113. Tel: 504-527-5760; Fax: 504-527-5799. Email: charper@catholicmutual.org; Ms. SUE FOSTER, Contracts/Risk Mgmt. Email: sfoster@catholicmutual.org.

Internal Audit/Special Assignments—Ms. CORINNE CADIS-MARCH, Financial Review Officer, 7887 Walmsley Ave., New Orleans, 70125-3496. Tel: 504-861-6203; Fax: 504-866-2906.

Information Technology—Mr. JUSTIN GIBSON, Dir., 1000 Howard Ave., Ste. 700, New Orleans, 70113-1903. Tel: 504-596-3064; Fax: 504-566-9718. Email: isd@archdiocese-no.org.

New Orleans Archdiocesan Cemeteries and New Orleans Cemeteries Trust—Mr. JODY C. ROME, Dir., 1000 Howard Ave., Ste. 500, New Orleans, 70113-1903. Tel: 504-596-3050; Fax: 504-596-3055. Email: jrome@archdiocese-no.org.

Property and Building Management—Ms. ELIZABETH LACOMBE, Dir., 1000 Howard Ave., Ste. 107, New Orleans, 70113-1903. Tel: 504-596-3070; Fax: 504-596-3073. Email: llacombe@archdiocese-no.org.

Parish Sites & Boundaries Committee—Rev. Msgr. FRANK J. GIROIR, Chm.

Property Records Office—Mrs. EMILY MORRIS, 7887 Walmsley Ave., New Orleans, 70125-3496. Tel: 504-861-6323; Fax: 504-866-2906.

School Food Services—Mrs. PATRICIA H. FARRIS, Dir., 1000 Howard Ave., Ste. 300, New Orleans, 70113-1925. Tel: 504-596-3434; Fax: 504-596-3459; 504-596-6901. Email: pfarris@schoolcafe.org.

Department of Pastoral Services

Executive Director—Deacon JESSE A. WATLEY, 7887 Walmsley Ave., New Orleans, 70125-3496. Tel: 504-861-6294; 504-861-9521; Fax: 504-866-2906. Email: pservices@archdiocese-no.org.

Black Catholic Ministries—Dr. JOYCE F. GILLIE CRUSE, Dir., 7887 Walmsley Ave., New Orleans, 70125-3496. Tel: 504-861-6207; 504-861-9521; Fax: 504-866-2906.

Center of Jesus the Lord—Rev. LANCE J. CAMPO, S.T.L., Dir., 1236 N. Rampart St., New Orleans, 70116-2497. Tel: 504-529-1636; Fax: 504-529-5003.

Charismatic Renewal—Liaisons: Mr. AL MANSFIELD; Mrs. PATTI MANSFIELD, 1901 Division St., Metairie, 70001-2716. Tel: 504-828-1368; Fax: 504-831-5810. Email: info@ccrno.org; Mailing Address: P.O. Box 7515, Metairie, 70010-7515.

Ecumenical Officer—Rev. STANLEY P. KLORES, M.A., M.Div., S.T.L., S.T.D., 724 Camp St., New Orleans, 70130. Tel: 504-525-4413; Fax: 504-568-1324.

Family Life Apostolate—Deacon ANDREA CAPACI, Dir., 7887 Walmsley Ave., New Orleans, 70125-3496. Tel: 504-861-6243; 504-861-9521; Fax: 504-866-2906. Email: familylife@archdiocese-no.org.

Commission for Persons with Disabilities—Mrs. SHIRLEY BERTUCCI, 7887 Walmsley Ave., New Orleans, 70125-3496. Tel: 504-861-6243; Fax: 504-866-2906. Email: familylife@archdiocese-no.org.

Filipino Catholic Ministry—Dr. ADLAI DEPANO, Coord.; Rev. ROBUSTIANO D. MORGIA, Spiritual Advisor, 7411 Sussex Pl., New Orleans, 70126. Tel: 504-280-7370.

Hanmaum Korean Catholic Chapel—Rev. JUN-HYUK PARK, Chap., 4812 W. Napoleon Ave., Metairie, 70001-2364. Tel: 504-888-8772; Fax: 504-888-2366.

Hispanic Apostolate Pastoral Services—Rev. LANCE J. CAMPO, S.T.L., Coord., 4309 Williams Blvd., Kenner, 70063. Mailing Address: P.O. Box 640577, Kenner, 70064. Tel: 504-467-2550; Fax: 504-467-2552.

Mensaje, Inc.—Rev. PEDRO NUNEZ, P.O. Box 1817, Kenner, 70063-1817. Tel: 504-456-2077; Fax: 504-456-2076. Email: mensaje@mensaje1.com. Web: www.mensaje.com.

Prisons Apostolate—Deacon WILLIAM B. JARRELL, Archdiocesan Dir., Mailing Address: P.O. Box 388, Gretna, 70054-0388. Tel: 504-374-7709, Ext. 3109. Email: dcbillctk@bellsouth.net.

Renovacion Carismatica Catolica Hispana—Deacon DAVID CALDERO, Dir., Mailing Address: P.O. Box 640057, Kenner, 70064. Tel: 985-764-6187.

Vietnamese Catholics Office—Rev. VIEN THE NGUYEN, J.C.L., M.Div., Liaison, 5069 Willowbrook Dr., New Orleans, 70129-0745. Tel: 504-254-5660; Fax: 504-254-9250. Mailing Address: P.O. Box 29745, New Orleans, 70189-0745.

Worship Office—Very Rev. PHILIP G. LANDRY, V.F., Dir., 7887 Walmsley Ave., New Orleans, 70125-3496. Tel: 504-861-6300; 504-861-9521; Fax: 504-866-2906. Email: worship@archdiocese-no.org.

Liturgical Commission—Very Rev. PHILIP G. LANDRY, V.F., Coord., 7887 Walmsley Ave., New Orleans, 70125-3496. Tel: 504-861-6300; 504-861-9521; Fax: 504-866-2906. Email: worship@archdiocese-no.org.

Department of Religious

Executive Director—Sr. SYLVIA THIBODEAUX, S.S.F. Liaison between the Archbishop and all religious congregations of sisters and brothers, with third orders and secular institutes, and with leadership conferences of women and men religious. 7887 Walmsley Ave., New Orleans, 70125-3496. Tel: 504-861-6281; 504-861-9521; Fax: 504-866-2906. Email: rpersonnel@archdiocese-no.org.

Archdiocesan Offices and Corporations

Bernard A. Grehan Trust—7887 Walmsley Ave., New Orleans, 70125-3496. Tel: 504-861-9521.

Catholic Charities Children's Day Care Centers Inc.—Registered Office, 1000 Howard Ave., Ste. 1000, New Orleans, 70113-1942.

Mental Health Association Development Corporation—7887 Walmsley Ave., New Orleans, 70125-3496. Tel: 504-861-9521.

St. Elizabeth's Home Registered Office—1000 Howard Ave., Ste. 1000, New Orleans, 70113-1942.

St. Gertrude's Retirement Center—

St. Mary's Catholic Orphan Boys' Asylum Board—1000 Howard Ave., Ste. 1000, New Orleans, 70113-1916.

St. Michael Special School—1522 Chippewa St., New Orleans, 70130. Registered Office: 7887 Walmsley Ave., New Orleans, 70125. Tel: 504-524-7285; Fax: 504-524-5883. Web: www.archdiocese-no.org/stmichael. Mrs. JANE SILVA, Dir. & Prin.

St. Vincent's Infant and Maternity Home Registered Office—1000 Howard Ave., Ste. 1000, New Orleans, 70113-1916.

Catholic Organizations

Apostles of Divine Mercy, New Orleans—Mrs. MARGARET BIESER, Dir., 17531 Barrett Lane, Baton Rouge, 70817-7540. Tel: 504-577-0385.

Archconfraternity of St. Ann—4920 Loveland St., Metairie, 70006.

Beginning Experience—Ms. TAMMY GILMER, Pres., 7887 Walmsley Ave., New Orleans, 70125.

Blue Army of Our Lady of Fatima—Very Rev. WARREN L. COOPER, V.F., Spiritual Dir., 4401 Seventh St., Marrero, 70072. Tel: 504-341-9516.

Catholic Charities Association Inc.—1000 Howard Ave., Ste. 1000, New Orleans, 70113-1916.

The Christ Committee of New Orleans—123 Iroquois Dr., Abita Springs, 70420. Tel: 985-893-0169. Email: kcicno@bellsouth.net.

Chateau de Notre Dame Guild—Rev. ROYCE J. MITCHELL, Spiritual Dir. (Retired), 2820 Burdette St., Apt. 706, New Orleans, 70125-2596. Tel: 504-861-3481.

Closer Walk Ministries—Rev. M. JEFFERY BAYHI, Dir., Mailing Address: P.O. Box 87279, Baton Rouge, 70879-8279. Tel: 225-615-7085; Fax: 225-615-7086. Email: admin@closerwalkministries.com.

Come, Lord Jesus Program of Prayer and Scripture—Rev. CONLEY BERTRAND, Dir., 1804 W. University, Lafayette, 70506-2544. Tel: 337-233-6144. Email: comelord@bellsouth.net.

Community of John the Evangelist—Ms. VIVIEN MICHALS, Contact, 2639 DeSoto St., New Orleans, 70119. Tel: 504-944-4000.

Confraternity of the Holy Face—1050 Robert Blvd., Slidell, 70458.

Council of Catholic Men—Mr. BEN RAPHAEL, Dir., 7887 Walmsley Ave., New Orleans, 70125-3496. Tel: 504-202-1061.

Council of Catholic School Cooperative Clubs—Rev. Msgr. ROBERT D. MASSETT, Spiritual Moderator, 6425 W. Metairie Ave., Metairie, 70003. Tel: 504-733-0922; Fax: 504-733-0869.

Council of Catholic Women—VACANT.

The Cursillo Movement—Mr. BILLY APP, Lay Dir., Mailing Address: P.O. Box 741745, New Orleans, 70174-1745. Tel: 504-464-0181, Ext. 111. Web: www.neworleanscursillo.org.

Engaged Encounter—Executive Couple: GARY LEVY; CLAUDIA LEVY.

Holy Name Societies—Mr. BEN RAPHAEL, Exec. Sec., Mailing Address: P.O. Box 6644, Metairie, 70009-6644. Tel: 504-202-1061.

Jesus Caritas Fraternity of Priests—Rev. Msgr. ROBERT I. GUSTE, 1908 Short St., Kenner, 70062-7599. Tel: 504-464-0413; Fax: 504-465-0930.

Ladies of Charity of the Archdiocese—Sr. JULIANNE BLANCHARD, D.C., Spiritual Dir., 1025 Napoleon Ave., New Orleans, 70115-2898. Tel: 504-899-1378.

Lay Carmelites of Our Lady of Mount Carmel—1609 Elise Ave., Metairie, 70003. Tel: 504-888-3461.

Legion of Mary—Rev. JOSEPH E. CAZENAVETTE, Spiritual Dir., New Orleans Comitium, 312 Lafitte St., Mandeville, 70448-5827. Tel: 985-626-5671.

Living Waters Program (Radio Ministry)—Rev. Msgr. ROBERT I. GUSTE, Dir., 1908 Short St., Kenner, 70062. Tel: 504-464-0413; Fax: 504-465-0930.

Magnificat, Ministry to Catholic Women—Mrs. PETER QUIRK, Pres. Central Svc. Team, 1201 Beverly Garden Dr., Metairie, 70002. Tel: 504-834-0057.

Magnificat Chapters—

Metairie Chapter—Mrs. DONNA MC NAMARA, Coord., 3416 Metairie Court, Metairie, 70002-1916. Tel: 504-833-3562.

New Orleans Chapter—Mrs. CLAUDIA MARSHALL, Coord., 2230 Soniat St., New Orleans, 70115-6426. Tel: 504-899-0390.

Slidell Chapter—Mrs. EDOLIA BARROS, Coord., 35300 Laurent Rd., Slidell, 70460-3644. Tel: 985-641-2585.

West Bank Chapter—Ms. BEVERLY TRAHAN, Coord., 2254 S. VonBraun Ct., Harvey, 70058-3083. Tel: 504-368-0869.

West St. Tammany Chapter—BETH MONTELEPRE, Coord., 83400 Pine Dr., Folsom, 70437-3260. Tel: 985-796-1274.

Marians of Metairie—Mrs. ROSE LYNNE LILJEBERG, 3908 Wheat Dr., Metairie, 70002-1302. Tel: 504-455-6608.

Marians of New Orleans—Mrs. MERRILL T. (CATHY) LANDWEHR, Pres., 3900 N. Arnoult Rd., Metairie, 70002-1566. Tel: 504-884-9637.

Marriage Encounter—Mr. GARY DAIGLE; Mrs. MARCIA DAIGLE. Tel: 985-649-0999.

Maryknoll Mission Education Center (Promotion of Missionary Work)—Mr. MATTHEW F. ROUSSO, Dir., 7730 Walmsley Ave., New Orleans, 70125. Tel: 504-866-8516.

Mary's Children—Mrs. NORA LAMBERT, Pres., 631 St. Charles Ave., New Orleans, 70130-3411. Tel: 504-218-8739.

Mary's Helpers (Medjugorje Information)—Mrs. MARGARET TROSCLAIR, Dir., Mailing Address: P.O. Box 1853, Marrero, 70073-1853. Tel: 504-348-7729; 800-573-4130.

Medjugorje Star—Rev. CHARLES SELLARS, O.M.I., Spiritual Dir. Email: medjugorje@mindspring.com. Web: medjugorje.home.mindspring.com. Directors: HUBIE MULE; KAY MULE, 2627 David Dr., Metairie, 70003-4599. Tel: 504-889-1713; Fax: 504-889-1714.

MIR Group (Medjugorje Information Center)—Ms. MIMI KELLY, 1 Galleria Blvd., Ste. 744, Metairie, 70001-2081. Tel: 504-849-2570; Fax: 504-849-2574. Email: themirgroup@aol.com.

Missionaries of St. Therese—Rev. JAMES J. JEANFREAU JR., Spiritual Moderator, 1000 Howard Ave., Ste. 1213, New Orleans, 70113. Tel: 504-527-5771.

Naim Conference—Ms. JUNE CASTRO DERMODY, 1035 W. William David Pkwy., Metairie, 70005. Tel: 504-828-8313. Email: familylife@archdiocese-no.org.

National Council of Catholic Men—Mr. BEN RAPHAEL, Dir., Mailing Address: P.O. Box 6644, Metairie, 70009-6644. Tel: 504-202-1061.

National Council of Catholic Women—VACANT.

Pax Christi New Orleans—Chairpersons: Mr. TOM EGAN; Mrs. JEANNIE EGAN, Mailing Address: P.O. Box 50304, New Orleans, 70150-0304. Tel: 504-522-3751. Email: jeanegan@tulane.edu.

Priests for Life—Rev. Msgr. ROGER A. SWENSON, Coord., 105 Bonnabel Blvd., Metairie, 70005-3798. Tel: 504-835-9343; Fax: 504-835-1525.

Retrouvaille/Rediscovery—JUDI DIEDLING; MIKE DIEDLING. Tel: 985-641-3802.

Rosary Congress Committee—Very Rev. NEAL W. MCDERMOTT, O.P., Spiritual Dir., 4640 Canal St., New Orleans, 70119. Tel: 504-488-2651. Web: www.rosarycongress.org.

St. Elizabeth's Guild—Mrs. DEBORAH B. ALCIATORE, Pres., c/o 1000 Howard Ave., Ste. 1000, New Orleans, 70113-1942.

St. Margaret's Daughters—Mr. LARRY STANSBERRY, CEO, 3419 St. Claude Ave., New Orleans, 70117-6144. Tel: 504-279-6414.

St. Thomas More Catholic Lawyers Association—Rev. JOSEPH S. PALERMO JR., J.D., 2901 S. Carrollton Ave., New Orleans, 70118-4391. Tel: 504-866-7426, Ext. 3335; Fax: 504-866-3119.

St. Vincent de Paul Society—Mr. CLAIBORNE PERRILLIAT, Pres.; Deacon RUDOLPH J. RAYFIELD SR., Exec. Dir., Mailing Address: P.O. Box 792880, New Orleans, 70179. Tel: 504-822-9288; Fax: 504-822-1964.

St. Vincent's Infant and Maternity Home Guild—1000 Howard Ave., Ste. 1000, New Orleans, 70113-1942.

Scouting—Deacon DANIEL FLYNN, Pastoral Min., 251 Halsey Dr., Harahan, 70123-4401. Tel: 504-737-8370; Ms. BARBARA WICK, Pres. Girl Scouts, 1508 Belmont Pl., Metairie, 70001-3715. Tel: 504-378-3751.

Serra Clubs—

Serra Club of New Orleans—Rev. LUIS F. RODRIGUEZ, Chap., 7887 Walmsley Ave., New Orleans, 70125-3496. Tel: 504-861-6298; Fax: 504-866-2906.

Serra Club of Downtown New Orleans—Rev. Msgr. ANDREW C. TAORMINA, J.D., V.F., Chap., 448 Metairie Rd., Metairie, 70005-4371. Tel: 504-834-0340.

Serra Club of East Jefferson—Rev. Msgr. ROBERT D. MASSETT, Chap., 6425 W. Metairie Ave., Metairie, 70003-4327. Tel: 504-733-0922.

Serra Club of West St. Tammany—Rev. Msgr. FRANK J. GIROIR, Chap., P.O. Box 40, Madisonville, 70447-0040. Tel: 985-845-7342; Mr. LARRY BUCKLEY, Pres. Tel: 985-892-7898 Serra Club of West Bank.

The Theresians International—Mrs. SALLY DUPLANTIER, Pres., 6311 St. Bernard Ave., New Orleans, 70122. Tel: 504-288-1897.

Woman's New Life Center—Ms. SUSAN M. MIRE, M.A., Founder & CEO, 3017 N. Causeway Blvd., Ste. 100, Metairie, 70002. Tel: 504-831-3117; Fax: 504-831-3155. Email: info@womansnewlife.com. Web: www.womansnewlife.com.

CLERGY, PARISHES, MISSIONS AND PAROCHIAL SCHOOLS

CITY OF NEW ORLEANS

(ORLEANS CIVIL PARISH)

1—ST. LOUIS CATHEDRAL (1720), (A Minor Basilica) Rev. Msgr. Crosby W. Kern, Rector; Deacons Ronald Guidry, Master of Ceremonies; Richard Brady; A. David Warriner Jr.; Larry D. Oney. In Res., Rev. William F. Maestri.

Res.: 615 Pere Antoine Alley, 70116-3291. Tel: 504-525-9585; Fax: 504-525-9583. Email: saintlouiscathedral-no@archdiocese-no.org. Web: www.stlouiscathedral.org.

School—Cathedral Academy, 820 Dauphine St., 70116-3089. Tel: 504-525-3860; Fax: 504-525-3193. Web: cathedralacademyno.org. Sr. Mary Andrew Hession, O.P., Prin. Nuns 7; Lay Teachers 13; Students 169.

Mission—Our Lady of Guadalupe, Orleans Civil Parish. Tel: 504-525-1551; Fax: 504-525-1827. Email: judeshrine@aol.com.

Shrine—International Shrine of St. Jude Rev. Anthony Rigoli, O.M.I.

Res.: 411 N. Rampart St., 70112-3594.

St. Jude Community Center—400 N. Rampart St., 70112-3594. Tel: 504-553-5790.

2—ALL SAINTS (1919), (African American), Rev. Michael Saah-Buckman, S.S.J.; Deacon Larry L. Calvin.

Res.: 1441 Teche St., 70114-5899. Tel: 504-361-8835; Fax: 504-361-9802.

Catechesis/Religious Program—Students 69.

3—ST. ALPHONSUS (1847), (Irish), Revs. Gregory Schmitt, C.Ss.R.; Eugene Harrison, C.Ss.R; Sr. Jane Briseno, R.S.M., Pastoral Assoc. In Res., Revs. Gerard B. LaPorte, C.Ss.R.; Byron J. Miller, C.Ss.R.

Res.: 2030 Constance St., 70130-5099. Tel: 504-522-6748; Fax: 504-523-3734. Email: stalphonsusoffice@parishmail.com. Web: www.stalphonsusneworleans.com.

School—2001 Constance St., 70130-5094. Tel: 504-523-6594. Sr. Monica Ellerbusch, R.S.M., Prin. Lay Teachers 10; Students 181.

Catechesis/Religious Program—Students 71.

4—ST. ANDREW THE APOSTLE (1952) Very Rev. Paul S. Hart; Rev. Edward J. Lauden, Parochial Vicar; Deacons James C. Ardoin; John J. Walker IV.

Res.: 3101 Eton St., 70131-5399. Tel: 504-393-2334; Fax: 504-392-0635.

School—3131 Eton St., 70131. Tel: 504-394-4171; Fax: 504-391-3627. Sisters 2; Lay Teachers 51; Students 740.

Catechesis/Religious Program—Tel: 504-393-0140; Fax: 504-393-0334. Students 41.

5—ANNUNCIATION (1844) Merged with St. Cecilia, St. Gerard, SS. Peter & Paul & St. Vincent de Paul to form Blessed Francis Xavier Seelos, New Orleans.

6—ST. ANTHONY OF PADUA (1915), Assumed parish territory of Sacred Heart of Jesus, New Orleans. Revs. Orlando Cardozo, O.P.; John E. Lydon, O.P.; Jeffery M. Ott, O.P.; Very Rev. Emiliano Zapata, O.P.; Revs. David G. Caron, O.P.; Michael M. Burke, O.P.; Gustavo Montanez, O.P.; Charles L. Latour, O.P.; Very Rev. Neal W. McDermott, O.P.; Rev. Jairo Sandoval, O.P., Parochial Vicar; Bro. Herman D. Johnson, O.P.

Res.: 4640 Canal St., 70119-5808. Tel: 504-488-2651; Fax: 504-488-1842. Email: stantno@archdiocese-no.org.

School—4601 Cleveland Ave., 70119-5813. Tel: 504-488-4426; Fax: 504-488-5373. Email: paduastars@archdiocese-no.org. Web: www.stanthonypadua.net. Sr. Ruth Angelette, O.P., Prin. Dominican Sisters - Congregation of Saint Mary 2; Lay Teachers 18; Students 196.

Catechesis/Religious Program—Students 19.

7—ST. AUGUSTINE (1841), (African American), Rev. Quentin E. Moody.

Res.: 1210 Gov. Nicholls St., 70116-2324. Tel: 504-525-5934; Fax: 504-523-2473.

Catechesis/Religious Program—Students 10.

8—BLESSED FRANCIS XAVIER SEELOS (2001) [CEM] Rev. Joseph A. Benson; Deacons Jesse A. Watley; Jose A. Sierra; Ms. Arthine T. Vicks, Pastoral Assoc.

Res.: 3053 Dauphine St., 70117-6724. Tel: 504-943-5566; Fax: 504-943-5501.

Catechesis/Religious Program—Students 64.

9—BLESSED SACRAMENT (1915), (African American), Merged See Blessed Sacrament-St. Joan of Arc, New Orleans. For inquiries about sacramental records, contact Blessed Sacrament-St. Joan of Arc parish.

10—BLESSED SACRAMENT-ST. JOAN OF ARC (2008), Merger of Blessed Sacrament & St. Joan of Arc, New Orleans, worshipping at St. Joan of Arc Church, which was establised in 1909. Rev. Charles Andrus, S.S.J.; Deacon Irvin Stewart Sr.

8321 Burthe St., 70118-1195. Tel: 504-866-7330; Fax: 504-866-1319. Email: bssj@josephite.com. Web: www.josephite.com/parish/la/bssj.

School—St. Joan of Arc School, 919 Cambronne St., 70118-1199. Tel: 504-861-2887; Fax: 504-866-9588. Email: stjoanno@archdiocese-no.org. Ms. Dionne Frost, Prin.

Catechesis/Religious Program—Lynn Buggage, D.R.E. Students 50.

11—BLESSED TRINITY (2008), Merger of St. Matthias, Our Lady of Lourdes and St. Monica, New Orleans, worshipping at St. Matthias Church, which was established in 1920. Rev. John Asare-Dankwah (Ghana).

4230 S. Broad St., 70125-3699. Tel: 504-822-3394; Fax: 504-822-3397. In Res., Rev. Frederick Asuming.

12—ST. BRIGID (1977) Closed. See Mary Queen of Vietnam, New Orleans. For inquiries regarding sacramental records, contact Archives.

13—ST. CECILIA (1897) Merged with Annunciation, St. Gerard, SS. Peter & Paul & St. Vincent de Paul to form Blessed Francis Xavier Seelos, New Orleans.

14—CORPUS CHRISTI (1916), (African American), Merged See Corpus Christi-Epiphany. For inquiries regarding sacramental records, contact Corpus Christi-Epiphany parish.

15—CORPUS CHRISTI-EPIPHANY (2008), Merger of Corpus Christi & Epiphany, New Orleans, worshipping at Corpus Christi Church, which was established in 1916. Rev. John G. Harfmann, S.S.J.
2022 St. Bernard Ave., 70116-1388. Tel: 504-945-8931; Fax: 504-947-5347. Email: cce@josephite.com.
Catechesis/Religious Program—Students 46.

16—ST. DAVID (1937), (African American), Assumed territory of St. Maurice, New Orleans. Rev. Joseph J. Campion, S.S.J.
Res.: 5617 St. Claude Ave., 70117-2533. Tel: 504-947-2853; Fax: 504-943-0577.

17—ST. DOMINIC (1924) Rev. Sergio Serrano, O.P.; Very Revs. Martin J. Gleeson, O.P.; Val A. McInnes, O.P.; Michael O'Rourke, O.P.; Revs. David G. Caron, O.P.; Raymond C. Finn, O.P.; Daniel Shanahan, O.P.; Bros. Roger Shondel, O.P.; Richard J. Bontempo, O.P.; Deacon John Pippenger.
Res.: 775 Harrison Ave., 70124-3192. Tel: 504-482-4156; Fax: 504-488-0906. Web: www.stdominicnola.org.
School—6326 Memphis St., 70124. Tel: 504-482-4123; Fax: 504-486-3870. Sisters 2; Lay Teachers 37; Students 493.
Catechesis/Religious Program—6361 Memphis St., 70124. Tel: 504-486-9731. Students 47.

18—EPIPHANY (1948), (African American), Merged See Corpus Christi-Epiphany. For inquiries regarding sacramental records, contact Corpus Christi-Epiphany parish.

19—ST. FRANCES XAVIER CABRINI (1952) Merged with St. Raphael the Archangel & St. Thomas the Apostle, New Orleans to form Transfiguration of the Lord, New Orleans. For inquiries regarding sacramental records, contact the archives office.

20—ST. FRANCIS DE SALES (1870), (African American), Merged with Holy Ghost, New Orleans to form St. Katharine Drexel. For inquiries regarding sacramental records, contact St. Katharine Drexel parish.

21—ST. FRANCIS OF ASSISI (1890) Very Rev. Philip G. Landry; Rev. Jeffrey A. Montz, Parochial Vicar; Deacon Wilbur A. Toups.
Res.: 631 State St., 70118-5899. Tel: 504-891-4479; Fax: 504-891-4470. Email: sfa@stfrancisuptown.com. Web: www.stfrancisuptown.com.
Catechesis/Religious Program—Students 61.

22—ST. GABRIEL THE ARCHANGEL (1954), (African American), Rev. Msgr. Douglas A. Doussan.
Office: 4700 Pineda St., 70126-3599. Tel: 504-282-0296; Fax: 504-288-8585. Web: www.stgabe.net.
Catechesis/Religious Program—Students 17.

23—ST. GERARD (1971) Merged with Annunciation, St. Cecilia, SS. Peter & Paul & St. Vincent de Paul to form Blessed Francis Xavier Seelos, New Orleans.

24—GOOD SHEPHERD (2008) Rev. Msgr. Christopher Nalty.
1025 Napolean Ave., 70115-2898. Tel: 504-899-1378; Fax: 504-899-0480. Email: ststephenpar@archdiocese-no.org. In Res., Revs. Douglas C. Brougher; Donald J. Ours, C.M.; Joseph Thottamkara, C.M.
School—St. Stephen Central School, 1027 Napoleon Ave., 70115-2899. Tel: 504-891-1927; Fax: 504-891-1928. Email: ststephen@archdiocese-no.org. Ms. Peggy LeBlanc, Prin.
Catechesis/Religious Program—Philip Bellini, D.R.E. Students 220.

25—ST. HENRY (1856) Merged with Our Lady of Good Counsel & St. Stephen, New Orleans to form Good Shepherd. For inquiries reagrding sacramental records, contact Good Shepherd parish.

26—HOLY GHOST (1915), (African American), Merged See St. Katharine Drexel. For inquiries regarding sacramental records contact St. Katharine Drexel parish.

27—HOLY NAME OF JESUS (1892), Assumed parish territory of St. Thomas More, New Orleans. Revs. Donald A. Hawkins, S.J.; Paul Schott, S.J.; Robert A. Hagan, S.J., Parochial Vicar.
Office & Mailing Address: 6220 LaSalle Pl., 70118-6236. Tel: 504-865-7430; Fax: 504-866-3391. Church: 6367 St. Charles Ave., 70118.
School—6325 Cromwell Pl., 70118-6299. Tel: 504-861-1466; Fax: 504-861-1480. Courtney Wolbrette, Prin. Sisters of Mercy 5; Lay Teachers 50; Students 485.
Catechesis/Religious Program—Tel: 504-572-2469. Students 61.

28—HOLY NAME OF MARY (ALGIERS) (1848) [CEM 2] [JC 2] Rev. Patrick Gannon; Deacon Dean D. Herrick.
Res.: 500 Eliza St., 70114-1098. Tel: 504-362-5511; Fax: 504-367-3504. Email: hnmary@bellsouth.net.
Catechesis/Religious Program—Students 42.

29—HOLY SPIRIT (1972) Rev. Msgr. Allen J. Roy; Deacon Daniel F. Reynolds; Pam Kamphuis, Music Ministry Coord.
Res.: 6201 Stratford Pl., 70131-7397. Tel: 504-394-5492; Fax: 504-398-0901. Web: www.holyspirit-no.org.
Catechesis/Religious Program—Theresa Donnelly, D.R.E. Students 57.

30—HOLY TRINITY, Closed. For inquiries for parish records contact the chancery.

31—IMMACULATE CONCEPTION (1851) Revs. Stephen J. Sauer, S.J.; Paul Osterle, S.J. In Res., Very Rev. Mark Lewis, S.J.; Revs. Francis X. Pistorius, S.J.; Michael D. Dooley, S.J.
Res.: 130 Baronne St., 70112-2304. Tel: 504-529-1477; Fax: 504-524-0155. Email: admini@jesuitchurch.net. Web: www.jesuitchurch.net.
Catechesis/Religious Program—Valerie Robinson, D.R.E. Students 17.

32—IMMACULATE HEART OF MARY (1954) Closed. See St. Maria Goretti. For inquiries regarding sacramental records, contact Archives.

33—INCARNATE WORD (1922) Closed. See Mater Dolorosa, New Orleans. For inquiries regarding sacramental records, contact Mater Dolorosa. Also known as St. Theresa of the Little Flower.

34—ST. JAMES MAJOR (1920) Rev. Richard N. Maughan; Deacon Glenn J. Wiltz.
Res.: 3736 Gentilly Blvd., 70122-6128. Tel: 504-304-6750; Fax: 504-304-6807. Email: stjamesmajor@cox.net.
Catechesis/Religious Program—Students 35.

35—ST. JOAN OF ARC (1909) Merged with Blessed Sacrament, New Orleans to form Blessed Sacrament-St. Joan of Arc parish. For inquiries regarding sacramental records, contact Blessed Sacrament-St. Joan of Arc parish.

36—ST. JOHN THE BAPTIST (1851), (Irish), Open for weddings and funerals only. Church under care of pastor of St. Patrick, New Orleans. For inquiries regarding sacramental records, contact Archives., Mailing Address: 724 Camp St., 70130-3757. Tel: 504-525-4413; Fax: 504-568-1324.
Res.: 1139 Oretha Castle Haley Blvd., 70113-1215.

37—ST. JOSEPH (1844) Revs. Donald J. Ours, C.M.; Joseph Thottamkara, C.M. (India).
(Legal Title: St. Joseph Roman Catholic)
Res.: 1802 Tulane Ave., 70112-2246. Tel: 504-522-3186, Ext. 141; Fax: 504-522-3171. Email: stjoseph@bellsouth.net. Web: www.stjosephchurch-no.org.
Catechesis/Religious Program—

38—ST. JULIAN EYMARD (1952) Closed. Parish territory assigned to Holy Name of Mary, New Orleans. For inquiries regarding sacramental records, contact Holy Name of Mary parish.

39—ST. KATHARINE DREXEL (2008), Merger of Holy Ghost and St. Francis de Sales, New Orleans, worshipping at Holy Ghost Church, which was established in 1915. Rev. John Cisewski.
2015 Louisiana Ave., 70115-5294. Tel: 504-891-3172; Fax: 504-891-9284.
School—Holy Ghost School, 2035 Toledano St., 70115-5295. Tel: 504-899-6782; Fax: 504-899-6782. Email: holyghost@archdiocese-no.org. Sr. M. Angela Smith, S.S.F., Prin. Sisters 4; Lay Teachers 6; Students 310.

40—ST. LEO THE GREAT (1920), (African American), Merged with St. Raymond, New Orleans to form St. Raymond-St. Leo the Great. For inquiries regarding sacramental records, contact St. Raymond-St. Leo the Great.

41—ST. MARIA GORETTI (1965), Assumed parish territory of Immaculate Heart of Mary & St. Simon Peter, New Orleans. For inquiries about sacramental records for Immaculate Heart of Mary, St. Maria Goretti or St. Simon Peter, contact Archives. Rev. Msgr. L. Earl Gauthreaux; Rev. Robustiano D. Morgia (Philippines); Deacons Ildefonso R. DeLeon; Oscar G. Foster III.
Mailing Address: 7300 Crowder Blvd., 70127-1599. Tel: 504-242-7554; Fax: 504-242-0755. In Res., Rev. Victor H. Cohea.
School—Tel: 504-242-1313.
Catechesis/Religious Program—Students 55.

42—ST. MARY OF THE ANGELS (1925), (African American), Rev. Joseph Rigali, O.F.M.; Bros. Mark Gehert; Phillips Robinette, O.F.M.
Res.: 3501 N. Miro St., 70117-5899. Tel: 504-945-3186; Fax: 504-945-9115.
Catechesis/Religious Program—Students 25.

43—MARY, QUEEN OF VIETNAM (1983), (Vietnamese), [JC], Assumed St. Nicholas of Myra & St. Brigid, New Orleans. Revs. Vien The Nguyen; Luke Hungdung Nguyen, Parochial Vicar; Nguyen Van Nguyen. Mailing Address: P.O. Box 29745, 70189-0745.
Res.: 5069 Willowbrook Dr., 70129-1047. Tel: 504-254-5660; Fax: 504-254-9250.
Catechesis/Religious Program—Tel: 504-254-5247. Students 915.
Mission—Our Lady of La Vang 6054 Vermillion Blvd., Orleans Civil Parish 70122-4296. Tel: 504-283-0559; Fax: 504-286-1937. Rev. Dominic Huyen Duc Nguyen.
Chapel—Vietnamese Martyrs 14400 Peltier Dr., New Orleans East, 70129-1713. Tel: 504-254-5660.
Shrine—Vietnamese Martyrs Shrine of the Archdiocese of New Orleans

44—MATER DOLOROSA (1848), Assumed Incarnate Word, New Orleans & St. Theresa of the Child Jesus, also known as St. Theresa of the Little Flower. Rev. John T. Hinton. In Res., Rev. John J. Marse.
Res.: 8128 Plum St., 70118-2012. Tel: 504-866-3669; Fax: 504-866-2349.
Catechesis/Religious Program—Tel: 504-866-5641. Dee Collura, D.R.E. Students 50.

45—ST. MATTHIAS (1920), (African American), Merged with Our Lady of Lourdes & St. Monica, New Orleans to form Blessed Trinity. For inquiries regarding sacramental records, contact Blessed Trinity parish.

46—ST. MAURICE (1852) Closed. Assumed by St. David, New Orleans. For inquiries regarding sacramental records, contact Archives.

47—ST. MONICA (1924) [CEM] Merged with Our Lady of Lourdes & St. Matthias to form Blessed Trinity. For inquiries regarding sacramental records, contact Blessed Trinity parish.

48—ST. NICHOLAS OF MYRA (1971) [CEM] Closed. Assigned to St. Brigid, New Orleans, which was assigned to Mary Queen of Vietnam. For inquiries regarding sacramental records, contact Archives.

49—OUR LADY OF GOOD COUNSEL (1887) Merged with St. Henry & St. Stephen. See Good Shepherd. For inquiries regarding sacramental records, contact Good Shepherd.

50—OUR LADY OF GUADALUPE /INTERNATIONAL SHRINE OF ST. JUDE (1826), (African American), Rev. Anthony Rigoli, O.M.I.
Res.: 411 N. Rampart St., 70112. Tel: 504-525-1551; Fax: 504-525-1827.
Catechesis/Religious Program—Tel: 504-522-8546. Students 78.

51—OUR LADY OF LOURDES (1905), (African American), Merged with St. Monica & St. Matthias, New Orleans to form Blessed Trinity worshipping at St. Matthias. For inquiries regarding sacramental records, contact Blessed Trinity parish.

52—OUR LADY OF THE ROSARY (1907) Very Rev. David J. Robicheaux; Deacons James Bialas; Michael G. Zaiontz.
1322 Moss St., 70119-2998. Tel: 504-488-2659; Fax: 504-488-6741. Web: www.ourladyoftherosary-no.com. In Res., Most Rev. Shelton J. Fabre.
High School—Holy Rosary High School, 3368 Esplanade Ave., 70119. Tel: 504-464-4747; Fax: 504-301-3974. Web: www.hra-hrhs.org. Mr. Len Enger, Prin.; Dawn Held, Librarian. Lay Teachers 17.
Catechesis/Religious Program—Program in conjunction with St. Dominic Church. Students 225.

53—OUR LADY STAR OF THE SEA (1911) [CEM] Rev. Rodney Anthony Ricard; Deacons Melvin C. Jones Sr.; Brian A. Gabriel.
Res.: 1835 St. Roch Ave., 70117-8199. Tel: 504-944-0166; Fax: 504-948-9555. Email: starofthecity@aol.com. Web: www.olss-no.com.
Catechesis/Religious Program—Students 43.

54—ST. PATRICK (1833), (Irish), Assumed St. John the Baptist, New Orleans. Rev. Stanley P. Klores; Deacon Chris DiGrado.
Res.: 724 Camp St., 70130-3757. Tel: 504-525-4413; Fax: 504-568-1324. Email: stpatrick@archdiocese-no.org. Web: www.oldstpatricks.org.
Catechesis/Religious Program—Robert Ramirez, D.R.E.

55—ST. PAUL THE APOSTLE (1947), (African American), [CEM] Rev. Alfred A. Ayem, S.V.D.; Deacon Graylin J. Miller.
Res.: 6828 Chef Menteur Hwy., 70126-5297. Tel: 504-242-8820; Fax: 504-242-8806.
Catechesis/Religious Program—Students 95.

56—SS. PETER AND PAUL (1848) Merged with Annunciation, St. Cecilia, St. Gerard & St. Vincent de Paul to form Blessed Francis Xavier Seelos, New Orleans.

57—ST. PETER CLAVER (1920), (African American), Very Rev. Michael P. Jacques, S.S.E.; Deacons Rudolph Rayfield; Terrel J. Broussard; Allen Stevens; Pearl Dupart, Assoc. Dir. Social Apostolate; Garmanne Mack, Office Mgr.; Henri Reed, Family Life Dir.; Mary Boutte, Youth Minister; Veronica Downs-Dorsey, Music Dir.
1923 St. Philip St., 70116-2199. Tel: 504-822-8059; 504-821-3146; Fax: 504-822-9251. Web: www.stpeterclaver.org.

School—St. Peter Claver Central School, 1020 N. Prieur St., 70116-2194. Tel: 504-822-8191; Fax: 504-822-2692. Web: spclaver.eduk12.net. Ms. Vanessa Chavis, Prin. Lay Teachers 23; Students 280.
Catechesis/Religious Program—Alena Boucree, D.R.E.; Sr. Jannette Pruitt, O.S.F., D.R.E. Students 202.

58—ST. PHILIP THE APOSTLE (1949), (African American), Closed. Assigned to St. Mary of the Angels, New Orleans, under the care of Franciscans. Buildings are under the care of the Archdiocese of New Orleans. For inquiries regarding sacramental records, contact Archives.

59—ST. PIUS X (1953) Very Rev. Patrick J. Williams; Deacons William A. Glennon; Christopher A. Bertucci. In Res., Rev. Msgr. Clinton J. Doskey (Retired).
Res.: 6666 Spanish Fort Blvd., 70124-4398. Tel: 504-282-3332; Fax: 504-283-8984. Email: spxrectory@archdiocese-no.org. Web: www.stpiusxnola.org.
School—6600 Spanish Fort Blvd., 70124-4399. Tel: 504-282-2811; Fax: 504-282-3043. Email: spxsch@archdiocese-no.org. Lay Teachers 24; Students 342.
Catechesis/Religious Program—Students 44.

60—ST. RAPHAEL THE ARCHANGEL (1947) Merged with St. Frances Cabrini & St. Thomas the Apostle, New Orleans to form Transfiguration of the Lord New Orleans. For inquiries regarding sacramental records, contact Archives.

61—ST. RAYMOND (1927), (African American), Merged with St. Leo the Great, New Orleans to form St. Raymond-St. Leo the Great. For inquiries regarding sacramental records, contact St. Raymond-St. Leo the Great parish.

62—ST. RAYMOND-ST. LEO THE GREAT (2008), Merger of St. Leo the Great & St. Raymond, New Orleans, worshipping at St. Leo the Great Church, which was established in 1920. Rev. Anthony Bozeman, S.S.J.; Deacons Royal C. Shelton; Dwight Alexander.
2916 Paris Ave., 70119. Tel: 504-945-8750; Fax: 504-309-1691. Email: crivera@archdiocese-no.org. In Res., Revs. Bedemoore Udechukuu; Howard W. Byrd, S.S.J.
School—St. Leo the Great Central School, 1501 Abundance St., 70119-2098. Tel: 504-943-1482; Fax: 504-944-5895. Mrs. Carmel Mire, Prin.

63—THE RESURRECTION OF OUR LORD (1963) Rev. Michael Joseph Vinh Ngoc Nguyen.
Res.: 9701 Hammond St., 70127-3519. Tel: 504-242-8669; Fax: 504-242-8767.
School—Resurrection of Our Lord Central School, 4861 Rosalia Dr., 70127-3598. Tel: 504-243-2257; Fax: 504-241-5532. Email: resurrection@archdiocese-no.org. Dr. Si Nguyen, Prin. Lay Teachers 41; Students 460.
Catechesis/Religious Program—Students 28.

64—ST. RITA (1921) Rev. Dennis J. Hayes III. In Res., Rev. Ray A. Hymel.
Res.: 2729 Lowerline St., 70125-3599. Tel: 504-866-3621; Fax: 504-861-0338. Email: stritachurchno@archdiocese-no.org.
School—St. Rita Central School, 65 Fontainebleau Dr., 70125-3495. Tel: 504-866-1777; Fax: 504-861-8512. Email: stritano@archdiocese-no.org. Sr. Annette Baxley, Prin. Marianites of Holy Cross 7; Lay Teachers 12; Students 264.
Catechesis/Religious Program—

65—ST. ROSE OF LIMA (1857) Closed. Assigned to Our Lady of the Rosary, New Orleans. Buildings are under the care of the Archdiocese of New Orleans. For inquiries regarding sacramental records, contact Archives.

66—SACRED HEART OF JESUS (1879) [CEM] Closed. Parish territory assigned to St. Anthony of Padua, New Orleans. For inquiries for sacramental records, contact the archives office.

67—ST. SIMON PETER (1986) Closed. Assigned to St. Maria Goretti, New Orleans. For inquiries regarding sacramental records, contact Archives.

68—ST. STEPHEN (1849) Merged with Our Lady of Good Counsel & St. Henry, New Orleans to form Good Shepherd. For inquiries regarding sacramental records, contact Good Shepherd parish.

69—ST. THERESA OF AVILA (1848), Special care to the Hispanic Community. Revs. Teodoro Agudo, O.F.M.Cap. (Spain); Eutiquiano Miguel, O.F.M.Cap.
Res.: 1404 Erato St., 70130-4387. Tel: 504-525-4226; Fax: 504-525-6014.
Catechesis/Religious Program—Students 18.

70—ST. THERESA OF THE CHILD JESUS (1929) Closed. Parish territory entrusted to Incarnate Word, New Orleans. For inquiries regarding sacramental records, contact the archives office.

71—ST. THOMAS MORE (1970) Closed. Became a campus ministry center (Tulane Catholic Center) serving Tulane University. For inquiries regarding sacramental records, contact Holy Name of Jesus parish.

72—ST. THOMAS THE APOSTLE (1974) Merged Became a campus ministry center (UNO Newman Center) serving the University of New Orleans. For inquiries regarding sacremental records, contact Archives.

73—TRANSFIGURATION OF THE LORD (2008), Merger of St. Frances Cabrini, St. Raphael the Archangel & St. Thomas the Apostle, New Orleans, temporarily worshipping at the UNO Newman Center until renovation of the former St. Raphael the Archangel Church is completed. Rev. Paul H. Desrosiers; Deacon Peter C. Rizzo.
Mailing Address: UNO Newman Center, 2000 Lakeshore Dr., 70148-0001. Tel: 504-288-6336; Fax: 504-288-6344. Email: newmancenter@uno.edu.

74—ST. VINCENT DE PAUL (1838) Merged with Annunciation, St. Cecilia, St. Gerard & SS. Peter & Paul to form Blessed Francis Xavier Seelos, New Orleans.

OUTSIDE THE CITY OF NEW ORLEANS

ABITA SPRINGS, ST. TAMMANY PARISH, ST. JANE DE CHANTAL (1887) [JC] Revs. Robert C. Cavalier; Raymond Joseph Guillot; Deacons Frans Labranche Jr.; Donald E. Bourgeois; Mark C. Coudrain; Michael J. Talbot.
Res.: 22122 Main St., P.O. Box 1870, 70420-1870. Tel: 985-892-1439; Fax: 985-871-9547.
Catechesis/Religious Program—72040 Maple St., 70420-3931. Tel: 985-893-3914. Students 300.
Mission—St. Michael the Archangel Bush, St. Tammany Parish. Fax: 985-886-0302.

AMA, ST. CHARLES PARISH, ST. MARK (1974) Rev. James Nguyen Bach.
Res.: P.O. Box 556, 70031-0556. Tel: 504-431-8505; Fax: 504-431-8506. Email: stmarkama@yahoo.com.
Catechesis/Religious Program—Tel: 504-431-8507. Mrs. Tammy Cantrelle, D.R.E. Students 68.

ARABI, ST. BERNARD PARISH

1—ST. LOUISE DE MARILLAC (1954) Closed. Assigned to Our Lady of Prompt Succor, Chalmette. For inquiries regarding sacramental records, contact Archives.

2—ST. ROBERT BELLARMINE (1964) Closed. Assigned to Our Lady of Prompt Succor, Chalmette. For inquiries regarding sacramental records, contact Archives.
Res.: 408 Cougar Dr., 70032-2098.

AVONDALE, JEFFERSON PARISH, ST. BONAVENTURE (1965) Rev. Curtis Thomas; Deacons Brian J. Klause; J. Vernon Insley.
Res.: 329 S. Jamie Blvd., 70094-2821. Tel: 504-436-1279; Fax: 504-436-1300.
Catechesis/Religious Program—Tel: 504-436-0744. Tina Adams, D.R.E. Students 72.

BELLE CHASSE, PLAQUEMINES PARISH, OUR LADY OF PERPETUAL HELP (1928) [CEM] Rev. William O'Riordan; Deacons Leslie D. Vincent; Robert Beaumont. In Res., Rev. Terence Hayden (Ireland).
Res.: 8968 Hwy. 23, 70037-2296. Tel: 504-394-0314; Fax: 504-394-0376. Email: churchoffice@olphbc.org. Web: www.olphbc.org.
School—8970 Hwy. 23. Tel: 504-394-0757; Fax: 504-394-1627. Sr. Elizabeth Hebert, S.L.W., Prin. Sisters 1; Lay Teachers 15; Students 247.
Catechesis/Religious Program—Dolly Roy, D.R.E. Students 350.

BOGALUSA, WASHINGTON PARISH, ANNUNCIATION CATHOLIC CHURCH (1906) [JC 3] Rev. Patrick Collum.
Res.: 517 Avenue B, 70427-3711. Tel: 985-732-4280; Fax: 985-735-1042.
202 W. 5th St., 70427-3723.
School—511 Avenue C, 70427-3797. Tel: 985-735-6643; Fax: 985-735-6119. Email: annunciationsch@archdiocese-no.org. Web: www.acs-bogalusa.org. Lay Teachers 17; Students 162.
Catechesis/Religious Program—Students 33.

BRIDGE CITY, JEFFERSON PARISH, HOLY GUARDIAN ANGELS (1963) Closed. Mission of Our Lady of Prompt Succor, Westwego.

BURAS, PLAQUEMINES PARISH, OUR LADY OF GOOD HARBOR (1864) [CEM] Closed. Parish & mission territory assigned to St. Patrick, Port Sulphur. For inquiries regarding sacramental records, contact Archives.

CHALMETTE , ST. BERNARD PARISH

1—ST. MARK (1964) Closed. Assigned to Our Lady of Prompt Succor, Chalmette. For inquiries regarding sacramental records, contact Archives.

2—OUR LADY OF PROMPT SUCCOR (1951), Parish assumed territory of Prince of Peace, Chalmette, St. Bernard Parish; St. Louise de Marillac, Arabi, St. Bernard Parish; St. Mark, Chalmette, St. Bernard Parish; & St. Robert Bellarmine, Arabi, St. Bernard Parish. Very Rev. Danilo C. Digal; Deacons Rodrigo A. Fonseca; Lino G. Parulan.
Res.: 2320 Paris Rd., 70043-5098. Tel: 504-271-3441; Fax: 504-271-2927. Email: olpschal@archdiocese-no.org; ourladysuccor@bellsouth.net. Web: www.olps-chalmette.org.
School—Our Lady of Prompt Succor Central School, 2305 Fenelon St., 70043-4951. Tel: 504-271-2953; Fax: 504-271-1490. Email: scoll8312@aol.com. Web: www.olpsschool.org. Sharon Coll, Prin. Lay Teachers 25; Students 420.
Catechesis/Religious Program—Tel: 504-271-1217. Brenda Tromatore, D.R.E. Students 335.
Mission—Chapel of St. Lawrence St. Bernard Parish Prison, St. Bernard Parish 70043. Tel: 504-278-7645; Fax: 504-278-7785.

3—PRINCE OF PEACE (1977) Closed. See Our Lady of Prompt Succor, Chalmette. For inquiries regarding sacramental records, contact Archives.

COVINGTON, ST. TAMMANY PARISH

1—MOST HOLY TRINITY (2006) Rev. Rodney P. Bourg. 4465 Hwy. 190 E. Service Rd., 70433-4957. Tel: 985-892-0642; Fax: 985-893-9287. Email: office@mostholytrinityano.org. In Res., Rev. Dean L. Robins.
Res.: 285 Ponchitolawa Dr., 70433-6203.
Catechesis/Religious Program—Patricia Hebert, D.R.E. Students 164.

2—ST. PETER (1843) Revs. Paul Van Tung Nguyen; Robert T. Cooper, Parochial Vicar; Deacon Charles Heine.
Res.: 125 E. 19th St., 70433-3195. Tel: 985-892-2422; Fax: 985-898-1998. Email: stpeterchurch@charter.net. Web: www.stpeterparish.com.
School—Tel: 985-892-1831; Fax: 985-898-2185. Email: lodwyer@stpetercov.org. Miss Lana O'Dwyer, Prin. Lay Teachers 35; Students 726.
Catechesis/Religious Program—Tel: 985-893-2446; Fax: 985-892-7567. Email: stpeterore@bellsouth.net. Students 364.

CROWN POINT, JEFFERSON PARISH, ST. PIUS X (1971) Closed. Mission of St. Anthony, Lafitte.

DES ALLEMANDS , ST. CHARLES PARISH, ST. GERTRUDE (1955) [CEM] Rev. Joseph Duc Dzien.
Res.: P.O. Box 767, 70030-0767. Tel: 985-758-7542; Fax: 985-758-7591. Email: stg_office@yahoo.com.
Catechesis/Religious Program—Tel: 985-758-1332. Tina Montz, C.R.E. Students 149.

DESTREHAN, ST. CHARLES PARISH, ST. CHARLES BORROMEO (1723), (German), [CEM] Rev. Msgr. Henry J. Bugler; Rev. Daniel E. Brouillette, Parochial Vicar; Deacons Harry Schexnayder; Michael Stohlman; Theodore J. Roussel.
Res.: 13396 River Rd., P.O. Box 428, 70047-0428. Tel: 985-764-6383; Fax: 985-764-3948.
School—Tel: 985-764-9232; Fax: 985-764-3726. Lay Teachers 37; Students 468; Preschool 74.
Catechesis/Religious Program—Students 472.

DIAMOND, PLAQUEMINES PARISH, ST. JUDE (1981) Closed. Parish territory entrusted to St. Patrick, Port Sulphur. For inquiries regarding sacramental records, contact Archives.

EDGARD , ST. JOHN THE BAPTIST PARISH, ST. JOHN THE BAPTIST (1770), (African American), [CEM] Rev. Joel P. Cantones; Deacon Warren R. Pierre.
Res.: 2361 Hwy. 18, 70049-9101. Tel: 985-497-3412; 985-497-8470; Fax: 985-497-3965.
Catechesis/Religious Program—Students 157.

FLORISSANT, ST. BERNARD PARISH, SAN PEDRO PESCADOR (1966), (Islenos), Closed. Parish territory assigned to St. Bernard, St. Bernard. For inquiries regarding sacramental records, contact St. Bernard parish.

FOLSOM, ST. TAMMANY PARISH, ST. JOHN THE BAPTIST (1921) Rev. Timothy J. Burnett, O.S.B.; Deacon Julius T. Zimmer.
Res.: 11345 St. John Church Rd., 70437-7155. Office: Tel: 985-796-3806; Fax: 985-796-9554.
Catechesis/Religious Program—Tel: 985-796-5507. Students 107.

FRANKLINTON, WASHINGTON PARISH, HOLY FAMILY (1982) Rev. Peter E. Hammett, O.S.B.
Res.: 1213 14th Ave., 70438. Tel: 985-839-4040; Fax: 985-839-2429.
Catechesis/Religious Program—Tel: 985-839-2428. Students 64.

GARYVILLE, ST. JOHN THE BAPTIST PARISH, ST. HUBERT (1907) Rev. William H. Blank; Deacon Garland J. Roussel Jr.
Res. & Office: 176 Anthony Monica St., P.O. Box K, 70051-0851. Tel: 985-535-3312; Fax: 985-535-1849. Email: sthubertch@rtconline.com.
Catechesis/Religious Program—Students 47.

GRETNA, JEFFERSON PARISH

1—ST. ANTHONY (1920) Closed. Mission of St. Joseph, Gretna.

2—ST. CLETUS (1965) Rev. Eugene F. Jacques; Deacon Patrick L. Dempsey.
Res.: 3600 Claire Ave., 70053-7699. Tel: 504-367-7951; Fax: 504-367-7928.
School—Tel: 504-366-3538; Fax: 504-366-0011. Ms. Mary Margaret Stepleton-Hitt, Prin. Lay Teachers 40; Students 581.
Catechesis/Religious Program—Tel: 504-361-4805. Students 230.

3—ST. JOSEPH (1857) Rev. James Richard Day.
Res.: 610 Sixth St., 70053-6098. Tel: 504-368-1313;

Fax: 504-368-6841.
Catechesis/Religious Program—Students 10.
Mission—St. Anthony Mission 924 Monroe St., Jefferson Parish 70053-2299. Tel: 504-368-6161.
School—St. Anthony School, 900 Franklin Ave., 70053-2224. Tel: 504-367-0689; Fax: 504-361-9054. Mrs. Marie K. Cannon, Prin.

HAHNVILLE , ST. CHARLES PARISH, OUR LADY OF THE HOLY ROSARY (1877) [CEM] Rev. Bernard C. Francis.
Res.: #1 Rectory Ln., 70057. Tel: 985-783-1199; Fax: 985-783-1974. Email: olrhahn@aol.com.

HARAHAN, JEFFERSON PARISH, ST. RITA (1950) Revs. Herbert J. Kiff Jr.; Clayton "Beau" Charbonnet, Parochial Vicar; Deacons Danny Flynn; Gary J. Borne.
Mailing Address: 7100 Jefferson Hwy., 70123-4928. Fax: 504-737-2921.
Res.: 160 Imperial Woods Dr., 70123-4998. Tel: 504-737-2915; Fax: 504-737-2921.
School—194 Ravan Ave., 70123-4999. Tel: 504-737-0744; Fax: 504-738-2184. Theresa Faucheux, Prin. Lay Teachers 32; Students 545.
Catechesis/Religious Program—Email: anconstant@archdiocese-no.org. Ms. Anna Maria Constant, Faith Life Coord. Students 65.

HARVEY, JEFFERSON PARISH

1—INFANT JESUS OF PRAGUE (1969) Closed. Mission of St. Martha, Harvey.

2—ST. JOHN BOSCO (1983) Revs. Sidney Figlia, S.D.B.; Joseph Vien Hoang, S.D.B.; Deacon Tyrell Manieri.
Res.: 2114 Oakmere Dr., 70058-2275. Tel: 504-340-0444; Fax: 504-340-9521. Email: church1010@boscosjb.com. Web: www.archdiocese-no.org/sjbc.
Catechesis/Religious Program—Matthew LaGrange, Youth Min. Students 26.

3—ST. MARTHA (1973) Rev. Lich Van Nguyen; Deacon Gerard L. Labadot.
Res.: 2555 Apollo Dr., 70058-5813. Tel: 504-366-1604; Fax: 504-366-1100.
Catechesis/Religious Program—Tel: 504-366-4142. Students 88.
Mission—Infant Jesus of Prague 700 Maple St., Jefferson Parish 70058-4008. Tel: 504-368-1397; Fax: 504-368-0662.

4—ST. ROSALIE (1949) Revs. Jonathan Parks, S.D.B.; James Curran, S.D.B.
Parish Offices—600 2nd Ave., 70058-2728. Tel: 504-340-1962; Fax: 504-340-1546.
Res.: 608 1st Ave., 70058-2799. Tel: 504-341-5656.
School—617 Second Ave., 70058-2798. Tel: 504-341-4342; Fax: 504-347-0271. Mary C. Wenzel, Prin. Lay Teachers 60; Students 1,200.
Catechesis/Religious Program—Tel: 504-349-7896. Students 73.

JEFFERSON, JEFFERSON PARISH, ST. AGNES (1931) Rev. Bac-Hai Viet Tran; Deacons Piero Caserta; Frank G. DiFulco.
Res.: 3310 Jefferson Hwy., 70121-2699. Tel: 504-833-3366; Fax: 504-834-1532. Email: stagneschurch@nocoxmail.com.
School—Tel: 504-835-6486; Fax: 504-835-4295. Web: www.mystagnes.com. Lay Teachers 16; Students 185.
Catechesis/Religious Program—Students 248.

KENNER, JEFFERSON PARISH

1—DIVINE MERCY (2009), Merger of Nativity of Our Lord and St. Elizabeth Ann Seton, Kenner. Temporarily worshipping at Nativity of Our Lord and St. Elizabeth Ann Seton churches until completion of a new parish church. All sacramental records located at Divine Mercy parish office. Revs. David W. Dufour; Hoai Thanh Nguyen, Parochial Vicar; Deacons Andrea Capaci; Noel W. Martinsen.
Parish Office: 3325 Loyola Dr., 70065-2567. Tel: 504-466-5016; Fax: 504-467-8575. Email: office@divinemercyparish.org. Web: divinemercyparish.org.
School—St. Elizabeth Ann Seton, 4119 St. Elizabeth Dr., 70065. Tel: 504-468-3524; Fax: 504-469-6014. Web: www.seasparish.com/school. Joan Kathmann, Prin. Lay Teachers 29; Students 485.
Catechesis/Religious Program—Carlos L. Gamundi, D.R.E. (Elementary); Maria Jose Bermudez, D.R.E. (High School). Students 76.

2—ST. ELIZABETH ANN SETON (1981) Merged with Nativity of Our Lord, Kenner to form a new parish, Divine Mercy. For inquiries regarding sacramental records, contact Divine Mercy parish office.

3—ST. JEROME (1963) Revs. James J. Jeanfreau Jr.; Alberto Bermudez; Deacons Daniel J. Cordes; Luis Campuzano Sr.
Res.: 2400 33rd St., 70065-3899. Tel: 504-443-3174; Fax: 504-443-5499.
Catechesis/Religious Program—Gail Bordelon, D.R.E. Students 144.

4—NATIVITY OF OUR LORD (1977) Merged with St. Elizabeth Ann Seton, Kenner to form Divine Mercy parish. For inquiries regarding sacramental records, contact Divine Mercy parish.

5—OUR LADY OF PERPETUAL HELP (1869) Rev. Richard M. Miles; Rev. Msgr. Robert I. Guste. Tel: 504-464-0413; Deacons Jeffrey Fariss; Greg A. Gross; Norbert Gubert; Sr. M. Michaeline Green, O.P., Pastoral Assoc.
Res.: 1908 Short St., 70062-7599. Tel: 504-464-0361; Fax: 504-465-0930.
School—Tel: 504-464-0531; Fax: 504-464-0725. Email: srglaeser@olphla.org. Web: www.olphla.org. Sr. Julie Glaeser, F.S.Sp.J., Prin. Franciscan Sisters 1; Lay Teachers 18; Students 218.
Catechesis/Religious Program—531 Williams Blvd., 70062. Tel: 504-464-0147. Email: tlabauve@olphla.org. Web: www.perpetualhelp.org. Students 70.

LA PLACE, ST. JOHN THE BAPTIST PARISH

1—ASCENSION OF OUR LORD (1979) Rev. Walter J. Austin; Deacon Thomas J. St. Pierre.
Res.: 799 Fairway Dr., 70068-2007. Tel: 985-652-2615; Fax: 985-652-7291. Email: rascension@comcast.net. Web: ascension.catholic.org.
School—1809 Greenwood Dr., 70068-2098. Tel: 985-652-4532; Fax: 985-651-5151. Email: aoloffice@catholic.org. Lay Teachers 29; Students 337.
Catechesis/Religious Program— Debbie Berns, Coord. Rel. Educ. Students 55.

2—ST. JOAN OF ARC (1947) [JC] Very Rev. John-Nhan Tran; Rev. Michael M. Thanh Ngoc Nguyen, Parochial Vicar; Deacons Dominic J. Arcuri; Paul Cimino; Kenneth Madere.
Res.: 529 W. 5th St., 70068. Tel: 985-652-9100; Fax: 985-651-2920. Email: secretary@sjachurch.com. Web: www.sjachurch.com.
School—412 Fir St., 70068-4310. Tel: 985-652-6310; Fax: 985-652-6390. Web: www.archdiocese-no.org/stjoanofarclp. Mr. Larry J. Bourgeois Jr., Prin. Lay Teachers 40; Students 706.
Convent—Daughters of Divine Providence, 386 Fir St., 70068-3941. Tel: 985-359-3163.
Catechesis/Religious Program— Helena Cupit, D.R.E. Students 105.

LACOMBE, ST. TAMMANY PARISH

1—ST. JOHN OF THE CROSS (1984) Rev. Gilmer Martin; Deacon Ricky J. Suprean; Margaret Zinser, Office Admin.
Res.: 61051 Brier Lake Dr., 70445-2911. Tel: 985-882-3779; Fax: 985-882-9282. Email: sjc1286@bellsouth.net. Web: home.catholicweb.com/stjohnofthecross/.
Community Center—61038 Brier Lake Dr., 70445-2911. Tel: 985-882-6625.
Catechesis/Religious Program—Tel: 985-882-6225. Liz Loga, D.R.E. Students 42.

2—SACRED HEART (1890) Rev. Kyle V. Dave; Deacon William P. Curry Jr.
Res.: P.O. Box 1080, 70445-1080. Tel: 985-882-5229; Fax: 985-882-9034.
Catechesis/Religious Program—Tel: 985-882-8041. Students 117.

LAFITTE, JEFFERSON PARISH, ST. ANTHONY (1936) [CEM], Assumed parish territory of St. Pius X, Crown Point which became a mission of the parish. Rev. John Ryan. In Res., Rev. Donald Duffy (Retired).
Res.: 2653 Jean Lafitte Blvd., 70067. Tel: 504-689-4101; Fax: 504-689-4102.
Catechesis/Religious Program—Tel: 504-689-0069. Mrs. Mary Smith, D.R.E. Students 320.
Mission—St. Pius 8151 Barataria Blvd., Crown Point, 70072-9704.

LULING, ST. CHARLES PARISH

1—ST. ANTHONY OF PADUA (1961) Rev. James Nguyen Bach.
Res.: 234 Angus Dr., 70070-4427. Tel: 985-785-8885; Fax: 985-785-8882.
Catechesis/Religious Program—Tel: 504-785-0050. Students 73.

2—HOLY FAMILY (1980) Rev. John M. Perino.
Res.: 155 Holy Family Ln., 70070-6103. Tel: 985-785-8585; Fax: 985-785-4983. Email: hlyfamilystaff@bellsouth.net.
Catechesis/Religious Program—Tel: 985-331-9100. Mrs. Andrea Alday, C.R.E. (High School); Mrs. Fran M. Petit, C.R.E. (Elementary). Students 487.

MADISONVILLE, ST. TAMMANY PARISH, ST. ANSELM (1962) Rev. Msgr. Frank J. Giroir; Rev. Hoang Minh Tuong, Parochial Vicar; Deacons John Glover; Louis Mire; Charles Read Jr.
Res.: P.O. Box 40, 70447-0040. Tel: 985-845-7342; Fax: 985-845-3076.
Catechesis/Religious Program—Tel: 985-845-9309. Kathryn Richard, D.R.E. Students 688.

MANDEVILLE, ST. TAMMANY PARISH

1—MARY QUEEN OF PEACE (1988) Very Rev. Ronald L. Calkins; Deacons Anthony J. Ferretti; John J. Finn; George (Butch) Shartle; Edward Beckendorf.
Res.: 1501 W. Causeway Approach, 70471-3047. Tel: 985-626-6977; Fax: 985-626-6971. Email: mqop@maryqueenofpeace.org. Web: www.maryqueenofpeace.org.
School—1515 W. Causeway Approach, 70471. Tel: 985-674-2466; Fax: 985-674-1441. Email: school@maryqueenofpeace.org. Web: www.m-qop.org. Dr. Jan Lancaster, Prin. Students 482.
Catechesis/Religious Program—Tel: 985-674-9794. Students 630.

2—OUR LADY OF THE LAKE ROMAN CATHOLIC CHURCH (1850) [JC] Revs. John Talamo; Joseph E. Cazenavette, Parochial Vicar; Deacons Steven Ferran; Ed Kelly.
Res.: 312 Lafitte St., 70448-5827. Tel: 985-626-5671; Fax: 985-626-5422. Email: oll@bellsouth.net. Web: www.ollparish.info.
School—316 LaFitte St., 70448. Tel: 985-626-5678; Fax: 985-626-4337. Email: pjohnson@ourladyofthelakeschool.org. Web: www.ourladyofthelakeschool.org. Frank Smith, Headmaster. Lay Teachers 44; Students 804.
Catechesis/Religious Program—Tel: 985-626-5671, Ext. 105. Email: lindaoll@bellsouth.net. Linda Simeon, C.R.E. Students 690.

MARRERO, JEFFERSON PARISH

1—ST. AGNES LE THI THANH (1995), (Vietnamese), [JC], (Personal Parish for Southeast Asians) Rev. Joseph Pham Van Tue.
Mailing Address, Office & Rectory: 1000 Westwood Dr., 70072-2415. Tel: 504-347-4725; Fax: 504-340-2476.
Church: 6851 St. Le Thi Thanh St., 70072-2556.
Mission—Assumption of Mary 172 Noel Dr., Avondale, Jefferson Civil Parish 70094-2900. Rev. Andrew Tran Cao Tuong, Admin.
Mission—St. Joseph 6450 Kathy Ct., Orleans Civil Parish 70131-7515. Rev. Peter Tran Van Nam, Admin.
Catechesis/Religious Program—Students 921.

2—IMMACULATE CONCEPTION (1924) Very Rev. Warren L. Cooper; Deacons Cesar C. Carillo; James A. Venturella; Robert Chauvin, Business Mgr.; Janel Ockman, Music Dir.
Res.: 4401 7th St., 70072-2099. Tel: 504-341-9516; Fax: 504-341-9517. Email: icchurchparish@aol.com. Web: www.icchurchparish.org.
School—601 Avenue C, 70072-2098. Tel: 504-347-4409; Fax: 504-341-2766. Email: iconception@archdiocese-no.org. Web: icschargers.org. Sr. Lise Parent, F.M.A., Prin. (Grade School). Salesian Sisters 2; Lay Teachers 53; Students 808.
Catechesis/Religious Program—Ashley Brumfield, D.R.E. Students 116.

3—ST. JOACHIM (1985) Rev. G. Amaldoss.
Res.: 5505 Barataria Blvd., 70072-6660. Tel: 504-341-9226; Fax: 504-348-0093.
Catechesis/Religious Program—Cynthia Duhe, D.R.E.; Wendy Baughman, D.R.E. Students 70.

4—ST. JOSEPH THE WORKER (1955) Rev. Otis W. Young Jr.
Res.: 455 Ames Blvd., 70072-1599. Tel: 504-347-8438; Fax: 504-340-9538.
Catechesis/Religious Program—Tel: 504-348-4784; Fax: 504-347-0852. Students 103.

5—THE VISITATION OF OUR LADY (1963) Revs. Michael J. Kettenring, Admin.; Steven V. Bruno, Parochial Vicar; Deacon James P. Rooney Jr.
Res.: 3500 Ames Blvd., 70072-5699. Tel: 504-347-2203; Fax: 504-347-2223. Email: volchurch@vol.org. Web: www.vol.org.
School—3520 Ames Blvd., 70072-5698. Tel: 504-347-3377; Fax: 504-341-5378. Email: volschool@vol.org. Mrs. Carolyn Levet, Prin. Lay Teachers 39; Students 773.
Catechesis/Religious Program—Tel: 504-341-8477; Fax: 504-347-2223. Cheryl Tourelle, D.R.E. Students 151.

METAIRIE, JEFFERSON PARISH

1—ST. ANGELA MERICI (1964) Rev. Msgr. Kenneth J. Hedrick; Rev. Peter A. Tomczak, Parochial Vicar; Deacons Gilbert R. Schmidt; Nicholas Chetta; Raymond E. Heap.
Res.: 901 Beverly Garden Dr., 70002-5085. Tel: 504-835-0324; Fax: 504-834-9709. Web: www.stangela.org.
School—835 Melody Dr., 70002-5095. Tel: 504-835-8491; Fax: 504-835-4463. Web: www.stangelaschool.org. Mrs. Colleen Remont, Prin. Lay Teachers 27; Students 460.
Catechesis/Religious Program—Tel: 504-837-9347. Students 509.

2—ST. ANN CHURCH AND SHRINE (1971) Revs. Michael J. Schneller; Michael J. Mitchell, Parochial Vicar; Deacons Philip E. Doolen; Raymond J. Bertin; Thomas H. Fox.
4940 Meadowdale St., 70006-4040.
Res.: 4841 Meadowdale St., 70006-4037. Tel: 504-324-6028; Fax: 504-455-7076. Email: stannmet@bellsouth.net (Church Office). Web: stannchurchandshrine.org.
School—4921 Meadowdale St., 70006-4098. Tel: 504-455-8383; Fax: 504-455-9572. Email: stann@stannschool.org. Web: www.stannschool.org. Lay Teachers 53; Students 855.

Catechesis/Religious Program—Email: stannreled@bellsouth.net. Students 132.

3—St. Benilde (1964) Revs. Patrick B. Wattigny; John P. Grenham; Deacons August B. Mendel; Clifford S. Wright; Biaggio DiGiovanni. In Res., Rev. John P. Grenham.
Res.: 1901 Division St., 70001-2798. Tel: 504-834-4980; Fax: 504-831-5810.
School—1801 Division St., 70001-2799. Tel: 504-833-9894; Fax: 504-834-4380. Web: www.stbenilde.com. Mrs. Vicky G. Helmsetter, Prin. Lay Teachers 20; Students 298.
Catechesis/Religious Program—Students 40.

4—St. Catherine of Siena (1921) Rev. Msgr. Roger A. Swenson; Deacons Michael Coney; Jere Crago, Pastoral Assoc.; Don M. Richard. In Res., Rev. Nicholas P. Pericone.
Res.: 105 Bonnabel Blvd., 70005-3736. Tel: 504-835-9343; Fax: 504-835-1525. Email: stcatherine@archdiocese-no.org. Web: www.stcatherineparish.com.
School—400 Codifer Blvd., 70005-3797. Tel: 504-831-1166; Fax: 504-833-8982. Web: www.stcatherine.k12.la.us. Mrs. Frances Dee Tarantino, Prin. Sisters of Charity of the Incarnate Word 3; Lay Teachers 67; Students 873.
Catechesis/Religious Program—Tel: 504-835-6648. Students 67.

5—St. Christopher the Martyr (1947) Revs. Frank Candalisa; Kevin T. DeLerno, Parochial Vicar; Deacons Charles Duke; Gerald J. Martinez.
Res.: 309 Manson Ave., 70001-4898. Tel: 504-837-8214; Fax: 504-837-8303. Email: scmrectory@bellsouth.net.
School—(Grades PreK-8), 3900 Derbigny St., 70001-4999. Tel: 504-837-6871; Fax: 504-834-0522. Email: arnochrist@archdiocese-no.org. Web: www-.stchristopherschool.org. Ruth Meche, Prin. Lay Teachers 41; Students (PreK) 134; Students (K-8) 637.
Catechesis/Religious Program—Doris Marse, D.R.E. Students 122.

6—St. Clement of Rome (1965) Revs. Luis F. Rodriguez; Nile C. Gross, Parochial Vicar; Deacons Kenneth Boe; David Caldero; Frank Minor; Thomas P. Lotz.
Res.: 4317 Richland Ave., 70002-3097. Tel: 504-887-7821; Fax: 504-454-3906.
School—3978 W. Esplanade Ave., 70002-3099. Tel: 504-888-0386; Fax: 504-885-8273. Lay Teachers 27; Students 514.
Catechesis/Religious Program—Students 140.

7—St. Edward the Confessor (1964) Very Rev. Gerald L. Seiler Jr.; Rev. John J. Payne Jr., Parochial Vicar; Deacons Gerard J. Fasullo Sr.; Steven J. Koehler.
Parish Office:—4921 W. Metairie Ave., 70001-4466. Tel: 504-888-0703; Fax: 504-455-5443. Email: stedward@steddy.org. Web: www.steddy.org.
School—Tel: 504-888-6353; Fax: 504-456-0960. Sr. Mary de Lourdes Charbonnet, S.L.W., Prin. Sisters of the Living Word 2; Lay Teachers 29; Students 547.
Catechesis/Religious Program—Sr. Mary de Lourdes Charbonnet, S.L.W., D.R.E. Students 36.
Chapel—Hanmaum Korean Catholic Chapel 4812 W. Napoleon Ave., 70001-2364. Tel: 504-888-8772; Fax: 504-888-2366.

8—St. Francis Xavier (1924) Rev. Msgr. Andrew C. Taormina; Deacons Robert D. Normand; Arthur G. Kingsmill.
Res.: 105 Vincent Ave., 70005. Tel: 504-834-0340 (Office); 504-837-4733 (Res./Rectory); Fax: 504-837-8735 (Office). Web: www.stfrancisxavier.com.
School—215 Betz Pl., 70005-4167. Tel: 504-833-1471; Fax: 504-833-1498. Barbara Martin, Prin. Lay Teachers 34; Students 430.
Catechesis/Religious Program—Tel: 504-834-0348. Students 68.

9—St. Lawrence the Martyr (1958) Closed. Parish territory assigned to Our Lady of Divine Providence, Metairie. For inquiries regarding sacramental records, contact Our Lady of Divine Providence parish.

10—St. Louis King of France (1947) Rev. Burnick J. Terrebonne; Deacons Wilbur Martinez; Paul G. Hauck.
Res.: 1609 Carrollton Ave., 70005-1498. Tel: 504-834-9977; Fax: 504-834-9979.
School—1600 Lake Ave., 70005-1499. Tel: 504-833-8224; Fax: 504-838-9938. Pamela Schott, Prin. Lay Teachers 22; Students 260.
Catechesis/Religious Program—Students 35.

11—St. Mary Magdalen (1955) Rev. Msgr. Robert D. Massett; Rev. Martin J. Smullen; Deacons Angeles Robin; Uriel Durr.
Res.: 6425 W. Metairie Ave., 70003-4327. Tel: 504-733-0922; Fax: 504-733-0869. Email: magdalen@smm.nocoxmail.com. Web: www.stmarymagdalenchurch.com.
School—6421 W. Metairie Ave., 70003-4395. Tel: 504-733-1433; Fax: 504-736-0727. Email: stmarymag@archdiocese-no.org. Mrs. Kim Downes, Prin. Lay Teachers 28; Students 420.
Catechesis/Religious Program—Tel: 504-733-8980. Linda Earle, D.R.E. Students 90.

12—Our Lady of Divine Providence (1965), Assumed parish territory of St. Lawrence the Martyr, Metairie. Rev. Michael Roberson; Deacons Fred C. Memleb Jr.; Roberto Angeli; Javier Olondo, Music Min. In Res., Rev. Pablo Fuentes.
Res.: 1000 N. Starrett Rd., 70003-5899. Tel: 504-466-4511; Fax: 504-466-4858. Web: www.oldp.org.
School—917 N. Atlanta St., 70003-5898. Tel: 504-466-0591; Fax: 504-466-0671. Email: oldp@archdiocese-no.org. Web: www.oldpschool.org. Mrs. Elvina DiBartolo, Prin. Lay Teachers 30; Students 304.
Catechesis/Religious Program— Mrs. Mickie Morris, D.R.E.; Katie Brandstetter, Youth Min. Students 141.

13—St. Philip Neri (1960) Rev. Lee John Saloy; Deacon Edward R. Cannon; Mr. Joseph E. Murray Sr., Business Mgr. In Res., Rev. Harry J. Adams.
Res.: 6500 Kawanee Ave., 70003-3298. Tel: 504-887-5535; Fax: 504-885-6259. Web: www.archdiocese-no.org/stphilipnerichurch.
School—6600 Kawanee Ave., 70003-3199. Tel: 504-887-5600; Fax: 504-456-6857. Web: www.stphilipneri.org. Dr. Carol Stack, Prin. Lay Teachers 35; Students 678.
Catechesis/Religious Program—Tel: 504-889-0089. Ruby Kirsch, Coord. Rel. Educ. Students 56.

Norco, St. Charles Parish, Sacred Heart of Jesus (1959) Rev. Msgr. Terry B. Becnel.
Res.: 401 Spruce St., 70079-2137. Tel: 985-764-6503; Fax: 985-725-0512. Email: shn@archdiocese-no.org. Web: www.sacredheartchurchnorco.org.
School—453 Spruce St., 70079. Tel: 985-764-9958; Fax: 985-764-0041. Email: sacredhrtjesus@archdiocese-no.org. Web: sacredheartschoolnorco.org. Cheryl Orillion, Prin. Lay Teachers 17; Students 157.
Catechesis/Religious Program—Students 209.

Paradis, St. Charles Parish, St. John the Baptist (1971) Rev. Joseph Duc Dzien; Deacon Garland Bourgeois Jr.
Res.: P.O. Box 1498, 70080-1498. Tel: 985-758-2668; Fax: 985-758-2901. Email: stjohnch@bellsouth.net.
Catechesis/Religious Program—Tel: 985-758-1593. Students 125.

Pearl River, St. Tammany Parish, SS. Peter and Paul (1970) Rev. Thomas M. McCann III; Deacons John Patrick Downey; Francis W. Drake; Richard W. Calkins; Eugene P. Templet.
Res.: 66192 St. Mary Dr., 70452-5705. Tel: 985-863-7935; Fax: 985-863-5431. Email: info@sppcprla.com. Web: www.sppcprla.com.
Catechesis/Religious Program—Students 129.

Pointe a la Hache, Plaquemines Parish, St. Thomas (1844) [CEM 2] Rev. Joseph M. Tran.
17605 Hwy. 15, 70082.
Catechesis/Religious Program—Students 55.
Mission—Assumption of Our Lady 6951 Hwy. 39, Braithwaite, Plaquemines Parish 70040-0063. Tel: 504-682-5607; Fax: 504-682-5617.

Port Sulphur, Plaquemines Parish, St. Patrick (1870) [CEM], Assumed St. Jude, Diamond and Our Lady of Good Harbor, Buras and its missions, St. Ann, Empire and St. Anthony, Boothville-Venice. Rev. Gerard P. Stapleton; Deacon Patrick R. Becnel.
Res.: 28698 Hwy. 23, 70083-9623. Tel: 504-564-6792; Fax: 504-564-9760.
Catechesis/Religious Program—Students 100.

Reserve, St. John the Baptist Parish

1—Our Lady of Grace (1937), (African American), Revs. Joseph C. Rodney Jr., S.S.J.; Julius Olinoyo, Parochial Vicar; Deacon Larry D. Oney.
Res.: 772 Hwy. 44, P.O. Box 464, 70084-0464. Tel: 985-536-2613; Fax: 985-536-1819.
School—Tel: 985-536-4291; Fax: 985-536-4250. Mrs. Carnille Treaudo, Prin. Lay Teachers 9; Students 229.
Catechesis/Religious Program—Tel: 985-536-2028. Myrtle Ann Lucas, D.R.E. Students 85.

2—St. Peter (1864) [CEM] Rev. Tuan Anh Pham; Deacon David W. Farinelli.
Res.: 1550 Hwy. 44, P.O. Box 435, 70084-0435. Tel: 985-536-2887; Fax: 985-536-7078.
School—Tel: 985-536-4296; Fax: 985-536-4305. Mrs. Theresa Jacob, Prin. Lay Teachers 18; Students 223.
Catechesis/Religious Program—Tel: 985-536-2886. Students 213.

River Ridge, Jefferson Parish, St. Matthew the Apostle (1959) Rev. Nghiem Van Nguyen; Deacons Dan Dorsey; Wayne A. Lobell; Nathan F. Simoneaux Jr.
Res.: 10021 Jefferson Hwy., 70123-2498. Tel: 504-737-4537; Fax: 504-737-4033.
School—Tel: 504-737-4604; Fax: 504-738-7985. Email: church@stmatthew.nocoxmail.com. Web: www.stmatthew-riverridge.4lpi.com. Lay Teachers 41; Students 621.
Catechesis/Religious Program—Students 110.

St. Benedict, St. Tammany Parish, St. Benedict (1970) Rev. Jonathan M. DeFrange, O.S.B.; Deacon Nelvin Luke.
Res.: 20370 Smith Rd., Covington, 70435. Tel: 985-892-5202; Fax: 985-892-4211.
Catechesis/Religious Program—Students 202.

St. Bernard, St. Bernard Parish, St. Bernard (1787) [CEM], Assumed parish territory of San Pedro Pescador, Florissant. Rev. John C. Arnone.
Mailing Address: P.O. Box 220, Saint Bernard, 70085. Tel: 504-281-2667; Fax: 504-281-2268.
Church: 2805 Bayou Rd., Saint Bernard, 70085-9748.

Slidell, St. Tammany Parish

1—St. Genevieve (1968) Rev. Jose Roel G. Lungay; Deacons Daniel Haggerty Jr.; Paul Mumme Sr.; Reginald J. Seymour; Ryan Rhodes, Music Min.
Res. and Mailing Address: 58203 Hwy. 433, 70460-3121. Tel: 985-643-6389 (Rectory); 985-643-3832 (Office); 985-641-6771 (Office); Fax: 985-649-5294 (Office). Email: stgenevieve@charterinternet.com.
Catechesis/Religious Program—(Combined with St. Margaret Mary, Slidell) Ona New, D.R.E. Students 90.
Mission—Edolia Barros 35300 Laurent Rd., 70460. Tel: 985-641-2585. Email: edoliabarros@charter.net.

2—St. Luke the Evangelist (1982) Very Rev. Mark Lomax; Revs. Thang Tran, Parochial Vicar; Joseph Thang Dinh Tran, Parochial Vicar; Deacons Robert Binney, (Retired); Harold Burke; Robert Trainor, (Retired); Ronald C. LeBlanc; Paul G. Augustin.
Office:—910 Cross Gates Blvd., 70461-8414. Tel: 985-641-6429; Fax: 985-847-0742. Email: office@stlukeslidell.org. Web: www.stlukeslidell.org.
Catechesis/Religious Program—Tel: 985-641-2570; Fax: 985-641-6570. Students 639.

3—St. Margaret Mary (1965) Rev. Msgr. Lanaux J. Rareshide; Revs. Thomas Kilasara; Luis Henao; Deacons John C. Weber; Carlos A. Ramirez; Louis F. Bauer.
Res.: 1050 Robert Blvd., 70458-2098. Tel: 985-643-6124; Fax: 985-643-6126.
School—Tel: 985-643-4612; Fax: 985-643-4659. Mr. Bobby Ohler, Prin. Lay Teachers 40; Students 752.
Catechesis/Religious Program—Tel: 985-649-3055. Students 450.

4—Our Lady of Lourdes (1890) [CEM], New church will open in 2010 at 400 Westchester Blvd., Slidell. Rev. Msgr. Frank J. Lipps; Deacons Charles B. Faler Jr.; Robert Dunbar.
Res.: 3924 Berkley St., 70458-5198. Tel: 985-643-4137; Fax: 985-643-1675. Email: mguidry@ollourdes.org. Web: www.ollparish-slidell.com; www.ollonline.com.
School—345 Westchester Pl., 70458-5299. Tel: 985-643-3230; Fax: 985-645-0648. Mr. Robert V. Kiefer Jr., Prin. Sisters 1; Lay Teachers 30; Students 575.
Catechesis/Religious Program—Tel: 985-643-4128. Email: pandrews@ollourdes.org. Mrs. Patricia S. Andrews, D.R.E. Students 250.

Terrytown, Jefferson Parish, Christ the King (1963) Rev. Michael Nam Hoang Nguyen; Deacons William B. Jarrell; Walfredo Corral; Kevin M. Steel.
Res.: 535 Deerfield Rd., 70056-2899. Tel: 504-361-1500; Fax: 504-361-0632. Email: ckchurch@bellsouth.net. Web: www.ctkterrytown.parishesonline.com.
School—2106 Deerfield Rd., 70056-2899. Tel: 504-367-3601; Fax: 504-208-4927. Email: christkingsch@archdiocese-no.org. Web: www.archdiocese-no.org/ctk. Lay Teachers 30; Students 411.
Catechesis/Religious Program—Students 108.

Violet, St. Bernard Parish, Our Lady of Lourdes (1916), For inquiries about sacramental records, contact St. Bernard parish. Rev. John C. Arnone.
Mailing Address: P.O. Box 220, Saint Bernard, 70085. Tel: 504-281-2667; Fax: 504-281-2268.
Church: 2621 Colonial Blvd., 70092.

Waggaman, Jefferson Parish, Our Lady of the Angels (1978) [CEM] Rev. Curtis Thomas.
Res.: 139 Herman St., 70094-2404. Tel: 504-436-4459; Fax: 504-436-8465.
Catechesis/Religious Program—Students 71.

Westwego, Jefferson Parish, Our Lady of Prompt Succor (1920) [CEM] Rev. Edward M. Grice; Deacon Wilfred Robichaux Jr. In Res., Rev. David L. Rabe.
Res.: 146 Fourth St., 70094-4297. Tel: 504-341-9522; Fax: 504-341-5957. Email: olpschurch@olps.nocoxmail.com.
School—531 Avenue A, 70094-4294. Tel: 504-341-9505; Fax: 504-341-9508. Sr. Deborah Walker, F.M.A., Prin. & Supr. Sisters 3; Lay Teachers 15; Students 229.
Catechesis/Religious Program—Students 100.

Mission—Holy Guardian Angels Mission 1701 Bridge City Ave., Bridge City, Jefferson Parish 70094. Web: www.hgaparish.org.

Non-Parochial Churches & Chapels

NEW ORLEANS, ORLEANS PARISH

1—CHAPEL OF THE VIETNAMESE MARTYRS (1978), (Vietnamese), Revs. Vien The Nguyen; Nguyen Luke Hung Dung, Parochial Vicar. In Res., Rev. Nguyen Van Nguyen.
Church: 14400 Peltier Dr., 70129-1713. Tel: 504-254-5660; Fax: 504-254-9250.
Catechesis/Religious Program—Students 545.

2—ST. JOSEPH CHAPEL (1895) Mailing Address: *c/o Archdiocesan Cemeteries Office*, 1000 Howard Ave, Ste. 500, 70113-1903. Tel: 504-596-3050; Fax: 504-596-3055. St. Joseph Cemetery, 2220 Washington Ave., 70113-2647. Tel: 504-488-4989; 504-488-5200.

3—ST. MARY CHAPEL (1845), (Shrine of St. Lazarus of Jerusalem); Temporarily closed due to Hurricane Katrina., Mailing Address: 1100 Chartres St., 70116-2596.
Church: 1116 Chartes St., 70116-2596. Fax: 504-525-9583.

4—ST. MARY'S ASSUMPTION (1858), (German), Revs. Gregory Schmitt, C.Ss.R.; Eugene Harrison, C.Ss.R.
Church: 2030 Constance St., 70130-5099. Tel: 504-522-6748; Fax: 504-523-3734.
Catechesis/Religious Program—Students 55.

5—ST. MARY'S CHAPEL Revs. Gregory Schmitt, C.Ss.R.; Eugene Harrison, C.Ss.R.
1516 Jackson Ave., 70130. Tel: 504-522-6748.

6—OUR LADY OF PROMPT SUCCOR NATIONAL SHRINE (1926) Mailing Address: 2734 Nashville Ave., 70115.
Church: 2701 State St., 70118-6399. Tel: 504-866-0200; Fax: 504-866-8300.

7—ST. ROCH CHAPEL, St. Roch Cemetery, St. Roch Ave. & Music St., 70117-8223. Tel: 504-488-8681; 504-482-5065. Mailing Address: *c/o Archdiocesan Cemeteries Office*, 1000 Howard Ave., Ste. 500, 70113. Tel: 504-596-3050; Fax: 504-596-3055.

MANDEVILLE, ST. TAMMANY PARISH, ST. DYMPHNA CATHOLIC CENTER AND CHAPEL (1971) Rev. Raphael Barousse, O.S.B., Chap.; Deacons Louis F. Bauer; Ronald C. LeBlanc; Ricky J. Suprean, Dir. Pastoral Care.
Southeast Louisiana Hospital, P.O. Box 3850, 70470-3850. Tel: 504-626-6317.

METAIRIE, JEFFERSON PARISH, HANMAUM KOREAN CATHOLIC CHAPEL (1990) Rev. Jun-Hyuk Park (Korea, South), Chap.
4812 W. Napoleon Ave., 70001-2364. Tel: 504-888-8772; Fax: 504-888-2366. Email: franco4369@hanmail.net. Web: www.geocities.com/hanmaumcatholic.

Pilgrimage Shrines

NEW ORLEANS, ORLEANS PARISH

1—NATIONAL SHRINE OF BLESSED FRANCIS XAVIER SEELOS (2000) Rev. Byron J. Miller, C.Ss.R., Dir.
919 Josephine St., 70130-5004. Tel: 504-525-2495; Fax: 504-581-9181. Web: www.seelos.org.

2—OUR LADY OF PROMPT SUCCOR NATIONAL SHRINE (1926) Sr. Carolyn Brockland, O.S.U., Prioress.
Mailing Address: *Ursuline Convent*, 2734 Nashville Ave., 70115.
Res.: 2701 State St., 70118-6399. Tel: 504-866-0200; Fax: 504-866-8300.

3—SHRINE OF ST. JUDE THADDEUS (1826), (African American), Rev. Anthony Rigoli, O.M.I.
411 N. Rampart St., 70112-3594. Tel: 504-525-1551; Fax: 504-525-1827.
Catechesis/Religious Program—Tel: 504-522-8546. Students 80.

4—SHRINE OF ST. LAZARUS OF JERUSALEM Rev. Msgr. Crosby W. Kern, Rector.
Mailing Address: 1100 Chartres St., 70116-2596.
Church: 1116 Chartres St., 70116-2596. Tel: 504-529-3040, Ext. 21; Fax: 504-525-9583.

METAIRIE, JEFFERSON PARISH, ST. ANN NATIONAL SHRINE (1971) Rev. Michael J. Schneller.
Church: 4940 Meadowdale St., 70006-4040. Tel: 504-455-7071; Fax: 504-455-7076. Email: stannmet@bellsouth.net. Web: stannchurchandshrine.org.
Catechesis/Religious Program—Students 132.

Non-Parochial Community

NEW ORLEANS, ORLEANS PARISH, BYZANTINE CATHOLIC MISSION (1978), Ruthenian Rite Jurisdiction. Rev. James M. Deshotels, S.J.; Deacon Gregory Haddad, Mission Admin.
Mailing Address: P.O. Box 1359, Gray, 70359-1359.
Church: 2435 S. Carrollton Ave., 70118. Tel: 504-861-0806; Fax: 985-872-9123. Email: stnicholasnola@yahoo.com.

Chaplains of Public Institutions

Hospitals

NEW ORLEANS. *Children's Hospital*, 200 Henry Clay Ave., 70118. Tel: 504-899-9511. Deacons Thomas P. Lotz, Pastoral Min., Glenn Wiltz Sr., Pastoral Min.
Kindred Hospital, 3601 Coliseum St., 70115-3687. Tel: 504-899-1555; Fax: 504-899-1509. Deacons Frank G. DiFulco, Pastoral Min., Daniel F. Reynolds, Pastoral Min.
Ochsner Baptist Medical Center, 2700 Napoleon Ave., 70115-6996. Tel: 504-899-9311. Vacant. Baptist Campus
Touro Infirmary, 1401 Foucher St., 70115-3593. Tel: 504-897-7011. Rev. Douglas C. Brougher, Chap. Tel: 504-897-7011; 504-899-1378.
University Hospital, 2021 Perdido St., 70112-1396. Tel: 504-903-3000. Rev. Eutiquiano Miguel, O.F.M.Cap., Chap.

COVINGTON. *Lakeview Regional Medical Center*, 95 E. Fairway Dr., 70433. Tel: 504-867-3800. Deacon Edward F. Kelley, Pastoral Min.
St. Tammany Hospital, 1202 S. Tyler St., 70433. Tel: 504-898-4000. Attended by Priests and Deacons from West St. Tammany Deanery.

GRETNA. *Ochsner Medical Center, West Bank*, 2500 Belle Chasse Hwy., 70056-7127. Tel: 504-392-3131. Rev. Terence Hayden (Ireland), Chap., Deacons James C. Ardoin, Pastoral Min., James P. Rooney Jr., Pastoral Min., Leslie D. Vincent, Dir. Pastoral Care.

JEFFERSON. *Ochsner Foundation Hospital*, 1516 S. Clearview Pkwy., 70121-2484. Tel: 504-842-3000.

MANDEVILLE. *Southeast Louisiana Hospital*, P.O. Box 3850, 70470-3850. Tel: 504-626-6317; Fax: 504-626-6658. Rev. Raphael Barousse, O.S.B., Chap., Deacons Louis F. Bauer, Pastoral Min., Ronald C. LeBlanc, Dir. Pastoral Ministry, Ricky J. Suprean, Pastoral Min.

MARRERO. *West Jefferson General Hospital*, 4500 11th St., 70072-3191. Tel: 504-347-5511. Rev. Denver B. Pentecost, Chap.
Wynhoven Health Care Center, 1050 Medical Center Blvd., 70072-3170. Tel: 504-347-0777. Rev. Denver B. Pentecost, Chap.

METAIRIE. *East Jefferson General Hospital*, 4200 Houma Blvd., 70002-2970. Tel: 504-454-4000. Rev. John J. Marse, Chap., Deacons Raymond E. Heap, Pastoral Min., Gary J. Borne, Pastoral Min., Joseph G. Casanova, Pastoral Min., Steven J. Koehler, Pastoral Min.
Tulane Lakeside Hospital, 4700 S.1-10 Service Rd. West, 70001. Tel: 504-780-8282. Deacon August Mendel, Pastoral Min.

SLIDELL. *Greenbriar Nursing & Convalescent Home*, 505 Robert Rd., 70458-1699. Tel: 985-643-6900. Revs. Luis Henao, Thomas Kilasara, Chap.
Guest House of Slidell Nursing Home, 1051 Robert Rd., 70458-2011. Tel: 985-643-5630. Revs. Luis Henao, Thomas Kilasara, Chap.
Live Oak Village Assisted Living Community, 2200 Gause Blvd. E., 70461-8414. Tel: 985-781-4545. Chaplain: Priests and Deacons of St. Luke the Evangelist, Slidell.
North Shore Living Center, 106 Medical Center Dr., 70461-7833. Tel: 985-643-0307. Attended by St. Luke the Evangelist, Slidell.
North Shore Regional Medical Center, 100 Medical Center Dr., 70461-7833. Tel: 985-649-7070. Attended by St. Luke the Evangelist, Slidell.
Slidell Memorial Hospital, 1001 Gause Blvd., 70458-2987. Tel: 985-643-2200. Attended by St. Margaret Mary, Slidell.
Trinity Neurologic Rehabilitation Center at Slidell, 1400 W. Lindberg Dr., 70458-3193. Tel: 985-641-4985. Revs. Luis Henao, Thomas Kilasara, Chap.

Colleges and Universities

NEW ORLEANS. *Delgado College*, 615 City Park Ave., 70119. Tel: 504-288-6336.
Delgado Community College, School of Nursing, 1450 Claiborne Ave., 70112.
Louisiana State University Medical Center.
Southern University in New Orleans, 6400 Press Dr., 70126. Tel: 504-288-6336.
Tulane Catholic Center, 1037 Audubon St., 70118-5294. Tel: 504-866-0984. Rev. John E. Lydon, O.P., Dir. Ministry.
University of New Orleans, UNO Newman Center, 2000 Lakeshore Dr., 70148-0001. Tel: 504-288-6336. Rev. Paul H. Desrosiers, Chap.

Prisons

NEW ORLEANS. *Orleans Parish Criminal Sheriff's Office Community Correctional Center*, 2800 Gravier St., 70119. Tel: 504-826-7050. Rev. Theodore M. Kalamaja, S.J., Chap., Deacon Graylin Miller, Pastoral Min.

ANGIE. *Rayburn Correctional Center*, 27268 Hwy. 21, 70426-3030. Tel: 985-848-5232. Deacon Michael J. Talbot, Pastoral Min. (Dedicated to Sen. Rayburn)

ANGOLA. *Louisiana State Penitentiary*. 17544 Tunica Trace, 70712. Tel: 225-655-4411.

CHALMETTE. *St. Bernard Parish Prison*, St. Bernard Courthouse, 70043-4793. Tel: 504-279-8823. (Vacant)

GRETNA. *Jefferson Parish Correctional Center*, P.O. Box 388, 70054-0388. Tel: 504-374-7700, Ext. 3109. Rev. Robert J. Ratchford, S.J., Chap. (Retired), Deacons William B. Jarrell, Pastoral Min., James A. Venturella, Pastoral Min.

HARVEY. *Rivarde Juvenile Detention Home*, 1525 Manhattan Blvd., 70058-3405. Tel: 504-392-2097. Deacon Tyrell Manieri, Chap.

MANDEVILLE. *St. Tammany Parish Prison*, Tel: 985-892-8324. Deacons George (Butch) Shartle, Pastoral Min., Eugene P. Templet, Pastoral Min.

On Special Assignment:
Revs.—
Allen, Kenneth, Diocesan Assignment
Maestri, William F., M.Div., M.A., Special Projects, Archdiocesan/Moderator of the Curia

---

On Duty Outside the Archdiocese:
Rev. Msgr.—
Calkins, Arthur B., Villa Stritch, Via della Nocetta, 63, 00164, Rome, Italy.
Revs.—
deWater, Joseph M., Riinsburgerweg, 4W59A 2215 RA, Woor Hout, The Netherlands.
Paysse, Wayne C., Black and Indian Mission Office, 2021 H St., N.W., Washington, DC 20006.
Picado, Rodrigo, 50 VS. E. Cortell, Curridabat, San Jose, Costa Rica, CA.
Planea, John (Philippines), Holy Infant Mission, Santo Nino, W. Samar 6711 Philippines.

Graduate Studies:
Revs.—
Luu, Vinh Dinh, Casa Santa Maria, Via Dell'Umilta 30, Rome, Italy.
Phan, Minh Cong, Pontifical North American College, 00120, Vatican City State.

Unassigned:
Rev.—
Nguyen, Joseph Dau Van

On Administrative Leave:
Revs.—
Fraser, Michael B., V.F.
Kinane, Gerard P.
Roux, Randy P.
Sanders, Patrick B., V.F.

On Medical Leave of Absence:
Revs.—
Berner, Francis
Mongeon, Peter M.

Retired:
Most Revs.—
Hughes, Alfred C., S.T.D., 7887 Walmsley Ave., 70125-3425.
Carmon, Dominic, S.V.D., D.D., 3270 Continental Dr., Kenner, 70065-2663.
Rev. Msgrs.—
Bilinsky, William, 84031 Pine Dr., Folsom, 70437.
Boeshans, Francis G., P.O. Box 6328, Diamondhead, MS 39525-6006.
Byrnes, Donald M., 2832 Burdette St., Apt. 416, 70125.
Carroll, Ralph E., 3724 Whitney Pl., Metairie, 70002.
Duke, Charles J., 3513 Lemon St., Metairie, 70006.
Glasgow, T. Gaspard, St. John Vianney Villa, 4701 Wichers Dr., Apt. B, Marrero, 70072.
Hebert, Ray P., St. John Vianney Villa, 4701 Wichers Dr., Apt. D, Marrero, 70072.
Hecker, Lawrence A., St. John Vianney Villa, 4701 Wichers Dr. Apt. H, Marrero, 70072.
Hotard, Howard H., 75352 River Rd., Covington, 70435.
LeBourgeois, Louis P., 70212 Nancy Rd., 70471.
Lorio, Joseph O., The Haven, 8215 YMCA Plaza Dr., Apt. 257, Baton Rouge, 70810.
Luminais, J. Anthony, 13755 County Rd. 747, Hanceville, AL 35077.
O'Reilly, Alvin J., 2820 Burdette St., Apt. 506, 70125.
Reisch, Milton L., St. John Vianney Villa, 4701 Wichers Dr., Apt. A, Marrero, 70072.
Roeten, Winus, 9512 Kuepferle Ct., River Ridge, 70123.
Roppolo, Ignatius M., 2820 Burdette St., Apt. 707, 70125.
Schutten, Marion F., 19392 Crawford Rd., Covington, 70434.
Tomasovich, John A., 69 Lake Lynn Dr., Harvey, 70058.

Van der Werff, Martin, 2820 Burdette St., Apt. 416, 70125.
Vincent, Robert G., P.O. Box 459, LaPlace, 70069-0459.

Revs.—
Barattini, John H., Casella Postale 79, 16043, Chiavari, Italy.
Boileau, David A., Chateau de Notre Dame, 2820 Burdette St., 70125.
Brignac, H. L., 1400 Haring Rd., La Place, 70068.
Caluda, Charles J., 3205 Bayou Rd., Saint Bernard, 70085.
Carabello, Francis J., 840 Oakwood Dr., Terrytown, 70056.
Dabria, Jerry J., 1117 Melody Dr., Metairie, 70002.
De La Pinera, Fernando, Casa Sacerdotal, de la Catedral S/N, Plaza, Almeria 04001 Spain.
Dixon, James R., St. Anthony Rectory, 901 N.E. 2nd St., Fort Lauderdale, FL 33301.
Duffy, Donald, 2653 Jean Lafitte Blvd., Lafitte, 70067.
Fagot, Hacker J., S.J., Ignatius Residence, 6321 Stratford Pl., 70131-7325.
Fernandez, Luis J., VA Medical Center, 6863 S.W. 16th St., Miami, FL 33155-1709.
Ferrie, Francis, 8316 Apricot St., 70118-3199.
Finn, John P., 122 Oak Ln., Luling, 70070.
Gillen, Thomas M., Our Lady of Wisdom Healthcare Center, 5600 Gen. DeGaulle Dr., 70131.
Hall, Adrian B., 3310 Jefferson Hwy., Jefferson, 70121.
Heffner, Carroll
Highfill, Brian H., 1271 Mound House St., Las Vegas, NV 89110-5900. (Retired Military)
Jenniskens, Thomas J., S.J., Ignatius Residence, 6321 Stratford Pl., 70131-7325.
Kennedy, Patrick J. R., 924 Monroe St., Gretna, 70053-2299.
Kennelly, Michael F., S.J., Ignatius Residence, 6321 Stratford Pl., 70131-7325.
Kissinger, Rodney T., S.J., Ignatius Residence, 6321 Stratford Pl., 70131-7325.
Lobo, Raul Venust, St. John Vianney Villa, 4701 Wichers Dr., Apt. F, Marrero, 70072.
McGough, William J., 309 W. 9th Ave., Covington, 70433.
Mead, James Herbert, S.J., Ignatius Residence, 6321 Stratford Pl., 70131-7325.
Meyer, Leo A., 805 Rue Decatur, Metairie, 70005.
Mitchell, Royce J., 2820 Burdette St., Apt. 706, 70125.
Monzillo, Oneil, 532 Indian Bluff, Apt. #104, Las Vegas, NV 89145.
Morgan, Brendan P., P.O. Box 73128, Metairie, 70033.
O'Donnell, William J., J.C.L.
O'Grady, Peter, 411 Shrewsbury Rd., Jefferson, 70121.
O'Neill, Charles E., S.J., Ignatius Residence, 6321 Stratford Pl., 70131-7325.
Pearce, Donald, S.J., Ignatius Residence, 6321 Stratford Pl., 70131-7325.
Perera, Denzil M., 1236 N. Rampart St., 70116.
Perkovic, Anton, 444 Adair St., 70448.
Pijoan, L. Adrian M. Figuerola, St. Augustine Home, 2349 W. 86th St., Indianapolis, IN 46260.
Piovan, Benjamin, Mission San Miguel Archangel, Ave. Central 4649 Y Calle 44, Col Vista Hermosa, C.P. 25010, Saltillo Coahuila, Mexico.
Poche, Louis, S.J., Ignatius Residence, 6321 Stafford Pl., 70131.
Qui, Vincent, 21 Pat Dr., Avondale, 70094.
Racivitch, Herve P., S.J., Ignatius Residence, 6321 Stratford Pl., 70131-7325.
Ratchford, Robert J., S.J., Ignatius Residence, 6321 Stratford Pl., 70131-7325.
Scherer, Donald R., P.O. Box 764, Robert, 70455.
Schmaltz, Bernard
Schott, James E., 501 Lake Ave., Apt. 3A, Metairie, 70005.
Schroder, John F., S.J., Ignatius Residence, 6321 Stratford Pl., 70131.
Serio, Anthony, 3809 Hudson St., Metairie, 70006.
Texada, David Ker, 1923 Salem St., Alexandria, 71301-3840.
Tranchina, Joseph, 2820 Burdette St., Apt. 418, 70125.
Trinchard, Paul, 7117 Edgewater Dr., 70471.
Vitte, Jules, Le Grand Angle, 9 Rue Jean Dollfus, 90.000 Belfort, France.
Vu, J.B Han, 12772 Louise St., Garden Grove, CA 92841.
Walsh, Laurence, Lyrattin, Ballinamult, Co. Waterford, Ireland.
White, Anthony J., St. John Vianney Villa, 4701 Wichers Dr. Apt. E, Marrero, 70072.
Young, Bernard L., 590 Central Dr., Apt. A-24, Southern Pines, NC 28387.

Permanent Deacons:
Alexander, Dwight, St. Raymond & St. Leo the Great, New Orleans
Angeli, Santiago Roberto, Pastoral Min., Ozanam Inn, New Orleans; Our Lady of Divine Providence, Metairie
Arcuri, Dominic Joseph, St. Joan of Arc, La Place
Ardoin, James C., St. Andrew the Apostle, New Orleans; Pastoral Min., Ochsner Medical Center-West Bank, Gretna
Arendt, Elliott, Sr., (Retired)
Armshaw, Cornelius, (Retired)
Attaway, Charles, (On Leave)
Augustin, Paul G., St. Luke the Evangelist, Slidell; Pastoral Min, Reconcile New Orleans/Cafe Reconcile
Balderas, Robert, Sr., (Retired)
Bauer, Louis F., St. Margaret Mary, Slidell; Pastoral Min., Southeast Louisiana Hospital, Mandeville
Beaumont, Robert G., Sr., Master of Ceremonies, Our Lady of Perpetual Help, Belle Chasse
Beckendorf, Edward, Mary Queen of Peace, Mandeville
Becnel, Patrick R., St. Patrick, Port Sulphur; Pastoral Min., Plaquemines Parish Sheriff's Office
Bertin, Raymond J., St. Ann Church and Shrine, Metairie
Bertucci, Christopher A., St. Piusx, New Orleans
Beyer, Walter L., (Retired)
Bialas, James, Diaconate Formation, Our Lady of the Rosary, New Orleans
Bienvenu, Roland, (Retired)
Binney, Robert, (Retired)
Blanchard, John, (Retired)
Boe, Kenneth, St. Clement of Rome, Metairie
Borne, Gary J., St. Rita, Harahan; Pastoral Min, East Jefferson General Hospital
Bourgeois, Donald E., St. Jane de Chantal, Abita Springs
Bourgeois, Garland, Jr., St. John the Baptist, Paradis; St. Gertrudes, Des Allemands; Pastoral Min., St. Charles Parish Prison
Brady, Richard, Perm. Diaconate Adv. Bd., St. Louis Cathedral; Master of Ceremonies
Broussard, Terrel J., St. Peter Claver
Burke, Harold, St. Luke the Evangelist; Pastoral Min., Pope John Paul II High School; Pastoral Min., Northshore Regional Medical Center; Slidell
Caffery, Thomas E., Jr., Perm. Diaconate Adv. Bd., Most Holy Trinity, Covington
Caldero, David, St. Clement of Rome, Metairie
Calkins, Richard W., Chap., SS. Peter & Paul, Pearl River
Calvin, Larry Lee, All Saints, New Orleans; Permanent Diaconate Personnel Board
Campeaux, Barry G., (On Duty Outside the Diocese)
Campuzano, Luis A., St. Jerome, Kenner; Hispanic Apostolate Pastoral Ministry
Cannon, Edward, St. Philip Neri, Metairie
Capaci, Andrea, Dir., Family Life Apostolate; Divine Mercy, Kenner; Appointed Special Advocate, Metropolitan Tribunal; Pastoral Min., Archbishop Chapelle High School
Carrillo, Cesar Cornelio, Immaculate Conception, Marrero
Casanova, Joseph Glen, Pastoral Min., East Jefferson Hospital
Caserta, Piero, St. Agnes, Jefferson; Pastoral Min., Covenant House
Cassou, Henry A., Jr., (Retired)
Chetta, Nicholas, St. Angela Merici, Metairie
Cimino, Paul, St. Joan of Arc, La Place
Coney, Michael, St. Catherine of Siena, Metairie
Cordes, Daniel J., St. Jerome, Kenner
Corral, Walfredo, Christ the King, Terrytown; Pastoral Min., Ozanam Inn
Coudrain, Mark C., St. Jane de Chantal, Abita Springs
Crago, Jere, Pastoral Assoc., St. Catherine of Siena, Metairie
Curry, William P., Jr., Sacred Heart, Lacombe
Daigle, Irving J., (On Duty Outside the Archdiocese)
Deichmann, Richard, (Retired)
DeLeon, Ildefonso R., St. Maria Goretti, New Orleans
Dempsey, Patrick L., St. Cletus, Gretna; Co-Dir., Apostleship of the Sea & Stella Maris Ministry
DiFulco, Frank G., St. Agnes, Jefferson; Pastoral Min., Kindred Hospital
DiGiovanni, Biaggio, St. Benilde, Metairie; Admin., Ozanam Inn, New Orleans
DiGrado, Chris, Master of Ceremonies; Perm. Diaconate Adv. Bd., St. Patrick, New Orleans
Donnaud, Paul J., (Retired)
Doolen, Philip E., Pastoral Assoc., St. Ann Church & Shrine, Metairie
Dorsey, Dan, St. Matthew the Apostle, River Ridge; Archdiocesan Spirituality Center
Dorvin, Edwin, (Retired)
Downey, John Patrick, SS Peter and Paul, Pearl River; Pastoral Min., Southeast Louisiana State Hospital, Mandeville
Drake, Francis W., SS. Peter and Paul, Pearl River
Duet, Ferris J., Jr., (On Leave of Absence)
Duffy, Peter E., J.D., (Retired)
Duke, Charles, St. Christopher the Martyr, Metairie
Dunbar, Robert, Our Lady of Lourdes, Slidell
Duplechain, Raphael, Jr., Permanent Diaconate, Asst. Dir.
Durbin, Oscar A., (Retired)
Durr, Uriel Andrew, St. Mary Magdalen, Metairie; Pastoral Min. Cabrini High School
Elfer, Ernest C., Jr., (On Leave of Absence)
Engel, Randall L., (On Duty Outside the Archdiocese)
Faler, Charles B., Jr. Our Lady of Lourdes, Slidell
Farinelli, David W., Coord. Marriage Preparation & Enrichment, Family Life Apostolate; St. Peter, Reserve
Fariss, Jeffrey, Our Lady of Perpetual Help, Kenner
Fasullo, Gerard, Sr., St. Edward the Confessor, Metairie; Appointed Special Advocate, Metropolitan Tribunal; Master of Ceremonies
Ferran, Steven, Our Lady of the Lake, Mandeville
Ferretti, Anthony J., (Retired)
Finn, John Joseph, Mary Queen of Peace, Mandeville
Flynn, Dan, St. Rita, Harahan; Catholic Committee on Boy Scouting
Fonseca, Rodrigo Alonso, Our Lady of Prompt Succor, Chalmette
Foster, Oscar G., III, St. Maria Goretti; Pastoral Min., Ozanam Inn
Fox, Thomas H., St. Ann Church & Shrine; Pastoral Min., Holy Cross High School
Fray, Ralph, (Retired)
Frilot, George H., II, Most Holy Trinity, Covington
Gabriel, Brian A., Our Lady Star of the Sea, New Orleans
Gaiennie, Richard M., Dir., Bridge House
Gamble, Eric, (On Leave)
Garon, Henry A., (Retired)
Gittens, Peter W., (Retired)
Glapion, Lloyd St. Clair, (Retired)
Glennon, William A., Jr., St. Pius X, New Orleans
Glover, John A., St. Anselm, Madisonville
Gross, Greg Andrew Nicholas, Our Lady of Perpetual Help, Kenner; Pastoral Min., Ozanam Inn
Gubert, Norbert, Our Lady of Perpetual Help, Kenner
Guidry, Ronald, Master of Ceremonies, St. Louis Cathedral, New Orleans
Guitterez, Clayton J., (On Leave)
Guntherberg, Thomas James, (On Leave)
Haggerty, Daniel, Jr., Dir. Pastoral Care, F.B.I. & Slidell Police Dept.; St. Genevieve, Slidell
Hamm, John David, (On Duty Outside the Diocese)
Hartman, Charles, (On Duty Outside Archdiocese)
Hauck, Paul G., St. Louis King of France, Metairie; Pastoral Min., Ozanam Inn
Heap, Raymond E., Pastoral Min., East Jefferson Hospital, Metairie; St. Angela Merici, Metairie
Heine, Charles, St. Peter, Covington
Herrick, Dean D., Holy Name of Mary, Algiers; Pastoral Min., Ozanam Inn
Howard, John, (Retired)
Hull, Samuel Petrus, (On Duty Outside the Diocese)
Insley, J. Vernon, St. Bonaventure, Avondale; Spir. Dir., Legion of Mary
Jackson, Earl D., Sr., (On Duty Outside Archdiocese)
Jarrell, William B., Christ the King, Terrytown; Dir., Archdiocese Prisons Ministry
Johnson, David L., (On Duty Outside the Diocese)
Johnson, Dwight J., (On Leave)
Jones, Melvin C., Sr., Our Lady Star of the Sea, New Orleans
Keller, Lawrence, (Retired)
Kelley, Edward Francis, Our Lady of the Lake, Mandeville; Pastoral Min., Lakeview Regional Hospital
Kingsmill, Arthur George, St. Francis Xavier, Metairie & Archdiocesan Metropolitan Tribunal, New Orleans
Klause, Brian Joseph, St. Bonaventure, Avondale; Pastoral Min., Jefferson Parish Correctional Center, Gretna
Koehler, Steven J., St. Edward the Confessor, Metairie; Pastoral Min., East Jefferson General Hospital
Labadot, Gerard L., St. Martha, Harvey; Permanent Diaconate Personnel Board
Labranche, Frans, Jr., J.D., St. Jane de Chantal, Abita Springs; Assoc. Judge, Metropolitan Tribunal

Landry, Coy, (Retired)
LeBlanc, Ames P., Jr., (Retired)
LeBlanc, Nolen J., (Retired)
LeBlanc, Ronald C., St. Luke the Evangelist, Slidell; Pastoral Min., Southeast Louisiana Hospital
LeBlanc, Russell T., (Retired)
LeDoux, John, (On Leave)
LeRose, Joseph R., Pastoral Min., Chateau Living Center
Levy, Albert A., III, (On Duty Outside the Archdiocese)
Lewis, Raymond, (Retired)
Lobell, Wayne A., St. Matthew the Apostle, River Ridge; Stella Maris Port Ministry
Lorenz, Fallon Herbert, (On Duty Outside the Archdiocese)
Lotz, Thomas P., St. Clement of Rome, Metairie; Pastoral Min., Children's Hospital
Luke, Nelvin, St. Benedict Church, St. Benedict
Madere, Kenneth P., St. Joan of Arc, La Place
Mallerich, Walton J., (On Leave)
Mamou, Joseph, (On Leave)
Manieri, Tyrell, St. John Bosco, Harvey; Pastoral Min., Rivarde Juvenile Detention Center, Gretna
Martinez, Gerald J., Dir. Archdiocese Stewardship, St. Elizabeth Ann Seton, Kenner
Martinez, Wilbur, (Retired)
Martinsen, Noel W., Divine Mercy, Kenner; Pastoral Min., St. Charles Parish Correctional Center
Matherne, Landry, (Retired)
Mathews, Michael Schmid, (On Leave)
Memleb, Fred C., Jr., Our Lady of Divine Providence, Metairie
Mendel, August B., St. Benilde, Metairie; Pastoral Min., Tulane Lakeside Hospital, Metairie
Mendieta, Roberto, (Retired)
Miester, Alvin C., Jr., (On Duty Outside the Archdiocese)
Miller, Graylin J., St. Paul the Apostle, New Orleans; Pastoral Min., Orleans Parish Correctional Center
Minor, Francis M., Pastoral Assoc., St. Clement of Rome, Metairie
Mire, Louis N., St. Anselm, Madisonville; Pastoral Min., Lakeview Reg. Medical Center
Mistretta, Nicholas L., (Retired)
Moragas, Lucien F., Archdiocese for the Military-Keesler A.F.B. (On Duty Outside the Diocese)
Morales, G. Ernesto, (Retired), St. Jerome, Kenner
Mumme, Paul, Sr., St. Genevieve, Slidell
Murphy, Larry, Adv. Formation Program
Normand, Robert D., St. Francis Xavier, Metairie; Advocate, Metropolitan Tribunal
Nunez, Charles R., Sr., (Retired)
Nuss, Henry, (On Leave)
Ohlmeyer, Sterling, (Retired)
Oney, Larry D., St. Louis Cathedral & Our Lady of Grace, Reserve
Parulan, Lino G., Our Lady of Prompt Succor, Chalmette; Pastoral Min., Stella Maris Port Ministry
Perez, Jose D., (Duty Outside)
Pierre, Warren R., St. John the Baptist, Edgard; Pastoral Min., Nelson Coleman Correctional Center, St. Charles Parish
Pippenger, John, St. Dominic, New Orleans; Permanent Diaconate Personnel Board
Ramirez, Carlos Alfredo, St. Margaret Mary, Slidell; E. Northshore Hispanic Apostolate
Rayfield, Rudolph J., Sr., St. Peter Claver , New Orleans, Exec. Dir., Society of St. Vincent de Paul
Read, Charles, Jr., St. Anselm, Madisonville
Reeson, Curles P., (On Duty Outside the Archdiocese)
Reynolds, Daniel F., Holy Spirit; Pastoral Min., Kindred Hospital, New Orleans
Rhodes, Frank W., Jr., (On Duty Outside the Archdiocese)
Richard, Don Michael, St. Catherine of Siena, Metairie
Richardson, Ray, (On duty Outside Archdiocese)
Rivere, Raymond H., (Retired)
Rizzo, Peter C., Transfiguration of the Lord
Robicheaux, Wilfred, Jr., Our Lady of Prompt Succor, Westwego; Holy Guardian Angels Mission, Bridge City
Robin, Angelas, St. Mary Magdalen, Metairie
Rooney, James P., Jr., Visitation of Our Lady; Pastoral Min., Ochsner Medical Center, Westbank
Rosato, Joseph R., Tulane Catholic Center; Pastoral Min., Christ the Healer Prog.
Rougelot, Sidney, (Retired)
Roussel, Garland Joseph, Jr., St. Hubert, Garyville; St. John Parish Correctional Facility
Roussel, Theodore J., St. Charles Borromeo, Destrehan
Scalise, Bertrand, Jr., (On Duty Outside the Archdiocese)
Schexnayder, Harry, St. Charles Borromeo, Destrehan
Schlette, Peter B., (On Duty Outside the Archdiocese)
Schmidt, Gilbert R., St. Angela Merici, Metairie; Master of Ceremonies
Seruntine, Alex J., Jr., (Retired)
Seymour, Reginald John, St. Genevieve, Slidell
Shartle, George (Butch), Mary Queen of Peace, Mandeville; St. Tammany Parish Prison
Shelton, Royal C., St. Raymond-St. Leo the Great, New Orleans
Sierra, Jose A., Blessed Francis Xavier Seelos, New Orleans; Master of Ceremonies
Simoneaux, Nathan F., Jr., St. Matthew the Apostle, River Ridge; Advocate, Metropolitan Tribunal
Smith, Charles J., (On Leave)
Smith, Gilbert W., (Retired)
St. Pierre, Thomas Joseph, Ascension of Our Lord, La Place
Stahl, Rudolph W., (On Duty Outside the Archdiocese)
Stall, Louis W., (Retired)
Steel, Kevin M., Christ the King, Terrytown; Advocate, Metropolitan Tribunal
Stevens, Allen, Pastoral Assoc., St. Peter Claver
Stewart, Irvin, Sr., St. Joan of Arc, New Orleans
Stohlman, Michael H., St. Charles Borromeo, Destrehan
Strahan, Douglas H., (Retired)
Suprean, Ricky J., St. John of the Cross, Lacombe; Pastoral Min., Southeast Louisiana Hospital
Swiler, James W., Dir. Office of Permanent Diaconate
Talbot, Michael J., St. Jane de Chantal; Pastoral Min., Raymond Correctional Center, Angie
Templet, Eugene P., SS. Peter & Paul, Pearl River; Pastoral Min., St. Tammany Parish Prison
Toups, Wilbur A., St. Francis of Assisi, New Orleans
Trainor, Robert, (Retired)
Venturella, James A., Immaculate Conception, Marrero; Pastoral Min., Jefferson Parish Correctional Center, Gretna
Vicroy, Clarence, (Retired)
Vincent, Daniel S., (On Duty Outside Archdiocese)
Vincent, Harold A., Dir. of Pastoral Care, Xavier University of Louisiana; Perm. Dioconate Personnel Board
Vincent, Leslie D., Our Lady of Perpetual Help, Cellechasse; Pastoral Min., Ochsner Medical Center-West Bank, Gretna
Walker, John J., IV, St. Andrew the Apostle, New Orleans; Pastoral Min., Jefferson Parish Correctional Center, Gretna
Warriner, A. David, Jr., Master of Ceremonies, St. Louis Cathedral; Coord., Court of Second Instance, Metropolitan Tribunal; Vice Chancellor; Archdiocese Liturgical Commission; Delegate, Dispensations & Permissions; Defender of the Bond
Watley, Jesse A., Exec. Dir., Dept. of Pastoral Services, Blessed Francis Xavier Seelos, New Orleans; Master of Ceremonies
Weber, John C., St. Margaret Mary, Slidell
Webre, Milton G., (On Duty Outside Archdiocese)
White, Alfred, (On Leave)
Williams, Everett, (Retired)
Williams, Herman J., Pastoral Assoc., St. Joseph, Gretna
Williams, John B., (Retired)
Wilson, Earl McMahon, Jr., (On Leave)
Wiltz, Glenn J., St. James Major, New Orleans; Pastoral Min., Children's Hospital
Wright, Clifford S., St. Benilde, Metairie
Zaiontz, Michael G., Our Lady of the Rosary, New Orleans; Advocate, Metropolitan Tribunal
Zeringue, Alfred, (On Duty Outside the Archdiocese)
Zimmer, Julius T., St. John the Baptist, Folsom

INSTITUTIONS LOCATED IN THE ARCHDIOCESE

[A] SEMINARIES, ARCHDIOCESAN

NEW ORLEANS. *Notre Dame Seminary Graduate School of Theology* (1923) 2901 S. Carrollton Ave., 70118-4391. Tel: 504-866-7426; Fax: 504-866-3119. Email: illjmb@nds.edu. Web: www.nds.edu. Priests 9; Laymen 4; Women Religious 3; Seminarians 70.

Administration: Rev. David Kelly, Dir. Pastoral Field Education; Dr. David Liberto, M.A., Ph.D., Academic Dean; Rev. Jose I. Lavastida, S.T.D., S.T.L., N.D.S., Pres. & Rector; Sr. Cecilia Castillo, S.T.J., B.A., Registrar; Mr. George Dansker, M.P.H., M.L.I.S., Librarian; Mr. Wayne Trosclair, B.S., Dir. of Facilities & Student Services; Ms. Michelle W. Klein, Business Mgr.; Sisters Janet Bodin, M.S.C., M.A., Ph.D., Dir. Pre-Theology/Phil.; Theresa Marie Tran, S.S.C., Assoc. Dir. Pastoral Field Educ.

Faculty: Revs. Joseph M. Krafft; Donald Martin, S.J., M.A., Ph.D.; Vien The Nguyen, J.C.L., M.Div.; Mark S. Raphael; Very Rev. Patrick J. Williams; Sisters Janet Bodin, M.S.C., M.A., Ph.D.; Elizabeth Fitzpatrick, O.Carm., M.A.; Rev. Joseph S. Palermo Jr., J.D.; Dr. Mark Barker; Dr. Basil Davis, M.A., Ph.D.; Dr. James M. Jacobs, M.A., Ph.D.; Dr. David Liberto, M.A., Ph.D.; Mr. Angelo Lupinetti; Mr. Kevin Redmann; Mr. George Dansker, M.P.H., M.L.I.S., Librarian; Dr. Chris Baglow, Ph.D.; Dr. Brant Pitre, Ph.D.

ST. BENEDICT. *St. Joseph Seminary College* (1890) 70457-9999. Tel: 504-892-1800; Fax: 504-867-2270. Email: rector@sjasc.edu. Web: www.sjasc.edu. Very Rev. Gregory M. Boquet, O.S.B., M.A., Pres. & Rector; Rt. Rev. Justin Brown, O.S.B., Abbot; Friar Vincent Dufresne, S.T.L.; Revs. Scott J. Underwood, O.S.B., M.T.S., M.Ed.; Matthew R. Clark, O.S.B., M.A., Vice Rector; Vanessa Crouere, Dir. Devel.; Kit Friedrichs-Baumann, Dir. Grants & Devel. Assoc.; George J. Binder, Registrar & Dir. Fin. Aid; Revs. Augustine E. Foley, O.S.B., M.A.Th.; Thomas L. Gwozdz, S.B.D., Ph.D.; Very Rev. Thomas C. Ranzino (BR); Dr. Jude Lupinetti, Ph.D., Academic Dean; Rev. Killian Tolg, B.A., M.A., Dean of Students; Bro. Simon Stubbs, O.S.B., Communications Dir.; Ms. Judith Gaubert, Dir. Finance. Benedictine Monks. Conducted by Provinces of New Orleans and Mobile and Monks of St. Joseph's Abbey. Priests 23; Brothers 13; Novices 2; Sisters 2; Lay Teachers 10; Seminarians 77; Total Enrollment 179; Lay Staff 15.

Faculty: Rev. Charles J. Benoit, O.S.B., M.A.Th.; Daniel Burns; Richard Moore; Revs. Josh Rodrigue; Basil Burns; Matthew R. Clark, O.S.B., M.A.; Augustine E. Foley, O.S.B., M.A.Th.; Thomas L. Gwozdz, S.B.D., Ph.D.; Sr. Jeanne d'Arc Kernion, O.S.B.; Ms. Josette Beaulieu-Grace, M.A.; Jeffrey Bell, Ph.D.; Al Dranguet; Peter M. Emerson, Ph.D.; Agnieszka Gutthy, Ph.D.; John E. Hebert, Ph.D.; Harry McMurray, Ph.D.; Dr. Ann K. Nauman, Ph.D.; Francie Rich.

Religious Studies Institute: Revs. Chris Decker; Vincent Dufresne; David Jamin; Tom Ranzino; Brenda Atkinson, M.A.; Rick Beben; Elizabeth Bourgeois, M.R.E.; Thomas Eldringhoff, M.A.; Mr. Charles Jumonville, M.R.E.; Rev. Chris Redden; Mr. Kenneth J. Thevenet, M.Mus.

Diaconate Program: Revs. Paul Counce, M.A., M.C.L.; Joel LaBauve; Robert Stine.

Professional Lay Staff: Todd Russell, Dir. Institute Technology; Carole Bryant, Academic Sec.; Janice Lewis, Sec. to President-Rector; Nicole D'Argeneaux, Accounting; Pamela Egan, R.N., N.P., Dir., Student Health Svcs.; Beverly Krieger, Sec.; Bonnie Wood, Librarian.

[B] SEMINARIES, RELIGIOUS OR SCHOLASTICATES

NEW ORLEANS. *St. John of the Cross, Discalced Carmelite House of Studies*, 2925 S. Carrollton Ave., 70118-4301. Tel: 504-861-9102; Fax: 504-865-1751. Email: samocd@cox.net. Web: www.carmelitesok.org. Revs. Gregory S. Ross, O.C.D., M.Div., S.T.L., Prov. Supr. in Res.; Sam Anthony Morello, O.C.D., Rector & Student Master; Bonaventure Sauer, O.C.D., Prov. Delegate to Secular Order. Priests 3.

Josephite House of Studies, 2000 St. Bernard Ave., 70116-1390. Priest Candidates 1.

METAIRIE. *Congregation of the Mother Coredemptrix Formation House* (1991) 112 Lilac St., 70005-1817. Tel: 504-835-9746; Fax: 504-835-9746. Email: hvmvncmc@yahoo.com. Priests 1; Brothers 9.

[C] COLLEGES AND UNIVERSITIES

NEW ORLEANS. *Loyola University New Orleans* (1912) 6363 St. Charles Ave., 70118-6195. Tel: 504-865-2011 (General); 504-865-3847 (Pres. Office); Fax: 504-865-3851. Email: ghoward@loyno.edu. Web: www.loyno.edu. Revs. Kevin Wildes, S.J., Pres.; Theodore A. Dziak, S.J., Jesuit Center Dir.; Dr. Edward Kvet, Provost/Vice Pres. for Academic Affairs; Revs. Michael A. Bouzigard, S.J., M.A., M.Div., M.Phil; James C. Carter, S.J.; Gerald M. Fagin, S.J.; Ernest Ferlita, S.J.; Marvin C. Kitten, S.J.; Lawrence Moore, S.J.; Leo A. Nicoll, S.J.; Peter S. Rogers, S.J.; Peter J. Bernardi, S.J.; Very Rev. Alfred C. Kammer, S.J., B.A., M.A., J.D., Prov. (New Orleans Society of Jesus); Revs. William J. Farge, S.J.; Robert S.

Gerlich, S.J.; Stephen C. Rowntree, S.J., B.A., M.A., M.Div., M.Th.; Bros. Gebhard R.M. Frohlich, S.J., (Retired); Lawrence J. Lundin, S.J., B.A., M.B.A., Treas. (New Orleans Society of Jesus); Rev. Kenneth P. Keulman; Jo Ann Cruz, Interim Dean College of Humanities & Natural Sciences; Anthony A. Decuir, Interim Dean College of Music; William B. Locander, Dean College of Business; Brian Bromberger, Dean Law School; Mary Lee Sweat, Dean Univ. Library; Dr. Luis Miron, Dean College of Social Studies Svcs.; Revs. John F. Armstrong, S.J., Formation Asst. (New Orleans Province of the Society of Jesus); Edward B. Arroyo, S.J., Exec. Dir. Jesuit Social Research Institute; James M. Caime, S.J., Dir. Liturgy & Music; Thomas P. Greene, S.J., Research Fellow, Jesuit Social Research Institute. Priests 22; Brothers 1; Sisters 1; Lay Teachers 467; Students 4,585.

Our Lady of Holy Cross College, 4123 Woodland Dr., 70131-7399. Tel: 504-394-7744; Fax: 504-391-2421. Email: admissions@olhcc.edu. Web: www.olhcc.edu. Rev. Anthony J. DeConciliis, C.S.C., Ph.D., Pres.; Raymond Gitz, Ph.D., Vice Pres. Academic Affairs; Jennifer Winters, Vice Pres. Fin. Affairs; Debbie Panepinto, Registrar; Sr. Helen Fontenot, M.S.C., Librarian. Priests 2; Brothers 1; Congregation of the Sisters Marianites of Holy Cross 6; Sisters 2; Lay Teachers 36; Students 1,300; Total Staff 160.

Xavier University of Louisiana (Coed), One Drexel Dr., 70125-1098. Tel: 504-486-7411; Fax: 504-520-7904. Email: apply@xula.edu. Web: www.xula.edu. Dr. Norman C. Francis, Pres.; Dr. Loren Blanchard, Vice Pres. Academic Affairs; Mrs. Lisa Lewis McClain, Dir. Office of Campus Ministry; Mr. Robert Skinner, Librarian. Priests 1; Brothers 1; Lay Teachers 202; Students 3,236.

[D] HIGH SCHOOLS, ARCHDIOCESAN

COVINGTON. *Archbishop Hannan High School*, 71324 Hwy. 1077, 70433. Tel: 985-249-6363; Fax: 985-249-6370. Email: info@hannanhigh.org. Mr. John A. Cavell Jr., Prin.; Rory R. Rafferty Jr., M.Ed., Asst. Prin.; Susan Yates, Librarian. Priests 1; Sisters 1; Lay Teachers 21; Students 270.

St. Scholastica Academy, P.O. Box 1210, 70434-1210. Tel: 985-892-2540; Fax: 985-893-5256. Email: mkv@ssacad.com. Web: www.ssacad.com. Mrs. Marguerite S. Celestin, Pres.; Mary Kathryn Villere, Prin.; Bobbie Landry, Librarian. Sisters 2; Lay Teachers 54; Students 751.

LA PLACE. *St. Charles Catholic High School*, 100 Dominican Dr., 70068-3499. Tel: 985-652-3809; Fax: 985-652-2609. Email: stcharlescath@archdiocese-no.org. Web: www.stcharlescatholic.org. Mr. Andrew C. Cupit, Prin.; Angie Louque, Librarian. Lay Teachers 33; Students 455.

MARRERO. *Academy of Our Lady* (2007) 537 Ave. D, 70072-2027. Tel: 504-341-6217; Fax: 504-341-6229. Email: ourlady@theacademyofourlady.org. Web: www.theacademyofourlady.org. Sr. Maria Colombo, F.M.A., Prin.; Michelle Maher, Librarian; Linda Todd, Librarian. Merger of Archbishop Blenk High School, Gretna & Immaculata High School, Marrero. Sisters 3; Lay Teachers 39; Girls 575.

Archbishop Shaw High School, 1000 Barataria Blvd., 70072-3052. Tel: 504-340-6727; Fax: 504-347-9883. Email: arnoshaw@archdiocese.org. Web: www.archbishopshaw.org. Revs. James McKenna, S.D.B., Pres. & Dir.; Louis Konopelski, S.D.B., Prin.; Mr. John Corb, Financial Admin.; Revs. John DiFiore, S.D.B., Youth Min.; Thomas McGahee, S.D.B.; Emil Fardellone, S.D.B.; Bros. Joseph Tortorici; Dave Verrett; Mrs. Susan LaHaye, Librarian. Salesians of St. John Bosco. Priests 5; Brothers 2; Lay Teachers 44; Boys 413.

METAIRIE. *Archbishop Chapelle High School*, 8800 Veterans Blvd., 70003-5235. Tel: 504-467-3105; Fax: 504-466-3191. Email: achs@archbishopchapelle.org. Web: www.archbishopchapelle.org. Mrs. Jane Ann Frosch, Pres.; Ms. Cathy Yaeger, Prin.; Annette Thibodeaux, Librarian. Priests 1; Lay Teachers 65; Girls 900.

Archbishop Rummel High School, 1901 Severn Ave., 70001. Tel: 504-834-5592; Fax: 504-832-4016. Email: info@rummelraiders.com. Web: www.rummelraiders.com. Mr. Michael Begg, Pres.; Mr. Thomas G. Moran, Prin.; Mr. Michael Scalco, Vice Pres. Facilities & Construction; Ms. Deborah Lobrano, Librarian. Lay Teachers 70; Boys 1,000.

SLIDELL. *Pope John Paul II Catholic High School* (1980) 1901 Jaguar Dr., 70461-9098. Tel: 985-649-0914; Fax: 985-649-5494. Email: pjp@pjp.org. Web: www.pjp.org. Mr. Richard Berkowitz, M.Ed., Prin. Lay Teachers 26; Students 373.

[E] HIGH SCHOOLS, PRIVATE

NEW ORLEANS. *Academy of the Sacred Heart "The Rosary"* (1887) 4521 St. Charles Ave., 70115-9990. Tel: 504-891-1943; Fax: 504-891-9939. Email: ash@ashrosary.org. Web: www.ashrosary.org. Dr. Timothy Burns, Ph.D., B.A., M.A., Headmaster; Yvonne S. Adler, Ph.D., Prin.; Mrs. Josephine Schloegel, Librarian. Religious of the Sacred Heart 1; Carmelites 1; Lay Teachers 30; Girls 216.

St. Augustine High School (1951) (Grades 7-12), 2600 A.P. Tureaud Ave., 70119-1299. Tel: 504-944-2424; Fax: 504-947-7712. Email: staughs@archdiocese-no.org. Web: purpleknights.com. Revs. Joseph M. Doyle, S.S.J., Pres.; John J. Raphael, S.S.J., Prin.; Wilbur J. Atwood, S.S.J., Librarian. Josephite Community., (See Separate Listing for Residence.) Priests 5; Lay Teachers 56; Boys 650.

Brother Martin High School (1869) (Grades 8-12), 4401 Elysian Fields Ave., 70122-3898. Tel: 504-283-1561; Fax: 504-286-8462. Email: gmrando@cox.net. Web: brothermartin.com. Mr. John J. Devlin III, Pres.; Mr. Gregory Rando, Prin. Brothers of the Sacred Heart 3; Sisters 1; Lay Teachers 96; Boys 1,202.

Cabrini High School (1959) (Grades 8-12), 1400 Moss St., 70119-2904. Tel: 504-482-1193; Fax: 504-483-8671. Ardley Hanemann Jr., Pres.; Mrs. Yvonne L. Hrapmann, Prin.; Helene Tucker, Academic Asst. Prin. Missionary Sisters of the Sacred Heart 1; Marianites of the Holy Cross 1; Lay Teachers 48; Girls 506.

Cabrini High School, Inc. Tel: 504-482-1193; Fax: 504-483-8673. Web: cabrinihigh.com.

De La Salle High School (1949) (Grades 10-12), (Coed), 5300 St. Charles Ave., 70115-4999. Tel: 504-895-5717; Fax: 504-895-1300. Email: delasalle@delasallenola.com. Web: www.delasallenola.com. Mr. Kenneth Tedesco, Pres.; Regina F. Hall, A.F.S.C., Prin. Brothers of the Christian Schools 2; Sisters 2; Lay Teachers 43; Students 305.

Holy Cross School (1879) (Grades 5-12), 5500 Paris Ave., 70122-2659. Tel: 504-942-3100; Fax: 504-286-5665. Email: contacthc@holycrosstigers.com. Web: www.holycrosstigers.com. Dr. Joseph H. Murry Jr., High School Prin.; Teresa Billings, Middle School Prin.; Mr. Charles DiGange, Headmaster; Very Rev. Patrick J. Williams, Chap. Brothers of the Congregation of Holy Cross, Southwest Province 1; Lay Teachers 63; Boys 821.

Jesuit High School (1847) (Boys), 4133 Banks St., 70119-6883. Tel: 504-486-6631; Fax: 504-483-3816. Email: principal@jesuitnola.org. Web: www.jesuitnola.org. Rev. Anthony F. McGinn, S.J., Rector; Mr. Michael Giambelluca, Prin.; Revs. Norman B. O'Neal, S.J.; Nicholas T. Schiro, S.J.; Donald E. Saunders, S.J. Priests 4; Brothers 1; Lay Teachers 90; Boys 1,102. In Res. Rev. Raymond R. Fitzgerald, S.J.

Office: 710 Baronne St., 70113-1064. Tel: 504-571-1055; Fax: 504-571-1744. Priests 4; Brothers 2; Lay Teachers 92; Boys 1,113.

St. Mary's Academy of the Holy Family, Mailing Address: 6905 Chef Menteur Blvd., 70126-5215. Tel: 504-245-0200; Fax: 504-245-0318. Email: smaoffice@archdiocese-no.org. Web: www.smaneworleans.com. Sr. Jennie Jones, S.S.F., Prin.; Michelle Ochillo, Librarian. Sisters 12; Lay Teachers 42.

St. Mary's Dominican High School (1860) 7701 Walmsley Ave., 70125-3494. Tel: 504-865-9401; Fax: 504-866-5958. Email: president@stmarysdominican.org. Web: www.stmarysdominican.org. Dr. Cynthia A. Thomas, Ed.D., Pres.; Mrs. Carolyn Favre, Prin. Priests 1; Sisters 6; Brothers 1; Lay Teachers 70; Students 916; Personnel Total 108.

Mount Carmel Academy (1833) 7027 Milne Blvd., 70124-2395. Tel: 504-288-7626; Fax: 504-288-7629. Email: mca@mcacubs.org. Web: www.mtcarmelcubs.org. Sr. Camille Anne Campbell, O.Carm., Pres. & Prin.; Very Rev. Patrick J. Williams, Chap.; Sr. Celeste Lehman, D.C., Librarian. Congregation of Our Lady of Mount Carmel. Sisters 5; Lay Teachers 115; Girls 1,167.

Ursuline Academy, (Grades 8-12), Secondary Dept. Day School College Prep., 2635 State St., 70118-6399. Tel: 504-861-9150; Fax: 504-861-7392. Email: admissions@ursulineneworleans.org. Web: www.ursulineneworleans.org. Gretchen Z. Kane, B.S., M.S., Pres.; John Gabriel, Prin.; Susan Young, Librarian. Lay Teachers 40; Girls 421.

Xavier University Preparatory School, 5116 Magazine St., 70115-1899. Tel: 504-899-6061, Ext. 310; Fax: 504-891-8766. Email: xavierprep@xavierprep.com. Web: www.xavierprep.com. Sr. Eileen Sullivan, S.B.S., Pres.; Mrs. Carolyn Oubre, Prin.; Sr. Nathalee Bryant, S.B.S., Librarian. Sisters 5; Lay Teachers 24; Girls 268.

COVINGTON. *The St. Paul's School* (1911) (Grades 8-12), P.O. Box 928, 70434-0928. Tel: 985-892-3200; Fax: 985-892-4048. Email: stpauls@stpauls.com. Web: www.stpauls.com. Bro. Raymond Bulliard, F.S.C., Prin. Day School for Young Men Brothers of the Christian Schools of the New Orleans-Santa Fe Province 6; Lay Teachers 60; Boys 800.

[F] HIGH SCHOOLS, PAROCHIAL

NEW ORLEANS. *Holy Rosary Academy* (1996) 3368 Esplanade Ave., 70119-3132. Tel: 504-482-7173; Fax: 504-482-7229. Email: holyrosaryaca@archdiocese-no.org. Michael J. Binder, Prin. Lay Teachers 18; Students 114.

[G] ELEMENTARY SCHOOLS, ARCHDIOCESAN

MARRERO. *Archbishop Shaw Junior High School*, (Grades 8-9), 1000 Barataria Blvd., 70072-3052. Tel: 504-340-6727; Fax: 504-347-9883. Email: arnoshaw@archdiocese-no.org. Web: www.archbishopshaw.org. Rev. James McKenna, S.D.B., Dir. & President; Cheryl Welch, Prin., Jr. High; Rev. Louis Konopelski, S.D.B., Prin.; Mrs. Susan LaHaye, Librarian. Priests 5; Brothers 2; Lay Teachers 44; Students 200.

[H] ELEMENTARY SCHOOLS, PRIVATE

NEW ORLEANS. *Academy of the Sacred Heart* (1887) (Grades Toddler-12), 4521 St. Charles Ave., 70115-4831. Tel: 504-891-1943; Fax: 504-891-9939. Email: ash@ashrosary.org. Web: www.ashrosary.org. Dr. Timothy Burns, Ph.D., B.A., M.A., Headmaster; Yvonne S. Adler, Ph.D., U.S. Div. Head; Kay Higginbotham, L.S. Div. Head; Kim Duckworth, M.S. Div. Head; Phina Schloegel, Librarian; Libby Adams, Librarian. Religious of the Sacred Heart 3; Lay Teachers 92; Girls 799.

St. Augustine High School, (Grades 7), 2600 A.P. Tureaud Ave., 70119-1299. Tel: 504-944-2424; Fax: 504-947-7712. Email: sdavidson@purpleknights.com. Web: purpleknights.com. Revs. Joseph M. Doyle, S.S.J., Pres.; John J. Raphael, S.S.J., Prin.; Wilbur J. Atwood, S.S.J., Librarian. Priests 5; Religious Brothers 1; Lay Teachers 55; Boys 700.

St. Benedict the Moor School (1998) (Grades PreK-4), 5010 Piety Dr., 70126. Tel: 504-288-2745; Fax: 504-282-9386. Email: stbenmoor@archdiocese-no.org. Drue Dumas, Prin. Sisters 1; Lay Teachers 5; Students 85.

Brother Martin High School (Grade 8), 4401 Elysian Fields Ave., 70122-3898. Tel: 504-283-1561; Fax: 504-286-8462. Web: brothermartin.com. Thomas E. Mavor, Prin.; Keiren Aucoin, Librarian. Lay Teachers 24; Boys 222.

Cabrini High School (1959) (Grades 8-12), 1400 Moss St., 70119-2904. Tel: 504-482-1193; Fax: 504-483-8671. Web: cabrinihigh.com. Ardley Hanemann Jr., Pres.; Mrs. Yvonne L. Hrapmann, Prin.; Helene Tucker, Asst. Academic Prin. Sisters 2; Lay Teachers 48; Students 460.

Christian Brothers School, (Grades 5-7), City Park, #8 Fredericks Ave., 70124-4602. Tel: 504-486-6770; Fax: 504-486-1053. Email: school@cbs-no.org. Web: www.cbs-no.org. Bro. Laurence Konersmann, Pres.; Mr. Joey M. Scaffidi, Prin.; Mrs. Carol Maquar, Librarian. Brothers 3; Lay Teachers 17; Boys 287.

De La Salle Junior High School, (Grades 8-9), (Coed), 5300 St. Charles Ave., 70115-4999. Tel: 504-895-5717; Fax: 504-895-1300. Email: peggys@delasallenola.com. Web: www.delasallenola.com. Mr. Kenneth Tedesco, Pres.; Regina F. Hall, A.F.S.C., Prin. Brothers 1; Lay Teachers 43; Students 156.

Holy Cross School, (Grades 5-12), 5500 Paris Ave., 70122. Tel: 504-942-3100; Fax: 504-286-5665. Email: contacthc@holycrosstigers.com. Web: www.holycrosstigers.com. Dr. Joseph H. Murry Jr., High School Prin.; Teresa Billings, Middle School Prin.; Mr. Charles DiGange, Headmaster; Mrs. Pam Falgoust, Librarian; Very Rev. Patrick J. Williams, Chap. Lay Teachers 54; Boys 750.

Jesuit High School, (Grades 8), 4133 Banks St., 70119-6883. Tel: 504-486-6631; Fax: 504-483-3816. Email: principal@jesuitnola.org. Web: www.jesuitnola.org. Rev. Anthony F. McGinn, S.J., Pres.; Mr. Michael A. Giambelluca, Prin. Priests 1; Lay Teachers 19; Boys 256.

St. Mary's Academy, (Grades PreK-12), 6905 Chef Menteur Blvd., 70126. Tel: 504-245-0200; Fax: 504-245-0422. Email: smaoffice@archdiocese-no.org. Web: www.smaneworleans.com. Sr. Jennie Jones, S.S.F., Prin.; Michelle Ochillo, Librarian. Priests 1; Sisters of the Holy Family 12; Lay Teachers 42; Students 653.

Stuart Hall School for Boys, 2032 S. Carrollton Ave., 70182. Tel: 504-861-1954; Fax: 504-861-5389.

Email: claforge@stuarthall.org. Web: www.stuarthall.org. Dr. Cissy LaForge, B.S., M.Ed., Ph.D., Prin.; Nancy Dunphy, Librarian. Lay Teachers 40.

Ursuline Academy, (Grades Toddler-7), 2635 State St., 70118-6399. Tel: 504-861-9150; Fax: 504-866-5293. Email: admissions@ursulineneworleans.org. Web: www.ursulineneworleans.org. Gretchen Z. Kane, B.S., M.S., Pres.; Kimberly Harper, Prin.; Pat Prudhomme, Librarian. Lay Teachers 36; Students 343.

COVINGTON. *The St. Paul's School*, (Grades 8-12), P.O. Box 928, 70434-0928. Tel: 985-892-3200; Fax: 985-892-4048. Email: stpauls@stpauls.com. Web: www.stpauls.com. Bro. Raymond Bulliard, F.S.C., Prin.; Trevor Watkins, Asst. Prin. Brothers of the Christian Schools., (See St. Paul's School under High Schools, Private) Brothers 6; Lay Teachers 60; Boys 800.

[I] SPECIAL EDUCATION

NEW ORLEANS. *St. Gerard Majella Alternative School* (1991) 1941 Dauphine St., 70116-1609. Tel: 504-309-9543; Fax: 504-309-9542. Email: majellaalt@archdiocese-no.org. Sr. Rose Elaine Kessler, S.S.N.D., Prin. Sisters 1; Lay Teachers 4; Students 25.

Good Shepherd Nativity School (2001) 353 Baronne St., 70112-1628. Tel: 504-598-9399; Fax: 504-598-9346. Email: epaul@thegoodshepherdschool.org. Web: www.thegoodshepherdschool.org. Mrs. Emily Paul, Prin.; Wendy Ruckman, Librarian. Lay Teachers 12; Total Staff 21; Students 83.

St. Michael Special School, 1522 Chippewa St., 70130. Tel: 504-524-7285; Fax: 504-524-5883. Email: stmichspecial@archdiocese-no.org. Mrs. Jane Silva, Prin. Religious 1; Lay Teachers 23; Students 191.

[J] DAY CARE CENTERS, CAMPS AND PRESCHOOLS

NEW ORLEANS. *Cub Corner* (1975) Pre-School, 420 Robt E. Lee Blvd., 70124. Tel: 504-286-8673; Fax: 504-286-8676. Web: www.home.bellsouth.net/p/pwp-mountcarmel. Elizabeth Coe, Child Care Dir.; Sr. Gwen Grillot, O.Carm., Exec. Dir. (A Ministry of the Sisters of Mount Carmel). Religious 3; Lay Staff 30.

St. John Berchmans Child Development Center (Not open at this time. Contact the Sisters of the Holy Family for information.), Mailing Address: 6901 Chef Menteur Hwy., 70126-5290. 2710 Gentilly Blvd., 70182-8623.

Lafon Child Development Center (1965) (Not open at this time. Contact the Sisters of the Holy Family for information.), 7024 Chef Menteur Hwy., 70126-5295. Mailing Address: 6901 Chef Menteur Hwy., 70126-5290.

Leslie Early Head Start Center, 2126 Constance St., 70130-5044. Tel: 504-522-2725. Total Staff 5.

Louise Early Head Start Center, 1205 Louisiana Ave., 70115-2488. Tel: 504-891-2871; Fax: 504-895-3129.

Rosary Child Development Center (2000) 5100 Willowbrook Dr., 70129-1047. Tel: 504-254-1528; Fax: 504-254-1531. Email: rosarycdc@yahoo.com. Sr. Thien-An Nguyen, F.M.S.R., Dir. Total Staff 15; Children (Daily Average) 95.

St. John the Baptist Head Start Program, 1920 Clio St., 70113-1214. Tel: 504-529-2557 (Preschool); Fax: 504-581-2028 (Center). Lay Staff 11; Children 57.

El Y Yo Head Start/Early Head Start, 735 Gen. Pershing St., 70115. Tel: 504-899-6165.

Incarnate Word Head Start/Early Head Start, 8326 Apricot St., 70115. Tel: 504-866-8918.

[K] HOMES FOR CHILDREN AND YOUTH

NEW ORLEANS. *Boys Hope Girls Hope* (1980) Group Homes for Boys and Girls., P.O. Box 19307, 70179-0307. Tel: 504-484-7744; Fax: 504-484-6120. Web: www.bhghnola.org. Cory J. Howat, Executive Director; Stephanie Strain, Office Mgr. Total Staff 8; Boys 8; Girls 8; Total Assisted 25.

**Covenant House New Orleans* (1987) Home for Runaway, Abused & Homeless Youth aged 16-21., 611 N. Rampart St., 70112-3540. Tel: 504-584-1111; 800-999-9999 (Hotline); Fax: 504-584-1171. Email: dlouque@covenanthouse.org. Web: covenanthouseno.org. Stacy Horn Koch, Exec. Dir. Total Assisted 1,300; Total Staff 100.

BELLE CHASSE. *Padua Pediatric Program* Facility for Severely-Profoundly Retarded and Multihandicapped Children, 200 Beta St., 70037-1499. Tel: 504-392-0502; Fax: 504-392-5411.

[L] RESIDENCES, ADULT

NEW ORLEANS. *Baronne Street Transitional Housing*, 2407 Baronne St., 70113-1621. Tel: 504-269-9311. Mrs. Connie Andry, Dir., Homeless Svcs. Crisis & Residential Emergency Center.

Ciara House, c/o 1000 Howard Ave., Ste. 1000, 70113. Ms. Monetta Clark, Admin. Housing for Chronically Mentally Ill Adults.

Ozanam Inn Shelter for Homeless Men, 843 Camp St., 70130-3751. Tel: 504-523-1184; Fax: 504-523-1187. Web: www.ozanaminn.org. Deacon Biaggio DiGiovanni, Admin. Sponsored by Society of St. Vincent de Paul. Total Staff 12; Total Assisted 35,040; Bed Capacity 96.

Project Lazarus (1986) Residential Program for Persons with AIDS, P.O. Box 3906, 70177-3906. Tel: 504-949-3609; Fax: 504-944-7944. Email: info@projectlazarus.net. Web: www.projectlazarus.net. Mr. Eric Oleson, Exec. Dir. Total in Residence 24; Total Assisted Annually 95; Total Staff 25.

GRETNA. *St. Jude the Apostle*, c/o 1000 Howard Ave., Ste. 1000, 70113. Community Home for Developmentally Disabled Adults.

Ocean Avenue, c/o 1000 Howard Ave., Ste. 1000, 70113. Community Home for Developmentally Disabled Adults.

St. Rosalie, c/o 1000 Howard Ave., Ste. 1000, 70113. Community Home for Developmentally Disabled Adults.

MARRERO. *Jefferson CARE Center*, c/o 1000 Howard Ave., Ste. 1000, 70113. Ms. Patricia G. Jones, Prog. Dir. Temporary Residence for Homeless Families.

METAIRIE. *Ss. Mary & Elizabeth*, c/o 1000 Howard Ave., Ste. 1000, 70113. Community Home for Developmentally Disabled Adults.

SLIDELL. *St. Peter the Fisherman*, c/o 1000 Howard Ave., Ste. 1000, 70113. Community Home for Developmentally Disabled Adults.

[M] DAY CARE CENTERS (ADULT)

NEW ORLEANS. *New Directions Adult Day Health Care Center*, 1523 N. Dorgenois St., 70119-2419. Tel: 504-943-9418; Fax: 504-948-3633. c/o 1000 Howard Ave., Ste. 1000, 70113.

People Program (1974) 2240 Lake Shore Dr., 70122. Tel: 504-284-7678; Fax: 504-284-7840. Email: info@peopleprogram.org. Web: www.peopleprogram.org. LaVerne Kappel, Exec. Dir.

Westbank Program, 6201 Stratford Pl., 70131. Tel: 504-394-5433.

Metairie Program, 6017 Camphor St., Metairie, 70003.

COVINGTON. *Alpha House Adult Day Health Care Center*, 20127 Hwy. 36, 70433-8658. Tel: 985-892-7074; Fax: 985-893-1962.

KENNER. *The Greenwalt Center for Alzheimer's Day Care and Research*, 1926 18th St., 70062-6208. Tel: 504-461-5889; Fax: 504-461-5795.

NORCO. *Norco Adult Day Care*, 425 Spruce St., 70079-8464. Tel: 985-764-9084; Fax: 985-764-8464. Maida Botts-Camp, Coord.

[N] HOMES AND RESIDENCES FOR FAMILIES AND SENIOR CITIZENS

NEW ORLEANS. *Annunciation Inn*, 1220 Spain St., 70117-8369. Tel: 504-944-0512; Fax: 504-944-0575. Dechaun Hicks, Community Mgr. Residence for Elderly Units 106.

The Apartments at Mater Dolorosa, 1226 S. Carrollton Ave., 70118. Tel: 504-865-7222; Fax: 504-861-9225. Total Staff 3.

Chateau de Notre Dame Residence and Nursing Home, 2832 Burdette St., 70125-2596. Tel: 504-866-2741; Fax: 504-866-2861. Email: wplaisance@archdiocese-no.org. Web: cdnd.org. Mr. Wayne Plaisance, CEO; Rev. Royce J. Mitchell, Chap. (Retired). Residential Units 100; Nursing Beds 171; Priests 1; Sisters 2; Lay Staff 210.

Christopher Inn Apts. Private Nonprofit Residence for Senior Citizens Sponsored by the Archdiocese, 2110 Royal St., 70116-1693. Tel: 504-949-0312; Fax: 504-945-2634. Deacon Graylin Miller, Community Mgr. Residents 144; Total Staff 8.

DeLille Inn (1987) 6924 Chef Menteur Hwy., 70126-5260. Tel: 504-245-8660; Fax: 504-245-8677.

The 1540 House Not currently open due to Hurricane Katrina, 1000 Howard Ave., Ste. 100, 70113. Tel: 504-596-3460; Fax: 504-596-3466.

St. John Berchmans Manor, 3400 St. Anthony St., 70122-3098. Tel: 504-943-9331; Fax: 504-943-9380. Units 149; Total Staff 5.

Lafon Nursing Facility of the Holy Family, 6900 Chef Menteur Blvd., 70126. Tel: 504-240-2288. Sr. Augustine McDaniel, S.S.F., Admin. Sisters of the Holy Family. Sisters 6; Residents 155; Total Staff 145.

St. Margaret's (1931) 3419 St. Claude Ave., 70117-6144. Tel: 504-279-6414; Fax: 504-277-1834. Email: lstansberry@stmargaretsno.org. Web: www.stmargaretsno.org. Mr. Larry Stansberry, CEO; Manda Mountain, Admin. Bed Capacity 112; Total Staff 165; Total Assisted Annually 160.

St. Martin Manor Not currently open due to Hurricane Katrina, 1000 Howard Ave., Ste. 100, 70113. Residential Units 140.

Nazareth II, 9640 Hayne Blvd., 70127-4725. Tel: 504-246-9640; Fax: 504-245-4273. Teresa Poche, Community Mgr. Apartments 120.

Nazareth Inn, 9630 Hayne Blvd., 70127-1260. Tel: 504-246-9630; Fax: 504-241-9631. Teresa Poche, Community Mgr.

Nazareth Manor, Inc. Apartments 150; Total Staff 12.

Our Lady of Wisdom Healthcare Center (Inter-Community Health Care, Inc.), 5600 Gen. de Gaulle Dr., 70131. Tel: 504-394-5991; Fax: 504-304-5421. Web: www.olwhealth.org. Bob Laster, Admin. Inter-community healthcare facility for Archdiocesan clergy and Religious Men: Order of Preachers, Society of Jesus, Society of Mary (Marists), Vincentian, Christian Brothers and Brothers of the Sacred Heart; Religious Women: Sisters of St. Joseph of Medaille, Sisters of Mercy, Sisters of the Living Word, Dominican Sisters of Peace, Sisters of the Immaculate Conception, Marianites of the Holy Cross, Sisters of Mount Carmel, Order of Saint Clare (Poor Clares) and Daughters of Charity. Total Staff 150; Bed Capacity 138; Total Assisted Annually 200.

Villa St. Maurice Not currently open due to Hurricane Katrina, 500 St. Maurice Ave., 70117-1568. Residence for Senior Citizens & Handicapped Residential Units 110.

Villa St. Maurice II (Villa Additions) Not currently open due to Hurricane Katrina, 6101 Douglas St., 70117-2100. Residence for Senior Citizens & Handicapped Residential Units 75.

LA PLACE. *Place Dubourg, Inc.* (1981) 201 Rue Dubourg, 70068-2433. Tel: 985-652-1981; Fax: 985-651-6147. Email: lrichard@christopherhomesinc.org. Mrs. Lynn Williams, Community Mgr. Units 115; Total Staff 6; Total in Residence 116.

MANDEVILLE. *Roquette III* (1998) 4300 Hwy. 22, 70448-2824. Tel: 985-626-5217; Fax: 985-626-9226. Residential Units 61; Total Staff 3.

Rouquette Lodge (1979) St. Tammany Manor, Inc.; Residence for Senior Citizens, 4300 Hwy. 22, 70448-2824. Tel: 985-626-5217; Fax: 985-626-9226. Brenda Schouest, Community Mgr. Residential Units 119; Total in Residence 119; Total Staff 18.

Rouquette II (1983) 4300 Hwy. 22, 70448-2824. Tel: 985-626-5217; Fax: 985-626-9226. Residential Units 51; Total in Residence 51; Total Staff 3.

MARRERO. *Wynhoven Apartments and Wynhoven II* Private Non-Profit Residence for Senior Citizens Sponsored by the Archdiocese, 4600-10th St., 70072-3048. Tel: 504-347-8442; Fax: 504-340-6076. *Wynhoven II*, 4606-10th St., 70072. Tel: 504-347-3285; Fax: 504-340-6076. Jackie lynch, Community Mgr. Residents 351; Total Staff 15.

Wynhoven Health Care Center, 1050 Medical Center Blvd., 70072-3170. Tel: 504-347-0777; Fax: 504-341-7240. Web: www.wynhoven.org. Jane Fockler, Admin.; Mr. Wayne Plaisance, Exec. Dir. Bed Capacity 188; Total Assisted 183; Total Staff 201.

MERAUX. *St. Bernard Manor* Not currently open due to Hurricane Katrina, 1000 Howard Ave., Ste. 100, 70113. Tel: 504-596-3460; Fax: 504-596-3466.

St. Bernard II, 2300 Archbishop Hannan Blvd., 70075-2640.

St. Bernard III, 2440 Archbishop Hannan Blvd., 70075-2640.

METAIRIE. *Metairie Manor*, 4929 York St., 70001-1013. Tel: 504-456-1467; Fax: 504-887-3718. Flo Ronan, Community Mgr. Residential Units 369.

Metairie II

Metairie III

[O] CATHOLIC HEALTH SERVICES

NEW ORLEANS. *Daughters of Charity Services of New Orleans*, 4164 Canal St., 70119. Tel: 504-482-2080; Fax: 504-483-6016. Email: jfirstley@dcsno.org. Michael G. Griffin, Pres. & CEO. Total Staff 60.

Health Center-Metairie, 111 N. Causeway Blvd., Metairie, 70001-4540. Tel: 504-482-0084. Email: rarnaud@dcsno.org. Mr. Vincent Sessoms.

Health Center-Carrollton, 3201 S. Carrollton Ave., 70118. Tel: 504-207-3060. Email: vsessoms@dcsno.org.

Health Center-St. Cecilia, 4201 N. Rampart St., 70117-5334. Tel: 504-941-6041.

Daughters of Charity Neighborhood Health Partnership, 3201 S. Carrollton Ave., 70118. Tel: 504-231-8193; Fax: 504-483-7833. Email: alandrum@dcsno.org. Ms. Aziza Landrum, Dir. Community Care.

March of Dimes Mom & Baby Mobile Unit I, 3201 S. Carrollton Ave., 70118. Tel: 504-906-3020; Fax: 504-483-7833. Email: rforest@dcsno.org; alandrum@dcsno.org.

March of Dimes Mom & Baby Mobile Unit II, 3201 S. Carrollton Ave., 70118. Tel: 504-231-5840; Fax: 504-483-7833. Email: alandrum@dcsno.org.

Seton Center for Child & Adolescent Development, 3201 S. Carrollton Ave., 70118. Tel: 504-207-3063; Fax: 504-483-7833. Email: nmorris@dcsno.org. Nancy Morris, Prog. Dir.

CHALMETTE. *St. Bernard Health Center, Inc.*, 7718 W. Judge Perez, Arabi, 70032. Tel: 504-271-8952; Fax: 504-278-4692. Frank A. Folino, Admin.

METAIRIE. *Sisters of Mercy Ministries dba Mercy Family Center* Psychological and psychiatric evaluation, counseling and tutorial services., 110 Veterans Memorial Blvd., Ste. 425, 70005. Tel: 504-838-8283; Fax: 504-838-9799. Email: sengro@mercyfamilycenter.com. Web: www.mercyfamilycenter.com.

1445 W. Causeway Approach, Mandeville, 70471. Tel: 985-727-7993; Fax: 985-727-7016. Email: dwalker1@mercyfamilycenter.com. Elaine Moore, Pres.; Stephen J. Engro, Dir. Devel. Total Assisted 2,800; Total Staff 34.

[P] MONASTERIES AND RESIDENCES OF PRIESTS AND BROTHERS

NEW ORLEANS. *Brothers of the Sacred Heart* (1821) *Provincial Office, New Orleans Province*, 4600 Elysian Fields Ave., 70122-3826. Tel: 504-301-4758; Fax: 504-301-4843. Email: noprovince@hotmail.com. Bros. Ronald Talbot, S.C., Prov.; Ivy LeBlanc, S.C., Treas.; Chris Sweeney, S.C., Vocation Dir. *Brothers of the Sacred Heart Foundation of the New Orleans Province, Inc.* (1977) 4600 Elysian Fields Ave., 70122. Tel: 504-301-4758; Fax: 504-301-4843. Bro. Ivy LeBlanc, S.C., Exec. Dir., 1156 Park Ave., 70122. Tel: 504-488-1353. Email: bileblanc@hotmail.com.

New Orleans Residences: Bros. Chris Sweeney, S.C., 1156 City Park Ave., 70122. Tel: 504-488-1353; Francis David, S.C. Thibodaux, LA; Carl Bouchereau, S.C., 4671 Painters St., 70122. Tel: 504-324-4508; Louis Couvillon, S.C., 4671 Painters St., 70122. Tel: 504-324-4508; Neal Golden, S.C., 4671 Painters St., 70122. Tel: 504-324-4508; William Boyles, S.C., 4671 Painters St., 70122. Tel: 504-324-4508; Bosco Faget, S.C., Our Lady of Wisdom Healthcare Center, 5600 Gen. DeGaulle Dr., 70131. Tel: 504-394-5991; Warren Laudumiey, S.C. Baton Rouge, LA; Neri Falgout, S.C.

Congregation of the Mission Western Province (Vincentians), DePaul Residence, 812 Constantinople St., 70115-2726. Tel: 504-897-3976; Fax: 504-899-7603; 504-899-3603. Revs. George Weber, C.M. (Retired); Louis Arceneaux, C.M.; Donald J. Ours, C.M.; Joseph Thottamkara, C.M.

Congregation of the Mission Western Province, Louisiana

Dominican Friars, Southern Dominican Province of St. Martin de Porres (1979) *Provincial Headquarters*, 1421 N. Causeway Blvd., Ste. 200, Metairie, 70001-4144. Tel: 504-837-2129; Fax: 504-837-6604. Email: provincial@opsouth.org. Web: www.opsouth.org. Very Revs. Martin J. Gleeson, O.P., Prov.; Emiliano Zapata, O.P., Socius & Vicar Prov.; Rev. Charles L. Latour, O.P., Steward & Promoter of Vocations; Very Rev. Robert U. Perry, O.P., Promoter for Community Life & Permanent Formation. Priests in the Archdiocese 22; Brothers in the Archdiocese 3.

Assigned but working elsewhere: Revs. Armando Ibanez, O.P., Producer Dir. Chicago, IL; George Boudreau; Gustavo Montanez, O.P.

Working Abroad: Revs. James Linus Dolan, O.P., Provincia Dominicana de San Juan Bautista del Peru, Apartado 4169, Lima 1, Peru. Tel: 427-7426 (011-51-1); Fax: 427-6791 (011-51-1); Rafael Proenza, O.P., Iglesia Parroquia de la Santisima, Calle 19 #258, 70 IYJ, Vedada, Plaza 16400, Habana, Cuba. Tel: 53-7832-7329; Fax: 53-755-3724; Christopher Eggleton, O.P. (Ecuador); Charles K. Johnson, O.P.; Leobardo Almazan, O.P.; Jose D. Padilla, O.P.; Philip Neri Powell, O.P.; Marcos Ramos, O.P.; Bro. Angel Mendez (Mexico). *Dominican Vocation Sponsors*, 1421 N. Causeway Blvd., Ste. 200, Metairie, 70001-4144. Tel: 504-837-2129; Fax: 504-837-6604.

DePorres Property Corporation, 1421 N. Causeway Blvd., Ste. 200, Metairie, 70001-4144. Tel: 504-837-2129; Fax: 504-837-6604. *Southern Dominican Foundation*, 1421 N. Causeway Blvd., Ste. 200, Metairie, 70001-4144. Tel: 504-837-2129; Fax: 504-837-6604. Very Revs. Martin J. Gleeson, O.P., Pres.; Emiliano Zapata, O.P., Vice Pres. & Sec.; Revs. Charles L. Latour, O.P., Treas.; Scott O'Brien, O.P., Promoter of Devel. *Southern Dominican Global Missions*, 4640 Canal St., 70119. Tel: 504-488-2652. Bro. Herman D. Johnson, O.P., Dir.

Ignatius Residence, 6321 Stratford Pl., 70131-7325. Tel: 504-394-2411; Fax: 504-433-2882. Email: ratch123@jesuits.net. Revs. James P. Bradley, S.J., Supr.; Kenneth A. Buddendorff, S.J., Asst. Dir.; Claude P. Boudreaux, S.J. (Retired); Hacker J. Fagot, S.J. (Retired); Thomas M. Gillin, S.J. (Retired); Ernest J. Jacques, S.J.; Thomas J. Jenniskens, S.J. (Retired); Theodore M. Kalamaja, S.J.; Michael F. Kennelly, S.J. (Retired); Rodney T. Kissinger, S.J. (Retired); Roland J. Lesseps, S.J., B.S., Ph.D.; Robert M. McCown, SJ (Retired); Joseph P. McGill, S.J.; James Herbert Mead, S.J. (Retired); B. Henry Miller, S.J.; Charles E. O'Neill, S.J. (Retired); Vincent A. Orlando, S.J.; Austin N. Park, S.J. (Retired); John F. Paul, S.J.; Donald Pearce, S.J. (Retired); Louis Poche, S.J. (Retired); Herve P. Racivitch, S.J. (Retired); Robert J. Ratchford, S.J. (Retired); Fred G. Reynolds, S.J.; Bros. Charles J. Blouin, S.J., (Retired); Anthony S. Coco, S.J.; George A. Murphy, S.J., (Retired); Joseph J. Remich, S.J., (Retired); Terence N. Todd, S.J. Priests 24; Brothers 4.

Jesuit Provincial Office (1907) New Orleans Province, 710 Baronne St., Ste. B, 70113. Tel: 504-571-1055; Fax: 504-571-1744. Email: noprovsj@norprov.org. Very Rev. Mark Lewis, S.J., Ph.D., M.Div., S.T.L., Ph.L., M.A., Prov.; Mary Baudouin, Provincial Asst. for Social Min.; Revs. Stephen C. Rowntree, S.J., B.A., M.A., M.Div., M.Th., Provincial Asst. for Intl. Min.; Michael D. Dooley, S.J., B.A., M.Div., M.Ed., Provincial Asst. for Secondary Ed.; Warren J. Broussard, S.J., M.Div., M.S.W., Asst. for Pastoral and Retreat Min.; Bro. Lawrence J. Lundin, S.J., B.A., M.B.A., Treas.; Revs. Gregory Lucey, S.J., Prov. Asst. for Higher Ed.; John F. Armstrong, S.J., Prov. Asst. for Formation; Michael S. Bourg, Dir. Devel.; Revs. Paul Deutsch, S.J., Vocation Promoter; Raymond R. Fitzgerald, S.J., Socius to the Provincial.

Catholic Society of Religious and Literary Education Priests 7; Brothers 1.

Priests of the Province Abroad: Revs. Charles B. Thibodeaux, S.J., M.Div., Casa Parroquial, Santa Rosa (Misiones), Paraguay. Tel: 595-858-221; Fax: 595-858-221; Edward G. Benya, S.J., B.S., S.T.L., CP 3910, Teresina, PI 64-051-971 Brazil. Tel: 55-86-237-0666; Fax: 55-51-590-4895; A. Gerard Fineran, S.J., S.T.L., Vila Kostka C.P. 9, Indaiatuba, SP 13330-970 Brazil. Tel: 55-193-894-8555; Fax: 55-19-3894-8866; David H. Romero, S.J., B.A., M.A., CP 3937 Noviciado Ir. Vincente Canas, Manaus-AM 69085-970 Brazil. Tel: 011-55-92-682-2033; Patrick S. Madigan, S.J., B.A., M.A., S.T.L., Arrupe College, POB MP 320, Mt. Pleasant, Harare, Zimbabwe. Tel: 2634-745-411; Fax: 263-4-745-904; John R. Stacer, S.J., M.A., Ph.D., S.T.L., Arrupe College, POB MP 320, Mt. Pleasant, Harare, Zimbabwe. Tel: 2634-745-411; Fax: 2634-745-904; Joseph A. Carola, S.J., B.A., M.Div., S.T.L., S.T.D., Pontifical Gregorian Univ., Piazza della Pilotta 4, Rome 00187 Italy. Tel: 39-06-6701-5226; Fax: 39-06-6701-5419; Michael S. Gallagher, S.J., B.A., M.A., J.D., M.Div., S.T.M., Luwisha House, Plot 5880 Great East Rd., Lusaka, Zambia. Tel: 260-1-293320; Fax: 260-1-290912; David A. Brown, S.J., B.S., M.A., M.Div., Campion Hall, Oxford OX1 1QS England. Tel: 44 1865 286 135; Anthony J. Corcoran, S.J. *Jesuit Health Trust* Tel: 504-571-1055; Fax: 504-571-1744. Bro. Lawrence J. Lundin, S.J., B.A., M.B.A., Sec. *Jesuits of Pohnpei*, P.O. Box 160, Pohnpei, FM 96941-0160. Tel: 691-320-2317. Rev. David L. Andrus, S.J., B.S., M.Div. *Arrupe International Residence*, P.O. Box 216 UP 1144, Quezon City, Philippines. Tel: 632-426-5911; Fax: 632-426-5964.

Josephite Fathers and Brothers 70119. Tel: 504-944-2424. (See Separate Listing for School) *The Josephite Faculty House of St. Augustine High School*, 2600 A.P. Tureaud, 70119. Tel: 504-944-2424. Rev. Wilbur J. Atwood, S.S.J., Rector; Bro. Laurence E. Price, S.S.J., Vice Rector; Revs. Joseph M. Doyle, S.S.J.; John J. Raphael, S.S.J.; Joseph McKinley, S.S.J.

Loyola Jesuit Community, 1575 Calhoun St., 70118-6153. Tel: 504-865-3448; Fax: 504-895-0179. Rev. James P. Bradley, S.J., Pres.

Marist Fathers, 1706 Jackson Ave., 70113. Tel: 504-524-5192; Fax: 504-524-9796. Revs. Peter R. Blanchard, S.M.; Edward Fuss, S.M.; Mariano J. Rizzuto, S.M.

ST. BENEDICT. *St. Joseph Abbey* (1890) 75376 River Rd., 70457. Tel: 985-892-1800; Fax: 985-867-2270. Web: www.sjasc.edu. Rt. Revs. Justin Brown, O.S.B., Abbot; Patrick Regan, O.S.B. (Retired); Revs. Raphael Barousse, O.S.B.; Adam Begnaud, O.S.B., M.S.; Charles J. Benoit, O.S.B., M.A.Th.; Very Rev. Gregory M. Boquet, O.S.B., M.A.; Revs. Basil David Burns, O.S.B.; Matthew R. Clark, O.S.B., M.A.; Cyril K. Crawford, O.S.B., B.A., M.Div.; Jonathan M. DeFrange, O.S.B.; Sean B. Duggan, O.S.B.; Augustine E. Foley, O.S.B., M.A.Th.; Peter E. Hammett, O.S.B.; Michael Jung, O.S.B.; Aelred Kavanagh, O.S.B., M.T.S., S.T.M., S.T.D.; Killian Tolg, B.A., M.A.; William J. MacCandless, O.S.B.; Paul Miranne, O.S.B.; Lawrence J. Phelps, O.S.B.; Scott J. Underwood, O.S.B., M.T.S., M.Ed.; Ambrose G. Wathen, O.S.B. Priests 25; Brothers 13.

[Q] CONVENTS AND RESIDENCES FOR SISTERS

NEW ORLEANS. *Congregation of Divine Providence, C.D.P.* (1912) 504 Fern, 70118-3830. Tel: 504-861-0284. Web: www.cdptexas.org. Email: tabilleaud@yahoo.com.

Congregation of St. Joseph, C.S.J., 4030 Delgado Ave., 70119-3807. Web: www.csjoseph.org. Total Sisters in Archdiocese 13.

Congregation of St. Joseph Ministry Against the Death Penalty, 3009 Grand Rt. St. John #6, 70122. Tel: 504-948-6557; Fax: 504-948-6558. Web: www-.prejean.org. Sr. Geraldine Riendeau, C.S.J., Sec. & Treas.

Congregation of the Marianites of the Holy Cross (1841) 1011 Gallier St., 70117-6111. Tel: 504-945-1620; Fax: 504-944-0756. Email: mscsec@marianites.org. Web: www.marianites.org. Sr. Suellen Tennyson, M.S.C., Congregational Leader. Total Sisters in Archdiocese 55.

Congregation of the Sisters of the Holy Faith, C.H.F., 1063 Moss St., 70119. Web: www.holyfaithsisters.net. Total Sisters in Archdiocese 4.

Daughters of Charity of St. Vincent de Paul, D.C., Sisters' Residence, 1016 Eleonore St., 70115. Tel: 504-891-3102. Email: sranthony@archdiocese-no.org. Sr. Anthony Barczykowski, D.C., Sister Servant. Total Sisters in Archdiocese 37.

Daughters of Our Lady of the Holy Rosary Queen of Peace Province (1967) 1492 Moss St., 70119-2904. Tel: 504-486-0039; Fax: 504-483-7910. Email: fmsrusa@dongmancoi.org. Web: www.dongmancoi.org. Sr. Mary James Hang-Nga Thi Tran, F.M.S.R., Prov. Supr. Total Sisters in Archdiocese 55.

Dominican Sisters (Cabra, Ireland) O.P., 916 St. Andrew St., 70130. Tel: 504-522-5974. Web: www.cabraop.org. Sr. Jeanne McLoughlin, Area Prioress. Total Sisters in Archdiocese 3.

Dominican Sisters of Peace, 5660 Bancroft Dr., 70122. Tel: 504-283-1122; Fax: 504-283-1217. Email: srsueop@aol.com. Total Sisters in Archdiocese 6.

Dominican Sisters of Peace, 580 Broadway, 70118-3564. Tel: 504-865-7302; Fax: 504-865-8079. Email: srpeace@oppeace.org. Web: www.oppeace.org. 5660 Bancroft Dr., 70122-1306. Tel: 504-283-1122. Sr. Theresa Fox, O.P., Mission Group Coord. Total Sisters in Archdiocese 33.

Franciscan Poor Clares (1885) 720 Henry Clay Ave., 70118-5891. Tel: 504-895-2019; Fax: 504-899-6218. Email: sisterct@juno.com. Web: www.poorclarenuns.com. Sr. Charlene Toups, O.S.C., Abbess. Nuns of the Order of St. Clare. Solemn Professed Nuns 9.

Missionary Sisters of the Sacred Heart (Cabrini) M.S.C., 3443 Esplanade Ave., Apt. 314, 70119. Tel: 504-377-7561.

Presentation Sisters of the Blessed Virgin Mary (1968) 1802 Tulane Ave., 70112. Tel: 504-273-5573; Fax: 504-598-4297. Email: vbutler15@cox.net. Web: www.pbvmunion.org.

Union of Sisters of the Presentation of the Blessed Virgin Mary (United States Prov.)

Lantern Light, Inc. Ministry of the Union of Sisters of the Presentation of the Blessed Virgin Mary (United States Prov.), 1802 Tulane Ave., 70112. Tel: 504-273-5573; Fax: 504-598-4297. Email: vbutler7@bellsouth.net. Web: www.lanternlight-.org.

Religious of the Sacred Heart, R.S.C.J. (1800) 2545 Bayou Rd., 70119. Tel: 504-309-2828. Email: mcameron@rscj.org. Web: www.rscj.org. Sisters 9.

4600 Carondelet St., 70115-4822. Tel: 504-899-6210. Sr. Muriel Cameron, R.S.C.J., Dir. Sisters 2; Total Sisters in Archdiocese 9.

Sisters of Mercy of the Americas, R.S.M., 6024 Freret St., 70118. Tel: 504-899-4780. Email: jcarey@mercysc.org. Web: www.mercysc.org.

Sisters of Mercy of the Americas, South Central Community, Inc. Total Sisters in Archdiocese 27.

Sisters of the Blessed Sacrament, S.B.S., 3812 Pine St., 70125-1105. Tel: 504-482-0917, Ext. 31. Xavier University Convent, 3812 Pine St., 70125. Tel: 504-482-0917; Fax: 504-482-6219. *Xavier Prep*, 5116 Magazine St., 70115. Tel: 504-897-0235. *Umoja*, 5014 Howard Ave., 70125. Tel: 504-304-8991. Total Sisters in the Archdiocese 15.

Sisters of the Holy Family Motherhouse, S.S.F. (1842) 6901 Chef Menteur Hwy., 70126-5290. Tel: 504-241-3088; Fax: 504-241-9774. Email: emartinssfd@aol.com. Web: www.sistersoftheholyfamily.org. Sr. Eva Regina Martin, S.S.F., Congregational Leader; Rev. Victor H. Cohea, Chap. Total Sisters in Archdiocese 53.

Sisters, Servants of Mary, S.de.M., 5001 Perlita St., 70122-1999. Tel: 504-282-5549; Fax: 504-282-5550. Email: ssm2@cox.net. Web: sisterservantsofmary.com. Sr. Elvia Navarro, S.de.M., Supr. Total Home Nursing Sisters in Archdiocese 13.

Tau House, 1029 Gov. Nicholls St., 70116-2432. Tel: 504-529-3569. Email: roddyssnd@aol.com; margmary27@hotmail.com. Sisters Ann Roddy, S.S.N.D, B.A., M.A., Admin.; Margaret Mary Friesenhahn, S.S.N.D., B.A., M.A. Center for the Empowerment of those infected with or affected by HIV/AIDS. Total in Residence 2; Total Staff 3.

Ursuline Sisters of the Roman Union, O.S.U. (1727) 2734 Nashville Ave., 70115. Tel: 504-866-1472; Fax: 504-866-8300. Sr. Carolyn Brockland, O.S.U., Prioress. Total Sisters in Archdiocese 8.

COVINGTON. *Carmelite Nuns, Discalced, O.C.D., Monastery of St. Joseph and St. Teresa* (1877) 73530 River Rd., 70435-2206. Tel: 985-898-0923; Fax: 985-871-9333. Email: covingtoncarmel@yahoo.com. Web: www.covingtoncarmelite.org. Professed Nuns 7; Junior Professed 1; Novices 1; Postulants 1.

Daughters of Divine Providence, F.D.P. (1832) 74684 Airport Rd., 70435-5621. Tel: 985-809-8854; Fax: 985-809-8854. Email: divineprovidence@netzero.net. Total Sisters in Archdiocese 13.

Teresian Sisters (Society of St. Teresa of Jesus), S.T.J., Provincial Office, 18080 St. Joseph's Way, 70435-5623. Tel: 985-893-1470; Fax: 985-893-2476. Email: teresians@aol.com. Web: www.teresians.org. Sr. Gina Marie Geraci, S.T.J., Prov. Sisters 13.

Formation House, 18158 St. Joseph's Way, 70435-5624. Tel: 985-893-1557; Fax: 985-871-0724. Email: claricestj@excite.com. Sr. Clarice Suchy, S.T.J., Community Coord.

LACOMBE. *Congregation of Our Lady of Mount Carmel, O.Carm.* (1833) *Generalate*, P.O. Box 476, 70445-0476. Tel: 985-882-7577; 504-524-2398; Fax: 504-524-5011. Sr. Elizabeth Fitzpatrick, O.Carm., M.A., Pres. Sisters 82. *Mount Carmel Development Office*, P.O. Box 1160, 70445-1160. Tel: 985-882-7577; 504-524-2398; Fax: 504-524-5011.

Cub Corner Tel: 504-286-8673; Fax: 504-286-8676. Sr. Gwen Grillot, O.Carm., Exec. Dir. Total Staff 17; Total Enrollment 52.

Carmelite Spirituality Center (2004) 62292 Fish Hatchery Rd., P.O. Box 130, 70445-0130. Tel: 985-882-7579; Fax: 504-524-5011; 985-882-6563. Email: carmelcenter@bellsouth.net. Web: www.carmelitespirituality.org.

MARRERO. *Salesian Sisters (Daughters of Mary Help of Christians) F.M.A.*, 2605 Crestwood Rd., 70072-2016. Tel: 504-347-4887. Email: fmamarrero@aol.com. Web: www.salesiansisters.org. Sisters in Archdiocese 5.

METAIRIE. *Daughters of St. Paul Convent, F.S.P.*, Pauline Book & Media Center, 4403 Veterans Memorial Blvd., 70006-5321. Tel: 504-887-7631; Fax: 504-887-1357. Email: neworleans@pauline.org. Total Sisters in Archdiocese 5.

Incarnate Word Sisters, C.C.V.I., 80 Metairie Ct., 70001-3032. Tel: 504-833-7972. Total Sisters in Archdiocese 4.

Religious of Our Lady of the Retreat in the Cenacle, R.C., The Cenacle Retreat House, 5500 St. Mary St., 70006. Tel: 504-887-1420; Fax: 504-887-6624. Email: cenacle2@aol.com. Web: www.cenaclesisters.org/metairie. Sr. Ann Wylder, R.C., Coord. Sisters 6; Total Staff 18.

Sisters of the Living Word, S.L.W., 4900 Park Dr., 70001-3237. Tel: 504-888-6676. Email: srstump@steddy.org. Web: www.slw.org. Sisters 2; Total Sisters in Archdiocese 9.

[R] RETREAT HOUSES

NEW ORLEANS. *Archdiocesan Spirituality Center*, 2901 S. Carrollton Ave., 70118-4391. Tel: 504-861-3254; Fax: 504-861-0584. Sr. Noel Toomey, O.P., M.A., Exec. Dir.

Center of Jesus the Lord, 1236 N. Rampart St., 70116-2497. Tel: 504-529-1636; Fax: 504-529-5003. Email: office@centerofjesusthelord.org. Web: www.centerofjesusthelord.org. Total Assisted 318; Total Staff 9; Total in Residence 2.

Sophie Barat House, 1719 Napoleon Ave., 70115-4809. Tel: 504-899-6027; Fax: 504-899-6210. Email: jmckinlay@rscj.org. Sisters Mary Blish, R.S.C.J.; Jane McKinlay, R.S.C.J. Total Staff 6; Total in Residence 4.

LACOMBE. *Carmelite Spirituality Center*, 62292 Fish Hatchery Rd., P.O. Box 130, 70445-0130. Tel: 985-882-7579; Fax: 985-882-6563. Email: carmelcenter@bellsouth.net. Web: www.carmelitespirituality.org. Sisters Barbara Breaud, O.Carm., Exec. Dir.; Terry Falco, R.S.M., Program Dir.; Lena Collins, O.Carm., House Dir.

METAIRIE. *Cenacle Retreat House* (1958) 5500 St. Mary St., 70006. Tel: 504-887-1420; Fax: 504-887-6624. Email: cenacle2@aol.com. Web: www.cenaclesisters.org/metairie. Sr. Ann Wylder, R.C., Retreat House Admin. Religious 6; Total Staff 22.

PONCHATOULA. *Magnificat Center of the Holy Spirit*, 23629 Faith Rd., 70454. Tel: 985-386-5815; 800-531-9710; Fax: 504-200-7771. Total in Residence 90; Total Staff 4.

ST. BENEDICT. *Abbey Christian Life Center*, 75276 River Rd., Saint Benedict, 70457-9900. Tel: 985-892-3473; 985-892-1800; Fax: 985-892-3448. Conducted by Benedictine Monks

[S] MISCELLANEOUS

NEW ORLEANS. *Christian Brothers Foundation*, 8 Friederichs Ave., 70124-4602. Tel: 504-488-2802; Fax: 504-486-1053. Email: foundation@cbs-no.org.

Jesuit Seminary and Mission Fund, 710 Baronne St., Ste. B, 70113-1064. Tel: 504-571-1055; Fax: 504-571-1744. Email: jesuits@norprov.org. Web: www.norprov.org. Michael S. Bourg, Exec. Dir., Devel.

**Pan African Roman Catholic Clergy Conference* (1999) 4230 S. Broad St., 70125-3660. Tel: 504-822-3394; Fax: 504-822-3397. Revs. Christopher Coleman, Ph.D., Pres.; Victor H. Cohea, Treas.

The Patrons of the Vatican Museums in the South, Inc. (1985) 775 Harrison Ave., 70124-3192. Tel: 504-482-4158; Fax: 504-485-0906. Email: vmcinnes@att.net. Very Rev. Val A. McInnes, O.P., Founder & Pres. Emeritus; Dr. Rudolph H. Ehrensing, Pres.

Pierre Toussaint Foundation of New Orleans, Inc. (1995) 2600 A.P. Tureaud Ave., 70119-1299. Tel: 504-949-3113; Fax: 504-945-4134. Email: josmdoyle@netscape.net. Rev. Joseph M. Doyle, S.S.J., Pres.

**Second Harvest Food Bank of Greater New Orleans and Acadiana* (1982) 1201 Sams Ave., 70123-2236. Tel: 504-734-1322; Fax: 504-733-8336. Web: www.no-hunger.org. Total Staff 30.

Stella Roman Foundation, Inc., 1010 Common St., Ste. 3010, 70112. Tel: 504-522-4756; Fax: 504-568-0783. Email: cidlaw@bellsouth.net. Rev. Msgr. Francis G. Boeshans, Pres. (Retired).

ABITA SPRINGS. *The Christ in Christmas Committee of New Orleans*, 123 Iroquis Dr., 70420. Tel: 985-893-0169. Email: kcicno@bellsouth.net. Stephen F. Hart, Chm.

LACOMBE. *MCA Foundation*, P.O. Box 476, 70445-0476. Tel: 504-288-7626, Ext. 137; Fax: 504-288-7629. Email: mca@mcacubs.org. Web: www.mtcarmelcubs.org. Sr. Elizabeth Fitzpatrick, O.Carm., M.A., Pres.

METAIRIE. *Equestrian Order of the Holy Sepulchre* (of Jerusalem, Southeastern Lieutenancy of the U.S.), 2955 Ridgelake Dr., Ste. 205, 70002. Tel: 504-832-0892; Fax: 504-832-1929. Email: office@sleohs.com. Anthony J. Capritto, Lieutenant.

International Dominican Foundation (2002) One Galleria Blvd., Ste. 710-B, 70001. Tel: 504-836-8180; Fax: 504-836-8189. Email: info@idfla.org. Most Rev. Donald W. Wuerl, S.T.D., Chm. Bd.; Very Revs. Mark Edney, O.P., Pres.; Val A. McInnes, O.P., Pres. Emeritus.

124 Airline Drive, Inc., 124 Airline Dr., 70001. Tel: 504-486-6631; Fax: 504-483-3816. Rev. Anthony F. McGinn, S.J., Pres.

Southern Dominican Foundation, 1421 N. Causeway Blvd., Ste. 200, 70001-4144. Tel: 504-837-2129; Fax: 504-837-6604. Email: provincial@opsouth.org. Web: www.opsouth.org. Very Revs. Martin J. Gleeson, O.P., Pres.; Emiliano Zapata, O.P., Vice Pres. & Sec.; Revs. Charles L. Latour, O.P., Treas.; Scott O'Brien, O.P., Promoter Devel.

Southern Dominican Global Missions, 4640 Canal St., 70119. Tel: 504-488-2652. Bro. Herman D. Johnson, O.P., Dir.

**Willwoods Community* (1978) 3330 N. Causeway Blvd., Ste. 345, 70002. Tel: 504-830-3700; Fax: 504-840-9838. Email: t.chambers@willwoods.org. Web: www.willwoods.org. Rev. Thomas E. Chambers, C.S.C., Ph.D., Pres.

**WLAE-TV, Educational Broadcasting Foundation, Inc.*, 3330 N. Causeway Blvd., Ste. 345, 70002. Tel: 504-866-7411; Fax: 504-840-9838. Email: info@wlae.com. Web: www.wlae.com.

SECULAR INSTITUTES

ABITA SPRINGS. *Caritas* (1950) *Administration Center*, P.O. Box 308, 70420-0308. Tel: 985-892-4345. Email: caritas11r@aol.com.

Daraja House (1980) P.O. Box 524, Covington, 70434. Tel: 985-893-2261.

RELIGIOUS INSTITUTES OF MEN REPRESENTED IN THE ARCHDIOCESE

For further details refer to the corresponding bracketed number in the Religious Institutes of Men or Women section.

[0200]—*Benedictine Monks*—O.S.B.
[0330]—*Brothers of the Christian Schools* (New Orleans Prov.)—F.S.C.
[0470]—*The Capuchin Friars*—O.F.M.Cap.
[]—*Congregation of Christian Brothers (Edmund Rice)*—C.F.C.
[1330]—*Congregation of the Mission of St. Vincent de Paul Fathers & Brothers* (Southern Prov.)—C.M.
[]—*Congregation of the Mother Coredemptrix*—C.M.C.
[0260]—*Discalced Carmelite Friars*—O.C.D.
[0520]—*Franciscan Friars*—O.F.M.
[0690]—*Jesuit Fathers and Brothers* (New Orleans)—S.J.
[0780]—*Marist Fathers and Brothers* (USA Prov.)—S.M.
[0910]—*Oblates of Mary Immaculate* (Southern American Prov.)—O.M.I.
[0430]—*Order of Preacher-Dominicans* (St Martin de Porres/Southern Prov.)—O.P.
[1100]—*Priests and Brothers of the Sacred Heart* (Metuchen, NJ)—S.C.
[0610]—*Priests of the Congregation of Holy Cross* (Southern Prov.; Indiana Prov.)—C.S.C.
[1070]—*Redemptorist Fathers and Brothers* (New Orleans)—C.Ss.R.
[1190]—*Salesians of Don Bosco*—S.D.B.
[0440]—*Society of St. Edmund*—S.S.E.
[0420]—*Society of the Divine Word* (St. Augustine Prov.)—S.V.D.
[0700]—*St. Joseph's Society of the Sacred Heart* (Baltimore, MD)—S.S.J.

RELIGIOUS INSTITUTES OF WOMEN REPRESENTED IN THE ARCHDIOCESE

[0230]—*Benedictine Sisters of Pontifical Jurisdiction* (Colorado)—O.S.B.
[0400]—*Congregation of Our Lady of Mount Carmel*—O.Carm.
[3110]—*Congregation of Our Lady of the Retreat in the Cenacle*—R.C.
[1940]—*Congregation of Sisters of the Holy Faith*—C.H.F.
[2410]—*Congregation of the Marianites of Holy Cross*—M.S.C.
[0460]—*Congregation of the Sisters of Charity of the Incarnate Word*—C.C.V.I.
[3832]—*Congregation of the Sisters of St. Joseph*—C.S.J.
[1950]—*Congregation of the Sisters of the Holy Family*—S.S.F.
[0800]—*Daughters of Divine Providence*—F.D.P.
[0850]—*Daughters of Mary Help of Christians*—F.M.A.
[0895]—*Daughters of Our Lady of the Holy Rosary*—F.M.S.R.
[0760]—*Daughters of St. Vincent de Paul*—D.C.
[0420]—*Discalced Carmelite Nuns*—O.C.D.
[1110]—*Dominican Sisters of Our Lady of the Rosary and of Saint Catherine of Siena, Cabra, Ireland*—O.P.
[]—*Dominican Sisters of Peace*—O.P.
[1115]—*Dominican Sisters of Peace*—O.P.
[]—*Lovers of the Holy Cross Sisters at Cho Quan*—L.H.C.
[2860]—*Missionary Sisters of the Sacred Heart*—M.S.C.
[0950]—*Pious Society Daughters of St. Paul*—F.S.P.
[3760]—*Poor Clare Nuns, Order of St. Clare*—O.S.C.
[2970]—*School Sisters of Notre Dame* (Dallas & Mankato)—S.S.N.D.
[0660]—*Sisters of Christian Charity* (Wilmette, IL)—S.C.C.
[1010]—*Sisters of Divine Providence of San Antonio, Texas*—C.D.P.
[2575]—*Sisters of Mercy of the Americas* (Brooklyn; St. Louis)—R.S.M.
[2630]—*Sisters of Mercy of the Holy Cross*—S.C.S.C.
[1670]—*Sisters of St. Francis of Savannah*—O.S.F.
[1530]—*Sisters of St. Francis of the Congregation of Our Lady of Lourdes, Sylvania, Ohio*—O.S.F.
[0260]—*Sisters of the Blessed Sacrament for Indians and Colored People*—S.B.S.
[2050]—*Sisters of the Holy Spirit and Mary Immaculate*—S.H.Sp.
[2120]—*Sisters of the Immaculate Conception*—C.I.C.
[2350]—*Sisters of the Living Word*—S.L.W.

[3600]—*Sisters Servants of Mary*—S.de.M.
[4020]—*Society of St. Teresa of Jesus*—S.T.J.
[4060]—*Society of the Holy Child Jesus*—S.H.C.J.
[4070]—*Society of the Sacred Heart*—R.S.C.J.
[3330]—*Union of the Sisters of the Presentation of the Blessed Virgin Mary*—P.B.V.M.
[4110]—*Ursuline Nuns*—O.S.U.

NECROLOGY

✠ D'Antonio, Most Rev. Nicholas, Prelate Emeritus, Ordinary of Olancho, Honduras, C.A.—Died Aug. 1, 2009

An asterisk (*) denotes an organization that has established tax-exempt status directly with the IRS and is not covered by the USCCB Group Ruling.

Diocese of New Ulm

(Dioecesis Novae Ulmae)

Most Reverend

JOHN M. LEVOIR

Bishop of New Ulm; ordained May 30, 1981; appointed Bishop of New Ulm July 14, 2008; ordained September 15, 2008. *Office: 1400 6th St. N., New Ulm, MN 56073-2099.*

Diocesan Pastoral Center: 1400 6th Street North, New Ulm, MN 56073-2099. Tel: 507-359-2966; Fax: 507-354-3667.

Web: www.dnu.org

Email: dnu@dnu.org

ESTABLISHED NOVEMBER 18, 1957.

Square Miles 9,863.

Comprises the Counties of Big Stone, Brown, Chippewa, Kandiyohi, Lac Qui Parle, Lincoln, Lyon, McLeod, Meeker, Nicollet, Redwood, Renville, Sibley, Swift, and Yellow Medicine in the State of Minnesota.

For legal titles of parishes and diocesan institutions, consult the Diocesan Pastoral Center.

STATISTICAL OVERVIEW

Personnel	
Bishop	1
Priests: Diocesan Active in Diocese	42
Priests: Diocesan in Foreign Missions	2
Priests: Retired, Sick or Absent	22
Number of Diocesan Priests	66
Total Priests in Diocese	66
Extern Priests in Diocese	3
Permanent Deacons in Diocese	3
Total Sisters	62
Parishes	
Parishes	76
With Resident Pastor:	
Resident Diocesan Priests	39
Without Resident Pastor:	
Administered by Priests	26
Administered by Religious Women	7
Administered by Lay People	4
Closed Parishes	1
Professional Ministry Personnel:	

Sisters	11
Lay Ministers	54
Welfare	
Catholic Hospitals	1
Total Assisted	8,718
Health Care Centers	2
Total Assisted	9,054
Homes for the Aged	6
Total Assisted	292
Residential Care of Disabled	2
Educational	
Diocesan Students in Other Seminaries	9
Total Seminarians	9
High Schools, Diocesan and Parish	3
Total Students	389
Elementary Schools, Diocesan and Parish	16
Total Students	1,918
Catechesis/Religious Education:	
High School Students	2,719

Elementary Students	5,445
Total Students under Catholic Instruction	10,480
Teachers in the Diocese:	
Sisters	3
Lay Teachers	157
Vital Statistics	
Receptions into the Church:	
Infant Baptism Totals	849
Minor Baptism Totals	35
Adult Baptism Totals	15
Received into Full Communion	76
First Communions	914
Confirmations	932
Marriages:	
Catholic	198
Interfaith	128
Total Marriages	326
Deaths	690
Total Catholic Population	63,011
Total Population	281,802

Former Bishops—Most Revs. ALPHONSE J. SCHLADWEILER, D.D., ord. June 9, 1929; appt. Nov. 28, 1957; cons. Jan. 29, 1958; installed Jan. 30, 1958; retired Dec. 23, 1975; died April 3, 1996; RAYMOND A. LUCKER, S.T.D., ord. June 7, 1952; appt. Titular Bishop of Meta and Auxiliary Bishop of St. Paul & Minneapolis July 12, 1971; cons. Sept. 8, 1971; appt. Bishop of New Ulm, Dec. 23, 1975; installed Feb. 19, 1976; retired Nov. 17, 2000; died Sept. 19, 2001; JOHN C. NIENSTEDT, ord. July 27, 1974; appt. Auxiliary Bishop of Detroit June 12, 1996; ord. July 9, 1996; appt. Bishop of New Ulm June 12, 2001; installed Aug. 6, 2001; appt. Coadjutor Archbishop of Saint Paul and Minneapolis April 24, 2007.

Diocesan Officials

Diocesan Pastoral Center—Most Rev. JOHN M. LEVOIR, 1400 6th Street North, New Ulm, 56073-2099. Tel: 507-359-2966; Fax: 507-354-3667.

Vicar General—Rev. Msgr. DOUGLAS L. GRAMS, J.C.L., 1400 6th St. N., New Ulm, 56073-2099. Tel: 507-359-2966; Fax: 507-354-3667.

Chancellor—Rev. Msgr. EUGENE L. LOZINSKI, Diocesan Pastoral Center, 1400 6th St. N., New Ulm, 56073-2099. Tel: 507-359-2966, Ext. 315; Fax: 507-354-3667.

Vice-Chancellor—Rev. JOHN G. BERGER, Church of St. Gregory the Great, 440 6th St., P.O. Box 5, Lafayette, 56054-0005. Tel: 507-228-8298.

Diocesan Tribunal—

Judicial Vicar (Officialis)—Rev. JOHN G. BERGER, Church of St. Gregory the Great, 440 6th St., P.O. Box 5, Lafayette, 56054-0005. Tel: 507-228-8298.

Moderator—MICHELLE FLOOD, Diocesan Pastoral Center, 1400 6th St. N., New Ulm, 56073-2099. Tel: 507-359-2966; Fax: 507-354-3667.

Associate Judges—Rev. Msgr. EUGENE L. LOZINSKI; Rev. PAUL L. WOLF; Rev. Msgr. DOUGLAS L. GRAMS, J.C.L.

Defender of the Bond—Rev. MARK S. MALLAK.

Office Manager—JANELLE BOYUM. Tel: 507-359-2966.

Notary—JANELLE BOYUM.

Diocesan Boards and Councils

Building Committee—Revs. GEORGE V. SCHMIT JR., Chm., Church of St. Mary, 220 S. 10th St., P.O. Box 500, Bird Island, 55310-0500. Tel: 320-365-3593; Fax: 320-365-3142; MICHAEL M. DOYLE; KAY OSBORNE; Mr. JOE EIKMEIER; Mr. RAYMOND MARTIN; ANN PRZYBILLA; Mr. RICHARD GREENE.

College of Consultors—Rev. Msgrs. DOUGLAS L. GRAMS, J.C.L.; EUGENE L. LOZINSKI; Revs. ANTHONY R. HESSE; JEROME E. PAULSON; STEVEN J. VERHELST; PAUL H. VAN DE CROMMERT.

Priests' Council—Rev. Msgrs. DOUGLAS L. GRAMS, J.C.L.; EUGENE L. LOZINSKI; Revs. KEITH R. SALISBURY; ANDREW J. MICHELS; ROBERT J. MRAZ; JAMES W. DEVORAK; PAUL H. VAN DE CROMMERT; BRIAN W. OESTREICH; ANTHONY R. HESSE; JEROME E. PAULSON; STEVEN J. VERHELST.

Committee on Parishes—Revs. PAUL D. TIMMERMAN; ANTHONY J. STUBEDA; BRIAN W. OESTREICH; Rev. Msgr. DOUGLAS L. GRAMS, J.C.L.; Revs. GEORGE V. SCHMIT JR.; RONALD V. HUBERTY, Chm.; DOLORES BERG; Sr. MARY KAY MAHOWALD, O.S.F.; CHRISTIE FOX; LAURIE YACKLEY; WAYNE CARLSON; SHIRLEY NOWAK; Sr. VIVIAN PETERSEN, O.S.B.; DAN J. ROSSINI, (Staff Liaison). On Call Members: KARLA CROSS; Sr. ANNA MARIE REHA, S.S.N.D.

Property Committee—ANDY RHODE, Chm.; Rev. JOHN H. BRUNNER; PHILIP LIESCH; BILL BRENNAN; MICHAEL H. BOYLE; DAN J. ROSSINI; THOMAS J. HOLZER, Staff Liaison.

Corporate Board—Most Rev. JOHN M. LEVOIR; Rev. Msgr. EUGENE L. LOZINSKI; MICHAEL H. BOYLE; Mr. PAUL A. ZINS; Rev. Msgr. DOUGLAS L. GRAMS, J.C.L.

Diocesan Pastoral Council—ROSE MARY KIRTZ, Chm., 520 2nd St. E., Hector, 55342. Tel: 320-848-2167; TOM GREEN, Vice Chm.; LINDA BUSCH, Sec. Members: Sr. CAROLE FREKING, O.S.F.; JERRY BROWN; MICHAEL BREDECK; JOANNE GREEN; DARREL BREYFOGLE; BARB KLOSTER; MARY SCHMITZ; ARLYCE ANDERSON; Sr. ANN CAROL KAUFENBERG, S.S.N.D.; RON POLMAN; JAN RAUENHORST; BRUCE BOT; Sr. JUDI ANGST, O.S.F.; JIM HUBLEY; DIANA KROELLS.

Finance Council—Rev. JEFFREY P. HOREJSI; DAVID CZECH; JERRY REITER; CHRIS HEIDERSCHEIDT; LORI THUL; DON CLASEMANN; DAVID LYNN; STEVE SCHREIBER; THOMAS J. HOLZER, Staff Liaison.

Sisters' Council—Sisters CARMEN SONNEK, O.S.F., Chm.; CAROLE FREKING, O.S.F., Vice Chm.; LUCILLE HASS, O.S.F., Sec. & Treas.; ANN CAROL KAUFENBERG, S.S.N.D., Diocesan Pastoral Council Rep.; THERESE COLLISON, S.S.N.D., E & C Rep.; MARY KAY MAHOWALD, O.S.F., Committee on Parishes Rep.

Diocesan Pastoral Center

Coordinator of Diocesan Staff— Pastoral Planning and Human Resources DAN J. ROSSINI, Diocesan Pastoral Center, 1400 6th St. N., New Ulm, 56073-2099. Tel: 507-359-2966, Ext. 322; 507-233-5322; Fax: 507-354-3667. Email: drossini@dnu.org.

Office of Finance and Cemeteries—THOMAS J. HOLZER, Dir., Diocesan Pastoral Center, 1400 6th St. N., New Ulm, 56073-2099. Tel: 507-359-2966, Ext. 309; 507-233-5309; Fax: 507-354-3667. Email: tomholzer@dnu.org.

Office of Development and Diocesan Foundation—Mr. WAYNE A. PELZEL, Dir., Diocesan Pastoral Center, 1400 6th St. N., New Ulm, 56073-2099. Tel: 507-359-2966, Ext. 310;

507-233-5310; Fax: 507-354-3667. Email: wpelzel@dnu.org.

Evangelization and Catechesis—

Religious Education and Faith Formation—BRYAN REISING, D.R.E. Tel: 507-359-2966, Ext. 324; 507-233-5324. Email: breising@dnu.org.

Catholic Schools—KARLA CROSS. Tel: 507-359-2966, Ext. 323; 507-233-5323. Email: kcross@dnu.org.

Lay Ecclesial Certification—KARLA CROSS, Coord.

Youth Ministry and Vocation Awareness—Sr. MARGARET MCHUGH, Dir., Diocesan Pastoral Center, 1400 6th St. N., New Ulm, 56073-2099. Tel: 507-359-2966, Ext. 327; 507-233-5327; Fax: 507-354-3667. Email: mmchugh@dnu.org.

Riverbend TEC (Together Encounter Christ)—Rev. DENNIS C. LABAT, Coord., Church of St. Raphael, 112 W. Van Dusen, Springfield, 56087-1396. Tel: 507-723-4141. Email: riverbendtec@newulmtel.net. Web: www.riverbendtec.org.

Committee for Evangelization & Catechesis—Sr. JUDI ANGST, O.S.F., Chm.; DIANA M. MCCARNEY; BRENDA LENERTZ; Sr. THERESE COLLISON, S.S.N.D.; RON SKJONG; Rev. PAUL D. TIMMERMAN. Ex Officio Members: KARLA CROSS; Sr. MARGARET MCHUGH; BRYAN REISING.

Communications and Advancement—Sr. MARY CHARLES MAYER, R.S.M., Dir. Tel: 507-359-2966, Ext. 333; 507-233-5333.

"Prairie Catholic"—Co Editors: Sr. MARY CHARLES MAYER, R.S.M. Tel: 507-359-2966, Ext. 333; 507-233-5333. Email: smcmayer@dnu.org; CHRISTINE CLANCY, Diocesan Pastoral Center, 1400 6th St. N., New Ulm, 56073-2099. Tel: 507-359-2966, Ext. 332; 507-233-5332; Fax: 507-354-3667. Email: cclancy@dnu.org.

Office of Worship and Lay Ministry—ANGELA J. PRZYBILLA, Dir. Tel: 507-359-2966, Ext. 320; 507-233-5320. Email: aprzybilla@dnu.org.

Worship Committee—Sr. JOANNE BACKES, O.S.B.; SARAH JIRAK; MARY BOLEK; LESLIE BRINKMAN; MARGE MARTIN; Sr. ELIZABETH GRUENES, O.S.B.; Rev. ANTHONY R. HESSE; ANN PRZYBILLA, Staff Liaison.

Charismatic Renewal—JAN CROWE, Diocesan Liaison, 21907 705th Ave., Dassel, 55325. Tel: 320-275-2424.

Ecumenism and Interreligious Affairs—Rev. PAUL D. TIMMERMAN, 636 1st Ave. N., Sleepy Eye, 56085-1004. Tel: 507-794-4171. Email: fatherpaultimmerman@gmail.com.

Office of Social Concerns and Family Life—CHRISTOPHER A. LOETSCHER, Dir., Diocesan Pastoral Center, 1400 6th St. N., New Ulm, 56073-2099. Tel: 507-359-2966, Ext. 338; 507-233-5338; Fax: 507-354-3667. Email: cloetscher@dnu.org.

Social Concerns Committee—Rev. JEFFREY P. HOREJSI; PAUL HAYDEN; Sr. DONNA WERMUS, S.S.N.D.; EILEEN WALLACE; JIM HUBLEY; THOMAS P. KEAVENY. Ex Officio: Sr. ANNA MARIE REHA, S.S.N.D.; Rev. PHILIP M. SCHOTZKO; CHRISTOPHER A. LOETSCHER, Staff Liaison.

Catholic Charities—Tel: 507-359-2617; 866-670-5163. THOMAS P. KAEVENY, Consultant. Tel: 320-359-2966; 320-233-5349; SAM RICKERTSEN, Counselor. Tel: 507-233-5344. Catholic Charities Advisors: BARB DIETZ; MEG DWYER-LEE; Sr. CAROLE FREKING, O.S.F.; NOEL "CHUCK" KOENIGS; CINDY NELSON; Rev. PAUL A. SCHUMACHER; SUE SERBUS; THOMAS P. KEAVENY, Staff Liaison. Ex Officio: Diocesan Staff: Sr. ANNA MARIE REHA, S.S.N.D.; CHRISTOPHER A. LOETSCHER; THOMAS J. HOLZER; Mr. WAYNE A. PELZEL.

Family Life—CHRISTOPHER A. LOETSCHER, Dir., Diocesan Pastoral Center, 1400 6th St. N., New Ulm, 56073-2099. Tel: 507-359-2966, Ext. 338; 507-233-5338; Fax: 507-354-3667. Email: cloetscher@dnu.org. Marriage Preparation, Natural Family Planning, Resources & Referral for Marriage & Family Concerns, Divorced/Separated.

Retrouvaille—Tel: 800-470-2230.

Family Life Education—Sr. CANDACE FIER, I.S.S.M., 1400 6th St. N., New Ulm, 56073-2099. Tel: 507-359-2966; Fax: 507-354-3667. Email: cfier@dnu.org.

AIDS Ministry—Rev. PAUL A. SCHUMACHER, Church of St. Dionysius, P.O. Box 310, Tyler, 56178-0310. Tel: 507-247-3464; Fax: 507-247-3286.

Propagation of the Faith/Holy Childhood Association—Rev. PHILIP M. SCHOTZKO, Diocesan Pastoral Center, 1400 6th St. N., New Ulm, 56073-2099. Tel: 507-359-2966; Fax: 507-354-3667.

San Lucas Mission Office—Rev. Msgr. GREGORY T. SCHAFFER; KATHY HUEBERT, Diocesan Pastoral Center, 1400 6th St. N., New Ulm, 56073-2099. Tel: 507-359-2966, Ext. 304; Fax: 507-354-3667. Email: khuebert@dnu.org.

Hispanic Ministry—Sr. ANNA MARIE REHA, S.S.N.D., Diocesan Pastoral Center, 1400 6th St. N., New Ulm, 56073-2099. Tel: 507-359-2966, Ext. 321; 507-233-5321; Fax: 507-354-3667. Email: areha@dnu.org.

Office of Personnel—

Priest Personnel—Rev. Msgr. DOUGLAS L. GRAMS, J.C.L., Exec. Dir., Diocesan Pastoral Center, 1400 6th St. N., New Ulm, 56073-2099. Tel: 507-359-2966, Ext. 303; Fax: 507-354-3667.

Priest Personnel Board—Rev. Msgr. DOUGLAS L. GRAMS, J.C.L., Exec. Dir.; Rev. DENNIS C. LABAT; Rev. Msgr. EUGENE L. LOZINSKI; Revs. TODD J. PETERSEN; GEORGE V. SCHMIT JR.; RONALD V. HUBERTY; Rev. Msgr. JOHN A. RICHTER.

Pastoral Administrators—Rev. DENNIS C. LABAT, Supvr., Diocesan Pastoral Center, 1400 6th St. N., New Ulm, 56073-2099. Tel: 507-359-2966, Ext. 316; Fax: 507-354-3667. Email: dlabat@newulmtel.net.

Victim Assistance Coordinator—CHRISTOPHER A. LOETSCHER. Tel: 507-359-2966, Ext. 338; 507-233-5338; Fax: 507-354-3667. Email: cloetscher@dnu.org.

Bishop's Delegate in Matters Pertaining to Sexual Misconduct—Rev. Msgr. DOUGLAS L. GRAMS, J.C.L., Diocesan Pastoral Center, 1400 6th St. N., New Ulm, 56073-2099. Tel: 507-359-2966; Fax: 507-354-3667.

Bishop's Delegate for the Permanent Diaconate—Rev. Msgr. EUGENE L. LOZINSKI. Tel: 320-864-5162; 320-864-2963 (Rectory); Fax: 320-864-5163.

Safe Environment Coordinator—Sr. CANDACE FIER, I.S.S.M., 1400 6th St. N., New Ulm, 56073. Tel: 507-359-2966; Fax: 507-354-3667. Email: cfier@dnu.org.

Office of Conciliation—MICHELLE FLOOD, Dir., 1400 6th St. N., New Ulm, 56073-2099. Tel: 507-359-2966; Fax: 507-354-3667.

Vocations Team—Most Rev. JOHN M. LEVOIR, Team Chm.; Revs. TODD J. PETERSEN, Dir., Diocesan Pastoral Center, 1400 6th St. N., New Ulm, 56073-2099. Tel: 507-359-2966, Ext. 331; 507-233-5331; 507-342-5155; Fax: 507-354-3667. Email: toddpetersen@mac.com; CRAIG A. TIMMERMAN, Asst. Dir., Diocesan Pastoral Center, 1400 6th St. N., New Ulm, 56073. Tel: 507-359-2966; Fax: 507-354-3667. Email: fathercraig@gmail.com; Sr. MARGARET MCHUGH, Coord., Vocation Fairs & Other Program Events, Diocesan Pastoral Center, 1400 6th St. N., New Ulm, 56073-2099. Tel: 507-359-2966, Ext. 327; 507-233-5327; Fax: 507-354-3667. Email: mmchugh@dnu.org.

Continuing Education—KARLA CROSS, Dir., Diocesan Pastoral Center, 1400 6th St. N., New Ulm, 56073-2099. Tel: 507-359-2966, Ext. 323; Fax: 507-354-3667.

Committee for Continuing Education of Clergy—Revs. JOHN A. PEARSON; MARK S. STEFFL; CRAIG A. TIMMERMAN; Sr. DONNA WERMUS, S.S.N.D.

Board of Trustees for Pension Plan for Priests—Most Rev. JOHN M. LEVOIR; Rev. Msgrs. DOUGLAS L. GRAMS, J.C.L.; EUGENE L. LOZINSKI; Revs. ROBERT P. GOBLIRSCH; STEVEN J. VERHELST; DONALD GUGGEMOS JR.; MICHAEL SCHWARTZ; THOMAS J. HOLZER, Staff Liaison.

Vicar for Retired Priests—Rev. Msgr. FRANCIS J. GARVEY, 57482 CSAH 3, Grove City, 56243-9786. Tel: 320-693-8900; Fax: 320-693-8900. Email: frgarvey@meltel.net.

Organizations in the Diocese of New Ulm

Diocesan Council of Catholic Women—JEANE APPEL, Pres., 109 S. Harrison, Lake Benton, 56149. Tel: 507-368-4341. Email: jappel@itctel.com; Rev. Msgr. EUGENE L. LOZINSKI, Diocesan Moderator.

Girl Scouts—MARY HAUSER, 4313 N.E. 15th St., Willmar, 56201. Tel: 320-235-3471.

Boy Scouts—Rev. ANDREW J. MICHELS, Chap., St. Mary, 636 1st Ave. N., Sleepy Eye, 56085-1004. Tel: 507-794-4171; Fax: 507-794-5871.

Marriage Encounter—JEFF KODET; RONDI KODET, 34814 280th St., Redwood Falls, 56283. Tel: 507-644-3523.

CLERGY, PARISHES, MISSIONS AND PAROCHIAL SCHOOLS

CITY OF NEW ULM

(BROWN COUNTY)

1—CATHEDRAL OF THE HOLY TRINITY (1856) [CEM] [JC], Holy Cross area faith community with St. Gregory the Great, Lafayette; St. George, West Newton Township; St. John the Baptist, Searles; St. Mary's, New Ulm. Rev. Msgr. John A. Richter, Rector; Rev. Mark S. Steffl, Parochial Vicar.
Res. & Mailing Address: 605 N. State St., 56073-1898. Tel: 507-354-4158; Fax: 507-354-2563. Email: newulmcathedral@hotmail.com. Web: cathedralht.org.
See New Ulm Area Catholic Schools, New Ulm under New Ulm Area Catholic Schools located in the Institution section.
Catechesis/Religious Program—Students 157.

2—ST. MARY (1911) [JC], Area faith community with Cathedral, New Ulm; Searles; Lafayette, West Newton Township. Rev. Msgr. Douglas L. Grams; Revs. Edward J. Ardolf. Tel: 507-232-3857; John C. Ekwoanya, Parochial Vicar.
Res. & Church: 417 S. Minnesota St., 56073-2120. Tel: 507-233-9500; Fax: 507-354-8414. Email: stmarys@newulmtel.net. Web: www.stmarys-newulm.com.
See New Ulm Area Catholic Schools, New Ulm under New Ulm Area Catholic Schools located in the Institution section.
Catechesis/Religious Program—Tel: 507-233-9505; Fax: 507-354-8414. Students 208.

OUTSIDE THE CITY OF NEW ULM

APPLETON, SWIFT CO., ST. JOHN (1880) [CEM 2] [JC 2], Area faith community with Madison, Dawson. Rev. Revocatus L. Mwakera.
Mailing & Res. Address: 450 S. Gaulke St., 56208-1516. Tel: 320-289-1146 (Office); 320-289-1211 (Rectory); Fax: 320-289-1146. Email: sjapton@fedtel.net.
Church: 350 S. Edquist St., 56208-1516.
Catechesis/Religious Program—Tel: 320-289-1146. Students 88.

ARLINGTON, SIBLEY CO., ST. MARY (1864) [CEM], Clustered with Gaylord and Green Isle. Rev. Jerome E. Paulson.
Res. & Mailing Address: 504 7th Ave., N.W., P.O. Box 392, 55307-0392. Tel: 507-964-5413; Fax: 507-964-5425. Email: stmararl@frontiernet.net.
Catechesis/Religious Program—Tel: 507-964-5425. Jane Steinborn, D.R.E. (Elem K-6); Anne Ballalatak, D.R.E. (Jr. & Sr. High 7-12). Students 160.

BARRY, BIG STONE CO., ST. BARNABAS, Closed. For sacramental records contact Holy Rosary, Graceville.

BEARDSLEY, BIG STONE CO., ST. MARY (1884) [CEM], Clustered with Graceville Sr. Rebecca Littel, O.S.B., Pastoral Assoc.
Res. & Mailing Address: P.O. Box 299, 56211-0299. Tel: 320-265-6113 (Rectory); Fax: 320-265-6133 (Call First). Email: saintmary@centurytel.net.
Church: 510 S. Forest St., 56211. Tel: 320-265-6916.
Catechesis/Religious Program—Students 25.

BECHYN, RENVILLE CO., ST. MARY, Closed. For sacramental records contact St. Aloysius, Olivia.

BELGRADE, NICOLLET CO., ST. MICHAEL, Closed. For sacramental records contact St. Paul, Nicollet.

BENSON, SWIFT CO., ST. FRANCIS (1881) [CEM], Area faith community with Clontarf, Danvers, De Graff & Murdock. Revs. William A. Sprigler. Tel: 320-843-2342; Samuel Perez Tax, Parochial Vicar (Murdock) Tel: 320-875-2246. Area Pastoral Leaders:, Christine Pinto, Dir. Faith Formation.
Area Office—Tel: 320-842-4271; Fax: 320-843-2264. Email: stfran@embarqmail.com. Web: www.catholicareaparishes.org.
Church: 508 13th St. N., 56215-1228. Tel: 320-842-4271; Fax: 320-843-2264.
Catechesis/Religious Program—Students 213.

BIRCH COOLIE, RENVILLE CO., ST. PATRICK, Closed. For sacramental records contact Sacred Heart, Franklin. Earlier records located at St. John, Morton.

BIRD ISLAND, RENVILLE CO., ST. MARY (1879) [CEM], Heart of Jesus area faith community with Hector, Olivia, Renville. Rev. George V. Schmit Jr.
Mailing Address: P.O. Box 500, 55310-0500. Email: stmarybi@yahoo.com.
Parish Offices & Rectory: 220 S. 10th St., P.O. Box 500, 55310-0500. Tel: 320-365-3593; Fax: 320-365-4510.
Res.: 240 S. 8th St., P.O. Box 500, 55310-0500. Tel: 320-365-3828.
School—(Grades K-8), 140 S. 10th St., P.O. Box 500, 55310-0500. Tel: 320-365-3693. Email: principal@stmarysschoolbirdisland.com. Web: www.stmarysschoolbirdisland.com. Mrs. Tracy Bertrand, Prin.; Mrs. Karen Smith, Librarian. Lay Teachers 13; Students 126.
Catechesis/Religious Program—Students 85.

CANBY, YELLOW MEDICINE CO., ST. PETER (1897) [CEM], Area faith community with St. Leo, Ghent & Minneota. Rev. Craig A. Timmerman.
Res.: 307 W. 4th St., 56220-1211. Tel: 507-223-7304; Fax: 507-223-5776. Email: churchofstpeters@canby.mntm.org.
School—(Grades K-6), 410 Ring Ave. N., 56220-1237.

Tel: 507-223-7729; Fax: 507-223-7178. Ms. Sandra Kollar, Prin. Lay Teachers 6; Students 52.
Catechesis/Religious Program—Students 119.

CLARA CITY, CHIPPEWA CO., ST. CLARA (1890), Holy Family area faith community with Granite Falls & Montevideo. Sr. Carole Freking, O.S.F., Pastoral Admin.
Church: 414 N. Main St., P.O. Box 310, 56222-0310. Tel: 320-847-2256; Fax: 320-847-2445. Email: stclara@hcinet.net. Web: saintsjac.org.
Catechesis/Religious Program—Tel: 320-847-2445. Email: bstrommer@hcinet.net. Students 94.

CLARKFIELD, YELLOW MEDICINE CO., ST. ISIDORE, Closed. For sacramental records contact St. Joseph, Montevideo.

CLEMENTS, REDWOOD CO., ST. JOSEPH (ORATORY) (1902) [CEM] Rev. Msgr. Robert J. Wyffels, Parochial Admin. Tel: 507-249-3643 (Morgan-St. Michaels).
Mailing & Physical Address: P.O. Box 459, Morgan, 56266-0459. Tel: 507-249-3643. Email: stmichaels@redred.com.

CLONTARF, SWIFT CO., ST. MALACHY (1878), Area faith community with Benson, Danvers, DeGraff & Murdock. Rev. William A. Sprigler, (Benson). Area Pastoral Leaders:, Christine Pinto, Dir. Faith Formation.
Res.: 508 13th St. N., Benson, 56215. Tel: 320-842-4271 (Area Office).
Church: 300 Armagh St., S.W., 56226.
Catechesis/Religious Program—Students 24.

COMFREY, BROWN CO., ST. PAUL (1900) [CEM], Area faith community with Leavenworth & Sleepy Eye. Sr. JoAnne Backes, O.S.B., Pastoral Admin.
Res. & Mailing Address: 209 N. Field St., P.O. Box 277, 56019-0277. Tel: 507-877-2361; Fax: 507-877-2361. Email: stpcomfrey@yahoo.com.
Catechesis/Religious Program—Tel: 507-877-9800. Students 57.

COTTONWOOD, LYON CO., ST. MARY (1902) [CEM], Area faith community with Green Valley & Marshall. Rev. Jack (John) A. Nordick.
Res. & Mailing Address: 255 W. 4th St. S., P.O. Box 228, 56229-0228. Tel: 507-423-5220; Fax: 507-423-5275. Email: stmarys.cottonwood@frontiernet.net. Web: www.holy-redeemer.com.
Catechesis/Religious Program—Students 112.

DANVERS, SWIFT CO., CHURCH OF THE VISITATION (ORATORY) (1885) [CEM] Rev. William A. Sprigler. Tel: 320-842-2342 (Benson).
Mailing Address: 508 13th St. N., Benson, 56215-1228. Email: stfran@embarqmail.com.

DARWIN, MEEKER CO., ST. JOHN (1861) [CEM], Clustered with Forest City. Rev. Patrick L. Casey, (Darwin).
Res. & Mailing: 106 N. 4th St., 55324-6016. Tel: 320-275-2915; 320-693-6878; Fax: 320-275-0198. Email: rectory@stjohnscatholic-darwin.com. Web: www.stjohnscatholic-darwin.com.
Catechesis/Religious Program—Tel: 320-286-2800. Email: shellymendiola@hotmail.com. Students 171.

DAWSON, LAC QUI PARLE CO., ST. JAMES (1898) [CEM], Area faith community with Appleton & Madison. Sr. Vivian Petersen, O.S.B., Pastoral Admin.
Res. & Mailing Address: 10th & Locust, P.O. Box 270, 56232-0270. Tel: 320-769-4465. Email: stjames@frontiernet.net.
Catechesis/Religious Program—Students 50.

DE GRAFF, SWIFT CO., ST. BRIDGET (1876) [CEM], Area faith community with Benson, Clontarf, Danvers & Murdock. Rev. William A. Sprigler. Tel: 320-843-2342.
Mailing Address & Res.: 508 13th St. N., Benson, 56215-1228. Tel: 320-842-4271; Fax: 320-843-2264.
Church: Email: stfran@embarqmail.com. Web: www.catholicareaparishes.org.
Area Office—Tel: 320-842-4271; Fax: 320-843-2264.
Catechesis/Religious Program—St. Bridget Activity Center, 508 13th St. N., Benson, 56215. Tel: 320-843-2005. Christine Pinto, Dir. Faith Formation. Tel: 320-843-4271. Students 30.

EDEN VALLEY, MEEKER CO., ST. PETER (1903) Closed. For inquiries for parish records contact Assumption Church, Eden Valley, Diocese of St. Cloud.

FAIRFAX, RENVILLE CO., ST. ANDREW (1871) [CEM], Area faith community with Franklin, Gibbon & Winthrop. Rev. Ronald V. Huberty.
Res. & Mailing Address: 15 S.E. First St., P.O. Box C, 55332-0903. Tel: 507-426-7125. Email: ffgw@centurytel.net.
Catechesis/Religious Program—Tel: 507-426-7739; 507-426-7742. Connie Serbus, D.R.E. Students 89.

FAXON TOWNSHIP, SIBLEY CO., ST. JOHN-ASSUMPTION (1859) [CEM 2], Clustered with Henderson, Jessenland. Rev. Keith R. Salisbury. Tel: 507-248-3550.
Mailing Address: 213 S. 6th, P.O. Box 427, Henderson, 56044.
Church: 26523 200th St., Belle Plaine, 56011-9302. Tel: 952-873-4390. Email: stjos@frontiernet.net.
Catechesis/Religious Program—Students 136.

FOREST CITY, MEEKER CO., ST. GERTRUDE (1857) [CEM], Clustered with Darwin. Rev. John A. Pearson, Sacramental Min. Tel: 320-693-6878 (Darwin); Mr. Michael P. McNeil, Pastoral Admin.
Res. & Church: 31608 650th Ave., Litchfield, 55355-4410. Tel: 320-693-7801; Fax: 320-693-5877. Email: stgert@xtratyme.com. Web: www.forministry.com/usmnrcathsgccs.
Res.: 106 N. 4th St., Darwin, 55324-6016.
Catechesis/Religious Program—Students 28.

FRANKLIN, RENVILLE CO., SACRED HEART (1898) [CEM 2], Area faith community with Fairfax, Gibbon, & Winthrop. Rev. Ronald V. Huberty. Tel: 507-426-7739.
Mailing Address: P.O. Box 175, 55333-0175. Email: ffgw@centurytel.net.
Res.: 15 S.E. First St., P.O. Box C, Fairfax, 55332-0903. Tel: 507-426-7125.
Church: E. Main St., 55333-0175.
Catechesis/Religious Program—Connie Serbus, D.R.E. Students 52.

GAYLORD, SIBLEY CO., ST. MICHAEL (1882), Clustered with Arlington and Green Isle. Rev. Jerome E. Paulson. Tel: 507-964-5413; Fax: 507-964-5425 (Arlington).
Res. & Mailing Address: 411 Court Ave., P.O. Box 357, 55334-0357. Tel: 507-237-2851; Fax: 507-237-2383. Email: stmichael@myclearwave.net.
Catechesis/Religious Program—P.O. Box 357, 55334-0357. Ann Whalen, D.R.E.; Misty Utendorfer, D.R.E. Students 91.

GHENT, LYON CO., ST. ELOI (1883) [CEM], Area faith community with Canby, St. Leo & Minneota. Mr. Michael A. Pekar Jr., Pastoral Admin.
Church: 306 W. McQuestion, 56239-9750. Tel: 507-428-3285. Email: steloi@starpoint.net.
Catechesis/Religious Program—Students 94.

GIBBON, SIBLEY CO., ST. WILLIBRORD (1886) [CEM], Area faith community with Fairfax, Franklin, Winthrop. Rev. Ronald V. Huberty. Tel: 507-426-7125 (Fairfax); Sr. Mary Ann Kuhn, S.S.N.D., Parish Min.
Res. & Mailing Address: 1032 Ash Ave., P.O. Box 436, 55335-0436. Tel: 507-834-6461. Email: stwill@centurytel.net.
Catechesis/Religious Program—Tel: 507-834-6659. Students 55.

GLENCOE, MCLEOD CO.
1—ST. GEORGE, Closed. For sacramental records, contact St. Pius X, Glencoe.
2—SS. PETER AND PAUL, Closed. For sacramental records, contact St. Pius X, Glencoe.
3—ST. PIUS X (1983) [CEM] Rev. Anthony J. Stubeda.
Res., Church & Mailing Address: 1014 Knight Ave., N., 55336-2300. Tel: 320-864-5162; 320-864-2963 (Rectory); Fax: 320-864-5163. Email: stpiusx@stpiusxglencoe.org.
School—(Grades PreK-6), 1103 E. 10th St., 55336-2399. Tel: 320-864-3214. Email: school@stpiusxglencoe.org. Kathryn Morgan, Prin. Sisters 2; Lay Teachers 6; Students 80.
Catechesis/Religious Program—Tel: 320-864-5162. Students 126.

GRACEVILLE, BIG STONE CO., HOLY ROSARY (1878) [JC], Clustered with Beardsley. Rev. David L. Breu; Deacon Art D. Abel. Tel: 320-748-7573 (Home).
Res. & Mailing Address: 511 Studdart Ave., P.O. Box 7, 56240-0007. Tel: 320-748-7313. Email: choly000@centurytel.net.
Catechesis/Religious Program—517 Studdart Ave., 56240. Tel: 320-748-7501. Students 138.

GRANITE FALLS, YELLOW MEDICINE CO., ST. ANDREW (1885) [CEM], Holy Family area faith community with Montevideo & Clara City. Rev. James W. Devorak. Fax: 320-269-7555 (Montevideo).
Mailing Address: 1094 Granite St., 56241-1355.
Res.: 521 Eureka Ave., Montevideo, 56241. Tel: 320-269-8623; Fax: 320-269-7555. Email: standrew@mvtvwireless.com. Web: www.saintsjac.org.
Catechesis/Religious Program—1056 Fourth St., 56241. Tel: 320-564-2336. Students 115.

GREEN ISLE, SIBLEY CO., ST. BRENDAN (1854) [CEM], Clustered with Arlington & Gaylord. Rev. Jerome E. Paulson. Tel: 507-248-3550.
Res. & Mailing Address: 221 McGrann St., S., P.O. Box 85, 55338-0085. Tel: 507-326-5111. Email: stbrendan@frontiernet.net.
Catechesis/Religious Program—Students 27.

GREEN VALLEY, LYON CO., ST. CLOTILDE (1912) [CEM], Area faith community with Cottonwood & Marshall. Rev. Paul L. Wolf.
Res.: 503 W. Lyon St., Marshall, 56258-1390. Tel: 507-532-5711 (Office). Email: linda@stclotilde.com.
Church: 3272-270th Ave., Marshall, 56258-0228. Tel: 507-532-2841.
Catechesis/Religious Program—Students 40.

GREENLEAF, MEEKER CO., ST. COLUMBAN, Closed. For inquiries for sacramental records contact St. Philip, Litchfield.

HECTOR, RENVILLE CO., CHURCH OF ST. JOHN (1878) [CEM], Heart of Jesus area faith community with Bird Island, Olivia, & Renville. Donald A. Clasemann, Pastoral Admin.
Church: 301 Cedar Ave. E., P.O. Box 295, 55342-0295. Tel: 320-848-6437; Fax: 320-848-2407. Email: stjohnshector@frontiernet.net.
Catechesis/Religious Program—Students 88.

HEGBERT, SWIFT CO., ST. AGNES, Closed. For sacramental records, contact St. John, Appleton.

HENDERSON, SIBLEY CO., ST. JOSEPH (1859) [CEM], Clustered with Faxon Township & Jessenland. Rev. Keith R. Salisbury.
Res. & Mailing Address: 213 S. 6th St., P.O. Box 427, 56044-7735. Tel: 507-248-3550. Email: stjos@frontiernet.net.
Catechesis/Religious Program—Students 60.

HOLLOWAY, SWIFT CO., ST. JOSEPH, Closed. For sacramental records, contact St. John, Appleton.

HUTCHINSON, MCLEOD CO., CHURCH OF ST. ANASTASIA (1866) [CEM], Clustered with Stewart. Revs. Gerald S. Meidl; Patrick E. Okonkwo.
Mailing Address: 460 Lake St., S.W., 55350-2349. Email: stanastasia@stanastasia.net. Web: www.stanastasia.net.
Church: 400 Lake St., S.W., 55350-2349. Email: stanastasia@stanastasia.net. Web: www.stanastasia.net.
Res.: 1016 Roe Ave., 55350-2117. Tel: 320-587-6507; Fax: 320-234-6756.
School—(Grades PreK-6) Tel: 320-587-2490. Email: jstoffels@stanastasia.net. Jody Stoffels, Prin. Lay Teachers 11; Students 145.
Catechesis/Religious Program—Tel: 320-234-6129. Students 391.

IVANHOE, LINCOLN CO., SS. PETER & PAUL (1900) [CEM], Clustered with Wilno. Rev. Paul A. Schumacher; Sr. M. Ellen Hoemberg, I.S.S.M., Pastoral Assoc. & D.R.E., (Wilno Ivanhoe).
Res. & Mailing Address: 111 N. Sherwood, P.O. Box 49, 56142-0049. Tel: 507-694-1402; Fax: 507-694-1437.
Catechesis/Religious Program—P.O. Box 49, 56142. Students 54.

JESSENLAND, SIBLEY CO., ST. THOMAS (ORATORY) (1855) [CEM] Rev. Keith R. Salisbury.
Mailing Address: P.O. Box 427, Henderson, 56044-0427. Email: stjos@frontiernet.net.
Church: 31624 Scenic Byway Rd., Henderson, 56044. Tel: 507-248-3550.

KANDIYOHI, KANDIYOHI CO., ST. PATRICK (1868) [CEM], Area faith community with Lake Lillian, Willmar & Spicer. Rev. Brian L. Mandel.
Mailing Address: 245 N. 2nd St., P.O. Box 164, 56251-0164.
Res. & Mailing Address: P.O. Box 164, 56251-0164. Tel: 320-382-6424. Email: stpatmn@charter.net. Web: ourlivingwater.org.
Catechesis/Religious Program—Students 69.

LAFAYETTE, NICOLLET CO., ST. GREGORY THE GREAT (1942) [CEM], Holy Cross area faith community with Cathedral & St. Mary's, New Ulm; St. John's, Searles; St. George, West Newton Township; St. Gregory the Great, Lafayette. Rev. John G. Berger.
Res. & Mailing Address: 440 6th St., P.O. Box 5, 56054-0005. Tel: 507-228-8298; Fax: 507-228-8298. Email: stsgg@centurytel.net.
Catechesis/Religious Program—Students 58.

LAKE BENTON, LINCOLN CO., ST. GENEVIEVE (1897) [CEM], Clustered with Tyler. Rev. Paul A. Schumacher.
Res. & Mailing Address: P.O. Box 310, Tyler, 56178. Tel: 507-247-3464; Fax: 507-247-3286.
Church: 119 S. Sherman St., 56149. Tel: 507-368-4232.
Catechesis/Religious Program—Fax: 507-247-3286. Students 64.

LAKE LILLIAN, KANDIYOHI CO., ST. THOMAS MORE (1934) [CEM], Area faith community with Kandiyohi, Willmar & Spicer. Rev. Brian L. Mandel.
Res. & Mailing Address: P.O. Box 164, Kandiyohi, 56251-0164. Tel: 320-382-6424. Email: stpatmn@charter.net. Web: ourlivingwater.org/stthomas.html.
Church: 781 Second St. E., 56253. Tel: 320-664-4810.
Catechesis/Religious Program—Students 28.

LAMBERTON, REDWOOD CO., ST. JOSEPH (1895) [CEM], Area faith community with Clements, Morgan, Sanborn & Springfield. Sr. Judi Angst, O.S.F., Pastoral Admin.
Mailing Address: P.O. Box 458, 56152-0458.
Res. & Mailing Address: 400 W. 2nd Ave., P.O. Box 458, 56152-0458. Tel: 507-752-7269. Email: stjoe@rrcnet.org.
Catechesis/Religious Program—Students 27.

LEAVENWORTH, BROWN CO., CHURCH OF THE JAPANESE MARTYRS (1867) [CEM], Area faith community with Comfrey & Sleepy Eye. Sr. JoAnne Backes, O.S.B., Pastoral Admin.
Office: 30881 County Rd. 24, Sleepy Eye, 56085-4361. Tel: 507-794-6974. Email: jmartyrs@sleepyeyetel.net.
Catechesis/Religious Program—Students 39.

LESTER PRAIRIE, MCLEOD CO., ST. CONRAD, Closed. Incorporated but never organized. No sacramental records.

LITCHFIELD, MEEKER CO., ST. PHILIP (1859) [CEM], Area faith community with Manannah. Rev. Joseph A. Steinbeisser.
Parish Offices: 306 N. Holcombe Ave., 55355-2223. Tel: 320-693-3313; Fax: 320-593-4783. Email: stphilip@hutchtel.net. Web: www.thechurchofstphilip.org.
Church: 821 E. 5th St., 55355-2223.
School—(Grades K-5), 225 E. 3rd St. Tel: 320-693-6283. Email: mccarney@stphilipsschool.com. Diana M. McCarney, Prin. Lay Teachers 7; Students 82.
Catechesis/Religious Program—Tel: 320-593-4776. Students 174.

LUCAN, REDWOOD CO., OUR LADY OF VICTORY (1889) [CEM], Area faith community with Wabasso, Seaforth and Wanda. Rev. Todd J. Petersen, (Wabasso).
Res. & Mailing Address: P.O. Box 96, 56255-0096. Tel: 507-747-2231; Fax: 507-747-2233. Email: ourlady@means.net.
Church: 303-Third St., 56255.
Catechesis/Religious Program—Students 15.

MADISON, LAC QUI PARLE CO., ST. MICHAEL (1884) [CEM], Area faith community with Dawson, Appleton. Rev. Revocatus L. Mwakera.
Res.: 450 S. Gaulke St., Appleton, 56208-1516. Tel: 320-289-1146 (Office).
Church: 412 3rd St., 56256-1494. Tel: 320-598-3690; Fax: 320-598-3619. Email: stmike2@frontiernet.net.
Catechesis/Religious Program—Students 66.

MANANNAH, MEEKER CO., CHURCH OF OUR LADY (1876) [CEM], Area faith community with Litchfield. Rev. Msgr. Francis J. Garvey.
Res.: 57482 CSAH 3, Grove City, 56243-9786. Tel: 320-693-8900; 320-453-7526; Fax: 320-693-8900. Email: ourlady@meltel.net.
Catechesis/Religious Program—Students 108.

MARSHALL, LYON CO., HOLY REDEEMER (1883) [CEM], Area faith community with Cottonwood & Green Valley. Revs. Paul L. Wolf; Jack (John) A. Nordick, Parochial Vicar.
Res. & Mailing Address: 503 W. Lyon St., 56258-1311. Tel: 507-532-5711; Fax: 507-532-3262. Email: pwolf@holy-redeemer.com. Web: www.holy-redeemer.com.
School—(Grades K-8), 501 S. Whitney. Tel: 507-532-6642; Fax: 507-532-2636. Email: cdesmet@holy-redeemer.com. Carol J. DeSmet, Prin. Lay Teachers 21; Students 279.
Catechesis/Religious Program—503 S. Whitney St., 56258-1995. Tel: 507-532-3602. Lori Timmerman, D.R.E. Students 394.
Mission—*St. Clotilde* 3272 270th Ave., 56258. Tel: 507-532-2841.

MIDDLE LAKE, NICOLLET CO., ST. NICHOLAS, Closed. Incorporated but never organized. No sacramental records.

MILROY, REDWOOD CO., ST. MICHAEL (1904) [CEM], Area faith community with Tracy & Walnut Grove. Mr. Richard Hamsa, Pastoral Admin.
200 Euclid Ave., 56263.
Res.: 400 Cedar St., P.O. Box 117, 56263-0117. Tel: 507-336-2505. Email: stmichael@means.net.
Catechesis/Religious Program—Students 88.

MINNEOTA, LYON CO., ST. EDWARD (1880) [CEM], Area faith community with Ghent, Canby & St. Leo. Rev. Jeremy G. Kucera.
Church & Res.: 409 N. Adams St., 56264-9801. Tel: 507-872-6346; Fax: 507-872-5263.
School—210 W. 4th St. Tel: 507-872-6391. Email: stedward@centurytel.net. Web: stedwardcatholicschool.com. Lori Rangaard, Prin. Lay Teachers 11; Students 120.
Catechesis/Religious Program—Tel: 507-428-3285. Students 130.

MONTEVIDEO, CHIPPEWA CO., ST. JOSEPH (1882) [CEM], Holy Family area faith community with Granite Falls & Clara City. Rev. James W. Devorak.
Res.: 521 Eureka Ave., 56265-1899. Tel: 320-269-8623. Email: stjoseph@saintsjac.org. Web: www.saintsjac.org.
Church: 512 Black Oak Ave., 56265-1874. Tel: 320-269-5954; Fax: 320-269-7555.
Catechesis/Religious Program—Students 126.

MORGAN, REDWOOD CO., ST. MICHAEL (1890) [CEM], Area faith community with Clements, Lamberton, Sanborn & Springfield. Rev. Msgr. Robert J. Wyffels.
Res., Church & Mailing Address: 510 W. 3rd St., P.O. Box 459, 56266-0459. Tel: 507-249-3643. Email: stmichaels@redred.com.
School—(Grades PreK-6), 612 W. 3rd St., P.O. Box 459, 56266-0459. Tel: 507-249-3192; Fax: 507-249-2557. Email: stmichaels@redred.com. Ms. Patty McCauley, Prin.; Mrs. Ruth Hacker, Librarian. Lay Teachers 4; Students 36.
Catechesis/Religious Program—Email: jlmadsen@redred.com. Students 58.

MORTON, RENVILLE CO., ST. JOHN (1873) [CEM], Clustered with Redwood Falls. Sr. Jodelle Zimmerman, O.S.B., Pastoral Admin.
331 W. 3rd St., P.O. Box 88, 56270-0088.
Res. & Mailing Address: 341 W. 3rd St., P.O. Box 88, 56270-0088. Tel: 507-697-6120. Email: stjohnsmorton@mchsi.com.
Catechesis/Religious Program—Students 46.

MURDOCK, SWIFT CO., CHURCH OF THE SACRED HEART (1879) [CEM], Area faith community with Benson, Clontarf, Danvers & De Graff. Rev. Samuel Perez Tax (Benson); Christine Pinto, Faith Formation.
Res., Church & Mailing Address: 201 Orleans, P.O. Box 9, 56271. Tel: 320-875-2246; 320-842-4271 (Area Office); Fax: 320-843-2264. Email: stfran@embarqmail.com. Web: www.catholicareaparishes.org.
Catechesis/Religious Program—Tel: 320-875-2451. Students 71.

NASSAU, LAC QUI PARLE CO., ST. JAMES (1902) [CEM], Clustered with Ortonville and Rosen. Rev. Robert P. Goblirsch, (Ortonville).
Res. & Mailing Address: 421 Madison Ave., Ortonville, 56278-2713. Tel: 320-839-2772; Fax: 320-839-2873. Email: secbkpr.stjohns@midconetwork.com.
Catechesis/Religious Program—Students 3.

NICOLLET, NICOLLET CO., ST. PAUL (1907) [CEM 4], Area faith community with St. Peter. Rev. Edward J. Ardolf.
Church & Mailing Address: 410 5th St., P.O. Box 248, 56074-0248. Tel: 507-232-3857.
Catechesis/Religious Program—Students 83.

NORTH MANKATO, NICOLLET CO., HOLY ROSARY (1924) Rev. Peter C. Nosbush.
Res. & Mailing Address: 525 Grant Ave., 56003-2939. Tel: 507-387-6501; Fax: 507-387-7365. Email: hros2@hickorytech.net.
School—546 Grant Ave., 56003-2937. Tel: 507-345-6765. Email: bblaisdell@macsmn.com. Web: www.loyolacatholicschools.org. Mrs. Bette Blaisdell, Pres. & High School Prin. School is part of Mankato Area Catholic Schools, Diocese of Winona. Numbers are reported by the Winona Diocese. Students 599.
Catechesis/Religious Program—Students 254.

OLIVIA, RENVILLE CO., ST. ALOYSIUS (1888) [CEM 2] [JC], Area faith community with Renville, Hector & Bird Island. Rev. Paul H. van de Crommert.
Church: 302 S. 10th St., 56277-1288. Tel: 320-523-2030 (Office); 320-523-1271 (Rectory); Fax: 320-214-2419. Email: saintaloysiuschurch@msn.com.
Catechesis/Religious Program—Tel: 320-523-2030. Students 75.

ORTONVILLE, BIG STONE CO., ST. JOHN (1879), Clustered with Nassau & Rosen. Rev. Robert P. Goblirsch.
Res.: 421 Madison Ave., 56278-2713. Tel: 320-839-2772; Fax: 320-839-2873. Email: secbkpr.stjohns@midconetwork.com. Web: www.bordermissionchain.com.
Catechesis/Religious Program—Tel: 320-839-2873. Email: dre.stjohns@midconetwork.com. Students 103.

RAYMOND, KANDIYOHI CO., SACRED HEART, Closed. For sacramental records, contact St. Clara, Clara City.

REDWOOD FALLS, REDWOOD CO., ST. CATHERINE (1870) [CEM], Clustered with Morton. Rev. Michael M. Doyle.
Church & Mailing Address: 900 E. Flynn St., P.O. Box 383, 56283-0383. Tel: 507-644-2278; Fax: 507-644-2643. Email: stcath@redred.com.
Res.: 904 E. Flynn St., P.O. Box 383, 56283-0383. Tel: 507-644-8114.
Catechesis/Religious Program—Students 256.

REGAL, KANDIYOHI CO., ST. ANTHONY (MISSION) (1933) [CEM] Closed. Records at Our Lady of the Lakes, Spicer.

RENVILLE, RENVILLE CO., HOLY REDEEMER (1891) [CEM], Heart of Jesus area faith community with Olivia, Bird Island & Hector. Sr. Donna Wermus, S.S.N.D., Pastoral Admin.
Church & Mailing Address: 106 S.E. 3rd St., P.O. Box 401, 56284-0401. Tel: 320-329-3884; Fax: 320-329-3884. Email: hrchurch@centurytel.net. Web: www.afcheartofjesus.org.
Catechesis/Religious Program—Tel: 320-329-8219. Students 73.

ROSEN, LAC QUI PARLE CO., ST. JOSEPH (1885) [CEM], Clustered with Nassau & Ortonville Rev. Robert P. Goblirsch. Tel: 320-839-2772 (Ortonville).
Mailing Address: 421 Madison Ave., Ortonville, 56278-2713. Tel: 320-839-2772; Fax: 320-839-2873. Email: secbkpr.stjohns@midconetwork.com. Web: www.bordermissionchain.com.
Catechesis/Religious Program—Tel: 320-568-2428. Students 46.

ST. LEO, YELLOW MEDICINE CO., ST. LEO (1881) [CEM], Area faith community with Canby, Ghent & Minneota. Rev. Craig A. Timmerman. Tel: 507-223-7304 (Canby).
Church & Mailing Address: 202 W. Church St., 56264. Tel: 507-224-2289. Email: churchofstpeter@canby.mntm.org.
Catechesis/Religious Program—Tel: 507-223-7729. Students 35.

ST. PETER, NICOLLET CO.
1—CHURCH OF ST. PETER (1856) [CEM], Area faith community with Nicollet. Rev. Philip M. Schotzko. Tel: 507-931-1628; Sr. Therese Collison, S.S.N.D., Pastoral Assoc.; Kay Osborne, Pastoral Assoc.
Church & Mailing Address: 1801 W. Broadway, P.O. Box 522, 56082-0522. Tel: 507-931-1628; Fax: 507-931-2977. Email: office@churchofstpeter.org. Web: www.churchofstpeter.org.
School—*John Ireland School*, (Grades K-6) Tel: 507-931-2810; Fax: 507-931-9179. Email: therese.collison@churchofstpeter.org. Web: www-.churchofstpeter.org. Sr. Therese Collison, S.S.N.D., Prin. Sisters 1; Lay Teachers 9; Students 295.
2—IMMACULATE CONCEPTION, Closed. For sacramental records, contact St. Peter's, St. Peter.
Catechesis/Religious Program—Tel: 507-931-3662. Connie Bollum, D.R.E. Students 295.

SANBORN, REDWOOD CO., ST. THOMAS (ORATORY) (1902), Area faith community with Springfield, Lamberton & Morgan. Sr. Judi Angst, O.S.F., Pastoral Admin.
301 E. Winona St., P.O. Box 176, 56083-0176. Tel: 507-752-7269.

SEAFORTH, REDWOOD CO., ST. MARY (1880) [CEM 2] [JC 2], Area faith community with Wabasso, Lucan & Wanda. Rev. Todd J. Petersen, (Wabasso).
Mailing Address: P.O. Box 239, Wabasso, 56293-0239. Tel: 507-342-5190 (Office); Fax: 507-342-5156. Email: stannesschool@wabassostannesschool.com.
Catechesis/Religious Program—Students 33.

SEARLES, BROWN CO., ST. JOHN THE BAPTIST (1905) [CEM], Holy Cross area faith community with Cathedral, New Ulm; St. Mary's, New Ulm; Lafayette; West Newton Township. Rev. Msgr. John A. Richter, Parochial Admin.
Res. & Mailing Address: 18241 First Ave. S., 56073-5171. Tel: 507-359-4244; Fax: 507-359-4244. Email: sjs@newulmtel.net. Web: www.stjohnssearles.catholicweb.com.
See New Ulm Area Catholic Schools, New Ulm under New Ulm Area Catholic Schools located in the Institution section.
Catechesis/Religious Program—Students 11.

SILVER LAKE, MCLEOD CO.
1—ST. ADALBERT, Closed. For sacramental records, contact Holy Family, Silver Lake.
2—CHURCH OF THE HOLY FAMILY (1993) [CEM 4] Rev. Brian W. Oestreich.
Res. & Mailing Address: 720 W. Main St., 55381-0326. Tel: 320-327-2261 (Rectory); 320-327-2910 (Church); Fax: 320-327-2261. Email: office@holyfamilysilverlake.org.
School—(Grades PreK-5), 700 W. Main St., 55381-0346. Tel: 320-327-2356. Email: principal@holyfamilysilverlake.org. Cathy Millerbernd, Prin. Lay Teachers 4; Students 48.
Catechesis/Religious Program—Tel: 320-327-2931. Email: HFRE@holyfamilysilverlake.org. Students 143.
3—ST. JOSEPH, Closed. For sacramental records, contact Holy Family, Silver Lake.

SLEEPY EYE, BROWN CO., ST. MARY (1876) [CEM], Area faith community with Comfrey & Leavenworth. Rev. Msgr. Eugene L. Lozinski; Revs. Paul D. Timmerman, Parochial Vicar; Mark S. Mallak, Chaplain. Tel: 507-794-6532; Deacon Mark D. Kober. Tel: 507-794-4682.
Res.: 636 First Ave. N., 56085-1004. Tel: 507-794-4171; Fax: 507-794-5871. Email: saintmaryse@sleepyeyetel.net. Web: www.stmarys-sleepyeye.com.
School—(Grades PreK-6), 104 St. Mary St. N.W. Tel: 507-794-6141; Fax: 507-794-4841. Email: thelget@sesmschool.com. Web: www.sesmschool-.com. Mrs. Mary Gangelhoff, Prin.; Mrs. Cindy Rieke, Librarian. Lay Teachers 20; Students 201.
High School—(Grades 7-12) Tel: 507-794-4121; Fax: 507-794-4841. Email: jneubauer@sesmschool.com. Mr. Jerry Neubauer, Prin.; Miss Jenny Blick, Librarian. Lay Teachers 19; Students 209.
Catechesis/Religious Program—Tel: 507-794-7600; Fax: 507-794-5871. Shauna Molden, D.R.E. Students 130.

SPICER, KANDIYOHI CO., OUR LADY OF THE LAKES (1962) [CEM], Area faith community with Willmar, Kandiyohi & Lake Lillian. Rev. Jeffrey P. Horejsi.
Res.: 15525 69th St., N.E., 56288-9659. Tel: 320-796-5664; Fax: 320-796-6310. Email: ourlady@tds.net. Web: www.olol.ourlivingwater.org.
Church & Mailing Address: 6680 153rd Ave. N.E., 56288-9659.
Catechesis/Religious Program—Tel: 320-796-5968. Students 266.

SPRINGFIELD, BROWN CO., ST. RAPHAEL (1874) [CEM], Area faith community with Lamberton, Morgan, Clements & Sanborn. Rev. Dennis C. Labat.
Res.: 112 W. Van Dusen St., 56087-1396. Tel: 507-723-4137 (Office); 507-723-4141 (Rectory). Email: straphael@newulmtel.net. Web: www.straphaelmn.org.
School—(Grades PreK-6), 20 W. VanDusen St. Tel: 507-723-4135; Fax: 507-723-5409. Email: strays@newulmtel.net. John DeZeeuw, Prin. Tel: 507-723-4136. Lay Teachers 8; Students 65.
Catechesis/Religious Program—Tel: 507-723-4138. Monica Simmons, Youth Min. & Faith Formation. Students 202.

STEWART, MCLEOD CO., CHURCH OF ST. BONIFACE (1877) [CEM], Clustered with Hutchinson. Rev. Gerald S. Meidl. Tel: 320-234-6756 (Hutchinson).
Mailing Address: 551 Main St., P.O. Box 202, 55385-0202. Tel: 320-562-2344. Email: stbcc@hutchtel.net.
Catechesis/Religious Program—Students 48.

SWAN LAKE, NICOLLET CO.
1—THE CHURCH OF THE VISITATION, Closed. For sacramental records, contact St. Paul, Nicollet.
2—VISITATION, Closed. For sacramental records, contact St. Paul, Nicollet.

TAUNTON, LYON CO., SS. CYRIL AND METHODIUS (1895) [CEM 2] Closed. For inquiries for parish records contact the chancery.

TRACY, LYON CO., ST. MARY (1885) [CEM], Area faith community with Walnut Grove & Milroy. Rev. Robert J. Mraz.
249 6th St., 56175-1114.
Res. & Mailing Address: 600 3rd St., P.O. Box 602, Walnut Grove, 56180. Tel: 507-629-4075 (Office); 507-859-2164 (Home); Fax: 507-629-3667 (Office). Email: stmary@iw.net. Web: www.stmarytracy.org.
Church: 285 6th St., 56175. Tel: 507-629-3841 (Church Hall); Fax: 507-629-3518.
School—(Grades K-6), 225 6th. St., 56175-1114. Tel: 507-629-3270; Fax: 507-629-3518. Email: stmarys@iw.net. Web: www.stmaryschooltracy.org. Mrs. Juliana Neuman, Prin. Lay Teachers 5; Students 36.
Catechesis/Religious Program—Tel: 507-629-3667. Email: saintmaryre@iw.net. Students 84.

TYLER, LINCOLN CO., ST. DIONYSIUS (1880) [CEM], Clustered with Lake Benton. Rev. Paul A. Schumacher.
Res. & Parish Office: 213 Linwood St., P.O. Box 310, 56178-0310. Tel: 507-247-5807 (Church); 507-247-3464 (Office); Fax: 507-247-3286. Email: bjthooft@frontiernet.net.
Church: 203 Linwood St., 56178.
Catechesis/Religious Program—Students 135.

VESTA, REDWOOD CO., HOLY NAME, Closed. For sacramental records, contact St. Catherine's, Redwood Falls.

WABASSO, REDWOOD CO., ST. ANNE (1900) [CEM] [JC], Area faith community with Lucan, Wanda, Seaforth. Rev. Todd J. Petersen.
Mailing Address: 1052 Cedar St., P.O. Box 239, 56293-0239.
Church Address: 950 North St., 56293-0239. Tel: 507-342-5190 (Office); 507-342-5155 (Rectory); Fax: 507-342-5156.
School—(Grades K-6), 1054 Cedar St., 56293-0239. Tel: 507-345-5389; Fax: 507-342-5156. Email: mail@wabassostanneschool.com. Web: inetteacher.com/school/201229. Mary Franta, Prin. Lay Teachers 9; Students 89.
Catechesis/Religious Program—Tel: 507-342-5190. Students 85.

WALNUT GROVE, REDWOOD CO., ST. PAUL (1902) [CEM], Area faith community with Tracy & Milroy. Rev. Robert J. Mraz. Tel: 507-859-2164 (Walnut Grove).
Mailing Address: 600 3rd St., P.O. Box 236, 56180-0236. Tel: 507-859-2164; Fax: 507-859-2375. Email: fatherbob@iw.net. Web: www.smstracy.org.
Catechesis/Religious Program—Tel: 507-629-4075; Fax: 507-629-3667. Students 9.

WANDA, REDWOOD CO., ST. MATHIAS (1871) [CEM], Area faith community with Seaforth, Lucan, Wabasso. Rev. Todd J. Petersen, (Wabasso).
Mailing Address: P.O. Box 239, Wabasso, 56293-0239.
Church: 308 St. Mathias Blvd., 56293. Tel: 507-342-5190 (Office); 507-342-5155 (Rectory); Fax: 507-342-5156. Email: stanneschool@wabassostanneschool.com.
Catechesis/Religious Program—Students 52.

WATKINS, MEEKER CO., CHURCH OF ST. ANTHONY (1889) [CEM] Rev. John H. Brunner.
Res. & Mailing Address: 170 Meeker Ave. S., P.O. Box 409, 55389-0409. Tel: 320-764-2755; Fax: 320-764-2755. Email: stanthony@meltel.net. Web: www.diversicommunity.com/watkins.
Church: 201 Central Ave. S., 55389-0409.
Catechesis/Religious Program—Tel: 320-764-5722. Students 177.

WEST NEWTON TOWNSHIP, NICOLLET CO., ST. GEORGE (1858) [CEM], Holy Cross area faith community with Lafayette; Searles; Cathedral-NewUlm; St. Mary's-New Ulm. Rev. John G. Berger. Tel: 507-228-8298 (Lafayette).
Mailing Address: 440 6th St., P.O. Box 5, Lafayette, 56054-0005. Tel: 507-228-8298.
Church: 63105 Fort Rd. Tel: 507-228-8298; Fax: 507-228-8298. Email: stsgg@centurytel.net. Web: www.churchofstgeorge.com.
Catechesis/Religious Program—Students 26.

WILLMAR, KANDIYOHI CO., ST. MARY (1871) [CEM], Area faith community with Spicer, Kandiyohi & Lake Lillian. Rev. Steven J. Verhelst.
Church & Mailing Address: 713 12th St., S.W., 56201-3099. Tel: 320-235-0118; Fax: 320-235-0153. Email: parishoffice@stmaryswillmar.org. Web: www.stmaryswillmar.org.
Catechesis/Religious Program—Tel: 320-235-3982. Students 480.

WILNO, LINCOLN CO., ST. JOHN CANTIUS (1883) [CEM], Clustered with Ivanhoe. Rev. Paul A. Schumacher.
Mailing Address: P.O. Box 49, Ivanhoe, 56142-0049.
Church: 3069 Kowno St., Ivanhoe, 56142-0049. Tel: 507-694-1402; Fax: 507-694-1437. Email: ellenh1@frontiernet.net.
Catechesis/Religious Program—Fax: 507-694-1548. Students 105.

WINSTED, MCLEOD CO., HOLY TRINITY (1869) [CEM 2] Rev. Anthony R. Hesse; Deacon Michael Thoennes.
Res. & Mailing Address: 111 Winsted Ave. W., P.O. Box 9, 55395-0009. Tel: 320-485-4421; Fax: 320-485-4283. Email: frtony@tds.net. Web: www.winstedholytrinity.org.
School—Holy Trinity Elementary School, (Grades PreK-6), 211 2nd St. N., 55395-0038. Tel: 320-485-2182, Ext. 2160. Email: cmillerbernd@tds.net. Mailing Address: P.O. Box 38, 55395-0038. Cathy Millerbernd, Prin. Lay Teachers 9; Students 96.
High School—Holy Trinity High School, (Grades 7-12), 110 Winsted Ave., P.O. Box 38, 55395-0038. Tel: 320-485-2182; Fax: 320-485-4283. Email: htprincipal@tds.net. Lay Teachers 12; Students 99.
Catechesis/Religious Program—Tel: 320-485-2182, Ext. 2155; Fax: 320-485-4283. Email: maryjeanhagar@yahoo.com. Students 185.

WINTHROP, SIBLEY CO., ST. FRANCIS DE SALES (1906), Area faith community with Fairfax, Gibbon & Franklin. Rev. Ronald V. Huberty. Tel: 507-426-7125 (Fairfax).
Church & Mailing Address: 510 N. Brown St., P.O. Box 447, 55396-0447. Tel: 507-647-5334. Email: ffgw@centurytel.net.
Catechesis/Religious Program—Box C, Fairfax, 55332. Fax: 507-426-7742. Connie Serbus, D.R.E. Students 20.

Chaplains of Public Institutions

APPLETON. *Prairie Correctional Facility*. Vacant.
IVANHOE. *Divine Providence Hospital & Home*.
ST. PETER. *St. Peter Regional Treatment Center*. Rev. John G. Berger, Chap.
WILLMAR. *Regional Treatment Center*. Rev. Jeffrey P. Horejsi, Chap.
WINSTED. *St. Mary's Care Center*. Rev. Eugene M. Brown, Chap. (Retired).

On Special or Other Diocesan Assignment:
Rev. Msgrs.—
Grams, Douglas L., J.C.L.
Lozinski, Eugene L.
Revs.—
Berger, John G.
Labat, Dennis C.
Petersen, Todd J.
Schotzko, Philip M.
Timmerman, Craig A.
Timmerman, Paul D.

On Duty Outside the Diocese:
Rev. Msgr.—
Schaffer, Gregory T., Parroquia San Lucas Toliman, Depto. Solola 07013, Guatemala. Tel: 011-502-7722-0112; Fax: 011-502-7722-0112
Rev.—
Goggin, John T., Parroquia San Lucas Toliman, Depto. Solola 07013 Guatemala. Tel: 011-502-7722-0112; Fax: 011-502-7722-0112

Military Chaplains:
Rev.—
Wagener, John M., Lt. Col. (Retired), 117 E. Summit Ave., San Antonio, TX 78212-2953. Tel: 210-738-3481

Retired:
Revs.—
Adrian, Stephen J., 10410 E. Twilight Dr., Sun Lakes, AZ 85248-6851. Tel: 602-895-0465
Barry, James D., 9300 Collegeville Rd., Apt. 305, Bloomington, 55437. Tel: 952-846-0551. Email: jdbarry35@yahoo.com
Becker, Dennis E., 11208 Co. Rd. 12 N.W., Garfield, 56332. Tel: 320-834-2100
Gross, Richard C., P.O. Box 6, Watkins, 55389. Tel: 320-764-2856
Hackert, Eugene C., 18906 US Hwy. 14 W., 56073. Tel: 507-354-7308
Hadusek, Paul J., 1009 Dano Circle, #2, Marshall, 56258-0721. Tel: 507-401-3215
Hansen, Lawrence H., 151 S. Bishop Ave., Unit B13, Secane, PA 19018. Tel: 484-469-4250
Irrgang, Kenneth E., 740 14th St. S. Apt. 13, St. Cloud, 56301-5518. Tel: 320-654-1008. Email: irrgang@charter.net
Jenniges, Leonard J. (STP), Divine Providence Community Home, 700-3rd Ave. N.W., Sleepy Eye, 56085-1099.
Krystosek, Robert H. (GI), P.O. Box 425, Clara City, 56222-0425. Tel: 320-847-2615
Martinka, Stanley V., 11267 W. 75th Ave., Arvada, CO 80005. Tel: 303-422-9457
Mead, Leland C., 22295 Lakewood Dr., Madison Lake, 56063-9706. Tel: 507-243-3868
Plathe, Anthony H., 1381 Mission Hills Blvd., Clearwater, FL 33759-2767. Tel: 727-773-7225
Rademacher, Germain P., 60297 402nd Ln., 56073. Tel: 507-359-5157; Fax: 507-359-5157
Schaefer, Roman J., Kasper Life Center, P.O. Box 1, Donaldson, IN 46513-0001. Tel: 574-935-1741
Siebenand, Ambrose F., St. Benedict Senior Community, 1810 Minnesota Blvd. S.E., Rm. 126, St. Cloud, 56304-2423. Tel: 320-252-0010

INSTITUTIONS LOCATED IN THE DIOCESE

[A] NEW ULM AREA CATHOLIC SCHOOLS

NEW ULM. *New Ulm Area Catholic Schools*, 515 N. State St., 56073-1897. Tel: 507-354-2719; Fax: 507-354-7071. Email: pgroebner@nuacs.com. Web: www.nuacs.com. Consolidated: The three schools consolidated under the above title are as follows:
St. Anthony Elementary School (Grades PreK-4), 514 N. Washington St., 56073. Tel: 507-354-2928; Fax: 507-359-7029. Email: shelly.bauer@nuacs.com. Shelly Bauer, Prin., (Grades Pre K-4). Lay Teachers 13; Students 215.
Holy Trinity Middle School, 515 N. State St., 56073-1897. Tel: 507-354-4311; Fax: 507-354-7071. Email: shelly.bauer@nuacs.com. Shelly Bauer, Prin., (Grades 5-8). Lay Teachers 11; Students 131.
Cathedral High School, 600 N. Washington St., 56073-1897. Tel: 507-354-4511; Fax: 507-354-5711. Email: peter.roufs@nuacs.com. Peter Roufs, Prin., (Grades 9-12). Priests 1; Sisters 1; Lay Teachers 14; Students 176.

[B] GENERAL HOSPITALS

GRACEVILLE. *Graceville Health Center* DBA: Holy Trinity Hospital, Graceville Health Center Clinic, Graceville Health Center Home Health, Grace Home, Grace Village., 115 W. 2nd St., P.O. Box 157, 56240-0157. Tel: 320-748-7223; Fax: 320-748-7225. Email: thowell@ghealth.net. Sr. Pia Rottinghaus, O.S.B., Board Pres.; Todd Howell, CEO. Inpatient Bed Capacity 15; Inpatients 284; Outpatients 8,434; Total Staff 170; Clinic Visits 6,550; Home Health Visits 1,918; Nursing Home 50; Assisted Living 16.
Graceville Health Center dba Chokio Medical Center 101 S. Main St., Chokio, 56221. Tel: 320-324-7500; Fax: 320-324-7563. Email: thowell@ghealth.net. Sr. Pia Rottinghaus, O.S.B., Board Pres.; Todd Howell, CEO. Clinic Visits 586; Total Staff 5.

[C] HOMES FOR AGED

GRACEVILLE. *Graceville Health Center dba Grace Home (SNF) and Grace Village (ALF)* 116 W. 2nd St., P.O. Box 638, 56240. Tel: 320-748-7261; Fax: 320-748-8238. Email: thowell@ghealth.net. Sr. Pia Rottinghaus, O.S.B., Board Pres.; Todd Howell, CEO. GH Bed Capacity 50; Grace Village Number of Rooms 16; Total Staff 80.

IVANHOE. *Divine Providence Apartments*, 312 E. George St., P.O. Box 136, 56142-0136. Tel: 507-694-1414; Fax: 507-694-1191. Cheryl Verschelde, Admin. Total Apartments 7.

SAINT PETER. *Benedictine Living Community of St. Peter*, 1907 Klein St., 56082. Tel: 507-934-2203; Fax: 507-934-8392. Email: linda.nelsen@bhshealth.org. Web: www.bhshealth.org. Long Term Care Beds 80; Total Staff 135.

SLEEPY EYE. *Divine Providence Community Home & Lake Villa Maria Senior Apts.*, 700 3rd Ave. N.W.,

56085-1099. Tel: 507-794-3011; 507-794-5333 (Lake Villa); Fax: 507-794-3020. Email: divine@sleepyeyetel.net. Sisters Lucy Tardivo, D.S.M.P., Supr.; Janet Kosman, Admin.; Rev. Mark S. Mallak, Chap. Daughters of St. Mary of Providence. Sisters 6; Lay Workers 94; Aged Residents 58; Tenants 19; Bed Capacity 58; Total Assisted Annually 110; Total Staff 105.

WINSTED. *St. Mary's Care Center* (1959) 551 4th St. N., Ste. 101, 55395-0750. Tel: 320-485-2151; Fax: 320-485-4241. Email: andy.opsahl@bhshealth.org. Web: www.stmaryscarecenter.org. Rev. Eugene M. Brown, Chap. (Retired); Andrew D. Opsahl, Admin. & CEO. Subsidiary of the Benedictine Health System. Bed Capacity 70; Total Staff 150.

[D] RETREAT HOUSES

NEW ULM. *St. Alphonsus Retreat House*, 1400 6th St. N., 56073-2099. Tel: 507-359-2966; Fax: 507-354-3667. Email: dnu@dnu.org.

SLEEPY EYE. *Schoenstatt Sisters of Mary (Secular Institute)* (1926) 27762 County Rd. 27, 56085-9801. Tel: 507-794-7727; 507-794-5622; Fax: 507-794-7727. Email: schoenstattonthelake@schsrsmary.org. Sr. Rita Marie Otto, Supr.; Miriam Lopez, Youth & Family Min.; Sisters M. Alice Kunz, Librarian; M. Deanne Niehaus, Youth Min.; M. Ellen Hoemberg, I.S.S.M., D.R.E.; M. Candace Fier, M.T.S., B.S.N., R.N., Dir. Office of Family Life Educ. & Safe Environment Dio NU; M. Elizabeth Dingloaum, Receptionist. Total Staff 7.

[E] YOUTH CENTERS

RENVILLE. *Center for Youth Ministry*, Diocesan Pastoral Center, 1400 6th St. N., 56073-2099. Tel: 507-359-2966; Fax: 507-354-3667. Sr. Margaret Mc Hugh, Dir. Youth Ministry.

[F] MISCELLANEOUS

ST. PETER. *St. Peter Regional Treatment Center*, 100 Freeman Dr., 56082-1599. Tel: 507-931-7100; Fax: 507-931-7711. Rev. John G. Berger, Chap.; Robert Wieber, (Protestant) Chap. Mental Health and Chemical Dependency: Patients Assisted Annually 825; Bed Capacity 530; Total Staff 1,256.

WILLMAR. *Willmar Regional Treatment Center*, 1550 Hwy. 71 N.E., 56201-1128. Tel: 320-231-5100; Fax: 320-231-5329. Sr. Cecile Schueller, S.S.N.D., Chap.; Rev. Jeffrey P. Horejsi, Chap.; Sr. Nadine Touhey, S.S.N.D., Chap. Mental Health and Chemical Dependency: Patients Assisted Annually 900; Bed Capacity 114; Total Staff 430.

RELIGIOUS INSTITUTES OF MEN REPRESENTED IN THE DIOCESE

For further details refer to the corresponding bracketed number in the Religious Institutes of Men or Women section.

[0200]—*Benedictine Monks* (Collegeville, MN)—O.S.B.

RELIGIOUS INSTITUTES OF WOMEN REPRESENTED IN THE DIOCESE

[]—*Benedictine Sisters of Pontifical Jurisdiction* (Crookston, MN)—O.S.B

[]—*Benedictine Sisters of Pontifical Jurisdiction* (Watertown, SD)—O.S.B.

[]—*Benedictine Sisters of Pontifical Jurisdiction* (Yankton, SD)—O.S.B.

[]—*Benedictine Sisters of Pontifical Jurisdiction* (St. Joseph, MN)—O.S.B.

[0940]—*Daughters of St. Mary of Providence* (Immaculate Conception Province, Chicago, IL)—D.S.M.P.

[]—*Franciscan Clarist Congregation* (Nirmal Pani Providence, Kerala State, India)—F.C.C.

[0210]—*Missionary Benedictine Sisters of Pontifical Jurisdiction* (Norfolk, NE)—O.S.B.

[]—*Presentation of the Blessed Virign Mary* (Fargo, ND)—P.B.V.M.

[]—*Religious Sisters of Mercy* (Alma, MI)—R.S.M.

[]—*Schoenstatt Sisters of Mary* (Waukesha, WI)

[2970]—*School Sisters of Notre Dame* (Mankato Province, Mankato, MN) —S.S.N.D.

[1680]—*School Sisters of St. Francis* (Milwaukee, WI)—S.S.S.F.

[]—*Sisters of St. Francis of the Congregation of Our Lady of Lourdes* (Sylvania, OH)—O.S.F.

[1570]—*Sisters of St. Francis of the Holy Family* (Dubuque, IA)—O.S.F.

[3840]—*Sisters of St. Joseph of Carondelet* (St. Paul, MN)—C.S.J.

[3830-03]—*Sisters of St. Joseph of Orange* (Orange, CA)—C.S.J.

[1720]—*Sisters of the Third Order Regular of St. Francis of the Congregation of Our Lady of Lourdes* (Rochester, MN)—O.S.F.

NECROLOGY

† Ward, Rev. Msgr. John C., (Retired)—Died Jan. 17, 2009

† Pistulka, Celestine C., (Retired)—Died March 16, 2009

† Schreiner, Bernard P., (Retired)—Died March 15, 2009

An asterisk (*) denotes an organization that has established tax-exempt status directly with the IRS and is not covered by the USCCB Group Ruling.

Archdiocese of New York

Archdiocese of New York

(Archidioecesis Neo-Eboracensis)

His Eminence

EDWARD CARDINAL EGAN, J.C.D., D.D.

Archbishop Emeritus of New York; ordained December 15, 1957; appointed Titular Bishop of Allegheny and Auxiliary Bishop of New York April 1, 1985; consecrated May 22, 1985; appointed Bishop of Bridgeport November 8, 1988; installed December 14, 1988; appointed Archbishop of New York May 11, 2000; installed June 19, 2000; elevated to Cardinal February 21, 2001; retired February 23, 2009. *Res.: 452 Madison Ave., New York, NY 10022.*

Most Reverend

PATRICK V. AHERN, D.D.

Retired Auxiliary Bishop of New York; ordained January 27, 1945; appointed Titular Bishop of Najiera and Auxiliary Bishop of New York February 3, 1970; consecrated March 19, 1970; retired April 26, 1994. *Res.: John Cardinal O'Connor Clergy Residence, 5665 Arlington Ave., Bronx, NY 10471.*

Most Reverend

ROBERT A. BRUCATO, D.D.

Retired Auxiliary Bishop of New York; ordained June 1, 1957; appointed Titular Bishop of Temuniana and Auxiliary Bishop of New York July 1, 1997; consecrated August 25, 1997; retired October 31, 2006. *Res.: John Cardinal O'Connor Clergy Residence, 5655 Arlington Ave., Bronx, NY 10471.*

Most Reverend

JOSU IRIONDO, D.D.

Auxiliary Bishop of New York; ordained December 23, 1962; appointed Titular Bishop of Alton and Auxiliary Bishop of New York October 30, 2001; consecrated December 12, 2001. *Res.: St. Anthony of Padua, 832 E. 166 St., Bronx, NY 10459.*

Most Reverend

DOMINICK J. LAGONEGRO, D.D.

Auxiliary Bishop of New York; ordained May 31, 1969; appointed Titular Bishop of Modrus and Auxiliary Bishop of New York October 30, 2001; consecrated December 12, 2001. *Res.: Sacred Heart, 301 Ann St., Newburgh, NY 12550.*

Most Reverend

JAMES F. McCARTHY, D.D.

Retired Auxiliary Bishop of New York; ordained June 1, 1969; appointed Titular Bishop of Verrona and Auxiliary Bishop of New York May 11, 1999; consecrated June 29, 1999; retired June 15, 2002.

Most Reverend

TIMOTHY M. DOLAN

Archbishop of New York; ordained June 19, 1976; appointed Auxiliary Bishop of St. Louis June 19, 2001; installed August 15, 2001; appointed Archbishop of Milwaukee June 25, 2002; installed as Tenth Archbishop August 28, 2002; appointed Archbishop of New York February 23, 2009; installed April 15, 2009. *Office: 1011 First Ave., New York, NY 10022.*

Chancery: 1011 First Ave., New York, NY 10022. Tel: 212-371-1000; Fax: 212-813-9538.

Web: www.ny-archdiocese.org

Most Reverend

WILLIAM J. McCORMACK, D.D.

Retired Auxiliary Bishop of New York; ordained February 21, 1959; appointed Titular Bishop of Nicives and Auxiliary Bishop of New York December 23, 1986; consecrated January 6, 1987; retired October 30, 2001. *Res.: 142 E. 29th St., New York, NY 10016.*

Most Reverend

ANTHONY F. MESTICE, D.D.

Retired Auxiliary Bishop of New York; ordained June 4, 1949; appointed Titular Bishop of Villanova and Auxiliary Bishop of New York March 5, 1973; consecrated April 27, 1973; retired October 30, 2001. *Res.: Our Lady of Consolation Residence, 3103 Arlington Ave., Ste. 8, Bronx, NY 10463.*

Most Reverend

PATRICK J. SHERIDAN, D.D.

Retired Auxiliary Bishop of New York; ordained March 1, 1947; appointed Titular Bishop of Curzola and Auxiliary Bishop of New York October 30, 1990; consecrated December 12, 1990; retired January 15, 2001. *John Cardinal O'Connor Clergy Residence, 5655 Arlington Ave., Bronx, NY 10471.*

Most Reverend

DENNIS J. SULLIVAN, D.D., V.G.

Auxiliary Bishop of New York; ordained May 29, 1971; appointed Titular Bishop of Enera and Auxiliary Bishop of New York June 28, 2004; consecrated September 21, 2004. *Res.: 452 Madison Ave., New York, NY 10022.*

Most Reverend

GERALD T. WALSH, D.D.

Auxiliary Bishop of New York; ordained May 27, 1967; appointed Auxiliary Bishop and Titular Bishop of Altiburus June 28, 2004; consecrated September 21, 2004. *Res.: St. Joseph's Seminary, 201 Seminary Ave., Yonkers, NY 10704.*

SEE ERECTED APRIL 8, 1808.

Square Miles 4,683.

Created an Archdiocese July 19, 1850.

Comprises the Boroughs of Manhattan, Bronx, and Richmond of the City of New York, and the Counties of Dutchess, Orange, Putnam, Rockland, Sullivan, Ulster and Westchester in the State of New York.

Legal Title: Archdiocese of New York.

STATISTICAL OVERVIEW

Personnel	
Retired Cardinals	1
Archbishops	1
Auxiliary Bishops	4
Retired Bishops	5
Priests: Diocesan Active in Diocese	460
Priests: Diocesan Active Outside Diocese	42
Priests: Retired, Sick or Absent	135
Number of Diocesan Priests	637
Religious Priests in Diocese	868
Total Priests in Diocese	1,505
Extern Priests in Diocese	295
Ordinations:	
Diocesan Priests	3
Religious Priests	2
Transitional Deacons	7
Permanent Deacons	6
Permanent Deacons in Diocese	374
Total Brothers	324
Total Sisters	2,799
Parishes	
Parishes	371
With Resident Pastor:	
Resident Diocesan Priests	287
Resident Religious Priests	75
Without Resident Pastor:	
Administered by Priests	9
Professional Ministry Personnel:	
Brothers	28
Sisters	110
Lay Ministers	389
Welfare	
Catholic Hospitals	7
Total Assisted	862,000
Health Care Centers	2
Total Assisted	4,800
Homes for the Aged	17
Total Assisted	136,000
Residential Care of Children	31
Total Assisted	2,617
Day Care Centers	375
Total Assisted	4,856
Specialized Homes	26
Total Assisted	1,964
Special Centers for Social Services	629
Total Assisted	293,664
Residential Care of Disabled	52
Total Assisted	614
Other Institutions	460
Total Assisted	10,104
Educational	
Seminaries, Diocesan	2
Students from This Diocese	52
Students from Other Diocese	33
Diocesan Students in Other Seminaries	1
Seminaries, Religious	8
Students Religious	125
Total Seminarians	178
Colleges and Universities	10
Total Students	43,252
High Schools, Diocesan and Parish	12
Total Students	4,418
High Schools, Private	43
Total Students	23,202
Elementary Schools, Diocesan and Parish	187
Total Students	51,290
Elementary Schools, Private	29
Total Students	4,820
Non-residential Schools for the Disabled	8
Total Students	153
Catechesis/Religious Education:	
High School Students	7,810
Elementary Students	96,623
Total Students under Catholic Instruction	231,746
Teachers in the Diocese:	
Priests	18
Brothers	33
Sisters	104
Lay Teachers	4,310
Vital Statistics	
Receptions into the Church:	
Infant Baptism Totals	23,494
Minor Baptism Totals	1,841
Adult Baptism Totals	938
Received into Full Communion	828
First Communions	21,638
Confirmations	18,273
Marriages:	
Catholic	3,914
Interfaith	765
Total Marriages	4,679

Deaths........................ 13,180 Total Catholic Population............ 2,608,299 Total Population.................. 5,796,221

Succession of Prelates—Most Rev. R. LUKE CONCANEN, O.P., D.D., first Bishop; cons. April 24, 1808; died June 19, 1810; Rt. Revs. JOHN CONNOLLY, O.P., D.D., second Bishop; cons. Nov. 6, 1814; died Feb. 6, 1825; JOHN DUBOIS, S.S., D.D., third Bishop; cons. Oct. 29, 1826; died Dec. 20, 1842; Most Rev. JOHN HUGHES, D.D., cons. Titular Bishop of Basileopolis and coadjutor to the Bishop of New York, Jan. 7, 1838; succeeded to the See of New York, Dec. 20, 1842; created first Archbishop, July 19, 1850; died Jan. 3, 1864; His Eminence JOHN CARDINAL MCCLOSKEY, D.D., second Archbishop; cons. Titular Bishop of Axiere, and coadjutor to the Bishop of New York, March 10, 1844; translated to the See of Albany, May 21, 1847; promoted to the See of New York, May 6, 1864; created first U.S. Cardinal, Cardinal Priest of the Holy Roman Church, March 15, 1875 under the title of Sancta Maria Supra Minervam; died Oct. 10, 1885; Most Rev. MICHAEL AUGUSTINE CORRIGAN, D.D., third Archbishop; cons. Bishop of Newark, NJ May 4, 1873; promoted to the Archiepiscopal See of Petra and made coadjutor to His Eminence Cardinal McCloskey, Archbishop of New York, with the right of succession, Oct. 1, 1880; succeeded to the See of New York, Oct. 10, 1885; made Assistant at the Pontifical Throne, April 19, 1887; died May 5, 1902; His Eminence JOHN CARDINAL FARLEY, fourth Archbishop of New York; ord. June 11, 1870; cons. Titular Bishop of Zeugma and Auxiliary to the Archbishop of New York, Dec. 21, 1895; promoted to this See, Sept. 15, 1902; preconized June 22, 1903; made Assistant at the Pontifical Throne, Dec. 4, 1904; created Cardinal Priest of the Holy Roman Church under the Title of Sancta Maria Supra Minervam, Nov. 27, 1911; died Sept. 17, 1918; PATRICK CARDINAL HAYES, fifth Archbishop of New York; ord. Sept. 8, 1892; appt. Auxiliary to the Archbishop of New York, July 3, 1914; cons. Titular Bishop of Tagaste, Oct. 28, 1914; appt. Bishop Ordinary of U.S. Army and Navy Chaplains by the Holy See, Nov. 24, 1917; promoted to the See of New York, March 10, 1919; created Cardinal Priest of the Holy Roman Church under the title of Sancta Maria in Via, March 24, 1924; died Sept. 4, 1938; FRANCIS CARDINAL SPELLMAN, sixth Archbishop of New York; ord. May 14, 1916; appt. Auxiliary Bishop of Boston, July 30, 1932; cons. Sept. 8, 1932; appt. to the See of New York, April 15, 1939; appt. Military Vicar for the Armed Forces of the United States, Dec. 11, 1939; created and proclaimed Cardinal Priest under the title of SS. John and Paul in the Consistory, Feb. 18, 1946; died Dec. 2, 1967; TERENCE CARDINAL COOKE, seventh Archbishop of New York; ord. Dec. 1, 1945; appt. Auxiliary Bishop of New York, Sept. 15, 1965; cons. Dec. 13, 1965; appt. to the See of New York, March 8, 1968; installed and appt. Military Vicar of the United States Armed Forces, April 4, 1968; created and proclaimed Cardinal Priest under the title of SS. John and Paul in the Consistory, April 28, 1969; died Oct. 6, 1983; JOHN CARDINAL O'CONNOR, eighth Archbishop of New York; ord. Dec. 15, 1945; appt. Titular Bishop of Curzola and Auxiliary Bishop to the Military Vicar, April 24, 1979; cons. May 27, 1979; appt. Bishop of Scranton, May 10, 1983; installed June 29, 1983; appt. Archbishop of New York, Jan. 31, 1984; installed March 19, 1984; created Cardinal Priest, May 25, 1985; died May 3, 2000; EDWARD CARDINAL EGAN, J.C.D., D.D., ord. Dec. 15, 1957; appt. Titular Bishop of Allegheny and Auxiliary Bishop of New York April 1, 1985; cons. May 22, 1985; appt. Bishop of Bridgeport Nov. 8, 1988; installed Dec. 14, 1988; appt. Archbishop of New York May 11, 2000; installed June 19, 2000; elevated to Cardinal Feb. 21, 2001; retired Feb. 23, 2009.

Vicar General—Most Rev. DENNIS SULLIVAN, D.D., V.G. Fax: 212-826-6020.

Retired Bishops—Most Revs. ROBERT A. BRUCATO, D.D., V.G. (Retired); PATRICK V. AHERN, D.D. (Retired); JAMES F. MCCARTHY, D.D.; WILLIAM J. MCCORMACK, D.D. (Retired); ANTHONY F. MESTICE, D.D. (Retired); PATRICK J. SHERIDAN, D.D. (Retired).

Episcopal Vicars of the Archdiocese—

South Bronx—Most Rev. JOSU IRIONDO, S.T.L., D.D., Church of St. Anthony of Padua, 832 E. 166 St., Bronx, 10459. Tel: 718-542-7293.

Orange, Sullivan, Ulster, Northern Westchester/Putnam, Dutchess—Most Rev. DOMINICK J. LAGONEGRO, D.D., Church of the Sacred Heart, 301 Ann St., Newburgh, 12550. Tel: 845-561-2264.

Regional Vicars of the Archdiocese—

Manhattan (West)—Rev. Msgr. THOMAS P. LEONARD, Holy Trinity Church, 213 W. 82nd St., New York, 10024. Tel: 212-787-0634.

Manhattan (North)—Rev. Msgr. GABRIEL LA PAZ, J.C.L., Incarnation Church, 1290 St. Nicholas Ave., New York, 10033. Tel: 212-927-7474.

Manhattan (South)—Rev. Msgr. KEVIN J. NELAN, Our Lady of Guadalupe/St. Bernard Church, 328 W. 14th St., New York, 10014. Tel: 212-243-0265.

Manhattan (East)—Rev. Msgr. THOMAS A. MODUGNO, St. Monica Church, 413 E. 79th St., New York, 10021. Tel: 212-288-6250.

Manhattan (Central Harlem)—Rev. FREDERICK J. PELLEGRINI, S.J., Church of St. Aloysius, 219 W. 132nd St., New York, 10027. Tel: 212-234-2848.

Bronx (Northwest)—Rev. Msgr. JOHN J. JENIK, Our Lady of Refuge, 290 E. 196th St., Bronx, 10458. Tel: 718-367-4690.

Bronx (Northeast)—Rev. Msgr. EDWARD M. BARRY, St. Barnabas Church, 409 E. 241st St., Bronx, 10470. Tel: 718-324-1478.

Bronx (East)—Rev. Msgr. DONALD M. DWYER, Our Lady of the Assumption Church, 1634 Mahan Ave., Bronx, 10461. Tel: 718-824-5454.

Staten Island—Rev. Msgrs. JAMES J. DORNEY, Co Vicar, St. Peter's Church, 53 St. Mark's Pl., New Brighton, Staten Island, 10301. Tel: 718-727-2672; PETER G. FINN, M.Div., M.S., M.Ed., Co Vicar, Blessed Sacrament Church, 30 Manor Rd., Staten Island, 10310. Tel: 718-442-1581.

Central Westchester—Rev. Msgr. PATRICK J. BOYLE, Church of the Resurrection, 910 Boston Post Rd., Rye, 10508. Tel: 914-967-0142.

Northern Westchester and Putnam—Rev. Msgr. GEORGE P. THOMPSON, St. Patrick Church, 7 Pound Ridge Rd., Bedford, 10506. Tel: 914-234-3668.

Westchester (Yonkers)—Rev. Msgr. HUGH J. CORRIGAN, Immaculate Conception Church, 103 S. Broadway, Yonkers, 10701. Tel: 914-963-0156.

Westchester (South Shore)—Rev. Msgr. HOWARD W. CALKINS, Sacred Heart Church, 115 Sharp Blvd., Mt. Vernon, 10550. Tel: 914-668-7440.

Orange—Rev. Msgr. GEORGE J. VALASTRO, Co Vicar (Retired), St. Joseph Church, 149 Cottage St., Middletown, 10940. Tel: 845-343-6013; Most Rev. DOMINICK J. LAGONEGRO, D.D., Co Vicar, 301 Ann St., Newburgh, 12550. Tel: 845-561-2264; Fax: 845-562-7144.

Rockland—Rev. Msgr. EDWARD J. WEBER, St. Francis of Assisi Church, 128 Parrott Rd., West Nyack, 10994. Tel: 845-634-4957.

Dutchess—Rev. Msgr. FRANCIS P. BELLEW, St. Mary's Church, 11 Clinton St., Wappingers Falls, 12590.

Ulster—Rev. Msgr. WILLIAM E. WILLIAMS, St. John the Evangelist Church, 915 Rte. 212, Saugerties, 12477. Tel: 914-246-9581.

Sullivan—Rev. Msgr. EDWARD F. STRAUB, St. Peter's Church, 264 N. Main St., Liberty, 12754. Tel: 845-292-4525.

Vicar for Development—Most Rev. GERALD T. WALSH, D.D., 1011 First Ave., New York, 10022. Tel: 212-371-1000, Ext. 3320.

Vicars for Religious—Sisters CATHERINE CLEARY, P.B.V.M., 1011 First Ave., New York, 10022. Tel: 212-371-1000, Ext. 2576; ROSAMOND BLANCHETT, R.S.H.M. Tel: 212-371-1000, Ext. 2575.

Vicar for Hispanic Affairs— (Vicario, Asuntos Hispanos), Most Rev. JOSU IRIONDO, S.T.L., D.D., St. Anthony of Padua, 832 E. 166 St., Bronx, 10459.

Archbishopric of New York—1011 First Ave., New York, 10022. Tel: 212-371-1000. (Cable Address: Curia New York).

Chancery—1011 First Ave., New York, 10022. Tel: 212-371-1000; Fax: 212-813-9380.

Chancellor and Moderator of the Curia—Rev. Msgr. GREGORY MUSTACIUOLO.

Vice-Chancellors—Rev. Msgr. DOUGLAS J. MATHERS, J.D., J.C.D.; Sr. EILEEN CLIFFORD, O.P.

Secretary to the Archbishop—Rev. JAMES A. CRUZ.

Archbishop's Delegate for Healthcare—KARL P. ADLER, M.D.

Chief Financial Officer—Mr. WILLIAM E. WHISTON.

General Counsel—JAMES P. MCCABE, J.D.

Canon 1742 Panel of Pastors—Rev. WILLIAM B. COSGROVE; Rev. Msgrs. JOSEPH R. GIANDURCO, J.C.D.; JOHN K. GRAHAM; Revs. ROBERT F. GRIPPO; GEORGE W. HOMMEL; MICHAEL F. KEANE; Rev. Msgr. ROBERT W. LARKIN; Rev. THOMAS F. MADDEN; Rev. Msgr. FRANCIS J. MCAREE, S.T.D.; Rev. ROBERT F. MCKEON; Rev. Msgrs. KEVIN P. O'BRIEN, Ph.D.; EDMUND J. WHALEN, S.T.D.

Archdiocesan Consultors—Most Revs. ROBERT A. BRUCATO, D.D., V.G. (Retired); DOMINICK LAGONEGRO, D.D.; JOSU IRIONDO, D.D.; GERALD T. WALSH, D.D.; Rev. Msgrs. THOMAS J. BERGIN; PETER G. FINN, M.Div., M.S., M.Ed.; THOMAS E. GILLEECE; WALLACE A. HARRIS; LESLIE J. IVERS; JAMES R. MOORE; GREGORY MUSTACIUOLO; Rev. CARLOS RODRIGUEZ.

Metropolitan Tribunal—

Judicial Vicar—Rev. WILLIAM S. ELDER, J.C.D.

Associate Judicial Vicar—Rev. RICHARD L. WELCH, C.Ss.R., J.C.D., M.R.E., M.Div.

Judges—Rev. WILLIAM S. ELDER, J.C.D.; Rev. Msgr. OSCAR A. AQUINO, J.C.D.; Rev. GEORGE OONNOONNY, J.C.L.; Rev. Msgr. KENNETH J. SMITH, M.A., S.T.B.; Revs. RICHARD L. WELCH, C.Ss.R., J.C.D., M.R.E., M.Div.; MAREK SUCHOCKI, J.C.D., M.Th.; Ms. SILVANA USANDIVARAS, J.D., L.L.M.; Revs. RAYMOND DALY, J.C.D.; ANTHONY OMENIHU, J.C.L.; Rev. Msgr. DESMOND J. VELLA, J.C.D., S.T.L., M.S.

Defenders of the Bond—Very Rev. ROBERT HOSPODAR, J.C.L.; Rev. JOSE MARABE, J.C.D.

Promoter of Justice—Very Rev. ROBERT HOSPODAR, J.C.L.

Office Manager—Sr. MARY DANIEL BAUER, F.S.P., B.A.

Tribunal Coordinator—Ms. SILVANA USANDIVARAS, J.D., L.L.M.

Advocates—Ms. CATHERINE A. BARRETT; Rev. RAFAEL G. CORNIEL, J.C.L., M.A.; Ms. LYDIA MARTINEZ; Ms. INGRID PENA; Ms. MARIA BELARDO.

Regional Offices—

Mt. Kisco Office—12 Green St., Mount Kisco, 10549. Tel: 914-666-2583. *Judge*, Rev. JOHN A. VIGILANTI, J.C.L., Ph.D., 12 Green St., Mt. Kisco, 10549. Tel: 914-666-2583. *Canonical Consultant*, PATRICIA GREENBAUM.

Poughkeepsie Office—240 Church St., Poughkeepsie, 12601. Tel: 845-452-1400; Fax: 845-452-2227. *Advocate*, Ms. PATRICIA KOMAN.

Interdiocesan Tribunal of New York State—201 Seminary Ave., Yonkers, 10704. Tel: 914-968-4301.

Judicial Vicar—Rev. MICHAEL T. MARTINE, J.C.L.; Sr. JOAN DUMBROWSKI, Sec. & Notary.

Censors Librorum—Rev. Msgr. FRANCIS J. MCAREE, S.T.D.; Rev. DONALD F. HAGGERTY, S.T.D.; Rev. Msgr. MICHAEL F. HULL, S.T.D.

Archdiocesan Offices and Directors

Apostleship of Prayer—VACANT.

Apostleship of the Sea—Rev. Msgr. KEVIN J. NELAN, Dir., Stella Maris Maritime Center for Seamen, Pier 52, New York, 10019. Tel: 212-265-5020.

Archivist—Sr. MARGUERITA SMITH, St. Joseph's Seminary, 201 Seminary Ave., Yonkers, 10704. Tel: 914-476-6333.

Black Ministry, Office of—Bro. TYRONE DAVIS, C.F.C., Dir., 1011 First Ave., New York, 10022. Tel: 212-371-1000.

Building Commission—St. Joseph's Seminary, 201 Seminary Ave., Yonkers, 10704. Tel: 914-476-1058.

Director—Mr. DAVID MADDOX.

Assistant Director—KEVIN SHAUGHNESSY.

Consultants—JASON GAYNOR; Deacon JOHN LARKIN; MARK LABATE.

Cardinal's Archdiocesan Appeal—TERENCE CURLEY, 1011 First Ave., New York, 10022. Tel: 212-371-1000.

Catechetical Office—Sr. JOAN CURTIN, C.N.D. Tel: 212-371-1000, Ext. 2849.

Catholic Charismatic Center— (Centro Carismatico Catolico) Most Rev. JOSU IRIONDO, S.T.L., D.D., Center Dir., 826 E. 166th St., Bronx, 10460. Tel: 212-378-1734.

Catholic Charities—Rev. Msgr. KEVIN L. SULLIVAN, Exec. Dir., 1011 First Ave., New York, 10022. Tel: 212-371-1000 (Consult separate listing).

Catholic Health Care System—KARL P. ADLER, M.D., Chm. Bd. Trustees, 1011 First Ave., New York, 10022. Tel: 212-371-1000; Fax: 212-751-4655.

Catholic Health Care Foundation of the Archdiocese of New York, Inc.—KARL P. ADLER, M.D., Chm., 1011 First Ave., New York, 10022.

Catholic High School Association—1011 First Ave., New York, 10022.

Catholic New York— (See Ecclesiastical Communications Corp.), JOHN WOODS, Editor; Mr. JOSEPH ZWILLING, Assoc. Publisher.

Catholic World Wide Web Corporation—1011 First Ave., New York, 10022.

Cemeteries— (The Trustees of St. Patrick's Cathedral in the City of New York, Inc.) Mr. GEORGE BORRERO, Exec. Dir., 1011 First Ave., New York, 10022. Tel: 212-753-4883.

Center for Spiritual Development at Archbishop Stepinac High School—ANN MARIE WALLACE, Ph.D., Dir., 950 Mamaroneck Ave., White Plains, 10605. Tel: 914-946-5729; Fax: 914-946-6073.

Central Services— Archdiocese of New York *1011 First Ave., New York, 10022*. Tel: 212-371-1000.

Charismatic Renewal Office—Rev. WILLIAM B. COSGROVE; Sr. PAULINE CINQUINI, S.C., 194 Gaylor Rd., Scarsdale, 10583. Tel: 914-725-1773; Fax: 914-725-5227. Email: charismny@juno.com.

Communications Office (Bureau of Information for the Media)—Mr. JOSEPH ZWILLING, Dir.; Ms. WANDA VASQUEZ, Asst. Dir., Spanish Communications; Rev. LORENZO ATO, 1011 First Ave., New York, 10022. Tel: 212-371-1000, Ext. 2990.

Conciliation and Arbitration, Office of—Rev. Msgr. DOUGLAS J. MATHERS, J.D., J.C.D., Dir., 1011 First Ave., New York, 10022. Tel: 212-371-1000, Ext. 2929.

Coordinator for Special & Pastoral Ministries—Rev. EMILE FRISCHE, M.H.M., 1011 First Ave., New York, 10022. Tel: 212-371-1000, Ext. 2925.

Coordinator of Priest Retiree Affairs—Deacon DONALD QUIGLEY, 201 Seminary Ave., Yonkers, 10704. Tel: 914-968-6200, Ext. 8107; Mrs. MARY B. LYNCH, R.N., Our Lady of Consolation, 3103 Arlington Ave., Bronx, 10463. Tel: 718-548-0888.

Criminal Justice, Office of—Mr. KENNETH HOFFARTH, Dir., 1011 First Ave., New York, 10022. Tel: 212-371-1000, Ext. 3166.

Data Systems Center and Telecommunication Office—Mr. ANDREW J. DONNELLY, Dir., 1011 First Ave., New York, 10022. Tel: 212-371-1000.

Deaf, Catholic Center for—Rev. Msgr. PATRICK P. MCCAHILL, Dir., 1011 First Ave., New York, 10022. Tel: 212-988-8563.

Development, Archdiocesan Office of—Most Rev. GERALD T. WALSH, D.D., Vicar for Devel.; HELEN T. LOWE, Exec. Dir., 1011 First Ave., New York, 10022. Tel: 212-371-1000.

Ecclesiastical Assistance Corporation—1011 First Ave., New York, 10022. Tel: 212-371-1000.

Ecclesiastical Communications Corp.—1011 First Ave., New York, 10022. Tel: 212-371-1000.

Ecclesiastical Maintenance Services, Inc.—Mr. CHRISTOPHER RODRIGUEZ, Gen. Mgr. Area Supvrs.: JOSEPH ROCH. Tel: 917-560-3916; Mr. ROBERT SCULLY, 1011 First Ave., New York, 10022. Tel: 212-371-1000.

Ecclesiastical Properties Corporation—1011 First Ave., New York, 10022.

Office of Ecumenical and Interreligious Affairs—Rev. ROBERT J. ROBBINS, Dir., 1011 First Ave., New York, 10022. Tel: 212-371-1000, Ext. 3076.

Educational Services of the Archdiocese of New York, Inc.—1011 First Ave., New York, 10022.

Education, Department of, Archdiocese of New York—1011 First Ave., New York, 10022. Tel: 212-371-1000. (Consult separate listing)

Family Life/Respect Life Office—Sr. VERONICA MARY, S.V., Dir., 1011 First Ave., New York, 10022. Tel: 212-371-1000, Ext. 3185.

Hispanic Affairs, Office of— (Vicario, Asuntos Hispanos), JUAN LULIO BLANCHARD, 1011 First Ave., New York, 10022. Tel: 212-371-1000, Ext. 2980.

Holy Childhood Association—Sr. PAULINE CHIRCHIRILLO, P.B.V.M., Mission Educ. Dir., 1011 First Ave., New York, 10022. Tel: 212-371-1000, Ext. 2700.

Holy Name Society Archdiocesan Union of New York—Rev. JAMES P. CONNOLLY, Dir.; Mr. ANTHONY J. MEROLLA, Exec. Sec., 1011 First Ave., New York, 10022. Tel: 718-931-9239.

Information, Bureau of and Radio-T.V. Communications— See Communications

Inner City Scholarship Fund, Inc.—1011 First Ave., New York, 10022. Tel: 212-371-1000.

Institutional Commodity Services Corporation—ALFRED A. SMITH, Acting Dir.; ROBERT SCHIAVI, Dept. Mgr., 1011 First Ave., New York, 10022. Tel: 212-371-1000.

Intercultural Institute—Most Rev. JOSU IRIONDO, S.T.L., D.D., Dir. Tel: 212-371-1000, Ext. 2982.

Instructional T.V. Communications Center—Mr. MICHAEL LAVERY, Dir., St. Joseph's Seminary, 201 Seminary Ave., Yonkers, 10704. Tel: 914-968-7800.

Insurance Division—DANNY HOLTSCLAW, Oper. Mgr., 1011 First Ave., New York, 10022. Tel: 212-371-1000, Ext. 3024.

Inter-Parish Financing, Commission for—Rev. BRIAN P. MCCARTHY, Chm., 1011 First Ave., New York, 10022. Tel: 212-371-1000.

Italian Apostolate, Office of the—Rev. ROBERT J. AUFIERI, Dir., 1011 First Ave., New York, 10022. Tel: 212-371-1000, Ext. 3055.

Justice and Peace, Archdiocesan Office of—Mr. GEORGE HORTON, Dir., 1011 First Ave., New York, 10022. Tel: 212-371-1000.

Legal Affairs, Office of—JAMES P. MCCABE, J.D., Gen. Counsel; RODERICK J. CASSIDY, J.D., Assoc. Gen. Counsel, 1011 First Ave., New York, 10022. Tel: 212-371-1000, Ext. 2440; Fax: 212-826-8795.

Language Institute—1011 First Ave., New York, 10022. Tel: 212-371-1000, Ext. 2982.

Legion of Mary—Rev. GERALD E. MURRAY, Dir., 1011 First Ave., New York, 10022.

Light and Life Evangelization Program— (Luz y Vida) *St. Joseph's Cursillo Center, 523 W. 142nd St., New York, 10031*. Tel: 212-926-7433.

Liturgical Commission, Archdiocesan—Sr. JANET BAXENDALE, S.C., M.A., St. Joseph's Seminary, 201 Seminary Ave., Yonkers, 10704.

**The Malta Human Services Foundation, 1011 First Ave., Rm. 1350, New York, 10022*. Tel: 212-371-1522. Web: www.maltausa.org. Deacon JEFFREY TREXLER, Exec. Dir. & Contact Person.

Pastoral Life Conference—Revs. THOMAS P. DEVERY. Tel: 212-371-1000, Ext. 2930; THOMAS P. D'ANGELO, Asst., 1011 First Ave., New York, 10022. Tel: 212-371-1000.

Pastoral Services, Archdiocese of New York—1011 First Ave., New York, 10022. Tel: 212-371-1000.

Pension Office, Archdiocesan—Mr. ARTHUR MONTEGARI, Exec. Sec., 1011 First Ave., New York, 10022. Tel: 212-371-1000.

Permanent Diaconate Formation Program—(Programa de Formacion para Diaconos) Deacon ANTHONY CASSANETO, Dir., St. Joseph's Seminary, 201 Seminary Ave., Yonkers, 10704. Tel: 914-968-6200, Ext. 8269.

Human Resources—Mrs. EILEEN F. EGAN, Dir., 1011 First Ave., New York, 10022. Tel: 212-371-1000, Ext. 2906; Fax: 212-838-0637.

Priest Personnel, Office of—Rev. THOMAS P. DEVERY, Dir., 1011 First Ave., New York, 10022. Tel: 212-371-1000, Ext. 2930; Fax: 212-826-8173.

Adjunct and International Clergy Office—Deacon JOSEPH SOLANTO, Coord., St. Joseph's Seminary, 201 Seminary Ave., Yonkers, 10704. Tel: 914-968-6200, Ext. 8122.

Priest Personnel Board—Rev. THOMAS P. DEVERY, Chm.

Priest Wellness Office—Sr. MONICA WALSH, R.S.H.M., Coord., St. Joseph's Seminary. Tel: 914-968-6200, Ext. 8246.

Priest Retiree Affairs—Deacon DONALD QUIGLEY, Coord., St. Joseph's Seminary, Bishop Fearns Bldg., 201 Seminary Ave., Yonkers, 10704. Tel: 914-968-6200, Ext. 8107; Fax: 914-375-7148.

Priests Council of the Archdiocese of New York—Most Rev. TIMOTHY M. DOLAN, Pres.; Rev. JOSEPH P. LAMORTE, Chm.; Rev. Msgr. JOHN J. JENIK, Vice Chm.; Rev. WILLIAM J. LUCIANO, Recording Sec., 1011 First Ave., New York, 10022. Tel: 212-371-1000, Ext. 2932.

Prison Apostolate—Rev. Msgr. LESLIE J. IVERS, Dir., Church of the Epiphany, 239 E. 21st St., New York, 10010. Tel: 212-475-1966.

Propagation of the Faith, Society for the—Archdiocesan Office, Sr. PAULINE CHIRCHIRILLO, P.B.V.M., Archdiocesan Dir., 1011 First Ave., New York, 10022. Tel: 212-371-1000, Ext. 2700.

Propagation of the Faith, National Office—Rev. Msgr. JOHN E. KOZAR, Natl. Dir., National Office: 366 Fifth Ave., New York, 10001. Tel: 212-563-8700.

Retirement Plan for Priests—Rev. Msgr. PATRICK J. BOYLE, Chm., 1011 First Ave., New York, 10022. Tel: 212-371-1000, Ext. 2934.

Safe Environment Program—Mr. EDWARD MECHMANN, Dir.

St. Joseph's Cursillo Center—Rev. FRANK PELUSO, O.A.R., Dir., 275 West 230th St., Bronx, 10463. Tel: 718-796-4340.

Schools, Superintendent of—Dr. TIMOTHY J. MCNIFF, 1011 First Ave., New York, 10022. Tel: 212-371-1000, Ext. 2802.

**Sovereign Military Hospitaller Order of Saint John of Jerusalem of Rhodes and of Malta* American Association, U.S.A. *1011 First Ave., Rm. 1350, New York, 10022*. Tel: 212-371-1522. Web: www.maltausa.org. Deacon JEFFREY TREXLER, Exec. Dir. & Contact Person.

Spiritual Development, Office of—Rev. EUGENE J. FULTON, Dir., One Pryer Manor Rd., Larchmont, 10538. Tel: 914-235-6839.

Trustees of St. Patrick's Cathedral in the City of New York, Inc.—Rev. Msgr. JAMES K. VAUGHEY, Exec. Dir., Cemeteries; Mr. GEORGE BORRERO, Asst. Exec. Dir., Cemeteries.

Victim Assistance Coordinators—Sr. EILEEN CLIFFORD, O.P. Tel: 212-371-1000, Ext. 2949. Email: victimsassistance@archny.org; Deacon LAWRENCE O'TOOLE, Coord. Safe Environment. Cell: 914-419-0017.

CLERGY, PARISHES, MISSIONS AND PAROCHIAL SCHOOLS

NEW YORK CITY

BOROUGH OF MANHATTAN

1—CATHEDRAL OF ST. PATRICK (Old, 1809; New, 1879) Rev. Msgr. Robert Ritchie, Rector; Revs. Joseph J. Tyrrell, Master of Ceremonies; Jose G. Marabe (Philippines), Parochial Vicar; Christopher Pliauplis, Parochial Vicar; Deacons Edmundo Ramos; Anthony Gostkowski. In Res., Rev. Msgr. James P. Cassidy (Retired); Revs. William M. Shelley (Retired); Richard Seagraves (Retired).
Rectory—460 Madison Ave., 10022. Tel: 212-753-2261; Fax: 212-755-4128.
(Archbishop's Residence), Res.: 452 Madison Ave., 10022. Most Revs. Timothy M. Dolan; Dennis Sullivan, Vicar Gen.; Rev. Msgrs. William J. Belford, Vicar for Clergy; Gregory Mustaciuolo, Chancellor; Rev. James A. Cruz, Sec. to Archbishop.
Chapel—New York, Sts. Faith, Hope and Charity, Records at St. Patrick Cathedral.

2—ST. AGNES (1873) Revs. Richard Adams; Dempsey Acosta; Joseph Braganza; Anastarsio Tarsio; Catalino S. Villaviza.
Res.: 143 E. 43rd St., 10017. Tel: 212-682-5722; Fax: 212-370-5791. Email: churchofstagnes@aol.com.

3—ST. ALBERT (1916) Closed. Parochial records at Sacred Heart.

4—ALL SAINTS (1879) Rev. Steven Pavignano, O.F.M. In Res., Rev. Francis K. Kim, O.F.M., Exec. Vice Pres., Franciscan Missionary Charities, Inc.; Bros. Charles F. Gilmartin, O.F.M., Vol. Pastoral Assoc., St. Francis of Assisi Church; Glenn W. Humphrey, O.F.M., School Psychologist, Rice High School.
Res.: 47 E. 129th St., 10035. Tel: 212-534-3535; Fax: 212-987-1930.
School—(1900) 52 E. 130th St., 10037. Tel: 212-534-0558; Fax: 212-831-6343. Geneine Morris, Prin. Lay Teachers 10; Students 191.
Catechesis/Religious Program— Participant in Harlem Tri Parish Religious Education Program (All Saints, St. Aloysius, St. Mark the Evangelist); Office at All Saints School. Students 7; Whole Tri Parish Program 135.

5—ST. ALOYSIUS (1899), (Jesuit) Revs. Frederick J. Pellegrini, S.J.; Thomas P. Green, S.J.
Res.: 219 W. 132nd St., 10027. Tel: 212-234-2848; Fax: 212-234-6495.
School—(1940) 223 W. 132nd St., 10027. Tel: 212-283-0921; Fax: 212-234-4198. Carol McCarthy, Prin.; Joe Lavagnino, Pres. Religious 2; Lay Teachers 20; Students 275.
Catechesis/Religious Program—Students 20.

6—ST. ALPHONSUS (1847) Closed. Records at St. Anthony of Padua.

7—ST. AMBROSE (CHAPEL CENTRO MARIA) (1897) Closed. Records at Sacred Heart Church.

8—ST. ANDREW (1842) Revs. James Hayes, S.S.S.; Gooe Iwele, O.M.I., Parochial Vicar. Blessed Sacrament Fathers and Brothers.
Res.: 20 Cardinal Hayes Pl., 10007. Tel: 212-962-3972; 212-962-3973; Fax: 212-962-1012. Email: churchofsaintandrewnyc@verizon.net. Web: www.saintandrewnyc.org.
Catechesis/Religious Program—
Station—New York Infirmary Beekman Downtown Hospital 170 William St., 10007. Tel: 212-312-5000.
Station—St. Margaret's House 49 Fulton St., 10007. Tel: 212-766-8122.

9—ST. ANN (1911), (Don Orione Fathers) Revs. Mario Guarino, F.D.P.; Pasquale Ruggieri, F.D.P. (Italy).
Res.: 312 E. 110th St., 10029.
School—(1926) 314-318 E. 110th St., 10029. Tel: 212-722-1295; Fax: 212-722-8267. Web: www-.stannsnyc.org. Sr. Josephine Cioffi, Prin. Priests 2; Sisters, Servants of the Immaculate Heart of Mary 1; Lay Teachers 12; Students 340.
Catechesis/Religious Program—Students 210.
Chapel—St. Ann's Convent 319 E. 109 St., 10029. Tel: 212-534-8321.

10—ST. ANN'S ROMAN CATHOLIC CHURCH (1852), Administered from and records located at Immaculate Conception, 414 E. 14th St., New York, NY 10009. Tel: 212-254-0200., 110 E. 12th St., 10003.

11—ANNUNCIATION (1853), (Hispanic), (Piarist Fathers) Revs. Jose M. Clavero, Sch.P. (Spain); Felix Ganuza, Sch.P. (Spain), Assoc. Pastor/Supr.; Marcel Ayuni Toh, Sch.P. (Cameroon); Fernando Negro, Sch.P. (Spain); Javier Renteria, Sch.P. (Spain).
Res.: 88 Convent Ave., 10027. Tel: 212-234-1919; Fax: 212-281-7205. Email: annunciationchurchnyc@yahoo.com.
School—(1858) 461 W. 131st St., 10027. Tel: 212-281-7174; Fax: 212-281-1732. Theresa Cetinski, Prin. Lay Teachers 13; Students 216.
Catechesis/Religious Program—Students 263.

12—ST. ANTHONY OF PADUA (Org. 1859; Re-org. 1866), (Italian), (Franciscan) Revs. Joseph F. Lorenzo,

O.F.M.; Francis A. Hanudel, O.F.M.; Bro. Courtland Campbell, O.F.M., Pastoral Min.
Res. & Chapel: 154 Sullivan St., 10012. Tel: 212-777-2755; Fax: 212-673-6684. Email: stanthonychurch@aol.com. Web: www.stanthonynyc.org.
Catechesis/Religious Program—Sr. Annette Seiter, O.S.F., D.R.E. Students 51.

13—ASCENSION (1895) Revs. John P. Duffell; Sixto Quezada (Dominican Republic).
Res.: 221 W. 107th St., 10025. Tel: 212-222-0666; Fax: 212-961-1086.
School—(1912) 220 W. 108th St., 10025. Tel: 212-222-5161; Fax: 212-280-4690. Lay Teachers 13; Students 320.
Catechesis/Religious Program—Tel: 212-749-5938; Fax: 212-749-8658. Students 250.
Chapel—Riverside Study Center 330 Riverside Dr., 10025. Tel: 212-222-3285; Fax: 212-316-3629. (Opus Dei)

14—ASSUMPTION (1858) Closed. Records at Sacred Heart Church.

15—ST. BENEDICT THE MOOR (1883) Attended by Sacred Heart of Jesus, New York Rev. Jose Gabriel Piedrahita, M.X.Y.
Res.: 457 W. 51st St., 10019. Tel: 212-265-5020; Fax: 212-977-4116.

16—ST. BERNARD (1868) Closed. Records at Our Lady of Guadalupe-St. Bernard.
Res.: 328 W. 14th St., 10014. Tel: 212-243-0265; Fax: 212-255-8466.
Catechesis/Religious Program—Tel: 212-243-5317; Fax: 212-255-8466. Students 100.

17—BLESSED SACRAMENT (1887) Rev. Msgr. Robert B. O'Connor; Rev. Alfredo Balinong, S.J. (Philippines); Rev. Msgr. William J. Toohy; Rev. Alexis Bastidas (Venezuela).
Res.: 152 W. 71st St., 10023. Tel: 212-877-3111; Fax: 212-799-6233. Web: www.blessedsacramentnyc.com.
School—(1902) 147-151 W. 70th St., 10023. Tel: 212-724-7561; Fax: 212-724-7561. Imella Engel, Prin. Lay Teachers 11; Students 270.
Catechesis/Religious Program—Students 150.
Chapel—Convent of Blessed Sacrament 133 W. 70th St., 10023.
Chapel—St. Agnes' Home 237 W. 74th St., 10023. Tel: 212-874-9203.
Chapel—Archdiocese Teachers Residence 22 W. 70th St., 10023.

18—ST. BONIFACE (1858) Closed. Records at Holy Family Church.

19—ST. BRIGID (1848; 1955), Records at St. Emeric, 185 Ave. D, New York, NY 10009. Tel: 212-228-4494. Rev. Lorenzo Ato, Admin.
Res.: 119 Avenue B, 10009. Tel: 212-228-5400; Fax: 212-254-0334.
School—185 E. Seventh St., 10009. Tel: 212-677-5210; Fax: 212-260-2262. Donna Vincent, Prin. Students 132.
Catechesis/Religious Program—Students 125.

20—ST. CATHERINE OF GENOA (1887) Rev. Msgr. Kenneth J. Smith; Rev. Ricardo Fajardo (Dominican Republic).
Res.: 506 W. 153rd St., 10031. Tel: 212-862-6130; Fax: 212-491-6272. Email: scg@yahoo.com.
Catechesis/Religious Program—Students 355.

21—ST. CATHERINE OF SIENA (1897), (Dominican), Very Rev. Edward M. Gorman, O.P., Prior/Pastor; Revs. John Thaddeus Murphy, O.P.; Michael Trainor, O.P.; Gabriel Gillen, O.P.; Stephen Francis Carmody, O.P., Hospital Chap.; Louis Mason, O.P., Hospital Chap.; Carlos-Bartolome Quijano, O.P., Hospital Chap. & Sub-Prior; Sean J. McConway, O.P., Hospital Chap.; Bro. Ignatius Perkins, O.P.; Sr. Margaret Oettinger, O.P., Hospital Chap.
Res.: 411 E. 68th St., 10021. Tel: 212-988-8300; Fax: 212-988-6918.

22—ST. CECILIA (1873), (Apostles of Jesus) Rev. Peter Mushi, A.J.; Deacon Alejandro Lugo.
125 E. 105th St., 10029.
Res.: Tel: 212-534-1350; Fax: 212-410-6177.
Catechesis/Religious Program—Students 166.

23—ST. CHARLES BORROMEO (1888) Revs. Philip Amankwah-Danquah, Interim Admin.; Thomas Mestriparampil; Telamaque Florvil (Haiti); Deacons Rodney Beckford; Kenneth L. Radcliffe.
Res.: 211 W. 141st St., 10030. Tel: 212-281-2100; Fax: 212-862-1881.
School—(1904) 214 W. 142 St., 10030. Tel: 212-368-6666; Fax: 212-281-1323. Sr. Marianne Poole, S.B.S., Prin. Sisters of the Blessed Sacrament 3; Lay Teachers 13; Students 250.
Catechesis/Religious Program—Students 50.
Mission—Resurrection 276 W. 151st St., New York Co. 10039. Tel: 212-690-7555; Fax: 212-690-6590.

24—CHURCH OF THE RESURRECTION (1907), Mission of St. Charles Borromeo. Records at St. Charles Borromeo, 211 W. 141st St., New York, NY 10030 (212-281-2100)., 211 W. 141st St., 10030.
Catechesis/Religious Program—Mrs. Marisa Rivera, C.R.E. Students 75.
Mission—Chapel of the Resurrection 276 W. 151st St., 10039. Tel: 212-690-7555; Fax: 212-690-6590. Email: scbharlem211@yahoo.com. Web: www.churchofstcharlesborromeoharlem.com.

25—ST. CLARE (1903) Closed. Records at St. Raphael's Church.

26—ST. CLEMENS MARY (1909) Closed. Records at Holy Cross Church, Manhattan.

27—ST. COLUMBA (1845) Rev. Arthur A. Golino. In Res., Rev. James C. Sheehan.
Res.: 343 W. 25th St., 10001. Tel: 212-807-8876; Fax: 212-989-6548. Email: saintcolumba@verizon.net.
Chapel—Sisters of Congregation of Notre Dame 329 W. 25th St., 10001. Tel: 212-243-1760.
Catechesis/Religious Program—Email: saintcolumbaccd@verizon.net. Students 40.

28—CORPUS CHRISTI (1906) Revs. Raymond M. Rafferty; William L. Wizeman, S.J. In Res., Rev. Msgr. Kevin L. Sullivan.
Res.: 529 W. 121st St., 10027. Tel: 212-666-9350; Fax: 212-531-2487. Email: corpus-christi-nyc@nyc.rr.com. Web: www.corpus-christi-nyc.org.
School—(1907) 535 W. 121st St., 10027. Tel: 212-662-9344; Fax: 212-662-2725. Web: www.ccschool-nyc.org. Dorothy Valla, Prin. Lay Teachers 11; Students 185.
Catechesis/Religious Program—Students 25.

29—ST. CYRIL (1916), (Slovenian), (Franciscan) Rev. Krizolog Cimerman, O.F.M.
Res.: 62 St. Mark's Pl., 10003. Tel: 212-674-3442; Fax: 212-674-3442.

30—SS. CYRIL AND METHODIUS - ST. RAPHAEL (1913; 1886), (Croatian), (Franciscan) Revs. Nikola Pasalic, O.F.M.; Stipe Renic, O.F.M.
Res.: 502 W. 41st St., 10036. Tel: 212-563-3395; Fax: 212-868-1203. Email: crkva.nyc@verizon.net.
Catechesis/Religious Program—Students 75.

31—ST. ELIZABETH (1869) Revs. Daniel S. Kearney; Evaristus Ohuche, Parochial Vicar; Osiris Salcedo, S.D.B. (Dominican Republic), Parochial Vicar; Emmanuel Udoh (Nigeria), Parochial Vicar.
Res.: 268 Wadsworth Ave., 10033. Tel: 212-568-8803; Fax: 212-781-2754.
School—(1936) 612 W. 187th St., 10033. Tel: 212-568-7291; Fax: 212-928-2515. Web: www.steliznyc.org. Sisters 4; Lay Teachers 18; Students 417.
Catechesis/Religious Program—Tel: 212-923-4900; Fax: 212-781-2754. Students 381.
Chapel—Sisters Residence 612 W. 187th St., 10033.
Chapel—Cabrini Chapel 701 Ft. Washington Ave., 10040. Tel: 212-923-3536; Fax: 212-923-1871. Email: st.francescabrinishrine@verizon.net.
Isabella Geriatric Center—515 Audubon Ave., 10040. Tel: 212-342-9245.

32—ST. ELIZABETH OF HUNGARY (1891), (Slovak), Rev. Msgr. Patrick P. McCahill.
Res.: 211 E. 83rd St., 10028-2854. Tel: 212-734-5747; 212-988-1903 (TTY); 866-810-3394 (VP); Fax: 212-988-1903. Email: MO65@archny.org. Web: www.stelizabethofhungarynyc.org.
Catechesis/Religious Program—Students 60.

33—ST. EMERIC (1949) Rev. Lorenzo Ato, Admin.
Res.: 185 Avenue D, 10009. Tel: 212-228-4494; Fax: 212-375-1163.
Catechesis/Religious Program—Students 139.

34—EPIPHANY (1868) Rev. Patrick Curley; Rev. Msgrs. Walter J. Niebrzydowski, Pastor Emeritus (Retired); Harry J. Byrne, Pastor Emeritus (Retired).
Res.: 239 E. 21st St., 10010. Tel: 212-475-1966; Fax: 212-477-0537. Web: www.epicchurch.us.
School—(1869) 234 E. 22nd St., 10010. Tel: 212-473-4128; Fax: 212-473-4392. Web: www.theepiphanyschool.org. Sisters 1; Lay Teachers 35; Students 500.
Catechesis/Religious Program—Students 184.

35—ST. FRANCES CABRINI (1973) Rev. Peter A. Miqueli.
Res.: 564 Main St., Roosevelt Island, 10044. Tel: 212-832-6778 (office).
Catechesis/Religious Program—Students 75.

36—ST. FRANCIS DE SALES (1894), (Don Orione Fathers) Rev. Victor Muzzin, F.D.P. (Italy). In Res., Rev. John A. Kamas, S.S.S.
Res.: 135 E. 96th St., 10128. Tel: 212-289-0425; Fax: 212-996-2028. Email: sfds.church@yahoo.com.

37—ST. FRANCIS OF ASSISI (1844), (Franciscan. For priests and brothers not listed here, see St. Francis Monastery under Monasteries and Residences of Priests and Brothers.) Revs. Jerome Massimino, O.F.M., Guardian; Michael Carnevale, O.F.M.; Anthony M. Carrozzo, O.F.M.; Joseph F. Cavoto, S.A.; John M. Felice, O.F.M.; R. Patrick Fitzgerald, O.F.M.; Robert A. Gavin, O.F.M.; Hugh Hines, O.F.M.; Joseph Kim (Korea, South); Pio Kim, O.F.M.; Vincent A. Laviano, O.F.M., Vicar; Felix P. McGrath, O.F.M.; John J. McVean, O.F.M.; Stephen D. Mimnaugh, O.F.M.; Timothy J. Shreenan, O.F.M.; Alan J. Thomas, Vicar; Kevin Tortorelli, O.F.M.; Thomas Walters, O.F.M.; Bro. Anthony LoGalbo, O.F.M. In Res., Very Rev. John F. O'Connor, O.F.M., Min. Provincial; Revs. James R. O'Connell, O.F.M., Hospital Chap.; Dominic Monti, O.F.M., Vicar Provincial; Brian E. Smail, O.F.M., Vocation Dir.; Bro. Michael Harlan, O.F.M., Sec. of the Province.
Res.: *St. Francis of Assisi Friary*, 135 W. 31st St., 10001. Tel: 212-736-8500; Fax: 212-736-8545. Web: www.stfrancisnyc.org.
Catechesis/Religious Program—Christine Moon, D.R.E. Students 29.

38—ST. FRANCIS XAVIER (1847), (Jesuit) Revs. Joseph S. Costantino, S.J.; Peter E. Fink, S.J.; Ms. Luz Marina Diaz, Dir. Faith Formation; Cassandra Agredo, Dir. Outreach Mission; Jacqueline Falco, Business Mgr.; John Uehlein, Dir. Music Min.
Office: 55 W. 15th St., 10011. Tel: 212-627-2100; Fax: 212-675-6997. Email: stfrancisxavier@sfxavier.org. Web: http:www.sfxavier.org.

39—ST. GABRIEL (1867) Closed. Records at Church of Sacred Hearts of Jesus and Mary.

40—GOOD SHEPHERD (1912), (Capuchin Franciscans) Revs. Robert Abbatiello, O.F.M.Cap., Guardian; Philip Bohan, O.F.M.Cap.; Arlen Harris, O.F.M-.Cap.; Deacon Rafael Then. In Res., Bro. Timothy Jones, O.F.M.Cap.
Res.: 608 Isham St., 10034. Tel: 212-567-1300; Fax: 212-567-1476. Web: www.goodshepherdnyc.org.
School—(1925) 620 Isham St., 10034. Tel: 212-567-5800; Fax: 212-567-5839. Lay Teachers 12; Students 148.
Catechesis/Religious Program—Students 150.
Chapel— 630 Isham St., 10034. Tel: 212-567-1600. (Private)

41—ST. GREGORY (1907) Rev. Msgr. Michael Crimmins; Rev. Nelson Pichardo.
Res.: 144 W. 90th St., 10024. Tel: 212-724-9766; 212-724-9767; Fax: 212-579-3380.
School—(1913) 138 W. 90th St., 10024. Tel: 212-362-5410; Fax: 212-362-5062. Ms. Donna Gabella, Prin. Lay Teachers 10; Students 210.
Catechesis/Religious Program—Email: stgregnyc@aol.com. Students 34.

42—GUARDIAN ANGEL (1888) Rev. Msgr. Michael F. Hull. In Res., Rev. Philip S. Phan.
Res.: 193 Tenth Ave., 10011-4709. Tel: 212-929-5966; Fax: 212-929-5966.
School—(1911)Tel: 212-989-8280; Fax: 212-352-1467. Maureen McElduff, Prin. Lay Teachers 10; Students 210.

43—ST. HEDWIG (1934) Closed. Parochial records at St. Stanislaus Church.

44—HOLY AGONY (1930), (Spanish), (Vincentian) Revs. Victor Elia, C.M.; Candido Arrizurieta, C.M.; Jesus Eguaras, C.M.; Jesus Arellano, C.M.
Res.: 1834 Third Ave., 10029. Tel: 212-289-5589; Fax: 212-289-8321. Email: milag2@verizon.net.
Catechesis/Religious Program—Students 135.

45—HOLY CROSS (1852) Revs. Peter M. Colapietro; Thomas Del Valle; Mr. Edward Greene, LAMP Min.
Res.: 329 W. 42nd St., 10036. Tel: 212-246-4732; Fax: 212-307-5033.
School—(1864) 332 W. 43rd St., 10036. Tel: 212-246-0923; Fax: 212-246-0923. Sr. Mary Theresa Dixon, O.P., Prin. Sisters of St. Dominic of Blauvelt 1; Lay Teachers 16; Students 400.
Convent—Dominican Convent, 460 W. 44th St., 10036. Tel: 212-246-9768.
Chapel—St. Joseph's Home 425 W. 44th St., 10036. Tel: 212-246-5363.

46—HOLY FAMILY (1924) Revs. Robert J. Robbins; Julito A. Cabatuan, Parochial Vicar; Bro. Robert V. Fontaine, C.S.C., Pastoral Assoc. In Res., Rev. Emile Frische, M.H.M.
Res.: 315 E. 47th St., 10017-2318. Tel: 212-753-3401; Fax: 212-753-3428. Email: pastor@churchholyfamily.org. Web: www.churchholyfamily.org.
Catechesis/Religious Program—Students 18.

47—HOLY INNOCENTS (1866) Revs. Thomas Kallumady; Owen J. Lafferty. In Res., Revs. William J. Delaney; Oliver Chanama.
Res.: 128 W. 37th St., 10018. Tel: 212-279-5861; Fax: 212-714-9313. Email: pastor@innocents.com. Web: www.innocents.com.

48—HOLY NAME OF JESUS (1868), (Franciscan) Revs. Daniel T. Kenna, O.F.M.; Michael McDonnell, O.F.M.; Gonzalo De Jesus Torre, O.F.M.; Lawrence D. Ford, O.F.M.; Evariste Ouedraogo. In Res., Revs. Brian Jordan, O.F.M.; Matthew A. Pravetz, O.F.M.; Deacon Andre Alexandre.
Res.: 207 W. 96th St., 10025. Tel: 212-749-0276; Fax: 212-749-2045. Email: holyname.nyc@aol.com.
School—(1905) Amsterdam Ave. & 97th St., 10025. Tel: 212-749-1240; Fax: 212-749-4363. Mr. John Joven, Prin. Sisters 1; Lay Teachers 17; Students 375.
Catechesis/Religious Program—Tel: 212-749-0276, Ext. 16. Students 155.

49—HOLY ROSARY (1884), (Augustinian) Revs. Gilbert Luis R. Centina III, O.S.A.; Abel Alvarez,

O.S.A., Parochial Vicar; Basilio S. Alava, O.S.A., Parochial Vicar.
Res.: 444 E. 119th St., 10035. Tel: 212-534-0740; Fax: 212-534-7572.
School—(1949) 371 Pleasant Ave., 10035. Tel: 212-876-7555; Fax: 212-876-0152. Lay Teachers 10; Students 252.
Catechesis/Religious Program—Students 35.

50—HOLY TRINITY (1898) Rev. Msgr. Thomas P. Leonard. In Res., Revs. James Yeakel, O.S.F.S.; William R. Dailey, C.S.C.
Res.: 213 W. 82nd St., 10024. Tel: 212-787-0634; Fax: 212-787-4917. Email: holy213@earthlink.net. Web: www.htcny.org.
Catechesis/Religious Program—Students 141.
Chapel—Chinese Catholic Information Center 86 Riverside Dr., 10024. Tel: 212-787-6969; Fax: 212-787-0351.

51—ST. IGNATIUS LOYOLA (1851), (Jesuit) Revs. George M. Witt, S.J.; William J. Bergen, S.J.; James L. Dugan, S.J.; Ugo R. Nacciarone, S.J.; Sr. Kathryn King, Pastoral Assoc.; Ms. Joanne F. Cunneen, Pastoral Assoc.
Res.: 980 Park Ave., 10028. Tel: 212-288-3588; Fax: 212-734-3671.
School—(1854) 48 E. 84th St., 10028. Tel: 212-861-3820; Fax: 212-879-8248. Lay Teachers 33; Students 527.
Day Nursery—240 E. 84th St., 10028. Tel: 212-734-6427; Fax: 212-734-6972. Lay Assistants 31; Capacity 125.
School—Loyola School, Tel: 212-288-3522; Fax: 212-861-1021.
School—Marymount School, 1026 Fifth Ave., 10028. Tel: 212-744-4486; Fax: 212-744-0163.
High School—Regis High School, 55 E. 84th St., 10028. Tel: 212-288-1100; Fax: 212-794-1221.
Catechesis/Religious Program—Tel: 212-861-4764. Ms. Joanne Cunneen, D.R.E. Students 490.

52—IMMACULATE CONCEPTION (1855) Revs. Joy Mampilly; Francis X. Buu. In Res., Rev. Msgr. Desmond J. Vella; Rev. Lorenzo Ato.
Res.: 414 E. 14th St., 10009. Tel: 212-254-0200; Fax: 212-505-7610. Web: www.immaculateconception-nyc.org.
School—(1864) 419 E. 13th St., 10009. Tel: 212-475-2590; Fax: 212-777-2818. Sisters 1; Lay Teachers 9; Students 230.
Catechesis/Religious Program—Students 65.

53—INCARNATION (1908), (Hispanic), Rev. Msgr. Gabriel La Paz; Revs. Felino Reyes Nin; Aroldo Guerra.
Res.: 1290 St. Nicholas Ave., 10033. Tel: 212-927-7474; Fax: 212-928-0315. Web: www.incarnation-nyc.org.
School—(1910) 568-570 W. 175th St., 10033. Tel: 212-795-1030; Fax: 212-795-1564. Lay Teachers 21; Students 552.
Catechesis/Religious Program—Maria Minaya, D.R.E. Students 574.

54—ST. JAMES (1827) Rev. Walter Tonelotto, C.S., Admin.
Rectory—23 Oliver St., 10038. Tel: 212-233-0161; Fax: 212-233-1210.
School—(1854) 37 St. James Place, 10038. Tel: 212-267-9289; Fax: 212-227-0065. Mrs. Anne Marie McGoldrick, Prin. Lay Teachers 10; Students 210.
Catechesis/Religious Program—Tel: 212-233-0161; Fax: 212-233-1210. Elba Feliciano, D.R.E. Students 15.

55—ST. JEAN BAPTISTE (1882), (Blessed Sacrament Fathers) Revs. Anthony Schueller, S.S.S.; Ernest R. Falardeau, S.S.S.; Bernard J. Camire, S.S.S.; Sujith Tillekeratne, S.S.S., Chap.; Deacons Richard Russo; Joseph Pino.
Res.: 184 E. 76th St., 10021. Tel: 212-288-5082; Fax: 212-717-8397. Email: sjbrcc@aol.com. Web: www.sjbrcc.net.
High School—173 E. 75th St., 10021. Tel: 212-288-1645; Fax: 212-288-6540. Email: information@stjean.org. Web: www.stjean.org. (Girls High School) Sisters of the Congregation of Notre Dame 5; Lay Teachers 30; Students 340.
Catechesis/Religious Program—Tel: 212-472-2853, Ext. 6. Email: robinscott@yahoo.com. Students 70.
Chapel—Sisters' Convent, Tel: 212-472-1230 (Apt. A); 212-472-8821 (Apt. B); Fax: 212-396-2025. Web: www.cnd-m.com.

56—ST. JOACHIM (1888), (Italian), Closed. Parochial records are at Church of St. Joseph.

57—ST. JOHN NEPOMUCENE (1895), (Slovak), Revs. Martin Svitan; Stefan Chanas, Parochial Vicar.
Res.: 411 E. 66th St., 10065. Tel: 212-734-4613; Fax: 212-734-2483. Email: slovakchurch@gmail.com. Web: www.stjohnnepomucene.org.
Chapel—Sisters' Convent 320 E. 66th St., 10065. Tel: 212-737-0221.

58—ST. JOHN THE BAPTIST (1840), (Capuchin) Revs. Philip Fabiano, O.F.M.Cap.; Edward Conway, O.F.M.Cap., Parochial Vicar; Thomas Franks, O.F.M.Cap., Parochial Vicar; John B. Riordan, O.F.M.Cap.; Bro. Luke Benbrook, O.F.M.Cap., Pastoral Assoc.; Deacon Salvatore P. Patricola, O.F.M.Cap., Pastoral Assoc. & Guardian. In Res., Revs. John Clermont, O.F.M.Cap., Missionary Apostolate; Valerian D'Silva, O.F.M.Cap. (India); Francis Gasparik, O.F.M.Cap., Dir. Office of Mission & Devel.; Leonard Glavin, O.F.M.Cap. (Retired); Thomas R. Houle, O.F.M.Cap., Chap., NYS Corrections; Matthias Wesnofske, O.F.M.Cap., Spiritual Asst. of Secular Order of St. Francis; Ramon Frias, O.F.M.Cap.; Bro. George McCloskey, O.F.M.Cap., Mission & Devel. & Communications Office.
Res.: 210 W. 31st St., 10001-2876. Tel: 212-564-9070; Fax: 212-564-3964.

59—ST. JOHN THE EVANGELIST (1840) [CEM] Rev. Msgr. Douglas J. Mathers; Revs. James P. Connolly, Senior Priest; Daniel J. Kyom.
Res.: 348 E. 55th St., 10022. Tel: 212-753-8418; Fax: 212-826-1848. Email: churchofstjohn@cs.com.
Catechesis/Religious Program—Students 3.

60—ST. JOHN THE MARTYR (1903) Revs. Sean R. Harlow, O.Carm.; Sunny John, O.Carm. (India), Parochial Vicar. In Res., Revs. Paul Feeley, O.Carm. (Retired); Raymond Maher, O.Carm.; Sunny Mathew, O.Carm. (India).
Res.: 259 E. 71st St., 10021-4596. Tel: 212-744-4880; 212-744-4881; Fax: 212-628-6662. Email: sjtm@nyc.rr.com.
Catechesis/Religious Program— Regional. See St. Ignatius Loyola, New York.

61—ST. JOSEPH (1829), (Dominican) Revs. John Patrick McGuire, O.P.; Vincent G. DeLucia, O.P.; John Davis, O.P.
Res.: 371 Sixth Ave., 10014. Tel: 212-741-1274; Fax: 212-741-2147. Web: www.stjoseph-village.com.
Catechesis/Religious Program—Thomas Sabatelli, D.R.E. Students 43.

62—ST. JOSEPH (1924), (Scalabrinian) Revs. Walter Tonelotto, C.S.; Joseph Ruan (Hong Kong), (Chinese Apostolate).
Res.: 5 Monroe St., 10002. Tel: 212-267-8376; Fax: 212-964-0132. Email: sjch5@aol.com. Web: www.stjosephnyc.org.
School—(1926) One Monroe St., 10002. Tel: 212-233-5152; Fax: 212-267-4357. Sisters (Apostles of the Sacred Heart of Jesus) 4; Lay Teachers 11; Students 235.
Catechesis/Religious Program—Students 40.
Convent—83 Madison St., 10002. Tel: 212-233-5670. Sisters (Apostles of the Sacred Heart of Jesus) 2.

63—ST. JOSEPH (1873) Revs. James Boniface Ramsey; Matthew Yatkauskas.
Res.: 404 E. 87th St., 10128. Tel: 212-289-6030; Fax: 212-348-8075. Email: sjosephyorkville@aol.com. Web: www.stjosephsyorkville.org.
School—(1880) 420 E. 87th St., 10128. Tel: 212-289-3057; Fax: 212-289-7239. Lay Teachers 13; Students 325.
Catechesis/Religious Program—Tel: 212-861-4764; Fax: 212-734-3671. Regional. See St. Ignatius Loyola, New York. Students 14.

64—ST. JOSEPH OF THE HOLY FAMILY (1860) Revs. Philip J. Kelly; Neil J. O'Connell, O.F.M.
Res.: 405 W. 125th St., 10027. Tel: 212-662-9125.
School—(1862) 168 Morningside Ave., 10027. Tel: 212-662-1736; Fax: 212-662-1490. Lay Teachers 10; Students 134.
Catechesis/Religious Program—Students 40.
Convent—400 W. 126th St., 10027.

65—ST. JUDE (1949) Rev. Elias Isla; Deacon Porfirio Rodriguez.
Res.: 431 W. 204th St., 10034. Tel: 212-569-3000; Fax: 212-304-4545.
School—(1953) 433 W. 204th St., 10034. Tel: 212-569-3400; Fax: 212-304-4479. Lay Teachers 16; Students 400.
Catechesis/Religious Program—Tel: 212-569-3002. Students 510.
Chapel—New York, St. Jude Convent

66—ST. LEO (1880) Closed. Parochial records at St. Stephen's Church.

67—ST. LUCY (1900) Rev. Msgr. Oscar A. Aquino, Admin. In Res., Rev. Esviardo Palomino, Pastor Emeritus (Retired).
Res.: 344 E. 104th St., 10029. Tel: 212-534-1470.
School—(1942) 340 E. 104th St., 10029. Tel: 212-534-4021; Fax: 212-354-4130. Consolidated with St. Francis de Sales School to form St. Francis de Sales-St. Lucy Academy (1993).
Catechesis/Religious Program—Diana Naranjo, D.R.E. Students 46.

68—ST. MALACHY'S (1902), (The Actors' Chapel) Revs. Richard D. Baker; Tomas Del Valle-Reyes; Regina Marino, Parish Mgr.
Res.: 239 W. 49th St., 10019. Tel: 212-489-1340; Fax: 212-262-6224. Email: info@actorschapel.org. Web: www.actorschapel.org.
Encore Community Services—Tel: 212-581-2910; 212-664-8628; Fax: 212-757-0244. Web: www.encorecommunityservices.org. Sisters Elizabeth Hasselt, O.P., Exec. Dir.; Lillian McNamara, O.P., Dir.; Peggy Gearity, Controller.
Encore Community Center & Programs—Tel: 212-581-2910.
Catechesis/Religious Program—Students 45.

69—ST. MARK THE EVANGELIST (1907), (Holy Spirit Fathers) Rev. Simon Lobon, C.Ss.P.
Res.: 65 W. 138th St., 10037. Tel: 212-281-4931; Fax: 212-491-6803.
School—(1912) 55 W. 138th St., 10037. Tel: 212-283-4848; Fax: 212-926-0419. Web: www.saintmarkschool.org. Sr. Catherine Hagan, D.C., Prin. Daughters of Charity of St. Vincent de Paul 1; Lay Teachers 12; Students 252.
Catechesis/Religious Program—Students 18.
Chapel—St. Mark's Convent, Tel: 212-283-4966.

70—ST. MARY (1826) Rev. Msgr. Neil A. Connolly; Rev. Robert J. O'Neil, M.H.M. In Res., Rev. Peter Ma (Retired), (Chinese Apostolate), (Retired).
Res.: 28 Attorney St., 10002. Tel: 212-674-3266; Fax: 212-539-0216. Email: stmaryparish@aol.com.
Catechesis/Religious Program—Students 155.

71—MARY HELP OF CHRISTIANS (1908) Unassigned. (Salesian); Records at: Immaculate Conception, 414 E. 14th St., New York, NY 10009 (212-254-0200)
Res.: 440 E. 12th St., 10009.

72—ST. MARY MAGDALEN (1873), (German), Closed. Parochial records at Immaculate Conception Church.

73—ST. MATTHEW (1902) Closed. Parochial records at Blessed Sacrament Church.

74—ST. MICHAEL (1857) Rev. Myles P. Murphy, S.T.L.
Res.: 424 W. 34th St., 10001. Tel: 212-563-2575; Fax: 212-563-4087.
High School—(1866-1874) 425 W. 33rd St., 10001. Tel: 212-563-2547. Mrs. Clotilde Dillou, Prin. Sisters of the Presentation 1; Lay Teachers 21; Girls 260.
Catechesis/Religious Program—Students 260.
Chapel—Sacred Heart 419 W. 33rd St., 10001. Tel: 212-947-7668.

75—ST. MICHAEL CHAPEL (1936), (Russian), Rt. Rev. Roman V. Russo, (Newton); Very Protodeacon Christopher LiGreci.
Church: 266 Mulberry St., 10012. Tel: 212-226-2644 (Church); 718-836-7311 (Residence); Fax: 718-921-5290.
Catechesis/Religious Program—Students 13.

76—ST. MONICA (1879) Rev. Msgr. Thomas A. Modugno; Revs. Joseph A. Francis, O.P.; Thomas Mankamthanath. In Res., Rev. Apolinari J. Ngirwa (Tanzania).
Res.: 413 E. 79th St., 10075. Tel: 212-288-6250; Fax: 212-570-1562. Email: info@churchofstmonica.org. Web: www.churchofstmonica.org.
Chapel—St. Monica Convent 404 E. 80th St., 10075. Tel: 212-288-1986.

77—MOST HOLY CRUCIFIX (1925), (Italian), Unassigned. Records at St. Patrick's Old Cathedral, 263 Mulberry St., New York, NY 10012. Tel: 212-226-8075.
Res.: 378 Broome St., 10013. Tel: 212-226-2556.

78—MOST HOLY REDEEMER (1844), (Redemptorist) Revs. Charles P. McDonald, C.Ss.R.; Blas Caceres, C.Ss.R. In Res., Revs. Lenin Delgado, C.Ss.R.; Arthur G. Wendel, C.Ss.R., Vicar.
Res.: 173 E. Third St., 10009. Tel: 212-673-4224.
Catechesis/Religious Program—Students 47.

79—MOST PRECIOUS BLOOD (1891), (Italian), [CEM], (Franciscan) Rev. Fabian Grifone, O.F.M., Supr.; Friar Dominic Poirier, O.F.M.
Res.: 109 Mulberry St., 10013. Tel: 212-226-6427; Fax: 212-226-1837. Email: fgrifone@aol.com. Web: www.mostpreciousbloodchurch.net.

80—NATIVITY (1842), (Mission of St. Teresa). Records at St. Teresa, 141 Henry St., New York, NY 10002. Tel: 212-233-0233. Rev. Donald C. Baker; Deacon Arnaldo Rodriguez.
Res.: 44 Second Ave., 10003. Tel: 212-674-8590; Fax: 212-674-8789.
Catechesis/Religious Program—Students 50.
Nativity Mission Center—204 Forsyth St., 10002. Tel: 212-477-2472; Fax: 212-473-0538.

81—ST. NICHOLAS (1833), (German), Closed. Parochial records at Most Holy Redeemer Church.

82—NOTRE DAME (1910), (Dominican) Revs. Andrzej J. Fornal, O.P.; Romuald Jedrejko, O.P.; Jacek Kopera, O.P.; Lukasz Misko, O.P.; Marek Pienkowski, O.P.
Res.: 405 W. 114th St., 10025. Tel: 212-866-1500; Fax: 212-222-5704. Email: parish@ndparish.org. Web: www.ndparish.org.
Catechesis/Religious Program—Students 12.
St. Luke's Hospital—Tel: 212-523-4000.
Amsterdam Nursing Home—Tel: 212-316-7700.

83—OUR LADY OF ESPERANZA (1912), (Spanish), Revs. Edward Russell, Admin.; Carlos Acosta Lopez.
Res.: 624 W. 156th St., 10032. Tel: 212-283-4340; Fax: 212-283-4388. Email: vze4s75z@verizon.net.
Catechesis/Religious Program—Students 270.

84—OUR LADY OF GOOD COUNSEL (1886) Revs. Kazimierz A. Kowalski; Richard Terga, C.I.C.M. In

Res., Revs. William S. Elder; Jakub Ciolak.
Res.: 230 E. 90th St., 10128. Tel: 212-289-1742; Fax: 212-427-5643.
Catechesis/Religious Program—Students 78.

85—OUR LADY OF GRACE (Stanton St.) (1907) Closed. Parochial records at Church of the Nativity.

86—OUR LADY OF GUADALUPE AT ST. BERNARD'S (1869) Rev. Msgr. Kevin J. Nelan; Rev. Lino Gonsalves (India); Deacon Rene Garcia. In Res., Rev. Joseph O'Meara.
Res.: 328 W. 14th St., 10014. Tel: 212-243-0265; Fax: 212-255-8466.
Catechesis/Religious Program—Students 150.
Mission—St. Monica 149 Christopher St., New York Co. 10014.

87—OUR LADY OF LORETO (1891), (Sicilian), Rev. Msgr. John B. Ahern (Retired).
Res.: 309 Elizabeth St., 10012. Tel: 212-431-9840; Fax: 212-625-9096.
Holy Name Centre for Homeless Men—Tel: 212-226-5848.

88—OUR LADY OF LOURDES (1901) Revs. Fabian Lopez; Gonzalo Arias Cardenas; Deacon Pedro O'Brien. In Res., Rev. Lawrence E. Lucas.
Res.: 472 W. 142nd St., 10031. Tel: 212-862-4380, Ext. 10; Fax: 212-862-4126.
School—(1903) 462-468 W. 143rd St., 10031. Tel: 212-926-5820, Ext. 11; Fax: 212-491-6034. Cathy M. Hufnagel, Prin. Lay Teachers 11; Students 225.
Catechesis/Religious Program—Tel: 212-862-4380, Ext. 10; Fax: 212-862-4126. Students 250.
Chapel—Convent of Our Lady of Lourdes 463 W. 142nd St., 10031. Tel: 212-862-4380; Fax: 212-862-4126.

89—OUR LADY OF MT. CARMEL (1884), (Italian), (Pallotine) Revs. Anthony Kelly, S.A.C.; Carlos Cardoso, S.A.C.
Res.: 448 E. 116th St., 10029-0614. Tel: 212-534-0681; Fax: 212-534-0629.
School—Mt. Carmel-Holy Rosary, 371 Pleasant Ave., 10035. Tel: 212-876-7555; Fax: 212-876-0152. Sisters 1; Lay Teachers 10; Students 180.
Catechesis/Religious Program—Students 300.
Convent—456 E. 116th St., 10029-0614. Tel: 212-427-2381. Sisters of Charity 5.

90—OUR LADY OF PEACE (1918), (Italian), Rev. Bartholomew Daly, M.H.M., Admin. In Res., Rev. Andrew Bielak (Poland).
Res.: 237 E. 62nd St., 10065. Tel: 212-838-3189; Fax: 212-308-4819. Email: olpnyc@aol.com.
Catechesis/Religious Program—Students 20.

91—OUR LADY OF PERPETUAL HELP (1887) Closed. For inquiries for parish records please see Our Lady of Peace.

92—OUR LADY OF POMPEII (1892), (Italian), (Scalabrinian) Revs. John Charles Massari, C.S.; Romulo Montero (Philippines), Pastoral Assoc.; Bro. Michael La Mantia, C.S.
Res.: 25 Carmine St., 10014. Tel: 212-989-6805; Fax: 212-727-3139. Email: pompeiny@aol.com.
School—(1930) 240 Bleecker St., 10014. Tel: 212-242-4147; Fax: 212-691-2361. Email: no34@adnyeducation.org. Web: www.ladyofpompeii.org. Sisters (Apostles of the Sacred Heart of Jesus) 3; Lay Teachers 19; Students 232.
Catechesis/Religious Program—Students 28.

93—OUR LADY OF SORROWS (1867), (Capuchin) Revs. Thomas Faiola, O.F.M.Cap.; Thomas McNamara, O.F.M.Cap.; Bro. Robert Gerdin, O.F.M.Cap., Pastoral Assoc.; Deacon Wallace Zambrana. In Res., Rev. Michael Marigliano, O.F.M.Cap.; Bros. Terence Taffe, O.F.M.Cap.; John Conway, O.F.M.Cap.
Res.: 213 Stanton St., 10002-1898. Tel: 212-475-2321; Fax: 212-475-2452. Email: oloschurch@yahoo.com. Web: www.ourladyofsorrowsny.4lpi.com.
Church: 103 Pitt St., 10002. Tel: 212-673-0900; Fax: 212-982-0166.
School—(1867) 219 Stanton St., 10002. Tel: 212-473-0320; Fax: 212-420-0285. Lay Teachers 12; Students 205.
Catechesis/Religious Program—Tel: 212-673-0900, Ext. 306. Students 90.

94—OUR LADY OF THE MIRACULOUS MEDAL (1926) Closed. For inquiries for parish records, see Holy Agony, New York.

95—OUR LADY OF THE ROSARY (1883), Shrine of St. Elizabeth Ann Seton. Rev. Peter Meehan; Rev. Msgr. Timothy Collins, Pastor Emeritus (Retired); Rev. Edward G. Zogby, S.J. In Res., Rev. Robert A. Jeffers (Retired).
Res.: 7 State St., 10004. Tel: 212-269-6865; Fax: 212-809-6850. Email: setonshrine05@netscape.com. Web: www.setonshrine.com.

96—OUR LADY OF THE SCAPULAR AND ST. STEPHEN (1869; 1848) Rev. Msgr. Lawrence M. Connaughton; Rev. Rafael G. Corniel, Parochial Vicar. In Res., Most Rev. William J. McCormack (Retired); Rev. Msgr. Walter J. Niebrzydowski (Retired); Revs. Anthony Nwachukwu (Nigeria); Stephen Okeke (Nigeria); Damian Umeokeke.
Res.: 142 E. 29th St., 10016. Tel: 212-683-1675; Fax: 212-683-7921. Email: olsss142@aol.com. Web: www.churchofststephen.com.
Catechesis/Religious Program—Web: www.epiphanyrcchurch.us. Students 16.
Mission—Sacred Hearts of Jesus and Mary 325 E. 33rd St., New York Co. 10016. Tel: 212-213-6027; Fax: 212-213-9136. Rev. Msgr. Lawrence M. Connaughton, Admin. In Res., His Eminence Edward Cardinal Egan; Rev. Michael K. Holleran.
Chapel—Bellevue Hospital, Chapel of Our Lady Helper of the Sick, Tel: 212-561-4440. Rev. Frederick O. Nyanguf, A.J.

97—OUR LADY OF VICTORY (1944) Rev. Msgrs. Marc A. Filacchione; Edward J. Mitty, Pastor Emeritus (Retired); Revs. Socorro Braganca, O.C.D.; Reynaldo Domagas (Philippines), (Hospital Chap.); Romeo Hontiveros (Philippines). In Res., Rev. John E. Fanning.
Res.: 60 William St., 10005. Tel: 212-422-5535; Fax: 212-785-4457. Web: www.ourladyofvictorychurch.org.

98—OUR LADY OF VILNIUS (1905), (Lithuanian), Closed. For inquiries for Sacramental records contact St. Anthony of Padua, 154 Sullivan St., New York, NY 10012.

99—OUR LADY QUEEN OF ANGELS (1886), Closed. Records at: Our Lady of Mt. Carmel, 448 E. 116th St., New York, NY 10029 (212-534-0681)
Res.: 226 E. 113th St., 10029.
School—(1886 and 1955) 229-231 E. 112th St., 10029. Tel: 212-722-9277; Fax: 212-987-8837. Lay Teachers 12; Students 235.
Catechesis/Religious Program—Tel: 212-860-7618; Fax: 212-828-0506. Students 65.
Convent—(Franciscan Sisters of the Renewal), 232 E. 113th St., 10029. Tel: 212-831-3334; Fax: 212-831-3339. Web: www.franciscansisterscfr.com. Sr. Francis O'Donnell, C.F.R., Local Servant.

100—OUR LADY QUEEN OF MARTYRS (1927) Revs. Antonio Almonte; Jean-Paul Soler, Parochial Vicar; Marco Antonio Ortega, Parochial Vicar; Deacons Narciso Hernandez; Manuel Cespedes; Luis Feliz; Delio Fernandez; Bienvenido Valdez.
Res.: 91 Arden St., 10040. Tel: 212-567-2637; Fax: 212-567-1305.
School—(1932) 71 Arden St., 10040. Tel: 212-567-3190; Fax: 212-304-8587. Andrew Woods, Prin. Lay Teachers 14; Students 350.
Catechesis/Religious Program—Students 250.

101—OUR SAVIOUR (1955) Rev. George W. Rutler.
Res.: 59 Park Ave., 10016. Tel: 212-679-8166; Fax: 212-213-0352. Email: info@oursaviournyc.org. Web: www.oursaviournyc.org.
Catechesis/Religious Program—Students 81.

102—ST. PATRICK'S OLD CATHEDRAL (1809) Rev. Msgr. Donald Sakano; Rev. Andrew Thi.
Res.: 263 Mulberry St., 10012. Tel: 212-226-8075; Fax: 212-226-1219. Email: oldstpats@yahoo.com. Web: www.oldsaintpatricks.com.
School—Boys & Girls Depts. (1817) 233-239 Mott St., 10012. Tel: 212-226-3984; Fax: 212-226-4469. Lay Teachers 10; Students 110.
Catechesis/Religious Program—Students 50.
Chapel—St. Michael (Russian—Other), [JC] 266 Mulberry St., 10012. Tel: 212-226-2644; Fax: 212-226-1219.

103—ST. PAUL (1834), (Institute of The Incarnate Word) Revs. Claudio Stewart; Gustavo Nieto.
Res.: 113 E. 117th St., 10035. Tel: 212-534-4422; Fax: 212-996-5588. Email: par.newyork@ive.org. Web: www.stpaulchurchive.org.
School—(1870) 114-122 E. 118th St., 10035. Tel: 212-534-0619; Fax: 212-534-3990. Email: stpaul@email.com. Lay Teachers 14; Students 335.
Catechesis/Religious Program—Tel: 212-534-4481. Email: ssvm@stpaulchurchive.org. Students 298.
Convent—(Sisters of The Servants of the Lord and The Virgin of Matara), St. Paul Convent, 149 E. 117th St., 10035. Tel: 917-492-3668. Email: c.marywalsh@servidoras.org. Web: www.ssvmusa.org.

104—ST. PAUL THE APOSTLE (1858), (Paulist. See also Paulist Fathers' Motherhouse under Monasteries located in the Institution section.) Revs. Gilbert S. Martinez, C.S.P.; Ronald A. Franco, C.S.P.; Deacon Waldemar Sandoval.
Mailing Address & Office: 405 W. 59th, 10019. Tel: 212-265-3495; Fax: 212-262-9239. Email: webmaster@stpaultheapostle.org. Web: www.stpaultheapostle.org.
Catechesis/Religious Program—Students 150.
Chapel—Oblates of Jesus the Priest, Tel: 212-265-3209; Fax: 212-265-4154.

105—ST. PETER (1785) Revs. Kevin Madigan; Donald T. Fussner (Retired); Alex Joseph (India); Arthur Leone (Retired).
Mailing Address: 22 Barclay St., 10007.
Res.: 18 Vesey St., 10007. Tel: 212-233-8355 (Church); 212-608-4709 (Res.); Fax: 212-285-0497. Email: st.peterschurch1785@verizon.net.
Catechesis/Religious Program—James O'Connor, D.R.E. Students 96.
Chapel—St. Joseph's Chapel 385 South End Ave., 10280. Tel: 212-466-0131. Web: www.sjchapel.org.

106—ST. RAPHAEL (1886) Closed. See Sts. Cyril and Methodius.

107—ST. ROSE (1868) Closed. Parochial records at St. Mary Church.

108—ST. ROSE OF LIMA (1902) Revs. Edward Russell; George Seans. In Res., Rev. Melchor Ferrer, S.D.B.
Res.: 510 W. 165th St., 10032. Tel: 212-568-0091.
School—(1924) 517 W. 164th St., 10032. Lay Teachers 10; Students 300.
Catechesis/Religious Program—Sr. Ramona Liriano, D.R.E. Students 297.
Chapel—St. Rose of Lima Convent 509 W. 164th St., 10032.
Medical Centre—

109—SACRED HEART OF JESUS (1876) Revs. Jose Gabriel Piedrahita, M.X.Y.; David A. DeSimone.
Res.: 457 W. 51st, 10019. Tel: 212-265-5020; Fax: 212-977-4116. Email: sacredheart51@nyc.rr.com. Web: www.shjsnyc.org.
School—(1892) 456 52nd St., 10019. Tel: 212-246-4784; Fax: 212-707-8382. Congregation of Christian Brothers 1; Lay Teachers 15; Students 210.
Chapel—Centro Maria 539 W. 54th St., 10019. Tel: 212-757-6989; Fax: 212-307-5687.
Chapel—Convent of Sacred Heart 450 W. 51st St., 10019. Tel: 212-397-1396; Fax: 212-397-1397.
Catechesis/Religious Program—Tel: 212-265-5020, Ext. 16; Fax: 212-977-4116. Students 70.

110—SACRED HEARTS OF JESUS AND MARY (1914), (Italian), Mission of Our Lady of Scapular and St. Stephen. Records at Our Lady of the Scapular and St. Stephen, 142 E. 29th St., New York, NY 10016. Tel: 212-683-1675. In Res., His Eminence Edward Cardinal Egan; Rev. Michael K. Holleran.
Res.: 325 E. 33rd St., 10016. Tel: 212-213-6027; Fax: 212-213-9136.
Station—N.Y.U. Medical Center, Tel: 212-889-3886.

111—ST. SEBASTIAN (1915) Closed. Parochial records at Epiphany Church.

112—ST. STANISLAUS BISHOP AND MARTYR (1872), (Polish), (Pauline Fathers) Revs. Bogdan Mikolaj Socha, O.S.P.P.E.; Dominik Pawel Libiszewski, O.S.P.P.E.
Res.: 101 E. Seventh St., 10009. Tel: 212-475-4576; Fax: 212-674-4894. Email: rectory@stanislauschurch.com. Web: www.stanislauschurch.com.
Catechesis/Religious Program—

113—ST. STEPHEN (1848) Consolidated in 1990. See Our Lady of Scapular/St. Stephen for details.

114—ST. STEPHEN OF HUNGARY (1902), (Franciscan) Revs. Angelus Gambatese, O.F.M., Guardian; Eric Carpine, O.F.M.; Ms. Jayne Porcelli, Pastoral Assoc. In Res., Revs. Kyle Hayden, O.F.M.; Christopher B. Keenan, O.F.M.; Jacques La Pointe, O.F.M.; Allan G. Von Kobs, O.F.M.; Dennis M. Wilson, O.F.M.; Bro. Timothy Miskowski, O.F.M.
Res.: 414 E. 82nd St., 10028. Tel: 212-861-8500; Fax: 212-535-9221. Web: www.saintstephenofhungary.org.
School—(1918) 408 E. 82nd St., 10028. Tel: 212-288-1989; Fax: 212-517-5877. Rev. Sean McCaughley (Ireland), Prin. Lay Teachers 11; Students 200.
Catechesis/Religious Program—Religious Education Program
Dewitt Nursing Home—211 E. 79th St., 10021. Tel: 212-879-1600.

115—ST. TERESA (1863) Revs. Donald C. Baker; Miguelito Lagrimas (Philippines); Sr. Diane Olmstead, M.S.C., Pastoral Assoc. In Res., Rev. Msgr. John E. Kozar.
Res.: 141 Henry St., 10002. Tel: 212-233-0233; Fax: 212-619-4538.
Church: 141 Henry St., 10002. Tel: 212-233-0233; Fax: 212-619-4538. Email: teresa141henry@hotmail.com. Web: www.teresa141henry.org.
Catechesis/Religious Program—Students 82.

116—ST. THOMAS MORE (1950) Rev. Msgr. John A. Boehning; Revs. Jose Tentativa; Edwin Diaz. In Res., Rev. Msgr. Thomas J. Shelley.
Res.: 65 E. 89th St., 10128. Tel: 212-876-7718; Fax: 212-831-5756. Email: m106@archny.org. Web: www.thomasmorechurch.org.
Catechesis/Religious Program—Narnia Clubs, 163 E. 81st St., 10150. Tel: 212-535-9329; Fax: 212-628-8409. Email: info@narniaclubs.com. Web: www.narniaclubs.com. Students 318.

117—ST. THOMAS THE APOSTLE (1889), (African American), [CEM], Records at St. Joseph of the Holy Family, 405 W. 125th St., NY, NY 10027.
Res.: 262 W. 118th St., 10026. Tel: 212-662-2693; Fax: 212-662-4560.
Catechesis/Religious Program—Students 127.

118—TRANSFIGURATION (1827), (Chinese-English), Rev. Raymond J. Nobiletti, M.M.
Res.: 29 Mott St., 10013-5006. Tel: 212-962-5157;

Fax: 212-962-5217. Email: transparish@aol.com. Web: www.transfigurationnyc.org.
School—(1832)Tel: 212-962-5265; Fax: 212-964-8965. Email: m110@adnyeducation.org. Web: www.transfigurationschoolnyc.org. Dr. Patrick Taharally, Prin. Lay Teachers 12; Students 267.
School—Kindergarten (1954) 10 Confucius Pl., 10002. Tel: 212-431-8769; Fax: 212-431-8917. Email: eieng@adnyschools.org. Ms. Emily Eng, Prin. Lay Teachers 18; Students 155.
Catechesis/Religious Program—Students 88.

119—ST. VERONICA (1887), Mission of Our Lady of Guadalupe at St. Bernard. Records at Our Lady of Guadalupe at St. Bernard, 328 W. 14th St., New York, NY 10014. Tel: 212-243-0265., 328 W. 14th St., 10014.

120—ST. VINCENT DE PAUL (1841), (French), Rev. Gerald E. Murray. In Res., Revs. Robert J. Poveromo; Gerard Messier, A.A.
Res.: 116 W. 24th St., 10011. Tel: 212-243-4727; Fax: 212-675-0528.
Church: 123 W. 23rd St., 10011.
Catechesis/Religious Program—Students 390.

121—ST. VINCENT FERRER (1867), (Dominican) Revs. Carlton P. Jones, O.P.; Bernard Lawrence Keitz, O.P.; Jeremy Aquinas Guilbeau, O.P.; Bro. John Damian McCarthy, O.P.
Res.: 869 Lexington Ave., 10065-6648. Tel: 212-744-2080; Fax: 212-327-3011. Web: www.csvf.org.
High School—151 E. 65th St., 10065-6607. Tel: 212-535-4680; Fax: 212-988-3455. Web: www.saintvincentferrer.com. Sr. Gail Morgan, O.P., Prin. Sisters of St. Dominic (Columbus, OH) 6; Lay Teachers 31; Girls 500.
Catechesis/Religious Program—Students 16.
Chapel—Sisters of St. Dominic 152 E. 66th St., 10065. Tel: 212-744-2375; Fax: 212-249-5355.
Chapel—Dominican Academy 44 E. 68th St., 10065. Tel: 212-744-0195; Fax: 212-744-0375.

BOROUGH OF BRONX

1—ST. ADALBERT (1898), (Polish), Closed. For inquiries for parish records contact the chancery.

2—ST. ANGELA MERICI (1899), (Apostles of Jesus) Revs. Peter Mushi, A.J.; John Kalungi, A.J.; Deacon Felipe Sin-Garciga.
Res.: 917 Morris Ave., Bronx, 10451. Tel: 718-293-0984; Fax: 718-293-7325. Email: pmushi@saintangelamerici.net. Web: www.saintangelamerici.net.
Church: E. 163rd St., Bronx, 10451.
School—(1917) 266 E. 163rd St., Bronx, 10451. Tel: 718-293-3365; Fax: 718-293-6617. Lay Teachers 24; Students 500.
Catechesis/Religious Program—Fax: 718-293-0984. Students 163.

3—ST. ANN (1927) Rev. Francis P. Scanlon. In Res., Revs. Misael Bacleon (Philippines); Andrew Ovienloba (Nigeria).
Res.: 3519 Bainbridge Ave., Bronx, 10467. Tel: 718-547-9350; Fax: 718-547-1718. Email: saintannchurch@aol.com.
School—(1928) Bainbridge Ave. & Gun Hill Rd., Bronx, 10467. Tel: 718-655-3449; Fax: 718-547-4020. Mrs. Cecile Rodriguez, Prin. Students 280.
Catechesis/Religious Program—Tel: 718-655-3449; Fax: 718-547-2020. Students 100.

4—ST. ANSELM (1892), (Augustinian Recollects) Revs. Antonio Palacios, O.A.R.; Jose Martinez, O.A.R.; Jose Antonio Rodrigalvarez, O.A.R.; Deacon Apolonio Mejia.
Res.: 685 Tinton Ave., Bronx, 10455. Tel: 718-585-8666; Fax: 718-401-6686.
School—(1908)Tel: 718-993-9464; Fax: 718-292-3496. Ms. Teresa M. Lopes, Prin. Lay Teachers 21; Students 475.
Catechesis/Religious Program—Tel: 718-585-8542. Students 340.

5—ST. ANTHONY (1908) Revs. Joseph J. Kelly; John J. Piderit, S.J.; Deacon Frankie Vazquez.
Res.: 1496 Commonwealth Ave., Bronx, 10460. Tel: 718-931-4040; 718-931-4041; Fax: 718-863-0202. Email: st.commonwealth@yahoo.com.
School—(1931) 1776 Mansion St., Bronx, 10460. Tel: 718-892-1244; Fax: 718-892-4656. Email: B224@adnyschools.org. Lay Teachers 12; Students 204.
Catechesis/Religious Program—Students 75.

6—ST. ANTHONY (1919) Mission of St. Francis of Rome. Records at Saint Frances of Rome, 4307 Barnes Ave., Bronx, NY 10466. Phone: 718-324-5340; Fax: 718-324-5373.
Res.: 4307 Barnes Ave., Bronx, 10466.
School—(1953) 4520 Matilda Ave., Bronx, 10470. Tel: 718-324-5104. Dina Monti, Prin. Lay Teachers 11; Students 279.
Catechesis/Religious Program—Attendance at Saint Frances of Rome Sunday school.

7—ST. ANTHONY OF PADUA (1903), (African American—Hispanic), [CEM] Most Rev. Josu Iriondo; Rev. Benjamin Palacios, D.V.M., Parochial Vicar; Deacon Nelson Duran.
Res.: 832 E. 166th St., Bronx, 10459. Tel: 718-542-7293; Fax: 718-378-1819. Email: stanthony832@aol.com.
Catechesis/Religious Program—Students 108.

8—ST. ATHANASIUS (1907) Revs. John O. Grange; Pompilio Alvarez (Spain); Deacons Alejandro Rosado; Fernando Vazquez.
Res.: 878 Tiffany St., Bronx, 10459. Tel: 718-328-2558; Fax: 718-328-3121. Email: sachurch878verizon@verizon.net.
School—(1913) 830 Southern Blvd., Bronx, 10459. Tel: 718-542-5161; Fax: 718-542-7584. Email: b227@adnyschools.org. Web: www.athschool.org. Marianne Kraft, Prin. Sisters 1; Lay Teachers 13; Students 354.
Catechesis/Religious Program—Sr. Louise Mileski, O.P., D.R.E. Students 286.

9—ST. AUGUSTINE (1849) Rev. Thomas B. Fenlon; Sr. Dorothy Hall, O.P., Pastoral Assoc.; Rita Velez, Sec. In Res., Rev. Joseph Bernardine Onyia (Nigeria), Chap., Bronx Lebanon Hospital.
Res.: 1183 Franklin Ave., Bronx, 10456. Tel: 718-893-0072; Fax: 718-861-3080. Email: staugbx@optonline.net.
Church: E. 167th St., Bronx, 10456.
School—(1887) 1176 Franklin Ave., Bronx, 10456. Tel: 718-542-3633; Fax: 718-542-7871. Cathryn Trapp, Prin. Lay Teachers 10; Students 212.
Catechesis/Religious Program—Students 135.

10—ST. BARNABAS (1910), (Irish—Italian), Rev. Msgr. Edward M. Barry; Revs. Patrick McCarthy; John Francis Antony; Deacons Vincent Laurato; Cornelius Manning. In Res., Rev. Cyprian Onyeihe (Nigeria).
Res.: 409 E. 241st St., Bronx, 10470. Tel: 718-324-1478; Fax: 718-324-1479. Email: stbarnabasbronx@aol.com. Web: www.stbarnabasbronx.org.
School—(1912) 413 E. 241st St., Bronx, 10470. Tel: 718-324-1088; Fax: 718-324-2397. Email: B229@adnyschools.org. Web: www.stbarnabasschool.org. Lay Teachers 16; Students 327.
High School—High School for Girls (1924)*St. Barnabas High School*, 425 E. 240th St., Bronx, 10470. Tel: 718-325-8800; Fax: 718-325-8820. Web: www.stbarnabashighschool. Sisters 3; Lay Teachers 18; Students 223.
Catechesis/Religious Program—Tel: 718-324-0865. Students 298.
Convent—(Sisters of Life), 445 E. 240th St., Bronx, 10470. Tel: 718-708-6742; Fax: 718-708-6744. Sisters 6.
Chapel—St. Barnabas High School Chapel Yonkers.

11—ST. BENEDICT (1923) Revs. Richard G. Smith; John Thawale; Angelo Palermo, S.A.C.; James B. Collins.
Res.: 2969 Otis Ave., Bronx, 10465-2198. Tel: 718-828-3403; Fax: 718-829-1304. Email: stbenedict@optonline.net.
School—(1923) 1016 Edison Ave., Bronx, 10465. Tel: 718-829-9557; Fax: 718-319-1898. Sisters 3; Lay Teachers 14; Students 328.
Catechesis/Religious Program—Tel: 718-829-1200. Students 357.
Chapel—St. John 1082 Edison Ave., Bronx, 10465.

12—BLESSED SACRAMENT (1927) Rev. Msgr. James E. White; Revs. Gilberto Angel-Neri; Fidel Cruz; Deacon Epi Portalatin.
Res.: 1170 Beach Ave., Bronx, 10472. Tel: 718-892-3214; Fax: 718-892-3907. Email: blsacramentchurch@yahoo.com.
School—(1929) 1160 Beach Ave. & 1141 Taylor Ave., Bronx, 10472. Tel: 718-892-0433; Fax: 718-892-3337. Email: b200@adnyschools.org. Miss Herminia Roman, Prin. Lay Teachers 10; Students 275.
Catechesis/Religious Program—Tel: 718-863-4620. Students 135.

13—ST. BRENDAN (1908) Revs. George R. Stewart; Santiago Rubio Clemente; Sancho Garrote; Sr. Catherine Naughton, O.P., Senior Outreach Coord.; Deacons Paul Hveem; Orlando Pascal.
Res.: 333 E. 206th St., Bronx, 10467. Tel: 718-547-6655; Fax: 718-547-6579.
School—(1912) 268 E. 207th St., Bronx, 10467. Tel: 718-653-2293; Fax: 718-653-3234. Miss Michele Pasquale, Prin. Lay Teachers 15; Students 345.
Catechesis/Religious Program—Tel: 718-654-6424. Judith Cordero, D.R.E. Students 235.

14—CHRIST THE KING (1926) Revs. Eric Cruz; Abraham Berko-Attah. In Res., Rev. George Oonnoonny.
Res.: 141 Marcy Pl., Bronx, 10452. Tel: 718-538-5546; Fax: 718-538-3081.
School—Tel: 718-538-5959; Fax: 718-538-6369. Lay Teachers 24; Students 491.
Catechesis/Religious Program—Tel: 718-538-5546; Fax: 718-538-3081. Students 364.
Mission—Ghanaian Mass & Pilgrims

15—ST. CLARE OF ASSISI (1929), (Italian), Revs. Richard Guarnieri; Dennis Cagantas (Philippines).
Res.: 1918 Paulding Ave., Bronx, 10462. Tel: 718-863-8974; Fax: 718-931-6909. Email: stclareofassisi@aol.com. Web: www.rc.net/newyork/stclare.
Church: 1027 Rhinelander Ave., Bronx, 10461.
School—(1951) 1911 Hone Ave., Bronx, 10461. Tel: 718-892-4080; Fax: 718-239-1007. Email: b232@adnyschools.org. Janice Desmond, Prin. Lay Teachers 25; Students 474.
Catechesis/Religious Program—Tel: 718-829-9624. Students 166.
Chapel—Brothers, Morningside House Chapel 1000 Pelham Pkwy., Bronx, 10461. Tel: 718-409-8200.

16—ST. DOMINIC (1924), (Italian), Rev. Robert P. Badillo, M.Id.; Deacon Reynaldo Rosado.
Res.: 1739 Unionport Rd., Bronx, 10462. Tel: 718-828-2424; Fax: 718-828-9725.
School—(1953) 1684 White Plains Rd., Bronx, 10462. Tel: 718-829-4837; Fax: 718-792-6912. Sr. Josefa Curcio, C.S.J.B., Prin. Sisters of St. John the Baptist 6; Lay Teachers 12; Students 340.
Catechesis/Religious Program—Our Lady of Solace, 1808 Holland Ave., Bronx, 10462. Tel: 718-823-9044. Students 150.
Convent—1710 Unionport Rd., Bronx, 10462. Tel: 718-824-2580. Sisters 9.

17—ST. FRANCES DE CHANTAL (1927) Rev. Msgr. Leslie J. Ivers; Revs. Michael K. Holleran; Epifanio Marcaida (Philippines); Deacons John Murphy; George Coppola.
Res.: 190 Hollywood Ave., Bronx, 10465. Tel: 718-792-5500; Fax: 718-792-1824. Web: www.sfdchantal.org. Email: sfdchantal@aol.com.
School—(1929) 2962 Harding Ave., Bronx, 10465. Tel: 718-892-5359; Fax: 718-892-6937. Email: sfdcbronxny@aol.com. Miss Debra Trignani, Prin. Lay Teachers 10; Students 275.
Catechesis/Religious Program—Students 210.
Convent—Convent of Sisters of Life, 198 Hollywood Ave., Bronx, 10465. Tel: 718-863-2264.
Chapel—House of the Holy Family 2780 Schurz Ave., Bronx, 10465. Tel: 718-863-9134.

18—ST. FRANCES OF ROME (1898) Revs. Francis J. Corry; John P. Sheehan; James P. Clark (Retired); Sr. Ellen Hublitz, O.P., Pastoral Assoc.
Res.: 4307 Barnes Ave., Bronx, 10466. Tel: 718-324-5340; Fax: 718-324-5373.
Church: 761 E. 236th St., Bronx, 10466.
Catechesis/Religious Program—Sr. Mary Gregory West, P.B.V.M., D.R.E. Students 98.
Mission—St. Anthony 4505 Richardson Ave., Bronx, 10470.
Mission—St. Francis of Assisi 4330 Baychester Ave., Bronx, 10466.

19—ST. FRANCIS OF ASSISI (1928), Mission of Sacred Heart. Records at Sacred Heart, 1253 Shakespeare Ave., Bronx, NY 10452. Tel: 718-293-2766., 1544 Shakespeare Ave., Bronx, 10452. Tel: 718-731-6840; 718-731-6841. Mailing Address: P.O. Box 520013, Bronx, 10452. Fax: 718-731-6841.

20—ST. FRANCIS OF ASSISI (1949) Mission of St. Frances of Rome. Records at Saint Frances of Rome, 4307 Barnes Ave., Bronx, NY 10466. Phone: 718-324-5340; Fax: 718-324-5373.
Res.: 4307 Barnes Ave., Bronx, 10466.
School—4300 Baychester Ave., Bronx, 10466. Tel: 718-994-4650. Mary Jane Helmrich, Prin. Lay Teachers 13; Students 314.
Catechesis/Religious Program—Attendance at Saint Frances of Rome.

21—ST. FRANCIS XAVIER (1928) Revs. Matthew J. Furey; Francis Gayam (India); Hippolytus Duru (Nigeria).
Res.: 1703 Lurting Ave., Bronx, 10461. Tel: 718-892-3330; Fax: 718-931-6890.
School—(1930) 1711 Haight Ave., Bronx, 10461. Tel: 718-863-0531; Fax: 718-319-1152. Mrs. Angela Deegan, Prin. Lay Teachers 16; Students 297.
Catechesis/Religious Program—Students 136.
Chapel—St. Francis Xavier Convent 1661 Haight Ave., Bronx, 10461. Tel: 718-892-9466; Fax: 718-829-1488.

22—ST. GABRIEL (1939) Revs. John M. Knapp; Raju Anthony (India); Deacon Eugene Burke. In Res., Revs. George H. Hill; Antony Siviramatu.
Res.: 3250 Arlington Ave., Bronx, 10463. Tel: 718-548-4470; 718-548-4471; Fax: 718-548-6451.
Church: 235th & Netherland Ave., Bronx, 10463. Fax: 718-548-0444.
School—590 W. 235th St., Bronx, 10463. Tel: 718-548-0444; Fax: 718-796-2638. Deborah D. Pitula, Prin. Lay Teachers 11; Students 226.
Catechesis/Religious Program—Tel: 718-548-6585. Mr. Glenn A. McCarthy, D.R.E. Students 90.

23—ST. HELENA (1940) Rev. Msgr. Thomas B. Derivan; Revs. Edmundo Gomez; Francis Xavier Reginald (Sri Lanka); Joseph Ligory (Sri Lanka).
Res.: 1315 Olmstead Ave., Bronx, 10462. Tel: 718-892-3232; Fax: 718-892-3078. Email: sthelenarc@yahoo.com. Web: www.sthelenabronxny.org.
School—(1941) 2050 Benedict Ave., Bronx, 10462.

Tel: 718-892-3234; Fax: 718-892-3924. Richard Meller, Prin. Lay Teachers 19; Students 505.
High School—Msgr. Scanlan High School (1949), (Coed), 915 Hutchinson River Pkwy., Bronx, 10465. Tel: 718-430-0100; Fax: 718-892-8845. Sr. Annmarie Fisher, O.P., Prin. Sisters of St. Dominic (Sparkill, NY) 8; Lay Teachers 35; Students 571.
Catechesis/Religious Program—Tel: 718-892-5557. Students 105.

24—HOLY CROSS (1921), (Franciscan) Revs. Todd Carpenter, O.F.M.; Robert J. Ginel; Peter A. Pomposello; Deacons Valentin Acabeo; Jaime A. Bello.
Res.: 620 Thieriot Ave., Bronx, 10473. Tel: 718-893-5550; Fax: 718-378-3655. Email: holycross@holycrossbronx.org. Web: www.holycrossbronx.org.
School—(1923 and 1955) 1846 Randall Ave., Bronx, 10473. Tel: 718-842-4492; Fax: 718-842-4052. Lay Teachers 12; Students 283.
Catechesis/Religious Program—Students 224.
Chapel—Chapel of St. Anthony at Holy Cross

25—HOLY FAMILY (1896) Revs. James D. Flanagan; Andrew M. O'Connor; Deacon Dhoel Canals. In Res., Rev. Kevin Sandberg, C.S.C.
Res.: 2158 Watson Ave., Bronx, 10472. Tel: 718-863-9156; Fax: 718-597-5560.
School—(1913) 2169 Blackrock Ave., Bronx, 10472. Tel: 718-863-7280; Fax: 718-931-8690. Lay Teachers 20; Students 414.
Catechesis/Religious Program—2169 Black Rock Ave., Bronx, 10472. Tel: 718-822-8030. Students 201.
Chapel—Holy Family 2155 Blackrock Ave., Bronx, 10472.

26—HOLY ROSARY (1925) Revs. Robert A. Quarato; Edwin Erhimeyoma (Nigeria); Deacon Joseph Solanto.
Res.: 1510 Adee Ave., Bronx, 10469. Tel: 718-379-4432; 718-379-4654; Fax: 718-379-9028. Email: holyrosarybx@verizon.net.
School—(1927; 1955) 1500 Arnow Ave., Bronx, 10469. Tel: 718-652-1838; Fax: 718-515-9872. Mrs. Maryann Fusco, Prin. Lay Teachers 25; Students 625.
Catechesis/Religious Program—Tel: 718-654-9381. Students 100.
Chapel—Holy Rosary Convent 2755 Woodhull Ave., Bronx, 10469. Tel: 718-798-6435.

27—HOLY SPIRIT (1901) Revs. Joseph Vijayan (India), Admin.; Raul Miguez (Italy).
Res.: 1940 University Ave., Bronx, 10453. Tel: 718-583-0120; Fax: 718-583-1444. Email: holyspiritbx@yahoo.com.
School—(1913) 1960 University Ave., Bronx, 10453. Tel: 718-583-1570; Fax: 718-583-3378. Lay Teachers 12; Students 300.
Catechesis/Religious Program—Students 271.

28—IMMACULATE CONCEPTION (1853), (German), (Redemptorist) Rev. Francis G. Skelly, C.Ss.R.; Deacon Cristobal Rodriguez. In Res., Revs. Tat-Thang Hoang, C.Ss.R.; Patrick Keyes, C.Ss.R.; Tom McCluskey, C.Ss.R.; Bros. Laurence J. Lujun; Jeffrey Rolle.
Res.: 389 E. 150th St., Bronx, 10455. Tel: 718-292-6970; Fax: 718-292-4603.
School—(1854) 378 E. 151st St., Bronx, 10455. Tel: 718-585-4843; Fax: 718-585-6846. Sisters of Christian Charity 4; Lay Teachers 22; Students 565.
Catechesis/Religious Program—Tel: 718-292-6970, Ext. 15. Mrs. Vilma Mattei, C.R.E. Students 114.
Chapel—Sisters of Christian Charity 365 E. 150th St., Bronx, 10455. Tel: 718-585-8981.

29—IMMACULATE CONCEPTION (1903), (Capuchin) Revs. John Lo Sasso, O.F.M.Cap.; Peter Napoli, O.F.M-.Cap.; Robert Williams, O.F.M.Cap.; Bro. Jesu Perez, O.F.M.Cap., Pastoral Assoc.; Deacons Carlos Mercado; Victor Tosi.
Capuchin Friary: 754 E. Gun Hill Rd., Bronx, 10467. Tel: 718-653-2200; Fax: 718-882-0054.
School—Tel: 718-547-3346; Fax: 718-547-5505. Sr. Latecia Aviles, O.B.T., Prin. Priests 4; Brothers 2; Oblates to the Blessed Trinity 4; Franciscan Missionary Sisters 2; Missionary Sisters of the Catechism 4; Lay Teachers 13; Students 895.

30—ST. JEROME'S (1869) Revs. Gustavo Nieto; Fortunato Romero (Peru).
Res.: 230 Alexander Ave., Bronx, 10454. Tel: 718-665-5533; Fax: 718-665-5875. Email: stjeromech@aol.com.
School—(1871) 222 Alexander Ave., Bronx, 10454. Tel: 718-292-4920; Fax: 718-292-3111. Lay Teachers 10; Students 300.
Catechesis/Religious Program—Mrs. Carmen Acevedo, D.R.E. Students 175.

31—ST. JOAN OF ARC (1949) Revs. Paul J. LeBlanc; Carlos A. Ruiz; Deacons Ismael Camacho; Angel Alvarez.
Res.: 1372 Stratford Ave., Bronx, 10472. Tel: 718-842-2233; Fax: 718-842-4720.
Catechesis/Religious Program—Students 284.

32—ST. JOHN CHRYSOSTOM (1899) Rev. Carlos Rodriguez.
Res.: 985 E. 167th St., Bronx, 10459. Tel: 718-542-6164; Fax: 718-542-0448.
School—(1914) 1144 Hoe Ave., Bronx, 10459. Tel: 718-328-7226; Fax: 718-378-5368. Sr. Mary Elizabeth Mooney, O.P., Prin. Sisters of St. Dominic (Sparkill, NY) 11; Lay Teachers 19; Students 611.
Catechesis/Religious Program—Tel: 718-328-7723. Students 367.

33—ST JOHN NAM (1989), (Korean), Revs. Simon Nam; Andrew H. Lee (Korea, South).
Res.: 3663 White Plains Rd., Bronx, 10467. Tel: 718-231-2414; Fax: 718-405-0053. Email: church_of_st_john_nam@hotmail.com.
Catechesis/Religious Program—Students 69.

34—ST. JOHN VIANNEY, CURE OF ARS (1960) Rev. Jose I. Serrano; Deacons Al Leasiolagi; Andes Almanzar; Edwin Cruz.
Res.: 715 Castle Hill Ave., Bronx, 10473. Tel: 718-863-4411; Fax: 718-863-1673.
School—2141 Seward Ave., Bronx, 10473. Tel: 718-892-4400; Fax: 718-931-0865. Email: b244@adnyschools.org. Lay Teachers 13; Students 180.
Catechesis/Religious Program—Students 51.

35—ST. JOHN'S (1886) Revs. Antonio Zabala, O.A.R.; Edward J. Fagan, O.A.R., Parochial Vicar; John Oldfield, O.A.R., Parochial Vicar; Francis A. Cregan, O.A.R., Parochial Vicar; Deacon Andrew Rivera. In Res., Rev. Francisco Sandoval, O.A.R.; Bro. Ramiro Munoz, O.A.R.
Res.: 3021 Kingsbridge Ave., Bronx, 10463. Tel: 718-548-1221; Fax: 718-548-7774. Email: oarbx@aol.com.
School—(1903) 3143 Kingsbridge Ave., Bronx, 10463. Tel: 718-548-0255; Fax: 718-548-0864. Mr. Ray Vitiello, Prin. Sisters 2; Lay Teachers 12; Students 248.
Catechesis/Religious Program—Tel: 718-884-2627. Students 201.
Convent—Religious of Jesus and Mary, 3029 Godwin Ter., Bronx, 10463. Tel: 718-548-4902; 718-543-2454.

36—ST. JOSEPH (1873) Revs. Salvatore Sportino; Clement Umoenoh.
Res.: 1949 Bathgate Ave., Bronx, 10457. Tel: 718-731-2504; Fax: 718-731-0478.
School—(1922) 1946 Bathgate Ave., Bronx, 10457. Tel: 718-583-9432; Fax: 718-299-0780. Janine A. Hughes, Prin. Lay Teachers 20; Students 465.
Catechesis/Religious Program—Students 22.

37—ST. LUCY (1927) Revs. Nikolin Pergjini; Neil Kelly. In Res., Rev. Msgr. Frederick J. Becker.
Church: 833 Mace Ave., Bronx, 10467. Tel: 718-882-0710; Fax: 718-882-8876.
School—(1955) 830 Mace Ave., Bronx, 10467. Tel: 718-882-2203; Fax: 718-547-8351. Mrs. Jane Stefanini, Prin. Lay Teachers 15; Students 410.
Catechesis/Religious Program—Tel: 718-652-0295. Students 326.

38—ST. LUKE (1897) Rev. Msgr. Gerald J. Ryan; Rev. Cesar Rafael Bejarano, O.F.M. (Venezuela); Mary Kay Louchart, Pastoral Assoc.; Sharon Joslyn, Pastoral Assoc.
Res.: 623 E. 138th St., Bronx, 10454. Tel: 718-665-6677; Fax: 718-665-0898. Email: stlukes138@aol.com.
School—(1910) 608 E. 139th St., Bronx, 10454. Tel: 718-585-0380; Fax: 718-665-3407. Email: b247@adnyeducation.org. Sisters of St. Dominic (Blauvelt) 1; Lay Teachers 16; Students 330.
Catechesis/Religious Program—Tel: 718-801-5512. Students 224.
Chapel—St. Luke Convent 621 E. 138th St., Bronx, 10454. Tel: 718-292-3016.

39—ST. MARGARET MARY (1923) Rev. Robert P. Arce. In Res., Revs. Nixon Andres Herrera-Diaz (Colombia); Jose Ambooken (India).
Res.: 1914 Morris Ave., Bronx, 10453-5904. Tel: 718-299-4233; Fax: 718-583-3726.
School—(1923) 121 E. 177th St., Bronx, 10453. Tel: 718-731-5905; Fax: 718-731-8924. Sisters of Mercy of the Americas 1; Lay Teachers 13; Students 370.
Catechesis/Religious Program—Students 400.

40—ST. MARGARET OF CORTONA (1887) Rev. Brian P. McCarthy; Rev. Msgr. Daniel A. Peake, Pastor Emeritus (Retired); Revs. Andrew J. Walsh; Efrem Pottamplackal, M.C.B.S.; David Manvelpillai (Sri Lanka).
Res.: 6000 Riverdale Ave., Bronx, 10471. Tel: 718-549-8053; Fax: 718-543-3432. Email: smcchurch@optonline.net.
School—(1926) 452 W. 260th St., Bronx, 10471. Tel: 718-549-8580; Fax: 718-884-3298. Email: b248@adnyschools.org. Web: www.stmargaretschool-riverdale.com. Sr. Kathleen Marie Gerritse, C.R., Prin. Sisters 1; Lay Teachers 16; Students 286.
Catechesis/Religious Program—Tel: 718-884-9777. Sr. Joan Dombrowski, D.R.E. Students 106.

41—ST. MARTIN OF TOURS (1897) Revs. John C. Flynn; Cosme S. Fernandes (India); Deacon Frankie Lopez. In Res., Rev. Msgr. Thomas McGarry (Retired).
Res.: 664 Grote St., Bronx, 10457. Tel: 718-295-0913; Fax: 718-295-2344. Email: stmartinoftoursparish@yahoo.com.
School—(1926) E. 182nd St. & Crotona Ave., Bronx, 10457. Tel: 718-733-0347; Fax: 718-733-5142. Web: www.saintmartinoftoursschool.org. Dominican Sisters (Sparkill, NY) 2; Lay Teachers 9; Students 109.
Catechesis/Religious Program—Ana Batista, D.R.E. Students 233.
Chapel—Dominican Convent 695 E. 182nd St., Bronx, 10457.

42—ST. MARY (1866) Unassigned. Records at: Our Lady of Grace, 3985 Bronxwood Ave., Bronx, NY 10466 (718-652-4817).
Church: White Plains Rd., Bronx, 10466-3932.
School—(1950) 3956 Carpenter Ave., Bronx, 10466-3932. Tel: 718-547-0500; Fax: 718-547-0532. Lay Teachers 14; Students 300.
Catechesis/Religious Program—Tel: 718-231-2569. Students 100.
Chapel—Convent 3961 Carpenter Ave., Bronx, 10466. Tel: 718-652-2873.
School Chapel—E. 224th St., Bronx, 10466.

43—ST. MARY STAR OF THE SEA (1887) Rev. Michael F. Challinor; Sr. Bernadette Hannaway, O.S.U., Pastoral Assoc. In Res., Rev. Augustas Onwubiko (Nigeria).
Res.: 595 Minneford Ave., Bronx, 10464-1118. Tel: 718-885-1440; Fax: 718-885-9498. Email: smssci@verizon.net.
Church: 600 City Island Ave., Bronx, 10464.
School—(1931) 580 Minneford Ave., Bronx, 10464. Tel: 718-885-1527; Fax: 718-885-1552. Email: b252@adnycschools.org. Dominican Sisters of Blauvelt 1; Lay Teachers 10; Students 212.
Catechesis/Religious Program—Students 150.
Chapel—Daughters of Mary 176 Kilroe St., Bronx, 10464. Tel: 718-885-1842.

44—ST. MICHAEL (1969) Revs. Pat F. Rossi; Benedict Paul, Parochial Vicar.
Res.: 765 Co-Op City Blvd., Bronx, 10475-1601. Tel: 718-671-8050; Fax: 718-320-3776.
Catechesis/Religious Program—

45—NATIVITY OF OUR BLESSED LADY (1924) Rev. Jaime H. Duenas (Retired).
Rectory—1531 E. 233rd St., Bronx, 10466. Tel: 718-324-3531; Fax: 718-798-0628. Email: natychurch@aol.com.
School—(1953) 3893 Dyre Ave., Bronx, 10466. Tel: 718-324-2188; Fax: 718-324-1128. Lay Teachers 20; Students 318.
Catechesis/Religious Program—Students 30.
Convent—1534 E. 233rd St., Bronx, 10466. Tel: 718-325-5355.

46—ST. NICHOLAS OF TOLENTINE (1906), (Augustinian) Revs. Joseph F. Girone, O.S.A.; Joseph Tran; Robert Terranova, O.S.A. In Res., Revs. William J. Wallace, O.S.A.; Richard Nahman, O.S.A.
Res.: 2345 University Ave., Bronx, 10468. Tel: 718-295-6800; Fax: 718-367-7411.
School—(1907) 2336 Andrews Ave., Bronx, 10468. Tel: 718-364-5110; Fax: 718-561-3964. Lay Teachers 10; Students 350.
Catechesis/Religious Program—Tel: 718-295-6800, Ext. 19. Mr. Jesus de La Rosa, Coord. Faith Formation. Students 396.
Convent—Convent of St. Nicholas of Tolentine, 2341 University Ave., Bronx, 10468. Tel: 718-367-3102.

47—OUR LADY OF ANGELS (1924) Revs. Thomas A. Lynch; Vincent Druding, Parochial Vicar; Deacon Carlos Sanchez.
Res.: 2860 Webb Ave., Bronx, 10468. Tel: 718-548-3005; Fax: 718-884-2450. Email: ourladyofangels@hotmail.com.
Church: 2860 Sedgwick Ave., Bronx, 10468.
School—(1928) 2865 Claflin Ave., Bronx, 10468. Tel: 718-549-3503. Web: www.ourladyofangelsschool.org. Sr. Mary Ann Cleary, S.C., Prin. Sisters of Charity of St. Vincent de Paul 3; Lay Teachers 19; Students 290.
Catechesis/Religious Program—Email: ourladyofangels/religioused@hotmail.com. Sisters Maria Corona, P.C., D.R.E.; Maria Eleazar, P.C., C.R.E.; Sylvia Santiago, C.R.E. Students 260.

48—OUR LADY OF GRACE (1924) Revs. Levelt Germain; Manuel Victor Herrera, Parochial Vicar; Cyprien Emille, Parochial Vicar; Charles Udokang; Deacons W. Joseph Mulryan; Salvatore Mazzella.
Res.: 3985 Bronxwood Ave., Bronx, 10466. Tel: 718-652-4817; Fax: 547-652-2996.
School—Tel: 718-547-9918; Fax: 718-547-7602. Daphne Lewis, Prin. Lay Teachers 18; Students 136.
Catechesis/Religious Program—Students 379.

49—OUR LADY OF MERCY (Fordham) (1852-1892) Revs. Ambiorix Rodriguez; Damian Ekete (Nigeria).

Res.: 2496 Marion Ave., Bronx, 10458. Tel: 718-933-4400; Fax: 718-933-5904. Email: office@ourladyofmercyny.org. Web: www.ourladyofmercyny.org.
School—(1907) 2512 Marion Ave., Bronx, 10458. Tel: 718-367-0237; Fax: 718-367-0529. Lay Teachers 12; Students 250.
Catechesis/Religious Program—Sr. Maria Manuela Villarroel, F.M.S.C., D.R.E. Students 195.

50—OUR LADY OF MT. CARMEL (1906), (Italian), Revs. Eric Rapaglia; James L. Miara; Oscar Munoz.
Res.: 627 E. 187th St., Bronx, 10458. Tel: 718-295-3770; Fax: 718-367-2240. Email: FrRapaglia@yahoo.com. Web: www.ourladymtcarmelbx.org.
School—(1925) 189th St. & Bathgate Ave., Bronx, 10458. Tel: 718-295-6080; Fax: 718-561-5205. Frank Borzelleri, Prin. Lay Teachers 14; Students 223.
Catechesis/Religious Program—2380 Belmont Ave., Bronx, 10458. Tel: 718-295-7397; Fax: 718-295-7656. Students 492.
Convent—Suore Missionarie del Catechismo, 2410 Hughes Ave., Bronx, 10458. Tel: 718-329-0390; Fax: 718-329-0390. Sisters 4; Lay Ministers 1.

51—OUR LADY OF PITY (1908), (Hispanic), Records at Sts. Peter & Paul, 833 St. Ann's Ave., Bronx, NY 10456. Rev. Matthew Morreale, O.F.M., Guardian & Pastor; Friar Dominic Poirier, O.F.M.
Res.: 276 E. 151st St., Bronx, 10451. Tel: 718-665-3880.

52—OUR LADY OF REFUGE (1923) [JC] Rev. Msgr. John J. Jenik; Deacon Ronald Sequeria.
Res.: 290 E. 196th St., Bronx, 10458. Tel: 718-367-4690; Fax: 718-365-7644. Web: www.ourladyofrefuge.com.
School—(1923) 2708 Briggs Ave., Bronx, 10458. Tel: 718-367-3081; Fax: 718-367-0741. Lay Teachers 10; Students 300.
Catechesis/Religious Program—Tel: 718-367-3384. Students 250.

53—OUR LADY OF SOLACE (1903) Revs. Robert P. Badillo, M.Id.; Ruben Cammayo (Philippines).
Res.: 731 Morris Park Ave., Bronx, 10462. Tel: 718-863-3282; Fax: 718-792-4950. Email: ols1@verizon.net.
Catechesis/Religious Program—Tel: 718-823-9044. Students 100.

54—OUR LADY OF THE ASSUMPTION (1923) Rev. Msgr. Donald M. Dwyer, Regional Vicar, E. Bronx; Revs. Anthony Mizzi-Gili; Gnana Prakash (India).
Res.: 1634 Mahan Ave., Bronx, 10461. Tel: 718-824-5454; Fax: 718-824-5456. Email: olaprsh@optonline.net.
School—(1928) 1617 Parkview Ave., Bronx, 10461. Tel: 718-829-1706; Fax: 718-931-2693. Katy Feeney, Prin. Lay Teachers 11; Students 341.
Catechesis/Religious Program—Tel: 718-904-8464. Students 335.
Chapel—Convent 1639 Parkview Ave., Bronx, 10461. Tel: 718-829-7980.

55—OUR LADY OF VICTORY (1909) Rev. Julio Vasquez (El Salvador).
Res.: 1512 Webster Ave., Bronx, 10457. Tel: 718-583-4044; Fax: 718-583-4764.
Catechesis/Religious Program—Students 185.

56—OUR SAVIOUR (1912), (Yarumal Missionaries) Revs. Jairo A. Valbuena, M.X.Y. (Colombia); David Guzman Perez, M.X.Y. (Colombia).
Res.: 2317 Washington Ave., Bronx, 10458. Tel: 718-295-9600; Fax: 718-295-9607.
Catechesis/Religious Program—Students 157.

57—ST. PETER AND ST. PAUL (1897) Rev. Richard Mederich Marcelino Cisneros.
Res.: 833 St. Ann's Ave., Bronx, 10456. Tel: 718-665-3924; Fax: 718-292-5159. Email: ssppchurch@verizon.net.
School—(1911) 838 Brook Ave., Bronx, 10456. Tel: 718-665-2056. Sisters 2; Lay Teachers 15; Students 342.
Catechesis/Religious Program—Students 155.

58—SS. PHILIP AND JAMES (1949) Rev. Steven Masinde; Deacon Albert V. Welhous.
Res.: 1160 E. 213th St., Bronx, 10469. Tel: 718-547-2203; Fax: 718-231-8160. Email: church@stsphilipandjames.com. Web: www.stsphilipandjames.com.
School—(1953) 1160 E. 213th St., Bronx, 10469. Tel: 718-882-4576; Fax: 718-653-6167. Email: school@stsphilipandjames.com. Web: www.stsphilipandjamesschool.com. Sisters of St. Dominic (Blauvelt) 1; Lay Teachers 11; Students 300.
Catechesis/Religious Program—Students 30.
Chapel—Dominican Sisters Convent 1180 E. 214th St., Bronx, 10469.

59—ST. PHILIP NERI (1898) Rev. Msgr. Kevin P. O'Brien; Rev. Nelson Couto (India).
Res.: 3025 Grand Concourse, Bronx, 10468. Tel: 718-733-3200; Fax: 718-733-4390.
School—(1913) 3031 Grand Concourse, Bronx, 10468. Tel: 718-365-8806. Mrs. Janet E. Heed, Prin. Lay Teachers 11; Students 354.
Catechesis/Religious Program—Students 222.
Chapel—Convent of Mount St. Ursula Marion Ave. & 200th St., Bronx, 10468. Tel: 718-365-7410.
Chapel—Kolping Residence Kolping Society, 2916 Grand Concourse, Bronx, 10468. Tel: 718-733-6119.
Chapel—Ursuline Residence 2850 Marion Ave., Bronx, 10468. Tel: 718-295-6094.
St. Mary's Hall—323 E. 198th St., Bronx, 10468. Tel: 718-933-9894. (Ursuline).

60—ST. PIUS V (1907) Rev. Adolfo Romero-Rios (Argentina); Deacons Raul Padron; Luis A. Torres. In Res., Rev. Fortunato Romero (Peru).
Res.: 420 E. 145th St., Bronx, 10454. Tel: 718-665-6642; Fax: 718-665-4007. Email: st_piusv@hotmail.com. Web: www.freewebs.com/saintpiuschurch.
High School—500 Courtlandt Ave., Bronx, 10454. Tel: 718-292-3636; Fax: 718-402-1704. Email: pius1045@aol.com. Web: www.stpiushs.org. Lay Teachers 14; Students 210.
Catechesis/Religious Program—Students 65.

61—ST. RAYMOND (1842) [CEM 2] Rev. Msgr. John K. Graham; Rev. Ramon Lopez. In Res., Revs. Stephen Adu-Kwaning (Ghana); William Brogan; Joseph Darbouze; Joey Francisco (Philippines).
Res.: 1759 Castle Hill Ave., Bronx, 10462. Tel: 718-792-4044; Fax: 718-863-8509. Email: strayoffice@yahoo.com.
School—(1860) 2380 E. Tremont Ave., Bronx, 10462. Tel: 718-597-3232; Fax: 718-892-4449. Email: b258@adnyeducation.org. Web: www.strayelem.org. Sr. Patricia Brito, R.J.M., Prin. Lay Teachers 30; Students 664.
High School—(Boys), 2151 St. Raymond Ave., Bronx, 10462. Tel: 718-824-5050; Fax: 718-863-8808. Bro. Daniel Gardner, F.S.C., Prin. Brothers of the Christian Schools 7; Lay Teachers 56; Students 711.
High School—(Girls), 1725 Castle Hill Ave., Bronx, 10462. Tel: 718-824-4220; Fax: 718-829-3571. Email: rayacad@adnyschools.org. Web: www.saintraymondacademy.org. Sr. Mary Ann D'Antonio, S.C., Prin. Sisters 4; Lay Teachers 30; Students 373.
Catechesis/Religious Program—Tel: 718-792-4044, Ext. 238. Sr. Teresa Marie Diaz, P.C.I., D.R.E. Students 210.
Family Outreach Program—1720 Metropolitan Ave., Bronx, 10462. Tel: 718-931-0095.
Chapel—Brothers Residence 1754 Castle Hill Ave., Bronx, 10462. Tel: 718-829-1417; Fax: 718-863-8392. Brothers of the Christian Schools 7.

62—ST. RITA OF CASCIA SHRINE CHURCH (1900), (Spanish), Revs. Jose Gregorio Gutierrez, Admin.; Ramon S. Manrique.
Res.: 448 College Ave., Bronx, 10451. Tel: 718-585-5900; Fax: 718-585-5901. Email: saintritaschurch@aol.com.
Catechesis/Religious Program—452 College Ave., Bronx, 10451. Students 199.

63—ST. ROCH (1899), (Augustinian Recollects) Rev. Jose Martinez, Admin.
Res.: 525 Wales Ave., Bronx, 10455. Tel: 718-292-3833; Fax: 718-292-3834.
Catechesis/Religious Program—Jeanette Guzman, D.R.E. Students 79.

64—SACRED HEART (1875) Rev. Msgr. Robert M. Trainor, Senior Priest; Revs. Joseph E. Franco, Parochial Admin.; Rufino Lecumberri, Senior Priest; Santiago Rubio, Parochial Vicar; Deacons Alfonso Ramos; Juan Chaparro.
Res.: 1253 Shakespeare Ave., Bronx, 10452. Tel: 718-293-2766; Fax: 718-293-1581.
School—Sacred Heart School (1950) 95 W. 168th St., Bronx, 10452. Tel: 718-293-4288; Fax: 718-293-4886. Rachel Suarez, Prin.; Abigal Akano, Asst. Prin. (Middle); Patricia Maldonado, Asst. Prin. (Primary). Lay Teachers 26; Students 655.
School—Middle School (1926) 1248 Nelson Ave., Bronx, 10452. Tel: 718-293-6040. Lay Teachers 15; Students 350.
Catechesis/Religious Program— Ms. Migdalia Colon, D.R.E. Students 230.
Mission—St. Francis of Assisi 1544 Shakespeare Ave., Bronx, 10452. Tel: 718-731-6840.

65—SANTA MARIA (1926), (Idente Missionaries) Revs. Fernando Real, M.Id.; Cristobal Martin, M.Id., Parochial Vicar. In Res., Revs. Antimo Fiorillo, Pastor Emeritus (Retired); Martin Esguerra, M.Id.; Bro. Marek Wasilewski, M.Id.
Res.: 2352 St. Raymond Ave., Bronx, 10462. Tel: 718-828-2380; Fax: 718-828-4296. Email: b265@archny.org. Web: www.santamariaparish.us.
School—(1951) 1510 Zerega Ave., Bronx, 10462. Tel: 718-823-3636; Fax: 718-823-7008. Sr. Diane Mastroianni, A.S.C.J., Prin. Sisters Apostles of the Sacred Heart of Jesus 2; Lay Teachers 13; Students 293.
Catechesis/Religious Program—Students 100.
Chapel—Santa Maria Convent 1460 Zerega Ave., Bronx, 10462.

66—ST. SIMON STOCK (1919), (Carmelite) Revs. Nelson Belizario, O.Carm.; Christopher J. Iannizzotto, O.Carm., Parochial Vicar.
Res.: 2191 Valentine Ave., Bronx, 10457. Tel: 718-367-1251; Fax: 718-933-8822. Web: www.stsimonstockschool.org.
Church: E. 182nd St. & Ryer Ave., Bronx, 10457.
School—2195 Valentine Ave., Bronx, 10457. Tel: 718-367-0453; Fax: 718-733-1441. Web: www.stsimonstockschool.org. Lay Teachers 9; Students 230.
Catechesis/Religious Program—Students 180.

67—ST. THERESA OF THE INFANT JESUS (1927), (Italian), Revs. Robert F. Grippo; Jacob Thumma (India), Parochial Vicar; Deacon Anthony P. Cassaneto. In Res., Rev. Antony Roja Ignaci.
Res.: 2855 St. Theresa Ave., Bronx, 10461. Tel: 718-892-1900; Fax: 718-892-1146.
School—(1954) 2872 St. Theresa Ave., Bronx, 10461. Tel: 718-792-3688; Fax: 718-892-9441. Mrs. Josephine Fanelli, Prin. Lay Teachers 25; Students 340.
Catechesis/Religious Program—Tel: 718-792-8434. Sr. Martha Otterstedt, D.R.E. Students 144.

68—ST. THOMAS AQUINAS (1890) Rev. Jose Giunta, I.V.E.
Res.: 1900 Crotona Pkwy., Bronx, 10460. Tel: 718-589-5235; Fax: 718-861-3638. Email: secretary@saintthomasaquinasbronx.org. Web: www.stthomasaquinasbronx.org.
School—(1907) 1909 Daly Ave., Bronx, 10460. Tel: 718-893-7600; Fax: 718-378-5531. Lay Teachers 10; Students 229.
Catechesis/Religious Program—1900 Crotona Pkwy., Bronx, 10460. Students 151.
Convent—1899 Daly Ave., Bronx, 10460.

69—ST. VALENTINE (1891), (Polish), Closed. For information for sacramental records, please contact Our Lady of Grace, Bronx.

70—VISITATION (1928) Rev. Msgr. Robert W. Larkin; Rev. John F. Lauri.
Res.: 160 Van Cortlandt Park S., Bronx, 10463. Tel: 718-548-1455; Fax: 718-548-0289.
School—(1932) 171 W. 239th St., Bronx, 10463. Tel: 718-543-2250; Fax: 718-543-3665. Priests 1; Sisters 3; Lay Teachers 7; Students 204.
Catechesis/Religious Program—Students 110.

BOROUGH OF RICHMOND

STATEN ISLAND

1—ST. ADALBERT (Elm Park) (1901), (Polish), Revs. Eugene J. Carrella; James P. Nieckarz, M.M.; Deacon Joseph J. Rentkowski.
Res.: 337 Morningstar Rd., 10303. Tel: 718-442-8476; Fax: 718-727-1241. Email: stadalbert311@aol.com.
School—(1905) 355 Morningstar Rd., 10303. Tel: 718-442-2020; Fax: 718-447-2012. Priests 1; Lay Teachers 10; Students 295.
Catechesis/Religious Program—Students 50.

2—ST. ANN (1914) Revs. John S. Kostek; Abraham K. George, Parochial Vicar; Jacek Wozny.
Res.: 101 Cromwell Ave., 10304. Tel: 718-351-0270; Fax: 718-980-4731.
School—(1955) 125 Cromwell Ave., 10304. Tel: 718-351-4343. Mrs. Bernadette Ficchi, Prin. Presentation Nuns 1; Lay Teachers 12; Students 234.
Catechesis/Religious Program—Mrs. Kathleen Daly, C.R.E. Students 255.

3—ST. ANTHONY (1908) Rev. John J. Wroblewski. 24 Shelly Ave., 10314.
Res.: 24 Shelly Ave., 10314. Tel: 718-761-6660; Fax: 718-761-1029.
Church: 4055 Victory Blvd., 10314.
Catechesis/Religious Program—Students 103.

4—ASSUMPTION/ST. PAUL (1922), (Italian), Records at: 718-447-6362; Fax 718-720-0106. Rev. Michael W. Cichon.
Res.: 145 Clinton Ave., 10301. Tel: 718-727-4594.
Catechesis/Religious Program—Students 63.

5—ST. BENEDICTA (1925) Closed. For inquiries for parish records contact Our Lady of Mount Carmel.

6—BLESSED SACRAMENT (1910) Rev. Msgrs. Peter G. Finn; Francis V. Boyle, Pastor Emeritus (Retired); Revs. Michael Moon; Francisco Lanzaderas.
Res.: 30 Manor Rd., 10310. Tel: 718-442-1581; Fax: 718-442-1398.
Church: Manor Rd. & Forest Ave., 10310.
School—(1917) 830 Delafield Ave., 10310. Tel: 718-442-3090; Fax: 718-442-9654. Mrs. Linda Magnusson, Prin. Lay Teachers 23; Students 600.
Catechesis/Religious Program—Tel: 718-448-0378. Students 477.

7—ST. CHARLES (1960) Rev. Msgr. Thomas J. Bergin; Revs. James B. Hynes; Albin Roby Antony (India); Deacons Michael Calafiore; Lawrence Droge; Stephen Tobon.
Res.: 644 Clawson St., 10306. Tel: 718-987-2670; Fax: 718-987-7950. Email: stcharles@verizon.net. Web: www.stcharles.e-paluch.com.
School—200 Penn Ave., 10306. Tel: 718-987-0200; Fax: 718-987-8158. Email: si314@adnyschools.org. Lay Teachers 30; Students 695.
Catechesis/Religious Program—Tel: 718-979-6800.

Email: mpetrides@stcharlessch.org. Students 453.

8—ST. CHRISTOPHER (1926) Revs. Joseph M. McLafferty; Richard J. Enegbuma.
Res.: 130 Midland Ave., 10306. Tel: 718-351-2452; Fax: 718-351-1174.
School—(1930) 15 Lisbon Pl., 10306. Tel: 718-351-0902; Fax: 718-351-0975. Catherine Falabella, Prin. Lay Teachers 14; Students 202.
Catechesis/Religious Program—130 Midland Ave., 10306. Tel: 718-351-2480; Fax: 718-351-1174. Gloria DePietro, D.R.E. Students 101.

9—ST. CLARE (1921) Rev. Msgr. Richard J. Guastella; Revs. James Essuon (Ghana), Parochial Vicar; John McCarthy, Parochial Vicar; Joseph Karikunnel (India), Parochial Vicar; Deacon Richard Mitchell.
Res.: 110 Nelson Ave., 10308. Tel: 718-984-7873; Fax: 718-966-8420.
School—151 Lindenwood Rd., 10308. Tel: 718-984-7091. Jo Rossicone, Prin. Lay Teachers 21; Students 643.
Catechesis/Religious Program—Tel: 718-948-4829. Seton Harney, C.R.E. Students 1,360.

10—ST. CLEMENT (1910) Rev. Msgr. Nicholas J. Soares.
Res.: 207 Harbor Rd., 10303. Tel: 718-442-1688; Fax: 718-442-4689.
Church: 126 Van Pelt Ave., 10303.
Catechesis/Religious Program—Tel: 718-727-6442. Students 301.

11—HOLY CHILD (1966) Revs. Alan Travers; Wilfred Y. Dodo (Nigeria); Edwin H. Cipot; Deacon Alfred Thompson; Sr. Jean Wagner, P.B.V.M., Pastoral Assoc.; Anne Lukasiewicz, Music Min.
Res.: 4747 Amboy Rd., 10312. Tel: 718-356-5890; Fax: 718-356-5995.
Preschool Office—4747 Amboy Rd., 10312. Tel: 718-356-5159; Fax: 718-356-1933.
School—*School of Religion*, Tel: 718-356-5277; Fax: 718-227-0898. Marie Ferro, D.R.E. Lay Teachers 112; Students 1,100.
Catechesis/Religious Program—Students 1,083.

12—HOLY FAMILY (1966) [JC] Revs. Austin E. Titus; John M. Mensah (Ghana).
Mailing Address: 366 Watchogue Rd., 10314. Tel: 718-761-6671. In Res., Rev. Alfred Pucci (Retired).
Catechesis/Religious Program—Students 380.

13—HOLY ROSARY (1927) Revs. Robert J. Aufieri; Bernal Stainwall; Stephen G. Challman; Deacon Rosario Tirella. In Res., Rev. Eduardo Amora (Philippines).
Res.: 80 Jerome Ave., 10305. Tel: 718-727-3360; Fax: 718-876-6183. Web: www.hrosarychurch.com.
School—(1955), (Grades PreK-8), 100 Jerome Ave., 10305. Tel: 718-447-1195; Fax: 718-815-5862. Diane R. Murphy, Prin. Lay Teachers 14; Students 342.
Catechesis/Religious Program—Tel: 718-273-6695. Laurel Fulcher, C.R.E. Students 254.
Mission—*Holy Rosary* 207 Sand Ln., 10305.

14—IMMACULATE CONCEPTION (1887) Rev. Peter J. Byrne; Deacon Hector Espinal. In Res., Rev. Peter J. West.
Res.: 128 Targee St., 10304. Tel: 718-447-2165; Fax: 718-447-4835. Email: i303@archny.org.
School—(1908) 104 Gordon St., 10304. Tel: 718-447-7018; Fax: 718-447-4365. Email: si303@adnyschools.org. Ms. Kathleen Curatolo, Prin. Lay Staff 23; Students 240.
Catechesis/Religious Program—Students 153.

15—ST. JOHN NEUMANN (1982) Revs. Robert W. Dillon; Lucito T. Purawan.
Res.: 1380 Arthur Kill Rd., 10312. Tel: 718-984-8535; Fax: 718-984-6948. Email: rectory@sjneumann.org.
Catechesis/Religious Program—Tel: 718-966-7327. Students 339.

16—ST. JOHN THE BAPTIST DE LA SALLE (1900), Records at: Immaculate Conception, 128 Targee St., Staten Island, NY 10304. Tel: 718-447-2165.
Res.: 128 Targee St., 10304. Tel: 718-447-2165; Fax: 718-447-4835.
Church: 76 Jackson St., 10304.

17—ST. JOSEPH (1902), (Italian), Rev. Michael T. Martine.
Parish Office—463 Tompkins Ave., 10305. Tel: 718-816-0047; Fax: 718-816-4529.
Res.: 171 St. Mary's Ave., 10305.
Church: 466 Tompkins Ave., 10305.
School—139 St. Mary's Ave., 10305. Tel: 718-447-7686; Fax: 718-447-7687. Linda Bilotti, Prin. Lay Teachers 157; Students 195.
Catechesis/Religious Program—Students 70.

18—ST. JOSEPH, ST. THOMAS (1848) [CEM] Rev. Msgr. Edmund J. Whalen; Revs. John F. Palatucci; Evangelio R. Suaybaguio; Arnel Ranada (Philippines).
Res.: 6097 Amboy Rd., 10309. Tel: 718-356-0294; Fax: 718-948-3885. Web: www.stjstparish.org.
School—50 Maguire Ave., 10309. Tel: 718-356-3344; Fax: 718-227-9531. Joanne DelGeorge, Prin. Lay Teachers 11; Students 338.
Catechesis/Religious Program—Tel: 718-984-1156. Elizabeth Brim, D.R.E. Students 1,600.

19—ST. MARGARET MARY (1926) Rev. Keith Fennessy; Deacon Patrick Graham.
Res.: 560 Lincoln Ave., 10306. Tel: 718-351-2612; Fax: 718-987-0446. Email: mmaryrectory@si.rr.com.
School—(1925) 556 Lincoln Ave., 10306. Tel: 718-351-4778; Fax: 718-351-3786. Mrs. Rita Vallebuono, Prin. Lay Teachers 8; Students 135.
Catechesis/Religious Program—Students 124.

20—ST. MARY (1852) [CEM] Rev. Victor J. Buebendorf. In Res., Rev. Michael Arputham.
Res.: 1101 Bay St., 10305. Tel: 718-727-0671; Fax: 718-815-7393. Email: stmaryrosebank@verizon.net.
School—(1853) 1124 Bay St., 10305. Tel: 718-447-1842; Fax: 718-447-0986. Virginia Savarese, Prin. Lay Teachers 10; Students 215.
Catechesis/Religious Program—Students 98.

21—ST. MARY OF THE ASSUMPTION (1853) [CEM], (Jesuit) Rev. D. Michael Flynn, S.J.; Deacon James Stahlnecker. In Res., Revs. John R. Hyatt, S.J.; Thomas J. Quinn, S.J. (Retired).
Res.: 2230 Richmond Ter., 10302. Tel: 718-442-6372; Fax: 718-448-2159. Email: stmaryassumption@hotmail.com.
Catechesis/Religious Program—Students 317.
Mission—*Christ the King* 182 Park Ave., Richmond Co. 10302.

22—ST. MICHAEL (1922) Rev. Msgr. Nicholas J. Soares.
Res.: 207 Harbor Rd., 10303. Tel: 718-442-1688; Fax: 718-442-4689.
Church: 211-213 Harbor Rd., 10303.
Catechesis/Religious Program—Tel: 718-727-6442. Students 301.

23—OUR LADY HELP OF CHRISTIANS (1898) Revs. Jarlath Quinn; Francis Maurice; Jerry Del Prado (Philippines); Deacons Edward J. Wetherall; John Singler; Richard Salhany.
Res.: 7396 Amboy Rd., 10307. Tel: 718-317-9772; Fax: 718-317-0038. Email: olhcpastor@aol.com. Web: wwwolhcparish.org.
School—(1910 and 1955) 23 Summit St., 10307. Tel: 718-984-1360; Fax: 718-966-9356. Email: olhcprincipal@aol.com. Mrs. M. Chiappchino, Prin. Lay Teachers 10; Students 300.
Catechesis/Religious Program—Tel: 718-356-3888. Students 800.

24—OUR LADY OF GOOD COUNSEL (1898), (Augustinian) Revs. John F. Dello Russo, O.S.A.; Joseph X. O'Connor, O.S.A.; Jorge Luis Cleto, O.S.A.
Res.: 10 Austin Pl., 10304. Tel: 718-447-1503; Fax: 718-447-7361. Email: ologc@verizon.net. Web: www.ologc.catholicweb.com.
School—(1923) 42 Austin Pl., 10304. Tel: 718-447-7260; Fax: 718-815-7262. Email: si304@adnyschools.org. Web: www.goodcounselsch.org. Mrs. Frances Santangelo, Prin. Lay Teachers 16; Students 300.
Catechesis/Religious Program—Tel: 718-816-0542. Linda Affatato, D.R.E. Students 300.

25—OUR LADY OF MT. CARMEL-ST. BENEDICTA (1913) Rev. D. Michael Flynn, S.J.; Deacon Anthony A. Lagotta, (Retired). In Res., Revs. Hernan Peredes, S.J.; Edward J. Quinnan, S.J.; Matthew F. Roche, S.J.
Res.: 1265 Castleton Ave., 10310. Tel: 718-442-3411; Fax: 718-442-3997. Email: mountcarmelsi@verizon.net.
School—285 Clove Rd., 10310. Tel: 718-981-5131; Fax: 718-981-0027. Email: si306@adnyedu.org.
Catechesis/Religious Program—Students 117.

26—OUR LADY OF PITY (1923) Rev. Msgr. Philip J. Franceschini; Rev. Edwin C. Lanuevo (Philippines); Sr. Eugene Sanita, Pastoral Assoc.; Deacon Michael Venditto.
Res.: 1616 Richmond Ave., 10314. Tel: 718-761-5421; Fax: 718-983-6225.
Catechesis/Religious Program—Catherine Arcuri, D.R.E. Students 262.

27—OUR LADY STAR OF THE SEA (1916) Rev. Msgr. Jeffrey Conway; Revs. Michael Sullivan, Parochial Vicar; Panimayakumar Gaspar (India), Parochial Vicar; Robert J. Poveromo, Parochial Vicar; Sr. Line Rioux, C.S.J., Pastoral Assoc.; Mrs. Debra Emigholz, Business Mgr.
Res.: 5371 Amboy Rd., Huguenot Park, 10312. Tel: 718-984-0593; Fax: 718-984-5203. Web: www.olssparish.org.
School—(1959) 5411 Amboy Rd., 10312. Tel: 718-984-5750. Irma Cummings, Prin.; Josephine Tortorella, Asst. Prin. Lay Teachers 24; Students 876.
Catechesis/Religious Program—5411 Amboy Rd., 10312. Tel: 718-984-1885. Camille Quaglia, D.R.E. Students 1,023.

28—OUR LADY, QUEEN OF PEACE (1922) Revs. Pancrose Kalist; William J. Damroth III; Mario Ramirez.
Res.: 90 Third St., 10306. Tel: 718-351-1093; Fax: 718-351-1784. Email: olqpchurch@verizon.net.
School—(1924) 22 Steele Ave., 10306. Tel: 718-351-0370; Fax: 718-351-0950. Theresa Signorile, Prin. Lay Teachers 18; Students 550.
Catechesis/Religious Program—Tel: 718-979-0989. Students 330.
Mission—*Our Lady of Lourdes* Cedar Grove Ave., New Dorp Beach, Richmond Co. 10306.

29—ST. PATRICK (1862) Rev. Msgr. John M. McCarthy; Revs. Joseph Victor Maynigo-Arenas (Philippines); Arnulfo Tiplaca. In Res., Rev. Ronelo Anung (Philippines).
Parish Office:—3560 Richmond Rd., 10306. Tel: 718-979-4227; Fax: 718-979-7637. Email: parishadmin@stpatrickssi.org.
Res.: 53 St. Patrick's Pl., 10306. Tel: 718-351-0044; Fax: 718-351-0824.
School—(1919) 3560 Richmond Rd., 10306. Tel: 718-979-8815; Fax: 718-979-4984. Web: www.stpatrickssi.org. Deborah Brochin, Prin. Lay Teachers 22; Students 526.
Catechesis/Religious Program—Tel: 718-979-1272. Students 290.

30—ST. PAUL (1924), Records for Assumption/St. Paul, 145 Clinton Ave., Staten Island, NY 10301 (718-447-6362; Fax 718-720-0106) Rev. Michael W. Cichon.
Res. & Mailing Address: 145 Clinton Ave., 10301. Tel: 718-447-6362; Fax: 718-720-0106.
Catechesis/Religious Program—
Christian Brothers Residence—148 Cassidy Pl., 10301.

31—ST. PETER (1839) [CEM] Rev. Msgr. James J. Dorney; Rev. E. Pablito Maghari (Philippines).
Res.: 53 St. Mark's Pl., 10301. Tel: 718-727-2672; Fax: 718-720-9269.
School—300 Richmond Ter., 10301. Tel: 718-447-1796; Fax: 718-447-4240. Miss Margaret Annunziata, Prin. Lay Teachers 13; Students 202.
High School—*St. Peter's Boys High School*, 200 Clinton Ave., 10301. Tel: 718-447-1676; Fax: 718-447-4027. Mr. John Fodera, Prin.; Bro. James Kelly, F.S.C., Pres. Sisters 2; Brothers of the Christian Schools 4; Lay Teachers 34; Students 660.
High School—*Girls High School*, Tel: 718-447-0304; Fax: 718-447-0832. Mrs. Paula McKeown, Prin. Lay Teachers 15; Students 124.
Catechesis/Religious Program—Students 42.
St. Joseph, Brothers' House—Tel: 718-447-2815.

32—ST. RITA (1921) Revs. Richard Veras; John F. Reardon, Pastor Emeritus (Retired); Anthony Gonzalez (Philippines), Parochial Vicar.
Res.: 281 Bradley Ave., 10314. Tel: 718-698-3746; Fax: 718-698-4670. Email: mg@si.rr.com. Web: www.churchofstrita.com.
School—(1922) 30 Wellbrook Ave., 10314. Tel: 718-761-2504; Fax: 718-761-0014. Web: www.stritaschoolsi.com. Adele Kosinski, Prin. Sisters 1; Lay Teachers 15; Students 376.
Catechesis/Religious Program—Email: ccd@si.rr.com. Mary Gillespie, C.R.E. Students 278.
Convent—*Dominican Sisters*, 61 Wellbrook Ave., 10314. Tel: 718-761-1171. (Roman Congregation of St. Dominic)

33—ST. ROCH (1922) Rev. Leo R. Prince.
Res.: 602 Port Richmond Ave., 10302. Tel: 718-442-4755; Fax: 718-981-4455. Email: strochs@si.rr.com.
School—465 Villa Ave., 10302. Tel: 718-448-2424. Sr. Mary Patricia, Prin. Sisters of St. John the Baptist 4; Lay Teachers 13; Students 197.
Catechesis/Religious Program—Students 101.

34—SACRED HEART (1875) Revs. Louis Jerome; Deogracias Lingao, Parochial Vicar. In Res., Rev. Robert J. Navins (Retired).
Res.: 981 Castleton Ave., 10310. Tel: 718-442-0058; Fax: 718-816-8006. Email: sacredheart310@yahoo.com. Web: www.sacredheartsi.com.
School—(1875) 301 N. Burgher Ave., 10310. Tel: 718-442-0347; Fax: 718-440-6978. Web: www.shschool.info. Cynthia A. Reimer, Prin. Lay Teachers 11; Students 305.
Catechesis/Religious Program—Tel: 718-448-1536; Fax: 718-448-1526. Students 220.

35—ST. STANISLAUS KOSTKA (1923), (Polish), Rev. Marek Suchocki.
Res.: 109 York Ave., 10301. Tel: 718-447-3937; Fax: 718-815-5733.
Catechesis/Religious Program—Students 64.

36—ST. SYLVESTER (1921) Rev. Jacob Thumma (India).
Res.: 854 Targee St., 10304-4517. Tel: 718-727-4639; Fax: 718-273-2950. Email: stsylvesterchr@aol.com.
School—(1930) 884 Targee St., 10304. Tel: 718-442-4938; Fax: 718-442-8177. Email: si331@adnyschools.org. Evelyn M. Lacagnino, Prin. Lay Teachers 9; Students 136.
Catechesis/Religious Program—Tel: 718-442-1374. Students 40.

37—ST. TERESA (1926) Revs. John J. O'Hara; Patrick Buckley; Arul Xavier Raj, O.F.M.Cap. (India);

Deacon Phillip J. Maroon.
Res.: 1634 Victory Blvd., 10314. Tel: 718-442-5412; Fax: 718-442-9041. Email: rectory@saintteresasi.org. Web: www.saintteresasi.org.
School—(1955) 1632 Victory Blvd., 10314. Tel: 718-448-9650; 718-447-6426; Fax: 718-447-6462. Email: si332@education.org. Lay Teachers 16; Students 357.
Catechesis/Religious Program—Tel: 718-981-2632; Fax: 718-981-0026. Students 294.
Mission—St. Nicholas Northern Blvd., Staten Island Co. 10301.
Chapel—St. Nicholas La Bau Ave. & Northern Blvd., 10314.

OUTSIDE THE CITY OF NEW YORK

AMENIA, DUTCHESS CO., IMMACULATE CONCEPTION (1868) [CEM] Revs. John L. Durkin; Charles Heston. In Res., Deacon David Weinstein.
Res.: 4 Lavelle Rd., Box 109, 12501. Tel: 845-373-8193; Fax: 845-373-8194.
Catechesis/Religious Program—Students 77.
Mission—St. Patrick [CEM] Church St., Millerton, Dutchess Co. 12546.

ARDSLEY, WESTCHESTER CO., OUR LADY OF PERPETUAL HELP (1929) Revs. Philip J. Gagliano; Robert J. Duane, Pastor Emeritus (Retired).
Res.: One Cross Rd., 10502. Tel: 914-693-0030. Email: olphardsley@aol.com.
Catechesis/Religious Program—Tel: 914-693-0037. Email: olphccd@aol.com. Students 396.

ARMONK, WESTCHESTER CO., ST. PATRICK (1966) Rev. John F. Quinn.
Res.: 29 Cox Ave., P.O. Box 6, 10504. Tel: 914-273-9724. Email: armagh@bestweb.net. Web: www.stpatrickinarmonk.org.
Catechesis/Religious Program—Tel: 914-273-8226; Fax: 914-273-4901. Email: patrreled@optonline.net. Diane McManus, Mod. Rel. Educ. Students 578.

BANGALL, DUTCHESS CO., IMMACULATE CONCEPTION (1919) [CEM] Rev. William A. White, Admin. In Res., Rev. John A. Bida.
Res.: 64 Hunns Lake Rd., P.O. Box 623, 12506-0623. Tel: 845-868-1923; Fax: 845-868-1593. Email: iccrectory@optonline.net.
Catechesis/Religious Program—Students 29.

BARRYTOWN, DUTCHESS CO., SACRED HEART, Closed. Parochial records at St. Christopher, Red Hook.

BEACON, DUTCHESS CO.
1—ST. JOACHIM (Records at St. John the Evangelist).
2—ST. JOHN THE EVANGELIST Revs. David E. Nolan; Fabian Eghiabumhe; Irenaeus Ikhane.
Res.: 2 Oak St., 12508. Tel: 845-838-0915; Fax: 834-838-0919. Email: stsjoachimjohn@optonline.net.
Catechesis/Religious Program—Tel: 845-831-6550. Students 360.

BEDFORD, WESTCHESTER CO., ST. PATRICK (1929) Rev. Msgr. George P. Thompson; Rev. Joseph Domfeh-Boateng (Ghana); Deacon Louis Santore.
Parish Office: 485 State Rd., 10506. Tel: 914-234-3344. Email: patrick485@optonline.net. Web: www.hereintown.com/ny/bedford/stpats.
Res.: 7 Pound Ridge Rd., Box 303, 10506. Tel: 914-234-3668; Fax: 914-234-9126. Email: stpatsgt@optonline.net.
School—(1956) State Rd., 10506. Tel: 914-234-7914. Email: w406@adnyschools.org. Web: www.st-patricksschoolbedford.org. Dr. Elizabeth Frangella, Prin. Lay Teachers 11; Students 165.
Catechesis/Religious Program—Tel: 914-234-3775; Fax: 914-234-0579. Mrs. Pat Perlstein, D.R.E.; Mrs. Karen Schmidt, D.R.E. Students 620.

BLAUVELT, ROCKLAND CO., ST. CATHARINE (1868) [CEM] Rev. Msgr. Emmet R. Nevin; Revs. Nicholas E. Callaghan; Abraham Vallayil, C.M.I.; Deacon John C. Kelleher.
Res.: 523 Western Hwy., 10913. Tel: 845-359-0542; Fax: 845-365-2387.
Catechesis/Religious Program—Tel: 845-359-4014. Mrs. Audrey Angelini, C.R.E. Students 767.
Chapel—Our Lady Queen of Peace 140 Old Orangeburg Rd., Orangeburg, 10962. Tel: 845-359-1000, Ext. 3588.

BREWSTER, PUTNAM CO., ST. LAWRENCE O'TOOLE (1878) [CEM] Revs. Robert F. McKeon; Eric Twene (Ghana); Andrew Gyabbah (Ghana); Alfredo Monteiro (India); Deacons Mark Shkreli; John Baffa.
Res.: 31 Prospect St., 10509. Tel: 845-279-2021; Fax: 845-279-7441.
Catechesis/Religious Program—Tel: 845-279-6098; Fax: 845-279-8165. Theresa Scorca, D.R.E.; Maryellen Tiernan, Curriculum Coord. Students 690.

BRIARCLIFF MANOR, WESTCHESTER CO., ST. THERESA (1926) Rev. Msgr. James K. Vaughey; Rev. L. Praxid DeSilva (Sri Lanka).
Res.: 1394 Pleasantville Rd., 10510. Tel: 914-941-1646; Fax: 914-944-9503. Email: stchurch@optonline.net. Web: www.sainttheresa.org.
School—Tel: 914-762-1050; Fax: 914-941-9483. Lay Teachers 10; Students 200.
Catechesis/Religious Program—Tel: 914-923-3286; Fax: 914-944-9503. Students 468.
Mission—Our Lady of the Wayside Rte. 100, Millwood, Westchester Co. 10546.

BRONXVILLE, WESTCHESTER CO., ST. JOSEPH (1922) Rev. Msgrs. James F. Doyle; Guy Vinci; Rev. Brian P. Taylor. In Res., Revs. Dawson Ambosta (India); Joachim Adione.
Res.: 15 Cedar St., 10708. Tel: 914-337-1660; Fax: 914-337-1342.
School—(1951) 30 Meadow Ave., 10708. Tel: 914-337-0261; Fax: 914-395-1192. Nancy Langehennig, Prin. Lay Teachers 25; Students 260.
Catechesis/Religious Program—28 Meadow Ave., 10708. Tel: 914-337-6383; Fax: 914-779-8103. Mrs. Antoinette Gilligan, D.R.E. Students 950.

BUCHANAN, WESTCHESTER CO., ST. CHRISTOPHER (1929) Rev. Msgr. Donald W. Hendricks; Rev. Gonzalo Morocho, S.D.B. (Ecuador); Deacon Ronald J. Schlitt.
Res.: 3094 Albany Post Rd., 10511. Tel: 914-737-1046; Fax: 914-737-9320. Email: stchristopher@optonline.net.
Catechesis/Religious Program—Tel: 914-737-1437. Email: olivell@optonline.net. Catherine M. Garnsey, D.R.E. Students 462.

CALLICOON, SULLIVAN CO., HOLY CROSS (1870) [CEM] [JC 2] Rev. Ignatius E. Smith, O.F.M.
Res.: 9719 Rte. 97, P.O. Box 246, 12723. Tel: 845-887-5450; Fax: 845-887-5873. Email: deusmeus@in4web.com.
Catechesis/Religious Program—Students 60.
Mission—St. Patrick, Long Eddy, 12760.
Chapel—Callicoon, Holy Cross Rectory

CARMEL, PUTNAM CO., ST. JAMES THE APOSTLE (1913) Revs. Anthony D. Sorgie; Vincent DePaul Howley; John A. DeBellis; Deacons Charles T. Borsavage; Gerard Cartwright; Anthony Gruerio.
Res.: 14 Gleneida Ave., 10512. Tel: 845-225-2079; Fax: 845-225-5566. Email: stjoll@aol.com.
School—(1954)Tel: 845-225-9365; Fax: 845-228-2859. Lay Teachers 10; Students 264.
Catechesis/Religious Program—Tel: 845-225-6504. Students 1,850.
Mission—Our Lady of the Lake/Mt. Carmel [JC] 1 Doherty Dr., Lake Carmel, Putnam Co. 10512. Tel: 845-228-1235.
Mission—Chapel of Life, Carmel

CHAPPAQUA, WESTCHESTER CO., ST. JOHN AND ST. MARY (1922) Rev. Msgrs. Thomas E. Gilleece; Patrick Barry; Deacons Charles Devlin; Walter Brady; Mrs. Joan Corso Ferroni, Pastoral Assoc.
Res.: 15 St. John's Pl., 10514. Tel: 914-238-3274; Fax: 914-238-3354. Web: www.sjmchap.com.
Catechesis/Religious Program—30 Poillon Rd., 10514. Tel: 914-238-3696. Email: kidsrelig@optimum.net. Students 704.

CHESTER, ORANGE CO., ST. COLUMBA (1875) [CEM] Rev. John S. Bonnici.
Res.: 27 High St., 10918. Tel: 845-469-2108; Fax: 845-469-6165.
Catechesis/Religious Program—Tel: 845-469-9503. Students 196.

COLD SPRING-ON-HUDSON, PUTNAM CO., OUR LADY OF LORETTO (1833) Revs. Brian T. McSweeney; Gabriel Awuafor (Ghana).
Res.: 24 Fair St., 10516. Tel: 845-265-3718; Fax: 845-265-4309.
Catechesis/Religious Program—Tel: 845-265-2594. Email: ollreled@verizon.net. Catherine Garnsey, D.R.E. Students 289.
Mission—St. Joseph's Chapel Garrison, Putnam Co. 10524.

CONGERS, ROCKLAND CO., ST. PAUL (1896) [CEM] Revs. Arthur Mastrolia; Brendan Gormley; Deacons Dominick Buonocore, Parish Mgr.; John W. McSherry; James Gorman; Mark Czerwinski.
Res.: 82 Lake Rd. W., 10920. Tel: 845-268-4464; Fax: 845-268-6790. Web: www.stpaulcongers.net.
School—365 Kings Hwy., Valley Cottage, 10989. Tel: 914-268-6506; Fax: 914-268-1809. Sr. Stephen Gerard, O.P., Prin. Sisters 2; Lay Teachers 10; Students 220.
Catechesis/Religious Program—Tel: 845-268-5442. Rowena Hoblin, C.R.E. Students 800.
Chapel—Congers, Sisters' Convent and School

CORNWALL-ON-HUDSON, ORANGE CO., ST. THOMAS OF CANTERBURY (1870) [CEM] Rev. Bernard P. Heter; Rev. Msgr. Francis X. Duffy, Pastor Emeritus (Retired); Deacons John V. Pelella; William Stafford.
Res.: 10 Second St., 12520. Tel: 914-534-2547; Fax: 914-534-1357. Email: stthomascanterbury@hvc.rr.com.
School—(1913) Hudson St., 12520. Tel: 914-534-2019. Mrs. Agnes Maleakas, Prin. Lay Teachers 6; Students 96.
Catechesis/Religious Program—Tel: 914-534-9393. Email: stthomasdre@aol.com. Mrs. Judy Valentine, D.R.E. Students 568.

CORTLANDT MANOR, WESTCHESTER CO.
1—ST. COLUMBANUS (Van Cortlandtville) (1950) Rev. Msgr. Patrick J. Keenan; Revs. Francis J. Samoylo; Rayappa Thumma; Deacon John J. Coppola.
Res.: 122 Oregon Rd., 10567. Tel: 914-737-4705; Fax: 914-736-7476.
School—122 Oregon Rd., 10567. Tel: 914-739-1200; Fax: 914-739-1109. Lay Teachers 10; Students 209.
Catechesis/Religious Program—Tel: 914-739-2441. Students 295.
Mission—North American Martyrs 55 Oscawana Lake Rd., Putnam Valley, Putnam Co. 10579. Tel: 845-528-6433.
2—HOLY SPIRIT (1966) Rev. Thomas P. Kiely; Deacon Ray Parchen.
Res.: 1969 Crompond Rd., 10567-4113. Tel: 914-737-2316; Fax: 914-737-6882. Email: holyspiritchurch1969@verizon.net.
Catechesis/Religious Program—Tel: 914-734-9243. Email: re_holyspiritchurch@att.net. Students 620.
Chapel—Cortlandt Manor

CRESTWOOD, WESTCHESTER CO., CHURCH OF THE ANNUNCIATION (1931) Rev. Msgr. Dennis P. Keane; Rev. Ivan Lovric (Croatia).
Res.: 470 Westchester Ave., 10707. Tel: 914-779-7345; Fax: 914-961-5688.
School—(1943) 465 Westchester Ave., 10707. Tel: 914-337-8760; Fax: 914-337-8878. Sr. Anne Massell, P.B.V.M., Prin. Sisters 3; Lay Teachers 25; Students 557.
Catechesis/Religious Program—Tel: 914-779-2374. Students 140.

CROTON FALLS, WESTCHESTER CO., ST. JOSEPH (1845) Rev. Msgr. James R. Moore; Revs. Jude Aguwa (Nigeria); Matthew C. Newcomb.
Res.: 10 Croton Falls Rd., P.O. Box 719, 10519. Tel: 914-277-3765; 914-277-3877; Fax: 914-277-1823.
School—(1949), (Grades PreK-8) Tel: 914-277-3783; Fax: 914-277-3238. Lay Teachers 10; Students 175.
Catechesis/Religious Program—14 Croton Falls Rd., 10519. Tel: 914-276-1067. Students 1,091.
Mission—St. Michael Park Ave., Goldens Bridge, Westchester Co. 10526.
Mission—St. John [CEM] Rte. 116, North Salem, Westchester Co. 10560.

CROTON-ON-HUDSON, WESTCHESTER CO., HOLY NAME OF MARY (1874) Revs. Michael F. Keane; Loyola Amalraj; Deacon Albert Mazza.
Res.: 110 Grand St., 10520. Tel: 914-271-4797; Fax: 914-271-6841.
School—Tel: 914-271-5182.
Catechesis/Religious Program—114 Grand St., 10520. Tel: 914-271-4254. Students 356.
Mission—Church of the Good Shepherd Benedict Blvd. and Young Ave., Harmon, Westchester Co. 10520.

DOBBS FERRY, WESTCHESTER CO.
1—OUR LADY OF POMPEII (1922), (Italian), Rev. Timothy J. Scannell, Admin.
Rectory—95 Palisade St., 10522. Tel: 914-693-0119; Fax: 914-693-3408.
Catechesis/Religious Program—
2—SACRED HEART (1862) Revs. Timothy J. Scannell; Emmanuel Poovathinal, C.M.I. (India); Deacon Patrick D. Troy.
Res.: 18 Bellewood Ave., 10522. Tel: 914-693-0119; Fax: 914-693-3408. Email: shrectory@aol.com.
Church: Broadway and Ashford Ave., 10522.
Catechesis/Religious Program—Tel: 914-479-1045. Mrs. Mary Perillo, D.R.E.; Ann Kinnally, Business Mgr. Students 320.

DOVER PLAINS, DUTCHESS CO., ST. CHARLES BORROMEO (1859) [CEM] Rev. John J. Backes; Deacon James Lawlor.
Res.: 83 Mill St., P.O. Box 9, 12522. Tel: 845-877-9934; Fax: 845-877-9936. Email: stcharlesdover@aol.com.
Catechesis/Religious Program—Tel: 845-832-6989; Fax: 845-832-6989. Students 151.
Mission—Our Lady of Solace Mission Wingdale, Dutchess Co.

EAST KINGSTON, ULSTER CO., ST. COLMAN (1904) Revs. James E. Borstelmann, Admin.; John C. McGuire, Pastor Emeritus (Retired); Luke W. McCann, Pastor Emeritus (Retired).
Res.: 18 Brigham St., Kingston, 12401. Tel: 914-336-8237; Fax: 914-382-1488.
Catechesis/Religious Program—Email: stcolemanff@yahoo.com. Students 71.

ELLENVILLE, ULSTER CO., ST. MARY AND ST. ANDREW (1850) Revs. John W. Lynch; Chinnappa Reddy Aduri.
Res.: 137 S. Main St., 12428. Tel: 845-647-6080; Fax: 845-647-2486.
Catechesis/Religious Program—Bruce Santiago, C.R.E. Students 160.
Mission—Our Lady of Lourdes Kerhonkson, Ulster Co. 12446.

ELMSFORD, WESTCHESTER CO., OUR LADY OF MT. CARMEL (1904) Revs. Jude Arogundade (Nigeria); Andrew Oni (Nigeria).
Res.: 59 E. Main St., 10523. Tel: 914-592-6789; Fax: 914-592-3898.
School—(1929)Tel: 914-592-7575; Fax: 914-345-1591. Web: www.olmc.ws. Sisters of Divine

Compassion 4; Lay Teachers 8; Students 214.
Catechesis/Religious Program—Tel: 914-592-4280. Students 160.

FISHKILL, DUTCHESS CO., CHURCH OF ST. MARY, MOTHER OF THE CHURCH (1953) Rev. Msgr. Joseph A. Martin; Revs. Robert B. Repenning; Adolfo Occeno (Philippines); Deacons Joseph R. Hafeman; Michael Decker; John O'Reilly.
Res.: 103 Jackson St., P.O. Box 780, 12524-0499. Tel: 845-896-6400; Fax: 845-896-4575. Email: stmaryfishkill@aol.com.
School—(1955)Tel: 845-896-9561; Fax: 845-896-8477. Mrs. Ellen Anderson, Prin. Lay Teachers 9; Students 285.
Catechesis/Religious Program—100 Jackson St., P.O. Box 780, 12524. Tel: 845-896-6430; Fax: 845-896-6764. Mrs. Eileen Budnik, D.R.E. Students 750.

FLORIDA, ORANGE CO., ST. JOSEPH (1895), (Polish), [CEM] Rev. Joseph M. Tokarczyk.
Res.: 14 Glenmere Ave., 10921. Tel: 845-651-7792; Fax: 845-651-7793. Email: saintjoseph@optonline.net.
Catechesis/Religious Program—19 Glenmere Ave., 10921. Tel: 845-651-4240. Students 256.
Mission—St. Stanislaus 17 Pulaski Hwy., Pine Island, Orange Co. 10969. Tel: 845-258-4426.

FORESTBURGH, SULLIVAN CO., ST. THOMAS AQUINAS (1900) [CEM] Rev. Ivan L. Csete; Deacon Paul A. Rausch.
Res. & Rectory: One Forestburgh Rd., 12777. Tel: 845-791-7400; Fax: 845-794-3685.
Catechesis/Religious Program—Email: ebrasington@hvc.rr.com. Students 50.

GARDINER, ULSTER CO., ST. CHARLES BORROMEO (1883) [CEM] Rev. Robert M. Panek.
Res.: 2212 Rte. 44/55, 12525. Tel: 845-255-1374; Fax: 845-256-9050.
Catechesis/Religious Program—Tel: 845-895-2532. Students 159.

GARNERVILLE, ROCKLAND CO., ST. GREGORY BARBARIGO (1961) Revs. Thomas L. Kreiser; Kuriakose Poovathumkudy; Deacons Augustine A. Pappalardo; Roland Dowen; John Kelly.
Res.: 21 Cinder Rd., 10923. Tel: 845-947-1873; Fax: 845-947-8256.
School—29 Cinder Rd., 10923. Tel: 845-947-1330; Fax: 845-947-4392. Mrs. Cathleen Cassel, Prin. Sisters of St. Dominic (Sparkill) 2; Lay Teachers 12; Students 292.
Catechesis/Religious Program—Tel: 845-429-2775. Mr. Donald Ruzzi, C.R.E.; Mrs. Janine Friscoe, Sacramental Coord. Students 700.

GLASCO, ULSTER CO., ST. JOSEPH (1919) Rev. Msgr. Charles F. Zanotti.
Res.: 61 Glasco Tpke., P.O. Box 208, 12432. Tel: 845-246-5453; Fax: 845-247-9343.
A-Villa St. Dominic—Tel: 914-246-5610, Ext. 51. Rest House for Ladies. Dominican Sisters (Sparkill). Also Known as Corazon Center.
Catechesis/Religious Program—Tel: 845-246-4598. Students 150.

GOSHEN, ORANGE CO., ST. JOHN THE EVANGELIST (1837) [CEM] Revs. Thomas Dicks; Niranjan Rodrigo, S.S.S.; Deacons Luis Baerga; Vincent Cookingham.
Res.: 71 Murray Ave., 10924. Tel: 845-294-5328; Fax: 845-294-2577.
School—77 Murray Ave., 10924. Tel: 845-294-6434; Fax: 845-294-7303. Sr. Patricia Langton, O.P., Prin. Sisters 1; Lay Teachers 8; Students 190.
Catechesis/Religious Program—Tel: 914-294-6847. Students 782.
Chapel—Immaculate Conception Convent 73 Murray Ave., 10924.
Chapel—John S. Burke H. S. Chapel 81 Fletcher St., 10924. Tel: 845-294-5481.
Station—Orange County Home and Infirmary, Tel: 845-294-7971.
Station—Orange County Jail, Tel: 845-294-6166.
Station—Campbell Hall Nursing Facility Orange. Tel: 845-294-8154.
Arden Hill Hospital—Tel: 845-294-5441.

GREENWOOD LAKE, ORANGE CO., HOLY ROSARY (1954) Rev. Robert J. Sweeney.
Res.: 41 Windermere Ave., 10925-2105. Tel: 845-477-8378; Fax: 845-477-7238. Email: holy_rosary_gwl@yahoo.com.
Catechesis/Religious Program—Tel: 845-477-0906; Fax: 845-477-0906. Students 190.

HARRIMAN, ORANGE CO., ST. ANASTASIA (1899) [CEM] Rev. Msgr. Joseph F. Reynolds; Rev. Eder Tamara (Colombia); Deacons Eugene E. Bormann; James Faulkner.
Res.: 21 N. Main St., P.O. Box 942, 10926. Tel: 845-238-3844; Fax: 845-238-3846. Email: parish.office@saintanastasiachurch.org. Web: www.saintanastasiachurch.org.
Catechesis/Religious Program—Tel: 845-782-5099. Students 563.

HARRISON, WESTCHESTER CO., ST. GREGORY THE GREAT (1911) Rev. Msgr. Francis J. McAree.
Res.: 215 Halstead Ave., 10528. Tel: 914-835-0677; Fax: 914-835-5152. Email: stgreggreat@aol.com. Web: www.stgregorythegreat.com.
Catechesis/Religious Program—94 Broadway, 10528. Tel: 914-835-1278; Fax: 914-835-2070. Students 521.

HARTSDALE, WESTCHESTER CO.

1—CHURCH OF OUR LADY OF SHKODRA (1989), (Albanian), [CEM] Rev. Peter Popovich.
Res.: 361 W. Hartsdale Ave., 10530. Tel: 914-761-3523; Fax: 914-949-2690.

2—SACRED HEART (1926) Rev. Msgr. Patrick J. Carney; Revs. Wenceslaus Rodrigues; Philip P. Tah. In Res., Rev. Peter Bleeser.
Res.: 10 Lawton Ave., 10530. Tel: 914-949-0028; Fax: 914-289-0398.
School—(1953) 59 Wilson St., 10530. Tel: 914-946-7242; Fax: 914-946-7323. Mrs. Virginia Salamone, Prin. Sisters 1; Lay Teachers 9; Students 215.
Catechesis/Religious Program—Tel: 914-428-5043; Fax: 914-428-5043. Email: sacredheart.re@aol.com. Sr. Mary Landon, F.S.P., D.R.E. Students 151.
Convent—11 Lawton Ave., 10530. Tel: 914-946-2581.

HASTINGS-ON-HUDSON, WESTCHESTER CO.

1—ST. MATTHEW (1892) Rev. Matthew F. Fernan. In Res., Rev. James Smyth.
Res.: 616 Warburton Ave., 10706. Tel: 914-478-2822; Fax: 914-478-3681.
Catechesis/Religious Program—Students 161.

2—ST. STANISLAUS KOSTKA (1912), (Polish), Records at: St. Matthew, 616 Warburton Ave., Hastings-on-Hudson, NY 10706 (914-478-2822).
Res.: 616 Warburton Ave., 10706.
Church: 52 Main St., 10706.

HAVERSTRAW, ROCKLAND CO.

1—ST. MARY OF THE ASSUMPTION (1899), (Slovak), Rev. Msgr. Robert J. McCabe, Admin.
Res.: 46 Conklin Ave., 10927. Tel: 845-429-2245; Fax: 845-429-1350. Email: havermar46@optimum.net.
Catechesis/Religious Program—Students 65.

2—ST. PETER (1848) [CEM] [JC] Revs. Thomas F. Madden; Miguel Castillo (Mexico).
Res.: 115 Broadway, 10927. Tel: 914-429-2196; Fax: 914-947-4564. Email: pastor@saintpeterschurch.us. Web: www.saintpeterschurch.us.
School—(1863) 21 Ridge St., 10927. Tel: 914-429-5311; Fax: 845-429-5140. Mrs. Margaret Hamilton, Prin. Lay Teachers 11; Students 248.
Catechesis/Religious Program—21 Ridge St., 10927. Tel: 914-429-8824; Fax: 845-429-2721. Students 705.
Station—Green Hills Home, Tel: 914-429-8411.
Station—Northern Riverview Health Care Center, Tel: 914-429-5381.

HAWTHORNE, WESTCHESTER CO., HOLY ROSARY (1901) Rev. John Fraser. In Res., Rev. Thomas Kamau.
Res.: 170 Bradhurst, 10532. Tel: 914-769-0030; Fax: 914-769-3326.
School—(1955) 180 Bradhurst Ave., 10532. Tel: 914-769-0030, Ext. 25.
Catechesis/Religious Program—Tel: 914-769-0030, Ext. 23. Deacon Richard McLaughlin, D.R.E. Students 602.

HIGHLAND FALLS, ORANGE CO., SACRED HEART OF JESUS (1870) [CEM] Rev. Jack Arlotta.
Res.: 353 Main St., 10928. Tel: 845-446-4609; Fax: 845-446-4610. Email: frjack-a@hvc.rr.com. Web: www.sacredheart-highlandfalls.org.
School—(1930) 7 Cozzens Ave., 10928. Tel: 845-446-2674; Fax: 845-446-3713. Web: www.sacredheartofjesushf.org. Lay Teachers 15; Students 145.
Catechesis/Religious Program—Tel: 845-446-2071. Maryann Brigham, D.R.E. Students 125.
Mission—Blessed Sacrament Rte 9W, Fort Montgomery, Orange Co. 10922.

HIGHLAND MILLS, ORANGE CO., ST. PATRICK (1957) Revs. Gerard P. Travers; John Palaparambil (India); Deacon Paul Weireter.
Res.: 26 Hunter St., 10930. Tel: 845-928-6027; Fax: 845-928-2982. Web: www.stpatrickshm.org.
Catechesis/Religious Program—Tel: 845-928-6688; Fax: 845-928-3189. Louise Pisano, D.R.E. Students 925.

HIGHLAND, ULSTER CO., ST. AUGUSTINE (1899) Revs. Lawrence Paolicelli; George Kyeremeh (Ghana); Deacons John Bellacicco; Frank S. Ottaviano.
Res.: 55 Main St., 12528. Tel: 845-691-7673; Fax: 845-691-6680.
School—(1958) 35 Phillips Ave. and Elting Pl., 12528. Tel: 845-691-2338; Fax: 845-691-2338. Ms. Pat O'Connor, Prin. Lay Teachers 12; Students 166.
Catechesis/Religious Program—Students 339.

HOPEWELL JUNCTION, DUTCHESS CO.

1—ST. COLUMBA (1992) Rev. Msgr. Gerardo J. Colacicco; Revs. Thomas V. Berg, Parochial Vicar; Justin S. Cinnante, Parochial Vicar; Deacons William Alvarado; John Reilly; Warren Testa.
Res.: 835 Rte. 82, P.O. Box 428, 12533. Tel: 845-227-8380; Fax: 845-227-8390. Email: stcolumba@frontiernet.net. Web: stcolumba-hopewelljunction.e-paluch.com.
School—St. Denis-St. Columba, Tel: 845-227-7777; Fax: 845-226-8470. Email: stcoll@aol.com. Web: stcolumba-hopewelljunction.e-paluch.com/school.asp. Sr. Anne Daniel, O.P., Prin. Sisters 1; Lay Teachers 16; Students 435.
Catechesis/Religious Program—P.O. Box 368, Hopewell Jct., 12533. Tel: 845-221-4900. Web: stcolumba-hopewelljunction.e-paluch.com /religiouseducation.htm. Mrs. Jo Ann Griffin, D.R.E. Students 1,204.

2—ST. DENIS (1899) [CEM] Rev. Stephen P. Norton; Deacons Walter Dauerer; Stanley Aviles; Enrico Messina; Robert Pelech.
Res. & Office: 598 Beekman Rd., P.O. Box 10, 12533. Tel: 845-227-8382; Fax: 845-227-3951. Email: stdenischurch@optonline.net. Web: www.stdenischurch.org.
The Ark and The Dove Preschool:—604 Beekman Rd., P.O. Box 1139, 12533. Tel: 845-227-5232; Fax: 845-227-0435. Email: noah1@stdenischurch.org.
School—St. Denis-St. Columba, See St. Columba for details., Tel: 845-227-7777; Fax: 845-226-8470. Email: stcol1@aol.com. Web: www.stcolumba.net. Students 435.
Catechesis/Religious Program—604 Beekman Rd., P.O. Box 1139, 12533. Tel: 845-227-3949; Fax: 845-227-0435. Email: stdenisre@stdenischurch.org. Students 597.

HYDE PARK, DUTCHESS CO., REGINA COELI (1863) Revs. Michael L. Palazzo; Raphael Amoako Tawiah; Deacons Frank J. Gohl; Gerard Lindley; Mark O'Sullivan; Peter Dalmer. In Res., Rev. John M. Lagiovane.
Res.: 2 Harvey St., 12538. Tel: 845-229-2134; Fax: 845-229-1668. Email: reginacoeli@verizon.net. Web: www.reginacoeli-hydepark-ny.org.
School—(1955) Albany Post Rd., 12538. Tel: 845-229-8589; Fax: 845-229-1388. Email: coeli@verizon.net. Lay Teachers 17; Students 152.
Catechesis/Religious Program—Tel: 845-229-9139; Fax: 845-229-1668. Students 150.
Mission—St. Paul (1851) Mulford Ave., Staatsburg, Dutchess Co. 12580.

IRVINGTON-ON-THE-HUDSON, WESTCHESTER CO., IMMACULATE CONCEPTION (1873) Rev. Msgr. Raymond J. Byrne; Rev. Ted Onumaegbu.
Res.: 16 N. Broadway, 10533. Tel: 914-591-7480; Fax: 914-591-7806. Email: immacon@optonline.net. Web: www.iccirvington.net.
Catechesis/Religious Program—Tel: 914-591-7740. Email: ccdicc@optonline.net. Students 250.

JEFFERSONVILLE, SULLIVAN CO.

1—ST. GEORGE (1963) [CEM] Merged with St. Francis of Assisi to form St. George-St. Francis, Jeffersonville.
Res.: 12748. Tel: 845-482-4640; Fax: 845-482-3276.
Catechesis/Religious Program—Students 110.

2—ST. GEORGE-ST. FRANCIS, [CEM] Rev. Ignatius Vu.
Res.: 97 Schoolhouse Hill Rd., P.O. Box 672, 12748. Tel: 845-482-4640; Fax: 845-482-3276. Email: stgeorge123@pronetisp.net.
Catechesis/Religious Program—Students 92.
Mission—St. Francis of Assisi 4020 State Rte. 52, Youngsville, Sullivan Co. 12791.

KATONAH, WESTCHESTER CO., ST. MARY OF THE ASSUMPTION (1908) Revs. Edmund P. Connors; Paul M. Waddell; Stephen Brenyah (Ghana); Deacon George Chiu.
Res.: 117 Valley Rd., 10536. Tel: 914-232-3356; Fax: 914-232-5736. Email: stmarysparish@yahoo.com. Web: www.catholic-church.org/stmary.
Catechesis/Religious Program—99 Valley Rd., 10536. Tel: 914-232-4648. Mrs. Susan Gmuer, C.R.E. Students 658.
Mission—St. Matthias (1909) 107 Babbitt Rd., Bedford Hills, Westchester Co. 10507.
Mission—The White Church 111 Spring St., South Salem, Westchester Co. 10590.

KINGSTON, ULSTER CO.

1—HOLY NAME OF JESUS (1884) Closed.

2—IMMACULATE CONCEPTION (1896), (Polish), [CEM] Rev. John W. Borzuchowski.
Res.: 467 Delaware Ave., 12401. Tel: 845-331-0846; Fax: 845-331-7647. Email: kbh62@prodigy.net.
Catechesis/Religious Program—Tel: 845-331-7352. Students 45.

3—ST. JOSEPH (1868) Revs. Frank J. Damis; Uldarico De la Pena (Philippines) (MO); George Devamapalle (India); Deacons Richard Frohmiller; Robert Winrow; John Peters; Joseph Doherty.
Res.: 242 Wall St., 12401. Tel: 845-338-1554; Fax: 845-340-1961. Email: sjcr240@earthlink.net.
School—(1869) Wall & Pearl Sts., 12401. Tel: 845-339-4390; Fax: 845-339-7001. Lay Teachers 14; Students 225.
Catechesis/Religious Program—Tel: 845-339-4391; Fax: 845-339-4391. Students 339.

Mission—Msgr. O'Reilly Chapel Zandhoeck Rd., Hurley, 12443.

4—ST. MARY (1842) [CEM] Rev. Edmund M. Burke. In Res., Rev. John Audu (Nigeria), Chap., Kingston Hospital & Parochial Vicar.
Res.: 160 Broadway, 12401. Tel: 845-331-0301; Fax: 845-339-6165.
School—Kingston Catholic School (1867) 159 Broadway, 12401. Tel: 845-331-9318; Fax: 845-331-2674. Jill Albert, Prin. Lay Teachers 12; Students 220.
Catechesis/Religious Program—Students 161.

5—ST. PETER (1858), (German), [CEM] Rev. Edmund M. Burke, Admin. In Res., Rev. Marc K. Oliver.
Res.: 93 Wurts St., 12401-6328. Tel: 914-331-0436; Fax: 914-331-7149.
Catechesis/Religious Program—(Spanish) Students 58.

LAGRANGEVILLE, DUTCHESS CO., BLESSED KATERI TEKAKWITHA (2002) Rev. Msgr. Desmond O'Connor; Rev. Ronald Perez; Deacons John Barone; Andrew Daubman; Robert Horton; Theodore Van De Ven.
Res.: 1925 Rte. 82, 12540. Tel: 845-227-1710; Fax: 845-227-1734. Email: blessedkateri@optonline.net. Web: www.blessedkateriparish.com.
Catechesis/Religious Program—Tel: 845-223-3767; Fax: 845-226-6150. Email: bktfaithform@optonline.net. Students 956.

LAKE KATRINE, ULSTER CO., ST. CATHERINE LABOURE (1957) Rev. John T. Kearney; Rev. Msgr. Eugene A. Fowler, Pastor Emeritus (Retired); Deacon John M. Sullivan, (Retired).
Res.: 200 Tuytenbridge Rd., P.O. Box 271, 12449. Tel: 914-382-1133; Fax: 914-382-1051.
Catechesis/Religious Program—Students 113.

LARCHMONT, WESTCHESTER CO.

1—ST. AUGUSTINE (1892) Rev. Msgrs. Thomas R. Kelly; Walter F. Kenny, Pastor Emeritus (Retired); Rev. Joseph Karimatton (India).
Res.: 18 Cherry Ave., 10538. Tel: 914-834-1220; Fax: 914-833-2130. Email: staugustineny@verizon.net. Web: www.staugustineny.org.
Catechesis/Religious Program—Tel: 914-834-9523. Sr. Suzanne Duzen, SS.C.M., D.R.E. Students 470.

2—SS. JOHN AND PAUL (1949) Revs. Thomas F. Petrillo; Salvatore DeStefano; Mariasoosai Benjamin (India); Deacon James Brown.
Res.: 280 Weaver St., 10538. Tel: 914-834-5458; Fax: 914-833-5081.
School—(1952)Tel: 914-834-6332; Fax: 914-834-6332. Colleen R. Pettus, Prin. Lay Teachers 12; Students 273.
Catechesis/Religious Program—Tel: 914-834-4597; Fax: 914-834-7493. Students 823.

LIBERTY, SULLIVAN CO., ST. PETER (1894) [CEM] Rev. Msgr. Edward F. Straub; Deacon John Riley.
Res.: 264 N. Main St., 12754. Tel: 914-292-4525; Fax: 914-292-1627.
Catechesis/Religious Program—Students 151.

LIVINGSTON MANOR, SULLIVAN CO., ST. ALOYSIUS (1899) [CEM] Rev. Msgr. William J. Collins; Rev. Alfred M. Croke, Pastor Emeritus (Retired).
Res.: Church St., Box 206, 12758. Tel: 914-439-5625; Fax: 914-439-5188.
Mission—Sacred Heart (1906) P.O. Box 206, De Bruce, Sullivan Co. 12758.
Mission—Gate of Heaven (1901) Highland Ave., Roscoe, Sullivan Co. 12776.
Catechesis/Religious Program—Students 41.

MAHOPAC, PUTNAM CO., ST. JOHN THE EVANGELIST (1889) Revs. Brian C. Brennan; Miroslaw Pawlaczyk (Poland); Deacons John Armo; Bernard Moran; John Scarfi.
Res.: 221 E. Lake Blvd., 10541. Tel: 845-628-2006; Fax: 845-628-5970. Email: info@stemahopac.org.
School—(1955) 239 E. Lake Blvd., 10541. Tel: 845-628-6464; Fax: 845-628-6469. Religious of the Divine Compassion 1; Lay Teachers 16; Students 131.
Catechesis/Religious Program—Students 1,641.
Chapel—Convent of Religious of the Divine Compassion, Tel: 914-628-6497.

MAMARONECK, WESTCHESTER CO.

1—MOST HOLY TRINITY (1874) Revs. Joseph F. Irwin; Joseph Kahumburu (Kenya); Mathew Pazhoor (India); Deacon Augustine DiFiore.
Res.: 320 E. Boston Post Rd., 10543. Tel: 914-698-5944; Fax: 914-698-5274. Email: courtneymht@yahoo.com.
Catechesis/Religious Program—Tel: 914-698-1868. Email: mhtdb@aol.com. Students 196.

2—ST. VITO (1911), (Italian), Revs. James F. Healy; Edward O'Neil.
Res.: 816 Underhill Ave., 10543. Tel: 914-698-2648; Fax: 914-698-6081. Email: stvitochurch@optonline.net.
Catechesis/Religious Program—826 Underhill Ave., Mamaronek, 10543. Tel: 914-698-2949. Students 301.

MARLBORO, ULSTER CO., ST. MARY (1900) [CEM] Rev. Edward Bader; Deacons Thomas Cornell; Vincent Porcelli; John T. Repke.
Res.: 71 Grand St., P.O. Box 730, 12542. Tel: 845-236-4340; Fax: 845-236-3183.
Catechesis/Religious Program—Tel: 845-236-7791. Mrs. Paula Marton, C.R.E. Students 470.
Mission—Our Lady of Mercy 977 River Rd., Newburgh/Roseton, Orange Co. 12550.

MAYBROOK, ORANGE CO., CHURCH OF THE ASSUMPTION (1907) Revs. Daniel M. O'Hare, Admin.; William F. Woodruff, Co-Admin. & Parochial Vicar; Benjamin Zirra; Deacon Edward M. Grosso.
Res.: 211 Homestead Ave., P.O. Box 320, 12543. Tel: 845-427-2046.
Catechesis/Religious Program—Tel: 845-427-5318. Students 134.

MIDDLETOWN, ORANGE CO.

1—HOLY CROSS (1999) Rev. Robert Porpora; Deacon Robert Buckner. In Res., Rev. Vincent I. Odikanoro.
Res.: 626 County Rte. 22, 10940. Tel: 845-355-4439; Fax: 845-355-4709.
Catechesis/Religious Program—Tel: 845-355-6255. Students 613.
Mission—Our Lady of the Scapular 125 Main St., Unionville, Orange Co. 10988. Tel: 845-726-3222.

2—ST. JOSEPH (1865) [CEM] Rev. Dennis Nikolic; Rev. Msgr. John J. Budwick, Parochial Vicar; Deacons Richard Trapani; Albert Loeffler. In Res., Rev. Msgr. George J. Valastro (Retired).
Res.: 149 Cottage St., 10940. Tel: 914-343-6013; Fax: 914-344-4735.
School—(1889) 113 Cottage St., 10940. Tel: 914-343-3139; Fax: 914-346-4647. Jennifer Langford, Prin. Lay Teachers 11; Students 170.
Catechesis/Religious Program—111 Cottage St., 10940. Tel: 845-343-4415. Mary Ellen Schwartz, C.R.E. Students 429.

3—OUR LADY OF MT. CARMEL (1912) Revs. Francis F. Dixon, O.Carm.; Raymond Bagdonis, O.Carm.; Patrick McGuigan, O.Carm.; Stephen Huytran, O.Carm.; Deacons Edward Woods, Pastoral Assoc.; John Frohbose, Pastoral Assoc. In Res., Revs. Alfred Isacsson, O.Carm.; Robert Greco, O.Carm.; John Logan, O.Carm.
Res.: 90 Euclid Ave., 10940. Tel: 845-343-4121; Fax: 845-343-4433.
School—205 Wawayanda Ave., 10940. Tel: 845-343-8836; Fax: 845-342-1404. Lay Teachers 16; Students 221.
Catechesis/Religious Program—Tel: 845-342-1510. Students 801.
Mission—Our Lady of the Assumption P.O. Box 527, Bloomingburg, Sullivan Co. 12721-0527. Tel: 845-733-1477; Fax: 845-733-6691.
Mission—St. Paul Rte. 17K, Bullville, Orange Co. 10915. Tel: 845-361-3107; Fax: 845-361-4201.

MILLBROOK, DUTCHESS CO., ST. JOSEPH (1890) [CEM] Rev. Msgr. James T. O'Connor; Revs. John Kyeremeh (Ghana); Anthony Kemetse (Ghana).
Res.: 15 North Ave., P.O. Box 439, 12545. Tel: 845-677-3422; Fax: 845-677-3423. Email: stjosephmil@aol.com.
School—(1957)Tel: 845-677-3670. Lay Teachers 10; Students 163.
Catechesis/Religious Program—Tel: 845-677-3273. Students 270.
Mission—(1883) Clinton Corners, Dutchess Co. 12514.
Chapel—Millbrook, Cardinal Hayes Home for Children
Station—Green Briar Home, Tel: 845-677-9997.

MILTON, ULSTER CO., ST. JAMES (1874) Rev. Fred Kempfirl.
Res.: 12 Main St., 12547. Tel: 914-795-2255; Fax: 914-795-1008.
Catechesis/Religious Program—Teresa Green, C.R.E. Students 83.

MONROE, ORANGE CO., SACRED HEART CHURCH (1957) Rev. Thomas J. Byrnes; Rev. Msgr. Bayani Valenzuela; Revs. George Pulparayil (India); Jeffrey E. Maurer; Christopher Argano; Deacons Peter Brockmann; Richard McCarthy, (Retired); Angelo Corsaro; Robert Duncan.
Res.: 26 Still Rd., 10950. Tel: 845-782-8510; Fax: 845-782-3593. Email: info@sacredheartchurch.org. Web: www.sacredheartchurch.org.
School—(1964)Tel: 845-783-0365; Fax: 845-782-0354. Catherine Muenkel, Prin. Sisters 1; Lay Teachers 11; Students 216.
Catechesis/Religious Program—Tel: 845-782-7420; Fax: 845-782-5192. Sr. Rose O'Rourke, D.R.E. Students 1,239.
Convent—Still Rd., 10950.
Mission—Sacred Heart Chapel Millpond Pkwy./Stage Rd., 10950.

MONTGOMERY, ORANGE CO., HOLY NAME OF MARY (1868) [CEM] Revs. Daniel O'Hare; Robert Geissler, Pastor Emeritus (Retired); Joseph D. Sullivan, Pastor Emeritus (Retired); Deacon Thomas Jordan.
Res.: 89 Union St., 12549. Tel: 845-457-5276.
Catechesis/Religious Program—Tel: 845-457-1738. Email: hnm469@frontiernet.net. Linda Hummel, D.R.E. Students 32.

MONTICELLO, SULLIVAN CO., ST. PETER (1874) [CEM] Revs. John Tran; Gonzalo Arias (Colombia). In Res., Rev. Stanislaus Ogbonna, C.S.Sp. (Nigeria).
Res.: 10 Liberty St., 12701. Tel: 845-794-5577; Fax: 845-791-1210.
Catechesis/Religious Program—Tel: 845-791-7172. Students 252.
Mission—St. Joseph Mongaup Valley, Sullivan Co.
Mission—St. Anne White Lake, Sullivan Co.

MT. KISCO, WESTCHESTER CO., ST. FRANCIS OF ASSISI (1868) [CEM] Rev. Steven E. Clark. In Res., Rev. Francis Anane.
Res.: 2 Green St., 10549. Tel: 914-666-5986; Fax: 914-666-3859. Email: sanfrankisco@earthlink.net. Web: www.sfamountkisco.org.
Catechesis/Religious Program—12 Green St., Mount Kisco, 10549. Tel: 914-666-3161; Fax: 914-666-5474. Students 315.

MT. VERNON, WESTCHESTER CO.

1—ST. MARY (1894) Rev. Msgr. John T. Meehan; Rev. Michael McDonnell, O.F.M.
Res.: 23 S. High St., 10550. Tel: 914-664-5855; Fax: 914-663-6097. Email: stmarymv@aol.com. Web: www.stmarys-church.com.
Catechesis/Religious Program—Students 182.

2—OUR LADY OF MOUNT CARMEL (1897), (Italian), Rev. Lawrence J. Quinn.
Res.: 10550. Tel: 914-668-3540; Fax: 914-668-4393.
Catechesis/Religious Program—Victoria Liconia, D.R.E. Students 170.

3—OUR LADY OF VICTORY (1871), Comunidade Catolica de Brasileiros (Missionaries of St. Charles-Scalabrinians) Rev. Luis Antonio Diaz Lamus, C.S.
Res.: 28 W. Sidney Ave., 10550. Tel: 914-668-5861; Fax: 914-668-0161. Email: w475@archny.org. Web: www.churcholv.org.
School—(1898) 38 N. Fifth Ave., 10550. Tel: 914-667-4063; Fax: 914-665-3135. Helena Castilla, Prin. Lay Teachers 14; Students 192.
Catechesis/Religious Program—Students 55.

4—SS. PETER AND PAUL (1929) Revs. John P. McDonagh; Jaison Mundanmany, C.M.I. In Res., Rev. Msgr. Thomas F. Scanlon (Retired).
Res.: 129 Birch St., 10552. Tel: 914-668-9815; Fax: 914-668-6052. Email: sppcmvny@gmail.com.
School—125 Birch St., Mount Vernon, 10552. Tel: 914-664-1321; Fax: 914-664-2951. Email: w478@adnyschools.org. Lay Teachers 13; Students 175.
Catechesis/Religious Program—Tel: 914-668-9880. Students 80.

5—SACRED HEART (1872) Rev. Msgr. Howard W. Calkins; Rev. Benjamin Uzbuegbuman (Nigeria).
Res.: 115 S. Fifth Ave., 10550. Tel: 914-668-7440; Fax: 914-668-1177. Email: sacredheart115@verizon.net.
School—(1895) Second St. & S. Fifth Ave., 10550. Tel: 914-667-1734; Fax: 914-667-1497. Lay Teachers 9; Students 320.
Catechesis/Religious Program—Mrs. Alison Nicholas, D.R.E. Students 320.
Chapel—Sacred Heart Convent 67 S. Fifth Ave., 10550.

6—ST. URSULA (1908) Rev. John T. McLoughlin; Deacons Thomas J. Abbamont; Carl Degenhardt.
Res.: 214 E. Lincoln Ave., 10552. Tel: 914-668-0085; Fax: 914-668-4228.
Catechesis/Religious Program—Tel: 914-699-7964. Ms. Mona Parkinson, C.R.E. Students 60.

NANUET, ROCKLAND CO., ST. ANTHONY (1897) [CEM] Revs. Joseph J. Deponai; Frank W. Bassett Jr.; Ferdinando Caindec; Deacon John R. Maloney. In Res., Rev. Joseph A. DeSanto (Retired).
Res.: 36 W. Nyack Rd., 10954. Tel: 845-623-2138; Fax: 845-623-5556. Email: stanthonys.church@verizon.net.
School—(1953) 32-34 West Nyack Rd., 10954. Tel: 845-623-2311; Fax: 845-623-2406. Email: stanthonysoffice@verizon.net. Joanne Fratello, Prin. Sisters 3; Lay Teachers 8; Students 221.
Catechesis/Religious Program—Tel: 845-624-2230. Email: st.anthony.prep@gmail.com. Ms. Anne Malloy, D.R.E. Students 825.
Mission—St. Anthony Shrine Church 38 W. Nyack Rd., Rockland Co. 10954.

NARROWSBURG, SULLIVAN CO., ST. FRANCIS XAVIER (1862) [CEM 2], (Franciscan) Rev. William Scully, O.F.M.
Res.: 151 Bridge St., 12764. Tel: 845-252-6681; Fax: 845-252-6519. Web: www.stfrancisxavier.net.
Catechesis/Religious Program—Students 24.
Mission—Our Lady of the Lake Rte. 52, Lake Huntington, Sullivan Co. 12752. Tel: 845-252-6681.

NEW CITY, ROCKLAND CO., ST. AUGUSTINE (1957) Revs. William B. Cosgrove; Michael Cedro; Varghese I. Chethipuzha; Deacons Michael G. McCabe; Lawrence O'Toole.
Res.: 140 Maple Ave., 10956. Tel: 845-634-3641;

Fax: 845-639-6118. Email: staug@optonline.net. Web: www.staugnewcity.org.
School—Tel: 845-634-7060; Fax: 845-634-8725. Web: www.saintaugustineparishschool.com. Katharine Murphy, Prin. Lay Teachers 10; Students 204.
Catechesis/Religious Program—Tel: 845-634-8462. Email: staugustinereo@yahoo.com. Students 750.

NEW PALTZ, ULSTER CO., ST. JOSEPH (1894), (Capuchin Franciscans) Revs. Bernard M. Maloney, O.F.M.Cap.; Barnabas Keck, O.F.M.Cap., Parochial Vicar; Raphael Iannone, O.F.M.Cap.
Res.: 34 S. Chestnut St., 12561. Tel: 845-255-5635; Fax: 845-255-5679. Email: stjoenp@csdsl.net. Web: www.stjosephnewpaltz.org.
Catechesis/Religious Program—Tel: 845-255-0237; Fax: 845-256-0687. Sr. Philomena Fleck, O.S.B., D.R.E. Students 500.

NEW ROCHELLE, WESTCHESTER CO.

1—BLESSED SACRAMENT (1848) [CEM] Rev. Msgr. William J. Bradley; Rev. Charles Imokhai (Nigeria); Deacons Charles Rizzo; Frank Orlando.
Res.: 15 Shea Pl., 10801. Tel: 914-632-3700; Fax: 914-632-0732.
High School—24 Shea Pl., 10801. Tel: 914-632-2595; Fax: 914-632-3321. Edward Sullivan, Prin. (Coed) Lay Teachers 25; Students 352.
Catechesis/Religious Program—Tel: 914-235-7311. Ms. Gina Rocas-Gardon, D.R.E. Students 312.

2—ST. GABRIEL (1893) Rev. Msgr. Patrick V. McNamara.
Res.: 120 Division St., 10801. Tel: 914-632-0211; Fax: 914-637-8991.
Catechesis/Religious Program—Mrs. Maria Elena Marquez, D.R.E. Students 220.

3—HOLY FAMILY (1913) Rev. Msgrs. Ferdinando D. Berardi; John Mescall, Pastor Emeritus (Retired); Revs. Joseph Okech Aolhunga (Kenya); George K. Nedumaruthumchalil (India); Deacons Donald Gray; Raymond Hall; Sr. Connie Koch, O.P., Pastoral Asst. for Faith Formation.
Res.: 83 Clove Rd., 10801. Tel: 914-632-0673; Fax: 914-576-8556.
Church: Mayflower Ave. & Mt. Joy Pl., 10801.
Catechesis/Religious Program—Tel: 914-636-6758. Students 350.
Chapel—Ursuline Sisters 1352 N. Ave., 10804. Tel: 914-636-3456; Fax: 914-576-2620.
Chapel—Iona Grammar and Preparatory Schools 173 Stratton Rd., 10804. Tel: 914-633-7744; 914-632-2727; Fax: 914-235-6338.
Chapel—Iona College 715 N. Ave., 10801. Tel: 914-633-2000; Fax: 800-633-2329.
Chapel—New Rochelle, St. Patrick Prov. 30 Montgomery Circle, 10801. Tel: 914-633-6851; Fax: 914-633-5579.
Chapel—New Rochelle, St. Joseph Chapel, Tel: 914-632-6592; Fax: 914-533-4264.
Chapel—Edmond Rice Hall 33 Pryer Ter., 10804. Tel: 914-636-6194; Fax: 914-636-0021.
Chapel—Opus Dei 99 Overlook Cir., 10804. Tel: 914-235-1201; Fax: 914-235-7805.
Chapel—Holy Cross Brothers Provincialate 85 Overlook Cir., 10804. Tel: 914-632-4468; Fax: 914-632-2490.

4—HOLY NAME OF JESUS (1929) Revs. Martin J. Biglin; Francis Maurice, O.F.M.Cap. (Pakistan); Deacons Carmine DeMarco; Robert Gontcharuk.
Res.: 75 Lispenard Ave., 10801. Tel: 914-636-4856; Fax: 914-636-8474.
Church: Petersville Rd. and Halligan St., 10801.
School—(1954) 70 Petersville Rd., 10801. Tel: 914-576-6672; Fax: 914-576-6676. Mr. Albert D'Angelo, Prin. Lay Teachers 10; Students 195.
Catechesis/Religious Program—Tel: 914-576-6038. Students 145.
Chapel—Sisters of Charity Convent 78 Petersville Rd., 10801. Tel: 914-636-4354.

5—ST. JOSEPH (1901), (Italian), Revs. Philip J. Caruso; Cosimo R. Fazio, Pastor Emeritus (Retired); Rev. Msgr. John A. Ruvo.
Res.: 280 Washington Ave., 10801. Tel: 914-632-0675; Fax: 914-633-4264.
Catechesis/Religious Program—St. Joseph School of Religion, 53 Sixth St., 10801. Tel: 914-632-3458. Email: stjoenr@aol.com. Antoinette Rossetti, D.R.E. Students 230.

NEW WINDSOR, ORANGE CO., ST. JOSEPH (1962) Rev. Robert G. Hilfiker; Deacons Joseph Lieby; Anthony Ferraiuolo.
Res.: 4 St. Joseph Pl., 12553. Tel: 845-561-8467; Fax: 845-562-3269. Email: stjoseph@choiceonemail.com.
School—148 Windsor Hwy., 12553. Tel: 845-565-5110; Fax: 845-565-6321. Sisters 1; Lay Teachers 9; Students 167.
Catechesis/Religious Program—Tel: 845-561-8475. Students 230.

NEWBURGH, ORANGE CO.

1—ST. FRANCIS OF ASSISI (1909), (Polish), [CEM] Rev. John J. Vondras.
Res.: 145 Benkard Ave., 12550. Tel: 845-561-1317; Fax: 845-561-1337.
School—Now Sacred Heart School, Merged in Sept. 1992., 24 S. Robinson Ave., 12550. Tel: 845-561-1433.
Catechesis/Religious Program—Tel: 845-561-6697. Students 435.

2—ST. MARY (1875) Rev. William A. Scafidi, M.Ss.A.; Deacons John L. Seymour; Rocco Damiano; William Castellane.
Res.: 180 South St., 12550. Tel: 845-562-0862; Fax: 845-562-0876. Web: www.stmary.org.
Catechesis/Religious Program—Maria Castellane, D.R.E. Students 186.

3—ST. PATRICK (1836) [CEM 2] Revs. Fernando A. Hernandez; Louis Van Thanh; Tomas Bobadilla (Mexico), Hispanic Apostolate; Sr. Helen Raynor, Spanish Apostolate; Deacons Fred Steup; Donald Halter; William Glover; Dennis White.
Res.: 55 Grand St., 12550. Tel: 914-561-0885; Fax: 914-561-8629.
Catechesis/Religious Program—Tel: 914-561-6470. Sr. Martha Hernandez, D.R.E., Hispanic Prog.; Ms. Mary Jane Newman, D.R.E. Students 660.
Mission—Our Lady of the Lake Lakeside & Rte. 52, Orange Lake, Orange Co. 12550. Tel: 914-561-9537.

4—SACRED HEART (1912), (Italian), Revs. William A. Scafidi, M.Ss.A.; Mark Connell, Parochial Vicar; Deacons Dominick Casadone; Peter Haight; Lawrence Kawula.
Res.: 301 Ann St., 12550. Tel: 914-561-2264; Fax: 914-562-7144. Email: sacredheart.newburgh@verizon.net. Web: www.sacredheart-newburgh.e-paluch.com.
School—(1951) 24 S. Robinson Ave., 12550. Tel: 914-561-1433; Fax: 914-561-4383. Religious 2; Lay Teachers 9; Students 136.
Catechesis/Religious Program—24 S. Robinson Ave., 12550. Tel: 914-561-2589. Students 437.

NYACK, ROCKLAND CO., ST. ANN (1869) Rev. Rees W. Doughty; Rev. Msgr. Seth Agyemano (Ghana); Revs. Emil Bettley; Alexander Agyepong (Ghana); Deacons Thomas Luke Conroy; Charles DeGroat.
Res.: 16 Jefferson St., 10960. Tel: 845-358-4707; Fax: 845-358-3246. Email: st_ann@msn.com. Web: www.stann-nyack.org.
Catechesis/Religious Program—Tel: 845-358-3758. Email: julielepore@verizon.net. Ms. Julie LePore, D.R.E. Students 208.
Parish Center—150 Third Ave., 10960.

OBERNBURG, SULLIVAN CO., ST. MARY (1854) [CEM], (Franciscan) Rev. Joseph Juracek, O.F.M.; Deacon Lawrence Knack.
Res.: 388 Obernburg Rd., 12767. Tel: 914-482-5541; Fax: 914-482-9340. Email: saintmarys@bcc.net. Web: http://members.bccnet/saintmarys.
Catechesis/Religious Program—Students 25.

OSSINING, WESTCHESTER CO.

1—ST. ANN (1927) Revs. Edward G. Byrne; Nito Bundac; Franklin Pantoja; Deacon Jose DeJesus.
Res.: 25 Eastern Ave., 10562. Tel: 914-941-2556; Fax: 914-923-9239. Email: saccc25ea@aol.com.
School—16 Elizabeth St., 10562. Tel: 914-941-0312; Fax: 914-941-3514. Jayson Bock, Prin. Lay Teachers 10; Students 131.
Catechesis/Religious Program—Tel: 914-941-2420. Students 567.
Convent—

2—ST. AUGUSTINE (1853) [CEM] Rev. Msgr. Hilary Franco; Rev. Slawomir Ciszkowski (Poland); Deacons Timothy Slominski; Steven DeMartino.
Res.: Eagle Park Rte. 9, 10562. Tel: 914-941-0067; Fax: 914-944-0828.
School—(1893)Tel: 914-941-3849; Fax: 914-941-4342. Sr. Mary Elizabeth Donoghue, Prin. Priests 2; Dominican Sisters of Our Lady of the Springs, Bridgeport, CT 2; Lay Teachers 25; Students 474.
Catechesis/Religious Program—Students 305.

OTISVILLE, ORANGE CO., HOLY NAME (1969) [CEM] Rev. Msgr. Peter Tran Van Phat.
Res.: 45 Highland Ave., P.O. Box 597, 10963. Tel: 845-386-1320; Fax: 845-386-6105. Email: hnojotisville@frontiernet.net.
Catechesis/Religious Program—Tel: 845-386-2327. Mrs. Jennifer Logedo, Coord. Students 282.

PATTERSON, PUTNAM CO., SACRED HEART (1957) Revs. Thomas Lutz; Ponnachan Georgekutty.
Res.: 414 Haviland Dr., 12563. Tel: 845-279-4832; Fax: 845-278-0432.
Catechesis/Religious Program—Mrs. Margaret Cairney, C.R.E. Students 360.

PAWLING, DUTCHESS CO., ST. JOHN THE EVANGELIST (1848) [CEM] Revs. John J. Duff; Vincent Paul Dassanayake (Sri Lanka); Vincent Paul Dassanayake (Sri Lanka).
Res.: 39 E. Main St., 12564. Tel: 845-855-5488; Fax: 845-855-1273.
Catechesis/Religious Program—Tel: 845-855-9408. Students 467.

PEARL RIVER, ROCKLAND CO.

1—ST. AEDAN (1966) Rev. Msgr. Joseph P. Penna; Rev. Hrudayaraju Sunkara; Deacon James F. Maher.
Res.: 23 Reld Dr., 10965. Tel: 845-735-7405; Fax: 845-735-4125. Email: staedan@optonline.net.
Catechesis/Religious Program—Tel: 845-735-2036. Email: staedan3@optonline.net. Students 643.

2—ST. MARGARET OF ANTIOCH (1895) Rev. Msgr. John J. O'Keefe. In Res., Revs. Joy Mankulam Devassy (India); Joseph Kuzhichalil (India); Paul Osei-Fosu (Ghana).
Res.: 33 N. Magnolia St., 10965. Tel: 845-735-4746; Fax: 845-735-4744.
School—(1953) 34 N. Magnolia St., 10965. Tel: 845-735-2855; Fax: 845-735-0131. Email: rk499@adnyschools.org. Mrs. Carolyn Slattery, Prin. Lay Teachers 14; Students 248.
Catechesis/Religious Program—Tel: 845-735-5489. Email: smprep@hotmail.com. Mrs. Brenda Lattuca, D.R.E. Students 846.

PEEKSKILL, WESTCHESTER CO., ASSUMPTION (1859) [CEM] Rev. John J. Higgins; Rev. Msgr. Francis J. Ansbro, Pastor Emeritus (Retired); Revs. Vernon P. Wickrematunge (Sri Lanka), Parochial Vicar; Louis Anderson, Parochial Vicar; Deacon James F. Roberts.
Res.: 131 Union Ave., 10566. Tel: 914-737-2071; Fax: 914-737-1633. Email: info@assumptionpeekskill.org. Web: www.assumptionpeekskill.org.
School—(1907) 920 Msgr. Ansbro Way, 10566. Tel: 914-737-0680; Fax: 914-737-1322. Email: school@assumptionpeekskill.org. Lay Teachers 16; Students 201.
Catechesis/Religious Program—Tel: 914-737-2231; Fax: 914-737-2353. Email: ccd@assumptionpeekskill.org. Students 352.
Chapel—Mount St. Francis, Tel: 914-737-3373; Fax: 914-736-9614.

PELHAM MANOR, WESTCHESTER CO., OUR LADY OF PERPETUAL HELP (1954) Revs. Robert J. DeJulio; Oliver Offor; Abraham Vettiyolil; Deacons Joseph McQuade; Daniel Murphy.
Res.: 559 Pelham Manor Rd., 10803. Tel: 914-738-1449; Fax: 914-738-9454. Email: olph@msn.com.
School—(1957) 575 Fowler Ave., 10803. Tel: 914-738-5158. Mrs. Susan Cotronei, Prin. Lay Teachers 12; Students 215.
Catechesis/Religious Program—Tel: 914-738-0670. Students 611.

PELHAM, WESTCHESTER CO., ST. CATHARINE (1896) Rev. Peter F. Bannan.
Res.: 25 Second Ave., 10803. Tel: 914-738-1491; Fax: 914-738-0398.
Catechesis/Religious Program—Tel: 914-738-1332. Students 325.

PHOENICIA, ULSTER CO., ST. FRANCIS DE SALES (1902) [CEM] Revs. George W. Hommel, Admin.; Matthew Azhakath, Parochial Vicar.
Res.: 109 Main St., P.O. Box 25, 12464. Tel: 845-688-5617; Fax: 845-688-5630.
Catechesis/Religious Program—Students 7.

PIERMONT, ROCKLAND CO., ST. JOHN THE BAPTIST (1852) Rev. Msgr. John T. Mulligan.
Res.: 895 Piermont Ave., 10968. Tel: 845-359-0078; Fax: 845-359-2976. Email: stjohnrectory2@optonline.net. Web: www.stjohnspiermont.org.
Catechesis/Religious Program—Students 194.

PINE BUSH, ORANGE CO., THE INFANT SAVIOUR (1951) Rev. Kevin M. Gallagher; Deacon Joseph N. Guglielmo.
Res.: 22 Holland Ave., 12566. Tel: 845-744-2391; Fax: 845-744-5938.
Catechesis/Religious Program—Tel: 845-744-9944. Students 420.
Mission—Our Lady of the Valley Walker Valley, Ulster Co. 12588.

PINE ISLAND, ORANGE CO., ST. STANISLAUS (1912), (Polish), [CEM], Mission of St. Joseph. Records at St. Joseph, 14 Glenmare Ave., Florida, NY 10921. Rev. Joseph M. Tokarczyk, Admin.
Res.: 17 Pulaski Hwy., P.O. Box 248, 10969. Tel: 845-651-7792.

PINE PLAINS, DUTCHESS CO., ST. ANTHONY (1958) Revs. William A. White; John A. Bida, Parochial Vicar.
Church: 68 Poplar Ave., 12567-5531. Tel: 518-398-7115; Fax: 518-398-9146. Email: stanthonys58@fairpoint.net.
Catechesis/Religious Program—Students 24.

PLATTEKILL, ULSTER CO., OUR LADY OF FATIMA (1960), (Theatine) Rev. John Jaume, C.R.
Res.: 1250 State Rt. 32, P.O. Box 700, 12568. Tel: 845-564-4972; Fax: 845-566-1954. Email: parishoffatima@aol.com.
Catechesis/Religious Program—Students 160.

PLEASANT VALLEY, DUTCHESS CO., ST. STANISLAUS KOSTKA (1903) Revs. Brian E. McWeeney; Francis Perry Yawo Azah (Ghana); Deacon John Dunn.
Res.: 1590 Main St., P.O. Box 558, 12569. Tel: 845-635-1700; Fax: 845-635-8675. Email: emmettre@optonline.net. Web: www.saintstanislaus.net.
Catechesis/Religious Program—Students 352.

PLEASANTVILLE, WESTCHESTER CO., HOLY INNOCENTS (1894) [CEM], (Dominican) Revs. Donald P. Thibault, O.P.; Daniel Davies, O.P.; Martin Connors, O.P., Chap.; Terence Quinn, O.P.; Hugh Burns, O.P.
Res.: 431 Bedford Rd., 10570. Tel: 914-769-0025; Fax: 914-747-2476.
Catechesis/Religious Program—Tel: 914-769-3297. Students 725.
Mission—Our Lady of Pompeii Saragota and Garrigan, Pleasantville Park, Westchester Co. 10570.

POCANTICO HILLS, WESTCHESTER CO., THE MAGDALENE (1894) Revs. Joseph Dietz; Kenneth Chigbo (Nigeria).
Res.: 525 Bedford Rd., Pocantico Hills, Sleepy Hollow, 10591-1216. Tel: 914-631-0529; Fax: 914-332-7958. Email: thmagdalene@archny.org.
Catechesis/Religious Program—Students 200.

PORT CHESTER, WESTCHESTER CO.

1—CORPUS CHRISTI (1925), (Salesians) Revs. Thomas E. Ruekert, S.D.B.; Peter Granzotto, S.D.B.; Donald Delaney, S.D.B., Vicar; Vincent Paczkowski, S.D.B., Coord. Youth Min.
Res.: 136 S. Regent St., 10573. Tel: 914-939-3169; Fax: 914-939-7249.
School—Corpus Christi - Holy Rosary School (1959) 135 S. Regent St., 10573. Tel: 914-937-4407; Fax: 914-937-6904. Sr. Karen Deenn, F.M.A., Prin. Sisters, Daughters of Mary Help of Christians 5; Lay Teachers 13; Students 250.
Catechesis/Religious Program—Sr. Margaret Rose Buonaiuto, F.M.A., D.R.E. Students 120.

2—OUR LADY OF MERCY (1854) [CEM] Revs. Robert J. Staar; Christopher Johnson, O.C.D. (India), Parochial Vicar; Lawrence Naskar, S.D.B. (India), Parochial Vicar.
Res.: 260 Westchester Ave., 10573. Tel: 914-939-0612; Fax: 914-939-2807. Email: olmoffice@optonline.net.
Catechesis/Religious Program—Tel: 914-937-5288. Miss Antoinette Rossetti, D.R.E. Students 245.

3—OUR LADY OF THE ROSARY (1904), (Salesian) Revs. Stephen Schenck, S.D.B.; Richard Alejunas, S.D.B., Coord. Youth Ministry; Raul Acosta, S.D.B.; William F. Keane, S.D.B., Novice Dir.; Deacon William Vaccaro, Admin. In Res., Rev. Philip Pascucci, S.D.B. (Retired).
Church & Mailing Address: 22 Don Bosco Pl., 10573. Tel: 914-939-0547; Fax: 914-937-0692.
Res.: 23 Nicola Pl., 10573. Tel: 914-937-5532.
Catechesis/Religious Program—Students 313.
Chapel—Adoration Chapel

4—SACRED HEART OF JESUS (1917) Rev. Msgr. Peter Gelsomino.
Res.: 229 Willett Ave., 10573. Tel: 914-939-1497; Fax: 914-937-6232.
Catechesis/Religious Program—Frank W. Noriega, D.R.E. Students 75.

PORT EWEN, ULSTER CO., PRESENTATION OF THE BLESSED VIRGIN MARY (1874) Rev. Carl D. Johnson; Deacon John J. Larkin.
Res.: 209 Hoyt St., Box 904, 12466. Tel: 845-331-0053; Fax: 845-331-3836. Email: presentationbvm@aol.com.
Catechesis/Religious Program—Students 45.
Mission—Sacred Heart [JC] 1055 Broadway, P.O. Box 200, Esopus, Ulster Co. 12429. Tel: 845-384-6828; Fax: 845-384-6234. Rev. Eugene J. Grohe, C.Ss.R.

PORT JERVIS, ORANGE CO.

1—IMMACULATE CONCEPTION (1851) Revs. George Hafemann; Clifford Ekwueme (Nigeria).
Res.: 50 Ball St., Box 712, 12771. Tel: 845-856-8212; Fax: 845-858-8375. Email: st-marys-rectory@hvc.rr.com.
Catechesis/Religious Program—Tel: 845-858-4208. Students 170.

2—MOST SACRED HEART (1899) [CEM], Records at: Immaculate Conception, P.O. Box 712, 50 Ball St., Port Jervis, NY 12771 (845-856-8212/5924), Mailing Address: 12 McAllister St., P.O. Box 712, 12771-0712. Tel: 845-856-8212; Fax: 845-858-8375.

POUGHKEEPSIE, DUTCHESS CO.

1—HOLY TRINITY (1921) Rev. Joseph P. LaMorte. In Res., Rev. Gamini E. Fernando (Sri Lanka).
Res.: 775 Main St., 12603. Tel: 845-452-1863; Fax: 845-485-7569. Email: htpok@hvc.rr.com. Web: www.holytrinitypoughkeepsie.org.
School—(1952) 20 Springside Ave., 12603. Tel: 845-471-0520; Fax: 845-471-0309. Email: d520@adnyschools.org. Mrs. Mary Ann McGivney, Prin. Sister Servants of the Immaculate Heart of Mary 2; Lay Teachers 9; Students 165.
Catechesis/Religious Program—Tel: 845-471-5838; Fax: 845-471-0309. Email: htre@hvc.com. Mrs. Lisa P. Timm, D.R.E. Students 305.
Chapel—Holy Trinity Convent 769 Main St., 12603. Tel: 845-452-3484.

2—ST. JOHN THE BAPTIST (1923), Records at: Our Lady of Mt. Carmel, 11 Mt. Carmel Pl., Poughkeepsie, NY 12601 (845-454-0340).
Res.: 1 Grand St., 12601. Tel: 845-454-0340; Fax: 845-486-8154.

3—ST. JOSEPH (1901), (Polish), (Society of Christ) Rev. Edward W. Traczyk, S.Ch.
Res.: 9 Lafayette Pl., 12601. Tel: 845-452-2333; Fax: 845-452-6686.
Catechesis/Religious Program—Students 18.
Chapel—Poughkeepsie, Rectory
Chapel—Cemetery Chapel 42 Evergreen Ave., 12601.

4—ST. MARTIN DE PORRES (1962) [CEM] Rev. Msgr. James P. Sullivan; Revs. Douglas Y. Crawford; Anthony Kemetse (Ghana); Deacons Robert Jarmick, Pastoral Assoc., (Retired); Franklin Hung, Pastoral Assoc.; Victor Salamone, Pastoral Assoc.; Patrick Hogan, Pastoral Assoc.
Res.: 118 Cedar Valley Rd., 12603. Tel: 845-473-4222; Fax: 845-473-4223. Email: smdppok@optonline.net. Web: www.stmartindeporres.org.
School—122 Cedar Valley Rd., 12603. Tel: 845-452-4428; Fax: 845-452-9013. Web: stmartindeporresschool.org. Mrs. Kathleen Leahy, Prin. Lay Teachers 12; Students 329.
Catechesis/Religious Program—Tel: 845-471-8728. Janet McGuirk, D.R.E.; Ellen Farina, Asst. D.R.E. Students 764.

5—ST. MARY (1873) Rev. Msgr. John J. Brinn; Rev. Jose Mena, Parochial Vicar. In Res., Rev. Msgr. John J. Farley.
Res.: 231 Church St., 12601-4200. Tel: 845-452-8250; Fax: 845-452-8266.
Catechesis/Religious Program—Tel: 845-471-4747; Fax: 845-471-4747. Students 290.

6—OUR LADY OF MT. CARMEL (1910), (Italian), Revs. Peter J. Kihm; Francis Mfodwo (Ghana); Deacon George F. Cacchione; Mr. Kevin Martin, Parish Mgr.
Res.: 11 Mt. Carmel Pl., 12601. Tel: 845-454-0340; Fax: 845-486-8154.
Catechesis/Religious Program—Email: mtcfaithform@hvc.rr.com. Mrs. Katherine Hamilton, D.R.E. Students 380.

7—ST. PETER (1837) [CEM] Revs. James A. Garisto; David A. DeSimone, (Chap. Vassar Hospital).
Res.: 6 Father Cody Plaza, Hyde Park, 12601. Tel: 845-452-8580; Fax: 845-471-4800. Web: www.stpeterparishny.org.
Church: *Administration Bldg.*, 171 Salt Point Rd., 12603. Fax: 845-471-4800.
School—(1844)Tel: 845-471-6600; Fax: 845-454-1674. Email: schooladminassistant@stpetersparishny.org. Lay Teachers 12; Students 175.
Catechesis/Religious Program—Tel: 845-452-8580, Ext. 205. Students 120.
Mission—Our Lady of the Rosary 185 Hudson View Dr., 12601.
Chapel—Poughkeepsie, Convent of St. Peter
Chapel—Hyde Park, P.J. Kenedy Memorial Chapel of Our Lady of the Way Culinary Institute of America, Albany Post Rd., Hyde Park, 12538. Rev. Marc Oliver, Chap.
Chapel—Our Lady Health of the Sick Hudson River Psychiatric Center, Ross Bldg., State Hospital, 12601. Rev. Augustin Graap, Chap.

RED HOOK, DUTCHESS CO., ST. CHRISTOPHER (1875) [CEM] Rev. Thomas J. Curley; Rev. Msgrs. Charles P. Coen, Pastor Emeritus; Joaquim J. Olendzki; Rev. Xavier S. Santiago (India).
Res.: 7411 S. Broadway, 12571. Tel: 845-758-3732; Fax: 845-758-1214. Email: saintchristopher@earthlink.net.
Catechesis/Religious Program—30 Benner Rd., 12571. Tel: 845-758-5506; Fax: 845-758-5682. Students 308.

RHINEBECK, DUTCHESS CO., THE GOOD SHEPHERD (1901) [CEM] Revs. Jeffrey R. Galens; Michael Soosairaj (India).
Res.: 3 Mulberry St., 12572. Tel: 845-876-4583; Fax: 845-876-7884. Web: www.goodshepherdrhinebeckny.org. Email: goodshep1@frontiernet.net.
Catechesis/Religious Program—Tel: 845-876-7298. Email: gsreligioused@frontiernet.net. Students 189.
Mission—St. Joseph Church St., Rhinecliff, Dutchess Co. 12574.
Rhinebeck, Ferncliff Nursing Home—Tel: 845-876-2011; Fax: 845-876-4810.
Rhinebeck, Sisters of St. Ursula, Linwood Retreat House—Tel: 845-876-4178; Fax: 845-876-6544.

ROSENDALE, ULSTER CO., ST. PETER (1855) [CEM] Rev. Andrew Florez; Deacon Robert Repke.
Res.: 1017 Keator Ave., P.O. Box 471, 12472. Tel: 845-658-3117; Fax: 845-658-3540.
Catechesis/Religious Program—Tel: 845-658-8911. Students 156.
Mission—Our Lady Help of Christians J.F.K. Ln., High Falls, Ulster Co. 12440.

RYE, WESTCHESTER CO., RESURRECTION (1880) Rev. Msgr. Patrick J. Boyle; Revs. Robert J. Verrigni; Zacharias Nadackal, C.M.I. (India). In Res., Rev. Msgrs. John Mescall (Retired); Edward D. O'Donnell (Retired).
Res.: 910 Boston Post Rd., 10580. Tel: 914-967-0142; Fax: 914-967-0254; Fax: 914-925-2751. Web: www.resurrectionrye.com.
School—(1906) 116 Milton Rd., 10580. Tel: 914-967-1218; Fax: 914-925-3511. Lay Teachers 37; Students 606.
Catechesis/Religious Program—Tel: 914-925-2754; Fax: 914-925-2758. Email: resprep@optonline.net. Students 1,115.
Chapel—Seton Hall Convent of the Sisters of Charity, Tel: 914-967-7085.

SAUGERTIES, ULSTER CO.

1—ST. JOHN THE EVANGELIST (1886) Rev. Msgr. William E. Williams; Deacon Edwin R. Topple.
Res.: 915 Rte. 212, 12477. Tel: 845-246-9581; Fax: 845-246-9582.
Catechesis/Religious Program—Students 132.

2—ST. MARY OF THE SNOW (1833) [CEM] Rev. Christopher H. Berean; Deacons Perry Bunyar; Donald Trees; Karl Pietkiewicz; Arnie Hyland; Hank Smith.
Res.: 36 Cedar St., 12477. Tel: 845-246-4913; Fax: 845-246-4996.
School—(1881) 25 Cedar St., 12477. Tel: 845-246-6381. Miss Christine M. Molinelli, Prin. Lay Teachers 10; Students 94; Preschool 9.
Catechesis/Religious Program—Tel: 845-246-7534. Mrs. Kelly Myers, Coord. Students 149.
Chapel—Saugerties, Parish Center

SCARSDALE, WESTCHESTER CO.

1—IMMACULATE HEART OF MARY (1912) Rev. Msgr. John T. Ferry; Revs. Robert P. Henry, Parochial Vicar; Thomas Valavanickal, C.M.I. (India), Parochial Vicar; Paul I. Nwambu (Nigeria), Parochial Vicar; Deacons Ernest F. Salomone; Robert di Targiani.
Res.: 8 Carman Rd., 10583. Tel: 914-723-0276; Fax: 914-722-0628. Email: w534@archny.org.
School—(1928) 201 Boulevard, 10583. Tel: 914-723-5608; Fax: 914-723-8004. Email: w534@adnyeducation.org. Web: www.ihmscarsdale.org. Mrs. Patricia Gatti, Prin. Lay Teachers 17; Students 293.
Catechesis/Religious Program—Tel: 914-723-7593; Fax: 914-723-7209. Email: ihmsor@aol.com. Mrs. Diane Meade, D.R.E. Students 850.

2—OUR LADY OF FATIMA (1948) Rev. Msgr. Hugh F. McManus; Deacons Michael J. Fox; John J. Kollar; Irene Ingham Kollar, Pastoral Assoc.
Res.: 5 Strathmore Rd., 10583. Tel: 914-723-7421; Fax: 914-723-7229. Web: www.olfchurchscarsdale.org.
School—(1950) 963 Scarsdale Rd., 10583. Tel: 914-723-0460; Fax: 914-722-4571. Email: w525@adnyschools.org. Web: www.olfschoolscarsdale.org. Mrs. Sharyn O'Leary, Prin. Lay Teachers 12; Students 185.
Catechesis/Religious Program—Tel: 914-472-6604; Fax: 914-472-6679. Email: olfreled@aol.com. Students 200.

3—ST. PIUS X (1954) Rev. Francisco Bacatan (Philippines); Deacons Theodore A. Gaskin; William J. Hill.
Res.: 91 Secor Rd., 10583. Tel: 914-725-2755; Fax: 914-725-2782. Email: saintpiusx@optoline.net. Web: www.saintpiusxchurch.com.
Catechesis/Religious Program—Tel: 914-472-5594; Fax: 914-725-2782. Email: stpiusxreled@yahoo.com. Students 235.

SHRUB OAK, WESTCHESTER CO., SAINT ELIZABETH ANN SETON (1963) Rev. Msgr. Thomas P. Sandi; Revs. George C. Lodi; S. Kulandairajan (India); Deacons G. Frank Bruno; Michael Wilson.
Res.: 1377 E. Main St., 10588. Tel: 914-528-3547; Fax: 914-528-4216. Email: seton@bestweb.net. Web: www.seton-parish.org.
School—1375 E. Main St., 10588. Tel: 914-528-3563; Fax: 914-528-0341. Sr. Gabriel Miriam, S.C., Prin. Sisters 1; Lay Teachers 25; Students 350.
Catechesis/Religious Program—Tel: 914-528-8553. Email: setonre@bestweb.net. Sara Koshofer, C.R.E. Middle School; Louise Frangella, C.R.E. Elementary School. Students 1,422.

SLEEPY HOLLOW, WESTCHESTER CO.

1—HOLY CROSS (1921), (Slovak—Polish), Unassigned. Records at: St. Teresa of Avila, 130 Beekman Ave., Sleepy Hollow, NY 10591 (914-631-0720).
Res.: 118 Beekman Ave., 10591.

2—IMMACULATE CONCEPTION (1917) Rev. Msgr. Louis J. Mazza.
Res.: 199 N. Broadway, 10591. Tel: 914-631-0446; Fax: 914-631-4157. Email: iccshny@aol.com.

3—ST. TERESA OF AVILA (1853) Rev. Msgr. Francis P. Gorman; Revs. Jude Egbeji (Nigeria); Asuramonil F. Peri (Sri Lanka).
Res.: 130 Beekman Ave., 10591. Tel: 914-631-0720; Fax: 914-366-6459.
Catechesis/Religious Program—Tel: 914-631-1831. Students 300.

SLOATSBURG, ROCKLAND CO., ST. JOAN OF ARC (1966), (Italian—Irish), Revs. D. Francis Dias; John J. McKenna, Pastor Emeritus (Retired).
Res.: 32 Eagle Valley Rd., 10974. Tel: 845-753-5239; Fax: 845-753-5341. Email: joanofarcsloats@optonline.net. Web: www.stjoansparish.org.
Catechesis/Religious Program—Tel: 845-753-5193. Students 200.

SPRING VALLEY, ROCKLAND CO., ST. JOSEPH (1894) Revs. Rudolph F. Gonzalez; Patrick Adekola (Nigeria); Jose Soto (Colombia); Dessier Predelus (Haiti); Peter Bakwaph (Nigeria).
Res.: 333 Sneden Pl. W., 10977. Tel: 845-356-0311; Fax: 845-352-8126.
Catechesis/Religious Program—Tel: 845-356-0054. Maureen Foley, D.R.E. Students 800.

STONY POINT, ROCKLAND CO., IMMACULATE CONCEPTION (1889) Rev. Msgr. William J. Foley; Revs. James H. Hauver; Reji Joseph, C.M.I.; Deacons Philip Marino; John Crapanzano; John Sadowski.
Res.: 26 John St., 10980. Tel: 845-786-2742; Fax: 845-942-2614. Email: r547@archny.org. Web: www.immaculatestonypoint.org.
Catechesis/Religious Program—24 E. Main St., 10980. Tel: 845-786-5298. Email: immaculatereled@verizon.net. Students 556.
Mission—Immaculate Conception 5 Buckberg Rd., Tomkins Cove, Rockland Co. 10986.

SUFFERN, ROCKLAND CO., SACRED HEART (1868) Rev. Msgr. Joseph R. Giandurco; Revs. Angelo J. Micciulla; Cresus Fernando (Sri Lanka); Deacon Joseph A. Witt. In Res., Rev. Brian Coffey, M.H.M.
Res. & Office: 129 Lafayette Ave., 10901. Tel: 845-357-0035; Fax: 845-368-0393.
School—(1909) 60 Washington Ave., 10901. Tel: 845-357-1684; Fax: 845-357-0318. Mrs. Kathleen Grande, Prin. Lay Teachers 11; Students 257.
Catechesis/Religious Program—Tel: 845-357-6044. Janis Batewell, Acting C.R.E. Students 515.
Chapel—Good Samaritan Hospital 255 Lafayette Ave., 10901. Tel: 845-368-5000.
Chapel—Tagaste Monastery 220 Lafayette Ave., 10901. Tel: 845-357-0067; Fax: 845-369-0625.

TAPPAN, ROCKLAND CO., OUR LADY OF THE SACRED HEART (1952) Revs. George J. Torok, C.O.; John F. Dwyer, Senior Priest; Francis Conka, C.O., Parochial Vicar. In Res., Revs. Vladimir Chripko, C.O.; Martin Kertys, C.O.
Res.: 120 King's Hwy., 10983. Tel: 845-359-1230; Fax: 845-359-1410. Email: marywarner@optonline.net.
Catechesis/Religious Program—Tel: 845-365-2141. Email: olshre@optonline.net. Students 512.

TARRYTOWN, WESTCHESTER CO., TRANSFIGURATION (1896), (Carmelite) Revs. Lucian W. Beltzner, O.Carm.; Philip Marani, O.Carm.
Res.: 268 S. Broadway, 10591. Tel: 914-631-1672; Fax: 914-524-9352. Web: www.transfiguration-church.org.
School—(1949) 40 Prospect Ave., 10591. Tel: 914-631-3737; Fax: 914-631-6640. Web: www.transfigurationschool.org. Audrey J. Woods, Prin. Lay Teachers 13; Students 214.
Catechesis/Religious Program—Tel: 914-631-2380; Fax: 914-631-1052. Students 200.

TIVOLI, DUTCHESS CO., ST. SYLVIA (1890) [CEM] Revs. Thomas J. Curley, Admin.; H. Theriault, Pastor Emeritus; Rev. Msgr. Joaquim J. Olendzki, Parochial Vicar.
Res.: 104 Broadway, P.O. Box 95, 12583-0095. Tel: 845-757-2442; Fax: 845-757-3553.
Catechesis/Religious Program— At St. Christopher, Red Hook. Students 80.

TUCKAHOE, WESTCHESTER CO.

1—ASSUMPTION (1911), (Italian), Rev. Eric P. Raaser.
Res.: 53 Winterhill Rd., 10707. Tel: 914-961-3643; Fax: 914-961-0283. Web: www.assumption-immaculate.org.
Catechesis/Religious Program— Clustered with Immaculate Conception, Tuckahoe.

2—IMMACULATE CONCEPTION (1853) [CEM] Revs. Eric P. Raaser; Joseph Emmanuel; Kevin M. Malick; Deacon Anthony Viola.
Res.: 53 Winterhill Rd., 10707. Tel: 914-961-3643; Fax: 914-961-0283. Web: www.assumption-immaculate.org.
School—(1913)Tel: 914-961-3785; Fax: 914-961-6054. Web: www.icschoolonline.org. Ms. Maureen J. Harten, Prin. Sisters 1; Lay Teachers 22; Students 310.
Catechesis/Religious Program—Tel: 914-961-1076; Fax: 914-961-4765. Lynn Callahan, D.R.E. Students 780.
Chapel—Sisters Convent, Tel: 914-961-3970.

TUXEDO, ORANGE CO., OUR LADY OF MT. CARMEL (1895) Rev. Msgr. John F.X. Smith.
Res.: 5 Tobin Way, Rte. 17, P.O. Box 697, 10987. Tel: 914-351-5284; Fax: 914-351-4866. Email: sm8j04@aol.com; olmc@aol.com.
Catechesis/Religious Program—Students 66.

VALHALLA, WESTCHESTER CO., HOLY NAME OF JESUS (1896) Revs. Joseph A. Blenkle; Philip T. Persico.
Res.: Two Broadway, 10595. Tel: 914-949-2323; Fax: 914-686-6325.
School—Tel: 914-948-1744; Fax: 914-948-1749. Web: www.hnjschool.net. Toni Corso, Prin. Lay Teachers 12; Students 145.
Catechesis/Religious Program—Tel: 914-949-1422. Email: hnjre@aol.com. Students 625.

VERPLANCK, WESTCHESTER CO., ST. PATRICK (1843) [CEM] Rev. Andrew E. Kurzyna.
Res.: 240 11th St., P.O. Box 609, 10596. Tel: 914-737-0635; Fax: 914-788-0584.
Catechesis/Religious Program—Church of St. Christopher, 3094 Albany Post Rd., Buchanan, 10511. Tel: 914-737-1437; Fax: 914-737-9320. Students 52.

WALDEN, ORANGE CO., MOST PRECIOUS BLOOD (1894) Rev. Joseph Fallon.
Res.: 42 Walnut St., 12586. Tel: 845-778-5719; Fax: 845-778-5659. Email: mpbparish@frontiernet.net.
School—180 Ulster Ave., 12586. Tel: 845-778-3028; Fax: 845-778-3785. Email: or554@adnyschools.org. Sisters of St. Dominic (Sparkill) 1; Lay Teachers 9.
Catechesis/Religious Program—Tel: 914-778-7081. Email: mpbreled@aol.com. Students 387.
Mission—St. Benedict Wallkill, Ulster Co. 12589.

WAPPINGERS FALLS, DUTCHESS CO., ST. MARY (1850) [CEM] Rev. Msgr. Francis P. Bellew; Rev. Gnanadhas George Michael (India).
Res.: 11 Clinton St., 12590. Tel: 845-297-6261; 845-297-6262; Fax: 845-297-3227. Email: churchstmary@aol.com. Web: www.catholic-church.org/saintmarys.
School—(1890 and 1955) Convent Ave., 12590. Tel: 845-297-7500; Fax: 845-297-0886. Email: officestmary@yahoo.com. Web: www.stmarywf.org. Mrs. Mary Ellen LaRose, Prin. Lay Teachers 18; Students 170.
Catechesis/Religious Program—Tel: 845-297-7586. Email: sm_ore@yahoo.com. Patricia Manuli, D.R.E. Students 315.
Chapel—Mt. Carmel

WARWICK, ORANGE CO., ST. STEPHEN (1865) [CEM] Rev. Michael P. McLoughlin; Rev. Msgr. Bernard J. Corrigan, Pastor Emeritus (Retired); Rev. Robert Bubel; Deacons Thomas MacDougall; Emmet Noonan.
Res.: 75 Sanfordville Rd., 10990. Tel: 845-986-4028; Fax: 845-986-4109. Web: www.warwickinfo.net/ststephen.
School—Tel: 845-986-3533; Fax: 845-986-7023. Web: ststephen-stedward.org. Lay Teachers 13; Students 263.
Catechesis/Religious Program—Tel: 845-986-2231; Fax: 845-986-5939. Web: warwickinfo.net. Students 901.

WASHINGTONVILLE, ORANGE CO., ST. MARY (1902) [CEM] Revs. Jeffrey E. Maurer; Paul Dmoch; Anthony Omenihu; Deacon Timothy Curran.
Res.: 2 Fr. Tierney Cir., 10992. Tel: 914-496-3730; Fax: 914-496-3159.
Catechesis/Religious Program—Tel: 845-496-4101. Students 1,400.

WEST HARRISON, WESTCHESTER CO., ST. ANTHONY OF PADUA (1952) Revs. Christopher W. Monturo; Peter C. Scaramuzzo.
Res.: 85 Harrison St., 10604. Tel: 914-948-1480; Fax: 914-948-0488. Email: stanthony@optonline.net. Web: www.stanthonyonline.org.
School—(1957) Gainsborg Ave., 10604. Tel: 914-949-6986; Fax: 914-328-1981. Web: www.rc.net/newyork/stanthonyschool/. Sisters of Divine Compassion 2; Students 350.
Catechesis/Religious Program—Tel: 914-949-0212; Fax: 914-949-6669. Email: stanthonyreled@optonline.net. Students 330.

WESLEY HILLS, ROCKLAND CO., ST. BONIFACE (1966) Rev. Hugh R. Grace; Deacon Peter Venezia.
Res.: 5 Willow Tree Rd., 10952. Tel: 845-354-7307; Fax: 914-354-9046.
Catechesis/Religious Program—Tel: 845-354-7039. Students 100.

WEST HURLEY-WOODSTOCK, ULSTER CO., ST. JOHN (1860) Rev. George W. Hommel.
Res.: 12 Holly Hills Dr., Woodstock, 12498. Tel: 914-679-7696; Fax: 914-679-8393.
Catechesis/Religious Program—Tel: 914-679-2869. Students 138.
Mission—St. Augustine Watson Hollow Rd., West Shokan, Ulster Co. 12494. Tel: 914-657-2190.

WEST NYACK, ROCKLAND CO., ST. FRANCIS OF ASSISI (1964) Rev. Msgr. Edward J. Weber; Deacon Farrell J. Hopkins; Sr. Patricia Hogan, O.P., Pastoral Assoc. In Res., Rev. Gerard F. Rafferty, S.S.L.
Res.: 128 Parrott Rd., 10994. Tel: 845-634-4957; Fax: 845-639-6629. Email: stfrancisassisi@optonline.net. Web: www.stfrancis-assisi.org.
Catechesis/Religious Program—Tel: 845-638-4215. Email: stfrancisprep@optonline.net. Mrs. Nancy Doran, D.R.E. Students 1,338.

WEST POINT, ORANGE CO., CATHOLIC CHAPEL OF THE MOST HOLY TRINITY (1899), Most Holy Trinity is being served under the Archdiocese for Military Services. For inquiries for sacramental records before Jan. 1, 1999, please contact Sacred Heart, Highland Falls. Revs. Matthew Pawlikowski; Edson J. Wood, O.S.A., Chap. U.S. Corps of Cadets; Timothy Valentine, S.J., Regimental Chap.
United States Military Academy, Bldg. 699, 10996. Tel: 845-938-8760; Fax: 845-938-8763.
Catechesis/Religious Program—Tel: 845-938-8761. Cindy Ragsdale, D.R.E. Students 209.

WHITE PLAINS, WESTCHESTER CO.

1—ST. BERNARD (1926) Rev. Robert J. Morris, Admin.; Deacon Daniel Pellegrin. In Res., Rev. Louis Maram Reddy (India).
Res.: 51 Prospect St., 10606. Tel: 914-949-2111; Fax: 914-949-6044. Email: stbernardwp@aol.com. Web: www.stbernardswp.com.
Catechesis/Religious Program—Tel: 914-686-8145. Students 501.

2—ST. JOHN THE EVANGELIST (1868) [CEM] Rev. Msgr. Neil Graham; Revs. Timothy S. Wiggins; Paul Chemplamparampil Joseph, C.M.I.; Jaccius Jean Pierre; Vincent E. Eut.
Res.: 148 Hamilton Ave., 10601. Tel: 914-949-0439; Fax: 914-421-1202.
Catechesis/Religious Program—Tel: 914-437-5144. Students 249.

3—OUR LADY OF MT. CARMEL (1902), (Italian), (Stigmatine) Rev. Albert Azrak, C.S.S.
Res.: 92 S. Lexington Ave., 10606. Tel: 914-948-5909; Fax: 914-328-1946. Web: www.ourladyofmountcarmelwp.org.
Catechesis/Religious Program—Fax: 914-948-5909. Students 223.

4—OUR LADY OF SORROWS (1929) Revs. Philip J. Quealy; Thomas DeSimone.
Res.: 920 Mamaroneck Ave., 10605. Tel: 914-949-9819; Fax: 914-949-4148. Email: olswp@optonline.net.
School—(1957) 888 Mamaroneck Ave., 10605. Tel: 914-761-0124; Fax: 914-761-0176. Email: w561@adnyschools.org. Web: www.olscc.com. Sr. Marie Cecile, Prin. Lay Teachers 15; Students 212.
Catechesis/Religious Program—Tel: 914-949-3896. Students 382.

WOODBOURNE, SULLIVAN CO., IMMACULATE CONCEPTION (1957) [CEM] Rev. John J. Lynch.
Res.: 6317 Rte. 42, P.O. Box 66, 12788. Tel: 845-434-7643; Fax: 845-436-7370. Email: s5640@bestweb.net.
Catechesis/Religious Program—Tel: 845-436-7370. Students 101.

WURTSBORO, SULLIVAN CO., ST. JOSEPH (1880) [CEM] Rev. Peter J. Madori; Deacon Edward Czerwinski. In Res., Rev. Matthias Ndulaka.
Res.: 180 Sullivan St., P.O. Box 277, 12790. Tel: 845-888-4522; Fax: 845-888-5072.
Catechesis/Religious Program—Students 105.

YONKERS, WESTCHESTER CO.

1—ST. ANN (1947) Revs. Andrew P. Carrozza; John Carson, Parochial Vicar; Thaddeus Obba (Nigeria), Parochial Vicar.
Res.: 854 Midland Ave., 10704. Tel: 914-965-1555; 914-965-5584; Fax: 914-965-0678.
School—40 Brewster Ave., 10701. Tel: 914-965-4333; Fax: 914-965-1778. Mr. Michael Vicario, Prin. Lay Teachers 10; Students 170.
Catechesis/Religious Program—Students 94.

2—ST. ANTHONY (Nepera Park) (1923) Revs. Karl A. Bauer; Robert Ashman.
Res. & Church: 10 Squire Ave., 10703. Tel: 914-965-2733; Fax: 914-963-2285. Web: www.stanthonys-catholic.org.
School—1395 Nepperhan Ave., 10703. Tel: 914-476-8489; Fax: 914-965-7939. Mrs. Elizabeth Carney, Prin. Lay Teachers 11; Students 241.
Catechesis/Religious Program—Tel: 914-965-5535. Students 91.

3—ST. ANTHONY (Willow St.) Closed. For inquiries for parish records contact Our Lady of Mt. Carmel, Yonkers.

4—ST. BARTHOLOMEW (1910), (Missionaries of St. Paul of Nigeria) Revs. Anthony Bassey, M.S.P. (Nigeria); Francis Oroffa, M.S.P., Parochial Vicar; Deacon Robert A. Clemens.
Res.: 15 Palmer Rd., 10701. Tel: 914-965-0566; Fax: 914-965-9046.
School—(1958) 278 Saw Mill River Rd., 10701. Tel: 914-476-7949; Fax: 914-476-7957. Mark Valentinetti, Prin. Lay Teachers 14; Students 183.
Catechesis/Religious Program—Tel: 914-476-6676. Students 125.

5—ST. CASIMIR (1899), (Polish), (Pauline) Revs. Krzysztof Drybka, O.S.P.P.E.; Mariusz Andrej Dymek, O.S.P.P.E.; Deacon John Radzilowicz.
Res.: 239 Nepperhan Ave., 10701. Tel: 914-963-1254; Fax: 914-969-5204. Email: rectory@saintcasimir.org. Web:

www.saintcasimir.org.
School—(1906) 259 Nepperhan Ave., 10701-3461. Tel: 914-965-2730; Fax: 914-965-3347. Helen DiNoia, Prin. Lay Teachers 11; Students 160.
Catechesis/Religious Program—Students 9.

6—CHRIST THE KING (1927) Revs. William J. Luciano; Anthony J. Giuliano, Parochial Vicar. In Res., Rev. Nicholas Nwagwu, Hospital Chap.
Res.: 740 N. Broadway, 10701. Tel: 914-963-7474; 914-963-7564; Fax: 914-963-7548. Email: ctkrectory@optonline.net.
School—(1955) 750 N. Broadway, 10701. Fax: 914-423-4101. Email: ctheking@optonline.net. Mrs. Bridget Browne, Prin. Lay Teachers 13; Students 195.
Catechesis/Religious Program—Email: rel.ed.ctk@verizon.net. Students 60.

7—ST. DENIS (1910) Revs. Edward P. O'Halloran; George Spiteri (Peru).
Res.: 470 Van Cortlandt Park Ave., 10705. Tel: 914-963-8468; Fax: 914-963-7354.
Catechesis/Religious Program—73 Lawrence St., 10705. Rev. Edward P. O'Halloran, D.R.E. Students 88.

8—ST. EUGENE (1949) Revs. Leonard F. Villa; Michael D. Morrow; Samson Imhangbe.
Rectory—32 Massitoa Rd., 10710. Tel: 914-779-5460; Fax: 914-793-8913. Email: rectory32@optonline.net. Web: www.steugene.com.
Parish Office: 31 Massitoa Rd., 10710. Tel: 914-961-2590; Fax: 914-961-2881.
School—(1951) 707 Tuckahoe Rd., 10710. Tel: 914-779-2956; Fax: 914-779-7668. Email: w577@adnyeducation.org. Lay Teachers 17; Students 320.
Catechesis/Religious Program—Tel: 914-793-2158; Fax: 914-337-9868. Marisela DeVictoria, D.R.E. Tel: 914-337-9868. Students 101.

9—IMMACULATE CONCEPTION (1848), (Spanish—Arabic), [CEM] Rev. Msgr. Hugh J. Corrigan; Revs. Sami Totah (Jordan); Virgilio Compentente (Philippines). In Res., Rev. Osvaldo Franklin (Angola).
Res.: 103 S. Broadway, 10701. Tel: 914-963-0156; Fax: 914-963-1803. Email: marys103@optonline.net.
School—(1857) 15 St. Mary's St., 10701. Tel: 914-965-7048; Fax: 914-423-2826. Patricia Raczy, Prin. Sisters 2; Lay Teachers 12; Students 160.
Catechesis/Religious Program—Tel: 914-963-1053. Students 155.
Good Shepherd Arabic Community of St. Mary—Rev. Sami Totah (Jordan), Admin.

10—ST. JOHN THE BAPTIST (1903) Rev. Msgr. J. Christopher Maloney; Revs. Thomas Valenti; Daniel Ulloa, O.P. (Mexico); Deacon Martin J. Olivieri.
Res.: 670 Yonkers Ave., 10704. Tel: 914-963-1486; Fax: 914-375-1115.
School—(1954)Tel: 914-965-2356. Sisters 2; Lay Teachers 14; Students 300.
Catechesis/Religious Program—Tel: 914-965-2338. Sr. Mary Beth Read, O.S.U., D.R.E. Students 185.
Chapel—Convent 176 Sweetfield Circle, 10704. Tel: 914-965-1837.

11—ST. JOSEPH PARISH (1871), (Hispanic), [CEM] Rev. George J. Kuhn; Deacon Abraham Santiago.
Res.: 141 Ashburton Ave., 10701. Tel: 914-963-0730; Fax: 914-964-5833.
Catechesis/Religious Program—Students 175.
Convent—Sisters of Charity, Tel: 914-423-1351. Sisters 6.

12—ST. MARGARET OF HUNGARY (1928) Unassigned. Records at: St. Joseph, 141 Ashburton Ave., Yonkers, NY 10701 (914-963-0730)
Res.: 76 Locust Hill Ave., 10701.

13—MOST HOLY TRINITY (1894), (Slovak), Rev. George Oonnooney.
Res.: 18 Trinity Pl., 10701. Tel: 914-963-0720; Fax: 914-709-0224.
Chapel—Franciscan Friars of the Renewal 15 Trinity Pl., 10701. Tel: 914-476-7279; Fax: 914-476-5033. Bro. Crispin Mary Rinaldi, C.F.R.

14—OUR LADY OF FATIMA (1977), (Portugese Center) Rev. Osvaldo Franklin (Angola), Admin.
Portuguese R.C. Center—355 S. Broadway, 10705. Tel: 914-423-9688; Fax: 914-423-8271. Email: fatima1305@verizon.net. Web: www.fatima-port-church.com.
Catechesis/Religious Program—Neide Pires, D.R.E. Students 91.

15—OUR LADY OF MT. CARMEL (1913), (Italian), (Pallottine) Revs. Terzo Vinci, S.A.C.; Chris Salvatori, S.A.C.; Deacons Alfred R. Impallomeni; Nick A. Mazzei Jr.
Res.: 70 Park Hill Ave., 10701. Tel: 914-963-4766; Fax: 914-963-4766. Email: tervinci@optonline.net.
Catechesis/Religious Program—Tel: 914-476-8888; Fax: 914-476-8888. Email: olmcreled@juno.com. Students 320.

16—OUR LADY OF THE ROSARY (1907) Unassigned. Records At: Immaculate Conception/St. Mary, 103 S. Broadway, Yonkers, NY 10701 (914-963-0156).
Res.: 226 Warburton Ave., 10701.

17—ST. PAUL THE APOSTLE (1923) Rev. Msgr. John A. Gallagher; Sr. Eileen Treanor, P.B.V.M., Parish Ministry; Deacons James J. Hamilton; Rudolfo Teng.
Res.: 602 McLean Ave., 10705. Tel: 914-963-7330; Fax: 914-963-1952. Email: w581@adny.org.
Church: Lincoln Park, 10705.
School—(1949) 77 Lee Ave., 10705. Tel: 914-965-2165; Fax: 914-965-5792. Grace Mallardi, Prin. Lay Teachers 10; Students 241.
Catechesis/Religious Program—Sr. Eileen Treanor, P.B.V.M., D.R.E. Students 101.

18—ST. PETER (1894) Revs. Joseph Espaillat; Julio Vasquez (El Salvador), Parochial Vicar; Deacon Pedro Irizarry.
Res.: 91 Ludlow St., 10705. Tel: 914-963-0822; Fax: 914-968-9305.
School—(1894 and 1955) 204 Hawthorne Ave., 10705. Tel: 914-963-2314; Fax: 914-966-8822. Email: principal@stpetersny.com. Web: www.stpetersny-.com. Sisters 1; Lay Teachers 9; Students 171.
Catechesis/Religious Program—Students 321.

19—SACRED HEART (1891), (Capuchin) Rev. Maurice Moreau, O.F.M.Cap.; Bro. Roger Deguire, O.F.M-.Cap.; Revs. Christopher Dietrich, O.F.M.Cap.; Cyprian Murray, O.F.M.Cap.; Charles Sammons, O.F.M.Cap., Parochial Vicar. In Res., Rev. Thomas Murphy, O.F.M.Cap.; Bro. Michael Loerch, O.F.M.Cap.
Res.: 110 Shonnard Pl., 10703. Tel: 914-963-4205; Fax: 914-476-4960.
School—(1893)Tel: 914-963-5318; Fax: 914-709-0250. Web: www.shgsyonkers.org. Lay Teachers 15; Students 180.
High School—34 Convent Ave., 10703. Tel: 914-965-3114; Fax: 914-965-4510. Religious 1; Lay Teachers 26; Students 383.
Sacred Heart Parish High School Foundation, Inc.—34 Convent Ave., 10703. Tel: 914-963-4205; Fax: 914-476-4960.
Catechesis/Religious Program—Students 91.
Convent—27 Convent Ave., 10703. Tel: 914-476-4602.

YORKTOWN HEIGHTS, WESTCHESTER CO., ST. PATRICK (1898) Revs. Joseph Bisignano; Herbert P. Degaris; Rev. Msgr. Dermot R. Brennan, Pastor Emeritus (Retired); Rev. Augustine Addai (Ghana); Deacons Kevin T. Byrnes; Gregory Osgood.
Res.: 137 Moseman Rd., 10598. Tel: 914-962-5050; 914-962-5051; Fax: 914-962-0595. Email: w583@archny.org. Web: www.stpatricks-yorktown.org.
School—(1953) 117 Moseman Rd., 10598. Tel: 914-962-2211; Fax: 914-243-4814. Lay Teachers 23; Students 359.
Catechesis/Religious Program—Tel: 914-962-5586; Fax: 914-962-3207. Students 2,216.

YOUNGSVILLE, SULLIVAN CO., ST. FRANCIS OF ASSISI (1963) Merged with St. George, Jeffersonville to form St. George-St. Francis, Jeffersonville.

YULAN, SULLIVAN CO., ST. ANTHONY OF PADUA (1907) [CEM], (Franciscan) Rev. Anthony F. Moore, O.F.M.
Res.: 12792. Tel: 845-557-8512; Fax: 845-557-3527. Email: afmofm@hvc.rr.com.
Catechesis/Religious Program—Students 75.
Mission—Sacred Heart Berme Church Rd., Pond Eddy, Sullivan Co. 12770. Tel: 845-557-8122.

Chaplains of Public Institutions
Military Installations

NEW YORK. *National Catholic Community Service*, 487 Park Ave., 10022. Rev. Msgr. Richard Cahill, Dir. (Cardinal Spellman Servicemen's Club)
New York City Veterans Administration Hospital, 406 First Ave., 10022. Revs. Pasquale V. Laghezza, SS.CC., Jose A. Salazar.

BRONX. *Veterans Administration Hospital*, 130 W. Kingsbridge Rd., 10460. Rev. Paul F. O'Connor, O.S.B.

MONTROSE. *Franklin D. Roosevelt Hospital*.

WEST POINT. *Stewart Field*. Rev. Nash P. Geany.
West Point.
U.S. Military Academy 10966. Vacant.

Societies

NEW YORK. *Marine and Aviation Department*. Vacant.
New York Fire Department. Rev. Msgr. Marc A. Filacchione.
New York Police Department. Rev. Msgr. Joseph J. Zammit.
New York Postal Service.
New York Sanitation Department. Rev. Peter M. Colapietro.

YONKERS. *Yonkers Fire Department*. Rev. Thomas F. McDonald (Retired).
Yonkers Police Department.

Prisons

CITY. *Adolescent Remand & Detention Center*, 11 Hazen St., East Elmhurst, 11370. Tel: 718-546-7223. Sr. Margaret McCabe.
Anna M. Kross Center, 18-18 Hazen St., East Elmhurst, 11370. Tel: 718-546-3654. Rev. George J. Dash, O.F.M.Cap.
Correctional Institution for Men, 10-10 Hazen St., East Elmhurst, 11370. Tel: 718-546-5796. Rev. Michael Concik.
George M. Motchan Detention Center, 15-15 Hazen St., East Elmhurst, 11370. Tel: 718-546-4543. Rev. Thomas Mestriparampil.
George Vierno Center, 09-09 Hazen St., East Elmhurst, 11370. Tel: 718-204-5079, Ext. 2254. Rev. Lawrence E. Lucas.
Manhattan Detention Center, 125 White St., 10013. Tel: 212-225-1367. Deacon Kenneth L. Radcliffe.
North Infirmary Command, 15-00 Hazen St., East Elmhurst, 11370. Tel: 718-546-1256. Rev. Hyacinth Njoku (Nigeria), Sr. Amy Henry.
Otis Bantum Correctional Center, 16-00 Hazen St., East Elmhurst, 11370. Tel: 718-546-6617. Revs. Oliver Chanama, Thomas Mestriparampil.
Rose M. Singer Center, 19-19 Hazen St., East Elmhurst, 11370. Sr. Eileen.
Spofford Juvenile Center, 1221 Spofford Ave., Bronx, 10474. Tel: 718-579-0100. Vacant.
VCBC, 1 Halleck, Bronx, 10474. Tel: 718-579-4371. Deacon Miguel Granda.

COUNTY. *Dutchess County Jail*, Poughkeepsie, 12601. Tel: 845-297-5706.
Orange County Jail. Attended from St. John, Goshen. Tel: 845-294-5328.
Putnam County Jail. Attended by St. James, Carmel. Tel: 845-225-2079.
Rockland County Jail. Attended by St. Augustine, New City. Tel: 845-634-3641.
Sullivan County Jail. Attended by St. Peter, Monticello. Tel: 845-794-5577.
Ulster County Jail, Kingston, 12401. Tel: 845-338-1554. Deacon John Bellacicco.
Westchester County Jail, Box 389, Valhalla, 10595. Tel: 914-347-6132. Rev. Paul Tolve, O.F.M.Cap.

FEDERAL. *Federal Correctional Institution*, Otisville, 10963. Tel: 845-386-5855, Ext. 291.
Metropolitan Correctional Center, 150 Park Row, 10007-1779. Tel: 212-240-9656, Ext. 6454. Rev. Michael O'Hara, O.M.I.

STATE. *Arthur Kill Correctional Facility*, 2911 Arthur Kill Rd., Staten Island, 10309-1197. Tel: 718-356-7333. Rev. Frank Naccarato.
Bayview Correctional Facility, 550 W. 20th St., 10011-2878. Tel: 212-255-7590. Rev. Matthew Uguoji.
Beacon Correctional Facility, Box 780, Beacon, 12508-0780. Tel: 845-831-4200. Deacon Frank Gohl.
Bedford Hills Correctional Facility, 247 Harris Rd., Bedford Hills, 10507-2499. Tel: 914-241-3100. Rev. Ronald D. Lemmert, M.Div., Sr. Mary Anne Collins.
Downstate Correctional Facility, Box 445, Fishkill, 12524-0445. Tel: 845-831-6600. Rev. Arecio Dormido.
Eastern Correctional Facility, Napanoch, 12458-0338. Tel: 845-647-7400. Rev. Thomas E. Smith, S.J., Deacon Joseph Doherty.
Edgecombe Correctional Facility, 611 Edgecombe Ave., 10032-4398. Tel: 212-923-2575. Rev. Matthew Uguoji.
Fishkill Correctional Facility, Box 307, Beacon, 12508. Tel: 845-831-4800. Rev. George J. Dash, O.F.M-.Cap., Deacon Frank Gohl.
Fulton Correctional Facility, 1511 Fulton Ave., Bronx, 10457-8398. Tel: 718-583-8000. Rev. Matthew Uguoji.
Green Haven Correctional Facility, Stormville, 12582. Tel: 845-221-2711. Rev. Gamini E. Fernando (Sri Lanka), Deacon Robert Buchner.
Lincoln Correctional Facility, 31-33 W. 110 St., 10026-4398. Tel: 212-860-9400. Rev. Matthew Uguoji.
Mid-Orange Correctional Facility, Warwick, 10990-0990. Tel: 845-986-2291. Deacon Ricardo Rosado, Rev. Augustine Graap, O.Carm.
Otisville Correctional Facility, Box 8, Otisville, 10963-0008. Tel: 845-386-1490, Ext. 4830. Rev. Augustine Graap, O.Carm., Deacon Eugene Bormann.
Shawangunk Correctional Facility, Box 750, Wallkill, 12589-0750. Tel: 845-895-2081. Rev. Thomas E. Smith, S.J., Deacon Angelo Corsaro.
Sing Sing Correctional Facility, 354 Hunter St., Ossining, 10562-5442. Tel: 914-941-0108, Ext. 4810. Rev. Ronald J. Lemmert, Deacon John Dunn.
Sullivan Correctional Facility, P.O. Box AG, Fallsburg, 12733-0116. Tel: 845-434-2080. Rev. Stanislaus Ogbonna, C.S.Sp. (Nigeria).
Taconic Correctional Facility, 250 Harris Rd., Bedford Hills, 10507-2498. Tel: 914-241-3010. Sr. Antonia Maguire.
Ulster Correctional Facility, Berne Rd., P.O. Box 800, Napanoch, 12458. Tel: 914-647-1670, Ext. 4800. Rev. Thomas E. Smith, S.J., Deacon James Faulkner.
Wallkill Correctional Facility, Box G, Wallkill, 12589-0286. Tel: 845-895-2021. Rev. Thomas E. Smith, S.J., Deacon Angelo Cosaro.

Woodbourne Correctional Facility, Pouch 1, Woodbourne, 12788. Tel: 845-434-7730. Rev. Matthias Ndylaka.

Hospitals

BRONX. *St. Barnabas Hospital*, Tel: 718-960-9000. Rev. Msgr. Thomas McGarry (Retired), Sr. Miriam Hanratty, O.P., Deacon Victor Pino.

Bronx Municipal Hospital Center, Abraham Jacobi Hospital, Nathan B. VanEtten Hospital. Revs. Sancho G. Garrote, Hippolytus Duru (Nigeria), Chap., Sr. Rosemary Sullivan, F.M.M., Chap.

Bronx Psychiatric Center, Tel: 718-931-0600. Rev. Sancho E. Garrote (Philippines).

Bronx-Lebanon Hospital Center, Tel: 718-590-1800; 718-518-5059. Revs. Ishamel Iwuala, Joseph Bernardine Onyia (Nigeria).

Calvary Hospital, Tel: 718-518-2114. Revs. Chux Okochi, Dir. Pastoral Svcs., Antonyraja Ignaci (India), Victor Mbanisi (BRK).

Lincoln Medical and Mental Health Center, Tel: 718-579-5000; 718-579-5059.

Montefiore Medical Center, Tel: 718-920-4997. Revs. Misael Bacleon (Philippines), Andrew Ovienloba, Ephrem Pottamplackal, M.C.B.S.

Montefiore Medical Center - North Division. Rev. Msgr. Frederick J. Becker, Vice Pres. Pastoral Svcs., Sr. Catherine McVicar, S.M.

New York Westchester Square Medical Center, Tel: 718-828-2380. Serviced by Santa Maria Parish.

North Central Bronx Hospital, Tel: 718-519-5000. Rev. Hippolytus Duru (Nigeria). Serviced by Jacobi Medical Chaplain.

U.S.V.A. Medical Center. Rev. Paul F. O'Connor, O.S.B.

Union Hospital, Tel: 718-200-2020. Serviced by St. Barnabas Hospital.

BRONXVILLE. *Lawrence Hospital*. Rev. Joachim Adione, Sr. Florence Mallon, S.C.

CALLICOON. *Community General Hospital*, Tel: 845-887-5530. Serviced by Holy Cross, Callicoon.

CARMEL. *Putnam Hospital Center*, Tel: 845-279-5711. Serviced by St. James the Apostle, Carmel.

CASTLE POINT. *V.A. Hudson Valley Healthcare*, Tel: 845-831-2000, Ext. 5453. Revs. Raymond A. Pavlick, Richard DeLaPena, Joseph W. Hickey (Retired).

COLD SPRING. *Julia L. Butterfield Memorial Hospital*, Tel: 914-265-3642. Serviced by Our Lady of Loretto, Cold Spring.

CORNWALL. *The Cornwall Hospital*, Tel: 845-534-2547. Rev. Peter Claver, Chap. Serviced by St. Thomas of Canterbury, Cornwall-on-Hudson.

DOBBS FERRY. *St. Cabrini Nursing Home*, Tel: 914-693-6800. Sr. Maryann Calabrese, Rev. Edwin F.D. Robinson, O.F.M., Dir. Pastoral Care.

Community Hospital of Dobbs Ferry, Tel: 914-693-0700. Serviced by Sacred Heart, Dobbs Ferry.

ELLENVILLE. *Ellenville Regional Hospital*, Tel: 845-647-6080. Serviced by the Church of St. Mary & St. Andrew, Ellenville.

GOSHEN. *Arden Hill Hospital*, Tel: 914-294-5441. Serviced by St. John, Goshen.

HARRIS. *Community General Hospital of Sullivan County*, Tel: 845-292-4525. Serviced by St. Peter, Monticello.

HARRISON. *Saint Vincent's Westchester*, Tel: 914-967-6500. Rev. James Yeakel, O.S.F.S., Dir. Pastoral Care.

HAWTHORNE. *Rosary Hill Home*, Tel: 914-769-0114. Rev. Martin Connors, O.P., B.A., S.T.B.

KINGSTON. *Benedictine Hospital*, Tel: 845-338-2500. Sisters M. Dorothy Huggard, O.S.B., Dir. Pastoral Care, Mary Feehan, O.S.B., Rev. Louis Yaya.

Kingston City Hospital, Tel: 845-331-3131. Rev. Edmund Burke.

MANHATTAN. *Bellevue Hospital*. Revs. Frederick O. Nyanguf, A.J., Chrisanth S. Mugasha, A.J.

Beth Israel Medical Center, Tel: 212-420-2759, Ext. 3. Revs. Francis Okoli (Nigeria), Damian Umeokeke.

Bird S. Coler Memorial Hospital and Home, Tel: 212-838-8155. Revs. Andrew Bielak (Poland), Harold F.X. O'Donnell, S.J.

Goldwater Memorial Hospital, Tel: 212-318-8000; 212-318-4738. Rev. Andrew Bielak (Poland).

Gouverneur Hospital, Tel: 212-374-4000. Serviced by St. Teresa, NYC.

Gracie Square, Tel: 212-988-4400. Serviced by St. Jean Baptiste.

Harlem Hospital, Tel: 212-281-4931. Rev. Emmanuel Okpalauwaekwe. Serviced by St. Mark.

Hospital for Special Surgery, Tel: 212-606-1757. Sr. Margaret Oettinger, O.P., Revs. Kevin Gillen, O.P., Carl Mason, Sean J. McConway, O.P., Michael Trainor, O.P.

Lenox Hill Hospital, Tel: 212-439-2547. Rev. Ralph Tillerkerante, S.S.S.

St. Luke's-Roosevelt Hospital Center, Tel: 212-523-4000.

Roosevelt Site. Revs. Lionel A. DeSilva, C.S.P. Tel: 212-523-6920, James F. McQuade, C.S.P.

St. Luke's Site. Serviced by Notre Dame, NYC

Manhattan Eye, Ear & Throat Hospital, Tel: 212-838-9200. Serviced by St. Vincent Ferrer.

Manhattan Psychiatric Center, Tel: 212-369-0500, Ext. 2530.

Medical Arts Center Hospital, Tel: 212-755-0200. Serviced by St. Patrick Cathedral.

Memorial Sloan Kettering Cancer Center, Tel: 212-639-5982. Revs. Kevin Gillen, O.P., Louis Mason, O.P., Sean J. McConway, O.P., Michael Trainor, O.P.

Metropolitan Hospital. Rev. Michael J. Sala, S.J.

Mount Sinai Medical Center. Revs. Apolinari J. Ngirwa (Tanzania), Matthew Abba.

New York Downtown Hospital - New York Infirmary, Tel: 212-312-5000; 212-233-5300. Rev. Reynaldo Domagas (Philippines). Serviced by St. Andrew, NYC.

New York Eye & Ear Infirmary, Tel: 212-673-3480. Serviced by Immaculate Conception, 414 E. 14th St., NY, NY 1009.

New York Presbyterian Hospital, Tel: 212-746-4690. Revs. Melchor Ferrer, S.D.B., Kevin Gillen, O.P., Louis Mason, O.P., Sean J. McConway, O.P., Carlos-Bartolome Quijano, O.P., Michael Trainor, O.P.

New York University Medical Center, Tel: 212-263-7300. Revs. Anthony Nwachukwu (Nigeria), Stephen Okeke (Nigeria).

Hospital for Joint Disease. Vacant. Serviced by Immaculate Conception Church, 414 E. 14th St., NY, NY 10009, Tel: 212-254-0200.

North General Hospital, Tel: 212-862-4380; 212-423-4511. Rev. Lawrence E. Lucas. Serviced by All Saints.

Presbyterian Medical Center, Tel: 212-305-3101. Rev. Michael M. Ferrer, S.D.B.

Allen Pavilion. Rev. Thomas McDonald.

Rockefeller University, Tel: 212-570-8000. Serviced by St. Catherine of Siena.

St. Vincent Hospital & Medical Center, Tel: 212-604-7858. Revs. Christopher B. Keenan, O.F.M., B.A., M.A., D.Min., James O'Connell, O.F.M.

Terence Cardinal Cooke Health Care Center, Tel: 212-360-3993. Cherilyn Frei, M.S., M.A., Dir. Pastoral Care.

U.S.V.A. Medical Center, Tel: 212-686-7500. Revs. Jose A. Salazar, Pasquale V. Laghezza, SS.CC., Andrew Sioleti, O.F.M.

MIDDLETOWN. *Horton Memorial Hospital*, Tel: 845-343-2424. Serviced by St. Joseph, Middletown.

MONTROSE. *FDR DVA Hospital*. Rev. Robert D. Tracy, O.Carm.

MOUNT KISCO. *Northern Westchester Hospital*, Tel: 914-666-1200. Rev. Francis Anane. Serviced by St. Francis of Assisi, Mt. Kisco.

MOUNT VERNON. *Mount Vernon Hospital*, Tel: 914-664-8000. Rev. Isaac Aganbi.

NEW HAMPTON. *MID Hudson Psychiatric Center*. Serviced by visiting priests.

NEW ROCHELLE. *Sound Shore Medical Center*, Tel: 914-632-5000. Revs. Andrew Bielak (Poland), Andres Fernandez-Lopez Pelaez. Chaplain, contact hospital operator.

NEWBURGH. *St. Luke Hospital*, Tel: 845-561-4400. Rev. Peter Claver. Serviced by St. Patrick, Newburgh.

NORTH TARRYTOWN. *Phelps Memorial Hospital*, Tel: 914-631-0720. Serviced by St. Theresa's, Sleepy Hollow.

NYACK. *Nyack Hospital*, Tel: 845-358-6200. Deacon James Gorman, Dir., P.C. Serviced By St. Ann, Nyack.

ORANGEBURG. *Rockland Psychiatric Center*. Serviced by area parishes.

OSSINING. *Stony Lodge Hospital*, Tel: 914-941-7400. Serviced by St. Augustine, Ossining.

PEEKSKILL. *Hudson Valley Hospital Center*, Tel: 914-737-9000. Vacant. Serviced by Holy Spirit, Cortlandt Manor.

POMONA. *Dr. Robert L. Yeager Health Center*. Serviced by St. Boniface, Monsey, NY

PORT JERVIS. *Bon Secours Community Hospital*, Tel: 845-856-5351. Deacons Albert W. Perroult, Dir. Pastoral Care, John Nash.

POUGHKEEPSIE. *St. Francis Hospital*, Tel: 845-471-2000. Sr. Marie Bernadette Wyman, Dir. Pastoral Care, Rev. Zeverin Emagalit, Pastoral Care Assoc., Sisters Alice Howley, Pastoral Care Assoc., Marie Colette, O.S.F., Pastoral Care Assoc., Patricia Nugent, Pastoral Care Assoc., Cathy O'Shea, Pastoral Care Assoc., Deacons Frank S. Ottaviano, Pastoral Care Assoc., (Beacon), Dennis White, Pastoral Care Assoc., (Beacon), Rev. Joseph Mali (Nigeria).

Hudson River Psychiatric Center, Tel: 845-452-7378. Rev. Augustine Graap, O.Carm.

Vassar Brothers Hospital 12601. Tel: 845-454-8500. Rev. Msgr. John Farley, Rev. David A. DeSimone. Serviced by St. Mary's Church, 231 Church St., Poughkeepsie, NY 12601, Telephone: 845-452-8250.

RHINEBECK. *Northern Dutchess Hospital*, Tel: 845-876-4583. Serviced by Good Shepherd, Rhinebeck.

RYE. *Rye Psychiatric Hospital Center*, Tel: 914-967-4567. Serviced by Church of the Resurrection, Rye.

STATEN ISLAND. *Bayley Seton Campus*, Tel: 718-354-6000. Serviced through St. Vincent's Hospital.

Richmond University Medical Center, Tel: 718-818-1234. Revs. Ralph Dawis, Chap., Clement Kalu.

Seaview Hospital Rehabilitation Center and Home, Tel: 718-371-3000, Ext. 3284. Rev. Edward Costello, O.F.M.Conv.

Staten Island University Hospital North. Revs. John DeLora, Eduardo Amora (Philippines).

Staten Island University Hospital South, Tel: 718-260-2000. Revs. John DeLora, Deogracias Linago, Pastoral Care, Joseph Raj (India).

SUFFERN. *Good Samaritan Hospital*, Tel: 914-357-3300. Sr. Margaret Strauch, S.S.N.D., Mgr. of Pastoral Care, Revs. Brian Coffey, M.H.M., Chap., Frank T. Wilder, O.A.R., Sr. Sheila Mullins, O.P., Chap.

TUXEDO PARK. *Tuxedo Memorial Health Care Center*, Tel: 914-351-4751. Vacant.

VALHALLA. *Blythdale Children's Hospital*, Tel: 914-592-7555. Serviced by Holy Name of Jesus.

Westchester Medical Center, Tel: 914-347-7000. Rev. Kenneth Chigbo (Nigeria). Night coverage by The Magdalene Pocantico Hills.

The Magdalene Pocantico Hills Night Coverage: Revs. Kenneth Chigbo (Nigeria), Joseph Dietz, Deacon Cecil Kenesic.

WARWICK. *St. Anthony Community Hospital*, Tel: 845-986-2276. Rev. Henry Tonto, S.M.M.M.

WASSAIC. *Taconic, D.D.S.O.* Serviced by Immaculate Conception Armenia.

WEST HAVERSTRAW. *Helen Hayes Hospital*, Tel: 845-947-2200. Serviced by Marion Shrine, Salesians.

WHITE PLAINS. *Burke Rehabilitation Center*, Tel: 914-948-0050. Rev. John Bauman, Sr. Laura Morgan, F.M.S.C.

New York Hospital - Cornell Medical Center Westchester Division, Tel: 914-949-9819. Served by Our Lady of Sorrows, Mamaroneck, NY.

White Plains Hospital, Tel: 914-681-0600. Rev. Louis Maram Reddy (India).

YONKERS. *St. John's Riverside Hospital*, Tel: 914-964-4444. Rev. Nicholas Nwagwu. Park Care Pavillion (formerly Yonkers General); Night Call-Christ the King, Yonkers, (914-963-7474). Serviced by St. Joseph's, Yonkers.

St. Joseph's Medical Center, Tel: 914-378-7000. Sr. Dolores Doyle, P.B.V.M., Dir. Pastoral Care, Rev. Thomas Murphy, O.F.M.Cap., Sr. Margaret Kelly, S.C.

On Duty Outside the Archdiocese:

Rev. Msgrs.—

Brown, Charles, Congregation Pro, Doctrina Fidei

Irwin, Kevin W., Catholic University of America, Washington, DC.

Meier, John P., Notre Dame Univ., South Bend, IN.

Shelley, Thomas J., Fordham

Stern, Robert L., Catholic Near East Welfare Association, 1011 First Ave., 10022-4195.

Revs.—

Altrui, Ronald P., Pennsylvania

Dillon, Richard J., University of Milan.

Hartmann, Edward J., Archdiocese of Fairbanks, Fairbanks, AK 99701.

Imbelli, Robert P., Boston College, Boston, MA.

Martin, William F., Christian Foundation for Children & Adults, P.O. Box 65, Warren, VT 05674.

Quinn, John L., Cross International Catholic Outreach, Pompano Beach, FL.

Sandstrom, Philip, American College, Louvain, Belgium.

Serra, Dominic, Catholic University of America, Washington, DC 20261.

Smarsh, Charles F., University of Maryland.

Graduate Studies:

Revs.—

Cleary, William

D'Alliessi, Daniel

Ernest, Matthew S.

Military Chaplains:

Rev. Msgr.—

Hill, Philip W., Office of the Chief of Chaplains, 2700 Army Pentagon, Washington, DC.

Revs.—

Lindblad, Karl-Albert, 2031 Nicklaus Dr., Suffolk, VA 23435. U.S.N.

Mandato, Kieran, 7437 Heatherfield Ln., Box 1799, Alexandria, VA 22315.

McGeory, Peter, US Navel Academy Chaplain's Office, 101 Cooper Rd., Annapolis, MD 21402.

Muhm, William M., 4499 Brisbane Way #4, Oceanside, CA 92054.

O'Reilly, Edward M. (Retired)

Pugliese, Francis A., PSC 557, Box 1921, Fpo, AP 96379-1921.

Absent on Sick Leave:
Revs.—
Adams, Walter C. (Retired)
D'Angelo, Thomas P.
D'Incecco, Alfred
Kosnik, Eugene
Leo, Arthur R.
Ross, Brendan
Ryan, Stephen M.
Welton, Arthur T.

On Leave of Absence:
Revs.—
Altrui, Ronald P.
Betances-Torres, Martin
Borkowski, Francis
Selvaraj, Peter

Retired:
Most Revs.—
Ahern, Patrick V., D.D., John Cardinal O'Connor Clergy Residence, 5655 Arlington Ave., Bronx, 10471.
Brucato, Robert A., D.D., V.G., John Cardinal O'Connor Clergy Residence, 5655 Arlington Ave., Bronx, 10471.
McCormack, William J., D.D., Our Lady of the Scapular and St. Stephen, 142 E. 29, 10016.
Mestice, Anthony F., D.D., Our Lady of Consolation Residence, 3103 Arlington Ave., Bronx, 10463.
Sheridan, Patrick J., D.D., John Cardinal O'Connor Clergy Residence, 5655 Arlington Ave., Bronx, 10471.
Rev. Msgrs.—
Ahern, John B., Our Lady of Loreto, 309 Elizabeth St., 10012.
Ansbro, Francis J., Assumption, 131 Union Ave., Peekskill, 10566.
Bardes, George F., John Cardinal O'Connor Clergy Residence, 5655 Arlington Ave., Bronx, 10471.
Birkle, Walter A., St. John the Baptist, 670 Yonkers Ave., 10704.
Boyle, Francis V., John Cardinal O'Connor Clergy Residence, 5655 Arlington Ave., Bronx, 10471.
Brennan, Dermot R., John Cardinal O'Connor Clergy Residence, 5655 Arlington Ave., Bronx, 10471.
Byrne, Harry J., John Cardinal O'Connor Clergy Residence, 5655 Arlington Ave., Bronx, 10471.
Clyne, Vincent F., 376 Baden Pl., Staten Island, 10306.
Collins, Timothy, John Cardinal O'Connor Clergy Residence, 5655 Arlington Ave., Bronx, 10471.
Corrigan, Bernard J., St. Stephen, 75 Sanfordville Rd., Warwick, 10990.
Cox, James, 999 Shapley Rd., Bainbridge, 13733.
Curran, Hugh D., St. Catherine's Parish, 25 Second Ave., Pelham, 10803.
Doherty, John T., John Cardinal O'Connor Clergy Residence, 5655 Arlington Ave., Bronx, 10471.
Duffy, Francis X., John Cardinal O'Connor Clergy Residence, 5655 Arlington Ave., Bronx, 10471.
Dunne, Joseph A., Our Lady of Consolation Residence, 3103 Arlington Ave., Bronx, 10463.
Ford, Robert A., John Cardinal O'Connor Clergy Residence, 5655 Arlington Ave., Bronx, 10471.
Fowler, Eugene A., Ferncliff Nursing Home, 21 Ferncliff Rhinebeck, Rock Tavern, 12575.
Gerathy, Kenneth A., Our Lady of Consolation Residence, 3103 Arlington Ave., Bronx, 10463.
Gillen, John J., St. Benedict, 2969 Otis Ave., Bronx, 10465.
Kenny, Walter F., S.T.D., St. Augustine, 18 Cherry Ave., Larchmont, 10538.
Loughman, Kenneth M., Most Precious Blood, 42 Walnut St., Walden, 12586.
Marinacci, Nicolas, St. Patrick's Old Cathedral, 263 Mulberry St., 10012.
McCormack, Robert, Convent of St. Brigitta, 4 Runkenhage Rd., Danien, CT 06830.
McCorry, Edward J., 5 Daisy Ct., Suffern, 10901.
Mitty, Edward J., John Cardinal O'Connor Residence, 5655 Arlington Ave., Bronx, 10471.
Narkun, Peter P., Cardinal Hayes High School, 650 Grand Concourse, Bronx, 10451.
O'Brien, William, 142 Garth Rd., Apt. 4T, Scarsdale, 10583.
O'Donnell, Peter C., John Cardinal O'Connor Clergy Residence, 5655 Arlington Ave., Bronx, 10471.
Oliverio, Francis E., 214 Grove St., Cedarhurst, 11516.
Pavis, Victor S., John Cardinal O'Connor Clergy Residence, 5655 Arlington Ave., Bronx, 10471.
Peake, Daniel A., John Cardinal O'Connor Clergy Residence, 5655 Arlington Ave., Bronx, 10471.
Plo, John, c/o Luis Bolinches, 23-9 Pta 27, Valencia 46023 Spain.
Scanlon, Thomas F., Sts. Peter & Paul, 129 Birch St., Mt. Vernon, 10552.
Revs.—
Arold, Richard J., 422 Ocean Blvd., Unit 4B, Long Branch, NJ 07740.
Carroll, Patrick, 49 E. 73rd. St., 10021.
Chiang, John B., 264 Chung Cheng Rd. Shihlin, Taipai 111 Taiwan.
Ciaravolo, Ronald, 213 Fairview Ave., Box 898, Montauk, 11954.
Coleman, John J., Regeis Residence, 3200 Baychester Ave., Bronx, 10475.
Conte, James W., 2156 Catalina Blvd., San Diego, CA 92107.
Conti, John P., 537 Third St., Brooklyn, 11215.
Croke, Alfred M., John Cardinal O'Connor Clergy Residence, 5655 Arlington Ave., Bronx, 10471.
Crotty, John M., John Cardinal O'Connor Clergy Residence, 5655 Arlington Ave., Bronx, 10471.
Daly, Christopher H., John Cardinal O'Connor Clergy Residence, 5655 Arlington Ave., Bronx, 10471.
Darby, Thomas J., John Cardinal O'Connor Clergy Residence, 5655 Arlington Ave., Bronx, 10471.
Delaney, John J., J.D., Mary Manning Walsh Nursing Home, 1339 York Ave., 10021.
Derrenbacher, James W., John Cardinal O'Connor Clergy Residence, 5655 Arlington Ave., Bronx, 10471.
DeSanto, Joseph A., 6 Lennox Ct., Bon Aire, Apt. 709, Suffern, 10901.
Dibble, Michael, 5 Corte de la Canada, Martinez, CA 94553.
DiNola, Leonard J., 16 Green St., Somersworth, NH 03878.
DiSenso, Gerard, John Cardinal O'Connor Clergy Residence, 5655 Arlington Ave., Bronx, 10471.
Doyle, Philip R., Box 1088, Carmel, 10512.
Driscoll, Donald, 160 Locust Ave., Scarsdale, 10583.
Duane, Robert J., John Cardinal O'Connor Clergy Residence, 5655 Arlington Ave., Bronx, 10471.
Dumpson, Roland J., Franciscans Handmaids of Mary Convent, 15 W. 124th St., 10027.
Dwyer, John, Our Lady of the Sacred Heart, 120 Kings Hwy., Tappan, 10983.
Fazio, Cosimo R., Box 1895, New Smyrna Beach, FL 32170.
Fiorillo, Antimo, Santa Maria Parish, 2352 St. Raymond's Ave., Bronx, 10462.
Fussner, Donald T., St. Peter, 18 Barclay St., 10007.
Gallagher, Eugene P., 207 Kings Hwy., Warwick, 10990.
Geissler, Robert, 196 Azalea Cir., Jackson, NJ 08527.
Gigante, Louis R., P.O. Box 820, Philmont, 12565.
Gussoni, Lino, Via Rodini Tedeschi 19, Piacenza 29100 Italy.
Halborg, John T., 90 LaSalle St., Apt. 9C, 10027.
Hammer, Jefferson J., P.O. Box 589, Pine Bush, 12566.
Hickey, Joseph W., 297 S. Broadway, Apt. 5C, Tarrytown, 10591.
Holihan, John W., Our Lady of Consolation Residence, 3103 Arlington Ave., Bronx, 10463.
Jeffers, Robert A., Our Lady of the Rosary, 7 State St., 10004.
Kennedy, Robert T., J.U.D., J.D., 400 Symphony Cir., Hunt Valley, MD 21030.
Kuolt, Benedict J., John Cardinal O'Connor Clergy Residence, 5655 Arlington Ave., Bronx, 10471.
Lancellotti, Vincent A., John Cardinal O'Connor Clergy Residence, 5655 Arlington Ave., Bronx, 10471.
Leone, Arthur, Our Lady of Good Counsel, 230 E. 90th St., 10128.
Ma, Peter, St. Mary's Parish, 28 Attorney St., 10002.
McAndrew, Joseph P., 5 Crescent Dr., Apt. 45, Warwick, 10990.
McCann, Luke W., Ph.D., 65 Viola Ave., Leonardo, NJ 07737.
McDonald, Bernard J., 160 E. Main St., Port Jervis, 12771.
McDonald, Thomas F., John Cardinal O'Connor Clergy Residence, 5655 Arlington Ave., Bronx, 10471.
McGuire, John C., 65 Viola Ave., Leonardo, NJ 07737.
McKenna, John J., 196 Azalea Cir., Jackson, NJ 08527.
McMahon, Bernard, 301 E. 63 St., 10021.
Mulloy, Matthew, Our Lady of Consolation Residence, 3103 Arlington Ave., Bronx, 10463.
Navins, Robert J., Sacred Heart, 981 Castleton Ave., Staten Island, 10310.
Neilson, Richard J., P.O. Box 999, South Orleans, MA 02662.
Nielson, Thomas A., 19B Monmouth Ln., Whiting, NJ 08759.
O'Meara, Joseph P., St. Patrick's Old Cathedral, 263 Mulberry St., 10012.
O'Reilly, Edward M., P.O. Box 5592, Hudson, FL 34674.
O'Shea, Gerard, Rt. A1A, Apt. 920, Atlantic Beach, FL 32233.
Palomino, Esviardo, St. Lucy, 344 E. 104 St., 10029.
Pane, Andrew, 9 Pasadena Rd., Bronxville, 10708.
Pizzuto, Alfred, John Cardinal O'Connor Clergy Residence, 5655 Arlington Ave., Bronx, 10471.
Pucci, Alfred, Holy Family, 366 Watchogue Rd., Staten Island, 10314.
Reardon, John F., John Cardinal O'Connor Clergy Residence, 5655 Arlington Ave., Bronx, 10471.
Reinheimer, George E., Our Lady of Consolation Residence, 3103 Arlington Ave., Bronx, 10463.
Smolinski, Joseph J., 11 Dale Ave., Apt. 21, Highland Falls, 10928.
Smyth, James, St. Matthew, 616 Warburton Ave., Hastings-on-Hudson, 10706.
Sullivan, Frederick J., Our Lady of Consolation Residence, 3103 Arlington Ave., Bronx, 10463.
Sullivan, Joseph D., 603 Mill Pl., Montgomery, 12549.
Tiercelin, Harry, Bethanie 7 Rue Dupanloup, Orleans 45057 France.
Tos, Aldo J., 1 Columbus Cir., Apt. 529A, 10019.
Tou, John B., St. Bernadette, 12 Zion Rd., Singapore.
Tubridy, James J., John Cardinal O'Connor Clergy Residence, 5655 Arlington Ave., Bronx, 10471.
Walsh, Ronald J., 87 Star Crest, Sand Lake, 12153.
Whitson, Robley E., 73 W. Shore Rd., New Preston, CT 06777.

Permanent Deacons:
Abbamont, Thomas J., St. Ursula, Mount Vernon
Abels, Gregory, (Leave of Absence)
Acabeo, Valentin, Holy Cross, Bronx
Ackerman, Henry, (Leave of Absence)
Aglietti, Richard, St. Joseph, Millbrook
Alexandre, Andre, Holy Name, Manhattan
Almanzar, Andres A., St. John Vianney, Bronx
Alvarado, William, St. Columba, Hopewell Junction
Alvarez, Angel, St. Joan of Arc, Bronx
Alvarez, Robert, (On Leave)
Armo, John, St. John Evangelist, Mahopac
Attridge, James C., St. Peter & Paul the Apostle Parish, Brandenton, FL
Aviles, Stanley, St. Denis, Hopewell Junction
Baerga, Luis, St. John the Evangelist, Goshen
Baffa, John, St. Lawrence O'Toole, Brewster
Banker, Howard A., (Medical Leave)
Barone, John, Blessed Kateri Tekakwitha, La Grangeville
Battersby, William L., St. Mary, Mount Vernon
Beckford, Rodney, St. Charles Borromeo, Manhattan
Bellacicco, John A., St. Augustine, Highland
Bello, James, Holy Cross, Bronx
Bello, Rafael J., (Medical Leave)
Bernal, Enrique, Fort Mill, SC
Biasotti, John C., (Leave of Absence)
Blake, George W., St. Martha, Sarasota, FL
Bormann, Eugene, St. Anastasia, Harriman
Borsavage, Charles T., St. James the Apostle, Carmel
Bouwmans, Philip R., Lords Valley, PA
Brady, Walter, St. John & St. Mary, Chappaqua
Brockmann, Peter, Sacred Heart, Monroe
Brown, James A., SS. John & Paul, Larchmont
Bruno, G. Frank, St. Elizabeth Ann Seton, Shrub Oak
Buckley, John J., Sacred Heart Parish, Pinellas Park, FL
Buckner, Robert, Holy Cross, (Middletown) South Centerville
Bunyar, Perry A., St. Mary of the Snow, Saugerties
Buonocore, Dominick, St. Paul, Congers
Burke, Eugene F., St. Gabriel, Bronx
Burnett, Robert V., Antigua, WI
Burns, James T., St. Francis Assisi, Englewood, FL
Byrne, Kevin, St. Patrick, Yorktown Heights
Cacchione, George F., Our Lady of Mt. Carmel, Poughkeepsie
Calafiore, Michael R., St. Charles, Staten Island
Camacho, Ismael, St. Joan of Arc, Bronx
Camacho, Vidal J., St. Elizabeth of Hungary, Pompano Beach, FL
Canals, Dhoel M., Holy Family, Bronx
Cartwright, Gerard, St. James the Apostle, Carmel
Carvajal, Rafael, Christ the King, Bronx
Casadone, Dominick G., Sacred Heart, Newburgh
Cassaneto, Anthony P., St. Theresa of the Infant Jesus, Bronx
Castellane, William, St. Mary's, Newburgh
Chaparro, Juan, Sacred Heart, Bronx
Charbonneau, Andre, St. Elizabeth, Manhattan
Charlesworth, Myles J., Our Lady of Lourdes Parish, Raleigh, NC
Chiu, George, St. Mary of the Assumption, Katonah

Clemens, Robert A., St. Bartholomew, Yonkers
Collins, George J., St. Thomas More, Boynton Beach, FL
Colton, Thomas, Albany, NY
Conroy, Luke, St. Ann, Nyack, NY
Cookingham, Vincent, St. John the Evangelist, Goshen, NY
Coppola, George, St. Frances de Chantal, Bronx
Coppola, John J., St. Columbanus, Cortlandt Manor
Corsaro, Angelo, Sacred Heart, Monroe
Cosme, Felix, Gainsville, GA
Cotto, Angel L., Caguas, Puerto Rico
Crapanzano, John, Immaculate Conception, Stony Point, NY
Cruz, Edwin J., St. John Vianney, Bronx
Curran, Timothy, St. Mary, Washingtonville
Czerwinski, Edward, St. Joseph, Wurtsboro
Czerwinski, Mark, St. Paul, Congers
D'Aiello, Joseph, St. Vincent de Paul, Milford, PA
Da Costa, Orlindo, Our Lady of Fatima, Yonkers
Dalmer, Peter, Regina Coeli, Hyde Park
Damiano, Rocco, St. Mary's, Newburgh
Darlestin, Leones J., St. Catherine of Genoa, Manhattan
Daubman, Andrew, Blessed Kateri Takakwitha, La Grangeville
Dauerer, Walter P., St. Denis, Hopewell Junction
De Jesus, Jose L., St. Ann, Ossining
De Maio, Donald J., St. Peter the Apostle, Naples, FL
De Marco, Carmine J., Holy Name of Jesus, New Rochelle
De Meis, John, Our Lady of Grace, Staten Island
De Vivo, Michael, St. Patrick's, York, PA
Decker, Michael, St. Mary, Mother of the Church, Fishkill
Degenhardt, Carl, St. Ursula, Mount Vernon
DeGroat, Charles, St. Ann's, Nyack
DeMartino, Steven, St. Augustine, Ossining
Deschler, Bernard M., St. Thomas More; St. Edmund, Rockaway Pt., NY
Devlin, Charles, SS. John and Mary, Chappaqua
Di Fiore, Augustine, Most Holy Trinity, Mamaroneck
Di Targiani, Robert, (Medical Leave)
Dickson, Donald, (Leave of Absence)
Dingee, Richard D., Holy Family, Port St. Lucie, FL
Doherty, Joseph, St. Joseph, Kingston
Donovan, William, (Medical Leave)
Dowen, Roland, St. Gregory Barbarigo Parish, Garnerville
Dringus, William L., Holy Spirit, Albany, NY
Droge, Lawrence, St. Charles Borromeo, Staten Island
Droulette, Donald L., Beltsville, MD
Duncan, Robert, Sacred Heart, Monroe
Dunn, John, St. Stanislaus, Pleasant Valley, NY
Duran, Nelson, St. Anthony of Padua, Bronx
Edgerton, John M., Tarpon Springs, FL
Espinal, Hector, Immaculate Conception, Staten Island
Esposito, Robert A., The Villages, FL
Estela, Jorge, St. Peter's, Haverstraw
Fama, Arthur, St. Anthony of Padua, Redbank, NJ
Farmer, Leonard, St. Joseph, New Windsor
Faulkner, James, St. Anastasia, Harriman
Feliz, Luis J., Our Lady Queen of Martyrs, NYC
Fernandez, Delio, Our Lady Queen of Martyrs, Manhattan
Fernandez, Roberto, (Medical Leave)
Ferraiuolo, Anthony P., St. Joseph, New Windsor
Fontánez, Luis, Orlando, FL
Forte, Joseph, (Leave of Absence)
Fox, Michael J., Our Lady of Fatima, Scarsdale
Francis, James, Sts. Peter and Paul, Bronx
Frohbose, John M., St. Paul, Bullville
Frohmiller, Richard J., St. Joseph, Kingston
Garcia, Rene, Our Lady of Guadalupe, Manhattan
Gaskin, Theodore A., St. Pius X, Scarsdale
Glover, William, St. Patrick, Newburgh
Gohl, Frank, Regina Coeli, Hyde Park
Gomas, Kelly, (Leave of Absence)
Gontcharuk, Robert, Holy Name of Jesus, New Rochelle
González, Faustino, La Coruna, Spain
González, Ismael, Nuestra Senora de la Asuncion, Caguas, Puerto Rico
Gorman, James, St. Paul, Congers
Gorzka, Stephen S., (Leave of Absence)
Grady, Paul, (Leave of Absence)
Graham, Patrick, St. Margaret Mary, SI
Granda, Miguel E., St. Gabriel, Bronx
Gray, Donald, Holy Family, New Rochelle
Grosso, Edward, Assumption, Maybrook
Gruerio, Anthony G., St. James, Carmel
Guglielmo, Joseph N., Infant Savior, Pine Bush
Hafeman, Joseph R., St. Mary Mother of the Church, Fishkill
Haight, Peter R., Sacred Heart, Newburgh
Hall, Raymond, Holy Family, New Rochelle
Halter, Donald, St. Patrick, Newburgh
Hamilton, Eugene R., St. Peter, Haverstraw
Hamilton, James J., Our Lady of the Springs, Ocala, FL
Hanson, Lee, Sun City, AZ
Hayes, James R., Regina Coeli, Hyde Park, NY
Hernandez, Narcisco, Our Lady Queen of Martyrs, Manhattan
Hill, William J., St. Pius X, Scarsdale
Hogan, Patrick J., St. Martin de Porres, Poughkeepsie
Hopkins, Farrell J., St. Francis of Assisi, West Nyack
Horton, Robert, Blessed Kateri Tekakwitha, La Grangeville
Horvath, Robert J., Sarasota, FL
Hung, Franklin, St. Martin de Porres, Poughkeepsie
Hveem, Paul, St. Brendan's, Bronx
Hyland, Arnold, St. Mary of the Snow, Saugerties
Impallomeni, Alfred R., Our Lady of Mount Carmel, Yonkers
Irizarry, Pedro, St. Peter, Yonkers
Jarmick, Robert E., St. Martin de Porres, Poughkeepsie
Jean-Gilles, Gabriel, Miami, FL
Jesselli, Stephen, (On Leave)
Johnson, Robert Joseph, (Leave of Absence)
Jordan, Thomas, Holy Name of Mary, Montgomery
Juhasz, Lajos, (Unassigned)
Kawula, Lawrence, Sacred Heart, Newburgh
Kazimir, Martin, Albany, NY
Kelleher, John C., St. Catharine, Blauvelt
Kelly, John, St. Gregory Barbarigo, Garnerville
Kenefick, Cecil, St. Theresa, Briarcliff Manor
Klein, John P., St. William, Ward, SC
Knack, Lawrence F., St. Mary, Obernberg
Knight, Charles C., Our Lady of the Lourdes Parish, Marysville, OH
Koch, George J., Our Lady of the Lourdes, Sun City West, AZ
Kollar, John J., Our Lady of Fatima, Scarsdale
Lagotta, Anthony A., (Medical Leave)
Larkin, John J., Presentation of the Blessed Virgin Mary, Port Ewen
Laurato, Vincent I., St. Barnabas, Bronx
Lawlor, James, St. Charles Borromeo, Dover Plains, NY
Le Blanc, Vincent F., Westchester Medical Center, West Harrison
Leasiolagi, Taulafoga, St. John Vianney, Bronx
Li Greci, Christopher, St. Michael Chapel, Manhattan
Lieby, Joseph, St. Joseph, New Windsor
Liegey, Gabriel, Holy Redeemer, Brewster, MA
Lindley, Gerard, Regina Coeli, Hyde Park
Loeffler, Albert, St. Joseph, Middletown
Longo, Ralph D., Annunciation, Crestwood
Lopez, Francisco Javier, St. Martin of Tours, Bronx
Lousa, Pedro, (Leave of Absence)
Lugo, Alejandro, St. Cecilia, Manhattan
Mac Dougall, Thomas, St. Stephen The Martyr, Warwick, NY
Maher, James, St. Aedans, Pearl River
Maldonado, Eusebio, Holy Cross, Manhattan
Maloney, John R., St. Anthony, Nanuet
Man, Chi Sum, Transfiguration, Manhattan
Mangino, Charles, (Leave of Absence)
Manning, Cornelius J., St. Barnabas, Bronx
Marino, Philip A., (On Leave)
Maroon, Phillip J., St. Teresa of the Infant Jesus, Staten Island
Martinez, Luis A., Holy Rosary, Manhattan
Mayeski, Martin, St. Joachim & St. John the Evangelist, Beacon
Mazza, Albert, Holy Name of Mary, Croton-on-Hudson
Mazzei, Nicholas A., Our Lady of Mt. Carmel, Yonkers
Mazzella, Salvatore, Our Lady of Grace, Bronx
McCabe, Michael G., St. Augustine, New City
McCarthy, Richard, Sacred Heart, Monroe
McGarry, James, St. Catherine of Siena, Sebring, FL
McLaughlin, Richard, Holy Rosary, Hawthorne
McQuade, Joseph, Our Lady of Perpetual Help, Pelham Manor
McSherry, John W., St. Paul, Congers
Meier, Anthony C., Raleigh, NC
Mejia, Apolonio, St. Anselm's, Bronx
Mercado, Carlos V., Immaculate Conception, Bronx
Messina, Enrico, St. Denis, Hopewell Junction
Mitchell, Richard F., St. Clare, Staten Island
Mojica, Jose, St. Martin of Tours, Bronx
Monegro, Juan, Incarnation, Manhattan
Moran, Bernard, St. John the Evangelist, Mahopac
Morillo, Felix M., Good Shepherd, Orlando, FL
Mueller, William J., St. Mary Star of the Sea, Bronx
Mulryan, W. Joseph, Our Lady of Grace, Bronx
Munoz, Frankie, St. Philip Neri, Bronx
Munoz, Jose, Mt. Pocono, PA
Murphy, Daniel, Our Lady of Perpetual Help, Pelham Manor
Murphy, John G., St. Frances de Chantal, Bronx
Nash, John J., Bon Secours Community Hospital, Port Jervis
Nolasco, Rolando, Our Lady of Mercy, Bronx
Noonan, Emmet, St. Stephen the Martyr, Warwick, NY
Nunez, Acadio, (Leave of Absence)
O'Brien, Donald F., Scranton, PA
O'Brien, Henry F., St. Lawrence, Fairhope, AL
O'Brien-Lambert, Pedro, Our Lady of Lourdes, Manhattan
O'Connor, Gerard R., Clifton Park, NY
O'Reilly, John F., St. Mary, Mother of the Church, Fishkill
O'Sullivan, Mark, Regina Coeli, Hyde Park
O'Toole, Lawrence, St. Augustine, New City
Olivieri, Martin J., St. John the Baptist, Yonkers
Orlando, Francis B., Blessed Sacrament, New Rochelle
Ortíz, Louis, Ponce, Puerto Rico
Ortíz, Pablo, (Unassigned)
Osgood, Kevin, St. Patrick, Yorktown Heights
Ottaviano, Frank S., St. Augustine, Highland
Pacheco, Angel, St. Isaac Jogues Parish, Orlando, FL
Padron, Jose R., St. Pius V, Bronx
Palladino, Joseph, St. Joseph, New Paltz
Pappalardo, Augustine A., St. Gregory Barbarigo, Garnerville
Parchen, Raymond, Holy Spirit, Cortlandt Manor
Patricola, Salvatore P., O.F.M.Cap., St. John the Baptist, NYC
Pelech, Robert, St. Denis, Hopewell Junction
Pelella, John V., St. Thomas of Canterbury, Cornwall-on-Hudson
Pellegrin, Daniel, St. Bernard, White Plains
Pellegrini, Guy A., Annunciation, Crestwood
Pena, Jose, St. Joseph, Spring Valley
Pereira, Joaquim, St. Margaret of Cortona, Riverdale
Perez, Primitivo, Ocala, FL (Unassigned)
Peters, John, St. Joseph, Kingston
Pietkiewicz, Karl J., St. Mary of the Snow, Saugerties
Pino, Joseph, St. Jean Baptiste, Manhattan
Pino, Victor M., (Unassigned)
Pipher, Jesse E., Our Lady Queen of Martyrs, Sarasota, FL
Porcel, Carlos M., (Medical Leave)
Porcelli, Vincent, St. Mary, Marlboro, NY
Portalatin, Epimegnio, Blessed Sacrament, Bronx
Powers, John, St. John the Evangelist, Manhattan
Powers, William, (Leave of Absence)
Quigley, Donald M., St. Margaret of Cortona, Bronx
Radcliffe, Kenneth L., Resurrection, Central Harlem
Radzilowicz, John, St. Casimir, Yonkers
Ramos, Alfonso, Sacred Heart, Bronx
Ramos, Edmundo A., St. Patrick's Cathedral, Manhattan
Ramos, Epifanio, Puerto Rico
Ramos, Rafael, Puerto Rico
Rausch, Paul A., St. Thomas Aquinas, Forestburg
Reilly, John P., St. Columba, Hopewell Junction
Rentkowski, Joseph, St. Adalbert, Staten Island
Repke, John W., St. Mary, Marlboro
Repke, Robert, St. Peter's, Rosendale
Rescildo, Ralph J., Southbury, CT
Rettino, P. Robert, Lord's Valley, PA (Medical Leave)
Reynolds, Peter E., St. Columba, Chester
Riley, John M., St. Peter, Liberty
Rivera, Andrew A., St. John, Bronx
Rivera, José A., Aquas Buenas, Puerto Rico
Rizzo, Charles A., Blessed Sacrament, New Rochelle
Rodgers, James, Richmond, VA
Rodriguez, Arnaldo, Nativity, Manhattan
Rodriguez, Cristobal, Immaculate Conception, Bronx
Rodriguez, Hector R., St. Patrick's Old Cathedral, Manhattan
Rodriguez, Hector L., St. John Fisher, Richmond, TX
Rodriguez, Porfirio, St. Jude, Manhattan
Rodríguez, Jacinto, San Antonio, Guayama, PR
Romagosa, Guillermo P., (Medical Leave)
Rosado, Alejandro, St. Athanasius, Bronx
Rosado, Odalis R., (Leave of Absence)
Rosado, Reynaldo, St. Dominic, Bronx
Rosado, Ricardo, Mid-Orange Correctional Facility, Warwick
Rush, James J., Harrisburg, PA
Russell, Franklyn R., St. Patrick, Newburgh
Russo, Richard J., St. Jean Baptist, Manhattan
Sadowski, John, Immaculate Conception, Stony Point
Sakowicz, Albert, Albany, NY
Salamone, Victor A., St. Martin de Porres, Poughkeepsie

Salhany, Richard, Our Lady Help of Christians, Staten Island
Salomone, Ernest F., Immaculate Heart of Mary, Scarsdale
Sanchez, Carlos, Our Lady of Angels, Bronx
Sanchez, Oscar, Puerto Rico
Sandoval, Waldemar, St. Paul the Apostle, Manhattan
Santana, Richard, Palm Beach, FL
Santana, Robert, (Medical Leave)
Santiago, Abraham, St. Joseph, Yonkers
Santore, Louis, St. Patrick, Bedford
Scarfi, John, St. John the Evangelist, Mahopac
Schimpf, Robert, St. Joseph, Bronxville
Schlitt, Ronald, St. Christopher, Buchanan
Scott, John, St. Ann's, Nyack
Sepulveda, Miguel A., Puerto Rico
Sequeira, Ronald, O.L. of Refuge, Bronx
Serrano, Jose I., St. Jude, Marion Oaks, FL
Seymour, John L., St. Mary, Newburgh
Shiel, Thomas P., Palm Harbor, FL
Shkreli, Marash, St. Lawrence O'Toole, Brewster
Sin-Garciga, Felipe, St. Angela Merici, Bronx
Singler, John A., Our Lady Help of Christians, Staten Island
Slominski, Timothy, St. Augustine, Ossining
Smith, Henry, St. Mary of the Snow, Saugerties
Smith, John A., St. Edmond's, Rehoboth Beach, DE
Solanto, Joseph P., Holy Rosary, Bronx
Stafford, William, St. Thomas of Canterbury, Cornwall on Hudson, NY
Stahlnecker, James J., St. Mary of the Assumption, Staten Island
Steup, Fredrick C., St. Patrick, Newburgh
Stewart, George, Jay, NY
Suarez, Israel, Guaynabo, Puerto Rico
Sullivan, John D., Lady Lake, FL
Sullivan, John M., (Medical Leave)
Sweeney, Walter F., Sacred Heart of Jesus, Boulder, CO
Tayco, Renato, (Medical Leave)
Taylor, Victor, Atlanta, Georgia
Teng, Rudolph, St. Paul the Apostle, Yonkers
Testa, Warren, St. Columba, Hopewell Junction
Then, Rafael, Good Shepherd, Manhattan
Thomas, Jordan, Holy Name of Mary, Montgomery
Thompson, Alfred, Holy Child, Staten Island
Tirella, Rosario J., Holy Rosary, Staten Island
Tobin, William D., (Medical Leave)
Tobon, Stephen, St. Charles Borromeo, Staten Island
Tola, Vincente, Sunrise, FL
Topple, Edwin R., St. John the Evangelist, Saugerties
Torres, Luis A., Mayaguez, Puerto Rico
Torres, Luis J., St. Pius V., Bronx
Tosi, Victor, Immaculate Conception, Bronx
Trapani, Richard, St. Joseph, Middletown, NY
Trees, Donald F., St. Mary of the Snow, Saugerties
Treiling, John F., St. Lawrence O'Toole, Brewster
Troy, Patrick D., Sacred Heart, Dobbs Ferry
Vaccaro, William N., Our Lady of the Rosary, Port Chester
Valdez, Bienvenido, Our Lady Queen of Martyrs, Manhattan
Vargas, Thomas A., (Leave of Absence)
Vasquez, Domingo, Davie, FL
Vazquez, Fernando, St. Athenasius, Bronx
Vazquez, Juan F., St. Anthony, Bronx
Velez, Randy, Roseboom, NY
Venditto, Michael, Our Lady of Pity, Staten Island
Venezia, Ignatius, St. Boniface, Wesley Hills
Verboys, Joseph, Our Lady of Peace, Hewitt
Villanueva, Engracio G., St. Joseph-St. Thomas, Staten Island
Viola, Anthony, Immaculate Conception & Assumption, Tuckahoe
Weinstein, David, Immaculate Conception, Amenia
Weir, John E., (Medical Leave)
Weireter, Paul J., St. Patrick, Highland Mills
Weiss, Robert W., Coatesville, PA
Welhous, Albert V., SS. Philip & James, Bronx
Wengeroth, Edward, (Medical Leave)
White, Dennis, St. Patrick, Newburgh
Whiteman, Robert, J.D., Ed.D., (Leave of Absence)
Wilson, Michael, St. Elizabeth Ann Seton, Shrub Oak, NY
Winrow, Robert P., St. Joseph, Kingston
Witt, Joseph A., Sacred Heart, Suffern
Woods, Edward J., Our Lady of Mt. Carmel, Middletown
Zambrana, Wallace, Our Lady of Sorrows, Manhattan
Zatarga, Michael, St. Joan of Arc, Boca Raton, FL

INSTITUTIONS LOCATED IN THE ARCHDIOCESE

[A] SEMINARIES, ARCHDIOCESAN

YONKERS. *Cathedral Prep Program* (1963) 201 Seminary Ave., 10704. Tel: 914-968-1340; Fax: 914-968-6671. Email: cprep@dunwoodie.edu. Web: www.cathedralprep.com. Revs. Luke M. Sweeney, S.T.L., Dir. of Vocations; Luis F. Saldana, S.T.D (Cand.), Asst. Vocation Dir. Hispanic Vocations; Andrew King, S.T.D. (Cand.).

St. John Neumann Seminary College At St. Joseph's Seminary Dunwoodie (1977) 201 Seminary Ave., 10704-1896. Tel: 914-964-3025; Fax: 914-968-6671. Email: sjnrh@archny.org. Web: www.archny.org; www.archnyvocations.org. Revs. Luis F. Saldana, S.T.D (Cand.), Rector; Luke M. Sweeney, S.T.L., Dir. Vocations & Formation Advisor; Daniel O'Reilly, M.A., Spiritual Dir. Priests 3.

St. Joseph's Seminary (1896) Archdiocesan Major Seminary, 201 Seminary Ave., 10704-1896. Tel: 914-968-6200; Fax: 914-376-2019. Email: sjs@archny.org. Web: www.ny-archdiocese.org/pastoral/seminary.cfm. Most Rev. Gerald T. Walsh, M.S.W., D.D., Rector; Revs. Donald F. Haggerty, S.T.D., Asst. Spiritual Dir.; Joseph Henchey, C.S.S.; Andrew King, S.T.D. (Cand.), Dean of Students & Admissions, Grad. Studies, Washington, DC; Kevin O'Reilly, S.T.D., Academic Dean; Luke M. Sweeney, S.T.L., Vocation Dir.; Luis F. Saldana, S.T.D (Cand.), Rector, St. John Neumann Seminary College; Michael Morris, M.A., Faculty Sec.; Daniel O'Reilly, M.A., Spiritual Dir., St. John Neumann Seminary College; Charles Szinos, M.Div., Spiritual Dir.; Sr. Sara Butler, M.S.B.T., Ph.D. Non-Resident Faculty: Priests 9; Sisters 4; Lay Teachers 5; Students 45.

Non-Resident Faculty: Rev. Msgr. John A. Radano; Revs. Andrew D. Apostoli, C.F.R., M.S.; Peter Dugandzic; Benedict Joseph Groeschel, C.F.R., Ed.D.; Rev. Msgr. Michael F. Hull, S.T.D.; Revs. Joseph T. Lienhard, S.J., Dr. Theol. Habil.; Michael T. Martine, J.C.L.; Gerard F. Rafferty, S.S.L.; Timothy J. Scannell, Ph.D.; Dr. John Tricamo; Dr. Stephen Buglione, Ph.D., Psychologist; Dr. Richard Gallagher, M.D., Psychiatrist; Sisters Janet Baxendale, S.C., M.A.; Marie Pappas, C.R., Ph.D. (Cand); Monica Wood, S.C., M.A., M.L.S., Dir. Library Svcs.; Mary Frances Mills, O.S.F., M.S., Registrar; Ms. Marie Dundon, M.A.; Ms. Jennifer Pascual, D.M.A., Dir. Music.

[B] SEMINARIES, RELIGIOUS OR SCHOLASTICATES

BEACON. *St. Lawrence of Brindisi Friary, Province of the Stigmata of St. Francis,* 180 Sargent Ave., 12508-3993. Tel: 845-831-0394; 845-838-0759 (Infirmary); Fax: 845-831-0918; 845-838-1352 (Infirmary). Bros. Julius Tkaczyk, O.F.M.Cap., Vicar; Douglas Soik, O.F.M.Cap.; Tom Burns, C.S.C., (Retired); Antonine Lizama, O.F.M.Cap.; Revs. Gerard De Leonardis, O.F.M.Cap. (Retired); Sylvester Catallo, O.F.M.Cap.; Robert Brennan (Retired); James W. Jones, O.F.M.Cap. (Retired); Sigmund Klimowicz, O.F.M.Cap.; Robert Grix, O.F.M.Cap.; Luke Guastella, O.F.M.Cap.; Gabriel Massaro, O.F.M.Cap. (Friary and Infirmary) Priests 8; Brothers 8; Lay Staff 19.

BRONX. *Ciszek Hall* Residence for Jesuit Scholastics and Brothers engaged in Philosophy and Theology Studies at Fordham University., 2502 Belmont Ave., 10458-6282. Tel: 347-329-5857; Fax: 718-365-3166. Revs. Vincent B. Sullivan, S.J., Rector; Richard Zanoni, S.J., Asst. Rector. Scholastics 24; Priests 3. In Res. Rev. Inacio Jussa, S.J.

STATEN ISLAND. *Society of St. Paul,* 2187 Victory Blvd., 10314. Tel: 718-761-0047; Fax: 718-761-0057. Email: provincialoffice@stpauls.us. Web: www.stpauls.us. Bros. Kevin J. Cahill, S.S.P., Book Store Coord.; Lawrence H. Schubert, S.S.P., Bursar's Office; Rev. Edmund C. Lane, S.S.P., Editor-in-Chief; Very Rev. Ernesto Tigreros, S.S.P., Prov. Supr.; Rev. Francis J. Parella, S.S.P. (Retired); Bros. Edward Donaher, S.S.P., Art Dir.; Robert Konrad, S.S.P., Mktg.; Peter Lyne, S.S.P., Mktg.; Joseph Dubois, S.S.P., Mailing; Vincent Minj, S.S.P., Parish Exhibits; Benedict Santoro, S.S.P., Book Store Coord.; Rev. Matthew Roehrio, S.S.P., Dir. Mktg.; Bros. Jerome Bauer, S.S.P., Graphics Dept./Junior Professed; Richard Brunner, S.S.P., Voc. Dir.; Emmanuel Cana, S.S.P., Bookstore Dir.; Revs. Joseph Eruppakkatt, S.S.P., Dir. of the Apostolate; Joseph Javillo, S.S.P., Prov. Bursar; Arthur Palisada, S.S.P., Translator; Tony Bautista, Formation Dir.; Bros. Frank Sadowski, S.S.P., Editorial Office; Joshua Seidl, S.S.P., Parish Exhibits. Priests 8; Brothers 13.
In Res. Bro. Antonio Paredes.

SUFFERN. *Tagaste Monastery* Major Seminary of the Province of St. Augustine of the Augustinian Recollect Fathers & Brothers. , 220 Lafayette Ave., 10901. Tel: 845-357-0067; Fax: 845-369-0625. Email: tagaste@optonline.net. Web: www.tagastemonastery.org. Revs. Ramon Gaitan, O.A.R., Prior; Frank T. Wilder, O.A.R., Prior; Marlon Beof, O.A.R., Prefect of Students; John Gruben, O.A.R., Novice Master; Bros. Joseph Joly, O.A.R.; Jorge Valdivia, O.A.R. Priests 5; Brothers 3; Simple Professed 3.

[C] COLLEGES AND UNIVERSITIES

NEW YORK. *College of Mount Saint Vincent* (Coed); Founded by the Sisters of Charity of Saint Vincent de Paul. Chartered by the University of the State of New York., 6301 Riverdale Ave., 10471-1093. Tel: 718-405-3200; Fax: 718-549-2603. Email: carol.finegan@mountsaintvincent.edu. Web: www.mountsaintvincent.edu. Charles L. Flynn Jr., Ph.D., Pres.; Bro. Daniel Adams, Dean, Undergraduate College; Madeline Melkonian, Vice Pres. Institutional Advancement and College Relations; Dr. Guy Lometti, Provost. Brothers 2; Sisters 4; Lay Faculty 69; Total Enrollment 1,980.

Marymount Manhattan College Chartered by the Univ. of the State of NY., 221 E. 71st St., 10021. Tel: 212-517-0400. Email: vdorgan@mmm.edu. Web: www.mmm.edu. Dr. Judson Shaver, Pres.; Dawn Webber, Vice Pres. Academic Affairs; Christy Gaiti, Vice Pres. Student Affairs (Acting); Paul Ciraulo, Vice Pres. Business & Financial Affairs; Mary Kay Demetry-Jeynes, Dean Courses for Adults; Jeanne Evans, Dir. College Rels. & Institutional Advancement; Sr. Virginia Dorgan, R.S.H.M., Campus Min. Sisters 3; Students 2,330.

BRONX. **Fordham University* (1841) Second campus and Branch campus at Lincoln Center, New York, NY 10023 and 400 Westchester Ave., West Harrison, NY 10528. Chartered by the Legislature of the State of New York., 441 E. Fordham Rd., 10458. Tel: 718-817-3040; Fax: 718-817-3050. Web: www.fordham.edu. Rev. Joseph M. McShane, S.J., Pres.; Mr. John J. Lordan, Senior Vice Pres., CFO & Treas.; Dr. Stephen Freedman, Senior Vice Pres. & Chief Academic Officer; Al Checcio, Vice Pres. Devel. & Univ. Rels.; Rev. Msgr. Joseph Quinn, Vice Pres. Mission & Min.; Mr. Frank Simio, Vice Pres. Finance; Dr. Frank J. Sirianni, Vice Pres. Information Technology; Mr. Jeffrey L. Gray, Vice Pres. Students Affairs; Dr. Brian Byrne, Vice Pres. Lincoln Center; Dr. Peter Stace, Vice Pres. for Enrollment; Mr. Marco Valera, Vice Pres. Facilities Mgmt.; John P. Harrington, Dean, Arts & Sciences Faculty; Dr. Nancy Busch, Dean, Graduate School of Arts & Sciences; Dr. Michael Latham, Interim Dean, Fordham College at Rose Hill; Dr. Donna Rapaccioli, Dean, College of Business Admin.; Dr. Robert Himmelberg, Interim Dean, Graduate School Business Admin.; Dr. James Hennessy, Dean, Graduate School Educ.; William Treanor, L.L.B., Dean, School of Law; Dr. Peter B. Vaughan, Dean, Graduate School of Social Svc.; Rev. Robert R. Grimes, S.J., Dean, Fordham College at Lincoln Center; Dr. Isabelle Frank, Dean, Fordham College of Liberal Studies; Rev. Anthony J. Ciorra, Dean, Graduate School of Religion & Religious Educ.; Mr. Thomas A. Dunne, Vice Pres. Govt. Rels. & Urban Affairs. Priests 45; Sisters 8; Total Staff 2,961; Total Enrollment 14,666.

Manhattan College (1853) 4513 Manhattan College Pkwy., Riverdale, 10471. Tel: 718-862-7200; 800-622-9235; Fax: 718-862-8019. Email: admit@manhattan.edu. Web: www.manhattan.edu. Dr. Brennan O'Donnell, Pres. Priests 1; Brothers 6; Sisters 1; Lay Staff 168; Administrators 176; Total Enrollment 3,500.

MT. KISCO. *Legion of Christ College, Inc.*, 773 Armonk Rd., 10549. Tel: 914-773-1368; Fax: 914-773-1438. P. O. Box 162, Thornwood, 10594. Rev. Jose Felix Ortega, L.C., Contact Person.

NEW ROCHELLE. **The College of New Rochelle* (1904) Founded in 1904 by the Religious of the Order of St. Ursula. Chartered by the Regents of the University of the State of New York. The College is composed of four schools: School of Arts and Sciences (Women); Graduate School; School of New Resources; School of Nursing (Coed)., 29 Castle Pl., 10805. Tel: 914-654-5000; Fax: 914-654-5980. Email: info@cnr.edu. Web: www.cnr.edu. Dr. Stephen J. Sweeny, Ph.D., Pres. Tel: 914-654-5430; Fax: 914-654-5980; Dr. Ellen Curry Damato, Exec. Vice Pres.; Dr. Dorothy Escribano, Senior Vice Pres. Academic Affairs; Dr. Richard Thompson, Ph.D., Dean School of Arts & Sciences; Dr. Marie Ribarich, Acting Dean, Graduate School; Dr. Mary Alice Donius, Dean School of Nursing; Ms. Elza Dinwiddie-Boyd, Dean of School of New Resources; Judith Huntington, Vice Pres. Financial Affairs; Rev. J. Joseph Flynn, O.F.M.Cap., Chap.; Ana Fontura, Dean, Gill Library; Helen Wolf, Dir. Campus Ministry. Priests 1; Sisters 5; Total Faculty & Staff 438; Students 4,670.

Iona College (Coed); Education in the tradition of the Christian Brothers. Independent College, 715 North Ave., 10801. Tel: 914-633-2000; Fax: 914-633-2018. Email: webmaster@iona.edu. Web: www.iona.edu. Priests 1; Brothers 8; Sisters 4; Lay Teachers 377; Students 4,248.

Iona College Rockland Graduate Center, 2 Blue Hill Plaza-Concourse Level, P.O. Box 1522, Pearl River, 10965-8522. Tel: 845-620-1350; Fax: 845-620-1260. Bro. James A. Liguori, C.F.C., Ed.D., Pres.; Dr. Warren Rosenberg, Vice Pres. for Academic Affairs & Provost; Ms. Kelli Hudson, Vice Pres. Finance & Admin.; Mr. Charles Carlson, Vice Provost for Student Devel.; Dr. Rich Petriccione, Vice Pres. for Advancement & External Affairs; Dr. Brian Nickerson, Dean of School of Arts & Sciences; Dr. Vincent Calluzzo, Dean, Hagan School of Business; Mr. Richard Palladino, Dir. Libraries.

NEWBURGH. *Mt. St. Mary College* (1954) (Coed), 330 Powell Ave., 12550. Tel: 845-561-0800; Fax: 845-562-6762. Email: williams@msmc.edu. Web: www.msmc.edu. Rev. Kevin Mackin, O.F.M., Pres.; Dr. Iris Turkenkopf, Ph.D., Vice Pres. of Academic Affairs; Darlene Benzenberg, Registrar; Sr. Kathleen Hickey, C.S.J., Dir. Campus Min.; Barbara Pertuzzelli, Library Dir. Divisions: Arts & Letters; Education; Business; Nursing; Natural Sciences; Mathematics & Information Technology; Philosophy & Religious Studies; Social Sciences. Sisters 3; Lay Teachers 78; Students 2,712.

ORANGEBURG. *Dominican College* (1952) Chartered by University of the State of New York., 470 Western Hwy., 10962. Tel: 845-848-7800; Fax: 845-359-2313. Email: admissions@dc.edu. Web: www.dc.edu. Sisters Mary Eileen O'Brien, O.P., Ph.D., Pres.; Kathleen Sullivan, O.P., Chancellor; Dr. Thomas Nowak, Vice Pres. Academic Affairs & Academic Dean; John Burke, Vice Pres. Student Devel. & Dean of Students; Anthony Cipolla, Vice Pres. Financial Affairs & Chief Fiscal Officer; Dorothy Filoramo, Vice Pres. Institutional Advancement; Brian Fernandes, Vice Pres. Enrollment Mgmt.; Mary McFadden, Registrar; Dr. William Stagmeyer, Institutional Research; Mr. Joseph Clinton, Athletics; Sr. Barbara McEneany, O.P., Campus Min.; Mr. John Barrie, M.A., M.L.S., Librarian. Sisters 10; Lay Teachers 72; Students 2,014.

Divisions: Dr. Sandra Countee, Allied Health; Dr. Mark Meachem, C.D.R., Arts & Sciences; Dr. Clare Pennino, Business Admin.; Dr. Maureen Creegan, Nursing; Dr. Barbara Socor, Social Sciences; Dr. Roger Tesi, Educ. Teacher; Rev. Ronald Stanley, O.P., Chap.

SPARKILL. *St. Thomas Aquinas College* 10976. Tel: 845-398-4000; Fax: 845-359-8136. Web: www.stac.edu. Sr. Margaret M. Fitzpatrick, S.C., Ed.D., Pres.; Dr. L. John Duvney, Vice Pres. Academic Affairs. Founded by Dominican Sisters of Sparkill in 1952. Senior coed college, chartered by Univ. of the State of New York. Sisters 2; Lay Professors 65; Students 2,700.

STATEN ISLAND. *St. John's University Staten Island Campus*, 300 Howard Ave., 10301. Tel: 718-390-4545; Fax: 718-390-4520. Web: www.stjohns.edu. Very Rev. Donald J. Harrington, C.M., Pres.; Rev. Patrick J. Griffin, C.M., Exec. Vice Pres. Mission & Branch Campuses, Staten Island; Sharon Lynch-Norton, Vice Provost; Donna Narducci, Assoc. Dean & Dir. Peter J. Tobin College of Business; James O'Keefe, Assoc. Dean College of Professional Studies; Stephen Kuntz, Assoc. Dean, School of Education, Graduate Div.; Denise Hopkins, Dean, Office of Student Affairs; Kelly Rocca, Assoc. Dean, St. John's College; Mark Meng, Librarian. Vincentian Community. Students 2,215.

VALHALLA. **New York Medical College, Administration Bldg.*, 40 Sunshine Cottage Rd., 10595. Tel: 914-594-4600. Web: www.nymc.edu.

[D] DEPARTMENT OF EDUCATION

NEW YORK. *Department of Education, Superintendent of Schools Office*, 1011 First Ave., 10022. Tel: 212-371-1000, Ext. 2800; Fax: 212-317-9236. Email: suptny@adnyeducation.org. Web: www.nycatholicschools.org. Dr. Timothy J. McNiff, Supt. Schools; Margot Pfohl, Chief of Staff; Mrs. Doreen DePaolis, Admin. Asst.

Office of Finance Tel: 212-371-1011, Ext. 2819; Fax: 212-758-3018. Mr. John Coyne, Exec. Dir.

Vocations Office, 1011 First Ave., 10022. Tel: 212-371-1011, Ext. 2803; Fax: 212-758-3018. Sr. Deanna Sabetta, C.N.D., Vocations Dir. for Rel. Life.

University Apostolate -Campus Ministry, St. Joseph Seminary, 201 Seminary Ave., Yonkers, 10704. Tel: 914-968-6200, Ext. 8252. Rev. Daniel O'Reilly, M.A., Dir.

Associate Superintendents: Sisters Anne Massell, P.B.V.M., Assoc. Supt. Personnel; Marie Pappas, C.R., Ph.D. (Cand), Assoc. Supt. Mission Effectiveness; Dr. Susan Abelein, Ph.D., Assoc. Supt. Professional Recruitment; Mrs. Fran Davies, Assoc. Supt. Communications & Public Relations; Mr. Michael Deegan, Assoc. Supt. Urban Education; Ms. Joanne DeMizio, Assoc. Supt. Curriculum & Staff Devel.; Mr. Henry Fortier, Assoc. Supt. Govt. Progs. & Public Policy; Dr. Joseph Gerics, Assoc. Supt. Secondary Educ.

Assistant Superintendents: Sr. Marie Morris, S.C., Asst. Supt. Special Educ.; Mr. Michael Borges, Asst. Supt. Religious Ed.; Mrs. Madeline Mitrevski, Asst. Supt. Student Information Svcs.; Ms. Dorothea Muccigrosso, Asst. Supt. Early Childhood.

Directors: Sr. Alice Kirk, O.P., Dir., Technology Staff Devel.; Mr. David DiCerto, Asst. Dir. Student Recruitment; Ms. Lucia DiJusto, C.F.P., Admin. Asst.; Mrs. Oneeka Jordan, SIS Helpdesk; Ms. Theresa Simmonds, Catechist Formation; Ms. Lillian Valentin, Data Collections.

District Superintendents: Mrs. Roseann Carotenuto, District Supt., Bronx; Mrs. Zoilita Herrera, District Supt., Staten Island; Mrs. Mary Jane Daley, District Supt., Rockland, Orange, Sullivan, Duchess, & Ulster; Sr. June Clare Tracy, O.P., Ph.D., District Supt., Manhattan; Mr. Philip Gorrasi, District Supt., Westchester/Putnam.

Archdiocesan Drug Abuse Prevention Program, 2789 Schurz Ave., 10465. Tel: 718-904-1333; Fax: 718-823-2177. Mrs. Frances Maturo, Dir.

Cooke Center for Learning and Development, 475 Riverside Dr., Ste. 730, 10115. Tel: 212-280-4477. Dr. Michael Termini.

Mother Franciska Elementary School, 850 Hylan Blvd., Staten Island, 10304. Tel: 718-447-1750; Fax: 718-447-8022. Patricia Cirbos, Education Supvr.

John Cardinal O'Connor School, 16 N. Broadway, Irvington, 10533. Tel: 914-591-9330; Fax: 914-231-7688. Mrs. Donna Taylor, Education Dir.

Joan Ann Kennedy Memorial Preschool, 26 Sharpe Ave., Staten Island, 10302. Tel: 718-876-0939; Fax: 718-816-6507. Dr. Kathryn Meyer, Education Dir.

The Therese Program for Children on the Autistic Spectrum

Bishop Patrick V. Ahern High School, 315 Arlene St., Staten Island, 10314. Tel: 718-982-5084; Fax: 718-982-5114. Mrs. Diane Cunningham, Exec. Dir.

Family Life/Respect Life Office, 1011 First Ave., 10022. Tel: 212-371-1000, Ext. 3185; Fax: 212-371-3382. Sr. Mary Elizabeth, S.J., Dir.

Archdiocesan Catechetical Office, 1011 First Ave., 10022. Tel: 212-371-1000, Ext. 2849; Fax: 212-980-1035. Sr. Joan Curtin, C.N.D., Archdiocesan Dir.; Ms. Ivelisse Sanchez, Asst. to Dir. Tel: 212-371-1000, Ext. 2859; Mrs. Nancy Doran, Dir. Catechist Formation. Tel: 212-371-1000, Ext. 2867; Sr. Teresita Morse, R.J.M., Dir. Formation of Catechetical Leaders. Tel: 212-371-1000, Ext. 2858; Mr. Oscar Cruz, Dir. Adult Catechesis/Catechumenate. Tel: 212-371-1000, Ext. 2851; Mrs. Kathleen Alonzo, Co-Dir. Catholic Youth Ministry. Tel: 212-371-1000, Ext. 2864; Mrs. Linda Sgammato, Dir. Special & Early Childhood Rel. Educ. Tel: 212-371-1000, Ext. 2852; Ms. Maureen McKew, Dir. Communications. Tel: 212-371-1000, Ext. 2855; Miss Ann Kearney, Financial Advisor. Tel: 212-371-1000, Ext. 2857; Ms. Anne Malloy, Co-Dir. New York Catholic Bible School. Tel: 212-371-1000, Ext. 2831; Mrs. Linda De Markey, Registrar: New York Catholic Bible School. Tel: 212-371-1000, Ext. 2860; Ms. Cynthia Martinez, Asst. Dir. Catholic Youth Ministry. Tel: 212-371-1000, Ext. 2831; Mr. James Connell, Webmaster. Tel: 212-371-1000, Ext. 2808.

Child Nutrition and School Management Service, 1011 First Ave., 10128. Tel: 212-371-1000, Ext. 2760; Fax: 212-421-3760. Mr. Edward Albano, Child Nutrition Dir.

Catechetical Regional Offices

Bronx, 4505 Richardson Ave., Bronx, 10470. Tel: 718-547-4212; Fax: 718-547-4231. Ms. Jeannette Chishibanji, Regional Director, Bronx.

Manhattan, c/o Mother Cabrini High School, 701 Fort Washington Ave., 10040. Tel: 212-923-0950; Fax: 212-543-3190. Sr. Catherine Ryan, F.S.P., Regional Dir., Manhattan.

Staten Island, 203 Sand Ln., Staten Island, 10305. Tel: 718-273-3833; Fax: 718-273-9602. Sr. Mary Crucifix Pandullo, C.S.J.B., Regional Director, Staten Island.

Dutchess/Ulster Counties, 26 S. Hamilton Ave., Poughkeepsie, 12601-2599. Tel: 845-471-5427; Fax: 845-471-5427. Mrs. Linda Fitzsimmons, Regional Dir., Dutchess/Ulster.

Central & Southern Westchester/Yonkers, 56 Dunston Ave., Yonkers, 10701. Tel: 914-965-0490; Fax: 914-965-0896. Sr. Zelide M. Ceccagno, M.S.C.S., Regional Dir, Yonkers, SCW & Adult Media Library.

Orange/Sullivan Counties, 19 Glenmere Rd., Florida, 10921. Tel: 845-728-0495; Fax: 845-728-0495.

Blessed Kateri Tekakwitha Center, P.O. Box 1011, Liberty, 12754. Tel: 845-292-9100; Fax: 845-292-9100. Sr. Kevin John Shields, O.P., Regional Dir., Orange/Sullivan Counties.

Rockland/Northern Westchester/Putnam Counties, 24 E. Main St., Stony Point, 10980. Tel: 845-429-4297; Fax: 845-429-4163. Mrs. Peg Hoblin, Regl. Dir., No. Westchester/Putnam/Rockland Counties. Tel: 845-624-3190 (Westchester/Putnam); Fax: 845-624-3190; Sr. Anne Ryan, P.B.V.M., Consultant. Tel: 845-534-3755.

Center for Spiritual Development, 96 Milton Rd., Rye, 10580. Tel: 914-967-7328; Fax: 914-967-7387. Anne Marie Wallace, Ph.D., Dir.

Instructional Television Tel: 914-968-7800; Fax: 914-968-2075. Mr. Michael Lavery, Admin. Dir.

215 Seminary Ave., Yonkers, 10704. Elementary School: Full-Time Sisters 142; Part-Time Sisters 51; Full-Time Brothers 10; Part-Time Brothers 1; Full-Time Order Priests 2; Part-Time Order Priests 3; Full-Time Lay Teachers 3,870; Part-Time Lay Teachers 988; Total Parish Enrollment 76,387; Total Inter-Parish Enrollment 1,709; Total Private Enrollment 4,250; High School: Full-Time Sisters 86; Part-Time Sisters 39; Full-Time Brothers 37; Part-Time Brothers 5; Full-Time Order Priests 27; Part-Time Order Priests 4; Full-Time Diocesan Priests 26; Full-Time Lay Teachers 2,304; Part-Time Lay Teachers 191; Total Diocesan Enrollment 10,588; Parish Enrollment 4,664; Private Enrollment 12,359.

[E] HIGH SCHOOLS, ARCHDIOCESAN

NEW YORK. *Cathedral High School* (Girls), 350 E. 56th St., 10022. Tel: 212-688-1545; Fax: 212-754-2024. Email: cathedhs@adnyeducation.org. Web: www.cathedralhs.org. Ms. Joan M. Close, Prin.; Rev. Robert J. Poveromo, Chm. Religion Dept.; Mrs. Rosemary Eivers, Asst. Prin. Priests 1; Sisters 5; Lay Teachers 41; Students 620.

BRONX. *Cardinal Hayes High School* (Boys)., 650 Grand Concourse, 10451. Tel: 718-292-6100; Fax: 718-292-9178. Email: hayes@adnyeducation.org. Web: www.cardinalhayes.org. Mr. Christopher J. Keogan, Prin.; Revs. Joseph P. Tierney, M.Div., Pres.; Harry Burke; Robert Harrison. Priests 3; Brothers 5; Sisters 1; Lay Teachers 62; Students 1,100. In Res. Rev. Msgr. Peter P. Narkun (Retired).

Cardinal Spellman High School, One Cardinal Spellman Pl., 10466. Tel: 718-881-8000; Fax: 718-515-6615. Email: spellman@cardinalspellman.org. Web: www.cardinalspellman.org. Neil McCarthy, Ph.D., Prin.; Revs. Trevor Nicholls, Pres.; John R. Kraljic; John T. Monaghan; James J. O'Shaughnessy; Peter R. Pilsner; Francis J. Principe. Priests 6; Sisters 2; Lay Teachers 80; Students 1,480. In Res. Revs. Thomas P. D'Angelo; Richard F. Gorman.

GOSHEN. *John S. Burke Catholic High School*, 80 Fletcher St., 10924. Tel: 845-294-5481; Fax: 845-294-0817. Email: jbyrnes@burkecatholic.org. Web: www.burkecatholic.org. Rev. Msgr. James T. Byrnes, Ph.D., Prin.; Ms. Sandra Jean, Asst. Prin. for Academics; Mr. Kevin Canty, Asst. Prin. for Student Affairs; Mr. John Dolan, Asst. Prin. for Operations; Mrs. Joanne Fitzpatrick, Procurator; Mrs. Joe L. Ruiz, Librarian. Priests 1; Lay Teachers 40; Students 504.

HARTSDALE. *Maria Regina High School*, 500 W. Hartsdale Ave., 10530. Tel: 914-761-3300; Fax: 914-761-0860. Email: mariareg@adnyeducation.org. Web: www.mariaregina.org. Sisters Danielle M. Baran, C.R., Pres., Prin. & Supr.; Mary Krystyna Kobielus, C.R., Librarian. Sisters of the Resurrection, Franciscan Sisters, Dominican Sisters. Sisters 8; Lay Teachers 31; Students 540.

HURLEY. *John A. Coleman Catholic High School* (1967) 430 Hurley Ave., 12443. Tel: 845-338-2750; Fax: 845-388-0250. Email: office@colemancatholic.net. Web: www.colemancatholic.org. Mr. Louis L. Tullo, Prin.; Doreen Kondratowicz, Librarian. Priests 1; Sisters 1; Lay Teachers 28; Students 192.

POUGHKEEPSIE. *Our Lady of Lourdes High School* (1954) 131 Boardman Rd., 12603. Tel: 845-463-0400; Fax: 845-463-0174. Email: lourdes@adnyschools.org. Web: www.ollchs.org. Rev. John M. Lagiovane, Prin.; Mr. Michael Krieger, Asst. Prin., Academics; Mr. Matthew Burke, Campus Min.; Bros. Henry Sawicki, F.M.S., Chm. Science Dept.; Gregory DelaNoy, F.M.S., Dir. Guidance & Asst. Prin. Faculty; James Stevens, F.M.S., Math Teacher; Mr. Charles Junjulas Jr., Dean of Men; Bro. Gregory DelaNoy, F.M.S., Asst. Principal, Faculty; Rev. John M. Lagiovane, Admissions; Mrs. Maureen Myers, Dean of Women; Ms. Judith Mletzko, Librarian. Brothers 2; Sisters 2; Lay Teachers 53; Students 726.

SOMERS. *John F. Kennedy Catholic High School*, 54 Rte. 138, 10589. Tel: 914-232-5061; Fax: 914-232-3416. Email: jfkhs@adnyeducation.org. Web: www.kennedycatholic.org. Rev. Mark G. Vaillancourt, Ph.D., Pres. & Prin.; Mr. Stephen T. Schmidt, Vice Prin. Academics; Deacon Alfred R. Impallomeni, Vice Prin. Faculty & Student Affairs; Sr. Barbara Heil, R.D.C., Dir. Admissions. Diocesian Priests, Sisters of the Divine Compassion. Priests 3; Sisters 7; Lay Teachers 29; Students 597.

STATEN ISLAND. *Monsignor Farrell High School*, 2900 Amboy Rd., 10306. Tel: 718-987-2900; Fax: 718-987-4241. Email: farrell@adnyeducation.org. Web: www.msgrfarrellhs.org. Rev. Msgr. John N. Paddack, Prin.; Rev. John P. Comiskey. Priests 2; Brothers 2; Sisters 2; Lay Teachers 64; Students 1,150.

Moore Catholic High School, 100 Merrill Ave., 10314. Tel: 718-761-9200; Fax: 718-982-7779. Email: moorecats@adnyeducation.org. Web: www.moorecatholichs.org. Douglas McManus, Prin.; Rev. Edmund P. Connors. Daughters of Our Lady of the Garden 2; Lay Teachers 55; Students 800.

WHITE PLAINS. *Archbishop Stepinac High School*, 950 Mamaroneck Ave., 10605. Tel: 914-946-4800; Fax: 914-684-2591. Email: stepinac@adnyeducation.org. Web: www.stepinac.org. Rev. Msgr. Anthony D. Marchitelli, Pres.; Mr. Paul Carty, Prin.; Rev. Thomas E. Collins, Assoc. Dean of Students. Priests 5; Sisters 2; Lay Teachers 45; Students 873.

Staff of School: Revs. Richard Vieras; Philip J. Quealy; Nathan Vail, F.S.S.P.

[F] HIGH SCHOOLS, PRIVATE

NEW YORK. *St. Agnes Boys High School*, 555 West End Ave., 10024-2795. Tel: 212-873-9100; Fax: 212-873-9292. Email: agneshs@adnyeducation.org. Web: www.staghs.org. Bro. Richard Van Houten, F.M.S., Prin. Brothers 3; Lay Teachers 19; Total Enrollment 300.

All Hallows Institute aka All Hallows High School (1909) (Boys), 111 E. 164th St., Bronx, 10452. Tel: 718-293-4545; Fax: 718-410-8298. Email: hallows@adnyeducation.org. Web: www.allhallows.org. Mr. Sean J. Sullivan, Prin.; Mr. Paul Krebbs, Pres. Congregation of Christian Sisters & Brothers 6; Lay Teachers 34; Students 640.

Aquinas High School (Girls), 685 E. 182nd St., Bronx, 10457. Tel: 718-367-2113; Fax: 718-295-5864. Email: aquinashs@adnyeducation.org. Web: www.aquinashs.org. Sisters Margaret Ryan, O.P., Pres.; Catherine Rose Quigley, O.P., Prin.; Rosalyn Fatigate, Librarian. Sisters 10; Lay Teachers 40; Students 675.

Convent of the Sacred Heart (Girls), One E. 91st St., 10128-0689. Tel: 212-722-4745; Fax: 212-996-1784. Email: coshhs@adnyeducation.org. Web: www.cshnyc.org. Dr. Joseph J. Ciancaglini, Head of School. Religious of the Sacred Heart. Sisters 2; Faculty 57; High School Students 254.

Cristo Rey New York High School, Inc. (2004) 112 E. 106th St., 10029. Tel: 212-996-7000; Fax: 212-427-7444. Web: www.cristoreyny.org. Rev. Joseph P. Parkes, S.J., Pres.; William P. Ford III, Prin. Sisters 2; Jesuit 2; Lay Teachers 25; Students 320.

**Cristo Rey New York High School, Inc.*, 112 E. 106th St., 10029. Tel: 212-996-7000; Fax: 212-427-7444. Email: cristorey@adnyeducation.org. Web: www.cristoreyny.org. Rev. Joseph P. Parkes, S.J., Pres.; William P. Ford III, Prin. Sisters 2; Jesuits 2; Lay Teachers 25; Students 320.

Dominican Academy (Girls), 44 E. 68th St., 10021. Tel: 212-744-0195; Fax: 212-744-0375. Email: dominica@adnyeducation.org. Web: www.dominicanacademy.org. Sisters Barbara Kane, O.P., Prin.; Geraldine Milbert, O.P., Librarian. Lay Teachers 18; Students 222.

La Salle Academy (Boys), 44 E. Second St., 10003. Tel: 212-475-8940; Fax: 212-529-3598. Email: lasalle@adnyeducation.org. Web: www.lasalleacademy.org. Dr. William B. Hambleton, Pres.; Bros. James Furlong, F.S.C.; Timothy Jones, F.S.C.; Mrs. Candace D. Hammonds, Prin.; Ms. Patricia Toney, Librarian. Brothers of The Christian Schools. Brothers 5; Lay Teachers 35; Students 400.

In Res. Bros. John Bassett, F.S.C.; Raymond Buck, F.S.C., (Retired); Stephen Caplice, F.S.C., (Retired); Leonard Wojtanowski, C.F.X.

Loyola School (Coed), 980 Park Ave., 10028. Tel: 212-288-3522; Fax: 212-861-1021. Email: loyola@adnyeducation.org. Web: www.loyola-nyc.org. Mr. James F. X. Lyness, Headmaster; Mr. Robert Sheehy, Bd. Chm.; Revs. Stephen N. Katsouros, S.J., Pres.; James J. Curry, S.J.; Michael E. Sehler, S.J. Society of Jesus. Priests 3; Lay Teachers 47; Students 209.

Mother Cabrini High School (1899) (Girls), 701 Ft. Washington Ave., 10040. Tel: 212-923-3540; Fax: 212-781-2051. Email: cabrini@adnyeducation.org. Web: www.cabrinihs.com. Brian Donahue, Head of School; Ms. Joan M. Close, Dean of Academics; Susan Fraleigh, Dean of Students; Mr. Matthew Bizzaro, Campus Min.; Erin A. Cicalese, Dir. Advancement; Mr. Daniel Gabriele, Librarian. Sisters 3; Lay Teachers 20; Students 350.

Notre Dame School of Manhattan (1912) (Girls), 327 W. 13th St., 10014. Tel: 212-620-5575; Fax: 212-620-0432. Email: ntdamehs@adnyeducation.org. Web: www.cheznous.org. Mrs. Maureen Noonan, Prin.; Dr. Virginia O'Brien, Pres. Sisters 5; Lay Teachers 18; Students 300.

Regis High School (1914) (Boys), 55 E. 84th St., 10028. Tel: 212-288-1100; Fax: 212-794-1221. Email: regishs@adnyeducation.org. Web: www.regis-nyc.org. Rev. Philip G. Judge, S.J., Pres.; Dr. Gary J. Tocchet, Prin.; Ms. Kristin Ross, Asst. Prin.; Mr. Nicholas de Spoelberch, Dean of Students; Revs. Anthony Andreassi, C.O.; Arthur C. Bender, S.J.; Edward F. Salmon, S.J. Society of Jesus. Priests 4; Lay Teachers 59; Students 532.

Res.: 53 E. 83rd St., 10028.

Rice High School (Boys), 74 W. 124th St., 10027. Tel: 212-369-4100; Fax: 212-348-4631. Email: ricehs@adnyeducation.org. Web: www.ricehs.org. Bro. Christopher D. Hall, C.F.C., Head of School. Congregation of Christian Brothers. Brothers 5; Lay Teachers 25; Students 259.

Xavier High School (Boys), 30 W. 16th St., 10011. Tel: 212-924-7900; Fax: 212-924-0303. Email: xavierhs@adnyeducation.org. Web: www.xavierhs.org. Rev. Daniel J. Gatti, S.J., Pres.; Mr. Michael Livigni, Headmaster; Mr. Joseph Sweeney, Asst. Prin.; Miss Janet Bonica, Registrar; Revs. James R. Van Dyke, S.J.; Robert V. O'Hare, S.J.; Bro. John Mulreany, S.J., Teacher Religion Dept.; Revs. Pierce A. Brennan, S.J.; Louis Garaventa, S.J.; Tracy Tong, Librarian; Michael McCabe, Dean of Students. Society of Jesus., (See listing for Xavier Jesuit Community for additional names of priests and brothers.) Priests 5; Jesuit Scholastics 1; Lay Teachers 71; Students 911.

BARDONIA. *Albertus Magnus*, 798 Rte. 304, 10954. Tel: 845-623-8842; Fax: 845-623-0009. Email: albertus@adnyeducation.org. Web: www.albertusmagnus.net. Joseph Troy, Pres. & Prin. Sisters of St. Dominic (Sparkill) 2; Lay Teachers 38; Students 454.

BRONX. *Academy of Mount St. Ursula* (1855) (Girls), 330 Bedford Park Blvd., 10458. Tel: 718-364-5353; Fax: 718-364-2354. Email: mtstursu@adnyeducation.org. Web: www.amsu.org. Rev. John A. Vigilanti, J.C.L., Ph.D., Pres.; Lisa Harrison, Prin.; Haydee Comacho, Librarian. Ursuline Nuns. Sisters 1; Lay Teachers 25; Students 350.

St. Catharine Academy (1889) (Girls), 2250 Williamsbridge Rd., 10469-4891. Tel: 718-882-2882; Fax: 718-231-9099. Email: catherin@adnyeducation.org. Web: www.scahs.org. Sisters Ann M. Welch, R.S.M., Prin.; Patricia Wolf, R.S.M., Pres. Sisters 8; Lay Teachers 4; Students 720.

Fordham Preparatory School (1841) (Boys), E. Fordham Rd., 10458. Tel: 718-367-7500; Fax: 718-367-7598. Web: www.fordhamprep.org. James J. Ryan, Bd. Chm.; Rev. Kenneth J. Boller, S.J., M.Div., Pres.; Mr. Robert J. Gomprecht, Prin.; Mr. Dennis M. Ahern, Asst. Prin.; Mrs. Theresa Napoli, Asst. Prin.; Mr. Steven Pettus, Dean of Students; Mr. Michael Lacinak, Dir. Guidance; Revs. John M. Costello, S.J.; Donald G. Devine, S.J.; Mallick J. Fitzpatrick, S.J.; Matthew C. Flood, S.J.; Joseph J. Kamienski, S.J.; John J. Leonard, S.J.; Stanley J. O'Konsky, S.J.; William J. O'Malley, S.J.; Charles D. Sullivan, S.J.; Raymond M. Sweitzer, S.J.; Susan Andrews, M.A., Librarian. Priests 1; Lay Teachers 72; Students 950.

Mount St. Michael Academy (Boys), 4300 Murdock Ave., 10466. Tel: 718-515-6400; Fax: 718-994-7729. Email: mount@adnyschools.org. Web: www.mountstmichael.org. Dr. Anthony Miserandino, Pres.; Bro. Larry Gordon, F.M.S., Prin. Brothers 8; Lay Teachers 55; Students 873.

Junior High School Tel: 718-515-6400; Fax: 718-994-7729. Web: www.mountstmichael.org. Mrs. Lillian Dippolito, Prin. Lay Teachers 7; Students 168.

Preston High School (1947) (Girls), 2780 Schurz Ave., 10465. Tel: 718-863-9134; Fax: 718-863-6125. Email: preston@adnyeducation.org. Web: www.prestonhs.org. Jane Grendell, Prin.; Linda Youngren, Asst. Prin.; Sisters Laura Donovan, R.D.C., Asst. Prin.; Loretta Marie Schollhamer, R.D.C., Librarian. Sisters of the Divine Compassion 3; Lay Teachers 40; Students 600.

DOBBS FERRY. *Our Lady of Victory Academy* (1945) (Girls), 565 N. Broadway, 10522. Tel: 914-693-1633; Fax: 914-693-5250. Email: olvictor@adnyeducation.org. Web: www.victoryhs.org. Sr. Joan Agro, O.P., Prin.; Patricia Wolf, Pres.; Sonia Brown, Librarian/Media/Computer Ed. Sisters of Mercy. Sisters 4; Lay Teachers 23; Students 400.

KATONAH. **The Montfort Academy*, 99 Valley Rd., 10536. Tel: 914-767-0325. Email: sterenzio@themontfortacademy.org. Web: www.themontfortacademy.org. Steven Terenzio, Headmaster.

NEW ROCHELLE. *Iona Preparatory School* (1916) (Boys), 255 Wilmot Rd., 10804. Tel: 914-632-0714; Fax: 914-632-9760. Web: www.ionaprep.org. Mr. Jim Irzyk, Pres.; Mr. George Teasdale, Prin.; Mr. Kieran Daly, Dean; Ms. Susan Natale, Dean; Mrs. Barbara Robertson, Chief Advancement Officer; Mrs. Dorothy Lamonaca, Dir. Fin. & Opers.; Kevin Kavanah, Librarian; Bros. James J. Adams, C.F.C.; William R. Harris, C.F.C.; Carmine P. Pellegrino; John A. Reynolds; Robert J. Roepke, C.F.C. Edmund Rice Christian Brothers North America. Brothers 5; Sisters 1; Lay Teachers 55; Students 725.

Salesian High School, 148 Main St., 10801. Tel: 914-632-0248; Fax: 914-632-1362. Email: salesian@adnyeducation.org. Web: www.salesianhigh.org. Revs. Patrick Angelucci, S.D.B., Dir. & Pres.; James Mulloy, S.D.B.; Thomas Provanzano, S.D.B., Coord. of Youth Ministry; Bros. Donald Caldwell, S.D.B., Guidance; Michael Equino, S.D.B.; Miguel Suarez, S.D.B.; James Zettel, S.D.B.; Sr. Barbara Wright, O.P., Asst. Prin.; John Flaherty, M.A., Prin.; Mr. Christopher Beal, Business Mgr.; Mr. Robert Molinaro, Dean of Students; Mr. Steven Sallustio, Vice Pres. Institutional Advancement; Paul Zaccagnino, Librarian. Priests 3; Brothers 3; Sisters 1; Lay Teachers 36; Students 503.

Ursuline School (1897) (Grades 6-12), (Girls), 1354 North Ave., 10804. Tel: 914-636-3950; Fax: 914-636-3949. Email: ursuline@adnyeducation.org. Web: www.ursuline.pvt.ny.us. Sr. Joan Woodcomb, O.S.U., Treas.; Mrs. Eileen Davidson, Prin.; Kathy Freeman, Librarian. Priests 1; Sisters 7; Lay Teachers 86; Students 815.

RYE. *School of the Holy Child*, (Grades 5-12), (Girls), 2225 Westchester Ave., 10580. Tel: 914-967-5622; Fax: 914-967-6476. Email: holychild@adnyeducation.org. Web: www.holychildrye.org. Ann F. Sullivan, Head of School; Joli Moniz, Admissions Dir.; Helen Kostelas, Librarian. Society of the Holy Child Jesus 1; Lay Teachers 52; Students (Upper School) 255; (Middle School) 89.

STATEN ISLAND. *St. John Villa Academy High School* (1932) 26 Landis Ave., 10305-3729. Tel: 718-442-6240; Fax: 718-447-6729. Email: sjva@adnyeducation.org. Web: www.sjva.org. Sr. Antonia Zuffante, C.S.J.B., Prin. Brothers 1; Sisters 12; Lay Teachers 33; Girls 579.

St. Joseph by the Sea, High School (Coed), 5150 Hylan Blvd., 10312. Tel: 718-984-6500; Fax: 718-984-6503. Email: josbysea@adnyeducation.org. Rev. Msgr. Joseph C. Ansaldi, Prin.; Rev. Michael P. Reilly. Priests 3; Sisters 6; Lay Teachers 69; Students 1,367.

St. Joseph Hill Academy (Girls), 850 Hylan Blvd., 10305-2095. Tel: 718-447-1374; Fax: 718-447-3041. Email: joshill@adnyeducation.org. Web: stjosephhill.org. Sr. M. Raimonde Bartus, F.D.C., Pres.; Angela T. Ferrando, Prin. Daughters of Divine Charity. Sisters 3; Lay Teachers 30; Students 435.

Notre Dame Academy High School, 134 Howard Ave., 10301. Tel: 718-447-8878; Fax: 718-447-2926. Email: ntdameac@adnyeducation.org. Web: www.notredameacademy.org. Sr. Patricia Corley, C.N.D., Pres.; Dr. Gregory Rossicone, Prin. Congregation of Notre Dame. Sisters 2; Lay Teachers 35; Girls 460.

WHITE PLAINS. *Academy of Our Lady of Good Counsel (High School)* (1922) (Girls), 52 N. Broadway, 10603. Tel: 914-949-0178; Fax: 914-682-3531. Email: cpeterson@goodcounselacademyhs.org. Web: www.goodcounselacademyhs.org. Sisters Carol Peterson, R.D.C., M.S., M.S.W., Prin.; Mary Alice O'Brien, R.D.C., Librarian. Sisters of the Divine Compassion 6; Dominican Sisters of Hope 1; Lay Teachers 26; Students 300.

[G] SPECIAL SCHOOLS

NEW YORK. *Grace Institute*, 1233 Second Ave., 10021. Tel: 212-832-7605; Fax: 212-486-2869. Email: info@graceinstitute.org. Web: www.graceinstitute.org. Dr. Mary Mulvihill. Sisters of Charity, Mt. St. Vincent. Sisters 4; Lay Teachers 4; Students 300.

John A. Coleman School, 590 Avenue of the Americas, 10011. Tel: 646-459-3401; Fax: 646-459-3689. Email: sharon.herl@setonpediatric.org. Web: www.setonpediatric.org. Ms. Sharon Herl, Prin.

Lavelle School for the Blind, E. 221st St. and Paulding Ave., 10469. Tel: 718-882-1212; Fax: 718-882-0005. Web: www.lavelleschool.org. William F. Simpson, Supt. Sisters of St. Dominic of Blauvelt. Capacity 183; Lay Teachers 24; Total Staff 132; Total Enrollment 160.

Mount St. Ursula Speech Center, 2885 Marion Ave., Bronx, 10458. Tel: 718-584-7679; Fax: 718-584-7954. Email: msuspeech@aol.com. Sr. Bernadette Hannaway, O.S.U., Admin. Bd. Dirs. Ursuline Nuns. Sisters 1; Lay Clinicians 8; Support Staff 5; Total Staff 13; Total Enrollment 140; Total Assisted Annually 234.

Seton Foundation for Learning, Inc. (1985) 315 Arlene St., Staten Island, 10314. Tel: 718-982-5084; Fax: 718-982-5114. Email: seton@adnyschools.org. Web: www.setonfoundation.net. Rev. Msgrs. James Dorney, Chm.; Peter Finn, Co-Chm.; Mrs. Diane Cunningham, Exec. Dir.; Thomas J. Vazzana, M.D., Pres. Lay Teachers 13; Assistants 28; Total Enrollment 110.

BRONX. *St. Joseph's School for the Deaf*, 1000 Hutchinson River Pkwy., 10465. Tel: 718-828-9000; 718-828-1671 (TDD); Fax: 718-792-6631. Email: darles@SJSDNY.org. Debra Arles, Exec. Dir. Directed by Daughters of the Heart of Mary. Capacity 160; Enrollment 125.

MILLBROOK. *Cardinal Hayes School for Special Children* (1984) 3374 Franklin Ave., P.O. Box CH, 12545. Tel: 845-677-6363; Fax: 845-677-6691. Email: fapers@cardinalhayeshome.org. Web: www.cardinalhayeshome.org. Fred Apers, Exec. Dir. Educational programs for multi-handicapped children. Lay Teachers 7; Capacity 60; Total Enrollment 55.

[H] ELEMENTARY SCHOOLS, PRIVATE

NEW YORK. *Academy of St. Joseph*, 111 Washington Pl., 10014. Tel: 212-243-5420; Fax: 212-414-4526. Ms. Angela Coombs, Prin.

Convent of the Sacred Heart (Girls), 1 E. 91st St., 10128. Tel: 212-722-4745; Fax: 212-996-1784. Web: cshnyc.org. Dr. Joseph J. Ciancaglini, Head of School. Sisters 2; Faculty 94; Elementary School Students 441.

St. John Villa Academy Elementary School, Mailing Address: 57 Cleveland Pl., Staten Island, 10305. Sr. Lucita Bacat, C.S.J.B., Prin. Sisters 9; Lay Teachers 10; Students 418.

Marymount School, (Grades N-12), 1026 Fifth Ave., 10028. Tel: 212-744-4486; Fax: 212-794-5205. Email: calvar@marymountnyc.org. Web: www.marymountnyc.org. Concepcion Alvar, B.S., M.A., Head of School; Elizabeth Clarke, Librarian; Robin Walker, Business Mgr. Religious of the Sacred Heart of Mary. Sisters 2; Lay Teachers 94; Students 605.

Nativity Mission Center, Inc. (1971) 204 Forsyth St., 10002. Tel: 212-477-2472; Fax: 212-473-0538. Email: keenan@nynativity.org. Web: www.nativitymission.org. Rev. James F. Keenan, S.J., Pres. & Contact Person. Brothers 2; Priests 1; Sisters 1; Total Staff 11; Students 60.

BRONX. *Saint Ignatius School*, 740 Manida St., 10474-5420. Tel: 718-861-9084; Fax: 718-861-9096. Email: info@nynativity.org. Web: www.nynativity.org. Dr. Jennifer Gallagher, Prin.

Villa Maria Academy (1887) 3335 Country Club Rd., 10465. Tel: 718-824-3260; Fax: 718-824-7315. Email: villa@adnyschools.org. Web: www.vma-ny.org. Sr. Teresa Barton, C.N.D., Prin.; Claudia Canzone, Librarian. Congregation of Notre Dame. Sisters 3; Lay Teachers 25; Students 475.

NEW ROCHELLE. *Iona Grammar School*, (Grades K-8), (Boys), 173 Stratton Rd., 10804. Tel: 914-633-7744; Fax: 914-235-6338. Email: pmborchetta@ionagrammer.com. Web: www.ionagrammar.com. Peter M. Borchetta, Pres. & Headmaster; Diana Gooljar, Librarian. Lay Teachers 18; Students 195.

NEWBURGH. *Bishop Dunn Memorial School*, 50 Gidney Ave., 12550. Tel: 845-569-3494; Fax: 845-569-3303. Email: bishdunn@adnyeducation.org. Web: www.bdms.org. Mr. James Delviscio, Prin.; Sr. Frances Irene Fair, Dir. Devel.; Donna Del Conte, Librarian. Dominican Sisters of Hope. Sisters 2; Lay Teachers 15; Students 290.

Nora Cronin Presentation Academy, 120 South St., 12550. Tel: 845-567-0708; Fax: 845-567-0709. Email: presentationacad@aol.com. Web: www.noracroninpresentationacademy.com. Sr. Yliana Hernandez, P.B.V.M., Contact Person, Pres., Prin.

San Miguel Academy of Newburgh, 241 Liberty St., 12550. Tel: 845-561-2822; Fax: 845-561-0312. Email: connell.sanmiguel@yahoo.com. Web: www.newburghsanmiguel.org. Rev. Mark J. Connell, Pres.; Mr. James Delviscio, Prin.

STATEN ISLAND. *Academy of St. Dorothy* (1932) 1305 Hylan Blvd., 10305. Tel: 718-351-0939; Fax: 718-351-0661. Email: dorothy@adnysch.org. Sr. Sharon A. McCarthy, S.S.D., Prin. Sisters of St. Dorothy 2; Lay Teachers 10; Students 288.

St. Joseph Hill Academy Elementary (1919) 850 Hylan Blvd., 10305. Tel: 718-981-1187; Fax: 718-448-7016. Email: joshiles@adnyschools.org. Web: www.stjosephhill.org. Mrs. Dorothy Zissler, Prin. Lay Teachers 32; Students 515.

Notre Dame Academy-Elementary School (1903) 78 Howard Ave., 10301. Tel: 718-273-9096; Fax: 718-273-1093. Email: ntdames@adnyeducation.org. Web: www.notredameacademy.org. Sr. Rose Mary Galligan, C.N.D., Prin. Congregation of Notre Dame. Lay Teachers 14; Students 277.

WHITE PLAINS. *Academy of Our Lady of Good Counsel* (Elementary Dept.), 52 N. Broadway, 10603. Tel: 914-761-4423; Fax: 914-997-4195. Email: gdounes@adrysch.org. Sr. Clare Arenholz, R.D.C., Prin. Sisters 3; Lay Teachers 14; Students 190.

[I] THE CATHOLIC CHARITIES OF THE ARCHDIOCESE OF NEW YORK

NEW YORK. *Catholic Charities Alliance*, 1011 First Ave., 10022. Tel: 212-371-1011, Ext. 2400. Rev. Msgr. Kevin L. Sullivan, Pres.

The Catholic Charities of the Archdiocese of New York, 1011 First Ave., 10022. Tel: 212-371-1000; Fax: 212-755-1526. Web: wwwcatholiccharitiesny.org. Rev. Msgr. Kevin L. Sullivan, Exec. Dir.; Joseph Buttigieg, Assoc. Exec. Dir.; Mr. Kenneth Dempsey, CFO; Mr. George B. Horton; Ms. Luz Taverez-Salazar, Special Asst.; Ms. Margaret King, Dir. Inst. Advancement; Mr. Joseph Becker, Agency Relations Liaison; Ms. Mary Ellen Ros, Catholic Charities Dir. Hudson Valley; Mr. Joseph Panepinto, Catholic Charities Dir. Staten Island; Mr. Philip Dorian, Dir. Agency Svcs.

The Ladies of Charity of the Catholic Charities of the Archdiocese of New York, 1011 First Ave., 10022. Tel: 212-371-1000, Ext. 2540; Fax: 212-319-8265. Ms. Dorothea A. McElduff, Exec. Dir.; Rev. Msgrs. William J. Toohy, Spiritual Dir.; Peter G. Finn, M.Div., M.S., M.Ed., Spiritual Dir.

Catholic Charities Community Services, Archdiocese of New York, 1011 First Ave., 10022. Tel: 212-371-1000; Fax: 212-826-8795. Ms. Beatriz Diaz, Exec. Dir.; Ms. Anne Tommaso, Dir. Beacon of Hope Svcs. Div.; Ms. Raluca Oncioiu, Dir. Migration & Refugee Svcs.; Mr. Alfred Peck, Dir. Community Outreach Svcs. Div.; Mr. Alec McAuley, Dir. CYO Div.; Ms. Mary Marshall, Dir. Hudson Valley Reg. Svcs.; Ms. Joy Jasper, Dir. Human Resources.

Roman Catholic Fund for Children and Other Purposes, 1011 First Ave., 10022. Tel: 212-371-1000; Fax: 212-826-8795. Rev. Msgr. Kevin L. Sullivan.

Holy Name Centre for Homeless Men, Inc., 18 Bleeker St., 10012. Tel: 212-226-5848. Rev. Msgr. John B. Ahern, Dir. (Retired).

Providence Health Services, 1249 Fifth Ave., 10029. Karl Adler, Pres.

St. Michael's Home, c/o The Catholic Charities of the Archdiocese of New York, 1011 First Ave., 10022. Tel: 212-371-1000. Web: cathwww.org. Bernard E. Reidey, Vice Pres.

GOSHEN. *Catholic Charities Community Services of Orange County*, Administrative Offices: 224 Main St., 10924. Tel: 845-294-5124. Dr. Dean Scher, COO, Exec. Dir.; Sr. Joanne Dress, CEO, Exec. V.P.

Early Learning Center, 59 St. John St., 10924. Tel: 845-294-7502. Montessori-based day care for 60 2.9-5 year olds.

Chemical Dependency Clinics: Medically supervised, outpatient clinics for chemically dependent adults and their families.

224 Main St., 10924. Tel: 845-294-5888; Fax: 845-294-1402.

21 Centre St., Middletown, 10940. Tel: 845-343-7675; Fax: 845-343-2501.

520 Rte. 17M, Monroe, 10950. Tel: 845-782-0295; Fax: 845-782-5164.

62 Grand St., Newburgh, 12550. Tel: 845-562-8255; Fax: 845-562-4140.

Gateway Clinic, 46 Roe St., Newburgh, 12550. Tel: 845-569-0034; Fax: 845-569-0047.

17-19 Sussex St., Port Jervis, 12771. Tel: 845-856-6344; Fax: 845-856-4091.

8 Scofield St., Walden, 12586. Tel: 845-778-5628; Fax: 845-778-5168.

Housing Resource Center, 280 Broadway, Newburgh, 12550. Tel: 845-561-1665; Fax: 845-561-2825. Provides eviction prevention services as part of a collaborative effort among Catholic Charities Community Services of Orange County and the Orange County Department of Social Services.

Student Assistance Services, 10 Orchard St., Middletown, 10940. Tel: 845-344-5565; Fax: 845-344-6982. Chemical dependency awareness, prevention, life skills education; Counseling, assessment, and referral services for students in Pine Bush School District.

Employee Assistance Program: Employee Assistance Programs for 45 corporations, businesses, governments, groups, etc. Provides confidential counseling assessment, and referral services for employees on a self-initiated or supervisor-recommended basis. Training programs and related consultative services provided.

10 Orchard St., Middletown, 10940. Tel: 845-344-5565; Fax: 845-344-6982.

Community Outreach Services--Immigration Services: Provides services to immigrants in need of assistance.

149 Cottage St., Middletown, 10940. Tel: 845-341-1978.

319 Broadway, Newburgh, 12550. Tel: 845-561-3452.

Community Outreach Services-Social Services: Provides information and referral, case management/service coordination, emergency assistance for rent, utilities, transportation, food and clothing (limited by available resources), entitlement assistance and advocacy. Also available to help parishes with CYO programs and to assess needs, evaluate existing service programs, recruit and train volunteers to meet parish needs and facilitate service to the parish.

21 Centre St., Middletown, 10940. Tel: 845-344-4242; Fax: 845-343-2501.

319 Broadway, Newburgh, 12550. Tel: 845-561-3451; Fax: 845-561-2825.

Maternity and Adoption Services: Offers maternity and adoption services to married and unmarried parents including those experiencing an unplanned pregnancy.

224 Main St., 10924. Tel: 845-294-5124, Ext. 302; Fax: 845-294-1369.

Health Insurance: Tel: 845-534-4894; Fax: 845-226-1369. Offers free or low cost health insurance through Family Health Plus and Child Health Plus programs. Coverage includes: check-ups, prenatal care, screenings and preventive care, well-child visits, immunizations, lab tests, x-rays, hospitalization and emergency treatment. (Appointments are set up at various sites in Orange County)

[J] HOUSING

NEW YORK. *Catholic Charities Department of Housing, Housing Development Institute, Inc.*, 1011 First Ave., 10022. Tel: 212-371-1000. Rev. Msgr. Kevin L. Sullivan, Pres.

[K] MENTAL HEALTH SERVICES

NEW YORK. *Catholic Charities Community Services, Beacon of Hope*, 1011 First Ave., 10022. Tel: 212-371-1000, Ext. 3608; Fax: 212-421-0021. Email: anne.tommaso@archny.org. Web: www.archny.org. Ms. Anne Tommaso, M.B.A., M.P.A., Dir., Beacon of Hope.

SVCMC Health Services Inc., 130 W. 12th St., Ste. 6-E, 10011. Tel: 212-604-7536. Email: estclair@svcmcny.org. Elizabeth St. Clair Esq., Contact Person.

[L] IMMIGRATION SERVICES

NEW YORK. *Catholic Charities Department of Immigrant Services*, 1011 First Ave. 12th Fl., 10022. Tel: 212-419-3700; Fax: 212-751-3197. Web: www.archny.org. Ms. Raluca Oncioiu, Dept. Dir.

Refugee Resettlement, 1011 First Ave., 12th Fl., 10022. Tel: 212-419-3726; Fax: 212-688-4178.

Project Irish Outreach, 1011 First Ave., 11th Fl., 10022. Tel: 212-371-1000, Ext. 3640; Fax: 212-755-1526. Ms. Patricia O'Callaghan, Coord.

New York Immigration Hotline, 1011 First Ave., 12th Fl., 10022. Tel: 212-419-3737; 800-566-7636. Lindita Berdynaj, Coord.

Asylum Information and Referral Hotline, 1011 First Ave., 12th Fl., 10022. Tel: 212-419-3737; Fax: 800-354-0365.

[M] COMMUNITY OUTREACH SERVICES DIVISION

NEW YORK. *Catholic Charities Community Services, Community Outreach Services Division*, 1011 First Ave., 10022. Tel: 212-371-1000, Ext. 2039; Fax: 212-317-8719.

Case Management/Social Services:

Central Office, 1011 First Ave., 10022. Tel: 212-371-1000, Ext. 2035; 888-744-7900 (Catholic Charities Helpline).

Central Harlem, 34 W. 134th St., 10030. Tel: 212-862-6401; Fax: 212-862-6421.

Lower Manhattan, 213 Stanton St., 10002. Tel: 212-673-0900.

East Manhattan, St. Cecilia's Church, 125 E. 105th St., 10029. Tel: 212-348-0488; Fax: 212-876-1827.

Washington Hts., 4111 Broadway, 10033. Tel: 212-795-6860; Fax: 212-781-2935.

South Bronx, 402 E. 152nd St., Bronx, 10455. Tel: 718-292-1485; Fax: 718-742-9754.
Staten Island, 120 Anderson Ave., Staten Island, 10302. Tel: 718-448-5757; Fax: 718-448-6749.
Westchester County/Peekskill, Our Lady of the Rosary, 22 Don Bosco Pl., Port Chester, 10573. Tel: 914-939-0547; Fax: 914-965-4241.
Westchester County/Yonkers, 204 Hawthorne Ave., Yonkers, 10701. Tel: 914-476-2700; Fax: 914-965-4241.
Dutchess County, 218 Church St., Poughkeepsie, 12601. Tel: 845-452-1400; Fax: 845-452-3336.
66 Bennett St., Middletown, 10943. Tel: 845-344-4244.
Rockland County, 78 Hudson Ave., Haverstraw, 10927. Tel: 845-942-5791; Fax: 845-429-2938.
Sullivan County, P.O. Box 395, Monticello, 12701. Tel: 845-791-6023; Fax: 845-791-6104.
Ulster County, 59 Pearl St., Kingston, 12401. Tel: 845-340-9170; Fax: 845-340-9596.
Emergency Food Services, 1011 First Ave., 10022. Tel: 212-371-1000, Ext. 2481; Fax: 212-317-8719. Ms. Jeanne McGettigan.
Homelessness Prevention Services:
1011 First Ave., 6th Fl., 10022. Tel: 212-371-1011, Ext. 2030; Fax: 212-753-7827. 2155 Blackrock Ave., Bronx, 10472. Tel: 718-414-1050; Fax: 718-414-1058. Antonio Garcia, Dir.
Hamilton Job Center, 530 W. 135th St., 3rd Fl., 10031. Tel: 212-690-9345; Fax: 212-690-9344.
St. Nicholas Job Center, 132 W. 125th St., Rm. 301, 10027. Tel: 212-666-3124; Fax: 212-666-8406.
Waverly Job Center, 12 W. 14th St., 4th Fl., 10011. Tel: 212-337-0213; Fax: 212-337-0211.
Employment Services, 1011 First Ave., 12th Fl., 10022. Tel: 212-371-1011, Ext. 3719; Fax: 212-319-8719.
Manhattan: Lt. Joseph P. Kennedy, Jr. Memorial Center, 34 W. 134th St., 10037. Tel: 212-862-6401; Fax: 212-862-6421.
Hudson Valley Regional Services:
Catholic Charities Community Services Hudson Valley Regional Services, Poughkeepsie Catholic Center, 218 Church St., Poughkeepsie, 12601. Tel: 845-452-1400; Fax: 845-452-3336. Ms. Mary Marshall, Dir.
Regional Offices:
Dutchess, Poughkeepsie Catholic Center, 218 Church St., Poughkeepsie, 12601. Tel: 845-452-1400; Fax: 845-452-3336. Ms. Mary Marshall.
Rockland, 78 Hudson Ave., Haverstraw, 10927. Tel: 845-942-5791; Fax: 845-429-2938.
Westchester, 22 Don Bosco Pl., Port Chester, 10573. Tel: 914-939-0547; Fax: 914-965-4241.
Sullivan, P.O. Box 395, Monticello, 12701. Tel: 845-791-6023; Fax: 845-791-6104. Rhetta Eason, Regl. Admin.
Ulster, 59 Pearl St., Kingston, 12401. Tel: 845-340-9170; Fax: 845-340-9596. Rhetta Eason, Regl. Admin.
Putnam, 235 Monsignor O'Brien Blvd., Mahopac, 10541. Tel: 845-628-2006, Ext. 115; Fax: 845-628-5970. John Scarfi, Parish Social Min.

[N] SOCIAL AND COMMUNITY DEVELOPMENT

NEW YORK. *Catholic Charities Department of Social and Community Development*, 1011 First Ave., Room 1287, 10022. Tel: 212-371-1000, Ext. 2480; Fax: 212-319-0405. Mr. George B. Horton, Dir. Tel: 212-371-1000, Ext. 2475.
Offices and Staff:
Criminal Justice Ministry Email: kenneth.hoffarth@archny.org. Mr. Kenneth Hoffarth, Dir. Tel: 212-371-1000, Ext. 3166.
Justice and Peace Ministry Thomas Dobbins Jr., Outreach Coord. Tel: 212-371-1000, Ext. 2473.
Education Outreach Program Alison Hughes-Kelsick, Dir. Tel: 212-371-1000, Ext. 2450.
Institute for Human Development Melissa Pavone, Dir.
Community Development and The Guild for Dorothy Day Ms. Lourdes Ferrer. Tel: 212-371-1000, Ext. 2474.
Deaf Apostolate Rev. Msgr. Patrick P. McCahill, Dir.

[O] SPECIAL SERVICES FOR THE ELDERLY/HANDICAPPED

BEACON. *Metropolitan Association of Contemplative Communities, Inc.*, 89 Hiddenbrooke Dr., 12508. Tel: 845-831-5572; Fax: 845-831-5579. Web: macc.catholic.org. Sr. Rita Donahue, O.C.D., Contact Person.

[P] SERVICES TO THE DISABLED

NEW YORK. *Catholic Charities Community Services Beacon of Hope House Division, Catholic Charities*, 1011 First Ave., 10022. Tel: 212-371-1000; Fax: 212-421-0021. Email: anne.tommaso@archny.org. Web: www.archny.org. Ms. Joy Jasper, Dir. Human Resources; Ms. Anne Tommaso, M.B.A., M.P.A., Dir. of Behavioral Health.
Beacon of Hope House Bronx Congregate Services, 1400 Waters Pl., Bronx, 10461. Tel: 718-892-3494; Fax: 718-892-5507. Ms. Jacqueline Rosario-Perez, M.S.W., Dir. Bronx Congregate Progs.
Terence Cardinal Cooke Residence, 2467 Bathgate Ave., Bronx, 10458. Tel: 718-367-6990; 718-367-5405 (TTY); Fax: 718-365-2544. Koren McLaughlin, Prog. Supvr.
Beacon of Hope House Staten Island Supervised Programs, 777 Seaview Ave., Bldg. D, 2nd Fl., Staten Island, 10305. Tel: 718-980-1072; Fax: 718-980-1077. Mr. Dennis Scimone, M.S.W., M.P.A., Dir. of Residential Svcs.; Ms. Karen Volpe, Admin. Sec.; Ms. Sandy Mormile, Dir. Staten Island Svcs.
Staten Island Apartment Programs Tel: 718-979-6241; Fax: 718-979-6941. Heather Bonilla, Prog. Mgr.
90-92 Hancock St., Staten Island, 10305. Tel: 718-979-6241; Fax: 718-979-6941.
Highbridge Neighborhood Supported Housing Program, 1484 Nelson Ave., Suite A, Bronx, 10452. Tel: 718-503-8106; Fax: 718-293-0939. Adriane Paniagua, Prog. Supvr.
Kingsborough Intensive Supported Apartment Program, 647 Vanderbilt Ave., Brooklyn, 11238. Tel: 718-398-4556; Fax: 718-398-4807. Ms. Michelle Foster, Prog. Supvr.
East Bronx Supported Housing, 690 Mace Ave., Bronx, 10467. Tel: 718-654-2731; Fax: 718-655-2101. Simone Williams, Dir. Bronx Supported Housing.
The Clubhouse, 512 Southern Blvd., Bronx, 10455. Tel: 718-993-1078; Fax: 718-993-0216. Ms. Sharon George, Prog. Dir.
New York Catholic Deaf Center, St. Elizabeth of Hungry Church, 211 E. 83rd St., 10028. Tel: 212-988-8563 (Voice); 212-988-1903 (TTY); 866-810-3394 (Video Phone); Fax: 212-988-1903. Web: www.deafcathnyc.org. Rev. Msgr. Patrick P. McCahill, Dir. Total Assisted Annually 5,871.
BARRYVILLE. *New Hope Manor*, 35 Hillside Rd., 12719. Tel: 845-557-8353; Fax: 845-557-6603. Email: newhopemnr@aol.com. Web: www.newhopemanor.org. Nicholas A. Roes, Ph.D., Dir.; Sr. Joanne Maloney, O.P., Bd. of Directors; Bro. Charles Kinney, S.A., Bd. of Directors. See listing in the Miscellaneous section for further details. Bed Capacity 56; Total Assisted Annually 90; Total Staff 50.
Staff: An all-female substance abuse treatment center Sisters Maureen Conway, O.P., Dir. of Education, Housemother, Counselor & Teacher; Patricia Conway, O.P., Housemother, Counselor & Teacher.

[Q] YOUTH SERVICES

NEW YORK. *Catholic Youth Organization of the Archdiocese of New York Inc.*, Executive Office, 1011 First Ave., 10022-4187. Tel: 212-371-1000; Fax: 212-826-3347. Chris Gallagher, Pres.; Mr. Alec McAuley, Exec. Dir.; Mrs. Judith Trancucci, Dir. Operations.
Archdiocesan Committee on Scouting Tel: 914-499-4840; Fax: 212-826-3347. Mr. John Kiernan, Chm.
CYO Bronx County Tel: 212-371-1000; Fax: 212-826-3347. Mr. Anthony D'Angelo, County Dir.
Grace Youth Ministry Tel: 212-371-1000, Ext. 3619. Mrs. Carmen Castro, Coord.
Lt. Joseph P. Kennedy, Jr., Memorial Center Tel: 212-862-6401; Fax: 212-862-6421.
34 W. 134th St., 10037. Tel: 212-862-6401; Fax: 212-862-6421.
CYO Staten Island County Tel: 718-448-4949; Fax: 718-448-0576.
120 Anderson Ave., Staten Island, 10302. Tel: 718-448-4950; Fax: 718-448-0576.
Staten Island Center Tel: 718-448-4949; Fax: 718-273-8361. Gayle Murphy, Center Dir.
120 Anderson Ave., Staten Island, 10302. Tel: 718-448-4949; Fax: 718-448-0576.
CYO Westchester/Putnam Offices Tel: 845-623-2785; Fax: 845-624-0889. Frank Magaletta, County Dir.
9 Brookview Blvd., Chestnut Ridge, 10977. Tel: 845-623-2785; Fax: 845-624-0889.
Blair Lodge Youth Ministry Center, Peekskill Rd., Putnam Valley, 10579. Tel: 845-528-5005; Fax: 845-528-6137.
1011 First Ave., 10022. Tel: 845-783-1254; Fax: 212-826-3347.
CYO Orange Office Mr. John Smith, Sports Coord. P.O. Box 234, Highland Mills, 10930. Tel: 845-534-7700; Fax: 212-826-3347.
CYO Rockland Office Tel: 845-620-1662. Thomas F. Collins.
34 Graney Ct., Pearl River, 10965. Tel: 845-620-1662; Fax: 845-452-3336.
CYO Dutchess Office Tel: 845-452-1400; Fax: 845-452-3336. David Kotchie, County Dir.
Catholic Center, 240 Church St., Poughkeepsie, 12601. Tel: 845-452-1400; Fax: 845-452-3336.
CYO Ulster/Sullivan County Tel: 845-340-9170; Fax: 845-340-9596.
59 Pearl St., Kingston, 12401. Tel: 845-340-9170; Fax: 845-340-9596. Tom Kelly, County Dir.
BRONX. *St. Francis Youth Center, Inc.*, 420 E. 156th St., 10455. Tel: 718-993-3405; 718-402-6235; Fax: 718-993-9997. Bro. Joachim Joseph, C.F.R., Dir.; Yvette Torres, Admin. Brothers 3; Priests 1; Lay Missionaries 1.
GARRISON. *Capuchin Youth and Family Ministries*, 781 Rte. 9D, 10524. Tel: 845-424-3609; Fax: 845-424-4403. Email: cyfm@cyfm.org. Web: www.cyfm.org. P.O. Box 192, 10524. Thomas Brinkmann, Exec. Dir.; Rev. Fred Nickle, O.F.M.Cap., Chap.; Bro. Luke Herman, O.F.M.Cap., Chap. A ministry of the Capuchin Franciscan Province of St. Mary.

[R] SOCIETY OF ST. VINCENT DE PAUL

NEW YORK. *Society of St. Vincent De Paul, Archdiocesan Central Council of New York* Territory: Archdiocese of New York., 1011 First Ave., 10022. Tel: 212-755-8615; Fax: 212-755-0151. Email: svdpny@stjohns.edu. James Young, Pres.; Rev. Robert T. Ritchie, Spiritual Advisor.
The Society of St. Vincent de Paul of the Archdiocese of New York, Inc.
District Council of Manhattan (1846) 1011 First Ave., Ste. 607, 10022. Tel: 212-755-8615; Fax: 212-755-0151. Email: ssvpny@gmail.com. Mrs. Leona James, Pres.; Mr. Vincent D. Reilly, Exec. Sec.
The Society of St. Vincent de Paul in the City of New York, Territory: Manhattan.
District Council of the Bronx, 611 Minneford Ave., City Island, 10464. Tel: 718-885-1197. Tom McMahon, Pres.
District Council of Staten Island, 445 Decatur Ave., Staten Island, 10314. Tel: 718-698-7874. Gary Malandro, Pres.
BRONX. *District Council of the Bronx* Territory: Borough of The Bronx & Lower Westchester., 402 E. 152nd St., 10455. Tel: 718-292-9090; Fax: 718-993-6130. Rev. Tom Dicks; Dominick Galdieri, Pres.
The Society of St. Vincent de Paul, District Council of the Bronx, Inc.

[S] INSTITUTIONS FOR DEPENDENT CHILDREN

NEW YORK. *Covenant House Under 21* (Runaway and Homeless Youth.), 460 W. 41st St., 10036. Tel: 212-727-4000; Fax: 212-727-4992. Mr. James M. White, Pres.; Mr. Jerome Kilbane, Exec. Dir. Total Assisted 8,593; Total Staff 539.
Rights of Passage Transition Housing. Bed Capacity 200.
Crisis Center Emergency Shelter. Bed Capacity 242.
Vincent J. Fontana Center for Child Protection, 27 Christopher St., 10014. Tel: 212-660-1323; Fax: 212-660-1319. Email: chuck.caputo@nyfoundling.org. Children & Families 250; Total Staff 12.
BLAUVELT. *Saint Dominic's Home* (1878) 500 Western Hwy., 10913. Tel: 845-359-3400; Fax: 845-359-4253. Email: judyk@stdominicshome.org. Web: www.stdominicshome.org. Judith D. Kydon, Exec. Dir. In Foster Homes 350.
New York Offices, 853 Longwood Ave., Ste. 202, Bronx, 10459. Tel: 917-645-9100; Fax: 917-645-9095. Web: www.stdominicshome.org.
St. Dominic's School Tel: 845-359-3400, Ext. 243; Fax: 845-359-5286. Web: www.stdominicshome-.org. (Serves children and adolescents with emotional disabilities, K-8th grade.) Capacity 80.
Community residences for developmentally disabled Tel: 845-359-3400; Fax: 845-359-3673. Capacity 150.
Community residences for mentally ill Tel: 845-359-3400; Fax: 845-359-7361. Capacity 36.
TORCH (To Reach Children), 2340 Andrews Ave., Bronx, 10468. Tel: 718-365-7238; Fax: 718-584-3057. Web: www.stdominicshome.org.
Friends of St. Dominic's Inc., 500 Western Hwy., 10913. Tel: 845-359-3400; Fax: 845-398-0466. Email: sjm@stdominicshome.org. Web: www.stdominicshome.org/friends. Sr. Joseph Mary Mahoney, O.P., Pres. Capacity 52.
BRONX. *Saint Dominic's Home - Prevention Program (ASTAAN)* Parent Aide Counseling Advocacy Information and Referral., 2345 University Ave., 10468. Tel: 718-584-4407; Fax: 718-584-4540. Email: annettet@stdominicshome.org. Web: www.stdominicshome.org. Families 100; Families Served 200.
NANUET. *St. Agatha Home of the New York Foundling Hospital* (Residential.), 135 Convent Rd., 10954. Tel: 914-623-3461. Sisters of Charity of St. Vincent de Paul of New York., Runaway Youth Program.; Refugee Assistance Program.; Ulster

County Prevention. Bed Capacity 126; Diagnostic Facilities 26; In Foster Homes 38; Group Homes 81; Non-Secure Detention 8; Adult Intermediate Care Facilities 65; Family Support/Respite 10.

OSSINING. *Cardinal McCloskey Emergency Residential School* (1980) 155 N. Highland Ave., 10562. Tel: 914-762-5302; Fax: 914-762-7844. Total Staff 7; Capacity 20; Total Assisted 45.

SPRING VALLEY. *Good Counsel, Inc.*, 22 Linden Ave., 10977. Tel: 845-356-0517; 800-723-8331 (Info & Referrals); Fax: 845-356-0406. Web: www.goodcounselhomes.org; www.postabortionhelp.org. Rev. Benedict Joseph Groeschel, C.F.R., Ed.D., Chm.; Christopher Bell, Exec. Dir.; Nannette Morris, House Mgr.

Good Counsel, Inc., 38 N. Clinton St., Poughkeepsie, 12601. Tel: 845-452-2944; 800-723-8331 (Info. & Referrals); Fax: 845-452-6390. Web: www.goodcounselhomes.org; www.postabortionhelp.org. Christopher Bell, Exec. Dir.; Sheri Johnson, Case Mgr., Exodus.

Good Counsel, Inc., 38 Wiman Pl., Staten Island, 10305. Tel: 718-727-8266; 800-723-8331 (Info. & Referrals); Fax: 718-447-6625. Web: www.goodcounselhomes.org; www.postabortionhelp.org. Christopher Bell, Exec. Dir.; Claudia Marroquin, House Mgr.

Good Counsel, Inc., 1157 Fulton Ave., Bronx, 10456. Tel: 718-312-3980, Ext. 10; 800-723-8331 (For Info & Referrals); Fax: 718-312-3991. Email: delores_morgan@goodcounselhomes.org. Web: www.goodcounselhomes.org. Christopher Bell, Exec. Dir.; Delores Morgan, House Mgr.

Good Counsel/Daystar Program, 275 North St., Harrison, 10528. Tel: 914-925-9834; 800-723-8331 (Info. & Referrals); Fax: 914-925-9101. Web: www.goodcounselhomes.org; www.postabortionhelp.org. Christopher Bell, Exec. Dir.; Gisette Anderson, House Dir. Bed Capacity 41; Total Assisted 315; Total Staff 60.

WEST PARK. *St. Cabrini Home* (1890) 12493. Tel: 845-384-6500; Fax: 845-384-6001. Email: info@cabrinihome.com. Web: cabrinihome.com. Tony Cortese, Exec. Dir. Served by Missionary Sisters of the Sacred Heart Children 80; Agency Operated Boarding Home 1; Group Homes 6; Missionary Sisters of Sacred Heart 5.

St. Cabrini Home, Inc. Tel: 845-384-6500; Fax: 845-384-6001. Email: infor@cabrinihome.com. Web: www.cabrinihome.com. Residents 210.

WHITE PLAINS. *Cardinal McCloskey Services* (1946) Two Holland Ave., 10603. Tel: 914-997-8000; Fax: 914-997-2166. Email: bfinnerty@cardinalmccloskey.org. Web: www.cardinalmccloskeyservices.org. Mrs. Beth Finnerty, Pres. & CEO. Statistical Information: Sisters 2; Hayden House Capacity: 20, Total Assisted: 39, Total Staff: 20; Foster Boarding Home Program Capacity: 350 Beds, Total Assisted: 437; Group Home Capacity: 8, Total Assisted: 8; Therapeutic Foster Boarding Home Program Capacity: 60 Beds, Total Assisted: 69; General Preventative Services Capacity: 225, Total Assisted: 934 children/319 families; Family Rehabilitation Services: 120, Total Assisted: 443 children/319 families; In Day Care: Site I Capacity: 850 (Family), Total Assisted: 1,451, Site II Capacity: 80 (Group), Total Assisted: 121 children/118 families; Site III CMS, University Heights DC: 77 (Group) - 102 (Family), Total Assisted: 263 children/240 families, MRDD Residences Capacity: 80, Total Staff: 487

Little Angels Head Start Program

[T] SPECIALIZED CHILD CARING HOMES

NEW YORK. *Good Shepherd Services*, 305 7th Ave., 9th Fl., 10001. Tel: 212-243-7070; Fax: 212-929-3412. Email: plomonaco@goodshepherds.org. Web: www.goodshepherds.org. Sr. Paulette LoMonaco, R.G.S., Exec. Dir. Provides foster care and adoption services and five residential programs for at risk adolescents, a training program for social service workers and a comprehensive range of neighborhood family services to individuals and youth in the Bronx and in Brooklyn. These services include a range of educational support, counseling, after school program, crisis intervention, and advocacy services. Sisters 3; Total Assisted 18,000; Total Staff 850.

Kennedy Child Study Center (1958) 151 E. 67th St., 10065. Tel: 212-988-9500; Fax: 212-570-6690. Email: ppg@kenchild.org. Web: www.kenchild.org. Peter P. Gorham, B.A., M.S.W., M.B.A., Exec. Dir. Preschool Special Education 120; Infant/Parent Services 23.

Case Management Services Tel: 212-988-9500; Fax: 212-327-2601. Family Support Services 20; Clinic Program 485.

Bronx Site, 1028 E. 179th St., Bronx, 10460. Tel: 718-842-0200; Fax: 718-842-1328. Preschool Special Education 160; Infant/Parent Services 100.

Case Management Services Tel: 718-842-0200; Fax: 718-842-1328. Family Support Services 40.

Mission of the Immaculate Virgin (1871) 6581 Hylan Blvd., Staten Island, 10309. Tel: 718-317-2803; 718-317-2600; Fax: 718-317-2830. Email: srynn@mountloretto.org. Web: www.mountloretto.org. Stephen Rynn, Exec. Dir.

Mission of the Immaculate Virgin for the Protection of Homeless and Destitute Children In Res. Rev. Msgr. Joseph C. Ansaldi; Rev. Michael P. Reilly.

Intermediate Care Facility Tel: 718-966-6185. Capacity 12.

Day Care Center & Universal Pre-K Tel: 718-317-2849. Capacity 85.

Individual Residential Alternatives

Individual Residential Alternatives (I.R.A.) Tel: 718-317-2803; Fax: 718-317-2830. Capacity 36.

Day Habilitation Program Tel: 718-317-2676. Capacity 8.

Residential & Day Care Tel: 718-317-2600; 718-317-2803; Fax: 718-317-2830. Total Assisted 297; Total Staff 162.

New York Foundling Charitable Corp., 590 Avenue of the Americas, 10011. Tel: 212-633-9300. Web: www.nyfoundling.org. Mr. William Baccaglini, Exec. Dir.

**New York Foundling Hospital Center for Pediatric, Medical and Rehabilitative Care, Inc. dba Elizabeth Seton Pediatric Center* (1987) 590 Avenue of the Americas, 10011. Tel: 646-459-3600; Fax: 646-459-3636. Email: patricia.tursi@setonpediatric.org. Web: www.setonpediatric.org. Patricia A. Tursi, CEO. Sponsored by Sisters of Charity of St. Vincent de Paul of New York. Bed Capacity 136; Total Assisted Annually 195; Total Staff 560.

New York Foundling Hospital, The (Children from Infancy to 21), 590 Avenue of the Americas, 10011. Tel: 212-633-9300; Fax: 212-886-4086. Email: info@nyfoundling.org. Web: www.nyfoundling.org. Mr. William Baccaglini, Exec. Dir. Children & Families 13,000; Total Staff 1,200.

Sr. Una McCormack Maternity Services, Inc. (1997) 1011 First Ave., 10022. Tel: 212-371-1000, Ext. 2100; Fax: 212-755-4110. Email: pgeorgini@cgshb.org. Philip Georgini, Exec. Dir.

MILLBROOK. *Cardinal Hayes Home for Children* (1941) Residential care for developmentally disabled children and young adults., St. Joseph Dr., P.O. Box CH, 12545. Tel: 845-677-6363; Fax: 845-677-6691. Email: fapers@cardinalhayeshome.org. Web: www.cardinalhayeshome.org. Fred Apers, Exec. Dir. Franciscan Missionaries of Mary 5; Capacity of Residential Facilities: Millbrook Intermediate Care Facility 60; Community Intermediate Care Facilities 50.

RHINEBECK. *Astor Home for Children, The* Residential Treatment Facility for severe emotionally disturbed-mentally ill boys and girls, ages 5-12., 6339 Mill St., P.O. Box 5005, 12572-5005. Tel: 845-871-1000; Fax: 845-876-2020. Email: jmcguirk@astorservices.org. Web: www.astorservices.org. James McGuirk, Ph.D., Exec. Dir. & CEO. Bed Capacity 20.

Residential Treatment Center (Rhinebeck) Bed Capacity 27; Therapeutic Foster Boarding Homes 30; Family-Based Treatment 10.

Counseling Centers: Red Hook, Poughkeepsie, Beacon and Bronx (Ages birth-18)

Day Treatment Programs (Ages 3-12) Capacity Dutchess Co. 56; Bronx 181; Therapeutic Nursery, Bronx 40; Adolescent Day Treatment 120.

Astor Family Services Program, Bronx (Ages birth-18) Capacity 90.

Head Start-Day Care Centers: Poughkeepsie, Beacon, Millerton, Wingdale, Wappingers Falls, Pine Plains Capacity 418.

Day Care Centers: Beacon, Wingdale Capacity 50.

Special Class Integrated Services (Ages 3-5) Capacity 32.

Early Head Start Capacity 135; Total Assisted 5,515; Total Staff 718.

Astor Learning Center, The The Astor Learning Center provides individualized special education for children with emotional disturbances in conjunction with the mental health services of the Residential Treatment programs. The ALC serves children between the ages of 5-11 at time of admission., 6339 Mill St., P.O. Box 5005, 12572-5005. Tel: 845-871-1032; Fax: 845-876-2020. Email: skeegan@astorservices.org. Web: www.astorservices.org. Sue Keegan, Prin. Capacity 75; Total Assisted 107; Total Staff 50.

[U] CHILDREN'S AGENCIES & PROTECTIVE INSTITUTIONS

NEW YORK. *Catholic Guardian Society and Home Bureau* (1908) 1011 First Ave., 10022. Tel: 212-371-1000; Fax: 212-935-7820. Email: jfrein@cgshb.org. Mr. John Frein, Exec. Dir. Intermediate care facilities, individual residential alternatives and family respite support programs for mentally retarded and developmentally disabled adults and adolescents. Group home program for boys and girls, ages 13-21 years; foster and kinship family care and adoption services for boys and girls, ages 0-21; provides regular and therapeutic foster homes for boys and girls ages 0-21; and specialized foster homes for children with AIDS and special medical conditions; Child abuse and neglect prevention programs; Specialized group care programs for mother-child population, children with special needs, and assessment services for PINS youth and their families; and juvenile justice non-secure detention facilities for adolescents; pregnancy support services; international adoption services; post-adoption services; homeless shelter and aftercare services for women with children; family day care services. Total Assisted 3,863; Total Staff 1,077.

LINCOLNDALE. *Lincoln Hall*, P.O. Box 600, 10540. Tel: 914-248-7474; Fax: 914-248-8391. Email: pt.lincolnhall@worldnet.att.net. Jack Flavin, Exec. Dir.

City Office, 220 E. 23rd St., 10010. Capacity (Boys) 207; Total Staff 351; Total Assisted 421.

[V] CATHOLIC CHARITIES - CHILD CARING AGENCIES

OSSINING. *The Cardinal McCloskey Emergency Residential School*, 155 N. Highland Ave., 10562. Tel: 914-762-5302; Fax: 914-762-7844. Email: jfedele@cardinalmccloskey.org. Teachers 4; Assistants 2.

STATEN ISLAND. *Sisters of Charity Healthcare System Nursing Home, Inc. dba Saint Elizabeth Anns Health Care & Rehabilitation Center* 91 Tompkins Ave., 10304. Tel: 718-876-1099; Fax: 718-876-1393. Email: pmcgrann@svcmcny.org. Patricia McGrann, Contact Person.

THORNWOOD. *Catholic World Mission, Inc.* (1998) 590 Columbus Ave., 10594. Tel: 914-773-1368; Fax: 914-773-1438. Web: www.catholicworldmission.org. Rev. Thomas Moylan, Contact Person.

[W] DAY NURSERIES

NEW YORK. *St. Benedict's Day Nursery, Day Care Center*, 21 W. 124th St., 10027. Tel: 212-423-5715; Fax: 212-423-5917. Email: stben124@aol.com. Ms. Carmina Cayanan, Dir. Handmaids of the Most Pure Heart of Mary 2; Lay Teachers 11; Children 76.

Nazareth Nursery (1901) Montessori Day Care., 214-216 W. 15th St., 10011-6501. Tel: 212-243-1881; Fax: 212-243-1881 (Call First). Web: www.nazarethnursery.org. Sisters Lucy Sabatini, O.S.F., Admin., Educ. Dir. & Prin.; Eleanore Therese Vargas, O.S.F., Asst. Admin. Capacity 55; Total Staff 14.

Providence Rest Child Day Care Center, Inc. (1991) 3310 Campbell Dr., 10465. Tel: 718-823-3588; Fax: 718-823-3588. Sisters 1; Total Assisted 25; Total Staff 7.

San Jose Day Nursery, 432 W. 20th St., 10011. Tel: 212-929-0839; Fax: 212-924-0891. Sisters Haydee Luisa Fernandez, Supr.; Trinidad Fernandez, Dir. Mothers of the Helpless 6; Children 57.

YONKERS. *Queen's Daughters Day Care Center, Inc.* (1903) 73 Buena Vista Ave., 10701. Tel: 914-969-4491; Fax: 914-969-4491. Email: qddcc@excite.com. Barbara Berrios, Dir. Children 125; Total Staff 20.

[X] GENERAL HOSPITALS

NEW YORK. *Cabrini Medical Center (Cabrini Development Council, Inc.)*, 227 E. 19th St., 10003. Tel: 212-995-6000; Fax: 212-995-6568. Mr. Robert S. Chaloner, Pres. & CEO; Sr. Arlene Primus, M.S.C., Exec. Dir. for Mission & Ministry. Bed Capacity Acute Hospital 467; Available for Use 329; Skilled Nursing Facility at Dobbs Ferry 306; New York City, Beds 240; Missionary Sisters of the Sacred Heart 10; Patients Assisted Annually (includes Homecare Visits) 66,832; Cabrini Hospice Program (Home Care) 900; Total Staff 2,376.

Stuyvesant Polyclinic, Inc. Tel: 212-674-0220; Fax: 212-533-2251. Patients Assisted Annually 62,891.

Sisters of Charity Health Care System Corp., 75 Vanderbilt Ave., Staten Island, 10304. Tel: 718-354-5080. Web: www.schcs.com. Bed Capacity 866; Total Assisted Annually 29,794; Total Staff 4,000.

Bayley Seton Campus Tel: 718-354-6000; Fax: 718-876-1234.

St. Vincent's Medical Center of Richmond

Saint Vincent Catholic Medical Centers of New York, 130 W. 12 St., 10011. Tel: 212-604-2300; Fax: 212-604-7533. Email: mfagan@svcmcny.org. Web:

svcmc.org. Henry Amoroso, Pres. & CEO; Lowell Johnson, CFO; Ms. Catherine Callagy, Senior Vice Pres. Fund Devel.; Arthur Webb, COO; Paul Goebel, Chief Administrative Officer. Bed Capacity 662; Total Assisted Annually 300,000; Total Staff 4,545.

St. Vincent's Manhattan, 170 W. 12th St., 10011. Tel: 212-604-7000.

St. Vincent's Westchester, 275 North St., Harrison, 10528. Tel: 914-967-6500; Fax: 914-925-5157.

BEACON. *St. Francis Hospital*, 11 Hastings Dr., 12508. Tel: 845-838-4500; Fax: 845-831-8131. Email: CDeFreest@SFHHC.org. Web: sfhhc.org. Constance DeFreest, M.S., R.N., Vice Pres. This Facility is a 100 bed facility for the treatment of chemical dependency, and is a division of St. Francis Hospital, North Rd., Poughkeepsie, NY. Bed Capacity 100; Total Assisted Annually 2,050; Total Staff 148.

KINGSTON. *Benedictine Hospital* (1901) 105 Mary's Ave., 12401. Tel: 914-338-2500; Fax: 914-334-3149. Web: www.benedictine.org. Sisters Mary Feehan, O.S.B., Senior Vice Pres., Mission Effectiveness; Mary Dorothy Huggard, O.S.B., Dir., Pastoral Care. Sisters of St. Benedict (Federation of St. Scholastica) 4; Capacity 222; Patients Assisted Annually 96,561; Total Staff 863.

PORT JERVIS. *Bon Secours Community Hospital* (1915) 160 E. Main St., 12771. Tel: 845-858-7000; Fax: 845-858-7415. Email: leah-cerkvenik@bshsi.org. Web: www.bonsecourscommunityhosp.org. Leah Cerkvenik, R.N., Exec. Vice Pres. & Admin. Capacity 141; SNF Beds 46; Patients Assisted Annually 81,802; Total Staff 474.

POUGHKEEPSIE. *St. Francis Hospital*, 241 North Rd., 12601. Tel: 845-483-5000; Fax: 845-485-3762. Web: www.sfhhc.org. Robert L. Savage, Pres. & CEO; Sr. Marie Bernadette Wyman, Dir. Pastoral Care; Revs. Zeverin Emagalit, Pastoral Care Assoc.; Joseph Mali (Nigeria), Pastoral Care Assoc. Sisters of St. Francis of Hastings-on-Hudson, New York.Sisters of St. Francis of the Neumann Communities - Syracuse, NY Capacity 300; Outpatient Visits 208,609; Admissions 10,018; Total Staff 1,533.

St. Francis Health Care Foundation, 241 North Rd., 12601. Tel: 845-431-8707; Fax: 845-483-5097.

SUFFERN. *Good Samaritan Hospital of Suffern* 10901. Tel: 845-368-5000; Fax: 845-368-5430. Web: www.GoodSamHosp.org. Terence O'Brien, CEO, Bon Secours Charity Health System; Philip A. Patterson, Exec. Vice Pres. & COO Bon Secours Charity Health System; Rev. Jamie Bono, Dir. Pastoral Care; Sr. Sheila M. Mullins, O.P., Chap. Sisters of Charity of St. Elizabeth 2; Capacity 370; Patients Assisted Annually 165,000; Total Staff 1,575.

WARWICK. *St. Anthony Community Hospital, Inc.* Franciscan System of Warwick, Inc., 15-19 Maple Ave., 10990. Tel: 845-986-2276; Fax: 845-986-2687. Leah Cerkvenik, R.N., EVP; Pam Corbett, Dir. Pastoral Care; Rev. Joseph P. McAndrew, Chap. (Retired). Capacity 73; Patients Assisted Annually 34,262.

YONKERS. *St. Joseph's Medical Center* (1888) 127 S. Broadway, 10701. Tel: 914-378-7000; Fax: 914-965-4838. Email: public.relations@saintjosephs.org. Web: saintjosephs.org. Mr. Michael J. Spicer, Pres.; Rev. Thomas Murphy, O.F.M.Cap.; Sr. Dolores Doyle, P.B.V.M., Dir. of Pastoral Care. Bed Capacity 394; Nursing Home Beds 200; Sisters of Charity of St. Vincent de Paul 7; Patients Assisted Annually 340,407; Total Staff 1,411.

[Y] SPECIAL HOSPITALS AND SANATORIA FOR INVALIDS

NEW YORK. *Calvary Hospital* (1889) For advanced cancer patients., 1740 Eastchester Rd., Bronx, 10461. Tel: 718-863-6900; Fax: 718-518-2674. Email: DLattarulo@calvaryhospital.org. Web: www.calvaryhospital.org. Frank A. Calamari, Pres. & CEO; Rev. Chux Okochi, Chap.; Eileen Pesek, Asst. Admin. & Dir. Pastoral Svcs. Pastoral Staff 14; Accommodations for 225; Patients Assisted Annually 4,700.

Terence Cardinal Cooke Health Care Center, 1249 Fifth Ave., 10029. Tel: 212-360-1000; Fax: 212-289-2739. Email: lgaffney@chcsnet.org. Web: www.tcchcc.org. Laura P. Gaffney, Exec. Dir. Hospital for developmentally disabled. Bed Capacity 50.

Developmental Disabilities Clinic, 1249 Fifth Ave., 10029. Tel: 212-360-3703; Fax: 212-360-3842. Comprehensive Outpatient medical, therapeutic and educational services. On site and off site OMRDD Article 16 services. Patients Assisted Annually 44,000.

Hemodialysis, 1249 Fifth Ave., 10029. Tel: 212-360-3860; Fax: 212-860-3862. 22 End Stage Renal Dialysis Stations; (For information concerning nursing home see Homes for Aged category.) Patients Assisted Annually 22,000.

BRONX. *St. Eleanora's Home for Convalescents* (1901) Sisters of Charity Center, 6301 Riverdale Ave., 10471. Tel: 718-549-9200, Ext. 261; Fax: 718-884-3013. Email: ghanley@scny.org. Web: scny.org. Total Assisted Annually 30; Total Staff 10.

HARRISON. *St. Vincent's Hospital Westchester* (1879) 275 North St., 10528. Tel: 914-967-6500; Fax: 914-925-5157. Web: www.svcmc.org. Bernadette Kingham-Bez. Psychiatric Hospital.; Clergy Consultation Program; Inpatient and outpatient mental health and substance abuse services for adults, adolescents, children and their families. Sites in Harrison, Tuckahoe & White Plains. Services available in Spanish. Capacity 133; Inpatients Assisted Annually 2,891; Sisters of Charity of St. Vincent de Paul 3; All outpatient program admissions 165,000; Partial Hospital 50; Opiod Maintenance Treatment Program 43.

HAWTHORNE. *Rosary Hill Home* (1901) Free home for incurable cancer patients., 10532. Tel: 914-769-0114; Fax: 914-769-3916. Web: www.hawthorne.dominicans.org. Sisters Mary Joseph, O.P., Admin.; Maureen, O.P., Supr. *The Servants of Relief for Incurable Cancer* Professed Sisters of St. Dominic 29; Capacity 72; Patients Assisted Annually 183.

[Z] ORDERS OF NURSING SISTERS

NEW YORK. *Little Sisters of the Assumption Family Health Service, Inc.* (1958) 333 E. 115th St., 10029. Tel: 646-672-5200; Fax: 212-348-8284. Email: gcarter@lsafhs.org. Gary Carter, Exec. Dir.

BRONX. *Convent of the Sisters Servants of Mary* Mission: Private nursing in the homes., 3305 Country Club Rd., 10465-1296. Tel: 718-829-0428; Fax: 718-829-2346. Email: servantsmaryny@optonline.com. Web: sistersservantsofmary.org. Sr. Elvia Navarro, S.deM., Mother Supr. Sisters 21.

OSSINING. *Dominican Sisters Family Health Service, Inc. (Central Services/Administration)* (1974) Community-based, certified, voluntary Home Health Agency and Long Term Home Health Care and AIDS Programs serving all of Westchester, Suffolk and the South Bronx. Unique community outreach programs., 299 N. Highland Ave., 10562. Tel: 914-941-1710; Fax: 914-941-0518. Email: VHanrahan@dsfhs.org. Web: www.dsfhs.org. Sisters Virginia Hanrahan, O.P., B.S.N., M.S.N., Ph.D., Pres./CEO; Margaret Flood, O.P., B.S.N., M.A., M.P.A., COO. Total Staff 423; Total Patients 14,000; Total Visits 197,000.

Bronx Office, 279 Alexander Ave., Bronx, 10454. Tel: 718-665-6557; Fax: 718-292-9113. Ana Collado, Admin.

Westchester Office, 299 N. Highland Ave., 10562. Tel: 914-941-1654; Fax: 914-941-1556. Email: EBobb@dsfhs.org. Evelyn Bobb, B.S.N., M.P.A., Admin.

Suffolk County Offices (4 Offices in Suffolk), 103-6 W. Montauk Hwy., Box 209, Hampton Bays, 11946. Tel: 631-728-0181; Fax: 631-728-2943. Email: pash@dsfhs.org. Web: www.dsfhs.org.

Box 678, Wainscott, 11975. Tel: 631-537-6759; Fax: 631-537-7187. Email: pash@dsfhs.org. Web: www.dsfhs.org. Pamella Ash, B.S.N., M.A., Admin., Suffolk Offices.

3237 Rte. 112, Ste. 1, Medford, 11763. Tel: 631-207-1170; Fax: 631-207-0149.

**Family Home Health Care, Inc.* (Licensed Home Health Care Affiliate), 65 S. Broadway, Tarrytown, 10591. Tel: 914-631-7200; Fax: 914-631-2382. Email: dozure@dsfhs.org. Diane Ozure, Admin.

Family Home Health Care, Inc. (Licensed Home Health Care Affiliate), 3237 Rte. 112, Ste. 1, Medford, 11763. Tel: 631-207-1170; Fax: 631-207-0149. Email: pash@dsfhs.org. Pamella Ash, B.S.N., M.A., Admin., Suffolk Offices.

STATEN ISLAND. *Pax Christi Hospice* Hospice Care Services for the terminally ill., 1200 South Ave., Ste. 306, 10314. Tel: 718-876-1022; Fax: 718-876-1803.

[AA] NURSING HOMES

NEW YORK. *Cabrini Center for Nursing & Rehabilitation*, 542 E. 5th St., 10009. Tel: 212-358-3000; Fax: 212-358-6269. Email: mdevlin@cabrini-eldercare.org. Web: www.cabrini-eldercare.org. Rev. Konaku Kuusegmeh, C.S.Sp., Chap.; Mary Devlin, COO. Total SNF Beds 240; Total Assisted Annually 1,832; Total Staff 305.

Kateri Residence (1981) Skilled Nursing Care/Residential Health Care Facility for the Elderly., 150 Riverside Dr., 10024-2201. Tel: 646-505-3500; Fax: 212-873-0658. Email: lbond@chcsnet.org. Web: www.kateriresidenceny.org. Lascelles L. Bond, Exec. Dir.; Janet Levine, R.N., Asst. Admin.; Derrick Watson, Dir. Res. Services; Jacqueline Edwards-Morris, Dir. Quality Mgmt. & Corp. Compliance Officer; Jocelyn Ronquillo, M.D., Medical Dir.; Ronie Rusea-Robinson, Dir. Nursing Svcs.; Eileen Donovan, Dir., Resident Assessment; Wanda Taylor, Dir. Admissions; Lisa Orriola, Dir., Recreation & Fundraising; Mary B. Fisher, Dir., Volunteers; Ms. Carmela Cantone, Dir. Pastoral Care; Sisters Miriam Poveda, R.S.H.M., Pastoral Care Assoc.; Padraic Mary McGuinness, O.P., Pastoral Care Assoc.; Patricia Nickerson, Dir. of Social Services; Cheryl Ben-David, Dir. Rehabilitation Svcs.; Rev. Anthony J. Pleho, Chap. Bed Capacity 520; Total Assisted Annually 1,625; Total Staff 648.

Mary Manning Walsh Home, 1339 York Ave., 10021. Tel: 212-628-2800; Fax: 212-585-3896. Email: mmwhome@msn.com. Sr. Sean William O'Brien, O.Carm., Admin. Carmelite Sisters for the Aged and Infirm. Total Staff 480; Bed Capacity 362; Total Assisted 724.

Terence Cardinal Cooke Health Care Center Skilled Nursing Facility; Skilled Nursing Facility AIDS Program, 1249 Fifth Ave., 10029. Tel: 212-360-1000; Fax: 212-289-2739. Email: lgaffney@chcsnet.org. Web: www.tcchcc.org. (See Special Hospitals Category for additional services offered from this Health Care Center.) Bed Capacity 523; Bed Capacity 156.

BRONX. *Bon Secours New York Health System, Inc.*, 2975 Independence Ave., 10463-4699. Tel: 718-548-1700; Fax: 718-601-3384. Email: ajones@fhsny.org. Web: scherviercares.org. James T. Higgins, CEO; Sr. Sheila Moroney, P.B.V.M., Dir. of Pastoral Care.

Schervier Nursing Care Center

Frances Schervier Housing Development Fund Corporation

Bon Secours Health System, Inc., 1505 Marriottsville Rd, Marriottsville, MD 21104. Tel: 410-442-5511; Fax: 410-442-1082. Total Staff 520; Chaplains 4; Total Assisted Annually 830.

Jeanne Jugan Residence (1903) 2999 Schurz Ave., 10465. Tel: 347-329-1800; Fax: 347-329-1815. Email: bxmothersuperior@littlesistersofthepoor.org. Web: www.jjbronx.org. Sr. Genevieve Nugent, Pres.; Rev. Robert M. Dunn, Chap. Low Income Apartments 20; Skilled 30; Dayshare 20; Bed Capacity 47; Total Staff 60; Total Assisted Annually 90.

Medical Missionaries of Mary, 563 Minneford Ave., 10464-1118. Tel: 718-885-0945; Fax: 718-885-0010. Email: minniefordmmm@verizon.net. Web: www.mmmusa.org. Sisters Siobhan Corkery, M.M.M., Congregational Leader; Therese McDonough, M.M.M., USA Area Leader.

St. Patrick's Home for the Aged and Infirm (1931) 66 Van Cortlandt Park S., 10463. Tel: 718-519-2800; Fax: 718-304-1817. Email: www.admissions@stpatrickshome.org. Web: www.stpatrickshome.org/. Sr. M. Patrick Michael, O.Carm., Admin. Carmelite Sisters for the Aged and Infirm. Sisters 13; Bed Capacity 264; Total Assisted Annually 429; Total Staff 350.

Providence Rest (1922) 3304 Waterbury Ave., 10465. Tel: 718-931-3000; Fax: 718-514-8447. Email: prnh@providencerest.org. Web: www.providencerest.org. Sisters Seline Mary Flores, C.S.J.B., Admin.; Michele Sinnona, Supr. Sisters of St. John the Baptist 19; Bed Capacity 200; Total Assisted 174; Total Staff 310.

St. Vincent de Paul Residence (1992) 900 Intervale Ave., 10459. Tel: 917-645-9200; Fax: 718-589-7010. Email: fcianciotto@chcsnet.org. Web: www.svdpres.org. Mr. Frank Cianciotto, CEO.

DOBBS FERRY. *Cabrini of Westchester*, 115 Broadway, 10522. Tel: 914-693-6800; Fax: 914-693-1731. Web: www.cabrini-eldercare.org. Patricia Krasnausky, Pres. & CEO; Rev. Edwin Robinson, O.F.M., Dir. Pastoral Care. Missionary Sisters of the Sacred Heart 5; Bed Capacity 304; Home Health Care 250; Total Staff 465.

Cabrini Care at Home, 115 Broadway, 10522. Tel: 914-693-6800, Ext. 500. Email: pkrasnausky@cabrini-eldercare.org. Web: www.cabrini-eldercare.org. Patricia Krasnausky, Contact Person.

MIDDLETOWN. *St. Teresa's Nursing Home*, 120 Highland Ave., 10940. Tel: 845-342-1033; Fax: 845-344-5631. Email: mchaiken@chcsnet.org. Bed Capacity 98; Total Assisted 98; Total Staff 122.

RHINEBECK. *Ferncliff Nursing Home* (1973) 21 Ferncliff Dr., 12572. Tel: 845-876-2011; Fax: 845-876-4810. Sr. Sean Damien Flynn, O.Carm., B.S., M.B.A., Admin. Member: Catholic Health Care System. Bed Capacity 328; Total Assisted 410; Total Staff 450.

STATEN ISLAND. *Carmel Richmond Healthcare and Rehabilitation Center* (1969) 88 Old Town Rd., 10304-4299. Tel: 718-979-5000; Fax: 718-979-8027. Sr. Maureen T. Murray, O.Carm., Pres. & CEO. Carmelite Sisters for the Aged and Infirm. Bed Capacity 300; Total Assisted Annually 330; Total Staff 350.

Friends of Carmel Richmond, Inc. (1981) Tel: 718-979-5000; Fax: 718-979-8027. Adult Daycare Program. Total Assisted 330; Total Staff 350; Adult Day Healthcare Program Rehabilitation Unit 30.

WARWICK. *Villa Frances at the Knolls* Franciscan Health Partner, Inc., 22 Van Duzer Pl., 10990. Tel: 914-987-5717; Fax: 914-986-1231. Leah Cerkvenik, R.N., Exec. Vice Pres., Warwick Campus; Rev. Joseph P. McAndrew, Chap. (Retired). Capacity 120.

[BB] ADULT RESIDENCES

NEW YORK. *St. Agnes' Residence* For students and working women., 237 W. 74th St., 10023. Tel: 212-874-1361. Nancy Clifford, Admin. Franciscan Fathers of St. Francis Monastery. Daughters of Mary of the Immaculate Conception 2; Accommodations for 99; Total Assisted 104; Total Staff 6.

Centro Maria, Inc. For young students and working women., 539 W. 54th St., 10019. Tel: 212-757-6989; Fax: 212-307-5687. Email: cenmariany@mindspring.com. Web: www.religiosasdemariainmaculada. Sr. Hilda Ramirez, R.M.I., Local Supr. Religious of Mary Immaculate 8; Total Assisted Annually 667; Bed Capacity 86.

Cor Mariae, c/o 1011 First Ave., Rm. 1130, 10022. Tel: 212-371-1000, Ext. 2435. Residence for formerly homeless senior women.

The Dwelling Place (1977) For homeless women., 409 W. 40th St., 10018. Tel: 212-564-7887; Fax: 212-695-3642. Sr. Nancy Chiarello, O.S.F., Admin. Bed Capacity 15; Dinner Program 60; Total Assisted 80,000; Total Staff 6.

El Carmelo Residence, 249 W. 14th St., 10011. Tel: 212-242-8224; Fax: 212-242-7233. Sr. Modesta Perez, Supr.

The Jeanne d'Arc Residence (1896) 253 W. 24th St., 10011. Tel: 212-989-5952; Fax: 212-691-0257. Email: jdresidence@gmail.com. Sr. Marlene Rust, Admin. Women. Accommodations for 140; Sisters of Divine Providence 7; Lay Staff 11; Total Assisted Annually 200.

St. Joseph's Immigrant Home For students and working women., 425 W. 44th St., 10036-4402. Tel: 212-246-5363. Sr. Mary Celine, D.M., Admin. Daughters of Mary of the Immaculate Conception 2; Accommodations for 90.

Kolping Society of New York Men's Residence (Catholic Kolping Society New York, Inc.) (1888) For young Catholic men., 165 E. 88th St., 10128. Tel: 212-369-6647; Fax: 212-987-5652. Email: residence@kolpingny.org. Ernst Endrich, Mgr. Bed Capacity 88; Total Assisted Annually 350; Total Staff 10.

The Leo House (1889) Clergy, Sisters & Other Travelers., 332 W. 23rd St., 10011. Tel: 212-929-1010; Fax: 212-366-6801. Mr. Frank Castro, Exec. Dir. Total Staff 32.

St. Mary's Residence (1913) For students and young working women., 225 E. 72nd St., 10021. Tel: 212-249-6850; Fax: 212-249-4336. Email: St.MarysRes72@aol.com. Sr. Almaisa Brito, F.D.C., Admin.; Mrs. Lisa Rodriguez, Dir. of Admissions. Daughters of Divine Charity 6; Bed Capacity 150; Total Staff 6.

Sacred Heart Residence Working or studying young ladies ages 19-29., 432 W. 20th St., 10011. Tel: 212-929-5790; Fax: 212-924-0891. Email: sacredheartresidence@hotmail.com. Web: www.sacredheartresidence.com. Sr. Haydee Luisa Fernandez, Admin. Congregation of Mothers of the Helpless. Capacity 30; Total Staff 3.

Thorpe Family Residence, Inc. (1988) 2252 Crotona Ave., 10457. Tel: 718-933-7312; Fax: 718-933-7311. Email: SrBarbTFR@aol.com. Web: www.bronxmall.com/com/thorpe. Sr. Barbara Lenniger, O.P., Exec. Dir. Residents 65; Total Assisted 130; Total Staff 12.

The Crotona-Thorpe Housing Development Fund Corporation Tel: 914-359-6400; Fax: 914-359-6503. Sr. Muriel Cooney, O.P., Pres. (Sub of Thorpe Family Residence, Inc.)

BRONX. *St. Elizabeth House*, 427 E. 155th St., 10455. Tel: 212-234-9089. Web: www.franciscanfriars.com. Rev. Bernard Marie Murphy, C.F.R., Dir.

Kolping-on-Concourse, 2916 Grand Concourse, 10458. Tel: 718-733-6119. Web: www.kolpingresidence.com. Jorge Paris, Mgr. (Catholic Kolping Society New York, Inc.) Total in Residence 96; Total Assisted Annually 125; Total Staff 11.

DOBBS FERRY. *Cabrini Housing Development Fund Corporation*, c/o of St. Cabrini Nursing Home, Inc., 115 Broadway, 10522. Tel: 914-693-6800, Ext. 500; Fax: 914-693-1731. Email: pkrasnausky@cabrini-eldercare.org. Web: www.cabrini-eldercare.org.

GARRISON. *St. Christopher's Inn* (1908) Temporary shelter for homeless men. Outpatient chemical dependency services & primary healthcare., 21 Franciscan Way, P.O. Box 150, 10524-0150. Tel: 845-335-1000; Fax: 845-335-1017. Email: bpalka@atonementfriars.org. Web: www.stchristophersinn-graymoor.org. Rev. Bernard Palka, S.A., Pres. & CEO. Atonement Friars. Total Assisted 1,200; Total Staff 60; Bed Capacity 147; Volunteers 8.

MONTROSE. *Kolping-on-Hudson* (Catholic Kolping Society New York, Inc.), 95 Montrose Point Rd., 10548. Tel: 914-736-0117. Total Assisted 2,000; Total Staff 10.

MOUNT VERNON. *St. Theresa's Residence*, 30 S. 10th Ave., 10550. Tel: 914-664-5900; Fax: 914-664-6733. John Schroeder, Exec. Dir. Bed Capacity 12.

[CC] CATHOLIC CAMPS

NEW YORK. *The Catholic Camp Association Inc.*, 1011 First Ave., 10022. Tel: 212-371-1000.

John V. Mara CYO Camps, Putnam Valley, 10579.

Hill Camp Capacity 120.

Valley Camp Capacity 120; Total Assisted 147; Total in Residence 271; Total Staff 48.

THORNWOOD. *Challenge NA, Inc.* (1997) 590 Columbus Ave., 10594. Tel: 914-773-1368; Fax: 914-773-1438. Rev. Jose Felix Ortega, L.C., Contact Person.

[DD] COMMUNITY CENTERS

NEW YORK. *Cardinal Spellman Center, Inc.*, 137 E. Second St., 10009. Tel: 212-677-6600; Fax: 212-995-8537. Community Centers foster and promote the positive development of children, youth, their families and other adults by providing or hosting various wholesome activities.

Casita Maria Inc. (1934) 928 Simpson St., 6th Fl., Bronx, 10459. Tel: 718-589-2230; Fax: 718-842-4622. Email: info@casita.us. Web: www.casita.us. Sarah Calderon, Exec. Dir.; Mrs. Jacqueline Weld, Chm. Serves the Bronx, East Harlem, and greater New York City; Casita Maria serves over 5,000 individuals each year through arts, education, and community programs.

Casita Maria-Carver Community Center, 55 E. 102nd St., 10029. Tel: 212-289-2708; 718-589-2230; Fax: 212-360-1947; 718-589-5714. Email: info@casita.us. Lue Ann Eldar, Exec. Dir.; Diana Ayala, Dir. Serves Carver Houses and adjacent areas of East Harlem.

Casita Maria Inc., 928 Simpson St., Bronx, 10459. Tel: 718-589-2230; Fax: 718-589-5714.

Drew-Hamilton CYO Center, 220 W. 143rd St., 10030. Serves Central Harlem.

Lieut. Joseph P. Kennedy, Jr. Memorial Community Center, 34 W. 134th St., 10037. Community Centers foster and promote the positive development of children, youth, their families and other adults by providing or hosting various wholesome activities.

Life Experience and Faith Sharing Association, 45 E. 126th St., 10035. Tel: 212-987-0959; Fax: 212-987-0958. Email: lefslitera@aol.com. James Addison, LEFS Team - Mission Co-Coord.; Deborah Byrd, LEFS Team; Deborah Canty, LEFS Team; Timothy Dunnington, LEFS Team; Sr. Dorothy Gallant, S.C., LEFS Team - Mission Co-Coord.; Georgia James, LEFS Team; Vaughn McLamb, LEFS Team; Sr. Cecilia Palange, I.C.M., LEFS Team; Ann Quintano, LEFS Team. LEFSA - Ministry among people who are homeless and formerly homeless. Total Assisted 1,500.

Staten Island CYO Center Serves residents of Port Richmond and surrounding areas.
120 Anderson Ave., Port Richmond, Staten Island, 10302. Fax: 718-273-8361.

HAVERSTRAW. *Catholic Community Services of Rockland, Inc.*, 78 Hudson St., 10927. Tel: 845-942-5791; Fax: 845-429-2938. Email: marth.robles@archny.org. Martha Robles, Exec. Dir. Provides emergency services to those in need.

PORT CHESTER. *Don Bosco Community Center of Port Chester, Inc.*, Office of the Pres., 22 Don Bosco Pl., 10573. Tel: 914-939-0323, Ext. 11; Fax: 914-939-3490. Email: boscoalive@yahoo.com. Web: www.donboscocenter.com. Rev. Richard P. Alejunas, Exec. Dir.

YONKERS. *Casa Juan Diego, Inc.*, 97 Yonkers Ave., 10701. Tel: 914-963-0250; Fax: 914-476-5033. Rev. Lawrence Schrodel, Dir. Services to the needy; especially Spanish Speaking immigrants, day laborers.

[EE] MONASTERIES AND RESIDENCES OF PRIESTS AND BROTHERS

NEW YORK. *All Saints Friary* (2002) (Order of Friars Minor-The Franciscans-Province of the Most Holy Name of Jesus), 47 E. 129th St., 10035. Tel: 212-534-3535; Fax: 212-534-7832. Bros. Charles F. Gilmartin, O.F.M.; Glenn W. Humphrey, O.F.M., B.A., M.A., Ph.D.; Revs. Francis K. Kim, O.F.M., B.A., M.Div.; Steven Pavignano, O.F.M. Priests 2; Brothers 2.

"America;" Residence and publication office of the America Press, 106 W. 56th St., 10019. Tel: 212-581-4640; Fax: 212-399-3596. Email: jesuits@americamagazine.org. Web: www.americamagazine.org. Revs. Andrew J. Christiansen, S.J., Editor-in-Chief; Robert C. Collins, S.J.; James J. DiGiacomo, S.J.; Charles A. Frederico, S.J.; Daniel J. Gatti, S.J.; Roger D. Haight, S.J.; Thomas J. Massaro, S.J.; Walter J. Modrys, S.J.; James J. Martin, S.J.; Leo J. O'Donovan, S.J.; Joseph A. O'Hare, S.J.; Robert F. O'Toole, S.J.; Joseph P. Parkes, S.J.; Edward F. Salmon, S.J., Supr.; Michael E. Sehler, S.J.; Thomas R. Slon, S.J.; Michael V. Teuth, S.J.; Charles M. Whelan, S.J.; Bro. Francis W. Turnbull, S.J. Priests 20; Brothers 1; Scholastics 2.

Atonement Friars, 138 Waverly Pl., 10014-3845. Tel: 212-243-4692; Fax: 212-675-6160. Web: www.atonementfriars.org. Revs. James Loughran, S.A.; Timothy I. MacDonald, S.A., Admin. & Guardian; Elias D. Mallon, S.A.; Charles Sharon, S.A., Admin.; Wilfred Tyrrell, S.A.

Brothers of the Christian Schools of Manhattan College, Inc., 4415 Post Rd., Bronx, 10471. Tel: 718-884-0613; Fax: 718-884-3500. Bros. Timothy Murphy, Pres./Dir.; Charles Barbush, F.S.C., Sub Dir. Total Staff 3; Total in Residence 24. In Res. Rev. Rinaldo Borzaga, A.F.S.C.

Calasanzian Fathers (Piarists), 88 Convent Ave., 10027. Tel: 212-234-1919; Fax: 212-281-7205. Email: annunciationchurchnyc@yahoo.com. Revs. Felix Ganuza, Sch.P. (Spain), Supr.; Jose M. Clavero, Sch.P. (Spain); Marcel Ayuni Toh, Sch.P. (Cameroon); Javier Vanejas, Sch.P. (Nicaragua); Igor Galindo, Sch.P. (Mexico); Fernando Negro, Sch.P. (Spain); Javier Renteria, Sch.P. (Spain).

St. Catherine of Siena Priory, 411 E. 68th St., 10021. Tel: 212-988-8300; Fax: 212-988-6918. Email: stcatsiena@aol.com. Revs. Christopher Johnson, O.P., Prior; Vincent Ferrer McHenry, O.P.; John Jerome Conroy, O.P.; David Aloysius Butler, O.P., Subprior; John Thaddeus Murphy, O.P.; Robert Philip Fitzsimmons, O.P.; George Lawrence Concordia, O.P., Ph.D.; Scott Matthew Erickson, O.P., S.T.B., M.Div.

St. Clare Friary, 440 W. 36th St., 10018-6326. Tel: 212-594-4108. Email: sground440@aol.com. Web: www.solidgroundministry.com. Rev. James Goode, O.F.M., Local Minister, Pastoral Dir., Solid Ground Ministry; Harold Williams Jr., Affiliate, Solid Ground Prog. Coord.; James P. Newson Jr., Black Catholic Apostolate for Life Asst. *Shrine of Saint Josephine Bakhita* In the Holy Mother of God Chapel, Tel: 212-868-1847. Web: www.solidgroundministry.com. *Solid Ground Ministry: A Franciscan Ministry with African American Families* (1996) Tel: 212-868-1847. Email: sground440@aol.com. Web: www.solidgroundministry.com. *National Black Catholic Apostolate for Life* (1997) Tel: 212-594-4108; Fax: 212-563-0787. Email: tnbcalife@aol.com. Web: www.blackcatholicsforlife.org.

St. Crispin Friary (1987) 420 E. 156th St., Bronx, 10455. Tel: 718-665-2441; Fax: 718-993-4754. Web: www.franciscanfriars.com. *Franciscan Friars of the Renewal* (1987) 420 E. 156th St., Bronx, 10455. Tel: 718-402-8255; Fax: 718-402-5556. Revs. Richard Roemer, C.F.R., Local Servant; Agustino Miguel Torres, C.F.R., Local Vicar; Benedict Joseph Groeschel, C.F.R., Ed.D., Community Council; Bernard Marie Murphy, C.F.R., Community Servant; Bros. Simon Dankowski, C.F.R.; Mariano Joseph Demma, C.F.R.; Roch Mary Greiner, C.F.R.; Nicholas Maria White, C.F.R. Priests 3; Brothers 6.

Saint Francis Monastery, Inc., 135W. 31 St., 10001. Tel: 212-736-8500. Rev. Jerome Massimino, O.F.M., Contact Person.

Franciscan Friars, Holy Name Province, Holy Name Province Provincialate, 129 W. 31st St., 2nd Fl., 10001-3403. Tel: 646-473-0265; Fax: 800-420-1078; 800-605-8542. Email: hnp@hnp.org. Web: www.hnp.org. Revs. John F. O'Connor, O.F.M., Pres. & Min. Prov.; Dominic Monti, O.F.M., Vicar Prov.; Bro. Michael Harlan, O.F.M., Prov. Sec.; Rev. Dennis M. Wilson, O.F.M., Prov. Treas.

The Order of Friars Minor of the Province of the Most Holy Name

Priests of the Province in Residences not listed elsewhere: Revs. David M. Bossman, O.F.M., Seton Hall University, 400 S. Orange Ave., South Orange, NJ 07079-2696. Tel: 973-761-9770; Fax: 973-275-2333; J. Patrick Kelly, O.F.M., FrancisCare, Elmwood Park Plaza, 475 Market St., Elmwood Park, NJ 07407-3104. Tel: 201-791-1499; Fax: 201-791-3529; Leonard Lencewicz, O.F.M., St. Anthony Hermitage, 8817 Brys Dr., Tampa, FL 33635. Tel: 813-888-5616; Fax: 813-886-3624; Rene F. Phillips, O.F.M., 850 Thomas Ln., Angola, 14006-9572. Tel: 716-549-7930; Benedict M. Taylor, O.F.M., Create

Inc., 73 Lenox Ave., 10026. Tel: 212-663-1975; Fax: 212-663-1293; Alfonso Guzman Alfaro, O.F.M., Arzobispado de San Juan, P.O. Box 9021967, San Juan 00902-1967 Puerto Rico. Tel: 787-725-4975; Fax: 787-723-4040; Lawrence A. Burke, O.F.M., Chap., Mount Saint Francis, 474 Sloatsburg Rd., Ringwood, NJ 07456; Kenneth R. Himes, O.F.M., Dean, School of Theology, Boston College, 140 Commonwealth Ave., Chestnut Hill, MA 02467; Joseph J. Nangle, O.F.M., Clare House, 708 Rock Creek Church Rd., N.W., Washington, DC 20010; Thomas F. Sheehan, O.F.M., 24 Parkdale Dr., Lancaster, 14086.

Priests Abroad: For Information Regarding Vocations to the Brotherhood & Priesthood, write Franciscan Vocation Office, 129 W. 31st St., 2nd Fl., New York, NY 10001-3403. Revs. Howard O'Shea, O.F.M., 34, Rue Roux Alpheran, Aix-En-Provence 13100, France. Tel: 011-33-4-4226-7789; Fax: 011-33-4-4226-7789; Joseph G. Rozansky, O.F.M., JPIC Office of the Order, Curia Generalizia dei Frati Minori, Via S. Maria Mediatrice 25, Rome 00165 Italy; Emerson Rodriguez-Delgado, O.F.M.

Franciscan Province of the Immaculate Conception, 125 Thompson St., 10012. Tel: 212-674-4388; Fax: 212-533-8034. Revs. Robert M. Campagna, O.F.M., Min. Prov.; Patrick Boyle, O.F.M., Vicar Prov.; James Goode, O.F.M., Promoter Missions; Bro. Ronald Bolfeta, O.F.M., Prov. Treas. & Prov. Sec. *Friars Minor of the Order of St. Francis, Incorporated, New York, 1871* Franciscan Province of the Immaculate Conception of New York City. Priests 123; Brothers 22; Permanent Deacons 2; Bishops 3. *Franciscan Mission Associates*, 274-280 W. Lincoln Ave., Mt. Vernon, 10550. Tel: 914-664-5604; Fax: 914-664-3017. Ms. Madeline Bonnici, Exec. Dir.; Rev. Vit Fiala, O.F.M., Dir. of Secular Franciscans. *Pious League of Saint Anthony*, 151 Thompson St., P.O. Box 700, 10012-0700. Tel: 212-674-4388; Fax: 212-533-8034.

Priests of the Province Abroad: Revs. Primo Piscitello, O.F.M., Guardian, Convento S. Francesco, Via Nicolo V, 35, Rome 00165 Italy; Francis Walter, O.F.M., General Definitor, Convento S. Francesco, Via Nicolo V, 35, Rome 00165 Italy; Edwin Paniagua, O.F.M., Translator; Antonio Riccio, O.F.M., Guardian.

Military Chaplains: Rev. Michael Travaglione, O.F.M., 23 Bassett St., Fort Bragg, NC 28307.

Retired Military Chaplains: Revs. Edwin Bobrek, O.F.M., 1427 Ave. de las Adelsas, Encinitas, CA 92024. Tel: 619-436-5355; Sigmund Brambilla, O.F.M., 97 Franklin St., Northampton, MA 01060. Tel: 413-584-4482; Jack Hoak, O.F.M., St. Rose of Lima Friary, 35 Center St., Meriden, CT 06450-5685. Tel: 518-273-8622; Fax: 518-273-2731; Charles Soto, O.F.M. (Retired), P.O. Box 4051, Steubenville, OH 43952. Tel: 740-424-9434.

Priests of the Province Residing Elsewhere: Revs. Romano S. Almagno, O.F.M., Sts. Peter & Paul Cathedral Res., 30 Fenner St., Providence, RI 02903; Lucius Annese, O.F.M., 201 E. 19th St., Apt. 8F, 10003. Tel: 212-995-6056; Marion Cascino, O.F.M.; John-Marie Cassese, O.F.M., Mary Manning Walsh Home, 1339 York Ave., 10021; Roderick Crispo, O.F.M.; Louis D. De Tommaso, O.F.M.; Simeon C. Distefano, O.F.M., Chap., 1339 York Ave., 10021. Tel: 212-628-2800; Frederick Fusco, O.F.M., 1939 Antietam St., Pittsburgh, PA 15206; Stephen Galambos, O.F.M., 21077 Quarry Hill Rd., Winona, MN 55987. Tel: 507-454-8000; Ronald Gliatta, O.F.M., 3301 N.E. 32nd Ave., Apt. 203, Fort Lauderdale, FL 33308; Ciro Iodice, O.F.M., 1111 Langley St., Fall River, MA 02720. Tel: 508-679-2105; Januarius Izzo, O.F.M., Marian Manor, 130 Dorchester St., South Boston, MA 02127; Richard Martignetti, O.F.M.; Alban V. Montella, O.F.M., Mary Manning Walsh Home, 1339 York Ave., 10021; Edwin Paniagua, O.F.M., General Curia of Friars Minor, Via S. Maria Mediatrice, 25, Rome 00165 Italy; Emery Parillo, O.F.M.; Clement Procopio, O.F.M., 306 S. 18th St., Cottonwood, AZ 86326. Tel: 928-639-4583; Roberto Siguere, O.F.M., Iglesia de S. Francisco, Barrio Latina, Jutiapa, Jutiapa Guatemala; Michael Travaglione, O.F.M., 4-25 BCT, FOB Salerno, APO AE 0314.

Residing in Canada: Revs. Yusuf Bagh, O.F.M., St. Jane Frances de Chantal Friary, 2747 Jane St., Downsview ON M3L 2E8 Canada. Tel: 416-741-1463; Fax: 416-741-1469; Gregory Botte, O.F.M., St. Francis Friary, 72 Mansfield Ave., Toronto ON M6J 2B2 Canada. Tel: 416-536-8195; Fax: 416-531-6883; Celestino Canzio, O.F.M., St. Charles Borromeo Friary, 811 Lawrence Ave., Toronto ON M6A 1C3 Canada. Tel: 416-787-0369; Fax: 416-256-4466; Michael D'Cruz, O.F.M., St. Charles Borromeo Friary, 811 Lawrence Ave., Toronto ON M6A 1C3 Canada. Tel: 416-787-0369; Fax: 416-256-4466; Gregory E. Imbroll, O.F.M., St. Charles Borromeo Friary, 811 Lawrence Ave., Toronto ON M6A 1C3 Canada. Tel: 416-787-0369; Fax: 416-256-4466; Frederick Mazzarella, O.F.M., St. Francis Friary, 72 Mansfield Ave., Toronto ON M6J 2B2 Canada. Tel: 416-536-8195; Fax: 416-531-6883; Amedeo Nardone, O.F.M., St. Jane Frances de Chantal Friary, 2747 Jane St., Downsview ON M3L 2E8 Canada. Tel: 416-741-1463; Fax: 416-741-1469; Peter Nguyen Van Quy, O.F.M.; Rohwin Pais, O.F.M., St. Jane Frances de Chantal Friary, 2747 Jane St., Downsview ON M3L 2E8 Canada. Tel: 416-741-1463; Fax: 416-741-1469; Ralph Paonessa, O.F.M., St. Lawrence Friary, 2210 Lawrence Ave. E., Scarborough ON M1P 2P9 Canada. Tel: 416-759-9359; Fax: 416-759-6725; Orlando Ruiz, O.F.M.; Blaise Tranchida, O.F.M., House of Providence, 3276 St. Clair Ave., E., Toronto ON M1L 1W1 Canada; Jimmy Zammit, O.F.M., Immaculate Conception Friary, 2 Richardson Ave., Toronto ON M6M 3R4 Canada. Tel: 416-651-1787; Fax: 416-651-7881. *St. Francis Center for Religious*, 208501 Hwy. #9, Caledon ON L7K 0A8 Canada. Tel: 519-941-1747; Fax: 519-941-6961. Revs. Lawrence Parent, O.F.M., Parochial Vicar, Immaculate Conception Friary, 2 Richardson Ave., Toronto ON M6M 3R4 Canada; Michael Della Penna, O.F.M., Valle de los Angeles, Aldeas San Jose El Manzano, Muknicipio de Santa Catalina Pinula, Guatemala; Bro. Philip Adamo, O.F.M. *St. Peter Friary*, 100 Bainbridge Ave., Woodbridge ON L4L-3YL Canada. Tel: 905-851-3600; Fax: 905-856-0171. Revs. Claudio Moser, O.F.M.; James Wells, O.F.M.; Michael Corcione, O.F.M.

The Franciscan Vocation Ministry of Holy Name Province (1901) 129 W. 31st St., 2nd Fl., 10001-3403. Tel: 212-924-1451; 646-473-0265; 800-677-7788; Fax: 800-793-7649. Email: vocation@hnp.org. Web: www.beafranciscan.org. Rev. Brian E. Smail, O.F.M., HNP Vocation Dir.

St. Ignatius Loyola Residence (1866) 53 E. 83rd St., 10028. Tel: 212-288-6200; Fax: 212-606-3460. Revs. James R. Van Dyke, S.J., Rector; Arthur C. Bender, S.J.; William J. Bergen, S.J.; Vincent L. Biagi, S.J.; Bro. John J. Campbell, S.J.; Revs. Kenneth J. Caufield, S.J.; James J. Curry, S.J.; Vincent P. DeCola, S.J.; Thomas F. Denny, S.J.; James L. Dugan, S.J.; John F. Garvey, S.J.; Mark C. Hallinan, S.J.; Philip G. Judge, S.J.; Stephen N. Katsouros, S.J.; Joseph W. Lux, S.J.; Ugo R. Nacciarone, S.J.; Robert E. O'Brien, S.J.; Daniel G. O'Hare, S.J.; Steven J. Pugliese, S.J.; Michael J. Sala, S.J.; Ramon A. Salomone, S.J., Min.; John R. Sheehan, S.J.; George M. Witt, S.J.; Bros. Christopher Derby, S.J.; Edward L. McCarthy, S.J.; Jerome P. Menkhaus, S.J.; Mr. U. Alejandro Baez, S.J.; Mr. James T. Donovan, S.J.; Mr. Brent H. Otto, S.J.

Immaculate Conception Friary, 754 E. Gun Hill Rd., 10467. Tel: 212-653-2200. Revs. John LoSasso, O.F.M.Cap.; Peter Napoli, O.F.M.Cap.; Robert Williams, O.F.M.Cap. Capuchin Friars of the Province of the Stigmata of St. Francis. Total Assisted 190; Total Staff 20; Priests 3; Brothers 2.

Institute of the Incarnate Word, Inc., 113 E. 117th St., 10035. Tel: 212-534-5257; Fax: 212-534-5258. Web: www.iveamerica.org. Rev. Gustavo Nieto, Pres.

Jesuit Community at Fordham University (1846) 441 E. Fordham Rd., 10458. Tel: 718-817-5322; Fax: 718-733-4456. Rev. John J. Cecero, S.J., Rector/Supr., Jesuit Community at Cardinal Spellman Hall. *Loyola Hall, Jesuit Community* (1929) Tel: 718-817-5322; Fax: 718-733-4456. Revs. Thomas E. Smith, S.J., Supr.; Thomas R. Marciniak, S.J., Minister; John D. Alexander, S.J.; Pierce A. Brennan, S.J.; Vincent E. Butler, S.J.; Robert H. Cousineau, S.J.; James H. Dahlinger, S.J.; Robert R. Dobbins, S.J.; Joseph V. Dolan, S.J., Sub Min.; John W. Donohue, S.J.; Edward T. Dowling, S.J.; Rev. Msgr. Charles J. Fahey (SY); Revs. James J. Fedigan, S.J.; Alfred L. Fiorino, S.J.; Daniel J. Fitzpatrick, S.J.; Matthew C. Flood, S.J.; Gabriel Jose T. Gonzalez, S.J.; John R. Keating, S.J.; Donald J. Keefe, S.J.; George C. McCauley, S.J.; John J. McDonald, S.J.; Donald J. Moore, S.J.; Thomas Murphy, S.J.; Vincent M. Novak, S.J.; Donald V. O'Brien, S.J.; David O. Ogun, S.J. (Nigeria); Louis B. Pascoe, S.J.; Richard J. Regan, S.J.; James A. Sadowsky, S.J.; Victor Salanga, S.J.; Daniel J. Sullivan, S.J.; Jose Vilaplana, S.J. (Spain); Joachim Von Kerssenbrock, S.J.; Bros. Sebastian A. Boccabella, S.J.; Gerard W. Schade, S.J.; Gilbert J. Scott, S.J. *Jesuit Community, Kohlmann Hall* Tel: 718-584-1638; Fax: 718-584-0760. Revs. Charles D. Sullivan, S.J., Supr.; Kenneth J. Boller, S.J., M.Div., Pres., Fordham Prep.; Donald G. Devine, S.J.; Mallick J. Fitzpatrick, S.J.; Joseph J. Kamiensky, S.J.; John J. Leonard, S.J., Sub Min.; Stanley J. O'Konsky, S.J.; William J. O'Malley, S.J.; Michael T. Siconolfi, S.J.; Raymond M. Sweitzer, S.J. *Cardinal Spellman Hall, Jesuit Community* (1995) Tel: 718-817-5330; Fax: 718-817-5717. Revs. John J. Cecero, S.J., Rector/Supr.; R. Bentley Anderson, S.J.; Bernard J. Barry, S.J.; Charles J. Beirne, S.J.; Henry J. Bertels, S.J.; Claudio M. Burgaleta, S.J.; Martin Chase, S.J.; Christopher M. Cullen, S.J.; Joseph A. Currie, S.J., Dir. of Campus Ministry; John T. Dzieglewicz, S.J.; Robert R. Grimes, S.J.; Anton T. Harris, S.J., Min. & Asst. to Rector; George Hunt, S.J.; Aloysius P. Kelley, S.J.; Joseph W. Koterski, S.J.; Joseph T. Lienhard, S.J.; Nicholas D. Lombardi, S.J.; David P. Marcotte, S.J.; Mark S. Massa, S.J.; Thomas M. McCoog, S.J.; Paul D. McNelis, S.J.; Joseph M. McShane, S.J., Pres., Fordham Univ.; Mark S. Mossa, S.J.; Joseph A. Novak, S.J.; Daniel J. O'Brien, S.J.; Gerard Reedy, S.J.; Patrick J. Ryan, S.J.; Thomas J. Scirghi, S.J.; Gregory S. Waldrop, S.J.; Mr. Todd R. Keough, S.J. Priests 72; Brothers 3; Scholastics 1; Total in Residence 76.

St. Joseph's Friary (Franciscan Friars of the Renewal); (Postulancy), 523 W. 142nd St., 10031. Tel: 212-234-9089; Fax: 212-234-8871; 212-281-4355 (Vocation Office). Web: www.franciscanfriars.com. Revs. Luke Mary Fletcher, C.F.R., Local Servant & Postulant Dir.; Gabriel Mary Bakkar, C.F.R., Vocation Dir.; Robert Lombardo, C.F.R.; Bro. Pius Marie Gagne, C.F.R., Asst. Voc. Dir. Postulants 10.

The Little Brothers of the Gospel (1956) 58 E. Fourth St., #10, 10003. Tel: 212-982-2431. *St. Mary Church*, 17 Pompton Ave., Pompton Lakes, NJ 07442. Tel: 973-835-0374; Fax: 973-835-8173.

Maryknoll House Catholic Foreign Mission Society., 121 E. 39th St., 10016. Tel: 212-697-4470; Fax: 212-697-4472. Email: mklnyc@aol.com. Web: www.maryknoll.org. Bro. Anthony Lopez, M.M., Dir.; Rev. Clyde Phillips, M.M.

Murray-Weigel Hall, 515 E. Fordham Rd., 10458-5004. Tel: 718-430-4900; Fax: 718-365-8650. Email: jmcostello@hotmail.com. Revs. Robert W. Dahlke, S.J.; Erwin G. Beck, S.J.; John B. Breslin, S.J., M.A., M.Div., Ph.D.; James R. Carney, S.J.; William B. Cogan, S.J.; Richard P. Grogan, S.J.; John M. Costello, S.J., Min.; John M. Doolan, S.J.; Garrett J. Fitzgerald, S.J., B.A., M.A.; John Gallen, S.J.; Joseph P. Kane, S.J.; Joseph V. Landy, S.J.; John M. McConnell, S.J.; Louis A. Mounteer, S.J.; Edward J. Murphy, S.J.; Anthony F. LaBau, S.J.; Richard J. Pendergast, S.J.; Thomas S. Prout, S.J.; Francis V. Rooney, S.J.; Peter J. Roslovich, S.J.; Louis E. Soloman, S.J.; John P. St. George, S.J.; Patrick J. Sullivan, S.J.; John G. Marzolf, S.J., Supr.; Richard F. Timone, S.J.; Francis P. Valentino, S.J.; James J. Wheeler, S.J.; Patrick T. Sullivan, S.J.; James A. McDonough, S.J.; Joseph F. Fitzpatrick, S.J.; Alfredo S. Quevedo, S.J.; Eugene J. Quigley, S.J.; William J. Scanlon, S.J., Chap. Health Care Facility; Brendan T. Scott, S.J.; William Sullivan, S.J.; Gerald E. Braun, S.J.; Neil J. Carr, S.J.; Robert E. Carter, S.J.; Martin A. Hegyi, S.J., B.A., Ph.D. (Hungary); Thomas C. Hennessy, S.J., M.A., M.S., Ph.D.; Robert G. Kelly, S.J., M.A.T., B.A., S.T.B.; Lawrence X. McCaffrey, S.J.; John J. Rohr, S.J. Priests 60; Brothers 6; Scholastics 1.

Scholastics: Bro. Raymond V. Whalen, S.J.

Our Lady of Consolation Residence Tel: 718-548-0888; Fax: 718-548-7824. 3103 Arlington Ave., Bronx, 10463-3305. Tel: 718-548-0889; 718-548-0889; Fax: 718-548-7824. Email: mblolc@aol.com. Mrs. Mary B. Lynch, R.N., Residence Dir.; Most Rev. Anthony F. Mestice, D.D. (Retired); Rev. Msgrs. Joseph A. Dunne (Retired); Kenneth A. Gerathy (Retired); Victor S. Pavis (Retired); Revs. Thomas J. Darby (Retired); John W. Holihan (Retired); Matthew Mulloy (Retired); Frederick J. Sullivan (Retired).

Padua Friary (1866) 147-151 Thompson St., 10012-3110. Tel: 212-254-9553; Fax: 212-254-9644. Bro. Courtland Campbell, O.F.M., Capitular, Guardian, Sec. & Mission Dir. J.P.I.C.; Revs. John-Marie Cassese, O.F.M.; Sebastian Buccellato, O.F.M., FMU Prom. & Parochial Ministry; Louis Troiano, O.F.M., Parochial Ministry; Adolph Giorda, O.F.M., Parochial Ministry; Louis D. De Tommaso, O.F.M., Provincial Treasurer; Bros. Luke Storino, O.F.M., Prov. Bookkeeper, Prov. Curia Staff; Paschal De Mattia, O.F.M., Provincial Curia Staff.

Pallottine Fathers, Society of the Catholic Apostolate, 448 E. 116th St., 10029. Tel: 212-534-0681; Fax: 212-534-0629. Revs. Tony Kelly, S.A.C., Spanish Apostolate; Carlos Cardoso, S.A.C., Assoc. Admin. Total Assisted 300; Total Staff 15.

Passionist Spiritual Center, 5801 Palisade Ave., Riverdale, 10471. Tel: 718-549-6500; Fax: 718-884-9732. Email: Passpiritctr@passionists.org. Web: www.passionist.org. Rev. Paul R. Fagan, C.P., Retreat Dir & Local Leader; Bro. James Johnson, C.P., Hosted & Special Events Coord.; Rev.

Michael Greene, C.P., Assoc. Retreat Dir.; Bro. Andre Mathieu, C.P., Itinerant Preacher; Rev. John Powers, C.P., Itinerant Preacher; Bro. August Parlavechio, C.P., Province Devel. Office & Part-time Retreat Staff.

Paulist Fathers' Motherhouse, 415 W. 59th St., 10019. Tel: 212-265-3209; Fax: 212-265-4154. Email: Paulist59@cs.com. Web: www.paulist.org. Revs. Gerald J. Aylward, C.S.P. (Retired); Donald Campbell, C.S.P.; John E. Collins, C.S.P., Preaching Apostolate; Kevin A. Devine, C.S.P.; Francis X. Diskin, C.S.P. (Retired); James M. DiLuzio, C.S.P., Preaching Apostolate; David P. Dwyer, C.S.P., Dir. Young Adult Ministries; Lionel A. DeSilva, C.S.P., Hosp. Chap.; David E. Farnum, C.S.P., Vocation Dir.; John J. Foley, C.S.P.; Ronald A. Franco, C.S.P., Assoc. Pastor St. Paul the Apostle; James A. Haley, C.S.P., Supr. & General Treas.; Dennis W. Hickey, C.S.P.; James B. Lloyd, C.S.P. (Retired); Kevin A. Lynch, C.S.P., Emeritus Publisher Paulist Press; Joseph F. Mahon, C.S.P. (Retired); Gilbert S. Martinez, C.S.P., Pastor St. Paul the Apostle; Lawrence V. McDonnell, C.S.P. (Retired); James F. McQuade, C.S.P., Hospital Chap.; Robert A. O'Donnell, C.S.P. (Retired); Frank Sabatté, C.S.P., Arts Ministry; Jeremiah D. Sullivan, C.S.P. (Retired); Francis M. Sweeney, C.S.P. (Retired); Timothy P. Tighe, C.S.P., Preaching Apostolate; Rudolph T. Vorisek, C.S.P. (Retired). See also St. Paul the Apostle Parish

Redemptorist Priests and Brothers, C.Ss.R. (1887) (Prov. of Baltimore), Redemptorist Residence, 323 E. 61st St., 10065-8204. Tel: 212-838-1324; Fax: 212-838-4154. Very Rev. Alfred Bradley, C.Ss.R., Local Supr.; Revs. Russell J. Abata, C.Ss.R., B.A., S.T.D.; Carlyle R. Blake, C.Ss.R.; Michael Hopkins, C.Ss.R., Consultor & Treas.; Michael Koncik, C.Ss.R., Chap.-Rikers Island, Otis Bateman No. 49 Infirmary Command; James P. Lundy, C.Ss.R.; Raymond P. McCarthy, C.Ss.R., M.Div.; Lawrence J. Murphy, C.Ss.R., B.A.; Francis J. O'Rourke, C.Ss.R., B.A., Consultor & Vicar; Robert Pagliari, C.Ss.R., B.A., M.A., Ph.D.; Richard L. Welch, C.Ss.R., J.C.D., M.R.E., M.Div., Tribunal Judge & Assoc. Judicial Vicar; Bro. Christopher A. Colarossi, C.Ss.R. *Society of Jesus, New York Province aka New York Province of the Society of Jesus* 39 E. 83rd St., 10028-0810. Tel: 212-774-5500; Fax: 212-794-1036. Email: nykprov@nysj.org. Web: www.nysj.org. Very Rev. David S. Ciancimino, S.J., Prov.; Revs. Vincent L. Biagi, S.J., Asst. for Secondary & Presecondary Educ. & Lay Formation; Rocco C. Danzi, S.J., Province Dir. Vocation Promotion; Thomas H. Feely, S.J., Asst. for Formation for the Maryland & New York Provinces; Charles A. Frederico, S.J., Vocation Dir. for Maryland & New York Provinces; Mark C. Hallinan, S.J., Asst. Social Min.; James F. Keenan, S.J., Dir. Devel.; Walter J. Modrys, S.J., Province Treas.; Ramon A. Salomone, S.J., Asst. to Provincial for Intl.; J. Peter Schineller, S.J., Archivist; Thomas R. Slon, S.J., Exec. Asst. to Prov.; James J. Yannarell, S.J., Province Health Care Coord. a.k.a. Jesuit Seminary and Mission Bureau, Inc.

Jesuit Provincial's Office (1540) 39 E. 83rd St., 10028. Tel: 212-774-5500; Fax: 212-794-1036. Email: nykprov@nysj.org. Web: www.nysj.org.

Priests of the Province Abroad: Revs. Michael P. Hilbert, S.J., Pontificia Universita Gregoriana, Piazza della Pilotta 4,00187, Rome, Italy. Tel: 39-06-6701-5452; Fax: 39-06-6701-5412; Keith F. Pecklers, S.J., Coll Bellarmino, Via del Seminario 120, 00186, Rome, Italy. Tel: 39-06-69527-6638; Fax: 39-06-6701-5413.

Priests of the Province in Residences Not Listed Elsewhere: Revs. George H. Belgarde, S.J., P.O. Box 429, Hogansburg, 13655. Tel: 613-575-2066; Gerard P. Bell, S.J., 15107 Interlachen Dr., Apt. 722, Silver Spring, MD 20906. Tel: 301-438-3753; Gerard H. Ettlinger, S.J., 10-01 162nd St., Apt. 5-D, Whitestone, 11357. Tel: 718-767-5895; Edward J. Mally, S.J., 1S 150 Spring Rd., Apt. 2E, Oakbrook Terrace, IL 60181. Tel: 630-833-0645; Fax: 708-756-6863; Walter J. Smith, S.J., 370 First Ave., Apt. 12C, 10010. Tel: 646-215-5347.

St. Vincent de Paul Residence, 900 Intervale Ave., 10459. Tel: 718-589-6965; Fax: 718-589-7010. Email: svdpres@chcn.org. Web: www.svdpres.org. Total Assisted 3,120; Total Staff 8.

St. Vincent Ferrer Priory (1867) Dominican Friars Provincial House (Province of St. Joseph)., 869 Lexington Ave., 10065-6648. Tel: 212-744-2080; Fax: 212-327-3011. Very Revs. David Dominic Izzo, O.P., S.T.L., Prior Prov.; E. Raymond Daley, O.P., Archdiocesan Tribunal; Carleton Parker Jones, O.P., S.T.D., Pastor; Revs. John Farren, O.P., S.T.D., Fundraising; William Robert Gannon, O.P., S.T.L., M.S.W.; Jeremy Aquinas Guilbeau, O.P., Parish Staff; Raymond Ferrer Halligan, O.P., S.T.L., Fundraiser; Bernard Lawrence Keitz, O.P., S.T.L.; Bernard Lawrence Keitz, O.P., S.T.L., Parish Staff; Antoninus Niemiec, O.P.; Bros. Martin Michael Downey, O.P., M.A., Guestmaster; John Damian McCarthy, O.P., Sexton & Sacristan.

Jesuit Community of the Immaculate Conception (1974) 147 Thompson St., 10012. Tel: 212-663-4615; Fax: 212-866-3241. Email: robjkeck@aol.com. Revs. Robert J. Keck, S.J., Supr.; George M. Anderson, S.J.; Daniel J. Berrigan, S.J.; W. Alan Briceland, S.J.; Gerald T. Huyett, S.J.; John G. McSherry, S.J.; Enrico Raulli, S.J.; Joseph C. Towle, S.J.; Edward G. Zogby, S.J.

Priests assigned but serving elsewhere: Revs. Ronald Henery, O.P, Itinerant Preacher; Frederick Damien Hoesli, O.P.; John Aedan McKeon, O.P., S.T.B., Itinerant Preacher; J. Albert Paretsky, O.P., S.S.L., S.T.D.; Jacob Restrick, O.P., Chap.; Robert William Vaughn, O.P., S.T.B., M.Ed., Itinerant Preacher.

Vincentian Fathers, 1834 Third Ave., 10029. Tel: 212-289-5589; Fax: 212-289-8321. Email: milagha2@verizon.net. Revs. Victor Elia, C.M., Supr.; Candido Arrizurieta, C.M.; Jesus Eguaras, C.M., Vicar; Jesus Arellano, C.M.

Padres Paules Community (Vincentians) Inc.

Xavier Jesuit Community, 30 W. 16th St., 10011. Tel: 212-924-7900; Fax: 212-337-7545. Email: hzen@juno.com. Rev. Pierce A. Brennan, S.J., Rector; Brian Altenhofen, S.J.; Very Rev. David S. Ciancimino, S.J., Admin.; Revs. Joseph S. Costantino, S.J., Pastor; Thomas H. Feely, S.J., Admin.; Peter E. Fink, S.J., Asst. Pastor; Daniel Hendrickson, S.J.; James F. Keenan, S.J., Admin.; Edward J. McMahon, S.J.; Harold F. O'Donnell, S.J., Hospital Chap.; James L. Pierce, S.J.; Steven A. Schoenig, S.J.; William L. Wizeman, S.J.; James J. Yannarell, S.J., Admin.; Henry J. Zenorini, S.J., Treas.; Rocco C. Danzi, S.J., Admin.; John E. Fagan, S.J., Admin.; Mateusz Janya, S.J., Teacher. (For list of faculty see the high school listing for Xavier High School)

BEACON. *St. Joachim Friary*, 61 Leonard St., 12508. Tel: 845-838-0000; Fax: 845-838-0004. Email: friarfred.cap@net.net. Web: www.cyfm.org. Revs. Fred Nickle, O.F.M.Cap., Chap.; Bernard Smith, O.F.M.Cap., Chap.; Bros. Lake Herman, O.F.M.Cap., Guardian; Carlos Hernandez, O.F.M.Cap. Serving Capuchin Youth and Family Ministries, Garrison, NY

BRONX. *Idente Missionaries - Santa Maria Residence*, 2352 St. Raymond Ave., 10462. Tel: 718-828-2380; Fax: 718-828-4296. Revs. Fernando Real, M.Id., Ph.D., Prov. Supr.; Robert P. Badillo, M.Id., Ph.D.; Martin I. Esquerra, D.Min.; Cristobal Martin, M.Id., Ph.D., Prov. Sec.; Bro. Marek Wasilewski, M.Id., B.A.

John Cardinal O'Connor Residence, 5655 Arlington Ave., 10471. Tel: 718-581-0070. Most Revs. Robert A. Brucato, D.D., V.G. (Retired); Patrick J. Sheridan, D.D. (Retired); Rev. Msgrs. George F. Bardes (Retired); Francis V. Boyle (Retired); Dermot R. Brennan (Retired); Harry J. Byrne (Retired); Timothy Collins (Retired); John T. Doherty (Retired); Francis X. Duffy (Retired); Robert A. Ford (Retired); Edward J. Mitty (Retired); Peter C. O'Donnell (Retired); Daniel A. Peake (Retired); Revs. Alfred M. Croke (Retired); John Crotty; Christopher H. Daly (Retired); James W. Derrenbacher (Retired); Gerard DiSenso (Retired); Robert J. Duane (Retired); Benedict J. Kuolt (Retired); Vincent A. Lancellotti (Retired); Thomas F. McDonald (Retired); Alfred Pizzuto (Retired); John F. Reardon (Retired); James J. Tubridy (Retired), Cardinal O'Connor Residence, 5655 Arlington Ave., 10471.

Saint Lawrence Friary, 1027 Grand Concourse, 10452. Tel: 718-293-9180; Fax: 718-293-3384. Revs. Anthony Marie Baetzold, C.F.R., Local Vicar; Bernard Marie Murphy, C.F.R., Local Servant; Bros. Matthew Youssef Hawkins, C.F.R.; Innocent Mariae Montgomery; Ignatius Mary Shin, C.F.R.

Our Lady of the Angels Friary (Franciscan Friars of the Renewal), 427 E. 155th St., 10455. Tel: 718-993-3405; Fax: 718-993-9997. Web: www.franciscanfriars.com. Revs. Stanley Fortuna, C.F.R.; Pio Maria Hoffman, C.F.R., Dir. St. Padre Pio Shelter; Bros. Joachim Joseph Bellavance, C.F.R., Dir. St. Francis Ctr.; John Joseph Brice, C.F.R., Asst. Community Steward; Cyril Joseph Grandell, C.F.R.; John Baptist Jordan, C.F.R.; Timothy Pio Sgoutas, C.F.R.; Maximilian Mary Stelmachowski, C.F.R., Local Servant, Community Steward.

Passionist Residence, 5801 Palisade Ave., 10471. Tel: 718-548-1182; Fax: 718-548-2945. Revs. James R. Gillette, C.P.; Xavier Hayes, C.P.; Columkille Regan; Bro. Michael Moran, C.P., Local Supr. Priests 3; Brothers 1; Total in Residence 4.

Yarumal Mission Society, Inc. (1997) Office of the Pres., 2317 Washington Ave., 10458. Tel: 718-561-8248; Fax: 718-295-9607. Email: imeyusa@aol.com. Web: www.yarumal.org. Revs. David Guzman, M.X.Y., Pres.; Jairo A. Valbuena, M.X.Y. (Colombia).

CORNWALL. *Jogues Retreat Center*, P.O. Box 522, 12518-0522. Tel: 845-534-7570; Fax: 845-534-3276. Email: conroyp48@hotmail.com. Revs. Edward J. Coughlin, S.J., Supr.; J. Peter Conroy, S.J., Asst. to Supr., Sabbatical.

ESOPUS. *Marist Brothers F.M.S. (Province of U.S.A.)* (1942) P.O. Box 197, 12429. Tel: 845-384-6625; Fax: 845-384-6277. Email: brohen@aol.com. Bros. Todd Patenaude, F.M.S., Supr.; Michael Mullin, F.M.S., Dir.; Henry J. Sawicki, F.M.S.; Gregory De LaNoy, F.M.S. Brothers 3.

Redemptorist Priests and Brothers C.Ss.R. (Province of Baltimore), Mount Saint Alphonsus, Rte. 9W, P.O. Box 219, 12429. Tel: 845-384-8000; Fax: 845-384-8088. Email: gkeav@aol.com. Web: www.msaretreat.com. Rev. Thomas Travers, C.Ss.R.; Bros. Gerard St. Hilaire, C.Ss.R.; Robert Skinner, C.Ss.R. Priests 6; Brothers 3. In Res. Revs. Dennis Billy, C.Ss.R.; Eugene J. Grohe, C.Ss.R.; John Kiwus, C.Ss.R.; Raymond Weithman, C.Ss.R.

GARRISON. *St. Christopher's Friary*, Box 150, 10524-0150. Tel: 845-335-1000; Fax: 845-424-3786. Web: www.stchristophersinn-graymoor.org. Revs. Charles Angell, S.A.; William Drobach, S.A.; Robert Warren, S.A., Guardian; Bro. James Daly, S.A.; Rev. Daniel Sylvain, S.A.; Bros. Benedict Terasawa, S.A.; Charles Kenny, S.A.; Robert Taylor, S.A. Total Staff 60; Total Assisted 1,200.

Franciscan Friars of the Atonement (1898) Graymoor, P.O. Box 300, 10524-0300. Tel: 845-424-3671; 845-424-3672; 845-424-3674; Fax: 845-424-2166. Email: glucrezia@atonementfriars.org. Web: www.atonementfriars.org. Revs. Fred Alvarez, S.A.; Norman Boyd, S.A.; Alban Carroll, S.A.; Martin Carter, S.A.; Joseph F. Cavoto, S.A.; Kenneth Cienik, S.A.; John W. Coppinger, S.A.; Bro. Kieran Cullen, S.A., (Retired); Revs. Gerald DiGiralamo, S.A., 4 Buttercup Dr., Bohemia, 11716; Joseph Di Mauro, S.A.; David L. Doerner, S.A. (Retired); Walter Gagne, S.A., Dir. Archives & Record Ctr., Guardian St. Paul's Friary; James Gardiner, S.A., Dir. Spiritual Life Center; Carmen Giuliano, S.A.; Bros. Francis Gutman, S.A.; Stephen Hanley, S.A., (Retired); Daniel Houde, S.A.; Rev. Robert Langone, S.A., Retreat Dir.; Bros. Alan LeMay, S.A.; Pius MacIsaac, S.A.; Dominic McDonnell, S.A.; Rev. Owen Murphy, S.A. (Retired); Bro. Theodore Novak, S.A.; Revs. Mark O'Connor, S.A.; Thomas Orians, S.A., Assoc. Dir. of Campus Min., Felician College, NJ; Bro. DePorres Poncia, S.A.; Revs. Georger Ribeiro, S.A.; Emil Tomaskovic, S.A.; Peter Taran; Bro. Edmund Sheridan, S.A., (Retired); Revs. Emmanuel Sullivan, S.A.; Daniel Sylvain, S.A.; Bro. Robert Taylor, S.A., (Retired); Rev. Wilfred Tyrell, S.A.; Bro. Liam Young, S.A., Mass Dept. *St. Francis of Assisi Novitiate*, Graymoor, P.O. Box 300, 10524-0300. Tel: 845-424-4055; Fax: 845-424-4673. Rev. Conan Hall, S.A.; Bro. Leo Hall, S.A. *St. Christopher's Inn*, Graymoor, P.O. Box 150, 10524-0150. Tel: 845-424-3616; Fax: 845-424-3786. Revs. Bernard Palka, S.A., Pres. & CEO; Charles Angell, S.A.; Bro. James Daly, S.A.; Rev. William Drobach, S.A., Vice Pres.; Bro. Charles Kenney, S.A.; Rev. John Kiesling, S.A., St. Joan of Arc Parish, Toronto ON M6P 1B1 Canada. Tel: 416-762-1026; Fax: 416-762-4194; Bro. Benedict Terasawa, S.A.; Rev. Robert Warren, S.A., Guardian, St. Christopher's Inn. *Graymoor Ecumenical and Interreligious Institute*, 475 Riverside Dr., Rm. 1960, 10115-1999. Tel: 212-870-2330; Fax: 212-870-2001. Rev. James Loughran, S.A., Dir. Tel: 212-807-9694; Fax: 212-870-2001. *Atonement Friars*, 138 Waverly Pl., 10014. Revs. Wilfred Tyrrell, S.A.; Henry Marchese, S.A. (Retired).

Priests of the Province Serving Elsewhere: Revs. David Fitzgerald, S.A., Pastor, St. Andrew the Apostle, Apex, NC; Thomas Gumprecht, S.A., St. Andrew the Apostle, Apex, NC; Francis Eldridge, S.A., St. Odilia's Parish, 522 Hooper Ave., Los Angeles, CA 90011; Bro. Gerard Hand, S.A.; Rev. Henry Mair, S.A., Chapel of Our Savior, 475 Westgate Dr., Brockton, MA 02301; Bro. Louis Marek, S.A.; Revs. Malcolm Martin, S.A., Chapel of Our Savior, 475 Westgate Dr., Brockton, MA 02301; V. Paul Ojibway, S.A., Santa Maria Parish, 20 Santa Maria Way, Orinda, CA 94563; Daniel O'Shea, S.A.; Boniface Riedmann, S.A. (Retired), Chapel of Our Savior, 475 Westgate Dr., Brockton, MA 02301; Bros. Savio McNiece, S.A., Chapel of Our Savior, 475 Westgate Dr., Brockton, MA 02301; Thomas Banacki, S.A.

Franciscan Friars of the Atonement, Minister General Office (1898) Graymoor, P.O. Box 300, 10524-0300. Tel: 845-424-2113; Fax: 845-424-2166. Email: ministergen@atonementfriars.org. Web: www.atonementfriars.org. Very Rev. James F. Puglisi, S.A., Min. Gen.; Rev. Timothy I. MacDonald, S.A., Vicar Gen. & 1st Gen. Counselor; Bro. Kevin Goss, S.A., Sec. Gen. & 3rd Gen. Counselor; Revs. Elias D. Mallon, S.A., 2nd Gen. Counselor; V. Paul Ojibway, S.A., 4th Gen. Councilor; Charles Sharon, S.A., Personnel Dir. & Assoc. Treas.

Friar-Priests serving in Japan, Diocese of Yokohama: Tel.: 011-81-45-581-6374; Fax: 011-81-45-581-9068. Revs. Pacificus Von Essen, S.A.; Fidelis Fujihara, S.A. (Japan); Charles Brozat, S.A.; Joseph Hiramatsu, S.A. (Japan), Regional Minister; Raymond Rodriquez Luis, S.A.; Bro. Ignatius Kobayashi, S.A. (Japan).

Friars on assignments or studies: Tel.: 845-424-3671; Fax: 845-424-2166. Revs. Joseph Scerbo, S.A.; Edward Gallagher, S.A. (Retired).

Friars stationed in England: Tel.: 011-44-171-828-4163; Fax: 011-44-171-798-9090. Bro. Denis Burgelin, S.A., (England); Revs. Robert Mercer, S.A. (England); Michael Seed, S.A. (England).

Friars stationed in Canada, Archdiocese of Vancouver: Tel.: 604-277-8353; Fax: 604-275-4034. Revs. Arthur Gouthro, S.A., St. Joseph the Worker Parish, 4451 Williams Rd., Richmond BC V7E 1J7 Canada. (Canada); William Linakis, S.A., 1127 Barclay St., Apt. 1202, Vancouver BC V6E 4C6. (Canada); David Poirier, S.A., St. Joseph the Worker Parish, 4451 Williams Rd., Richmond BC V7E 1J7 Canada. (Canada); Bros. Timothy MacDonald, S.A., St. Joseph the Worker Parish, 4451 Williams Rd., Richmond BC V7E 1J7 Canada. (Canada); Hugh MacIsaac, S.A., (Canada).

Archdiocese of Toronto, Canada: Revs. Damian MacPherson, S.A. (Canada), Dir. Ecumenical & Interfaith Affairs, St. Michael's Rectory, 200 Church St., Toronto ON M5B 1Z2 Canada. Tel: 416-694-0382; Fax: 416-934-3445; Daniel Callahan, S.A.; Patrick Cogan, S.A., Dir. of Formation & Guardian Paul Wattson Friary, Paul Wattson Friary, 15 Laxton Ave., Toronto ON M6K 1K8 Canada. Tel: 416-537-0327; Fax: 416-532-8472; Bro. John Baptist Hildreth, S.A., Paul Wattson Friary, 15 Laxton Ave., Toronto ON M6K 1K8 Canada. Tel: 416-537-0327; Fax: 416-532-8472.

Friars residing in Italy: Tel.: 011-39-06-687-9552; Fax: 011-39-06-683-3631. Bro. Simon Peter Ango, S.A.; Rev. Edward Boes, S.A., Rector, Church of Sant'Onofrio; Bros. Gregory Lucrezia, S.A., Proc. Gen.; Joseph O'Gara, S.A.; Very Rev. James F. Puglisi, S.A., Minister General; Rev. Brian Terry, S.A. *Graymoor Ecumenical & Interreligious Institute*, 475 Riverside Dr., Rm. 1960, 10115-1999. Tel: 212-870-2330; Fax: 212-870-2001. Email: lmnygeii@aol.com. Web: www.geii.org.

Friars of the Atonement, Inc.
St. Christopher's Inn, Inc.
Union That Nothing Be Lost, Inc.
Paul Wattson Human Resources Fund, Inc., (G.E.I.I.)

HARTSDALE. *Mill Hill Fathers Residence*, 222 W. Hartsdale Ave., 10530-1667. Tel: 914-682-0645; Fax: 914-682-0862. Email: mhmnyoffice@aol.com. Web: www.millhillmissionaries.com. Revs. Terence J. Lee, M.H.M., Admin.; Matthew Grier, M.H.M.; Bartholomew Daly, M.H.M., Regl. Representative; Emile Frische, M.H.M.; James Brian Coffey, M.H.M.; Gregory P. Rice, M.H.M.; Bro. Theodore Tolboom, M.H.M., (Retired); Revs. Lester Lonergan, M.H.M. (Retired), 1415 Abbey Pl., Apt. 14, Charlotte, NC 28209; Peter Major, M.H.M.

JAMAICA ESTATES. *Paulist Fathers Generalate*, 86-11 Midland Pkwy., 11432. Tel: 718-291-5995; Fax: 718-291-6646. Web: www.paulist.org. Very Rev. John F. Duffy, C.S.P., Pres.; Revs. Michael J. Kallock, C.S.P.; James W. Moran, C.S.P.; Francis P. Desiano, C.S.P.; James A. Haley, C.S.P., Treas.

Paulist Priests at Paulist Foundations outside the U.S.: Tel.: 011-3906-488-2748; Fax: 011-3906-474-0236. Revs. Gregory Apparcel, C.S.P., Via Venti Settembre 14, Rome 00187 Italy. Tel: 011-3906-488-2748; Fax: 011-3906-474-0236; Thomas J. Holahan, C.S.P.; Thomas R. Marshall, C.S.P., 659 Markham St., Toronto ON M6G 2M1 Canada. Tel: 416-534-4219; Fax: 416-534-4219; Thomas P. Murphy, C.S.P., 659 Markham St., Toronto ON M6G 2M1 Canada. Tel: 416-534-4219; Fax: 416-534-4219; James F. McCabe, C.S.P., 659 Markham St., Toronto ON M6G 2M1 Canada. Tel: 416-534-4219; Fax: 416-534-4219; Deacon Richard J. Boudreau, C.S.P., 659 Markham St., Toronto ON M6G 2M1 Canada. Tel: 416-534-4219; Fax: 416-534-4219.

Military Chaplains: Rev. Thomas P. Hall, C.S.P.

On Special Assignment in the U.S. and Abroad: Revs. Justin J. McCormick, C.S.P.; Thomas A. Kane, C.S.P.; James Kolb, C.S.P.; Michael B. McGarry, C.S.P.; Thomas F. Stransky, C.S.P.

Retired: Revs. George R. Fitzgerald, C.S.P.; Lawrence V. McDonnell, C.S.P. (Retired); James R. O'Gara, C.S.P.; Frank M. Sweeney, C.S.P.; Robert T. Scott, C.S.P.; Robert W. Baer, C.S.P.; Edward R. Donovan, C.S.P.; Wilfred A. Brimley, C.S.P.; William J. Cantwell, C.S.P.; Wilfred Dewan, C.S.P.; Francis X. Diskin, C.S.P. (Retired); Harry J. Dooley, C.S.P.; Thomas J. Dove; William J. Kenney, C.S.P.; James B. Lloyd, C.S.P. (Retired); Edward J. McDonald, C.S.P.; Kenneth H. McGuire, C.S.P.; Louis F. McKernan, C.S.P.; Robert P. Michele, C.S.P.; Ernest C. Mort, C.S.P.; Thomas P. Murphy, C.S.P.; Robert A. O'Donnell, C.S.P. (Retired); Robert F. Quinn, C.S.P.; Rudolph T. Vorisek, C.S.P. (Retired); Edward D. Wroblewski, C.S.P.

MARYKNOLL. *M.M.A.F. Charitable Trust, Treasury Office*, P.O. Box 306, 10545-0306. Tel: 914-941-7590; Fax: 914-941-3619. Email: rcallahan@maryknoll.org. Rev. Richard B. Callahan, M.M., Contact Person.

Maryknoll Fathers and Brothers 10545-0305. Tel: 914-941-7590; Fax: 914-944-3605. Email: generalcouncil@maryknoll.org. Web: www.maryknoll.org.

General Council: Most Rev. William J. McNaughton, M.M. (Retired); Revs. Edward M. Dougherty, M.M., Supr. Gen. & Pres.; Jose A. Aramburu, M.M., Vicar Gen. & Vice Pres.; Edward J. McGovern, M.M., Asst. Gen.; Paul R. Masson, M.M., Asst. Gen.; John F. Ahearn, M.M.; Thomas A. Ahearn, M.M. (Retired); Joseph B. Arsenault, M.M. (Retired); Richard Aylward, M.M. (Retired); Paul D. Belliveau, M.M. (Retired); Lionel A. Bouffard, M.M. (Retired); Francis J. Breen, M.M.; J. Ernest Brunelle, M.M. (Retired); Richard B. Callahan, M.M., Treas. Gen.; Charles H. Cappel, M.M. (Retired); John J. Casey, M.M.; Dennis W. Cleary, M.M.; George C. Cotter, M.M.; William J. Coy, M.M. (Retired); Wayman P. Deasy, M.M.; Robert L. Depinet, M.M. (Retired); Robert W. Donnelly, M.M. (Retired); Michael A. Duggan, M.M.; Miguel F. d'Escoto, M.M. (Retired); Lawrence W. Flynn, M.M. (Retired); William B. Frazier, M.M.; Herbert T. Gappa, M.M. (Retired); James M. Gilligan, M.M. (Retired); Donald F. Glover, M.M. (Retired); Ronald L. Green, M.M.; Kevin J. Hanlon, M.M.; Joseph A. Heim, M.M. (Retired); James L. Hilgeman, M.M. (Retired); Robert A. Jalbert, M.M.; David J. Jones, M.M. (Retired); John M. Kaserow, M.M.; Thomas H. Keefe, M.M. (Retired); John E. Keegan, M.M. (Retired); Martin P. Keegan, M.M. (Retired); David C. Kelly, M.M.; Leo R. Kennedy, M.M (Retired); Leo R. Kennedy, M.M (Retired); John R. King, M.M. (Retired); David E. LaBuda, M.M.; Joseph P. LaMar, M.M., Asst. Treas. (Retired); Peter M. Le Jacq, M.M.; James W. Lehr, M.M. (Retired); Lawrence J. Lewis, M.M.; Robert J. Lloyd, M.M. (Retired); Martin J. Lowery, M.M.; Ernest C. Lukaschek, M.M.; William T. Madden, M.M. (Retired); Joseph V. McCabe, M.M.; Gerard T. McCrane, M.M. (Retired); Lawrence F. McCulloch, M.M. (Retired); Thomas P. McDonnell, M.M. (Retired); Joseph J. McGahren, M.M. (Retired); Francis T. McGourn, M.M. (Retired); Charles J. McPadden, M.M. (Retired); Carl P. Meulemans, M.M.; Edward F. Moore, M.M.; Dennis Moorman, M.M.; John J. Moran, M.M.; Gerald J. Nagle, M.M. (Retired); John B. Northrop, M.M.; Paul A. O'Brien, M.M. (Retired); Fernand Paquet, M.M. (Retired); Thomas E. Pesaresi, M.M.; Edward J. Phillips, M.M.; George H. Ratermann, M.M. (Retired); Robert J. Reiley, M.M. (Retired); Peter L. Ruggere, M.M.; Thomas C. Saunders, M.M. (Retired); J. Daniel Schneider, M.M. (Retired); William L. Senger, M.M.; Michael A. Simone, M.M. (Retired); John C. Sivalon, M.M.; John F. Soltis, M.M. (Retired); Romane St. Vil, M.M.; Raymond F. Sullivan, M.M. (Retired); J. Edward Szendrey, M.M.; Joseph W. Towle, M.M. (Retired); James M. Travis, M.M. (Retired); Joseph R. Veneroso, M.M.; Robert W. Vujs, M.M. (Retired); Edward F. Waick, M.M. (Retired); John J. Walsh, M.M.; Michael P. Walsh, M.M.; Edward M. Wroblewski, M.M. (Retired); Maurice J. Zerr, M.M. (Retired); Juan M. Zuniga, M.M.; Michael O. Zunno (Retired); Bros. John E. Argauer, M.M., (Retired); John J. Blazo, M.M.; Gordon M. Burns, M.M., (Retired); Eugene E. Casper, M.M., (Retired); Brendan J. Corkery, M.M.; Kevin F. Dargan, M.M.; Wayne J. Fitzpatrick, M.M.; Vianney R. Flick, M.M., (Retired); Thomas A. Hickey, M.M.; Anthony Lopez, M.M.; Victor E. Marshall, M.M., (Retired); Andrew E. Marsolek, M.M.; David E. McKenna, M.M., (Retired); Donald R. Miriani, M.M., (Retired); Frank J. Norris, M.M., (Retired); DePorres Stilp, M.M., (Retired); Raymond C. Tetrault, M.M.; Alexander J. Walsh, M.M., (Retired). *Maryknoll St. Teresa's Residence*, 10545-0321. Tel: 914-941-4240; 914-941-4247; Fax: 914-923-3407.

Staff: Revs. Richard A. Bell, M.M. (Retired); John P. Hudert, M.M. (Retired) In Res. Revs. Frederick J. Allen, M.M. (Retired); Anthony B. Brodniak, M.M.; Richard L. Brooker, M.M. (Retired); Ralph F. Christman, M.M.; Robert F. Crohan, M.M. (Retired); Gilbert J. De Ritis, M.M. (Retired); Daniel D. Dolan, M.M. (Retired); Patrick J. Donovan, M.M. (Retired); Thomas F. Gibbons, M.M. (Retired); Charles F. Girnius, M.M. (Retired); Fernand L. Goeselin, M.M. (Retired); Robert Golish, M.M. (Retired); John P. Grady, M.M. (Retired); Frederick J. Hegarty, M.M.; John P. Hudert, M.M. (Retired); Charles T. Huegelmeyer, M.M. (Retired); Daniel P. Jensen, M.M. (Retired); Walter W. Johnson, M.M. (Retired); Richard S. Kardian, M.M. (Retired); John B. Keaney, M.M. (Retired); Walter T. Kelleher, M.M. (Retired); Edward R. Killackey, M.M. (Retired); Joseph R. Lang, M.M. (Retired); Robert R. Lefebvre, M.M. (Retired); William F. Marley, M.M. (Retired); William E. McCarthy, M.M. (Retired); Francis S. Meccia, M.M.; Laurence T. Murphy, M.M. (Retired); James P. Nieckarz, M.M.; James K. Nishimuta, M.M. (Retired); Howard E. O'Brien, M.M. (Retired); John J. O'Brien, M.M. (Retired); Frank T. O'Donnell, M.M. (Retired); James W. O'Neill, M.M. (Retired); Joseph J. O'Neill, M.M. (Retired); George F. Painter, M.M. (Retired); Peter J. Petrucci, M.M. (Retired); Arthur J. Prall, M.M. (Retired); James R. Roy, M.M. (Retired); John J. Ruessmann, M.M.; James M. Scanlon, M.M. (Retired); Steven S. Scherrer, M.M. (Retired); Charles J. Schmidt, M.M. (Retired); J. David Sullivan, M.M. (Retired); John C. Tynan, M.M. (Retired); Norbert M. Verhagen, M.M. (Retired); Donald J. Vittengl, M.M. (Retired); James R. Whitmore, M.M. (Retired); C. Thomas Wilcox, M.M. (Retired); Louis J. Wolken, M.M. (Retired); Robert R. Zahn, M.M. (Retired); Richard E. Zeimet, M.M. (Retired); Bros. Peter Agnone, M.M., (Retired); George Carlonas, M.M, (Retired); Jude M. Conniff, M.M.; Leon J. Cook, M.M., (Retired); Augustine J. Horkan, M.M, (Retired); Kieran J. Stretton, M.M., (Retired); John J. Wohead, M.M., (Retired); Goretti A. Zilli, M.M.

Special Assignments: Revs. Patrick A. Bergin, M.M. (Retired); Roy L. Bourgeois, M.M.; Curtis R. Cadorette, M.M.; John P. Casey, M.M. (Retired); Donald J. Doherty, M.M. (Retired); Daniel A. Lanza, M.M. (Retired); Francis J. Leong, M.M. (Retired); Robert A. Lilly, M.M. (Retired); Manuel J. Mejia, M.M. (Retired); Richard T. Ouellette, M.M. (Retired); Richard E. Paulissen, M.M. (Retired); Raymond G. Pierini, M.M.; Joseph S. Pulaski, M.M. (Retired); John A. Rich, M.M. (Retired); Daniel J. Sherman, M.M. (Retired); David J. Schwinghamer, M.M.; Gerald M. Wickenhauser, M.M. (Retired); Arthur H. Willie, M.M. (Retired); John F. Wymes, M.M. (Retired).

Maryknoll Fathers and Brothers Charitable Trust, P.O. Box 306, 10545-0306. Tel: 914-941-7590, Ext. 2422; Fax: 914-944-3628. Web: www.maryknoll.org. Revs. Thomas A. Ahearn, M.M., Trustee (Retired); Richard B. Callahan, M.M., Trustee; Wayman P. Deasy, M.M., Trustee; William T. Madden, M.M., Trustee (Retired); Thomas P. McDonnell, M.M. (Retired); J. Edward Szendrey, M.M., Trustee; Susan J. Dahl, Trustee.

MIDDLETOWN. *St. Albert's Priory*, 72 Carmelite Dr., P.O. Box 908, 10940-0908. Tel: 914-344-2220; Fax: 914-342-4412. Revs. Garth Eversley, O.Carm.; Vincent McDonald, O.Carm.; Thomas Zalewski, O.Carm.; Bros. Michael Garraghan, O.Carm.; Dominic Dang Nguyen, O.Carm. *The National Shrine of Our Lady of Mount Carmel*, 710 Carmelite Dr., P.O. Box 2163, 10940-2163. Tel: 845-343-1879; Fax: 845-343-1912. Rev. Thomas Zalewski, O.Carm., Dir.

Brandsma Priory, Carmelite Novitiate, 1 Carmelite Dr., P.O. Box 2127, 10940-0439. Tel: 845-343-2959; Fax: 845-344-1808. Rev. Quinn Connors, O.Carm., Novice Dir. Carmelite Friars (North American Prov. of St. Elias and Most Pure Heart of Mary Province). Novices 5.

Carmelite Friars (North American Province of St. Elias) (1931) 68 Carmelite Dr., P.O. Box 3079, 10940-0890. Tel: 845-344-2223; 845-344-2225 (Vocation phone); Fax: 845-344-2210. Email: proelias@frontiernet.net. Web: www.carmelites.com. Very Rev. Mario Esposito, O.Carm., Prior Prov.; Rev. Patrick McGuigan, O.Carm., Prov. Procurator. Tel: 914-344-2224; Bro. Robert Bathe, O.Carm., Vocation Dir. *Office of Lay Carmelites*, 70 Carmelite Dr., P.O. Box 3079, 10940-0890. Tel: 845-344-2474; Fax: 845-956-2474. Email: jsoreth@aol.com. Rose Mary Lancellotti, Provincial Delegate Lay Carmelite.

MOUNT VERNON. *St. Bernardine of Siena Friary*, 25 Laurel Ave., 10552-1018. Tel: 914-699-1221; Fax: 914-668-6143. Rev. James Villa, O.F.M., Admin. & Guardian. Franciscan Friars, Province of Immaculate Conception. Priests 3. In Res. Revs. Andre Cirino, O.F.M.; Roderick Crispo, O.F.M.

Kolbe Friary, 274-280 W. Lincoln Ave., 10550. Tel: 914-664-7169. Bro. Angelo Monti, O.F.M.,

Guardian. Franciscan Friars, Province of the Immaculate Conception.

NEW PALTZ. *St. Joseph Friary*, 34 S. Chestnut St., 12561. Tel: 914-255-5635; Fax: 914-255-5679. Revs. Bernard M. Maloney, O.F.M.Cap.; Raphael Iannone, O.F.M.Cap., Province Property Mgr.; Barnabas Keck, O.F.M.Cap. Capuchin Franciscans, Province of St. Mary.

NEW ROCHELLE. *Brothers of Holy Cross of the Eastern Province of the United States of America, Inc.* (1958) 85 Overlook Cir., 10804-4501. Tel: 914-632-4468; 914-632-4469; Fax: 914-632-2490. Email: tdzie@aol.com. Web: www.holycrossbrothers.org. Bros. Thomas A. Dziekan, C.S.C., Prov.; Jonathan Beebe, C.S.C., B.A., M.A., M.S.W., Councillor; Edward Boyer, C.S.C., B.A., M.A., Councillor; James J. Branigan, C.S.C., B.A., M.S., Councilor; Jerome Donnelly, C.S.C., B.A., M.A., Councilor; Mark Knightly, C.S.C., B.A., M.S.W., Councilor; Stephen J. LaMendola, C.S.C., B.A., M.A., B.S., P.D., Councilor; George Schmitz, C.S.C., B.A., M.A., Steward; William Zaydak, C.S.C., B.A., M.A., Asst. Prov. Professed Brothers (Total in Province) 110. In Res. Bros. Robert Russo, C.S.C.; James Rio, C.S.C.

Congregation of Christian Brothers New Rochelle (1906) 21 Pryer Ter., 10804. Tel: 914-636-6194; Fax: 914-636-0021. Email: alb@cbinstitute.org. Brothers Living in Community 5. *Saint Joseph Residence* (1986) 30 Montgomery Cir., 10804. Tel: 914-633-6851; Fax: 914-633-5579. Email: rmcgcfc@yahoo.com. Bro. Michael L. Colasuonno, Pastoral Care Coord. Limited care facility for male religious. Total in Residence 20; Total Staff 8.

Holy Cross Brothers, Eastern Province, Charitable Trust, 85 Overlook Cir., 10804. Tel: 914-632-4468; Fax: 914-632-2490. Email: TDzie@aol.com. Web: www.holycrossbrothers.org. Bros. Thomas A. Dziekan, C.S.C., Pres. & Trustee; Peter Martin, C.S.C., B.A., M.A., Treas. & Trustee; Renatus Foldenauer, C.S.C., Trustee; Richard Kiniry, C.S.C., B.A., M.A., Trustee; Stephen J. LaMendola, C.S.C., B.A., M.A., B.S., P.D., Trustee.

Saint Joseph's Residence, Inc., 30 Montgomery Cir., 10804-4413. Tel: 914-633-6851; Fax: 914-633-5579. Email: jbm@atgnet.com. Bros. Thomas F. Feerick, Vice Pres. Finance; Kevin M. Griffith, C.F.C.; Thomas C. Higgins, Sec.; James B. Moffett, C.F.C., Vice Pres. Admin. Congregation of Christian Brothers., A facility of limited care for male religious. Total in Residence 20; Total Staff 5.

Salesian Cooperators of St. John Bosco, 148 Main St., 10801-5396. Tel: 914-636-4225. Email: tdunnesdb@aol.com. Mr. James Dolan, Prov. Coord.; Very Rev. Thomas Dunne, S.D.B., Prov. Delegate.

Salesian Provincial House (1959) 148 Main St., P.O. Box 639, 10802-0639. Tel: 914-636-4225; Fax: 914-636-0159. Email: sdbsue@aol.com. Web: www.salesians.org. Very Rev. James Heuser, S.D.B., Prov.; Revs. Edward Cappelletti, S.D.B.; James L. Cerbone, S.D.B.; Thomas Brennan, S.D.B.; Michael Mendl, S.D.B.; Terrence O'Donnell, S.D.B.; Sean Rooney, S.D.B.; Robert Savage, S.D.B., Archives; Frank Wolfram, S.D.B., Supr.; Bros. Bruno Busatto, S.D.B.; Thomas Dion, S.D.B.; Emile Dube, S.D.B.; Thomas Higgs, S.D.B.; Andrew Lacombe, S.D.B.; John Zito, S.D.B. Priests 10; Brothers 6.

PELHAM. *Marist Brothers* (1994) 2 Eden Ter., Poughkeepsie, 12601-4803. Tel: 845-471-8354. Bros. James Stevens, Dir.; John Malich, F.M.S.; Augustine Martin; John Nash.

Marist Brothers Champagnat Hall Community (1926) 4300 Murdock Ave., Bronx, 10466. Tel: 718-994-4227; 718-994-4676; Fax: 718-994-0145. Bros. James Devine, Dir.; Gerard Brereton; Nicholas Caffrey; Denis Caverley; Valerian Doiron; Luke Driscoll; James Gaffney, F.S.C.; Lawrence Gordon; Thomas Kelly; Augustine Landry; Lawrence Lavallee; Godfrey Robertson; Victor Serna; Matthew Snowden; Vincent Xavier.

Marist Brothers Community (1993) 26 First Ave., 10803. Tel: 914-738-1218. Bros. John Bantz, F.M.S., Dir.; Larry Gordon, F.M.S.; James McKnight, F.M.S.; Donnell Neary, F.M.S.; Sean Sammon, F.M.S.; Michael Sheerin, F.M.S.

Marist Brothers-St. Benedict Community, 1082 Edison Ave., Bronx, 10465. Tel: 718-931-3744. Bros. Gerald Doherty, Dir.; Frederick Sambor, Dir.; Eugene Birmingham; Armand Lamagna, F.M.S.; Thomas Schady, F.M.S.

Marist Residence, 272 W. 91st St., 10024. Tel: 212-769-4951; Fax: 212-769-4951. Email: FMS91@aol.com. Bros. James Adams, F.M.S., Dir.; Richard Van Houten, F.M.S., Prin.; Emil Denworth, F.M.S.; James Kearney, F.M.S.; George Kopper, F.M.S.

PELHAM MANOR. *St. Vincent's Residence*, 190 Mt. Tom Rd., 10803-3309. Tel: 914-738-6138; Fax: 914-738-6138. Email: msalvagna@cpprov.org. Revs. Edward L. Beck, C.P., Supr. & Dir.; Robert Joerger, C.P.; Michael J. Salvagna, C.P.; Melvin Shorter, C.P. The Passionists.

SCARBOROUGH. *Carmelite Fathers, NY Prov. of St. Elias, Carmelite Priory*, c/o St. Albert's Priory, P.O. Box 908, Middletown, 10940. Tel: 845-344-2220.

STATEN ISLAND. *St. Francis Friary*, 500 Todt Hill Rd., 10304. Tel: 718-981-3131; Fax: 718-981-2742. Email: bjfarleo@aol.com. Revs. Brennan-Joseph Farleo, O.F.M.Conv., Guardian, Supr. & Preaching Min.; Philip Blaine, O.F.M.Conv., Spiritual Center Dir.; Edward Costello, O.F.M.Conv., Chap.; Shawn Nolan, O.F.M.Conv. (Retired); Stephen Valenta, O.F.M.Conv. (Retired); Bros. Edward Handy, O.F.M.Conv., Social Svc.; Damian Pinault, O.F.M.Conv., (Retired). *Friars Minor Conventual Immaculate Conception Province Charitable Trust* Tel: 718-981-3131; Fax: 718-981-2742. Priests 6; Brothers 2.

Scalabrinian Missionaries Scalabrinian Mission Office, The Center for Migration Studies; St. Charles Residence., 209 Flagg Pl., 10304. Tel: 718-351-0232; Fax: 718-979-1241. Email: cms@cmsny.org. Web: www.scalabrini.org. Revs. Rene Manenti, C.S., Dir., Center for Migration Studies & St. Charles Devel. Office; Ezio Marchetto, Asst. Dir., Center for Migration Studies.

THORNWOOD. *Legionaries of Christ*, 582 Columbus Ave., 10594. Tel: 914-749-3900; Fax: 914-749-3939. Email: twlc@legionaries.org. Web: www.legionofchrist.org.

WEST PARK. *Congregation of Christian Brothers*, Santa Maria-on-Hudson, 12493. Tel: 845-384-6750; Fax: 845-750-6290. Bros. D. D. Crimmins, Contact Person; J. Laurence Heathwood; R.J. Lasik. Total in Residence 4.

WHITE PLAINS. *Capuchin Friars of North America*, 30 Gedney Park Dr., 10605-3599. Tel: 914-761-3008; Fax: 914-948-6429. Email: jmchugh@juno.com. Revs. John Pavlik, O.F.M.Cap., Pres.; Charles Polifka, O.F.M.Cap., Vice Pres.; Jerome McHugh, O.F.M.Cap., Sec. & Treas.

St. Conrad Friary (1882) Provincial Headquarters of the Province of St. Mary of the Capuchin Order., 30 Gedney Park Dr., 10605-3599. Tel: 914-761-3008; Fax: 914-948-6429. Email: stmaryprov@juno.com. Web: www.capuchin.org. Revs. John Gallagher, O.F.M.Cap., Min. Prov.; John McHugh, O.F.M.Cap., Vicar Prov.; Jerome McHugh, O.F.M.Cap., Sec. & Treas.; Mr. David LeGare, Dir. Finance; Rev. Gabriel Massaro, O.F.M.Cap., Senior Care; Bros. Richard Therrien, O.F.M.Cap., Prof. Theology at Stepinac H.S.; John Shento, O.F.M.Cap., Dir. Communications; Sr. Anna Daly, S.H.C.J., B.S., M.S., Archivist; Bro. Pius Blandino, O.F.M.Cap., Plant Mgr.; Revs. Paul Engel, O.F.M.Cap., Dir. Downey Side, New York, NY; Joseph Flynn, O.F.M.Cap., Chap., College of New Rochelle.

The Province of St. Mary of the Capuchin Order, (Nature of Apostolate: Provincial Administration, Parishes, Capuchin Food Pantries, Hospital & Prison Chaplains, Preaching, Recruitment). Total in Residence 8; Total Staff 11. *Capuchin Friars International, Inc.* (1984) St. Conrad Friary, 30 Gedney Park Dr., 10605-3599. Tel: 914-761-3008, Ext. 21; Fax: 914-948-6429. Web: www.ofmcap.org. Revs. Luis Eduardo Rubiano, O.F.M.Cap., Treas.; Giampiero Gambaro, O.F.M.Cap., Sec.; Jerome McHugh, O.F.M.Cap., Asst. Sec. Treas. *St. Francis of Assisi Foundation*, St. Conrad Friary, 30 Gedney Park Dr., 10605-3599. Tel: 914-761-3008, Ext. 21; Fax: 914-948-6429. Dr. Livio Camozzi, Pres.; Bro. Mark Schenk, O.F.M.Cap., Vice Pres.; Revs. Giampiero Gambaro, O.F.M.Cap., Treas.; Jerome McHugh, O.F.M.Cap., Asst. Sec. Treas.

St. Francis of Assisi Foundation

YONKERS. *Cathedral Preparatory Seminary High School Formation Program* (1903) 201 Seminary Ave., 10704-1896. Tel: 914-968-6200, Ext. 8182; Fax: 914-376-2019. Rev. Thomas A. Lynch, Ph.D. (Cand.), Dean. Priests 1; Students 30.

St. Clare Friary Residence for Senior Friars., 110 Shonnard Pl., 10703. Tel: 914-423-2392. Revs. Michael Connolly, Guardian; Senan Taylor, O.F.M.Cap., Vicar; Joel Daniels, O.F.M.Cap.; Darius Devito, O.F.M.Cap.; Andrew Drew, O.F.M.Cap. (Retired); Raymond Hand, O.F.M.Cap.; Knute Kenlon, O.F.M.Cap.; James McIntyre, O.F.M.Cap.; Eymard McKinnon; John Proppe, O.F.M.Cap.; Charles Repole, O.F.M.Cap. Capuchin Franciscan Friars, Province of St. Mary. Total in Residence 11; Total Staff 3.

St. Felix Friary (Franciscan Friars of the Renewal), 15 Trinity Plaza, 10701. Tel: 914-476-7279; Fax: 914-476-5033. Web: FranciscanFriars.com. Revs. James Atkins; Terrence Messer, C.F.R.; Louis Leonelli, C.F.R.; Bro. Crispin Mary Rinaldi, C.F.R., Servant; Rev. Lawrence Schroedal; Bros. Paul Raniero Donnelly, C.F.R.; Nathanael Mary Lysinger, C.F.R.; Isaac Spinharney, C.F.R.

St. Leopold's Friary (Franciscan Friars of the Renewal); (House of Studies), 259 Nepperhan Ave., 10701-3461. Tel: 914-965-8143. Web: www.ewtn.com/renewal. Revs. Andrew Apostoli; Joseph Mary Deane, C.F.R., M.Div.; Luke Mary Fletcher, C.F.R.; Conrad Osterhout, C.F.R., Servant; Juniper Mary Sistare, C.F.R.; Bros. Ephraim Marie Ali; Anthony Marie Baetzold, C.F.R.; Gabriel Mary Bakker; Solanhs Maria Benfatti; John Anthony Boughton, C.F.R., Vicar; Augustine Conner; Leo Fisher, C.F.R.; Rev. Jacob Hausman, C.F.R.; Bros. Michael Kmlotek; Sylvester Mary Mann, C.F.R.A; Christopher Paul Metzger, C.F.R.; Albert Maria Osewski; Lawrence Joseph Schroedel, C.F.R.; Robert Stanion; Juan Diego Sutherland; Paulus Marie Tautz.

[FF] CONVENTS AND RESIDENCES OF SISTERS

NEW YORK. *Academy of St. Dorothy* (1932) 1305 Hylan Blvd., Staten Island, 10305. Tel: 718-987-0677; 718-351-0939; Fax: 718-351-0661. Email: dorothy@adnyschools.org. Sr. Mary Ann Keegan, S.S.D., Admin. Sisters of St. Dorothy. Sisters 8.

Blessed Trinity Missionary Cenacle, 414 E. 14th St., 10009. Tel: 212-475-1450; Fax: 212-254-8565. Web: MSBTNYC.com. Sr. Sara Butler, M.S.B.T., Ph.D. Missionary Social Work and Parish & Community Services, and Catholic Charities of New York; Nazareth Housing-Work with homeless; seminary education. Missionary Servants of the Most Blessed Trinity 4. *Catholic Charities*, 213 Stanton St., 10002. Tel: 212-777-3111; Fax: 212-677-9057. Email: msbtnyc1@aol.com.

Carmelite Sisters Teresas of St. Joseph, Inc., 249 W. 14th St., 10011. Tel: 212-242-8224; Fax: 212-242-7233. Email: hnascarmelitaj@aol.com. Sr. Angela Perez, Supr.

Convent of Our Lady of the Presentation (1775) 419 Woodrow Rd., 10312. Tel: 718-356-2121; Fax: 718-948-4115. Email: rosemarypssi@aol.com. Motherhouse and Novitiate of the Sisters of the Presentation. Sisters 18.

Corpus Christi Monastery, 1230 Lafayette Ave., 10474-5399. Tel: 718-328-6996; Fax: 718-328-1974. Email: corpuschristiny@bronxop.org. Sr. Maria Pia of the Eucharist, O.P., Prioress. Solemnly Professed 10.

The Dwelling Place of New York, Inc., 409 W. 40th St., 10018. Tel: 212-564-7887; Fax: 212-695-3642. Email: nancydpny@aol.com. Sr. Nancy Chiarello, O.S.F., Admin. For Homeless Women Sisters 2.

Franciscan Handmaids of Mary Convent Generalate of the Franciscan Handmaids of Mary., 15 W. 124th St., 10027. Tel: 212-289-5655; Fax: 212-987-5447. Email: handmaidsofmary@aol.com. Web: www.fhm.members.aol.com/fhm.nyc. Sisters Loretta Theresa Richards, F.H.M., Congregation Min.; Maria Goretti Mannix, F.H.M., Asst. Cong. Minister Formation, Dir.; Vincent Marie Wilson, F.H.M., Dir. Vocations. Sisters 22; Total Assisted 100.

Other Convents: *St. Edward Food Pantry*, 6581 Hylan Blvd., Staten Island, 10309. Tel: 718-984-1625; Fax: 718-996-0814. Sr. Vincent Marie Wilson, F.H.M., Dir.

Handmaids of Mary Altar Bread Distribution Service, 6581 Hylan Blvd., Staten Island, 10309. Tel: 718-984-1625; Fax: 718-966-0814. Sr. Maria Goretti Mannix, F.H.M., Dir., Formation. Associates 35.

Most Pure Heart of Mary Convent, 63 Bayside Ln., Staten Island, 10309. Tel: 718-966-5998.

Franciscan Missionaries of Mary, 3305 Wallace Ave., Bronx, 10467-6519. Tel: 718-547-4693; Fax: 718-325-5102. Email: palfmm@aol.com. Web: www.fmmusa.org.

FMM Provincialate, 3305 Wallace Ave., Bronx, 10467-6519. Tel: 718-547-4693; Fax: 718-325-5102. Email: palfmm@aol.com. Web: www.fmm.org or www.fmmusa.org.

Holy Name of Jesus Convent, 204 W. 97th St., 10025-5620. Tel: 212-678-6901; Fax: 212-678-6865. Email: fmmny97@aol.com. Web: www.fmmusa.org.

Our Lady of Millbrook Convent, Box K, Millbrook, 12545. Tel: 845-677-6739; Fax: 845-677-6530. Email: fmmch@aol.com. Web: www.fmmusa.org.

Franciscan Sisters of the Poor Foundation, Inc., 708 Third Ave., Ste. 1858, 10017. Tel: 212-818-1987; Fax: 212-808-0096. Email: lchristian@franciscanfoundation.org. Web: www.franciscanfoundation.org.

International Presentation Association of the Sisters of the Presentation of the Blessed Virgin Mary, 211 E. 43rd St., Ste. 1207, 10017-4707. Tel: 212-370-0075; Fax: 212-370-0075. Email: pbvmipa@msn.com. Web: www.ipa.ozehosting.com. Sr. Fatima Rodrigo, Contact Person.

St. Joseph Provincialate (1921) 850 Hylan Blvd., Staten Island, 10305. Tel: 718-981-4402; Fax: 718-556-3550. Email: sisterwilliam@gmail.com. Web: www.godslovefdc.org. Provincialate of the Daughters of Divine Charity (St. Joseph Province). In Province 30.

Missionary Sisters of Our Lady of Perpetual Help, Inc. (1934) *Office of the President*, 371 E. 150th St., Bronx, 10455. Tel: 718-742-2509; Fax: 718-742-2503. Sr. Isaura Flores, M.P.S., Acting Mother Supr.; Melissa Garza, Agent Residence.

Missionary Sisters of the Immaculate Heart of Mary (1897) District House, 238 E. 15th St., Apt. 5, 10003-3901. Tel: 212-677-2959; Fax: 212-475-7455. Email: icmusdist@juno.com. Sr. Flotilda Lape, I.C.M., Dist. Leader. *St. Joseph Convent* (1948) 238 E. 15th St., 10003-3901. Tel: 212-254-0658; Fax: 212-475-7455. Sisters 15.

Parish Visitors of Mary Immaculate (1920) 2151 Watson Ave., Bronx, 10472-5401. Tel: 718-823-0350; Fax: 718-823-0350. Sr. Linda Giovanelly, P.V.M.I., Supr. Sisters 5.

**Servants of the Lord and Virgin of Matara, Inc.*, 226 E. 113th St., 10029. Tel: 212-534-4063. Web: ssvmusa.org. Sr. Mary Mother of Mercy McDunnough, Pres.

Shalom Convent, 714 W. 231st St., 10463. Tel: 718-884-1663. Email: kerr714sweeney@verizon.net. Franciscan Sisters of the Poor 3.

Sisters of Charity Center, 6301 Riverdale Ave., 10471-1093. Tel: 718-549-9200, Ext. 230; Fax: 718-884-3013. Web: www.scny.org. Sr. Dorothy Metz, Pres.

The Sisters of Charity of Saint Vincent de Paul of New York
Sisters of Charity Center
Mount Saint Vincent on Hudson
The Sisters of Charity of Saint Vincent de Paul of New York Pension Trust Total in Congregation 367; In Archdiocese 361.

Sisters of Charity Novitiate, 149 Convent Rd., Nanuet, 10954. Tel: 845-623-1134 (Novitiate); 845-623-1071 (House). Sr. Anne Denise Brennan, Formation/Novice Dir.

The Elizabeth Seton Federation, Inc. (1995) Sisters of Charity Center, 6301 Riverdale Ave., Bronx, 10471. Tel: 718-549-9200, Ext. 268; Fax: 718-884-3013. Web: www.sisters-of-charity-federation.org.

Sisters of the Good Shepherd, 337 E. 17th St., 10003-3804. Tel: 212-475-4245; Fax: 212-777-9260.

Sisters of the Good Shepherd-New York City Sisters 3.

Society of Helpers, 385 W. 263rd St., Bronx, 10471. Tel: 718-884-3100. Email: nyhelper@rcn.com. Web: www.helpers.org. Sr. Geraldine Finan, Supr. Sisters 4.

Society of the Sacred Heart, R.S.C.J., 515 E. 118th St., 10035. Tel: 212-876-2895; 212-987-4422; Fax: 212-348-8284. Email: jcagney@rscj.org. Web: www.RSCJ.org.
Other Residences: *Society of the Sacred Heart, R.S.C.J.*, 501 W. 52nd St., #4E, 10019. Tel: 212-581-3894. *Society of the Sacred Heart, R.S.C.J.*, 222 E. 93rd St., 10128. Tel: 212-876-2276; Fax: 212-996-5277. *Society of the Sacred Heart, R.S.C.J.*, 406 E. 80th St., 10021. Tel: 212-288-1986; 212-288-5116 (East River Community); Fax: 212-861-8851. *Society of the Sacred Heart, R.S.C.J.*, 400 W. 126th St., Apt. 2, 10027-2503. Tel: 212-749-8438.

Visitation Convent (Sisters of Life), 320 E. 66th St., 10021. Tel: 212-737-0221. Sisters 5.

BEACON. *Carmelite Monastery* (2000) 89 Hiddenbrooke Dr., 12508-2230. Tel: 845-831-5572; Fax: 845-831-5579. Email: beaconcarmel@optonline.net. Web: www.carmelitesbeacon.org. Sr. Michaelene Devine, O.C.D., Prioress. Professed Nuns 18.

BLAUVELT. *Congregation of Sisters of St. Dominic of Blauvelt*, 496 Western Hwy., 10913. Tel: 845-359-5600; Fax: 845-359-5773. Email: mmalone@opblauvelt.org. Web: www.opblauvelt.org. Sisters Mary Malone, O.P., Pres.; Catherine Howard, O.P., Asst. to the Pres.
The Sisters of St. Dominic of Blauvelt, New York Sisters 157.

BRONX. *The Congregation of The Daughters of Mary, Inc.*, 176 Kilroe St., 10464. Tel: 718-885-1842; Fax: 718-885-1842. Email: dmcityisland@optimum.net. Sr. Agnes Jose, D.M., Sec. & Treas.

Franciscan Sisters of the Renewal (Franciscan Sisters of the Renewal), *Convent of San Damiano*, 1661 Haight Ave., 10461. Tel: 718-829-9466; Fax: 718-829-1488. Web: www.franciscansisterscfr.com. Sisters Lucille Cutrone, C.F.R., Community Servant; Agnes Mary Holtz, C.F.R. (Mother House, Novitiate House, Convent of San Damiano) Sisters 13.

Missionaries of Charity, Inc., 335 E. 145th St., 10451. Tel: 718-292-0019; Fax: 718-292-2929. Sisters M. Leticia, M.C., Regl. Supr.; M. Rose Clara, M.C., Supr. 406 W. 127th St., 10027. Tel: 212-222-7229. Sr. M. Manorama, M.C., Supr. 657 Washington St., 10014. Tel: 212-645-0587. Sr. M. Tonia, M.C., Supr.

Our Lady of Guadalupe Convent, 3537 Bainbridge Ave., 10467. Tel: 718-547-9840; Fax: 718-547-0995. Sr. Clare Marie Matthiass, C.F.R., Local Servant. (Franciscans Sisters of the Renewal) Sisters 16.

Sisters of St. John the Baptist, Provincial Residence, 3308 Campbell Dr., 10465-1358. Tel: 718-518-7820; Fax: 718-518-8930. Email: srmcecile@hotmail.com. Web: baptistines.org. Sr. Mary Cecile Swanton, C.S.J.B., Prov. Supr. In Province 100; In Archdiocese 92.

Mt. St. John Convent, 150 Anderson Hill Rd., Purchase, 10577. Tel: 914-761-7965; Fax: 914-761-2315. Sr. Mary Faith Chanda, C.S.J.B., Supr. (Retired Sisters' Residence) Sisters in Residence 22.

ESOPUS. *Mother of Perpetual Help Monastery*, P.O. Box 220, 12429. Tel: 845-384-6533; Fax: 845-384-6654. Email: rednuns@juno.com. Web: www.redemptoristinenunsofnewyork.org/. Sr. Paula Schmidt, O.SS.R., Prioress. Redemptoristine Nuns. Professed Sisters 10.

GARRISON. *Motherhouse and Novitiate of the Franciscan Sisters of the Atonement* (1898) St. Francis Convent - Graymoor, 41 Old Highland Tpke., 10524. Tel: 845-424-3623; Fax: 845-424-3298. Email: nconboy@graymoor.org. Web: www.graymoor.org. Sisters Nancy Conboy, S.A., Min. Gen.; Mary Electa Barber, S.A., Coord.
Franciscan Sisters of the Atonement, Inc. Sisters 82.

Our Lady of the Atonement Retreat House, St Francis Convent, 41 Old Highland Tpk., 10524. Tel: 845-424-3300; Fax: 845-424-3971. Email: retreathouse@graymoor.org. Web: www.graymoor.org. Sr. Eleanor White, S.A., Directress. Franciscan Sisters of the Atonement, Graymoor. Sisters 2.

GRAYMOOR. *Mother Lurana House* Adult Social Day Center., 166 Old W. Point Rd., E., Garrison, 10524. Tel: 845-424-3184; Fax: 845-424-4137. Web: www.graymoor.org. Sr. Eileen Waldron, S.A., Admin. Franciscan Sisters of the Atonement.

HARTSDALE. *Institute of the Sisters of Mercy of the Americas, Mid-Atlantic Community*, 150 Ridge Rd., 10530-2205. Tel: 914-328-3200; Fax: 914-328-3761. Email: cmccann@mercymidatlantic.org. Web: www.mercymidatlantic.org. Sr. Christine McCann, R.S.M., Pres.
The Sisters of Mercy, Inc. Sisters of Mercy. Sisters of Mercy of the Americas 1,071.

HASTINGS-ON-HUDSON. *Sisters of St. Francis of the Neumann Communities* (1893) 49 Jackson Ave., 10706-3217. Tel: 914-478-3930; Fax: 914-478-5470. Email: msalerno@sosf.org. Web: www.sosf.org. Sr. Maria Salerno, O.S.F., Leadership; Rev. Knute Kenlon, O.F.M.Cap., Chap. Sisters of St. Francis, Hastings-on-Hudson. Sisters 89.

HAVERSTRAW. *Sisters of St. Francis of Peace* (1986) *Congregation Center*, 20 Ridge St., 10927-1198. Tel: 845-942-2527; Fax: 845-429-8141. Email: jgilligan@fspnet.org. Web: www.fspnet.org. Sr. Jeanne Gilligan, F.S.P., Congregation Min.

HAWTHORNE. *Motherhouse & Novitiate of the Sisters of St. Dominic, Congregation of St. Rose of Lima* (1900) 10532. Tel: 914-769-0114; Fax: 914-769-0827. Web: www.hawthorne-dominicans.org. Sr. Mary Francis, O.P., Supr. Gen.; Rev. Martin Connors, O.P., B.A., S.T.B., Chap.
Motherhouse and Dominican Sisters of St. Dominic, Congregation of St. Rose of Lima. Professed Sisters 29; Sisters in Community 57; In Archdiocese 29.

HIGHLAND MILLS. *Religious of Jesus and Mary* (1911) 15 Bethany Dr., 10930-1003. Tel: 845-928-2213; Fax: 845-928-9437. Email: RJMClaireD@aol.com. Web: www.bethanyspiritualitycenter.org. Sr. Claire Dandeneau, R.J.M., Supr. Sisters 12.

HOPEWELL JUNCTION. *St. Aloysius Novitiate*, Beekman Rd., P.O. Box 98, 12533. Tel: 914-226-5671; Fax: 914-226-5671. Email: jstab35097@aol.com. Web: www.staloysius.ny.org. Sr. Gloria Castro, Supr. Gen. Oblates to the Blessed Trinity. Sisters 9; Postulants 2; Total in Residence 37; Total Staff 31.

LIBERTY. *Blessed Kateri Tekakwitha Religious Education Center*, Box 1011, 12754. Tel: 845-292-9100; Fax: 845-292-9100. Email: BKT4@verizon.net. Dominican Sisters.

LIVINGSTON MANOR. *Monastic Sisters of Bethlehem and of the Assumption of the Virgin* (1951) Grooville Rd., 12758. Tel: 845-439-4300; Fax: 845-439-3069. Sr. Amena Figeat, M.S.B.A.V., Supr. Total in Residence 15.

MARYKNOLL. *Maryknoll Communities, Inc.*, 77 Ryder Rd., P.O. Box 133, 10545-0133. Tel: 914-941-7590; Fax: 914-944-3628. Email: rcallahan@maryknoll.org. Web: www.maryknoll.org.

Maryknoll Residential Care Skilled Nursing home for the Maryknoll sisters only., Maryknoll Sisters Center, 10545-0311. Tel: 914-941-9230; Fax: 914-941-0213. Email: pedmiston@mksisters.org. Web: www.maryknoll.org. Sr. Patricia Edmiston, Admin. Bed Capacity 42; Sisters 33.

Maryknoll Sisters Charitable Trust, Treasury Office, P.O. Box 306, 10545-0306. Tel: 914-941-7590; Fax: 914-944-3628. Email: rcallahan@maryknoll.org. Web: www.maryknoll.org. Rev. Richard B. Callahan, M.M., Trustee.

Maryknoll Sisters Contemplative Community Contemplative Community of the Maryknoll Sisters of St. Dominic., P.O. Box 311, 10545-0311. Tel: 914-941-7575; Fax: 914-923-0733. Email: mkcontemplativecom@juno.com. Sr. Grace Myerjack, M.M., Coord. Sisters 8.

Maryknoll Sisters of St. Dominic Inc. (1912) P.O. Box 311, 10545-0311. Tel: 914-941-7575; Fax: 914-923-0733. Email: secretariat@mksisters.org. Web: www.maryknoll.org. Sr. Marcelline Yurkovic, M.M., Center-Rogers Coord. Professed Sisters 524; Total in Residence 225.

MILLBROOK. *Franciscan Missionaries of Mary* (1941) P.O. Box K, 12545. Tel: 845-677-6739; Fax: 845-677-9530. Email: fmmch@aol.com. Web: fmmusa.org. Sisters Anne Turbini, F.M.M.; Jacqueline LaVie, F.M.M.; Martha Vu, F.M.M. Sisters 4.

MONROE. *Parish Visitors of Mary Immaculate* (1920) *Marycrest*, 164 Quaker Hill Rd., P.O. Box 658, 10949-0658. Tel: 845-783-2251; Fax: 845-783-2085. Sisters Carole Marie Troskowski, Gen. Supr.; Mary Remias, Juniorate Dir.; Maria Catherine, Novice Dir. A contemplative-missionary community serving the Church by person-to-person evangelization through visiting parish families on behalf of their priests; religious education for children and adults not connected with the Catholic schools, giving spiritual counsel and serving as a liaison for social service needs of family members. Total in Community 60.

Queen of Apostles Convent Provincial Retirement Home and Provincialate of the Sisters of the Catholic Apostolate (Pallottine)., 98 Harriman Heights Rd., 10950. Tel: 845-492-5000. Email: qoaconvent@hotmail.com. Web: www.apostle-csac.org. Sisters Ann Joachim Firneno, Supr.; Olivia Reginella, C.S.A.C., Prov.; Rev. Msgr. Joseph F. Reynolds, Chap. Sisters 36.

MONSEY. *St. Zita's Villa* Motherhouse and Novitiate of Sisters of Reparation of the Congregation of Mary., 50 Saddle River Rd., N., 10952. Tel: 845-356-2011; Fax: 914-352-5209. Sr. Maureen Francis, S.R.C.M., Supr. Sisters 6.

NEW ROCHELLE. *Ursuline Bedford Park Convent* (1855) 1338 North Ave., 10804. Tel: 914-636-3456; Fax: 914-576-2620. Email: bedfordpark@aol.com. Sr. Pascal Conforti, O.S.U. Sisters 9.

Ursuline Communities, Inc. (1997) 1338 North Ave., 10804. Tel: 914-712-0060; Fax: 914-712-3134. Email: ursruepr@aol.com.

Ursuline Convent of St. Teresa's, 39 Willow Dr., 10805. Tel: 914-632-1199; Fax: 914-633-5281. Sr. Ann Peterson, O.S.U., Supr.
Ursuline Convent of St. Teresa's, New York Sisters 33.

Ursuline Provincialate, 1338 North Ave., 10804-2121. Tel: 914-712-0060; Fax: 914-712-3134. Email: ursruepr@aol.com. Provincialate of the Ursulines of the Roman Union, Eastern Province. Sisters in Province 131.

Ursuline Sisters of Andrews Avenue, Inc. (1995) 1338 North Ave., 10804. Tel: 914-712-0060; Fax: 914-712-3134.

Ursuline Residence, Inc., 1338 North Ave., 10804. Tel: 914-712-0060; Fax: 914-712-3134.

NEW WINDSOR. *Mt. St. Joseph* (1775) Administration Center of the Sisters of the Presentation of the Blessed Virgin Mary of New Windsor., 84 Presentation Way, 12553. Tel: 914-564-0513; Fax: 914-567-0219. Email: pbvmadministration@hvc.rr.com. Web: sistersofthepresentation.org. Sisters Patricia Anastasio, P.B.V.M., Pres.; Margaret Muller, P.B.V.M., Community Archivist. Ministry in the field of academic education in parochial elementary and high schools; pastoral services; health care; social services. Sisters 138.

NEWBURGH. *Center of Hope Sisters' Residence*, 320 Powell Ave., 12550. Tel: 845-561-6520; Fax: 845-569-8139. Email: jmarkiewica@ophope.org. Web: www.ophope.org. Exec. Office: 299 N. Highland Ave., Ossining, 10562. Tel: 914-941-4420 (Exec. Office). Sr. Maura Schefter, O.P., Admin. Dominican Sisters of Hope.

Daughters of Mary Immaculate (1898) Italian Apostolate in Sacred Heart Church., 15 Stori Rd., 12550. Tel: 845-565-5034. Sr. Alba Danese, F.M.I., Supr. Total Assisted 210; Total Staff 2.

Sisters of St. Dominic Charitable Trust, 320 Powell Ave., 12550. Tel: 845-561-6520; Fax: 845-569-8748.

Email: hdowney@ophope.org. Hugh R. Downey, Trustee.

NYACK. *Sisters of Our Lady of Christian Doctrine aka Institute of Christian Doctrine* Visitation House, 629 N. Midland Ave., 10960-1032. Tel: 845-358-7663; Fax: 845-358-7663. Email: agnesrcdpres@aol.com. Web: www.sistersrcd.org. Sr. Agnes O'Connor, R.C.D., Pres. Sisters 25.

Marydell Faith & Life Center, 640 N. Midland Ave., 10960. Tel: 845-358-5399; Fax: 845-358-1671. Email: marydell@netzero.net.

OSSINING. *Dominican Sisters of Hope* (1995) 299 N. Highland Ave., 10562-2327. Tel: 914-941-4420; Fax: 914-941-1125. Email: lelcock@ophope.org. Web: www.ophope.org. Sr. Lorelle Elcock, O.P., Prioress. Total in Community 215.

Dominicare, Inc. (2001) Office of the President, 299 N. Highland Ave., 10562-2327. Tel: 914-941-4420; Fax: 914-941-1125. Email: lelcock@ophope.org. Web: www.ophope.org.

PEEKSKILL. *Mt. St. Francis, Motherhouse & Infirm of Franciscan Missionary Sisters of Sacred Heart* Canonical Name: Franciscan Missionary Sisters of the Sacred Heart., 250 South St., 10566. Tel: 914-737-5409; Fax: 914-736-9614. Email: sajfmsc@mail.com. Sr. Anne James Guerin, F.M.S.C., Prov. Supr.

Missionary Sisters of the Third Order of St. Francis

RHINEBECK. *Linwood Spiritual Center*, 50 Linwood Rd., 12572-2507. Tel: 845-876-4178; Fax: 845-876-1920. Email: rboyle@st-ursula.org; msteeley@st-ursula.org. Web: www.linwoodspiritualctr.org. Sr. Maureen Steeley, S.U., Dir. Spiritual Center. Society of St. Ursula.

RYE. *Convent of the Holy Child*, 25 Convent Ln., 10580-1904. Tel: 914-967-5544; Fax: 914-925-2575. Email: holychildd@aol.com. Sisters of the Holy Child Jesus 20.

SCARSDALE. *Blessed Sacrament Monastery*, 86 Dromore Rd., 10583-1706. Tel: 914-722-1657; Fax: 914-722-1665. Email: obsny@optonline.net. Web: www.catholic.org/macc. Sr. Mary Veronica Kiley, Prioress. Sacramentine Nuns. Sisters 11.

SLOATSBURG. *St. Mary's Villa, Spiritual & Educational Center*, 150 Sisters Servants Ln., P.O. Box 9, 10974-0009. Tel: 845-753-5100; Fax: 845-753-1956. Email: ssminy@aol.com. Sisters Servants of Mary Immaculate.

SPARKILL. *Dominican Convent of Our Lady of the Rosary* (1876) Motherhouse and General Novitiate of Dominican Sisters of Congregation of Our Lady of the Rosary., 175 Rte. 340, 10976-1047. Tel: 845-359-4088; Fax: 845-359-4083. Email: lorraine.larocca@sparkill.org. Web: www.sparkill.org. Sr. Maryann Summa, O.P., Pres.; Rev. George Torak, Chap. Sisters 353.

STATEN ISLAND. *Daughters of St. Paul, Pious Society* (1915) 840 Delafield Ave., 10310. Tel: 718-447-5071; Fax: 718-816-1332. Email: statenisland@pauline.org. Web: www.pauline.org. Sr. Mary Thecla Paolini, Supr. Missionary Sisters of the Communications Media. Sisters 7.

Pious Disciples of the Divine Master, Regional and Formation House, 60 Sunset Ave., 10314. Tel: 718-761-2323; 718-494-8597; Fax: 718-494-2123. Email: srnieves@aol.com. Web: www.pddm.us. Sr. M. Nieves Salinas, P.D.D.M., Regl. Supr. Sisters 10.

TARRYTOWN. *Provincial Center, Religious Sacred Heart of Mary*, 50 Wilson Park Dr., 10591-3023. Tel: 914-631-8872; Fax: 914-631-7803. Email: mod@rshmeap.org. Web: www.rshm.org. Sisters Kathleen Fagan, R.S.H.M., Prov. Supr.; Joanne Safian, R.S.H.M., Prov. Counselor; Margaret Ellen Flannelly, R.S.H.M., Prov. Counselor; Martina Crowley, R.S.H.M., Treas.; Mary Alice Young, R.S.H.M., Dir. of Advancement; Lucia Kenny, R.S.H.M., Archivist; Loretta Ruvo, R.S.H.M., Dir. Vocation Promotion; Ms. Shirley Ann Solivan, Provincial Team Sec. Total Staff 16.

WALDEN. *Convent of Most Precious Blood*, 100 Ulster Ave., 12586. Tel: 845-778-7616. Sisters 2.

Little Sisters of the Assumption, Provincial House, 100 Gladstone Ave., 12586. Tel: 845-778-0667; Fax: 845-778-0676. Email: provsec@littlesisters.org. Web: www.littlesisters.org. Sr. Annette Allain, L.S.A., Prov. Sisters in Province 31.

Other residences in New York: *Little Sisters of the Assumption*, 475 E. 115th St., 10029. Tel: 212-369-2097. *Little Sisters of the Assumption*, 310 E. 120th St., 10035. Tel: 917-668-4738; Fax: 212-427-6096. *Little Sisters of the Assumption*, 2 Donner Dr., 12586. Tel: 845-778-1867.

Little Sisters of the Assumption, 98 Gladstone Ave., 12586-0677. Tel: 845-778-7252; Fax: 845-778-0676. Sr. Annette Allain, L.S.A., Prov. Sisters 14.

WAPPINGERS FALLS. *Monastery of St. Clare - Franciscan Poor Clare Nuns* (1915) 70 Nelson Ave., 12590-1121. Tel: 845-297-1685; Fax: 845-297-7657. Email: claresny@gmail.com. Web: www.poorclaresny.com. Sr. Mary Michael Boisseau, O.S.C., Abbess.

Franciscan Poor Clare Nuns Sisters 11; Novices 1.

WARWICK. *Mt. Alverno Center, Bon Secours Charity Health System*, 20 Grand St., 10990. Tel: 845-986-2267; Fax: 845-986-9269. Email: Ann-Lombardi@bshsi.org. Web: www.stanthonycommunityhosp.org. Thomas R. Brunelle, FACHE, Warwick Campus; Michael Deyo, Admin., Mt. Alverno Center, Adult Home/Assisted Living Program; Rosemarie Zlotnick, Pastoral Care; Rev. Henry Tanto, Chap. (Retired). St. Francis Center at the Knolls, Villa Francis at the Knolls.

WHITE PLAINS. *Convent of Our Lady of Good Counsel* Motherhouse of the Sisters of the Divine Compassion., 52 N. Broadway, 10603. Tel: 914-798-1300; Fax: 914-949-5169. Email: smerritt@divinecompassion.org. Web: divinecompassion.org. Sr. Susan Merritt, R.D.C., Pres. Sisters 27.

RDC Center for Counseling and Human Development, Inc. (1991) 52 N. Broadway, 10603. Tel: 914-949-0504; Fax: 914-997-1979. To provide counseling services for laity, religious and clergy. Individual and group counseling are offered as well as marital and family therapy.

YONKERS. *St. Paul the Apostle*, 586 McLean Ave., 10705. Tel: 914-968-8094; Fax: 914-968-0462. Sisters Agnes Mary, S.V., Supr.; Mary Rose, S.V., Vicar Gen.; Elizabeth Ann, S.V.; John Mary, S.V.; Theresa Elizabeth, S.V.; Dorothy Guadalupe, S.V.; Mariea Dolorosa, S.V.

Our Lady of New York, 1955 Needham Ave., Bronx, 10466. Tel: 718-881-8008; Fax: 718-654-2911.

Sacred Heart of Jesus (1991) 450 W. 51st St., 10019. Tel: 212-397-1396; Fax: 212-397-1397. Sisters Brigid Ancille Marie, S.V.; Mary, S.V.; Rose Clairvaux, S.V.; Mary Kolbe, S.V.; Rita Marie, S.V.

Villa Maria Guadalupe, 159 Skymeadow Dr., Stamford, CT 06903. Tel: 203-329-1492; Fax: 203-329-1495. Sisters Mary Karen, S.V., Local Supr.; Rosario John, S.V.; Josamarie Perpetua, S.V.; Marija Joseph, S.V.; Maria Emmanuel, S.V.; Mary Teresa, S.V.; Ave Maria, S.V.; John Joseph, S.V.

St. Francis de Chantal, 198 Hollywood Ave., Bronx, 10465. Tel: 718-863-2264; Fax: 718-792-9645. Sisters Mary Gabriel, S.V., Dir. of Vocations; Giovanna Mariae, S.V.; Mariam Caritas, S.V.; Antoniana Maria, S.V.; Loretto Michael, S.V.; Mary Louise Concepta, S.V.

Sisters of Life, 586 McLean Ave., 10705. Tel: 914-968-8094; Fax: 914-968-0462. Sr. Agnes Mary Donovan, S.V., Supr. Gen. Professed Sisters 37; Novices 12; Postulants 12.

[GG] RETREAT HOUSES

BRONX. *St. Joseph's Center*, 275 W. 230th St., 10463. Tel: 718-796-4340. Rev. Jose Luis Martinez, O.A.R., Dir.; Bro. Mario Alvarez, O.A.R., Admin. (Spanish Cursillo Center) Total in Residence 1; Total Staff 2.

The Passionist Spiritual Center/Cardinal Spellman Retreat House, 5801 Palisade Ave., 10471. Tel: 718-549-6500; Fax: 718-884-9732. Email: PassSpiritCtr@passionists.org. Web: www.passionists.org & www.preacherman.org. Rev. Paul R. Fagan, C.P., Dir. & Local Coord.; Mr. William J. Gilberg, Admin.; Bro. James Johnson, C.P., Coord. of Special Events; Rev. Michael Greene, C.P., Assoc. Retreat Dir.; Bro. Andre Mathieu, C.P., Itinerant Preacher; Rev. John Powers, C.P., Itinerant Preacher; Bro. August Parlavechio, C.P., Province Devel. Office & Part-time Retreat Team.

ESOPUS. *Marist Brothers of Ulster County* (1994) Mid Hudson Valley Camp - Summer camp for disadvantaged children/Retreat house for youth. Winter youth retreat facility., P.O. Box 197, 12429. Tel: 845-384-6106 (residence); 845-384-6620 (office); Fax: 845-384-6479. Email: esopusdon1@aol.com. Web: www.maristretreathouse.com. Bro. Donald Nugent, F.M.S., Dir. Total Staff 2.

Mount St. Alphonsus Redemptorist Retreat Center, 1001 Broadway, P.O. Box 219, 12429. Tel: 845-384-8000; Fax: 845-384-8088. Web: www.msaretreat.com. Very Rev. John G. Kingsbury, C.Ss.R., Rector; Bros. Robert Skinner, C.Ss.R.; Gerard St. Hilaire, C.Ss.R.; Revs. John Murray, C.Ss.R.; Joseph Freund, C.Ss.R. Redemptorist Fathers and Brothers., Groups and individual retreats, conferences, workshops, and days of prayer. Available for Religious Chapters. Capacity 106; Bed Capacity 161.

HIGHLAND MILLS. *Bethany Spirituality Center, Inc.*, 202 County Rte. 105, P.O. Box 1003, 10930-3130. Tel: 845-928-2213; Fax: 845-928-2320. Email: info@bethanyspiritualitycenter.org. Web: www.bethanyspiritualitycenter.org. Sr. Eileen Reid, R.J.M., Pres.; Richard C. Green, Dir. Religious of Jesus and Mary. Total in Residence 12.

LARCHMONT. *St. Francis Retreat, Inc.*, 1 Pryer Manor Rd., 10538. Tel: 914-235-6839; Fax: 914-576-6540. Rev. Benedict Joseph Groeschel, C.F.R., Ed.D. Tel: 914-632-3743.

Trinity Retreat, 1 Pryer Manor Rd., 10538. Tel: 914-235-6839; Fax: 914-576-6540. Email: trinityret@aol.com. Revs. Eugene J. Fulton, Dir.; Benedict Joseph Groeschel, C.F.R., Ed.D., Assoc. Dir.

MIDDLETOWN. *National Shrine of Our Lady of Mount Carmel*, 70 Carmelite Dr., P.O. Box 2163, 10940-2163. Tel: 845-343-1879; Fax: 845-343-1912. Email: nsolmc@warwick.net. Web: www.ourladyofmtcarmelshrine.com. Rev. Thomas Zalewski, O.Carm., Dir. Total Staff 4.

SLOATSBURG. *St. Mary's Villa*, 150 Sisters Servants Ln., P.O. Box 9, 10974-0009. Tel: 845-753-5100; Fax: 845-753-1956. Email: ssminy@aol.com. Sisters Servants of Mary Immaculate., Spiritual and Educational Center. (Retreats) Total in Residence 6; Total Staff 9.

STATEN ISLAND. **Mount Manresa Jesuit Retreat House* (1911) 239 Fingerboard Rd., 10305. Tel: 718-727-3844; Fax: 718-727-4881. Email: info@mountmanresa.org. Web: www.mountmanresa.org. Rev. Edward J. Quinnan, S.J., M.A., M.Div., Ph.D., S.T.M., Supr.; Sr. Maureen Skelly, S.C., Retreat Min.; Mr. Fred Herron, Interim Dir.; Ms. Arlene Volsario, Admin.; Rev. Matthew F. Roche, S.J., Retreat Min. Society of Jesus. Total in Residence 4; Total Staff 6.

STONY POINT. *Don Bosco Retreat Center and Marian Shrine* Founded 1947., 174 Filors Ln., 10980-2620. Tel: 914-947-2200; Fax: 914-947-2203. Email: marianshrine@aol.com. Web: www.marianshrine.org. Revs. George Atok, S.D.B.; Augustine Baek, S.D.B., RYC Korean Min.; Paul Bedard, S.D.B.; James Berning, S.D.B., Retreats Coord.; William Bucciferro, S.D.B., Shrine Coord. & Delegate for Cooperator Salesians; John Cosgrove, S.D.B.; Joseph Doran, S.D.B., Chap. Marycrest Convent, Monroe; Peter Sang Yun Kim, S.D.B.; Peter Malloy, S.D.B.; John Puntino, S.D.B., Dir.; Waclaw Swierzbiolek, S.D.B., Polish Min.; Chester Szemborski, S.D.B.; Vincent Zuliani, S.D.B.; Bros. Michael Brinkman, S.D.B.; John Cauda, S.D.B.; Jerome Cincotta, S.D.B.; Charles Mayer, S.D.B.; Richard Pasiak, S.D.B.; Henry van der Velden, S.D.B.; Bernard Zdanowicz, S.D.B. Total in Residence 20; Total Staff 23.

Marian Shrine (1947) 174 Filors Ln., 10980-2660. Tel: 845-947-2200; Fax: 845-947-2203. Email: marianshrine@aol.com. Web: www.marianshrine.org. Revs. George Atok, S.D.B.; Augustine Baek, S.D.B., RYC Korean Min.; Paul Bedard, S.D.B.; James Berning, S.D.B., Retreats Coord. CYM; William Bucciferro, S.D.B., Shrine Coord. & Delegate for Cooperator Salesians; John Cosgrove, S.D.B.; Joseph Doran, S.D.B., Chap. Marycrest Convent, Monroe; Peter Sang Yun Kim, S.D.B.; Peter Malloy, S.D.B.; John Puntino, S.D.B., Dir.; Waclaw Swierzbiolek, S.D.B., Polish Min.; Chester Szemborski, S.D.B.; Vincent Zuliani, S.D.B.; Bros. Michael Brinkman, S.D.B.; John Cauda, S.D.B.; Jerome Cincotta, S.D.B.; Charles Mayer, S.D.B.; Richard Pasaik, S.D.B.; Henry van der Velden, S.D.B.; Bernard Zdanowicz, S.D.B. Total in Residence 20; Total Staff 23.

WAPPINGERS FALLS. *Mt. Alvernia Retreat House* 12590. Tel: 845-297-5706; Fax: 845-298-0309. Email: mtalverniarh@optonline.net. Revs. Michael Nappo, O.F.M., Guardian, Retreat Staff; Roch Ciandella, O.F.M., Dir. Retreats; Thomas Garone, O.F.M., Assoc. Dir., Retreats; Sebastian Buccellato, O.F.M., Spanish Apostolate; Armand Padula, O.F.M., Librarian, Parochial Ministry; Bro. Thomas Hollowood, O.F.M., Dir. Maintenance.

WARWICK. *Franciscan Sisters of the Poor Convent*, 24 Grand St., 10990. Tel: 914-986-2267. Miss Jean Wetstine, Exec. Dir.; Sr. Paula Adelman, Local Community Min.; Rev. Edward Sullivan, O.F.M., Chap. Franciscan Sisters of the Poor.

YONKERS. *Sisters of Mary Reparatrix*, 287 Hayward St., 10704. Tel: 914-376-3245; Fax: 914-423-5721. Sisters Judy Frasietti, S.M.R.; Geraldine McCullagh, S.M.R. Sisters 2.

[HH] UNIVERSITY APOSTOLATES

YONKERS. *University Apostolate* 201 Seminary Ave., 10704. Tel: 914-968-6200, Ext. 8252; Fax: 914-968-6671. Rev. Daniel O'Reilly, M.A., Dir.

Bronx Community College Loew Hall-Room 422, University Ave. & W. 181st St., Bronx, 10453. Tel: 718-289-5954. Web: www.bcc.cuny.edu. Rev. James Sheehan, Campus Min.

City College of New York Baskerville, 204, 137th St. & Convent Ave., 10031. Tel: 212-650-5866. Web: www.ccny.cuny.edu. Mr. Gregory Pope, Campus Min.

Columbia University 110 Earl Hall, 10027. Tel: 212-854-5110. Web: www.columbia.edu. Revs. Andrzej J. Fornal, O.P., Campus Min.; Jacek Kopera, O.P., Campus Min.; Marek Pienkowski, O.P., Campus Min.

Culinary Institute of America 93 Wurts St., Kingston, 12401. Tel: 845-331-0436; Fax: 845-340-9596. Email: chaplains@bestweb.net. Web: www.ciachef.edu. Rev. Marc K. Oliver, Campus Min.

Dutchess Community College 93 Wurts St., Kingston, 12401-4509. Tel: 845-331-0436. Web: www.cuny-dutchess.edu. Rev. Marc K. Oliver, Campus Min.

Vassar College St. Raymond Ave., Poughkeepsie, 12604. Tel: 845-437-7000. Web: www.vassar.edu. Ms. Linda Tuttle, Campus Min.

Dominican College 470 Western Hwy., Orangeburg, 10962. Tel: 845-359-7800. Sr. Barbara McEneany, O.P., Dir. Campus Min.; Rev. Ronald Stanley, O.P., Chap., Campus Min.

Fashion Institute of Technology (SUNY) 227 W. 27th St., 10001. Tel: 212-564-9070, Ext. 237. Web: www.fitnyc.edu. Rev. John B. Riordan, O.F.M.Cap., Campus Min.

Fordham University at Rosehill 441 E. Fordham Rd., Bronx, 10458. Tel: 718-817-4500; Fax: 718-817-4505. Email: currie@fordham.edu. Web: www.fordham.edu/cm. Rev. Joseph Currie, S.J.; Sr. Regina DeVitto, C.N.D., Faith Formation; Randy Jerome, Retreats & CLC; Mr. Denis Kelly; Mr. Robert Minotti, Dir. Music; Lisandro Pena, Liturgy Coord.; Gil Severiano, Sec.; Rev. Erika Crawford, Interfaith Coord.

Fordham Lincoln Center 113 W. 60th St., Lowenstein 217, 10023. Tel: 212-636-6267; 212-636-6268. Rev. Damian O'Connell, S.J., Liturgy Coord.; Ms. Joan Cavanagh, Assoc. Dir.; Mr. Patrick Callaghan, Sec.

Herbert H. Lehman College Student Life Bldg., 250 Bedford Park Blvd. W. (222E), Bronx, 10468. Tel: 718-960-4979. Web: www.lehman.cuny.edu. Rev. Neil J. O'Connell, O.F.M., B.A., S.T.B., M.A., Ph.D., Campus Min.

Borough of Manhattan 199 Chambers St., 10009. Tel: 212-220-8000. Web: www.bmcc.cuny.edu. Rev. Neil J. O'Connell, O.F.M., B.A., S.T.B., M.A., Ph.D., Campus Min.

Hostos Community College 475 Grand Concourse (Rm. C371), Bronx, 10451. Tel: 718-518-6873 (Mon-Tues). Web: www.hostos.cuny.edu. Rev. James Sheehan, Campus Min.

Hunter/Baruch College Newman Catholic Center, 695 Park Ave., Rm. 1317 E. Bldg., 10021. Tel: 212-772-4752 (Hunter); 646-312-4762 (Baruch). Web: www.hunter.cuny.edu; www.baruch.cuny.edu. Sr. Barbara Ann Mueller, O.P., Campus Min.

Iona College 715 North Ave., New Rochelle, 10801. Tel: 914-633-2632; Fax: 914-633-2363. Web: www.iona.edu. Mr. Carl Procario-Foley, Dir. Campus Min.; Rev. Francis F. Dixon, O.Carm., Campus Min.; Tiffany Di Nomi, Campus Min.; Jeanne McDermott, Campus Min.

John Jay College 445 W. 59th St., Rm. 2311, 10019-1128. Tel: 212-237-8281; Fax: 212-237-8465. Web: www.jjay.cuny.edu.

Manhattan College 4513 Manhattan College Pkwy., Bronx, 10471. Tel: 718-862-7972; Fax: 718-862-8073. Email: lois.harr@manhattan.edu. Web: www.manhattan.edu.
Campus Ministry and Social Action Lois Harr, M.A., Dir. Campus Min.; Rev. George H. Hill, M.Div., M.A., Chap. Tel: 718-862-7972; Mr. Kevin McCloskey, Campus Min.; Jennifer Edwards, M.A., Campus Min.

Manhattanville College 2900 Purchase St., Purchase, 10577. Tel: 914-323-5150, Ext. 447; Fax: 914-694-2496. Rev. William Tyrrell, S.A., Campus Min.

Marist College 3399 North Rd., Poughkeepsie, 12601. Tel: 845-575-3130; 845-575-3000, Ext. 2275; Fax: 845-575-3299. Email: francis.kelly@marist.edu. Rev. Richard LaMorte, Chap.; Bro. Frank Kelly, F.M.S., Campus Min.

Mt. St. Mary College 330 Powell Ave., Newburg, 12550. Tel: 845-569-3517. Web: www.msmc.edu. Sr. Kathleen Hickey, C.S.J., Campus Min.; Carol Gibney, Campus Min.

College of Mt. St. Vincent 6301 Riverdale Ave., Riverdale, 10471. Tel: 718-405-3200; 718-405-3215; 718-405-3216. Web: www.cmsv.edu. Sisters Cecilia Harriendorff, S.C., Campus Min.; Theresa Capria, S.C.

College of New Rochelle 29 Castle Pl., New Rochelle, 10805. Tel: 914-654-5052; 914-654-5867; Fax: 914-654-5958. Email: hwolf@cnr.edu. Web: www.cnr.edu. Helen Wolf, Dir.; Rev. John Joseph Flynn, O.F.M.Cap., Chap.

New York Maritime College 6 Pennyfield Ave., Fort Schuyler, Bronx, 10465-4198. Tel: 718-409-7200. Web: www.sunymaritime.edu. Rev. Daniel O'Reilly, M.A., Campus Min.

New York Medical College Valhalla, 10595. Tel: 914-594-4646; Fax: 914-594-4421. Web: www.nymc.edu. Deacon Lawrence O'Toole, Campus Min.

New York University Catholic Center at NYU, 58 Washington Sq. S., 10012. Tel: 212-741-1274. Email: john.mcquire-op@nyu.edu. Web: www.nyu.edu. Revs. Vincent G. DeLucia, O.P., Dir. NYU Catholic Center; John Davis, O.P., Campus Min.; John McGuire, O.P., Campus Min.
Office: *St. Joseph's Rectory*, 371 - 6th Ave., 10014. Tel: 212-741-1274; Fax: 212-473-2971.

Pace University One Pace Plaza, 20 Cardinal Hayes Pl., 10038. Tel: 212-962-3972. Web: www.pace.edu. Rev. John McGuire, O.P., Campus Min.

Pace University/Westchester SUNY/Purchase 105 Arden St., Apt. 5D, 10040. Tel: 914-543-3340. Web: www.pacewestchester.edu; www.purchase.edu. William Mulligan, Campus Min.

Rockland Community College 145 College Rd., Suffern, 10901. Tel: 845-574-4531; Fax: 845-574-4552. Web: www.sunyrockland.edu. Mr. Michael Ver'Schneider, Campus Min.

St. John's University 300 Howard Ave., Rm. B9, Staten Island, 10301. Tel: 718-390-4473. Web: www.stjohns.edu. Sr. Joan Mahoney, C.N.D., Dir. Campus Min. Tel: 718-390-4473; James Behan Jr., Campus Min.; Melissa Gibilaro, Campus Min.

St. Thomas Aquinas 125 Rte. 340, Sparkill, 10976. Tel: 845-398-4062; Fax: 845-398-4061. Web: www.stac.edu. Sr. Madeleine Murphy, O.P., Campus Min.

SUNY/New Paltz 75 S. Manheim Blvd., New Paltz, 12561. Tel: 845-691-7151. Web: www.newpaltz.edu. Mr. Henry Grimsland, Campus Min.

Wagner College & The College of Staten Island One Campus Rd., Staten Island, 10301. Tel: 718-390-3461 (Wagner); 718-982-2652 (College of Staten Island). Email: elaine.schenk@verizon.net. Web: www.wagner.edu; www.csi.cuny.edu. Sr. Elaine R. Schenk, M.Id., Campus Min.

[II] MISCELLANEOUS

NEW YORK. *Alfred E. Smith Memorial Foundation, Inc., The* (1946) 1011 First Ave., 10022-4134. Tel: 212-371-1000, Ext. 3315; Fax: 212-753-5980.

America Press, Inc. (1909) The Business & Editorial Offices, 106 W. 56th St., 10019. Tel: 212-581-4640; Fax: 212-399-3596. Email: america@americamagazine.org. Web: www.americamagazine.org. Rev. Andrew J. Christiansen, S.J., Pres. & Editor-in-Chief; Ms. Jan Attridge, Publisher; Mr. Albert C. Pierce, Chm. Bd. of Trustees.

American Committee on Italian Migration, Inc., 25 Carmine St., 10014. Tel: 212-247-7373; Fax: 212-265-5793. Email: acimny@aol.com. Web: www.aciminnigra.org. Rev. Joseph Fugolo, C.S., Natl. Exec. Sec. To insure fair immigration policy favoring reunion of families and cultural integration of Italian Americans. Total Staff 3.

American Compassion Services, Inc., 1356 Madison Ave., 3S, 10128. Tel: 646-264-2680. Email: info@fidesco-usa.org. Herve Dutiel, Pres.

St. Ansgar Scandinavian Catholic League (1910) 3 E. 28th St., 8th Fl., 10016. Tel: 212-675-0400; Fax: 201-433-3355. Email: viggor@rambusch.com. Web: www.saintansgars.org. Dr. Astrid M. O'Brien, Pres.; Revs. Thomas A. Nielson, Chap. (Retired); John T. Halborg, Dir. Programs, Editor of the Bulletin (Retired); Mr. Viggo B. Rambusch, Chm.

Apostolate for Family Consecration, Inc., St. Joseph East Coast Center, 350 5th Ave., Suite 5900, PMB #26N, 10118-0069. Tel: 212-971-1370. Email: jconiker@familyland.org. Web: www.familycatechism.com. Jerome Coniker, Pres.

Benefice Advantage, 155 E. 56th St., 2nd Fl., 10022. Tel: 718-518-2168; Fax: 718-518-2690. Email: vsampugnaro@chcsnet.org. Vincent Sampugnaro, Human Resources.

Brooklyn Prep Alumni Association (1964) Loyola Hall, Fordham Univ., 10458. Tel: 718-817-5454; Fax: 718-733-4456. Web: www.brooklynprep.org. Rev. Daniel J. Fitzpatrick, S.J., Moderator. Membership 4,780.

Calvary Fund, Inc., 1740 Eastchester Rd., Bronx, 10461. Tel: 718-518-2077; Fax: 718-518-2477. Email: webmaster@calvaryhospital.org. Web: calvaryhospital.org. Frank A. Calamari, Pres.; Richard E. Meyer, Chm.

The Cardinal Cooke Guild, 1011 First Ave., 10022. Tel: 212-371-1000, Ext. 2740; Fax: 212-371-1011 Ext. 2478. Email: abbeykkmoy@aol.com. Web: www.terencecardinalcooke.org. Official organization for the promotion of the Cause of Canonization of the Servant of God Terence Cardinal Cooke. Cause: Dr. Avv. Andrea Ambrosi, Roman Postulator; Rev. Msgr. Joseph R. Giandurco, J.C.D., Vice Postulator; Rev. Benedict Joseph Groeschel, C.F.R., Ed.D., Consultant Guild: Patricia Handal, Coord.

Cardinal Cooke Memorial Foundation, 1011 First Ave., Rm. 1940, 10022. Tel: 212-371-1000; Fax: 212-813-9538.

Cardinal's Fund for Children, 1011 First Ave., Rm. 1130, 10022.

Carmel Housing Development Fund Co., Inc., 1011 First Ave., 10022. Tel: 212-371-1000; Fax: 212-826-8795. Rev. Msgr. Kevin L. Sullivan, Pres.

Catholic Alumni Club of the Archdiocese of New York, 83 Christopher St., 10014. Tel: 212-243-6513. Email: marydplaza@yahoo.com. Web: www.caci.org/cac/newyorkcac.html. Marguerite Cronin, Pres.

Catholic Big Sisters and Big Brothers, 137 E. 2nd St., 2nd Fl., 10009. Tel: 212-475-3291; Fax: 212-475-0280. Email: director@cbsbb.org. Web: www.cbsbb.org. Total Assisted 1,029.

Catholic Daughters of the Americas and Its Courts, 10 W. 71st St., 10023. Tel: 212-877-3041; Fax: 212-724-5923. Email: cdofanatl@aol.com. Web: www.catholicdaughters.org. Librada Ramirez, Natl. Regent; Mrs. Margaret O'Brien, Contact Person.

Catholic Family and Human Rights Institute, 866 United Nations Plaza, Ste. 495, 10017. Tel: 212-754-5948; Fax: 212-754-9291. Email: c-fam@c-fam.org. Web: www.c-fam.org. Austin Ruse, Pres.; Susan Yoshihara, Ph.D., Exec. Vice Pres.

Catholic Health Care Foundation of the Archdiocese of New York, Inc., 205 Lexington Ave., 3rd Fl., 10016. Tel: 212-752-4735. Email: poconnor@archcare.org. Web: www.archcare.org. Mrs. Patricia O'Connor, Contact Person.

Catholic Health Care System, 205 Lexington Ave., 3rd Fl., 10016. Tel: 212-752-4735. Email: slarue@chcsnet.org. Web: www.chcsnet.org. Karl P. Adler, M.D., Archbishop's Delegate for Health Care.

Catholic High School Association of New York (1928) 1011 First Ave., Rm. 1856, 10022. Tel: 212-371-1000; Fax: 212-758-3018. Email: supt@adnyschools.org. Web: www.ny-archdiocese.org.

Catholic High Schools' Athletic Association of the Archdiocese of New York, 650 Grand Concourse, 10451. Tel: 718-585-5556.
4300 Murdock Ave., Bronx, 10466. Tel: 718-325-6423. Mr. Richard Tricario, Pres.

Catholic Indemnity Insurance Company, c/o 1011 First Ave., 10022. Tel: 212-371-1000; Fax: 212-838-0841. Email: edward.reigadas@archny.org. Edward Reigadas, Sec.

Catholic Interracial Council of N.Y., The, 899 10th Ave., 10019. Tel: 212-237-8600. Gerard W. Lynch, Pres.

**Catholic League for Religious and Civil Rights*, 450 Seventh Ave., 34th Fl., 10123. Tel: 212-371-3191; Fax: 212-371-3394. Email: cl@catholicleague.org. Web: www.catholicleague.org. Dr. William A. Donohue, Pres.; Bernadette Brady, Vice Pres. Total Staff 12.

Catholic Medical Mission Board, Inc., National Headquarters, 10 W. 17th St., 10011-5765. Tel: 212-242-7757; Fax: 212-807-9161; 212-242-0930. Email: info@cmmb.org. Web: www.cmmb.org.
Officers: Most Rev. Joseph M. Sullivan, D.D., Chm.; Frank J. Sasinawski Esq., Vice Chm.; Mary Colleen Scanlon, R.N., J.D., Sec.; Michael Doring Connelly, Treas.
Members: Rev. J. Peter Schineller, S.J.; Sr. Patricia Eck, C.B.S.; Chris Allen; Nicholas D'Agostino Jr.; John E. Celentano; John F. Galbraith; Jean Marie C. Grisi; John D. Herrick; Bradley P. Holmes Esq.; Clarion E. Johnson, M.D.; Henry W. Mann Esq.; Patrick D. Mutchler; Mario J. Paredes; E. Anne Petersen, M.D., M.P.H.; Robert E. Robotti; F. William Smullen III.

Catholic Near East Welfare Association (CNEWA) (1926) 1011 First Ave., 10022. Tel: 212-826-1480; Fax: 212-826-8979. Email: cnewa@cnewa.org. Web: www.cnewa.org. Most Rev. Timothy M. Dolan, Pres. & Treas.; His Eminence Marc Cardinal Ouellet, P.S.S., Vice Pres.; Rev. Msgr. Robert L. Stern, Sec. Gen.; Rev. Guido Gockel, M.H.M., Under Sec. Gen.; Mr. Omar Delgadillo, Sec. for Admin.; Mr. Michael La Civita, Asst. Sec. for Communications; Mrs. Tresool Singh, Asst. Sec. for Fin.

Catholic Resources, Inc., 1339 York Ave., 10021. Tel: 646-475-4835. Email: kmcguire@chcsnet.org. Kathryn McGuire, Sr. Vice Pres.

Catholic Spiritual Family, The Work, Inc., 123 E. 38th St., 10016. Tel: 212-725-8316, Ext. 108. Email: theworkinc@catholic.org. Web: www.thework-fso.org. Sr. Monika Mader, F.S.O., M.B.A., Treas.

Catholic Women's Union of New York, Inc. (1916) *c/o Eunice Vasile*, 2664 Salt Point Tpke., Clinton Corners, 12514. Tel: 845-266-3074; Fax: 845-266-3666. Eunice Vasile, M.P.A., R.N., Pres.; Anna K. Weisz, B.A., Vice Pres.; Hilda Dengler McGlew,

J.D., Treas.; Mary Sophie Ruedi, B.A., Sec.; Rev. Arthur Wendell, C.Ss.R., Moderator.

The Catholic World Wide Web Corporation, 1011 First Ave., 10022. Tel: 212-371-1000. Email: bernard.reidy@archny.org. Web: www.archny.org. Bernard E. Reidy, Archbishop's Delegate for Admin. & Fin.

Centro Altagracia de Fe y Justicia, Inc. (Altagracia Center of Faith and Justice, Inc.), 39 E. 83rd St., 10028. Tel: 212-568-2115; Fax: 212-568-2118. Email: info@centroaltagracia.org. Web: www.centroaltagracia.org. Rev. Mark C. Hallinan, S.J., Sec.; Richard Espinal, Exec. Dir.

Centro Carismatico Catolico Hispano De La Arquidiocesis De Nueva York, 826 E. 166th St., Bronx, 10459. Tel: 718-378-1734; Fax: 718-378-1819. Email: centro826@aol.com. Web: www.centrocatolicocarismatico.com. Most Rev. Josu Iriondo, S.T.L., D.D., Dir.

Chapel San Lorenzo Ruiz (Philippine Pastoral Center), 378 Broome St., 10013. Tel: 212-966-1019; Fax: 212-966-1034. Email: chapelofsanlorenzoruiz@gmail.com. Web: www.chapelofsanlorenzo.com. Rev. Erno Diaz, Dir.

Chinese Catholic Information Center, 86 Riverside Dr., 10024. Tel: 212-787-6969. Rev. Paul Chan (Taiwan), Dir. Total in Residence 7; Total Staff 4.

Christ House, Inc. Shared Residence for Religious and Young Men Lacking Family Support., 432 E. 142nd St., Bronx, 10454. Tel: 718-665-8740; Fax: 718-665-1665. Email: christhouse@earthlink.net. Mr. Raul Morales, Dir.

The Christophers (1945) 5 Hanover Sq., 10004. Tel: 212-759-4050; Fax: 212-838-5073. Email: mail@christophers.org. Web: www.christophers.org. Mary Ellen Robinson, COO. A multi-media organization reaching millions with the Gospel message. Total Staff 30.

CNEWA UNITED STATES (2003) 1011 First Ave., 10022. Tel: 212-826-1480; Fax: 212-826-8979. Email: cnewa.us@cnewa.org. His Eminence William Cardinal Keeler, D.D., J.C.D., Pres.; Mr. Gabriele Delmonaco, National Sec.

Committee for Mission Responsibility Society, Inc. The Propagation of the Faith, 1011 First Ave., 10022. Tel: 212-371-1000, Ext. 2700; Fax: 212-371-7220. Email: pchirchirillo@aol.com. Sr. Pauline Chirchirillo, P.B.V.M.

Community of St. Egidio, U.S.A., Inc., P.O. Box 250299, 10025-1534. Tel: 212-663-1483. Email: ppiscitelli@hotmail.com. Web: www.santegidio.org. Paola Piscitelli, Pres.

Cor Mariae Development Fund Corporation, 1011 First Ave., 10022. Rev. Msgr. Kevin L. Sullivan, Pres. & Contact Person.

Cor Mariae Housing Development Fund, Inc., 1101 First Ave., 10022. Tel: 212-371-1000, Ext. 2400. Rev. Msgr. Kevin L. Sullivan, Pres.

Cornelia Connelly Center for Education, Holy Child Middle School, 220 E. 4th St., 10009. Tel: 212-982-2287; Fax: 212-982-0547. Email: mscerbo@connellycenter.org. Web: www.holychild.com. Mary Claire Scerbo, Dir.; Sr. Marcia Sichol, S.H.C.J., Contact Person.

Courage International, Incorporated, Church of St. John the Baptist, 210 W. 31st St., 10001. Tel: 212-268-1010; Fax: 212-268-7150. Email: NYcourage@aol.com. Web: couragerc.net. Rev. John F. Harvey, O.S.F.S., Dir. Total Staff 4.

Descubriendo El Siglo XXI, Inc. (Discovering XXI Century Inc.) (2001) *Holy Cross Church*, 329 W. 42nd St., 10036. Tel: 212-244-4778; Fax: 212-868-6997. Email: radiosigloxxi@aol.com. Web: www.descubriendoelsiglo21.org. Rev. Tomas Del Valle-Reyes, Pres.

The Dominican Foundation of Dominican Friars, Province of St. Joseph, Inc., 141 E. 65th St., 10065. Tel: 212-535-3664; Fax: 775-542-5511. Rev. John Farren, O.P., S.T.D., Dir. Advancement.

Dominican Friars' Guilds, 141 E. 65th St., 10065. Tel: 212-744-2410; Fax: 212-737-3875. Web: www.op-stjoseph.org.

St. Jude Dominican Missions, 141 E. 65th St., 10065. Tel: 212-744-2410; Fax: 212-737-3875. Email: advancement@opfriars.org. Rev. John Farren, O.P., S.T.D., Dir.

Dominican Rosary Apostolate, 141 E. 65th St., 10065. Tel: 212-744-2410; Fax: 212-737-3875.

Deserving Poor Boys Priesthood Association, 141 E. 65th St., 10065. Tel: 212-744-2410; Fax: 212-737-3875.

St. Martin de Porres Guild, 141 E. 65th St., 10065. Tel: 212-744-2410; Fax: 212-737-3875.

Dominican Shrine of St. Jude, Inc., St. Catherine of Siena Priory, 411 E. 68th St., 10065. Tel: 212-249-6067; 212-988-8300; Fax: 212-988-8920. Email: concog@ prodigy.net. Web: www.ophomily.org. Very Rev. Edward M. Gorman, O.P.; Rev. George Lawrence Concordia, O.P., Ph.D., Admin. Dir.

**The Elizabeth Seton Housing Development Fund Corporation*, 1991 Lexington Ave., 10035. Tel: 212-348-1655; Fax: 212-348-1822. Email: epfeldmann@att.net. Sr. Elizabeth Vermaelon, Pres. Total Assisted 87; Total Staff 3.

Felix Varela Foundation, Inc., The, 1011 First Ave., 10022. Tel: 718-229-8001, Ext. 677; 718-281-9677; Fax: 917-522-9707. Most Rev. Octavio Cisneros, Pres.

Focolare Movement-Manhattan, 429 E. 12th St., 10009. Tel: 212-388-9498. Email: focmny@yahoo.com. Web: www.focolare.org. Flavio Pedroni, Local Dir.

Foundation of the Order of Friars Minor of the Province of the Most Holy Name, 129 W. 31st St., 2nd Fl., 10001-3403. Tel: 212-924-1451; Fax: 800-420-1078. Email: hnp@hnp.org. Web: www.hnp.org. Very Rev. John F. O'Connor, O.F.M., Pres.

St. Frances Cabrini Shrine, Inc., 701 Fort Washington Ave., 10040. Tel: 212-923-3536. Web: www.mothercabrini.com.

St. Francis Counseling Center, Inc., 135 W. 31st St., 10001. Tel: 212-736-8500; Fax: 212-736-8545. Web: www.stfrancisnyc.org. Julie Berwick, L.C.S.W., Dir.

St. Francis Monastery Breadline for the Poor, Inc., 135 W. 31st St., 10001-3439. Tel: 212-736-8500; Fax: 212-736-8545. Email: stfra135@aol.com. Rev. Jerome Massimino, O.F.M., Contact Person.

Franciscan Missionary Charities, Inc. (1997) 14 E. 129th St., 10035. Tel: 917-797-8890; 646-685-7788. Email: cowofm@hanmail.net. Revs. Ronald P. Stark, O.F.M., Pres.; Francis K. Kim, O.F.M., B.A., M.Div., Exec. Vice Pres.

Franciscan Missionary Union, Province of the Most Holy Name Headquarters, St. Francis Friary, 135 W. 31st St., 10001-3439. Tel: 888-372-6478. Email: nyce1999@msn.com. Rev. Russell C. Becker, O.F.M., Dir.; Bro. Thomas J. Cole, O.F.M., Mission Promoter. The Franciscan Missionary Union also maintains 3 Medical Clinics in Lima, Peru and assisting the Prelacy of Itaituba and the Diocese of Mirecema. Various social services in Bolivia; local assistance in Vietnam, Taiwan, Japan, Brazil, East Africa and Southern US Missions. Friar Missionaries 46.

Franciscans International, Inc., 246 E. 46th St., #1F, 10017-2937. Tel: 212-490-4624; Fax: 212-490-4626. Email: newyork@fiop.org. Web: www.franciscansinternational.org. Sr. Denise Boyle, F.M.D.M., Exec. Dir.; Rev. Elias D. Mallon, S.A., Office Mgr. Advocacy; Sr. Kathleen L. Uhler, O.S.F., Advocacy.

Franciscans of Holy Name Province Benevolence Trust, Inc., 129 W. 31st St., 2nd Fl., 10001-3403. Tel: 212-924-1451; Fax: 800-420-1078. Email: hnp@hnp.org. Web: hnp.org. Rev. David Hyman, O.F.M., Trustee.

Franciscans of Holy Name Province Sick, Aged and Retired Trust, 129 W. 31st St., 2nd Fl., 10001-3403. Tel: 646-473-0265; Fax: 800-420-1078. Email: hnp@hnp.org. Web: www.hnp.org.

Franciscans of Holy Name Province Education and Formation Trust, 129 W. 31st St., 2nd Fl., 10001-3403. Tel: 646-473-0265; Fax: 800-420-1078. Email: hnp@hnp.org. Web: www.hnp.org. Bro. Christopher Coccia, O.F.M., Trustee.

The Fratecelli Corporation, 129 W. 31st St., 2nd Fl., 10001-3403. Tel: 646-473-0265; Fax: 800-420-1078. Email: hnp@hnp.org. Web: www.hnp.org. Rev. Kevin Mullen, O.F.M., Pres.

Friends of American Art in Religion, Inc., 143 E. 43rd St., 10017. Tel: 212-682-5722; Fax: 212-370-5791. His Eminence Edward Cardinal Egan, Pres.; Rev. Msgr. Eugene V. Clark, P.A., Sec. & Treas.

The Good Shepherd Volunteers, Inc., 337 E. 17th St., 10003. Tel: 212-475-4245, Ext. 718; Fax: 212-979-8604. Email: gsv@goodshepherds.org. Web: www.gsvolunteers.org. Michele G. Gilfillan, M.A., Dir.

Gregorian University Foundation, The, 106 W. 56th St., 10019. Tel: 212-582-5433; Fax: 212-956-2921. Email: o'tooler@mindspring.com. Web: www.the-gregorian.com. Rev. Robert F. O'Toole, S.J., Pres.

Guild of Catholic Lawyers, The (1928) 101 Park Ave., 30th Fl., 10178. Tel: 212-808-7847; Fax: 212-808-7897. Rev. George W. Rutler, Spiritual Dir.

Healing Through God Word Ministries, Inc., 320 Powell Ave., Newburgh, 12550. Tel: 307-864-3941. Sr. Jean Marie Timko, O.P., Pres.

Healing Through God Word Ministries, Inc./ Apostolate of Intercession Healing & Teaching the Word of God, An evangelistic ministry of teaching the scriptures, intercession, and healing. Involves missions, retreats, days of renewal, healing services, and Bible studies.

Hispanic Catholic Charismatic Center of the Archdiocese of New York, 826 E. 166th St., Bronx, 10459. Tel: 718-378-1734; Fax: 718-378-1819. Email: centro826@aol.com. Web: wwwcentrocatolicocarismatico.com. Most Rev. Josu Iriondo, S.T.L., D.D.

The Housing Fund of the Archdiocese of New York, 1011 First Ave., 10022. Tel: 212-371-1000. Rev. Msgrs. Kevin L. Sullivan, Vice. Pres.; Donald Sakano, Sec. & Treas.

The Human Adventure Corp. Doing Business for Communion and Liberation, 125 Maiden Ln., 15th Fl., 10038. Tel: 212-337-3580; Fax: 212-337-3585. Email: riro@clhac.com. Web: www.clonline.org/us. Maurizio Maniscalco, Vice Pres.

Hungarian Catholic League of America, Inc., 414 E. 82 St., 10028. Tel: 212-327-2959; Fax: 212-535-9221. Rev. Msgr. William I. Varsanyi, P.A., Bd. Chm.; A. Petrak, Sec.

Incarnation Children's Center Fund, Inc. (1988) 142 Audubon Ave., 10032. Tel: 212-928-2590, Ext. 32; Fax: 212-928-1500. Email: ccastro@incarnationchildrenscenter.org. Web: www.incarnationchildrenscenter.org. Carolyn Castro, Exec. Dir. Capacity 21.

Institute of the Helpers, 385 W. 263rd St., Bronx, 10471. Tel: 718-884-3100. Sr. Maryellen Moore.

International Catholic Organizations Information Center, Inc., 323 E. 47 St., 10017. Tel: 212-355-5557; Fax: 212-355-9865. Email: ico_center@yahoo.com. Frederic L. Gannon, M.D., Pres. of Board; Dorothy Farley, Exec. Dir.

**The Jesuit Collaborative*, c/o New York Province of the Society of Jesus, 38 E. 83rd St., 10028-0810.

Jesuit Seminary and Mission Bureau, Inc., 39 E. 83rd St., 10028. See Jesuit Provincial's office.

St. Joseph's Union of Staten Island, New York Inc., 108 Bedell St., Staten Island, 10309. Tel: 718-984-9296. Sr. Una McCormack, O.P., Treas.

LAMP Ministries, Inc. (1982) 2704 Schurz Ave., Bronx, 10465. Tel: 718-409-5062; Fax: 718-904-0048. Email: tscheuring@lampministries.org. Web: www.lampministries.org. Tom Scheuring, Ph.D., Co-Dir.; Lyn Scheuring, Ph.D., Co-Dir.; Marybeth Greene, Assoc. Dir.; Ed Greene, Assoc. Dir.

LaSalle New York City, Inc., 44 E. 2nd St., 10003. Tel: 212-475-8940; Fax: 212-529-3598. Web: www.lasalleacademy.org. Bros. Franc Byrnes, F.S.C., Chm.; Michael Farrell, F.S.C., Pres. Total Assisted 370; Total Staff 45.

The Lay Fraternity of St. Dominic, Inc., 141 E. 65th St., 10021-6618. Tel: 212-744-2080. Email: top@opfriars.org. Ms. Dorothy Murphy, Pres.

Legion of Mary, Office, 1011 First Ave., 10022. Tel: 212-752-7966. Email: ny.senatus@worldnet.att.net. Web: legion-of-mary-NY.home.att.net.

**Life Athletes, Inc.*, 1011 First Ave., 10022. Tel: 574-237-9000. Email: chris@lifeathletes.org. Web: www.lifeathletes.org. Christopher J. Godfrey, Pres.

Lumen Dei, 340 W. 53rd St., 10019. Tel: 212-586-4447; Fax: 212-586-1640. Email: newyork@lumendei.org. Web: www.lumendei.org. Rev. Wilberto Reyes Garced, L.D., Regl. Supr. Priests of Lumen Dei 1; Sisters of Lumen Dei 5.

Manhattan North Community Services, Inc., 91 Arden St., 10040. Niki Montaluo, Pres.

Maria Droste Services (1982) 386 Park Ave. S., Ste. 903, 10016-8804. Tel: 212-889-4042; Fax: 212-889-3936. Email: srros@mariadrosteservices.com. Web: www.mariadrosteservices.com. Betsy Selman-Babinecz, D.C.S.W., L.C.S.W. Dir.

St. Germaine's Services

**Monsignor Robert Fox Memorial Shelter Housing Development, Inc.*, Fox House, 111 E. 117th St., 10035. Tel: 212-534-6634; Fax: 212-427-8507. Email: foxshelter@aol.com. Sr. Florence Speth, Exec. Dir. Total Assisted 565; Total Staff 17.

National Federation for Life, 1011 First Ave., Rm. 1417, 10022.

National Office of the Devotees of Padre Pio, Inc., 1154 1st Ave., 10065. Tel: 212-838-6549. Mr. Mario Bruscki, Dir.

**Nazareth Housing, Inc.* (1983) 519 E. 11th St., 10009. Tel: 212-777-1010; Fax: 212-777-1867. Web: www.nazarethhousingnyc.org.

New York Catholic Continuum Care, Inc. (NYCCC), 1011 First Ave., 11th Fl., 10022. Tel: 212-371-1011, Ext. 2462. Doug Sansted, Contact Person.

New York Catholic Foundation, Inc., 1011 First Ave., 10022. Tel: 212-371-1000. Email: helen.lowe@archny.org. Web: archny.org. Helen Lowe, Exec. Dir. Devel.

New York Catholic Homes, Inc., 1011 First Ave., 10022. Tel: 212-371-1000, Ext. 2939. Email: william.whiston@archny.org. Mr. William E. Whiston, Treas. & Contact Person.

New York Society of the John Paul II Foundation, Inc. (1997) 101 E. 7th St., 10009. Tel: 718-383-8030; Fax: 718-349-2773. Email: polstar.shop@verizon.net. Mr. Michael Pajak, Pres. Tel: 718-383-9587.

Nocturnal Adoration Society of the United States (1900) 184 E. 76th St., 10021. Tel: 212-288-5082; Fax: 212-717-8397. Email: sjbrcc@aol.com. Web:

www.sjbrcc.net. Congregation of the Blessed Sacrament.

North American College of Rome, Alumni Assoc. of, Church of St. Joseph-St. Thomas, 6097 Amboy Rd., Staten Island, 10309. Tel: 718-356-0294; Fax: 718-948-3885. Rev. Msgr. Edmund J. Whalen, S.T.D.

Northeast Hispanic Catholic Center, 1011 First Ave., 10022. Tel: 212-751-7045; Fax: 212-753-5321. Email: nhcc1011@aol.com. Rudy Vargas IV, Exec. Dir.

**Partnership for Global Justice*, 211 E. 43rd St., Ste. 708, 10017. Tel: 212-682-6481. Email: partnershipforglobaljustice@gmail.com. Web: www.partnershipforglobaljustice.com. Sr. Lucianne Siers, O.P., Dir.

St. Patrick's International Inc., c/o Cullen & Dykman, 44 Wall St., 10005-2407. Tel: 212-732-2000; Fax: 212-742-8260. Email: spsbur@iol.ie. Web: www.spms.org. Rev. Seamus O'Neill, Pres.

Patrons of the Arts in Vatican Museums, 404 E. 87th St., 10128. Tel: 212-289-6030; Fax: 212-348-8075. His Eminence Edward Cardinal Egan, J.C.D., D.D., Chm.; Rev. James Boniface Ramsey, Mod. Staff 2.

St. Paul's Guild, Inc., 1011 First Ave., Rm. 1940, 10022. Tel: 212-371-1000; Fax: 212-813-9538.

Pauline Books & Media, 64 W. 38th St., 10022. Tel: 212-754-1110; Fax: 212-754-2268. Web: www.pauline.org.

Pauline Books & Media Total Staff 5.

Pax Christi Metro New York (1983) 371 Sixth Ave., 10014. Tel: 212-420-0250; Fax: 212-420-1628. Email: nypaxchristi@igc.org. Web: www.nypaxchristi.org. Rosemarie Pace, B.A., Ed.D., M.S., Dir. We are a regional chapter of Pax Christi USA, the national Catholic movement for peace.

Perpetual Help Center, 294 E. 150th St., Bronx, 10451. Tel: 718-585-3678; Fax: 718-993-5870. Web: www.perpetualhelpcenter.org. Rev. Daniel Francis, C.Ss.R. Redemptorist Fathers of New York.

Polish Dominicans, Inc., 405 W. 114th St., 10025. Tel: 212-866-1500. Email: afflo@dominikanie.pl. Web: ndparish.org. Revs. Romuald Jedrejko, O.P., Pres.; Jacek Buda, O.P.; Andrzej J. Fornal, O.P., Sec.; Jacek Kopera, O.P.; Marcin Mankowski, O.P.; Lukasz Misko, O.P.; Maciej Okonski, O.P.; Marek Pienkowski, O.P.

Regina Coeli Society First Friday Club for the Catholic Women of New York City Police Dept., P.O. Box 939, 10272-0604. Tel: 646-610-6169. Det. Gloria Felix, Pres.

St. Rose's Settlement, 1011 First Ave., Rm. 1940, 10022. Tel: 212-371-1000; Fax: 212-813-9538.

Scalabrini International Migration Network, 27 Carmine St., 10014-4423. Tel: 212-675-3993. Email: development@simn-cs.net. Web: www.simn-cs.net. Rev. Leonir Mario Chiarello, Dir.

Shrine of St. Jude, Inc., St. Stephen of Hungary Parish, 414 E. 82nd St., 10028. Tel: 800-688-JUDE; Fax: 212-535-9221. Web: www.saintstephenofhungary.org. Revs. John F. O'Connor, O.F.M., Pres.; Angelus Gambatese, O.F.M., Spiritual Dir.; Sr. Natalie M. Runfola, R.S.C.J., Exec. Sec.

Sisters of Charity of New York Charitable Trust (1988) 6301 Riverdale Ave., Bronx, 10471-1093. Tel: 718-549-9200; Fax: 718-884-3013. Web: www.scny.org.

Sisters of Charity Center (1971) 6301 Riverdale Ave., Bronx, 10471-1093. Tel: 718-549-9200, Ext. 261; Fax: 718-884-3013. Web: www.scny.org.

**The Elizabeth Seton Women's Center, Inc.* (1996) 133 W. 70th St., 10023. Tel: 212-579-3657; Fax: 212-579-3659. Email: eswc@aol.com. Sisters Dorothy Metz, Pres.; Arleen Ketchum, S.C., Dir.

St. Thomas Aquinas Foundation National Headquarters (Order of Preachers, St. Joseph Prov.), 141 E. 65th St., 10065. Tel: 212-737-5757; Fax: 212-861-4216. Email: provincial@opfriars.org. Web: www.op-stjoseph.org. Very Rev. David Dominic Izzo, O.P., S.T.L., Pres.

St. Thomas Aquinas Foundation of the Dominican Fathers of the United States (STAF)

Thorpe Family Residence, Inc. (1988) 2252 Crotona Ave., Bronx, 10457. Tel: 718-933-7312; Fax: 718-933-7311. Total Assisted Families 16; Total Staff 10.

Trust for the Center for Migration Studies in New York, 27 Carmine St., 10014-4423. Tel: 212-255-1111; Fax: 212-255-1771. Web: www.cmsny.org. Rev. Rene Manenti, C.S.

Saint Vincent's Catholic Medical Centers Foundation, Inc., 170 W. 12th St., Smith 5, 10011. Tel: 212-604-2276; Fax: 212-604-7533. Email: ccallagy@svcmcny.org. Ms. Catherine Callagy, Sr. Vice Pres. Fund Devel.

Xavier Society for the Blind (1900) 154 E. 23rd St., 10010. Tel: 212-473-7800. Rev. John R. Sheehan, S.J., Chm. Bd.

BARRYVILLE. *New Hope Manor*, 35 Hillside Rd., 12719. Tel: 845-557-8353; Fax: 845-557-6603. Email: newhopemnr@aol.com. Web: www.newhopemanor.org. Nicholas A. Roes, Ph.D., Exec. Dir.; Sisters Patricia Conway, O.P., Counselor, House Mother & Teacher; Maureen Conway, O.P., Dir. Education, Counselor & Teacher; Joanne Malone, O.P., Bd. Member; Marianne Morelli, O.P., Bd. Member; Margaret Murphy, O.P., Bd. Member; Bro. Charles Kinney, S.A., Bd. Member. Sparkill Dominican Sisters, Sisters of Christian Charity, Franciscan Friars of the Atonement, A live-in therapeutic community for the substance abuse rehabilitation of women, pregnant women, and infants.

BEACON. *Carmelite Communion, Inc.* (2000) 89 Hiddenbrooke Dr., 12508-2230. Tel: 845-831-5572; Fax: 845-831-5579. Email: beaconcarmel@optonline.net. Web: www.carmelitesbeacon.org. Sr. Michaelene Devine, O.C.D., Prioress & Contact Person. Professed Sisters 18.

Metropolitan Association of Contemplative Communities, Inc. (1967) 89 Hiddenbrooke Dr., 12508. Tel: 845-831-5572; Fax: 845-831-5579. Web: macc.catholic.org. Sr. Rita Donahue, O.C.D., Contact Person.

BRONX. *Abraham House, Inc.*, 340 Willis Ave., P.O. Box 305, 10454. Tel: 718-292-9321; Fax: 718-292-5925. Email: information@abrahamhouse.org. Robert Murphy, Pres. Total Assisted 6,000; Total Staff 35.

American St. Boniface Society, Incorporated, P.O. Box 1352, 10466-1352. Tel: 718-994-0989; Fax: 718-994-6119. Rev. Joachim Von Kerssenbrock, S.J., Exec. Dir.

St. Anthony Shelter for Renewal, 420 E. 156th St., 10455. Tel: 718-665-2441. Rev. Richard Roemer, C.F.R., Pres.

Calvary Holding Company, Inc., 1740 Eastchester Rd., 10461. Tel: 718-518-2251; Fax: 718-518-2674. Frank A. Calamari, Pres.; Thomas J. Fahey Jr., M.D., Chm.

Focolare Movement, 179 Robinson Ave., 10465. Tel: 718-828-1969; Fax: 718-828-6929. Email: czfny@optonline.net. Donna Kempt, Local Dir.

Focolare Movement Formation Fund, 179 Robinson Ave., 10465. Tel: 212-636-7328; Fax: 212-636-6899. Web: www.focolare.us. Amelia J. Uelmen Esq., Contact Person.

Foundation of Christ the Redeemer Institute Id of Christ the Redeemer, Men & Women Idente Missionaries., 2352 St. Raymond Ave., 10462. Tel: 718-828-2380; Fax: 718-828-4296.

**Francesco Productions Inc.* (2003) 420 E. 156th St., 10455. Tel: 718-401-1589; Fax: 718-401-8984. Web: www.francescoproductions.com. Kim Yu, Mng. Dir.; Rev. Stanley Fortuna, C.F.R., Founder.

Franciscan Mission Outreach, Inc., 420 E. 156th St., 10455. Tel: 718-402-8255; Fax: 718-402-5556. Rev. Bernard Marie Murphy, C.F.R., Contact Person. Priests 2; Total Staff 2.

Franciscan Renewal Ministries, Inc., 420 E. 156th St., 10455. Tel: 718-665-2441. Rev. Bernard Marie Murphy, C.F.R., Sec. & Contact Person.

St. Joseph's Center (1994) For the development of Lay Leaders, Cursillo Center, Marriage Encounter. (Spanish), 275 W. 230th St., 10463. Tel: 718-796-4340; Fax: 718-796-4340. Rev. Jose Luis Martinez, O.A.R., Dir. Total in Residence 2; Total Staff 4; Capacity 45.

St. Joseph's School for the Deaf Childrens Fund, Inc., 1000 Hutchinson River Pkwy., 10465. Tel: 718-792-8308; Fax: 718-792-2532. Email: dorothydhm@aol.com. The Children's Fund assists St. Joseph's School for the Deaf in meeting the needs of the children and their educational experiences.

Saint Jutta Foundation, Inc. (1956) c/o Rev. Martin A. Hegyi, S.J., Murray-Weigal Hall, 515 E. Fordham Rd., 10458-5029. Tel: 718-817-3671; Fax: 718-365-8650. Email: hegyi@fordham.edu. Rev. Martin A. Hegyi, S.J., B.A., Ph.D. (Hungary), Contact Person.

**Mercy Center, Inc.* (1990) 377 E. 145th St., 10454-1006. Tel: 718-993-2789; Fax: 718-402-1594. Email: administration@mercycenterbronx.org. Web: www.mercycenterbronx.org. Joseph S. Dirr, Co-Dir.; Sr. Mary Galeone, R.S.M., Co-Dir. Parenting skills courses, business training, support groups, spirituality groups, & ESL. Sisters 4; Total Assisted 2,500; Total Staff 21.

Metro New York Christian Life Communities, Inc., Loyola Faber Hall, Fordham University, 10458. Tel: 718-817-5454; Fax: 718-733-4456. Email: frfitz@juno.com. Web: www.fordham.edu/clc. Rev. Daniel J. Fitzpatrick, S.J., Moderator & Contact Person.

The Saint Padre Pio Shelter Corporation, 427 E. 155th St., 10455. Tel: 718-292-3713; Fax: 718-402-5556. Web: www.franciscanfriars.com. Rev. Pio Maria Hoffmann, C.F.R.; Bros. John Joseph Brice, C.F.R.; Timothy Pio Sgoutas, C.F.R. Total Assisted 18.

Preston Center of Compassion, Inc. (2003) *Office of the President*, 2780 Schurz Ave., 10465. Tel: 718-892-8977. Donna Santarpia, Pres.; Sr. Patricia Warner, R.D.C., Dir.

Rosalie Hall, Inc., 4150 Bronx Blvd., 10466. Tel: 718-920-9800; Fax: 718-920-9896. (Home for Unwed Mothers)

**Tolentine-Zeiser Community Life Center, Inc.*, 2345 University Ave., 10468. Tel: 718-933-6935; Fax: 718-733-1653. Total Assisted 172; Total Staff 12.

Youth Ministries for Peace & Justice, Inc. (1994) 1384 Stratford Ave., 10472. Tel: 718-328-5622; Fax: 718-328-5630. Email: atorres.fleming@ympj.org. Web: www.ympj.org. Alexie Torres-Fleming, Exec. Dir.

BRONXVILLE. *Polish Knights of Malta, Inc.* (1986) 1 Stoneleigh Plaza, #4-E, 10708. Tel: 914-793-4596; Fax: 914-771-4034. Email: witoldsulimirski@cs.com. Mr. Witold S. Sulimirski, Pres.

CORNWALL. *Contemplative Outreach, Ltd.*, 10 Landmark Dr., Ste. 117, P.O. Box 208, 12518. Tel: 845-534-5180. Email: office@coutreach.org. Web: www.contemplativeoutreach.org. Rt. Rev. Thomas Keating, O.C.S.O., Chairperson; Gail Fitzpatrick-Hopler, Pres. Total Staff 12.

ELMSFORD. *Leviticus 25:23 Alternative Fund, Inc.* (1983) 33 W. Main St., Rm. 205, 10523. Tel: 914-606-9003; Fax: 914-606-9006. Email: info@leviticusfund.org. Web: www.leviticusfund.org. David C. Raynor, Exec. Dir.; Sr. Margaret Murphy, O.P., Finance Officer; Maryann Sorese, Bus. Devel. Office.

GARRISON. *House of Nazareth Life Institute Ltd. (Nazareth Life Center)* (1979) 20 Nazareth Way, Box 242, 10524. Tel: 845-424-3116. Sr. Marita Paul, F.S.P., Dir. Total in Residence 8; Total Staff 2.

HARTSDALE. *Marian Woods, Inc* (2001) 152 Ridge Rd., 10530. Tel: 914-750-6000; Fax: 914-750-6100. Frances A. Brooks, Exec. Dir.

Mercy Education Support Fund, Inc., 150 Ridge Rd., 10530. Tel: 914-328-3200, Ext. 410; Fax: 914-328-3761. Email: srpwolf@optonline.net. Sr. Patricia Wolf, R.S.M., Pres. & Contact Person.

HAVERSTRAW. *Franciscan Sisters of Peace*, 20 Ridge St., 10927-1198. Tel: 845-942-2527; Fax: 845-429-8141. Email: jgilligan@fspnet.org. Web: www.fspnet.org. Sr. Jeanne Gilligan, F.S.P., Congregation Minister.

Ladycliff College Alumnae Association, Inc., c/o Franciscan Sisters of Peace, 20 Ridge St., 10927-1198. Tel: 914-446-2973; 914-446-5921.

HAWTHORNE. *Blessed Margaret's Cancer Relief Fund, Inc.*, Rosary Hill Home, 600 Linda Ave., 10532. Tel: 914-769-0114; Fax: 914-769-0827. Sr. Mary Francis, O.P., Pres.

The Rose Hawthorne Guild, 600 Linda Ave., 10532. Tel: 914-769-0114; Fax: 914-769-0827. Sr. Mary Francis, O.P., Pres. & Contact Person.

HIGHLAND MILLS. *Thevenet Montessori School*, (Grades PreK-1), 202 Country Rte. 105, 10930. Tel: 845-928-6981; Fax: 845-928-3179. Email: thevenet@frontiernet.net. Sr. Norene Costa, Prin. Religious of Jesus and Mary. Sisters 2; Lay Teachers 10; Students 122.

HYDE PARK. *Focolare Movement National Center (Women's Branch)* (1943) Women's Branch, *Mariapolis Luminosa with offices of Focolare magazine "Living City"*, 200 Cardinal Rd., 12538. Tel: 845-229-0230, Ext. 135; Fax: 845-229-1770. Email: czf.luminosa.ny@focolare.us. Web: livingcitymagazine.com. Marigen Lohla, Co-Dir. Tel: 845-229-9712; Fax: 845-229-1770. Founded in Trent, Italy in 1943. International Headquarters are in Rome, Italy. Movement was approved in March 1962 with the aim of working toward the fulfillment of Christ's prayer for unity, that all may be one. More than four million people, in all walks of life, married and single, are committed in or connected with the Movement. Centers in over fifty countries. Call for additional information.

Focolare Movement National Center (Men's Branch) (Men), *Mariapolis Luminosa with publishing house New City Press*, 7 Intellect Way, 12538. Tel: 845-229-0307; Fax: 845-229-0269. Email: czmlumi@optonline.net. Web: rc.net/focolare. Rev. Terence Gunn.

Focolare Movement, Mariapolis Luminosa (Work of Mary), 200 Cardinal Rd., 12538. Tel: 845-229-0307; Fax: 810-222-0307. Web: www.focolare.us. Amelia J. Uelmen Esq., Contact Person.

Focolare Movement, Women's Branch (East Coast) (Work of Mary), 257 Peace Ave., 12538. Tel: 845-229-9712; Fax: 845-229-1770. Web: www.focolare.us. Amelia J. Uelmen Esq., Contact Person.

Living City of the Focolare Movement, Inc., 202 Comforter Blvd., 12538. Tel: 845-229-0496; Fax: 845-220-1770. Web: www.livingcitymagazine.com. Amelia J. Uelmen Esq., Contact Person.

New City Press of the Focolare Movement, Inc., 202 Comforter Blvd., 12538. Tel: 845-229-0335; Fax: 845-229-0351. Web: www.newcitypress.com. Amelia J. Uelmen Esq., Contact Person.

JAMAICA. *The Fellowship of the Beloved Disciple* (1980) *Immaculate Conception Monastery*, 86-45 Edgerton Blvd., 11432. Tel: 718-739-6502; Fax: 718-739-7770. Email: lallycp@aol.com. Web: www.unityincommunity.org. Rev. Owen Lally, C.P., Chap.; Yvonne Zeller, Dir.

LARCHMONT. *The Oratory of Divine Love, Inc.*, 1 Pryer Manor Rd., 10538. Tel: 914-643-3743. Email: ycleffi@aol.com. Web: www.oratoryofdivinelove.com. Rev. Benedict Joseph Groeschel, C.F.R., Ed.D., Pres.

LIVINGSTON MANOR. *The Monastic Family of Bethlehem* (1987) 393 Our Lady of Lourdes Camp Rd., 12758. Tel: 845-439-4300; Fax: 845-439-3069.

MARYKNOLL. *The Asian Catholic News Fund*, P.O. Box 306, 10545-0306. Tel: 914-941-7590; Fax: 914-944-3628. Email: rcallahan@maryknoll.org. Web: www.maryknoll.org. Rev. Richard B. Callahan, M.M., Contact Person.

Friends of St. Maria Goretti, U.S.A., Inc., P.O. Box 0043, 10545-0043. Tel: 914-941-6372; Fax: 914-945-0715. Email: gzilli@maryknoll.org. Web: www.mariagoretti.org. Bro. Goretti A. Zilli, M.M., Pres. Tel: 914-941-6372; 914-941-7590; Rev. William T. Madden, M.M., Treas. (Retired); Mr. Ronald Finn, Vice Pres.; Mrs. Marie Finn, Sec.

Maryknoll Fathers and Brothers Apostolic Trust, P.O. Box 306, 10545-0306. Tel: 914-941-7590; Fax: 914-941-3619. Web: www.maryknoll.org. Mr. Richard B. Callahan, Contact Person.

Maryknoll Lay Missioners Foundation, P.O. Box 307, 10545-0307. Tel: 914-762-6364; Fax: 914-762-7362. Email: sstanton@mklm.org. Sam Stanton, Contact Person.

Maryknoll Mission Association of the Faithful (1994) P.O. Box 307, 10545-0307. Tel: 914-762-6364; Fax: 914-944-3576. Email: info@mklm.org. Web: www.mklm.org. Sam Stanton, Exec. Dir.; Alicia Butkiewicz, Dir. Mission. Purpose: Maryknoll Lay Missioners (MKLM) is a Catholic organization, comprising single men and women, couples and families, inspired by the mission of Jesus to live and work with poor communities in Africa, Asia and the Americas, responding to basic needs and helping to create a more just and compassionate world. MKLM applies skills and knowledge to respond to the basic needs of the poor, raising the quality of life, and restoring hope, by making lasting improvements in the areas of justice and peace, education, health, pastoral care and sustainable development. MKLM recruits, trains and financially supports its Catholic missioners solely by public donation.

Maryknoll Missionary Education Trust, P.O. Box 306 Ryder Rd., 10545. Tel: 914-631-2979.

MOUNT VERNON. *St. Dymphna Devotion* (1961) 274-280 W. Lincoln Ave., P.O. Box 598, 10551-0598. Tel: 914-664-5604; Fax: 914-664-3017. Rev. Robert M. Campagna, O.F.M., Prov.; Ms. Madeline Bonnici, Exec. Dir. Province of the Immaculate Conception.

Franciscan Mission Associates (1961) 274-280 W. Lincoln Ave., P.O. Box 598, 10550. Tel: 914-664-5604; Fax: 914-664-3017. Web: www.franciscanmissionassoc.org. Rev. Robert M. Campagna, O.F.M., Prov.; Ms. Madeline Bonnici, Exec. Dir. Province of the Immaculate Conception.

MT. KISCO. *Regina Apostolorum, Inc.*, 773 Armonk Rd., 10549. Tel: 914-773-1368; Fax: 914-773-1438. Rev. Jose Felix Ortega, L.C., Contact Person.

NEW ROCHELLE. *The Center for Spirituality and Justice*, 39 Willow Dr., 10805. Tel: 914-633-8667; Fax: 914-633-5281. Email: miriamcosu@juno.com. Web: www.centerforspiritualityandjustice.org. Sr. Miriam Cleary, O.S.U., M.A., M.S., MTk., Pres. & Treas.; Rev. Michael Wastag, O.Carm., M.S., M.Div., Sec. Total Assisted 14; Total Staff 3.

Christian Brothers Foundation, Inc., 33 Pryer Ter., 10804. Tel: 914-636-6194; Fax: 914-636-0021. Bro. Hugh B. O'Neill, C.F.C., Contact Person.

Holy Cross International, Inc., 85 Overlook Cir., 10804-4501. Tel: 508-565-1301; 508-565-1301. Email: mtccsc@aol.com. Web: www.holycrosscongregation.org. Rev. Mark T. Cregan, C.S.C., Esq.

Marian Residence Fund (1997) 1338 North Ave., 10804. Tel: 914-712-0060; Fax: 914-712-3134. Email: ursruepr@aol.com.

O.S.U. Charitable Trust (1997) 1338 North Ave., 10804. Tel: 914-712-0060; Fax: 914-712-3134. Email: ursruepr@aol.com.

Songcatchers, Inc., 44 Liberty Ave., 10801. Tel: 914-654-1178 (Day); 914-576-6774 (Eve.); Fax: 914-654-1178. Email: bdowdmus@aol.com. 50 Washington Ave., 10801. Web: www.songcatchers.info. Sr. Beth Dowd, O.S.U., Dir. Program activities for elementary school children, including Choir Camp, Concert Choir, and an After-School Music Program, Early Childhood Music Program. Young adults: volunteer staff of after-school program and camp.

Ursuline Social Outreach, Inc. (1996) 138 Centre Ave., 10801. Tel: 914-633-7298; Fax: 914-633-7393. Email: usoalc@aol.com. Sr. Eileen Fane, O.S.U., Ph.D., Exec. Dir. Ursuline Outreach sponsors The Adult Learning Center, 572B Main St., New Rochelle, NY 10801. Sisters 3; Volunteers 60; Total Assisted Annually 1,000.

NEWBURGH. **Newburgh Ministry* (1983) 9 Johnston St., P.O. Box 1449, 12551. Tel: 845-561-0070; Fax: 845-561-5087. Sr. Margaret Anderson, O.P., Chairperson, Bd. of Dir.; James McElhinney, Exec. Dir.

Newburgh San Miguel Program dba Newburgh San Miguel Program P.O. Box 284, Chappaqua, 10514. Tel: 914-861-9222. Email: gk@sonocap.com. Rev. Mark J. Connell, Pres.& Project Coord.; Greg Kiernan, Dir. Devel.; Sr. Lois Dee, O.P., Prin.

Our Lady of Comfort Women's Center, 91 Ann St., 12550. Tel: 845-561-6267; Fax: 914-565-0572. Nina Faulkner, Treas. Shelter for Women & Children.

Presentation Educational Foundation, Inc., 157 Liberty St., 12550. Tel: 845-567-0708; Fax: 845-567-0709. Web: noracroninpresentationacademy.com. Sr. Yliana Hernandez, P.B.V.M., Pres.

OSSINING. *Dominican Sisters of Hope Ministry Trust*, 299 N. Highland Ave., 10562. Tel: 914-941-4420; Fax: 914-941-1125. Email: ministrytrust@ophope.org. Web: www.ophope.org. Esther K. Erkins, Chairperson.

PELHAM. *Passionist Communications, Inc.*, P.O. Box 8600, 10803-0440. Tel: 914-738-3344; Fax: 914-738-7652. Email: contact@TheSundayMass.org. Web: www.thesundaymass.org. Rev. Edward L. Beck, C.P.

Passionist Communications Center, P.O. Box 8600, 10803-1417. Tel: 914-738-3344; Fax: 914-738-7652. Email: contact@TheSundayMass.org. Web: www.thesundaymass.org. Rev. Edward L. Beck, C.P., Exec. Producer.

RHINEBECK. **The Astor Home for Children Foundation, Inc.*, 6339 Mill St., P.O. Box 5005, 12572-5005. Tel: 845-871-1117; Fax: 845-876-2020. Email: smoorhead@astorservices.org. Web: www.astorservices.org. Sonia Barnes-Moorhead, Exec. Vice Pres.

RIVERDALE. *Holy Innocents Foundation*, 5272 Post Rd., 10471. Fax: 718-593-0248. Kevin T. O'Reilly, Pres.

RYE. *Catholic Women@Work Inc.*, 815 Boston Post Rd., 10580. Tel: 203-795-2800; Fax: 203-281-6051. Rev. Anthony Bannon, L.C.

Center for Spiritual Development (1979) *Archbishop Stepinac H.S.*, 950 Mamaroneck Ave., White Plains, 10605. Tel: 914-946-5729; Fax: 914-946-6073. Ann Marie Wallace, Ph.D., Dir.

Legion of Christ North America, Inc., 815 Boston Post Rd., 10580. Tel: 914-773-1368. Rev. Jose Felix Ortega, L.C., Contact Person.

Pastoral Support Services, Inc., 815 Boston Post Rd., 10580. Tel: 914-773-1368. Rev. Jose Felix Ortega, L.C., Sec.

The Resurrection School Foundation, Inc., 910 Bost Post Rd., 10580. Tel: 914-925-2732; Fax: 914-925-3527. Email: info@resurrectionschoolfoundation.com. Web: www.resurrectionschoolfoundation.com. Michael Iuliano, Dir.

SALT POINT. *Camp Veritas*, 1653 Salt Point Tpke., 12578. Tel: 845-266-5784. Email: ryan1@campveritas.com. Web: www.campveritas.com. Ryan Young, Bd. Chairperson.

SCARSDALE. *Catholic Charismatic Renewal Office*, 194 Gaylor Rd., 10583. Tel: 914-725-1773; Fax: 914-725-5227. Email: charismny@optonline.net. Web: www.catholiccharismaticny.org. Sr. Pauline Cinquini, S.C., Co-Liaison; Rev. William B. Cosgrove, Co-Liaison.
Tel: 845-634-3641; Fax: 845-639-6118. Email: frbill@optonline.net.

SLEEPY HOLLOW. *RSHM Life Center, Inc* (1995) 32-34 Beekman Ave., 10591. Tel: 914-366-9710; Fax: 914-366-9713. Email: susan@rshmlifecenter.org. Web: www.rshmlifecenter.org. Sacred Heart of Mary. Total Assisted 500; Adults 240; Children 260; Total Staff 7.

SLOATSBURG. *St. Mary's Villa, Inc.*, 150 Sisters Servants Ln., P.O. Box 9, 10974-0009. Tel: 845-753-5100; Fax: 845-753-1956. Email: ssminy@aol.com. Sisters Michele Yakymovitch, S.S.M.I., Pres.; Consolata Trudick, S.S.M.I., Sec.

The Blessed Josaphata Fund (2001) 9 Emmanuel Dr., P.O. Box 9, 10974-0009. Tel: 845-753-2840; Fax: 845-753-1956. Email: rmulcahey@sbcq.com; ssminy@aol.com. Richard T. Mulcahey Jr., Esq., Contact Person; Sr. Michele Yakymovitch, S.S.M.I., Provincial Supr.

SPARKILL. *Hallel Institute* (1974) 175 Rte. 340, 10976-1047. Tel: 845-365-2277; Fax: 845-365-2279. Email: hallel@hallel.net. Web: hallel.net. Rev. George J. Torok, C.O., Pres. Total in Residence 37; Total Staff 9.

New York Oratory of St. Philip Neri, Inc., 175 Rte. 340, 10976. Tel: 845-365-2277; Fax: 845-365-2279. Rev. George J. Torok, C.O., Pres.

One to One Learning, Inc. (1997) Office of the President, 175 Rte. 340, 10976. Tel: 845-512-8176; Fax: 845-512-8178. Email: clpangel@aol.com. Sr. Cecilia LaPietra, O.P., Executive Dir.

STATEN ISLAND. *Chait Housing Development Corporation*, 75 Vanderbilt Ave., Bldg. 3, 10304. Tel: 718-818-5055. Email: mditommaso@svcmcny.org. Marianne DiTommaso, Asst. Sec. Bd. Dirs.

Emmaus Ministries, Ltd., c/o Church of St. Clare, 110 Nelson Ave., 10308. Tel: 718-984-7873; Fax: 718-966-8420. Web: www.stclares.com. Monica Brown, Pres.; Rev. Msgr. Joseph P. Murphy, Vice Pres. & Contact Person.

Fort Place Housing Corporation, 78 Fort Place, 10301. Tel: 718-818-5055. Email: mditommaso@svcmcny.org. Marianne DiTommaso, Asst. Sec. Bd. Dirs.

Indian Knanaya Catholic Community of Greater NY, Inc., 94 Wilcox St., 10303. Tel: 914-494-7571; Fax: 914-494-9183. Email: ikcc@hotmail.com. Jose Chummar, Pres.

Pax Christi Hospice, 1200 South Ave., Ste. 306, 10314. Tel: 718-876-1022. Email: mackermann@svcmcny.orgFax: 718-876-1803.

Pax Christi Hospice, 227 E. 19th St., 10003. Tel: 212-995-6480 (Inpatient); 212-995-7474 (Home Care).

Schoenstatt Sisters of Mary, Secular Institute, 337 Cary Ave., 10310-2041. Tel: 718-727-8005; Fax: 718-727-3155. Email: sistersofmaryny@schsrsmary.org. Sisters 6; Total Staff 3.

**Sisters of Charity Housing Development, Corp.*, 150 Brielle Ave., 10314-6400. Tel: 718-477-6803; Fax: 718-477-1356. Email: epfeldmann@worldnet.att.net. Eric Feldmann, Exec. Dir.

SUFFERN. *Good Samaritan Foundation for Better Health, Inc.*, 255 Lafayette Ave., 10901-4869. Tel: 845-368-5151; Fax: 845-368-5596. Email: stacey_kirschenbaum@bshsi.org. Web: goodsamhosp.org. Sr. Mary Louise Moran, S.C., Pres.; Stacey Kirschenbaum, Exec. Vice Pres. Fundraising arm of Good Samaritan Hospital, Suffern, NY.

TARRYTOWN. *Religious of the Sacred Heart of Mary Charitable Trust*, 50 Wilson Park Dr., 10591. Tel: 914-631-2979; Fax: 914-332-4735. Sr. Bernadette Kenny, Contact Person.

THORNWOOD. *Alpha Omega Family Center, Inc.* (1993) 582 Columbus Ave., 10594. Tel: 914-749-3900; Fax: 914-749-3939. Rev. Richard Gill, L.C., Contact Person.

Arke, Inc., 590 Columbus Ave., 10594. Tel: 914-773-1368. Rev. Jose Felix Ortega, L.C., Contact Person.

Catholic Net, Inc. (1997) 590 Columbus Ave., 10594. Tel: 914-773-1368; Fax: 914-773-1438. Rev. Jose Felix Ortega, L.C., Contact Person.

Consolidated Catholic Administrative Services, Inc. (1999) 590 Columbus Ave., 10594. Tel: 914-773-1368; Fax: 914-773-1438. Rev. Jose Felix Ortega, L.C., Contact Person.

Familia USA, Inc. (1997) 590 Columbus Ave., 10594. Tel: 914-773-1368; Fax: 914-773-1438. Rev. Jose Felix Ortega, L.C., Contact Person.

Helping Hands Medical Missions, Inc. (1997) 590 Columbus Ave., 10594. Tel: 914-749-3900; Fax: 914-749-3939. Rev. Emilio Diaz Torre, L.C.

Legion of Christ and Consecrated Regnum Christi Members Assistance Foundation (2002) 590 Columbus Ave., 10594. Tel: 914-773-1368; Fax: 914-773-1438. Rev. Jose Felix Ortega, L.C., Contact Person.

Legion of Christ, Incorporated (1978) 590 Columbus Ave., 10594. Tel: 914-773-1368; Fax: 914-773-1438. Rev. Peter Hopkins, L.C., Contact Person.

Mission Network Programs USA, Inc. (1997) 590 Columbus Ave., 10594. Tel: 914-773-1368; Fax: 914-773-1438. Email: cknet@flash.net. Web: catholickidsnet.org. Rev. Jose Felix Ortega, L.C., Contact Person.

Nueva Primavera Inc., 590 Columbus Ave., 10594. Tel: 914-773-1368. Rev. Jose Felix Ortega, L.C., Contact Person.

Youth and Family Encounter, Inc. (1998) 590 Columbus Ave., 10594. Tel: 914-773-1368; Fax:

914-773-1438. Rev. Jose Felix Ortega, L.C., Contact Person.

TUCKAHOE. *Peace Through Divine Mercy, Inc.* (1988) 50 Columbus Ave., #410, 10707. Tel: 914-771-7717; Fax: 914-750-6100. Email: kathleenkeefe@optonline.net. Web: www.peacethroughmercy.com. Kathleen Keefe, Contact Person. Apostolate for priestly and family renewal.

WALDEN. *Family Lifeline Volunteers, Inc.*, 100 Gladstone Ave., 12586. Tel: 845-778-8529; Fax: 845-778-4437. Email: srannamarie@familylifelinevolunteers.org. Web: www.familylifelinevolunteers.org. Sr. Annette Allain, L.S.A., Prog. Coord.

WHITE PLAINS. *Company of St. Paul*, 52 Davis Ave., 10605. Tel: 914-946-1019; Fax: 914-946-1019. Rev. Stuart Sandberg, Pres.

Concerts at the Chapel, Inc., White Plains Center of Compassion, 52 N. Broadway, 10603. Tel: 914-798-1201. Web: www.divinecompassion.org. Paula Caracappa, Coord.

Deutschsprachige Katholische Gemeinde New York-German Speaking Catholic Congregation New York, 106 Greenacres Ave., 10606. Tel: 914-831-3165. Rev. Peter Bleeser, Contact Person.

Religious of Divine Compassion Charitable Trust, 52 N. Broadway, 10603. Tel: 914-798-1300; Fax: 914-949-5169. Email: smerritt@divinecompassion.org. Web: divinecompassion.org.

WOODBOURNE. *Heart's Home USA* (2003) 2299 Ulster Heights Rd., 12788. Tel: 718-522-2922. Email: info@heartshomeusa.org. Web: www.heartshomeusa.org. Laetitia Pallaut De Bessett, Pres.

YONKERS. *Finian Sullivan Corporation*, One Father Finian Sullivan Dr., 10703. Tel: 914-287-6102. Email: pbassano@bpslaw.com. Peter Bassano, Esq., Contact Person.

Jesus Caritas Fraternity, Inc., 4 Curran Ct., 1R, 10710. Tel: 914-961-0050. Email: margebaker@secularinstitutes.org. Mary D. Christensen, Corresponding Sec.

NACAR, Inc., 27 Convent Ave., 10703. Tel: 914-597-4022; Fax: 914-597-4053. Email: eocsc@aol.com. Web: www.catholic-church.org/nacar. Sr. Ellen Rose O'Connell, S.C., Pres., Emeritus/Archivist.

[JJ] PERSONAL PRELATURES

NEW YORK. *Prelature of the Holy Cross and Opus Dei* (1928) 139 E. 34th St., 10016. Tel: 646-742-2700; Fax: 646-742-2747. Email: newyork@opusdei.org. Web: www.opusdei.org. Rev. Msgrs. Thomas G. Bohlin, Ph.D., S.T.D., Regl. Vicar for the U.S.; Javier Garcia de Cardenas; Revs. Deogracias Rosales; Robert A. Brisson; James W. Albrecht; John C. Agnew.

Overlook Study Center Tel: 914-235-0199; Fax: 914-637-9597. Revs. Bradley K. Arturi, J.C.D.; John R. Waiss; Oreste Gonzalez.

99 Overlook Cir., New Rochelle, 10804. Tel: 914-235-6128. Rev. Malcolm M. Kennedy.

330 Riverside Dr., 10025. Tel: 212-222-3285; Fax: 212-316-3629.

RELIGIOUS INSTITUTES OF MEN REPRESENTED IN THE ARCHDIOCESE

For further details refer to the corresponding bracketed number in the Religious Institutes of Men or Women section.

[0130]—*Assumptionists*—A.A.
[0140]—*The Augustinians* (Prov. of St. Joseph)—O.S.A.
[0330]—*Brothers of the Christian Schools* (New York Prov.)—F.S.C.
[0600]—*Brothers of the Congregation of Holy Cross*—C.S.C.
[0400]—*Canons Regular of the Order of the Holy Cross* (Prov. of St. Odilia, Minneapolis, MN)—O.S.C.
[0470]—*The Capuchin Friars* (St. Mary Prov.)—O.F.M.Cap.
[0270]—*Carmelite Fathers & Brothers* (St. Elias Prov.)—O.Carm.
[0310]—*Congregation of Christian Brothers* (Eastern U.S.)—C.F.C.
[0220]—*Congregation of the Blessed Sacrament*—S.S.S.
[1330]—*Congregation of the Mission*—C.M.
[1210]—*Congregation of the Missionaries of St. Charles*—C.S.
[1000]—*Congregation of the Passion* (St. Paul Prov.)—C.P.
[0480]—*Conventual Franciscans* (Immaculate Conception Prov.)—O.F.M.Conv.
[0520]—*Franciscan Friars* (Provs. of Most Holy Name of Jesus, Immaculate Conception; Commissariats of Holy Cross, Holy Family)—O.F.M.
[0530]—*Franciscan Friars of the Atonement*—S.A.
[0690]—*Jesuit Fathers and Brothers* (New York Prov.)—S.J.
[0730]—*Legionaries of Christ*—L.C.
[]—*Little Brothers of the Gospel*
[0770]—*The Marist Brothers*—F.M.S.
[0780]—*Marist Fathers* (Northeastern Prov.)—S.M.
[0800]—*Maryknoll*—M.M.
[0830]—*Mill Hill Missionaries*—M.H.M.
[0720]—*The Missionaries of Our Lady of La Salette*—M.S.
[0910]—*Oblates of Mary Immaculate* (Eastern Prov.)—O.M.I.
[0430]—*Order of Preachers-Dominicans* (St. Joseph Prov.)—O.P.
[0150]—*Order of the Augustinian Recollects*—O.A.R.
[1030]—*Paulist Fathers*—C.S.P.
[1040]—*Piarist Fathers*—Sch.P.
[1070]—*Redemptorist Fathers* (Baltimore Prov.)—C.SS.R.
[1190]—*Salesians of Don Bosco* (St. Philip Prov.)—S.D.B.
[1020]—*Society of St. Paul*—S.S.P.
[0990]—*Society of the Catholic Apostolate*—S.A.C.
[1280]—*Stigmatine Fathers and Brothers*—C.S.S.
[1300]—*Theatine Fathers*—C.R.
[0560]—*Third Order Regular of Saint Francis*—T.O.R.

RELIGIOUS INSTITUTES OF WOMEN REPRESENTED IN THE ARCHDIOCESE

[0130]—*Apostles of the Sacred Heart of Jesus*—A.S.C.J.
[0230]—*Benedictine Sisters of Pontifical Jurisdiction*—O.S.B.
[0330]—*Carmelite Sisters for the Aged and Infirm*—O.Carm.
[3110]—*Congregation of Our Lady of the Retreat in the Cenacle*—R.C.
[2410]—*Congregation of the Marianites of Holy Cross*—M.S.C.
[3710]—*Congregation of the Sisters of Saint Agnes*—C.S.A.
[1920]—*Congregation of the Sisters of the Holy Cross*—C.S.C.
[1710]—*Congregation of the Third Order of St. Francis of Mary Immaculate*—O.S.F.
[0760]—*Daughters of Charity of St. Vincent de Paul*—D.C.
[0790]—*Daughters of Divine Charity* (St. Joseph Prov.)—F.D.C.
[0850]—*Daughters of Mary Help of Christians*—F.M.A.
[0860]—*Daughters of Mary of the Immaculate Conception*—D.M.
[0950]—*Daughters of St. Paul*—F.S.P.
[0810]—*Daughters of the Heart of Mary*—D.H.M.
[0420]—*Discalced Carmelite Nuns*—O.C.D.
[1050]—*Dominican Contemplative Nuns*—O.P.
[1070-03]—*Dominican Sisters*—O.P.
[1070-11]—*Dominican Sisters*—O.P.
[1070-05]—*Dominican Sisters*—O.P.
[1070-06]—*Dominican Sisters*—O.P.
[1070-13]—*Dominican Sisters*—O.P.
[1070-16]—*Dominican Sisters*—O.P.
[1070-23]—*Dominican Sisters*—O.P.
[1070-15]—*Dominican Sisters*—O.P.
[1115]—*Dominican Sisters of Peace*—O.P.
[1120]—*Dominican Sisters of the Roman Congregation*—O.P.
[1170]—*Felician Sisters*—C.S.S.F.
[1260]—*Franciscan Handmaids of the Most Pure Heart of Mary*—F.H.M.
[1370]—*Franciscan Missionaries of Mary*—F.M.M.
[1400]—*Franciscan Missionary Sisters of the Sacred Heart* (Peekskill, NY)—F.M.S.C.
[1180]—*Franciscan Sisters of Allegany, New York*—O.S.F.
[1310]—*Franciscan Sisters of Little Falls, Minnesota*—O.S.F.
[1425]—*Franciscan Sisters of Peace*—F.S.P.
[1190]—*Franciscan Sisters of the Atonement*—S.A.
[1440]—*Franciscan Sisters of the Poor*—S.F.P.
[2070]—*Holy Union Sisters*—S.U.S.C.
[]—*Idente Missionaries*—M.Id.
[3790]—*Institute of the Sisters of St. Dorothy*—S.S.D.
[2310]—*Little Sisters of the Assumption*—L.S.A.
[2340]—*Little Sisters of the Poor*—L.S.P.
[2470]—*Maryknoll Sisters of St. Dominic*—M.M.
[2480]—*Medical Missionaries of Mary*—M.M.M.
[2680]—*Misericordia Sisters*—S.M.
[2720]—*Mission Helpers of the Sacred Heart*—M.H.S.H.
[2710]—*Missionaries of Charity*—M.C.
[1360]—*Missionary Franciscan Sisters of the Immaculate Conception*—O.S.F.
[2790]—*Missionary Servants of the Most Blessed Trinity*—M.S.B.T.
[2900]—*Missionary Sisters of St. Charles Borromeo*—M.S.S.C.B.
[2750]—*Missionary Sisters of the Immaculate Heart of Mary*—I.C.M.
[2860]—*Missionary Sisters of the Sacred Heart*—M.S.C.
[2920]—*Mothers of the Helpless*—M.D.
[3030]—*Oblates of the Most Holy Redeemer*—O.SS.R.
[3035]—*Oblates of the Mother of Orphans*—O.M.O.
[3760]—*Order of St. Clare*—O.S.C.
[2010]—*Order of the Most Holy Redeemer*—O.SS.R.
[3160]—*Parish Visitors of Mary Immaculate*—P.V.M.I.
[3450]—*Religious of Jesus-Mary*—R.J.M.
[3460]—*Religious of Mary Immaculate*—R.M.I.
[3465]—*Religious of the Sacred Heart of Mary* (Eastern North American Prov.)—R.S.H.M.
[2519]—*Religious Sisters of Mercy, Alma, MI*—R.S.M.
[3490]—*Sacramentine Nuns*—O.S.S.
[2970]—*School Sisters of Notre Dame*—S.S.N.D.
[1680]—*School Sisters of St. Francis*—O.S.F.
[0980]—*Sister Disciples of the Divine Master*—P.D.D.M.
[1830]—*Sister of the Good Shepherd*—R.G.S.
[3020]—*Sisters Oblates of the Blessed Trinity*—O.B.T.
[0590]—*Sisters of Charity of Saint Elizabeth, Convent Station*—S.C.
[0650]—*Sisters of Charity of St. Vincent de Paul, New York*—S.C.
[0660]—*Sisters of Christian Charity*—S.C.C.
[2360]—*Sisters of Loretto*—S.L.
[2575]—*Sisters of Mercy of the Americas*—R.S.M.
[3000]—*Sisters of Notre Dame de Namur*—S.N.D.deN.
[3080]—*Sisters of Our Lady of Christian Doctrine*—R.C.D.
[3740]—*Sisters of St. Casimir*—S.S.C.
[1510]—*Sisters of St. Francis of the Mission of the Immaculate Virgin*—O.S.F.
[3820]—*Sisters of St. John the Baptist*—C.S.J.B.
[3830-05]—*Sisters of St. Joseph*—C.S.J.
[3890]—*Sisters of St. Joseph of Peace*—C.S.J.P.
[0260]—*Sisters of the Blessed Sacrament for Indians and Colored People*—S.B.S.
[3140]—*Sisters of the Catholic Apostolate (Pallottine)*—C.S.A.C.
[2980]—*Sisters of the Congregation de Notre Dame*—C.N.D.
[0970]—*Sisters of the Divine Compassion*—R.D.C.
[1000]—*Sisters of the Divine Providence of Kentucky*—C.D.P.
[1990]—*Sisters of the Holy Names of Jesus & Mary*—S.N.J.M.
[3320]—*Sisters of the Presentation of the B.V.M.* (Newburgh; Staten Island)—P.B.V.M.
[3320]—*Sisters of the Presentation of the B.V.M.* (Aberdeen, SD)—P.B.V.M.
[3470]—*Sisters of the Reparation of the Congregation of Mary*—S.R.C.M.
[3480]—*Sisters of the Resurrection*—C.R.
[1490]—*Sisters of the Third Franciscan Order (Syracuse)*—O.S.F.
[3600]—*Sisters, Servants of Mary*—S.M.
[2160]—*Sisters, Servants of the Immaculate Heart Of Mary*—I.H.M.
[1890]—*Society of Helpers*—H.H.S.
[2460]—*Society of Mary Repartrix*—S.M.R.
[4040]—*Society of St. Ursula*—S.U.
[4060]—*Society of the Holy Child Jesus*—S.H.C.J.
[4070]—*Society of the Sacred Heart*—R.S.C.J.
[4110]—*Ursuline Nuns*—O.S.U.
[4130]—*Ursuline Sisters (Tildonk)*—O.S.U.
[4230]—*Xaverian Missionary Sisters*—X.M.M.

ARCHDIOCESAN CEMETERIES

AIRMONT. *Cemetery of the Ascension*
HAWTHORNE. *Cemetery of the Gate of Heaven*
LONG ISLAND CITY. *Calvary*
STATEN ISLAND. *Cemetery of the Resurrection*

NECROLOGY

† Boyd, Rev. Msgr. Joseph J., Wesley Hills, NY St. Boniface; Larchmont, NY SS. John & Paul—Died Dec. 20, 2009
† Gavigan, Rev. Msgr. Peter J., Bronx, NY Our Lady of Victory—Died March 17, 2009
† Guido, Rev. Msgr. William F., New York, NY Our Savior—Died April 30, 2009
† Harrington, Rev. Msgr. John, Pearl River, NY St. Margaret of Antioch—Died Aug. 22, 2009
† Malley, Rev. Msgr. James, (Retired)—Died March 28, 2009
† Meehan, Rev. Msgr. Joseph P., (Retired)—Died Dec. 18, 2009
† Quinn, Rev. Msgr. John J., (Retired)—Died Sept. 24, 2009

† Servodidio, Rev. Msgr. John T., Staten Island, NY St. Joseph—Died March 22, 2009
† Smith, Rev. Msgr. William B., Yonkers, NY St. Joseph's Seminary—Died Jan. 24, 2009
† Basile, Nicholas F., Mount Vernon, NY St. Francis of Assisi—Died April 6, 2009
† Buttinelli, Antonio, (Retired)—Died Feb. 12, 2009
† Cassiero, Daniel A., Chap., U.S. Air Force—Died Oct. 31, 2009
† Fogarty, Daniel F., (Retired)—Died Aug. 21, 2009
† Jacimerski, Jan, (Retired)—Died July 22, 2009
† McGinn, Sylvester P., (Retired)—Died May 15, 2009
† Mercer, John E., Staten Island, NY Our Lady of Pity—Died Nov. 30, 2009
† Mulvanerty, Thomas M., New York, NY St. Monica; Bronx, NY Christ the King & Our Lady of Solace—Died April 2, 2009
† Neuhaus, Richard J., New York, NY Immaculate Conception—Died Jan. 8, 2009
† O'Brien, John P., Scarsdale, NY St. Pius X—Died Dec. 9, 2009
† O'Connor, Maurice, (Retired)—Died March 29, 2009
† Resta, Vincent Anthony, (Retired)—Died July 19, 2009
† Sepp, Michael P., Bronx, NY Sacred Heart—Died March 13, 2009
† Tubridy, James M., West Point, NY Most Holy Trinity—Died Oct. 17, 2009

An asterisk (*) denotes an organization that has established tax-exempt status directly with the IRS and is not covered by the USCCB Group Ruling.

Diocese of Norwich

(Dioecesis Norvicensis)

Most Reverend

MICHAEL R. COTE, D.D.

Bishop of Norwich; ordained June 29, 1975; appointed Titular Bishop of Cebarades and Auxiliary Bishop of Portland May 9, 1995; ordained July 27, 1995; appointed Bishop of Norwich March 11, 2003; installed May 14, 2003. *Res.: 274 Broadway, Norwich, CT 06360.*

Chancery: 201 Broadway, Norwich, CT 06360. Tel: 860-887-9294; Fax: 860-886-1670.

Web: www.norwichdiocese.org

ESTABLISHED AUGUST 6, 1953.

Square Miles 1,978.

Corporate Title: The Norwich Roman Catholic Diocesan Corporation.

Comprises the Counties of Middlesex, New London, Tolland and Windham in the State of Connecticut and Fishers Island, a portion of Suffolk County in the State of New York.

For legal titles of parishes and diocesan institutions, consult the Chancery Office.

STATISTICAL OVERVIEW

Personnel	
Bishop	1
Priests: Diocesan Active in Diocese	67
Priests: Diocesan Active Outside Diocese	8
Priests: Retired, Sick or Absent	40
Number of Diocesan Priests	115
Religious Priests in Diocese	52
Total Priests in Diocese	167
Extern Priests in Diocese	12
Ordinations:	
Diocesan Priests	1
Transitional Deacons	1
Permanent Deacons in Diocese	72
Total Brothers	24
Total Sisters	203
Parishes	
Parishes	76
With Resident Pastor:	
Resident Diocesan Priests	55
Resident Religious Priests	12
Without Resident Pastor:	
Administered by Priests	9
Missions	6
Pastoral Centers	10
Professional Ministry Personnel:	
Sisters	1
Lay Ministers	17
Welfare	
Homes for the Aged	2
Total Assisted	239
Special Centers for Social Services	1
Total Assisted	85
Educational	
Diocesan Students in Other Seminaries	5
Seminaries, Religious	1
Students Religious	30
Total Seminarians	35
High Schools, Diocesan and Parish	3
Total Students	1,892
High Schools, Private	2
Total Students	411
Elementary Schools, Diocesan and Parish	19
Total Students	2,839
Catechesis/Religious Education:	
High School Students	1,688
Elementary Students	14,974
Total Students under Catholic Instruction	21,839
Teachers in the Diocese:	
Priests	2
Brothers	7
Sisters	27
Lay Teachers	325
Vital Statistics	
Receptions into the Church:	
Infant Baptism Totals	1,706
Minor Baptism Totals	69
Adult Baptism Totals	67
Received into Full Communion	304
First Communions	2,327
Confirmations	2,107
Marriages:	
Catholic	330
Interfaith	119
Total Marriages	449
Deaths	2,004
Total Catholic Population	238,388
Total Population	697,653

Former Bishops—Most Revs. BERNARD J. FLANAGAN, D.D., J.C.D., ord. Dec. 8, 1931; cons. Nov. 30, 1953; installed Dec. 9, 1953; transferred to See of Worcester, Aug. 12, 1959; retired March 31, 1983; died Jan. 28, 1998; VINCENT J. HINES, D.D., J.C.D., ord. May 2, 1937; appt. Nov. 27, 1959; cons. March 17, 1960; retired June 17, 1975; died April 23, 1990; DANIEL P. REILLY, D.D., ord. May 30, 1953; appt. June 17, 1975; cons. Aug. 6, 1975; transferred to See of Worcester, Oct. 27, 1994; installed Dec. 8, 1994; retired March 9, 2004; DANIEL A. HART, D.D., ord. Feb. 2, 1953; cons. Auxiliary Bishop of Boston Oct. 18, 1976; appt. Sept. 12, 1995; installed Bishop of Norwich Nov. 1, 1995; retired March 11, 2003; died Jan. 14, 2008.

Office of the Bishop—Most Rev. MICHAEL RICHARD COTE, D.D. Tel: 860-887-9294. Email: bpcote@norwichdiocese.net; Mrs. ALICE PUDVAH, Administrative Asst. Tel: 860-887-9294, Ext. 234. Email: alice@norwichdiocese.net; Rev. KEVIN M. REILLY, Sec. to Bishop. Tel: 860-887-9294, Ext. 259.

The Chancery

Chancery—201 Broadway, Norwich, 06360. Tel: 860-887-9294; Fax: 860-886-1670.

Vicar General—Rev. Msgr. THOMAS R. BRIDE, P.A., K.C.H.S., V.G. Tel: 860-887-9294, Ext. 231. Email: vicargeneral@norwichdiocese.net; Mrs. CHRISTINE SIART, Sec. Tel: 860-887-9294, Ext. 246. Email: sec.voc@norwichdiocese.net.

Chancellor—Rev. Msgr. ROBERT L. BROWN. Tel: 860-887-9294, Ext. 232; Cell: 860-303-6080. Email: chancellor@norwichdiocese.net; Mrs. BECKY CADY, Sec. Tel: 860-887-9294, Ext. 235. Email: becky@norwichdiocese.net; Mrs. REBECCA MCDOUGAL, Receptionist. Tel: 860-887-9294, Ext. 100.

Vicar for Clergy—Rev. Msgr. RICHARD P. LAROCQUE. Tel: 860-887-9294, Ext. 258. Email: vicarclergy@norwichdiocese.net; Deacon MICHAEL C. BERSTENE, Dir. Deacon Personnel; Mrs. LIZ MISAMORE, Sec. Tel: 860-887-9294, Ext. 265. Email: lizm@norwichdiocese.net.

Diocesan Attorney—MICHAEL E. DRISCOLL ESQ., 22 Courthouse Sq., Norwich, 06360. Tel: 860-889-3321.

Diocesan Attorney Emeritus—JAMES J. DUTTON JR., Esq., K.S.G., 22 Courthouse Sq., Norwich, 06360. Tel: 860-889-3321.

Diocesan Finance Office—Tel: 860-887-9294; Fax: 860-885-1512. Mr. WILLIAM J. RUSSELL, CPA, Diocesan Finance Officer. Tel: 860-887-9294, Ext. 241; Mrs. SUSAN GARDINER, Administrative Asst. Tel: 860-887-9294, Ext. 261; Mr. VICTOR WELTIG, Internal Auditor. Tel: 860-887-9294, Ext. 242; Ms. JANET WEST, Finance Analyst. Tel: 860-887-9294, Ext. 243; Mrs. ANN MARIE OSOWSKI, Benefits Admin. Tel: 860-887-9294, Ext. 245; Ms. KAREN HUFFER, Accountant. Tel: 860-887-9294, Ext. 244; Ms. ROBIN HOLTSCLAW, Risk Mgr. (CMRS). Tel: 800-331-2561; Fax: 860-726-9412.

College of Consultors—Rev. Msgrs. HENRY N. ARCHAMBAULT, P.A., J.C.D., V.F.; THOMAS R. BRIDE, P.A., K.C.H.S., V.G.; ROBERT L. BROWN; RICHARD P. LAROCQUE; ANTHONY S. ROSAFORTE; Very Revs. MICHAEL T. DONOHUE; LAURENCE A.M. LAPOINTE; Revs. MARK D. O'DONNELL; ROBERT WASHABAUGH.

Presbyteral Council—Most Rev. MICHAEL RICHARD COTE, D.D., Pres.; Very Rev. LAURENCE A.M. LAPOINTE, Chm. Members: Rev. Msgrs. HENRY N. ARCHAMBAULT, P.A., J.C.D., V.F.; THOMAS R. BRIDE, P.A., K.C.H.S., V.G.; ROBERT L. BROWN; RICHARD P. LAROCQUE; ANTHONY S. ROSAFORTE; Rev. ROLAND C. CLOUTIER, L.C.S.W.; Very Revs. MICHAEL T. DONOHUE; GREGOIRE J. FLUET, Ph.D., V.F., K.H.S.; JAMES P. CARINI; MICHAEL L. PHILLIPPINO; Revs. V. ANTONY ALAHARASAN, M.A., Ph.D.; GRZEGORZ P. BROZONOWICZ; ROBERT W. CRONIN (Retired); GREGORY P. GALVIN; LESZEK T. JANIK, J.C.L.; PAUL J. MURDOCK; MARK D. O'DONNELL; WILLIAM J. OLESIK; DENNIS M. PERKINS; RICHARD J. RICARD; MICHAEL S. SMITH; TED F. TUMICKI, S.T.L., J.C.L., Sec.; ROBERT WASHABAUGH, Vice Chm.; JOSEPH B. WHITTEL.

Deans—Very Revs. LAURENCE A.M. LAPOINTE, Willimantic; JAMES P. CARINI, Vernon; Rev. Msgr. HENRY N. ARCHAMBAULT, P.A., J.C.D., V.F., Norwich; Very Revs. CHARLES R. LEBLANC, Putnam; GREGOIRE J. FLUET, Ph.D., V.F., K.H.S., Old Saybrook; MICHAEL T. DONOHUE, New London; MICHAEL L. PHILLIPPINO, Middletown.

Diocesan Pastoral Council—Most Rev. MICHAEL RICHARD COTE, D.D., Chm.; Rev. Msgrs. HENRY N. ARCHAMBAULT, P.A., J.C.D., V.F.; THOMAS R. BRIDE, P.A., K.C.H.S., V.G.; ROBERT L. BROWN; Rev. WALTER M. NAGLE; Mr. TODD POSTLER; Ms. HELENE LABELLE; Mr. JAMES LANDHERR; Sr. ELISSA RINERE, C.P., J.C.D.; Mrs. ESPERANZA NUGENT; Mr. STEPHEN ST. JOHN; Mrs. ELAINE TRUDO.

The Tribunal

Diocesan Tribunal—

Judicial Vicar—Rev. LESZEK T. JANIK, J.C.L.

Adjutant Judicial Vicar—VACANT.

Defenders of the Bond—Revs. ROGER J. LAMOUREUX, O.M.I.; JOSEPH CASTALDI, J.C.L.

Coordinator of the Tribunal—SALLY J. TOLLES Cons. Sec. D.H.S., J.D., J.C.L.

Judges—Rev. Msgr. HENRY N. ARCHAMBAULT, P.A., J.C.D., V.F.; Revs. GEORGE J. RICHARDS JR., J.C.L.; TED F. TUMICKI, S.T.L., J.C.L.; SALLY J. TOLLES Cons. Sec. D.H.S., J.D., J.C.L.;

Sr. ELISSA RINERE, C.P., J.C.D.

Archivist—Very Rev. GREGOIRE J. FLUET, Ph.D., V.F., K.H.S.

Auditor/Assessors—Full Time: BEATRICE L. THEROUX Consecrated Secular, D.H.S.; Sr. ELISSA RINERE, C.P., J.C.D. Part Time: Rev. Msgr. RICHARD P. LAROCQUE; Revs. DENNIS G. CAREY; RUSSELL F. KENNEDY; Very Revs. GREGOIRE J. FLUET, Ph.D., V.F., K.H.S.; CHARLES R. LEBLANC; Revs. RICHARD J. RICARD; ROBERT WASHABAUGH; Deacon MELVIN G. NYGAARD.

Administrative Assistant of the Tribunal—VACANT.

Notaries—Rev. Msgrs. THOMAS R. BRIDE, P.A., K.C.H.S., V.G.; ROBERT L. BROWN.

Diocesan Offices, Ministries and Societies

Vicar for Ministry—Rev. JOSEPH B. WHITTEL, Bishop Flanagan Ministry Center, 1595 Norwich New London Tpke., Uncasville, 06382. Tel: 860-848-2237, Ext. 309. Email: jbwhittel@hotmail.com.

Advisory Ministry Evaluation Committee—Rev. Msgrs. THOMAS R. BRIDE, P.A., K.C.H.S., V.G.; ROBERT L. BROWN, Chm.; Mr. WILLIAM J. RUSSELL, CPA, D.F.O.; Revs. DENNIS M. PERKINS; JOSEPH B. WHITTEL; Deacon LAWRENCE HILL; Sr. MARY A. MCCARTHY, R.S.M.; SALLY J. TOLLES Cons. Sec. D.H.S., J.D., J.C.L.; Mrs. NANCY MIGNAULT; Mrs. RELLA BERNABUCCI; Mr. WILLIAM JUZWIC; Dr. JEREMIAH LOWNEY; Dr. ROBERT MILLER, Ph.D.

Annual Bishop's Appeal (ABA)— See Development, Diocesan Office.

Bishop's Liaison with Retired Clergy—Rev. Msgr. RICHARD P. LAROCQUE, The Chancery, 201 Broadway, Norwich, 06360-4458. Tel: 860-887-9294, Ext. 258.

Bishop's Delegate for Safe Environments—Rev. TED F. TUMICKI, S.T.L., J.C.L.

Delegate for Consecrated Life—SALLY J. TOLLES Cons. Sec. D.H.S., J.D., J.C.L. The Tribunal, Diocese of Norwich, 201 Broadway, Norwich, 06360-4419. Tel: 860-887-9294, Ext. 255.

Diocesan Finance Council—Most Rev. MICHAEL RICHARD COTE, D.D., Chm.; Rev. Msgr. THOMAS R. BRIDE, P.A., K.C.H.S., V.G.; Mr. JAMES CRONIN; Mr. PETER LAMALFA; Mr. FRED PERKINS, CPA; Mr. BERNARD PHANEUF; Mr. WILLIAM MCGURK; Mr. TERRENCE CAHILL; Mr. VINCENT ROEMMELE; Mr. PETER SIPPLES, Attorney.

Diocesan Panel of Pastors, Canon 1742—Rev. Msgr. ANTHONY S. ROSAFORTE; Revs. DENNIS M. PERKINS; RICHARD J. RICARD.

Diocesan Pastoral Council— See Chancery listing.

Board of Education— See School Office.

Board of Conciliation and Arbitration—SALLY J. TOLLES Cons. Sec. D.H.S., J.D., J.C.L.

Building Commission—Very Rev. MICHAEL F. DONOHUE, Chm.; Rev. ROBERT A. MURPHY, M.S.A.; Mr. GEORGE SCHILLER; Mr. PAUL LUSSIER.

Campaigns—

Campaign for Human Development—Very Rev. MICHAEL T. DONOHUE, Diocesan Dir., St. Matthias Church, 317 Chesterfield Rd., P.O. Box 25, East Lyme, 06333-0025. Tel: 860-739-5208; Fax: 860-739-0524.

Catholic Relief Services—Rev. Msgr. ROBERT L. BROWN, Dir.; Mrs. BECKY CADY, 201 Broadway, Norwich, 06360-4328. Tel: 860-887-9294, Ext. 236.

Campus Ministry—Very Rev. LAURENCE A.M. LAPOINTE, Diocesan Dir., Newman Hall, 290 Prospect St., Willimantic, 06226. Tel: 860-423-0856; Fax: 860-456-8083 (See separate category under Institutions for details).

Middletown—Rev. HALBERT WEIDNER, C.O., Wesleyan University - The University Chaplains, 171 Church St., Middletown, 06459-3625. Tel: 860-685-2777, Ext. 2706; Fax: 860-685-2821.

New London—Very Rev. LAURENCE A.M. LAPOINTE, Catholic Chap., Connecticut College, P.O. Box 5203, New London, 06320-5203. Tel: 860-439-2452; Fax: 860-439-2463.

Storrs—Chaplains: Revs. GREGORY C. MULLANEY; JOHN N. ANTONELLE; ANTHONY J. DIMARCO; Sr. ANNMARIE O'CONNOR, St. Thomas Aquinas Chapel, 46 N. Eagleville Rd., Storrs, 06268-1710. Tel: 860-429-6436; Fax: 860-429-2809. Email: office@stthomasuconn.org.

Willimantic—Very Rev. LAURENCE A.M. LAPOINTE, Campus Min., Eastern Connecticut State University, Newman Hall, 290 Prospect St., Willimantic, 06226-2304. Tel: 860-423-0856; Fax: 860-456-8083.

Catechetical Ministry— See Faith Formation Office

Catholic Charities, Diocese of Norwich, Inc.—

Executive Director—Mr. MAREK KUKULKA, L.M.F.T., 331 Main St., Norwich, 06360. Tel: 860-889-8346; Fax: 860-889-2658.

Adolescent Subtance Abuse Treatment Program—DIANE SVENNING, L.C.S.W., Prog. Supvr., Norwich Office.

Adoption Program—Mrs. SUSAN SEDENSKY, J.D., Prog. Coord.

Behavioral Health Clinic—HOLLY DREGER, L.C.S.W., Dir. Clinic, Norwich Office.

Emergency Financial Service—ROSALINDA BAZINET, B.A., Supvr. New London Office, 22 Masonic St., Ste. 202, New London, 06320. Tel: 860-443-5328; Fax: 860-443-6013; SYLVIA LAUDETTE, M.S.W., Mgr., Norwich Office, 331 Main St., Norwich, 06360. Tel: 860-889-8346; Fax: 860-889-2658; DIANNE LAMBERT, M.P.H., Social Worker, Willimantic Office, 115 Ash St., Willimantic, 06226. Tel: 860-423-7065; Fax: 860-456-1098.

Empowering People for Success Program—COLETTA WILSON, Social Worker, New London Office, 22 Masonic St., New London, 06320. Tel: 860-443-5328; Fax: 860-443-6013; GERALDO HEREDIA, M.A., Willimantic Office, 115 Ash St., Willimantic, 06226. Tel: 860-423-7065; Fax: 860-456-1098.

Housing Counseling—BARBARA R. CROUCH, Norwich Office, 331 Main St., Norwich, 06360. Tel: 860-889-8346; Fax: 860-889-2658.

Mentoring Program—LISA ELLISON, Prog. Coord., New London Office, 22 Masonic St., New London, 06320. Tel: 860-443-5328; Fax: 860-443-6013.

Office of Family Life— Marriage preparation, marriage support and enrichment, natural family planning, parenting education, True Love Waits (chastity/abstinence), Project Rachel (post abortion), separation and divorce, bereavement, singles and singles-again. SEAN FEENEY, Norwich Office, 331 Main St., Norwich, 06360. Tel: 860-889-8346; Fax: 860-889-2658.

Parish of Social Ministry—SEAN FEENEY, Norwich Office, 331 Main St., Norwich, 06360. Tel: 860-889-8346; Fax: 860-889-2658.

Pregnancy Program—YAMILA DIAZ, D.M., Coord., Norwich Office, 331 Main St., Norwich, 06360. Tel: 860-889-8346; Fax: 860-889-2658.

Catholic Mutual Relief Society— Diocesan Property and Liability Insurance, Ms. ROBIN HOLTSCLAW, Claims/Risk Mgr. Email: rholtsclaw@catholicmutual.org; Office for all claims: Catholic Mutual Group, 467 Bloomfield Ave., Bloomfield, 06002. Tel: 800-331-2561; Fax: 860-726-9412. National Office: Catholic Mutual Relief Society, 10843 Old Mill Rd., Omaha, NE 68154. Tel: 800-228-6108; Fax: 402-551-2943.

Catholic Youth Organization (CYO)— See Faith Formation, Office for

Cemetery Corporation and Subsidiaries, Diocesan Cemeteries—SHIRLEY MCGRATH, Cemetery Mgr., Office, 815 Boswell Ave., Norwich, 06360-2536. Tel: 860-887-1019; Fax: 860-889-4804 (For details on individual cemeteries see separate listing); The following cemeteries are subsidiaries of the Norwich Diocesan Cemetery Corp.

Moosup—All Hallows Cemetery, Green Hallow Rd., Moosup, 06354. Cemetery Office: 815 Boswell Ave., Norwich, 06360-2536. Tel: 860-887-1019.

New London—St. Mary Cemetery of New London Corp., 600 Jefferson Ave., New London, 06320-2412. Tel: 860-443-3465 (Office).

Norwich—St. Mary & St. Joseph Cemetery Corp., 815 Boswell Ave., Norwich, 06360-2536. Tel: 860-887-1019.

Taftville—Sacred Heart Cemetery Corp., Harland Rd., Taftville, 06380. Cemetery Office, 815 Boswell Ave., Norwich, 06360-2536. Tel: 860-887-1019.

Uncasville—St. Patrick Cemetery, Depot Rd., Uncasville, 06382. Cemetery Office, 815 Boswell Ave., Norwich, 06360-2536. Tel: 860-887-1019.

Wauregan—Sacred Heart Cemetery, Wauregan Rd., Wauregan, 06387. Cemetery Office: 815 Boswell Ave., Norwich, 06360-2536. Tel: 860-887-1019.

Westbrook—Resurrection Cemetery Corp., Rte. 145, Westbrook, 06498. Tel: 860-399-6503 (Cemetery Office).

Censor of Books—Rev. ROBERT W. CRONIN (Retired), 11 Middlefield Dr., West Hartford, 06107. Tel: 860-232-1886; Very Rev. LAURENCE A.M. LAPOINTE, Newman Hall, 290 Prospect St., Willimantic, 06226. Tel: 860-423-0856.

Communications, Office of—31 Perkins Ave., Norwich, 06360-3613. Tel: 860-887-3933; Fax: 860-859-1253. Web: www.norwichdiocese.org. Mr. MICHAEL R. STRAMMIELLO, Dir. Email: com@norwichdiocese.net; Ms. MEREDITH MORRISON, Administrative Asst.

Four County Catholic— Official monthly newspaper of the Diocese of Norwich: (No July issue).

Publisher—Most Rev. MICHAEL RICHARD COTE, D.D., Bishop of Norwich.

News Editor—LAURA MURKETT, 31 Perkins Ave., Norwich, 06360-3613. Tel: 860-886-1281; Fax: 860-859-1253. Email: comlaura@norwichdiocese.net.

Theological Advisor—Rev. TED F. TUMICKI, S.T.L., J.C.L.

Community Ministries—

Middletown—Mr. RONALD KROM, Exec. Dir.; FRED TOLLI, Mgr. Meals Prog.; TERRY CARBONE, Svc. Coord., St. Vincent dePaul Place, 617 Main St., P.O. Box 398, Middletown, 06457-0398. Tel: 860-344-0097; Fax: 860-343-0023.

Norwich—JILLIAN CORBIN, Exec. Dir.; Ms. BETTY ROARTY, Administrative Asst., St. Vincent dePaul Place, 10 Railroad Pl., Norwich, 06360. Tel: 860-889-7374.

Connecticut Catholic Conference—MICHAEL CARROLL CULHANE, Exec. Dir.; Deacon DAVID REYNOLDS, Legislative Liaison, Connecticut Catholic Conference, 134 Farmington Ave., Hartford, 06105-3784. Tel: 860-524-7882; Fax: 860-525-0750. Email: ccc@ctcatholic.org. Web: www.ctcatholic.org.

Continuing Education and Formation Commission for the Clergy—Revs. MARK D. O'DONNELL, Chm.; GRZEGORZ P. BROZONOWICZ; ROLAND C. CLOUTIER, L.C.S.W.; PETER B. LISZEWSKI; DENNIS M. PERKINS; MICHAEL S. SMITH.

Council of Catholic Women—Mrs. JUDY PAPPAGALLO, Pres.; Very Rev. CHARLES R. LEBLANC, Diocesan Moderator, Mailing Address: St. Patrick Rectory, P.O. Box 177, East Hampton, 06424-0177. Tel: 860-267-6644. District Moderators: Revs. CHRISTOPHER J. ZMUDA, Th.Psy.D., Willimantic Deanery; EUGENE L. PILATOWSKI, Norwich Deanery (Retired); JOSEPH F. DECOSTA, New London Deanery; WILLIAM J. MCNULTY, Putnam Deanery (Retired); Very Rev. JAMES P. CARINI, Rockville Deanery; Rev. PAUL J. GAUMOND, Shoreline Deanery.

The Deaf, Ministry to—The Chancery, 201 Broadway, Norwich, 06360. Tel: 860-887-9294.

Ecclesia Dei Ministry (Tridentine Rite)—

Director and Chaplain—Very Rev. GREGOIRE J. FLUET, Ph.D., V.F., K.H.S., St. Bridget of Kildare, P.O. Box 422, Moodus, 06469-0422. Tel: 860-873-8623.

Development, Diocesan Office of (DOD)—Mr. THOMAS P. O'BRIEN, Exec. Dir. Tel: 860-886-1928, Ext. 13; Fax: 860-886-2651. Email: thomas.obrien@norwichdiocese.net. Administrative Assistants: SUSAN UNDERHILL. Tel: 860-886-1928, Ext. 12; MARLENE PEER, 197 Broadway, Norwich, 06360-4407. Tel: 860-886-1928, Ext. 11.

Annual Bishop's Appeal—Mr. THOMAS P. O'BRIEN, Exec. Dir., 197 Broadway, Norwich, 06360. Tel: 860-886-1928, Ext. 13; Fax: 860-886-2651. Email: thomas.obrien@norwichdiocese.net.

Planned Giving Office—Mr. THOMAS P. O'BRIEN, 197 Broadway, Norwich, 06360. Tel: 860-886-1928, Ext. 13. Email: thomas.obrien@norwichdiocese.net.

Stewardship Office—Mr. THOMAS P. O'BRIEN, 197 Broadway, Norwich, 06360. Tel: 860-886-1928, Ext. 13. Email: thomas.obrien@norwichdiocese.net.

Disabilities-People with— See His Able People, Ministry of

Ecumenism—

Diocesan Commission for Ecumenical and Interreligious Affairs—Deacon LEO N. BERNARD; Ms. KATHLEEN BURTON; SANDRA CALABRO; Mr. CHARLES HENRY SR.; Sr. BARBARA HOBBS, P.B.V.M.; Mr. MARK KRISTOFF; Very Rev. CHARLES R. LEBLANC; Rev. MARK D. O'DONNELL; MICHAEL OLOCK; RAFAEL ORTIZ; Rev. FRANCIS C. ROULEAU.

Ecumenical and Interreligious Affairs, Office of—VACANT, Bishop Flanagan Ministry Center, 1595 Norwich-New London Tpke., Uncasville, 06382-1319. Tel: 860-848-2237, Ext. 204; Fax: 860-848-2816. Email: ecuminter@norwichdiocese.net.

Evangelization & Catechumenate (RCIA), Office of—See Office of Faith Events

Faith Events, Office of—Bishop Flanagan Ministry Center, 1595 Norwish-New London Tpke., Uncasville, 06382-1319. Tel: 860-848-2237, Ext. 312; Fax: 860-848-2816. MARGE VANNER, Interim Coord. Advisory Board: Sr. MARY JUDE LAZARUS, S.C.M.C., Co Chair; Deacon GERALD L. SHAW, Co Chair; Rev. GREGORY BROZONOWICZ; Sr. MARIA ROSA CAMPOS, R.O.D.A.; Deacon CHRISTOPHER DESKUS; Rev. LESZEK T. JANIK, J.C.L.; Mrs. DOROTHY KING; Mrs. NANCY MIGNAULT.

Faith Formation, Office for— See Office of Faith Events

"Four County Catholic"— See Newspaper

Haitian Ministries—EMILY SMACK, Dir., Bishop Flanagan Ministry Center, 1595 Norwich-New London Tpke., Uncasville, 06382-1319. Tel: 860-848-2237, Ext. 206. Email: haiti.ministry@snet.net. Web: www.haitianministries.org. Haitian Ministries Board: DOLORES DEL VECHIO; PETER HARDING; PETER LODEN; BARBARA WYSOCKI; Sr.

MARY LYNN HEALY, R.S.M.; JEAN M. AQUILA; Rev. MICHAEL JONES, O.F.M.

Hospice St. Joseph for the Diocese of Norwich, Inc.—1595 Norwich - New London Tpke., Uncasville, 06382. Tel: 860-848-2237, Ext. 304; Fax: 860-848-2816. Email: hsj33haiti@aol.com. GERALDINE O'HARE, Chm. Bd.

Local Haitian Apostolate/Apostola Ayisyun—Rev. JOHN MORIN, O.M.I., Ministry to Local Haitians, 331 Main St., Norwich, 06360. Tel: 860-460-0794; Fax: 860-889-2658 Haitian Creole Mass: Sun. 12 pm.

Hispanic Ministry—Sr. MARY JUDE LAZARUS, S.C.M.C., Diocesan Dir., Hispanic Apostolate Office, 61 Club Rd., Windham, 06280-1007. Tel: 860-456-3349; Fax: 860-423-4157. Email: aposthispano@juno.com.

Evangelization—Sisters SANDRA BELLO, H.M.S.P.; MINERVA SALGADO, H.M.S.P., St. Mary Star of Sea Convent, 22 Huntington St., New London, 06320. Tel: 860-444-9673. Hispanic Ministry Board: Mrs. ROSA MARIA LEMUS, New London; Mrs. CLAUDIA SCHKEEPER, New London; Mr. GEBERTH GAMBOA, Norwich; Mrs. ZULMA GAMBOA, Norwich; Mrs. GUSTAVO VIVEROS, Willimantic; Mrs. EVA SANTIAGO, Willimantic; Mrs. AURORA SANTOSTEFANO, Middletown.

Clinton—

St. Mary of the Visitation Church - Spanish Apostolate—Rev. MICHAEL SEQUEIRA, Pastor; Sr. MARIA CECILIA QUEZADA, R.O.D.A., Pastoral Assoc., 54 Grove St., Clinton, 06413-1999. Tel: 860-669-8512; Fax: 860-669-9052.

Middletown—

St. Francis of Assisi Church - Spanish Apostolate—Sr. MARIA CECILIA QUEZADA, R.O.D.A., Pastoral Assoc., 10 Elm St., Middletown, 06457-4426. Tel: 860-347-4684; Fax: 860-347-7669.

New London—

St. Mary, Star of the Sea Church - Spanish Apostolate—Rev. ROBERT WASHABAUGH, Pastor; Sr. ROSA M. CAMPOS, R.O.D.A., Pastoral Assoc.; Deacons JESUS DIEZ-CANSECO, 10 Huntington St., New London, 06320-6198. Tel: 860-447-1431; Fax: 860-437-1889. Email: stmarysnl@aol.com; MARIO RAMOS, Residence: 20 Old Colony Ln., Ledyard, 06339. Tel: 860-536-8870.

Norwich—

St. Mary Church - Spanish Apostolate—Rev. RUSSELL F. KENNEDY; Sr. FRANCISCA CANDELARIA, R.O.D.A., Pastoral Assoc., 70 Central Ave., Norwich, 06360-4794. Tel: 860-887-2565.

Windham—

Iglesia del Sagrado Corazon de Jesus—Rev. PAUL J. MURDOCK, Pastor, Res.: 310 Elizabeth Lane, Stonegate Manor, North Windham, 06256. Pastoral Associates: Sr. FRANCISCA CANDELARIA, R.O.D.A.; VIRGINIA RODRIGUEZ; Deacon FELIPE SILVA, 61 Club Rd., Windham, 06280-1007. Tel: 860-423-8617; Fax: 860-423-4157.

Holy Childhood— See Pontifical Association of the Holy Childhood.

Holy Name Societies— Address all mail to: *Holy Name Societies, 201 Broadway, Norwich, 06360-4328.* Tel: 860-887-9294.

Office of Internal Affairs—201 Broadway, Norwich, 06360-4480. Tel: 800-624-7407; 860-889-4455. Mr. VIC LENDA JR., Bishop's Delegate for Internal Investigations; Mrs. MARIE TWOMEY, Assistance Coord. Tel: 800-624-7407.

Insurance— See Catholic Mutual Relief Society (C.M.R.S.)

Justice & Peace, Catholic Action for—Rev. JOSEPH B. WHITTEL, Vicar for Ministry, Bishop Flanagan Ministry Center, 1595 Norwich-New London Tpke., Uncasville, 06382-1319. Tel: 860-848-2237; Fax: 860-848-2816. Email: jbwhittel@hotmail.com.

His Able People, Ministry of— A ministry for persons with disabilities. *Inquiries should be made to: 201 Braodway, Norwich, 06360.* Tel: 860-887-9294, Ext. 100.

Lawyers, Guild of Catholic—Mailing Address: 201 Broadway, Norwich, 06360-4328. Tel: 860-887-9294, Ext. 246. MICHAEL E. DRISCOLL ESQ., Pres.; Rev. Msgr. HENRY N. ARCHAMBAULT, P.A., J.C.D., V.F., Chap.; Mrs. CHRISTINE SIART, Sec. Tel: 860-887-9294, Ext. 246.

Legion of Mary—Rev. ROBERT B. LYNCH, Diocesan Spiritual Dir. (Retired), St. Mary Rectory, 70 Central Ave., Norwich, 06360-4794. Tel: 860-887-2565.

Worship, Office of—Sr. ELISSA RINERE, C.P., J.C.D., Dir., Bishop Flanagan Ministry Center, 1595 Norwich-New London Tpke., Uncasville, 06382-1319. Tel: 860-848-2237, Ext. 209; Fax: 860-848-2816. Email: rinere@norwichdiocese.net. Liturgical Commission: Very Rev. JAMES P. CARINI; CONSTANCE BUTLER; Mrs. SANDY RUSSO; SUSAN MYSHRALL; Deacon PETER L. GILL; Rev. PAUL J. MURDOCK; Mrs. NANCY MIGNAULT; Dr. SUSAN BERRY.

Marriage Encounter/Catholic Charities/Family Life Office—SUSAN WILLIAMS, 331 Main St., Norwich, 06360. Tel: 860-889-8346; Fax: 860-889-2658.

Mercy Xavier Fund—Bro. BRIAN DAVIS, C.F.X., Pres., 181 Randolph Rd., Middletown, 06457. Tel: 860-347-2343; 860-346-7735.

Ministry Formation, Office of—The Bishop Flanagan Ministry Center, 1595 Norwich-New London Tpke., Uncasville, 06382-1319. Tel: 860-848-2237, Ext. 308; Fax: 860-848-2816.

Newspaper— Official monthly newspaper of Diocese of Norwich--"Four County Catholic" LAURA MURKETT, News Editor. Tel: 860-886-1928. Email: comlaura@norwichdiocese.net; Rev. TED F. TUMICKI, S.T.L., J.C.L., Theological Advisor.

Pastoral Planning, Office of—Sr. ELISSA RINERE, C.P., J.C.D., Bishop Flanagan Ministry Center, 1595 Norwich-New London Tpke., Uncasville, 06382-1319. Tel: 860-848-2237, Ext. 203; Fax: 860-848-2816. Email: rinere@norwichdiocese.org. Advisory Board: Very Rev. JAMES P. CARINI; DAVID GRAFT; Sr. MARY JUDE LAZARUS, S.C.M.C.; Rev. MARK D. O'DONNELL; SUSAN MYSHRALL; Rev. MICHAEL S. SMITH; Mrs. JANET WALSH; Rev. ROBERT WASHABAUGH; Deacon DAVID G. YOUNG.

People with Disabilities— See His Able People, Ministry of

Permanent Diaconate, Office of—The Chancery, 201 Broadway, Norwich, 06360-4458. Web: www.norwichdeacons.org. Deacon MICHAEL C. BERSTENE, Diocesan Dir., Deacon Personnel. Tel: 860-887-9294; Fax: 860-886-1670. Email: director@norwichdeacons.org; Mrs. LIZ MISAMORE, Sec. Tel: 860-887-9294, Ext. 265; Fax: 860-886-1670. Email: lizm@norwichdiocese.net.

Planned Giving Office— See Development, Diocesan Office of

Pontifical Association of the Holy Childhood—Rev. WILLIAM J. OLESIK, St. Mary Church, 34 N. Main St., Jewett City, 06351. Tel: 860-376-2044.

Pontifical Society for the Propagation of the Faith—Rev. WILLIAM J. OLESIK, Dir., St. Mary Church, 34 N. Main St., Jewett City, 06351. Tel: 860-376-2044.

Prison Ministry for Diocese of Norwich—Ms. SHEREE L. ANTOCH, Dir., Bishop Flanagan Ministry Center, 1595 Norwich-New London Tpke., Uncasville, 06382-1319. Tel: 860-848-2237, Ext. 212; Fax: 860-848-2816. Email: prison@norwichdiocese.net.

Brooklyn—

Brooklyn Correctional Institution—59 Hartford Rd., Brooklyn, 06234. Tel: 860-779-4568. Sr. PATRICIA COOK, R.S.M., Chap., Siena House, 100 Rte. 165, Preston, 06365-8417.

Niantic—

Gates Correctional Institution—131 N. Bridebrook Rd., Niantic, 06357. Tel: 860-691-4756. Deacon THOMAS J. CASEY, Chap.

York Correctional Institution—201 W. Main St., Niantic, 06357. Tel: 860-691-6544; 860-691-6673. Deacon DENNIS F. DOLAN, Chap.

Somers—

Northern Correctional Institution—287 Bilton Rd., Somers, 06071. Tel: 860-763-8686. Deacon ROBERT BERND, Chap., 159 Brainard Rd., Apt. 23, Enfield, 06082.

Osborn Correctional Institution—100 Bilton Rd., Somers, 06071. Tel: 860-749-8391, Ext. 5476. Deacon GERALD GERACI, Chap.

Willard-Cybulski Correctional Institution—391 Shaker Rd., Enfield, 06082. Tel: 860-763-6106. Deacon LEO B. CONRAD, Chap.

Storrs—

Bergin Correction Institution—251 Middle Tpke., Storrs Mansfield, 06268. Tel: 860-487-1724; Fax: 860-487-2737. Sr. MARY LYNN HEALY, R.S.M., Chap.

Uncasville—

Corrigan Correctional Institution—986 Norwich-New London Tpke., Uncasville, 06382. Tel: 860-848-5764. Sr. PATRICIA COOK, R.S.M., Chap., Siena House, 100 Rte. 165, Preston, 06365-8417.

Radgowski Correctional Institution—982 Norwich-New London Tpke., Uncasville, 06382. Tel: 860-848-5032. Chaplains: Sr. PATRICIA COOK, R.S.M., Siena House, 100 Rte. 165, Preston, 06365-8417; Deacon DENNIS DOLAN.

Commission for Human Life and Justice—Rev. JOSEPH B. WHITTEL, Vicar for Ministry, Bishop Flanagan Ministry Center, 1595 Norwich-New London Tpke., Uncasville, 06382-1319. Tel: 860-848-2237, Ext. 309; Fax: 860-848-2813. Email: jbwhittel@hotmail.com.

Project Northeast— A program of Evangelization for the unchurched poor. Rev. RICHARD L. ARCHAMBAULT, Dir., 81 Church St., Putnam, 06260-1809. Tel: 860-928-4078; 860-928-0105; Sr. ELEANOR BALDONI, D.H.S., Assoc. Dir., 22 Pearl Ave., Putnam, 06260-1625. Tel: 860-928-5965.

RCIA— See Evangelization & Catechumenate, Office of

Religious— See Delegate for Consecrated Life

Retirement—

Priests' Retirement Plan Board—Most Rev. MICHAEL RICHARD COTE, D.D.; Revs. DENNIS M. PERKINS; JOSEPH CASTALDI, J.C.L.; Mr. JAMES CRONIN; Rev. DENNIS G. CAREY; Mrs. ROSEMARY STREKEL; Mr. CHARLES HAYES.

Safe Environments, Office of—Bishop Flanagan Ministry Center, 1595 Norwich-New London Tpke., Uncasville, 06382. Tel: 860-848-2237. Rev. TED F. TUMICKI, S.T.L., J.C.L., Bishop's Delegate; Ms. SHEREE L. ANTOCH, Admin. Tel: 860-848-2237, Ext. 212; Mrs. JUDY PAPPAGALLO, Admin. Asst. Tel: 860-848-2237, Ext. 301.

School Office, Diocesan—43 Perkins Ave., Norwich, 06360-4480. Tel: 860-887-4086; Fax: 860-887-9371. Web: www.norwichdso.org. Dr. JOHN F. SHRINE, Ph.D., K.M., Supt. Email: superintendentdso@norwichdiocese.net; Sr. BARBARA GOULD, R.S.M., Asst. Supt. Email: asstsuperdso@norwichdiocese.net; Ms. LOIS PEGG, Sec. Email: secretarydso@norwichdiocese.net.

Diocesan School Technology Consultant—Ms. SHEILA CERJANEC, Technology Coord. Email: technologydso@norwichdiocese.net.

Board of Education—Most Rev. MICHAEL RICHARD COTE, D.D., Ex Officio; Rev. Msgr. THOMAS R. BRIDE, P.A., K.C.H.S., V.G.; Dr. JOHN F. SHRINE, Ph.D., K.M., Supt.; Mrs. ANN ALFIERO; Rev. Msgr. HENRY ARCHAMBAULT, P.A., J.C.D.; Mrs. SHARON BRIERE; Rev. Msgr. ROBERT BROWN; Mrs. MARILYN EBBITT; Mr. WILLIAM JUZWIC; Dr. ROBERT MILLER, Ph.D.; Mr. WILLIAM J. RUSSELL, CPA, D.F.O.; Mrs. MARIE TWOMEY.

Scouting— See Faith Events, Office of

Sick, Ministry to the—Sr. RITA JOHNSON, S.S.N.D., Dir., W.W. Backus Hospital, 326 Washington St., Norwich, 06360-2742. Tel: 860-889-8331; 860-886-6948. Res.: 7 Otis St., Norwich, 06360. Tel: 860-886-6948.

Soup Kitchen— See Community Ministries, Saint Vincent de Paul Place Email: svdpp@sbcglobal.net.

Spanish Speaking Apostolate— See Hispanic Ministry

Spiritual Renewal Services—Co-Directors: Rev. RAYMOND D. INTOVIGNE, Rectory: 1600 Main St., P.O. Box 250, Coventry, 06238-0250. Tel: 860-742-0681; Mrs. JUDITH HUGHES, Office, 11 Bath St., P.O. Box 6, Norwich, 06360-5836. Tel: 860-887-0702; 860-887-7667 Prayer Line; Fax: 860-859-1366. Email: srs1223@sbcglobal.net.

Victim Assistance Coordinator—Mrs. MARIE TWOMEY. Tel: 860-848-2237, Ext. 314.

Vocations—

Director of Vocations—Rev. GREGORY P. GALVIN, Res.: St. Thomas Aquinas, 46 N. Eagleville Rd., Storrs, 06268; Mrs. CHRISTINE SIART, Sec. to Rev. Gregory P. Galvin, 201 Broadway, Norwich, 06360-4328. Tel: 860-887-9294, Ext. 246. Res.: St. Thomas Aquinas, 46 N. Eagleville Rd., Storrs, 06268. Email: vocations@norwichdiocese.net; sec.voc@norwichdiocese.net.

Seminarian Advisory Board—Rev. GREGORY P. GALVIN; Very Rev. MICHAEL L. PHILLIPPINO; Revs. LESZEK T. JANIK, J.C.L.; KEVIN M. REILLY; MICHAEL C. GIANNITELLI; RICHARD RICARD.

CLERGY, PARISHES, MISSIONS AND PAROCHIAL SCHOOLS

CITY OF NORWICH

(NEW LONDON COUNTY)

1—ST. PATRICK CATHEDRAL (1879) Rev. Msgr. Anthony S. Rosaforte, Rector; Rev. P. Gregorz Jednaki. In Res., Rev. Joseph E. Nichols (Retired).

School—211 Broadway, 06360. Tel: 860-889-4174; Fax: 860-889-0040. Email: stpatrick.cath.sch@snet.net. Catherine Reed, Prin. Sisters of Charity of Our Lady, Mother of the Church 1; Lay Teachers 13; Students 193.

Catechesis/Religious Program—Agnes Carver, D.R.E. Students 172.

2—ST. JOSEPH (1904), (Polish), Rev. Tomasz Sztuber, Admin. In Res., Rev. Eugene L. Pilatowski (Retired); Deacon Thomas A. Lewis.

Res.: 120 Cliff St., 06360-5134. Tel: 860-887-1565; Fax: 860-889-3560.

School—Tel: 860-887-4565; Fax: 860-886-6468. Sr.

M. Rafael Allen, S.C.M.C., Prin. Sisters of Charity 2; Lay Teachers 15; Students 130.
Catechesis/Religious Program—Tel: 860-887-4565. Students 16.

3—ST. MARY (1845) Rev. Gerald S. Kirby; Sr. Francisca Candelaria, R.O.D.A., Pastoral Assoc. Hispanic Min. In Res., Rev. Robert B. Lynch, Pastor Emeritus (Retired).
Res.: 70 Central Ave., 06360-4794. Tel: 860-887-2565; Fax: 860-892-1692. Email: secretary@stmarys1845.org.
Catechesis/Religious Program—Students 16.

4—SS. PETER AND PAUL (1938) Revs. George J. Richards Jr.; Christopher Zmuda, Parochial Vicar.
Res.: 181 Elizabeth St., 06360-6199. Tel: 860-887-9857; Fax: 860-886-4728. Email: ssppnorwich@netscape.net.
Catechesis/Religious Program—Students 40.

5—SACRED HEART (Norwichtown) (1902) Rev. Michael J. Gill; Deacon Wayne Sinclair.
Res.: 52 W. Town St., Norwichtown, 06360-2296. Tel: 860-887-1030; Fax: 860-887-6550. Email: campal@sbcglobal.net.
Catechesis/Religious Program—Tel: 860-887-1715. Paula Wiencek, C.R.E. Students 81.
Mission—St. John 190 Fitchville Rd., Bozrah, New London Co. 06334.

OUTSIDE THE CITY OF NORWICH

ASHFORD, WINDHAM CO., ST. PHILIP THE APOSTLE (1921) [CEM 2], Yoked with St. Jude, Willington. Rev. Russell F. Kennedy, Admin.
Res.: 64 Pompey Hollow Rd., 06278-1540. Tel: 860-429-2860; Fax: 860-487-5703. Email: church7227@sbcglobal.net. Web: www.saintphilipsaintjude.org.
Catechesis/Religious Program—Tel: 860-429-1921; Fax: 860-487-5703. Laura Lankford, D.R.E. Students 151.

BALLOUVILLE, WINDHAM CO., ST. ANNE (1882) Closed. For inquiries for parish records contact St. Joseph, Dayville.

BALTIC, NEW LONDON CO., ST. MARY OF THE IMMACULATE CONCEPTION (1866) [CEM] Rev. Joseph Tito.
Res.: 70 W. Main St., 06330-1348. Tel: 860-822-6378; Fax: 860-822-6378.
School—St. Joseph, 10 School Hill Rd. Tel: 860-822-6141; Fax: 860-822-1479. Sr. Mary Patrick Mulready, S.C.M.C., Prin. Sisters of Charity of Our Lady, Mother of the Church 3; Lay Teachers 6; Students 100.
Catechesis/Religious Program—Students 80.

BOLTON, TOLLAND CO., ST. MAURICE (1954), Yoked with Sacred Heart, Vernon. Rev. Stanley J. Szczapa.
Res.: 32 Hebron Rd., 06043-7606. Tel: 860-643-4466; Fax: 860-643-4466. Email: stmauricechurch@sbcglobal.net. Web: www.stmauricekofc.org.
Catechesis/Religious Program—Tel: 860-643-8374. Email: stmaurice@aol.com. Mrs. Rella Bernabucci, D.R.E. Students 55.

BROOKLYN, WINDHAM CO., OUR LADY OF LA SALETTE (1968) Rev. Daniel J. Scott, M.S.
Res.: 21 Providence Rd., P.O. Box 211, 06234-0211. Tel: 860-774-6275; Fax: 860-774-0679. Email: ourlady@snet.net. Web: www.lasalette-lourdes.org.
Catechesis/Religious Program—Students 154.
Mission—Our Lady of Lourdes 41 Cedar Swamp Rd., Hampton, Windham Co. 06247.

CANTERBURY, WINDHAM CO., ST. AUGUSTINE (1978), Yoked with St. John the Apostle, Plainfield. Rev. Arul Rajan Peter, Admin.; Deacon Timothy M. Marshall.
Res.: 144 Westminster Rd., 06331-1417. Tel: 860-546-6074; Fax: 860-546-6074. Email: staugus@charter.net. Web: www.staugustine-canterbury.org.
Catechesis/Religious Program—Tel: 860-546-6225. Students 67.

CHESTER, MIDDLESEX CO., ST. JOSEPH (1885) [CEM] Rev. Robert Murphy, M.S.A.; Deacon Lawrence Moneypenny.
Res.: 48 Middlesex Ave., 06412-1309. Tel: 860-526-5495; Fax: 860-526-7880. Web: www.stjosephchester.parishesonline.com.
Catechesis/Religious Program—Tel: 860-526-2152. Students 232.

CLINTON, MIDDLESEX CO., ST. MARY OF THE VISITATION (1934) [CEM] Rev. Michael Sequeira; Deacon Paul Weber; Sr. Cecilia Quezada, R.O.D.A., Pastoral Assoc.
Res.: 54 Grove St., 06413-1999. Tel: 860-669-8512; Fax: 860-669-9052. Email: godsquad@snet.net. Web: www.stmarysclinton.com.
Catechesis/Religious Program—Tel: 860-669-7375. Email: reledof@snet.net. Andrea Tuthill, D.R.E. & Youth Min. Students 411.

COLCHESTER, NEW LONDON CO., ST. ANDREW (1860) [CEM 2] [JC 2] Revs. Michael C. Giannitelli; Martin J. Jones; Deacon Dennis Dolan.
Res.: 128 Norwich Ave., 06415-1269. Tel: 860-537-2355; Fax: 860-537-2356. Email: standrew.rectory@sbcglobal.net.
Catechesis/Religious Program—Tel: 860-537-5415. Email: standrewccd@sbcglobal.net. Students 659.

COLUMBIA, TOLLAND CO., ST. COLUMBA (1960) Rev. Daniel C. Cronin.
Res.: 328 Junction Rtes. 66 & 87, P.O. Box 146, 06237-0146. Tel: 860-228-3735; Fax: 860-228-8777. Email: sec.stcolumba@sbcglobal.net.
Catechesis/Religious Program—Tel: 860-228-3727. Students 149.

COVENTRY, TOLLAND CO., ST. MARY (1877) [CEM] Revs. Victor Chaker; Raymond D. Intovigne, Parochial Vicar.
Res.: 1600 Main St., P.O. Box 250, 06238-0250. Tel: 860-742-0681; Fax: 860-742-1318.
Catechesis/Religious Program—Tel: 860-742-1092. Students 388.
Mission—St. Joseph Eagleville, Tolland Co.

CROMWELL, MIDDLESEX CO., ST. JOHN (1882) Revs. Raymond Borkowski, O.F.M.Conv.; Mitchell Sawicki, O.F.M.Conv.
Res.: 5 St. John Ct., 06416-2118. Tel: 860-635-5590; Fax: 860-635-5591.
Catechesis/Religious Program—Tel: 860-635-5156. Email: faithformationsjc@sbcglobal.net. Web: www.saintjohn-cromwell.org. Students 422.

DANIELSON, WINDHAM CO., ST. JAMES (1869) [CEM] Revs. John J. O'Neill, M.S.; Thomas Sickler, M.S.; Deacon Rene N. Barbeau Jr. In Res., Revs. John E. Welch, M.S. (Retired); Joseph Whalen, M.S. (Retired).
Res.: 12 Franklin St., 06239. Tel: 860-774-3900; Fax: 860-774-4205.
School—Tel: 860-774-3281; Fax: 860-779-2137. Ms. Cheryl Veilleux, Prin. Lay Teachers 13; Students 215.
Catechesis/Religious Program—Tel: 860-774-8459. Students 200.
Mission—Our Lady of Peace

DAYVILLE, WINDHAM CO., ST. JOSEPH (1874) [CEM] Rev. Leon J. Susaimanickam, Admin.
Res.: 350 Hartford Pk., Box 487, 06241-2109. Tel: 860-774-8656; Fax: 860-774-8656.
Catechesis/Religious Program—Alyce Chartier, D.R.E.; Norma Pokoski, D.R.E. Students 100.

DURHAM, MIDDLESEX CO., NOTRE DAME (1955) Rev. Mariadas J. Lipton, Admin.; Deacon Ronald Blank.
Res.: 272 Main St., 06422-1611. Tel: 860-349-3058; Fax: 860-349-8949. Email: officendc@comcast.net. Web: www.churchofnotredame.org.
Catechesis/Religious Program—Email: drendc@comcast.net. Kum Cha Soja, D.R.E. Students 450.

EAST HAMPTON, MIDDLESEX CO., ST. PATRICK (1879), (Irish), [CEM] Rev. Walter M. Nagle; Sr. Dominic Joseph Valla, A.S.C.J., Pastoral Assoc. In Res., Rev. Dennis J. Mercieri.
Res.: 47 W. High St., P.O. Box 177, 06424-0177. Tel: 860-267-6644; Fax: 860-267-7807. Email: stpatrick47@sbcglobal.net. Web: www.stpatrickeh.org.
Catechesis/Religious Program—Students 524.

EAST LYME, NEW LONDON CO., ST. MATTHIAS (Flanders) (1939) Very Rev. Michael T. Donohue; Sr. M. Rita Clare, R.S.M.; Deacons Steven Reed; Gerald L. Shaw.
Church: 317 Chesterfield Rd., P.O. Box 25, 06333-0025. Tel: 860-739-5208; Fax: 860-739-0524.
Catechesis/Religious Program—Tel: 860-739-5208; Fax: 860-739-0524. Students 370.

ELLINGTON, TOLLAND CO., ST. LUKE (1961) Revs. Thomas Plathottam, C.S.T.; George Villamthanam, C.S.T.; Deacons Harry Grospitch; Frank Hann.
Rectory—141 Maple St., P.O. Box 246, 06029-0246. Tel: 860-875-8552; Fax: 860-872-6548. Email: stluke_ellington@comcast.net. Web: www.rc.net/norwich/stluke.
Church: 139 Maple St., 06029.
Catechesis/Religious Program—Tel: 860-875-4951. Email: stluke_dre@comcast.net. Mrs. Nancy Rudek, D.R.E.; Beth Dionne, Youth Min. Students 500.
Convent—St. Luke Convent, 8 Berr Ave., 06029-0246. Tel: 860-944-6921.

ESSEX, MIDDLESEX CO., OUR LADY OF SORROWS (1926) Rev. Paul J. Gaumond; Deacon William Kaiser Jr.
Res.: 14 Prospect St., 06426-1049. Tel: 860-767-1284; Fax: 860-767-7874. Web: www.oloschurch.com.
Catechesis/Religious Program—Tel: 860-767-1074. Students 325.

FISHERS ISLAND, SUFFOLK CO., OUR LADY OF GRACE (1902), (Irish), Rev. Wojciech Pelczarski, S.D.S.
Res.: Alpine Ave., Box 425, NY 06390-0425. Tel: 631-788-7353; Fax: 631-788-7312. Email: olog@fishersisland.net.
Catechesis/Religious Program—Students 11.

GALES FERRY, NEW LONDON CO., OUR LADY OF LOURDES (1960) Rev. Joseph F. DeCosta; Deacon R. Philip Hayes.
Res.: 1650 Rte. 12, 06335-1534. Tel: 860-464-7251; Fax: 860-464-7252. Email: frjoe@ololgf.org. Web: www.ololgf.org.
Catechesis/Religious Program—Tel: 860-464-6676. Email: ffo@ololgf.org. Monika de Andrade, C.R.E. Students 255.

GROTON, NEW LONDON CO.

1—ST. MARY MOTHER OF THE REDEEMER (1964) Rev. Grzegorz P. Brozonowicz; Deacons Peter H. Danesi III; Paul Wallen; Douglas A. Hoffman.
Res.: 69 Groton Long Point Rd., 06340. Tel: 860-445-1446; Fax: 860-448-7269. Email: st.marys.top@comcast.net. Web: stmarymr.catholicweb.com.
Catechesis/Religious Program—Tel: 860-448-0529. Mrs. Barbara Simoncini, D.R.E.; Mrs. Theresa Seals, D.R.E. Students 324.

2—SACRED HEART (1905) Rev. Dariusz Dudzik.
Res.: 56 Sacred Heart Dr., 06340-4431. Tel: 860-445-2905; 860-445-6648; Fax: 860-445-6648. Web: www.sacredheartgroton.org.
School—Sacred Heart School, (Grades PreK-8), 50 Sacred Heart Dr., 06340-4431. Tel: 460-445-0611; Fax: 860-448-4999. Soraya Betancourt-Calle, Prin. Lay Teachers 16; Aides 6; Students 214.
Catechesis/Religious Program—Tel: 860-445-2905, Ext. 12. Students 77.

HEBRON, TOLLAND CO., THE CHURCH OF THE HOLY FAMILY (1987) Rev. Michael S. Smith; Deacon Thomas J. Casey.
Mailing Address: P.O. Box 146, 06248-0146. Tel: 860-228-0096; Fax: 860-228-1629.
Catechesis/Religious Program—Tel: 860-228-0096, Ext. 3. Mrs. Rachel Casey, D.R.E. Students 693.

HIGGANUM, MIDDLESEX CO., ST. PETER (1958) Revs. Jan Swiderski; George Mattathilanickal.
Res.: 30 St. Peter Ln., P.O. Box 707, 06441-0707. Tel: 860-345-8018; Fax: 860-345-4067.
Catechesis/Religious Program—Tel: 860-345-4726. Students 168.

JEWETT CITY, NEW LONDON CO., ST. MARY (1870), (Polish), [CEM 2] Rev. William Olesik; Deacons Paul R. Baillargeon; Anthony Dombrowski.
Res.: 34 N. Main St., 06351-2012. Tel: 860-376-2044; Fax: 860-376-5771. Email: stmary.church@snet.net. Web: www.stmaryjc.4lpi.com.
School—54 N. Main St., 06351. Tel: 860-376-0446; Fax: 860-376-4200. Richard B. Woodworth, Prin. Lay Teachers 10; Students 51.
Catechesis/Religious Program—Fax: 860-376-5771. Email: psrstmary@hotmail.com. Students 201.

KILLINGWORTH, MIDDLESEX CO., ST. LAWRENCE (1978) Revs. Jan Swiderski; George Mattathilanickal; Deacons John A. Balchus; Robert Ferraro.
Res.: 7 Hemlock Dr., 06419-2227. Tel: 860-663-2576; Fax: 860-663-4238. Email: stlawrencec@yahoo.com. Web: www.stlawrencechurch.com.
Catechesis/Religious Program—Tel: 860-663-2943. Students 311.

LEBANON, NEW LONDON CO., ST. FRANCIS OF ASSISI (1945) Rev. Robert F. Buongirno; Deacon Michael L. Puscas.
Res.: 67 W. Town St., 06249. Tel: 860-642-6711; Fax: 860-642-4032. Email: stfrancisassisi@catholic.org.
Catechesis/Religious Program—M. James Hay, D.R.E.; Mrs. Joann Hay, C.R.E. Students 231.

MIDDLEFIELD, MIDDLESEX CO., ST. COLMAN (1890) Rev. Anthony J. DiMarco, Admin.; Deacon Peter L. Gill.
Res.: 145 Hubbard St., P.O. Box 457, 06455-0457. Tel: 860-349-3868; Fax: 860-349-3150.
Catechesis/Religious Program—Tel: 860-347-1725. Ms. Barbara-Jean DiMauro, D.R.E. Students 180.

MIDDLETOWN, MIDDLESEX CO.

1—ST. FRANCIS OF ASSISI (1903) Rev. Halbert Weidner, C.O.
Res.: 10 Elm St., 06457-4426. Tel: 860-347-4684; Fax: 860-347-7669. Email: stfrancis10elm@snet.net. Web: saintfrancisofassisi.com.
Catechesis/Religious Program—Tel: 860-347-4684, Ext. 18. Students 63.

2—ST. JOHN (1843) [CEM] Very Rev. Michael L. Phillippino; Deacon John Hancock.
Res.: 19 John's Sq., 06457-2201. Tel: 860-347-5626; Fax: 860-638-3633. Web: www.saintjohnchurchmiddletown.com.
School—Tel: 860-347-3202; Fax: 860-347-3537. Email: kathleenoking@comcast.net. Kathleen King, Prin. Lay Teachers 19; Students 165.
Catechesis/Religious Program—Lynellan Willard, D.R.E. Students 53.

3—ST. MARY OF CZESTOCHOWA (1903), (Polish), [CEM] Rev. Marek Masnicki.
Res.: 79 S. Main St., 06457-3606. Tel: 860-347-2365; Fax: 860-347-2110. Email: stmarymdtln@yahoo.com.
School—87 S. Main St., 06457. Tel: 860-347-2978; Fax: 860-347-7267. Web: www.stmarymiddletown-.com. Mrs. Kathleen Dutil, Prin. Lay Teachers 10; Students 226.

Catechesis/Religious Program—Email: stmaryccd@yahoo.com. Susan Ferriaolo, D.R.E. Students 150.

4—ST. PIUS X (1957) Revs. Gerard Mulvey, O.F.M-.Cap.; Samuel Fuller, O.F.M.Cap.; Bro. Eugene Sheehan, O.F.M.Cap. In Res., Revs. Bruce Quinn, O.F.M.Cap. (Retired); Ephrem Karwowski, O.F.M.Cap.
Res.: 310 Westfield St., 06457-2047. Tel: 860-347-4441; 860-347-4442; Fax: 860-347-3001. Email: stpiusfriars@snet.net. Web: www.stpius-x.org.
Catechesis/Religious Program—Tel: 860-346-9100. Carol Butler, C.R.E. (6th); Kimberly Molski, C.R.E. (PreK-5th). Students 522.

5—ST. SEBASTIAN (1930), (Italian), [CEM] Rev. James Thaikoottathil, Admin.
Res.: 155 Washington St., 06457-2800. Tel: 860-347-2638; Fax: 860-347-6736 (Office). Email: church6892@att.net. Web: stsebastianct.org.
Catechesis/Religious Program—Students 177.

MONTVILLE, NEW LONDON CO., ST. JOHN THE EVANGELIST (1881) [CEM] Rev. Stephen S. Gulino; Deacon Melvin Nygaard. In Res., Rev. Msgr. Robert L. Brown, Chancellor. Tel: 860-887-9294 (Chancery); 860-848-3771 (Private); Cell: 860-303-6080.
Res.: 22 Maple Ave., Uncasville, 06382-2327. Tel: 860-848-1257; Fax: 860-848-1258. Email: stjhh@sbcglobal.net. Web: www.stjohnsuncasville.com.
Catechesis/Religious Program—Tel: 860-848-1409; Fax: 860-848-1258. Sara Waters, D.R.E. Students 203.

MOODUS, MIDDLESEX CO., ST. BRIDGET OF KILDARE (1914) [CEM] Very Rev. Gregoire J. Fluet.
Res.: 75 Moodus-Leesville Rd., P.O. Box 422, 06469-0422. Tel: 860-873-8623; Fax: 860-873-9407.
Catechesis/Religious Program—Students 344.

MOOSUP, WINDHAM CO., ALL-HALLOWS (1859) [CEM], Yoked with Sacred Heart, Wauregan. Rev. Damian Tomiczek, S.D.S.
Res.: 130 Prospect St., 06354-1499. Tel: 860-564-2668; Fax: 860-564-3941. Email: ahcmoosup@yahoo.com. Web: www.ahcmoosup.com.
Catechesis/Religious Program—Tel: 860-230-0141. Lisa Krauss, D.R.E. (Grades 1-5). Students 106.
Mission—St. Joseph

MYSTIC, NEW LONDON CO., ST. PATRICK (1870) [CEM] Rev. Brian J. Romanowski.
Res.: 32 E. Main St., P.O. Box 236, 06355-0236. Tel: 860-536-1800; Fax: 860-572-1513. Email: stpatrick@snet.net.
Catechesis/Religious Program—Tel: 860-536-6808; Fax: 860-572-1513. Susan Waters, D.R.E. & Youth Min. Students 163.

NEW LONDON, NEW LONDON CO.

1—ST. JOSEPH (1907) Revs. Joseph Castaldi; Prodeep Chandra Nayak; Texie Dissanayake; Deacon Gerard Gaynor Jr.
Res.: 17 Squire St., 06320-4891. Tel: 860-443-5393; Fax: 860-443-0113.
School—Tel: 860-442-1720; Fax: 860-443-5247. Lay Teachers 10; Students 208.
Catechesis/Religious Program—Students 200.

2—ST. MARY, STAR OF THE SEA (1870), (Spanish), Rev. Robert Washabaugh; Deacons Jesus A. Diez Canseco; Mariano Ramos; Sr. Rosa Maria Campos, R.O.D.A., Pastoral Assoc. Tel: 860-443-5870; Deborah McCann-Connors, Pastoral Assoc. The Oblate Sisters to Divine Love; Missionary Sisters of the Divine Word.
Res.: 10 Huntington St., 06320-6198. Tel: 860-447-1431; Fax: 860-437-1889. Email: information@stmarynewlondon.net. Web: www.stmarynl.org.
School—(1879) 16 Huntington St., 06320. Tel: 860-443-7758; Fax: 860-444-2465. Web: www.stmary-schoolnewlondon.com. Regina Ferrante, Prin. Priests 1; Lay Teachers 9; Students 119.
Catechesis/Religious Program—Tel: 860-447-1431; Fax: 860-437-1889. Ms. Alvania Hilario, Rel. Educ. Sec. Students 124.

NIANTIC, NEW LONDON CO., ST. AGNES (1922) [JC] Revs. Mark D. O'Donnell; Tomasz Albrecht, Parochial Vicar; Deacons Maurice J. Walsh; James Delaney.
Res.: 22 Haigh Ave., 06357-3129. Tel: 860-739-9722; Fax: 860-691-2187. Email: saintagnesparish@sbcglobal.net. Web: www.saintagnescatholicchurch.com.
Catechesis/Religious Program—Tel: 860-739-9992. Email: dre.st.agnes@sbcglobal.net. Lorraine Morrone, D.R.E. Students 198.
Chapel—Crescent Beach, St. Francis Chapel (Summer) [JC]

NORTH GROSVENORDALE, WINDHAM CO., ST. JOSEPH (1872) [CEM], Yoked with St. Stephen, Quinebaug. Very Rev. Charles R. LeBlanc; Rev. Richard D. Breton.
Res.: 12 Main St., P.O. Box 897, 06255-0897. Tel: 860-923-2361; Fax: 860-923-3396. Email: stjoseph18@sbcglobal.net. Web: stjoseph-sacred.net.
School—26 Main St., P.O. Box 137, 06255-0897. Tel: 860-923-2090; Fax: 860-923-3609. Mrs. Sharon Briere, Prin. Lay Teachers 13; Students 108.
Catechesis/Religious Program—Tel: 860-923-0155. Students 200.
Mission—Sacred Heart

NORTH STONINGTON, NEW LONDON CO., ST. THOMAS MORE (1967) Rev. V. Antony Alaharasan.
Res.: 87 Mystic Rd., 06359. Tel: 860-535-1601; Fax: 860-535-2828. Email: smchurch01@snet.net.
Catechesis/Religious Program—Fax: 860-535-2828. Michael Lloyd, Dir. Faith Formation. Students 116.

OAKDALE, NEW LONDON CO., OUR LADY OF THE LAKES (1966) Rev. Tadeusz Zadorozny (Poland) (Nor); Deacon William T. Herrmann. In Res., Rev. Kevin M. Reilly.
Res.: 752 Norwich-Salem Tpke., 06370. Tel: 860-859-1575; Fax: 860-859-3273. Email: our.lady@snet.net. Web: ourladyofthelakes-oakdale.e-paluch.com.
Catechesis/Religious Program—Tel: 860-859-8733. Email: faith.formation@att.net. Students 189.

OCCUM, NEW LONDON CO., ST. JOSEPH (1878) Rev. Ted F. Tumicki; Deacon Lawrence E. Hill.
Res.: 11 Baltic Rd., 06360. Tel: 860-822-8020; Fax: 860-822-8007.
Catechesis/Religious Program—Tel: 860-822-6963. Mrs. Monica Bernier, D.R.E. Students 90.
Saint Society Church— (Corporate Title: St. Joseph Church Society of Occum, CT, Inc.)

OLD LYME, NEW LONDON CO., CHRIST THE KING (1934) Rev. Msgr. Thomas R. Bride; Deacon Julius Periera. In Res., Rev. Thomas W. Ahern (Retired).
Office: 1 McCurdy Rd., 06371-1629. Tel: 860-434-1660 (Rectory); 860-434-1669 (Office); Fax: 860-434-7140. Web: christthekingchurch.net.
Catechesis/Religious Program—Tel: 860-434-9873. Louise Young, D.R.E. Students 103.

OLD SAYBROOK, MIDDLESEX CO., ST. JOHN (1884) [CEM] Revs. Joseph C. Ashe; Joseph Kaipayil, M.C.B.S.; Deacon Joseph Giuliano.
Res.: 161 Main St., 06475-2367. Tel: 860-388-3787; Fax: 860-388-6008. Web: www.stjohnchurchos.com.
School—42 Maynard Rd., 06475. Tel: 860-388-0849; Fax: 860-388-6265. Web: stjohnschoolos.org. Sr. M. Martin, S.C.M.C., Prin. Sisters 2; Lay Teachers 15; Students 243.
Catechesis/Religious Program—Sherri Potter, D.R.E. Students 362.

PAWCATUCK, NEW LONDON CO., ST. MICHAEL (1861) [CEM 2] Rev. Dennis M. Perkins.
Res.: 60 Liberty St., 06379. Tel: 860-599-5580; Fax: 860-599-8079. Email: saint.michael@sbcglobal.net.
School—Tel: 860-599-1084; Fax: 860-599-2817. Doris S. Messina, Prin. Lay Teachers 9; Students 171.
Catechesis/Religious Program—Mrs. Crystal F. Wilcox, D.R.E. Students 296.

PLAINFIELD, WINDHAM CO., ST. JOHN THE APOSTLE (1907) [CEM], Yoked with St. Augustine, Canterbury. Rev. Arul Rajan Peter, Admin.; Deacon Leo N. Bernard.
Res.: 10 Railroad Ave., 06374-1215. Tel: 860-564-3313; Fax: 860-564-3314. Email: stjohnplainfield@ct.metrocast.net.
Catechesis/Religious Program—12 Railroad Ave., 06374. Tel: 860-564-8380. Students 100.

POMFRET, WINDHAM CO., MOST HOLY TRINITY (1886) Rev. Richard Sliwinski, S.D.B.; Deacon Jorge Escalona.
Res.: 568 Pomfret St., P.O. Box 235, 06258-0235. Tel: 860-928-5830; Fax: 860-928-4035. Email: mhtoffice@sbcglobal.net. Web: www.mostholytrinitypomfret.parishesonline.com.
Catechesis/Religious Program—Email: tcalabrese@jwu.edu. Students 209.

PORTLAND, MIDDLESEX CO., ST. MARY (1872) [CEM] Rev. John F. Ashe; Sisters Mary Ida Dolan, R.S.M., Pastoral Assoc.; Laura Marie Meskill, R.S.M., Pastoral Assoc.; Deacon Dana Garry.
Res.: 51 Freestone Ave., 06480. Tel: 860-342-2328; Fax: 860-342-1433. Email: st.mary.rectory@sbcglobal.net.
Catechesis/Religious Program—Tel: 860-342-2308. Students 444.

PRESTON, NEW LONDON CO., ST. CATHERINE OF SIENA (1975) Rev. Joseph Chacko, Admin.; Mrs. Nancy Mignault, Pastoral Assoc.
Res.: 243 Rte. 164, 06365-8726. Tel: 860-887-9966; Fax: 860-889-7640.
Catechesis/Religious Program—Students 142.

PUTNAM, WINDHAM CO., ST. MARY CHURCH OF THE VISITATION (1866) [CEM] Rev. Roland C. Cloutier; Deacon Pierre M. Desilets.
Res.: 218 Providence St., 06260-1514. Tel: 860-928-6535; Fax: 860-928-7246. Email: stmarychurchputnam@snet.net. Web: www.stmaryputnam.org.
School—23 Marshall St., 06260. Tel: 860-928-7046; 860-928-3847; Fax: 860-928-9379. Email: info@smsputnam.org. Web: www.smsputnam.com. Mr. Steven Guilbault, Prin.
Catechesis/Religious Program—15 Marshall St., 06260. Tel: 860-928-2032. Mrs. Carol Paul, Dir. Faith Formation. Students 125.

QUAKER HILL, NEW LONDON CO., OUR LADY OF PERPETUAL HELP (1904), (Polish), Rev. Joseph B. Whittel; Deacon Ronald S. Kitlinski.
Res.: 63 Old Norwich Rd., P.O. Box 329, 06375-0329. Tel: 860-443-1875; Fax: 860-437-9869. Web: ourladyph.org.
Catechesis/Religious Program—59 Old Norwich Rd., 06375. Tel: 860-447-3550. Sr. Michelle Sokol, S.S.J.-T.O.S.F., D.R.E. Students 67.
Convent—Sisters of St. Joseph of Third Order of St. Francis, 59 Old Norwich Rd., P.O. Box 329, 06375. Tel: 860-447-3550.

QUINEBAUG, WINDHAM CO., ST. STEPHEN (1955), Yoked with St. Joseph, North Grosvenordale. Very Rev. Charles R. LeBlanc.
Res.: 130 Old Turnpike Rd., P.O. Box 222, 06262-0222. Tel: 860-935-5205; Fax: 860-497-0027. Email: ststephenquinebaug@charter.net.
Catechesis/Religious Program—Students 46.

ROCKVILLE, TOLLAND CO.

1—ST. BERNARD (1854) [CEM] Revs. Richard J. Ricard; Karl Christopher Schuh; Deacons Michael Berstene; Alexander Saunders, (Retired).
Res.: 25 St. Bernard Ter., 06066-3217. Tel: 860-875-0753; Fax: 860-871-7460. Email: rectory@saintbernardchurch.org. Web: www.saintbernardchurch.org.
School—20 School St., P.O. Box 177, 06066. Tel: 860-875-0475; Fax: 860-872-2444. Mrs. Ann Aulerich, Prin. Sisters 1; Lay Teachers 14; Students 66.
Catechesis/Religious Program—22 School St., 06066. Tel: 860-875-3828. Email: kmarganella@snet.net. Kimberly Manganella, D.R.E. Students 325.
Cemetery Office—Tel: 860-872-6601.

2—ST. JOSEPH (1905), (Polish), Revs. Krysztof Wieliczko, O.S.P.P.E.; Gabriel Suleimanovs, O.S.P.P.E., Parochial Vicar; Deacon Benjamin Cortese.
Res.: 33 West St., 06066-6154. Tel: 860-871-1970; Fax: 860-872-0333. Email: sjcrockville@hotmail.com. Web: www.rc.net/norwich/st_joseph/.
School—41 West St., 06066. Tel: 860-875-4943; Fax: 860-870-4532. Email: sjro@norwichdiocesecs.org. Mrs. Lucia Trudeau, Prin. Lay Teachers 11; Students 155.
Catechesis/Religious Program—Students 124.

ROGERS, WINDHAM CO., ST. IGNATIUS (1939) Closed. For inquiries for parish records contact St. Joseph, Dayville.

SOMERSVILLE, TOLLAND CO., ALL SAINTS (1915) Rev. David P. Choquette; Deacons James J. Burgess; Walter B. Williams; John J. Abdalla.
Res.: 25 School St., P.O. Box M, 06072-0913. Tel: 860-749-8625; Fax: 860-763-1890. Email: alstchurch@yahoo.com. Web: www.somersallsaints.org.
Catechesis/Religious Program—Tel: 860-763-0348. Sandy E. Russo, D.R.E. Students 453.

STAFFORD SPRINGS, TOLLAND CO., ST. EDWARD (1869) [CEM] Revs. Richard-Jacob Forcier, O.F.M.Conv.; Jude Surowiec, O.F.M.Conv.; David Kashen, O.F.M-.Conv.
Mailing Address: 6 Benton St., 06076-0433. Tel: 860-684-2705; Fax: 860-684-0757. Email: stedwardparish@stedward-stafford.org. Web: www.stedward-stafford.org.
Res.: 55 High St., 06076.
School—(Grades PreK-8), 25 Church St., 06076. Tel: 860-684-2600; Fax: 860-684-4030. Maryanne Pelletier, Prin. Lay Teachers 10; Students 123.
Catechesis/Religious Program—Students 279.
Mission—St. Joseph, (Summer Chapel), 6 Benton St., Tolland Co. 06076.

STONINGTON, NEW LONDON CO., ST. MARY (1850) [CEM] Rev. Msgr. Richard P. LaRocque.
Res.: 95 Main St., 06378-1219. Tel: 860-535-1700; Fax: 860-535-3433.
Catechesis/Religious Program—Tel: 860-535-4252. Matthew West, D.R.E. Students 137.

STORRS, TOLLAND CO., ST. THOMAS AQUINAS (1947) Revs. Gregory C. Mullaney; John N. Antonelle, Parochial Vicar; Jane Froglay, Music Dir.; Joanne Cichocki, Business Mgr. In Res., Rev. Gregory P. Galvin.
Res.: 46 N. Eagleville Rd., Storrs Mansfield, 06268. Tel: 860-429-6436.
Catechesis/Religious Program—Tel: 860-429-6436; Fax: 860-429-2809. Email: reled.sta@charterinternet.com. Elizabeth Ashe, D.R.E. Students 120.

TAFTVILLE, NEW LONDON CO., SACRED HEART (1883) Rev. Msgr. Henry N. Archambault. In Res., Rev. William J. Flynn (Retired).
Res.: 156 Providence St., P.O. Box 208, 06380. Tel: 860-887-3072; Fax: 860-204-9338. Email: sacred.heart@sbcglobal.net.
School—15 Hunters Ave., 06380-0208. Tel: 860-887-1757; Fax: 860-889-7276. Email: principal.shta@norwichdioceseos.org. Web: www.sacredhearttaftville.org. Sr. David Riguier, S.C.M.C., Prin. Sisters of Charity of Our Lady, Mother of the Church 3; Lay Teachers 11; Students 188.
Catechesis/Religious Program—Tel: 860-887-3072. Students 60.

TOLLAND, TOLLAND CO., ST. MATTHEW (1964) Very Rev. James P. Carini; Rev. James Sucholet; Deacon Ronald Freedman.
Mailing Address: P.O. Box 100, 06084-0100. Tel: 860-872-0200; Fax: 860-875-4413. Email: parishoffice@stmatthewct.org. Web: www.stmatthewct.org.
Catechesis/Religious Program—Email: faithformation@stmatthewct.org. Mrs. Cynthia Yaconiello, D.R.E. (Grades K-6); Mrs. Heidi Kay, Youth Min. (Grades 7-12); Mrs. Ann Marie Galdau, Dir. (Preschool). Students 798.

VERNON, TOLLAND CO., SACRED HEART (1958) [JC], Yoked with St. Maurice, Bolton. Rev. Stanley J. Szczapa; Mrs. Rella Bernabucci, Pastoral Asst.; Ernest Golnik, Liturgy and Music Dir.; Deacon Lawrence W. Deraleau.
Church: 550 Hartford Tpke., 06066-5000. Tel: 860-875-4563; Fax: 860-872-2535. Email: info@sacredheartchurch.net. Web: www.sacredheartchurch.net.
Catechesis/Religious Program—Students 113.

VOLUNTOWN, NEW LONDON CO., ST. THOMAS THE APOSTLE (1892) [CEM] [JC] Rev. Augustine Naduvilekoot.
Res.: 61 Preston City Rd., P.O. Box 99, 06384-0099. Tel: 860-376-2293; Fax: 860-376-0287. Web: www.stthomasvoluntown.org.
Catechesis/Religious Program—49 Preston City Rd., 06384. Tel: 860-376-8352. Cathy Becotte, D.R.E. Tel: 860-376-8665. Students 39.
Mission—St. Anne (1891) Rte. 201, Glasgo, New London Co.

WATERFORD, NEW LONDON CO., ST. PAUL (1960) Rev. Dennis G. Carey; Deacon Richard K. Walker.
Res.: 170 Rope Ferry Rd., 06385-2609. Tel: 860-443-5587; Fax: 860-442-9308. Email: stpaulwtfd@sbcglobal.net.
Catechesis/Religious Program—Tel: 860-443-3375. Mrs. Roseann Ward, C.R.E. Students 242.

WAUREGAN, WINDHAM CO., SACRED HEART (1889), (French), [CEM], Yoked with All Hallows, Moosup. Rev. Damian Tomiczek, S.D.S.
Res.: 620 Wauregan Rd., P.O. Box 468, 06387-0468. Tel: 860-564-2668; Fax: 860-564-3941. Email: shcbulletinnews@hotmail.com.
Catechesis/Religious Program—120 Prospect St., Moosup, 06354.

WEST WILLINGTON, TOLLAND CO., ST. JUDE (1981), Yoked with St. Philip, Ashford. Rev. Russell F. Kennedy, Admin.; Deacon Christopher Deskus.
Res.: 25 Old Farms Rd., P.O. Box 240, Willington, 06279-0240. Tel: 860-429-9655; Fax: 860-429-9655. Email: church7227@scbglobal.net. Web: www.saintphilipsaintjude.org.
Catechesis/Religious Program—Tel: 860-429-8604. Students 80.

WESTBROOK, MIDDLESEX CO., ST. MARK (1962) Rev. Peter B. Liszewski; Deacon Thomas E. Rymut.
Res.: 222 McVeagh Rd., 06498-1512. Tel: 860-399-9207; Fax: 860-399-7751.
Catechesis/Religious Program—Tel: 860-399-6208. Students 244.

WILLIMANTIC, WINDHAM CO.
1—ST. JOSEPH (1859) [CEM] Revs. Leszek T. Janik; Benjamin V. Soosaimanickam; Deacon Lawrence Goodwin.
Res.: 99 Jackson St., 06226-3077. Tel: 860-423-8439; Fax: 860-423-6825. Email: stjosephwilli@yahoo.com. Web: stjosephwilli.com.
School—St. Mary-St. Joseph, 35 Valley St., 06226. Tel: 860-423-8479; Fax: 860-423-8365. Sr. Elaine Moorcroft, Prin.
Catechesis/Religious Program—Students 230.
Convent—88 Jackson St., 06226. Tel: 203-423-5122.
Mission—St. Margaret Rte. 14, Scotland, Windham Co. 06264. Tel: 203-423-1791.
2—ST. MARY (1903), (French), Rev. Roger J. Lamoureux, O.M.I. In Res., Rev. Edward C. Poulin (Retired).
Res. & Parish Center: 80 Maple Ave., 06226-2733. Tel: 860-423-5835; Fax: 860-423-9933. Email: stmary06226@charter.net. Web: stmarywillimantic.4lpi.com.
Church: 46 Valley St., 06226-2733.
School—St. Mary-St. Joseph, 35 Valley St., 06226. Tel: 860-423-8479; Fax: 860-423-8365. Email: smsj@charterinternet.com. Web: www.smsjschool.org. Sr. M. Elaine Moorcraft, S.C.M.C., Prin. Sisters 2; Lay Teachers 15; Students 147.
Catechesis/Religious Program—Tel: 860-423-9700. Students 63.
Convent—Sisters of Charity of Our Lady, 88 Jackson St., 06226. Tel: 860-423-5122.
Faith Formulation—Tel: 860-423-9700.

WINDHAM, WINDHAM CO., SAGRADO CORAZON DE JESUS (1991), (Hispanic), Rev. Paul J. Murdock; Sr. Francisca Candelaria, R.O.D.A., Pastoral Assoc.; Deacon Felipe Silva; Virginia Rodriguez, Pastoral Assoc.
Mailing Address: 61 Club Rd., 06280-1007. Tel: 860-423-8617; Fax: 860-423-4157. Email: sagradocor@sbcglobal.net.
Catechesis/Religious Program—Students 104.

Chaplains of Public Institutions

NORWICH. *William W. Backus Hospital* 06360. Tel: 860-889-8331. Sr. Rita Johnson, S.S.N.D., Chaplaincy Svcs.

GROTON. *U.S. Submarine Base-New London* 06349-5013. Tel: 860-694-3232. Rev. Joseph Koch, Chap., C.H.C., U.S.N.

MIDDLETOWN. *Connecticut Valley Hospital*, Eastern Dr., P.O. Box 351, 06457. Tel: 860-262-5900; Fax: 860-262-5900. Deacon Peter L. Gill, Chap.
Middlesex Memorial Hospital, 28 Crescent St., 06457-0822. Tel: 860-347-9471, Ext. 6725. Rev. Dennis J. Mercieri, Chap.

NEW LONDON. *Lawrence and Memorial Hospitals*, Montauk Ave., 06320. Tel: 860-442-0711, Ext. 2609. Deacon William H. McGann.
U.S. Coast Guard Memorial Chapel, U.S. Coast Guard Academy, 15 Mohegan Ave., 06320-4195. Tel: 860-444-8482; Fax: 960-701-6729. Rev. Daniel Mode, Lieutenant, L.C.D.R., C.H.C., U.S.N.

On Duty Outside the Diocese:
Rev. Msgr.—
Randall, Kevin S., 3339 Massachusetts Ave., N.W., Washington, DC 20008-3687.
Revs.—
Angelo, Thomas M.
Boudreau, C. Paul
Caiazzo, Nicholas
Gwudz, John S.
Maltese, James L., Parish of Saints Philip and James, 1 Carow Pl, St. James, NY 11780.
Martin, Patrick A., P.O. Box 16, Stafford Springs, 06076.
Smith, Thomas J., St. Joseph, 242 Wall St., Kingston, NY 12401-3838.

Military Chaplains:
Rev.—
Angelo, Thomas M., Ch. Capt., 23 Wg/MC, Pope AFB, NC 28308.

Absent on Leave:
Revs.—
Bolieau, Henry G.
Dempsey, Edward M., 75 Bushnell St., Hartford, 06114.
Valliere, Timothy C.

Retired:
Rev. Msgrs.—
Malanowski, Thaddeus F., 908 S. Prospect Ave., Clearwater, FL 34616.
West, Willis W.
Revs.—
Ahern, Thomas W.
Almendra, Leoncio T., St. Catherine of Sienna, 18115 Sherman Way, Reseda, CA 91335.
Archer, Arthur
Cronin, Robert W., 11 Middlefield Dr., West Hartford, 06107.
Davis, Edward J., 179 Train St., Dorchester, MA 02122. Tel: 617-282-0479
Drummond, Elsyn J.
Flint, Kenneth, P.O. Box 399, Mystic, 06355.
Flynn, William J.
Giaquinto, Albert C., Theological College, 401 Michigan Ave., N.E., Washington, DC 20064.
Gruber, Anthony P.
Klein, Theodore J., Ph.D., 140 Greemanville Ave., Apt. 2, Mystic, 06355.
Konopka, Edward M.
Kuzdal, Anthony P., 22 Moulton Ct., Willimantic, 06226.
LeCours, Sylva P., 40 Hartford Pike, Dayville, 06241.
Liszewski, Francis A.
Lynch, Robert B.
Marciniak, John, 70 W. 18th Rd., Broad Channel, NY 11693.
McGrail, Charles A., 468 Main St., Apt. 218, Niantic, 06357.
McNulty, Robert E., 65 Beach St., P.O. Box 356, Green Harbor, MA 02041.
McNulty, William J., 66 Brown St., Hamden, 06518.
Nichols, Joseph E., Cathedral of St. Patrick, 213 Broadway, 06360.
Pilatowski, Eugene L., St. Joseph Church, 120 Cliff St., 06360-5198.
Poulin, Edward C., S.M., 13 Blissville Rd., Lisbon, 06351. Tel: 860-887-3689
Pupsys, Adam, 89 Mill Rock Rd., E., Old Saybrook, 06475.
Ramen, Paul F., 350 Pond Hill Rd., Moosup, 06354. Tel: 860-887-2565
Smilga, Zenon, Matulaitis Nursing Home, 10 Thurber Rd., #2, Putnam, 06260-2522.
Vaillancourt, Raymond, M.S.
Wisneski, Edward, S.T.D., Ph.D., 78 E. Ridge Rd., Middletown, 06457.

Permanent Deacons:
Abdalla, John, (Retired)
Bachand, Francis J., (Retired)
Baillargeon, Paul R., St. Mary, Jewett City
Balchus, John A., St. Lawrence, Killingworth
Barbeau, Rene N., Jr., St. James, Danielson
Barlow, Robert C., St. Andrew, Colchester
Bernard, Leo N., (Retired)
Berstene, Michael C., Diocesan Dir. of Deacon Personnel, St. Bernard, Rockville
Blank, Ronald E., Notre Dame, Durham
Burgess, James J., All Saints, Somersville
Burke, John J., Jr., Flat Rock, NC
Cannata, Nicholas J., (Retired)
Cartier, L. Roger, Pinellas Park, FL
Casey, Thomas J., Church of the Holy Family, Hebron
Cortese, Benjamin, St. Joseph, Rockville
Cote, Albert J., (Retired)
Cyr, Warren, Prison Ministry, Niantic
Danesi, Peter H., III, St. Mary, Groton
Delaney, James, St. Agnes, Niantic
Deraleau, Lawrence W., Sacred Heart, Vernon
Desilets, Pierre M., St. Mary, Putnam
Deskus, Christopher, St. Juse, Willington
Diez Conseco, Jesus A., St. Mary, Hispanic Apostolate, New London
Dolan, Dennis F., Prison Ministry, Niantic
Dombrowski, Anthony, St. Mary, Jewett City
Doyle, Dennis A., III, SS. Peter & Paul, Norwich
Escalona, Jorge, Most Holy Trinity, Pomfret
Fecteau, Al R., (Retired)
Ferraro, Robert, St. Lawrence, Killingworth
Freedman, Ronald, St. Matthew, Tolland
Garry, Dana, St. Mary, Portland
Gaynor, Gerard J., Saint Joseph, New London
Gill, Peter L., St. Colman, Middlefield
Giuliano, Joseph, St. John, Old Saybrook
Goodwin, Lawrence M., St. Joseph, Williamantic; St. Margaret Mission, Scotland
Grospitch, Harry J., St. Luke, Ellington
Hancock, John, St. John, Middletown
Hann, Frank, St. Luke, Ellington
Hayes, Robert P., Our Lady of Lourdes, Gales Ferry
Herrmann, William, Our Lady of Lakes, Oakdale
Hill, Lawrence, St. Joseph, Occum
Hoffman, Douglas A., St. Mary, Groton
Jolin, Joseph, North Fort Meyers, FL
Kaiser, William, Jr., Our Lady of Sorrows, Essex
Kitlinski, Ronald S., Our Lady Perpetual Help, Quaker Hill
LaCasse, Roland J., (Retired)
LaPlante, Joseph A., Southwest Harbor, ME
Lewis, Thomas A., St. Joseph, Norwich
Marshall, Timothy M., St. Augustine, Canterbury
McGann, William H., Our Lady of Lourdes, Gales Ferry
McMahon, James R., Sr., Spring Hill, FL
Melendez, Carlos, Port St. Lucie, FL
Moneypenny, Lawrence, St. Joseph, Chester
Nygaard, Melvin G., St. John, Uncasville
O'Reilly, Henry E., (Retired)
Osuba, Jose, Columbia
Pereira, Julias A., Christ the King, Old Lyme
Phaneuf, Bernard A., St. Mary, Putnam
Puscas, Michael L., St. Francis of Assisi, Lebanon
Ramos, Mariano, St. Mary, New London
Reed, Steven W., St. Matthias, East Lyme
Rymut, Thomas E., St. Mark, Westbrook
Saunders, Alexander, (Retired)
Shaw, Gerald L., St. Matthias, East Lyme
Silva, Felipe, Sagrado Corazon de Jesus, Windham
Sinclair, Wayne, Sacred Heart, Norwichtown
Tynan, Thomas M., Alexandria, VA
Walker, Richard K.
Wallen, Paul A., (Retired)
Walsh, Maurice, St. Agnes, Niantic
Weber, F. Paul, St. Mary of the Visitation, Clinton
Williams, Walter B., All Saints, Somersville

INSTITUTIONS LOCATED IN THE DIOCESE

[A] SEMINARIES, RELIGIOUS OR SCHOLASTICATES

CROMWELL. *Holy Apostles College and Seminary* (1956) 33 Prospect Hill Rd., 06416-2005. Tel: 860-632-3010; 860-632-3012 (Admissions); Fax: 860-632-3030. Email: rector@holyapostles.edu. Web: www.holyapostles.edu. Very Rev. Douglas L. Mosey, C.S.B., Ph.D., Pres. & Rector; Revs. Maurice Sheehan, O.F.M.Cap., Academic Dean; Michel Legault, M.S.A.; Very Revs. Gregoire J. Fluet, Ph.D., V.F., K.H.S., Vice Pres.; Addison Hallock, M.S.A., Spiritual Dir.; Revs. Bradley Pierce, M.S.A.; Ronan P. Callahan, C.P.; Rev. Msgr. David Q. Liptak (HRT); Revs. Luis Luna, M.S.A.; David Zercie, M.S.A.; Joseph M. Olczak, O.S.P.P.E.; Jude Surowiec, O.F.M.Conv.; John Hillier, Vice Rector; Rev. Msgr. James Turro; Sr. Mary Anne Linder, F.S.E., Dir. Field Educ.; Dr. Cynthia Toolin, Registrar; Mr. William J. Russell, CPA, D.F.O., Finance Officer; Rev. Jean-Paul Roy, M.S.A.; Clare Adamo, M.S.L.S., Library Dir. Priests 19; Brothers 2; Sisters 3; Lay Teachers 11; Seminarians 83; College Division Lay Students 202.

[B] HIGH SCHOOLS, DIOCESAN

MIDDLETOWN. *Mercy High School* (1963) 1740 Randolph Rd., 06457-5155. Tel: 860-346-6659; Fax: 860-344-9887. Email: info@mercyhigh.com. Web: www.mercyhigh.com. Sr. Mary A. McCarthy, R.S.M., Prin.; Mrs. Virginia Sullivan, Vice Prin. Student Life; Sr. Patty Moriarty, R.S.M., Dir. Admissions; Mrs. Jennifer Kensel, Vice Prin. Strategic Planning & Mktg.; Mr. Steven Brickey, Vice Prin. Academics; Sr. Peggy O'Neill, R.S.M., Vice Prin. & Registrar; Miss Ann Derbacher, Campus Min.; Mrs. Patricia Boothroyd, Librarian. Sisters 5; Lay Teachers 65; Students 693; Total Staff 88.

Xavier High School (1963) 181 Randolph Rd., 06457-5635. Tel: 860-346-7735; Fax: 860-346-6859. Email: donnaj@xavierhighschool.org. Web: www.xavierhighschool.org. Bros. Brian Davis, C.F.X., Headmaster; James Boyle, C.F.X., Community Dir.; Mr. Andrew T. Gargano, Academic Dean; Mr. Brendan Donohue, Academic Dean; Mr. Nicholas Cerreta, Dean, Students; Mr. David Sizemore, Dean Faculty Formation. Brothers of St. Francis Xavier. Brothers 7; Lay Teachers 62; Students 868.

UNCASVILLE. *Saint Bernard School*, 1593 Norwich-New London Tpke., 06382-1399. Tel: 860-848-1271; Fax: 860-848-1274. Email: info@saint-bernard.com. Web: www.saint-bernard.com. Mr. William McKenna, Headmaster. Tel: 860-848-1271, Ext. 146; Rev. Brian J. Romanowski, Chap.

Grades 9-12 Tel: 860-848-1271, Ext. 159 (Prin.); Fax: 860-848-1274. Mrs. Deborah Fitzgerald, Prin.

Grades 6-8 Tel: 860-848-1271, Ext. 250; Fax: 860-848-0261. Ms. Mary C. Dillman, Prin.

[C] HIGH SCHOOLS, PRIVATE

BALTIC. *Academy of the Holy Family* (1874) 54 W. Main St., P.O. Box 691, 06330-0691. Tel: 860-822-9272; Fax: 860-822-1318. Email: principal@ahfbaltic.org. Web: www.ahfbaltic.org. Sr. Mary Loreto Beckstein, S.C.M.C., Prin.; Barbara Gozzo, Librarian. Sisters of Charity of Our Lady Mother of the Church. Sisters 10; Lay Teachers 9; Students 62.

THOMPSON. *Marianapolis Preparatory School*, P.O. Box 304, 06277-0304. Tel: 860-923-9565; Fax: 860-923-3730. Email: mebbitt@marianapolis.org. Web: www.marianapolis.org. Mrs. Marilyn Ebbitt, Headmistress; Rev. Timothy Roth, M.I.C., Chap.; Douglas Daniels, Chief Fin. Operating Officer; Ms. Cheryl Wakely, Librarian. Priests 1; Lay Teachers 40; Students 323.

Congregation of Marians of the Immaculate Conception, P.O. Box 368, 06277-0368. Tel: 860-923-2220; Fax: 860-923-1884. Rev. John Petrauskas, M.I.C.

[D] CHILDREN, RESIDENTIAL CARE FOR

DEEP RIVER. *Mount St. John*, 135 Kirtland St., 06417-1816. Tel: 860-343-1340; Fax: 860-343-1394. Email: decerbod@mtstjohn.org; mckenneyv@mtstjohn.org. Web: www.mtstjohn.org. Mr. Douglas DeCerbo, Exec. Dir.; Mrs. Kathy White, Prin. Boys 32; Bed Capacity 32; Total Assisted Annually 85; Lay Staff 116; Total Staff 116.

[E] HOMES FOR AGED

WINDHAM. *St. Joseph Living Center* (1988) 14 Club Rd., 06280-1000. Tel: 860-456-1107; Fax: 860-450-7114. Email: liverson@wcmh.org. Geralyn Hines-Iversen, Admin.; Dr. Stephen J. Leach, Medical Dir.; Patricia Duffy, R.N., Dir. Nursing Svcs.; Valerie Oliver, R.N., Case Mgr.; Paula Haney, R.P.T., Dir. Rehabilitation Svcs.; Rev. George Mattathilanickal, Chap. Sisters 8; Capacity 120; Total Assisted 120; Lay Staff 200; Total Staff 210.

[F] SPECIAL CARE FACILITIES

WILLIMANTIC. *Holy Family Home and Shelter, Inc.*, 88 Jackson St., P.O. Box 884, 06226-0884. Tel: 860-423-7719; Fax: 860-423-3770. Email: sisterpeter@holyfamilywillimantic.org. Web: www.holyfamilywillimantic.org. Bonnie Reilein, Exec. Dir. Email: bonnie7@mindspring.com; Sr. M. Peter Bernard, S.C.M.C., Dir. Public Rels. Total Staff 15; Bed Capacity 32; Residents 32; Total Assisted 175. In Res. Rev. Stephen Fronckewicz, O.S.B.

[G] MONASTERIES AND RESIDENCES OF PRIESTS AND BROTHERS

CROMWELL. *Society of the Missionaries of the Holy Apostles* (1956) 22 Prospect Hill Rd., 06416-2005. Tel: 860-632-3039; Fax: 866-344-8134 (Internal Fax). Rev. Edward C. Doherty, M.S.A.; Very Rev. Addison Hallock, M.S.A., Prov. Supr.; Revs. Daniel Karempelis, M.S.A.; William McCarthy, M.S.A.; Robert Murphy, M.S.A.; Bradley Pierce, M.S.A.; George Realmuto, M.S.A.; Robert Sickler, M.S.A.; Thomas Simon, M.S.A.; Richard Skarbek, M.S.A.; Pasquale Taliercio, M.S.A. Society of the Missionaries of the Holy Apostles.

Working Outside the Diocese: Revs. Humberto Almazan, M.S.A.; James Anderson, M.S.A.; Robert Anello, M.S.A.; Charles Bak, M.S.A.; Patrick Biegler, M.S.A.; J. Patrick Boyhan, M.S.A.; William Broome, M.S.A.; Robert Burk, M.S.A.; James Downs, M.S.A.; Harold Dunn, M.S.A.; Francis Fajella, M.S.A.; Richard Gray, M.S.A.; Stanley Grove, M.S.A.; Richard Hite, M.S.A.; Vincent Kilidjian, M.S.A.; Benedict Klucinec, M.S.A.; Peter Kucer, M.S.A.; John R. Lyons, M.S.A.; Michael Nofi, M.S.A.; Maximo Asencios Pablo, M.S.A.; Gerard Petta, M.S.A.; Laurence Preston, M.S.A.; Edward Przygocki, M.S.A.; Martin Rooney, M.S.A.; Vincent Salamoni, M.S.A.; Jose Salazar, M.S.A.; David Zercie, M.S.A.

GRISWOLD. *Marian Friary of Our Lady of Guadalupe*, 199 Colonel Brown Rd., 06351. Tel: 860-376-6840; Fax: 860-376-6848. Email: friars@figuadalupe.com. Web: www.figuadalupe.com. Revs. Angelo Mary Geiger, F.I., American Supr.; Ignatius Mary Manfredonia, F.I., Guardian, Novice Master; Bonaventure M. McGuire, F.I., Vicar; Friars Augustine M. Arts, F.I.; Davide Michael Mary Bianchini, F.I.; Roderic Mary Burke, F.I.; Didacus Mary Cortes, F.I.; Isaac Joseph Mary Haas, F.I.; David Lawrence Houseal, F.I.; Jude Mary McFeely, F.I.; Joseph Paul Mary Parackal John, F.I.; Gabriel Marc Mary Reyes, F.I. Brothers 4; Priests 3; Novices 4; Postulants 1.

MIDDLETOWN. *Congregation of the Brothers of St. Francis Xavier*, 181 Randolph Rd., 06457-5635. Tel: 860-346-8585; Fax: 860-346-6859. Bros. Brian Davis, C.F.X., Headmaster; James Boyle, C.F.X., Dir.; Eugene Behenna, C.F.X.; Labre Dillon, C.F.X.; Thomas Fahey, C.F.X.; J. Robert Houlihan, C.F.X.; Thomas Ryan, C.F.X. Total in Residence 7.

THOMPSON. *Marian Fathers* (1673) Marianapolis Prep School, 06277-0368. Tel: 860-923-2220; Fax: 860-923-1884. Email: timothy.roth@snet.net. P.O. Box 368, 06277-0368. Email: timothy.roth@snet.net. Rev. Timothy Roth, M.I.C., First Councillor, & Vice Prov.; Bros. Donald Schaefer, M.I.C., Prov. Treas. & Second Councillor; Brian Manian, M.I.C., Supr., Fourth Prov. Councilor; Rev. John Petrauskas, M.I.C. Total in Residence 5.

WILLIMANTIC. *Missionary Oblates of Mary Immaculate*, 289 Windham Rd., P.O. Box 55, 06226-0055. Tel: 860-423-8484; Fax: 860-456-5583. Revs. Roger Couture, O.M.I., Supr.; Salvador Gonzalez, O.M.I.; Roger E. Lamoureux, O.M.I.; John Morin, O.M.I.; Ronald Meyer, O.M.I.; Bro. Andrew Lawlor, O.M.I. Total in Residence 6; Total Staff 12.

[H] CONVENTS AND RESIDENCES FOR SISTERS

NORWICH. *School Sisters Notre Dame*, 7 Otis St., 06360. Tel: 860-886-6948.

BALTIC. *Holy Family Motherhouse*, 54 W. Main St., 06330-0691. Tel: 860-822-8241; Fax: 860-822-9842. Email: academythe@sbcglobal.net. Web: www.sistersofcharity.com. Sr. M. Anthony, Supr. Gen. Sisters of Charity of Our Lady, Mother of the Church. Professed 60; Junior Professed 4; Novices 3.

Sacred Heart Educational Center-Tutoring Tel: 860-822-6508. Sr. M. Mercedes, Admin.

DANIELSON. *Sisters of Adoration of the Blessed Sacrament, St. Joseph Convent*, 26 Franklin St., 06239. Tel: 860-774-3748. Email: sabs.sister@yahoo.com. Sisters 9.

GALES FERRY. *Society of the Sisters for the Church*, P.O. Box 295, 06335. Tel: 860-423-8484 (Work); 860-464-4023 (Home).

HIGGANUM. *Apostles of the Sacred Heart of Jesus* (1894) Sacred Heart on the Lake, 529 Brainard Hill Rd., 06441-4010. Tel: 860-345-4653; Fax: 860-345-4469. Total in Residence 3.

MIDDLETOWN. *Sisters of Mercy of the Americas, Northeast Community*, 421 High St., 06457. Tel: 860-346-6619. Email: RTGarneau@aol.com. Other residences located in Middletown, Norwich, Portland, Preston & Quaker Hill Sisters 2.

Sisters of Our Lady of the Garden (1829) Convent and Nursery School., 67 Round Hill Rd., 06457-6119. Tel: 806-346-5765; Fax: 806-346-6361. Sr. Donna Beauregard, F.M.H., Supr. Total Assisted 82; Total Staff 9.

Sisters of St. Joseph, T.O.S.F. (1901) 46 Camp St., Apt. 2, 06457-2445. Tel: 860-347-8936.

PUTNAM. *Holy Spirit Provincial House*, 72 Church St., 06260-1810. Tel: 860-928-0891; Fax: 860-928-6496. Sr. Norma Bourdon, D.H.S., Prov.; Rev. Richard L. Archambault, Chap. Daughters of the Holy Spirit. Sisters 57.

Other Locations: *Notre Dame Community*, 4 Ravine St., 06260. Tel: 860-928-6163. *Provincialate Community*, 31 Ravine St., 06260. Tel: 860-928-7072; 860-928-3882. *All Hallows Convent*, 152 Prospect St., Moosup, 06354. Tel: 860-564-5409.

351 Church St., 06260. Tel: 860-963-0311.

70 Proulx St., Apt. G21, Brooklyn, 06234. Tel: 860-779-0790.

27 Primrose Village, Dayville, 06241-2154. Tel: 860-779-2115.

218 Woodstock Ave., Apt. 8, 06260. Tel: 860-928-5894.

70 Proulx St., Apt. C13, Brooklyn, 06234. Tel: 860-779-1291.

Immaculate Conception Convent, Spiritual Renewal Center and Novitiate, 600 Liberty Hwy., 06260-2503. Tel: 860-928-7955; Fax: 860-928-1930. Rev. Arvydas Zygas, Chap.; Sr. Igne Marijosius, M.V.S., Prov. Supr. Sisters of the Immaculate Conception of the Blessed Virgin Mary 6; Total in Residence 9; Total Staff 12.

Matulaitis Nursing Home Inc., 10 Thurber Rd., 06260-2522. Tel: 860-928-7976; Fax: 860-963-2378. Email: mnhadm@yahoo.com. Web: matulaitisnh.org. Jane Logan, Admin.; Rev. Izydor Sadowski, S.D.B., Chap. Sisters of the Immaculate Conception of the Blessed Virgin Mary. Sisters 7; Residents 119.

Provincialate Community of the Daughters of the Holy Spirit, 31 Ravine St., 06260-1817. Tel: 860-928-7072. Web: www.fillesstesprit.org. Sisters Norma Bourdon, D.H.S., Prov. Tel: 860-928-7072; Bonnie Morrow, D.H.S., Prov. Councillor & Treas. Tel: 860-928-3882.

QUAKER HILL. *Emmaus Community* (1976) 1A Burlake Rd., 06375-1202. Tel: 860-447-1512. Total in Residence 2; Total Staff 2.

WILLIMANTIC. *Sisters of Charity of Our Lady, Mother of the Church*, St. Joseph Convent, 88 Jackson St., 06226. Tel: 860-423-5122. Total in Residence 4; Total Staff 4.

[I] RETREAT HOUSES

NORWICH. *Ministry of His Able People*, 201 Broadway, 06360-4328. Tel: 860-887-9294, Ext. 100.

MYSTIC. *St. Edmund's Retreat*, P.O. Box 399, 06355-0399. Tel: 860-536-0565; Fax: 860-572-7655. Email: admin@endersisland.com. Web: www.endersisland.com. Rev. Thomas F.X. Hoar, S.S.E., Pres.; Mr. Jeffrey L. Anderson, Exec. Dir.; Mrs. Claire St. Clair, Finance Dept.; John J. Foley II, Chair of Board of Trustees; Robert Wilson, Chair Finance Committee. Total in Residence 2; Total Staff 20.

WILLIMANTIC. *Immaculata Retreat House*, 289 Windham Rd., P.O. Box 55, 06226-0055. Tel: 860-423-8484; Fax: 860-423-5285. Email: immaculata@omict.org. Web: www.immaculataretreat.org. Revs. Roger Couture, O.M.I., Supr.; John Morin, O.M.I.; Mrs. Paulette Bard, Dir. Missionary Oblates of Mary Immaculate: U.S. Province. Total in Residence 5; Total Staff 12.

[J] RENEWAL CENTERS

PORTLAND. *Affirmation Counseling Center* (1990) 553 Portland Cobalt Rd., 06480-1968. Tel: 860-342-0760; Fax: 860-342-4226. Mr. Marek Kukulka, L.M.F.T., Exec. Dir.; Silvia Colavito, Admin.; Revs. Roland C. Cloutier, L.C.S.W., Consultant; Stanley Kennedy, L.P.C., Psychotherapist; Donna Grisham, L.A.D.C., Psychotherapist; Ann D. Cady, L.P.C., Psychotherapist; Sheila Chunis, L.P.C., Psychotherapist; Julie S. Dudek, M.A., L.P.C., Psychotherapist; Robert Malafronte, L.C.S.W.,

Psychotherapist; Laura Jakabauski, L.P.C., Psychotherapist; Michele Binezewski, L.P.C., Psychotherapist; Susan Hameline-Kasznay, L.M.F.T., Psychotherapist. Total Assisted 711; Total Staff 10.

UNCASVILLE. *Emmaus-Diocesan Spiritual Life Services* (1976) 1595 Norwich-New London Tpke., 06382-1319. Tel: 860-848-2237; Fax: 860-848-2816. Sisters Agnes Therrien, S.S.Ch., Co-Dir.; Mary Ann De Francesco, R.S.M., Co-Dir. Sisters 2; Total Staff 2.

[K] SECULAR INSTITUTES

WINDHAM. *Secular Branch of the Daughters of the Holy Spirit* (2003) 80 Tuckie Rd., 06280. Tel: 860-456-2778. Email: stolles428@aol.com. Sally J. Tolles, Consecrated Secular, D.H.S., Regl. Mod.

[L] CAMPUS MINISTRY

WILLIMANTIC. *Campus Ministry* , Eastern Connecticut State University, Newman Hall., 290 Prospect St., 06226. Tel: 860-423-0856; Fax: 860-456-8083. Email: lapointel@easternct.edu. Web: www.norwichdiocese.org. Very Rev. Laurence A.M. LaPointe, Diocesan Dir. Campus Ministry.

Wesleyan University-The University Ministry Office of the University Chaplains, 171 Church St., Middletown, 06459-3625. Tel: 860-685-2277; Fax: 860-685-2821. Rev. Halbert Weidner, C.O., College Chap.

Connecticut College Harkness Chapel, 270 Mohegan Ave., New London, 06320-4196. Tel: 860-439-2452; Fax: 860-439-2463. Email: lalap@conncoll.edu; lapointel@easternet.edu. Very Rev. Laurence A.M. LaPointe, College Chap.

University of Connecticut St. Thomas Aquinas Chapel, 46 N. Eagleville Rd., Storrs, 06268-1710. Tel: 860-429-6436; Fax: 860-429-2809. Email: stthoffice@worldnet.att.net. Revs. John J. Walsh, S.J., Chap.; Gerard R. McKeon, S.J., Chap.; Anne Marie O'Conner, Pastoral Min.

[M] MISCELLANEOUS

NORWICH. *The Annual Bishop's Appeal of the Diocese of Norwich, Inc.*, 197 Broadway, 06360. Tel: 860-886-1928; Fax: 860-886-2651. Email: thomas.obrien@norwichdiocese.net. Web: www.norwichdiocese.org. Mr. Thomas P. O'Brien, Exec. Dir. & Dir. Planned Giving.

The Catholic Foundation of the Diocese of Norwich, Inc., 197 Broadway, 06360. Tel: 860-886-1928; Fax: 860-886-2651. Email: thomas.obrien@norwichdiocese.net. Web: www.norwichdiocese.org. Mr. Thomas P. O'Brien, Exec. Dir.

Diocese of Norwich Assisted Living Services, Inc., 201 Broadway, 06360-4480. Tel: 860-887-9294; Fax: 860-886-1670.

The Donor Advised Funds of the Diocese of Norwich, Inc., 201 Broadway, 06360. Tel: 860-887-9294; Fax: 860-886-1670.

CROMWELL. *Basilian Fathers of Connecticut, Inc.* (1987) 33 Prospect Hill Rd., 06416. Tel: 860-632-3010; Fax: 860-632-3030. Email: fr_mosey@juno.com. Very Rev. Douglas L. Mosey, C.S.B., Ph.D., Pres. & Rector.

Marian Housing Corporation, 213 Broadway, 06360-4328. Tel: 860-632-1688; 860-859-0527; Fax: 860-889-2978.

DEEP RIVER. *Edmund Rice Charitable Foundation, Inc.*, 135 Kirtland St., 06417. Tel: 860-343-1340; Fax: 860-343-1394. Email: decerbod@mtstjohn.org.

Mount Saint John Foundation for Charitable Works, Inc., 135 Kirtland St., 06417. Tel: 860-343-1303; Fax: 860-526-1636. Email: decerbod@mtstjohn.org.

MIDDLETOWN. *Mercy Alumnae and Development Office*, 1740 Randolph Rd., 06457. Tel: 860-347-8957; Fax: 860-344-9887. Email: bmiller@mercyhigh.com. Web: www.mercyhigh.com. Barbara P. Miller, Dir. Alumnae & Devel.

Mercy-Xavier Fund Corporation, 181 Randolph Rd., 06457. Tel: 860-346-7735; Fax: 860-346-6859.

Xavier Advancement Office, 181 Randolph Rd., 06457. Tel: 860-347-6079; Fax: 860-346-6859. Email: advancement@xavierhighschool.org. Web: www.xavierhighschool.org. Mr. Michael Tommasi, Dir.; Mr. Joseph E. Lane, Asst. Devel. Office; Mr. John Guerin, Communications Dir. Total Staff 4.

MYSTIC. *St. Edmund's of Connecticut, Inc.*, P.O. Box 399, 06355-0399. Tel: 860-536-0565; Fax: 860-572-7655. Email: admin@endersisland.com. Web: www.endersisland.com. Most Revs. Michael Richard Cote, D.D., Pres.; Thomas Tobin; Very Rev. Michael Cronouge, S.S.E., Supr. General; Rev. Thomas F.X. Hoar, S.S.E., Sec.

UNCASVILLE. *Hospice St. Joseph for the Diocese of Norwich Inc.*, 1595 Norwich-New London Tpke., 06382. Tel: 860-848-2237, Ext. 304; Fax: 860-848-2816. Email: hsj33haiti@aol.com. Web: hospicesaintjoseph.org. Alexandre Jean Raynald Carre, Chm. Bd.

PUTNAM. *The Daughters of the Holy Spirit Charitable Trust* (1985) 72 Church St., 06260-1810. Tel: 860-928-0891; Fax: 860-928-6496. Email: bmorrow@snet.net. Sr. Bonnie Morrow, Trustee & Contact Person.

The Holy Spirit Health Care Center, Inc., 72 Church St., 06260. Tel: 860-928-0891; Fax: 860-928-1312. Sr. Norma Bourdon, D.H.S., Prov. & Contact Person; Mrs. Annemarie Shiroka, Admin.

WILLIMANTIC. *Saint Joseph's Home for the Aged, Inc.* (1991) 88 Jackson St., 06226. Tel: 860-887-9294; Fax: 860-885-1512. Email: dfo@norwichdiocese.net.

WINDHAM. *Sagrado Corazon de Jesus, Inc. of Windham*, 61 Club Rd., 06280. Tel: 860-423-8617; Fax: 860-423-4157. Email: sagradocor@sbcglobal.net.

RELIGIOUS INSTITUTES OF MEN REPRESENTED IN THE DIOCESE

For further details refer to the corresponding bracketed number in the Religious Institutes of Men or Women section.

[]—*Basilian Fathers*—C.S.B.

[]—*Benedictine Monks*—O.S.B.

[1350]—*Brothers of St. Francis Xavier* (St. Joseph Prov.)—C.F.X.

[0610]—*Brothers of the Congregation of Holy Cross*—C.S.C.

[0470]—*The Capuchin Friars* (Prov. of St. Mary)—O.F.M. Cap

[0740]—*Congregation of Marians of the Immaculate Conception*—M.I.C.

[]—*Congregation of the Oratory of St. PhilipNeri*—C.O.

[0480]—*Conventual Franciscans*—O.F.M.Conv

[0533]—*Franciscan Friars of the Immaculate*—F. I.

[0690]—*Jesuit Fathers and Brothers*—S.J.

[]—*Little Flower Congregation*—C.S.T.

[0720]—*The Missionaries of Our Lady of La Salette* (Prov. of Our Lady of the Americas)—M.S.

[]—*Missionary Congregation of the Blessed Sacrament*—M.C.S.B.

[0910]—*Oblates of Mary Immaculate* (Missionary Oblates of Mary Immaculate, U.S. Prov.)—O.M.I.

[]—*Order of St. Paul the First Hermit, Pauline Fathers*—O.S.P.P.E.

[1190]—*Salesians of Don Bosco*—S.D.B.

[]—*Salvatorian Fathers*—S.D.S.

[1260]—*Society of Mary*—S.M.

[0440]—*Society of St. Edmund*—S.S.E.

[0590]—*Society of the Missionaries of the Holy Apostles*—M.S.A.

RELIGIOUS INSTITUTES OF WOMEN REPRESENTED IN THE DIOCESE

[0130]—*Apostoles of the Sacred Heart of Jesus*—A.S.C.J.

[]—*Congregation of Notre Dame*—C.N.D.

[]—*Daughters of Our Lady of the Garden*—F.M.H.

[0820]—*Daughters of the Holy Spirit*—D.H.S.

[]—*Franciscan Apostolic Sisters*—F.A.S.

[1190]—*Franciscan Sisters of Atonement*—S.A.

[1180]—*Francisican Sisters of Allegany*—O.S.F.

[2575]—*Institute of the Sisters of Mercy of the Americas*—R.S.M.

[]—*Missionary Servants of the Word*—H.M.S.P.

[3465]—*Religious of the Sacred Heart of Mary*—R.S.H.M.

[2970]—*School Sisters of Notre Dame*—S.S.N.D.

[]—*Sisters Oblates to Divine Love*—R.O.D.A.

[0530]—*Sisters of Charity of Our Lady, Mother of the Church*—S.C.M.C.

[3000]—*Sisters of Notre Dame de Namur* (Connecticut Prov.)—S.N.D.deN.

[3750]—*Sisters of St. Chretienne*—S.S.Ch.

[3830]—*Sisters of St. Joseph*—S.S.J.

[]—*Sisters of St. Joseph*—C.S.J.

[3930]—*Sisters of St. Joseph of the Third Order of St. Francis*—S.S.J.-T.O.S.F.

[]—*Sisters of St. Martha*—C.S.M.

[]—*Sisters of the Adoration of the Blessed Sacrament*—S.A.B.S.

[]—*Sisters of the Cross and Passion*—C.P.

[2140]—*Sisters of the Poor of the Immaculate Conception of the Blessed Virgin Mary (Lithuanian)*—M.V.S.

[3320]—*Sisters of the Presentation of the B.V.M.*—P.B.V.M.

NECROLOGY

† Gadarowski, Rev. Msgr. Bronislaw A., (Retired)—Died Nov. 10, 2009

† Morris, Lester G., (Retired)—Died March 24, 2009

† Roughan, Richard F., (Retired)—Died Oct. 5, 2009

† Surprenant, John L., (Inactive)—Died Nov. 14, 2009

An asterisk (*) denotes an organization that has established tax-exempt status directly with the IRS and is not covered by the USCCB Group Ruling.

Diocese of Oakland

(Dioecesis Quercopolitana)

Most Reverend

SALVATORE J. CORDILEONE

Bishop of Oakland; ordained July 9, 1982; appointed Auxiliary Bishop of San Diego and Titular Bishop of Natchesium July 5, 2002; ordained August 21, 2002; appointed Bishop of Oakland March 23, 2009; installed May 5, 2009. *Office: 2121 Harrison St., Ste. 100, Oakland, CA 94612-3788.*

Most Reverend

JOHN S. CUMMINS, D.D.

Retired Bishop of Oakland; ordained January 24, 1953; appointed Titular Bishop of Lambesi and Auxiliary Bishop of Sacramento February 26, 1974; consecrated May 16, 1974; appointed Bishop of Oakland May 3, 1977; installed June 30, 1977; retired September 30, 2003. *Office: 617 Prospect Ave., Oakland, CA 94610.* Tel: 510-832-5037.

Chancery Office: 2121 Harrison St., Ste. 100, Oakland, CA 94612-3788. Tel: 510-893-4711; Fax: 510-893-0945.

Email: chancellor@oakdiocese.org

Web: www.oakdiocese.org

ESTABLISHED JANUARY 13, 1962.

Square Miles 1,467.

Comprises two Counties in the State of California--viz., Alameda and Contra Costa.

Legal Title: The Roman Catholic Bishop of Oakland, a Corporation Sole.
For legal titles of parishes and diocesan institutions, consult the Chancery Office.

STATISTICAL OVERVIEW

Personnel	
Bishop	1
Retired Bishops	1
Priests: Diocesan Active in Diocese	96
Priests: Diocesan Active Outside Diocese	10
Priests: Retired, Sick or Absent	54
Number of Diocesan Priests	160
Religious Priests in Diocese	200
Total Priests in Diocese	360
Extern Priests in Diocese	43
Ordinations:	
Diocesan Priests	1
Transitional Deacons	1
Permanent Deacons in Diocese	120
Total Brothers	92
Total Sisters	336
Parishes	
Parishes	84
With Resident Pastor:	
Resident Diocesan Priests	47
Resident Religious Priests	14
Without Resident Pastor:	
Administered by Priests	22
Administered by Lay People	1
Missions	1
Pastoral Centers	17
Professional Ministry Personnel:	
Sisters	23
Lay Ministers	132
Welfare	
Homes for the Aged	2
Total Assisted	213
Day Care Centers	1
Total Assisted	462
Specialized Homes	6
Total Assisted	20,304
Special Centers for Social Services	4
Total Assisted	664,718
Residential Care of Disabled	1
Total Assisted	865
Educational	
Diocesan Students in Other Seminaries	24
Seminaries, Religious	4
Students Religious	375
Total Seminarians	399
Colleges and Universities	2
Total Students	5,149
High Schools, Diocesan and Parish	3
Total Students	1,792
High Schools, Private	6
Total Students	4,131
Elementary Schools, Diocesan and Parish	45
Total Students	11,776
Elementary Schools, Private	2
Total Students	121
Catechesis/Religious Education:	
High School Students	6,005
Elementary Students	19,870
Total Students under Catholic Instruction	49,243
Teachers in the Diocese:	
Priests	48
Brothers	37
Sisters	50
Lay Teachers	1,933
Vital Statistics	
Receptions into the Church:	
Infant Baptism Totals	8,415
Minor Baptism Totals	490
Adult Baptism Totals	297
Received into Full Communion	398
First Communions	8,443
Confirmations	4,755
Marriages:	
Catholic	902
Interfaith	171
Total Marriages	1,073
Deaths	2,478
Total Catholic Population	431,212
Total Population	2,517,141

Former Bishops—Most Revs. FLOYD L. BEGIN, S.T.D., cons. May 1, 1947; appt. Bishop of Oakland on Feb. 21, 1962; died April 26, 1977; JOHN S. CUMMINS, D.D. (Retired), ord. January 24, 1953; appt. Titular Bishop of Lambesi and Auxiliary Bishop of Sacramento February 26, 1974; cons. May 16, 1974; appt. Bishop of Oakland May 3, 1977; installed June 30, 1977; retired Sept. 30, 2003; ALLEN HENRY VIGNERON, D.D., ord. July 27, 1975; appt. Auxiliary Bishop of Detroit and Titular Bishop of Sault Ste. Marie June 12, 1996; cons. July 9, 1996; appt. Coadjutor Bishop of Oakland Jan. 10, 2003; installed Feb. 26, 2003; succeeded to See Oct. 1, 2003; appt. Archbishop of Detroit Jan. 5, 2009; installed Jan. 28, 2009.

Chancery Office—2121 Harrison St., Ste. 100, Oakland, 94612-3788. Tel: 510-893-4711; Fax: 510-893-0945. Office Hours: 8:30-4:45.

Office of the Bishop—Most Rev. SALVATORE J. CORDILEONE, Bishop; Rev. DAVID E. STAAL, Dir.; KAREN LEACH, Administrative Asst.

Moderator of the Curia and Vicar General—Rev. GEORGE E. MOCKEL.

Chancellor—Sr. GLENN ANNE MCPHEE, O.P.

Chief Financial Officer—Mr. MICHAEL P. CANIZZARO.

Judicial Vicar—Rev. RAYMOND G. BRETON, J.C.L.

Director of Communications—Mr. MICHAEL BROWN.

Bishop's Representative for Eastern Rite Catholics—Rev. DAVID LINK.

Bishop's Representative for Permanent Deacons—Deacon DAVID REZENDES.

Bishop's Representative for Catholic Charismatics (English)—Ms. ROSEMARIE MULLINS.

Bishop's Representative for Catholic Charismatics (Spanish)—Rev. FRANCISCO J. FIGUEROA ESQUER.

Catholic Cathedral Corporation of the East Bay (CCEB)—Mr. MICHAEL P. CANIZZARO, Contact, 2121 Harrison St., Ste. 100, Oakland, 94612-3788. Tel: 510-267-8323; Fax: 510-446-7401. Email: mcanizzaro@oakdiocese.org. Officers: Mr. JOHN L. MCDONNELL, Pres.; Rev. DAVID E. STAAL, Vice Pres.; Mr. WILLIAM UTIC, Sec.; Mr. MICHAEL P. CANIZZARO, CFO/Treas.

Christ the Light Cathedral Corporation—Mr. MICHAEL P. CANIZZARO, Contact, 2121 Harrison St., Ste. 100, Oakland, 94612-3788. Tel: 510-267-8323; Fax: 510-446-7401. Email: mcanizzaro@oakdiocese.org. Officers: Mr. JOHN L. MCDONNELL, Pres.; Rev. DAVID E. STAAL, Vice Pres.; Mr. MICHAEL P. CANIZZARO, Treas.; Mr. WILLIAM UTIC, Sec.

John Paul II High School, a California nonprofit religious corporation—Mr. MICHAEL P. CANIZZARO, Incorporator, 2121 Harrison St., Ste. 100, Oakland, 94612-3788. Tel: 510-267-8323; Fax: 510-446-7401. Email: mcanizzaro@oakdiocese.org.

The Roman Catholic Welfare Corporation of Oakland—2121 Harrison St., Ste. 100, Oakland, 94612-3788. Tel: 510-893-4711.

Consultors—Revs. SEAMUS J. FARRELL; ROBERT M. HERBST, O.F.M.Conv., J.C.D.; GEORGE E. MOCKEL; PAULSON MUNDANMANI; PAUL SCHMIDT; LARRY E. YOUNG.

Presbyteral Council—Revs. RAYMOND G. BRETON, J.C.L., Chm.; SEAMUS J. FARRELL; ROBERT M. HERBST, O.F.M.Conv., J.C.D.; DAVID LAWRENCE, S.J.; JOSE M. LEON; RUBEN MORALES; PAULSON MUNDANMANI; JESUS NIETO-RUIZ; JOSEPH PHAN; PAUL J. SCHMIDT; RONALD SCHMIT; LARRY E. YOUNG. Ex Officio: Rev. GEORGE E. MOCKEL.

Diocesan Pastoral Council—Region 1: Ms. JANET COOK; Ms. MARY FAIR. Region 2: Mr. CHUCK

WOODS; Ms. ELSA VEGA; Mr. JULIO CASTENADA. Region 3: Ms. JO BERNING. Region 4: Ms. YVONNE ALGER-ROUNDS. Region 5: Mr. MARKUS MULLARKY. Deacon Representative: Deacon ERNEST JARAMILLO. Women Religious Representative: VACANT. Priest Representatives: Revs. SEAMUS J. FARRELL; JAY MATTHEWS. Ex Officio: Rev. GEORGE E. MOCKEL; Sr. GLENN ANNE MCPHEE, O.P.

Diocesan Planning Board—Mr. J. J. WEST; Ms. MARY FAIR; Mr. MIKE HENDERSHOT; Ms. JOANN MASS; Rev. JOSE ARONG, O.M.I.; Ms. RITA MITCHELL; Rev. GEORGE E. MOCKEL.

Deacon Council—Deacons WILLIAM GALL, Pres.; TIMOTHY MOORE, Past Pres.; RONALD HORAN, Pres.-elect; DAVE REZENDES; Revs. GEORGE ALENGADAN, S.D.B.; LAWRENCE C. D'ANJOU; RAYMOND SACCA.

Lay Ecclesial Ministers Council (LEMC)—Region 1: Ms. PAULINE PORTER; Ms. ANNETTE ROUX. Region 2: Mrs. JACKIE HOOKE. Region 3: Ms. ANNE MARIE FOURRE; Ms. SUZY SILVA. Region 4: Ms. ROBYN LANG; Ms. MICHELE IDIART WALSH. Region 5: Ms. LAUREN AGUAYO; Ms. FRANCES ROJEK. Special Works: VACANT. Priest Representative: Rev. JOHN PROCHASKA. Ex Officio: Mr. KEITH BORCHERS; Sr. GLENN ANNE MCPHEE, O.P.

Diocesan Finance Council—Mr. DAVID L. ASH; Mr. WILLIAM ATKINSON; Mr. PAUL BONGIOVANNI; Mr. JOHN CALLAGY; Mr. RICHARD CAMPBELL; Mr. MICHAEL P. CANIZZARO; Mr. PATRICK DEVINE; Mr. GLEN HENTGES; Rev. GEORGE E. MOCKEL; Mr. DONALD G. SAVAGE; Mr. WILLIAM UTIC; Mr. KIP WIXSON.

Pastoral Leadership Placement Board (PLPB)—Revs. ROBERT J. MCCANN, J.C.L., Chm.; RAYMOND G. BRETON, J.C.L.; Sr. ANNE BURGARD; Rev. ISMAEL GUTIERREZ; Mrs. KATHLEEN MURPHY; Sr. ROSALINE NGUYEN, L.H.C.; Revs. JOHN PROCHASKA; FRED RICCIO; Rev. Msgr. ANTONIO VALDIVIA (Retired). Ex Officio: Revs. GEORGE E. MOCKEL; RAYMOND SACCA.

Deans—Deanery #1: Rev. ROBERT MENDONCA. Deanery #2: Rev. RAYMOND ZIELEZIENSKI. Deanery #3: Rev. JOSEPH PAREKKATT, S.D.B. Deanery #4: Rev. JOHN KASPER, O.S.F.S. Deanery #5: Rev. LEO ALBAN ASUNCION. Deanery #6: Rev. OLMAN SOLIS. Deanery #7: Rev. RICHARD J. CULVER. Deanery #8: Rev. RICHARD A. MANGINI. Deanery #9: Rev. FRED RICCIO. Deanery #10: Rev. TIMOTHY K. JOHNSON. Deanery #11: Rev. JESUS NIETO-RUIZ. Deanery #12: Rev. JAMES MATTHEWS. Deanery #13: Rev. QUANG MINH DONG. Deanery #14: Rev. JOHN PROCHASKA. Deanery #15: Rev. GEOFFREY BARAAN. Deanery #17: Rev. RAMON GOMEZ. Deanery #18: Rev. MICHAEL LACEY. Deanery #19: Rev. THUONG NGUYEN. Deanery #20: Rev. DAVID J. FARRUGIA, O.P. Deanery #21: Rev. GARY KLAUER, O.F.M.Conv. Deanery #22: Rev. JOHN R. BLAKER. Deanery #23: Rev. JAMES J. THOTTAPALLY.

Diocesan Departments

Apostleship of the Sea—Rev. JOSEPH DUONG PHAN, Port Chap., 4001 Seventh St., Oakland, 94607. Tel: 510-444-7885.

Archivist/Records Management—Ms. CARRIE MCCLISH, 2121 Harrison St., Ste. 100, Oakland, 94612-3788. Tel: 510-893-5339; Fax: 510-893-4734.

Canon Law Department—

Judicial Vicar & Director—Rev. RAYMOND G. BRETON, J.C.L.

Adjutant Judicial Vicars—Revs. ROBERT M. HERBST, O.F.M.Conv., J.C.D.; ROBERT J. MCCANN, J.C.L.

Promoter of Justice—Rev. FRANCISCO V. VICENTE, O.P., J.C.D.

Defenders of the Bond—Rev. DAVID K. O'ROURKE, O.P.; Mr. ROBERT FLUMMERFELT, J.C.L.

Judges—Revs. RAYMOND G. BRETON, J.C.L.; ROBERT M. HERBST, O.F.M.Conv., J.C.D.; ROBERT J. MCCANN, J.C.L.; HERMAN LEONG, J.C.L.

Notaries of the Tribunal—JACQUELINE COMPTON; MARY O'SULLIVAN; Mr. MARCOS POZO.

Auditor—Mrs. CAROL IZO.

Case Instructors—AUDRA COMPTON; THERESA KOBAK; KAREN LAIBLE; ESPERANZA MAGALLANES-QUINTEROS; JENNIFER PRYON; MARTHA QUANT; RHONDA SERVIN; Deacon PETER DAC TA; ANHNGUYET TRONG.

Court of Second Instance—Rev. ROBERT M. HERBST, O.F.M.Conv., J.C.D., Presiding Judge; Mrs. CAROL IZO, Notary.

Catholic Schools Office—Sr. BARBARA BRAY, S.N.J.M., Supt., 2121 Harrison St., Oakland, 94612-3787. Tel: 510-628-2152; Ms. KATHLEEN RADECKE, Asst. Supt. Tel: 510-628-2164; Mrs. LINDA BASMAN, Asst. Supt. Tel: 510-628-2167; Sr. BARBARA DAWSON, R.S.C.J., Consortium Dir. (part-time)Tel: 510-628-2163; Mr. STEVE RAMMEL, Controller. Tel: 510-628-2165.

Catholic Youth Organization—Mr. BILL FORD, Dir., 2121 Harrison St., Ste. 100, Oakland, 94612-3788. Tel: 510-893-5154; Fax: 510-834-5498.

Censor—Rev. ROBERT J. MCCANN, J.C.L., 2121 Harrison St., Ste. 100, Oakland, 94612-3788. Tel: 510-267-8330.

Clergy Services—Rev. RAYMOND SACCA, Dir., 2121 Harrison St., Ste. 100, Oakland, 94612-3788. Tel: 510-267-8307.

Development—Mr. JOHN NEUDECKER, Dir., 2121 Harrison St., Ste. 100, Oakland, 94612-3788. Tel: 510-267-8314.

FACE (Family Aid Catholic Education, Tuition Assistance)—Ms. KRISTA ROSA BRENNAN, Dir., 2121 Harrison St., Ste. 100, Oakland, 94612-3788. Tel: 510-628-2169.

Department for Evangelization and Catechetics—Mr. KEITH BORCHERS, Dir., 2121 Harrison St., Ste. 100, Oakland, 94612-3787. Tel: 510-893-4711; Mr. DENNIS PURIFICACION, Assoc. Dir.

Associate Director for Spanish Programming—Mr. JUAN CARLOS GAVIRIA.

Marriage and Family Life Ministry—Mr. EDWARD HOPFNER.

Social Ministry: Culture of Life and Social Justice—Mr. JOHN WATKINS.

Youth and Young Adult Ministry—Mr. JOE MURRAY.

Evangelization and Catechetical Resource Ministry for Latinos—Ms. MARY ANN WIESINGER.

St. Joseph Center for the Deaf Catechetical and Faith Formation—Ms. KATA STRAWN, D.R.E., 25580 Campus Dr., Hayward, 94542-1137. Tel: 510-881-2245 (Voice); 510-881-2248 (Video Phone); 510-881-2247 (TTY); Fax: 510-881-2248. Email: sjcd@sjcd.org. Web: www.sjcd.org.

Special Religious Education Department (SPRED)—Sr. AURORA PEREZ, Dir., 3705 Dorisa Ave., Oakland, 94605. Tel: 510-635-7252; Fax: 510-632-7045. Email: spredoakdiocese@igc.org.

Episcopal Liturgies—Rev. PAUL D. MINNIHAN, S.T.D., Coord. Tel: 510-271-1945. Email: pminnihan@oakdiocese.org.

Ethnic Pastoral Centers—

Director of Ethnic & Cultural Services Division—Sr. FELICIA SARATI, C.S.J., 2121 Harrison St., Ste. 100, Oakland, 94612-3788. Tel: 510-273-4998.

Asian/Indian Pastoral Center—Ms. BELLA COMELO, 2048 Juneau St., San Leandro, 94577. Tel: 510-357-0940.

Brazilian Pastoral Center—Mr. JOSE FREITAS, 1500 Elm St., El Cerrito, 94530. Tel: 510-232-4328.

Chinese Pastoral Center—Rev. PAUL FENG CHEN, Dir., 707 C St., Union City, 94587. Tel: 510-471-2609.

Fijian Pastoral Center—Rev. PETER L. CHONG, 30 Mandalay Rd., Oakland, 94618. Tel: 510-547-2777.

Eritrean Pastoral Center—Rev. GEBRIEL WOLDAI, Bay Area Regl. Dir., 1640 Addison St., Berkeley, 94703. Tel: 510-549-3620.

Indonesian Pastoral Center—Mr. BEN LIEM, 4013 Yolo Dr., San Jose, 95136-1986. Tel: 408-221-9262.

Kenyan Pastoral Center—Rev. JAMES K. KARIU, 5641 Esmond Ave., Richmond, 94805. Tel: 510-860-2299.

Kmhmu/Laotian Pastoral Center—Rev. DONALD MACKINNON, C.Ss.R., 2215 Rose St., Berkeley, 94709. Tel: 510-582-8888.

Korean Pastoral Center—Rev. DOMINIC KIM, Dir., St. Andrew Kim Korean Catholic Pastoral Center, 6226 Camden St., Oakland, 94605. Tel: 510-562-3843.

Nigerian Pastoral Center—Prof. CHRISTIAN OKEKE, 4320 Mink Court, Antioch, 94531. Tel: 925-755-2994.

Polish Pastoral Center—Deacon WITOLD CHICHON, Dir., 4593 Ridgeline Dr., Antioch, 94531-9393. Tel: 925-779-1027.

Tongan Pastoral Center—Ms. MELE MAUSIA, 1135 83rd Ave., Oakland, 94621. Tel: 510-927-7131.

Vietnamese Pastoral Center—Sr. ROSALINE NGUYEN, L.H.C., 2121 Harrison St., Ste. 100, Oakland, 94612-3788. Tel: 510-628-2153.

Facilities, Planning and Services—Mr. ALEX HERNANDEZ, Dir.; Mr. JAMES H. MCCANN, Assoc. Dir.

Financial Services—Mr. PAUL BONGIOVANNI, Controller, 2121 Harrison St., Ste. 100, Oakland, 94612-3788. Tel: 510-267-8321.

Catholic Funeral and Cemetery Services—Mr. ROBERT W. SEELIG, Dir., 1965 Reliez Valley Rd., P.O. Box 488, Lafayette, 94549. ANTIOCH, Contra Costa County, Holy Angels/Holy Cross Cemetery; HAYWARD, Alameda County, Holy Angels Funeral and Cremation Center/Holy Sepulchre Cemetery and Mausoleum, Holy Angels/Sorensen's Chapel; LAFAYETTE, Contra Costa County, Holy Angels/Queen of Heaven Cemetery; LIVERMORE, Alameda County, Holy Angels/St. Michael's Cemetery; OAKLAND, Alameda County, Cathedral of Christ the Light Mausoleum, Holy Angels/St. Mary's Cemetery; SAN PABLO, Contra Costa County, Holy Angels/St. Joseph's Cemetery and Mausoleum.

Legal Title: The Roman Catholic Cemeteries of the Diocese of Oakland, a California nonprofit religious corporation, dba Catholic Funeral and Cemetery Services

Holy Childhood—Mr. JOHN NEUDECKER, Dir., 2121 Harrison St., Ste. 100, Oakland, 94612-3788. Tel: 510-267-8357.

Hospital Ministry—Rev. MATTHEW VANISSERY, Dir.

Human Resources—Dr. PENNY PENDOLA, Dir., 2121 Harrison St., Ste. 100, Oakland, 94612-3788. Tel: 510-267-8359.

Safe Environment for Children—MARILYN MARCHI, Prog. Coord.

Latino Ministry Department—Mr. HECTOR D. MEDINA, Dir., 2121 Harrison St., Ste. 100, Oakland, 94612-3788. Tel: 510-628-2180; Fax: 510-834-5498.

Newspaper: "The Catholic Voice"—Ms. MONICA CLARK, Editor, 2121 Harrison St., Ste. 100, Oakland, 94612-3788. Tel: 510-893-5339.

"El Heraldo Catolico"—JOSE LUIS AGUIRRE, Assoc. Editor, 2121 Harrison St., Ste. 100, Oakland, 94612-3788. Tel: 510-893-5339.

Pastoral Planning and Stewardship—Ms. DEBRA GUNN, Dir., 2121 Harrison St., Ste. 100, Oakland, 94612-3788. Tel: 510-267-8368.

Office of Priest and Deacon Formation—Rev. GEORGE ALENGADAN, S.D.B. Tel: 510-267-8364.

Propagation of the Faith—Mr. JOHN NEUDECKER, Dir., Legal Title: Oakland Society for the Propagation of the Faith.

Provost— Cathedral of Christ the Light Rev. PAUL D. MINNIHAN, S.T.D. Tel: 510-271-1945.

St. Peter the Apostle Society—Mr. JOHN NEUDECKER, Dir.

Vicars for Religious—Revs. RAYMOND G. BRETON, J.C.L.; ROBERT M. HERBST, O.F.M.Conv., J.C.D.

Vocations—Rev. LAWRENCE C. D'ANJOU, Priestly and Relg. & Dir. for Seminarians, 2121 Harrison St., Ste. 100, Oakland, 94612-3788. Tel: 510-267-8345.

Organizations—

Confraternity of Eucharistic Devotion (CEDDO)—Mr. DICK DUCKART, Moderator; Mrs. BRIGITTE DESIMONE, Asst. Moderator; Mrs. PAMELA HAMILTON, Sec.; Mr. RALPH DESIMONE, Treas.; Rev. LAWRENCE C. D'ANJOU, Chap., 2121 Harrison St., Ste. 100, Oakland, 94612-3788. Tel: 925-676-8248. Email: ceddo@oakdiocese.org. Web: www.eucharisticdevotion.org.

Courage - Oakland Chapter—Chaplains: Revs. JOHN DIREEN; FRANCISCO FIGUEROA.

Cursillo Movement—Rev. LEO J. EDGERLY JR., Spiritual Dir.

Diocesan Council of Catholic Women—STEFFIE SILVIA, 5521 Columbia Ave., Richmond, 94804-5627. Tel: 510-525-7829.

St. Vincent de Paul Society—

Alameda County, Executive Director—Mr. PHILIP ARCA, 9235 San Leandro St., Oakland, 94603. Tel: 510-636-4246; 510-638-7600.

Contra Costa, Executive Director—Mr. RON WESTON, 2210 Gladstone Dr., Pittsburg, 94565. Tel: 925-439-5060, Ext. 19.

CLERGY, PARISHES, MISSIONS AND PAROCHIAL SCHOOLS

CITY OF OAKLAND

(ALAMEDA COUNTY)

1—CATHEDRAL PARISH OF CHRIST THE LIGHT (2008) Revs. Quang Minh Dong; Ismael Gutierrez, Parochial Vicar; Deacons Eugene Stelly; Rey Encarnacion; Peter Ta.

Res.: 2121 Harrison St., 94612. Tel: 510-832-5057; Fax: 510-832-0212. Email: cpctl@oakdiocese.org. Web: www.cpctl.org.

Catechesis/Religious Program—Sr. Kim Trong Nguyen, S.S.N.D., D.R.E. Students 135.

2—ST. ANDREW-ST. JOSEPH (1965), (African American), Merged into Cathedral Parish of Christ the Light, Oakland.

3—ST. ANTHONY (1871) Revs. Jesus Nieto-Ruiz; Peter Son Vo, Parochial Vicar. In Res., Rev. Sergio Mora.

Res.: 1535 16th Ave., 94606-4425. Tel: 510-534-2117; Fax: 510-534-2119. Email: sanantonio-oakland@comcast.net. Web: www.stanthonyoakland.parishesonline.com.

School—(Grades K-8), 1500 E. 15th St., 94606. Tel: 510-534-3334; Fax: 510-534-3378. Sr. Barbara Flannery, C.S.J., Prin. Lay Teachers 10; Students 154.

Catechesis/Religious Program—Carmen Hernandez, C.R.E. Students 425.

4—St. Augustine (1907) Rev. Mark Wiesner; Ms. Karen Miller, Pastoral Assoc.; Robbie Valentine, Office & Facility Admin.; James Gilman, Music Dir.; Mr. Walt Sears, Adult Formation. In Res., Rev. Gonzague Leroux (France).
Res.: 400 Alcatraz Ave., 94609-1106. Tel: 510-653-8631; Fax: 510-653-4256. Email: saintaugustinechurch@comcast.net.
Catechesis/Religious Program—Tel: 510-653-8631, Ext. 103; Fax: 510-653-4256. Email: saintaugustinechurch@comcast.net. Rebecca Pelle, D.R.E. Students 41.

5—St. Benedict (1930), (African American), Rev. James Matthews; Deacon Ronald Tutson. In Res., Rev. Cuthbert Aronyu (Uganda).
Res.: 2245 82nd Ave., 94605-3407. Tel: 510-632-1847; Fax: 510-633-2092. Email: saintbenedictcrh@aol.com.
Catechesis/Religious Program—Students 17.

6—St. Bernard (1912), (Hispanic—African American), Revs. Roberto Flores, S.V.D.; Edmund Kofi Afagbegee, S.V.D. (Ghana), Parochial Vicar; Deacon Javier Fuentes. In Res., Rev. Stephen Ernest, S.V.D.
Res.: 1620-62nd Ave., 94621-4221. Tel: 510-632-3013; Fax: 510-632-5286. Email: st.bernard.church@sbcglobal.net.
School—(Grades K-8), 1630-62nd Ave., 94621-4221. Tel: 510-632-6323; Fax: 510-632-6110. Ellen Spencer, Prin. Lay Teachers 10; Students 75.
Catechesis/Religious Program—Students 225.

7—Cathedral of St. Francis de Sales (1886) Merged with St. Mary, Immaculate Conception to form Catholic Parish of Christ the Light.

8—St. Columba (1898), (African American), Rev. Aiden McAleenan, Parochial Admin.; Rawn Harbor, Pastoral Assoc.
Res.: 6401 San Pablo Ave., 94608-1233. Tel: 510-654-7600; Fax: 510-654-7615. Email: stcolumba@sbcglobal.net. Web: www.stcolumbao.com.
Catechesis/Religious Program—Students 42.

9—St. Cyril (1926), (Korean), Merged with St. Lawrence O'Toole, Oakland to form St. Lawrence O'Toole-St. Cyril of Jerusalem, Oakland. For parish records contact St. Lawrence O'Toole-St. Cyril of Jerusalem, Oakland.

10—St. Elizabeth (1892), (Hispanic), Revs. Oscar A. Mendez, O.F.M.; Martin Ibarra, O.F.M., Parochial Vicar.
Res.: 1500 34th Ave., 94601-3024. Tel: 510-536-1266; Fax: 510-536-8560. Email: stelizabethchurch@yahoo.com. Web: www.stelizabethoak.org.
School—(Grades PreK-8), 1516 33rd Ave., 94601-3016. Tel: 510-532-7392; Fax: 510-532-0321. Sr. Rose Marie Hennessy, O.P., Prin.; Joseph Peterson, Vice Prin. Sisters 2; Lay Teachers 22; Students 317.
Catechesis/Religious Program—Students 400.

11—St. Jarlath (1910) Rev. Francisco J. Figueroa Esquer, Admin. In Res., Rev. Thomas Martin (Australia).
Res.: 2620 Pleasant St., 94602-2125. Tel: 510-532-2068; Fax: 510-532-3745. Email: sjarlath@sbcglobal.net.
School—(Grades K-8), 2634 Pleasant St., 94602-2125. Tel: 510-532-4387; Fax: 510-532-1001. Web: www.stjarlath.org. Ellen Spencer, Prin. Sisters 1; Lay Teachers 10; Students 107.
Catechesis/Religious Program—Students 154.

12—St. Lawrence O'Toole, Merged with St. Cyril, Oakland to form St. Lawrence O'Toole-St. Cyril of Jerusalem, Oakland. For parish records contact St. Lawrence O'Toole-St. Cyril of Jerusalem, Oakland.

13—St. Lawrence O'Toole-St. Cyril of Jerusalem (1916) Rev. Nicholas Glisson; Deacon Jeffrey Burns. In Res., Revs. Anthony Lam Phan; Ken Hamilton, S.V.D.; George Byarugaba (South Africa).
Res.: 3725 High St., 94619-2107. Tel: 510-530-0761; Fax: 510-530-0974. Email: slotsjc@sbcglobal.net. Web: www.stlawrenceotoole.net.
School—(Grades K-8) Tel: 510-530-0266; Fax: 510-530-7568. Email: bmccullough@csdo.org. Web: www.stlawrenceotoole.com. Barbara McCullough, Prin.; Michelle Collier, Librarian. Sisters 1; Lay Teachers 10; Students 169.
Catechesis/Religious Program—Tel: 510-530-0775; Fax: 510-530-0775. Email: srmaria@earthlink.net. Web: www.stlawrenceotoole.net. Students 105.

14—St. Leo the Great (1911) Rev. Timothy K. Johnson. In Res., Revs. Thomas Ng (Retired); Anatole A. Tiendrebeogo (Burkina Faso).
Res.: 176 Ridgeway Ave., 94611-5122. Tel: 510-654-6177; Fax: 510-654-4203. Email: stleo@pacbell.net. Web: www.stleothegreat.org.
School—(Grades PreK-8), 4238 Howe St., 94611-4705. Tel: 510-654-7828; Fax: 510-654-4057. Email: sleo@csdo.org. Web: www.stleothegreat.org. Sonya Simril, Prin. Lay Teachers 15; Students 219.
Catechesis/Religious Program—Email: stleo@pacbell.net. Web: www.stleothegreat.org. Students 15.

15—St. Louis Bertrand (1908), (Hispanic—African American), Rev. Jesus Hernandez Vidal, Admin.; Deacon Earl Johnson.
Res.: 1410-100th Ave., 94603-2506. Tel: 510-568-1080; Fax: 510-635-8618. Email: slbchurch@comcast.net.
Catechesis/Religious Program—Tel: 510-632-2865. Students 644.

16—St. Margaret Mary (1922) Rev. Stanislaw Zak. In Res., Rev. Jean-Marie Moreau.
Res.: 1219 Excelsior Ave., 94610-2830. Tel: 510-482-0596; Fax: 510-482-2093. Email: stmargaretm@yahoo.com. Web: www.stmargmaryoak.org.
Catechesis/Religious Program—Students 78.

17—Mary Help of Christians Church (1915), (Spanish), Rev. Sergio Mora, Parochial Admin.; Reyna Pina Lupian, Admin.; Deacon Gabriel Hernandez.
Res.: 2611 E. Ninth St., 94601-1404. Tel: 510-534-3501. Email: maryhelpofchrist@aol.com.
Catechesis/Religious Program—Students 167.

18—St. Mary, Immaculate Conception, Merged into the Cathedral Parish of Christ the Light, Oakland.

19—St. Mary, Immaculate Conception-St. Francis de Sales (1993) Merged into the Cathedral Parish of Christ the Light, Oakland.

20—Our Lady of Lourdes (1921) Rev. Seamus D. Genovese.
Res.: 2808 Lakeshore Ave., 94610-3613. Tel: 510-451-1790; Fax: 510-893-6443. Email: lourdesoakland@aol.com. Web: www.lourdesoakland.com.
Catechesis/Religious Program—Students 35.

21—St. Paschal Baylon (1955) Rev. Michael Norkett.
Res.: 3700 Dorisa Ave., 94605-4941. Tel: 510-636-0335; Fax: 510-636-0287. Email: stpaschalbaylon@juno.com.

22—St. Patrick (1879), (African American—Hispanic), Revs. Gregory Chisholm, S.J.; David H. Gill, S.J., Parochial Vicar.
Res.: 1023 Peralta St., 94607-1927. Tel: 510-444-1081; Fax: 510-444-1113. Email: howard1023@sbcglobal.net.
School—St. Martin de Porres, St. Patrick Campus, (Grades 6-8), 1630 10th St., 94607-1426. Tel: 510-832-1757; Fax: 510-832-6481. Sr. Barbara Dawson, R.S.C.J., Pres.; Maurice Harper, Vice Prin. Lay Teachers 3; Students 64.
Catechesis/Religious Program—Students 58.

23—Sacred Heart (1876) Revs. Karl Davis, O.M.I.; Jose Arong, O.M.I., Parochial Vicar. In Res., Revs. Nicanor Sarmiento, O.M.I.; Philip Singarayar, O.M.I.; Scott Hill, O.M.I.
Res.: 4025 Martin Luther King Jr. Way, 94609-2317. Tel: 510-655-9209; Fax: 510-652-1958.
School—St. Martin de Porres, Sacred Heart Campus, (Grades K-5), 675 41st St., 94609-2380. Tel: 510-652-2220; Fax: 510-652-2294. Sr. Barbara Dawson, R.S.C.J., Pres.; Maurice Harper, Vice Prin. Lay Teachers 7; Students 149.
Catechesis/Religious Program—Students 30.

24—St. Theresa of the Infant Jesus (The Little Flower) (1925) Rev. Patrick Goodwin. In Res., Rev. Peter L. Chong (Fiji).
Res.: 30 Mandalay Rd., 94618. Tel: 510-547-2777; Fax: 510-653-3575. Email: debbie@sttheresaoakland.org. Web: www.sttheresaoakland.org.
School—(Grades K-8), 4850 Clarewood Dr., 94618. Tel: 510-547-3146; Fax: 510-547-3253. Web: www.sttheresaschool.org. Email: jkoneffklatt@yahoo.com. Judith KoneffKlatt, Prin. Lay Teachers 38; Students 281.
Catechesis/Religious Program—Tel: 510-547-2777, Ext. 25. Email: kristine@sttheresaoakland.org. Students 119.

OUTSIDE THE CITY OF OAKLAND

Alameda, Alameda Co.

1—St. Albert (1976) Revs. Joy Kumarthusseril, M.F. (India); Jojo Puthussery, M.F. (India), Parochial Vicar.
Res.: 1022 Holly St., 94502-7038. Tel: 510-522-2185; Fax: 510-522-1055. Email: bookkeeper@stalbertsalameda.org.
Catechesis/Religious Program—Students 47.

2—St. Barnabas (1925) Rev. Dana P. Michaels, Parochial Admin. In Res., Revs. Robert Herbst, O.F.M.Conv.; Herman Leong.
Res.: 1427 Sixth St., 94501-3760. Tel: 510-522-8933; Fax: 510-522-8380. Email: sbparishoffice@comcast.net. Web: www.rc.net/oakland/st-barnabas.
Catechesis/Religious Program—Tel: 510-337-8962. Students 50.

3—St. Joseph Basilica (1885) Rev. Fred A. Riccio; Deacon David Young. In Res., Rev. Raymond Sacca.
Res.: 1109 Chestnut St., 94501-4212. Tel: 510-522-0181; Fax: 510-522-2864. Email: parish@st-joseph-community.org. Web: www.st-joseph-community.org.
School—St. Joseph Elementary School, (Grades K-8), 1910 San Antonio Ave., 94501-4216. Tel: 510-522-4457; Fax: 510-522-2890. Monica O'Callaghan, Prin. Sisters 1; Lay Teachers 18; Students 266.
Please see Saint Joseph Notre Dame High School under High Schools Parochial located in the Institution section.
Catechesis/Religious Program—Tel: 510-522-0181, Ext. 9409. Ms. Anne Marie Fourre, Dir. Faith Formation. Students 190.

4—St. Philip Neri (1925) Revs. Joy Kumarthusseril, M.F. (India); Jojo Puthussery, M.F. (India), Parochial Vicar.
Res.: 3108 Van Buren St., 94501-4840. Tel: 510-522-2299; Fax: 510-522-8123. Email: spirit_ruah@yahoo.com. Web: www.saspn.org.
School—(Grades K-8), 1335 High St., 94501-3165. Tel: 510-521-0787; Fax: 510-521-2418. Vikki Wojcik, Prin. Lay Teachers 18; Students 245.
Catechesis/Religious Program—Tel: 510-865-2626, Ext. 19. Email: cffoffice@saspn.org. Students 65.

Antioch, Contra Costa Co.

1—St. Ignatius of Antioch (1979) [CEM] Rev. Robert Rien, Parochial Admin.; Deacons Gary Hack; Gerald Waters. In Res., Rev. Thomas Bonacci, C.P.
Office: 3351 Contra Loma Blvd., 94509-5468. Tel: 925-778-0768; Fax: 925-778-0845. Email: st.ignatius@sbcglobal.net. Web: www.stignatiusofantioch.com.
Res.: 209 Tanganyika Ct., 94509.
Catechesis/Religious Program—3351 Contra Loma Blvd., 94509-5468. Tel: 925-778-1631. Students 216.

2—Most Holy Rosary (1874), (Hispanic), [CEM] [JC] Very Rev. Roberto Corral, O.P.; Revs. Dismas Sayre, Parochial Vicar; Francisco V. Vicente, O.P., Parochial Vicar; Sisters Sylvia Enriquez, O.P., Hispanic Ministry; Monica Terraza, O.P., Hispanic Ministry; Deacons Charles Silvernale; Jerry Grigg; Mrs. Jackie Hooke, Pastoral Assoc. & Business Admin. In Res., Rev. Edward Krasevac, O.P.
Res.: 1313 A St., 94509-2328. Tel: 925-757-4020; Fax: 925-757-6828.
School—(Grades PreK-8), 25 E. 15th St., 94509. Tel: 925-757-1270; Fax: 925-757-9309. Susana Lapeyrade-Drummond, Prin.; Dee Voight, Librarian. Lay Teachers 66; Students 600.
Catechesis/Religious Program—1313 A St., 94059-2328. Tel: 915-757-9515; Fax: 925-757-9638. Web: holyrosaryca.org. Students 679.

Bay Point, Contra Costa Co., Our Lady, Queen of the World (1962) Rev. Richard J. Culver.
Res.: 3155 Winterbrook Dr., 94565-3264. Tel: 925-458-4718; Fax: 925-458-3161. Email: wanda@olqw.org. Web: www.olqw.org.
Catechesis/Religious Program—Tel: 925-458-4574; Fax: 925-458-3161. Email: olqw@sbcglobal.net. Students 150.

Berkeley, Alameda Co.

1—St. Ambrose (1909) Revs. Joseph Fernandez, S.D.B. (India), Parochial Admin.; Bosco Ponthokkan, S.D.B. (India), Parochial Vicar.
Res.: 1145 Gilman St., 94706-2252. Tel: 510-525-2620; Fax: 510-525-5399.
Catechesis/Religious Program—Students 90.

2—Holy Spirit Parish/Newman Hall (1967) Revs. Bernie Campbell, C.S.P.; Albert Moser, C.S.P., Parochial Vicar; William L. Edens, C.S.P., Parochial Vicar. (Newman Center 1899). In Res., Rev. Brett C. Hoover, C.S.P.
Res.: 2700 Dwight Way, 94704-3113. Tel: 510-848-7812; Fax: 510-848-0179. Email: email@calnewman.org. Web: www.calnewman.org.
Catechesis/Religious Program—Ms. Frances Rojek, D.R.E. Students 135.

3—St. Joseph the Worker (1879) Revs. John Direen; George E. Crespin, Pastor Emeritus (Retired); Deacon Noe Gonzalez. In Res., Revs. Matthew Vanissery; Joseph Thieu Nguyen; Gebriel Woldai.
Res.: 1640 Addison St., 94703-1404. Tel: 510-843-2244; Fax: 510-843-2730. Email: sjwchurch@sbcglobal.net. Web: www.stjtwc.org.
Catechesis/Religious Program—Tel: 510-843-2244. Students 210.

4—St. Mary Magdalen (1923) Revs. David J. Farrugia, O.P.; Bruno Gibson, O.P., Parochial Vicar. In Res., Revs. Paul C. Raftery, O.P.; Albert Paretsky, O.P.; Michael J. Dodds, O.P.; Michael Sweeney, O.P.
Res.: 2005 Berryman St., 94709-1920. Tel: 510-526-4811; Fax: 510-525-3638.
School—School of the Madeleine, (Grades K-8), 1225 Milvia St., 94709-1932. Tel: 510-526-4744; Fax: 510-526-5152. Catherine Deehan, Prin. Lay

Teachers 21; Students 306.
Catechesis/Religious Program—Students 40.

BRENTWOOD, CONTRA COSTA CO., IMMACULATE HEART OF MARY (1949), (English—Spanish), Revs. Jerry W. Brown; Carl Tacuyan Arcosa, Parochial Vicar; Deacons John Kortuem; Ed Spano; Ron Horan.
Office: 500 Fairview Ave., 94513-1742. Tel: 925-634-4154; Fax: 925-516-9340.
Rectory—1361 Downey Point Dr., 94513-1870. Tel: 925-516-3189.
Catechesis/Religious Program—Students 721.

BYRON, CONTRA COSTA CO., ST. ANNE (1916) Rev. Ronald G. Schmit.
Mailing Address: P.O. Box 476, 94514-0476. Tel: 925-634-6625; Fax: 925-634-4194.
Catechesis/Religious Program—Tel: 925-634-6625, Ext. 224. Email: srbarbara@stannechurchbyron.com. Web: www.stannechurchbyron.com. Students 297.

CASTRO VALLEY, ALAMEDA CO.

1—OUR LADY OF GRACE (1947) Revs. Kevin C. Mullins, O.S.A.; Paul E. Quante, O.S.A., Parochial Vicar; Deacon Matthew Dulka.
Res.: 3433 Somerset Ave., 94546-54. Tel: 510-537-0806; Fax: 510-537-6281. Email: olgcv@sbcglobal.net. Web: www.olgcv.org.
School—(Grades K-8), 3427 Somerset Ave., 94546. Tel: 510-581-3155; Fax: 510-581-1059. Web: www.olg-school.org. Colleen F. Wahl, Prin. Lay Teachers 16; Students 190.
Catechesis/Religious Program—Tel: 510-582-9266; Fax: 510-537-6281. Email: olgrec@sbcglobal.net. Ms. Robyn Lang, D.R.E. Students 155.

2—TRANSFIGURATION (1961) Rev. Mario L. Borges; Deacons Timothy Moore; Burton Rigley; Martin Leach. In Res., Rev. David Link.
Res.: 4000 E. Castro Valley Blvd., 94552-4908. Tel: 510-538-7941; Fax: 510-538-7983. Email: transfig_office@sbcglobal.net. Web: www.transfigchurch.com.
Catechesis/Religious Program—Tel: 510-537-1502. Email: transfigccd@aol.com. Students 304.

CONCORD, CONTRA COSTA CO.

1—ST. AGNES (1964) Rev. Vincent Cotter; Deacon Richard Gierak.
Res.: 3966 Chestnut Ave., 94519-1955. Tel: 925-689-0838; Fax: 925-689-7899. Email: stagnesoffice@comcast.net. Web: www.stagnesparish.net.
School—(Grades K-8), 3886 Chestnut Ave., 94519-1907. Tel: 925-689-3990; Fax: 925-689-3455. Web: www.stagnesconcord.com. Karen Mangini, Prin. Sisters 2; Lay Teachers 29; Students 349.
Catechesis/Religious Program—Students 156.

2—ST. BONAVENTURE (1957) Revs. Richard A. Mangini; David Lawrence, S.J., Parochial Vicar; Deacons William Gall; Mariano Preza, Latino Ministry; Christa L. Fairfield, Parish Life Dir.
Res.: 5562 Clayton Rd., 94521-4158. Tel: 925-672-5800; Fax: 925-672-4606. Web: www.stbonaventure.net.
Catechesis/Religious Program— Rosann Halick, D.R.E. Students 497.

3—ST. FRANCIS OF ASSISI (1984), (Formerly Most Precious Blood, 1955) Revs. Hugo Hernandez, M.G. (Mexico), Admin.; Glenn A. Naguit, Parochial Vicar; Deacons Charles Palomares; John Mazibrook; Fred Schaub, Business Mgr.
Res.: 860 Oak Grove Rd., 94518-3461. Tel: 925-682-5447; Fax: 925-682-5491. Web: www.sfaconcord.org.
School—(Grades K-8), 866 Oak Grove Rd., 94518-3461. Tel: 925-682-5414; Fax: 925-682-5480. Web: www.sfaconcord.org. Sr. James M. Dyer, C.S.J., Prin. Sisters 2; Lay Teachers 27; Students 303.
Catechesis/Religious Program—Ms. Kathleen M. DeLemos, Youth Min.; Mrs. Scarlett Salaverria, D.R.E. Students 505.

4—QUEEN OF ALL SAINTS (1923) [CEM] Revs. Michael Cunningham; Enrique Ballesteros, Parochial Vicar.
Res.: 2390 Grant St., 94520-2245. Tel: 925-825-0350; Fax: 925-825-6975. Email: gaschurch@yahoo.com. Web: www.qaschurch.org.
School—(Grades K-8), 2391 Grant St., 94520-2244. Tel: 925-685-8700; Fax: 925-685-2034. Patrick Cook, Prin. Lay Teachers 18; Students 160.
Catechesis/Religious Program—Tel: 925-685-8707. Email: nancytomsic@yahoo.com. Nancy Tomsic, D.R.E. Students 575.

CROCKETT, CONTRA COSTA CO., ST. ROSE OF LIMA (1912) Rev. Ciarian Dillon, O.M.I.
Res.: 555 Third Ave., 94525-1114. Tel: 510-787-2052; Fax: 510-787-1199.
Catechesis/Religious Program—Tel: 510-787-1203. Students 16.
Mission—St. Patrick 2nd St. & School St., Port Costa, Contra Costa Co. 94525.

DANVILLE, CONTRA COSTA CO., ST. ISIDORE (1910) Revs. Gerard K. Moran; Paul Coleman (Ireland), Parochial Vicar; Deacons Adam J. Pietras; John Jee. In Res., Rev. Msgrs. Daniel E. Cardelli, Pastor Emeritus (Retired); John T. McCracken, Pastor Emeritus (Retired); Rev. James E. Driscoll (Retired).
Parish Office:—440 LaGonda Way, 94526-2562. Tel: 925-837-2122; Fax: 925-362-1919. Email: office@st-isidore-danville.org. Web: www.st-isidore-danville.org.
Res.: 445 LaGonda Way, 94526-2522. Tel: 925-837-2122.
School—(Grades K-8), 435 La Gonda Way, 94526. Tel: 925-837-2977; Fax: 925-837-2407. Web: www-.stisidore.org. Jean Schroeder, Prin. Lay Teachers 36; Students 640.
Catechesis/Religious Program—Tel: 925-362-1900; Fax: 925-362-1909. Students 875.
Kids Connection—432 La Gonda Way, 94526-2562. Tel: 925-820-7753. Before and after school child care.
Youth Ministry—440 La Gonda Way, 94526-2562. Tel: 925-362-1904; Fax: 925-362-1929. Students 160.

DUBLIN, ALAMEDA CO., ST. RAYMOND (1961) Revs. Robert J. McCann; Terence O'Malley, S.C.J., Parochial Vicar; Deacons Joe Sicat; John Archer Jr.; David Cloyne.
Res.: 11555 Shannon Ave., 94568. Tel: 925-828-2460; Fax: 925-828-8610. Email: office@st-raymond-dublin.org. Web: www.st-raymond-dublin.org.
School—(Grades K-8), 11557 Shannon Ave., 94568-1376. Tel: 925-574-7425; Fax: 925-828-2454. Madeleine de la Fontaine, Prin. Lay Teachers 17; Students 287.
Catechesis/Religious Program—Tel: 925-574-7414. Email: julie@st-raymond-dublin.org. Students 489.

EL CERRITO, CONTRA COSTA CO.

1—ST. JEROME (1941) Rev. Dante Tamayo; Deacon Benjamin Agustin. In Res., Rev. George R. Vargas (Philippines).
Res.: 308 Carmel Ave., 94530-3735. Tel: 510-525-0876; Fax: 510-526-2721. Email: saintjeromechurch@comcast.net. Web: www.stjeromecc.org.
School—(Grades K-8), 320 San Carlos Ave., 94530. Tel: 510-525-9484; Fax: 510-525-5227. Marla Korte, Prin. Lay Teachers 25; Students 200.
Catechesis/Religious Program—Students 59.

2—ST. JOHN THE BAPTIST (1925) Revs. John Maxwell; Rolando Bartolay, Parochial Vicar; Deacon Thomas McGowan. In Res., Rev. Raymond Ogbemure (Nigeria).
Res.: 11150 San Pablo Ave., 94530-2131. Tel: 510-234-2244; Fax: 510-234-3726.
School—(Grades K-8), 11156 San Pablo Ave., 94530-2131. Web: www.stjohn-elcerrito.org. Teresa Barber, Prin. Lay Teachers 27; Students 254.
Catechesis/Religious Program—Students 32.

EL SOBRANTE, CONTRA COSTA CO., ST. CALLISTUS (1952) Rev. James J. Thottapally, Admin.
Res.: 3580 San Pablo Dam Rd., 94803-2822. Tel: 510-223-1153; Fax: 510-223-1137. Email: st.callistus@sbcglobal.net.
Catechesis/Religious Program—Tel: 510-222-2538. Students 145.

FREMONT, ALAMEDA CO.

1—CORPUS CHRISTI (1914) Rev. Salvador Macias. In Res., Deacons Jorge Angel; Alfonso Perez.
Res.: 37891 Second St., 94536-2926. Tel: 510-790-3207; Fax: 510-790-3227.
Catechesis/Religious Program—Tel: 510-790-3226. Email: ccreled@sbcglobal.net. Students 200.

2—HOLY SPIRIT (1886) [CEM] [JC] Revs. Mathew Vellankal, S.D.B. (India), Admin.; Joseph Tran, Parochial Vicar; Thomas Khue, Parochial Vicar; Deacons Rudolph Brazil; William Drobick; Richard Yee; Stephen Taylor; Charles Glover. In Res., Rev. Johnson C. Abraham (India).
Res.: 37588 Fremont Blvd., 94536-3707. Tel: 510-797-1660; Fax: 510-797-7080. Email: hsparish@gmail.com. Web: www.holyspiritfremont.org.
School—(Grades PreK-8), 3930 Parish Ave., 94536. Tel: 510-793-3553; Fax: 510-793-2694. Email: hss@me.com. Web: holysspiritfmt.com. Susan Buchanan, Prin. Lay Teachers 20; Students 332.
Catechesis/Religious Program—Tel: 510-456-4974; Fax: 510-456-4991. Email: jenniferhsc@aol.com. Web: www.hscfaithformation.com. Students 590.

3—ST. JAMES THE APOSTLE (1972) Rev. Antony Vazhappilly, S.D.B. (India), Admin.; Deacon Ernesto Dandan.
Res.: 34700 Fremont Blvd., 94555. Tel: 510-792-1962; Fax: 510-796-5494. Email: stjamesapostle@att.net.
Catechesis/Religious Program—Students 42.

4—ST. JOSEPH (OLD MISSION SAN JOSE) (1797) [CEM] Rev. Msgr. Manuel C. Simas; Rev. Joseph Nguyen, Parochial Vicar; Sr. Mary Teresa Parker, Pastoral Assoc.; Deacon Lance Vivet.
Res.: P.O. Box 3276, 94539-0327. Tel: 510-656-2364; Fax: 510-656-2438. Email: stjomisssj@aol.com. Web: www.stjosephmsj.org.
School—(Grades K-8), 43222 Mission Blvd., 94539-5827. Tel: 510-656-6525; Fax: 510-656-3608. Jan Cooper, Prin. Dominican Sisters of San Jose 1; Lay Teachers 16; Students 274.
Catechesis/Religious Program—Tel: 510-657-0905; Fax: 510-657-4165. Students 245.

5—ST. LEONARD (1959) Merged with Santa Paula, Fremont to form Our Lady of Guadalupe, Fremont.

6—OUR LADY OF GUADALUPE (2000) Revs. John Prochaska; Juan Franco, Parochial Vicar; James Sullivan, Parochial Vicar; Deacons Ovide Guesnon; Steven Budnik Sr.; Jorge Lara; Michael Cantlon.
Office: 41933 Blacow Rd., 94538. Tel: 510-657-4043; Fax: 510-657-4055. Email: office@guadalupe-parish.org. Web: www.guadalupe-parish.org.
Res. & Church: 40382 Fremont Blvd., 94538-3409. Tel: 510-656-4921; Fax: 510-226-0714.
School—(Grades K-8), 40374 Fremont Blvd., 94538-3409. Tel: 510-657-1674; Fax: 510-657-3659. Linda Parini, Prin.; Traci Colon, Librarian. Priests 1; Lay Teachers 10; Students 215.
Catechesis/Religious Program—Tel: 510-651-4966. Students 633.

7—SANTA PAULA (1965) Merged with St. Leonard, Fremont to form Our Lady of Guadalupe, Fremont.

HAYWARD, ALAMEDA CO.

1—ALL SAINTS (1898) [CEM] Revs. Carl H. Seewald, S.V.D., Parochial Vicar; Anthony W. Herrera, Parochial Vicar; Deacons Nelson Gonsalves; Lawrence Quinn; Mr. Stephen P. Mullin, Parish Life Dir. In Res., Rev. Luke Ssemakula (Uganda).
Church: 22824 Second St., 94541-5217. Tel: 510-581-2570; Fax: 510-581-9538.
School—(Grades K-8), 22870 Second St., 94541. Tel: 510-582-1910; Fax: 510-582-0866. Email: allsaints_elemschool@csdo.org. Web: www.all-saints-school.org. Jocelyn Pierre-Antoine, Prin. Lay Teachers 12; Students 225.
Catechesis/Religious Program—Students 226.

2—ST. BEDE (1955) Revs. Seamus J. Farrell; Rosendo R. Manalo, Parochial Vicar; Jesus Manuel Galvez, O.F.M. Conv., Parochial Vicar; Deacon Denis Ryken, (Retired).
Res.: 26950 Patrick Ave., 94544-3851. Tel: 510-782-2171; Fax: 510-782-9712. Email: st.bedechurch@yahoo.com.
School—(Grades K-8), 26910 Patrick Ave., 94544-3851. Tel: 510-782-3444; Fax: 510-782-2243. Web: www.stbedehay.com. Antoinette Cosentino, Prin. Lay Teachers 18; Students 233.
Catechesis/Religious Program—Tel: 510-782-4292. Students 600.

3—ST. CLEMENT (1951) Revs. Ramon Gomez; Kenneth Sales, Parochial Vicar.
Office & Res.: 750 Calhoun St., 94544-4202. Tel: 510-582-7282; Fax: 510-582-1875. Email: saintclement@comcast.net.
School—(Grades K-8), 790 Calhoun St., 94544-4202. Tel: 510-538-5885; Fax: 510-538-1643. Mrs. Lana Jang Rocheford, Prin. Lay Teachers 14; Students 271.
Catechesis/Religious Program—Students 531.

4—ST. JOACHIM (1950) Revs. Zbignew Fraszczak, S.V.D.; Hieu Trong Nguyen, S.V.D., Parochial Vicar; Deacons Rigoberto Cabezas; Ernest Jaramillo.
Res.: 21250 Hesperian Blvd., 94541-5809. Tel: 510-783-2766; Fax: 510-783-2760. Web: stjoachimcatholicchurch.org.
School—(Grades PreK-8) Tel: 510-783-3177; Fax: 510-783-2161. Web: www.stjoachimschool.org. Armond Seishas, Prin. Lay Teachers 34; Students 351.
Catechesis/Religious Program—Tel: 510-785-1818. Students 803.

LAFAYETTE, CONTRA COSTA CO., ST. PERPETUA (1952) Rev. John Kasper, O.S.F.S., Parochial Admin.; Deacon Luis Rivilla.
Res.: 3454 Hamlin Rd., 94549-5019. Tel: 925-283-0272; Fax: 925-283-6534. Email: office@stperpetua.org. Web: www.stperpetua.org.
School—(Grades K-8), 3445 Hamlin Rd., 94549-5018. Tel: 925-284-1640; Fax: 925-284-5676. Karen Goodshaw, Prin.; Mari Pongkhamsing, Librarian. Lay Teachers 25; Students 246.
Catechesis/Religious Program—Tel: 925-283-0272, Ext. 204. Students 345.

LIVERMORE, ALAMEDA CO.

1—ST. CHARLES BORROMEO (1964) [JC] Rev. Augusto Acob, Parochial Admin.; Deacons John Durden Jr.; Gilbert Pesqueira. In Res., Rev. Richard McCafferty, S.J. (Retired).
Res.: 1315 Lomitas Ave., 94550-6441. Tel: 925-447-4549; Fax: 925-373-7088. Email: office@stcharlesborromeo.org. Web: www.stcharlesborromeo.org.
Catechesis/Religious Program—Students 319.

2—ST. MICHAEL (1878), (Spanish), [CEM] Revs. Robert Mendonca; Ruben Morales, Parochial Vicar; David E. Staal; Deacons David Rezendes; William Archer, Bus. Admin. & Pastoral Assoc.; Manuel Moya. In Res., Revs. Augustine Koilparampil; Walter W. Mayer (Retired).
Res.: 458 Maple St., 94550-3238. Tel: 925-447-1585;

Fax: 925-447-0520.
School—(Grades K-8), 345 Church St., 94550-3205. Tel: 925-447-1888; Fax: 925-447-6720. Sr. Emmanuel Cardinale, O.P., Prin. Sisters 1; Lay Teachers 14; Students 267.
Catechesis/Religious Program—Tel: 925-447-8814; Fax: 925-447-6720. Patty Malhiot, D.R.E. Students 425.

MARTINEZ, CONTRA COSTA CO., ST. CATHERINE OF SIENA (1873) [CEM] Rev. Leonardo Asuncion (Philippines), Parochial Admin.; Deacons Alberto Dizon; David Holland.
Parish Office & Mailing Address: 1125 Ferry St., 94553-1720.
Res.: 1100 Estudillo St., 94553-1707. Tel: 925-228-2230; Fax: 925-228-1318. Email: frleostcath@yahoo.com. Web: www.stcatherineofsienamartinez.org.
School—(Grades PreK-8), 604 Mellus St., 94553-1639. Tel: 925-228-4140; Fax: 925-228-0697. Mr. Andrew Von Haunalter, Prin. Lay Teachers 25; Students 187.
Catechesis/Religious Program—1125 Ferry St., 94553-1720. Tel: 925-228-2230, Ext. 7. Students 204.

MORAGA, CONTRA COSTA CO., ST. MONICA (1965) Rev. Wayne Campbell.
Res.: 1001 Camino Pablo, 94556-1831. Tel: 925-376-6900; Fax: 925-376-9796. Email: office@stmonicamoraga.com. Web: www.stmonicamoraga.com.
Catechesis/Religious Program—Students 374.

NEWARK, ALAMEDA CO., ST. EDWARD (1920) Revs. Jeffrey R. Keyes, C.PP.S.; James Franck, C.PP.S., Parochial Vicar; Jerard Raj Irudayanathan Irudeya, C.PP.S. (India), Parochial Vicar; Sr. Mary Mark Schoenstein, O.P., Pastoral Assoc.; Deacons Ernest Perez, (Retired); Rolito C. Roque; Nick Bruckner, (Retired); Roger Wedl; Antonio Barreto, (Retired).
Res.: 5788 Thornton Ave., 94560-3826. Tel: 510-797-0241; Fax: 510-797-4557. Email: parishoffice@stedwardcatholic.org.
School—(Grades K-8) Tel: 510-793-7242; Fax: 510-793-3189. Sr. Diane Aruda, O.P., Prin. Lay Teachers 21; Students 295.
Catechesis/Religious Program—Tel: 510-797-5588. Email: faithformation@stedwardcatholic.org. Students 510.

OAKLEY, CONTRA COSTA CO., ST. ANTHONY (1925) [JC] Revs. Olman Solis, Parochial Admin.; Giopre Prado, Parochial Vicar; Ms. Joann Mass, Business Mgr.; Deacons Joseph Tovar; Alan Layden; Frank Bustos, (Retired).
Res.: 971 O'Hara Ave., 94561-5785. Tel: 925-625-2048; Fax: 925-625-4433. Email: jmassstanthony@aol.com. Web: www.stanthonyoakley.org.
Catechesis/Religious Program—Tel: 925-625-2077. Students 602.

ORINDA, CONTRA COSTA CO., SANTA MARIA (1892) Rev. Msgr. Theodore W. Kraus; Deacons Maurice Custodio, (Retired); Clement Chen. In Res., Revs. Paul Ojibway, S.A.; George Alengadan, S.D.B.
Res.: 40 Santa Maria Way, 94563-2605. Tel: 925-254-2426; Fax: 925-254-2468. Email: smoffice@smparish.org. Web: www.santamariaparish.info.
Catechesis/Religious Program—Students 252.
Convent—50 Santa Maria Way, 94563-2605. Tel: 925-253-0831.

PIEDMONT, ALAMEDA CO., CORPUS CHRISTI (1929) Rev. Leo J. Edgerly Jr. In Res., Revs. Basil DePinto (Retired); Daniel E. Danielson (Retired).
Res.: 322 St. James Dr., 94611-3627. Tel: 510-530-4343; Fax: 510-530-6824. Email: rectory@corpuschristipiedmont.org. Web: www.corpuschristipiedmont.org.
School—(Grades K-8), One Estates Dr., 94611-3341. Tel: 510-530-4056; Fax: 510-530-5926. Web: www-.corpuschristischool.com. Mrs. Kathleen Murphy, Prin.; Alexandra Walton, Librarian. Lay Teachers 29; Students 277.
Catechesis/Religious Program—Students 140.

PINOLE, CONTRA COSTA CO., ST. JOSEPH (1947) Revs. Paul J. Schmidt; Kenneth Nobrega, Parochial Vicar; Mark Amaral, Parochial Vicar; Deacons Leslie Miyashiro; Donaciano Perez. In Res., Rev. Richard Gagliardi (Retired).
Parish Center, Office & Mailing Address: 2100 Pear St., 94564-1711. Tel: 510-741-4900; Fax: 510-724-9185. Email: info@sjcpinole.org. Web: www.sjcpinole.org.
Church: 837 Tennent Ave., 94564-1723.
School—(Grades K-8), 1961 Plum St., 94564. Tel: 510-724-0242; Fax: 510-724-9886. Arlene Marseille, Prin. Lay Teachers 20; Students 300.
Catechesis/Religious Program—Students 516.

PITTSBURG, CONTRA COSTA CO.
1—GOOD SHEPHERD (1965) Rev. Helmut W. Richter; Deacon Ken Wedge.
Res.: 3200 Harbor St., 94565-5444. Tel: 925-432-6404; Fax: 925-432-6748. Web: www.goodshepherdpittsburg.org.
Catechesis/Religious Program—Tel: 925-439-1091. Students 218.
2—ST. PETER, MARTYR OF VERONA (1914) Revs. Ricardo A. Chavez; Jesus Salvador Quiroz, Parochial Vicar. In Res., Rev. William Johnson.
Res.: 740 Black Diamond St., 94565-2148. Tel: 925-432-4771; Fax: 925-432-3389.
School—(Grades PreK-8), 425 W. 4th St., 94565-1968. Tel: 925-439-1014; Fax: 925-439-1506. Joseph Siino, Prin. Lay Teachers 14; Students 290.
Catechesis/Religious Program—Tel: 925-432-7200. Students 608.

PLEASANT HILL, CONTRA COSTA CO., CHRIST THE KING (1951) Revs. Brian Joyce; Declan Deane, Parochial Vicar; Deacon John Ashmore. In Res., Revs. Brian Timony (Retired); Michael Dibble.
Res.: 199 Brandon Rd., 94523-3220. Tel: 925-682-2486; Fax: 925-682-5021. Email: webmaster@ctkph.org. Web: www.ctkph.org.
School—(Grades K-8), 195 Brandon Rd., 94523. Tel: 925-685-1109; Fax: 925-685-1289. Email: info@ctkschool.org. Web: www.ctkschool.org. Mrs. Kathy Gannon-Briggs, Prin. Lay Teachers 21; Students 321.
Catechesis/Religious Program—Tel: 925-686-1017; Fax: 925-686-6325. Web: www.ctkph.org. Students 1,101.

PLEASANTON, ALAMEDA CO.
1—ST. AUGUSTINE (1901) Merged with St. Elizabeth Seton, Pleasanton to form The Catholic Community of Pleasanton.
2—THE CATHOLIC COMMUNITY OF PLEASANTON (1901) [CEM] Revs. Padraig Greene, Admin.; William Rozario (India), Parochial Vicar; Jerrold F. Kennedy, Parochial Vicar; Deacons Richard Martin; Ernest Freeman; Gary Wortham.
Res.: 3999 Bernal, P.O. Box 817, 94566-7264. Tel: 925-846-4489; Fax: 925-426-5061. Web: www.catholicsofpleasanton.org.
Catechesis/Religious Program—Tel: 925-846-3531; Fax: 925-846-3543. Students 1,400.
3—ST. ELIZABETH SETON (1991) Merged with St. Augustine, Pleasanton to form The Catholic Community of Pleasanton.

POINT RICHMOND, CONTRA COSTA CO., OUR LADY OF MERCY (1902) Rev. David K. O'Rourke, O.P., Parochial Admin.
Res.: 301 W. Richmond Ave., 94801-3862. Tel: 510-232-1843. Email: dkorop@sbcglobal.net. Web: www.pointrichmondcatholic.org.

RICHMOND, CONTRA COSTA CO.
1—ST. CORNELIUS (1952) [CEM] Rev. Filiberto Barrera, Admin. In Res., Rev. Edmund Coppinger (WIL) (Retired).
Res.: 205-28th St., 94804-3001. Tel: 510-233-5215; Fax: 510-233-7342.
School—(Grades K-8), 201-28th St., 94804-3001. Tel: 510-232-3326; Fax: 510-232-4071. Ms. Sherri Moradi, Prin. Lay Teachers 9; Students 176.
Catechesis/Religious Program—Students 430.
2—ST. DAVID OF WALES (1952) Revs. John R. Blaker; James Kimani Kairu (Kenya), Parochial Vicar.
Res.: 5641 Esmond Ave., 94805-1112. Tel: 510-237-1531; Fax: 510-237-3801. Email: davidofwales@gmail.com.
School—(Grades PreK-8), 871 Sonoma St., 94805-1122. Tel: 510-232-2283; Fax: 510-231-0484. Web: home.catholicweb.com/stdavidschool. Ann Pires, Prin. Lay Teachers 16; Students 170.
Catechesis/Religious Program—Students 22.
3—ST. MARK (1912) Rev. Ramiro Flores, Admin.
Res.: 159 Harbour Way, 94801-3553. Tel: 510-234-5886; Fax: 510-236-5711.
Catechesis/Religious Program—Tel: 510-234-5886, Ext. 222. Students 452.

RODEO, CONTRA COSTA CO., ST. PATRICK (1923) Revs. Larry E. Young; Weerasak Chompoochan, Parochial Vicar.
Res.: 902 Spruce Ct., 94572-1549. Tel: 510-313-0829; Fax: 510-799-5681.
Office: 825 Seventh St., 94572-1549. Tel: 510-799-4406. Web: www.stpatrickrodeo.org.
School—(Grades PreK-8), 907 Seventh St., 94572-1549. Tel: 510-799-2506; Fax: 510-799-6781. Kelly Stevens, Prin. Lay Teachers 27; Students 303.
Catechesis/Religious Program—Tel: 510-799-4434. Students 300.

SAN LEANDRO, ALAMEDA CO.
1—ST. ALPHONSUS LIGUORI (1955) [CEM] Merged with Our Lady of Grace, Castro Valley. For parish records contact OUr Lady of Grace, Castro Valley.
2—ASSUMPTION OF THE BLESSED VIRGIN MARY (1951) Revs. Vincent J. Scott; Christopher Berbena, Parochial Vicar; Deacons Dac Cao; Harry Clyde; George Peters. In Res., Rev. Joseph Duong Phan.
Res.: 1100 Fulton Ave., 94577-6210. Tel: 510-352-1537; Fax: 510-352-9155. Email: slassumption@sbcglobal.net. Web: www.churchoftheassumption.net.
School—(Grades K-8), 1851 136th Ave., 94578-1661. Tel: 510-357-8772; Fax: 510-357-7018. Pamela Lyons, Prin.; Alice Ganski, Librarian. Lay Teachers 23; Students 282.
Catechesis/Religious Program—Students 42.
3—ST. FELICITAS (1952) Rev. Augustine Joseph, Parochial Admin.; Deacon Jose Prado, (Retired). In Res., Revs. Tran Thuc Dinh (Vietnam) (Retired); Joseph Pathiyil, M.F. (India).
Res.: 1662 Manor Blvd., 94579-1509. Tel: 510-351-5244; Fax: 510-351-5730. Email: stfelicitaschurch@comcast.net.
School—(Grades K-8), 1650 Manor Blvd., 94579-1509. Tel: 510-357-2530; Fax: 510-357-5358. Web: www.stfelicitas-school.org. Rodney Pierre-Antoine, Prin. Lay Teachers 14; Students 278.
Catechesis/Religious Program—Tel: 510-483-4880. Sandi Walton, D.R.E. Students 250.
4—ST. LEANDER (1864) Revs. Paul R. Vassar; Mel Serraon, Parochial Vicar; Fernando Cortez, Parochial Vicar; Deacons Dennis Davis; Victor Silveira. In Res., Rev. Thomas Lester (Retired).
Office: 474 W. Estudillo Ave., 94577-3610. Tel: 510-895-5631; Fax: 510-352-3578. Email: stleander@sbcglobal.net.
School—(Grades PreK-8), 451 Davis St., 94577. Tel: 510-351-4144; Fax: 510-483-6060. Lynne Mullen, Prin. Lay Teachers 15; Students 242.
Catechesis/Religious Program—Students 388.
5—OUR LADY OF GOOD COUNSEL (1966) [JC] Rev. Thuong Nguyen. In Res., Rev. Andrews Amritharaj, S.D.B. (India).
Rectory—14112 Azores Pl., 94577-6402. Tel: 510-614-2765; Fax: 510-614-2876. Email: ourladycounsel@yahoo.com.
Church: 2500 Bermuda Ave., 94577-5436.

SAN LORENZO, ALAMEDA CO., ST. JOHN THE BAPTIST (1925) Revs. Michael Lacey; Hugo Franca (Brazil), Parochial Vicar; Deacons Leonard J. Bettencourt, (Retired); Arturo Jimenez.
Res.: 264 E. Lewelling Blvd., 94580-1736. Tel: 510-351-5050; Fax: 510-276-0397. Email: stjohnsrectory@hotmail.com. Web: www.stjohnsparishslz.org.
School—(Grades PreK-8), 270 E. Lewelling Blvd., 94580-1736. Tel: 510-276-6632; Fax: 510-276-5645. Web: www.stjohnslz.org. Elizabeth Guneratne, Prin.; Louise Bettencourt, Librarian. Lay Teachers 19; Students 267.
Catechesis/Religious Program—Tel: 510-351-5050, Ext. 16; Fax: 510-276-0397. Kathleen Kennedy, D.R.E. Students 487.

SAN PABLO, CONTRA COSTA CO., ST. PAUL (1864) Revs. Gary Klauer, O.F.M.Conv.; Luke Van Vu, O.F.M.Conv., Parochial Vicar; Jacob Carazo, O.F.M.Conv., Parochial Vicar.
Res.: 1845 Church Ln., 94806-3705. Tel: 510-232-5931; Fax: 510-232-1846.
School—(Grades K-8) Tel: 510-233-3080; Fax: 510-231-8776. Web: www.stpaulofsanpablo.org. Connie Howard, Prin. Lay Teachers 19; Students 197.
Catechesis/Religious Program—1825 Church Ln., 94806. Students 455.

SAN RAMON, CONTRA COSTA CO., ST. JOAN OF ARC (1979) Rev. Raymond Zielezienski; Deacons Ruben Gomez; Charles Stanton, Parish Mgr.; Hock Chuan Oey.
Office: 2601 San Ramon Valley Blvd., 94583-1630. Tel: 925-830-0600. Email: parishoffice@sjasr.org. Web: www.sjasr.org.
Res.: 2421 Cuenca Dr., 94583.
Catechesis/Religious Program—Tel: 925-830-4710. Students 1,188.

UNION CITY, ALAMEDA CO.
1—ST. ANNE (1973) Revs. Geoffrey Baraan; Richard Boyle, O.S.M., Parochial Vicar; Deacons Benigno Calub; Carlos Rabuy.
Res.: 32223 Cabello St., P.O. Box 292, 94587-0292. Tel: 510-471-7766; Fax: 510-487-6540. Email: stanne@sbcglobal.net. Web: www.sainteannecatholic.org.
Catechesis/Religious Program—Tel: 510-489-2080. Students 935.
2—HOLY FAMILY CATHOLIC ETHNIC MISSION (1933) Deacon Witold Cichon, Admin. Polish Center.
Parish Office: 25580 Campus Dr., Hayward, 94542. Fax: 510-881-2248.
Church: 3880 Smith St., 94587-2614. Tel: 510-881-2245.
Center for the Deaf—Email: sjcd@sjcd.org. Web: www.sjcd.org.
Catechesis/Religious Program—Ms. Kata Strawn, D.R.E. Students 4.
Polish Center—Tel: 510-282-4875; Fax: 925-754-8056. Email: witoldpt@aol.com. Web: www.polish-pastoralcenter.org. Grazyna Koralewski, Polish School Prin.; Halina Fiutek, Youth Ministry; Revs. Dominik Ciolek, S.J. (Poland), Chap.; Marek Kruszynski, S.J. (Poland), Chap.

Catechesis/Religious Program—Students 35.

3—OUR LADY OF THE ROSARY (1951) Rev. Jose M. Leon; Deacons Federico Ceja, (Retired); Richard Folger; Gustaaf Roemers; Luis Trucios.
Res.: 703 C St., 94587-2195. Tel: 510-471-2609; Fax: 510-471-4601. Email: admin@olrchurch.org. Web: www.olrchurch.org.
School—(Grades K-8), 678 B St., 94587-2141. Tel: 510-471-3765. Email: admin@olrschool.org. Web: www.olrschool.org. Gloria Galarsa, Prin. Lay Teachers 9; Students 151.
Catechesis/Religious Program—Tel: 510-471-7419. Email: reled@olrchurch.org. Web: www.olrchurch.org. Students 346.

WALNUT CREEK, CONTRA COSTA CO.

1—ST. ANNE (1965) Rev. Joseph Parekkatt, S.D.B. (India), Parochial Admin.
Res.: 1600 Rossmoor Pkwy., 94595-2507. Tel: 925-932-2324; Fax: 925-932-4628.

2—ST. JOHN VIANNEY (1965) Revs. James J. McGee; Clarence Zamora, Parochial Vicar; Deacon Herb Casey.
Res.: 1650 Ygnacio Valley Rd., 94598-3123. Tel: 925-939-7911; Fax: 925-939-0450. Email: staff@sjvianney.org. Web: www.sjvianney.org.
Catechesis/Religious Program—Tel: 925-939-9544. Students 509.

3—ST. MARY (1941) [JC] Revs. Paulson Mundanmani, Admin.; Javier Aguilar, Parochial Vicar; Deacon Antonio Reyes.
Res.: 1201 Alpine Rd., 94596-4403. Tel: 925-891-8937; Fax: 925-934-1358. Email: rectory@stmary-wc.org. Web: www.stmary-wc.org.
School—(Grades PreK-8), 1158 Bont Ln., 94596. Tel: 925-935-5054; Fax: 925-935-5063. Web: www.stmary.net. Suzanne Edwards, Prin. Lay Teachers 38; Students 291; Sisters 1.
Catechesis/Religious Program—2039 Mt. Diablo Blvd., 94596. Tel: 925-891-8930. Web: www.stmary-wc.org. Students 264.

4—ST. STEPHEN (1966) Rev. Denis A. Des Rosiers.
Res.: 525 Madonna Ln., 94597-2917. Tel: 925-939-3826; Fax: 925-988-0417. Email: keavenyct@sbcglobal.net. Web: saintstephenparish.org.
Church: 1101 Keaveney Ct., 94597-2465.
Catechesis/Religious Program—Students 25.

Chaplains of Public Institutions

Hospitals

OAKLAND. *Children's Hospital*, Tel: 510-655-9209. Sr. Bernice Gotelli, P.B.V.M. Tel: 510-428-3385, Ext. 2676. Attended by Sacred Heart Parish.
Highland Hospital, Tel: 510-482-0596. Attended by St. Margaret Mary Parish.
Kaiser-Permanente Medical Center. Pastoral Care., Tel: 510-752-6281; 510-654-6177 (Parish). Attended by St. Leo the Great Parish.
Summit Campus of the Alta Bates Summit Medical Center. Pastoral Care, Tel: 510-869-6784; 510-655-9209 (Parish). Attended by Sacred Heart Parish.

ANTIOCH. *Delta Memorial Hospital*, Tel: 925-757-4020 (Parish). Attended by Holy Rosary Parish.

ALAMEDA. *Alameda Hospital*, Tel: 510-522-0181. Attended by St. Joseph Basilica.

BERKELEY. *Alta Bates Campus of the Alta Bates Summit Medical Center*. Pastoral Care., Tel: 510-204-6730. Rev. Michael Guimon, O.S.M., Chap. Tel: 510-204-6733; 510-801-0426.
Herrick Campus of the Alpha Bates Summit Medical Center, Tel: 510-843-2244. Rev. Michael Guimon, O.S.M., Chap. Tel: 510-204-6733; 510-801-0426. Attended by St. Joseph the Worker Parish, Berkeley.

CASTRO VALLEY. *Eden Hospital*, Tel: 510-537-0806. Attended by Our Lady of Grace Parish.

CONCORD. *Mount Diablo Hospital Medical Center*. Director of Pastoral Care, Tel: 925-674-2133. Rev. William Johnson, Chap. Tel: 925-947-5281; Pager: 925-920-8420. Attended by St. Peter Martyr Church.

FREMONT. *Kaiser Permanente Medical Center*, Tel: 510-657-4043 (Our Lady of Guadalupe Parish); 510-797-0241 (St. Edward Parish); 510-656-2364 (St. Joseph Parish). Attended by Our Lady of Guadalupe Parish; St. Edward Parish; St. Joseph Parish.
Washington Hospital. Revs. Johnson C. Abraham (India), Chap. Tel: 510-557-9845, Jeffrey Finley, C.PP.S. Tel: 510-797-1111, Ext. 4153 (Dir. Pastoral Care).

HAYWARD. *Kaiser Permanente Medical Center*, Tel: 510-781-2171. Attended by St. Bede Parish.
St. Rose Hospital. Pastoral Care.

LIVERMORE. *VA Palo Alto Health Care System Home*. Livermore Division., Tel: 925-447-2560. Rev. Augustine Koilparampil. Tel: 925-447-2560.
Valley Memorial Hospital, Tel: 925-447-4549. Attended by St. Charles Borromeo Parish.

MARTINEZ. *Contra Costa Regional Medical Center and VA Administrative Skilled Nursing Center*, Tel: 925-370-4178. Rev. William Johnson. Tel: 925-432-4771, Sr. Moira McPherson, O.P. Tel: 925-228-2230, Ext. 8. Attended by St. Catherine of Siena Parish.

PITTSBURG. *Delta Memorial Hospital*, Tel: 925-432-6404. Attended by Good Shepherd Parish.

PLEASANTON. *Valley Care Medical Center*, Tel: 925-846-4489 (Catholic Community of Pleasanton); 425-447-4549 (Parish). Attended by The Catholic Community of Pleasanton & St. Borromeo Parish.

RICHMOND. *Kaiser-Permanente Medical Center*, Tel: 510-233-5215 (St. Cornelius Parish); 510-234-5886 (St. Mark Parish); 510-232-5931 (St. Paul Parish).

SAN LEANDRO. *All Saints Hospital*, Tel: 510-352-1537. Attended by Assumption Parish.
Fairmont Hospital, Tel: 510-352-1537. Attended by Assumption Parish.
George Mark Children's House, Tel: 510-352-1537. Attended by Assumption Parish.
John George Psychiatric Pavillion, Tel: 510-352-1537. Attended by Assumption Parish.
Kindred Hospital, Tel: 510-352-1537. Attended by Assumption Parish.
San Leandro Hospital, Tel: 510-895-5631. Attended by St. Leander Parish.

SAN PABLO. *Doctors Medical Center*, Tel: 510-232-5931 (St. Paul Parish); 510-223-1153 (St. Callistus Parish). Attended by St. Paul Parish & St. Callistus Parish.

SAN RAMON. *San Ramon Regional Medical Center*, Tel: 925-830-0600. Attended by St. Joan of Arc Parish.

WALNUT CREEK. *John Muir Memorial Hospital*. Pastoral Care., Tel: 925-947-5281 (St. John Vianney Parish); 925-939-7911.
Kaiser-Permanente Medical Center, Tel: 925-891-8900. Attended by St. Mary Parish.

Prisons and Jails

OAKLAND. *Glenn E. Dyer Detention Facility*, Tel: 510-268-2777 (Chap. Jennings).

CLAYTON. *Marsh Creek Detention Facility*. Kathleen Barrere, Chap. Tel: 925-674-9140.

DUBLIN. *Alameda County Santa Rita Jail*. Richard Denoix, Detention Min. Tel: 925-426-1857.
Federal Correctional Institution. Peggy Ashforth, Chap. Tel: 925-833-7500, Ext. 385, Hans Nhoch, Dept. Head. Tel: 925-833-7500, Ext. 384.

MARTINEZ. *John A. Davis Juvenile Hall*. Mr. Ed Cichon, Chap. Tel: 510-758-1469.
Martinez Detention Facility. Deacon Charles Silvernale, Chap. Tel: 925-754-1959.

RICHMOND. *West County Detention Facility*. Vishnu Ramrattan, Chap. Tel: 510-262-4330. (formerly Richmond Jail)

SAN LEANDRO. *Juvenile Hall Facility*. Mr. Michael Wharton. Tel: 510-701-0685, Mr. Byrne Sherwood. Tel: 925-283-0462.

On Duty Outside the Diocese:
Revs.—
Nguyen, Hy, S.S.
Thurston, Anthony
Tompkins, Terry
Wydeven, John L.

Study Leave:
Rev.—
Kappler, Stephan

Military Chaplains:
Revs.—
Clemens, Neal, Chap., 407 AEG/HC, Ali Air Force Base, AE 09331.
Dinh, Van, Chap., Spanghalem Air Base, 52 FW/HC. Unit 3680, Box 70, Apo, AE 09126-8070 Germany.
Tran, Joseph, Chap., 60 AMW/HC, Hacket St., Travis Afb, 94535-1110.

Graduate Studies:
Revs.—
Lopez, Sergio, J.C.D. (Cand.), (Studying in Rome)
Nguyen, Bich, (Studying in Rome)

On Sabbatical:
Revs.—
Fiedorowicz, Joseph
Landeza, Jayson J.
Rudzewicz, Jan

Retired:
Rev. Msgrs.—
Adams, Robert
Cardelli, Daniel E.
Ferraro, Joseph
McCracken, John T.
Valdivia, Antonio
Revs.—
Andrade, Bernardino
Atwood, Ronald E.
Brainard, Ernest B.
Brylka, Vincent R.
Charm, Robert
Cleu, Paul
Crespin, George E.
Danielson, Daniel E.
DePinto, Basil
Devine, Paul
Dinh, Tran Thuc (Vietnam)
Driscoll, James E.
Fernandes, John
Gagliardi, Richard
Jaques, Domingos
Joyce, Michael
Kozina, Vladimir
Lester, Thomas
Lima, John H.
Marshall, William
Mayer, Walter W.
Mifsud, Carmelo
Ng, Thomas
Osuna, E. Donald
Palis, Theo
Peiris, Richard
Phan, Anthony Lam
Pickett, James B.
Poon, Stanislaus
Ruffing, Norman
Russell, Kenneth
Schexnayder, James
Snyder, Alexander
Starbuck, James
Timony, Brian

Permanent Deacons:
Agustin, Benjamin, St. Jerome, El Cerrito
Angel, Jorge, Corpus Christi, Freemont
Archer, John, St. Raymond Penafort, Dublin
Archer, William, St. Michael, Livermore
Arteaga, Gustavo, (On duty outside diocese)
Ashmore, John, Christ the King, Pleasant Hill
Baptista, Antonio, (On duty outside diocese)
Barnes, James, (Retired)
Barreto, Antonio, (Retired)
Beltran, Juan
Bettencourt, Leonard, (Retired)
Bothe, William, (Retired)
Brazil, Rudolph, Holy Spirit, Fremont
Bruckner, Nick, (Retired), St. Edward, Newark
Budnik, Steven, Sr., Our Lady of Guadalupe, Fremont
Burns, Jeffrey, St. Lawrence O'Toole, Oakland
Bustos, Frank, (Retired), St. Anthony, Oakley
Cabezas, Rigoberto, St. Joachim, Hayward
Calub, Benigno, St. Ann, Union City
Cantlon, Michael, Our Lady of Guadalupe, Fremont
Cao, Dac, Church of the Assumption, San Leandro
Casey, Herb, St. John Vianney, Walnut Creek
Ceja, Federico, (Retired)
Chen, Clement, Santa Maria, Orinda
Chichon, Witold, Polish Pastoral Center, Union City
Cloyne, David, St. Raymond, Dublin
Clyde, Harry, Church of the Assumption, San Leandro
Custodio, Maurice, Santa Maria, Orinda
Dandan, Ernesto, St. James, Fremont
Davis, Dennis, St. Leander, San Leandro
DeLeon, Joseph L., (Out of Diocese)
Dizon, Alberto, St. Catherine of Siena, Martinez
Drobick, William, Holy Spirit, Fremont
Duhe, Gaston J., (Retired)
Dulka, Matthew, Our Lady of Grace, Castro Valley
Durden, John, Jr., St. Charles, Livermore
Ehling, Rex, (Retired)
Encarnacion, Rey, Cathedral Parish of Christ the Light, Oakland
Evans, Garry, (On Duty Outside the Diocese)
Folger, Richard, Our Lady of the Rosary, Union City
Freeman, Ernest, Catholic Community of Pleasanton
Frumkin, Paul, (Retired)
Fuentes, Javier, St. Bernard, Oakland
Gall, William, St. Bonaventure, Concord
Garcia, James, (On Duty Outside the Diocese)
Gierak, Rich, St. Agnes, Concord
Glover, Chuck, Holy Spirit, Freemont
Gomes, Joseph, (On Duty Outside the Diocese)
Gomez, Ruben, St. Joan of Arc, San Ramon
Gonsalves, Nelson, All Saints, Hayward
Gonzalez, Noe, St. Joseph the Worker, Berkeley
Grigg, Jerry, Most Holy Rosary, Antioch
Guesnon, Ovide, Our Lady of Guadalupe, Fremont
Hack, Gary, St. Ignatius, Antioch

Hernandez, Gabriel, Mary Help of Christians
Hoblitzell, Ross, (Retired)
Holland, David, St. Catherine of Siena, Martinez
Horan, Ronald, Immaculate Heart of Mary, Brentwood
Jaramillo, Ernest, (Retired)
Jee, John, St. Isidore, Danville
Jimenez, Arturo, St. John the Baptist, San Lorenzo
Johnson, Earl, St. Louis Bertrand, Oakland
Kortuem, John, Immaculate Heart of Mary, Brentwood
Lara, Jorge, Our Lady of Guadalupe, Fremont
Layden, Alan, St. Anthony, Oakley
Leach, Marty, Transfiguration, Castro Valley
Lee, Stanley, (On Duty Outside the Diocese) Philippines
Lewandowski, Daniel, (On Duty Outside the Diocese)
Macachor, Oscar, St. Joachim, Hayward (On Leave)
Madrigal, Ysidro, (Retired)
Martin, Richard, Catholic Community of Pleasanton
Mazibrook, John, St. Francis of Assisi, Concord
McGowan, Thomas, St. John, El Cerrito
Miyashiro, Leslie, St. Joseph, Pinole
Molloy, Ernest, (On Duty Outside the Diocese)
Moore, Timothy, Transfiguration, Castro Valley
Moya, Manuel, St. Michael, Livermore
Nguyen, John, (Unassigned)
Oey, Hock Chuan, St. Joan of Arc, San Ramon
Palomares, Charles, St. Francis of Assisi, Concord
Pearce, James, (On Duty Outside the Diocese)
Perez, Alfonso, Corpus Christi, Fremont
Perez, Donaciano, St. Joseph, Pinole
Perez, Ernest, (Retired)
Perez, Jose, (Retired)
Pesqueira, Gil, St. Charles Borromeo, Livermore
Peters, George, Church of the Assumption, San Leandro
Pietras, Adam J., St. Isidore, Danville
Prado, Jose, (Retired), St. Felicitas, San Leandro
Preza, Mariano, St. Bonaventure, Concord
Quigley, Edward, (On Duty Outside the Diocese)
Quinn, Lawrence, All Saints, Hayward
Rabuy, Carlos, St. Anne, Union City
Reyes, Antonio, St. Mary, Walnut Creek
Rezendes, David, St. Michael, Livermore
Rigley, Burton, Transfiguration, Castro Valley
Rivilla, Luis, St. Perpetua, Lafayette
Roemers, Gustaaf, Our Lady of the Rosary, Union City
Roque, Rolito C., St. Edward, Newark
Ryken, Denis, (Retired)
Sicat, Joe, St. Raymond, Dublin
Silveira, Victor, St. Leander, San Leandro
Silvernale, Charles, Holy Rosary, Antioch
Spano, Edward, Immaculate Heart of Mary, Brentwood
Stanton, Charles, St. Joan of Arc, San Ramon
Stelly, Eugene, Cathedral Parish of Christ the Light, Oakland
Ta, Peter, Cathedral Parish of Christ the Light, Oakland
Taylor, Stephen, Holy Spirit, Fremont
Tovar, Joseph, St. Anthony, Oakley
Trucios, Luis, Our Lady of the Rosary, Union City
Tutson, Ron, St. Benedict, Oakland
Victoria, Hector, (Retired)
Vivet, Lance, St. Joseph the Mission, Fremont
Waters, Gerald, St. Ignatius, Antioch
Wedge, Ken, Good Shepherd, Pittsburg
Wedl, Roger, St. Edward, Newark
Wong, Danny, Chinese Ministry Center, Oakland
Wortham, Gary, Catholic Community of Pleasanton
Yee, Richard, Holy Spirit, Fremont
Young, David, St. Joseph Basilica, Alameda

INSTITUTIONS LOCATED IN THE DIOCESE

[A] SEMINARIES, RELIGIOUS OR SCHOLASTICATES

OAKLAND. *School of Applied Theology Graduate Theological Union-Berkeley* An Affiliate of the Graduate Theological Union, Berkeley; SAT Sabbatical, 5890 Birch Ct., 94618-1627. Tel: 510-652-1651; Fax: 510-420-0542. Email: satgtu@aol.com. Web: www.satgtu.org. Bro. Stanislaus Sobczyk, F.S.C., Pres. & Dean; Sr. Maureen Therese McGroddy, R.S.H.M., Dean Students & Admissions. Brothers 4; Sisters 6; Lay Teachers 27; Students 69; Total Staff 3.

Trustees: J. Randall Andrada; Mary V. Clemency; Ron Courtney; Sr. Barbara Dawson, R.S.C.J.; James A. Donahue, Ph.D.; Kathleen Gannon Briggs; Sr. Mary T. Grove, I.H.M.; Alan Holloway; Bro. Stanislaus Sobczyk, F.S.C.; Edward Tywoniak, Ed.D.; Mr. Robert Mallon; John McMahon.

BERKELEY. *Dominican School of Philosophy and Theology* (Dominican House of Studies at the Graduate Theological Union), 2301 Vine St., 94708-1816. Tel: 510-849-2030; Fax: 510-849-1372. Email: info@dspt.edu. Web: www.dspt.edu. Rev. Michael Sweeney, O.P., Pres.; Peter MacLeod, Vice Pres., Administration, CFO; Mr. Mariciel Mahoney, Vice Pres. of Advancement; Rev. Christopher J. Renz, O.P., Academic Dean; John Knutsen, Dir. Admissions; Rev. Michael Fones, O.P., Co-Dir., Catherine of Siena Inst.; Sherry Anne Weddell, Co-Dir., Catherine of Siena Inst.; Teresa Olson, Registrar; Colleen Powers, Office Admin. & Dir. Student Svcs. Priests 17; Sisters 3; Lay Teachers 2; Students 86.

Faculty (Regular): Revs. Joseph Boenzi, S.D.B.; Michael Dodds, O.P.; Edward Krasevac, O.P.; Bryan Kromholtz, O.P.; Eugene Ludwig, O.F.M.Cap.; Michael T. Morris, O.P.; Albert Paretsky, O.P.; Anselm Ramelow, O.P.; Richard Schenk, O.P.; Augustine Thompson, O.P.; Sisters Marianne Farina, C.S.C.; Barbara Green, O.P.; Margarita Vega, Ph.D.

Faculty (Adjunct): Revs. Brett C. Hoover, C.S.P.; Arthur Lenti, S.D.B.; Hilary Martin, O.P.; Brendan McAnerney, O.P.; Henry Ormond, O.Carm.; Sergius Propst, O.P.; John J. Roche, S.D.B.; Sr. Mary Greenan, F.M.A.; Sharon Girard, Ph.D.

Franciscan School of Theology (1968) 1712 Euclid Ave., 94709-1208. Tel: 510-848-5232; Fax: 510-549-9466. Email: info@fst.edu. Web: www.fst.edu. Revs. Mario DiCicco, O.F.M., Pres.; Faustino M. Cruz, S.M., Academic Dean; Joyce McConeghey, Admin. Asst. Dean; Patricia Morgan, Admissions Coord.; Jenna Neilson, Registration Coord.; Ms. Clare Ronzani, Dir. Spiritual Formation; Mary Smith, Business Mgr. Priests 10; Brothers 2; Sisters 3; Deacons 1; Lay Teachers 3; Total Enrollment 80.

Faculty: Revs. Joseph P. Chinnici, O.F.M.; Faustino M. Cruz, S.M.; Michael D. Guinan, O.F.M.; Richard Gula, S.S.; Joseph Hartzler, S.M., S.T.L., Ph.D., Th.M.; Kenneth J. Laverone, O.F.M.; Kenan B. Osborne, O.F.M.; Louis Vitale, O.F.M.; Thomas West, O.F.M.; Bros. John Kiesler, O.F.M.; William J. Short, O.F.M.; Sisters Joanne Doi, M.M.; Eva Lumas, S.S.S.; Mary McGann, R.S.C.J.; Deacon Jeffrey Burns, Ph.D.; Ronald Harbor; Darleen Pryds; Mr. Andrew Utiger.

Jesuit School of Theology at Santa Clara University An Ecclesiastical Faculty of Theology under statutes approved by the Holy See. One of two theological centers of the U.S. Jesuit Conference, Society of Jesus. A graduate school of Santa Clara University located at Berkeley. A Member of the Graduate Theological Union (GTU), Berkeley., 1735 LeRoy Ave., 94709-1115. Tel: 510-549-5000; Fax: 510-841-8536. Email: ltran@jstb.edu. Web: jstb.edu. Revs. Kevin F. Burke, S.J., Exec. Dean; Robert W. McChesney, S.J., Dir. Sabbatical Prog.; George R. Murphy, S.J., Coord. Formation Programs; Dr. Bruce Lescher, Assoc. Academic Dean; Sr. Grace A. Hogan, O.P., Interim Exec. Dir. Enrollment Mgmt.; Margi English, Exec. Dir. Devel.; Ms. Lorna Wallace McKeown, Asst. Academic Dean & In-House Registrar; Rosemary Moore, Dean Students; Lan Tran, Bus. Mgr. & Treas. Priests 12; Sisters 5; Lay Teachers 10; Faculty 21; Students 140.

Faculty (Emeriti): Rev. Donald L. Gelpi, S.J.; Sr. Sandra M. Schneiders, I.H.M.

Faculty: (See listing for The Jesuit Community at The Jesuit School of Theology at Berkeley) Revs. Thomas E. Buckley, S.J.; Kevin F. Burke, S.J.; Gregory Chisholm, S.J.; John C. Endres, S.J.; Eduardo C. Fernandez, S.J.; David H. Gill, S.J.; George E. Griener, S.J.; Francis X. McAloon, S.J.; William R. O'Neill, S.J.; T. Howland Sanks, S.J.; Sr. Mary Ann Donovan, S.C.; Dr. Jerome P. Baggett; Dr. Thomas Cattoi; Dr. Lisa Fullam; Dr. Alejandro Garcia-Rivera; Dr. Gina Hens-Piazza; Dr. Bruce Lescher; Dr. Mia M. Mochizuki; Dr. Jean-Francois Racine; Ms. Jill K. Marshall.

Part-time Emeritus Faculty: Rev. Donald L. Gelpi, S.J.; Sr. Sandra M. Schneiders, I.H.M.

Part-time Adjunct Faculty: Revs. David W. Johnson, S.J.; George R. Murphy, S.J.; Sisters Jane Ferdon, O.P.; Gloria Inez Loya, P.B.V.M.; Julia Prinz, V.D.M.F.; Ms. Clare Ronzani.

[B] COLLEGES AND UNIVERSITIES

OAKLAND. *Holy Names University* (1868) Chartered 1868. Residence and Non-Residence Students., 3500 Mountain Blvd., 94619-1627. Tel: 510-436-1000; Fax: 510-436-1199. Web: www.hnu.edu.

Sisters of the Holy Names of Jesus and Mary, A Corporation

Holy Names University, A Corporation Sisters of the Holy Names of Jesus and Mary. Priests 1; Sisters 5; Lay Professors 36; Students 1,149.

Administration: Sr. Rosemarie Nassif, S.S.N.D., Pres.; Lizbeth Martin, Vice Pres. Academic Affairs; Michael Miller, Vice Pres. Student Affairs; Stuart Koop, Vice Pres. Finance & Admin.; Sr. Carol Sellman, S.N.J.M., Vice Pres.; Davorka Cvitkovic, Vice Pres. Inst. Advancement; Jeanette Calixto, Registrar; Carrie Rehak, Ph.D., Dir. Campus Ministry; Karen Schneider, Dir. Library Svcs.

Religious Faculty: Sisters Marcia Frideger, S.N.J.M.; Maureen Hester, S.N.J.M.; Christine Patrinos, S.N.J.M.; JoAnne Quinlivan, S.N.J.M.; Nancy Teskey, S.N.J.M.

Religious Staff: Rev. James Conlon.

MORAGA. *St. Mary's College* (1963) Coed. Resident and Non-Resident Students., 1928 St. Mary's Rd., 94556-2715. Tel: 925-631-4000; Fax: 925-376-1847. Web: www.stmarys-ca.edu. Bro. Ronald Gallagher, F.S.C., Pres.

Saint Mary's College of California Brothers of the Christian Schools, District of San Francisco. Priests 4; Brothers 23; Professors 443; Total Enrollment 4,000.

Saint Mary's College Community: Bro. Donald Mansir, F.S.C., Dir., Chair - Bishop Cummins Institute.

Alemany Community: Bro. Michael Meister, F.S.C., Dir., Prof. Rel. Studies & Theology.

Campus Ministers: Revs. Thomas McElligott, Campus Min.; Salvatore Ragusa, S.D.S., Campus Min.

Faculty: Revs. John Morris, O.P.; Michael A. Russo; Bros. Mel Anderson, F.S.C., Pres. Emeritus; Michael S. Avila, F.S.C., Prof. Rel. Studies & Theology; William Beatie, F.S.C., Prof. Philosophy; Dominic Berardelli, F.S.C., Spec. Asst. to Pres.; Glenn Bolton, F.S.C., Career Counseling; Kenneth W. Cardwell, F.S.C., Prof. Internal Prog.; Camillus Chavez, F.S.C., Campus Min.; Myron Collins, F.S.C., Prof. Chemistry; Charles Hilken, F.S.C., Prof. History; Richard Lemberg, F.S.C., Librarian, Instructional Svcs.; Bernard LoCoco, F.S.C.; Brenden Madden, F.S.C., Career Counseling; Mark McVann, F.S.C., Prof. Rel. Studies & Theology; Bertrand Nguyen, F.S.C., (Retired); Raphael Patton, F.S.C., Prof. Mathematics; Casimir Reichlin, F.S.C., Spec. Asst. to Pres.; Augustus Rosin, F.S.C., Prof. Chemistry; Dominic Ruegg, F.S.C., Librarian; Clarence Schenk, F.S.C., Media Svcs.; Martin Yribarren, F.S.C.

[C] HIGH SCHOOLS, DIOCESAN

OAKLAND. *Bishop O'Dowd High School* (1951) 9500 Stearns Ave., 94605-4720. Tel: 510-577-9100; Fax: 510-638-3259. Email: sphelps@bishopodowd.org. Web: www.bishopodowd.org. Stephen Phelps, Ed.D., Pres.; Joseph Salamack, Prin.; Annette Counts, Librarian. Lay Teachers 100; Students 1,199.

St. Elizabeth High School, 1530-34th Ave., 94601. Tel: 510-532-8947; Fax: 510-532-9754. Email: lbrock@stliz-hs.org. Web: www.stliz-hs.org. Sr. Mary Liam Brock, O.P., Prin. Sisters 1; Lay Teachers 22; Students 201.

[D] HIGH SCHOOLS, PAROCHIAL

ALAMEDA. *Saint Joseph Notre Dame High School*, 1011 Chestnut St., 94501-4315. Tel: 510-523-1526; Fax: 510-523-2181. Email: toconnor@sjnd.org. Web: www.sjnd.org. Mr. Simon Chiu, Prin.; Catherine Cook, Asst. Prin. Academics; Jennifer Dlugosh, Librarian. Lay Teachers 37; Total Staff 55; Students 392.

[E] HIGH SCHOOLS, PRIVATE

OAKLAND. *Holy Names High School* (1868) 4660 Harbord Dr., 94618-2211. Tel: 510-450-1110; Fax: 510-547-3111. Email: sslyngstad@hnhsoakland.org. Web: www.hnhsoakland.org. Sally Slyngstad, S.N.J.M., Prin.; Julia Haverstock, Librarian. Sisters of the Holy Names of Jesus and Mary. Sisters 3; Lay Teachers 36; Students 200.

BERKELEY. *Saint Mary's College High School* (1863) 1294 Albina Ave., 94706-2599. Tel: 510-526-9242; Fax: 510-559-6277. Web: www.saintmaryschs.org. Bro. Edmond Larouche, F.S.C., Pres.; Mr. Peter Imperial, Prin.; Mr. Brian Thomas, Librarian. Brothers of the Christian Schools. Brothers 2; Lay Teachers 46; Students 617.

CONCORD. *Carondelet High School* (1965) 1133 Winton Dr., 94518-3527. Tel: 925-686-5353; Fax: 925-671-9429. Email: chs@carondeleths.org. Web: www.carondelet.pvt.k12.ca.us. Sr. Kathleen Lang, C.S.J., Pres.; Dr. Teresa Hurlbut, Prin.; Mrs. Joan Tracy, M.L.S., Librarian. Sisters of St Joseph of Carondelet. Sisters 4; Lay Teachers 58; Students 811.

Convent: Tel: 925-686-9697.

De La Salle High School of Concord, Inc. dba De La Salle High School (1965) (Boys), 1130 Winton Dr., 94518-3528. Tel: 925-288-8100; Fax: 925-686-3474.

Email: higakic@dlshs.org. Web: www.dlshs.org. Mr. Mark DeMarco, Pres.; Bro. Christopher Brady, F.S.C., Prin.; Ms. Elaine Seed, Librarian. Brothers of the Christian Schools Brothers 1; Lay Teachers 81; Students 1,051.

Co-Assistant Principals: Mr. Jack Dyer, Student Life; Mr. Roger Hassett, Dir. Campus Ministry; Mrs. Mary Ann Lemire Mattos, Academic Life.

HAYWARD. *Moreau Catholic High School* (1965) 27170 Mission Blvd., 94544. Tel: 510-881-4300; Fax: 510-581-5669. Email: tlee@moreaucatholic.org. Web: www.moreaucatholic.org. Terrence Lee, Pres.; Lauren Lek, Prin.; Catherine Wickboldt, Corp. Treas.; Susan Geiger, Librarian; Rev. Tito Bonoan, Chap. Congregation of Holy Cross. Priests 1; Lay Teachers 53; Students 900.

RICHMOND. *Salesian High School*, 2851 Salesian Ave., 94804. Tel: 510-234-4433; Fax: 510-236-4636. Email: jwilks@salesian.com. Web: www.salesian.com. Rev. Nicholas J. Reina, S.D.B., Dir. & Pres.; Mr. Timothy Chambers, Prin.; Revs. John Malloy, S.D.B.; Jerry Bonjean, S.D.B., Chap.; Bros. Patrick Maloney, S.D.B., (Retired); Anthony Matse, S.D.B., (Retired); Ricardo Ramos, S.D.B.; Rev. Kristian Laygo, S.D.B.; Sr. Mary Greenan, F.M.A., Coord. Youth Min.; Janet Wilks, Dir. Devel. Salesians of St. John Bosco. Priests 2; Brothers 4; Sisters 1; Lay Teachers 37; Students 552. In Res. Bros. Jerry Weirich, S.D.B.; Michael Touchstone, S.D.B.

[F] ELEMENTARY SCHOOLS, PRIVATE

CONCORD. *Wood Rose Academy*, (Grades K-8), 4347 Cowell Rd., 94518-1807. Tel: 925-825-4644; Fax: 925-825-4645. Web: www.woodroseacademy.org. Email: woodroseacad@sbcglobal.net. Ellen Crnkovich, Prin.; Rosemarie Ramirez, Librarian. Lay Teachers 10; Students 85.

[G] EARLY CHILDHOOD EDUCATION CENTERS

FREMONT. *Dominican Kindergarten*, 43326 Mission Blvd., 94539-5829. Tel: 510-651-7978; Fax: 510-657-1734. Email: sjanemarie@aol.com. Web: msjdominicans.org/kinder.html. Sr. Jane Marie Estoesta, O.P., Dir. & Teacher. Sisters 1; Students 36.

[H] CATHOLIC CHARITIES OF THE DIOCESE OF OAKLAND

OAKLAND. *Catholic Charities of the Diocese of Oakland*, 433 Jefferson St., 94607-3539. Tel: 510-768-3100; Fax: 510-451-6998. Email: info@cceb.org. Web: www.cceb.org. Solomon Belette, CEO; Colleen Miller, Dir. Devel. & Public Affairs; Susana Mullen, Controller; Michael Radding, Dir. Programs.

Catholic Charities of the Diocese of Oakland. Total Assisted Annually 17,000.

Counseling for the Deaf and Hard of Hearing, 25580 Campus Dr., Hayward, 94542-1137. Tel: 510-881-2248 (Video Phone); Teletype: 510-881-2247; Fax: 510-881-2248. Ms. Lorraine Wilson, Counselor.

Oakland Family Service Center, 433 Jefferson St., 94607-3539. Tel: 510-768-3100; Fax: 510-451-6998. Web: www.cccb.org. Carol Leahy, Dir. Family Support Svcs. Tel: 510-768-3165; Carla Salazar, Housing Case Mgr. Oakland. Tel: 510-768-3105.

Office and School Counseling Tel: 510-768-3103. Roy Hammond, Dir.

Immigration Services Tel: 510-768-3122. Raquel Aguirre, Dir. Immigration Svcs.

Refugee Resettlement Tel: 510-768-3106. Sr. Elisabeth Lang, Dir. Refugee Resettlement.

Multicultural Senior Service Network Tel: 510-768-3159. Bau Ta, Dir.

Development and Public Affairs Tel: 510-768-3115. Email: cmiller@cceb.org. Colleen Miller, Dir. Devel. & Public Affairs.

Concord Family Service Center, 3540 Chestnut St., Concord, 94519. Tel: 925-825-3099; Fax: 925-825-5503. Dora Segura, Housing Case Mgr.

Richmond Family Service Center, 2369 Barrett Ave., Richmond, 94804. Tel: 510-234-5110, Ext. 313; Fax: 510-237-6778. Lisa Raffel, Dir., Richmond Family Svc. Center.

[I] SOCIETY OF ST. VINCENT DE PAUL

PITTSBURG. *Society of St. Vincent de Paul of Contra Costa County* (1958) 2210 Gladstone Dr., 94565-5101. Tel: 925-439-5060; Fax: 925-439-7863. Email: svdpccc@stvincen.org. Web: www.svdp.contracosta.org. Mr. Jim Noe, Pres.; Mr. Ron Weston, Exec. Dir. Total Assisted Annually 19,839.

[J] DAY NURSERIES

OAKLAND. *Saint Vincent's Day Home, Inc.* (1911) 1086 Eighth St., 94607-2616. Tel: 510-832-8324; Fax: 510-832-5021. Email: info@svdh.org. Web: www.svdh.org. Corinne M. Mohrmann, Exec. Dir.

Saint Vincent's Day Home, A Corporation, Purpose: Since 1911, Saint Vincent's Day Home's (SVDH) mission has been to serve and act on behalf of the needs, rights and well-being of all young children by offering educational and developmental services and resources to families struggling toward self-sufficiency. SVDH strives to achieve high-quality services while promoting excellence in the field of Child Development and Family Services. Religious 1; Lay Staff 50; Capacity 230; Total Assisted 462; Total Staff 51.

[K] ORGANIZATIONS FOR DEAF AND HARD OF HEARING

HAYWARD. *St. Joseph's Center for Deaf and Hard of Hearing*, 25580 Campus Drive, 94542-1137. Tel: 510-881-2245 (Voice); 866-720-9221 (Video Phone); 510-881-2247 (TDD); Fax: 510-881-2248. Email: sjcd@sjcd.org. Web: www.sjcd.org.

St. Joseph's Center for the Deaf and Hard of Hearing, A Corporation. Total Assisted Annually 200; Total Staff 3.

[L] RETIREMENT AND CARE FACILITIES

OAKLAND. *Bishop Begin Villa* (Retired Priests), 3418 E. 18th St., 94601-3004. Tel: 510-536-0719; Fax: 510-261-4516. Revs. Joseph A. Ferreira (Retired); Tom J. Edwards; Vincent R. Brylka (Retired). Residents 3; Total Assisted 3.

Mercy Retirement and Care Center (1822) (Affiliated with Elder Care Alliance), 3431 Foothill Blvd., 94601-3129. Tel: 510-534-8540; Fax: 510-261-7551. Email: pcreedon@eldercarealliance.org. Web: www.mercyretirementcenter.org. Sr. Patricia Creedon, Admin. Sponsored by the Sisters of Mercy. Sisters of Mercy 5; Employees 160; Residents 103; Bed Capacity 106.

Bishop Begin Villa, Retirement Facility for Priests in the Oakland Diocese Extensive community services.

Convalescent Hospital - Skilled Nursing Facility Tel: 510-534-8540; Fax: 510-261-4516. Web: www-.mercyretirementcenter.org. Residential Care, Assisted Living, and Skilled Nursing. Bed Capacity 59; Residents 59.

[M] MONASTERIES AND RESIDENCES OF PRIESTS AND BROTHERS

OAKLAND. *Franciscan Friars (Province of Santa Barbara)*, St. Elizabeth Friary, 1500 34th Ave., 94601-3024. Tel: 510-536-1287; Fax: 510-536-3578. Email: stefriary@mail.com. Web: www.sbfranciscans.org. Revs. William Brand, O.F.M.; Rigoberto Caloca-Rivas, O.F.M., Ph.D.; Sebastian Drake, O.F.M.; Franklin Fong, O.F.M.; Peter Krieg, O.F.M.; Kenny Scott, O.F.M.; Louis Vitale, O.F.M.; Bros. Robert Brady, O.F.M.; Eric Burke, O.F.M.; Javier Diaz, O.F.M.; Thomas More Ganmy, O.F.M.; Jan Honchosky, O.F.M.; Vincent Nguyen, O.F.M.; Eric Pilarcik, O.F.M.; Joe Sury, O.F.M.; Victor Vega, O.F.M.; Rufino Zaragoza, O.F.M. *Franciscan Friars (Province of St. Barbara), Provincial Office*, 1500-34th Ave., 94601-3092. Tel: 510-536-3722; Fax: 510-536-3970. Email: ofmcamain@att.net. Web: www.sbfranciscans.org. Revs. John Hardin, O.F.M., Prov. Min.; Alberto Villafan, O.F.M., Vocation Coord.; Ken Lavarone, O.F.M., Prov. Vicar; Bro. Peter Boegel, O.F.M., Assoc. Treas. & Prov. Sec.; Ms. Guadalupe Aceves, Treas. Priests 3; Total Staff 20.

On Duty Outside the Province: Revs. Garrett Edmunds, O.F.M., Jerusalem; David Gaa, O.F.M., Russia; John Gibbons, O.F.M., Russia; Bro. Leo Gonzales, O.F.M., Holy Land; Revs. Tommy King, O.F.M., Peru; Finian McGinn, O.F.M., San Francisco, CA; Rodrigo Ortiz, O.F.M., Colombia; Sergio Santo, O.F.M., Philippines; Bro. Gerard Saunders, O.F.M., Peru; Revs. Gary Swirczynski, O.F.M., Arizona; Michael Weldon, O.F.M. Franklin, WI; Robert Young, O.F.M., Florida. *Franciscan Friars (Province of Santa Barbara)*, 1508 Arch St., Berkeley, 94708-1829. Tel: 510-845-1124. Rev. Joseph P. Chinnici, O.F.M.; Bro. Garrett Galvin, O.F.M., Guardian; Rev. Joseph Goh, O.F.M.; Bros. Raul Diaz, O.F.M.; Rami Fodda, O.F.M.; Nghia Phan, O.F.M. *Franciscan Friars (Province of Santa Barbara)*, 1559 33rd Ave., 94601. Tel: 510-479-7741. Revs. Martin Ibarra, O.F.M.; Oscar A. Mendez, O.F.M.; Bro. David Cobian, O.F.M., M.Div.

Jesuit Fathers and Brothers (1972) *Murray Residence Community*, 171 Santa Rosa Ave., 94610-1316. Tel: 510-655-8334; Fax: 510-655-4816. Revs. John A. Baumann, S.J.; Thomas C. Weston, S.J., Supr.; Tri M. Dinh, S.J.; Stephen M. Kelly, S.J.; Lester E. Love, S.J.; Gregory Chisholm, S.J.

Missionary Oblates of Mary Immaculate United States Province (1953) 290 Lenox Ave., 94610-4625. Tel: 510-452-1550; Fax: 510-893-1272. Email: omi290@comcast.net. Web: www.omiusa.org. Rev. Anthony Dummer, O.M.I.

Oblate Fathers Western Province Inc.; Western Oblates Support Trust Fund Total in Residence 3; Total Staff 1. In Res. Revs. Don Arel, O.M.I.; William Hallahan, O.M.I., Dir.; Maynard Kegler, O.M.I.; Umberto Nespolo, O.M.I.

Order of Preachers (Province of the Most Holy Name of Jesus - Western Dominican Province) (1914) 5877 Birch Ct., 94618-1626. Tel: 510-658-8722; Fax: 510-658-1061. Email: wdp@opwest.org. Web: www.opwest.org. Very Rev. Emmerich W. Vogt, O.P., Prior Prov.; Revs. Dominic DeDomenico, O.P., Treas.; Jude Eli, O.P., Dir. Western Dominican Preaching; John Evans, O.P., Dir. Province Web Site; Thomas Hayes, O.P., Promoter Holy Name Society, (Knight Commander of the Holy Sepulcher); Kieran J. Healy, O.P., Student Master; Xavier Lavagetto, O.P., Promoter Parish Min.; Steven Maekawa, O.P., Dir. Vocations; Reginald Martin, O.P., Dir. Promoter Rosary Confraternity; John Morris, O.P., Promoter Social Justice; Mark Padrez, O.P., Socius & Vicar to Prov.; Daniel Rolland, O.P., Promoter Campus Min.; Anthony Rosevear, O.P., Novice Master; Richard Schenk, O.P., Promoter Permanent Formation & Regent of Studies; Vincent Serpa, O.P., Promoter, Media & Dominican Laity; Martin Walsh, O.P., Dir. Dominican Mission Foundation & Dir. St. Jude Shrine. Province of the Most Holy Name of Jesus. Total in the Province 152.

Serving in Latin America: Revs. David Bello, O.P. (Mexico); Timothy Conlan, O.P. (Guatemala); Bartholomew dela Torre, O.P. (Mexico); Michael Rolland, O.P.; Bro. Martin Walsh, O.P.

Serving in Rome: Revs. Luke D. Buckles, O.P., Prof. Pontificia Universita San Tommaso; Robert Christian, O.P., Prof. Pontificia Universita San Tommaso; Alejandro Crosthwaite, O.P., Prof. Pontificia Universita San Tommaso.

Serving in Israel: Rev. Gregory T. Tatum, O.P., Assoc. Prof. Ecole Biblique et Archeologique Francaise.

Serving in Australia: Rev. Hilary Martin, O.P., Visiting Prof.

Serving in Africa: (Kenya) Bro. Daniel Thomas, O.P.

Serving in Switzerland: Revs. Michael S. Sherwin, O.P., Assoc. Prof. Univ. Freibourg; Bernard Blankenhorn, O.P., Doctoral Studies; Bros. Stephen Maria Lopez, O.P., Studies; John Marie Bingham, O.P., Studies.

Order of Preachers (Province of the Most Holy Name of Jesus - Western Dominican Province) (1932) *St. Albert Priory*, Dominican House of Formation, 5890 Birch Ct., 94618-1627. Tel: 510-596-1800; Fax: 510-596-1860. Web: www.op.org/opwest/sap. Very Revs. Gerald Buckley, O.P., Prior; Emmerich W. Vogt, O.P.; Revs. Dominic Briese, O.P.; Michael Carey, O.P.; Dominic DeDomenico, O.P., Province Trustee; Finbarr Hayes, O.P.; Kieran J. Healy, O.P., Student Master; Bryan Kromholtz, O.P.; Steven Maekawa, O.P., Dir. Vocations; Hilary Martin, O.P.; Brendan McAnerney, O.P., DominICON Ministry Sacramento, CA; Mark O'Leary, O.P.; Samuel Parsons, O.P.; Sergius Propst, O.P.; Christopher J. Renz, O.P.; Edmund K. Ryan, O.P.; Richard Schenk, O.P., Subprior, Regent of Studies; Augustine Thompson, O.P.; Antoninus Wall, O.P.; Janko Zagar, O.P.; Bros. Michael Augustine Amabisco, O.P.; Raymond Bertheaux, O.P.; John Marie Bingham, O.P.; Joseph Mary Do, O.P.; Christopher Fadok, O.P.; Justin Gable, O.P.; Lupe Gonzalez, O.P., Residing in Mexico City.; Mark Gorski, O.P.; Peter Junipero Hannah, O.P.; Simon Kim, O.P.; Stephen Maria Lopez, O.P.; Corwin Saxon Low, O.P.; Richard Maher, O.P.; Dominic Maichrowicz, O.P.; Pasquale Manalio-Passarelli, O.P.; Mark Francis Manzano, O.P.; Matthew Augustine Miller, O.P.; Isaiah Mary Molano, O.P, Residing in Washington, DC; Gabriel Mosher, O.P.; Dominic Tuan Ngo, O.P.; Michael James Rivera, O.P.; Ambrose Sigman, O.P.; Emmanuel Taylor, O.P.; Tap Vu, O.P.; Boniface Willard, O.P.; Peter Yost, O.P. *Order of Preachers (Province of Holy Name of Jesus - Western Dominican Province), Siena House*, 5730 Presley Way, 94618-1633. Tel: 510-654-8735; Fax: 510-654-8735. Revs. Jerome Cudden, O.P., Province Dir. Devel.; Michael Morris, O.P., Dominican School of Philosophy and Theology; David K. O'Rourke, O.P., Parish Admin., (Our Lady of Mercy, Richmond, CA); Mark Padrez, O.P., Socius & Vicar to Prov. & Supr.; Terence Reilly, O.P.; Leo Tubbs, O.P.; Samuel Parsons, O.P. Priests 7.

Redemptorist Fathers (Denver Province), 8945 Golf Links Rd., P.O. Box 5007, 94605-4124. Tel: 510-562-9740; Fax: 510-562-1406. Email: POBCSS@aol.com. Rev. Patrick O'Brien, C.Ss.R., Pres.

Redemptorist Society of California; Redemptorists of Oakland.

BERKELEY. *Capuchin Franciscan Friars, House of Studies*, 1534 Arch St., 94708-1829. Tel: 510-841-2229; Fax: 510-849-0809. Email: piusofmcap@hotmail.com. *Saint Conrad Friary* Tel: 510-841-2229; Fax: 510-849-0809. Revs. Christopher Kearney, O.F.M.Cap.; Peter Vong Mai (Vietnam); Bros. Peter Ciolino, O.F.M.Cap.; Alex Escalera, O.F.M.Cap.; Hai Ho, O.F.M.Cap. Friars in Residence 5; Friars in Formation 2; Total Staff 4.

Incarnation Monastery, Camaldolese Benedictines (1979) 1369 La Loma Ave., 94708-2031. Tel: 510-845-0601; Fax: 510-845-0601. Email: facolnaghi@aol.com. Web: www.contemplation.com. Rev. Andrew Colnaghi, Prior. Tel: 510-548-0965; Fax: 510-548-6439. Total in Residence 3. In Res. Revs. Thomas Matus, O.S.B.Cam.; Arthur Poulin, O.S.B.Cam.

Jesuit Fathers and Brothers, Jesuit Community at Jesuit School of Theology, 1756 LeRoy Ave., 94709-1157. Tel: 510-225-6200; Fax: 510-549-1114. Email: rector@jstb.edu. Web: www.jstbjesuits.org. Revs. Patricius Mutiara Andalas, S.J. (Indonesia); David J. Ayotte, S.J.; Thomas E. Buckley, S.J.; Kevin F. Burke, S.J., Exec. Dean; Dominik Ciolek, S.J. (Poland); James Dabhi, S.J. (India); Kurt M. Denk, S.J.; Saturnin Tsayem Dongmo, S.J. (Cameroon); John C. Endres, S.J.; Eduardo C. Fernandez, S.J.; Emmanuel Foro, S.J. (Burkina Faso); Donald L. Gelpi, S.J.; Fausto Gianfreda, S.J. (Italy); David H. Gill, S.J.; George E. Griener, S.J.; Xavier Jeong-yeon Hwang, S.J. (Korea, South); David W. Johnson, S.J.; Vimal Kishore, S.J. (India); Jacques Cyprien Ranaivotratra Maminirina, S.J. (Madagascar); Francis X. McAloon, S.J.; Robert W. McChesney, S.J.; John T. Mitchell, S.J., Min.; Jean Willy Moka Mubelo, S.J. (Democratic Republic of Congo); George R. Murphy, S.J.; Sess Julien N'Guessan, S.J. (Cote d'Ivoire); Thao N. Nguyen, S.J.; Robert J. Ochs, S.J.; William R. O'Neill, S.J.; Fulgence Ratsimbazafy, S.J. (Madagascar); Deogratias Mutayoba Rwezaura, S.J. (Tanzania); T. Howland Sanks, S.J.; Anthony E. Scholander, S.J., Rector; Rodrigo Esteban Zarazaga, S.J.; Marek Kruszynski, S.J. (Poland); Joseph Loic Mben, S.J. (Cameroon); Hanh Duc Pham, S.J.; Jacques Randrianary, S.J. (Madagascar); Innocent Balthazary Rugaragu, S.J. (Rwanda); Ignatius Sasmita, S.J.; Richard Tambwe Mutibula, S.J. (Democratic Republic of Congo). (See also listing for The Jesuit School of Theology at Berkeley). Priests 39; Brothers 1; Deacons 4; Total in Residence 76; Scholastics 32.

Marist Fathers and Brothers, 2335 Warring St., 94704-1839. Tel: 510-486-1232; 510-486-1276; Fax: 510-848-7204. Web: www.maristsociety.org. Rev. Thomas E. Ellerman, S.M., Dir. Postulants; Mr. Jack Ridout, Vocations Dir. & Business Mgr. *Marist Society Inc.*, Seminary Name: St. Peter Chanel Seminary - Marist Pre-novitate Program.

Priests of the Congregation of Holy Cross, Holy Cross Center, 2597 Virginia St., 94709-1108. Tel: 510-548-8515. Revs. Jeffrey A. Cooper, C.S.C.; Harry Cronin, C.S.C., Dir.; Brent A. Kruger, C.S.C.

Redemptorist Fathers (Denver Province), St. Clemens Maria House, Redemptorist Asian Pacific Ministry Center, 2215 Rose St., 94709-1430. Tel: 510-981-9005; Fax: 510-981-9004. Email: kunpah@aol.com. Web: www.kmhmu-catholic.org. Revs. Donald MacKinnon, C.Ss.R.; Richard Ochiltree, C.Ss.R.; Richard Schiblin, C.Ss.R.; David Tobin, C.Ss.R.; Deacon Dennis Lee, C.S.S.P.

The Redemptorists of Berkeley

Salesians of Don Bosco, Don Bosco Hall, 1831 Arch St., 94709-1309. Tel: 510-204-0800; Fax: 510-843-4335. Email: sulsdbfam@aol.com. Web: www.donboscowest.org. Total in Residence 16; Total Staff 5.

Core Team: Revs. Joseph Boenzi, S.D.B., Councilor; Arthur Lenti, S.D.B., Councilor; John Roche, S.D.B., Prof.; Gael E. Sullivan, S.D.B., Dir.; Steven Whelan, S.D.B., Economer; Bro. John Rasor, S.D.B., Councilor.

Students in Residence: Revs. Tresphord Chisanga, S.D.B. (Zambia); James Heuser, S.D.B.; Taisali Leuluia, S.D.B.; Joseph Pampackal, S.D.B.; David Purdy, S.D.B.; Seung Yong Yi, S.D.B.

Servites (United States of America Province), 2406 Virginia St., 94709-1206. Tel: 510-849-2726. Revs. Bruce J. Klikunas, O.S.M., (Retired); Michael Guimon, O.S.M., Alta-Bates Summit Hospital Chap. Total in Residence 2.

Society of the Precious Blood (Province of Kansas City) (1985) 2800 Milvia St., 94703-2209. Tel: 510-841-2777. Revs. David Matz, C.PP.S.; James D. Sloan, C.PP.S.; Joseph Nassal, C.PP.S.; Matt Link, C.PP.S. Priests 2.

CASTRO VALLEY. *Conventual Franciscans (Province of St. Joseph of Cupertino), Holy Family Friary*, 19697 Redwood Rd., 94546-3456. Tel: 510-582-7314; Fax: 510-582-7455. Revs. Stephen Bejo, O.F.M.Conv.; Paul Fazio, O.F.M.Conv.; Thomas Hamilton, O.F.M.Conv.; Stephen King, O.F.M.Conv.; Francisco Nahoe, O.F.M.Conv.; Allen Ramirez, O.F.M.Conv.; Bros. Francisco Cabral, O.F.M.Conv.; Joseph Kim, O.F.M.Conv.; Patrick Lytell, O.F.M.Conv.; Tammylee Ngo, O.F.M.Conv.; James Phan, O.F.M.Conv.

[N] CONVENTS AND RESIDENCES FOR SISTERS

OAKLAND. *Adrian Dominican Sisters (Congregation of the Most Holy Rosary)*, 3693 High St., 94619-2105. Tel: 510-530-2621. Adrian Dominican Sisters 3; San Rafael Dominican Sisters 1; Sisters of The Holy Family 1.

Congregation of the Queen of the Holy Rosary (Dominican Sisters of Mission San Jose), St. Elizabeth Convent, 1555-34th Ave., 94601-3062. Tel: 510-532-8344; Fax: 510-533-2365. Web: www.msjdominicans.org. Sisters 14.

Dominican Sisters of Oakford, Bethany House, 919 Aileen St., 94608-2805. Tel: 510-652-0986. Email: bethanyop@earthlink.net. Web: www.oakford.op.org. Sisters 2.

Sisters of Mercy of the Americas (West Midwest Community), Mercy Retirement and Care Center, 3431 Foothill Blvd., 94601-3129. Tel: 510-534-8540; Fax: 510-261-7551. Web: www.mercyretirementcenter.org. Sisters 5.

Sisters of Notre Dame de Namur (California Province), 3431 Foothill Blvd., 94601-3129. Tel: 510-893-4094. 3431 Foothill Blvd., 94601-3129. Tel: 510-533-3162. Sisters 12.

Sisters of Sacred Hearts of Jesus and Mary, 2150 Lakeshore Ave., 94606-1189. Tel: 510-839-3231; Fax: 510-839-5256. Sisters 9.

Sisters of St. Joseph of Carondelet

St. Francis Community, 2668 Concord Blvd., Concord, 94519. Tel: 925-691-9313. Sisters 2.

Carondelet Community, 1133 Winton Dr., Concord, 94518-3527. Tel: 925-686-9697; Fax: 925-671-9429. Sisters 2. *Kwanza House Community*, 529 Jean St., 94610-1906. Tel: 510-655-2382; Fax: 510-655-0249. Sisters 2. *Christ the King Community*, 3095 Diablo View Rd., Pleasant Hill, 94523-4535. Tel: 925-280-1562; Fax: 925-685-1289. Sisters 3. *St. Anthony Community*, 428 Coral Reef Rd., Alameda, 94501. Tel: 510-995-8604. Sisters 2.

Bethany Community, 2203 Colonial Ct., Walnut Creek, 94598-1125. Tel: 925-932-2004. Sisters 3. *Via del Sol Community*, 720 N. Gate Rd., Walnut Creek, 94598. Tel: 925-287-9611. Sisters 2.

Sisters of the Holy Names of Jesus and Mary (U.S. - Ontario Province), 3500 Mountain Blvd., 94619. Tel: 510-436-1265; Fax: 503-675-7138. Web: www.snjmusontario.org. Sisters 45.

Sisters of the Presentation of the Blessed Virgin Mary (1854) 11 Warren Ave., No. 7, 94611-5457. Tel: 510-420-4556.

BERKELEY. *Congregation of the Queen of the Holy Rosary (Dominican Sisters of Mission San Jose)*, St. Mary Magdalen Community, 2004 Eunice St., 94709-1932. Tel: 510-527-4817; Fax: 510-527-4818. Email: maryb@msjdominicans.org. Web: www.msjdominicans.org. Sisters 4.

Sisters of Charity of the Blessed Virgin Mary, 1746 Addison St., 94703-1567. Tel: 510-841-8791. Email: helen.thompson@comcast.net. Web: www.bvmcong.org.

BRENTWOOD. *Religious Missionary Sisters of the Blessed Sacrament and Mary Immaculate*, 636 - 3rd St., 94513-1357. Tel: 925-513-8154; Fax: 925-516-4847. Email: jabeleno@sbcglobal.net. Sisters 3.

CONCORD. *Quinhon Missionary Sisters of the Holy Cross*, Provincial House, 1685 Humphrey Dr., 94519-2810. Tel: 925-674-9639; Fax: 925-676-9320. Sr. Rosaline Lieu Nguyen, L.H.C., Novice Directress. *Aspirant House*, 50 Santa Maria Way, Orinda, 94563-2605. Tel: 925-253-0831. Sr. Mary Anh Cong, L.H.C., Aspirants Directress.

St. Felicitas Convent, 1604 Manor Dr., San Leandro, 94579. Tel: 510-351-5577. Sr. Josefa Ngoc Nguyen, L.H.C., Supr.

Sisters of St. Joseph of the Third Order of St. Francis, 2301 Mt. Diablo St., 94520-2213. Tel: 925-825-2091; Fax: 925-825-2439. Sisters 6.

EL CERRITO. *Sisters of Mercy (U.S. Province)*, St. John the Baptist Convent, 11154 San Pablo Ave., 94530-2131. Tel: 510-233-6769; Fax: 510-233-6058. Sisters 2.

EMERYVILLE. *Sisters of St. Francis of Penance and Christian Charity* (1835) *Casa Guadalupe*, 1231 40th St., Apt. 223, 94608. Tel: 510-655-5944. Web: www.stfrancisprovince.org. *Sophia House*, 3877 Howe St., #210, 94611. Tel: 510-601-8132. Sr. Patricia Rayburn, O.S.F., Provincial. Sisters 3.

FREMONT. *Congregation of the Queen of the Holy Rosary (Dominican Sisters of Mission San Jose)* (1876) 43326 Mission Blvd., 94539-5829. Tel: 510-657-2468; Fax: 510-657-1734. Web: www.msjdominicans.org. Sr. Gloria Marie Jones, O.P., Congregational Prioress. Generalate Motherhouse and Novitiate of the Dominican Sisters of Mission San Jose, Congregation of The Queen of the Holy Rosary. Sisters 101.

Queen of Peace Community Tel: 510-657-2468; Fax: 510-657-1734. Sr. Carmel Marie Silva, O.P., Community Prioress.

St. Joseph Priory Tel: 510-657-2468; Fax: 510-657-1734. Sr. Mary Kidder, O.P., Community Prioress.

St. Martin Residence Tel: 510-657-2468; Fax: 510-657-1734. Sr. Jennifer Daniels, O.P., Community Prioress.

Siena Community (1977) Tel: 510-657-2468; Fax: 510-657-1734. Sr. Katherine Jean Cowan, O.P., Community Prioress.

St. Edward Convent (1969) 37088 Arden St., Newark, 94560-3702. Tel: 510-793-9447; Fax: 510-793-3189. Sr. Diane Aruda, O.P., Community Prioress.

St. Elizabeth Convent, 1555-34th Ave., 94601-3062. Tel: 510-532-8344; Fax: 510-533-2365. Sr. Mary Liam Brock, O.P., Community Prioress.

St. Mary Magdalen Convent (1937) 2004 Eunice St., Berkeley, 94709-1926. Tel: 510-527-4817; Fax: 510-527-4818. Sr. Mary Brennan, O.P., Community Prioress.

Our Lady of Guadalupe Convent, 46752 Crawford St., 94539-7164. Tel: 510-490-6902. Sr. Denise Lazaro, O.P., Community Prioress.

San Domenico Community Tel: 510-657-2468; Fax: 510-657-1734. Sr. Jarlath McGrath, O.P., Community Prioress.

Sisters of the Holy Family, Motherhouse, 159 Washington Blvd., P.O. Box 3248, 94539-0324. Tel: 510-624-4500; Fax: 510-624-4550. Email: info@holyfamilysisters.org. Web: www.holyfamilysisters.org. Sr. Gladys Guenther, S.H.F., Congregational Pres. Sisters 56.

HERCULES. *Congregation of the Mother of Carmel* (1866) 142 Weiss Ct., 94547-3750. Tel: 510-724-4178. Email: weisscarmel@yahoo.com. Sisters 3.

KENSINGTON. *Discalced Carmelite Nuns* (1950) 68 Rincon Rd., 94707-1047. Tel: 510-526-5050. Solemn Professed 4.

LIVERMORE. *Congregation of the Most Holy Name (Dominican Sisters of San Rafael)* (1912) St. Michael Convent, 375 Maple St., 94550-3235. Tel: 925-443-1666; Fax: 925-447-6720. Email: ecardinale@csdo.org. Sisters 2.

NEWARK. *Congregation of the Queen of the Holy Rosary (Dominican Sisters of Mission San Jose)*, St. Edward Convent, 37088 Arden St., 94560-3702. Tel: 510-793-9447; Fax: 510-793-3189 (School). Email: diane@msjdominicans.org. Sisters 4.

RICHMOND. *Franciscan Sisters of Little Falls, MN*, 1635 Butte St., 94804-5213. Tel: 510-524-6476; Fax: 510-524-6476. Sisters 3.

Sisters of Social Service, 3175 Southampton Ct., #19, 94806. Tel: 510-223-3665. Email: elumas@fst.edu. Web: www.sistersofsocialservice.com.

SAN LEANDRO. *Dominican Sisters of Oakford*, Our Lady of Guadalupe House of Formation, 327 Woodland Park, 94577-3732. Tel: 510-569-9189. Email: sisterjodiop@yahoo.com. Total in Residence 4; Sisters 4.

Our Lady of Oakford Regional Center, 980 Woodland Ave., 94577. Tel: 510-638-2822; Fax: 510-633-9734.

Marist Missionary Sisters, 1515 Boxwood Ave., 94579-1303. Tel: 510-357-7816. Email: missionarymaryss@comcast.net. Web: www.maristmissionarysmsm.org. Sr. Antonina Lafaele, S.M.S.M. Sisters 3.

SAN LORENZO. *Union of Sisters of the Presentation of the Blessed Virgin Mary (Kildare, Ireland)*, St. John the Baptist Convent, 16642 Ashland Ave., 94580-1710. Tel: 510-278-7128; Fax: 510-278-5145. Email: sjcnv@aol.com. Web: www.gnofn.org/~presis. Sisters 3.

WALNUT CREEK. *Sisters of the Holy Family* (1962) 1823 Sunnyvale Ave., 94597-1811. Tel: 925-935-6151; Fax: 925-935-6151. Email: mfaheyshf@aol.com. Web: www.holyfamilysisters.org.

[O] PASTORAL CENTERS

OAKLAND. *Holy Redeemer Center* Spiritual hospitality center., 8945 Golf Links Rd., P.O. Box 5007, 94605-4124. Tel: 510-635-6341; Fax: 510-562-1406. Email: hrcoakland@aol.com. Rev. Patrick O'Brien, C.Ss.R., Dir.

DANVILLE. *San Damiano Retreat* (1961) Retreat House for men, women and married couples., *Franciscan Retreat House*, 710 Highland Dr., P.O. Box 767, 94526-3704. Tel: 925-837-9141; Fax: 925-837-0522. Email: info@sandamiano.org. Web: www.sandamiano.org. Rev. Raymond J. Bucher,

O.F.M., Dir. Tel: 925-837-9141; Fax: 925-837-0522. Total in Residence 5; Total Staff 24. In Res. Revs. Rusty Shaughnessey, O.F.M., Retreat Master; Evan Arthur Howard, O.F.M. (Retired); Josef Prochnow, O.F.M.; Bros. Marion Alfonso, O.F.M.; Dennis Duffy, O.F.M.

LAFAYETTE. *Diocesan Youth Retreat Center*, 1977 Reliez Valley Rd., 94549-1505. Tel: 925-934-5802; Fax: 925-934-0642. Email: youthretreat@sbcglobal.net. Web: www.oakdiocese.org/youthretreat. P.O. Box 1505, 94549. Total in Residence 1; Total Staff 1.

WALNUT CREEK. *Holy Family Center* (1982) 1823 Sunnyvale Ave., 94597-1811. Tel: 945-935-6151. Email: mfaheyshf@aol.com. Sr. Marietta Fahey, S.H.F., Dir. Ministries: Personal Growth Programs, Counseling, Spiritual Direction, Adult Faith Formation.

[P] NEWMAN CENTERS

OAKLAND. *Holy Names University Campus Ministry* (1868) 3500 Mountain Blvd., 94619-1627. Tel: 510-436-1081; Fax: 510-436-1199. Email: rehak@hnu.edu. Web: www.hnu.edu. Carrie Rehak, Ph.D., Dir. Campus Min.

MORAGA. *St. Mary's College Mission and Ministry Center* P.O. Box 4777, 94575-4777. Tel: 925-631-4366. Web: www.stmarys-ca.edu. Revs. Thomas J. McElligott (SFR), Chap.; Salvatore Ragusa, S.D.S., Asst. Dir., Liturgy & Prayer; Bro. Camillus Chavez, F.S.C., Meditation Coord.; Joanne Angerame, Administrative Asst.; Mr. Leo Guardado, Asst. Dir., Justice & Educ.; Ms. Marie Lawler, Dir.; Ms. Rebecca Sallee, Assoc. Dir.; Ms. Pamela Thomas, Asst. Dir., Residential Min.; Mr. Anthony Artega, Asst. Dir. Music Ministry.

[Q] PERSONAL PRELATURES

BERKELEY. *Opus Dei* Prelature of the Holy Cross and Opus Dei, *Garber House*, 1827 Oxford St., 94709-1800. Tel: 510-548-2819; Fax: 510-644-3898. Rev. Jerome L. Jung.

[R] MISCELLANEOUS LISTINGS

OAKLAND. *Adventus, a California nonprofit public benefit corporation*, 2121 Harrison St., 94612-3787. Tel: 510-893-4711; Fax: 510-893-0945. Email: mcanizzaro@oakdiocese.org. Purpose: To support the mission of the Roman Catholic Diocese of Oakland.

The Benilde Religious & Charitable Trust, c/o Plageman, Lund and Cannon LLP, 1999 Harrison St., Ste. 1670, 94612-3500. Tel: 510-899-6100; Fax: 510-899-6101. Email: wplageman@plagemanlund.com. Web: www.plagemanlund.com. Mr. William H. Plageman Jr., Contact Person. Charitable trust fund to benefit the educational activities of the Brothers of the Christian Schools of San Francisco. Lasallian Education Opportunities.

Casa Vincentia Home for single pregnant women, 18-25 yrs., 3210 62nd Ave., 94605-1614. Tel: 510-729-0316; Fax: 510-729-0319. Web: www.casavincentia.org. Barbara Jackson, Exec. Dir. Total in Residence 6; Total Staff 1; Total Assisted Annually 23.

Dominican Community Support Charitable Trust, 5877 Birch Ct., 94618-1626. Tel: 510-658-8722; Fax: 510-658-1061. Very Rev. Emmerich W. Vogt, O.P., Trustee; Rev. Dominic DeDomenico, O.P., Trustee.

Dominican Missionaries for the Deaf Apostolate, 2121 Harrison St., 94612-3787. Tel: 210-627-6303. Email: tomcoughlin@juno.com. Web: www.dominicanmissionaries.org.

Dominican Sisters Vision of Hope (2000) 1555 34th Ave., 94601-3062. Tel: 510-533-5768; Fax: 510-533-2365. Email: osd@msjdominicans.org. Web: www.visionofhope.org. Sr. John Martin Fixa, O.P., Exec. Dir.

Franciscan Charities, Inc., 1500 34th Ave., 94601-3024. Tel: 510-536-3772; Fax: 510-536-3970.

A Friendly Manor/A Friendly Place, 2298 San Pablo Ave., 94612-1321. Tel: 510-451-8923; Fax: 510-451-8920. Email: afriendlymanor@bcglobal.net. Sr. Maureen Lyons, C.S.J. Purpose: Daytime hospitality center for homeless women. Total Staff 7; Number Served Annually 17,680.

**The Gamelin-California Association* (1991) Apartment building designed for disabled persons and persons with AIDS., Providence House, 540-23rd St., 94612-1718. Tel: 510-444-0839; Fax: 510-465-5420. Email: barbara.cook@providence.org. Web: www.providence.org/oakland. Barbara Cook, Dir. Units 40; Number Served Annually 40.

Italian Catholic Federation (1924) 8393 Capwell Dr., Ste. 110, 94621-2117. Tel: 510-633-9058; 888-423-1924; Fax: 510-633-9758. Email: info@icf.org. Web: www.icf.org. Rev. Msgr. Daniel E. Cardelli, Diocesan Chap. & Spiritual Dir. (Retired).

Lasallian Educational Opportunities, Inc. (1994) 710 40th St., 94609-2372. Tel: 510-450-0747; Fax: 510-548-1343. Email: ngonza1230@gmail.com. Web: home.pacbell.net. Deacon Noe Gonzalez, Dir. Total Assisted 210; Total Staff 7.

Missionaries of the Kingship of Christ A Franciscan Secular Institute for Women, Men, Priests., 1500-34th Ave., 94601-3024. Tel: 510-536-3722.

**Next Step Learning Center, Inc.*, 2222 Curtis St., 94607. Tel: 510-251-1731; Fax: 510-251-8028. Web: www.nextsteplc.org. George Schopf, Pres.; Sisters Rosemarie Delaney, S.N.J.M., Vice Pres.; Cynthia Canning, S.N.J.M., Sec.

**Oakland Elizabeth House* (1991) 6423 Colby St., 94618-1309. Tel: 510-658-1380; Fax: 510-658-3160. Email: oakehouse@oakehouse.org. Web: www.oakehouse.org. Lori Ottolini Geno, Dir. Purpose: Transitional house and program for women and their children. Total Assisted Annually 150.

PICO National Network (1972) 171 Santa Rosa Ave., 94610-1316. Tel: 510-655-2801; Fax: 510-655-4816. Email: jbaumann@piconetwork.org. Web: www.piconetwork.org. Revs. John A. Baumann, S.J., Founder & Dir. Special Projects; Michael Mandala, S.J.; Mr. Hank Goldstein, Vice Chm.

Province of Saint Barbara Fraternal Care Trust, 1500 34th Ave., 94601. Tel: 510-536-3722.
Trustees Very Rev. Melvin A. Jurisich, O.F.M., Chm.; Revs. John Hardin, O.F.M.; Michael Hill, O.F.M.; Bro. Peter Boegel, O.F.M., Sec.; Mr. Edward J. Dantzig.

Redemptorist Vice Province Initiative, 8945 Golf Links Rd., 94605. Tel: 312-739-0900; Fax: 312-782-3773. Email: mjsamis4@aol.com. Michael J. Samis, Asst. Sec.

Religious Communities Investment Fund, Inc., 462 Elwood Ave., Ste. 2, 94610. Tel: 510-836-7556; Fax: 510-836-7556. Web: www.rcif.org. Sr. Corinne Florek, O.P., Dir. & Contact Person.

BERKELEY. *Academy of American Franciscan History*, 1712 Euclid Ave., 94709-1208. Tel: 510-548-1755; Fax: 510-549-9466. Email: acadafh@fst.edu. Web: www.aafh.org. Total Staff 1.

Inter-Friendship House Association, Friendship Center, 1646 Addison St., 94703-1404. Tel: 510-843-7675; Fax: 510-843-7675. Web: www.fuyou-berkeley.org. Ken Wong, Chm. Total Staff 1.

Multicultural Institute (1991) 1920 Seventh St., 94710-2011. Tel: 510-848-4075; Fax: 510-848-4095. Email: rcaloca@mionline.org. Web: www.mionline.org. Board of Directors: Revs. William M. Cieslak, O.F.M.Cap., Ph.D.; James Lockman, O.F.M., Ph.D.; Rigoberto Caloca Rivas, O.F.M., Ph.D.; Jon M. Balousek, Treas. Tel: 925-254-8373; John Matzger, Sec.; Philip J. Murphy, M.B.A., Pres.
Administrative Staff: Rev. Rigoberto Caloca-Rivas, O.F.M., Ph.D., Exec. Dir.; Dr. Paula Worby, Ph.D., Assoc. Dir.; Bro. David Cobian, O.F.M., M.Div., Life Skills Prog. Dir.; Rey Gonzalez, Life Skills Prog. Asst.; Rodolfo Lara, Life Skills Prog. Dir.; Cesar Meza-Esviele, Life Skills Prog. Dir.; Enrique Moreno, Life Skills Prog. Asst.

CONCORD. *Carondelet High School Foundation* (1999) 1133 Winton Dr., 94518-3527. Tel: 925-686-5353, Ext. 180; Fax: 925-686-4901. Email: KML@carondeleths.org. Web: www.carondelet.pvt.k12.ca.us. Patricia Larsen, Exec. Dir.; Sr. Kathleen Lang, C.S.J., Pres. Carondelet High School.

East Bay Services to the Developmentally Disabled (1984) 1870 Adobe St., 94520. Tel: 925-825-2091; Fax: 925-825-2439. Nonresidence Serves 800; Residence 65; Total Staff 70.

DANVILLE. *Catholic Professional & Business Breakfast Club of the Diocese of Oakland*, 440 LaGonda Way, 94526. Tel: 925-683-5263; Fax: 925-831-0887. Email: aliyount@sbcglobal.net. Web: www.catholicsatwork.org. Attila Bardos, Pres.; John Dunican, Treas.

EL CERRITO. *Divine Mercy Eucharistic Society*, 11152 San Pablo Ave., 94530-2131. Tel: 510-412-4715; Fax: 510-412-3537. Email: divinemercyjesus@comcast.net. Web: divinemercywestcoast.org. Thelma Orias, Pres.

Mary's House aka Mary's House of Mercy 1850 Church Ln., San Pablo, 94806-3706. Tel: 510-236-0383; Fax: 510-236-0395. Email: divinemercyjesus@comcast.net. Web: marys-house.org. (ministry of Divine Mercy Eucharistic Society) Total Assisted Annually 11.

FREMONT. *Dominican Sisters of Mission San Jose Foundation (A Nonprofit Corp.)*, 43326 Mission Blvd., 94539-5829. Tel: 510-657-2468; Fax: 510-657-1733. Email: development@msjdominicans.org. Web: www.msjdominicans.org. Michael Botello, Pres.; Janice Caldwell, Sec. & Treas.; Dominique Mintz, Exec. Vice Pres.

Pia Backes Support Trust, Dominican Sisters of Mission San Jose, 43326 Mission Blvd., 94539-5829. Tel: 510-657-2468; Fax: 510-683-0712. Email: jarcher@msjdominicans.org. Sr. Mary Liam Brock, O.P., Pres.

RELIGIOUS INSTITUTES OF MEN REPRESENTED IN THE DIOCESE

For further details refer to the corresponding bracketed number in the Religious Institutes of Men or Women section.

[0140]—*The Augustinians*—O.S.A.
[0330]—*Brothers of the Christian Schools* (Prov. of San Francisco)—F.S.C.
[0200]—*Camaldolese Benedictines*—O.S.B.Cam.
[0470]—*The Capuchin Friars*—O.F.M.Cap.
[0270]—*Carmelite Fathers and Brothers*—O.Carm.
[1000]—*Congregation of the Passion*—C.P.
[1130]—*Congregation of the Priests of the Sacred Heart*—S.C.J.
[0480]—*Conventual Franciscans*—O.F.M.Conv.
[0520]—*Franciscan Friars* (Prov. of Santa Barbara)—O.F.M.
[0530]—*Franciscan Friars of the Atonement*—S.A.
[]—*Guadalupe Missioners*—M.G.
[0305]—*Institute of Christ the King Sovereign Priest*—I.C.
[0690]—*Jesuit Fathers and Brothers*—S.J.
[0780]—*Marist Fathers and Brothers*—S.M.
[]—*Missionaries of Faith*—M.F.
[0910]—*Oblates of Mary Immaculate* (US Prov.)—O.M.I.
[920]—*Oblates of St. Francis de Sales*—O.S.F.S.
[0430]—*Order of Preachers-Dominicans* (Prov. of the Most Holy Name of Jesus, Western Dominican Prov.)—O.P.
[1030]—*Paulist Fathers*—C.S.P.
[0610]—*Priests of the Congregation of Holy Cross*—C.S.C.
[1070]—*Redemptorist Fathers* (Denver Prov.)—C.SS.R.
[1190]—*Salesians of Don Bosco* (San Francisco Prov.)—S.D.B.
[1240]—*Servites*—O.S.M.
[1290]—*Society of Priests of St. Sulpice*—S.S.
[1200]—*Society of the Divine Savior*—S.D.S.
[0420]—*Society of the Divine Word*—S.V.D.
[1060]—*Society of the Precious Blood* (Prov. of the Pacific)—C.PP.S.

RELIGIOUS INSTITUTES OF WOMEN REPRESENTED IN THE DIOCESE

[0100]—*Adorers of the Blood of Christ*—A.S.C.
[1070-13]—*Adrian Dominican Sisters* (Congregation of the Most Holy Rosary)—O.P.
[]—*Congregation of Mother of Carmel*—C.M.C.
[1070-04]—*Congregation of the Most Holy Name* (Dominican Sisters of San Rafael)—O.P.
[1070-12]—*Congregation of the Queen of the Holy Rosary* (Dominican Sisters of Mission San Jose)—O.P.
[]—*Congregation of the Sacred Word*—C.S.W.
[0850]—*Daughters of Mary Help of Christians*—F.M.A.
[0420]—*Discalced Carmelite Nuns*—O.C.D.
[1070-30]—*Dominican Sisters of Oakford*—O.P.
[]—*Dominican Sisters of the Christian Doctrine*—O.P.
[1070-30]—*Dominican Sisters (Sinsinawa-Congregation of the Most Holy Rosary)*—O.P.
[1310]—*Franciscan Sisters of Little Falls, Minnesota*—O.S.F.
[2470]—*Maryknoll Sisters of St. Dominic*—M.M.
[2710]—*Missionaries of Charity*—M.C.
[]—*Missionary Sisters of Our Lady of Perpetual Help*—M.P.S.
[2420]—*Missionary Sisters of the Society of Mary, Marist Missionary Sisters*—S.M.S.M.
[]—*Quinhon Missionary Sisters of the Holy Cross*—L.H.C.
[]—*Religious Missionary Sisters of the Blessed Sacrament and Mary Immaculate*—M.S.S.
[3465]—*Religious of the Sacred Heart of Mary*—R.S.H.M.
[2970]—*School Sisters of Notre Dame*—S.S.N.D.
[0440]—*Sisters of Charity of Cincinnati, Ohio*—S.C.
[0430]—*Sisters of Charity of the Blessed Virgin Mary* (Mt. Carmel, Dubuque, IA)—B.V.M.
[1930]—*Sisters of Holy Cross*—C.S.C.
[2360]—*Sisters of Loretto at the Foot of the Cross*—S.L.
[2516]—*Sisters of Mercy* (U.S. Prov.)—S.M.
[2570]—*Sisters of Mercy of the Americas West Midwest Community* (Regional Community of Burlingame, CA)—S.M.
[3000]—*Sisters of Notre Dame de Namur* (California Prov.)—S.N.D.deN.
[1650]—*Sisters of St. Francis of Philadelphia*—O.S.F.
[4080]—*Sisters of Social Service of Los Angeles, Inc.*—S.S.S.

[1630]—*Sisters of St. Francis of Penance and Christian Charity*—O.S.F.

[3840]—*Sisters of St. Joseph of Carondelet* (Los Angeles Prov.)—C.S.J.

[3830-03]—*Sisters of St. Joseph of Orange*—C.S.J.

[3930]—*Sisters of St. Joseph of the Third Order of St. Francis*—S.S.J.-T.O.S.F.

[1960]—*Sisters of the Holy Family*—S.H.F.

[1990]—*Sisters of the Holy Names of Jesus and Mary* (U.S. - Ontario Prov.)—S.N.J.M.

[3320]—*Sisters of the Presentation of the B.V.M.* (San Francisco, CA)—P.B.V.M.

[3680]—*Sisters of the Sacred Hearts of Jesus and Mary*—S.H.J.M.

[]—*Sisters of the Third Order of St. Dominic Congregation of the Most Holy Name*—O.P.

[2150]—*Sisters, Servants of the Immaculate Heart of Mary*—I.H.M.

[4070]—*Society of the Sacred Heart*—R.S.C.J.

[1070-13]—*Third Order of St. Dominic Congregation of the Most Holy Rosary*—O.P.

[3330]—*Union of the Sisters of the Presentation of the Blessed Virgin Mary*—P.B.V.M.

NECROLOGY

† Macchi, William, (Retired)—Died Oct. 9, 2009

An asterisk (*) denotes an organization that has established tax-exempt status directly with the IRS and is not covered by the USCCB Group Ruling.

Diocese of Ogdensburg

(Dioecesis Ogdensburgensis)

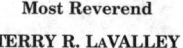

Most Reverend

TERRY R. LAVALLEY

Bishop of Ogdensburg; ordained September 24, 1988; appointed Bishop of Ogdensburg February 23, 2010; installed April 30, 2010. *Mailing Address: P.O. Box 369, Ogdensburg, NY 13669.*

Chancery Office: P.O. Box 369, Ogdensburg, NY 13669. Tel: 315-393-2920; Fax: 866-314-7296.

Web: www.dioogdensburg.org

Square Miles 12,036.

Erected by His Holiness Pius IX, February 16, 1872.

Incorporated by a special act of the Legislature of the State of New York, April 10, 1945, with the title: The Roman Catholic Diocese of Ogdensburg, New York.

Comprises that part of Herkimer and Hamilton Counties north of the northern line of the townships of Ohio and Russia as existing in 1872 with the entire Counties of Lewis, Jefferson, St. Lawrence, Franklin, Clinton and Essex in the State of New York.

For legal titles of parishes and diocesan institutions, consult the Chancery Office.

STATISTICAL OVERVIEW

Personnel	
Bishop	1
Priests: Diocesan Active in Diocese	72
Priests: Diocesan Active Outside Diocese	5
Priests: Retired, Sick or Absent	53
Number of Diocesan Priests	130
Religious Priests in Diocese	5
Total Priests in Diocese	135
Extern Priests in Diocese	3
Ordinations:	
Permanent Deacons	12
Permanent Deacons in Diocese	70
Total Brothers	8
Total Sisters	113
Parishes	
Parishes	105
With Resident Pastor:	
Resident Diocesan Priests	64
Resident Religious Priests	2
Without Resident Pastor:	
Administered by Priests	37
Administered by Deacons	1
Administered by Religious Women	1
Missions	10
Professional Ministry Personnel:	
Sisters	18
Lay Ministers	832
Welfare	
Homes for the Aged	1
Total Assisted	128
Special Centers for Social Services	4
Total Assisted	30,000
Educational	
Students from Other Diocese	2
Diocesan Students in Other Seminaries	5
Total Seminarians	5
High Schools, Diocesan and Parish	2
Total Students	352
Elementary Schools, Diocesan and Parish	13
Total Students	2,020
Catechesis/Religious Education:	
High School Students	1,552
Elementary Students	6,016
Total Students under Catholic Instruction	9,945
Teachers in the Diocese:	
Priests	2
Sisters	10
Lay Teachers	186
Vital Statistics	
Receptions into the Church:	
Infant Baptism Totals	1,075
Minor Baptism Totals	55
Adult Baptism Totals	32
Received into Full Communion	32
First Communions	1,039
Confirmations	990
Marriages:	
Catholic	241
Interfaith	119
Total Marriages	360
Deaths	1,668
Total Catholic Population	108,078
Total Population	491,438

Former Bishops—Rt. Revs. EDGAR P. WADHAMS, D.D., ord. Jan. 15, 1850; cons. May 5, 1872; died Dec. 5, 1891; HENRY GABRIELS, D.D., ord. Sept. 21, 1861; cons. May 5, 1892; died April 23, 1921; Most Revs. JOSEPH H. CONROY, D.D., LL.D., ord. June 11, 1881; cons. May 1, 1912; succeeded to the See, Nov. 21, 1921; died March 20, 1939; FRANCIS J. MONAGHAN, S.T.D., LL.D., ord. May 29, 1915; cons. June 29, 1936; succeeded to the See, March 20, 1939; died Nov. 13, 1942; BRYAN J. MCENTEGART, D.D., LL.D., ord. Sept. 8, 1917; cons. Aug. 3, 1943; transferred to Titular See of Aradi, Aug. 19, 1953; appt. June 26, 1953; to Rectorship of Catholic University of America, Washington, D.C.; appt. Bishop of Brooklyn, April 16, 1957; installed June 13, 1957; appt. Archbishop, April 15, 1966; retired and appt. Titular Archbishop of Gabii, July 17, 1968; died Sept. 30, 1968; WALTER P. KELLENBERG, D.D., ord. June 2, 1928; cons. Oct. 5, 1953; appt. to Ogdensburg, Jan. 19, 1954; transferred to See of Rockville Centre, April 16, 1957; installed May 27, 1957; died Jan. 11, 1986; JAMES J. NAVAGH, D.D., ord. Dec. 21, 1929; cons. Sept. 24, 1952; appt. to Ogdensburg, May 8, 1957; transferred to Paterson, Feb. 12, 1963; died in Rome, Oct. 2, 1965; LEO R. SMITH, D.D., ord. Dec. 21, 1929; appt. Auxiliary Bishop of Buffalo, July 9, 1952; cons. Sept. 24, 1952; appt. Bishop of Ogdensburg, Feb. 12, 1963; died in Rome Oct. 9, 1963; THOMAS A. DONNELLAN, D.D., ord. June 3, 1939; appt. March 4, 1964; cons. April 9, 1964; appt. to Atlanta, May 29, 1968; transferred to Archdiocese of Atlanta, July 16, 1968; died in Atlanta, Oct. 15, 1987; STANISLAUS J. BRZANA, S.T.D., LL.D, ord. June 7, 1941; appt. Titular Bishop of Cufruta and Auxiliary of Buffalo, May 24, 1964; cons. June 29, 1964; transferred to Ogdensburg, Oct. 22, 1968; retired Nov. 11, 1993; died March 1, 1997; PAUL S. LOVERDE, D.D., S.T.L., J.C.L., ord. Dec. 18, 1965; appt. Titular Bishop of Ottabia and Auxiliary Bishop of Hartford, Feb. 3, 1988; cons. April 12, 1988; transferred to Ogdensburg, Nov. 11, 1993; installed Jan. 17, 1994; appt. Bishop of Arlington, Jan. 25, 1999; installed March 25, 1999; GERALD M. BARBARITO, D.D., J.C.L., ord. Jan. 31, 1976; appt. Titular Bishop of Gisipa and Auxiliary Bishop of Brooklyn June 28, 1994; cons. Aug. 22, 1994; transferred to Ogdensburg Oct. 26, 1999; installed Jan. 7, 2000; appt. Bishop of Palm Beach July 1, 2003; installed Aug. 28, 2003; ROBERT J. CUNNINGHAM, D.D., J.C.L., ord. May 24, 1969; appt. Bishop of Ogdensburg March 9, 2004; ord. and installed May 18, 2004; appt. Bishop of Syracuse April 21, 2009; installed May 26, 2009.

Diocesan Offices

Unless otherwise noted, all mail for the following offices to go to: *Spratt Memorial Bldg., 604 Washington St., P.O. Box 369, Ogdensburg, 13669.* Office Hours: Mon.-Fri. 8:15-4 (Sept.-June); Summer Hours: 8:45-4.

Office of the Bishop—Most Rev. TERRY R. LAVALLEY, 604 Washington St., P.O. Box 369, Ogdensburg, 13669.

Secretary to the Bishop—VACANT.

Bishop's Office Secretary—LINDA ROSS. Fax: 315-393-2150.

Episcopal Vicar for Diocesan Service and Director of Seminarians and Vocations—Rev. DOUGLAS J. LUCIA, J.C.L., Mailing Address: P.O. Box 369, Ogdensburg, 13669. Tel: 315-393-2920; Fax: 866-314-7296. Associate Vocations Director: Rev. BRYAN D. STITT, S.T.L.

Department of Worship—Rev. DOUGLAS J. LUCIA, J.C.L., Dir.

Fiscal Officer—Mr. MICHAEL J. TOOLEY. Fax: 315-393-5911.

Parish Administrative Services Coordinator—Mr. VINCE THOUIN.

Human Resources Director—Ms. KIMBERLY SNOVER.

Insurance Claims and Risk Management Department—Mr. JACK CARTER, Mgr. Tel: 315-393-0441; Fax: 866-519-6423; RITA TULIP, Claims Svc. Representative.

Unless otherwise noted, all mail for the following offices to go to: *Bishop Stanislaus J. Brzana Diocesan Pastoral Center, 622 Washington St., P.O. Box 369, Ogdensburg, 13669.* Office Hours: Mon.-Fri. 8:15-4 (Sept.-June); Summer Hours: 8:45-4.

Episcopal Vicar for Pastoral Services and Moderator of the Curia—Rev. Msgr. JOHN R. MURPHY, S.T.L., M.A.

Chancellor—Sr. JENNIFER VOTRAW, S.S.J.

Episcopal Vicar for Clergy and Director Priest Personnel and Deacons—Rev. JAMES W. SEYMOUR.

Matrimonial Tribunal and Office of Canonical Affairs—

Judicial Vicar and Vicar for Canonical Affairs—Rev. Msgr. HARRY K. SNOW, M.A., J.C.L., V.F.

Moderator of the Tribunal—Mrs. ELAINE SEYMOUR.

Adjutant Judicial Vicars—Most Rev. TERRY R. LAVALLEY; Revs. PHILIP T. ALLEN; DOUGLAS J. LUCIA, J.C.L.

Promoter of Justice—Rev. Msgr. PETER R. RIANI, V.F., S.T.D., M.Ed.

Defenders of the Bond—Revs. LAWRENCE E. COTTER, S.T.L., B.S., M.S. (Retired); RAYMOND J. MOREAU; JOSEPH A. MORGAN; ALAN D. SHNOB; JOHN R. YONKOVIG.

Judges—Rev. Msgrs. BERNARD E. CHRISTMAN (Retired); ANTHONY A. MILIA (Retired); Revs. ROBERT L. COTTER (Retired); DANIEL T. KEEFE (Retired); CLYDE A. LEWIS; GILBERT B. MENARD (Retired).

Notary—Mrs. DIANNA L. SHAVER.

Advocates—Sr. MARY PATRICK MURPHY, S.S.J., M.S.; Rev. Msgrs. DENNIS J. DUPREY, V.F.; JOHN R.

MURPHY, S.T.L., M.A.; Revs. DOUGLAS A. DECKER; GARVIN J. DEMARAIS; GARRY B. GIROUX, J.C.L.; ALBERT J. HAUSER; ALAN J. LAMICA; WILLIAM G. REAMER.

Bishop's Delegate for Religious—Sr. ELLEN DONAHUE, S.A.

Development Office— Planned Giving; Stewardship Office Mrs. JANICE SHOEN, Exec. Dir.; Mrs. VALERIE MATHEWS, Asst. Dir.

Bishops' Fund Appeal—Mrs. VALERIE MATHEWS, Dir.

The Foundation of the Roman Catholic Diocese of Ogdensburg, New York—Mrs. JANICE SHOEN, Exec. Dir.

Evangelization—Sr. MARY EAMON LYNG, S.S.J., Dir.

Formation for Ministry—VACANT, Dir.

Mission Aid Societies—Sr. MARY ELLEN BRETT, S.S.J., Dir. Fax: 315-393-0981 Society for The Propagation of the Faith; Holy Childhood Association; Society of St. Peter the Apostle; Missionary Union of Clergy and Religious; Ogdensburg Peruvian Apostolate.

Office of Planning—Sr. JENNIFER VOTRAW, S.S.J., Dir.

Department of Communications—Sr. JENNIFER VOTRAW, S.S.J., Dir., Mailing Address: P.O. Box 369, Ogdensburg, 13669. Tel: 315-393-2920; Fax: 866-314-7296.

Bureau of Information—Sr. JENNIFER VOTRAW, S.S.J., Mailing Address: P.O. Box 369, Ogdensburg, 13669. Tel: 315-393-2920; Fax: 866-314-7296.

Newspaper— "The North Country Catholic" Mrs. MARY LOU KILIAN, Editor; CHRISTINE WARD, Editorial Asst., Mailing Address: P.O. Box 326, Ogdensburg, 13669. Tel: 315-608-7556.

Bureau of Media—Mrs. LINDA J. KELLEY, 1900 State Hwy. 11B, Potsdam, 13617. Tel: 315-265-0261; Fax: 315-268-7104.

Cemeteries—Sr. JENNIFER VOTRAW, S.S.J., Mailing Address: P.O. Box 369, Ogdensburg, 13669. Tel: 315-393-2920; Fax: 866-314-7296.

Unless otherwise noted, all mail for the following offices to go to: *Bishop Paul S. Loverde Center for Education and Formation, 100 Elizabeth St., P.O. Box 369, Ogdensburg, 13669*. Fax: 866-314-7296. Office Hours: Mon.-Fri. 8:15-4 (Sept.-June); Summer Hours: 8:45-4.

Episcopal Vicar for Catholic Education—Rev. Msgr. ROBERT H. AUCOIN, S.T.L., M.Ed., Seton Catholic Central, 206 New York Rd., Plattsburgh, 12901. Email: raucoin@dioogdensburg.org.

Diocesan Director of Christian Formation—Sr. ELLEN ROSE COUGHLIN, S.S.J. Tel: 315-393-4231; Fax: 866-314-7296.

Department of Christian Formation—

Ogdensburg Regional Center—Mrs. HEIDI MACKO, Dir.

Plattsburgh Regional Center—Sr. ELIZABETH MENARD, O.P., Dir., 114A Cornelia St., Plattsburgh, 12901. Tel: 518-563-2022; Fax: 518-563-2138.

Watertown Regional Center—Mr. MICHAEL WAGNER, Dir., 866 Arsenal St., Watertown, 13601. Tel: 315-782-3620; Fax: 315-782-2009.

Department of Youth Ministry—JAMES LUNDY.

Catholic Scouting—Rev. BRYAN D. STITT, S.T.L., Diocesan Liaison.

Department of Education—Sisters ELLEN ROSE COUGHLIN, S.S.J., Supt. & Dir. Educ.; SHIRLEY ANNE BROWN, S.S.J., Catholic School Supvr.; VACANT, Dir. Faith Formation.

Family Life Department and Pre-Cana—Directors: Deacon GARY FRANK; Mrs. GAYLE FRANK.

Consultative Bodies

Deans—Rev. THOMAS E. KORNMEYER, V.F., Adirondack; Rev. Msgrs. LEEWARD J. POISSANT, V.F., Clinton; PETER R. RIANI, V.F., S.T.D., M.Ed., Essex; DENNIS J. DUPREY, V.F., Franklin; Revs. SONY G. PULICKAL, V.F., Hamilton-Herkimer; ARTHUR J. LABAFF, V.F., Jefferson; VACANT, Lewis; Rev. Msgr. HARRY K. SNOW, M.A., J.C.L., V.F., St. Lawrence.

Diocesan Consultors—Rev. Msgrs. ROBERT L. LAWLER, P.A.; ROBERT H. AUCOIN, S.T.L., M.Ed.; Revs. DOUGLAS G. COMSTOCK; PIERRE AUBIN, M.S.C.; ARTHUR J. LABAFF, V.F.; DONALD J. MANFRED; JOSEPH A. MORGAN; KEVIN J. O'BRIEN; DOUGLAS J. LUCIA, J.C.L.

Council of Religious—Sisters MIRIAM NAJIMY, D.H.M., B.A., M. Rel. Studies, Pres.; EUNICE LALONDE, G.N.S.H., Vice Pres.; MARY RITA MORRISSETTE, O.S.M., Sec.; BERNADETTE DUCHARME, S.C.L., Treas.

Committee on Assignments—Rev. Msgrs. ROBERT L. LAWLER, P.A.; JOHN R. MURPHY, S.T.L., M.A.; Revs. DOUGLAS J. LUCIA, J.C.L.; JAY W. SEYMOUR; RAYMOND J. MOREAU; CHRISTOPHER C. CARRARA; CLYDE A. LEWIS; ARTHUR J. LABAFF, V.F.; MICHAEL GAFFNEY.

Other Diocesan Offices and Directors

Diocesan Archivist— (see Chancellor's Office) Ms. SALLY RUSAW, Assoc. Archivist.

Apostleship of Prayer—Rev. ALBERT J. HAUSER, Dir., Mailing Address: P.O. Box 369, Ogdensburg, 13669.

Building Commission—Sr. JENNIFER VOTRAW, S.S.J., Mailing Address: P.O. Box 369, Ogdensburg, 13669.

Campus Ministry—*John XXIII College Community, 90 Broad St., Plattsburgh, 12901*. Rev. TIMOTHY G. CANAAN, Dir.; JACKIE ROBERTSEN; Rev. THOMAS E. KORNMEYER, V.F.; Sr. CAROL KRAEGER, S.S.J.; Revs. ROBERT L. DECKER; GARRY B. GIROUX, J.C.L.; Mr. ALAN KNACK; Deacon PHILIP GIARDINO; RITA MAWN; Rev. DOUGLAS J. LUCIA, J.C.L.; Sisters JULIANA RAYMOND, S.S.J.; BETHANY FITZGERALD, S.S.J.

Catholic Charities—Sr. DONNA FRANKLIN, D.C., Diocesan Dir., Wadhams Hall, 6866 State Hwy. 37, Ogdensburg, 13669. Tel: 315-393-2255; Fax: 315-393-2402. Ogdensburg Office: TRENTON CLARK, 716 Caroline St., Ogdensburg, 13669. Tel: 315-393-2660; Fax: 315-393-9362. Watertown Office 812 State St., Watertown, NY 13601. Tel: 315-788-4330; Fax: 315-786-0539.: Plattsburgh Office: PORTIA TURCO, Dir., 4914 S. Catherine St., Plattsburgh, 12901. Tel: 315-561-0470; Fax: 315-561-0472. Malone Office: JOELLE LAMICA, Dir., Rennie St., Malone, 12953. Tel: 518-483-1460; Fax: 518-483-1478. Lowville Office Satellite office of Watertown, NY. 7514 S. State St., Lowville, NY 13367. Tel: 315-376-4141; Fax: 315-376-4141.: Tupper Lake Office - Foster Grandparent Program: VIVIAN SMITH, 80 Park St., Ste. 2, P.O. Box 701, Tupper Lake, 12986. Tel: 518-359-7688; Fax: 518-359-3927.

RSVP of Clinton County—JOYCE ST. GERMAIN, 46 Flynn Ave., Plattsburgh, 12901. Tel: 518-566-0944; Fax: 518-566-0945.

RSVP of Essex County—PATRICIA MCCAUGHIN, Project Dir., 38 Park Pl., Ste. 3, Port Henry, 12974. Tel: 518-546-3565.

Seaway House—CAROL WHITCOMBE, Dir., 212 Caroline St., Ogdensburg, 13669. Tel: 315-393-3133.

Catholic Relief Services—Sr. DONNA FRANKLIN, D.C., Mailing Address: P.O. Box 296, Ogdensburg, 13669. Tel: 315-393-2255; Fax: 315-393-2402.

Censor Librorum—Rev. LAWRENCE E. COTTER, S.T.L., B.S., M.S. (Retired), Mailing Address: P.O. Box 369, Ogdensburg, 13669.

Charismatic Renewal—Rev. FRANCIS J. CORYER, Liaison, Mailing Address: 1413 Military Tpke., P.O. Box 2223, Plattsburgh, 12901.

Committee for the Continuing Education of Clergy—Rev. SCOTT D. FOBARE, Chm., Mailing Address: St. Patrick's Church, 12 St. Patrick Pl., Port Henry, 12974. Tel: 518-846-7254; Fax: 518-375-3624.

Ecumenical Commission—Rev. DANIEL L. CHAPIN, Chm., Mailing Address: St. Stephen's Church, P.O. Box 38, Croghan, 13327-0038. Tel: 315-346-6958; Fax: 315-346-1200.

Legion of Mary—VACANT.

Natural Family Planning Services—Mr. ANGELO PIETROPAOLI; Mrs. SUZANNE PIETROPAOLI, 36 First St., Malone, 12953.

Permanent Diaconate Program—

Director of Deacon Formation—Rev. Msgr. ROBERT H. AUCOIN, S.T.L., M.Ed., Seton Catholic Central, 206 New York Rd., Plattsburgh, 12901.

Priests' Eucharistic League—Rev. ALBERT J. HAUSER, Dir., Mailing Address: P.O. Box 369, Ogdensburg, 13669. Tel: 315-393-2920; Fax: 315-394-7401.

Respect Life Office—Mr. JOHN MINER; COLLEEN MINER.

St. Vincent de Paul Society—VACANT.

Young Adult Ministry—GIB PATENAUDE, Dir., 5673 Cascade Rd., Lake Placid, 12946. Tel: 518-523-2553; Fax: 518-523-2448.

CLERGY, PARISHES, MISSIONS AND PAROCHIAL SCHOOLS

CITY OF OGDENSBURG

(ST. LAWRENCE COUNTY)

1—ST. MARY'S CATHEDRAL (1748) [CEM] Sr. Mary Theresa La Brake, G.N.S.H., Pastoral Assoc.; Deacons Francis F. Bateman; David J. Sandburg; John L. White. In Res., Rev. Vicente F. Jazmines.
Res.: 415 Hamilton St., 13669. Tel: 315-393-3930; Fax: 315-393-6680. Email: gbouchard@saintmaryscathedral.net. Web: www.saintmaryscathedral.net.
Catechesis / Religious Program—214 Morris St., 13669. Tel: 315-393-1820; Fax: 315-393-1670. Email: bishopconroydre@verizon.net. Web: www.bishopconroyschool.org. Mrs. Celina Burns, D.R.E. Students 227.

2—NOTRE DAME (1859), (French), [CEM] Rev. F. James Shurtleff; Deacons Thomas Kilian; Mark A. LaLonde; Elizabeth J. Bernhard, Pastoral Assoc. In Res., Rev. Msgrs. George M. Phillips (Retired); John R. Murphy.
Res.: 125 Ford Ave., 13669. Tel: 315-393-5050; Fax: 315-393-5962. Email: notredame@lttfilsp.com. Web: www.notredame-ogdensburg.com.
School—*St. Marguerite D'Youville Academy*, (Grades PreK-6), 315 Gates St., 13699. Tel: 315-393-0165; Fax: 315-394-0499. Mrs. Celina Burns, Prin. Lay Teachers 14; Students 102.
Catechesis / Religious Program—Bishop Conroy Christian Formation Program, 214 Morris St., 13669. Tel: 315-393-1820; Fax: 315-393-1670. Mrs. Celina Burns, D.R.E. Students 128.

OUTSIDE CITY OF OGDENSBURG

ADAMS, JEFFERSON CO., ST. CECILIA (1870) [CEM] Rev. Douglas A. Decker.
Mailing Address: 17 Grove St., 13605. Email: stcec@frontiernet.net. Web: www.stceciliaadams.org.
Catechesis / Religious Program—Students 216.
Mission—*Queen of Heaven* 8900 NYS Rte. 3, Henderson, Jefferson Co. 13650. Tel: 315-232-2392; Fax: 315-232-2817.

ALEXANDRIA BAY, JEFFERSON CO., ST. CYRIL OF ALEXANDRIA (CATHOLIC COMMUNITY OF ALEXANDRIA) (1000 Islands) (1885) [CEM] Rev. Douglas G. Comstock; Deacon Bernard E. Slate.
Catholic Community of Alexandria
Res.: 17 Rock St., 13607. Tel: 315-482-2670; Fax: 815-301-1901. Email: pastor@stcyrils.org. Web: www.stcyrils.org.
Catechesis / Religious Program—Students 80.

ALTONA, CLINTON CO., HOLY ANGELS (1865), (Irish—French Canadian), [CEM] Rev. Gilbert O. Boisvert.
Res.: P.O. Box 113, 12910. Tel: 518-236-5848; Fax: 518-236-4249. Email: holyangels@primelink1.net.
Oratory—*Jericho, St. Alexis*
Catechesis / Religious Program—Tel: 518-236-4249. Students 171.

AU SABLE FORKS, CLINTON CO.

1—CATHOLIC COMMUNITY OF HOLY NAME AND ST. MATTHEW Rev. Kris C. Lauzon; Deacon John J. Ryan.
Res.: 10 Church Ln., P.O. Box 719, 12912. Tel: 518-647-8225; Fax: 518-647-5394.
Worship Site:—
St. Matthew—
School—(Grades PreK-6), 5 Pleasant St., 12912. Tel: 518-647-8444. Mrs. Jean Pulsifer, Prin. Sisters 1; Lay Teachers 7; Students 68.
Catechesis / Religious Program—Students 46.
Mission—*St. Margaret*

2—HOLY NAME (1848) [CEM] Merged with St. Matthew, Black Brook to form Catholic Community of Holy Name and St. Matthew, Au Sable Forks.

BLACK BROOK, CLINTON CO., ST. MATTHEW (1848) [CEM] Merged Now a worship site of Catholic Community of Holy Name and St. Matthew.

BLACK RIVER, JEFFERSON CO., ST. PAUL (1901) Rev. Andrew R. Mulvaney; Deacon William S. Raven.
Res.: 208 LeRay St., 13612. Tel: 315-773-5672.
Church: 210 LeRay St., 13612.
Catechesis / Religious Program—Students 38.

BLOOMINGDALE, ESSEX CO., ST. PAUL (1897) [CEM 2] Revs. Thomas E. Kornmeyer; Paul J. Kelly, Parochial Vicar.
Res.: 1636 NYS Rte. 3, P.O. Box 356, 12913. Tel: 518-891-0144; Fax: 518-891-5259.
Mission—*Assumption of the B.V.M.* 826 NYS Rte. 86, Gabriels, Franklin Co. 12939.
Catechesis / Religious Program—Tel: 518-891-3111. Mary Kay Benham, D.R.E.; Ronald Burke, D.R.E.; Darci Hart, D.R.E. Students 105.

BOMBAY, FRANKLIN CO., ST. JOSEPH (1912) [CEM] Rev. Martin E. Cline; Mrs. Carol Pulsifer, Pastoral Assoc. In Res., Rev. Edward E. Papp (Retired).
Res.: 20 County Rte. 4, P.O. Box 156, 12914. Tel: 518-358-2500; Fax: 518-358-2500.
Office & Mailing Address: P.O. Box 499, Fort Covington, 12937. Tel: 518-358-2500.
Catechesis / Religious Program—Students 28.

BRASHER FALLS, ST. LAWRENCE CO., ST. PATRICK (1830), (Irish—French), [CEM] Rev. Patrick A. Ratigan.
Res.: P.O. Box 208, 13613. Tel: 315-389-5401; Fax: 315-389-4066. Email: parish@twcny.rr.com.
Parish Center—Email: parish@twcny.rr.com. Web: www.stpatrick-stlawrence.org.
Catechesis / Religious Program— Patty Eldridge, D.R.E. Students 73.

BROWNVILLE, JEFFERSON CO., ROMAN CATHOLIC COMMUNITY OF BROWNVILLE AND DEXTER formerly

Immaculate Conception of the B.V.M. (1874), (Irish—Italian), Rev. Kevin J. O'Brien.
Res.: 119 W. Main St., P.O. Box 99, 13615. Tel: 315-782-1143; Fax: 315-782-0231. Email: icses@twcny.rr.com.
Immaculate Conception—Worship Site: 13615.
Catechesis/Religious Program—Tel: 315-788-7240. Mrs. Christina M. Corey, D.R.E. Students 160.

BRUSHTON, FRANKLIN CO., ST. MARY'S CHURCH (1870) [CEM] Rev. Christopher J. Looby.
Res.: 1317 Washington St., 12916-0249. Tel: 518-529-7433. Email: office@stmarysbrushton.org.
Catechesis/Religious Program—Tel: 518-529-6580; Fax: 518-529-7433. Ernest Russell Jr., D.R.E. Students 77.

BURKE, FRANKLIN CO., ST. GEORGE (1874) [CEM] Merged with St. Patrick, Chateaugay to form Catholic Community of Burke and Chateaugay.

CADYVILLE, CLINTON CO., ST. JAMES CHURCH (1854) [CEM] Rev. Msgr. Lawrence M. Deno.
Res.: 26 Church Rd., P.O. Box 117, 12918-0117. Tel: 518-293-7026; Fax: 518-293-8246. Web: www.stjamescadyville.org.
Catechesis/Religious Program—Students 86.

CANTON, ST. LAWRENCE CO.

1—ST. MARY (1868) [CEM] Rev. Douglas J. Lucia; Deacon James M. Snell.
Res.: 68 Court St., 13617. Tel: 315-386-2543; Fax: 315-386-8870.
School—(Grades PreK-6), 2 Powers St., 13617. Tel: 315-386-3572. Mrs. Marianne Jadlos, Prin. Lay Teachers 11; Students 125.
Catechesis/Religious Program—Ms. Jamie Burns, C.R.E. Students 66.
Oratory—St. Henry-DeKalb Junction
Oratory—St. Paul-Pyrites 24 Pestle St., Russell, St. Lawrence Co. 13684.

2—NEWMAN MINISTRY OF ST. MARY'S PARISH: NEWMAN CENTER (1959), (Campus Parish) Rev. Douglas J. Lucia; Sr. Bethany Fitzgerald, S.S.J., Assoc. Campus Min.
Res.: 39 Court St., P.O. Box 424, 13617. Tel: 315-386-8425.
Catechesis/Religious Program—

CAPE VINCENT, JEFFERSON CO.

1—THE CATHOLIC COMMUNITY OF CAPE VINCENT, ROSIERE AND CHAUMONT Rev. Pierre Aubin, M.S.C.; Sr. Anne Hogan, S.S.J., Pastoral Assoc.
Box 288, 13618.
Res.: Box 288, 13618. Tel: 315-654-2662; Fax: 315-654-4721.
Catechesis/Religious Program—Students 74.

2—ST. VINCENT OF PAUL (1832) [CEM 2] Merged with St. Vincent de Paul, Rosiere & All Saints, Chaumont to form The Catholic Community of Cape Vincent, Rosiere and Chaumont, Cape Vincent.

CARTHAGE, JEFFERSON CO., ST. JAMES MINOR (1818) [CEM 2] [JC] Revs. George F. Maroun; John J. Cosmic (Retired); Sisters Mary Rita Kempney, S.S.J., Pastoral Assoc.; Marie Angele Ellis, S.S.J., Pastoral Assoc.; Deacon Richard J. Staab.
Res.: 327 West St., 13619. Tel: 315-493-3224; Fax: 315-493-3280. Email: stjames@twcny.rr.com.
School—Augustinian Academy, (Grades PreK-8), 317 West St., 13619. Tel: 315-493-1301; Fax: 315-493-0632. Sr. Annunciata Collins, S.S.J., Prin. Sisters of St. Joseph 1; Lay Teachers 12; Students 112.
Catechesis/Religious Program—Students 80.
Convent—Tel: 315-493-1672.

CHAMPLAIN, CLINTON CO., ST. MARY (1861) [CEM 2] Rev. James A. Delbel; Deacon Leonard Patrie.
Res.: 86 Church St., P.O. Box 368, 12919. Tel: 518-298-8244; Fax: 518-298-2879. Email: churchofstmary@yahoo.com.
School—(Grades PreK-6) Tel: 518-298-3372; Fax: 518-298-3886. Email: smaoffice@primelink1.net. Web: www.stmarysacademy.net. Sr. Marie Cordata Kelly, S.S.J., Prin.; Mrs. Linda Seymour, Librarian. Sisters of St. Joseph 2; Lay Teachers 8; Students 55.
Catechesis/Religious Program—Students 87.

CHASM FALLS, FRANKLIN CO., ST. HELEN (1881) [CEM], Malone Catholic Parishes - see detailed information under Notre Dame, Malone., 306 W. Main St., P.O. Box 547, Malone, 12953. Email: mcp@twcny.rr.com. Web: malonecatholic.com.
Oratory—St. Mary, Malone Catholic Parishes -see detailed information under Notre Dame, Malone., Lake Titus, Franklin Co. 12953.
Oratory—St. Joseph, Malone Catholic Parishes - see detailed information under Notre Dame, Malone., Owl's Head, Franklin Co. 12953.
Catechesis/Religious Program—Ms. Tamra Murphy, D.R.E.

CHATEAUGAY, FRANKLIN CO., CATHOLIC COMMUNITY OF BURKE AND CHATEAUGAY formerly St. Patrick's Church (1848) [CEM] Rev. John J. Looby; Mary Emily Lauzon, Pastoral Assoc.
Res.: 132 W. Main St., P.O. Box 908, 12920. Tel: 518-497-6673; Fax: 518-497-6165. Email: ccbc@twcny.rr.com.
Catechesis/Religious Program—Students 180.
Oratory—St. Jude Brainardsville, Franklin Co. 12920.

CHAUMONT, JEFFERSON CO., ALL SAINTS (1922) Merged with St. Vincent de Paul, Cape Vincent & St. Vincent de Paul, Rosiere to form The Catholic Community of Cape Vincent, Rosiere and Chaumont, Cape Vincent.

CHAZY, CLINTON CO., SACRED HEART (1898) [CEM 2] Rev. L. William Gordon.
Res.: 27 Church St., P.O. Box 459, 12921. Tel: 518-846-7650; Fax: 518-846-7655. Email: csacredheart@twcny.rr.com. Web: home.twcny.rr.com/sacredheart.
Catechesis/Religious Program—Tel: 518-846-7180. Email: religion@westelcom.com. Students 151.

CHURUBUSCO, CLINTON CO., IMMACULATE HEART OF MARY (1880) [CEM 2] Rev. Howard McCasland, Admin. (Retired).
Res.: Rte. 189, 12923. Tel: 518-497-9956.
Catechesis/Religious Program—St. Edmund's Center, Ellenburg. Tel: 518-594-3907. Students 38.

CLAYTON, JEFFERSON CO., ST. MARY'S OF CLAYTON (1838) [CEM 2] Rev. Arthur J. LaBaff; Deacon Gary A. Frank.
Res.: 521 James St., 13624. Tel: 315-686-3398 (Rectory); 315-686-2638 (Rel. Educ. Office); Fax: 315-686-2700. Email: stmarysclayton@westelcom.com.
Catechesis/Religious Program—Tel: 315-686-2638. Students 91.

COLTON, ST. LAWRENCE CO., ST. PATRICK (1864) [CEM] [JC] Revs. Bryan D. Stitt; Lawrence E. Cotter, Pastor Emeritus (Retired).
Res.: P.O. Box 315, 13625. Tel: 315-262-2871; Fax: 315-262-2188.
Church: 4897A SH56, 13625.
Catechesis/Religious Program—Students 59.
Mission—St. Paul South Colton, St. Lawrence Co. 13687.
Mission—St. Michael Parishville, St. Lawrence Co. 13625.

CONSTABLE, FRANKLIN CO., THE CATHOLIC COMMUNITY OF CONSTABLE, WESTVILLE AND TROUT RIVER (1872) [CEM] Rev. Francis J. Flynn; Deacon Garry N. Burnell.
Res.: 1197 State Rte. 122, P.O. Box 78, 12926. Tel: 518-483-2775 (Rectory); 518-483-0486 (Parish Office); Fax: 518-483-0486.
Catechesis/Religious Program—Students 79.
Mission— 4326 State Rte. 37, Westville, Franklin Co. 12926.

CONSTABLEVILLE, LEWIS CO., ST. MARY (1820) [CEM] [JC 2] Rev. Lawrence E. Marullo.
Rectory—3200 N. Main St., P.O. Box 382, 13325. Tel: 315-397-2556. Email: srectory1@twcny.rr.com.
Catechesis/Religious Program—Students 26.

COOPERSVILLE, CLINTON CO., ST. JOSEPH (1790) [CEM] Revs. Clyde A. Lewis; Normand C. Cote, Pastor Emeritus (Retired).
Mailing Address: P.O. Box 217, Rouses Point, 12979. 74 Mason Rd., Champlain, 12919. Tel: 518-297-7361; Fax: 518-297-3181. Email: stpats@twcny.rr.com.
Catechesis/Religious Program—Tel: 518-846-7180; Fax: 518-846-7655. Email: csacredheart@twcny.rr.com. Students 6.

COPENHAGEN, LEWIS CO., ST. MARY (1901), (Irish—French), [CEM 2] Rev. George F. Maroun; Sr. Mary Rita Kempney, S.S.J., Pastoral Assoc.; Deacon Richard J. Staab.
Res.: 9790 NYS Rte. 12, P.O. Box 12, 13626-0012. Tel: 315-688-2683. Email: stmarycope@westelcom.com.
Catechesis/Religious Program—Students 34.

CROGHAN, LEWIS CO., ST. STEPHEN (1869) [CEM] [JC 3] Rev. Daniel L. Chapin.
Res.: 9748 State Rte. 812, P.O. Box 38, 13327-0038. Tel: 315-346-6958; Fax: 315-346-1200.
Catechesis/Religious Program—Tel: 315-346-6963. Mr. Thomas Schneeberger, D.R.E. Students 171.
Oratory—Belfort, St. Vincent de Paul
Oratory—New Bremen, St. Peter [CEM 3]

CROWN POINT, ESSEX CO., SACRED HEART CHURCH (1874) [CEM] Rev. William G. Muench; Sr. Carol Daul, S.A., Pastoral Assoc.; Deacon Elliott A. Shaw.
Mailing Address: c/o 22 Father Jogues Pl., Ticonderoga, 12883.
Church: 12928. Tel: 518-597-3924. Email: tipastor@verizon.net. Web: www.smsh.org.
Catechesis/Religious Program—Students 30.

DANNEMORA, CLINTON CO., ST. JOSEPH (1853) [CEM 2] Rev. Donald F. Kramberg; Deacon Edward Mazuchowski. In Res., Rev. Guy F. Edwards. Tel: 518-492-2511, Ext. 4800.
Res.: 179 Smith St., Box 418, 12929-0418. Tel: 518-492-7118; Fax: 518-492-7742. Email: st.joe@charterinternet.com.
Catechesis/Religious Program—Tel: 518-492-2524. Email: llelynch@aol.com. Lynn Lynch, C.R.E. Students 157.

DEFERIET, JEFFERSON CO., ST. RITA (1900) Rev. Andrew R. Mulvaney.
Res.: 208 Leray St., Black River, 13612. Tel: 315-773-5672.
Church: 31 Riverside Dr., 13628.

ELIZABETHTOWN, ESSEX CO., ST. ELIZABETH (1881) [CEM] Rev. Msgr. Peter R. Riani.
Res.: 8434 NYS Rte. 9N, P.O. Box 368, 12932. Tel: 518-873-6760; Fax: 518-873-6530.
Catechesis/Religious Program—Students 20.

ELLENBURG, CLINTON CO., ST. EDMUND (1869) [JC 2] Rev. John J. Looby; Deacon John A. Levison.
Res. & Church: 5526 Rte. 11, P.O. Box 119, 12933-0119. Tel: 518-594-8843 (Rectory); 518-594-3907 (Office); Fax: 518-594-3222. Email: stedmund@twcny.rr.com. Web: stedmunds.grainofwheat.net.
Catechesis/Religious Program—Fax: 518-594-3222. Mona LaBombard, D.R.E. Students 93.

ESSEX, ESSEX CO., ST. JOSEPH, [CEM] [JC] Merged with St. Philip of Jesus, Willsboro to form Catholic Community of St. Philip of Jesus and St. Joseph of Willsboro.

EVANS MILLS, JEFFERSON CO., ST. MARY (1847) [CEM] Rev. Mark R. Reilly.
Res.: 8408 S. Main St., 13637. Tel: 315-629-4425; Fax: 315-782-4678. Email: cstmarys@twcny.rr.com.
Catechesis/Religious Program—Students 65.
Mission—St. Joseph Philadelphia, Jefferson Co.
Mission—St. Theresa of Avila Theresa, Jefferson Co.
Oratory—St. Michael (1849) [CEM] Antwerp, Jefferson Co. Tel: 315-659-8372. Rev. Mark R. Reilly. Antwerp, NY

FORT COVINGTON, FRANKLIN CO., ST. MARY (1837) [CEM 2] Rev. Martin E. Cline.
Res.: P.O. Box 156, Bombay, 12914. Tel: 518-358-2500; Fax: 518-358-2500.
Office & Mailing Address: P.O. Box 499, 12937.
Catechesis/Religious Program—Tel: 518-358-2500. Jocelyn Kelly, D.R.E. Students 52.

GLENFIELD, LEWIS CO., ST. MARY (1919) [CEM] Rev. Christopher C. Carrara.
Res.: 5457 Shady Ave., Lowville, 13367. Tel: 315-376-6662; Fax: 315-376-6663.
Catechesis/Religious Program—Tel: 315-376-6662. Students 14.
Mission—St. Thomas (1876) [CEM] Greig, Lewis Co.

GOUVERNEUR, ST. LAWRENCE CO.

1—ST. HENRY (1893) [CEM] Closed. Now an Oratory under St. Mary's, Canton.

2—ST. JAMES (1875) [CEM 2] Rev. Stephen Rocker.
Res.: 164 E. Main St., 13642. Tel: 315-287-0114; Fax: 315-287-0606. Web: stjamesgouv.com.
School—(Grades PreSchool-6), 20 S. Gordon St., 13642. Tel: 315-287-0130; Fax: 315-287-0054. Mrs. Bridgette LaPierre, Prin. Lay Teachers 13; Students 129.
Catechesis/Religious Program—Debra Wand, D.R.E. Students 25.

3—SACRED HEART (1894) Rev. Stephen Rocker; Deacon Peter J. Lawless.
Res. & Mailing Address: 164 E. Main St., 13642. Tel: 315-287-0114; Fax: 315-287-0606. Email: catholic@twcny.rr.com.
Parish Hall: 6 Trout Lake Rd., Edwards, 13635.
Catechesis/Religious Program—Mary Anne Lawless, D.R.E. Students 10.

HAMMOND, ST. LAWRENCE CO., ST. PETER (1905), (French—Irish), [CEM] Merged with The Roman Catholic Community of Morristown, Hammond & Rossie. Now a worship site.

HARRISVILLE, LEWIS CO., ST. FRANCIS SOLANUS (1879), (French—Irish), [CEM] Rev. Robert L. Decker; Deacon Ken Seymour.
Res.: 14355 Maple St., P.O. Box 208, 13648. Tel: 315-543-2421; Fax: 315-543-2421.
Catechesis/Religious Program—Students 14.
Oratory—St. Rita Lake Bonaparte.
Oratory—St. Henry Natural Bridge, Jefferson Co. 13665. Tel: 315-543-2431.

HEUVELTON, ST. LAWRENCE CO., ST. RAPHAEL'S (1880) Rev. James W. Seymour; Deacon Richard L. Van Kirk.
Res.: 5 Clinton St., P.O. Box 377, 13654. Tel: 315-344-2383. Email: saintraphael@twcny.rr.com.
Catechesis/Religious Program—Students 68.

HOGANSBURG, FRANKLIN CO., ST. PATRICK (1834), (Irish), [CEM] [JC] Rev. Martin E. Cline; Mrs. Carol Pulsifer, Pastoral Assoc.
Office & Mailing Address: P.O. Box 499, Fort Covington, 12937.
Res.: 20 County Rte. 4, P.O. Box 156, Bombay, 12914. Tel: 518-358-2500; Fax: 518-358-2500.
Catechesis/Religious Program—Jocelyn Kelly, D.R.E.

HOPKINTON, ST. LAWRENCE CO., CHURCH OF THE HOLY CROSS (1877) [CEM] Rev. Alfred H. Fish.

Res.: P.O. Box 288, St. Regis Falls, 12980. Tel: 518-856-9456.
Catechesis/Religious Program—Students 7.

HOUSEVILLE, LEWIS CO., ST. HEDWIG (1922), (Polish), Rev. Christopher C. Carrara.
St. Peter's Church: 5457 Shady Ave., Lowville, 13367-1615. Tel: 315-376-6662; Fax: 315-376-6663.
Catechesis/Religious Program—

INDIAN LAKE, HAMILTON CO., ST. MARY'S (1958) [CEM] Rev. Sony G. Pulickal.
Res.: Rte. No. 28, P.O. Box 332, 12842. Tel: 518-648-5422; Fax: 518-648-0323.
Catechesis/Religious Program—Students 28.
Mission—St. Paul P.O. Box 332, Blue Mountain Lake, Hamilton Co. 12842.

INLET, HAMILTON CO., ST. ANTHONY OF PADUA (1929) Rev. Joseph W. Giroux; Deacon Ronald Ste.-Marie.
Mailing Address: P.O. Box 236, Old Forge, 13420. Tel: 315-357-2811; Fax: 315-369-2049.
Catechesis/Religious Program—Students 18.
St. William—, Seasonal Chapel, Raquette Lake, 13436.

KEENE, ESSEX CO., ST. BRENDAN (1868) Rev. Joseph A. Morgan; Deacon Bruce Carley Wadsworth.
Res.: P.O. Box 130, 12942-0130. Tel: 518-576-4434; Fax: 518-576-9318.
Catechesis/Religious Program—Students 3.

KEESEVILLE, CLINTON AND ESSEX COS.
1—CHURCH OF THE IMMACULATE CONCEPTION (THE ROMAN CATHOLIC COMMUNITY OF KEESEVILLE) (1835), (Irish—French), [CEM] Consolidated with St. John the Baptist, Keeseville to form The Roman Catholic Community of Keeseville.
2—ST. JOHN THE BAPTIST (THE ROMAN CATHOLIC COMMUNITY OF KEESEVILLE) (1853), (French—Irish), [CEM 2] Rev. Msgr. Leeward J. Poissant.
Res.: 1804 Main St., 12944-3745. Tel: 518-834-7100; Fax: 518-834-4612. Email: rcckparish@charter.net.
Immaculate Conception— (1835) Worship Site: Tel: 518-834-2070.
St. John the Baptist— (1853) Worship Site: Tel: 518-834-7600.
Catechesis/Religious Program—1806 Main St., 12944-3745. Tel: 518-578-5632. Students 111.

LAFARGEVILLE, JEFFERSON CO., ST. JOHN THE EVANGELIST (1848) [CEM] Rev. Arthur J. LaBaff.
Res. & Mailing Address: 521 James St., Clayton, 13624. Tel: 315-686-3398; Fax: 315-686-2700.
Church: 35923 Rte.180, 13656. Email: stmarysclayton@westel.com.com.
Catechesis/Religious Program—Students 19.

LAKE CLEAR, FRANKLIN CO., ST. JOHN IN THE WILDERNESS (1887) [CEM] [JC] Revs. Thomas E. Kormeyer; Paul J. Kelly, Parochial Vicar; Sr. Carol Kraeger, S.S.J., Pastoral Assoc.
Mailing Address: 6148 State Rte. 30, P.O. Box 260, 12945. Tel: 518-891-2286. Email: srcarolk@yahoo.com.
Res.: 27 St. Bernard's St., Saranac Lake, 12983. Tel: 518-891-4616; Fax: 518-891-4619. Email: stbernard@roadrunner.com. Web: stbernards-saranaclake.catholicexchange.com.
Catechesis/Religious Program—Pius X Inter-Parish Religious Education Center, 61 River St., Saranac Lake, 12983. Tel: 518-891-3111. Email: piusxyouth@yahoo.com. Students 5.
Summer Station—Fish Creek, State Campsite. Tel: 518-891-3239.
Oratory—St. Gabriel Pickett Hall, #105, Paul Smiths, Franklin Co. 12970. Tel: 518-327-6225.

LAKE PLACID, ESSEX CO., ST. AGNES (1896) [CEM] Rev. Joseph A. Morgan; Deacon Bruce Carley Wadsworth.
Res.: 169 Hillcrest Ave., 12946. Tel: 518-523-2200; Fax: 518-523-2203. Email: stagnesch@roadrunner.com.
School—(Grades PreK-6), 2322 Saranac Ave., 12946. Tel: 518-523-3771. Ms. Rebecca Marlow, Prin. Lay Teachers 11; Students 90.
Catechesis/Religious Program—Tel: 518-523-3202. Mrs. Mary Lawrence, D.R.E. Students 165.

LAKE PLEASANT, HAMILTON CO., ST. JAMES MAJOR (1924) Rev. Shane M. Lynch.
Res.: 2781 NYS Rte. 8, P.O. Box 214, Speculator, 12164. Tel: 518-548-6275. Email: sjcsac@frontiernet.net.
Catechesis/Religious Program—Students 1.

LISBON, ST. LAWRENCE CO., SS. PHILIP AND JAMES (1872) Rev. James W. Seymour; Sr. Mary Frances Barnes, D.C., Pastoral Assoc.; Elaine Craig, Lay Min.; Marlene Watson, Lay Min.
Mailing Address: 6892 County Rt. 10, P.O. Box 175, 13658. Tel: 315-393-3796. Email: ssp&j@centralny.twcbc.com.
Catechesis/Religious Program—Tel: 315-393-3796. Students 37.

LONG LAKE, HAMILTON CO., ST. HENRY (1899) [JC] Rev. Peter M. Berg.
Res.: 18 Adams Ln., Newcomb, 12852-1701. Tel: 518-582-3671; Fax: 518-582-5483. Email: therese@capital.net.
Catechesis/Religious Program—Students 15.

LOUISVILLE, ST. LAWRENCE CO., ST. LAWRENCE (1930) [CEM] Rev. Donald J. Manfred; Sr. Evelyn McCarte, D.C., Pastoral Assoc.
Res.: 30 Willard Rd., Massena, 13662. Tel: 315-769-3120. Email: stlawr@northnet.org.
Catechesis/Religious Program—Students 27.

LOWVILLE, LEWIS CO., ST. PETER (1870) Rev. Christopher C. Carrara; Sr. Lucille Beaulieu, O.S.M., Pastoral Assoc.; Deacon Ronald J. Pominville.
Res.: 5441 Shady Ave., 13367. Tel: 315-376-6662; Fax: 315-376-6663. Email: stpeters@centralny.twcbc.org. Web: www.stpeters-lowville.org.
Catechesis/Religious Program—Web: stpeters-lowville.org. Margaret Martin, D.R.E. Students 125.

LYON MOUNTAIN, CLINTON CO., ST. BERNARD (1875) [CEM] [JC] Rev. Theodore A. Crosby; Deacon Francis Siskavich.
Res.: 10 Church Pond Rd., P.O. Box 23, 12952. Tel: 518-735-4357; Fax: 518-735-4357. Email: stbernardchurch@starband.net.
Catechesis/Religious Program—Students 30.
Mission—St. Michael [CEM 2] Standish, Clinton Co.

MADRID, ST. LAWRENCE CO., ST. JOHN THE BAPTIST (1869) [CEM] Rev. Msgr. Robert L. Lawler; Sr. Constance Sylver, S.S.J., Pastoral Assoc. In Res., Sr. Constance Sylver, S.S.J.
Pastor's Residence: 34 Oak St., P.O. Box 187, Waddington, 13694. Tel: 315-388-4466; Fax: 315-388-4722. Email: stmarywadd@aol.com.
Res. & Church Address: 3715 Co. Rte. 14, 13660-0068. Fax: 315-322-5661.
Church Mailing Address: P.O. Box 68, 13660. Tel: 315-322-5661.
Catechesis/Religious Program—Students 35.

MALONE, FRANKLIN CO.
1—ST. JOHN BOSCO (1935) [CEM], Malone Catholic Parishes - see detailed information under Notre Dame., 306 W. Main St., P.O. Box 547, 12953.
2—ST. JOSEPH'S (1849), (Irish), [CEM 2], Malone Catholic Parishes - see detailed information under Notre Dame., 306 W. Main St., P.O. Box 547, 12953.
3—NOTRE DAME (1868), (French-Canadian), [CEM] Rev. Msgr. Dennis J. Duprey; Rev. Bernard D. Menard; Sisters Mary Elizabeth Looby, G.N.S.H., Pastoral Assoc.; Barbara Schiavoni, G.N.S.H., Pastoral Assoc.
Priest's Res.: 11 Church Pl., P.O. Box 547, 12953. Tel: 518-483-4074; Fax: 518-483-4185. Email: mcp@twcny.rr.com. Web: malonecatholic.com.
Office: 306 W. Main St., P.O. Box 547, 12953. Tel: 518-483-1300; Fax: 518-483-1307.
School—Holy Family, (Grades PreK-8), Joint venture Malone Catholic Parishes and 5 other rural parishes., 12 Homestead Pk., 12953. Tel: 518-483-4443; Fax: 518-481-6762. Anne Marie Wiseman, Prin. Sisters 1; Lay Teachers 13; Students 171.
Catechesis/Religious Program—Ms. Tamra Murphy, D.R.E. Combined with St. Joseph, Malone; St. John Bosco, Malone; St. Helen, Chasm Falls, Malone. Students 343.
Holy Family Foundation Board—Mr. Brian McKee, Pres.

MASSENA, ST. LAWRENCE CO.
1—ST. JOSEPH (1947) [JC] Merged with St. Mary's to form The Catholic Community of St. Mary's & St. Joseph's.
2—ST. MARY (1913) [JC] Merged with St. Joseph's to form The Catholic Community of St. Mary's & St. Joseph's.
3—SACRED HEART (1874) [CEM] Rev. Donald J. Manfred; Sr. Juliana Fitzpatrick, O.S.M., Pastoral Assoc.; Deacons James J. Hotte; Thomas E. Proulx.
Res.: 212 Main St., P.O. Box 329, 13662. Tel: 315-769-2469; Fax: 315-769-6973. Email: sacredh@nnymail.com. Web: www.catholic-church.org/massenasacredheart.
Catechesis/Religious Program—Sr. Edward Marie Tesiero, S.A., Dir. Christian Formation. Students 233.
Convent—188 Main St., P.O. Box 91, 13662. Tel: 315-769-6238.
4—THE CATHOLIC COMMUNITY OF ST. MARY'S & ST. JOSEPH'S Rev. J. Michael Gaffney; Sr. Maureen Sweeney, S.S.J., Pastoral Assoc.
105 Cornell Ave, P.O. Box 609, 13662. Tel: 315-764-0239; Fax: 315-796-5526. Email: stsmaryandjoseph@twcny.rr.com. Web: www.stmarymassena.catholicweb.com.
School—Trinity Catholic School, (Grades PreK-6), 188 Main St., 13662. Tel: 315-769-5911; Fax: 315-769-6973. Email: principal@twcny.rr.com. Web: www.trinitycatholicschool.net. Joan Rufa, Prin. Sisters of Saint Joseph and Servants of Mary 2; Lay Teachers 10; Students 220.
Catechesis/Religious Program—Anne Borsellino, D.R.E. (Grades K-12). Students 126.

MINEVILLE, ESSEX CO., THE CHURCH OF ALL SAINTS (1872) [CEM] Rev. Scott D. Fobare.
Res.: 12 St. Patrick's Pl., Port Henry, 12974. Tel: 518-546-7254; Fax: 518-375-3624.
Church: 23 Bartlett Pond Rd., 12956.
Catechesis/Religious Program—Tel: 518-942-3326. Students 43.

MOOERS FORKS, CLINTON CO., ST. ANN (1860), (French-Canadian), [CEM] Rev. Gerald A. Cerank; Deacons Tyrone A. Rabideau; Dennis Monty.
Res.: 3062 Rte. 11, P.O. Box 89, 12959. Tel: 518-236-5632; Fax: 518-236-4446.
Catechesis/Religious Program—Tel: 518-236-4436. Students 129.

MOOERS, CLINTON CO., ST. JOSEPH (1910), (French-Canadian), [CEM] Rev. Gerald A. Cerank.
Mailing Address: P.O. Box 89, Mooers Forks, 12959-0089. Tel: 518-236-5632; Fax: 518-236-4446.
83 Maple St., 12958.
Catechesis/Religious Program—73 Maple St., 12958. Tel: 518-236-4436. Students 104.

MORRISONVILLE, CLINTON CO., THE ROMAN CATHOLIC COMMUNITY OF ST. ALEXANDER AND ST. JOSEPH formerly St. Alexander (1897) [CEM] Rev. Scott R. Seymour; Deacon Marvin M. Connor.
Rectory—1349 Military Tpke., Plattsburgh, 12901. Tel: 518-563-6301.
Church: 1 Church St., P.O. Box 159, 12962. Tel: 518-561-5039; Fax: 518-561-5040.
Catechesis/Religious Program— Mrs. Pamela J. Ballantine, D.R.E. Students 130.

MORRISTOWN, ST. LAWRENCE CO., THE ROMAN CATHOLIC COMMUNITY OF MORRISTOWN, HAMMOND AND ROSSIE formerly St. John the Evangelist (1941) Rev. Kevin D. McEwan.
Res.: P.O. Box 216, 13664. Tel: 315-375-6571; Fax: 315-375-4832. Email: stjohns@centralny.twcbc.com.
Worship Site:—
St. Peter—
Catechesis/Religious Program—Students 17.
Oratory—Our Lady of Grace Brier Hill, St. Lawrence Co. 13664.

NEWCOMB, ESSEX CO., ST. THERESE (1950) [CEM] Rev. Peter M. Berg.
Res.: 18 Adams Ln., 12852-1701. Tel: 518-582-3671; Fax: 518-582-5483. Email: stetherese@frontiernet.net.
Catechesis/Religious Program—

NORFOLK, ST. LAWRENCE CO., VISITATION OF THE B.V.M. (1880) [CEM] Rev. Andrew J. Amyot. In Res., Deacon Lawrence A. Connelly.
Church & Rectory: 3 Morris St., P.O. Box 637, 13667. Tel: 315-384-3575. Email: maryelizabeth@westelcom.com.
Catechesis/Religious Program—Tel: 315-384-4242. Students 62.

NORTH BANGOR, FRANKLIN CO., ST. AUGUSTINE (1887) [CEM] Rev. Christopher J. Looby, Priest Mod.; Sr. Sheila Jane Moran, S.S.J., Parish Life Dir.
Res.: 2472 S.R. 11, 12966. Tel: 518-483-6674; Fax: 518-483-6674.
Catechesis/Religious Program—Students 63.

NORTH LAWRENCE, ST. LAWRENCE CO., ST. LAWRENCE (1875), (Irish—French), [CEM] Rev. Patrick A. Ratigan.
Res.: P.O. Box 208, Brasher Falls, 13613. Tel: 315-389-5401; Fax: 315-389-4066. Email: parish@twcny.rr.com. Web: www.stpatrick-stlawrence.org.
Catechesis/Religious Program— Clustered with St. Patrick, Brasher Falls. Students 8.

NORWOOD, ST. LAWRENCE CO., ST. ANDREW (1876) [CEM] Rev. Msgr. Harry K. Snow; Deacon Frederick A. Brousseau.
Res.: 2 Park Ave., 13668. Tel: 315-353-7303; Fax: 315-353-4650.
Catechesis/Religious Program—Students 62.

OLD FORGE, HERKIMER CO., ST. BARTHOLOMEW (1897) Rev. Joseph W. Giroux.
Res.: P.O. Box 236, 13420. Tel: 315-369-3554; Fax: 315-369-2049. Email: stbarts@frontiernet.net.
Catechesis/Religious Program—Students 41.

OLMSTEDVILLE, ESSEX CO., ST. JOSEPH (1871) [CEM 2] Rev. Richard S. Sturtz.
Mailing Address: P.O. Box 368, Schroon Lake, 12870. Tel: 518-251-2565; 518-532-7100; Fax: 518-532-7100.
Rectory—639 Church Rd., P.O. Box 1, 12857.
Catechesis/Religious Program—Tel: 518-251-2565. Students 8.

PERU, CLINTON CO., ST. AUGUSTINE (1883) [CEM] Rev. Alan D. Shnob; Deacons George Grady Benson; Jonathan L. Votraw.
Res.: 3035 Main St., 12972. Tel: 518-643-2439 (Office); 518-643-6759 (Rectory); Fax: 518-643-0960. Email: staugrec@verizon.net. Web: www.peruparish.org.
Catechesis/Religious Program—Tel: 518-643-9498. Students 183.
Oratory—St. Patrick [CEM 2] West Peru, Clinton Co. 12972.

PLATTSBURGH, CLINTON CO.

1—ST. JOHN THE BAPTIST (1837), (Irish), [CEM 3] Revs. Timothy G. Canaan; Normand C. Cote (Retired).
Res.: 7 Margaret St., 12901. Tel: 518-563-0730; Fax: 518-563-0754. Email: office@stjohnsplatsburgh.org.
See Seton Academy Elementary School, Plattsburgh under Elementary Schools, Private in the Institution Section.
Catechesis/Religious Program—Students 70.

2—ST. JOSEPH (Treadwells Mill) (1935) Merged with St. Alexander, Morrisonville to form The Roman Catholic Community of St. Alexander and St. Joseph.

3—ST. MARY OF THE LAKE (Cumberland Head) (1965) [CEM] Rev. Albert J. Hauser.
Res.: 1202 Cumberland Head Rd., 12901. Tel: 518-561-2488; Fax: 518-561-3732. Email: ahauser@dioogdensburg.org.
Catechesis/Religious Program—Leslie Marvel, Rel. Coord. Students 64.

4—NEWMAN PARISH, JOHN XXIII COLLEGE COMMUNITY (1970) Rev. Timothy G. Canaan.
Res.: 90 Broad St., 12901. Tel: 518-563-0730 (Res.); 518-561-7545 (Office); Fax: 518-561-1004.

5—OUR LADY OF VICTORY (1907), (French), Rev. Albert J. Hauser.
Res.: 4919 S. Catherine St., 12901. Tel: 518-561-1842; Fax: 518-561-2269.
Catechesis/Religious Program—Students 43.
Convent—4907 S. Catherine St., 12901. Tel: 518-563-7419; Fax: 518-563-0383. Sr. Bernadette Ducharme, S.C.S.L., Supr.

6—ST. PETER (1853) [CEM] Rev. John R. Yonkovig; Deacons Mark Bennett, Spiritual Life Dir.; Frank A. Bushey Jr. In Res., Rev. Msgrs. Joseph G. Aubin (Retired); Robert H. Aucoin.
Res.: 114 Cornelia St., 12901. Tel: 518-563-1692; Fax: 518-566-9420. Email: spchurch1692@primelink1.net. Web: www.saintpeterschurch.org.
See Seton Academy Elementary School, Plattsburgh under Elementary Schools, Private in the Institution Section.
Convent—St. Peter's Convent, 5 Caitlin Way, 12903. Tel: 518-566-7315. Email: dshope2@charter.net. Sr. Mary Stephanie Frenette, O.P., Contact Person. Dominican Sisters of Hope Total in Residence 2.
Catechesis/Religious Program—Tel: 518-563-3278. Therese Moen, D.R.E.; Alison Crystler, Youth Min. Students 271.

PORT HENRY, ESSEX CO., ST. PATRICK (1854), (Irish), [CEM] Rev. Scott D. Fobare.
Res.: 12 St. Patrick's Pl., 12974. Tel: 518-546-7254; Fax: 518-375-3624.
Catechesis/Religious Program—Tel: 518-546-3374. Students 74.

PORT LEYDEN, LEWIS CO., ST. MARTIN (1879) [CEM] Rev. Stephen H. Gratto.
Res.: 7108 North St., P.O. Box 431, 13433. Tel: 315-348-6104; Fax: 315-348-6353. Email: smartins@frontiernet.net.
Catechesis/Religious Program—Students 56.
Mission—St. John Lyons Falls, Lewis Co. Tel: 315-348-6599.

POTSDAM, ST. LAWRENCE CO., ST. MARY (1841) [CEM] Rev. Garry B. Giroux.
Res.: 17 Lawrence Ave., 13676. Tel: 315-265-9680; Fax: 315-268-1443. Email: stmarypot@twcny.rr.com. Web: www.potsdamcatholic.org.
Catechesis/Religious Program—Tel: 315-265-9520. Email: ajkane@potsdamcatholic.org. Students 88. 41 Elm St., 13676. Email: campusministry@potsdamcatholic.org. Serving SUNY Potsdam and Clarkson Univerities.

RAQUETTE LAKE, HAMILTON CO., ST. WILLIAM (1890), Seasonal chapel of St. Anthony of Padua in Inlet, N.Y. Rev. Joseph W. Giroux.
Mailing Address: P.O. Box 236, Old Forge, 13420. Tel: 315-369-3554; Fax: 315-369-2049.

RAYMONDVILLE, ST. LAWRENCE CO., ST. RAYMOND (1920) [CEM] Rev. Andrew J. Amyot.
P.O. Box 637, Norfolk, 13667.
Res.: 8828 Rte. 56, 13678-0178. Tel: 315-384-4242; Fax: 315-384-3575.
Catechesis/Religious Program—Students 9.

REDFORD, CLINTON CO., CHURCH OF THE ASSUMPTION (1853) [CEM] Rev. Donald F. Kramberg; Deacon Edward Mazuchowski.
Res.: 78 Clinton St., 12978. Tel: 518-293-6259; Fax: 518-293-6435. Email: carousel1850@charter.net.
Catechesis/Religious Program—Kris Bowman, C.R.E. Students 69.

REDWOOD, JEFFERSON CO., ST. FRANCIS XAVIER (1848) [CEM] Consolidated Worship site of Catholic Community of Alexandria.

ROSIERE, JEFFERSON CO., ST. VINCENT DE PAUL (1871) [CEM] Merged with St. Vincent de Paul, Cape Vincent & All Saints, Chaumont to form The Catholic Community of Cape Vincent, Rosiere and Chaumont, Cape Vincent.

ROUSES POINT, CLINTON CO., ST. PATRICK (1857), (Irish), [CEM] [JC] Rev. Clyde A. Lewis; Deacon Noel A. Hinerth; Jo Anne Ryan, Business Mgr.
Res.: 136 Lake St., P.O. Box 217, 12979. Tel: 518-297-7361; Fax: 518-297-3181. Email: stpats@twcny.rr.com. Web: www.saintpatricks.ws.
Catechesis/Religious Program—9 Liberty St., P.O. Box 217, 12979. Tel: 518-297-3188. Kathy Guay, D.R.E. Students 94.

SACKETS HARBOR, JEFFERSON CO., ST. ANDREW (1886) Rev. Kevin J. O'Brien; Deacon Norman Hunneyman, (Serves at Mercy Health Care Center, Watertown, NY).
Res.: 112 E. Main St., Box 530, 13685. Tel: 315-646-3341.
Catechesis/Religious Program—Students 31.

SAINT REGIS FALLS, FRANKLIN CO., ST. ANN (1883) [CEM] Rev. Alfred H. Fish.
Res.: P.O. Box 288, St. Regis Falls, 12980. Tel: 518-856-9456.
Catechesis/Religious Program—Students 27.
Oratory—St. Peter Santa Clara.

SARANAC LAKE, FRANKLIN CO., ST. BERNARD (1888) [CEM] [JC] Revs. Thomas E. Kornmeyer; Paul J. Kelly, Parochial Vicar; Sr. Carol Kraeger, S.S.J., Pastoral Assoc.; Deacons Frederick R. Oberst; Joseph Szwed; Jerome A. Cheney.
Res.: 27 St. Bernard St., 12983. Tel: 518-891-4616; Fax: 518-891-4619. Email: stbernard@adelphia.net. Web: www.stbernardssaranaclake.com.
School—(Grades N-5) Tel: 518-891-2830. Web: www.sbssl.com. Anne Bayruns, Prin. Lay Teachers 7; Students 74.
Catechesis/Religious Program—Pius X Center Mary Kay Benham, D.R.E.; Cherie Raleth, D.R.E. Students 100.

SCHROON LAKE, ESSEX CO., OUR LADY OF LOURDES (1883) [CEM] Rev. Richard S. Sturtz.
Res.: 1114 Main St., P.O. Box 368, 12870. Tel: 518-532-7100; Fax: 518-532-7100. Email: ollsjc@verizon.net. Web: www.schroonlakecatholicchurch.com.
Rectory—1114 U.S. Rte. 9, 12870.
Catechesis/Religious Program—Students 40.

SCIOTA, CLINTON CO., ST. LOUIS (1899), (French-Canadian), [CEM] Rev. Gilbert O. Boisvert.
Res.: P.O. Box 113, Altona, 12910. Tel: 518-236-5848; Fax: 518-236-4249.
Catechesis/Religious Program—Tel: 518-236-4436. Students 18.

STAR LAKE, ST. LAWRENCE CO., ST. HUBERT (1893), (French—Irish), [JC] Rev. Robert L. Decker; Deacon Philip F. Giardino.
Res.: 1046 Oswegatchie Trail Rd., P.O. Box 9, 13690. Tel: 315-848-3612; Fax: 315-848-2510. Email: sthubertschurch@gmail.com.
Catechesis/Religious Program—Students 35.
Oratory—St. Anthony of Padua P.O. Box 9, Newton Falls, St. Lawrence Co. 13690.
Oratory—St. Michael P.O. Box 9, Fine, St. Lawrence Co. 13690.

TICONDEROGA, ESSEX CO., ST. MARY (1852) [CEM] Rev. William G. Muench; Sr. Carol Daul, S.A., Pastoral Assoc.; Deacon Elliott A. Shaw.
Res.: 22 Father Jogues Pl., 12883. Tel: 518-585-7144; Fax: 518-585-3632. Email: tipastor@verizon.net. Web: www.smsh.org.
School—(Grades K-8), 64 Amherst Ave., 12883. Tel: 518-585-7433; Fax: 518-585-3632. Email: sschoo3@nycap.rr.com. Web: home.nycap.rr.com/tistmarys. Sr. Sharon Anne Dalton, S.S.J., Prin. Sisters 2; Lay Teachers 8; Students 105.
Catechesis/Religious Program—Tel: 518-597-3924. Students 50.

TROUT RIVER, FRANKLIN CO., ST. BRIDGET'S ORATORY (1865) [CEM] Rev. Francis J. Flynn; Deacon Garry Burnell.
Res.: 1197 State Rte. 122, P.O. Box 78, Constable, 12926. Tel: 518-483-2775 (Rectory); 518-483-0486 (Office); Fax: 518-483-1618.

TUPPER LAKE, FRANKLIN CO.

1—ST. ALPHONSUS (1890) [CEM] Rev. Raymond J. Moreau; Deacons James T. Ellis; Gerald H. Savage; James R. Keough.
Res.: 48 Wawbeek Ave., 12986. Tel: 518-359-3405; Fax: 518-359-2364. Email: stalphon@verizon.net. Web: www.mysite.verizon.net/stalphon.
Catechesis/Religious Program—Combined with Holy Name of Jesus, Tupper Lake., Tel: 518-359-2551. Students 129.

2—HOLY NAME OF JESUS (Faust) (1904) [CEM] Rev. Raymond J. Moreau; Deacons James T. Ellis; Gerald H. Savage; James R. Keough.
Res.: 114 Main St., 12986. Tel: 518-359-9194; Fax: 518-359-9360. Email: holyname3@verizon.net.
Church: 114 Main St., 12986.
Catechesis/Religious Program—Combined with St. Alphonsus, Tupper Lake., Tel: 518-359-2551. Cheryl Tarbox, D.R.E. Students 144.

WADDINGTON, ST. LAWRENCE CO., ST. MARY (1826) [CEM 3] Rev. Msgr. Robert L. Lawler.
Res.: 34 Oak St., P.O. Box 187, 13694. Tel: 315-388-4466; Fax: 315-388-4722. Email: rlawler9@twcny.rr.com.
Catechesis/Religious Program—Msgr. Arquett Parish Center, Tel: 315-388-4423. Students 50.

WATERTOWN, JEFFERSON CO.

1—ST. ANTHONY (1913), (Italian), [JC] Rev. Donald A. Robinson; Deacons Richard C. Warner Sr.; John R. Murray.
Res.: 850 Arsenal St., 13601. Tel: 315-782-1190; Fax: 315-786-3489.
Catechesis/Religious Program—Students 75.

2—HOLY FAMILY (1895) Rev. Steven M. Murray; Deacons Edward R. Miller; Michael J. Allan; Patrick J. Bates, Pastoral Assoc. In Res., Rev. Msgr. Paul E. Whitmore (Retired); Rev. Leo A. Wiley (Retired).
Res.: 129 Winthrop St., 13601. Tel: 315-782-2468; Fax: 315-782-4684. Email: hfchurch@twcny.rr.com. Web: www.holyfamilywatertown.org.
Catechesis/Religious Program—Holy Family Religious Education Office, Sterling Pl., 13601. Tel: 315-782-6750. Email: religioused@twcny.rr.com. Students 180.

3—OUR LADY OF THE SACRED HEART (1876) [CEM] Rev. Richard Kennedy, M.S.C.; Sr. Diane Marie Ulsamer, S.S.J., Pastoral Assoc.; Deacons William Michael Johnston; John J. Trombly.
Parish Office—320 W. Lynde St., 13601. Tel: 315-782-1474; Fax: 315-782-4939. Email: rwkpng03@mscparish.com. Web: www.olshparish.org.
Preschool and Day Care—Tel: 315-782-3060. Ms. Shannon Turner, Day Care Dir.
Catechesis/Religious Program—Sr. Diane Ulsamer, S.S.J., D.R.E. Students 50.

4—ST. PATRICK (1854) [CEM], (Linked with St. Anthony) Deacon Kevin Mastellon, Parish Life Coord.; Sr. Mary William Argy, S.S.J., Pastoral Assoc.; Deacon William G. Schmidt.
Res. & Mailing Address: 123 S. Massey St., 13601-3201. Tel: 315-782-6086 (Pastoral Center); Fax: 315-788-4059. Email: pastoralcenter@stpatswtn.org. Web: stpatrickwatertownny.org.
Catechesis/Religious Program—Mrs. Elizabeth Bamann, D.R.E. Students 45.

WELLS, HAMILTON CO., ST. ANN'S (1890) [CEM] Rev. Shane M. Lynch.
Mailing Address: P.O. Box 214, Speculator, 12164. Tel: 518-548-6275. Email: sjcsac@frontiernet.net.
Catechesis/Religious Program—Students 9.

WEST CHAZY, CLINTON CO., ST. JOSEPH (1884) [CEM] Rev. J. Roger McGuinness.
Res.: 60 W. Church St., P.O. Box 224, 12992. Tel: 518-493-4521; Fax: 518-493-5880. Email: stjosephs@westelcom.com.
Catechesis/Religious Program—Students 62.

WEST LEYDEN, LEWIS CO., ST. MARY'S NATIVITY (1900) [CEM] Rev. Lawrence E. Marullo.
Mailing Address: 1183 State Rte. 26, P.O. Box 305, 13489.
Res.: 1175 State Rte. 26, P.O. Box 382, Constableville, 13325. Tel: 315-397-2556.
Catechesis/Religious Program—Students 35.
Oratory—SS. Peter & Paul

WESTPORT, ESSEX CO., ST. PHILIP NERI (1879) [CEM] Rev. Msgr. Peter R. Riani.
Res.: 8434 NYS Rte. 9N, P.O. Box 368, Elizabethtown, 12932. Tel: 518-873-6760; Fax: 518-873-6530.
Catechesis/Religious Program—Students 9.

WILLSBORO, ESSEX CO.

1—CATHOLIC COMMUNITY OF ST. PHILIP OF JESUS OF WILLSBORO (1909) & ST. JOSEPH OF ESSEX (1872), [CEM] Rev. Joseph W. Elliott.
Mailing Address: P.O. Box 607, 12996.
Res.: 3746 Main St., 12996. Tel: 518-963-4524; Fax: 518-963-7719. Email: stphilip@willex.com.
Catechesis/Religious Program—Students 30.

2—ST. PHILIP OF JESUS (1909) [CEM] Merged with St. Joseph, Essex to form Catholic Community of St. Philip of Jesus and St. Joseph of Willsboro.

WITHERBEE, ESSEX CO., ST. MICHAEL (1911) Closed. For inquiries for parish records contact the chancery.

Chaplains of Public Institutions

FORT DRUM. *U.S. Army Headquarters*. Revs. Ned Blick, Simon Obeng, Mathias Rendon, O.F.M.

Military and Medical

OGDENSBURG. *St. Lawrence Psychiatric Center*, St. Vincent's Chapel, 13669. Tel: 315-541-2001, Ext. 2414; Fax: 315-541-2049. Rev. Vicente F. Jazmines, Chap.

FORT DRUM. *U.S. Army Headquarters Fort Drum*, Tel: 315-772-5591; Fax: 315-772-6725.

PLATTSBURGH. *Champlain Valley Physicians Hospital Medical Center*, 75 Beekman St., 12901. Tel: 518-561-2000. Rev. William G. Reamer, Chap.

TUPPER LAKE, (SUNMOUNT). *Sunmount Developmental Center*, 403 Park St., 12986. Tel: 518-359-3311; Fax: 518-359-4133. Rev. Alan J. Lamica, Chap., Deacon Richard L. Van Kirk, Chap.

WATERTOWN. *Samaritan Medical Center*, 830 Washington St., 13601. Tel: 315-785-4000; Fax: 315-785-4195. Bro. John Paul Paradis, M.S.C., Chap. & Coord., Casey Shortt, Chap. & Coord.

Prisons

OGDENSBURG. *Ogdensburg Correctional Facility*, One Correction Way, 13669. Tel: 315-393-0281. Deacon Thomas F. Kilian, Rev. James W. Seymour.

Riverview Correctional Facility, Box 158, 13669. Tel: 315-393-8400. Rev. James W. Seymour, Deacon Mark A. LaLonde.

ALTONA. *Altona Correctional Facility*, P.O. Box 125, 12910. Tel: 518-236-7841; Fax: 518-236-6235. Rev. Guy F. Edwards, Deacon John A. Levison.

CAPE VINCENT. *Cape Vincent Correctional Facility* 13618. Tel: 315-654-4100, Ext. 548. Deacon Robert V. Ruddy, Rev. Richard Huber, M.S.C.

DANNEMORA. *Clinton Correctional Facility*, P.O. Box 798, 12929-0798. Tel: 518-492-2511, Ext. 4800. Deacon Larry R. Debiec, Rev. Guy F. Edwards. Tel: 518-492-7118.

GABRIELS. *Gabriel's Correctional Facility*, P.O. Box 100, 12939. Tel: 518-327-3111, Ext. 258. Rev. Victor E. Lamore, Chap.

GOUVERNEUR. *Gouverneur Correctional Facility*, Scotch Settlement Rd., P.O. Box 370, 13642. Tel: 315-287-7351; Fax: 315-287-2533. Deacons Bruce Dougherty, Thomas F. Kilian.

LYON MOUNTAIN. *Lyon Mountain Correctional Facility*, P.O. Box 23, 12952. Tel: 518-735-4540. Vacant.

MALONE. *Barehill Correctional Facility*, Cady Rd., 12953. Tel: 518-483-8411, Ext. 409. Deacon Richard L. Van Kirk, Rev. Alan J. Lamica.

Franklin Correctional Facility, P.O. Box 10, 12953-9720. Tel: 518-483-6040, Ext. 2402. Deacon Joseph R. Szwed, Rev. Garvin J. Demarais.

Upstate Correctional Facility, P.O. Box 2000, 12953. Tel: 518-483-6997. Deacon Bryan J. Bashaw, Rev. Garvin J. Demarais. Tel: 518-483-6997.

MORIAH. *Moriah Shock Incarceration Correctional Facility*, Fisher Hill Rd., P.O. Box 999, Mineville, 12956-0999. Tel: 518-942-7531. Rev. James A. Delbel, Deacon Elliott Shaw.

RAY BROOK. *Adirondack Correctional Facility*, Box 110, 12977-0110. Tel: 518-891-1343. Rev. Victor E. Lamore.

Res.: Star Rte., Box 152, Saranac Lake, 12983. Tel: 518-891-6540.

Federal Correctional Institution, P.O. Box 300, 12977. Tel: 518-891-5400. Rev. Alan J. Lamica.

WATERTOWN. *Watertown Correctional Facility* 13601. Tel: 315-782-7490, Ext. 445. Deacon Bruce Dougherty.

On Duty Outside the Diocese:
Revs.—
Hubbard, Jeffrey A., St. Patrick's Seminary & University, 320 Middlefield Rd, Menlo Park, CA 94025.
Kennehan, John P., St. John's Mercy Hospital, Springfield, MO.
Ledermann, Paul F., Veterans Home, P.O. Box 7, Yountville, CA 94599.
Sestito, Joseph N., 100 Van Tassal Ln., Rome, 13440.
Wertman, Raymond, 2292 Costa Rican Dr., Brahmin #56, Clearwater, FL 34623.

Absent on Sick Leave, Disabled:
Revs.—
Demers, Richard D., St. Augustine's Rectory, 3035 State Rte. 22, Peru, 12972.
Giroux, Harry E. (Retired), St. Joseph's Home, 950 Linden St., 13669.
Gonyo, Roland G., St. Joseph's Home, 950 Linden St., 13669.
Helfrich, Peter G., 10 Knoll Brook Rd., Apt. 3, Rochester, 14610.
Wheelock, Joseph P.

Retired:
Rev. Msgrs.—
Aubin, Joseph G., St. Peter's Rectory, 114A Cornelia St, Plattsburgh, 12901.
Christman, Bernard E., Indian Harbor Beach, FL 32937.
McAvoy, C. John, 51 Willow Way, Apt. 19, Saranac Lake, 12983.
McCarthy, Robert J., 324 Pratt St., 13601.
Milia, Anthony A., 866 Arsenal St., 13601.
Phillips, George M., Notre Dame Rectory, P.O. Box 149, 13669.
Whitmore, Paul E., Holy Family Rectory, 129 Winthrop St., 13601.

Revs.—
Beyette, Paul V., HC, Box 218, Loon Lake, 12989.
Chase, Charles E., 115 Beaver Pond Tr., Sugar Hill, NH 03585.
Cosmic, John J., 39 Anderson Ave., P.O. Box 117, Deferiet, 13628.
Cote, Norman J., St. John the Baptist Rectory, 7 Margaret St., Plattsburgh, 12901.
Cotter, Lawrence E., S.T.L., B.S., M.S., P.O. Box 606, 13669. United Helpers, 8103 State Hwy. 68, 13669.
Cotter, Robert L., 1425 Washington St., 13601.
Crable, John M., Samuel F. Vilas Home, 61 Beckman St., Plattsburgh, 12901.
DeRoche, Wilfred L., South Meadow Village, #26-5, Carver, MA 02330.
Downs, John L., 8828 State Hwy. 56, Raymondville, 13678.
Hart, Rolland A., 224 Stone Hill Rd., Williston, VT 05495.
Jarecki, Michael S., P.O. Box 627, Winchester, NH 03470.
Keefe, Daniel T., 9290 State Rte. 3, Loon Lake, 12989.
Lamitie, James F., 1772 Bar Harbor Dr., Fort Pierce, FL 34945.
Lamitie, Robert O., Star Rte., Box 35 C, Saranac Lake, 12983.
McCasland, Howard, Immaculate Heart of Mary, Rt. 189-560, Churubusco, 12923.
Menard, Gilbert B., 2 Garrett Way, Schuyler Falls, 12985.
Moody, Thomas A., Samaritan Keep Home, 830 Washington St., 13601.
O'Reilly, Patrick J., 89 Greenwood St., Lake Placid, 12946.
Papp, Edward E., P.O. Box 156, Bombay, 12914.
Patterson, Terrence R., Box 288, Potsdam, 13676. Tel: 315-265-2986
Poupore, Norman E., P.O. Box 824, Pierrepont Manor, 13674.
Silver, John E., 2705 Sagittarius Dr., Myrtle Beach, SC 29575.
Tobin, George W., 10 Aiken Ct., Plattsburgh, 12901.
Wiley, Leo A., Holy Family Church, 129 Winthrop St., 13601.

Permanent Deacons:
Allen, Michael J., Holy Family, Watertown
Bashaw, Bryan J., Malone
Bateman, Francis F., Ogdensburg
Bennett, Mark E., Spritual Life Director, 95 Brinkerhoff St., Plattsburgh, 12901. Church of St. Peter, Plattsburg
Benson, George Grady, Peru
Brousseau, Frederick A., St. Mary, Potsdam
Burnell, Garry N., St. Francis of Assisi, Constable
Bushey, Frank A., Jr., 7 Addoms St., Plattsburgh, 12901. Church of St. Peter, Plattsburg
Chaufty, James W., P.O. Box 43, Port Leyden, 13433. St. Martin's Church, Port Leyden; St. John's Church, Lyons Falls
Cheney, Jerome A., Saranac Lake
Cogan, John A., 108 Sunrise Dr., Plattsburgh, 12901. Our Lady of Victory, Plattsburg; St. Mary's of the Lake in Cumberland Head
Connelly, Lawrence A., Norfolk
Connor, Marvin M., 459 Irish Settlement Rd., P.O. Box 325, Schuyler Falls, 12985. Roman Catholic Community of St. Alexander and St. Joseph, Morrisonville & Treadwells Mill
Crosby, Patrick, Clayton (Summers Only) (Syracuse Diocese)
Dashnaw, Donald, (Retired Outside Diocese)
Daugherty, Bruce Wayne, Clayton & LaFargeville
Debiec, Larry, Clinton Correctional Facility, Dannemora
Defayette, Gerald R., (Retired), St. Joseph, West Chazy
Diehl, Robert, (Retired), 8 B Wyoming Ave, Whiting, NJ 08759.
Dwyer, Brian T., 543 County Rte. 52, Chateaugay, 12920. Catholic Community, Burke & Chateaugay
Ellis, James T., St. Alphonsus, Tupper Lake
Frank, Gary A., St. Mary, Clayton
Giardino, Philip F., St. Hubert, Star Lake
Gilbert, Joseph H., (Retired)
Gillen, James, Jonesboro, ME
Gilner, Gerard, (Retired), St. Mary, Indian Lake
Hennigan, David N., Our Lady of the Sacred Heart, Watertown
Hinerth, Noel A., St. Patrick, Rouses Point
Hotte, James J., Sacred Heart, Massena
Hunneyman, Norman L., St. Andrew's, Sackets Harbor; Mercy Center, Watertown
Johnston, William Michael, Our Lady of the Sacred Heart, Watertown
Keough, James R., St. Alphonsus, Tupper Lake
Kilian, Thomas F., Gouverneur Correctional Facility, Gouverneur; Notre Dame, Ogdensburg; Ogdensburg Correctional Facility
King, Robert A., (Retired), St. Peter, Plattsburgh
LaLonde, Mark A., Notre Dame, Ogdensburg; Riverview Correctional Facility, Ogdensburg
Lawless, Peter J., Sacred Heart, Edwards
LeClair, Robert J., Sacred Heart, Chazy
Levison, John A., Altona Correctional Facility, Altona
Looby, Phillip M., St. Francis, Solanus, Harrisville
Lukasiewicz, Jack M., 357 Cemetery Rd., Plattsburgh, 12901. Our Lady of Victory, Plattsburg; St. Mary's of the Lake in Cumberland Head
Mader, Frederick J., (Retired), St. Paul, Bloomingdale
Mastellon, Kevin, Watertown
Mazuchowski, Edward, St. Joseph, Dannemora
Miller, Edward R., Holy Family, Watertown
Moltz, David, (Retired), 700 E. Brighten Ave., Syracuse, 13205.
Monty, Dennis, St. Ann's, Mooers Forks
Murray, John R., St. Anthony's, Watertown (Syracuse Diocese)
Oberst, Frederick R., St. Bernard, Saranac Lake
Patrie, Leonard L., St. Mary, Champlain
Pominville, Ronald J., St. Peter, Lowville
Proulx, Thomas E., 21 Douglas Rd., Massena, 13662. Church of Sacred Heart, Massena; St. Lawrence Church, Louisville
Rabideau, Tyrone, St. Ann, Mooers Forks
Raven, William S., St. Paul, Black River
Ruddy, Robert V., St. Vincent of Paul & Cape Vincent Correctional Facility, Cape Vincent
Ryan, John J., Holy Name, Ausable Forks
Sandburg, David J., 9535 State Hwy. 37, 13669. St. Mary's Cathedral, Ogdensburg
Savage, Gerald H., St. Alphonsus, Tupper Lake
Schmidt, William G., St. Patrick, Watertown
Seymour, Kenneth A., Harrisville; Star Lake
Sharrow, Thomas D., Schenectady
Shaw, Elliott A., St. Mary's, Ticonderoga; Moriah Shock Incarceration Facility, Mineville
Siskavich, Francis, St. Bernard, Lyon Mountain
Slate, Bernard E., Alexandria Bay
Snell, James M., 10 Morningside Dr., Potsdam, 13676. St. Mary's Church, Canton
Staab, Richard J., St. James, Carthage
Ste.-Marie, Ronald, St. Anthony, Inlet
Stewart, George, St. Margaret, Wilmington; Au Sable Forks (New York Diocese)
Szwed, Joseph, St. Bernard, Saranac Lake; Franklin Correctional Facility, Malone
Trombly, John J., 678 Grant St., 13601.
Van Kirk, Richard L., Heuvelton
Votraw, Jonathan L., 10 Belmont Ave., Plattsburgh, 12901. St. Augustine's Church, Peru
Wadsworth, Bruce Carley, Lake Placid
Warner, Richard C., Sr., St. Anthony, Watertown
White, John L., 928 Caroline St., 13669. St. Mary's Cathedral, Ogdensburg
Yarchuk, Andrew, (Retired), 30 Wellington Rd., Webster, 14580.

INSTITUTIONS LOCATED IN THE DIOCESE

[A] HIGH SCHOOLS, INTERPAROCHIAL

PLATTSBURGH. *Seton Catholic Central*, 206 New York Rd., 12903. Tel: 518-561-4031; Fax: 518-563-1193. Email: raucoin@setoncatholic.net. Web: www.setoncatholic.net. Rev. Msgr. Robert H. Aucoin, S.T.L., M.Ed., Prin.; Andrew Lauria, Librarian. Lay Teachers 23; Students 179.

WATERTOWN. *Immaculate Heart Central High School*, (Grades 7-12), 1316 Ives St., 13601. Tel: 315-788-4670; Fax: 315-788-4672. Email: ihcadmin@ihchs.org. Web: www.ihcschools.org. Mr. Pat A. Fontana, Prin.; Rev. Mark R. Reilly, Spiritual Dir.; Eleanor Percy, Librarian. Priests 2; Sisters 3; Lay Teachers 25; Students 315.

[B] ELEMENTARY SCHOOLS, PRIVATE

PLATTSBURGH. *Seton Academy Elementary School*, (Grades PreK-6), St. Charles St., 12901. Tel: 518-825-7386. Sr. Helen Hermann, S.S.J., Prin.; Kathleen Toner, Asst. Prin. Religious 1; Lay Teachers 16; Students 207.

WATERTOWN. *Immaculate Heart Central School*, 122 Winthrop St., 13601. Tel: 315-788-7011; Fax: 315-788-7011. Email: ihcelemadmin@twcny.rr.com. Gail Graham, Prin.; Annette Connolly, Vice-Prin.

Immaculate Heart (Central Elementary) (Grades PreK-6) Gail Graham, Prin.; Annette Connolly, Vice-Prin. Sisters 1; Lay Teachers 17.

[C] RELIGIOUS EDUCATION

OGDENSBURG. *Bishop Conroy School of Religion*, 214 Morris St., 13669-1714. Tel: 315-393-1820; Fax: 315-393-1670. Email: bishopconroydre@verizon.net. Mrs. Celina Burns, D.R.E. Lay Teachers 40; Total Staff 1; Students 290.

SARANAC LAKE. *Pius X Center*, (Grades K-12), 27 St. Bernard St., 12983. Tel: 518-891-4616, Ext. 27; Fax: 518-891-4619. Email: piusxyouth@yahoo.com. Mary Kay Benham, Dir. Total Staff 2; Students 125.

WATERTOWN. *Watertown Catechetical Office*, Sterling Pl., 13601. Tel: 315-782-0030. Sisters Diane Marie Ulsamer, S.S.J., Coord.; Noel Chabanel, S.S.J., Outreach Coord. Sisters 2; Students 140.

Special Religious Education Tel: 315-782-0030. Sr. Diane Marie Ulsamer, S.S.J., Coord.

[D] CONFERENCE AND RETREAT CENTER

OGDENSBURG. *Wadhams Hall*, 6866 State Hwy. 37, 13669-4420. Tel: 315-393-4231; Fax: 315-393-4249. Email: inquiry@wadhams.edu. Web: www.wadhams.edu. Mr. Jeffrey Ward, A.A.S., Bus. Mgr. Total Staff 6.

[E] SPECIAL HOSPITALS AND HOMES FOR INVALIDS AND AGED

OGDENSBURG. *St. Joseph's Home* (1960) 950 Linden St., 13669. Tel: 315-393-3780; Fax: 315-393-3847. Email: administrator@stjh.org. Web: www.stjh.org. Andrew Peterson, Admin. Total Staff 114; Total Assisted 139; Bed Capacity 82.

[F] MONASTERIES AND RESIDENCES OF PRIESTS AND BROTHERS

SARANAC LAKE. *St. Joseph's Friary*, P.O. Box 470, 12983. Tel: 518-891-3494. Bros. Alan Lemay, S.A.; Paschal Steen, T.S.A. Total in Residence 2.

WATERTOWN. *Missionaries of the Sacred Heart*, 668 Thompson St., 13601. Tel: 315-782-3480; Fax: 315-782-0473. Email: rwkpng03@mscparish.com. Revs. Pierre Aubin, M.S.C.; David DeLuca, M.S.C.; Vincent T. Freeh, M.S.C.; Richard Huber, M.S.C.; Richard Kennedy, M.S.C.; Bros. Peter Marceau, M.S.C.; Jean-Paul Paradis, M.S.C.

[G] CONVENTS AND RESIDENCES FOR SISTERS

OGDENSBURG. *Sisters of St. Joseph*, 251 Proctor Ave., 13669. Tel: 315-393-6511. Total in Residence 3.

CARTHAGE. *St. James Convent, Sisters of St. Joseph*, 317 West St., 13619. Tel: 315-493-1672. Email: smacollinsssj@yahoo.com. Total Staff 2; Total in Residence 2.

ELLENBURG CENTER. *Our Lady of the Adirondack's Inc. House of Prayer* (1972) 7270 Star Rd., Rte. 190, 12934-2501. Tel: 518-594-3253; Fax: 518-594-7143. Email: oadirond@twcny.rr.com. Web: www.ourladyoftheadirondackshouseofprayer.catholicweb.com. Our Lady of the Adirondacks Community. Total Staff 3.

Our Lady of the Adirondacks Community (1990) Email: oadirond@twcny.rr.com. Web: www.ourladyoftheadirondackshouseofprayer.catholicweb.com. Rev. Alan J. Lamica, Spiritual Dir. Tel: 518-529-7433.

Our Lady of the Adirondacks Prayer Association (1972) Tel: 518-594-3253; Fax: 518-594-7143. Email: oadirond@twcny.rr.com. Web: www.ourladyoftheadirondackhouseofprayer.catholicweb.com. Members 170.

LAKE PLACID. *St. Margaret Convent*, 185 Old Military Rd., 12946. Tel: 518-523-2929; Fax: 518-523-5449. Email: mokeefersm@mercymidatlantic.org. Sr. M. Camillus O'Keefe, R.S.M., B.A., B.S., Supr. Sisters of Mercy.

MALONE. *St. Joseph's Ursuline Nuns*, 49 Morton St., 12953. Tel: 518-483-2880; Fax: 518-483-5356. Email: ursulmal@verizon.net. Sisters 2.

MASSENA. *St. Joseph's Convent, Sisters of St. Joseph*, 72 Malby Ave., 13662. Tel: 315-764-0379. Total in Residence 2; Sisters of St. Joseph 2.

Sacred Heart Convent, 188 Main St., P.O. Box 91, 13662. Tel: 315-769-6238. Email: mas-osm@verizon.net. Total in Residence 4.

PLATTSBURGH. *Sisters of Charity of St. Louis* (1910) 4907 S. Catherine St., 12901-3658. Tel: 518-563-7410. Email: p.burg@scslnys.org.

Sisters of Mercy, 62-64 Court St., 12901. Tel: 518-561-9689; Fax: 518-563-4553. Email: sisterb@gmail.com. Sisters of Mercy Sisters of Mercy 4.

SARANAC LAKE. *Sisters of Mercy of the Americas* (1831) 35 Trudeau Rd., 12983-5635. Tel: 518-891-3234. Email: srmcarolyn@roadrunner.com.

TICONDEROGA. *St. Mary's Convent, Sisters of St. Joseph* (1959) 145 Lake George Ave., 12883. Tel: 518-585-6547; Fax: 518-585-7505. Email: sschoo3@nycap.rr.com. Sr. Sharon Anne Dalton, S.S.J. Total in Residence 2.

TUPPER LAKE. *Dominican Sisters of Hope, Ossining* (1995) 37 Lake St., Apt. 2, 12986. Tel: 518-359-9632.

WATERTOWN. *Precious Blood Monastery, Sister Adorers of the Precious Blood*, 400 Pratt St., 13601. Tel: 315-788-1669; Fax: 315-779-9046. Email: smarilyn@twcny.rr.com. Web: sisterspreciousblood.org. Sisters Martha R. Emery, A.P.B., Supr.; Marilyn McGillan, A.P.B., Asst. Supr. Total Staff 6; Total in Residence 6.

Sisters of St. Joseph Motherhouse (1880) 1425 Washington St., 13601-4533. Tel: 315-782-3460; Fax: 315-788-2794. Email: bcollinsssj@yahoo.com. Web: www.ssjwatertown.org. Sisters Mary Ellen Brett, S.S.J., Motherhouse Supr.; Bernadette Marie Collins, S.S.J., Major Supr.; Mr. Randy Belina, Motherhouse Admin. Total Staff 26; Total in Residence 28.

[H] RETREAT HOUSES

PLATTSBURGH. *Regina Maria Spiritual Life Center* (1959) 90 Maine Rd., 12903-4001. Tel: 518-561-3421; Fax: 518-561-3816. Email: reginamaria90@aol.com. Sr. Miriam Najimy, D.H.M., B.A., M. Rel. Studies, Supr. Daughters of the Heart of Mary 2.

[I] INCORPORATED CEMETERIES

BRASHER FALLS. *St. Patrick's Cemetery Association of Brasher Falls, N.Y.*, Box 208, 13613. Tel: 315-389-5401; Fax: 315-389-4066. Email: parish@twcny.rr.com. Web: www.stpatrick-stlawrence.org. Rev. Patrick A. Ratigan.

CARTHAGE. *St. James Cemetery Corporation*, 327 West St., 13619. Tel: 315-493-3224; Fax: 518-493-3280. Email: stjames@twcny.rr.com.

CROGHAN. *St. Stephen's Cemetery Association, Inc.*, 9748 State Rte. 812, Box 38, 13327. Tel: 315-346-6958; Fax: 315-346-1200. Email: cschnee@twcny.rr.com.

MALONE. *St. Joseph's Cemetery of Malone, N.Y., Inc.*, 306 W. Main St., 12953. Tel: 518-483-1300; Fax: 518-483-1307. Email: mcp@twcny.rr.com. Web: malonecatholic.com.

Notre Dame Cemetery of Malone, N.Y., Inc., Office: 306 W. Main St., 12953. Tel: 518-483-1300; Fax: 518-483-1307. Email: mcp@twcny.RR.com. Web: malonecatholic.com.

PLATTSBURGH. *Mount Carmel Cemetery*, St. John the Baptist Church, 7 Margaret St., 12901. Tel: 518-563-0730; Fax: 518-563-0754. Email: office@stjohnsplattsburgh.org.

WATERTOWN. *Calvary Cemetery Association of Watertown, N.Y.*, 320 W. Lynde St., 13601. Tel: 315-782-1474; Fax: 315-782-4939. Email: rwkpng03@mscparish.com. Priests 1; Total Staff 1.

[J] MISCELLANEOUS LISTINGS

OGDENSBURG. *St. Joseph's Foundation, Inc.*, 950 Linden St., 13669. Tel: 315-394-0463; Fax: 315-393-3847. Email: stjhfoundation@nnymail.com. Web: www.stjh.org.

CAPE VINCENT. *Mission Project Service*, 139 N. Kanady St., P.O. Box 288, 13618. Tel: 315-654-2447; Fax: 315-654-4721. Email: misprojser@aol.com. Web: www.missionprojectservice.org. Beverly Hennigan, Exec. Dir.; Rev. Pierre Aubin, M.S.C., Dir.

HOGANSBURG. *St. Regis Mission* , (Akwesasne); Reservation and parish on both sides of U.S.-Canadian border, Box 429, 13655. Tel: 613-575-2066. Rev. George H. Belgarde, S.J., Pastor. Priests 1; Brothers 1.

Roman Catholic Community Center, Inc. (Kateri Tekakwitha Center) Mrs. Lucille Peters, Rel. Educ. Coord. Tel: 518-358-2931.

LAKE PLACID. *Mercy Care for the Adirondacks, Inc.*, 185 Old Military Rd., 12946. Tel: 518-523-5580; Fax: 518-523-5449. Email: dbeal@adkmercy.org. Web: www.adkmercy.org. Donna Beal, Exec. Dir.

SARANAC LAKE. *Guggenheim Center for Religious Programs*, P.O. Box 664, 12983. Tel: 518-891-0809 (Lodge); 518-891-3323 (Dorm). Mr. Ralph Bennett, Dir. Tel: 518-327-3545.

Res.: P.O. Box 5, Rainbow Lake, 12976. Tel: 518-327-3545.

WATERTOWN. *Sacred Heart Foundation* (1967) 668 Thompson St., 13601. Tel: 315-782-3344; Fax: 315-782-0473. Email: mail@sacredheartfoundation.com. Web: www.sacredheartfoundation.com. Nicholas J. Buduson, Foundation Mgr.

The Federation of Sisters of the Precious Blood, Inc. (1969) 400 Pratt St., 13601. Tel: 315-788-1669; Fax: 315-779-9046. Email: srm1@twcny.rr.com. Web: www.sisterspreciousblood.org. Sr. Mary Jo Divney, A.P.B., Pres. Sisters 55.

RELIGIOUS INSTITUTES OF MEN REPRESENTED IN THE DIOCESE

For further details refer to the corresponding bracketed number in the Religious Institutes of Men or Women section.

[0320]—*Brothers of Christian Instruction* (Alfred, ME)—F.I.C.

[0530]—*Franciscan Friars of the Atonement*—S.A.

[0690]—*Jesuit Fathers and Brothers* (French Canadian Prov. of Montreal)—S.J.

[1110]—*Missionaries of the Sacred Heart*—M.S.C.

RELIGIOUS INSTITUTES OF WOMEN REPRESENTED IN THE DIOCESE

[]—*Congregation of the Sisters of the Cross of Chavanod* (India)

[0760]—*Daughters of Charity of St. Vincent de Paul*—D.C.

[0750]—*Daughters of the Charity of the Sacred Heart of Jesus*—F.C.S.C.J.

[0810]—*Daughters of the Heart of Mary*—D.H.M.

[1070-03]—*Dominican Sisters*—O.P.

[1105]—*Dominican Sisters of Hope*—O.P.

[1190]—*Franciscan Sisters of the Atonement*—S.A.

[1840]—*Grey Nuns of the Sacred Heart*—G.N.S.H.

[2575]—*Institute of the Sisters of Mercy of the Americas* (New York, NY)—R.S.M.

[3580]—*Servants of Mary* (Servite Sisters)—O.S.M.

[0110]—*Sisters Adorers of the Precious Blood*—A.P.B.

[0620]—*Sisters of Charity of St. Louis*—S.C.S.L.

[3840]—*Sisters of St. Joseph of Carondelet*—C.S.J.

[3830-12]—*Sisters of St. Joseph of Watertown*—S.S.J.

[4110]—*Ursuline Nuns*—O.S.U.

Incorporated Cemeteries

CARTHAGE. *St. James Cemetery*

Croghan

St. Stephen's Cemetery Association, Inc.

Malone

St. Joseph's Cemetery of Malone, NY, Inc.

Notre Dame Cemetery of Malone, NY, Inc.

Plattsburgh

Mount Carmel Cemetery

Watertown

Calvary Cemetery Association of Watertown, NY

NECROLOGY

† Gefell, Rev. Msgr. Gerard J., (Retired)—Died Feb. 6, 2010

† Robillard, Rev. Msgr. Thomas J., Norfolk, NY Church of the Visitation—Died March 19, 2009

† Bleaux, Floyd J. Jr., Bombay, NY St. Joseph; Fort Covington, NY St. Mary; Hogansburg, NY St. Patrick—Died Sept. 2, 2009

† Menard, Francis A., (Retired)—Died Jan. 17, 2009

† Soucy, Timothy J., Lowville, NY St. Peter's—Died March 14, 2009

An asterisk (*) denotes an organization that has established tax-exempt status directly with the IRS and is not covered by the USCCB Group Ruling.

Archdiocese of Oklahoma City

(Archidioecesis Oklahomapolitana)

Most Reverend

EUSEBIUS J. BELTRAN, D.D.

Archbishop of Oklahoma City; ordained May 14, 1960; appointed Bishop of Tulsa February 28, 1978; installed April 20, 1978; appointed Archbishop of Oklahoma City November 24, 1992; installed January 22, 1993. *Res.: P.O. Box 32180, Oklahoma City, OK 73123.*

Catholic Pastoral Center: 7501 Northwest Expwy., P.O. Box 32180, Oklahoma City, OK 73123. Tel: 405-721-5651; Fax: 405-721-5210.

ESTABLISHED FEBRUARY 6, 1973.

Square Miles 42,470.

Erected into a Vicariate Apostolic by Brief of May 29, 1891. Erected into the Diocese of Oklahoma with the See in Oklahoma City by a Brief of Pope Pius X, August 17, 1905. Name changed to Diocese of Oklahoma City and Tulsa by Bull of Pope Pius XI, November 14, 1930. Erected into Archdiocese of Oklahoma City by a Bull of Pope Paul VI, December 13, 1972. The Province includes the Dioceses of Tulsa and Little Rock.

Comprises the following 46 Counties: Alfalfa, Beaver, Beckham, Blaine, Caddo, Canadian, Carter, Cimarron, Cleveland, Comanche, Cotton, Custer, Dewey, Ellis, Garfield, Garvin, Grady, Grant, Greer, Harmon, Harper, Jackson, Jefferson, Johnston, Kay, Kingfisher, Kiowa, Lincoln, Logan, Love, McClain, Major, Marshall, Murray, Noble, Oklahoma, Pontotoc, Pottawatomie, Roger Mills, Seminole, Stephens, Texas, Tillman, Washita, Woods and Woodward.

For legal titles of parishes and archdiocesan institutions, consult the Pastoral Office.

STATISTICAL OVERVIEW

Personnel	
Archbishops	1
Abbots	1
Retired Abbots	3
Priests: Diocesan Active in Diocese	60
Priests: Diocesan Active Outside Diocese	1
Priests: Retired, Sick or Absent	26
Number of Diocesan Priests	87
Religious Priests in Diocese	27
Total Priests in Diocese	114
Extern Priests in Diocese	20
Ordinations:	
Diocesan Priests	2
Permanent Deacons	12
Permanent Deacons in Diocese	100
Total Brothers	8
Total Sisters	97
Parishes	
Parishes	67
With Resident Pastor:	
Resident Diocesan Priests	57
Resident Religious Priests	8
Missions	44
Closed Parishes	1
Professional Ministry Personnel:	
Brothers	1
Sisters	11
Lay Ministers	70
Welfare	
Catholic Hospitals	5
Total Assisted	289,950
Health Care Centers	1
Total Assisted	108
Homes for the Aged	6
Total Assisted	385
Day Care Centers	2
Total Assisted	122
Residential Care of Disabled	1
Total Assisted	30
Educational	
Diocesan Students in Other Seminaries	18
Total Seminarians	18
Colleges and Universities	1
Total Students	709
High Schools, Diocesan and Parish	2
Total Students	1,033
Elementary Schools, Diocesan and Parish	18
Total Students	4,175
Elementary Schools, Private	2
Total Students	391
Catechesis/Religious Education:	
High School Students	3,394
Elementary Students	10,065
Total Students under Catholic Instruction	19,785
Teachers in the Diocese:	
Priests	6
Brothers	2
Sisters	7
Lay Teachers	384
Vital Statistics	
Receptions into the Church:	
Infant Baptism Totals	2,313
Minor Baptism Totals	317
Adult Baptism Totals	210
Received into Full Communion	501
First Communions	2,593
Confirmations	1,393
Marriages:	
Catholic	401
Interfaith	224
Total Marriages	625
Deaths	720
Total Catholic Population	108,871
Total Population	2,998,568

Former Bishops—Rt. Rev. THEOPHILE MEERSCHAERT, D.D., ord. Dec. 23, 1871; appt. first Vicar-Apostolic of Indian Territory and Titular Bishop of Sidyma by Bulls of June 2, 1891; cons. in Natchez, Sept. 8, 1891; appt. first Bishop of Oklahoma, Aug. 23, 1905; made assistant at the pontifical throne, Nov. 30, 1916; died Feb. 21, 1924; Most Revs. FRANCIS C. KELLEY, D.D., LL.D., Ph.D., Litt.D., Bishop of Oklahoma City & Tulsa; ord. Aug. 24, 1893; appt. Bishop of Oklahoma, June 25, 1924; cons. Holy Name Cathedral, Chicago, IL, Oct. 2, 1924; died Feb. 1, 1948; EUGENE J. MCGUINNESS, D.D., Bishop of Oklahoma City & Tulsa; ord. May 22, 1915; cons. Bishop of Raleigh, Dec. 21, 1937; appt. Coadjutor, Oklahoma City and Tulsa "cum jure successionis," Nov. 11, 1944; installed Jan. 10, 1945; succeeded to the See, Feb. 1, 1948; died Dec. 27, 1957; VICTOR J. REED, D.D., Bishop of Oklahoma City & Tulsa; ord. Dec. 21, 1929; cons. March 5, 1958; died Sept. 8, 1971; JOHN R. QUINN, D.D., ord. July 19, 1953; appt. Auxiliary Bishop of San Diego and Titular Bishop of Thisiduo, Oct. 21, 1967; Episcopal ordination, Dec. 12, 1967; transferred to Oklahoma City and Tulsa, Nov. 18, 1971; appt. as Archbishop of the Archdiocese of Oklahoma City, Dec. 13, 1972; installed as Archbishop of Oklahoma City, Feb. 6, 1973; transferred to Archbishop of San Francisco, April 26, 1977; CHARLES A. SALATKA, D.D., ord. Feb. 24, 1945; appt. Titular Bishop of Cariana and Auxiliary of Grand Rapids Dec. 9, 1961; cons. March 6, 1962; appt. Bishop of Marquette Jan. 10, 1968; installed March 25, 1968; appt. Archbishop of Oklahoma City Sept. 27, 1977; installed Dec. 15, 1977; retired Nov. 24, 1992; died March 17, 2003.

Vicar General—Rev. Msgr. EDWARD J. WEISENBURGER, V.G., M.A., J.C.L.

Regional Vicars—Region I-A: Rev. MICHAEL L. CHAPMAN, B.A., 317 N. Blackwelder, Oklahoma City, 73106. Region I-B: Rev. EDWARD T. MENASCO, Mailing Address: P.O. Box 1227, Norman, 73070. Region II-A: Rev. WILLIAM L. NOVAK, Mailing Address: P.O. Box 850249, Yukon, 73085. Region II-B: Rev. WILBUR E. MOORE (Retired), Mailing Address: P.O. Box 368, Nicoma Park, 73066. Region III: Rev. THOMAS O'TOOLE, 125 E St., S.W., Ardmore, 73401. Region IV: Rev. JAMES A. GOIN, Mailing Address: P.O. Box 748, Chickasha, 73023. Region V: Rev. CARL WILLIAM JANOCHA, 3001 E. Hwy. 66, Elk City, 73644. Region VI: Rev. BILL PRUETT, Mailing Address: P.O. Box 731, Guymon, 73942. Region VII: Rev. KEVIN J. RATTERMAN, 211 N. Cherokee, Hennessey, 73742. Region VIII: Rev. JOHN MICHALICKA, Mailing Address: P.O. Box 1330, Ponca City, 74602. Region IX: Rev. STEPHEN V. HAMILTON, S.T.L., 406 S. 6th St., Kingfisher, 73750.

Catholic Pastoral Center—7501 Northwest Expwy., P.O. Box 32180, Oklahoma City, 73123. Tel: 405-721-5651; Fax: 405-721-5210. Office Hours: Mon.-Fri. 8:30-4:30.

Chancellor—Mrs. LOUTITIA D. EASON.

Vicar General—Rev. Msgr. EDWARD J. WEISENBURGER, V.G., M.A., J.C.L.

Vicar for Ministries—VACANT.

Archdiocesan Tribunal—7501 Northwest Expwy., P.O. Box 32180, Oklahoma City, 73123. Tel: 405-721-5651.

Judicial Vicar—Rev. RICHARD D. STANSBERRY JR., M.A., M.Div., J.C.L.

Judge—Ms. ANNE KIRBY, J.C.L.

Defenders of the Bond—Revs. LOWELL STIEFERMAN; GERARD MACAULAY (Retired).

Advocate—Mrs. JUDY REILLY.

Notary—Ms. MARILYN NEWMAN.

Interdiocesan Tribunal of Second Instance for the Province of Oklahoma City—Mailing Address: P.O. Box 32180, Oklahoma City, 73123. Tel: 405-721-5651.

Judicial Vicar—Rev. ROBERTO QUANT, J.C.L.

Adjutant Judicial Vicars—Rev. Msgr. FRANCIS I. MALONE, J.C.L.; Rev. TAM NGUYEN, J.C.L.

Judges—Sr. KATHRYN OLSEN, I.H.M., J.C.L.; Rev. Msgr. EDWARD J. WEISENBURGER, V.G., M.A., J.C.L.

Defenders of the Bond—Mr. GEORGE RIGAZZI, J.C.L. (2nd instance); Revs. ELMER C. SCHWARZ, J.C.L. (Retired) (2nd instance); PETER QUANG LE, J.C.L.; STEPHEN V. HAMILTON, S.T.L.

Notaries—Mrs. TONI NICHOLLS; Mrs. LIZ PARKER; Ms. SUZI BLANCO.

Consultors Archdiocesan—Revs. BRUCE K. NATSUHARA, B.A., S.T.B., S.T.L.; JOSEPH A. JACOBI; Rev. Msgr. EDWARD J. WEISENBURGER, V.G., M.A., J.C.L.; Revs. JOACHIM SPEXARTH, O.S.B.; RICHARD D. STANSBERRY JR., M.A., M.Div., J.C.L.

Council of Priests Archdiocesan—Revs. JOHN R. METZINGER; BRUCE K. NATSUHARA, B.A., S.T.B., S.T.L., Sec.; TIMOTHY D. LUSCHEN; SCOTT A. BOECKMAN; JOACHIM SPEXARTH, O.S.B.; RAYMOND K. ACKERMAN; CHARLES R. MURPHY, B.S., M.Ed., M.Div., Vice Chm.; Rev. Msgr. EDWARD J. WEISENBURGER, V.G., M.A., J.C.L.; Revs. JOSEPH A. JACOBI; STEPHEN V. HAMILTON, S.T.L.; RAYMOND K. ACKERMAN; JAMES A. GOIN.

Health Panel, Archdiocesan—Rev. WILLIAM B. ROSS, Chm. (Retired), 1506 W. Walnut, El Reno, 73036. Tel: 405-527-3077.

Personnel Committee—Revs. THOMAS J. BOYER; RAYMOND K. ACKERMAN; CHARLES R. MURPHY;

JOSEPH R. ROSS.

Archdiocesan Offices and Directors

Office of Stewardship and Development—VACANT, Dir., Mailing Address: P.O. Box 32180, Oklahoma City, 73123. Tel: 405-721-5651.

Archdiocesan Development Fund— formerly Diocesan Development Fund; also formerly known as Diocesan Fund, Bishop's Fund for Diocesan Development, Mr. THOMAS MAXWELL, Dir., 7501 N.W. Expwy., P.O. Box 32180, Oklahoma City, 73123. Tel: 405-721-5651.

Archdiocese of Oklahoma City Educational Trust Fund—Sr. CATHERINE POWERS, C.N.D., Dir., 7501 N.W. Expwy., P.O. Box 32180, Oklahoma City, 73123.

Catholic Charities of the Archdiocese of Oklahoma City, Inc.—Mr. TIMOTHY O'CONNOR, Dir., 1501 N. Classen Blvd., Oklahoma City, 73106. Tel: 405-523-3000; Fax: 405-523-3030.

Archdiocesan Finance Council—Most Rev. EUSEBIUS JOSEPH BELTRAN, D.D.; Revs. RICHARD D. STANSBERRY JR., M.A., M.Div., J.C.L.; TIMOTHY M. FULLER; Mr. JOHN TORBETT; Mr. FLOYD ANDERSON; Mrs. ELLEN FLEMING; Mr. LARRY KUNZ; Mr. MICHAEL MILLIGAN; Ms. THERESA HILD; Mr. MICHAEL R. STERKEL; Mr. DAVID JOHNSON, Business Mgr., Mailing Address: Business Office, P.O. Box 32180, Oklahoma City, 73123. Tel: 405-721-5651.

Building Committee—Mr. DAVID JOHNSON, Mailing Address: P.O. Box 32180, Oklahoma City, 73123. Tel: 405-721-5651.

Catholic Foundation of Oklahoma, Inc.—VACANT, 7501 Northwest Expwy., P.O. Box 32180, Oklahoma City, 73123. Tel: 405-721-5651.

Catholic Lawyers Guild—Mailing Address: P.O. Box 32180, Oklahoma City, 73123. Tel: 405-721-5651. VACANT, Mailing Address: P.O. Box 1585, Ada, 74821. Tel: 580-332-4811.

Catholic Physicians Guild—Rev. DANIEL MCCAFFREY, Chap., Mailing Address: P.O. Box 32180, Oklahoma City, 73123. Tel: 405-942-4084.

Catholic Social Services—Mr. TIM O'CONNOR, 1501 N. Classen Blvd., Oklahoma City, 73106. Tel: 405-523-3000; Fax: 405-523-3030.

Charismatic Renewal—Rev. MARVIN F. LEVEN, Episcopal Moderator (Retired), Mailing Address: P.O. Box 404, Okarche, 73762. Tel: 405-263-7798.

Communications, Archdiocesan Department of—Mailing Address: P.O. Box 32180, Oklahoma City, 73123. Tel: 405-721-1810; 405-721-5651.

Correction Related Ministry—VACANT.

Council of Catholic Women, Archdiocesan—Rev. ROBERT T. WOOD.

Ecumenical and Interreligious Affairs, Office for Archdiocesan Dir.—VACANT.

Education—Sr. CATHERINE POWERS, C.N.D., Archdiocesan Dir., Mailing Address: P.O. Box 32180, Oklahoma City, 73123. Tel: 405-721-4202; 405-721-5651.

Catholic Schools, Office of—Sr. CATHERINE POWERS, C.N.D., Supt.; Mrs. CRIS CARTER, Assoc. Supt., Mailing Address: P.O. Box 32180, Oklahoma City, 73123. Tel: 405-721-4202; 405-721-5651.

Religious Education, Office of—Ms. PATRICIA KOENIG, Dir.; Ms. ANGELA SCHMIDT, Assoc. Dir., Mailing Address: P.O. Box 32180, Oklahoma City, 73123. Tel: 405-721-1415; 405-721-5651.

Pastoral Ministry Office—Sr. M. DIANE KOORIE, R.S.M., Dir., Mailing Address: P.O. Box 32180, Oklahoma City, 73123. Tel: 405-721-1415; 405-721-5651 Affiliated with Kansas Newman College, Wichita, KS and Aquinas Institute, St. Louis, MO.

Campus Ministry, Department of—Rev. RAYMOND K. ACKERMAN, Mailing Address: 100 E. Stinson, Norman, 73072. Tel: 405-321-0990.

Clergy Education, Department of—Mailing Address: P.O. Box 32180, Oklahoma City, 73123. Tel: 405-721-5651.

Victim Assistance Coordinator—Mrs. JENNIFER GOODRICH, Mailing Address: P.O. Box 32180, Oklahoma City, 73123. Tel: 405-721-5651, Ext. 150. Email: jgoodrich@catharchdioceseokc.org.

Family Life Department—Mr. GEORGE RIGAZZI, J.C.L., Mailing Address: P.O. Box 32180, Oklahoma City, 73123. Tel: 405-721-8943; 405-721-5651.

Justice and Human Development, Commission for—VACANT.

Legal Counsel—Mr. DOUG EASON, 14000 Quail Springs Pkwy., Ste. 200, Oklahoma City, 73118. Tel: 405-841-6000.

Master of Ceremonies—Revs. ROBERT T. WOOD; TIMOTHY M. FULLER, Asst.

Ministry to Priests Program—Rev. JOSEPH R. ROSS, Mailing Address: P.O. Box 2546, Lawton, 73502. Tel: 580-355-2054.

Mission "Micatokla"--Archdiocesan Mission of Santiago Atitlan, Guatemala—Mr. DAVID JOHNSON, Mailing Address: P.O. Box 32180, Oklahoma City, 73123. Tel: 405-721-5651; Fax: 405-721-5210.

Newspaper— "The Sooner Catholic" Ms. RAY DYER, Editor, Mailing Address: P.O. Box 32180, Oklahoma City, 73123. Tel: 405-721-1810; 405-721-5651.

Permanent Diaconate—Deacon MAX SCHWARZ, Dir., Mailing Address: P.O. Box 32180, Oklahoma City, 73123. Tel: 405-721-5651.

Priests' Medical Fund— formerly known as Infirm Priest Fund. Rev. Msgr. EDWARD J. WEISENBURGER, V.G., M.A., J.C.L., Mailing Address: P.O. Box 32180, Oklahoma City, 73123. Tel: 405-721-5651.

Priests' Retirement Board—Most Rev. EUSEBIUS JOSEPH BELTRAN, D.D.; Revs. EDWARD T. MENASCO, Mailing Address: P.O. Box 1227, Norman, 73070; MICHAEL L. CHAPMAN, B.A., 317 N. Blackwelder, Oklahoma City, 73106.

Propagation of the Faith, Holy Childhood Assoc., Missionary Cooperation Plan—VACANT, Mailing Address: P.O. Box 32180, Oklahoma City, 73123. Tel: 405-721-5651.

Rural Life—VACANT.

Scouting—Rev. MICHAEL WHEELAHAN, Mailing Address: P.O. Box 360, Medford, 73759. Tel: 580-395-2148.

St. Ann's Home, Inc.—Mrs. DOROTHY JOYCE, Admin., 9400 St. Ann Dr., Oklahoma City, 73162. Tel: 405-728-7888.

St. Francis de Sales Seminary (Legal Title)—Most Rev. EUSEBIUS JOSEPH BELTRAN, D.D., Pres.; Mr. DAVID JOHNSON, Treas., Mailing Address: P.O. Box 32180, Oklahoma City, 73123.

Vocations and Seminarians—Rev. WILLIAM L. NOVAK, Dir.

Worship and Spiritual Life, Office of—Rev. STEPHEN J. BIRD, Dir.

Youth and Young Adult Ministry, Office of—Mrs. NANCY HOUSH, Dir. Tel: 405-721-5651; Mrs. BECKY JAIME, Assoc. Dir., Mailing Address: P.O. Box 32180, Oklahoma City, 73123. Tel: 405-721-9220; 405-721-5651.

CLERGY, PARISHES, MISSIONS AND PAROCHIAL SCHOOLS

OKLAHOMA CITY

(OKLAHOMA COUNTY)

1—CATHEDRAL OF OUR LADY OF PERPETUAL HELP (1919) [JC] Rev. Msgr. Edward J. Weisenburger; Rev. Thanh Van Nguyen; Deacons William Enos; Paul Lewis; Anthony Le; Sang Ninh.
Res.: 3214 Lake Ave., 73118. Tel: 405-525-2349; Fax: 405-525-3628. Email: olph@cathedralokc.org. Web: www.cathedralokc.org.
School—Bishop John Carroll, 1100 N.W. 32, 73118. Tel: 405-525-0956 (Office); Fax: 405-523-3053. Lay Teachers 15; Students 190.
Catechesis/Religious Program—Tel: 405-525-2349, Ext. 140. Students 215.

2—ST. ANDREW DUNG-LAC (1994), (Vietnamese), [JC] Rev. Dominic Hung Hoang; Deacons Ty V. Nguyen; Kha Nguyen; Sr. Mary Quy Truong.
Mailing Address: 3000 S.W. 55th St., P.O. Box 891584, 73119.
Church: 3000 S.W. 55th St., 73119. Tel: 405-681-2665; 405-681-6918; Fax: 405-681-7951.
Catechesis/Religious Program—Students 344.

3—ST. CHARLES BORROMEO (1954) [JC] Revs. Philip M. Seeton; James A. Wickersham; Arul Pudhota; Deacons John Pitt, (Retired); Marc LeWand; Bill Gorden; Thomas Phan; Bill King; Alfonso Lopez.
Res.: 5024 N. Grove St., 73122. Tel: 405-789-2595; Fax: 405-789-4394.
School—5000 N. Grove St., 73122. Tel: 405-789-0224; Fax: 405-789-3583. Lay Teachers 22; Students 224.
Catechesis/Religious Program—Students 338.

4—CHRIST THE KING (1949) [JC] Rev. Richard D. Stansberry Jr.; Deacons James Smith; Richard L. Boothe III.
Mailing Address: 8005 Dorset Dr., P.O. Box 20508, 73156-0508. Tel: 405-842-1481; Fax: 405-843-0539. Web: www.ckokc.org.
Rectory—1900 Elmhurst Ave., 73120. Tel: 405-841-6680.
Church: 8005 Dorset Dr., 73120.
School—1905 Elmhurst, 73120. Tel: 405-843-3909; Fax: 405-843-6519. Web: www.ckschool.com. Mrs. Karen Carter, Prin. Lay Teachers 28; Students 427.
Catechesis/Religious Program—Tel: 405-843-4766. Students 265.

5—CHURCH OF THE EPIPHANY OF THE LORD (1976) Revs. Stephen J. Bird; Anthony Raj Ram; Alveria Kopp, Pastoral Assoc.; Mrs. Judy Reilly, Pastoral Assoc.; Deacons Robert Heskamp; Richard Fahy.
Res.: 7336 W. Britton Rd., 73132. Tel: 405-722-2110; Fax: 405-722-6719. Email: epiphany@epiphanyokc.com. Web: www.epiphanyokc.com.
Catechesis/Religious Program—Tel: 405-722-0051. Email: redirector@epiphanyokc.com. Roxann Lackner, D.R.E.; Tracy Osterman, Youth Dir. Students 393.

6—CORPUS CHRISTI (1924), (African American), [JC] Rev. John Zupez, S.J.; Deacons Dunn Cumby; Bernard Hollier.
Res.: 1005 N.E. 15th St., 73117. Tel: 405-239-2854; Fax: 405-235-2122. Email: jzupez@jesuits.net.
Catechesis/Religious Program—Students 28.
Mission—St. Robert Bellarmine

7—ST. EUGENE'S (1958) [JC] Revs. Joseph A. Jacobi; William B. Ross (Retired); Deacons Bill Bawden, Dir. Admin.; Duane Descher, (Retired); Alejandro Randolph; Thomaas O. Goldsworthy.
Res.: 2400 W. Hefner Rd., P.O. Box 20930, 73156. Tel: 405-751-7115; Fax: 405-751-8722. Web: www.steugenes.org.
School—Tel: 405-751-0067; Fax: 405-302-4254. Lay Teachers 27; Students 347.
Catechesis/Religious Program—Students 236.

8—ST. FRANCIS OF ASSISI (1925) [JC] Rev. Charles R. Murphy; Deacon Joe Forgue.
Res.: 1901 N.W. 18th St., P.O. Box 60569, 73106. Tel: 405-528-0485; Fax: 405-524-1260. Web: www.stfrancisokc.com.
School—Rosary, 1910 N.W. 19th St., 73106. Tel: 405-525-9272; Fax: 405-525-5643. Web: www.rosaryschool.com. Mrs. Karen Lynn, Prin. Lay Teachers 25; Students 206.
Catechesis/Religious Program—Students 150.

9—HOLY ANGELS (1924), (Hispanic), [JC] Rev. Michael L. Chapman; Deacons Lucio Nieto; Santos Hernandez.
Res.: 317 N. Blackwelder St., 73106. Tel: 405-232-6572; Fax: 405-235-8334.
Convent—Carmelite Missionaries of St. Teresa, 1522 N.W. Third St., 73106. Tel: 405-231-1935.
Catechesis/Religious Program—Students 361.

10—IMMACULATE CONCEPTION (1892) [CEM] Rev. George Pupius; Deacon James Keene.
Res.: 3901 S.W. 29th St., 73119. Tel: 405-685-4224; Fax: 405-685-4483.
Catechesis/Religious Program—Tel: 405-685-4806. Students 75.

11—ST. JAMES THE GREATER (1954) Rev. Robert T. Wood; Deacon Marti Gulikers.
Church: 4201 S. McKinley, 73109. Tel: 405-636-6800; Fax: 405-636-6848.
Res.: 4308 S. Blackwelder, 73119. Tel: 405-636-6802; Fax: 405-636-6807.
School—1224 S.W. 41st St., 73109. Tel: 405-636-6810; Fax: 405-636-6818. Lay Teachers 17; Students 176.
Catechesis/Religious Program—Tel: 405-636-6840. Students 157.

12—ST. JOSEPH (1889) [JC], (Old Cathedral) Rev. Bruce K. Natsuhara. In Res., Rev. George Parackal.
Res.: 307 N.W. 4th St., 73102. Tel: 405-815-6650; Fax: 405-815-6644. Email: stjosephs1@coxinet.net.
Church: 307 N.W. 4th St., 73102.
Catechesis/Religious Program—Students 220.

13—KOREAN MARTYRS (1996), (Korean), Rev. Jinsu Lawrence Kim.
Res.: 7517 S. Lynn, 73159. Tel: 405-688-5585; Fax: 405-688-5586.
Church: 2600 S.W. 74th St., 73159. Tel: 405-681-6464; Fax: 405-688-5586.
Catechesis/Religious Program—Students 3.

14—OUR LADY OF MOUNT CARMEL AND ST. THERESE LITTLE FLOWER (1921) [JC] Revs. Raul Reyes, O.C.D.; Luis Castañeda, O.C.D., Supr.; Juan Evangelista Cabrera, O.C.D.
Mailing Address: 1125 S. Walker Ave., 73101-1196. Tel: 405-235-2037; Fax: 405-235-7023.
Catechesis/Religious Program—Tel: 405-236-5259. Students 647.

15—ST. PATRICK (1950) Rev. Thomas McSherry; Deacons Duane Fischer; Forrest T. Simpson Jr.
Res.: 2121 N. Portland, 73107. Tel: 405-946-4441; Fax: 405-946-4894. Email: info@stpatrickokc.org. Web: www.stpatrickokc.org.
Catechesis/Religious Program—Students 180.

16—ST. PAUL, APOSTLE (1956) [JC] Rev. Lowell Stieferman; Deacon Raymond LaChance.
Res.: 3901 S. Sunnylane Rd., Del City, 73115. Tel: 405-677-4873; Fax: 405-619-0596.
Mission— Del City, Mission Co.
Catechesis/Religious Program—Students 107.

17—ST. PHILIP NERI (Midwest City) (1946) [CEM] Rev. Timothy M. Fuller; Deacon James G. Young.
Church & Mailing Address: 1107 Felix Pl., Midwest

City, 73110-5331. Tel: 405-737-4476; Fax: 405-741-0531. Email: parish@spnok.org.
Rectory—301 Wilson Dr., Midwest City, 73110-5346.
School—1121 Felix Pl., Midwest City, 73110. Tel: 405-737-4496; Fax: 405-732-7823. Lay Teachers 14; Students 182.
Catechesis/Religious Program—Tel: 405-737-4476, Ext. 108. Email: dre@spnok.org. Students 154.

18—SACRED HEART (1911) [JC] Revs. Joseph H. Arledge; Rayanna Pudota.
Res.: 2706 S. Shartel Ave., 73109. Tel: 405-634-2458; Fax: 405-634-2459. Email: sacredheartokc@yahoo.com. Web: www.sacredheartokc.org/parish.
School—2700 S. Shartel Ave., 73109. Tel: 405-634-5673; Fax: 405-634-7011. Web: www.sacredheartokc.org. Joana Camacho, Prin. Lay Teachers 12; Students 145.
Catechesis/Religious Program—Tel: 405-634-6448. Email: sacredheartrosamz@cox.net. Students 768.

OUTSIDE OKLAHOMA CITY

ADA, PONTOTOC CO., ST. JOSEPH (1902) Rev. Russell L. Hewes; Deacons Michael Radosevich, (Retired); Dennis D. Fine.
Res.: 1300 E. Beverly St., P.O. Box 1585, 74821. Tel: 580-332-4811; Fax: 580-436-1226.
Catechesis/Religious Program—Students 135.
Mission—St. Francis Xavier 1313 E. 7th St., Sulphur, Murray Co. 73086. Tel: 580-622-3070.

ALTUS, JACKSON CO., PRINCE OF PEACE (1964) Rev. Joseph Sundar Raju Pudota.
Res.: 1500 Falcon Rd., 73521. Tel: 580-482-3363; Fax: 580-482-6657. Email: princeofpeace1766@cableone.net.
Mission—St. Helen Church 507 E. Highview, Frederick, 73542. Tel: 580-335-3298; Fax: 580-335-3953. Email: sthelenchurch@pldio.net.
Catechesis/Religious Program—Students 169.

ALVA, WOODS CO., SACRED HEART (1897) [CEM] Rev. Damian Lawrence.
Res.: 627 12th St., 73717. Tel: 580-327-0339; 580-327-3006 (office); Fax: 580-327-0710. Email: sacredheart1@itlnet.net.
Mission—Our Mother of Mercy 210 S. Main St., Waynoka, Woods Co. 73860.
Mission—St. Cornelius (1895) 404 S. Massachusetts, Cherokee, Alfalfa Co. 73728. Tel: 580-596-3328.
Catechesis/Religious Program—Tel: 580-327-3006. Students 28.

ANADARKO, CADDO CO., ST. PATRICK'S (1892), (Native American), [JC 5] Rev. Samineni Stanislaus (India); Stephanie Fleshman, Music Dir.
Res.: 1115 W. Petree Rd., Box 628, 73005. Tel: 405-247-5255; Fax: 405-247-5249. Email: stpats@sbcglobal.net.
Mission—Our Lady of the Most Holy Rosary Binger. Hwy. 152, Binger, Caddo Co. 73009.
Mission—St. Richard Hwy. 9, Carnegie, Caddo Co. 73015. Tel: 580-654-2177.
Catechesis/Religious Program—Students 62.

ARDMORE, CARTER CO., ST. MARY (1898) [CEM] Rev. Thomas O'Toole.
Mailing Address: 101 E St., S.W., 73401. Email: stmaryardmore@hotmail.com. Web: stmaryardmoreok.org.
Res.: 125 E St. S.W., 73401. Tel: 580-223-0231; Fax: 580-226-2129.
Mission—St. Cecilia 300 E. Lincoln Ave., Healdton, Carter Co. 73438.
Mission—St. Anthony 305 E. Wilson St., Tishomingo, Johnston Co. 73460-3124.
Catechesis/Religious Program—Students 176.

BETHANY, OKLAHOMA CO., LATIN MASS COMMUNITY (2000) Revs. Howard L. Remski, F.S.S.P., Chaplain; Howard L. Remski, F.S.S.P.
Mailing Address: 4701 N. McMillion Ave., 73008. Tel: 405-440-9168; Fax: 405-782-0767.
Church & Chapel: 4703 N. McMillian Ave., 73008.

BLACKWELL, KAY CO., ST. JOSEPH'S (1901) Rev. Martin Larok Obwona, F.C. (Uganda); Deacons Bart Brashears; Francisco Estrada.
Res.: 315 W. Blackwell Ave., P.O. Box 578, 74631. Tel: 580-363-2096; Fax: 580-363-2096.
Catechesis/Religious Program—Tel: 580-363-0441; Fax: 580-363-0441. Students 21.

CALUMET, CANADIAN CO., IMMACULATE HEART OF MARY (1940), (German—Irish), See separate listing. Now a mission of Holy Trinity, Okarache.

CHANDLER, LINCOLN CO., OUR LADY OF SORROWS (1894) [CEM] Rev. James J. Mickus; Deacon Rusty Wooden.
Res.: 409 Price Ave., P.O. Box 543, 74834. Tel: 405-258-1239; Fax: 405-258-0010.
Mission—St. Louis Hwy. 99 & Eighth Ave., Stroud, Lincoln Co. 74079.
Catechesis/Religious Program—Students 53.

CHICKASHA, GRADY CO., HOLY NAME (1895) [CEM] Rev. James A. Goin.
Res.: 210 S. Seventh St., Box 748, 73023-0748. Tel: 405-224-7513; Fax: 405-224-4434.
Catechesis/Religious Program—Tel: 405-224-6068. Students 126.

CLINTON, CUSTER CO., ST. MARY'S (1944) Rev. Rex Arnold; Deacons Pedro Maldonado; William A. Hough.
Res.: 714 S. 12th St., P.O. Box 1295, 73601. Tel: 580-323-0309; 580-323-0345 (Office); Fax: 580-323-1351. Email: frrex@sbcglobal.net. Web: stmarysclintonok.org.
Mission—St. Anne 522 E. 3rd, Cordell, Washita Co. 73632.
Catechesis/Religious Program—1218 Knox Ave., P.O. Box 1295, 73601. Tel: 580-323-0345; Fax: 580-323-0345. Email: k.hubbard@stmarysclintonok.org. Students 224.

DUNCAN, STEPHENS CO., ASSUMPTION (1902) [CEM] Revs. Joseph M. Irwin; Christopher H. Tran; Deacon James Conway.
Res.: 711 Hickory Ave., 73533. Tel: 580-255-0590; Fax: 580-252-1597. Web: www.assumptiononline.org.
Mission—Immaculate Conception Fourth & Comanche, Marlow, Stephens Co. 73055. Tel: 580-658-2365.
Mission—St. Patrick Church 3rd & Ohio, Walters, Cotton Co. 73572.
Mission—San Jose 1117 Lincoln Ave., Ryan, Jefferson Co. 73565. Tel: 580-757-2830.
Mission—St. Thomas Aquinas Chapel 400 E. 'D' St., Stephens Co. 73533.
Catechesis/Religious Program—Lori Jech, D.R.E. Students 176.

EDMOND, OKLAHOMA CO.

1—ST. JOHN THE BAPTIST (1889) Rev. John R. Metzinger; Very Rev. Louis Vanderley, O.S.B.; Revs. Daniel J. Letourneau; Long N. Phan; Deacons Bill Coyle, Business Mgr.; Gary Peterson, Outreach; Roy Forsythe, Prison Ministry.
Res.: 900 S. Littler Ave., P.O. Box 510, 73083-0510. Tel: 405-340-0691; Fax: 405-340-5715.
School—St. Elizabeth Ann Seton School, 925 South Blvd., 73034-4710. Tel: 405-348-5364; Fax: 405-340-9627. Email: seas@stjohn-catholic.org. Web: www.stjohn-catholic.org/s_e_a_s_.htm. Lay Teachers 26; Students 480.
Catechesis/Religious Program—Tel: 405-340-9871; Fax: 405-340-3260. Web: www.stjohn-catholic.org/re.htm. Students 667.

2—ST. MONICA (1993) [CEM] Rev. Timothy D. Luschen.
Mailing Address: 2001 N. Western, 73012. Tel: 405-359-2700; Fax: 405-341-0023.
Res.: 1121 N.W. 199th St., 73012. Tel: 405-330-2699; Fax: 405-330-2699.
Catechesis/Religious Program—Students 471.

EL RENO, CANADIAN CO., SACRED HEART (1890) [CEM] Rev. Frank J. Schmitt, S.J.
Res.: 208 S. Evans Ave., 73036-3636. Tel: 405-262-1405; Fax: 405-262-2251; 405-262-2818. Email: elreno@sacredheart.com.
School—Sacred Heart School, 210 S. Evans, 73036. Tel: 405-262-2284; Fax: 405-262-3818. Shannon Statton, Prin. Teachers 11; Students 89.
Catechesis/Religious Program—Tel: 405-262-2273. Students 105.

ELGIN, COMANCHE CO., ST. ANN (1914), (German), [CEM] Rev. Madineni Prakash; Deacon Thomas E. Biles.
Res.: 8492 St. Hwy. 17, P.O. Box 10, 73538. Tel: 580-492-5914; Fax: 580-492-5908. Email: stann@tds.net.
Mission—Our Lady of Perpetual Help 220 N. A St., Sterling, Comanche Co. 73567.
Mission—Mother of Sorrows 521 E. Wallace, Apache, Caddo Co. 73006.
Catechesis/Religious Program—Students 77.

ELK CITY, BECKHAM CO., ST. MATTHEW'S (1970), (German), [CEM] [JC 3] Rev. Carl William Janocha; Deacons Paul Albert; Jim E. Warnke; Kathy Noble, Music Min.
Mailing Address: 3001 E. Hwy. 66, 73644-9607. Tel: 580-225-0066; Fax: 580-225-3522. Email: stmatthew@cableone.net.
Res.: 2900 E. Highway 66, 73644. Tel: 580-225-3980; Fax: 580-225-3522. Email: stmatthew@cableone.net.
Mission—Queen of All Saints 914 N. 5th St., Sayre, Beckham Co. 73662. Tel: 580-928-5124. Deacon Sherman McKaskle.
Catechesis/Religious Program—Celia Spitz, D.R.E. Students 129.

ENID, GARFIELD CO.

1—ST. FRANCIS XAVIER (1893) [CEM] [JC] Rev. Kevin J. Ratterman; Deacon Anthony Crispo.
Res.: 110 N. Madison, P.O. Box 3527, 73702. Tel: 580-237-0812; Fax: 580-237-0909.
School—St. Joseph Catholic School, (Grades PreK-6) Tel: 580-242-4449; Fax: 580-242-3541. Lay Teachers 9; Students 92.
Catechesis/Religious Program—Students 461.

2—ST. GREGORY THE GREAT (1971) Rev. Lawrence T. Kowalski.
Res.: 2045 Lantern Ln., 73703. Tel: 580-233-1845. Email: stgregorys@sbcglobal.net. Web: www.stgregoryenid.com.
Church: 1924 W. Willow, 73703. Tel: 580-233-4589; Fax: 580-233-4590.
Mission—St. Michael [CEM] Main St., Goltry, Alfalfa Co. 73739.
Catechesis/Religious Program—Fax: 580-233-4589. Students 115.

FREDERICK, TILLMAN CO., ST. HELEN (1927) Consolidated St. Helen is now a mission listed under Prince of Peace, Altus.

GUTHRIE, LOGAN CO., ST. MARY'S (1889) [CEM] Rev. Denis G. Hanrahan; Deacons Roy Ellison; Richard Washko, (Retired).
Mailing Address: 411 N. Elm St., P.O. Box 1556, 73044.
Res.: 411 N. Elm St., P.O. Box 1556, 73044. Tel: 405-282-4239; Fax: 405-282-5610. Email: stmarys@coxinet.net.
School—502 E. Warner Ave., 73044. Tel: 405-282-2071; Fax: 405-282-2924. Email: stmaryscatholic@sbcglobal.net. Lay Teachers 12; Students 168.
Mission—St. Margaret Mary P.O. Box 632, Crescent, Logan Co. 73028. Tel: 405-969-2351.
Catechesis/Religious Program—Students 68.

GUYMON, TEXAS CO., ST. PETER'S (1906), (Hispanic), [CEM] Revs. Bill Pruett; Raul Sanchez; Balaswamy Konka; Deacons Joe Cruz; Simon Guerra.
Res.: 1220 N. Quinn St., P.O. Box 731, 73942. Tel: 580-338-7212; Fax: 580-338-8746. Email: stpeter@ptsi.net. Web: www.saintpeterapostle.com.
Mission—St. Frances Cabrini 101 Ave. C, Beaver, Beaver Co. 73932. Tel: 580-256-5305.
Mission—Sacred Heart 106 N. Albright, P.O. Box 468, Hooker, Texas Co. 73945. Tel: 580-652-2320.
Mission—Good Shepherd S. Ellis at Second, P.O. Box 966, Boise City, Cimarron Co. 73933. Tel: 580-544-3443.
Catechesis/Religious Program—Tel: 405-454-9940. Students 302.

HARRAH, OKLAHOMA CO., ST. TERESA OF AVILA (1907), (Polish), [CEM] See separate listing. Now a mission of St. Vincent de Paul, McLoud.

HENNESSEY, KINGFISHER CO., ST. JOSEPH'S (1890), (Hispanic), [CEM] Rev. Roberto Quant.
Res.: 211 N. Cherokee St., 73742. Tel: 405-853-4425; Fax: 405-853-2166.
Mission—St. Joseph 101 First St., P.O. Box 117, Bison, Garfield Co. 73720.
Catechesis/Religious Program—Tel: 405-853-2158; Fax: 405-853-2158. Students 130.

HITCHCOCK, BLAINE CO., SACRED HEART MISSION, Closed. For inquiries for parish records contact St. Anthony of Padua Church, Okeene.

KINGFISHER, KINGFISHER CO., SS. PETER AND PAUL (1896) [CEM] Rev. Stephen V. Hamilton; Deacon Terrence R. Rice.
Mailing Address: 309 S. Main, 73750.
Res.: 410 S. 6th St., 73750. Tel: 405-375-4581; Fax: 405-375-3858. Web: www.stspeterandpaul.org.
School—Tel: 405-375-4616; Fax: 405-375-5296. Lay Teachers 10; Students 68.
Catechesis/Religious Program—Students 104.
Mission—St. Rose of Lima 900 N. Clarence Nash Blvd., Watonga, Blaine Co. 73772.

KONAWA, POTTAWATOMIE CO., SACRED HEART (1876) [CEM] Rev. Adrian Vorderlandwehr, O.S.B.
Mailing Address: Rte. 1, Box 101, 74849.
Res.: 47943 Abbey Rd., 74849. Tel: 580-925-2145; Fax: 580-925-2145.
Mission—St. Mary Wanette, Pottawatomie Co.
Catechesis/Religious Program—Students 32.

LAWTON, COMANCHE CO.

1—BLESSED SACRAMENT (1902) Rev. Joseph R. Ross; Deacon Bill Adamson. In Res., Rev. James D.M. Stafford.
Res.: 12 S.W. Seventh St., Box 2546, 73502. Tel: 580-355-2054; Fax: 580-355-2055. Email: blessedsaclawton@sbcglobal.net.
School—St. Mary's, 611 A Ave., 73501. Tel: 580-355-5288; Fax: 580-355-4336. Email: saintmarysknights@juno.com. Lay Teachers 18; Students 161.
Catechesis/Religious Program—Tel: 580-353-8182. Students 77.

2—HOLY FAMILY (1959), (Formerly St. Barbara) Rev. Kirk S. Larkin; Deacons Michael J. Romaka; Jim Coe; David Bunch.
Res.: 1010 N.W. 82nd St., 73505. Tel: 580-536-6351; Fax: 580-536-6352. Email: holyfamilyoffice@sbcglobal.net. Web: www.holyfamilylawton.org.
Catechesis/Religious Program—Tel: 580-536-6355; Fax: 580-536-6352. Email: holyfamilydre@sbcglobal.net. Students 296.

LEXINGTON, CLEVELAND CO., ST. JOHN THE BAPTIST, Closed. For parish records contact Our Lady of Victory, Purcell.

LOYAL, KINGFISHER CO., ST. JOSEPH MISSION, Closed. For inquiries for parish records contact Sts. Peter

& Paul Church, Kingfisher.

MADILL, MARSHALL CO., HOLY CROSS CHURCH (1948) Rev. Oby Zunmas.
14 W. Francis St., 73446-3234. Tel: 580-795-3721; Fax: 888-696-2593.
Mission—Good Shepherd 200 N.W. 8th, P.O. Box 127, Marietta, 73448. Tel: 580-276-9604.
Catechesis/Religious Program—Kitty Walker, D.R.E. (Holy Cross); Carol Steinbock, D.R.E. (Good Shepherd). Students 286.

MANGUM, GREER CO., SACRED HEART (1902) Rev. Jude Shayo, A.J.
Mailing Address: P.O. Box 310, 73554. Tel: 580-782-2657; Fax: 580-782-3297.
Res.: 409 N. Byers, 73554. Tel: 580-726-3925.
Mission—Sts. Peter and Paul 324 SS. Randlett, Hobart, Kiewa Co. 73651. Fax: 580-726-3486. Web: www.stspeter-paul.com.
Mission—Our Lady of Guadalupe 524 E. Chestnut, Hollis, Harmon Co. 73550. Tel: 580-688-2233.
Catechesis/Religious Program—Students 82.

MCLOUD, POTTOWATOMIE CO., ST. VINCENT DE PAUL (1904) Rev. Lucas Raj Pinapati (India).
Res.: 122 S. 10th St., P.O. Box 585, 74851. Tel: 405-964-5606 (Res.); Fax: 405-964-5606.
Catechesis/Religious Program—Students 19.
Mission—St. Teresa of Avila 1576 Tim Holt Dr., Harrah, Oklahoma Co. 73045. Tel: 405-454-2819; Fax: 405-454-0981. Web: www.stteresaharrah.org.

MEDFORD, GRANT CO., ST. MARY'S (1940) [CEM 3] Rev. Michael Wheelahan.
Res.: 214 W. Cherokee, Box 360, 73759. Tel: 580-741-1056; Fax: 580-395-2148.
Mission—St. Mary's Assumption Main & Birch, Wakita, Grant Co. 73771. Tel: 580-594-2541.
Mission—St. Joseph's S. Hwy. 81, Pond Creek, Grant Co. 73766.
Catechesis/Religious Program—Tel: 580-395-2290. Students 40.

MOORE, CLEVELAND CO., ST. ANDREW'S (1962) [CEM] Rev. John W. Feehily; Deacons Jerome Caplinger; Angus Watford.
Res.: 800 N.W. Fifth St., 73160. Tel: 405-799-3334; Fax: 405-799-4880. Web: www.standrewmoore.com.
Catechesis/Religious Program—Tel: 405-799-3334, Ext. 305. Email: linda@standrewmoore.com. Linda Hartley, D.R.E. Students 319.

MUSTANG, CANADIAN CO., CHURCH OF THE HOLY SPIRIT (1983) Rev. James A. Greiner.
Church: 1100 N. Sara Rd., P.O. Box 246, 73064. Tel: 405-376-9435 (Parish Office); 405-376-5218 (Rectory); Fax: 405-376-4929. Email: lonelk67@sbcglobal.net. Web: www.mustangcatholic.com.
Catechesis/Religious Program—Tel: 405-376-5633. Martin Weaver, D.R.E. Students 147.

NEWKIRK, KAY CO., ST. FRANCIS OF ASSISI (1894) Rev. Joseph S. Vas (Retired).
Res.: 610 W. Ninth St., P.O. Box 11, 74647. Tel: 580-362-3320; Fax: 580-362-2830. Email: sfcnewkirk@sbcglobal.net.
Catechesis/Religious Program—Students 62.

NICOMA PARK, OKLAHOMA CO., OUR LADY OF FATIMA (1949) Rev. Shane I. Tharp.
Res.: 2255 W. Meyer Cir., Box 368, 73066. Tel: 405-769-2490; Fax: 405-769-9113.
Catechesis/Religious Program—Tel: 405-769-2655. Students 65.

NORMAN, CLEVELAND CO.

1—CHURCH OF ST. MARK THE EVANGELIST (1991) Rev. Thomas J. Boyer; Deacon Byron Jacobson.
Mailing Address: 3939 W. Tecumseh Rd., 73072-1708. Tel: 405-366-7676; Fax: 405-366-7842.
Res.: 3701 Castlerock Rd., 73072. Tel: 405-447-3085.
Catechesis/Religious Program—Students 308.

2—ST. JOSEPH'S (1896) [CEM] Revs. Edward T. Menasco; William M. Lewis; Deacons Larry Sousa; Patrick Gabrish; Jeff Willard, Pastoral Assoc.; Steve Lewis; Richard Montedoro.
Mailing Address: 421 E. Acres, P.O. Box 1227, 73070.
Res.: 422 E. Tonhawa, P.O. Box 1227, 73070. Tel: 405-321-8080; Fax: 405-321-4360. Web: www.stjosephsok.org.
Church: 211 N. Porter, 73071.
Catechesis/Religious Program—Tel: 405-321-8084. Students 361.

3—ST. THOMAS MORE UNIVERSITY PARISH (1979) [JC] Rev. Raymond K. Ackerman; Deacon John D. Pigott; Jon Roberts, Music Dir.; Erin Cleto, Campus Min.; Christy Meiser, Business Mgr.
Res.: 1501 Lincoln Ave., 73072. Tel: 405-329-5319. Web: www.stm-ou.org.
Church: 100 E. Stinson St., 73072. Tel: 405-321-0900; Fax: 405-321-0964. Web: www.stm-ou.org.
Catechesis/Religious Program—Michelle Breedlove, D.R.E. & Youth Ministry Coord. Students 128.

OKARCHE, KINGFISHER CO., HOLY TRINITY (1893) [CEM] Rev. David M. Lafferty; Deacon Max Schwarz.
Res.: 211 W. Missouri, Box 185, 73762-0185. Tel: 405-263-7930; Fax: 405-263-4518.
School—Box 485, 73762. Tel: 405-263-4422; Fax: 405-263-9753. Tamara Grimes, Prin. Teachers 1; Lay Teachers 12; Students 93.
Catechesis/Religious Program—Tel: 405-263-4640. Students 72.
Mission—Immaculate Heart of Mary 107 Freehome, Calumet, Canadian Co. 73014.

OKEENE, BLAINE CO., ST. ANTHONY'S (1901) [CEM] Rev. Prabhakar Kalivela.
Res.: P.O. Box 767, 73763. Tel: 580-822-3511 (Rectory); 580-822-3544 (Office); Fax: 580-822-3542. Email: stanthony@pldi.net.
Rectory—220 E. Grant, 73763.
Mission—St. Thomas P.O. Box 624, Seiling, Dewey Co. 73663. Tel: 580-922-4376.
Mission—St. Ann 424 S. 6th, P.O. Box 55, Fairview, Major Co. 73737. Tel: 580-227-2270.
Catechesis/Religious Program—Tel: 580-822-3507. Students 36.

PAULS VALLEY, GARVIN CO., ST. CATHERINE OF SIENA (1949) [JC] Rev. Michael Vaught.
Res.: 205 W. Bert St., 73075. Tel: 405-238-3741.
Mission—St. Peter's E. Second & Quapah, Lindsay, Garvin Co. 73052.
Catechesis/Religious Program—Students 65.

PERRY, NOBLE CO., ST. ROSE OF LIMA (1893) [CEM] Rev. Thomas Dowdell; Sandy Soulek, Pastoral Assoc.
Mailing Address: P.O. Box 603, 73077-0603.
Res.: 421 Ninth St., 73077. Tel: 580-336-9300; Fax: 580-336-9795. Email: stroseperry@sbcglobal.net. Web: www.saintroseperry.com.
Mission—Sacred Heart Broadway & Lowe, Billings, Noble Co. 74630.
Catechesis/Religious Program—Students 42.

PONCA CITY, KAY CO., CHURCH OF ST. MARY (1893) [CEM] [JC] Revs. John J. Michalcka; Joseph Patrick Schwarz; Deacon Richard Robinson.
Res.: 707 E. Ponca St., Box 1330, 74602. Tel: 580-765-6031; Fax: 580-765-1327. Email: stmarysponcacity@sbcglobal.net. Web: www.stmarypc.com.
School—St. Mary, 415 S. 7th, 74601. Tel: 580-765-4387. Web: www.stmarypc.com/school/school/htm. Teachers 18; Students 158.
Catechesis/Religious Program—Tel: 580-765-7794. Email: stmarydre@sbcglobal.net. Students 98.

PRAGUE, LINCOLN CO., ST. WENCESLAUS, NATIONAL SHRINE OF THE INFANT JESUS OF PRAGUE (1899), (Czech), [CEM] Rev. M. Price Oswalt.
Res.: 304 Jim Thorpe Blvd., Box 488, 74864. Tel: 405-567-3404; Fax: 405-567-0365.
Mission—St. Michael 217 S. Koonce, P.O. Box 684, Meeker, Lincoln Co. 74855.
Catechesis/Religious Program—Students 26.

PURCELL, MCCLAIN CO., OUR LADY OF VICTORY (1886), (Hispanic), [CEM] Rev. Michael Vaught.
Office: 316 W. Jefferson St., Box 1280, 73080. Tel: 405-527-3077; Fax: 405-527-7842; 405-527-6817 (Office). Email: ourladyofvictory@cebridge.net.
Office: 307 W. Jefferson St., P.O. Box 1280, 73080.
Catechesis/Religious Program—Students 153.

SEMINOLE, SEMINOLE CO., IMMACULATE CONCEPTION (1928) Rev. Basil Keenan, O.S.B.
Mailing Address: P.O. Box 164, 74818-0164.
Res.: 811 W. Wrangler Blvd., 74868. Tel: 405-382-3602; Fax: 405-382-3602. Email: basilosb@hotmail.com.
Chapel—St. Joseph Chapel 702 S. Seminole, Wewoka, 74884.
Catechesis/Religious Program—Students 51.

SHAWNEE, POTTAWATOMIE CO., ST. BENEDICT (1895) [CEM] Revs. Donald J. Wolf; Chinnapa Reddy Konkala; Deacons David Schrupp; William T. Thurman.
Res.: 632 N. Kickapoo, 74801. Tel: 405-275-0001; Fax: 405-214-9181. Email: st.benedict.office@sbcglobal.net. Web: www.stbenedictchurch.net.
Catechesis/Religious Program—Tel: 405-275-5399. Students 189.

SULPHUR, MURRAY CO., ST. FRANCIS XAVIER (1974) See separate listing. Became a mission of St. Joseph, Ada.

TONKAWA, KAY CO., ST. JOSEPH'S (1909) [JC] Rev. Martin Larok Obwona, F.C. (Uganda).
Res.: 320 W. North St., P.O. Box 525, 74653. Tel: 580-628-2416; Fax: 580-363-2096.
Catechesis/Religious Program—Students 32.

UNION CITY, CANADIAN CO., ST. JOSEPH'S (1893) [CEM] Rev. Frank J. Schmitt, S.J. (Missouri Province of Jesuits); Deacon Lloyd Menz, Pastoral Assoc.
Res.: 403 N. Kate Boevers Ave., Box 100, 73090. Tel: 405-483-5329; Fax: 405-483-5183.
Catechesis/Religious Program—Tel: 405-381-2569. Students 62.

WEATHERFORD, CUSTER CO., ST. EUGENE'S (1960) [CEM 3] Rev. Mark E. Mason; Deacon Joseph Dubey.
Res.: 704 N. Bryan, 73096. Tel: 580-772-3209; Fax: 580-772-3541. Email: st-secretary@itlnet.net. Web: steugenecatholicchurch.org.
Mission—Blessed Sacrament 520 N. Oklahoma, Thomas, Custer Co. 73669.
Mission—Sacred Heart 204 N. Clark Ave., Hinton, Caddo Co. 73047.
Catechesis/Religious Program—Students 175.

WOODWARD, WOODWARD CO., ST. PETER'S (1905), (German), Rev. Scott A. Boeckman.
Res.: 2020 Oklahoma Ave., 73801. Tel: 580-256-8505; Fax: 580-256-5840. Web: stpeternwok.com.
Mission—Sacred Heart 301 N. Main, Mooreland, Woodward Co. 73852.
Mission—Holy Name 600 S. Main, Shattuck, Ellis Co. 73858.
Mission—St. Joseph 325 S.W. 2nd, Buffalo, Harper Co. 73834.
Catechesis/Religious Program—Tel: 580-256-2966. Email: stpeterdre@sbcglobal.net. Students 251.

YUKON, CANADIAN CO., ST. JOHN NEPOMUK (1889) Rev. William L. Novak; Deacons Jeffrey Kelly; John Teague; Daniel Lombardi.
Mailing Address: 600 Garth Brooks Blvd., P.O. Box 850249, 73085.
Church: 600 S. Garth Brooks Blvd., 73099. Tel: 405-354-2743; Fax: 405-354-2770. Email: parishsecretary@sjnok.org.
School—(Grades PreK-8) Tel: 405-354-2509; Fax: 405-354-8192. Web: www.sjnok.org. Diane Floyd, Prin.; Sue Parizek, Librarian. Lay Teachers 17; Students 201.
Catechesis/Religious Program—Students 452.

Special Assignment:
Revs.—
Bird, Stephen J., Dir., Office of Worship & Spiritual Life, P.O. Box 32180, 73123. Tel: 405-721-5651
Leven, Marvin F., Chap. (Retired), Mercy Health Center, 4300 W. Memorial, 73120.
McCaffrey, Daniel, Natural Family Planning Outreach, 3366 N.W. Expressway, Bldg. D, #630, 73112.
Menasco, Edward T., Diaconate Program, P.O. Box 32180, 73123.
Paracka1, George, Chap. St. Anthony Hospital, 1000 N. Lee St., P.O. Box 205, 73101. Tel: 405-272-6263
Ross, Joseph R., P.O. Box 2546, Lawton, 73502. Tel: 580-355-2054

Military Chaplains:
Rev.—
Creider, Philip B., Command Chap., U.S.S. Tarawa (LHA-1), FPD AP.

Absent on Sick Leave:
Revs.—
Grimes, Price D., Jr., P.O. Box 32180, 73123. Tel: 405-720-9871
Parker, Rick, 26245 Ocean View Ave., Carmel, CA 93923.

Retired:
Revs.—
Bao, Anthony, Belleview Health Center, 6500 N. Portland #674, 73116.
Bash, Cletus, Saint Ann Nursing Home, 400 Saint Ann's Dr. E13, 73162.
Beckman, Richard J., 1601 Academy Rd., Ponca City, 74604.
Burger, Joseph, Saint Ann Nursing Home, 9400 Saint Ann's Dr. #C13, 73162.
Devlin, Kevin, 1044 W. 80th Ave., Conway Spring, KS 67031.
Donohoe, Philip M., 301 Wade St., #205, El Reno, 73036.
Gallatin, Paul H., 5700 N.W. 50th St., 73122.
Kolb, Joseph C., P.O. Box 32180, 73123.
Lamb, Louis J., Saint Ann Retirement Center, 7501 W. Britton Rd., #338, 73132.
Leven, Marvin F., P.O. Box 464, Okarche, 73762.
MacAulay, Gerard, Saint Ann Retirement Center, 7501 W. Britton Rd., #238, 73132.
Monahan, David F., 9400 Saint Ann's Dr., 73162.
Moore, Wilbur E., P.O. Box 32180, 73123.
Roberson, Henry, 1141 Pinehurst Dr., Norman, 73072.
Ross, William B., 1506 W. Walnut, El Reno, 73036.
Schwarz, Elmer C., J.C.L., P.O. Box 32180, 73123.
Vas, Joseph S.
Vrana, John P.
Wrigley, Franklin, Saint Ann Nursing Home, 9400 Saint Ann's Dr., D-9, 73162. Tel: 405-728-7888

Permanent Deacons:
Adamson, Bill, Blessed Sacrament, Lawton
Albert, Paul, St. Matthew, Elk City
Bartlett, Chester A., St. Charles Borromeo, Oklahoma City

Barton, James D., St. Joseph Old Cathedral, Oklahoma City
Bawden, William, St. Eugene, Oklahoma City
Best, David, (Retired)
Brashers, Bart, St. Joseph, Blackwell
Bunch, David, Holy Family, Lawton
Caplinger, Jerome, St. Andrew, Moore
Coe, James, Holy Family, Lawton
Conway, James, Immaculate Conception, Marlow
Coyle, William St. John the Baptist, Edmond
Crispo, Anthony, St. Francis Xavier, Enid
Cruz, Joseph M., St. Peter, Guymon
Cumby, Dunn, Corpus Christi, Oklahoma City
Descher, Duane, (Retired)
Dubey, Joseph, St. Eugene, Weatherford
Duclos, Edward, St. Joseph Old Cathedral, Oklahoma City
Ellison, Roy, St. Mary's, Guthrie
Enos, William, Our Lady's Cathedral, Oklahoma City
Fahy, Richard, Epiphany of the Lord, Oklahoma City
Fischer, Duane, St. Patrick, Oklahoma City
Forgue, Joseph, St. Francis of Assisi, Oklahoma City
Forsythe, Roy, St. John the Baptist, Edmond
Frazier, Dennis, St. Patrick, Oklahoma City
Gabrish, Patrick, St. Joseph, Norman
Gorden, William, St. Charles, Oklahoma City
Guerra, Simon, St. Peter, Guymon
Gulikers, Marti, St. James, Oklahoma City
Guoladdle, Bobby, (Retired)
Hernandez, Santos, Holy Angels, Oklahoma City
Heskamp, Robert, Epiphany of the Lord, Oklahoma City
Hollier, Bernie, Corpus Christi, Oklahoma City
Hunt, Lee, St. Monica, Edmond
Jacobsen, Byron, St. Mark, Norman
Keene, James, Immaculate Conception Church, Oklahoma City
Kelly, Jeffrey, St. John Nepomuk Church, Yukon
Kenny, Philip, St. Peter, Woodward
King, William, St. Charles, Oklahoma City
LaChance, Raymond, St. Paul, Del City
Le, Anthony, Our Lady's Cathedral, Oklahoma City
Leal, George, Sacred Heart Church, Oklahoma City
LeWand, Mark, (Retired)
Lewis, Paul, Our Lady's Cathedral, Oklahoma City
Lewis, Steve, St. Joseph, Norman
Lopez, Alfonso, Saint Charles Borromeo, Oklahoma City
Maldonado, Pedro, St. Mary, Clinton
Martinez, Leopoldo, (Retired)
Martinez, Mariano, Sacred Heart, Oklahoma City
McKaskle, Sherman, Queen of All Saints, Sayre
Means, Gary, St. Cornelius, Cherokee
Mejstrik, Norman, St. Philip Neri, Midwest City
Menz, Lloyd, St. Joseph, Union City
Mobley, Eulis, Prince of Peace, Altus
Montedoro, Richard, St. Joseph, Norman
Nguyen, Manh San, Chap., Oklahoma County Jail
Nieto, Lucio, (Retired)
Ninh, Sang, Our Lady's Cathedral, Oklahoma City
O'Loughlin, Bernard, (Retired)
Ontiveros, Santiago, St. Peter, Woodward
Ortiz, Jose, Our Lady of Victory, Purcell
Painter, Richard, St. Philip, Midwest City
Peterson, Gary, St. John the Baptist, Edmond
Phan, Thomas, St. Charles, Oklahoma City
Pigott, John, St. Thomas More, Norman
Pitt, John, (Retired)
Radosevich, Michael, St. Joseph, Ada
Rakosky, Gerald St. Monica, Edmond
Randolph, Alejandro, St. Eugene, Oklahoma City
Robinson, Richard, St. Mary, Ponca City
Rossow, Larry, St. Joseph, Norman
Schott, Thomas, St. Thomas More, Norman
Schrupp, David, St. Benedict, Shawnee
Schwarz, Max, Holy Trinity, Okarche
Smith, James, Christ the King, Oklahoma City
Smits, Robert, St. Patrick, Anadarko
Sousa, Lawrence, St. Joseph, Norman
Teague, John, St. John Nepomuk, Yukon
Vance, Herbert Reeves, Chap., Oklahoma Medical Complex, Oklahoma City
Wade, James Lee, St. Mary, Ardmore
Walker, Rod, Holy Cross, Madill
Wallace, Wenum Ray, Prince of Peace, Altus
Warnke, Jim E., St. Matthew, Elk City
Warren, John, Our Lady of Victory Church, Purcell
Washko, Richard, (Retired)
Watford, Angus, St. Andrew, Moore
Willard, Jeff, St. Joseph, Norman
Wooden, Rusty, Our Lady of Sorrows, Chandler
Young, James G., St. Philip Neri, Midwest City

INSTITUTIONS LOCATED IN THE ARCHDIOCESE

[A] COLLEGES AND UNIVERSITIES

SHAWNEE. *St. Gregory's University* (Coed); Liberal Arts and Sciences, 1900 W. MacArthur Dr., 74804. Tel: 405-878-5100; Fax: 405-878-5198. Email: president@stgregorys.edu. Web: www.stgregorys.edu. Rt. Rev. Lawrence R. Stasyszen, O.S.B., S.T.D., Chancellor; Rev. Robert A. Busch, Ph.D., Dean, College of Arts & Sciences; David Marker, Ph.D., Interim Pres. Priests 5; Brothers 2; Sisters 1; Lay Teachers 29; Total Staff 69; Students 668.

[B] HIGH SCHOOLS, ARCHDIOCESAN

OKLAHOMA CITY. *Bishop McGuinness Catholic High School* (1950) (Coed), 801 N.W. 50th St., 73118. Tel: 405-842-6638; Fax: 405-858-9550; 405-858-9550 (Prin. Office). Email: development@bmchs.org. Web: bmchs.org. Mr. David Morton, Pres. & Prin.; Revs. Daniel J. Letourneau; Thanh Van Nguyen; James A. Wickersham; Ms. Katherine Marquis, Librarian. Sisters 1; Lay Teachers 59; Students 701.

[C] HIGH SCHOOLS, PRIVATE

OKLAHOMA CITY. *Mount St. Mary High School* (1903) (Coed), 2801 S. Shartel Ave., 73109. Tel: 405-631-8865; Fax: 405-631-9209. Email: themount@mountstmary.org. Web: mountstmary.org. Rev. Rayanna Pudota, Chap.; Mrs. Talita DeNegri, Prin.; Mr. Brian Boeckman, Chm., Rel. Studies Dept.; Mrs. Geraldine Adams, Librarian. Sisters of Mercy of the Americas, Archdiocese of Oklahoma City. Priests 1; Lay Teachers 32; Students 334.

[D] ELEMENTARY SCHOOLS, PRIVATE

OKLAHOMA CITY. *Villa Teresa* (1933) (Grades PreK-4), 1216 Classen Dr., 73103. Tel: 405-232-4286; Fax: 405-552-2658. Email: principal@coxinet.net. Web: villateresaschool.com. Sisters Veronica Higgins, Prin.; Joseph Marie Gibbons, Librarian. Carmelite Sisters of St. Therese of the Infant Jesus. Sisters 5; Lay Teachers 17; Total Staff 31; Students 244.

Villa Teresa Moore, (Grades N-K), 13501 S. Western Ave., 73170. Tel: 405-691-7737; Fax: 405-691-7981. Email: villateresamoore3@hotmail.com. Sr. Veronica Higgins, Prin.; Ann M. Grover, Dir. Carmelite Sisters of St. Therese of the Infant Jesus. Lay Teachers 7; Students 96.

NORMAN. *All Saints Catholic School, Inc.* (1996) 4001 36th Ave., N.W., 73072. Tel: 405-447-4600; Fax: 405-447-7227. Email: lschmitt@ascsn.org. Web: www.ascsn.org. Leslie Schmitt, Prin.; Felicia Kizer, Librarian. Lay Teachers 29; Students 450; PreK Students 37; Total Staff 42.

[E] GENERAL HOSPITALS

OKLAHOMA CITY. *St. Anthony Hospital*, 1000 N. Lee St., P.O. Box 205, 73101. Tel: 405-272-7000; Fax: 405-272-7075. Web: www.saintsok.com. Joe Hodges, Pres.; Rev. George Parackal, Chap. A member of SSM Health Care. Bed Capacity 601; Total Staff 2,646; Patients Assisted Annually 123,462.

Saint Anthony South Hospital, 2129 S.W. 59th St., 73119. Tel: 405-713-5751; Fax: 405-680-4149. Mr. Christopher Howard, CEO. A member of SSM Health Care. Bed Capacity 124.

Mercy Health Center Owned and operated by Sisters of Mercy Health System, St. Louis., 4300 W. Memorial Rd., 73120. Tel: 405-755-1515; Fax: 405-752-3811. Email: tomedelstein@mercy.net. Web: www.mhso.okla.smhs.com. Di Smalley, Pres. & CEO; Paul Lewis, Dir. Pastoral Svcs. Sisters 2; Bed Capacity 381; Total Staff 3,088; Patients Assisted Annually 19,500.

ARDMORE. *Mercy Memorial Health Center, Inc. (MMHC)*, 1011 14th Ave., N.W., 73401. Tel: 580-220-6611; Fax: 580-220-6580. Email: mindy.burdick@mercy.net. Web: www.mercyok.net. Ms. Mindy Burdick, Pres. Total Staff 950; Bed Capacity 175; Patients Assisted Annually 140,000.

[F] SPECIAL CARE FACILITIES

OKLAHOMA CITY. *St. Ann's Home, Inc.* (1950) 9400 St. Ann's Dr., 73162. Tel: 405-728-7888; Fax: 405-728-1302. Mrs. Dorothy Joyce, Exec. Dir. Sisters 2; Total Staff 115; Bed Capacity 120; Total Assisted 108.

[G] ECUMENICAL CENTERS

OKLAHOMA CITY. *Catholic Pastoral Center*, 7501 Northwest Expwy., 73132. Tel: 405-721-5651; Fax: 405-721-5210. Email: tmaxwell@catharchdioceseokc.org. Web: www.catharchdioceseokc.org. Mr. Thomas Maxwell, Dir.; Mrs. Jeanine McFall, Events Coord. Used for Archdiocesan Chancery; ecumenical activities; retreat-meeting center for ecumenical and nonprofit organizations; and retired priests' residence.

[H] HOMES FOR THE AGED

OKLAHOMA CITY. *Saint Ann Retirement Center, Inc.*, 7501 W. Britton Rd., 73132. Tel: 405-721-0747; Fax: 405-721-0492. Email: djohnson@catharchdioceseokc.org. Mr. David J. Johnson, Business Mgr. Total Assisted 50; Total Staff 60; Total Independent 120.

Trinity Gardens Apartments, 1501 N. Classen Blvd., 73106. Tel: 405-523-3000; Fax: 405-523-3030. Email: toconnor@catholiccharitiesok.org. Mr. Timothy O'Connor, Contact Person. 58 low income apartments for senior citizens. Affordable Housing Units 58; Total Assisted Annually 66; Total Staff 1.

Catholic Charities, 3825 N.W. 19th St., 73107. Tel: 405-523-3000; Fax: 405-523-3030. Residents 67.

Villa Isenbart, Inc. (1970) c/o Catholic Charities, 1501 Classen Blvd., 73106. Tel: 405-523-3000; Fax: 405-523-3030. Email: toconnor@catholiccharitiesok.org. 40 Apartment Residences for Low-Income Elderly. Apartments (Low-Income) 40; Total Assisted Annually 43; Total Staff 1.

3801 N.W. 19th St., 73107. Tel: 405-947-4143; Fax: 405-947-4199. Mr. Timothy O'Connor, Dir. Residents 41.

EL RENO. *Saint Katharine Drexel Retirement Center, Inc.*, 301 W. Wade, 73036. Tel: 405-262-2920 (Legal Counsel); Fax: 405-295-1950. Email: skdblm@gmail.com. Brenda Miller, Exec. Dir. Bed Capacity 54; Total Assisted Annually 50; Total Staff 18.

PONCA CITY. *St. Mary's Housing Foundation*, P.O. Box 1330, 74602. Tel: 580-765-7794; Fax: 580-765-1327. Email: stmarysponcacity@sbcglobal.net. 408 S. 8th St., 74601. Rev. John J. Michalicka, Pres. Senior Citizens Residences 6.

Westminster Village, Inc. (1985) (Formerly The Retirement Community Devel. Corp.); Sisters of St. Joseph/Sisters of the Sorrowful Mother of Broken Arrow, OK, 1601 Academy Rd., 74604. Tel: 580-762-0927. Web: www.via-christi.org. Michelle D. Jernigan, CEO. Continuum of care for the aged. Total Staff 106; Residents 151; Total Assisted 170.

[I] MONASTERIES AND RESIDENCES OF PRIESTS AND BROTHERS

OKLAHOMA CITY. *Monastery of Our Lady of Mount Carmel and Little Flower*, 1125 S. Walker Ave., 73109. Tel: 405-235-2037; Fax: 405-235-7035. Order of Discalced Carmelites (Oklahoma Province)., Little Flower Clinic: Free medical service for the poor. Total Assisted Annually 1,500.

SHAWNEE. *St. Gregory's Abbey* (1875) Order of St. Benedict, including University, Novitiate, and Mabee-Gerrer Museum of Art., 1900 W. MacArthur Dr., 74804. Tel: 405-878-5491; Fax: 405-878-5189. Email: abbotlawrence@stgregorys.edu. Web: www.monksok.org. Rt. Revs. Lawrence R. Stasyszen, O.S.B., S.T.D., Abbot & University Chancellor; Martin Lugo, O.S.B., Novice Master; Adrian R. Vorderlandwehr, O.S.B., CPA, Business Mgr; Very Rev. Louis Vanderley, O.S.B., Prior & Chap.; Revs. Nicholas K. Ast, O.S.B.; Matthew J. Brown, O.S.B.; Charles J. Buckley, O.S.B., Ph.D., Vocation Dir.; Boniface T. Copelin, O.S.B.; Brendan Helbing, O.S.B.; Maurus P. Jaeb, O.S.B.; Basil Keenan, O.S.B.; Manuel Magallanes, O.S.B.; Eugene C. Marshall, O.S.B.; Rt. Rev. Charles Massoth, O.S.B., Guest Master (Retired); Rev. Patrick McCool, O.S.B.; Bro. Andrew C. Raple, O.S.B.; Revs. Joachim Spexarth, O.S.B., Subprior; Paul J. Zahler, O.S.B., Ph.D.; Bros. Benet S. Exton, O.S.B.; Isidore D. Harden, O.S.B.; George A. Hubl, O.S.B.; Kevin E. McGuire, O.S.B.; Joseph L. Niichel, O.S.B.; Dominic J. Ramirez, O.S.B.; Damian S. Whalen, O.S.B.

Benedictine Fathers of Sacred Heart Mission, Inc. Priests 17; Brothers 8. *Saint Gregory's Abbey Benefit Trust*, 1900 W. MacArthur St., 74804-2404. Tel: 405-878-5463; Fax: 405-878-5400. Rt. Rev. Lawrence R. Stasyszen, O.S.B., S.T.D., Trustee & Contact Person.

[J] CONVENTS AND RESIDENCES FOR SISTERS

OKLAHOMA CITY. *Carmelite Sisters of St. Therese of the Infant Jesus Motherhouse* (1917) 1300 Classen Dr., 73103. Tel: 405-232-7926; Fax: 405-236-3170. Email: pmillerok@hotmail.com. Web: www.oksister.com. Sr. Patricia Ann Miller, Gen. Supr. Sisters in Community 20; Resident Sisters 16.

Villa Teresa School
Dominican Sisters of Our Lady of the Rosary, 7501 NW Expwy., P.O. Box 32180, 73123.
Medical Sisters of St. Joseph, Little Flower Province, c/o 7217 N.W. 121st. St., 73162. Tel: 405-721-4390; Fax: 405-721-4390. Email: oklittleflower@att.net. Sr. Rosemilla Michael, Supr. Sisters 4.
Sisters of Mercy of the Americas (1831) Retirement Center for Sisters of Mercy of Oklahoma., Mercy Health Center Convent, 4300 W. Memorial Rd., 73120. Tel: 405-755-1515; Fax: 405-936-5498. Email: rpower@mercysc.org. Web: www.mercyok.com. Sr. M. Rose Elizabeth Power, R.S.M., Coord. Sisters 17; Staff 18.

PIEDMONT. *Carmel of St. Joseph* (1939) 20,000 N. County Line Rd., 73078-9123. Tel: 405-348-3947; Fax: 405-348-4916. Email: dcn@okcarmel.org. Web: www.okcarmel.org. Sr. Donna Ross, O.C.D., Prioress. Discalced Carmelite Nuns (Cloistered). Professed Sisters 11.
Sisters of Benedict, 728 Richland Rd., S.W., 73078-9324. Tel: 405-373-4565; Fax: 405-373-3392. Email: redplains@mountosb.org. Web: www.mountosb.org/redplains. Sisters Jan Futrell, O.S.B., Prioress; Marie Ballmann, O.S.B., Contact Person. Tel: 405-373-4739. Professed Sisters 9.

[K] CAMPUS MINISTRY & NEWMAN CENTERS

NORMAN. *Campus Ministry for the Archdiocese of Oklahoma City* 100 E. Stinson, 73072. Tel: 405-321-0990; Fax: 405-321-0964. Web: www.stm-ou.org/students. Rev. Raymond K. Ackerman, Pastor & Dir.; Miss K. Erin Cleto, Campus Min. Tel: 405-321-0990, Ext. 205.
University of Oklahoma 100 E. Stinson, 73072. Tel: 405-321-0990; Fax: 405-321-0964. Web: www.stm-ou.org/students. Miss K. Erin Cleto, Campus Min.
East Central State University P.O. Box 1585, Ada, 74820. Tel: 580-332-4811; Fax: 580-436-1226. Rev. Russell L. Hewes.
Northwestern Oklahoma State College 627 12th St., Alva, 73717. Tel: 580-327-0339; Fax: 580-327-0710. Rev. Shane I. Tharp.
University of Science & Arts of Oklahoma P.O. Box 748, Chickasha, 73023. Tel: 405-224-7513; Fax: 405-224-4434. Rev. Elmer C. Schwarz, J.C.L. (Retired).
University of Central Oklahoma 321 E. Clegern, Edmond, 73034. Tel: 405-340-6300; Fax: 405-340-5715. Very Rev. Louis Vanderley, O.S.B.
Oklahoma Panhandle State University P.O. Box 277, Goodwell, 73942. Tel: 580-338-7212; Fax: 580-338-5584. Rev. Bill Pruett.
Cameron University P.O. Box 7948, Lawton, 73506. Tel: 580-536-6351. Rev. Philip M. Seeton.
Northern Oklahoma College P.O. Box 525, Tonkawa, 74653. Tel: 580-628-2416; Fax: 580-531-2607. Rev. Larok Martin.
Southwestern Oklahoma State University P.O. Box 407, Weatherford, 73096. Tel: 580-772-3209; Fax: 580-772-3541. Rev. Mark E. Mason; Deacon Joe Dubey.

[L] MISCELLANEOUS

OKLAHOMA CITY. *St. Anthony Hospital Foundation, Inc., Oklahoma City, Oklahoma* Member of SSM Health Care, P.O. Box 205, 73101. 826 N.W. 11, 73106. Tel: 405-272-7070; Fax: 405-270-7607. Email: saintsfoundation@ssmhc.com. Web: www.givetosaints.com. Sherry Rhodes, Pres.
Bishop McGuinness Catholic High School Building Trust (2003) 14000 Quail Springs Pkwy., Ste. 200, 73134. Tel: 405-936-0990; Fax: 405-248-4111. Email: dgeason@telepath.com. Douglas G. Eason, Contact Person.
Sister BJ's Pantry, Inc., 1300 Classen Dr., 73103. Tel: 405-340-9281. Sr. Barbara Joseph Foley, C.S.T., Contact Person. An apostolate of the Oklahoma Carmelite Sisters of St. Theresa of the Infant Jesus, Oklahoma City, OK.
SSM Health Care of Oklahoma, Inc. (For staff listings please see St. Anthony Hospital located under General Hospitals), 1000 N. Lee, P.O. Box 205, 73101. Tel: 405-272-7000; Fax: 405-272-6477. Chris Howard, Pres. & CEO.

ARDMORE. *Mercy Memorial Health Center Foundation*, 1011 Fourteenth Ave., N.W., 73401. Tel: 580-220-6712; Fax: 580-220-6170. Email: mindy.burdick@mercy.net. Ms. Mindy Burdick, Pres. & Contact Person; Andre Moore, Exec. Dir.
Healdton
Healdton Mercy Hospital Corporation, 918 S. 8th St., Healdton, 73438. James Newman, CFO, Mercy Memorial Health Center Inc. Tel: 405-752-3724.

LAWTON. *Columbia Square, Inc. dba Villanova Apartments* 1501 N. Classen, 73106. Tel: 405-523-3000; 580-248-2550; Fax: 580-248-2550. Email: toconnor@catholicharities.org.
304 W. 4th, 73505. Tel: 405-523-3000; Fax: 405-523-3030. Mr. Tim O'Connor, Pres. Bd. of Dirs.

OKARCHE. *New Leaven Ministries Foundation*, 511 Hunter Dr., P.O. Box 464, 73762. Tel: 405-263-7798. Email: frsamxi@pldi.net. Rev. Marvin F. Leven (Retired).

PIEDMONT. *Red Plains Spirituality Center* Location at Red Plains Monastery, 728 Richland Rd., S.W., 73078-9324. Tel: 405-373-4565; Fax: 405-373-3392. Email: redplains@mountosb.org. Web: www.mountosb.org/redplains. Operated by Benedictine Sisters.

PRAGUE. *National Shrine of the Infant Jesus of Prague St. Wenceslaus Church*, P.O. Box 488, 74864. Tel: 405-567-3080; Fax: 405-567-0364. 304 Jim Thorpe Blvd., 74864. Tel: 405-567-3404; 405-567-3080; Fax: 405-567-0364; 405-567-3404. Email: shrine_iop@hotmail.com. Novena to the Infant Jesus of Prague takes place the 17th through 25th of each month. Pilgrimages take place on Sunday prior to the 25th of the month.

SHAWNEE. *St. Gregory's University Endowment Foundation*, 1900 W. MacArthur, 74804. Tel: 405-878-5157; Fax: 405-878-5198. Email: hbmccann@stgregorys.edu. Web: www.stgregorys.edu. Hannah B. McCann, Contact Person.
National Institute on Development Delays, Inc., 1900 W. MacArthur, 74804. Tel: 405-878-5288; Fax: 405-878-5302. Email: frpaul@stgregorys.edu. Web: www.nidd.org. Rev. Paul J. Zahler, O.S.B., Ph.D., Founder/Dir.
Early Developmental Integration Center Tel: 405-878-5289; Fax: 405-878-5302.
C. Harold and Connie Brand Early Child Development Center Tel: 405-878-5289; Fax: 405-878-5302.
Native American Home Start Program formerly Kickapoo Home Start Program Tel: 405-878-5289; Fax: 405-878-5302. Overnight Camp (adults) 30; Child Development Center 45.
Lyle H. Boren Child Development Center Tel: 405-878-5289; Fax: 405-878-5302.
Home Integration, Inc. Tel: 405-878-5289; Fax: 405-878-5302.
St. Michael Foundation, Inc. Tel: 405-878-5289; Fax: 405-878-5302.

RELIGIOUS INSTITUTES OF MEN REPRESENTED IN THE ARCHDIOCESE

For further details refer to the corresponding bracketed number in the Religious Institutes of Men or Women section.

[0200]—*Benedictine Monks*—O.S.B.
[0260]—*Discalced Carmelite Friars* (Oklahoma Prov.)—O.C.D.
[0690]—*Jesuit Fathers* (Missouri Prov.)—S.J.

RELIGIOUS INSTITUTES OF WOMEN REPRESENTED IN THE ARCHDIOCESE

[0100]—*Adorers of the Blood of Christ*—A.S.C.
[0230]—*Benedictine Sisters of Pontifical Jurisdiction*—O.S.B.
[0380]—*Carmelite Sisters of St. Therese of the Infant Jesus*—C.S.T.
[0390]—*Congregation of Missionary Carmelites of St. Therese* (Houston, TX)—C.M.S.T.
[0420]—*Discalced Carmelite Nuns*—O.C.D.
[1070-13]—*Dominican Sisters* (Adrian, MI)—O.P.
[1070-06]—*Dominican Sisters* (Newburgh, NY)—O.P.
[1070-03]—*Dominican Sisters* (Sinsinawa, WI)—O.P.
[1115]—*Dominican Sisters of Peace*—O.P.
[1900]—*Eucharistic Missionaries of St. Theresa* (Mexico)—M.E.S.T.
[1415]—*Franciscan Sisters of Mary*—F.S.M.
[]—*Hermanas Catequistas Guadalupanas*—H.C.G.
[2500]—*Medical Sisters of St. Joseph*—M.S.J.
[1680]—*School Sisters of St. Francis*—S.S.S.F.
[2980]—*Sisters of Congregation de Notre Dame*—C.N.D.
[2575]—*Sisters of Mercy of the Americas*—R.S.M.
[3360]—*Sisters of Providence of St. Mary-of-the-Woods*—S.P.
[3840]—*Sisters of St. Joseph of Carondelet*—C.S.J.
[2150]—*Sisters, Servants of the Immaculate Heart of Mary*—I.H.M.

CEMETERIES

OKLAHOMA CITY. *Resurrection Memorial Cemetery, Inc.*, 7500 W. Britton Rd., 73132. Tel: 405-721-4191; Fax: 405-721-3238. Email: cristford@aol.com. Christina T. Ford, Dir.

NECROLOGY

† Kaylor, Gary, (Retired)—Died Jan. 4, 2009
† Moore, Donald C., (Retired)—Died Oct. 7, 2009
† Schettler, Charles H., (Retired)—Died Dec. 17, 2009

Archdiocese of Omaha

(Archidioecesis Omahensis)

Most Reverend

GEORGE J. LUCAS

Archbishop of Omaha; ordained on May 24, 1975; appointed Bishop of the Diocese of Springfield in Illinois on October 19, 1999; ordained a Bishop and installed December 14, 1999; appointed Archbishop of Omaha June 3, 2009; installed July 22, 2009. *Chancery Office: 100 N. 62nd St., Omaha, NE 68132-2795.*

Most Reverend

ELDEN FRANCIS CURTISS

Retired Archbishop of Omaha; ordained May 24, 1958; appointed Bishop of Helena March 4, 1976; consecrated April 28, 1976; appointed Archbishop of Omaha May 4, 1993; installed June 25, 1993; retired June 3, 2009. *Chancery Office: 100 N. 62nd St., Omaha, NE 68132-2795.*

ESTABLISHED AS A VICARIATE-APOSTOLIC JANUARY 6, 1857.

Square Miles 14,051.

Erected a Diocese October 2, 1885; Archdiocese August 7, 1945.

Comprises the Counties of Boyd, Holt, Merrick, Nance, Boone, Antelope, Knox, Pierce, Madison, Platte, Colfax, Stanton, Wayne, Cedar, Dixon, Dakota, Thurston, Cuming, Dodge, Burt, Washington, Douglas and Sarpy in the State of Nebraska.

For legal titles of parishes and archdiocesan institutions, consult the Chancery Office.

Chancery Office: 100 N. 62nd St., Omaha, NE 68132-2795. Tel: 402-558-3100; Fax: 402-558-3026.

Web: www.archomaha.org

Email: archbishop@archomaha.org

STATISTICAL OVERVIEW

Personnel	
Archbishops	1
Retired Archbishops	1
Retired Bishops	1
Abbots	1
Retired Abbots	2
Priests: Diocesan Active in Diocese	133
Priests: Diocesan Active Outside Diocese	8
Priests: Retired, Sick or Absent	55
Number of Diocesan Priests	196
Religious Priests in Diocese	80
Total Priests in Diocese	276
Extern Priests in Diocese	5
Ordinations:	
Transitional Deacons	1
Permanent Deacons	8
Permanent Deacons in Diocese	237
Total Brothers	23
Total Sisters	288
Parishes	
Parishes	132
With Resident Pastor:	
Resident Diocesan Priests	92
Resident Religious Priests	3
Without Resident Pastor:	
Administered by Priests	35
Administered by Deacons	1
Administered by Lay People	1
Missions	16
Closed Parishes	1
Professional Ministry Personnel:	
Sisters	25
Lay Ministers	106
Welfare	
Catholic Hospitals	4
Total Assisted	239,337
Homes for the Aged	3
Total Assisted	284
Day Care Centers	31
Total Assisted	4,166
Specialized Homes	2
Total Assisted	9,127
Special Centers for Social Services	11
Total Assisted	98,231
Other Institutions	1
Total Assisted	78,387
Educational	
Diocesan Students in Other Seminaries	28
Total Seminarians	28
Colleges and Universities	2
Total Students	8,485
High Schools, Diocesan and Parish	13
Total Students	3,167
High Schools, Private	5
Total Students	2,576
Elementary Schools, Diocesan and Parish	55
Total Students	14,201
Elementary Schools, Private	1
Total Students	72
Non-residential Schools for the Disabled	1
Total Students	57
Catechesis/Religious Education:	
High School Students	3,631
Elementary Students	15,428
Total Students under Catholic Instruction	47,645
Teachers in the Diocese:	
Priests	18
Scholastics	2
Brothers	4
Sisters	20
Lay Teachers	1,539
Vital Statistics	
Receptions into the Church:	
Infant Baptism Totals	4,271
Minor Baptism Totals	176
Adult Baptism Totals	160
Received into Full Communion	483
First Communions	4,181
Confirmations	3,712
Marriages:	
Catholic	814
Interfaith	495
Total Marriages	1,309
Deaths	1,728
Total Catholic Population	224,920
Total Population	909,580

Former Bishops—Rt. Revs. JAMES O'GORMAN, O.C.S.O., D.D., ord. Dec. 21, 1843; Vicar-Apostolic and Titular Bishop of Raphanea; cons. May 8, 1859; died July 4, 1874; JAMES O'CONNOR, D.D., ord. March 25, 1848; Vicar-Apostolic and Titular Bishop of Dibona; cons. Aug. 20, 1876; appt. first Bishop of Omaha, Oct. 2, 1885; died May 27, 1890; RICHARD SCANNELL, D.D., ord. Feb. 26, 1871; cons. Bishop of Concordia, Nov. 30, 1887; transferred to Omaha, Jan. 30, 1891; died Jan. 8, 1916; Most Revs. JEREMIAH J. HARTY, D.D., ord. April 28, 1878; cons. Archbishop of Manila, P.I., Aug. 15, 1903; transferred to Omaha, May 16, 1916; died Oct. 29, 1927; FRANCIS J. L. BECKMAN, S.T.D., D.D. Bishop of Lincoln and Apostolic Administrator of Omaha from June 1, 1926 to July 4, 1928; JOSEPH FRANCIS RUMMEL, D.D., Bishop of Omaha; appt. March 30, 1928; cons. May 29, 1928; installed July 4, 1928; transferred to the Archdiocese of New Orleans, March 9, 1935; died Nov. 8, 1964; JAMES H. RYAN, D.D., appt. Titular Bishop of Modra, Aug. 15, 1933; cons. Oct. 25, 1933; transferred to See of Omaha, Aug. 3, 1935; installed Nov. 21, 1935; elevated to Archepiscopal dignity, Aug. 7, 1945; died Nov. 23, 1947; GERALD T. BERGAN, D.D., ord. Oct. 28, 1915; appt. Bishop of Des Moines, March 24, 1934; cons. June 13, 1934; promoted to Omaha, Feb. 7, 1948; retired June 18, 1969; made Titular Archbishop of Tacarata; died July 12, 1972; DANIEL E. SHEEHAN, D.D., J.C.D., ord. May 23, 1942; appt. Titular Bishop of Capsu and Auxiliary, Jan. 4, 1964; cons. March 19, 1964; succeeded to See, June 11, 1969; retired May 14, 1992; died Oct. 24, 2000; ELDEN FRANCIS CURTISS, ord. May 24, 1958; appt. Bishop of Helena March 4, 1976; cons. April 28, 1976; appt. Archbishop of Omaha May 4, 1993; installed June 25, 1993; retired June 3, 2009.

Vicar General—Very Rev. MICHAEL W. GREWE, V.G.

Chancery Office—100 N. 62nd St., Omaha, 68132-2795. Tel: 402-558-3100; Fax: 402-558-3026. Email: archbishop@archomaha.org. Office Hours: Mon.-Fri. 8:30-5.

Chancellor—Rev. JOSEPH C. TAPHORN, J.C.L.

Vice Chancellor—Deacon TIMOTHY F. MCNEIL.

Moderator of the Curia—Rev. GREGORY P. BAXTER, S.T.L.

Finance Director (canonical)—Mr. HERBERT L. KARRER.

Metropolitan Tribunal—100 N. 62nd St., Omaha, 68132.

Judicial Vicar—Rev. PATRICK C. HARRISON, J.C.L.

Judges—Rev. RYAN P. LEWIS, J.C.L., S.T.L.; Deacon ROBERT J. OVERKAMP, J.C.L.; Rev. JOSEPH C. TAPHORN, J.C.L.

Promoter of Justice—Rev. R. MICHAEL FITZPATRICK, J.C.L., S.T.L.

Defenders of the Bond—Revs. R. MICHAEL FITZPATRICK, J.C.L., S.T.L.; MICHAEL F. GUTGSELL, J.C.L.

Appeal Court— The Tribunal of the Archdiocese of St. Louis, MO is the Appeal Court for Omaha.

Consultors—Very Rev. MICHAEL W. GREWE, V.G.; Revs. THOMAS E. BAUWENS; R. MICHAEL FITZPATRICK, J.C.L., S.T.L.; NORMAN F. HUNKE; DANIEL L. WITTROCK; MICHAEL F. GUTGSELL, J.C.L.

Deans—Revs. JAMES M. BUCKLEY, U.S.E.; ALFRED J. SALANITRO, U.S.C.; FRANK J. BAUMERT, U.N.E.; GREGORY P. BAXTER, S.T.L., U.W.C.; DENNIS A. HANNEMAN, Sub. S.; FRANKLIN A. DVORAK, Sub. N.; THOMAS W. WEISBECKER, R.S.W.; JOHN S. ANDREWS, R.N.C.; PATRICK A. MCLAUGHLIN, R.S.E.; DERMOT J. DUNNE, R.C.; JAMES V. KRAMPER, R.N.W.; DAVID F. LIEWER, R.N.E.

Finance Council—Rev. R. MICHAEL FITZPATRICK, J.C.L., S.T.L.; Very Rev. MICHAEL W. GREWE, V.G.; Rev. GREGORY P. BAXTER, S.T.L.; Mr. HERBERT L. KARRER; Rev. JOSEPH C. TAPHORN, J.C.L.; Mr. RICK WITT; Rev. DAMIAN ZUERLEIN; Mr. HERMAN D. WEIST.

Archdiocesan Offices and Directors

Cemeteries—VACANT, Dir.

Censor Librorum—Rev. JOSEPH C. TAPHORN, J.C.L.

Omaha Priests Retirement Plan and Trust, The—Most Rev. GEORGE J. LUCAS; Rev. Msgr. JAMES R. CAIN, J.C.D. (Retired); Very Rev. MICHAEL W. GREWE, V.G.; Mr. JAMES KINEEN; Mr. JOSEPH BEVERIDGE; Mr. HERBERT L. KARRER.

Ecumenical Officer—Rev. RYAN P. LEWIS, J.C.L., S.T.L.

Worship Office—Bro. WILLIAM WOEGER, F.S.C., Dir.

Council of Catholic Women, Archdiocesan—Rev. JAMES V. KRAMPER, Archdiocesan Moderator, Mailing Address: P.O. Box 37, Ewing, 68735. Tel: 402-626-7605.

Diaconate Program—RALPH B. O'DONNELL, Urban Dir., 4112 S. 26th St., Omaha, 68107. Tel: 402-733-8811; Rev. KEITH D. REZAC, Rural Dir., 118 W. Willow St., Pierce, 68767. Tel: 402-329-4200.

Catholic Schools Office—Rev. Msgr. JAMES E. GILG, Supt. Schools, 3212 N. 60th St., Omaha, 68104. Tel: 402-554-8493.

Catholic Faith Formation Office—3212 N. 60th St., P.O. Box 4130, Omaha, 68104. Rev. MATTHEW J. GUTOWSKI, Dir.

Administrative Services Office—Mr. HERBERT L. KARRER, Dir., 100 N. 62nd St., Omaha, 68132. Tel: 402-558-3100; Fax: 402-561-1210.

Information Technology Office—Mr. SHAWN M. BAAS, Dir., 3300 N. 60th St., Omaha, 68104. Tel: 402-557-5500; Fax: 402-827-3793.

Stewardship & Development Office—Mrs. MARY JEWELL, Dir., Mailing Address: P.O. Box 4130, Omaha, 68104-0130. Tel: 402-554-8493; Fax: 402-551-3426.

Family Life Office—Mrs. VALERIE CONZETT, D.Min., L.P.C., Dir., 3214 N. 60th St., Omaha, 68104-3495. Tel: 402-551-9003; 888-800-8352; Fax: 402-551-3050. Email: vhconzett@archomaha.org. Areas of Ministry: Aging, Black Catholics, Disabilities, Hispanic Marriage and Family Life, Marriage and Family Life, Media Center, Natural Family Planning, Respect Life Apostolate, & Rural Life.

Newspaper— "The Catholic Voice" Mr. CHARLIE WIESER, Editor, 6060 N.W. Radial Hwy., P.O. Box 4010, Omaha, 68104. Tel: 402-558-6611; Fax: 402-558-6614.

Propagation of the Faith—Rev. GREGORY P. BAXTER, S.T.L., Dir., 100 N. 62nd St., Omaha, 68132. Tel: 402-558-3100; Fax: 402-558-3026.

Priests' Council—

Officers—Revs. MICHAEL F. GUTGSELL, J.C.L., Pres.; DERMOT J. DUNNE, Vice Pres.; PATRICK A. MCLAUGHLIN, Sec.; DAMIAN J. ZUERLEIN, Treas.

Age Groups—Rev. Msgr. JAMES E. GILG; Revs. GARY L. OSTRANDER; DAMIAN J. ZUERLEIN; FRANK J. BAUMERT; DANIEL L. WITTROCK; JOHN L. PIETRAMALE; MARK T. BERAN; JOHN P. BROHEIMER.

Religious Orders—Revs. MICHAEL DODD, S.S.C.; THOMAS AQUINAS LEITNER, O.S.B.; GEORGE SULLIVAN, S.J.

Deans—Revs. ALFRED J. SALANITRO, (USC); JAMES M. BUCKLEY, (USE); FRANK J. BAUMERT, (UNE); THOMAS W. WEISBECKER, (RSW); JOHN S. ANDREWS, (RNC); JAMES V. KRAMPER, (RNW); PATRICK A. MCLAUGHLIN, (RSE); DAVID F. LIEWER, (RNE); DERMOT J. DUNNE, (RC); DENNIS A. HANNEMAN, (Sub. S.); FRANKLIN A. DVORAK, (Sub.N.); GREGORY P. BAXTER, S.T.L., (UWC).

Archbishop's Appointees—Revs. GREGORY P. BAXTER, S.T.L.; PATRICK C. HARRISON, J.C.L.; JOSEPH C. TAPHORN, J.C.L.

Ex Officio (Consultors)—Very Rev. MICHAEL W. GREWE, V.G., Vicar Gen.; Revs. THOMAS E. BAUWENS, Consultor; NORMAN F. HUNKE; DANIEL L. WITTROCK; MICHAEL F. GUTGSELL, J.C.L.; R. MICHAEL FITZPATRICK, J.C.L., S.T.L.

St. Cecilia Institute for Laity Formation—Bro. WILLIAM J. WOEGER, F.S.C., Provost, 3900 Webster St., Omaha, 68131. Tel: 402-553-5524; Fax: 402-558-1325. Web: www.archomaha.org/education/sci.

Omaha. Archdiocesan Deposit and Loan Fund, Inc.— A pool of funds from archdiocesan parishes providing low interest loans for capital improvements and new construction by archdiocesan parishes. This nonprofit religious, charitable and educational corporation, whose president is the Archdiocese of Omaha, is duly constituted under the laws of the State of Nebraska. Mr. LEE KARRER, Finance Dir., 100 N. 62nd St., Omaha, 68132. Tel: 402-558-3100; Fax: 402-561-1210.

Omaha. Archdiocesan Retreat and Conference Centers— Located in renovated Sheehan Center; overnight, day and weekend accommodations for teens, young adults and adult groups, large and small meeting space, chapel and food service area. *3330 N. 60th St., Omaha, 68104.* Tel: 402-558-1442; Fax: 402-551-1482. GARY BOSANEK, Dir.

Servant Minister—Rev. THOMAS A. GREISEN.

Victim Assistance Coordinator—MARY BETH HANUS, Dir., Mailing Address: P.O. Box 4130, Omaha, 68104-0130. Tel: 402-827-3798; 888-808-9055. Email: mbhanus@archomaha.org.

Vocations Office—Rev. PAUL C. HOESING, 100 N. 62nd St., Omaha, 68132. Tel: 402-558-3100; Fax: 402-558-3026. Email: pchoesing@archomaha.org. Web: www.archomaha.org/vocations.

CLERGY, PARISHES, MISSIONS AND PAROCHIAL SCHOOLS

CITY OF OMAHA

(DOUGLAS COUNTY)

1—ST. CECILIA CATHEDRAL (1888) Revs. Michael F. Gutgsell; Mark J. McKercher.
Res.: 701 N. 40 St., 68131. Tel: 402-551-2313; Fax: 402-551-2306. Email: stceciliacathedral@stceciliacathedral.org. Web: www.stceciliacathedral.org.
School—Tel: 402-556-6655; Fax: 402-502-3048. Paulette Rourke, Prin. Lay Teachers 24; Students 295.
Catechesis/Religious Program—Students 42.

2—ST. ADALBERT (1919) Rev. William D. L'Heureux. In Res., Rev. Carl F. Sodoro.
Res.: 2617 S. 31st St., 68105. Tel: 402-345-1621.
Catechesis/Religious Program—2124 S. 32nd Ave., 68105. Tel: 402-341-5604. Students 4.

3—ST. AGNES (1889), (Irish—Spanish), Merged with Our Lady of Guadalupe, Omaha to form Our Lady of Guadalupe - St. Agnes Parish, Omaha.

4—ST. ANDREW KIM TAEGON CATHOLIC COMMUNITY Rev. Paul Saewan Oh.
2617 S. 31st St., 68105. Tel: 402-345-1621.
Catechesis/Religious Program—Rosa Hwang Po, D.R.E. Students 9.

5—ST. ANN (1917), (Italian—Hispanic), Closed. For inquiries for parish records contact St. Peter, Omaha.

6—ST. ANTHONY (1907), (Lithuanian), Rev. Frank A. Partusch.
Res.: 5401 S. 33rd St., 68107. Tel: 402-733-2423.
Catechesis/Religious Program—Students 3.

7—ASSUMPTION, B.V.M. (1894), (Czech), Rev. James E. Keiter.
Res.: 5434 S. 22nd St., 68107. Tel: 402-734-4500; Fax: 402-734-4501. Email: jkeiter@assumptionguadalupe.com.
Catechesis/Religious Program—Participate in Our Lady of Guadalupe/St. Agnes program., 4930 S. 23rd St., 68107. Tel: 402-731-2196; Fax: 402-827-6764.

8—ST. BENEDICT THE MOOR (1919) Revs. Albert R. Thelen, S.J.; Kenneth P. Vavrina; Deacons Frank Barbour; Ernie Spicer.
Res.: 2423 Grant St., 68111. Tel: 402-348-0631; Fax: 402-342-4451. Email: stbenedictthemoor.oma@archomaha.org.
Catechesis/Religious Program—Students 56.

9—ST. BERNARD (1905) Rev. Gerald P. Melchior; Deacons Donald Kemp, (Retired); Charles Baughman; Edwin Osterhaus; Paul Dreismeier; Timothy F. McNeil; David Christensen. In Res., Rev. Matthew J. Gutowski.
Res.: 3601 N. 65 St., 68104. Tel: 402-551-0269; Fax: 402-551-2311. Web: stbernardomaha.org.
School—Tel: 402-553-4993; Fax: 402-551-4939. Ellie Seward, Prin. Lay Teachers 13; Students 184.
Catechesis/Religious Program—Tel: 402-556-1679. JoAnne Raleigh, D.R.E.; Deb Waskowiak, Dir. Youth Min. Tel: 402-934-3599. Students 83.

10—BLESSED SACRAMENT (1919) Rev. Craig J. Loecker, Admin.
Res.: 3020 Curtis Ave., 68111. Tel: 402-455-5200; Fax: 402-455-6699. Email: admin@blessedsacrament.ohmcoxmail.com. Web: www.blessedsacramentomaha.org.
School—6316 N. 30th St., 68111. Tel: 402-455-4030; Fax: 402-455-6699. Lay Teachers 12; Students 153.
Catechesis/Religious Program—Students 9.

11—ST. BRIDGET (1887), (Irish), Rev. Ralph B. O'Donnell.
Res.: 4112 S. 26th St., 68107. Tel: 402-733-8811; Fax: 402-731-9937.
Catechesis/Religious Program—Tel: 402-734-5227. Students 5.

12—ST. CHARLES BORROMEO (2005) Rev. Norman F. Hunke.
P. O. Box 625, Gretna, 68028. Tel: 402-916-9730; Fax: 402-916-9740. Email: parish@scbccomaha.org. Web: www.stcharlesomaha.org.
Catechesis/Religious Program—Amanda Hoeke, D.R.E.; Jackie Schuler, D.R.E. Students 169.

13—CHRIST THE KING (1953) Revs. Steven J. Stillmunks; Bert Boschert, S.J.; Diane Sullivan, Dir. of Adult Faith Formation.
Res.: 654 S. 86th St., 68114. Tel: 402-391-3606; Fax: 402-391-1498. Email: troiac@ctkomaha.org. Web: www.ctkomaha.org.
School—831 S. 88th St., 68114. Tel: 402-391-0977; Fax: 402-391-2418. Email: ctkschool@ctkomaha.org. Lay Teachers 27; Students 363.
Catechesis/Religious Program—Tel: 402-391-3624. Email: warnera@ctkomaha.org. Ann Warner, D.R.E. Students 125.

14—ST. ELIZABETH ANN (1981) Revs. Franklin A. Dvorak; Bernard Starman, Asst.; Deacons Jack Finney; Ernie Gencarelli; Martin Crowley; Dennis Connor; John Dagerman; Duane Karmazin; David Klein.
Res.: 5419 N. 114th St., 68164. Tel: 402-493-2186; Fax: 402-493-0630.
See St. James-Seton School, Omaha under Elementary Schools, Interparochial located in the Institution section.
Catechesis/Religious Program—Tel: 402-572-0369; Fax: 402-572-0347. Ms. Jo Kusek, D.R.E. Students 208.

15—ST. FRANCES CABRINI (1856) Rev. James F. Clifton, S.J.
Res.: 1334 S. 9th St., 68108. Tel: 402-342-2464; Fax: 402-342-2470. Email: stfrancescabrini.oma@archomaha.org.
Catechesis/Religious Program—Students 16.
See All Saints Catholic School, Omaha under Elementary Schools, Interparochial located in the Institution section.

16—ST. FRANCIS ASSISI, (Polish—Spanish), Rev. William E. Sanderson.
Res.: 3529 Q St., 68107. Tel: 402-731-0204.
Catechesis/Religious Program—Students 237.

17—HOLY CROSS (1922) Rev. Carl A. Salanitro; Deacons George Elster; Timothy A. Mulcahy.
Res.: 4803 William St., 68106. Tel: 402-553-7500; Fax: 402-553-7735.
School—Tel: 402-551-3773; Fax: 402-556-1896. Lay Teachers 18; Students 290.
Catechesis/Religious Program—Students 67.

18—HOLY FAMILY (1876) Deacon Ralph L. Hueser, Admin.
Res.: 1715 Izard St., 68102. Tel: 402-345-1062; Fax: 402-344-8136. Email: holyfamilyomaha@cox.net.
Catechesis/Religious Program—Students 1.

19—HOLY GHOST (1918) Rev. Gregory Benkowski; Deacons Tom Schulte; Paul Eubanks; Andy Sommer; Al Aulner; Tim Leininger.
Res.: 5219 S. 53rd St., 68117. Tel: 402-731-3176; Fax: 402-738-1409. Email: parishsecretary@holyghostomaha.org. Web: www.holyghostomaha.com.
School—(Grades PreK-8), 5203 Q St., 68117. Tel: 402-731-5161; Fax: 402-731-5174. Mrs. Dana Martin, Prin. Lay Teachers 13; Students 168.
Catechesis/Religious Program— Eleanor Morley, D.R.E. Students 68.

20—HOLY NAME (1917) Rev. Frank J. Baumert.
Res.: 3014 N. 45th St., 68104. Tel: 402-451-6622; Fax: 402-457-6901. Email: holynameparish@holynameomaha.org. Web: www.holynameomaha.org.
School—(Grades PreSchool-8) Tel: 402-451-5403; Fax: 402-453-7950. Sofia Kock, Prin. Lay Teachers 19; Students 187.
Catechesis/Religious Program—Students 14.

21—IMMACULATE CONCEPTION, B.V.M. (1897), (Polish), Revs. John A. Brancich, F.S.S.P.; Terrence Gordon, F.S.S.P., Parochial Vicar.
Res.: 2708 S. 24th St., 68108. Tel: 402-342-1074; Fax: 402-505-7616.
See All Saints Catholic School, Omaha under Elementary Schools, Interparochial located in the Institution section.
Catechesis/Religious Program—Students 39.

22—ST. JAMES (1963) Revs. Richard J. Reiser; Roger Kalscheuer; Deacons Jerry Gau; Stan Kurtz; Pat Lenz; Wayne Young; Richard Hopkins; Randy Grosse; William Hecht.
Res.: 9025 Larimore Ave., 68134. Tel: 402-572-0499; Fax: 402-573-9345. Email:

rectory@stjamescatholicchurch.org. Web: www.stjamescatholicchurch.org.
See St. James-Seton School, Omaha under Elementary Schools, Interparochial located in the Institution section.
Catechesis/Religious Program—Tel: 402-572-0369; Fax: 402-572-0347. Ms. Jo Kusek, D.R.E. Students 227.

23—St. Joan of Arc (1955) Rev. Daniel F. Soltys; Deacon Ronald R. Ryan. In Res., Rev. Patrick C. Harrison.
Res.: 3122 S. 74th St., 68124. Tel: 402-393-2005; Fax: 402-398-9438.
School—7430 Hascall St., 68124. Tel: 402-393-2314; Fax: 402-393-4405. Lay Teachers 13; Students 111.
Catechesis/Religious Program—Tel: 402-391-1906; 402-393-2315. Marilyn Opitz, D.R.E. Students 96.

24—St. John (1897) Revs. Bert Thelen, S.J.; Philip R. Amidon, S.J.; Paul A. Mahowald, S.J.; Deacon Ken Kalkowski.
Office: 2500 California Pl., 68178. Tel: 402-280-3031; Fax: 402-280-2465.
Catechesis/Religious Program—Students 10.

25—St. John Vianney (1974) Rev. R. Patrick McCaslin; Deacons Frank Telich; John Kronschnabel; Harold Sawtelle; Joseph Choi; Chuck Luczynski. In Res., Rev. Paul L. Vasquez.
Res.: 5801 Oak Hills Dr., 68137. Tel: 402-895-0808. Web: www.sjvomaha.org.
Catechesis/Religious Program—Tel: 402-895-0896; Fax: 402-932-1336. Sr. Marietta Kerkvliet, O.S.B. Students 347.

26—St. Joseph (1887), (German—Hispanic), Rev. William D. Bond.
Church: 1723 S. 17th St., 68108. Tel: 402-342-1618; Fax: 402-342-2640.
See All Saints Catholic School, Omaha under Elementary Schools, Interparochial located in the Institution section.
Catechesis/Religious Program—Tel: 402-502-1392. Students 373.

27—St. Leo (1978) Revs. Harold J. Buse; An Duy Phan; Deacons George Knockenhauer; Jerry Steenson; Ira Miller; Reinold ter Kuille.
1920 N. 102nd St., 68114. Tel: 402-397-0407; Fax: 402-397-2887. Email: dina_turco@stleo.net. Web: www.stleo.net.
See St. Pius X-St. Leo School, Omaha under Elementary Schools, Interparochial located in the Institution section.
Catechesis/Religious Program—Tel: 402-397-0407, Ext. 206. Students 402.

28—St. Margaret Mary (1919) Revs. Gregory P. Baxter; Jeffrey J. Mollner. In Res., Revs. Paul C. Hoesing; Joseph C. Taphorn.
Res.: 6116 Dodge St., 68132-2114. Tel: 402-558-2255; Fax: 402-551-6644. Web: www.smmomaha.org.
School—123 N. 61st St., 68132. Tel: 402-551-6663; Fax: 402-551-5631. Lay Teachers 24; Students 570.
Catechesis/Religious Program—Tel: 402-558-9119; Fax: 402-551-5631. Students 116.

29—St. Mary (1901) Rev. William E. Sanderson.
Res.: 3529 Q St., 68107. Tel: 402-731-0204; Fax: 402-731-0793.
Catechesis/Religious Program—

30—St. Mary Magdalene (1868) Rev. Msgr. James E. Gilg. In Res., Rev. James F. Schwertley (Retired).
Res.: 109 S. 19th St., 68102. Tel: 402-342-4807; Fax: 402-344-0941.
See All Saints Catholic School, Omaha under Elementary Schools, Interparochial located in the Institution section.

31—Mary Our Queen (1963) Revs. Robert K. English; Christopher N. Onuoha; Francis D. Valerio; Deacons Paul Rooney; Steve Floersch; Robert Hamilton.
Res.: 3535 S. 119th St., 68144. Tel: 402-333-8662; Fax: 402-333-4504. Email: pastor.maryourqueen.oma@archomaha.org. Web: www.maryourqueenchurch.com.
Church: 3504 S. 118th St., 68144.
School—3405 S. 119th St., 68144. Tel: 402-333-8663; Fax: 402-334-3948. Web: www.mogschool.org. Lay Teachers 31; Students 514.
Catechesis/Religious Program—Tel: 402-333-8231, Ext. 225. Barb Eastridge, D.R.E. Students 279.

32—Mother of Perpetual Help (1975), (Church of the Deaf) Marlene Rowe, Lay Coord. Tel: 402-493-7220.
Res.: 5215 Seward St., 68104. Tel: 402-558-4214.
Our Lady of Fatima Catholic Community—Rev. Nguyen Loi.
Rectory—709 S. 28th St., 68105-1511. Tel: 402-341-4560; Fax: 402-341-6483.

33—Our Lady of Guadalupe (1927), (Spanish), Merged with St. Agnes, Omaha to form Our Lady of Guadalupe - St. Agnes Parish, Omaha.

34—Our Lady of Guadalupe - St. Agnes Parish Revs. Carl J. Zoucha; Jose Mendoza (Venezuela); Deacons Joe Ramirez; Duane Bronk; Luis Valadez; Jesus Herrera; Martin Franco.
4930 S. 23rd St., 68107. In Res., Revs. Bill Bernardo Schmitt; Charles "Chuck" Lintz.
Res.: 2221 "Q" St., 68107. Tel: 402-731-0100.
Res.: 2310 O St., 68107. Tel: 402-731-2196; Fax: 402-827-6764.
Catechesis/Religious Program—Tel: 402-738-8240. Marcella Cervantes, D.R.E. Students 850.
Convent—St. Agnes, 5225 S. 23rd St., 68107. Tel: 402-731-1005.

35—Our Lady of Lourdes (1917) Rev. William D. L'Heureux; Deacons Frank Hilt; Robert Pickett.
Res.: 2110 S. 32nd Ave., 68105. Tel: 402-346-0900; Fax: 402-344-3315. Email: ourladyoflourdesoma@archomaha.org.
School—2124 S. 32nd Ave., 68105. Tel: 402-341-5604. Web: www.omahaourladyoflourdes.com. William Kelly, Prin. Lay Teachers 20; Students 257.
Catechesis/Religious Program—Students 294.

36—St. Patrick (1883) Rev. James M. Buckley.
Res.: 1404 Castelar St., 68108. Tel: 402-341-1305; Fax: 402-342-5510. Email: stpatricko@cox.net. Web: www.stpatrickomaha.com.
See All Saints Catholic School, Omaha under Elementary Schools, Interparochial located in the Institution section.
Catechesis/Religious Program—Students 45.

37—St. Patrick (Elkhorn) formerly St. Patrick (1868) [CEM] Revs. Ronald S. Wasikowski; Rodney T. Adams.
Res.: 20500 W. Maple Rd., P.O. Box 10, 68022. Tel: 402-289-4289; Fax: 402-763-9530. Web: www.stpatselkhorn.org.
School—(Grades PreK-8) Tel: 402-289-5407. Donald Ridder, Prin. Lay Teachers 33; Students 695.

38—St. Peter (1887) Revs. Damien Cook; S. Anthony Weidner; Deacon John Zak.
Catechesis/Religious Program—Tel: 402-289-4947. Mary McMahon, D.R.E. Students 649.
Res.: 709 S. 28th St., 68105-1511. Tel: 402-341-4560; Fax: 402-341-6483. Email: secretary@stpeterchurch.net. Web: www.stpeterchurch.net.
Catechesis/Religious Program—Students 380.

39—SS. Peter and Paul (1917), (Croatian), Rev. Frank A. Partusch.
Res.: 5912 S. 36th St., 68107. Tel: 402-731-4578; Fax: 402-738-8808.
School—Tel: 402-731-4713; Fax: 402-731-2633. Richard Leimbach, Prin. Lay Teachers 12; Students 158.
Catechesis/Religious Program—Tel: 402-733-3344; Fax: 402-731-2633. Bernice Pfeifer, D.R.E. Students 160.

40—St. Philip Neri (1904) Rev. Craig J. Loecker; Sr. Susan Ivis, Pastoral Min. Tel: 402-451-6921; Deacon Fred Hendrick.
Res.: 8200 N. 30th St., 68112. Tel: 402-455-1289; Fax: 402-455-8398. Web: www.spnomaha.org.
School—8202 N. 31st St., 68112. Tel: 402-455-8666; Fax: 402-453-3620. Richard Cuva, Prin. Lay Teachers 13; Students 175.
Catechesis/Religious Program—Tel: 402-455-2190. Email: reducation@hotmail.com. Marsha Moon, D.R.E. Students 43.

41—St. Pius X (1954) Revs. John L. Pietramale; Anthony Nkyi (Ghana).
Res.: 6905 Blondo St., 68104. Tel: 402-558-8446; Fax: 402-558-4986. Web: www.stpiusxomaha.org.
See St. Pius X-St. Leo School, Omaha under Elementary Schools, Interparochial located in the Institution section.
Catechesis/Religious Program—Tel: 402-558-1898. Patty Griffith, D.R.E. Students 84.

42—St. Richard (1963) Closed. for inquiries for parish records, please contact Holy Name Parish, Omaha.

43—St. Robert Bellarmine (1966) Revs. Donald W. Shane; Marc Lim; Deacons Larry Sampier; Thomas Murphy; Michael Fletcher; Robert Jergovie; Jack Miller; Robert Jergovic.
Res.: 11802 Pacific St., 68154. Tel: 402-333-8989; Fax: 402-333-5489. Web: www.stroberts.com.
School—(Grades PreK-8), 11900 Pacific St., 68154. Tel: 402-334-1929; Fax: 402-333-7188. Sandra Suiter, Prin. Lay Teachers 29; Students 595.
Catechesis/Religious Program—Tel: 402-333-1959. Deb Poledna, D.R.E. Students 294.

44—St. Rose (1919) Rev. Ralph B. O'Donnell. In Res., Rev. Thomas A. Greisen.
Res.: 4102 S. 13th St., 68107. Tel: 402-733-9327; Fax: 402-731-9937. Email: st.roseomaha@cox.net.
Catechesis/Religious Program—Students 1.

45—Sacred Heart (1890) Rev. Thomas M. Fangman; Deacons Charles Weskirchen; James Chambers; Richard Crotty.
Res.: 2218 Binney St., 68110. Tel: 402-451-5755; 402-451-7897; Fax: 402-451-1731.
School—Tel: 402-451-5858; Fax: 402-451-7480. Lay Teachers 15; Students 158.
Catechesis/Religious Program—2207 Wirt St., 68110. Students 115.

46—St. Stanislaus (1919), (Polish), Rev. R. Michael Fitzpatrick; Deacons Daniel Saniuk; James Staroski.
Res.: 4002 J St., 68107. Tel: 402-731-4152; Fax: 402-731-4389. Email: rfitzk@aol.com.
School—(Grades K-8) Tel: 402-731-0484; Fax: 402-733-4898. Lay Teachers 8; Students 108.
Catechesis/Religious Program—At and with SS. Peter & Paul, Omaha. Students 18.

47—St. Stephen the Martyr (1989) Revs. James R. Tiegs; Andrew L. Sohm; Gerald "Chi" Igboanusi; Deacons Ernest Abbott Jr.; Dennis Dethlefs; Paul Tomaso; C. Martin Warwick; Daniel F. Blanton; Jerry Kozney.
Res.: 16701 S St., 68135. Tel: 402-895-1811; Fax: 402-896-1990. Email: stephen.martyr@stephen.org. Web: www.stephen.org.
Church: 16701 S St., 68135. Tel: 402-896-9675; Fax: 402-896-1990.
School—Tel: 402-896-0754; Fax: 402-861-4640. Dr. David Peters, Prin. Lay Teachers 39; Students 892.
Catechesis/Religious Program—Tel: 402-896-5683; Fax: 402-861-4590. Mary Maguire, D.R.E. Students 1,298.

48—St. Therese of the Child Jesus (1918) Rev. Kenneth P. Vavrina.
Res.: 2423 Grant St., 68111. Tel: 402-348-0631; Fax: 402-342-4451. Email: stbenedictthemoor.oma@archomaha.org.
Church: 1423 Ogden St., 68110.
Catechesis/Religious Program—Felix Cortes, D.R.E. Students 67.

49—St. Thomas More (1958) Revs. Ryan P. Lewis; Kizito Raphael Okhuoya (Nigeria).
Res.: 4804 Grover St., 68106. Tel: 402-556-1456; Fax: 402-556-1395.
School—3515 S. 48th Ave., 68106. Tel: 402-551-9504; Fax: 402-551-9507. Web: www.stmbengals.org. Lay Teachers 18; Students 200.
Catechesis/Religious Program—Tel: 402-551-9507; Fax: 402-551-9507. Students 56.

50—St. Vincent de Paul (1991) Revs. Daniel J. Kampschneider; Joseph G. Broudou; Deacons Donald K. Clausen; William J. Barnes; Gary J. Hennessey; Richard Jizba; James G. Bollman; Jay Reilly; Mike Poulin, Pastoral Min.; Wendy Everson, Pastoral Min.; Steve Nespor, Dir. Youth Min.; Kathy Mayer, Dir. Worship; Bob Verkuilen, Dir. Devel.
Mailing Address: 14330 Eagle Run Dr., 68164.
Res.: 14217 Eagle Run Dr., 68164. Tel: 402-496-7988 (Pastoral Center); 402-498-8425 (Rectory); Fax: 402-496-9933 (Pastoral Center). Web: www.svdpomaha.org.
School—Tel: 402-492-2111. Web: www.svdpomaha.org. Dr. Barbara Marchese, Prin. Lay Teachers 39; Students 785.
Catechesis/Religious Program—Tel: 402-493-1642; Fax: 402-496-9933. Vicki Smith, D.R.E. Students 524.

51—St. Wenceslaus (1877), (Czech), Revs. Melvin J. Merwald; Michael Swanton; Deacons Donald Cowles; Joe Kulus; Michael J. DeSelm.
Res.: 15353 Pacific St., 68154. Tel: 402-330-0304; Fax: 402-330-1476. Web: www.stwenceslaus.org.
School—(Grades K-8) Tel: 402-330-4356. William Huben, Prin. Sisters 1; Lay Teachers 37; Students 782.
Catechesis/Religious Program—Tel: 402-330-1889. Joan Fleming, D.R.E. Students 606.

OUTSIDE THE CITY OF OMAHA

Albion, Boone Co., St. Michael (1877) [CEM] Rev. Stanley T. Schmit.
Res.: 524 W. Church St., 68620. Tel: 402-395-2393.
School—Tel: 402-395-2926; Fax: 402-395-2926. Lay Teachers 7; Students 131.
Catechesis/Religious Program—Students 132.

Aloys, Cuming Co., St. Aloysius (1891), (German), [CEM] Rev. Gerald E. Gonderinger.
Mailing Address: 343 N. Monitor St., West Point, 68788.
Res. & Church: 700 Hwy. 32, West Point, 68788. Tel: 402-372-2188; Fax: 402-372-3563. Email: stmary@yahoo.com. Web: myweb.cableone.net/stmary.
Catechesis/Religious Program—Students 2.

Atkinson, Holt Co., St. Joseph (1886) [CEM] Rev. LuVerne W. Steffes.
Res.: 317 W. State St., P.O. Box 220, 68713. Tel: 402-925-2122.
School—Tel: 402-925-2104; Fax: 402-925-2104. Email: stjoeschool@esu8.org. Lay Teachers 5; Students 41.
Catechesis/Religious Program—Students 83.

Bancroft, Cuming Co., Holy Cross (1884), (German), [CEM] Rev. Paul R. Ortmeier.
Res.: P.O. Box 524, Lyons, 68038. Tel: 402-687-2102; Fax: 402-687-2102. Web: www.stjoseph-holycross.com.
Catechesis/Religious Program—Students 49.

BATTLE CREEK, MADISON CO., ST. PATRICK'S (1875) [CEM] Rev. Joseph M. Wray; Deacon Tom Hughes.
Res.: 107 N. Third St., P.O. Box 40, 68715. Tel: 402-675-2485. Email: stpatrick@frontier.com.
Catechesis/Religious Program—Tel: 402-675-6345. Teresa Wilkinson, D.R.E. Students 104.
Mission—St. Francis de Sales Schoolcraft, Madison Co.

BEEMER, CUMING CO., HOLY CROSS (1913) [CEM] Rev. William J. Safranek.
Res.: 517 Fraisier St. N., P.O. Box 212, 68716. Tel: 402-528-3475; Fax: 402-528-3475. Email: hcbeemer@gpcom.net.
Catechesis/Religious Program—Students 32.

BELLEVUE, SARPY CO.

1—ST. BERNADETTE (1963) Rev. Alfred J. Salanitro; Deacons Ron Casart; Gary Chladek; Pete Digilio, (Retired); Sebastian Enzolera. In Res., Most Rev. Anthony Milone (Retired).
Res.: 7600 S. 42nd St., 68147. Tel: 402-731-4694; Fax: 402-733-4890. Email: terriamac@gmail.com. Web: www.stbernadetteparish.org.
School—Tel: 402-731-3033; Fax: 402-731-8735. Mrs. Therese Nelson, Prin. Lay Teachers 18; Students 270.
Catechesis/Religious Program—Fax: 402-733-4890. Jacquelyn Diane Van Ornam, D.R.E. Students 110.

2—ST. MARY (1921) Revs. Dennis A. Hanneman; Mark M. Bridgman; Deacons Ralph Hueser; Duane Iwanski; Chuck L'Archevesque; Andy Foray; John Huck; John Wacha; Lee Mayhan; Al Belcher.
Res.: 811 W. 23rd Ave., 68005. Tel: 402-291-1350; Fax: 402-291-1375. Email: rectory@stmarysbellevue.com. Web: www.stmarysbellevue.com.
School—(Grades PreK-8), 903 W. Mission Ave., 68005. Tel: 402-291-1694; Fax: 402-291-9667. Cheryl Castle, Prin.; Mary Ellen Reckmeyer, Librarian. Lay Teachers 15; Students 229.
Catechesis/Religious Program—Tel: 402-291-7222; Fax: 402-291-3964. Elizabeth Tomaso, D.R.E. Students 311.

3—ST. MATTHEW THE EVANGELIST CHURCH OF BELLEVUE (1996) Rev. Dennis R. Stolinski. In Res., Rev. Msgr. Thomas D. Furlong (Retired).
Res.: 3605 Looking Glass Dr., 68123. Tel: 402-292-7418; Fax: 402-292-7421. Email: saintmatthew@stmatthewsomaha.org. Web: www.homestead.com/stmatthewschurch.
School—(Grades PreSchool-8), 12210 S. 36th St., 68123. Tel: 402-291-2030; Fax: 402-291-2047. Web: www.stmatthewsschool.net. Donna Blazek, Prin. Lay Teachers 14; Students 178.
Catechesis/Religious Program—Students 179.

BLAIR, WASHINGTON CO., ST. FRANCIS BORGIA (1865) [CEM] Rev. Mario D. Rapose; Rebecca Crotty, Bookkeeper.
Res.: 2005 Davis Dr., 68008. Tel: 402-426-3823; Fax: 402-426-5131. Email: office@stfrancisborgia.org.
Catechesis/Religious Program—Tel: 402-426-5145. Deborah Lager, D.R.E. Students 289.

BLOOMFIELD, KNOX CO., ST. ANDREW (1892) Rev. Michael D. Schmitz.
Res.: 1316 W. 5th St., Crofton, 68730. Tel: 402-388-4814; Fax: 402-388-2680. Email: strosecrofton@gpcom.net.
Catechesis/Religious Program—Tel: 402-373-2696; Fax: 402-373-2233. Barb Jackson, D.R.E. Students 81.

BOW VALLEY, CEDAR CO., SS. PETER AND PAUL, Merged with Sacred Heart, Wynot; Ss. Philip and James, St. James and Immaculate Conception, St. Helena to form Holy Family Church of Cedar County, Hartington.

BOYS TOWN, DOUGLAS CO., IMMACULATE CONCEPTION B.V.M. (1936) Revs. Steven Boes; Valentine J. Peter.
Mailing Address: 13703 Dowd Dr., 68010. In Res., Rev. Msgr. Peter F. Dunne (Retired); Revs. Eugene McReynolds, O.S.B.; Clifford J. Stevens (Retired).
Parish Center: 13900 Dowd Dr., 68010. Tel: 402-498-1464; Fax: 402-493-9575.
Catechesis/Religious Program—Tel: 402-498-1030. Students 346.

BUTTE, BOYD CO, SACRED HEART PARISH OF BOYD COUNTY (1906) [JC 4] Rev. Timothy Podraza.
Res. & Office: 921 Gale St., P.O. Box 8, 68722. Tel: 402-775-2452; 402-775-0067 (Office).
Catechesis/Religious Program—Tel: 402-775-2622. Students 115.

CEDAR RAPIDS, BOONE CO., ST. ANTHONY (1884) [CEM] Rev. Ralph J. Steffensmeier.
Res.: P.O. Box 56, 68627. Tel: 308-358-0773; Fax: 308-358-0773.
Catechesis/Religious Program—Students 61.
Mission—St. Mary [CEM] Primrose, Boone Co. 68627.

CENTRAL CITY, MERRICK CO., ST. MICHAEL (1910) Rev. Msgr. Nelson A. Newman; Deacons Robert Flesch; Richard Larson; Donald Placke.
Res.: 2402 20th Ave., 68826. Tel: 308-946-2855; Fax: 308-946-2214.
Catechesis/Religious Program—Kendra Jefferson, D.R.E. Students 80.

CLARKS, MERRICK CO., ST. PETER (1918) [CEM] Rev. Richard J. Whiteing.
Res.: 315 N. Esther, Box 368, Fullerton, 68638. Tel: 308-536-2574; Fax: 308-536-2574.
Church: 302 N. Dixon St., 68628.
Catechesis/Religious Program—Tel: 308-548-2870. Students 39.

CLARKSON, COLFAX CO.

1—SS. CYRIL AND METHODIUS (1901), (Czech), [CEM] Rev. Timothy W. Forget.
Res.: 120 Cherry St., P.O. Box 457, 68629. Tel: 402-892-3464 (Church Office); 402-892-3064 (Father's Office); Fax: 402-892-9879.
School—St. John Neumann, Tel: 402-892-3474; Fax: 402-892-3090. Lay Teachers 5; Students 35.
Catechesis/Religious Program—Students 75.

2—HOLY TRINITY (1878), (Czech), [CEM] Rev. Leo Rigatuso.
Res.: 614 Center St., Howells, 68641. Tel: 402-986-1627; Fax: 402-986-1627.
School— See Elementary Schools, Interparochial under Institutions located in the Archdiocese.
Catechesis/Religious Program—Students 43.

COLERIDGE, CEDAR CO., ST. MICHAEL (1886), (German—Irish), [CEM] Rev. Jeffrey S. Loseke.
Mailing Address: P.O. Box 278, Hartington, 68739.
Res.: 315 S. Madison, 68727. Tel: 402-254-6559; Fax: 402-254-6553. Email: trinitymichael@hartel.net.
Catechesis/Religious Program—Students 28.

COLUMBUS, PLATTE CO.

1—ST. ANTHONY (1913) Rev. Lydell T. Lape; Deacons Michael Placzek; Michael McGuire; Kelly McGowan.
Res.: 562 17th Ave., 68601. Tel: 402-564-3313; Fax: 402-563-1005.
School—1719 6th St., 68601. Tel: 402-564-4767; Fax: 402-564-5530. Web: teachers.esu7.org/stanthony. Norma Cremers, Prin. Lay Teachers 7; Students 151.
Catechesis/Religious Program—Lori Olson, D.R.E. Students 148.

2—ST. BONAVENTURE (1877) [CEM] Revs. Thomas W. Weisbecker; Michael P. Keating. In Res., Rev. Andrew J. Roza; Deacons Arthur Spenner; Lawrence Mielak.
Res.: 1565 18th Ave., 68601. Tel: 402-564-7151; Fax: 402-562-6025. Email: stbons@esu7.org. Web: www.stbons.com.
School—Tel: 402-564-7153; Fax: 402-564-2587. Cheryl Zoucha, Prin. Lay Teachers 15; Students 223.
Catechesis/Religious Program—Gail Benesch, D.R.E.; Belinda Keiter, Youth Min. Students 280.

3—ST. ISIDORE (1963) [JC] Rev. Joseph A. Miksch.
Res.: 3921 20th St., 68601. Tel: 402-564-8993; Fax: 402-564-8955. Email: isidore@mychurch.com. Web: www.saintisidores.com.
School—3821 20th St., 68601. Tel: 402-564-2604. Lay Teachers 16; Students 213.
Catechesis/Religious Program—Tel: 402-246-5455. Students 157.

CONSTANCE, CEDAR CO., ST. JOSEPH (1896) [CEM], (Mission of Fordyce) Rev. David L. Fulton.
Mailing Address: P.O. Box 170, Fordyce, 68736. Tel: 402-357-3506. Email: frfulton@hotmail.com. Web: www.stbonifaceparish.org.
See West Catholic Elementary, Fordyce under Elementary Schools, Interparochial located in the Institution section.
Catechesis/Religious Program—Students 8.

CREIGHTON, KNOX CO., ST. LUDGER (1885), (German—Czech), [JC] Rev. Walter L. Nolte.
Res.: 410 Bryant Ave., 68729-2917. Tel: 402-358-3596; Fax: 402-358-3559.
School—Lay Teachers 4; Students 34.
Catechesis/Religious Program—Tel: 402-358-3501. Karen Boyle, D.R.E.; Ellen Huigens, D.R.E.; Darla Frisch, D.R.E. Students 64.
Mission—St. Ignatius Brunswick, Antelope Co.

CROFTON, KNOX CO., ST. ROSE OF LIMA (1906) [CEM] Rev. Michael D. Schmitz.
Res.: 1316 W. Fifth St., 68730. Tel: 402-388-4814; Fax: 402-388-2680. Email: strosecrofton@gpcom.net.
School—1302 W. 5th St., 68730. Tel: 402-388-4393; Fax: 402-388-4393. Email: strose@esu1.org. Web: www.stroseschool.us. Lay Teachers 9; Students 101.
Catechesis/Religious Program—Terry Mueller, D.R.E., (Grades 1-8); Leslie Donner, D.R.E., (Grades 9-12). Students 90.

DELOIT TOWNSHIP, HOLT CO., ST. JOHN THE BAPTIST (1910) [CEM] Rev. James V. Kramper.
Res.: P.O Box 37, Ewing, 68735. Tel: 402-626-7605; Fax: 402-626-7605.
Catechesis/Religious Program—Students 12.

DODGE, DODGE CO., ST. WENCESLAUS (1883), (Czech), [CEM 2] [JC] Rev. Patrick A. McLaughlin.
Res.: 743 Second St., 68633. Tel: 402-693-2235; Fax: 402-693-2236. Web: www.stwenc.org.
School—212 N. Linden St., 68633. Tel: 402-693-2819; Fax: 402-693-2347. Stacy Littecht, Headmistress. Lay Teachers 5; Students 59.
Catechesis/Religious Program—Tel: 402-693-2347. Joan Ruskamp, D.R.E. Students 62.
Mission—Sacred Heart (1874) [CEM] Olean, Colfax Co. Tel: 402-693-2356.
Catechesis/Religious Program—Students 9.

DUNCAN, PLATTE CO., ST. STANISLAUS, [CEM] Rev. Rodney V. Kneifl.
Mailing Address: P.O. Box 155, Platte Center, 68653-0155.
Church: 1120 8th St., 68634. Tel: 402-897-2625; Fax: 402-246-2045. Email: stsjoemike@aol.com.
Catechesis/Religious Program—Students 25.

ELGIN, ANTELOPE CO., ST. BONIFACE (1902), (German), [CEM] Rev. Daniel R. Andrews; Deacons Dennis Wiehn; Bill Camp.
Res.: 301 S. 2nd St., P.O. Box B, 68636-0433. Tel: 402-843-2345; Fax: 402-843-2253. Email: stboniface.elg@archomaha.org.
School—Tel: 402-843-5460; Fax: 402-843-5842. Email: saintbon@esu8.org. Lay Teachers 7; Students 104.
Catechesis/Religious Program—Students 51.

EMERSON, DAKOTA CO., SACRED HEART (1886) [CEM] Rev. Michael B. Malloy.
Res.: 601 N. Main St., P.O. Box 250, 68733. Tel: 402-695-2342; Fax: 402-695-2505. Email: sacredheartchurch_1@msn.com.
Catechesis/Religious Program—Students 52.

EWING, HOLT CO., ST. PETER DE ALCANTARA (1886) [CEM] Rev. James V. Kramper.
Res.: P.O. Box 37, 68735. Tel: 402-626-7605; Fax: 402-626-7605.
Catechesis/Religious Program—Students 52.
Mission—Mission of St. Theresa of Avila, Clearwater, NE 509 Nebraska St., Clearwater, 68726.

FORDYCE, CEDAR CO., ST. JOHN THE BAPTIST (1909), (German), [CEM] Rev. David L. Fulton; Deacons Marcus Potts; Brian Heine.
Res.: P.O. Box 170, 68736. Tel: 402-357-3506; Fax: 402-357-3795. Email: frfulton@hotmail.com. Web: www.stbonifaceparish.org.
See West Catholic Elementary, Fordyce under Elementary Schools, Interparochial located in the Institution section.
Catechesis/Religious Program—Mary Jean Zavadil, D.R.E. Students 8.
Mission—St. Joseph, Cedar Co. Tel: 402-388-4814.

FORT CALHOUN, WASHINGTON CO., ST. JOHN THE BAPTIST (1883) Rev. Robert F. Preisinger.
Res.: 215 N. 13th St., P.O. Box 148, 68023. Tel: 402-468-5348; Fax: 402-468-4619. Email: sjcc@huntel.net.
Catechesis/Religious Program—Tel: 402-468-5659. Email: religioused@huntel.net. Students 99.

FREMONT, DODGE CO., ST. PATRICK (1858) [CEM] Revs. Owen W. Korte; James R. de Anda; Ronald A. Battiato; Deacons Robert Chapman; Edward Gentrup; LeRoy Spieker; Vic Henry; Dan Mueller; Joe Uhlik; David Krueger; David A. Probst; Andy Kresha; Craig Steel.
Rectory—422 E. Fourth St., 68025. Tel: 402-721-6611; Fax: 402-727-8167. Email: stpatsfremont@yahoo.com. Web: www.stpatsfremont.org.
Church: 3400 E. 16th St., 68025. Tel: 402-727-6500.
High School—Archbishop Bergan, Tel: 402-721-9683; Fax: 402-721-5366. Web: www.berganknights.org. Ron Beacom, Prin. Lay Teachers 13; Students 112.
School—Bergan Middle School, (Grades 6-8) Tel: 402-721-9766; Fax: 402-721-5366. Mary Riggert, Librarian. Lay Teachers 7; Students 100.
School—Archbishop Bergan Elementary formerly ABC Elementary (Grades K-4) Kate Hurst, Librarian. Teachers 7; Students 130.
Catechesis/Religious Program—Tel: 402-721-9710. Email: stpatsfremontrf@yahoo.com. Margaret Iossi, D.R.E. Students 375.

FULLERTON, NANCE CO., ST. PETER (1917), (Polish), [CEM] Rev. Richard J. Whiteing.
Res.: 315 N. Esther, P.O. Box 368, 68638-0368. Tel: 308-536-2574; Fax: 308-536-2574.
Church: 315 N. Esther St., 68638.
Catechesis/Religious Program—Tel: 308-536-3379. Students 105.
Mission— 302 N. Dixon St., Clarks, Merrick Co. 68628.

GENOA, NANCE CO., ST. ROSE OF LIMA (1900) [JC] Rev. Frank E. Jindra.
Res.: 116 N. Elm St., P.O. Box 490, 68640-0490. Tel: 402-993-2323; Fax: 402-993-9962. Email: st.rose@frontiernet.net.
Catechesis/Religious Program—Students 113.

GRETNA, SARPY CO., ST. PATRICK (1858), (Irish), [CEM] Very Rev. Michael W. Grewe; Deacons Joseph Krajicek; Larry Heck; Kent Boettger; Steve

Grandinetti.
Res.: 214 No. Cherokee Dr., 68028. Tel: 402-332-4428. Church: 508 Angus St., 68028. Tel: 402-332-4444; Fax: 402-332-5107. Email: parishoffice@msn.com. Web: www.stpatsgretna.org.
Catechesis/Religious Program—Tel: 402-332-3454. Email: religiouseddirector@msn.com. Students 680.

HARTINGTON, CEDAR CO., HOLY TRINITY (1886), (German—Irish), [CEM] [JC] Rev. Jeffrey S. Loseke.
Res.: 404 S. Broadway Ave., P.O. Box 278, 68739. Tel: 402-254-6559; Fax: 402-254-6553. Email: trinitymichael@hartel.net.
School—(Grades K-6) Tel: 402-254-6496. Adaline Dreesen, Librarian. Lay Teachers 10; Students 144.
Catechesis/Religious Program—Students 114.

HOOPER, DODGE CO., ST. ROSE OF LIMA, [CEM] Rev. Vitalis E. Anyanike.
Res.: 405 Elk St., P.O. Box 443, 68031. Tel: 402-654-3449; Fax: 402-654-3449. Email: parishroselaw@gmail.com.
Catechesis/Religious Program—Students 38.
Mission—St. Lawrence [CEM] Grant St., Box 443, Scribner, Dodge Co. 68031. Tel: 402-654-3449.
Catechesis/Religious Program—Students 74.

HOWELLS, COLFAX CO.
1—ST. JOHN NEPOMUCENE (1893) [CEM] Rev. Leo Rigatuso.
Res.: 614 Center St., 68641. Tel: 402-986-1653; Fax: 402-986-0882.
See Howells Community Catholic School, Howells under Elementary Schools, Interparochial located in the Institution section.
Catechesis/Religious Program—Students 29.
2—SS. PETER AND PAUL (1890), (German), [CEM] Rev. Leo Rigatuso.
Res.: 614 Center St., 68641. Tel: 402-986-1653.
See Howells Community Catholic School, Howells under Elementary Schools, Interparochial located in the Institution section.
Catechesis/Religious Program—Students 43.
Mission—Holy Trinity 1733 Rd. 12, Clarkson, Colfax Co. 68629. Tel: 402-986-1627; Fax: 402-986-1627.

HUMPHREY, PLATTE CO., ST. FRANCIS (1883) [CEM] [JC 2] Revs. Thomas E. Bauwens; Wayne Pavela.
Res.: 203 S. 5th, P.O. Box 116, 68642. Tel: 402-923-0913; Fax: 402-923-1931.
School—(Grades K-12) Tel: 402-923-0611; Fax: 402-923-1590. Julie Huettner, Librarian. Lay Teachers 22; Students 227.
Catechesis/Religious Program—Students 64.

JACKSON, DAKOTA CO., ST. PATRICK (1856) [CEM] Rev. Paul M. Albenesius.
Res.: 203 E. Elk St., P.O. Box 87, 68743. Tel: 402-632-4292.
Catechesis/Religious Program—Tel: 402-632-4258; Fax: 402-632-4312. Claudette Albenesius, D.R.E. Students 67.
Mission—St. Mary [CEM 2] 200 Iowa St., P.O. Box 126, Hubbard, Dakota Co. 68741. Tel: 402-632-4283.

KRAKOW, NANCE CO., SS. PETER AND PAUL (1893), (Polish), [CEM] Rev. Frank E. Jindra.
Res.: R.R. 2, P.O. Box 490, Genoa, 68640. Tel: 402-993-2323; Fax: 402-993-9962. Email: fjindra@frontiernet.net.
Catechesis/Religious Program—Students 35.

LAUREL, CEDAR CO., ST. MARY (1894) Rev. James F. McCluskey.
Res.: 406 Elm St., P.O. Box 828, 68745. Tel: 402-256-3303; Fax: 402-256-3019. Email: maryann68745@yahoo.com.
Catechesis/Religious Program—Shirley Haahr, D.R.E. Students 68.
Mission—St. Anne [CEM] Dixon, Dixon Co.

LEIGH, COLFAX CO., ST. MARY (1900) [CEM] Rev. Timothy W. Forget.
Res.: 220 W. Third St., P.O. Box 385, 68643. Tel: 402-487-2666; Fax: 402-487-2666. Email: smarlei@frontiernet.net.
Catechesis/Religious Program—Laurie Urban, D.R.E. Students 45.

LINDSAY, PLATTE CO., HOLY FAMILY (1895) [CEM] Rev. James F. Novotny.
Res.: 103 E. 3rd St., P.O. Box 68, 68644. Tel: 402-428-2455; Fax: 402-428-5205. Email: lhfp@megavision.com. Web: www.megavision.net/lhf.
School—(Grades 1-6) Tel: 402-428-3455; Fax: 402-428-3231. Email: dschindler@esu7.org. Web: www.lhf.esu7.org. Patty Hemmer, Librarian. Lay Teachers 4; Students 42.
High School—(Grades 7-12) Tel: 402-428-3215; Fax: 402-428-3231. Lay Teachers 9; Students 84.
Catechesis/Religious Program—Students 126.

LYNCH, BOYD CO., ASSUMPTION B.V.M. (1892) [CEM] Merged with Ss. Peter and Paul, Butte and St. Mary, Spencer to form Sacred Heart Parish of Boyd Co.

LYONS, BURT CO., ST. JOSEPH (1884) Rev. Paul R. Ortmeier.
Res.: 430 Lincoln St., P.O. Box 524, 68038. Tel: 402-687-2102; Fax: 402-687-2102. Web: www.stjoseph-holycross.com.
Catechesis/Religious Program—Students 69.
Mission—Holy Cross

MADISON, MADISON CO., ST. LEONARD (1885) [CEM] Rev. Dermot J. Dunne; Deacon Lawrence F. Throener.
Res.: 504 S. Nebraska St., P.O. Box 368, 68748. Tel: 402-454-3529; Fax: 402-454-6533.
School—Tel: 402-454-3525; Fax: 402-454-6653. Lay Teachers 4; Students 60.
Catechesis/Religious Program—Tel: 402-454-6533. Students 179.

MENOMINEE, CEDAR CO., ST. BONIFACE (1882), (German), [CEM] Rev. David L. Fulton; Deacon Clarence Jansen.
Res.: P.O. Box 170, Fordyce, 68736. Tel: 402-357-3506; Fax: 402-357-3795. Email: frfulton@hotmail.com. Web: www.stbonifaceparish.org.
See West Catholic Elementary, Fordyce under Elementary Schools, Interparochial located in the Institution section.
Catechesis/Religious Program—Tel: 402-357-3308. Email: stjohnbon1@gpm.com. Mary Jean Zavadil, D.R.E. Students 48.

MONTEREY, CUMING CO., ST. BONIFACE (1905), (German), [CEM] Rev. Gerald E. Gonderinger, Admin.
343 N. Monitor St., West Point, 68788.
Res.: 450 12th Rd., West Point, 68788. Tel: 402-372-2188; Fax: 402-372-3563. Email: wpstmary@yahoo.com. Web: myweb.cableone.net/stmary.
Catechesis/Religious Program—Students 5.

NELIGH, ANTELOPE CO., ST. FRANCIS Rev. John P. Broheimer; Deacon Bernard Burbach.
Res.: 702 W. 11th St., P.O. Box 259, 68756. Tel: 402-887-4521; Fax: 402-843-2297. Email: stfrancisc@frontiernet.net.
Catechesis/Religious Program—Students 155.

NEWCASTLE, DIXON CO., ST. PETER (1873) [CEM] Rev. David F. Liewer; Deacon Dennis Knudsen.
Mailing Address: 421 Second St., P.O. Box 898, Ponca, 68770-0898. Tel: 402-755-2773; Fax: 402-755-2525.
Res.: 405 Annie St., P.O. Box 127, 68757. Tel: 402-355-2620 (Rectory).
Catechesis/Religious Program—Tel: 402-355-2280. Susie Day, D.R.E. Students 43.

NORFOLK, MADISON CO., SACRED HEART (1881), (German), Revs. David D. Belt; Scott A. Hastings; Deacons Jim Doolittle; Irving St. Arnold; Roger D. Pribnow; Donald M. Seamann.
Office: 204 S. Fifth St., 68701.
Res.: 202 S. Fifth St., 68701. Tel: 402-371-2621; Fax: 402-371-0403. Web: www.shpo.org.
Church: 200 S. 5th St., 68701.
St. Mary's Catholic Church—2300 Madison Ave., 68701.
School—Sacred Heart Elementary School, (Grades PreSchool-6), 2301 Madison Ave., 68701. Tel: 402-371-4584 (Pre-School-6); Fax: 402-379-8129 (Pre-School-6). Web: www.ncknights.org. Troy Berryman, Prin. (Pre-School-6); Sherry Stuifbergen, Librarian. Priests 2; Lay Teachers 25; Students 406.
High School—Norfolk Catholic High School (1925), (Grades 7-12), 2300 Madison Ave., 68701. Tel: 402-371-2784 (7-12); Fax: 402-379-2929 (7-12). Email: jeffbellar@ncknights.org. Mr. Jeff Bellar, Prin. & Contact (7-12). Priests 2; Lay Teachers 24; Students 322.
Catechesis/Religious Program—Tel: 402-371-8658. Marilyn Kathol, D.R.E. (Pre-School-12); Philip Zimmerman, Adult Formation. Students 385.

NORTH BEND, DODGE CO., ST. CHARLES BORROMEO (1892) [JC] Rev. Donald M. Cleary.
Res.: 831 Locust St., P.O. Box 457, 68649. Tel: 402-652-8484; Fax: 402-652-3418. Email: stcharles.nbe@archomaha.org.
Catechesis/Religious Program—Tel: 402-652-8437. Jody Mullally, D.R.E. (Grades K-6). Students 97.

O'NEILL, HOLT CO., ST. PATRICK (1877) Revs. Francis A. Nigli; Jeffrey Lorig.
Res.: 301 E. Adams, 68763. Tel: 402-336-1602; Fax: 402-336-1533.
School—(Grades PreSchool-6) Tel: 402-336-2664; Fax: 402-336-2055. Lay Teachers 10; Students 133.
High School—(Grades 7-12) Tel: 402-336-4455; Fax: 402-336-1533. Sisters 1; Lay Teachers 13; Students 110.
Catechesis/Religious Program—Tel: 402-336-1602; Fax: 402-336-1533. Georgia Blumenstock, D.R.E. Students 150.
Mission—St. Joseph Amelia, Holt Co. Tel: 402-482-5283.

OSMOND, PIERCE CO., ST. MARY OF THE SEVEN DOLORS (1904) [CEM] Rev. John S. Andrews.
509 Hill St., P.O. Box 397, 68765.
Res.: 208 E. 5th St., P.O. Box 397, 68765. Tel: 402-748-3340; Fax: 402-748-3433.
School—Tel: 402-748-3433. Email: cconley_stmarys@huntel.net. Lay Teachers 4; Students 30.
Catechesis/Religious Program—Students 58.

PAPILLION, SARPY CO., ST. COLUMBKILLE (1897) Revs. Damian J. Zuerlein; Damien E. Wee; Deacons Eldon Lauber, Pastoral Assoc.; Frank Mascarello; Jerry Overkamp; William Hill; Russ Perry; Duane Thome; Steve Jordan; Bob Stier; John J. Zurek; Eric VandeBerg; Brian Thomas.
Office: 200 E. Sixth St., 68046. Tel: 402-339-3285; Fax: 402-592-4753. Web: www.saintcolumbkille.org.
School—224 E. 5th St., 68046. Tel: 402-339-8706; Fax: 402-592-4147. Lay Teachers 24; Students 501.
Catechesis/Religious Program—Tel: 402-339-0990; Fax: 402-339-3977. Students 720.

PENDER, THURSTON CO., ST. JOHN (1889) [JC] Rev. Michael B. Malloy.
Res.: 108 N. 5th, P.O. Box 96, 68047. Tel: 402-385-3258; Fax: 402-385-3400. Email: catholic@inebraska.com.
Catechesis/Religious Program—Students 61.

PETERSBURG, BOONE CO., ST. JOHN THE BAPTIST (1896) [CEM] Rev. Stanley T. Schmit.
Mailing Address: 4th & Norman Sts., P.O. Box 608, 68652.
Res.: 524 W. Church St., Albion, 68620. Tel: 402-395-2393.
School—Tel: 402-386-5472. Web: teachers.esu7.orglstjb. Lay Teachers 2; Students 11.
Catechesis/Religious Program—Students 38.

PIERCE, PIERCE CO., ST. JOSEPH (1905), (German), [CEM] Rev. Keith D. Rezac.
Res.: 118 W. Willow St., 68767. Tel: 402-329-4200; Fax: 402-329-4579.
Catechesis/Religious Program—Tel: 402-329-6655. Students 120.

PLAINVIEW, PIERCE CO., ST. PAUL (1912) [CEM] Rev. Keith D. Rezac.
Res.: *St. Joseph*, 118 W. Willow, Pierce, 68767. Tel: 402-329-4200; Fax: 402-329-4579.
Catechesis/Religious Program—Students 42.

PLATTE CENTER, PLATTE CO., ST. JOSEPH (1884), (German—Irish), [CEM] [JC] Rev. Rodney V. Kneifl.
Res.: 155 A St., P.O. Box 155, 68653-0155. Tel: 402-246-2255; Fax: 402-246-2045. Email: stsjoemike@aol.com.
Catechesis/Religious Program—Tel: 402-246-5700. Email: stjopre@megavision.com. Angela Dolezal, D.R.E.; Lisa Hoadley, D.R.E. Students 65.

PONCA, DIXON CO., ST. JOSEPH (1890) [CEM] Rev. David F. Liewer.
Mailing Address: 421 Second St., P.O. Box 898, 68770.
Res.: 421 Annie St., P.O. Box 127, Newcastle, 68757. Tel: 402-355-2620; 402-755-2773 (Office); Fax: 402-755-2525.
Catechesis/Religious Program—Wendy Masin, D.R.E.; Jamie Hamar, D.R.E. Students 92.

RAEVILLE, BOONE CO., ST. BONAVENTURE (1882), (German), [CEM] Rev. Daniel R. Andrews.
Res.: 301 S. 2nd St., Box B, Elgin, 68636. Tel: 402-843-2345; Fax: 402-843-2253. Email: stbonaventure.rae@archomaha.org.
Catechesis/Religious Program—Students 5.

RALSTON, DOUGLAS CO., ST. GERALD (1957) Revs. Gary L. Ostrander; Perry L. Robinson, S.J.; Deacon Michael Conzett.
Res.: 7859 Lakeview St., 68127. Tel: 402-331-1955; Fax: 402-339-8733. Email: office@stgerald.org. Web: www.stgerald.org.
Church: 9602 Q St., 68127.
School—Tel: 402-331-4223; Fax: 402-331-4523. David Garland, Prin. Lay Teachers 26; Students 393.
Catechesis/Religious Program—Tel: 402-331-4223. Students 1,348.

RANDOLPH, CEDAR CO., ST. FRANCES DE CHANTAL (1892), (German), [CEM] Rev. John S. Andrews; Deacon Doug Tunink.
Rectory—402 N. Bridge St., 68771. Tel: 402-337-0644. Email: stjane@cableone.net.
Res.: *St. Mary's*, 208 E. 5th St., P.O. Box 397, Osmond, 68765. Tel: 402-748-3340.
Catechesis/Religious Program—Tel: 402-337-0341. Sandy Thies, D.R.E. Students 130.

ST. CHARLES, CUMING CO., ST. ANTHONY (1862), (German), [CEM] Rev. Gerald E. Gonderinger.
343 N. Monitor St., West Point, 68788.
Res.: 449 15th Rd., West Point, 68788. Tel: 402-372-2188; Fax: 402-372-3563. Email: wpstmary@yahoo.com. Web: myweb.cableone.net/stmary.
Catechesis/Religious Program—Students 5.

ST. EDWARD, BOONE CO., ST. EDWARD (1888) [CEM] Rev. James F. Novotny.
Res.: 805 Washington St., P.O. Box A, 68660-0136. Tel: 402-678-2642; Fax: 402-678-2341. Email: stedward@gpcom.net.
Catechesis/Religious Program—Elizabeth Czarnick,

D.R.E. (Elementary); Erica Werts, D.R.E. (Jr.-Sr. High). Students 66.

St. Helena, Cedar Co., Immaculate Conception, Merged with Ss. Philip & James, St. James; Ss. Peter & Paul, Bow Valley & Sacred Heart, Wynot to form Holy Family Church of Cedar County.

St. James, Cedar Co., Ss. Philip and James, Merged with Immaculate Conception, St. Helena; Ss. Peter and Paul, Bow Valley and Sacred Heart, Wynot to form Holy Family Church of Cedar County.

Schuyler, Colfax Co.

1—St. Mary (1914) Merged with St. Augustine, Schuyler to form Divine Mercy, Schuyler.

2—St. Augustine (1878), (Irish—German), Merged with St. Mary, Schuyler to form Divine Mercy, Schuyler.

3—Divine Mercy Revs. Gerald A. Leise; Anthony L. Espinosa; Deacons Carl Perrin; Marvin Capoun; James DeBlauw; Danny Hastings.
Res.: 308 W. 10 St., 68661. Tel: 402-352-3540; Fax: 402-352-5971.
Catechesis/Religious Program—320 W. 10th St., 68661. Tel: 402-352-2149. Sara Rojo, D.R.E. Students 366.

Silver Creek, Merrick Co., St. Lawrence (1902), (Polish), [CEM] Rev. Frank E. Jindra.
407 Vine St., P.O. Box 332, 68663.
Res.: 116 N. Elm St., P.O. Box 490, Genoa, 68640. Tel: 402-993-2323; Fax: 402-993-9962.
Catechesis/Religious Program—Tel: 308-773-2430. Kris Zelasney, D.R.E. Students 54.

Snyder, Dodge Co., St. Leo, [CEM] Rev. Donald M. Cleary.
P.O. Box 188, 68664.
Res.: 831 Locust St., P.O. Box 457, North Bend, 68649. Tel: 402-652-8484; Fax: 402-652-3418. Email: stleo.sny@archomaha.org.
Catechesis/Religious Program—Tel: 402-568-2586. Betty Marxsen, D.R.E. Students 31.

South Sioux City, Dakota Co., St. Michael (1898) [CEM] Revs. Daniel L. Wittrock; Oscar A. Perez (Venezuela).
Office:—P.O. Box 128, 68776.
Res.: 1405 First Ave., 68776. Tel: 402-494-5423; Fax: 402-494-6342.
School—Tel: 402-494-1526; Fax: 402-494-4283. Lay Teachers 14; Students 115.
Catechesis/Religious Program—1414 Third Ave., 68776. Tel: 402-494-2827. Students 130.

Spencer, Boyd Co., St. Mary (1892) [CEM 2] Merged with Ss. Peter and Paul, Butte and Assumption B.V.M., Lynch to form Sacred Heart Parish of Boyd Co.

Springfield, Sarpy Co., St. Joseph (1980) [JC] Rev. Charles F. Swanson. In Res., Rev. Raphael B. Librea (Retired).
Res.: 102 S. Ninth St., 68059. Tel: 402-253-2889; Fax: 402-253-2949.
Catechesis/Religious Program—Tel: 402-253-2949. Sherry Huntwork, D.R.E. Students 120.

Stanton, Stanton Co., St. Peter (1893) [JC] Rev. Gerald A. Connealy.
Res.: 1504 Ivy St., P.O. Box 557, 68779. Tel: 402-439-2147; Fax: 402-439-2149. Email: stpeters@stanton.net.
Catechesis/Religious Program—Tel: 402-379-1234; 402-439-2331. Valerie Morfeld, D.R.E.; Karen Petersen, D.R.E. Students 77.

Stuart, Holt Co., St. Boniface (1899) [CEM] Rev. LuVerne W. Steffes.
Res.: 106 E. Fourth, P.O. Box 190, 68780. Tel: 402-924-3262; Fax: 402-924-3262. Email: stboniface@elkhorn.net.
Catechesis/Religious Program—Students 89.

Tarnov, Platte Co., St. Michael (1884), (Polish), [CEM] Rev. Rodney V. Kneifl.
Res.: P.O. Box 155, Platte Center, 68653. Tel: 402-246-2255; Fax: 402-246-2045. Email: stsjoemike@aol.com.
Catechesis/Religious Program—Tel: 402-923-1308. Email: rbrand1@megavision.com. Students 24.

Tekamah, Burt Co., St. Patrick (1889) [JC] Rev. Mark A. Tomasiewicz.
Res.: 1323 R St., 68061-1542. Tel: 402-374-1692; Fax: 402-808-2004.
Catechesis/Religious Program—Tel: 402-374-2616. Carrie Braniff, D.R.E. Students 80.
Mission—Holy Family [CEM] 2801 Co. Rd. U, Decatur, Burt Co. 68020.

Tilden, Madison Co., Our Lady of Mt. Carmel (1887) [CEM] Rev. John P. Broheimer.
Res.: P.O. Box 458, 68781. Tel: 402-368-7710; Fax: 402-368-7710.
Catechesis/Religious Program—Tel: 402-368-5919. Corinne Frey, D.R.E. Students 66.

Valley, Douglas Co., St. John (1917) Rev. Lloyd A. Gnirk.
Res.: 209 E. Sunset, P.O. Box 587, 68064. Tel: 402-359-5783; Fax: 402-359-5217.
Catechesis/Religious Program—Tel: 402-625-2717. Connie Schnoes, D.R.E. Students 91.

Verdigre, Knox Co., St. Wenceslaus (1884), (Czech—Bohemian), [CEM] Rev. Douglas P. Scheinost.
Res.: 409 S. Third St., P.O. Box 9, 68783-0009. Tel: 402-668-2331; Fax: 402-668-2375.
Catechesis/Religious Program—Students 60.
Mission—St. William 262 Buckeye Rd., P.O. Box 9, Knox Co. 68783-0009. Tel: 402-857-3438. Rev. Douglas P. Scheinost.

Walthill, Thurston Co., St. Joseph (1912), (Native American), Revs. Michael P. Eckley; David M. Korth.
Mailing Address: P.O. Box GG, Winnebago, 68071-0766.
Res.: 501 Main St., 68067. Tel: 402-846-5550; Fax: 402-878-2760.
Catechesis/Religious Program—Students 8.
Mission—Our Lady of Fatima Box 404, Macy, Thurston Co. 68067. Revs. Michael P. Eckley; David M. Korth.

Wayne, Wayne Co., St. Mary (1881) Rev. Mark T. Beran.
Res.: 412 E. 8th St., 68787. Tel: 402-375-2000; Fax: 402-375-5782.
School—St. Mary's Catholic School, 420 E. 7th St., 68787. Tel: 402-375-2337; Fax: 402-375-2337. Lay Teachers 6; Students 34.
Catechesis/Religious Program—Students 178.

West Point, Cuming Co., Assumption B.V.M. (1875) [CEM] Revs. Gerald E. Gonderinger; Francis W. Lordemann; Deacons Vincent Maly; Kenneth Batenhorst; Francis Meiergerd.
Res.: 343 N. Monitor St., 68788. Tel: 402-372-2188; Fax: 402-372-3563. Email: wpstmary@yahoo.com. Web: myweb.cableone.net/stmary.
School—Guardian Angel, Tel: 402-372-5328. Web: gacatholicschool.org. Sr. Mary Ann Tupy, Prin. Priests 2; Sisters 1; Lay Teachers 16; Students 237.
Catechesis/Religious Program—Email: ccdstmaryswp@yahoo.com. Lisa Hunke, D.R.E. Students 124.

Winnebago, Thurston Co.

1—St. Augustine's, (Native American), (Indian Mission) Revs. Michael P. Eckley; David M. Korth.
Res.: P.O. Box GG, 68071. Tel: 402-878-2577; Fax: 402-878-2760. Web: staugustinemission.org.
School—St. Augustine Indian Mission School, (Grades K-8), 1 Mission Rd., P.O. Box GG, 68071. Tel: 402-878-2402; Fax: 402-878-2760. Email: dmkorth@archomaha.org. Web: www.staugustinemission.org. Donald Blackbird Jr., Prin.; Sr. Frances Betz, Librarian. Missionary Benedictine Sisters 4; Lay Teachers 9; Students 120.
Mission—St. Cornelius Homer, Dakota Co. 68030. Revs. Michael P. Eckley; David M. Korth.
Catechesis/Religious Program—Students 21.

2—Our Lady of Fatima of Macy, Closed. This is a mission of St. Joseph, Walthill.

Wisner, Cuming Co., St. Joseph (1879), (Irish—German), [CEM] [JC] Rev. William J. Safranek.
Res.: 1318 G Ave. W., P.O. Box 623, 68791. Tel: 402-529-3531. Email: stjoes@gpcom.net.
Catechesis/Religious Program—Tel: 402-529-3891. Anne McManigal, D.R.E. Students 101.
Mission—Holy Cross 517 Fraisier St., Beemer, Cuming Co. 68716. Tel: 402-528-3475; Fax: 402-528-7234. Email: hcbeemer@gpcom.net.

Wynot, Cedar Co.

1—Holy Family Church of Cedar County (2000), (German), [JC 4] Rev. Eric S. Olsen.
Parish Office—P.O. Box 65, 68792-0065. Tel: 402-254-3311; 402-357-2465; Fax: 402-357-2766. Email: holyfamily@gpcom.net.
Catechesis/Religious Program—Tel: 402-254-6980. Students 213.

2—Sacred Heart, Merged see Holy Family of Cedar Country.

Special Assignment:
Rev.—
Vasquez, Paul L., Mass Supply and Archives

On Duty Outside the Archdiocese:
Revs.—
Hanefeldt, Joseph G., Faculty, North American College, Rome
Kasun, Paul L., O.S.B., Christ the King Priory, Schuyler, NE
LaPlante, David W., Archdiocese of Milwaukee
Parrinello, Frank P., Fraternity of St. Peter (F.S.S.P.)

Graduate Studies:
Rev.—
Burkhalter, Ross C., Graduate Theological Studies, Catholic University of America

---

Military Chaplains:
Revs.—
DeGuzman, Dennis U., U.S.A.F.
Dillon, Jerome V., Chap., U.S.N.R.
Hall, Douglas C., U.S.A.F.
Reeson, David G., U.S.A.F.

On Medical Leave:
Revs.—
Keller, Daniel E., St. Robert Bellarmine, 11802 Pacific St., 68154.
Wray, Joseph M.

On Leave of Absence:
Revs.—
Gutgsell, Stephen J.
Welsh, Garry A.

Retired:
Rev. Msgrs.—
Brodersen, Charles F., 7323 Shirley St. #303, 68124.
Cain, James R., J.C.D., 7323 Shirley St. #206, 68124.
Dunne, Peter F., Boys Town Center, Boys Town, 68010.
Furlong, Thomas D., 3605 Looking Glass Dr., Bellevue, 68123.
Gass, Robert J., 14948 G St., 68137.
Krejci, Albert L., 7323 Shirley St. #306, 68124.
Kubart, Francis E., 7323 Shirley St. #105, 68124.
Meister, Andrew H., 2952 Bluff Rd., Cedar Bluffs, 68015.
Michalak, John S., Via Christe, 3636 California St. #319, 68131.
Nienaber, Robert H., 7323 Shirley St. #312, 68124.
O'Donnell, Edward C., 6809 N. 68th Plz., 68152.
Werner, Cyril J., P.O. Box 562, Hartington, 68739.
Whelan, William S., 7323 Shirley St. #101, 68124.
Wiese, Melvern A., 320 E. Decatur St., West Point, 68788.
Wolbach, Richard A., 4001 S. 36th St., 68107.

Revs.—
Adams, Thomas J., 3330 S. 104th Ave., 68124.
Astuto, Lucian S., 15676 Webster St., 68118.
Bartek, William C., 7323 Shirley St. #204, 68124.
Beacom, John F., 757 E. Decatur, West Point, 68788.
Benliro, Fernando C., 9620 W. Russell Rd. #1105, Las Vegas, NV 89148.
Ciurej, Richard S., 4107 S. 38th St., 68107.
Conley, Martin P., 7323 Shirley St. #315, 68124.
Fangman, Paul J., Wolf Memorial Home, P.O. Box 271, Albion, 68620.
Finch, Joseph E., St. Theresa Mortherhouse, 600 Woods Rd., Germantown, NY 12526.
Fitzgerald, William J., 7655 East Main, Scottsdale, AZ 85251.
Hunkeler, Edward J., 7323 Shirley St. #309, 68124.
Kenny, James E., New Cassell, 900 N. 90th St. #155, 68114.
Kros, Donald M., 50241 Edgewater Rd., Box 51, Lynch, 68748.
Lammers, Ralph A., 7323 Shirley St. #201, 68124.
Lange, Timothy J., 200 Benedictine Ln., Yankton, SD 57078.
Librea, Raphael B., 102 S. 9th St., Springfield, 68059.
McCaslin, John O., 7323 Shirley St. #305, 68124.
McKamy, Eldon J., 22426 N. Homestead Ln., Sun City West, AZ 85375.
McMahon, Aloysius J., Immanuel Fontenelle Home, 6809 N. 68th Plaza, #128A, 68152.
Meyer, Emmett F., 411 NW 20 Ter., Cape Coral, FL 33993.
Peschel, Roland A., 7323 Shirley St. #210, 68124.
Petrasic, Martin J., 7323 Shirley St. #207, 68124.
Printy, Michael G., 7323 Shirley St. #304, 68124.
Richling, Theodore L., 7323 Shirley St. #102, 68124.
Ryberg, James C., 7323 Shirley St. #212, 68124.
Schlautman, Wayne W., 7323 Shirley St. #301, 68124.
Schmitz, Robert A., 7323 Shirley St. #213, 68124.
Schwartz, Hugh F., 7323 Shirley St. #205, 68124.
Schwertley, James F., 109 S. 19th St., 68102.
Smith, Robert J., 7323 Shirley St. #302, 68124.
Spenner, Jerome I., 7323 Shirley St. #203, 68124.
Stevens, Clifford J., 14100 Crawford St., HQ Bldg., Boys Town, 68010.
Stortz, Donald L., 626 N. 44th St., 68131.
Wessling, Floyd A., Via Christe, 3636 California St. #303, 68131.
Wilwerding, Anthony P., 7323 Shirley St. #208, 68124.

Permanent Deacons:
Abbott, Ernest, Jr.
Adams, Chuck
Anderson, Andy
Anderson, Dennis

Archbold, Steve
Archibald, Joseph
Aulner, Al
Barbour, Frank
Barnes, William J.
Bartman, Frank
Batenhorst, Kenneth F.
Baughman, Charles
Belcher, Roger A.
Berger, Bill, (On Duty Outside the Diocese)
Bevan, Edward J.
Blanton, Dan
Boettger, Kent
Bollman, James G.
Bond, Ken, (On Duty Outside the Diocese)
Brich, James
Bronk, Duane
Burbach, Bernie
Camp, William J.
Cantrell, Charles D.
Capoun, Marvin
Carl, Robert J.
Casart, Ronald
Casner, James
Cerio, Paul M.
Cerveny, John
Chambers, James
Chapman, Robert, (Retired)
Chladek, Gary F.
Choi, Joseph
Christensen, Dave
Clausen, Donald
Connor, Dennis
Conrad, James J., Jr.
Conzett, Michael
Cowles, Donald
Crotty, Richard
Crowley, Martin
Dagerman, John
Dahlseid, John
DeBlauw, James L.
DeSelm, Michael J.
Dethlefs, Dennis
DiGiacomo, Yano
Digilio, John J.
Digilio, Peter, (Retired)
Dineen, Lonnie
Dohmen, Louis
Doolittle, James
Dreismeier, Paul
Drueke, Dick
Dunn, Donald, (Retired)
Elster, George
Emerson, William
Enzolera, Sebastian
Eubanks, Paul
Ficenic, Terry
Filipcic, Anthony, (Retired)
Finney, Jack
Fisher, Ed
Fitzgerald, Thomas
Flesch, Robert
Fletcher, Michael
Floersch, Steve
Foray, Andrew
Franco, Martin
Frankenfield, Thomas H.
French, Don
French, Gary
Gau, Jerome
Gencarelli, Ernest, (Retired)
Gentrup, Edward
Goldsmith, Edwin G.
Graff, Francis
Grandinetti, Steve
Gross, Patrick
Grosse, Randy
Gurney, David
Guzman, Luis
Hamilton, Robert
Hanson, Chris
Hastings, Danny
Hecht, William
Heck, Lawrence
Heffeman, John, (On Duty Outside the Diocese)
Heine, Brian
Hendricks, Fred
Hennessey, Gary
Henry, Victor R.
Herrara, Jesus
Hesson, Ronald W.
Hill, William H., Jr.
Hills, Lyle, (Retired)
Hilt, Frank
Hopkins, Richard
Huck, John
Hueser, Ralph
Hughes, Thomas J.
Hunke, Melvin
Iwanski, Duane
Janda, Dave
Janik, Norman
Jansen, Clarence
Jergovic, Robert
Jizba, Richard
Johnson, Donald
Jordan, Steve
Joyce, Kevin
Kaiser, Roland, (On Duty Outside the Diocese)
Kalkowski, Kenneth
Karmazin, Duane
Keating, James
Kemp, Donald, (Retired)
Klein, David
Knockenhauer, George F.
Knudsen, Dennis
Kober, Mark, (On Duty Outside the Diocese)
Koziel, Timothy J.
Kozney, Jerry
Krajicek, Joseph
Kramper, Jim, (On Duty Outside the Diocese)
Kresha, Andrew
Krieski, Timothy, (On Duty Outside the Diocese)
Kronschnabel, John, (Retired)
Krueger, David
Kube, Norman
Kuchar, Stephen, (On Duty Outside the Diocese)
Kuehl, Joseph
Kulus, Joe
Kurtz, Stanley
L'Archevesque, Charles
Larson, Rick
Lauber, Eldon
Leick, Mike
Leininger, Tim
Lenz, Patrick
Livingston, Tom, (Retired)
Luczynski, Chuck
Lukowski, Ray
Maly, Vince
Marsh, Douglas
Mascarello, Frank
Matukewicz, Paul
Mayhan II, Leo
McGowan, Kelly
McGuire, Michael
McNeil, Richard, (Retired)
McNeil, Tim
Meiergerd, Francis
Metzinger, Roger
Mielak, Lawrence
Miller, Carl, (On Duty Outside the Diocese)
Miller, Ira
Miller, Jack
Morello, Carl
Mouton, Gregory
Mruz, Lawrence F.
Mueller, Daniel D.
Mueting, Richard, (On Duty Outside the Diocese)
Mulcahy, Timothy A.
Murphy, James
Murphy, Thomas
Narducci, Warren, (On Duty Outside the Diocese)
Nelson, Richard
Newell, Mike
Nordick, John, (On Duty Outside the Diocese)
O'Donnell, William L., (On Duty Outside the Diocese)
Olsenholler, Jeffery
Osterhaus, Edwin
Overkamp, Jerry, J.C.L.
Palmer, Quentin, (On Duty Outside the Diocese)
Pavlik, Keith
Perchal, Daniel E.
Perrin, Carl A.
Perry, Russ
Pickett, Robert
Placke, Donald
Placzek, Michael
Potts, Marcus
Poulosky, Paul, (On Duty Outside the Diocese)
Powers, Paul, (On Duty Outside the Diocese)
Preister, Tim
Pribnow, Otto
Pribnow, Roger D.
Probst, David A.
Ramirez, Joseph, (Retired)
Reese, Mike, (On Duty Outside the Diocese)
Reilly, James L.
Reynolds, Mike
Ridder, Frederick
Rooney, Paul
Ryan, Ronald R.
Rzewnicki, Philip
Sampier, Larry D.
Sanders, Thomas, (On Duty Outside the Diocese)
Saniuk, Daniel
Sawtelle, Harold
Schimonitz, Eugene, (Retired)
Schindel, James
Schlautman, William
Schmit, Vincent
Schulte, Thomas
Schultz, Charles J.
Schumacher, Allan
Seamann, Donald M.
Simmonds, Bud
Smith, Marty
Sommer, Andrew
Sommer, Fred, (Retired)
Spenner, Arthur
Spicer, Ernest
Spieker, LeRoy
St. Arnold, Skip
Staroski, Jim
Steel, Craig
Steenson, Gerald
Steffen, Andrew
Steffen, Paul
Stier, Robert A.
Sukup, Charles
Tardy, Jim
Telich, Frank
ter Kuille, Reinold
Tharp, Bud, (Retired)
Thoene, Sylvan
Thomas, Brian
Thome, Duane, (Retired)
Throener, Lawrence F.
Tomaso, Paul
Tunink, Douglas G.
Tylutki, Glenn, (On Duty Outside the Diocese)
Uhlik, Joseph R.
Valadez, Luis
Valasek, Thomas W.
VandeBerg, Eric
Villemure, Arthur
Wacha, John
Warwick, Marty
Watson, James
Weskirchen, Charles, (Retired)
Wiehn, Dennis
Young, William
Zak, John J., Jr.
Zurek, John J.

INSTITUTIONS LOCATED IN THE ARCHDIOCESE

[A] COLLEGES AND UNIVERSITIES

OMAHA. *College of Saint Mary* (1923) 7000 Mercy Rd., 68106. Tel: 402-399-2400; Fax: 402-399-2342. Email: enroll@csm.edu. Web: www.csm.edu. Dr. Maryanne Stevens, Pres.; Dr. Christine Pharr, Vice Pres. Academic Affairs; Robert Gass, Chap.; Carmen Steele, Public Rels.; Melissa Tiemann, Librarian. Sisters 8; Lay Teachers 54; Students 1,100.

**Creighton University* (1878) 2500 California Plaza, 68178. Tel: 402-280-2700; Fax: 402-280-2727. Email: jpschlegel@creighton.edu. Web: www.creighton.edu. Rev. John P. Schlegel, S.J., Pres. & Contact; Michael J. LaCroix, M.L.S., M.B.A., Dir., Reinert Alumni Memorial Library. Priests 30; Brothers 1; Sisters 6; Lay Teachers 767; Total Enrollment 7,385; Total Staff 2,776.

The University is comprised of the following schools:

College of Arts and Sciences Tel: 402-280-2431; Fax: 402-280-4729. Dr. Robert Lueger, Dean, College Arts and Sciences.

College of Business Administration Tel: 402-280-2852; Fax: 402-280-2172. Dr. Anthony Hendrickson, Dean, College of Business Admin.

Graduate School and University College/Summer Sessions Tel: 402-280-2424; 402-280-2870; Fax: 402-280-2423; 402-280-5762. Dr. Barbara J. Braden, Ph.D., Dean; Dr. Gail Jensen, Dean, Graduate School.

School of Law Tel: 402-280-2874; Fax: 402-280-3161. Eric Chiappinelli, J.D., Dean School of Law.

School of Dentistry Tel: 402-280-5061; Fax: 402-280-5094. Dr. Wayne W. Barkmeier, D.D.S., Dean, School of Dentistry.

School of Medicine Tel: 402-280-2600; Fax: 402-280-4027. Dr. Rowen Zetterman, Interim Dean, School of Medicine.

School of Nursing Tel: 402-280-2004; Fax: 402-280-2045. Dr. Eleanor Howell, Dean, School of Nursing.

School of Pharmacy and Health Professions Tel: 402-280-1828; Fax: 402-280-5738. Dr. J. Christopher Bradberry, Ph.D., Dean, School of Pharmacy & Health Professions.

[B] HIGH SCHOOLS, ARCHDIOCESAN

OMAHA. *Daniel J. Gross Catholic High School of Omaha*, 7700 S. 43rd St., 68147. Tel: 402-734-2000; Fax: 402-734-4270. Email: cleve@grosscatholic.org. Web: www.grosscatholic.org.

Rev. Steve Emanuel, Chap., Campus Min.; Rebecca Cleveland, Pres. & Contact; Dorothy Ostrowski, Prin. Priests 1; Lay Teachers 43; Students 432; Total Staff 62.

St. Peter Claver Cristo Rey Catholic High School of Omaha, 5301 S. 36th St., 68107. Tel: 402-734-1802; Fax: 402-734-1835. Email: mmoecker@spccristorey.org. Web: www.spccristorey.org. Rev. James E. Keiter, Pres.; Leigh McKeechan, Prin.; Jerry Jacobs, Librarian. Lay Teachers 16; Students 186.

Roncalli Catholic High School of Omaha (1964) 6401 Sorensen Pkwy., 68152. Tel: 402-571-7670; Fax: 402-571-3216. Email: elgn52@cox.net; choltz@roncallicatholic.org. Web: www.roncallicatholic.org. Mr. Chad Holtz, Dean & Asst. Prin.; Rev. Bernard Starman, Chap., Pastoral Min.; Mr. James Meister, Dean of Academics, Activities Dir.; Margie Hladik, Media Specialist; Rev. Lloyd A. Gnirk, Pres. & Prin. Priests 2; Lay Teachers 28; Students 329; Total Staff 42.

V.J. & Angela Skutt Catholic High School (1993) 3131 S. 156th St., 68130. Tel: 402-333-0818; Fax: 402-333-1790. Email: skuttcatholic@gmail.com. Web: www.skuttcatholic.com. Patrick Slattery, Pres. & Prin.; Rob Meyers, Asst. Prin.; Michael McMahon, Activities Dir.; Isele Padilla, Librarian. Priests 1; Sisters 1; Lay Teachers 49; Students 702; Total Staff 75.

COLUMBUS. *Scotus Central Catholic High School*, (Grades 7-12), 1554 18th Ave., 68601. Tel: 402-564-7165; Fax: 402-564-6004. Email: wmorfel@esu7.org. Web: www.scotuscc.org. Mr. Wayne Morfeld, Pres.; Rev. Andrew J. Roza, Chap. & Teacher; Mrs. Cathy Podliska, Librarian. Priests 1; Lay Teachers 27; Students 368.

ELGIN. *Pope John XXIII Central Catholic High School at Elgin*, 303 Remington St., P.O. Box 179, 68636. Tel: 402-843-5325; Fax: 402-843-2297. Email: bgetzfre@esu8.org. Betty Getzfred, Prin.; Revs. Daniel R. Andrews, Pres.; John P. Broheimer, Theology Teacher; Joan Stuhr, Librarian. Priests 2; School Sisters of St. Francis 1; Lay Teachers 11; Students 95.

HARTINGTON. *Cedar Catholic High School* (1964) 401 S. Broadway, P.O. Box 15, 68739-0015. Tel: 402-254-3906; Fax: 402-254-3976. Email: cbernard@esu1.org. Web: www.cedarcatholic.org. Mr. Chris Bernard, Prin.; Rev. Jeffrey S. Loseke, Pres.; Marilyn Rastede, Librarian. Priests 3; Sisters 1; Lay Teachers 19; Students 208; Total Staff 22.

WEST POINT. *Central Catholic High School*, 419 E. Decateur, 68788. Tel: 402-372-5326; Fax: 402-372-5327. Web: www.westpointcentralcatholic.org. Matthew R. Richardson, Prin.; Mary Jo Kempschneider, Librarian. Priests 2; Franciscan Sisters of Christian Charity 1; Lay Teachers 16; Students 100.

[C] HIGH SCHOOLS, PRIVATE

OMAHA. *Creighton Preparatory School*, 7400 Western Ave., 68114. Tel: 402-393-1190; Fax: 402-393-0260. Email: tmerk@prep.creighton.edu. Web: www.creightonprep.creighton.edu. Rev. Thomas Merkel, S.J., Pres., Supr.; Mr. John Naatz, Prin.; Revs. William J. Doran, S.J.; William F. O'Leary, S.J.; Kevin C. Schneider, S.J.; James A. Sinnerud, S.J.; George Sullivan, S.J.; Robert J. Tillman, S.J.; Bro. Edward Gill, S.J.; Mrs. Diane Sands, Librarian; Christopher Johnson; Michael Lex. Priests 6; Scholastics 2; Lay Teachers 69; Students 1,039.

Duchesne Academy of the Sacred Heart (1881) 3601 Burt St., 68131. Tel: 402-558-3800; Fax: 402-558-0051. Email: shaggas@duchesneacademy.org. Web: www.duchesneacademy.org. Mrs. Sheila K. Haggas, Head of School & Contact; Laura Hickman, Prin.; Suzanne Rose, Librarian. Society of the Sacred Heart 3; Lay Teachers 32; Girls 299.

Marian High School, 74th and Military Ave., 68134. Tel: 402-571-2618, Ext. 114; Fax: 402-571-1952. Email: stoohey@marian.creighton.edu. Web: marianhighschool.net. Susan Toohey, Head of School, Prin. & Contact. Servants of Mary. Lay Teachers 50; Girls 643.

Mercy High School (1955) 1501 S. 48th St., 68106. Tel: 402-553-9424; Fax: 402-553-0394. Email: burnellj@mercyhigh.org. Web: www.mercyhigh.org. Sr. Delores Hannon, R.S.M., Pres. & Contact; Carolyn Jaworski, Prin.; Kathy Redding, Librarian. Sisters of Mercy of the Americas 2; Lay Teachers 36; Girls 390.

ELKHORN. *Mount Michael Benedictine School*, 22520 Mt. Michael Rd., 68022-3400. Tel: 402-289-2541; Fax: 442-289-4539. Email: tridder@mountmichael.org. Web: www.mountmichaelhs.com. Rt. Revs. Michael Liebl, O.S.B., Abbot; Raphael Walsh, O.S.B., Pres.; Thomas H. Ridder, Prin.; Revs. Richard Thell, O.S.B.; John Hagemann, O.S.B.; Daniel Lenz, O.S.B.; Louis L. Sojka, O.S.B.; Stephen J. Plank, O.S.B.; Bro. Luke Clinton, Librarian. Priests 7; Sisters 1; Professed Brothers 4; Lay Teachers 19; Students 205.

[D] ELEMENTARY SCHOOLS, INTER-PAROCHIAL

OMAHA. *All Saints Catholic School*, 1335 S. 10th St., 68108. Tel: 402-346-5757; Fax: 402-346-8794. Email: allsts@cathschls.creighton.edu. Marlan Burki, Prin. & Contact. Serving parishes of St. Frances Cabrini, St. Joseph, St. Mary Magdalene Immaculate Conception, St. Patrick and also St. Peter, St. Rose, St. Bridget Lay Teachers 15; Students 160.

Assumption-Guadalupe Grade School, 5602 S. 22nd St., 68107. Tel: 402-734-4504; Fax: 402-734-4505. Web: www.assumptionguadalupe.com. Rev. James E. Keiter, Pres.; Nicole Lanum, Prin.; Monica Brown, Librarian. Priests 1; Lay Teachers 17; Students 209; Preschool 13.

St. James-Seton School, 4720 N. 90th St., 68134. Tel: 402-572-0339; Fax: 402-572-0347. Email: sjsprin@sjsomaha.org. Web: sjsomaha.org. Terry Crum, Prin. & Contact; Nan Forman, Librarian. Lay Teachers 35; Students 718; Total Staff 66.

St. Pius X/St. Leo School (1956) 6905 Blondo St., 68104. Tel: 402-551-6667; Fax: 402-551-8123. Email: joyce.gubbels@spsl.net. Web: www.spsl.net. Mrs. Joyce Gubbels, Prin. & Contact; Mrs. Christy Vogel, Librarian. Sisters 2; Lay Teachers 52; Students 755.

FORDYCE. *West Catholic Elementary*, (Grades 1-6), 303 Omaha St., P.O. Box 167, 68736-0167. Tel: 402-357-3507; Fax: 402-357-3551. Email: csbrewer@schools.archomaha.com. Dianne Becker, Librarian; Mary Pinkelman, Office Mgr.; Minette Platz, 1-2 Grade Teacher; Teresa Aarens, 3-4 Grade Teacher; Connie Brewer, 5-6 Grade Teacher & Head Teacher. Serving parishes in Constance, Fordyce & Menominee Lay Teachers 3; Students 34.

HARTINGTON. *East Catholic Elementary* Serving parishes in Bow Valley, St. Helena & Wynot, 108 W. 889th Rd., 68739-6079. Tel: 402-357-2146; Fax: 402-357-3758. Email: mjklug@schools.archomaha.org. Mary Jean Klug, Head Teacher. Lay Teachers 5; Students 50.

HOWELLS. *Howells Community Catholic School*, 114 N. 6th St., 68641. Tel: 402-986-1689; Fax: 402-986-1689. Carrie Gall, Head Teacher; Rev. Leo Rigatuso; Pat Recker, Librarian. Serving parishes in Howells, Olean, Heun, Aloys & Tabor Lay Teachers 4; Students 59.

[E] ELEMENTARY SCHOOLS, PRIVATE

OMAHA. *The Jesuit Middle School of Omaha* (1996) 2311 N. 22nd St., 68110. Tel: 402-346-4464; Fax: 402-341-1817. Email: ski@jesuit.coxatwork.com. Web: www.jesuitmso.org. Rev. James L. Michalski, S.J., Pres. & Contact; Anthony Connelly, Prin. Lay Teachers 5; Students 72; Total Staff 11.

[F] SPECIAL EDUCATION

OMAHA. *Madonna School*, 6402 N. 71st Plaza, 68104. Tel: 402-556-1883; Fax: 402-556-7332. Email: madonnaschool@cov.net. Web: www.madonnaschool.org. Sr. Michelle Faltus, S.F.C.C., Exec. Dir. Serving Special Needs Children. Lay Teachers 9; Para Teachers 7; Administrators 4; Students 57.

Madonna Shop, 15683 Spaulding St., 68116. Tel: 402-551-5441; Fax: 402-551-6910. Email: rdm7911@aol.com. Robin Moses, Mgr. Workshop for physical and mental disabilities Total Staff 9; Total Enrollment 41.

[G] GENERAL HOSPITALS

OMAHA. **Archbishop Bergan Mercy Medical Center* (1910) 7500 Mercy Rd., 68124. Tel: 402-398-6060; Fax: 402-398-6920. Web: alegent.com. Marie Knedler, Admin.; Revs. Carl F. Sodoro, Chap.; Ron Elliott, Chap. & Pastoral Care Mgr.; Mary Mason, Chap.; Sr. Dorothy Rolf, Chap.; Rev. Kit Billings, Chap.; Rev. Jodi Wangsness, Chap.; Marian Standeven, Operations Leader Mission Svcs./Community Affairs. Affiliate of Catholic Health Initiatives. Priests 1; Sisters 1; Bed Capacity 400; Patients Assisted Annually 100,292; Total Staff 1,875.

**Bergan Mercy Foundation, Inc.* Tel: 402-343-4438; Fax: 402-343-4316. Shane Seymour, Chief Devel. Officer; Beth Llewellyn, Vice Pres. Mission Integration.

Boys Town National Research Hospital, 555 N. 30 St., 68131. Tel: 402-498-6511; Fax: 402-498-6357. Web: www.boystownhospital.org. Dr. Patrick Brookhouser, Dir. Bed Capacity 155; Total Assisted Annually 48,844; Total Staff 841.

O'NEILL. *Avera St. Anthony's Hospital* (1952) 300 N. 2nd St., 68763. Tel: 402-336-2611; Fax: 402-336-5135. Email: Ron.Cork@avera-sta.org. Web: www.avera-sta.org. Ronald J. Cork, Pres. & CEO. Sponsored by Sisters of the Presentation of the B.V.M. of Aberdeen, SD & Benedictine Sisters of Sacred Heart Monastery, Yankton, SD., Attended by St. Patrick Church. Bed Capacity 25; Bassinets 6; Patients Assisted Annually 23,556; Total Staff 243.

WEST POINT. *Franciscan Care Services, Inc. dba St. Francis Memorial Hospital* 430 N. Monitor St., 68788-1595. Tel: 402-372-2404; Fax: 402-372-2360. Email: rbriggs@fcswp.org. Web: www.fcswp.org. Ronald O. Briggs, CEO & Contact; Deacon Vince Maly, Chap. Franciscan Sisters of Christian Charity. Sisters 4; Bed Capacity 25; Patients Assisted Annually 66,645; Total Staff 230.

[H] NURSING AND CONVALESCENT HOMES

OMAHA. *Mercy Villa*, 1845 S. 72nd St., 68124. Tel: 402-391-6224; Fax: 402-390-8691. Email: mreichmuth@mercywmw.org. Sr. Monica Marie Reichmuth, R.S.M., Community Care Coord. Retirement Home for the Sisters of Mercy of the Americas for the West Midwest Community. Resident Sisters 47; Total Assisted 40; Total Staff 55.

New Cassel Retirement Center, 900 N. 90th St., 68114. Tel: 402-393-2277; Fax: 402-393-3784. Web: www.newcassel.org. Mr. Joseph H. Schulte, Admin.; Rev. Bob Smith; Mary Kerres, Dir. Pastoral Care. School Sisters of St. Francis. Sisters 4; Aged Residents 179; Total Staff 75.

WEST POINT. *Franciscan Care Services, Inc. dba St. Joseph Retirement Community* (1905) 320 E. Decatur, 68788. Tel: 402-372-3477; Fax: 402-372-6600. Web: www.fcswp.org. Jerry Wordekemper, Admin. Franciscan Sisters of Christian Charity (Manitowoc, WI) 3; Residents 75; Total Assisted Annually 65; Total Staff 37.

[I] PROTECTIVE INSTITUTIONS

BOYS TOWN. **Father Flanagan's Boys' Home*, 14100 Cranford Dr., 68010. Tel: 402-498-1000; Fax: 402-498-1010. Email: peterv@boystown.org. Web: www.boystown.org. Rev. Steven Boes, Exec. Dir. & Pres.; Dr. Dan Daly, Exec. Vice Pres. Youth Care; Robert Pick, Vice Pres., Nebraska - Iowa; Rev. Eugene McReynolds, O.S.B.; Robert Gehringer, High School Prin.; Cathy DeSalvo, Grade School Prin. Priests 4; High School: Teachers 28; Students 399; Grade School: Teachers 14; Students 89.

Boys Town USA (1986) Tel: 402-498-1928; Fax: 402-498-1010. Jim Gross, Vice Pres., Training & Evaluation; Dr. Jerry Davis, Vice Pres., Nat'l Advocacy & Public Policy; John Mollison, Spec. Liaison Alumni; Rev. Valentine J. Peter, S.T.D., J.C.D., Senior Assoc. Pastor.

Boys Town National Research & Training Center (1989) Tel: 402-498-1560; Fax: 402-498-1500. Stacy Young, Senior Vice Pres. Human Resources; Lori Susie, Senior Vice Pres., Devel.

Boys Town National Research Hospital for Children (1975) Tel: 402-498-6501; Fax: 402-498-6357. Dr. Patrick Brookhouser, Exec. Vice Pres. Health Care; John Arch, Vice Pres., Admin.; Pat Connell, Vice Pres., Behavioral Health.

Boys Town Crisis Hotline (1986) Tel: 800-448-3000; Fax: 402-498-6357. Ginny Gohr, Coord.

Boys Town Center for Adolescent & Family Spirituality (1998) Tel: 402-498-1009; Fax: 402-493-9575. Laura Budenberg, Co-Dir.; Kathy McGee, Co-Dir. Total Assisted For All Programs 46,213; Total Staff 2,204.

[J] FAMILY SERVICE CENTERS

OMAHA. *Catholic Charities*, Daniel E. Sheehan Center, 3300 N. 60th St., 68104. Tel: 402-554-0520; Fax: 402-554-0365. Email: catholiccharities@ccomaha.org. Web: www.ccomaha.org.

Catholic Charities, Inc. Satellite Offices and Services:

Christ Child Center, 1248 S. 10th St., 68108. Tel: 402-342-4566; Fax: 402-342-4541. Email: ChristChildMain@ccomaha.org. Shelley Schrader, J.D., Senior Dir.; Monroe Evans, Prog. Dir. Services: Community Services administration; After-School programs; Health and recreation: gym and pool; Senior Services Health and recreation: bingo, pool, socialization, classes; summer camp.

Columbus Center, 3020 18th St., Columbus, 68601. Tel: 402-563-3833; Fax: 402-562-8714. Email: ColumbusClinic@ccomaha. org. Steve Johnson, LMHP, CPC, Dir. Services: Assessments, Mental health/substance abuse: adult and youth; Columbus Center administration; Community reintegration and support; Outpatient treatment, Medication management: adult, Mental health: adult & youth, Substance abuse: adult & youth; Residential treatment, co-occurring: adult.

Christ Child Learning Center, 2201 S. 11th St., 68108. Tel: 402-341-1880; Fax: 402-933-2941. Email: ChristChildLearning@ccomaha.org. Karen Bluvas, Dir. Services: Day care; Pre-School.

Domestic Violence Services - The Shelter Tel: 402-558-5700. Email: FrancesH@ccomaha.org. Terese Holm, R.N., M.S.N., Dir.; France Hauptman, L.M.H.P., L.C.S.W., Prog. Dir. Services: 24-hour crisis line; counseling & advocacy; emergency shelter & temporary housing.

Father Kelligar House, 4439 S. 33rd St., 68107. Tel: 402-827-3495; Fax: 402-827-3595. Email: KHouse@ccomaha.org. Joanie Huss, L.M.H.P., L.A.D.C., Clinical Mgr. Services: Intermediate residential treatment.

Journeys Tel: 402-898-4135; Fax: 402-898-4139. Email: JourneysBldg@ccomaha.org. Teri Speck, Dir. Services: Assessments, Substance abuse/ mental health: adolescent; Community reintegration and support; Education, Substance abuse: adolescent, Outreach; Outpatient treatment, Intensive group therapy: adolescent, Family therapy, Routine outpatient: adolescent; Residential treatment, Adolescent, Family therapy.

Journeys (West Office), 10806 Prairie Hills Dr., 68144. Tel: 402-504-4099; Fax: 402-898-4139. Email: JourneysBldg@ccomaha.org. Teri Speck, Dir. Services: Assessments, Substance abuse/ mental health: adolescent; Community reintegration & support; Education, Substance abuse: adolescent, Outreach; Outpatient treatment, Intensive group therapy: adolescent, Family therapy, Routine outpatient: adolescent.

Juan Diego Center, 5211 S. 31st St. (SONA Bldg.), 68107. Tel: 402-731-5413; Fax: 402-731-5865. Email: JuanDiegoCenter@ccomaha.org. John Synowiecki, Dir. Govt. Rels.; Elisha Novak, Dir. Immigration Legal Assistance; Ana Barrios, Dir. Juan Diego Prog.; Karen Mavropoulos, Dir. Microbusiness Training & Devel. Services: Government Relations and Public Policy.; Immigration Legal Assistance: Family-based consultation & representation; Naturalization clinics; Outreach & education: Justice for Immigrants; Refugee adjustment of status; VAWA/U-Visa immigration benefit.; Juan Diego Program: Domestic Violence Services, counseling & advocacy; Family Enrichment Program, basic skills education, financial family planning, nutrition & health, parenting classes; Food Assistance, Christmas & Thanksgiving meals, emergency food pantry, perishable daily food distribution, share food buying.; Latina Resource Center: community referral services; domestic violence counseling; English as a Second Language classes (ESL); GED classes.; Microbusiness Training & Development: business financing; business resource center & computer lab; continuing education & consultation; training & development.

North Center, 2111 Emmet St., 68110. Tel: 402-453-6363; Fax: 402-934-5313. Email: ChristChildNorth@ccomaha.org. Monroe Evans, Dir. Services: After school programs; summer camp.

Omaha Campus for Hope, 1490 N. 16th St., 68102. Tel: 402-827-0570; Fax: 402-827-0580. Email: OCHBLdg@ccomaha.org. Michael Phillips, Dir.; Madonna Licht, L.M.H.P., L.C.S.W., Asst. Dir. Services: Community reintegration & support - adults; Emergency detoxification services - adults, involuntary detox program, protective custody services, sustance abuse assessments; Residential treatment - adults, short term, intermediate, co-occurring substance abuse & mental health disorders.

Sheehan Center, 3300 N. 60th St., 68104. Tel: 402-554-0520; Fax: 402-554-0365. Email: SheehanCenterCampus@ccomaha.org. Joseph V. Rysavy, Senior Dir. Admin.; Terese Holm, R.N., M.S.N., Dir. Assessments & Outpatient Treatment & Dir. Pregnancy Counseling & Adoption; Mel Brestel, L.M.H.P., M.S.W., Prog. Mgr. Assessments & Outpatient Treatment; Jean Sassatelli, Senior Dir. Behavioral Health; Shelley Schrader, J.D., Senior Dir. Community Svcs.; Kathy Fitzgerald Grandsaert, Senior Dir. Devel.; Anne Steinhoff, Interim Dir.; Theresa Ross, Dir. Fin.; Kaisha Harris, Dir. Human Resources; Scott Morris, Dir. Information Tech.; Teri Hautzinger, Dir. Mktg.; Sue Malloy, Prog. Mgr. Pregancy Counseling & Adoption. Services: Assessments, mental health/ substance abuse: adult; Outpatient treatment, medication management, mental health: adult, substance abuse: adult, family therapy; Pregnancy Counseling & Adoption, pregnancy counseling, Mentoring Moms, adoption services & counseling, post-adoption services.

St. James Manor, 3102 N. 60th St., 68104. Tel: 402-551-4243; Fax: 402-558-8013. Email: StJamesManor@ccomaha.org. Deb Lang, Dir. Services: affordable housing.

St. Martin de Porres Center, 2417 Burdette St., 68111. Tel: 402-341-4004; Fax: 402-341-1130. Email: StMartinDePorresBldg@ccomaha.org. Marilyn Sims, Dir. Services: Community Forums: Friends & families of inmates, neighborhood association meetings. Family Enrichment & Support: family activities, family enrichment program, basic skills education, financial family planning, nutrition & health, parenting classes. Food Assistance: Christmas & Thanksgiving meals, emergency food pantry, perishable daily food distribution, share food buying. Senior Services: health & recreation, bingo, pool, socialization, classes.

[K] MONASTERIES AND RESIDENCES OF PRIESTS AND BROTHERS

OMAHA. *Jesuit Community at Creighton University*, 2500 California Plaza, 68178. Tel: 402-280-2700; Fax: 402-280-5590. Email: jesuits@creighton.edu. Web: www.creighton.edu. Revs. Robert F. O'Connor, S.J., Rector; Philip R. Amidon, S.J.; Andrew Alexander, S.J.; Thomas E. Bannantine, S.J.; Charles R. Baumann, S.J.; Burnell B. Bisbee, S.J.; Hubert G. Boschert, S.J.; Raymond A. Bucko, S.J.; Robert O. Burns, S.J.; Gregory I. Carlson, S.J.; James F. Clifton, S.J.; Paul Coelho, S.J.; John D. Cuddigan, S.J., Pastoral Ministry; Donald A. Doll, S.J.; Michael J. Flecky, S.J.; William F. Gerut, S.J.; Lawrence D. Gillick, S.J.; M. Dennis Hamm, S.J.; William J. Harmless, S.J.; Richard J. Hauser, S.J.; Bro. James F. Heidrick, S.J.; Revs. John P. Horn, S.J.; Eugene J. Jakubek, S.J.; William T. Johnson, S.J.; Howard E. Kalb, S.J.; Charles T. Kestermeier, S.J.; Paul A. Mahowald, S.J.; Patrick J. Malone, S.J.; Dennis P. McNeilly, S.J.; Thomas S. McShane, S.J., Prof.; James L. Michalski, S.J.; Michael G. Morrison, S.J.; Richard W. Ott, S.J.; Anand Pereira, S.J.; Francis A. Prokes, S.J.; Perry L. Robinson, S.J.; John P. Schlegel, S.J., Pres., Creighton Univ.; Thomas J. Shanahan, S.J.; Thomas A. Simonds, S.J.; David L. Smith, S.J.; Bro. Robert E. Smith, S.J.; Revs. Paul J. Strittmatter, S.J.; Albert R. Thelen, S.J.; Robert J. Tillman, S.J.; Bro. James Edema, S.J.; Rev. Neal J. Wilkinson, S.J.; Bro. Michael R. Wilmot, S.J.; Revs. M. John Wymelenberg, S.J.; John D. Zuercher, S.J.

Jesuit Community at Creighton University Priests 48; Brothers 4; Jesuit Scholastics 1.

ELKHORN. *Mount Michael Benedictine Abbey* (1954) 22520 Mount Michael Rd., 68022-3400. Tel: 402-289-2541; Fax: 402-289-4539. Email: abbot@mountmichael.org. Web: www.mountmichael.org. Rt. Revs. Theodore Wolff, O.S.B.; Michael Liebl, O.S.B., Abbot; Raphael Walsh, O.S.B., Pres. School; Bro. Jerome Kmiecik, O.S.B.; Revs. Adrian Liable, O.S.B.; Nathanael Foshage, O.S.B.; Eugene McReynolds, O.S.B.; Richard Thell, O.S.B., Prior; John Hagemann, O.S.B.; Daniel Lenz, O.S.B.; Louis L. Sojka, O.S.B., Subprior & Contact; Stephen J. Plank, O.S.B. Mount Michael Benedictine Abbey Priests 11; Professed Brothers 12; Total Assisted 210; Total Staff 60.

ST. COLUMBANS. *Missionary Society of St. Columban* (Corporate Title: Missionary Society of St. Columban), 68056. Tel: 402-291-1920; Fax: 402-291-8693. Email: directorusa@columban.org. Web: www.columban.org. Revs. Arturo Aguilar, S.S.C., Regl. Dir.; Salvatore Caputo, S.S.C., Ph.D.; Michael Dodd, S.S.C.; Edward Dolan, S.S.C.; Charles Lintz, S.S.C.; Anthony Mortell, S.S.C.; Donal O'Farrell, S.S.C.; Charles O'Rourke, S.S.C.; Edward Quinn, S.S.C.; William Schmitt, S.S.C.; Thomas Shaughnessy, S.S.C.; Colm Stanley, S.S.C.; Richard Steinhiber, S.S.C.; Paul White, S.S.C. Regional Headquarters and Administration Offices of the Columban Fathers in the United States Priests 12.

Other Assignments: Revs. Donald Kelley, S.S.C. (Retired), Brownsville; Peter Cronin, S.S.C., Buffalo; Vincent McCarthy, S.S.C., Buffalo; James Michaels, S.S.C., Buffalo; Thomas Walsh, S.S.C., Buffalo; Charles Flaherty, S.S.C., Boston; Leo Distor, S.S.C., Chicago; Charles Duster, S.S.C., Chicago; Thomas Glennon, S.S.C., Chicago; Francis Grady, S.S.C., Chicago; Timothy Mulroy, S.S.C., Chicago; Francis Roger, S.S.C., Chicago; John Smith, S.S.C., Chicago; John Wanaurny, S.S.C., Chicago; Clarence Beckley, S.S.C. (Retired), Dubuque; Michael Donnelly, S.S.C., El Paso; William Morton, S.S.C., El Paso; Kevin Mullins, S.S.C., El Paso; Dennis O'Mara, S.S.C., El Paso; Albert Utzig, S.S.C., El Paso; Robert Burke, S.S.C. (Retired), Joliet; John Brannigan, S.S.C., Los Angeles; Yong Hoon Choi, S.S.C., Los Angeles; Thomas Cusack, S.S.C., Los Angeles; George DaRoza, S.S.C., Los Angeles; Gerard Dunne, S.S.C., Los Angeles; Peter Kenny, S.S.C., Los Angeles; Francis Manion, S.S.C., Los Angeles; Thomas Reynolds, S.S.C., Los Angeles; James Shiffer, S.S.C., Los Angeles; Edward Roberts, S.S.C., Palm Beach; Denis Bartley, S.S.C., Providence; John Buckley, S.S.C., Providence; Francis Carroll, S.S.C., Providence; Charles Degnan, S.S.C., Providence; James Dwyer, S.S.C.; Howard Eisel, S.S.C., Providence; Norbert Feld, S.S.C., Providence; Victor Gaboury, S.S.C. (Retired), Providence; Brian Gallagher, S.S.C., Providence; Michael Harrison, S.S.C., Providence; John Hogan, S.S.C., Providence; Francis Keaney, S.S.C., Providence; Oliver Kennedy, S.S.C., Providence; John Marley, S.S.C., Providence; Daniel McGinn, S.S.C., Providence; Joseph McSweeney, S.S.C., Providence; Joseph McSweeny, S.S.C., Providence; John Moran, S.S.C., Providence; Paul O'Malley, S.S.C. (Retired), Providence; Robert O'Rourke, S.S.C. (Retired), Providence; Paul Richardson, S.S.C., Providence; John Roche, S.S.C., Providence; Alban Sueper, S.S.C. (Retired), Providence; William Sullivan, S.S.C., Providence; William Sweeney, S.S.C., Providence; John Lagomarsino, S.S.C., Sacramento; Gerard O'Shaughnessy, S.S.C., San Bernardino; Brendan O'Sullivan, S.S.C., San Bernardino; Bernard Toal, S.S.C., San Bernardino; Robert Clark, S.S.C., San Diego; Finbar Maxwell, S.S.C., San Jose; William Brunner, S.S.C., Sioux City; Cathal Gallagher, S.S.C., Sioux Falls; Mark Mengel, S.S.C., Springfield, MA; Robert Mosher, S.S.C., St. Louis; Thomas Vaughan, S.S.C. (Retired), St. Paul; Gerald Wilmsen, S.S.C. (Retired), Superior.

SCHUYLER. *Benedictine Mission House*, 1123 Rd. I, P.O. Box 528, 68661-0528. Tel: 402-352-2177; Fax: 402-352-2176. Email: monastery@benedictinemissionhouse.com. Web: www.benedictinemissionhouse.com. Revs. German Neubert, O.S.B., Prior & Contact; Volker Futter, O.S.B., Subprior; Thomas Aquinas Leitner, O.S.B.; Paul L. Kasun, O.S.B. Brothers 4.

[L] CONVENTS AND RESIDENCES FOR SISTERS

OMAHA. *Monastery of St. Clare* (1878) 3626 N. 65th Ave., 68104. Tel: 402-558-4916; Fax: 402-558-5046. Web: www.omahapoorclare.com. Sr. Mary Clare Brown, Contact. Poor Clares (Second Order of St. Francis)., Attended by Jesuit Fathers. Sisters 8.

Motherhouse of the Servants of Mary, Convent of Our Lady of Sorrows, 7400 Military Ave., 68134. Tel: 402-571-2547; Fax: 402-573-6055. Web: www.osms.org. Sisters Virginia Silvestri, O.S.M., Prov. & Contact; Margaret Stratman, O.S.M., Asst. Prov. Professed 87; Sisters in Motherhouse 34.

Provincial Motherhouse and Novitiate of the Notre Dame Sisters (1853) 3501 State St., 68112. Tel: 402-455-2994; Fax: 402-455-3974. Email: notredamesisters@notredamesisters.org. Web: www.notredamesisters.org. Sr. Celeste Wobeter, N.D., Prov. Pres. Professed 49; Sisters in Motherhouse 21.

Sisters of Mercy of the Americas West Midwest Community, Inc. (2008) 7262 Mercy Rd., 68124-2389. Tel: 402-393-8225; Fax: 402-393-8145. Email: info@mercywmw.org. Web: www.mercywestmidwest.org. Sisters Norita Cooney, R.S.M., Pres.; Judith Frikker, R.S.M., Substitute Pres.; Sheila Megley, R.S.M., Treas.; Judith Cannon, R.S.M., Sec.; Kathy Thornton, R.S.M., Leadership Team; Michelle Gorman, R.S.M., Leadership Team; Kim Kinsel, Community Operating Officer; Carol Kelley, Community Fin. Officer; Sandy Goetzinger-Comer, Dir. Communications. Sisters of Mercy of the Americas West Midwest Community, Inc., (As of July 1, 2008 the Sisters of Mercy of the Americas Regional Communities of Auburn, CA; Burlingame, CA; Cedar Rapids, IA; Chicago, IL; Detroit, MI; and Omaha, NE, merged to create Sisters of Mercy of the Americas West Midwest Community, Inc.) Sisters 810; Associates 565.

Knowles Mercy Spirituality Center, 2304 Campanile Rd., Waterloo, 68069. Tel: 402-359-4288; Fax: 402-359-4843. Email: kmscenter@mercywmw.org. Web: www.kmscenter.org. Sr. Jean Sitter, R.S.M., Dir.; Marisa Gilbert, Assoc. Dir. Overnight Capacity 15; Daytime Capacity 60; Staff 6.

Sisters of the Good Shepherd (R.G.S.), 1106 N. 36th St., 68131. Tel: 402-551-2966; Fax: 402-292-2046. Email: ellen.dolan@stmarysbellevueebm. Web: www.goodshepherdsisters.org.

NORFOLK. *Immaculata Monastery* (1923) 300 N. 18th St., 68701-3687. Tel: 402-371-3438; Fax: 402-379-2877. Email: khermsen@norfolk-osb.org. Web: www.norfolk-osb.org. Sr. Kevin Hermsen, O.S.B., Prioress & Contact.

Immaculata Monastery, Priory Motherhouse and Novitiate of the Missionary Benedictine Sisters Sisters 35; Personnel 15.

[M] SECULAR INSTITUTES

OMAHA. *Cor Unum Family Inc.*, 7323 Shirley St., #101, 68124. Tel: 402-933-9812. Email: bwhelanl@cox.net. Rev. Msgr. William S. Whelan, Contact Person (Retired).

Institute of the Apostolic Oblates (1950) 6762 Western Ave., 68132. Tel: 402-553-4418; Fax: 402-553-1388. Email: aoomaha@prosanctity.org. Web: www.prosanctity.org. Teresa J. Monaghen, Natl. Moderator; Franca Salvo, Local Moderator, & Contact Person; Jessica L. Kary, Vocation Dir. A secular institute for women with the aim of promoting the apostolate of interior life, the universal call to holiness, and the Pro Sanctity Movement.

Apostolic Sodales formerly Apostolic Sodales - Secular Institute (1962) 11002 N. 204 St., Elkhorn, 68022. Tel: 402-731-2196; Fax: 402-731-2196. Web: http://apostolic-sodales.org. Revs. Thomas W. Weisbecker, First Natl. Bro.; Frank E. Jindra, Spiritual Dir.; Carl J. Zoucha, Contact Person. A Secular Institute for priests with the aim of promoting the spirituality of the Cenacle, brotherhood among priests, and forming the Church as a family.

ELKHORN. *Pro Sanctity Movement* (1947) 11002 N. 204th St., 68022. Tel: 402-289-2670; Fax: 402-289-1938. Email: psm@prosanctity.org. Web: www.prosanctitate.org. Teresa Monaghen, Natl. Dir. & Contact. Tel: 402-289-2670. Ecclesial organization: Promotes apostolates of holiness; teaches, supports and guides people seeking to deepen their spiritual life.

[N] FOUNDATIONS AND TRUST FUNDS

OMAHA. *The Institute for Priestly Formation Foundation*, 2500 California Plaza, 68178. Tel: 402-546-6384. Mr. P. Thomas Pogge, Exec. Dir.

The Omaha Archdiocesan Educational Foundation, Inc.

The Office of Stewardship and Development formerly The Office of Stewardship, Planning and Development 3212 North 60th St., P.O. Box 4130, 68104-0130. Tel: 402-554-8493; Fax: 402-554-8402. Email: mejewell@archomaha.org.

Archbishop Sheehan Adult Education Endowment Trust

All Saints Catholic School Educational Endowment Trust

Black Students Catholic Educational Endowment Trust

Black Student Catholic Scholarship Trust Fund, 68104. A trust for the purpose of providing eligible black Catholic students scholarships and assistance for Catholic high school education. The board of 10 trustees for a nonprofit religious and educational corporation, whose president is the Archbishop of Omaha oversees the affairs of this trust.

Music in Catholic Schools Endowment Trust

Roncalli Catholic High School Educational Endowment Trust

Roncalli Catholic High School Scholarship Endowment Trust

Religious Education Evangelization Commission Endowment Trust

The Catholic Voice Educational Endowment Trust

Marian High School Scholarship Endowment Trust

Marian High School Endowment Trust

The Omaha Archdiocesan Parish Foundation, Inc.

St. Michael Church Endowment Trust, Albion.

St. Michael Church Educational Endowment Trust, Albion.

St. Aloysius Parish Endowment Trust, Aloys.

St. Aloysius Parish Educational Endowment Trust Aloys, NE

St. Joseph Parish Endowment Trust, Amelia.

St. Joseph Parish Educational Endowment Trust, Amelia.

St. Joseph Parish Endowment Trust, Atkinson.

St. Joseph Church Educational Endowment Trust, Atkinson.

Holy Cross Parish Endowment Trust, Bancroft.

Holy Cross Parish Educational Endowment Trust, Bancroft.

St. Patrick Parish Endowment Trust, Battle Creek.

St. Patrick Parish Educational Endowment Trust, Battle Creek.

Holy Cross Parish Endowment Trust, Beemer, 68716.

Holy Cross Parish Educational Endowment Trust, Beemer.

St. Mary Church Endowment Trust, Bellevue.

St. Mary Church Educational Endowment Trust, Bellevue.

St. Matthew the Evangelist Parish Endowment Trust, Bellevue, 68123.

St. Francis Borgia Parish Endowment Trust, Blair.

St. Francis Borgia Parish Educational Endowment Trust, Blair.

St. Andrew Parish Endowment Trust, Bloomfield.

St. Andrew Parish Educational Endowment Trust, Bloomfield.

SS. Peter and Paul Parish Endowment Trust, Bow Valley.

SS. Peter and Paul Parish Educational Endowment Trust, Bow Valley.

East Catholic Elementary School Educational Endowment Trust, Bow Valley.

St. Ignatius Parish Endowment Trust, Brunswick.

St. Ignatius Parish Educational Endowment Trust, Brunswick.

SS. Peter and Paul Parish Endowment Trust, Butte.

SS. Peter and Paul Parish Educational Endowment Trust, Butte.

St. Anthony Parish Endowment Trust, Cedar Rapids.

St. Anthony Parish Educational Endowment Trust, Cedar Rapids.

St. Michael Catholic Church Parish Endowment Trust, Central City.

St. Michael Parish Educational Endowment Trust, Central City.

St. Peter Parish Endowment Trust, Clarks.

St. Peter Parish Educational Endowment Trust, Clarks.

SS. Cyril and Methodius Parish Endowment Trust, Clarkson.

SS. Cyril and Methodius Parish Educational Endowment Trust, Clarkson.

Holy Trinity Church of Colfax, County Parish and Cemetery Endowment Trust Fund, Clarkson, 68629.

St. Theresa of Avila Parish Endowment Trust, Clearwater.

St. Theresa of Avila Parish Educational Endowment Trust, Clearwater.

St. Theresa Church of Clearwater Cemetery Endowment Trust Fund, Clearwater, 68726.

St. Michael Parish Endowment Trust, Coleridge.

St. Michael Parish Educational Endowment Trust, Coleridge.

St. Anthony Parish Endowment Trust, Columbus.

St. Anthony Parish Educational Endowment Trust, Columbus.

St. Anthony Elementary School Endowment Trust, Columbus.

St. Bonaventure Church Endowment Trust, Columbus.

St. Isidore Church Endowment Trust, Columbus.

St. Isidore Parish Educational Endowment Trust, Columbus.

St. Isidore Elementary School Endowment Trust, Columbus.

Scotus Central Catholic High School Endowment Trust, Columbus.

St. Joseph Parish Endowment Trust, Constance.

St. Joseph Parish Educational Endowment Trust, Constance.

St. Ludger Parish Endowment Trust, Creighton.

St. Ludger Parish Educational Endowment Trust, Creighton.

St. Ludger Elementary School Endowment Trust, Creighton.

St. Joseph Church of Constance Endowment Trust Fund, Crofton, 68730. Rev. Joseph G. Broudou, Contact Person.

St. Rose Church Cemetery Endowment Trust Fund, Crofton, 68730. Rev. Joseph G. Broudou, Contact Person.

St. Rose of Lima Parish Endowment Trust, Crofton.

St. Rose of Lima Parish Educational Endowment Trust, Crofton.

Holy Family Parish Endowment Trust, Decatur.

Holy Family Parish Educational Endowment Trust, Decatur.

St. Anne Parish Endowment Trust, Dixon.

St. Anne Parish Educational Endowment Trust, Dixon.

St. Anne Church of Dixon Cemetery Endowment Trust Fund, Dixon, 68732.

St. Wenceslaus Parish Endowment Trust, Dodge.

St. Wenceslaus Church Educational Endowment Trust, Dodge.

St. Stanislaus Parish Endowment Trust, Duncan.

St. Stanislaus Parish Educational Endowment Trust, Duncan.

St. Boniface Parish Endowment Trust, Elgin.

St. Boniface Parish Educational Endowment Trust, Elgin.

St. Boniface School Endowment Trust, Elgin.

Pope John XXIII Central Catholic High School Endowment Trust, Elgin.

St. Patrick Parish Endowment Trust, Elkhorn.

St. Patrick School Endowment Trust, Elkhorn.

St. Patrick School Tuition Assistance Endowment Trust, Elkhorn.

Mt. Michael Foundation, Inc., Elkhorn.

Sacred Heart Parish Endowment Trust, Emerson.

Sacred Heart Parish Educational Endowment Trust, Emerson.

St. Peter de Alcantara Parish Endowment Trust, Ewing.

St. Peter de Alcantara Parish Educational Endowment Trust, Ewing.

St. Theresa Church of Clearwater Cemetery Endowment Trust Fund, Ewing, 68735. Rev. William J. Safranek, Contact.

St. John the Baptist Parish Endowment Trust, Fordyce.

St. John the Baptist Parish Educational Endowment Trust, Fordyce.

West Catholic Educational Endowment Trust, Fordyce.

St. John the Baptist Parish Endowment Trust, Fort Calhoun.

St. John the Baptist Church Educational Endowment Trust, Fort Calhoun.

St. Patrick Catholic Church Endowment Trust, Fremont.

St. Patrick Parish Educational Endowment Trust, Fremont.

Archbishop Bergan Jr./Sr. Catholic High School Educational Endowment Trust, Fremont.

St. Peter Catholic Church Endowment Trust, Fullerton.

St. Peter Parish Educational Endowment Trust, Fullerton.

St. Rose of Lima Parish Endowment Trust, Genoa.

St. Rose of Lima Parish Educational Endowment Trust, Genoa.

St. Patrick Parish Endowment Trust, Gretna.

St. Patrick Parish Educational Endowment Trust, Gretna.

Holy Trinity Parish Endowment Trust, Hartington.

Holy Trinity Parish Educational Endowment Trust, Hartington.

Holy Trinity Grade School Endowment Trust, Hartington.

Cedar Catholic High School Educational Endowment Trust, Hartington.

Holy Trinity Parish Endowment Trust, Heun.

Holy Trinity Parish Educational Endowment Trust, Heun.

Holy Trinity Parish of Colfax County Parish and Cemetery Endowment Trust Fund Heun, NE

St. Cornelius Parish Endowment Trust, Homer.

St. Cornelius Parish Educational Endowment Trust, Homer.

St. Rose of Lima Parish Endowment Trust, Hooper.

St. Rose of Lima Parish Educational Endowment Trust, Hooper.

St. John Nepomucene Parish Endowment Trust, Howells.

St. John Nepomucene Parish Educational Endowment Trust, Howells.

SS. Peter and Paul Parish Endowment Trust, Howells.

SS. Peter and Paul Parish Educational Endowment Trust, Howells.

SS. Peter and Paul Catholic Church Endowment for Howells Community Catholic School, Howells.

St. Mary Parish Endowment Trust, Hubbard.

St. Mary Parish Educational Endowment Trust, Hubbard.

St. Francis Parish Endowment Trust, Humphrey.

St. Francis Parish Educational Endowment Trust, Humphrey.

St. Francis Church of Humphrey Cemetery Endowment Trust Fund, Humphrey, 68642.

St. Patrick Parish Endowment Trust, Jackson.

St. Patrick Parish Educational Endowment Trust, Jackson.

SS. Peter and Paul Parish Endowment Trust, Krakow.

SS. Peter and Paul Parish Educational Endowment Trust, Krakow.

St. Ann Church of Dixon Cemetery Endowment Trust Fund, Laurel, 68745. Rev. James F. McCluskey.

St. Mary Parish Endowment Trust, Laurel.

St. Mary Parish Educational Endowment Trust, Laurel.

St. Mary Parish Endowment Trust, Leigh.

St. Mary Parish Cemetery Endowment Trust, Leigh.

Holy Family Parish Endowment Trust, Lindsay.

Holy Family Parish Educational Endowment Trust, Lindsay.

Assumption Parish Endowment Trust, Lynch.

Assumption Parish Educational Endowment Trust, Lynch.

Assumption Parish Cemetery Endowment Trust, Lynch.

St. Joseph Parish Endowment Trust, Lyons.

St. Joseph Parish Educational Endowment Trust, Lyons.

Our Lady of Fatima Parish Endowment Trust, Macy.

Our Lady of Fatima Parish Educational Endowment Trust, Macy.

St. Leonard Parish Endowment Trust, Madison.

St. Leonard Parish Educational Endowment Trust, Madison.

St. Boniface Parish Endowment Trust, Menominee.

St. Boniface Parish Educational Endowment Trust, Menominee.

St. Boniface's Church Cemetery Endowment Fund Menominee, NE

St. Boniface Parish Endowment Trust, Monterey.

St. Boniface Parish Educational Endowment Trust, Monterey.

Sacred Heart Parish Endowment Trust, Naper.

Sacred Heart Parish Educational Endowment Trust, Naper.
St. Francis of Assisi Parish Endowment Trust, Neligh.
St. Francis of Assisi Parish Educational Endowment Trust, Neligh.
St. Peter Parish Endowment Trust, Newcastle.
St. Peter Parish Educational Endowment Trust, Newcastle.
St. William Parish Endowment Trust, Niobrara.
St. William Parish Educational Endowment Trust, Niobrara.
Sacred Heart Parish Endowment Trust, Norfolk.
Sacred Heart Parish Religious Education Endowment Trust, Norfolk.
Sacred Heart Elementary School Educational Endowment Trust, Norfolk.
Norfolk Catholic High School Educational Endowment Trust, Norfolk.
St. Charles Borromeo Parish Endowment Trust, North Bend.
St. Charles Borromeo Parish Educational Endowment Trust, North Bend.
Sacred Heart Parish Endowment Trust, Olean.
Sacred Parish Educational Endowment Trust, Olean.
Church of the Assumption Endowment Trust
Church of the Assumption Educational Endowment Trust
Church of the Assumption Scholarship Educational Endowment Trust
Blessed Sacrament Parish Endowment Trust
Blessed Sacrament Parish Educational Endowment Trust
Blessed Sacrament School Educational Endowment Trust
Christ the King Parish Endowment Trust
Christ the King Educational Endowment Trust
Holy Cross Parish Endowment Trust
Holy Family Parish Endowment Trust
Holy Family Parish Educational Trust
Holy Ghost Parish Endowment Trust
Holy Ghost Parish Educational Endowment Trust
Holy Name Parish Endowment Trust
Holy Name Parish Educational Endowment Trust
Holy Name Elementary School Endowment Trust Omaha, NE
Immaculate Conception Parish Endowment Trust
Immaculate Conception Parish Educational Endowment Trust
Mary Our Queen Educational Endowment Trust
Mary Our Queen Parish Endowment Trust, 68198.
Mother of Perpetual Help Parish Endowment Trust
Mother of Perpetual Help Parish Educational Endowment Trust
Our Lady of Fatima Parish Endowment Trust
Our Lady of Fatima Parish Educational Endowment Trust
Our Lady of Guadalupe Parish Endowment Trust
Our Lady of Guadalupe Educational Endowment Trust, 68131.
Our Lady of Lourdes Parish Endowment Trust Tel: 402-346-0900.
Our Lady of Lourdes Parish Educational Endowment Trust Tel: 402-346-0900.
Our Lady of Lourdes School Educational Endowment Trust
Sacred Heart Parish Endowment Trust
Sacred Heart Parish Educational Endowment Trust

St. Adalbert Parish Endowment Trust
St. Adalbert Parish Educational Endowment Trust
St. Agnes Parish Endowment Trust
St. Agnes Parish Educational Endowment Trust
St. Ann Parish Endowment Trust
St. Ann Parish Educational Endowment Trust
St. Anthony Parish Endowment Trust
St. Anthony Parish Educational Endowment Trust
St. Benedict Parish Endowment Trust
St. Benedict Parish Educational Endowment Trust
St. Bernadette Parish Endowment Trust
St. Bernadette Parish Educational Endowment Trust

St. Bernard Parish Memorial Endowment Trust
St. Bernard Parish Religious Education Endowment Trust
St. Bridget Parish Endowment Trust
St. Bridget Parish Educational Endowment Trust
St. Cecilia Cathedral Endowment Trust
St. Elizabeth Ann Parish Endowment Trust
St. Elizabeth Ann Parish Educational Endowment Trust
St. Francis of Assisi Church of South Omaha Endowment Trust
St. Francis of Assisi Church of South Omaha Educational Endowment Trust
St. Frances Cabrini Parish Endowment Trust
St. Frances Cabrini Parish Educational Endowment Trust
St. James Parish Endowment Trust
St. James Parish Educational Endowment Trust
St. James/Seton School Educational Endowment Fund
St. Joan of Arc Parish Endowment Trust
St. Joan of Arc Parish Educational Endowment Trust
St. Joan of Arc Grade School Educational Endowment Trust
St. John Vianney Church of Millard Parish Endowment Trust
St. John Vianney Parish Educational Endowment Trust
St. Joseph Parish Endowment Trust
St. Joseph Parish Educational Endowment Trust
St. Leo Parish Endowment Trust
St. Leo Parish Educational Endowment Trust
St. Margaret Mary Parish Endowment Trust
St. Margaret Mary Parish Educational Endowment Trust
St. Margaret Mary School Educational Endowment Trust
St. Mary's Church of Tabor Parish and Cemetery Endowment Trust Fund, 100 North 62nd St., 68132. Tel: 402-986-1627; Fax: 402-986-1627.
St. Mary Parish Endowment Trust
St. Mary Parish Educational Endowment Trust
St. Mary Elementary School Endowment Trust
St. Patrick Parish Endowment Trust
St. Patrick Church Educational Endowment Trust
St. Peter Parish Endowment Trust
St. Peter Parish Educational Endowment Trust
SS. Peter and Paul Church Endowment Trust
SS. Peter and Paul Parish Educational Endowment Trust
SS. Peter and Paul Elementary School Educational Endowment Trust
St. Philip Neri Church Endowment Trust
St. Philip Neri Parish Educational Endowment Trust
St. Pius X Parish Endowment Trust
St. Pius X Parish Educational Endowment Trust
St. Pius X/St. Leo School Educational Endowment Trust
St. Richard Parish Endowment Trust
St. Richard Parish Educational Endowment Trust
St. Richard Grade School Educational Endowment Trust
St. Robert Bellarmine Parish Endowment Trust
St. Rose Parish Endowment Trust
St. Rose Parish Educational Endowment Trust
St. Stanislaus Parish Endowment Trust
St. Stanislaus Parish Educational Endowment Trust

St. Stephen the Martyr Parish Endowment Trust
St. Stephen the Martyr Parish Educational Endowment Trust
St. Stephen the Martyr Elementary School Educational Endowment Trust
Teachers' Salary Endowment Trust Fund of St. Stephen Church of Omaha, 68198.
St. Therese of the Child Jesus Parish Endowment Trust
St. Therese of the Child Jesus Parish Educational Endowment Trust
St. Thomas More Parish Endowment Trust
St. Thomas More Parish Educational Endowment Trust
St. Thomas More School Educational Endowment Trust
St. Vincent de Paul Parish Endowment Trust
St. Vincent de Paul Parish Educational Endowment Trust
St. Wenceslaus Parish Endowment Trust
St. Wenceslaus Parish Educational Endowment Trust

St. Patrick Foundation, Inc., O'Neill.
St. Mary School Foundation, Inc., O'Neill.
St. Patrick Parish Educational Endowment Trust, Oneill, 68763.
St. Mary of the Seven Dolors Parish Endowment Trust, Osmond.
St. Columbkille Parish Endowment Trust, Papillion.
St. Columbkille Educational Endowment Trust, Papillion.
St. John the Baptist Parish Endowment Trust, Pender.
St. John the Baptist Parish Educational Endowment Trust, Pender.
St. John the Baptist Parish Endowment Trust, Petersburg.
St. John the Baptist Parish Educational Endowment Trust
St. John the Baptist Center Maintenance Endowment Trust, Petersburg.
St. John the Baptist Church of Petersburg Cemetery Endowment Trust, Petersburg, 68652.
St. Joseph Parish Endowment Trust, Pierce.
St. Joseph Parish Educational Endowment Trust, Pierce.
St. Paul Parish Endowment Trust, Plainview.
St. Paul Parish Educational Endowment Trust, Plainview.
St. Joseph Parish Endowment Trust, Platte Center.
St. Joseph Parish Educational Endowment Trust, Platte Center.
St. Joseph Parish Endowment Trust, Ponca.
St. Joseph Parish Educational Endowment Trust, Ponca.
St. Mary Parish Endowment Trust, Primrose.
St. Mary Parish Educational Endowment Trust, Primrose.
St. Bonaventure Parish Endowment Trust, Raeville.
St. Bonaventure Parish/Pope John XXIII High School Educational Endowment Trust, Raeville.
St. Gerald Parish Endowment Trust, Ralston.
St. Gerald Parish Educational Endowment Trust, Ralston.
St. Gerald School Educational Endowment Trust, Ralston.
St. Frances de Chantal Parish Endowment Trust, Randolph.
St. Frances de Chantal Parish Educational Endowment Trust, Randolph.
St. Frances de Chantal of Randolph Cemetery Endowment Trust Fund, Randolph, 68771.
St. Anthony Parish Endowment Trust, St. Charles.
St. Anthony Parish Educational Endowment Trust, St. Charles.
St. Edward Parish Endowment Trust, St. Edward.
St. Edward Parish Educational Endowment Trust, St. Edward.
St. Edward's Church of St. Edward Cemetery Endowment Trust Fund, St. Edward, 68660.
Immaculate Conception Parish Endowment Trust, St. Helena.
Immaculate Conception Parish Educational Endowment Trust, St. Helena.
SS. Philip and James Parish Endowment Trust, St. James.
SS. Philip and James Parish Educational Endowment Trust, St. James.
St. John Parish Endowment Trust, St. John.
St. Francis de Sales Parish Endowment Trust, Schoolcraft.
St. Augustine Parish Endowment Trust, Schuyler.
St. Augustine Parish Educational Endowment Trust, Schuyler.
St. Mary Parish Endowment Trust, Schuyler.
St. Mary Parish Educational Endowment Trust, Schuyler.
St. Lawrence Parish Endowment Trust, Scribner.
St. Lawrence Parish Educational Endowment Trust, Scribner.
St. Lawrence Parish Endowment Trust, Silver Creek.
St. Lawrence Parish Educational Endowment Trust, Silver Creek.
St. Lawrence Church of Silver Creek Cemetery Endowment Trust Fund, Silver Creek, 68663.
St. Leo Parish Endowment Trust, Snyder.
St. Leo Parish Educational Endowment Trust, Snyder.
St. Michael Parish Endowment Trust, South Sioux City.
St. Michael Educational Endowment Trust, South Sioux City.
St. Mary Catholic Church Endowment Trust, Spencer.
St. Mary Parish Educational Endowment Trust, Spencer.
St. Mary Cemetery Endowment Trust, Spencer.
St. Joseph Parish Endowment Trust, Springfield.
St. Joseph Parish Educational Endowment Trust, Springfield.
St. Peter Parish Endowment Trust, Stanton.
St. Peter Parish Educational Endowment Trust, Stanton.
St. Boniface Parish Endowment Trust, Stuart.
St. Boniface Parish Educational Endowment Trust, Stuart.
St. Boniface Elementary School Endowment Trust, Stuart.
St. Mary Parish Endowment Trust, Tabor.
St. Mary Parish Educational Endowment Trust, Tabor.
St. Mary's Church of Tabor Parish and Cemetery Endowment Trust Fund
St. Michael Parish Endowment Trust, Tarnov.
St. Michael Parish Educational Endowment Trust, Tarnov.
St. Patrick Parish Endowment Trust, Tekamah.
St. Patrick Parish Educational Endowment Trust, Tekamah.
Our Lady of Mt. Carmel Parish Endowment Trust, Tilden.
Our Lady of Mt. Carmel Parish Educational Endowment Trust, Tilden.
St. John the Evangelist Parish Endowment Trust, Valley.
St. John the Evangelist Parish Educational Endowment Trust, Valley.
St. Wenceslaus Church Parish Endowment Trust, Verdigre.

St. Wenceslaus Parish Educational Endowment Trust, Verdigre.
St. Joseph Parish Endowment Trust, Walthill.
St. Joseph Parish Educational Endowment Trust, Walthill.
St. Mary Parish Endowment Trust, Wayne.
St. Mary Parish Educational Endowment Trust, Wayne.
Church of the Assumption of the B.V.M. Parish Endowment Trust, West Point.
Church of the Assumption of the B.V.M. Parish Educational Endowment Trust, West Point.
Guardian Angels Grade School Educational Endowment Trust, West Point.
West Point Central Catholic High School Educational Endowment Trust, West Point.
West Point Central Catholic High School Activity Center Endowment Trust
St. Augustine Indian Mission Endowment Trust, Winnebago.
St. Augustine Indian Mission Educational Endowment Trust, Winnebago.
St. Augustine Indian Mission Tuition Relief Educational Endowment Trust, Winnebago.
FEATHERS, Winnebago, 68071. Rev. David M. Korth, Contact & Dir. An endowment, duly constituted under the laws of the State of Nebraska as a nonprofit religious, charitable and educational corporation, to provide scholarships to Native American children of the Winnebago nation to attend high school, grade school, college.
St. Joseph Parish Endowment Trust, Wisner.
St. Joseph Parish Educational Endowment Trust, Wisner.
Sacred Heart Parish Endowment Trust, Wynot.
Sacred Heart Parish Educational Endowment Trust, Wynot.

ELKHORN. *Mount Michael Foundation*, 22520 Mount Michael Rd., 68022-3400. Tel: 402-289-2541; Fax: 402-289-4539. Rt. Rev. Michael Liebl, O.S.B., Abbot.

FORDYCE. *Cemetery Endowment for St. Boniface Church*, Box 170, 68736. Tel: 402-357-3506. Rev. David L. Fulton, Contact Person, Pastor.

ST. COLUMBANS. *Columban Fathers Regional Administration*, P.O. Box 10, 68056-0010. Tel: 402-291-1920; Fax: 402-291-8693. Email: stcolneus@aol.com. Web: www.columban.org. Veronica Dayhuff, Treas.
St. Columban's Central Administration Web: columban.org.
St. Columban's Medical and Retirement Tel: 402-291-1920; Fax: 402-291-4984.
St. Columban's Gift Annuity Trust Tel: 402-291-1920; Fax: 402-291-4984.
St. Columban's Education Trust Tel: 402-291-1920; Fax: 402-291-4984.
St. Columban's Priests Health Program Trust Tel: 402-291-1920; Fax: 402-291-4984.
St. Columban's Retirement Fund Trust Tel: 402-291-1920; Fax: 402-291-4984.
St. Columban's Masses in Trust Tel: 402-291-1920; Fax: 402-291-4984.
St. Columban's Donors/Personal Trust Tel: 402-291-1920; Fax: 402-291-4984.
St. Columban's Regional Trust Tel: 402-291-1920; Fax: 402-291-4984.
St. Columban's Burse Estate Trust Tel: 402-291-1920; Fax: 402-291-4984.
St. Columban's Gift Annuity Trust California Tel: 402-291-1920; Fax: 402-291-4984.

NORFOLK. *Missionary Benedictine Sisters Foundation, Immaculata Monastery*, 300 N. 18th St., 68701. Tel: 402-379-3438. Email: mashonosb@conpoint.com. Web: www.norfolkosb.org. Sr. Marie Andre Shon, O.S.B., Contact Person.

SCHUYLER. *St. Benedict Center Endowment Fund* (2000) 1126 Rd. "I", P.O. Box 528, 68661-0528. Tel: 402-352-8819; Fax: 402-352-8884. Email: Retreats@StBenedictCenter.com. Web: www.StBenedictCenter.com. Rev. Germar Neubert, O.S.B., Contact at Benedictine Mission House/Christ the King Priory. An endowment for the purpose of providing for the support and benefit of development, maintenance and supplemental funding of programs and services of St. Benedict Center and the receipt and management of gifts and bequests to the same center. The nonprofit, charitable and educational corporation is duly constituted under the laws of the State of Nebraska.
St. Benedict Center A nonprofit, ecumenical retreat and conference center, founded by the Missionary Benedictines of Christ the King Priory, Schuyler, NE. As Benedictines we share our hospitality and spirituality with those who search for personal and spiritual growth. We welcome individuals and groups of all Christian denominations, as they seek God in a peaceful and quiet setting. We provide an atmosphere that is conducive to prayer, rest and renewal for laity, clergy and religious., 1126 Rd. I, P.O. Box 528, 68661-0528. Tel: 402-352-8819; Fax: 402-352-8884. Email: Retreats@StBenedictCenter.com. Web: www.StBenedictCenter.com.
Benedictine Mission House Endowment Trust, 1123 Rd. "I", P.O. Box 528, 68661-0528. Tel: 402-352-2177. Email: monastery@benedictinemissionhouse.com. Web: www.benedictinemissionhouse.com. Rev. Germar Neubert, O.S.B., Contact Person.

[O] MISCELLANEOUS

OMAHA. *Archdiocese of Omaha Youth Camp*, 100 N. 62nd St., 68132. Tel: 402-332-3384; Fax: 402-332-3384.
Beginning Experience of Omaha, Inc., 3214 N. 60th St., 68104-3495. Tel: 402-557-5514; 888-800-8352. Email: paseier@archomaha.org. Pat Seier, Coord.
Bethlehem House (2002) 2301 S. 15th St., 68108. Tel: 402-502-9224; Fax: 402-884-0586. Email: wcchdir@wcch.omhcoxmail.com. Web: www.bethlehemhouseomaha.com. Gina Freimuth, Exec. Dir., 1404 Castelar St., 68108. Tel: 402-341-1305; Fax: 402-342-5511. Provides housing, spiritual and pastoral support to women facing crisis pregnancy for up to 8 weeks after delivery. Staff 4.
C.M.G. Agency, Inc., 10843 Old Mill Rd., 68154-2600. Tel: 800-228-6108, Ext. 2413; Fax: 402-551-2943. Email: ppeterson@catholicmutual.org. Paul Peterson, Contact & Sec. An insurance agency supporting the religious and business activities of the Catholic Mutual Relief Society of America and The Catholic Relief Insurance Company of America.
Cathedral Arts Project, Inc., 100 N. 62nd St., 68132. Tel: 402-558-3100, Ext. 243; Fax: 402-558-3026. Email: WJWOEGER@archomaha.org. Web: www.cathedralartsproject.org. Bro. William J. Woeger, F.S.C., Exec. Dir. & Contact.
**Catholic Charities Foundation*, 3300 N. 60th, 68104-3402. Tel: 402-554-0520; Fax: 402-829-9268. Email: catholiccharities@ccomaha.org. Web: www.ccomaha.org. John J. Griffith, Pres. & Contact.
Catholic Jail and Prison Ministry (1998) 701 S. 28th St., 68105-1511. Tel: 402-342-7142; Fax: 402-330-5842. Email: RPVON@prodigy.net. Richard P. Vondenkamp, Dir.
Catholic Mutual of Canada, 10843 Old Mill Rd., 68154-2600. Tel: 800-228-6108, Ext. 2413; Fax: 402-551-2943. Email: ppeterson@catholicmutual.org. Paul Peterson, Contact Person & Vice Pres. To support the religious and business activities of the Catholic Mutual Relief Society of America and its subsidiary Catholic Relief Insurance Company of America.
Catholic Umbrella Pool (1987) 10843 Old Mill Rd., 68154-2600. Tel: 402-551-8765; Fax: 402-551-2943. Email: mab@aohct.org. Mr. Matthew A. Byrne, Pres.
Christ Child Society of Omaha (1906) 1248 S. 10th St., 68108. Tel: 402-342-4566; Fax: 402-342-4541. Web: www.christchildofomaha.com. For programming, see Catholic Charities.
Christian Family Movement (CFM), 3514 N. 63rd St., 68104. Tel: 402-558-1710. Deacon Edwin Osterhaus, Contact; Sheila Osterhaus, Contact.
Christian Urban Education Service (1974) 2207 Wirt St., 68110. Tel: 402-451-5755; Fax: 402-451-1731. Email: sacredheart@sacredheart-cues.org. Web: www.sacredheart-cues.org. Rev. Thomas M. Fangman, Exec. Dir. of CUES.
Christians Encounter Christ, 1938 S. 149th Cir., 68144. Tel: 402-334-2597. Rick Ekstrom, Contact. Purpose: To promote the transferring of environments through Christian leaders who are willing to live and share their principles of being Christian. Through the ongoing development of their Christian Personality, strengthened by their 4th Day, these leaders strive to instill the spirit and sense of gospel to all environments in which they are actively involved.
Cristo Rey Work/Study Program of Omaha, 5301 S. 36th St., 68107. Tel: 402-734-1802; Fax: 402-734-1835. Email: jpogge@spccristorey.org. Web: www.spccristorey.org. Rev. James E. Keiter, Contact Person.
Equestrian Order of the Holy Sepulchre of Jerusalem, Northern Lieutenancy, 10306 Regency Parkway Dr., 68114. Tel: 402-397-7300; Fax: 402-397-7824. Email: tburke@lo.mlaw.com. Thomas R. Burke, Vice Pres.
FOCCUS, Inc. USA formerly FOCCUS, Inc. (1986) 3214 N. 60th St., 68104. Tel: 402-827-3735; 877-883-5422 (Toll free); Fax: 402-551-3050. Email: foccus@foccusincusa.com. Web: www.foccusincusa.com. Mrs. Valerie Conzett, D.Min., L.P.C., Dir., Family Life Office; Lynda Madison, Dir., FOCCUS, Inc. USA. A marriage education ministry offering research-based marriage preparation and marriage enrichment materials and services supporting family life around the world.
Francis House-Men's Shelter (1975) 1702 Nicholas St., 68102. Tel: 402-341-1821; Fax: 402-341-5270. Email: siena1702@sienafrancis.omhcoxmail.com. Web: www.sienafrancis.org. Mike Saklar, Exec. Dir. (Men's Sheltering) Total Assisted Monthly 700; Total Staff 15.
Heart of Mary Publishing Company, Incorporated (1991) 2216 Poppleton Ave., 68108-3436. Tel: 402-342-9265; Fax: 402-342-9094. Email: srmlucy@cox.net. Web: www.heartofmaryministry.com. Sr. Mary Lucy Astuto, D.E.F., M.S., Pres.
Holy Name Housing Corp., 3014 N. 45th St., 68104. Tel: 402-453-6100; Fax: 402-451-7187. Sr. Marilyn Ross, R.S.M., Exec. Dir. & Contact.
IXIM, Spirit of Solidarity, 200 E. 6th St., Papillion, 68046. Tel: 402-339-3285; Fax: 402-592-4753. Web: ixim.org. Rev. Damian J. Zuerlein, Contact Person.
St. James Manor, Inc., 3102 No. 60th St., 68104. Tel: 402-551-4243; Fax: 402-558-8023. Email: JoeR@ccomaha.org. Joseph V. Rysavy, Pres. & Contact.
Latino Catholic Scholarship Fund, P.O. Box 7448, 68107. Tel: 402-554-8493; Fax: 402-551-3426. Email: mejewell@archomaha.org. Web: www.archomaha.com. Mrs. Mary Jewell, Contact Person. Receives and distributes funds as financial aid to Latino students attending Catholic schools.
Legion of Mary, 702 W. 11th St., Neligh, 68756. Tel: 402-887-4521. Rev. John P. Broheimer, Spiritual Dir.
Marriage Encounter, 11140 Y St., 68137. Tel: 402-592-1788. Web: www.archomaha.com/lunks/wwme. Todd & Deb Banchor, Local Contact.
McAuley Ministry Fund (1995) 7262 Mercy Rd., 68124-2389. Tel: 402-393-8225; Fax: 402-393-8145. Email: info@mercywmw.org. Web: www.mercywestmidwest.org. Sr. Judith Frikker, R.S.M., Pres. (Provides support to the mission of the Sisters of Mercy of the Americas West Midwest Community Inc.).
Mercy Holdings (1979) 7262 Mercy Rd., 68124-2389. Tel: 402-393-8225; Fax: 402-393-8145. Email: info@mercywmw.org. Web: www.mercywestmidwest.org. Sr. Norita Cooney, R.S.M., Contact.
Mercy Housing Midwest, 7262 Mercy Rd., 68124. Tel: 303-830-3371; Fax: 303-830-3301. Email: poroark@mercyhousing.org.
Mercy House, 2904 N. 45th St., 68104. Tel: 303-830-3371; Fax: 303-830-3301.
Mercy Northglen, 7262 Mercy Rd., 68124. Tel: 303-830-3371; Fax: 303-830-3301.
Mercy Western Manor, 7262 Mercy Rd., 68124. Tel: 303-830-3371; Fax: 303-830-3301.
Mercy Crestview Village, 7300 Edna Ct., La Vista, 68128. Tel: 303-830-3371; Fax: 303-830-3301.
Mercy Oakwood Gardens, 7262 Mercy Rd., 68124. Tel: 303-830-3371; Fax: 303-830-3301. To provide affordable housing to the economically poor.
The Most AMYable Roman Catholic Lending Library, Inc. (2001) 5404 William St., 68106-2355. Tel: 402-553-1837. Email: rogjud@yahoo.com. Roger Elliott, Pres.; Judy Elliott, Vice Pres. Purpose: a nonprofit religious, charitable and educational corporation is duly constituted under the laws of the State of Nebraska and operated by a Board of Directors for the purpose of collecting and lending orthodox Catholic books and magazines, videos and audiotapes, compact and video discs, prayer petitions and Rosary Decade Group.
New Cassel Foundation, 900 N. 90th St., 68114-2704. Tel: 402-393-2277; Fax: 402-393-3784. Web: www.newcassel.org. Ric Miller, Pres. & Contact. A nonprofit religious, charitable and educational corporation, duly constituted under the laws of the State of Nebraska, to provide support and benefit for the New Cassel Retirement Center and the Franciscan Centre.
New Covenant Center: Education for Justice and Peace (1982) 2830 Caldwell St., 68131. Tel: 402-345-1368. Email: mcosssf@juno.com. Sr. Maureen Connolly, S.S.S.F., M.Div., Prog. Coord.
Notre Dame Housing, Inc. (1996) 3501 State St., 68112-1709. Tel: 402-455-2994; Fax: 402-455-3974. Email: janiceludvik@yahoo.com. Web: www.notredamesisters.org. Sr. Janice Ludvik, N.D., Contact. Purpose: To provide housing for elderly and persons of low-income or otherwise unable to afford market rate housing.
Notre Dame Living Center, Inc. (1996) 3501 State St., 68112-1709. Tel: 402-455-2994; Fax: 402-455-3974. Email: janiceludvik@yahoo.com. Web: www.notredamesisters.org. Sr. Janice Ludvik, N.D., Contact. Purpose: Provides affordable

housing to the elderly, particularly those of low-income status.

Pope Paul VI Institute for the Study of Human Reproduction (1982) 6901 Mercy Rd., 68106. Tel: 402-390-6600; Fax: 402-390-9851. Email: popepaul@popepaulvi.com. Web: www.popepaulvi.com. Thomas W. Hilgers, M.D., Dir.

Project Welcome, 4801 California St., #2, 68132. Tel: 402-709-0505. Sr. Joan Mueller, O.S.C., Ph.D., CEO.

Siena House-Women's Shelter (1975) 1702 Nicholas St., 68102. Tel: 402-341-1821; Fax: 402-341-5270. Email: siena1702@sienafrancisomhcoxmail.com. Web: www.sienafrancis.org. Mike Saklar, Exec. Dir. (Women's Sheltering) Total Staff 15; Total Assisted Monthly 65.

Siena/Francis House Recovery Program (1975) D.T.S., P.O. Box 217, 68101. Tel: 402-341-1821; Fax: 402-341-5270. Email: siena1702@sienafrancis.omhcoxmail.com. Web: www.sienafrancis.org. Mike Saklar, Dir. & Contact. Total Staff 22; Total Assisted Monthly 85.

Teachers' Salary Endowment Trust Fund of St. Stephen Church of Omaha, St. Stephen Church of Omaha, 16701 "S" St., 68135. Tel: 402-896-9675; Fax: 402-896-1990. Email: t.jorgensen@stephen.org. Web: www.stephen.org. Purpose: providing endowment support for teachers employed by St. Stephen Church of Omaha. Priests 2.

TEC, Box 4130, 68104. Tel: 402-554-8493; Fax: 402-554-8402. Email: rmramos@archomaha.org. Web: www.archomaha.com/tec/tec.htm. Ms. Rita Ramos, Coord. Youth Ministry.

St. Vincent de Paul Society, 4320 Fort St., 68111. Tel: 402-346-5445. Email: svdpomaha@qwestoffice.net. Web: svdpomaha.com/home. Rev. Harold J. Buse, Spiritual Dir.; Joan DeSelm, Pres.

St. Vincent de Paul Store, Inc., 2101 Leavenworth St., 68102. Tel: 402-341-1688; 402-341-4942; Fax: 402-341-9079. Web: www.svdpomaha.org.

GRETNA. *Holy Family Shrine* Mailing Address: P.O. Box 507, 68028. Tel: 402-332-4565. Email: holyfamilyshrine@hotmail.com. Web: www.holyfamilyshrine.com. 23132 Pflug Rd., 68028. Matthew Sakowski, Caretaker. A place of pilgrimage, prayer and resource for the public and private prayer. This nonprofit religious, charitable and educational corporation is duly constituted under the laws of the State of Nebraska and operated by a Board of Trustees.

LYNCH. *Niobrara Valley House of Renewal*, P.O. Box 163, 68746. Tel: 402-569-3433. Rev. Douglas P. Scheinost, Pastor.

OAKDALE. *Tintern Retreat and Resource Center*, 52619 843 Rd., 68761. Tel: 402-776-2188. Email: tintern@gpcom.net. Web: www.tintern.homestead.com. Becky Kerkman, Mgr. & Contact.

PLATTE CENTER. *Servants of the Heart of the Father*, P.O. Box 218, 68653. Tel: 402-246-9214; Fax: 402-246-9217. Email: sothotf@aol.com. Web: www.sothotf.org. Rev. Rodney V. Kneifl, Contact Person.

[P] PUBLIC ASSOCIATIONS OF THE CHRISTIAN FAITHFUL

OMAHA. *Christian Life Community-North Central Region (CLC)* (1998) 2500 California Plaza, 68178. Tel: 402-280-2692; Fax: 402-280-5590. Email: jzsj@creighton.edu. Rev. John D. Zuercher, S.J., Contact & Regional Ecclesial Asst. A public association of the Christian faithful of Pontifical Right providing spiritual support and guidance in the Jesuit tradition of the Spiritual Exercises.

Franciscan Sisters of Joy, Santa Chiara Monastery, 4801 California St., #2, 68132. Tel: 402-551-0347. Email: jmueller@creighton.edu. Sr. Joan Mueller, O.S.C., Ph.D., Clare Sister.

Institute for Priestly Formation formerly INSTITUTE FOR PRIESTLY FORMATION, CREIGHTON UNIVERSITY 2500 California Plaza, 68178. Tel: 402-546-6384; Fax: 402-280-3529. Email: ipf@creighton.edu. Web: www.creighton.edu/ipf. Rev. Richard J. Gabuzda, Exec. Dir. Purpose: To offer programs and support for the integration of theological study, spiritual growth and direction, and retreat experiences for diocesan seminarians and priests.

Intercessors of the Lamb, 11811 Calhoun Rd., 68152. Tel: 402-455-5262; Fax: 402-455-1323. Email: bellwether@novia.net. Web: www.bellwetheromaha.org. Sr. Nadine Brown, Foundress & Contact. A community of consecrated hermits and a contemplative center of formation with the charism of intercessory prayer; provides retreats, conferences and resources for contemplative charismatic, marian and spiritual warfare spirituality. Consecrated Hermit Brothers and Sisters 65; Priests 5.

[Q] PRIVATE ASSOCIATIONS OF THE FAITHFUL

OMAHA. *Daughters of the Eternal Father* (2002) 2216 Poppleton Ave., 68108-3436. Tel: 402-342-1032; Fax: 402-342-9094. Email: srmlucy@cox.net. Web: www.omahadef.org. Sr. Mary Lucy Astuto, D.E.F., M.S., Foundress.

Seraphic Sisters of the Eucharist, 705 S. 28th St., 68105. Tel: 402-346-6845; Fax: 402-341-6483. Email: seraphicsisters@yahoo.com. Sisters Clara Maria Acosta-Millan, S.S.E., Supr.; Lourdes Candida-Cano, Asst.

RELIGIOUS INSTITUTES OF MEN REPRESENTED IN THE ARCHDIOCESE

For further details refer to the corresponding bracketed number in the Religious Institutes of Men or Women section.

[0200]—*Benedictine Monks*—O.S.B.

[0330]—*Brothers of the Christian Schools* (St. Louis, MO)—F.S.C.

[0690]—*Jesuit Fathers and Brother* (Wisconsin Prov.)—S.J.

[1065]—*Priestly Fraternity of St. Peter*

[0370]—*Society of St. Columban*—S.S.C.

RELIGIOUS INSTITUTES OF WOMEN REPRESENTED IN THE ARCHDIOCESE

[0230]—*Benedictine Sisters of Pontifical Jurisdiction*—O.S.B.

[1070-03]—*Dominican Sisters*—O.P.

[1115]—*Dominican Sisters of Peace*—O.P.

[1230]—*Franciscan Sisters of Christian Charity*—O.S.F.

[1430]—*Franciscan Sisters of Our Lady of Perpetual Help*—O.S.F.

[2575]—*Institute of the Sisters of Mercy of the Americas*—R.S.M.

[0210]—*Missionary Benedictine Sisters*—O.S.B.

[2690]—*Missionary Catechists of Divine Providence*

[2960]—*Notre Dame Sisters*—N.D.

[3760]—*Order of St. Clare*—O.S.C.

[2970]—*School Sisters of Notre Dame*

[1680]—*School Sisters of St. Francis* (Our Lady of Angels Prov.)—O.S.F.

[3580]—*Servants of Mary*—O.S.M.

[0430]—*Sisters of Charity of the Blessed Virgin Mary*—C.S.J.

[1630]—*Sisters of St. Francis of Peace and Christian Charity* (Denver Prov.)—O.S.F.

[1640]—*Sisters of St. Francis of Perpetual Adoration* (Colorado Springs, CO)—O.S.F.

[1830]—*Sisters of the Good Shepherd*—R.G.S.

[3270]—*Sisters of the Most Precious Blood* (O'Fallon, MO)—C.PP.S.

[3320]—*Sisters of the Presentation of the B.V.M.*—P.B.V.M.

[4070]—*Society of the Sacred Heart*—R.S.C.J.

ARCHDIOCESAN CEMETERIES

OMAHA. *Calvary*

Holy Sepulchre

St. Mary

St. Mary Magdalene

Resurrection

NECROLOGY

† Mickells, Rt. Rev. Msgr. Anthony B., (Retired)—Died March 20, 2009

† Kerwin, Rev. Msgr. Eugene H., (Retired)—Died June 23, 2009

† Golik, Stanislaus, (Retired)—Died Sept. 7, 2009

An asterisk (*) denotes an organization that has established tax-exempt status directly with the IRS and is not covered by the USCCB Group Ruling.

Diocese of Orange in California

(Arausicanae in California)

Most Reverend

TOD DAVID BROWN, D.D.

Bishop of Orange; ordained May 1, 1963; appointed Bishop of Boise December 27, 1988; Episcopal Ordination April 3, 1989; appointed Bishop of Orange June 29, 1998; installed September 3, 1998. *Office: Marywood Center, 2811 E. Villa Real Dr., Orange, CA 92867.*

Chancellor's Office: 2811 E. Villa Real Dr., P.O. Box 14195, Orange, CA 92863-1595. Tel: 714-282-3000; Fax: 714-282-3029.

Web: www.rcbo.org

Email: sgiacomi@rcbo.org

Most Reverend

NORMAN F. McFARLAND, D.D., J.C.D.

Retired Bishop of Orange; ordained June 15, 1946; appointed Titular Bishop of Bida and Auxiliary of San Francisco June 5, 1970; consecrated September 8, 1970; appointed Apostolic Administrator December 6, 1974; appointed Bishop of Reno-Las Vegas February 10, 1976; installed March 31, 1976; appointed Bishop of Orange December 29, 1986; installed February 24, 1987; retired June 30, 1998. *Res.: 200 W. La Veta Ave., Orange, CA 92866. Office: Marywood Center, 2811 E. Villa Real Dr., Orange, CA 92867.*

Most Reverend

DOMINIC MAI LUONG

Auxiliary Bishop of Orange; ordained May 21, 1966; appointed Auxiliary Bishop of Orange April 25, 2003; installed June 11, 2003.

Most Reverend

CIRILO FLORES

Auxiliary Bishop of Orange; ordained June 8, 1991; appointed Auxiliary Bishop of Orange and Titular Bishop of Quiza January 5, 2009; ordained March 19, 2009. *Office: Marywood Center, 2811 E. Villa Real Dr., Orange, CA 92867.*

ESTABLISHED JUNE 18, 1976.

Square Miles 782.

Comprises the County of Orange in the State of California.

Diocesan Patron: Our Lady of Guadalupe.

Legal Titles: (Prot. No. CD 528-76)
The Roman Catholic Bishop of Orange, a Corporation Sole.
Diocese of Orange Education and Welfare Corporation.
Catholic Charities of Orange.
For legal titles of parishes and diocesan institutions, consult the Diocesan Pastoral Service Office

STATISTICAL OVERVIEW

Personnel	
Bishop	1
Auxiliary Bishops	2
Retired Bishops	1
Abbots	1
Priests: Diocesan Active in Diocese	117
Priests: Diocesan Active Outside Diocese	8
Priests: Retired, Sick or Absent	50
Number of Diocesan Priests	175
Religious Priests in Diocese	84
Total Priests in Diocese	259
Extern Priests in Diocese	30
Ordinations:	
Diocesan Priests	6
Religious Priests	1
Transitional Deacons	1
Permanent Deacons	12
Permanent Deacons in Diocese	101
Total Brothers	12
Total Sisters	323
Parishes	
Parishes	57
With Resident Pastor:	
Resident Diocesan Priests	44
Resident Religious Priests	6
Without Resident Pastor:	
Administered by Priests	7
Missions	5

Pastoral Centers	5
Closed Parishes	1
Professional Ministry Personnel:	
Sisters	21
Lay Ministers	626
Welfare	
Catholic Hospitals	3
Total Assisted	796,750
Health Care Centers	5
Total Assisted	26,973
Homes for the Aged	1
Total Assisted	57
Day Care Centers	2
Total Assisted	150
Specialized Homes	5
Total Assisted	331
Special Centers for Social Services	13
Total Assisted	501,899
Other Institutions	1
Total Assisted	98
Educational	
Diocesan Students in Other Seminaries	30
Total Seminarians	30
High Schools, Diocesan and Parish	3
Total Students	4,381
High Schools, Private	4
Total Students	2,294

Elementary Schools, Diocesan and Parish	32
Total Students	11,752
Elementary Schools, Private	3
Total Students	1,328
Catechesis/Religious Education:	
High School Students	11,214
Elementary Students	32,061
Total Students under Catholic Instruction	63,060
Teachers in the Diocese:	
Priests	17
Brothers	6
Sisters	29
Lay Teachers	1,681
Vital Statistics	
Receptions into the Church:	
Infant Baptism Totals	14,806
Minor Baptism Totals	712
Adult Baptism Totals	487
Received into Full Communion	1,618
First Communions	11,920
Confirmations	6,309
Marriages:	
Catholic	1,785
Interfaith	427
Total Marriages	2,212
Deaths	2,763
Total Catholic Population	1,280,159
Total Population	3,010,759

Former Bishops—Most Revs. WILLIAM R. JOHNSON, appt. Titular Bishop of Biera and Auxiliary Bishop of Los Angeles, Feb. 9, 1971; cons. March 25, 1971; installed as first Bishop of Orange, June 18, 1976; died July 28, 1986; NORMAN F. McFARLAND, D.D., J.C.D. (Retired), ord. June 15, 1946; appt. Titular Bishop of Bida and Auxiliary of San Francisco, June 5, 1970; cons. Sept. 8, 1970; appt. Apostolic Administrator, Dec. 6, 1974; appt. Bishop of Reno-Las Vegas, Feb. 10, 1976; installed March 31, 1976; appt. Bishop of Orange, Dec. 29, 1986; installed Feb. 24, 1987; retired June 30, 1998.

Vicar General—Rev. Msgr. MICHAEL HEHER, V.G., Office: Marywood Center.

Chancellor—Mrs. SHIRL GIACOMI, Office: Marywood Center.

Moderator of the Curia—Rev. Msgr. MICHAEL HEHER, V.G., Office: Marywood Center.

Director of Clergy Personnel—Rev. Msgr. TUAN JOSEPH PHAM, J.C.L., Office: Marywood Center.

Secretary to the Bishop—Rev. Msgr. TUAN JOSEPH PHAM, J.C.L., Office: Marywood Center.

Vicar for Religious Communities—Sr. EYMARD FLOOD, O.S.C., Office: Marywood Center.

Vicar for Priests—Rev. CHRISTOPHER SMITH, Office: Marywood Center.

Vicar for Faith Formation—Rev. GERALD M. HORAN, O.S.M., Office: Marywood Center.

Diocesan Pastoral Service Office—2811 E. Villa Real Dr., P.O. Box 14195, Orange, 92863-1595. Tel: 714-282-3000; Fax: 714-282-3029. Office Hours: Mon.-Fri. 9-5.

Office of Canonical Services—2811 E. Villa Real Dr., P.O. Box 14195, Orange, 92863-1595. Tel: 714-282-3080; Fax: 714-282-3087. Rev. Msgr. DOUGLAS COOK, J.C.L., Dir. Canonical Svcs.

Judicial Vicar—Rev. Msgr. DOUGLAS COOK, J.C.L.

Adjutant Judicial Vicars—Rev. Msgr. TUAN JOSEPH PHAM, J.C.L.; Revs. THOMAS KELLER, M.S.C., J.C.L.; SY NGUYEN, J.C.L.; STEPHEN DOKTORCZYK, J.C.L.; MINH CONG BUI, J.C.L.; VIET PETER HO, J.C.L.

Promoter of Justice—Rev. STEPHEN DOKTORCZYK, J.C.L.

Judges—Rev. Msgrs. JOHN G. CAMPBELL, J.C.L.; ARTHUR A. HOLQUIN, S.T.L.; Rev. JAMES HARTNETT; Rev. Msgr. DOUGLAS COOK, J.C.L.; Revs. JOSEPH M. NETTEKOVEN; THEODORE OLSON; JOHN CARONAN, O.Praem., J.C.L.; JACK SEWELL, J.C.L.; MINH CONG BUI, J.C.L.; FERNANDO ENGEL, J.C.L.; Sisters MARGARET ANNE RAMSDEN, S.F.C.C., J.C.L.; ANNE GIBLIN, R.S.C., J.C.L.; Ms. PEGGY JEAN PAOLI, J.C.L.; Rev. STEVE DOKTORCZYK.

Defenders of the Bond—Revs. THOMAS KELLER, M.S.C., J.C.L.; VIET PETER HO, J.C.L.

Ecclesiastical Notaries—AIDEE MALDONADO; LINDA BRAUN; PAULA LYNN; LILLIAN ESQUIVEL; SUSAN STANKIS; KIM BUI.

Newman Apostolate—Rev. JOHN FRANCIS VU, S.J., Mailing Address: P.O. Box 6030, Irvine, 92616. Tel: 714-856-0211.

Diocesan Pastoral Council—Mrs. SHIRL GIACOMI, Chancellor. Tel: 714-282-3115.

Parish Councils and Parish Development—Mrs. SHIRL GIACOMI, Chancellor, Office: Marywood Center.

Diaconate—Deacon FRANK CHAVEZ, Office: Marywood Center.

Clergy Personnel Board—Revs. TIMOTHY FREYER;

ENRIQUE J. SERA; EFRAIN FLORES; VINCENT PHAM; MICHAEL ST. PAUL; Rev. Msgrs. MICHAEL HEHER, V.G.; DONALD ROMITO; TUAN JOSEPH PHAM, J.C.L., Auditor, Office: Marywood Center.

Sexual Misconduct and Oversight Review Board (SMORB)—RON LOWENBERG, Chm.; JOSEPH M. CERVANTES, Ph.D., ABPP; PAUL COBLE ESQ.; WILLIAM J. COLLINS, M.D.; GENE HOWARD; Sr. KATHLEEN MARIE PUGHE, C.S.J.; DARLYNE PETTINICHIO; Rev. ENRIQUE J. SERA; Honorable MICHAEL BRENNER; DIANE GOMEZ-VALENZUELA, M.S.W. Staff: Rev. STEPHEN DOKTOCZYK, Promoter of Justice; MARIA RULLO SCHINDERLE ESQ.; MARIANNE BUNGCAG.

Media Relations—RYAN LILYENGREN, Office: Marywood Center.

Orange Diocesan Council of Catholic Women—Sr. EYMARD FLOOD, O.S.C., Moderator; PHYLLIS FIORENTINO, Pres., Office: Marywood Center.

General Counsel—Ms. MARIA RULLO SCHINDERLE.

Priests' Relief—Rev. . CHRISTOPHER SMITH, Office: Marywood Center.

Council of Priests—Most Revs. TOD DAVID BROWN, D.D.; DOMINIC M. LUONG, D.D., V.G.; Rev. CIRILO FLORES; Rev. Msgrs. J. MICHAEL MCKIERNAN; DOUGLAS COOK, J.C.L.; TUAN JOSEPH PHAM, J.C.L., Auditor; Rev. BRUCE PATTERSON; Rev. Msgr. MICHAEL HEHER, V.G.; Revs. JOHN E. JANZE; STEVEN SALLOT; ARMANDO VIRREY; EDWARD POETTGEN, Chm.; THEODORE OLSON; SY NGUYEN, J.C.L.; MICHAEL P. HANIFIN; KENNETH A. SCHMIT; STEVEN CORREZ; JOSEPH ROBILLARD; JOHN W. MONEYPENNY; JOSEPH KNERR; BRENDAN DAVID MANSON; STEVEN CORREZ; JOHN FRANCIS VU, S.J.; Rev. Msgr. ARTHUR A. HOLQUIN, S.T.L.; Revs. MICHAEL L. HARVEY, O.F.M.; RICHARD A. DELAHUNTY; CHARBEL GRBAVAC, O.Praem.

Observers—Mrs. SHIRL GIACOMI, Chancellor; Deacon FRANK CHAVEZ.

Consultors—Rev. Msgrs. DOUGLAS COOK, J.C.L.; J. MICHAEL MCKIERNAN; MICHAEL HEHER, V.G.; Rev. CIRILO FLORES; Most Rev. DOMINIC M. LUONG, D.D., V.G.; Rev. STEVEN SALLOT; Rev. Msgr. ARTHUR A. HOLQUIN, S.T.L.; Revs. THEODORE OLSON; JOHN E. JANZE; SY NGUYEN, J.C.L.; MICHAEL L. HARVEY, O.F.M.; EDWARD POETTGEN.

Propagation of the Faith—Sr. ERNESTINE VELARDE, O.D.N., Dir., Office: Marywood Center.

Council for Religious—Sisters EYMARD FLOOD, O.S.C., Dir.; BRID O'SHEA, R.S.C.; FRANCESCA TRAN, L.H.C.; IRMA GOMEZ, M.E.S.S.T.; MARGARET ANNE RAMSDEN, S.F.C.C., J.C.L.; CHRISTOPHER MILLER, O.P.; SHARON MARIA LAMPRECHT, O.D.N.; ELIA CARO, O.S.F.

Office for Faith Formation—Rev. GERALD HORAN, O.S.M.

Children's Faith Formation Advisory Council—Mrs. MARIA BARRIENTOS; Mrs. BARBARA LATILLER; Mrs. PAM BENDER; Ms. RENATE GOUTIER; Mrs. KATHY HERNANDEZ; Mrs. ROSE ANTOGNOLI; Sr. CECILIA TRANG PHAM, L.H.C.; Ms. SHERRI OLDHAM; Ms. SILVIA MANDRAGON; Ms. STELLA HEUMANN; Mrs. SANDY COUSINS. Staff: Rev. GERALD M. HORAN, O.S.M.; Dr. KATHLEEN SCHINHOFEN, Assoc. Dir., Office of Faith Formation; Mrs. NANCY HARDY.

Catholic Schools and Parish Faith Formation—Rev. GERALD M. HORAN, O.S.M., Supt. & Vicar; Mrs. SALLY TODD, Assoc. Supt., Office: Marywood Center; Mrs. NANCY HARDY, Dir. Parish Faith Formation; SUSAN IGLESIAS, Dir. Elementary School Finances.

Safe Environment Coordinator—DIANE MURRAY.

Young & Young Adult Ministries—Mr. ARMANDO CERVANTES, Coord. Office: Marywood Center.

Diocesan Consultative Schools Board— Office: Marywood Center Membership: Rev. GERALD M. HORAN, O.S.M., Ex Officio; Mrs. SALLY TODD, Ex Officio; Mr. RANDY REDWITZ, Chm.; Mr. ROBERT ANDERSON; THOMAS DELANEY; KENNETH LARSON; Mrs. TRUDY MAZZARELLA; Ms. MICHELE NGUYEN; Rev. STEVEN SALLOT; Mr. CHUCK PACKARD; Ms. ADRIANNA LOPEZ, Recording Sec.; Mr. FRANK TALARICO.

Vocations Office—Rev. JOHN NENEMAN, Dir., Office: Marywood Center.

Catholic Campaign for Human Development—Local Board: Deacon JAMES MERLE, Chm.; JOYCE COTTAGE; Deacons GARY MUCHO; DENIS ZAUN; ROBERT SOIKKELI; Ms. JUDY DONCKELS; Ms. JEANNIE MOLLENAUER.

Diocesan Offices and Directors

Apostleship of Prayer—Rev. JOSEPH M. NETTEKOVEN, 2050 W. Ball Rd., Anaheim, 92804. Tel: 714-774-2595.

Archivist—Rev. WILLIAM KREKELBERG, Office: Mission Basilica San Juan Capistrano, 31522 Camino Capistrano, San Juan Capistrano, 92675-0691.

Boy Scouts/Girl Scouts—Rev. MICHAEL P. HANIFIN, Office: Santa Clara de Asis Church, 22005 Avenida de la Paz, Yorba Linda, 92887-2745.

Liturgical Commission—Rev. Msgr. ARTHUR A. HOLQUIN, S.T.L., Ex Officio; Mr. JAIME ROMERO; Rev. Msgr. J. MICHAEL MCKIERNAN, Chm.; Deacon FRANK CHAVEZ; Ms. LESA TRUXAW, Ex Officio; Dr. JOAN H. TIMMERMAN; Revs. TUAN PHAM, J.C.L., Ex Officio; CRAIG M. BUTTERS; Mr. MARK PURCELL; Rev. EUGENE LEE; Mr. JOSEPH BAZYOUROS; Deacon TOM MCGUIRE.

Building and Renovation Committee of the Liturgical Commission—Rev. Msgrs. J. MICHAEL MCKIERNAN; ARTHUR A. HOLQUIN, S.T.L.; TUAN JOSEPH PHAM, J.C.L.; Ms. LESA TRUXAW, Chm., Office: Marywood Center.

Land Advisory Board—Most Rev. TOD DAVID BROWN, D.D.; Rev. EDWARD POETTGEN; Mr. ARTHUR BIRTCHER; Mr. TERENCE K. BARRY, Chm.; Ms. SHARON HENNESSEY; Mr. R. RAND SPERRY; Rev. Msgr. MICHAEL HEHER, V.G.; Mr. J. BARNEY PAGE. Staff: Mr. PHIL RIES; LILY FUNK; Rev. Msgr. TUAN JOSEPH PHAM, J.C.L.; JOE NOVOA; Mrs. SHIRL GIACOMI; Ms. MARIA RULLO SCHINDERLE.

Diocesan Construction Board—Most Rev. TOD DAVID BROWN, D.D.; JACK W. FLEMING; Rev. KENNETH A. SCHMIT; Mr. ARTHUR BIRTCHER, Chm.; Mr. MARKO E. BOTICH; Mr. EDWARD REYNOLDS; Mr. HARRY G. KREIDER; Mr. RICHARD HEIM; Ms. MARY WESTBROOK. Staff: Rev. Msgr. MICHAEL HEHER, V.G.; Mr. PHIL RIES; JOE NOVOA, Dir. Construction; Rev. Msgr. TUAN JOSEPH PHAM, J.C.L.; Mrs. SHIRL GIACOMI; LOY GIBSON, Comm. Sec.

Diocesan Finance Council—Most Rev. TOD DAVID BROWN, D.D.; Rev. Msgr. LAWRENCE J. BAIRD, P.A.; Rev. CIRILO FLORES; Rev. Msgr. MICHAEL HEHER, V.G.; Mr. TIMOTHY BUSCH; Ms. MAUREEN FLANAGAN, C.F.A.; Sr. MARY BERNADETTE MCNULTY, C.S.J.; Mr. JEFFREY D. LITTELL; Mr. RALPH SABIN; Mr. GUY WILSON, Chm.; Mr. ROGER KIRWAN; Mr. PAUL SCHLOEMER; Mr. THANG KIEU; Mrs. SHIRL GIACOMI, Chancellor. Staff: Mr. PHIL RIES, Dir.; IMELDA CHAN; Rev. Msgr. TUAN JOSEPH PHAM, J.C.L.; Mr. KEVIN LARSON; Ms. MARIA RULLO SCHINDERLE.

Director of Finance—Mr. PHIL RIES, Dir.; Mr. KEVIN LARSON, Controller, Office: Marywood Center.

Catholic Charities of Orange—THERESA SMITH, M.S.W., L.C.S.W., Exec. Dir., 1820 E. 16th St., Santa Ana, 92701. Tel: 714-347-9605; Fax: 714-542-3020.

Cemeteries—Mr. MICHAEL WESNER, Dir., Office: Marywood Center.

Ministry to Priests—Rev. CHRISTOPHER SMITH, Vicar for Priests.

Cursillo Movement—Deacon DOUG COOK, Exec. Spiritual Dir.; Revs. DAVID VUELVAS-ARIAS, Spiritual Dir., Hispanic Cursillo; SY NGUYEN, J.C.L., Spiritual Dir., Vietnamese Cursillo, Office: Marywood Center.

Deaf Ministry—NANCY LOPEZ, Dir.; Deacon FRANK LUNA, 1800 E. McFadden Ave., Ste. 130, Santa Ana, 92705. Tel: 714-547-7316 (TTY); 714-547-0824 (Voice); Fax: 714-558-7103. Email: nlopez@rcbo.org. Web: www.rcbo.org.

Detention Ministry—Deacon PHILLIP GOODMAN, 1820 W. Orangewood Ave., Ste. 101, Orange, 92868. Tel: 714-634-9909; Fax: 714-634-9910.

Library/Media Center—APRIL CIPO, Coord.

Institute of Pastoral Ministry—Mrs. OLIVIA CORNEJO, Dir. Office: Marywood Center.

Ecumenical and Interreligious Affairs—Rev. AL BACA, Chm.; Ms. MARY SUSA; Very Rev. HUGH C. BARBOUR, O.Praem.; Mr. FEDERICO SAYRE; Mr. BRAD HAWKINS; Mr. DONALD ROSS; Mr. EUGENE O'TOOLE; Mr. JAMES NIELSON; Mr. HOWARD YOUNG; Rev. JOHN MONESTERO; Mr. ANTHONY VULTAGGIO; Mr. DARREL KING; Mrs. ORALIE ENOS; Dr. H. MICHAEL HERSH; Sr. JEANNE FALLON, C.S.J.; Ms. IRMA ESPINOSA; Ms. RENATE GOUTIER; Ms. SUE FENWICK; Mr. GREG KELLEY; Honorable FINGAL SHULTE; Judge DAVID MCEACHEN; Mr. BRIAN WOODS; Rev. CHRISTIAN MONDOR, O.F.M.; Mrs. ADRIANNE WITTHOEFT.

Natural Family Planning—Ms. MARY OFFENHEISER, M.S.N., Coord., Office: Catholic Charities of Orange County, Inc., 1800 McFadden Ave., Santa Ana, 92705. Tel: 714-347-9600.

Engaged Encounter—TOM HARRISON; LISA HARRISON.

Marriage Encounter - English—JIM SKUDLARSKI; CHERYL SKUDLARSKI.

Marriage Encounter - Spanish—SANTOS VASQUEZ; MARIA LUISA VASQUEZ.

Vietnamese Community Couples Retreat—Mr. KY VU; Mrs. CAY DINH VU, 24862 Branch Ave., Lake Forest, 92630. Tel: 949-472-5083.

Retrouvaille - English—VICTOR ORTIZ; KATHERINE ORTIZ.

Retrouvaille - Spanish—LUIS GONZALES; VIRGINIA GONZALES.

Office of Hispanic Ministry—Deacon GUILLERMO TORRES, Dir., Office: Marywood Center.

Holy Childhood—Sr. ERNESTINE VELARDE, O.D.N., Dir., Office: Marywood Center.

Catholic Relief Services—Mrs. SHIRL GIACOMI, Chancellor.

Risk Management and Insurance Services—Mr. MICHAEL SHAFFER, Dir., Office: Marywood Center.

Legion of Mary—

English—TERI FODOR, Pres. Tel: 714-533-1550.

Vietnamese—THACH LUU, Pres.

Worship—Ms. LESA TRUXAW, Dir., Office: Marywood Center.

Respect Life, Justice and Peace—GEORGEANN LOVETT, Dir. Office: Marywood Center.

Catecumenate—Ms. LESA TRUXAW, Dir., Office: Marywood Center.

Advancement (Orange Catholic Foundation)—VACANT, Pres., Office: Marywood Center.

Victim Assistance Coordinator—HERMINIA SHEA-MARTINEZ, Ph.D. Tel: 800-364-3064. Email: hershea@verizon.net.

CLERGY, PARISHES, MISSIONS AND PAROCHIAL SCHOOLS

CITY OF ORANGE

1—CATHEDRAL OF THE HOLY FAMILY (1921) Rev. Msgr. Douglas Cook, Rector; Revs. Bao Q. Thai, Parochial Vicar; Joseph Thuong Tran, Parochial Vicar; Deacons Richard Lovett; Tom McGuine. In Res., Rev. Rafael Luevano.
Res.: 566 S. Glassell St., 92866. Tel: 714-639-2900; Fax: 714-639-8022. Email: parish@hfcathedral.org. Web: www.hfcathedral.org.
School—530 S. Glassell St., 92866. Tel: 714-538-6012; Fax: 714-633-5892. Lay Teachers 29; Students 521.
Catechesis/Religious Program—Tel: 714-639-2900, Ext. 235; Fax: 714-516-9949. Students 493.

2—HOLY TRINITY (2005) Rev. Reynold Furrell; Deacon Randall McMahon; Andy Albritton, Music & Media Dir.
1600 Corporate Dr., Ladera Ranch, 92694. Tel: 949-218-6675; 949-218-3131; Fax: 949-388-1311. Email: frreynold@holytrinityladera.org. Web: www.holytrinityladera.org.
Catechesis/Religious Program—Kathie Wickham, D.R.E.; Patti Wieckert, Youth Min., Confirmation & Jr. High. Students 535.

3—LA PURISIMA (1964) Revs. Vincent Hung Pham, Admin.; Avelino Orozco; Deacons Anthony Bube; Juan Espinoza; Paul Amorino.
Res.: 11712 N. Hewes, 92869. Tel: 714-633-5800; Fax: 714-633-8364. Email: info@lapurisima.net. Web: www.lapurisima.net.
School—Tel: 714-633-5411; Fax: 714-633-1588. Email: lps@lpcs.net. Web: www.lpcs.net. Mrs. Debbie Vallas, Prin. Lay Teachers 19; Students 225.
Catechesis/Religious Program—Tel: 714-633-5344. Students 947.

4—ST. NORBERT (1963) Revs. Patrick Rudolph; Agustin Escobar; Benedict Yang; Deacon Joseph Esparza; Janine Kilgore, Liturgy Director.
Res.: 300 E. Taft Ave., 92865. Tel: 714-637-4360; Fax: 714-637-4311. Email: info@stnorbertchurch.org. Web: www.stnorbertchurch.org.
School—Tel: 714-637-6822; Fax: 714-637-1604. Email: sshaia@stnorbertchurch.org. Lay Teachers 15; Students 302.
Catechesis/Religious Program—Tel: 714-998-1070. Mrs. Carmen Estrada, D.R.E.; Edith Marik, D.R.E.; Ms. Charlene Dumitru, D.R.E.; Kirsten King, Youth Min. Students 762.

ORANGE COUNTY OUTSIDE THE CITY

ALISO VIEJO, CORPUS CHRISTI (1999) Rev. Fred K. Bailey.
27231 Aliso Viejo Pkwy., 92656. Tel: 949-389-9008; Fax: 949-831-6540. Email: corpuschristi@corpuschristialisoviejo.org. Web: www.avcatholics.org.
Catechesis/Religious Program—Students 409.

ANAHEIM

1—ST. ANTHONY CLARET (1955) Revs. Rudolph J. Preciado; Binh T. Nguyen; Michael St. Paul; Deacon August Mones.
Res.: 1450 E. La Palma Ave., 92805. Tel: 714-776-0270; Fax: 714-776-6022. Email: stanthonyclaret@yahoo.com.

Catechesis/Religious Program—Tel: 714-778-1399; Fax: 714-956-2701. Margarita Navarro, D.R.E. Students 1,387.

2—ST. BONIFACE (1860) Revs. Timothy Freyer; Gregory Marquez; Augustine Bich Vu.
Res.: 120 N. Janss St., 92805. Tel: 714-956-3110; Fax: 714-399-0566. Email: stboniface120@aol.com. Web: www.rc.net/orange/stboniface.
Catechesis/Religious Program—Tel: 714-772-3060; Fax: 714-399-0568. Students 1,466.

3—ST. JUSTIN MARTYR (1958) Revs. Joseph Robillard; Thomas Paul K. Naval, Parochial Vicar; Francis Ng, Parochial Vicar; Deacons Raymond Duthoy; Jose Ferreras; Kalini Folau; Ramon Leon; Louis Liu. In Res., Rev. John Monestero.
Res.: 2050 W. Ball Rd., 92804. Tel: 714-774-2595; Fax: 714-774-9849. Web: www.saintjustin.org.
Church: Ball Rd. and Empire, 92804.
School—2030 W. Ball Rd., 92804. Tel: 714-772-4902; Fax: 714-772-2092. Lay Teachers 12; Students 186.
Catechesis/Religious Program—Students 691.
Mission—Sacred Heart 10852 Harcourt, Orange Co. 92804. Tel: 714-821-3133; Fax: 714-821-1498.

4—SAN ANTONIO DE PADUA DEL CAÑON CHURCH (1977) Revs. Joseph M. Nettekoven; Seamus A. Glynn, Pastor Emeritus (Retired); Viet Peter Ho, Parochial Vicar; Deacon Doug Cook.
Res.: 5800 E. Santa Ana Canyon Rd., 92807. Tel: 714-974-1416; Fax: 714-974-9630. Web: sanantonioparish.org.
See St. Francis of Assisi School, Yorba Linda under Multi-Parish Schools located in the Institution section.
Catechesis/Religious Program—Tel: 714-974-2053. Carolyn Buehler, D.R.E. Students 1,115.

BREA, ST. ANGELA MERICI (1962) Revs. Michael-Dwight Colin Galinada; Douglas Dale; Martin Nguyen; Deacons Jim Merle; Benjamin Flores.
Res.: 585 Walnut St., 92821. Tel: 714-529-1821; Fax: 714-529-0569. Email: office@stangelabreachurch.org. Web: stangelabreachurch.org.
Church: Walnut and Fir, 92821.
School—575 S. Walnut Ave., 92821. Tel: 714-529-6372; Fax: 714-529-7755. Religious 1; Lay Teachers 14; Students 295.
Catechesis/Religious Program—Tel: 714-529-2311. Students 643.

BUENA PARK, ST. PIUS V (1948) Revs. Theodore Olson; Khoi Phan, Parochial Vicar; Antonio Lopez; Deacons Rey Marin; William Yang.
Res.: 7691 Orangethorpe Ave., 90621. Tel: 714-522-2193; Fax: 714-522-1730. Web: stpius5.org.
School—7681 Orangethorpe Ave., 90621. Tel: 714-522-5313; Fax: 714-522-1767. Web: stpius5school.net. Lay Teachers 20; Students 508.
Catechesis/Religious Program—Tel: 714-522-3971. Email: sre@stpius5.org. Students 1,059.

CAPISTRANO BEACH, SAN FELIPE DE JESUS (1950), (Hispanic), Rev. Steven Sallot, Admin.; Deacon Victor Samano.
Mailing Address: *c/o St. Edward the Confessor*, 33926 Calle La Primavera, Dana Point, 92629.
Res.: 26010 Domingo Ave., 92624. Tel: 949-496-1307; Fax: 949-496-1557.
Church: Domingo St. & Sepulveda, 92624.
Catechesis/Religious Program—Tel: 949-493-8918. Students 237.

COSTA MESA

1—ST. JOACHIM (1947) Revs. Enrique J. Sera; Stephen Doktorczyk; Gilberto Escobedo.
Mailing Address: 1964 Orange Ave., 92627.
Res.: 1943 Orange Ave., 92627. Tel: 949-574-7400; Fax: 949-574-7407. Email: tstuddert@stjoachimparish.com. Web: www.stjoachimparish.com.
School—Tel: 949-574-7411; Fax: 949-646-8948. Lay Teachers 16; Students 280; Teacher Aides 7; Day Care Personnel 2.
Catechesis/Religious Program—Tel: 949-574-7400; Fax: 949-575-7407. Students 703.

2—ST. JOHN THE BAPTIST (1960) Revs. Hildebrand Garceau, O.Praem.; Augustine R. Puchner, O.Praem.; Philip T. Smith, O.Praem.; Andrew Tran, O.Praem. In Res., Revs. Robert Hodges, O.Praem.; Norbert J. Wood, O.Praem.
Res.: 1015 Baker St., 92626. Tel: 714-540-2214; Fax: 714-540-5902. Email: info@sjboc.org. Web: www.sjbcostamesa.org.
School—1021 Baker St., 92626. Tel: 714-557-5060; Fax: 714-557-9263. Web: www.sjbschool.net. Sr. M. Vianney Ennis, S.M., Prin. Sisters of Mercy 1; Lay Teachers 22; Students 600.
Catechesis/Religious Program—Tel: 714-546-4102. Christina Ford, D.R.E. (English); Sisters Linh Magdalene Dinh, L.H.C., D.R.E. (Vietnamese); Bertha Rafael, M.C., D.R.E. (Spanish). Students 705.

CYPRESS, ST. IRENAEUS (1961) Revs. Patrick Moses, Admin.; Matthew Munoz; Venancio Amidar; Deacon Jose Campos.
Res.: 5201 Evergreen Ave., 90630. Tel: 714-826-0760; Fax: 714-826-1608. Email: parish@sticypress.org. Web: www.sticypress.org.
School—9201 Grindlay St., 90630. Tel: 714-827-4500; Fax: 714-827-2930. Email: office@stischoolcypress.org. Sisters 1; Lay Teachers 28; Students 398.
Catechesis/Religious Program—9211 Grindlay St., 90630. Tel: 714-826-1140; Fax: 714-826-1608. Email: rbradley@sticypress.org. Students 800.

DANA POINT, ST. EDWARD THE CONFESSOR (1969) Revs. Steven Sallot; Loc Tran; Mario Juarez, Parochial Vicar; Christopher Heath; Deacons Jesse Michel; Ron Tiberi.
Res.: 33926 Calle La Primavera, 92629. Tel: 949-496-1307; Fax: 949-496-1557. Web: www.stedward.com.
School—33866 Calle La Primavera, 92629. Tel: 949-496-1241; Fax: 949-496-1819. Lay Teachers 25; Students 630.
Catechesis/Religious Program—Tel: 949-496-6011. Students 672.

FOUNTAIN VALLEY, HOLY SPIRIT (1972) Revs. Martin Duc Tran, Admin.; Winnie "Wayne" Adajar; Raphael Xuan Nguyen; Deacon Phillip Goodman.
Mailing Address: 17270 Ward St., 92708.
Res.: 16806 Mt. Olsen Cir., 92708. Tel: 714-963-1811; Fax: 714-968-1775. Email: office@hsccfv.org. Web: www.hsccfv.org.
Catechesis/Religious Program—Tel: 714-963-7871; 714-964-8767 (Vietnamese); Fax: 714-968-1775. Email: re@hsccfv.org; vietre@hsccfr.org (Vietnamese). Sisters Lucia Tu, S.D.S.H., D.R.E.; Theresa Trang Nguyen, L.H.C., D.R.E. Students 893.

FULLERTON

1—ST. JULIANA FALCONIERI (1965) Revs. Frank Falco, O.S.M.; Patrick Donovan, O.S.M., Chap. (California State Univ. - Newman Club); Paul M. Gins, O.S.M., Parochial Vicar; Deacons Gerhard P. Stadel; William Schlater.
Res.: 1316 N. Acacia Ave., 92831. Tel: 714-879-1965; Fax: 714-526-6673. Email: info@stjulianachurch.org. Web: www.stjulianachurch.org.
School—1320 N. Acacia Ave., 92831. Tel: 714-871-2829; Fax: 714-871-8465. Web: www.stjulianaschool.org. Lay Teachers 16; Part-Time Teachers 4; Students 284.
Catechesis/Religious Program—Students 298.

2—ST. MARY'S (1912) Revs. James C. Ries; Juan B. Navarro, Parochial Vicar; Deacons Carlos Gonzalez; Manuel Chavira.
Res.: 400 W. Commonwealth Ave., 92832. Tel: 714-525-2500; Fax: 714-525-3837. Web: saintmarysfullerton.catholicweb.com.
See school listing under St. Philip Benizi, Fullerton for details.
Catechesis/Religious Program—Students 500.

3—ST. PHILIP BENIZI (1958) Revs. David Gallegos, O.S.M.; Justin M. Pisciotta, O.S.M.; Alvaro Mejia Agudelo, O.S.M.; Deacons Richard Glaudini; Fidel Rodriguez. In Res., Rev. Gerald M. Horan, O.S.M.
Parish Office: 235 S. Pine Dr., 92833. Tel: 714-871-3610; Fax: 714-871-5827. Email: philipbenizi@aol.com. Web: benizi.us.
Res.: 5210 Somerset, Buena Park, 90621.
School—Annunciation Catholic School, 215 S. Pine Dr., 92833-3293. Tel: 714-871-6121; Fax: 714-992-4167. Web: annunciationcs.org. Mrs. Clancy Habich, Prin. Lay Teachers 12; Students 158.
Catechesis/Religious Program—Tel: 714-870-0561. Mrs. Maria Barrientos, Dir. Faith Formation; Kathleen O'Leary, Youth Min. & Confirmation Coord. Students 580.

GARDEN GROVE

1—ST. CALLISTUS (1961) Revs. Tuyen Nguyen; Joseph Long Kim Nguyen; Jude Lucier O. Praem; Ismael Silva; Benjamin Philip Tran, Parochial Vicar; Deacons Joseph Khiet Nguyen; Jose Serrano; Guillermo Torres.
Res.: 12921 Lewis St., 92840. Tel: 714-971-2141; Fax: 714-971-9112.
Church: Garden Grove Blvd. and Lewis St., 92840.
St. Callistus Preschool—12132 Haster St., 92840. Tel: 714-750-6777.
School—(Grades PreSchool-8), 12901 Lewis St., 92840. Tel: 714-971-2023; Fax: 714-971-2031. Sisters 1; Lay Teachers 12; Students 190.
Catechesis/Religious Program—Tel: 714-971-2091. Maureen Ross, D.R.E. Students 1,646.

2—ST. COLUMBAN (1953) Revs. Juan Caboboy; Steven Correz; Joseph Thai Nguyen; Kiem Van Tran; Deacon Anthony Carrasco. In Res., Rev. Msgr. Michael Heher.
Res.: 10801 Stanford Ave., 92840. Tel: 714-534-1174; Fax: 714-534-1937. Web: www.saintcolumbanchurch.org.
School—10855 Stanford Ave., 92840. Tel: 714-534-3947; Fax: 714-590-9153. Religious Sisters of Charity 1; Lay Teachers 12; Students 207.
Catechesis/Religious Program—Tel: 714-537-2015. Students 1,325.

HUNTINGTON BEACH

1—ST. BONAVENTURE (1965) Revs. Bruce Patterson; Angelos Sebastian, Parochial Vicar; Joseph Hoang, Parochial Vicar; Deacons Jim Andersen; Scott Ford; Vincent Tran. In Res., Rev. John R. Keller (Retired).
Res.: 16400 Springdale St., 92649. Tel: 714-846-3350; 714-846-3359; Fax: 714-840-0480. Email: email@stbonaventure.org. Web: www.stbonaventure.org.
School—16377 Bradbury Ln., 92647. Tel: 714-846-2472; Fax: 714-840-0498. Judy Luttrell, Prin. Union of the Sisters of the Presentation of the Blessed Virgin Mary 6; Lay Teachers 27; Students 616.
Catechesis/Religious Program—Tel: 714-846-2472. Laraine Soule, D.R.E. Students 1,372.

2—ST. MARY'S BY THE SEA (1977) Rev. Joseph Luan Nguyen, Admin. In Res., Rev. Eamon Mackin, C.H.S.
Res.: 321 10th St., 92648. Tel: 714-536-6913; Fax: 714-536-2464. Email: officesmbs@bizla.rr.com. Web: stmarysbythesea.net.
Catechesis/Religious Program—Students 61.

3—SS. SIMON AND JUDE (1912) Revs. Michael L. Harvey, O.F.M.; Richard Juzix, O.F.M.; Deacon Bill Cobbett; Sr. Maureen Sheehan, B.V.M., Pastoral Assoc.; Patsi Wagner, Pastoral Assoc.; Christina Sumpter, Pastoral Admin. In Res., Rev. Christian Mondor, O.F.M.
Res.: 20444 Magnolia St., 92646. Tel: 714-962-3333; Fax: 714-965-6456. Email: ssj@ssj.org. Web: www.ssj.org.
School—20400 Magnolia St., 92646. Tel: 714-962-4451; Fax: 714-968-1329. Web: www.ssj.org/school/. Lay Teachers 35; Students 579.
Catechesis/Religious Program—Tel: 714-963-0014. Web: www.ssj.org/faith/index.html. Richard Ballesteros, D.R.E. Students 750.

4—ST. VINCENT DE PAUL (1977) Revs. Jerome T. Karcher; Antonio Zapata; Deacon Fernando Mezquita.
Res.: 8345 Talbert Ave., 92646. Tel: 714-842-3000; Fax: 714-842-6780. Email: svdp@svdphb.org. Web: www.svdphb.org.
Catechesis/Religious Program—Tel: 714-842-3000; Fax: 714-842-6780. Email: reled@svdphb.org. Students 579.

IRVINE

1—ST. ELIZABETH ANN SETON (1976) Rev. Thomas Pado; Deacon Steve Greco.
Res.: 9 Hillgate, 92612-3265. Tel: 949-854-1000; Fax: 949-854-0079. Web: www.seasirvine.org.
Catechesis/Religious Program—Students 105.

2—ST. JOHN NEUMANN (1978) Rev. Msgr. Donald Romito; Rev. Anthony Hien T. Vu, Parochial Vicar. In Res., Revs. John M. Joyce (Retired); Michael Tung Nguyen.
Res.: 5101 Alton Pkwy., 92604-8605. Tel: 949-559-4006; Fax: 949-857-4788. Email: parishoffice@sjnirvine.org. Web: www.sjnirvine.org.
Catechesis/Religious Program—Tel: 949-786-6105; Fax: 949-786-6102. Email: religioused@sjnirvine.org. Kellie De Leo, D.R.E.; Juliana Gerace, Dir. Youth Min. Students 635.

3—ST. THOMAS MORE (1996) [CEM] Revs. John E. Janze; George Blais; Deacon Tony Patronite; Theresa Nawlt, Business Mgr.; Cari Maas, Music Dir. In Res., Rev. William Krekelberg.
Res.: 14010 Remington, 92620-3212. Tel: 949-551-8601; Fax: 949-551-5879.
Catechesis/Religious Program—Barbara Catiller, D.R.E.; David Calavitta, Youth Min. Students 675.

LA HABRA, OUR LADY OF GUADALUPE (1947) Revs. Justin H. MacCarthy; William Hubbard, Parochial Vicar; Brendan David Manson, Parochial Vicar; Deacon Carlos Navarro.
Res.: 900 W. La Habra Blvd., 90631. Tel: 562-691-0533; Fax: 562-694-8328. Web: www.olglahabra.org.
School—Tel: 562-697-9726; Fax: 562-905-0095. Web: www.olgvikings.com. Lay Teachers 22; Students 387.
Catechesis/Religious Program—Tel: 562-691-2104; Fax: 562-697-6391. Students 589.

LAGUNA BEACH, ST. CATHERINE OF SIENA (1923) Revs. Eamon T. O'Gorman; Marito F. Rebamontan, Senior Priest.
Res.: 1042 Temple Ter., 92651. Tel: 949-494-9701; Fax: 949-497-2610. Email: info@stcathlagunabeach.org. Web: www.stcathlagunabeach.org.
School—30516 S. Coast Hwy., 92651. Tel: 949-494-7339; Fax: 949-376-5752. Web: www.saintcatherinelaguna.com. Lay Teachers 14; Students 173.
Catechesis/Religious Program—Tel: 949-494-9701, Ext. 119. Students 180.

LAGUNA NIGUEL, ST. TIMOTHY (1980) Rev. Msgr. John Urell; Rev. Timothy Nguyen, Parochial Vicar.
Rectory—29182 Via San Sebastian, 92677.
Church: 29102 Crown Valley Pkwy., 92677. Tel: 949-249-4091; Fax: 949-249-4094. Web: www.st-timsrc.org.

Catechesis/Religious Program—Tel: 949-495-4126. Students 441.

LAGUNA WOODS, ST. NICHOLAS (1965) Revs. Richard A. Delahunty; Thai Paul Minh Trinh. In Res., Rev. Timothy MacCarthy (Retired).
Res.: 24252 El Toro Rd., 92637. Tel: 949-837-1090; Fax: 949-837-9510.
Catechesis/Religious Program—Tel: 949-837-7676. Students 200.

LAKE FOREST, SANTIAGO DE COMPOSTELA (1979) Revs. David Gruver; William Barman; Deacons Carlos Euyoque; Don Jensen. In Res., Rev. Rosendo Silva, L.C.
Res.: 21682 Lake Forest Dr., 92630. Tel: 949-951-8599; Fax: 949-951-2687. Email: admin@santiagodecomp.com. Web: www.santiago-catholicchurch.org.
See Serra Catholic School, Rancho Santa Margarita under Multi-Parish Schools located in the Institution section.
Catechesis/Religious Program—Tel: 949-951-0792; Fax: 949-951-2687. Email: re@santiagodecomp.com. Students 762.

LOS ALAMITOS, ST. HEDWIG (1960) Revs. Kenneth A. Schmit; Christopher Tuan Pham; Deacons Larry Hurst; Gary Mucho.
Res.: 11482 Los Alamitos Blvd., 90720. Tel: 562-296-9000; Fax: 562-296-9099. Web: sainthedwigparish.org.
School—3591 Orangewood Ave., 90720. Tel: 562-296-9060; Fax: 562-296-9089. Email: parishschool@sainthedwigparish.org. Lay Teachers 25; Students 446.
Catechesis/Religious Program—Tel: 562-296-9040. Students 440.

MISSION VIEJO, ST. KILIAN (1970) Rev. James P. Dunning; Deacon Bob Kelleher.
26872 Estanciero Dr., 92691. Email: gmoonll@cox.net.
Res.: 25672 Morales, 92691. Tel: 949-586-4440; Fax: 949-454-1043. Email: stkilians@cox.net. Web: stkilianchurch.org.
See Serra Catholic School, Rancho Santa Margarita under Multi-Parish Schools located in the Institution section.
Catechesis/Religious Program—Tel: 949-586-4550; Fax: 949-454-1043. Email: skre@cox.net. Marcia Burns, D.R.E. Students 759.

NEWPORT BEACH

1—OUR LADY OF MOUNT CARMEL (1923) Rev. Msgr. Lawrence J. Baird; Rev. Robert Tan Pham, S.J., Parochial Vicar; Deacons Stephen Mutz; Glenn Erwin. In Res., Revs. Sean Condon (Ireland), Senior Priest (Retired); John Weling, S.J.
Res.: 1441 W. Balboa Blvd., 92661-1010. Tel: 949-673-3775; Fax: 949-673-3137. Email: olmc@olmc.net. Web: www.olmc.net.
Catechesis/Religious Program—Tel: 949-673-2719; Fax: 949-673-3137. Students 225.
Chapel—St. John Vianney 314 Marine Ave., Balboa Island, 92662-1206. Tel: 949-675-2221; Fax: 949-673-3801.

2—OUR LADY QUEEN OF ANGELS (1961) Revs. Kerry Beaulieu; Joseph D. Nguyen; David Klunk, Parochial Vicar; Deacon Jim Arnold. In Res., Most Rev. Dominic M. Luong; Rev. Msgr. Wilbur Davis (Retired).
Res.: 2046 Mar Vista Dr., 92660. Tel: 949-644-0200; Fax: 949-644-1349. Web: www.olqa.org.
School—Tel: 949-644-1166; Fax: 949-644-6213. Email: info@olqa.org. Web: www.olqaschool.org. Lay Teachers 28; Students 447.
Catechesis/Religious Program—Tel: 949-219-1497; Fax: 949-644-1349. Students 570.

PLACENTIA, ST. JOSEPH (1953) Revs. Timothy Ramaekers; Robert Capone; Deacons Ed Faulk; Jorge Ramirez. In Res., Rev. Thomas Keller, M.S.C.
Res.: 717 N. Bradford Ave., 92870-4514. Tel: 714-528-1487; Fax: 714-579-3791.
School—801 N. Bradford Ave., 92870-4515. Tel: 714-528-1794; Fax: 714-528-0668. Email: mail@sjsplacentia.org. Web: www.sjsplacentia.org. Lay Teachers 16; Students 305.
Catechesis/Religious Program—Tel: 714-528-1487; Fax: 714-579-3791. Teri Kleckner, D.R.E.; Eloisa Ramirez, D.R.E. (Spanish). Students 613.
Mission—Santa Teresita 636 Van Buren Ave., Atwood, Orange Co. 92811.

RANCHO SANTA MARGARITA, SAN FRANCISCO SOLANO CHURCH (1989) Revs. Craig M. Butters; John R. LeVecke, S.J.; Deacon Carl Swanson.
Res.: 22082 Antonio Pkwy., 92688-1993. Tel: 949-589-7767; Fax: 949-589-7768. Email: information@sfsolano.org. Web: www.sfsolano.org.
See Serra Catholic School, Rancho Santa Margarita under Multi-Parish Schools located in the Institution section.
Catechesis/Religious Program—Tel: 949-589-1709; Fax: 949-589-2840. Mrs. Mary Ann Taeger, D.R.E. Students 1,012.

SAN CLEMENTE, OUR LADY OF FATIMA (1947) Revs. Jack Sewell; Sergio Ramos. In Res., Rev. Msgr. Anthony McGowan, Pastor Emeritus (Retired).
Res.: 105 La Esperanza, 92672. Tel: 949-492-4101; Fax: 949-492-4856. Email: lrojas@olfchurch.net. Web: www.olfchurch.net.
School—Tel: 949-492-7320; Fax: 949-492-3793. Web: school.ourladyoffatima.net. Lay Teachers 13; Students 211.
Catechesis/Religious Program—Tel: 949-492-4101; Fax: 949-492-4856. Students 530.

SAN JUAN CAPISTRANO, MISSION BASILICA - SAN JUAN CAPISTRANO (1776) [CEM] Rev. Msgr. Arthur A. Holquin, Pastoral Rector; Rev. Armando Virrey, Parochial Vicar; Deacon David Sire. In Res., Rev. Michael M. Pontarelli, O.S.M.
Res.: 31522 Camino Capistrano, 92675. Tel: 949-234-1360; Fax: 949-248-2008 (Parish Office). Web: www.missionparish.org.
School—31641 El Camino Real, 92675. Tel: 949-234-1385; Fax: 949-248-2178. Lay Teachers 15; Students 294.
Catechesis/Religious Program—Tel: 949-234-1370; Fax: 949-248-2056. Mrs. Linda Berkshire, D.R.E. Students 670.

SANTA ANA

1—CHRIST OUR SAVIOR CATHEDRAL (2005) Rev. Msgr. J. Michael McKiernan, Rector.
3337 S. Bristol #119, 92704. Tel: 714-444-1500. Email: parishoffice@christoursaviorcathedral.com. Web: christoursaviorcathedral.com. In Res., Rev. Minh Bui; Deacon Frank Chavez.
Catechesis/Religious Program—Mr. Luis Ramirez, D.R.E. Students 140.

2—ST. ANNE'S (1923), (Hispanic), Revs. Salvador Landa; Ramon Cisneros; Randy Guillen (NEW); Deacon Francisco Martinez.
Res.: 109 W. Borchard Ave., P.O. Box 2425, 92707. Tel: 714-835-7434; 714-835-7435; Fax: 714-835-4506.
School—Tel: 714-542-9328; Fax: 714-542-3431. Sisters 1; Lay Teachers 18; Students 233.
Catechesis/Religious Program—Tel: 714-542-1213; Fax: 714-542-6608. Students 780.

3—ST. BARBARA CATHOLIC CHURCH (1962) Revs. Richard C. Kennedy; Tuan John Nguyen; Michael Mai Khai Hoan, Senior Priest; Paul Flynn, O.S.A. (Ireland); Deacon Joseph Anh Nguyen. In Res., Rev. Jose Luis Jimenez, O.A.R. (Retired).
Res.: 730 S. Euclid St., 92704. Tel: 714-775-7733; Fax: 714-775-9467. Email: st_barbara_church@hotmail.com.
School—5306 W. McFadden Ave., 92704. Tel: 714-775-9477; Fax: 714-775-9468. Email: sbs@stbarbara.com. Web: www.stbarbara.com. Lay Teachers 30; Students 418.
Catechesis/Religious Program—Tel: 714-775-9475. Students 1,528.

4—ST. GEORGE (CHALDEAN CATHOLIC) Rev. Zuhair G. Toma (LA).
Mailing Address: 4807 W. McFadden, 92704. Tel: 714-531-7760; Fax: 714-775-1442.

5—IMMACULATE HEART OF MARY (1960) Revs. Edward Poettgen; Hector Bedoya; Carlos Leon; Deacons Gerardo de Santos; Adolfo Ramirez. In Res., Rev. Ignatius Lau (Retired).
Res.: 1100 S. Center St., 92704. Tel: 714-751-5335; Fax: 714-662-0130. Email: m40manuela@msn.com.
School—Tel: 714-545-8185; Fax: 714-545-2362. Lay Teachers 9; Students 188.
Catechesis/Religious Program—Tel: 714-546-5186. Students 1,835.

6—ST. JOSEPH (1887) Revs. John W. Moneypenny; Leonel M. Vargas.
Res.: 727 Minter St., 92701. Tel: 714-542-4411; Fax: 714-542-9770. Email: sjpostmaster@stjosephsa.org. Web: www.stjosephsa.org.
School—608 Civic Center Dr. E., 92701. Tel: 714-542-2704; Fax: 714-542-2132. Email: bsnyder@stjoesa.org. Web: www.stjoesa.org. Lay Teachers 9; Students 242.
Catechesis/Religious Program—717 N. Minter St., 92701. Tel: 714-550-8096; Fax: 714-245-2319. Students 580.

7—OUR LADY OF GUADALUPE (1927), (Hispanic), Rev. David Vuelvas-Arias, Admin.
Res.: 541 E. Central Ave., 92707. Tel: 714-540-0902; Fax: 714-540-3053.
Catechesis/Religious Program—Tel: 714-540-9231. Rosa Castro, D.R.E. Students 600.

8—OUR LADY OF GUADALUPE (1938), (Hispanic), Revs. Alfredo de Dios, O.A.R.; Juan Jose Guzman, O.A.R.; Deacons Ulises Feliciano, O.A.R.; Miguel Gonzalez.
Res.: 1322 E. Third St., 92701. Tel: 714-836-4142; Fax: 714-836-7417. Email: olguadalupesa@hotmail.com.
Catechesis/Religious Program—Tel: 714-973-0279. Margarita Garza, D.R.E. Students 1,529.

9—OUR LADY OF LA VANG (2006) Revs. Bill T. Cao, Admin.; Anthony Phuc Nguyen; Deacons Rigoberto Maldonado; Jerry Dao. In Res., Revs. J. Duc Minh Nguyen; Sergio Ramos.
Res.: 288 S. Harbor Blvd., 92704. Tel: 714-775-6200. Email: lavangparish@yahoo.com. Web: www.ourladyoflavang.org.
Catechesis/Religious Program—Students 512.

10—OUR LADY OF THE PILLAR (1965), (Hispanic), Revs. Anthony Palos, O.A.R.; Euben Capacillo; Jose Luis Martinez, O.A.R.; Gabino Perez, O.A.R.; Deacon Luis Gallardo. In Res., Rev. Joachim Goni, O.A.R. (Retired).
Res.: 1622 W. 6th St., 92703. Tel: 714-543-1700; Fax: 714-543-9640.
Catechesis/Religious Program—Tel: 714-542-4684. Students 750.

SEAL BEACH

1—ST. ANNE'S (1921) Rev. Robert S. Vidal; Rev. Msgr. Michael Collins, Pastor Emeritus (Retired); Deacon Gary Mucho.
Res.: 340 Tenth St., 90740. Tel: 562-431-0721; Fax: 562-431-3050. Email: stannesealbeach@yahoo.com. Web: www.stannesealbeach.org.
Catechesis/Religious Program—Tel: 562-431-8524; Fax: 562-431-3050. Sr. Samuel Marie Settar, O.S.F., D.R.E. Students 104.

2—HOLY FAMILY (1969) Rev. James Hartnett. In Res., Rev. Msgrs. Brian Coghlan (Retired); James J. Pierse (Retired).
Res.: 13900 Church Pl., 90740. Tel: 562-430-8170; Fax: 562-493-4643.

STANTON, ST. POLYCARP (1961) Revs. Quang Vinh Chu; Miguel A. Hernandez; Deacons Binh Chu; Larry Leone; Ramiro Lopez. In Res., Rev. Joseph C. Nguyen.
Res.: 8100 Chapman Ave., 90680. Tel: 714-893-2766; Fax: 714-898-6675. Web: www.stpolycarp.org.
School—8182 Chapman Ave., 90680. Tel: 714-893-8882; Fax: 714-897-3357. Web: www.saintpolycarp-school.com. Lay Teachers 10; Students 169.
Catechesis/Religious Program—Tel: 714-892-3158. Students 870.

TUSTIN, ST. CECILIA (1957), (Spanish—Vietnamese), Revs. Alfred Baca; Thomas De Nguyen-Dang; Deacons Don Ngo; Martin Ruiz.
Res.: 1301 Sycamore, 92780. Tel: 714-544-3250; Fax: 714-838-1996. Web: www.stcecilia.org.
School—1311 Sycamore, 92780. Tel: 714-544-1533; Fax: 714-544-0643. Email: school@stceciliak8.org. Lay Teachers 18; Students 315.
Catechesis/Religious Program—Tel: 714-838-4466. Students 1,058.

WESTMINSTER, BLESSED SACRAMENT (1947) Revs. Tuan Ngoc Pham; Joseph Droessler; Efrain Flores; Danh Ngoc Trinh; Deacons Matt Calabrese; Arturo Gimenez; Hao Nguyen; Joseph Stripling.
Res.: 14072 S. Olive St., 92683. Tel: 714-892-4489; Fax: 714-892-5560. Email: bscparishoffice@socal.rr.com. Web: www.blessedsacramentparish.com.
School—14146 S. Olive St., 92683. Tel: 714-893-7701; Fax: 714-891-7186. Email: blsdsacramentsch@covet.net. Roisin McAree, Prin. Lay Teachers 16; Students 297.
Catechesis/Religious Program—14144 S. Olive St., 92683. Tel: 714-897-2142; Fax: 714-892-5560. Ana Marie Gimenez, D.R.E. Students 1,276.

YORBA LINDA

1—ST. MARTIN DE PORRES (1970) Revs. Joseph Knerr; Ian Bustonera; Deacon Denis F. Zaun.
Mailing Address: 19767 Yorba Linda Blvd., 92886. Tel: 714-970-2771; Fax: 714-970-5654. Web: www.smdpyl.org.
School—St. Francis of Assisi, 5330 Eastside Cir., 92887. Tel: 714-695-3700; Fax: 714-695-3704. Web: www.stfrancis-yorbalinda.com. Kathleen Falcone, Prin. Lay Teachers 51; Students 479; Total Staff 51.
Catechesis/Religious Program—Tel: 714-970-2521; Fax: 714-970-5654. Mrs. Pam Bender, D.R.E.; Cindy Piszyk, D.R.E. (Adult); Shannon Kwan, D.R.E. (Youth). Students 596.

2—SANTA CLARA DE ASIS (2001) Rev. Michael P. Hanifin; Deacon Robert Soikkeli.
Mailing Address & Office: 22005 Avenida de la Paz, 92887. Tel: 714-970-7885; Fax: 714-970-2618. Email: santaclarachurch@yahoo.com. Web: www.santaclarachurch.org.
Catechesis/Religious Program—Students 330.

Chaplains Of Public Institutions

ORANGE. *UCI Medical Center*, 101 The City Dr. S., 92868. Tel: 714-634-5678. Rev. Joseph Son Nguyen. (Served by St. Callistus Parish.)
12921 Lewis St., Garden Grove, 92840. Tel: 714-971-2141.

COSTA MESA. *Fairview Developmental Center*, 2501 Harbor, 92626. Tel: 714-545-9331. Mary Brosseau.

SANTA ANA. *All Adult and Juvenile Jail Facilities,* 2112 N. Main St., Ste. 290, 92868. Tel: 714-634-9909; Fax: 714-634-9910. Deacon Phillip Goodman, Dir. Email: pgoodman@rcbo.org, Rev. Adrian Sanchez, O.Praem., Chap., Sr. Claudia Romero, Juvenile Facilites, Fred Lapuza, Adult Facilities, Deacon Martin Ruiz, Hispanic Ministry.

Special Assignment:
Most Rev.—
Luong, Dominic M., D.D., V.G.
Rev. Msgrs.—
Cook, Douglas, J.C.L.
Heher, Michael, V.G.
Pham, Tuan Joseph, J.C.L.
Revs.—
Bui, Minh Cong, J.C.L.
Doktorczyk, Steve
Flores, Cirilo
Grace, John, O.S.A.
Horan, Gerald M., O.S.M.
Keller, Thomas, M.S.C., J.C.L.
Krekelberg, William
Luevano, Rafael
Moreland, J. Gordon, S.J., Dir., House of Prayer for Priests, 7734 Santiago Canyon Rd., 92869.
Neneman, John
Philbin, Patrick, House of Prayer for Priests
Smith, Christopher

On Duty Outside the Diocese:
Revs.—
Hopcus, Daniel, St. Mary of the Woods, IN 47876-1089.
Hopping, John Paul
Shimotsu, John M., Military
Sweeney, Kevin, Military

Military Chaplains:
Revs.—
Shimotsu, John M.
Sweeney, Kevin

Absent on Sick Leave:
Revs.—
DiStefano, Joseph
Justice, Joseph Charles
Kinzer, Gary
Kolberg, Lawrence R.
Monestero, John

Inactive Leave:
Revs.—
Kim, Roy
McAndrew, John P. (Retired)

Education Leave:
Revs.—
Becker, Edward
Droessler, Jeffrey A.
Peters, Timothy J.
Sun Kim, Simon Chung, Washington, D.C.

Administrative Leave:
Rev. Msgr.—
Murray, Daniel J., J.C.L.
Revs.—
Henson, Jerome
Nguyen, Anh Tuan
Nguyen, Dominic
Salazar, Cesar

Retired:
Most Rev.—
McFarland, Norman F.
Rev. Msgrs.—
Caceres, Alonso
Campbell, John
Coghlan, Brian
Collins, Michael
Davis, Wilbur
Keenan, John C.
McGowan, Anthony
McLaughlin, William
Pierse, James J.
Tanilong, Gerardo J.
Revs.—
Bebek, Dominic
Benedicto, Benjamin
Block, John
Bradley, John A.
Buckman, Frank
Chen, Rafael
Condon, Sean (Ireland)
Conlon, Colmbanus
Croal, Thomas
Fee, Pat
Fry, James Q.
Ha, Thomas Do Thanh
Ho, Matthias
Huynh, Andrew
Johnson, Dan
Joyce, John M.
Keller, J. Rod
Lau, Ignatius
Luongo, John
Lyons, Denis
MacCarthy, Timothy
McAndrew, John P.
Nguyen, Tien Duc
Patrick, William
Po, Thanh Ha
Sheahan, John A.
Shetter, John
Skonezny, Raymond
Vu, Joachim

Permanent Deacons:
Amorino, Paul, La Purisima, Orange
Anderson, James, St. Bonaventure, Huntington Beach
Arnolds, James, Our Lady Queen of Angels, Newport Beach
Barth, John, (On Duty Outside the Diocese)
Bourne, Scotty, (On Duty Outside the Diocese)
Boyer, Charles, St. John Neuman, Irvine
Brenes-Rios, Anthony, (On Duty Outside the Diocese)
Bube, Anthony, La Purisima, Orange
Calabrese, Matt, Blessed Sacrament, Westminster
Campos, Jose, St. Ireaneus, Cypress
Canlas, Fred, St. Joachim, Costa Mesa
Carrasco, Anthony, St. Columban, Garden Grove
Carver, Timothy, (On Leave)
Chavez, Frank, Christ Our Savior Cathedral, Santa Ana
Chavira, Manuel, St. Mary, Fullerton
Chu, Binh, St. Polycarp, Stanton
Chung, Peter, St. Thomas Korean Center, Anaheim
Cobbett, William, SS. Simon and Jude, Huntington Beach
Cook, Douglas, San Antonio de Padua, Anaheim Hills
Dao, Jerry, Our Lady of La Vang, Santa Ana
Davis, Clyde, (On Duty Outside the Diocese)
Dennis, Irving, (On Duty Outside the Diocese)
DeSantos, Gerardo, Immaculate Heart of Mary, Santa Ana
Devore, Robert, Corpus Christi, Aliso Viejo
Duthoy, Raymond, St. Justin Martyr, Anaheim
Erwin, Glenn, Our Lady of Mt. Carmel, Newport Beach
Esparza, Joseph, St. Norbert, Orange
Espinoza, Juan, La Purisima, Orange
Esposito, Robert, (On Duty Outside Diocese)
Euyoque, Carlos, Santiago de Compostela, Lake Forest
Faulk, Edward, St. Joseph, Placentia
Ferreras, Jose, St. Justin Martyr, Anaheim
Fletcher, Michael, St. Nicholas, Laguna Woods
Flores, Benjamin, St. Angela Merici, Brea
Folau, Kalini, Tongan Community
Ford, Scott, St. Bonaventure, Huntington Beach
Gallardo, Luis
Garza, Domingo
Gimenez, Arturo, Blessed Sacrament, Westminster
Glaudini, Richard, St. Philip Benizi, Fullerton
Gonzales, Carlos, St. Mary, Fullerton
Gonzalez, Miguel, Our Lady of Guadalupe, Santa Ana
Goodman, Phillip, Holy Spirit, Fountain Valley
Greco, Steve, Elizabeth Ann Seton, Irvine
Griffin, Gary, Our Lady of the Pillar, Santa Ana
Hurst, Larry, St. Hedwig, Los Alamitos
Jensen, Don, Santiago de Compostela, Lake Forest
Kelleher, Robert, St. Kilian, Mission Viejo
Kim, Peter, Korean Martyrs Catholic Center, Westminster
Lechner, Joel, (On Duty Outside Diocese)
Lee, Moon Chul, Korean Martyrs
Leon, Ramon, St. Justin Martyr, Anaheim
Leone, Larry, St. Polycarp, Stanton
Leuta, Filipo, Samoan Community
Liu, Louis, Chinese Catholic Community, Santa Ana
Lopez, Ramiro, St. Polycarp, Stanton
Lovett, Richard, Holy Family Cathedral, Orange
Luna, Frank, (Retired)
Maldonado, Rigoberto, Our Lady of La Vang, Santa Ana
Marin, Reynaldo, St. Pius V, Buena Park
Martinez, Francisco, St. Anne, Santa Ana
McGuine, Thomas, Holy Family Cathedral, Orange
McMahon, Randall, Holy Trinity, Ladera Ranch
Melton, Harold, (On Duty Outside the Diocese)
Merle, James, St. Angela Merici, Brea
Meyer, Leon, (Retired)
Michel, Jesse, St. Edwards, Dana Point
Milam, Jay, St. Boniface, Anaheim
Miller, Gerald, (On Duty Outside the Diocese)
Mones, August, St. Anthony Claret, Anaheim
Mucho, Richard "Gary", St. Hedwig, Los Alamitos
Mutz, Stephen, Our Lady of Mt. Carmel, Newport Beach
Naumann, Richard, (Retired)
Navarro, Carlos, Our Lady of Guadalupe, La Habra
Ngo, Dong Dinh, St. Cecilia, Tustin
Nguyen, Anh Phuong, St. Barbara, Santa Ana
Nguyen, Hao, Blessed Sacrament, Westminster
Nguyen, Joseph Khiet, St. Callistus, Garden Grove
Patronite, Tony, St. Thomas More, Irvine
Porcella, Roger, (On Duty Outside the Diocese)
Pyne, Gerald, St. Iranaeus, Cypress
Ramirez, Adolfo, Immaculate Heart of Mary, Santa Ana
Ramirez, Jorge, St. Joseph, Placentia
Reynoso, Jose Luis, Pius V, Buena Park
Richeson, James, (On Duty Outside the Diocese)
Rodriguez, Fidel, St. Philip Benizi, Fullerton
Rodriguez, Jose Luis, St. Boniface, Anaheim
Romero, Rafael, St. Joseph, Santa Ana
Ruiz, Martin, St. Cecilia, Tustin
Salgado, Eddie, St. Catherine of Siena, Laguna Beach
Samano, Victor, San Felipe de Jesus, Capistrano Beach
Schlater, William, St. Juliana Falconieri, Fullerton
Schlemmer, Jon, (Retired)
Serrano, Jose, St. Callistus, Santa Ana
Sire, David, Mission Basilica San Juan Capistrano, San Juan Capistrano
Sokkeli, Bob, Santa Clara de Asis, Yorba Linda
Song, Thomas, St. Thomas Korean Center, Anaheim
Stadel, Gerhard P., St. Juliana Falconieri, Fullerton
Stripling, Joseph, Blessed Sacrament, Westminster
Sullivan, Neill, Our Lady Queen of Angels, Newport Beach
Swanson, Carl, San Francisco Solano, Rancho Santa Margarita
Swift, Bernard, (Retired)
Thompson, Wayne, St. Nicholas, Laguna Woods
Tiberi, Ron, St. Edward the Confessor, Dana Point
Torres, Guillermo, St. Callistus, Garden Grove
Tran, Vincent, St. Bonaventure, Huntington Beach
Yang, William, Hmong Community, Buena Park
Zaun, Denis, St. Martin de Porres, Yorba Linda

INSTITUTIONS LOCATED IN THE DIOCESE

[A] SEMINARIES AND SCHOLASTICATES FOR RELIGIOUS

MIDWAY CITY. *St. Patrick's Novitiate,* 7820 Bolsa Ave., 92655. Tel: 714-897-8181; Fax: 714-898-9020. Email: BrosStPatrick@aol.com. Web: www.patricianbrothers.com. Bro. Aquinas Cassin, F.S.P., Supr. Conducted by the Brothers of St. Patrick. Brothers 5.

SILVERADO. *St. Michael's Norbertine Postulancy, Novitiate and Juniorate* (1959) 19292 El Toro Rd., 92676. Tel: 949-858-0222; Fax: 949-858-4583. Rt. Rev. Eugene J. Hayes, O.Praem., Abbot; Revs. Thomas W. Nelson, O.Praem., Dir. Formation; Ambrose Criste, O.Praem., Novice Master; Very Rev. Hugh C. Barbour, O.Praem., Prof. Philosophy; Revs. Gregory M. Dick, O.Praem., Prof. Scripture; Sebastian A. Walshe, O.Praem., Prof. Philosophy. Conducted by the Norbertine Fathers., For listing of other Norbertine priests working in the Diocese, refer to St. Michael College Prep High School. Priests 6; Total Enrollment 19.

[B] COLLEGES AND UNIVERSITIES

ORANGE. *St. Joseph College, Orange* Branch Campus of University of San Francisco; St. Joseph Library., 480 S. Batavia St., 92868. Tel: 714-633-8121; Fax: 714-744-3166. Sisters Jane DeLisle, C.S.J., Gen. Sec.; Christine Hilliard, C.S.J., Librarian.

[C] HIGH SCHOOLS, DIOCESAN

FULLERTON. *Rosary High School* (Girls), 1340 N. Acacia Ave., 92831. Tel: 714-879-6302; Fax: 714-879-0853. Email: rosary@rosaryhs.org. Web: www.rosaryhs.org. Mrs. Trudy Mazzarella, Pres.; Terry Gonzales, Prin.; Winnie Stokes, Librarian. Lay Teachers 42; Students 692; Total Staff 46.

RANCHO SANTA MARGARITA. *Santa Margarita Catholic High School,* 22062 Antonio Pkwy., 92688. Tel: 949-766-6000; Fax: 949-766-6005. Email: information@smhs.org. Web: www.smhs.org. Mr. Paul Carey, Pres.; Mr. Raymond R. Dunne, Prin. & Contact Person; Joan Zelarney, Librarian. Priests 1; Lay Teachers 98; Students 1,699.

SANTA ANA. *Mater Dei High School* (1950) (Coed), 1202 W. Edinger Ave., 92707-2191. Tel: 714-754-7711; Fax: 714-754-1880. Email: admissions@materdei.org. Web: www.materdei.org. Ms. Frances Clare, Prin. & Contact; Mr. Patrick Murphy, Pres.; Rev. John Weling, S.J.; Nancy Ryan, Librarian. Priests 1; Sisters 1; Lay Teachers 151; Students 2,177; Total Staff 186.

[D] HIGH SCHOOLS, PRIVATE

ANAHEIM. *Cornelia Connelly School of the Holy Child* (1961) (Girls), 2323 W. Broadway, 92804. Tel: 714-776-1717; Fax: 714-776-2534. Email: cornelia@connellyhs.org. Web: www.connellyhs.org. Sr. Francine Gunther, S.H.C.J., Head of School; Martha Izabal Serrano, Asst. Head; Donna Greenhut, Librarian. Society of the Holy Child Jesus. Lay Teachers 24; Students 260; Total Staff 43.

Servite High School, A California Corporation, 1952 W. La Palma, 92801. Tel: 714-774-7575; Fax: 714-774-1404. Email: mail@servitehs.org. Web: www.servitehs.org. Mr. Peter S. Bowen, Pres.; Mr. Michael P. Brennan, Prin.; Dr. Edward Galvez, Asst. Prin. Academic Affairs; Mr. Andrew A. Katnic, Asst. Prin. Student Affairs; Jacqui Engelman, Librarian. Servite Friars. Priests 1; Lay Teachers 60; Students 840; Total Staff 101.

SAN JUAN CAPISTRANO. *JSerra Catholic High School*, 26351 Junipero Serra Rd., 92675. Tel: 949-493-9307; Fax: 949-493-9308. Web: www.jserra.org. Thomas R. Waszak, Prin.; Mr. Eric Stroupe, Vice Pres. Academics; Dr. Sharon Anderson, Vice Pres. Student Svcs.; Jeanne Swedo, Librarian. Priests 3; Lay Teachers 63.

SILVERADO. *St. Michael's Preparatory School* (Boarding school for boys), 19292 El Toro Rd., 92676-9710. Tel: 949-858-0222; Fax: 949-858-7365. Email: stmichaelsprep@juno.com. Web: www.stmichaelsprep.org. Revs. Gabriel D. Stack, O.Praem., Headmaster; Chrysostum Anthony Baer, O.Praem, Dean Students; Claude Williams, O.Praem., Asst. Dean Students; John Henry Hanson, O.Praem.; Alphonsus B. Hermes, O.Praem.; Jerome M. Molokie, O.Praem.; Justin S. Ramos, O.Praem.; James G. Smith, O.Praem., Treas.; Hubert S. Szanto, O.Praem.; Sebastian Walsh, O.Praem. Priests 10; Seminarians 6; Lay Teachers 6; Students 64; Total Staff 23.

[E] ELEMENTARY SCHOOLS AND DAY NURSERIES, PRIVATE

ANAHEIM. *St. Catherine's Military Academy* (1889) 215 N. Harbor Blvd., 92805. Tel: 714-772-1363; Fax: 714-772-3004. Email: admissions@stcatherinesmilitaryacademy.org. Web: stcatherinesmilitaryacademy.org. Sr. Johnellen Turner, O.P., Admin. & Prin.; Angela Ippolito, Dir. Admissions & Mktg.

St. Catherine's Military Academy, a Corp. Dominican Sisters of Mission San Jose 11; Lay Teachers 13; Students 130; Total Staff 23.

SANTA ANA. *Santa Clara Day Nursery and Kindergarten*, 1021 N. Newhope, 92703. Tel: 714-554-8850; Fax: 714-554-5886. Email: clarisas@netzero.net. Sisters Susana Guzman, M.C., Contact; Maria Socorro Miranda, Prin. Poor Clare Missionary Sisters (M.C.). Sisters 13; Children 95; Total Staff 13.

TUSTIN. *Saint Jeanne de Lestonnac School* (1961) 16791 E. Main, 92780. Tel: 714-542-4271; Fax: 714-542-0644. Email: srsharon@sjdlschool.com. Web: www.sjdlschool.com. Sr. Sharon Maria Lamprecht, O.D.N., Prin.; Catherine Zimmerman, Librarian. Sisters of the Company of Mary 6; Adrian Dominican 1; Lay Teachers 37; Students 450; Total Staff 45.

[F] MULTI-PARISH SCHOOLS

RANCHO SANTA MARGARITA. *Serra Catholic School* (1995) 23652 Antonio Pkwy., 92688-1993. Tel: 949-888-1990; Fax: 949-635-1921. Email: serra@serraschool.org. Web: www.serraschool.org. Angeline Trudell, Prin.; Mrs. Cathy Muzzy, Asst. Prin. (Gr. 5-8); Mr. Tony Napoli, Asst. Prin. (Gr. K-4); Mrs. Carol Reiss, Asst. Prin. Student Svcs. Lay Teachers 57; Students 995; Total Staff 133.

YORBA LINDA. *St. Francis of Assisi School* (1998) 5330 East Side Cir., 92887. Tel: 714-695-3700; Fax: 714-695-3704. Email: office@stfayl.org. Web: www.stfayl.org. Kathleen B. Falcone, Prin.; Avelina Oliver, Librarian. Lay Teachers 28; Students 476; Total Staff 52.

[G] GENERAL HOSPITALS

ORANGE. *St. Joseph Hospital of Orange* (1929) 1100 W. Stewart Dr., 92868. Tel: 714-771-8000, Ext. 8020; Fax: 714-744-8600. Larry Ainsworth, Pres. & CEO; Alan Garrett, Exec. Vice Pres. & COO; Linda Simon, Vice Pres. Mission Integration; Rev. Elly S. Tavarro. Inpatients 97,225; Outpatients 240,119; Beds 412; Other Employees 2,311; Nurses 1,000.

FULLERTON. *St. Jude Medical Center* (1957) 101 E. Valencia Mesa Dr., 92835-3875. Tel: 714-871-3280; Fax: 714-446-5067. Email: cdesfor@stjoe.org. Web: www.stjudemedicalcenter.org. Revs. William Caffrey, S.V.D., Chap.; Ignacio Estrada, S.V.D., Chap.; Timothy Freyer, Chap.; Gregory Marquez, Chap.; Alvin Smith, Chap.; Sisters Claudette Des Forges, C.S.J., Vice Pres. Mission Integration; Judy Eugenio, C.S.J., Chap.; Josepha Ha, C.H.C., Chap.; Bill Boylan, Chap.; Lawrence G. Ehren, Dir., Mission Svcs., Chap.; Rosa Perez Williams, Chap. Bed Capacity 384; Nurses 656; Total Staff 2,600; Total Assisted Inpatient & Outpatient 400,000.

LAGUNA BEACH. *Mission Hospital Laguna Beach (MHLB)*, 31872 Coast Hwy., 92651. Tel: 949-499-7225; Fax: 949-499-5789. St. Joseph Health System. Bed Capacity 159; Patients Assisted: Inpatients 18,980; Outpatients 16,046.

MISSION VIEJO. *Mission Hospital Regional Medical Center (MHMV)*, 27700 Medical Center Rd., 92691. Tel: 949-364-1400; Fax: 949-364-2056. Email: peter.bastone@stjoe.org. Web: www.mission4health.com. Peter Bastone, Pres. & CEO; Cynthia H. Mueller, Vice Pres., Mission Integration; Michael Moran, Chap. St. Joseph Health System. Total Staff 2,100; Patients Assisted: Inpatient Days 76,085; Outpatients 29,719; Bed Capacity 279.

[H] SPECIAL SERVICES

ORANGE. *Loyola Institute for Spirituality*, 480 S. Batavia St., 92868. Tel: 714-997-9587; Fax: 714-997-9588. Email: office@loyolainstitute.org. Web: www.loyolainstitute.org. Revs. Stephen Corder, S.J., Exec. Dir.; Felix N.W. Just, S.J., Dir. Biblical Studies; David C. Robinson, S.J., Assoc. Dir.; Bro. Charles Jackson, S.J., Assoc. Dir.; Sr. M. Barbra Ostheimer, S.N.D., Assoc. Dir.; Wini Chuidan, Fin. Officer; Cynthia Galvez, Office Mgr.; Elisa Leon, Dir. Devel.

ANAHEIM. *St. Thomas Korean Catholic Center*, 412 N. Crescent Way, 92801. Tel: 714-772-3995; Fax: 714-772-3636. Email: stthomas@stkcc.org. Web: www.stkcc.org. Revs. Alex K. Kim, Dir.; Eugene Lee, Assoc. Dir.; Deacons Peter Chung; Thomas Song.

SANTA ANA. *St. Francis Home for the Aged* (1944) 1718 W. 6th St., 92703. Tel: 714-542-0381; Fax: 714-542-4654. Email: stfrancishome@sbcglobal.net. Web: www.st-francis-home.org. Sr. Elia Caro, O.S.F., Admin. & Contact Person. Franciscan Sisters of the Immaculate Conception, Inc. Sisters 14; Bed Capacity 70; Total Assisted 56; Total Staff 22.

Vietnamese Catholic Center, 1538 N. Century Blvd., 92703. Tel: 714-554-4211; 714-554-5565; Fax: 714-265-1161. Email: srtuoi.tran@vnco.org; sy.nguyen@vncatholic.org. Web: www.vncatholic.org. Rev. Sy Nguyen, J.C.L., Dir. & Contact Person. Total in Residence 1; Total Staff 5.

SILVERADO. *St. Michael's Summer Camp* Boys aged 7-12 years., St. Michael's Abbey, 19292 El Toro Rd., 92676-9701. Tel: 949-858-0222, Ext. 226; Fax: 949-858-4583. Rev. Patrick D. Foutts, O.Praem., Contact. Capacity 120; Total in Residence 95; Total Staff 25.

WESTMINSTER. *Korean Catholic Ministry*, 7655 Trask Ave., 92683. Tel: 714-897-6510; Fax: 714-897-0832. Email: church@kmccoc.org. Web: www.kmccoc.org. Rev. John Hogan, S.S.C., Dir. Korean Martyrs Center & Contact Person.

YORBA LINDA. *Pope John Paul II Polish Center*, 3999 Rose Dr., 92886. Tel: 714-996-8161; Fax: 714-996-8161. Web: www.polishcenter.org. Revs. Henry Noga, S.V.D., Dir.; David C. Robinson, S.J., Assoc. Dir.; John Francis Vu, S.J., Chap., U.C. Irvine.

[I] MONASTERIES AND RESIDENCES OF PRIESTS AND BROTHERS

ANAHEIM. *Manresa Jesuit Residence*, 401 W. Leonora St., 92805-2634. Tel: 714-991-7765; Fax: 714-991-7798. Email: loyinst@pacbell.net. Web: loyolainstitute.org. Rev. Stephen Corder, S.J., Exec. Dir., Loyola Institute for Spirituality; Bro. Charles Jackson, S.J., Assoc. Dir.; Revs. Felix N.W. Just, S.J., Dir. Biblical Studies; David C. Robinson, S.J., Assoc. Dir.; John Francis Vu, S.J., Vocation Dir. & Chap., U.C. Irvine.

Servite Fathers and Brothers Servite Friars, Servite Priory, 1922 W. La Palma Ave., 92801-3544. Tel: 714-774-8869; Fax: 714-774-6792. Web: www.servite.org. Revs. Thomas M. Crotty, O.S.M.; Paul M. Gins, O.S.M.; Perry McCoy, O.S.M.; Edward M. Penonzek, O.S.M.; Michael M. Pontarelli, O.S.M.; Eugene M. Smith, O.S.M.; Bro. Christopher M. Moran, O.S.M. *Servite High School*, 1952 W. La Palma Ave., 92801-3595. Tel: 714-774-7575; Fax: 714-774-1401. Web: www.servitehs.org.

FULLERTON. *Servite Fathers and Brothers*, St. Juliana Falconieri, 1316 N. Acacia, 92831. Tel: 714-879-1971; Fax: 714-526-6673. Email: info@stjulianachurch.org. Web: www.stjulianachurch.org. Rev. Frank Falco, O.S.M., Contact Person. Total in Residence 3; Total Staff 3. *St. Philip Benizi*, 235 S. Pine Dr., 92833-3294. Tel: 714-871-3613.

HUNTINGTON BEACH. *Franciscan Friars*, SS. Simon and Jude, 20444 Magnolia St., 92646. Tel: 714-962-3333; Fax: 714-965-6456. Email: ssj@ssj.org. Web: www.ssj.org. Rev. Dan Lackie, O.F.M., Contact Person.

MIDWAY CITY. *Brothers of St. Patrick, St. Patrick's Novitiate*, 7820 Bolsa Ave., 92655. Tel: 714-897-8181; Fax: 714-898-9020. Bros. Aquinas Cassin, F.S.P., Supr. (Retired); Joseph Anoop, F.S.P.; Benedict Mavelil, F.S.P.; Kevin Minihan, F.S.P.; Matthew Regan, F.S.P., (Retired).

SANTA ANA. *Augustinian Recollects*, Our Lady of Guadalupe, 1322 E. 3rd St., 92701-5104. Tel: 714-836-4142; Fax: 714-836-7417. Rev. Alfredo de Dios, O.A.R., Contact Person. *Our Lady of the Pillar*, 1622 6th St., 92703. Tel: 714-543-1700; Fax: 714-543-9640. Rev. Anthony Palos, O.A.R.

SILVERADO. *Norbertine Fathers of Orange Inc.* (1959) For detailed information regarding the high school and seminary, please refer to High Schools, Private and Seminaries and Scholastics for Religious in the Institution section., St. Michael's Abbey (O.Praem.), 19292 El Toro Rd., 92676-9710. Tel: 949-858-0222; Fax: 949-858-4583. Rt. Revs. Eugene J. Hayes, O.Praem., Abbot; Ladislas K. Parker, O.Praem., Abbot Emeritus (Retired); Very Rev. Hugh C. Barbour, O.Praem., Prior; Revs. James G. Smith, O.Praem., Subprior; Jordan S. Anderson, O.Praem.; Chrysostum Anthony Baer, O.Praem; Godfrey E. Bushmaker, O.Praem.; John E. Caronan, O.Praem.; Leo J. Celano, O.Praem.; Ambrose Criste, O.Praem.; Gregory M. Dick, O.Praem.; Paul L. Gelencser, O.Praem. (Retired); Vincent M. Gilmore, O.Praem.; Francis M. Gloudeman, O.Praem.; Charbel Grbavac, O.Praem.; John Henry Hanson, O.Praem.; Alphonsus B. Hermes, O.Praem.; Joseph K. Horn, O.Praem.; Gerlac A. Horvath, O.Praem. (Retired); Bernard M. Johnson, O.Praem.; Jerome M. Molokie, O.Praem.; Peter D. Muller, O.Praem.; Thomas W. Nelson, O.Praem.; Augustine R. Puchner, O.Praem.; Justin S. Ramos, O.Praem.; Adrian Sanchez, O.Praem.; Gabriel D. Stack, O.Praem.; Hubert S. Szanto, O.Praem.; Victor S. Szcurek, O.Praem.; Xavier Trebels, O.Praem.; Sebastian A. Walshe, O.Praem.; Charles W. Willingham, O.Praem. For detailed information concerning St. Michael's Abbey and St. Michael's College Preparatory High School please refer to the Seminary and High School categories in this diocese. Priests 48; Clerics 14; Postulants 2; Deacons 1.

WESTMINSTER. *Columban Fathers, Korean Martyrs Catholic Center*, 7655 Trask Ave., 92683. Tel: 714-897-6510; Fax: 714-897-0832. Email: church@kmccoc.org. Web: www.kmccoc.org. Rev. John Hogan, S.S.C. Tel: 714-897-2825.

[J] CONVENTS AND RESIDENCES FOR SISTERS

ORANGE. *Congregation of the Sisters of the Holy Cross, Inc.*, 540 S. LaVeta Park Cir., Apt. 49, 92868. *Sisters of the Holy Cross, Inc.*

Sisters of St. Joseph of Orange Motherhouse Community, 480 S. Batavia, 92868. Tel: 714-633-8121; Fax: 714-744-3165. Email: csjomhi@csjorange.org. Sr. Jane DeLisle, C.S.J., Gen. Sec. & Contact Person. Sisters 23. *Regina Residence Community*, 430 S. Batavia St., 92868. Tel: 714-744-3109; Fax: 714-744-3163. Email: rreginares@earthlink.net. Sisters 55. *Nazareth Community*, 940 W. Palmyra, 92868. Tel: 714-771-4706. Email: nazarethcommunity@yahoo.com. Sisters 4. *Casa Esperanza Community*, 954 W. Palmyra, 92868. Tel: 714-639-1030. Email: casaesperanzacsj@yahoo.com. Sisters 2. *St. Joseph Hospital Community*, P.O. Box 5600, 92863-5600. Tel: 714-771-8000; 714-771-8040. Email: cnvntsjo@corp.stjoe.org. Sisters 9. *Greengrove Community*, 2075 Greengrove St., 92865. Tel: 714-974-9079. Email: csjgr@earthlink.net. Sisters 2. *Valencia Community*, 5742 E. Valencia Dr., 92869. Tel: 714-639-2665. Email: csjval@yahoo.com. Sisters 3. *Palmyra Community*, 1000 W. Palmyra St., 92868-3812. Tel: 714-997-0590. Email: sisters@sbcglobal.net. Sisters 3.

Westwood Community, 2014 N. Westwood Ave., Santa Ana, 92706-3542. Tel: 714-689-8667. Email: csjwestwood@gmail.com. Sisters 4.

Union of Sisters of the Presentation of the Blessed Virgin Mary, 343 E. Chestnut, 92867. Tel: 714-283-2496; Fax: 714-283-4159. Email: orangePBVM@aol.com. Web: pbvmunion.org. Sr. Marilyn Omieczynski, Contact Person. Sisters 2.

ANAHEIM. *Dominicans, Mission San Jose, St. Catherine Military Academy*, 215 N. Harbor Blvd., 92805-2596. Tel: 714-772-1363; Fax: 714-772-3004. Email: scms@msjdominicans.org. Web: www.stcatherinesmilitary.com. Sr. Johnellen Turner, O.P., Admin., Prin. & Contact Person. Sisters 17.

BREA. *Sisters of St. Clare*, 446 S. Poplar Ave., 92821-6649. Tel: 714-256-1278. Sr. Anne Otter, Contact Person. Sisters 2. St. Clare's Garden, 449 S. Pine Ave., 92821-6649. Tel: 714-257-1113; Fax: 714-257-1068. Sr. Briegeen Moore, O.S.C., Contact Person.

BUENA PARK. *Sisters of Our Lady of Perpetual Help* (1932) 6751 Western Ave., 90621. Tel: 714-521-1345; Fax: 714-521-7611. Email: solphca@hanmail.net. Sr. Maura Cho, S.O.L.P.H., Pres. & Contact. Sisters 8.

COSTA MESA. *Sisters of Mercy of Ireland* (1959) St. John the Baptist Convent, 2960 Mendoza Dr., 92626. Tel: 714-545-2116; Fax: 714-557-9263. Email: mvianney@sjbschool.net. Sr. Mary Vianney, S.M., Prin. & Contact Person.

Sisters of St. Joseph of Orange (1946) *St. Joachim School*, 1964 Orange Ave., 92627. Tel: 949-547-7411, Ext. 409; Fax: 949-646-8948. Email: skm@stjoachimparish.com. Sr. Kathleen Marie, Prin.

CYPRESS. *Union of the Sisters of the Presentation of the Blessed Virgin Mary*, 5151 Evergreen Ave., 90630. Tel: 714-527-4844; Fax: 714-527-5189. Sr. Mary Dunlea, P.B.V.M., Contact Person. Sisters 6.

DANA POINT. *Sisters of St. Joseph of Orange* (1912) Dana Point Community, 33392 Via Lenita, 92629. Tel: 949-488-0433. Email: csjdana@earthlink.net. Sr. Martha Ann Fitzpatrick, Contact Person. Sisters 2.

FULLERTON. *Sisters of St. Joseph of Orange*, East Alto Community, 1601 E. Alto Ln., 92831. Tel: 714-526-3141. Email: csjoalto@adelphia.net. Sr. Judith Fergus, Contact Person. Sisters 3. *St. Jude Hospital Community*, 3642 Coronado Dr., 92835. Tel: 714-879-7159. Sisters 2.

GARDEN GROVE. *Eucharistic Missionaries of the Most Holy Trinity*, 11892 E. Lampson Ave., 92840. Tel: 714-530-5727; Fax: 714-636-5192. Email: orangemest@aol.com. Sisters Virginia Herrera, M.E.S.S.T., Local Supr.; Irma Gomez, M.E.S.S.T., Contact. Sisters 5.

Religious Sisters of Charity, St. Columban Convent, 12555 Westlake St., 92840. Tel: 714-534-1003. Email: rscgg@aol.com. Sr. Bernadette Moran, Contact Person. Sisters 3.

Sisters of St. Joseph of Orange, Garden Grove Community, 9731 Acacia Ave., 1- C, 92841. Tel: 714-530-4695. Sr. Rebecca Rodriguez, Contact Person.

HUNTINGTON BEACH. *Sisters of Charity of the Blessed Virgin Mary*, SS. Simon & Jude Convent, 20512 Tobermory Cir., 92646-5837. Tel: 714-968-2237; Fax: 714-965-6456. Web: www.bvmcong.org. Sr. Maureen Sheehan, B.V.M., Contact Person.

Sisters of the Presentation of the Blessed Virgin Mary, St. Bonaventure Convent, 16441 Bradbury Ln., 92647. Tel: 714-846-6212; Fax: 714-840-0480. Email: presentation@linkline.com. Web: www.gnofn.org/~presis/. Sr. Annunciata Murtagh, P.B.V.M., Contact. Sisters 5.

LAKE FOREST. *School Sisters of St. Francis* (1874) 24162 Laulhere Pl., 92630-4418. Tel: 949-951-8681. Email: generalate@sssf.org. Web: www.sssf.org. Sisters Agnes Steiner, S.S.S.F., Contact Person; Paula Jane Tupa, S.S.S.F., Admin. & Dir. Education, Escalade Academy. Sisters 2.

SANTA ANA. *Franciscan Missionary Sisters of the Immaculate Conception* (1944) St. Francis Home for the Aged, 1718 W. 6th St., 92703. Tel: 714-542-0381; 714-542-8352; Fax: 714-542-4654. Email: stfrancishome@sbcglobal.net. Web: www.st-francis-home.org. Sisters 14; Total Staff 22; Total Assisted 60.

Poor Clare Missionary Sisters of the Blessed Sacrament, 1019 N. Newhope St., 92703-1534. Tel: 714-554-8850; Fax: 714-554-5886. Email: clarisas@netzero.net. Sr. Susana Guzman, M.C., Contact Person. Sisters 14.

Sisters of St. Joseph of Carondelet, Hogar de San Jose, 507 N. Linwood Ave., 92701. Tel: 714-541-6480. Email: adcsj@sbcglobal.net; marta-1@sbcglobal.net. Sr. Mary McKay, C.S.J., Prov. Sisters 2. *St. Joseph*

Sisters of St. Joseph of Orange, Casa Guadalupe Community, 414 S. Broadway, 92701. Tel: 714-834-9381. Email: csj414@yahoo.com. Mailing Address: 480 S. Batavia St., 92868. Sisters 4. *Bethany*, 480 S. Batavia, 92868. Tel: 714-289-6761; Fax: 714-289-6760. Email: csjbeth@csjorange.org. Sr. Louise Ann Micek, Dir. Sisters 4. *Olive Street Community*, 2109 N. Olive St., 92706. Tel: 714-542-3380. Email: 2109csj@sbcglobal.net. Sisters 4.

Taller San Jose, 801 N. Broadway, 92707. Tel: 714-543-5105; Fax: 714-543-5032. Email: ssmith@tallersanjose.org. Shawna Smith, Exec. Dir. Sisters 2.

Sisters of the Company of Mary, St. Anne Convent, 1339 S. Broadway, 92707. Tel: 714-558-1340; Fax: 714-542-3431. Email: saintanneschool@sbcglobal.net. Sisters 5.

Sisters of the Lovers of the Holy Cross, 1401 S. Sycamore St., 92707. Tel: 714-973-1951; Fax: 714-667-0711. Web: www.lhcla.org. Sisters 8. 920 N. Bewley St., 92703. Tel: 714-554-9385; Fax: 714-554-5925. Email: srmonicalhc@yahoo.com. Web: www.lhcla.org. Sr. Monica Phi Tran, L.H.C., Contact Person. Sisters 17.

Society Devoted to the Sacred Heart, Heart of Jesus Retreat Center, 2927 S. Greenville St., 92704. Tel: 714-557-4538; Fax: 714-668-9780. Email: rcconvent@sbcglobal.net. Web: www.sdsh.org. Sisters 7. *Sacred Heart Convent*, 2911 S. Greenville St., 92704. Tel: 714-751-6335; Fax: 714-546-0873. Sisters 5.

SEAL BEACH. *Franciscans, Syracuse*, 328 1/2 10th St., 90740. Tel: 562-493-4630. Email: sealbeachsam@yahoo.com.

SILVERADO. *Rosarian Dominicans* (1972) St. Michael's Convent, 19292 El Toro Rd., 92676. Tel: 949-858-0487. Sisters 8.

TUSTIN. *Adrian Dominicans*, St. Jeanne de Lestonnac Convent, 16791 E. Main St., 92780. Tel: 714-541-3125; Fax: 714-835-0648. Email: srterry@sjdlschool.com. Web: www.sjdlschool.com.

Sisters of the Company of Mary (1607) Provincial House, 16791 E. Main St., 92780-4034. Tel: 714-541-3125; Fax: 714-835-0648. Email: elviraodn@yahoo.com. Web: www.lestonnac.org. Sr. Elvira Rios, O.D.N., Prov. Sec. & Contact Person. Sisters 17.

Lestonnac Retreat Center: (1961) Tel: 714-542-2496; Fax: 714-835-0648.

Lestonnac Residence: (1980) Tel: 714-541-3125; Fax: 714-835-0648.

WESTMINSTER. *Korean Sisters of Our Lady of Perpetual Help*, 7655 Trask Ave., 92683. Tel: 714-373-2556; Fax: 714-897-0832.

[K] CATHOLIC CHARITIES

SANTA ANA. *Catholic Charities of Orange County, Inc.* (1976) 1820 E. 16th St., 92701. Tel: 714-347-9600; Fax: 714-542-3020. Email: tsmith@ccoc.org. Web: www.ccoc.org. Theresa Smith, M.S.W., L.C.S.W., Exec. Dir. & CEO; Rev. Cirilo Flores, Vicar for Charities. Total Staff 51; Total Assisted 94,675.

Columbian Disability Camps Orange, CA.; Weekend getaway and ACE camp., 5140 Box Canyon Ct., Yorba Linda, 92887. Tel: 714-347-9627; Fax: 714-542-8482. Web: recreationcampoc.com. Mailing Address: 2811 E. Villa Real Dr., 92867. Meghan Schinderle, Co-Dir.; Katie Webb, Co-Dir.

Casa Santa Maria, 7551 Orangethorpe Ave., Buena Park, 90621. Tel: 714-523-1734; Fax: 714-542-3020. Ofelia Aranda, Advocate. Independent senior housing living project.

Counseling Services, 1820 E. 16th St., 92701. Tel: 714-347-9643; Fax: 714-542-3020.

Doris Cantlay Drop In Center Tel: 714-668-1130; Fax: 714-957-2523. Xang Yang, Dir.

Employment Services, Anaheim. Tel: 714-347-9664; Fax: 714-635-9896. Thu Tran, Contact Person.

Independent Senior Housing Living Project Casa Santa Maria, 7551 Orangethorpe Ave., Buena Park, 90621-1015. Tel: 714-523-1734; Fax: 714-542-3020. Ofelia Aranda, Advocate.

Resettlement, Immigration & Citizenship Services Tel: 714-347-9664; Fax: 714-542-3541. Thu Tran, Prog. Dir.

[L] RETREAT HOUSES

ORANGE. *Center for Spiritual Development*, 434 S. Batavia St., 92868-3907. Tel: 714-744-3175, Ext. 4421; Fax: 714-744-3176. Email: csdinfo@csjorange.org. Web: www.thecsd.com. Sr. Mary Anne Huepper, C.S.J., Exec. Dir.; Julie Mussche, Dir. & Contact. Total Staff 13.

House of Prayer for Priests (1983) 7734 E. Santiago Canyon Rd., 92869. Tel: 714-639-9740; Fax: 714-639-9313. Email: jgmhop@yahoo.com. Rev. J. Gordon Moreland, S.J., Dir. & Contact Person. Total in Residence 2; Total Staff 1; Total Assisted 1,500. In Res. Rev. Patrick B. Philbin, S.M.

Marywood Retreat Center, 2811 E. Villa Real Dr., 92867. Tel: 714-282-3098 (Days Mon-Fri); 714-282-3099 (Evenings & Weekends); Fax: 714-282-3029. Email: esandoval@rcbo.org. Web: www.rcbo.org. Elizabeth Sandoval, Reservations & Facilities Coord., Contact Person. Maywood serves as an educational facility and retreat center. Facilities include a chapel, auditorium, gymnasium, kitchen, accommodations for overnight stays, meeting rooms and classrooms. Overnight Guest Accommodations 107.

FULLERTON. *Pro Sanctity Spirituality Center, Retreat House* (1979) 205 S. Pine Dr., 92833. Tel: 714-956-1020. Email: psmcal@aol.com. Web: prosanctity.org. Agnes Rus, Dir. Capacity: 26 overnight, 32 day use

Pro Sanctity Movement (1947) Tel: 714-956-1020; Fax: 714-525-8948. Renee Jarecki, Dir.; Palmira Tafani, Counselor.

LA HABRA. *Villa Maria House of Prayer* (1978) 1252 N. Citrus Dr., 90631-2652. Tel: 562-691-5838; Fax: 562-691-2572. Sr. Grace Ann Loperena, C.S.J., Contact Person. Sisters of St. Joseph of Carondelet. Sisters 3.

SANTA ANA. *Heart of Jesus Retreat Center, Heart of Jesus Retreat Center Convent*, 2927 S. Greenville St., 92704. Tel: 714-557-4538; Fax: 714-668-9780. Email: rcconvent@sbcglobal.net. *Sacred Heart Convent*, 2911 S. Greenville St., 92704. Tel: 714-751-6335; Fax: 714-546-0873. Web: www.sdsh.org. Society Devoted to the Sacred Heart. Heart of Jesus Retreat Center Convent 7; Sacred Heart Convent 5; Total Staff 7.

[M] NEWMAN CENTERS

FULLERTON. *California State University Fullerton, Newman Center* (1966) St. Juliana Falconieri, 1316 N. Acacia Ave., 92831-1202. Tel: 714-871-1086; Fax: 714-526-6673. Email: donovanpj7@roadrunner.com. Web: www.newman-csuf.com. Rev. Patrick Donovan, O.S.M., Chap., Dir., Treas., Newman Catholic Club. Tel: 714-871-1086.

IRVINE. *U.C.I. Interfaith Center* P.O. Box 6030, 92616-6030. Tel: 949-856-0211; 949-753-3373; Fax: 714-639-9313. Email: pphilbin@sbcglobal.net. Web: spirit.dos.uci.edu/ucc. Revs. Patrick B. Philbin, S.M., Chap. & Diocesan Dir. Campus Ministry; John Francis Vu, S.J., Assoc. Chap.

[N] SECULAR INSTITUTES

FULLERTON. *Institute of the Apostolic Oblates, Inc. House of Formation of the Professed Apostolic Oblates* (1950) 2125 W. Walnut Ave., 92833. Tel: 714-956-1020. Email: ApostolicO@aol.com. Agnes Rus, Local Moderator. House of Formation for Professed Apostolic Oblates. Secular Institute of the Apostolic Oblates, Inc.

[O] MISCELLANEOUS LISTINGS

ORANGE. *American Federation Pueri Cantores*, 615 E. Chapman Ave., #200, 92866. Tel: 714-633-7554; Fax: 714-516-1531. Email: info@pcchoirs.org. Web: www.pcchoirs.org. Jan Schmidt, Exec. Dir.

Christ Our Savior Cathedral Fund, Inc., c/o Diocese of Orange, 2811 E. Villa Real Dr., 92867. Tel: 714-282-3024.

The Diocese of Orange Church Facilities Fund, Inc., c/o Diocese of Orange, 2811 E. Villa Real Dr., 92867. Tel: 714-282-3024.

St. Joseph Health System, 500 S. Main St., Ste. 1000, 92868. Tel: 714-347-7500; Fax: 714-347-7501. Web: www.stjhs.org. William Noce, Bd. Chm.; Ms. Deborah Proctor, Pres. & CEO.

St. Joseph Health System Foundation, 500 S. Main St., Ste. 1000, 92868. Tel: 714-347-7500; Fax: 714-347-7501. Gabriela Robles, Dir., Community Outreach.

St. Jude Hospital Yorba Linda, St. Joseph Health System, 500 S. Main St., 92868-4515. Tel: 714-347-7579; Fax: 714-347-7590. Robert J. Frashetti.

Orange Catholic Foundation (2000) 2811 E. Villa Real Dr., 92867-1999. Tel: 714-282-3021; Fax: 714-282-3029. Web: www.oc-foundation.org.

Orange County Catholic Alumni Club, P.O. Box 6054, 92863-6054. Tel: 714-502-8086. Email: orangecountyCAC@juno.com. Web: www.occaci.com.

Sisters of St. Joseph Healthcare Foundation, 480 S. Batavia St., 92868. Tel: 714-633-8121; Fax: 714-744-3135. Email: rfox@csjorange.org. Sr. Mary Rogers, C.S.J., Exec. Dir.

St. Joseph Health Ministry, 500 S. Main St., Ste. 1000, 92868. Tel: 714-347-7778; 714-347-7586; Fax: 714-347-7501.

FULLERTON. *St. Jude Memorial Foundation*, P.O. Box 4138, 92834. Tel: 714-992-3033; Fax: 714-446-5430. Lynne Bolen, Contact Person.

Western Catholic Educational Association, 2651 E. Chapman Ave., Ste. 216, 92831. Tel: 714-447-9834; Fax: 714-447-9846. Email: wcea214@sbcglobal.net. Web: westwcea.org. Bro. William Carriere, F.S.C., Exec. Dir.

IRVINE. *Our Lady of Peace Korean Catholic Center*, 6789 Quail Hill Pkwy., #206, 92603.

SANTA ANA. *Project SUCCESS*, 5306 W. McFadden Ave., 92704. Tel: 714-775-9485; Fax: 714-531-5868.

Email: info@project-success.org. Web: www.project-success.org.

RELIGIOUS INSTITUTES OF MEN REPRESENTED IN THE DIOCESE

For further details refer to the corresponding bracketed number in the Religious Institutes of Men or Women section.

[]—*Alagard Ni Maria*—A.M.
[0140]—*Augustinian Fathers*—O.S.A.
[0150]—*Augustinian Recollects*—O.A.R.
[]—*Claretian Missionaries*—C.M.F.
[]—*Congregation of the Mission*—C.M.
[]—*Congregation of the Most Holy Redeemer*—C.Ss.R.
[]—*Crusade of the Holy Spirit*—C.H.S.
[]—*Divine Word*—S.V.D.
[0520]—*Franciscan Fathers*—O.F.M.
[0690]—*Jesuit Fathers and Brothers*—S.J.
[]—*Legionnaires of Christ*—L.C.
[0780]—*Marist Fathers*—S.M.
[0660]—*Missionaries of the Holy Spirit*—M.Sp.S.
[1110]—*Missionaries of the Sacred Heart*—M.S.C.
[0900]—*Norbertine Fathers*—O.Praem.
[1190]—*Salesians of Don Bosco*—S.D.B.
[1240]—*Servite Fathers and Brothers*—O.S.M.

RELIGIOUS INSTITUTES OF WOMEN REPRESENTED IN THE DIOCESE

[1920]—*Congregation of Sisters of the Holy Cross*—C.S.C.
[3832]—*Congregation of the Sisters of St. Joseph*—C.S.J.
[1070-13]—*Dominican Sisters* (Adrian, MI)—O.P.
[]—*Dominican Sisters* (Mission San Jose)—O.P.
[]—*Dominican Sisters* (Western Australia)—O.P.
[]—*Eucharistic Missionaries of the Most Holy Trinity*—M.E.S.S.T.
[]—*Family of Mary of the Visitation*—F.M.V.
[1350]—*Franciscan Missionary Sisters of the Immaculate Conception*—O.S.F.
[1540]—*Franciscan Sisters* (Syracuse, IA)—O.S.F.
[]—*Korean Order of Discaled Carmelites*—O.C.D.
[2390]—*Lovers of the Holy Cross Sisters*—L.H.C.
[2490]—*Medical Missionary Sisters*—M.M.S.
[]—*Missionaries of the Holy Spirit*—M.S.P.S.
[2840]—*Poor Clare Missionaries of Blessed Sacrament*—M.C.
[3280]—*Presentation Sisters of Blessed Virgin Mary*—P.B.V.M.
[3400]—*Religious Sisters of Charity*—R.S.C.
[2575]—*Religious Sisters of Mercy of the Americas*—R.S.M.
[]—*Religious Sisters of the Sacred Heart of Mary*—R.S.H.M.
[]—*Rosarian Dominican Sisters*—O.P.
[]—*School Sisters of Notre Dame*—S.S.N.D.
[1680]—*School Sisters of St. Francis*—S.S.S.F.
[]—*Sisters for Christian Community*—S.F.C.C.
[0430]—*Sisters of Charity of the Blessed Virgin Mary*—B.V.M.
[]—*Sisters of Mercy of Ireland*—R.S.M.
[]—*Sisters of Notre Dame*—S.N.D.
[]—*Sisters of Our Lady of Perpetual Help*—S.O.L.P.H.
[3340]—*Sisters of Providence IN*—S.P.
[]—*Sisters of Providence* (Seattle)—S.P.
[3770]—*Sisters of St. Clare*—O.S.C.
[3830-03]—*Sisters of St. Joseph* (Orange)—C.S.J.
[3840]—*Sisters of St. Joseph of Carondelet*—C.S.J.
[3840]—*Sisters of St. Joseph of Carondelet* (Albany Prov.)—C.S.J.
[]—*Sisters of St. Joseph of Concordia*—C.S.J.
[3935]—*Sisters of St. Louis*—S.S.L.
[0700]—*Sisters of the Company of Mary*—O.D.N.
[1990]—*Sisters of the Holy Names of Jesus and Mary*—S.N.J.M.
[2270]—*Sisters of the Little Company of Mary*—L.C.M.
[4050]—*Sisters of the Society Devoted to the Sacred Heart*—S.D.S.H.
[]—*Sisters, Servants of the Immaculate Heart of Mary*—I.H.M.
[]—*Society of Jesus*—S.J.
[4060]—*Society of the Holy Child Jesus*—S.H.C.J.

DIOCESAN CEMETERIES

ORANGE. *Holy Sepulcher*, 7845 Santiago Canyon Rd., 92869. Tel: 714-532-6551; Fax: 714-288-8441. Email: holysepulcher@rcbo.org. Kevin Haynes, Supt.

ANAHEIM. *Holy Cross*, 619 S. Euclid, 92802. Tel: 714-532-6551.

HUNTINGTON BEACH. *Good Shepherd Cemetery and Mausoleum*, 8301 Talbert Ave., 92646. Tel: 714-847-8546; Fax: 714-842-9979. Email: goodshepherd@rcbo.org. Guadalupe Ramirez, Mgr.

LAKE FOREST. *Ascension*, 24754 Trabuco Rd., 92630. Tel: 949-837-1331; Fax: 949-837-9013; 949-837-9013. Email: ascension@rcbo.org. John D. Callaghan Jr., Supt.

NECROLOGY

(No Deaths)

An asterisk (*) denotes an organization that has established tax-exempt status directly with the IRS and is not covered by the USCCB Group Ruling.

Diocese of Orlando

(Dioecesis Orlandensis)

Most Reverend

THOMAS G. WENSKI, D.D.

Bishop of Orlando; ordained May 15, 1976; appointed Titular Bishop of Kearney and Auxiliary Bishop of Miami June 24, 1997; consecrated September 3, 1997; appointed Coadjutor Bishop of Orlando July 1, 2003; installed August 22, 2003; appointed Fourth Bishop of Orlando November 13, 2004. *Office: 50 E. Robinson St., Orlando, FL 32801.* Tel: 407-246-4815. *Mailing Address: P.O. Box 1800, Orlando, FL 32802-1800.*

Most Reverend

NORBERT L. DORSEY, C.P., D.D., S.T.D.

Bishop Emeritus of Orlando; ordained April 28, 1956; appointed Auxiliary Bishop of Miami January 10, 1986; ordained Titular Bishop of Mactaris and Auxiliary Bishop of the Archdiocese of Miami March 19, 1986; appointed Bishop of Orlando March 20, 1990; installed as Third Bishop of Orlando May 25, 1990; retired November 13, 2004. *Office: 50 E. Robinson St., Orlando, FL 32801. Mailing Address: P.O. Box 1800, Orlando, FL 32802.*

ESTABLISHED JUNE 18, 1968.

Square Miles 9,611.

Comprises the Counties of Brevard, Lake, Marion, Orange, Osceola, Polk, Seminole, Sumter and Volusia in the State of Florida.

For legal titles of parishes and diocesan institutions, consult the Chancery.

Chancery: 50 E. Robinson St., Orlando, FL 32801. Mailing Address: P.O. Box 1800, Orlando, FL 32802. Tel: 407-246-4800; Fax: 407-246-4942.

Web: www.orlandodiocese.org

Email: eworley@orlandodiocese.org

STATISTICAL OVERVIEW

Personnel	
Bishop	1
Retired Bishops	1
Priests: Diocesan Active in Diocese	96
Priests: Diocesan Active Outside Diocese	4
Priests: Diocesan in Foreign Missions	1
Priests: Retired, Sick or Absent	35
Number of Diocesan Priests	136
Religious Priests in Diocese	37
Total Priests in Diocese	173
Extern Priests in Diocese	35
Ordinations:	
Diocesan Priests	1
Transitional Deacons	1
Permanent Deacons	14
Permanent Deacons in Diocese	181
Total Brothers	7
Total Sisters	87
Parishes	
Parishes	79
With Resident Pastor:	
Resident Diocesan Priests	70
Resident Religious Priests	9
Missions	12
Pastoral Centers	2
Professional Ministry Personnel:	
Brothers	3
Sisters	27
Lay Ministers	202
Welfare	
Health Care Centers	1
Total Assisted	148
Day Care Centers	12
Total Assisted	564
Specialized Homes	1
Total Assisted	18
Special Centers for Social Services	7
Total Assisted	58,620
Residential Care of Disabled	1
Total Assisted	64
Educational	
Diocesan Students in Other Seminaries	25
Total Seminarians	25
High Schools, Diocesan and Parish	5
Total Students	2,653
Elementary Schools, Diocesan and Parish	31
Total Students	11,438
Non-residential Schools for the Disabled	1
Total Students	60
Catechesis/Religious Education:	
High School Students	3,861
Elementary Students	22,359
Total Students under Catholic Instruction	40,396
Teachers in the Diocese:	
Priests	1
Brothers	4
Sisters	10
Lay Teachers	979
Vital Statistics	
Receptions into the Church:	
Infant Baptism Totals	6,286
Minor Baptism Totals	462
Adult Baptism Totals	334
Received into Full Communion	557
First Communions	6,260
Confirmations	4,740
Marriages:	
Catholic	775
Interfaith	330
Total Marriages	1,105
Deaths	3,540
Total Catholic Population	413,643
Total Population	4,074,074

Former Bishops—Most Revs. WILLIAM D. BORDERS, D.D., ord. May 18, 1940; appt. Bishop of Orlando, May 2, 1968; cons. June 14, 1968; transferred to Baltimore, March 25, 1974 as Archbishop; THOMAS J. GRADY, D.D., ord. April 23, 1938; appt. Second Bishop of Orlando, Nov. 9, 1974; installed Dec. 16, 1974; retired May 25, 1990; died April 21, 2002; NORBERT L. DORSEY, C.P., D.D., S.T.D., ord. April 28, 1956; appt. Titular Bishop of Mactaris and Auxiliary Bishop of Miami Jan. 10, 1986; cons. March 19, 1986; appt. Bishop of Orlando March 20, 1990; installed as Third Bishop of Orlando May 25, 1990; retired Nov. 13, 2004.

Chancery—50 E. Robinson St., Orlando, 32801. Tel: 407-246-4800; Fax: 407-246-4942. Email: eworley@orlandodiocese.org. Web: www.orlandodiocese.org. *Mailing Address: P.O. Box 1800, Orlando, 32802.*

Vicar General—Rev. Msgr. PATRICK J. CAVERLY, P.A., V.G., Mailing Address: P.O. Box 1800, Orlando, 32802. Tel: 407-246-4800.

Vicar General and Chancellor for Canonical Affairs—Very Rev. GREGORY PARKES, J.C.L., Mailing Address: P.O. Box 1800, Orlando, 32802. Tel: 407-246-4846. Email: gparkes@orlandodiocese.org.

Chancellor for Administration and Chief Operating Officer—Sr. ELIZABETH ANNE WORLEY, S.S.J., Mailing Address: P.O. Box 1800, Orlando, 32802. Tel: 407-246-4899. Email: eworley@orlandodiocese.org.

Chief Financial Officer—BRYAN JOSEPH, Mailing Address: P.O. Box 1800, Orlando, 32802. Tel: 407-246-4831. Email: bjoseph@orlandodiocese.org.

Marriage Tribunal—50 E. Robinson St., Orlando, 32801. Tel: 407-246-4850.

Judicial Vicar—Very Rev. FERNANDO GIL, J.D., J.C.D., 50 E. Robinson St., Orlando, 32801. Tel: 407-246-4854.

Director of Tribunal—Very Rev. FERNANDO GIL, J.D., J.C.D.

Promoter of Justice—Sr. LUCY VAZQUEZ, O.P., J.C.D.

Defenders of the Bond—Very Rev. GREGORY PARKES, J.C.L.; Rev. JOSE BAUTISTA, J.C.L.; Sr. LUCY VAZQUEZ, O.P., J.C.D.

Judges—Revs. PAIGE BLAKELY, J.C.L.; RONALD KRISMAN, J.C.L.; JOSE BAUTISTA, J.C.L.; TITO NELS ROJAS, J.C.L.; JOSEPH V. BELLERIVE, J.C.D.; CROMWELL CABRISOS, J.C.L.; Very Revs. JOHN GIEL, V.F., J.C.L.; FERNANDO GIL, J.D., J.C.D.

Regional Advocates—Sr. PATRICIA O'MALLEY, S.N.D.deN. Tel: 386-668-1426; MIREYA MCCANN. Tel: 407-246-4856; Sr. JOYCE ROHLIK, B.V.M., Resurrection, Lakeland, 33813. Tel: 863-646-3556.

Deans—Very Revs. JOHN GIEL, V.F., J.C.L., Northern Deanery; ESAU GARCIA, V.F., Central Deanery South; STEPHEN D. PARKES, V.F., Central Deanery North; STAN MURRAY, V.F., Eastern Deanery; PETER PUNTAL, V.F., Western Deanery; SEAN HESLIN, V.F., Southern Deanery.

Presbyteral Council— (Term 2008-2010)

President—Most Rev. THOMAS WENSKI, Bishop of Orlando.

Chairman—Rev. CHRISTOPHER HOFFMANN, V.F.

Vice Chairman—Rev. BENJAMIN A. BERINTI, C.PP.S., V.F.

Secretary—Rev. JORGE TORRES.

Ex Officio Members—Rev. Msgr. PATRICK J. CAVERLY, P.A., V.G.; Very Revs. GREGORY PARKES, J.C.L., Chancellor; PAUL HENRY, Vicar for Clergy; JOHN C. GIEL, V.F. (Northern Dean); SEAN HESLIN, V.F. (Southern Dean); STAN MURRAY, V.F. (Eastern Dean); PETER PUNTAL, V.F. (Western Dean); STEPHEN D. PARKES, V.F. (Central North Dean); ESAU GARCIA, V.F. (Central South Dean).

Representatives by Deanery—Northern: Rev. RALPH DUWELL. Southern: Rev. LEO HODGES. Eastern: Rev. THOMAS CONNERY. Western: Rev. CHARLES VIVIANO. Central North: Rev. RICHARD WALSH. Central South: Rev. JOHN M. MCCORMICK.

Representatives by Age Group—25-45: Rev. KARL BERGIN. 46-55: Very Rev. FERNANDO GIL, J.D., J.C.D. 56-63: Rev. ROBERT J. HOEFFNER. 64+: Very Rev. SEAN HESLIN, V.F.

Representative for Incardinated Priests—Rev. PETER J. HENRY.

Representative for Unincardinated Priests—Rev. ANDREZEJ JURKIEWICZ.

Representative for Religious Priests—Rev. PATRICK QUINN, T.O.R. (Retired).

Representative for Retired Priests—Rev. SEAN K. COONEY (Retired).

Appointed Members—Revs. JOSE BAUTISTA, J.C.L.; BENJAMIN A. BERINTI, C.PP.S., V.F.; JORGE TORRES; CHAU J. NGUYEN; CHRISTOPHER HOFFMANN, V.F.

Vicar for Clergy—Very Rev. PAUL HENRY.

Vicar for Religious—Sr. ROSEMARY HICKMANN, O.P., Mailing Address: P.O. Box 1800, Orlando, 32802. Email: rhickmann@orlandodiocese.org.

Sister's Council—Sr. ROSEMARY HICKMANN, O.P., Pres., Mailing Address: P.O. Box 1800, Orlando, 32802.

Diocesan Offices and Organizations

Archivist and Librarian—HYUN PETERSON, Dir., Mailing Address: P.O. Box 1800, Orlando, 32802. Tel: 407-246-4920.

Catholic Charities of Central Florida, Inc.—PAMELA GILARDI, Chm., Bd. Directors; ARNE NELSON, Capt., US Navy (retired), Pres. & CEO, Central Office: 1819 N. Semoran Blvd., Orlando, 32807-3598. Tel: 407-658-1818; Fax: 407-282-2891. Email: arne.nelson@cflcc.org. Web: www.cflcc.org/index.php.

Cemetery, San Pedro—Rev. PATRICK QUINN, T.O.R., Dir. (Retired), Mailing Address: San Pedro Center, 2400 Dike Rd., Winter Park, 32792. Tel: 407-671-6322.

Censor of Books—Rev. STEVEN OLDS, St. Vincent de Paul Seminary, 10701 S. Military Trail, Boynton Beach, 33436.

Liturgy—Rev. ROBERT E. WEBSTER, Dir. (Retired), Mailing Address: P.O. Box 1800, Orlando, 32802. Tel: 407-246-4861.

Liturgical Music—GLENN OSBORNE, Dir., Mailing Address: P.O. Box 1800, Orlando, 32802. Tel: 407-246-4862.

Propagation of the Faith—Rev. JOHN M. MCCORMICK, Dir., St. James Cathedral, 215 N. Orange Ave., Orlando, 32801. Tel: 407-422-2005.

Victim Assistance Coordinator—HEIDI PECKHAM, Mailing Address: P.O. Box 1800, Orlando, 32802. Tel: 407-246-4866; 407-246-7179 (HOTLINE). Email: hpeckham@orlandodiocese.org.

Secretariat for Administration—BRYAN JOSEPH, Sec. & CFO, Mailing Address: P.O. Box 1800, Orlando, 32802. Tel: 407-246-4831. Email: bjoseph@orlandodiocese.org.

Diocesan Finance Committee—JOSEPH F. BERT, Chm., Mailing Address: P.O. Box 1800, Orlando, 32802.

Fiscal Management—BRYAN JOSEPH, CFO.

Comptroller—ROGER BARNES, Mailing Address: P.O. Box 1800, Orlando, 32802. Tel: 407-246-4832.

Design and Construction Services—ANTONIO AGUERREVERE, Sr. Dir., Mailing Address: P.O. Box 1800, Orlando, 32802. Tel: 407-246-4870. Email: taguerrevere@orlandodiocese.org.

Human Resources—THERESA SIMON, Sr. Dir., Mailing Address: P.O. Box 1800, Orlando, 32802. Tel: 407-246-4830. Email: tsimon@orlandodiocese.org.

Information Technology—JACK PAIGE, Sr. Dir., Mailing Address: P.O. Box 1800, Orlando, 32802. Tel: 407-246-4839. Email: jpaige@orlandodiocese.org.

Insurance Committee—Dr. MARGARET CURRAN, Chm., Mailing Address: P.O. Box 1800, Orlando, 32802. Tel: 407-246-4835.

Secretariat for Evangelization—CAROL BRINATI, Sec., Mailing Address: P.O. Box 1800, Orlando, 32802. Tel: 407-246-4814. Email: cbrinati@orlandodiocese.org.

Advocacy and Justice - Respect Life—DEBORAH STAFFORD SHEARER, Dir., Mailing Address: P.O. Box 1800, Orlando, 32802. Tel: 407-246-4819; Fax: 407-246-4942.

Communications—CAROL BRINATI, Dir., Mailing Address: P.O. Box 1800, Orlando, 32802. Tel: 407-246-4814. Email: cbrinati@orlandodiocese.org.

Hispanic Communications— (Buena Nueva FM; El Clarin) TOMAS EVANS, Dir., Mailing Address: P.O. Box 1800, Orlando, 32802. Tel: 407-246-4926.

Media Center—DANIEL HARDESTER, Dir., 50 E. Robinson St., Orlando, 32801. Tel: 407-246-4895; Fax: 407-246-4935.

Mission Office, Sister Diocese—Sr. BERNADETTE MACKAY, O.S.U., Dir., Mailing Address: P.O. Box 1800, Orlando, 32802. Tel: 407-246-4890; Fax: 407-246-4892.

Newspaper— "The Florida Catholic" TANYA GOODMAN, Orlando Editor, Mailing Address: P.O. Box 1800, Orlando, 32802. Tel: 407-246-4924.

Secretariat for Faith Formation—NICHOLAS WOLSONOVICH, Ph.D., Sec. & Supt. Schools, Mailing Address: P.O. Box 1800, Orlando, 32802. Tel: 407-246-4904; Fax: 407-246-4940. Email: nwolsonovich@orlandodiocese.org.

Diocesan School Board—JOSEPH STANTON, Chm. Bd., Mailing Address: P.O. Box 1800, Orlando, 32802. Tel: 407-246-4904; Fax: 407-246-4940.

Religious Education—Sr. LINDA L. GAUPIN, C.D.P., Ph.D., Sr. Dir., Mailing Address: P.O. Box 1800, Orlando, 32802. Tel: 407-246-4910; Fax: 407-246-4935. Email: lgaupin@orlandodiocese.org.

Schools—NICHOLAS WOLSONOVICH, Ph.D., Supt. Schools, Mailing Address: P.O. Box 1800, Orlando, 32802. Tel: 407-246-4904; Fax: 407-246-4940. Email: nwolsonovich@orlandodiocese.org.

Secretariat for Pastoral Ministries—HEIDI PECKHAM, Sec., Mailing Address: P.O. Box 1800, Orlando, 32802. Tel: 407-246-4866. Email: hpeckham@orlandodiocese.org.

Campus Ministry—MICHELLE FISCHER, Dir., Mailing Address: P.O. Box 1800, Orlando, 32802. Tel: 407-246-4867.

Catholic Campus Ministry at University of Central Florida—Mailing Address: P.O. Box 677145, Orlando, 32867. Tel: 407-382-7063. Very Rev. STEPHEN D. PARKES, V.F., Campus Min.

Ethnic Ministries—Rev. JOHN M. MCCORMICK, Dir. Tel: 407-422-2005.

African Ministry—Rev. EMMANUEL AKALUE.

Portuguese/Brazilian Ministry—Rev. ADEMIR GUERINI, C.S.

Filipino Ministry—Rev. PEDRO (PETER) PUNTAL.

Haitian Ministry—Rev. JEAN GAETAN BOURSIQUOT.

Hispanic Ministry—Rev. YBAIN F. RAMIREZ, Dir., Mailing Address: P.O. Box 1800, Orlando, 32802. Tel: 407-246-4931.

Korean Ministry—Rev. MICHAEL YANG-GWON PYO.

Polish Ministry—Rev. ANDREZEJ JURKIEWICZ.

Vietnamese Ministry—Rev. CHAU J. NGUYEN.

Family Life and Pastoral Care—VACANT, Dir., Mailing Address: P.O. Box 1800, Orlando, 32802. Tel: 407-246-4881.

Farmworker Ministry and Hope CommUnity Center—Sisters GAIL GRIMES, S.N.D.deN., Admin.; ANN KENDRICK, S.N.D.deN., Community Rels. Coord., 1016 N. Park Ave., Apopka, 32712. Tel: 407-880-4673; Fax: 407-464-0854. Web: www.hcc-offm.org.

Permanent Diaconate—Deacons DAVID GRAY, Dir.; MARSHALL GIBBS, Co Dir., Mailing Address: P.O. Box 1800, Orlando, 32802. Tel: 407-246-4875; Fax: 407-246-4942.

Priestly Life and Ministry—Rev. RICHARD W. TROUT, Dir., P.O. Box 1800, Orlando, 32802. Tel: 407-246-4875.

Priest Personnel—Rev. RICHARD WALSH, Dir., Mailing Address: P.O. Box 1800, Orlando, 32802. Tel: 407-246-4875.

San Pedro Spiritual Development Center—Rev. PATRICK QUINN, T.O.R. (Retired), San Pedro Center, 2400 Dike Rd., Winter Park, 32792. Tel: 407-671-6322.

Cursillos de Cristiandad—Rev. DAVID KACZMAREK, T.O.R., San Pedro Center, 2400 Dike Rd., Winter Park, 32792. Tel: 407-671-6322.

Foundations for Lay Ministry Program—Rev. PATRICK QUINN, T.O.R., Dir. (Retired), Mailing Address: San Pedro Center, 2400 Dike Rd., Winter Park, 32792. Tel: 407-671-6322.

Tourism Ministry—

Apostleship of the Sea Chaplain— Port Canaveral: Deacon WILLIAM WANCA SR., 720 Mullet Rd., Ste. N, Cape Canaveral, 32920. Tel: 321-431-2700.

Airport Ministry, Orlando International Airport—Rev. ROBERT F. SUSANN, M.S., Airport Chap. Tel: 407-947-5453.

Vocations—Rev. MIGUEL GONZALEZ, Dir., Mailing Address: P.O. Box 1800, Orlando, 32802. Tel: 407-246-4875; Fax: 407-246-4937. Email: mgonzalez@orlandodiocese.org.

Youth and Young Adult Ministry—MICHELLE FISCHER, Dir., Mailing Address: P.O. Box 1800, Orlando, 32802. Tel: 407-246-4911; Fax: 407-246-4935. Email: mfischer@orlandodiocese.org.

Girl Scouting—MICHELLE FISCHER, Mailing Address: P.O. Box 1800, Orlando, 32802. Tel: 407-246-4867.

Other Diocesan Organizations

Catholic Charities of Central Florida, Inc.—PAMELA GILARDI, Chm., Bd. Directors; ARNE NELSON, Capt., US Navy (retired), Pres. & CEO, Mailing Address: Central Office, 1819 N. Semoran Blvd., Orlando, 32807-3598. Tel: 407-658-1818; Fax: 407-282-2891. Web: www.cflcc.org/index.php; Central Regional Office: 1771 N. Semoran Blvd., Orlando, 32807-3598. Tel: 407-658-1818. Southern Regional Office: 817 Dixon Blvd., Cocoa, 32922-5808. Tel: 321-636-6144. Eastern Regional Office: 207 White St., Daytona Beach, 32114-3427. Tel: 386-255-6521. Western Regional Office: 1801 E. Memorial Blvd., Lakeland, 33801-5528. Tel: 863-686-7153.

Immigration Services—

Refugee Resettlement—RICHARD LOGUE, Dir., 1771 N. Semoran Blvd., Ste. C, Orlando, 32807-3598. Tel: 407-658-0110; Fax: 407-249-5699.

Criminal Justice Office—THOMAS GILLAN, Dir., Mailing Address: 1819 N. Semoran Blvd., Orlando, 32807-3544. Tel: 407-658-1818.

**Pathways to Care, Inc.*JANE MARKHEIM, Admin., Mailing Address: 430 Plumosa Ave., Casselberry, 32707. Tel: 407-388-0245. Web: pathwaystocare.org/.

Catholic Foundation of Central Florida, Inc.—WILLIAM OROSZ, Chm., Bd. Directors; Mrs. MARILYN L. BLANCHETTE, Pres., Mailing Address: P.O. Box 4905, Orlando, 32801-4905. 50 E. Robinson St., Orlando, 32801. Tel: 407-246-4841; Fax: 407-246-4939. Email: mblanchette@orlandodiocese.org.

**Hope Community Center, Inc.* Sisters GAIL GRIMES, S.N.D.deN., Admin.; ANN KENDRICK, S.N.D.deN., Community Rels. Coord., Mailing Address: 1016 N. Park Ave., Apopka, 32712. Tel: 407-880-4673; Fax: 407-464-0854. Web: www.hcc-offm.org.

CLERGY, PARISHES, MISSIONS AND PAROCHIAL SCHOOLS

CITY OF ORLANDO

(ORANGE COUNTY)

1—ST. JAMES CATHEDRAL (1881) Revs. John M. McCormick, Rector; Ybain F. Ramirez; Scott M. Circe.
Church: 215 N. Orange Ave., 32801. Tel: 407-422-2005; Fax: 407-422-2009. Email: info@stjcc.net. Web: www.stjcc.net.
School—505 E. Ridgewood St., 32803. Tel: 407-841-4432; Fax: 407-648-4603. Email: stjcs@stjcs.com. Web: www.stjcs.com. Mrs. Gerri Gendall, Prin. Lay Teachers 30; Students 468.
Catechesis/Religious Program—Students 258.
Mission—*St. Ignatius Kim Korean Mission* 1518 E. Muriel St., Orange Co. 32806. Tel: 407-897-6587; Fax: 407-893-4381. Rev. Michael Yang-Gwon Pyo.

2—ST. ANDREW (1957) Revs. Vigny Joseph Bellerive; Gaetan Boursiquot, Haitian Ministry; Deacons Jose Cruz; Rafael Hernandez.
Res.: 801 Hastings, 32808. Tel: 407-293-0730; Fax: 407-293-0739. Email: lstandrewcatho@cfl.rr.com. Web: www.standrew-orlando.org.
School—877 Hastings St., 32808. Tel: 407-295-4230; Fax: 407-290-0959. Email: sand@doschool.org. Web: www.standrewcatholicschool.org. Lay Teachers 20; Students 346.
Catechesis/Religious Program—Students 109.

3—BLESSED TRINITY (1965) Revs. Roland Nadeau, M.S.; Juan Daniel Petrino, Parochial Vicar. In Res., Rev. Robert F. Susann, M.S., Airport Chap.
Res.: 4545 E. Anderson Rd., 32812. Tel: 407-277-1702; Fax: 407-277-1973. Email: info@blessedtrinityorlando.org. Web: blessedtrinityorlando.org.
Catechesis/Religious Program—Tel: 407-277-1702; Fax: 407-277-1973. Students 270.

4—ST. CHARLES BORROMEO (1954) Revs. Augustine Clark; Fernando Ramirez, Parochial Vicar; Deacon Paul Volkerson.
Res.: 4001 Edgewater Dr., 32804. Tel: 407-293-9556; Fax: 407-293-9213. Web: www.stcharlesorlando.org.
School—4005 Edgewater Dr., 32804. Tel: 407-293-7691; Fax: 407-295-9839. Web: www.stcharles-orlando.org. Lay Teachers 30; Students 478.
Preschool—Students 24.
Catechesis/Religious Program—Tel: 407-293-9556, Ext. 121. Students 52.

5—GOOD SHEPHERD (1956) Revs. Brian R. Sheridan, M.S.; Stephen J. Krisanda, M.S.; Baiju Augustine Avittappally, M.S.; Terry Niziolek, M.S.; Deacons Jose "Manny" Garcia; John T. Crotty; Confesor De Jesus; Vincente Rivera.
Mailing Address: 5900 Oleander Dr., 32807. Tel: 407-277-3939; Fax: 407-273-5148.
Res.: 567 Hewett Dr., 32807. Tel: 407-275-6381.
School—Tel: 407-277-3973; Fax: 407-277-2605. Email: pmcnamee@goodshepherd.org. Web: www.goodshepherd.org. Lay Teachers 31; Students 589.
Good Shepherd Early Childhood Educational Ctr.—Tel: 407-277-3939, Ext. 220. Email: dmcmeekin@goodshepherd.org. Sisters 1; Lay Teachers 14; Students 56.
Catechesis/Religious Program—Tel: 407-277-3939, Ext. 211. Email: lmediavilla@goodshepherd.org. Laura Mediavilla, C.R.E. Students 539.

6—HOLY CROSS (1992) Very Rev. Esau Garcia; Revs. John Walsh; Peter Cordeno; Deacons Celso Diaz; Ramon Morales; Kenneth N. Money; Hector Lopez, Music Min.; Mary Shelton, Liturgy Dir.; Dennis Cote, Business Mgr.
Res.: 12600 Marsfield Ave., 32837. Tel: 407-438-0990; Fax: 407-438-4090.
Catechesis/Religious Program—Rachel Mannix, D.R.E. (K-5); Tina Shannon, Middle School & Senior High Youth Coord. Students 879.

7—HOLY FAMILY (1975) [JC] Revs. William Ennis; Waldemar Maciag (Poland); Francisco Aquino (Philippines); Deacons Charles Mallon; Patrick McAvoy; Robert Pleus; John R. Martin; Carl Orbon; Carl L. Brockman.
Res.: 5125 S. Apopka-Vineland Rd., 32819. Tel: 407-876-2211; Fax: 407-876-1167. Email: hfoffice@hfcchurch.com. Web: www.holyfamilyorlando.org.
School—5129 S. Apopka-Vineland Rd., 32819. Tel: 407-876-9344; Fax: 407-876-8775. Web: www.hfcschool.com. Sr. Dorothy Sayers, M.P.F., Prin. Sisters 1; Lay Teachers 30; Students 687.
Catechesis/Religious Program—Tel: 407-876-6331; Fax: 407-876-8775. Students 1,082.

8—ST. ISAAC JOGUES (1987) Rev. Jose Munoz; Deacons Robert Kloznick; Pedro Laboy; Orlando Lendoiro; Angel Pacheco; Rafael Mejia; Felix Montanez; Jose Miguel Gonzalez.
Mailing Address: 4301 S. Chickasaw Tr., 32829. Tel: 407-249-0906; Fax: 407-273-3236. Email: stisaac@st-isaac.org. Web: st-isaac.org.
Catechesis/Religious Program—Students 952.

9—ST. JOHN VIANNEY (1959) Revs. Paul J. Henry; Tomas Hurtado; Rex Familar; Deacons Ovidio Ossa; Thomas P. Breaud; Angel Gonzalez.
Res.: 6200 S. Orange Blossom Tr., 32809. Tel: 407-855-5391; Fax: 407-859-3631. Web: www.sjvorlando.org.
School—Tel: 407-855-4660; Fax: 407-857-7932. Web: www.sjvs.org. Sr. Elizabeth Murphy, Prin. Sisters of St. Francis of Philadelphia 2; Lay Teachers 36; Students 625.
Catechesis/Religious Program—Tel: 407-855-5391, Ext. 235. Isabel Villamil-Gonzalez, D.R.E. Students 305.

10—ST. JOSEPH (1962), (Polish—Filipino), Revs. Robert W. Brown; Larry Lossing (Retired); Andrzej Jurkiewicz.
Res.: 1501 N. Alafaya Tr., 32828. Tel: 407-275-0841; Fax: 407-275-0841.
Catechesis/Religious Program—Students 500.

11—ST. MAXIMILIAN KOLBE Rev. David Scotchie.
4013 Alcott Cir., 32828-4886. Email: office@avaloncatholic.org. Web: www.avaloncatholic.org.
Catechesis/Religious Program—Denise Kriscunas, D.R.E. Students 244.

12—ST. PHILIP PHAN VAN MINH CATHOLIC CHURCH (2004) Revs. Chau J. Nguyen; Chien Nguyen.
Mailing Address: 15 W. Par St., 32804. Email: vanphong@philipminhparish.org. Web: philipminhparish.org.
Catechesis/Religious Program—Students 365.

OUTSIDE THE CITY OF ORLANDO

ALTAMONTE SPRINGS, SEMINOLE CO.

1—ANNUNCIATION (1982) Rev. Msgr. Patrick J. Caverly; Revs. Mark R. Wajda; Charles J. Deeney, O.M.I.; Stephen A. Baumann.
Mailing Address: P.O. Box 915887, Longwood, 32791-5887. Tel: 407-869-9472; Fax: 407-869-4661. Web: www.churchofannunciation.org.
Res.: 1020 Montgomery Rd., 32714.
School—Annunciation Catholic Academy, (Grades K-8) Tel: 407-774-2801; Fax: 407-774-2826. Lay Teachers 30; Students 506.
Catechesis/Religious Program—Tel: 407-869-0934. Students 908.

2—ST. MARY MAGDALEN (1959) Revs. Charles I. Mitchell; Edward J. Thompson; Thomas Smith (Retired); Gilbert Medina; Deacons Henry Libersat, (Retired); Jerry Kelly; Marshall Gibbs; Juan Cruz; Lois Locey, Pastoral Assoc.
Res.: 861 Maitland Ave., 32701. Tel: 407-831-1212; Fax: 407-831-1560. Email: office@stmarymagdalen.org. Web: www.stmarymagdalen.org.
School—869 Maitland Ave., 32701. Tel: 407-339-7301; Fax: 407-339-9556. Email: stmarymagdalen@smmschool.org. Web: www.smmschool.org. Sisters 1; Lay Teachers 33; Students 469.
Catechesis/Religious Program—Tel: 407-831-1212, Ext. 233. Email: larannw@stmarymagdalen.org. Students 360.

APOPKA, ORANGE CO., ST. FRANCIS OF ASSISI (1966) Revs. Timothy P. Labo; Percival P. Devera, Parochial Vicar; Jesus Arroyave (Colombia); Deacons Frank Diaz; Laurence Herbert; Jim G. Shelley.
Res.: 834 S. Orange Blossom Trail, 32703-6560. Tel: 407-886-4602; Fax: 407-886-9758. Email: stfrancisofassisi@catholicweb.com. Web: home.catholicweb.com/stfrancisofassisi/.
Catechesis/Religious Program—Students 617.

BAREFOOT BAY, BREVARD CO., ST. LUKE (1986) [JC] Revs. Patrick J. O'Carroll; Yuon Hachi (Canada); Deacon John Dunlop.
Res.: 5055 Micco Rd., 32976. Tel: 772-664-9310; Fax: 772-664-3374.
Catechesis/Religious Program—Students 34.

BARTOW, POLK CO., ST. THOMAS AQUINAS (1956) Rev. Peter Mitchell.
Res.: 1305 E. Mann Rd., 33830. Tel: 863-533-8578; Fax: 863-533-5090.
Catechesis/Religious Program—Tel: 863-533-4514. Students 80.
Mission—St. Elizabeth Ann Seton, Tel: 863-285-7390.
Mission—Our Lady of Guadalupe 2150 State Rd. 559, Wahneta, Polk Co. 33880. Tel: 863-299-3854; Fax: 863-299-8247. Rev. Norman Farland.

BELLEVIEW, MARION CO., ST. THERESA (1951) Rev. David P. Vivero Jr.
Res. & Church: 11528 S.E. U.S. Hwy. 301, 34420-4430. Tel: 352-245-4506; Fax: 352-245-1521. Web: www.sttheresacatholicchurch.org.
Catechesis/Religious Program—Tel: 352-245-5300; Fax: 352-245-1521. Email: sttheresare@cfl.rr.com. Students 112.

BUSHNELL, SUMTER CO., ST. LAWRENCE (1959) Rev. Pedro Zapata; Deacon Bruno Wiencek.
Office & Mailing Address: 320 E. Dade Ave., 33513. Tel: 352-793-7788; Fax: 352-793-4787. Email: stlawbush@gmail.com.
Res.: 223 E. Vermont Ave., 33513. Tel: 352-399-1631 (Emergency Phone).
Catechesis/Religious Program—Students 82.

CANDLER, MARION CO., IMMACULATE HEART OF MARY (1983) Rev. Felicito S. Baybay.
Mailing Address: P.O. Box 310, 32111. Tel: 352-687-4031; Fax: 352-687-1811.
Catechesis/Religious Program—Tel: 352-687-8818. Students 82.

CASSELBERRY, SEMINOLE CO., ST. AUGUSTINE (1969) Revs. Luis Barrera; James MacLoughlin, Vicar (Retired); William J. Neumann, Vicar.
Office & Church: 375 N. Sunset Dr., 32707. Tel: 407-695-3262; Fax: 407-699-8998. Email: samainoffice@embarqmail.com. Web: www.staugustinecc.org.
Rectory—
Catechesis/Religious Program—Students 197.

CELEBRATION , OSCEOLA CO., CORPUS CHRISTI (2005) Very Rev. Gregory Parkes.
Mailing Address: 1050 Celebration Ave., 34747. Tel: 321-939-1491; Fax: 321-939-1494. Web: www.celebrationcatholic.org.
Catechesis/Religious Program—Students 220.

CLERMONT, LAKE CO.

1—BLESSED SACRAMENT (1961) Revs. Robert Webster; Raul Adrain Valdez; Cromwell Cabrisos; Deacons Rafael Gonzales; Fred Molina; Mike Shortell; Fred Grant; Louis Roman.
720 12th St., 34711. Email: frbob@blessedsacramentcc.com. Web: www.blessedsacramentcc.com.
Res.: 1675 Grandiflora Ave., 34711. Tel: 352-394-3562; 352-242-9047; Fax: 352-241-0062. Email: frbob@blessedsacramentcc.com. Web: www.blessedsacramentcc.com.
Catechesis/Religious Program—Tel: 352-394-3562, Ext. 103. Students 652.
Mission—Mission Outreach - Santo Toribio Romo Mascotte, 34753. Fax: 352-241-0064.

2—ST. FAUSTINA CATHOLIC CHURCH (2006) Rev. Jean Hugues Desir.
Mailing Address: P.O. Box 135576, 34713-5576. Web: stfaustina.org.
Catechesis/Religious Program—Students 106.

COCOA BEACH, BREVARD CO., CHURCH OF OUR SAVIOUR (1956) Very Rev. Sean Heslin; Rev. Robert Brennan, C.S.C.
Res.: 5301 N. Atlantic Ave., 32931. Tel: 321-783-4554; Fax: 321-868-6743. Email: oursaviourchurch@cfl.rr.com. Web: www.oursavioursparish.com.
School—Tel: 321-783-2330; Fax: 321-784-6330. Web: www.oursaviour-school.org. Lay Teachers 16; Students 170.
Catechesis/Religious Program—Students 209.

COCOA, BREVARD CO., BLESSED SACRAMENT (1967) Rev. Anthony F. Quinlivan, C.Ss.R.; Deacons Richard J. Basso; Eugene O'Hern.
5135 N. U.S. Hwy. 1, 32927.
Office: 5135 N. Cocoa Blvd., 32927. Tel: 321-632-6333; Fax: 321-631-2560. Email: blessedchurch@bellsouth.net. Web: www.blessedsacramentcocoa.org.
Catechesis/Religious Program—Students 94.

DAYTONA BEACH, VOLUSIA CO.

1—BASILICA OF SAINT PAUL (1881) Revs. Timothy P. Daly; Charles Nabwana, Hospital Chap.; Deacons Robert Landers; Vernon Hart; Rick Ferranti.
Res.: 317 Mullally St., 32114. Tel: 386-252-5422; Fax: 386-252-1936. Web: www.basilicaofsaintpaul.com.
School—Tel: 386-252-7915; Fax: 386-238-7903. Web: www.stpaulpanthers.org. Lay Teachers 15; Students 156.
Catechesis/Religious Program—Students 40.

2—OUR LADY OF LOURDES (1953) Rev. Philip J. Egitto.
Res.: 201 University Blvd., 32118. Tel: 386-255-0433; Fax: 386-238-1175. Web: www.ourladyoflourdesdaytona.com.
School—1014 N. Halifax, 32118. Tel: 386-252-0391; Fax: 386-238-1175. Email: prandlovoll@yahoo.com. Web: lourdesacademy.net. Lay Teachers 19; Students 275.
Catechesis/Religious Program—Students 76.

DELAND, VOLUSIA CO., ST. PETER'S CHURCH (1883) Revs. Thomas Connery; James Patrick Morgan; Jesus Tovar-Encinas; Deacons Chester DeMarsh; Robert LaPlante; Gerard Smith; Robert Kinsey; Ronald Keehner.
Mailing Address: 359 New York Ave., P.O. Box 3700, 32721.
Res.: 359 W. New York Ave., De Land, 32720. Tel: 386-822-6000; Fax: 386-822-6034.
School—Tel: 386-822-6010; Fax: 386-822-6013. Mrs. Mary Martin, Prin. Lay Teachers 28; Students 260.
Catechesis/Religious Program—Rick Grinstead, D.R.E. & Youth Min. Students 400.
Mission—San Jose Mission 165 Emporia Rd., Barberville, Volusia Co. 32005. Tel: 386-749-9372.

DEBARY, VOLUSIA CO., ST. ANN'S (1961) Revs. Peter J. Henry; David C. Gillis, Parochial Vicar; Deacon Jim Lathan.
Mailing Address: P.O. Box 530218, 32753-0218.
Office: 26 Dogwood Tr., 32713. Tel: 386-668-8270; Fax: 386-668-8471. Email: stannsdebary@comcast.net. Web: home.catholicweb.com/stannsdebary/.
Res.: 10 Larkspur Ln., 32713. Tel: 386-668-8619.
Catechesis/Religious Program—Email: religiousedkid@comcast.net. Students 295.

DELTONA, VOLUSIA CO.

1—ST. CLARE (1989), (Anglo—Hispanic), Rev. Carlos Bedoya; Deacons Joseph Robert; Leonard LaPointe.
2961 Day Rd., 32738. Tel: 386-789-9990; Fax: 386-789-2430.
Catechesis/Religious Program—Students 106.

2—OUR LADY OF THE LAKES (1970) Revs. Joseph L. Roberts III; Alvaro Jimenez; Frank Cerio; Deacon Ricardo Gonzalez.
Res.: 1310 Maximilian St., 32725. Tel: 386-574-2131; Fax: 386-860-0074. Email: olladmin@cfl.rr.com.
Catechesis/Religious Program—Tel: 386-574-4620. Students 320.

DUNNELLON, MARION CO., ST. JOHN THE BAPTIST (1976) Rev. Emmanuel Akalue; Deacons Fred Crawford Jr.; Joseph Interlandi.
Res.: 7545 S. Hwy. 41, 34432. Tel: 352-489-3166; Fax: 352-489-3156. Email: mail@stjohncc.com. Web: www.stjohncc.com.
Catechesis/Religious Program—Students 68.

EUSTIS, LAKE CO., ST. MARY OF THE LAKES (1912) Rev. Manuel A. Fernandez.
Res.: 218 Ocklawaha Ave., 32726-4840. Tel: 352-483-3500; Fax: 352-483-1370. Email: stmary27@mpinet.com.
Catechesis/Religious Program—Tel: 352-483-3500, Ext. 13. Students 275.

HAINES CITY, POLK CO., ST. ANN (1969), (Anglo—Hispanic), [JC], (Formerly Transfiguration) Revs. Robert W. Mitchell; Pawel Pazdzioch (Poland); Deacons Jose Ramos; Hector Colon; Noe Monat; Robert Demming.
Mailing Address: 1311 E. Robinson Dr., P.O. Box 1285, 33845. Tel: 863-422-4370; Fax: 863-421-2522. Email: office@stannhc.org. Web: www.stannhc.org.
Catechesis/Religious Program—Students 328.

INDIALANTIC, BREVARD CO., HOLY NAME OF JESUS (1959) Revs. David Page; Joseph Bui; Anthony R. Welle; Deacons Charles Foy; Joseph Richiuso; Vincent Trunzo; Joseph Gassman; John Farrell.

Res.: 3050 Hwy. A1A, 32903. Tel: 321-773-2783; Fax: 321-777-0929. Email: hnjparish@hnj.org. Web: www.hnj.org.
School—Tel: 321-773-1630; Fax: 321-773-7148. Email: hnj@hnj.org. Ms. Mary Ellen Massey, Prin. Pre-School: 3-4 years. Lay Teachers 25; Students 265.
Catechesis/Religious Program—Tel: 321-773-2783, Ext. 120. Students 520.

KISSIMMEE, OSCEOLA CO.
1—ST. CATHERINE OF SIENA (1994) Revs. Jose Bautista (Colombia); Nazaire Massillon, Parochial Vicar; Deacons Juan Vargas; Eliezer Maldonado; Esteban Cruz; Ernesto Nunez.
Office: 2750 E. Osceola Pkwy., 34743. Tel: 407-344-9607; Fax: 407-344-9160. Email: stcatherineofsiena@cfl.rr.com. Web: homecatholicweb.com/stcatherineofsiena.
Res. & Mailing Address: P.O. Box 450698, 34745-0698.
Catechesis/Religious Program—Students 228.
2—HOLY REDEEMER (1917) Very Rev. Christopher Hoffmann; Revs. Longin Buhake; Hector Vazquez Saad; Deacons Manuel Lacsamana; Tommy Tate; Susano Neris.
Res.: 1603 N. Thacker Ave., 34741. Tel: 407-847-2500; 407-846-3700; Fax: 407-847-9687. Email: info@hredeemer.org. Web: hredeemer.org.
School—(1993), (Grades PreK-8), 1800 W. Columbia Ave., 34741. Tel: 407-870-9055; Fax: 407-870-2214. Mrs. Colleen Ehlenbeck, Prin.; Sr. Eileen Fichtner, Librarian. Sisters of St. Joseph 1; Lay Teachers 19; Students 262.
Catechesis/Religious Program—Tel: 407-870-8196; Fax: 407-870-2214. Email: re@hredeemer.org. Mrs. Rose Dzejak, D.R.E. Students 560.

LADY LAKE, LAKE CO., ST. TIMOTHY (1985) Revs. Edward Waters; Gerald Shovelton (Retired); Ralph DuWell; Eugene R. Weis (ROC) (Retired); Deacons Russell Anderberg, (Retired); John Sullivan; Frederick Giel; Nicholas Deutsch, (Retired); Ronald L'Huillier; George Mattison; Richard R. Kaseta.
1351 Paige Pl., 32159. Tel: 352-753-0989; Fax: 352-753-9602. Web: www.sttimothycc.com. In Res., Rev. Gerard M. Cunningham (WDC).
Catechesis/Religious Program—Students 100.

LAKE WALES, POLK CO., HOLY SPIRIT (1927) Rev. Anthony Bluett; Rev. Msgr. Leo Dobosiewicz (Retired); Deacons Donald E. Raymond; John Avery; Samuel Knight.
Res.: 644 S. 9th St., P.O. Box 232, 33853. Tel: 863-676-1556; Fax: 863-676-2962.
Catechesis/Religious Program—Tel: 863-678-1083. Students 263.
Mission—St. Leo the Great Nalcrest, Polk Co. 33856. Tel: 863-679-1919. 10721 E. Leisure, 33898.

LAKELAND, POLK CO.
1—ST. ANTHONY CATHOLIC CHURCH (1982) Revs. Nicholas J. O'Brien; Franklin Salazar, Hispanic Ministry; Deacon Francisco Hernandez.
Church: 820 Marcum Rd., 33809-4306. Tel: 863-585-8047; Fax: 863-859-1036. Web: www.stanthonyparish.com.
School—(Grades PreK-8), 924 Marcum Rd., 33809. Tel: 863-858-0671; Fax: 863-858-0876. Web: www-.saintanthonycatholicschool.com. Mrs. Janet Peddecord, Prin. Lay Teachers 12; Students 182.
Catechesis/Religious Program—Students 78.
2—CHURCH OF THE RESURRECTION (1963) Revs. Matthew Mello; Gabriel Ipasu; Domingo N. Gonzalez (Retired); Deacons Joseph Wortman; Antonio Martinez.
Res.: 3855 S. Florida Ave., 33813-1109. Tel: 863-646-3556; Fax: 863-644-8697. Email: office@churchoftheres.net. Web: www.churchoftheres.net.
School—(1990), (Grades PreK-8), 3720 Old Hwy. 37, 33813. Tel: 863-644-3931; Fax: 863-648-0625. Email: office@resurrectioncatholicschool.org. Web: www.resurrectioncatholicschool.org. Debbie Petrigala, Librarian. Lay Teachers 33; Students 480.
Catechesis/Religious Program—Tel: 863-644-0585. Email: lmalthaner@churchoftheres.net. Students 322.
3—ST. JOHN NEUMANN (1988) Rev. Frank Buck.
Res. & Church: 501 E. Carter Rd., 33813. Tel: 863-647-3400; Fax: 863-647-0888. Email: mailbox@sjncc.org. Web: www.sjncc.org.
Catechesis/Religious Program—Students 218.
4—ST. JOSEPH'S (1898) [JC] Revs. John Caulfield; Ramon Bolatete; Franklin Salazar. In Res., Rev. Felix Banos (Retired).
Res.: 210 W. Lemon St., P.O. Box 30, 33802. Tel: 863-682-0555; Fax: 863-686-9546.
School—310 McDonald St., 33803. Tel: 863-686-6415; Fax: 863-687-8074. Web: www.stjosephlakeland.org. Lay Teachers 18; Students 183.
Catechesis/Religious Program—Students 316.

LEESBURG, LAKE CO., ST. PAUL'S (1954) Very Rev. John C. Giel; Rev. Gianni Agostinelli, C.S.; Deacons Michael McGinnity; Sam Damiano; George Lenhardt.
Res.: 1330 Sunshine Ave., 34748. Tel: 352-787-6354; Fax: 352-787-5971.
School—1304 Sunshine Ave., 34748. Tel: 352-787-4657; Fax: 352-787-0324. Lay Teachers 15; Students 168.
Catechesis/Religious Program—Tel: 352-787-6354; Fax: 352-787-5971. Students 89.

LONGWOOD, SEMINOLE CO., CHURCH OF THE NATIVITY (1960) Revs. Thomas G. Barrett; Justin Vakko, O.C.D., Parochial Vicar; Deacons John Gravois; Walter A. Skinner Jr.
Res.: 3255 N. Ronald Reagan Blvd., 32750. Tel: 407-322-3961; Fax: 407-322-3981. Email: info@nativity.org. Web: nativity.org.
Catechesis/Religious Program—Students 425.

MELBOURNE BEACH, BREVARD CO., IMMACULATE CONCEPTION (1978) Rev. Joseph A. Nolan; Deacons Howard Pettengill Jr.; Michael J. Biennas.
Res.: 3780 S. Hwy. A1A, 32951. Tel: 321-725-0552; Fax: 321-727-8218.
Catechesis/Religious Program—Tel: 321-726-8111. Students 71.

MELBOURNE, BREVARD CO.
1—ASCENSION (1959) Rev. Eamon Tobin; Deacons Michael McElwee; Sergio Colon; Tom Stauffacher.
Mailing Address: 2950 N. Harbor City Blvd., 32935-6259. Tel: 321-254-1595; Fax: 321-255-3490. Web: www.ascensioncatholic.net.
School—Tel: 321-254-5495; Fax: 321-259-0993. Web: www.ascensioncatholicsch.org. Lay Teachers 29; Students 500.
Catechesis/Religious Program—Tel: 321-254-1595, Ext. 3080. Students 315.
2—OUR LADY OF LOURDES (1931), (Hispanic), Rev. William Hanley; Deacons Richard Beauton; Arcelio Perez; Edward Stives; Vincent Accardi. In Res., Revs. Carl Feil, O.S.M. (Retired); Joseph J. Rimshaw, S.S.J. (Retired).
Res.: 1626 Oak St., 32901-4517. Tel: 321-723-3636; Fax: 321-951-8029. Email: admin@oll-church.com. Web: oll-church.com.
School—420 E. Fee Ave., 32901. Tel: 321-723-3631; Fax: 321-723-7408. Email: school@ollmelbourne.org. Web: www.ollmelbourne.org. Lay Teachers 16; Students 162.
Catechesis/Religious Program—Email: carolynziarno@oll-church.com. Students 170.

MERRITT ISLAND, BREVARD CO., DIVINE MERCY CATHOLIC COMMUNITY (1964) Revs. Michael A. Farrell; Karl Bergin.
Res.: 1940 N. Courtenay Pkwy., 32953. Tel: 321-452-5955; Fax: 321-455-2268.
School—Tel: 321-452-0263; Fax: 321-453-7573. Lay Teachers 25; Students 187.
Catechesis/Religious Program—Students 280.
Convent—1930 N. Courtenay Pkwy., 32953. Tel: 321-452-1279.

MIMS, BREVARD CO., HOLY SPIRIT (1967) Rev. Andrezj Wojtan.
Office & Res.: 2399 Holder Rd., 32754-2103. Tel: 321-269-2282; Fax: 321-269-2252.
Catechesis/Religious Program—Tel: 321-269-7785. Students 144.

MOUNT DORA, ORANGE CO., ST. PATRICK'S (1973), (Hispanic), [CEM] Revs. Robert D'Aversa, T.O.R.; Blase Romano, T.O.R.; Gianni Agostinelli, C.S.; Deacon William Fisher Jr.
Res.: 6801 Old Hwy. 441 S., 32757. Tel: 352-383-8556; Fax: 352-383-8443.
Catechesis/Religious Program—Tel: 352-383-8556, Ext. 34. Students 240.

NEW SMYRNA BEACH, VOLUSIA CO.
1—OUR LADY STAR OF THE SEA (1973) Rev. John S. Murray.
Res.: 4000 S. Atlantic Ave., 32169. Tel: 386-427-4530; Fax: 386-427-1331.
Catechesis/Religious Program—Tel: 386-427-4530, Ext. 11. Students 35.
2—SACRED HEART (1926) Revs. Glenn D. Parker, C.Ss.R.; John G. Barry, C.Ss.R.; Edward J. Gray, C.Ss.R.; Francis Nelson, C.Ss.R.; John F. Murray, C.Ss.R.; Deacon Thomas Murray.
Mailing Address: P.O. Box 729, 32170.
Res.: 998 Father Donlan Dr., 32168. Tel: 386-428-6426; Fax: 386-423-4088. Email: r_sacred@bellsouth.net. Web: sacredheartnsb.org.
School—1003 Turnbull St., 32168. Tel: 386-428-4732; Fax: 386-428-4087. Email: labboud@sacredheartcatholic.com. Web: sacredheartcatholic.com. Sisters of Notre Dame (Toledo) 3; Lay Teachers 10; Students 248.
Catechesis/Religious Program—Tel: 386-427-8372. Email: abaker@sacredheartcatholic.com. Andy Baker, D.R.E. & Youth Min. Students 217.
Mission—St. Gerard 3171 S. Ridgewood Ave., Edgewater, Volusia Co. 32141. Tel: 386-428-6930.

OCALA, MARION CO.
1—BLESSED TRINITY (1922) Revs. Patrick J. Sheedy; Roy V. Eco; Alfonso Cely; Deacons James Schwartz; James Boerstler; Heriberto Berrios. In Res., Rev. Michael O'Keeffe.
Res.: 5 S.E. 17th St., 34471. Tel: 352-629-8092; Fax: 352-351-8872. Email: mail@blessedtrinity.org. Web: blessedtrinity.org.
School—Tel: 352-622-5808; Fax: 352-622-1660. Email: btschool@btschool.org. Web: btschool.org. Lay Teachers 39; Students 680.
Catechesis/Religious Program—Students 269.
Mission—Christ the King 14045 N. U.S. Hwy. 301, P.O. Box 129, Citra, 32113. Tel: 352-595-5605.
2—ST. JUDE'S CATHOLIC COMMUNITY (1983) Rev. Lemier Guillaume; Deacons Santos Santiago; Jose Serrano; Edward Wilson; Ruth Sutherland, Business Mgr.
Church: 443 Marion Oaks Dr., 34473-3203. Tel: 352-347-0154; Fax: 352-347-5211.
Catechesis/Religious Program—Elba Santiago, C.R.E.; Cathy O'Donnell, Music Min. Students 103.
3—OUR LADY OF THE SPRINGS (1982) Revs. Andrew Mallick; George Maniangattu, Parochial Vicar; Deacons James Hamilton, (Retired); John Howell.
Office: 4047 N.E. 21st St., 34470. Tel: 352-236-2230; Fax: 352-236-1475. Email: ourladyofthespringsocala@embarqmail.com. Web: www.ourladyofthesprings.org.
Catechesis/Religious Program—Students 41.
Mission—St. Joseph of the Forest Silver Springs. 17301 E. Hwy. 40, Ocala National Forest, Marion Co. 34488. Tel: 352-625-4222; Fax: 352-625-4922. Email: stjoeforest@aol.com.
Mission—St. Hubert of the Forest 55600 Veterans Dr., Astor, Lake Co. 32102. Tel: 352-759-3983; Fax: 352-759-3982. Web: www.sthubertsmission.com. P.O. Box 715, Astor, 32102.
4—QUEEN OF PEACE (1987) Revs. Patrick J. O'Doherty; Alex Panakal, O.C.D., Curate.
Res.: 6455 S.W. State Rd. 200, 34476. Tel: 352-854-2181; Fax: 352-854-7840. Email: queen_of_peace@embarqmail.com.
Catechesis/Religious Program—Students 90.

ORMOND BEACH, VOLUSIA CO.
1—ST. BRENDAN (1960) Rev. John J. Ryan.
Res.: 1000 Ocean Shore Blvd., 32176. Tel: 386-441-1505; Fax: 386-441-0774. Email: stbrendanormond@aol.com. Web: stbrendanbythesea.com.
School—Tel: 386-441-1331. Email: stb@stbrendanormond.org. Web: stbrendanormond.org. Lay Teachers 28; Students 200.
Catechesis/Religious Program—Tel: 386-441-1505, Ext. 307. David Sikorra, D.R.E.; Stanley Zerkowski, Liturgy Dir. Students 43.
2—PRINCE OF PEACE (1966) Revs. Bill Zamborsky; Ronald E. Oser, Parochial Vicar; Deacon Bruce Gesinski.
Res.: 600 S. Nova Rd., 32174. Tel: 386-672-5272; Fax: 386-677-3224. Web: www.princeofpeaceormond.org.
Catechesis/Religious Program—Tel: 386-672-5272, Ext. 26. Email: popdre@cfl.rr.com. Students 291.

OVIEDO, SEMINOLE CO., MOST PRECIOUS BLOOD CATHOLIC CHURCH (2005) Very Rev. Stephen D. Parkes; Rev. Jorge Torres, Parochial Vicar.
Mailing Address: P.O. Box 622288, 32762-2288. Tel: 407-365-3231; Fax: 407-365-3313. Email: sparkes@oviedocatholic.org. Web: www.oviedocatholic.org.
Catechesis/Religious Program—Students 963.

PALM BAY, BREVARD CO.
1—ST. JOSEPH (1914) [CEM] Rev. Robert J. Hoeffner; Deacons Alfred P. Somma; James Stokes; Michael Mintern.
Res.: 5330 Babcock St., N.E., 32905. Tel: 321-727-1565; Fax: 321-676-2579. Email: hoeffnerr@st-joe.org. Web: www.st-joe.org.
School—Tel: 321-723-8866; Fax: 321-727-1181. Email: adama@st-joe.org. Lay Teachers 19; Students 220.
Catechesis/Religious Program—Email: wyattl@st-joe.org. Students 212.
2—OUR LADY OF GRACE (1989) Revs. Leo Hodges; Robert Markunas; Deacons William T. Wanca Sr., Pastoral Assoc.; Jack Rhine; Albert Gutierrez; Kevin Crawford.
Church & Mailing Address: 300 Malabar Rd. S.E., 32907-3005. Tel: 321-725-3066; Fax: 321-725-9534. Email: ourladyofgrace@cfl.rr.com. Web: www.ourladyofgracechurch.com.
Res.: 949 Haas St., 32907. Tel: 321-726-8742.
Catechesis/Religious Program—Students 330.

POINCIANA, KISSIMMEE CO., ST. ROSE OF LIMA (1994) Unassigned.
Rectory—3860 Pleasant Hill Rd., Kissimmee, 34746. Tel: 407-932-5004; Fax: 407-932-0407. Email: office@fl-saintroseoflima.com. Web: www.fl-saintroseoflima.com.
Catechesis/Religious Program—Students 422.

PORT ORANGE, VOLUSIA CO.
1—EPIPHANY (1962) Very Rev. Michael E. Giglio; Rev. J. Michael Nugent.

Res.: 201 Lafayette St., 32127. Tel: 386-767-6111; Fax: 386-767-0017. Email: epiphanychurch@cfl.rr.com. Web: home.catholicweb.com/EpiphanyCatholicChurch.
Catechesis/Religious Program—Students 110.

2—OUR LADY OF HOPE (1981) [CEM] Revs. Joseph Pinchock; Stephen Ogonwa (Nigeria), Parochial Vicar; Deacons Thomas A. Tagye, Pastoral Assoc.; Michael Pettit.
Res.: P.O. Box 290216, 32129. Tel: 386-788-6144; Fax: 386-761-8840.
Catechesis/Religious Program—Tel: 386-788-6747. Email: hopedre@cfl.rr.com. Maureen Kealhoffer, C.R.E. Students 339.

ROCKLEDGE, BREVARD CO., ST. MARY'S (1917) [JC] Rev. Nicholas King; Rev. Msgr. Terence J. Farrelly, Pastor Emeritus (Retired); Rev. Luis Osorio.
Mailing Address: 75 Barton Ave., 32955. Tel: 321-636-6834; Fax: 321-632-4301. Email: secretary@stmarysrockledge.org. Web: www.stmarysrockledge.org.
School—Tel: 321-636-4208; Fax: 321-636-0591. Email: info@stmarys-school.org. Web: www.stmarys-school.org. Lay Teachers 19; Students 349.
Catechesis/Religious Program—Tel: 321-633-9985. Email: faithformation@stmarysrockledge.org. Students 89.

ST. CLOUD, OSCEOLA CO., ST. THOMAS AQUINAS (1968) Revs. Fabian G. Gimeno; Kent A. Walker, Parochial Vicar.
Mailing Address: P.O. Box 700368, 34770-0368.
Res.: 721 Brown Chapel Rd., 34769. Tel: 407-957-4495; Fax: 407-957-1771. Email: stthomasaquinas@cfl.rr.com. Web: www.stthomasaquinasstcloud.org.
Church: 700 Brown Chapel Rd., 34769.
School—800 Brown Chapel Rd., 34769. Tel: 407-957-1772; Fax: 407-957-8700. Web: www.staschool.info. Lay Teachers 20; Students 359.
Catechesis/Religious Program—Tel: 407-957-4057. Students 448.

SANFORD, SEMINOLE CO., ALL SOULS (1911) [CEM] Revs. Richard W. Trout; Mark Christopher (Retired); Ken Metz; Tito Nels Rojas; Mr. Jon Trout, Dir. Opers.
Res.: 301 W. 8th St., 32771. Tel: 407-322-3795; Fax: 407-322-1131. Web: www.allsoulssanford.org.
School—810 S. Oak Ave., 32771. Tel: 407-322-7090; Fax: 407-321-7255. Email: office@allsoulscatholicschool.org. Web: allsoulscatholicschool.org. Lay Teachers 15; Students 261.
Catechesis/Religious Program—Email: mlfess@allsoussanford.org. Students 318.

SUMMERFIELD, MARION CO., ST. MARK THE EVANGELIST (2005) Revs. Simon Shaner, O.S.P.P.E.; Tadeuz Olzacki, Parochial Vicar; Deacon Robert A. Esposito, Pastoral Assoc.; Don Curtis, Business Mgr.; Nancy Kiser, Music Min.
7081 S.E. Hwy. 42, 34491. Tel: 352-347-9317; Fax: 352-347-9749. Email: simonsay109@hotmail.com. Web: www.stmarkrcc.com.
Catechesis/Religious Program—Twinned with St. Timothy's. Students 9.

TITUSVILLE, BREVARD CO., ST. TERESA (1958) Revs. Eugeniusz Grytner; Krzysztof Bugno, S.D.S.; Deacon Donald Boland.
Res.: 203 Ojibway Ave., 32780. Tel: 321-268-3441; Fax: 321-268-3270. Web: home.catholicweb.com/saintteresa/index.cfm.
School—Tel: 321-267-1643; Fax: 321-268-5124. Email: jzackel@steresa-titusville.org. Web: www.stteresa-titusville.org. Sisters of Mercy (Gort, Ireland) 1; Lay Teachers 17; Students 270.
Catechesis/Religious Program—Tel: 321-268-0440. Students 171.
Convent—Sisters of Mercy, 3380 Muirfield Dr., 32780. Tel: 321-267-1610; Fax: 321-267-1610. Sisters 2.
Convent—Sisters of Notre Dame, Chardon, Ohio, 1735 Harrison #130, 32780. Tel: 321-264-4274. Sisters 4.

VIERA, BREVARD CO., ST. JOHN THE EVANGELIST (2001) Revs. R. Bradley Beaupre, C.S.C.; Louis Manzo, C.S.C.; Donald G. Mainardi (Retired); Robert McBride, Dir. Liturgy & Music; Deacons Hugh W. Muller; James Seidel; Claudia A. Stokes, Dir. Faith Formation.
Mailing Address: 5655 Stadium Pkwy., 32940. Tel: 321-637-9650; Fax: 321-637-9651. Email: office@stjohnviera.org. Web: www.stjohnviera.org.
Catechesis/Religious Program—Students 347.

WILDWOOD, SUMTER CO.

1—SAN PEDRO DE JESUS MALDONADO MISSION (2006) Unassigned. 210 Wonders St., 34785. Tel: 352-787-9208.
Catechesis/Religious Program—Cecilia Montavlo, D.R.E. Students 19.

2—ST. VINCENT DE PAUL (2005) Rev. Peter A. Sagorski; Deacons John Claude Curtin; Miguel Beltran; Joseph Mador; Dana McCarthy; Byron Otradovec; Frank Campione; Daniel Pallo; Richard Radford.
5323 E. CR 462, 34785. Tel: 352-330-0220; Fax: 352-748-6106. Web: www.sumtercatholic.org.
Catechesis/Religious Program—Celines Sanchez, C.R.E. Students 30.

WINTER GARDEN, ORANGE CO., RESURRECTION (1967) Revs. Alex Dalpiaz, C.S.; Ademir Guerini, C.S., Parochial Vicar.
Res.: 358 Floral Ave., 34787.
Church & Mailing Address: 1211 Winter Garden Vineland Rd., 34787. Tel: 407-656-3113; Fax: 407-654-4935. Email: resurrectionwg@earthlink.net. Web: www.resurrectionwg.org.
Catechesis/Religious Program—Students 721.

WINTER HAVEN, POLK CO.

1—ST. JOSEPH'S (1923) Rev. Pedro (Peter) Puntal; Deacons Nuoc Van Dang; John Landry.
Res.: 532 Ave. M N.W., 33881. Tel: 863-294-3144; Fax: 863-299-9709. Web: www.stjosephwh.org.
School—535 Avenue M, N.W., 33881. Tel: 863-293-3311; Fax: 863-299-7894. Web: www.stjosephwh-school.org. Lay Teachers 34; Students 385.
Catechesis/Religious Program—Students 340.

2—ST. MATTHEW (1973) [CEM 2] Rev. Charles Viviano.
Res.: 558 Cody Caleb Dr., 33884.
Church: 1991 Overlook Dr., 33884. Tel: 863-324-3040; Fax: 863-324-9181. Email: stmatthew@stmatthewwh.com. Web: stmatthewwh.com.
Catechesis/Religious Program—Tel: 863-324-3559. Students 340.

WINTER PARK, ORANGE CO., ST. MARGARET MARY (1947) Revs. Richard Walsh; Vilaire Philius; Francis X.J. Smith (Retired); Deacons Robert Kreps; Nemsy Gubatan.
Res.: 526 N. Park Ave., 32789. Tel: 407-647-3392; Fax: 407-647-4492. Web: www.stmargaretmary.org.
School—142 E. Swoope Ave., 32789. Tel: 407-644-7537; Fax: 407-644-7357. Web: www.smmknight-.org. Lay Teachers 37; Students 577.
Catechesis/Religious Program—Tel: 407-647-5171; Fax: 407-647-4492. Students 500.

WINTER PARK, SEMINOLE CO., SAINTS PETER AND PAUL (1967) Revs. Derk Schudde; Fidel Rodriguez; Deacons Al Castellana; Norman Levesque; James Campbell, (Retired); Donald Warner; Jerry Vaughan; Nick Nichols.
Res.: 5300 Old Howell Branch Rd., 32792. Tel: 407-657-6114; Fax: 407-657-9375. Email: mail@stspp.net. Web: www.stspp.net.
Catechesis/Religious Program—Fax: 407-657-9530. Students 600.

WINTER SPRINGS, SEMINOLE CO., ST. STEPHEN (1985) Revs. John J. Bluett; George W. Dunne, S.S.S. (Ireland).
Res.: 575 Tuskawilla Rd., 32708. Tel: 407-699-5683; Fax: 407-699-8408. Email: ststephen@st-stephen.com. Web: st-stephen.com.
Catechesis/Religious Program—Students 1,050.

SHRINES, BASILICA OF THE NATIONAL SHRINE OF MARY QUEEN OF THE UNIVERSE (1986) Very Rev. Edward J. McCarthy; Revs. Martin Gerber; Barry Dowd; Joseph Buranosky, Dir. Opers.; Sharon Mayer, Dir. Devel.; William Picher, Dir. Music.
Mailing Address: 8300 Vineland Ave., 32821.
Res.: 7468 Lake Willis Dr., 32821. Tel: 407-239-8631. Email: shrine@maryqueenoftheuniverse.org. Web: maryqueenoftheuniverse.org.

Special Assignment:
Revs.—
Bui, Phong, Prison Chap.
Gohring, William, Fire Dept. & Hospital Chap.

On Duty Outside the Diocese:
Revs.—
Mueller, Michael, U.S. Military
Olds, Steven, St. Vincent de Paul Seminary, Boynton Beach, FL
Payne, Jeremiah L., Graduate Studies Rome
Ruse, Fred R.
Stahl, Allen M. (Retired), U.S. Military

Retired:
Rev. Msgrs.—
Farrelly, Terence J., 56 Barton Ave., Rockledge, 32955. Tel: 321-636-9099
Harte, F. Joseph, P.O. Box 691805, 32869.
Kamide, Paul T., 750 Ridge Blvd., S., Daytona Beach, 32119.
Revs.—
Arboleda, Vidal, 10237 Chorlton Circle, 32832.
Banos, Felix, P.O. Box 30, Lakeland, 33802-0030.
Benitez, Eduardo, P.O. Box 1524, Davenport, 33837.
Bonar, Clyde A., 2235 Coldstream Dr., Winter Park, 32792. Tel: 407-622-6237
Cooney, Sean K., 9610 Abbot Ct., 32817. Tel: 407-657-1961
Finley, William, 2501 Q. St., N.W., Apt. 426, Washington, DC 20007.
Fucheck, Robert, 1444 Highland Pl., Lady Lake, 32162.
Garcia, Emilio, P.O. Box 1757, Dunnellon, 34430.
Gonzalez, Domingo N., P.O. Box 5756, Lakeland, 33807. Tel: 863-644-2461
Hamilton, Edward A., 400 Alderbrook Dr., Wayne, PA 19087. Tel: 610-949-0443
Hannon, Michael, 210 Gretchen Ct., Oldsmar, 34677. Tel: 727-781-7619
Joseph, William, Flat 42 The Lumiere Bldg., 544 Romford Rd, London E7 8AY, United Kingdom.
Kurber, Robert, 12204 Manado St., 32837. Tel: 407-240-1642
Londono, Hugo, P.O. Box 1496, Ormond Beach, 32175. Tel: 386-441-6548
Lossing, Larry, 1702 Elaine St., Altamonte Springs, 32701.
MacLoughlin, James, St. Augustine Catholic Church, 375 N. Sunset Dr., Casselberry, 32707. Tel: 407-695-3262
Mainardi, Donald G., 1025 Rockledge Dr., #505, Rockledge, 32955. Assisting Divine Mercy
McMackin, Thomas P., Prince of Peace, 1103 Monticello Ln., #2, Port Orange, 32129. Tel: 386-846-5578
McNicholas, Stephen, 990708, 29 West Beach, Cobh, CO Cork Ireland.
Mitzi, John, 410 Marsh Point Cir., Saint Augustine, 32084.
Mutsko, Frank J., P.O. Box 1800, 32802.
O'Leary, Raymond J., 2555 S. Atlantic Ave., Daytona Beach, 32118. Tel: 386-788-6144
Pagan, Antonio, 1009 First St., Rockville, MD 20850.
Palmese, Anthony, 443 Marion Oaks Dr., Ocala, 34473-3203.
Quinn, Peter, 2967 S. Atlantic Ave., #907, Daytona Beach, 32116.
Reagan, Robert, P.O. Box 1471, Greenville, ME 04441. Tel: 207-695-2092
Schneider, Edward
Sheedy, Val, Oceans 3, 3043 S. Atlantic Ave., Apt. 202, Daytona Beach, 32118.
Smith, Francis X.J., 526 Park Ave., N., Winter Park, 32789.
Traupman, Robert, 2999 N.W. 48th Ave., #251, Lauderdale Lakes, 33313. Tel: 954-533-4478
Wawrzycki, Andrew, 15015 Broadway Ave., Snohomish, WA 98296.
Zammit, Francis X., P.O. Box 291242, Port Orange, 32129. Tel: 386-761-1388

Permanent Deacons:
Abrew, Rosendo, St. Augustine, Casselberry
Accardi, Vince, Holy Name of Jesus, Indialantic
Agers, Allen, (Retired), Holy Spirit, Mims
Anderberg, Russell, St. Timothy, Lady Lake
Andrew, Donald, Resurrection, Lakeland
Avery, John, Holy Spirit, Lake Wales
Barbieri, Robert, St. Peter, Deland
Basso, Richard, Blessed Sacrament, Sharpes
Beauton, Richard, Our Lady of Lourdes, Melbourne
Beltran, Miguel, St. Vincent de Paul, Wildwood
Berrios, Heriberto, Blessed Trinity, Ocala
Biennas, Michael, Immaculate Conception, Melbourne
Boerstler, James, Blessed Trinity, Ocala
Boland, Donald, St. Teresa, Titusville
Bonneau, Louis, Immaculate Heart of Mary, Candler
Breaud, Thomas P., St. John Vianney, Orlando
Brockman, Carl L., Holy Family, Orlando
Campbell, James, Sts. Peter & Paul, Winter Park
Castellana, Al, Sts. Peter & Paul, Winter Park
Colon, Hector, St. Ann, Haines City
Colon, Sergio, Ascension, Melbourne
Contreras, Juan, St. Rose of Lima, Poinciana
Crawford, Fred J., Jr., St. John the Baptist, Dunnellon
Crawford, Kevin, Our Lady of Grace, Palm Bay
Crotty, John, Good Shepherd, Orlando
Cruz, Estaban, St. Catherine of Siena, Kissimmee
Cruz, Jose F., St. Andrew, Orlando
Cruz, Juan, St. Mary Magdalen, Orlando
Curtin, Claude J., St. Vincent de Paul, Wildwood
Daidone, Salvatore, Most Precious Blood, Oviedo
Damiano, Samuel, St. Paul, Leesburg
Dang, Nuoc Van, St. Joseph, Winter Haven
DeJesus, Confesor, Good Shepherd, Orlando
DeJesus, Edwin, St. Maximilian Kolbe, Orlando
DelGiudice, John, St. Thomas Aquinas, St. Cloud
DeMarsh, Chester, St. Peter, DeLand
Demming, Robert, St. Ann, Haines City
Deutsch, Nicholas, St. Timothy, Lady Lake
Diaz, Celso, Holy Cross, Orlando
Diaz, Frank, St. Francis of Assisi, Apopka
Drummer, Kenneth L., St. Anthony Catholic Church
Dunlop, John, St. Luke, Barefoot Bay
Durden, Don L., Divine Mercy, Merritt Island
Dwyer, Bruce, Holy Spirit, Mims
Espinoza, Alan, St. Isaac Jogues, Orlando

Esposito, Robert A., St. Timothy, Lady Lake
Falotico, Francis E., Our Lady of Grace, Palm Bay
Farrell, John, Holy Name of Jesus, Indialantic
Ferranti, Richard, Basilica of St. Paul, Daytona
Ferriola, Constantino, Nativity, Longwood
Fisher, William, Jr., St. Patrick, Mount Dora
Foy, Les, Holy Name of Jesus, Indialantic
Garcia, Jose M., Good Shepherd, Orlando
Gassman, Joseph, Holy Name of Jesus, Indialantic
Gaucher, Paul, St. Patrick, Mt. Dora
Gaudioso, Robert D., St. Rose of Lima, Poinciana
Gibbs, Marshall, St. Mary Magdalen, Altamonte Springs
Giel, Frederick, St. Timothy, Lady Lake
Gil, Luis, St. Rose of Lima, Poinciana
Giron, Jose, St. Lawrence, Bushnell
Gonzales, Rafael, Blessed Sacrament, Clermont
Gonzalez, Jose, St. Isaac Jogues, Orlando
Gonzalez, Ricardo, Our Lady of the Lakes, Deltona
Grant, Frederick, Blessed Sacrament, Clermont
Gravois, John, Nativity, Longwood
Gray, David, Cathedral of St. James, Orlando
Gubatan, Nemsy, St. Margaret Mary, Winter Park
Gutierrez, Albert, Our Lady of Grace, Palm Bay
Hamilton, James J., Our Lady of the Springs, Ocala
Hart, Vernon, Basilica of St. Paul, Daytona
Herbert, Larry, St. Francis of Assisi, Apopka
Hernandez, Francisco, St. Joseph, Lakeland
Hernandez, Rafael, St. Andrew, Orlando
Howell, John, Our Lady of the Springs, Ocala
Humphrey, Frank, Our Lady Star of the Sea, New Symrna Beach
Interlandi, Joseph, St. John the Baptist, Dunnellon
Kasetta, Richard, St. Timothy, Lady Lake
Keehner, Ron, St. Peter, DeLand
Kelly, Gerard, St. Mary Magdalen, Altamonte Springs
Kinsey, Robert, St. Peter, DeLand
Kloznick, Robert, St. Isaac Jogues, Orlando
Knight, Samuel, Holy Spirit, Lake Wales
Kreps, Bob, St. Margaret Mary, Winter Park
L'Huillier, Ron, St. Timothy, Lady Lake
L'Huillier, Ron, St. Timothy, Lady Lake
Laboy, Pedro, St. Isaac, Jogues, Orlando
Lacsamana, Manuel, Holy Redeemer, Kissimmee
Lafleur, Normand, St. Theresa, Belleview
Lammers, Jack, St. Joseph of the Forest Mission, Silver Springs
Landers, Robert, St. Paul, Daytona Beach
Landry, John, St. Joseph, Winter Haven
LaPlante, Robert, St. Peter, DeLand
LaPointe, Leonard, St. Clare, Deltona
Lathan, Jim, St. Ann, DeBary
Lendoiro, Orlando, St. Isaac Jogues, Orlando
Leonhardt, George, Jr., St. Paul, Leesburg
Levesque, Norman, St. Peter, Winter Park; St. Paul, Winter Park
Libersat, Henry, St. Mary Magdalen, Altamonte Springs
Lysaght, Evan, Our Lady of Lourdes, Daytona
Mador, Joseph, St. Vincent de Paul, Wildwood
Maldonado, Eliezer, St. Catherine of Siena, Kissimmee
Mallon, Charles A., Holy Family, Orlando
Martin, James, Holy Spirit, Lake Wales
Martin, John R., Holy Family, Orlando
Martinez, Antonio, Resurrection, Lakeland
Mattison, George, St. Timothy, Lady Lake
McAvoy, Patrick, Holy Family, Orlando
McCarthy, Dana G., St. Vincent de Paul Mission, Wildwood
McDonald, Francis L., St. Mary of the Lakes, Eustis
McElwee, Michael, Ascension, Melbourne
McGinnity, Michael, St. Paul, Leesburg
Mejia, Rafael, St. Isaac, Jogues, Orlando
Michels, Alan, St. Joseph, Palm Bay
Molina, Fred, Blessed Sacrament, Clermont
Monat, Noe, St. Ann, Haines City
Money, Kenneth, Holy Cross, Orlando
Montanez, Felix, St. Isaac Jogues, Orlando
Morales, Angel, St. John Vianney, Orlando
Morales, Ramon, Holy Cross, Orlando
Morillo, Felix M., Good Shepherd Parish, Orlando
Muller, Hugh W., St. John the Evangelist, Viera
Multeri, James R., All Souls, Sanford
Murello, Andrew, St. Mary's, Rockledge
Murphy, Mike, St. Mary's, Rockledge
Murray, Thomas A., Sacred Heart, New Smyrna Beach
Neris, Susano, Holy Redeemer, Kissimmee
Nevarez, Ramon, St. Clare, Deltona
Nichols, Nick, Sts. Peter & Paul, Winter Park
Nugent, Michael J., Epiphany, Port Orange
Nunez, Ernesto, St. Catherine of Siena, Kissimmee
O'Hern, Eugene J., Blessed Sacrament, Cocoa
Orbon, Carl, Holy Family, Orlando
Ossa, Ovidio, St. John Vianney, Orlando
Otradovec, Byron, St. Vincent de Paul, Wildwood
Oullette, Lucain, St. Matthew, Winter Haven
Oyola, Angel, St. Catherine of Siena, Kissimmee
Pacheco, Angel, St. Isaac Jogues, Orlando
Pagan, Miguel A., St. Maximilian Kolbe, Orlando
Pallo, Daniel, St. Vincent de Paul, Wildwood
Perez, Arcelio, Our Lady of Lourdes, Melbourne
Pettengill, Howard, Jr., Immaculate Conception, Melbourne Beach
Pettit, Michael, Our Lady of Hope, Port Orange
Pineiro, Ismael, Blessed Sacrament, Clermont
Pleus, Robert, Holy Family, Orlando
Radford, Richard, St. Vincent de Paul, Wildwood
Ramos, Jose Vidal, St. Rose of Lima, Poinciana
Ramos, Jose A., St. Ann, Haines City
Raymond, Donald, Holy Spirit, Lake Wales
Reilly, Eugene, Hospital Chaplain
Rhine, Jack, Our Lady of Grace, Palm Bay
Richiuso, Joseph, Holy Name of Jesus, Indialantic
Rinderle, Edward, St. Peter, Deland
Rivera, Vincente, Good Shepherd, Orlando
Robert, Joseph, St. Clare, Deltona
Rodriguez, Diego N., Resurrection, Lakeland
Roe, Robert, St. Joseph, Lakeland
Roman, Luis, Blessed Sacrament, Clermont
Rumplasch, John, St. Mark the Evangelist, Summerfield
Santiago, Santos, St. Jude, Ocala
Schneider, Paul A., Blessed Sacrament, Clermont
Schwartz, James, Blessed Trinity, Ocala
Seidel, James, Holy Name of Jesus, Indialantic
Serrano, Jose, St. Jude, Ocala
Shelley, Jim G., St. Francis of Assisi. Apopka
Shortell, Mike, Blessed Sacrament, Clermont
Skinner, Walter A., Jr., Nativity Catholic Church, Longwood
Smith, Gerard F., St. Peter, DeLand
Somma, Alfred P., St. Joseph, Palm Bay
Stauffacher, Thomas, Ascension, Melbourne
Stokes, James, St. Joseph, Palm Bay
Sullivan, John, St. Timothy, Lady Lake
Tagye, Thomas A., Our Lady of Hope, Port Orange
Tate, Tommy L., Holy Redeemer, Kissimmee
Thomas, Walther, St. Vincent de Paul, Wildwood
Torres, Gilberto, St. Clare, Deltona
Trunzo, Vincent, Holy Name of Jesus, Indialantic
Vargas, Juan, St. Catherine of Siena, Kissimmee
Vaughn, Jerry, Sts. Peter & Paul, Winter Park
Volkerson, Paul, St. Charles Borromeo, Orlando
Wanca, William T., Sr., Our Lady of Grace, Palm Bay; Tourism Ministry
Warner, Donald, Sts. Peter & Paul, Winter Park
Whale, William, Epiphany, Port Orange
Wiencek, Bruno, St. Lawrence, Bushnell
Wilson, Edward, St. Jude, Ocala
Wortman, Joseph, Resurrection, Lakeland

INSTITUTIONS LOCATED IN THE DIOCESE

[A] HIGH SCHOOLS, DIOCESAN AND PAROCHIAL

ORLANDO. *Bishop Moore Catholic High School Inc.* (1954) 3901 Edgewater Dr., 32804. Tel: 407-293-7561; Fax: 407-296-8135. Email: kanem@bishopmoore.org. Web: www.bishopmoore.org. Revs. Vilaire Philius, Chap.; Gilbert Medina, Chap.; Maureen Kane, Prin. & Pres.; Gail Boudreaux, Librarian. Lay Teachers 86; Students 1,170; Total Staff 16.

DAYTONA BEACH. *Father Lopez Catholic High School, Inc.*, 3918 LPGA Blvd., 32124. Tel: 386-253-5213; Fax: 386-252-6101. Email: gpressey@fatherlopez.org. Web: www.fatherlopez.org. Mr. George Pressey, Prin.; E. Lee Phillips, Media Specialist. Lay Teachers 25; Total Staff 43; Students 325.

LAKELAND. *Santa Fe Catholic High School, Inc.* (1960) 3110 Highway 92 E., 33801. Tel: 863-665-4188; Fax: 863-665-4151. Email: gcote@santafecatholic.org. Web: www.santafecatholic.org. Gwen Cote, Pres.; Cheryl Newhouse, Librarian. Sisters 1; Lay Teachers 24; Students 253; Brothers 1.

MELBOURNE. *Central Catholic High School, Inc.*, 100 E. Florida Ave., 32901. Tel: 321-727-0793; Fax: 321-727-1134. Email: rauchs@melbournecc.org. Web: melbournecc.org. Rev. Michael Di Renzo; Ms. Susan Rauch, Prin.; Mrs. Bonnie Priester, Librarian; Matt Gifford. Priests 1; Lay Teachers 32; Students 350.

OCALA. *Trinity Catholic High School, Inc.* (2000) 2600 S.W. 42nd St., 34471. Tel: 352-622-9025; Fax: 352-861-8164. Email: daubin@tchs.us. Web: www.trinitycatholichs.org. Bro. Daniel Aubin, F.S.C., Pres.; Rev. Patrick J. Sheedy, School Pastor; Mrs. Lila Vivi, Librarian. Brothers 3; Lay Teachers 42; Students 553.

[B] SPECIAL SCHOOLS

ORLANDO. *Morning Star School* (1960) 954 Leigh Ave., 32804-2299. Tel: 407-295-3077; Fax: 407-522-1700. Email: mss954@aol.com. Kathryn Harding, Ph.D., Prin. School for Exceptional Children. Sisters of St. Joseph of St. Augustine 1; Lay Teachers 8; Students 60.

[C] HOUSING ACCOMMODATIONS FOR THE ELDERLY

ORLANDO. *St. Joseph's Garden Court, Inc.*, 1515 N. Alafaya Trail, 32828. Tel: 407-382-0808; 407-470-1357 (Catholic Charities); Fax: 407-382-0812; 407-657-5648.

Monsignor Bishop Manor, Inc., 815 Borders Cir., Ste. 144, 32808. Tel: 407-293-3339; Fax: 407-293-0085. Total Staff 5; Total in Residence 215.

DAYTONA BEACH. *Casa San Pablo*, 401 N. Ridgewood Ave., 32114. Tel: 386-253-2828; Fax: 386-253-0842. Barbara D. Mitchell, Admin. Total in Residence 64; Total Staff 7.

MELBOURNE. *Ascension Manor* (1995) 2960 Pineapple Ave., 32935. Tel: 321-757-9828; Fax: 321-752-9437; Teletype: 800-955-8771. Email: ascensionmanor@carteretmgmt.com. Josephine Stratford, Mgr. Total in Residence 80; Total Staff 9.

OCALA. *Trinity Villas I, Inc.*, 3728 N.E. 8th Pl., 34470-1093. Tel: 352-694-5507; Fax: 352-694-1434. Email: dcrawford@trinityvilla.cfcoxmail.com. Debra Crawford, Mgr. Total in Residence 98; Total Staff 5.

Trinity Villas II, Inc., 3728 N.E. 8th Pl., 34470-1093. Tel: 352-694-5507; Fax: 352-694-1434. Email: dcrawford@trinityvilla.cfcoxmail.com. Debra Crawford, Mgr. Total in Residence 64; Total Staff 3.

ORMOND BEACH. *Prince of Peace Housing, Inc. dba Prince of Peace Villas* (1996) 664 S. Nova Rd., 32174. Tel: 386-673-5080; Fax: 386-673-2008. Email: cmartin@carteretmgmt.com. Carol Martin-Ryan, Mgr. Total in Residence 70; Total Staff 5.

PORT ORANGE. *Epiphany Manor* (1989) 4792 S. Ridgewood Ave., 32127. Tel: 386-767-2556; Fax: 386-761-0490. Email: cstefano@carteretmgmt.com. Cheryl Stefano, Mgr. Total Residence 75; Total Staff 5; Apartment Units 72.

WINTER HAVEN. *Episcopal Catholic Apartments* (1974) 500 Ave. L, N.W., 33881. Tel: 863-299-4481; Fax: 863-299-5719. Haley Alam, Admin. Apartments 199; Total Staff 15.

[D] FAMILY CARE FACILITIES

SAINT CLOUD. *Bishop Grady Villas* (2004) 401 Bishop Grady Ct., 34769. Tel: 407-892-6078; Fax: 407-892-3081. Web: www.bishopgradyvillas.org. Kevin Johnson, Exec. Dir. Bed Capacity 48; Total Assisted Annually 74; Total Staff 39.

[E] RETREAT CENTERS

WINTER PARK. *San Pedro Spiritual Development Center*, 2400 Dike Rd., 32792. Tel: 407-671-6322; Fax: 407-671-3992. Email: info@sanpedrocenter.org. Web: www.sanpedrocenter.org. Rev. J. Patrick Quinn, Admin. Total in Residence 5; Total Staff 16.

Friars on Staff: Revs. David Kaczmarek, T.O.R.; John Vianney Cunningham, T.O.R.; Bro. Truong Tello Vu, T.O.R.; Rev. Benjamin A. Berinti, C.PP.S., V.F.

Friars in Residence: Rev. Patrick Seelman, T.O.R. (Retired).

[F] MONASTERIES AND RESIDENCES OF PRIESTS AND BROTHERS

COCOA BEACH. *Congregation of Holy Cross, Eastern Province*, 325 Arthur Ave., 32931-4065. Tel: 321-799-8383; Fax: 321-783-6312. Email: thelodge@cfl.rr.com. Revs. Robert Brennan, C.S.C.; Joseph J. Long, C.S.C. (Retired); James Murphy, C.S.C., Asst. Supr.; Laurence Olszewski, C.S.C.; Bros. William Farrell, C.S.C.; Dennis Fleming, C.S.C., Supr.; Herman Zaccarelli, C.S.C.; Gerard Suddick, C.S.C., (Retired); Joseph Umile, C.S.C.; Revs. Gorge B. Mulligan, C.S.C.; Kenneth J. Silvia, C.S.C.; Frank A. Taste, C.S.C. Priests 7; Brothers 5; Total Staff 4.

DELAND. *Augustinian Monks of the Primitive Observance*, 2075 Mercers Fermery Rd., 32720. Tel: 386-736-4321. Email: monks@augustinianmonks.com. Web: www.augustinianmonks.com. Rev. Seamus, O.S.A.Prim., Abbot/Pres.

KISSIMMEE. *Presentation Brothers*, 1602 Pettis Blvd., 34741-3117. Tel: 407-846-2033; Fax: 407-846-7473. Email: fpm1802@Juno.com. Web: www.presentationbrothers.com. Bros. Francis Sebo, F.P.M.; Gerard Despathy, F.P.M., Prov. Supr.; Francis Schafer, F.P.M., Community Leader; James Needham, F.P.M.

NEW SMYRNA BEACH. *St. Alphonsus Villa-Redemptorist Fathers and Brothers*, 318 N. Riverside Dr., P.O. Box 548, 32170-0548. Tel: 386-428-6481. Very Rev. Jerome L. Chavarria, C.Ss.R., Rector; Revs. George F. Kelly, C.Ss.R. (Retired); Vincent Douglass, C.Ss.R. (Retired); Joseph Gorney, C.Ss.R. (Retired); Karl Aschmann, C.Ss.R. (Retired); Donald J. Winter, C.Ss.R. (Retired); Eugene Daigle, C.Ss.R. (Retired); Bros. Frank Roberts, C.Ss.R.; Christopher Walsh, C.Ss.R., Admin.; Rev. David Skarda, C.Ss.R. Total in Residence 10; Total Staff 8.

Redemptorist Fathers of the Vice Province of Richmond, 313 Hillman St., P.O. Box 1529, 32170. Tel: 386-427-3094; Fax: 386-423-1270. Email: vprichmond@aol.com. Very Rev. Jerome L. Chavarria, C.Ss.R., Vice Prov. & Supr.; Revs. Glenn D. Parker, C.Ss.R., Consultor; Peter Sousa, C.Ss.R., Vice Prov. Vicar.

Redemptorists Fathers of Florida, Inc.; Redemptorists Fathers of South Carolina; Redemptorists Fathers of North Carolina, Inc.; Redemptorists Fathers of Virginia, Incorporated; Redemptorists Fathers of Georgia, Incorporated. Total in Residence 1; Total Staff 1.

Villa Madonna, 4385 Saxon Dr., 32169. Tel: 386-427-4660. Email: seraphintor@aol.com. Very Rev. Seraphin J. Conley, T.O.R. (Retired). Email: seraphintor@aol.com; Rev. Emile A. Gentile, T.O.R., Contact Person (Retired).

OCALA. *Congregation of Christian Brothers* (1802) (Congregation) (Edmund Rice Christian Brothers North America), 1384 S.E. 54th Pl., 34480-5760. Tel: 352-622-1374; Fax: 352-861-8164. Email: daubin@tchs.org. Web: www.trinitycatholichs.org. Bros. Daniel Aubin, F.S.C., Pres.; F. Damian Ryan, C.F.C.; Francis Gammaro, C.F.C. Edmund Rice Brothers 2; De La Salle Christian Brothers 1.

WINTER PARK. *Franciscan Friars, T.O.R., San Pedro Friary*, 2400 Dike Rd., 32792. Tel: 407-671-6322; Fax: 407-671-3992. Email: info@sanpedrocenter.org. Web: www.sanpedrocenter.org. Revs. J. Patrick Quinn; David Kaczmarek, T.O.R.; Vianney Cunningham, T.O.R.; Bro. Truong Tello Vu, T.O.R.; Rev. Benjamin A. Berinti, C.PP.S., V.F. For detailed information of staff and residences in this diocese, please see Retreat Centers in the Institution section. Priests 4; Brothers 1; Total in Residence 5; Total Staff 16. In Res. Rev. Patrick Seelman, T.O.R. (Retired).

[G] CAMPUS MINISTRY

ORLANDO. *Catholic Campus Ministry at the University of Central Florida* 12094 Collegiate Way, 32817. Tel: 407-382-7063; Fax: 407-382-7073. Email: info@ccmknights.com. Web: www.ccmknights.com. Mailing Address: P.O. Box 677145, 32867. Very Rev. Stephen D. Parkes, V.F., Campus Min.; Rev. Jorge Torres, Campus Min.; Tony Marco, Assoc. Campus Min.; Michelle Ducker, Admin. & Communications.

Embry-Riddle Aeronautical University (1926) *Office of Campus Ministry-Interfaith Chapel*, Interfaith Chapel, 600 S. Clyde Morris Blvd., Daytona Beach, 32114-3900. Tel: 386-226-6580; Fax: 386-226-7370. Email: dbcsu@erau.edu. Web: www.dbcsu.org.

600 S. Clyde Morris Blvd., Daytona Beach, 32114-3900. Tel: 386-226-6581; Fax: 386-226-7370. Email: dalyt@erau.edu. Rev. Timothy P. Daly, Catholic Chaplain, Catholic Ministry.

DELAND. *Stetson University Catholic Campus Ministry* 359 W. New York Ave., 32720. Tel: 386-822-6000; Fax: 386-822-6034. Web: www.stpeterdeland.net. Rev. Thomas Connery; Rick Grinstead, Campus Min. Total Staff 2.

LAKELAND. *Florida Southern College Newman Center* c/o St. Joseph, 210 W. Lemon St., 33815. Tel: 863-682-0555; Fax: 863-686-9546. Email: rayboletti@msn.com. Web: www.stjosephlakeland.org. Rev. Ramon Bolatete, Chap. Total in Residence 1; Total Staff 1.

MELBOURNE. *Florida Institute of Technology Campus Ministry* (1958) 150 W. University Blvd., 32901-6988. Tel: 321-674-8045; Fax: 321-674-8938. Email: dbailey@fit.edu. Web: www.fit.edu. Rev. Douglas S. Bailey, S.D.S. Total Staff 1.

WINTER PARK. *Rollins College Campus Ministry* c/o St. Margaret Mary, 526 Park Ave. N., 32789. Tel: 407-647-3392; Fax: 407-647-4492. Web: stmargaretmary.org.

[H] MISCELLANEOUS

ORLANDO. **Catholic Volunteers in Florida, Inc.*, P.O. Box 536476, 32853-6476. Tel: 407-382-7071; Fax: 407-382-7073. Email: volunteer@cvif.org. Web: www.cvif.org. Sr. Florence Bryan, S.S.J., Dir. Site Placements/Formation; Candance Thompson, Dir. Prog./Opers.; Ms. Elaine Fowler, Exec. Dir. National recruitment for statewide (FL) placement of full-time volunteers in one-year service assignments. Co-sponsored by Florida's bishops, Sisters of St. Joseph of St. Augustine, FL, and New Hope Charities. The Episcopal Advisor is Most Reverend John H. Ricard, S.S.J. of the Diocese of Pensacola-Tallahassee. Lay Volunteers 19; Total Staff 3.

The Florida Catholic Serving the Dioceses of Orlando, Palm Beach & Venice., Mailing Address: P.O. Box 4993, 32802. Tel: 407-373-0075; Fax: 407-373-0087. Carol Brinati, Acting Associate Publisher.

APOPKA. **Diocesan Council of Orlando, Society of St. Vincent DePaul, Inc.*, 770 S. Orange Blossom Trail, 32703. Tel: 407-880-3126; Fax: 407-886-0030. James Barbarino, Business Mgr.

RELIGIOUS INSTITUTES OF MEN REPRESENTED IN THE DIOCESE

For further details refer to the corresponding bracketed number in the Religious Institutes of Men or Women section.

[]—*Congregation of Christian Brothers* (Eastern U.S. American Province)—C.F.C.
[0220]—*Congregation of the Blessed Sacrament*—S.S.S.
[0610]—*Congregation of the Holy Cross (Southern Province)*—C.S.C.
[]—*Congregation of the Holy Spirit*
[1000]—*Congregation of the Passion*—C.P.
[0520]—*Franciscan Fathers*—O.F.M.
[]—*Legionaries of Christ*—L.C.
[0760]—*Marist Fathers Society of Mary*—S.M.
[0720]—*Missionaries of Our Lady of LaSalette*—M.S.
[]—*Missionaries of St. Charles*—C.S.
[]—*Missionhurst Congregation of the Immaculate Heart of Mary*—C.I.C.M.
[0910]—*Oblates of Mary Immaculate*—O.M.I.
[]—*Order of Discalced Carmelites*
[]—*Order of Preachers*
[]—*Order of St. Paul the First Hermit*
[]—*Presentation Brothers*—F.P.M.
[1070]—*Redemptorist Fathers (Baltimore Province)*—C.SS.R.
[]—*Society of African Missions*—S.M.A.
[1200]—*Society of the Divine Savior*—S.D.S.
[]—*Society of the Divine Savior (Polish Province)*
[1060]—*Society of the Precious Blood (Cincinnati Province)*—C.PP.S.
[]—*St. Joseph Society of the Sacred Heart*—S.S.J.
[0560]—*Third Order Regular of Saint Francis (Province of the Immaculate Conception)*—T.O.R.

RELIGIOUS INSTITUTES OF WOMEN REPRESENTED IN THE DIOCESE

[]—*Congregation of Divine Providence*
[]—*Immaculate Heart of Mary Reparatrix*
[]—*Incarnatio Consecratio Mission*
[]—*Irish Sisters of Mercy*
[]—*Mission Helpers of Sacred Heart*
[]—*Order of St. Ursula*
[3320]—*Presentation Sisters of the Blessed Virgin Mary*—P.B.V.M.
[]—*Religious Sisters Filippini*
[]—*Servants of Mary*
[]—*Sisters of Charity of Seton Hall*
[]—*Sisters of Charity of the Blessed Virgin Mary*
[]—*Sisters of the Good Shepherd*
[]—*Sisters of Mercy of the Americas*
[]—*Sisters of Notre Dame-Chardon*
[]—*Sisters of Notre Dame de Namur*
[]—*Sisters of St. Benedict of St. Agnes (African)*
[]—*Sisters of St. Dominic (Adrian)*
[]—*Sisters of St. Dominic (St. Catherine de Ricci)*
[]—*Sisters of St. Dominic (Sinsinawa)*
[]—*Sisters of St. Francis of Christian Charity*
[]—*Sisters of St. Francis of the Holy Family*
[]—*Sisters of St. Joseph*
[]—*Sisters of St. Joseph (St. Augustine)* St. Augustine, Fl
[]—*Sisters of the Holy Names of Jesus and Mary*
[]—*Sisters of the Immaculate Heart of Mary*

NECROLOGY

(No Deaths)

An asterisk (*) denotes an organization that has established tax-exempt status directly with the IRS and is not covered by the USCCB Group Ruling.

Diocese of Owensboro

(Dioecesis Owensburgensis)

Most Reverend

WILLIAM F. MEDLEY

Bishop of Owensboro; ordained May 22, 1982; appointed Bishop of Owensboro December 15, 2009; ordained February 10, 2010. *Mailing Address: 600 Locust St., Owensboro, KY 42301.*

Catholic Pastoral Center: 600 Locust St., Owensboro, KY 42301. Tel: 270-683-1545; Fax: 270-683-6883.

Web: www.owensborodio.org

Email: ja@pastoral.org

Most Reverend

JOHN J. MCRAITH, D.D.

Bishop Emeritus of Owensboro; ordained February 21, 1960; appointed October 23, 1982; consecrated December 15, 1982; retired January 5, 2009. *Res. & Mailing: 501 W. Fifth St., Owensboro, KY 42301.*

CREATED DECEMBER 9, 1937.

Square Miles 12,502.

Erected February 23, 1938.

Comprises the following thirty-two Counties in the western part of the State of Kentucky: Allen, Ballard, Breckinridge, Butler, Caldwell, Calloway, Carlisle, Christian, Crittenden, Daviess, Edmonson, Fulton, Graves, Grayson, Hancock, Henderson, Hickman, Hopkins, Livingston, Logan, Lyon, McCracken, McLean, Marshall, Muhlenberg, Ohio, Simpson, Todd, Trigg, Union, Warren and Webster.

For legal titles of parishes and diocesan institutions, consult the Catholic Pastoral Center.

STATISTICAL OVERVIEW

Personnel	
Bishop	1
Retired Bishops	1
Priests: Diocesan Active in Diocese	52
Priests: Diocesan Active Outside Diocese	1
Priests: Retired, Sick or Absent	20
Number of Diocesan Priests	73
Religious Priests in Diocese	18
Total Priests in Diocese	91
Extern Priests in Diocese	13
Ordinations:	
Diocesan Priests	2
Permanent Deacons in Diocese	3
Total Brothers	1
Total Sisters	179
Parishes	
Parishes	79
With Resident Pastor:	
Resident Diocesan Priests	38
Resident Religious Priests	12
Without Resident Pastor:	
Administered by Priests	25
Administered by Religious Women	1
Administered by Lay People	3
Professional Ministry Personnel:	
Sisters	12
Lay Ministers	60
Welfare	
Catholic Hospitals	1
Total Assisted	268,590
Homes for the Aged	2
Total Assisted	210
Day Care Centers	3
Total Assisted	218
Specialized Homes	1
Total Assisted	16
Special Centers for Social Services	2
Total Assisted	9,469
Educational	
Diocesan Students in Other Seminaries	16
Seminaries, Religious	1
Total Seminarians	16
Colleges and Universities	1
Total Students	719
High Schools, Diocesan and Parish	3
Total Students	732
Elementary Schools, Diocesan and Parish	15
Total Students	3,267
Catechesis/Religious Education:	
High School Students	1,155
Elementary Students	3,274
Total Students under Catholic Instruction	9,163
Teachers in the Diocese:	
Priests	2
Sisters	16
Lay Teachers	325
Vital Statistics	
Receptions into the Church:	
Infant Baptism Totals	908
Minor Baptism Totals	112
Adult Baptism Totals	110
Received into Full Communion	240
First Communions	1,023
Confirmations	947
Marriages:	
Catholic	211
Interfaith	153
Total Marriages	364
Deaths	553
Total Catholic Population	51,241
Total Population	867,967

Former Bishops—Most Revs. FRANCIS R. COTTON, D.D., First Bishop of Owensboro; ord. June 17, 1920; appt. Dec. 16, 1937; cons. Feb. 24, 1938; died Sept. 25, 1960; HENRY J. SOENNEKER, D.D., Second Bishop of Owensboro; ord. May 26, 1934; appt. March 10, 1961; cons. April 26, 1961; installed May 9, 1961; retired June 17, 1982; died Sept. 24, 1987; JOHN J. MCRAITH, ord. Feb. 21, 1960; appt. Oct. 23, 1982; cons. Dec. 15, 1982; retired Jan. 5, 2009.

Catholic Pastoral Center—600 Locust St., Owensboro, 42301. Tel: 270-683-1545; Fax: 270-683-6883. Refer all official business to this address.

Vicar General—VACANT.

Clergy Personnel Director—Rev. DARRELL VENTERS, St. Jerome, 20 State Rte. 339 N., Fancy Farm, 42039. Mailing Address: P.O. Box 38, Fancy Farm, 42039-0038.

Chancellor—Sr. JOSEPH ANGELA BOONE, O.S.U.

Archivist—Sr. EMMA CECILIA BUSAM, O.S.U.

Diocesan Tribunal—

Judicial Vicar—Very Rev. J. MICHAEL CLARK, J.C.L.

Adjutant Judicial Vicar—VACANT.

Defenders of the Bond—Rev. JOSEPH M. MILLS, J.C.L. (Retired); Sr. MARGARET ALOKAN, O.S.F., J.C.L.

Judges—Revs. LEONARD J. ALVEY; JOHN R. VAUGHAN, J.C.D.; RICHARD MEREDITH; TITUS AHABYONA, J.C.L.; MAXWELL OKELLO, J.C.L.; CHARLES ZMUDZINSKI, C.P.M., J.C.L.

Advocates— Priests and pastoral ministers of the diocese.

Auditor and Case Promoter—Ms. LOUANNE PAYNE.

Notaries—Mrs. MARY ANN KURZ; Ms. LOUANNE PAYNE; Ms. SANDY MORRIS.

Clinical Psychologists (Periti)—Sr. VIVIAN MARIE BOWLES, O.S.U., Ed.D.; WILLIAM G. BACH, M.D.

Diocesan Boards and Councils

Diocesan Pastoral Council—

Consultors—Revs. ANTHONY BICKETT; D. ANDREW GARNER; BRUCE MCCARTY; JERRY RINEY; GERALD CALHOUN; DARRELL VENTERS; MICHAEL WILLIAMS.

Deans/Coordinators—Revs. FRANK RUFF, G.H.M., Bowling Green; BRIAN JOHNSON, Eastern; BENJAMIN F. LUTHER, Hopkinsville; ANTHONY J. SHONIS, Central; JOHN R. VAUGHAN, J.C.D., Owensboro West; PATRICK M. BITTEL, Owensboro East; BRIAN ROBY, Paducah; JASON MCCLURE, The Lakes; KENNETH MIKULCIK, Fancy Farm.

Age Group Six Representative—Rev. Msgr. GEORGE H. HANCOCK.

Priests' Council—

Council of Religious—Sisters PAM MUELLER, O.S.U., Pres.; EULA JOHNSON, S.C.N., Treas.; DEBRA A. BAILEY, A.D.; ELAINE BURKE, O.S.U., Sec.; MARGARET ALOKAN, O.S.F., J.C.L.; SHARON MILLER, G.H.M.S.

Pastoral Office for Administration—Sr. JOSEPH ANGELA BOONE, O.S.U., Dir.; KAY HARDIN, Assoc. Dir.; ERNIE TALIAFERRO, Asst. Dir.

Pastoral Office for Stewardship—Mr. KEVIN KAUFFELD, Dir.

Committee for Administration—Mr. HOMER BARTON; Ms. JANET BERRY; Sr. BARBARA JEAN HEAD, O.S.U.; CHRIS D. MELTON; Mr. CHARLES KAMUF; Mr. JOSEPH HANCOCK; Mr. BOB OGLE; Revs. BRAD WHISTLE; GERALD CALHOUN; MARTIN E. HAYES; Mr. BRYAN BORDERS; Mr. MIKE THOMPSON.

Pastoral Office for Education—

Superintendent of Schools—Mr JAMES P. MATTINGLY.

Director of Office for Faith Formation—Ms. PATTY BLAIR, Dir. Lay Ministry & Formation; Ms. ELAINE ROBERTSON, Assoc. Dir. Faith Formation.

Committee for Education—Revs. GERALD CALHOUN; LARRY HOSTETTER, S.T.D.; Ms. SANDY MCALLISTER; Sisters MARY CELINE WEIDENBENNER, O.S.U.; KARLA KAELIN, O.S.U.; Mr. PAUL O'REILLY; Ms. ANN O'REILLY; Mr. GARY ERVIN; Ms. PAULA PAYNE; Mr. GEORGE BARBER; Ms. DUSTI BENSON; Ms. KIM HARDESTY; Ms. VICKIE STUMPH; Ms. ELLEN ANDERSON; Ms. DONNA FAVORS; Ms. MARIE NIMMO.

Director of Ecumenism—Very Rev. J. MICHAEL CLARK, J.C.L.
Youth Ministry—Ms. MELINDA PRUNTY, Dir.
Gasper River Catholic Youth Camp and Retreat Center—Mr. BEN WARRELL, Dir.
Director of Communications and Editor of the Diocesan Newspaper— "Western Kentucky Catholic" MEL HOWARD.
Television and Radio Broadcast Communications—Rev. JOHN R. MEREDITH, Dir.; Mr. CLIFF RUSSELL, Broadcast Consultant.
Pastoral Office for Worship—Rev. LARRY MCBRIDE, Dir.; Ms. MARTHA HAGAN, Assoc. Dir.; Mr. MIKE BOGDAN, Dir. Office for Music.
Diocesan Liturgical Committee—Revs. CARL MCCARTHY; LARRY MCBRIDE; ANTHONY BICKETT; Ms. MARTHA HAGAN; Ms. PATTY BROWN; Mr. MICHAEL BOGDAN; Ms. CLEO HIGDON; Sr. ALICIA COOMES, O.S.U.
Pastoral Office for Spiritual Life—Sr. AMELIA STENGER, O.S.U., Dir., Mount St. Joseph, 8001 Cummings Rd., Maple Mount, 42356. Tel: 270-229-0200; Fax: 270-229-0279.
Cursillo—Sr. ELAINE BURKE, O.S.U., Mount St. Joseph, 8001 Cummings Rd., Maple Mount, 42356. Tel: 270-229-4103, Ext. 720; Fax: 270-229-0279; CECILIA HAMILTON, Lay Dir., 4324 Landsdowne N., Owensboro, 42303. Tel: 270-926-4176.
Catholic Charities—RITA HEINZ, Dir. Programs, 600 Locust St., Owensboro, 42301. Tel: 270-683-1545. Board Members: MARK PFIEFER; Revs. ED BRADLEY; C. PHILLIP RINEY; Sisters LUCY BONIFAS, O.S.F.; JOSEPH ANGELA BOONE, O.S.U.; Ms. MARIANNE POTINA; PEGGY HOWARD; EDIE KEENEY; ROSE LOWERY; DAN FORTIER; TIM HAMMOND; ERIC HICKS; KATHLEEN BAUMGARTEN; JANE BROOKS; MARGARET FENWICK; VANCE WEBB; IGNATIUS C. PAYNE JR.
Catholic Campaign for Human Development—RICHARD MURPHY, Dir.
Catholic Relief Service—RICHARD MURPHY, Dir.
Pastoral Office for Social Concerns—RICHARD MURPHY, Dir.
Social Concerns Committee—RICHARD MURPHY; LIZ FRANCIS; SHEILA HOWARD; Ms. MARILYN CHANDLER; MARTHA CRABTREE; BERNADETTE HOWARD; SUZANNE ROSE; VERONICA WILHITE; Ms. DONNA FAVORS; MARTHA HOUSE; Sr. SUZANNE SIMS, O.S.U.; DARRELL HOWARD.
Office for Safe Environment for the Protection of Children and Young People—Ms. MOLLY THOMPSON, Coord.
Respect Life Office—RICHARD MURPHY.
African-American Office—VERONICA WILHITE, Dir.
Hispanic Office—LUIS AJU, Dir.
Justice for Immigrants—PATTI GUTIERREZ, Coord. Tel: 270-852-8372. Email: pattigutierrez@pastoral.org.
Pastoral Office of Family Life—BETTY MEDLEY, Dir.
Family Life Committee—BETTY MEDLEY; Mr. TOM HAYDEN; Ms. JOYCE HAYDEN; Ms. JUDY KAPELSOHN; Ms. GAIL CRITCHELOW; Mr. JERRY CRITCHELOW; Mr. DENNY MANN; Ms. TONYA BARR.
Natural Family Planning—Billings Ovulation Method: MICHELLE ROBERTS, Owensboro; MARTHA WINN, Bowling Green; RONI MUDD, Leitchfield. Creighton Model Method: SUZANNE PADGETT, Owensboro; PATTI GUTIERREZ, Owensboro; AMANDA REFFITT, Owensboro.
Society for the Propagation of the Faith—Rev. RAY CLARK.
Clergy Personnel Director—Rev. ANTHONY BICKETT.
Vicar of Clergy—Rev. DARRELL VENTERS.
Priest Personnel Committee—Revs. GERALD CALHOUN, Vicar Gen.; D. ANDREW GARNER, Dir. Vocations; LARRY HOSTETTER, S.T.D.; JOHN M. THOMAS; BENJAMIN F. LUTHER; JERRY RINEY; JASON WAYNE MCCLURE; DARRELL VENTERS, Vicar of Clergy.
Vocations Office—Rev. D. ANDREW GARNER, Dir., Catholic Pastoral Center, 600 Locust St., Owensboro, 42301-2130. Tel: 270-314-8152; Fax: 270-683-6883.
Ongoing Formation of Priests—Rev. RICHARD MEREDITH, St. Pius Tenth Parish, 3814 U.S. 60 E., Owensboro, 42303. Tel: 270-684-4745; Fax: 270-684-2709.
**Roman Catholic Diocese of Owensboro Charitable Trust Fund, Inc.*Sr. JOSEPH ANGELA BOONE, O.S.U.; Most Rev. JOHN JEREMIAH MCRAITH; Rev. PAUL POWELL, J.C.L. (Retired); Mr. BOB OSBORNE; Mr. KEVIN KAUFFELD; Rev. C. PHILLIP RINEY.

Organizations

St. Vincent de Paul Society—IGNATIUS C. PAYNE JR., Diocesan Council Pres., 3880 Bordeaux Loop, S., Owensboro, 42303. Tel: 270-683-6525.
Scouting Activities—Rev. KENNETH MIKULCIK, Chap., St. Joseph Parish, 702 W. Broadway, Mayfield, 42066. Tel: 270-247-2843.
Holy Childhood Association—Rev. RAY CLARK.
Teens Encounter Christ—Rev. ERIC D. RILEY, Mailing Address: Holy Redeemer Parish, P.O. Box 106, Beaver Dam, 42320. Tel: 270-274-3414.
Legion of Mary—Rev. BENJAMIN F. LUTHER, Dir. Marian Chapters.
Serra Club—Rev. BRUCE MCCARTY, Chap.
Owensboro Chapter—GARY JACKSON, Pres. Tel: 270-926-4221.
Holy Name, Henderson Chapter—LARRY DENTON, Pres. Tel: 270-827-1368.
Mercy Health Partners - Lourdes, Inc.—1530 Lone Oak Rd., P.O. Box 7100, Paducah, 42002-7100. Tel: 270-444-2444; Fax: 270-444-2980. STEVEN GRINNELL, Pres. & CEO.
Victim Assistance Coordinator—RITA HEINZ. Tel: 270-683-1545. Email: heinzr@pastoral.org.
Birthright—TERRI LAHUGH, Dir., 512 W. 7th St., Owensboro, 42301. Tel: 270-683-1103. Email: birthright839@bellsouth.net. Hours: Mon.-Fri. 9am-noon.
Daughters of Isabella—Very Rev. Msgr. BERNARD POWERS, State Chap. (Retired); ANN NEWBY, State Regent. Tel: 270-685-4001; SHEILA THOMSON, Owensboro Circle #241 Regent. Tel: 270-683-2397; MARTHA FLOYD, Paducah Circle #258 St. Francis de Sales. Tel: 270-443-1640.

CLERGY, PARISHES, MISSIONS AND PAROCHIAL SCHOOLS

CITY OF OWENSBORO

(DAVIESS COUNTY)

1—ST. STEPHEN CATHEDRAL (1839) Revs. John R. Vaughan; Joshua A. McCarty, Parochial Vicar; Sr. Therese Francis Walker, M.S.B.T., Pastoral Assoc. & Dir. Faith Formation; Mr. Michael Conley, Dir. Music Ministry; Mr. Larry Lyon, Business Mgr.
Res.: 610 Locust St., 42301. Tel: 270-683-6525; Fax: 270-683-3621. Web: www.ststephencathedral.org.
Catechesis/Religious Program—Students 44.
Chapel—Blessed Sacrament [CEM] 602 Sycamore St., 42301. Tel: 270-926-4741. Veronica Wilhite, Admin.

2—BLESSED MOTHER (1948) Rev. John Meredith; Brett Ballard, Dir. Music; Jan Storm, Business Mgr. & Admin.; Darlene Quinn, Office Asst.
Office: 601 E. 23rd St., 42303. Tel: 270-683-8444; Fax: 270-683-6423.
Res.: 515 E. 22nd St., 42303. Tel: 270-688-9040.
Catechesis/Religious Program—Nicholas Hardesty, D.R.E.; Christina Best, Youth Min. Students 88.

3—THE IMMACULATE (1954) Rev. Anthony Jones; Kathy Rasp, Office Admin.
Parish Office—2516 Christie Pl., 42301. Tel: 270-683-0689; Fax: 270-926-9016.
Res.: 2601 Christie Pl., 42301.
Catechesis/Religious Program—Sr. Julia Head, O.S.U., D.R.E. Students 98.

4—SS. JOSEPH AND PAUL (1887) Revs. Carl McCarthy; Jean Rene Kalombo.
Res.: 609 E. 4th St., 42303. Tel: 270-683-5641; Fax: 270-685-4766. Web: www.stjpc.org.
Catechesis/Religious Program—423 Clay St., 42303. Tel: 270-683-5641. Students 84.
Mission—Good Samaritan Refugee Home 1601 Pearl St., Daviess Co. 42303.

5—OUR LADY OF LOURDES (1959) Rev. Brad Whistle.
Res.: 4029 Frederica St., 42301. Tel: 270-684-5369; Fax: 270-683-8008. Web: www.lourdescatholicchurch.com.
Catechesis/Religious Program—Drew Hardesty, D.R.E. Students 102.
Our Lady of Lourdes Day Care—4005 Frederica St., 42301. Tel: 270-926-6516. Children 69.

6—ST. PIUS TENTH (1957) Revs. Richard Meredith; Titus Ahabyona (Uganda), Parochial Vicar.
Mailing Address: 3418 US 60 E., 42303.
Res.: 3512 E. Sixth St., 42303. Tel: 270-684-5517; 270-684-4745 (Office); Fax: 270-684-2709. Web: stpiustenthparish.org.
Catechesis/Religious Program—Students 172.
St. Pius Tenth Day Care—Tel: 270-684-7456. Children 76.

7—PRECIOUS BLOOD (1960) Rev. Bruce McCarty.
3306 Fenmore St., 42301. Tel: 270-684-6888; Fax: 270-684-1304.
Catechesis/Religious Program—Sr. Rosanne Spalding, O.S.U., D.R.E. Students 43.
Precious Blood Day Care—3400 Fenmore St., 42301. Tel: 270-683-3012. Children 73.

8—ST. RAPHAEL (1842) [CEM] Closed. Records at Diocesan Archives, 600 Locust St., Owenboro, Tel: 270-683-1545. St. Raphael Cemetery, est. 1847, became interparochial when church burned in 1983.

OUTSIDE THE CITY OF OWENSBORO

AURORA, MARSHALL CO., ST. HENRY (1967) [CEM] Rev. Babu Kulathumkal (India).
Church: 16097 U.S. Hwy. 68 E., Hardin, 42048. Tel: 270-474-8058; Fax: 270-474-9867. Web: sainthenryparish.com.
Catechesis/Religious Program—Students 15.

AXTEL, BRECKINRIDGE CO., ST. ANTHONY (1812) [CEM] Rev. Maxwell Okello (Kenya).
Res.: 1654 S. Hwy. 79, Hardinsburg, 40143. Tel: 270-257-2132; Fax: 270-257-2137. Email: stanthony@bbtel.com.
Catechesis/Religious Program—Students 58.

BARDWELL, CARLISLE CO., ST. CHARLES (1891) [CEM] Rev. Masilamani Suvakkin, H.G.N. (India).
Res.: 6922 State Rte. 408, 42023. Tel: 270-642-2586; Fax: 270-642-2222. Email: ssdcpastor@wk.net. Web: www.stcharles-bardwell.org.
Catechesis/Religious Program—Students 39.

BEAVER DAM, OHIO CO., HOLY REDEEMER (1962) Rev. Eric D. Riley.
13th & Madison Sts., P.O. Box 106, 42320. Tel: 270-274-3414.
Office: P.O. Box 106, 42320. Tel: 270-274-3414; Fax: 270-274-4245.
Catechesis/Religious Program—Students 63.

BIG CLIFTY, GRAYSON CO., ST. MARY, Closed. Records kept at St. Paul's Church, 1821 St. Paul Rd., Leitchfield, KY 42754. Tel: 270-242-7436.

BOWLING GREEN, WARREN CO.

1—HOLY SPIRIT (1970) Revs. W. Jerry Riney; J. Raymond Goetz, Parochial Vicar.
Office: 4754 Smallhouse Rd., 42104. Tel: 270-842-7777. Web: www.holyspiritcatholic.org.
Catechesis/Religious Program—Lori Lewis, D.R.E. Students 763.

2—ST. JOSEPH'S (1859) Rev. Stan Puryear; John McAllister, Dir. Faith Formation; Deacon Robert Imel. In Res., Rev. Maurice J. Tiell (Retired).
Office: 434 Church Ave., 42101. Tel: 270-842-2525; Fax: 270-843-9624. Web: www.stjosephbg.com.
Res.: 401 Church Ave., 42101. Tel: 270-843-7568.
Catechesis/Religious Program—Students 89.

BROWN'S VALLEY, DAVIESS CO., ST. ANTHONY (1902) [CEM] Very Rev. J. Michael Clark, Pastor/Diocesan Admin.
Church: 261 St. Anthony Rd., Utica, 42376. Tel: 270-733-4341. Email: stabv@bellsouth.net. Web: www.stanthony.church-builder.com.
Catechesis/Religious Program—Students 68.

CADIZ, TRIGG CO., ST. STEPHEN (1966) Rev. Babu Kulathumkal (India); Ms. April Washer, C.R.E.
Res.: 1698 Canton Rd., 42211. Tel: 270-522-3801; Fax: 270-522-3901. Email: ststephencath387@bellsouth.net.
Catechesis/Religious Program—Students 33.

CALHOUN, MCLEAN CO., ST. SEBASTIAN (1871) [CEM] Rev. John Okoro (Nigeria).
180 State Rte. 136 W., 42327-9521.
Res.: 445 Main St., 42327-9521. Tel: 270-273-9268; Fax: 270-273-3185.
Catechesis/Religious Program—Students 60.

CALVERT CITY, MARSHALL CO., ST. PIUS TENTH (1954) Rev. Roy Anthony Stevenson.
Office: 777 Fifth Ave., P.O. Box 495, 42029. Tel: 270-395-4727; Fax: 270-395-5747. Email: stpiusx@newwavecomm.net. Web: www.stpiusx.us.
Res.: 723 Fifth Ave., 42029.
Church: 777 Fifth Ave., 42029.
Catechesis/Religious Program—Betty Lou Derry, D.R.E. Students 56.

CENTRAL CITY, MUHLENBERG CO., ST. JOSEPH (1886) Rev. Benjamin F. Luther; Sisters Rose Karen Johnson, O.S.U., Pastoral Assoc.; Rose Theresa Johnson, O.S.U., Pastoral Assoc.
Res.: 113 S. Third St., 42330. Tel: 270-754-1164; Fax: 270-754-1164.
Catechesis/Religious Program—Students 31.

CLARKSON, GRAYSON CO., ST. ELIZABETH OF HUNGARY (1906) [CEM] Rev. Martin E. Hayes.
Res.: 1821 St. Paul Rd., Leitchfield, 42754. Tel: 270-242-7436.
Church: 306 Clifty Ave., 42726. Tel: 270-242-4414. Email: stpaulgrayson@msn.com.
Catechesis/Religious Program—Students 29.

CLINTON, HICKMAN CO., ST. JUDE Rev. Shijo Vadakumkara, H.G.N. (India).
Mailing Address: 304 Mayfield Rd., 42031. Email: stjudeclinton@hotmail.com.
Church: 306 Mayfield Rd., 42031. Tel: 270-653-6869.
Catechesis/Religious Program—Students 11.

CLOVERPORT, BRECKINRIDGE CO., ST. ROSE (1857) [CEM] Rev. Gregory G. Trawick.
Res.: 118 Chestnut St., 40111. Tel: 270-788-6422; Fax: 270-788-6930.

Catechesis/Religious Program—Students 48.

CURDSVILLE, DAVIESS CO., ST. ELIZABETH Rev. Richard Powers (Retired); Judy Schadler, Contact Person.
Mailing Address: 6143 First St., P.O. Box 9-A, 42334. Tel: 270-229-4134. Email: selizabethville@gmail.com.

DAWSON SPRINGS, HOPKINS CO., RESURRECTION Rev. Bruce Fogle.
Church: 530 Industrial Park Rd., 42408. Tel: 270-383-4743; 270-797-8665.
Catechesis/Religious Program—Students 13.

EARLINGTON, HOPKINS CO., IMMACULATE CONCEPTION (1847) Rev. Bruce Fogle.
Res.: 112 S. Day St., 42410. Tel: 270-383-4743. Email: immaculatecc@bellsouth.net.
Catechesis/Religious Program—Students 13.

EDDYVILLE, LYON CO., ST. MARK CHURCH (1990) Rev. Thomas Shaiju, H.G.N. (India).
Res.: 302 Peachtree Ln., 42038. Tel: 270-365-6786.
Catechesis/Religious Program—Students 15.

ELKTON, TODD CO., ST. SUSAN (1965) Rev. Frank Ruff, G.H.M., Sacramental Min.; Jose Gallegos, Pastoral Assoc.; Ms. B. J. Asher, Parish Life Coord.
221 Allensville St., P.O. Box 788, 42220. Tel: 270-265-5263 (Office); Fax: 270-265-5288 (Office).
Catechesis/Religious Program—Students 6.

FANCY FARM, GRAVES CO., ST. JEROME (1836) [CEM] Rev. Darrell Venters.
Res.: P.O. Box 38, 42039. Tel: 270-623-8181; Fax: 270-623-6341. Email: stjerome@wk.net. Web: stjeromefancyfarm.org.
Catechesis/Religious Program—Students 187.

FANCY FARM, HICKMAN CO., ST. DENIS (1914) [CEM] Rev. Masilamani Suvakkin, H.G.N. (India).
Mailing Address: 6922 State Rte. 408, Bardwell, 42023. Tel: 270-642-2586; Fax: 270-642-2222.
Catechesis/Religious Program—Students 10.

FORDSVILLE, OHIO CO., ST. JOHN THE BAPTIST (1893) Rev. Eric D. Riley; Sr. Marie Michael Hayden, O.S.U., Pastoral Assoc.
66 Smith St., 42343. P.O. Box 127, 42343. Tel: 270-276-3619. Email: sjbccfordsville@bellsouth.net.
Catechesis/Religious Program—Students 14.

FRANKLIN, SIMPSON CO., ST. MARY (1880) [CEM] Rev. Robert Drury.
Res.: 403 N. Main St., P.O. Box 388, 42135-0388. Tel: 270-586-4515; Fax: 270-586-4549. Email: ccfk@bellsouth.net.
Catechesis/Religious Program—Students 50.

FULTON, FULTON CO., ST. EDWARD Rev. Shijo Vadakumkara, H.G.N. (India).
Res.: 504 Eddings St., 42041. Tel: 270-472-2742. Email: stedwardky@bellsouth.net.
Catechesis/Religious Program—Students 19.

GRAND RIVERS, LIVINGSTON CO., ST. ANTHONY OF PADUA (1986) Rev. Roy Anthony Stevenson.
Res.: 1518 J.H. O'Bryan Ave., P.O. Box 447, 42045. Church: Tel: 270-362-7121. Email: stpiusx@newwavecomm.net.
Catechesis/Religious Program—Students 6.

GRAYSON SPRINGS, GRAYSON CO., ST. AUGUSTINE (1815) [CEM] Rev. Brian A. Johnson.
Res. & Mailing Address: c/o St. Anthony Church, 1256 St. Anthony Church Rd., Clarkson, 42726. Tel: 270-242-4791; Fax: 270-242-2601.
Catechesis/Religious Program—Students 16.

GUTHRIE, TODD CO., STS. MARY & JAMES (1950) Rev. Frank Ruff, G.H.M., Sacramental Min.; Ms. B. J. Asher, Parish Life Coord.
313 3rd St., 42234. P.O. Box 325, 42234. Tel: 270-483-2571. Email: saintsusan@bellsouth.net.
Catechesis/Religious Program—Students 15.

HARDINSBURG, BRECKINRIDGE CO., ST. ROMUALD (1811) [CEM] Rev. Anthony Bickett. In Res., Rev. Dan Kreutzer.
Res.: 394 N. Hwy. 259, 40143. Tel: 270-756-2356; Fax: 270-756-2099. Email: stromuald@bbtel.com. Web: www.stromuald.org.
Catechesis/Religious Program—Students 95.

HAWESVILLE, HANCOCK CO., IMMACULATE CONCEPTION (1871) [CEM] Rev. Chrispin Q. B. Oneko (Kenya).
430 Main Cross, P.O. Box 219, 42348.
Res.: 190 Judith Lynn, P.O. Box 219, 42348. Tel: 270-927-8419; Fax: 270-927-6783.
Catechesis/Religious Program—Students 61.

HENDERSON, HENDERSON CO., HOLY NAME OF JESUS, [CEM] Revs. J. Edward Bradley; Anthony J. Shonis, Parochial Vicar; Sr. Margaret Ann Aull, O.S.U., Pastoral Assoc.
Res.: 511 Second St., 42420. Tel: 270-826-2096; Fax: 270-827-1494. Web: www.holynameparish.net.
School—(Grades PreK-8), 628 Second St., 42420. Tel: 270-827-3425; Fax: 270-827-4027. Web: www.holynameschool.org. Daryl Hagan, Prin. Ursuline Sisters 1; Lay Teachers 29; Students 514.
Catechesis/Religious Program—Students 218.

HENSHAW, UNION CO., ST. AMBROSE (1832) [CEM] Rev. Larry McBride.
Res.: *c/o St. Francis Borgia*, P.O. Box 256, Sturgis, 42459. Tel: 270-333-5915; Fax: 270-333-4342.
Church: 5914 S.R. 270 W., Morganfield, 42437. Tel: 270-333-1832; Fax: 270-333-1833. Email: ambrose1832@bellsouth.net. Web: www.saintambrosekentucky.org.
Catechesis/Religious Program—Tel: 270-333-2806. Students 13.

HICKMAN, FULTON CO., SACRED HEART (1853) Rev. Shijo Vadakumkara, H.G.N. (India); Butch Busby, Contact Person.
Res.: 411 Moulton St., 42050-1327. Tel: 270-236-2071.
Catechesis/Religious Program—1203 Lattus Rd., 42050. Tel: 270-236-4604. Students 8.

HOPKINSVILLE, CHRISTIAN CO., SS. PETER AND PAUL (1872) Revs. John M. Thomas; Jose Carmelo Jimenez (Mexico); Anthoni Ottagan, H.G.N.
Res.: 902 E. Ninth St., 42240. Tel: 270-885-8522; Fax: 270-885-5296. Web: www.stsppchurch.org.
Catechesis/Religious Program—Students 73.
School—(Grades PreK-8) Tel: 270-886-0172; Fax: 270-887-9924. Web: www.stsppschool.org. Sarah Kranz, Prin. Lay Teachers 10; Students 200.

IRVINGTON, BRECKINRIDGE CO., HOLY GUARDIAN ANGELS (1898) [CEM] Rev. Gregory G. Trawick.
301 W. High St., 40146. Tel: 270-547-2137. Email: holyguardianangel@hotmail.com.
Catechesis/Religious Program—Students 11.

KNOTTSVILLE, DAVIESS CO., ST. WILLIAM (1887) [CEM] Rev. Patrick M. Bittel.
Res.: 6007 St. Lawrence Rd., Philpot, 42366. Tel: 270-281-4802; Fax: 270-281-9556.
School—Mary Carrico Memorial School, (Grades K-8) Tel: 270-281-5526; Fax: 270-281-9556. Email: mcarrico144@yahoo.com. Mike Clark, Prin. Lay Teachers 9; Students 76.
Catechesis/Religious Program—Students 91.

LACENTER, BALLARD CO., ST. MARY (1907) [CEM] Rev. Julian Ibemere (Nigeria); Sr. Teresa Riley, O.S.U., Pastoral Assoc.
Church: 624 Broadway, P.O. Box 570, 42056. Tel: 270-665-5551 (Office); 270-665-5654 (Res.); Fax: 270-665-5551. Email: stmcc@brtc.net.

LEITCHFIELD, GRAYSON CO., ST. JOSEPH'S, [CEM] Rev. Randy Howard.
Res.: 109 W. Walnut St., 42754. Tel: 270-259-3028; Fax: 270-259-9860.
Catechesis/Religious Program—Students 70.

LEWISPORT, HANCOCK CO., ST. COLUMBA (1850) [CEM] Rev. Chrispin Q. B. Oneko (Kenya).
815 Pell St., 42351.
Res.: 190 Judith Lynn, P.O. Box 219, Hawesville, 42348. Tel: 270-927-8419; Fax: 270-927-6783.
Catechesis/Religious Program—Students 40.

LIVERMORE, MCLEAN CO., ST. CHARLES Rev. John Okoro (Nigeria).
Mailing Address: 180 Hwy. 136 W., Calhoun, 42327. Church: 506 Hill Ave., 42352. Tel: 270-273-3185; 270-273-9268 (Res.); Fax: 270-273-3185. Email: stsebch@bellsouth.net.

MADISONVILLE, HOPKINS CO., CHRIST THE KING (1969) Rev. Gerald Calhoun; Patricia L. Brown, Pastoral Assoc.
Res.: 1600 Kingsway Dr., 42431. Tel: 270-821-5494; Fax: 270-825-8612. Email: christthekingchu@bellsouth.net. Web: www.vci.net/~ctk.
School—(Grades PreK-8) Tel: 270-821-8271. Email: christschool@bellsouth.net. Larry Bishop, Prin.; SuzAnne Wilson, Librarian. Lay Teachers 8; Students 85.
Catechesis/Religious Program—Students 40.
Preschool—Tel: 270-821-3954. Students 62.

MARION, CRITTENDEN CO., ST. WILLIAM (1962) [CEM] Rev. Larry McBride.
Mailing Address: P.O. Box 343, 42064.
Res.: 1308 N. Adams, Sturgis, 42459.
Church: 860 S. Main St., 42064. Tel: 270-965-2477. Email: stwilliam@vci.net. Web: www.stwilliam-church.org.

MAYFIELD, GRAVES CO., ST. JOSEPH (1887) [CEM] Rev. Kenneth Mikulcik; Sr. Esperanza Rivera Gomez, M.A.G., Hispanic Ministry.
Res.: 702 W. Broadway St., 42066. Tel: 270-247-2843; Fax: 270-247-6835. Web: www.stjosephcatholic.com.
School—St. Joseph Catholic School, (Grades PreK-6), 112 S. 14th St., 42066. Tel: 270-247-4420; Fax: 270-247-2612. Susan Brinkley, Prin. Lay Teachers 5; Students 56.
Catechesis/Religious Program—Students 59.

MCQUADY, BRECKINRIDGE CO., ST. MARY-OF-THE-WOODS (1870) [CEM 2] Rev. Maxwell Okello (Kenya).
1654 Hwy. 79 S., Hardinsburg, 40143.
Church: 4711 Hwy. 105 S., Hardinsburg, 40143. Tel: 270-756-2093; Fax: 270-257-2137. Email: tmalewitz@mac.com.
Catechesis/Religious Program—Mr. Tom Malewitz, D.R.E. Students 40.

MORGANFIELD, UNION CO., ST. ANN (1877) [CEM] Revs. Gerald H. Baker; Richard Cash.
Res.: 304 Church St., 42437. Tel: 270-389-2287; Fax: 270-389-0219.
Catechesis/Religious Program—Students 49.

MORGANTOWN, BUTLER CO., HOLY TRINITY (1958) Rev. Eric D. Riley.
766 Logansport Rd., P.O. Box 222, 42261.
Res.: 117 13th Rd., P.O. Box 106, Beaver Dam, 42320. Tel: 270-274-3414.
Catechesis/Religious Program—Students 2.

MURRAY, CALLOWAY CO., ST. LEO (1933) Rev. Jason Wayne McClure; Deacon Joseph R. Ohnemus, Pastoral Assoc.; Sr. Esperanza Rivera Gomez, M.A.G., Hispanic Ministry.
Res.: 401 N. 12th St., 42071. Tel: 270-753-3876; Fax: 270-759-2074.
Catechesis/Religious Program—Allison Loomis, D.R.E. & Campus Min. Students 145.

OAK GROVE, CHRISTIAN CO., ST. MICHAEL THE ARCHANGEL (1995) Rev. David W. Kennedy; Deacon Jack Cheasty.
Church: 448 State Line Rd., P.O. Box 505, 42262. Tel: 270-640-9850; Fax: 931-552-5518. Email: stmichael1@bellsouth.net. Web: www.stmichael-archangel.org.
Catechesis/Religious Program—Students 121.

PADUCAH, MCCRACKEN CO.

1—ST. FRANCIS DE SALES (1848) [CEM] Rev. Brian Roby.
Church: 116 S. Sixth St., 42001. Tel: 270-442-1923; Fax: 270-443-4616. Email: sfds@vci.net. Web: www.stfrancisdesalespaducah.org.
Catechesis/Religious Program—Sr. Martha Keller, O.S.U., D.R.E. Students 46.

2—ST. JOHN THE EVANGELIST (1839) Rev. Tom Buckman; Hazel Wurth, Contact Person.
Parish Office: 6705 Old U.S. Hwy. 45, 42003. Tel: 270-554-3810; Fax: 270-534-9163. Web: www.stjohnspaducah.com.
Catechesis/Religious Program—Paducah Faith Formation, 1241 Elmdale Rd., 42003. Tel: 270-443-0295; Fax: 270-443-0295. Students 54.

3—ROSARY CHAPEL Revs. Brian Roby; Julian Ibemere (Nigeria), Parochial Vicar.
Catechesis/Religious Program—Students 9.
Chapel— 711 Ohio St., P.O. Box 1481, 42001. Tel: 270-444-6383; Fax: 270-444-0553. Email: rosary@bellsouth.net.

4—ST. THOMAS MORE (1944) [CEM] Revs. J. Patrick Reynolds; Daniel C. Dillard, Parochial Vicar; James Hess, Liturgy & Music Dir.; Sr. Imelda Quechol, M.A.G., Hispanic Ministry; Danny Thomas, Youth Min.; Donna Tarantino, Dir. Ministries & Volunteers; Missy Eckenberg, Dir. Devel.
Church: 5645 Blandville Rd., 42001-8722. Tel: 270-534-9000; Fax: 270-534-4339. Email: bulletin@stmore.org. Web: www.stmore.org.
Catechesis/Religious Program—Faith Formation, 1241 Elmdale Rd., 42003. Tel: 270-443-0295. Students 94.

PEONIA, GRAYSON CO., ST. ANTHONY (1822) [CEM] Rev. Brian A. Johnson.
Res.: 1256 St. Anthony Church Rd., Clarkson, 42726. Tel: 270-242-4791. Email: stanthony@usdol.net.
Catechesis/Religious Program—Students 35.

PHILPOT, DAVIESS CO., ST. LAWRENCE (1821) [CEM] Rev. Patrick M. Bittel.
Res.: 6007 St. Lawrence Rd., 42366. Tel: 270-281-4802; Fax: 270-281-9556. Web: www.swsl.org.

PRINCETON, CALDWELL CO., ST. PAUL (1874) [CEM] Rev. Thomas Shaiju, H.G.N. (India).
Res.: 813 S. Jefferson, 42445. Tel: 270-365-6786 (Rectory); 270-365-3645 (Office). Email: pesolomon@bellsouth.net.
Catechesis/Religious Program—Students 18.

PROVIDENCE, WEBSTER CO., HOLY CROSS Rev. Bruce Fogle.
112 S. Day St., Earlington, 42410.
Church: 730 North Highway 41A, 42450. Tel: 270-383-4743.
Catechesis/Religious Program—Students 7.

REED, HENDERSON CO., ST. AUGUSTINE (1896) [CEM] Rev. Suresh Bakka (India).
Res.: 81 Church St., 42301. Tel: 270-764-1691; Fax: 270-764-0444.
Church: 16777 Hwy. 60 E., 42451. Tel: 270-764-5599. Web: www.gus-n-pete.org.
Catechesis/Religious Program—Students 13.

ROME, DAVIESS CO., ST. MARTIN (1885) Rev. Peter Hughes.
Church: 5856 Kentucky 81, 42301. Tel: 270-685-0339; Fax: 270-684-5444. Email: stmartinrome@gmail.com.

RUSSELLVILLE, LOGAN CO., SACRED HEART (1873) Rev. Peter R. Stryker, C.P.M.
Res.: 296 W. 6th St., 42276. Tel: 270-726-6963; Fax: 270-726-2232. Email: email@sacredheartrussellville.org. Web: www.sacredheartrussellville.org.
Catechesis/Religious Program—Students 67.

ST. JOSEPH, DAVIESS CO., ST. ALPHONSUS (1854) [CEM] Rev. Richard Powers (Retired).
Mailing Address: 7925 KY 500, 42301. Tel:

270-229-4164.
Res.: 10500 McIntyre Rd, 42301. Fax: 270-229-4164. Email: st.alphonsus@netzero.net.
Catechesis/Religious Program—Students 60.

ST. PAUL, GRAYSON CO., ST. PAUL (1810) [CEM] Rev. Martin E. Hayes.
Res.: 1821 St. Paul Rd., Leitchfield, 42754. Tel: 270-242-7436. Email: stpaulgrayson@msn.com.
School—(Grades K-8), 1812 St. Paul Rd., Leitchfield, 42754. Tel: 270-242-7483. Email: saintpaulschool@windstream.net. Sr. Anne Michelle Mudd, O.S.U., Prin. Lay Teachers 3; Students 29.
Catechesis/Religious Program—Students 31.

SCOTTSVILLE, ALLEN CO., CHRIST THE KING (1964) Rev. Dennis Holly, G.H.M.; Catherine Grapes, Office Admin.
Res.: 298 Bluegrass Dr., P.O. Box 463, 42164. Tel: 270-237-4404. Email: christtheking@nctc.com. Web: www.scottsvilleky.catholicweb.com.
Catechesis/Religious Program—Students 22.

SEBREE, WEBSTER CO., ST. MICHAEL (1977) Rev. Al Bremer; Patti Gutierrez, Parish Life Coord.
Office: P.O. Box 705, 42455. Tel: 270-835-2584; Fax: 270-835-2584. Email: stmichaelsebree@gmail.com.
Catechesis/Religious Program—Students 22.

SORGHO, DAVIESS CO., ST. MARY MAGDALENE (1907) [JC] Rev. Mark A. Buckner.
Office: 7232 Kentucky 56, 42301. Tel: 270-771-4436; Fax: 270-771-4478. Email: pattibartley@yahoo.com.
Res.: Tel: 270-771-0729.
Catechesis/Religious Program—Tel: 270-771-4438. Debi Hopkins, D.R.E. Students 63.

STANLEY, DAVIESS CO., ST. PETER OF ALCANTARA (1873) [CEM 2] Rev. Suresh Bakka (India).
Res.: 81 Church St., 42301. Tel: 270-764-1983; Fax: 270-764-0444. Web: www.gus-n-pete.org. Email: stanette@gus-n-pete.org.
Catechesis/Religious Program—Students 13.

STURGIS, UNION CO., ST. FRANCIS BORGIA (1952) Rev. Larry McBride.
Mailing Address: P.O. Box 256, 42459.
Church: 1317 N. Main St., 42459. Tel: 270-333-5915; Fax: 270-333-4342. Email: saintfrancisborgia@yahoo.com.
Catechesis/Religious Program—1317 N. Main St., 42459. Tel: 270-333-2806; Fax: 270-333-4342. Students 9.

SUNFISH, EDMONSON CO., ST. JOHN THE EVANGELIST (1830) [CEM] Rev. Randy Howard.
Church: 430 St. John Church Rd., 42284. Tel: 270-259-3028; Fax: 270-259-9860.

UNIONTOWN, UNION CO., ST. AGNES (1859) [CEM] Rev. Terry Devine.
Mailing Address: P.O. Box 607, 42461.
Office: 504 Mulberry St., 42461.
Res.: 407 Fifth St., 42461. Tel: 270-822-4416; 270-822-4780 (Rectory); Fax: 270-822-5316. Email: stagnes@owens.twcbc.com.
Church: 413 Fifth St., 42461.
Catechesis/Religious Program—Students 86.

WAVERLY, UNION CO.
1—ST. PETER (1909) [CEM] Rev. Freddie Byrd.
Res.: 201 E. Market St., 42462. Tel: 270-389-4224. Email: stpeter.sacredheart@gmail.com.
Catechesis/Religious Program—Students 56.
2—SACRED HEART (1812) [CEM] Rev. Freddie Byrd.
201 E. Market St., 42462. Tel: 270-389-4224.
Church: 674 St. Rt. 141 N., Morganfield, 42437. Tel: 270-389-4224. Email: stpeter.sacredheart@gmail.com.
Catechesis/Religious Program—Students 7.

WAX, GRAYSON CO., ST. BENEDICT (1830) [CEM] Rev. Brian A. Johnson.
Mailing Address: 1256 St. Anthony Church Rd., Clarkson, 42726.
Catechesis/Religious Program—Students 17.
St. Anthony Church—Wax Rd., 42726. Tel: 270-242-4791.

WHITESVILLE, DAVIESS CO., ST. MARY OF THE WOODS (1845) [CEM] Rev. David P. Johnson.
Res.: 10503 Franklin St., 42378. Tel: 270-233-4529.
Church: 10534 Main Cross, P.O. Box 1, 42378. Tel: 270-233-4196; Fax: 270-233-5557.
School—St. Mary's Grade School, (Grades PreSchool-8) Tel: 270-233-5253; Fax: 270-233-9360. Sr. Suzanne Sims, O.S.U., Prin.; Peggy Clark, Librarian. Lay Teachers 11; Students 177.
Catechesis/Religious Program—Students 160.

Non-Parochial Assignments:
Revs.—
Alvey, Leonard J., Brescia University, 717 Frederica St., 42301.
Clark, Ray, Chap., Passionist Monastery, 8564 Crisp Rd., 42378. Prison Ministry
Garner, Andy, Diocesan Vocation Dir., 600 Locust St., 42301-2130. Tel: 270-683-1545, Ext. 368
Hostetter, Larry, S.T.D., Pres., Brescia University, 717 Frederica St., 42301.
Riney, Maury D., Chap., Owensboro Medical Health System, 42301. Carmel Home, 2501 Old Hartford Rd., 42303.
Roof, Frank, Chap., Lourdes Hospital, 2496 Lakewood Dr., Paducah, 42003.

On Duty Outside the Diocese:
Rev.—
Patterson, Ralph, St. Mary Parish, 2211 E. Lakeview Dr., Johnson City, TN 37601.

Absent on Leave:
Revs.—
Arflack, Gregory A.
Ausenbaugh, J. Andrew
Hayes, Gary
Karl, Kevin
Payne, Gary
Ulrich, Steve
Weider, Henry

Retired:
Very Rev. Msgrs.—
Hancock, George, Bishop Cotton Apts, 2501 1/2 Old Hartford Rd., Apt. 6, 42303.
Powers, Bernard, 10534 Main Cross St., 42378.
Revs.—
Clemons, Delma
DeNardi, Charles A., Carmel Home, 2501 Old Hartford Rd., 42303.
Glahn, Carl, Carmel Home, 2501 Old Hartford Rd., 42303.
Miller, Joseph C., 20333 Fairwood Dr., Neves, MN 56467.
Mills, Joseph M., J.C.L., Bishop Cotton Apts, 2501 1/2 Old Hartford Rd., 42303.
Powell, Paul, J.C.L., St. Martin Parish, 5856 KY 81, 42301.
Powers, Aloysius, Bishop Cotton Apts, 2501 1/2 Old Hartford Rd., Apt. 6, 42303.
Reisz, Leonard, 617 E. 23rd St., 42303.
Rhodes, Joseph, Carmel Home, 2501 Old Hartford Rd., 42303.
Riney, Philip C., Bishop Cotton Apts, 2501 1/2 Old Hartfort Rd., 42303.
Tiell, Maurice J., St. Joseph Parish, 434 Church Ave., Bowling Green, 42101-1810.
Wheatley, Carroll, 185 Greenfield, Jackson, TN 38305.

INSTITUTIONS LOCATED IN THE DIOCESE

[A] COLLEGES AND UNIVERSITIES

OWENSBORO. *Brescia University*, 717 Frederica St., 42301. Tel: 270-685-3131; Fax: 270-686-6422. Web: www.brescia.edu. Rev. Larry Hostetter, S.T.D., Pres.; Sisters Sharon Sullivan, O.S.U., Ph.D., Vice Pres. Academic Affairs & Academic Dean; Helena Fischer, O.S.U., Registrar; Rev. Leonard J. Alvey, Prof. & Counselor; Todd Butler, Dir. Ministry Formation; Sr. Judith Riney, O.S.U., Dir. Library Svcs. Priests 2; Sisters 12; Administrators 29; Lay Teachers 35; Students 719.

[B] HIGH SCHOOLS, INTER-PAROCHIAL

OWENSBORO. *Owensboro Catholic High School*, 1524 W. Parrish Ave., 42301. Tel: 270-684-3215; Fax: 270-684-7050. Email: harold.staples@owensborocatholic.org. Web: www.owensborocatholic.org/schools/ochs. Mr. Harold Staples, Prin.; Mr. Kurt Osborne, Asst. Prin.; Ms. Sherry Orth, Rel. Dept. Chair; Ms. Amy Lambert, Dean of Students; Mr. Keith Osborne, Devel. Dir.; Ms. Marilyn Pace, Librarian. Lay Teachers 36; Students 434.

PADUCAH. *St. Mary High School*, 1243 Elmdale Rd., 42003. Tel: 270-442-1681, Ext. 232; Fax: 270-442-7920. Email: tburkeen@smss.org. Web: www.smss.org. Mr. Tony Burkeen, Prin.; Rhonda Webb, Librarian. Lay Teachers 17; Students 163.

WHITESVILLE. *Trinity High School* 42378. Tel: 270-233-5533; Fax: 270-233-9293. Web: www.trinityhs.com. Mr. Bill Hagan, Prin. Lay Teachers 15; Students 137.

[C] ELEMENTARY SCHOOLS, INTER-PAROCHIAL

OWENSBORO. *Owensboro Catholic Elementary 4-6 Campus*, (Grades 4-6), 525 E. 23rd St., 42303. Tel: 270-683-6989; Fax: 270-684-5956. Email: tracy.conkright@owensborocatholic.org. Ms. Tracy Conkright, Prin.; Susie Alvey, Librarian. Lay Teachers 15; Students 256.

Owensboro Catholic Elementary K-3 Campus, (Grades K-3), 4017 Frederica St., 42301. Tel: 270-684-7583; Fax: 270-684-4938. Email: lori.whitehouse@owensborocatholic.org. Web: www.owensborocatholic.org. Ms. Lori Whitehouse, Prin.; Sherry Durham, Librarian. Religious 1; Lay Teachers 23; Students 389.

Owensboro Catholic Middle School, (Grades 7-8), (Owensboro Catholic Middle School), 2540 Christie Pl., 42301. Tel: 270-683-0480; Fax: 270-683-0495. Email: ann.flaherty@owensborocatholic.org. Web: www.owensborocatholic.org. Ms. Ann Flaherty, Prin.; Ms. Margie Ebelhar, Librarian. Lay Teachers 18; Students 192.

BOWLING GREEN. *St. Joseph Interparochial School*, (Grades PreSchool-8), 416 Church Ave., 42101-1887. Tel: 270-842-1235; Fax: 270-842-9072. Email: janlange@stjosephschoolbg.org. Web: stjosephschoolbg.org. Janice Lange, Prin.; Sally Jackson, Librarian. Lay Teachers 28; Students 342.

HARDINSBURG. *St. Romuald School*, (Grades PreK-8), 408 N. Hwy. 259, 40143. Tel: 270-756-5504; Fax: 270-756-2099. Email: srissecretary@hotmail.com. Mr. Rob Cox, Prin. Lay Teachers 18; Students 312.

MORGANFIELD. *St. Ann Interparochial School*, (Grades PreK-8), 320 S. Church St., 42437-1600. Tel: 270-389-1898; Fax: 270-389-1834. Email: beth.hendrickson@st-ann.com. Web: www.st-ann.com. Gail Ciecorka, Prin.; Ms. Charlotte Hollis, Librarian. Lay Teachers 13; Students 227.

PADUCAH. *St. Mary Elementary*, (Grades PreK-5), 377 Highland Blvd., 42003. Tel: 270-442-1681, Ext. 251; Fax: 270-442-7920. Email: triegling@smss.org. Web: www.smss.org. Tony Riegling, Prin.; Lisa Jett, Media Specialist. Lay Teachers 20; Students 328.

St. Mary Middle School, (Grades 6-8), 1243 Elmdale Rd., 42003. Tel: 270-442-1681, Ext. 232; Fax: 270-442-7920. Web: www.smss.org. Mr. Tony Burkeen, Prin.; Rhonda Webb, Librarian. Lay Teachers 9; Students 144.

[D] GENERAL HOSPITALS

PADUCAH. *Mercy Health Partners-Lourdes, Inc.*, 1530 Lone Oak Rd., P.O. Box 7100, 42002-7100. Tel: 270-444-2444; Fax: 270-444-2980. Web: www.elourdes.com. Steven Grinnell, Pres. & CEO; Ms. Marianne Potina, Vice. Pres. of Mission Integration. Catholic Healthcare Partners. Bed Capacity 260; Patients Assisted Annually 268,590; Total Staff 1,400.

McAuley Manor, Inc. Tel: 270-575-0050; Fax: 270-415-9165. Email: lmidyett@mercyhousing.org. Housing for Elderly.

Mercy Manor, Inc. Tel: 270-415-9166; Fax: 270-415-9165. Email: lmidyett@mercyhousing.org. Apartments for Elderly.

Dublin Manor, Inc. Apartments for the Elderly, Tel: 270-441-0026; Fax: 270-444-2980. Email: lmidyett@mercyhousing.org.

Lourdes Foundation, Inc., 1530 Lone Oak Rd., 42002-7100. Tel: 270-444-2205; Fax: 270-444-2732. Web: www.elourdes.com.

Mercy Regional Emergency Medical System Tel: 270-443-6529; Fax: 270-444-9128.
Mercy Regional Emergency Medical System

[E] HOMES FOR AGED

OWENSBORO. *Carmel Home*, 2501 Old Hartford Rd., 42303. Tel: 270-683-0227; Fax: 270-688-0630. Sr. M. Francis Teresa Scully, Carmel., D.C.J., Admin. & Supr.; Rev. Maury D. Riney, Chap. Carmelite Sisters of the Divine Heart of Jesus. Sisters 5; Residents 113; Bed Capacity 115; Total Staff 104; Total Assisted Annually 142.

KNOTTSVILLE. *Bishop Soenneker Home* Residential Care of the Handicapped/Disabled Ederly., 42366. Tel: 270-281-4881; Fax: 270-281-5804. Residents 53; Total Staff 29; Total Assisted Annually 68.

[F] MONASTERIES AND RESIDENCES OF PRIESTS AND BROTHERS

AUBURN. *Fathers of Mercy*, 806 Shaker Museum Rd., 42206. Tel: 270-542-4146; Fax: 270-542-4147. Email: missions@fathersofmercy.com. Web: www.fathersofmercy.com. Very Rev. William Casey, C.P.M., 2nd Councillor; Revs. John Molloy, C.P.M., 2501 Old Hartford Rd., 42301; Peter R. Stryker, C.P.M., 296 W. 6th St., Russellville, 42276 In Res. Revs. Ben Cameron, C.P.M., 1st Councillor, Asst. Gen. Mission Dir.; Louis Caporiccio, C.P.M., House Superior, Novice Master; James P. Costigan, C.P.M.; Christopher Crotty, C.P.M.; Francis Fusare, C.P.M.; Louis Guardiola, C.P.M.; Wade Menezes, C.P.M.; George L. McInnis, C.P.M.; Frank Sherry, C.P.M.; Anthony M. Stephens, C.P.M., Vocations Dir., Student Master, 3rd Councillor; Thomas Sullivan,

C.P.M., 4th Councillor; David M. Wilton, C.P.M., Supr. Gen.; Charles Zmudzinski, C.P.M., J.C.L., Treas. Gen.

[G] CONVENTS AND RESIDENCES FOR SISTERS

OWENSBORO. *The Glenmary Center*, P.O. Box 22264, 42304-2264. Tel: 270-686-8401; Fax: 270-686-8759. Web: www.glenmarysisters.org. Sr. Sharon Miller, G.H.M.S., Pres. Home Mission Sisters of America, Inc. aka Glenmary Sisters. Professed Sisters in Community 10.

Service to the Home Missions Total Assisted Annually 10,000; Total Staff 9.

MAPLE MOUNT. *Mount St. Joseph*, 8001 Cummings Rd., 42356. Tel: 270-229-4103; Fax: 270-229-4127. Email: michele.morek@maplemount.org. Web: www.ursulinesmsj.org. Sisters Michele Morek, O.S.U., Congregational Leader; Vickie Cravens, O.S.U., Archivist. Motherhouse and Convent of the Ursuline Nuns of the Congregation of Paris. Professed Sisters in Community 176.

WHITESVILLE. *Passionist Nuns/St. Joseph's Monastery*, 8564 Crisp Rd., 42378-9782. Tel: 270-233-4571; Fax: 270-233-4356. Email: nunsp@bellsouth.net. Web: www.passionistnuns.org. Sr. Catherine Marie Schuhmann, C.P., Supr. Religious of the Passion of Jesus Christ, (Passionist Nuns, Cloistered Contemplative). Postulants 1; Junior Professed 2; Final Vows 12; Affiliate 1.

[H] RETREAT CENTERS

BOWLING GREEN. *Gasper River Catholic Youth Camp & Retreat Center*, 2695 Jackson Bridge Rd., 42101. Tel: 270-781-2466. Web: www.gasperriverretreatcenter.org. Mr. Ben Warrell, Dir. (A diocesan-owned entity)

MAPLE MOUNT. *Mount Saint Joseph Conference and Retreat Center, Inc.*, 8001 Cummings Rd., 42356. Tel: 270-229-0200; Fax: 270-229-0279. Email: msj.center@maplemount.org. Web: www.msjcenter.org. Sr. Amelia Stenger, O.S.U., Dir.

[I] NEWMAN CENTERS

BOWLING GREEN. *Western Kentucky University Newman Center St. Thomas Aquinas Chapel*, 1403 College St., P.O. Box 10170, 42102-4770. Tel: 270-843-3638; Fax: 270-843-3326. Email: mew_62@hotmail.com. Web: www.wkucatholiccenter.com. Rev. Michael E. Williams, Dir. Students 1,651.

MURRAY. *Murray State University Newman House* 401 N. 12th St., 42071. Tel: 270-753-3876; Fax: 270-759-2074. Email: allie@stleoky.org. Web: www.newmanhouse.org. Allison Loomis, Campus Min.; Rev. Jason McClure, Chap. Students 800.

[J] MISCELLANEOUS LISTINGS

OWENSBORO. *Cathedral Preschool*, 600 Locust St., 42301. Tel: 270-926-1652; Fax: 270-683-3621. Email: pam.weafer@pastoral.org. Pam Weafer, Dir. Teachers 4; Students 132.

The Catholic Foundation of Western Kentucky, 600 Locust St., 42301. Tel: 270-683-1545; Fax: 270-683-6883. Email: ja@pastoral.org. Web: www.rcdok.org. Mr. Kevin Kauffeld, Contact Person.

Centro Latino, 524 Locust St., 42301. Tel: 270-683-2541; Fax: 270-684-5819. Email: ocentrolatino@aol.com. Total Staff 4; Total Assisted Annually 9,000.

**Daniel Pitino Shelter, Inc.*, 501 Walnut St., 42301. Tel: 270-688-9000; Fax: 270-688-0093. Email: dpsjim@hotmail.com. Web: www.pitinoshelter.org. Provides soup kitchen seven days a week, shelter for 65 homeless, education facilities and medical services for those unable to pay. Total Assisted Annually 469; Employees 11; Volunteers 210.

St. Gerard Life Home, 600 Locust St., 42301. Tel: 270-852-8328. Email: adoptions@pastoral.org. Rita Heinz, Catholic Charities Dir. Birthmother housing and pregnancy outreach.

Gideon Productions, Inc., 515 E. 22nd St., 42303. Tel: 270-688-9040; Fax: 270-688-9040. Email: frjohn@gideonproductions.com. Web: www.gideonproductions.com. Rev. John R. Meredith, Dir.; Mr. Cliff Russell, Broadcast Consultant.

**Glenmary Sisters Charitable Trust*, P.O. Box 22264, 42301. Tel: 270-686-8401; Fax: 270-686-8759.

Interparish Deposit Loan Fund Corp., 600 Locust St., 42301-2130. Tel: 270-683-1545; Fax: 270-683-6883. Email: ja@pastoral.org. Web: www.owensborodio.org. Sr. Joseph Angela Boone, O.S.U., Contact Person.

Owensboro Catholic Consolidated School System, 1524 W. Parrish Ave., 42301. Tel: 270-686-8896; Fax: 270-686-8997. Email: ken.rasp@owensborocatholic.org. Web: www.owensborocatholic.org. Ken Rasp, Dir.

**The Roman Catholic Diocese of Owensboro Kentucky Charitable Trust Fund, Inc.*, 600 Locust St., 42301. Tel: 270-683-1545; Fax: 270-683-6883. Email: ja@pastoral.org. Web: www.owensborodio.org. Sr. Joseph Angela Boone, O.S.U.

BOWLING GREEN. *Diocesan Shrine of Mary Mother of the Church and Model of all Christians*, St. Joseph, 434 Church St., 42101. Tel: 270-842-2525; Fax: 270-754-1164.

HORSE BRANCH. *St. Francis Community Center*, 768 Horsebranch Loop, 42349. Tel: 270-274-4385. Sr. Luisa Bickett, O.S.U., Pastoral Outreach Min.

PADUCAH. *St. Mary School System*, 1243 Elmdale Rd., 42003. Tel: 270-442-1681, Ext. 273; Fax: 270-442-7920. Email: learn@smss.org. Web: www.smss.org. Patrick Cairney.

St. Mary School System Benefit Fund, 1243 Elmdale Rd., 42003. Tel: 270-442-1681, Ext. 273; Fax: 270-442-7920. Email: learn@smss.org. Web: www.smss.org. Patrick Cairney, Contact Person.

PRINCETON. *Heralds of Good News of St. Paul, Inc.*, 813 S. Jefferson St., 42445. Tel: 270-365-6786. Rev. Thomas Shaiju, H.G.N. (India), Dir. & Contact Person.

RELIGIOUS INSTITUTES OF MEN REPRESENTED IN THE DIOCESE

For further details refer to the corresponding bracketed number in the Religious Institutes of Men or Women section.

[0820]—*Congregation of the Fathers of Mercy*—C.P.M.

[0570]—*Glenmary Home Missioners* (Glendale OH)—G.H.M.

[]—*Heralds of Good News* (India)—H.G.N.

RELIGIOUS INSTITUTES OF WOMEN REPRESENTED IN THE DIOCESE

[]—*Africa Province of the Franciscan Sisters of the Immaculate Conception* (Glasgow, Scotland, Nigeria Province)—O.S.F.

[0360]—*Carmelite Sisters of the Divine Heart of Jesus*—Carmel D.C.J.

[]—*Holy Cross Sisters USA Provinces*—S.C.S.C.

[2080]—*Home Mission Sisters of America*—G.H.M.S.

[2575]—*Institute of the Sisters of Mercy of the Americas* (Cincinnati, OH; Detroit, MI)—R.S.M.

[2790]—*Missionary Servants of the Most Blessed Trinity*—M.S.B.T.

[]—*Missioneras del Sagrado Corazon de Jesus Ad Gentes*—M.A.G.

[3170]—*Religious of the Passion of Jesus Christ*—C.P.

[1070-03]—*Sinsinawa Domincan Sisters*—O.P.

[0500]—*Sisters of Charity of Nazareth*—S.C.N.

[]—*Sisters of St. Benedict*—O.S.B.

[2260]—*Sisters of the Lamb of God*—A.D.

[1760]—*Sisters of the Third Order of St. Francis of Penance and Charity* (Tiffin, OH)—O.S.F.

[1720]—*Sisters of the Third Order Regular of St. Francis of the Congregation of Our Lady of Lourdes* (Rochester, MN)—O.S.F.

[4120]—*Ursuline Nuns, of the Congregation of Paris*—O.S.U.

INTERPAROCHIAL CEMETERIES

OWENSBORO. *Mater Dolorosa*, 1860 W. 9th St., 42301. 5404 Leitchfield Rd., 42303. Tel: 270-926-8097; Fax: 270-926-8038. Email: dolorosa3@juno.com. Mr. Art Hodde, Dir. Staff 5.

St. Raphael Cemetery Est. 1847, 6025 Hayden Bridge Rd., 42301. 600 Locust St., 42301-2130. Tel: 270-683-1545.

Resurrection, 5404 Leitchfield Rd., 42303. Tel: 270-926-8097; Fax: 270-926-8038. Email: dolorosa3@juno.com. Mr. Art Hodde, Dir.

BOWLING GREEN. *St. Joseph Interparochial Cemetery, Inc., St. Joseph Cemetery Foundation*, P.O. Box 10334, 42102. Tel: 270-842-2525 (St. Joseph Parish); 270-842-7777 (Holy Spirit Parish). Mr. Ray Grudzielanek, Chief Oper. Mgr.

PADUCAH. *Mt. Carmel Interparochial Cemetery* (1893) 116 S. 6th St., 42001. Tel: 270-442-1923. Rev. Brian Roby, Dir.

NECROLOGY

(No Deaths)

An asterisk (*) denotes an organization that has established tax-exempt status directly with the IRS and is not covered by the USCCB Group Ruling.

Diocese of Palm Beach

(Dioecesis Litoris Palmensis)

Most Reverend

GERALD M. BARBARITO

Bishop of Palm Beach; ordained January 31, 1976; appointed Auxiliary Bishop of Brooklyn June 28, 1994; installed August 22, 1994; appointed Bishop of Ogdensburg October 26, 1999; appointed Bishop of Palm Beach July 1, 2003; installed August 28, 2003. *Office: 9995 N. Military Tr., Palm Beach Gardens, FL 33410.*

The Pastoral Center Office: 9995 N. Military Tr., Palm Beach Gardens, FL 33410. Tel: 561-775-9500; Fax: 561-775-9556. *Mailing Address: P.O. Box 109650, Palm Beach Gardens, FL 33410-9650*

Web: diocesepb.org

Email: info@diocesepb.org

ESTABLISHED OCTOBER 24, 1984.

Square Miles 5,115.

Comprises the Counties of Palm Beach, Martin, Indian River, Okeechobee and St. Lucie in the State of Florida.

Legal Corporate Title: The Diocese of Palm Beach.

For legal titles of parishes and diocesan institutions, consult the Chancery.

STATISTICAL OVERVIEW

Personnel	
Bishop	1
Retired Bishops	1
Priests: Diocesan Active in Diocese	81
Priests: Diocesan Active Outside Diocese	4
Priests: Retired, Sick or Absent	35
Number of Diocesan Priests	120
Religious Priests in Diocese	32
Total Priests in Diocese	152
Extern Priests in Diocese	4
Ordinations:	
Diocesan Priests	2
Transitional Deacons	2
Permanent Deacons	41
Permanent Deacons in Diocese	91
Total Brothers	2
Total Sisters	115
Parishes	
Parishes	50
With Resident Pastor:	
Resident Diocesan Priests	44
Resident Religious Priests	6
Missions	3
Professional Ministry Personnel:	
Brothers	2
Sisters	29
Lay Ministers	81
Welfare	
Homes for the Aged	5
Total Assisted	435
Day Care Centers	5
Total Assisted	700
Special Centers for Social Services	18
Total Assisted	17,500
Other Institutions	1
Total Assisted	80
Educational	
Seminaries, Diocesan	1
Students from This Diocese	15
Students from Other Diocese	51
Diocesan Students in Other Seminaries	2
Total Seminarians	17
High Schools, Diocesan and Parish	3
Total Students	1,573
Elementary Schools, Diocesan and Parish	14
Total Students	4,501
Elementary Schools, Private	2
Total Students	543
Catechesis/Religious Education:	
High School Students	4,598
Elementary Students	11,987
Total Students under Catholic Instruction	23,219
Teachers in the Diocese:	
Sisters	16
Lay Teachers	545
Vital Statistics	
Receptions into the Church:	
Infant Baptism Totals	4,043
Minor Baptism Totals	244
Adult Baptism Totals	180
Received into Full Communion	415
First Communions	3,966
Confirmations	2,656
Marriages:	
Catholic	539
Interfaith	147
Total Marriages	686
Deaths	2,395
Total Catholic Population	279,823
Total Population	1,970,000

Former Bishops—Most Revs. THOMAS V. DAILY, D.D., ord. Jan. 10, 1952; appt. Titular Bishop of Bladia and Auxiliary Bishop of Boston, Dec. 31, 1974; cons. Feb. 11, 1975; appt. first Bishop of Palm Beach, July 17, 1984; installed Oct. 24, 1984; transferred to Bishop of Brooklyn, Feb. 20, 1990; J. KEITH SYMONS, D.D., ord. May 18, 1958; appt. Auxiliary Bishop of St. Petersbury, Jan. 16, 1981; cons. March 19, 1981; appt. second Bishop of Pensacola-Tallahassee, Sept. 29, 1983; installed Nov. 8, 1983; appt. second Bishop of Palm Beach, June 2, 1990; installed July 31, 1990; resigned June 2, 1998; ANTHONY J. O'CONNELL, D.D., ord. March 30, 1963; appt. Bishop of Knoxville, May 27, 1988; ord. and installed Sept. 8, 1988; appt. Bishop of Palm Beach Nov. 6, 1998; resigned March 8, 2002; SEAN P. O'MALLEY, O.F.M.Cap., Ph.D., ord. Aug. 29, 1970; appt. Coadjutor May 30, 1984; appt. Bishop of St. Thomas, Virgin Islands; ord. Aug. 2, 1984; installed Oct. 16, 1985; appt. Bishop of Fall River June 16, 1992; installed Aug. 11, 1992; appt. Bishop of Palm Beach Sept. 3, 2002; installed Oct. 19, 2002; appt. Archbishop of Boston July 1, 2003; installed July 30, 2003.

The Pastoral Center—Mailing Address: P.O. Box 109650, Palm Beach Gardens, 33410-9650. Tel: 561-775-9500; Fax: 561-775-9556. *9995 N. Military Tr., Palm Beach Gardens, 33410.*

Vicar General—Very Rev. CHARLES E. NOTABARTOLO, V.G.

Moderator of Curia—Very Rev. CHARLES E. NOTABARTOLO, V.G.

Episcopal Secretary—Rev. BRIAN KING.

Executive Secretary to Bishop—Mrs. ANNETTE RUSSELL.

Chancellor—Mrs. LORRAINE SABATELLA, B.A.

Coordinator of Archives and Records—Mrs. MERKE BARONI.

Matrimonial Tribunal—

Judicial Vicar—Rev. Msgr. THOMAS J. KLINZING, J.C.L.

Adjutant Judicial Vicar—Rev. GLEN J. POTHIER, J.C.L., D.Th.

Judges—Rev. Msgr. THOMAS J. KLINZING, J.C.L.; Revs. GLEN J. POTHIER, J.C.L., D.Th.; FRANCISCO JAVIER OSORIO, J.C.L.

Defenders of the Bond—Rev. Msgrs. RONALD BESHARA, S.T.L., J.C.L.; RAYMOND BLAIR, S.T.L., J.C.D.

Assessors—Rev. Msgr. JAMES M. BURKE (Retired); Very Rev. MICHAEL W. EDWARDS, V.F.; Rev. KEVIN NELSON, M.A., M.Div.

Promoter of Justice—Rev. DAMIAN TOWEY, C.P., J.C.D.

Notaries—Mrs. LORRAINE SABATELLA, B.A.; Mr. SANDI MARTINEZ, M.A.; Mrs. HELEN COUGHTER, B.A.; Mrs. DEBORAH DUXBURY, B.A.; Ms. ALICE RIVERA.

Director of the Tribunal—Mr. SANDI MARTINEZ, M.A.

Case Directors & Secretaries—Mr. SANDI MARTINEZ, M.A.; Mrs. HELEN COUGHTER, B.A.; Mrs. DEBORAH DUXBURY, B.A.; Ms. ALICE RIVERA.

Advocates—Rev. Msgr. JAMES M. BURKE (Retired); Deacon SAM BARBARO; Rev. GERALD GRACE, S.T.D.; Deacons MARTIN SERRAES; DENNIS DEMES, Ph.D.; Rev. KEVIN NELSON, M.A., M.Div.; Mr. BERNARD CONKO, B.M.M., J.D.; Mr. JAMES CIOFFI; Mr. MARTIN KNECHT JR.

Vicars Forane—Very Revs. MICHAEL W. EDWARDS, V.F., Northern Deanery; ALFREDO HERNANDEZ, V.F., Central Deanery; THOMAS J. SKINDELESKI, V.F., Southern Deanery; AIDAN HYNES, V.F., Cathedral Deanery.

Vocations—Rev. YVES FRANCOIS, Dir. Tel: 561-775-9555.

Religious—Rev. JOSEPH SANTA-BIBIANA, S.D.B., Episcopal Delegate; Sr. MARGARET JEANNE KELLER, S.S.J., Assoc. Dir. Tel: 561-775-9554.

Diaconate—VACANT, Episcopal Delegate; Deacon DENNIS DEMES, Ph.D., Dir. Formation. Tel: 561-775-9540.

Chief Financial Officer—Mr. DENIS HAMEL. Tel: 561-775-9518.

Consultative Bodies

Consultors—Rev. Msgr. THOMAS J. KLINZING, J.C.L.; Very Revs. MICHAEL W. EDWARDS, V.F.; CHARLES E. NOTABARTOLO, V.G.; Revs. GERALD GRACE, S.T.D.; FRANCIS J. LECHIARA; RICHARD MURPHY; JAMES MURTAGH; ARTHUR VENEZIA.

Presbyteral Council—Ex Officio: Very Rev. CHARLES E. NOTABARTOLO, V.G., Vicar Gen.; Rev. Msgr. THOMAS J. KLINZING, J.C.L., Judicial Vicar; Very Revs. MICHAEL W. EDWARDS, V.F., Vicar Forane - Northern Deanery; AIDAN HYNES, V.F., Vicar Forane - Cathedral Deanery; ALFREDO HERNANDEZ, V.F., Vicar Forane - Central Deanery; THOMAS J. SKINDELESKI, V.F., Vicar Forane - Southern Deanery. Elected Members: Very Rev. THOMAS E. BARRETT; Revs. JOHN A. CROWLEY (Retired); JAIME DORADO; RICHARD E. GEORGE;

LOUIS GUERIN; GERALD GRACE, S.T.D.; FRANCISCO OSORIO; JOSEPH M. PAPES; NESTOR RODRIGUEZ; ELIFETE ST. FORTE; Very Rev. PAUL WIERICHS, C.P.

Diocesan Offices

Background Screening—KELLIE JOHNSON-PETRUZZI. Tel: 561-775-9530.

Black Catholic Ministry—LORRAINE LYLES, Dir. Tel: 561-844-5971, Ext. 108.

Building, Construction, Real Estate Office—Rev. RICHARD MURPHY, Episcopal Delegate. Tel: 561-775-9514; MICHAEL LOCKWOOD, Dir. Tel: 561-775-9523.

Campus and Young Adult Ministry—TERENCE MCCORRY, Dir. Tel: 561-775-9524.

Catholic Charities Administrataive Offices—VACANT, Episcopal Delegate; NANCY MONICATTI, A.C.S.W., Exec. Dir. Tel: 561-775-9573; DIANN JASINSKI, Assoc. Dir. Tel: 561-775-9567; JUDY EVANS, Mgr. Human Resources. Tel: 561-775-9564.

Cemetery: Our Lady Queen of Peace—10941 Southern Blvd., West Palm Beach, 33411. Rev. ZBIGNIEW A. RUDNICKI, Dir. Tel: 561-798-5661; Mr. THOMAS JORDAN, Admin. Tel: 561-793-0711.

Communications—ALEXIS WALKENSTEIN, Dir. Tel: 561-775-9529. Email: awalkenstein@diocesepd.org; LINDA REEVES, Florida Catholic Editor. Tel: 561-775-9528. Email: flcath@diocesepb.org; SCOTT LOMBARDI, Web Devel. Tel: 561-775-9505.

Diocesan Services Appeal/Fundraising—LYNDSAY VONBOKERN, Devel. Coord. Tel: 561-775-9590; LYNN WELLS, Administrative Asst.

Ecumenism—Deacon DENNIS DEMES, Ph.D., Episcopal Delegate. Tel: 561-775-9540.

Education—

Schools Office—Sr. JOAN DAWSON, O.S.F., Supt. Tel: 561-775-9546; Mrs. MARIE PRIVUZNAK, Asst. Supt. Tel: 561-775-9532.

Office of Catechetical Leadership and Youth Ministry Formation—Mr. ANTHONY MARCHICA, Dir. Tel: 561-775-9548; MARIE DRIVER, Sec. & Media Coord. Tel: 561-775-9549.

School of Christian Formation (English & Spanish)—Deacon JAIME ZAPATA, Dir. Tel: 561-775-9506.

Employee Services— (see also Insurance Services) Mrs. ANA JAROSZ, Dir. Tel: 561-775-9525; GRETCHEN CARD, Human Resources Asst. Tel: 561-775-9503.

Family Life/Marriage—Mrs. JANICE PETERSEN MINSHEW, Coord. Tel: 561-775-9557.

Finance—Mr. DENIS HAMEL, CFO. Tel: 561-775-9518; CHRIS GRANT, Controller. Tel: 561-775-9515.

Haitian Ministry—Rev. YVES GEFFRARD, Episcopal Delegate. Tel: 561-466-9617.

Hispanic Ministry—Deacon JAIME ZAPATA, Dir. Tel: 561-775-9506.

Information Technology—CARLOS MESA, Network Admin. Tel: 561-775-9542; STEPHEN MEEKER, Systems Support Technician. Tel: 561-775-9578; MIKE IRISH, Programmer. Tel: 561-775-9504.

Insurance Services— (see also Employee Services) Mrs. ANA JAROSZ, Dir. Tel: 561-775-9525; DONISE JACQUES, Benefits Asst. Tel: 561-775-9574.

Internal Services—Ms. MARIAN LOYND, Dir. Tel: 561-630-2694.

Liturgy—Rev. MICHAEL DRISCOLL, O.Carm., Dir. Tel: 561-392-8172; Mrs. MARGARET OWERS, Sec. Tel: 561-775-9539.

Mayan Ministry—Sr. RACHEL SENA, O.P. Tel: 561-533-8130.

Permanent Diaconate/Diaconate Formation Program—Deacons SAM BARBARO, Episcopal Delegate. Tel: 561-775-9540; DENNIS DEMES, Ph.D., Dir. Formation. Tel: 561-775-9541; ANA DAZA-JALLER, Permanent Diaconate & Diaconate Formation Asst. Tel: 561-775-9540.

Prison Ministry—Mr. THOMAS LAWLER, Dir. Tel: 561-775-9553.

Propagation of the Faith & Missionary Cooperative Plan—Very Rev. MICHAEL W. EDWARDS, V.F., Dir. Tel: 772-567-5129; Mrs. BETTY MCKINLEY, Sec. Tel: 561-775-9598.

Real Estate—Rev. RICHARD MURPHY, Episcopal Delegate. Tel: 561-775-9514.

Religious Men and Women—Episcopal Delegates: Rev. JOSEPH SANTA-BIBIANA, S.D.B.; Sr. MARGARET JEANNE KELLER, S.S.J. Tel: 561-775-9554.

Respect Life—Mr. DONALD KAZIMIR, Coord.; DONNA GARDNER, Post Abortion Healing & Project Rachel. Tel: 561-775-9565.

Safe Environments—Mrs. KATHRYN JOHANSEN, Coord. Tel: 561-775-9593.

Seminarians—Rev. YVES FRANCOIS, Dir. Tel: 561-775-9555.

Substance Addiction—Mr. ERIK A. VAGENIUS, MHS, CAP, Coord. Tel: 561-775-9527.

Vocations—Rev. YVES FRANCOIS, Dir. Tel: 561-775-9555.

Catholic Charities Services and Offices

Episcopal Delegate for Catholic Charities—VACANT.

Executive Director—NANCY MONICATTI, A.C.S.W.

Associatie Director—DIANN JASINSKI.

Catholic Charities Administrative Offices—9995 N. Military Trail, Palm Beach Gardens, 33410-9650. Tel: 561-775-9560; Fax: 561-625-5906. *Mailing Address: P.O. Box 109650, Palm Beach Gardens, 33410-9650.*

After-School Programs—

Glades Kids Activity Center—Mailing Address: P.O. Box 196, Belle Glade, 33430. Tel: 561-993-0066; Fax: 561-993-0061.

Good to Grow—100 W. 20th St., Riviera Beach, 33404. Tel: 561-844-5971; Fax: 561-844-0665. *Mailing Address: P.O. Box 9966, Riviera Beach, 33419.*

Pahokee Pals—1200 E. Main St., Pahokee, 33476. Tel: 561-924-5677; Fax: 561-924-3595. *Mailing Address: P.O. Box 664, Pahokee, 33476.*

Counseling Services—

Counseling—VAUGHN HOHREITER, Delray Beach. Tel: 561-504-5097; DONNA ROSS. Tel: 561-847-5131; GLORIA STEVENSON, 900 54th St., West Palm Beach, 33407. Tel: 561-254-6558; Fax: 561-863-5379. Mailing Address: P.O. Box 8246, West Palm Beach, 33407; HELEN KELLY, 1111 S. Federal Hwy., Ste. 110, Stuart, 34995. Tel: 772-283-0541; Fax: 772-220-9894; MOLLY MCGUIRE, St. Edward Catholic Church, 144 N. County Rd., Palm Beach, 33480-3916. Tel: 561-891-0379; Fax: 561-514-3582; MARY LAMARR, 3300 S.W. Chartwell St., Port Saint Lucie, 34953. Tel: 772-204-9566. St. Helen Cathoilc Church, 2025 20th Ave., Vero Beach, 32960. Tel: 772-778-5411; Fax: 772-562-2209. Mailing Address: P.O. Box 2927, Vero Beach, 32960.

Elder Services—

Elder Affairs—900 54th St., West Palm Beach, 33407. Tel: 561-842-2406; Fax: 561-863-5379. *Mailing Address: P.O. Box 8246, West Palm Beach, 33407.* AMY FARIELLO.

Health Related Services—

Interfaith Health & Wellness/Wellness Ministry—900 54th St., West Palm Beach, 33407. Tel: 561-842-2406; Fax: 561-863-5379. *Mailing Address: P.O. Box 8246, West Palm Beach, 33407.* BERNADETTE MACY.

Immigration Services—

Immigration Legal Services—TIMOTHY KEOHANE, 900 54th St., West Palm Beach, 33407. Tel: 561-494-0928; Fax: 561-202-2310. Mailing Address: P.O. Box 8246, West Palm Beach, 33407; RENEE ARNAO, 1111 S. Federal Hwy., Ste. 216, Stuart, 34995. Tel: 772-463-0445; Fax: 772-872-0311; MARIA CRISTINA MARQUEZ, 15305 W. Adams Ave., Indiantown, 34956. Tel: 772-597-2812; Fax: 772-597-2813. Mailing Address: P.O. Box 67, Indiantown, 34956.

Pregnancy Services—

Birthline—1040 S. Federal Hwy., Ste. 101, Delray Beach, 33483. Tel: 561-278-0894; Fax: 561-274-7056. *3452 W. Boynton Beach Blvd., Boynton Beach, 33436.* Tel: 561-738-2060; Fax: 561-732-0750. MARY RODRIGUEZ.

Lifeline—900 54th St., West Palm Beach, 33407. Tel: 561-842-5301; Fax: 561-842-5302. *Mailing Address: P.O. Box 8246, West Palm Beach, 33407.* MARY RODRIGUEZ.

Refugee Services—

Refugee and Resettlement—900 54th St., West Palm Beach, 33407. Tel: 561-863-9255; Fax: 561-863-1680. *Mailing Address: P.O. Box 8246, West Palm Beach, 33407.* MARY LYNN AYMOND-GONZALEZ.

Transitional Housing—

Samaritan Center—3650 41st St., Vero Beach, 32967. Tel: 772-770-3039; Fax: 772-567-0812. TRACEY SEGAL.

Organizations and Movements

Charismatic Movement—

English—Tel: 561-392-0007. Rev. JOHN GALLAGHER, Spiritual Dir.

Spanish—Tel: 561-793-8544. Rev. MARIO CASTANEDA, Spiritual Dir.

Christ Child Society—

Boca Raton—AGNES GREGORY. Tel: 561-482-3067.

North Palm Beach—MARY BISHOP. Tel: 561-795-0134.

Stuart—CHERYL MACKIE. Tel: 772-299-7852.

Con El, Healthcare Ministry to the Third World—DOROTHY MARTIN. Tel: 561-659-2822.

Council of Catholic Women—Rev. CLEMENS HAMMERSCHMITT, Spiritual Moderator. Tel: 561-966-8878; JEAN WADDINGTON, Pres. Tel: 561-641-5153.

Cursillo Movement—

English—Tel: 561-747-9330. Deacon JOSEPH POLLOCK, Spiritual Advisor; JANICE COLLINS, Lay Dir.

Spanish—Tel: 561-964-4168. Sr. MARGARITA GOMEZ, R.M.I., S.T.L., D.Min., Spiritual Advisor; ALICIA M. FERNANDEZ, Lay Dir.

Damas Catolicas en Acion—Rev. NESTOR RODRIGUEZ, Spiritual Moderator; LILIA MARIA GIBBONS, Founder & Dir.

Knights of Columbus—Very Rev. THOMAS J. SKINDELESKI, V.F. Tel: 561-276-6892; PETER J. BISHOP, Membership Admin. Tel: 561-795-0134.

Legion of Mary, Palm Beach Curia—Rev. DANIS RIDORE, Spiritual Moderator. Tel: 561-276-6892; GLORIA PAT STEWART, Pres. Tel: 561-659-4160.

CLERGY, PARISHES, MISSIONS AND PAROCHIAL SCHOOLS

CITY OF PALM BEACH GARDENS

(PALM BEACH GARDENS), CATHEDRAL OF ST. IGNATIUS LOYOLA (1984) Very Rev. Thomas E. Barrett, Rector; Revs. Andrew Brierley; Edgar Mazariegos.
Res.: 9999 N. Military Tr., 33410. Tel: 561-622-2565; Fax: 561-624-9489. Web: www.stignatiuspb-.com. Email: office@stignatiuspb.com.
See All Saints Catholic School, Jupiter under Interparochial Schools located in the Institution section.
Catechesis/Religious Program—Students 308.

OUTSIDE THE CITY OF PALM BEACH GARDENS

BELLE GLADE, PALM BEACH CO., ST. PHILIP BENIZI (1961) Revs. Joseph Santa-Bibiana, S.D.B.; Jeremiah Reen, S.D.B.; Quesnel Delvard, S.D.B.; Bros. Robert Metell, S.D.B.; Robert Malusa, S.D.B.
Res.: 710 S. Main St., 33430-4202. Tel: 561-996-3870; Fax: 561-996-1281. Email: philip710@comcast.net.
Catechesis/Religious Program—Tel: 561-996-5928; Fax: 561-996-1281. Students 347.

BOCA RATON, PALM BEACH CO.

1—ASCENSION (1968) Revs. Charles Hawkins; Peter Van Nguyen; Deacon Lon Phillips.
Res.: 7250 N. Federal Hwy., 33487-1606. Tel: 561-997-5486; Fax: 561-997-5862. Email: ascensioncatholicchurch@ascensioncatholicchurch.net. Web: ascensioncatholicchurch.net.
Catechesis/Religious Program—Students 194.

2—ST. JOAN OF ARC (1956) Rev. Msgr. Michael D. McGraw, M.Ss.A.; Revs. David C. Downey; Jimmy Hababag (Philippines).
Res.: 370 S.W. 3rd St., 33432. Tel: 561-392-0007; Fax: 561-392-0074. Web: www.stjoan.org.
School—501 S.W. 3rd Ave., 33432. Tel: 561-392-7974; Fax: 561-368-6671. Sr. Ellen Murphy, R.S.M., Prin. Sisters 3; Lay Teachers 30; Students 590.
Catechesis/Religious Program—Tel: 561-391-4345; Fax: 561-962-6002. Students 575.
Convent—500 S.W. 4th Ave., 33432. Tel: 561-368-6655 (Sisters of Mercy).

3—ST. JOHN THE EVANGELIST (1992) Rev. Michael O'Flaherty.
Res.: 10300 Yamato Rd., 33498. Tel: 561-488-1373; Fax: 561-488-5562. Email: stjohnbocaraton@bellsouth.net.
Catechesis/Religious Program—Students 411.

4—ST. JUDE (1979) Revs. Michael Driscoll, O.Carm.; Richard Champigny, O.Carm.; Emiel Abalahin, O.Carm.
Church: 21689 Toledo Rd., 33433. Tel: 561-392-8172. Web: www.stjudeboca.org.
Rectory & Priory: 2235 S.W. 16th Pl., 33486-8560. Tel: 561-750-1937.
Preschool—Tel: 561-392-9579; Fax: 561-362-0845. Total Staff 18; Students 70.
School—Tel: 561-392-9160; Fax: 561-392-5815. Miss Debbie Armstrong, Prin. & Preschool Dir. Lay Teachers 34; Students 353.
Catechesis/Religious Program—Tel: 561-362-8597; Fax: 561-362-0845. Email: linda@stjudeboca.org. Students 410.

5—OUR LADY OF LOURDES (1977) Rev. Francis Reardon.
Res.: 22094 Lyons Rd., 33428. Tel: 561-483-2440.
Catechesis/Religious Program—Tel: 561-483-2440, Ext. 1429; Fax: 561-558-1434. Email: rdannunzio@lourdesboca.org. Students 606.

BOYNTON BEACH, PALM BEACH CO.

1—ST. MARK (1952) Revs. Richard T. Florek, O.F.M-.Conv.; Samuel Zebron, O.F.M.Conv.; Germain Kopaczynski, O.F.M.Conv.; Sr. Mary Joan Millecan, Contact Person, St. Mark Pastoral Care.
Res. & St. Mark Pastoral Care: 643 St. Mark Pl., 33435. Tel: 561-734-9330; 561-735-3530 (Pastoral

Care); Fax: 561-735-3463.
School—730 N.E. 6th Ave., 33435. Tel: 561-732-9934; Fax: 561-732-0501. Dr. Joseph Finley, Prin. Lay Teachers 25; Students 216.
Catechesis/Religious Program—Students 160.

2—ST. THOMAS MORE (1972) Revs. Julian P. Harris; Alex J. Vargas; Peter Truong; Deacons George Collins; William Cresswell; Silvio Menendez.
Res.: 10935 S. Military Tr., 33436. Tel: 561-737-3095; Fax: 561-737-8697. Web: stthomasmoreboynton.org.
Catechesis/Religious Program—Tel: 561-737-3521; Fax: 561-737-3596. Email: gdvenas@stmbb.org. Students 837.

DELRAY BEACH, PALM BEACH CO.

1—EMMANUEL (1983) Revs. Timothy Sockol; Raymond P. Hubert, Pastor Emeritus (Retired).
Res.: 15700 S. Military Tr., 33484. Tel: 561-496-2480; Fax: 561-496-5755.
Catechesis/Religious Program—Students 85.

2—OUR LADY OF PERPETUAL HELP MISSION (1987) Rev. Roland Desormeaux, C.S.
Church & Res.: 510 S.W. Eighth Ave., 33444-2448. Tel: 561-276-4880; Fax: 561-276-7036. Email: perpetualchurch@aol.com.
Catechesis/Religious Program—Students 181.

3—OUR LADY QUEEN OF PEACE (1963) Revs. Carlos Anklan, C.S.; Vincenzo Ronchi, C.S. In Res., Rev. Hector Sartori, C.S.
Res.: 9600 W. Atlantic Ave., 33446. Tel: 561-499-6234; Fax: 561-499-5513. Email: hanklan@aol.com. Web: www.queenofpeacemission.org.
Catechesis/Religious Program—Students 257.

4—ST. VINCENT FERRER (1941) Very Rev. Thomas J. Skindeleski; Revs. John A. Skehan, Pastor Emeritus (Retired); Danis Ridore (Canada); Deacons Lee Levenson; Joseph Nick Nowak; Bruce Turnbull. In Res., Rev. Michael Parrotta.
Res.: 840 George Bush Blvd., 33483. Tel: 561-276-6892; Fax: 561-276-8068. Email: svfoffice@bellsouth.net. Web: www.stvincentferrer.com.
School—810 George Bush Blvd., 33483. Tel: 561-278-3868; Fax: 561-279-9508. Mrs. M. Vikki Delgado, Prin. Little Servant Sisters of the Immaculate Conception 2; Lay Teachers 19; Students 272.
Catechesis/Religious Program—Tel: 561-279-8041; Fax: 561-276-6274. Students 160.

FELLSMERE, INDIAN RIVER CO., OUR LADY OF GUADALUPE MISSION (1991) Revs. John Morrissey; Raciel Trevino.
Catechesis/Religious Program—Students 230.
Mission— Rte. 512, P.O. Box 9, Indian River Co. 32948. Tel: 772-571-9875; Fax: 772-571-8321. Email: olg@bellsouth.net.

FORT PIERCE, ST. LUCIE CO.

1—ST. ANASTASIA (1911) Revs. Richard E. George; Mark Mlay, A.L.C.P. (Tanzania).
Res.: 407 S. 33rd St., 34947. Tel: 772-461-2233; Fax: 772-461-2242. Web: www.stanastasiachurch.org.
School—401 S. 33 St., 34947. Tel: 772-461-2232; Fax: 772-468-2037. Email: info@stanna.org. Web: www.stanna.org. Mr. Kevin Hoeffner, Prin. Sisters 1; Lay Teachers 44; Students 578.
Catechesis/Religious Program—Email: kfrank@stanastasiachurch.org (Youth); susan.elizabeth.smith@gmail.com (Religious Ed.). Students 50.

2—ST. MARK THE EVANGELIST (1972) Revs. Michael J. McNally; Sean de Leis, C.S.Sp.
Res.: 1924 Zephyr Ave., 34982. Tel: 772-461-8150; Fax: 772-464-2367. Email: stmarkssecretary@bellsouth.com.
Catechesis/Religious Program—Tel: 772-464-8955. Email: drestmark@bellsouth.net. Students 70.

3—NOTRE DAME MISSION (1995) Revs. Richard E. George; Yves Geffrard (Haiti).
Res.: 217 N. U.S. Hwy. #1, 34950. Tel: 561-466-9617; Fax: 561-466-4075.
Catechesis/Religious Program—Tel: 772-335-9540. Students 16.

HIGHLAND BEACH, PALM BEACH CO., ST. LUCY (1968) Rev. Gerald Grace.
Res.: 3510 S. Ocean Blvd., 33487. Tel: 561-278-1280; Fax: 561-278-8509. Email: stlucys@bellsouth.net.
Catechesis/Religious Program—Students 6.

HOBE SOUND, MARTIN CO., ST. CHRISTOPHER (1960) Very Rev. Aidan Hynes.
Res.: 12001 S.E. Federal Hwy., 33455. Tel: 772-546-5150; Fax: 772-546-8820. Email: stchris@bellsouth.net. Web: stchrishobesound.com.
See All Saints Catholic School, Jupiter under Interparochial Schools located in the Institution section.
Catechesis/Religious Program—Students 245.

INDIANTOWN, MARTIN CO., HOLY CROSS (1960) Revs. Nestor Rodriguez; Juan de la Calle, Pastor Emeritus.
Mailing Address: 15927 S.W. 150th St., P.O. Box 999, 34956. Tel: 772-597-2798; Fax: 772-597-2741. Email: holcros1@onearrow.net.
Res.: 15670 Famel Blvd., 34956. Tel: 772-597-3935.
Catechesis/Religious Program—Students 109.

JENSEN BEACH, MARTIN CO., ST. MARTIN DE PORRES (1973) Revs. James Molgano; Thomas J. Rynne, Pastor Emeritus (Retired); Marco Tulio DeLeon.
Res.: 2555 N.E. Savanna Rd., 34957. Tel: 772-334-4214; Fax: 772-334-8627. Email: info@stmartindp.com. Web: www.stmartindp.com.
Catechesis/Religious Program—Tel: 772-334-4492. Email: religiousedu@stmartindp.com. Students 172.

JUPITER, PALM BEACH CO., ST. PETER (1987) Revs. Donald T. Finney; Sabas Mallya; Eduardo Medina; Deacons Stephen McMahon; Donald Battison; Joseph Pollock; Byron Champagne; Stephen Scienzo.
Res.: 1701 Indian Creek Pkwy., 33458. Tel: 561-575-0837; Fax: 561-575-6784. Email: parish@stpetercatholicchurch.com. Web: stpetercatholicchurch.com.
See All Saints Catholic School, Jupiter under Interparochial Schools located in the Institution section.
Catechesis/Religious Program—Students 600.

LAKE WORTH, PALM BEACH CO.

1—ST. MATTHEW (1992) Rev. Clemens Hammerschmitt.
Res. & Mailing: 6090 Hypoluxo Rd., 33463-7312. Tel: 561-966-8878; Fax: 561-968-1238.
Catechesis/Religious Program—Tel: 561-966-1538. Students 353.

2—SACRED HEART (1917) Revs. Joseph M. Papes; Peter Van Nguyen, Pastor Emeritus; Francis X. Fenech, Pastor Emeritus (Retired); Duvan Bermudez.
Res.: 425 N. M St., 33460. Tel: 561-582-4736; Fax: 561-588-5238.
School—410 N. M St., 33460. Tel: 561-582-2242; Fax: 561-547-9699. Candace Tamposi, Prin. Sisters 1; Lay Teachers 19; Students 178.
Catechesis/Religious Program—Tel: 561-582-4736, Ext. 200. Students 141.

LANTANA, PALM BEACH CO., HOLY SPIRIT (1964) Revs. Kevin Nelson; Ronald Schulz, Pastor Emeritus (Retired).
Res. and Mailing: 1000 Lantana Rd., P.O. Box 3978, 33465. Tel: 561-585-5970; Fax: 561-575-8482. Email: hspiritlantana@gmail.com. Web: holyspiritlantana.com.
Catechesis/Religious Program—Tel: 561-585-5970, Ext. 301. Students 113.

NORTH PALM BEACH, PALM BEACH CO.

1—ST. CLARE (1960) Revs. William D. O'Shea; Giuseppe Savaia.
Res.: 821 Prosperity Farms Rd., 33408. Tel: 561-622-7477; Fax: 561-624-0022. Email: stclare821@aol.com.
School—Tel: 561-622-7171; Fax: 561-627-4426. Web: stclareschool.com. Mr. Andrew J. Houvouras, Prin. Lay Teachers 35; Students 447.
Catechesis/Religious Program—Students 105.

2—ST. PAUL OF THE CROSS (1970) Rev. Arthur Venezia.
Res.: 10970 Jack Nicklaus Dr., 33408. Tel: 561-626-1873; Fax: 561-626-4383. Email: paulcross@bellsouth.net. Web: paulcross.org.
See All Saints Catholic School, Jupiter under Interparochial Schools located in the Institution section.
Catechesis/Religious Program—Email: joannereled@bellsouth.net. Students 149.

OKEECHOBEE, OKEECHOBEE CO., SACRED HEART (1964) Rev. Hugh Duffy.
Mailing Address: P.O. Box 716, 34973.
Res.: 901 S.W. 6th St., 34974. Tel: 863-763-3727; Fax: 863-763-9334. Email: heartokeechobee@earthlink.net.
Catechesis/Religious Program—Tel: 863-763-2745. Students 528.

PAHOKEE, PALM BEACH CO., ST. MARY (1933) Rev. John J. Mericantante.
Res.: 1200 E. Main St., 33476. Tel: 561-924-7305; Fax: 561-924-9394. Web: www.stmaryofpahokee.com.
Catechesis/Religious Program—Tel: 561-924-5888. Students 350.

PALM BEACH, PALM BEACH CO., ST. EDWARD (1926) Rev. Francis J. Lechiara.
Res.: 144 N. County Rd., 33480. Tel: 561-832-0400; Fax: 561-833-3359.
Catechesis/Religious Program—Students 71.

PALM BEACH GARDENS, PALM BEACH CO., ST. PATRICK (1987) Revs. Brian Flanagan; Brian Campbell.
Res.: 13591 Prosperity Farms Rd., 33410. Tel: 561-626-8626; Fax: 561-622-6471. Email: stpatpbg@yahoo.com. Web: www.stpatrickchurch.org.
See All Saints Catholic School, Jupiter under Interparochial Schools located in the Institution section.
Catechesis/Religious Program—Students 150.

PALM CITY, MARTIN CO., HOLY REDEEMER (1983) Revs. Martin B. Mulqueen; John A. Kasparek.
Mailing Address: P.O. Box 916, 34991. Web: www.holyredeemer.org.
Catechesis/Religious Program—Tel: 772-463-1579; Fax: 772-286-8792. Email: religed@bellsouth.net. Students 540.

PALM SPRINGS, PALM BEACH CO., ST. LUKE (1961) Revs. Adrian Torres; Paul Chung Nguyen; Thomas LaFreniere.
Res.: 2892 S. Congress Ave., 33461. Tel: 561-965-8980; Fax: 561-965-1384. Email: stluke00@bellsouth.net. Web: www.stlukeparish.com.
School—Tel: 561-965-8190; Fax: 561-965-2404. Suzanne Sandelier, Prin. Lay Teachers 16; Students 178.
Catechesis/Religious Program—Tel: 561-969-1242. Students 715.

PORT ST. LUCIE, ST. LUCIE CO.

1—ST. BERNADETTE (2001) Revs. Victor A. Ulto; Son Linh Hoang.
Church: 350 N.W. California Blvd., 34986. Tel: 772-336-9956; Fax: 772-336-5266. Email: stbernadetteslw@aol.com. Web: stbernadettescatholicchurch.org.
Catechesis/Religious Program—Students 210.

2—ST. ELIZABETH ANN SETON (1993) Revs. Edmund L. Szpieg; Carl Hellwig.
Church: 930 S.W. Tunis Ave., 34953-3351. Tel: 772-336-0282; Fax: 772-336-1494.
Catechesis/Religious Program—Tel: 772-336-0363; Fax: 772-336-1494. Students 450.

3—HOLY FAMILY (1987) Revs. Thomas F. Cauley; Eduardo Medina.
Mailing Address: 2330 Mariposa Ave., 34952. Tel: 772-335-2385; Fax: 772-335-2517.
Catechesis/Religious Program—Tel: 772-337-4313. Students 336.

4—ST. LUCIE (1961) Rev. Mark Szanyi, O.F.M.Conv.; Rev. Msgr. James M. Burke, Pastor Emeritus (Retired); Revs. Peter C. Dolan, Pastor Emeritus (Retired); Michael Englert, O.F.M.Conv.; Vincent Rubino, O.F.M.Conv.; Deacons Richard Moser; Carlos Melendez.
Res.: 425 S.W. Irving St., 34983. Tel: 772-878-1215; Fax: 772-878-1299. Web: www.stlucie.cc.
Catechesis/Religious Program—290 S.W. Prima Vista, Port Saint Lucie, 34983. Students 372.

RIVIERA BEACH, PALM BEACH CO., ST. FRANCIS OF ASSISI (1948) Revs. Arthur Obin, O.M.I.; Gilmond Boucher; Deacon Richard Lyles.
Res.: 200 W. 20th St., 33404-6160. Tel: 561-842-2482; Fax: 561-863-2985.

ROYAL PALM BEACH, PALM BEACH CO., OUR LADY QUEEN OF THE APOSTLES (1988) Revs. Zbigniew A. Rudnicki; Elifete St. Forte; Deacons Stephen Hayes; Luis J. Castellanos.
Res.: 100 Crestwood Blvd. S., 33411. Tel: 561-798-5661; Fax: 561-798-5663. Web: www.olqaroyalpalm.com.
Catechesis/Religious Program—Students 470.

SEBASTIAN, INDIAN RIVER CO., ST. SEBASTIAN (1981) Rev. John Morrissey; Deacon Steven Guess.
Mailing Address: 13075 U.S. Hwy. 1, 32978. Tel: 772-589-5790; Fax: 772-388-0084. Email: office@stsebastian.com. Web: www.stsebastian.com.
Catechesis/Religious Program—Tel: 772-589-4147. Students 260.

STUART, MARTIN CO.

1—ST. ANDREW (1999) Rev. John A. Barrow.
Church & Mailing: 2100 S.E. Cove Rd., 34997. Tel: 772-781-4415; Fax: 772-781-2906.
Catechesis/Religious Program—Students 70.

2—ST. JOSEPH (1916) Revs. Noel McGrath (Ireland); Juan Raul Cardenas.
Res.: 1200 E. 10th St., 34996. Tel: 772-287-2727; Fax: 772-287-4998. Email: maritam@sjcflorida.org. Web: sjcflorida.org.
School—Tel: 772-287-6975; Fax: 772-287-4733. Mrs. Mary Preston, Prin. Lay Teachers 35; Students 279.
Catechesis/Religious Program—Tel: 772-287-2727, Ext. 109. Glen Aitken, D.R.E. Students 355.

TEQUESTA, PALM BEACH CO., ST. JUDE (1962) Very Rev. Charles E. Notabartolo; Revs. Thomas Vengayil, Pastor Emeritus; Benedict Ndeyekiyo Mosha, A.L.C.P. (Tanzania).
Mailing Address: P.O. Box 3726, 33469.
Res.: 204 U.S. Hwy. One, 33469. Tel: 561-746-7974; Fax: 561-743-6127. Email: infostjude@bellsouth.net. Web: www.stjudecatholicchurch.com.
See All Saints Catholic School, Jupiter under Interparochial Schools located in the Institution section.
Catechesis/Religious Program—Tel: 561-746-1890; Fax: 561-743-6127. Students 189.

VERO BEACH, INDIAN RIVER CO.

1—ST. HELEN (1919) Very Rev. Michael W. Edwards; Rev. Msgr. Irvine Nugent, Pastor Emeritus (Retired); Revs. Tri Pham; Jean Wesner Boulin; Rodney Titus.
Res.: 2085 Tallahassee Ave., P.O. Box 2927, 32961. Tel: 772-567-5129; Fax: 772-567-1061. Email: sthelenchurch@hotmail.com. Web: sthelenvero.org.

School—2050 Vero Beach Ave., 32960. Tel: 772-567-5457; Fax: 772-567-4823. Howard Avril, Prin. Lay Teachers 17; Students 281.
Catechesis/Religious Program—2025 20th Ave., 32960. Tel: 772-562-5954; Fax: 772-562-2209. Email: sthelenre@bellsouth.net. Students 260.

2—HOLY CROSS (1981) Revs. Richard Murphy; Michael Massaro, C.S.C.; John B. O'Hare, Pastor Emeritus (Retired).
Res.: 500 Iris Ln., 32963. Tel: 772-231-0671; Fax: 772-234-5653.
Catechesis/Religious Program—Students 217.

3—ST. JOHN OF THE CROSS (1989) Revs. John J. Pasquini; John A. Crowley, Pastor Emeritus (Retired); Deacons Charles Mallory; Eugene Hoch; Joseph Verboys.
Res.: 950 82nd Ave., 32966. Tel: 772-563-0057; Fax: 772-563-9176.
Catechesis/Religious Program—Email: stjohnofthecross@bellsouth.net. Students 30.

WELLINGTON, PALM BEACH CO.

1—ST. RITA (1980) Revs. Donald Munro; Francisco Osorio.
Res.: 13645 Paddock Dr., 33414. Tel: 561-793-8544; Fax: 561-793-4082. Email: saintrita@bellsouth.net. Web: www.saintrita.com.
Catechesis/Religious Program—Whole Community Catechesis Faith Formation, Tel: 561-795-4321; Fax: 561-795-5478. Email: stritadonna@bellsouth.net. Students 1,600.

2—ST. THERESE DE LISIEUX (2000) Rev. Brian Lehnert; Deacons Alfred C. Payne; Bill Jacobs.
Mailing Address: 11800 Lake Worth Rd., 33449.
Rectory—3760 Cypress Edge Dr., Lake Worth, 33467. Tel: 561-784-0689; Fax: 561-784-8346.
Catechesis/Religious Program—Students 320.

WEST PALM BEACH, PALM BEACH CO.

1—ST. ANN (1895) Revs. James Murtagh; John D'Mello; Andre Dumarsais Pierre-Louis.
Our Lady Faith Haitian Center—Tel: 561-805-7712.
Res.: 310 N. Olive Ave., 33401. Tel: 561-832-3757; Fax: 561-659-1465.
School—Tel: 561-832-3676; Fax: 561-832-1791. Dr. Patrice A. Scheffler, Prin. Lay Teachers 22; Students 232.
Catechesis/Religious Program—Tel: 561-659-7026; Fax: 561-659-7024. Students 45.
St. Ann Place Outreach to the Homeless—2107 N. Dixie Hwy., 33407. Tel: 561-805-7708. Sr. Carleen Cekal, S.S.N.D., Dir.

2—HOLY NAME OF JESUS (1954) Revs. Gavin Badway; Ducasse Francois, I.V. Dei. (Haiti); Jaime Dorado (Colombia).
Res.: 345 S. Military Tr., 33415. Tel: 561-683-3555; Fax: 561-683-1051. Email: hnjchurch@aol.com. Web: www.holynameofjesuschurch.net.
School—Tel: 561-683-2990; Fax: 561-683-0803. Web: holynameofjesusschool.org. Michael Smith, Prin. Lay Teachers 9; Students 206.
Catechesis/Religious Program—Tel: 561-683-3555, Ext. 19. Email: sranne@holynameofjesuschurch.net. Students 350.

3—ST. JOHN FISHER (1963) Rev. Mario Castaneda.
Res.: 4001 N. Shore Dr., 33407. Tel: 561-842-1224; Fax: 561-842-8750. Email: stjohnfisher4001@aol.com.
Catechesis/Religious Program—Students 54.

4—ST. JULIANA (1949) Very Rev. Alfredo Hernandez; Revs. Camillus Temba, A.L.C.P.; Jose Crucet.
Res.: 4500 S. Dixie Hwy., 33405. Tel: 561-833-9745; Fax: 561-833-4992. Web: www.stjulianacatholicchurch.com.
School—4355 S. Olive Ave, 33405. Tel: 561-655-1922; Fax: 561-655-8552. Email: info@saintjuliana.org. Web: www.saintjuliana.org. Dr. Serena Brasco, Prin. Sisters of St. Joseph 1; Lay Teachers 22; Students 317.
Catechesis/Religious Program—Tel: 561-833-1278; Fax: 561-833-4992. Students 380.

5—MARY IMMACULATE (1974) Revs. Tomasz Makowski; Glen J. Pothier.
Res.: 390 Sequoia Dr., 33409. Tel: 561-686-8128; Fax: 561-686-6893.
Catechesis/Religious Program—Students 68.

Released from Diocesan Assignment:
Revs.—
Euteneuer, Thomas J., Human Life International, 4 Family Life, Front Royal, VA 22630.
Gallagher, John, Evangelization study and writing
Guerin, Louis T., M.Div., St. Vincent de Paul Regional Seminary, Boynton Beach, 33436-4899.
Horgan, Daniel B., US Airforce Chap.
Lacy, Aidan, St. Mary's Medical Center, P.O. Box 24620, 33416-4620.
O'Flanagan, Thomas P., US Navy Chap.
O'Toole, Timothy, Cross International Catholic Outreach

Retired:
Rev. Msgrs.—
Burke, James M.
McMahon, John
Nugent, Irvine
Revs.—
Block, John G.
Calle, Juan de la
Christopher, Mark
Crowley, John A.
Devereaux, Martin C.
Dockerill, Walter
Dolan, Peter C.
Fenech, Francis X.
Guinan, Frank
Hubert, Raymond P.
MacGabhann, Kevin
Murphy, Richard
O'Hare, John B.
O'Loughlin, Frank
Otto, Thomas
Powell, Bernard F.
Profeta, Salvatore
Rynne, Thomas J.
Schulz, Ronald
Skehan, John A.

Permanent Deacons:
Ambroise, Emile
Baker, Philip
Barbaro, Sam
Battison, Donald
Beaudoin, John
Beres, Ronald
Blake, Richard
Bloom, David
Breitfelder, Edward
Brooks, James
Caceres, Edgard
Castellanes, Luis
Champagne, Byron
Collins, George
Crary, Lawrence
Cresswell, William
Culhane, Neil
Cuseo, Anthony
Delgado, Alberto
Demes, Dennis, Ph.D.
DiMauro, Joseph
Dingee, Richard
Draughon, Woodworth R., Jr.
Ervin, Martin
Fathauer, Ronald
Ferguson, William
Fisher, Edward
Garamella, Robert
Gaucher, Paul
Gluhosky, Frank
Golden, Robert
Guess, Steven
Hamilton, Jack
Hankle, David
Hayes, Stephen
Hoch, Eugene
Jacobs, William
Klimazewski, Norbert
Lacey, James
Leone, Charles
Levenson, Lee
Lizardi, Mark
Loafman, Frank
Lopez, Jesus
Lucente, Salvatore
Lyles, Richard
Mallory, Charles
Mancuso, Terry
Matos, William
Mazzella, Peter
McBride, Peter
McMahon, Stephen
Melendez, Carlos
Menendez, Silvio
Meyer, James
Mieyal, Denis
Moser, Richard
Mostler, John
Munoz, Miguel
Murray, Paul
Nowak, Nick
O'Connell, Joseph
Ortiz, Jose
Pagliara, Daniel
Parlee, Charles W.
Payne, Alfred C.
Phillips, Lon
Pierce, Jack
Plucinski, Andrew
Pollock, Joseph
Pope, Robert
Powell, David R.
Raisch, Jack
Santana, Richard
Sawney, Ira (Grenada)
Schopfer, Richard
Scienzo, Stephen
Seppanen, Henry
Serraes, Martin
Sherman, Gregory
Sullivan, John
Turnbull, Bruce
Venezia, Richard
Verboys, Joseph
Voegele, Richard
Watzek, William
Wesley, Albert
Whalen, Charles
White, George
Wildes, William
Zapata, Jaime
Zatarga, Michael
Ziemianski, Lawrence L.

INSTITUTIONS LOCATED IN THE DIOCESE

[A] SEMINARIES, RELIGIOUS OR SCHOLASTICATES

BOYNTON BEACH. *St. Vincent de Paul Regional Seminary*, 10701 S. Military Tr., 33436. Tel: 561-732-4424; Fax: 561-737-2205. Web: svdp.edu. Rev. Msgr. Keith R. Brennan, J.C.D. (STA), Rector & Pres.; Revs. Steven Olds (ORL), Dean Spiritual Formation; Guillermo Arias, S.J., M.Ed.; Dr. Sixto Garcia, Ph.D.; Dr. Antonio Lopez, Ph.D.; Mr. Art Quinn, B.A., M.A., M.S., Ed.S., Library Dir.; Most Rev. Raymond Lessard, D.D., S.T.L., J.C.L.; Revs. Michael Muhr, S.P., M.Div., M.A.; Steven O'Hala, S.T.D. (MIA), Vice Rector, Dean of Academic Formation; Jose Juan Quijano, S.T.L., S.T.D. (MIA); Louis T. Guerin, M.Div., Dean Pastoral Formation; Rev. Msgr. Stephen Bosso, M.Div., S.S.L.; Revs. Jose N. Alfaro, H.E.B., H.E.L. (MIA), Dean of Students, Human Formation; Michael J. Flynn, M.Div., S.T.L. (PT), Liturgy Dir.; Sr. Margarita Gomez, R.M.I., S.T.L., D.Min.; Dr. Emilio Chavez, S.T.D., Ph.D.; Dr. Carol Razza; Sr. Joyce Lavoy, O.P., M.A., M.M.Ed.; Mr. Stanton Cadow, Dir., Inst. Devel.; Mr. Keith Parker, Campus Admin.; Mrs. Joyce Martinez, B.A., M.Ed., Dir. Language.

[B] HIGH SCHOOLS, DIOCESAN AND PAROCHIAL

BOCA RATON. *Pope John Paul II High School, Inc.*, 4001 N. Military Tr., 33431. Tel: 561-314-2100; Fax: 561-989-8582. Email: pjphs@pjpii.org. Web: www.pjpii.org. Dr. Michael J. Coury, Pres.; Sr. Eileen Sullivan, O.P., Prin.; Ms. Diane DeMarco, Campus Min.; Mr. Christopher Kilian, Asst. Prin.; Mrs. Susan Hanley, Media Specialist. Sisters 2; Lay Teachers 35; Students 463.

FORT PIERCE. *John Carroll High School, Inc.* (1962) 3402 Delaware Ave., 34947-6116. Tel: 772-464-5200; Fax: 772-464-5233. Email: jcchs@johncarrollhigh.com. Web: www.johncarrollhigh.com. Very Rev. Thomas E. Barrett, Pres.; Mr. Ben C. Hopper, Prin.; Elaine Welker, Media Specialist. Priests 1; Lay Teachers 29; Students 424.

WEST PALM BEACH. *Cardinal Newman High School, Inc.*, 512 Spencer Dr., 33409-3616. Tel: 561-683-6266; Fax: 561-683-7307. Email: jclarke@cardinalnewman.com. Web: www.cardinalnewman.com. Rev. David W. Carr, Pres.; John F. Clarke, Prin.; Ms. Susan Stephenson, Asst. Prin. Student Life; Ms. Theresa Fretterd, Asst. Prin. Academics; Rev. Andre Dumarsais Pierre-Louis, Chap.; Nelle Martin, Media Specialist. Priests 2; Deacons 1; Lay Teachers 53; Students 686.

[C] INTERPAROCHIAL SCHOOLS

JUPITER. *All Saints Catholic School*, 1759 Indian Creek Pkwy., 33458. Tel: 561-748-8994; Fax: 561-748-8979. Email: ascs@allsaintsjupiter.org. Web: www.allsaintsjupiter.org. Mrs. Mary Beth Quick, Prin.; Mrs. Kim Maihack, Librarian. Lay Teachers 38; Total Enrollment 442.

[D] SCHOOLS, PRIVATE

INDIANTOWN. *Hope Rural School*, (Grades PreK-5), 15929 S.W. 150th St., 34956. Tel: 772-597-2203; Fax: 772-597-2259. Email: hopesch@onearrow.net. Sisters Mary Dooley, S.S.N.D., Dir.; Katherine Kinnally, S.S.N.D., Prin. Sisters 2; Lay Teachers 14; Students 115.

WEST PALM BEACH. *Holy Cross Catholic Preschool & Center*, 930 Southern Blvd., 33405. Tel: 561-366-8026; Fax: 561-366-8577. Email: holycrosscpc@aol.com. Ana M. Fundora, Exec. Dir. Sisters 2; Lay Teachers 19; Students 100.

**Rosarian Academy*, (Grades PreK-8), 807 N. Flagler Dr., 33401. Tel: 561-832-5131; Fax: 561-820-8750. Email: info@rosarian.org. Web: www.rosarian.org. Sr. Corinne Sanders, O.P., Prin.; Betty Sayer, Librarian. Sisters of St. Dominic (Adrian, MI). Sisters 4; Lay Teachers 41; Students 422.

[E] GENERAL HOSPITALS

WEST PALM BEACH. *St. Mary's Hospital, Inc.*, 901 45th St., 33407-2495. Affiliated Support Organizations: *Women's Health Services, Inc.*

[F] HOMES FOR AGED

WEST PALM BEACH. *Lourdes-Noreen McKeen Residence for Geriatric Care*, 315 Flagler Dr. S., 33401. Tel: 561-655-8544; Fax: 561-650-8952. Web: www.lnmr.org. Sr. Mary Anne Dennehy, O.Carm., Admin.; Rev. Chinnappan M. Devaraj, O.F.M., Chap.

[G] PERSONAL PRELATURES

DELRAY BEACH. *Prelature of the Holy Cross and Opus Dei*, 4409 Frances Dr., 33445. Tel: 561-498-1249; Fax: 561-498-0054. Rev. Victor Cortes.

[H] MONASTERIES AND RESIDENCES OF PRIESTS AND BROTHERS

NORTH PALM BEACH. *Our Lady of Florida Spiritual Center*, 1300 U.S. Hwy. No. 1, 33408. Tel: 561-626-1300; Fax: 561-627-3956. Email: malbee@cpprov.org. Web: www.ourladyofflorida.org. Very Rev. Paul Wierichs, C.P., Dir.; Revs. Damian Towey, C.P., J.C.D.; Emmanuel Gardon, C.P.; Fidelis Connelly, C.P.; Patrick Daugherty, C.P.; Vincent Youngberg, C.P. Priests 4.

VERO BEACH. *Paulist Fathers Residence*, 1225 20th Ave., 32960. Tel: 772-562-0500; Fax: 772-794-9810. Revs. William J. Cantwell, C.S.P.; Charles A. Martin, C.S.P.; Michael J. Martin, C.S.F.

[I] CONVENTS AND RESIDENCES FOR SISTERS

DELRAY BEACH. *Christ the King Monastery of St. Clare* (Solemn Vows, Papal Enclosure), 3900 Sherwood Blvd., 33445-5699. Tel: 561-498-3294; Fax: 561-498-2281. Email: ctkmdelray@aol.com. Sr. Leanna Chrostowski, O.S.C., Abbess. Cloistered Sisters 9.

STUART. *Congregation of the Sisters of the Most Holy Soul of Christ*, 1042 E. 9th St., 34996. Tel: 772-286-5720. Email: sschusa@yahoo.com. Web: sistersofthemostholysoulofchrist.com. Sr. Martina Bednarz, C.A.C.H., Supr.

WEST PALM BEACH. *Adrian Dominican Sisters, Florida Mission Chapter*, 810 N. Olive Ave., 33401-3710. Tel: 561-832-6521; Fax: 561-832-0365. Email: alees@adriandominicans.org. Web: www.adriandominicans.org. Sr. Anne Liam Lees, O.P., Chapter Prioress.

Congregation of the Sisters of the Holy Cross, 2335 Edgewater Dr., 33406. Tel: 561-434-7593.

[J] RETREAT HOUSES

LANTANA. *The Cenacle Spiritual Life Center*, 1400 S. Dixie Hwy., 33462-5492. Tel: 561-582-2534; Fax: 561-582-8070. Email: cenaclefl@aol.com. Web: www.cenaclesisters.org. Spiritual Life Center for laity and religious. Sisters 6.

NORTH PALM BEACH. *Our Lady of Florida Spiritual Center*, 1300 U.S. Hwy. No. 1, 33408. Tel: 561-626-1300; Fax: 561-627-3956. Email: malbee@cpprov.org. Web: www.ourladyofflorida.org.

[K] MISCELLANEOUS LISTINGS

PALM BEACH GARDENS. *Catholic Charities Foundation of the Diocese of Palm Beach, Inc.*, 9995 N. Military Tr., 33410.

Catholic Charities of the Diocese of Palm Beach, Inc., P.O. Box 109650, 34410-9650. 9995 N. Military Tr., 34410. Tel: 561-775-9560; Fax: 561-625-5906.

Con El, Inc., P.O. Box 109650, 33410-9650.

Diocesan Council of Catholic Women, c/o P.O. Box 109650, 33410. Rev. Clemens Hammerschmitt, Diocesan Moderator; Jean Waddington, Pres. Tel: 561-641-5153.

Diocese of Palm Beach, Inc., P.O. Box 109650, 33410-9650.

Diocese of Palm Beach Burse Fund Trust

Diocese of Palm Beach Endowment Trust

Diocese of Palm Beach Health Plan Trust Very Rev. Charles E. Notabartolo, V.G., Chm.; Rev. Louis T. Guerin, M.Div., Chm.

Diocesan Pension Plan Trust Very Rev. Charles E. Notabartolo, V.G., Chm.

Diocese of Palm Beach Savings Fund Trust, Diocese of Palm Beach, P.O. Box 109650, 33410-9650. Mr. Denis Hamel, Chm.

Diocesan Property & Liability Insurance Committee Rev. Richard Murphy, Chm.

The Florida Catholic of Palm Beach, Inc., P.O. Box 109650, 33410-9650. Linda Reeves, Editor.

Helping Hands Scholarship Fund, Diocese of Palm Beach, Tel: 561-775-9547. P.O. Box 109650, 33410-9650.

BOCA RATON. *Christ Child Society of Boca Raton*, P.O. Box 811025, 33481-1025. Tel: 561-482-3067; Fax: 561-482-3087. Email: agnesgreg@aol.com.

Cross International Catholic Outreach, Inc., 370 W. Camino Gardens Blvd., 33432. Tel: 561-392-9212, Ext. 104; Fax: 561-367-0564. Email: info@crossinternational.org. Web: www.crosscatholic.org. Mr. James J. Cavnar, Pres.

Friends of Newman, Inc., 370 S.W. 3rd St., 33432.

BOYNTON BEACH. *St. Vincent de Paul Regional Seminary Endowment Trust*, 10701 S. Military Tr., 33436.

GREENACRES. *Villa Madonna*, 4809 Lake Worth Rd., 33463-3455. Tel: 561-963-1900; Fax: 561-963-1476. Email: thirdvilla@aol.com. Rosemary McMahon, Resident Mgr.

JENSEN BEACH. *Villa Assumpta, Inc.*, 2539 N.E. Mission Dr., 9-8, 34957. Tel: 561-334-0009; Fax: 561-334-2168. Email: villaassumpta1994@hotmail.com. Janice Foci, Resident Mgr.

NORTH PALM BEACH. *Christ Child Society of Palm Beach*, P.O. Box 14441, 33408. Tel: 561-795-0134. Email: mbishop110@aol.com.

PORT ST. LUCIE. *Villa Seton, Inc.*, 3300 S.W. Chartwell St., 34953. Tel: 772-344-6969; Fax: 772-344-7822. Lauren Feeney, Resident Mgr.

RIVIERA BEACH. **St. Vincent de Paul Salvage Store of West Palm Beach, Inc.*, 2647 Old Dixie Hwy., West Palm Beach, 33404-4119. Tel: 561-967-9699. Email: svdppalmbeach@att.net. Richard Persek, Pres.

Villa Franciscan, Inc., 2101 Avenue F, 33404. Tel: 561-840-0444; Fax: 561-840-9444. Email: vfan@bellsouth.net. Web: villafranciscan.catholicweb.com.

STUART. *Christ Child Society of Stuart*, P.O. Box 2007, 34995. Tel: 772-299-7852. Cheryle Mackie, Pres.

VERO BEACH. **St. Sebastian Conference of St. Vincent de Paul Society, Inc.*, 5480 85th St., 32967-5544.

WELLINGTON. *Magnificat Palm Beach Center, Inc.*, 1420 Sailboat Cir., 33414. Tel: 561-793-0343; Fax: 561-793-0343. Diane Bailey, Treas.; Dr. Carol Razza, Coord.

WEST PALM BEACH. *Villa Regina*, 2660 Haverhill Rd. N., 33417. Tel: 561-478-3900; Fax: 561-478-9787. Fay Smith-Williams, Resident Mgr.

RELIGIOUS INSTITUTES OF MEN REPRESENTED IN THE DIOCESE

For further details refer to the corresponding bracketed number in the Religious Institutes of Men or Women section.

[]—*Apostolic Life Community of Priests in the Opus Spiritus Sancti* (Tanzania)—A.L.C.P.
[0030]—*Congregation of St. Paul*—C.S.P.
[0610]—*Congregation of the Holy Cross*—C.S.C.
[0650]—*Congregation of the Holy Ghost of Ireland*—C.S.Sp.
[1000]—*Congregation of the Passion*—C.P.
[0260]—*Discalced Carmelite Friars*—O.C.D.
[0520]—*Franciscan Friars* (Holy Name Prov.)—O.F.M.
[0470]—*Franciscan Friars, Capuchin (Province of St. Augustine)*—O.F.M.Cap.
[0480]—*Franciscans Friars, Conventual*—O.F.M.Conv.
[0590]—*Missionaries of Holy Apostles*—M.S.A.
[1210]—*Missionaries of St. Charles Borromeo*—C.S.
[0910]—*Oblates of Mary Immaculate*—O.M.I.
[0920]—*Oblates of St. Francis de Sales*—O.S.F.S.
[0270]—*Order of Carmelites*—O.Carm.
[1040]—*Piarist Fathers*—Sch.P.
[1050]—*Pontifical Institute for Foreign Missions*—P.I.M.E.
[0700]—*St. Joseph Society of the Sacred Heart*—S.S.J.
[1190]—*Salesians of Don Bosco*—S.D.B.
[0690]—*Society of Jesus*—S.J.
[0370]—*Society of St. Columban*
[0590]—*Society of the Missionaries of Holy Apostles*—M.S.A.
[1060]—*Society of the Precious Blood*—C.PP.S.

RELIGIOUS INSTITUTES OF WOMEN REPRESENTED IN THE DIOCESE

[0330]—*Carmelite Sisters for the Aged and Infirm*—O.Carm.
[0685]—*Claretian Missionary Sisters*—R.M.I.
[3710]—*Congregation of St. Agnes*—C.S.A.
[1930]—*Congregation of the Sisters of the Holy Cross*—C.S.C.
[1710]—*Congregation of the Third Order of St. Francis of Mary Immaculate*—O.S.F.
[]—*Consecrated Virgin*—C.V.
[1070-03]—*Dominican Sisters* (Sinsinawa, WI)—O.P.
[1070-13]—*Dominican Sisters* (Adrian, MI)—O.P.
[]—*Dominican Sisters of Blawville* (New York)
[1070-16]—*Dominican Sisters of Hope*—O.P.
[1115]—*Dominican Sisters of Peace*—O.P.
[]—*Dominican Sisters of Peace*
[1070-17]—*Dominican Sisters of St. Catherine de Ricci*—O.P.
[1180]—*Franciscan Sisters of Allegany, NY*—O.S.F.
[1845]—*Guadalupan Missionaries of the Holy Spirit*—M.G.Sp.S
[]—*Hermitage of the Diocese of Palm Beach*
[2300]—*Little Servant Sisters of the Immaculate Conception*
[2470]—*Maryknoll Sisters of St. Dominic*—M.M.
[2490]—*Medical Mission Sisters*—M.M.S.
[3760]—*Order of St. Clare*—O.S.C.
[3110]—*Religious of Our Lady of the Cenacle*—R.C.
[3465]—*Religious of the Sacred Heart of Mary*—R.S.H.M.
[2970]—*School Sisters of Notre Dame*—S.S.N.D.
[]—*Sisters for Christian Community*—S.F.C.C.
[0590]—*Sisters of Charity of St. Elizabeth* (Convent Station, NJ)—S.C.
[2110]—*Sisters of Humility of Mary*—H.M.
[2560]—*Sisters of Mary Reparatrix*—S.M.R.
[2520]—*Sisters of Mercy* (Dublin, Ireland)—R.S.M.
[2575]—*Sisters of Mercy of the Americas*—R.S.M.
[1630]—*Sisters of St. Francis of Penance and Christian Charity*—O.S.F.
[3840]—*Sisters of St. Joseph of Carondelet*—C.S.J.
[3900]—*Sisters of St. Joseph of St. Augustine*—S.S.J.
[0260]—*Sisters of the Blessed Sacrament*—S.B.S.
[1990]—*Sisters of the Holy Names of Jesus and Mary*—S.N.J.M.
[]—*Sisters of the Most Holy Soul of Jesus*—S.S.C.H.
[2150]—*Sisters, Servants of the Immaculate Heart of Mary*—I.H.M.

DIOCESAN CEMETERIES

ROYAL PALM BEACH. *Our Lady Queen of Peace Catholic Cemetery, Inc.*, 10941 Southern Blvd., 33406. Tel: 561-793-0711; Fax: 561-793-0182. Email: info@ourqueen.org. Web: www.ourqueen.org. Rev. Zbigniew A. Rudnicki, Dir.; Mr. Thomas Jordan, Admin.

NECROLOGY

(No Deaths)

Diocese of Paterson

(Dioecesis Patersonensis)

Most Reverend

ARTHUR J. SERRATELLI

Bishop of Paterson; ordained December 20, 1968; appointed Titular Bishop of Enera and Auxiliary Bishop of Newark July 3, 2000; Episcopal ordination September 8, 2000; appointed Bishop of Paterson June 1, 2004.

Most Reverend

FRANK J. RODIMER, D.D., J.C.D.

Retired Bishop of Paterson; ordained May 19, 1951; appointed Bishop of Paterson December 13, 1977; ordained and installed February 28, 1978; retired June 1, 2004. *Res.: 1082 Greenpond Rd., Green Pond, NJ 07435.*

Diocesan Center: 777 Valley Rd., Clifton, NJ 07013. Tel: 973-777-8818; Fax: 973-777-8976.

Web: www.patersondiocese.org

ESTABLISHED DECEMBER 9, 1937.

Square Miles 1,214.

Comprises the Counties of Passaic, Morris and Sussex in the State of New Jersey.

For legal titles of parishes and diocesan institutions, consult the Chancery Office.

STATISTICAL OVERVIEW

Personnel	
Bishop	1
Retired Bishops	1
Abbots	2
Retired Abbots	5
Priests: Diocesan Active in Diocese	152
Priests: Diocesan Active Outside Diocese	16
Priests: Retired, Sick or Absent	80
Number of Diocesan Priests	248
Religious Priests in Diocese	126
Total Priests in Diocese	374
Extern Priests in Diocese	22
Ordinations:	
Diocesan Priests	8
Religious Priests	1
Transitional Deacons	7
Permanent Deacons	12
Permanent Deacons in Diocese	212
Total Brothers	30
Total Sisters	728
Parishes	
Parishes	111
With Resident Pastor:	
Resident Diocesan Priests	99
Resident Religious Priests	8
Without Resident Pastor:	
Administered by Priests	4
Pastoral Centers	5
Professional Ministry Personnel:	
Brothers	2
Sisters	26
Lay Ministers	120
Welfare	
Catholic Hospitals	3
Total Assisted	949,712
Homes for the Aged	6
Total Assisted	440
Residential Care of Children	1
Total Assisted	70
Day Care Centers	6
Total Assisted	1,600
Specialized Homes	2
Total Assisted	1,500
Special Centers for Social Services	12
Total Assisted	64,000
Residential Care of Disabled	12
Total Assisted	90
Educational	
Diocesan Students in Other Seminaries	41
Seminaries, Religious	2
Students Religious	4
Total Seminarians	45
Colleges and Universities	2
Total Students	2,156
High Schools, Diocesan and Parish	4
Total Students	2,518
High Schools, Private	4
Total Students	1,342
Elementary Schools, Diocesan and Parish	41
Total Students	10,130
Elementary Schools, Private	3
Total Students	521
Catechesis/Religious Education:	
High School Students	9,572
Elementary Students	33,344
Total Students under Catholic Instruction	59,628
Teachers in the Diocese:	
Priests	16
Brothers	8
Sisters	60
Lay Teachers	838
Vital Statistics	
Receptions into the Church:	
Infant Baptism Totals	6,977
Minor Baptism Totals	93
Adult Baptism Totals	128
Received into Full Communion	219
First Communions	6,998
Confirmations	4,942
Marriages:	
Catholic	1,025
Interfaith	264
Total Marriages	1,289
Deaths	3,216
Total Catholic Population	424,722
Total Population	1,129,405

Former Bishops—Most Revs. THOMAS H. MCLAUGHLIN, S.T.D., LL.D., cons. July 25, 1935; transferred to Paterson, Dec. 16, 1937; died March 17, 1947; THOMAS A. BOLAND, S.T.D., LL.D., cons. July 25, 1940; transferred to Paterson, June 21, 1947; transferred to Newark as Archbishop, Nov. 15, 1952; died March 16, 1979; JAMES A. MCNULTY, D.D., appt. Auxiliary Bishop of Newark, Aug. 2, 1947; cons. Oct. 7, 1947; appt. Bishop of Paterson, April 9, 1953; transferred to Diocese of Buffalo, Feb. 12, 1963; died Sept. 4, 1972; JAMES J. NAVAGH, D.D., cons. Sept. 24, 1952; appt. Bishop of Ogdensburg, May 8, 1957; transferred to Bishop of Paterson, Feb. 12, 1963; died Oct. 2, 1965; LAWRENCE B. CASEY, D.D., appt. Auxiliary Bishop of Rochester, Feb. 10, 1953; cons. May 5, 1953; appt. Bishop of Paterson, March 9, 1966; died June 15, 1977; FRANK J. RODIMER, D.D., J.C.D. (Retired), appt. Bishop of Paterson Dec. 13, 1977; ord. Feb. 28, 1978; resigned June 1, 2004.

Vicar General and Moderator of the Curia—Rev. Msgr. JAMES T. MAHONEY, Ph.D., V.G.

Chief Operating Officer—Mr. THOMAS A. BARRETT.

Chief Financial Officer—Mr. PAUL I. RUBACKY.

Episcopal Vicars—

Education—Rev. PAUL S. MANNING.

Evangelization—Rev. GENO SYLVA, S.T.D., Vicar for Evangelization.

Pastoral Administration—Rev. Msgr. WILLIAM P. STOBER.

Deans—Revs. ANTONIO RODRIGUEZ, Passaic; JOHN T. CONNOLLY, M.Div., Clifton; JOSEPH J. GARBARINO, Northeast Morris; Rev. Msgr. MARK J. GIORDANI, Paterson; Rev. JOHN P. PILIPIE, Sussex; Rev. Msgrs. T. MARK CONDON, J.C.L., S.T.L., Mid-Passaic; JOSEPH J. GOODE, M.Ch.A., Southwest Morris; RAYMOND J. KUPKE, Ph.D., Southeast Morris; Revs. ROBERT J. MITCHELL, Western Morris; JUDE S. SALUS, O.S.B., Eastern Morris; MARC MANCINI, J.C.L., Northern Morris; FREDERICK WALTERS, Northern Passaic.

Chancellor/Delegate for Religious—Sr. MARY EDWARD SPOHRER, S.C.C.

Vice Chancellors—Revs. MARC MANCINI, J.C.L.; T. KEVIN CORCORAN.

Archivist—Rev. Msgr. RAYMOND J. KUPKE, Ph.D.

Priest Secretary to the Bishop—Rev. T. KEVIN CORCORAN.

Secretary to the Bishop—Mrs. BARBARA FIERRO.

Secretary to the Vicar General and Chancellor—Mrs. ARLINE PERRO.

Secretary to the Vice Chancellors—Mrs. KERRY TIMONEY.

Diocesan Counsel—KENNETH F. MULLANEY JR.

Diocesan Tribunal—

Judicial Vicar—Rev. Msgr. EDWARD J. KURTYKA, P.A., J.C.D.

Adjutant Judicial Vicar—Rev. Msgr. JOSEPH T. ANGINOLI, J.C.L.

Judge—Rev. MARK A. MANCINI, M.Div.

Advocates—Revs. JOHN T. CONNOLLY, M.Div.; VINCENT B. GROGAN, O.F.M., J.C.D.

Auditors—Revs. PAUL IOVINO (Retired); JOHN P. HANLEY (Retired).

Defenders of the Bond—Rev. Msgrs. T. MARK CONDON, J.C.L., S.T.L.; GEORGE F. HUNDT, J.C.L.

Canonical Advisor—Rev. Msgr. JOSEPH J. GOODE, M.Ch.A.

Pro-Synodal Judges—Rev. MICHAEL J. BURKE, S.T.M., J.D.; Rev. Msgr. JOHN J. CARROLL, Ed.D.; Rev. JOHN T. CATOIR, J.C.D. (Retired); Rev. Msgrs. JOHN E. HART; JOHN J. DEMKOVICH; HERBERT K. TILLYER, P.A., M.Ch.A.; THOMAS J. TRAPASSO, S.T.L. (Retired); Rev. REGIS P. WALLACE, O.S.B.

Administrative Assistants and Notaries—Mrs. SHAWN VACCA; Mrs. MARY BETH LEONHARD.

Consulting Psychologist—THOMAS E. KAVANAGH, Psy.D.; Revs. RICHARD MUCOWSKI, O.F.M.; GREGORY A. BATTAFARANO, O.Carm., M.S., L.P.C.
Minister to Priests—Rev. Msgr. PETER J. DOODY.
Vocations Office—737 Valley Rd., Clifton, 07013. Tel: 973-777-2955; Fax: 973-777-4597. Revs. THOMAS H. FALLONE, Dir.; T. KEVIN CORCORAN, Asst. Dir.
Vocations Board—Revs. STANLEY C. BARRON; WILLIAM B. COLLINS; MARK OLENOWSKI; ANTONIO GAVIRIA; MARC MANCINI, J.C.L.; STEFAN LAS.
Consultative Bodies—
Presbyteral Council—Rev. Msgr. JOHN E. HART, Chm.; Rev. PATRICK RICE, Vice Chm.; Rev. Msgr. RICHARD A. STEIGER; Rev. EIDER REYES; Rev. Msgrs. LOUIS J. BIHR; JOHN J. CARROLL, Ed.D.; Revs. FRANK P. AGRESTI; BRIAN SULLIVAN; Rev. Msgrs. JAMES H. O'RORKE (Retired); GEORGE F. HUNDT, J.C.L.; JAMES T. MAHONEY, Ph.D., V.G.; Revs. MICHAEL RODAK; ANTONIO RODRIGUEZ; JUDE S. SALUS, O.S.B.
College of Consultors—Rev. Msgr. JOHN E. HART, Chm.; Rev. PATRICK RICE, Vice Chm.; Rev. Msgrs. RICHARD A. STEIGER; JAMES H. O'RORKE (Retired); Revs. EIDER REYES; MICHAEL RODAK; Rev. Msgr. LOUIS J. BIHR; Rev. BRIAN SULLIVAN; Rev. Msgrs. GEORGE F. HUNDT, J.C.L.; JAMES T. MAHONEY, Ph.D., V.G.; Revs. MARC MANCINI, J.C.L.; ANTONIO RODRIGUEZ.
College of Deans—Rev. ROBERT J. MITCHELL, Chm.
Finance Council—LORRAINE HRICIK-DEL GUERCIO, Chm.; Sr. MARY EDWARD SPOHRER, S.C.C.; Mr. STANTON J. FEELEY; Mr. THOMAS A. BARRETT; Mr. PAUL I. RUBACKY; Mr. JOHN BERGER; Mr. JAMES GARIBALDI; Mr. CHARLES PASCARELLA; Mr. MICHAEL RESCOE; Rev. Msgr. JAMES T. MAHONEY, Ph.D., V.G.; Mr. WILLIAM MCLAUGHLIN; Mr. EUGENE R. SYLVA.
Theological Commission—Rev. Msgrs. JOHN E. HART; T. MARK CONDON, J.C.L., S.T.L.; Sr. KATHLEEN FLANAGAN, S.C., Ph.D.; Dr. JAMES INCARDONA, Ph.D.; Rev. ALEKSY KOWALSKI, Ph.D.; Rev. Msgr. RAYMOND J. KUPKE, Ph.D.; Revs. ANTHONY J. MASTROENI, S.T.D., J.D.; CHARLES J. PARR, Ph.D.; Rev. Msgr. HERBERT K. TILLYER, P.A., M.Ch.A.; Dr. DIANNE TRAFLET, J.D., S.T.D.
Pastoral Council—Mrs. JANET HOVEN, Chm.
Justice and Peace Commission—Rev. PATRICK RICE, Chm.
Liturgical Commission—VACANT, Chm.
Hispanic Commission—Mr. RAUL E. PAMPLONA, Chm.
Black Catholic Ministries Commission—Mrs. RUTH LAWSON, Chm.
Education Council—Mr. EDWIN PETERSON, Chm.

Diocesan Secretariats

Communications Secretariat—Mailing Address: 597 Valley Rd., P.O. Box 1887, Clifton, 07015. Tel: 973-278-3202; Fax: 973-279-2265. Mr. RICHARD A. SOKERKA, Exec. Sec.; VACANT, Communications; Mr. JOSEPH CECE, Webmaster. Email: cecej@infonetdev.com.
Diocesan Newspaper, "The Beacon"—Tel: 973-279-8845. Mr. RICHARD A. SOKERKA, Editor & Gen. Mgr.; Mr. MICHAEL WOJCIK, News Editor.
Catholic Campus Ministry Television—Tel: 973-595-6184. Directors: Rev. LOUIS J. SCURTI; Mr. RUSSELL MYERS III.
Media Resource Center—777 Valley Rd., Clifton, 07013. Tel: 973-777-8818. Ms. MARYANNE NILAN, Consultant.
Secretariat for Evangelization—777 Valley Rd., Clifton, 07013. Tel: 973-777-8818. Rev. GENO SYLVA, S.T.D., Vicar for Evangelization; Mr. PHILIP A. RUSSO, Exec. Sec.
Office of Family Life—Mrs. MARIE RYAN, Consultant.
Respect Life—Dr. MARY MAZZARELLA, Consultant.
Parish Catechetics Office—Mr. THOMAS BROWN, Consultant.
Catechetical Leaders Association—SUE REILLY.
Office of Multicultural Ministries—Rev. ENRIQUE CORONA, Consultant.
Commission for Hispanic Catholic Ministry—Ms. YADIRA MOHARITA.
Office of Worship and Spirituality—Rev. Msgr. T. MARK CONDON, J.C.L., S.T.L., Dir.
Liturgical Commission—Rev. Msgr. T. MARK CONDON, J.C.L., S.T.L.
Environment and Architecture Committee—VACANT.
Initiation Committee—Ms. JOANNE CALAFIORE.
Diocesan Chapter, National Pastoral Musicians—Mr. PAUL CUSTLER.
Diocesan Choir—Mr. PAUL CUSTLER.
Office of Youth Ministry—Mr. PHILIP A. RUSSO, Consultant.
Catholic Scouting—
Boy Scouting—Rev. PETER J. CLARKE, Chap.
Girl Scouting—Rev. FRANK P. AGRESTI, Chap.
Office of Campus Ministry—Rev. LOUIS J. SCURTI, Coord. Tel: 973-595-6184.
Ecumenical Officer—Rev. CHARLES J. PARR, Ph.D., 597 Valley Rd., Clifton, 07013. Tel: 973-777-5651.
Related Organizations—
Catholic Deaf Society—Rev. Msgrs. JOSEPH J. GOODE, M.Ch.A., Moderator, 24 Ann Rd., Long Valley, 07853. Tel: 908-850-0263; THOMAS J. TRAPASSO, S.T.L., Asst. Moderator (Retired).
Charismatic Renewal—Rev. NICHOLAS BOZZA, Liaison. Tel: 973-347-0032.
English Cursillos—Mr. MIKE WILSON, Lay Dir.; Rev. RAYMOND ORAMA, Spiritual Advisor.
Spanish Cursillos—LUIS SALERNA, Lay Dir.; WILLIAM TORRES; Rev. BRANDO IBARRA, Spiritual Advisor.
Retrouvaille—Contact Couple: PAT GALLO; TOM GALLO. Tel: 732-238-0234.
World Wide Marriage Encounter—Executive Couple: MICHAEL MORGAN; EILEEN MORGAN. Tel: 973-827-9606. Registration Couple: EILEEN PEREZ; RALPH PEREZ. Tel: 800-499-6552.
Secretariat for Pastoral Administration—737 Valley Rd., Clifton, 07013. Tel: 973-777-2955.
Vicar for Pastoral Administration—Rev. Msgr. WILLIAM P. STOBER.
Clergy Personnel Office—Rev. Msgrs. RAYMOND M. LOPATESKY, Dir.; THOMAS J. COLETTA, Asst. Dir.; Mrs. ROSEMARY J. DONNELLY, Administrative Asst.
Deacon Internship Program—Rev. Msgr. FRANCIS J. DUFFY, Dir., 250 Speedwell Ave., Morris Plains, 07950. Tel: 973-538-1418.
Ministry for Priestly Formation and Education—VACANT.
Priestly Life Committee—Revs. HERNAN ARIAS; PAWEL F. SZUREK; MARK OLENOWSKI; STANLEY C. BARRON; DAVID MCDONNELL.
Mission Office—24 DeGrasse St., Paterson, 07505. Tel: 973-278-3491. Rev. Msgr. JOHN J. DEMKOVICH, Dir.; Rev. STANLEY C. BARRON, Assoc. Dir.
Office of Health Care Ministry—205 Madison Ave., Madison, 07940. Tel: 973-443-9300. VACANT.
Office of the Permanent Diaconate—205 Madison Ave., Madison, 07940. Tel: 973-443-9300; Fax: 973-443-4140; 973-777-8976. Rev. EUGENE R. SYLVA, Dir.; Deacon KEVIN CLEARY, Asst. Dir.
Victim Assistance Coordinator—Ms. PEGGY ZANELLO. Tel: 973-879-1489.
Division of Finance and Budget—777 Valley Rd., Clifton, 07013. Tel: 973-777-8818. Mr. THOMAS A. BARRETT, COO.
Division of Finance and Budget—Mr. PAUL I. RUBACKY, CFO; Ms. JOLANTA LONDENE, Controller; Mr. TIMOTHY POTTER, Dir. Devel.; Ms. ISAMARIE LOPEZ, Asst.
Diocesan Cemeteries Office—58 McLean Blvd., Paterson, 07513. Tel: 973-279-2900. Rev. Msgr. HERBERT K. TILLYER, P.A., M.Ch.A., Dir.; Mr. JOHN M. CAVANAUGH, Asst. Dir.
Office of Business Administration—Deacon ROBERT AYERS, Business Mgr.; Mr. JAMES FIERRO, Diocesan Facilities Mgr.; REBECA RUIZ, Diocesan Architect.
Office of Human Resources—Ms. JOAN VALK, Dir.; Mrs. VIRGINIA EMAUS, Employee Benefits; Mr. RICHARD ZICCARDI, Risk Mgr.
Youth and Protection—VACANT, Coord.
School Division—777 Valley Rd., Clifton, 07013. Tel: 973-777-8818. Rev. PAUL S. MANNING, Vicar for Educ.; Mr. JOHN R. ERIKSEN, Supt. Assistant Superintendents Elementary Education: Mrs. SHEILA O'LEARY; Mrs. LINDA KOSTENKO; Sr. RITA MARIE FRITZEN, O.S.F.; Mr. JOHN FANELLI, Asst. Supt. Technology; Mr. PATRICK PEACE, Dir. School Admin. Svcs.; Mr. EDWIN PETERSON, Educ. Council Pres.; Sr. JUNE MORRISSEY, S.C., Pres. Elementary Principals' Assoc.
Secretariat for Catholic Charities—24 DeGrasse St., Paterson, 07505. Tel: 973-279-7100; Fax: 973-523-1150. Mr. JOSEPH F. DUFFY, Exec. Sec.; Rev. EDWARD LAMBRO, Dir. Devel. & Public Rels.
Hispanic Information Center—270 Passaic St., Passaic, 07055. Tel: 973-779-7022. Mr. LORENZO HERNANDEZ, Dir.
Catholic Family and Community Services—Mr. JOSEPH F. DUFFY, Exec. Dir.; Mr. ROBERT JACOB, Assoc. Dir. & CFO; Ms. CATHERINE SPINA, Admin. Asst.; Rev. MICHAEL J. BURKE, S.T.M., J.D., Staff Attorney.
Aging Services—Tel: 973-279-4300. Ms. LINDA WARD, Sussex County. Tel: 973-209-0123; Ms. RITA KELLY, Passaic County. Tel: 973-279-7100, Ext. 33.
Adoption and Counseling Services—476 17th Ave., Paterson, 07504. Tel: 973-523-9595. Rev. THOMAS MCGRATH, Dir.
Friendship Corner—279 Carroll St., Paterson, 07509. Tel: 973-569-0001. Ms. ELLEN TULLY, Dir.
Italian Catholic Center—24 DeGrasse St., Paterson, 07501. Tel: 973-278-4955. Miss PHILOMENA DESOPO, Dir.
Mount Saint Joseph Children's Center—124 Shepherd Ln., Totowa, 07512. Tel: 973-595-5720. Ms. PATRICIA S. VERDUIN, Dir.
Multi-Lingual Center—24 DeGrasse St., Paterson, 07501. Tel: 973-279-7100. Ms. ROSE KARADASHIAN, Dir.
Partnership for Social Services—48 Wyker Rd., Franklin, 07416. Tel: 973-827-4702. Sr. THOMASINA GEBHARD, S.S.M., Dir.
Marian Aids Ministry—Sr. MARIA ELIZABETH WHILIFER, Dir.
Father English Multi-Purpose Community Center—435 Main St., Paterson, 07501. Tel: 973-881-0280. Mr. JOSEPH MELOSH, Dir.
Preschool Day Care Center Programs— A Child's World-El Mundo del Nino; Ms. EUNICE RAMIREZ, Dir.
El Mundo de Colores—44 Ward St., Paterson, 07505. Tel: 973-523-0919. Ms. LAURA ZARIFE, Dir.
After School Programs—Ms. AIDA ZARATE, Dir.
Teenage After School Program—Mr. JUAN GONZALEZ, Dir.
Work Assistance Program—Mr. JUAN GONZALEZ, Dir.
Senior and Disabled Transportation—MICHAEL DRAKEFORD, Dir.
Emergency Food and Clothing Programs—Mr. CARLOS ROLDAN, Dir.
Passaic Teen Center—228 Hope Ave., Passaic, 07055. Tel: 973-473-5755. VACANT, Dir.
Youth Haven— (Shelter-Crisis Intervention) *212 Slater St., Paterson, 07501.* Tel: 973-881-1661. VACANT, Dir.
Hope House— (Catholic Social Services of Morris County, Inc.) *19-21 Belmont Ave., Dover, 07801.* Tel: 973-361-5555. Mrs. DIANE SIBERNAGEL, Exec. Dir.; Ms. ANGELA VANCE, Dir. Devel. & Publicity; Mrs. JUDI WESLEY, Dir. Prevention Svcs.; Ms. KRIS ERNST, Dir. Behavioral Health Svcs.; JIJU KOTTARTHIL, Chief Accountant.
Department for Persons with Disabilities—1049 Weldon Rd., Oak Ridge, 07438. Tel: 973-697-4394. Ms. JULIE TATTI, Exec. Dir.; Mr. SCOTT MILLIKEN, Asst. Exec. Dir.; Ms. JOANNA MILLER, Asst. Exec. Dir.; Sr. JOAN KATHLEEN GERCKE, S.S.J., Staffing & Pastoral Care Coord.; Mr. ROCCO ZAPPILE, CFO; Mr. ROY DE FRANCO, Dir. Devel.
Group Homes—Murray House, 86 Allwood Place, Clifton, 07015. Tel: 973-470-5694. Ms. PAMELA VANECK, Dir. *Barnet House, 52 Lenox Ave., Pompton Lakes, 07442.* Tel: 973-409-2764. MARIA CASTNER, Dir. *Finnegan House, 1049 Weldon Rd., Oak Ridge, 07438.* Tel: 973-697-1246. Ms. LYNNE ROCKSTROH, Dir. *Alexander House, 1049 Weldon Rd., Oak Ridge, 07438.* Tel: 973-697-1812. Ms. CLARA BECK, Dir. *Columbus House, 1048 Weldon Rd., Oak Ridge, 07438.* Tel: 973-697-1644. Ms. CHERYL SLATE, Dir. *Fitzpatrick House, 215 Mountain Ave., Pompton Lakes, 07442.* Tel: 973-248-1569. Mr. CHRISTOPHER BRANCATO, Dir. *Wehrlen House, 18 Bisset Dr., West Milford, 07480.* Tel: 973-208-1883. MARCIA WYNNE, Dir. *Gruenert Employment Center, 725 Rte. 15 S., Lake Hopatcong, 07849.* Tel: 973-663-9102. Mrs. KATHY DE YOUNG, Dir. *Basile Apartment, Brittany Chase, Wayne, 07470.* Tel: 973-694-9591. Mr. JEFFREY ONDIMU. *Calabrese House, 829 Littleton Rd., Parsippany, 07054.* Tel: 973-299-8360. LORI EVANS, Dir. *Wallace House, 447 Glen Rd., Sparta, 07871.* Tel: 973-276-3470. Ms. KIM WALTER, Dir. *Keleher Apartments, 124 Barrister Dr., Butler, 07405.* Tel: 973-283-8475. Ms. ISABEL MARTE, Dir.
Straight and Narrow, Inc.—508 Straight St., Paterson, 07503. Tel: 973-345-6000. Mr. DAVID J. MACTAS, Exec. Dir.; Dr. JUDITH HERSCHLAG, Ph.D., Dir. Clinical Svcs.; Ms. SARA PASQUINO, Dir. Alpha-II Prog.; Dr. HAYMAN RAMBARAN, Dir. Straight and Narrow Detox/Medical Unit; Ms. KAREN ROCCISANO, Dir., Alpha I & III Programs; Mr. VITO ANDRISANI, Out-Patient Svcs.; LILIKO OGOSOWARA, Dir. Adolescent Treatment; Rev. Msgr. LOUIS J. BIHR, Dir. Pastoral Care Unit. *Family Success Center*, Ms. REINA RIVAS, Dir. *Adult Medical Day Care Center, 182 First St., Passaic, 07055.* Ms. MARIE BROWN, Dir. In Res.: Rev. Msgr. WILLIAM M. NAUGHTON.
Migrant Ministry—Shrine of St. Joseph, 1050 Long Hill Rd., Stirling, 07980. Tel: 973-896-0444. Bro. JOHN SKRODINSKY, S.T., Esq., Dir.; LUIS ARIAS, Asst. Dir.; Rev. RAFAEL PIRROS, S.T.
Affiliated Organizations—
Apostleship of Prayer—Rev. Msgr. CHRISTOPHER C. DILELLA, Dir., 26 Green Village Rd., Madison, 07040. Tel: 973-377-4000.
Diocesan Council of Catholic Women—Rev. Msgr. JOSEPH A. CIAMPAGLIO, Dir.; Mrs. MAUREEN JOYCE, Pres., 8 Glenwood Mountain Rd., Sussex, 07461.

Diocesan Holy Name Federation—Mr. FRANK STEINER, Pres.
Legion of Mary—Rev. Msgr. JOHN J. DEMKOVICH, Spiritual Dir.; Mrs. LUCY LEONE, Pres., 63 Monroe St., Passaic, 07055. Tel: 973-779-0427.
Priests Eucharistic League—Rev. Msgr. CHRISTOPHER C. DILELLA, Dir.

CLERGY, PARISHES, MISSIONS AND PAROCHIAL SCHOOLS

CITY OF PATERSON

(PASSAIC COUNTY)

1—CATHEDRAL OF ST. JOHN THE BAPTIST (1820) [CEM] Rev. Msgr. Mark J. Giordani; Revs. Ruben Dario Castillo (Colombia); Misael Jaramillo; Deacons Jose Pomales; Guido Pedraza; Hector Castellanos.
Res.: 381 Grand St., 07505. Tel: 973-345-4070; Fax: 973-345-7831.
Catechesis / Religious Program—Students 291.

2—ST. AGNES (1883) Rev. Luis A. Rendon, Admin.; Deacons Gilberto Vazquez; Pedro Cruz.
Res.: 681 Main St., 07503. Tel: 973-279-0250; Fax: 973-357-1218.
Catechesis / Religious Program—Students 130.

3—ST. ANTHONY'S (1909), (Italian), Rev. Eider Reyes.
Res.: 138 Beech St., 07501. Tel: 973-742-9695; Fax: 973-881-0522.
Catechesis / Religious Program—Students 110.

4—BLESSED SACRAMENT (1911), (Italian), Revs. J. Patrick Ryan; Heriberto Guerra.
Res.: 224 E. 18th St., 07524. Tel: 973-523-5002; Fax: 973-523-3766.
School—(1953) 289-Sixth Ave., 07524. Tel: 973-278-8787; Fax: 973-278-6436. Sr. Noreen Holly, S.C., Prin. Maestre Pie Filippini (Religious Teachers Filippini) 4; Lay Teachers 8; Students 200.
Catechesis / Religious Program—Students 100.

5—ST. BONAVENTURE (1877) Revs. Daniel P. Grigassy, O.F.M.; Christian F. Camadella, O.F.M.; Christopher VanHaight, O.F.M., Parochial Vicar; Deacons Joseph Balough; Anthony Fierro.
Res.: 174 Ramsey St., 07501. Tel: 973-279-1016; Fax: 973-279-2507.
Catechesis / Religious Program—Students 220.

6—ST. CASIMIR'S (1911), (Lithuanian), Rev. John P. Hanley, Admin. (Retired).
Res.: 501 W. Broadway, 07522. Tel: 973-595-8446; Fax: 973-790-0778.

7—ST. GEORGE (1897) Revs. John J. Klein; Nelson Betancur; Deacons William Hussey, (Retired); Eugenio Morales.
Res.: 408 Getty Ave., 07503. Tel: 973-742-0350; Fax: 973-754-0657.
Catechesis / Religious Program—Students 89.

8—ST. GERARD MAJELLA (1962) Revs. Ezio Antunes, S.D.V.; Lorenzo Gomez, S.D.V., Parochial Vicar; Robert Vass, S.D.V., Parochial Vicar. In Res., Rev. Charles J. Waller.
Res.: 501 W. Broadway, 07522. Tel: 973-595-8446; Fax: 973-790-0778.
School—(1965)Tel: 973-595-5640; Fax: 973-595-5475. Sisters 1; Lay Teachers 9; Students 205.
Catechesis / Religious Program—Students 88.

9—ST. JOSEPH'S (1867) Rev. Robert W. Wisniefski; Deacons Ronald Romano; Hector Casillas.
Res.: 399 Market St., 07501. Tel: 973-278-0030.
See Pope John Paul II School, Clifton under Elementary Schools, Diocesan located in the Institution section.
Catechesis / Religious Program—Students 163.

10—ST. MARY'S (1873), (Auxilium Christianorum) Rev. Jorge I. Rodriguez; Deacons Antonio Salierno; Juan Carlos Carnero; Jose Trinidad.
Res.: 410 Union Ave., 07502. Tel: 973-790-8651; Fax: 973-790-8534.
School—(1874) 95 Sherman Ave., 07502. Tel: 973-956-1542; Fax: 973-956-1759. Salesian Sisters of St. John Bosco 3; Lay Teachers 11; Students 200.
Catechesis / Religious Program—Students 160.

11—ST. MICHAEL THE ARCHANGEL (1903), (Italian), Revs. Ezio Antunes, S.D.V.; Lorenzo Gomez, S.D.V., Parochial Vicar; Robert Vass, S.D.V., Parochial Vicar.
Res.: 70 Cianci St., 07501-1831. Tel: 973-523-8413. Email: ezantunes@yahoo.com. Web: stmichaelpaterson.org.
Catechesis / Religious Program—Combined with St. Gerard, Majella Students 8.

12—OUR LADY OF LOURDES (1882) Rev. John-Jairo Suarez, Admin.; Deacons Mario Munoz; Raul Pamplona.
Res.: 440 River St., 07524-1902. Tel: 973-742-2142; Fax: 973-345-9136. Email: blessedpastor@aol.com. Web: www.miracleoflourdes.org.
Catechesis / Religious Program—Students 125.

13—OUR LADY OF POMPEI (1916), (Italian), Rev. Sal J. Panagia; Deacon Henry Gallo.
Res.: 70 Murray Ave., 07501. Tel: 973-742-1969; Fax: 973-742-1335.
Catechesis / Religious Program—Students 65.

14—OUR LADY OF VICTORIES (1882) Rev. Msgr. Thomas J. Coletta; Deacon Maximo Paulino. In Res., Rev. Janusz Rzadca.
Res.: 100 Fair St., 07501. Tel: 973-279-0487; 973-279-0527; Fax: 973-977-8506. Email: olvjude@verizon.net. Web: www.olvjude.org.
Catechesis / Religious Program—Students 150.

15—ST. STEPHEN'S (1903), (Polish), Rev. Dariusz K. Kaminski; Deacon Candelario Espinal.
Res.: 86 Martin St., 07501. Tel: 973-742-2822; Fax: 973-742-1679.
Catechesis / Religious Program—Students 90.

16—ST. THERESE (1926) Revs. Luciano Cruz; Patrick Magee, F.L.H.F.; Deacons Nicholas Varsalona; Raul Pamplona; Luis Ramirez.
Res.: 80 13th Ave., 07504. Tel: 973-881-0400; Fax: 973-881-7638.
School—(1953) 765-14th Ave., 07504. Tel: 973-278-4135; Fax: 973-278-3228. Deacon Nicholas Varsalona, Prin. Lay Teachers 10; Students 320.
Catechesis / Religious Program—Students 50.

OUTSIDE THE CITY OF PATERSON

ANDOVER, SUSSEX CO., GOOD SHEPHERD (1979) [CEM] Rev. Msgr. Richard A. Steiger; Deacons Thomas Sullivan; Edmund Galinski; Keith Harris; Mrs. Sharon Matuza, Pastoral Assoc.
Office: Rte. 517 (48 Tranquility Rd.), P.O. Box 464, 07821. Tel: 973-786-6631; 973-786-5520 (Res.); 973-786-5811 (CEM); Fax: 973-786-5233.
Catechesis / Religious Program—Tel: 973-786-6632. Students 550.

BOONTON, MORRIS CO.

1—SS. CYRIL AND METHODIUS (1907), (Slovak), [CEM] Rev. Zbigniew Tyburski.
Res.: 215 Hill St., 07005. Tel: 973-334-0139; Fax: 973-402-9512. Web: stcyrilboonton.org.
Catechesis / Religious Program—Students 73.

2—OUR LADY OF MOUNT CARMEL (1847) [CEM] Rev. A. Richard Carton.
Res.: 910 Birch St., 07005. Tel: 973-334-1017; Fax: 973-689-2731.
School—(1868) 205 Oak St., 07005. Tel: 973-334-2777; Fax: 973-334-0975. Lay Teachers 12; Students 140.
Catechesis / Religious Program—Students 339.

BRANCHVILLE, SUSSEX CO., OUR LADY QUEEN OF PEACE (1951) Rev. Msgr. William P. Stober.
Res.: 209 Rte. 206, 07826. Tel: 973-948-3185; Fax: 973-948-4799.
Catechesis / Religious Program—Tel: 973-948-2741. Students 246.

BUDD LAKE, MORRIS CO., ST. JUDE (1946) Rev. Robert J. Mitchell; Deacons Anthony C. Siino; Paul M. Wisniewski; John M. Sanker; Joanne Lawlar, Pastoral Assoc.
Res.: 17 Mt. Olive Rd., 07828. Tel: 973-691-1561; Fax: 973-691-9060. Web: www.stjudeparish.org.
Catechesis / Religious Program—Students 670.

BUTLER, MORRIS CO., ST. ANTHONY (1878) [CEM] Revs. John Alderson, O.F.M.; John J. Leonard, O.F.M. In Res., Rev. Jude Murphy, O.F.M.
Res.: 65 Bartholdi Ave., 07405. Tel: 973-838-0031; Fax: 973-838-0649.
School—(1882)Tel: 973-838-0854; Fax: 973-838-1460. Lay Teachers 11; Students 207.
Catechesis / Religious Program—Students 325.
Parish House—71 Bartholdi Ave., 07405. Tel: 973-838-8585.

CEDAR KNOLLS, MORRIS CO., NOTRE DAME OF MT. CARMEL (1917) Revs. Jude S. Salus, O.S.B.; Justin Capato, O.S.B.; Deacons Joseph Harris; Victor Lupi; Ronald Forino; Matthew McMahon; Alfredo Fanelli; David Collins; Henry de Mena; James Butkus.
Office: 75 Ridgedale Ave., 07927. Tel: 973-538-1358; Fax: 973-538-7403.
Catechesis / Religious Program—Students 850.

CHATHAM TOWNSHIP, MORRIS CO., CORPUS CHRISTI (1966) Rev. Msgr. James T. Mahoney.
Res.: 234 Southern Blvd., 07928. Tel: 973-635-0070; Fax: 973-635-5518. Email: jmahoney@corpuschristi.org. Web: www.corpuschristi.org.
Catechesis / Religious Program—Students 1,420.

CHATHAM, MORRIS CO., ST. PATRICK'S (1874) Rev. Owen B. Moran, Temporary Admin.; Deacons Joseph A. Wisneski; Mark Nixon.
Parish Office: 41 Oliver St., 07928.
Res.: 85 Washington Ave., 07928. Email: info@st-pats.org. Web: www.st-pats.org.
School—(1872) 45 Chatham St., 07928. Tel: 973-635-4623; Fax: 973-635-2311. Lay Teachers 30; Students 411.
Catechesis / Religious Program—Students 855.

CHESTER, MORRIS CO., ST. LAWRENCE THE MARTYR (1950) Rev. Msgr. Paul F. Knauer; Deacon Frank Owens.
Res.: Main St., P.O. Box 730, 07930. Tel: 908-879-5371; Fax: 908-879-7701.
Catechesis / Religious Program—Main St., P.O. Box 31, 07930. Tel: 908-879-6714; Fax: 908-879-7701. Students 926.

CLIFTON, PASSAIC CO.

1—ST. ANDREW THE APOSTLE (Allwood) (1938) Rev. Msgr. Richard A. Rusconi; Deacons Robert G. Ayers; Richard J. Goglia.
Res.: 400 Mt. Prospect Ave., 07012. Tel: 973-779-6873; Fax: 973-779-0573.
School—(1953) 418 Mt. Prospect Ave., 07012. Tel: 973-473-3711; Fax: 973-473-6611. Sisters of the Presentation 1; Lay Teachers 10; Students 200.
Catechesis / Religious Program—Tel: 973-779-6873; Fax: 973-779-0573. Students 134.

2—ST. BRENDAN (1945) Rev. Frank W. Weber. In Res., Rev. Msgr. Francis Matarazzo (Retired).
Res.: 154 E. First St., 07011. Tel: 973-772-1115; Fax: 973-772-0497. Email: weber01@aol.com. Web: www.st-brendan.org.
School—(1946) 154 E. First St., 07011. Tel: 973-772-1149; Fax: 973-772-5547. Sisters 1; Lay Teachers 16; Students 368.
Catechesis / Religious Program—Tel: 973-772-6775; Fax: 973-772-6213. Students 170.

3—ST. CLARE'S (1913) Revs. Peter V.B. Wells, Admin.; Thomas J. Fitzgerald.
Res.: 69 Allwood Rd., 07014. Tel: 973-777-7588; Fax: 973-249-6825.
School—(1959)Tel: 973-777-7582; Fax: 973-473-0127. Lay Teachers 19; Students 183.
Catechesis / Religious Program—Students 109.

4—SS. CYRIL AND METHODIUS (1913), (Slovak), Revs. Paul O'Donnell Duggan; Hector Melendez.
Res.: 218 Ackerman Ave., 07011. Tel: 973-546-4390; Fax: 973-546-3269. Email: cyrilmethodius1@verizon.net.
Catechesis / Religious Program—Students 88.

5—ST. JOHN KANTY (1930), (Polish), Revs. Raphael Zwolenkiewicz, O.F.M.Conv.; Michael I. Socha, O.F.M. Conv.; Roger Haas, O.F.M.Conv.; Deacon Robert Altilio.
Res.: 49 Speer Ave., 07013. Tel: 973-779-0564; 973-779-4102 (Office); Fax: 973-773-0857. Email: sjkrcch@optonline.net. Web: www.saintjohnkanty.org.
Catechesis / Religious Program—Tel: 973-779-6214. Students 217.

6—ST. PAUL (1914) Rev. Victor J. Mazza; Deacons Joseph Puskas; Peter Casamento. In Res., Rev. Clement Cardillo, S.D.B.
Res.: 124 Union Ave., 07011. Tel: 973-546-2746; Fax: 973-340-2083.
Catechesis / Religious Program—Students 200.

7—ST. PHILIP THE APOSTLE (1943) Revs. Paul S. Manning; Pawel F. Szurek, Parochial Vicar; Deacon Nicholas Veliky. In Res., Rev. Msgr. P. Kevin Flanagan (Retired).
Res.: 797 Valley Rd., 07013. Tel: 973-779-6200; Fax: 973-779-2959. Web: www.stphilip.org.
School—(1954)Tel: 973-779-4700; Fax: 973-779-0932. Email: bzito@stphilip.org. Web: www.saint-philipschool.org. Lay Teachers 25; Students 418.
Catechesis / Religious Program—Tel: 973-779-1439. Students 355.

8—SACRED HEART (1897), (Italian), Rev. John T. Connolly; Rev. Msgr. Julian B. Varettoni, Pastor Emeritus (Retired); Rev. Andrew T. Perretta.
Res.: 145 Randolph Ave., 07011. Tel: 973-546-6012; Fax: 973-546-1814. Email: church@sacredheartclifton.com.
School—(1953) 43 Clifton Ave., 07011. Tel: 973-546-4695; Fax: 973-546-8774. Sisters 1; Lay Teachers 13; Students 205.
Catechesis / Religious Program—Students 41.

CONVENT STATION, MORRIS CO., ST. THOMAS MORE (1966) Rev. Joseph G. Farias, Admin.
Res.: Madison Ave., Box 286, 07961. Tel: 973-267-5330.
Catechesis / Religious Program—Tel: 973-267-5585. Students 15.

DENVILLE, MORRIS CO., ST. MARY'S (1926) Revs. Martin G. Glynn; Richard V. Tartaglia; Deacons Al Klose; Michael Allgaier; John Flynn.
Res.: 15 Myers Ave., 07834. Tel: 973-627-0269; Fax: 973-627-6355.
School—(1954)Tel: 973-627-2606; Fax: 973-627-9316. Lay Teachers 16; Students 150; Sisters 143.
Catechesis / Religious Program—Tel: 973-627-8276. Students 629.

DOVER, MORRIS CO.

1—ST. MARY'S (1845) [CEM] Rev. John DeMattia; Deacons Thomas P. Beirne; Stuart Hartnett. In Res., Rev. Ifeanyi Iwu.
Res.: 425 W. Blackwell St., 07801. Tel: 973-366-0184; Fax: 973-366-5377.
Catechesis / Religious Program—Students 322.

2—OUR LADY QUEEN OF THE MOST HOLY ROSARY (1959), (Hispanic), Revs. Brendan J. Murray, Admin.; Enrique Corona, Parochial Vicar.
Res.: 77 Richards Ave., 07801. Tel: 973-361-2725; Fax: 973-361-4058. Email: holyrosary@verizon.net.
Catechesis/Religious Program—Students 239.

3—SACRED HEART (1904) Revs. Brendan J. Murray; Enrique Corona, Parochial Vicar. In Res., Rev. Carmen Buono.
Res.: 4 Richards Ave., 07801. Tel: 973-366-0060; Fax: 973-366-8636. Web: sacredheart-dover.com.
Catechesis/Religious Program—Students 163.

EAST HANOVER, MORRIS CO., ST. ROSE OF LIMA (1957) Revs. Owen B. Moran; Hubert Jurjewicz; Deacons Frank Para, Pastoral Assoc.; Vincent Leo Jr.
Res.: 312 Ridgedale Ave., 07936. Tel: 973-887-5572; Fax: 973-884-0476. Web: saintroseoflimachurch.org.
School—(1961)Tel: 973-887-6990; Fax: 973-887-8655. Lay Teachers 10; Students 188.
Catechesis/Religious Program—Tel: 973-887-0357. Students 565.

FLANDERS, MORRIS CO., ST. ELIZABETH ANN SETON (1985) Rev. Stanley C. Barron; Deacons Dennis King; Frank Puglia; Stephen P. Natafalusy.
Res.: 61 Main St., 07836. Tel: 973-927-1629; Fax: 973-927-0327. Email: steliz@hughes.net. Web: stelizabethschurch.org.
Catechesis/Religious Program—Tel: 973-927-7077; Fax: 973-927-0093. Students 900.

FLORHAM PARK, MORRIS CO., HOLY FAMILY (1951) Rev. Msgr. Raymond J. Kupke; Rev. William J. Mooney; Deacons William F. Ward; Peter Flore; Mrs. Barbara Froetscher, Pastoral Assoc.; Mrs. Patricia Danishek, Pastoral Assoc.; Mrs. Virginia Akhoury, Pastoral Assoc.; Mrs. Mary Jane McGuire, Pastoral Assoc.
Res.: 1 Lloyd Ave., 07932. Tel: 973-377-1817; Fax: 973-377-6350.
School—(1954)Tel: 973-377-4181; Fax: 973-377-0273. Sisters of Christian Charity 1; Lay Teachers 16; Students 165.
Catechesis/Religious Program—Tel: 973-377-3101. Students 631.

FRANKLIN, SUSSEX CO., IMMACULATE CONCEPTION (1867) [CEM] Rev. Boguslaw Kobus; Deacon Jerome Schenker.
Res.: 75 Church St., 07416. Tel: 973-827-9575; Fax: 973-827-7375. Web: immaculateconceptionparish.org. Email: church@icrschool.com. Students 364.
Catechesis/Religious Program—Tel: 973-827-9501. Email: church@icrschool.com. Students 342.

GREEN POND, MORRIS CO., ST. SIMON THE APOSTLE (Rockaway Twp.) (1942) Rev. Marc Mancini.
Res.: 1010 Green Pond Rd., 07435. Tel: 973-697-4699; Fax: 973-697-1784.
Catechesis/Religious Program—Students 118.

HAMBURG, SUSSEX CO., ST. JUDE THE APOSTLE (1966) Rev. William B. Collins.
Res.: 4-24 Beaver Run Rd., P.O. Box 1, 07419. Tel: 973-827-8030; Fax: 973-827-8382. Email: stjudehamburg@embarqmail.com. Web: www.stjudehamburg.org.
Catechesis/Religious Program—Tel: 973-827-2280. Students 351.

HASKELL, PASSAIC CO., ST. FRANCIS OF ASSISI (1905) Rev. Lancelot Reis; Deacon Jose Rivera.
Res.: 868 Ringwood Ave., 07420. Tel: 973-835-0480; Fax: 973-835-3277. Email: stfrancis@optonline.net. Web: stfrancishaskell.org.
School—(1912)Tel: 973-835-3268; Fax: 973-616-7644. Lay Teachers 11; Students 162.
Catechesis/Religious Program—Tel: 973-835-1946. Students 253.

HAWTHORNE, PASSAIC CO., ST. ANTHONY'S (1908) Rev. Msgr. Martin McDonnell; Rev. Brian Sullivan; Deacons Richard J. Brudzynski; George Forshay; Anthony E. Bernardine; Gerald Fadlalla.
Res.: 276 Diamond Bridge Ave., 07506. Tel: 973-427-1478; Fax: 973-427-4826. Email: info@stanthony-hawthorne.org. Web: www.stanthony-hawthorne.org.
School—(1912) 270 Diamond Bridge Ave., 07506. Tel: 973-423-1818; Fax: 973-423-6065. Sisters 3; Lay Teachers 12; Students 204.
Catechesis/Religious Program—Tel: 973-427-7873. Students 747.

HEWITT, PASSAIC CO., OUR LADY QUEEN OF PEACE (1921) Revs. Frederick Walters; Adam Muda; Deacons Charles Roche; Joseph Verboys; Philip Thiuri.
Res.: 1911 Union Valley Rd., 07421. Tel: 973-728-8162; Fax: 973-728-4650. Web: www.olqp.com.
School—(1960)Tel: 973-728-9339; Fax: 973-728-6850. Franciscan Sisters 1; Lay Teachers 14; Students 152.
Catechesis/Religious Program—Students 653.

HIGHLAND LAKES, SUSSEX CO., OUR LADY OF FATIMA (1954) Rev. Msgr. Robert B. Carroll; Rev. Abuchi Nwosu, Parochial Vicar.
Mailing Address: 184 Breakneck Rd, P.O. Box 242, 07422. Tel: 973-764-4457; Fax: 973-764-4504. Email: olfatima@warwick.net. Web: olfatima-highlandlksnj.catholicweb.com.
Catechesis/Religious Program—Students 304.

HOPATCONG, SUSSEX CO., ST. JUDE'S (1931) Revs. George J. Gothie; John J. McGuigan; Deacon Thomas Friel.
Res.: 40 Maxim Dr., 07843. Tel: 973-398-6377; Fax: 973-398-0121. Email: reled@stjudehopatcong.org. Web: www.stjudehopatcong.org.
Catechesis/Religious Program—Students 225.

KINNELON, MORRIS CO., OUR LADY OF THE MAGNIFICAT (1961) [CEM] Rev. Msgr. John J. Carroll; Rev. Raymond Orama, Parochial Vicar.
Res.: 2 Miller Rd., 07405. Tel: 973-838-6838; Fax: 973-838-0710. Web: olmchurch.org.
School—(1964)Tel: 973-838-6222; Fax: 973-838-0409. Mrs. Phyllis Sisco, Prin. Lay Teachers 18; Students 148.
Catechesis/Religious Program—Tel: 973-838-0567. Sr. Ellen Denise O'Connor, F.S.P. Students 849.

LAKE HOPATCONG, MORRIS CO., OUR LADY STAR OF THE SEA (Jefferson Twp.) (1910) Rev. P. Christopher Muldoon; Deacon Alberto R. Totino.
Res.: 237 Espanong Rd., P.O. Box 337, 07849. Tel: 973-663-0211; Fax: 973-663-4302. Email: olsos@optonline.net. Web: www.olsoslh.org.
Catechesis/Religious Program—Tel: 973-663-0124; Fax: 973-663-2118. Students 378.

LINCOLN PARK, MORRIS CO., ST. JOSEPH'S (1922) Revs. Philip A. LeBeau; Robert J. Norton, O.F.M., Parochial Vicar; Deacons Stephen J. Marabeti; Joseph Parlapiano.
Res.: 216 Comly Rd., 07035. Tel: 973-696-4411; Fax: 973-305-8466. Email: stjoelp@optonline.net. Web: www.stjosephsonline.org.
Catechesis/Religious Program—Students 320.

LITTLE FALLS, PASSAIC CO., OUR LADY OF THE HOLY ANGELS (1883) Rev. Msgr. T. Mark Condon; Rev. David Pickens; Deacon Joseph Sisco; Sr. Nancy Grassia, O.S.F., Pastoral Assoc.
Res.: 473 Main St., 07424. Tel: 973-256-5200; Fax: 973-256-0185.
Catechesis/Religious Program—Tel: 973-256-5200. Students 478.

LONG VALLEY, MORRIS CO.

1—ST. LUKE (1982) Rev. Michael J. Drury.
Res.: P.O. Box 416, 07853. Tel: 908-876-3515; Fax: 908-876-5277.
Church: 265 W. Mill Rd., 07853.
Catechesis/Religious Program—Students 1,109.

2—ST. MARK THE EVANGELIST (1986) Rev. Msgr. Joseph J. Goode.
Office: 59 Spring Ln., 07853.
Res.: 24 Ann Rd., 07853. Tel: 908-850-0652; 908-850-0263; Fax: 908-850-0648. Email: frjoe.stm@comcast.net.
Catechesis/Religious Program—Students 468.

MADISON, MORRIS CO., ST. VINCENT MARTYR (1805) [CEM] Rev. Msgr. George F. Hundt; Rev. Jesus A. Gaviria.
Res.: 26 Green Village Rd., 07940. Tel: 973-377-4000; Fax: 973-377-8242.
School—(1848)Tel: 973-377-1104; Fax: 973-377-2632. Lay Teachers 29; Students 417.
Catechesis/Religious Program—Tel: 973-966-1771. Students 715.

MCAFEE, SUSSEX CO., ST. FRANCIS DE SALES (1963) Rev. Msgr. John V. Boland.
Mailing Address: P.O. Box 785, 07428. Tel: 973-827-3248; Fax: 973-827-7534.
Catechesis/Religious Program—Tel: 973-827-8300. Email: stfrancisdesales@earthlink.net. Web: www-.stfrancisvernon.org. Students 800.

MENDHAM, MORRIS CO., ST. JOSEPH'S (1853) [CEM] Rev. Msgr. Joseph T. Anginoli; Rev. Frank P. Agresti, Parochial Vicar; Deacon Robert F. Santos. 6 New St., 07945. Tel: 973-543-5950; Fax: 973-543-6025.
School—(1963)Tel: 973-543-7474; Fax: 973-543-7817. Lay Teachers 18; Students 230.
Catechesis/Religious Program—Students 720.

MONTAGUE, SUSSEX CO., ST. JAMES THE GREATER (1943) Rev. Wayne F. Varga; Deacon Wayne Von Doehren.
Res.: 75 River Rd., 07827. Tel: 973-948-2296; Fax: 973-948-4634. Email: stjamesthomas@aol.com.
Catechesis/Religious Program—122 C.R. 645, Sandyston, 07826. Tel: 973-948-7064. Students 70.

MONTVILLE, MORRIS CO., ST. PIUS X (1959) Rev. Joseph J. Garbarino; Deacons Jack Callahan; Patrick Mann.
Parish Ministry Office—Tel: 973-335-2894; Fax: 973-394-0069.
Res.: 24 Changebridge Rd., 07045. Tel: 973-331-1706.
School—(1963)Tel: 973-335-1253; Fax: 973-335-2392. Sr. June Morrissey, S.C., Prin. Religious 2; Lay Teachers 12; Students 260.
Catechesis/Religious Program—24 Changebridge Rd., 07045. Students 1,084.

MORRIS PLAINS, MORRIS CO., ST. VIRGILIUS (1881) Rev. Msgr. Francis J. Duffy; Rev. Richard Kilcomons; Deacons Sylvester Mazzoccoli; Thomas Harenchar; Merle Sisler; Rich Pinto; Frank Para; Ken Rado.
Res.: 250 Speedwell Ave., 07950. Tel: 973-538-1418; Fax: 973-538-2992. Email: parishoffice@stvirgil.org. Web: www.stvirgil.org.
School—(1910) 238 Speedwell Ave., 07950. Tel: 973-539-7267; Fax: 973-292-5157. Mrs. Cathy Condon. Lay Teachers 14; Students 150.
Catechesis/Religious Program—Tel: 973-267-1366. Students 615.

MORRISTOWN, MORRIS CO.

1—ASSUMPTION OF THE BLESSED VIRGIN MARY (1848) [CEM] Rev. Msgr. John E. Hart; Rev. Dennis J. Crowley; Deacons P. Michael Hanly; William Harty; Brian D. Beyerl. In Res., Rev. Geno Sylva.
Res.: 91 Maple Ave., 07960. Tel: 973-539-2141; Fax: 973-984-0632. Email: assumption@assumptionparish.org. Web: assumptionparish.org.
School—(1850) 63 MacCulloch Ave., 07960. Tel: 973-538-0590; Fax: 973-984-3632. Sisters of Charity 2; Lay Teachers 45; Students 532.
Catechesis/Religious Program—Tel: 973-267-5638; Fax: 973-984-0632. Students 719.

2—ST. MARGARET OF SCOTLAND (1885) Revs. Hernan Arias; Brian Ditullio; Deacon Tim Holden.
Res.: 6 Sussex Ave., 07960. Tel: 973-538-0874; Fax: 973-538-4581. Email: stmargaret07960@yahoo.com.
Catechesis/Religious Program—Tel: 973-267-8354. Students 262.

MOUNT ARLINGTON, MORRIS CO., OUR LADY OF THE LAKE (1888) Revs. Hugh P. Murphy; Desmond O'Connor, S.P.S.
Res.: One Park Ave., 07856. Tel: 973-398-0240; Fax: 973-398-3667.
Catechesis/Religious Program—Tel: 973-601-1475. Students 317.

MOUNT HOPE, MORRIS CO., ST. BERNARD'S (1855) Rev. Alfred J. Lampron, Admin.
Res.: 446 Mt. Hope Rd., Wharton, 07885-2814. Tel: 973-627-0066; Fax: 973-627-3631. Email: stbernardsmth@verizon.net.
Catechesis/Religious Program—Students 10.

MOUNTAIN LAKES, MORRIS CO., ST. CATHERINE OF SIENA (1956) Rev. Thomas Mangieri, Temporary Admin.
Res.: 10 N. Pocono Rd., 07046. Tel: 973-334-7131; Fax: 973-334-3202.
Catechesis/Religious Program—Tel: 973-334-5257. Students 742.

NETCONG, MORRIS CO., ST. MICHAEL'S (1873) [CEM] Rev. Nicholas Bozza; Deacons Joseph Keenan; Stuart Murphy; Richard F. Bias.
Res.: 4 Church St., 07857. Tel: 973-347-0032; Fax: 973-347-1560.
School—(1922), (Grades PreK-8), 10 Church St., 07857. Tel: 973-347-0039; Fax: 973-347-0054. Lay Teachers 15; Students 236.
Catechesis/Religious Program—Tel: 973-347-1465. Students 395.

NEW VERNON, MORRIS CO., CHRIST THE KING (1956) Rev. Patrick G. O'Donovan.
Res.: Blue Mill Rd., P.O. Box 368, 07976. Tel: 973-539-4955; Fax: 973-267-7070. Web: www.churchofchristtheking.org.
Catechesis/Religious Program—Students 403.

NEWTON, SUSSEX CO., ST. JOSEPH (1854) [CEM] Rev. Peter Filipkowski; Deacons Gerald Hanifan; Alfred Kucinski; Arthur Van Vleet; Larry D'Amico; Thomas Zayac.
Res.: 17 Elm St., 07860. Tel: 973-383-1985; Fax: 973-383-8164. Email: stjoseph727@yahoo.com.
Catechesis/Religious Program—Tel: 973-383-8413. Students 370.

OAK RIDGE, MORRIS CO., ST. THOMAS, THE APOSTLE (1949) [CEM] Rev. Msgr. John E. Fitzpatrick.
Res.: 5635 Berkshire Valley Rd., 07438. Tel: 973-208-0090; Fax: 973-208-0092.
Catechesis/Religious Program—Tel: 973-208-0096. Students 201.

OGDENSBURG, SUSSEX CO., ST. THOMAS OF AQUIN (1881) [CEM] Rev. John P. Pilipie; Deacons Edward Reading; Dominic Zampella.
Res.: 53 Kennedy Ave., 07439. Tel: 973-827-3190; Fax: 973-827-2885. Email: stthomasofaquin@embarqmail.com. Web: www.stthomasofaquin.org.
Catechesis/Religious Program—Students 125.

PARSIPPANY, MORRIS CO.

1—ST. ANN (1982) Rev. Timothy Dowling; Sr. Frances Sanzo, S.S.C., Pastoral Assoc.; Mrs. Ginny Bissig, Pastoral Assoc.; Deacons Alfred Frank; Leonard Deo.
Res.: 781 Smith Rd., 07054. Tel: 973-884-1986; Fax: 973-884-0940.
Catechesis/Religious Program—Students 318.

2—ST. CHRISTOPHER (1944) Revs. Joseph G. Buffardi; Marcin Walka; Deacons John J. Kelly; John Bernero; Henry Rohrman; Richard A. Gaydo; Alan Lucibello. In Res., Rev. Msgr. Frank B. Ferraioli (Retired).

Res.: 1050 Littleton Rd., 07054. Tel: 973-539-7050; Fax: 973-539-3601.
See separate listing under Elementary Schools, Diocesan in the Institution section.
Catechesis/Religious Program—Tel: 973-539-6208. Students 350.

3—ST. PETER THE APOSTLE (1938) Rev. Msgr. Herbert K. Tillyer; Revs. L. Richard Hardy; William Santeliz, Parochial Vicar; Sr. Sylvia Berzinski, S.S.C., Pastoral Assoc.; Deacons Louis Chiocco; Robert A. Lang; Joseph Marsicovete; Peter Cistaro.
Res.: 179 Baldwin Rd., 07054. Tel: 973-334-2090; Fax: 973-334-5397. Email: stpeterpar@optonline.net. Web: saintpetertheapostle.org.
See separate listing under Elementary Schools, Diocesan in the Institution section.
Catechesis/Religious Program—189 Baldwin Rd., 07054. Tel: 973-335-9713; Fax: 973-334-5397. John Cammarata, D.R.E. Students 595.

PASSAIC, PASSAIC CO.

1—ST. ANTHONY OF PADUA (1917), (Italian), Revs. Brando Ibarra; Vidal Gonzalez.
Res.: 101-103 Myrtle Ave., 07055. Tel: 973-777-4793; Fax: 973-779-6864. Email: info@stanthonypassaic.com. Web: stanthonypassaic.com.
School—St. Anthony - Passaic Catholic (1960) 40 Tulip St., 07055. Tel: 973-773-0970; Fax: 973-473-4681. Sr. Joselle Ratka, C.S.S.F., Prin. Sisters 2; Lay Teachers 12; Students 105.
Day Care Center: 101-103 Myrtle Ave., 07055. Tel: 973-777-5018.
Catechesis/Religious Program—Students 400.

2—ASSUMPTION OF THE BLESSED VIRGIN MARY (1891), (Slovak), Rev. Msgr. John J. Demkovich; Rev. Edgar Ruiz, Parochial Vicar.
Res.: 63 Monroe St., 07055. Tel: 973-779-0427; Fax: 973-472-5033.
Catechesis/Religious Program—Students 42.

3—HOLY ROSARY (1918), (Polish), Revs. Stefan Las; Marek Miarecki; Gregorz Golba.
Res.: 6 Wall St., 07055. Tel: 973-473-1578; Fax: 973-473-1773. Email: holyrosarypass@optonline.net.
Catechesis/Religious Program—Students 328.

4—HOLY TRINITY (1900), (German), Revs. Antonio Rodriguez; Bernardo Velasquez, Parochial Vicar.
Res.: 226 Harrison St., 07055. Tel: 973-778-9763; Fax: 973-778-7582.
Catechesis/Religious Program—Students 575.

5—ST. JOSEPH'S (1892), (Polish), Revs. Stanley Lesniowski; Andrzej Puchalski.
Res.: 7 Parker Ave., 07055. Tel: 973-473-2822; Fax: 973-473-2855.
Catechesis/Religious Program—Students 214.

6—ST. NICHOLAS (1868) [CEM] Rev. Msgr. Felipe N. Carvajal.
Res.: 153 Washington Pl., 07055. Tel: 973-779-7867; Fax: 973-815-1893. Email: stnicholasrc@prodigy.net.
Catechesis/Religious Program—Tel: 973-779-7867; Fax: 973-815-1893. Students 46.

7—OUR LADY OF FATIMA (1954), (Hispanic), Revs. Gilberto Gutierrez; Bernardo Velasquez, Parochial Vicar.
Res.: 32 Exchange Pl., 07055. Tel: 973-472-0815; Fax: 973-472-0250.
Catechesis/Religious Program—Students 215.

8—OUR LADY OF MT. CARMEL (1902), (Italian), Rev. Ignatius Zampino, O.F.M.Cap. In Res., Revs. Vincent Liuzzo, O.F.M.Cap.; Francis Majewski, O.F.M.Cap.
Res.: 10 St. Francis Way, 07055. Tel: 973-473-0246; Fax: 973-473-3404. Email: ladyofmtcarmel@verizon.net. Web: ladyofmtcarmel.org.
School—(1954)Tel: 973-473-8183; Fax: 973-473-0937. Franciscan Sisters 2; Lay Teachers 6; Students 110.
Catechesis/Religious Program—Students 49.

9—ST. STEPHEN'S (1902), (Magyar), Rev. Laszlo Vas.
Res.: 223 Third St., 07055. Tel: 973-779-0332; Fax: 973-778-4263.
Catechesis/Religious Program—Students 17.

PEQUANNOCK, MORRIS CO.

1—HOLY SPIRIT (1949) Rev. John F. Tarantino; Deacons Michael Scruggs; Gary Zack.
Res.: 318 Newark-Pompton Tpke., 07440. Tel: 973-696-1234; Fax: 973-305-9390. Email: info@holyspiritchurchnj.org.
School—(1956) 330 Newark-Pompton Tpke., 07440. Tel: 973-835-5680; Fax: 973-835-1757. Maestre Pie Filippini (Religious Teachers Filippini) 1; Lay Teachers 20; Students 220.
Catechesis/Religious Program—330 Newark-Pompton Tpke., 07440. Tel: 973-835-5696. Students 160.
Convent—Tel: 973-694-2111.

2—OUR LADY OF FATIMA CHAPEL (TRIDENTINE) (1994) Revs. Benoit Guichard, F.S.S.P.; Paul J. McCambridge, F.S.S.P.; Joseph Howard, F.S.S.P. In Res., Rev. Kenneth Baker, S.J.
Res.: 32 West Franklin Ave., 07440. Tel: 973-694-6727. Web: www.olfchapel.org.
School—St. Maximilian Kolbe School, 18 First St., 07440. Tel: 973-694-1034; Fax: 973-694-1304. Mrs. Mary Lou Bednar, Prin. Lay Teachers 11; Students 60.
Catechesis/Religious Program—Students 32.

POMPTON LAKES, PASSAIC CO., OUR LADY OF THE ASSUMPTION (1906) Revs. Kevin Downey, O.F.M.; Francis Gunn, O.F.M., Parochial Vicar; Lawrence Anderson (O.F.M); Deacons Thomas Kimak; Hal Clark.
Parish Office—17 Pompton Ave., 07442. Tel: 973-835-0374; Fax: 973-835-8173.
St. Mary's Friary: 37 Pompton Ave., 07442. Tel: 973-839-1975. Email: smc@stmarys-pompton.org. Web: www.stmarys-pompton.org.
School—(1951) 25 Pompton Ave., 07442. Tel: 973-835-2010; Fax: 973-835-7529. Sr. Mary Byrnes, P.B.V.M., Prin. Lay Teachers 11; Students 281.
Catechesis/Religious Program—Tel: 973-835-7750; Fax: 973-616-6307. Students 1,732.

POMPTON PLAINS, MORRIS CO., OUR LADY OF GOOD COUNSEL (1962) Rev. Msgr. Patrick J. Scott; Deacons Edward Jaroszewski; Herb D. Coyne; Carmen Restaino. In Res., Rev. Richard H. Oliveri (Retired).
Res.: 155 W. Pkwy., P.O. Box 218, 07444. Tel: 973-839-2447; Fax: 973-839-9492.
Catechesis/Religious Program—Tel: 973-839-3311. Students 760.

PROSPECT PARK, PASSAIC CO., ST. PAUL'S (1924) Rev. Msgr. Edward J. Kurtyka. In Res., Rev. Michael A. Burke.
Res.: 286 Haledon Ave., 07508. Tel: 973-790-8169.
Catechesis/Religious Program—Tel: 973-790-8135. Students 82.

RANDOLPH, MORRIS CO.

1—ST. MATTHEW THE APOSTLE (1988) Rev. Daniel W. Murphy; Deacons Edward Keegan; Richard A. Brady; John Dugger; Jim Hackett.
Res.: 335 Dover-Chester Rd., 07869. Tel: 973-584-1101; Fax: 973-584-0499. Email: st.matthews@st.matthewsrandolph.org. Web: www.stmatthewsrandolph.org.
Catechesis/Religious Program—Students 790.

2—RESURRECTION (1978) Rev. John Andrew Connell; Deacons Roger Lacouture; Kenneth Weaver; Raymond Latour; Richard Reck; Richard Van Glahn.
Res.: 651 Millbrook Ave., 07869. Tel: 973-895-4224; Fax: 973-895-3224. Web: www.resurrectionparishnj.org.
Catechesis/Religious Program—Tel: 973-895-4226. Students 1,020.

RINGWOOD, PASSAIC CO., ST. CATHERINE OF BOLOGNA (1917) Rev. Msgr. Patrick G. Panos; Rev. Paul Barboutz; Deacons James Elliott; Richard Michalski.
Res.: 112 Erskine Rd., 07456. Tel: 973-962-7032; Fax: 973-962-1776. Email: stcathringwood@optonline.net. Web: www.scobp.org.
School—(1948)Tel: 973-962-7131; Fax: 973-962-0585. Franciscan Sisters of Philadelphia 1; Lay Teachers 14; Students 265.
Catechesis/Religious Program—Tel: 973-962-6081. Students 465.

ROCKAWAY, MORRIS CO.

1—ST. CECILIA'S (1869) [CEM] Revs. Sigmund A. Peplowski; Peter S. Glabik, Parochial Vicar; Jean-Claude St. Martin, Parochial Vicar; Deacons John F. Taylor; Paul D. Willson.
Res.: 70 Church St., 07866. Tel: 973-627-0313; 973-627-0316; Fax: 973-627-4811. Email: stcec@optonline.net. Web: www.st-cecilia.org.
School—(1958) Halsey Ave., 07866. Tel: 973-627-6003; Fax: 973-627-5217. Sisters of Christian Charity 2; Lay Teachers 12; Students 261.
Catechesis/Religious Program—Tel: 973-252-0760. Students 696.
Convent—90 Church St., 07866. Tel: 973-627-6533.

2—SACRED HEART (1923), (Slovak), Revs. Sigmund A. Peplowski; Peter S. Glabik, Parochial Vicar; Jean-Claude St. Martin, Parochial Vicar. In Res., Rev. Volodymyr Baran.
Res.: 63 E. Main St., 07866. Tel: 973-627-0422; Fax: 973-627-6249.
School—(1965) 40 E. Main St., 07866. Tel: 973-627-7689. Sisters of the Sorrowful Mother 1; Lay Teachers 10; Students 230.
Catechesis/Religious Program—Students 51.

ROCKAWAY TOWNSHIP, MORRIS CO., ST. CLEMENT, POPE AND MARTYR (1964) Rev. James J. Termyna; Deacons Harry Dachisen; Robert Morton.
Res.: 154 Mt. Pleasant Ave., Dover, 07801. Tel: 973-366-7095; Fax: 973-366-6083. Email: parishoffice@stclement-rtwp.org. Web: www.stclement-rtwp.org.
Catechesis/Religious Program—Tel: 973-366-7547. Students 306.

SANDYSTON, SUSSEX CO., ST. THOMAS THE APOSTLE (1941) Rev. Wayne F. Varga; Deacon Wayne Von Doehren.
Mailing Address: 210 Rte. 206 N., 07826. Tel: 973-948-2296. Email: stjamesthomas@aol.com.
Catechesis/Religious Program—122 C.R. 645, 07826. Fax: 973-948-7004. Students 657.

SCHOOLEY'S MOUNTAIN, MORRIS CO., OUR LADY OF THE MOUNTAIN (1954) [CEM] Rev. Mark Olenowski, Admin.
Res.: 2 E. Springtown Rd., Long Valley, 07853. Tel: 908-876-4395; Fax: 908-876-3744.
Catechesis/Religious Program—Tel: 908-876-4003. Students 839.

SPARTA, SUSSEX CO.

1—BLESSED KATERI TEKAKWITHA (1988) Rev. Patrick Rice; Deacons Andrew Calandriello; Gerard Leary; Charles Mathias; Tony Chiocco; Barry O'Brien; Joseph Cote; Glen P. Murphy.
Office: 427 Stanhope Rd., 07871. Tel: 973-729-1682; Fax: 973-729-0702. Email: office@blessedkateri.org. Web: www.blessedkateri.org.
Res.: 11 Cherry Tree Ln., 07871. Tel: 973-729-2892.
Catechesis/Religious Program—Tel: 973-729-0489. Students 1,050.

2—OUR LADY OF THE LAKE (1935) Revs. David McDonnell; Michael Rodak, Parochial Vicar; Deacon Edward Maron.
Res.: 294 Sparta Ave., 07871. Tel: 973-729-6107; Fax: 973-729-7203. Email: info@ourladyofthelake.org. Web: www.ourladyofthelake.org.
School—(1954)Tel: 973-729-9174; Fax: 973-729-0318. Dr. Catherine Duncan, Librarian. Lay Teachers 38; Students 541.
Catechesis/Religious Program—Tel: 973-729-2918. Students 968.

STIRLING, MORRIS CO., ST. VINCENT DE PAUL (1886) [CEM] Rev. Msgr. Patrick E. Brown; Rev. Leonardo Jaramillo, Parochial Vicar; Deacons Peter J. O'Neill; Brian F. Mather.
Res.: Bebout Ave., 07980. Tel: 908-647-0118; Fax: 908-647-5992.
School—(1955)Tel: 908-647-0421; Fax: 908-647-3878. Sisters 1; Lay Teachers 19; Students 204.
Catechesis/Religious Program—Tel: 908-647-6772. Students 637.

STOCKHOLM, SUSSEX CO., ST. JOHN VIANNEY (1958) Rev. Matthew J. Twiggs; Deacon James Camarrano.
Res.: 2823 Rte. 23, P.O. Box 505, 07460. Tel: 973-697-6550; Fax: 973-697-6882. Web: www.sjvianneyparish.org.
Catechesis/Religious Program—Tel: 973-764-7071. Students 392.

SUCCASUNNA, MORRIS CO., ST. THERESE (1957) Revs. Joseph P. Davis; Robert K. Hooper; Luis Carlos Moreno; Deacons Anthony Signorelli; Bruce Olsen.
Res.: 7 Hunter St., 07876. Tel: 973-584-8271; Fax: 973-584-0684. Email: sttheresеoffice@optonline.net.
School—(1963) 135 Main St., 07876. Tel: 973-584-0812; Fax: 973-584-2029. Sisters 1; Lay Teachers 9; Students 263.
Catechesis/Religious Program—Tel: 973-584-9444; Fax: 973-584-9492. Students 760.

SUSSEX, SUSSEX CO., ST. MONICA (1881) Rev. Charles A. Perricone; Carol Bezak, Pastoral Assoc.; Deacon Richard Nolan.
Res.: 33 Unionville Ave., 07461. Tel: 973-875-4521; Fax: 973-875-7538.
Catechesis/Religious Program—Tel: 973-875-2252; Fax: 973-875-5531. Students 250.

SWARTSWOOD, SUSSEX CO., OUR LADY OF MT. CARMEL (1951) Rev. John J. Quinlan; Deacons Ellis F. Schweitzer; Anthony P. Barile Jr.; Robert T. Davis; Edward J. Muller; Debra M. Tripi, Pastoral Assoc.
Mailing Address: P.O. Box 124, 07877. Tel: 973-383-3566; Fax: 973-383-3831.
Catechesis/Religious Program—Tel: 973-579-2355. Students 223.

TOTOWA BOROUGH, PASSAIC CO., ST. JAMES OF THE MARCHES (1926) Rev. Joseph E. Murphy, Admin. (Retired). In Res., Rev. Marek Biegun.
Res.: 32 St. James Pl., 07512. Tel: 973-790-0288; Fax: 973-790-7064. Email: stjameschurch@optonline.net.
Catechesis/Religious Program—31 St. James Pl. Tel: 973-790-4860; Fax: 973-790-4644. Students 410.

WAYNE, PASSAIC CO.

1—ANNUNCIATION (1963) Rev. Msgr. Peter J. Doody; Deacons Andrew Kostic; Joseph Crowley. In Res., Rev. Msgr. Christopher Lella.
Res.: 45 Urban Club Rd., 07470. Tel: 973-694-5700; Fax: 973-694-5706. Web: www.abumwayne.org.
Catechesis/Religious Program—Tel: 973-694-0787. Students 124.

2—HOLY CROSS (1925) Rev. Charles J. Parr. In Res., Rev. Joseph J. Orlandi.
Res.: 17 Van Duyne Ave., 07470. Tel: 973-696-1065; Fax: 973-696-3641. Email: holycrosswayne@verizon.net.
Catechesis/Religious Program—Tel: 973-696-3500. Students 59.

3—IMMACULATE HEART OF MARY (1956) Rev. Daniel A. Kelly; Sr. Maureen Corcoran, S.C.; Deacon Daniel Galvin.

Res.: 580 Ratzer Rd., 07470. Tel: 973-694-3400; Fax: 973-694-3459. Email: ihmchurch@aol.com. Web: www.ihmwaynenj.org.
School—(1958)Tel: 973-694-1225; Fax: 973-872-9043. Lay Teachers 16; Students 200.
Catechesis/Religious Program—Tel: 973-694-4891. Students 627.

4—OUR LADY OF CONSOLATION (1963) Rev. Michael D. Lombardo; Deacons Robert Pringle; John Schuler.
Res.: 1799 Hamburg Tpke., 07470. Tel: 973-839-3444; Fax: 973-839-9695.
School—(1967)Tel: 973-839-2323; Fax: 973-839-2428. Lay Teachers 26; Students 190.
Catechesis/Religious Program—Students 351.

5—OUR LADY OF THE VALLEY (1960) Rev. Frank Hreno, S.D.V., Temporary Admin.; Deacons Vincent Cocilovo; Michael J. Malecki. In Res., Rev. James Moss.
Office: 630 Valley Rd., 07470. Tel: 973-694-4585; Fax: 973-696-4430.
Res.: 614 Valley Rd., 07470. Web: www.olvwayne.org.
Catechesis/Religious Program—630 Valley Rd. Tel: 973-696-8307. Students 805.

WEST MILFORD TOWNSHIP, PASSAIC CO., ST. JOSEPH (1765) Rev. Steven Shadwell, Admin.; Deacons Milton Smilek; Anthony Curcio; Benjamin LoParo; Harry White; David Cedrone.
Res.: 454 Germantown Rd., 07480. Tel: 973-697-6100; Fax: 973-697-3716. Web: www.stjoseph-nj.org.
Catechesis/Religious Program—Tel: 973-208-0636. Students 371.

WHIPPANY, MORRIS CO., OUR LADY OF MERCY (1854) [CEM] Revs. Sean McDonnell; Daniel Staniskis.
Res.: 9 Parsippany Rd., 07981. Tel: 973-887-0050; Fax: 973-887-0991. Email: olmchwhip@aol.com. Web: www.ourladyofmercyparish.com.
School—90 Whippany Rd., 07981. Tel: 973-887-2611; Fax: 973-887-6629. Ms. Elizabeth Ventola, Prin. Lay Teachers 17; Students 200.
Catechesis/Religious Program—94-96 Whippany Rd. Tel: 973-887-0767. Students 284.

Chaplains of Public Institutions
Hospitals

PATERSON. *St. Joseph Hospital*, 703 Main St., 07503. Tel: 973-754-2000; 973-754-2060 (Office). Mr. William McDonald, Pres. & CEO, Revs. Martin Rooney, Francis Enrico Conde, Chap., Edward A. Collins, Thomas G. Rainforth, Christopher Anyanwu.
Preakness Hospital, P.O. Box V, 07509. Tel: 973-278-6800. Rev. James Moss.

DENVILLE. *St. Clare Hospital*, Pocono Rd., 07834. Tel: 973-627-3000. Rev. Ethel Iwu Ifeanyi, Chap.

DOVER. *Dover General Hospital*, Jardine St., 07801. Tel: 973-939-3000. Revs. Volodymyr Baran, Henry Tanto.

MORRIS PLAINS. *Greystone Park Psychiatric Hospital* 07950. Tel: 973-538-1800. Rev. Simon P. Gallagher, O.S.B.

MORRISTOWN. *Morristown Memorial Hospital*, 100 Madison Ave., 07960. Tel: 973-540-5307. Revs. Volodymyr Baran, Zbigniew Kluba, Sr. Jo Mascera, S.S.C.

NEWTON. *Newton Memorial Hospital*, 175 High St., 07860. Tel: 973-383-2121. Vacant.

PASSAIC. *St. Mary Hospital*, 211 Pennington Ave., 07055. Tel: 973-473-1000. Revs. Sam Frapaul, O.F.M.Cap., Vincent Liuzzo, O.F.M.Cap.

POMPTON PLAINS. *Chilton Memorial Hospital* 07444. Tel: 973-831-5000. Rev. Robert J. Norton, O.F.M., Chap., Deacons Edward Jaroszewski, Gil Leifer.

TOTOWA. *North Jersey Developmental Center*. Rev. Louis J. Scurti.

WAYNE. *St. Joseph's Wayne Hospital*, Hamburg Tpke., 07470. Tel: 973-942-6900. Rev. Robert J. Norton, O.F.M.

Correctional Facilities

PATERSON. *Passaic County Jail*. Rev. Msgr. Mark J. Giordani, Rev. Luis A. Rendon.

MORRISTOWN. *Morris County Jail*. Rev. Msgr. Patrick E. Brown.

NEWTON. *Sussex County Jail*. Rev. Thomas H. Fallone.

Special Assignment:
Rev. Msgr.—
Bihr, Louis J., 296 Straight St., 07501.
Revs.—
Corcoran, T. Kevin, 179 Derrom Ave., 07504.
Lambro, Edward, 476 17th Ave., 07504. Tel: 973-523-4456
McGrath, Thomas, 476 17th Ave., 07504. Tel: 201-523-9595

On Duty Outside the Diocese:
Revs.—
Bono, James P., Suffern, NY
Briganti, Philip J., El Paso, TX
Grasso, Richard, Daytona Beach, FL
Holterhoff, Edward G., Monterey, CA
Joly, Michael D., Yorktown, VA
Kanzic, Gerald, Pittsburgh, PA
McLoughlin, Brendan, Denville, NJ
Pavlick, Raymond A., Walden, NY
Reading, Edward, Ortley Beach, NJ
Savitt, Alan F., Clifton, NJ
Stephenson, Alphonse J., Point Pleasant, NJ
Vitillo, Robert J., Geneva, Switzerland
Weis, John H., Sebewaing, MI

Graduate Studies:
Revs.—
Tangorra, Philip-Michael
Waller, Charles J.

Military Chaplains:
Rev. Msgr.—
Cusack, John J., USAF
Revs.—
O'Grady, Frank, USA
Parisi, Michael, USN

Unassigned:
Rev. Msgr.—
Naughton, William M.
Revs.—
Bay, Richard
Biegun, Marek
Mastroeni, Anthony J., S.T.D., J.D.
McLaughlin, Anthony J.
Scolamiero, Dominic A.

Sabbatical:
Rev. Msgr.—
Tamayo, Elias

Absent on Leave:
Revs.—
Cramer, William N.
Erwin, Patrick O.
Long, David P., S.T.L., J.C.L.
Mabango, Ashiono Anthony
Scott, James C.
Treglio, Vincent

Medical Leave:
Rev. Msgr.—
DiLella, Christopher C.
Rev.—
Drogon, Greg

Retired:
Most Rev.—
Rodimer, Frank J., D.D., J.C.D., 1082 Green Pond Rd., Green Pond, 07435.
Rev. Msgrs.—
Amandolare, Ronald J., 34 Timberline Dr., Little Egg Harbor Twp, 08087.
Boland, Eugene, 2 Tulip Crescent, Unit 1A, Little Falls, 07424.
Carey, Leo P., Nazareth Village, Main St., Box 635, Chester, 07930.
Cassidy, Charles C., 15 Sea Girt Ln., Waretown, 08758.
Ciampaglio, Joseph M., 32 Greenways Ln., Lakewood, 08701.
Conway, Michael, 2510 S.W. 81st Ave., Apt. 308, Davie, FL 33328.
Corr, John F., 83 Primose Tr., Morristown, 07960.
Dericks, John H., 288 Lackawanna Dr., Andover, 07821.
Diachak, Robert, Nazareth Village, 11 Meadow Ln., P.O. Box 745, Chester, 07930.
Dudak, George A., Nazareth Village, Main St., Chester, 07930.
Feenan, J. Francis, P.O. Box 2121, West Paterson, 07424.
Ferraioli, Frank B., 1050 Littleton Rd., Parsippany, 07054.
Ferrito, Joseph L., 15 Sea Girt Ln., Waretown, 08758.
Flanagan, P. Kevin, 797 Valley Rd., Clifton, 07013.
Introini, Elso C., 34 San Carlos St., Toms River, 08757.
Lasch, Kenneth E., J.C.D., 41 Elm St., Apt. 2-E, Morristown, 07960.
Lee, Thaddeus, P.O. Box 2044, Beach Haven, 08008.
Longua, Paul A., The Atrium at Wayne, 1120 Alps Rd., Wayne, 07470.
Madden, Brendan P., Nazareth Village, Main St., Chester, 07930.
Matarazzo, Francis, 154 E. 1st St., Clifton, 07011.
McBride, Peter A., Nazareth Village, Main St., Chester, 07930.
McCarthy, William, 3 Winding Wood Dr., Sayreville, 08872.
Murray, James H., 19 Pocono Rd., Apt. 83, Denville, 07834.
O'Rorke, James H., 58 Portsmouth Ct., Hamburg, 07419.
Puma, Vincent E., Cedar Crest Village, Parkview 603, Pompton Plains, 07444.
Rauscher, Martin F., 41 Elm St., Apt. 4E, Morristown, 07960.
Russo, Charles J., 27 Livingston Rd., Morristown, 07960.
Ryan, Leo P., Main St., Box 635, Chester, 07930.
Schinski, Stanley E., Main St., Box 635, Chester, 07930.
Trapasso, Thomas J., S.T.L., Main St., Box 635, Chester, 07930.
Varettoni, Julian B., 486 Rt. 46, Hackettstown, 07840.
Wehrlen, John B., 11 8th Ave., Seaside Park, 08752.
Revs.—
Casey, Joseph M., 11 Cattano Ave., Morristown, 07960.
Catoir, John T., J.C.D., Nazareth Village, Main St., Chester, 07930.
Costigan, George, 37 Windemere Ave., Mount Arlington, 07856.
Coutinho, Absalom, Bradenton, FL 34282.
Davey, Edward M., Nazareth Village, Main St., Chester, 07930.
Dillon, Edward J., 1754 River Rd., Upper Black Eddy, PA 18972.
Hanley, John P., 501 W. Broadway, 07524.
Heekin, John M., 3912 S. Ocean Blvd., Apt. 505, Highland Beach, FL 33487.
Hertel, James R., J.C.D., 2 Ann St., Unit F112, Clifton, 07013.
Heusser, John F., 509 Goffle Hill Rd., Hawthorne, 07506.
Hewitt, Kenneth R., 490 Windemere Ave., Mount Arlington, 07856.
Iovino, Paul, 23 Mission Way, Barnegat, 08005.
Jacobs, Richard A., 157 Bridge St., Catskill, NY 12414.
Klim, Vincent, Nazareth Village, Main St., Chester, 07930.
Krajewski, Paul A., 10 Prime Rose Ln., Mount Arlington, 07856.
Kuzhippallil, George, P.O. Box 164, Broadway, 08808.
LoGatto, Joseph J., Via Fontanella, Cosenza, Italy.
Lugo, Joseph W., 78 Chestnut St., Bridgewater, 08807.
McHugh, Dennis, Our Lady's Shrine, Knock, County Mayo, Ireland.
McLeod, David, 726 Newell Ave., Manahawkin, 08050.
Mullan, Patrick, Nazareth Village, Main St., Box 635, Chester, 07930.
Murphy, Joseph E., Nazareth Village, Main St., Box 635, Chester, 07930.
Mushinsky, John E., 22 Boston Rd., Neptune, 07753.
Nix, Albert P., P.O. Box 564, Sparta, 07871.
O'Connor, John H., 6 Condict St., Morris Plains, 07950.
O'Kielty, James P. (ARL), 134 Christendom Dr., Front Royal, VA 22630.
O'Riordan, Jeremiah, Nazareth Village, Main St., Chester, 07930.
Oliveri, Richard H., 155 W. Pkwy., Pompton Plains, 07444.
Pisarcik, John G., 302 Regent St., Dover, DE 19904-3392.
Rento, Richard G., 33 Murray Ln., Lavalette, 08735.
Sella, Donald J., P.O. Box 1108, Fajardo, PR 00738.
Shema, George T., Nazareth Village, Main St., Box 635, Chester, 07930.
Smith, James, Nazareth Village, Main St., Box 635, Chester, 07930.
Sordillo, Ronald, 306 Mountain Ave., New Providence, 07974.
Stepien, Allen F., 5 New Briar Ln., Clifton, 07012.

Permanent Deacons:
Acevedo, Pedro, St. Agnes, Paterson
Allgaier, Michael, St. Mary, Denville
Altilio, Robert M., St. John Kanty, Clifton
Ayers, Robert, St. Andrew, Clifton
Balough, Joseph, St. Bonaventure, Paterson
Bandel, Arthur
Barile, Anthony P., Jr., Our Lady of Mount Carmel, Swartswood
Beirne, Thomas P., St. Mary, Dover
Bernardine, Anthony E., St. Anthony, Hawthorne
Beyerl, Brian D., Assumption, Morristown
Bianchi, Roland, Archdiocese of Newark
Bias, Richard F., St. Michael, Netcong
Biersbach, Raymond, St. Mark, Long Valley
Boscia, Edward F., St. Thomas, Ogdensburg
Brady, Richard A., St. Matthew, Randolph
Brudzynski, Richard, St. Anthony, Hawthorne
Butkus, James A., Notre Dame, Cedar Knolls

Calandriello, Andrew, Blessed Kateri Tekakwitha, Sparta
Callahan, Jack, St. Pius X, Montville
Cammarano, James, St. John Vianney, Stockholm
Carnero, Juan Carlos, St. Mary, Paterson
Carraro, Joseph, Our Lady of the Mountain, Schooleys Mountain
Casamento, Peter, St. Mary, Pompton Lakes
Casillas, Hector, St. Joseph, Paterson
Cassidy, Joseph, (Retired)
Castellanos, Hector, St. John Cathedral, Paterson
Cedrone, David, Our Lady Queen of Peace, West Milford
Chimileski, Raymond J., St. Luke, Long Valley
Chiocco, Anthony F., Blessed Kateri Tekakwitha, Sparta
Chiocco, Louis, St. Peter the Apostle, Parsippany
Cistaro, Peter, St. Peter the Apostle, Parsippany
Clark, Hal G., St. Mary, Pompton Lakes
Cleary, Kevin, St. Luke, Long Valley
Cocilovo, Vincent, Our Lady of the Valley, Wayne
Collins, David, Notre Dame, Cedar Knolls
Combs, Kevin L., St. Francis De Sales, McAfee
Cortes, Jesus, Our Lady of Fatima, Passaic
Cote, Joseph, Blessed Kateri Tekakwitha, Sparta
Coyne, Herb D., Our Lady of Good Counsel, Pompton Plains
Crowley, Joseph C., Jr.
Cruz, Pedro, St. Agnes, Paterson
Curcio, Anthony, Jr., St. Joseph, West Milford
D'Amico, Larry, St. Joseph, Newton
Dachisen, Harry, St. Clement Pope and Martyr, Rockaway Township
DaSilva, Joao, Morristown Memorial Hospital
Davila, Jesus, Our Lady of Victories, Paterson
Davis, Robert T., Our Lady of Mount Carmel, Swartswood
de Mena, Henry, Notre Dame, Cedar Knolls
Delgado, Alberto, Our Lady of Lourdes, Paterson
Deo, Leonard, St. Ann, Parsippany
DiLorenzo, Anthony
Dolan, Eugene P., (Unassigned)
Drury, Brian, Sacred Heart, Dover
Duarte, Hildebrando A.
Dugger, John, St. Matthew, Randolph
Elliott, James, St. Catherine of Bologna, Ringwood
Espinal, Candelario, St. Stephen, Paterson
Fadalla, Gerald J., St. Anthony, Hawthorne
Fanelli, Alfredo, Notre Dame of Mt. Carmel, Cedar Knolls
Ferry, Daniel F.
Fierro, Anthony O., St. Bonaventure, Paterson
Fiore, Peter M., Holy Family, Florham Park
Flynn, Jack, St. Mary, Denville
Forino, Ronald, Notre Dame of Mount Carmel, Cedar Knolls
Forshay, George W., St. Anthony, Hawthorne
Frank, Alfred E., St. Ann, Parsippany
Friel, Thomas, St. Jude, Hopatcong
Galinski, Edmund V., Good Shepherd, Andover
Gallo, Henry, Our Lady of Pompei, Paterson
Galvin, Daniel
Gardner, Leo, (Retired)
Gaydo, Richard A., St. Christopher, Parsippany
Gibbons, Thomas P., Our Lady of the Mountain, Schooley's Mountain
Gil, Luis
Goglia, Richard J., St. Andrew, Clifton
Gordon, Gary, Morristown Memorial Hospital
Gunther, Stephen A.
Hackett, Jim, St. Matthew the Apostle, Randolph
Hanifen, Gerald B., St. Joseph, Newton
Hanly, P. Michael, Assumption, Morristown
Harenchar, Thomas G., St. Virgil, Morris Plains
Harris, Joseph, Notre Dame, Cedar Knolls
Harris, Keith, Good Shepherd, Andover
Hartnett, Stuart, St. Mary, Dover
Harty, William, (Retired)
Head, Robert C., Our Lady of the Mountain, Schooley's Mountain
Healy, Philip, (Retired)
Healy, Thomas F., Jr., St. Luke, Long Valley
Higgins, Edward J., St. Mary, Pompton Lakes
Holden, Timothy M., St. Margaret, Morristown
Hussey, William E., (Retired)
Hyle, Henry, (Retired)
Jaroszewski, Edward, Our Lady of Good Counsel Church, Pompton Plains
Keegan, Edward, St. Matthew, Randolph
Keenan, Joseph, St. Michael, Netcong
Kelly, John, St. Christopher, Parsippany
Kimak, Thomas J., St. Mary, Pompton Lakes
King, Dennis, St. Elizabeth Ann Seton, Flanders
Klose, Albert P., (Retired)
Kostic, Andrew, (Retired)
Kronyak, Thomas, (Unassigned)
Kucinski, Al, St. Joseph, Newton.
Lacouture, Roger, Resurrection, Randolph
Lally, Edward J., St. Clare's Hospital, Denville
Lang, Robert A., St. Peter the Apostle, Parsippany
Latour, Raymond, Resurrection, Randolph
Leary, Gerard, Blessed Kateri Tekakwitha, Sparta
Lebron, Florencio G.
Leo, Vincent, Jr., St. Rose of Lima, East Hanover
Llibre, John, (Unassigned)
Lo Paro, Ben, St. Joseph, West Milford
Long, William P., (Retired)
Lucibello, Allan J., St. Christopher, Parsippany
Lupi, Victor, Notre Dame, Cedar Knolls
Malecki, Michael J., Our Lady of the Valley, Wayne
Mallory, Charles
Mann, Patrick, St. Pius X, Montville
Marabeti, Stephen J., St. Joseph Church, Lincoln Park
Maron, Edward, Our Lady of the Lake, Sparta
Marsicovete, Joseph, St. Peter the Apostle, Parsippany
Mather, Brian F., St. Vincent de Paul, Stirling
Mathias, Charles T., Bl. Kateri Tekakwitha, Sparta
Mazzaccoli, Sylvester A., St. Virgil Church, Morris Plains
McCabe, Mark, (Retired)
McMahon, Matthew, Notre Dame of Mount Carmel, Cedar Knolls
Meyer, John, St. Mark, Long Valley
Michalski, Richard, St. Catherine of Bologna, Ringwood
Morales, Eugenio, SS. Cyril and Methodius, Clifton
Morris, James, (Unassigned)
Morton, Robert, St. Clement, Rockaway Twp.
Muller, Edward J., Our Lady of Mount Carmel, Swartswood
Munoz, Mario, Our Lady of Lourdes, Paterson
Murphy, Glen P., Blessed Kateri Tekakwitha, Sparta
Murphy, Stuart, St. Michael, Netcong
Natafalusy, Stephen P., St. Elizabeth Ann Seton, Flanders
Nixon, Mark G., St. Patrick, Chatham
Nolan, Richard
O'Brien, Barry, Blessed Kateri Tekakwitha, Sparta
O'Leary, Donald
O'Neill, Peter J., St. Vincent de Paul, Stirling
Ochner, Ronald
Olsen, Bruce, St. Therese, Succasunna
Owens, Frank, St. Lawrence the Martyr, Chester
Pamplona, Raul
Para, Frank, St. Virgil, Morris Plains
Parlapiano, Joseph J., St. Joseph, Lincoln Park
Paulino, Maximo, Our Lady of Victories, Paterson
Pedraza, Guido, St. John the Baptist, Paterson
Pilek, John F., (Unassigned)
Pinto, Richard, St. Virgil, Morris Plains
Pisano, Vincent F.
Pomales, Jose, St. John Cathedral, Paterson
Pringle, Robert H., Consolation, Wayne
Puglia, Frank, St. Elizabeth Ann Seton, Flanders
Puleo, Paul A., (Retired)
Puskas, Joseph, St. Paul, Clifton
Quinn, Joseph, Notre Dame of Mt. Carmel, Cedar Knolls
Rado, Kenneth, St. Virgil, Morris Plains
Ramirez, Edward, St. Nicholas, Passaic
Ramirez, Luis, St. Therese, Paterson
Reading, Edward J., St. Thomas of Aquin, Ogdensburg
Reck, Richard, Resurrection, Randolph
Restaino, Carmen, Our Lady of Good Counsel, Pompton Plains
Richardson, Joseph, Our Lady of Magnificat, Kinnelon
Rivera, Jose M., St. Francis of Assisi, Haskell
Roche, Charles, Our Lady Queen of Peace, Hewitt
Rohrman, Harry, St. Christopher, Parsippany
Romano, Ron, St. Joseph, Paterson
Salierno, Anthony, St. Mary, Paterson
Sanchez, Armando
Sanker, John M., St. Jude, Budd Lake
Santiago, Manuel
Santos, Robert F., St. Joseph, Mendham
Schenker, Jerome, Immaculate Conception, Franklin
Schuler, John, Our Lady of Consolation, Wayne
Schwietzer, Ellis F.
Scrone, Daniel
Scruggs, Michael K., Holy Spirit, Pequannock
Sheehan, Patrick, St. Matthew, Randolph
Signorelli, Anthony, St. Therese, Succasunna
Siino, Anthony C., St. Jude, Budd Lake
Silva, Percy, (Unassigned)
Simeone, Enio
Sisco, Joseph
Sisler, Merle F., St. Virgil, Morris Plains
Sisson, Stanley
Smilek, Milton, St. Joseph, West Milford
Spruiell, Thomas, (Retired)
Sullivan, Thomas, Good Shepherd, Andover
Taylor, John F., St. Cecilia, Rockaway
Tenga, Charles, St. Jude the Apostle, Hamburg
Thiuri, Phillipe, Our Lady Queen of Peace, Hewitt
Totino, Alberto R., Our Lady Star of the Sea, Lake Hopatcong
Trinidad, Jose M., St. Mary, Paterson
Turner, John, Leave of Absence
Van Glahn, Richard, Resurrection, Randolph
Van Orman, Patrick, Our Lady of the Mountain, Schooleys Mountain
Varsalona, Nicholas, St. Therese Church, Paterson
Vazquez, Gilberto, St. Agnes, Paterson
Veliky, Nicholas, St. Philip the Apostle, Clifton
Verboys, Joseph R., Our Lady Queen of Peace, Hewitt
Vesota, Robert, Father English Center, Paterson
Von Doehren, Wayne, St. James, Montague; St. Thomas, Hainesville
Walker, John, (Unassigned)
Wallace, Michael J., Passaic County Youth Detention Center
Ward, William, Holy Family, Florham Park
Weaver, Kenneth, Resurrection, Randolph
White, Harry, St. Joseph, West Milford
Willson, Paul D., St. Cecelia, Rockaway
Wisneski, Joseph A., St. Patrick, Chatham
Wisniewski, Paul M., St. Jude, Budd Lake
Zack, Gary, Holy Spirit, Pequannock
Zampella, Dominic, St. Thomas of Aquin, Ogdensburg
Zayac, Thomas, St. Joseph, Newton

INSTITUTIONS LOCATED IN THE DIOCESE

[A] SEMINARIES, RELIGIOUS OR SCHOLASTICATES

BOONTON. *Domus Bartimaeus* (Diocesan House of Discernment), 913 Birch St., 07005. Tel: 973-588-7814. Rev. Thomas H. Fallone. Seminarians 4. In Res. Rev. Richard Bay.

OAK RIDGE. *Paulist Novitiate*, 243 Mount Paul Rd., 07438-9512. Tel: 973-697-6341; Fax: 973-697-7814. Email: mountpaulnj@c.s.com. Rev. John J. Foley, C.S.P., J.C.D., Dir. Ministries. Missionary Society of St. Paul the Apostle (Paulist Fathers). Enrollment 4.

[B] COLLEGES AND UNIVERSITIES

MENDHAM. *Assumption College for Sisters*, 350 Bernardsville Rd., 07945-2923. Tel: 973-543-6528; Fax: 973-543-1738. Email: acs@acs350.org. Web: www.acs350.org. Sisters Mary Joseph Schultz, S.C.C., Pres.; Gerardine Tantsits, S.C.C., Academic Dean & Registrar; Theresa Bower, S.C.C., Librarian; Patricia McGrady, Treas. Conducted by Sisters of Christian Charity. Religious 8; Lay Staff 3; Students 42.

MORRISTOWN. *College of Saint Elizabeth*, 2 Convent Rd., 07960-6989. Tel: 973-290-4000; 973-290-4475; Fax: 973-290-4485. Web: www.cse.edu. Rev. Msgr. Thomas J. McDade (NEW), Scholar in Res.; Sr. Francis Raftery, S.C., Pres.; Katherine Buck, Vice Pres. Student Life; Maria Cammarata, Vice Pres. Finance & Admin. and Treas.; Anthony Colabraro, Comptroller; James Dlugos, Vice Pres. & Dean Academic Affairs; Dr. Carol Strobeck, Dean, Women's College & Undergraduate Studies; Mrs. Donna Tatarka, Dean Admissions; Amira Unver, Librarian. Sisters of Charity., Full-time Admin. and Faculty: Priests 4; Religious 17; Lay Teachers 207; Students 2,111.

[C] HIGH SCHOOLS, DIOCESAN

PATERSON. *Paterson Catholic Regional High School*, 764 11th Ave., 07514. Tel: 973-278-1024; Fax: 973-684-7244. Email: principal@patersoncatholic.org. Web: www.patersoncatholic.org. Mary Debra Baier, Pres.; Michele R. Neves, Asst. Prin.; Rev. Janusz Rzadca, Chap.; Gwen Noubuisi, Librarian. Priests 1; Brothers 1; Sisters 1; Lay Teachers 31; Students 304.

DENVILLE. *Morris Catholic High School* 07834. Tel: 973-627-6674; Fax: 973-627-4351. Email: mchs@morriscatholic.org. Web: www.morriscatholic.org. Michael St. Pierre, Pres.; Dr. Jeanne Gradone, Prin.; Rev. Carmen Buono, Chap. Priests 1; Sisters 3; Lay Teachers 38; Students 458.

SPARTA. *Pope John XXIII High School* 07871. Tel: 973-729-6125; Fax: 973-729-4313. Email: pjhs@popejohn.org. Rev. Msgr. Kieran A. McHugh, Pres. Lay Teachers 70; Students 914.

WAYNE. *De Paul High School*, 1512 Alps Rd., 07470. Tel: 973-694-3702; Fax: 973-633-5381. Email: asciaino@dpchs.org. Web: depaulcatholic.org. Rev. Michael Donovan, Pres.; Anthony J. Sciaino, Prin.; Rev. Peter J. Clarke, Chap. Sisters 1; Brothers 2; Lay Teachers 72; Students 822.

[D] HIGH SCHOOLS, PRIVATE

CONVENT STATION. *Academy of St. Elizabeth* 07961. Tel: 973-290-5200; Fax: 973-290-5232. Sr. Patricia Costello, O.P, Prin. Sisters of Charity. Sisters 3;

Lay Teachers 25; Students 225.

MORRISTOWN. *Delbarton School*, 230 Mendham Rd., 07960. Tel: 973-538-3231; Fax: 973-538-8836. Email: homepage@delbarton.org. Web: www.delbarton.org. Bro. Paul J. Diveny, O.S.B., Headmaster; Mr. Charles Ruebling, Asst. Headmaster; Mrs. Anne Leckie, Dean of Faculty; Dr. David Donovan, Dir. Admissions; Mr. David Hajduk, Dir. Campus Min. Day School for Boys. (Grades 7-12) Monks 10; Laymen 68; Students 542.

Villa Walsh Academy 07960. Tel: 973-538-3680; Fax: 973-538-6733. Email: villawalsh@aol.com. Web: www.villawalsh.org. Sr. Patricia Pompa, M.P.F., Prin. College Preparatory for girls (Grades 7-12). Conducted by Religious Teachers Filippini Sisters 5; Lay Teachers 32; Students 255.

NORTH HALEDON. *Mary Help of Christians Academy*, 659-723 Belmont Ave., 07508. Tel: 973-790-6200; Fax: 973-790-6125. Email: principal@maryhelp.org. Web: www.maryhelp.org. Sr. Kim Keraitis, F.M.A., Prin.; Lillian Brunetti, Librarian. Daughters of Mary Help of Christians (Salesian Sisters). Sisters 11; Lay Teachers 26; Students 320.

[E] ELEMENTARY SCHOOLS, DIOCESAN

PARSIPPANY. *All Saints Regional School*, 189 Baldwin Rd., 07054. Tel: 973-334-4704. Ms. Judy Berg, Pres.

TOTOWA. *Academy of Saint Francis of Assisi*, 400 Totowa Rd., 07512. Tel: 973-956-8824; Fax: 976-956-9430. Email: office@academyofstfrancis.org. Web: www.academyofstfrancis.org. Mrs. Carol La Salle, Prin. Serves Our Lady of the Holy Angels, Little Falls & St. James, Totowa Lay Teachers 11; Students 247.

[F] REGIONAL ELEMENTARY SCHOOLS

FRANKLIN. *Immaculate Conception Regional School*, (Grades PreK-8), 65 Church St., 07416. Tel: 973-827-3777; Fax: 973-827-8728. Email: dispagna@icrschool.com. Web: www.icrschool.com. Ms. Diane Di Spagna, Prin. Serves Immaculate Conception, Franklin; Our Lady of Fatima, Highland Lakes; St. John Vianney, Stockholm; St. Monica, Sussex; St. Thomas of Aquin, Ogdensburg; St. Francis De Sales, McAfee; St. Jude, Hamburg Lay Teachers 16; Students 216.

NEWTON. *St. Joseph Regional School*, Jefferson St., 07860. Tel: 973-383-2909; Fax: 973-383-6353. Email: sjrs@nac.net. Web: www.sjccsorg. Ms. Jo-Ann M. Higgs, Prin. Serves St. Joseph, Newton; Our Lady Queen of Peace, Branchville; Our Lady of Mount Carmel, Swartswood Lay Teachers 12; Students 195.

[G] PRIVATE PRESCHOOL

FLORHAM PARK. *Magic Kingdom Day Nursery*, 88 Brooklake Rd., 07932. Tel: 973-966-9762; Fax: 973-377-3994. Email: magickingdom2008@yahoo.com. Sr. M. Antonietta Raucci, S.D.V., Prin. Vocationist Sisters. Sisters 13; Lay Teachers 1; Students 54.

NEWTON. *Camp Auxilium Learning Center*, 14 Old Swartswood Rd., 07860. Tel: 973-383-2621; Fax: 973-383-3214. Email: campauxilium@nac.net. Web: www.campauxilium.org. Sr. Theresa Samson, F.M.A., Prin. Salesian Sisters. Sisters 5; Lay Teachers 9; Students 241.

PARSIPPANY. *St. Elizabeth Nursery and Montessori School, Inc.*, 499 Park Rd., 07054. Tel: 973-540-0721; Fax: 973-540-9186. Email: saintelizabeths@yahoo.con. Web: www.stelizabethschool.com. Sisters Gina Maria Amico, F.S.S.E., Delegate General; Cathy Lynn Cummings, F.S.S.E., Prin. Students 327.

[H] EVANGELIZATION CENTERS

MADISON. *St. Paul Inside The Walls: The Catholic Center for Evangelization at Bayley-Ellard*, 205 Madison Ave., 07940. Tel: 973-377-1004; Fax: 973-377-1952. Rev. Geno Sylva, S.T.D., Dir.

[I] CHILDREN'S CENTERS

TOTOWA. *Mt. St. Joseph Children's Center*, 124 Shepherds Ln., 07512. Tel: 973-595-5720; Fax: 973-595-1930. Ms. Patricia S. Verduin, Dir. Residential school for classified emotionally disturbed boys, 6-14, referred from public school districts. Under the direction of Catholic Family and Community Services. Residents 37.

[J] RETREAT HOUSES & HOUSES OF PRAYER

BRANCHVILLE. *Sanctuary of Mary-Our Lady of the Holy Spirit*, 252 Wantage Ave., 07826. Tel: 973-875-7625. Revs. James Mulligan, S.O.L.T.; Paul Johnson, S.O.L.T.

CHESTER. *Hermits of Bethlehem in the Heart of Jesus*, 82 Pleasant Hill Rd., 07930. Tel: 908-879-7059; Fax: 908-879-7059. Rev. Eugene C. Romano, Desert Father. Priests 2; Sisters 6; Brothers 3.

CONVENT STATION. *Xavier Center* A retreat & conference center., 07961-0211. Tel: 973-290-5100; Fax: 973-290-5121. Email: xaviercenter@scnj.org. Web: www.xaviercenter.org. Sr. Barbara Garland, S.C., Admin.

FLORHAM PARK. *Vocationist Fathers Retreat Center*, 90 Brooklake Rd., 07932. Tel: 973-966-6262; Fax: 973-593-8381. Email: info@vocationist.org. Web: www.vocationist.org.

MENDHAM. *Quellen Spiritual Center*, 350 Bernardsville Rd., 07945. Tel: 973-543-6528, Ext. 217; Fax: 973-543-9459. Email: quellen@scceast.org. Web: www.quellenspiritualcenter.org. Sr. Teresa Marie Skierkowski, S.C.C., Dir.

Villa Pauline 07945. Tel: 973-543-9058. Retreat House for Men & Women Sisters of Christian Charity 5.

MORRISTOWN. *Loyola House of Retreats*, 161 James St., 07960. Tel: 973-539-0740; Fax: 973-898-9839. Email: retreathouse@loyola.org. Web: www.loyola.org. Revs. Gerald J. McIntyre, S.J., Supr.; Charles Moutenot, S.J., Pres. & Dir. Spiritual Progs.; Edmund W. Nagle, S.J.; William P. Poorten, S.J.; William J. Rakowicz, S.J.; Kirk R. Reynolds, S.J.; Thomas F. Walsh, S.J. Society of Jesus. Priests 7.

St. Mary's Abbey Retreat Center, 230 Mendham Rd., 07960. Tel: 973-538-5231, Ext. 2100; Fax: 973-538-7109. Email: abbeyretreat@juno.com. Web: delbarton.org. Rev. Patrick M. Hurley, O.S.B., Dir. & Guestmaster.

MOUNT ARLINGTON. *Claremount Retreat Center*, 35 Windemere Ave., 07856. Tel: 973-601-1475; Fax: 973-234-5292. Email: claremount@optonline.net. Sr. Alexandra Marie Kolat, C.S.S.F., Dir.

NEWTON. *Sacred Heart Retreat Center*, 20 Old Swartswood Rd., 07860. Tel: 973-383-2620; Fax: 973-383-3083. Email: shcenter@nac.net. Sr. Theresa Kelly, F.M.A., Dir. Daughters of Mary Help of Christians (Salesian Sisters of St. John Bosco). Sisters 4.

OAK RIDGE. *Mount Paul Retreat Center*, 243 Mount Paul Rd., 07438-9512. Tel: 973-697-6341; Fax: 973-697-7814. Email: mtpaulnj@aol.com. Rev. John J. Foley, C.S.P., J.C.D., Dir. Ministries.

RINGWOOD. *Franciscan Spiritual Center-Ringwood*, 474 Sloatsburg Rd., 07456-1798. Tel: 973-962-9778; Fax: 973-962-1160. Email: msfretreat@optonline.com. Web: www.franciscanspiritualcenternj.com. Sr. Rosemary Napolitano, O.S.F., Dir. Sisters of St. Francis of Philadelphia.

[K] GENERAL HOSPITALS

PATERSON. *St. Joseph's Hospital and Medical Center*, 703 Main St., 07503. Tel: 973-754-2000; Fax: 973-754-3273. Mr. William McDonald, Pres. & CEO; Sr. Maryanne Campeotto, S.C., Vice Pres., Mission; Revs. Martin Rooney, Dir. Mission Svcs.; Christopher Anyanwu; Edward A. Collins, Chap.; Thomas G. Rainforth, Chap. Sisters of Charity of St. Elizabeth 35; Bed Capacity 1,000; Patients Assisted Annually 315,607.

DENVILLE. *Saint Clare's Health Services, Inc. dba Saint Clare's Health System* 400 W. Blackwell St., Dover, 07801. Tel: 973-989-3525; Fax: 973-989-3430. Email: ikaler@saintclares.org. Web: www.saintclares.org. Edward J. McManus, Chm.; Mr. Leslie D. Hirsch, M.D., Pres. & CEO. Affiliates:

Saint Clare's Hospital, Inc. Tel: 973-625-6194; Fax: 973-625-6184.

Saint Clare's Foundation, Inc. Tel: 973-983-5300.

St. Francis Life Care Corporation

Visiting Nurse Association of Saint Clare's, Inc. Tel: 973-729-7078.

Saint Clare's Community Care, Inc., Sparta, 07834. Tel: 973-983-1540; Fax: 973-983-1530.

Saint Clare's Hospital, Inc., 25 Pocono Rd., 07834. Tel: 973-625-6194; Fax: 973-625-6184. Email: ikaler@saintclares.org. Web: www.saintclares.org. Edward J. McManus, Chm.; Mr. Leslie D. Hirsch, M.D., Pres. & CEO. (Parent Corp.: Saint Clare's Health Services) Patients Assisted Annually 314,152; Bed Capacity 579.

Campuses:

Saint Clare's Hospital-Denville Tel: 973-625-6045; Fax: 973-625-6184.

Saint Clare's Hospital-Boonton Township Tel: 973-316-1808; Fax: 973-316-1815.

Saint Clare's Hospital-Sussex Tel: 973-702-2980; Fax: 973-702-2893.

Saint Clare's Hospital-Dover Tel: 973-989-3525; Fax: 973-989-3560.

Pastoral Care Department: Revs. Henry Tanto; Victor Rezumov; Sisters Catherine M. Belongia, S.S.M.; Susan Evelyn; Mary Joan Phillips, S.S.M.; Frances Renn, S.M.M.; Juanita Williams; Deacon Joseph Marsicovete.

PASSAIC. *St. Mary's Hospital*, 350 Blvd., 07055. Tel: 973-365-4300; Fax: 973-471-5531. Email: sniffenm@smh-passaic.org. Web: www.smh-passaic.org. Michael J. Daniel, Pres. & CEO; Revs. Stephen Hoyt, O.F.M.Cap.; Sam Fra Paul, O.F.M.Cap.; Sr. Dolores Cervi, S.S.D. Sisters of Charity of St. Elizabeth 3; Bed Capacity 292; Patients Assisted Annually 257,139.

St. Mary's Health Corporation

St. Mary's Hospital Foundation Tel: 973-365-9605. Bruce Byrne, Exec. Dir.

[L] HOMES FOR AGED

PATERSON. *St. Joseph Rest Home for Aged Women* Conducted by Daughters of Charity of the Most Precious Blood, 46 Preakness Ave., 07522. Tel: 973-956-1921; Fax: 973-956-1582. Sr. Josephine Alderuccio, D.C.P.B., Supr. Residents 18.

DENVILLE. *St. Francis Health Resort*, 122-126 Diamono Spring Rd., 07834. Tel: 973-627-5000; Fax: 973-627-6389. Email: jthone@saintclares.org. Web: www.saintfrancisres.com. Sr. M. Johnice Thone, S.S.M., Exec. Dir. Senior Living Community Sisters of the Sorrowful Mother 6; Bed Capacity 100; Apartments 62; Guests 150.

Franciscan Oaks Independent Living Units & Health Center, 21 Pocono Rd., 07834. Tel: 973-586-5000; Fax: 973-586-5039. Sponsored by Sisters of the Sorrowful Mother.

TOTOWA. *St. Joseph's Home for the Elderly*, 140 Shepherd Ln., 07512. Tel: 973-942-0300; Fax: 973-942-7201. Email: info@littlesistersofthepoor.org. Sr. Gerard Marie, L.S.P., Admin./Supr.; Rev. Evan Greco, O.F.M., Chap. Conducted by Little Sisters of the Poor Sisters 14; Residents 110.

[M] RESIDENCES FOR WOMEN

WAYNE. *Bethany Residence*, 738 Rte. 23, 07470. Tel: 973-628-8109. Cora Ladung, Admin. Residents 12.

[N] MONASTERIES AND RESIDENCES OF PRIESTS AND BROTHERS

BUTLER. *St. Anthony Friary*, 63 Bartholdi Ave., 07405. Tel: 973-838-4080; Fax: 973-492-5483. Revs. Bernard R. Creighton, O.F.M., Vicar; Kevin M. Cronin, O.F.M.; Edward Donohue, O.F.M.; Hugh Eller, O.F.M.; Vincent B. Grogan, O.F.M., J.C.D.; John J. Kull, O.F.M.; Claude T. Lenahan, O.F.M.; Stephen Lynch, O.F.M.; Revs. Gerald McCaffrey, O.F.M.; Jeremiah V. McGinley, O.F.M.; Anthony McGuire, O.F.M.; Emmet Murphy, O.F.M.; John J. Pierce, O.F.M.; John M. Richardson, O.F.M.; Leon C. Ristuccia, O.F.M.; Edwin F.D. Robinson, O.F.M.; Rayner F. Williams, O.F.M.; Bros. Peter X. Ahlheim, O.F.M.; Robert M. Frazetta, O.F.M.; John P. Mahon, Guardian; William P. Mann, O.F.M.; Frank Waywood, O.F.M. Order of Friars Minor. Priests 17; Brothers 5. *Franciscan Ministry of the Word* Tel: 973-838-4093. Web: www.franmow.org. Rev. Kevin M. Cronin, O.F.M.

CLIFTON. *Holy Face of Jesus Monastery*, 1697 State Hwy. 3, P.O. Box 691, 07012. Tel: 973-778-1177; Fax: 973-778-3809. Email: holyface@worldnet.att.net. Revs. Bernard Schinn, O.S.B., Supr.; Louis-Marie Navaratne, O.S.B. Sylvestrine Benedictine Monks. Priests 2.

FLORHAM PARK. *Father Justin Vocationary*, 90 Brooklake Rd., 07932. Tel: 973-966-6262; Fax: 973-593-8381. Email: info@vocationist.org. Web: www.vocationist.org. Revs. Ignatius Okoroji, S.D.V., Supr.; Vernon Kohlmann, S.D.V.

MORRISTOWN. *St. Mary's Abbey*, Delbarton, 230 Mendham Rd., 07960. Tel: 973-538-3231; Fax: 973-538-7109. Email: osbmonks@delbarton.org. Web: www.osbmonks.org. Rt. Revs. Giles P. Hayes, O.S.B., Abbot; Brian H. Clark, O.S.B., Abbot Emeritus; Thomas J. Confroy, O.S.B., Abbot Emeritus; Gerard P. Lair, O.S.B., Abbot Emeritus; Revs. Jerome Borski, O.S.B.; Benet W. Caffrey, O.S.B.; Gabriel M. Coless, O.S.B.; Richard F. Cronin, O.S.B.; Edward Seton Fittin, O.S.B.; Donal R. Fox, O.S.B.; Simon P. Gallagher, O.S.B.; John E. Hesketh, O.S.B.; Patrick M. Hurley, O.S.B.; Beatus T. Lucey, O.S.B.; James O'Donnell, O.S.B., Treas.; Hilary O'Leary, O.S.B., Novice Master; Rembert F. Reilly, O.S.B.; Wilfred G. Schulz, O.S.B.; Joachim B. Schweitzer, O.S.B.; Andrew T. Smith, O.S.B.; Luke L. Travers, O.S.B., Subprior; Very Rev. Bruno A. Ugliano, O.S.B., Prior; Revs. Basil J. Wallace, O.S.B.; Regis P. Wallace, O.S.B.; Bros. John Babicz, O.S.B.; Paul J. Diveny, O.S.B.; Jeremiah R. Grosse, O.S.B.; Tarcisius Hoang-Hoa, O.S.B.; Jonathan M. Hunt, O.S.B.; Kieran M. Shiek, O.S.B.; Kevin M. Tidd, O.S.B.; James Konchalski, O.S.B. Priests 35; Serving Outside the Diocese 10; Brothers 8.

Resident Outside the Abbey: Revs. Damian B. Breen, O.S.B.; Timothy J. Brennan, O.S.B.; Justin Capato, O.S.B.; Elias R. Lorenzo, O.S.B.; Karl J.

Roesch, O.S.B.; Anthony G. Sargent, O.S.B.; Jude S. Salus, O.S.B.; Benedict M. Worry, O.S.B.; Bro. Brendan A. Tumulty, O.S.B.

NEWTON. *St. Paul's Abbey*, 289 Rte. 206 S, P.O. Box 7, 07860-0007. Tel: 973-383-2470; Fax: 973-383-5782. Email: osbnewton@catholic.or.kr. Rt. Revs. Justin E. Dzikowicz, O.S.B., (Resigned); Augustine J. Hinches, O.S.B., (Resigned); Very Rev. Samuel Kim, O.S.B., Prior; Revs. Peter Ahn, O.S.B.; Odilo Yi, O.S.B. Order of St. Benedict, Congregation of St. Ottilien., (Formerly the Little Flower Monastery) Priests 9; Lay Monks 7.
Priests Residing Outside the Monastery: Rt. Rev. Joel P. Macul, O.S.B., Abbot; Revs. Peter W. Blue, O.S.B., Inkamana Abbey, P/Bag X9333, Vryheid, 3100, South Africa. Tel: 27-34-982-2577; Patrick J. Bonner, O.S.B., Florida; Damian J. Milliken, O.S.B., P.O. Box 213, Lushoto. Tel: 255-2726-40210; Fax: 255-2726-40212.

OAK RIDGE-MILTON. *St. Stanislaus B. M. Friary*, 2 Manor Dr., 07438. Tel: 973-697-7757. Deacon Jerzy P. Krzyskow. Capuchin Fathers. Brothers 1.

RINGWOOD. *Holy Name Friary, Inc.*, 2 Morris Rd., 07456. Tel: 973-962-7200; Fax: 973-962-9766. Email: hnfringwood@netscape.net. Revs. A. Francis Soucy, O.F.M., Supr. & Contact Person; Giles Bello, O.F.M.; Matthew L. Gaskin, O.F.M.; Depaul Genska, O.F.M.; Robert Grix, O.F.M.Cap.; Martin Hanhauser, O.F.M.; Bonaventure Hayes, O.F.M.; Joseph Kiernan, O.F.M.; Eric F. Kyle, O.F.M.; Brian Linehan, O.F.M.; Robert Lynch, O.F.M.; Henry Madden, O.F.M.; Theodore A. McNally, O.F.M.; Kenan Morris, O.F.M.; Joel Munzing, O.F.M.; Owen Murphy, S.A.; Robert Nee, O.F.M.; Cassian A. Miles, O.F.M.; Boniface Riedman, S.A.; Finian A. Riley, O.F.M.; Peter Sheridan, O.F.M.; Aloysius Siracus, O.F.M.; Lambert F. Valentine, O.F.M.; Bros. Kieran Cullen, S.A.; Fintan Duffy, O.F.M.; Brian Hart, O.F.M.; Ennis Thomas, O.F.M.; Joseph P. Trunk, O.F.M.; Rosario Vieira, O.F.M. Priests 25; Brothers 6.

STIRLING. *Holy Spirit Missionary Cenacle*, 1050 Long Hill Rd., 07980. Tel: 908-647-0208; Fax: 908-647-5770. Email: religious@stshrine.org. Web: stshrine.org. Revs. Peter Krebs, S.T., Dir.; Gary Banks, S.T.; Ralph Frisch, S.T.; Conrad Schmitt, S.T.; Bros. Martin Pacholek, S.T.; Gerardo Ramirez, S.T. Missionary Servants of the Most Holy Trinity. Priests 4; Brothers 2.
Shrine of St. Joseph, 1050 Long Hill Rd., 07980. Tel: 908-647-0208; Fax: 908-647-5770. Email: religious@stshrine.org. Web: stshrine.org. Rev. Peter Krebs, S.T., Custodian. Priests 4; Brothers 2; Sisters 7.

WAYNE. *P.I.M.E. Missionaries Residence*, 34 Grandview Dr., 07470. Tel: 973-694-1790; Fax: 973-694-0444. Email: pimenj@optonline.net. Web: www.pimeusa.org. Revs. Luigi Acerbi, P.I.M.E.; Giancarlo Ghezzi, P.I.M.E.
Xaverian Missionary Fathers, Provincial House, 12 Helene Court, 07470. Tel: 973-942-2975; Fax: 973-942-5012. Email: xavwayne@optonline.net. Web: www.xaviermissionaries.org. Revs. Carl S. Chudy, S.X., Prov.; Frank B. Grappoli, S.X., Rector & Treas.
Mission Assignments: Makeni, Sierra Leone: Most Rev. George Biguzzi, S.X., Bishop of Makeni; Revs. Luigi Brioni, S.X.; Eugene Montesi, S.X.; Luciano Peterlini, S.X.
Belem, Brazil: Revs. Francis Gugliotta, S.X.; Danilo Lago, S.X.
Burundi: Rev. Pierino Zoni, S.X.
Cameroon: Revs. Rene Lovat, S.X.; Fernandes de Araujo Herondi, S.X.
Sao Paulo, Brazil: Rev. Gino Nasini, S.X.
Jakarta, Indonesia: Revs. Bruno Orru, S.X.; Franco Qualizza, S.X.
Bogota, Colombia: Revs. Mauro Loda, S.X.; Mark Marangone, S.X.
Torreon, Mexico: Revs. Dan Boschetto, S.X.; Ramon Cerratos, S.X.; Pablo Nieves, S.X.
Taiwan: Revs. Edi Foschiatto, S.X.; Martino Roia, S.X.; Joe Vignato, S.X.
Japan: Revs. Renato Filippini, S.X.; Frank Sottocornula, S.X.
Mozambique: Revs. Horacio Perez, S.X.; Dario Maso, S.X.

[O] CONVENTS AND RESIDENCES FOR SISTERS

PATERSON. *Daughters of Charity of the Most Precious Blood*, 46 Preakness Ave., 07522. Tel: 973-956-1921; Fax: 973-956-1582. Sr. Josephine Alderuccio, D.C.P.B., Supr. Sisters 10.
Missionary Sisters of the Immaculate Conception of the Mother of God, 779 Broadway, 07514-1329. Tel: 973-279-3790; Fax: 973-742-8231. Email: smiconti@optonline.net. Sr. Kathryn Conti, S.M.I.C., Prov. Coord.
Missionary Sisters of the Immaculate Conception of the Mother of God, 396 E. 38th St., 07504-1414. Tel: 973-279-2885; Fax: 973-742-8281. Email: smcketa@optonline.net. Sisters 4.
Missionary Sisters of the Immaculate Conception of the Mother of God, St. Bonaventure Convent, 146 Danforth Ave., 07501. Tel: 973-357-1915. International House for Studies
Missionary Sisters of the Immaculate Conception of the Mother of God, 374-18th Ave., 07504-1333. Tel: 973-523-4988. Sisters 3.
Missionary Sisters of the Immaculate Conception, Inc., 779 Broadway, 07514. Tel: 973-279-3790; Fax: 973-742-8231.

BOONTON. *Society of the Sisters of the Church*, 24 Deer Hill Ct., 07005. Tel: 973-299-8365; Fax: 973-884-0940. Email: SRBW@ssoc.org. Web: www.ssoc.org. Sr. Frances Sanzo, S.S.C., Coord. Sisters 12.

CHESTER. *Carmel of the Immaculate Heart of Mary*, 80 Pleasant Hill Rd., 07930-2135. Tel: 908-879-4990; Fax: 908-879-0884. Email: hermcarm@gti.net. Sr. Mary of Jesus and St. Joseph, O.Carm., Desert Mother. Hermits of Our Lady of Mt. Carmel Sisters 4.

CONVENT STATION. *Motherhouse of the Sisters of Charity*, P.O. Box 476, 07961-0476. Tel: 973-290-5000; Fax: 973-290-5335. Email: escharity@aol.com. Web: www.scnj.org. Sr. Maureen Shaughnessy, S.C., Gen. Supr. Professed Sisters 60.

DENVILLE. *Our Lady of Sorrows Convent, Sisters of Sorrowful Mother*, 9 Pocono Rd., 07834. Tel: 973-627-9008; Fax: 973-625-9245. Email: olsconventnj@aol.com. Web: www.ssmfranciscans.org.
Residences: *Our Lady of Sorrows Convent, Sisters of Sorrowful Mother*, 4 Pocono Rd., 07834. Tel: 973-983-8456; Fax: 973-270-0187. *Our Lady of Sorrows Convent, Sisters of Sorrowful Mother*, 45 N. Shore Dr., 07834. Tel: 973-625-8433. *Our Lady of Sorrows Convent, Sisters of Sorrowful Mother*, 40 E. Main St., Rockaway, 07866. Tel: 973-627-4643.
Our Lady of Sorrows Convent, 9 Ulysses St., Parsippany, 07054. Tel: 973-331-1471.

FLORHAM PARK. *St. Anne Villa*, P.O. Box 476, Convent Station, 07961. Tel: 973-867-1502; Fax: 973-867-1560. Email: rcaiazzo@saintannevilla.org. Sr. Marian Farrell, S.C., Admin.; Rev. Jerome Borski, O.S.B., Chap. Sisters of Charity of St. Elizabeth., Home for retired and infirm Sisters Bed Capacity 101.
Sister Joanna House of Formation, 88 Brooklake Rd., 07932. Tel: 973-966-9762; Fax: 973-377-3994. Email: vocationist@yahoo.com. Sisters Gelsomina Mosca, Supr. & Prin.; Louisa Garcione, S.D.V., Delegate. Sisters 15.

GLADSTONE. *Mt. St. John Convent*, 22 St. John's Dr., 07934. Tel: 908-234-0640; Fax: 908-781-7814. Email: baptistines@worldnet.att.net. Web: www.baptistines.home.att.net. Sr. Angelita Vazzano, C.S.J.B., Admin. Sisters of St. John the Baptist. Sisters 3.

HALEDON. *Institute of the Daughters of Mary Help of Christians*, 655 Belmont Ave., 07508. Tel: 973-790-7963; Fax: 973-790-6482. Email: secretarysua@aol.com. Web: www.salesiansisters.org. Sisters Phyllis Neves, F.M.A., Prov.; Carmen Pena, F.M.A., Supr.; Rev. Armindo Simao Laranjinha, S.D.B., Chap. Provincialate of Daughters of Mary Help of Christians Daughters of Mary Help of Christians (Salesian Sisters) 100.

MENDHAM. *Mallinckrodt Convent-Motherhouse and Novitiate of the Sisters of Christian Charity* 07945. Tel: 973-543-6528; Fax: 973-543-9459. Web: scceast.org. Sr. Joan Daniel Healy, S.C.C., Prov. Supr. Daughters of the Blessed Virgin Mary of the Immaculate Conception. Sisters 45; Novices 2; Postulants 1.

MORRISTOWN. *St. Lucy Provincialate of the Religious Teachers Filippini, Novitiate, Villa Walsh Academy*, 455 Western Ave., 07960-4928. Tel: 973-538-2886; Fax: 973-538-6107. Email: bjtakacs@filippiniusa.org. Web: www.filippiniusa.org. Sisters Betty Jean Takacs, M.P.F., Prov.; Rita Tassinari, M.P.F., Supr.; Lillian Ernest, M.P.F., Dir. Formation.
Pontifical Institute of the Religious Teachers Filippini Sisters 87; Junior Professed 2; Novices 1.
Monastery Discalced Carmelite Nuns of the Most Blessed Virgin Mary of Mt. Carmel, 189 Madison Ave., 07960. Tel: 973-539-0773. Sr. Therese Katulski, O.C.D., Prioress. Professed Nuns 9; Novices 2.

MOUNT ARLINGTON. *Felician Sisters of St. Francis of Assisi Convent*, 37 Windemere Ave., 07856. Sr. Mary Josita, C.S.S.F., Local Supr. Professed Sisters 7.

PARSIPPANY. *St. Francis of Assisi Novitiate-Franciscan Sisters of St. Elizabeth*, 499 Park Rd., 07054. Tel: 973-539-3857; Fax: 973-539-3347. Email: srcathylynn@yahoo.com. Web: www.franciscansisters.com. Sr. Gina Maria Amico, F.S.S.E., Delegate Gen. Perpetually Professed Sisters 54; Temporarily Professed Sisters 16.

PASSAIC. *Our Lady of Mt. Carmel Convent, Sisters of Saint Francis of Philadelphia*, 47 Reid Ave., 07055. Tel: 973-471-6352; Fax: 973-473-0937. Sr. M. Berard, O.S.F., Supr. Sisters 2.

RINGWOOD. *Sisters of St. Francis of Philadelphia, Mt. St. Francis Convent*, 474 Sloatsburg Rd., 07456. Tel: 973-962-7411; Fax: 973-962-0445. Email: mgurley@osfphila.org. Sr. Mary C. Gurley, O.S.F., Admin. Sisters of St. Francis 2.
Sisters of St. Francis of Philadelphia, St. Clare Convent, 474 Sloatsburg Rd., 07456. Tel: 973-962-4705.
Sisters of St. Francis of Philadelphia, 474 Sloatsburg Rd., 07456. Tel: 973-962-6416. Sr. Francis Paul Torre, O.S.F., Admin. Total in Residence: Sisters of St. Francis of Philadelphia 9; Missionary Sisters of the Immaculate Conception 5.

STIRLING. *Holy Trinity Convent*, 1026 Long Hill Rd., 07980. Tel: 908-647-6584. Sr. Sophia Kozikowska, Supr. Servants of Jesus 7.

WEST PATERSON. *Missionary Sisters of the Immaculate Conception of the Mother of God*, Generalate, 47 Garden Ave., 07424-3337. Tel: 973-279-1484; Fax: 973-279-2991. Email: smicgen@optonline.net. Sr. Veronica Lee, S.M.I.C., Coord. Gen. Sisters 6.
The Society of Sisters for the Church, 396 Rifle Camp Rd., 07424. Tel: 718-894-8564. Web: www.ssc-usa.org. Sr. Loretta Rybacki, S.S.C., Pres. Sisters 22.

[P] NEWMAN CENTERS

HALEDON. *William Paterson University of New Jersey* 219 Pompton Rd., 07508. Tel: 973-720-3524; 973-595-6184; 973-720-3849 (Studio); Fax: 973-595-5312. Email: scurti@wpunj.edu. Web: www.princeofpeacechapel.com. Rev. Louis J. Scurti, Dir. Jesus Christ, Prince of Peace Chapel & Bishop Frank J. Rodimer Catholic Campus Ministry Center & CCM Communications.

MADISON. *Drew University Catholic Campus Ministry* 07940. Tel: 973-408-3027. Email: jfarias@drew.edu. Rev. Joseph G. Farias. Tel: 973-443-8496; Fax: 973-267-4425.
Res.: P.O. Box 286, Convent Station, 07961-0387. Tel: 973-267-5330; Fax: 973-267-4425.
Fairleigh Dickinson University
Catholic Campus Ministry Fairleigh Dickinson University, 285 Madison Ave., 07940. Tel: 973-443-8651; Fax: 973-287-5330. Email: madisonccm@aol.com. Rev. Joseph G. Farias.
Res.: P.O. Box 387, Convent Station, 07961-0387. Tel: 973-443-8496; Fax: 973-443-8651.

[Q] MISCELLANEOUS LISTINGS

PATERSON. *St. Anthony's Guild* 07509. Tel: 973-777-3737; Fax: 212-594-2769. Email: anthonian@aol.com. Web: www.anthonian.org. Rev. Joseph M. Hertel, O.F.M.; Bro. Thomas J. Cole, O.F.M., Asst. Dir. Membership organization supports the work of The Franciscan Friars of Holy Name Province.
The Association of the Marian Apostolate of Mercy, Inc., 31 St. James Pl., Totowa, 07512. Tel: 973-956-5969; Fax: 973-956-5971. Email: marianassociates@gmail.com. Sr. Maria Elizabeth Whilifer, Pres.; Judith A. Bonnesen, Treas.; Rev. Msgr. Paul L. Bochicchio, V.F. (NEW).
Cor Jesu Mission Fund Inc, 1048 E. 26th St., 07513. Tel: 973-278-2540. Revs. Anthony J. Mastroeni, S.T.D., J.D., Pres.; Charles MacIsaac, Vice Pres.; Sr. Mary Taylor, R.S.C.J., Treas.
Martin de Porres Village Corporation, Green St., 07501. Tel: 973-881-8022; Fax: 973-881-0149. Rev. Msgr. Herbert K. Tillyer, P.A., M.Ch.A., Pres. Sponsoring Martin De Porres, Vill.
Province of the Immaculate Conception of the Missionary Sisters of the Immaculate Conception 1996 Trust Fund, 779 Broadway, 07514. Tel: 973-279-3790; Fax: 973-742-8231. Email: smicmissionarysisters@yahoo.com. Sr. Joanne Riggs, S.M.I.C., Trustee.
Riese Corporation, c/o R.P. Marzulli Co., 264 Belleville Ave., Bloomfield, 07003. Tel: 973-279-2262; Fax: 973-279-8625. Rev. Msgr. Herbert K. Tillyer, P.A., M.Ch.A., Pres. Sponsoring Governor Paterson Towers, Maurice Brick Residence, Brestel Residence, William F. Hinchcliffe Pavilion, Ralph J. Diverio Residence, Murray M. Bisgaier Residence, William Levine Residence.

CHESTER. *Nazareth Village* Retirement residence for diocesan priests., 11 Meadow Ln., Box 635, 07930. Tel: 908-879-6991; Fax: 908-879-7461. Email: nazarethvillage@hotmail.com. Web: www.nazarethvillage.com. Rev. Msgr. Raymond M. Lopatesky, Dir. In Res. Rev. Msgrs. Leo P. Carey

(Retired); George A. Dudak (Retired); Brendan P. Madden (Retired); Peter A. McBride (Retired); Peter J. McHugh; Leo P. Ryan (Retired); Stanley E. Schinski (Retired); Revs. Marek Biegun; John T. Catoir, J.C.D. (Retired); Edward M. Davey (Retired); Vincent Klim (Retired); Patrick Mullan (Retired); Joseph E. Murphy (Retired); Jeremiah O'Riordan (Retired); George T. Shema (Retired); James A.D. Smith; Rev. Msgrs. Robert M. Diaghek; Thomas J. Trapasso, S.T.L. (Retired).

CLIFTON. *Consortium of Catholic Schools of the Roman Catholic Diocese of Paterson, Inc.*, 777 Valley Rd., 07013. Tel: 973-777-8818. Most Rev. Arthur J. Serratelli, S.T.D., S.S.L., D.D., Pres.; Rev. Msgr. James T. Mahoney, Ph.D., V.G., Vice Pres.; Mary Debra Baier, Dir.; Sr. Mary Edward Spohrer, S.C.C., Sec. & Treas.

CONVENT STATION. *Seton Health Care, Inc.*, *Convent of Saint Elizabeth*, P.O. Box 476, 07961. Tel: 973-290-5450; Fax: 973-290-5335. Email: mshaughnessy@scnj.org. Web: www.scnj.org. Sr. Maureen Shaughnessy, S.C., Pres.

MORRISTOWN. *College of St. Elizabeth, Center for Theological and Spiritual Development* 2 Convent Rd., 07960. Tel: 973-290-4354; Fax: 973-290-4312. Email: ibaratte@cse.edu. Web: www.cse.edu/center.

PASSAIC. *St. Jude Media Ministries*, 63 Monroe St., 07055. Tel: 908-879-1460; Fax: 908-879-7461. Email: jcatoir@aol.com. Web: www.messengerofjoy.com. Rev. John T. Catoir, J.C.D., Dir. (Retired).

POMPTON LAKES. *Pathways Counseling Center, Inc.*, 16 Pompton Ave., 07442. Tel: 973-835-6337; Fax: 973-616-4688. Email: pegb@pathwayscounseling.org. Web: www.pathwayscounseling.org. Ms. Mathilda Catarina, Ph.D., Clinic Dir.; Ms. Peg Buczek, Admin. Mgr.

SPARTA. *The Catholic Academy of Sussex County, Inc.*, 28 Andover Rd., 07871. Tel: 973-729-6125. Most Rev. Arthur J. Serratelli, S.T.D., S.S.L., D.D., Pres.; Rev. Msgr. James T. Mahoney, Ph.D., V.G., Vice Pres.; Sr. Mary Edward Spohrer, S.C.C., Sec. & Treas.; Rev. Msgr. Kieran A. McHugh, Dir.

Pope John XXIII High School Special Project Foundation, Inc, 28 Andover Rd., 07871. Most Rev. Arthur J. Serratelli, S.T.D., S.S.L., D.D., Pres.; Rev. Msgr. Kieran A. McHugh, Agent.

WAYNE. *Siena Village*, 1000 Siena Village, 07470. Tel: 973-696-2811; Fax: 973-696-2721. Email: aldors@aol.com. Sr. Alice Matthew, O.P., Dir.

RELIGIOUS INSTITUTES OF MEN REPRESENTED IN THE DIOCESE

For further details refer to the corresponding bracketed number in the Religious Institutes of Men or Women section.

[0200]—*Benedictine Monks* (St. Mary, St. Paul Abbeys; Holy Face of Jesus Monastery)—O.S.B.
[0470]—*The Capuchin Friars*—O.F.M.Cap
[0480]—*Conventual Franciscans*—O.F.M.Conv
[0520]—*Franciscan Friars* (Holy Name Prov.)—O.F.M.
[0690]—*Jesuit Fathers and Brothers* (New York Prov.)—S.J.
[0840]—*Missionary Servants of the Most Holy Trinity* (Silver Spring, MD)—S.T.
[1050]—*Pontifical Institute for Foreign Missions*—P.I.M.E.
[1190]—*Salesians of Don Bosco* (Turin, Italy)—S.D.B.
[1340]—*Vocationist Fathers*—S.D.V.
[1360]—*Xaverian Missionary Fathers* (Wayne)—S.X.

RELIGIOUS INSTITUTES OF WOMEN REPRESENTED IN THE DIOCESE

[0230]—*Benedictine Sisters of Pontifical Jurisdiction*—O.S.B.
[0740]—*Daughters of Charity of the Most Precious Blood*—D.C.P.B.
[0850]—*Daughters of Mary Help of Christians*—F.M.A.
[]—*Daughters of the Most Pure Heart of the Most Holy Virgin Mary* (Passaic)
[0420]—*Discalced Carmelite Nuns*—O.C.D.
[1070-06]—*Dominican Sisters*—O.P.
[1070-18]—*Dominican Sisters*—O.P.
[1115]—*Dominican Sisters of Peace*—O.P.
[1170]—*Felician Sisters*—C.S.S.F.
[1400]—*Franciscan Missionary Sisters of the Sacred Heart* (Peekskill)—F.M.S.C.
[]—*Hermits of Our Lady of Mt. Carmel*—H.O.Carm.
[2340]—*Little Sisters of the Poor*—L.S.P.
[2760]—*Missionary Sisters of the Immaculate Conception of the Mother of God*—S.M.I.C.
[3430]—*Religious Teachers Filippini*—M.P.F.
[1700]—*School Sisters of the Third Order of St. Francis*—O.S.F.
[3560]—*Servants of Jesus* (Starling)—S.J.
[3580]—*Servants of Mary*—O.S.M.
[0590]—*Sisters of Charity of Saint Elizabeth, Convent Station*—S.C.
[0660]—*Sisters of Christian Charity*—S.C.C.
[3820]—*Sisters of St. John the Baptist*—C.S.J.B.
[3830]—*Sisters of St. Joseph* (Chestnut Hill, PA)—C.S.J.
[3890]—*Sisters of St. Joseph of Peace*—C.S.J.P.
[1830]—*Sisters of the Good Shepherd*—R.G.S.
[3320]—*Sisters of the Presentation of the B.V.M.*—P.B.V.M.
[4100]—*Sisters of the Sorrowful Mother (Third Order of St. Francis)*—S.S.M.
[]—*The Society of the Sisters of the Church* (Passaic)
[4210]—*Vocationist Sisters*—S.D.V.

NECROLOGY

† Busch, Rev. Msgr. Aloysius J., (Retired)—Died Oct. 19, 2009
† McQuaid, Rev. Msgr. Eugene, (Retired)—Died Dec. 20, 2008
† Morris, Rev. Msgr. John E., (Retired)—Died Sept. 17, 2009
† Colaiacovo, Arthur J., Convent Station, NJ Saint Thomas More—Died March 16, 2009
† Fanning, Leo M., (Retired)—Died Dec. 29, 2008
† Freeswick, William J., Denville, NJ Saint Francis Health Resort—Died Sept. 12, 2009
† Hinds, Edward J., Chatham, NJ St. Patrick's—Died Oct. 22, 2009

An asterisk (*) denotes an organization that has established tax-exempt status directly with the IRS and is not covered by the USCCB Group Ruling.

Diocese of Pensacola-Tallahassee

(Dioecesis Pensacolensis-Tallaseiensis)

Most Reverend

JOHN H. RICARD, S.S.J.

Bishop of Pensacola-Tallahassee; ordained May 25, 1968; ordained Auxiliary Bishop of Baltimore July 2, 1984; appointed Bishop of Pensacola-Tallahassee January 21, 1997.

Monsignor James Amos Pastoral Center: 11 North B St., Pensacola, FL 32502. Tel: 850-435-3500; Fax: 850-436-6424. *Mailing Address: P.O. Drawer 13284, Pensacola, FL 32591*

Web: www.ptdiocese.org

Email: chancellor@ptdiocese.org

ESTABLISHED NOVEMBER 6, 1975.

Square Miles 14,044.

Comprises the following Counties: Bay, Calhoun, Escambia, Franklin, Gadsden, Gulf, Holmes, Jackson, Jefferson, Leon, Liberty, Madison, Okaloosa, Santa Rosa, Taylor, Wakulla, Walton and Washington Counties.

For legal titles of parishes and diocesan institutions, consult the Pastoral Center.

STATISTICAL OVERVIEW

Personnel	
Bishop	1
Priests: Diocesan Active in Diocese	49
Priests: Diocesan Active Outside Diocese	7
Priests: Retired, Sick or Absent	14
Number of Diocesan Priests	70
Religious Priests in Diocese	18
Total Priests in Diocese	88
Extern Priests in Diocese	16
Ordinations:	
Transitional Deacons	3
Permanent Deacons	17
Permanent Deacons in Diocese	67
Total Brothers	5
Total Sisters	27
Parishes	
Parishes	49
With Resident Pastor:	
Resident Diocesan Priests	39
Resident Religious Priests	5
Without Resident Pastor:	
Administered by Priests	5
Missions	8
Professional Ministry Personnel:	
Brothers	5
Sisters	11
Lay Ministers	60
Welfare	
Catholic Hospitals	1
Total Assisted	44,631
Homes for the Aged	2
Total Assisted	893
Special Centers for Social Services	4
Total Assisted	21,000
Other Institutions	2
Total Assisted	42
Educational	
Diocesan Students in Other Seminaries	11
Total Seminarians	11
High Schools, Diocesan and Parish	2
Total Students	680
Elementary Schools, Diocesan and Parish	7
Total Students	1,891
Catechesis/Religious Education:	
High School Students	1,081
Elementary Students	3,915
Total Students under Catholic Instruction	7,578
Teachers in the Diocese:	
Priests	3
Sisters	9
Lay Teachers	201
Vital Statistics	
Receptions into the Church:	
Infant Baptism Totals	976
Minor Baptism Totals	120
Adult Baptism Totals	107
Received into Full Communion	225
First Communions	1,063
Confirmations	923
Marriages:	
Catholic	158
Interfaith	118
Total Marriages	276
Deaths	538
Total Catholic Population	62,420
Total Population	1,381,566

Former Bishops—Most Revs. RENE H. GRACIDA, D.D., ord. May 23, 1959; appt. Titular Bishop of Masuccaba and Auxiliary of Miami, Dec. 6, 1971; cons. Jan. 25, 1972; appt. first Bishop of Pensacola-Tallahassee, Oct. 1, 1975; installed Nov. 6, 1975; transferred to Bishop of Corpus Christi, May 19, 1983; J. KEITH SYMONS, D.D., Bishop of Pensacola-Tallahassee; ord. May 18, 1958; Titular Bishop of Siguritanus and Auxiliary of St. Petersburg; appt. Jan. 16, 1981; cons. March 19, 1981; Bishop of Pensacola-Tallahassee; appt. Sept. 29, 1983; installed Nov. 8, 1983; transferred to Bishop of Palm Beach, June 2, 1990; JOHN M. SMITH, J.C.D., D.D., Bishop of Pensacola-Tallahassee; ord. May 27, 1961; Titular Bishop of Tre Taverne and Auxiliary of Newark; appt. Dec. 1, 1987; cons. Jan. 25, 1988; Bishop of Pensacola-Tallahassee; appt. June 25, 1991; installed July 31, 1991; transferred to Coadjutor Bishop of Trenton, Nov. 21, 1995; appt. Bishop of Trenton July 1, 1997.

Monsignor James Amos Pastoral Center—11 North B St., Pensacola, 32501. Tel: 850-435-3500; Fax: 850-436-6424. *Mailing Address: P.O. Drawer 13284, Pensacola, 32591.*

Office of the Bishop—TEENA EASTER, Exec. Sec. Tel: 850-435-3511.

Chancellor—Rev. Msgr. MICHAEL V. REED, J.C.L.

Moderator of the Curia—Rev. Msgr. MICHAEL V. REED, J.C.L.

Vicar for Priests—Rev. Msgr. JOHN T. CASSIDY.

Vicar for Permanent Deacons and Chairman—Rev. JOSEPH P. CALLIPARE.

Vicar for Religious—Rev. Msgr. MICHAEL V. REED, J.C.L.

Vicars Forane—Very Revs. DENNIS J. O'BRIEN, Northwest Vicariate Forane; EUGENE D. CASSERLY, M.Ch.A., V.F., Southwest Vicariate Forane; Rev. Msgr. MICHAEL A. CHERUP, West Central Vicariate Forane; Very Revs. PETER LAWRENCE ZALEWSKI, V.F., East Central Vicariate Forane; KEVIN JOHNSON, Eastern Vicariate Forane.

Vicar General—Rev. Msgr. LUKE HUNT, V.G.

Diocesan Tribunal—Mailing Address: P.O. Drawer 13284, Pensacola, 32591. Tel: 850-436-6454; Fax: 850-436-6457.

Judicial Vicar—Rev. Msgr. JAMES J. FLAHERTY, J.C.L., J.V.

Associate Judicial Vicar—VACANT.

Advocate—Rev. CRAIG SMITH.

Judges—Rev. Msgr. JAMES J. FLAHERTY, J.C.L., J.V.; Rev. T. JOSEPH FOWLER, J.C.L.; Deacon DANIEL M. MCAULIFFE, J.C.L.

Promoter of Justice—Rev. Msgr. MICHAEL V. REED, J.C.L.

Auditors—RUBY B. RIVAIS; Rev. CRAIG SMITH.

Defender of the Bond—Very Rev. EUGENE D. CASSERLY, M.Ch.A., V.F.

Notary—RUBY B. RIVAIS.

College of Consultors—Rev. Msgr. JAMES J. FLAHERTY, J.C.L., J.V.; Very Rev. DENNIS J. O'BRIEN; Rev. Msgr. MICHAEL W. TUGWELL; Very Rev. PETER LAWRENCE ZALEWSKI, V.F.; Rev. Msgrs. MICHAEL V. REED, J.C.L.; LUKE HUNT, V.G.

Administrative Council—Rev. Msgrs. JAMES J. FLAHERTY, J.C.L., J.V.; MICHAEL V. REED, J.C.L., Chancellor; Very Rev. DENNIS J. O'BRIEN; JOHN GODLEWSKI; Mr. KEVIN VICKERY; MARK DUFVA; JOHN KENNEDY.

Council of Priests—Most Rev. JOHN H. RICARD, S.S.J., Pres. Members Ex Officio: Rev. Msgrs. LUKE HUNT, V.G.; MICHAEL V. REED, J.C.L. Members Elected by Deanery: Rev. NICHOLAS FRANK SCHUMM, NW; Rev. Msgr. JAMES J. FLAHERTY, J.C.L., J.V., Pres., SW; Rev. ROBERT F. MORRIS, WC; Rev. Msgr. FRANCIS S. SZCZYKUTOWICZ, E; Rev. EDWARD T. JONES, EC. Members At Large: Revs. THOMAS GUIDO; PATRICK FOLEY. Members Appointed: Rev. Msgr. MICHAEL W. TUGWELL; Rev. ROY C. MARIEN; Very Rev. PETER LAWRENCE ZALEWSKI, V.F., Sec.

Executive Committee of Permanent Deacons—Most Rev. JOHN H. RICARD, S.S.J.; Rev. JOSEPH P. CALLIPARE, Vicar for Permanent Deacons & Chm.; Deacons PAUL GRAAFF; STEPHEN WULF; DANIEL M. MCAULIFFE, J.C.L.; ROGER GALLAGHER; LOU FETE; SANTIAGO MOLINA; RICHARD LURTON.

Council of Sisters—Sisters MAUREEN JOSEPH KIRWAN, S.C., Pres.; MARGUERITE GIBBS, I.H.M., Vice Pres.

Priests' Pension Plan, Board for—Most Rev. JOHN H. RICARD, S.S.J.; Rev. Msgrs. LUKE HUNT, V.G.; MICHAEL V. REED, J.C.L.; MICHAEL P. MOONEY; Very Rev. EUGENE D. CASSERLY, M.Ch.A., V.F.; Rev. JOHN F. KELLY; Rev. Msgrs. JOHN T. CASSIDY; JOHN O'SULLIVAN. Consultants: JOHN GODLEWSKI; ROBERT EMMANUEL ESQ.

Priest Personnel Board—Rev. Msgr. JOHN T. CASSIDY, Ex Officio; Rev. JOSEPH FOWLER, Northwest; Rev. Msgrs. JOHN O'SULLIVAN, East; MICHAEL CHERUP, West Central; FRANCIS S. SZCZYKUTOWICZ, East

Central; Rev. JAMES PAUL VALENZUELA, Southwest, Mailing Address: P.O. Drawer 13284, Pensacola, 32591. Tel: 850-435-3500.

Diocesan Commissions, Departments, and Offices

Apostleship of the Sea, Office of the—Rev. PETER MCLAUGHLIN, Chap., Mailing Address: P.O. Box 12423, Pensacola, 32591-2423. Tel: 850-435-3500.

Archivist—CARLISLE SEMMES, Ed.D., Mailing Address: P.O. Box 13284, Pensacola, 32591. Tel: 850-435-3500.

Commission for African American Catholics—GABRIEL M. BROWN, Chm., Mailing Address: P.O. Drawer 13284, Pensacola, 32591. Tel: 850-435-3500.

Building & Renovation, Diocesan Commission for—Rev. Msgrs. LUKE HUNT, V.G.; MICHAEL V. REED, J.C.L.; JOHN GODLEWSKI; JOHN KENNEDY; Rev. PAUL T. WHITE; THEODORE J. RUCKSTUHL; J. PATRICK REMICH; ROBERT BENNETT, Chm.; JAN L. VIAU, Mailing Address: P.O. Drawer 13284, Pensacola, 32591. Tel: 850-435-3500.

Campus Ministry—Mailing Address: P.O. Drawer 13284, Pensacola, 32591. Tel: 850-435-3500. Rev. JAMES PAUL VALENZUELA, Pensacola-University of West Florida: Nativity of Our Lord Parish, 9945 Hillview Dr., Pensacola, 32514. Tel: 850-477-3221. Tallahassee-Florida Agricultural & Mechanical University, St. Eugene Chapel: Rev. EJIOFOR UGWU, M.S.P., Dir. & Chap., 701 Gamble St., Tallahassee, 32310. Tel: 850-222-6482. Florida State University: Rev. EDWARD T. JONES, Dir., Mailing Address: P.O. Box 2395, Tallahassee, 32316. Tel: 850-222-9630.

Catholic Daughters of the Americas—Rev. ROBERT F. MORRIS, Court Chap.; Mrs. JOYCE PFEIFFER, Regent, 304 N. Sunset Blvd., Gulf Breeze, 32507.

Catholic Women, Diocesan Council of—CAROL GIGUERE, Pres., Mailing Address: P.O. Drawer 13284, Pensacola, 32591. Tel: 850-435-3500.

Catholic Charities of Northwest Florida—MARK DUFVA, Exec. Dir., Mailing Address: 1000 W. Garden St., Pensacola, 32502. Tel: 850-435-3516.

Pensacola Office—VACANT, Regl. Dir., 1815 N. 6th Ave., Pensacola, 32503. Tel: 850-436-6410; Fax: 850-436-6439. Email: cathchar@cc.ptdiocese.org. Fort Walton Beach Office: CAROLYN KETCHEL, Regl. Dir., 11 First St., S.E., Fort Walton Beach, 32548. Tel: 850-244-2825; Fax: 850-664-9146. Email: ketchelc@cc.ptdiocese.org. Panama City Office: DIANE WILLIAMS, Regl. Dir., 3128 E. 11th St., Panama City, 32401. Tel: 850-763-0475; Fax: 850-763-2969. Email: williamsd@cc.ptdiocese.org. Tallahassee Office: DEBRA HERMAN, Regl. Dir., Mailing Address: P.O. Box 20165, Tallahassee, 32316. Tel: 850-222-2180; Fax: 850-681-6963. Email: cathchartal@cc.ptdiocese.org.

Campaign for Human Development, Office of—Ms. CAROLINE BUSH, Dir., 1000 W. Garden St., Pensacola, 32502. Tel: 850-435-5569.

Justice and Peace, Office of—Catholic Charities, 1000 W. Garden St., Pensacola, 32502. Tel: 850-435-3500.

Liaison for Diocesan Disaster Relief—

Charismatic Renewal, Diocesan Commission for—Rev. EUGENE PATHE, Moderator; HELEN FREELAND, Chm., 9186 Deer Ln., Navarre, 32566. Tel: 850-939-7164. Email: hsonfish@aol.com.

Cursillo Movement—Rev. SEAN VINCENT KNOX, Spiritual Dir.; CATHY CURRIER, Diocesan Lay Dir., 102 Jamie Ct., Crestview, 32539. Tel: 850-689-0190.

Ecumenical & Interreligious Affairs, Office of—Rev. JOHN GRAY, Dir. (Retired), 5200 Saufley Field Rd., Pensacola, 32526. Tel: 850-456-5966; Fax: 850-453-3138.

Finance, Department of—JOHN GODLEWSKI, Dir., Mailing Address: P.O. Drawer 13284, Pensacola, 32591. Tel: 850-435-3500.

Human Resources—DAWN GAGNON.

Internal Review—MIKE NOWLAN.

Communications— "The Catholic Compass" PEGGY DEKEYSER.

Real Estate/Construction—ROBERT BENNETT.

Information Technology—CELESTE DURAND.

Accounting—PAULA BEAUCHAMP.

Cemetery, Office of—Deacon STEPHEN WULF, Dir., Holy Cross Cemetery, 1300 E. Hayes St., Pensacola, 32503. Tel: 850-432-0878; Fax: 850-434-9032; FRED MCEVOY, Dir., Calvary Cemetery, 4298 Country Club Blvd., Sunny Hills, 32428. Tel: 850-773-2165.

Finance, Diocesan Commission for—Most Rev. JOHN H. RICARD, S.S.J.; ROBERT EMMANUEL ESQ., Chm.; Rev. Msgrs. LUKE HUNT, V.G., Sec.; MICHAEL V. REED, J.C.L.; JOHN T. CASSIDY; BLAISE ADAMS; DENNIS MCKINNON; ROBERT HAMEL; ERIC NICKELSEN; J. PATRICK REMICH; JOHN GODLEWSKI, Mailing Address: P.O. Drawer 13284, Pensacola, 32591. Tel: 850-435-3500.

Holy Name Society—Rev. Msgr. MICHAEL V. REED, J.C.L., Mailing Address: P.O. Drawer 13284, Pensacola, 32591. Tel: 850-435-3500.

Independent Review Board—Mailing Address: P.O. Drawer 13284, Pensacola, 32591. Tel: 850-435-3500; Fax: 850-436-6424. Rev. DOUGLAS G. HALSEMA; Mrs. STEPHANIE ALFT; Mrs. ANGELA GUILLAUME; Dr. ANITA NUSBAUM; ROBERT EMMANUEL ESQ.; SHELLY REYNOLDS CLAUBAUGH; KELLY MEEK; PAUL JANSEN; Deacon DONALD KREHELY.

Knights of Columbus—Rev. Msgr. LUKE HUNT, V.G., Diocesan Chap., Mailing Address: P.O. Box 1057, Gulf Breeze, 32562. Tel: 850-934-0222; Fax: 850-934-2804.

Legion of Mary—Rev. HECTOR R.G. PEREZ, S.T.D., Diocesan Spiritual Dir., 900 W. Garden St., Pensacola, 32501. Tel: 850-432-9362.

Liturgy, Office of—Rev. PAUL T. WHITE, Dir., 100 Francis St., Mary Esther, 32569. Tel: 850-581-2556.

Ministries, Department of—

Ministry Support—Mr. KEVIN VICKERY, Dir., Mailing Address: P.O. Drawer 13284, Pensacola, 32591. Tel: 850-435-3500; Fax: 850-436-6424. Email: vickeryk@ptdiocese.org.

Catechetics—Sr. MARGARET KUNTZ, A.S.C.J. Email: kuntzm@ptdiocese.org.

Adult Faith Formation—STEPHANIE MCNEILL. Email: mcneills@ptdiocese.org.

Youth—LISA KURNIK, Scouting. Email: kurnikl@ptdiocese.org.

Marriage—MARIO SACASA. Tel: 850-201-0254. Email: sacasam@ptdiocese.org.

Child and Youth Protection—

Ethnic Concerns—

Hispanic Ministry, Office of—Very Rev. DENNIS J. O'BRIEN, Dir.

Orders & Ministries, Commission for—Mailing Address: P.O. Drawer 13284, Pensacola, 32591. Tel: 850-435-3500; Fax: 850-436-6424. Rev. Msgr. SLADE CRAWFORD; Rev. THOMAS J. GUIDO; Very Rev. DENNIS J. O'BRIEN; Rev. JOSEPH FOWLER, J.C.L.; Rev. Msgrs. JOHN O'SULLIVAN; MICHAEL V. REED, J.C.L.

Office of the Permanent Diaconate and Permanent Deacon Formation—Rev. JOSEPH P. CALLIPARE, Vicar for Permanent Deacons, 11 N. "B" St., Pensacola, 32502. Tel: 850-435-3552; Fax: 850-435-3565. Email: calliparej@ptdiocese.org.

Permanent Deacon Formation Team—Revs. JOSEPH P. CALLIPARE, Dir.; DOUGLAS G. HALSEMA, Spiritual Formation; Deacon TIMOTHY M. WARNER, Esq., Pastoral Formation; Rev. PAUL T. WHITE, Liturgical Formation.

Permanent Deacon Formation Board— Committee for Admissions and Scrutinies Ms. CAROLINE BUSH; Ms. JANE BRIM; Rev. JOSEPH P. CALLIPARE, Chm.; Deacon JOHN DURKIN; Rev. DOUGLAS G. HALSEMA; Mrs. BETTY ANN LURTON; Deacons GARY MCBRIDE; JOHN PARNHAM; TIMOTHY M. WARNER, Esq.; Rev. PAUL WHITE.

Permanent Deacon Deanery Representatives—Deacons DANIEL M. MCAULIFFE, J.C.L., West Central; LOU FETE, Eastern; ROGER GALLAGHER, East Central; PAUL GRAAFF, Northwest; RICHARD LURTON, At-Large; SANTIAGO MOLINA, At-Large; STEPHEN WULF, Southwest.

Continuing Education & Formation—Rev. Msgr. JAMES J. FLAHERTY, J.C.L., J.V., Dir., 307 Beach Dr., Destin, 32541. Tel: 850-654-5422.

Propagation of the Faith, Office of—Rev. Msgr. FRANCIS S. SZCZYKUTOWICZ, Dir., 2056 Sunny Hills, Sunny Hills, 32428-2929. Tel: 850-773-3406.

Respect Life Committee—Co Chairmen: Deacons ROGER GALLAGHER. Email: rogercrna@aol.com; MARK SCHNEIDER. Email: maslas1@embarqmail.com.

St. Vincent de Paul Society— Pensacola Particular Council, VIVIAN KRUMEL, Pres., 2200 W. Desoto St., Pensacola, 32505. Tel: 850-434-6615; Deacon ROBERT LEBLANC, Spiritual Dir.

Schools, Department of—Mr. KEVIN VICKERY, Supt. Schools; DONNA BASS, Administrative Asst.; EVALINE JONES, Teacher Certification, Mailing Address: P.O. Drawer 13284, Pensacola, 32591. Tel: 850-435-3500; Fax: 850-436-6424. Email: ptschools@ptdiocese.org.

Holy Childhood Association—VACANT, Dir.

Catholic Youth Sports League—LEONARDO CRUZ, Dir.

Seminarian Candidate Review Board—Rev. ROY C. MARIEN; Rev. Msgr. C. SLADE CRAWFORD; Very Rev. DENNIS J. O'BRIEN; Rev. JOSEPH FOWLER; Rev. Msgr. MICHAEL W. TUGWELL; WILLIAM NADICKSBERND; Sr. SUSAN MARIE KRUPP, A.S.C.J.; Mrs. LINDA BARRETT; ROSEMARY MASON, Mailing Address: P.O. Drawer 13284, Pensacola, 32591. Tel: 850-435-3500.

Seminarians, Office of—Rev. Msgr. C. SLADE CRAWFORD, Dir.; MICHELE JOHNSTON, Staff Asst., Mailing Address: P.O. Drawer 13284, Pensacola, 32591. Tel: 850-435-3552. Email: johnstonm@ptdiocese.org.

Vocations, Office of—Rev. Msgr. MICHAEL W. TUGWELL, Dir.; MICHELE JOHNSTON, Staff Asst., Mailing Address: P.O. Drawer 13284, Pensacola, 32591. Tel: 850-435-3552. Email: johnstonm@ptdiocese.org.

Serra Club—Pensacola: Rev. DOUGLAS G. HALSEMA, Chap.; JAMES DAIGLE, Pres. Tallahassee: REINALDO MANZO, Pres.

Stewardship & Development, Office of—JOHN KENNEDY, Dir.

Victim Assistance Coordinators—DANIELLE MALONE, L.M.H.L. Tel: 850-438-3131, Ext. 17. Email: maloned@ptdiocese.org; Dr. JAMES GAGNON, M.S.W., L.C.S.W. Tel: 850-877-0205.

CLERGY, PARISHES, MISSIONS AND PAROCHIAL SCHOOLS

GREATER PENSACOLA

(ESCAMBIA COUNTY)

1—CATHEDRAL OF THE SACRED HEART (1905) Rev. Msgr. Michael V. Reed, Rector; Revs. James Thoyalil (India), Parochial Vicar; George Sammut, Parochial Vicar; Deacons Jean White, (Retired); John Durkin; John Parnham; Paul Graaff.
Mailing Address: 1212 E. Moreno St., 32503.
Apostles of the Sacred Heart. In Res., Rev. Msgr. George Sindik (Retired).
Res.: 1101 E. Mallory St., 32503. Tel: 850-438-3131; Fax: 850-436-6428. Email: reedm@sch.ptdiocese.org. Web: www.shc.ptdiocese.org.
School—Sacred Heart Cathedral School, (Grades K-8), 1603 N. 12th Ave., 32503. Tel: 850-436-6440; Fax: 850-436-6444. Sr. Elizabeth Knight, A.S.C.J., Prin.; Mary Fritz, Librarian.
Catechesis/Religious Program—Tel: 850-438-3131; Fax: 850-436-6428. Students 114.
Convent—3531 Monteigne Dr., 32503. Tel: 850-438-0560.

2—ST. ANNE (Brownsville) (1953) Closed. For inquiries for Sacramental records, please see the Cathedral of the Sacred Heart, Pensacola.

3—ST. ANNE'S (Bellview) (1964) Rev. John J. Licari; Deacons Thomas Gordon; Donald Krehely.
Res.: 5200 Saufley Field Rd., 32526-1626. Tel: 850-456-5966; Fax: 850-453-3138. Web: www.stannebv.org.
Catechesis/Religious Program—Students 104.

4—ST. ANTHONY OF PADUA (1941), (African American), Rev. Msgr. Michael V. Reed; Deacons Jean White, (Retired); John Durkin; John Parnham; Paul Graaff.
Mailing Address: c/o 1212 E. Moreno St., 32503. Tel: 850-324-5655; Fax: 850-944-5299. Email: reedm@ptdiocese.org. Web: www.ptdiocese.org.
Res. & Church: 1804 N. Davis Hwy., 32503. Tel: 850-436-6422.
Catechesis/Religious Program—Twinned with The Cathedral of the Sacred Heart., *Community Center*, 1805 N. 6th Ave., 32503.

5—HOLY SPIRIT (1976) Rev. Msgr. James J. Flaherty; Deacon Lloyd Krueger.
Res.: 1145 Freeboard Blvd., 32507. Tel: 850-324-5159. Church: 10650 Gulf Beach Hwy., 32507. Tel: 850-492-0837; Fax: 850-492-4968.
Catechesis/Religious Program—Tel: 852-492-0837, Ext. 211. Students 125.

6—ST. JOHN THE EVANGELIST (1851) [CEM] Rev. Joseph P. Callipare; Deacon Gerard Williamson.
Res.: 303 S. Navy Blvd., 32507. Tel: 850-455-0356; Fax: 850-453-5109. Email: office@stjohn.ptdiocese.org. Web: www.stjohn.ptdiocese.org.
School—(Grades K-8), 325 S. Navy Blvd., 32507. Tel: 850-456-5218; Fax: 850-456-5956. Web: www.sjsw.ptdiocese.org. Sr. Isabel Garza, F.M.A., Prin. Sisters 3; Lay Teachers 16; Students 180.
Catechesis/Religious Program—Email: reled@stjohn.ptdiocese.org. Students 65.
Convent—Tel: 850-456-3046.

7—ST. JOSEPH (1891) [CEM] Rev. Patrick Foley; Sr. Maureen Joseph Kirwan, S.C., Pastoral Assoc.; Deacon Eugene Pallone.
Mailing Address: P.O. Box 13566, 32591. Tel: 850-436-6461; Fax: 850-436-6462. Email: admin@stjoseph.ptdiocese.org. Web: www.stjosephchurchpensacola.parishonline.com.
Res.: 141 W. Intendencia St., 32502. Tel: 850-436-6461; Fax: 850-436-6462. Email: admin@stjoseph.ptdiocese.org. Web: www.stjosephchurchpensacola.parishesonline.com.
Catechesis/Religious Program—Tel: 850-436-6461;

Fax: 850-436-6462. Email: rothschildg@stjoseph.ptdiocese.org. Gail Rothschild, D.R.E. Students 55.

8—LITTLE FLOWER (1945) Very Rev. Eugene D. Casserly; Deacons Reymond Castellano; Stephen Wulf.
Res.: 6495 Lillian Hwy., P.O. Box 3009, 32516. Tel: 850-455-5641; Fax: 850-455-4508. Email: office@ptlittleflower.org.
School—(Grades K-8) Tel: 850-455-4851; Fax: 850-457-8982. Sr. Barbara Zipoli, A.S.C.J., Prin.; Spencer Davis, Librarian. Lay Teachers 18; Students 181.
Catechesis/Religious Program—Tel: 850-455-8434. Students 91.

9—ST. MARY (1941) Revs. Dominic Phan Sa; Robert Jules Johnson, Parochial Vicar; Deacon Herman Lux.
Res. & Mailing Address: 401 Van Pelt Ln., 32505. Tel: 850-478-2797; Fax: 850-478-2739. Email: stmaryca@bellsouth.net. Web: www.stmaryqapensacola.parishesonline.com.
Catechesis/Religious Program—Tel: 850-478-2797; Fax: 850-478-2739. Students 60.

10—ST. MICHAEL (1781) Rev. Peter A. McLaughlin (CAM).
Mailing Address: P.O. Box 12423, 32591-2423.
Res.: 19 N. Palafox St., 32501. Tel: 850-438-4985; Fax: 850-433-9758. Email: foster1@stmichael.ptdiocese.org. Web: www.stmichael.ptdiocese.org.
Catechesis/Religious Program—Students 15.

11—NATIVITY OF OUR LORD (1969) Rev. Msgr. Michael P. Mooney; Rev. James Paul Valenzuela, Parochial Vicar; Deacons Randall Comeau, (Retired); Dennis Dobransky; John Bartoszewicz. In Res., Rev. Msgr. Raymond Mullins (Retired).
Res.: 9945 Hillview Dr., 32514-5702. Tel: 850-477-3221; Fax: 850-478-5584.
Catechesis/Religious Program—Tel: 850-477-3221, Ext. 5. Email: mzeni@nativityofourlordcc.org. Web: nativityofourlordcc.org. Students 277.

12—OUR LADY QUEEN OF MARTYRS, MISSION (1977), (Vietnamese), Rev. Mau Ho, S.D.D.
Res.: 3295 S. Barrancas Ave., 32507. Tel: 850-455-2712; Fax: 850-455-0264. Email: ourladyqueenofmartyrs@gmail.com.
Catechesis/Religious Program—Tel: 850-455-2712; Fax: 850-455-0264. Students 65.

13—ST. PAUL (1963) Revs. Douglas G. Halsema; Joseph Fowler, Parochial Vicar; Deacons John P. Morgan, (Retired); Robert Leblanc; Richard Lurton; Charles Lee.
Res.: 1700 Conway Dr., 32503. Tel: 850-434-2551; Fax: 850-436-6449. Email: parishoffice@stpaulcatholic.net. Web: www.stpaulcatholic.net.
School—3121 Hyde Park Rd., 32503. Tel: 850-436-6435; Fax: 850-436-6437. Ms. Louise West, Prin. Lay Teachers 19; Students 214.
Catechesis/Religious Program—Fax: 850-436-6449. Email: whibbse@stpaulcatholic.net. Students 209.
Mission—Church of Our Savior 6700 Old Spanish Tr., Escambia Co. 32504. Tel: 850-434-2551; Fax: 850-436-6449.

14—ST. STEPHEN (1922) Rev. Hector R.G. Perez.
Res.: 900 W. Garden St., 32502. Tel: 850-432-9362; Fax: 850-435-9946.
Catechesis/Religious Program—Tel: 850-432-9362; Fax: 850-435-9946. Email: fhrgp3@cox.net. Students 37.

15—ST. THOMAS MORE (1954) Rev. Msgr. John T. Cassidy; Deacon Kenneth McClure.
Mailing Address: 510 Bayshore Dr., 32507. Tel: 850-456-2543; Fax: 850-455-5203. Email: bayshore@stm.gccoxmail.com.
Catechesis/Religious Program—Tel: 850-456-0001; Fax: 850-455-5203. Students 15.

CITY OF TALLAHASSEE

(LEON COUNTY)

1—CO-CATHEDRAL OF ST. THOMAS MORE (1968) Rev. Msgr. Michael W. Tugwell, Rector; Rev. Edward T. Jones, Parochial Vicar; Deacon Santiago Molina.
Res.: 900 W. Tennessee St., P.O. Box 2395, 32316. Tel: 850-222-7371; 850-222-9630 (Office); Fax: 850-222-6430.
For a complete listing, see John Paul II Catholic High School located under High Schools, Diocesan in the Institution section.
Catechesis/Religious Program—Students 140.
Chapel—St. Eugene, Florida A&M University [JC] 701 W. Gamble St., 32310. Tel: 850-222-6482; Fax: 850-222-6482. Rev. Ejiofor Ugwu, M.S.P.

2—BLESSED SACRAMENT (1845) Revs. John V. O'Sullivan; Richard Lee Schamber, Parochial Vicar; Deacons Charles Fete; Rudolph Raymaker; Patrick Dallet; Michael Nixon.
Res.: 624 Miccosukee Rd., 32308. Tel: 850-222-1321; Fax: 850-222-9772. Web: www.bsc.ptdiocese.org.
School—Trinity Catholic, (Grades K-8), 706 E. Brevard St., 32308. Tel: 850-222-0444; Fax: 850-224-5067. Mrs. Janet Gendusa, Prin. Lay Teachers 28; Students 505.
For a complete listing, see John Paul II Catholic High School located under High Schools, Diocesan in the Institution section.
St. John Neumann Retreat Center—685 Miccosukee Rd., 32308. Tel: 850-224-2971. Sr. Christine Kelly, S.S.J., Dir.
Catechesis/Religious Program—Students 160.

3—GOOD SHEPHERD (1973) Revs. Michael Foley; James Christian Winkeljohn, Parochial Vicar; William Philip Ganci, Parochial Vicar; Deacons Marcus Hepburn; Edward Melvin III; Gerald Haynes; Thomas McBrearty; Mark Schneider.
4665 Thomasville Rd., 32309-2512. Tel: 850-893-1837; 850-893-2381; Fax: 850-894-6912. Email: goodshepherd@gs.ptdiocese.org. Web: www.goodshepherdparish.org.
For a complete listing, see John Paul II Catholic High School located under High Schools, Diocesan in the Institution section.
Catechesis/Religious Program—Bette Scaringe, D.R.E. Students 820.

4—ST. LOUIS (1979) Very Rev. Kevin Johnson; Deacons Nelson Madera; Robert Macko.
Res.: 4151 Miraflores Ln., 32303. Tel: 850-562-5140. Email: stlouischurch@embarqmail.com.
Catechesis/Religious Program—Tel: 850-562-5140; Fax: 850-562-3117. Students 117.

OUTSIDE THE CITIES OF PENSACOLA AND TALLAHASSEE

APALACHICOLA, FRANKLIN CO., ST. PATRICK (1851) [JC] Rev. Roger Latosynski.
Res.: 27 Sixth St., P.O. Box 550, 32329. Tel: 904-653-9453; Fax: 850-653-4528. Email: stpatcath@gtcom.net. Web: www.stpatrickmass.com.
Catechesis/Religious Program—Sr. Jeanne Drea, O.P., Dir., Faith Formation. Students 28.

BAYOU GEORGE, BAY CO., OUR LADY OF THE ROSARY Rev. W. P. Brown.
Res.: 5622 Julie Dr., Panama City, 32404. Tel: 850-769-5067; Fax: 850-769-1229.
Catechesis/Religious Program—Tel: 850-769-5067; Fax: 850-769-1227. Students 16.
Mission—Our Lady Queen of Peace P.O. Box 213, Fountain, Bay Co. 32438. Tel: 850-722-0466; Fax: 850-722-0466.

BLOUNTSTOWN, CALHOUN CO., ST. FRANCIS OF ASSISI (1972) [CEM] Rev. Kurian Manikuttiyil.
Res.: 16498 S.W. Gaskin St., 32424. Tel: 850-674-4482; Fax: 850-674-4482. Email: stfrancisassisi@gtcom.net.
Catechesis/Religious Program—Students 7.

BONIFAY, HOLMES CO., BLESSED TRINITY (1979) Rev. Richard Dawson.
Res.: 2331 Hwy. 177A, 32425. Tel: 850-547-3735; Fax: 850-547-7477. Email: btbonifay@embarqmail.com.
Catechesis/Religious Program—Students 10.

CANTONMENT, ESCAMBIA CO., ST. JUDE THADDEUS (1945) [CEM] [JC] Revs. Thomas Koyickal; George Thekkummatthil; Deacon Thomas Simard.
Res.: 303 Rocky Ave., 32533. Tel: 850-968-6189; Fax: 850-968-1578. Email: stjudethaddeusch@bellsouth.net. Web: stjudecantonment.com.
Mission—St. Elizabeth of Hungary 303 Rocky Ave., Escambia Co. 32533. Tel: 850-587-2550.
Catechesis/Religious Program—Students 2.

CHATTAHOOCHEE, GADSDEN CO., HOLY CROSS PARISH (1979) Rev. Kurian Manikuttiyil.
Res.: 4034 Memorial Blue Star Hwy., 32324. Tel: 850-663-4610.

CHIPLEY, WASHINGTON CO., ST. JOSEPH THE WORKER (1968) Rev. Sean Vincent Knox.
Res.: P.O. Box 266, 32428. Tel: 850-638-7654.
Catechesis/Religious Program—Students 23.

CRAWFORDVILLE, WAKULLA CO., ST. ELIZABETH ANN SETON (1975) [CEM] Rev. James B. MacGee, O.M.I.
Mailing Address: 3609 Coastal Hwy., 32327. Tel: 850-926-1797; Fax: 850-926-1737.
Catechesis/Religious Program—Students 55.
Mission—St. Stephen the Protomartyr 1997 Natural Bridge Rd., P.O. Box 208, Woodville, Leon Co. 32362-0208. Tel: 850-421-9094.

CRESTVIEW, OKALOOSA CO., OUR LADY OF VICTORY (1954) Revs. John B. Cayer; Florencio Lagura; Deacon Kenneth Mayfield.
Office: 550 Adams Dr., 32536. Tel: 850-682-4622; Fax: 850-689-0335. Email: olvadmin@olv.ptdiocese.org. Web: www.olv.ptdiocese.org.
Catechesis/Religious Program—Tel: 850-682-4622, Ext. 15; Fax: 850-689-0335. Students 248.

DE FUNIAK SPRINGS, WALTON CO., ST. MARGARET (1931) Rev. Richard Dawson; Deacon Walter Harris.
Mailing Address: P.O. Box 590, 32435-0590. Tel: 850-892-9247; Fax: 850-892-2065.
Res.: 247 U.S. Hwy. 331 N., Box 590, 32435. Tel: 850-892-9247; Fax: 850-892-2065. Email: stmargaret@embarqmail.com.
Catechesis/Religious Program—Tel: 850-892-9247; Fax: 850-892-2065. Students 24.

DESTIN, OKALOOSA CO., CORPUS CHRISTI (1977) Rev. Robert F. Morris.
Res.: 307 Beach Dr., 32541. Tel: 850-654-5422; Fax: 850-837-3807. Email: corpuschristic@aol.com.
Catechesis/Religious Program—Tel: 850-654-5423; Fax: 850-837-3807. Students 66.

FORT WALTON BEACH, OKALOOSA CO., ST. MARY CHURCH (1914) Rev. Msgr. Michael A. Cherup; Rev. Craig Smith, Parochial Vicar; Deacons Robert J. Saxer; Charles Wolf; Walter Richardson; Daniel M. McAuliffe; Charles Hartman III.
Res.: 110 St. Mary Ave., S.W., 32548. Tel: 850-243-3742; Fax: 850-243-1271. Email: smcfwb@saintmarychurchfwb.org. Web: www.saintmarychurchfwb.org.
School—(Grades K-8), 110 Robinwood Dr., 32548. Tel: 850-243-8913; Fax: 850-243-7895. Mrs. Regina Nadicksbernd, Prin. Lay Teachers 24; Students 405.
Catechesis/Religious Program—Tel: 850-244-1833; Fax: 850-243-1271. Students 234.

FOUNTAIN, BAY CO., OUR LADY QUEEN OF PEACE MISSION Rev. William P. Brown.
Mailing Address: 5622 Julie Dr., Panama City, 32404. Tel: 850-722-0466; Fax: 850-722-0466.
Church: 18005 Lazy Ln., 32438. Tel: 850-769-5067; Fax: 850-769-1227.
Catechesis/Religious Program—Students 19.

FREEPORT, WALTON CO., CHRIST THE KING MISSION (1984) Rev. Thomas S. Collins; Deacon Dave Casey.
Mailing Address: c/o St. Rita, P.O. Box 1223, Santa Rosa Beach, 32459.
Church: 15542 U.S. Hwy. 3315, 32439. Tel: 850-267-2558; Fax: 850-267-3711.

GULF BREEZE, SANTA ROSA CO.

1—ST. ANN (1948) Rev. Msgr. Luke Hunt; Rev. Paul Francis Lambert, Parochial Vicar; Deacon John Scott.
Res.: 100 Daniel Dr., P.O. Drawer 1057, 32561. Tel: 850-932-2859; Fax: 850-934-2804. Email: info@stanngulfbreeze.org. Web: www.stanngulfbreeze.org.
School—St. Ann Discovery School, Tel: 850-932-9330; Fax: 850-934-2804. Jean Jones, Dir. (Learning Center) (Age 1-Pre-K) Teachers 33; Students 140.
Catechesis/Religious Program—Tel: 850-932-2859, Ext. 234; Fax: 850-934-2804. Students 307.
Mission—Our Lady of the Assumption Pensacola Beach. 920 Via de Luna, P.O. Box 1057, Santa Rosa Co. 32561. Tel: 850-934-0222; Fax: 850-934-6020.

2—SAINT SYLVESTER (1979) Revs. John F. Kelly; Alvaro Pio Gonzalez (Colombia), Parochial Vicar.
Church & Office: 6464 Gulf Breeze Pkwy, 32563. Tel: 850-939-3020; Fax: 850-936-5366. Email: saintsylv@stsylv.org. Web: www.stsylv.org.
Rectory—7083 Brighton Oaks Blvd., Navarre, 32566. Tel: 850-936-1215.
Catechesis/Religious Program—Sandra Nicholas, D.R.E. Students 267.

LANARK VILLAGE, FRANKLIN CO., SACRED HEART OF JESUS (1960) Rev. Yozefu B. Ssemakula.
Res.: 109 Elm St., P.O. Box 729, 32323. Tel: 850-697-3445.

MADISON, MADISON CO., ST. VINCENT DE PAUL (1907) Rev. Viet Tan Huynh. In Res., Rev. Joseph C. Schwab, O.M.I.
Res.: 186 N.W. Sumter St., 32340-2048. Tel: 850-973-2428; Fax: 850-973-2825.
Catechesis/Religious Program—Students 19.

MARIANNA, JACKSON CO., ST. ANNE (1947) [JC] Rev. Sean Vincent Knox.
Res.: 3009 Fifth St., P.O. Box 1547, 32447. Tel: 850-482-3734; Fax: 850-482-7241.
Catechesis/Religious Program—Tel: 850-482-3734; Fax: 850-482-7241. Students 45.

MARY ESTHER, OKALOOSA CO., ST. PETER (1975) Rev. Paul T. White; Deacon David P. Robinson.
Res.: 100 Francis St., 32569. Tel: 850-581-2556; Fax: 850-581-2640. Email: office@stpeter.ptdiocese.org. Web: www.stpeter.ptdiocese.org.
Catechesis/Religious Program—Tel: 850-581-7263. Students 81.

MEXICO BEACH, BAY CO., OUR LADY OF GUADALUPE MISSION (1980) Closed. For inquiries for parish records contact the chancery.

MILTON, SANTA ROSA CO., ST. ROSE OF LIMA (1957) [JC] Very Rev. Dennis J. O'Brien; Rev. Nicholas Frank Schumm, Parochial Vicar; Deacons Thomas Kennell; Chris Christopher; Jeffrey Massey.
Church: 6451 Park Ave., 32570. Tel: 850-623-3600; Fax: 850-983-3043. Email: srlparish@srl.ptdiocese.org. Web: www.stroselima.parishesonline.com.
Res.: 5965 Sleepy Hollow, 32570. Tel: 850-983-1449.

Catechesis/Religious Program—Students 192.

MIRAMAR BEACH, WALTON CO., CHURCH OF THE RESURRECTION (1981) Rev. Thomas J. Guido; Rev. Msgr. Slade Crawford, Senior Priest; Deacon Matthew Rezmer.
Rectory—
Church: 259 Miramar Beach Dr., 32550. Tel: 850-837-0357; Fax: 850-837-2062.
Catechesis/Religious Program—Tel: 850-837-0357; Fax: 850-837-2062. Email: marilyn@rcc-destin.org. Marilyn Austin, D.R.E. & Youth Ministry; Steve McCown, Music Min. Students 121.

MONTICELLO, JEFFERSON CO., ST. MARGARET (1917) Rev. Viet Tan Huynh.
Res.: c/o 186 Sumter St., Madison, 32340. Tel: 850-973-2428; Fax: 850-973-9311.
Church: U.S. Hwy. 90 E., 32344. Tel: 850-997-3622; Fax: 850-973-2825.
Catechesis/Religious Program—Students 46.

NICEVILLE, OKALOOSA CO.

1—CHRIST OUR REDEEMER (1989) Rev. Roy C. Marien; Deacons Joaquin Trevino; James Murray; William E. Schaal; Miguel Nolla; Susan Marco, Youth Min.; Adam Ubowski, Music Min.
Res.: 1028 White Point Rd., 32578. Tel: 850-897-7797; Fax: 850-897-2422. Email: coroffice@gmail.com. Web: www.ptdiocese.cor.org.
Catechesis/Religious Program—Tel: 850-897-2974; Fax: 850-897-2422. Email: coreducate@gmail.com; coryouth@gmail.com. Web: www.corcatholic.org. Lisa Hall, D.R.E. Students 250.

2—HOLY NAME OF JESUS (1960) Rev. Dominic Dat Tran; Deacons Louis Marini; Willie O'Neal; James Cox; Gary McBride; Thomas Fraites; John Shin.
Res.: 1200 Valparaiso Blvd., 32578-2946. Tel: 850-678-7813; Fax: 850-678-5775. Email: holyname@holynamechurch.org. Web: www.holynamechurch.org.
Catechesis/Religious Program—Tel: 850-678-6790; Fax: 850-678-5775. Email: hnjdre@holynamechurch.org. Students 201.

PANAMA CITY BEACH, BAY CO., ST. BERNADETTE (1956) Rev. Ted Sosnowski, C.R. (Poland); Deacons Conrad Provencher; Dale Johnson; Juli Roock, Business Mgr.; Yvette Valenti, Youth Min.
Res.: 1214 Moylan Rd., 32407. Tel: 850-249-4100; Fax: 850-233-1177. Web: www.stbernadette.com.
Child Development Center—Tel: 850-230-0009; Fax: 850-230-6989. Juli Roock, Dir. Lay Teachers 29; Students 118.
Catechesis/Religious Program—Tel: 850-234-3266. Stephen M. Kaats, D.R.E. Students 104.
St. Bernadette John Lee Outreach Center— (2003) 1329 Moylan Rd., 32407. Tel: 850-236-5252. Email: stbernadette@knology.net.

PANAMA CITY, BAY CO.

1—ST. DOMINIC (1890) Very Rev. Peter Lawrence Zalewski; Revs. Benedict Klucinec, M.S.A.; Charles Reid Collins; Anthony Tin Nguyen, S.D.D.; Deacons Salvatore Cirabisi; Roger Gallagher; Estal Daron, (Retired). In Res., Rev. John Selleck.
Res.: 3308 E. 15th St., 32405-7414. Tel: 850-785-4574; Fax: 850-872-0800. Web: www.stdominic.ptdiocese.org.
Catechesis/Religious Program—Tel: 850-763-7393; Fax: 850-872-0800. Students 321.

2—ST. JOHN THE EVANGELIST (1945) Rev. Jerzy W. Zieba, C.R. (Poland); Deacons Timothy M. Warner; Earl C. Mirus; George Walters.
Res.: 1008 Fortune Ave., 32401. Tel: 850-763-1821; Fax: 850-784-1739. Email: stj.office@knology.net. Web: www.stjohnpc.ptdiocese.org.
School—1005 Fortune Ave., 32401. Tel: 850-763-1775; Fax: 850-784-4461. Email: stjohns@knology.net. Web: www.stjohncatholicschool-.com. Dr. Kathy Kidd, Prin. Lay Teachers 15; Students 178.
Catechesis/Religious Program—Email: stj.dre@knology.net. Mary Fry, D.R.E. Students 65.

3—SS. PETER & PAUL MISSION (1981), (Vietnamese), [JC] Rev. Anthony Tin Nguyen, S.D.D., Parochial Vicar.
Mailing Address: P.O. Box 3627, 32401. Tel: 850-785-4574.
Res.: 3308 E. 15th St., 32405. Tel: 850-785-4574.
Catechesis/Religious Program—Students 55.

PENSACOLA BEACH, ESCAMBIA CO., OUR LADY OF THE ASSUMPTION MISSION (1979) Mailing Address: P.O. Box 1057, Gulf Breeze, 32562. Tel: 850-934-0222; Fax: 850-934-6020. Web: www.stanngulfbreeze.org. See St. Ann, Gulf Breeze.
920 Via de Luna, 32561. Tel: 850-934-0222.
Catechesis/Religious Program—Tel: 850-934-0222; Fax: 850-934-6020. Students 12.

PERRY, TAYLOR CO., IMMACULATE CONCEPTION (1914) Rev. Bernard Jakubco, M.S.C.
Res.: 2750 S. Byron Butler Pkwy., 32348. Tel: 850-584-3169; Fax: 850-584-3169. Email: immac@fairpoint.net.
Catechesis/Religious Program—Tel: 850-584-8853. Students 36.
Center—Tel: 850-584-8853.

PORT ST. JOE, GULF CO., ST. JOSEPH (1925) Rev. Philip Fortin.
Res.: 2006 Monument Ave., P.O. Box 820, 32457-0820. Tel: 850-229-1922; Fax: 850-229-1585. Email: stjoseph@fairpoint.net.
Church: 20th & Monument Sts., 32457-0820.
Catechesis/Religious Program—Tel: 850-227-1417. Students 39.
Mission—San Blas Catholic Mission C30E, Gulf Co. 32456.
Mission—St. Lawrence Mission Wewahitchka, Gulf Co. Tel: 850-639-5787.

QUINCY, GADSDEN CO., ST. THOMAS THE APOSTLE (1957) Rev. Juan Pedro Hernandez.
Res. & Mailing Address: Hwy. 90 & 27 N. Shadow St., P.O. Box 549, 32351. Tel: 850-627-2350; Fax: 850-627-6755. Email: st_thomas@tds.net. Web: www.stthomas-quincy.parishesonline.com.
Catechesis/Religious Program—Tel: 850-627-2350; Fax: 850-627-6755. Students 39.
Hispanic Ministry Office of St. Thomas—Religious Education Office. Tel: 850-627-8807; Fax: 850-627-6755.

SANTA ROSA BEACH, WALTON CO., ST. RITA (1982) Rev. Thomas S. Collins; Deacon David Casey.
Mailing Address: 137 Moll St., 32459. Tel: 850-267-2558; 850-622-2751 (Rectory); Fax: 850-267-3711. Email: saintritacatholic.church@mchsi.com. Web: saintritaparish.org.
Res.: Tel: 850-267-2558; Fax: 850-267-3711.
Catechesis/Religious Program—Students 148.
Mission—Christ the King Catholic Mission Freeport, Walton Co.

SUNNY HILLS, WASHINGTON CO., ST. THERESA (1972) Rev. Msgr. Francis S. Szczykutowicz.
Res.: 2056 Sunny Hills Blvd., 32428. Tel: 850-773-3406; Fax: 850-773-7008. Email: fr_frank@bellsouth.net.
Catechesis/Religious Program—Tel: 850-773-3406; Fax: 850-773-7008.

WEWAHITCHKA, GULF CO., ST. LAWRENCE MISSION, Mailing Address: P.O. Box 820, Port St. Joe, 32457. Email: stjoseph@gtcom.net.

WOODVILLE, LEON CO., ST. STEPHEN THE PROTOMARTYR (1979) Rev. James B. MacGee, O.M.I.
Mailing Address: P.O. Box 208, 32363. Tel: 850-421-9094. See St. Elizabeth Ann Seton, Medart.
Res.: 3609 Coastal Hwy., Crawfordville, 32327. Tel: 850-926-1797; Fax: 850-926-1737. Email: seascp@aol.com.
Catechesis/Religious Program—Students 3.

Chaplains of Public Institutions

PENSACOLA. *Escambia County Jail*. Deacon Dennis Dobransky.
Saufley Field Federal Prison Camp. Rev. J. Deffenbaugh.

TALLAHASSEE. *Federal Correctional Institution*. Deacon Ted Horbowy.

CHATTAHOOCHEE. *Florida State Hospital*. Rev. Kurian Manikuttiyil.

CHIPLEY. *Washington Correctional Institution*. Rev. John Selleck.

CRAWFORDVILLE. *Wakulla Correctional Institution*. Deacons Marcus Hepburn, Santiago Molino, Madera Nelson.

CRESTVIEW. *Okloosa Correctional Facility*. Deacon James Cox.

EGLIN. *Eglin Federal Prison Camp Eglin Air Force Base*. Deacon Gary McBride.

MARIANNA. *Florida Correctional Institutions*.

SNEADS. *Apalachee Correctional Institution*.

WEWAHITCHKA. *Gulf Coast Institution*. Rev. John Selleck.

On Duty Outside the Diocese:
Rev. Msgr.—
Bosso, Stephen C., 10701 E. Military Tr., Boynton Beach, 33436.
Rev.—
Flynn, Michael J., M.Div., S.T.L., St. Vincent de Paul Regional Seminary, Boynton Beach, FL

Military Chaplains:
Revs.—
Krzywicki, Lance P., Chap., ILVA, 1, 07029, Tempio Paosania, Italy.
McClanahan, Robert P., Jr., Chap., Cmdr.
Stewart, Paul, MacDill AFB.
Voyt, Stephen A., Lt. Col., Hickam AFB, HI 96853.

On Leave of Absence:
Revs.—
Bluett, James K., Fort Richardson, Fort Richardson, AK 99505-5999.
Castillo, Richard

Retired:
Rev. Msgrs.—
Bowles, Richard J., V.F.
Mullins, Raymond
Sindik, George
Revs.—
Altenbaugh, Richard L.
Cregan, James F.
Dolan, Hugh
Gray, John
Hevia, Todd O.
Hogarty, Paul
Jorden, James A.
Joseph, William
Kiem, Anthony
Kirby, Edward A.
Lambert, James J.
O'Shea, David T.

Permanent Deacons:
Barrows, Stanley, (On Duty Outside Diocese)
Bartoszewicz, John M., Nativity of Our Lord Parish, Pensacola
Brinkworth, Gary, (On Duty Outside Diocese)
Casey, David R., St. Rita, Santa Rosa Beach
Castellano, Reymond, Little Flower, Pensacola
Christopher, Chris, St. Rose of Lima, Milton
Cirabisi, Sal, St. Dominic, Panama City
Comeau, Randall O., (Retired), Nativity of Our Lord, Pensacola
Cox, James, Holy Name of Jesus, Niceville
Dallet, Patrick, Blessed Sacrament, Tallahassee
Daron, Estal, (Retired), St. Dominic, Panama City (Extern)
Dobransky, Dennis, Nativity of Our Lord, Pensacola
Durkin, John, Cathedral of the Sacred Heart, Pensacola
Fete, Charles, Blessed Sacrament, Tallahassee
Fraites, Thomas J., Holy Name of Jesus, Niceville
Gallagher, Roger, St. Dominic, Panama City
Gardner, James L., (Retired)
Gordon, Thomas, St. Anne, Pensacola
Graaff, Paul, Cathedral of the Sacred Heart, Pensacola
Harris, Walter, St. Margaret, Defuniak Springs
Hartman, Charles, III, (Retired), St. Mary Church, Fort Walton Beach (Archdiocese of New Orleans) (Extern)
Haynes, Gerald, Good Shepherd, Tallahassee
Hepburn, Marcus, Good Shepherd, Tallahassee
Horbowy, Thadeous, Blessed Sacrament, Tallahassee (Extern)
Howell, John, (On Duty in Diocese of Orlando)
Johnson, Dale R., (Retired), St. Bernadette, Panama City Beach
Kennell, Thomas H., St. Rose of Lima, Milton
Krehely, Donald, St. Anne, Pensacola
Kreppein, John, (On Duty Outside Diocese)
Krueger, Lloyd, Holy Spirit, Pensacola
L'Huillier, Ron, (On Duty Outside Diocese)
Landry, Alduce, (Retired)
Leblanc, Robert, St. Paul, Pensacola
Lee, Charles, St. Paul, Pensacola
Lurton, Richard, St. Paul, Pensacola
Lux, Herman, St. Mary, Pensacola (Diocese of Altoona-Johnstown) (Extern)
Macko, Richard, St. Louis, Tallahassee
Madera, Nelson I., St. Louis, Tallahassee
Marini, Louis, (Retired), Holy Name of Jesus, Niceville
Massey, Jeffrey, St. Rose of Lima, Milton
Mayfield, Kenneth, Our Lady of Victory, Crestview (Archdiocese of Los Angeles) (Extern)
Mc Auliffe, Daniel, St. Mary, Ft. Walton Beach
McBrearty, Thomas, Good Shepherd, Tallahassee
McBride, Gary, Holy Name of Jesus, Niceville
McClure, Kenneth, St. Thomas More, Pensacola
Melvin, Edward, III, Good Shepherd, Tallahassee
Mirus, Earl C., St. John the Evangelist, Panama City
Molina, Santiago, St. Thomas More, Tallahassee
Morgan, John P., (Retired), St. Paul, Pensacola
Murphy, Michael, (On Duty Outside Diocese)
Murray, James, Christ Our Redeemer, Blue Water Bay
Nixon, Michael, Blessed Sacrament, Tallahassee
Nolla, Miguel, Christ Our Redeemer, Niceville
O'Neal, Willie, Holy Name of Jesus, Niceville
Pallone, Eugene, St. Joseph, Pensacola
Parnham, John, Cathedral of the Sacred Heart, Pensacola
Provencher, Conrad, (Retired), St. Bernadette, Panama City Beach (Diocese of Trenton) (Extern)
Raymaker, Rudolph, Blessed Sacrament, Tallahassee
Renick, John, M.D., On Duty Outside the Diocese
Rezmer, Matthew, Resurrection, Miramar Beach
Richardson, Walter H., (Retired), St. Mary, Fort Walton Beach

Robinson, David P., (Retired), St. Peter, Mary Esther
Saxer, Robert J., St. Mary, Fort Walton Beach
Schaal, William E., (Retired), Christ Our Redeemer, Blue Water Bay
Schneider, Mark, Good Shepherd, Tallahassee
Scott, John, St. Ann, Gulf Breeze
Seabrook, Bradley M., (Retired), St. Jude, Cantonment
Shin, John, Holy Name of Jesus, Niceville
Simard, Thomas, St. Jude; St. Elizabeth, Cantonment
Trevino, Joaquin D., (Retired), Christ Our Redeemer, Blue Water Bay
Walters, George, St. John the Evangelist, Panama City
Warner, Timothy M., Esq., St. John the Evangelist, Panama City
White, Jean, (Retired)
Williamson, Gerard, (Retired), St. John the Evangelist, Pensacola
Wolf, Charles R., (Retired), St. Mary, Fort Walton Beach
Wulf, Stephen, Little Flower, Pensacola
Zmuda, Henry, (Serving in Diocese of St. Augustine)

INSTITUTIONS LOCATED IN THE DIOCESE

[A] HIGH SCHOOLS, DIOCESAN

PENSACOLA. *Pensacola Catholic High School*, 3043 W. Scott St., 32505. Tel: 850-436-6400; Fax: 850-436-6405. Email: kmartin@pensacolachs.org. Web: pensacolachs.org. Sr. Kierstin Martin, A.S.C.J., Prin.; Rebecca Frandsen, Librarian. Sisters 1; Lay Teachers 50; Students 563; Total Staff 59.

TALLAHASSEE. *John Paul II Catholic High School* (2001) 5100 Terrebone Dr., 32311-7848. Tel: 850-201-5744; Fax: 850-205-3299. Email: srecronan@jpiichs.org. Web: www.jpiichs.org. Sr. Ellen Cronan, A.S.C.J., Prin.; MaryAnn Hensarling, Librarian. Sisters 3; Lay Teachers 16; Students 119; Total Staff 4.

[B] GENERAL HOSPITALS

PENSACOLA. *The Mother Seton Guild of Sacred Heart Hospital, Inc.*, 5151 N. 9th Ave., 32504. Ms. Janet Shelby, Pres.

Sacred Heart Foundation, Inc. (1984) 5151 N. 9th Ave., 32504. Tel: 850-416-4660; Fax: 850-416-4664. Email: hroberts@shhpens.org. Web: sacred-heart.org. P.O. Box 2700, 32513-2700. Tel: 850-416-4660; Fax: 850-416-4664. Roger Webb, Chm. Bed Capacity 458; Total Assisted Annually 2,493; Total Staff 9.

Sacred Heart Health System, Inc. dba Sacred Heart Hospital of Pensacola; Sacred Heart Hospital on the Emerald Coast 5151 N. Ninth Ave., 32504. Tel: 850-416-7000; Fax: 850-416-6119. Email: pmadden@shhpens.org. Web: sacred-heart.org. Patrick J. Madden, Pres. & CEO. Annual Admissions 26,824; Total Staff (SHHP) 4,108; Total Staff (SHHEC) 717; Total Number of Admissions & Outpatient Encounters 344,631; Bed Capacity (SHHP) 493; Bed Capacity (SHHEC) 74.

Sacred Heart Health Ventures, Inc., 5151 N. Ninth Ave., 32504. Tel: 850-416-6500; Fax: 850-416-6119. Email: kemmanue@shhpens.org. Karen Emmanuel, Gen. Counsel.

[C] HOMES FOR AGED

PENSACOLA. *Haven of Our Lady of Peace, Inc.* (2000) 1900 Summit Blvd., 32503. Tel: 850-436-5900; Fax: 850-436-5959. Email: miperez@shhpens.org. Martha Perez, Vice Pres./Admin. Bed Capacity 120; Total Staff 198; Total Assisted Annually 782.

[D] APARTMENTS FOR THE ELDERLY AND HANDICAPPED

TALLAHASSEE. *Casa Calderon, Inc.*, 800 W. Virginia St., 32304. Tel: 850-222-4026; Fax: 850-561-6868. Email: karkoel@aol.com. Rev. Msgr. Michael W. Tugwell, Pres.; Ms. Barbara Bolden, Mgr. Total Assisted 111; Total Staff 5.

[E] MONASTERIES AND RESIDENCES FOR PRIESTS AND BROTHERS

TALLAHASSEE. *Brotherhood of Hope*, 2302 Mission Rd., 32304-2629. Tel: 850-580-3553; Fax: 850-576-2384. Web: www.brotherhoodofhope.net. Bros. Allen Marquez; Stephen Quense; Clinton Reed; Jason Zink.

Missionary Servants of the Most Holy Trinity, 7997 Mahan Dr., P.O. Box 10429, 32302-2429. Tel: 850-224-4955. Email: fvrst@mail.instal.com. Revs. Dennis M. Berry, S.T., Custodian; Walter O'Donnell, S.T.; Allen Rodrigues, S.T.; Bro. Raymond Calixte, S.J.

[F] CONVENT AND RESIDENCES FOR SISTERS

PENSACOLA. *Sacred Heart Hospital Administration*, 5151 N. 9th Ave., 32504. Tel: 850-416-7910; Fax: 850-416-6119. Web: www.shhint.net.

APALACHICOLA. *Martin House* (1982) 149 10th St., 32320. Tel: 850-653-8774. Email: jdreaop@hotmail.com. Sisters Jeanne Drea, O.P.; Mary Alice Neylon, O.P.; Leonius Skaar, O.P. Sisters (Sinsinawa Dominican Congregation of the Most Holy Rosary) 3.

SUNNY HILLS. *Vestiarki Sisters of Jesus (Poland)* (1882) 3919 Vistula Dr., 32428. Tel: 850-773-3302. Sisters 4; Total Assisted 3.

[G] HOMELESS SHELTERS

PANAMA CITY. *St. Barnabas House*, 2943 E. 11th St., 32401. Tel: 850-763-0475; Fax: 850-763-2969. Email: catholicchari@comcast.net. c/o Catholic Charities, 3128 E. 11th St., 32401. Deborah Walton, Coord. Bed Capacity 16; Total in Residence 20; Total Staff 3; Total Assisted Annually 34.

Naomi House, 2941 E. 11th St., 32401. Tel: 850-763-0475; Fax: 850-763-2969. Email: catholicchari@comcast.net. c/o Catholic Charities, 3128 E. 11th St., 32401. Bed Capacity 4; Total Staff 3; Total Assisted Annually 8.

[H] RETREAT HOUSES

TALLAHASSEE. *The Saint John Neumann Spiritual Renewal Center*, 685 Miccosukee Rd., 32308. Tel: 850-224-2971; Fax: 850-224-2941. Sr. Christine Kelly, S.S.J., Dir. Sisters 3.

[I] MISCELLANEOUS

PENSACOLA. *The Catholic Foundation of Northwest Florida, Inc.*, P.O. Drawer 13284, 32591. Tel: 850-435-3500; Fax: 850-435-3568. Web: www.ptdiocese.org. John Godlewski, Dir. Fin.

Diocese of Pensacola-Tallahassee Education Foundation, Inc., 11 N. B St., 32501. Tel: 850-435-3500; Fax: 850-436-6424. Email: ptschools@ptdiocese.org. Web: www.ptdiocese.org.

St. Michael Cemetery Foundation, Inc., P.O. Box 13602, 32561. Tel: 850-436-4643. Web: www.stmichaelcemetery.org.

TALLAHASSEE. *Florida Catholic Conference* (1969)Office: 201 W. Park Ave., 32301-7760. Tel: 850-222-3803; Fax: 850-681-9548. Email: flacathconf@flacathconf.org. Web: www.flacathconf.org. D. Michael McCarron, Ph.D., Exec. Dir.

Martyrs of La Florida Missions, Incorporated, 1230 Archangel Way, 32317. Tel: 850-894-1304. Robin Fennema, Vice Pres.

RELIGIOUS INSTITUTES OF MEN REPRESENTED IN THE DIOCESE

For further details refer to the corresponding bracketed number in the Religious Institutes of Men or Women section.

[]—*Brothers of Hope* (Benedictine - St. Meinrad, IN)

[1080]—*Congregation of the Resurrection* (Chicago Prov.)—C.R.

[]—*Missionaries of the Sacred Heart*—M.S.C.

[0840]—*Missionary Servants of the Most Holy Trinity*—S.T.

[]—*Missionary Society of St. Paul of Nigeria* (Gwagwalda-Abuja)—M.S.P.

[0910]—*Oblates of Mary Immaculate* (Eastern American Prov.)—O.M.I.

[0520]—*Order of Friars Minor, Franciscans*—O.F.M.

[0975]—*Society of our Lady of the Most Holy Trinity*—S.O.L.T.

[0420]—*Society of the Divine Word*—S.V.D.

[1335]—*Vincentian Congregation*—V.C.

RELIGIOUS INSTITUTES OF WOMEN REPRESENTED IN THE DIOCESE

[0130]—*Apostles of the Sacred Heart of Jesus*—A.S.C.J.

[1070-03]—*Dominican Sisters*—O.P.

[1070-13]—*Dominican Sisters*—O.P.

[]—*Salesian Sisters of St. John Bosco*—F.M.A.

[0590]—*Sisters of Charity of Saint Elizabeth, Convent Station*—S.C.

[2575]—*Sisters of Mercy of the Americas* (Baltimore, MD)—R.S.M.

[3830-06]—*Sisters of St. Joseph of Buffalo*—S.S.J.

[3830-14]—*Sisters of St. Joseph of Rochester*—S.S.J.

[3900]—*Sisters of St. Joseph of St. Augustine, Florida*—S.S.J.

[2150]—*Sisters, Servants of the Immaculate Heart of Mary*—I.H.M.

[]—*Vestiarki Sisters of Jesus* (Poland)—V.S.J.

NECROLOGY

† Kerr, Rev. Msgr. William A., Tallahassee, FL Pres., Casa Calderon, Inc.—Died May 13, 2009
† Caffrey, Joseph, (Retired)—Died July 22, 2009
† Condren, William, (Retired)—Died Nov. 3, 2009
† Nguyen, Augustine Hue, (Retired)—Died May 12, 2009

An asterisk (*) denotes an organization that has established tax-exempt status directly with the IRS and is not covered by the USCCB Group Ruling.

Diocese of Peoria

(Dioecesis Peoriensis)

Most Reverend

DANIEL R. JENKY, C.S.C.

Bishop of Peoria; ordained April 6, 1974; appointed Auxiliary Bishop of Fort Wayne-South Bend and Titular Bishop of Amantia October 21, 1997; consecrated December 16, 1997; appointed Bishop of Peoria February 12, 2002; installed April 10, 2002. *Office: 419 N.E. Madison Ave., Peoria, IL 61603.*

Chancery: 419 N.E. Madison Ave., Peoria, IL 61603. Tel: 309-671-1550; Fax: 309-671-1576.

ESTABLISHED 1877.

Square Miles 16,933.

A cross-section of Illinois, bounded on the north by the Counties of Whiteside, Lee, De Kalb, Grundy and Iroquois, and on the east by Kendall, Grundy, Kankakee and Ford, and on the south by Adams, Brown, Cass, Menard, Sangamon, Macon, Moultrie, Douglas and Edgar; comprising the Counties of Bureau, Champaign, Dewitt, Fulton, Hancock, Henderson, Henry, Knox, La Salle, Livingston, Logan, Marshall, Mason, McDonough, McLean, Mercer,Peoria, Piatt, Putnam, Rock Island, Schuyler, Stark, Tazewell, Vermilion, Warren and Woodford.

For legal titles of parishes and diocesan institutions, consult the Chancery.

STATISTICAL OVERVIEW

Personnel	
Bishop	1
Abbots	2
Retired Abbots	1
Priests: Diocesan Active in Diocese	138
Priests: Diocesan Active Outside Diocese	15
Priests: Retired, Sick or Absent	45
Number of Diocesan Priests	198
Religious Priests in Diocese	30
Total Priests in Diocese	228
Extern Priests in Diocese	15
Ordinations:	
Diocesan Priests	2
Transitional Deacons	2
Permanent Deacons in Diocese	158
Total Brothers	9
Total Sisters	215
Parishes	
Parishes	159
With Resident Pastor:	
Resident Diocesan Priests	129
Resident Religious Priests	20
Without Resident Pastor:	
Administered by Priests	10
Missions	28
Pastoral Centers	5
Professional Ministry Personnel:	
Sisters	13
Lay Ministers	24
Welfare	
Catholic Hospitals	9
Total Assisted	3,861,879
Homes for the Aged	4
Total Assisted	410
Day Care Centers	2
Total Assisted	244
Specialized Homes	1
Total Assisted	22
Special Centers for Social Services	1
Total Assisted	36,746
Educational	
Diocesan Students in Other Seminaries	29
Total Seminarians	29
Colleges and Universities	1
Total Students	425
High Schools, Diocesan and Parish	7
Total Students	2,734
Elementary Schools, Diocesan and Parish	42
Total Students	10,022
Catechesis/Religious Education:	
High School Students	1,037
Elementary Students	7,489
Total Students under Catholic Instruction	21,736
Teachers in the Diocese:	
Priests	13
Brothers	2
Sisters	10
Lay Teachers	990
Vital Statistics	
Receptions into the Church:	
Infant Baptism Totals	1,828
Adult Baptism Totals	213
Received into Full Communion	377
First Communions	2,056
Confirmations	2,434
Marriages:	
Catholic	336
Interfaith	248
Total Marriages	584
Deaths	1,463
Total Catholic Population	161,242
Total Population	1,465,840

Former Bishops—Most Revs. JOHN LANCASTER SPALDING, D.D., cons. May 1, 1877; resigned Sept. 11, 1908; Titular Archbishop of Scitopolis; appt. Oct. 14, 1908; died Aug. 25, 1916; EDMUND M. DUNNE, D.D., ord. June 24, 1887; cons. Sept. 1, 1909; died Oct. 17, 1929; JOSEPH H. SCHLARMAN, Ph.D., J.C.D., ord. June 29, 1904; cons. June 17, 1930; named Assistant at Papal Throne, Nov. 16, 1950; Archbishop ad personam; appt. June 27, 1951; died Nov. 10, 1951; WILLIAM E. COUSINS, D.D., ord. April 23, 1927; Titular Bishop of Forma and Auxiliary Bishop of Chicago; appt. Dec. 17, 1948; cons. March 7, 1949; Bishop of Peoria; appt. May 21, 1952; Archbishop of Milwaukee; appt. Dec. 17, 1958; died Sept. 14, 1988; JOHN B. FRANZ, D.D., ord. June 13, 1920; Bishop of Dodge City; appt. May 29, 1951; cons. Aug. 29, 1951; transferred to Peoria, Aug. 8, 1959; installed Nov. 4, 1959; retired June 1, 1971; died July 3, 1992; EDWARD W. O'ROURKE, D.D., ord. May 28, 1944; Bishop of Peoria; appt. May 24, 1971; cons. July 15, 1971; retired Jan. 23, 1990; died Sept. 29, 1999; JOHN J. MYERS, J.C.D., ord. Dec. 17, 1966; appt. Coadjutor Bishop of Peoria July 7, 1987; ord. Sept. 3, 1987; succeeded to Bishop of Peoria, Jan. 23, 1990; appt. Archbishop of Newark July 24, 2001; installed Oct. 9, 2001.

Bishop's Office—419 N.E. Madison Ave., Peoria, 61603. Tel: 309-671-1550; Fax: 309-671-1576. Please direct all calls for the Bishop's Office to this number; Office Hours: Mon.-Fri. 8:30-4:30.

Vicar General—Rev. Msgr. PAUL E. SHOWALTER, P.A., V.G., Ordinary, Mailing Address: Spalding Pastoral Center, 419 N.E. Madison Ave., Peoria, 61603. Tel: 309-671-1550; Fax: 309-671-1576.

Chancellor—Ms. PATRICIA GIBSON, J.C.L., Spalding Pastoral Center, 419 N.E. Madison Ave., Peoria, 61603. Tel: 309-671-1550; Fax: 309-671-1576.

Director of the Curia—Ms. PATRICIA GIBSON, J.C.L., Spalding Pastoral Center, 419 N.E. Madison Ave., Peoria, 61603. Tel: 309-671-1550; Fax: 309-671-1576.

Vice Chancellors—Rev. Msgr. JOSEPH A. ZUBE, J.C.L.; Deacons ROBERT POMAZAL; ROBERT SONDAG; Mr. CHRISTOPHER KREPS; Rev. Msgr. STANLEY L. DEPTULA, 419 N.E. Madison Ave., Peoria, 61603-3720. Tel: 309-671-1550; Fax: 309-671-1595.

Director of Development—Mr JOHN GIBSON, Spalding Pastoral Center, 419 N.E. Madison Ave., Peoria, 61603. Tel: 309-671-1550; Fax: 309-671-1595.

Director of Finance—Mr. JOHN BANNON, Spalding Pastoral Center, 419 N.E. Madison Ave., Peoria, 61603. Tel: 309-671-1550; Fax: 309-671-1597.

Legal Department—Ms. PATRICIA GIBSON, J.C.L., Spalding Pastoral Center, 419 N.E. Madison Ave., Peoria, 61603-3720. Tel: 309-671-1550; Fax: 309-671-1576.

Diocesan Tribunal—Sr. MARIANNE BURKHARD, O.S.B., J.C.L., Spalding Pastoral Center, 419 N.E. Madison Ave., Peoria, 61603. Tel: 309-671-1550; Fax: 309-677-6798.

Judicial Vicar—Rev. Msgr. JASON GRAY, J.C.L.

Defender of the Bond—Rev. Msgr. RICK J. OBERCH.

Promoter of Justice—Rev. Msgr. RICK J. OBERCH.

Adjutant Judicial Vicar—VACANT.

Director of the Tribunal—Sr. MARIANNE BURKHARD, O.S.B., J.C.L.

Judges—Sr. MARIANNE BURKHARD, O.S.B., J.C.L.; Ms. ADELA MARIA KIM, J.C.L.; Rev. Msgrs. J. BRIAN REJSEK, J.C.L.; JASON A. GRAY, J.C.L.

Advocates—Mrs. CHERYL CRISS; Mrs. COLLEEN MCCULLA; Mrs. LINDA THOMAS.

Notaries—Mrs. DEBRA WILLIAMS; Mrs. DIANE HAHN; DEBRA ANNE HILL.

Diocesan College of Consultors—Rev. Msgrs. PAUL E. SHOWALTER, P.A., V.G., Vicar Gen.; JOHN J. PRENDERGAST; JEROME HAM; DALE L. WELLMAN; Rev. THADDEUS PRACZ; Rev. Msgr. GERALD T. WARD; Rev. WILLIAM T. MILLER, I.C., Spalding Pastoral Center, 419 N.E. Madison Ave., Peoria, 61603. Tel: 309-671-1550; Fax: 309-671-1576.

Vicariates and Vicars—Rev. Msgrs. GERALD T. WARD, Bloomington-Lincoln; ALBERT W. HALLIN, P.A., Champaign; Revs. THADDEUS PRACZ, Danville; JAMES G. PALLARDY, Henry-Kewanee; ROBERT D. SPILMAN, La Salle; Rev. Msgrs. DALE L. WELLMAN, Rock Island; RICHARD A. PRICCO, Macomb; ERNEST E. PIZZAMIGLIO, Galesburg; RAYMOND J. BOYLE, P.A., Ottawa; Rev. TIMOTHY NOLAN, Pekin; Rev. Msgrs. MICHAEL C. BLISS, Peoria; THOMAS E. MACK, Pontiac.

Diocesan Offices and Directors

Finance Council (Canon 492)—Most Rev. DANIEL ROBERT JENKY, C.S.C.; Rev. Msgr. PAUL E. SHOWALTER, P.A., V.G.; Sr. DIANE MARIE MCGREW, O.S.F.; Revs. JAMES G. PALLARDY; ROBERT D. SPILMAN; Bro. WILLIAM DYGERT, C.S.C.; Mr. DAN DALY; Mr. LEON HINTON; Mr. VERNON WEGERER; Mr. DANIEL REYNOLDS; Mr. JOHN BANNON; Mr JOHN GIBSON; Ms. PATRICIA GIBSON, J.C.L.; Mr. DON WESTERN; Ms. RITA KRESS; Mr. ROBERT BRADY, Spalding Pastoral Center, 419 N.E. Madison Ave., Peoria, 61603. Tel: 309-671-1550; Fax: 309-671-1595.

Liturgy, Churches and Chapels—Rev. Msgr. STANLEY L. DEPTULA, 419 N.E. Madison Ave., Peoria, 61603. Tel: 309-671-1550; Fax: 309-671-1573.

Catholic Cemeteries—Deacon ROBERT W. MYERS SR., Spalding Pastoral Center, 419 N.E. Madison Ave., Peoria, 61603. Tel: 309-671-1550; Fax: 309-671-1595.

Catholic Education Office—Bro. WILLIAM DYGERT, C.S.C., Supt., Catholic Schools, Spalding Pastoral Center, 419 N.E. Madison Ave., Peoria, 61603. Tel: 309-671-1550; Fax: 309-671-1595. Associate Superintendents: PATRICIA KELLOGG; Mr. KENNETH J. SANDERSON; Mr. VINCENT MCCLEAN, Ph.D., Dir.,

Office of Catechetics.

Respect Life & Human Dignity—Ms. JEANNE WHALEN, Dir., Spalding Pastoral Center, 419 N.E. Madison Ave., Peoria, 61603. Tel: 309-671-1550; Fax: 309-671-1581.

Catholic Relief Services—Rev. Msgr. PAUL E. SHOWALTER, P.A., V.G., 419 N.E. Madison Ave., Peoria, 61603. Tel: 309-671-1550; Fax: 309-671-1576.

Catholic Women, Council of—Rev. Msgr. DALE L. WELLMAN, Moderator, 1608 13th St., Moline, 61265. Tel: 309-762-2362.

Censor Librorum—Rev. PHILIP HALFACRE, St. Patrick, 726 W. Jefferson St., Ottawa, 61350.

Clergymen's Aid, Inc.—Most Rev. DANIEL ROBERT JENKY, C.S.C., Trustee & Ex Officio; Rev. Msgrs. PAUL E. SHOWALTER, P.A., V.G., Trustee & Ex Officio; DOUGLAS HENNESSY, Pres.; Revs. GREG NELSON; ROBERT D. SPILMAN, Vice Pres.; MARK A. DESUTTER; DONALD HENDERSON; JEFFREY D. STIRNIMAN, Sec.; Rev. Msgr. DALE WELLMAN; Rev. PATRICK M. RIORDAN, 412 N.E. Madison Ave., Peoria, 61603. Tel: 309-671-1550; Fax: 309-671-1595.

Commission for Ecumenism—Rev. Msgr. ALBERT W. HALLIN, P.A., 416 County Rd. 1100 N., Seymour, 61875. Tel: 217-863-2190.

Communications, Diocesan Office of—VACANT, Spalding Pastoral Center, 419 N.E. Madison, Peoria, 61603. Tel: 309-671-1550; Fax: 309-671-1595.

Conciliation and Arbitration Process—Rev. Msgr. PAUL E. SHOWALTER, P.A., V.G., Spalding Pastoral Center, 419 N.E. Madison Ave., Peoria, 61603-2720. Tel: 309-671-1550; Fax: 309-671-1576.

Cursillo Program—Rev. TERRY A. CASSIDY, Spiritual Dir.; Deacon WILLIAM READ, Diocesan Dir., Spalding Renewal Center, 401 N.E. Madison Ave., Peoria, 61603. Tel: 309-676-5587.

Diocesan Office of Development and Stewardship—Mr JOHN GIBSON, Dir., Spalding Pastoral Center, 419 N.E. Madison Ave., Peoria, 61603. Tel: 309-671-1550; Fax: 309-671-1595.

Diocesan Evangelization Office—VACANT, Dir., St. Bernard's School, 512 E. Kansas, Peoria, 61603. Tel: 309-682-5823; Fax: 309-682-6030.

Diocesan Office of Finance—Mr. JOHN BANNON, Dir., Finance Office: Spalding Pastoral Center, 419 N.E. Madison Ave., Peoria, 61603. Tel: 309-671-1550; Fax: 309-671-1597.

Diocesan Hispanic Ministry Office—Rev. Msgr. J. BRIAN REJSEK, J.C.L., Dir., St. Bernard's School, 512 E. Kansas, Peoria, 61603. Tel: 309-682-5823; Fax: 309-682-6030.

Diocesan Office of Human Resources—KAREN SMALL, Dir., Spalding Pastoral Center, 419 N.E. Madison Ave., Peoria, 61603. Tel: 309-671-1550; Fax: 309-671-1583.

Diocesan Pastoral Council—Rev. Msgr. PAUL E. SHOWALTER, P.A., V.G., Spalding Pastoral Center, 419 N.E Madison Ave., Peoria, 61603. Tel: 309-671-1550; Fax: 309-671-1576.

Diocesan Personnel Board—Rev. Msgr. PAUL E. SHOWALTER, P.A., V.G., Spalding Pastoral Center, 419 N.E. Madison Ave., Peoria, 61603. Tel: 309-671-1550; Fax: 309-671-1576.

Diocesan Director of Music—SHERRY SECKLER, Ph.D. Tel: 309-672-6447.

Divine Worship, Office of—Rev. Msgr. STANLEY L. DEPTULA, 419 N.E. Madison Ave., Peoria, 61603. Tel: 309-671-1550; Fax: 309-671-1573.

Office of Marriage and Family—Mr. TIM RODER, Dir., Spalding Pastoral Center, 419 N.E. Madison Ave., Peoria, 61603. Tel: 309-671-1550; Fax: 309-671-1581.

Office of Pastoral Services—Ms. JEANNE WHALEN, Dir., Spalding Pastoral Center, 419 N.E. Madison Ave., Peoria, 61603. Tel: 309-671-1550; Fax: 309-671-1581.

Holy Childhood Association—Rev. Msgr. PAUL E. SHOWALTER, P.A., V.G., 419 N.E. Madison Ave., Peoria, 61603. Tel: 309-671-1550.

Office of Victims Assistance—Deacon ROBERT SONDAG, 419 N.E. Madison Ave., Peoria, 61603. Tel: 309-671-1550; Fax: 309-671-1576.

Newspaper--"The Catholic Post"—Mr. THOMAS DERMODY, Editor-in-Chief, 419 N.E. Madison Ave., Peoria, 61603. Tel: 309-671-1550; Fax: 309-671-1579.

Nurses, Council of—VACANT.

Permanent Diaconate, Office of—Rev. Msgr. CHARLES J. BEEBE, Spalding Pastoral Center, 419 N.E. Madison Ave., Peoria, 61603. Tel: 309-671-1550; Fax: 309-671-1581.

Priests' Eucharistic League—Rev. Msgr. JOSEPH A. ZUBE, J.C.L., Spalding Pastoral Center, 419 N.E. Madison Ave., Peoria, 61603. Tel: 309-671-1550; Fax: 309-677-6798.

Propagation of the Faith—Rev. Msgr. PAUL E. SHOWALTER, P.A., V.G., 419 N.E. Madison Ave., Peoria, 61603. Tel: 309-671-1550; Fax: 309-671-1576.

Priests' Purgatorial Society—Rev. Msgr. PAUL E. SHOWALTER, P.A., V.G., Spalding Pastoral Center, 419 N.E. Madison Ave., Peoria, 61603. Tel: 309-671-1550; Fax: 309-671-1576.

Rural Life Conference—Deacon WILLIAM GRAY, Dir., 1225 N. County Rd. 1000, Hamilton, 62341. Tel: 217-847-3818. Email: gfpltd@frontiernet.net.

Presbyteral Council—Rev. ROBERT RAYSON, Pres., Spalding Pastoral Center, 419 N.E. Madison, Peoria, 61603. Tel: 309-671-1550; Fax: 309-671-1576.

Catholic Charities—Ms. PEGGY A. ARIZZI, Exec. Dir.; TRICIA FOX, Asst. Exec. Dir., 2900 W. Heading Ave., Peoria, 61604. Tel: 309-636-8000; Fax: 309-671-0253. Bloomington Offices, 603 N. Center St., Bloomington, 61701. Tel: 309-829-6307; Fax: 309-829-3254. 502 S. Morris Ave., Bloomington, 61704. Tel: 309-820-7616; Fax: 309-820-7657. Champaign Office, 1315 A Curt Dr., Champaign, 61820. Tel: 217-352-5179; Fax: 217-352-0318. Danville Office, 102 N. Robinson, Danville, 61832. Tel: 217-443-1772; Fax: 217-443-1701. Galesburg Office, 292 N. Chambers, Galesburg, 61401. Tel: 309-342-1136; Fax: 309-342-1891. LaSalle Office, 542 Crosat, LaSalle, 61301. Tel: 815-223-4007; Fax: 815-223-4550. LaSalle Office, 548 Crosat, La Salle, 61301. Tel: 815-223-0318. Lincoln Office. Tel: 217-732-3771; Fax: 217-735-1738. Macomb Office, 310 E. Washington St., Macomb, 61455. Tel: 309-833-1791; Fax: 309-836-1462. Rock Island Office, 4703 44th St., Rock Island, 61201. Tel: 309-788-9581; Fax: 309-788-9608.

TEC—Sr. JACQUE SCHROEDER, O.S.F., Diocesan Spiritual Dir., Spalding Renewal Center, 401 N.E. Madison Ave., Peoria, 61603. Tel: 309-676-4001; Fax: 309-676-4022. Email: tecinfo@peoriacursillotec.com.

Vocations Office—Rev. BRIAN K. BROWNSEY, Dir., Spalding Pastoral Center, 419 N.E. Madison Ave., Peoria, 61603. Tel: 309-671-1550; Fax: 309-671-1581. Assistant Directors: Rev. Msgr. STANLEY L. DEPTULA; Revs. JAMES E. KRUSE; DAVID P. RICHARDSON, St. Philomena, 3300 N. Twelve Oaks Dr., Peoria, 61604.

Christ Child Society of Central Illinois—Mailing Address: P.O. Box 1563, Peoria, 61655. Tel: 309-677-7697. Email: christchildsociety@gmail.com. JOAN WEBER, Pres.

Christ Child Society of the Quad Cities—Mailing Address: P.O. Box 6184, Rock Island, 61201. Email: ccsqc@yahoo.com. SHELLY HUISKAMP.

CLERGY, PARISHES, MISSIONS AND PAROCHIAL SCHOOLS

CITY OF PEORIA

(PEORIA COUNTY)

1—ST. MARY'S CATHEDRAL (1846) Rev. Msgr. Paul E. Showalter, Rector; Most Rev. Daniel Robert Jenky, C.S.C.; Deacon Toby Tyler.
Office: 512 E. Kansas, 61603.
Res.: 607 N.E. Madison Ave., 61603. Tel: 309-682-5823; Fax: 309-682-6030.
Catechesis / Religious Program—Students 60.

2—ST. ANN (1994) Rev. Terry A. Cassidy; Deacons Joseph Koeppel; William Sloman; Stephen Cenek; Bruce Steiner; Sr. Judith Croegaert, O.S.B., Pastoral Assoc.
Mailing Address: 1010 S. Louisa St., 61605. Tel: 309-674-5072; Fax: 309-655-1566. Email: stann_parish@comcast.net.
Catechesis / Religious Program—Students 86.

3—ST. BERNARD'S (1903) Rev. Msgr. Paul E. Showalter; Rev. Geoffrey Horton, Parochial Vicar.
525 E. Kansas Ave., 61603.
Res.: 509 E. Kansas Ave., 61603. Tel: 309-682-1221; Fax: 309-682-3462. Email: b.stbernards@comcast.net.
Catechesis / Religious Program— In conjunction with St. Peter's Parish and St. Mary's Cathedral.

4—ST. BONIFACE'S (1881), (German), Closed. For inquiries for parish records contact St. Ann, Peoria.

5—ST. CECILIA'S, Closed. For Sacramental records write St. Philomena, 3300 N. Twelve Oaks Dr., Peoria, IL 61604.

6—HOLY FAMILY (1956) Revs. Michael J. Glastetter, O.F.M.Conv.; Alejandro Lopez, O.F.M.Conv.; Deacon Joseph Lahood.
Res.: 3720 N. Sterling Ave., 61615. Tel: 309-688-3427; Fax: 309-688-2174. Web: www.peoriaholyfamily.com.
School—2329 W. Reservoir, 61615. Tel: 309-688-2931; Fax: 309-681-5687. Sharon Zogby, Prin. Lay Teachers 15; Students 220.
Catechesis / Religious Program—Email: holyfamilydre@hotmail.com. Nicole Arendell, D.R.E. Students 50.

7—ST. JOHN'S (1890), (Irish), Closed. For inquiries for parish records contact St. Ann, Peoria.

8—ST. JOSEPH (1976) Revs. Lawrence W. Zurek, O.F.M.; Luis Aponte-Merced, O.F.M.; Bert Heise, O.F.M. (Retired); Robert Weakley, O.F.M.
Mailing Address: 504 Fulton St., 61602. Tel: 309-676-0726; Fax: 309-673-6330.
Church: 103 Richard Pryor Pl., 61605.
Southside Catholic Child Care Center—1010 W. Johnson, 61605. Tel: 309-674-7340.

9—ST. JUDE'S (1975) [CEM] Revs. R. Anthony Lee; Ryan Bredemeyer; Deacons Thomas Rapach; Roger Hunter.
Res.: 10811 N. Knoxville Ave., 61615. Tel: 309-243-7811; Fax: 309-243-7810. Email: stjude@stjudechurchpeoria.org. Web: www.stjudechurchpeoria.org.
Catechesis / Religious Program—Tel: 309-243-7811, Ext. 212; 309-243-7811, Ext. 213; Fax: 309-243-7810. Students 302.

10—ST. MARK'S (1891) Rev. Charles Klamut; Deacon John Skender. In Res., Revs. Joseph M. Mwinzi (Kenya); Geoffrey Horton.
Res.: 1113 W. Bradley Ave., 61606-1722. Tel: 309-673-1263; Fax: 309-637-1484. Email: stmark@mtco.com.
School—711 N. Underhill, 61606. Tel: 309-676-7131; Fax: 309-677-8060. Web: www.saint-mark.net. Steve Hagenbruch, Prin. Lay Teachers 17; Students 230.
Catechesis / Religious Program—Tel: 309-497-2838. Students 30.

11—ST. PETER'S (1897) Rev. Msgr. Paul E. Showalter; Rev. Geoffrey Horton, Parochial Vicar; Deacon Richard Zimmerman.
Res.: 2719 N.E. Madison Ave., 61603. Tel: 309-685-3861; Fax: 309-685-4523. Email: st.peterspeoria@comcast.net.
Catechesis / Religious Program—Anita Keck, D.R.E. Students 13.

12—ST. PHILOMENA (1945) [JC] Revs. David P. Richardson; Donald Henderson, Parochial Vicar.
Res.: 3300 N. Twelve Oaks Dr., 61604-1464. Tel: 309-682-8642; Fax: 309-682-8955. Email: rectory@stphils.com. Web: www.stphils.com.
School—3216 N. Emery Ave., 61604. Tel: 309-685-1208; Fax: 309-681-5676. Sisters of St. Francis of the Immaculate Conception 1; Lay Teachers 21; Students 387.
Catechesis / Religious Program—Tel: 309-685-1677, Ext. 202. Mrs. Judith Martin, D.R.E. Students 53.
St. Philomena Endowment Trust—

13—SACRED HEART (1879), (German), Revs. Lawrence W. Zurek, O.F.M.; Luis Aponte-Merced, O.F.M. In Res., Revs. Bert Heise, O.F.M. (Retired); Aquinas Schneider, O.F.M. (Retired).
Res.: 504 Fulton St., 61602. Tel: 309-494-9602 (Rectory); 309-673-6317 (Parish Offices); Fax: 309-673-6330. Email: sacredheart@comcast.net. Web: www.sacredheartpeoria.com.

14—ST. THOMAS (1937) Rev. Msgr. William A. Watson; Rev. Thomas Taylor; Sr. Rachel Bergschneider, O.S.B., Pastoral Assoc. & D.R.E.; Deacon Francis L. Eaton.
Res.: 904 E. Lake Ave., Peoria Heights, 61616. Tel: 309-688-3446; Fax: 309-688-3467.
School—4229 N. Monroe, Peoria Heights, 61616. Tel: 309-685-2533; Fax: 309-681-7262. Mrs. Maureen Bentley, Prin. Lay Teachers 26; Students 465.
Catechesis / Religious Program—Students 119.

15—ST. VINCENT DE PAUL (1962) Rev. Msgr. Jason A. Gray; Rev. Dustin P. Schultz; Deacons Robert W. Myers Sr.; Thomas DeBernardis.
Res.: 6001 N. University St., 61614. Tel: 309-691-3602; Fax: 309-691-3687. Email: svdppeoria@hotmail.com. Web: svdppeoria.com.
School—Tel: 309-691-5012; Fax: 309-683-1036. Mr. Michael Birdoes, Prin. Lay Teachers 28; Students 526.
Catechesis / Religious Program—Tel: 309-691-5012, Ext. 162. Students 153.

OUTSIDE THE CITY OF PEORIA

ABINGDON, KNOX CO., SACRED HEART (1924) Revs. William T. Miller, I.C.; Joseph Presley, I.C.
Res. & Mailing: 506 N. Main St., 61410. Tel: 309-462-3421. Email: scrdhrt@abingdon.net.
Catechesis / Religious Program—

ALEDO, MERCER CO., ST. CATHERINE'S CHURCH (1914) [CEM] Rev. John Thieryoung.
Res.: 106 N.E. Fourth, 61231. Tel: 309-582-7500; Fax: 309-582-5163.
Catechesis / Religious Program—Students 44.
Mission—St. Mary's

ALEXIS, WARREN CO., ST. THERESA'S (1877), (Swedish), [CEM] Rev. Dennis E. Spohrer, Admin.

Res.: 131 N. Main St., P.O. Box 26, 61412. Tel: 309-843-0000.
Catechesis/Religious Program—Students 14.

ANDALUSIA, ROCK ISLAND CO., ST. PATRICK CHURCH (1974) Rev. S. Stephen Engelbrecht.
Res.: Box 249, 61232. Tel: 309-798-2098; Fax: 309-798-2840. Email: stpt@mchsi.com. Web: stpatrickandalusia.org.
Catechesis/Religious Program—Students 164.

ANNAWAN, HENRY CO., SACRED HEART (1893) [CEM] Rev. Jerry Logan.
Res.: 305 W. South Ave., 61234. Tel: 309-935-6911.
Catechesis/Religious Program—Students 37.
Mission—St. Mary's St. Mary's Rd., Hooppole, Henry Co. 61258.

ARLINGTON, BUREAU CO., ST. PATRICK'S (1864) [CEM] Rev. Paul J. Meismer.
Mailing Address: 106 Church St., P.O. Box 78, 61312.
Res.: 212 S. Main St., Cherry, 61317. Tel: 815-894-2006.
Catechesis/Religious Program—Students 24.

ATKINSON, HENRY CO., ST. ANTHONY'S (1870), (Belgian), [CEM] Rev. Michael Monclova; Deacon Nicholas Simon.
Res.: 204 W. Main St., P.O. Box 210, 61235-0210. Tel: 309-936-7900; Fax: 309-936-7900. Web: www.catholic-church.org/stanthonys.
Catechesis/Religious Program—Students 22.

BARTONVILLE, PEORIA CO., ST. ANTHONY (1969) Rev. David C. Heinz; Deacon Louis Tomlianovich.
Res.: 2525 Skyway Rd., 61607. Tel: 309-697-0645; Fax: 309-697-2188. Email: saintanthony1@comcast.net.
Catechesis/Religious Program—Students 105.

BEMENT, PIATT CO., ST. MICHAEL Rev. Bruce Lopez; Deacon Gene Triplett.
Res.: 1301 N. Market St., Monticello, 61856. Tel: 217-762-2566; Fax: 217-762-8666. Web: www.stphilomenaonline.org.
Catechesis/Religious Program— (With St. Philomena)

BENSON, WOODFORD CO., ST. JOHN (1873) [CEM] Rev. Msgr. Charles J. Beebe.
Res.: 508 W. Randolph, Roanoke, 61561. Tel: 309-394-2615; Fax: 309-923-3031. Email: msgrbeebe@cdop.org.
Catechesis/Religious Program—Jennifer Peterson, D.R.E. Students 5.

BLACKSTONE, LIVINGSTON CO., ST. BERNARD, Closed. For inquiries for sacramental records contact Immaculate Conception, Streater.

BLOOMINGTON, MCLEAN CO.

1—HOLY TRINITY (1853) [CEM] Rev. Msgr. Douglas J. Hennessy; Rev. John F. Cyr; Deacons Brendan Carolan; Robert Hermes; James Gore.
Mailing Address: 711 N. Main St., 61701. Tel: 309-829-2197; Fax: 309-829-2243. Web: www.holytrinitybloomington.org.
School—Holy Trinity Elementary School, (Grades PreSchool-5), 1909 E. Lincoln, 61701. Tel: 309-662-3712; Fax: 309-663-9115. Students 450.
School—Holy Trinity Junior High, (Grades 6-8), 705 N. Roosevelt, 61701. Tel: 309-828-7151; Fax: 309-827-8131. Web: www.holytrinitycatholicschool.org. Mrs. Kay O'Brien, Prin. Lay Teachers 38; Students 181.
Catechesis/Religious Program—Tel: 309-828-8242. Students 200.

2—ST. MARY'S (1867), (German), [CEM] Revs. Ric Schneider, O.F.M.; Gregg Petri, O.F.M.; Dennet Jung, O.F.M.; Bro. Kevin Duckson, O.F.M.; Deacons Darrel Petri; Jerry Hozie; Jose Montenegro.
Res.: 527 W. Jackson St., 61701. Tel: 309-827-8526; Fax: 309-829-3061. Web: stmarysparish.catholicweb.com.
School—603 W. Jackson St., 61701. Tel: 309-828-5954. Web: www.stmarysschool.net. Lay Teachers 15; Students 172.
Catechesis/Religious Program—Students 282.

3—ST. PATRICK CHURCH OF MERNA (1890) [CEM] Rev. Msgr. Gerald T. Ward; Revs. Thomas Shea; John Cyr, Parochial Vicar; Sr. Rita Ann Bregenhorn, O.S.U., Pastoral Assoc.
Church: 1001 N. Towanda Barnes Rd., 61704. Tel: 309-662-7361; Fax: 309-664-6167. Email: office@stpatrickmerna.org. Web: www.stpatrickmerna.org.
Catechesis/Religious Program—Students 708.

4—ST. PATRICK'S (1892) [JC] Rev. David Whiteside.
Res.: 1209 W. Locust St., 61701. Tel: 309-829-1355; Fax: 309-828-0577. Email: s.patricks@comcast.net. Web: www.historicsaintpatricks.org.
Catechesis/Religious Program—Students 27.

BRADFORD, STARK CO., ST. JOHN THE BAPTIST (1876) [CEM] Rev. Vien Van Do.
Mailing Address: 303 N. Galena, Wyoming, 61491.
Res.: 218 First St., Box 310, 61421. Tel: 309-897-4081; Fax: 309-897-8007.
Catechesis/Religious Program—Students 38.

BRIMFIELD, PEORIA CO., ST. JOSEPH'S (1852), (Irish), [CEM] Rev. John M. Verrier.
Mailing Address: P.O. Box 199, 61517.
Res.: 314 W. Clay St., 61517. Tel: 309-446-3275; Fax: 309-446-9409.
Catechesis/Religious Program—Students 75.
Mission—St. James Williamsfield, Knox Co. 61489. Tel: 309-446-3275.

BUDD, LIVINGSTON CO., ST. BERNARD'S, Closed. For parish records contact Church of the Immaculate Conception, Streator.

BUSHNELL, MCDONOUGH CO., ST. BERNARD (1877) Rev. Thomas B. Holloway.
Res.: 376 W. Hail St., 61422. Tel: 309-772-2333; Fax: 309-772-2112.
Catechesis/Religious Program—Students 46.

CAMP GROVE, MARSHALL CO., ST. PATRICK (1866), (Irish), [CEM] Rev. Vien Van Do.
Mailing Address: 303 N. Galena, Wyoming, 61491.
Res.: 115 W. Camp St., 61424. Tel: 309-493-5261.
Catechesis/Religious Program— Attend St. Dominic, Wyoming.

CAMPUS, LIVINGSTON CO., SACRED HEART (1882), (Irish), [CEM] Rev. Peter A. Pilon.
205 N. Elm St., 60920.
Res.: 313 W. Hamilton, Odell, 60460. Tel: 815-998-2197; Fax: 815-998-2197.
Catechesis/Religious Program—Mrs. Joyce Ferrari, D.R.E. Students 22.

CANTON, FULTON CO., ST. MARY'S (1862) [CEM 2] Rev. Daniel Ebker.
Mailing Address: 139 E. Chestnut St., 61520-2728. Fax: 309-647-1580. Email: stmaryscn@sbcglobal.net.
Res.: 140 N. 2nd Ave., 61520. Tel: 309-647-1476.
Catechesis/Religious Program—Tel: 309-647-0261; Fax: 309-647-1580. Students 117.

CARTHAGE, HANCOCK CO., IMMACULATE CONCEPTION (1860) [CEM] Revs. Anthony J. Trosley; Thomas Szydlik.
Mailing Address: 190 N. Wells St., P.O. Box 147, Nauvoo, 62354.
Res.: 125 N. Fayette, 62321. Tel: 217-357-3087.
Catechesis/Religious Program—Todd Courtois, D.R.E.; Julie Courtois, D.R.E. Students 40.

CHAMPAIGN, CHAMPAIGN CO.

1—HOLY CROSS (1912) Rev. Stephen A. Willard; Deacons Henry Hart; Edward Mohrbacher; Robert J. Ulbrich.
Res.: 405 W. Clark St., 61820. Tel: 217-352-8748; Fax: 217-366-2929. Email: office@holycrosschampaign.org.
School—410 W. White St., 61820. Tel: 217-356-9521; Fax: 217-356-1745. Email: meyersm@holycrosselem.org. Web: www.holycrosselem.org. Mrs. Rose Costello, Prin. Lay Teachers 26; Students 360.
Catechesis/Religious Program—Tel: 217-352-8748; Fax: 217-366-2929. Marc Cardaronella, D.R.E. Students 65.

2—ST. JOHN'S CATHOLIC CHAPEL (1918), (For Catholic Students at the University of Illinois) Rev. Msgrs. Gregory K. Ketcham; Edward J. Duncan, Pastor Emeritus (Retired); Revs. Luke A. Spannagel; Anthony Co. In Res., Revs. Adolph Menendez, S.X.; Maurus Mount, O.S.B.
Newman Hall—604 E. Armory Ave., 61820. Tel: 217-344-1184; Fax: 217-344-4957. Email: info@sjcnc.org. Web: www.sjcnc.org.

3—ST. MARY'S (1854) [CEM] Rev. Thomas J. Royer.
Res.: 612 E. Park St., 61820. Tel: 217-352-8364; Fax: 217-352-6859. Email: stmary@stmary-cu.org. Web: stmary-cu.org.
Catechesis/Religious Program—Students 22.

4—ST. MATTHEW (1965) Rev. Msgr. Mark J. Merdian; Revs. Robert Lampitt; Mark O. Miller.
Res.: 1303 Lincolnshire Dr., 61821. Tel: 217-359-4224; Fax: 217-359-9846. Web: www.stmatt.net.
School—1307 Linconshire Dr., 61821. Tel: 217-359-4114; Fax: 217-359-8319. Mrs. Kathleen Scherer, Prin. Lay Teachers 25; Students 450.
Catechesis/Religious Program—Students 200.
Convent—Sisters of St. Francis of the Martyr St. George, 1719 Robert Dr., 61821. Tel: 217-351-5139.

CHATSWORTH, LIVINGSTON CO., SS. PETER AND PAUL (1877), (German—Irish), [CEM] Rev. Binh K. Tran.
Res.: 406 N. Fifth St., P.O. Box 546, 60921. Tel: 815-635-3127; Fax: 815-635-3756.
Mission—St. James Box 583, Forrest, Livingston Co. 61741.
Catechesis/Religious Program—Students 22.

CHENOA, MCLEAN CO., ST. JOSEPH'S (1859) [CEM] Rev. Carl LoPresti.
Res.: 225 W. Owsley, 61726. Tel: 815-945-2561; Fax: 815-945-7634.
Catechesis/Religious Program—Students 12.
Mission—St. Mary Lexington, McLean Co.

CHERRY, BUREAU CO., HOLY TRINITY (1904) [CEM] Rev. Paul J. Meismer.
Res.: 212 S. Main, P.O. Box 159, 61317. Tel: 815-894-2006; Fax: 815-894-2090.
Catechesis/Religious Program—Ladyne Huhn, D.R.E. Students 57.

CHILLICOTHE, PEORIA CO., ST. EDWARD'S (1900) [CEM] Rev. Glenn H. Harris; Deacons Gregory Serangeli; Bob Pomazal.
Res.: 1216 N. 6th St., 61523. Tel: 309-274-3809; Fax: 309-274-3834.
School—Tel: 309-274-2994; Fax: 309-274-4141. Ms. Jeannine McAllister, Prin. Lay Teachers 13; Students 187.
Catechesis/Religious Program—Students 81.

CLINTON, DE WITT CO., ST. JOHN THE BAPTIST CATHOLIC CHURCH (1879) Rev. James P. Henning, O.F.M.Conv.
Res.: 612 N. Plum, Farmer City, 61842. Tel: 309-928-3855; Fax: 309-928-9147.
Church: 502 N. Monroe St., 61727. Tel: 217-935-3727.
Catechesis/Religious Program—Fax: 217-935-4101. Students 69.

COAL VALLEY, ROCK ISLAND CO., ST. MARIA GORETTI (1972) Rev. James P. DeBisschop; Sr. Sandra Brunenn, O.S.B., Pastoral Assoc.; Deacon Charles Breeden.
Res.: 220 E. 22nd Ave., P.O. Box 159, 61240. Tel: 309-799-3414; Fax: 309-799-3436. Email: smg@smgcv.org. Web: www.smgcv.org.
Catechesis/Religious Program—Tel: 309-799-7283. Students 70.

COLFAX, MCLEAN CO., ST. JOSEPH'S (1850) Rev. Carl LoPresti.
Res.: 107 W. North, P.O. Box 169, 61728. Tel: 309-723-6229; Fax: 309-723-6229.
Catechesis/Religious Program—Students 22.

COLONA, HENRY CO., ST. PATRICK'S (1941) Rev. Duane C. Jack.
Res.: 201 First St., 61241. Tel: 309-792-3854; Fax: 309-792-8630. Email: stpatcolona@qconline.com.
Catechesis/Religious Program—Tel: 309-949-3700. Rose Roe, C.R.E. Students 138.

CREVE COEUR, TAZEWELL CO., SACRE COEUR (1954) Rev. Attilio Morelli.
Res.: 301 Roosevelt St., 61610. Tel: 309-282-2677; Fax: 309-282-2672.
Church: 601 Rusche Ln., 61610. Tel: 309-699-8511.
Catechesis/Religious Program—Ms. Maura Stone, D.R.E. Students 11.

CULLOM, LIVINGSTON CO., ST. JOHN'S (1881) [CEM], St. John's is served by clergy of St. Mary's, Pontiac Rev. Msgr. Thomas E. Mack; Rev. Glenn J. Fontana; Deacons George Wagner; R.J. Wallace.
Res.: 119 E. Howard, Pontiac, 61764. Tel: 815-844-7683.
Church: 113 W. Van Alstyne St., P.O. Box 376, 60929.
Catechesis/Religious Program—Students 25.

DALZELL, BUREAU CO., ST. THOMAS MORE (1934), (Italian), Rev. Robert Rayson, Admin.
Res.: 302 Chestnut, 61320. Tel: 815-663-6201.
Catechesis/Religious Program—Jyll Pozzi, D.R.E. Students 12.

DANVILLE, VERMILION CO.

1—HOLY FAMILY (1978) [CEM] Rev. Thaddeus Pracz; Deacon Richard Smith.
Church: 444 E. Main St., 61832. Tel: 217-431-5100; Fax: 217-431-5103.
School—Tel: 217-431-5108. Web: hfsdanv.org. Ms. Peggy Croy, Prin. Lay Teachers 19; Students 260.
Catechesis/Religious Program—Students 52.

2—ST. PAUL'S (1915) Rev. Greg Nelson; Sr. Charles Allen, Pastoral Assoc.
Res.: 1303 N. Walnut St., 61832. Tel: 217-442-5313; Fax: 217-442-5356. Web: www.sabre-net.org.
School—1307 N. Walnut St., 61832. Tel: 217-442-3880; Fax: 217-442-5852. Mrs. Mary Shepherd, Prin. Lay Teachers 19; Students 286.
Catechesis/Religious Program—Students 84.

DELAVAN, TAZEWELL CO., ST. MARY'S (1867) [CEM] Rev. Gerald J. Verdun.
Res.: 505 E. 4th St., P.O. Box 769, 61734. Tel: 309-244-8516.
Mission—St. Joseph's Hopedale, Tazewell Co.
Catechesis/Religious Program—Students 63.

DEPUE, BUREAU CO., ST. MARY'S (1908) [CEM] Rev. Kevin G. Creegan.
Res.: 312 Park St., Box 19, 61322. Tel: 815-447-2552; Fax: 815-447-2552.
Catechesis/Religious Program—Students 100.
Mission—St. Mary Main St., P.O. Box 271, Tiskilwa, Bureau Co. 61368. Tel: 815-646-4451.

DOWNS, MCLEAN CO., ST. MARY'S (1910) Rev. Msgr. Gerald T. Ward.
Church: 108 E. Washington St., P.O. Box 66, 61736. Tel: 309-378-4679; Fax: 309-378-4679. Email: churchofstmary@verizon.net.
Catechesis/Religious Program—Students 82.

DUNLAP, PEORIA CO., ST. CLEMENT'S, Closed. For inquiries for parish records contact St. Jude, 10811 N. Knoxville, Peoria, IL 61615.

DWIGHT, LIVINGSTON CO., ST. PATRICK'S (1862), (Irish), [CEM] Rev. James E. Rickey.
Res.: 126 W. Mazon Ave., P.O. Box 70, 60420. Tel: 815-584-3522; Fax: 815-584-3518.

Catechesis/Religious Program—Tel: 815-584-3110; Fax: 815-584-3518. Virginia Connor, D.R.E. Students 116.

EAGLE TOWNSHIP, LA SALLE CO., ANNUNCIATION OF BLESSED VIRGIN MARY (1869), (Irish), [CEM] Rev. Charles A. McCarthy, C.S.Sp.
Res.: Rte 1, 957 N. 17th Rd., Tonica, 61370. Tel: 815-856-2502; Fax: 815-856-2503.
Church: 1205 State Rte 18 E., Streator, 61364. Tel: 815-672-6500.
Catechesis/Religious Program— Attend Grand Ridge and St. Anthony's, Streator

EARLVILLE, LA SALLE CO., ST. TERESA OF AVILA (1904) [CEM 2] Rev. Chris G. Haake.
Res.: 221 W. Union St., 60518-8181. Tel: 815-246-4321; Fax: 815-246-4341. Email: st.teresa.earlville@mchsi.com. Web: st.teresa.earlville.home.mchsi.com.
Catechesis/Religious Program—Students 55.

EAST MOLINE, ROCK ISLAND CO.
1—ST. ANNE (1919) Rev. Keith A. Walder.
Res.: 555 18th Ave., 61244. Tel: 309-755-5071; Fax: 309-755-5343. Email: mbanaszek@olgca.us. Web: www.stanne-em.us.
School—Our Lady of Grace Catholic Academy, 602 17th Ave., 61244. Tel: 309-755-9771; Fax: 309-755-7407. Email: office@olgca.us. Web: www.olgca.us. Linda Vandervennet, Prin. Lay Teachers 14; Students 140.
Catechesis/Religious Program—Students 270.
2—ST. MARY'S (1907), (English—Spanish), Parish Suspended. Rev. Keith A. Walder.
Res.: 555 18th St., 61244. Tel: 309-755-4111; Fax: 309-755-2384. Email: stmaryschurch@mchsi.com.
School—Our Lady of Grace Catholic Academy, 602 17th Ave., 61244. Tel: 309-755-4352.
Catechesis/Religious Program—Twinned with St. Anne, East Moline and Our Lady of Guadalupe, Silvis., 800 17th St., Silvis, 61282. Tel: 309-792-3867; Fax: 309-792-2241.

EAST PEORIA, TAZEWELL CO., ST. MONICA CHURCH (1898) Rev. Kenneth L. Marchulones; Deacon Charles Robbins.
Res.: 303 Campanile Dr., 61611. Tel: 309-694-2061. Email: st_monicas@hotmail.com.
Catechesis/Religious Program—Tel: 309-699-8458. Marjorie Miesmer, D.R.E. Students 44.

EL PASO, WOODFORD CO., ST. MARY'S (1863) [CEM 2] Rt. Rev. Roger F. Corpus, O.S.B. (Retired).
Res.: 79 W. Third, P.O. Box 197, 61738. Tel: 309-527-4555; Fax: 309-527-7750.
Catechesis/Religious Program—Tel: 309-527-3958. Beth Miller, D.R.E. Students 84.

ELKHART, LOGAN CO., ST. PATRICK (1856) Rev. Thomas W. Shaw.
Res.: 213 S. Bogardus, P.O. Box 19, 62634. Tel: 217-947-2714; Fax: 217-947-2524. Email: st.patrickschurch@mchsi.com.
Catechesis/Religious Program—Students 25.
Mission—St. Thomas Aquinas Mount Pulaski, Logan Co.
Catechesis/Religious Program—Students 24.

ELMWOOD, PEORIA CO., ST. PATRICK'S (1870), (Irish), [CEM] Rev. Paul Stiene, I.C.
Res.: 802 W. Main St., P.O. Box 440, 61529. Tel: 309-742-4921; Fax: 309-742-4921.
Catechesis/Religious Program—Students 51.

EUREKA, WOODFORD CO., ST. LUKE (1982) [JC] Rev. Eugene A. Radosevich.
Church & Mailing Address: 904 E. Regan Dr., P.O. Box 226, 61530. Tel: 309-467-4855. Email: stluke@mtco.com.
Catechesis/Religious Program—Marcia Brogly, C.R.E. Students 28.

FAIRBURY, LIVINGSTON CO., ST. JOHN THE BAPTIST (1857) [CEM] Rev. Scott Archer.
Res.: 110 E. Ash, 61739. Tel: 815-692-2555.
Catechesis/Religious Program—Students 55.
Mission—St. Rose Strawn, Livingston Co.

FARMER CITY, DE WITT CO., SACRED HEART (1899) [CEM] Rev. James P. Henning, O.F.M.Conv.; Deacons John Leonard; Scott Whitehouse.
Res.: 612 N. Plum St., 61842. Tel: 309-928-3855; Fax: 309-928-9147. Email: shchurch@farmwagon.com.
Catechesis/Religious Program—Students 41.
Mission—St. John Bellflower, McLean Co.

FARMINGTON, FULTON CO., ST. MATTHEW'S (1904) Rev. Bruce King, I.C.; Deacon Gary Schultz.
Res.: 156 E. Vernon St., 61531. Tel: 309-245-4001; Fax: 309-245-4351.
Catechesis/Religious Program—Students 34.

GALESBURG, KNOX CO.
1—CORPUS CHRISTI (1885) [CEM] Revs. William T. Miller, I.C.; Joseph Presley, I.C.
Res.: 273 S. Prairie St., 61401. Tel: 309-343-8256; Fax: 309-343-4793. Email: gare2@galesburg.net.
School—Costa Catholic Academy, 2726 Costa Dr., 61401. Tel: 309-344-3151; Fax: 309-344-1594. James Kovac, Prin. Operates with Immaculate Heart and St. Patrick. Lay Teachers 18; Students 260.
Catechesis/Religious Program—Students 117.
2—IMMACULATE HEART OF MARY (1956) Rev. Msgr. Ernest E. Pizzamiglio; Deacons Michael Mannino; Rod Gray.
Mailing Address: P.O. Box 550, 61402. Tel: 309-344-3108; Fax: 309-344-1205. Web: www.parishesonline.com/ihomc.
Res.: 2401 N. Broad St., 61401. Email: ihomc@grics.net.
See Costa Catholic Academy, Galesburg under Corpus Christi, Galesburg for details.
Catechesis/Religious Program—Students 62.
3—ST. PATRICK'S (1863) [JC] Revs. William T. Miller, I.C.; Joseph Presley, I.C.; Deacon James D. Haneghan.
Res.: 858 S. Academy St., 61401. Tel: 309-343-9874; Fax: 309-343-9944. Email: stpatrickschurch@galesburg.net.
See Costa Catholic School, Galesburg under Corpus Christi, Galesburg for details.
Catechesis/Religious Program—Students 20.

GALVA, HENRY CO., ST. JOHN'S (1882), (Swedish), [CEM] Rev. John R. Burns; Deacon John V. Holevoet.
Church: 212 N.E. 1st St., 61434. Tel: 309-932-2409; 309-334-2180 (Office); Fax: 309-334-2137. Email: stjohnchurch@winco.net.
Catechesis/Religious Program—Students 48.

GENESEO, HENRY CO., ST. MALACHY'S (1866) Rev. Michael G. Pakula; Deacons Thomas Harley Chaffee; Harley Harris, (Retired); Thomas Wachtel; Larry Honzel; Robert O'Rourke; Arthur Ries.
Res.: 551 E. Ogden Ave., 61254. Tel: 309-944-2250; Fax: 309-944-5319. Email: office@saintmalachy.org. Web: saintmalachy.org.
School—595 E. Ogden Ave., 61254. Tel: 309-944-3230. Mr. Stan Griffin, Prin. Lay Teachers 7; Students 111.
Catechesis/Religious Program—Tel: 309-944-3518. M. Elizabeth Fristensky, D.R.E. Students 200.

GEORGETOWN, VERMILION CO., ST. ISAAC JOGUES (1942) Rev. John Paninski, M.S.
Res.: 109 W. Seventh St., 61846-1404. Tel: 217-662-6708.
Catechesis/Religious Program—Students 5.

GRANVILLE, PUTNAM CO., SACRED HEART OF JESUS (1908), (Italian), [CEM] Rev. Patrick DeMeulemeester.
Res.: 311 Hennepin St., P.O. Box 217, 61326. Tel: 815-339-2138; Fax: 815-339-2880. Email: shgsph@mchsi.com.
Catechesis/Religious Program—Students 64.

HAVANA, MASON CO., ST. PATRICK'S (1865) [CEM] Rev. Richard W. Brunskill; Deacons Stanley Buczko; Jon Dosher.
Res.: 545 S. Orange, 62644. Tel: 309-543-6373; Fax: 309-543-3241.
Catechesis/Religious Program—Students 85.
Mission—Immaculate Conception 505 S. Adams, Manito, Mason Co. 61546. Tel: 309-968-6826. Deacons William Meyer; Robert Sondag.

HENNEPIN, PUTNAM CO., ST. PATRICK'S (1865) [CEM] Rev. Patrick DeMeulemeester.
Res.: 10 St. & Dore, P.O. Box 217, Granville, 61326. Tel: 815-925-7500; 815-339-2138 (Office); Fax: 815-339-2880. Email: shgsph@mchsi.com.
Catechesis/Religious Program—Students 38.

HENRY, MARSHALL CO.
1—ST. JOSEPH'S (1878) [CEM 2] Rev. Thomas R. Mizeur.
1002 School St., P.O. Box 75, 61537. Email: iccc@grics.net. In Res., Sisters Anita Pauwels, O.S.F.; Alice Rogers, O.S.F.
Tri-Parish Offices: 415 N. High St., Lacon, 61540. Tel: 309-246-5145; Fax: 309-246-5417.
Church: 1002 N. School St., 61537. Tel: 309-364-2063 (Convent).
Catechesis/Religious Program—Students 8.
2—ST. MARY'S (1851) [CEM 2] Rev. Thomas R. Mizeur.
Tri-Parish Offices: 415 N. High St., Lacon, 61540. Tel: 309-246-5145.
Res.: 401 South St., 61537. Tel: 309-364-2525; Fax: 309-246-5417. Email: iccc@grics.net.
Church: 401 South St., P.O. Box 75, 61537. Tel: 309-364-2525; Fax: 309-246-5417.
Catechesis/Religious Program—Mary Ann Magnuson, D.R.E. Twinned with St. Joseph's, Henry Students 65.

HOOPESTON, VERMILION CO., ST. ANTHONY CHURCH (1877) Rev. Bowan M. Schmitt.
Church: 423 S. Third St., P.O. Box 414, 60942. Tel: 217-283-6211; Fax: 217-283-6252. Email: stanthonyhoopeston@cell1net.net.
Catechesis/Religious Program—Tel: 219-283-6249. Email: drestanthony@cell1net.net. Students 60.

HOOPPOLE, HENRY CO., ST. MARY'S, Attended by Annawan. Temporarily closed.

IVESDALE, CHAMPAIGN CO., ST. JOSEPH'S (1863), (Irish), [CEM] Rev. Msgr. Albert W. Hallin.
Church: P.O. Box 175, 61851.
Catechesis/Religious Program—James Brewer, D.R.E. Students 28.

KEWANEE, HENRY CO.
1—ST. FRANCIS OF ASSISI (1906) Rev. James G. Pallardy.
Res.: 410 W. Central Blvd., 61443. Tel: 309-852-2761; Fax: 309-852-0222.
Catechesis/Religious Program—Students 66.
2—ST. MARY'S CATHOLIC CHURCH (1855) [CEM 2] Rev. James G. Pallardy; Deacons Martin Van Meltebeck; John T. Mock; Raymond Van Wassenhove.
Res.: 406 W. Central Blvd., 61443-2010. Tel: 309-852-4549; Fax: 309-853-4106. Email: stmarykewanee@hotmail.com.
School—Visitation, 107 S. Lexington, 61443. Tel: 309-856-7451; Fax: 309-852-4259. Mr. David Hobin, Prin. Lay Teachers 13; Students 117.
Catechesis/Religious Program—Tel: 309-856-5451. Deacon Martin Van Meltebeck, D.R.E. Students 107.

KICKAPOO, (EDWARDS) PEORIA CO., ST. MARY OF KICKAPOO (1837) Rev. Joseph Dondanville.
Res.: 9910 W. Knox St., Kickapoo (Edwards), 61528. Tel: 309-691-2030 (Church); Fax: 309-691-2898.
School—Tel: 309-691-3015. Mr. Ron Dwyer, Prin. Lay Teachers 10; Students 141.
Catechesis/Religious Program—Students 45.

LA SALLE, LA SALLE CO.
1—ST. HYACINTH'S (1875) [CEM] Very Rev. Robert Rayson; Rev. Adam Stimpson, Parochial Vicar; Deacon Ronald Rager.
Res.: 913 Fifth St., 61301. Tel: 815-223-1459; Fax: 815-223-1580.
Church: 927 10th St., 61301.
School—Trinity Catholic Academy, 650 Fourth St., 61301. Tel: 815-223-8523; Fax: 815-223-5366. Mr. Roy Pesch, Prin. Lay Teachers 16; Students 168.
Catechesis/Religious Program— Attend at Resurrection, La Salle. Students 156.
2—ST. PATRICK'S (1838), (Irish), [CEM] Very Rev. Robert Rayson; Rev. Adam Stimpson, Parochial Vicar; Deacon Ronald Rager. In Res., Rev. Msgr. Deogratias Rweyongeza.
Res.: *c/o Resurrection Church*, 913 Fifth St., 61301. Tel: 815-223-1459.
Church: 725 Fourth St., 61301. Tel: 815-223-0641; Fax: 815-223-0523.
School—Trinity Catholic Academy, (Grades PreSchool-8) Tel: 815-223-1166; Fax: 815-223-7650. Mr. Roy Pesch, Prin. Lay Teachers 21; Students 210.
Catechesis/Religious Program— Attend at St. Hyacinth, La Salle.
3—RESURRECTION (1979), (Suspended) Very Rev. Robert Rayson; Rev. Adam Stimpson; Deacon Ronald Rager.
Res.: 913 Fifth St., 61301. Tel: 815-223-1459; Fax: 815-223-1580.
4—SHRINE OF QUEEN OF THE HOLY ROSARY (1925), (Italian), [JC], (Suspended) Very Rev. Robert Rayson. In Res., Rev. Msgr. Deogratias Rweyongeza.
Res.: *c/o Resurrection Church*, 913 5th St., 61301. Tel: 815-223-1459.
Church: 725 4th St., 61301. Tel: 815-233-7129.
Catechesis/Religious Program— Attend at Resurrection, La Salle.

LACON, MARSHALL CO., IMMACULATE CONCEPTION (1853) [CEM] Revs. Thomas R. Mizeur; Harold F. Schmitt; Ronald Enderlin; Deacon J. Robert Murphy. In Res., Rev. Arthur D. Meyer (Retired).
Office & Rectory: 415 High St., 61540. Tel: 309-246-5145; Fax: 309-246-5417. Email: iccc@grics.net.
Church: 418 N. Center St., 61540.
Catechesis/Religious Program—Katie Bogner, D.R.E. Students 28.

LADD, BUREAU CO., ST. BENEDICT'S (1893), Parish Suspended.
Res.: 314 Bureau St., 61329. Tel: 815-894-2319; Fax: 815-894-2265.

LEONORE, LA SALLE CO., SS. PETER AND PAUL'S (1860), (German), [CEM] Rev. Charles A. McCarthy, C.S.Sp.
Res.: 957 N. 17th Rd., Tonica, 61370. Tel: 815-856-2502; Fax: 815-856-2503.
Catechesis/Religious Program—Students 20.

LEWISTOWN, FULTON CO., ST. MARY'S (1865) [CEM] Rev. Msgr. Robert W. O'Connor.
Res.: 705 N. Broadway St., P.O. Box 106, 61542. Tel: 309-547-3226; Fax: 309-547-3226.
Catechesis/Religious Program—Students 6.
Mission—St. Michael St. David, Fulton Co.

LINCOLN, LOGAN CO., HOLY FAMILY (1857) [CEM 2] Revs. Jeffrey G. Laible; Huy (John) Quoc Pham.
Res.: 316 S. Logan St., 62656. Tel: 217-732-4019; Fax: 217-735-2650. Web: www.holyfamilylincoln.com.
School—Carroll Catholic School, (Grades PreSchool-8), 111 Fourth St., 62656. Tel: 217-732-7518; Fax: 217-732-7518. Web: www.carrollcatholic.com. John W. Link, Prin.; Vanessa Tibbs, Librarian. Lay Teachers 12; Students 114.

Catechesis/Religious Program—Holy Family Religious Education Center, Tel: 217-735-3520. Students 86.
Mission—St. Mary's Atlanta, Logan Co. 61723.

LORETTO, LIVINGSTON CO., ST. MARY'S (1873), (German), Closed. For inquiries contact St. Patrick, Dwight.

LOSTANT, LA SALLE CO., ST. JOHN THE BAPTIST'S (1862) [CEM] Rev. Luke Poczworowski, O.F.M.Conv.
Res.: P.O. Box 486, Wenona, 61377. Tel: 815-853-4558; Fax: 815-853-0111. Email: smary1867@mchsi.com.
Church: 301 S. Sheridan, 61334. Tel: 815-368-3339.
Catechesis/Religious Program—Dorothy Applebee, D.R.E. Combined with St. Mary's, Wenona

MACOMB, MCDONOUGH CO., ST. PAUL'S (1854) [CEM] Rev. Msgr. Richard A. Pricco; Deacon Lawrence Adams.
Res.: 309 W. Jackson, 61455. Tel: 309-833-2496. Web: www.stpaul.macomb.com.
School—(Grades PreK-6), 322 W. Washington St., 61455. Tel: 309-833-2470; Fax: 309-833-2470. Email: stpaul@macomb.com. Mrs. Barbara Shrode, Prin. Lay Teachers 8; Students (K-6) 118; Preschool 42.
Catechesis/Religious Program—325 W. Jackson St., 61455. Tel: 309-837-1024. Students 81.
Mission—Sacred Heart Tennessee, McDonough Co.

MAHOMET, CHAMPAIGN CO., OUR LADY OF THE LAKE (1981) Rev. John C. Horton; Deacon Edward Mueller.
Res.: 703 N. Craig Dr., P.O. Box 109, 61853. Tel: 217-586-5153; Fax: 217-586-5924.
Catechesis/Religious Program—Tel: 217-586-2798. Mr. Roger L. Phelps, D.R.E. Students 312.

MARSEILLES, LA SALLE CO., ST. JOSEPH'S (1881) Rev. Msgr. J. Brian Rejsek.
Res.: 200 Broadway St., 61341. Tel: 815-795-2240; Fax: 815-795-2240.
Catechesis/Religious Program—Tel: 815-795-2251. Students 73.

MATHERVILLE, MERCER CO., ST. ANTHONY'S CHURCH (1916) [CEM 2] Rev. John Thieryoung.
Office: c/o 106 N.E. 4th St., Aledo, 61231. Tel: 309-582-7500; Fax: 309-582-5163.
Catechesis/Religious Program—Students 74.
Mission—St. John Viola, Mercer Co. 61486. Tel: 309-596-2950.

MENDOTA, LA SALLE CO., HOLY CROSS (1863) [CEM] Revs. Fredi Gomez Torres, Admin.; Gary W. Blake, Parochial Vicar; Deacons Vincent Slomian; Raymond Fischer.
Res.: 1010 Jefferson St., 61342. Tel: 815-538-6151; Fax: 815-539-5014. Web: holycrossmendota.com.
School—1008 Jefferson St., 61342. Tel: 815-539-7003; Fax: 815-539-9082. Mrs. Anita Kobilsek, Prin. Lay Teachers 13; Students 127.
Catechesis/Religious Program— Karen Zolper, D.R.E. Students 195.

METAMORA, WOODFORD CO.

1—ST. MARY OF LOURDES (1831) [CEM] Rev. Neri Greskoviak, O.F.M.; Bro. Xavier Gedeon, O.F.M., Pastoral Assoc.; Deacons Jack Gaetz; Robert Heiple; William Read; Larry DeCapp.
Res.: 424 Lourdes Church Rd., 61548. Tel: 309-383-4460; Fax: 309-383-4467. Email: stmarylo@ontco.com. Web: www.germantownhills.com/lourdes.
Catechesis/Religious Program—Students 175.

2—ST. MARY'S (1864), (German), [CEM] Rev. Donald F. Roszkowski; Deacon Joseph Lowry; Sharon Elbert, Business Mgr.
Res.: 415 W. Chatham St., P.O. Box 319, 61548. Tel: 309-367-4407; Fax: 309-367-9456. Email: lselbert@mtco.com. Web: stmarysmetamora.com.
School—Tel: 309-367-2528; Fax: 309-367-2169. Ryan Bustle, Prin. Lay Teachers 15; Students 134.
Catechesis/Religious Program—Alan Anderson, D.R.E. Students 125.
Mission—St. Elizabeth Washburn, Woodford Co.

MILAN, ROCK ISLAND CO., ST. AMBROSE (1924) Rev. Anthony M. Ego.
Res.: 312 W. First St., 61264. Tel: 309-787-4593; Fax: 309-787-6403. Email: stambrosemilan@att.net. Web: ambroseparish.faithweb.com.
Catechesis/Religious Program—Tel: 309-787-6403. Diane Hansen, D.R.E. Students 67.

MINONK, WOODFORD CO., ST. PATRICK'S (1878) [CEM] Rev. Luke Poczworowski, O.F.M.Conv.
Res.: 207 W. Third St., Wenona, 61377.
Church & Office: 420 E. Sixth St., Box 107, 61760-0107. Tel: 309-432-2700; Fax: 815-432-3399.
Catechesis/Religious Program—Students 71.

MOLINE, ROCK ISLAND CO.

1—CHRIST THE KING (1967) Rev. Donald L. Levitt.
Parish Center—3205 60th St., 61265. Tel: 309-762-4634; Fax: 309-762-7848. Email: ctkenter@netexpress.net. Web: christtheking.org.
Catechesis/Religious Program—Tel: 309-762-4634, Ext. 206. Sharon Dodd, D.R.E. (PreK-6 & Junior High); Sr. Charlotte Seubert, F.S.P.A., D.R.E.; Paul Fritch, Youth Min.; Kim Van DeRostyne, Youth Min. Students 177.

2—ST. MARY'S (1875) [CEM] Rev. Francisco Trujillo; Deacon Russell W. Swim.
Res.: 412 10th St., 61265. Tel: 309-764-1562; Fax: 309-764-0317. Email: stmarysmolineil@hotmail.com. Web: www.parishesonline.com.
Catechesis/Religious Program—Tel: 309-762-6575. Meaghan Terry, D.R.E.; Bonnie Howard, D.R.E. Students 273.

3—SACRED HEART (1906), (Belgian), Rev. Msgr. Dale L. Wellman; Rev. Douglas A. Grandon; Sr. Kathleen Mullin, Pastoral Assoc.; Deacons Dennis De Vooght; Patrick Murphy.
Lee Parish Center—1608 13th St., 61265. Tel: 309-762-2362; Fax: 309-757-5502. Email: shchurch@netexpress.net.
School—Seton Catholic School, (Grades PreK-8), 1320 16th Ave., 61265. Tel: 309-757-5502; Fax: 309-762-0545. Sisters 1; Lay Teachers 34; Students 572.
Catechesis/Religious Program— Sara Tucker, D.R.E. Students 126.

MONMOUTH, WARREN CO., IMMACULATE CONCEPTION (1864) [CEM] Rev. Anthony Bernas; Deacon William Clark.
Church: 210 W. Broadway, 61462. Tel: 309-734-7533; Fax: 309-734-7120.
School—115 North B St., 61462. Tel: 309-734-6037; Fax: 309-734-6082. Kathryn Bennett, Prin. Lay Teachers 11; Students 139.
Catechesis/Religious Program—Rita Selby, D.R.E. Students 83.

MONTICELLO, PIATT CO., ST. PHILOMENA Rev. Bruce Lopez; Deacon Gene Triplett.
Res.: 1301 N. Market St., 61856. Tel: 217-762-2566; Fax: 217-762-8666. Web: www.stphilomenaonline.org.
Catechesis/Religious Program—Students 221.

MORTON, TAZEWELL CO., BLESSED SACRAMENT (1957) Rev. Mark A. DeSutter; Deacons Rick Miller; David Steeples; Kevin Zeeb.
Res.: 225 E. Greenwood St., 61550. Tel: 309-266-9721. Web: www.mortonblessedsacrament.org.
School—233 E. Greenwood St., 61550. Tel: 309-263-8442; Fax: 309-263-8443. Mr. James Eckhart, Prin. Lay Teachers 18; Students 274.
Catechesis/Religious Program—Tel: 309-266-6791. Students 248.

NAUVOO, HANCOCK CO., SS. PETER AND PAUL (1848), (German), [CEM 2] Revs. Anthony J. Trosley; Thomas Szydlik.
Res.: 190 N. Wells St., P.O. Box 147, 62354. Tel: 217-453-2428; Fax: 217-453-2015. Email: ssppnauvoo@gmail.com.
School—Tel: 217-453-2511. Email: sppskids@mchsi.com. Mrs. Therese Hayes, Prin. Lay Teachers 7; Students 57.
Catechesis/Religious Program—Students 25.
Mission—Sacred Heart Dallas City, Hancock Co. 62330.

NORMAL, MCLEAN CO., EPIPHANY (1966) [JC] Rev. Msgr. Eric S. Powell; Revs. Julius Turyatoranwa; Johndamasceni Zilimu (Tanzania).
Res.: 1006 E. College Ave., 61761. Tel: 309-452-2585; 309-452-3223; Fax: 309-452-4851. Email: admin@epiphanyparish.com.
School—1002 E. College Ave., 61761. Tel: 309-452-3268; Fax: 309-454-8087. Web: epiphanyschools.org. Mr. Richard Morehouse, Prin. Lay Teachers 24; Students 375.
Catechesis/Religious Program—Deacon Mark Cleary, D.R.E. Students 254.

ODELL, LIVINGSTON CO., ST. PAUL'S (1873), (Irish), [CEM 2] Rev. Peter A. Pilon.
Res.: 313 W. Hamilton, P.O. Box 307, 60460. Tel: 815-998-2197; Fax: 815-998-2197. Email: stpaul.odell@mchsi.com.
School—Tel: 815-998-2194; Fax: 815-998-1514. Email: stpaulodell@catholic.org. Sr. Maria Semonski, Prin. Lay Teachers 6; Students 68; Religious 1.
Catechesis/Religious Program—Students 3.
Mission—Sacred Heart 205 N. Elm St., P.O. Box 68, Campus, 60920.

OGLESBY, LA SALLE CO., HOLY FAMILY (1953) Rev. Michael J. Andrejek.
Res.: 311 N. Woodland Ave., 61348. Tel: 815-883-8233; Fax: 815-883-8771.
School—336 Alice Ave., 61348. Tel: 815-883-8916; Fax: 815-883-8943. Mrs. Jyll Jasick, Prin. Lay Teachers 14; Students 174.
Catechesis/Religious Program—Students 100.

OHIO, BUREAU CO., IMMACULATE CONCEPTION CHURCH (1875), (Irish), [CEM] Rev. Daniel J. Wilder.
Res.: *c/o St. John's*, 204 N. Main St., Walnut, 61376-0370. Tel: 815-379-2602; Fax: 815-379-2302.
Church: 101 N. Main St., P.O. Box 358, 61349.
Catechesis/Religious Program—Gayle Thomas, D.R.E. Students 24.

ORION, HENRY CO., MARY, OUR LADY OF PEACE (1960) Rev. James P. DeBisschop.
Res.: 1402 10th St., P.O. Box 175, 61273-0175. Tel: 309-526-8422; Fax: 309-526-8469.
Catechesis/Religious Program—Students 116.

OTTAWA, LA SALLE CO.

1—ST. COLUMBA (1844), (Irish), [CEM] Revs. David M. Kipfer; Raymond P. Guthrie.
Res.: 122 W. Washington St., 61350. Tel: 815-433-0700; Fax: 815-433-0305. Email: stcolumbaottawa@hotmail.com. Web: www.geocities.com/scsottawa/.
School—(Grades PreK-8), 1110 LaSalle St., 61350. Tel: 815-433-1199; Fax: 815-433-1219. Email: saintcolumbaschool@gmail.com. Michael I. Nadeau, Prin. Lay Teachers 13; Students 170.
Catechesis/Religious Program—Students 118.
Mission—St. Mary's 2098 E. 22nd Rd., Grand Ridge, La Salle Co. 61235. Tel: 815-433-0700.

2—ST. FRANCIS OF ASSISI (1858) [CEM] Rev. Msgr. Jerome Ham.
Res.: 820 Sanger St., 61350. Tel: 815-434-0969; Fax: 815-434-1073.
Catechesis/Religious Program—Mrs. Mary Beth Mann, D.R.E. Students 100.

3—ST. MARY'S (1927) Revs. Philip Halfacre, Admin.; Lourduraj Ignatius, S.A.C. (India).
Mailing Address: 2005 Center St., P.O. Box 2552, Ottawa (Naplate), 61350. Tel: 815-433-2404; Fax: 815-433-9458.
Catechesis/Religious Program—Students 40.
Convent—2005 Center St., 61350. Tel: 815-433-2637. Dominican Sisters 2.

4—ST. PATRICK'S (1893), (Irish), Revs. Philip Halfacre; Lourduraj Ignatius, S.A.C. (India).
Res.: 726 W. Jefferson St., 61350. Tel: 815-434-0768; Fax: 815-434-0793.
School—801 W. Jefferson St., 61350. Tel: 815-433-2889; Fax: 815-431-9419. Email: st.patrick@mchsi.com. Web: stpatrickottawa.catholicweb.com. Harold Garner, Prin. Lay Teachers 12; Students 197.
Catechesis/Religious Program—Mrs. Mary Jean Weihman, D.R.E. Students 115.
Convent—2005 Center St., 61350. Tel: 815-433-2637.

PEKIN, TAZEWELL CO., ST. JOSEPH'S (1863) [CEM 2] Revs. Timothy Nolan; Patrick Fixsen; Lawrence A. Morlan; Deacons Charles Murray; Martin Pogioli; Mark Wilder; Ernie Whited; Tim Blanchard.
Res.: 303 S. Seventh St., 61554. Tel: 309-347-6108; Fax: 309-347-6959.
School—300 S. Sixth St., 61554. Tel: 309-347-7194; Fax: 309-347-7196. Shannon Rogers, Prin. Lay Teachers 13; Students 192.
Catechesis/Religious Program—Tina Sondag, D.R.E. Students 200.

PENFIELD, CHAMPAIGN CO., ST. LAWRENCE'S (1898) [CEM] Rev. Michael Menner.
Res.: P.O. Box 49, 61862. Tel: 217-595-5560; 217-595-5620 (Office); Fax: 217-595-5439.
Catechesis/Religious Program—Students 27.
Mission—St. Charles Borromeo Homer, Champaign Co. 61849.

PERU, LA SALLE CO.

1—ST. JOSEPH'S (1854) [CEM] Rev. Harold L. Datzman, O.S.B.
Res.: 1925 5th St., P.O. Box 608, 61354. Tel: 815-223-0718; Fax: 815-223-5690.
Catechesis/Religious Program—Kristi Bejster, D.R.E. Students 130.

2—ST. MARY (1867), (Irish), Rev. William M. Gardner.
Mailing Address: P.O. Box 150, Spring Valley, 61362.
Res.: 1109 Pulaski St., 61354. Tel: 815-223-0315.
Church: 1325 Sixth St., 61354.
See Peru Catholic School System, Peru under St. Joseph's, Peru for details.
Catechesis/Religious Program—Students 12.

3—ST. VALENTINE (1891), (Polish), [CEM] Rev. William M. Gardner.
Res.: 1109 Pulaski St., 61354. Tel: 815-223-0315.
See Peru Catholic School System, Peru under St. Joseph's, Peru for details.
Catechesis/Religious Program—Students 89.

PESOTUM, CHAMPAIGN CO.

1—ST. JOSEPH (1904), (German), [CEM], (Suspended) Rev. Msgr. James K. Ramer.
Res.: P.O. Box 266, Philo, 61864. Tel: 217-684-2571; Fax: 217-684-2186.

2—ST. MARY (1875), (German), [CEM] Rev. Msgr. James K. Ramer.
Res.: P.O. Box 266, Philo, 61864. Tel: 217-684-2571; Fax: 217-684-2186. Email: churchstthomasphilo@comcast.net.
Catechesis/Religious Program— See St. Thomas, Philo

PETERSTOWN, LA SALLE CO., SS. PETER AND PAUL (1872) [CEM] Revs. Gary W. Blake; Fredi Gomez Torres.
Res.: 1010 Jefferson St., Mendota, 61342. Tel: 815-538-6151; Fax: 815-539-5014.

PHILO, CHAMPAIGN CO., ST. THOMAS (1869) [CEM] Rev. Msgr. James K. Ramer, Admin.
Res.: 310 E. Madison, P.O. Box 266, 61864. Tel:

217-684-2571; Fax: 217-684-2186.
School—Tel: 217-684-2309; Fax: 217-684-2217. Web: www.stthomasphilo.org. Mrs. Anita Crain, Prin. Lay Teachers 10; Students 80.
Catechesis/Religious Program— Combined with Immaculate Conception Mission and St. Mary, Pesotum. Students 90.
Mission—Immaculate Conception [CEM] Bongard, Champaign Co. 61864.

PONTIAC, LIVINGSTON CO., ST. MARY'S (1877) [CEM] Rev. Msgr. Thomas E. Mack; Rev. David Sabel, Parochial Vicar.
Res.: 119 E. Howard St., P.O. Box 374, 61764. Tel: 815-844-7683; Fax: 815-842-4345.
School—414 N. Main St., 61764. Tel: 815-844-6585; Fax: 815-844-6987. Mrs. Sharon Warfield, Prin. Lay Teachers 14; Students 198.
Catechesis/Religious Program—Students 90.
Mission—St. Joseph Flanagan, Livingston Co. 61740. Tel: 815-844-7683.

PRINCETON, BUREAU CO., ST. LOUIS (1865) Rev. Jeffrey D. Stirniman.
Res.: 616 S. Gosse Blvd., 61356. Tel: 815-879-0181; Fax: 815-879-0181. Email: rectory@stlchurch.comcastbiz.net.
School—(Grades PreSchool-8), 631 Park Ave. W., 61356. Tel: 815-872-8521; Fax: 815-879-8010. Email: stlouiscs@comcast.net. Web: www.stlschool.net. Mrs. Mary Paula Schmitt, Prin. Sisters 1; Lay Teachers 13; Students 107.
Catechesis/Religious Program—Tel: 815-872-7016. Students 100.

PRINCEVILLE, PEORIA CO., ST. MARY OF THE WOODS (1867) [CEM] Rev. Patrick M. Riordan; Deacon Frederick J. Kruse.
Res.: 119 Saint Mary St., 61559-9244. Tel: 309-385-4370; 309-385-2578 (Office); Fax: 309-385-1754. Email: smowmo@verizon.net.
Catechesis/Religious Program—Students 60.

RANSOM, LA SALLE CO., ST. PATRICK'S (1883) [CEM] Rev. Msgr. John J. Prendergast.
Res.: 404 N. Park St., Streator, 61364. Tel: 815-672-2034; Fax: 815-673-3796. Email: immaculateconceptionparish@verizon.net.
Church: 110 Wallace, P.O. Box 127, 60470. Tel: 815-672-2474; Fax: 815-672-2040.
Catechesis/Religious Program—Students 12.

RANTOUL, CHAMPAIGN CO., ST. MALACHY (1888) [CEM] Revs. Michael Bies; Stanley J. Malinowski, Pastor Emeritus (Retired).
Res.: 340 E. Belle Ave., Ste. 1, 61866. Email: stmalachychurch@catholicweb.com. Web: stmalachychurch.catholicweb.com.
School—340 E. Belle Ave., 61866. Tel: 217-892-2011; Fax: 217-892-5780. Email: stmalachyschool@catholicweb.com. Web: stmalachyschool.catholicweb.com. Mr. James Flaherty, Prin. Sisters 1; Lay Teachers 13; Students 151.
Catechesis/Religious Program—Sr. Sara Koch, O.P., C.R.E. Students 73.
Convent—Dominican Sisters (Springfield), 304 E. Belle Ave., 61866. Tel: 217-892-2870.

RAPIDS CITY, ROCK ISLAND CO., ST. JOHN THE BAPTIST (1857) [CEM] Rev. Steven P. Loftus.
Res.: 1416 Third Ave., P.O. Box 250, 61278. Tel: 309-496-2414. Email: stjohnrc@mchsi.com.
Catechesis/Religious Program—Fax: 309-496-3414. Students 65.
Mission—St. Mary 708 State Ave., Rte. 84, Hampton, Rock Island Co. 61256. Tel: 309-496-3414.

RARITAN, HENDERSON CO., CHURCH OF ST. PATRICK (1876), (Irish), Rev. Kenneth J. Hummel.
Res.: P.O. Box 24, 61471. Tel: 309-837-3989.
Catechesis/Religious Program—Students 33.

ROANOKE, WOODFORD CO., ST. JOSEPH (1874) Rev. Msgr. Charles J. Beebe.
Res.: 508 W. Randolph, 61561. Tel: 309-923-3031; Fax: 309-926-3031.
Catechesis/Religious Program—Jennifer Peterson, D.R.E. Students 45.

ROCK ISLAND, ROCK ISLAND CO.

1—ST. JOSEPH'S (1876), (Suspended) Rev. Gregory Jozefiak.
Res.: 2208-4th Ave., 61201. Tel: 309-788-3322; Fax: 309-788-9367.

2—ST. MARY (1851), (German), (Formerly Immaculate Conception) Revs. Gregory Jozefiak; George J. Schroeder, Pastor Emeritus (Retired).
Rectory—2208 4th Ave., 61201-8904. Tel: 309-788-3322; Fax: 309-788-9367.

3—ST. PIUS X (1955) Revs. R. Michael Schaab; Peter Zorjan; Deacons Timothy Granet; Paul Martin; Philip Sailer; Joseph Dockery-Jackson; Jack Kettering.
Res.: 2502 29th Ave., 61201. Tel: 309-793-7373; Fax: 309-793-7376.
See Jordan Catholic School of Rock Island, Inc., Rock Island under Elementary Schools, Inter-Parochial located in the Institution section.
Catechesis/Religious Program—Students 120.

4—SACRED HEART (1900) Rev. Gregory Jozefiak.
Res.: *St. Mary's Church*, 2208 4th Ave., 61201. Tel: 309-788-3322. Email: shrec@qconline.com.
School—Jordan Catholic School of Rock Island, Tel: 309-793-7350; Fax: 309-793-7361. Web: www.jordanschool.com. Lay Teachers 30; Students 537. See Jordan Catholic School of Rock Island, Inc., Rock Island under Elementary Schools, Inter-Parochial located in the Institution section.
Catechesis/Religious Program—Students 35.

RUSHVILLE, SCHUYLER CO., ST. ROSE (1870) [JC] Rev. Msgr. Richard A. Pricco, Admin. In Res., Rev. Thomas Tibainuguka (Tanzania).
Res.: 319 N. Franklin St., P.O. Box 194, 62681-0292. Tel: 217-322-3424; Fax: 309-833-1560.
Catechesis/Religious Program—Students 51.

RUTLAND, LA SALLE CO., SACRED HEART (1895), (Irish), [CEM] Closed. Now a mission of St. Ann, Toluca.

ST. AUGUSTINE, KNOX CO., ST. AUGUSTINE (1863) [CEM] Rev. Thomas B. Holloway.
Mailing Address: c/o 376 W. Hail, Bushnell, 61422. Tel: 301-462-3421; 309-772-2333.
Catechesis/Religious Program—Students 15.

SENECA, LA SALLE CO., ST. PATRICK'S (1856) [CEM] Rev. Msgr. Raymond J. Boyle.
Parish Center—176 W. Union, 61360. Tel: 815-357-6239; Fax: 815-357-6476.
Catechesis/Religious Program—Tel: 815-357-8509. Students 115.

SEYMOUR, CHAMPAIGN CO., ST. BONIFACE (1878) [CEM] Rev. Msgr. Albert W. Hallin.
Church & Res.: 416 County Rd., 1100 N., 61875. Tel: 217-863-2190; Fax: 217-863-2190.
Catechesis/Religious Program—

SHEFFIELD, BUREAU CO., ST. PATRICK'S (1854) [CEM] Rev. Jerry Logan.
Res.: 305 W. South Ave., Annawan, 61234. Tel: 309-935-6911.
Church: 231 W. Atkinson St., P.O. Box 338, 61361-0038.
Catechesis/Religious Program—Mary Jo Nelson, D.R.E. Students 36.

SILVIS, ROCK ISLAND CO., OUR LADY OF GUADALUPE (1927) Revs. Keith A. Walder; Raymond P. Guthrie.
Res.: 800 17th St., 61282. Tel: 309-792-3867; Fax: 309-792-2241. Web: www.olgsilvis.net.
Catechesis/Religious Program—Cheri Smith, D.R.E. Students 31.

SPRING VALLEY, BUREAU CO.

1—ST. ANNE'S, Closed. For sacramental records contact St. Anthony Church, Spring Valley.

2—ST. ANTHONY (1904), (Italian), Rev. Robert D. Spilman.
Res.: 510 Richard A. Mautino Dr., P.O. Box 150, 61362-0150. Tel: 815-663-3731; Fax: 815-663-0012.
Catechesis/Religious Program—Tel: 815-663-3731. Students 73.

3—IMMACULATE CONCEPTION (1884) [CEM] Rev. Robert D. Spilman.
Mailing Address: P.O. Box 150, 61362.
Res.: 510 Richard A. Mautino Dr., 61362. Tel: 815-663-3731; Fax: 815-663-0012.
Catechesis/Religious Program—

4—SS. PETER AND PAUL'S (1891), (Polish), [CEM], Parish Suspended. Rev. Robert Spilman.
Mailing Address: P.O. Box 150, 61362.
Mission—St. Gertrude

STREATOR, LA SALLE CO.

1—ST. ANTHONY OF PADUA (1881) [CEM] Rev. Msgr. John J. Prendergast; Rev. Ronald E. Dodd, Parochial Vicar.
Res.: 407 S. Park St., 61364. Tel: 815-672-4523; Fax: 815-672-0378. Email: gibbons@sasfriars.org. Web: sasfriars.org.
School—410 S. Park St., 61364. Tel: 815-672-3847; Fax: 815-673-3590. Email: stanthsc@sasfriars.org. Web: www.sasfriars.org. Sr. Carol Royston, Prin. Lay Teachers 16; Students 147.

2—ST. CASIMIR (1916), (Polish), [CEM], (Suspended) Rev. Msgr. John J. Prendergast, Admin.
Res.: 405 Illinois St., 61364. Tel: 815-672-2206.
Catechesis/Religious Program—

3—IMMACULATE CONCEPTION (1868) [CEM] Rev. Msgr. John J. Prendergast; Rev. Ronald E. Dodd, Parochial Vicar.
Res.: 404 N. Park St., 61364. Tel: 815-672-2034; Fax: 815-673-3796. Email: immaculateconceptionparish@verizon.net.
Catechesis/Religious Program—407 S. Park St., 61364. Tel: 815-672-5911. Students 41.

4—ST. STEPHEN'S (1884), (Slovak), [CEM 2] Rev. Msgr. John J. Prendergast; Rev. Ronald E. Dodd, Parochial Vicar.
Res.: 711 Lundy St., 61364. Tel: 815-672-2474; Fax: 815-672-2040. Email: ststephen@mchsi.com.
Catechesis/Religious Program—Tel: 815-672-5911. Students 91.

THOMASBORO, CHAMPAIGN CO., ST. ELIZABETH OF HUNGARY (1893) [CEM] Rev. Msgr. Albert W. Hallin; Rev. Stanley J. Malinowski, Pastor Emeritus (Retired).
Res.: 100 Church St., Box 307, 61878. Tel: 217-643-3395; Fax: 217-643-2217. Email: stelizabethparish@mchsi.com.
Catechesis/Religious Program—Students 16.

TISKILWA, BUREAU CO., ST. MARY'S (1881) [CEM] Closed. Now a mission of St. Mary, Depue.

TOLONO, CHAMPAIGN CO., ST. PATRICK'S (1859) [CEM] Rev. William Keebler.
Res.: 212 E. Washington St., P.O. Box K, 61880. Tel: 217-485-5194.
Catechesis/Religious Program—Email: stpatrickstolono@hotmail.com. Students 72.

TOLUCA, MARSHALL CO., ST. ANN'S (1895), (Italian), [CEM] Rev. Edward S. Kopec.
Res.: 311 W. Santa Fe Ave., Box 165, 61369. Tel: 815-452-2043.
Catechesis/Religious Program—Mrs. Rose Hansen, D.R.E.
Mission—Sacred Heart Rutland, La Salle Co. 61358.

URBANA, CHAMPAIGN CO., ST. PATRICK'S (1901) Rev. Joseph T. Hogan; Deacon Clifford Maduzia.
Res.: 708 W. Main St., 61801. Tel: 217-367-2665; Fax: 217-383-1002. Web: www.stpaturbana.org.
Catechesis/Religious Program—Carolyn McElrath, D.R.E. Students 297.

UTICA, LA SALLE CO., ST. MARY (1858) [CEM] Rev. Msgr. James J. Swaner.
Res.: 303 Division St., 61373. Tel: 815-667-4677; Fax: 815-667-4097. Email: stmaryutica@att.net.
Catechesis/Religious Program—Students 89.

WALNUT, BUREAU CO., ST. JOHN THE EVANGELIST (1912) Rev. Daniel J. Wilder.
Res.: 204 N. Main St., P.O. Box 370, 61376-0370. Tel: 815-379-2602; Fax: 815-379-2302. Email: stjohns1912@mchsi.com.
Catechesis/Religious Program—Students 36.

WAPELLA, DE WITT CO., ST. PATRICK CHURCH (1858) [CEM] Rev. Patrick Henehan.
Res.: 308 S. Locust St., 61777. Tel: 217-935-9242; Fax: 217-935-4101.
Catechesis/Religious Program—Students 50.

WARSAW, HANCOCK CO., SACRED HEART (1874), (German), [CEM] Rev. Michael L. Menner.
Res.: 245 S. 9th St., 62379. Tel: 217-256-3657. Email: shc@mchsi.com.
Catechesis/Religious Program—Students 21.
Mission—St. Mary 560 Lakeview Ave., Hamilton, Hancock Co. 62341. Deacon Greggory Golemo.

WASHBURN, WOODFORD CO., ST. ELIZABETH, [CEM] Closed. Now a mission of St. Mary, Metamora.

WASHINGTON, TAZEWELL CO., ST. PATRICK'S (1941) Rev. Joseph P. Donton; Deacons James Maubach; Joseph Venzon.
Res.: 705 E. Jefferson, 61571. Tel: 309-444-3524; Fax: 309-444-7070. Email: stpatrickchurch705@comcast.net. Web: www.stpatswashington.com.
School—100 N. Harvey, 61571. Tel: 309-444-4345; Fax: 309-444-7100. Email: stpatrickwashington@comcast.net. Dr. Sharon Weiss, Prin. Lay Teachers 20; Students 256.
Catechesis/Religious Program—Keo Thompson, C.R.E. Students 209.

WEDRON, LA SALLE CO., ST. JOSEPH'S (1947) Rev. John G. Waugh.
Mailing Address: Box 60, 60557.
Res.: 3609 E. 2351 Rd., Serena, 60549. Tel: 815-792-2622.
Catechesis/Religious Program—Students 35.

WENONA, MARSHALL CO., ST. MARY'S (1867) [CEM] Rev. Luke Poczworowski, O.F.M.Conv.
Res.: 207 W. Third St., P.O. Box 486, 61377. Tel: 815-853-4558; Fax: 815-853-0111. Email: smary1867@mchsi.com.
Catechesis/Religious Program—Students 106.
Mission—Immaculate Conception Mt. Palatine, La Salle Co. Closed temporarily.

WESTVILLE, VERMILION CO.

1—ST. MARY'S (1903) [CEM] Rev. Timothy J. Sauppe.
Res.: 231 N. State St., 61883. Tel: 217-267-3334; Fax: 217-267-3334. Email: stmary1903@yahoo.com.
School—225 N. State St., 61883. Tel: 217-267-7730; Fax: 217-267-3327. Web: stmaryswestville.com/school. Mr. David Bibb, Prin. Lay Teachers 11; Students 83.
Catechesis/Religious Program—Students 35.

2—SS. PETER AND PAUL, Closed. For inquiries for parish records contact St. Mary's, Westville.

WOODHULL, HENRY CO., ST. JOHN'S (1889), (Swedish), [CEM 2] Rev. John R. Burns; Deacon Joseph O'Tool.
Res.: 390 E. Highway Ave., P.O. Box 249, 61490. Tel: 309-334-2180; Fax: 309-334-2137. Email: stjohnchurch@winco.net.
Catechesis/Religious Program—Students 29.
Mission—St. John Vianney 313 S. West St., Cambridge, Henry Co. 61238. Email: stjohn@geneseo.net.

WYOMING, STARK CO., ST. DOMINIC'S (1881) [CEM] Rev. Vien Van Do.
Res.: 303 N. Galena Ave., 61491. Tel: 309-695-4031; Fax: 309-695-4412.
Catechesis/Religious Program—Students 32.

Chaplains of Public Institutions

DANVILLE. *Veterans' Administration Hospital*, Tel: 217-442-8000.
DWIGHT. *Dwight Correctional Center*, Tel: 815-584-3522. Rev. James E. Rickey. Attended from St. Patrick's, Dwight.
LINCOLN. *Logan Correctional Center*, Tel: 217-947-2714; 309-244-8516. Rev. Thomas W. Shaw, St. Patrick Parish, Elkhart.
PONTIAC. *Illinois State Penitentiary*. Attended from St. Paul, Odell
Res.: 811 Hill St., 61704. Tel: 815-842-1150.
SHERIDAN. *Illinois Industrial School for Boys*. Rev. John G. Waugh, Chap.

Special Residence:
Rev. Msgr.—
Zube, Joseph A., J.C.L.

On Duty Outside the Diocese:
Rev. Msgrs.—
Rohlfs, Steven P., S.T.D., V.G., Rector, Mt. St. Mary's Seminary, Emmitsburg, MD
Soseman, Richard, M.A., J.C.L., Rome, Italy
Swetland, Stuart W., S.T.D., Professor, Mt. St. Mary's Seminary, Emmitsburg, Md
Revs.—
Campbell, Dwight
Caster, Gary C.
Erickson, David
Henseler, J. Thomas, Diocese of Springfield, IL
Hochstatter, Theodore, East Africa
Myers, James E., 32 Middlefield Rd., Menlo Park, CA 94025.
Ohm, Edward U., (Military)
Reese, Benjamin
Vitaliano, Dominic J., (Military)

On Leave of Absence:
Revs.—
Bird, Steven
Gallagher, Francis
Morlan, Lawrence A.
Small, Jeffrey
Windy, Jeff

Retired:
Rev. Msgrs.—
Duncan, Edward J., 1206 S. Prospect Ave., Champaign, 61820.
Fitzpatrick, Donnelly J.
Fitzsimmons, Richard, 830 Garfield Ave., Batavia, 60510.
Higgins, E. Edward, P.O. Box 138, Hennepin, 61327.
Motsett, C. Bourke, 1806 Washington, Danville, 61832.
Very Rev.—
Flattery, John J., 20967 Walnut Hill Rd., Danville, 61834.
Revs.—
Anderson, Joseph W., 545 W. Paseo del Canto, Green Valley, AZ 85614.
Barclift, Richard L.
Brajkovich, Thomas R., 114 S. 2nd St. #3, Chillicothe, 61523.
Bresnahan, Richard F., 2435 - 29th St., Moline, 61265.
Carney, Edward, 1295 Millpoint Rd., East Peoria, 61611.
Collins, Patrick, 609 Campbell Rd., P.O. Box 221, Douglas, MI 49406.
Crawford, Richard E., 1414 S. Monroe, Streator, 61364.
Dietzen, John J., 2705 W. Willow Lake Dr., #82, 61614.
Enderlin, R. E.
Fritz, Henry H., O.S.B.
Gildner, Leo H., 801 E. Etna Rd., Apt. 207, Ottawa, 61350.
Harkrader, Edward O., 545 S. Fifth St., Princeton, 61356.
Heyd, Joseph J., O.S.B.
Hoffman, Robert, 343 Hickory Ct., Oakwood, 61858.
Horzen, Bernard A., O.S.B.
Kelly, Thomas F., W6881 W. Lake Shore Dr., Elkhorn, WI 53121.
King, John, Little Ireland Rd., R.R. 1 P.O. Box 1936, Starrucca, PA 18462.
Kolczaski, Richard, 1001 Monks Ave., Peru, 61354.
Kretz, James C.
Lukoskie, Raymond M., 2102 LeClaire St., Warsaw, 62379.
Mai-Chi-Than, Joseph M., 904 Switchgrass Ln., Champaign, 61822.
Malinowski, Stanley J., P.O. Box 307, Thomasboro, 61878.
Maloy, Dale, 1709 Char-Lu Dr., Mendota, 61342.
Mann, Robert G., 19614 Star Ridge Dr., Sun City West, AZ 85375.
Meyer, Arthur D.
Meyer, Gerald J.
Mullen, Richard, 2414 Heritage Dr., Champaign, 61822.
O'Connor, Robert D., Kahl Home, 1101 W. 9th St., Davenport, IA 52804.
O'Riley, Dennis H., 225 E. Autumn, Oakwood, 61858.
Onderko, John M., 2200 36th St., Rock Island, 61201.
Prendergast, Robert E., P.O. Box 548, Kewanee, 61443.
Raney, Richard E., 21460 Bay Village Dr., #236, Fort Myers Beach, FL 33931-4337.
Remm, George F., P.O. Box 6136, Champaign, 61826.
Roche, David, 413 E Second St., Minonk, 61760.
Ryan, Francis, 500 Centennial Dr., #549, East Peoria, 61611.
Ryan, William A., 610 E. First St., #2-6, Spring Valley, 61362.
Schladen, Robert, P.O. Box 6105, 61601.
Schroeder, George J., 16 Waverly Dr., Rock Island, 61201.
Thompson, George M., 3026 55th St., Moline, 61265.
Verhoye, Gerard A., 202 N. State, Box 603, Atkinson, 61235.

Permanent Deacons:
Adams, John L., St. Paul's, Macomb
An, Yi-Ning Michael, Epiphany, Normal
Angelo, Alfredo W., Jr., St. Patrick, Colona
Beltramini, Robert, St. Joseph's, Peru
Blanchard, Timothy, St. Joseph, Pekin
Bradford, Bruce, Sacred Heart, Peoria
Breeden, Charles, St. Maria Goretti, Coal Valley
Briggs, James W., St. Anne's, E. Moline
Buczko, Stanley, St. Patrick, Havana
Burton, John, St. Joseph's, Brimfield and St. James, Williamsfield
Buyck, Jerry, Christ the King, Moline
Carolan, Brendan, Holy Trinity, Bloomington
Cenek, Stephen, St. Ann, Peoria
Chaffee, Harley, St. Malachy, Genesco
Clark, William H., Immaculate Conception, Monmouth and St. Theresa's Alexis.
Cleary, Mark, Epiphany, Normal
Crutcher, Steven, St. Patrick of Merna, Bloomington
Curry, Dirck, Epiphany, Normal
DeBernardis, Thomas, St. Vincent de Paul, Peoria
DeCapp, Larry, St. Mary of Lourdes, Metamora
DeVooght, Dennis, Sacred Heart, Moline
Dockery-Jackson, Joseph, St. Pius X, Rock Island
Dosher, Jon, St. Patrick, Havana
Eaton, Francis, St. Thomas, Peoria Heights
Efinger, Donald, (Working Outside the Diocese)
England, Robert, (Retired)
Ensenberger, Tony, St. Paul, Macomb
Filzen, Bernard R., (Retired)
Fischer, Raymond, Holy Cross, Mendota
Gaetz, Dale, St. Mary, Lourdes
Golemo, Greggory, Sacred Heart, Warsaw; St. Mary, Hamilton
Gore, James, Holy Trinity, Bloomington
Granet, Timothy, St. Pius X, Rock Island
Gray, Rodney, Immaculate Heart of Mary, Galesburg
Gray, William, Dir. of Rural Life, Sts. Peter and Paul, Nauvoo
Grimler, Richard, (Working Outside the Diocese)
Hammond, Richard G., St. Anthony, Bartonville
Haneghan, James, St. Patrick, Galesburg
Harris, Harley, (Retired)
Hart, Henry, Holy Cross, Champaign; Spiritual Director Champaign Cursillo
Heckman, M. Andrew, St. Elizabeth, Thomasboro; Director of Worship, St. John's Chapel, Champaign
Heipel, Robert, St. Mary of Lourdes, Metamora
Hermes, Robert, Holy Trinity, Bloomington
Holevoet, John V., St. John, Woodhull; St. John, Galva
Honzel, Larry, St. Malachy, Geneseo
Hunter, Roger, St. Jude, Peoria
Kettering, Jack M., St. Pius X, Rock Island
Kim, Byung-Joon (Paul), St. Mary, Champaign
Koeppel, Joseph, St. Ann's, Peoria
Kovachevich, Victor, St. Patrick of Merna, Bloomington
Kruse, Frederick J., Dir. King's House, Henry, IL
La Hood, Joseph, Holy Family, Peoria; Prison Ministry
Lalande, John, (Working Outside the Diocese)
Landry, John, (Retired)
Leonard, John, St. John's, Bellflower; Sacred Heart, Farmer City
Levy, Matthew, Our Lady of Guadalupe, Silvis
Lowry, Joseph, St. Mary of Lourdes, Metamora
Maduzia, Clifford, St. Patrick, Urbana
Mannino, Michael, Immaculate Heart of Mary, Galesburg
Martin, Paul, St. Pius X, Rock Island
Maubach, James, St. Patrick, Washington
Meyer, William, Immaculate Conception, Manito; St. Patrick, Havana
Miller, Rick, Blessed Sacrament, Morton
Mock, John, (Retired)
Mohrbacher, Edward, Holy Cross, Champaign
Montenegro, Jose, St. Mary, Bloomington
Moran, Thomas, Blessed Sacrament, Morton
Mueller, Edward, Our Lady of the Lake, Mahomet
Murphy, John P., St. Louis, Princeton; St. Mary's, Tiskilwa
Murphy, John R., Immaculate Conception, Lacon
Murphy, Patrick, Sacred Heart, Moline
Murray, Charles, St. Joseph, Pekin
Myers, Robert, St. Vincent de Paul, Peoria; Executive Dir. Catholic Cemetery Assn. of Peoria
Neakrase, Paul, St. Patrick, Washington
O'Rourke, Robert, St. Malachy, Geneseo
O'Tool, Joseph, St. John, Woodhull
Petri, Darrel, St. Mary, Bloomington
Pinheiro, Edwin, (On Leave of Absence)
Pogioli, Martin, St. Joseph, Pekin
Pomazal, Robert, Vice Chancellor, St. Edward, Chillicothe
Pool, Michael, St. Patrick of Merna, Bloomington
Racki, Stephen, III, St. Patrick of Merna, Bloomington
Rager, Ronald L., IL Valley Community Hospital, Peru
Randazzo, Frank G.
Rapach, Thomas, St. Jude's, Peoria
Read, William, Diocese Dir., Cursillo-Tec; St. Mary's of Lourdes, Metamora
Reid, Michael, (On Leave of Absence)
Reising, David, St. Philomena, Peoria
Ries, Arthur, St. Malachy, Geneseo
Robbins, Charles, St. Monica, E. Peoria
Sailer, Philip, St. Pius X, Rock Island
Sandoval, Henry, (On Leave of Absence)
Schultz, Gary, St. Matthew, Farmington
Serangeli, Gregory, St. Edward's, Chillicothe; Director of Evangelization, Diocese of Peoria
Simon, Nicholas, St. Anthony, Atkinson
Sims, Fred, (Working Outside the Diocese)
Skender, John, St. Mark, Peoria
Sloman, William, St. Francis Medical Center & St. Ann, Peoria
Slomian, Vincent, Holy Cross, Mendota
Smith, Richard, Holy Family, Danville
Sondag, Robert, Immaculate Conception, Manito
Steeples, David, Blessed Sacrament, Morton
Steiner, Bruce, St. Ann, Peoria
Swim, Russ, St. Mary, Moline
Tomlianovich, Louis A., St. Anthony's, Bartonville
Triplett, Gene, St. Philomena, Monticello; St. Michael, Bement
Tyler, Raymond Toby, Cathedral of St. Mary of the Immaculate Conception, Peoria
Ulbrich, Robert J., Holy Cross, Champaign
Van Meltebeck, Martin, St. Mary, Kewanee
Van Wassenhove, Raymond, (Retired)
Vargas, Ausencio, Hispanic Ministry, St. Mary's Cathedral
Venzon, Joseph, St. Patrick, Washington
Vogelbaugh, Bob, Sacred Heart, Moline
Wachtel, Thomas, St. Malachy, Geneseo
Wagner, George, St. Mary's, Pontiac; St. John, Cullom; St. Joseph, Flanagan
Waldschmidt, Robert, (Retired)
Wallace, Ray, St. Mary's, Pontiac; St. John, Cullom; St. Joseph, Flanagan
Whited, Ernie, St. Joseph, Pekin
Whitehouse, Scott, Sacred Heart, Farmer City
Wilder, Mark, St. Joseph, Pekin
Zeeb, Kevin, Blessed Sacrament, Morton
Zimmerman, Richard, St. Peter, Peoria
Zulz, Charles, St. Mary's, Wenona; St. Patrick's Minonk; St. John's, Lostant

INSTITUTIONS LOCATED IN THE DIOCESE

[A] SEMINARIES, RELIGIOUS OR SCHOLASTICATES

PEORIA. *Rosminian Novitiate*, 2327 W. Heading Ave., 61604. Tel: 309-676-6341; Fax: 309-676-1087. Email: wtmic@juno.com. Revs. Paul Stiene, I.C., Novice Master; William T. Miller, I.C., Provincial Supr. Priests 2; Total Staff 2.

PERU. *St. Bede Abbey* (1891) 24 W. US Hwy 6, 61354. Tel: 815-223-3140; Fax: 815-223-8580. Email: cpeifer@juno.com. Web: stbedeabbey.org. Benedictine Fathers and Brothers. Priests 20; Brothers 6.
Staff: Rt. Revs. Claude J. Peifer, O.S.B., Abbot; Marion E. Balsavich, O.S.B. (Retired); Roger F. Corpus, O.S.B. (Retired); Very Rev. Dominic M. Garramone, O.S.B., Subprior & CFO; Revs. Gabriel G. Bullock, O.S.B.; Michael Calhoun, Prior; Harold L. Datzman, O.S.B.; Philip D. Davey, O.S.B., Junior Master; Patrick A. Fennell, O.S.B.; Henry H. Fritz, O.S.B. (Retired); Kevin D. Gorman, O.S.B. (Retired); Ambrose B. Hessling, O.S.B.; Joseph J. Heyd, O.S.B. (Retired); Bernard A. Horzen, O.S.B. (Retired); Ronald L. Margherio, O.S.B.; Matthew C. Mazzuchelli, O.S.B.; James M. Murray, O.S.B.; Samuel D. Pusateri, O.S.B.; Arthur G. Schmit, O.S.B.; Stephen J. Souse, O.S.B.; Bros. Nathaniel Grossman, O.S.B.; Gregory Jarzombek, O.S.B.; George J. Matsuoka, O.S.B., (Retired); Luke E. McLachlan, O.S.B.; Robert Pondant, O.S.B.; Anthony Shaughnessy, O.S.B.

[B] HIGH SCHOOLS, DIOCESAN AND INTER-PAROCHIAL

PEORIA. *Peoria Notre Dame High School*, 5105 N. Sheridan, 61614. Tel: 309-691-8741; Fax: 309-691-0875. Web: peorianotredame.com. Mr. Charlie Roy, Prin.; Sr. Margaret Schulz, C.S.J., Asst. Prin. Student Affairs; Mr. Michael Pryor, Asst. Prin. Academics; Mr. Tim Speck; Rev. Ryan Bredemeyer; Mrs. Maureen Vadis, Librarian. Priests 2; Sisters 1; Lay Teachers 55; Students 821.

Peoria Notre Dame Scholarship Trust, 5105 N. Sheridan Rd., 61614. Rev. Msgr. William A. Watson, Pres.

Peoria Notre Dame High School Foundation, St. Thomas Parish, 904 E. Lake Ave., Peoria Heights, 61616. Tel: 309-688-3446. Email: s.cicciarelli@pndhs.org. Most Rev. Daniel Robert Jenky, C.S.C., Contact Person.

BLOOMINGTON. *Central Catholic High School*, 1201 Airport Rd., 61704-2534. Tel: 309-661-7000; Fax: 309-661-7010. Email: jallen@blmcchs.org. Web: www.blmcchs.org. Mrs. Joy Allen, Prin.; Rev. Patrick Henehan; Ann Cox, Librarian. Priests 1; Lay Teachers 29; Students 414.

CHAMPAIGN. *High School of St. Thomas More*, 3901 N. Mattis Ave., 61822. Tel: 217-352-7210; Fax: 217-352-7213. Email: admin@hs-stm.org. Web: www.hs-stm.org. Tim Millage, Prin.; Rev. Joseph Dondanville, Chap.; Joy Mortensen, Librarian. Priests 1; Lay Teachers 40; Students 377.

DANVILLE. *Schlarman High School* 61832. Tel: 217-442-2725; Fax: 217-442-0293. Email: pstitt@schlarman.com. Web: www.schlarman.com. Mr. Robert Rice, Prin.; Rev. Bowan M. Schmitt, Chap. Lay Teachers 20; Students 180.

OTTAWA. *Marquette High School*, 1000 Paul St., 61350. Tel: 815-433-0125; Fax: 815-433-2632. Email: rjs@marquettehs.com. Web: marquettehs.com. Ronald Spandet, Prin.; Rev. Chris G. Haake, Chap. Priests 2; Lay Teachers 23; Students 202.

ROCK ISLAND. *Alleman High School* (1949) 1103 40th St., 61201. Tel: 309-786-7793; Fax: 309-786-7834. Email: allemanhs@mchsi.com. Web: www.allemanhighschool.org. Colin Letendre, Prin.; Revs. Daniel J. Mirabelli, C.S.V., Dir. of Devel.; Gregory Jozefiak, Campus Min.; Laurie Doyle, Librarian. Priests 3; Sisters 3; Deacons 2; Lay Teachers 29; Students 450.

[C] HIGH SCHOOLS, PRIVATE

PERU. *St. Bede Academy* (1890) 24 W. U.S. Hwy. 6, 61354-2903. Tel: 815-223-3140; Fax: 815-223-8580. Web: www.st-bede.com. Mrs. Michelle Mershon, Prin. Benedictine Fathers and Brothers. Benedictine Priests 3; Brothers 2; Lay Teachers 19; Students 309.
Administration: Dr. Ted Struck, Supt.; Mrs. Helen Klabel, Registrar; Rev. Ronald L. Margherio, O.S.B., Chap.; Very Rev. Dominic M. Garramone, O.S.B., CFO; Mr. Bernie Moore, Asst. Prin.; Mr. Robert Leclercq, Dir. Guidance; Mrs. Eve Postula, Treas. & Business Mgr.

[D] ELEMENTARY SCHOOLS INTER-PAROCHIAL

EAST MOLINE. *Our Lady of Grace Catholic Academy*, 602-17 Ave., 61244. Tel: 309-755-9771; Fax: 309-755-7407. Email: office@olgca.us. Web: www.olgca.us. Most Rev. Daniel Robert Jenky, C.S.C., Contact Person; Linda Vandervennet, Prin.; Sylvia Standaert, Librarian. Lay Teachers 11.

LA SALLE. *Trinity Catholic Academy*, 650 Fourth St., 61301. Tel: 815-223-8523; Fax: 815-223-7450. Email: trinitycatholic@insightbb.com. Web: www.asd.com. Mr. Roy Pesch, Prin. Lay Teachers 16; Students 211.

MOLINE. *Seton Catholic School*, (Grades PreK-8), 1320-16th Ave., 61265. Tel: 309-757-5500; Fax: 309-762-0545. Email: jbarrett@setonschool.com. Web: www.setonschool.com. Mrs. Jane Barrett, Prin. Sisters 1; Lay Teachers 35; Students 544.

ROCK ISLAND. *Jordan Catholic School of Rock Island, Inc.* Directs the Elementary School System for the Rock Island-Milan area, operating facilities at Sacred Heart and St. Pius X. Parishes in Rock Island., 2901-24th St., P.O. Box 3490, 61204-3490. Tel: 309-793-7350; Fax: 309-793-7361. Web: www.jordanschool.com. Michael Daly, Prin.; Gail Bain, Librarian. Lay Teachers 25; Students 467.

Commission on Education for Jordan Catholic School, P.O. Box 3490, 61204-3490. Tel: 309-793-7350; Fax: 309-793-7361.

WEST PEORIA. *Immaculate Conception Pre-Kindergarten*, 2408 W. Heading Ave., 61604-5096. Tel: 309-674-6168; Fax: 309-674-2006. Email: imfosf@yahoo.com. Web: westpeoriasisters.org. Sr. M. Elaine Haertjens, O.S.F., Dir. Sponsored by the Sisters of St. Francis of the Immaculate Conception. Students 9.

[E] CATHOLIC CHARITIES OF THE DIOCESE PEORIA

WEST PEORIA. *Catholic Charities of the Diocese of Peoria*, 2900 W. Heading Ave., 61604. Tel: 309-636-8000; Fax: 309-674-1664. Email: communications@ccdop.org. Web: www.ccdop.org. Ms. Peggy A. Arizzi, Exec Dir.; Ms. Tricia C. Fox, Asst. Exec. Dir. Total Institutional Staff 32; Other Staff 414; Total Assisted 36,746.

Catholic Charities Administration, 2900 W. Heading Ave., 61604. Tel: 309-636-8000; Fax: 309-674-1664. Web: www.ccdop.org. Adoption, abstinence education, child care, community organizing, crisis intervention, delinquency intervention, family counseling/behavioral health, family preservation, food pantry, foster care, Latino and immigrant outreach, pregnancy support services, residential care for youth and senior services.

Catholic Charities Branch Offices, 4806 N. Sheridan Rd., 61614. Tel: 309-682-6258; Fax: 309-682-6472. Web: www.ccdop.org.
Catholic Charities Branch Offices:
603 N. Center St., Bloomington, 61701. Tel: 309-829-6307; Fax: 309-829-3254. Web: www.c-cdop.org.
502 S. Morris Ave., Bloomington, 61701. Tel: 309-820-7617; Fax: 309-820-7657. Web: www.c-cdop.org.
1315A Curt Dr., Champaign, 61821. Tel: 217-352-5179; Fax: 217-352-7817. Web: www.ccdop.org.
102 N. Robinson, Danville, 61832. Tel: 217-443-1772; Fax: 217-443-1701. Web: www.ccdop.org.
292 N. Chambers, Galesburg, 61401. Tel: 309-342-1136; Fax: 309-342-1891. Web: www.ccdop.org.
815 2nd St., La Salle, 61301. Tel: 815-223-4007; Fax: 815-224-4550. Web: www.ccdop.org.
2100 W. 5th St., Lincoln, 62656. Tel: 217-732-5935; Fax: 217-735-1738. Web: www.ccdop.org.
123 S. McArthur St., Macomb, 61455-0355. Tel: 309-833-1791; Fax: 309-836-1462. Web: www.c-cdop.org.
Fort Armstrong, 4703 44th St., Ste. 4, Rock Island, 61201. Tel: 309-788-9581. Web: www.ccdop.orgFax: 309-788-9608.
Catholic Charities Outreach Offices:
Streator Outreach Office, 125 S. Vermillion St., Ste. 12, Streator, 61364.
2900 W. Heading Ave., 61604. Tel: 309-636-8000.

[F] CHILDREN'S HOMES

WEST PEORIA. *Catholic Charities Foster Care Program*, 2900 W. Heading Ave., 61604. Tel: 309-636-8000; Fax: 309-671-1046. Web: www.ccdop.org. Greg Westbrook, Program Admin.; Ms. Peggy A. Arizzi, Exec. Dir.; Ms. Trish Fox, Asst. Exec. Dir. Clients placed in Foster Care during year 1,302; Total Staff 175.

Guardian Angel Home, 2900 W. Heading Ave., 61604. Tel: 309-636-7500; Fax: 309-673-3405. Web: www.ccdop.org. Peggy Arizzi, Exec. Dir. Treatment for Abused and Neglected Youth. Total Staff 32; Capacity 16; Served 22.

[G] DAY CARE CENTERS

PEORIA. *South Side Catholic Child Care Center*, 1010 W. Johnson St., 61605. Tel: 309-674-7340; Fax: 309-497-3740. Friar Joyce Jackson, Dir. Children 128; Total Staff 20.

WEST PEORIA. *Jesu Children's Enrichment Centers*, 2900 W. Heading Ave., 61604. Tel: 309-636-7550; Fax: 309-671-8905. Email: jesu@rogys.com. Total Staff 25; Capacity 104; Served 116.

[H] GENERAL HOSPITALS

PEORIA. *Saint Francis Medical Center*, 530 N.E. Glen Oak Ave., 61637-0002. Mr. Keith Steffen, Admin.; Rev. Msgr. Michael C. Bliss, Dir., Pastoral Care. Sponsored and owned by the Sisters of the Third Order of St. Francis. Sisters of the Third Order of St. Francis 7; Bed Capacity 616; Patients Assisted Annually 471,700; Total Staff 5,888.

OSF Healthcare System (1880) 800 N.E. Glen Oak Ave., 61603-3200. Tel: 309-699-2852; Fax: 309-655-6869. Web: www.osfhealthcare.org. Sponsored and owned by the Sisters of the Third Order of St. Francis. Total Assisted Annually 2,205,762; Total Staff 12,715; Bed Capacity 1,469.

OSF Healthcare Foundation (1989) 800 N.E. Glen Oak Ave., 61603-3200. Tel: 309-655-4817. Mr. James Moore, CEO.

BLOOMINGTON. *OSF St. Joseph Medical Center*, 2200 E. Washington, 61701. Tel: 309-662-3311; Fax: 309-662-7143. Web: osfhealthcare.org. Mr. Kenneth J. Natzke, Pres.& CEO; Rev. Deogratias Kiwanuka, Dir., Pastoral Care. Sponsored and owned by the Sisters of the Third Order of St. Francis. Bed Capacity 143; Total Assisted Annually 321,788; Total Staff 987.

DANVILLE. *Provena United Samaritans Medical Center*, 812 N. Logan, 61832. Tel: 217-443-5000; Fax: 217-443-1965. Web: www.provena.org/usmc. David Bertauski, Pres. & CEO.
Provena Hospitals. Sisters 2; Capacity 210; Patients Assisted Annually 101,298; Total Staff 883.
Provena Medical Group

GALESBURG. *St. Mary Medical Center*, 3333 N. Seminary St., 61401-1299. Tel: 309-344-3161; Fax: 309-344-9498. Web: osfhealthcare.org. Mailing Address: 1175 St. Francis Ln., East Peoria, 61611. Mr. Richard S. Kowalski, Chief Exec. Officer; Rev. Deus-Dedit B. Byabato, Chap.; Deacon David Steeples, Dir., Pastoral Care. Sisters of the Third Order of St. Francis 2; Patients Assisted Annually 172,219; Capacity 138; Total Staff 689.

The Galesburg St. Mary Medical Center Foundation, 3333 N. Seminary St., 61401.

MONMOUTH. *OSF Holy Family Medical Center*, 1000 W. Harlem Ave., 61462-1099. Tel: 309-734-3141; Fax: 309-734-3029.

PONTIAC. *OSF Saint James-John W. Albrecht Medical Center*, 2500 W. Reynolds, 61764. Tel: 815-842-2828; Fax: 815-842-4912. Web: osfhealthcare.org. David T. Ochs, Pres. & CEO; Deacon George Wagner, Dir., Pastoral Care. Sponsored and owned by the Sisters of the Third Order of St. Francis. Capacity 42; Patients Assisted Annually 187,406; Total Staff 419.

SPRING VALLEY. *St. Margaret's Hospital*, 600 E. First St., 61362. Tel: 815-664-5311; Fax: 815-664-1335. Email: admin@aboutsmh.org. Web: www.aboutsmh.org. Timothy Muntz, Pres.; Deacon John Murphy, Pastoral Care Dir. Sisters of Mary of the Presentation 2; Bed Capacity 123; Patients Assisted Annually 238,604; Total Staff 625.

STREATOR. *St. Mary's Hospital*, 111 Spring St., 61364. Tel: 815-673-2311; Fax: 815-673-4541. Web: www.stmaryshospital.org. Sr. Laura Northcraft, Pastoral Care Dir. Hospital Sisters Third Order of St. Francis. Sisters 1; Patients Assisted Annually 49,687; Bed Capacity 251; Bassinets 28; Total Staff 555.

URBANA. *Provena Covenant Medical Center*, 1400 W. Park St., 61801. Tel: 217-337-2000; Fax: 217-337-4541. Web: www.provena.org/covenant. Sr. Mary Robert Morton, S.S.C.M., Supr.; David Bertauski, Pres. & CEO; Sr. Mary Robert Morton, S.S.C.M., Dir. & Pastoral Min.
Provena Covenant Medical Center. Sisters 7; Capacity 254; Patients Assisted Annually 113,415; Total Staff 1,016.

[I] SPECIAL HOSPITALS AND SANATORIA

LACON. *St. Joseph Nursing Home*, 401 Ninth St., 61540. Tel: 309-246-2175; Fax: 309-246-3609. Email: amehlbrech@stjosephnursinghome-lacon.com. Web: www.stjosephnursinghome-lacon.com. Mrs. Angela Mehlbrech, Admin.; Rev. Harold F. Schmitt, Chap. Daughters of St. Francis of Assisi. Bed Capacity 93; Total Assisted 130; Total Staff 107.

PEORIA HEIGHTS. *Saint Clare Home*, 5533 N. Galena Rd., 61614. Tel: 309-682-5428; Fax: 309-682-8478. Web: osfhealthcare.org. Rev. Msgr. Michael C. Bliss, Chap.; Kelly McGrath, Admin. Sponsored and owned by the Sisters of the Third Order of St. Francis., Skilled nursing facility. Bed Capacity 98; Total Assisted Annually 205; Total Staff 82.

[J] HOMES FOR AGED

PEORIA. *St. Augustine Manor*, 1301 N.E. Glendale Ave., 61603. Tel: 309-674-7069; Fax: 309-494-6547. Jeri Myers, Residential Mgr. Residents 40; Total Assisted Annually 55; Total Staff 4.

St. Joseph's Home of Peoria Home Care, 2408 W. Heading Ave., West Peoria, 61604. Tel: 309-673-7425; Fax: 309-674-2006. Email: sjhcoffice@yahoo.com. Web: osfsisterswpeoria.org. Sr. Mary Barbara Buckley, O.S.F., Admin. Tel: 309-673-7425; Fax: 309-673-7431. Sisters of St. Francis of the Immaculate Conception. Total Assisted Annually 20; Staff 9.

[K] MONASTERIES AND RESIDENCES FOR PRIESTS AND BROTHERS

GEORGETOWN. *La Salette Missionaries, c/o St. Isaac Jogues Parish*, 109 W. Seventh St., 61846-1404. Tel: 217-662-6708. Rev. John Paninski, M.S., c/o St. Isaac Jogues Parish, Georgetown.

La Salette Fathers, Inc. Priests 1; Total Staff 1.

PRINCEVILLE. *Congregation of St. John*, 11223 W. Legion Hall Rd., 61559. Tel: 309-385-1193; Fax: 309-385-1830. Web: www.stjean.com. Revs. Joseph Mary Brown, C.S.J., Prior; Nathan Cromley, C.S.J.; Antoine Thomas, C.S.J. Priests 3; Professed Brothers 5; Novices 3; Postulants 4.

[L] CONVENTS AND RESIDENCES FOR SISTERS

PEORIA. *St. Francis Medical Center Convent*, 1175 St. Francis Ln., East Peoria, 61611. Tel: 309-655-2083; 309-655-4840. Email: sistermaryjohn.harvey@osfhealthcare.org. Web: franciscansisterspeoria.org. Sr. Mary John Harvey, O.S.F., Supr. The Sisters of the Third Order of St. Francis 7.

Immaculate Conception Convent (1891) 2408 W. Heading Ave., 61604-5096. Tel: 309-674-6168; Fax: 309-674-2006. Email: imfosf@yahoo.com. Web: westpeoriasisters.org. Sr. Paula Vasquez, O.S.F., Pres. Motherhouse of the Sisters of St. Francis of the Immaculate Conception. Sisters 40; Professed Sisters 40.

Missionaries of Charity Convent (1991) 506 Hancock St., 61603. Tel: 309-495-9490. Sr. M. Jesusla, M.C., Supr. Sisters 4; Total Assisted 9,807; Total Volunteer Staff 2.

The Poor Clares Tel: 309-682-3182; Fax: 309-682-3182. Web: www.poorclaresjoliet.org. Sisters 4.

Our Lady of the Angels Convent, 3432 W. Baskin Ridge, 61604. Tel: 309-682-3182; Fax: 309-682-3182.

EAST PEORIA. *Motherhouse, The Sisters of the Third Order of St. Francis*, 1175 Saint Francis Ln., 61611-1299. Tel: 309-699-7215. Web: www.franciscansisterspeoria.org. Sr. Judith Ann Duvall, O.S.F., Major Supr. Sisters in Residence 22; Total Sisters in Community 34.

Mt. Alverno Novitiate, 1175 Saint Francis Ln., 61611-1299. Tel: 309-699-9313. Web: www.franciscansisterspeoria.org. Rev. Msgr. Rick J. Oberch, Chap. Novitiate of The Sisters of the Third Order of St. Francis., Members of the Novitiate are currently residing at St. Francis Medical Center Convent.

HENRY. *Servants of the Pierced Hearts of Jesus and Mary*, P.O. Box 165, 61537.

LACON. *St. Joseph Motherhouse and Novitiate* 61540. Tel: 309-246-2175; Fax: 309-246-2708. Email: sradriana@centurytel.net. Web: www.laconfranciscans.org. Sr. Adriana Zdila, Provincial Supr. Congregation of the Daughters of St. Francis of Assisi - American Province. Sisters 10; Sisters in Community (Professed) 14.

PEORIA HEIGHTS. *Franciscan Sisters of John the Baptist*, 1209 E. Lake Ave., 61616. Tel: 309-688-3500. Email: fsjpeoria@yahoo.com. Web: www.sistersofjohnthebaptist.org. Sr. M. Vaclava Ballon, F.S.J.B., Supr. Professed Sisters 9.

PRINCEVILLE. *Sisters of St. John* (1999) 11227 W. Legion Hall Rd., 61559. Tel: 309-385-2550; Fax: 309-385-2550. Sr. Marie Segolene, S.J., Supr. Sisters 18.

ROCK ISLAND. *St. Mary Monastery* (1874) 2200-88th Ave. W., 61201-7649. Tel: 309-283-2100; Fax: 309-283-2200. Email: benedictines@smmsisters.org. Web: www.smmsisters.org. Sr. Phyllis McMurray, O.S.B., Prioress. Benedictine Sisters. Sisters in Community 56.

Benet House Retreat Center Tel: 309-283-2108; Fax: 309-283-2200. Email: retreats@smmsisters.org. Web: www.smmsisters.org. Sr. Charlotte Sonneville, O.S.B., Dir.

WEST PEORIA. *Mother of Peace Home* (1970) 2408 W. Heading Ave., 61604. Tel: 309-673-4657. Email: iccmoph@yahoo.com. Web: osfsisterswpeoria.org. Sr. Mary Ann Mehuys, O.S.F., Admin. Total in Residence 7; Total Staff 15.

[M] NEWMAN CENTERS

PEORIA. *Newman Foundation at Bradley University & Illinois Central College* 1116 W. College Ave., 61606-1728. Tel: 309-674-0208 (Office); Fax: 309-497-3759. Email: info@bradleynewman.org. Web: bradleynewman.org. Total in Residence 1; Total Staff 7; Total Assisted 3,471.

CHAMPAIGN. *St. John's Catholic Newman Center at the University of Illinois, Urbana-Champaign* 604 E. Armory Ave., 61820. Tel: 217-344-1266; Fax: 217-344-4957. Email: info@sjcnc.org. Web: www.sjcnc.org. Rev. Msgrs. Edward J. Duncan, Emeritus (Retired); Gregory K. Ketcham, Dir. & Chap.; Revs. Adolph Menendez, S.X.; Maurus Mount, O.S.B.; Luke A. Spannagel; Anthony Co. Total in Residence 9; Newman Center Residence 582; Newman Center Staff 120; Total Staff 9.

MACOMB. *St. Francis of Assisi Newman Center* (1945) 1401 W. University Dr., 61455. Tel: 309-837-3988; Fax: 309-837-4179. Web: www.newmanonfire.org. Rev. Kenneth J. Hummel.

NORMAL. *St. Robert Bellarmine Catholic Newman Center, Illinois State Univ., Wesleyan Univ., Heartland Community* 501 S. Main St., 61761. Tel: 309-452-5046; Fax: 309-452-3845. Email: srsilvia@isucatholic.org. Web: www.isucatholic.org. Sr. Silvia Tarafa, S.C.T.J.M., Chap. Total Staff 2.

ROCK ISLAND. *Augustana College Catholic Campus Ministry* 639-38th St., 61201. Tel: 309-794-7272; Fax: 309-794-7422. Email: marilynring@augustana.edu. Sr. Marilyn Ring, O.S.B. Total Staff 1.

[N] PERSONAL PRELATURES

URBANA. *Opus Dei* Prelature of the Holy Cross and Opus Dei, Lincoln Green Foundation, 715 W. Michigan Ave., 61801. Tel: 217-367-6650; Fax: 217-344-2987. Email: pdowbor@juno.com. Web: www.opusdei.org. In Res. Rev. Barry Cole.

[O] MISCELLANEOUS

PEORIA. *Archbishop Fulton J. Sheen Foundation* (1996) P.O. Box 728, 61652-0728. Tel: 309-671-1550; Fax: 309-677-6798. Email: info@archbishopsheencause.org. Web: www.archbishopsheencause.org. Rev. Msgr. Stanley L. Deptula, Exec. Dir.; Sara Worrell, Public Rels.; Jane Peverly, Sec.

Family Resource Center, 419 N.E. Madison Ave., 61603. Tel: 309-673-1713. Most Rev. Daniel Robert Jenky, C.S.C.

Franciscan Spirituality and Resource Center 2408 W. Heading Ave., 61604. Tel: 309-674-6168; Fax: 309-674-2006. Web: westpeoriasisters.org. Sisters Betty Jean Haverback, O.S.F., Contact Person; Diane VandeVoorde, O.S.F., Contact Person.

Jordan Catholic School of Rock Island, Inc., 419 N.E. Madison Ave., 61603. Tel: 309-671-1550. Most Rev. Daniel R. Jenky, C.S.C., Contact Person.

Nazareth House, NFP, 419 N.E. Madison Ave., 61603. Tel: 309-671-1550. Most Rev. Daniel R. Jenky, C.S.C., Contact Person.

Notre Dame High School of Peoria, Inc. 61614. Tel: 309-691-8741; Fax: 309-691-0875. Email: c.roy@pndhs.org. Web: peorianotredame.com.

Seton Catholic School of Moline, Inc., 419 N.E. Madison Ave., 61603. Tel: 309-671-1550. Most Rev. Daniel R. Jenky, C.S.C., Contact Person.

SHARE Food Program of Central Illinois, Inc., 1825 N.E. Adams St., 61603. Tel: 309-637-0282; 800-637-5508; Fax: 309-637-0307. Total Staff 3; Assisted 136,000.

St. Vincent De Paul Society, 412 N.E. Madison Ave., 61603. Tel: 309-671-1550; Fax: 309-671-1576. Diocesan Council and Particular Council of Peoria.

ALEDO. *Family of Mary*, 1331 230th St., 61231. Tel: 309-372-4654. Email: triumph@winco.net.

BLOOMINGTON. *Central Catholic High School of Bloomington, Inc.* (1898) 61704. Tel: 309-661-7000; Fax: 309-661-7010. Mrs. Joy Allen, Contact Person, 1201 Airport Rd., 61704. Email: jallen@blmcchs.org. Web: www.blmcchs.org.

CHAMPAIGN. *Provena Home Care*, 1501 Interstate Dr., 61822. Tel: 217-355-4120; Fax: 217-355-4121. Email: Dianna.Moody@provena.org. Web: www.provenahealth.org. Thomas F. Nehring, System Vice Pres., Mission & Leadership Devel.

The High School of St. Thomas More of Champaign, Inc., 3901 N. Mattis, 61822. Tel: 217-352-7210; Fax: 217-352-7213. Email: tmillage@hs-stm.org. Web: www.hs-stm.org.

DANVILLE. *Schlarman High School of Danville, Inc.* (1946) 61832. Tel: 217-442-2725; Fax: 217-442-0293. Email: brice@schlarman.com. Web: www.schlarman.com.

LA SALLE. *Starved Rock-LaSalle Manor, Inc.*, 1135 S. 10th St., 61301. Tel: 815-223-0557; Fax: 815-223-0559. Ms. Susan Dillberg, Contact Person. Housing Units 48; Residents 97; Staff 2.

LACON. *St. Francis of Assisi Fund, NFP*, 507 N. Prairie St., 61540-1152. Tel: 309-246-2175; Fax: 309-246-2708. Web: www.laconfranciscans.org. Sr. Adriana Zdila, Pres.

Religious Sisters Aid, NFP, 507 N. Prairie St., 61540-1152. Tel: 309-246-2175; Fax: 309-246-2708. Web: laconfranciscans.org. Sr. Adriana Zdila, Pres.

MOLINE. *The Order of the Legion of Little Souls of the Merciful Heart of Jesus*, 428 39th St., 61265-1641. Tel: 309-797-8491; Fax: 309-643-6270. Email: littlesoul@ureach.com. Web: www.littlesouls.us. Teresa I. Huyten, Dir.; Revs. Michael L. Menner, Diocesan Chap.; John R. Burns, Natl. Chap.

NORMAL. *Homes of Hope, Inc.*, 401 Pine St., Ste. 1, 61761. Tel: 309-862-0607; Fax: 309-452-7131. Email: homesofhope1@verizon.net. Maureen McIntosh, Dir. Total Staff 30; Bed Capacity 16.

OTTAWA. *Marquette High School of Ottawa, Inc.* 61350.

ROCK ISLAND. *Alleman High School of Rock Island, Inc.* 61201. Tel: 309-786-7793; Fax: 309-786-7834. Email: allemanhs@mchsi.com. Web: www.allemanhighschool.org.

RELIGIOUS INSTITUTES OF MEN REPRESENTED IN THE DIOCESE

For further details refer to the corresponding bracketed number in the Religious Institutes of Men or Women section.

[]—*Apostles of Jesus - Peoria Community*
[0200]—*Benedictine Monks* (St. Bede Abbey)—O.S.B.
[]—*Congregation of St. John*—C.S.J.
[1320]—*Clerics of St. Viator*—C.S.V.
[0480]—*Conventual Franciscans*—O.F.M.Conv
[0520]—*Franciscan Friars* (Prov. of St. John the Baptist)—O.F.M.
[0300]—*Institute of Charity* (Rome, Italy)—I.C.
[0720]—*The Missionaries of Our Lady of La Salette*—M.S.

RELIGIOUS INSTITUTES OF WOMEN REPRESENTED IN THE DIOCESE

[0230]—*Benedictine Sisters of Pontifical Jurisdiction*—O.S.B.
[0920]—*Congregation of the Daughters of St. Francis of Assisi, (American Prov.)*—D.S.F.
[2100]—*Congregation of the Humility of Mary*—C.H.M.
[1920]—*Congregation of the Sisters of the Holy Cross*—C.S.C.
[1730]—*Congregation of the Sisters of the Third Order of St. Francis, Oldenburg, IN*—O.S.F.
[1710]—*Congregation of the Third Order of St. Francis of Mary Immaculate, Joliet, IL*—O.S.F.
[0760]—*Daughters of Charity of St. Vincent de Paul*—D.C.
[1070-03]—*Dominican Sisters*—O.P.
[1070-10]—*Dominican Sisters*—O.P.
[]—*Franciscan Sisters of John the Baptist*
[1450]—*Franciscan Sisters of the Sacred Heart*—O.S.F.
[1770]—*Hospital Sisters of the Third Order of St. Francis*—O.S.F.
[2575]—*Institute of the Sisters of Mercy of the Americas*—R.S.M.
[2710]—*Missionaries of Charity*—M.C.
[3230]—*Poor Handmaids of Jesus Christ*—P.H.J.C.
[2970]—*School Sisters of Notre Dame*—S.S.N.D.
[1680]—*School Sisters of St. Francis*—O.S.F.
[3520]—*Servants of the Holy Heart of Mary*—S.S.C.M.
[0430]—*Sisters of Charity of the Blessed Virgin Mary*—B.V.M.
[0660]—*Sisters of Christian Charity*—S.C.C.
[2450]—*Sisters of Mary of the Presentation*—S.M.P.
[3360]—*Sisters of Providence of Saint Mary-of-the-Woods, Indiana*—S.P.
[1540]—*Sisters of Saint Francis, Clinton, Iowa*—O.S.F.
[1705]—*The Sisters of St. Francis of Assisi*—O.S.F.
[1580]—*Sisters of St. Francis of the Immaculate Conception*—O.S.F.
[3840]—*Sisters of St. Joseph of Carondelet*—C.S.J.
[]—*Sisters of the Community of St. John*
[]—*Sisters of the Holy Cross*—C.S.C.
[1820]—*Sisters of the Third Order of St. Francis (East*

Peoria, Illinois)—O.S.F.

[]—*Sisters of the Visitation*

CEMETERIES/CEMETERY ASSOCIATIONS

PEORIA. *Catholic Cemetery Association of Peoria, IL,* 7519 N. Allen, 61614. Tel: 309-691-5889; Fax: 309-690-4737. Email: ccapeo@ameritech.net. Web: www.cdop.org/cemetery. Rev. Msgr. Paul E. Showalter, P.A., V.G. Operates St. Mary's Cemetery, St. Joseph's Cemetery and Resurrection Cemetery in Peoria.

BLOOMINGTON. *Bloomington-Normal Catholic Cemetery Association,* 1800 E. Eastland Dr., 61704. Tel: 309-663-1968.

DANVILLE. *Resurrection Catholic Cemetery Association of Danville, IL,* 818 Wendt, 61832. Tel: 217-431-5114; Fax: 217-431-0918.

FARMER CITY. *St. Joseph Cemetery Association of Farmer City, IL,* 612 N. Plum St., 61842. Tel: 309-928-3855; Fax: 309-928-9147. Email: shchurch@farmwagon.com.

GALESBURG. *St. Joseph's Cemetery Association of Galesburg, IL,* P.O. Box 539, 61402-0539. Tel: 309-342-6512.

PEKIN. *Catholic Cemetery Association of Pekin, IL* 61554. Tel: 309-347-6109; Fax: 309-347-6959.

ROCK ISLAND. *Calvary Cemetery Association of Rock Island, IL* 61201. Tel: 309-788-6197; Fax: 309-788-6734. Email: info@calvarycemetaryri.com. Web: www.calvarycemetaryri.com.

NECROLOGY

† Bolerasky, Rev. Msgr. Peter E., (Retired)—Died Oct. 30, 2009
† Maloney, Rev. Msgr. Thomas, (Retired)—Died Aug. 7, 2009
† Condon, Louis—Died Feb. 17, 2009
† Finnell, Eugene, (Retired)—Died Dec. 27, 2008
† Kane, Eugene J., (Retired)—Died July 28, 2009
† Morrissey, Lawrence P., (Retired)—Died Feb. 5, 2009
† Purcell, James, (Retired)—Died Oct. 19, 2009
† Reynolds, Robert E., (Retired)—Died Oct. 27, 2009
† Wuellner, George E., (Retired)—Died Aug. 8, 2009

An asterisk (*) denotes an organization that has established tax-exempt status directly with the IRS and is not covered by the USCCB Group Ruling.

Archdiocese of Philadelphia

(Archidioecesis Philadelphiensis)

His Eminence

ANTHONY CARDINAL BEVILACQUA, D.D., M.A., J.C.D., J.D.

Archbishop Emeritus of Philadelphia; ordained June 11, 1949; appointed Titular Bishop of Aquae Alba and Auxiliary Bishop of Brooklyn October 7, 1980; consecrated November 24, 1980; appointed Bishop of Pittsburgh October 7, 1983; installed December 12, 1983; installed Archbishop of Philadelphia February 11, 1988; Created Cardinal Priest June 28, 1991; retired July 15, 2003. *Office: St. Charles Borromeo Seminary, 100 E. Wynnewood Rd., Wynnewood, PA 19096.*

Most Reverend

MARTIN N. LOHMULLER, D.D.

Auxiliary Bishop Emeritus of Philadelphia; ordained June 3, 1944; appointed Auxiliary Bishop of Philadelphia and Titular Bishop of Ramsbury February 11, 1970; consecrated April 2, 1970; retired October 11, 1994. *Res.: 1410 Almshouse Rd., Jamison, PA 18929.*

Most Reverend

LOUIS A. DESIMONE, D.D.

Auxiliary Bishop Emeritus of Philadelphia; ordained May 10, 1952; appointed Auxiliary Bishop of Philadelphia and Titular Bishop of Cillio June 27, 1981; consecrated August 12, 1981; retired April 2, 1997. *Res.: St. Justin Martyr Rectory, 1222 Hagysford Rd., Narberth, PA 19072.*

Most Reverend

ROBERT P. MAGINNIS, D.D., V.G.

Auxiliary Bishop of Philadelphia; ordained May 13, 1961; appointed Auxiliary Bishop of Philadelphia and Titular Bishop of Siminia January 24, 1996; consecrated March 11, 1996. *Res.: St. Edmond Home for Children, 320 S. Roberts Rd., Rosemont, PA 19010. Office: 222 N. 17th St., Rm. 830, Philadelphia, PA 19103-1299.* Tel: 215-965-8190; Fax: 215-965-8193.

His Eminence

CARDINAL JUSTIN RIGALI

Archbishop of Philadelphia; ordained April 25, 1961; appointed Archbishop and President of the Pontifical Ecclesiastical Academy June 8, 1985; ordained September 14, 1985; appointed Archbishop of St. Louis January 25, 1994; installed March 15, 1994; appointed Archbishop of Philadelphia July 15, 2003; installed October 7, 2003; Created Cardinal Priest October 21, 2003. *Office: 222 North 17th St., Philadelphia, PA 19103.*

The Chancery: 222 N. 17th St., Philadelphia, PA 19103-1299. Tel: 215-587-4538; Fax: 215-587-3907.

Web: www.archphila.org

Email: chancery@adphila.org

Most Reverend

JOSEPH P. MCFADDEN, D.D., V.G.

Auxiliary Bishop of Philadelphia; ordained May 16, 1981; appointed Auxiliary Bishop of Philadelphia and Titular Bishop of Horreomargum June 8, 2004; consecrated July 28, 2004. *Res.: 13307 Proctor Rd., Philadelphia, PA 19116-1797. Office: 222 N. Seventeenth St., Rm. 530, Philadelphia, PA 19103-1299.* Tel: 215-965-8280; Fax: 215-965-8283.

Most Reverend

TIMOTHY C. SENIOR, M.S.W., M.A., M.DIV., M.B.A., V.G., D.D.

Auxiliary Bishop of Philadelphia; ordained May 18, 1985; appointed Auxiliary Bishop of Philadelphia and Titular Bishop of Floriana June 8, 2009; ordained July 31, 2009. *Office: 222 N. 17th St., Rm. 1200, Philadelphia, PA 19103-1299.* Tel: 215-587-4507; Fax: 215-587-4545.

Most Reverend

DANIEL E. THOMAS, D.D., S.T.L., V.G.

Auxiliary Bishop of Philadelphia; ordained May 18, 1985; appointed Auxiliary Bishop of Philadelphia and Titular Bishop of Bardstown June 8, 2006; ordained July 26, 2006. *Office: 222 N. 17th St., Rm. 930, Philadelphia, PA 19103-1299.* Tel: 215-965-8275; Fax: 215-965-8278.

DIOCESE ESTABLISHED APRIL 8, 1808.

Square Miles 2,183.

Erected an Archdiocese February 12, 1875.

Comprises all the City and County of Philadelphia, and the Counties of Bucks, Chester, Delaware and Montgomery in the State of Pennsylvania.

Patrons of the Diocese: I. Immaculate Conception B.V.M., December 8; II. Saints Peter and Paul, Apostles, June 29. This Archdiocese was solemnly consecrated to the Sacred Heart of Jesus on the Feast of Saint Teresa of Avila, October 15, 1873. On May 23, 1952, the Archdiocese of Philadelphia was solemnly consecrated to the Immaculate Heart of Mary at the Shrine of Our Lady of Fatima, Portugal.

For legal titles of parishes and archdiocesan institutions, consult The Chancery.

STATISTICAL OVERVIEW

Personnel	
Cardinals	1
Retired Cardinals	1
Auxiliary Bishops	4
Retired Bishops	2
Abbots	2
Priests: Diocesan Active in Diocese	433
Priests: Diocesan Active Outside Diocese	18
Priests: Retired, Sick or Absent	147
Number of Diocesan Priests	598
Religious Priests in Diocese	369
Total Priests in Diocese	967
Extern Priests in Diocese	31
Ordinations:	
Diocesan Priests	6
Permanent Deacons in Diocese	245
Total Brothers	101
Total Sisters	2,763
Parishes	
Parishes	267
With Resident Pastor:	
Resident Diocesan Priests	242
Resident Religious Priests	25
Missions	7
Pastoral Centers	17
Closed Parishes	1
Professional Ministry Personnel:	
Brothers	1
Sisters	127
Lay Ministers	227
Welfare	
Catholic Hospitals	7
Total Assisted	842,614
Health Care Centers	1
Total Assisted	153
Homes for the Aged	35
Total Assisted	5,911
Residential Care of Children	2
Total Assisted	530
Day Care Centers	1
Total Assisted	59
Specialized Homes	3
Total Assisted	1,943
Special Centers for Social Services	18
Total Assisted	108,279
Residential Care of Disabled	7
Total Assisted	895
Other Institutions	15
Total Assisted	20,879
Educational	
Seminaries, Diocesan	1
Students from This Diocese	46
Students from Other Diocese	98
Seminaries, Religious	1
Students Religious	14
Total Seminarians	60
Colleges and Universities	11
Total Students	41,151
High Schools, Diocesan and Parish	20
Total Students	17,903
High Schools, Private	15
Total Students	7,662
Elementary Schools, Diocesan and Parish	180
Total Students	54,677
Elementary Schools, Private	17
Total Students	4,669
Non-residential Schools for the Disabled	5
Total Students	226
Catechesis/Religious Education:	
High School Students	1,249
Elementary Students	52,643
Total Students under Catholic Instruction	180,240
Teachers in the Diocese:	
Priests	92
Brothers	35
Sisters	430
Lay Teachers	8,919
Vital Statistics	
Receptions into the Church:	
Infant Baptism Totals	13,918
Minor Baptism Totals	661
Adult Baptism Totals	431
Received into Full Communion	457
First Communions	12,750
Confirmations	12,772
Marriages:	
Catholic	3,202
Interfaith	1,253
Total Marriages	4,455
Deaths	11,369
Total Catholic Population	1,464,938
Total Population	3,892,194

Former Bishops—Most Revs. MICHAEL FRANCIS EGAN, O.F.M., D.D., cons. Oct. 28, 1810; died July 22, 1814; HENRY CONWELL, D.D., cons. Sept. 24, 1820; died April 22, 1842; FRANCIS PATRICK KENRICK, D.D., cons. June 6, 1830; transferred to Baltimore in 1851; died July 8, 1863; JOHN NEPOMUCENE NEUMANN, C.Ss.R., D.D., cons. March 28, 1852; died Jan. 5, 1860; Canonized June 19, 1977.; JAMES FREDERIC WOOD, D.D., cons. coadjutor, cum iure successionis, April 26, 1857; Bishop of Philadelphia, Jan. 5, 1860; appt. Archbishop Feb. 12, 1875; Sacred Pallium, June 17, 1875; died

June 20, 1883; PATRICK JOHN RYAN, D.D., cons. April 14, 1872; Bishop of Tricomia and Coadjutor with right of succession to the Archbishop of St. Louis; appt. Titular Archbishop of Salamis, Jan. 6, 1884; Archbishop of Philadelphia, June 8, 1884; died Feb. 11, 1911; EDMOND FRANCIS PRENDERGAST, D.D., cons. Feb. 24, 1897, Titular Bishop of Scillio; Auxiliary Bishop of Philadelphia; Archbishop of Philadelphia, May 27, 1911; died Feb. 26, 1918; His Eminence DENNIS CARDINAL DOUGHERTY, D.D., appt. Bishop of Nueva Segovia, P.I., April 7, 1903; cons. June 14, 1903; transferred to Jaro, P.I., April 19, 1908; transferred to Buffalo Nov. 30, 1915; transferred to Philadelphia April 30, 1918; installed as Archbishop of Philadelphia July 10, 1918; Pallium conferred May 6, 1919; created Cardinal Priest, March 7, 1921; died May 31, 1951; JOHN CARDINAL O'HARA, C.S.C., appt. Military Delegate of Armed Forces and Titular Bishop of Mylasa Dec. 11, 1939; cons. Jan. 15, 1940; transferred to Buffalo March 10, 1945; transferred to Philadelphia Nov. 28, 1951; installed as Archbishop of Philadelphia Jan. 9, 1952; Pallium conferred Jan. 12, 1953; created Cardinal Priest Dec. 15, 1958; died Aug. 28, 1960; JOHN CARDINAL KROL, D.D., J.C.D., ord. Feb. 20, 1937; appt. Titular Bishop of Cadi and Auxiliary Bishop of Cleveland July 11, 1953; cons. Sept. 2, 1953; appt. Archbishop of Philadelphia Feb. 11, 1961; created Cardinal Priest June 26, 1967; retired Feb. 11, 1988; died March 3, 1996; ANTHONY CARDINAL BEVILACQUA, D.D., M.A., J.C.D., J.D., ord. June 11, 1949; appt. Titular Bishop of Aquae Alba and Auxiliary Bishop of Brooklyn Oct. 7, 1980; cons. Nov. 24, 1980; appt. Bishop of Pittsburgh Oct. 7, 1983; installed Dec. 12, 1983; installed Archbishop of Philadelphia Feb. 11, 1988; Created Cardinal Priest June 28, 1991; retired July 15, 2003.

Vicars General—Most Revs. ROBERT P. MAGINNIS, D.D., V.G.; JOSEPH P. MCFADDEN, D.D., V.G.; DANIEL E. THOMAS, D.D., S.T.L., V.G.; TIMOTHY C. SENIOR, D.D., V.G., M.B.A., M.S.W., M.Div.

Office of the Cardinal—His Eminence CARDINAL JUSTIN RIGALI, Archbishop of Philadelphia; Rev. Msgr. JOHN J. MCINTYRE, Sec. to the Cardinal Archbishop, 222 N. 17th St., Philadelphia, 19103-1299. Tel: 215-587-3800.

Office of the Vicar for Administration—Most Rev. TIMOTHY C. SENIOR, D.D., V.G., M.B.A., M.S.W., M.Div. Assoc. to the Vicar Admin.: Mr. JAMES J. BOCK JR. Tel: 215-587-0518.

Regional Vicars—Rev. Msgrs. JOSEPH P. DUNCAN, M.Div., Vicar for Bucks County, 685 York Rd., Warminster, 18974. Tel: 215-957-1525; JOSEPH T. MARINO, M.Div., M.A., Vicar for Chester County, 2 Forest Lane, Strafford, 19087-2504. Tel: 610-995-9450; GEORGE A. MAJOROS, M.S., M.Div., Vicar for Delaware County, 1 Fatima Dr., Secane, 19018-4640. Tel: 610-534-9900; ARTHUR E. RODGERS, Ph.D., Vicar for Montgomery County, 120 Bryn Mawr Ave., Bala Cynwyd, 19004. Tel: 610-784-0092; JOSEPH L. LOGRIP, M.A., M.Div., Vicar for Philadelphia-North, 2918 E. Thompson St., Philadelphia, 19134. Tel: 215-739-1009; KEVIN C. LAWRENCE, M.Div., Vicar for Philadelphia-South, 2339 S. 3rd St., Philadelphia, 19148. Tel: 215-755-1003.

Office for Consecrated Life—

Vicar for Consecrated Life—Rev. Msgr. JOSEPH J. ANDERLONIS, S.T.D.

Coordinator for Vocations to the Consecrated Life—Sr. KATHLEEN LEARY, S.S.J., Office, 222 N. 17th St., Philadelphia, 19103-1299. Tel: 215-587-3795; Fax: 215-587-3790.

The Chancery—Rev. Msgr. GERARD C. MESURE, J.D., J.C.D., M.A., Chancellor; Rev. JAMES M. OLIVER, J.C.D., M.A., M.Div., Vice Chancellor, 222 N. 17th St., Philadelphia, 19103-1299. Tel: 215-587-4538; Fax: 215-587-3907.

Archivist—JOSEPH J. CASINO, M.A., M.S.L.S., Office, 100 E. Wynnewood Rd., Wynnewood, 19096-3001. Tel: 610-667-2125; Fax: 610-667-2730.

Metropolitan Tribunal—*222 N. 17th St., Philadelphia, 19103-1299*. Tel: 215-587-3750; Fax: 215-587-0508. Communications should be sent to the above address.

Judicial Vicar—Rev. Msgr. MICHAEL J. FITZGERALD, M.Div., J.C.D., J.D.

Assistant Judicial Vicars—Rev. SEAN P. BRANSFIELD, M.Div., M.A., J.C.L.; Rev. Msgr. PAUL A. DIGIROLAMO, J.C.D., M.A., M.Div.; Rev. EDUARDO G. MONTERO, J.C.L.

Archdiocesan Judges—Rev. JOSEPH C. DIECKHAUS, J.C.L.; Rev. Msgr. JAMES J. GRAHAM, J.C.D., M.Div.; Rev. STEVEN J. HARRIS, J.C.D.; Rev. Msgrs. SAMUEL E. SHOEMAKER, J.C.D.; VINCENT M. WALSH, J.C.D. (Retired).

Promoters of Justice—Rev. Msgr. GERARD C. MESURE, J.C.D., J.D.; Rev. JAMES M. OLIVER, J.C.D., M.A., M.Div.

Defenders of the Bond—Rev. Msgrs. JOHN P. BOLAND, M.A. (Retired); GERARD C. MESURE, J.C.D., J.D.; Rev. JAMES M. OLIVER, J.C.D., M.A., M.Div.; Rev. Msgr. ROBERT J. POWELL, D.M.A, M.A., M.Div.; Revs. JOHN D. REARDON, M.Div.; VINCENT F. WELSH, J.C.L., M.A.

Approved Advocates—Revs. JOSEPH W. BONGARD, M.A.; JOSEPH E. HOWARTH, M.A.L.S.; Rev. Msgrs. KENNETH P. MCATEER, M.Div.; JOSEPH J. NICOLO, M.Div.; Sr. CAROL MOCKUS, C.S.F.N.; Deacons JOHN M. BETZAL; EDWARD A. KONARSKI.

Notary—ADAM A. DICKERSON, M.A.

Office for General Counsel—TIMOTHY R. COYNE ESQ., Gen. Counsel. Tel: 215-587-0511; Fax: 215-587-0512.

Information Technology Services—Mr. BRUCE JENSEN, Dir. Tel: 215-587-3687; Fax: 215-587-3808.

Office for Audit Services—Mr. PHILIP H. GALLAGHER JR., CPA, Dir. Tel: 215-587-2474; Fax: 215-587-2430.

Office for General Services—Mr. GEORGE G. SHARRETTS, Dir. Tel: 215-587-3633; Fax: 215-965-7553.

Office for Special Projects/Closures—Rev. ZACHARY W. NAVIT, M.A., M.Div., Dir. Tel: 215-587-3519 (Special Projects); 215-587-3996 (Closures); Fax: 215-587-2481.

Office for Development and Business Leadership Organized for Catholic Schools—MARY ANN CARLISLE, Exec. Dir. BLOCS, 1001 E. Hector St., Ste. 100, Conshohocken, 19428. Tel: 484-684-1212; Fax: 484-684-1296; MARY CLARE RAMUNO, Exec. Admin. Email: info@blocs.org.

Office for Communications—DONNA FARRELL, Dir. Tel: 215-587-3747; Fax: 215-587-3875.

Newspaper - "The Catholic Standard and Times"—MATTHEW GAMBINO, Dir. & Gen. Mgr. Tel: 215-587-3698; Fax: 215-587-3979.

Office for Hispanic Catholics—

Vicar for Hispanic Catholics—Rev. Msgr. HUGH JOSEPH SHIELDS, M.Div.; ANNA C. VEGA, M.A., Dir., 222 N. 17th St., Philadelphia, 19103-1299. Tel: 215-667-2820; Fax: 215-667-2825.

Office for Research and Planning—ROBERT J. MILLER, Ed.D., Dir. Tel: 215-587-3545; Fax: 215-587-3817.

Secretariat for Catholic Education

All addresses are: 222 N. 17th St., Philadelphia, PA 19103-1299 unless otherwise indicated.

Secretary for Catholic Education—Dr. RICHARD MCCARRON JR. Tel: 215-587-3700; Fax: 215-587-5644.

Office of Catholic Education—Dr. RICHARD MCCARRON JR., Sec. for Catholic Educ.; Mr. THOMAS J. SMITH, Deputy Sec. Catholic Educ.; Ms. MARY E. ROCHFORD, Supt. Schools; ELLEN WEDEMEYER, Ed.D., M.B.A., Asst. Supt. Special Educ.; Ms. DEBORAH BACHOR, Asst. Supt. Elementary Educational Svcs. Directors: Mrs. EILEEN WILSON, Dir. Elementary Educational Svcs.; Sr. EDWARD WILLIAM QUINN, I.H.M., Dir. Elementary Curriculum & Instruction; Mrs. CAROL CARY, Dir. Secondary Curriculum & Instruction; JASON BUDD, Dir. Secondary School Svcs.; Sr. MARIE ESTHER HART, I.H.M., Coord. Science Initiatives; Mrs. REGINA DIGUILIO, Exec. Dir. for Institutional Advancement; Dr. ANGELINE M. GAMPICO, Dir. Elementary Staff Rel.; Ms. ROSELEE MADDALONI, Dir. Elementary Educational Svcs.; Mrs. THERESA RYAN-SZOTT, Dir. Secondary Personnel; Mrs. NANCY CARAMANICO, Dir. Technology K-12.

Office for Catechetical Formation—Rev. JOHN J. AMES, S.T.D., M.A., M.Div., Deputy Sec. Catechetical Formation; Mrs. ANN MENNA, Dir. Parish Elementary Relg. Educ.; Ms. ELIZABETH A. RIORDAN, Dir. Secondary Rel. Educ. & Staff Devel.

Office for Youth and Young Adults—Mr. JOHN J. TAGUE, M.A., M.B.A., Dir.; Ms. ANDREA MONTILLO, Asst. to Dir., 222 N. 17th St., Philadelphia, 19103-1299. Tel: 215-965-4637; Fax: 215-965-4629.

Parish Youth and Young Adult Ministry—Vicariate Coordinators: Mr. CHRISTOPHER JONES, Philadelphia North & South; Ms. ABBIE LANGSDORF, Chester & Delaware Counties; Ms. MARIA RICHARDSON, Bucks & Montgomery Counties.

Catholic Scouting—Ms. PATRICIA ANTONACCI, Coord.

Archdiocesan Boy Scouts—Rev. Msgr. JOHN B. WENDRYCHOWICZ, Chap.

Community Service Corps—KATHLEEN PFEFFER, Coord.

Athletic Ministry—Ms. CAROL BEAUSOLEIL, Coord.; Mr. VINCENT DREWICZ, Assoc. Coord.

Secretariat for Catholic Human Services

All addresses are: 222 N. 17th St., Philadelphia, PA 19103. Tel: 215-587-3900, unless otherwise indicated.

Secretary for Catholic Human Services—JOSEPH J. SWEENEY JR., M.B.A., N.H.A. Tel: 215-587-3908; GARY MILLER, CFO. Tel: 215-587-3892; EDWARD J. LIS, M.A., M.Div., Dir. Catholic Mission Integration. Tel: 215-965-1710; ANNE H. AYELLA, Dir. Catholic Relief Svcs., 111 S. 38th St., Philadelphia, 19104. Tel: 215-895-3470; SUZANNE O'GRADY-LAURITO, Coord. Catholic Campaign for Human Devel. Tel: 215-587-5656.

Catholic Charities of the Archdiocese of Philadelphia—JOSEPH J. SWEENEY JR., M.B.A., N.H.A., Sec. Catholic Human Svcs. Tel: 215-587-3908; JAMES AMATO, L.S.W., Deputy Sec. Catholic Social Svcs. Tel: 215-587-3754; GARY MILLER, CFO. Tel: 215-587-3892; AMY STONER, L.S.W., Dir. Community-Based Prevention Svcs. Tel: 215-587-3906; KATHLEEN EMERY, M.S.W., Dir. Community-Based & Specialized Svcs. Tel: 215-587-3590; DEBORAH WAGNER, L.S.W., Dir. Housing & Homeless Svcs. Tel: 215-587-3589; JOSEPH LAVORITANO, Dir., St. Gabriel's System, 227 N. 18th St., Philadelphia, 19103. Tel: 215-665-8777; MARK E. FITZGERALD, M.S.W., N.H.A., Dir. Developmental Progs. Div., Administrative Office, 1797 S. Sproul Rd., Springfield, 19064. Tel: 484-475-2469.

For detailed information please see Catholic Social Services of the Archdiocese of Philadelphia in the Institution Section (J).

Catholic Health Care Services—JOSEPH J. SWEENEY JR., M.B.A., N.H.A., Sec. Catholic Human Svcs. & Diocesan Coord. for Health Care Affairs. Tel: 215-587-3908; STUART K. SKINNER, R.N., M.B.A., N.H.A., Acting Deputy Sec. & CEO Catholic Health Care Svcs. and Dir. Facility-Based Svcs. Tel: 215-587-2436; 215-587-2496; MICHAEL CZEKNER, M.B.A., C.M.A., CFO. Tel: 215-242-2062; MARGARET M. FULLMER, M.H.A., N.H.A., Asst. Dir. Facility-Based Svcs. Tel: 215-587-3663; KELLY WRIGHT, M.S.W., N.H.A., Dir. Prog. Devel. & Administrative Support. Tel: 215-587-2487; JUDITH P. HORVATH, R.N., M.B.A., N.H.A., Dir. Clinical Oper. Tel: 215-587-3663; JOHN M. WAGNER, Dir. Project Devel. Tel: 215-587-3589.

For detailed information please see Catholic Social Services of the Archdiocese of Philadelphia in the Institution Section (J).

Nutritional Development Services—*111 S. 38th St., Philadelphia, 19104*. Tel: 215-587-3470. LORRAINE M. KNIGHT, M.Ed., Dir.

Office of Community Development—JOHN M. WAGNER, Dir. Tel: 215-587-3589.

Secretariat For Evangelization

All addresses are: 222 N. 17th St., Philadelphia, PA 19103-1299. Fax: 215-587-3561, unless otherwise indicated.

Administrative Director—Deacon DAVID B. SCHAFFER, M.A., M.S. Tel: 215-587-5666.

Office for Black Catholics—Rev. STEPHEN D. THORNE, M.A., M.Div., Dir. Tel: 215-587-3634.

Office for Ecumenical and Interreligious Affairs—Rev. Msgr. MICHAEL J. CARROLL, M.A. (Retired). Tel: 215-587-3624.

Office for Formation of the Laity—MARYANNE HARRINGTON, Dir. Tel: 215-587-0500.

RCIA/Adult Faith Formation—AUGUSTINE CARRILLO, Coord. Tel: 215-587-3685.

Church Ministry Institute—MARYANNE HARRINGTON, Dir.; Sr. MARY ELLEN DIEHL. Tel: 215-587-0551.

Parish Evangelization—Sr. LOUISE ALFF, O.S.F., Coord. Tel: 215-587-0547; CONSTANCE SCHARFF, Prog. Coord.

Parish Pastoral Councils Formation—MARTI HARRINGTON, Coord. Tel: 215-587-3694.

Family Life Office—DOMINIC LOMBARDI, M.A., S.T.L., Dir. Tel: 215-587-5639; ANN HANINCIK, M.T.S., Admin., Marriage Preparation. Tel: 215-587-3639; TARA SEYFER, M.T.S., Admin., Natural Family Planning.

Prison Ministry Program—Rev. GREGORY P. COZZUBBO, C.M., Chap.; LAURA FORD, Coord. Tel: 215-331-3640.

Office for Pastoral Care for Migrants and Refugees—Rev. JOSEPH G. WATSON, M.Div., M.A., Dir. Tel: 215-587-3540.

African Outreach—Rev. KIERAN O. UDEZE, Coord., Cathedral Basilica of SS. Peter & Paul, 18th St. & the Benjamin Franklin Pkwy., Philadelphia, 19103. Tel: 215-561-1313.

Apostleship of the Sea—Rev. DOMINIC ISAAC, J.C.D., Coord., Apostleship of the Sea, 475 N. Fifth St., Philadelphia, 19123. Tel: 215-922-2562.

Arab Outreach— Contact: Office for Pastoral Care for Migrants and Refugees Tel: 215-587-3540.

Cambodian Apostolate— Contact: Office for Pastoral Care for Migrants and Refugees Tel: 215-587-3540.

Chinese Apostolate—Rev. THOMAS BETZ, O.F.M.Cap., Coord. Tel: 215-592-7552.

Filipino Apostolate—Rev. EFREN V. ESMILLA, M.Div., Chap., Our Lady of Hope Rectory, 5200 N. Broad St., Philadelphia, 19141. Tel: 215-329-8100.

Haitian Apostolate—Rev. GARDY VILLARSON, O.M.I., Chap., Incarnation of Our Lord Rectory, 5105 N. 5th St., Philadelphia, 19120. Tel: 215-329-2320.

Hungarian Apostolate— Contact: Office for Pastoral Care for Migrants and Refugees Tel: 215-587-3540.

Indian Apostolate, Syro Malankara Rite—Rev. JOSEPH SUNDARAM, Chap., Maternity B.V.M., 9220 Bustleton Ave., Philadelphia, 19115.

Indian Apostolate-Knanayan Comm.—c/o Office for Pastoral Care for Migrants and Refugees. Tel: 215-587-3540.

Indian Apostolate, Latin Rite—Rev. RAJU B. SELVARAJ PILLA, Coord., Our Lady of Grace Rectory, 225 Bellevue Ave., Penndel, 19047. Tel: 215-757-7700.

Indonesian Apostolate—Rev. IGNATIUS SUPARNO, C.M., Chap., St. Thomas Aquinas, 1719 Morris St., Philadelphia, 19145. Tel: 215-334-2312.

Irish Apostolate— Contact: Office for Pastoral Care for Migrants and Refugees Tel: 215-587-3540.

Korean Apostolate—Revs. JOHN SUNG WOO PARK, Holy Angels, 7000 Old York Rd., Philadelphia, 19126. Tel: 215-548-5535; SIMON HYUNG-MIN HA, Coord., Holy Cross, Bishop & Springfield Rds., Springfield, 19064. Tel: 610-626-3321.

Laotian Apostolate—Rev. WILLIAM G. AYRES, St. Michael Rectory, 1445 N. 2nd St., Philadelphia, 19122. Tel: 215-739-2358.

Pakistani Apostolate—Rev. DOMINIC ISAAC, J.C.D., Coord., St. William, Rising Sun Ave. & Devereaux St., Philadelphia, 19111. Tel: 215-745-1389.

Polish Apostolate—Rev. Msgr. FRANCIS S. FERET, St. Adalbert, Allegheny Ave. & Thompson St., Philadelphia, 19134. Tel: 215-739-3500.

Portuguese and Brazilian Apostolates—Rev. GELSO DADATT, St. Martin of Tours, 5450 Roosevelt Blvd., Philadelphia, 19124. Tel: 215-533-0593.

Vietnamese Apostolate—Rev. Msgr. JOSEPH T. TRINH, St. Helena Rectory, 6161 N. 5th St., Philadelphia, 19120. Tel: 215-424-1300; Revs. JOSEPH DINH C. HUYNH, St. Thomas Aquinas Rectory, 1719 Morris St., Philadelphia, 19145. Tel: 215-334-2312; PETER N. QUINN, St. Alice Rectory, 150 Hampden Rd., Upper Darby, 19082. Tel: 610-352-1431; DOMINIC TRAN, St. Francis de Sales Rectory, 4625 Springfield Ave., Philadelphia, 19143. Tel: 215-222-5819; DOMINIC NGUYEN, C.Ss.R., Visitation Rectory, 2625 B St., Philadelphia, 19143. Tel: 215-634-1133.

Respect Life Office—SUSAN M. VADAS, Dir. Tel: 215-587-5661. Web: www.archdiocese-phl.org/evangelization/resplife/resplife.htm.

AIDS Ministry Program—SUSAN M. VADAS, Dir. Tel: 215-587-5661.

Department for Pastoral Care for Persons with Disabilities—Sr. KATHLEEN SCHIPANI, I.H.M., M.Ed., M.A., Admin. Tel: 215-597-3530 (Voice); 215-587-0510 (TTY).

Deaf Apostolate—Sr. KATHLEEN SCHIPANI, I.H.M., M.Ed., M.A., Admin. Tel: 215-587-3913 (Voice); 215-587-0510 (TTY); Rev. ANTHONY T. RUSSO, C.Ss.R., Coord., Visitation B.V.M. Tel: 215-423-9547. Web: www.archdiocese-phl.org/evangelization/resplife/deafapos.htm. For information on Mass schedule call office or visit our web site.

Department for Pro-Life Activities—SUSAN M. VADAS, Admin. Tel: 215-587-3703.

Pontifical Society for the Propagation of the Faith—Rev. Msgr. JAMES T. MCDONOUGH, M.S.W., L.L.D., Dir. (Retired); MICHELE MEIERS, Admin. Tel: 215-587-3944.

Pontifical Society of St. Peter Apostle—Rev. Msgr. JAMES T. MCDONOUGH, M.S.W., L.L.D., Dir. (Retired). Tel: 215-587-3944.

Pontifical Missionary Society of the Holy Childhood (Holy Childhood Assoc.)—MAUREEN RILLING, Mission Coord. Tel: 215-587-3945.

Pontifical Missionary Union—Rev. Msgr. JAMES T. MCDONOUGH, M.S.W., L.L.D., Dir. (Retired). Tel: 215-587-3944.

Office for Worship—Rev. G. DENNIS GILL, M.Div., S.L.L. Tel: 215-587-3537.

Secretariat For Clergy

All addresses are: 222 N. 17th St., Philadelphia, PA 19103-1299 unless otherwise indicated.

Office of the Vicar for Clergy—Rev. Msgr. DANIEL J. SULLIVAN, M.Div.; Revs. BRIAN P. HENNESSY, M.Div., J.C.L., Asst. to Vicar for Clergy; CHARLES ZLOCK, M.A., M.Div., M.I.B.S., Assoc. to Vicar for Clergy for Ongoing Formation.

Priests' Personnel Board—Most Revs. TIMOTHY C. SENIOR, D.D., V.G., M.B.A., M.S.W., M.Div.; ROBERT P. MAGINNIS, D.D., V.G.; JOSEPH P. MCFADDEN, D.D., V.G.; DANIEL E. THOMAS, D.D., S.T.L., V.G.; Rev. Msgrs. JOSEPH P. DUNCAN, M.Div.; MICHAEL J. FITZGERALD, M.Div., J.C.D., J.D.; JOSEPH T. MARINO, M.Div., M.A.; WILLIAM J. J. O'DONNELL, M.A. (Retired); ARTHUR E. RODGERS, Ph.D.; Rev. CHARLES J. SULLIVAN; Rev. Msgrs. DANIEL J. SULLIVAN, M.Div.; KEVIN C. LAWRENCE, M.Div.; Revs. WILLIAM F. MCGEOWN; BRIAN A. IZZO, M.A., M.Div.; PAUL M. KENNEDY, M.A., M.Div.; Rev. Msgrs. JOSEPH L. LOGRIP, M.A., M.Div.; GEORGE A. MAJOROS, M.S., M.Div.

Department Retired Clergy—Rev. Msgr. WILLIAM A. DOMBROW, M.Div.

Permanent Diaconate Department—Rev. Msgr. GREGORY J. PARLANTE, M.A., M.Div., Assoc. to Vicar for Clergy; Deacon JAMES T. OWENS, Dir.; Sr. SANTA MARIA D'ANGELO, R.S.M., Asst. Dir. Associates to the Administrator: Deacons WILLIAM L. HICKEY; PAUL J. MCBLAIN.

St. Charles Borromeo Seminary—Rev. Msgr. JOSEPH G. PRIOR, M.Div., M.A., S.S.L., S.T.D., Rector, 100 E. Wynnewood Rd., Wynnewood, 19096. Tel: 610-667-3394.

Vocation Office for Diocesan Priesthood—Rev. CHRISTOPHER B. ROGERS, M.A., St. Charles Borromeo Seminary, 100 E. Wynnewood Rd., Wynnewood, 19096. Tel: 610-667-5778.

Secretariat For Temporal Services

All addresses are: 222 N. 17th St., Philadelphia, PA 19103-1299 unless otherwise indicated.

Temporal Services—Mr. GLENN J. MASAKOWSKI, M.MGT., Sec. & CFO. Tel: 215-587-3959; Fax: 215-965-1711; Ms. ANITA GUZZARD, M.B.A., Deputy Sec. & Controller. Tel: 215-587-3943; Fax: 215-587-3939; Mrs. MARLENE M. LOGLISCI, M.B.A., S.P.H.R., Deputy Sec. & Dir. Tel: 215-587-3910; Fax: 215-587-3572.

Investment Services—Mr. ROBERT J. GUNN, Dir. Tel: 215-587-3969; Fax: 215-965-1711.

Catholic Cemeteries Office—Mr. ROBERT WHOMSLEY, Dir., 111 S. 38th St., Philadelphia, 19104. Tel: 215-895-3450; Fax: 215-895-3458.

Human Resources Office—Mrs. MARLENE M. LOGLISCI, M.B.A., S.P.H.R., Deputy Sec. & Dir. Tel: 215-587-3910; Fax: 215-587-3572.

Office for Insurance Services—CHARLES J. DEBEVEC, C.P.C.U., Dir. Tel: 215-587-3644; Fax: 215-587-2498.

Office for Accounting Services—ANITA GUZZARDI, M.B.A., Deputy Sec. & Controller. Tel: 215-587-3943; Fax: 215-587-3939.

Educational Financial Services—DAVID J. MAGEE, M.B.A., Ed.D., Dir. Tel: 215-587-3755; Fax: 215-587-3525.

Office of Property Services—Mr. ARTHUR FRIEDMAN, M.S., Coord. Tel: 215-587-3560; Fax: 215-587-0599.

Archdiocesan Offices, Boards, Commissions and Committees

All addresses are: 222 N. 17th St., Philadelphia, PA 19103-1299 unless otherwise indicated.

Blind, Guild for all the—Rev. EDMUND J. MAHER (Retired). Tel: 610-586-8535.

Board of Trustees of Lay Employees Retirement Plan—His Eminence CARDINAL JUSTIN RIGALI, Chm.; Mr. GLENN J. MASAKOWSKI, M.MGT., Vice Chm.

Diocesan Priests' Compensation and Benefits Committee—Rev. Msgr. DANIEL J. SULLIVAN, M.Div., Chm.; Revs. JOSEPH J. KELLEY; EDWARD H. BELL, M.Div.; WILLIAM G. DONOVAN, Ph.D., M.Div.; WILLIAM B. DOONER, M.Div.; Rev. Msgr. JOHN P. BOLAND, M.A. (Retired); Revs. VICTOR J. ESCHBACH; TIMOTHY M. JUDGE, M.Div.; Mr. GLENN MASAKOWSKI; Mr. ROBERT J. SIMS; Rev. Msgr. PAUL A. DIGIROLAMO, J.C.D., M.A., M.Div.

Building Committee—Rev. ROBERT C. VOGAN, Chm., (Drawings of building plans are reviewed by this committee).

Censores Librorum—Rev. Msgr. JOSEPH G. PRIOR, M.Div., M.A., S.S.L., S.T.D.; Revs. J. BRIAN BRANSFIELD, M.Div., M.A., S.T.L.; ROBERT A. PESARCHICK, M.A., S.T.L., S.T.D.; JOSEPH T. SHENOSKY, S.T.L., M.A., M.Div.

College of Consultors—Most Revs. ROBERT P. MAGINNIS, D.D., V.G.; JOSEPH P. MCFADDEN, D.D., V.G.; DANIEL E. THOMAS, D.D., S.T.L., V.G.; TIMOTHY C. SENIOR, D.D., V.G., M.B.A., M.S.W., M.Div.; Rev. Msgrs. MICHAEL J. FITZGERALD, M.Div., J.C.D., J.D.; DANIEL J. SULLIVAN, M.Div.; CHARLES L. SANGERMANO, M.Div.; Rev. EFREN V. ESMILLA, M.Div.; Rev. Msgr. JOSEPH L. LOGRIP, M.A., M.Div.; Revs. KEVIN J. MOLEY, C.Ss.R.; STEPHEN D. THORNE, M.A., M.Div.

Council of Priests—His Eminence CARDINAL JUSTIN RIGALI; Most Revs. ROBERT P. MAGINNIS, D.D., V.G.; JOSEPH P. MCFADDEN, D.D., V.G.; DANIEL E. THOMAS, D.D., S.T.L., V.G.; TIMOTHY C. SENIOR, D.D., V.G., M.B.A., M.S.W., M.Div.; Rev. Msgrs. DANIEL J. SULLIVAN, M.Div.; JOSEPH P. GARVIN, M.S.W., M.Div.; MICHAEL K. MAGEE, M.Div., M.A., S.S.L., S.T.L., S.T.D.; WILLIAM J. J. O'DONNELL, M.A. (Retired); MICHAEL C. PICARD, M.A.; STEPHEN P. MCHENRY, Ph.D., M.A., M.Div.; Revs. MICHAEL J. DAVIS, M.Div.; JOSEPH L. FARRELL, M.Div.; WILLIAM C. KAUFMAN, M.Div.; MICHAEL J. LEE, O.Praem.; JOHN R. DIORIO, M.A., M.Div.; MATTHEW W. GUCKIN, M.Div.; THOMAS M. HIGGINS, M.Div.; ROLAND D. SLOBOGIN, M.Div.

Educational Fund— Office of the Chief Financial Officer. Tel: 215-587-3959.

Information Line, Archdiocesan—Tel: 215-587-3600.

Interparochial Cooperation, Commission for—Rev. PAUL M. KENNEDY, M.A., M.Div., Chm., St. Katherine of Siena Rectory, 9700 Frankford Ave., Philadelphia, 19114-2896. Tel: 215-637-7548.

Legion of Mary—Rev. FRANCIS G. LENDACKY, St. Agnes-St. John Nepomucane Rectory, 319 Brown St., Philadelphia, 19123-2228. Tel: 215-627-0340.

Parish Sites and Boundaries, Commission for—Rev. Msgr. JAMES P. MCCOY, Chm.

Pastors Review Board—Revs. THOMAS M. HIGGINS, M.Div.; WILLIAM C. KAUFMAN, M.Div.; Rev. Msgrs. JOSEPH L. LOGRIP, M.A., M.Div.; STEPHEN P. MCHENRY, Ph.D., M.A., M.Div.; THOMAS M. MULLIN, S.S.L., M.A., M.Div.; Rev. ROLAND D. SLOBOGIN, M.Div.

Pennsylvania Catholic Conference— (Harrisburg) Board of Governors: His Eminence CARDINAL JUSTIN RIGALI. Administrative Board: Most Rev. TIMOTHY C. SENIOR, D.D., V.G., M.B.A., M.S.W., M.Div.; TIMOTHY R. COYNE ESQ. Department on Communications: DONNA FARRELL; MATTHEW GAMBINO. Education Department: Dr. RICHARD MCCARRON JR.; Ms. MARY E. ROCHFORD. Social Concerns: JOSEPH J. SWEENEY JR., M.B.A., N.H.A.; Deacon DAVID B. SCHAFFER, M.A., M.S.

Office for Child and Youth Protection—KAREN BECKER, L.S.W., Dir. Tel: 215-965-1743; Fax: 215-587-2466.

CLERGY, PARISHES, MISSIONS AND PAROCHIAL SCHOOLS

CITY OF PHILADELPHIA

(PHILADELPHIA COUNTY)

1—CATHEDRAL BASILICA OF SS. PETER AND PAUL (1846) Rev. Msgr. Michael T. McCulken; Revs. Edward P. Burke; Philip M. Forlano; Kieran O. Udeze. In Res., Rev. G. Dennis Gill; Deacons Epifanio DeJesus; Joseph A. Micucci.
Res.: 1723 Race St., 19103. Tel: 215-561-1313; 215-561-1314; Fax: 215-561-1580. Web: www.sspeterpaulcathedral.catholicweb.com.
Chapel—Our Lady of the Miraculous Medal 1903 Spring Garden St., 19130.

2—ST. ADALBERT (1904), (Polish), Rev. Msgr. Francis S. Feret; Rev. Thaddeus Gorka.
Res.: 2645 E. Allegheny Ave., 19134. Tel: 215-739-3500; Fax: 215-739-5706.
See Our Lady of Port Richmond Regional School, Philadelphia under Regional Parish Schools located in the Institution Section.

3—ST. AGATHA-ST. JAMES (1976), Consolidated. Revs. Steven J. Marinucci; Philip A. Florio, S.J.; Vincent R. Morabito; George Strausser.
Res.: 3728 Chestnut St., 19104. Tel: 215-386-9732; Fax: 215-386-9734. Web: saintsaj.org.

4—ST. AGNES-ST. JOHN NEPOMUCENE (1907), (Slovak), Consolidated January 1, 1980. Rev. Francis G. Lendacky.
Res.: 319 Brown St., 19123. Tel: 215-627-0340.

5—ALL SAINTS (Bridesburg) (1860) [CEM] Rev. William E. Grogan.
Res.: 2651 Buckius St., 19137. Tel: 215-535-4411; Fax: 215-744-6533. Email: allsaintsphl@aol.com.
See Pope John Paul II Regional Catholic School, Philadelphia under Regional Parish Schools located in the Institution section.
Catechesis/Religious Program—Students 56.

6—ALL SAINTS CHAPEL, Closed. (1877-1977) Formerly located at Philadelphia General Hospital, 700 Civic Center Blvd. Spiritual records are kept at St. Agatha-St. James Church. Tel: 215-386-9732; 386-9733.

7—ST. ALOYSIUS (1894-2003), (German), Closed. Formerly located at 26th & Tasker Sts. Spiritual records are kept at worship site of St. Gabriel Church, Tel: 215-463-4060.

8—ST. ALPHONSUS, Closed. (1852-1972) Formerly located at 1400 S. Fourth St. Spiritual records are kept at Sacred Heart of Jesus Church. Tel: 215-465-4050; 465-4051.

9—St. Ambrose (1923) Revs. James N. Catagnus; John M. Harkins; Deacon Jose M. Mendez.
Res.: 405 E. Roosevelt Blvd., 19120. Tel: 215-329-7900; 215-329-7901; Fax: 215-329-9206.
Church: C St. & Roosevelt Blvd., 19120.
Catechesis/Religious Program—Tel: 215-455-8160. Students 24.

10—St. Andrew (1924), (Lithuanian), Rev. Peter M. Burkauskas.
Res.: 1913 Wallace St., 19130. Tel: 215-765-2322; Fax: 215-765-0124.

11—St. Anne (1845) [CEM] Revs. Joseph D. Brandt; Joseph M. Arnholt.
Res.: 2328 E. Lehigh Ave., 19125. Tel: 215-739-4590; Fax: 215-739-0983. Email: stannephil@aol.com. Web: www.saintanne.net.
School—2343 E. Tucker St., 19125. Tel: 215-634-4231; Fax: 215-427-0608. Timothy Archer, Prin. Lay Teachers 10; Students 210.
Catechesis/Religious Program—Cedar & Tucker Sts. Students 52.

12—Annunciation B.V.M. (1860) Rev. Gary Pacitti. In Res., Rev. James R. Casey.
Res.: 1511 S. 10th St., 19147. Tel: 215-334-0159; Fax: 215-462-5065.
School—12th & Wharton Sts., 19147. Tel: 215-465-1416; Fax: 215-465-0308. Lay Teachers 11; Students 226.
Catechesis/Religious Program—Mary Ellen Carroll, D.R.E. Students 50.

13—St. Anselm (1962) Revs. Thomas J. Dunleavy; Keith J. Chylinski. In Res., Rev. John E. Fitzgerald (Retired); Deacon Gerald J. Whartenby.
Res.: 12670 Dunks Ferry Rd., 19154. Tel: 215-637-3525; Fax: 215-637-4915. Email: stanselm.church@verizon.net. Web: www.stanselmparish.org.
School—12650 Dunks Ferry Rd., 19154. Tel: 215-632-1133; Fax: 215-632-3264. Mrs. Geraldine Murphy, Prin. Lay Teachers 24; Students 433.
Catechesis/Religious Program—Students 175.

14—St. Anthony of Padua (1886) Closed. Formerly located at 2321 Fitzwater St. Spiritual records are kept at St. Charles Borromeo Church. Tel: 215-735-0600.

15—Ascension of Our Lord (1899) Rev. Michael A. Chapman; Deacon Leo Gladnick.
Res.: 725 E. Westmoreland St., 19134. Tel: 215-739-1670; Fax: 215-739-1455.
School—735 E. Westmoreland St., 19134. Tel: 215-739-6226; Fax: 215-739-7317. Teresa Richardson, Prin. Sisters 1; Lay Teachers 11; Students 164.
Catechesis/Religious Program— Deacon Leo Gladnick, D.R.E. Students 50.

16—Assumption B.V.M. (1848) Closed. (1848-1995) Formerly located at 1131 Spring Garden St. Spiritual records are kept at St. John the Evangelist Church. Tel: 215-563-4145.

17—St. Athanasius (1928) Rev. Joseph F. Okonski; Deacon Fred Poellnitz. In Res., Rev. Anayo Naa, C.Ss.R. (Nigeria).
Res.: 2050 Walnut Ln., 19138. Tel: 215-548-2700; Fax: 215-548-7453.
See St. Athanasius-Immaculate Conception School, Philadelphia under Regional Parish Schools located in the Institution section.
Catechesis/Religious Program—Students 36.

18—St. Augustine (1796) Rev. James D. McBurney, O.S.A. First foundation of Augustinian Order in U.S.A. In Res., Revs. Patrick B. McStravog, O.S.A.; Paul F. Morrisey, O.S.A.; James D. Paradis, O.S.A.
Res.: 243 N. Lawrence St., 19106-1195. Tel: 215-627-1838; Fax: 215-627-3911. Email: staug243@verizon.net. Web: www.st-augustinechurch.com.
See St. Mary Interparochial School, Philadelphia under Regional Parish Schools located in the Institution section.
Catechesis/Religious Program—Students 16.

19—St. Barbara (1921) Rev. Msgr. Wilfred J. Pashley.
Res.: 5359 Lebanon Ave., 19131. Tel: 215-473-1044; Fax: 215-473-5252. Email: saintbarbara5359@aol.com.
Catechesis/Religious Program—Students 1.
Convent—5336 Diamond St., 19131. Tel: 215-477-3839.

20—St. Barnabas (1919) Rev. John F. Babowitch; Deacons John J. Ellis; John J. Kreczkevich.
Res.: 6300 Buist Ave., 19142-3098. Tel: 215-726-1119; 215-726-1120; Fax: 215-726-1180.
Mary, Mother of Peace Area Catholic School. For further information see Regional Parish Schools in the Institution section.
Catechesis/Religious Program—Tel: 215-724-8728; Fax: 215-729-2315. Sr. Susan Bruno, I.H.M., D.R.E. Students 30.
Convent—6328 Buist Ave., 19142-3097. Tel: 215-729-1572.

21—St. Bartholomew (1919) Rev. James E. Goerner. In Res., Rev. Joseph C. McCaffrey.
Res.: 5600 Jackson St., 19124. Tel: 215-831-1224; 215-831-1225; Fax: 215-831-0467. Email: stbartrectory@yahoo.com. Web: stbartsparish.org.
Catechesis/Religious Program—Students 65.

22—St. Benedict (1922) Rev. George B. Moore; Deacons Stephen Hopkins; James L. Mahoney; Calvin C. Smith.
1942 E. Chelten Ave., 19138.
Res.: 1940 E. Chelten Ave., 19138. Tel: 215-924-4401; Fax: 215-924-4390. Email: saintbenedict@comcast.net.
Catechesis/Religious Program—Students 40.

23—St. Bernard (1927) Revs. Joseph N. Accardi; David B. Machain (Retired); Deacon Richard F. Hunter. In Res., Rev. Thomas M. Sodano.
Res.: 7341 Cottage St., 19136. Tel: 215-333-0446; Fax: 215-333-3215.
Catechesis/Religious Program—Students 55.

24—St. Bonaventure (1889-1993) Closed. Formerly located at 9th & Cambria Sts. Spiritual records are kept at St. Veronica Church. Tel: 215-228-4878.

25—St. Boniface (1865) Closed. Formerly located at 174 W. Diamond St. Spiritual records are kept at Visitation B.V.M. Church. Tel: 215-634-1133.

26—St. Brendan (1925-1934) Closed. Formerly located at 507 Manheim St. Spiritual records are kept at St. Francis of Assisi Church. Tel: 215-842-1287.

27—St. Bridget (1853) Rev. Joseph P. Devlin.
Res.: 3667 Midvale Ave., 19129. Tel: 215-844-4126; Fax: 215-842-2536. Email: stb@stbridgeteastfalls.org. Web: stbridgeteastfalls.org.
School—3636 Stanton St., 19129. Fax: 215-844-4089. Lay Teachers 17; Students 216.
Catechesis/Religious Program—Students 20.
Convent—3665 Midvale Ave., 19129.

28—St. Callistus (1921) Rev. John D. Harvey, O.F.M.Cap.
Res.: 700 N. 67th St., 19151-3614. Tel: 215-473-4417; Fax: 215-473-6728. Email: brojohn@stcallistusphilly.org. Web: stcallistusphilly.org.

29—St. Carthage (1915-2000) Closed. Formerly located at 525 Cobbs Creek Pkwy. Spiritual records are kept at St. Cyprian Church. Tel: 215-747-3250.

30—St. Casimir (1893), (Lithuanian), Rev. Peter M. Burkauskas.
Res.: 324 Wharton St., 19147. Tel: 215-468-2052; Fax: 215-468-0354.

31—St. Catherine of Siena (1910-1972) Closed. Formerly located at 436 W. Penn St. Spiritual records are kept at St. Vincent de Paul Church. Tel: 215-438-2925.

32—St. Cecilia (1911) Revs. Charles E. Bonner; James M. Cox; James T. McCabe; Deacon Patrick J. Diamond.
Res.: 535 Rhawn St., 19111. Tel: 215-725-1240; Fax: 215-725-2130. Email: stcecilia.swagner@verizon.net.
School—525 Rhawn St., 19111. Tel: 215-725-8588; Fax: 215-725-0247. Sisters of the Immaculate Heart of Mary 4; Lay Teachers 29; Students 690.
Catechesis/Religious Program—Tel: 215-725-2821. Students 149.

33—Chapel of Our Lady of the Miraculous Medal (La Milagrosa) (1912), (Spanish), Attended by Cathedral Basilica of SS. Peter and Paul, 1723 Race St., Philadelphia, PA 19103. Tel: 215-561-1313; 1314.
Church: 1903 Spring Garden St., 19130.
Catechesis/Religious Program—Students 16.

34—St. Charles Borromeo (1868) Rev. Edward P. Kuczynski; Deacon William C. Mayes.
Res.: 902 S. 20th St., 19146. Tel: 215-735-0600; Fax: 215-735-6630.
Church: 20th & Christian Sts., 19146.
Catechesis/Religious Program—Tel: 215-735-6898; Fax: 215-732-6253. Students 25.

35—Christ the King (1963) Rev. James A. Callahan. In Res., Rev. Joseph T. Shenosky.
Res.: 3252 Chesterfield Rd., 19114. Tel: 215-632-1144; Fax: 215-632-4933. Email: ctk@christthekingparish.net. Web: www.christthekingparish.net.
School—3205 Chesterfield Rd., 19114. Tel: 215-632-1375; 215-637-3838. Web: www.christthekingschool.net. Sisters of St. Joseph 2; Lay Teachers 22; Students 425.
Catechesis/Religious Program—Tel: 215-632-2144. Students 110.

36—St. Christopher (1950) Rev. Msgr. Joseph P. Garvin; Revs. Engelbert G. Michel; Robert C. Yetman; Deacon Edward J. Morris. In Res., Most Rev. Joseph P. McFadden; Rev. Msgr. John P. Boland (Retired); Rev. Dennis J.W. O'Donnell.
Res.: 13301 Proctor Rd., 19116. Tel: 215-673-5177; Fax: 215-698-0585. Web: www.stchrisparish.org.
School—13305 Proctor Rd., 19116. Tel: 215-673-5787; Fax: 215-673-8511. Web: www.saintchris.angelcities.com. Lay Teachers 32; Students 641.
Catechesis/Religious Program— Sr. Marie Notwick, S.S.J., D.R.E. Students 215.

37—St. Clement (1865) Closed. Spiritual records are kept at Divine Mercy Parish. Tel: 215-727-8300.

38—St. Columba (1895-1993) Closed. Formerly located at 2340 W. Lehigh Ave. Spiritual records are kept at St. Martin de Porres Church. Tel: 215-228-8330; 228-8331.

39—Corpus Christi, Closed. (1921-1987) Formerly located at 29th & Allegheny Ave. Spiritual records are kept at St. Martin de Porres Church. Tel: 215-228-8330; 228-8331.

40—Saint Cyprian (2000) Rev. Msgr. Federico A. Britto. In Res., Revs. John D. Hand; Stephen D. Thorne; Dominic Hoang Minh Tien.
Res.: 525 Cobbs Creek Pkwy., 19143. Tel: 215-747-3250; Fax: 215-747-2372. Email: sntcyprian@verizon.net. Web: www.saintcyprian.net.
School—6225 Cedar Ave., 19143. Tel: 215-748-4450; Fax: 215-747-7794. Paulla Jones-Hawkins, Prin. Lay Teachers 14; Students 242.
Catechesis/Religious Program—Students 15.

41—Divine Mercy Parish (2004) Rev. Michael S. Olivere.
Res.: 6667 Chester Ave., 19142-1397. Tel: 215-727-8300; Fax: 215-727-5932. Email: divinemercyparish@comcast.net. Web: divinemercyrc.com.
School—*Mary, Mother of Peace Regional Parish School*, 64th and Buist Ave., 19142. Tel: 215-729-3603. Sr. Janet Walters, I.H.M., Prin. For further information see Regional Parish Schools in the Institution section.
Catechesis/Religious Program—Mary Finnegan, C.R.E. Students 20.

42—St. Dominic (1849) [CEM] Revs. Edward T. Kearns; Michael J. Heim; Deacon Mark A. Salvatore.
Res.: 8504 Frankford Ave., 19136. Tel: 215-624-5502; 215-624-5503; Fax: 215-333-1750. Email: stdominicphila@hotmail.com. Web: stdominicphilapa.e-paluch.com.
School—8512 Frankford Ave., 19136. Tel: 215-333-6703; Fax: 215-333-9930. Sr. Shaun Thomas, I.H.M., Prin. Sisters, Servants of the Immaculate Heart of Mary 5; Lay Teachers 23; Students 415.
Catechesis/Religious Program—Tel: 215-624-5301. Students 70.
Convent—8510 Frankford Ave., 19136. Tel: 215-333-0144.

43—St. Donato (1910), (Italian), Rev. Ferdinand Buccafurni.
Res.: 403 N. 65th St., 19151. Tel: 215-747-4131; Fax: 215-747-7884.
School—405 N. 65th St., 19151. Tel: 215-748-2994; Fax: 215-748-0288. Amelia Luci, Prin. Lay Teachers 11; Students 225.
Catechesis/Religious Program—Students 2.

44—St. Edmond (1912) Rev. Thomas J. Rossi, O.Praem.; Deacon James J. Stewart.
Res.: 2130 S. 21st St., 19145. Tel: 215-334-3755; Fax: 215-334-2081.
Catechesis/Religious Program—Students 16.

45—St. Edward the Confessor (1865-1993) Closed. Spiritual records are kept at Visitation B.V.M. Church. Tel: 215-634-1133; 228-8331.

46—St. Elizabeth (1872-1993) Closed. Spiritual records are kept at St. Martin De Porres Church.

47—Epiphany of Our Lord (1889) Rev. John Pidgeon; Rev. Msgr. Richard T. Powers. In Res., Rev. Dennis J. Witalec; Deacon Frederick C. Druding.
Res.: 1121 Jackson St., 19148. Tel: 215-334-1035; Fax: 215-334-7885.
School—1248 Jackson St., 19148. Tel: 215-467-5385; Fax: 215-336-5103. Patricia Cody, Prin. Lay Teachers 15; Students 215.
Catechesis/Religious Program—Tel: 215-467-5621. Marge Jarman, C.R.E. Students 71.

48—St. Francis de Sales (1890) Rev. Louis C. Bier; Deacon Trac Mai Huynh; Barbara McGee, Business Mgr. In Res., Rev. Christal Rozario.
Res.: 4625 Springfield Ave., 19143. Tel: 215-222-5819; Fax: 215-222-5821. Web: www.saintfrancisdesales.net.
School—917 S. 47th St., 19143. Tel: 215-387-1749; Fax: 215-387-6605. Sr. Mary McNulty, I.H.M., Prin. Sisters, Servants of the Immaculate Heart of Mary 7; Lay Teachers 22; Students 501.
Catechesis/Religious Program—Tel: 215-222-3382. Sr. Alice Marie Daly, I.H.M., D.R.E. Students 43.
Convent—912 S. 47th St., 19143. Tel: 215-727-3929. Email: ihm912@comcast.net.

49—St. Francis of Assisi (1899) Rev. Eugene F. Sheridan, C.M. In Res., Revs. Joseph V. Cummins, C.M.; Jesus Guadarrama, C.M.; Timothy V. Lyons, C.M.
Res.: 4821 Greene St., 19144. Tel: 215-842-1287; Fax: 215-842-3338.
Catechesis/Religious Program—Students 20.

50—St. Francis Xavier (1839) Revs. Paul C. Convery, C.O.; Brian R. Gaffney, C.O.; Deacon Vincent J. Thompson. In Res., Very Rev. Georges G. Thiers,

C.O., Provost; Rev. Philip G. Bochanski, C.O.
Res.: 2319 Green St., 19130. Tel: 215-765-4568; Fax: 215-765-4049.
School—641 N. 24th St., 19130. Tel: 215-763-6564; Fax: 215-236-2818. Lay Teachers 12; Students 236.
Catechesis/Religious Program—Students 32.
Oratory— 2321 Green St., 19130.

51—ST. GABRIEL (1895) Rev. Michael J. Lee, O.Praem.; Sisters Marian Gregory, I.H.M., Pastoral Min.; Felice Marie, I.H.M., Pastoral Min.; Rev. Maurice C. Avicolli, O.Praem.
Res.: 2917 Dickinson St., 19146. Tel: 215-463-4060; Fax: 215-755-2680. Web: devoted.to/stgabes.
School—St. Gabriel School, 2917 Dickinson St., 19146. Tel: 215-468-7230; Fax: 215-468-2554. Sr. Noreen James Friel, I.H.M., Prin. Consolidated school for St. Gabriel Parish, St. Aloysius Parish & King of Peace Parish, Philadelphia, PA. Sisters 3; Lay Teachers 10; Students 206.
Catechesis/Religious Program—Tel: 215-334-0374. Mr. Chris Marano, Youth Min. Students 30.
Convent—2916 Dickinson St. Tel: 215-334-2620.

52—ST. GEORGE (1902), (Lithuanian), Rev. Msgr. Joseph J. Anderlonis.
Res.: 3580 Salmon St., 19134. Tel: 215-739-3102; Fax: 215-739-7217.
School—2700 E. Venango St., 19134. Tel: 215-634-8803. Lay Teachers 10; Students 212.
Convent—3570 Salmon St., 19134. Tel: 215-739-0472.

53—GESU (1868-1993) Closed. Formerly located at 18th & Thompson Sts. Spiritual records are kept at St. Malachy Church. Tel: 215-763-1305.

54—GOOD SHEPHERD (1925) Closed. Spiritual records are kept at Divine Mercy Parish. Tel: 215-727-8300.

55—ST. GREGORY, Closed. (1895-1981) Formerly located at 52nd & Warren Sts. Spiritual records are kept at St. Rose of Lima Church. Tel: 215-877-2991, 2992.

56—ST. HEDWIG (1907-2000), (Polish), Closed. Spiritual records are kept at St. Francis Xavier Church, Tel: 215-765-4568.

57—ST. HELENA (1924) Rev. Stephen B. Perzan; Rev. Msgr. Joseph T. Trinh; Deacons Victor Seda; Huan C. Tran. In Res., Rev. Edward A. Pelczar.
Res.: 6161 N. Fifth St., 19120-1422. Tel: 215-424-1300; Fax: 215-424-9152.
School—6101 N. Fifth St., 19120. Tel: 215-549-2947; Fax: 215-549-5947. Sisters of St. Joseph 1; Lay Teachers 20; Students 394.
Catechesis/Religious Program—Students 43.

58—ST. HENRY (1916-1993), (German), Closed. Formerly located at 4400 N. 5th St. Spiritual records are kept at Incarnation Church. Tel: 215-329-2320; 329-2321.

59—HOLY ANGELS (1906), (Korean), Revs. John Sung Woo Park; Abel Han Jun-Seok.
Res.: 7000 Old York Rd., 19126. Tel: 215-548-5535; 215-548-5536; Fax: 215-224-6615.
Catechesis/Religious Program—Bernard Suh, C.R.E. Students 200.

60—HOLY CHILD (1909-1993) Closed. Formerly located at 5200 N. Broad St. Spiritual records are kept at Our Lady of Hope Church. Tel: 215-329-8100; 329-8164.

61—HOLY CROSS (1890) Rev. Robert H. Mulligan; Deacon Francis B. Urmson.
Res.: 6440 Greene St., 19119. Tel: 215-438-2921; Fax: 215-848-7953.
Rectory—154 E. Mt. Airy Ave., 19119.
School—144 E. Mt. Airy Ave., 19119. Tel: 215-242-0414; Fax: 215-242-0414. Sisters of St. Joseph 1; Lay Teachers 12; Students 190.
Catechesis/Religious Program—Students 18.
Convent—148 E. Mt. Airy Ave., 19119. Tel: 215-247-0262.

62—HOLY FAMILY (1885) Rev. Francis X. McKee. In Res., Rev. Msgr. John E. Breslin (Retired).
Res.: 234 Hermitage St., 19127. Tel: 215-482-0450; Fax: 215-482-7531. Email: rectory234@aol.com.
School—Holy Child Catholic School, 242 Hermitage St., 19127. Tel: 215-487-2796; 215-483-0903; Fax: 215-242-0214. Web: holychildmyk.org. Michael J. Patterson, Prin. Regional school for Holy Family, St. John the Baptist, St. Josaphat, St. Lucy and St. Mary of the Assumption parishes. Lay Teachers 26; Students 390.
Catechesis/Religious Program—Interparochial C.C.D. Program - Holy Family, Tel: 215-483-4470; Fax: 215-483-4471. Students 46.

63—HOLY INNOCENTS (1927) Revs. Thomas M. Higgins; Vincent Tung The Pham.
Res.: 1337 E. Hunting Park Ave., 19124. Tel: 215-743-2600; Fax: 215-743-8041. Email: holyinnocents@comcast.net.
See Holy Innocents Area Catholic School, Philadelphia under Regional Parish Schools located in the Institution section.
Catechesis/Religious Program—Tel: 215-743-5909. Students 250.

64—HOLY NAME OF JESUS (Fishtown) (1904) Rev. Francis P. Groarke; Deacon John G. Boyle.
Res.: 701 E. Gaul St., 19125-2896. Tel: 215-739-3960; Fax: 215-739-7597. Web: www.holyname-fishtown.org.
Catechesis/Religious Program—Students 7.

65—HOLY REDEEMER (1941), (Chinese), Unassigned. Mission Chapel of the Church of St. John the Evangelist.
School—915 Vine St., 19107. Tel: 215-922-0999; Fax: 215-922-6674. Web: www.holyredeemer.cc. Lay Teachers 12; Students 301.
Catechesis/Religious Program—Students 41.
Parish House—916 Wood St., 19107. Tel: 215-592-7552.

66—HOLY SPIRIT (1964) Rev. John E. Calabro; Deacon Albert George.
Res.: 1900 Geary St., 19145. Tel: 215-334-4242; Fax: 215-334-8787. Web: www.holyspirit-phl.org.
School—1845 Hartranft St., 19145. Tel: 215-389-0715; Fax: 215-336-7719. Web: www.holyspiritschool-phl.org. Lay Teachers 11; Students 239.
Catechesis/Religious Program—Students 32.

67—HOLY TRINITY, (German), [CEM] Closed. (1788-2009) Formerly located at 6th & Spruce Sts. Spiritual records are kept at Worship Site of Old St. Mary's, Philadelphia. Tel: 215-923-7930.

68—ST. HUBERT (1924) Closed. Formally located at Torresdale and Cottman Aves. from 1924-1940. Spiritual records transferred to St. Bernard Church. Tel: 215-333-0446.

69—ST. HUGH OF CLUNY (1922) Revs. Andris Alexis Moronta, I.V.E.; Marcelo R. Lopresti, I.V.E.; Deacon Jose L. Lozada-Figueroa.
Res.: 145 W. Tioga St., 19140. Tel: 215-634-1800; Fax: 215-427-0303.
School—3501 N. Mascher St., 19140. Tel: 215-863-8048; Fax: 215-634-2690. Sisters of St. Joseph 3; Lay Teachers 6; Students 141.
Catechesis/Religious Program—Fax: 215-427-0303. Students 172.

70—ST. IGNATIUS OF LOYOLA (1893) Rev. James C. Otto.
Rectory—Res.: 636 N. 43rd St., 19104. Tel: 215-386-5065; Fax: 215-386-2832. Email: oms-si@yahoo.com. Web: www.oms-stignatius.com.
School—Our Mother of Sorrows-St. Ignatius School, 1008 N. 48th St., 19131. Tel: 215-473-5828. Sr. Owen Patricia Bonner, S.S.J., Prin.
Catechesis/Religious Program—Sr. Stephanie Henry, S.B.S., D.R.E. Students 20.
Convent—644 N. 43rd St., 19104. Tel: 215-386-0302.
Chaplaincy—St. Ignatius Nursing Home. Tel: 215-349-8800; Fax: 215-222-3078.

71—IMMACULATE CONCEPTION (1869) Rev. William G. Ayres, Admin., St. Michael Rectory, 1445 N. 2nd St., 19122. Tel: 215-739-2358.
Res.: 1020 N. Front St., 19123. Tel: 215-627-2702; Fax: 215-627-7344. Email: the-el-church@catholicweb.com. Web: the-el-church.catholicweb.com.
Catechesis/Religious Program—Students 2.

72—IMMACULATE CONCEPTION (1902) Rev. John J. Holliday, C.M.; Deacon Brouycie P. Isley. In Res., Revs. Michael J. Carroll, C.M.; Gregory P. Cozzubbo, C.M.; Carl L. Pieber, C.M.
Res.: 1020 E. Price St., 19138. Tel: 215-843-9468; Fax: 215-843-6570. Web: immaculateconception-phila.net.
See St. Athanasius-Immaculate Conception School, Philadelphia under Regional Parish Schools located in the Institution section.
Catechesis/Religious Program—Tel: 215-843-9468; Fax: 215-843-6570. Students 52.
Shrine—Our Lady of the Miraculous Medal 500 E. Chelten Ave., 19144. Tel: 215-848-1985. Web: www-.cammonline.org.

73—IMMACULATE HEART OF MARY (1952) Rev. Msgr. Joseph P. McGeown; Revs. Michael A. Filippello; Paul Obrimski; Deacon George W. Kletzel.
Res.: 819 Cathedral Rd., 19128. Tel: 215-483-1000; Fax: 215-483-1732. Email: ihmparish@comcast.net. Web: ihmchurch-andorra.e-paluch.com.
School—815 Cathedral Rd., 19128. Tel: 215-482-2029; Fax: 215-482-1075. Lay Teachers 33; Students 445.
Catechesis/Religious Program—Tel: 215-483-4266. Students 35.

74—INCARNATION OF OUR LORD (1900) Revs. Geraldo J. Pinero; Charles J. Kennedy; Deacons Felipe Cruz; Jose Hernandez. In Res., Rev. Gardy Villarson, O.M.I., (Haitian Apostolate).
Res.: 5105 N. Fifth St., 19120. Tel: 215-329-2320; Fax: 215-329-6149. Web: www.incarnationchurch.e-paluch.com.
School—Tel: 215-457-2779; Fax: 215-457-1328. Sisters Mary Anne Sweeney, I.H.M., Prin.; Mary Thomas, I.H.M., Vice Prin. Sisters, Servants of the Immaculate Heart of Mary 6; Lay Teachers 14; Students 372.
Catechesis/Religious Program—Students 165.
Convent—401 W. Lindley Ave., 19120. Tel: 215-329-0672.

75—SAINT IRENAEUS (1966) Closed. Spiritual records are kept at Divine Mercy Parish. Tel: 215-727-8300. Worship Site of Divine Mercy Parish.

76—ST. JAMES (1850-1976) Consolidated with St. Agatha to form St. Agatha-St. James. See separate listing for details.

77—ST. JEROME (1955) Revs. Joseph B. Graham; Dennis P. Boyle; Carl Graczyk, O.F.M.; Deacon Charles Pavonarius. In Res., Rev. Anthony W. Dieckhaus.
Res.: 8100 Colfax St., 19136. Tel: 215-333-4461; Fax: 215-333-6791. Email: stjeromeparish@aol.com. Web: www.stjeromeparish.com.
School—3031 Stamford St., 19136. Tel: 215-624-0637; Fax: 215-624-5711. Sharon Nendza, Prin. Lay Teachers 32; Students 676.
Catechesis/Religious Program—Students 64.

78—ST. JOACHIM (1845) [CEM] Rev. Steven P. Wetzel, O.S.F.S.
Res.: 1527 Church St., 19124. Tel: 215-535-0580; Fax: 215-831-1788.
See Holy Innocents Area Catholic School, Philadelphia under Regional Parish Schools located in the Institution section.
Catechesis/Religious Program—Students 29.

79—ST. JOAN OF ARC (1919) Rev. John J. Large. 1676 Ruan St., 19124. Tel: 215-535-4036; Fax: 215-535-1267.
Rectory—Res.: 2025 E. Atlantic St., 19134. Tel: 215-535-4641; Fax: 215-587-0508.
See Holy Innocents Area Catholic School, Philadelphia under Regional Parish Schools located in the Institution section.
Catechesis/Religious Program—Maggie Purr, D.R.E. Students 8.

80—ST. JOHN CANTIUS (1892), (Polish), Revs. Joseph J. Zingaro; Janusz Brembor. In Res., Rev. Marcel Kolakowski, O.F.M. (Retired).
Res.: 4415 Almond St., 19137. Tel: 215-535-6667; Fax: 215-535-7107. Email: sjc4415@comcast.net.
School—Pope John Paul II Regional Catholic, 4435 Almond St., 19137. Tel: 215-535-3446; Fax: 215-535-3858. Web: pjp2rcs.com. Regional school for St. John Cantius and All Saints parishes. Lay Teachers 21; Students 323.
Catechesis/Religious Program—Students 49.

81—ST. JOHN NEPOMUCENE, (Slovak), Consolidated with St. Agnes January 1, 1980. Spiritual records transferred to St. Agnes Church, 319 Brown St., Philadelphia, PA 19123. Tel: 215-627-0340.

82—ST. JOHN THE BAPTIST (1831) [CEM] Revs. James A. Lyons; Christopher D. Lucas; Deacon Gaspero P. Baratta.
Res.: 146 Rector St., 19127. Tel: 215-482-4600; Fax: 215-482-2976. Email: sjbphila@aol.com. Web: stjohnmanayunk.org.
Catechesis/Religious Program—Students 40.

83—ST. JOHN THE EVANGELIST (1830) [CEM] Revs. Francis Yacobi, O.F.M.Cap.; Senan Glass, O.F.M-.Cap.; Anselm Martin, O.F.M.Cap.; Matthew Palkowski, O.F.M.Cap.; Bro. James Gavin, O.F.M.Cap. In Res., Revs. Thomas Betz, O.F.M-.Cap.; Piotr Kwiatek, O.F.M.Cap; Benjamin Regotti, O.F.M.Cap.
Res.: 21 S. 13th St., 19107. Tel: 215-563-4145; Fax: 215-563-1770. Web: www.stjohnsphilly.com.
See St. Mary Interparochial School, Philadelphia under Regional Parish Schools located in the Institution section.
Mission—Holy Redeemer Chinese Church 915 Vine St., Philadelphia Co. 19107. Tel: 215-922-0999; Fax: 215-922-6674.

84—ST. JOSAPHAT (1898), (Polish), Rev. Leonard A. Lewandowski.
Res.: 124 Cotton St., 19127. Tel: 215-483-4470; Fax: 215-483-4037.
See Holy Child Catholic School, Philadelphia under Regional Parish Schools located in the Institution section.
Catechesis/Religious Program—Maryann Quinn, D.R.E. Students 37.

85—ST. KATHERINE OF SIENA (1922) Revs. Paul M. Kennedy; Ronald J. Ferrier; Armand D. Garcia; Deacon James J. Duffy; Carol Buchsbaum, Business Mgr. In Res., Rev. Msgr. Francis A. Carbine (Retired); Rev. Patrick Gitonga.
Res.: 9700 Frankford Ave., 19114-2896. Tel: 215-637-7548; Fax: 215-637-0146. Email: skschurch@skschurch.com. Web: www.skschurch.com.
School—9720 Frankford Ave., 19114. Tel: 215-637-2181; Fax: 215-637-4867. Web: www.sksgradeschool-.com. Sr. M. John, C.S.F.N., Prin. Sisters of the Holy Family of Nazareth 4; Lay Teachers 27; Students 589.
Catechesis/Religious Program—Tel: 215-637-1464. Email: prep@skschurch.com. Students 82.

86—King of Peace, (Italian), Closed. Spiritual records are kept at St. Gabriel Church, Tel: 215-463-4060.

87—St. Ladislaus (1906-2003), (Polish), Closed. Formerly located at 1650 W. Hunting Park Ave. Spiritual records are kept at St. Josaphat Church, Tel: 215-483-4470.

88—St. Laurentius (1882), (Polish), Rev. Francis A. Gwiazda.
Res.: 1608 E. Berks St., 19125. Tel: 215-739-1776; 215-739-9387; Fax: 215-739-9663. Email: stlaurentius@netzero.net.
School—1612 E. Berks St., 19125. Tel: 215-423-8834; Fax: 215-426-4675. Email: aplauren06@nni.com. Web: userweb.nni.com/aplauren06. Felician Sisters of St. Francis 1; Lay Teachers 10; Students 250.
Catechesis/Religious Program—Students 236.
Convent—1648 E. Berks St., 19125. Tel: 215-739-4447.

89—St. Leo (1884) Rev. Robert T. Feeney. In Res., Rev. Joseph E. O'Brien (Retired).
Res.: 6658 Keystone St., 19135. Tel: 215-333-0340; Fax: 215-333-7590. Email: stleotacony@hotmail.com. Web: www.saintleos.com.
Catechesis/Religious Program—Tel: 215-331-3399. Students 82.

90—St. Lucy (1905), (Italian), Rev. Francis J. Sabatini.
Res.: 4503 Smick St., 19127. Tel: 215-483-0554; Fax: 215-483-2450.
See Holy Child Catholic School, Philadelphia under Regional Parish Schools located in the Institution section.

91—St. Ludwig (1891-1975), (German), Closed. Formerly located at 28th & Master Sts. Spiritual records are kept at St. Francis Xavier Church. Tel: 215-765-4568.

92—St. Madeleine Sophie (1925) Rev. Robert H. Mulligan; Deacons Richard Coyne; Francis Urmson. In Res., Rev. Brian P. Hennessy.
Res.: 6440 Greene St., 19119. Tel: 215-438-2921; Fax: 215-848-7953. Email: smg0398@comcast.net.
See Holy Cross Parish School, Philadelphia.
Catechesis/Religious Program—Students 4.

93—St. Malachy (1850) Rev. Msgr. Kevin C. Lawrence.
Res.: 1429 N. 11th St., 19122. Tel: 215-763-1305; Fax: 215-763-2023. Email: ccsm@stmalachy.us. Web: www.saintmalachyparish.com.
School—1419 N. 11th St., 19122. Tel: 215-232-0696; Fax: 215-236-1434. Lay Teachers 12; Students 215.
Catechesis/Religious Program—Students 45.

94—Saint Martha (1966) Rev. Alexander Masluk; Rev. Msgr. John J. Miller; Deacon Raymond F. Gwynn Sr. In Res., Rev. James J. Collins.
Res.: 11301 Academy Rd., 19154-3304. Tel: 215-632-3720; Fax: 215-632-7737. Web: stmarthachurch.com.
School—11321 Academy Rd., 19154-3304. Tel: 215-632-0320; Fax: 215-632-5546. Lay Teachers 21; Students 436.
Catechesis/Religious Program—Students 90.

95—St. Martin De Porres (1993) Rev. Edward J. Hallinan; Deacons Edward J. Andrews; Thomas A. Shields. In Res., Rev. Shaun L. Mahoney.
Res.: 2340 W. Lehigh Ave., 19132. Tel: 215-228-8330; Fax: 215-221-6516.
School—23rd St. & Lehigh Ave., 19132. Tel: 215-223-6872; Fax: 215-223-4126. Sisters of St. Joseph 5; Lay Teachers 12; Students 390.
Catechesis/Religious Program—Students 21.

96—St. Martin of Tours (1923) Rev. Msgr. Edward M. Deliman; Revs. Christopher R. Cooke; Joseph L. DiGregorio; Deacon Stanley M. Zaleski; Sisters Elizabeth Ann Motz, I.H.M., Pastoral Assoc.; Ellen Maguire, S.S.J., Pastoral & Social Min. In Res., Rev. Gelso Dadatt.
Res.: 5450 Roosevelt Blvd., 19124. Tel: 215-535-2962; Fax: 215-535-3091. Email: stmartinsphila@aol.com. Web: www.smtparish.org.
School—Loretto Ave. & Sanger St., 19124. Fax: 215-533-1579. Sisters of the Immaculate Heart of Mary 6; Lay Teachers 28; Students 566.
Catechesis/Religious Program—Fax: 215-535-3091. Email: ccd@smtparish.org. Brenda Pineda, C.R.E. Students 83.

97—St. Mary Magdalen de Pazzi, (Italian), Closed. (1852-2000). Formerly located at 712 Montrose St. Spiritual records are kept at Saint Paul Church. Tel: 215-923-0355.

98—St. Mary of Czestochowa, (Polish), Closed. (1927-2000) Formerly located at 59th St. and Elmwood Ave. Spiritual records are kept at St. Barnabas Church. Tel: 215-726-1119; 1120.

99—St. Mary of the Assumption (1849), (German), [CEM] Rev. James T. McGuinn.
Res.: 176 Conarroe St., 19127. Tel: 215-482-4264; Fax: 215-508-1731. Web: www.stmarymanayunk.com.
See Holy Child Catholic School, Philadelphia under Regional Parish Schools located in the Institution section
Catechesis/Religious Program—Students 78.

100—St. Mary of the Eternal, (Italian), Closed. (1911-1976) Formerly located at 2222 W. Clearfield St. Spiritual records are kept at St. Martin de Porres. Tel: 215-228-8330; 228-8331.

101—Mater Dolorosa (1911), (Italian), Rev. John J. Large. In Res., Rev. Cornelius F. Kilty, O.S.F.S.
Res.: 1676 Ruan St., 19124. Tel: 215-535-4036; 215-743-4718; Fax: 215-535-1267. Email: materdolorosachurch@verizon.net. Web: materdolorosachurch.net.
See Holy Innocents Area Catholic School, Philadelphia under Regional Parish Schools located in the Institution section.
Catechesis/Religious Program—Students 25.

102—Maternity B.V.M. (1870) Rev. Paul S. Quinter; Rev. Msgr. Bernard E. Witkowski; Revs. John P. Hutter; Jaehwa John Lee; Deacons Phillip Heaney; Charles R. Lindsay. In Res., Rev. Joseph Sundaram.
Res.: 9220 Old Bustleton Ave., 19115-4686. Tel: 215-673-8127; 215-676-5144; Fax: 215-673-6597. Web: maternitybvm.catholicweb.com.
School—9322 Bustleton Ave., 19115. Tel: 215-673-0235; Fax: 215-671-1347. Lay Teachers 23; Students 556.
Catechesis/Religious Program—Tel: 215-673-4010. Sr. Mary Beth Geraghty, R.S.M., D.R.E. Students 163.
Convent—Tel: 215-673-8118.

103—St. Matthew (1927) Rev. Msgr. Charles E. McGroarty; Revs. Thomas J. Cavanaugh; Matthew C. Chadwick, O.F.M.Conv.; Deacon Robert Burns. In Res., Rev. Msgr. Thomas J. Kelley (Retired).
Res.: 3000 Cottman Ave., 19149. Tel: 215-333-0585; Fax: 215-333-0757. Web: www.stmattsparish.com.
School—3040 Cottman Ave., 19149. Tel: 215-333-3142. Sisters, Servants of the Immaculate Heart of Mary 10; Lay Teachers 39; Students 889.
Catechesis/Religious Program—Students 87.
Convent—3040 Cottman Ave., 19149. Tel: 215-333-8214.

104—St. Michael (1831) [CEM] Rev. William G. Ayres; Bonnie Hackett, Coord. Parish Svcs.; Deacon Zoilo Martes.
Res.: 1445 N. Second St., 19122. Tel: 215-739-2358; Fax: 215-739-5766. Web: www.saintmichael.catholicweb.com.
Catechesis/Religious Program—Students 39.

105—St. Michael Mission, Closed. Spiritual records are kept at Our Lady of Calvary Church. Tel: 215-637-7515.

106—St. Michael of the Saints, Closed. (1924-1982) Formerly located at 4811 Germantown Ave. Spiritual records kept at St. Francis of Assisi Church. Tel: 215-842-1287.

107—St. Monica (1895) Revs. Joseph J. Kelley; Ronald Check; Deacon Leonard D. DeMasi. In Res., Rev. Msgr. James E. Connelly (Retired); Rev. Clement Kurowski, O.F.M. (Retired).
Res.: 2422 S. 17th St., 19145. Tel: 215-334-4170; 215-334-4171; Fax: 215-389-6045. Web: www.saintmonicaparish.net.
School—Junior School, 1720 Ritner Ave., 19145. Tel: 215-334-3777; Fax: 215-389-0355.
School—Senior School, 2500 S. 16th St., 19145. Tel: 215-467-5338; Fax: 215-467-4599. Servants of the Immaculate Heart of Mary 6; Lay Teachers 23; Students 445.
Catechesis/Religious Program—Tel: 215-334-1659; Fax: 215-389-0355. Students 142.

108—Most Blessed Sacrament, Closed. (1901-2008) Formerly located at 56th St. & Chester Ave. Spiritual records are kept at St. Francis de Sales Church, Philadelphia. Tel: 215-222-5819.

109—Most Precious Blood of Our Lord (1907-1993) Closed. (1907-1993) Formerly located at 28th & Diamond Sts. Spiritual records are kept at St. Martin De Porres Church. Tel: 215-228-8330.

110—Mother of Divine Grace (1926), (Italian), Rev. Msgr. Joseph L. Logrip.
Res.: 2918 E. Thompson St., 19134. Tel: 215-739-0353; Fax: 215-739-9910.
School—2612 E. Monmouth St., 19134. Tel: 215-426-7325; Fax: 215-426-0753. Lay Teachers 11; Students 232.
Catechesis/Religious Program—Students 4.

111—Nativity of the Blessed Virgin Mary (1882) Revs. Dennis Z. Fedak; Richard P. Connors; James P. Gorman. In Res., Rev. Daniel J. Moriarity (Retired).
Res.: 2535 E. Allegheny Ave., 19134. Tel: 215-739-2735; Fax: 215-739-2748. Email: nativitybvm@aol.com. Web: www.nativityphiladelphia.4lpi.com.
Catechesis/Religious Program—Tel: 215-739-1173. Students 30.

112—St. Nicholas of Tolentine (1912), (Italian), Revs. Nicholas Martorano, O.S.A.; John Brynes, O.S.A.; James R. Keating, O.S.A. In Res., Revs. W. Howard McGraw, O.S.A.; Denis G. Wilde, O.S.A.
Res.: 910 Watkins St., 19148. Tel: 215-463-1326; Fax: 215-463-0888. Web: www.stnicksphila.com.
Church: Ninth St. below Morris St., 19148.
School—913 Pierce St., 19148. Tel: 215-468-0353; Fax: 215-334-9661. Religious Sisters Filippini 3; Religious 2; Lay Teachers 17; Students 347.
Catechesis/Religious Program—Students 73.

113—Old St. Joseph's (1733) Revs. Daniel M. Ruff, S.J.; Michael A. Hricko, S.J. In Res., Revs. James F. McAndrews, S.J. (Retired); Joseph J. McGovern, S.J. (Retired); Terrence Toland, S.J. (Retired).
Res.: 321 Willings Aly., 19106. Tel: 215-923-1733; 215-923-1734; Fax: 215-574-8529. Web: www.oldstjoseph.org.
See St. Mary Interparochial School, Philadelphia under Regional Parish Schools located in the Institution section.
Catechesis/Religious Program—Linda Robinson, D.R.E. Students 40.

114—Old St. Mary's (1763) [CEM] Rev. Msgr. Paul A. DiGirolamo.
Res.: 252 S. Fourth St., 19106. Tel: 215-923-7930.
See St. Mary Interparochial School, Philadelphia under Regional Parish Schools located in the Institution section.

115—Our Lady Help of Christians (1885), (German), Rev. Dennis Z. Fedak.
Res.: 3160 Gaul St., 19134. Tel: 215-739-2211; Fax: 215-739-9272.
See Our Lady of Port Richmond Regional School, Philadelphia under Regional Parish Schools located in the Institution Section.
Convent—Tel: 215-739-7890.

116—Our Lady of Angels (1907), (Italian), Closed. Formerly located at 4970 Master St. Spiritual records are kept at worship site of St. Donato Church. Tel: 215-747-4131.

117—Our Lady of Calvary (1958) Revs. John P. Paul; William S. Kirk; Quan M. Trinh.
Res.: 11024 Knights Rd., 19154. Tel: 215-637-7515; Fax: 215-637-7517. Web: www.ourladyofcalvary.org.
School—11023 Kipling Ln., 19154. Tel: 215-637-1648; Fax: 215-637-3810. Sisters of the Holy Family of Nazareth 5; Lay Teachers 34; Students 812.
Catechesis/Religious Program—Students 180.

118—Our Lady of Consolation (1917), (Italian), Rev. Dennis J. Carbonaro; Deacon Joseph M. Cella.
Res.: 7056 Tulip St., 19135. Tel: 215-333-0442; 215-333-5774; Fax: 215-333-2884. Web: www.olctacony.org.
School—Princeton & Edmund Sts., 19135. Tel: 215-624-0505. Web: www.olcschool.catholicweb.com. Mr. Stephen DiCicco, Prin. Religious 1; Lay Teachers 10; Students 226.
Catechesis/Religious Program—Students 50.

119—Our Lady of Good Counsel (1898-1932) Closed. Formerly located at 816 Christian St. Spiritual records are kept at St. Paul Church. Tel: 215-923-0355.

120—Our Lady of Hope (1993) Revs. Efren V. Esmilla; Rayford E. Emmons; Deacons William Champagne; Israel Rosario; Felipe Hernandez; Homer A. Panganiban.
Res.: 5200 N. Broad St., 19141-1628. Tel: 215-329-8100; 215-329-8164; Fax: 215-324-4660. Email: olhphiladelphia@aol.com.
Catechesis/Religious Program—Students 20.

121—Our Lady of Loreto (1932-2000), (Italian), Closed. Formerly located at 6214 Grays Ave. Spiritual records are kept at St. Barnabas Church. Tel: 215-726-1119; 1120.

122—Our Lady of Lourdes (1894) Revs. James W. Mayer, O.de.M.; Joseph K. Horvath, O.de.M.
Res.: 6315 Lancaster Ave., 19151. Tel: 215-473-2848; Fax: 215-473-2878. Email: dbaker@ourladylourdes.org. Web: www.ourladylourdes.org.
Parish Center: 1920 N. 63rd St., 19151. Tel: 215-473-1669; Fax: 215-473-1670.
School—1940 N. 63rd St., 19151. Tel: 215-877-2727; Fax: 215-877-6042. Sisters of Our Lady of Mercy 3; Lay Teachers 14; Students 245.
Catechesis/Religious Program—Students 52.

123—Our Lady of Mercy (1889-1984) Closed. Formerly located at Broad St. & Susquehanna Ave. Spiritual records are kept at St. Malachy Church. Tel: 215-763-1305.

124—Our Lady of Mt. Carmel (1896) Revs. Francis J. Cauterucci; Kevin B. McGoldrick; Augustus C. Puleo.
Res.: 2319 S. Third St., 19148. Tel: 215-334-7766; Fax: 215-334-3269. Web: olmc-sophilly.org.
School—2329 S. Third St., 19148. Tel: 215-334-0584; Fax: 215-336-4519. Sisters of Mercy 2; Lay Teachers 9; Students 193.
Catechesis/Religious Program—Students 24.
Convent—251 Ritner St., 19148. Tel: 215-334-6800.

125—Our Lady of Pompeii (1914-1993), (Italian), Closed. Formerly located at 6th St. & Erie Ave. Spiritual records are kept at St. Veronica Church.

Tel: 215-228-4878.

126—OUR LADY OF RANSOM (1955) Rev. Christopher Redcay; Deacon Ralph J. Shirley. In Res., Rev. Edward L. Rauch, O.S.F.S. (Retired); Rev. Msgr. Hugh Joseph Shields.
Res.: 6701 Calvert St., 19149. Tel: 215-332-6166; Fax: 215-332-6811. Email: olorbulletin@yahoo.com. Web: www.oloransom.org.
School—6740 Roosevelt Blvd., 19149. Tel: 215-332-4352. Lay Teachers 10; Students 225.
Catechesis/Religious Program—Tel: 215-708-2495. Students 60.
Convent—Tel: 215-624-1954.

127—OUR LADY OF THE BLESSED SACRAMENT (1910-1972) Closed. Formerly located at 712 N. Broad St. Spiritual records are kept at the Cathedral Basilica of SS. Peter and Paul. Tel: 215-561-1313; 561-1314.

128—OUR LADY OF THE BLESSED SACRAMENT (2005) Rev. Paul Kuppe, O.F.M.Cap.; Deacon Richard G. Nightingale.
Mailing Address: 345 N. 63rd St., 19139. Tel: 215-476-6511; Fax: 215-476-3230. Web: www.olobs.org.
School—344 N. Felton St., 19139. Tel: 215-474-4011; Fax: 215-474-7807.
Catechesis/Religious Program—Mark Gonzalez, Dir. Faith Formation. Students 33.

129—OUR LADY OF THE HOLY SOULS (1909-1993) Closed. Formerly located at 19th & Tioga Sts. Spiritual records are kept at Our Lady of Hope Church. Tel: 215-329-8100.

130—OUR LADY OF THE ROSARY (1886-2005) Closed. Formerly located at 345 N. 63rd St. Spiritual records are kept at Our Lady of the Blessed Sacrament Church. Tel: 215-476-6511.

131—OUR LADY OF THE ROSARY (Germantown) (1928-1977), (Italian), Closed. Formerly located at 528 E. Haines St. Spiritual records are kept at Immaculate Conception Church. Tel: 215-843-9468.

132—OUR LADY OF VICTORY (1899-2005) Closed. Formerly located at 5412 Vine St. Spiritual records are kept at Our Lady of the Blessed Sacrament Church. Tel: 215-476-6511.

133—OUR MOTHER OF CONSOLATION (1855) Very Rev. Robert L. Bazzoli, O.S.F.S.; Rev. David J. Devlin, O.S.F.S.; Deacon Clifford W. Brown. In Res., Revs. R. Douglas Smith, O.S.F.S.; Nicholas R. Waseline, O.S.F.S.
Res.: 9 E. Chestnut Hill Ave., 19118. Tel: 215-247-0430; Fax: 215-247-2506. Email: bbazzoli@omcparish.com. Web: omcparish.com.
School—17 E. Chestnut Hill Ave., 19118. Tel: 215-247-1060; Fax: 215-247-0590. Email: bhagy@omcparish.com. N. Bruce Hagy, Prin. Lay Teachers 12; Students 176.
Catechesis/Religious Program—Email: jrussell@omcparish.com. Students 115.
Convent—23 E. Chestnut Hill Ave., 19118. Tel: 215-247-0552.

134—OUR MOTHER OF SORROWS (1852) Rev. James C. Otto.
St. Ignatius of Loyola, 636 N. 43rd St., 19104. Tel: 215-386-5065.
Rectory—1030 N. 48th St., 19131. Tel: 215-878-0875; Fax: 215-878-7420. Email: oms-si@yahoo.com. Web: www.oms-stignatius.com.
School—Our Mother of Sorrows-St. Ignatius School, 1020 N. 48th St., 19131. Tel: 215-473-5828; Fax: 215-477-3096. Web: www.skdp.org. Sr. Owen Patricia Bonner, S.S.J., Prin. Sisters of St. Joseph 3; Lay Teachers 10; Students 310.
Catechesis/Religious Program— Mrs. Jennifer Simmons, D.R.E. Students 205.

135—ST. PATRICK (1839) Rev. Daniel E. Mackle. In Res., Rev. Msgrs. Louis A. D'Addezio; Michael J. Fitzgerald.
Res.: 242 S. 20th St., 19103. Tel: 215-735-9900; Fax: 215-732-0998. Email: stpatricksparish@aol.com.
School—St. Mary Interparochial School, Tel: 215-923-7522.
See St. Mary Interparochial School, Philadelphia under Regional Parish Schools located in the Institution section.
Catechesis/Religious Program—Students 25.

136—ST. PAUL (1843) Rev. Gerald P. Carey.
Res.: 808 S. Hutchinson St., 19147. Tel: 215-923-0355; Fax: 215-923-1803. Web: stpaulparishsouthphilly.com.
Worship Site:— Saint Mary Magdalen de Pazzi Church, 712 Montrose St.
Catechesis/Religious Program—Students 140.

137—ST. PETER CLAVER (1889-1985) Closed. Formerly located at 12th & Lombard Sts. Spiritual records are kept at St. John the Evangelist Church. Tel: 215-563-4145.

138—ST. PETER THE APOSTLE (1842) [CEM] Revs. Kevin J. Moley, C.Ss.R.; Robert Harrison, C.Ss.R.; Varghese Kocherry, C.Ss.R.; Arthur Gildea, C.Ss.R.; Mark Wise, C.Ss.R.; Deacons Jose Miguel Betancourt; Juan Ramos. In Res., Revs. Gerard Brinkman, C.Ss.R.; Donald Miniscalco, C.Ss.R.; Dennis J. Billy, C.Ss.R.; Rev. Msgr. George Tomichek, D.C.
Church, Rectory & Mailing Address: 1019 N. Fifth St., 19123. Tel: 215-627-2386; Fax: 215-627-2366.
School—1009 N. Fifth St., 19123. Tel: 215-922-5958. Sr. Rose Federici, S.S.N.D. School Sisters of Notre Dame 1; Lay Teachers 11; Students 250.
Catechesis/Religious Program— Sr. Clare Marsico, I.H.M., D.R.E. Students 60.
Convent—1005 N. 5th St., 19123. Tel: 215-627-3954.
Shrine—St. John Neumann, Tel: 215-627-3080; Fax: 215-627-3296. Mary Argenbright, Office Mgr.

139—ST. PHILIP NERI (1840) Revs. James M. Oliver; Francis Piro (Retired).
Res.: 218 Queen St., 19147. Tel: 215-468-1922; Fax: 215-465-3147. Email: stphilipneri@comcast.net. Web: churchofstphilipneri.org.

140—ST. RAPHAEL (1904-1989) Closed. Spiritual records are kept at Divine Mercy Parish. Tel: 215-727-8300.

141—ST. RAYMOND OF PENAFORT (1941) Rev. Christopher M. Walsh.
Res.: 1350 Vernon Rd., 19150. Tel: 215-549-3760; Fax: 215-549-1271. Email: saintraymondchurch@yahoo.com. Web: www.saintraymond.net.
School—7940 Williams Ave., 19150. Tel: 215-548-1919; Fax: 215-548-1925. Lay Teachers 10; Students 310.
Catechesis/Religious Program—Students 52.

142—RESURRECTION OF OUR LORD (1928) Revs. Joseph E. Howarth; Charles F. Engelhardt, O.S.F.S.; Deacon Dennis J. Friel. In Res., Rev. Joseph E. Tustin, O.S.F.S.
Res.: 2000 Shelmire Ave., 19152. Tel: 215-745-3211; Fax: 215-745-0587. Web: www.resurrectphila.org.
School—2020 Shelmire Ave., 19152. Tel: 215-742-1127; Fax: 215-742-0947. Email: resurrectionschool@yahoo.com. Web: www.resurrection.org/school. Mrs. Joan Stulz, Prin. Lay Teachers 26; Students 510.
Catechesis/Religious Program—Tel: 215-742-0947. Students 62.

143—ST. RICHARD (1924), (Italian), Rev. William C. Kaufman.
Res.: 3010 S. 18th St., 19145. Tel: 215-468-4777; Fax: 215-468-3161. Web: www.strichardchurch.org.
School—19th & Pollock Sts., 19145. Tel: 215-467-5430. Lay Teachers 11; Students 291.
Catechesis/Religious Program—Dennis Mueller, D.R.E. Students 46.
Convent—1827 Pollock St., 19145.

144—ST. RITA OF CASCIA (1907) Revs. Joseph A. Genito, O.S.A., Pastor & Shrine Dir.; Eugene DelConte, O.S.A., Shrine Ministry; William A. Recchuti, O.S.A. In Res., Revs. John R. Flynn, O.S.A.; Michael Scuderi, O.S.A.
Res. & Friary: 1166 S. Broad St., 19146. Tel: 215-546-8333; Fax: 215-732-3510. Email: ritashrine@aol.com. Web: www.saintritashrine.org.
Shrine—The National Shrine of St. Rita of Cascia 1166 S. Broad St., 19146. Tel: 215-546-8333; Fax: 215-732-3510.

145—ST. ROSE OF LIMA (1921) Rev. Msgr. Wilfred J. Pashley.
Res.: 1535 N. 59th St., 19151. Tel: 215-877-2991; Fax: 215-877-8255. Email: saintroseoflima@aol.com.
School—1522 N. Wanamaker St., 19131. Tel: 215-473-6030; Fax: 215-473-2338. Sisters, Servants of the Immaculate Heart of Mary 4; Lay Teachers 10; Students 220.

146—SACRED HEART (1913-1977), (Hungarian), Closed. Formerly located at Mascher & Master Sts. Spiritual records are kept at St. Michael Church. Tel: 215-739-2358.

147—SACRED HEART OF JESUS (1871) Revs. Michael J. Sheehan; William E. Dean. In Res., Rev. John J. Bradley (Retired).
Res.: 1404 S. Third St., 19147-6099. Tel: 215-465-4050; 215-465-4051; Fax: 215-465-0400. Web: www.sacredheartsp.com.
School—1329 Moyamensing Ave., 19147. Tel: 215-462-4129; Fax: 215-462-9429. Web: www.sacredheartsp.com. Sr. Patricia Mount, I.H.M., Prin. Sisters of the Immaculate Heart of Mary 4; Lay Teachers 9; Students 238.
Convent—1420 S. Third St., 19147. Tel: 215-463-8719. Sr. Kathleen Schipani, I.H.M., Supr.

148—ST. STANISLAUS (1891), (Polish), Closed. Formerly located at 242 Fitzwater St. Spiritual records are kept at worship site of St. St. Philip Neri Church. Tel: 215-468-1922.

149—STELLA MARIS (1954) Rev. Peter J. DiMaria; Rev. Msgr. George J. Mazzotta; Deacon James A. Thompson.
Res.: 2901 S. 10th St., 19148. Tel: 215-465-2336; 215-465-2337; Fax: 215-465-1061.
School—814 Bigler St., 19148. Tel: 215-467-6262; Fax: 215-389-6040. Sisters of St. Joseph 2; Lay Teachers 13; Students 181.
Catechesis/Religious Program—Students 100.
Convent—2929 S. 10th St., 19148. Tel: 215-462-1111.

150—ST. STEPHEN (1843-1993) Closed. Formerly located at Broad & Butler Sts. Spiritual records are kept at Our Lady of Hope Church. Tel: 215-329-8100.

151—ST. TERESA OF AVILA (1853-1972) Closed. Formerly located at Broad & Catherine Sts. Spiritual records are kept at St. Rita Church. Tel: 215-546-8333.

152—ST. THERESE OF THE CHILD JESUS (1925) Rev. Christopher M. Walsh, Admin.; Deacon Edward M. Purnell.
Res.: 6611 Ardleigh St., 19119. Tel: 215-438-5279; Fax: 215-438-8031.
Catechesis/Religious Program—Tel: 215-438-5279. Students 27.

153—ST. THOMAS AQUINAS (1885) Revs. Herbert J. Sperger; Joseph Dinh C. Huynh (Vietnam).
Res.: 1719 Morris St., 19145. Tel: 215-334-2312; Fax: 215-755-9369. Email: staparish@yahoo.com.
School—18th & Morris Sts., 19145. Tel: 215-334-0878; Fax: 215-334-2357. Email: sta.school@yahoo.com. Lay Teachers 13; Students 304.
Day Care—1700 Fernon St.; 1800 Morris St. Tel: 215-334-6480; Fax: 215-334-8221. Staff 15; Children 100.
Catechesis/Religious Program—Students 100.

154—ST. TIMOTHY (1928) Rev. Stephen F. Leva; Rev. Msgr. James J. Flood (Retired); Rev. John E. Donia; Deacon Edward F. Hanley. In Res., Revs. Patrick G. McCormick; Thomas J. Rooney.
Res.: 3001 Levick St., 19149. Tel: 215-624-6188; Fax: 215-624-1316. Web: www.st-tims.org.
School—3051 Levick St., 19149. Tel: 215-338-9797; Fax: 215-331-6457. Lucille Hillerman, Prin.; Margaret Presutti, Vice Prin. Lay Teachers 24; Students 539.
Catechesis/Religious Program—Tel: 215-338-9797, Ext. 123. Students 100.
Convent—3033 Levick St., 19149. Tel: 215-624-8333.

155—TRANSFIGURATION OF OUR LORD (1905-2000) Closed. Spiritual records are kept at St. Cyprian Church. Tel: 215-747-3250.

156—ST. VERONICA (1872) Rev. Eduardo Coll, I.V.E.; Deacon Rafael Maldonado.
Res.: 533 W. Tioga St., 19140. Tel: 215-228-4878; 215-225-5677; Fax: 215-228-0381. Email: par.philadelphi@ive.org.
School—Sixth & Tioga St., 19140. Tel: 215-225-1575; Fax: 215-225-2595. Sr. Mary Ann Bolger, I.H.M., Prin. Sisters, Servants of the Immaculate Heart of Mary 3; Lay Teachers 8; Students 203.
Catechesis/Religious Program—Tel: 215-228-4878. Sr. Maria de Foy, S.S.V.M., D.R.E. Students 190.
Convent—Sisters, Servants of the Immaculate Heart of Mary, 3521 N. Sixth St., 19140. Tel: 215-223-9107. Sr. Victoria Ferraro, I.H.M., Supr.
Convent—Kathareine Drexel Sisters, Servants of the Lord and the Virgin of Matara, 632 W. Erie Ave., 19140. Tel: 215-226-3507.

157—ST. VINCENT DE PAUL (1851) Rev. Richard J. Rock, C.M. In Res., Revs. Abel Osorio, C.M.; Ignatius Suparno, C.M. (Indonesia).
Res.: 109 E. Price St., 19144. Tel: 215-438-2925; Fax: 215-438-4856. Web: www.saint-vincent-church.org.
See the Depaul Catholic School, Philadelphia under Regional Parish Schools located in the Institution section.
Catechesis/Religious Program—Students 60.

158—VISITATION B.V.M. (1874) Revs. Bruce Lewandowski, C.Ss.R.; James Cascione, C.Ss.R.; Luyen Dau, C.Ss.R.; John Olenick, C.Ss.R.; Deacons Edwin Manzano; Jorge L. Vera. In Res., Revs. Kevin R. Murray, C.Ss.R.; Anthony T. Russo, C.Ss.R.
Res.: 2625 B St., 19125. Tel: 215-634-1133; Fax: 215-634-6662. Email: visitationchurch@visitationbvm.com. Web: www.visitationbvm.net.
School—300 E. Lehigh Ave., 19125. Tel: 215-634-7280; Fax: 215-634-4062. Sisters of St. Joseph 5; Lay Teachers 24; Students 500.
Catechesis/Religious Program—Sr. Linda Lukiewski, S.S.J., D.R.E. Students 434.

159—ST. WILLIAM (1920) Revs. Joseph G. Watson; Scott D. Brockson; Mardean E. Miller; Deacon Louis Malfara. In Res., Rev. Dominic Isaac, J.C.D.
Res.: 6200 Rising Sun Ave., 19111. Tel: 215-745-1389; Fax: 215-745-2650. Web: www.churchofstwilliam.org.
School—Main School, Rising Sun and Robbins St., 19111. Tel: 215-342-4488. Sr. Catherine Clark, I.H.M., Prin.
School—Middle School, Rising Sun and Devereaux Aves., 19111. Tel: 215-725-2574. Sisters, Servants of the Immaculate Heart of Mary 4; Lay Teachers 17; Students 410.

Catechesis/Religious Program—Tel: 215-745-0921. Sr. Maryan Chappetto, I.H.M., D.R.E. Students 107.
Convent—6226 Rising Sun Ave., 19111. Tel: 215-745-3513.
Pastoral Care Ministry—

OUTSIDE THE CITY OF PHILADELPHIA

ABINGTON, MONTGOMERY CO., OUR LADY HELP OF CHRISTIANS (1953) Rev. Anthony W. Janton; Deacon Joseph T. Rooney. In Res., Rev. John P. Melepuram.
Res.: 1500 Marian Rd., 19001. Tel: 215-886-3456; Fax: 215-886-7312. Web: www.olhc-parish.org.
Preschool—Tel: 215-887-8503. Lay Teachers 8; Students 49.
School—Elkins & Crater Rds., 19001. Tel: 215-887-3067; Fax: 215-887-3250. Lay Teachers 16; Students 259.
Catechesis/Religious Program—Tel: 215-672-7074. Dianne Donohue. Students 178.

AMBLER, MONTGOMERY CO.
1—ST. ANTHONY OF PADUA (1886) [CEM] Rev. Msgr. Stephen P. McHenry; Rev. John T. Lyons; Deacons David E. Jones; Kevin Gentilcore.
Res.: 259 Forest Ave., 19002-5903. Tel: 215-646-4742; Fax: 215-646-4864. Web: www.saintanthony-parish.org.
See St. Anthony - St. Joseph Elementary School, Ambler under Regional Parish Schools located in the Institution section.
Catechesis/Religious Program—260 Forest Ave., 19002. Tel: 215-646-6150. Students 279.
2—ST. JOSEPH (1920) Rev. Eugene M. Tully; Deacon Francis Clark.
Res.: 16 S. Spring Garden St., 19002-4797. Tel: 215-646-0494; Fax: 215-643-6389. Email: maccard@verizon.net.
Catechesis/Religious Program—Students 116.

ARDMORE, MONTGOMERY CO., ST. COLMAN (1907) Rev. James C. Sherlock; Deacon David B. Schaffer. In Res., Rev. Tadeusz Pacholczyk.
Res.: 11 Simpson Rd., 19003. Tel: 610-642-0545; 610-649-4775; Fax: 610-642-6853. Email: stcolmanchurch@gmail.com. Web: www.stcolman-church.org.
See SS. Colman-John Neumann School, Bryn Mawr under Regional Parish Schools located in the Institution section.
Catechesis/Religious Program—Students 84.

ARDSLEY, MONTGOMERY CO., QUEEN OF PEACE (1954) Rev. Lawrence F. Crehan; Joseph Costello, Business Mgr.
Res.: 820 North Hills Ave., 19038. Tel: 215-887-1838; Fax: 215-887-8328. Email: queenofpeaceparish@comcast.net. Web: www.queenofpeaceparish.net.
School—835 N. Hills Ave., 19038. Tel: 215-886-4782. Email: principal@qofpeace.org. Web: www.qof-peace.org. Sr. Patricia Healey, I.H.M., Prin. Sisters, Servants of the Immaculate Heart of Mary 2; Lay Teachers 13; Students 170.
Catechesis/Religious Program—Tel: 215-886-3014. Anna Olson, D.R.E.
Convent—825 North Hills Ave., 19038. Tel: 215-887-4785.

ASTON, DELAWARE CO., ST. JOSEPH (1947) Revs. Robert C. Vogan; William S. Lange; Rev. Msgr. Richard J. Skelly (Retired); Deacon John M. Betzal.
Res.: 3255 Concord Rd., 19014. Tel: 610-497-3340; Fax: 610-497-3383. Email: stjoseph256@comcast.net. Web: www.stjosephaston.org.
School—Tel: 610-494-0147. Email: stjosephschooloffice@comcast.net. Ms. Anne Cook, Prin. Lay Teachers 14; Students 219.
Catechesis/Religious Program—Tel: 610-494-4358. Email: cmaugeri@stjoseph.org. Ms. Catherine Maugeri, D.R.E. Students 375.

BALA CYNWYD, MONTGOMERY CO., ST. MATTHIAS (1906) Rev. Msgr. Arthur E. Rodgers; Mr. John Yura, Business Mgr.; Brandon Artman, Dir. Parish Svcs. In Res., Rev. Charles E. Gormley (Retired).
Res.: 128 Bryn Mawr Ave., 19004-3099. Tel: 610-664-0207; Fax: 610-664-3559. Email: aer@saintmatthias.org. Web: saintmatthias.org.
Catechesis/Religious Program—120 Bryn Mawr Ave., 19004-3098. Tel: 610-664-1942. Students 82.
Convent—108 Highland Ave., 19004. Tel: 610-667-1399.

BENSALEM, BUCKS CO.
1—ST. CHARLES BORROMEO (1903) Rev. Msgr. Joseph P. Duncan. In Res., Rev. Richard K. McFadden.
Res.: 1731 Hulmeville Rd., 19020. Tel: 215-638-3625; Fax: 215-245-8578. Web: stcharles-bensalem.e-paluch.com.
School—(Grades PreK-8), 1704 Bristol Pike, 19020. Tel: 215-639-3456; Fax: 215-639-0496. Web: stcharlesbensalem.org. Sisters, Servants of the Immaculate Heart of Mary 2; Lay Teachers 16; Students 302.
Catechesis/Religious Program—Tel: 215-638-3650. Students 120.
Convent—1080 Kings Ave., 19020. Tel: 215-639-0113. Sisters Servants of the Immaculate Heart of Mary 8.
2—ST. ELIZABETH ANN SETON (1976) Rev. Michael J. Lonergan; Deacon Stephen A. Guckin.
1200 Park Ave., 19020-4652. Tel: 215-245-6122; Fax: 215-245-4211. Web: www.seasparish.info.
Catechesis/Religious Program—Tel: 215-638-1498. Students 72.
3—SAINT EPHREM (1966) [CEM] Rev. Msgr. Kenneth P. McAteer; Revs. Stephen F. Katziner; Richard E. Rudy; Deacons Edward J. Dymek Jr.; James P. DeBow.
Res.: 5400 Hulmeville Rd., 19020. Tel: 215-245-1698; Fax: 215-245-4787.
School—5340 Hulmeville Rd., 19020. Tel: 215-639-9488; Fax: 215-639-0206. Sisters, Servants of the Immaculate Heart of Mary 4; Lay Teachers 25; Students 470.
Catechesis/Religious Program—Tel: 215-639-4895. Students 230.
Convent—5300 Hulmeville Rd., 19020. Tel: 215-638-1024.
4—OUR LADY OF FATIMA (1954) Revs. John F. Meyers; Victor P. Warkulwiz, M.S.S.; Deacon Adolfo Crespo.
Res.: Fatima Acres, 2933 Street Rd., 19020. Tel: 215-639-4254; Fax: 215-639-4589. Email: olf.pastor@verizon.net.
Early Childhood Center—Fatima Acres, 2913 Street Rd., 19020. Tel: 215-639-1916.
School—2915 Street Rd., 19020. Tel: 215-638-3256; Fax: 215-639-6424. Email: apolfat08@olfatimaschool.org. Web: olfatimaschool.org. Sisters, Servants of the Immaculate Heart of Mary 3; Lay Teachers 8; Students 170.
Catechesis/Religious Program—Tel: 215-639-8814. Sr. Mary Ann Fazakerley, I.H.M., D.R.E. Students 165.

BERWYN, CHESTER CO., ST. MONICA (1897) [CEM] Rev. William A. Trader.
Res.: 635 First Ave., 19312. Tel: 610-644-0110; Fax: 610-695-0850. Web: www.saintmonicachurch.org.
School—610 First Ave., 19312. Tel: 610-644-8848; Fax: 610-695-8515. Mrs. Diana Thompson, Prin. Lay Teachers 16; Students 197.
Catechesis/Religious Program—Tel: 610-647-4757; Fax: 610-647-4757. Mary Pizzano, D.R.E. Students 300.

BOOTHWYN, DELAWARE CO., ST. JOHN FISHER (1971) Rev. John A. Freeman; Deacon John J. DuBois.
Res.: 4225 Chichester Ave., 19061. Tel: 610-485-0441; Fax: 610-859-2109. Web: www.stjohnfisher-church.com.
See Holy Saviour-St. John Fisher School, Linwood under Regional Parish Schools located in the Institution section.
Catechesis/Religious Program—Tel: 610-485-0581. Students 280.

BRIDGEPORT, MONTGOMERY CO.
1—ST. AUGUSTINE (1892) [CEM] Rev. Charles Zlock.
Res.: 464 Ford St., 19405. Tel: 610-272-4088; Fax: 610-272-6396. Email: staugustine@comcast.net. Web: www.saintaugustinechurch.net.
Catechesis/Religious Program—Students 83.
Worship Site:—
Our Lady of Sorrows—421 Coates St., 19405.
2—OUR LADY OF MT. CARMEL (1924), (Italian), Rev. Salvatore J. Pronesti.
Res.: 502 Ford St., 19405. Tel: 610-272-3479; Fax: 610-272-5449. Email: olmcoffice@comcast.net. Web: www.olmcchurch.net.
Catechesis/Religious Program—Tel: 610-272-3479; Fax: 610-272-5449. Students 62.
3—OUR MOTHER OF SORROWS (1926), (Slovak), Closed. For inquiries for parish records contact the chancery.

BRISTOL, BUCKS CO.
1—ST. ANN (1906), (Italian), Very Rev. James R. Day, O.SS.T.; Rev. Thomas A. Morris, O.SS.T. In Res., Rev. Vincent Bechamps, O.SS.T.
Res.: 357 Dorrance St., P.O. Box 1175, 19007. Tel: 215-788-2128; Fax: 215-781-9782. Email: office@stannbristol.com. Web: www.stannbristol.com.
Catechesis/Religious Program—Tel: 215-788-2030; Fax: 215-788-2979. Students 95.
Convent—430 Jefferson Ave., 19907. Tel: 215-788-2531.
Mission—*Sacred Heart of Jesus* Main St., Tullytown, Bucks Co. 19007.
2—ST. MARK (1845) [CEM] Rev. Dennis M. Mooney.
Res.: 1025 Radcliffe St., 19007. Tel: 215-788-2493; Fax: 215-785-4121. Email: office@saintmarkchurch.net. Web: www.saintmarkchurch.net.
School—1024 Radcliffe St., 19007. Tel: 215-785-0973; Fax: 215-781-0268. Mrs. Angelina Clair, Prin. Lay Teachers 12; Students 186.
Catechesis/Religious Program—Tel: 215-788-2319. Mary Leonhauser, C.R.E. Students 133.

BROOKHAVEN, DELAWARE CO., OUR LADY OF CHARITY (1952) Rev. Msgr. Andrew J. Hanlon; Rev. Mark S. Gaspar. In Res., Rev. Lukas Runtu.
Res.: 231 Upland Rd., 19015. Tel: 610-872-6192; Fax: 610-872-1120.
School—249 Upland Rd., 19015. Tel: 610-874-0410; Fax: 610-874-5879. Lay Teachers 12; Students 184.
Catechesis/Religious Program—Tel: 484-480-5469. Students 195.

BROOKLINE, DELAWARE CO., ANNUNCIATION B.V.M. (1927) Rev. Mark J. Haynes; Deacon Francis J. Connors. In Res., Rev. Christopher B. Rogers.
Res.: 410 Sagamore Rd., Havertown, 19083. Tel: 610-449-1613; Fax: 610-449-7041. Web: www.annunciationparish.com.
School—411 Brookline Blvd., Havertown, 19083. Tel: 610-446-8430; Fax: 610-446-0627. Sisters of Mercy 1; Lay Teachers 14; Students 190.
Catechesis/Religious Program—Tel: 610-449-9858. Students 340.
Convent—421 Brookline Blvd., Havertown, 19083. Tel: 610-449-4065.

BROOMALL, DELAWARE CO., ST. PIUS X (1955) Revs. James Hutchins; Albert J. Santorsola; Rev. Msgr. John J. Jagodzinski; Deacons Joseph E. Iannucci; Stephen C. Kazanjian. In Res., Rev. Edward J. Casey.
Res.: 220 Lawrence Rd., 19008. Tel: 610-353-4880; Fax: 610-356-1084. Email: stpiusxbusinessoffice@comcast.net. Web: www.saintpius.net.
School—204 Lawrence Rd., 19008. Tel: 610-356-7222; Fax: 610-356-5380. Sisters, Servants of the Immaculate Heart of Mary 6; Lay Teachers 21; Students 451.
Catechesis/Religious Program—Tel: 610-353-6950; Fax: 610-356-1084. Students 452.

BRYN MAWR, DELAWARE CO., ST. JOHN NEUMANN (1964) Rev. James J. McKeaney; Sr. Carol Kelly, S.S.J., Dir. Parish Ministries. In Res., Rev. Marc F. Capizzi.
Res.: 380 Highland Ln., 19010. Tel: 610-525-3100; Fax: 610-525-6363. Email: sjnparish@verizon.net.
See SS. Colman-John Neumann School, Byrn Mawr under Regional Parish Schools located in the Institution section.
Catechesis/Religious Program—Students 125.
Convent—340 Highland Ln., 19010. Tel: 610-527-1220; 610-527-3115.

BRYN MAWR, MONTGOMERY CO., OUR MOTHER OF GOOD COUNSEL (1885) Revs. James E. Martinez, O.S.A.; Francis A. Sirolli, O.S.A. In Res., Revs. Anthony P. Burrascano, O.S.A.; Dennis M. McGowan, O.S.A.
Res.: 31 Pennswood Rd., 19010. Tel: 610-525-0147; Fax: 610-525-0157. Email: frjmartinez@omgcparish.org. Web: www.omgcparish.org.
Catechesis/Religious Program—Fax: 610-525-0157. Students 150.

BUCKINGHAM, BUCKS CO., OUR LADY OF GUADALUPE (2000) Rev. Msgr. Joseph P. Gentili; Deacon Robert P. Gohde.
Mailing Address: P.O. Box 406, 18912-0406.
Parish Office—5667 York Rd., Lahaska, 18931. Tel: 215-794-2004; Fax: 215-794-5004.
Res.: 3686 W. Long Ln., Doylestown, 18902-1292. Tel: 215-230-4625.
Catechesis/Religious Program—Tel: 215-794-4105; Fax: 215-794-4106. Students 563.

CENTER SQUARE, MONTGOMERY CO., ST. HELENA (1919) Rev. Msgr. Joseph J. Nicolo; Rev. George J. Szparagowski; Deacon A. Kenneth Belanger.
Res.: 1489 DeKalb Pike, Blue Bell, 19422. Tel: 610-275-7711; Fax: 610-275-7610. Web: www.sainthelena-centersquare.net.
School—1499 DeKalb Pike, Blue Bell, 19422. Tel: 610-279-3345. Web: www.sainthelenaschool.org. Sisters of Mercy 1; Lay Teachers 29; Students 447.
Catechesis/Religious Program—Tel: 610-279-3870. Students 254.
Convent—Tel: 610-272-1383.

CHADDS FORD, DELAWARE CO., ST. CORNELIUS (1963) Rev. Msgr. Gregory J. Parlante; Rev. Dominic M. Chiaravalle; Deacon Richard G. Wirth.
Res.: 160 Ridge Rd., 19317. Tel: 610-459-2502; Fax: 610-459-3942. Email: stcorn1@comcast.net. Web: saintcornelius.org.
School—*St. Cornelius School*, Tel: 610-459-8663; Fax: 610-459-7728. Students 254.
Catechesis/Religious Program—Tel: 484-840-9250; Fax: 610-459-3942. Students 700.

CHALFONT, BUCKS CO., ST. JUDE (1962) Rev. Msgr. James P. McCoy; Rev. Robert G. Suskey; Mr. Robert T. O'Sullivan, Business Mgr.; Deacons John T. Riordan; Claude B. Granese.
Res.: 321 W. Butler Ave., 18914-2329. Tel: 215-822-0179; Fax: 215-822-0638. Email: stjudeoffice@comcast.net. Web: www.stjudechalfont.org.
School—323 W. Butler Ave., 18914-2329. Tel: 215-822-9225; Fax: 215-822-0722. Email: semrsm@stjudeschool.com. Web: www.stjudeschool-.com. Sr. Elizabeth Marley, R.S.M., Prin. Sisters 1;

Lay Teachers 24; Students 374.
Catechesis/Religious Program—Tel: 215-822-7553. Email: prep@stjudeschool.com. Alice Patcella, D.R.E. Students 572.

CHELTENHAM, MONTGOMERY CO.

1—ST. JOSEPH (1953) Rev. William S. Harrison.
Res.: 7631 Waters Rd., 19012-1318. Tel: 215-635-5533; Fax: 215-635-4578.
Catechesis/Religious Program—Students 39.

2—PRESENTATION OF BLESSED VIRGIN MARY (1890) Revs. William S. Harrison; John R. McFadden; Sr. Joan B. Melley, S.S.J., Parish Svcs. Dir.
Res.: 100 Old Soldiers Rd., 19012. Tel: 215-379-1364; 215-379-1599; Fax: 215-379-2054.
School—Hasbrook Ave. & Old Soldiers Rd., 19012. Tel: 215-379-3798; Fax: 215-379-4430. Web: www.presentationbvm.org/school. Lay Teachers 14; Students 256.
Catechesis/Religious Program—Tel: 215-379-2054. Students 87.
Convent—107 Old Soldiers Rd., 19012. Tel: 215-379-8343.

CHESTER HEIGHTS, DELAWARE CO., ST. THOMAS THE APOSTLE (1729) [CEM] Revs. Richard C. Williams; John H. Roebuck.
Res.: 430 Valley Brook Rd., Glen Mills, 19342. Tel: 610-459-2224; Fax: 610-459-2677.
School—Tel: 610-459-8134; Fax: 610-459-8120. Lay Teachers 35; Students 404.
Catechesis/Religious Program—Tel: 610-459-3477. Mary Sassani, D.R.E. Students 545.
Chaplaincies— Glen Mills Schools; Delaware County Prison; Brinton Manor; Rosehill; Riddle Hospital; 4 Seasons Assisted Living.

CHESTER, DELAWARE CO.

1—ST. ANTHONY OF PADUA (1908-1993), (Italian), Closed. Formerly located at 308 W. 3rd St. Spiritual records are kept at Saint Katharine Drexel Church, Chester. Tel: 610-872-3731.

2—ST. HEDWIG (1902-1993), (Polish), Closed. Formerly located at 4th & Hayes Sts. Spiritual records are kept at Sacred Heart Church, Clifton Heights. Tel: 610-623-0409.

3—IMMACULATE HEART OF MARY (1873-1993) Closed. Formerly located at 2nd & Norris Sts. Spiritual records are kept at Saint Katharine Drexel Church, Chester. Tel: 610-872-3731.

4—SAINT KATHARINE DREXEL (1993) Rev. Msgr. Joseph C. McLoone; Rev. Peter J. Welsh; Deacons Michael J. Finn; John J. Pileggi.
1920 Providence Ave., 19013. Tel: 610-872-3731; Fax: 610-872-0545. Web: www.stkatharinedrexelparish.org.
Catechesis/Religious Program—Students 39.
Convent—1902 Providence Ave., 19013. Tel: 610-876-4916.
Saint Katharine Drexel Center—2nd & Norris St., 19013. Tel: 610-872-3731; Fax: 610-872-0545.

5—ST. MICHAEL (1842-1993) Closed. Formerly located at 7th St. & Avenue of the States. Spiritual records are kept at Saint Katharine Drexel Church, Chester. Tel: 610-872-3731.

6—OUR LADY OF VILNA (1924-1972), (Lithuanian), Closed. Formerly located at 4th & Madison Sts. Sacramental records are kept at Saint Katharine Drexel Church, Chester. Tel: 215-872-3731.

7—RESURRECTION OF OUR LORD (1911-1993) Closed. Formerly located at 9th St. & Highland Ave. Spiritual records are kept at Saint Katharine Drexel Church, Chester. Tel: 610-872-3731.

8—ST. ROBERT (1922-1993) Closed. Formerly located at 20th St. & Providence Ave. Spiritual records are kept at Saint Katharine Drexel Church, Chester. Tel: 610-872-3731.

CLIFTON HEIGHTS, DELAWARE CO., SACRED HEART (1910), (Polish), Rev. Jan Palkowski.
Res.: 316 E. Broadway, 19018. Tel: 610-623-0409; Fax: 610-623-2926. Email: shc316@aol.com. Web: www.sacredheart-cliftonheights.net.
Catechesis/Religious Program—Students 25.
Mission—St. Hedwig Chapel 4th & Hayes Sts., Chester, Delaware Co. 19013.

COATESVILLE, CHESTER CO.

1—ST. CECILIA (1869) [CEM] Revs. Francis J. Mulranen; Semanhyia Boateng-Mensah; Nicholas J. Dininni, Coord. Hispanic Ministry, N. Chester Co.; Deacon Frederick H. Kerr.
Res.: 99 N. 6th Ave., 19320. Tel: 610-384-0422; Fax: 610-384-4415.
See Pope John Paul II Regional Catholic Elementary School, West Brandywine under Regional Parish Schools located in the Institution section.
Regional Religious Education Program—Tel: 610-384-0900. Nancy Sanchez, D.R.E. Students 132.
Convent—603 E. Lincoln Hwy., 19320. Tel: 610-384-0733; Fax: 610-384-5730.

2—ST. JOSEPH (1924), (Slovak), Revs. John V. Oulds; Joseph S. Hasieber (ALX) (Retired).
Res.: 404 Charles St., 19320. Tel: 610-384-0360; Fax: 610-384-8545. Email: staff@stjosephcoatesville.org. Web: www.stjosephcoatesville.org.
See Pope John Paul II Regional Catholic Elementary School, West Brandywine under Regional Parish Schools located in the Institution section.
Catechesis/Religious Program—Students 54.

3—OUR LADY OF THE ROSARY (1917), (Italian), Rev. Thomas J. Brennan; Deacon Richard Stoughton.
Res.: 80 S. 17th Ave., 19320. Tel: 610-384-1415; Fax: 610-383-6592. Email: FatherB@olrcc.org. Web: www.olrcc.org.
See Pope John Paul II Regional Catholic Elementary School, West Brandywine under Regional Parish Schools located in the Institution section.
Catechesis/Religious Program—Tel: 610-384-1415. Students 123.
Regional Religious Education Program—2875 Manor Rd., West Brandywine. Tel: 610-384-3145; Fax: 610-384-1506. Email: rreppj2@yahoo.com. Students 479.

4—ST. STANISLAUS KOSTKA (1907), (Polish), [CEM] Rev. John V. Oulds.
Res.: 209 W. Lincoln Hwy., 19320. Tel: 610-384-1172; Fax: 610-384-8545. Email: ststanskostkacc@aol.com.
See Pope John Paul II Regional Catholic Elementary School, West Brandywine under Regional Parish Schools located in the Institution section.
Catechesis/Religious Program—Students 2.

COLLEGEVILLE, MONTGOMERY CO., ST. ELEANOR (1911) Rev. Msgrs. Patrick E. Sweeney; James J. Foley; Rev. Jonathan J. Dalin; Deacons Albert T. Derivan; Joseph DeRosa. In Res., Rev. Robert W. Povish.
Res.: 647 Locust St., 19426. Tel: 610-489-1647; Fax: 610-489-7469. Email: church@steleanor.com. Web: www.steleanor.com.
School—Tel: 610-489-9434; Fax: 610-489-6137. Email: mpaulhamus@steleanor.com. Web: www.steleanorschool.com. Lay Teachers 24; Students 490.
Catechesis/Religious Program—Tel: 610-489-4677. Email: religioused@steleanor.com. Students 1,130.

COLLINGDALE, DELAWARE CO., ST. JOSEPH (1916) Rev. James E. McVeigh; Deacon Paul McBlain.
Res.: 500 Woodlawn Ave., 19023. Tel: 610-583-4530; Fax: 610-583-7730. Email: parishrectory@stjoseph-collingdale.org. Web: www.saintjoseph-collingdale.com.
School—Bartram & Woodlawn Aves., 19023. Tel: 610-586-0356; Fax: 610-586-7710. Sr. Gerald Helene, O.S.F., Prin. Sisters of St. Francis of Philadelphia 1; Lay Teachers 13; Students 239.
Catechesis/Religious Program—Tel: 610-586-1520. Dolly Mount, D.R.E. Students 70.

CONSHOHOCKEN, MONTGOMERY CO.

1—SS. COSMAS AND DAMIAN (1912), (Italian), Rev. Gasper A. Genuardi. In Res., Rev. John J. McKenzie, O.S.A.; Deacons Armand J. Maresca; Joseph C. Carr.
Res.: 209 W. Fifth Ave., 19428. Tel: 610-828-0101; Fax: 610-828-5294. Email: sscdchurch@aol.com. Web: sscosmasanddamian.com.
See SS. Cosmas & Damian Primary Campus, Conshohocken under Regional Parish Schools located in the Institution section.
Catechesis/Religious Program—Students 70.

2—ST. MARY (1905), (Polish), [CEM] Rev. Msgr. Gerard C. Mesure.
Res.: 140 W. Hector St., 19428. Tel: 610-828-0260; Fax: 610-828-9665. Email: stmaryconshy@verizon.net.
Catechesis/Religious Program—Mrs. Kathleen Pulli, D.R.E.

3—ST. MATTHEW (1851) [CEM] [JC 2] Rev. James W. Donlon. In Res., Rev. John J. Ames.
Res.: 219 Fayette St., 19428. Tel: 610-828-0424; Fax: 610-825-5168.
See Conshohocken Catholic School, Conshohocken under Regional Parish Schools located in the Institution section.
Catechesis/Religious Program—Email: stmatthewdre@verizon.net. Web: www.stmatthewchurch.com. Students 141.
Convent—Third Ave. & Harry St., 19428. Tel: 610-828-0174.

CROYDON, BUCKS CO., ST. THOMAS AQUINAS (1922) Rev. Michael J. Davis; Deacon John J. Gallagher.
Res.: 126 Walnut Ave., 19021-5496. Tel: 215-788-2989; 215-788-5813; Fax: 215-788-7626.
School—130 Walnut Ave., 19021. Tel: 215-785-1130; Fax: 215-785-2564. Colleen Noone, Prin. Lay Teachers 12; Students 144.
Catechesis/Religious Program—Students 99.

DARBY, DELAWARE CO., BLESSED VIRGIN MARY (1913) Rev. Joseph Corley. In Res., Rev. Edward J. Kennedy.
Res.: 1101 Main St., 19023. Tel: 610-583-2128; Fax: 610-583-9829. Email: bvmrectory@rcn.com. Web: www.bvm-darby.com.
School—47 MacDade Blvd., 19023. Tel: 610-586-0638; Fax: 610-586-1582. Sisters, Servants of the Immaculate Heart of Mary 3; Lay Teachers 10; Students 209.
Catechesis/Religious Program—Tel: 610-586-2490. Students 28.

DOWNINGTOWN, CHESTER CO., ST. JOSEPH (1851) [CEM] Rev. Msgr. William J. Lynn; Rev. Brian M. Kean; Deacon Edward R. Schiappa. In Res., Revs. Edward J. Jablonski; Matthew W. Guckin.
Res.: 338 Manor Ave., 19335. Tel: 610-269-8294; Fax: 610-269-2487.
School—340 Manor Ave., 19335. Tel: 610-269-8999; Fax: 610-269-2252. Sisters, Servants of the Immaculate Heart of Mary 5; Lay Teachers 31; Students 627.
Catechesis/Religious Program—Tel: 610-873-8798; Fax: 610-873-5466. Mrs. Kathryn Thomas, D.R.E. Students 875.
Convent—336 Manor Ave., 19335. Tel: 610-269-8314.

DOYLESTOWN, BUCKS CO., OUR LADY OF MOUNT CARMEL (1850) [CEM] Rev. Msgr. Charles H. Hagan; Revs. Ronald M. Jakows; James J. Mulligan, S.T.L.; Paschal U. Onunwa (Nigeria); Deacons George Corwell; James J. Fowkes.
Res.: 235 E. State St., 18901. Tel: 215-348-4190; Fax: 215-348-3104. Web: www.ourladymtcarmel.org.
School—E. Ashland St., 18901. Tel: 215-348-5907; Fax: 215-348-5671. Sisters of St. Francis of Philadelphia 1; Lay Teachers 25; Students 390.
Catechesis/Religious Program—Tel: 215-345-7089; Fax: 215-345-4216. Cindy Balceniuk, D.R.E. Students 1,200.
Convent—209 E. State St., 18901. Tel: 215-348-4663.

DREXEL HILL, DELAWARE CO.

1—ST. ANDREW (1916) Rev. Msgr. Albin J. Grous; Revs. James F. Sullivan; Girard J. Cusatis (Retired); Deacon Daniel N. DeLucca.
Res.: 3500 School Ln., 19026. Tel: 610-259-1169; Fax: 610-259-0556. Email: info@standrewdh.com. Web: www.standrewdh.com.
School—529 Mason Ave., 19026. Tel: 610-259-5145; Fax: 610-284-6956. Sisters of St. Joseph 1; Lay Teachers 16; Students 268.
Catechesis/Religious Program—Students 230.
Convent—535 Mason Ave., 19026. Tel: 610-259-6130.

2—ST. BERNADETTE (1947) Revs. John J. Kelly; Robert F. Lucas; Deacons Frank B. Burke; Thomas P. Fitzpatrick.
Res.: 1035 Turner Ave., 19026. Tel: 610-789-7676; Fax: 610-789-9539. Web: stbernadette-drexelhill.e-paluch.com.
School—1015 Turner Ave., 19026. Tel: 610-449-6126; Fax: 610-789-0890. Oblate Sisters of St. Francis de Sales 2; Lay Teachers 13; Students 234.
Catechesis/Religious Program—Tel: 610-853-1740. John Blisard, D.R.E. Students 260.
Convent—Tel: 610-789-2325.

3—ST. CHARLES BORROMEO (1849) [CEM] Revs. Roland D. Slobogin; Daniel P. Devine; Deacon Francis Fabrizio.
Res.: 3422 Dennison Ave., 19026. Tel: 610-623-3800; Fax: 610-284-9583. Web: stcharlesdrexelhill.org.
Catechesis/Religious Program—Tel: 610-259-4389. Students 149.

4—ST. DOROTHY (1947) Revs. Michael D. Murphy; John D. Silcox Jr.; Deacon John J. Davaro.
Res.: 4910 Township Line Rd., 19026. Tel: 610-789-7788; 610-789-7338; Fax: 610-789-6936.
School—1225 Burmont Rd., 19026. Tel: 610-789-4100. Web: www.saintdorothy.org. Lay Teachers 20; Sisters of Mercy 2; Students 377.
Catechesis/Religious Program—Tel: 610-853-1499. Students 337.
Convent—1201 Burmont Rd., 19026. Tel: 610-789-4112.

EAST GOSHEN, CHESTER CO., SS. PETER AND PAUL (1967) Rev. Msgr. Daniel J. Kutys; Rev. James J. Whelan; Deacons Arthur G. Harrison; Thomas J. Horan; Robert F. Pierce.
Res.: 1325 Boot Rd., West Chester, 19380. Tel: 610-692-2216; Fax: 610-692-7103. Web: www.sspeterandpaulrc.org.
School—(Grades PreK-8), 1327 Boot Rd., West Chester, 19380-5901. Tel: 610-696-1000; Fax: 484-631-0181. Email: school@sspeterandpaulrc.org. Mrs. Margaret Egan, Prin. Lay Teachers 27; Students 457.
Catechesis/Religious Program—Tel: 610-692-5886; Fax: 484-631-0182. Email: lpjte@verizon.net. Patricia B. Ehrhart, D.R.E. Students 450.

EAST LANSDOWNE, DELAWARE CO., ST. CYRIL OF ALEXANDRIA (1928) Rev. Dominic Tran Minh Duc; Deacon James E. Dalton. In Res., Rev. James P. Olson.
Res.: 153 Penn Blvd., 19050-2698. Tel: 610-623-5160; Fax: 610-622-2479. Web: saintcyril.org.
School—716 Emerson Ave., 19050. Tel: 610-623-1113; Fax: 610-623-2427. Sr. Barbara Montague, I.H.M., Prin. Sisters, Servants of the Immaculate Heart of Mary 4; Lay Teachers 12; Students 218.

Catechesis/Religious Program—Fax: 610-622-2479. Students 50.
Convent—171 Penn Blvd., 19050. Tel: 610-623-6590.

EDDYSTONE, DELAWARE CO., ST. ROSE OF LIMA (1890) Rev. Gerald D. Canavan; Deacon Lawrence P. Schnepp.
Res.: 1901 Chester Pike, 19022. Tel: 610-876-6170; Fax: 610-876-6128.
See St. Madeline-St. Rose, Ridley Park under Consolidated Parish Schools located in the Institution section.
Catechesis/Religious Program—Students 157.

ELKINS PARK, MONTGOMERY CO., ST. JAMES (1923) Rev. J. Thomas Heron. In Res., Rev. Quan H. Tran.
Res.: 8320 Brookside Rd., 19027. Tel: 215-635-6210; Fax: 215-635-3346. Email: stjames8320@verizon.net. Web: www.stjamesparish.net.
School—8304 Brookside Rd., 19027. Tel: 215-635-4673; Fax: 215-635-3521. Lay Teachers 12; Students 145.
Catechesis/Religious Program—Students 95.

ESSINGTON, DELAWARE CO., ST. MARGARET MARY ALACOQUE (1921) Rev. Anthony F. Orth; Deacon Frederick M. Ryan.
Res.: 500 Wanamaker Ave., 19029. Tel: 610-521-9177; Fax: 610-595-0230. Email: stmarectory@comcast.net. Web: stmargaretmaryalacoque.net.
Catechesis/Religious Program—Students 43.

EXTON, CHESTER CO., SS. PHILIP AND JAMES (1959) Revs. Joseph C. Dieckhaus; Michael J. Reilly; Deacons Frank M. Bizal; James E. Bogdan; Charles W. Polley Jr.
Res.: 107 N. Ship Rd., 19341. Tel: 610-363-6536; Fax: 610-524-7359. Web: www.sspj.net.
School—721 E. Lincoln Hwy., 19341. Tel: 610-363-6530; Fax: 610-363-6495. Sr. Marita Kathryn Barber, I.H.M., Prin. Sisters, Servants of the Immaculate Heart of Mary 6; Lay Teachers 32; Students 642.
Catechesis/Religious Program—Tel: 610-363-1307. Sr. Eunice Marie, I.H.M., D.R.E. Students 425.
Convent—105 N. Ship Rd., 19341. Tel: 610-363-2263.

FAIRLESS HILLS, BUCKS CO., ST. FRANCES CABRINI (1953) Rev. Msgr. Michael P. McCormac; Deacons Mace M. Mazzoni; Louis F. Hoelzle.
Res.: 325 S. Oxford Valley Rd., 19030. Tel: 215-946-4040; Fax: 215-943-1116.
School—10 Goble Ct., 19030. Tel: 215-946-6334; Fax: 215-946-0316. Email: sfcoffice@comcast.net. Web: www.sfcaph.org. Mary E. Katz, Prin. Lay Teachers 9; Students 187.
Catechesis/Religious Program—Tel: 215-946-1115. Email: cabrinidre@live.com. Marybeth Curran, D.R.E. Students 160.

FALLSINGTON, BUCKS CO., ST. JOSEPH THE WORKER (1956) Rev. Donald G. Birch. In Res., Rev. Mark J. Hunt.
Res.: 9172 New Falls Rd., 19054. Tel: 215-945-4486; Fax: 215-945-3292. Web: www.sjtw.org.
School—9160 New Falls Rd., 19054. Tel: 215-945-4312; Fax: 215-945-8733. Web: www.sjtwschool.org. Lay Teachers 11; Students 172.
Catechesis/Religious Program—Tel: 215-945-4680. Students 166.

FEASTERVILLE, BUCKS CO., ASSUMPTION B.V.M. (1950) Revs. William F. McGeown; J. Jerome Wild; Deacon Robert J. Stewart; Sr. Diane Wolf, S.S.J., Pastoral Assoc.
Res.: 1900 Meadowbrook Rd., 19053. Tel: 215-357-1221; Fax: 215-357-2283. Web: www.abvmfeasterville.org.
School—Tel: 215-357-5499. Sisters, Servants of the Immaculate Heart of Mary 4; Lay Teachers 13; Students 231.
Catechesis/Religious Program—Tel: 215-357-3445. Mrs. Joyce Boag, C.R.E. Students 264.
Convent—55 Bristol Rd., 19053. Tel: 215-355-3898.

FLOURTOWN, MONTGOMERY CO., ST. GENEVIEVE (1953) Rev. Msgr. Michael J. Matz. In Res., Rev. Carl F. Janicki; Deacons Joseph Nines; Michael G. Conroy.
Res.: 1225 Bethlehem Pike, 19031. Tel: 215-836-2828; Fax: 215-836-7218. Email: rectory@stgensparish.com. Web: www.stgensparish.com.
School—1237 Bethlehem Pike, 19031. Tel: 215-836-5644; Fax: 215-836-0159. Web: www.stgens.com. Sisters of St. Joseph 3; Lay Teachers 18; Students 235.
Catechesis/Religious Program—Tel: 215-836-1994. Students 148.
Seven Dolors Church—Worship Site: 1200 E. Willow Grove Ave., Wyndmoor, 19038. Tel: 215-836-2828; Fax: 215-836-7218.

GLADWYNE, MONTGOMERY CO., ST. JOHN BAPTIST VIANNEY (1927) Rev. Msgr. Donald E. Leighton. In Res., Rev. Msgr. Joseph A. Shields (Retired).
Res.: 1110 Vaughans Ln., 19035. Tel: 610-642-0938; Fax: 610-642-1432.
Catechesis/Religious Program—350 Conshohocken State Rd., 19035. Sr. Mary Sarah, R.S.M., D.R.E. Students 75.

GLENOLDEN, DELAWARE CO., ST. GEORGE (1923) Rev. Christopher J. Papa.
Res.: 22 E. Cooke Ave., 19036-1497. Tel: 610-237-1633; Fax: 610-237-9626. Web: www.stgeorgeparish.org.
Catechesis/Religious Program—Students 107.
Convent—11 E. Lamont Ave., 19036-1497. Tel: 484-318-5092.

GLENSIDE, MONTGOMERY CO., ST. LUKE THE EVANGELIST (1905) Rev. Msgrs. J. Michael Flood; John F. O'Brien (Retired); Rev. John F. McBride; Deacon Thomas M. Croke.
Res.: 2316 Fairhill Ave., 19038. Tel: 215-572-0128; Fax: 215-572-0482. Email: stlukerc@aol.com. Web: www.stlukerc.org.
School—2336 Fairhill Ave., 19038. Tel: 215-884-0843; Fax: 215-884-4607. Sr. William Adele, S.S.J., Prin. Sisters of St. Joseph 4; Lay Teachers 22; Students 335.
Catechesis/Religious Program—2330 Fairhill Ave., 19038. Tel: 215-884-2080. Email: prep@stlukerc.org. Sharon D'Amore, D.R.E. Students 285.
Convent—2324 Fairhill Ave., 19038. Tel: 215-884-0225.

HATBORO, MONTGOMERY CO., ST. JOHN BOSCO (1953) Revs. Martin T. Cioppi; Gerald C. Ronan; Deacons Daniel J. Rouse; William F. Kruckenberger.
Res.: 235 E. County Line Rd., 19040. Tel: 215-672-7280; Fax: 215-672-1105. Web: www.saintjohnbosco.org.
School—215 E. County Line Rd., 19040-1244. Tel: 215-675-1484. Sisters, Servants of the Immaculate Heart of Mary 3; Lay Teachers 15; Students 150.
Catechesis/Religious Program—Tel: 267-803-0774; Fax: 215-675-7084. Email: cflack@saintjohnbosco.org. Students 361.
Convent—189 E. County Line Rd., 19040. Tel: 215-675-2301.

HATFIELD, MONTGOMERY CO., ST. MARIA GORETTI (1953) Revs. Leonard N. Peterson; Andrew C. Brownholtz; Joseph Rydzewski, Business Mgr.; Eileen Ericsson, Music Dir.
Res.: 1601 Derstine Rd., 19440. Tel: 215-721-0199; Fax: 215-721-4320. Web: www.stmariagoretti.net.
School—2980 Cowpath Rd., 19440. Tel: 215-721-9098; Fax: 215-721-3394. Lay Teachers 14; Students 178.
Catechesis/Religious Program—Tel: 215-721-6559. Julie Clymer, D.R.E.; Joseph Cruice, Youth Min. Students 596.

HAVERTOWN, DELAWARE CO., ST. DENIS (1825) [CEM] Rev. Msgr. James J. Graham; Rev. Michael V. Marrone; Deacon John F. Schlegel. In Res., Rev. Msgr. Bernard J. Trinity (Retired).
Res.: 2401 St. Denis Ln., 19083. Tel: 610-446-0200; Fax: 610-446-4638. Web: www.stdenishavertown.org.
School—300 E. Eagle Rd., 19083. Tel: 610-446-4608; Fax: 610-446-5705. Web: www.edline.net/pages/stdenis_es. Jacqueline Coccia, Prin. Lay Teachers 27; Students 388.
Catechesis/Religious Program—Tel: 610-449-7892; Fax: 610-446-5705. Students 328.
Convent—Tel: 610-446-1263.

HIGHLAND PARK, DELAWARE CO., ST. LAURENCE (1917) Rev. Michael J. Gerlach; Rev. Msgr. Richard Malone; Deacon Mark Wallace.
Res.: 30 St. Laurence Rd., Upper Darby, 19082. Tel: 610-449-0600; 610-449-0601; Fax: 610-449-4299.
School—8245 W. Chester Pike, 19082. Tel: 610-789-2670; Fax: 610-789-1128. Web: www.saintlaurence-.org. Sisters, Servants of the Immaculate Heart of Mary 13; Lay Teachers 21; Students 384.
Catechesis/Religious Program—Tel: 610-789-4854. Students 75.
Convent—Tel: 610-449-7042.
H.O.P.E. Program—Tel: 610-449-0600; Fax: 610-449-4299.

HILLTOWN, BUCKS CO., OUR LADY OF THE SACRED HEART (1919) [CEM] Rev. Michael J. Kelly; Deacons Vincent G. Ceneviva; J. Gerry Murphy. In Res., Rev. John D. Schiele.
Res.: 9 Broad St., 18927. Tel: 215-822-9224; Fax: 215-712-0278. Web: www.olsh-hilltown.org.
See St. Agnes-Sacred Heart School, Hilltown under Regional Parish Schools located in the Institution section.
Catechesis/Religious Program—Tel: 215-822-9020. Students 581.

HOLLAND, BUCKS CO., ST. BEDE THE VENERABLE (1965) Rev. Msgr. John C. Marine; Rev. Joseph C. Bordonaro. In Res., Rev. Msgr. Robert J. Grudowski (Retired).
Res.: 1071 Holland Rd., 18966. Tel: 215-357-5720; Fax: 215-396-0704. Web: www.st-bede.org.
School—1053 Holland Rd., 18966. Tel: 215-357-4720; Fax: 215-355-9526. Margi Slomiany, Prin. Lay Teachers 23; Students 354.
Catechesis/Religious Program—Tel: 215-357-2130; Fax: 215-357-0232. Students 779.

HORSHAM, MONTGOMERY CO., ST. CATHERINE OF SIENA (1963) Revs. Joseph F. Rymdeika; Jacob John; Deacon Timothy Urbanski. In Res., Rev. John C. Nguyen.
Res.: 321 Witmer Rd., 19044. Tel: 215-672-2881; Fax: 215-674-1025. Web: stcatherineschurch.org.
School—317 Witmer Rd., 19044. Tel: 215-674-1904; Fax: 215-674-1466. Lay Teachers 22; Students 252.
Catechesis/Religious Program—Tel: 215-674-8549. Students 383.
Convent—319 Witmer Rd., 19044. Tel: 215-672-7221.

HUNTINGDON VALLEY, MONTGOMERY CO., ST. ALBERT THE GREAT (1962) Rev. Msgr. Paul V. Dougherty; Revs. John J. LaRosa; Charles D. Smith; Deacon Michael J. Kolakowski; Sr. Marie Rachfalski, O.S.F., Parish Svcs. Dir.
Res.: 212 Welsh Rd., 19006. Tel: 215-947-3500; Fax: 215-938-9071. Email: rectory@stalberthegreat.org.
School—214 Welsh Rd., 19006. Tel: 215-947-2332; Fax: 215-938-9360. Cynthia Koons, Prin. Lay Teachers 26; Students 463.
Catechesis/Religious Program—Tel: 215-947-3641. Sr. Patricia Gannon, S.S.J., D.R.E. Students 270.

JAMISON, BUCKS CO., ST. CYRIL OF JERUSALEM (1965) Rev. Msgr. Robert J. Powell; Rev. Joseph L. Farrell; Deacons Joseph F. Windish; Joseph Owen. In Res., Most Rev. Martin N. Lohmuller.
Res.: 1410 Almshouse Rd., 18929. Tel: 215-343-1288; Fax: 215-343-3924.
Catechesis/Religious Program—Tel: 215-343-3139. Students 755.

JENKINTOWN, MONTGOMERY CO., IMMACULATE CONCEPTION (1866) Rev. Msgr. John J. Conahan; Deacons Paul Hagerty; Alvin Clay. In Res., Rev. Edward C. Kelly.
Res.: 604 West Ave., 19046-2708. Tel: 215-884-4022; 215-887-0181; Fax: 215-887-4163.
School—606 West Ave., 19046-2708. Tel: 215-887-1312; Fax: 215-887-5517. Diane Greco, Prin. Lay Teachers 18; Students 181.
Catechesis/Religious Program—Tel: 215-885-5586. Mrs. Nancy Grabowski, D.R.E. Students 132.

KENNETT SQUARE, CHESTER CO., ST. PATRICK (1869) [CEM] Rev. Victor F. Sharrett; Deacon James K. Madonna. In Res., Rev. Andres Garcia.
Res.: 218 Meredith St., 19348. Tel: 610-444-2128. Email: stpatkennett@verizon.net. Web: www.rc.net/philadelphia/st_patrick/.
Parish Office:—205 Lafayette St., 19348. Tel: 610-444-4364; Fax: 610-444-2129.
School—210 Meredith St., 19348. Tel: 610-444-3104; Fax: 610-444-3166. Web: www.stpatskennettsquare.org. Lay Teachers 22; Students 214.
Catechesis/Religious Program—Tel: 610-444-2214. Marianne Kane, D.R.E. Students 293.

KIMBERTON, CHESTER CO., ST. BASIL THE GREAT (1965) Rev. Robert A. McLaughlin.
Res.: 2300 Kimberton Rd., Box 637, 19442-0637. Tel: 610-933-2110; 610-933-4730; Fax: 610-933-0627. Email: stbasil@chesco.com. Web: www.stbasils.org/church.
School—Tel: 610-933-2453; Fax: 610-933-7590. Email: arufo@stbasils.org. Web: www.stbasils.org. Lay Teachers 12; Students 191.
Catechesis/Religious Program—Tel: 610-935-1261. Email: dre@stbasil.org. Students 250.
Convent—Sisters of St. Francis Residence, Tel: 610-933-2345.

KING OF PRUSSIA, MONTGOMERY CO., MOTHER OF DIVINE PROVIDENCE (1954) Rev. Msgr. John T. Conway; Deacon Mark H. Dillon. In Res., Rev. Msgr. Joseph W. Murray (Retired).
Res.: 333 Allendale Rd., 19406-1640. Tel: 610-265-4178; Fax: 610-265-1653. Email: mdpinfo@mdpparish.com. Web: mdpparish.com.
School—405 Allendale Rd., 19406. Tel: 610-265-2323; Fax: 610-265-1816. Web: www.mdpschool-.com. Lay Teachers 19; Students 238.
Catechesis/Religious Program—Tel: 610-337-2173. Students 270.

LAFAYETTE HILL, MONTGOMERY CO., ST. PHILIP NERI (1945) Rev. Msgr. Charles P. Vance; Deacon Salvatore R. Bianco. In Res., Revs. Joseph W. Bongard; Anthony J. DiGuglielmo.
Res.: 437 Ridge Pike, 19444. Tel: 610-828-5717; 610-834-1975; Fax: 610-834-0392.
School—3015 Chestnut St., 19444. Tel: 610-828-3082; Fax: 610-828-2943. Sisters of St. Joseph 2; Lay Teachers 26; Students 521.
Catechesis/Religious Program—Tel: 610-834-9868. Students 255.
Convent—Tel: 610-828-2866.

LANSDALE, MONTGOMERY CO., ST. STANISLAUS (1876) [CEM] Rev. Msgr. Joseph A. Tracy; Revs. Augusto M. Concha; John R. Weber; Deacons Mathieu Tielemans, (Retired); Charles G. Lewis; C. Stephens Vondercrone; Raymond C. Wellbank. In Res., Rev. Msgr. Thomas J. Duane.
Res.: 51 Lansdale Ave., 19446. Tel: 215-855-3133; Fax: 215-855-5478. Email: ststan@comcast.net. Web:

www.ststanislaus.com.
School—493 E. Main St., 19446. Tel: 215-368-0995; Fax: 215-393-4869. Diane McCaughan, Prin. Lay Teachers 26; Students 375.
Catechesis/Religious Program—Tel: 215-855-9893. Email: ststans@aol.com. Students 280.

LANSDOWNE, DELAWARE CO., ST. PHILOMENA (1898) Rev. Paul J. Castellani. In Res., Rev. Jason Kulczynski.
Res.: 41 E. Baltimore Ave., 19050. Tel: 610-622-2420; Fax: 610-622-1215. Web: www.saintphilomena.net.
School—21 N. Highland Ave., 19050. Tel: 610-259-6817; Fax: 610-259-5656. Email: stphilomenaoffice@juno.com. Patricia Walsh, Prin. Lay Teachers 13; Students 173.
Catechesis/Religious Program—Students 15.

LENNI, DELAWARE CO., ST. FRANCIS DE SALES (1894) [CEM] Rev. Michael A. Colagreco.
Res.: 35 New Rd., P.O. Box 97, 19052. Tel: 610-459-2203; Fax: 610-459-5029. Web: www.sfdschurch.org.
School—Tel: 610-459-0799; Fax: 610-558-3058. Sisters of St. Francis of Philadelphia 2; Lay Teachers 11; Students 169.
Catechesis/Religious Program—Tel: 610-459-0554. Students 223.
Convent—28 New Rd., Aston, 19014. Tel: 610-459-2501.
Station—Fair Acres Geriatric Center Lima. Tel: 610-891-5600.
Station—Granite Farms Est. Media. Tel: 610-358-3440.
Station—Riddle Village Media. Tel: 610-891-3777.
Station—The Residence at Glen Riddle Media. Tel: 610-358-9933.
Station—Riddle Hospital Media. Tel: 610-566-9400.
Station—Penn State Lima Campus Media. Tel: 610-892-1350.
Station—Williamson School Media. Tel: 610-566-1776.

LEVITTOWN, BUCKS CO.
1—IMMACULATE CONCEPTION B.V.M. (1954) Rev. Timothy F. O'Sullivan. In Res., Rev. Joseph P. Lea.
Res.: 5201 Emilie Rd., 19057-2505. Tel: 215-946-1638; 215-946-1639; Fax: 215-946-2149. Web: www.immaculateconceptionparish.com.
School—3810 Oxford Valley Rd., 19057. Tel: 215-949-2848. Sisters, Servants of the Immaculate Heart of Mary 1; Lay Teachers 11; Students 154.
Catechesis/Religious Program—Tel: 215-595-6096. Students 135.
Convent—Tel: 215-945-4664.
2—ST. MICHAEL THE ARCHANGEL (1953) Revs. Michael C. DiIorio; Charles J. Sullivan; Deacons Harry J. Simpson; William F. Shire.
Res.: 66 Levittown Pkwy., 19054. Tel: 215-945-1166; Fax: 215-945-6988. Web: www.stmichaellvt.org/church.
School—130 Levittown Pkwy., 19054. Tel: 215-943-0222; Fax: 215-943-9068. Web: www.stmichaellvt.org. Lay Teachers 15; Students 297.
Catechesis/Religious Program—Tel: 215-547-2518. Rita Danhardt, C.R.E. Students 380.
Convent—88 Levittown Pkwy., 19054. Tel: 215-943-0978.
3—QUEEN OF THE UNIVERSE (1955) Revs. Michael F. Hennelly; John J. Farry; Deacon Joseph Upcavage.
Res.: 2443 Trenton Rd., 19056. Tel: 215-945-8750; Fax: 215-945-0413. Web: www.quparish.org.
School—2477 Trenton Rd., 19056. Tel: 215-945-1866. Sisters of St. Joseph 1; Lay Teachers 12; Students 144.
Catechesis/Religious Program—Tel: 215-945-2704. Email: quprep@gmail.com. Students 386.
Convent—2505 Trenton Rd., Bucks Co. 19056. Tel: 215-945-6116.

LIMERICK, MONTGOMERY CO., BLESSED TERESA OF CALCUTTA (2006) Rev. Paul C. Brandt; Deacon David M. Kubczak.
Mailing Address: P.O. Box 229, 19468. Web: www.blteresacalcutta.org.
Office: 1228 Main St., Linfield, 19468. Tel: 610-287-2525; Fax: 610-495-9928.
Res.: 284 Swamp Pike, Schwenksville, 19473.
School—(Grades K-8), 256 Swamp Pike, Schwenksville, 19473. Tel: 610-287-2500; Fax: 610-287-2543.
Catechesis/Religious Program—Students 567.

LINFIELD, MONTGOMERY CO., ST. CLARE (1963) Closed. Formerly located at 1228 Main St., Linfield. Spiritual records are kept at Blessed Teresa of Calcutta Church. Tel: 610-287-2525.

LINWOOD, DELAWARE CO., HOLY SAVIOUR (1915) Revs. John J. Sibel; Philip J. Lowe.
Res.: 108 E. Ridge Rd., 19061-4327. Tel: 610-485-2520; 610-485-2521; Fax: 610-485-7727. Email: holysaviour@verizon.net.
See Holy Saviour-St. John Fisher, Linwood under Regional Parish Schools located in the Institution section.
Catechesis/Religious Program—Tel: 610-485-2520; Fax: 610-485-7727. Students 235.
Convent—122 E. Ridge Rd., 19061. Tel: 610-485-7320.

LOWER MAKEFIELD, BUCKS CO., ST. JOHN THE EVANGELIST (1964) Rev. Msgrs. James J. Fitzpatrick; David H. Benz; Deacon James E. Hartmann.
Res.: 752 Big Oak Rd., Morrisville, 19067. Tel: 215-295-4102; Fax: 215-295-3128. Email: rectoryoffice@stjohnpa.org. Web: www.stjohnpa.org.
School—728 Big Oak Rd., Morrisville, 19067. Tel: 215-295-0629; Fax: 215-295-6258. Lay Teachers 17; Students 227.
Catechesis/Religious Program—Tel: 215-295-9239. Students 350.
Convent—Tel: 215-295-8201.

MALVERN, CHESTER CO., ST. PATRICK (1915) Revs. James J. Ambrogi; Peter Talocci; Deacon Lawrence P. Froio. In Res., Rev. Kevin P. McCabe.
Res.: 126 Woodland Ave., 19355. Tel: 610-647-2345; Fax: 610-647-4997. Web: www.stpatrickmalvern.org.
School—115 Channing Ave., 19355. Tel: 610-644-5797; Fax: 610-647-0535.
Catechesis/Religious Program—118 Woodland Ave., 19355. Tel: 610-296-8899; Fax: 610-296-8384. Students 319.

MANOA, DELAWARE CO., SACRED HEART (1927) Rev. Henry J. McKee; Deacons John J. Suplee; Thomas J. Woods. In Res., Rev. Paul J. O'Donnell.
Res.: 105 Wilson Ave., Havertown, 19083. Tel: 610-449-3000; Fax: 610-449-2364. Email: shpmckee@comcast.net.
School—Tel: 610-446-9198; Fax: 610-446-4861. Sisters, Servants of the Immaculate Heart of Mary 2; Lay Teachers 12; Students 231.
Catechesis/Religious Program—Tel: 610-446-7597; Fax: 610-446-3176. Sr. Kathleen McCafferty, S.S.J., D.R.E. Students 330.
Convent—Tel: 610-446-7597.

MAPLE GLEN, MONTGOMERY CO., ST. ALPHONSUS (1963) Rev. Msgr. Thomas J. Owens; Rev. Stephen A. Moerman; Deacon Peter H. Burghart.
Res.: 33 Conwell Dr., 19002. Tel: 215-646-4600; Fax: 215-646-0180. Web: www.stalphonsusparish.com.
School—29 Conwell Dr., 19002. Tel: 215-646-0150; Fax: 215-646-7150. Lay Teachers 23; Students 420.
Catechesis/Religious Program—Tel: 215-643-7938. Web: www.stalphonsus.com. Students 223.
Convent—1563 Temple Dr., 19002. Tel: 215-646-6644.

MARCUS HOOK, DELAWARE CO., IMMACULATE CONCEPTION (1917), (Italian), Rev. Joseph A. Amalfitano.
Res.: 21 W. Eighth St., 19061. Tel: 610-485-1026; Fax: 610-485-7819.
Catechesis/Religious Program—Students 44.

MEDIA, DELAWARE CO.
1—ST. MARY MAGDALEN (1963) Rev. Msgr. Ralph J. Chieffo; Deacons E. Peter Zurbach; James A. DiFerdinand. In Res., Revs. William J. Chiriaco; John E. Mulgrew (Retired).
Res.: 2400 N. Providence Rd., 19063. Tel: 610-566-8821; Fax: 610-566-1005. Email: frralphsmm@verizon.net. Web: www.stmarymagdalen.net.
School—2430 N. Providence Rd., 19063. Tel: 610-565-1822; Fax: 610-627-9670. Email: smsoffice@comcast.net. Lay Teachers 25; Students 400.
Catechesis/Religious Program—Tel: 610-565-5782. Email: deaconjamessmm@verizon.net. Students 140.
2—NATIVITY OF THE BLESSED VIRGIN MARY (1868) [CEM] Rev. Edward H. Bell. In Res., Rev. Msgr. Charles V. Devlin (Retired); Rev. Daniel J. Cavanaugh, Senior Priest.
Res.: 30 E. Franklin St., 19063. Tel: 610-566-0185; Fax: 610-566-2873. Email: nativitybvm@comcast.net. Web: www.nativity-bvm.org.
School—Gayley St., 19063. Tel: 610-566-6881; Fax: 610-566-3910. Web: www.nativitybvmschool.org. Mrs. Mary Ann Johnston, Prin. Lay Teachers 18; Students 185.
Catechesis/Religious Program—Students 238.

MILMONT PARK, DELAWARE CO., OUR LADY OF PEACE (1922) Rev. Louis J. Kolenkiewicz.
Res.: 501 Belmont Ave., 19033-3308. Tel: 610-532-8081; 610-532-8082; Fax: 610-532-7402.
Catechesis/Religious Program—Students 85.

MORRISVILLE, BUCKS CO., HOLY TRINITY (1900) [CEM] Rev. John C. Eckert; Deacon Warren C. Leonard.
Res.: 201 N. Pennsylvania Ave., 19067. Tel: 215-295-3045; Fax: 215-295-8317. Email: holytrinityrcc@aol.com. Web: www.holytrinitymorrisville.org.
School—Osborne Ave. & Stockham Ave., 19067. Tel: 215-295-6900; Fax: 215-337-9079. Mrs. Elaine McDowell, Prin. Lay Teachers 11; Students 215.
Catechesis/Religious Program—Tel: 215-295-3079. Students 129.

MORTON, DELAWARE CO., OUR LADY OF PERPETUAL HELP (1907) Rev. Msgr. John M. Savinski; Rev. Richard Smith.
Res.: O.L.P.H. Ct., 2130 Franklin Ave., 19070. Tel: 610-543-1046; Fax: 610-543-6150. Email: olpho101@comcast.net. Web: www.olphmorton.org.
School—#5 O.L.P.H. Ct., 2130 Franklin Ave., 19070. Tel: 610-543-8350; Fax: 610-544-3203. Sisters of St. Francis of Philadelphia 1; Lay Teachers 19; Students 310.
Catechesis/Religious Program—Tel: 610-543-5448. Students 300.
Convent—#3 O.L.P.H. Ct., 2130 Franklin Ave., 19070. Tel: 610-543-0186.

NARBERTH, MONTGOMERY CO., ST. MARGARET (1900) Rev. Robert J. Chapman; Sr. Anne Marie Stegmaier, I.H.M., Parish Svcs. Dir. In Res., Rev. Stephen J. Dougherty.
Res.: 208 N. Narberth Ave., 19072. Tel: 610-664-3770; Fax: 610-664-5001. Email: stmargrectory@comcast.net. Web: www.saintmarg.org.
School—227 N. Narberth Ave., 19072. Tel: 610-664-2640; Fax: 610-664-4677. Email: secretary@saint-margaret.org. Web: www.saint-margaret.org. Sisters of Mercy 1; Lay Teachers 15; Students 270.
Catechesis/Religious Program—Tel: 610-664-5715. Carol Eichman, C.R.E. Students 160.

NEW GARDEN TOWNSHIP, CHESTER CO., ST. GABRIEL OF THE SORROWFUL MOTHER (1988) Rev. Richard J. Maisano.
Mailing Address: P.O. Box 709, Avondale, 19311. Tel: 610-268-0296; Fax: 610-268-5022. Email: stgabriel@kennett.net. Web: www.rc.net/philadelphia/st_gabriel.
Catechesis/Religious Program— Brian G. Jefferes, C.R.E. Students 215.

NEW HOPE, BUCKS CO., ST. MARTIN OF TOURS (1885) [CEM] Rev. W. Frederick Kindon.
Res.: 1 Riverstone Cir., 18938. Tel: 215-862-5472; Fax: 215-862-1829. Email: frkindon@stmartinoftours.org. Web: www.stmartinoftours.org.
School—Mrs. Anne Florian, Prin.
Catechesis/Religious Program—Kitty Formica, Dir. Faith Formation. Students 250.

NEWTOWN SQUARE, DELAWARE CO., ST. ANASTASIA (1912) Rev. Msgr. Philip J. Cribben; Rev. Michael G. Speziale; Deacon Frank Colgan. In Res., Revs. Stephen P. DeLacy; Edward A. Windhaus.
Res.: 3301 W. Chester Pike, 19073. Tel: 610-356-1613; Fax: 610-356-8332. Email: peribben@saintannies.org. Web: www.saintanastasia.net.
School—3309 W. Chester Pike, 19073. Tel: 610-356-6225; Fax: 610-356-5748. Web: www.saintannies.org. Sisters of St. Joseph 2; Lay Teachers 38; Students 625.
Catechesis/Religious Program—Tel: 610-356-5069. Students 435.
Convent—3305 W. Chester Pike, 19073. Tel: 610-356-0273.

NEWTOWN, BUCKS CO., ST. ANDREW (1880) [CEM] Rev. Msgr. Michael C. Picard; Revs. Daniel M. Kredensor; Richard B. Landry, M.S.; John F. Wackerman.
Res.: 81 Swamp Rd., 18940. Tel: 215-968-2262; Fax: 215-579-9344. Web: standrewnewtown.com.
School—51 Wrights Rd., 18940. Tel: 215-968-2685; Fax: 215-968-4795.
Preschool—51 Wrights Rd., 18940. Tel: 215-968-2685; Fax: 215-968-4795. Lay Teachers 42; Students 850.
Catechesis/Religious Program—Tel: 215-968-6929. Students 1,084.

NORRISTOWN, MONTGOMERY CO.
1—ST. FRANCIS OF ASSISI (1923) Rev. Vincent F. Welsh.
Res.: 600 Hamilton St., 19401. Tel: 610-272-0402; Fax: 610-272-1794. Web: www.saintfrancisnorristown.com.
School—Oak & Buttonwood Sts., 19401. Tel: 610-272-0501; Fax: 610-272-8011. Email: contact@sfacatholic.org. Web: www.sfacatholic.org. Sisters of St. Joseph 2; Lay Teachers 14; Students 176.
Catechesis/Religious Program—Email: pugh.katherine4@gmail.com. Students 87.
Convent—Tel: 610-272-3686.
2—HOLY SAVIOUR (1903), (Italian), Rev. Msgr. Charles L. Sangermano. In Res., Rev. Alan J. Okon Jr.
Res.: 407 E. Main St., 19401. Tel: 610-275-0958; Fax: 610-275-8464. Web: www.holysaviour.com.
School—Our Lady of Victory Regional School, 351 E. Johnson Hwy., 19401. Tel: 610-275-2990. Lay Teachers 12; Students 190.
Catechesis/Religious Program—Students 110.
Mission—Our Lady of Mount Carmel 460 Fairfield Rd., Plymouth Meeting, Montgomery Co. 19462. Tel: 610-277-7739.
3—ST. PATRICK (1835) [CEM] Rev. William S. Murphy; Jeff Mitchell, Business Mgr.; David Tague,

Operations Mgr.
Res.: 714 DeKalb St., 19401. Tel: 610-272-1408; Fax: 610-275-0238. Web: www.stpatrickchurch.com.
Catechesis/Religious Program—Religious Educ. Bldg., 703 Green St., 19401. Tel: 610-272-4500. Mary Ann Mitchell, D.R.E. Students 102.
Convent—Missionaries of Charity, 630 DeKalb St., 19401. Tel: 610-277-5962.

4—ST. PAUL (1963) Rev. Harry E. McCreedy; Sr. Rosellen Bracken, R.S.M., Parish Svcs. Dir.; Mary Rose Edmonds, Business Mgr.; Deacon Michael Dayoc. In Res., Rev. Msgr. Henry B. Degnan (Retired).
Res.: 2007 New Hope St., 19401. Tel: 610-279-6725; Fax: 610-275-6771. Web: www.saintpaulcatholicchurcheastnorriton.net.
School—Our Lady of Victory Catholic Regional School, 351 E. Johnson Hwy., 19401. Tel: 610-275-2990; Fax: 610-275-0470. Lay Teachers 12; Students 176.
Catechesis/Religious Program—Tel: 610-279-5330. Mrs. Meg Farrell, D.R.E. Students 70.

5—ST. TERESA OF AVILA (1918) Rev. Msgr. Andrew J. Golias; Deacon Francis C. Lally.
Res. & Mailing Address: 1260 S. Trooper Rd., 19403-3659. Tel: 610-666-5820; Fax: 610-666-7511. Email: starectory@comcast.net. Web: www.stteresaofavilaparish.com.
School—2550 S. Parkview Dr., 19403. Tel: 610-666-6069; Fax: 610-666-0195. Web: www.stteresaofavila.com. Janet Lazorcheck, Prin. Lay Teachers 14; Students 200.
Catechesis/Religious Program—Tel: 610-666-0644. Ms. Mary Katherine Roach, D.R.E. Students 243.

6—ST. TITUS (1962) Rev. Thomas P. Kletzel.
Res.: 3006 Keenwood Rd., East Norriton, 19403. Tel: 610-279-4990; Fax: 610-279-8640. Web: www.sttitus.org.
School—Keenwood Rd. & Norriton Dr., East Norriton, 19403. Tel: 610-279-6043; Fax: 610-279-8090. Mrs. Joanne Zinn, Prin. Lay Teachers 15; Students 187.
Catechesis/Religious Program—3000 Keenwood Rd., East Norriton, 19403. Tel: 610-279-5662. Mrs. Claire Boyle, C.R.E. Students 93.

NORTH WALES, MONTGOMERY CO.

1—MARY, MOTHER OF THE REDEEMER (1987) Rev. Msgrs. Philip C. Ricci; James J. Shields; Rev. William J. Teverzczuk; Deacons George H. Klinger; Joseph W. Lonergan; Charles Talaber, Business Mgr.
Res.: 1325 Upper State Rd., 19454. Tel: 215-362-7400; 215-362-8966; Fax: 215-362-4127. Web: mmredeemer.org.
School—1321 Upper State Rd., 19454. Tel: 215-412-7101; Fax: 215-412-7197. Mrs. Denise Judge, Prin.
Catechesis/Religious Program—Tel: 215-412-2251; Fax: 215-412-7197. Nancy Franks, D.R.E. Students 720.

2—ST. ROSE OF LIMA (1919) Rev. Msgr. Daniel A. Murray; Rev. Gerald S. Smith. In Res., Rev. Kevin J. Kelly; Deacon Edward A. Konarski.
Res.: 428 S. Main St., 19454-3224. Tel: 215-699-4617; Fax: 215-699-4452.
School—425 W. Pennsylvania Ave., 19454-3498. Tel: 215-699-8831; Fax: 215-661-1691. Lay Teachers 17; Students 167.
Catechesis/Religious Program—Tel: 215-699-4434. Joanne M. Tragesser, D.R.E. Students 192.

NORWOOD, DELAWARE CO., ST. GABRIEL (1891) Revs. Samuel A. Verruni; Thomas J. Donaghy (Retired); David A. Fernandes; Deacon Gary W. Guy.
Res.: 233 Mohawk Ave., 19074. Tel: 610-586-1225; Fax: 610-586-6068. Email: office2@stgabrielnorwood.org. Web: www.stgabrielnorwood.org.
School—20 E. Cleveland Ave., 19074. Tel: 610-532-3234; Fax: 610-532-5523. Lay Teachers 14; Students 226.
Catechesis/Religious Program—Tel: 610-532-5057. Email: religiousedu@stgabrielnorwood.org. Students 323.

ORELAND, MONTGOMERY CO., HOLY MARTYRS (1949) Rev. Michael J. Ryan. In Res., Revs. Charles J. Noone (Retired); Raymond F. Tribuiani.
Res.: 120 Allison Rd., 19075. Tel: 215-884-8575; Fax: 215-884-5924. Web: www.holymartyrschurch.net.
School—(Grades PreK-8), 121 Allison Rd., 19075. Tel: 215-887-2044; Fax: 215-887-0024. David Hayden, Prin. Lay Teachers 12; Students 139.
Preschool—207 Ulmer Ave., 19075. Tel: 215-572-8605.
Catechesis/Religious Program—Tel: 215-884-8575. Students 220.

OTTSVILLE, BUCKS CO., ST. JOHN THE BAPTIST (1743) [CEM] Revs. Raymond Diesbourg, M.S.C.; Anthony Ripp, M.S.C.; Deacons Ernest D'Angelo; Edward S. Jones.
Res.: 4050 Durham Rd., 18942. Tel: 610-847-5521. Web: www.stjohnsottsville.org.
School—Tel: 610-847-5523; Fax: 610-847-8549. Email: principal@stjohnsottsville.org. Lay Teachers 19; Students 183.
Catechesis/Religious Program—Tel: 610-847-5522; Fax: 610-847-5522. Students 230.

OXFORD, CHESTER CO., SACRED HEART (1914) Rev. Gregory J. Hamill; Deacon Francis Murphy. In Res., Rev. Sean F. O'Neill.
Res.: 203 Church Rd., 19363. Tel: 610-932-5040; Fax: 610-932-5041. Web: sacredheartchurchoxford.org.
School—Tel: 610-932-3633; Fax: 610-932-6051. Mr. Steven Brunner, Prin.
Catechesis/Religious Program—Tel: 610-932-5863. Mrs. Maryanne Fazio, Dir. Faith Formation. Students 370.

PAOLI, CHESTER CO., ST. NORBERT (1956) Revs. Domenic A. Rossi, O.Praem.; John C. Zagarella, O.Praem.; Deacons William Masapollo; John P. Lozano.
Res.: 50 Leopard Rd., 19301. Tel: 610-644-1655; Fax: 610-644-1928. Web: www.stnorbert.org.
School—Greenlawn & Leopard Rds., 19301. Tel: 610-644-1670; Fax: 610-644-0201. Lay Teachers 19; Students 185.
Catechesis/Religious Program—Tel: 610-644-1670, Ext. 122. Students 438.

PARKESBURG, CHESTER CO., OUR LADY OF CONSOLATION (1853) [CEM] Revs. Victor J. Eschbach; Ignatius Marneni; Deacon Eugene Favinger. In Res., Rev. John Van De Paer, C.I.C.M.
Res.: 603 W. Second Ave., 19365. Tel: 610-857-3510; Fax: 610-857-2353. Email: olc@comcast.net. Web: www.olcchurch.org.
See Coatesville Area Catholic Elementary School, Coatesville under Regional Parish Schools located in the Institution section.
Catechesis/Religious Program—603 W. 2nd Ave., 19365. Tel: 610-857-1003. Delores Cain, D.R.E. Students 400.
Mission—St. Malachy (1838) [CEM] 76 St. Malachi Rd., Cochranville, Chester Co. 19330. Tel: 610-857-3510; Fax: 610-857-2353.

PENN VALLEY, MONTGOMERY CO., ST. JUSTIN MARTYR (1964) Closed. Formerly located at 1222 Hagysford Rd., Narberth. For sacramental records, contact St. John Baptist Vianney, Gladstone. In Res., Most Rev. Louis A. DeSimone; Rev. Russell J. DeSimone, O.S.A.
Res.: 1222 Hagysford Rd., Narberth, 19072. Tel: 610-664-0165; Fax: 610-664-5612.

PENNDEL, BUCKS CO., OUR LADY OF GRACE (1908) [CEM] Revs. William B. Dooner; Eugene C. Wilson; Deacon Dominic A. Garritano. In Res., Rev. Raju Pilla.
Res.: 225 Bellevue Ave., 19047. Tel: 215-757-7700; 215-757-7786; Fax: 215-757-5377. Web: ourladyofgrace-penndel.org.
School—300 Hulmeville Ave., 19047. Tel: 215-757-5287; Fax: 215-757-6199. Web: olg1.org. Mrs. Denise Lewis, Prin. Lay Teachers 23; Students 409.
Catechesis/Religious Program—Tel: 215-757-5530. Students 430.
Parish Service Center—338 Hulmeville Ave., 19047. Tel: 215-757-5052; Fax: 215-757-5530.

PENNSBURG, MONTGOMERY CO., ST. PHILIP NERI (1919) [CEM] Rev. Robert A. Roncase; Deacon Michael J. Franks Sr. In Res., Rev. Raymond W. Smart (Retired).
Res.: 1325 Klinerd Rd., 18073. Tel: 215-679-9275; 215-679-9330; Fax: 215-679-0386. Email: spnofc@comcast.net. Web: www.spnparish.org.
School—Sixth & Washington Sts., East Greenville, 18041. Tel: 215-679-7481; Fax: 215-679-8370. Web: www.spnelementary.com. Students 137.
Catechesis/Religious Program—Tel: 215-541-3120; Fax: 215-541-1398. Students 225.

PHOENIXVILLE, CHESTER CO.

1—ST. ANN (1905) [CEM] Rev. John J. Newns.
Res.: 502 S. Main St., 19460. Tel: 610-933-3732; Fax: 610-935-7958. Email: stannphx@comcast.net. Web: www.churchofsaintann.org.
See Holy Family School, Phoenixville under Regional Parish Schools located in the Institution section.
Catechesis/Religious Program—Tel: 610-755-1077; Fax: 610-935-7958. Email: youthstann@comcast.net. Students 332.

2—HOLY TRINITY (1903), (Polish), [CEM] Rev. Michael W. Rzonca.
Res.: *Sacred Heart Rectory*, 148 Church St., 19460. Tel: 610-933-3830; Fax: 610-935-9261. Email: holytrinityphoenixville@verizon.net. Web: www.holytrinity-phoenixville.net.
Church: 217 Dayton St., 19460.
See Holy Family School, Phoenixville under Regional Parish Schools located in the Institution section.
Catechesis/Religious Program—Students 7.
Convent—Bernardine Sisters of the Third Order of St. Francis, 221 Dayton St., 19460. Tel: 610-983-9446.

3—ST. MARY OF THE ASSUMPTION (1840) [CEM 2] Rev. Gary J. Kramer.
Res.: 212 Dayton St., 19460. Tel: 610-933-2526; Fax: 610-935-1706. Web: www.stmaryassumption.org.
See Holy Family School, Phoenixville under Regional Parish Schools located in the Institution section.
Catechesis/Religious Program—Students 150.

4—SACRED HEART (1900), (Slovak), [CEM] Rev. Michael W. Rzonca.
Res.: 148 Church St., 19460. Tel: 610-933-3830; Fax: 610-935-9261. Email: sacredheartphoenixville@verizon.net. Web: www.sacredheart-phoenixville.net.
See Holy Family School, Phoenixville under Regional Parish Schools located in the Institution section.
Catechesis/Religious Program—Students 36.

PLYMOUTH MEETING, MONTGOMERY CO., EPIPHANY OF OUR LORD (1957) Rev. Joseph J. Quindlen; Deacons William R. Radetzky; Kenneth P. Clancy; Emil J. Wernert. In Res., Rev. James J. Kelly (Retired).
Res.: 3050 Walton Rd., 19462-2361. Tel: 610-828-8634; Fax: 610-828-1802. Email: epiphanych@comcast.net. Web: www.epiphanyofourlord.com.
School—3040 Walton Rd., 19462-2361. Tel: 610-825-0160; Fax: 610-825-0460. Web: www.eols.org. Miss Miriam A. Havey, Prin. Lay Teachers 16; Students 198.
Catechesis/Religious Program—Tel: 610-825-6790; Fax: 610-825-0460. Email: religious.education@eols.org. Web: www.eols.org. Lauren Farrell, D.R.E. Students 201.

POTTSTOWN, MONTGOMERY CO.

1—ST. ALOYSIUS (1856) [CEM 2] Revs. Walter J. Benn; Angelo Hernandez; Deacon James Anderson.
Parish Office: 223 Beech St., 19464.
Res.: 214 N. Hanover St., 19464. Tel: 610-326-5877; Fax: 610-326-0901. Web: saintaloysius.net.
School—220 N. Hanover St., 19464. Tel: 610-326-6167; Fax: 610-970-9960. Sisters of St. Francis of Philadelphia 1; Lay Teachers 23; Students 329.
Catechesis/Religious Program—Tel: 610-326-5877, Ext. 146. Students 225.
Convent—370 South St., 19464. Tel: 610-326-1498.

2—HOLY TRINITY (1899), (Slovak), Closed. Spiritual records are kept at St. Aloysius Church, Pottstown. Tel: 610-326-5877. Worship site of St. Aloysius Church, Pottstown.

3—ST. PETER (1924), (Polish), Closed. Formerly located at 1128 South St. Spiritual records are kept at Blessed Teresa of Calcutta Church. Tel: 610-287-2525.

PRIMOS, DELAWARE CO., ST. EUGENE (1955) Rev. Joseph M. McDermott; Deacon James V. Walsh. In Res., Rev. Msgr. Michael J. Burke (Retired); Rev. John B. Flanagan.
Res.: 200 S. Oak Ave., 19018. Tel: 610-626-2866; Fax: 610-626-1904. Email: steugene55@rcn.com. Web: www.sainteugenechurch.net.
School—110 S. Oak Ave., 19018. Tel: 610-622-2909; Fax: 610-622-6358. Web: sainteugeneschool.org. Lay Teachers 10; Students 223.
Catechesis/Religious Program—Students 102.

QUAKERTOWN, BUCKS CO., ST. ISIDORE (1886) [CEM] Revs. Frederick J. Riegler; Edward E. Brady; Deacon Richard S. Haddon.
Parish Office: 603 W. Broad St., 18951. Email: stisidorechurch@comcast.net. Web: www.stisidores.org.
Res.: 2545 W. Pumping Station Rd., 18951. Tel: 215-536-4389; Fax: 215-536-4137.
School—603 W. Broad St., 18951. Tel: 215-536-6052; Fax: 215-536-8647. Lay Teachers 15; Students 265.
Catechesis/Religious Program—Tel: 215-536-6498. Students 427.

RICHBORO, BUCKS CO., ST. VINCENT DE PAUL (1968) Revs. Joseph J. McLaughlin; George B. Cadwallader; Deacons John M. Golaszewski, Business Mgr.; William F. Iacobellis.
Res.: 654 Hatboro Rd., 18954-1039. Tel: 215-357-5905; Fax: 215-953-8190. Web: www.svdp-richboro.org.
Catechesis/Religious Program—Tel: 215-322-1932. Students 480.
Convent—624 Hatboro Rd., 18954-1039. Tel: 215-942-9152.

RIDLEY PARK, DELAWARE CO., ST. MADELINE (1908) Rev. Louis P. Bellopede; Deacon Gregory R. O'Brien.
Res.: 110 Park St., 19078. Tel: 610-532-6880; Fax: 610-532-6653.
Church: Penn St. & Morton Ave., 19078.
See St. Madeline-St. Rose School, Ridley Park under Regional Parish Schools located in the Institution section.
Catechesis/Religious Program—Tel: 610-583-6120.

Students 215.

RIEGELSVILLE, BUCKS CO., ST. LAWRENCE (1974) [JC] Rev. Gavin W. Muir.
Res.: 345 Elmwood Ln., 18077. Tel: 610-749-2684; Fax: 610-749-2695. Email: saintlawrence@verizon.net. Web: parishesonline.com/scripts/hostedsites/org.asp?ID=7320.
Catechesis/Religious Program—Students 96.

ROSLYN, MONTGOMERY CO., ST. JOHN OF THE CROSS (1953) Rev. John D. Reardon; Deacon Raymond Jacobucci. In Res., Rev. Aloysius Ochasi.
Res.: 2741 Woodland Rd., 19001. Tel: 215-659-4460; Fax: 215-659-2551. Web: www.stjohnofthecrossparish.org.
School—2805 Woodland Rd., 19001. Tel: 215-659-1365; Fax: 215-659-7996. Web: www.stjohnofthecross.org. Mrs. Marianne Garnham, Prin. Lay Teachers 10; Students 150.
Catechesis/Religious Program—Tel: 215-659-1451. Students 175.
Convent—Grey Nuns of the Sacred Heart, 2803 Woodland Rd., 19001. Tel: 215-659-4483.

ROYERSFORD, MONTGOMERY CO., SACRED HEART (1973) Rev. Timothy M. Judge; Deacon Joseph Houser.
Res.: 838 Walnut St., P.O. Box 64, 19468. Tel: 610-948-5915; 610-948-4087; Fax: 610-948-0573. Web: sacredheartroyersford.org.
School—Lewis Rd. & Washington St., 19468. Tel: 610-948-7206; Fax: 610-948-6508. Lay Teachers 14; Students 189.
Catechesis/Religious Program—Tel: 610-792-2997. Laura Hritz, C.R.E. Students 366.

RYDAL, MONTGOMERY CO., ST. HILARY OF POITIERS (1962) Rev. Kevin P. Murray; Deacon John K. Hunter.
Res.: 820 Susquehanna Rd., 19046. Tel: 215-884-3252; Fax: 215-884-5342. Email: sthilaryrydal@comcast.net.
School—920 Susquehanna Rd., 19046. Tel: 215-887-4520; Fax: 215-887-6337. Students 221.
Catechesis/Religious Program—Students 120.

SCHWENKSVILLE, MONTGOMERY CO., ST. MARY (1926) Revs. Charles J. McElroy; Thomas J. Furey.
Res.: 40 Spring Mount Rd., 19473. Tel: 610-287-8156; Fax: 610-287-4226. Web: www.churchofsaintmary.org.
School—Tel: 610-287-7757. Lay Teachers 24; Students 319.
Catechesis/Religious Program—Tel: 610-287-4517. Students 439.

SECANE, DELAWARE CO., OUR LADY OF FATIMA (1952) Rev. Msgr. George A. Majoros; Rev. John R. DiOrio. In Res., Rev. Thomas R. Urian.
Res.: 1 Fatima Dr., 19018. Tel: 610-532-5800; Fax: 610-532-6937. Web: www.olfchurchsecane.com.
School—10 Fatima Dr., 19018. Tel: 610-586-7539; Fax: 610-586-0117. Web: olfschool/secane.com. Sisters, Servants of the Immaculate Heart of Mary 6; Lay Teachers 17; Students 286.
Catechesis/Religious Program—Tel: 610-586-3633. Students 181.
Convent—5 Fatima Dr., 19018. Tel: 610-532-1190.

SELLERSVILLE, BUCKS CO., ST. AGNES (1919) [CEM] Rev. Msgr. John B. Wendrychowicz; Revs. Mark E. Fernandes; Jeffrey M. Stecz; Deacons Harry Tucker; Harry D. Antrim.
Res.: 445 N. Main St., 18960. Tel: 215-257-2128; Fax: 215-257-4561. Web: www.stagneschurch.org.
See St. Agnes-Sacred Heart School, Hilltown under Regional Parish Schools located in the Institution section.
Catechesis/Religious Program—Tel: 215-257-1811; Fax: 215-257-0525. Email: stagnesprep@aol.com. Web: www.stagnesprep.org. Students 390.

SHARON HILL, DELAWARE CO., HOLY SPIRIT (1892) Rev. Martin E. Woodeshick; Deacon Albert Rayner. In Res., Rev. Msgr. Daniel J. Kehoe, Pastor Emeritus (Retired).
Res.: 1028 School St., 19079. Tel: 610-583-2220; Fax: 610-583-5130.
Catechesis/Religious Program—Tel: 610-583-2220. Sr. Maureen Murray, R.S.M., D.R.E. Students 10.

SOUTH COVENTRY, CHESTER CO., ST. THOMAS MORE (1968) Rev. Hugh J. Dougherty.
Res.: 2101 Pottstown Pike, Pottstown, 19465. Tel: 610-469-9304; Fax: 610-469-9315.
Catechesis/Religious Program—Tel: 610-469-9302. Students 557.

SOUTHAMPTON, BUCKS CO., OUR LADY OF GOOD COUNSEL (1923) Rev. Msgr. Anthony J. D'Angelico; Revs. John J. Kilgallon; William J. Monahan.
Res.: 611 Knowles Ave., 18966-4198. Tel: 215-357-1300, Ext. 100; Fax: 215-357-4452. Web: www.olgc.org.
School—Tel: 215-357-1300, Ext. 101. Mr. Frank Mokriski, Prin. Lay Teachers 29; Students 433.
Catechesis/Religious Program—Tel: 215-357-1300, Ext. 107. Students 430.

SPRING CITY, CHESTER CO., ST. JOSEPH (1919) Rev. Charles R. O'Hara. In Res., Rev. Donato P. Silveri.
Res.: 3640 Schuylkill Rd., 19475. Tel: 610-948-7760; Fax: 610-948-8509. Email: st.joes@comcast.net. Web: www.stjosephspringcity.com.
Catechesis/Religious Program—Tel: 610-792-4535. Email: stjosephprep@comcast.net. Andrea Jackowski, D.R.E. Students 171.

SPRINGFIELD, DELAWARE CO.

1—ST. FRANCIS OF ASSISI (1923) Revs. Salvatore M. Riccio; Mark S. Kunigonis; Joseph J. Meehan (Retired); Deacons James D. Kane Sr.; Arthur M. McGuire; Timothy W. Baxter.
Res.: 136 Saxer Ave., 19064. Tel: 610-543-0848; Fax: 610-604-0283. Web: www.sfaparish.org.
School—112 Saxer Ave., 19064. Tel: 610-543-0546; Fax: 610-544-9431. Lay Teachers 17; Students 299.
Catechesis/Religious Program—Students 425.

2—HOLY CROSS (1948) Revs. John D. Gabin; Brian A. Izzo; Simon Hyung-Min Ha; Sr. Mary Carmela Sandusky, R.S.M., Pastoral Min.; Deacons Robert Frankenberger, (Retired); Joseph N. Gousie Sr. In Res., Rev. Msgr. Paul F. Curran (Retired).
Res.: 651 E. Springfield Rd., 19064. Tel: 610-626-3321; Fax: 610-622-2920.
School—Bishop & Springfield Rds., 19064. Tel: 610-626-1709; Fax: 610-626-1859. Lay Teachers 25; Students 403.
Catechesis/Religious Program—Tel: 610-626-1057; Fax: 610-626-8057. Students 240.
Convent—Tel: 610-626-2492.

3—ST. KEVIN (1955) Rev. John C. Moloney; Sr. Eleanor McFadden, S.S.J., Pastoral Assoc.; Deacons Thomas Eichman; Leonard Diana. In Res., Rev. Thomas P. Gillin.
Rectory—St. Kevin, 200 W. Sproul Rd., 19064-2016. Tel: 610-544-8777; 610-544-8778; Fax: 610-544-7832.
School—Tel: 610-544-4455; Fax: 610-544-7092. Lay Teachers 16; Students 215.
Catechesis/Religious Program—Tel: 610-544-3236; Fax: 610-544-7382. Students 212.
Convent—Tel: 610-544-4535.

STOWE, MONTGOMERY CO., ST. GABRIEL OF THE SORROWFUL MOTHER (1929) Rev. Thomas A. Nasta.
Parish Center—127 E. Howard St., 19464. Tel: 610-326-5127; Fax: 610-326-5749.
Res.: 421 Jefferson St., 19464.
Catechesis/Religious Program—Tel: 610-327-5376. Students 30.

STRAFFORD, CHESTER CO., OUR LADY OF THE ASSUMPTION (1908), (Italian), [CEM] Rev. Msgr. Joseph T. Marino; Deacon John P. Rose. In Res., Rev. Msgr. James T. McDonough (Retired); Rev. Daniel J. Hoy (Retired).
Res.: 35 Old Eagle School Rd., 19087-2577. Tel: 610-688-1178; 610-688-6147; Fax: 610-293-9680. Web: www.olastrafford.org.
Preschool—135 Fairfield Ln., 19087. Tel: 610-688-5277. Students 96.
Catechesis/Religious Program—Tel: 610-688-6590. Students 105.

SWARTHMORE, DELAWARE CO., NOTRE DAME DE LOURDES (1959) Rev. Karl A. Zeuner; Deacons James Basilio; Michael McAndrews.
Res.: 950 Michigan Ave., 19081. Tel: 610-544-1270; Fax: 610-544-4310. Email: rectory@notredamedelourdes.net.
School—990 Fairview Rd., 19081. Tel: 610-328-9330; Fax: 610-328-3955. Lay Teachers 14; Students 214.
Catechesis/Religious Program—Students 173.

SWEDESBURG, MONTGOMERY CO., SACRED HEART (1907), (Polish), Rev. Andrew McCormick; Rev. Msgr. Anthony E. Jaworowski (Retired).
Res.: 120 Jefferson St., 19405. Tel: 610-275-1750; Fax: 610-275-0480. Web: sacredheart-swedesburg.net.
Catechesis/Religious Program—Students 60.
Convent—635 E. Fourth St., 19405. Tel: 610-239-1785. Sr. Klara Slonina, Supr. Sisters Servants of the Most Sacred Heart

TROOPER, MONTGOMERY CO., VISITATION B.V.M. (1954) Rev. Msgr. Thomas A. Murray; Revs. Edward J. Kelly; Michael J. Saban. In Res., Rev. Msgr. Ignatius L. Murray (Retired).
Res.: 196 N. Trooper Rd., Norristown, 19403. Tel: 610-539-5572; Fax: 610-539-3240. Web: www.visitationbvm.org.
School—N. Trooper Rd., R.D. 1, Norristown, 19403. Tel: 610-539-6080; Fax: 610-630-7946. Sisters of the Holy Family of Nazareth 2; Lay Teachers 32; Students 668.
Catechesis/Religious Program—Tel: 610-539-6211. Roseanne Terranova, D.R.E. Students 530.
Convent—Tel: 610-539-5558.

UPPER DARBY, DELAWARE CO., ST. ALICE (1922) Rev. Peter N. Quinn.
Res.: 150 Hampden Rd., 19082. Tel: 610-352-1431; Fax: 610-352-1432.
Catechesis/Religious Program—Students 45.

UPPER GWYNEDD, MONTGOMERY CO., CORPUS CHRISTI (1964) Rev. Msgr. Thomas P. Flanigan; Revs. Kevin J. Gallagher; Richard J. McAndrews; Deacons Francis E. Langsdorf; William W. Evans; Sr. Eleanor McNichol, S.S.J., Parish Min. In Res., Rev. Benjamin Nwanonenyi.
Res.: 900 Sumneytown Pike, Lansdale, 19446. Tel: 215-855-1311; Fax: 215-855-3631. Web: corpuschristilansdale.org.
School—920 Sumneytown Pike, Lansdale, 19446. Tel: 215-368-0582; Fax: 215-361-5927. Email: ccsprin@fast.net. Sisters of St. Joseph 1; Lay Teachers 32; Students 540.
Catechesis/Religious Program—Tel: 215-362-2292. Trish Keen, D.R.E. Students 700.
Convent—1622 Supplee Rd., Lansdale, 19446. Tel: 215-368-0737.

UPPER UWCHLAN, CHESTER CO., SAINT ELIZABETH (2000) Rev. Msgr. Thomas M. Mullin; Deacons James E. Bogdan; Richard L. Fremont; Barry R. Midwood.
Parish Office & Church: 100 St. Elizabeth Dr., P.O. Box 695, Uwchlan, 19480-0695. Tel: 610-321-1200; Fax: 610-646-6513. Email: steuucc@stelizabethparish.org. Web: www.stelizabethparish.org.
Res.: 2 Fox Ridge Rd., Glenmoore, 19343-9546. Tel: 610-321-9616.
School—120 Saint Elizabeth Dr., P.O. Box 780, Uwchlan, 19480-0780. Tel: 610-646-6540; Fax: 610-646-6541. Email: bdougherty@stelizabethparish.org. Bernadette Dougherty, Prin. Students 326.
Catechesis/Religious Program—Tel: 610-646-6545. Email: religioused@stelizabethparish.org. Students 850.

VILLANOVA, DELAWARE CO., ST. THOMAS OF VILLANOVA PARISH (1848) Rev. Richard O'Leary, O.S.A. In Res., Revs. William J. Donnelly, O.S.A.; Allan Fitzgerald, O.S.A.
Res.: 1242 Montrose Ave., Rosemont, 19010. Tel: 610-525-4801. Web: www.stthomasofvillanova.org.
St. Thomas of Villanova Preschool—1236 Montrose Ave., Rosemont, 19010. Tel: 610-525-7554.
Catechesis/Religious Program—Students 269.

WALLINGFORD, DELAWARE CO., ST. JOHN CHRYSOSTOM (1952) Rev. James R. Bajorek; Deacons Raymond Vadino; Walter Lance.
Res.: 617 S. Providence Rd., 19086. Tel: 610-874-3418; Fax: 610-872-1741. Email: sjcparish@yahoo.com. Web: www.saintjohnchrysostom.net.
School—607 S. Providence Rd., 19086. Tel: 610-876-7110; Fax: 610-876-5923. Email: stjohnprincipal@comcast.net. Web: www.sjcschool-news.org. Lay Teachers 20; Students 150.
Catechesis/Religious Program—605 S. Providence Rd., 19086. Tel: 610-872-4673. Email: stjohnreligiouseducation@comcast.net. Students 390.
Convent—Tel: 610-872-7194.

WARMINSTER, BUCKS CO., NATIVITY OF OUR LORD (1956) Revs. Angelo R. Citino; Timothy J. Buckley.
Res.: 625 W. Street Rd., 18974. Tel: 215-675-1925; Fax: 215-674-3787. Email: frcitino@nativityofourlord.org.
Parish Office Center: 605 W. Street Rd., 18974. Fax: 267-803-1777. Web: www.nativityofourlord.org.
School—585 W. Street Rd., 18974. Tel: 215-675-2820; Fax: 215-675-9413. Email: sklunder@nativity-school.org. Web: www.nativity-school.org. Lay Teachers 26; Students 472.
Catechesis/Religious Program—Tel: 215-672-5316; Fax: 215-675-9413. Email: astolarik@nativity-school.org. Students 367.
Convent—605 W. Street Rd., 18974. Tel: 215-672-0147.

WARRINGTON, BUCKS CO.

1—ST. JOSEPH (1922) Revs. James A. Grant; John F. Bowe; Deacon Karl Hartmann.
Res.: 1795 Columbia Ave., 18976. Tel: 215-672-3020; Fax: 215-672-3114. Web: www.saintjoseph-church.us.
See St. Joseph-St. Robert Bellarmine School, Warrington under Regional Parish Schools located in the Institution section.
Catechesis/Religious Program—Tel: 215-672-9990. Mrs. Cathy Cain, D.R.E. Students 285.
Station—Willow Grove Joint Reserve Base Willow Grove. Tel: 215-443-6002.

2—ST. ROBERT BELLARMINE (1968) Rev. Msgr. James D. Beisel; Rev. Stephen H. Paolino; Deacon George E. Morris Jr.
Res.: 856 Euclid Ave., 18976. Tel: 215-343-0315; Fax: 215-343-8592.
School - See St. Joseph-St. Robert Bellarmine School, Warrington under Regional Parish Schools located in the Institution section.
Catechesis/Religious Program—850 Euclid Ave., 18976. Tel: 215-343-9433. Students 577.

WAYNE, CHESTER CO., ST. ISAAC JOGUES (1970) Rev. Steven J. Harris; F. Lee Parry, Business Mgr.; Mary D. Schachinger, Parish Svcs. Dir.
Res.: 50 W. Walker Rd., 19087. Tel: 610-687-3366; Fax: 610-293-9529. Email: rectory@stisaac.org. Web:

www.stisaac.org.
Preschool—Tel: 610-687-2481, Ext. 6; Fax: 610-293-9529. Email: anna@stisaac.org.
Catechesis/Religious Program—Tel: 610-687-2481, Ext. 4. Email: reled@stisaac.org. Louis M. Valenti, D.R.E. Students 203.
Youth Ministry—Tel: 610-687-2481, Ext. 5. Email: jaquilantr@stisaac.org.

WAYNE, DELAWARE CO., ST. KATHARINE OF SIENA (1893) Rev. Msgr. John A. Close; Rev. Thomas F. Doyle; Sisters Kathleen Callaghan, S.S.J., Dir. Parish Life & Ministry; Elizabeth O'Hara, S.S.J., Parish Svcs. Dir. In Res., Rev. Msgr. Michael J. Carroll (Retired).
Res.: 104 S. Aberdeen Ave., 19087. Tel: 610-688-4584; Fax: 610-688-7951. Email: rectory@stkatharineofsiena.org. Web: www.stkatharineofsiena.org.
School—229 Windermere Ave., 19087. Tel: 610-688-5451; Fax: 610-688-6796. Email: school@stkatharineofsiena.org. Frank Tosti, Prin. Lay Teachers 25; Students 414.
Catechesis/Religious Program—Tel: 610-688-7890. Email: religioused@stkatharineofsiena.org. Barbara Seaman, D.R.E. Students 515.
Convent—235 Windermere Ave., 19087. Tel: 610-688-0655.

WEST BRANDYWINE, CHESTER CO., ST. PETER (1963) Rev. Michael J. Fitzpatrick. In Res., Rev. Emmanuel K. Iheaka; Deacons Thomas C. Concitis; James T. McAvoy.
Parish Office: 2835 Manor Rd., 19344. Tel: 610-380-9045; Fax: 610-380-9049.
Res.: 1080 N. Manor Rd., Honey Brook, 19344-9610. Web: www.saintpeterchurch.net.
See Pope John Paul II Regional Catholic Elementary School, West Brandywine under Regional Parish Schools located in the Institution section
Regional Religious Education Program—2875 Manor Rd. Tel: 610-384-3145; Fax: 610-384-1506. Patrice A. Peterson, D.R.E. Students 419.

WEST CHESTER, CHESTER CO.

1—ST. AGNES (1793) [CEM] Rev. Msgr. Nelson J. Perez; Revs. Anthony J. Cossavella; Laurence J. Gleason; James J. Melle; Deacons Victor Gonzalez; Clement J. McGovern; Patrick M. Stokely.
Res.: 233 W. Gay St., 19380. Tel: 610-692-2990; Fax: 610-692-9623. Email: info@saintagnesparish.org. Web: saintagnesparish.org.
School—211 W. Gay St., 19380. Tel: 610-696-1260; Fax: 610-436-9631. Sisters, Servants of the Immaculate Heart of Mary 4; Lay Teachers 24; Students 355.
Catechesis/Religious Program—207 W. Gay St., 19380. Tel: 610-436-4640; Fax: 610-719-1961. Students 506.
Convent—205 W. Gay St., 19380. Tel: 610-692-9430.

2—SS. SIMON AND JUDE (1961) Rev. Msgr. Francis W. Beach; Rev. Jeffrey M. Rott; Mr. Ronald B. Avellino, Business Mgr.; Deacons James Lyon; Thaddeus C. Raczkowski. In Res., Revs. William Dickinson; Joseph M. Glatts.
Res.: 8 Cavanaugh Ct., 19382. Tel: 610-696-3624; Fax: 610-696-3971. Email: rectory@simonandjude.org. Web: www.simonandjude.org.
School—6 Cavanaugh Ct., 19382. Tel: 610-696-5249; Fax: 610-696-4682. Sisters, Servants of the Immaculate Heart of Mary 4; Lay Teachers 24; Students 414.
Catechesis/Religious Program—Tel: 610-692-3118. Sisters Barbara Jude Gentry, I.H.M., D.R.E.; Mary Beth Coyle, Coord. Evangelization & Adult Faith Formation. Students 545.
Convent—Tel: 610-692-4394.

WEST CONSHOHOCKEN, MONTGOMERY CO., ST. GERTRUDE (1888) Rev. Msgr. Gerard C. Mesure.
Res.: *St. Mary Rectory*, 140 W. Hector St., Conshohocken, 19428.
Church: 209 Merion Ave., Conshohocken, 19428. Tel: 610-828-0268; Fax: 610-828-7024. Email: stgerts1888@aol.com.

WEST GROVE, CHESTER CO., ASSUMPTION B.V.M. (1873) [CEM] Rev. Msgr. John W. Graf; Rev. Kenneth Putz; Joyce Malchione, Business Mgr.; Deacons Thomas Hannan; Michael DeGrasse. In Res., Rev. Msgr. Francis J. Depman.
Parish Office: 105 W. Evergreen St., 19390. Tel: 610-869-2722. Email: abvm@comcast.net. Web: www.assumptionbvmwestgrove.org.
Res.: 107 W. Evergreen St., 19390. Tel: 610-869-2722; Fax: 610-869-3252.
School—290 State Rd., 19390. Tel: 610-869-9576; Fax: 610-869-4049. Email: assumptionwestgrove@comcast.net. Danielle White, Prin. Lay Teachers 16; Students 222.
Catechesis/Religious Program—Tel: 610-869-8575. Kristine McNicholas, D.R.E. Students 842.
Mission—Santa Maria, Madra de Dios P.O. Box 1019, Avondale, Chester Co. 19311. Tel: 610-268-3365; Fax: 610-869-9395. Web: www.misionsantamaria.org.

WESTTOWN, CHESTER CO., ST. MAXIMILIAN KOLBE (1986) Rev. Msgr. Robert J. Carroll; Rev. Martin J. Ivanovich; Deacons Lawrence Brandon; Alfred Mauriello. In Res., Rev. John J. Nordeman.
Res.: 15 E. Pleasant Grove Rd., West Chester, 19382. Tel: 610-399-6936; Fax: 610-399-4828. Email: saintmax@comcast.net. Web: www.stmax.org.
School—(Grades PreK-8), 300 Daly Dr., West Chester, 19382. Tel: 610-399-8400; Fax: 610-399-4684. Students 392.
Catechesis/Religious Program—Tel: 610-399-9642. Students 547.

WILLOW GROVE, MONTGOMERY CO., ST. DAVID (1919) Rev. Msgr. Richard T. Bolger; Revs. Anthony T. Rossi; John J. Shelley (Retired); Deacon William F. Eliason.
Res.: 316 N. Easton Rd., 19090. Tel: 215-657-0252; Fax: 215-659-6516. Email: stdavidparish@comcast.net. Web: www.stdavidparish.org.
School—401 N. Easton Rd., 19090. Tel: 215-659-6393; Fax: 215-659-6377. Sisters, Servants of the Immaculate Heart of Mary 6; Lay Teachers 16; Students 248.
Catechesis/Religious Program—Tel: 215-659-4059. Students 282.
Convent—400 N. Easton Rd., 19090. Tel: 215-659-0445.

WYNDMOOR, MONTGOMERY CO., SEVEN DOLORS (1916-2003) Closed. Formerly located at 1200 E. Willow Grove Ave. Spiritual records are kept at St. Genevieve Church, Tel: 215-836-2828.

WYNNEWOOD, MONTGOMERY CO., PRESENTATION B.V.M. (1954) Rev. Eduardo G. Montero; Deacon Ernest W. Angiolollo.
Res.: 204 Haverford Rd., 19096. Tel: 610-642-8341; Fax: 610-896-1970. Web: www.presbvm.org.
Catechesis/Religious Program—Students 75.
Parish Center: 240 Haverford Rd., 19096. Tel: 610-642-8341.

YARDLEY, BUCKS CO., ST. IGNATIUS OF ANTIOCH (1920) [CEM] [JC] Rev. Msgr. Samuel E. Shoemaker; Rev. Bernard J. Taglianetti; Deacon Robert J. Skawinski.
Res.: 999 Reading Ave., 19067. Tel: 215-493-3377; Fax: 215-493-0450. Email: contact@stignatiusyardley.org. Web: www.stignatiusyardley.org.
School—997 Reading Ave., 19067. Tel: 215-493-3867; Fax: 267-573-3550. Web: www.sisschool.org. Lay Staff 23; Students 220.
Catechesis/Religious Program—Tel: 215-493-5204; Fax: 215-493-0956. Students 583.

YEADON, DELAWARE CO., ST. LOUIS (1928) Rev. John P. Collins; Deacon Charles R. Amen.
Res.: 821 W. Cobbs Creek Pkwy., 19050. Tel: 610-623-0553; Fax: 610-623-8191. Web: www.stlix.org; www.stlouischurchyeadon.org.
Catechesis/Religious Program—Students 16.

Chaplains of Public Institutions

PHILADELPHIA. *Philadelphia Prison System*, 8001 State Rd., 19136. Tel: 215-276-2288. Rev. Gregory P. Cozzubbo, C.M.
Veterans Administration Medical Center, University & Woodland Aves., 19104. Tel: 215-823-5800, Ext. 2776. Rev. Michael A. Lipareli.

COATESVILLE. *Veterans Administration Medical Center* 19320. Tel: 215-384-7711, Ext. 190. Rev. Emmanuel K. Iheaka.

GRATERFORD. *Graterford State Correctional Institution* 19426. Tel: 215-489-4151. Rev. Robert W. Povish.

NORRISTOWN. *Norristown State Hospital* 19401. Tel: 215-270-1104. Rev. Dominick F. Finn, O.S.F.S., Chap.

SPRING CITY. *Southeastern Pennsylvania Veterans Center* 19475. Tel: 215-948-2400. Rev. Donato P. Silveri.

On Special or Other Archdiocesan Assignment:
Most Revs.—
Maginnis, Robert P., D.D., V.G., Saint Edmond Home, 320 S. Roberts Rd., Bryn Mawr, 19010.
McFadden, Joseph P., D.D., V.G., Proctor Rd., 19116.
Senior, Timothy C., D.D., V.G., M.B.A., M.S.W., M.Div., Divine Providence Village, 686 Old Maple Rd., Springfield, 19064.
Thomas, Daniel E., D.D., S.T.L., V.G., 209 Merion Ave., West Conshohocken, 19428.
Rev. Msgrs.—
Anderlonis, Joseph J., S.T.D., Vicar, Office for Consecrated Life, Saint George Rectory, 3580 Salmon St., 19134.
D'Addezio, Louis A., M.A., Dir., Office for Special Projects & Closures, Saint Patrick Rectory, 242 S. 20th St., 19103.
Dombrow, William A., M.Div., Rector, Villa Saint Joseph, 1436 Landowne Ave., Darby, 19023.
Fitzgerald, Michael J., M.Div., J.C.D., J.D., Judicial Vicar, Metropolitan Tribunal, Saint Patrick Rectory, 242 S. 20th St., 19103.
McIntyre, John J., Admin. Sec., Office of the Archbishop, Cardinal's Residence, 5700 City Ave., 19131.
Mesure, Gerard C., J.C.D., J.D., Chancellor, Office of the Chancellor, Saint Mary Rectory, 140 West Hector St., Conshohocken, 19428.
Shields, Hugh Joseph, M.Div., Vicar for Hispanic Catholic, Our Lady of Ransom Rectory, 6701 Calvert St., 19149.
Sullivan, Daniel J., M.Div., Vicar for Clergy, Sisters of Mercy Convent, 515 Montgomery Ave., Merion Station, 19066.
Revs.—
Ames, John J., S.T.D., M.A., M.Div., Deputy Sec., Office for Catechetical Formation, Saint Matthew Rectory, 219 Fayette St., Conshohocken, 19428.
Bransfield, Sean P., M.Div., M.A., J.C.L., Archdiocesan Judge, Metropolitan Tribunal, Cardinal's Residence, 5700 City Ave., 19131.
Collins, James J., S.O.E.D., Faculty, Holy Family University, 9701 Frankford Ave., 19114.
Dieckhaus, Anthony W., Chap., Nazareth Hospital, Saint Jerome Rectory, 8100 Colfax St., 19136.
Farley, Bernard C., Chap., Saint John Neumann Nursing Home, 10400 Roosevelt Blvd., 19116.
Forlano, Philip M., M.A., Chap., La Milagrosa, Cathedral Basilica SS. Peter and Paul, 1723 Race St., 19103.
Gill, G. Dennis, M.Div., S.L.L., Dir., Office for Worship, Cathedral Basilica SS. Peter and Paul, 1723 Race St., 19103.
Hennessy, Brian P., M.Div., J.C.L., Asst. Vicar Clergy, St. Madeleine Sophie Rectory, 6440 Greene St., 19119-3298.
Hickey, Gregory J., M.A., Rector, St. Joseph's-in-the-Hills Retreat House, 315 S. Warren Ave., P.O. Box 315, Malvern, 19355.
Hunt, Mark J., M.A., S.T.L., Prof., Holy Family Univ. - Newtown Campus, Saint Joseph the Worker Rectory, 9172 New Falls Rd., Fallsington, 19054.
Kennedy, Edward J., Chap., St. Francis Country House, Blessed Virgin Mary Rectory, 1101 Main St., Darby, 19023.
Kloda, Marshall J., M.Div., Chap., Nazareth Hospital, 2601 Holme Ave., 19152.
Kuczynski, Edward P., M.Div., Chap., St. Monica Manor, Saint Philip Neri Rectory, 218 Queen St., 19147.
Lowe, Philip J., Ed.D., Faculty - Neumann College, Holy Saviour Rectory, 108 E. Ridge Rd., Marcus Hook, 19061.
Mahoney, Shaun L., S.T.D., Chap., Temple Univ. Newman Ctr., Saint Martin de Porres Rectory, 2340 W. Lehigh Ave., 19132.
Maloney, Joseph L., M.Div., Dir., Immaculata Univ. Campus Ministry, Immaculata University, 1145 King Rd., Immaculata, 19345-0663.
McKay, Douglas M., Chap., Holy Family Home, 5300 Chester Ave., 19143.
McKelvey, James P., M.Div., Chap., Camilla Hall, Camilla Hall, P.O. Box 100, Immaculata, 19345.
Morabito, Vincent R., M.Div., Chap., Drexel Univ. Newman Ctr., St. Agatha/St. James Rectory, 3728 Chestnut St., 19104-3188.
Nordeman, John J., M.A., Chap., West Chester Univ. Newman Ctr., Saint Maximilian Kolbe Rectory, 15 E. Pleasant Grove Rd., West Chester, 19382.
O'Donnell, Dennis J.W., Ph.D., Dir., Holy Redeemer Health System, Saint Christopher Rectory, 13301 Proctor Rd., 19116.
Oliver, James M., J.C.D., M.A., M.Div., Vice Chancellor, Office of the Chancellor, Saint Phillip Neri Rectory, 218 Queen St., 19147.
Pelczar, Edward A., Chap., Temple Univ. Hospital, Saint Helena Rectory, 6161 N. Fifth St., 19120.
Rogers, Christopher B., M.A., Dir., Vocation Office for Diocesan Priesthood, Annunciation B.V.M. Rectory, 410 Sagamore Rd., Havertown, 19083.
Swope, Mark G., Chap., Provincialate, Sisters of Holy Redeemer, 521 Moredon Rd., Huntingdon Valley, 19006.
Thorne, Stephen D., M.A., M.Div., Dir., Office for Black Catholics, Saint Cyprian Rectory, 525 Cobbs Creek Pkwy., 19143.
Tribuiani, Raymond F., M.Div., Chap., Chestnut Hill College, Holy Martyrs Rectory, 120 Allison Rd., Oreland, 19075.
Windhaus, Edward A., M.A., M.Div., Newman Chap., Bryn Mawr, Haverford & Swarthmore Colleges, Saint Anastasia Rectory, 3301 W. Chester Pike, Newtown Square, 19073.
Zlock, Charles, M.A., M.Div., M.I.B.S., Assoc. Vicar for Clergy for Ongoing Formation, Saint Augustine Rectory, 464 Ford St., Bridgeport, 19405.

On Duty Outside the Archdiocese:
Rev. Msgr.—
Burns, Vincent P., Glenmary Home Missioners, P.O. Box 465618, Cincinnati, OH 45246.
Revs.—
Benonis, Richard R., HC 33, Box 850, Barksdale, TX 78828.
Bonavitacola, John M., Our Lady of Mount Carmel Parish, 2121 S. Rural Rd., Tempe, AZ 85282.
Bozeman, Anthony M., Saint Joan of Arc Parish, 8321 Burthe St., New Orleans, LA 70118.
Bransfield, J. Brian, M.Div., M.A., S.T.L., U.S-.C.C.B. Secretariat of Evangelization and Catechesis, 3211 4th St., N.E., Washington, DC 20017.
Brouwers, Hans A.L., Office of the Grand Master, Order of the Holy Sepulchre of Jerusalem, Vatican City 00120.
Fairbanks, Gregory J., H.Ed., Pontifical Council for Promoting Christian Unity, Vatican City State 00120.
Funk, Peter C., Diocese of Beaumont, 9920 N. Major Dr., P.O. Box 3948, Beaumont, TX 77713.
Marczewski, Robert, S.T.L., M.Div., SS. Cyril and Methodius Seminary, 3535 Indian Trail, Orchard Lake, MI 48324.
Menei, Francis T., Saint Richard Parish, 201 Adele Ave., Manheim, 17545.

Military Chaplains:
Rev. Msgr.—
McManus, Gerald D.
Revs.—
Coffey, Joseph L.
Concha, Alfonso J.
Foley, Francis P.
McDermott, Stephen C.

Graduate Studies:
Revs.—
Crowley, John C., Casa Santa Maria Via dell, Umilta 30, Rome 00187 Italy.
DiGuglielmo, Anthony J., M.Div., Franciscan Monastery, 1400 Quincy St., N.E., Washington, DC 20017.
Kozak, Lawrence F., M.Div., Casa Santa Maria, Via dell'Umilta 30, Rome, Italy.

Absent on Sick Leave:
Revs.—
Dragon, Joseph W.
McLaughlin, James J.
Nguyen, Khoa M.
Oswald, Leo P.
Small, William T., M.A.
Stenson, Paul J.
Witalec, Dennis J.

Retired:
Rev. Msgrs.—
Barszczewski, Francis A., S.T.L., M.S.L.S., Villa Saint Joseph, 1436 Lansdowne Ave., Darby, 19023-1298.
Boland, John P., M.A., Saint Christopher Rectory, 13301 Proctor Rd., 19116-3716.
Breslin, John E., Holy Family Rectory, 234 Hermitage St., 19127.
Burke, Michael J., M.Div., Saint Eugene Rectory, 200 S. Oak Ln., Primos, 19018.
Busco, John J., Villa St. Joseph, 1436 Lansdowne Ave., Darby, 19023-1298.
Campbell, Hugh P., 40 Greenbriar Rd., Perryville, MD 21903.
Carbine, Francis A., M.A., Saint Katherine of Siena Rectory, 9700 Frankford Ave., 19114-2896.
Carroll, Michael J., M.A., Saint Katherine of Siena Rectory, 104 S. Aberdeen Ave., Wayne, 19087.
Connelly, James E., S.T.L., H.E.D., St. Monica Rectory, 2422 S. 17th St., 19145.
Cunningham, Joseph C., Villa Saint Joseph, 1436 Lansdowne Ave., Darby, 19023-1298.
Curran, Paul F., Holy Cross Rectory, 651 E. Springfield Rd., Springfield, 19064.
Degnan, Henry B., St. Paul Rectory, 2007 New Hope St., Norristown, 19401.
Devlin, Charles V., P.A., Nativity B.V.M. Rectory, 30 E. Franklin St., Media, 19063.
Dreger, Francis X., 2700 W. Brigantine Ave., Brigantine, NJ 08203.
Flood, James J., St. Timothy Rectory, 3001 Levick St., 19149.
Galyo, John M., St. Mary Magdalen Rectory, 2400 N. Providence Rd., Media, 19063-1998.
Grudowski, Robert J., Saint Bede the Venerable Rectory, 1071 Holland Rd., Holland, 18966.
Howard, James J., 9224 Grace Ln., 19115.
Jaworowski, Anthony E., Sacred Heart Rectory, 120 Jefferson St., Swedesburg, 19405.
Kane, Joseph T., Villa St. Joseph, 1436 Lansdowne Ave., Darby, 19023-1298.
Kehoe, Daniel J., Holy Spirit Rectory, 1028 School St., Sharon Hill, 19079.
Kelley, Thomas J., St. Matthew Rectory, 3000 Cottman Ave., 19149.
Matteo, James P., Villa Saint Joseph, 1436 Lansdowne Ave, Darby, 19023-1298.
McBride, James P., 10 E. Maple St., Tresckow, 18254.
McDonough, James T., M.S.W., L.L.D., Our Lady of the Assumption Rectory, 35 Old Eagle School Rd., Strafford, 19087.
McGuire, Anthony W., 400 E. Allens Ln., 19119-1103.
McManus, Robert T., 72 Parkridge Dr., Bryn Mawr, 19010.
Meehan, Francis X., S.T.D., St. Charles Seminary, Overbrook, 100 E. Wynnewood Rd., Wynnewood, 19096.
Menna, Francis A., Villa Saint Joseph, 1436 Lansdowne Ave., Darby, 19023-1298.
Monaghan, Charles J., Villa Saint Joseph, 1436 Lansdowne Ave., Darby, 19023-1298.
Mortimer, James E., 406 Solly Ave., 19111.
Murray, Ignatius L., Visitation B.V.M. Rectory, 196 N. Trooper Rd., Norristown, 19403-2665.
Murray, Joseph W., Mother of Divine Providence Rectory, 333 Allendale Rd., King Of Prussia, 19406-1640.
Nace, Arthur J., 106 Gabriel Ct., Broomall, 19008.
Nugent, Arthur W., 1341 Osbourne Ave., Roslyn, 19001.
O'Brien, Bartholomew J., Villa Saint Joseph, 1436 Lansdowne Ave., Darby, 19023-1298.
O'Brien, John F., St. Luke the Evangelist Rectory, 2316 Fairhill Ave., Glenside, 19038-4107.
O'Donnell, William J. J., M.A., Regina Coeli Residence for Priests, 685 York Rd., Warminster, 18974.
Scanlon, Thomas J., St. Mary's Manor, 701 Lansdale Ave., Lansdale, 19446-2900.
Schmidt, Francis X., 110 Nester Dr., Valley Forge Crossing, Norristown, 19403.
Sharkey, John A., Villa Saint Joseph, 1436 Lansdowne Ave., Darby, 19023-1298.
Shields, Joseph A., Saint John the Baptist, Vianney Rectory, 1110 Vaughan Ln., Gladwyne, 19035.
Skelly, Richard J., Saint Joseph Rectory, 256 Concord Rd., Aston, 19014-1905.
Statkus, Francis J., 208 E. Trenton Ave., Wildwood Crest, NJ 08260.
Trinity, Bernard J., Saint Denis Rectory, 2401 Saint Denis Ln., Havertown, 19083.
Walsh, Vincent M., J.C.D., Villa Saint Joseph, 1436 Lansdowne Ave., Darby, 19023-1298.
Wright, Richard J., Villa St. Joseph, 1436 Lansdowne Ave., Darby, 19023-1298.
Revs.—
Anziano, James J., M.D., Regina Coeli Residence for Priests, 685 York Rd., Warminster, 18974.
Barr, Philip R., 1040 Harmony Hill Rd., Downingtown, 19335-4008.
Bartos, Francis J., Villa Saint Joseph, 1436 Lansdowne Ave., Darby, 19023-1298.
Benischeck, Bernard J., M.A., Villa St. Joseph, 1436 Lansdowne Ave., Darby, 19023-1298.
Benonis, William J., St. Mary's Manor, 701 Lansdale Ave., Lansdale, 19446-2900.
Bowen, Joseph D., Saint Mary's Manor, 701 Lansdale Ave., Lansdale, 19446-2900.
Boyle, George J., Annunciation B.V.M. Rectory, 410 Sagamore Rd., Havertown, 19083-3998.
Bradley, John J., Sacred Heart of Jesus Rectory, 1404 S. Third St., 19147-6099.
Breen, Robert H., Villa Saint Joseph, 1436 Lansdowne Ave., Darby, 19023-1298.
Burgoyne, Sidney C., Ph.D., Villa Saint Joseph, 1436 Lansdowne Ave., Darby, 19023-1298.
Cahill, Edward B., M.A., Villa St. Joseph, 1436 Lansdowne Ave., Darby, 19023-1298.
Callahan, Joseph W., Villa Saint Joseph, 1436 Lansdowne Ave., Darby, 19023-1298.
Cellucci, Carl D., Villa St. Joseph, 1436 Lansdowne Ave., Darby, 19023-1298.
Chow, Luke L., 422 Black Matt Rd., Douglassville, 19518.
Chwieroth, Edward J., Salem Harbour Apartments, 106 Moorsgate, Andalusia, 19020.
Coates, John T., Saint Mary's Manor, 701 Lansdale Ave., Lansdale, 19446-2900.
Cornely, Francis J., Regina Coeli Residence for Priests, 685 York Rd., Warminster, 18974.
Crowe, George W., Saint John Vianney Center, 151 Woodbine Rd., Downingtown, 19335.
Cusatis, Girard J., St. Andrew Rectory, 3500 School Ln., Drexel Hill, 19026.
Cusick, Eugene G., Villa Saint Joseph, 1436 Lansdowne Ave., Darby, 19023.
Dinda, John J., Villa Saint Joseph, 1436 Lansdowne Ave., Darby, 19023-1298.
Donnelly, William P., Villa St. Joseph, 1436 Landsdowne Ave., Darby, 19023-1298.
Dougherty, Daniel J., 244 Baltimore Pike, Apt. 135, Glen Mills, 19342.
Doyne, David A., Villa St. Joseph, 1436 Landsdowne Ave., Darby, 19023-1298.
Duffy, Thomas J., Regina Coeli Residence for Priests, 685 York Rd., Warminster, 18974.
Durney, Charles W., 59 Catawissa St., Barnesville, 18214-2428.
Feeney, Thomas M., Villa St. Joseph, 1436 Lansdowne Ave., Darby, 19023-1298.
Fitzgerald, John E., St. Anselm Rectory, 12669 Dunks Ferry Rd., 19154.
Fitzgibbons, John A., St. John Vianney Center, 151 Woodbine Rd., Downingtown, 19335-3080.
Foley, Peter J., 430 82nd Ave., St. Pete Beach, FL 33706.
Foster, John J., Saint Mary's Manor, 701 Lansdale Ave, Lansdale, 19446-2900.
Franey, John A., P.O. Box 336, Perryville, MD 21903.
Gallagher, Daniel J., Villa Saint Joseph, 1436 Lansdowne Ave., Darby, 19023-1298.
Gallagher, Francis M., M.A., P.O. Box 597, Ambler, 19002-0597.
Gallagher, John P., Ph.D., Villa Saint Joseph, 1436 Lansdowne Ave., Darby, 19023-1298.
Gallagher, Joseph J., 2849 Hellerman St., 19149.
Gallen, Francis H., St. Martha Manor, 470 Manor Ave., Downingtown, 19335.
Garzarelli, Santo R., St. Francis Country House, 1412 Lansdowne Ave., Darby, 19023-1218.
Givey, David W., P.O. Box 641, Somers Point, NJ 08244-9998.
Gormley, Charles E., Saint Matthias Rectory, 128 Bryn Mawr Ave., Bala Cynwyd, 19004.
Gormley, James W., Villa St. Joseph, 1436 Lansdowne Ave., Darby, 19023-1298.
Graf, Henry C., Regina Coeli Residence for Priests, 685 York Rd., Warminster, 18974.
Graham, Thomas D., St. Francis Country House, 1412 Lansdowne Ave., Darby, 19023-1218.
Hagenbach, George G., Villa Saint Joseph, 1436 Lansdowne Ave., Darby, 19023-1298.
Herron, Francis X., 9 N. Pelham Ave., Longport, NJ 08403.
Hoy, Daniel J., Our Lady of the Assumption Rectory, 35 Old Eagle School Rd., Strafford, 19087.
Hughes, James F., 257 N. State Rd., Apt. 19A, Springfield, 19064.
Jung, Joseph B., Villa Saint Joseph, 1436 Lansdowne Ave., Darby, 19023-1298.
Kelly, Francis E., 4972 Skippack Pike, P.O. Box 259, Creamery, 19430-0259.
Kelly, James Joseph, Epiphany of Our Lord Rectory, 3050 Walton Rd., Norristown, 19462.
Krick, Howard K., Regina Coeli Residence for Priests, 685 York Rd., Warminster, 18974.
Lepleiter, Robert P., Regina Coeli Residence for Priests, 685 York Rd., Warminster, 18974.
Locke, James E., 31 Ocean Rd., Ocean City, NJ 08226.
Machain, David B., Saint Bernard Rectory, 7341 Cottage St., 19136.
Maguire, Connell J., 2800 N. Ocean Dr., Apt. B15 A, Riviera Beach, FL 33404.
Maher, Edmund J., Villa St. Joseph, 1436 Landsdowne Ave., Darby, 19023-1298.
Maloney, Wilfred F., 1007 Fownes Ave., Brigantine, NJ 08203.
Martin, James J., Saint Francis Country House, 1412 Lansdowne Ave., Darby, 19023-1218.
McCloskey, Joseph W., Villa St. Joseph, 1436 Lansdowne Ave., Darby, 19023-1298.
McCole, John F., Saint Francis Country House, 1412 Lansdowne Ave., Darby, 19023-1218.
McGee, Leo J., M.A., Villa Saint Joseph, 1436 Lansdowne Ave., Darby, 19023-1298.
McGinnis, James J., M.Div., Saint Francis Country Home, 1412 Lansdowne Ave., Darby, 19023-1218.
McKelvey, Thomas P., Saint Francis Country House, 1412 Lansdowne Ave., Darby, 19023-1218.
McNamara, Donald P., 618 Ashford Rd., Wilmington, DE 19803.
McNamee, John P., c/o Saint Malachy Rectory, 1429 N. 11th St., 19122.
Meehan, Joseph J., M.S., St. Francis of Assisi Rectory, 136 Saxer Ave., Springfield, 19064-2333.
Moriarity, Daniel J., Nativity B.V.M. Rectory, 2535 E. Allegheny Ave., 19134.
Mulgrew, John E., M.A., Saint Mary Magdalen Rectory, 2400 N. Providence Rd., Media, 19063-1998.
Murphy, James J., St. Francis Country House, 1412 Lansdowne Ave., Darby, 19023-1218.
Murphy, Joseph T., 812 Rowland Ave., Cheltenham, 19012.
Nevins, John J., Motherhouse, Grey Nuns of the Sacred Heart, 1750 Quarry Rd., Morrisville, 19067-3998.
Noone, Charles J., Holy Martyrs Rectory, 120 Allison Rd., Oreland, 19075-1896.

O'Brien, Joseph E., Saint Leo Rectory, 6658 Keystone St., 19135.
Piro, Francis, St. Philip Neri Rectory, 218 Queen St., 19147.
Pohl, Jerome H., 2982 Richmond St., 19134.
Romano, Harry A., Villa St. Joseph, 1436 Landsdowne Ave., Darby, 19023-1298.
Scarcia, John J., M.Div., P.O. Box 884, Eagle Lake, FL 33839.
Schifalacqua, Ildebrando E., 113 Eldredge Ave., West Cape May, NJ 08204.
Schlett, Francis J., 308 Merry Brook Dr., Havertown, 19083.
Shellem, John J., Villa Saint Joseph, 1436 Lansdowne Ave., Darby, 19023-1298.
Shelley, John J., St. David Rectory, 316 N. Easton Rd., Willow Grove, 19090-2501.
Smart, Raymond W., Saint Philip Neri Rectory, 1325 Klinerd Rd., Pennsburg, 18073.
Smith, William J., Saint Francis Country House, 1412 Lansdowne Ave., Darby, 19023-1218.
Speitel, Edmond J., 248A Wesley Ave., Ocean City, NJ 08226.
Stec, Joseph C., M.A., Saint Laurentius Rectory, 1608 East Berks St., 19125-2499.
Sweeney, Joseph J., M.Div., Saint Mary's Manor, 701 Lansdale Ave., Lansdale, 19446-2900.
Szal, Ignatius J., 460 Sunbury St., Minersville, 17954.
Walsh, John M., Villa Saint Joseph, 1436 Lansdowne Ave., Darby, 19023-1298.
Wesolowski, Edmund C., Villa Saint Joseph, 1436 Lansdowne Ave., Darby, 19023-1298.
White, Stephen C., J.D., 122 Marlin St., Folsom, 19033-1288.
Wiedmann, Paul A., Villa St. Joseph, 1436 Lansdowne Ave., Darby, 19023-1298.
Wilz, John C., M.A., Holy Trinity Rectory, 201 N. Pennsylvania Ave., Morrisville, 19067.

Permanent Deacons:
Amen, Charles R., Divine Mercy Church
Anderson, James, Jr., St. Aloysius Church, Pottstown
Andrews, Edward J., St. Martin De Porres Church
Angiolollo, Ernest W., Presentation B.V.M. Church, Wynnewood
Antrim, Harry D., St. Agnes Church, Sellersville
Arno, Michael R., Diocese of St. Petersburg, FL
Baratta, Gaspero P., St. John the Baptist Church
Basilio, James A., Notre Dame De Lourdes Church, Swarthmore
Baxter, William T., Saint Francis of Assisi Church, Springfield
Belanger, A. Kenneth, St. Helena Church, Blue Bell
Betancourt, Jose M., St. Peter the Apostle Church
Betzal, John M., St. Joseph Church, Aston
Bianco, Salvatore R., St. Philip Neri Church, Lafayette Hill
Bingham, Dennis J., Archdiocese of Baltimore, MD
Bizal, Francis M., SS. Philip and James Church, Exton
Bogdan, James E., SS. Philip and James Church, Exton
Bonilla, Victor M.
Boyle, John G., Holy Name of Jesus Church
Brandon, Lawrence G., St. Maximilian Kolbe Church, West Chester
Brown, Clifford W., Our Mother of Consolation Church
Burghart, Peter H., St. Alphonsus Church, Maple Glen
Burke, Francis B., St. Bernadette, Drexel Hill
Burns, James H.
Burns, Robert C., St. Matthew Church
Butcavage, Thomas E., St. Agnes Continuing Care Center, Philadelphia
Calabrese, Peter J., Archdiocese of Baltimore, MD
Campbell, John J.
Cantanese, Ralph M.
Carr, Joseph C., SS. Cosmas and Damian Church, Conshohocken
Cavaliere, Francis M., St. Robert Bellarmine Church, Warrington
Cella, Joseph M., Our Lady of Consolation Church
Ceneviva, Vincent G., Our Lady of Sacred Heart Church, Hilltown
Champagne, William E., Our Lady of Hope Church
Clancy, Kenneth P., Epiphany of Our Lord Church, Plymouth Meeting
Clark, Francis T., St. Joseph Church, Ambler
Clay, Alvin A., Immaculate Conception Church, Jenkintown
Colgan, Francis M., St. Anastasia Church, Newtown Square
Concitis, Thomas C., St. Peter Parish Office, West Brandywine
Connors, Francis J., Annunciation B.V.M. Church, Havertown
Conroy, Michael G., St. Genevieve Church, Flourtown
Corwell, George V., Our Lady of Mt. Carmel Church, Doylestown
Coyle, Joseph P.
Coyne, Richard C., Holy Cross Church
Crespo, Adolfo, Our Lady of Fatima Church, Bensalem
Croke, Thomas M., St. Luke the Evangelist Church, Glenside
Cruz, Felipe, Incarnation of Our Lord Church
D'Amico, John J., Diocese of Phoenix, AZ
D'Angelo, Ernest, St. John the Baptist Church, Ottsville
Dalton, James E., St. Cyril of Alexandria Church, East Lansdowne
Davaro, John J., St. Dorothy Church, Drexel Hill
Dayoc, Michael J., St. Paul Church, East Norristown
DeBow, James P., St. Ephrem Church, Bensalem
DeGrasse, Michael J., Assumption B.V.M. Church, West Grove
DeJesus, Epifanio, Cathedral Basilica of SS. Peter & Paul
DeLucca, Daniel N., St. Andrew Church, Drexel Hill
DeMasi, Leonard D., St. Monica Church
Derivan, Albert T., St. Eleanor Church, Collegeville
DeRosa, Joseph R., St. Eleanor Church, Collegeville
Diamond, Patrick J., Saint Cecilia Church, Philadelphia
Diana, Leonard J., St. Kevin Church, Springfield
DiFerdinand, James A., St. Mary Magdalen Church, Media
DiIenno, Anthony J., c/o Office of the Vicar for Clergy
Dillon, Mark H., Mother of Providence Church, King of Prussia
Druding, Frederick C., Epiphany of Our Lord Church
DuBois, John J., St. John Fisher Church, Boothwyn
Duffy, James J., St. Katherine of Siena
Dymek, Edward J., Jr., St. Ephrem Church, Bensalem
Eichman, Thomas E., St. Kevin Church, Springfield
Eliason, William F., St. David Church, Willow Grove
Ellis, John J., St. Barnabas Church
Evans, William W., Corpus Christi Church, Lansdale
Fabrizio, Francis S., St. Charles Borromeo Church, Drexel Hill
Favinger, M. Eugene, Our Lady of Consolation Church, Parkesburg
Ferreira, Joao A., Incarnation of Our Lord Church
Finn, Michael J., Saint Katharine Drexel Church, Chester
Fitzpatrick, Thomas P., St. Bernadette Church, Drexel Hill
Fontanez, Jose, c/o Vicar for Clergy
Fowkes, James J., Our Lady of Mount Carmel Church, Doylestown
Frankenberger, Robert
Franks, Michael J., Sr., St. Philip Neri Church, Pennsburg
Fremont, Richard L., St. Elizabeth Church, Uwchlan
Friel, Dennis J., Resurrection of Our Lord Church, Philadelphia
Froio, Lawrence P., St. Patrick Church, Malvern
Gallagher, John J., St. Thomas Aquinas Church, Croydon
Garritano, Dominic A., Our Lady of Grace Church, Penndel
Gellentien, Robert P.
Gentilcore, Kevin F., St. Anthony of Padua Church, Ambler
George, Albert J., Holy Spirit Church
Gladnick, Leo T., Ascension of Our Lord Church
Gohde, Robert P., Our Lady of Guadalupe Church, Buckingham
Golaszewski, John M., St. Vincent De Paul Church, Richboro
Gonzalez, Victor, St. Agnes Church, West Chester
Gousie, Joseph N., Sr., Holy Cross Church, Springfield
Granese, Claude B., St. Jude Church, Chalfont
Guckin, Stephen A., Saint Elizabeth Ann Seton Church, Bensalem
Guy, Gary W., St. Gabriel Church, Norwood
Gwynn, Raymond F., Sr., St. Martha Church
Haddon, Richard S., St. Isidore Church, Quakertown
Hagerty, Paul B., Immaculate Conception Church, Jenkintown
Hanley, Edward F., St. Timothy Church
Hannan, Thomas J., Assumption B.V.M. Church, West Grove
Harrison, A. Gerald, SS. Peter and Paul Church, West Chester
Hartmann, James E., St. John the Evangelist Church, Morrisville
Hartmann, Karl J., St. Joseph Church, Warrington
Heaney, Philip E., Maternity B.V.M. Church
Hernandez, Felipe, Our Lady of Hope Church
Hernandez, Jose, Incarnation of Our Lord Church
Hickey, William L., Office for Permanent Deacons, St. Charles Borromeo Seminary
Hoelzle, Louis F., Saint Francis Cabrini Church, Fairless Hills
Hopkins, Stephen, St. Benedict Church
Horan, Thomas J., SS. Peter & Paul Church, West Chester
Houser, Joseph F., Sacred Heart Church, Royersford
Hunter, John K., St. Hilary of Poitiers Church, Rydal
Hunter, Richard F., St. Bernard Church
Huynh, Trac Mai, St. Francis De Sales Church
Hynes, John
Iacobellis, William F., St. Vincent De Paul Church, Richboro
Iannucci, Joseph E., St. Pius X Church, Broomall
Isley, Brouycie P., Immaculate Conception Church
Jacobucci, Raymond, Saint John of the Cross Church, Roslyn
Jones, David E., St. Anthony of Padua Church, Ambler
Jones, Edward S., St. John the Baptist Church, Ottsville
Kane, James D., St. Francis of Assisi Church, Springfield
Kazanjian, Stephen C., St. Pius X Church, Broomall
Kern, Paul R.
Kerr, Frederick H., St. Cecilia Church, Coatesville
Klauder, Francis C., Archdiocese of Indianapolis, IN
Kletzel, George W., Immaculate Heart of Mary Church
Klinger, George H., Mary, Mother of the Redeemer Church, North Wales
Kolakowski, Michael J., Saint Albert the Great Church, Huntington Valley
Konarski, Edward A., St. Rose of Lima Church, North Wales
Kreczkevich, John J., St. Barnabas Church
Kretsch, Donald J.
Kruckenberger, William F., St. John Bosco Church, Hatboro
Kubczak, David M., Blessed Teresa of Calcutta Church, Limerick
Lally, Francis C., Saint Teresa of Avila Church, Norristown
Lance, Walter C., St. John Chrysostom Church, Wallingford
Langsdorf, Francis E., Corpus Christi Church, Lansdale
Leahy, Eugene R.
Leonard, Warren C., Holy Trinity, Morrisville
Leonhardt, George W., Jr., Diocese of Orlando, FL
Lewis, Charles G., St. Stanislaus Church, Lansdale
Lindsay, Charles R., Maternity B.V.M. Church
Lonergan, Joseph W., Mother of the Redeemer Church, North Wales
Lozada, Jose Luis, St. Hugh of Cluny Church
Lozano, John P., St. Norbert Church, Paoli
Luczkowski, Edward R., Holy Redeemer Health System, Inc., Huntington Valley
Lyon, James E., SS. Simon & Jude Church, West Chester
Madonna, James K., St. Patrick Church, Kennett Square
Mahoney, James L., St. Benedict Church
Makoid, Eric T., Diocese of St. Petersburg, FL
Maldonado, Rafael, St. Veronica Church
Malfara, Louis S., St. William Church
Manzano, Edwin R., Visitation B.V.M. Church
Maresca, Armand J., SS. Cosmas & Damian Church, Conshohocken
Martes, Zoilo, St. Michael Church
Masapollo, William M., St. Norbert Church, Paoli
Mauriello, Alfred J., St. Maximilian Kolbe, West Chester
Mayes, William C., St. Charles Borromeo Church
Mazzoni, Mace M., St. Frances Cabrini Church, Fairless Hills
McAndrews, Michael J., Notre Dame DeLourdes Church, Swarthmore
McAvoy, James T., St. Peter Church, Brandywine
McBlain, Paul J., St. Joseph Church, Collingdale
McGovern, Clement J., St. Agnes Church, West Chester
McGuire, Arthur M., St. Francis of Assisi Church, Springfield
Mendez, Jose M., St. Ambrose Church
Micucci, Joseph A., Cathedral Basilica SS. Peter & Paul
Midwood, Barry R., St. Elizabeth Church, Glenmoore
Morales, Jose A., Diocese of St. Petersburg, FL
Morris, Edward J., St. Christopher Church
Morris, George E., Jr., St. Robert Bellarmine

Church, Warrington
Murphy, Francis X., Sacred Heart Church, Oxford
Murphy, James G., Our Lady of the Sacred Heart Church, Hilltown
Nightingale, Richard G., Our Lady of the Blessed Sacrament Church
Niland, Joseph W.
Nines, Joseph L., St. Genevieve Church, Flourtown
O'Brien, Gregory R., St. Madeline Church, Ridley Park
Oliver, Joseph M.
Orlando, Joseph P., Diocese of Camden, NJ
Owen, Joseph T., St. Cyril of Jerusalem Church, Jamison
Owens, James T., Office for Permanent Deacons, St. Charles Seminary, Wynnewood
Panganiban, Homer A., Our Lady of Hope Church
Pavonarius, Charles A., St. Jerome Church
Pierce, Robert F., SS. Peter & Paul Church, West Chester
Pileggi, John J., Saint Katherine Drexel Church, Chester
Poellnitz, Fredrick E., St. Athanasius Church
Polley, Charles W., Jr., SS. Philip and James Church, Exton
Purnell, Edward M., St. Theresa of the Child Jesus Church
Raczkowski, Thaddeus C., SS. Simon & Jude Church, West Chester
Radetsky, William R., Epiphany of Our Lord Church, Plymouth Meeting
Ramos, Juan F., St. Peter the Apostle
Rayner, Albert E., Holy Spirit Church, Sharon Hill
Riordan, John T., St. Jude Church, Chalfont
Rooney, Joseph T., Our Lady Help of Christians Church, Abington
Rosario, Israel, Our Lady of Hope Church
Rose, John P., Our Lady of the Assumption Church, Strafford
Rouse, Daniel J., St. John Bosco Church, Hatboro
Ryan, Frederick M., St. Margaret Mary Alacoque Church, Essington
Salvatore, Mark A., St. Dominic Church
Schaffer, David B., M.A., M.S., Saint Colman Church, Ardmore
Schiappa, Edward R., St. Joseph Church, Downingtown
Schlegel, John F., St. Denis Rectory, Havertown
Schnepp, Lawrence P., St. Rose of Lima Church, Eddystone
Seda, Victor I., St. Helena Church
Sexton, Joseph F.
Shields, Thomas A., St. Martin De Porres Church
Shire, William F., St. Michael the Archangel Church, Levittown
Shirley, Ralph J., Our Lady of Ransom Church
Simpson, Harry J., St. Michael the Archangel, Levittown
Skawinski, Robert J., St. Ignatius Church, Yardley
Small, Michael C., c/o Vicar for Clergy
Smith, Calvin C., St. Benedict Church
Stam, Bernardus C., Diocese of Wilmington, DE
Stevens, Allen T., Jr., Archdiocese of New Orleans, LA
Stewart, James J., St. Edmond Church
Stewart, Robert J., Assumption B.V.M. Church, Feasterville
Stokely, Patrick M., St. Agnes Church, West Chester
Stoughton, Richard L., Our Lady of the Rosary Church, Coatesville
Suplee, John J., Sacred Heart Church, Havertown
Thompson, James A., Stella Maris
Thompson, Vincent J., St. Francis Xavier- The Oratory Church, Philadelphia
Tielemans, Mathieu M., St. Stanislaus Church, Lansdale
Tobin, Charles A., Diocese of Camden, NJ
Tormey, James M., Diocese of Wilmington, DE
Tran, Huan C., Saint Helena Church, Philadelphia
Tucker, Henry E., St. Agnes Church, Sellersville
Upcavage, Joseph R., Queen of the Universe Church, Levittown
Urbanski, Timothy E., St. Catherine of Siena Church, Horsham
Urmson, Francis B., Holy Cross Church
Vadino, Raymond M., St. John Chrysostom Church, Wallingford
Vera, Jorge L., Visitation B.V.M. Church
Vondercrone, C. Stephens, St. Stanislaus Church, Lansdale
Wagner, Anthony E., Temple University Newman Center
Walker, James
Wallace, Mark M., St. Laurence Church, Upper Darby
Walsh, James V., St. Eugene Church, Primos
Wellbank, Raymond C., St. Stanislaus Church, Lansdale
Wernert, Emil J., Epiphany of Our Lord, Plymouth Meeting
Whartenby, Gerald J., St. Anselm Church
Windish, Joseph F., St. Cyril of Jerusalem Church, Jamison
Wirth, Richard D., St. Cornelius Church, Chadds Ford
Wojewodka, Boleslaw S.
Woods, Thomas J., Sacred Heart Church, Havertown
Zaleski, Stanley M., St. Martin of Tours Church
Ziff, Joel M.
Zurbach, E. Peter, St. Mary Magdalen Church, Media

INSTITUTIONS LOCATED IN THE ARCHDIOCESE

[A] SEMINARIES, ARCHDIOCESAN

WYNNEWOOD. *Theological Seminary of St. Charles Borromeo, Overbrook*, Administration: 100 E. Wynnewood Rd., 19096. Tel: 610-667-3394; Fax: 610-667-7635. Email: seminary@adphila.org. Web: www.scs.edu. Rev. Msgr. Joseph G. Prior, M.Div., M.A., S.S.L., S.T.D., Rector; Rev. David E. Diamond, M.Div., M.A., Ph.D., Vice Rector & Provost; Elaine K. Rice, M.B.A., Vice Pres., Finance & Opers.; Rev. Robert A. Pesarchick, M.A., S.T.L., S.T.D., Academic Dean, Theology Division; Carmina M. Magnusen Chapp, M.A., Ph.D., Academic Dean, Rel. Studies Div.; Rev. Patrick J. Welsh, M.Div., M.A., S.S.L., Dean of Men, Theology Division; Jared Haselbarth, M.A., Asst. Dean Religious Studies Div.; Rev. Robert B. McDermott, M.Div., Dean of Men, College Division; David L. Osborne, M.A., M.B.A., Dir. Devel.; Revs. Joseph F. Gleason, M.Div., M.S., M.A., Dir. Spiritual Formation, Theology Division; Anthony J. Costa, M.Div., M.A., S.T.L., S.T.D., Dir. Spiritual Formation, College Division; Michael H. Spitzer, M.Div., M.A., S.T.L., S.T.D., Dir. Pastoral and Apostolic Formation; Mary D. D'Urso, M.B.A., Dir. Fin. Svcs.; Cait Kokolus, M.S.L.S., M.A., Vice Pres. Information Svcs. & Assessment; Lawrence A. Heyman, Ed.M., M.S., Registrar; James P. Gibbons, Dir. Dining & Guest Svcs.; James F. Growdon, M.A., Asst. Academic Dean, College Div.; Nicholas Mancini, Dir. Safety & Security; Stephen D. Sankey, Dir. Information Technology. Priests 22; Sisters 3; Lay Staff 28; Permanent Deacons 1; College and Theology Division Students 152; Religious Studies Division Students 98; Seminarians from Archdiocese 46; Seminarians from other Dioceses 98; Religious Communities 8.

Full Time Instructional Faculty: Rev. Msgrs. Michael K. Magee, M.Div., M.A., S.S.L., S.T.L., S.T.D.; Francis X. Meehan, S.T.D. (Retired); Revs. Patrick J. Brady, M.Div., S.S.L.; Dennis J. Billy, C.Ss.R., M.A., M.M.R.Sc., S.T.D., Th.D., D.Min.; William G. Donovan, Ph.D., M.Div.; Stephen J. Dougherty, M.Div., M.A.; Frank A. Giuffre, M.Div., M.A., S.S.L.; Kelly Anderson, M.A., S.T.L.; Ene Andrilli, M.L.S.; Candida Antonelli, M.Ed.D.; Peter J. Colosi, M.Phil., M.A., Ph.D.; James M. Despres, M.A.; Janet Haggerty, M.A., Ph.D.; James Humble, M.S.L.S.; Atherton C. Lowry, M.A., Ph.D.; Theodore E. Kiefer, M.A., D.M.A.; Nathaniel Schmiedicke, M.A., Ph.D.

Adjunct Faculty: Rev. Msgrs. Michael J. Fitzgerald, M.Div., J.C.D., J.D.; Charles L. Sangermano, M.Div.; Revs. Sean P. Bransfield, M.Div., M.A., J.C.L.; Augustine M. Esposito, O.S.A., M.Div., M.A., Ph.D.; Mark J. Hunt, M.A., S.T.L.; Daniel E. Mackle, M.Div., M.A.; James P. Olson, M.Div., M.A., S.T.L.; Deacon Daniel N. DeLucca, M.A., Ph.D.; Sisters Mary Elizabeth Kratzinger, S.S.J., M.A.; Kathleen Schipani, I.H.M., M.Ed., M.A.; S. Rita Small, R.S.M., M.A.; John H. Ahtes, M.A.; Anne D. Chavez, M.A.; Robert Crewalk, B.A.; Joan Dlugos, M.A., Ph.D.; Charles A. Gallagher, M.Ed.; Franklin Lane, M.A.; Joseph S. Pizza, M.A.

[B] SEMINARIES, RELIGIOUS OR SCHOLASTICATES

PHILADELPHIA. *Brothers of the Christian Schools*, Jeremy House, 6633 Ardleigh St., 19119-3824. Tel: 215-843-1884; Fax: 215-843-1617. Email: jeremyhouse@juno.com. Bro. Richard Buccina, F.S.C., Dir. Professed Brothers 4; Postulants 3.

DePaul Novitiate, 5710 Magnolia St., 19144. Tel: 215-843-1581; Fax: 215-844-9634. Rev. Charles P. Strollo, C.M., Dir. National Novitiate for the Congregation of the Mission (Vincentians). Priests 5; Brothers 1. In Res. Revs. Joseph V. Agostino, C.M.; William M. Allegretto, C.M.; Elmer Bauer III, C.M.; Miles J. Heinen, C.M.; Bro. Peter A. Campbell, C.M.

St. Vincent's Seminary, 500 E. Chelten Ave., 19144-1296. Tel: 215-713-2400; Fax: 215-844-2085. Email: cmphila88@aol.com. Web: www.cmeast.org. Very Rev. Msgr. Michael J. Carroll, C.M., Prov., Eastern Province; Revs. Charles P. Strollo, C.M., Asst. Prov.; Bernard M. Tracey, C.M., B.A., M.Div., Supr.; Elmer Bauer III, C.M., Prov. Treas. & Second Councillor; Carl L. Pieber, C.M., Dir. Miraculous Medal Association; John W. Carven, C.M., Prov. Archivist; Mr. Allen Andrews, Exec. Dir. Finance. Central House of the Eastern Province of the Congregation of the Mission, (Vincentians). Residence for retired priests & brothers.

PAOLI. *Daylesford Abbey*, 220 S. Valley Rd., 19301-1900. Tel: 610-647-2530; Fax: 610-651-0219. Email: nobertines@daylesford.org. Web: www.daylesford.org. Revs. Ronald J. Rossi, O.Praem., Abbot; Richard J. Antonucci, O.Praem., Abbot; Very Rev. Andrew D. Ciferni, O.Praem., Prior; Rev. William J. Kelly, O.Praem.; Very Rev. John Joseph Novielli, O.Praem., Vocations Dir.; Rev. Joseph A. Serano, O.Praem., Treas.

Norbertine Fathers, Inc. Priests 25; Brothers 6.

SPRINGFIELD. *Servants of Charity*, 1795 S. Sproul Rd., 19064. Tel: 610-328-3406; Fax: 610-328-1019. Email: servantsofcharity@comcast.net. Web: www.servantsofcharity.org. Revs. Silvio De Nard, S.C; Paul Oggioni, Sd.C; Dennis M. Weber, Sd.C. Congregation of the Servants of Charity. Priests 4; Candidates 1. In Res. Rev. Elie Saade.

[C] COLLEGES AND UNIVERSITIES

PHILADELPHIA. *Chestnut Hill College*, 9601 Germantown Ave., 19118-2693. Tel: 215-248-7000; Fax: 215-248-7155. Email: chcapply@chc.edu. Web: www.chc.edu. Sisters Carol Jean Vale, S.S.J., Ph.D., Pres.; Mary Josephine Larkin, S.S.J., Dean Library & Info. Resources. Sisters 20; Lay Teachers 59; Students 2,250.

Holy Family University (1954) 9801 Frankford Ave., 19114. Tel: 215-637-7700; Fax: 215-637-3787. Email: fonley@holyfamily.edu. Web: www.holyfamily.edu. Sr. Francesca Onley, C.S.F.N., Pres.; Revs. James MacNew, Chap. & Campus Min.; Mark J. Hunt, M.A., S.T.L., Dept. of Rel. Studies; Lori Schwabenbauer, Librarian. Congregation of the Sisters of the Holy Family of Nazareth. Sisters 6; Lay Faculty 92; Undergraduate Students 2,257; Graduate Students 1,088. In Res. Rev. James J. Collins, S.O.E.D., Dept. of Religious Studies.

St. Joseph's University Regis Hall, 5600 City Ave., 19131. Tel: 610-660-1000; Fax: 610-660-1201. Web: www.sju.edu. Under the direction of the Jesuit Fathers. Incorporated January 29, 1851. Priests 17; Sisters 1; Lay Teachers 649; Students 8,050.

Jesuit Fathers Tel: 610-660-1400; Fax: 610-664-6640. Revs. Timothy R. Lannon, S.J., Pres.; Nicholas J. Rashford, S.J.; Mark C. Aita, S.J., M.D.; Anthony J. Berret, S.J.; Bruce M. Bidinger, S.J.; Thomas J. Brennan, S.J.; William J. Byron, S.J.; Joseph F. Chorpenning, O.S.F.S., S.T.L., Ph.D.; Peter A. Clark, S.J.; Joseph J. Feeney, S.J.; Vincent J. Genovesi, S.J.; Joseph J. Godfrey, S.J.; Daniel R.J. Joyce, S.J.; Joseph L. Lombardi, S.J.; Dennis E. McNally, S.J.; James D. Redington, S.J.; Patrick H. Samway, S.J.; Deacon Joseph A. Koczera, S.J.; Sisters Ann Bernadette, G.N.S.H.; Elizabeth Ann Linehan, R.S.M.; Evelyn Minick, Librarian.

LaSalle University, 1900 W. Olney Ave., 19141. Tel: 215-951-1000; Fax: 215-951-1488. Bro. Michael J. McGinniss, F.S.C., Ph.D., Pres.; Richard A. Nigro, Ph.D., Provost; Matthew S. McManness, Vice Pres. Fin. & Admin.; R. Brian Elderton, M.Ed., Vice Pres. Univ. Advancement; John F. Dolan, Vice Pres. Enrollment Svcs.; James E. Moore, Vice Pres. Student Affairs, Dean Students; Thomas A. Keagy, Ph.D., Dean, School of Arts and Sciences; Paul R. Brazina, Dean, School of Business Admin.; Zane Robinson Wolf, Ph.D., Dean, School of Nursing; James C. Plunkett, Exec. Dir., Admissions; Yusuf J. Ugras, Dean, College Professional & Continuing Studies; Bro. Robert J. Kinzler, F.S.C., Dir. University Ministry & Svc.; John S. Baky, Dir. Connelly Library. (Incorporated under the auspices of the Brothers of the Christian Schools) Priests 4; Brothers 9; Sisters 3; Lay Teachers 221; Students 6,470.

ASTON. *Neumann College*, One Neumann Dr., 19014-1298. Tel: 610-459-0905; Fax: 610-459-1370. Email: neumann@neumann.edu. Web: www.neumann.edu. Dr. Rosalie M. Mirenda, Ph.D., Pres.; Rev. Jude Michael Krill, O.F.M.Conv., Chap.; John Michael Powell, Librarian. Sponsored by the Sisters of St. Francis of Philadelphia., Opened September 1965. Priests

2; Sisters 30; Administrators 125; Faculty and Staff 216; Adjuncts 204; Lay Teachers 187; Students 3,099.

GWYNEDD VALLEY. *Gwynedd-Mercy College* 19437. Tel: 215-646-7300; Fax: 215-641-5573. Email: dobbs.a@gmc.edu. Web: www.gmc.edu. Rev. John Collins, C.S.S.R., Chap. Sisters of Mercy 5; Sisters 1; Brothers 1; Lay Teachers 79; Students 2,554.

IMMACULATA. *Immaculata University* (1920) 19345. Tel: 610-647-4400; Fax: 610-647-7635. Web: www.immaculata.edu. Sisters R. Patricia Fadden, I.H.M., Pres.; Ann Heath, I.H.M., Ph.D., Vice Pres. for Academic Affairs; Dr. Stephen Pugliese, M.A., Interim Vice Pres. for Student Affairs; Dr. Thomas Ford, Vice Pres. for Financial Affairs; Theresa Grentz, Vice Pres. for Institutional Advancement; Janice Bates, M.A., Registrar; Dr. Samuel Wrightson, Dean College of Lifelong Learning; Dr. Janet Kane, Dean College of Graduate Studies; Sr. Elaine Glanz, I.H.M., Dean College of Undergraduate Studies; Marie Moughan, M.A., Exec. Dir. Public Rels. & Mktg.; Robert Forest, Dir. Financial Aid; Erin Ebersole, Dir. Inst. Research, Planning & Assessment; Jeffrey Rollison, Exec. Dir. Library. Conducted by Sisters, Servants of the Immaculate Heart of Mary. Sisters 21; Total Staff 100; Enrollment 4,137.

RADNOR. *Cabrini College* (1957) 610 King of Prussia Rd., 19087-3698. Tel: 610-902-8100; Fax: 610-902-8309. Email: lplummer@cabrini.edu. Web: www.cabrini.edu. Dr. Marie A. George, Pres.; Christa Angeloni, Campus Min.; Rev. Michael Bielecki, O.S.A., Campus Min. Missionary Sisters of the Sacred Heart. Priests 1; Sisters 1; Lay Teachers 307; Students 3,547.

ROSEMONT. *Rosemont College of the Holy Child Jesus* 19010-1699. Tel: 610-527-0200; Fax: 610-527-0341. Email: shirsh@rosemont.edu. Web: www.rosemont.edu. Sharon Latchaw Hirsh, Ph.D., Pres.; Jeanne Marie Hatch, S.H.C.J., Vice Pres., Mission; Elizabeth Small, Dir. Worship & Spirituality; Catherine M. Fennell, Exec. Dir. Library Svcs.; Joseph T. Rogers, Dir. Institutional Research. Sisters of the Holy Child Jesus 3; Lay Teachers 128; Students 1,200.

VILLANOVA. *Villanova University*, 800 Lancaster Ave., 19085. Tel: 610-519-7499; Fax: 610-519-5333. Email: Stephen.Merritt@Villanova.edu. Web: www.villanova.edu. Revs. Peter M. Donohue, O.S.A., Pres. & Bd. Trustee; Raymond F. Dlugos, O.S.A., Bd. Trustee; William T. Garland, O.S.A., Bd. Trustee; Gary N. McCloskey, O.S.A., Bd. Trustee; James D. Paradis, O.S.A., Bd. Trustee; Very Rev. Donald F. Reilly, O.S.A., Bd. Trustee; Revs. Bernard C. Scianna, O.S.A., Bd. Trustee; Luis A. Vera, O.S.A., Bd. Trustee; Bro. Robert Thornton, O.S.A., Bd. Trustee; James A. Anderson, Ph.D., Bd. Trustee; Herbert F. Aspbury, Bd. Trustee; Richard P. Brennan, Bd. Trustee; Kimble A. Byrd, Esq., Bd. Trustee; Tara S. Cortes, Ph.D., Bd. Trustee; James C. Curvey, Bd. Trustee; James D. Danella, Bd. Trustee; James C. Davis, Bd. Trustee; Denise L. Devine, Bd. Trustee; Nance K. Dicciani, Ph.D., Bd. Trustee; John G. Drosdick, Bd. Trustee; William B. Finnerman, Bd. Trustee; Daryl J. Ford, Ph.D., Bd. Trustee; William M. Gibson, Bd. Trustee; Patricia H. Imbesi, Bd. Trustee; John P. Jones III, Bd. Trustee; Catherine M. Keating, Bd. Trustee; Anne Welsh McNulty, Bd. Trustee; Thomas Mulroy, Bd. Trustee; James F. Orr III, Bd. Trustee; Terence M. O'Toole, Bd. Trustee; Michael B. Picotte, Bd. Trustee; Paul A. Tufano Esq., Bd. Trustee. Founded 1842 by the Augustinians, Province of St. Thomas of Villanova. Colleges of Liberal Arts and Sciences, Engineering, Commerce and Finance, Nursing, Part-time and Continuing Education, Graduate Studies and the School of Law and Continuing Education. Priests 16; Lay Teachers 556; Students 10,172; Clerical Faculty: Total Staff 15; Full-Time Enrollment 6,374; Part-Time Enrollment 583.

Administration: Ann Diebold, Vice Pres. Univ. Communications; Dr. John R. Johannes, Vice Pres. Academic Affairs; Rev. John P. Stack, O.S.A., Vice Pres. Student Life; Mr. Michael J. O'Neill, Vice Pres. Univ. Advancement; Barbara E. Wall, Vice Pres. Mission & Min.; Ms. Dorothy A. Malloy, Vice Pres. Univ. Counsel; Mr. Kenneth G. Valosky, Vice Pres. Admin. & Finance; Mr. Stephen Fugale, Vice Pres. & CIO Information Tech. Svcs.; Rev. George F. Riley, O.S.A., Special Asst. to Pres. External Affairs; Dr. Helen K. Lafferty, Univ. First College Prof.; Doris DelTosto Brogan Esq., Acting Dean & Prof. Law; Mr. James Danko, Dean Villanova School of Business; Rev. Kail C. Ellis, O.S.A., Dean of Liberal Arts & Sciences; Dr. Gary Gabriele, Dean of Engineering; Mr. Paul Pugh, Dean of Students; Dr. M. Louise Fitzpatrick, Dean College of Nursing; Mr. Stephen R. Merritt, Dean Office of Enrollment Mgmt.; Sr. Beth Hassel, P.B.V.M., Exec. Dir. Campus Min.; Mr. Vincent Nicastro, Dir. Athletics; Revs. Robert Hagan, O.S.A., Asst. Athletic Dir.; Joseph D. Calderone, O.S.A., Chap., Law School; John P. Betoni, O.S.A., Graduate Studies Asst.; Kevin DePrinzio, O.S.A., Campus Min.; Christopher J. Drennen, O.S.A., Campus Min.; Thomas Murnane, O.S.A., Office of Univ. Admission; Dennis J. Gallagher, O.S.A., Archivist; Joseph S. Mostardi, O.S.A., Campus Min.; Bro. Michael Duffy, O.S.A., Campus Min.

Clerical Faculty: Revs. Richard G. Cannuli, O.S.A., Dir. Art Gallery, Curator Univ. & Art Collection, Chair of Theatre Dept.; Francis J. Caponi, O.S.A., Office of Theology & Religious Studies; David A. Cregan, O.S.A., Theatre Production; Edmund J. Dobbin, O.S.A., Theology & Rel. Studies; Daniel E. Doyle, O.S.A., Theology & Rel. Studies; Edward Enright, O.S.A.; John J. Farrell, O.S.A. (Retired); Joseph L. Farrell, O.S.A., Dir. of Programming & External Outreach; Allan Fitzgerald, O.S.A.; John J. Hagen, O.S.A., Adjunct; Richard Jacobs, O.S.A.; Charles P. Laferty, O.S.A., Adjunct; Martin Laird, O.S.A.; Joseph Loya, O.S.A.; Lee J. Makowski, O.S.A.; Neil J. McGettigan, O.S.A., Adjunct; John J. McKenzie, O.S.A.; Robert J. Murray, O.S.A.; Joseph Ryan, O.S.A.; Michael J. Scanlon, O.S.A.; Joseph P. Lucia, Dir. Falvey Library.

[D] HIGH SCHOOLS, ARCHDIOCESAN

PHILADELPHIA. *Archbishop Ryan High School* Opened September 7, 1966., 11201 Academy Rd., 19154-3397. Tel: 215-637-1800; Fax: 215-637-8833. Email: information@archbishopryan.com. Web: www.archbishopryan.org. Mr. Michael J. McArdle, Pres.; Revs. Rene Barczak, O.F.M.; Richard K. McFadden; Joseph T. Shenosky, S.T.L., M.A., M.Div., School Min.; Helen T. Chaykowsky, Prin.; Mary Lorenzo Brelsford, Librarian. Franciscan Friars, Order of Friars Minor. Priests 3; Sisters 11; Lay Teachers 90; Total Staff 143; Students 1,803.

Cardinal Dougherty High School, 6301 N. 2nd St., 19120-1599. Tel: 215-276-2300; Fax: 215-276-2306. Email: info@cardinaldougherty.org. Web: www.cardinaldougherty.org. Rev. Carl F. Janicki, Pres.; Thomas F. Rooney Jr., Ed.D., Prin.; Deacon Stephen A. Guckin, School Min.; Marcia Cooper, Librarian. (Coed) Opened September 1956. Priests 2; Sisters 7; Lay Teachers 40; Students 785.

Father Judge High School for Boys Opened September 1954., 3301 Solly Ave., 19136-2396. Tel: 215-338-9494; Fax: 215-338-0250. Email: jcampellone@fatherjudge.net. Web: fatherjudge.com. Revs. Joseph G. Campellone, O.S.F.S., Pres.; Jack Kolodziej, O.S.F.S., Asst. Prin.; Gerard J. Mahoney, O.S.F.S.; Bro. James Williams, O.S.F.S.; Dr. Kathleen Herpich, Prin.; Sandra Kolander, Librarian. Oblates of St. Francis de Sales. Priests 4; Sisters 3; Brothers 1; Lay Teachers 6; Students 1,142.

St. Hubert's Catholic High School for Girls Opened September 1941., 7320 Torresdale Ave., 19136. Tel: 215-624-6840; Fax: 215-624-5940. Email: contactus@huberts.org. Web: www.huberts.org. Sr. Mary E. Smith, I.H.M., Pres.; Rev. Thomas M. Sodano, Dir. School Ministry; Ms. Regina Craig, Prin. Priests 1; Sisters 13; Lay Teachers 42; Students 792.

SS. John Neumann and Maria Goretti Catholic High School (Formerly Southeast Catholic High School, St. John Neuman High School for Boys, St. Maria Goretti High School for Girls); (Boys and Girls 2004), 1736 S. Tenth St., 19148-1694. Tel: 215-465-8437; Fax: 215-462-2410. Web: www.neumanngoretti.com. John Murawski Jr., Pres.; Rev. Jason Kulczynski, School Min.; Mrs. Patricia C. Sticco, Prin. Priests 1; Sisters 2; Lay Teachers 43; Students 832.

John W. Hallahan Catholic Girls High School Opened September 18, 1901., 311 N. 19th St., 19103-1198. Tel: 215-563-8930; Fax: 215-563-3809. Email: jhpres@adphila.org. Web: www.jwhallahan.org. Mrs. Margaret A. Gallagher, Pres.; Rev. Christopher D. Lucas, School Min.; Ms. Mary Kirby, Prin.; Rita Moore, Librarian. Priests 1; Sisters 3; Lay Teachers 27; Students 580.

Little Flower Catholic High School for Girls Opened September 1, 1939., 1000 W. Lycoming St., 19140. Tel: 215-455-6900; Fax: 215-329-0478. Web: www.LittleFlowerHighSchool.org. Sisters Kathleen Klarich, R.S.M., Prin.; Donna Shallo, I.H.M., Pres.; Rev. Joseph C. McCaffrey, M.B.A., M.Div., School Min.; Brooke Hauer, Librarian. Sisters 4; Lay Teachers 32; Students 735.

Northeast Catholic High School for Boys Opened September 7, 1926., 1842 E. Torresdale Ave., 19124-4418. Tel: 215-831-1234; Fax: 215-743-0926. Email: preznechs@aol.com. Web: www.northcatholic.com. Rev. Nicholas R. Waseline, O.S.F.S., Prin. Oblates of St. Francis de Sales. Priests 4; Sisters 1; Lay Faculty 32; Students 650.

Roman Catholic High School for Boys Opened September 8, 1890., 301 N. Broad St., 19107. Tel: 215-627-1270; 215-627-1570; Fax: 215-627-4979. Email: info@cahillite.com. Web: www.romancatholichs.com. Revs. Joseph W. Bongard, M.A., Rector; James R. Casey, School Min.; Mr. Robert O'Neill, Prin.; Eric Rosenberger, Librarian. Priests 2; Sisters 2; Lay Teachers 47; Students 990.

West Philadelphia Catholic High School West Catholic High School for Boys opened in 1916. West Catholic High School for Girls opened in 1926. Consolidated September, 1989., 4501 Chestnut St., 19139. Tel: 215-386-2244; Fax: 215-222-1651. Email: westcatholic@hotmail.org. Web: www.westcatholic.org. Bro. Timothy Ahern, F.S.C., Pres.; Sr. Mary E. Bur, I.H.M., Prin.; Mrs. Carol Tulba, Librarian. Priests 1; Sisters 7; Brothers 5; Lay Teachers 28; Students 488.

DOWNINGTOWN. *Bishop Shanahan High School*, 220 Woodbine Rd., 19335. Tel: 610-518-1300; Fax: 610-343-6220. Email: rplunkett@shanahan.org. Web: www.shanahan.org. Sisters Regina Plunkett, I.H.M., Pres.; Maureen L. McDermott, I.H.M., Prin.; Revs. Matthew W. Guckin, M.Div., School Min.; Kevin P. McCabe; Alice Dowling, Librarian. (Coed) Formerly St. Agnes High School opened in 1909; became diocesan high school September 1957, moved from West Chester to Downingtown in 1998. Sisters, Servants of the Immaculate Heart of Mary 9; Priests 2; Lay Teachers 67; Students 1,262.

DREXEL HILL. *Archbishop Prendergast High School* Opened September 1956. Restructured 2006. See Monsignor Bonner and Archbishop Prendergast Catholic High School.

Monsignor Bonner and Archbishop Prendergast Catholic High School, 401-403 N. Lansdowne Ave., 19026-1196. Tel: 610-259-0280; Fax: 610-259-1630. Web: www.bonnerhigh.com; www.prendie.com. Revs. James P. Olson, M.Div., M.A., S.T.L., Pres.; Thomas R. Urian; Matthew Wayock, Dir. School Min.; William Brannick, Prin.; Sr. Elizabeth Flavin, S.S.J., Librarian. (Boys) Opened September 1953 as Archbishop Prendergast High School for Boys. New name adopted September 1956. Restructured 2006. Priests 2; Sisters 8; Lay Teachers 77; Students 1,541.

FAIRLESS HILLS. *Conwell-Egan Catholic High School*, 611 Wistar Rd., 19030. Tel: 215-945-6200; Fax: 215-945-6206. Email: cecinfo@conwell-egan.org. Web: conwell-egan.org. Dr. Lorraine Rice, Pres.; Margaret Blanco, Prin.; Larine Lodise, Guidance Dir.; Rev. Joseph P. Lea, Campus Min.; Geraldine Brennan, Librarian. Formerly Bishop Egan High School, Fairless Hills, and Bishop Conwell High School, Levittown. Priests 2; Sisters 6; Brothers 1; Lay Teachers 41; Students 830.

LANSDALE. *Lansdale Catholic High School*, 700 Lansdale Ave., 19446-2995. Tel: 215-362-6160; 215-242-6160 (Philadelphia); Fax: 215-362-5746. Email: jcasey@lansdalecatholic.com. Web: www.lansdalecatholic.com. Timothy P. Quinn, Prin.; James W. Casey, Pres.; Rev. John D. Schiele; Tiffany Emrick, Librarian. Opened 1949. 1983 joined the System of Secondary Schools in Philadelphia. Priests 1; Lay Teachers 42; Students 815.

NORRISTOWN. *Kennedy-Kenrick Catholic High School*, 250 E. Johnson Hwy., 19401. Tel: 610-275-2846; Fax: 610-277-6699. Web: www.kkchs.org. Rev. Alan J. Okon Jr., Pres.; Sr. Janet Purcell, Prin.; Daniel McCarthy, Dir. Campus Min. Formerly Bishop Kenrick High School, Norristown, and Archbishop Kennedy High School, Conshohocken. Priests 2; Sisters 9; Lay Teachers 28; Students 520; Administrators 4.

POTTSTOWN. *St. Pius X High School* Opened 1954., 844 N. Keim St., 19464. Tel: 610-326-8990; Fax: 610-323-8594. Email: president@stpiusxhs.org. Web: www.stpiusxhs.org. Rev. Alan J. Okon Jr., Pres.; Judith M. Owens, Prin.; Rev. Thomas A. Nasta, Chap.; Thomas Phillips, School Min. Priests 2; Sisters 1; Lay Teachers 27; Students 539.

RADNOR. *Archbishop John Carroll High School* Opened September 1967., 211 Matson Ford Rd., 19087. Tel: 610-688-7610; Fax: 610-688-8326 (Prin.); 610-971-0827 (Pres.). Email: carroll@jcarroll.org. Web: www.jcarroll.org. Revs. Edward J. Casey, M.Div., Pres.; Stephen P. DeLacy, School Min.; David R. Dickens, Prin.; Charmane Gates, Librarian. Priests 3; Sisters 2; Lay Teachers 47; Students 976.

SPRINGFIELD. *Cardinal O'Hara High School* (Coed) Opened September, 1963., 1701 S. Sproul Rd., 19064. Tel: 610-544-3800; Fax: 610-544-1189. Web: cohs.com. William J. McCusker, Ed.D., Pres.;

George Stratts, Prin.; Revs. William J. Chiriaco; John B. Flanagan, School Min.; Paul J. O'Donnell, M.Div.; Joseph Konecki, Librarian. Priests 3; Sisters 1; Lay Teachers 78; Students 1,528.

WARMINSTER. *Archbishop Wood Catholic High School* Opened September 1964., 655 York Rd., 18974. Tel: 215-672-5050; Fax: 215-672-9572 (Academic Office); 212-672-5451 (Business Office). Email: infoabwhs@yahoo.com. Web: www.archwood.org. Dr. Frederick J. Ciao, Ph.D., Pres.; Mrs. Mary Harkins, M.A., Prin.; Revs. James F. Endres, Assoc. Disciplinarian; John C. Nguyen, School Min.; Barbara Schuster-Boer, Librarian. Priests 2; Sisters 2; Lay Teachers 60; Students 1,090.

WYNCOTE. *Bishop McDevitt High School*, 125 Royal Ave., 19095-1198. Tel: 215-887-5575; Fax: 215-887-1371. Email: bmcdhs1@nni.com. Web: www.mcdevitths.org. Salvatore DiNenna, Ed.D., Pres.; Revs. Edward C. Kelly; Quan H. Tran; Rosemary Naab, Prin.; Glenda Rieffel, Librarian. Opened September 1958. Priests 2; Sisters 3; Lay Teachers 35; Students 670.

[E] VOCATIONAL HIGH SCHOOLS

PHILADELPHIA. *Mercy Vocational High School*, 2900 W. Hunting Park Ave., 19129-1803. Tel: 215-226-1225; Fax: 215-228-6337. Email: generalinfo@mercyvhs.org. Web: www.mercyvocational.org. Sisters Rosemary Herron, R.S.M., Pres.; Susan Walsh, R.S.M., Prin.; Catherine Glatts, Vice Prin.; Sr. Emily Connor, R.S.M., School Min.; Frances Skiendzielewski, Librarian. Sisters of Mercy 13; Lay Teachers 31; Students 355.

[F] HIGH SCHOOLS, PRIVATE

PHILADELPHIA. *St. Joseph's Preparatory School*, Office of the President, 1733 W. Girard Ave., 19130. Tel: 215-978-1950; Fax: 215-765-1710. Web: www.sjprep.org. Rev. George W. Bur, S.J., Pres.; Mr. Michael Gomez, Prin.; Dennis Hart, Dean of Students; Mr. Timothy O'Shaughnessy, CFO; Mr. Joseph Nawn, Asst. Prin. Instruction & Learning; Mrs. Rose Marie Kettinger, Registrar/Asst. Prin. for Academic Programs & Records; Rev. Msgr. Bruce M. Maivelett, S.J., Dir. of Ignatian Identity; Rev. Francis E. Skechus, S.J.; Albert Zimmerman, Dir. Devel.; Mrs. Sonia Nelson, Librarian. Priests 3; Sisters 1; Lay Teachers 76; Students 980.

Nazareth Academy High School, 4001 Grant Ave., 19114-2999. Tel: 215-637-7676; Fax: 215-637-8523. Email: jacobs@nazarethacademyhs.org. Web: www.nazarethacademyhs.org. Sisters Mary Joan Jacobs, C.S.F.N., Ed.D., Prin.; M. Clarissa Mroz, C.S.F.N., Librarian. Sisters 12; Lay Teachers 43; Girls 467.

BENSALEM. *Holy Ghost Preparatory School*, 2429 Bristol Pike, 19020. Tel: 215-639-2102; Fax: 215-639-4225. Email: jduaime@holyghostprep.org. Web: www.holyghostprep.org. Revs. Jeffrey T. Duaime, C.S.Sp., Pres. Tel: 215-639-2102; Christopher H. McDermott, C.S.Sp., Chap.; Philip Agber, C.S.Sp.; Mr. Michael O'Toole, Prin.; Mr. Vincent Profy, Ed.D., Librarian. Spiritan Fathers 3; Lay Teachers 47; Males 516.

BRYN MAWR. *Country Day School of the Sacred Heart*, 480 Bryn Mawr Ave., 19010. Tel: 610-527-3915; Fax: 610-527-0942. Email: smacdonald@cdssh.org. Web: www.cdssh.org. Sr. Matthew Anita MacDonald, S.S.J., Head of School; Rev. Thomas P. Gillin, M.S.; Catherine Scholl, Librarian. Sisters 2; Lay Teachers 45; Students 340.

DEVON. *Devon Preparatory School* 19333. Tel: 610-688-7337; Fax: 610-688-2409. Email: info@devonprep.com. Revs. James J. Shea, Sch.P., Prin.; Richard S. Wyzykiewicz, Sch.P., Chap. & Rector; Ferdinand Negrillos, Sch.P.; Geza Pazmany, Sch.P.; Bro. Nelson Henao, Sch.P.; Mr. Paul J. Sanborn, Librarian. Piarist Fathers. Priests 2; Brothers 1; Lay Teachers 41; Students 285.

FLOURTOWN. *Mt. St. Joseph Academy*, 120 W. Wissahickon Ave., 19031. Tel: 215-233-3177; Fax: 215-233-4734. Email: kbrabson@msjacad.org. Web: www.msjacad.org. Sr. Kathleen Brabson, S.S.J., Pres.; Dr. Judith Caviston, Prin. Sisters of St. Joseph 10; Lay Teachers 52; Students 560.

GWYNEDD VALLEY. *Gwynedd-Mercy Academy*, 1345 Sumneytown Pike, 19437-0902. Tel: 215-646-8815; Fax: 215-646-4361. Email: skathleen@gmahs.com. Web: www.gmahs.com. Sr. Kathleen Boyce, R.S.M., Prin.; Marilyn Duffy, Librarian. Sisters 7; Lay Teachers 37; Girls 390.

HOLLAND. *Villa Joseph Marie High School*, 1180 Holland Rd., 18966. Tel: 215-357-8810; Fax: 215-357-2477. Email: dkoop@vjmhs.org. Web: www.vjmhs.org. Mary T. Michel, Pres.; Diana Koopman, Prin. Lay Teachers 35; Students 370.

MALVERN. *Malvern Preparatory School for Boys*, 418 S. Warren Ave., 19355-2707. Tel: 484-595-1194; Fax: 484-595-1118. Web: www.malvernprep.com. Revs. Stephen J. Baker, O.S.A., Prior Faculty; Francis J. Caponi, O.S.A.; Harry J. Erdlen, O.S.A., Campus Min.; Augustine M. Esposito, O.S.A., M.Div., M.A., Ph.D.; James R. Flynn, O.S.A., Headmaster; Thomas J. Meehan, O.S.A.; Mr. James Stewart, Pres.; Mrs. Elizabeth Driscoll, Librarian. Priests 5; Lay Teachers 75; Students 610.

Villa Maria Academy High School, 370 Old Lincoln Hwy., 19355. Tel: 610-644-2551; Fax: 610-644-2866. Email: info@vmahs.org. Web: www.vmahs.org. Sr. Marita Carmel, I.H.M., Prin.; Mrs. Celeste Dougherty, Librarian. Sisters, Servants of the Immaculate Heart of Mary 12; Lay Teachers 50; Girls 445.

MERION. *Merion Mercy Academy*, 511 Montgomery Ave., Merion Station, 19066. Tel: 610-664-6655; Fax: 610-664-6322. Email: mma@merion-mercy.com. Web: www.merion-mercy.com. Sr. Barbara Buckley, R.S.M., Prin.; Ashley Stang, Dir. Media Center. Day School for Girls. Sisters of Mercy 17; Lay Teachers 49; Students 492.

VILLANOVA. *Academy of Notre Dame de Namur*, 560 Sproul Rd., 19085. Tel: 610-687-0650; Fax: 610-687-1912. Web: www.ndapa.org. Veronica Collins Harrington, Pres.; Ms. Anne T. Carroll, Jr. School Dir.; Joseph D'Angelo, Prin.; Ms. Mary Buxton, Librarian. Sisters 1; Lay Teachers 71.

WYNDMOOR. *LaSalle College High School*, 8605 Cheltenham Ave., 19038. Tel: 215-233-2911; Fax: 215-233-1418. Email: admissions@lschs.org. Web: www.lschs.org. Bro. Richard Kestler, F.S.C., Pres.; Mr. Joseph Marchese, Prin.; Bro. James Rieck, Religious Supr.; Donna Long, Librarian. Priests 1; Brothers of the Christian Schools 10; Lay Teachers 89; Students 1,070.

[G] REGIONAL PARISH SCHOOLS

PHILADELPHIA. *St. Athanasius-Immaculate Conception School*, 7105 Limekiln Pike, 19138. Tel: 215-424-5045; Fax: 215-927-6615. Email: apathanic05@nni.com; saic@sa-ic.org. Sisters Joan Alminde, S.S.J., Prin.; Arleen McNicholas, S.S.J., Librarian. Regional school for St. Athanasius Parish and Immaculate Conception Parish. Sisters 3; Lay Teachers 11; Students 307.

Holy Child Catholic School, 242 Hermitage St., 19127. Tel: 215-487-2796; Fax: 215-487-9134. Email: hcchprincipal@gmail.com. Web: teacherweb.com/PA/HolyChildCatholicSchool/SchoolHomePage/SDHP1.stm. Michael J. Patterson, Prin. Regional school for Holy Family, St. Lucy and St. Mary of the Assumption parishes.

Holy Innocents Area Catholic School, 1312 E. Bristol St., 19124. Tel: 215-743-5909; Fax: 215-743-0199. Email: holyinnocentsaces@juno.com. Sr. Regina Mullen, I.H.M., Prin. Area School for St. Joan of Arc, St. Joachim, Mater Dolorosa, Holy Innocents. Sisters, Servants of the Immaculate Heart of Mary 9; Lay Teachers 14; Students 311.

St. Mary Interparochial School, 5th & Locusts Sts., 19106. Tel: 215-923-7522; Fax: 215-923-8502. Email: stmary@cavtel.net. Jeanne M. Meredith, Prin.; Barbara Brown, Librarian. Regional school for St. Stanislaus Parish, Old St. Joseph Parish, Old St. Mary Parish, St. John the Evangelist Parish, St. Augustine Parish, Holy Trinity Parish, St. Mary Magdalen de Pazzi and St. Patrick. Lay Teachers 10; Students 236.

Mary, Mother of Peace, 64th St. & Buist Ave., 19142. Tel: 215-729-3603; Fax: 215-729-2315. Sr. Janet Walters, I.H.M., Prin. Regional school for Divine Mercy and St. Barnabas. Sisters 2; Lay Teachers 15; Students 298.

Our Lady of Port Richmond Regional School, 3233 Thompson St., 19134. Tel: 215-739-1920; Fax: 215-739-0519. Sisters Mary Ripp, S.C.C., Prin.; Angela Abbruzzese, S.C.C., Librarian. Regional School for St. Adalbert, Nativity of the Blessed Virgin Mary and Our Lady Help of Christians. Sisters 3; Lay Teachers 24.

Pope John Paul II Regional School, (Grades PreK-8), 4435 Almond St., 19137. Tel: 215-535-3446; Fax: 215-535-3858. Web: pjp2rcs.com. Linda Osik-Milewski, Prin.; Anna Marie Kelly, Librarian. Regional School for St. John Cantius and All Saints Parishes. Lay Teachers 16; Students 231.

The DePaul Catholic School, 44 W. Logan St., 19144. Tel: 215-842-1266; Fax: 215-842-1400. Email: chillig@thedepaulcatholicschool.org. Web: thedepaulcatholicschool.org. Sr. Cheryl Ann Hillig, D.C., Prin. Regional school for St. Francis of Assisi Parish and Saint Vincent de Paul Parish. Sisters 3; Lay Teachers 33; Priests 2; Students 345.

AMBLER. *St. Anthony - St. Joseph Elementary School*, 260 Forest Ave., 19002. Tel: 215-646-6150; Fax: 215-654-5254. Email: kaleslie@stanthony-stjoseph.org. Web: www.sa-sj.org. Kathleen Dilts, Prin.; Rosa Costanzo, Librarian. Regional school for St. Anthony of Padua Parish and St. Joseph Parish. Sisters of St. Joseph 1; Lay Teachers 12; Students 192.

BRYN MAWR. *SS. Colman-John Neumann School*, 372 Highland Ln., 19010. Tel: 610-525-3266; Fax: 610-525-6103. Web: www.scjnschool.org. Catherine Blumstein, Prin. Regional school for St. Colman Parish and St. John Neumann Parish. Lay Teachers 19; Students 220.

CONSHOHOCKEN. *Conshohocken Catholic School*, 205 Fayette St., 19428. Tel: 610-828-2007; Fax: 610-825-8796. Email: conshohockencatholic@yahoo.com. Patricia J. Kaeser, Prin.; Sr. Mary Pat Watson, Librarian. Regional school for SS. Cosmas & Damian Parish and St. Matthew Parish.

St. Matthew Elementary Campus, 205 Fayette St., 19428. Tel: 610-828-2007; Fax: 610-825-8796.

SS. Cosmas & Damian Primary Campus (Grades PreK-K), 130 W. 5th Ave., 19428. Tel: 610-828-0755; Fax: 610-828-5191. Sisters 4; Lay Teachers 17; Students 200.

HILLTOWN. *St. Agnes-Sacred Heart School*, 100 Broad St., P.O. Box 31, 18927. Tel: 215-822-9174; Fax: 215-822-7942. Web: www.sashschool.com. Margaret Graham, Prin.; Joanne Roberts, Librarian (Hilltown); Patti Alber, Librarian (Sellersville). Regional School for St. Agnes, Sellersville and Sacred Heart, Hilltown. Lay Teachers 13.

LINWOOD. *Holy Saviour-St. John Fisher School*, 122 E. Ridge Rd., 19061. Tel: 610-485-0363; Fax: 610-485-7809. Email: hssjfprincipal@gmail.com. Mary Rose C. Worrilow, Ed.D. Regional school for Holy Saviour Parish and St. John Fisher Parish. Lay Teachers 14; Students 216.

NORRISTOWN. *Our Lady of Victory Regional Catholic School*, 351 E. Johnson Hwy., 19401. Tel: 610-275-2990; Fax: 610-275-0470. Angela Ciccanti, Prin.; Frances Luthy, Librarian. Regional school for Holy Saviour, St. Patrick and St. Paul parishes. Lay Teachers 16; Students 170.

PHOENIXVILLE. *Holy Family School*, 221 Third Ave., 19460. Tel: 610-933-7562; Fax: 610-933-8823. Email: info@myholyfamily.com. Web: www.myholyfamilyschool.org. Mrs. Ann Marie Braca, Prin.; Mrs. Josephine Bachi, Librarian. Regional school for St. Ann Parish, Holy Trinity Parish, St. Mary of the Assumption Parish, Sacred Heart Parish and St. Joseph, Spring City. Lay Teachers 24; Students 432.

RIDLEY PARK. *St. Madeline-St. Rose School*, 500 Tome St., 19078. Tel: 610-583-3662; Fax: 610-583-3683. Email: smsrprincipal@comcast.net. Web: www.smsr-central.net. Regional school for St. Madeline Parish and St. Rose of Lima Parish. Lay Teachers 14; Students 252.

WARRINGTON. *St. Joseph-St. Robert School*, 850 Euclid Ave., 18976. Tel: 215-343-5100; Fax: 215-343-7434. Web: stjstr.org. Mrs. Deborah R. Jaster, Prin.; Marie Orzechowski, Librarian. Regional school for St. Joseph Parish and St. Robert Bellarmine Parish. Lay Teachers 15; Students 263.

WEST BRANDYWINE. *Pope John Paul II Regional Catholic Elementary School*, 2875 Manor Rd., 19320. Tel: 610-384-5961; Fax: 610-384-5730. Email: abmcguire@yahoo.com. Web: www.popejohnpaul2sch.org. Sr. Anne B. McGuire, Prin.; Elizabeth Powell, Librarian. Area school for St. Cecilia, St. Joseph, St. Stanislaus and Our Lady of the Rosary, Coatesville, and St. Peter Parish, West Brandywine. Servants of the Immaculate Heart of Mary 3; Lay Teachers 26; Students 613.

[H] ELEMENTARY SCHOOLS, PRIVATE

PHILADELPHIA. *The Gesu School*, 1700 W. Thompson Sts., 19121. Tel: 215-763-3660; 215-763-9077 (Development); Fax: 215-763-9844. Email: neil@gesuschool.org. Web: www.gesuschool.org. Christine Beck, Pres.; Sr. Ellen Convey, I.H.M., Prin.; Rev. Neil L. Ver'Schneider, S.J., Vice Prin.; Sr. Patricia McGrenra, I.H.M. Priests, Society of Jesus 1; Sisters, Servants of the Immaculate Heart of Mary 2; Lay Teachers 30; Students 457.

**La Salle Academy*, (Grades 3-8), 1434 N. 2nd St., 19122. Tel: 215-739-5804; Fax: 215-739-1664. Email: jeannemcgowan2002@yahoo.com. Web: www.lasalleacademy.net. Sr. Jeanne McGowan, S.S.J., Pres.; Teresa Diamond, Prin. Sisters 1; Lay Teachers 11; Students 90.

Nazareth Academy Grade School, 4701 Grant Ave., 19114. Tel: 215-637-7777; Fax: 215-637-5696. Email: nazarethacademygradeschool@yahoo.com. Web: www.nazarethacademy.net. Sisters M. Martin Duffy, C.S.F.N., Pres.; Mary Ann Allton, C.S.F.N., Prin.; M. Anita Pasternak, C.S.F.N., Vice Prin.; M. Yvette Ortiz, C.S.F.N., Finance Dir.; Mrs. Nancy Lydon, Librarian. Sisters of the Holy

Family of Nazareth 6; Lay Teachers 16; Students 229.

Norwood-Fontbonne Academy, 8891 Germantown Ave., 19118. Tel: 215-247-3811; Fax: 215-247-8405; 215-248-9721. Email: jlaurich@norfon.org. Web: www.norwoodfontbonneacademy.org. Sr. Jean Laurich, S.S.J., Prin.; Mr. George Aspen, Asst. Prin.; Mrs. Deborah Wood, Asst. Prin.; Mr. William Dennis, Campus Min.; Theresa Hutsell, Campus Min.; Mrs. Joanne Baillie, Admissions Dir.; Ms. Stephanie Belzer, Devel. Dir; Ms. Shannon Craig, Librarian. Sisters of St. Joseph 5; Lay Teachers 40; Students 440.

BRYN MAWR. *St. Aloysius Academy*, (Grades PreK-8), 401 S. Bryn Mawr Ave., 19010. Tel: 610-527-0506; 610-525-1670; Fax: 610-525-5140. Email: soar@staloysiusacademy.org. Web: www.staloysiusacademy.org. Sr. Stephen Ann Roderiguez, I.H.M., Ed.D., Prin.; Mary Jane McGough, Librarian. Sisters, Servants of the Immaculate Heart of Mary 7; Lay Teachers 29; Students 192.

CHESTER. *Drexel Neumann Academy*, 1901 Potter St., 19013-5497. Tel: 610-872-7358; Fax: 610-872-7833. Sisters Margaret Gannon, O.S.F., Pres.; Catherine McGowan, S.S.J., Prin.

DREXEL HILL. *Holy Child Academy*, (Grades N-8), 475 Shadeland Ave., 19026. Tel: 610-259-2712; Fax: 610-259-1862. Email: acoll@holychildacademy.com. Web: holychildacademy.com. Mrs. Anita P. Coll, Head. Lay Teachers 27; Students 184.

IMMACULATA. *Villa Maria Academy*, 1140 King Rd., 19345-0600. Tel: 610-644-4864; Fax: 610-647-6403. Email: office@villamaria.org. Web: www.villamaria.org. Sr. Mary Ellen Tennity, I.H.M., Prin.; Sarah Connelly, Librarian. Sisters, Servants of the Immaculate Heart of Mary 6; Lay Teachers 35; Girls 360.

MERION. *Waldron Mercy Academy*, 513 Montgomery Ave., Merion Station, 19066. Tel: 610-664-9847; Fax: 610-664-6364. Email: wma@waldronmercy.org. Web: www.waldronmercy.org. Sr. Patricia Smith, R.S.M., Prin.; Mr. Stephen Stritch, Vice Prin. Advancement; Sisters Joellen McDonnell, R.S.M., Admissions Dir.; Mary Agnes Donnelly, R.S.M., Librarian. Private, co-educational elementary school with child care, preschool & Montessori programs. Sisters of Mercy 4; Lay Teachers 40; Students 515.

RADNOR. *Armenian Sisters Academy* Montessori for ages 3-6. Elementary for ages 7-14., 440 Upper Gulph Rd., 19087. Tel: 610-687-4100; Fax: 610-687-2430. Email: asaphila@aol.com. Web: www.asaphila.org. Sr. Louisa Kassarjian, Prin. Sisters 2; Lay Teachers 22; Students 155.

ROSEMONT. *Rosemont School of the Holy Child*, 1344 Montgomery Ave., 19010. Tel: 610-992-1000; Fax: 610-922-1030. Email: mbroderi@rosemontschool.org. Web: www.rosemontschool.org. Sr. Mary Broderick, S.H.C.J., Prin.; Catherine Stuart, Librarian. Sisters of the Holy Child Jesus 2; Lay Teachers 36; Students 322.

SPRING HOUSE. *Gwynedd-Mercy Academy Elementary School*, (Grades K-8), *Elementary School*, 816 Norristown Rd., P.O. Box 241, 19477. Tel: 215-646-4916; 215-646-2406 (Business Office); Fax: 215-646-7250. Email: mkenney@gmaelem.org. Web: www.gmaelem.org. Sr. Anne Crampsie, R.S.M., Prin.; Ms. Karen Czarny, Curriculum Coord.; Jean Bellavance, Librarian. Sisters of Mercy 1; Lay Teachers 44; Students 489; Total Staff 55.

WYNCOTE. *Ancillae-Assumpta Academy*, (Grades PreK-8), (Coed), 2025 Church Rd., 19095. Tel: 215-885-1636; Fax: 215-885-2740. Email: mdondero@ancillae.org; mgillespie@ancillae.org. Marian Dondero, Dir.; Sr. Maureen Gillespie, A.C.J., Prin.; Rosanne Zajko, Librarian. Handmaids of the Sacred Heart of Jesus 5; Lay Teachers 66; Students 571.

WYNDMOOR. *Regina Coeli Academy*, 1108 E. Willow Grove Ave., 19038-7663. Tel: 215-836-2208. Email: info@reginacoeliacademy.com. Web: www.reginacoeliacademy.com. Mr. Tim Murnane, Chm. Bd.; Mrs. Michele Fowler, Headmistress. A private independent school PreK-8. Classical curriculum and formation in the Catholic faith. Lay Faculty 15; Students 75.

YARDLEY. *Grey Nun Academy* (Coed Day School), 1750 Quarry Rd., 19067. Tel: 215-968-4151; Fax: 215-860-7418. Email: mfinnegan@gnaedu.org. Web: www.gnaedu.org. Marianne R. Finnegan, Prin.; Sr. Martha Moyle, G.N.S.H., Asst. Prin.; Linda Rowan, Librarian. Grey Nuns of the Sacred Heart 1; Lay Teachers 23; Students 180.

[I] SPECIAL EDUCATION

PHILADELPHIA. *St. Lucy Day School for Children with Visual Impairments and Archbishop Ryan Academy for the Deaf*, 4251 L St., 19124. Tel: 215-289-4220; Fax: 215-289-4229. Email: APLucy01@nni.com. Web: www.slds.org. Sr. M. Margaret Fleming, I.H.M., Prin. Sisters, Servants of the Immaculate Heart of Mary 5; Lay Teachers 6; Students 32.

Our Lady of Confidence Day School, Willow Grove. Tel: 215-657-9311; Fax: 215-657-9312. Email: apConf01@nni.com. Web: www.ourladyofconfidence.com. Mentally Challenged. Sisters Servants of the Immaculate Heart of Mary 2; Lay Teachers 8.

Main School and Office, 314 N. Easton Rd., Willow Grove, 19090-2506. Tel: 215-657-9311; Fax: 215-657-9312. Email: APConf01@nni.com.

High School Site, 6301 N. Second St., 19020-1599. Tel: 215-276-2300, Ext. 285; Fax: 215-967-3339. Sr. Judith Moeller, I.H.M., Prin.

LEVITTOWN. *Archangels Academy School of Special Education*, 3810 Bristol-Oxford Valley Rd., 19057. Tel: 215-269-1490; Fax: 215-269-1141. Email: office@archangelsacademy.org. Web: www.archangelsacademy.org. Sr. Angela Mastrangelo, I.H.M., Prin. Cognitively and Developmentally Delayed Students ages 4[00bd]-16. Sisters 2; Lay Teachers 6; Students 31.

WYNNEWOOD. *St. Katherine Day School*, 930 Bowman Ave., 19096. Tel: 610-667-3958; Fax: 610-667-3625. Email: APKath01@nni.com. Margaret Devaney, Prin. Children with Developmental Delay and/or Multiple Impairments. Lay Teachers 11; Students 86.

[J] CATHOLIC SOCIAL SERVICES OF THE ARCHDIOCESE OF PHILADELPHIA

PHILADELPHIA. *Catholic Social Services of the Archdiocese of Philadelphia*, 222 N. 17th St., 19103-1202. Tel: 215-587-3900; Fax: 215-587-2479. Email: CHSweb@chs-adphila.org. Web: www.css-phl.org. Joseph J. Sweeney Jr., M.B.A., N.H.A., Sec., Catholic Human Svcs. All addresses unless otherwise indicated.

St. Gabriel's System, 227 N. 18th St., 19103. Tel: 215-665-8777; Fax: 215-665-6621. Web: www.saint-gabrielsystem.org. Joseph Lavoritano, M.A., M.Ed., N.C.S.P., Dir. - Youth Svcs.

Developmental Programs Division Administrative Office, 1797 S. Sproul Rd., Springfield, 19064. Tel: 484-475-2469; Fax: 610-543-5397. Web: www.cssmrs-erv.org. Mark E. Fitzgerald, M.S.W., N.H.A., Dir. Devel. Programs Div.

Adoption Services Tel: 215-854-7050. Robert Montoro, M.S.W., Prog. Supvr.

Child Care/Foster Home Services Tel: 215-587-0529. Teresa Thompson, L.S.W., Dir. Community - Based Svcs.

Philadelphia County Programs/Family Svcs. Center Amy Stoner, L.S.W., Dir. Community Based Prevention Svcs.

Cardinal Bevilacqua Community Center, 2646 Kensington Ave., 19125. Tel: 215-426-9422. Estella Reyes-Bugg, B.S., Admin.

Casa del Carmen Family Services, 4440 N. Reese St., 19140. Tel: 215-329-5660. W. Giovanni Morante, M.A., Admin.

Northeast Philadelphia Family Service Center, 7340 Jackson St., 19136. Tel: 215-624-5920.

South Philadelphia Family Service Center, 1941 Christian St., 19146. Tel: 215-790-9530.

Southwest Philadelphia Family Service Center, 6214 Grays St., P.O. Box 16986, 19142. Tel: 215-724-8550. Renee Hudson-Small, L.S.W., Admin.

Suburban Counties-Family Service Centers Tel: 610-279-7372. Kathleen Emery, M.S.W., Dir.

Bucks County Family Service Centers, 100 Levittown Pkwy., Levittown, 19054. Tel: 215-945-2550.

Middle Bucks County, 607 W. Street Rd., Warminster, 18974. Tel: 215-957-6699.

Upper Bucks County, 427 N. Main St., Sellersville, 18960. Tel: 215-453-7098. Maryann Adams, L.C.S.W., Supvr.

Chester County Family Service Centers, 125 N. Darlington St., West Chester, 19380. Tel: 610-344-7028. 105 Prospect Ave., West Grove, 19390. Tel: 610-869-6500. 605 E. Lincoln Hwy., Coatesville, 19320. Tel: 610-344-7028. Mary Ann Nagel, M.S.S., L.C.S.W., Prog. Mgr.

Delaware County Family Service Center, 240 N. Bishop Ave., Springfield, 19064. Tel: 610-626-6550. Gail McCoach, L.C.S.W., Prog. Mgr.

130 E. 7th St., Chester, 19013. Tel: 610-876-7101. Alana Schafer, L.C.S.W., Admin.

Montgomery County Family Service Center, 353 E. Johnson Hwy., Norristown, 19401. Tel: 610-279-7372. Elizabeth Peteraf, M.A., Prog. Mgr.

Community-Based & Specialized Services Div., 227 N. 18th St., 19103. The offices are all located at the Holy Family Center unless otherwise noted.

Immigration and Resettlement Services Tel: 215-854-7019. Mark Shea Esq., Admin.

Senior Adult Services Tel: 215-854-7087. Kathleen Newman, Asst. Admin.

Volunteer & Community Relations Services Tel: 215-854-7058. William Tangradi, M.S.W., Mgr.

Housing/Homeless Services, 222 N. 17th St., 19103. Tel: 215-854-7080. Deborah Wagner, L.S.W., Admin.

Catholic Health Care Services

St. John Neumann Place, 2600 Moore St., 19145. Tel: 215-463-0410. Lorraine Yarborough, Property Mgr., NDC Real Estate Mgmt.

Information Technology Services (ITS) Division Franz Fruehwald, M.B.A., CIO. Tel: 215-965-1737; Michael Leiden, Dir. Information Systems. Tel: 215-854-7061; M. Lee Myers, Dir. Information Technology. Tel: 267-663-0031.

Nutritional Development Services, 111 S. 38th St., 19104. Tel: 215-895-3470. Lorraine M. Knight, M.Ed., Dir.

Office for Community Development John M. Wagner, Dir. Tel: 215-587-3589.

[K] RESIDENTIAL SERVICES FOR CHILDREN

PHILADELPHIA. *St. Vincent Homes, Administrative Office Building*, 1509 Church St., 19124. Tel: 215-992-5402; Fax: 215-992-5198. Richard Pytlewski, M.S.W., Admin.; Theresa Metz, Dir., Social Work. Operates the following programs for court adjudicated dependent females ages 12-21 who suffer from abuse and neglect. All facilities are staffed 24/7. Capacity 74; Total Staff 87.

St. Joachim's Hall Group Home (16 females ages 12-21), 1509 Church St., 19124. Tel: 215-992-5402; Cell: 267-574-1100; Fax: 215-992-5189.

St. Joseph's Hall Group Home (12 females ages 12-21), 477 E. Locust Ave., 19144. Tel: 215-849-1316; Cell: 215-300-2315; Fax: 215-842-0387.

St. Joan of Arc Hall (16 females ages 12-21), 7201 Milnor St., 19135. Tel: 215-992-5070; Cell: 215-275-4560; Fax: 215-624-8355.

Guardian Angel Mother/Baby Prog. (10 teen mothers ages 12-21 and 10 babies), 157 W. Carpenter Ln., 19111. Tel: 215-849-9029; Cell: 215-200-6651; Fax: 215-849-0651.

Maternity Group Home (10 females ages 12-21 who are pregnant), 104 E. Township Line Rd., Havertown, 19083. Tel: 610-446-0105; Cell: 215-200-6605; Fax: 610-446-1532.

AMBLER. *St. Mary's Villa for Children and Families*, 701 Bethlehem Pike, P.O. Box 388, 19002-0388. Tel: 215-643-7676; Fax: 215-542-9219. Email: fryer.diana@hfi-pgh.org. Web: www.hfi.org. Diana L. Fryer, Exec. Dir. Family centered organization providing residential care and treatment to youth ages 7-18. St. Mary's is committed to helping children, preserving families and strengthening communities by providing residential treatment and outpatient mental health counseling. It strives to empower children and families to lead responsible lives and develop healthy relationships built on faith, hope and love. Sisters of the Holy Family of Nazareth 1; Capacity 87; Total Staff 118; Total Assisted Annually 169.

BENSALEM. *St. Francis - St. Joseph Homes for Children*, 3400 Bristol Pike, 19020. Tel: 215-638-9310; Fax: 215-638-2498. Email: fswiack@chs-adphila.org. Web: www.sfsj.org. Francis E. Swiacki Jr., L.S.W., Admin. Provides residential treatment at 15 sites for boys, ages 12 to 21; also Supervised Living for boys 17 & older. Total Assisted 250; Capacity 158; Total Staff 202.

[L] RESIDENTIAL SCHOOLS FOR MENTALLY CHALLENGED CHILDREN AND ADULTS

SPRINGFIELD. *Cardinal Krol Center*, 1799 S. Sproul Rd., 19064. Tel: 484-475-2467; Fax: 610-544-1207. Web: catholicsocialservicesphilly.org; www.cssmrserv.org. Rev. Dennis M. Weber, Sd.C, Dir. of Mission Identity. A residential facility for 131 male adults with developmental/intellectual disabilities which provides an environment, both day and residential, that contributes to the individuals own growth and development by fulfilling their potential in the physical, mental, emotional, social, psychological, and spiritual areas of their lives. Priests 3; Residential Capacity 131; Day Program 45; Total Assisted Annually 200; Total Staff 200.

Divine Providence Village, 686 Old Marple Rd., 19064. Tel: 610-328-7730; Fax: 610-544-1710. Rosemary Bellenghi, M.S.W., Admin.; Rev. Paul Oggioni, Sd.C, Chap. Care & specialized training for developmentally disabled females. Capacity 96.

Don Guanella School, 1797 S. Sproul Rd., 19064-1195. Tel: 484-475-2474; Fax: 610-328-2136.

Email: fr.dweber@chs-adphila.org. Web: www.catholicsocialservicesphilly.org. Rev. Dennis M. Weber, Sd.C, Dir. of Mission Identity & Integration. Provides specialized care and residential treatment program for boys with developmental/intellectual disabilities ages 6-21. Capacity: Residents 40; Day Students 100.

[M] RESIDENTIAL HOMES FOR PHYSICALLY HANDICAPPED CHILDREN

ROSEMONT. *St. Edmond's Home for Children*, 320 S. Roberts Rd., 19010. Tel: 610-525-8800; Fax: 610-525-2693. Web: cssmrserv.org. Denise Clofine, M.Ed., Admin.; Rev. Silvio De Nard, S.C, Chap. Licensed I.C.F./M.R. Home for children ages birth to 21 with severe/profound intellectual and physical disabilities. Capacity 40; Total Staff 160.

[N] PROTECTIVE INSTITUTIONS

PHILADELPHIA. *St. Gabriel's System*, Administrative Offices, 227 N. 18th St., 19103. Tel: 215-665-8777; Fax: 215-665-8821. Email: jlavoritano@chs-adphila.org. Web: www.saintgabrielssystem.org. Joseph Lavoritano, M.A., M.Ed., N.C.S.P., Exec. Dir. Administrative and Intake services for residential treatment; Day Treatment for Court-committed delinquent boys, ages 12-17. (See St. Gabriel's Hall, De LaSalle in Towne, De LaSalle Vocational and St. Gabriel's System Reintegration Services and Brother Rousseau Academy). Total Staff 426; Total Assisted 3,000.

AUDUBON. *St. Gabriel's Hall*, Box 7280, 19407-7280. Tel: 215-247-2776 (Philadelphia); 610-666-7970 (Audubon); Fax: 610-666-1479. Email: jlavoritano@chs_adphila.org. Joseph Lavoritano, M.A., M.Ed., N.C.S.P., Exec. Dir.; Bro. Brian Henderson, F.S.C., Dir. Offers residential treatment for court-committed delinquent boys, ages 10-18.

[O] DAY TREATMENT CENTERS

PHILADELPHIA. *De La Salle-In-Towne Day Treatment Center*, 25 S. Van Pelt St., 19103. Tel: 215-567-5500; Fax: 215-567-6922. Email: cgaus@chs-adphila.org. Joseph Lavoritano, M.A., M.Ed., N.C.S.P., Exec. Dir.; Charles E. Gaus, Dir. A community-based day treatment program for court-committed delinquent boys, ages 14-17. Capacity 110; Total Staff 35; Total Assisted 260.

BENSALEM. *De La Salle Vocational Day Treatment Center*, Box 344, 19020. Tel: 215-464-0344; Fax: 215-638-3767. Email: jlogan@chs-adphila.org. Joseph Lavoritano, M.A., M.Ed., N.C.S.P., Exec. Dir.; Mr. James Logan, M.S.S., Dir. A community based day treatment program for court-committed delinquent boys, ages 15-18. Capacity 125; Total Staff 37.

[P] SENIOR COMMUNITY CENTERS

PHILADELPHIA. *St. Anne's Senior Community Center*, 2607 E. Cumberland St., 19125. Tel: 215-423-2772; Fax: 215-423-2423. Barbara Jo Hartzell, Center Coord. Total Staff 6; Total Assisted 11,288.

St. Charles Senior Community Center, 1941 Christian St., 19146. Tel: 215-790-9530; Fax: 215-790-9765. Kathy Boles, Coord.

Norris Square Senior Community Center, 2121 N. Howard St., 19133. Tel: 215-423-7241; Fax: 215-634-7751. Bethzaida Butler Lopez, Coord. Total Assisted 120; Total Staff 10.

Star Harbor Senior Community Center, 4700 Springfield Ave., 19143. Tel: 215-724-4414; Fax: 215-726-7496. Email: bjhartze@chs-adphila.org. Ernestine Patterson, Coord.

[Q] OUTREACH CENTERS

PHILADELPHIA. *Casa del Carmen*, 4400 N. Reese St., 19140. Tel: 215-329-5660; Fax: 215-329-6722. W. Giovanni Morante, M.A., Admin. Offers emergency crisis social services to the Spanish speaking community in Philadelphia and surrounding areas.

Drueding Center/Project Rainbow, 413 W. Master St., 19122. Tel: 215-769-1830; Fax: 215-787-0999. Email: acollins@holyredeemer.com. Web: www.holyredeemer.com. Anne Marie Collins, Exec. Dir. Sponsor: Sisters of the Holy Redeemer, C.S.R., Subsidiary of Holy Redeemer Health System; Provides transitional housing and support services for homeless women with children; daycare is provided for the children.

Marketing/Public Affairs Department, c/o 1602 Huntingdon Pike, Meadowbrook, 19046. Tel: 215-938-3226; Fax: 215-938-3232.

St. Francis Inn, 2441 Kensington Ave., 19125. Tel: 215-423-5845; Fax: 215-423-2289. Email: stfrancisinn@aol.com. Web: www.stfrancisinn.org. Rev. Michael A. Duffy, O.F.M., Contact Person. Hot meals for the poor. Priests 1; Brothers 3; Sisters 2; Lay Staff 8.

St. Benedict Thrift Store, 437 W. Girard Ave., 19122. Tel: 215-235-1848. A clothing and furniture thrift store operated by Franciscans.

Thea Bowman's Women's Center, 2858 Kensington Ave., 19134. Tel: 215-739-1137. Sr. Xavier Kozubal, C.S.F.N., Contact Person. Women's day activity center.

St. John's Hospice for Men, 1221 Race St., 19107. Tel: 215-563-7763; Fax: 215-563-0108. Web: www.saintjohnshospice.org. Kevin Barr, M.R.S., M.B.A., Prog. Dir. Staffed by Catholic Social Services Archdiocese of Philadelphia. Total Assisted 50,000; Total Staff 33.

Mercy Hospice, 334 S. 13th St., 19107. Tel: 215-545-5153; Fax: 215-545-1872. Yvonne Branch, Dir. Provides residential case management and referral services to homeless women, women in recovery who are single or are with their children. Mercy Hospice also provides lunch Monday thru Friday from 12:00 - 12:45 p.m. to homeless women and children. Showers, clothing and the use of a telephone are available on a limited basis. Total Staff 26.

Visitation Homes, 2638 Kensington Ave., 19125. Tel: 215-425-2080; Fax: 215-425-1412. Sara Frisby-Simms, Prog. Dir. Residential service program for families making the transition from homelessness to permanent housing. The program offers 18 furnished one to three bedroom apartments and on site case management and life skill services. Referrals come through the City's Office of Emergency Shelter and Services. For a period of up to 2 years, residents are helped to achieve economic self sufficiency and address the other issues which led to their homelessness.

Women of Hope, 251 N. Lawrence St., 19106. Tel: 215-592-9116; Fax: 215-592-0650. Sr. Maureen Crissy, R.S.M., Prog. Dir. Residential facility for chronically mentally ill homeless women. Capacity 22; Total Staff 21; Total Assisted 24.

Women of Hope Lombard, 1210 Lombard St., 19147. Tel: 215-732-1341; Fax: 215-732-0659. Susan Stier, Prog. Dir. Residential Facility for chronically mentally ill homeless women. Capacity 24.

CHESTER. *Bernardine Center*, 2625 W. Ninth St., 19013. Tel: 610-497-3225; Fax: 610-497-3659. Email: director@bernardinecenter.org. Web: www.bernardinecenter.org. Sr. Sandra Lyons, O.S.F., Dir. West Side Brunch, Emergency Food Cupboard, Supercupboard Program, Advocacy, Computer Lab, English as a Second Language (ESL), Citizenship Classes. Sisters 6.

[R] DAY CARE CENTERS

PHILADELPHIA. *Casa del Carmen Day Care Center*, 4400 N. 5th St., 19140. Tel: 215-457-4325; Fax: 215-457-4339. Mailing Address: 4400 N. Reese St., 19140. W. Giovanni Morante, M.A., Admin.

St. Monica Day Care Center, 1441 Porter St., 19145. Tel: 215-334-6001; Fax: 215-467-4599. Email: DOCIHM@aol.com. Web: stmonica.org. Sr. Colleen Dougherty, I.H.M., Admin. Sister, Servants of the Immaculate Heart of Mary. Total Staff 12; Total Assisted 120.

[S] GENERAL HOSPITALS

PHILADELPHIA. *St. Agnes Continuing Care Center*, 1900 S. Broad St., 19145. Tel: 215-339-4220. Web: www.mercyhealth.org. H. Ray Welch, Pres. & CEO Mercy Health System; Sr. Kate O'Donnell, O.S.F., Vice Pres. Mission & Healthy Comm. Opened May 15, 1888.; Affiliate of Catholic Health East/Mercy Health System. Bed Capacity 58; Total Staff 414; Total Assisted Annually 931.

Mercy Philadelphia Hospital, 501 S. 54th St., 19143. Tel: 215-748-9300; Fax: 215-748-9709. Web: www.mercyhealth.org. H. Ray Welch, Pres. & CEO, Mercy Health System; Kathryn C. Conallen, CEO; Sr. Megan Brown, R.S.M., Vice Pres., Mission Svcs. Opened July 2, 1918. Incorporated May 1, 1969. Affiliate of Catholic Health East/ Mercy Health System. Sisters of Mercy 11; Bed Capacity 214; Patients Assisted Annually 76,037; Total Staff 1,043.

Nazareth Hospital, 2601 Holme Ave., 19152. Tel: 215-335-6039; Fax: 215-335-6598. Web: www.mercyhealth.org. H. Ray Welch, Pres. & CEO, Mercy Health System; Christina Fitz-Patrick, CEO; Mary Ann Carter, Vice Pres. Comm. Outreach Mission. Affiliate of Catholic Health East & Mercy Health System. Bed Capacity 233; Total Staff 1,362; Patients Assisted Annually 153,852.

DARBY. *Mercy Fitzgerald Hospital*, 1500 Lansdowne Ave., 19023-1291. Tel: 610-237-4030; Fax: 610-237-4202. Web: www.mercyhealth.org. H. Ray Welch, Pres. & CEO Mercy Health Systems; Brian Finestein, F.A.C.H.E., CEO; Sr. Angela Fellin, R.S.M., Chap.; Revs. Paul J. DeAntoniis, O.Praem, Chap.; Joseph C. Laenen, O.Praem., Chap.; Christal Rozario, Chap. Opened July 1, 1933. Incorporated May 1, 1969.; Affiliate of Catholic Health East & Mercy Health System.

HUNTINGDON VALLEY. *Holy Redeemer Health Care Corporation and Foundation*, 667 Welsh Rd., 19006. Tel: 215-938-4650; Fax: 215-938-4671. Web: www.holyredeemer.com. Parent Corporation of Holy Redeemer Health System; Sponsor: Sisters of the Holy Redeemer, C.S.R. Total Staff 3,487; Total Assisted 212,000.

Marketing & Public Affairs Department, c/o 1602 Huntingdon Pike, Meadowbrook, 19046. Tel: 215-938-3226; Fax: 215-938-3232.

HRH Management Corporation, 667 Welsh Rd., 19006. Tel: 215-938-4650; Fax: 215-938-4671. Web: www.holyredeemer.com. Affiliate of Holy Redeemer Health System. Sponsor: Sisters of the Holy Redeemer, C.S.R.

LANGHORNE. *St. Mary Medical Center*, Langhorne-Newton Rd., 19047. Tel: 215-710-2000; Fax: 215-710-2298. Email: trivera@stmaryhealthcare.org. Web: www.stmaryhealthcare.org. Gregory T. Wozniak, Pres. & CEO; Richard Brochu, Admin., Spiritual Care. Opened February 21, 1973.; Affiliate of Catholic Health East. Bed Capacity 366; Patients Assisted Annually 210,220; Total Staff 2,734.

Langhorne MRI, Inc., Langhorne-Newton Rd., 19047. Tel: 215-710-2000; Fax: 215-710-2298.

MEADOWBROOK. *Holy Redeemer Hospital and Medical Center*, 1648 Huntingdon Pike, 19046. Tel: 215-947-3000; Fax: 215-938-3945. Email: kreilly@holyredeemer.com. Web: www.holyredeemer.com. Patrice Morris, Vice Pres. Mission Integration. Sponsor: Sisters of the Holy Redeemer, C.S.R., Subsidiary of Holy Redeemer Health System, Inc.; Acute care community hospital, providing a broad spectrum of services, including preventive, rehabilitative, emergency and obstetrical care plus pastoral counseling. Bed Capacity 244; Total Assisted 14,700; Total Staff 1,630.

NORRISTOWN. *Mercy Suburban Hospital* (1944) 2701 DeKalb Pike, 19401. Tel: 610-278-2002; Fax: 610-272-4642. Web: www.mercyhealth.org. H. Ray Welch, Pres. & CEO Mercy Health Systems; Jeffrey Snyder, FACHE, FHFMA, CEO; Sr. Ann O'Connell, R.S.M., Vice Pres. Mission Svcs. Affiliate of Catholic Health East/Mercy Health System Bed Capacity 129; Total Assisted Annually 96; Total Staff 1,000.

[T] SPECIALIZED HOSPITALS

PHILADELPHIA. *Mount Nazareth*, 2755 Holme Ave., 19152. Tel: 215-338-8992; Fax: 215-338-8752. Sr. Regina Wieczezynski, Supr. Sisters of the Holy Family of Nazareth., Home for retired and infirm sisters. Resident Sisters 33; Total Assisted Annually 30; Total Staff 19.

ASTON. *Assisi House*, 600 Red Hill Rd., 19014. Tel: 610-459-8990; Fax: 610-558-5344. Email: JLAMANNA@osfPHILA.org. Web: www.osfphila.org. Sr. Jane La Manna, O.S.F., Admin.; Rev. Francis Sariego, O.F.M.Cap. Home for retired Sisters of St. Francis of Philadelphia. Capacity 130; Total Assisted Annually 142; Total Staff 207.

DARBY. *Villa Saint Joseph*, 1436 Lansdowne Ave., 19023-1298. Tel: 610-586-8535; Fax: 610-586-2810. Rev. Msgr. William A. Dombrow, M.Div., Rector; Helen McConnell, R.N., M.S., Admin. Home for aged, infirm and convalescent priests of the Archdiocese of Philadelphia. Sisters 1; Total Staff 60; Residents 62.

DOWNINGTOWN. *St. John Vianney Center*, 151 Woodbine Rd., 19335. Tel: 610-269-2600; Fax: 610-873-8028. Web: www.sjvcenter.org. Mr. Edward Maguire, Admin. Center for Behavioral Healthcare for Priests, Brothers, and Sisters. Bed Capacity 50; Total Assisted Annually 122; Total Staff 63.

IMMACULATA. *Camilla Hall Nursing Home*, King and Frazier Rds., P.O. Box 100, 19345-0100. Tel: 610-644-1152; Fax: 610-695-0691. Email: ihmcamilla@worldnet.att.net. Sisters Margaret Gradl, I.H.M., Admin.; Patricia McGuigan, I.H.M., Supr.; Rev. James P. McKelvey, M.Div., Chap. Sisters, Servants of the Immaculate Heart of Mary. Bed Capacity 220; Skilled Care 75; Residents 165; Total Staff 155.

MERION STATION. *McAuley Convent*, 517 Montgomery Ave., 19066. Tel: 610-667-2775; Fax: 610-667-9650. Sisters Mary Anne Basile, Supr. & Admin.; Mary Bonaventure, R.S.M., Dir. of Nursing. Infirmary for Religious Sisters of Mercy. Total Staff 50; Total Assisted 36.

VENTNOR. *Villa St. Joseph by the Sea* Summer residence for aged, infirm, and convalescent priests of the Archdiocese of Philadelphia., 114 S. Princeton Ave., 08406. Tel: 609-823-9383. Email: hmcconnell@chs.adphila.org. Rev. Msgr. William

A. Dombrow, M.Div., Rector; Helen McConnell, R.N., M.S., Admin.

WARMINSTER. *Regina Coeli Residence for Priests*, 685 York Rd., 18974. Tel: 215-441-4642. Rev. James F. Endres, Admin.; Helen McConnell, R.N., M.S., Admin. Home for retired priests of the Archdiocese of Philadelphia. Total Staff 5; Total in Residence 11.

[U] AFFILIATED SERVICES

PHILADELPHIA. **Holy Redeemer Home Care and Hospice* Holy Redeemer Support Services, 12265 Townsend Rd., Ste. 400, 19154. Tel: 215-671-9200; Fax: 215-671-1950. Web: www.holyredeemer.com. Donald Friel, Exec. Vice Pres. Affiliate of Holy Redeemer Health System. Sponsor: Sisters of the Holy Redeemer; Medicare certified home health agency serving patients in their own homes; Medicare certified hospice program serving terminally ill patients and their families.

Marketing/Public Affairs Department, c/o 1602 Huntingdon Pike, Meadowbrook, 19046. Tel: 215-938-3226; Fax: 215-938-3232.

PHOENIXVILLE. *St. Mary's Franciscan Shelter*, 209 Emmett St., 19460. Tel: 610-933-3097; Fax: 610-917-9845. Email: stmarysfs@verizon.net. Web: stmarysfs.org. Total Staff 6; Families Assisted 30. Staff: Sr. Christine Kranichfeld, Exec. Dir.; Kate Garges.

[V] NURSING AND CONVALESCENT HOMES

PHILADELPHIA. *St. Ignatius Nursing Home*, 4401 Haverford Ave., 19104. Tel: 215-349-8800; Fax: 215-222-3078. Email: jmeacham@stignatiusnursinghome.org. Web: www.stignatiusnursinghome.org. John W. Meacham, Admin. Attended from St. Ignatius Church. Felician Sisters 3; Bed Capacity 176; Total Assisted 403; Total Staff 220; Total in Residence 176.

St. John Neumann Nursing Home, 10400 Roosevelt Blvd., 19116. Tel: 215-698-5600; Fax: 215-698-5755. Email: jchapman@chs-adphila.org. Web: SJN-PHL.org. John T. Chapman, N.H.A., Admin.; Rev. Bernard C. Farley, Chap. Sisters of the Holy Family of Nazareth. Bed Capacity 226; Total Assisted 477; Total Staff 330.

St. Monica Manor, 2509 S. 4th St., 19148. Tel: 215-271-1080; Fax: 215-271-6290. Web: www.smonicam-ph1.org. Jeffrey S. Cox, N.H.A., Admin. Bed Capacity 180; Total Assisted 294; Total Staff 267.

Sacred Heart Free Home for Incurable Cancer, 1315 W. Hunting Park Ave., 19140. Tel: 215-329-3222; Fax: 215-329-4197. Email: srmedward@aol.com. Web: www.sacredheartphila.org. Sisters Marie Edward, O.P., Supr.; Mary Barbara, O.P., Admin. *The Servants of Relief for Incurable Cancer* Dominican Sisters of Hawthorne., Opened April 27, 1930.; Attended by Oblates of St. Francis de Sales. Bed Capacity 37; Total Assisted 82; Total Staff 32.

DARBY. *St. Francis Country House*, 1412 Lansdowne Ave., 19023-1218. Tel: 610-461-6510; Fax: 610-461-3558. Web: www.sfch-ph1.org. Rev. Edward J. Kennedy, Chap. Opened June 30, 1913. Capacity 273; Total Assisted Annually 437; Total Staff 400.

DOWNINGTOWN. *St. Martha Manor*, 470 Manor Ave., 19335. Tel: 610-873-8490; Fax: 610-873-5927. Web: smartham-phl.org. Maureen Reisinger, N.H.A., Admin.; Rev. Edward J. Jablonski, Chap. Capacity 120; Total Assisted Annually 160; Total Staff 210.

FLOURTOWN. *St. Joseph Villa*, 110 W. Wissahickon Ave., 19031-1898. Tel: 215-836-4179; Fax: 215-248-7889. Email: apprichd@stjosephvilla.org. Web: www.stjosephvilla.org. Sr. Dorothy Apprich, S.S.J., Admin. Bed Capacity 324; Licensed Beds 106; Convent Beds 216; Total Staff 400.

[W] LONG TERM RESIDENCES FOR THE ELDERLY

PHILADELPHIA. *Holy Family Home*, 5300 Chester Ave., 19143-4993. Tel: 215-729-5153; Fax: 215-727-5332. Sr. Veronica Coyle, L.S.P., Admin.; Rev. Douglas M. McKay, Chap. Little Sisters of the Poor. Total Staff 100; Residents 97.

Immaculate Mary Home, 2990 Holme Ave., 19136-1829. Tel: 215-335-2100; Fax: 215-331-1016. Email: vgibbonne@chs-adphila.org. Web: IMH-PHL.org. Veronica Gibbone, Admin.; Sr. Patricia Bove, O.S.F., Pastoral Care Coord. Opened March 1976. Capacity 296; Total Assisted Annually 502; Total Staff 413.

St. Joseph Housing Corporation, Mount St. Joseph Convent, 9701 Germantown Ave., 19118-2694. Tel: 215-248-7200; Fax: 215-248-7277. Email: msjc@ssjphila.net. Web: www.ssjphila.org.

Staffed by the Sisters of St. Joseph. Total Staff 4; Total in Residence 107.

DARBY. *Little Flower Manor* All Skilled Nursing Care., 1201 Springfield Rd., 19023. Tel: 610-534-6000; Fax: 610-534-6039. Staffed by Sisters of the Divine Redeemer. Total Staff 185; Patients Assisted Annually 239.

DOWNINGTOWN. *Catholic Health Care Services-Villa Saint Martha*, 490 Manor Ave., 19335. Tel: 610-873-5300; Fax: 610-873-2855. Email: admissions.vsm@chs-adphila.org. Web: www.vsm-phl.org. Diane M. Fly, Admin.; Rev. Edward J. Jablonski, Chap. Independent Living, Assisted Living, Memory Support Assisted Living. Units 120; Total Staff 75; Total Assisted Annually 140.

ELVERSON. *St. Mary of Providence Center*, 227 Isabella Rd., 19520. Tel: 610-942-4166; Fax: 610-942-4259. Email: stmaryofprov@comcast.net. Web: stmaryofprov-pa.org. Sr. Noreen Franzina, D.S.M.P., Supr. Residence for Senior Citizens. Center of Spirituality, Retreats and Days of Recollection. Sisters 4; Capacity 39; Overnight and Day Retreats 110; Total Staff 17; Total in Residence 46.

FLOURTOWN. *Bethlehem Retirement Village*, 100 W. Wissahickon Ave., 19031. Tel: 215-233-0998; Fax: 215-233-9052. Email: joliverssj@yahoo.com. Sr. Judith Oliver, S.S.J., Mgr. Staffed by the Sisters of St. Joseph. Apartments 100; Total Staff 4; Total in Residence 102.

HUNTINGDON VALLEY. *Redeemer Village - Redeemer Village II*, 1551 Huntingdon Pike, 19006. Tel: 215-947-8168. Web: www.holyredeemer.com. *Marketing/Public Affairs Department*, Holy Redeemer Health System, c/o 1602 Huntingdon Pike, Meadowbrook, 19046. Joseph Munizza, Mgr., Redeemer Village. Sisters of the Holy Redeemer, C.S.R., Subsidiary of Holy Redeemer Health System. Low income housing for the elderly or handicapped, subsidized by HUD. Apartments 151.

Redeemer Village II, 1551 Huntingdon Pike, 19006. Tel: 215-947-8168. Sisters of the Holy Redeemer, C.S.R., Subsidiary of Holy Redeemer Health System, Inc. Low income housing for the elderly or handicapped, subsidized by HUD. Apartments 49.

LANSDALE. *St. Mary Manor*, 701 Lansdale Ave., 19446. Tel: 215-368-0900; Fax: 215-362-2891. Web: SMM_PHL.org. Maria GioVinco, Admin. Immaculate Heart of Mary Sisters. Total Assisted Annually 338; Total Staff 239.

YARDLEY. *D'Youville Manor*, 1750 Quarry Rd., 19067. Tel: 215-579-1750; Fax: 215-579-3054. Email: dyouvillemanor@greynun.org. Web: www.dyouvillemanor.org. Cecile F. Shocket, M.S.N., R.N., N.H.A., Admin. Operated by Grey Nuns of the Sacred Heart. Assisted living retirement residence for the elderly. Capacity 51; Total Staff 40; Total in Residence 40.

[X] RESIDENCES FOR WOMEN

PHILADELPHIA. *Saint Katharine Drexel Residence*, 7919 Forrest Ave., 19150. Tel: 215-549-5765; Fax: 215-549-2375. Patti Jo Bailey, Admin.

St. Mary's Residence, 247 S. 5th St., 19106. Tel: 215-922-4228; Fax: 215-922-0192. Kathleen Nelson, Prog. Dir. Catholic Social Services. Residents 36; Total Staff 7.

[Y] MONASTERIES AND RESIDENCES OF PRIESTS AND BROTHERS

PHILADELPHIA. *Augustinian Community (O.S.A.)*, 910 Watkins St., 19148. Tel: 215-463-1326; Fax: 215-463-0888. Web: www.stnicksphila.com. Revs. Nicholas Martorano, O.S.A., Prior; John Brynes, O.S.A.; James R. Keating, O.S.A.; Howard McGraw, O.S.A.; Denis G. Wilde, O.S.A. Priests 4; Total Staff 45; Total Assisted 150.

The Brothers of the Christian Schools, Roncalli Community, 6519 N. 12th St., 19126. Tel: 215-424-4032. Bros. Thomas McPhillips, F.S.C., Dir.; Joseph Burke, F.S.C.; Gerard Molyneaux, F.S.C.

Brothers of the Christian Schools, St. Mary's Community, 7018 Boyer St., 19119-1801. Tel: 215-248-2434; Fax: 215-248-4327. Email: st.maryshall@verizon.net. Bro. Hugh Albright, F.S.C., Dir. Total in Residence 3.

Congregation of the Mission, St. Vincent's Seminary, 500 E. Chelten Ave., 19144-1203. Tel: 215-713-2400; Fax: 215-844-2085. Email: cmphila88@aol.com. Web: www.cmeast.org. Central House of the Congregation of the Mission (Vincentian Community), Eastern Province. Novitiate, Central Shrine of the Miraculous Medal in the United States, The Central Association of the Miraculous Medal and St. Catherine's Infirmary, Assisted Living Facility, The Brother Bertrand Ducournau Archives of the Eastern Province of the Congregation of the Mission. Total in Residence 42.

Provincial Administration: Very Rev. Msgr. Michael J. Carroll, C.M., Prov.; Revs. Charles P. Strollo, C.M., Asst. Prov.; Elmer Bauer III, C.M., Prov. Treas.; Mr. Allen Andrews, Exec. Dir. Finance.

House Administration: Revs. Bernard M. Tracey, C.M., B.A., M.Div., Supr.; William J. Bamber, C.M., Asst. Supr.; William J. O'Brien, C.M., Treas. In Res. Revs. William J. Bamber, C.M.; Robert J. Brandenberger, C.M.; John J. Buckley, C.M.; John W. Carven, C.M., Prov. Archivist; John J. Cusack, C.M.; Gerald E. Deitzer, C.M.; Daniel E. Donovan, C.M.; William P. Finn, C.M.; Frederick J. Gaulin, C.M.; William P. Goff, C.M.; William J. Gormley, C.M.; Aloysius P. Grass, C.M.; John J. Hodnett, C.M.; Thomas J. Hynes, C.M.; Stephen J. India, C.M.; John V. Kennedy, C.M.; Thomas R. Kennedy, C.M.; Arthur J. Kolinsky, C.M.; Daniel J. Kramer, C.M.; John J. Lawlor, C.M.; Francis X. Maguire, C.M.; Thomas P. Mallaghan, C.M.; Joseph P. McClain, C.M.; John J. McDonnell, C.M.; Walter J. Menig, C.M.; John G. Nugent, C.M.; William J. O'Brien, C.M.; John S. Pearce, C.M.; Alfred R. Pehrsson, C.M.; Robert Prior, C.M.; Charles M. Shanley, C.M.; William W. Sheldon, C.M.; Harold G. Skidmore, C.M.; James E. Smith, C.M.; Robert J. Stone; Robert Swain, C.M.; Bernard M. Tracey, C.M., B.A., M.Div.; Louis P. Trotta, C.M; Michael J. Tumulty, C.M.; Robert R. Vignola, C.M.; Bros. Stephen Kennedy, C.M.; Francis Mallaghan, C.M.

Vincentian Fathers of the Eastern Province of the Congregation of the Mission serving on special assignments other than the Motherhouse:

Rome, Italy: Very Rev. G. Gregory Gay, C.M.; Rev. John W. Gouldrick, C.M.

District of Columbia: Revs. Robert P. Maloney, C.M.; David M. O'Connell, C.M.

Illinois: Rev. Dennis H. Holtschneider, C.M.

Mexico: Rev. Juan Chavarria, C.M.

Michigan: Revs. Thomas M. Finley, C.M.; Michael M. Shea, C.M.

Father Louis Brisson Residence, 3301 Solly Ave., 19136-2340. Tel: 215-624-1604; Fax: 215-332-3478. Revs. Robert D. Ashenbrenner, O.S.F.S. (Retired); Leon V. Bonikowski, O.S.F.S., Oblate Mission of Appeals; Joseph G. Campellone, O.S.F.S., Pres.; John J. Dennis, O.S.F.S. (Retired); John V. DiFilippo, O.S.F.S. (Retired); Eugene L. Kelly, O.S.F.S. (Retired); Jack Kolodziej, O.S.F.S.; Gerard J. Mahoney, O.S.F.S.; Robert G. Mulligan, O.S.F.S.; William Nessel, O.S.F.S. (Retired); Edward L. Rauch, O.S.F.S. (Retired); Vincent E. Smith, O.S.F.S.; John J. Sullivan, O.S.F.S.; Bro. James F. Williams, O.S.F.S., Rel. Supvr. Total Staff 7; Total in Residence 14.

Gesu School Jesuit Community and Outreach Center (S.J.), 1700 W. Thompson St., 19121. Tel: 215-763-3660; Fax: 215-763-9844. Email: neil@gesuschool.org. Rev. Neil L. Ver'Schneider, S.J., Contact Person. Total Assisted 500; Total Staff 1.

Jesuit Community, Arrupe House, 1226 N. 18th St., 19121. Tel: 215-765-1875; Fax: 215-978-1920. Email: bmaivelett@sjprep.org. Revs. George W. Bur, S.J., Pres. St. Joseph Prep.; Bruce A. Maivelett, S.J., Dir. Mission/Ministry St. Joseph's Prep; Neil L. Ver'Schneider, S.J., Admin. Gesu School; Jeffrey P. Putthoff, S.J., Dir. Hope Works; Mr. Michael C. Magree, S.J., Teacher St. Joseph's Prep. Residence of Jesuit Fathers and Brothers.

Monastery of Our Lady of Mercy, 6398 Drexel Rd., 19151-2596. Tel: 215-879-0594; Fax: 215-877-7625. Email: vocations@orderofmercy.org. Web: www.orderofmercy.org. Rev. Joseph K. Horvath, O.de.M., Local Supvr.; Bro. Martin Jarocinski, O.de.M., Archivist/Vocational Asst. Order of the B.V.M. of Mercy (Mercedarian Friars)., Pre-Novitiate House of Studies for the Order. Total in Residence 4.

Order of Friars Minor of the Province of the Most Holy Name aka Holy Name Province The Franciscans, 1802 E. Hagert St., 19125. Tel: 215-423-2859; Fax: 215-423-3875. Revs. William DeBiase, O.F.M.; Michael A. Duffy, O.F.M.; Patrick Sieber, O.F.M.; Bros. Xavier de la Huerta, O.F.M.; Fred Dilger, O.F.M.; John Gill, O.F.M.

The Philadelphia Congregation of The Oratory of St. Philip Neri, 2321 Green St., 19130-3196. Tel: 215-765-4568; Fax: 215-765-4049. Very Rev. Georges G. Thiers, C.O., Provost; Revs. Paul C. Convery, C.O., Vicar; Philip G. Bochanski, C.O.; Brian R. Gaffney, C.O.

St. Pius X Residence, 10821 Knights Rd., 19154. Tel: 215-632-1300. Revs. Rene Barczak, O.F.M.; Carl Graczyk, O.F.M.; Francis Berna, O.F.M. Order of Friars Minor, Assumption B.V.M. Province.

The Brothers of the Christian Schools Jeremy House, 6633 Ardleigh St., 19119-3824. Tel: 215-843-1884; Fax: 215-843-1617. Bro. Richard Buccina, F.S.C., Dir. Professed Brothers 4; Postulants 3.

AUDUBON. *Christian Brothers (F.S.C.), St. Gabriel Hall Community*, 1350 Pawlings Rd., P.O. Box 7280, 19407-7280. Tel: 215-247-2776; 610-666-7970; Fax: 610-666-0743.

BENSALEM. *Congregation of the Holy Spirit*, Spiritan Hall, 2401 Bristol Pike, 19020. Tel: 215-638-0845; Fax: 215-639-5438. Email: jduaime@aol.com. Web: www.spiritans.org. Revs. Jeffrey T. Duaime, C.S.Sp., Supr.; Philip Agber, C.S.Sp.; Christopher H. McDermott, C.S.Sp., Bursar. Faculty Residence for Priests Teaching at Holy Ghost Preparatory School.

BRYN MAWR. *Augustinians Friars (O.S.A.)*, Our Mother of Good Counsel Community, 31 Pennswood Rd., 19010-3475. Tel: 610-525-0327; Fax: 610-525-0157. Email: frjmartinez@omgcparish.org. Revs. James E. Martinez, O.S.A., Prior & Contact Person; Anthony P. Burrascano, O.S.A.; Dennis M. McGowan, O.S.A.; Francis A. Sirolli, O.S.A.

DEVON. *Piarist Fathers (Order of the Pious Schools)*, 363 Valley Forge Rd., 19333. Tel: 610-688-7337; Fax: 610-688-2409. Email: coeurdeleon@earthlink.net; richardwyzykiewicz@yahoo.com. Total Staff 8; Total in Residence 7.

Priests who teach at Devon Preparatory School: Revs. James J. Shea, Sch.P., Headmaster; Richard S. Wyzykiewicz, Sch.P., Rector; Kalman Miskolczy, Sch.P.; Ferdinand Negrillos, Sch.P.; Geza Pazmany, Sch.P.; Bro. Nelson Henao, Sch.P.

DOYLESTOWN. *Pauline Fathers Monastery, Shrine of Our Lady of Czestochowa*, 654 Ferry Rd., P.O. Box 2049, 18901. Tel: 215-345-0607; Fax: 215-348-2148. Email: info@czestochowa.us. Web: www.czestochowa.us. Office: Tel: 215-345-0600; 215-345-0601; Fax: 215-348-2148. Very Rev. Joseph M. Olczak, O.S.P.P.E., Prov.; Revs. Michael Czyzewski, O.S.P.P.E.; Sebastian Hanks; Jan Kolmaga, O.S.P.P.E.; Marek Lacki, O.S.P.P.E., Prov. Sec.; Tadeusz Lizinczyk, Prior; Jerzy Maj, O.S.P.P.E., Prov. Vicar; Jan Michalak, O.S.P.P.E., Subprior; Bartlomiej Marciniak, O.S.P.P.E.; Lucius Tyrasinski, O.S.P.P.E.; Rafal Walczyk, O.S.P.P.E., Shrine Dir.; Stephen Z. Wozniczka, O.S.P.P.E.; Bros. Tomasz Fabiszewski, O.S.P.P.E.; Kazimierz Kania, O.S.P.P.E.; Bernard Kluczkowki, O.S.P.P.E.; Piotr Lisiecki, O.S.P.P.E.; Casimir Pasnik.

DREXEL HILL. *Bellesini Friary*, 403 N. Lansdowne Ave., 19026. Tel: 610-259-7750. Revs. Joseph L. Farrell, O.S.A.; Kevin DePrinzio, O.S.A.

FAIRLESS HILLS. *St. Anthony Friary*, 607 Wistar Rd., 19030. Tel: 215-943-4810; Fax: 215-943-7410. Revs. Fidelis F. Weber, T.O.R., Guidance Dir. & Local Min.; Neil Saller, T.O.R.; Bro. Lawrence Hilferty, T.O.R. Franciscan Friars T.O.R., Faculty residence for priests and brothers who teach at Conwell-Egan Catholic High School. Total in Residence 3.

LAVEROCK. *Brothers of Charity (F.C.)*, Triest Hall, 7720 Doe Ln., 19038. Tel: 215-887-6361; Fax: 215-877-6372. Email: jfitzfc@aol.com. Web: www.brothersofcharity.org. Total Staff 4; Total in Residence 8.

MALVERN. *Augustinian Friars (O.S.A.), Malvern Prep School, St. Augustine Friary at Albers Hall*, 418 S. Warren Ave., 19355-2707. Tel: 484-595-1194; Fax: 484-595-5765. Web: www.augustinians.org. Revs. Stephen J. Baker, O.S.A., Prior; Francis J. Caponi, O.S.A., Assoc. Prof., Villanova Univ.; Harry J. Erden, O.S.A., Campus Min.; Augustine M. Esposito, O.S.A., M.Div., M.A., Ph.D.; James R. Flynn, O.S.A., Headmaster; Thomas J. Meehan, O.S.A. Total in Residence 6; Students 610.

MERION STATION. *Jesuit Community at St. Joseph's University*, 261 City Ave., 19066. Tel: 610-660-1400; Fax: 610-664-6640. Email: vgenoves@stu.edu. Web: www.sju.edu/jesuits. *Loyola Center and Manresa Hall* Revs. Mark C. Aita, S.J., M.D.; Joseph M. Alminde, S.J.; Bruce M. Bidinger, S.J.; Edward C. Bradley, S.J.; Patrick P. Brannan, S.J.; Thomas J. Brennan, S.J.; Francis F. Burch, S.J.; William J. Byron, S.J.; Peter A. Clark, S.J.; Jerome B. Coll, S.J.; Robert S. Curry, S.J.; Sean T. Dempsey; James A. Devereux, S.J.; Paul A. Donovan, S.J.; Henry J. Erhart, S.J.; Philip A. Florio, S.J.; Vincent J. Genovesi, S.J., Rector; Thomas F. Gleeson, S.J., Min.; Edgar Graham, S.J.; Frederick A. Homann, S.J.; Edward A. Jarvis, S.J.; Albert H. Jenemann, S.J.; Daniel R.J. Joyce, S.J.; John J. Kelly, S.J.; Timothy R. Lannon, S.J., Pres.; Joseph L. Lombardi, S.J.; Richard G. Malloy, S.J.; Clarence A. Martin, S.J.; Thomas D. Masterson, S.J.; John J. Mawhinney, S.J.; John W. McDaniel, S.J.; Gerald J. McGlone, S.J.; Dennis E. McNally, S.J.; Joseph F. Monaghan, S.J.; James W. Moore, S.J.; Edward H. Nash, S.J.; Vincent M. O'Brien, S.J.; Eugene J. Power, S.J.; Nicholas J. Rashford, S.J.; Anthony P. Roberts, S.J.; Francis E. Skechus, S.J.; Herbert F. Smith, S.J.; Martin R. Tripole, S.J.; John Woodward, S.J.; Bros. John J. McLane, S.J.; Gerald E. Peltz, S.J.; William J. Sudzina, S.J.; Mr. Joseph A. Koczerz, S.J. Priests 50; Brothers 4; Jesuits 1. *St. Alphonsus House*, 5800 Overbrook Ave., 19131. Tel: 215-477-9220; Fax: 215-477-1519. Revs. Anthony J. Berret, S.J.; Joseph J. Feeney, S.J.; Joseph J. Godfrey, S.J.; James D. Redington, S.J.; Patrick H. Samway, S.J.; Bro. Lee S. Colombino, S.J. Priests 5.

Residing Elsewhere: Rev. Thomas F.X. Wheeler, S.J., Infirmary Chap., McAuley Convent, 517 Montgomery Ave., 19066-1296. Tel: 610-660-7841; Fax: 610-667-9680.

PAOLI. *Daylesford Abbey*, 220 S. Valley Rd., 19301-1900. Tel: 610-647-2530; Fax: 610-651-0219. Email: norbertines@daylesford.org. Web: www.daylesford.org. Revs. Ronald J. Rossi, O.Praem., Abbot; Richard J. Antonucci, O.Praem., Abbot; Very Rev. John Joseph Novielli, O.Praem., Dir. Devel. & Vocation; Revs. Steven J. Albero, O.Praem., Subprior; Joseph A. Serano, O.Praem., Treas.; Very Rev. Andrew D. Ciferni, O.Praem., Prior; Revs. Joseph P. McLaughlin, O.Praem.; Theodore J. Antry, O.Praem.; Maurice C. Avicolli, O.Praem.; Michael T. Collins, O.Praem.; Francis X. Cortese, O.Praem.; William R. Craig, O.Praem.; Paul J. DeAntoniis, O.Praem; William J. Kelly, O.Praem.; Blaise R. Krautsack, O.Praem.; Joseph C. Laenen, O.Praem.; David T. Lawlor, O.Praem.; Michael J. Lee, O.Praem.; Thomas O. Meulemans, O.Praem.; James C. Rodia, O.Praem.; Domenic A. Rossi, O.Praem.; Thomas J. Rossi, O.Praem.; Nicholas R. Terico, O.Praem.; Charles T. Urban, O.Praem.; John C. Zagarella, O.Praem.; Bros. Blase G. Corso, O.Praem.; Francis Danielski, O.Praem.; John B. Ginder, O.Praem.; A. Gerard Jordan, O.Praem.; Joseph P. Mulholland, O.Praem.; Frater Carl Braschoss, O.Praem. *Norbertine Fathers, Inc.* Priests 25; Brothers 6.

ROSEMONT. *Saxony Hall*, 110 Montrose Ave., 19010-1509. Tel: 215-327-9497; Fax: 610-520-4510. Revs. James J. McCartney, O.S.A., Prior Treas.; Christopher J. Brennen; Daniel E. Doyle, O.S.A.; Joseph Loya, O.S.A.; Gordon E. Marcellus, O.S.A.; William A. McGuire, O.S.A.; John J. McKenzie, O.S.A. Total in Residence 7.

SPRINGFIELD. *Servants of Charity (S.C.)* Don Guanella Village, Cardinal Krol Center, 1799 S. Sproul Rd., 19064. Tel: 610-543-3380; Fax: 610-544-1207. Email: fr.dweber@chs-adphila.org. Rev. Dennis M. Weber, Sd.C, Prov. Counselor/U.S. Rep. Total in Residence 6.

VILLANOVA. *St. Augustine Friary*, 214 Ashwood Rd., 19085. Tel: 610-527-0325; Fax: 610-527-0575. Revs. T. Shawn Tracy, O.S.A., Prior; Thomas R. Cook, O.S.A.; Edward Dixey, O.S.A.; Patrick F. Leonard, O.S.A.; Daniel J. McLaughlin, O.S.A.; Alfred E. Murphy, O.S.A.; James V. Vitali, O.S.A.; Bro. Jack D. Stagliano, O.S.A. Priests 7; Brothers 1.

Fray de Leon Community, Burns Hall - West Campus, Villanova University, 19085. Tel: 610-519-5020; Fax: 610-519-7479. Revs. Joseph S. Mostardi, O.S.A., Prior; David A. Cregan, O.S.A.; Peter M. Donohue, O.S.A.; Robert Hagan, O.S.A.; Bro. Michael Duffy, O.S.A. Augustinians. Total in Residence 4. P.O. Box 340, 19085. Tel: 610-527-3330, Ext. 279; Fax: 610-527-0618.

St. John Stone Friary, 37 Aldwyn Ln., 19085. Tel: 610-527-7925. Revs. John E. Deegan, O.S.A.; Arthur B. Chappell, O.S.A.; Kail C. Ellis, O.S.A., Prior; Michael J. Scanlon, O.S.A.

Provincial Offices of the Order of St. Augustine, Province of St. Thomas of Villanova, P.O. Box 340, 19085-0340. Tel: 610-527-3330; Fax: 610-520-0618. Email: secretary@augustinian.org. Web: www.augustinian.org. Very Rev. Donald F. Reilly, O.S.A., Prior Prov. Tel: 610-527-3330, Ext. 225; Revs. William A. McGuire, O.S.A., Treas. & Mission Procurator. Tel: 610-527-3330, Ext. 226; John J. Sheridan, O.S.A., Prov. Archivist. Tel: 610-527-3330, Ext. 247; John R. Flynn, O.S.A., Contact Person, Prov. Sec. Tel: 610-527-3330, Ext. 223; Anthony P. Burrascano, O.S.A., Mission Office. Tel: 610-527-3330, Ext. 238; Kevin M. DePrinzio, O.S.A., Dir. Vocations. Tel: 610-527-3330, Ext. 284; James D. Paradis, O.S.A., Dir. Ongoing Formation & Personnel. Tel: 610-527-3330, Ext. 233; Joseph S. Mostardi, O.S.A., Dir. Office of the Augustinian Volunteers. Tel: 610-527-3330, Ext. 279.

St. Thomas Monastery, 800 E. Lancaster Ave., 19085. Tel: 610-519-7500; Fax: 610-519-5040. Revs. John P. Betoni, O.S.A.; John E. Bresnahan, O.S.A.; Donald X. Burt, O.S.A.; Angus N. Carney, O.S.A.; Thomas J. Casey, O.S.A.; Harry A. Cassel, O.S.A. (Retired); Francis E. Chambers; William M. Cleary, O.S.A.; Russell J. DeSimone, O.S.A.; Edmund J. Dobbin, O.S.A.; Edward C. Doherty, O.S.A.; Edward E. Doran, O.S.A.; John M. Driscoll, O.S.A.; Joseph A. Duffey (Retired); John J. Farrell, O.S.A. (Retired); Francis A. Farsaci, O.S.A.; John J. Ferrence, O.S.A.; John J. Fitzgerald, O.S.A.; Dennis J. Gallagher, O.S.A.; James L. Galligan, O.S.A.; Francis X. Gallogly; Raymond E. Geisser; Anthony M. Genovese, O.S.A., Prior; Karl A. Gersbach, O.S.A.; Adrian Gilligan, O.S.A.; James G. Glennon, O.S.A.; Edward V. Griffin, O.S.A.; John J. Hagen, O.S.A.; Roger M. Hanouille, O.S.A.; John R. Havener; Joseph A. Jordan, O.S.A.; Cherubin F. Kerr, O.S.A.; Charles P. Laferty, O.S.A.; Martin S. Laird, O.S.A.; John F. Lipp, O.S.A.; George P. Magee, O.S.A.; Gary N. McCloskey, O.S.A.; Neil J. McGettigan, O.S.A.; William A. McGuire, O.S.A.; Robert F. Andrews, O.S.A.; Robert M. Burke, O.S.A.; Lee J. Makowski, O.S.A.; Daniel J. Menihane; Ralph J. Monteiro, O.S.A.; Thomas M. Murnane, O.S.A., Subprior; Robert J. Murray, O.S.A.; James L. Nolan, O.S.A.; Bernard J. O'Dowd, O.S.A.; Walter J. Quinn, O.S.A.; George F. Riley, O.S.A.; Joseph G. Ryan, O.S.A.; Augustus C. Sandmann, O.S.A.; Joseph C. Schnaubelt, O.S.A.; John J. Sheridan, O.S.A.; Martin L. Smith, O.S.A., Treas.; Stanley C. Smith, O.S.A.; Joseph A. Spinelli, O.S.A.; John P. Stack, O.S.A.; Robert E. Steinman, O.S.A.; Michael P. Sullivan, O.S.A. Total Staff 72; Total in Residence 60.

St. Thomas of Villanova Friary, 109 Willowburn Rd., 19085-1313. Tel: 610-527-0856; Fax: 610-527-8812. Very Rev. Donald F. Reilly, O.S.A., Prior Prov.; Revs. Richard G. Cannuli, O.S.A.; Joseph D. Calderone, O.S.A., Prior; Bro. Robert Thornton, O.S.A.

WYNDMOOR. *Christian Brothers (F.S.C.)*, LaSalle High School Community, 8605 Cheltenham Ave., 19038. Tel: 215-233-3030; Fax: 215-233-0297. Email: rieck@lschs.org. Web: www.lschs.org. Bro. James F. Rieck, F.S.C., Contact Person. Total in Residence 16.

Oblates of St. Francis de Sales (O.S.F.S.) Villa de Sales Oblate Residence, 8501 Flourtown Ave., 19038. Tel: 215-836-1472; Fax: 215-836-7213. Rev. Joseph F. Chorpenning, O.S.F.S., S.T.L., Ph.D., Religious Supr. & Contact Person. Total in Residence 9.

Villa de Sales Oblate Residence, 8501 Flourtown Ave., 19038. Tel: 215-836-1472; Fax: 215-836-7213. Revs. Joseph F. Chorpenning, O.S.F.S., S.T.L., Ph.D.; Gerald M. Dunne, O.S.F.S.; Charles F. Engelhardt, O.S.F.S.; Thomas P. Gallagher, O.S.F.S.; William A. Guerin, O.S.F.S.; Very Rev. Richard T. Reece, O.S.F.S.; Revs. Robert G. Reece, O.S.F.S.; Albert J. Smith, O.S.F.S.; Bro. Robert J. Drelich, O.S.F.S. Total in Residence 9.

[Z] CONVENTS AND RESIDENCES OF SISTERS

PHILADELPHIA. *Assumption Hall*, Sisters of St. Joseph, 8900 Norwood Ave., 19118-2711. Tel: 215-247-3665; 215-248-2564. Sr. Marjorie Lawless, S.S.J., Contact. Residence for Norwood-Fontbonne Academy Faculty. Total Staff 15.

Assumption House, 1001 S. 47th St., 19143. Tel: 215-386-5016; Fax: 215-386-1780. Email: rabowman227@juno.com. Sr. Clare Teresa, R.A.

Blessed Trinity Mother Missionary Cenacle, 3501 Solly Ave., 19136. Tel: 215-335-7550; Fax: 215-335-7559. Email: msbtphl@msbt.org. Web: msbt.org. Sisters Joan Marie Keller, M.S.B.T., Gen. Custodian; Ellen Kieran, M.S.B.T., Gen. Sec. Generalate, Novitiate and Candidacy of the Missionary Servants of the Most Blessed Trinity. Mother Boniface Center. Total Staff 25; Total in Residence 75.

Carmelite Monastery, 66th Ave. and Old York Rd., 19126. Tel: 215-424-6143; Fax: 215-424-6143. Sr. Barbara of the Holy Ghost, O.C.D., Prioress.

Congregation of the Sisters of St. Felix, St. Ignatius Convent, 4401 Haverford Ave., 19104. Tel: 215-222-2296; Fax: 215-222-3078. Sr. Mary Agatha Cebula, C.S.S.F., N.H.A., Local Min.

Daughters of Charity, 449 E. Locust Ave., 19144-1323. Tel: 215-438-3536; Fax: 215-438-5232. Email: philadtrs@aol.com. Web: dc-northeast.org. Sr. Patricia Evanick, D.C., Supr. Total in Residence 5.

Daughters of St. Paul Convent, 9610 Evans St., 19115. Tel: 215-969-5068. Email: philadelphia@paulinemedia.com. Web: www.pauline.org. Sr. Patricia Maresca, F.S.P., Supr. Sisters 5.

Emmaus Convent, 5358 Cedar Ave., 19143. Tel: 215-471-7260. Email: rsmemmaus@aol.com. Sisters of Mercy (R.S.M.). Total in Residence 3.

St. Francis Convent, 1727 S. 11th St., 19148. Tel: 215-463-7343. Email: gpfrancia@verizon.net. Residence of Sisters of St. Francis of Philadelphia employed at SS. John Neumann and Maria Goretti Catholic High School and Hallahan High School, St. Nicholas Elementary School, St. Thomas Aquinas Elementary School, Childrens Aid Society, University of Pennsylvania, Assisi House (Retirement).

Franciscan Sisters of Allegany (O.S.F.), 2622 Potter St., 19125. Tel: 215-739-6441; Fax: 215-739-5607.

Handmaids of the Sacred Heart of Jesus, 1242 S. Broad St., 19146-3119. Tel: 215-468-6368; Fax: 215-271-1488. Email: cbanh1@juno.com. Web: acjusa.org. Sr. Cam Banh, A.C.J., Supr. Total in Residence 4.

Hannah House, Sisters of St. Joseph, 2458 N. 16th St., 19132. Tel: 215-221-0211; Fax: 215-228-7070. Email: ginjenkins@verizon.net. Sr. Virginia Jenkins, S.S.J., Contact Person. Sisters 2.

Immaculate Heart Convent, 7310 Torresdale Ave., 19136. Tel: 215-332-8299; Fax: 215-332-6077. Email: ihc@comcast.net. Sr. Mary Theresa Flynn, I.H.M., Supr. Faculty Residence for Sisters, Servants of the Immaculate Heart of Mary, teaching at St. Hubert High School. Total in Residence 14.

Immaculate Heart Convent, 4904 Chestnut St., 19139. Tel: 215-474-8971. Sr. Mary K. Lydon, I.H.M., Supr. Faculty Residence for Sisters, Servants of the Immaculate Heart of Mary, who teach at West Philadelphia Catholic High School. Total Staff 3; Total in Residence 6.

St. Joseph Convent, 7300 Torresdale Ave., 19136. Tel: 215-338-4884. Email: ssjtorr@netcarrier.com. Faculty Residence for Sisters of St. Joseph, who teach at St. Martin of Tours, St. Hubert High School and, St. Vincent's Homes.

Little Sisters of the Poor, Holy Family Home, 5300 Chester Ave., 19143. Tel: 215-729-5153; Fax: 215-729-5158.

Little Workers of the Sacred Hearts, Sacred Hearts Convent, 160 Carpenter Ln., 19119-2563. Tel: 215-843-2266.

Mary Immaculate Convent, 1731 S. 11th St., 19148. Tel: 215-468-9133; Fax: 215-336-7463. Email: maryim1731@yahoo.com. Sr. Dorothy Mayer, I.H.M., Supr. Faculty Residence for Sisters, Servants of the Immaculate Heart of Mary, who teach at SS. John Neuman and Maria Goretti Catholic High School and John W. Hallahan High School. Total in Residence 15; Total Staff 15.

Medical Mission Sisters, North American Sector, 8400 Pine Rd., 19111. Tel: 215-742-6100; Fax: 215-342-3948. Email: mmsorg@medicalmissionsisters.org. Web: www.medicalmissionsisters.org. Sisters Rosemary Ryan, M.M.S., Sector Coord., SNA Coord. Mission; Frances Vaughan, M.M.S., SNA Coord. Devel.; Rose Kershbaumer, M.M.S., SNA Coord. Sisters. Sisters in Sector 116; Total in Residence 74.

St. Michael Hall, 9001 Germantown Ave., 19118. Tel: 215-247-3698. Email: SSJsmhall@aol.com. Faculty Residence for Sisters of St. Joseph who staff Chestnut Hill College. Total in Residence 11.

Monastery of the Visitation Nuns, 5820 City Ave., 19131-1295. Tel: 215-473-5888; Fax: 215-473-7512. Email: viznunphil@aol.com. Sr. Antoinette Marie Walker, V.H.M., Supr. Jesuit priests from St. Joseph's University, Chaplains. Total Staff 6; Total in Residence 6.

Mother of Peace House, 2622 Potter St., 19125. Tel: 215-739-6441; Fax: 215-739-5607. Franciscan Sisters of Allegany.

Mt. St. Joseph Convent, 9701 Germantown Ave., 19118-2694. Tel: 215-248-7200; Fax: 215-248-7277. Email: msjc@ssjphila.org. Web: ssjphila.org. Sr. Anne Patricia Myers, S.S.J., Congregational Pres. Motherhouse of the Sisters of St. Joseph of Chestnut Hill, Philadelphia.

Nazareth Convent, Religious Sisters of Mercy, 6369 Woodbine Ave., 19151. Tel: 215-477-3022. Sr. Kathleen Lyons, R.S.M., Contact Person & Treas.

Peace Hermitage, 8400 Pine Rd., 19111. Tel: 215-342-2039; 215-742-6100; Fax: 215-342-3948. Society of Catholic Medical Missionaries (Medical Mission Sisters). Total in Residence 2.

School Sisters of Notre Dame, Visitation Community, 3978 Constance Rd., 19114. Tel: 215-824-0754. Email: sisterbernie@yahoo.com. Web: www.ssnd.org. Sr. Bernadette Marie Ravenstahl, S.S.N.D., Contact.

Sister Servants of the Holy Spirit of Perpetual Adoration (S.Sp.S.A.P.), Convent of Divine Love, 2212 Green St., 19130. Tel: 215-567-0123; Fax: 215-569-8314. Email: conventofdivinelove@verizon.net. Web: www.adorationsisters.org. Sr. Mary Caritas, S.Sp.S.A.P., Supr.; Rev. Philip G. Bochanski, C.O., Chap.

Sisters of St. Francis of Philadelphia, Santa Chiara, 2238 S. 12th St., 19148. Tel: 215-465-2227. Email: RRBARBAOSF@aol.com. Sisters Residence for those who work at Our Lady of Angels Convent, Aston and Epiphany Church.

Sisters of St. Francis of Philadelphia, Canticle House, 1624 Mifflin St., 19145. Tel: 215-551-2586. Web: www.osfphila.org.

Sisters of St. Joseph, Neumann House, 58 E. Northwestern Ave., 19118. Tel: 215-248-7200; Fax: 215-248-7277. Email: msjc@ssjphila.org. Web: ssjphila.org. Total in Residence 4.

Sisters of St. Joseph of Philadelphia, Immaculate Heart of Mary Convent, 823 Cathedral Rd., 19128. Tel: 215-482-8540. Sisters in Residence 5.

Sisters of St. Joseph of Philadelphia Convent, 6818 Cresheim Rd., 19119. Tel: 215-438-7515. Total in Residence 9.

Sisters of St. Joseph of Philadelphia Elizabeth House, 138 W. Carpenter Ln., 19119-2563. Tel: 215-849-3362. Sr. Mary Elizabeth Hamm, S.S.J., Contact Person.

Sisters of St. Joseph of Philadelphia, Fournier Community, Administration, 9701 Germantown Ave., 19118-2694. Tel: 215-248-7200; Fax: 215-248-7277. Email: msjc@ssjphila.org. Web: ssjphila.org. Sr. Mary Theresa Shevland, Contact Person. Sisters 3.

Sisters of the Good Shepherd, 5356 Chew Ave., 19138. Tel: 215-843-9411; Fax: 215-843-3141. Email: srnora@coraservices.org. Neighborhood ministry, mediation program.

Sisters of the Holy Child, 2362 E. York St., 19125-3029. Tel: 215-423-9514.

Sisters of the Holy Family of Nazareth, 4001 Grant Ave., 19114. Tel: 215-268-1050; Fax: 215-268-1075. Web: nazarethcsfn.org. Sr. Sally Marie Kiepura, C.S.F.N., Prov. Supr.

Sisters of the Holy Family of Nazareth, 9801 Frankford Ave., 19114. Tel: 267-341-3735; Fax: 267-341-3702.

Sisters of the Holy Family of Nazareth, Jesus of Nazareth Convent (aka Mount Nazareth), 2755 Holme Ave., 19152. Tel: 215-338-8992; Fax: 215-338-8752. Sr. Regina Wieczezynski, Supr. Staff 22; Total in Residence 33.

Sisters of the Holy Family of Nazareth, Infant Jesus Convent, 2723 Holme Ave., 19152-2015. Tel: 215-335-6380; Fax: 215-335-3764. Email: nazcon@aol.com. Web: www.csfn.org. Total in Residence 26.

Sisters of the Holy Redeemer, Angelus Community, 705 Medary Ave., 19126. Tel: 215-276-2187; Fax: 215-914-4111. Email: sranita@holyredeemer.com. Web: www.sistersholyredeemer.org. Total in Residence 3.

ARDMORE. *Missionary Sisters of the Holy Rosary (M.S.H.R.)*, 205 Cricket Ave., 19003. Tel: 610-896-1786. Web: holyrosarymissionarysisters.org. Total in Residence 3.

ASTON. *Anna Bachmann House*, 606 S. Convent Rd., 19014. Tel: 610-558-3240. Web: www.osfphila.org. Sr. Eileen Walsh, O.S.F., Contact Person.

Convent of Our Lady of Angels, 609 S. Convent Rd., 19014. Tel: 610-459-4125; Fax: 610-459-0195. Email: cljones@osfphila.org. Web: www.osfphila.org. Sr. Esther Anderson, Congregational Min. Motherhouse of the Sisters of St. Francis of Philadelphia.

Mt. Alvernia Convent, 602A S. Convent Rd., 19014. Tel: 610-459-5989. Email: hherberich@comcast.net. Sr. Helen St. Paul, O.S.F., Contact Person. Sisters of St. Francis of Philadelphia. Total in Residence 2.

Sisters of St. Francis, 607 S. Convent Rd., 19014. Tel: 610-358-5417. Email: cwright@osfphila.org. Web: www.osfphila.org. Sr. Donna Desien, O.S.F., Congregational Sec.

Sisters of St. Francis of Philadelphia, 6 Red Hill Rd., 19014. Tel: 610-459-1113.

Sisters of St. Francis of Philadelphia, Our Lady of the Valley Convent, 10 Red Hill Rd., 19014-1119. Tel: 610-358-4008. Web: www.osfphila.org. Sr. Ann David Strohminger, O.S.F., Contact. Total in Residence 4.

Sisters of St. Francis of Philadelphia, Assisi House, 600 Red Hill Rd., 19014. Tel: 610-459-8990; Fax: 610-558-5344. Email: jlamanna@osfphila.org. Web: www.osfphila.org. Total in Residence 86; Total Staff 207.

Sisters of St. Francis of Philadelphia, Portiuncula Convent, 610 Red Hill Rd., 19014. Tel: 610-558-5350; Fax: 610-558-5344. Email: portiuncula@hotmail.com. Sisters 10.

Sisters of St. Francis of Philadelphia (Assumption Convent), Assumption Convent, 609 S. Convent Rd., 19014. Tel: 610-558-7672. Web: www.osfphila.org. Sr. Donna Desien, O.S.F., Congregational Sec. Total in Residence 5.

Sisters of St. Francis of Philadelphia (Franciscan Formation House), 609 S. Convent Rd., 19014. Tel: 610-558-7731. Web: www.osfphila.org. Sr. Donna Desien, O.S.F., Congregational Sec. Total in Residence 4.

Sisters of St. Francis of Philadelphia, TAU Convent, 4000 Concord Rd., 19014. Tel: 610-494-7322. Sr. Helen Budzik, O.S.F., Contact. Total in Residence 4.

BENSALEM. *St. Michael Hall*, 1663 Bristol Pike, 19020. Tel: 215-244-9900; 215-638-0865; Fax: 215-244-6222. Email: stmichhall@aol.com.

Sisters of the Blessed Sacrament The Infirmary of the Sisters of the Blessed Sacrament.

Sisters of the Blessed Sacrament, 1663 Bristol Pike, 19020-5702. Tel: 215-244-9900; Fax: 215-244-8174. Web: www.katharinedrexel.org. Sr. Patricia Suchalski, S.B.S., Pres.

Sisters of the Blessed Sacrament for Indians and Colored People, Motherhouse of the Sisters of the Blessed Sacrament for Indians and Colored People. Total in Residence 80; Total Staff 80.

BROOKHAVEN. *Sisters of St. Francis of Philadelphia, Claddagh House*, 160 Meadowbrook Ln., 19015. Tel: 610-490-5367. Email: mirmurray@comcast.net. Web: www.osfphila.org. Total in Residence 3.

BRYN MAWR. *Missionary Sisters of the Holy Rosary*, 741 Polo Rd., 19010. Tel: 610-520-1974; Fax: 610-520-2002. Email: helenamcneill@comcast.net. Web: www.holyrosarymissionarysisters.com. Total in Residence 3.

Society of the Holy Child Jesus, 700 Old Lancaster Rd., 19010. Tel: 610-527-5076; Fax: 610-527-4671. Email: apenrose@juno.com. Retirement Residence for Sisters of the Holy Child Jesus. Total in Residence 5.

CHELTENHAM. *Sisters of the Good Shepherd (Contemplative)*, 7633 Waters Rd., 19012. Tel: 215-782-8627; Fax: 215-782-8741. Sr. Martha Cardenas, Supr. Total in Residence 9.

CHESTER. *Bernardine Sisters of St. Francis*, Sacred Heart Convent, 2601 W. Tenth St., 19013. Tel: 610-497-9788; Fax: 610-497-3659. Email: conlab1@juno.com. Total in Residence 11.

Missionaries of Charity, Gift of Mary, 2714 W. 9th St., 19013. Tel: 610-494-7424. Sr. M. Consuela, M.C., Supr. Total Assisted 300; Total Staff 5.

DREXEL HILL. *St. Joseph Convent*, 435 N. Lansdowne Ave., 19026-1190. Tel: 610-622-0440; Fax: 610-259-5606. Email: sosjdrexelhill@yahoo.com. Faculty residence for Sisters of St. Joseph who teach at Msgr. Bonner and Archbishop Prendergast Catholic High School and West Philadelphia Catholic High School.

ERDENHEIM. *Sisters of St. Joseph of Philadelphia*, Divine Shepherd Convent, 927 Bethlehem Pike, 19038. Tel: 215-836-2082. Total in Residence 6.

Sisters of St. Joseph of Philadelphia, Nazareth House, 931 Bethlehem Pike, 19038. Tel: 215-836-2613. Total in Residence 5.

ELVERSON. *Daughters of St. Mary of Providence (D.S.M.P.)*, 227 Isabella Rd., 19520. Tel: 610-942-4166; Fax: 610-942-4259. Email: stmaryofprov@comcast.net. Web: stmaryofprov-pa.org. Sr. Noreen Franzina, D.S.M.P., Supr. Total in Residence 4; Total Staff 17.

ESSINGTON. *Bernardine Sisters of St. Francis*, St. Margaret Mary Convent, 546 Wanamaker Ave., 19029. Tel: 610-521-3286; Fax: 610-521-3280. Email: jperose@aol.com.

FALLSINGTON. *Grey Nuns of the Sacred Heart, St. Joseph the Worker Convent*, 9168 New Falls Rd., 19054-1805. Tel: 215-269-9783. Total in Residence 5.

FLOURTOWN. *St. Rita Convent*, 1410 Bethlehem Pike, 19031. Tel: 215-836-1615. Email: smbi@verizon.net. Sisters Marianne Beatty, R.S.M., Admin.; Maureen B. McCann, R.S.M., Coord. Sisters of Mercy of the Americas. Total in Residence 2.

Sisters of St. Joseph of Philadelphia, Mt. St. Joseph Academy, 120 W. Wissahickon Ave., 19031-1922. Tel: 215-233-4368; Fax: 215-233-4734. Email: ssjmountcon@verizon.net. Total in Residence 14.

Sisters of St. Joseph of Philadelphia, St. Joseph Villa Staff Visitation Community, 110 W. Wissahickon Ave., 19031-1898. Tel: 215-836-4179; Fax: 215-248-7802. Email: visitationcommunity@msn.com. Total 11.

FOX CHASE MANOR. *Sisters of St. Basil the Great (O.S.B.M.)* Motherhouse of the Sisters of St. Basil., 710 Fox Chase Rd., 19046-4198. Tel: 215-663-9153; Fax: 215-379-4843. Email: province@stbasils.com. Web: www.stbasils.com. Sr. Laura Palka, O.S.B.M., Prov. Supr.

Basilian Spirituality Center, 710 Fox Chase Rd., Jenkintown, 19046-4198. Tel: 215-780-1227; Fax: 215-379-4843.

GLENSIDE. *Medical Mission Sisters* (Society of Catholic Medical Missionaries, Inc.), 15 E. Glenside Ave., 19038. Tel: 215-886-4036. Email: eunice@medicalmissionsisters.org. Web: medicalmissionsisters.org. Total in Residence 3.

GWYNEDD VALLEY. *Religious Sisters of Mercy - St. Joseph Convent*, 1349 Sumneytown Pike, P.O. Box 902, 19437-0902. Tel: 215-646-5259.

Religious Sisters of Mercy - Transfiguration Convent, 1325 Sumneytown Pike, P.O. Box 901, 19437-0901. Tel: 215-641-5512; Fax: 215-641-5509. Email: mcmahon.c@gmc.edu. Web: www.gmc.edu.

HAVERFORD. *Handmaids of the Sacred Heart of Jesus*, 616 Coopertown Rd., 19041. Tel: 610-642-5715;

Fax: 610-642-6788. Sr. Kathleenjoy Cooper, A.C.J., Local Coord.

HUNTINGDON VALLEY. *Sisters of the Holy Redeemer Provincialate*, 521 Moredon Rd., 19006. Tel: 215-914-4100; Fax: 215-914-4111; 215-914-4171. Email: amhaas@holyredeemer.com. Web: www.sistersholyredeemer.org. Sisters Anne Marie Haas, C.S.R., Prov. Supr.; Ellen M. Marvel, C.S.R., Formation Dir.; Revs. Dennis J.W. O'Donnell, Ph.D., Dir. Integrated Health Svcs.; Mark G. Swope, Chap. Holy Redeemer Health System. Total in Residence 16.

IMMACULATA. *Sisters, Servants of the Immaculate Heart of Mary (I.H.M.)*, Pacis Hall, P.O. Box 700, 19345-0700. Tel: 610-889-1668; Fax: 610-695-0691 (Camilla Hall). Email: pacishall03@netzero.net. Sr. Maria Patris Hogan, I.H.M., Supr. Total in Residence 35.

Sisters, Servants of the Immaculate Heart of Mary (I.H.M.), 1145 King Rd., P.O. Box 400, 19345-0400. Tel: 610-647-4400, Ext. 3660; Fax: 610-640-5890. Email: gillet@immaculata.edu. Web: www.ihmimmaculata.org. Total in Residence 48.

Sisters, Servants of the Immaculate Heart of Mary, (I.H.M.), King & Frazer Rds., P.O. Box 100, 19345. Tel: 610-644-1152; Fax: 610-695-0691. Email: ihmcamilla@worldnet.att.net.

Villa Maria House of Studies, 1140 King Rd., 19345-0200. Tel: 610-647-2160; Fax: 610-889-4874. Email: s.rita.lenihan@ihmimmaculata.org.

Villa Maria House of Studies, Motherhouse of the Sisters, Servants of the Immaculate Heart of Mary, Ministry in the field of Academic Education at all levels, Congregation Retirement and Health Care Center, Pastoral Ministry, Diocesan and Parish Administration, Literary Center, Spirituality Center, Directors of Religious Education, Guidance/Counseling, Ministry to Hispanics. Total in Congregation 904.

JENKINTOWN. *Sisters of the Holy Redeemer*, St. Elizabeth Convent, 615 Fox Chase Rd., 19046. Tel: 215-379-0112; Fax: 215-914-4111. Email: sranita@holyredeemer.com. Web: www.sistersholyredeemer.org. Total in Residence 2.

LANGHORNE. *Monastery of St. Clare, Poor Clares*, 1271 Langhorne-Newtown Rd., 19047-1297. Tel: 215-968-5775; Fax: 215-968-6254. Email: stclare@poorclarepa.org. Web: www.poorclarepa.org. Cloistered Contemplative Nuns., Prayer and Altar Bread Ministry.

San Damiano Convent, 104 Alberts Way, 19047. Tel: 215-860-7185.

Sisters of St. Francis of Philadelphia Total in Residence 4.

Sisters of St. Francis of Philadelphia, St. Mary Medical Center Convent, 1207 Langhorne-Newton Rd., 19047-1233. Tel: 215-757-9494. Total in Residence 8.

Sisters of St. Francis of Philadelphia, Franciscan Residence, 113 Alberts Way, 19047. Tel: 215-860-1059. Sisters serving at St. Mary Medical Center.

LANSDALE. *Religious of the Assumption, Assumption Convent*, 506 Crestview Rd., 19446. Tel: 215-362-6296; 215-368-4427; Fax: 215-368-4427. Email: ralansdale@verizon.net.

MALVERN. *Villa Maria Academy Convent*, 370 Old Lincoln Hwy., 19355. Tel: 610-647-4878; Fax: 610-644-2866. Email: info@vmahs.org. Web: www.vmahs.org. Sisters, Servants of the Immaculate Heart of Mary (I.H.M.). Total in Residence 13.

MEADOWBROOK. *Sisters of the Holy Redeemer*, Emmanuel Convent, 1616 Huntingdon Pike, 19046. Tel: 215-938-5650; Fax: 215-914-4111. Email: snicklaus@holyredeemer.com. Web: www.sistersholyredeemer.org. Total in Residence 4.

MERION. *Sisters of Mercy of the Americas, Mid-Atlantic Community, Sisters of Mercy Convent*, 515 Montgomery Ave., Merion Station, 19066. Tel: 610-664-6650; Fax: 610-664-3429. Email: MFK@mercymidatlantic.org. Web: www.sistersofmercymerion.org. Sisters Christine McCann, R.S.M., Pres.; Marian Francis Kelly, R.S.M., Local Coord. Sisters 86.

Sisters of Mercy of the Americas, Mid-Atlantic Community, St. Anne Convent, 276 Meeting House Ln., Merion Station, 19066. Tel: 610-667-4531. Web: www.mercymidatlantic.org.

Sisters of Mercy of the Americas, Mid-Atlantic Community, Inc., 515 Montgomery Ave., Merion Station, 19066. Tel: 610-664-6650; Fax: 610-664-3429. Web: www.mercymidatlantic.org. Sisters Christine McCann, R.S.M., Pres.; Carol Conly, R.S.M., Leadership Team; Catherine McGroarty, R.S.M., Leadership Team; Honora Nicholson, R.S.M., Leadership Team; Patricia Vetrano, R.S.M., Leadership Team; Mary Waters, R.S.M., Leadership Team. As of January 1, 2007 the Sisters of Mercy of the Americas, Regional Communities of Brooklyn, Dallas, Hartsdale, Merion and Watchung merged to create the Sisters of Mercy of the Americas, Mid-Atlantic Community, Inc. Sisters 1,071.

MORTON. *Sisters of St. Francis of Philadelphia (O.S.F.)*, 2130 Franklin Ave., Ct. No. 3, 19070-1217. Tel: 610-543-0186. Email: aboss@osfphila.org. Total in Residence 6; Total Staff 6.

NEWTOWN. *Grey Nuns of the Sacred Heart*, 4 Stockton Ct., 18940. Tel: 215-968-0735. Email: pgearygnsh@aol.com. Sisters Jean Liston, G.N.S.H.; Patricia Geary, G.N.S.H. Total in Residence 2.

NORRISTOWN. *Immaculate Heart Convent*, 1834 Arch St., 19401. Tel: 610-279-2616. Email: cnews1834@aol.com. Sr. Ann Raymond Welte, I.H.M, Supr. Faculty Residence for Sisters, Servants of the Immaculate Heart of Mary, who teach at Kennedy-Kenrick Catholic High School.

Missionaries of Charity, 630 DeKalb St., 19401-3944. Tel: 610-277-5962. Sr. M. Noreen, M.C., Supr. Services include Food Distribution and Emergency Night Shelter. Sisters 5.

RADNOR. *Armenian Sisters of the Immaculate Conception*, 440 Upper Gulph Rd., 19087. Tel: 610-688-9360; Fax: 610-687-2430. Email: asaphila@aol.com. Web: www.asaphila.org. Sr. Louisa Kassarjian, Supr. Total in Residence 2.

Missionary Sisters of the Sacred Heart of Jesus (Cabrini Sisters), Cabrini College Convent Gatehouse, 610 King of Prussia Rd., 19807-3698. Tel: 610-995-1210; Fax: 610-995-1210. Email: vandusen49@aol.com. Web: www.mothercabrini.org. Total in Residence 2.

ROSEMONT. *American Province Archives, Sisters of the Holy Child Jesus*, 1308 Wendover Rd., 19010. Tel: 610-525-8951; Fax: 610-525-8952. Email: hmayer@shcj.org. Web: www.shcj.org. Sr. Helena Mayer, S.H.C.J., Archivist.

Holy Child Center, 1341 Montgomery Ave., 19010. Tel: 610-525-9900; Fax: 610-527-2428. Email: mbryan@shcj.org. Web: www.shcj.org. Total in Residence 30; Total Staff 53.

Sisters of the Holy Child Jesus (S.H.C.J.), Gracemere Convent, 1316 Wendover Rd., 19010. Tel: 610-525-5601. Total in Residence 5.

Society of the Holy Child Jesus, Provincial Office, 1341 MontgomeryAve., 19010-1628. Tel: 610-626-1400; Fax: 610-525-2919. Email: hmcdonald@shcj.org. Web: www.shcj.org. Sr. Helen T. McDonald, S.H.C.J., Prov. Leader.

Society of the Holy Child Jesus American Province, Inc.

SPRINGFIELD. *St. Anthony Convent*, 1715 S. Sproul Rd., 19064. Tel: 610-544-4066. Residence for Sisters of St. Francis of Philadelphia who serve in various ministries of the Archdiocese. Total Staff 4; Total in Residence 4.

Immaculate Heart of Mary Convent, 1725 S. Sproul Rd., 19064. Tel: 610-544-0275. Email: ihspringfield@hotmail.com. Sr. Georgine Marie Williamson, I.H.M., Supr. Faculty Residence for Sisters, Servants of the Immaculate Heart of Mary, who teach in Cardinal O'Hara High School and Msgr. Bonner and Archbishop Prendergast High School.

St. Joseph Convent, 1705 S. Sproul Rd., 19064. Tel: 610-544-4198. Email: ssjoh@nni.com. Sr. Mary Beth Kratzinger, S.S.J. Sisters of St. Joseph Faculty House, Cardinal O'Hara High School. Total in Residence 9.

Our Lady of Mercy Convent, 1735 S. Sproul Rd., 19064. Tel: 610-544-0238. Faculty Residence for Sisters of Mercy who teach in Cardinal O'Hara and Mercy Vocational High Schools and who serve in other various ministries.

STRAFFORD. *Our Lady of the Assumption Convent*, 139 Fairfield Ln., 19087. Tel: 610-688-7889. Email: olaihm@comcast.net. Sr. Marie Jerome McHale, I.H.M., Supr. Sisters, Servants of the Immaculate Heart of Mary. Total in Residence 6.

UPPER DARBY. *Dominican Sisters Administrative Offices, Dominican Congregation of St. Catherine de Ricci*, 131 Copley Rd., 19082. Email: cgaekeop@verizon.net. Web: www.elkinsparkop.org. Sr. Carolyn Krebs, O.P., Pres.

WARMINSTER. *Sisters of St. Joseph of Philadelphia*, Nativity of Our Lord Convent, 605 W. Street Rd., 18974. Tel: 215-672-0147; Fax: 215-675-9413. Residence of Sisters St. Joseph.

WYNCOTE. *Handmaids of the Sacred Heart of Jesus Provincialate*, 2025 Church Rd., 19095. Tel: 215-576-6250; Fax: 215-576-8052. Email: mgillespie@ancillae.org. Web: www.ancillae.org. Sisters Dorothy Beck, A.C.J., Prov. Supr.; Maureen Gillespie, A.C.J., Local Supr. Total in Residence 10.

WYNNEWOOD. *Sisters of the Holy Child Jesus (S.H.C.J.)*, Connell House, 105 Old Forest Rd., 19096. Tel: 610-649-8462. Web: www.shcj.org. Total in Residence 3.

YARDLEY. *Motherhouse of the Grey Nuns of the Sacred Heart*, 1750 Quarry Rd., 19067-3998. Tel: 215-968-4236; Fax: 215-968-6656. Email: efahey@greynun.org. Web: greynun.org. Sisters Julia C. Lanigan, Pres.; Elaine Fahey, G.N.S.H., Coord., Motherhouse Community. Total in Residence 49.

[AA] RETREAT HOUSES

PHILADELPHIA. *Marianist Province of the United States dba NACMS* 1341 N. Delaware Ave., Ste. 406, 19125-4300. Tel: 215-634-4116; Fax: 215-634-4955. Email: mwyman@sm-usa.org. Web: www.nacms.org. The Marianist Center is committed to the spirit of Mary. This spirit mission fosters spiritual growth and formation, the building of lay faith/action communities and social justice according to the unique gifts of the Marianist tradition. Programs offered in Spirituality, Mary & Community Building for groups, staff, faculty, and parishes, as well as special day long programs specially designed for families. Total Staff 3; Total Assisted 600.

Mother Boniface Center, 3501 Solly Ave., 19136. Tel: 215-335-7541; Fax: 215-335-7541. Email: mbcretreat@msbt.org. Sponsored by Missionary Servants of the Most Blessed Trinity. Mid-week and weekend programs; retreats, days of recollection, scripture study, meetings, workshops and hosting programs. Capacity 57; Total Staff 6; Total in Residence 3.

ASTON. *Clare House*, 608 B. Legion Rd., 19014. Tel: 610-459-4077; Fax: 610-558-5377. Email: fsc@osfphila.org. Web: www.fscaston.org. Sr. Christa Thompson, O.S.F. Directed and Private Retreats. 5 Hermitages on property also. Staffed by Sisters of St. Francis of Philadelphia. Capacity 6; Total Staff 2; Total Guests 441; Total Guests at Hermitages 232.

Franciscan Spiritual Center, 609 S. Convent Rd., 19014. Tel: 610-558-6152; Fax: 610-558-5377. Email: fsc@osfphila.org. Web: www.fscaston.org. Sr. Christa Marie Thompson, O.S.F., Dir. Private, directed and group retreats. Spiritual, human development and holistic programs. Staffed by the Sisters of St. Francis Philadelphia.

DOYLESTOWN. *Shrine of Our Lady of Czestochowa*, 654 Ferry Rd., P.O. Box 2049, 18901. Tel: 215-345-0600; 215-345-0601; Fax: 215-348-2148. Email: info@czestochowa.us. Web: czestochowa.us.

HAVERFORD. *Saint Raphaela Center*, 616 Coopertown Rd., 19041. Tel: 610-642-5715; Fax: 610-642-6788. Email: acjhaverford1@aol.com. Web: straphaelacenter.org. Sr. Margaret Scott, A.C.J., Local Supr.

MALVERN. *St. Joseph's-in-the-Hills* (The Malvern Retreat House), 315 S. Warren Ave., P.O. Box 315, 19355-0315. Tel: 610-644-0400; Fax: 610-644-4363. Email: mail@malvernretreat.com. Web: malvernretreat.com. Rev. Gregory J. Hickey, M.A. Tel: 610-644-0400, Ext. 28; James A. Fitzsimmons, Pres.; Francis J. Marx, Chm. Owned and Operated by Catholic Laity since 1921, we serve the spiritual needs of lay men and women of all ages, clergy and religious of many denominations and provide a place of peaceful hospitality. Annual Retreatants over 21,000; Private Rooms 350.

[BB] NEWMAN APOSTOLATE

PHILADELPHIA. *Newman Apostolate for Archdiocese of Philadelphia* 222 N. 17th St., 19103. Tel: 215-587-4544; Fax: 215-964-1749. Email: frjames@adphila.org. Web: www.archdiocese-phl.org/offices/na.htm. Rev. John J. Ames, S.T.D., M.A., M.Div., Deputy Sec.

Full Time Chaplaincies:

University of Pennsylvania Newman Hall, 3720 Chestnut St., 19104-6189. Tel: 215-898-7575; Fax: 215-386-5899. Email: pflorio@newman.upenn.edu. Web: www.newman.upenn.edu. Rev. Philip A. Florio, S.J., Newman Chap.

Drexel University Newman Center, 30 S. 33rd St., 19104-2509. Tel: 215-590-8760; Fax: 215-587-8634. Email: frvinmorabito@gmail.com. Web: www.drexel.edu/newmancenter. Rev. Vincent R. Morabito, M.Div., Chap.

Temple University Newman Center, 2129 N. Broad St., 19122-1193. Tel: 215-232-3779; Fax: 215-235-7302. Email: shaun.mahoney@temple.edu. Web: www.templenewmancenter.org. Rev. Shaun L. Mahoney, S.T.D., Chap.; Sr. Helen Victor, S.S.J., Asst. to Chap.

West Chester University Newman Center, 409 Trinity Dr., West Chester, 19382-5362. Tel: 610-436-0891; Fax: 610-436-6247. Email: fathernordeman@yahoo.com. Web: www.wcunewman.org. Rev. John J. Nordeman, M.A., Chap.; Sarah Bacza, Asst. Dir.

Tri-College Newman Cluster-Bryn Mawr, Haverford and Swarthmore Colleges St. Anastasia, 3301

West Chester Pike, Newtown Square, 19073. Tel: 610-328-8578; Fax: 610-356-8332. Email: ewindha1@swarthmore.edu. Rev. Edward A. Windhaus, M.A., M.Div., Chap.

Part-time Chaplaincies:

Tenet Hahnemann (Center City Campus) Tel: 215-561-1313. Chaplaincy Vacant.

MCP Medical College of Pennsylvania (East Falls Campus) St. Bridget Church, 3667 Midvale Ave., 19129-1712. Tel: 215-844-4126.

Warminster Hospital St. John Bosco Church, 235 East County Line Rd., Hatboro, 19040-1298. Tel: 215-672-7280.

Moss Rehab Einstein at Elkins Park St. James Church, 8320 Brookside Dr., Elkins Park, 19027. Tel: 215-635-6210. Rev. Raymond J. Himsworth, Chap.

Arcadia University St. Luke the Evangelist Church, 2316 Fairhill Ave., Glenside, 19038-4107. Tel: 215-572-0128. Rev. Msgr. J. Michael Flood, Chap.

Bucks County Community College St. Andrew Church, 81 Swamp Rd., Newtown, 18940. Tel: 215-968-2262.

Cheney University Tel: 610-399-2353. Chaplaincy Vacant.

Community College of Philadelphia 19130. Chaplaincy Vacant.

Delaware County Community College St. Anastasia Church, 3301 W. Chester Pk., Newtown Square, 19073. Tel: 610-356-3303; 610-359-5206. Chaplaincy Vacant.

Delaware County Community College Math Science Dept., Media, 19063. Tel: 610-359-5206.

St. Anastasia Church 3301 West Chester Pike, Newtown Square, 19073. Tel: 610-356-1613; 610-356-3303; Fax: 610-356-8332.

Delaware Valley College of Science and Agriculture St. Jude Church, 321 W. Butler Ave., Chalfont, 18914-2329. Tel: 215-822-0179; Fax: 215-822-0638. Rev. James B. McCoy.

Harcum Junior College Our Mother of Good Counsel, 31 Pennswood Rd., Bryn Mawr, 19010. Tel: 610-526-6050. Sharon Watson, Dean of Student Affairs.

Harcum College , Chaplaincy Vacant.

Haverford College , Chaplaincy Vacant

Thomas Jefferson University , Chaplaincy Vacant.

Lincoln University Sacred Heart Church, 101 Church Rd., Oxford, 19363. Tel: 610-932-5040. Rev. John F. Hummell, Ed.D., Chap.

Montgomery County Community College St. Helena Church, P.O. Box 5085, Center Square, 19422. Tel: 610-275-7711. Chaplaincy Vacant.

Pennsylvania State University-Abington , Chaplaincy Vacant.

Pennsylvania State University - Ogontz Campus Our Lady Help of Christians, 1500 Marian Rd., Abington, 19001. Tel: 215-886-3456.

Pennsylvania State University - Delaware County Campus St. Francis de Sales Church, 33 New Rd., Box 97, Lenni, 19062. Tel: 610-459-2203.

Pennsylvania State University-Great Valley Campus 19104. Chaplaincy Vacant

Philadelphia College of Pharmacy and Science St. Francis de Sales Church, 4625 Springfield Ave., 19143. Tel: 215-222-5819.

Philadelphia College of Textiles and Science St. Bridget Church, 3667 Midvale Ave., 19129-1712. Tel: 215-844-4126.

Philadelphia University St. Bridget Church, 3667 Midvale Ave., 19129-1712. Tel: 215-844-4126.

Roxborough Memorial School of Nursing St. John the Baptist, 146 Rector St., 19107. Tel: 215-482-4600.

Temple University, Ambler Campus St. Alphonsus Church, 33 Conwell Dr., Maple Glen, 19002. Tel: 215-646-4600; Fax: 215-646-0180. Web: www.libertynet.org/~tunewman.

University of the Arts Assoc. Dean's Office, Broad and Pine Sts., 19102. Tel: 215-875-2236. Chaplaincy Vacant.

St. John the Evangelist Church 21 S. 13th St., 19107. Tel: 215-563-4145. Dr. Annelte DiMedio, Ph.D., Contact.

University of the Sciences in Philadelphia 600 S. 43rd St., 19104. Tel: 215-596-8800. Rev. Zachary W. Navit, M.A., M.Div., Chap., St. Francis de Sales.

Ursinus College St. Eleanor Church, 647 Locust St., Collegeville, 19426-2541. Tel: 610-489-1647; Fax: 610-489-7469. Rev. Msgr. Patrick E. Sweeney, Chap.

Widener University Blessed Katherine Drexel Church, 20th and Providence Ave., Chester, 19013-5695. Tel: 610-872-0545. Rev. Msgr. Joseph C. McLoone, M.A., Chap., St. Katharine Drexel.

[CC] MISCELLANEOUS LISTINGS

PHILADELPHIA. *Apostleship of Prayer*, St. Joseph's University, 5600 City Ave., 19131. Tel: 610-660-1400; Fax: 610-664-6640. Rev. Patrick H. Samway, S.J., Contact.

Br. Rousseau Academy, 7201 Milnor St., 19135. Tel: 215-624-5600; Fax: 215-624-3100. Larry Patrick, M.P.A., Dir.

Catholic Clinical Consultants, 222 N. 17th St., 19103-1299. Tel: 610-269-2600. Rev. Msgr. Michael T. McCulken, Pres.

Catholic Health Care Services, 222 N. 17th St., 19103. Tel: 215-587-3663; Fax: 215-587-3773. Web: www.catholichealthcareservices.org.

Catholic Heritage Center, c/o Archdiocese of Philadelphia, 222 N. 17th St., 19103-1299. The Catholic Heritage Center, a proposed state-of-the-art, multi-purpose facility is owned by the Archdiocese of Philadelphia. It will include a museum featuring both permanent and temporary exhibits on Catholic history, heritage, art and culture, a research library and archives, an education resource center, and a gift shop. The center will offer school groups, families and other visitors an opportunity to encounter their Catholic heritage with an experience which is both educational and entertaining. Project is currently on hold.

Catholic Kolping Society, 1285 Southampton Rd., 19116. P.O. Box 52651, 19115. Tel: 215-676-8977. Email: phlkolping@aol.com. Web: www.kolpingphilly.com. Rev. Engelbert G. Michel, Praeses; Frank Staub, Pres.; Mr. Earl Asimos, Treas.

Catholic League For Persons With Disabilities, 11621 Banes St., 19116. Tel: 215-725-9746; 215-676-0394. Rev. Edmund J. Maher, Spiritual Dir. (Retired).

Catholics United for the Faith (St. John Neumann Philadelphia Area Chapter), 183 Hillcrest Ave., 19118. Tel: 215-247-2585; Fax: 215-247-2585. Email: annemwilson@yahoo.com. Mrs. Anne M. Wilson, Chm.

The Central Association of the Miraculous Medal, 475 E. Chelten Ave., 19144-5785. Tel: 215-848-1010; 800-523-3674; Fax: 215-848-1014. Email: lizanne@cammonline.org. Web: www.cammonline.org. Rev. Carl L. Pieber, C.M.; James Pando, Dir. Opers.

Change for Change aka Change for Global Change 9701 Germantown Ave., 19118-2694. Tel: 215-248-7220; Fax: 215-248-7277. Email: changeforglobalchange@earthlink.net. Change for Global Change exists to address the global problem of sustainability through education, donations and grants to not-for-profit organizations for projects to aid those who have little or no means to provide a sustainable life for themselves.

CORA Services, 8540 Verree Rd., 19111. Tel: 215-342-7660; 215-535-2957 (Neumann Center); Fax: 215-745-9857. Email: info@coraservices.org. Web: www.coraservices.org. James F. Harron, CEO.

CORA Services, Inc., Philadelphia, Pennsylvania, Services provided for children, families and teen pregnancy. Programs available: counseling, speech and language, remediation and GED, Early Childhood, Drug & Alcohol. Total Assisted 19,000; Total Staff 205.

CSFN Mission & Ministry, Inc., Sisters of the Holy Family of Nazareth, Holy Family Prov., 4001 Grant Ave., 19114. Tel: 215-268-1035; Fax: 215-268-1075. Email: slorth@att.net.

Daughters of St. Paul, 9171 A Roosevelt Blvd., 19114. Tel: 215-676-9494; Fax: 215-676-9928. Email: philadelphia@paulinemedia.org. Web: www.pauline.org. Sr. Patricia Maresca, F.S.P., Supr.

**DePaul, USA*, 5725 Sprague St., 19138-1721. Tel: 215-438-1955; Fax: 215-438-1944. Email: eileen.smith@depaulusa.org. Web: www.depaulusa.org. Eileen Smith, Exec. Dir. DePaul USA offers homeless and disadvantaged people the opportunity to fulfill their potential and make positive, informed choices about their future. Depaul USA is part of Depaul International and works in the spirit of St. Vincent de Paul, believing that everyone should have a place to call home and a stake in their community.

Fournier Retirement Fund Corporation, Mount St. Joseph Convent, 9701 Germantown Ave., 19118-2694. Tel: 215-248-7205; Fax: 215-248-7277. Email: msjc@ssjphila.org. Web: www.ssjphila.org. Sr. Joanne Fehrenbach, S.S.J., Gen. Sec. & Contact Person.

Franciscan Volunteer Ministry, Inc., P.O. Box 29276, 19125. Tel: 215-427-3070; Fax: 215-427-3059. Email: fvmpd@aol.com. Web: www.franciscanvolunteerministry.org. Katie Sullivan, Prog. Dir. Purpose: To create and run a Franciscan lay volunteer program in the United States.

Good Shepherd Mediation Program, 5356 Chew Ave., 19138. Tel: 215-843-5413; Fax: 215-843-2080. Email: gsmediation@phillymediators.org. Web: www.phillymediators.org. Cheryl Cutrona, Exec. Dir.

Good Shepherd Corporation, Philadelphia, Pennsylvania

IHM Center for Literacy, 425 W. Lindley Ave., 19120. Tel: 215-457-2232; Fax: 215-457-1611. Email: ihmesl@verizon.net. Web: mysite.verizon.net/ihmesl/. Sisters Mary Regina Schuyler, I.H.M., Dir.; Janice Owen, I.H.M., Site Coord. Full-time program with courses in ABE; English for Speakers of Other Languages (ESOL) 929 S. Farragut St., 19143. Tel: 215-382-0292; Fax: 215-382-4662. Email: ihmesldesales@verizon.net.

**International Institute for Culture, Ivy Hall*, 6331 Lancaster Ave., 19151. Tel: 215-877-9910; Fax: 215-877-9911. Web: www.iiculture.org. John M. Haas, Ph.D., S.T.L., Pres. Purpose: for the evangelization of culture through international conferences, language and cultural programs, etc., which reflect the rich cultural heritage of the Catholic Church which serves to bring people to the Person of Jesus Christ.

Katherine Kiernan Chateau, Inc., c/o Catholic Social Services, 222 N. 17th St., Ste. 300, 19103. Tel: 215-587-3903; Fax: 215-587-2479. Email: CHSweb@chs-adphila.org.

Marianist Lay Network of North America (MLNNA), 1341 N. Delaware Ave., #406, 19125-4300. Tel: 215-634-4116; Fax: 215-634-4955. Email: aj@marianistfamily.org. Web: marianist.com/lay.

Medical Mission Sisters Supplemental Subsidy Fund, Inc., 8400 Pine Rd., 19111. Tel: 215-742-6100; Fax: 215-742-2602. Sr. Frances Vaughan, M.M.S., Pres. Bd.

Missionary Cenacle Apostolate, 3501 Solly Ave, 19136. Tel: 410-772-5799. Pat Regan, Treas.; Alma Robles, Gen. Custodian. The MCA is a branch of the Missionary Cenacle Family. Lay people called to be missionaries in the Church in the providence of everyday life. MCA members live and work in the United States, Mexico, Puerto Rico, Colombia, and Costa Rica.

National Shrine of Saint Rita of Cascia, 1166 S. Broad St., 19146. Tel: 215-546-8333; Fax: 215-732-3510. Email: ritashrine@aol.com. Web: www.saintritashrine.org. Rev. Joseph A. Genito, O.S.A., Dir. Center of Devotion to Saint Rita in the United States.

Sisters of Saint Joseph Welcome Center, 728 E. Allegheny Ave., 19134-2428. Tel: 215-634-1696; Fax: 215-634-0760. Email: emarnien@earthlink.net. Web: www.ssjwelcomecenter.org. Sisters Eileen Marnien, Dir.; Marian Behrle, Dir. Literacy Prog. Sisters 4.

Society of Catholic Medical Missionaries Generalate, Inc. (Effective 1991), 8400 Pine Rd., 19111. Tel: 215-742-6100; Fax: 215-342-3948. Email: generalate@medicalmissionsisters.org.uk. Web: www.medicalmissionsisters.org. Sisters Clarita Hackman, M.M.S., Contact Person; Agnes Lanfermann, H.H.S., Pres. Corporation collects funds for charitable and missionary work, for Medical Mission Sisters; Assists in operation of hospitals, clinics and primary health care programs; Assists in care of poor, sick and infirm, in U.S. and overseas; Assists in training and educating men and women in medicine and nursing, and other health professions; Trains candidates for the Community; Provides assisted living care to sick and elder Medical Mission Sisters.

Society of St. Vincent de Paul of Philadelphia, 901 E. Luzerne St., 19124. Tel: 215-288-9540; Fax: 215-288-9540. Email: careygroberts@comcast.net. Dom Visco, Pres.; Carey G. Roberts, Exec. Dir. Catholic Lay Organization serving those in need with spiritual, moral, material and financial support regardless of race, creed, etc.

The Saint Thomas More Society of Philadelphia, 2600 One Commerce Sq., 19103-7098. Tel: 215-564-8000; Fax: 215-564-8120. Email: momara@stradley.com. Web: www.stmsphl.org. John Duffy, Esquire. Purpose: The Society is an association of catholic lawyers organized to strengthen the religious and charitable commitment of its members and to promote high ethical standards in the legal profession, as exemplified by the life of Saint Thomas More.

The Warner Perpetual Trust for the Benefit of Catholic Charities, Provident National Bank, P.O. Box 7648, 19101. Tel: 610-585-5698; Fax: 610-358-4275.

The Warner Perpetual Trust for the Benefit of Catholic Charities of the Archdiocese of Philadelphia, (The "Perpetual" Trust)

ASTON. **Heartful Ministries, Inc.*, One Neumann Dr., 19014. Tel: 610-358-4210; Fax: 610-358-4530. Email: info@heartful-ministries.org. Web: www.heartfulministries.org. Sr. Mary Kay Kelley, S.S.J., M.A., Founding Co-Dir.; Catherine G. Johnson, M.A., M.S., Founding Co-Dir. Purpose: to serve the diverse needs of the Church for liturgical and spiritual formation offering youth and adult retreats; parish adult faith formation; workshops on prayer, liturgy, and music; liturgical preparation and music ministry for religious communities and other conferences.

Sisters of St. Francis Foundation, 609 S. Convent Rd., 19014. Tel: 610-558-7713; Fax: 610-558-5357. Email: mvdgeest@osfphila.org. Web: www.osfphila.org. Sr. Mary Vandergeest, O.S.F., Exec. Dir. Purpose: Raises funds to fulfill the needs of the Ministries and Retired Sisters of the Sisters of St. Francis of Philadelphia.

Sisters of St. Francis of Philadelphia, Charitable Trust II, Our Lady of Angels Convent, 19014. Tel: 610-558-7733; Fax: 610-459-0195. Email: cljones@osfphila.org. Web: www.osfphila.org. Sr. Esther Anderson, O.S.F., Congregational Min.

BALA CYNWYD. *The Papal Foundation*, 150 Monument Rd., 19004. Tel: 610-535-6340; 610-535-6341; Fax: 610-535-6343. Email: jcoffey@thepapalfoundation.com. Web: www.thepapalfoundation.com. Mr. James V. Coffey, M.A., Contact Person.

CONSHOHOCKEN. *Mercy Health System of Southeastern PA*, One West Elm St., 19428. Tel: 610-567-6106; Fax: 610-567-6150. Email: kkeenan@mercyhealth.org. Web: www.mercyhealth.org. H. Ray Welch, Pres. & CEO Mercy Health System; Sisters Mary Christine McCann, R.S.M., Bd. Chm.; Kathleen Keenan, R.S.M., Senior Vice Pres., Mission & Sponsorship. Mercy Health System is a regional health corporation of Catholic Health East, sponsored by the Sisters of Mercy.

The health care services operated by Mercy Health System include:

Mercy Philadelphia Hospital Tel: 215-748-9300; Fax: 215-748-9709.

Mercy Fitzgerald Hospital Tel: 610-237-4030; Fax: 610-237-4202.

Mercy Suburban Hospital Tel: 610-278-2002; Fax: 610-272-4642.

St. Agnes Continuing Care Center Tel: 215-339-4220; Fax: 215-339-5650.

St. Agnes Continuing Care Center Foundation Tel: 215-339-4220; Fax: 215-339-5650.

Nazareth Hospital Tel: 215-335-6039; Fax: 215-335-6598.

Nazareth Health Care Foundation Tel: 215-335-6159; Fax: 215-335-6265.

N.E. Physician Services, Inc. Tel: 215-335-6039; Fax: 215-335-6598.

Keystone Mercy Health Plan Tel: 215-937-8201; Fax: 215-937-8202.

Mercy Management Services Tel: 610-567-6106; Fax: 610-567-6150.

Mercy Health Foundation Tel: 610-567-5205; Fax: 610-567-6150.

Mercy Home Health Tel: 610-690-2526; Fax: 610-690-4644.

Mercy Court Tel: 610-623-3083; Fax: 610-259-1414.

EXTON. **Catholic Leadership Institute*, 750 Springdale Dr., Ste. 200, 19341. Tel: 610-363-1315; Fax: 610-363-3731. Email: info@CatholicLeaders.org. Web: www.CatholicLeaders.org. Most Rev. Gregory M. Aymond, D.D., M.Div., Episcopal Mod.; Timothy C. Flanagan, Founder & Chair; Matthew F. Manion, Pres. & CEO; Rev. William Dickinson, National Dir. Leadership Devel. Lay organization providing leadership training and personal development programs to help clergy, religious and lay leaders reach their God given potential as Catholic leaders and Christian witnesses in their family, workplace, community and Church.

**Theology of the Body Institute*, 479 Thomas Jones Way, Ste. 100, 19341. Tel: 215-302-8200; Fax: 215-302-8200. Web: tobinstitute.org. Maria D. Stumpf, Dir. Opers. & Programs. Purpose: To educate and train men and women to understand, live and promote the Theology of the Body and to ensure that the teachings of John Paul II are promoted faithfully and effectively.

FLOURTOWN. *Saint Joseph Guild*, 110 W. Wissahickon Ave., P.O. Box 36, 19031-0036. Tel: 215-248-7838; Fax: 215-248-7802. Email: sjguild19@aol.com. Web: www.ssjphila.org. Sr. Frances DeLisle, S.S.J., Coord.

FORT WASHINGTON. *John Paul II Foundation for Peace, Justice & Human Rights, The Copernicus House*, 1 Reiff Mill Rd., Ambler, 19001. Tel: 215-646-4420; Fax: 215-628-8944. Email: KEENCORNER@aol.com.

HUNTINGDON VALLEY. **Holy Redeemer Health System*, 1602 Huntingdon Pike, Meadowbrook, 19046. Tel: 215-938-4650; 215-938-3236. Web: www.holyredeemer.com. Michael B. Laign, Pres. & CEO. Sponsor: Sisters of the Holy Redeemer, C.S.R., Parent organization which maintains, manages, and operates the health care system composed of the various corporations sponsored and established by the Sisters of the Holy Redeemer, C.S.R. as follows: Holy Redeemer Health Care Corporation and Foundation; Holy Redeemer Health System; Holy Redeemer Hospital and Medical Center; St. Joseph's Manor; The Lafayette-Redeemer; Holy Redeemer Active and Retirement Living Communities; Holy Redeemer Home Care and Hospice; Holy Redeemer Transitional Care Unit; Holy Redeemer Physician and Ambulatory Services; Redeemer Village; Redeemer Village II; Drueding Center/Project Rainbow; HRH Management Corporation; Convents Provincialate; Angelus Convent; Emmanuel Convent; Our Lady of Peace Convent; St. Elizabeth Convent.

Holy Redeemer Hospital and Medical Center Tel: 215-947-3000. Web: www.holyredeemer.com.

St. Joseph's Manor Tel: 215-938-4000. Web: www.holyredeemer.com. Robin Frankwich, Vice Pres.

The Lafayette - Redeemer Tel: 215-214-2877. Benjamin Pieczynski, Vice Pres.

Holy Redeemer Health Care Corporation and Foundation Tel: 215-938-4650. Web: www.holyredeemer.com.

Holy Redeemer Home Care and Hospice Tel: 800-678-8678. Web: www.holyredeemer.com.

Holy Redeemer Transitional Care Unit Tel: 215-947-3000.

IMMACULATA. *Enserv Inc.*, 1145 King Rd., 19345. Tel: 610-647-4400, Ext. 3147; Fax: 610-251-1668.

JENKINTOWN. **PNFPN-Philadelphia Natural Family Planning Network*, P.O. Box 220, 19046. Tel: 215-885-8388. Web: pnfpn.org. Lester A. Ruppersberger, D.O., Pres. PNFPN is a network of persons dedicated to the promotion of Natural Family Planning (NFP). Our mission is to explain its practice, effectiveness, benefits and underlying moral principles as understood and taught by the Catholic Church.

KING OF PRUSSIA. *Rachel's Vineyard Ministries (International Headquarters)*, 808 N. Henderson Rd., 19406. Tel: 610-354-0555 Toll Free: 877-HOPE-4-ME (877-4673-3463); 877-467-3463 (877 HOPE-4-ME); Fax: 610-354-0311. Email: t.burke@rachelsvineyard.org; k.burke@rachelsvineyard.org. Web: www.rachelsvineyard.org. Theresa Burke, Ph.D., L.P.C., N.C.P., Founder & Exec. Dir.; Kevin Burke, M.S.S., L.S.W., Assoc. Dir. Purpose: to provide retreats offering emotional and spiritual healing after abortion; and continuing education for professionals, clergy and lay persons.

MEADOWBROOK. **Holy Redeemer Physician and Ambulatory Services*, 1648 Huntington Pike, 19046. Tel: 215-938-3713; Fax: 215-938-4610. Web: www.holyredeemer.com. Michele Urofsky, Exec. Vice Pres. Sponsor: Sisters of the Holy Redeemer C.S.R., Affiliate of Holy Redeemer Health System; Nonprofit corporation formed to establish, operate and maintain family health clinics and practices, laboratories, dispensaries, buildings, and facilities relating to these purposes, and provide the services of physicians and other health care professionals in connection with the provision of health care services at Holy Redeemer Hospital and Medical Center, and other hospitals, clinics and health care facilities.

MERION STATION. *Sisters of Mercy of the Americas Mid-Atlantic Community, Inc.*, 515 Montgomery Ave., 19066. Tel: 610-664-6650; Fax: 610-664-3429. Web: www.mercymidatlantic.org. Sr. Christine McCann, R.S.M., Pres.

NEWTOWN SQUARE. *Catholic Health East*, 3805 West Chester Pike, Ste. 100, 19073-2304. Tel: 610-355-2004; Fax: 610-271-9600. Email: sshare@che.org. Web: www.che.org. Mr. Robert V. Stanek, Pres. & CEO. Catholic Health East is a multi-institutional, Catholic health system co-sponsored by 9 religious congregations: Franciscan Sisters of Allegany in St. Bonaventure, NY; Sisters of Providence in Holyoke, MA; Sisters of Mercy of the Americas-Northeast Community; Sisters of Mercy of the Americas-Mid-Atlantic Community; Sisters of Mercy of the Americas-South Central Community; Sisters of Mercy of the Americas-New York, Pennsylvania, Pacific West Community; the Sisters of St. Joseph of St. Augustine, FL; Sisters of Charity of Seton Hill, Greensburg, PA; Sisters, Servants of the Immaculate Heart of Mary, Scranton, Pennsylvania; and Hope Ministries, a Public Juridic Person of Pontifical Right within Catholic Health East, Newtown Square, PA. Founded in 1997, Catholic Health East facilities serve communities through 19 regional systems in 11 eastern states.

Continuing Care Management Services Network, 3805 West Chester Pike, Ste. 100, 19073-2304. Tel: 610-355-2000; Fax: 610-355-2050. Email: jcapassol@che.org. Web: www.che.org. Mr. John Capasso, Pres. & CEO.

Global Health Ministry, 3805 West Chester Pike, Ste. 100, 19073-2304. Tel: 610-355-2003; Fax: 610-271-9600. Email: mmcginley@globalhealthministry.org. Web: www.globalhealthministry.org. Sr. Mary Jo McGinley, R.S.M., Pres. & Exec. Dir.

UPPER DARBY. *Dominican Pastoral Counseling*, 131 Copley Rd., 19082. Tel: 215-635-6027; Fax: 215-635-2017. Email: cgaekeop@verizon.net. Web: www.elkinsparkop.org. Sr. Ceal Warner, O.P., Gen. Councilor.

Lucy Eaton Smith Fund, 131 Copley Rd., 19082. Tel: 215-635-6027; Fax: 215-635-2017. Email: cealop1@verizon.net. Web: www.elkinsparkop.org. Sr. Ceal Warner, O.P., Gen. Councilor.

VILLANOVA. *Augustinian Volunteers*, Business Office: 214 Ashwood Rd., 19085. Tel: 610-527-3330, Ext. 291; Fax: 610-520-0618. Email: av@osavol.org. Web: www.osavol.org. April Gagne, Dir.; Patrick DiDomenico, Assoc. Dir.; Jane O'Connor, Asst. Dir. A faith-based lay volunteer program serving the poor in the Archdioceses of Chicago, Boston and New York and the Diocese of San Diego.

YEADON. *Mercy Court*, 550 S. Lansdowne Ave., 19050. Tel: 610-623-3083; Fax: 610-259-1414. Email: mercycourt@comcast.net. Paula S. Wisdo, Prog. Mgr. Sisters of Mercy., Low income apartments for independent living for older adults. Total Apartments 100; Total Staff 5.

RELIGIOUS INSTITUTES OF MEN REPRESENTED IN THE ARCHDIOCESE

For further details refer to the corresponding bracketed number in the Religious Institutes of Men or Women section.

[0140]—*Augustinians* (Prov. of St. Thomas Villanova)—O.S.A.
[0290]—*Brothers of Charity*—F.C.
[0330]—*Brothers of the Christian Schools* (Baltimore Prov.)—F.S.C.
[0900]—*Canons Regular of Premontre*—O.Praem.
[0470]—*Capuchin Friars*—O.F.M.Cap.
[0650]—*Congregation of the Holy Spirit* (Eastern Prov.)—C.S.Sp.
[0860]—*Congregation of the Immaculate Heart of Mary (Missionhurst)*—C.I.C.M.
[1330]—*Congregation of the Mission* (Eastern Prov.)—C.M.
[]—*Institute of the Incarnate Word*—I.V.E.
[]—*Legionaries of Christ*—L.C.
[0800]—*Maryknoll Fathers and Brothers*—M.M.
[0850]—*Missionaries of Africa*—M.Afr.
[0825]—*Missionaries of the Blessed Sacrament*—M.S.S.
[1110]—*Missionaries of the Sacred Heart* (American Prov.)—M.S.C.
[0840]—*Missionary Servants of the Most Holy Trinity*—S.T.
[0910]—*Oblate Missionaries of Mary Immaculate*—O.M.I.
[0920]—*Oblates of St. Francis de Sales*—O.S.F.S.
[0520]—*Order of Friars Minor* (Assumption B.V.M. & Most Holy Name Provs.)—O.F.M.
[0970]—*Order of Our Lady of Mercy*—O.deM.
[1310]—*Order of the Holy Trinity*—O.SS.T.
[1010]—*Pauline Fathers*—O.S.P.P.E.
[0950]—*The Philadelphia Congregation of the Oratory of Saint Philip Neri*—C.O.
[1040]—*Piarist Fathers*—Sch.P.
[1070]—*Redemptorist Fathers* (Baltimore Prov.)—C.SS.R.
[1220]—*Servants of Charity*—S.C.
[0690]—*Society of Jesus (Jesuits)* (Maryland Prov.)—S.J.
[0560]—*Third Order Regular of Saint Francis* (Prov. of the Most Sacred Heart)—T.O.R.

RELIGIOUS INSTITUTES OF WOMEN REPRESENTED IN THE ARCHDIOCESE

[1070-13]—*Adrian Dominican Sisters*—O.P.
[2120]—*Armenian Sisters of the Immaculate Conception*—C.I.C.
[1810]—*Bernardine Sisters of the Third Order of St. Francis*—O.S.F.
[0690]—*Comboni Missionary Sisters*—C.M.S.
[0760]—*Daughters of Charity of St. Vincent de Paul*—D.C.
[0940]—*Daughters of St. Mary of Providence*—D.S.M.P.
[0420]—*Discalced Carmelite Nuns*—O.C.D.
[1070-23]—*Dominican Sisters of Hawthorne*—O.P.
[1105]—*Dominican Sisters of Hope*—O.P.
[]—*Dominican Sisters of Our Lady of the Rosary*—O.P.
[1115]—*Dominican Sisters of Peace*—O.P.
[1070-17]—*Dominican Sisters of St. Catherine de Ricci*—O.P.
[1170]—*Felician Sisters*—C.S.S.F.
[1180]—*Franciscan Sisters of Allegany, New York*—O.S.F.

[1840]—*Grey Nuns of the Sacred Heart*—G.N.S.H.
[1870]—*Handmaids of the Sacred Heart of Jesus*—A.C.J.
[2310]—*Little Sisters of the Assumption*—L.S.A.
[2340]—*Little Sisters of the Poor*—L.S.P.
[2345]—*Little Workers of the Sacred Hearts*—P.O.S.C.
[2490]—*Medical Mission Sisters*—M.M.S.
[2710]—*Missionaries of Charity*—M.C.
[2790]—*Missionary Servants of the Most Blessed Trinity*—M.S.B.T.
[2730]—*Missionary Sisters of the Holy Rosary*—M.S.H.R.
[2800]—*Missionary Sisters of the Most Sacred Heart of Jesus of Hiltrup*—M.S.C.
[2860]—*Missionary Sisters of the Sacred Heart* (Eastern Prov.)—M.S.C.
[3060]—*Oblates Sisters of St. Francis de Sales*—O.S.F.S.
[3730]—*Order of St. Basil the Great*—O.S.B.M.
[3760]—*Order of St. Clare*—O.S.C.
[0950]—*Pious Society Daughters of St. Paul*—F.S.P.
[3390]—*Religious of the Assumption*—R.A.
[3430]—*Religious Teachers Filippini*—M.P.F.
[2970]—*School Sisters of Notre Dame*—S.S.N.D.
[]—*Servants of the Lord and of the Virgin of Matara*—S.S.V.M.
[3540]—*Sister Servants of the Holy Spirit of Perpetual Adoration*—S.Sp.S.deA.P.
[3630]—*Sister Servants of the Most Sacred Heart of Jesus*—S.S.C.J.
[0500]—*Sisters of Charity of Nazareth*—S.C.N.
[0660]—*Sisters of Christian Charity*—S.C.C.
[2575]—*Sisters of Mercy of the Americas, Merion, PA*—R.S.M.
[3000]—*Sisters of Notre Dame de Namur*—S.N.D.deN.
[2670]—*Sisters of Our Lady of Mercy*—S.O.L.M.
[3893]—*Sisters of Saint Joseph of Philadelphia*—S.S.J.
[1650]—*Sisters of St. Francis of Philadelphia*—O.S.F.
[]—*Sisters of St. Francis of the Martyr St. George*—F.S.G.M.
[0260]—*Sisters of the Blessed Sacrament for Indians and Colored People*—S.B.S.
[0970]—*Sisters of the Divine Compassion*—R.D.C.
[1830]—*Sisters of the Good Shepherd*—R.G.S.
[1970]—*Sisters of the Holy Family of Nazareth*—C.S.F.N.
[2000]—*Sisters of the Holy Redeemer*—C.S.R.
[2060]—*Sisters of the Most Holy Trinity*—O.SS.T.
[2160]—*Sisters Servants of the Immaculate Heart of Mary* (Scranton)—I.H.M.
[2170]—*Sisters, Servants of the Immaculate Heart of Mary (Immaculata)*—I.H.M.
[4060]—*Society of the Holy Child Jesus*—S.H.C.J.
[4120]—*Ursuline Sisters of the Immaculate Conception*—O.S.U.
[4190]—*Visitation Nuns*—V.H.M.

ARCHDIOCESAN CEMETERIES

PHILADELPHIA. *Cathedral*, 111 S. 38th St., 19104. 1032 N. 48th St., 19131. Tel: 215-477-8918; Fax: 215-477-8313.

Holy Sepulchre, 111 S. 38th St., 19104. Cheltenham Ave. & Ivy Hill Rd., 19150. Tel: 215-247-0691; Fax: 215-886-0298.

New Cathedral, 111 S. 38th St., 19104. 2nd & Butler Sts., 19140. Tel: 215-634-3212; Fax: 215-634-1733.

BENSALEM. *Resurrection*, 111 S. 38th St., 19104. 5201 Hulmeville Rd., 19020. Tel: 215-639-0965; Fax: 215-639-4532.

CHALFONT. *St. John Neumann*, 111 S. 38th St., 19104. 3797 County Line Rd., 18914. Tel: 215-822-0680; Fax: 215-822-5159.

COATESVILLE. *All Souls*, 111 S. 38th St., 19104. 3215 Manor Rd., 19320. Tel: 484-288-6140; Fax: 484-288-6147.

NEWTOWN. *All Saints*, 111 S. 38th St., 19104. 291 W. Durham Rd., 18940.

SPRINGFIELD. *SS. Peter and Paul*, 111 S. 38th St., 19104. 1600 S. Sproul Rd., 19064. Tel: 610-544-4933; Fax: 610-544-6467.

WEST CONSHOHOCKEN. *Calvary*, 111 S. 38th St., 19104. Gulph & Matsonford Rd., 19428. Tel: 610-525-2214; Fax: 610-525-6247.

WEST GROVE. *Holy Saviour* Penn Township

YEADON. *Holy Cross*, 111 S. 38th St., 19104. 626 Bailey Rd., 19050. Tel: 610-626-2206; 215-476-3656; Fax: 610-623-6247.

NECROLOGY

† Herron, Rev. Msgr. Bernard J., (Retired)—Died Aug. 29, 2009
† LaHart, Rev. Msgr. Richard T., (Retired)—Died Sept. 17, 2009
† Meehan, Rev. Msgr. James H., (Retired)—Died June 26, 2009
† Norrell, Rev. Msgr. Albert V., (Retired)—Died March 25, 2009
† Palmieri, Rev. Msgr. Alexander J., Chancellor, Diocese of Philadelphia—Died Aug. 1, 2009
† Carbone, Vito J., (Absent on Sick Leave)—Died April 17, 2009
† Homa, Thomas D., (Retired)—Died Sept. 16, 2009
† Kennedy, Joseph J., (Retired)—Died Dec. 22, 2008
† Kostelnick, Albert T., (Retired)—Died March 30, 2009
† O'Connor, John P., (Retired)—Died July 26, 2009
† Roedel, Robert H., (Retired)—Died April 5, 2009
† Senske, Joseph A., (Retired)—Died Jan. 1, 2009
† Walsh, Joseph E., (Retired)—Died Dec. 29, 2008
† Wright, William A., Drexel Hill, PA St. Bernadette—Died Dec. 24, 2008

An asterisk (*) denotes an organization that has established tax-exempt status directly with the IRS and is not covered by the USCCB Group Ruling.

Diocese of Phoenix

(Dioecesis Phoenicensis)

Most Reverend

THOMAS J. OLMSTED, J.C.D.

Bishop of Phoenix; ordained July 2, 1973; appointed Coadjutor Bishop of Wichita February 16, 1999; Episcopal ordination April 20, 1999; appointed Bishop of Wichita October 4, 2001; appointed Bishop of Phoenix November 25, 2003; installed December 20, 2003. *Office: 400 E. Monroe St., Phoenix, AZ 85004-2336.*

Most Reverend

THOMAS J. O'BRIEN

Bishop Emeritus of Phoenix; ordained May 7, 1961; consecrated January 6, 1982; installed January 18, 1982; retired June 18, 2003. *Mailing Address: 400 E. Monroe St., Phoenix, AZ 85004-2336.*

ESTABLISHED DECEMBER 2, 1969.

Square Miles 43,967.

Comprises the Counties of Maricopa; Mohave; Yavapai & Coconino not to include the territorial boundaries of the Navajo Indian Reservation; Pinal--that portion of land known as the Gila River Indian Reservation in the State of Arizona.

Patroness of Diocese: Our Lady of Guadalupe.

For legal titles of parishes and diocesan institutions, consult the Chancery Office.

Diocesan Pastoral Center: 400 E. Monroe St., Phoenix, AZ 85004-2336. Tel: 602-257-0030; 602-354-2000; Fax: 602-354-2427.

Web: www.diocesephoenix.org

Email: communications@diocesephoenix.org

STATISTICAL OVERVIEW

Personnel	
Bishop	1
Retired Bishops	1
Priests: Diocesan Active in Diocese	88
Priests: Diocesan Active Outside Diocese	2
Priests: Retired, Sick or Absent	57
Number of Diocesan Priests	147
Religious Priests in Diocese	95
Total Priests in Diocese	242
Extern Priests in Diocese	61
Ordinations:	
Diocesan Priests	3
Transitional Deacons	3
Permanent Deacons in Diocese	239
Total Brothers	17
Total Sisters	190
Parishes	
Parishes	92
With Resident Pastor:	
Resident Diocesan Priests	62
Resident Religious Priests	17
Without Resident Pastor:	
Administered by Priests	8
Administered by Deacons	2
Administered by Religious Women	1
Administered by Lay People	1
Administered by Pastoral Teams, etc.	1
Missions	23
Pastoral Centers	3
Professional Ministry Personnel:	
Brothers	6
Sisters	43
Lay Ministers	376
Welfare	
Catholic Hospitals	2
Total Assisted	590,420
Health Care Centers	1
Total Assisted	15,460
Homes for the Aged	15
Total Assisted	774
Residential Care of Children	1
Total Assisted	3
Day Care Centers	9
Total Assisted	777
Specialized Homes	28
Total Assisted	5,462
Special Centers for Social Services	27
Total Assisted	1,480,618
Residential Care of Disabled	20
Total Assisted	142
Other Institutions	1
Total Assisted	1,449
Educational	
Diocesan Students in Other Seminaries	23
Seminaries, Religious	3
Total Seminarians	23
High Schools, Diocesan and Parish	5
Total Students	3,761
High Schools, Private	1
Total Students	1,270
Elementary Schools, Diocesan and Parish	32
Total Students	9,581
Catechesis/Religious Education:	
High School Students	3,334
Elementary Students	24,768
Total Students under Catholic Instruction	42,737
Teachers in the Diocese:	
Priests	7
Brothers	3
Sisters	33
Lay Teachers	857
Vital Statistics	
Receptions into the Church:	
Infant Baptism Totals	7,640
Minor Baptism Totals	707
Adult Baptism Totals	354
Received into Full Communion	1,342
First Communions	8,233
Confirmations	10,474
Marriages:	
Catholic	891
Interfaith	239
Total Marriages	1,130
Deaths	2,737
Total Catholic Population	764,140
Total Population	4,494,940

Former Bishops—Most Revs. EDWARD A. MCCARTHY, D.D., installed Bishop of the Diocese of Phoenix, Dec. 2, 1969; transferred to Coadjutor Archbishop of Miami, July 7, 1976; installed Sept. 17, 1976; died June 7, 2005; JAMES S. RAUSCH, D.D., Ph.D., installed March 22, 1977; died May 18, 1981; THOMAS J. O'BRIEN, D.D. (Retired), ord. May 7, 1961; cons. Jan. 6, 1982; installed Bishop of the Diocese of Phoenix Jan. 18, 1982; retired June 18, 2003.

Moderator of the Curia—Rev. FREDRICK J. ADAMSON, V.G., Diocesan Pastoral Center, 400 E. Monroe, Phoenix, 85004. Tel: 602-354-2180.

Vicar General—Revs. FREDRICK J. ADAMSON, V.G.; DAVID SANFILIPPO, V.G., Diocesan Pastoral Center, 400 E. Monroe St., Phoenix, 85004. Tel: 602-354-2480.

Diocesan Office—400 E. Monroe St., Phoenix, 85004-2336. Tel: 602-257-0030; 602-354-2000; Fax: 602-354-2427.

Chancellor—Sr. JEAN STEFFES, C.S.A., 400 E. Monroe St., Phoenix, 85004-2336. Tel: 602-354-2470; Fax: 602-354-2427.

Assistant Chancellor—Rev. MICHAEL L. DISKIN, 400 E. Monroe St., Phoenix, 85004-2336. Tel: 602-354-2471; Fax: 602-354-2427.

College of Consultors—Revs. FREDRICK J. ADAMSON, V.G.; ROBERT ALIUNZI, A.J., V.F.; RICHARD R. FELT, V.F.; MICHAEL L. DISKIN; CHRISTOPHER J. FRASER, J.C.L.; DAVID SANFILIPPO, V.G.; JOHN A. HERMAN, C.S.C.; JOHN LANKEIT; DANIEL VOLLMER.

Finance and Administration—Rev. FREDRICK J. ADAMSON, V.G.; Mr. JOSEPH ANDERSON, Dir., 400 E. Monroe St., Phoenix, 85004-2336. Tel: 602-354-2185; Fax: 602-354-2448.

Diocesan Tribunal—Office: 400 E. Monroe St., Phoenix, 85004-2336. Tel: 602-354-2275; Fax: 602-354-2424.

Judicial Vicar—Rev. CHRISTOPHER J. FRASER, J.C.L. Email: frfraser@diocesephoenix.org.

Diocesan Judges—AMY M. ARNOLD, J.C.L.; Revs. CHARLES G. KIEFFER, V.F.; VALENTINE BOYLE, O.Carm.; Deacon WILLIAM FINNEGAN, J.C.L.; Rev. TIMOTHY R. DAVERN, J.C.L.

Defenders of the Bond—Revs. ROBERT J. CARUSO; PETER P. DOBROWSKI; Sr. ELLEN SINCLAIR, S.D.S.

Advocates—Rev. GARY R. REGULA; Sr. BRIDGET CHAPMAN, M.M.; Mrs. SANDRA J. CONSIGLIO, M.A.; DEBORAH MALATIN; WILLIAM AHEARN; CYNTHIA BENZING; Deacon ROBERT CAMPAS; MARILYN CRAWFORD; Rev. H. FRED LECLAIRE, C.M.F.; ASENCION MURGA; ANNIE PHILLIPPI; Deacon JAMES FOGLE; JOZETTE NELMS; Rev. MICAH MUHLEN, O.F.M.; Deacon MILFORD SUIDA; Revs. NICHOLAS A. FLORIDI; PATRICK FARLEY; Deacon PATRICK TOILOLO; SUSAN PIETRO.

Auditors—Sr. RUTH KARNITZ, S.S.N.D.; Ms. NICOLE LEE, J.C.L.; Mrs. JUSTINA SANCHEZ.

Promoter of Justice— per causam AMY M. ARNOLD, J.C.L.

Censor Librorum—Rev. TIMOTHY R. DAVERN, J.C.L.

Notaries—MARY LYN PYEATTE; PATRICIA FISCHER; Sr. RUTH KARNITZ, S.S.N.D.; TERESA VARGO; DEBORAH MALATIN.

Appellate Court Administrator-Diocese of Phoenix—Sr. RUTH KARNITZ, S.S.N.D.

Youth Protection Advocate—JEAN SOKOL, 400 E. Monroe, Phoenix, 85004. Tel: 602-354-2396; Fax: 602-354-2496.

Archives—MARIA BETERAN, Archivist, 400 E. Monroe St., Phoenix, 85004-2336. Tel: 602-354-2475.

Arizona Catholic Conference—Mr. RONALD JOHNSON, Exec. Dir., 400 E. Monroe St., Phoenix, 85004-2336. Tel: 602-354-2390; Fax: 602-354-2466; 602-354-2394.

Buildings & Property—JOHN MINIERI, Dir. Real Property & Facilities, Diocesan Center, 400 E. Monroe St., Phoenix, 85004-2336. Tel: 602-354-2161; Fax: 602-354-2440.

Catholic Community Foundation - Diocese of Phoenix—DONNA MARINO, Exec. Dir., 400 E. Monroe St., Phoenix, 85004-2336. Tel: 602-354-2400; Fax: 602-354-2423.

Catholic Cemeteries— St. Francis, Holy Redeemer, Holy Cross, Queen of Heaven, Calvary, All Souls Rev. MICHAEL L. DISKIN, Spiritual Advisor; GARY L. BROWN, Exec. Dir., Administrative Offices, 2033 N. 48th St., Phoenix, 85008. Tel: 602-267-1329; Fax: 602-685-1516. Calvary Cemetery, 201 W. University, Flagstaff, 86001. Tel: 928-220-2317; Fax: 928-774-1105 (Call First). St. Francis Cemetery, 2033 N. 48th St., Phoenix, 85008. Tel: 602-267-1329; Fax: 602-267-7942. Holy Redeemer Cemetery, 23015 N. Cave Creek Rd., Phoenix, 85040. Tel: 480-513-3243; Fax: 480-513-3293. Holy Cross Cemetery, 10045 W. Thomas Rd., Avondale, 85323. Tel: 623-936-1710; Fax: 623-936-6605. Queen of Heaven Cemetery, 1500 E. Baseline Rd., Mesa, 85204. Tel: 480-892-3729; Fax: 480-813-2826. All Souls Cemetery, 700 N. Bill Gray Rd., Cottonwood, 86326. Tel: 928-649-1998. Mortuary Location: Queen of Heaven Mortuary, 1562 E. Baseline Rd., Mesa, 85204. Tel: 480-892-3729; Fax: 480-813-2826.

"The Catholic Sun"— (Diocesan Newspaper) ROB DEFRANCESCO, Editor, 400 E. Monroe St., Phoenix, 85004-2336. Tel: 602-354-2130; Fax: 602-354-2429. Email: info@catholicsun.org. Web: www.catholicsun.org.

Public Information Officer—JAMES DWYER, 400 E. Monroe, Phoenix, 85004-2336. Tel: 602-354-2121; Fax: 602-354-2273.

Stewardship Office— (Charity & Development Appeal) KATHRYN MCLAUGHLIN, Dir.; Rev. GREGORY SCHLARB, Vicar, 400 E. Monroe St., Phoenix, 85004. Tel: 602-354-2215; Fax: 602-354-2432.

Ecumenical and Interreligious Affairs—Rev. MICHAEL L. DISKIN, Dir., 400 E. Monroe, Phoenix, 85004. Tel: 602-354-2471; Fax: 602-354-2427.

Division of Formation and Education—MARYBETH MUELLER, Exec. Dir., 400 E. Monroe, Phoenix, 85004. Tel: 602-354-2341; Fax: 602-354-2444.

Diaconate Ministry—Deacons JAMES TRANT, Dir., 400 E. Monroe, Phoenix, 85004. Tel: 602-354-2011; Fax: 602-354-2437; KEITH DAVIS, Assoc. Dir. Tel: 602-354-2012.

Vocations—Rev. PAUL G. SULLIVAN, Dir., 400 E. Monroe, Phoenix, 85004. Tel: 602-257-2004; Fax: 602-354-2442. Email: frsullivan@diocesephoenix.org.

Worship and Liturgy, Office of—Revs. KIERAN KLECZEWSKI, V.F., Exec. Dir. Tel: 602-354-2113; JOHN MUIR, Asst. Dir., 400 E. Monroe St., Phoenix, 85004. Tel: 602-354-2110.

Schools—MARYBETH MUELLER, Supt. Schools. Tel: 602-354-2341; Sr. MELITA M. PENCHALK, O.S.B.M., Asst. Supt. School. Tel: 602-354-2343; CECILIA FRAKES, Asst. Supt., 400 E. Monroe, Phoenix, 85004. Tel: 602-354-2342; Fax: 602-354-2432.

Family Catechesis—400 E. Monroe St., Phoenix, 85004. ERIC WESTBY, Dir. Tel: 602-354-2320; CARMEN PORTELA, Asst. Dir. Tel: 602-354-2031; RYAN HANNING, Assoc. Dir., Adult Catechesis. Tel: 602-354-2321.

Natural Family Planning—CINDY LEONARD, Coord., 400 E. Monroe St., Phoenix, 85004. Tel: 602-354-2122; Fax: 602-354-2124.

Youth-Young Adult Evangelization—BILL MARCOTTE, Dir., 400 E. Monroe, Phoenix, 85004. Tel: 602-354-2380; Fax: 602-354-2431.

The Catholic Scouting Program—Rev. DENNIS O'ROURKE, V.F., Liaison, St. Gabriel, 32648 N. Cave Creek Rd., Cave Creek, 85331. Tel: 480-595-0883; Fax: 480-595-0886.

Office of Marriage and Respect Life—MIKE PHALEN, Dir., 400 E. Monroe, Phoenix, 85004. Tel: 602-354-2355; Fax: 602-354-2431.

Mount Claret Center—Deacon JOHN MICKEL.

Office of Disability Ministry—ISABELLA RICE, Dir., 400 E. Monroe, Phoenix, 85004. Tel: 602-354-2370; 602-354-2369 (TTY); Fax: 602-354-2432.

Native American Ministry Office—Rev. DALE JAMISON, O.F.M., Dir., 400 E. Monroe St., Phoenix, 85004. Tel: 602-354-2050.

Native American Ministry - Field Office—Rev. DALE JAMISON, O.F.M., Dir.; CLISSENE LEWIS, Pastoral Admin., 120 Church St., Sacaton, 85247. Mailing Address: P.O. Box 545, Sacaton, 85247. Tel: 520-562-3716.

General Counsel—JOHN KELLY, Attorney, 400 E. Monroe, Phoenix, 85004. Tel: 602-354-2474; Fax: 602-354-2427.

Priests' Assurance Association—Rev. Msgr. RICHARD W. MOYER, Pres. (Retired), 3302 N. 7th St., #133, Phoenix, 85014. Tel: 602-277-0171.

Priest Personnel—Rev. DAVID SANFILIPPO, V.G., Vicar for Priests, 400 E. Monroe, Phoenix, 85004. Tel: 602-354-2473; Fax: 602-354-2427.

Advisory Board for the Continuing Formation of Priests—Rev. DAVID SANFILIPPO, V.G., 400 E. Monroe, Phoenix, 85004. Tel: 602-354-2473.

Priestly Life and Ministry Board—Rev. DAVID SANFILIPPO, V.G., 400 E. Monroe, Phoenix, 85004. Tel: 602-354-2473.

Priests' Placement Board—Rev. DAVID SANFILIPPO, V.G., 400 E. Monroe, Phoenix, 85004. Tel: 602-354-2473.

Prisons, Catholic Ministries To—Deacon PETER MURPHY, Dir., 400 E. Monroe St., Phoenix, 85004. Tel: 602-354-2485. Email: dcnmurphy@diocesephoenix.org.

Youth at Risk—KEVIN STARRS, Coord., 400 E. Monroe, Phoenix, 85004. Tel: 602-518-0377.

State Adult Facilities— Phoenix Prison Complex, Perryville Prison (Female), Lewis Prison, Yavapai County.

Native American Prisons— Sacaton, Salt River.

State Juvenile Facilities— Adobe Mountain, Black Canyon, S.W. Regional.

County Jails (Adult & Juvenile)— Durango Jail, Estrella Jail (Female), Towers Jail, Fourth Avenue Jail, Lower Buckeye Jail, Tents (Male & Female).

Federal Prison (Adult)— Federal Correction Institute (Male & Female).

Private Prison (Adult)— Phoenix West, Kingman.

County Juvenile Detention Center— Maricopa County Court System.

Propagation of the Faith—MARGO GONZALEZ, Dir., 400 E. Monroe, Phoenix, 85004. Tel: 602-354-2005; Fax: 602-354-2442.

Holy Childhood Association—MARGO GONZALEZ, Dir., 400 E. Monroe, Phoenix, 85004. Tel: 602-354-2005; Fax: 602-354-2442.

Office of Ethnic Ministries—Rev. DAVID SANFILIPPO, V.G., Dir. Tel: 602-354-2480; IGNACIO RODRIGUEZ, Assoc. Dir., 400 E. Monroe, Phoenix, 85004. Tel: 602-354-2042; Fax: 602-354-2459.

Office of Hispanic Ministry—JOSE ROBLES, Dir., 400 E. Monroe St., Phoenix, 85004. Tel: 602-354-2041.

Human Resources (Personnel and Benefits)—JOHN UNGVARY, Chief Human Resources Officer, 400 E. Monroe, Phoenix, 85004. Tel: 602-354-2200; Fax: 602-354-2428.

Religious, Office of—Sr. JEAN STEFFES, C.S.A., Dir., 400 E. Monroe, Phoenix, 85004. Tel: 602-354-2470; Fax: 602-354-2427.

Catholic Tuition Organization of the Diocese of Phoenix (CTODP)—WALLACE ESTFAN, Pres.; PAUL S. MULLIGAN, M.T.S., Exec. Dir., 2025 N. 3rd St., Ste. #165, Phoenix, 85004-1425. Tel: 602-218-6542; Fax: 602-218-6623.

Office of Black Catholic Ministry—KIT MARSHALL, Dir., Diocesan Center, 400 E. Monroe St., Phoenix, 85004. Tel: 602-354-2025.

Presbyteral Council—Revs. FREDRICK J. ADAMSON, V.G.; MICHAEL L. DISKIN; RICHARD R. FELT, V.F.; GREG MENEGAY; GREG SCHLARB; DANIEL VOLLMER; Most Rev. THOMAS J. OLMSTED, J.C.D.; Revs. CHRISTOPHER J. FRASER, J.C.L.; DAVID SANFILIPPO, V.G.; TIMOTHY R. DAVERN, J.C.L.; JOHN LANKEIT; JOHN D. EHRICH; BENOIT DRAPEAU, C.J.M.; GARY R. REGULA; MICHAEL STRALEY; ROBERT ALIUNZI, A.J., V.F.; JOHN A. HERMAN, C.S.C.; WILLIAM J. KOSCO; DAVID KELASH; HANS P. RUYGT.

Research and Planning Office—CARYN MERON, Dir., 400 E. Monroe St., Phoenix, 85004. Tel: 602-354-2484; Fax: 602-354-2431.

Victim Assistance Coordinator—JEAN SOKOL, 400 E. Monroe St., Phoenix, 85004. Tel: 602-354-2396. Email: jsokol@diocesephoenix.org.

Deans—Revs. ROBERT ALIUNZI, A.J., V.F., Northwest Deanery; RICHARD R. FELT, V.F., East Deanery; CHARLES G. KIEFFER, V.F., Central Deanery; KIERAN KLECZEWSKI, V.F., Southwest Deanery; DANIEL MCBRIDE, V.F., South Deanery; PATRICK MOWRER, V.F., North Deanery; DENNIS O'ROURKE, V.F., Northeast Deanery.

CLERGY, PARISHES, MISSIONS AND PAROCHIAL SCHOOLS

CITY OF PHOENIX

(MARICOPA COUNTY)

1—SS. SIMON AND JUDE ROMAN CATHOLIC CATHEDRAL (1953) Revs. Robert Clements, Rector; Raul Lopez Marzetti; Robert Bolding; Deacons Charles Shaw; Tony West; Juan Guzman. In Res., Most Rev. Thomas J. Olmsted.
Res.: 6351 N. 27th Ave., 85017. Tel: 602-242-1300; Fax: 602-249-3768.
School—(Grades K-8) Tel: 602-242-1299. Sr. Raphael Quinn, I.B.V.M., Prin. Sisters 1; Lay Teachers 20; Students 526.
Santa Rosa Hall—1903 W. Ocotillo Rd., 85017.
Convent—Tel: 602-242-2544.

2—ST. AGNES ROMAN CATHOLIC PARISH (1940) Revs. Bradley L. Peterson, O.Carm., Admin.; Patrick Gavin, O.Carm.
Church & Res.: 1954 N. 24th St., 85008. Tel: 602-244-0349; Fax: 602-244-0054.
School—(Grades PreSchool-8), 2311 E. Palm Ln., 85006. Tel: 602-244-1451. Denise Campbell, Prin. Lay Teachers 14; Students 214.

3—ST. ANTHONY ROMAN CATHOLIC PARISH (1943) Revs. Alfredo Frutades, I.V.E.; Librado Godinez Rivera, I.V.E.
Church & Res.: 909 S. First Ave., 85003. Tel: 602-252-1771; Fax: 602-258-4714.
Center-St. Pius X—, Closed 2004.
Convent—Missionaries of Charity, Gift of Mary Convent, 1414 S. 17th Ave., 85007. Tel: 602-258-5504.
Mission—Our Lady of Fatima 1418 S. 17th Ave., Maricopa Co. 85007. Tel: 602-254-4944. Rev. Francis A. Pecock, Admin.

4—ST. AUGUSTINE ROMAN CATHOLIC PARISH (1970) Revs. Carlos Gomez; Jose Garibaldi Ballesteros Urias; Deacons James Hamilton; Ernesto Ramirez; Lorenzo McKnight; Ricardo Gonzalez.
Church: 3630 N. 71st Ave., 85033. Tel: 623-849-3131; Fax: 623-849-5689.

5—ST. BENEDICT ROMAN CATHOLIC PARISH (1985) Rev. Gary R. Regula; Deacon John Benware.
Church: 16223 S. 48th St., 85048. Tel: 480-961-1610; Fax: 480-961-1794.
School—St. John Bosco Interparish School, (Grades PreSchool-8), 16035 S. 48th St., 85048. Tel: 480-219-4848; Fax: 480-219-5767. Email: sconner@sjbosco.org. Web: www.sjbosco.org. Shelley Conner, Prin.; Theresa Harvey, Librarian. Diocesan Intraparish School Lay Teachers 31; Students 562.

6—ST. CATHERINE OF SIENA ROMAN CATHOLIC PARISH (1947) Revs. Alonso Saenz; Alfredo Valdez Molina; Deacons Carlos Terrazas; Albert Gonzalez; Jesus Morales; Manuel Vasquez, (Retired).
Res.: 6401 S. Central Ave., 85040. Tel: 602-276-5581; Fax: 602-276-2119.
School—(Grades K-8), 6413 S. Central Ave., 85040. Tel: 602-276-2241, Ext. 251; Fax: 602-268-7886. Catherine Lucero, Prin. & Preschool Dir. Lay Teachers 10; Students 230.
School—Preschool Sisters 1; Lay Teachers 3; Students 36.

7—CORPUS CHRISTI ROMAN CATHOLIC PARISH (1985) Revs. Albert F.H. Hoorman; Rafael Bercasio; Deacons Alexander Gaudio; Patrick Flynn; Philip Simeone; Robert England.
Res.: 3550 E. Knox, 85044. Tel: 480-893-8770; Fax: 480-893-3291.

8—ST. EDWARD CONFESSOR ROMAN CATHOLIC PARISH (1976) Rev. Daniel McBride, Canonical Pastor; Deacon Peter Fejes, Admin. Pro Tem. In Res., Revs. Victor Yakubu; Thomas Kawai.
Res.: 4410 E. Southern Ave., 85040. Tel: 602-438-0043; Fax: 602-438-9305.

9—ST. FRANCIS XAVIER ROMAN CATHOLIC PARISH (1928) Revs. Daniel J. Sullivan, S.J.; John Auther, S.J.; John Martin; Deacons Jose Orozco; William DeMarco.
Church: 4715 N. Central Ave., 85012-1796. Tel: 602-279-9547; Fax: 602-248-8968.
School—(Grades K-8) Tel: 602-266-5364. Kim Cavnar, Prin. Lay Teachers 28; Students 548.

10—ST. GREGORY ROMAN CATHOLIC PARISH (1947) Revs. Emile Pelletier Jr.; Eugene Florea; Deacons Lee Kloft; Carmene Carbone; Edward Bolton, (Retired). In Res., Rev. David Sanfilippo.
Res.: 3424 N. 18th Ave., 85015. Tel: 602-264-4488; Fax: 602-266-5210.
School—(Grades PreSchool-8), 3440 N. 18th Ave., 85015. Tel: 602-266-9527. Ms. Maureen Fyan, Prin.

Lay Teachers 21; Students 326.

11—HOLY FAMILY ROMAN CATHOLIC PARISH (1968) Rev. Daniel McBride, Canonical Pastor; Deacon Peter Fejes, Admin. Pro Tem.
Res.: 6802 S. 24th St., 85040. Tel: 602-268-2632; Fax: 602-268-8909.

12—IMMACULATE HEART OF MARY ROMAN CATHOLIC PARISH (1924) Rev. Alfredo Frutades, I.V.E.; Deacons Richard Yanez; Lowell O'Grady.
Church: 909 E. Washington St., 85034. Tel: 602-253-6129; Fax: 602-253-4210.

13—ST. JEROME ROMAN CATHOLIC PARISH (1962) Revs. Andres Arango, C.J.M.; Benoit Drapeau, C.J.M.; Deacons Schubert Wenzel; Bill Bidleman, (Retired); Dick Rein.
Church: 10815 N. 35th Ave., 85029. Tel: 602-942-5555; Fax: 602-504-9115.
School—(Grades PreSchool-8) Tel: 602-942-5644. Carl Hodus, Prin. Lay Teachers 16; Students 258.

14—ST. JOAN OF ARC ROMAN CATHOLIC PARISH (1979) Revs. Donald J. Kline; John Muir; Nicholas A. Floridi; Deacons Michael Carlomagno; James Springer.
Church: 3801 E. Greenway Rd., 85032-4698. Tel: 602-867-9171; Fax: 602-482-7930.
School—Preschool, 2yrs.-PreK, Tel: 602-867-9179. Michelle Buxtin, Dir. Lay Teachers 1; Students 59.

15—ST. JOSEPH ROMAN CATHOLIC PARISH (1969) Rev. John Greb. In Res., Deacon James Trant.
Res.: 11001 N. 40th St., 85028. Tel: 602-996-5120; Fax: 602-996-4011.

16—ST. LUKE ROMAN CATHOLIC PARISH (1985) Rev. Richard A. Milligan.
Res.: 19644 N. Seventh Ave., 85027. Tel: 623-582-0561.

17—ST. MARK ROMAN CATHOLIC PARISH (1946) Revs. Charles Kieffer, Canonical Pastor; Fausto Penafiel.
Res.: 400 N. 30th St., 85008. Tel: 602-267-0503; Fax: 602-275-7261.

18—ST. MARTIN DE PORRES ROMAN CATHOLIC PARISH (1973) Revs. David Sanfilippo, Canonical Pastor; Thomas Kawai; Sr. Dorothy Deger, S.N.D.deN., Parish Life Coord.; Deacon Jose Olivarez.
Res.: 3851 W. Wier Ave., 85041. Tel: 602-276-2466 (Church); Fax: 602-232-2147.

19—ST. MARY'S ROMAN CATHOLIC BASILICA (1881) Revs. Vincent Mesi, O.F.M.; Micah Muhlen, O.F.M. In Res., Rev. Luis Baldonado, O.F.M. (Retired).
Res.: 231 N. Third St., 85004. Tel: 602-354-2100; Fax: 602-354-2060.

20—MATER MISERICORDIAE ROMAN CATHOLIC MISSION Rev. J. Terra, F.S.S.P.
2312 E. Campbell Ave., 85016-5597. Tel: 480-231-0573. Web: www.phoenixlatinmass.org.

21—ST. MATTHEW ROMAN CATHOLIC PARISH (1939) Rev. Raymond J. Ritari; Deacons Tony Beltran; Matias Valle.
Res.: 320 N. 20th Dr., 85009. Tel: 602-258-1789; Fax: 602-258-6507.
School—(Grades K-8), 2038 W. Van Buren, 85009. Tel: 602-254-0611. Gena McGowan, Prin. Brothers 1; Lay Teachers 10; Students 180.

22—MOST HOLY TRINITY ROMAN CATHOLIC PARISH (1951) Revs. Alphonsus Bakyil, S.O.L.T.; Richard Klepac, S.O.L.T.; Deacons Donald Fischer; J.R. Dalisay.
Res.: 8620 N. Seventh St., 85020. Tel: 602-944-3375; Fax: 602-943-2323.
School—(Grades PreSchool-8), 535 E. Alice Ave., 85020. Tel: 602-943-9058. Michael Brennan, Prin. & Dir. (Preschool). Lay Teachers 16; Students 180.

23—OUR LADY OF CZESTOCHOWA ROMAN CATHOLIC PARISH (2008) Rev. Eugeniusz Bolda, S.Ch.
Church: 2828 W. Country Gables Dr., 85053. Tel: 602-212-1172; Fax: 602-212-1173.
Convent—Missionary Sisters of Christ the King for Polonia, Tel: 602-680-7646. Sr. Weronika E. Ilnicka, M.Ch.R., Supr.

24—OUR LADY OF THE VALLEY ROMAN CATHOLIC PARISH (1973) Rev. Edward J. Kaminski, C.S.C., Admin.; Deacons Robert Manthie; Richard Meidl.
Church: 3220 W. Greenway Rd., 85053. Tel: 602-993-1213; Fax: 602-993-1223.

25—ST. PAUL ROMAN CATHOLIC PARISH (1976) Revs. Michael Straley; Robert Binta; Deacons Bill Vivio; Guy Goubeaux; Joseph Badame.
Res.: 330 W. Coral Gables Dr., 85023. Tel: 602-942-2608; Fax: 602-548-0708.

26—ST. PHILIP THE DEACON ROMAN CATHOLIC MISSION, A QUASI-PARISH Revs. Charles Kieffer, Canonical Pastor; Fausto Penafiel; Deacon Angel Guzman.
615 N. 20th St., Maricopa Co. 85006. Tel: 602-253-1076.

27—SACRED HEART ROMAN CATHOLIC PARISH (1962) Rev. Timothy Conlon, O.S.C.; Ms. Ann Conway, Parish Life Coord.
Church: 1421 S. 12th St., 85034. Tel: 602-258-2089.

28—ST. THERESA ROMAN CATHOLIC PARISH (1955) Revs. Charles G. Kieffer; Mathew Plathottam; Frank Fernandez; Deacons Colin Campbell; Sione Hola.
Church: 5045 E. Thomas Rd., 85018. Tel: 602-840-0850; Fax: 602-840-0871.
School—(Grades PreSchool-8), 5001 E. Thomas Rd., 85018. Tel: 602-840-0010. Sr. Patricia Gehling, S.S.N.D., Prin.; Catherine Downey, Dir. (Preschool). Sisters 2; Lay Teachers 27; Students 600.

29—ST. THOMAS THE APOSTLE ROMAN CATHOLIC PARISH (1950) Revs. John D. Ehrich; Arthur Nave; Deacons Thomas Bills; Douglas Bogart; Ken Miller, (Retired); Americo Gouveia, (Retired).
Church: 2312 E. Campbell Ave., 85016-5597. Tel: 602-954-9089; Fax: 602-956-3454.
School—(Grades K-8), 4510 N. 24th St., 85016. Tel: 602-954-9088. Mary Coffman, Prin. Sisters 2; Lay Teachers 24; Students 533.
Convent—4550 N. 24th St., 85016. Tel: 602-368-5238. Dominican Srs. of Mary, Mother of the Eucharist.

30—VIETNAMESE MARTYRS PARISH ROMAN CATHOLIC PARISH (2004) Rev. Joseph Nguyen, O.P.
8620 N. 7th St., 85020-3197. Tel: 602-395-0421.

31—ST. VINCENT DE PAUL ROMAN CATHOLIC PARISH (1957) Revs. Kilian McCaffrey; Alberto Vasquez Coloma; Craig Friedley; Deacons Bill Jenkins; Lorenzo Salazar.
Church: 3140 N. 51st Ave., 85031. Tel: 623-247-6871; Fax: 623-247-4457.
School—(Grades PreSchool-8), 3130 N. 51st Ave., 85031. Tel: 623-247-8595; Fax: 623-245-0132. Sr. Julie Kubsak, D.C., Prin. Sisters 3; Lay Teachers 17; Students 381.
Convent—Daughters of Charity, 3130 N. 51st Ave., 85031. Tel: 623-247-8916.

OUTSIDE THE CITY OF PHOENIX

ANTHEM, MARICOPA CO., ST. ROSE PHILIPPINE DUCHESNE ROMAN CATHOLIC PARISH (2004) Rev. Mark Harrington; Deacons William Clower; Daniel Peterson; John D'Amico.
2825 W. Rose Canyon Cir., 85086. Tel: 623-465-9740; Fax: 623-742-7031.
Mission—Catholic Community of the Good Shepherd, A Quasi-Parish 45033 N. 12th St., New River, 85087.

ASHFORK, YAVAPAI CO., ST. ANNE ROMAN CATHOLIC MISSION ASHFORK, A QUASI-PARISH Rev. Bruno Cuario, D.S.
47047 7th St., 86320. Mailing Address: P.O. Box 525, Ash Fork, 86320. Tel: 928-637-2458.

AVONDALE, MARICOPA CO., ST. THOMAS AQUINAS ROMAN CATHOLIC PARISH Revs. Kieran Kleczewski; Thielo Ramirez; Jorge Canez, Parochial Vicar; Deacons Al Scheller; Milford Suida; James Cascio.
Church: 13720 W. Thomas Rd., 85323. Tel: 623-935-2151; Fax: 623-935-5044.
School—(Grades PreSchool-8) Dr. James McDermott, Prin. Sisters 1; Lay Teachers 11; Students 250.

BAGDAD, YAVAPAI CO., ST. FRANCIS OF ASSISI ROMAN CATHOLIC PARISH (1959) Rev. Leonardo J. Vargas, Admin.
Mailing Address: P.O. Box 768, 86321.
Church & Rectory: 220 Cook St., 86321. Tel: 928-633-2389.
Mission—St. Mary Mediatrix, A Quasi Parish 17343 Hwy. 89, P.O. Box 706, Yarnell, Yavapai Co. 85362. Tel: 928-427-0276.

BAPCHULE, PINAL CO., ST. PETER'S (1950) Rev. Dale Jamison, O.F.M., Canonical Pastor.
Mailing Address: P.O. Box 545, Sacaton, 85147. Tel: 520-560-2690.
School—(Grades K-8), 1500 N. St. Peter Rd., P.O. Box 10840, 85151. Tel: 520-315-3835; Fax: 520-315-3963. Sr. Martha Mary Carpenter, O.S.F., Prin. Sisters 7; Lay Teachers 10; Students 203.
Convent—Franciscan Sisters of Christian Charity (Manitowoc, WI), P.O. Box 10840. Tel: 520-315-3645.
Missions of Gila River Catholic Community Team—
Mission—Holy Family Blackwater, Pinal Co.
Mission—Our Lady of Victory Sacaton Flats, Pinal Co.
Mission—St. Anne Santan, Pinal Co.
Mission—St. Anthony Sacaton, Pinal Co.
Convent—Sisters of the Blessed Sacrament
Mission—St. Francis 16657 N. Church St., Maricopa, Pinal Co. 85139. Tel: 480-440-4414.

BLACK CANYON CITY, YAVAPAI CO., ST. PHILIP BENIZI ROMAN CATHOLIC MISSION BLACK CANYON CITY, A QUASI-PARISH Deacons James Sejba; Leslie Stokes.
34621 Black Canyon Hwy., P.O. Box 138, 85324. Tel: 623-374-5392.

BUCKEYE, MARICOPA CO., SAINT HENRY ROMAN CATHOLIC PARISH (1956) Rev. William J. Kosco; Deacons George Cameron; John Bilinski; Mark Grabowski; Victor Leon.
Church: 128 S. Third St., 85326. Tel: 623-386-6407; Fax: 623-386-4328.

BULLHEAD CITY, MOHAVE CO., ST. MARGARET MARY ROMAN CATHOLIC PARISH (1947) Revs. Peter P. Dobrowski; Julius Kayiwa; Deacons Richard Eckert; John Del Quadro.
Church: 1691 N. Oatman Rd., 86442. Tel: 928-758-7117; Fax: 928-758-2345.

CAMP VERDE, YAVAPAI CO., ST. FRANCES CABRINI ROMAN CATHOLIC PARISH (1962) Revs. Reynaldo Clutario, S.O.L.T.; Alvin Cayetano, S.O.L.T.
Res.: P.O. Box 1677, 86322. Tel: 928-567-3543.
Church: 781 S. Cliffs Pkwy., 86322. Tel: 928-567-3543; Fax: 928-567-7058.

CAREFREE, MARICOPA CO., OUR LADY OF JOY ROMAN CATHOLIC PARISH (1972) Revs. Patrick Farley, Admin.; Herbert Hauck.
Mailing Address: P.O. Box 1359, 85377.
Res.: 36811 N. Pima Rd., 85377. Tel: 480-488-2229 (Church); 480-488-0469 (Rectory); Fax: 480-488-1085.
School—(Grades PreSchool-K) Tel: 480-595-6409. Deborah Allen, Dir. Lay Teachers 6; Students 80.

CASHION, MARICOPA CO., ST. WILLIAM ROMAN CATHOLIC PARISH (1973) Rev. Mario Garcia-Icedo, Admin.
Mailing Address: P.O. Box 329, 85329.
Church: 11003 W. Third St., 85329. Tel: 623-936-6115; Fax: 623-936-8308.
Chapel—Our Lady of Guadalupe Santa Maria. 6807 Lower Buckeye Rd., Maricopa Co. 85043.

CAVE CREEK, MARICOPA CO., ST. GABRIEL ROMAN CATHOLIC PARISH (2002) Revs. Dennis O'Rourke; Benedict Onegiu, Parochial Vicar; Deacon James Fogle.
32648 N. Cave Creek Rd., 85331. Tel: 480-595-0883; Fax: 480-595-0886.
School—Annunciation Catholic School, (Grades 1-2) Dr. Sharon Pristash, Prin. Lay Teachers 2; Students 25.

CHANDLER, MARICOPA CO.

1—ST. ANDREW THE APOSTLE ROMAN CATHOLIC PARISH (1985) Revs. John R. Coleman; Richard McGuire, O.S.C.; Deacons Ernest Garcia; Michael Carr; Donald Crawford.
Res.: 3450 W. Ray Rd., 85226. Tel: 480-899-1990; Fax: 480-917-8475.

2—ST. MARY ROMAN CATHOLIC PARISH (1937) Revs. Daniel McBride; Jesus G. Ty; Will Schmid; Braulio Valencia; Deacons Craig Hintze; Mike Kronschnabel; Manuel Olivas; Edward Hickcox.
Church: 230 W. Galveston, 85224. Tel: 480-963-3207; Fax: 480-814-9417.
School—St. Mary-Basha Catholic Elementary, (Grades K-8), 200 W. Galveston, 85224. Tel: 480-963-4951. Sr. Mary Norbert Long, S.C., Prin. Sisters of Charity of Seton Hill 2; Lay Teachers 25; Students 515.
Convent—Sisters of Charity, Seton Hill, 464 W. Ivanhoe, 85225. Tel: 480-963-5038.

CHINO VALLEY, YAVAPAI CO., ST. CATHERINE LABOURE ROMAN CATHOLIC MISSION CHINO VALLEY, A QUASI-PARISH Rev. H. Fred LeClaire, C.M.F., Admin.
2062 N. Hwy. 89, 86323. Mailing Address: P.O. Box 152, 86323-0152. Tel: 928-636-4071. Email: stcathlab@juno.com.

COTTONWOOD, YAVAPAI CO., IMMACULATE CONCEPTION ROMAN CATHOLIC PARISH (1966) Revs. David Kelash; Pawel Stawarczyk; Deacons James Brown; Ron Pelton; David Kaminsky; Onofre Duran, (Retired).
Church: 700 N. Bill Gray Rd., 86326. Tel: 928-634-2933; Fax: 928-634-3326.
School—St. Joseph Catholic School, (Grades PreSchool-8), 2715 E. Hwy. 89A, P.O. Box 370, 86326. Tel: 928-649-0624; Fax: 928-649-1191. Email: info@stjcmvv.com. Web: www.sjcms.net. Greg Kirkham, Prin. Lay Teachers 7; Students 80.
Mission—St. Cecilia Clarkdale, Yavapai Co. Site for Tridentine Mass. Closed 2002, for sacramental records contact Immaculate Conception, 928-634-2142.
Mission—Holy Family, (Closed 2004), Jerome, Yavapai Co.

EL MIRAGE, MARICOPA CO., SANTA TERESITA ROMAN CATHOLIC PARISH (1968) Rev. Stephen Schack.
P.O. Box 67, 85335. Tel: 623-583-8183; Fax: 623-583-2963.
Church: 14016 N. Verbena St., 85335.

FLAGSTAFF, COCONINO CO., SAN FRANCISCO DE ASIS ROMAN CATHOLIC PARISH (1997) Revs. Patrick Mowrer; Jude Uche, C.S.Sp.; Deacons Lawrence Whelan; James Bret; Robert Olberding; Dennis Revering; James Arnold, (Retired); Douglas Rade, (Retired).
Mailing Address: 2257 E. Cedar Ave., 86004-1918. Tel: 928-779-1341; Fax: 928-779-5124.
Holy Trinity Newman Center—520 W. Riordan Rd., 86002. Tel: 928-779-2903; Fax: 928-779-0698. Rev. Matthew Lowry, Chap.
School—San Francisco de Asis, (Grades PreSchool-8), 320 N. Humphrey, 86001. Tel: 928-779-1337; Fax: 928-774-1943. Mary Frances Malinoski, Prin. Lay Teachers 15; Students 203.
Convent—Institute of the Blessed Virgin Mary Loretto Sisters, 202 S. Kendrick, 86001. Tel: 520-744-3680.
Chapel—Nativity of B.V.M. 16 W. Cherry Ave., 86001.
Chapel—Our Lady of Guadalupe 224 S. Kendrick, 86001.

Chapel—St. Pius X 2257 E. Cedar Ave., 86004.

FOUNTAIN HILLS, MARICOPA CO., ASCENSION ROMAN CATHOLIC PARISH (1976) Rev. John T. McDonough; Deacons Richard Smith; Phillip LoCascio.
Church: 12615 Fountain Hills Blvd., 85268. Tel: 480-837-1066; Fax: 480-837-9093.
Mission—St. Dominic 25603 N. Danny Ln., Ste. 2, Rio Verde, Maricopa Co. 85263. Tel: 480-471-2112.

GILA BEND, MARICOPA CO., ST. MICHAEL ROMAN CATHOLIC PARISH (1963) Rev. Kieran Kleczewski, Parochial Admin.
Mailing Address: 13720 W. Thomas Rd., Avondale, 85323.
Church: 314 Dodson St., 85337.

GILBERT, MARICOPA CO., ST. ANNE ROMAN CATHOLIC PARISH (1943) Revs. Greg Schlarb; Jose Jesus Lopez; Timothy R. Davern; Deacons Joe Spadafino; Keith Boswell; Joseph Cady. In Res., Revs. Michael J. Boyle, C.M.; Stephen Adrian (Retired).
Church: 440 E. Elliot Rd., 85299-0228.
Convent—Carmelite Sisters, M.C.S.T.N.J., 419 E. Washington #3-D, 85234. Tel: 480-633-3729.

GLENDALE, MARICOPA CO.

1—ST. HELEN ROMAN CATHOLIC PARISH (1974) Revs. R. Bruce Downs; James J. Ferguson, C.S.C.; Deacons Joseph Shinske; Robert Campas; John Mickel.
Church: 5510 W. Cholla, 85304. Tel: 623-979-4202; Fax: 623-412-1226.

2—ST. JAMES ROMAN CATHOLIC PARISH (1982) Revs. Robert Aliunzi, A.J.; John R. Ssegawa, A.J.; Deacons Alan Bowslaugh; Frank Devine; Jack O'Connor, (Retired); Carl Sadlier.
Church: 19640 N. 35th Ave., 85308. Tel: 623-581-0707; Fax: 623-581-0110.
Res.: 18225 N. 35th Dr., 85308. Tel: 623-843-0421.

3—ST. LOUIS THE KING ROMAN CATHOLIC PARISH (1962) Revs. Michael L. Diskin, Canonical Pastor; Joseph Bui, P.I.M.E.; Deacons Joseph Stickney; George Valverde; Eduardo Zavala.
Church: 4331 W. Maryland Ave., 85301. Tel: 623-930-1127; Fax: 623-930-1129.
School—(Grades PreSchool-8) Tel: 623-939-4260. Jane Daigle, Prin.; Jennifer Weworski, Preschool Dir. Lay Teachers 13; Students 250.

4—OUR LADY OF PERPETUAL HELP ROMAN CATHOLIC PARISH (1947) Revs. Michael D. Accinni Reinhardt; Oscar Gutierrez; Deacons Anthony Lopez; Robert Myers; Eddie Molina; Dennis Raczkowski.
Church: 5614 W. Orangewood Ave., 85301. Tel: 623-939-9785; Fax: 623-934-8854.
School—(Grades PreSchool-8), 7521 N. 57th Ave., 85301. Tel: 623-931-7288. Mary Pat Waldman, Prin. Lay Teachers 18; Students 288.
Chapel—Our Lady of Guadalupe 55th Ave. & Lamar, 85301.

5—ST. RAPHAEL ROMAN CATHOLIC PARISH (1974) Rev. Edward J. Kaminski, C.S.C., Canonical Pastor; Deacons Richard Meidl; Robert Manthie.
5504 W. Acoma, 85306.
Church: 5525 W. Acoma, 85306. Tel: 602-938-4227; Fax: 602-978-0305.

6—ST. THOMAS MORE ROMAN CATHOLIC PARISH (1997) Rev. James Turner; Deacons Roy Drapeau; Keith Davis; Richard Kjewski.
6180 W. Utopia Rd., 85308-7111. Tel: 623-566-8222; Fax: 623-825-1468.

GOODYEAR, MARICOPA CO., SAINT JOHN VIANNEY ROMAN CATHOLIC PARISH (1956) Revs. John A. Herman, C.S.C.; Andrew Gawrych, C.S.C.; Deacons Nick Bonaito; Greg Galloway.
Church: 539 La Pasada Blvd., 85338. Tel: 602-932-3313; Fax: 602-932-1896.
School—(Grades PreSchool-8) Tel: 623-932-2434. Sr. Ignacia Carrillo, F.M.A., Prin.; Cindi Zulegu, Dir. Sisters 1; Lay Teachers 15; Students 253.
Convent—F.M.A., Salesian Sisters, 15 W. Loma Linda Blvd., Avondale, 85323. Tel: 623-932-2652; Fax: 623-932-1243.

GRAND CANYON, COCONINO CO., EL CRISTO REY ROMAN CATHOLIC PARISH (1960) Revs. Dindo Bruno Cuario, D.S., Canonical Pastor; Boniface Akara, C.M.F.
Mailing Address: P.O. Box 505, 86023. Tel: 928-638-2390.
Church: 44 Albright Ave., 86023.

GUADALUPE, MARICOPA CO., OUR LADY OF GUADALUPE ROMAN CATHOLIC PARISH (1970) Rev. Joseph A. Baur, O.F.M., Admin.; Deacon Santo Bernasconi.
Church: 5445 San Angelo St., 85283. Tel: 480-839-2860.
Res.: 9004 Calle Maravilla, 85283. Tel: 480-839-2376.

HIGLEY, MARICOPA CO., ST. MARY MAGDALENE ROMAN CATHOLIC PARISH Rev. Greg Menegay; Deacons Robert Carey; Gerald O'Toole; William Shea, (Retired).
Mailing Address: P.O. Box 849, 85236-0849. Tel: 480-279-6737; Fax: 480-279-6786.
Church: 2654 E. Williams Field Rd., Gilbert, 85296.

JEROME, YAVAPAI CO., HOLY FAMILY (1908) Closed. Now a mission of Immaculate Conception, Cottonwood.

KINGMAN, MOHAVE CO., ST. MARY ROMAN CATHOLIC PARISH (1906) Rev. Matthew Krempel, O.F.M., Admin. Pro-Tem.; Deacons Bruce Bennett; Bill Del Monaco; Philip Wisely.
Res.: 302 E. Spring St., 86401. Tel: 928-753-3359; Fax: 928-753-2581.
Mission—Our Lady of the Desert, A Quasi-Parish, 16041 N. Pierce Ferry Rd., Dolan Springs, Mohave Co. 86441. Tel: 928-767-3154. Rev. Thomas J. Hallsten.
Mission—La Santisima Trinidad Catholic Mission A Quasi-Parish 3735 Scenic Blvd., Scenic, Mohave Co. 86432. Sr. Maria Guadalupe Magana, H.J., Mission Coord.

LAKE HAVASU CITY, MOHAVE CO., OUR LADY OF THE LAKE ROMAN CATHOLIC PARISH (1969) Revs. Chauncey Winkler; Sylvester Modebei; Michael Ashibuogwu; Deacons Thomas C. Coe; Jeffrey Arner; Gilbert Lopez; John Navaretta; Patrick Toilolo; Thomas DeFilippis, (Retired); Robert Treichel, (Retired).
Church: 1975 Daytona Dr., 86403. Tel: 928-855-2685; Fax: 928-855-7172.
School—Preschool, (Grades PreK) Tel: 928-855-0154. Priests 1; Lay Teachers 2; Students 21.

LAVEEN, MARICOPA CO., ST. JOHN THE BAPTIST (1950) Deacon James Trant, Parish Life Coord.; Rev. Dale Jamison, Canonical Pastor; Deacon Ron Poulin.
Mailing Address: P.O. Box 693, 85339-0693. Tel: 520-550-2034; Fax: 520-550-4873.
Convent—Tel: 520-550-5522.
Mission—St. Catherine Santa Cruz, Pinal Co. Tel: 602-292-4466.
Mission—St. Francis of Assisi, Pime-Maricopa Indian Community, Salt River., Mailing Address: 3090 N. Longmore, Scottsdale, 85256.
Mission—San Lucy Gila Bend, Maricopa, Pinal Co. 85239. P.O. Box 2245, Gila Bend, 85337-2245.
Blessed Kateri Tekakwitha Spirituality Center—Deacon James Trant.
Chapel—St. Paschal Baylon Lehi.

MAYER, YAVAPAI CO., ST. JOSEPH ROMAN CATHOLIC MISSION MAYER, A QUASI-PARISH Rev. Reynaldo Clutario, S.O.L.T.
10901 S. Hwy. 69, 86333. Mailing Address: P.O. Box 171, 86333-0171. Tel: 928-632-4018.

MESA, MARICOPA CO.

1—ALL SAINTS ROMAN CATHOLIC PARISH (1972) Rev. Robert J. Caruso; Deacons T. Vincent Neely, (Retired); Reed Santa, (Retired); Gordon R. Aird; Bernard Filzen; Albro Wilson.
Church: 1534 N. Recker Rd., 85205. Tel: 480-985-7655; Fax: 480-396-0837.

2—ST. BRIDGET ROMAN CATHOLIC PARISH (1985) Rev. W. Scott Brubaker; Deacon Paul Hursh.
Res.: 2850 E. Lockwood St., 85213. Tel: 480-924-9138.
Church: 2213 N. Lindsay Rd., 85213. Tel: 480-924-9111; Fax: 480-924-3103.

3—CHRIST THE KING ROMAN CATHOLIC PARISH (1959) Revs. Steve Kunkel; Peter Dai Bui; Deacons Willard Capistrant; Ronald Ruiz; Tom Bishop; Neal Tift.
1505 E. Dana Ave., 85204.
Church: 1551 E. Dana Ave., 85204. Tel: 480-964-1719; Fax: 480-844-4498.
School—(Grades PreSchool-8) Tel: 480-844-4480. Don Graff, Prin. Lay Teachers 13; Students 221.

4—ST. COLUMBA KIM ROMAN CATHOLIC MISSION Rev. Min-ho Jang, Parochial Admin.
2211 S. Kachina Dr., Tempe, 85282.

5—HOLY CROSS ROMAN CATHOLIC PARISH (1978) Revs. Richard R. Felt; John Shetler, Parochial Vicar; Joshua Alvero, D.S.; Deacons Thomas Ferreira; James Gersitz; Gene Messer; Joe Scaccia; William Finnegan; Ignacio Ixta.
Church: 1244 S. Power Rd., 85206. Tel: 480-981-2021; Fax: 480-981-6844.

6—QUEEN OF PEACE ROMAN CATHOLIC PARISH (1934) Rev. Charles Goraieb; Deacons John Reidel; Richard Areyzaga; Santiago Rodriguez; Jamie Whitford; Thomas Phelan.
Church: 141 N. Macdonald St., 85201. Tel: 480-969-9166; Fax: 480-969-8102.
School—(Grades PreSchool-8), 109 N. Macdonald St., 85201. Tel: 602-969-0226. Priests 1; Lay Teachers 12; Students 191.

7—ST. TIMOTHY ROMAN CATHOLIC PARISH (1978) Revs. John D. Spaulding; Eric Houseknecht; Deacons Thomas Bolduc; Barry Smith; Richard Petersen; Kevin Bassett; Abram Calderon; Dutch Hurrish, (Retired); Oliver Babbits, (Retired). In Res., Rev. Oliver Mohan, O.M.I. (Retired).
Church: 1730 W. Guadalupe, 85202. Tel: 480-775-5200; Fax: 480-820-7984.
School—St. Timothy Preschool, Tel: 480-775-5237. Monica Glick, Dir. Lay Teachers 3; Students 102.
School—St. Timothy Catholic School, (Grades K-8), 2520 S. Alma School Rd., 85210. Tel: 480-775-2650. Maureen Vick, Prin. Lay Teachers 16; Students 177.

PEORIA, MARICOPA CO., ST. CHARLES BORROMEO ROMAN CATHOLIC PARISH (1968) Rev. Loren Gonzales; Deacon Gustavo Arteaga.
Mailing & Church: 8615 W. Peoria Ave., 85345-0819.
Res.: 8617 W. Peoria Ave., 85345. Tel: 623-979-3418.

PRESCOTT VALLEY, YAVAPAI CO., ST. GERMAINE ROMAN CATHOLIC PARISH (1984) Rev. Daniel Vollmer; Deacons Robert Palmer; Wayland Moncrief.
Church: 7997 E. Dana Dr., 86314. Tel: 928-772-6350; Fax: 928-772-4413.

PRESCOTT, YAVAPAI CO., SACRED HEART ROMAN CATHOLIC PARISH (1877) Revs. Arhtur Gramaje, C.M.F.; Daryl Olds, C.M.F.; Valentin Ramon; Gerald Caffrey, C.M.F.; Richard Wozniak, C.M.F.; Deacons Thomas Kayser, (Retired); John Lamon, (Retired); Tony Humphrey; Peter Balland; Thomas Gregory, (Retired); Joseph Bueti.
Church: 150 Fleury Ave., 86301. Tel: 928-445-3141; Fax: 928-717-1074.
School—(Grades PreSchool-8), 131 N. Summit Ave., 86301. Tel: 928-445-2621. Lynn Reuter, Prin. Sisters 2; Lay Teachers 15; Students 189.
Convent—Institute of the Blessed Virgin Mary, 229 N. Summit St., 86301. Tel: 928-445-7861.

QUEEN CREEK, MARICOPA CO., OUR LADY OF GUADALUPE ROMAN CATHOLIC PARISH Revs. Thomas Moylan, L.C.; Thomas Bennett, L.C.; Michael Goodyear, L.C.; Deacon David Barraza.
Mailing Address: P.O. Box 856, 85142-0856. Tel: 480-963-3207.
Church: 20615 E. Ocotillo Rd., 85242.
School—Our Lady of Guadalupe School, (Grades PreSchool-K) Anne Marie Romley, Dir. Lay Teachers 5; Students 71.

SCOTTSDALE, MARICOPA CO.

1—ST. BERNADETTE ROMAN CATHOLIC PARISH (1995) Revs. Peter Rossa; Jose D. Cornelia, D.S.; Deacons Ronald Little; James Hostutler; James Mickens.
Office: 16245 N. 60th St., 85254. Tel: 480-905-0221; Fax: 480-905-0249.
School—Blessed Pope John XXIII Catholic School Community, (Grades K-8), 16235 N. 60th St., 85254. Tel: 480-905-0939; Fax: 480-905-0955. Email: popejohnXXIII@diocesephoenix.org. Christina Bernier, Prin. Sisters 1; Lay Teachers 22; Students 604.

2—ST. BERNARD OF CLAIRVAUX ROMAN CATHOLIC PARISH (1994) Revs. Brian Bell; William W. Faiella, C.S.C.; Deacons Louis Cornille; Alan Hungate.
Church: 10755 N. 124th St., 85259. Tel: 480-661-9843; Fax: 480-614-8092.

3—BLESSED SACRAMENT ROMAN CATHOLIC PARISH (1974) Rev. Patrick Robinson; Deacons Bernard Rekiere; Clemens Czapinski, (Retired); Bob Evans. In Res., Rev. Thomas A. Walsh (Retired).
Church: 11300 N. 64th St., 85254. Tel: 480-948-8370; Fax: 480-951-3844.
School—Preschool, (Grades PreSchool-K) Tel: 480-998-9466. Heather Fraher, Dir. Lay Teachers 6; Students 58.

4—ST. DANIEL THE PROPHET ROMAN CATHOLIC PARISH (1961) Revs. Thaddeus McGuire; Pedro Velez Prensa; Deacons Martin Dippre; John Barelli; Roy Anderson, (Retired); Charles Raymond, (Retired). In Res., Rev. Paul Passant.
Church: 1030 N. Hayden Rd., 85257. Tel: 480-945-8437; Fax: 480-945-4335.
School—(Grades K-8) Tel: 480-949-8034. Rita Standerfer, Prin. Lay Teachers 7; Students 77.
Convent—Daughters of Mary, 7830 E. Roosevelt, 85257.

5—ST. MARIA GORETTI ROMAN CATHOLIC PARISH (1967) Rev. Douglas E. Lorig; Deacons Herve Lemire; Charles Voss; John Berger.
Res.: 8344 E. Edward Ave., 85250.
Church: 6261 N. Granite Reef Rd., 85250. Tel: 480-948-8380; Fax: 480-948-8815.
School—Preschool, (Grades PreSchool-K) Tel: 480-948-8815. Kathleen Bies, Dir. Lay Teachers 4; Students 95.

6—OUR LADY OF PERPETUAL HELP ROMAN CATHOLIC PARISH (1949) Rev. Msgr. Thomas Hever; Rev. Patrick Smith; Deacons Jack Ehrlich; Irving Fleming. In Res., Revs. William J. Fitzgerald (OM) (Retired); John Bernbrock, S.J.
Church & Res.: 7655 E. Main St., 85251. Tel: 480-947-4331; Fax: 480-874-3798.
School—(Grades K-8), 3801 N. Miller Rd., 85251. Tel: 480-874-3720. Sr. Marian Grace Brandt, S.C., Prin. Sisters 2; Lay Teachers 23; Students 457.
Convent—Sisters of Charity, 7634 E. Second St., 85251. Tel: 480-945-3867.

7—ST. PATRICK ROMAN CATHOLIC PARISH (1980) Rev. Eric Tellez; Rev. Msgr. George Schroeder; Deacons James Hoyt; Fred Giesner; John A. Meyer.
Church: 10815 N. 84th St., 85260. Tel: 480-998-3843; Fax: 480-998-5218.

SEDONA, YAVAPAI CO., ST. JOHN VIANNEY ROMAN CATHOLIC PARISH (1965) Rev. J.C. Ortiz; Deacons Ronald Martinez; Donald Henkiel.
Mailing Address: P.O. Box 3909, West Sedona, 86340.
Church: 180 Soldiers Pass Rd., West Sedona, 86340. Tel: 928-282-7545; Fax: 928-282-1798.
Chapel—Holy Cross 780 Chapel Rd., P.O. Box 1043, 86339. Tel: 928-282-4069; Fax: 928-282-3701. Dr. Charles E. Reaume, Admin.

SELIGMAN, YAVAPAI CO., ST. FRANCIS ROMAN CATHOLIC PARISH (1940) Rev. Bruno Cuario, D.S., Canonical Pastor.
P.O. Box 309, 86337. Tel: 928-422-3354.
Church: 104 Schoeny, 86337.

SUN CITY WEST, MARICOPA CO., OUR LADY OF LOURDES ROMAN CATHOLIC PARISH (1979) Rev. David M. Ostler; Deacons George Koch; Jerome Reicks, (Retired); Lee Hanson; Maurice Arnold, (Retired); Ronald TenBarge.
Business Office: 19002 N. 128th Ave., 85375. Tel: 623-344-7266; Fax: 623-214-1246.
Church: *Prince of Peace*, 14818 W. Deer Valley Dr., 85375. Tel: 623-344-7280; Fax: 623-214-2101.

SUN CITY, MARICOPA CO.
1—CHURCH OF ST. JOACHIM & ST. ANNE ROMAN CATHOLIC PARISH (1961) Rev. John Ebbesmier; Deacons Stephen Weiss; Charles Heeter, (Retired).
Mailing Address: P.O. Box 748, Youngtown, 85363.
Church: 11625 111th Ave., 85351-3746. Tel: 623-972-1179; Fax: 623-972-1170.
2—ST. CLEMENT OF ROME ROMAN CATHOLIC PARISH (1970) Revs. John Slobig; Augustine Ogumere, C.S.Sp.; Deacons Michael Phelan; Stanley Giza, (Retired); Irving Dennis, (Retired); Lee Beatrice.
Church: 15800 Del Webb Blvd., 85351. Tel: 623-974-5867; Fax: 623-974-0562.
3—ST. ELIZABETH SETON ROMAN CATHOLIC PARISH (1976) Revs. Franklin Bartel; Regidor Carreon (Retired); Deacons Forrest Briesch; Raymond Roger; Paul Csuy; Larry Grey.
Church: 9728 Palmeras Dr., 85373. Tel: 623-972-2129; Fax: 623-974-0654.

SUN LAKES, MARICOPA CO., ST. STEVEN ROMAN CATHOLIC PARISH (1988) Revs. L. Pierre Hissey; James Alling; Deacons Richard Corwin; Frank Danna; Louis Pardini.
Church: 24827 S. Dobson Rd., 85248. Tel: 480-895-9266; Fax: 480-895-9304.

SURPRISE, MARICOPA CO., ST. CLARE OF ASSISI ROMAN CATHOLIC PARISH Rev. Hans P. Ruygt; Deacons Stephen Martin; Donnan Lukaszewski; Joseph Wenzler; Ted Micek; Vincent Torres.
Church: 17111 W. Bell Rd., 85374. Tel: 623-546-3444; Fax: 623-975-5615.

TEMPE, MARICOPA CO.
1—ALL SAINTS ROMAN CATHOLIC NEWMAN CENTER Rev. James D. Thompson, O.P., Dir.
230 E. University Dr., 85281-3700. Tel: 480-967-7823; Fax: 480-967-1741. Web: www.newman-asu.org.
2—CHURCH OF THE RESURRECTION ROMAN CATHOLIC PARISH (1970) Revs. Joseph P. McGaffin; Romeo Dionisio; Deacons Richard Cuprak; Wayne Morten; William Malatin. In Res., Rev. Joseph G. Krynen (Retired).
Church: 3201 S. Evergreen Rd., 85282. Tel: 480-838-0207; Fax: 480-756-1501.
3—HOLY SPIRIT ROMAN CATHOLIC PARISH (1973) Rev. Thomas J. Hallsten, Parochial Admin.; Deacons Stephen Beard; Gary Johnson.
Rectory—1871 E. Libra Dr., 85283.
Church: 1800 E. Libra Dr., 85283.
4—ST. MARGARET ROMAN CATHOLIC PARISH (1972) Rev. Charles Goraieb, Canonical Pastor; Deacons Frank G. Galarza, Parish Life Coord.; Thomas Swisher; Pedro Mesa.
Church: 2435 E. McArthur Dr., 85281. Tel: 480-967-0379; Fax: 480-967-3825.
5—OUR LADY OF MT. CARMEL ROMAN CATHOLIC PARISH (1932) Revs. John Bonavitacola, Parochial Admin.; Bernard Green, S.D.S.; Deacons James Brett; Thomas Glenn.
Church: 2121 S. Rural Rd., 85282. Tel: 480-967-8791; Fax: 480-967-4919.
School—(Grades K-8), 2117 S. Rural Rd., 85282. Tel: 480-967-5567. Dr. Vincent Sheridan, Prin. Lay Teachers 24; Students 465.
School—Little Lambs Preschool, 3-4yrs., Tel: 480-966-1753. Molly Gorman, Dir. Lay Teachers 6; Students 46.

TOLLESON, MARICOPA CO., BLESSED SACRAMENT ROMAN CATHOLIC PARISH (1953) Rev. John Lankeit; Deacons Jose Garza; Peter Murphy; Sergio Estupinan; Anthony Chavez, (Retired).
Church: 512 N. 93rd Ave., 85353.
Res.: 312 N. 93rd Ave., 85353. Tel: 623-936-7107; Fax: 623-936-9536.

WICKENBURG, MARICOPA CO., ST. ANTHONY OF PADUA ROMAN CATHOLIC PARISH (1941) Rev. Msgr. George Highberger.
Church: 232 N. Tegner St., 85390. Tel: 928-684-2096; Fax: 928-684-3539.
Mission—Our Lady of Guadalupe 50627 Eagle Eye Rd., P.O. Box 294, Aguila, Maricopa Co. 85320. Tel: 928-685-2392.
Mission—Good Shepherd of the Desert, Quasi-Parish., P.O. Box 1134, Congress, Yavapai Co. 85332. Tel: 928-427-6328.

WILLIAMS, COCONINO CO., ST. JOSEPH'S ROMAN CATHOLIC PARISH (1928) Rev. Bruno Cuario, D.S.
Church: 900 W. Grant, 86046. Tel: 928-635-2430; Fax: 928-635-0177.

Chaplains of Public Institutions

PHOENIX. *Arizona State Hospital*, 2500 E. Van Buren St., 85008. Tel: 602-244-1331. Deacon James Cascio, M.P.S., Chap.
Banner Good Samaritan Medical Center, 1111 E. McDowell Rd., 85006. Tel: 602-239-2000. Rev. Vincent Mesi, O.F.M., Interim Chap.
John C. Lincoln Hospital - N. Mountain, 2500 E. Dunlap, 85020. Tel: 602-943-2381. Rev. Jose D. Cornelia, D.S., Chap.
St. Joseph's Hospital, P.O. Box 2071, 85001. Tel: 602-406-3275. Rev. Milton N. Adamson, C.S.C., Chap., Sr. Margaret McBride, R.S.M., Mission Svcs., Bonnie McCulley, Dir. Chap. Svcs.
St. Luke's Medical Center, 1800 E. Van Buren St., 85006. Tel: 602-251-8100. Vacant.
Maricopa Medical Center, 2601 E. Roosevelt St., 85008. Tel: 602-344-5011. Rev. Fidelis Igwenwanne, Chap.
Phoenix Indian Medical Center, 4212 N. 16th St., 85016. Tel: 602-263-1017. Vacant. (For Sacramental Records Contact St. Francis Xavier at 602-279-9547)
Sky Harbor Interfaith Chaplaincy, Sky Harbor International Airport, Terminal 4, Level 3. Tel: 602-683-3885. Web: phoenix.gov/skyharborairport/customer-service/travelers-in-crisis.html. Deacon Joseph Cady, Chap.
United States Veterans Affairs Medical Center, 650 E. Indian School Rd., 85012. Tel: 602-222-6422. Revs. Kenneth Kleiber, Chap., Matthias Crehan, O.F.M., Chap.

CHANDLER. *Chandler Regional Hospital*, 475 S. Dobson Rd., 85224. Tel: 480-728-5650. Rev. Tim Bushy, Chap.

GILBERT. *Mercy Gilbert Medical Center*, 3555 S. Val Vista Dr., 85296. Tel: 480-728-8000. Rev. Tim Bushy, Chap.

LUKE AIR FORCE BASE. *Luke Catholic Community*, 58 FW/HC, 13968 Shooting Star St., 85309-1932. Tel: 623-856-6211; Fax: 623-856-6968. Deacon James Pfleger, Chap.

MESA. *Banner Desert Medical Center*, 1400 S. Dobson Rd., 85202. Tel: 480-512-3199. Rev. Romeo Dionisio, Chap.

PRESCOTT. *United States Veterans Hospital (Prescott)*, 500 Hwy. No. 89, 86313. Tel: 928-445-4860. Rev. Gerald Caffrey, C.M.F., Chap.

SCOTTSDALE. *Scottsdale Healthcare Osborn*, 7400 E. Osborn Rd., 85251. Tel: 480-882-4000. Rev. Patrick Smith, Chap.

SUN CITY. *Banner Boswell Medical Center*, 10401 W. Thunderbird Blvd., 85351. Tel: 623-977-7211. Rev. Larry W. Weidner, Chap.

Special Assignment:
Revs.—
Fenlon, Brian, Hospice Chap., Hospice of the Valley, 6710 N. 79th Pl., Scottsdale, 85250-7921. Tel: 480-998-2557
Penafiel, Fausto, 5141 W. Burton Dr., 85043.
Rice, Gregory P., M.H.M., 5995 N. 78th St., #2098, Scottsdale, 85250.
Sotelo, Antonio, Prison Chap. (Retired), 700 W. University Dr., #154, Tempe, 85281. Tel: 480-967-0379

On Leave:
Rev. Msgr.—
Fushek, Dale J., V.G.
Revs.—
Briceno, Joseph C.
Carpenter, Christopher
Colleary, Patrick
Deptula, Michael
Draves-Arpaia, Cornelius
Gonzalez, Hugo
Goulet, Wayne F.
Hall, John
Lessard, Joseph M.
Madrid, Saul
Orel, Paul
Sherwood, Lan S.
Shetler, John
Wesolowski, Tomasz

Retired:
Most Rev.—
O'Brien, Thomas J., D.D., 400 E. Monroe, 85004.
Rev. Msgrs.—
Malone, Alan, Eyrecourt, Ballinasloe, Galway, Co. Ireland.
McKay, William E., 6457 E. Dodge St., Mesa, 85205.
McMahon, John J., Mt. Claret Center, 4633 N. 54th St., 85018.
Moyer, Richard W., 3302 N. 7th St., #133, 85014.
O'Grady, Michael, 6301 N. 34th Ln., 85017.
Revs.—
Baumann, Lawrence L., 4040 E. Comanche Dr., Cottonwood, 86326.
Bormann, Charles P., 5029 E. Smokehouse Tr., Cave Creek, 85331.
Boulanger, Andre, 2239 E. Cheery Lynn, 85016-4928.
Boyle, Thomas, 325 W. Holly St., 85003.
Brogan, Leo, 850 Beech St., Apt. 1503, San Diego, CA 92101.
Colton, Bernard, 122A Clanabogan Rd., Omagh, Co. Tyrone BT 7815 N Northern Ireland.
Cullinan, John F., 1694 W. Glendale Ave., #343, 85021.
Cunningham, John F., 16709 E. Frye Rd., Gilbert, 85297.
D'Eon, Earl, St. Clement of Rome, 15800 Del Webb Blvd., 85351-1698.
Feit, Matthias, 4633 N. 54th St., 85018.
Gauthier, John C., 8931 Ferry Rd., New Roads, LA 70760-2078.
Gillespie, Joseph, 715 W. Lynwood St., 85007-1912.
Graf, Harold P., 3655 N. 5th Ave., #110, 85013.
Groves, Edmund, St. Paul's Convent, Bushmount, Clonakilty, Co. Cork Ireland.
Hanley, John, 4633 N. 54th St., 85018.
Harnischfeger, William, 10626 Mimosa Dr., 85351.
Healy, William P., 8514 E. Via De Los Libros, Scottsdale, 85258.
Hennessy, Joseph I., 24418 S. Starcrest, Sun Lakes, 85248.
Kotnis, Gregory M., 15735 W. Arrowhead Dr., Suprise, 85374.
Krynen, Joseph G., Resurrection Parish, 3201 S. Evergreen Rd., Tempe, 85282.
Meyer, Blase G., 7145 E. Juanita Ave., Mesa, 85208-4024.
Minogue, Michael J., 13018 W. Rosewood Dr., El Mirage, 85335.
Mitchell, William J., 1675 Leisure World, Mesa, 85206.
Morales, Raul, 6124 E. Akron, Mesa, 85205.
O'Carroll, Eugene, 3609 W. Questa Dr., Glendale, 85310.
O'Dea, Thomas, Ballycanally, Ennis, Co. Clare, Ireland.
Parker, Charles, 8330 N. 21st Dr., Unit #207, 85021-9347.
Pirrung, George, P.O. Box 1144, Cottonwood, 86326.
Riccitelli, Dennis, 7145 E. Juanita Ave., Mesa, 85208.
Sigman, Louis A., 1272 E. La Costa Pl., Chandler, 85226.
Simlik, Frank P., 10713 W. El Dorado Dr., 85351.
Skagen, Robert, 3422 W. Del Monico Ln., 85051.
Sotelo, Antonio, 700 W. University Dr., #154, Tempe, 85281.
Van De Ven, Kenneth A., 10630 N. 46th Ave., Glendale, 85304.
Voss, Robert J., 10742 N. 140th Pl., Scottsdale, 85259.
Waldron, William, 10417 Saratoga Cir., 85351-2210.
Walsh, Thomas A., Blessed Sacrament Parish, 11300 N. 64th St., Scottsdale, 85254.
Wasielewski, Henry R., P.O. Box 939, Tempe, 85280-0939.
Zappitelli, Francis, P.O. Box 17906, Fountain Hills, 85269.

Permanent Deacons:
Aird, Gordon R., All Saints Catholic Church, Mesa
Anderson, Roy, (Retired), St. Daniel, Scottsdale
Anselmo, Clement
Anselmo, Thomas A., (Unassigned)
Areyzaga, Richard, Queen of Peace, Mesa
Arner, Jeffrey, Our Lady of the Lake, Lake Havasu City
Arnold, James, (Retired), San Francisco de Asis, Flagstaff
Arnold, Maurice, (Retired), Our Lady of Lourdes, Sun City West
Arteaga, Gustavo, St. Charles Borromeo, Peoria
Babbits, Oliver, (Retired), St. Timothy, Mesa
Badame, Joseph, St. Paul, Phoenix
Balland, Peter, Sacred Heart, Prescott
Barelli, John, St. Daniel the Prophet, Scottsdale
Barraza, David, Our Lady of Guadalupe, Queen Creek
Bassett, Kevin, St. Timothy, Mesa
Battista, James, (Retired)

Beard, Stephen, Holy Spirit, Tempe
Beatrice, Lee, St. Clement of Rome, Peoria
Beltran, Anthony N., St. Matthew's, Phoenix
Bennett, Bruce, Ed.D., St. Mary, Chandler
Benware, John, St. Benedict, Phoenix
Berger, John, St. Maria Goretti, Scottsdale
Bernasconi, Santino R., Our Lady of Guadalupe, Guadalupe
Bidleman, William, (Retired), St. Jerome, Phoenix
Bilinski, John, (Retired), St. Henry, Buckeye
Bills, Tom, St.Thomas the Apostle, Phoenix
Bishop, Thomas, Christ the King Parish, Mesa
Bogart, Douglas, St. Thomas the Apostle, Phoenix
Bolduc, Thomas, St. Timothy, Mesa
Bolton, Edward L., (Retired), St. Gregory, Phoenix
Bonaiuto, Dominick, St. John Vianney Parish, Goodyear
Boswell, Keith, St. Anne, Gilbert
Bowslaugh, Alan P., St. James, Glendale
Bret, James, San Francisco De Asis, Flagstaff
Brett, James, Our Lady of Mount Carmel, Tempe
Brown, James, Immaculate Conception, Cottonwood
Bueti, Joseph, Sacred Heart, Prescott
Burke, Edward, (Unassigned)
Cady, Joseph, St. Anne, Gilbert
Calderon, Abram, St. Timothy, Mesa
Cameron, George, St. Henry Parish, Buckeye
Campas, Robert, St. Helen, Glendale
Campbell, Colin, St. Theresa, Phoenix
Capistrant, Willard, Christ the King, Mesa
Carbone, Carmene, St. Gregory Parish, Phoenix
Carey, Robert, St. Mary Magdalene, Gilbert
Carlomagno, Michael, St. Joan of Arc, Phoenix
Carr, Michael, St. Andrew the Apostle, Chandler
Cascio, James, M.P.S., St. Thomas Aquinas, Avondale
Chavez, Antonio, (Retired), Blessed Sacrament, Tolleson
Clapham, Winfred, Queen of Peace, Mesa
Clower, William, St. Rose, Anthem
Coe, Tom, Our Lady of the Lake, Lake Havasu City
Cornille, Louis, St. Bernard of Clairvaux, Scottsdale
Corwin, Richard, St. Steven, Sun Lakes
Crawford, Don, St. Andrew, Chandler
Csuy, Paul E., (Retired), St. Elizabeth Seton, Sun City
Cummings, Jack, (Unassigned)
Cuprak, Richard, Resurrection, Tempe
Czapinski, Clemens, (Retired), Blessed Sacrament, Scottsdale
D'Amico, John, St. Rose Parish, Anthem
Dalisay, J.R., Most Holy Trinity, Phoenix
Danna, Frank, (Retired), St. Steven
Davis, Keith, St. Thomas More, Glendale
DeFelippis, Thomas, (Retired), Our Lady of the Lake
Del Monaco, William, (Retired), St. Mary
Del Quadro, John, St. Margaret Mary, Bullhead City
DeMarco, William, St. Francis Xavier, Phoenix
Dennis, Irving, (Retired), St. Clement of Rome, Sun City
Devine, Frank, St. James, Glendale
Dippre, Martin, St. Daniel the Prophet, Scottsdale
Drapeau, Roy, St. Thomas More, Glendale
Duran, Onofre, (Retired), Immaculate Conception, Cottonwood
Eckert, Dick, (Retired), St. Margaret Mary, Bullhead City
Ehrlich, Jacob, Our Lady of Perpetual Help, Scottsdale
Elmore, Michael, (Unassigned)
England, Robert, Corpus Christi, Phoenix
Estupinan, Sergio, Blessed Sacrament, Scottsdale
Evans, Robert, Blessed Sacrament Parish, Scottsdale
Fejes, Peter, St. Edward, Phoenix
Ferreira, Thomas, Holy Cross, Mesa
Filzen, Bernard, All Saints Catholic Church, Mesa
Finnegan, William, J.C.L., Holy Cross, Mesa
Fischer, Donald, Most Holy Trinity, Phoenix
Fleming, Irving, (Retired), Our Lady of Perpetual Help, Scottsdale
Flynn, Patrick F., (Retired), Corpus Christi, Ahwatukee
Fogle, James, St. Gabriel, Carefree
Galarza, Frank, St. Margaret, Tempe
Galloway, Gregory, St. John Vianney Parish, Goodyear
Garcia, Ernie, St. Andrew the Apostle, Chandler
Garza, Jose, Blessed Sacrament, Tolleson
Gaudio, Alexander L., (Retired), Corpus Christi, Phoenix
Gergosian, Edward, (Retired)
Gersitz, James, Holy Cross, Mesa
Giesner, Fred, (Retired), St. Patrick, Scottsdale
Giza, Stanley, (Retired), St. Clement of Rome, Sun City
Glenn, Thomas, Our Lady of Mount Carmel, Tempe
Gonzalez, Albert, St. Catherine of Siena, Phoenix
Gonzalez, Ricardo, St. Augustine, Phoenix
Gonzalez, Ronald, FCI Chapel
Goubeaux, Guy, St. Paul, Phoenix
Gouveia, Americo, (Retired), St. Thomas the Apostle, Phoenix
Grabowski, Martin, St. Henry, Buckeye
Gregory, Tom, (Retired), Sacred Heart, Prescott
Grey, Larry, St. Elizabeth Seton, Sun City
Guzman, Angel, St. Philip the Deacon, Phoenix
Guzman, Juan, (Retired), Ss. Simon & Jude, Phoenix
Hamilton, James, (Retired), St. Augustine, Phoenix
Hanson, Lee, Our Lady of Lourdes, Sun City West
Heeter, Charles, (Retired), St. Joachim & Anne, Sun City
Henkiel, Donald, St. John Vianney Catholic, West Sedona
Henn, Thomas
Hernandez, Jose, (Retired), St. Mark, Phoenix
Hickcox, Edward M., (Retired), St. Mary, Chandler
Hintze, Craig, St. Mary, Chandler
Hola, Sione, St. Theresa, Phoenix
Holmes, Michael, St. Catherine Laboure, Chino Valley
Hostutler, James, St. Bernadette, Scottsdale
Hoyt, James, St. Patrick, Scottsdale
Humphrey, Tony, Sacred Heart, Prescott
Hungate, Alan, St. Bernard of Clairvaux, Scottsdale
Hurrish, Dutch, (Retired), St. Timothy, Mesa
Hursh, Paul, St. Bridget, Mesa
Ixta, Ignacio, Holy Cross, Mesa
Jenkins, William, St. Vincent de Paul, Phoenix
Johnson, Gary, Holy Spirit, Tempe
Kaminsky, David, Immaculate Conception, Cottonwood
Kayser, Thomas E., Sacred Heart, Prescott
Kijewski, Richard, St. Thomas More, Glendale
Kloft, Lee, St. Gregory Parish, Phoenix
Koch, George, Our Lady of Lourdes, Sun City West
Kronschnabel, Michael, St. Mary, Chandler
Kuban, Donald
Kulinowski, Kenneth, St. Thomas Byzantine, Gilbert
Lamon, John, Sacred Heart Parish, Prescott
Lemire, Herve, St. Maria Goretti, Scottsdale
Leon, Victor, St. Henry, Buckeye
Lessard, Joseph M., (Retired), Mt. Claret, Scottsdale
Liszewski, Len
Little, Ronald, St. Bernadette, Scottsdale
LoCascio, Phillip, Ascension, Fountain Hills
Lopez, Anthony, Our Lady of Perpetual Help, Glendale
Lopez, Gilbert, Our Lady of the Lake, Lake Havasu City
Lukaszewski, Donnan, St. Clare of Assisi, Surprise
Malatin, William, Resurrection, Tempe
Manthie, Robert, St. Raphael, Glendale
Martin, Sidney, St. Peter, Bapchule
Martin, Stephen J., (Retired), St. Clare of Assisi, Surprise
Martinez, Ronald, St. John Vianney, Sedona
McKnight, Lorenzo, St. Augustine, Phoenix
Meidl, Richard, St. Raphael, Glendale
Mesa, Pedro, St. Margaret, Tempe
Messer, Gene, Holy Cross, Mesa
Meyer, John A., St. Patrick, Scottsdale
Micek, Theodore, St. Clare of Assisi, Surprise
Mickel, John, St. Helen Parish, Glendale
Mickens, James, St. Bernadette, Scottsdale
Miller, Kenneth, (Retired), St. Thomas the Apostle, Phoenix
Molina, Eddie, (Retired), Our Lady of Perpetual Help, Glendale
Moncrief, Wayland, St. Germaine, Prescott
Morales, Jesus, St. Catherine of Siena, Phoenix
Morton, Dwight, (Unassigned)
Morton, Wayne, Resurrection, Tempe
Murphy, Peter, Dir., Prison Ministry; Blessed Sacrament, Tolleson
Myers, Robert P., Our Lady of Perpetual Help, Glendale
Navaretta, John, Our Lady of the Lake, Lake Havasu City
Nazzal, James, St. Joseph, Phoenix
Neely, Theodore, (Retired), All Saints, Mesa
O'Connor, John, (Retired), St. James, Glendale
O'Grady, Lowell, Immaculate Heart, Phoenix
Olberding, Robert, San Francisco de Asis, Flagstaff
Olivarez, Jose D., St. Martin de Porres, Phoenix
Olivas, Manuel, St. Mary, Chandler
Orozco, Jose, St. Francis Xavier, Phoenix
Palmer, Robert, St. Germaine Parish, Prescott Valley
Pardini, Louis, Ph.D., (Retired), St. Steven, Sun Lakes
Pelton, Ron, (Retired)
Petersen, Richard, St. Timothy, Mesa
Peterson, Daniel L., St. Rose, Anthem
Pfleger, James, Luke Air Force Base, Litchfield
Phelan, Mike, St. Clement of Rome
Phelan, Thomas J., Queen of Peace, Mesa
Poulin, Ronald, St. John the Baptist, Laveen
Raczkowski, Dennis, Our Lady of Perpetual Help, Glendale
Rade, Douglas, (Retired), San Francisco de Asis, Flagstaff
Ramirez, Ernesto, St. Vincent de Paul, Phoenix
Raymond, Charles J., (Retired), St. Daniel
Reicks, Jerome, (Retired), Our Lady of Lourdes, Sun City West
Rein, Richard, St. Jerome, Phoenix
Rekiere, Bernard, Blessed Sacrament, Scottsdale
Revering, Dennis, San Francisco de Asis, Flagstaff
Riedel, John, Queen of Peace, Mesa
Rocha, Felix, (Unassigned)
Rodriguez, Santiago, Queen of Peace, Mesa
Roger, Ray, (Retired), St. Elizabeth Seton, Sun City
Rooker, Roy
Ruiz, Jesus, (Unassigned)
Ruiz, Ron, Christ the King, Mesa
Sadlier, Carl, St. James, Glendale
Salazar, Lorenzo, (Retired), St. Vincent de Paul, Phoenix
Sanchez, Jesse, St. Agnes, Phoenix
Santa, Reed, (Retired), All Saints, Mesa
Scaccia, Joseph, Holy Cross, Mesa
Scheller, Albert, St. Thomas Aquinas, Avondale
Sejba, Jim, St. Philip Benizi Mission, Black Canyon City
Shaw, Chuck, Ss. Simon & Jude, Phoenix
Shea, William, St. Mary Magdalene, Higley
Shinske, Joseph, St. Helen's, Glendale
Simeone, Philip, Corpus Christi, Phoenix
Smith, Barry, (Retired), St. Timothy, Mesa
Smith, Richard, Ascension, Fountain Hills
Spadafino, Joseph, St. Anne, Gilbert
Springer, James, St. Joan of Arc, Phoenix
Stickney, Joseph, St. Louis the King, Glendale
Stokes, Leslie, St. Philip Benizi, Black Canyon City
Suida, Milford, St. Thomas Aquinas, Avondale
Swisher, Thomas, St. Margaret, Mesa
Ten Barge, Ronald, Our Lady of Lourdes, Sun City West
Terrazas, Carlos, St. Catherine of Siena, Phoenix
Tift, Neal, Christ the King, Mesa
Toilolo, Patrick, Our Lady of the Lake, Lake Havasu City
Torres, Vincent, St. Clare of Assisi, Surprise
Trant, James, Dir. Office of Diaconate, St. Francis of Assisi Mission, Scottsdale
Treichel, Robert, (Retired), Our Lady of the Lake, Lake Havasu
Valle, Matias, St. Matthew, Phoenix
Valverde, W. George, (Retired)
Vasquez, Manuel, (Retired), St. Catherine of Siena, Phoenix
Vivio, William, St. Paul, Phoenix
Voss, Charles, St. Maria Goretti, Scottsdale
Weiss, Stephen, St. Joachim & St. Anne, Youngtown
Wenzel, Schubert, St. Jerome Parish, Phoenix
Wenzler, Joseph, St. Clare of Assisi, Surprise
West, Tony, SS. Simon & Jude Cathedral, Phoenix
Whelan, Laurence, San Francisco de Asis, Flagstaff
Whitford, Jaime, Queen of Peace Parish, Mesa
Wilson, Albro
Wisely, Phil, St. Mary, Kingman
Yanez, Richard, Immaculate Heart of Mary, Phoenix
Zavala, Eduardo, St. Louis the King, Glendale

INSTITUTIONS LOCATED IN THE DIOCESE

[A] HIGH SCHOOLS, DIOCESAN

PHOENIX. *Bourgade Catholic High School*, 4602 N. 31st Ave., 85017. Tel: 602-973-4000; Fax: 602-973-5854. Email: srmary@bourgade.org. Web: www.bourgade.org. Sisters Mary McGreevy, S.S.N.D., Prin.; Kathleen Janiak, R.S.M., Dir. of Studies; Lori Pieper, Dir. of Students; Rev. Eugene Florea, Chap.; Angela Moore, Librarian. Sisters 2; Lay Teachers 29; Students 386.

St. Mary's Roman Catholic High School, 2525 N. Third St., 85004. Tel: 602-251-2500; Fax: 602-251-2595. Email: sfessler@smknights.org. Web: www.smknights.org. Mrs. Suzanne Fessler, Prin.; Mr. Robert Rogers, Asst. Prin.; Rev. Robert Bolding, Chap.; Daniel T. Johansen, Academic Counselor; Catherine Clarke, Librarian. Priests 1; Sisters 2; Lay Teachers 40; Students 717.

Xavier College Preparatory Roman Catholic High School, 4710 N. Fifth St., 85012. Tel: 602-277-3772; Fax: 602-279-1346. Email: sjfphx@xcp.org. Web: www.xcp.org. Sisters M. Joan Fitzgerald, B.V.M., Prin.; Lynn Winsor, B.V.M., Vice Prin.; Rev. John Muir, Chap.; Mary Harkins, Librarian. Sisters 4; Lay Teachers 77; Students 1,178.

CHANDLER. *Seton Roman Catholic High School*, 1150 N. Dobson Rd., 85224. Tel: 480-963-1900; Fax: 480-963-1974. Email: pcollins@setonchs.org. Web: www.setoncatholic.org. Patricia Collins, Prin.; Patrick Reardon, Asst. Prin.; Rev. Will Schmid, Chap. Lay Teachers 44; Students 560.

SCOTTSDALE. *Notre Dame Preparatory Roman Catholic High School*, 9701 E. Bell Rd., 85260. Tel: 480-634-8200; Fax: 480-634-8299. David D. Gonsalves, Prin.; Preston Colao, Asst. Prin.; Dr. David Harris, Asst. Prin.; Rev. Michael Goodyear, L.C., Chap.; Lillian Vancel, Librarian. Priests 2; Brothers 1; Sisters 1; Lay Teachers 70; Students 920.

[B] HIGH SCHOOLS, PRIVATE

PHOENIX. *Brophy College Preparatory*, 4701 N. Central Ave., 85012. Tel: 602-264-5291; Fax: 602-234-1669. Web: www.brophyprep.org. Rev. Edward Reese, S.J., Pres.; Robert E. Ryan III, Prin.; Jeff Glosser, Asst. Prin. Student Activities; Seamus Walsh, Asst. Prin. Curriculum & Instruction; Jim Bopp, Dean Students; Mr. A. Joseph Helm Jr., Dir., Legacy; Carol Ford, Controller; Rev. E. Louis Bishop, S.J.; Jennie Oleksak, Librarian. Jesuit Fathers., Boys Day School. Priests 2; Brothers 1; Lay Teachers 80; Students 1,270.

[C] GENERAL HOSPITALS

PHOENIX. *St. Joseph's Hospital and Medical Center dba Catholic Healthcare West* 350 W. Thomas Rd., 85001. Tel: 602-406-3000; Fax: 602-406-6149. Web: www.stjosephs-phx.org. Ms. Linda Hunt, Pres. Sponsored by Sisters of Mercy of the Americas-West Midwest Community. Sisters 3; Bed Capacity 738; Patients Assisted Annually 480,712; Total Staff 5,380.

GILBERT. *Mercy Gilbert Medical Center dba Catholic Healthcare West* 3555 S. Val Vista Dr., 85296. Tel: 480-503-5440. Web: www.mercygilbert.org. Laurie Eberst, Pres. Mercy Gilbert. Sponsored by Sisters of Mercy of the Americas-West Midwest Community. Bed Capacity 206; Total Assisted Annually 109,708; Total Staff 1,131.

[D] HOMES FOR THE AGED & HANDICAPPED

PHOENIX. *Avondale Senior Village*, 10830 W. Apache St., Bldg. 1, Avondale, 85323. Tel: 623-936-5452; Fax: 623-936-5320. Web: www.mercyhousing.org. Mailing Address: P.O. Box 1180, Avondale, 85323. Shelly Winkley, Property Mgr. Units 41; Total Assisted Annually 80; Total Staff 3.

Camelot Casitas, 1907 E. Virginia, 85006. Tel: 602-276-7554; Fax: 602-276-7538. Web: www.mercyhousing.org. Sherry Nolen.

Casa De Merced, 62 N. 92nd Dr., Tolleson, 85353. Tel: 623-936-9668; Fax: 623-936-9658. Web: www.mercyhousing.org. Mary Camarena, Property Mgr.

El Mirage Senior Village, 12424 W. Thunderbird Rd., El Mirage, 85335. Tel: 623-875-1688; Fax: 623-875-1685. Web: www.mercyhousing.org. Units 41; Total Assisted Annually 80; Total Staff 3.

Guadalupe Senior Village, 9403 S. Avenida Del Yaqui, Guadalupe, 85283. Tel: 480-897-3273; Fax: 480-897-3274. Web: www.mercyhousing.org. Shelly Winkley, Property Mgr. Units 22; Total Assisted Annually 40; Total Staff 3.

Mesa Senior Meadows, 333 E. 6th St., Mesa, 85201. Tel: 480-615-7893; Fax: 480-615-7894. Web: www.mercyhousing.org. Jill Fuller, Property Mgr.; Heather Prentice, Resident Svcs. Coord. Units 41; Total Assisted Annually 80; Total Staff 3.

Peoria Place, 1525 N. 39th Ave., 85009. Tel: 480-820-5234; Fax: 480-755-2298. Web: www.mercyhousing.org. Sherry Nolen, Property Mgr.

Plazas de Merced, 5236 S. 5th St., 85040. Tel: 602-493-9294; Fax: 602-493-0307. Web: www.mercyhousing.org. Sherry Nolan, Property Mgr.; Alice Scott, Resident Svcs. Coord.

Roeser Senior Village Apartments, 454 E. Roeser Rd., 85040. Tel: 602-268-5100.

Sweetwater Gardens Apartments (Handicapped), 2035 E. Sweetwater, 85022. Tel: 602-867-4549. Total Assisted Annually 29.

Vista Alegre, 6515 W. Maryland Ave., Glendale, 85301. Tel: 623-937-0418; Fax: 623-937-0425. Web: www.mercyhousing.org. Janet Weidler, Property Mgr.

AVONDALE. *Vianney Villas Apartments* (Retirement)-HUD Rent Subsidized, 750 S. Fourth St., 85323. Tel: 623-932-2036; Fax: 623-932-1134. Total Assisted Annually 56.

KINGMAN. *Amy Neal Retirement Center*, 3700 Western Ave., 86401-3080. Tel: 928-757-7016. HUD rent subsidized.

Kingman Heights Apartments, 1020 Detroit Ave., 86401. Tel: 928-753-2425; Fax: 928-753-2425. (Retirement)- HUD rent subsidized. Total Assisted Annually 40.

LAKE HAVASU CITY. *Becket House Apartments* (Retirement), 865 Cashmere Dr., 86403. Tel: 928-855-7178. Total Assisted Annually 60.

PAYSON. *Pineview Manor Apartments*, 304 S. Clark Rd., 85541. Tel: 928-474-1317. Email: jgreene@fsl.org. Total Assisted Annually 29; Total Staff 1.

WICKENBURG. *Padua Hills Apartments* (Retirement)-HUD Rent Subsidized, 460 S. West Rd., 85390. Tel: 928-684-7034. Total Assisted Annually 27.

WILLIAMS. *St. Agnes Apartments* (Retirement), 200 S. Ninth, 86046. Tel: 928-635-2913. Total Assisted Annually (Apartments) 25; Total Assisted Annually (Food Bank) 5,200.

[E] CONVENTS AND RESIDENCES OF SISTERS

PHOENIX. *Institute of Blessed Virgin Mary (I.B.V.M.)* (Regional House), 2521 W. Maryland Ave., 85017. Tel: 602-433-0658; Fax: 602-864-8620. Email: maryward@qwest.net. Web: ibvm.org. Sr. Kay Foley, I.B.V.M., Provincial. Sisters 3.

Missionaries of Charity, 1414 S. 17th Ave., 85007. Tel: 602-258-5504. Sr. Clarita, M.C., Local Supr. Sisters 6.

Our Lady of Guadalupe Monastery Sisters of St. Benedict, 8502 W. Pinchot Ave., 85037. Tel: 623-848-9608; Fax: 623-846-4029. Email: bensrs@aol.com. Sr. Linda Campbell, O.S.B., Prioress. Sisters 2; Affiliate 1; Oblates 13.

Sisters of Charity of the Blessed Virgin Mary (Xavier Convent), 311 E. Highland Ave., 85012. Tel: 602-264-0445. Sr. Joan Nuckols, B.V.M., Community Representative. Sisters 7.

Sisters of Divine Savior, 323 E. Elm St., 85012-1703. Tel: 602-274-0228. Email: srgeorgene@yahoo.com. Web: www.sdssisters.org. Sr. Georgene Faust, S.D.S., Cluster Coord. for Region. Sisters 9.

Union of Sisters of the Presentation of the Blessed Virgin Mary, 729 W. Wilshire Dr., 85007. Tel: 602-271-9687; Fax: 602-253-9166. Email: teresa6085501@yahoo.com. Sisters 4.

BLACK CANYON CITY. *Poor Clares of Perpetual Adoration*, 19950 E. St. Joseph Rd., P.O. Box 92, 85324. Tel: 623-374-9204. Email: desertnuns@msn.com. Sisters 7.

MESA. *Sisters of Notre Dame de Namur* (Casa Guadalupe), 548 W. Third St., 85201. Tel: 480-964-3685; Fax: 480-655-9975. Email: mesasnd@aol.com. Sisters 8.

[F] MONASTERIES AND RESIDENCES OF PRIESTS AND BROTHERS

PHOENIX. *Carmelite Community*, 1717 W. Flower, 85015. Tel: 602-274-3189. Revs. Tiernan O'Callaghan, O.Carm., Prior (Retired); Silvan Boyle, O.Carm. (Retired). Priests 2.

Crosier Community of Phoenix (Canons Regular of the Order of the Holy Cross), P.O. Box 32705, 85064-2705. Tel: 602-224-0434; Fax: 602-224-0722. Email: swhenrich@crosier.org. Web: www.crosier.org. Rev. Thomas A. Enneking, O.S.C., Subprior, 454 E. Roeser Rd., 85040; Very Rev. Thomas R. Carkhuff, O.S.C.; Revs. Stephen Bauer, O.S.C.; John Christ, O.S.C.; David N Donney, O.S.C.; Louis R. Mraz, O.S.C. (Retired); Robert J. Rossi, O.S.C.; Philip Suehr, O.S.C.; Bros. James Lewandowski, O.S.C., 454 E. Roeser Rd., 85040; James Scher, O.S.C., Admin., Third Age Coord., 454 E. Roeser Rd., 85040. Priests 13; Brothers 7. 454 E. Roeser Rd., 85040. Tel: 602-243-9747. Very Rev. Steven Henrich, O.S.C., Prior; Revs. Timothy Conlon, O.S.C.; Richard McGuire, O.S.C.; Francis K. Scheets, O.S.C. (Retired); Gerald Thaar, O.S.C. (Retired); Bros. Neil Emon, O.S.C., (Retired); Gabriel Guerrero, O.S.C., (Retired), P.O. Box 32705, 85064; Gregory Madigan, O.S.C., (Retired); Gus Schloesser, O.S.C.; Timothy Tomczak, O.S.C., P.O. Box 32705, 85064.

Crosier Provincial House Province of St. Odilia, 4332 N. 24th St., 85016-6259. Tel: 602-443-7100; Fax: 602-443-7101. Email: provincial@crosier.org. Web: www.crosier.org. Very Rev. Thomas R. Carkhuff, O.S.C., Provincial; Revs. Michael Cotone, O.S.C.; Joseph Hennen, O.S.C., (On Exclaustration); Anna Thompson, Prov. Asst. Priests 2; Total Staff 8. In Res. Revs. William Deziel, O.S.C., (On Exclaustration); Dale Ettel, O.S.C., (On Exclaustration) Crosiers Serving Abroad Revs. Lyle Ehmke, O.S.C.; James Hentges, O.S.C.; James Herrmann, O.S.C.; Glen Lewandowski, O.S.C.; Virgil Petermeier, O.S.C.

Holy Cross Congregation/Casa Santa Cruz, 7126 N. Seventh Ave., 85021. Tel: 602-944-6000; Fax: 602-944-1221. Revs. Milton N. Adamson, C.S.C., Supr.; Duane Balcerski, C.S.C.; James R. Blantz, C.S.C.; William W. Faiella, C.S.C.; James J. Ferguson, C.S.C., Asst. Supr.; John P. Keefe, C.S.C.; Howard Kuhns, C.S.C. (Retired); Joseph F. O'Donnell, C.S.C. (Retired); Stephen J. Sedlock; James W. Thornton, C.S.C. (Retired); Bro. Ronald G. Whelan, C.S.C. Priests 10; Brothers 1.

Society of Jesus, 120 E. Mariposa St., 85012. Tel: 602-264-5291. Revs. John M. Martin, S.J., Supr.; E. Louis Bishop, S.J.; Harry T. Olivier, S.J.; Edward Reese, S.J., Pres., Brophy Prep.; Daniel J. Sullivan, S.J.; John Auther, S.J.; David J. Robinson.

St. Therese Priory, 75 E. Mariposa St., #3, 85012-1631. Tel: 602-604-2365; Fax: 602-274-3189. Revs. Valentine Boyle, O.Carm.; Charles Kurgan, O.Carm.

TEMPE. *Dominicans (Dominican Community-Jordan House)*, 1042 E. Campus, 85282. Tel: 480-967-7823. Revs. Miguel Rolland, O.P.; James D. Thompson, O.P. Priests 3.

[G] RETREAT HOUSES

PHOENIX. *Mount Claret Roman Catholic Retreat Center*, 4633 N. 54th St., 85018. Tel: 602-840-5066; Fax: 602-840-5732. Rev. Paul G. Sullivan, Dir.; Thomas McGuire, Assoc. Dir. Priests 5. In Res. Rev. Fredrick J. Adamson, V.G.; Rev. Msgr. John J. McMahon (Retired); Revs. John Hanley (Retired); Matthias Feit (Retired).

Our Lady of Guadalupe Retreat/Conference Center, 8502 W. Pinchot, 85037. Tel: 623-848-9608. Web: benedictinesistersphoenix.com. Conference Center Overnight Capacity 25; Conference Center Daytime Capacity 70; Scholastica House Daytime Capacity 30; Scholastica House Overnight Capacity 2.

CORNVILLE. *Living Water Retreat Center*, P.O. Box 529, 86325. Tel: 928-634-4421; Fax: 928-634-0005. Web: www.livingwaterretreatcenter.com. (Owned and operated by City of the Lord)

SCOTTSDALE. *Franciscan Renewal Center, Inc. (Casa de Paz Y Bien)*, 5802 E. Lincoln Dr., 85253. Tel: 480-948-7460; Fax: 480-948-2325. Email: casa@thecasa.org. Web: www.thecasa.org. Revs. Joseph Schwab, O.F.M., Exec. Dir.; Alonso De Blas, O.F.M.; Peter Kirwin, O.F.M.; Bro. Mario Vasquez, O.F.M. Priests 4; Brothers 1.

[H] NEWMAN CENTERS

PHOENIX. *Office of Youth and Young Adult Ministries* 400 E. Monroe, 85004. Tel: 602-354-2380; Fax: 602-354-2460. Email: bmarcotte@diocesephoenix.org. Web: www.diocesephoenix.org. Bill Marcotte, Dir. Mesa Community College, Chandler; Gilbert Community College; Scottsdale Community College; Paradise Valley Community College; ASU West.

Glendale Community College

Yavapai College, Emery Riddle Aeronautical University Sacred Heart Parish, 150 Fleury Ave., Prescott, 86301. Tel: 928-445-3141. Mr. Vincent Gallegos. (Prescott)

Arizona State University All Saints Catholic Newman Center, 230 E. University Dr., P.O. Box 1987, Tempe, 85281. Tel: 480-967-7823. Rev. James D. Thompson, O.P. (Tempe)

Holy Trinity Catholic Newman Center 520 W. Riordan Rd., Flagstaff, 86001. Tel: 928-779-2903; Fax: 928-779-0698. Email: info@naunewman.org. Web: www.naunewman.org. Michael Vollmer, Assoc. Dir.; Rev. Matthew Lowry, Chap.

John Paul II Catholic Newman Center ASU Polytechnic Campus in Mesa, c/o Our Lady of Guadalupe Parish, P.O. Box 856, Queen Creek, 85242-0856. Church Location: 20615 E. Ocotillo Rd., Queen Creek, 85242-8990. Tel: 480-987-0315; Fax: 480-888-1159. Rev. Michael Goodyear, L.C., Chap.

Catholic Committee on Scouting Tel: 480-595-0883. Rev. Dennis O'Rourke, V.F., Chap.

[I] ACADEMIES OF RELIGIOUS TEACHING

PHOENIX. *Kino Institute of Theology and Pastoral Ministry Formation*, 400 E. Monroe, 85004. Tel: 602-354-2300; Fax: 602-354-2251. Web: www.kinoinstitute.org. MaryBeth Mueller, Exec. Dir. Education & Evangelism; Sisters Maria Celia Molina, S.S.N.deN., M.Th., Coord. Spanish Progs.; Darcy Peletich, O.S.F., M.A., M.L.S., Librarian; Luz Lobato, Admin. Asst.; Gina Milligan, Admin. Asst. Tel: 602-906-9798.

[J] MISCELLANEOUS LISTINGS

PHOENIX. *Andre House of Arizona*, 213 S. 11th Ave., 85007-3132. Tel: 602-255-0580; Fax: 602-257-4415. Email: director@andrehouseaz.org. Web: www.andrehouseaz.org. P.O. Box 2014, 85001-2014. Tel: 602-255-0580; Fax: 602-257-4415. Rev. Eric Schimmel, C.S.C., Dir.; Bro. Richard Armstrong, C.S.C. Hospitality House, Indiana Province of the Congregation of Holy Cross.

Catholic Charities Community Services, 4747 N. 7th Ave., 85013. Tel: 602-285-1999; Fax: 602-285-0311. Web: www.catholiccharitiesaz.org. Steve Lasswell, Pres.; Paul Martodam, M.P.A., CEO; Kristen Schmidt, M.S.W., Ph.D., COO.

Regional Service Centers:

Catholic Charities Community Services, Phoenix, 1825 W. Northern Ave., 85021. Tel: 602-997-6105; Fax: 602-943-0377. Tom Egan, Dir. Prog. Opers.

Catholic Charities Community Services, Flagstaff, 460 N. Switzer Canyon Dr., Flagstaff, 86001. Tel: 928-774-9125; Fax: 928-774-0697. Victor Hudenko, Dir. Housing & Homeless Svcs.

Catholic Charities Community Services, Yavapai, 434 W. Gurley, Prescott, 86301. Tel: 928-778-2531; Fax: 928-771-9531.

Verde Valley Office, 736 N. Main St., Cottonwood, 86326. Tel: 928-634-4254; Fax: 928-639-4368. Cathy Peterson, Dir. Prog. Opers.

Catholic Charities Community Services, West Valley, 7400 W. Olive Ave., Ste. 10, Peoria, 85345. Tel: 623-486-9868; Fax: 623-486-9988. Cathy Tompkins, M.S., C.P.C., Dir. Prog. Opers. 51 Head Start Classrooms

Parish & Community Engagement, 4747 N. 7th Ave., 85013. Tel: 602-285-1999; Fax: 602-285-0311. Tricia Hoyt, Dir.

Residential Facilities:

DIGNITY HOUSE Tel: 602-274-3680. Rachel Irby, Prog. Supvr. Group living for homeless women leaving prostitution.

My Sister's Place Tel: 480-821-1024; Fax: 480-963-9532. Domestic Violence Shelter

The Catholic Retreat for Young Singles, Inc., P.O. Box 16064, 85011. Tel: 602-369-8018. Email: enanneman@hotmail.com. Eric Nanneman, Pres.

The Catholic Tuition Organization of the Diocese of Phoenix (CTODP), 2025 N. Third St., #165, 85004-1425. Tel: 602-218-6542; Fax: 602-218-6623. Email: pmulligan@catholictuition.org. Web: www.catholictuition.org. Paul S. Mulligan, M.T.S., Exec. Dir.; Wallace Estfan, Pres.

Christ Child Society, 4633 N. 54th St., 85018-1904. Tel: 602-667-3355. Alice Wold, Pres.; Bette Laatsch, Treas.

Crosier Missions, 4332 N. 24th St., 85016-6259. Tel: 602-443-7100; Fax: 602-443-7101. Email: athompson@crosier.org. Web: www.crosier.org. Bro. Albert Becker, O.S.C., Dir. Devel. Total Staff 1.

Cursillo Movement, 4633 N. 54th St., 85018. Tel: 602-840-5066; Fax: 602-840-5732. Rev. Donald Kline, Spiritual Dir.; Deacon Jesse Sanchez, Assoc. Spiritual Dir.; Rosa Maria Estrada, Assoc. Spiritual Dir.

Foundation for Senior Living, 1201 E. Thomas Rd., 85014. Tel: 602-285-1800. Email: gmikkelsen@fsl.org.

Affordable Services for Seniors, Inc., 1201 E. Thomas Rd., 85014. Tel: 602-285-1800. Email: shastings@fsl.org. Mr. Guy Mikkelsen, Pres.

Foundation for Senior Adult Living, Inc. Tel: 602-285-1800; Fax: 602-285-1838. Email: jgreene@fsl.org. Sweetwater Gardens (Apartments for the Handicapped), Phoenix; Kingman Heights Apartments, Kingman.

FSL Management Tel: 602-285-1800; Fax: 602-285-1838. Email: dpaddison@fsl.org.

FSL Programs Tel: 602-285-1800; Fax: 602-285-1838. Email: lmartin@fsl.org. Ms. Linda Martin, Dir. Adult Day Health Care Centers; In-Home Care Services; Home Safety & Repair Program; Community Action Programs/Senior Centers; Adult Foster Care; Oasis (Older Adult Service & Information System); Pathways Program (Resources and Referral-Care Management).

FSL Real Estate Services Tel: 602-285-1800; Fax: 602-285-1838. Email: shastings@fsl.org. Mr. Guy Mikkelsen, Contact Person.

FSL Rural Development Tel: 602-285-1800; Fax: 602-285-1838. Email: jgreene@fsl.org. Becket House Apartments, Lake Havasu City; Vianney Villas Apartments, Avondale; Padua Hills Apartments, Wickenburg; St. Agnes Apartments, Williams, Amy Neal Retirement Center, Kingman.

FSL Home Improvements, 1201 E. Thomas Rd., 85014. Tel: 602-285-1800; Fax: 602-285-1838. Email: ksmith@fsl.org.

FSL Pathways, 1201 E. Thomas Rd., 85014. Tel: 602-285-1800; Fax: 602-285-1838. Email: chill@fsl.org. Carolyn Hill, Contact Person. Assisted Group Living Program (11 Houses), Phoenix.

Payson Senior Living, Inc., 1201 E. Thomas Rd., 85014. Tel: 602-285-1800; Fax: 602-285-1838. Email: jgreene@fsl.org. (Pineview Manor Apartments, Payson)

St. Clair Senior Living, 1201 E. Thomas Rd., 85014. Tel: 602-285-1800. Email: shastings@fsl.org. Mr. Guy Mikkelsen, Pres.

St. Joseph the Worker (Job Service), P.O. Box 13503, 85002-3503. 1125 W. Jackson St, 85007. Tel: 602-417-9854; Fax: 602-258-4940. Email: info@sjwjobs.org. Web: www.sjwjobs.org. Peter Ziebron, Chm. Bd. & Pres.; Amy Caffarello, Exec. Dir.; Christopher A. Coury, Vice Chm. & Sec.; Pat Moroney, Treas. To assist homeless, low-income, and other disadvantaged individuals in their efforts to become self-sufficient through permanent, full-time employment.

Saint Mary's Scholarship & Benefit Fund, 2525 N. Third St., 85004. Tel: 602-256-4909; Fax: 602-251-2595. Email: kmankoski@smknights.org. Web: www.smknights.org. Ashley K. Ober, Pres.; Karen Mankoski, Exec. Dir.

Mercy Properties Arizona, 5236 S. 5th St., 85040. Tel: 303-830-3371; Fax: 303-830-3301. Web: www.mercyhousing.org.

**Natural Family Planning*, 4480 E. Lafayette Blvd., 85018. Tel: 602-952-9159. Email: pegfrei@cox.net. Web: www.phxnfp.org. Peggy Frei, Coord. Center provides Natural Family Planning Services, Instructional Series, Introductions to Natural Family Planning for Marriage Preparation. Program is endorsed by the Diocesan Development Plan for N.F.P., U.S. Conference of Catholic Bishops (USCCB).

**Southwest Catholic Health Network Corp.*, 4350 E. Cotton Center Blvd., 85040. Tel: 602-263-3000; Fax: 602-263-2098. Mark Fisher, Pres. & CEO.

St. Vincent De Paul Society, P.O. Box 13600, 85002. Tel: 602-254-3338; 602-266-4673; Fax: 602-261-6829. Web: www.stvincentdepaul.net. Joseph J. Riley, Pres.; Stephen J. Zabilski, Exec. Dir.

CHANDLER. *The Catholic Singles Ministry, Inc.*, 4589 W. Ivanhoe St., 85226. Tel: 480-961-4211. Email: kmp.email@att.net. Web: www.catholicsinglesministry.org. Karina Penaranda, Contact Person.

GOODYEAR. *St. John Vianney School Development Fund*, 539 La Pasada Blvd., 85338. Tel: 623-932-3313; Fax: 623-932-1896. Email: frherman@diocesephoenix.org. Web: www.stjohnvianneyparish.com. Rev. John A. Herman, C.S.C., Pres.

MESA. **Life Teen, Inc.*, 2222 S. Dobson Rd., Ste. 601, 85202. Tel: 480-820-7001; Fax: 480-820-8653. Email: randyr@lifeteen.com. Web: www.lifeteen.com. Randy Raus, Pres.

Paz de Cristo Community Center dba St. Timothy Catholic Community 424 W. Broadway Rd., 85210. Tel: 480-464-2370. Email: pazdecristo@qwest.net; pazfencinas@qwestoffice.net. Rev. John D. Spaulding, Pres.

SCOTTSDALE. *Mercy Housing Southwest*, Mailing Address: 4802 E. Ray Rd., Ste. 23, PMB 256, 85044. 401 W. Baseline Rd., Ste. 208, Tempe, 85283-5349. Tel: 602-952-9525; Fax: 480-755-2298. Email: swheelock@mercyhousing.org. Jennifer Erixon, Pres.

TEMPE. **City of the Lord*, 711 W. University Dr., 85281-3411. Tel: 480-968-5895; 480-968-5990; Fax: 480-921-9175. Email: rwcarmody@msn.com. Web: www.cityofthelord.org. Robert Carmody, Pres.; Thomas McGuire, Vice Pres.; James Hyde, Sec. & Treas.

**Friends of the Orphans*, 2222 S. Dobson Rd., Ste. 401, Mesa, 85202. Tel: 480-967-9449; Fax: 480-967-9288. Email: infosw@friendsus.org. P.O. Box 25507, 85285-5507. Tel: 480-967-9449; Fax: 480-967-9288. Web: www.friendsoftheorphans.org. Deacon James Hoyt, Regl. Dir. Deacons 1; Total Staff 5; Total Assisted 33,500.

**Youth Arise North America*, 711 W. University Dr., 85281-3411. Henry Cappello, CEO & Pres.; Bill Marcotte, Vice Pres.

RELIGIOUS INSTITUTES OF MEN REPRESENTED IN THE DIOCESE

For further details refer to the corresponding bracketed number in the Religious Institutes of Men or Women section.

[]—*Apostles of Jesus*—A.J.
[0200]—*Benedictine Monks* (St. Meinrad Archabbey)—O.S.B.
[0600]—*Brothers of the Congregation of Holy Cross*—C.S.C.
[0400]—*Canons Regular of the Order of the Holy Cross*—O.S.C.
[0270]—*Carmelite Fathers and Brothers* (Prov. of St. Elias)—O.Carm.
[0350]—*Cistercian Order of the Strict Observance (Trappists)*—O.C.S.O.
[0360]—*Claretian Missionaries* (Western Prov.)—C.M.F.
[0310]—*Congregation of Christian Brothers*—C.F.C.
[1330]—*Congregation of the Mission Western Province*—C.M.
[]—*Disciples of Hope*—D.S.
[0520]—*Franciscan Friars* (Prov. of Santa Barbara; Prov. of Our Lady of Guadalupe; Prov. of St. John the Baptist)—O.F.M.
[0650]—*Holy Ghost Fathers* (Western Prov.)—C.S.Sp.
[]—*Institute of the Incarnate Word*—I.V.E.
[0690]—*Jesuit Fathers and Brothers* (California & Milwaukee Provs.)—S.J.
[0730]—*Legionaries of Christ*—L.C.
[]—*Miles Jesu*—M.J.
[0830]—*Mill Hill Missionaries*—M.H.M.
[0910]—*Oblates of Mary Immaculate* (Our Lady of Hope)—O.M.I.
[0430]—*Order of Preachers (Dominicans)* (Western Prov.)—O.P.
[1050]—*Pontifical Institute for Foreign Missions*—P.I.M.E.
[1065]—*Priestly Fraternity of St. Peter*—F.S.S.P.
[0610]—*Priests of the Congregation of Holy Cross*—C.S.C.
[1260]—*Society of Christ*—S.Ch.
[0975]—*Society of Our Lady of the Most Holy Trinity*—S.O.L.T.
[1200]—*Society of the Divine Savior* (North American Prov.)—S.D.S.

RELIGIOUS INSTITUTES OF WOMEN REPRESENTED IN THE DIOCESE

[0230]—*Benedictine Sisters of Pontifical Jurisdiction* (Duluth, MN)—O.S.B.
[0990]—*Congregation of Divine Providence* (Pittsburgh, PA)—C.D.P.
[2715]—*The Congregation of Missionary Sisters of Christ the King for Polish Immigrants* (Poznan, Poland; Chicago, IL)—M.Chr.
[3710]—*Congregation of the Sisters of St. Agnes* (Fond du Lac, WI)—C.S.A.
[1710]—*Congregation of the Third Order of St. Francis of Mary Immaculate* (Joliet, IL)—O.S.F.
[0760]—*Daughters of Charity* (Los Altos Hills, CA)—D.C.
[0850]—*Daughters of Mary Help of Christians* (San Antonio, TX)—F.M.A.
[]—*Daughters of Mary Immaculate, Chaldean*—D.M.I.
[]—*Daughters of Mary, Mother of the Church* (Naga City, Philippines)—D.M.
[1070-03]—*Dominican Sisters* (Sinsinawa, WI)—O.P.
[1070-13]—*Dominican Sisters* (Adrian, MI)—O.P.
[1070-30]—*Dominican Sisters* (Oakford, S. Africa)—O.P.
[1115]—*Dominican Sisters of Peace*—O.P.
[1120]—*Dominican Sisters of Roman Congregation* (Lewiston, ME)—O.P.
[1170]—*Felician Sisters* (Chicago, IL)—C.S.S.F.
[1230]—*Franciscan Sisters of Christian Charity* (Manitowoc, WI)—O.S.F.
[1310]—*Franciscan Sisters of Little Falls, Minnesota* (Little Falls, MN)—O.S.F.
[1440]—*Franciscan Sisters of the Poor* (Brooklyn, NY)—F.S.P.
[1910]—*Hermanas Josefinas*—H.J.
[2370]—*Institute of the Blessed Virgin Mary (Loretto Sisters)* (Prov. Wheaton, IL)—I.B.V.M.
[2740]—*Maryknoll Sisters of St. Dominic* (Maryknoll, NY)—M.M.
[]—*Missionarias Carmelitas de Santa Teresa del Nino Jesus* (Pueblo, Mexico)—M.C.S.T.N.J.
[2710]—*Missionaries of Charity* (Calcutta, India)—M.C.
[]—*Missionaries of the Kingship of Christ, a Secular Institute* (Bethesda, MD)—S.I.M.
[3130]—*Our Lady of Victory Missionary Sisters* (Huntington, IN)—O.L.V.M.
[3210]—*Poor Clares of Perpetual Adoration*—P.C.P.A.
[2970]—*School Sisters of Notre Dame* (Milwaukee, WI; Mankato, MN; St. Louis, MO)—S.S.N.D.
[1680]—*School Sisters of St. Francis* (Milwaukee, WI)—S.S.S.F.
[1690]—*School Sisters of the Third Order of St Francis* (Pittsburgh, PA)—O.S.F.
[3590]—*Servants of Mary Servite Sisters* (Lady Smith, WI)—O.S.M.
[0570]—*Sisters of Charity of Seton Hill, Greensburg, Pennsylvania*—S.C.
[0430]—*Sisters of Charity of the B.V.M.* (Dubuque, IA)—B.V.M.
[2360]—*Sisters of Loretto at the Foot of the Cross* (Nerinx, KY)—S.L.
[2575]—*Sisters of Mercy of the Americas* (Buffalo, NY; Omaha, NE)—R.S.M.
[3000]—*Sisters of Notre Dame de Namur* (Cincinnati,

OH)—S.N.D.deN.
[1540]—*Sisters of St. Francis* (Clinton, IA)—O.S.F.
[1705]—*The Sisters of St. Francis of Assisi* (Milwaukee, WI)—O.S.F.
[1570]—*Sisters of St. Francis of the Holy Family* (Dubuque, IA)—O.S.F.
[3830-15]—*Sisters of St. Joseph* (Concordia, KS)—C.S.J.
[3840]—*Sisters of St. Joseph of Carondelet*—C.S.J.
[3930]—*Sisters of St. Joseph of the Third Order of St. Francis* (South Bend, IN)—S.S.J.-T.O.S.F.
[0260]—*Sisters of the Blessed Sacrament* (Bensalem, PA)—S.B.S.
[1030]—*Sisters of the Divine Savior* (Milwaukee, WI)—S.D.S.
[3730]—*Sisters of the Order of St. Basil the Great* (Uniontown, PA)—O.S.B.M.
[3260]—*Sisters of the Precious Blood* (Dayton, OH)—C.PP.S.
[2150]—*Sisters, Servants of the Immaculate Heart of Mary*—I.H.M.
[3330]—*Union of the Sisters of the Presentation of the B.V.M.* (Phoenix, AZ)—P.B.V.M.

NECROLOGY

(No Deaths)

An asterisk (*) denotes an organization that has established tax-exempt status directly with the IRS and is not covered by the USCCB Group Ruling.

Diocese of Pittsburgh

(Dioecesis Pittsburgensis)

Most Reverend

DAVID A. ZUBIK

Bishop of Pittsburgh; ordained May 3, 1975; appointed Auxiliary Bishop of Pittsburgh and Titular Bishop of Jamestown February 18, 1997; consecrated April 6, 1997; appointed Bishop of Green Bay October 10, 2003; installed December 12, 2003; appointed Bishop of Pittsburgh July 18, 2007; installed September 28, 2007. *Office: 111 Blvd. of the Allies, Pittsburgh, PA 15222-1618.*

Most Reverend

WILLIAM J. WINTER, V.G., S.T.D.

Retired Auxiliary Bishop of Pittsburgh; ordained December 17, 1955; appointed Auxiliary Bishop of Pittsburgh and Titular Bishop of Uthina December 27, 1988; consecrated February 13, 1989; retired May 20, 2005. *Res.: St. John Vianney Manor, 2600 Morange Rd., Pittsburgh, PA 15205.*

NOTHING IS IMPOSSIBLE WITH GOD

ESTABLISHED AUGUST 8, 1843.

Square Miles 3,754.

Comprises the Counties of Allegheny, Beaver, Lawrence, Washington, Greene, and Butler in the State of Pennsylvania.

Legal Title: The Diocese of Pittsburgh and each parish in the diocese are organized as separate Pennsylvania Charitable Trusts.

Pastoral Center: 111 Blvd. of the Allies, Pittsburgh, PA 15222-1618. Tel: 412-456-3000.

Web: www.diopitt.org

Email: communications@diopitt.org

STATISTICAL OVERVIEW

Personnel	
Bishop	1
Retired Bishops	1
Priests: Diocesan Active in Diocese	260
Priests: Diocesan Active Outside Diocese	15
Priests: Diocesan in Foreign Missions	1
Priests: Retired, Sick or Absent	111
Number of Diocesan Priests	387
Religious Priests in Diocese	98
Total Priests in Diocese	485
Extern Priests in Diocese	28
Ordinations:	
Diocesan Priests	4
Religious Priests	2
Transitional Deacons	3
Permanent Deacons in Diocese	41
Total Brothers	29
Total Sisters	1,143
Parishes	
Parishes	212
With Resident Pastor:	
Resident Diocesan Priests	174
Resident Religious Priests	8
Without Resident Pastor:	
Administered by Priests	29
Administered by Religious Women	1
Closed Parishes	2
Professional Ministry Personnel:	
Brothers	2
Sisters	57
Lay Ministers	232
Welfare	
Catholic Hospitals	1
Total Assisted	227,840
Homes for the Aged	9
Total Assisted	1,953
Day Care Centers	8
Total Assisted	1,723
Specialized Homes	5
Total Assisted	1,877
Special Centers for Social Services	7
Total Assisted	102,673
Residential Care of Disabled	1
Total Assisted	193
Other Institutions	1
Total Assisted	336
Educational	
Seminaries, Diocesan	1
Students from This Diocese	16
Diocesan Students in Other Seminaries	14
Total Seminarians	30
Colleges and Universities	3
Total Students	13,919
High Schools, Diocesan and Parish	8
Total Students	3,487
High Schools, Private	4
Total Students	720
Elementary Schools, Diocesan and Parish	95
Total Students	18,306
Elementary Schools, Private	4
Total Students	785
Non-residential Schools for the Disabled	2
Total Students	164
Catechesis/Religious Education:	
High School Students	4,648
Elementary Students	39,990
Total Students under Catholic Instruction	82,049
Teachers in the Diocese:	
Priests	2
Brothers	17
Sisters	66
Lay Teachers	1,793
Vital Statistics	
Receptions into the Church:	
Infant Baptism Totals	5,705
Minor Baptism Totals	196
Adult Baptism Totals	258
Received into Full Communion	553
First Communions	6,624
Confirmations	7,359
Marriages:	
Catholic	1,515
Interfaith	627
Total Marriages	2,142
Deaths	8,282
Total Catholic Population	673,801
Total Population	1,908,721

Former Bishops—Rt. Revs. MICHAEL J. O'CONNOR, S.J., D.D., ord. June 1, 1833; cons. Aug. 15, 1843; transferred to Erie and then to Pittsburgh Dec. 20, 1853; resigned May 23, 1860; entered the Society of Jesus Dec. 22, 1860; died at Woodstock College, MD, Oct. 18, 1872; MICHAEL DOMENEC, C.M., D.D., ord. June 30, 1839; cons. Dec. 9, 1860; transferred to Allegheny, Jan. 11, 1876; resigned July 29, 1877; died at Tarragona, Spain, Jan. 5, 1878; JOHN TUIGG, D.D., ord. May 14, 1850; cons. March 19, 1876; transferred to as Apostolic Administrator of Allegheny 1877; died at Altoona Dec. 7, 1889; RICHARD PHELAN, D.D., ord. May 4, 1854; cons. Aug. 2, 1885; Titular Bishop of Cibyra and Coadjutor to the Rt. Rev. John Tuigg; succeeded to Bishop Tuigg, Dec. 7, 1889; died at Idlewood Dec. 20, 1904; Most Revs. J. F. REGIS CANEVIN, D.D., ord. June 4, 1879; cons. Titular Bishop of Sabrata and Coadjutor, Feb. 24, 1903; succeeded to the See of Pittsburgh, Dec. 20, 1904; resigned Nov. 26, 1920; Titular Archbishop of Pelusium; appt. Jan. 9, 1921; died at Pittsburgh March 22, 1927; HUGH C. BOYLE, D.D., ord. July 2, 1898; succeeded to the See of Pittsburgh, June 16, 1921; cons. June 29, 1921; died at Pittsburgh Dec. 22, 1950; His Eminence JOHN CARDINAL DEARDEN, D.D., S.T.D., ord. Dec. 8, 1932; Titular Bishop of Sarepta and Coadjutor Bishop of Pittsburgh; appt. March 13, 1948; cons. May 18, 1948; succeeded to the See, Dec. 22, 1950; assistant at the Pontifical Throne, Oct. 15, 1957; installed at the Archdiocese of Detroit, Dec. 18, 1958; created Cardinal, April 28, 1969; died at Southfield, MI Aug. 1, 1988; JOHN CARDINAL WRIGHT, D.D., S.T.D., ord. Dec. 8, 1935; appt. May 10, 1947; cons. June 30, 1947; transferred to Bishop of Worcester, Jan. 28, 1950; transferred to Pittsburgh, Jan. 23, 1959; to the Roman Curia as Prefect of the Sacred Congregation for the Clergy; appt. April 23, 1969; created Cardinal, April 28, 1969; died at Cambridge, MA, Aug. 10, 1979; Most Rev. VINCENT M. LEONARD, D.D., ord. June 16, 1935; appt. Titular Bishop of Arsacal and Auxiliary, Feb. 28, 1964; cons. April 21, 1964; succeeded to the See, June 1, 1969; resigned June 30, 1983; died at Pittsburgh Aug. 28, 1994; His Eminence ANTHONY CARDINAL BEVILACQUA, D.D., J.C.D., J.D., ord. June 11, 1949; appt. Oct. 4, 1980; cons. Nov. 24, 1980; Bishop of Pittsburgh; appt. Oct. 10, 1983; installed Dec. 12, 1983; appt. Archbishop of Philadelphia, Feb. 11, 1988; created Cardinal, June 29, 1991; resigned Oct. 7, 2003; Most Rev. DONALD W. WUERL, S.T.D., ord. Dec. 17, 1966; appt. Titular Bishop of Rosemarkie and Auxiliary Bishop of Seattle Dec. 3, 1985; cons. Jan. 6, 1986; appt. and canonically installed Bishop of Pittsburgh Feb. 12, 1988; liturgically installed March 25, 1988; appt. Archbishop of Washington May 16, 2006; installed June 22, 2006.

Pastoral Center—111 Blvd. of the Allies, Pittsburgh, 15222-1618. Tel: 412-456-3000. All official correspondence should be directed to this office.

Vicars General—Very Revs. ROBERT F. GUAY, V.G., M.Div.; JOSEPH M. MELE, V.G., Ph.D.

Episcopal Vicars—

Vicar for Clergy—Very Rev. HARRY R. BIELEWICZ, V.E., M.Div.

Vicar for Canonical Services—Very Rev. LAWRENCE A. DINARDO, V.E., J.C.L.

Regional Vicars—

Vicariate 1—Very Rev. ROBERT F. GUAY, V.G., M.Div., Sisters of the Holy Spirit Motherhouse, 5246 Clarwin Ave., Pittsburgh, 15229. Tel: 412-456-5644.

Vicariate 2—Very Rev. FREDERICK L. CAIN, V.E., Sisters of Saint Francis of the Providence of God, 1401 Hamilton Rd., Pittsburgh, 15234. Tel: 412-456-5645.

Vicariate 3—Rev. Msgr. WILLIAM M. OGRODOWSKI, V.E., S.T.L., Saint Paul Seminary, 2900 Noblestown Rd., Pittsburgh, 15205. Tel: 412-456-5648.

Vicariate 4—Very Rev. PHILIP N. FARRELL, V.E., M.A., M.Div., Holy Sepulcher, 1304 E. Cruikshank Rd., Butler, 16002. Tel: 412-456-5649.

Chancellor—ARLENE M. MCGANNON, D.Min. Tel: 412-456-3129.

Vice Chancellor—Very Rev. BRIAN J. WELDING, V.J., J.C.D., S.T.L. Tel: 412-456-3135.

Bishop's Office—Most Rev. DAVID ALLEN ZUBIK, D.D.; Mrs. JUDITH A. STYPERK, Exec. Asst.

General Secretary—WILLIAM G. BATZ, Ph.D. Tel: 412-456-3131; Fax: 412-456-3197.

Associate General Secretary—ARLENE M. MCGANNON, D.Min. Tel: 412-456-3129.

Vicar for Canonical Services—Very Rev. LAWRENCE A. DINARDO, V.E., J.C.L., Address all correspondence to: 111 Blvd. of the Allies, Pittsburgh, 15222-1698. Tel: 412-456-3135; Fax: 412-456-3183.

Director, Department for Canon and Civil Law Services—Very Rev. LAWRENCE A. DINARDO, V.E., J.C.L., Address all correspondence to: 111 Blvd. of the Allies, Pittsburgh, 15222-1698. Tel: 412-456-3135; Fax: 412-456-3183.

Assistant Director, Department for Canon and Civil Law Services—Very Rev. BRIAN J. WELDING, V.J., J.C.D., S.T.L. Tel: 412-456-3135.

Moderator of the Tribunal—JAY CONZEMIUS, J.C.L.

Matrimonial Concerns, Office for—Revs. RICHARD M. LELONIS, J.C.L., Dir.; LOUIS L. DENINNO, J.C.L., M.Div., Canonical Consultant, Address all correspondence to: 2900 Noblestown Rd., Pittsburgh, 15205-4227. Tel: 412-456-3033; Fax: 412-456-3118.

Tribunal Office—Address all correspondence to: 2900 Noblestown Rd., Pittsburgh, 15205-4227. Tel: 412-456-3033; Fax: 412-456-3118.

Judicial Vicar—Very Rev. BRIAN J. WELDING, V.J., J.C.D., S.T.L.

Judges—Revs. ROBERT J. AHLIN, J.C.L.; JAMES R. BEDILLION, J.C.L.; LOUIS L. DENINNO, J.C.L., M.Div.; Very Rev. LAWRENCE A. DINARDO, V.E., J.C.L.; Rev. WILLIAM P. FEENEY, M.Div.; Very Rev. ROBERT F. GUAY, V.G., M.Div.; Mrs. RITA F. JOYCE, J.D., J.C.L.; Revs. JAMES E. KUNKEL, S.T.M.; RICHARD M. LELONIS, J.C.L.; JAMES P. MCDONOUGH, S.T.L., J.C.L.; THOMAS M. O'DONNELL, M.Div. (Retired); JOSEPH C. SCHEIB, J.C.L., M.Div., M.A.; CHARLES W. SPEICHER, Ph.D., S.T.M.; BENEDETTO P. VAGHETTO, J.C.L.

Promoter of Justice—Very Rev. LAWRENCE A. DINARDO, V.E., J.C.L.

Defender of the Bond—Rev. JAMES L. BRUNEY, M.Div.

Notaries—Ms. MARTHA J. BRAUN; Ms. SYLVIA VEHEC; Ms. PHYLLIS GEINZER.

Secretary for Catholic Education—Rev. KRIS D. STUBNA, S.T.D.

Secretary for Clergy—Very Rev. HARRY R. BIELEWICZ, V.E., M.Div.; Mrs. RITA E. FLAHERTY, M.S.W., Diocesan Assistance Coord., 111 Blvd. of the Allies, Pittsburgh, 15222-1618. Tel: 412-456-3060; Fax: 412-456-3188; Tel: 888-808-1235 (Toll Free Victim's Assistance Hotline).

Secretary for Evangelization and Social Concerns—Deacon ALEXANDER WHOBLICKY, 111 Blvd. of the Allies, Pittsburgh, 15222-1618. Tel: 412-456-3157; Fax: 412-456-3180.

Department for Consecrated Life—Sr. GERALDINE MARIE WODARCZYK, C.S.F.N., Delegate for Relg., 111 Blvd. of the Allies, Pittsburgh, 15222. Tel: 412-456-3067.

Priest Council—Most Rev. DAVID ALLEN ZUBIK, D.D.; Very Rev. HARRY R. BIELEWICZ, V.E., M.Div.; Revs. CHARLES S. BOBER, S.T.D.; THOMAS J. BURKE, M.Div.; Very Rev. FREDERICK L. CAIN, V.E.; Rev. JOHN DAYA, O.F.M.Cap.; Very Rev. LAWRENCE A. DINARDO, V.E., J.C.L.; Revs. MARK A. ECKMAN, M.Div.; REGIS M. FARMER, D.Min.; Very Rev. PHILIP N. FARRELL, V.E., M.A., M.Div.; Rev. WILLIAM P. FEENEY, M.Div.; Very Rev. JOHN FOGARTY, C.S.Sp.; Revs. JOSEPH M. FREEDY; ANTHONY GARGOTTA; Very Rev. ROBERT F. GUAY, V.G., M.Div.; Revs. JOHN R. HANEY, M.Div.; DANIEL J. LANGA; EUGENE F. LAUER (Retired); MATTHEW R. MCCLAIN; Very Rev. JOSEPH M. MELE, V.G., Ph.D.; Rev. Msgr. WILLIAM M. OGRODOWSKI, V.E., S.T.L.; Revs. JEREMIAH T. O'SHEA; JOHN W. SKIRTICH; THOMAS A. SPARACINO, M.Div.; BENEDETTO P. VAGHETTO, J.C.L.; DANIEL W. WHALEN, S.T.L., J.D.; Most Rev. WILLIAM J. WINTER, V.G., S.T.D. (Retired).

College of Consultors—Most Rev. DAVID ALLEN ZUBIK, D.D.; Very Revs. ROBERT F. GUAY, V.G., M.Div.; JOSEPH M. MELE, V.G., Ph.D.; FREDERICK L. CAIN, V.E.; PHILIP N. FARRELL, V.E., M.A., M.Div.; Rev. Msgr. WILLIAM M. OGRODOWSKI, V.E., S.T.L.; Revs. CHARLES S. BOBER, S.T.D.; THOMAS J. BURKE, M.Div.; MARK A. ECKMAN, M.Div.; REGIS M. FARMER, D.Min.; JOHN W. SKIRTICH; BENEDETTO P. VAGHETTO, J.C.L.

Diocesan Development Board—PATRICK M. JOYCE, Ph.D., Chm.; Mr. WAYNE C. BOETTCHER; Very Rev. ROBERT F. GUAY, V.G., M.Div.; (Ret.) Judge MAUREEN LALLY-GREEN; Mr. AMBROSE MURRAY; Mr. FREDERICK P. O'BRIEN; Ms. SUSAN L. RAUSCHER; Rev. KRIS D. STUBNA, S.T.D.

Diocesan Finance Council—Most Rev. DAVID ALLEN ZUBIK, D.D.; WILLIAM G. BATZ, Ph.D., Chm.; Mrs. KATHLEEN W. BUECHEL; Ms. KATHLEEN GEIS; Mr. HOWARD HANNA III; Mr. MICHAEL J. HANNON; Mr. CHRISTOPHER SOBEL; Mr. JAMES C. STALDER.

Clergy Personnel Board—Rev. FRANK D. ALMADE, Ph.D.; WILLIAM G. BATZ, Ph.D.; Very Rev. HARRY R. BIELEWICZ, V.E., M.Div., Chm.; Deacon STEPHEN J. BYERS; Very Rev. FREDERICK L. CAIN, V.E.; Rev. MARK A. ECKMAN, M.Div.; Very Revs. PHILIP N. FARRELL, V.E., M.A., M.Div.; ROBERT F. GUAY, V.G., M.Div.; Revs. JOHN R. HANEY, M.Div.; RONALD P. LENGWIN, M.Div.; Very Rev. JOSEPH M. MELE, V.G., Ph.D.; Rev. ROBERT M. MILLER, S.T.L.; Rev. Msgr. WILLIAM M. OGRODOWSKI, V.E., S.T.L.; Revs. TERRENCE P. O'CONNOR, M.Div., J.D.; JOHN W. SKIRTICH; DANIEL W. WHALEN, S.T.L., J.D.

Diocesan Administration

Administrative Procedures, Office for—Mrs. RITA F. JOYCE, J.D., J.C.L., Admin. Tel: 412-456-3135.

Adult and Family Faith Formation, Office for—Mrs. MAUREEN H. WOOD, M.R.E., Dir. Tel: 412-456-3160; Deacon STEPHEN J. BYERS, Asst. Tel: 412-456-3124.

Archives and Record Center—Mr. KENNETH A. WHITE, Dir.; Mr. BURRIS E. ESPLEN IV, Archivist, 4721 Fifth Ave., Pittsburgh, 15213-2915. Tel: 412-456-3158.

Diocesan Assistance Coordinator—Mrs. RITA E. FLAHERTY, M.S.W. Tel: 412-456-3060. Email: rflaherty@diopitt.org.

Auditors/Analysts, Office for the—Mr. JAMES E. STIERHEIM, Supvr. Tel: 412-456-3029.

Black Catholics, Ethnic and Cultural Communities, Dept. for—Mrs. MARGRETTA STOKES TUCKER, M.Ed., Dir. Tel: 412-456-3170.

Blind Persons— Refer to Disabilities, Dept. for Persons with

Educational Budget and Planning, Office for—Mr. ROY CARTIER, M.B.A., M.R.P., Dir. Tel: 412-456-3108.

Building Commission—WILLIAM G. BATZ, Ph.D., Chm.; Mr. JAMES J. ZIELINSKI, Exec. Sec. Tel: 412-456-3034.

Building Services, Office for—Mrs. DARLENE M. HOLZER, Dir. Tel: 412-456-3016.

Business Services, Dept. for—Mr. FREDERICK P. O'BRIEN, CFO & Dir. Tel: 412-456-3137.

Campus Ministry, Office for—Rev. W. PETER HORTON, M.A., M.Div., Dir., 1010 McNeilly Rd., Pittsburgh, 15226-2513. Tel: 412-456-3140.

Canon and Civil Law Services, Dept. for—Very Revs. LAWRENCE A. DINARDO, V.E., J.C.L., Dir.; BRIAN J. WELDING, V.J., J.C.D., S.T.L., Asst. Dir. Tel: 412-456-3135.

Canonical Services, Office for—Very Revs. LAWRENCE A. DINARDO, V.E., J.C.L., Vicar; BRIAN J. WELDING, V.J., J.C.D., S.T.L., Asst. Dir. Tel: 412-456-3135.

Catechetical Ministries and Catechesis, Office for—Mrs. SHARON T. TYBOROWSKI HACHMAN, Dir. Tel: 412-456-3110.

Catholic Charities—Ms. SUSAN L. RAUSCHER, Exec. Dir., 212 9th St., Pittsburgh, 15222. Tel: 412-456-6999. Allegheny County, 212 9th St., Pittsburgh, 15222. Tel: 412-456-6999. Beaver County, 3582 Brodhead Rd., Ste. 108, Monaca, 15601. Tel: 724-775-0758. Butler County, 407 A W. Jefferson St., Butler, 16001. Tel: 724-287-4011. Greene County, 72 E. High St., Waynesburg, 15370. Tel: 724-627-6410. Lawrence County, 413 Highland Ave., New Castle, 16101. Tel: 724-658-5526. Washington County, 331 S. Main St., Washington, 15301. Tel: 724-228-7722. Roselia Center, 624 Clyde St., Pittsburgh, 15213. Tel: 412-682-4410; 412-682-4411. St. Joseph's House of Hospitality, 1635 Bedford Ave., Pittsburgh, 15219. Tel: 412-471-0666.

Catholic Charities Health Care Center, Inc.—DIANE REDINGTON, Admin. & Contact Person, 212 Ninth St., Pittsburgh, 15222. Tel: 412-456-6911.

Challenges: Options in Aging—Shenley Square, 2706 Mercer Rd., New Castle, 16105-1422.

Catholic Cemeteries Assoc., The—Ms. ANNABELLE MCGANNON, Exec. Dir., 718 Hazelwood Ave., Pittsburgh, 15217-2807. Tel: 412-521-9133.

Catholic Schools, Dept. for—ROBERT L. PASERBA, Ed.D., Supt. Catholic Schools; Sr. MARY JO MUTSCHLER, S.C., Asst. Supt. Catholic Elementary Schools; Mr. DONALD A. TETI, M.Ed., Asst. Supt. Catholic Secondary Schools; RONALD T. BOWES, D.A., Asst. Supt. Public Policy & Devel. Tel: 412-456-3090.

Educational Consultants, Elementary, Office for—2900 Noblestown Rd., Pittsburgh, 15205. Tel: 412-456-3070. Mr. MICHAEL C. KILLMEYER, M.Ed., M.S.; Sisters CATHERINE ANN KOLLER, C.D.P., M.A.; LORETTA KRALL, C.S.J., M.A.; M. DENISE MAHER, C.S.J., M.A.; CECILIA GRANDILLO, M.A.

Educational Consultants, Secondary, Office for—2900 Noblestown Rd., Pittsburgh, 15205. Tel: 412-456-3070. EDWARD G. SCHEID, Ph.D.

Elementary and Secondary School Catechesis, Office for—111 Blvd. of the Allies, Pittsburgh, 15222. Tel: 412-456-3115. Mr. CHRISTOPHER J. CHAPMAN.

Chaplain Services, Office for—111 Blvd. of the Allies, Pittsburgh, 15222. Very Rev. HARRY R. BIELEWICZ, V.E., M.Div.

Charismatic Prayer Groups—Rev. JOHN P. SWEENEY, M.Div., Moderator, St. Bonaventure Parish, 2001 Mount Royal Blvd., Glenshaw, 15116-2099. Tel: 412-486-2606.

Chief Financial Officer—Mr. FREDERICK P. O'BRIEN. Tel: 412-456-3137.

Church Relations, Office for—Mrs. MAUREEN LALLY-GREEN, Dir.

Communications Commission—Mr. ROBERT P. LOCKWOOD, Chm. Tel: 412-456-3020.

Communications, Dept. for—Mr. ROBERT P. LOCKWOOD, Dir.; CRAIG T. MAIER, Ph.D., Sr. Staff Communicator. Tel: 412-456-3020.

Continuing Education of Clergy, Office for—Rev. DAVID G. POECKING, S.T.L., Dir., St. Paul Seminary, 2900 Noblestown Rd., Pittsburgh, 15205-4227. Tel: 412-456-3048.

Cultural Diversity, Commission—Mrs. BESS BIAMONTE, Chm. Tel: 412-456-3170.

Deaf Persons— Refer to Disabilities, Dept. for Persons with

Diaconate, Office for the—Deacon STEPHEN J. BYERS, Dir. Tel: 412-456-3124.

Diocesan National Black Catholic Congress Leadership Team—Ms. MARIE FRANCIS, Team Leader. Tel: 412-456-3170.

Disabilities, Dept. for Persons with—VACANT, Dir.; Rev. WALTER G. RYDZON, M.Div., Chap. to Deaf Persons; Deacon ROBERT BARTH, Asst. to Chap. Tel: 412-456-3119 (Voice); 412-456-3122 (TTY).

Ecumenical and Interfaith Commission—Rev. RONALD P. LENGWIN, M.Div., Chm. Tel: 412-456-3021.

Media and Technology, Dept. for—Mr. JEFFREY A. HIRST, Dir., St. Paul Seminary, 2900 Noblestown Rd., Pittsburgh, 15205-4227. Tel: 412-456-3120.

Envisioning Ministry, Dept. for—MARY ANN GUBISH, D.Min., Dir. Tel: 412-456-3047.

Ethnic Ministries, Office for—Chaplain to Korean Catholic Community: Rev. JANG WON CHOI. Chaplain to Latino Catholic Community: Rev. DANIELE VALLECORSA, S.T.L. Chaplain to Vietnamese Catholic Community: Rev. DAM D. NGUYEN, M.Div. Tel: 412-456-3170.

Financial Services, Office for—Mr. WAYNE C. BOETTCHER, Dir. Tel: 412-456-3025.

Central Accounting Services—Tel: 412-456-3030.

Parish Accounting Services—Tel: 412-456-3025.

Foundation, Catholic Diocese of Pittsburgh—PATRICK M. JOYCE, Ph.D., Dir. Tel: 412-456-3085.

Health Care Liaison, Office of the—Very Rev. LAWRENCE A. DINARDO, V.E., J.C.L. Tel: 412-456-3135.

Information Technology, Office for—VACANT, Dir. Tel: 412-456-3152.

Insurance/Benefits, Office for—Mr. DAVID S. STEWART, A.R.M., Dir. Tel: 412-456-3045.

Justice and Peace Commission—VERONICA C. MORGAN-LEE, Ph.D., Chm. Tel: 412-456-3162.

Lay Personnel, Office for—Mrs. DARLENE M. HOLZER,

Dir. Tel: 412-456-3016.

Learning Media Center—Mr. JEFFREY A. HIRST, Dir., St. Paul Seminary, 2900 Noblestown Rd., Pittsburgh, 15205-4227. Tel: 412-456-3120.

Legal Services, Office for—Mrs. RITA F. JOYCE, J.D., J.C.L., Gen. Counsel; KRISTIN M. BOOSE, J.D., Asst. Gen. Counsel; PAUL IURLAND, Legal Counsel; Mr. CHRISTOPHER G. PONTICELLO, J.D., Assoc. Gen. Counsel. Tel: 412-456-3126.

Legislative Advocacy and Respect Life, Office for—VACANT, Dir.

Matrimonial Concerns, Office for—Revs. RICHARD M. LELONIS, J.C.L., Dir.; LOUIS L. DENINNO, J.C.L., M.Div., Canonical Consultant, 2900 Noblestown Rd., Pittsburgh, 15205-4227. Tel: 412-456-3076.

Diocesan Review Board—Very Rev. LAWRENCE A. DINARDO, V.E., J.C.L., Exec. Sec. Tel: 412-456-3135.

Ministries, Institute for—Sr. MARY ANN CARR, S.C., Dir., 111 Blvd. of the Allies, Pittsburgh, 15222. Tel: 412-456-3068.

Mission Office—Rev. RONALD P. LENGWIN, M.Div., Dir. Tel: 412-456-3065.

Music, Office for—Rev. JAMES J. CHEPPONIS, M.Div., M.A., Dir.; Mr. DONALD FELLOWS, Assoc. Dir., St. Paul Seminary, 2900 Noblestown Rd., Pittsburgh, 15205-4227. Tel: 412-456-3042.

Natural Family Planning Advisory Committee—Deacon STEPHEN J. BYERS, Chm. Tel: 412-456-3124.

Newspaper— "Pittsburgh Catholic" Mr. ROBERT P. LOCKWOOD, Gen. Mgr.; Mr. WILLIAM CONE, Editor, 135 First Ave., #200, Pittsburgh, 15222-1506. Tel: 412-471-1252.

Parish Life and Lay Leadership, Secretariat for—Mr. JOHN P. FLAHERTY, M.A., Sec. Tel: 412-456-3146.

Pastoral Formation, Office for—Sr. CINDY ANN KIBLER, S.H.S. Tel: 412-456-3053.

Payroll, Office for—Mr. JOHN G. CVETIC, Dir. Tel: 412-456-3006.

Pilgrimage Office—Rev. RONALD P. LENGWIN, M.Div., Dir. Tel: 412-456-3065.

Pornography, Commission to Counter—Mrs. NORMA NORRIS, Chm. Tel: 412-456-3157.

Post-Ordination Formation, Department for—Very Rev. JOSEPH M. MELE, V.G., Ph.D., Dir., St. Paul Seminary, 2900 Noblestown Rd., Pittsburgh, 15205-4227. Tel: 412-456-3048.

Pre-Ordination Formation, Department for—Very Rev. DENNIS P. YUROCHKO, S.T.L., St. Paul Seminary, 2900 Noblestown Rd., Pittsburgh, 15205-4227. Tel: 412-456-3048.

Priestly Vocations, Office for—Rev. MATTHEW R. MCCLAIN, Dir.

Property Planning and Development, Office for—Mr. JAMES J. ZIELINSKI, Dir., 135 First Ave., Pittsburgh, 15222. Tel: 412-456-3034.

Protection of Children and Young People, Office for the—Mr. RONALD W. RAGAN, M.P.A., Dir., St. Paul Seminary, 2900 Noblestown Rd., Pittsburgh, 15205. Tel: 412-456-5633.

Public and Community Affairs, Office for—Rev. RONALD P. LENGWIN, M.Div., Dir. Tel: 412-456-3021.

Religious Education, Dept. for—Mrs. JUDITH A. KIRK, Dir. Tel: 412-456-3112.

Retired Priests, Office for—Rev. LEROY A. DIPIETRO, Delegate. Tel: 412-732-2797.

Retired Priests, Residences for—Mr. GLENN DELICH, Admin., Cardinal Dearden Center, 4721 Fifth Ave., Pittsburgh, 15213-2915. Tel: 412-687-8022. St. John Vianney Manor, 2600 Morange Rd., Pittsburgh, 15205-4268. Tel: 412-928-0825.

St. Paul Cathedral—Very Rev. DONALD P. BREIER, M.Div., Rector & Pastor, 108 N. Dithridge St., Pittsburgh, 15213-2694. Tel: 412-621-4951.

St. Paul Seminary—Very Revs. DENNIS P. YUROCHKO, S.T.L., Rector; JOSEPH M. MELE, V.G., Ph.D., Vice Rector, Dir. Spiritual Formation.

Society for the Propagation of the Faith—Rev. RONALD P. LENGWIN, M.Div., Dir. Tel: 412-456-3065.

Stewardship and Development, Office for—PATRICK M. JOYCE, Ph.D., Dir.; Mrs. DOLORES C. NYPAVER, Asst. Dir.; Mr. PAUL F. STABILE, Dir. Planned Giving. Tel: 412-456-3085.

Television and Radio Production— Refer to Media and Technology, Office for

Theological Commission—Rev. JOSEPH J. KLEPPNER, S.T.L., Ph.D., Chm. Tel: 412-456-3100.

Vision Impairments, Persons with— Refer to Disabilities, Dept. for Persons with

Worship Commission—Rev. JAMES R. GRETZ, Chm. Tel: 412-456-3041.

Worship, Dept. for—Rev. JAMES R. GRETZ, Dir., St. Paul Seminary, 2900 Noblestown Rd., Pittsburgh, 15205-4227. Tel: 412-456-3041.

Youth and Young Adult Ministry, Dept. for—Mrs. JOYCE A. GILLOOLY, M.Ed., Dir.; Mr. GARY M. SLIFKEY, M.A., M.S., Assoc. Dir.; Mr. GARY RONEY, Assoc. Dir.; Deacon VICTOR P. SATTER, 1010 McNeilly Rd., Pittsburgh, 15226-2513. Tel: 412-456-3140.

CLERGY, PARISHES, MISSIONS AND PAROCHIAL SCHOOLS

CITY OF PITTSBURGH, PROPER

(ALLEGHENY COUNTY)

1—ST. PAUL CATHEDRAL (1834) Very Rev. Donald P. Breier; Revs. Kim J. Schreck; Andrew C. Fischer, Parochial Vicar. In Res., Rev. Daniele Vallecorsa; Very Rev. Brian J. Welding.
Res.: 108 N. Dithridge St., 15213. Tel: 412-621-4951; Fax: 412-621-1079. Email: st.paul.cathedral@verizon.net. Web: www.stpaulcathedralpgh.org.
School—St. Agnes Diocesan School, 120 Robinson St., 15213. Tel: 412-682-1129; Fax: 412-687-8091. Patsy Coffield, Prin. Lay Teachers 11; Students 160.
Catechesis/Religious Program—125 N. Craig St., 15213. Tel: 412-621-9444. Students 40.

2—ST. AGNES, Closed. For sacramental records contact St. Paul Cathedral.

3—ST. ANN, (Hungarian), Closed. See St. Stephen.

4—ST. AUGUSTINE, (German), Closed. See Our Lady of the Angels.

5—ST. BEDE (1922) Rev. Edward M. Bryce; Sr. Mary Elizabeth Schrei, S.C., Pastoral Assoc. In Res., Revs. John Mary Mooka, A.J.; Leonard Chuwa, A.J.
Res.: 509 S. Dallas Ave., 15208. Tel: 412-661-7222; Fax: 412-661-9337. Web: www.catholic-church.org/stbedepgh.
School—6920 Edgerton Ave., 15208. Tel: 412-661-9425; Fax: 412-661-0447. Lay Teachers 23; Students 364.
Catechesis/Religious Program—Students 75.

6—ST. BENEDICT THE MOOR (1889), (African American), Revs. Carmen A. D'Amico, Team Ministry; Thomas A. Sparacino, Team Ministry Assoc.; Deacon Reynold Wilmer.
Mailing Address: 91 Crawford St., 15219.
Rectory—164 Washington Pl., 15219. Tel: 412-471-0257; Fax: 412-471-1345. Email: churchoffice@stbenedictthemoor.org. Web: www.stbenedictthemoor.org.
School—2900 Webster Ave., 15219. Tel: 412-682-3755; Fax: 412-682-4058. Email: stben@stbenedictthemoorschool.org. Web: www.stbenedictthemoorschool.org. Sisters of St. Joseph 5; Lay Teachers 13; Students 191.
Catechesis/Religious Program—Students 106.
Convent—Tel: 412-621-0519.

7—ST. CATHERINE OF SIENA (Beechview) (1902) Rev. James M. Bachner; Deacon Thomas O'Neill.
Res.: 1810 Belasco Ave., 15216. Tel: 412-531-2135; Fax: 412-531-8543. Email: saintcatherine15216@yahoo.com.
Catechesis/Religious Program—Tel: 412-561-0399. Students 80.

8—ST. CHARLES LWANGA PARISH (1992) Rev. David H. Taylor. Consolidated from the following churches: Corpus Christi, Holy Rosary, Mother of Good Counsel, Our Lady Help of Christians, Our Lady of the Most Blessed Sacrament, SS. Peter & Paul, and St. Walburga.
Res.: 7114 Kelly St., 15208. Tel: 412-731-3020; Fax: 412-731-1615. Email: fatdht@verizon.net.
School—Holy Rosary, 7120 Kelly St., 15208. Tel: 412-731-2567; Fax: 412-731-3476. Lay Teachers 9; Students 160.
Catechesis/Religious Program—Email: nadinepowell@verizon.net. Students 40.

9—CORPUS CHRISTI, Closed. See St. Charles Lwanga.

10—ST. ELIZABETH OF HUNGARY, (Slovak), Closed. See St. Patrick-St. Stanislaus Kostka.

11—EPIPHANY (1902), (Irish), Revs. Carmen A. D'Amico, Pastoral Team; Thomas A. Sparacino, Pastoral Team; John Walsh, Hospital Chap. & Sacramental Min.
Res.: 164 Washington Pl., 15219-3502. Tel: 412-471-0257; Fax: 412-471-1345. Email: churchoffice@epiphanychurch.net. Web: www.epiphanychurch.net.

12—HOLY FAMILY, (Polish), Closed. See Our Lady of the Angels.

13—HOLY ROSARY, Closed. See St. Charles Lwanga.

14—ST. HYACINTH, (Polish), Closed. See St. Regis.

15—IMMACULATE CONCEPTION (1905), (Italian), Merged with St. Joseph, Pittsburgh to form Immaculate Conception-St. Joseph, Pittsburgh.

16—IMMACULATE CONCEPTION-ST. JOSEPH (2001), (German), Revs. John E. Dinello; Bartley A. Sorensen.
Res.: 4712 Liberty Ave., 15224. Tel: 412-682-5353; Fax: 412-682-6766. Email: macsj2@verizon.net.
School—321 Edmond St., 15224. Tel: 412-621-5199; Fax: 412-621-5601.
Catechesis/Religious Program—Students 44.

17—IMMACULATE HEART OF MARY (1897), (Polish), Rev. Joseph E. Swierczynski.
Res.: 3058 Brereton Ave., 15219. Tel: 412-621-5170; Fax: 412-621-7445.
Catechesis/Religious Program—Tel: 412-682-2886; Fax: 412-682-6889. Twinned with Our Lady of Angels. Students 15.

18—ST. JOACHIM, Closed. See St. Rosalia.

19—ST. JOHN THE BAPTIST, Closed. See Our Lady of the Angels.

20—ST. JOSEPH (1872), (German), Merged with Immaculate Conception, Pittsburgh to form Immaculate Conception-St. Joseph, Pittsburgh.

21—ST. KIERAN, Closed. See St. Matthew.

22—ST. LAWRENCE O'TOOLE (East End) (1897) Rev. James G. Graham.
Res.: 5323 Penn Ave., 15224. Tel: 412-363-1771; Fax: 412-363-7552.
Catechesis/Religious Program—Students 18.

23—ST. MARTIN (West End) Closed. See Guardian Angels.

24—ST. MARY ASSUMPTION (Lawrenceville) Closed. See St. Matthew.

25—ST. MARY OF MERCY (1870) Revs. Carmen A. D'Amico, Moderator; Thomas A. Sparacino, Co-Pastor. In Res., Revs. Ronald P. Lengwin; Thomas M. O'Donnell (Retired).
Res.: 202 Stanwix St., 15222. Tel: 412-261-0110; Fax: 412-261-0113. Email: services_stmaryofmercy@verizon.net. Web: www.stmaryofmercy.org.

26—ST. MARY'S (Lawrenceville) Closed. See Our Lady of the Angels.

27—ST. MATTHEW (1993), Consolidated from St. Kieran and St. Mary Assumption. Rev. Joseph J. Janiszeski, T.O.R.
Res.: 5322 Carnegie St., 15201. Tel: 412-781-6701; Fax: 412-781-1331.
Catechesis/Religious Program— Combined with Our Lady of Angels. Students 25.

28—MOTHER OF GOOD COUNSEL, (Italian), Closed. See St. Charles Lwanga.

29—OUR LADY HELP OF CHRISTIANS, (Italian), Closed. See St. Charles Lwanga.

30—OUR LADY OF THE ANGELS (1993) [CEM], Consolidated from St. Augustine, Holy Family, St. John the Baptist and St. Mary. Rev. John Daya, O.F.M.Cap. In Res., Rev. Reginald Russo, O.F.M.Cap.; Bro. David Cira, O.F.M.Cap.
Res.: 225 37th St., 15201. Tel: 412-682-0929; Fax: 412-682-6889. Email: ola2@peoplepc.com. Web: www.oloapgh.org.
See St. John Neumann Regional, Catholic Elementary, Pittsburgh under Consolidated Schools located in the Institution section.
Catechesis/Religious Program—Web: www.oloapgh.org. Gene Ritter, D.R.E.; Faye Ritter, D.R.E. Students 76.

31—OUR LADY OF THE MOST BLESSED SACRAMENT, Closed. See St. Charles Lwanga.

32—ST. PATRICK (Strip District) Closed. See St. Patrick-St. Stanislaus Kostka.

33—ST. PATRICK-ST. STANISLAUS KOSTKA (1993), (Polish), Rev. Harry E. Nichols. Consolidated with St. Stanislaus, St. Patrick and St. Elizabeth of Hungary. In Res., Rev. Albert Schempp, M.I.
Res. & Parish Office: 57 21st St., 15222. Tel: 412-471-4767; Fax: 412-471-1209. Email: saintsinthestrip@comcast.net. Web: www.saintsinthestrip.org.
Catechesis/Religious Program—Students 8.

34—SS. PETER AND PAUL (East Liberty) Closed. See St. Charles Lwanga.

35—ST. PHILOMENA (Squirrel Hill) Closed. See St. Bede.

36—ST. RAPHAEL (1911) Revs. Benedetto P. Vaghetto; Gilbert Z. Puznakoski, Part-Time Parochial Vicar.
Res.: 1118 Chislett St., 15206. Tel: 412-661-3100; Fax: 412-661-4105. Email: straphaelchurch@verizon.net. Web: www.straphaelschurch.org.
School—(Grades PreSchool-8), 1154 Chislett St., 15206. Tel: 412-661-0288; Fax: 412-661-0428. Email: straph@verizon.net. Web: www.straphaelelementaryschool.net. Sisters of St. Joseph 2; Lay Teachers 9; Students 154.
Catechesis/Religious Program—Tel: 412-661-0290 (Sunday Only). Students 45.

37—ST. REGIS (1993), (Polish), Merged with St. Hyacinth. Rev. Daniele Vallecorsa.
Mailing Address: 3235 Parkview Ave., 15213.
Res.: 108 N. Dithridge St., 15213. Tel: 412-687-6292; 412-687-6292; Fax: 412-681-1175. Email: 51101@diopitt.org.

Catechesis/Religious Program—Students 85.
38—ST. ROSALIA (1993), Merged with St. Joachim. Rev. Joseph W. Reschick. In Res., Rev. Joseph C. Beck.
Res.: 411 Greenfield Ave., 15207. Tel: 412-421-5766; Fax: 412-421-4529. Email: strosaliaparish@verizon.net. Web: www.strosaliaparish.com.
School—Tel: 412-521-3005; Fax: 412-521-2763. Lay Teachers 11; Students 132.
Catechesis/Religious Program—Tel: 412-521-7836. Students 53.
39—SACRED HEART (1872) Revs. Robert J. Grecco; Mark J. Skertich, Parochial Vicar. In Res., Rev. Edward S. Litavec (Retired).
Res.: 310 Shady Ave., 15206. Tel: 412-661-0187; Fax: 412-661-7932. Email: sacredheartshadyside@comcast.net.
School—325 Emerson St., 15206. Tel: 412-441-1582; Fax: 412-441-2798. Email: info@shes-pgh.org. Web: www.shes-pgh.org. Sisters of Charity 1; Sisters of St. Joseph 1; Lay Teachers 23; Students 449.
Catechesis/Religious Program—Students 50.
40—ST. STANISLAUS (Strip District), (Polish), Closed. See St. Patrick-St. Stanislaus Kostka.
41—ST. STEPHEN (1993), Merged with St. Ann. Rev. Cornelius W. McCaulley (Retired).
Mailing Address: 5115 Second Ave., 15207. Tel: 412-421-9210; Fax: 412-421-6421. Email: ststephen@verizon.net. Web: www.ststephenhazelwood.org.
Res.: 131 E. Elizabeth St., 15207. Tel: 412-421-9210.
Catechesis/Religious Program—134 E. Elizabeth St., 15207. Tel: 412-421-4748; Fax: 412-421-4748. Students 45.

SOUTH SIDE
1—ST. ADALBERT, (Polish), Closed. See Prince of Peace.
2—ST. BASIL (1907) Rev. James R. Torquato. In Res., Rev. Joseph C. Scheib.
Res.: 1735 Brownsville Rd., 15210. Tel: 412-882-9763; Fax: 412-882-2476. Email: 06701@diopitt.org.
Catechesis/Religious Program—Students 135.
3—ST. CANICE (Knoxville) Closed. See St. John Vianney.
4—ST. CASIMIR, (Lithuanian), Closed. See Prince of Peace.
5—ST. GEORGE (Allentown) Closed. See St. John Vianney.
6—GUARDIAN ANGELS (West End) (1994) [CEM], Merged with St. James and St. Martin. Rev. Donald N. Buchleitner, Admin.
Res.: 1030 Logue St., 15220. Tel: 412-921-4077; Fax: 412-922-4945. Email: karen7113@aol.com.
Catechesis/Religious Program—Tel: 412-921-3223. Students 74.
7—ST. HENRY, Closed. See St. John Vianney.
8—HOLY ANGELS (1903) Rev. Robert J. Ahlin.
Res.: 408 Baldwin Rd., 15207. Tel: 412-461-6906; Fax: 412-461-0961. Email: cheryl@holyangelshays.com. Web: www.holyangelshays.com.
Catechesis/Religious Program—Tel: 412-461-6909, Ext. 23. Email: elaineocd@verizon.net. Students 299.
9—HOLY INNOCENTS (1900) Rev. Donald N. Buchleitner.
Res.: 3011 Landis St., 15204. Tel: 412-331-0268; Fax: 412-331-1219. Email: hiparish@verizon.net.
Catechesis/Religious Program—1030 Logue St., 15220. Tel: 412-921-3223. Email: jh0836@aol.com. Clustered with Guardian Angels, Pittsburgh Students 70.
10—ST. JAMES (West End) Closed. See Guardian Angels.
11—ST. JOHN THE EVANGELIST, Closed. See Prince of Peace.
12—ST. JOHN VIANNEY (Hilltop) (1994) [CEM], Consolidation of the following churches: St. Canice, St. George, St. Henry and St. Joseph. Rev. Thomas R. Wilson, Admin.
823 Climax St., 15210. Tel: 412-381-8300; Fax: 412-431-3790. Email: sjv@sjvpgh.org. Web: www.sjvpgh.org.
Catechesis/Religious Program—Tel: 412-381-5581. Students 110.
13—ST. JOSAPHAT, (Polish), Closed. See Prince of Peace.
14—ST. JUSTIN (Mt. Washington) (1917) Rev. Walter G. Rydzon.
Res.: 539 Boggs Ave., 15211. Tel: 412-381-9878; 412-381-9825 (TTY); Fax: 412-381-0371. Email: stjustinchurch@cs.com. Web: www.saintjustins.org. Catholic Deaf Community.
Catechesis/Religious Program—Tel: 412-381-3774; Fax: 412-381-0371. Students 98.
15—ST. MARY OF THE MOUNT (Mt. Washington) (1873) Rev. Michael J. Stumpf.
Res.: 403 Grandview Ave., 15211. Tel: 412-381-0212; Fax: 412-381-9921. Email: smom@smomp.org. Web: www.smomp.org.
School—Bishop Leonard-St. Mary of the Mount Academy, 115 Bigham St., 15211. Tel: 412-431-4645; Fax: 412-381-0770. Web: www.blsmma.org. Sisters of the Immaculate Heart of Mary 2; Lay Teachers 10; Students 190.
Catechesis/Religious Program—Tel: 412-381-3310. Students 63.
16—ST. MATTHEW, (Slovak), Closed. See Prince of Peace.
17—ST. MICHAEL, (German), Closed. See Prince of Peace.
18—OUR LADY OF LORETO (1959) Rev. Robert J. Miller; Sr. Anne Flynn, S.C., Parish Minister. In Res., Very Rev. Harry R. Bielewicz, Vicar for Clergy.
Res.: 1905 Pioneer Ave., 15226. Tel: 412-341-6161; Fax: 412-341-3399. Email: ollpari@aol.com.
Catechesis/Religious Program—Tel: 412-341-6163. Email: pscherwin@verizon.net. Students 100.
Convent—1901 Pioneer Ave., 15226. Tel: 412-343-1377.
19—ST. PAMPHILUS (1960) Rev. Alexis Anania, O.F.M.; Deacon Leon F. Miles. In Res., Friar John-Michael Pinto, O.F.M.
Res.: 948 Tropical Ave., 15216. Tel: 412-341-1000; 412-531-8449; Fax: 412-341-6956.
Church: 1000 Tropical Ave., 15216.
Catechesis/Religious Program—Tel: 412-561-0330. Students 40.
20—ST. PETER, Closed. See Prince of Peace.
21—ST. PIUS X (1954) Rev. Robert J. Miller.
Res.: 3040 Pioneer Ave., 15226. Tel: 412-563-5423; Fax: 412-561-3868. Email: saint.piusx@verizon.net. Web: www.spxchurch.org.
See Brookline Regional Catholic School, Pittsburgh under Consolidated Schools located in the Institution section.
Catechesis/Religious Program—Tel: 412-563-1588. Students 91.
22—PRINCE OF PEACE (1992) [CEM 6], Consolidated from the following churches: St. Adalbert, St. Casimir, St. John the Evangelist, St. Josaphat, St. Matthew, St. Michael and St. Peter. Rev. Bernard M. Harcarik.
Mailing Address: 81 S. 13th St., 15203-1897. In Res., Rev. Eugene F. Laver.
Res.: 162 S. 15th St., 15203-1897. Tel: 412-481-8380; Fax: 412-431-0209. Email: 49801@diopitt.org.
Catechesis/Religious Program—Tel: 412-381-5458. Students 61.
23—RESURRECTION (Brookline) (1909) Rev. Frank Mitolo. In Res., Rev. Victor J. Rocha (Retired).
Res.: 1100 Creedmoor Ave., 15226. Tel: 412-563-4400; Fax: 412-563-4403. Email: ressi@earthlink.net. Web: www.eressi.com.
Catechesis/Religious Program—Tel: 412-343-9551. Students 291.
24—ST. VINCENT (Esplen) Closed. See St. John of God, McKees Rocks.
25—ST. WENDELIN (Carrick) (1873) [CEM] Rev. Edwin J. Wichman.
Res.: 2728 Custer Ave., 15227. Tel: 412-882-1480; Fax: 412-884-2334.
Catechesis/Religious Program—Tel: 412-882-3414. Students 116.

NORTH SIDE
1—ST. AMBROSE, Merged with St. Boniface to form Holy Wisdom.
2—ANNUNCIATION, Closed. See Incarnation of the Lord.
3—ST. BONIFACE, Merged with St. Ambrose to form Holy Wisdom.
4—ST. CYRIL OF ALEXANDRIA (1924) Rev. James L. Bruney.
Res.: 3854 Brighton Rd., 15212. Tel: 412-761-1552; Fax: 412-761-3318. Email: saintcyrilchurch@yahoo.com.
School—Tel: 412-761-5043; Fax: 412-761-0840. Lay Teachers 13; Students 113; Preschool 25.
Catechesis/Religious Program—Tel: 412-734-0505. Email: stcyrilreled@yahoo.com. Students 110.
5—ST. FRANCIS XAVIER, Closed. See Risen Lord.
6—ST. GABRIEL ARCHANGEL, (Slovak), Closed. See Risen Lord.
7—HOLY WISDOM (1994) [CEM] Very Rev. Lawrence A. DiNardo. In Res., Revs. Louis L. DeNinno; Vincent F. Kolo.
Res.: 1025 Haslage Ave., 15212-3429. Tel: 412-231-1071; Fax: 412-231-1072. Email: office@holywisdomparish.org. Web: www.holywisdomparish.org.
Catechesis/Religious Program—Tel: 412-321-3186; Fax: 412-321-7807. Twinned with St. Peter, North Side. Students 75.
8—INCARNATION OF THE LORD (1993), Consolidated from Annunciation and Nativity of Our Lord. Rev. David D. DeWitt.
Res.: 4071 Franklin Rd., 15214. Tel: 412-931-2911; Fax: 412-931-2832. Email: jmbpgh@comcast.net.
Catechesis/Religious Program—Students 30.
9—ST. JOSEPH, Closed. See St. Peter.
10—ST. LEO, Closed. See Risen Lord.
11—MOST HOLY NAME OF JESUS (Troy Hill) (1868), (German), [CEM] Rev. Lawrence R. Smith; Deacon G. Gregory Jelinek.
Res.: 1700 Harpster St., 15212-4393. Tel: 412-231-2994; Fax: 412-231-7180. Email: mostholyhname@hotmail.com. Web: www.mostholynameofjesusparish15212.org.
See Cardinal Wright Regional School, Pittsburgh under Consolidated Schools located in the Institution section.
Catechesis/Religious Program—Tel: 412-231-3002; 412-759-9835. Students 170.
Chapel—St. Anthony's (1880)Tel: 412-323-9504. Sr. Margaret Liam Glenane, S.A., Asst. Dir.
12—NATIVITY OF OUR LORD, Closed. See Incarnation of the Lord.
13—OUR LADY QUEEN OF PEACE, Closed. See St. Peter.
14—ST. PETER (1993), (Polish), [CEM], Consolidated from St. Cyprian, St. Mary's, Mary Immaculate & Our Lady, Queen of Peace, St. Joseph, St. Peter and St. Wenceslaus. Revs. Ralph Tajak, O.S.B.; William A. Beaver, O.S.B., Senior Priest.
Res.: 720 Arch St., 15212. Tel: 412-321-0711; Fax: 412-321-7807. Email: stpeter@winbeam.com. Web: www.stpeterparish.org.
See Cardinal Wright Regional School, Pittsburgh under Consolidated Schools located in the Institution section.
Catechesis/Religious Program—711 W. Commons, 15212. Tel: 412-321-3186. Email: patkammersell@cardinalwrightregionalschool.org. Students 53.
15—REGINA COELI, (Italian), Closed. For sacramental records contact St. Cyril of Alexandria.
16—RISEN LORD (1993), Consolidated from the following churches: St. Francis Xavier, St. Gabriel Archangel, St. Leo and Our Lady of Perpetual Help. Rev. David D. DeWitt.
Rectory & Office: 3250 California Ave., 15212. Tel: 412-761-1507; Fax: 412-761-6454. Email: risenlord@choiceonemail.com.
Catechesis/Religious Program—Alda Walker, D.R.E.; Karen Smay, D.R.E. Students 14.
17—ST. WENCESLAUS, Closed. See St. Peter.

OUTSIDE THE CITY OF PITTSBURGH

ALEPPO TOWNSHIP, ALLEGHENY CO., ST. MARY (1852) [CEM] Rev. David J. Jastrab.
Mailing Address: 444 Glenfield Rd., Sewickley, 15143. Tel: 412-741-6460; Fax: 412-749-9271. Email: bcox@saintmaryaleppo.org. Web: www.saintmaryaleppo.org.
Catechesis/Religious Program—Tel: 412-741-3959. Email: b_venturella@saintmaryaleppo.org. Students 120.
ALIQUIPPA, BEAVER CO., ST. TITUS (1994) [CEM 2] [JC 2], Merged with St. Joseph, West Aliquippa. Rev. Paul C. Householder.
Res.: 952 Franklin Ave., 15001. Tel: 724-378-8561; Fax: 724-378-4851. Email: sttituschurch@comcast.net.
Catechesis/Religious Program—Tel: 724-375-7940. Students 96.
ALLISON PARK, ALLEGHENY CO., ST. URSULA (1908) Revs. Garrett D. Dorsey; Ernest Strelinski.
Res.: 3937 Kirk Ave., 15101. Tel: 412-486-6700; Fax: 412-486-2562. Email: ursula@stursula.com.
School—Tel: 412-486-5511; Fax: 412-492-7295. Sisters 1; Lay Teachers 14; Students 151.
Catechesis/Religious Program—Tel: 412-486-3374; Fax: 412-486-3374. Students 202.
AMBRIDGE, BEAVER CO.
1—CHURCH OF CHRIST THE KING, Closed. See Good Samaritan.
2—DIVINE REDEEMER, Closed. See Good Samaritan.
3—GOOD SAMARITAN (1994) [CEM], Consolidated from the following churches: St. Veronica, Divine Redeemer, St. Stanislaus, Christ the King and Holy Trinity. Revs. Terrence P. O'Connor; Joseph M. Freedy, Parochial Vicar.
725 Glenwood Ave., 15003. Web: www.goodsam1.org.
Res.: *Parsonage*, 923 Melrose Ave., 15003. Tel: 724-385-0356; Fax: 724-266-5570.
Catechesis/Religious Program—Tel: 724-266-6565. Email: rcurcio@goodsamaritanrcchurch.org. Students 156.
4—HOLY TRINITY, (Croatian), Closed. See Good Samaritan.
5—ST. STANISLAUS, Closed. See Good Samaritan.
6—ST. VERONICA, Closed. See Good Samaritan.
ASPINWALL, ALLEGHENY CO., ST. SCHOLASTICA (1903) Rev. Kenneth R. White.
Res.: 309 Brilliant Ave., 15215. Tel: 412-781-0186; Fax: 412-781-4316. Email: parish@saintscholastica.com. Web: www.saintscholastica.com.
See Christ the Divine Teacher Catholic Academy, Pittsburgh under Consolidated Schools located in the Institution section.

Catechesis/Religious Program—Tel: 412-781-0608. Students 510.

AVELLA, WASHINGTON CO., ST. MICHAEL (1917) [CEM] Rev. Pierre G. Sodini.
Res.: 95 Highland Ave., 15312. Tel: 724-587-3570; Fax: 724-587-5203. Email: stmike@hky.com.
Catechesis/Religious Program—Students 100.

BADEN, BEAVER CO., ST. JOHN THE BAPTIST (1866) [CEM] Revs. Terrence P. O'Connor; Joseph M. Freedy, Parochial Vicar.
Res.: 375 Linmore Ave., P.O. Box 171, 15005. Tel: 724-869-2280; Fax: 724-869-0305. Email: stjohnsbadenpa@yahoo.com.
Catechesis/Religious Program— This information is combined with Good Samaritan, Ambridge. Students 32.

BAIRDFORD, ALLEGHENY CO., ST. VICTOR (1919) Rev. Robert R. Coyne.
Res.: 527 Bairdford Rd., P.O. Box 149, 15006. Tel: 724-265-2070; Fax: 724-265-6316.
Catechesis/Religious Program—Tel: 724-265-4040. Students 500.

BALDWIN BORO, ALLEGHENY CO., ST. ALBERT THE GREAT (1956) Rev. James R. Orr.
Res.: 3198 Schieck St., 15227. Tel: 412-884-7744; Fax: 412-884-2300. Email: stalbert@choiceonemail.com.
Catechesis/Religious Program—Tel: 412-884-8282. Students 260.

BEAVER FALLS, BEAVER CO.

1—DIVINE MERCY (1994), (Polish), [CEM], Consolidated from St. Mary and Holy Trinity. Rev. James B. Farnan.
Mailing Address: 605 Tenth St., 15010.
Res.: 3908 6th Ave., 15010. Tel: 724-846-4585; Fax: 724-846-6868.
School—609 Tenth St., 15010. Tel: 724-846-5955; Fax: 724-846-1894. Web: www.dmacademy.com. Lay Teachers 9; Students 83.
Catechesis/Religious Program—3908 6th Ave., 15010. Tel: 724-843-7375; Fax: 724-843-7575. Email: saintphilomena@verizon.net. Web: stphilomenabeaverfalls.org. Students 25.

2—HOLY TRINITY, (Polish), Closed. See Divine Mercy.

3—ST. PHILOMENA (1948) Rev. James B. Farnan.
Res.: 3908 Sixth Ave., 15010. Tel: 724-843-7375; Fax: 724-843-7575. Email: saintphilomena@verizon.net. Web: www.stphilomenabeaverfalls.org.
Catechesis/Religious Program—Students 55.

BEAVER, BEAVER CO., SS. PETER AND PAUL (1830) [CEM] Rev. Michael W. Decewicz. In Res., Rev. William J. Schwartz.
Res.: 200 Third St., 15009. Tel: 724-775-4111; Fax: 724-775-1117. Email: office@ssppbeaver.org. Web: www.ssppbeaver.org.
School—370 E. End Ave., 15009. Tel: 724-774-4450; Fax: 724-774-5192. Email: school@ssppbeaver.org. Lay Teachers 16; Students 195.
Catechesis/Religious Program—Students 324.

BELLEVUE, ALLEGHENY CO., ASSUMPTION OF THE BLESSED VIRGIN MARY ON THE BEAUTIFUL RIVER (1903) Revs. Dennis M. Buranosky; Richard J. Tusky, Parochial Vicar.
Res.: 45 N. Sprague Ave., 15202. Tel: 412-766-6660; Fax: 412-766-4836. Email: parish@assumptionchurch.org. Web: www.assumptionchurch.org.
School—35 N. Jackson Ave., 15202. Tel: 412-761-7887; Fax: 412-761-7620. Web: www.assumptionchurch.org. Lay Teachers 13; Students 104.
Catechesis/Religious Program—Tel: 412-766-4046. Email: assumptionred@aol.com. Students 425.

BENTLEYVILLE, WASHINGTON CO.

1—AVE MARIA (1994) [CEM 2], Consolidated from St. Luke, St. Clement and St. Joseph. Rev. Gary W. Krummert.
Res.: 126 Church St., 15314-1406. Tel: 724-239-3591; Fax: 866-910-7782. Email: 06001@diopitt.org.
Catechesis/Religious Program—Students 142.
Ave Maria Religious Education Center—Oak St., P.O. Box 590, Ellsworth, 15331. Tel: 724-239-2226. Email: avemaria1278@fairpoint.net.

2—ST. LUKE, Closed. See Ave Maria, Ellsworth.

BESSEMER, LAWRENCE CO., ST. ANTHONY (1909) Merged with St. Lawrence, Hillsville to form Christ the King, Hillsville.

BETHEL PARK, ALLEGHENY CO.

1—ST. GERMAINE (1957) Rev. John J. Baver; Mary Beth Green, Pastoral Assoc.
Res.: 7003 Baptist Rd., 15102. Tel: 412-833-0661; Fax: 412-833-4036. Email: germaine@thesafety.net.
School—St. Katharine Drexel School, 7001 Baptist Rd., 15102. Tel: 412-833-0223; Fax: 412-347-0361. Email: principal@stkatharinedrexelschool.org. Web: www.stkatharinedrexelschool.org. Lay Teachers 12; Students 135.
Catechesis/Religious Program—Tel: 412-833-6662. Students 232.

2—ST. THOMAS MORE (1953) Revs. Mark A. Eckman; Michael S. Suslowicz.
Res.: 126 Fort Couch Rd., 15241. Tel: 412-833-0031; Fax: 412-833-5995. Email: parishoffice@stmpgh.org. Web: www.stmpgh.org.
School—134 Fort Couch Rd., 15241. Tel: 412-833-1412; Fax: 412-833-5597. Email: rileys@stmcs.org. Web: www.stmcs.org. Lay Teachers 22; Students 383.
Catechesis/Religious Program—Tel: 412-835-6996; Fax: 412-283-0256. Students 816.

3—ST. VALENTINE (1931) Revs. Alan E. Morris, Admin.; Jeremiah T. O'Shea, Parochial Vicar & Senior Priest.
Res.: 2710 Ohio St., 15102. Tel: 412-835-4415; Fax: 412-835-4417. Email: svoffice@comcast.net. Web: www.stvals.org.
Catechesis/Religious Program—2709 Mesta St., 15102. Tel: 412-835-3780. Students 540.

BLAWNOX, ALLEGHENY CO., ST. EDWARD (1938) Rev. Anthony Gargotta.
Res.: 450 Walnut St., 15238. Tel: 412-828-4066; Fax: 412-828-3084. Email: st.edwards@comcast.net.
Catechesis/Religious Program—Tel: 412-828-7310. Students 82.

BOBTOWN, GREENE CO., ST. IGNATIUS OF ANTIOCH (1924) Rev. Lawrence V. Holpp.
Res.: P.O. Box 63, 15315. Tel: 724-839-7122; Fax: 724-839-7315.
Catechesis/Religious Program—Students 30.

BOYERS, BUTLER CO., ST. ALPHONSUS (1841) [CEM] [JC 3], Merged with Epiphany, St. Paschal and St. Louis, West Sunbury. Rev. James R. Bedillion.
Mailing Address: P.O. Box 46, 16020. Tel: 724-791-2393; Fax: 724-791-9971.
Res.: 2709 W. Sunbury Rd., P.O. Box 46, 16020. Email: stalphparish@zoominternet.net.
Catechesis/Religious Program—Students 170.

BRADDOCK HILLS, ALLEGHENY CO., SACRED HEART (1897), (Polish), Merged with Good Shepherd, Braddock.

BRADDOCK, ALLEGHENY CO., GOOD SHEPHERD (1985), Merged with Sacred Heart, Braddock Hills. Rev. Thomas J. Burke.
Mailing Address: 1024 Maple Way, 15104. Email: gshepoffice@comcast.net. Web: www.goodshepherdbraddock.org. In Res., Rev. Douglas A. Boyd.
Res.: 1600 Brinton Rd., 15221. Tel: 412-271-1515; Fax: 412-271-1222.
School—1025 Braddock Ave., 15104. Tel: 412-271-2492; Fax: 412-271-3248. Email: goodshepfamily@verizon.net. Jacqueline Fazio, Prin. Sisters 2; Lay Teachers 10; Students 127.
Catechesis/Religious Program—Tel: 412-271-2630. Email: missjoan2@verizon.net. Students 55.
Convent—Tel: 412-271-1736.

BRENTWOOD, ALLEGHENY CO., ST. SYLVESTER (1924) Very Rev. John M. Bachkay.
Res.: 3754 Brownsville Rd., 15227. Tel: 412-882-8593; Fax: 412-882-0153. Email: office@stsylvesterparish.org. Web: www.saintsylvesterparish.org.
School—30 W. Willock Rd., 15227. Tel: 412-882-9900. Lay Teachers 15; Students 303.
Catechesis/Religious Program—Tel: 412-881-4142. Students 525.

BRIDGEVILLE, ALLEGHENY CO.

1—ST. AGATHA (1894) Closed. See Holy Child.

2—ST. ANTHONY (1915), (Lithuanian), Closed. See Holy Child.

3—ST. BARBARA (1894) [CEM] Rev. Richard E. Ward.
Res.: 45 Prestley Rd., 15017-1971. Tel: 412-221-5152; Fax: 412-221-7935. Email: stbarb@comcast.net.
Catechesis/Religious Program—Students 278.

4—HOLY CHILD (1994) [CEM], Consolidated from St. Agatha and St. Anthony. Revs. Richard C. Yagesh; Robert J. Meyer, Senior Priest; Paul W. Merkovsky.
Res.: 212 Station St., 15017. Tel: 412-221-5213; Fax: 412-257-2461. Email: holychildparish@verizon.net. Web: www.holychildparish.org.
School—Tel: 412-221-4720; Fax: 412-257-9742. Email: stholychild@comcast.net. Sisters 1; Lay Teachers 13; Students 147.
Catechesis/Religious Program—Tel: 412-221-6514. Students 538.

BULGER, WASHINGTON CO., ST. ANN (1917) Rev. Robert M. Staszewski.
Res.: 967 Grant St., Box 488, 15019-0488. Tel: 724-796-3791; 724-796-9151 (Social Hall); Fax: 724-796-5173. Email: annchurc@icubed.com.
Catechesis/Religious Program—Students 88.

BURGETTSTOWN, WASHINGTON CO., OUR LADY OF LOURDES (1916) [CEM] Rev. Robert P. Connolly.
Res.: 1109 Main St., 15021. Tel: 724-947-3363; Fax: 724-947-9348. Email: olol@verizon.net.
Catechesis/Religious Program—Tel: 724-947-5076. Email: ololccd@verizon.net. Students 75.

BUTLER, BUTLER CO.

1—ST. FIDELIS OF SIGMARINGEN (1995) Revs. James F. Murphy; George Palick.
Res.: 125 Buttercup Rd., 16001. Tel: 724-482-2690; Fax: 724-482-2315. Email: stfidel@aol.com. Web: www.saintfidelis.org.
Catechesis/Religious Program—Tel: 724-482-2362. Joan Pilat, D.R.E. Students 451.

2—ST. MICHAEL THE ARCHANGEL (1909), (Italian—French), [CEM] Rev. James W. Dolan.
Res.: 432 Center Ave., 16001. Tel: 724-282-4107; Fax: 724-282-3156. Email: stmikearchl@zoominternet.net.
See Butler Catholic School, Butler under Consolidated Schools located in the Institution section.
Catechesis/Religious Program—Tel: 724-282-9365. Students 75.

3—ST. PAUL (1867) Revs. Steven V. Neff; Nicholas J. Argentieri, Parochial Vicar; Deacon Mitchell M. Natali.
Res.: 128 N. McKean St., 16001. Tel: 724-287-1759; Fax: 724-287-2081. Email: stpaulchurch@zoominternet.net. Web: www.stpaulbutler.org.
See Butler Catholic School, Butler under Consolidated Schools located in the Institution section.
Catechesis/Religious Program—Students 280.

4—ST. PETER (1821), (German), [CEM] Rev. James W. Dolan.
Res.: 127 Franklin St., 16001. Tel: 724-287-2743; Fax: 724-287-3080. Email: office@specialandloved.com. Web: www.specialandloved.com.
See Butler Catholic School, Butler under Consolidated Schools located in the Institution section.
Catechesis/Religious Program—Students 160.

5—ST. WENDELIN (1863) [CEM] Revs. Steven V. Neff; Nicholas J. Argentieri, Parochial Vicar.
Res.: 210 Saint Wendelin Rd., 16002-1065. Tel: 724-287-0820; Fax: 724-287-6253. Email: parish@stwendelinbutler.org; 59201@diopitt.org. Web: www.stwendelinbutler.org.
Preschool—Tel: 724-285-4986. Students 32.
School—(Grades K-8), 211 Saint Wendelin Rd., 16002. Tel: 724-285-4986. Lay Teachers 8; Students 70.
Catechesis/Religious Program—Students 120.

CABOT, BUTLER CO., ST. JOSEPH (1904) Revs. Ward Stakem, O.F.M.Cap.; Mark Carter, O.F.M. Cap., Parochial Vicar.
Res.: 315 Stoney Hollow Rd., 16023. Tel: 724-352-2149; Fax: 724-352-7174. Email: stjosephcabot@zoominternet.net. Web: www.stjosephcabot.41pi.com.
Catechesis/Religious Program—Tel: 724-352-3030; Fax: 724-352-3443. Email: sjreled@zoominternet.net. Students 315.

CALIFORNIA, WASHINGTON CO., ST. THOMAS AQUINAS (1888) [CEM] Rev. George J. Moneck.
Res.: 213 Fourth St., 15419. Tel: 724-938-3204; Fax: 724-938-0434.
Catechesis/Religious Program—Tel: 724-938-7775. Students 86.

CANONSBURG, WASHINGTON CO.

1—ST. GENEVIEVE, (Polish), Closed. See St. Patrick.

2—ST. PATRICK (1993) [CEM], Merged with St. Genevieve. Revs. John J. Batykefer; Joseph B. Codori; Very Rev. Gabriel Badurina, T.O.R., Chap.; Deacon Joseph Cerenzia.
Res.: 317 W. Pike St., 15317. Tel: 724-745-6560; Fax: 724-746-1112. Email: stpatparish@verizon.net. Web: www.stpatrickparish.net.
School—Hutchinson & Murdock Sts., 15317. Tel: 724-745-7977; Fax: 724-746-9778. Email: stpat@pulsenet.com. Web: www.stpatschool.org. Priests 2; Lay Teachers 13; Students 224.
Catechesis/Religious Program—Tel: 724-745-3787. Students 567.

CARMICHAELS, GREENE CO., ST. HUGH (1951), (Polish), Rev. John M. Bauer.
Res.: 408 Rt. 88, 15320. Tel: 724-966-7270; Fax: 724-966-9118. Email: sthugholcpc@windstream.net.
Catechesis/Religious Program—Students 141.

CARNEGIE, ALLEGHENY CO.

1—ST. ELIZABETH ANN SETON (1992), (Italian—German), [CEM] [JC 4], Consolidated from the following churches: Holy Souls, St. Ignatius de Loyola, Immaculate Conception, St. Joseph, St. Luke and St. Vincent de Paul, Walkers Mill. Revs. David G. Poecking; Robin Evanish.
Mailing Address: 206 Mary St., 15106-2489.
Res.: 125 Finley Ave., 15106-2489. Tel: 412-276-1011; Fax: 412-276-0816.
Catechesis/Religious Program—127 Finley Ave., 15106. Tel: 412-279-8118. Students 269.

2—HOLY SOULS, Closed. See St. Elizabeth Ann Seton.

3—ST. IGNATIUS DE LOYOLA, (Polish), Closed. See St. Elizabeth Ann Seton.

4—IMMACULATE CONCEPTION, (Polish), Closed. See St. Elizabeth Ann Seton.

5—ST. JOSEPH, (German), Closed. See St. Elizabeth Ann Seton.
6—ST. LUKE, Closed. See St. Elizabeth Ann Seton.

CASTLE SHANNON, ALLEGHENY CO., ST. ANNE (1889) [CEM] Revs. Robert J. Cedolia; Michael A. Zavage, Parochial Vicar. In Res., Rev. Hugh J. Lang (Retired).
Res.: 400 Hoodridge Dr., 15234. Tel: 412-531-5964; Fax: 412-531-6901.
School—4040 Willow Ave., 15234. Tel: 412-561-7720; Fax: 412-561-7927. Lay Teachers 13; Students 168.
Catechesis/Religious Program—Tel: 412-561-0101. Students 450.

CECIL, WASHINGTON CO., ST. MARY (1909) [CEM] Rev. Stan M. Gregorek.
Res.: 10 St. Mary's Ln., 15321. Tel: 412-221-1560; Fax: 412-221-9544. Email: stmarysch@comcast.net. Web: www.stmarycecil.org.
Catechesis/Religious Program—Tel: 412-221-0595. Students 216.

CENTER TOWNSHIP, BEAVER CO., ST. FRANCES CABRINI (1961) Revs. Joseph J. Kleppner; Mariusz Mularczyk, Parochial Vicar; Ellen Cavanaugh, Pastoral Assoc.; Brenda Kostial, Music Dir.
Res.: 115 Trinity Dr. Center Twp., Aliquippa, 15001. Tel: 724-775-6363; Fax: 724-775-3848. Email: sfcabrini@comcast.net. Web: www.sfcabriniparish.org.
Catechesis/Religious Program—Tel: 724-774-4888. Deanna Stacho, D.R.E.; Robert Weaver, Youth Min. Students 600.

CENTER TOWNSHIP, BUTLER CO., ST. ANDREW (1964) Rev. James G. Salberg.
Res.: 1660 N. Main St. Ext., Butler, 16001. Tel: 724-287-7781; Fax: 724-287-7346.
Catechesis/Religious Program—Students 177.

CHARLEROI, WASHINGTON CO.
1—SS. CYRIL AND METHODIUS, (Slovak), Closed. See Mary Mother of the Church.
2—ST. JEROME, Closed. See Mary Mother of the Church.
3—MARY MOTHER OF THE CHURCH (1992) [CEM], Consolidated from SS. Cyril & Methodius, St. Jerome and Mother of Sorrows. Rev. David F. Dzermejko.
Res.: 624 Washington Ave., 15022-1932. Tel: 724-483-4572; 724-483-5533; Fax: 724-483-0122.
Catechesis/Religious Program—Students 160.
4—MOTHER OF SORROWS, (Italian), Closed. See Mary Mother of the Church.

CHICORA, BUTLER CO., MATER DOLOROSA (1875) Rev. Joseph P. Pudichery.
Res.: 409 N. Main St., P.O. Box 243, 16025. Tel: 724-445-2275; Fax: 724-445-7507. Email: materdol@zoominternet.net. Web: www.freewebs.com/materdolorosa/stjoe.
Catechesis/Religious Program—Email: stj@zoominternet.net. Combined with St. Joseph, North Oakland. Students 73.

CHIPPEWA TOWNSHIP, BEAVER CO., CHRIST THE DIVINE TEACHER (1969) Rev. Robert M. Franco.
Res.: 116 Thorndale Dr., Beaver Falls, 15010. Tel: 724-846-3818; Fax: 724-846-3819. Email: cdt-church@comcast.net.
Catechesis/Religious Program—Tel: 724-847-4750. Email: cdtreled@comcast.net. Students 294.

CHURCHILL BOROUGH, ALLEGHENY CO., ST. JOHN FISHER (1960) Rev. Carl J. Gentile.
Res.: 33 Lewin Ln., 15235. Tel: 412-241-4722; Fax: 412-241-4653.
Catechesis/Religious Program—Tel: 412-241-4653. Students 201.

CLAIRTON, ALLEGHENY CO.
1—ST. CLARE OF ASSISI (1994) [CEM], Consolidated from the following churches: St. Joseph, St. Paulinus and St. Clare. Rev. Richard J. Zelik, O.F.M.-Cap.
Mailing Address: 460 Reed St., 15025. Tel: 412-233-7870; Fax: 412-233-0742. Email: stclareparish2@comcast.net. Web: stclarepa.home-.comcast.net. In Res., Revs. Lester Knoll, O.F.M-.Cap. Tel: 412-233-7828; Angelus Shaughnessy, O.F.M.Cap. Tel: 412-233-4477; Bonaventure Stefun, O.F.M.Cap.
Catechesis/Religious Program—Students 30.
2—ST. JOSEPH, Closed. See St. Clare of Assisi.
3—ST. PAULINUS, Closed. See St. Clare of Assisi.

CLARKSVILLE, WASHINGTON CO., ST. THOMAS (1992), (Polish—Italian), Rev. J. Francis Frazer.
Res.: 30 Main St., 15322. Tel: 724-377-2588; Fax: 724-377-0707. Email: stthomas@windstream.net.
Catechesis/Religious Program—Students 60.

CONWAY, BEAVER CO., OUR LADY OF PEACE (1941) Revs. John P. Fitzgerald; William E. Dorner, Parochial Vicar.
Res.: 1000 3rd Ave., 15027. Tel: 724-869-3024; Fax: 724-869-3025. Email: olop@verizon.net.
Catechesis/Religious Program—Tel: 724-869-4723. Email: olopdre@verizon.net. Students 246.

CORAOPOLIS, ALLEGHENY CO., ST. JOSEPH (1891) [CEM] Rev. Richard S. Jones; Sr. Mary Elizabeth Brush, C.S.J., Pastoral Assoc.; Virginia Ambrose, Dir. Music; Mary Ellen Pendel, Business Mgr.
Res.: 1304 Fourth Ave., 15108. Tel: 412-264-6162; Fax: 412-264-5370. Email: st.josephparish@verizon.net.
School—Tel: 412-264-6141; Fax: 412-264-1518. Email: stjosephschool@gaggle.net. Felician Sisters 3; Lay Teachers 14; Aides 2; Students 112; Preschool 12.
Catechesis/Religious Program—Tel: 412-262-9252. Email: pastoralassociate@verizon.net. Students 108.

COYLESVILLE, BUTLER CO., ST. JOHN (1853) [CEM] Rev. Donald R. Bischof.
Res.: 668 Clearfield Rd., Fenelton, 16034-9743. Tel: 724-287-7590; Fax: 724-287-3550. Email: stjohnchurch@zoominternet.net.
Catechesis/Religious Program—Tel: 724-287-0426. Email: stjohnccd@zoominternet.net. Students 110.

CRAFTON, ALLEGHENY CO., ST. PHILIP (1839), (Irish), [CEM] Rev. Walter W. Dworak.
Res.: 50 W. Crafton Ave., 15205. Tel: 412-922-6300; Fax: 412-920-7310. Email: parishoffice@saintphilipchurch.org. Web: www.saintphilipchurch.org.
School—52 W. Crafton Ave., 15205. Tel: 412-928-2742. Web: www.spsangelway.org. Sisters of Charity 1; Lay Teachers 22; Students 411.
Catechesis/Religious Program—Tel: 412-928-2742, Ext. 8. Email: mlmcnam@aol.com. Students 125.

CRANBERRY TOWNSHIP, BUTLER CO.
1—ST. FERDINAND (1961) Revs. John P. Gallagher; Edward J. Kunco; George R. Dalton; Barbara McCarthy, Pastoral Assoc.
Res.: 2535 Rochester Rd., 16066-6496. Tel: 724-776-2888; Fax: 724-776-2378. Web: www.stferd.org.
Catechesis/Religious Program—Tel: 724-776-9177; Fax: 724-776-6640. Email: clara@stferd.org. Students 1,117.
Saint Ferdinand Parish Charitable Trust - A Pennsylvania Charitable Trust.
2—ST. KILIAN (1917) Revs. Charles S. Bober; Joseph A. Carr.
Res.: 7076 Franklin Rd., 16066-5302. Tel: 724-625-1665; Fax: 724-625-1922. Email: parish@saintkilian.org. Web: www.saintkilian.org.
School—Sr. Kathy Kudlac, O.S.C., Prin. Faculty 17; Students 490.
Catechesis/Religious Program—Students 1,087.

CREIGHTON, ALLEGHENY CO., HOLY FAMILY (East Deer Twp.) (1949) Rev. Miroslaw Stelmaszczyk.
Res.: 787 Freeport Rd., 15030. Tel: 724-224-1626; Fax: 724-224-0609.
Catechesis/Religious Program—Students 25.

CRESENT, ALLEGHENY CO., ST. CATHERINE OF SIENA (1959) Revs. Louis F. Vallone; Robert J. Zajdel.
Res.: 199 McGovern Blvd., Crescent, 15046. Tel: 724-457-7026; 724-457-0106 (Church Hall); Fax: 724-457-3292.
Catechesis/Religious Program—Students 155.

DARLINGTON, BEAVER CO., ST. ROSE OF LIMA (1854) [CEM] Rev. James B. Krah, Admin.
Res.: 3357 Constitution Blvd., 16115. Tel: 412-843-0152; Fax: 724-843-7810.
Catechesis/Religious Program—Students 200.

DONORA, WASHINGTON CO.
1—ST. CHARLES, Closed. See Our Lady of the Valley.
2—ST. DOMINIC, (Slovak), Closed. See Our Lady of the Valley.
3—HOLY NAME OF THE BLESSED VIRGIN MARY, Closed. See Our Lady of the Valley.
4—OUR LADY OF THE VALLEY (1992) [CEM], Consolidated from the following churches: St. Charles Borromeo, St. Dominic, Holy Name of the Blessed Virgin Mary and St. Philip Neri. Rev. Pierre M. Falkenhan.
Res.: 571 Thompson Ave., 15033. Tel: 724-379-4777; Fax: 724-379-6242.
Catechesis/Religious Program—Students 75.
5—ST. PHILIP NERI, (Italian), Closed. See Our Lady of the Valley.

DUQUESNE, ALLEGHENY CO.
1—CHRIST THE LIGHT OF THE WORLD (1994) [CEM 2], Consolidated from St. Hedwig and Holy Name. Rev. Dennis J. Colamarino.
Res.: 32 S. First St., 15110. Tel: 412-469-0196; Fax: 412-466-6845. Email: office@christthelightoftheworld.org. Web: www.christthelightoftheworld.org.
Catechesis/Religious Program—Students 119.
2—HOLY NAME, Closed. See Christ the Light of the World.
3—ST. JOSEPH (1897), (German), [CEM] Rev. Dennis J. Colamarino.
Res.: 817 W. Grant Ave., 15110. Tel: 412-466-1304; Fax: 412-466-3013. Email: stjosephchurch1@verizon.net.
Catechesis/Religious Program— Twinned with Christ the Light of the World. Students 28.

EAST MCKEESPORT, ALLEGHENY CO., ST. ROBERT BELLARMINE (1951) Rev. John D. Brennan.
Res.: 1313 Fifth Ave., 15035. Tel: 412-824-2644; Fax: 412-824-4786. Email: strobertbellarmine@comcast.net. Web: www.geocities.com/strobbel.
Catechesis/Religious Program—Tel: 412-824-3688; Fax: 412-824-5330. Email: srbcf@comcast.net. Students 250.

EAST PITTSBURGH, ALLEGHENY CO.
1—ST. HELEN, (Slovak), Closed. See Holy Cross.
2—HOLY CROSS (1994), Consolidated from St. William and St. Helen. Rev. Miroslaus A. Wojcicki.
Res.: 905 Main St., 15112. Tel: 412-829-1146; Fax: 412-816-2059.
3—ST. WILLIAM, Closed. See Holy Cross.

ELIZABETH, ALLEGHENY CO., ST. MICHAEL (1851) [CEM] Rev. Rudolph F. Smoley.
Res.: 101 McLay Dr., 15037. Tel: 412-751-0663; Fax: 412-751-2161. Email: stmichael1@libcom.com.
Catechesis/Religious Program—Students 190.

ELLWOOD CITY, LAWRENCE CO.
1—ST. AGATHA (1895), (Territorial), Merged with Purification of the Blessed Virgin Mary, Ellwood City to form Holy Redeemer, Ellwood City.
2—HOLY REDEEMER PARISH (2000) [CEM] Revs. Mark L. Thomas; Louis F. Pascazi; Joseph J. Dascenzo (Retired).
300 Crescent Ave., Ste. 1, 16117. Tel: 724-758-4411; Fax: 724-752-1466. Email: holydmrec@zoominternet.net. Web: www.holyredeemerparishpgh.com.
School—311 Lawrence Ave., 16117. Tel: 724-758-5591; Fax: 724-758-0705. Email: info@holyredeemerschool.com. Web: www.holyredeemerschool.com. Religious 3; Lay Teachers 14; Students 96.
Catechesis/Religious Program—603 Bridge St., 16117. Tel: 724-752-1271; 724-758-5562; Fax: 724-752-1271. Email: hrreledu@zoominternet.net. Web: www.holyredeemerparish.org. Students 508.
Convent—300 Crescent Ave., 16117. Tel: 724-758-3741.
3—PURIFICATION OF THE BLESSED VIRGIN MARY (1914) Merged with St. Agatha, Ellwood City to form Holy Redeemer, Ellwood City.

ELRAMA, ALLEGHENY CO., ST. ISAAC JOGUES (1950) Very Rev. Robert J. Boyle.
Mailing Address: 3609 Washington Ave., Finleyville, 15332.
Church: 1216 Collins Ave., Jefferson Hills, 15025. Tel: 412-384-4406; Fax: 412-384-5740. Email: stisaacjogues@msn.com.
Catechesis/Religious Program—Students 60.

EMSWORTH, ALLEGHENY CO., SACRED HEART (1891) Rev. John P. Skaj, C.S.Sp.
Res.: 154 Orchard Ave., 15202. Tel: 412-761-6651; Fax: 412-766-8298.
Catechesis/Religious Program—Tel: 412-761-3806. Students 140.

ETNA, ALLEGHENY CO., ALL SAINTS (1902) Rev. John L. Gudewicz.
Res.: 19 Wilson St., 15223-1798. Tel: 412-781-0530; Fax: 412-784-8769. Email: allsaintsetna@comcast.net.
Catechesis/Religious Program—Tel: 412-781-5183; Fax: 412-781-5273. Email: allsaintsreled@comcast.net. Students 189.
Social Service—Tel: 412-781-0530.

EVANS CITY, BUTLER CO., ST. MATTHIAS (1939) Rev. Robert M. Miller.
Res.: *St. Gregory*, 2 W. Beaver St., Zelienople, 16063. Tel: 724-452-7245; Fax: 724-452-4064.
Church: 417 E. Main St., P.O. Box 545, 16033-0545. Tel: 724-538-5331; Fax: 724-538-8237. Email: st.matthias.ec.pc@gmail.com. Web: www.ritzerthall.org.
Catechesis/Religious Program—Students 67.

FINLEYVILLE, WASHINGTON CO., ST. FRANCIS OF ASSISI (1893) [CEM] Very Rev. Robert J. Boyle; Deacon Victor P. Satter.
Res.: 3609 Washington Ave., 15332. Tel: 724-348-7145; Fax: 724-348-7522. Email: stfran2@verizon.net.
Catechesis/Religious Program—Tel: 724-348-6190. Students 205.

FOREST HILLS, ALLEGHENY CO., ST. MAURICE (1949) Revs. John W. Skirtich; Jeffrey T. Molnar, Parochial Vicar.
Res.: 2001 Ardmore Blvd., 15221. Tel: 412-271-0809; Fax: 412-271-2415. Email: parishoffice@stmauriceparish.org. Web: www.stmauriceparish.org.
School—Tel: 412-351-5403; Fax: 412-273-9114. Email: principal@stmauriceschool.org. Web: www-.stmauriceschool.org. Sisters 1; Lay Teachers 19; Students 266.
Catechesis/Religious Program—Tel: 412-271-6606; Fax: 412-271-2415. Students 92.

FRANKLIN PARK BOROUGH, ALLEGHENY CO.
1—ST. JOHN NEUMANN (1979) Rev. Albin C. McGinnis. Res.: 1543 Old Orchard Rd., 15237. Tel: 412-366-2020; Fax: 412-366-2866. Email: 25701@diopitt.org. Web: www.stjohnneumannpgh.org.
Catechesis/Religious Program—2230 Rochester Rd., 15237. Tel: 412-366-5885. Students 516.
2—SAINTS JOHN AND PAUL (1994) Rev. Joseph R. McCaffrey.
Res.: 2586 Wexford-Bayne Rd., Sewickley, 15143. Tel: 724-935-2104; Fax: 724-935-8320. Email: info@stsjohnandpaul.org. Web: www.stsjohnandpaul.org.
Catechesis/Religious Program—Students 1,014.
FREDERICKTOWN, WASHINGTON CO.
1—ST. MICHAEL THE ARCHANGEL, Closed. See St. Oliver Plunkett, Marianna.
2—ST. OLIVER PLUNKETT (1994) [CEM] Unassigned. Consolidated from Saints Mary & Ann, Marianna, and St. Michael Archangel, Fredericktown.
Res.: 73 Welcome St., Box 638, 15333. Tel: 724-377-0128; Fax: 724-377-0129. Email: stoliverplunkett@windstream.net.
Catechesis/Religious Program—Students 100.
FREEDOM, BEAVER CO., ST. FELIX (1906) [CEM] Rev. Michael P. Greb, O.F.M.Cap.
450 13th St., 15042. Tel: 724-775-1476; Fax: 724-775-5684. Email: stfelix@verizon.net.
Catechesis/Religious Program—Students 71.
GLADE MILLS, BUTLER CO., HOLY SEPULCHER (1955) Rev. Albert J. Semler.
Res.: 1304 E. Cruikshank Rd., Butler, 16002. Tel: 724-586-7610; Fax: 724-586-7247. Email: hsc.office@zoominternet.net. Web: www.holysepulcher.org.
School—6515 Old Rte. 8, Butler, 16002. Tel: 724-586-5022; Fax: 724-586-5073. Lay Teachers 13; Students 199.
Catechesis/Religious Program—Tel: 724-586-7276. Email: hsfaith/formation@zoominternet.net. Students 428.
GLASSPORT, ALLEGHENY CO.
1—ST. CECILIA, Closed. See Queen of the Rosary.
2—QUEEN OF THE ROSARY (1994), Consolidated from Holy Cross and St. Cecilia. Rev. Casimir Kedzierski.
Res.: 530 Michigan Ave., 15045. Tel: 412-672-7209; Fax: 412-672-6390. Email: gorglasspt@comcast.net. Web: www.queenoftherosaryparish.homestead.com.
School—St. Joseph Regional School 15045. Tel: 412-678-0659. See Consolidated Schools under Institutions located in the Diocese.
Catechesis/Religious Program—Students 53.
GLENSHAW, ALLEGHENY CO.
1—ST. BONAVENTURE (1957) Revs. John P. Sweeney; F. Raymond Trance.
Res.: 2001 Mt. Royal Blvd., 15116. Tel: 412-486-2606; Fax: 412-492-9329. Email: st_bonnie@hotmail.com.
School—Tel: 412-486-2606, Ext. 301; Fax: 412-487-8657. Lay Teachers 27; Students 300.
Catechesis/Religious Program—Tel: 412-486-2606, Ext. 200. Students 450.
2—ST. MARY OF THE ASSUMPTION (1834) [CEM] Revs. John A. Marcucci; Edward Schleicher; Deacon Francis J. Dadowski.
Res.: 2510 Middle Rd., 15116. Tel: 412-486-4100; Fax: 412-486-4150. Email: rectory@stmaryglenshaw.org. Web: www.stmaryglenshaw.org.
School—Tel: 412-486-7611; Fax: 412-487-9509. Sisters of Divine Providence 1; Lay Teachers 20; Students 297.
Catechesis/Religious Program—Tel: 412-486-5521; Fax: 412-486-5177. Students 497.
GREEN TREE, ALLEGHENY CO., ST. MARGARET (1938) Rev. Francis J. Murhammer.
310 Mansfield Ave., 15220.
Res.: 912 Alice St., 15220. Tel: 412-921-0745; Fax: 412-921-0707. Email: saintmargaret@verizon.net.
School—915 Alice St., 15220. Tel: 412-922-4765; Fax: 412-922-4647. Email: cmilitzer@stmargschool.com. Web: www.stmargschool.com. Lay Teachers 19; Students 301.
Catechesis/Religious Program—Tel: 412-921-1613; Fax: 412-921-0707. Email: smosdre@gmail.com. Students (K-8) 220.
HARMAR, ALLEGHENY CO., ST. FRANCIS OF ASSISI (1940) Rev. Anthony Gargotta.
Res.: 450 Walnut St., 15238. Tel: 412-828-4066; Fax: 412-828-3084. Email: stfrancisofassisi@verizon.net.
Catechesis/Religious Program—Students 20.
HARWICK, ALLEGHENY CO., OUR LADY OF VICTORY (1944) Rev. Albert L. Zapf.
Res.: 1319 Low Grade Rd., Box 198, 15049. Tel: 724-274-8575; Fax: 724-274-0529. Email: olov1@verizon.net.
Catechesis/Religious Program—Tel: 724-274-6445. Email: olovr.ed@verizon.net. Students 192.
HERMAN, BUTLER CO., ST. MARY OF THE ASSUMPTION (1842) [CEM] Revs. Ward Stakem, O.F.M.Cap.; Mark Carter, O.F.M. Cap.
Res.: 821 Herman Rd., Butler, 16002. Tel: 724-285-3285; Fax: 724-285-4715. Email: saintmaryinhermanfr@zoominternet.net.
Catechesis/Religious Program—Students 95.
HILLSVILLE, LAWRENCE CO.
1—CHRIST THE KING (2000) [CEM 2] Rev. James A. Downs.
Mailing Address: P.O. Box 23, 16132. Tel: 724-667-7721; Fax: 724-667-0827.
Catechesis/Religious Program—Students 202.
2—ST. LAWRENCE (1904), (Italian), Merged with St. Anthony, Bessemer to form Christ the King, Hillsville.
HOLIDAY PARK, ALLEGHENY CO., OUR LADY OF JOY (1968) Rev. David A. Driesch; Gregory Callaghan, Pastoral Assoc. In Res., Rev. Ladis Cizik.
Res.: 2000 O'Block Rd., 15239. Tel: 412-795-3388; Fax: 412-793-5308. Web: www.ourladyofjoy.org.
Catechesis/Religious Program—Tel: 412-795-4389. Students 440.
HOMESTEAD, ALLEGHENY CO.
1—ST. ANNE, Closed. See St. Maximilian Kolbe, Homestead.
2—ST. ANTHONY, Closed. See St. Maximilian Kolbe, Homestead.
3—ST. MARY MAGDALENE, Closed. See St. Maximilian Kolbe, Homestead.
4—ST. MAXIMILIAN KOLBE (1992) [CEM 3], Consolidated from the following churches: St. Anne, Homestead; St. Anthony, Homestead; St. Margaret, Homestead; St. Mary Magdalene, Homestead; St. Michael, Homestead; SS. Peter & Paul, Homestead. Rev. E. Daniel Sweeney. In Res., Revs. Mark W. Glasgow. Tel: 412-462-1807; Robert G. Turner (Retired).
Parish Center: 363 W. 11th Ave. Ext., 15120. Tel: 412-461-1054; Fax: 412-462-1744. Email: stmaximiliankolbe@comcast.net. Web: home.catholicweb.com/stmaximiliankolbe.
Catechesis/Religious Program—Students 48.
5—SS. PETER AND PAUL, (Lithuanian), Closed. See St. Maximilian Kolbe, Homestead.
HOPEWELL TOWNSHIP, BEAVER CO., OUR LADY OF FATIMA (1954) Rev. Howard W. Campbell.
Res.: 2270 Brodhead Rd., Aliquippa, 15001. Tel: 724-375-7626; Fax: 724-375-0219.
School—Tel: 724-375-7565. Lay Teachers 15; Students 180; Preschool 35.
Catechesis/Religious Program—Tel: 724-378-8020. Students 435.
IMPERIAL, ALLEGHENY CO., ST. COLUMBKILLE (1908) [CEM] Rev. Domenic Mancini.
Res.: 103 Church Rd., 15126. Tel: 724-695-7325; Fax: 724-695-9202.
Catechesis/Religious Program—101 Church Rd., 15126. Tel: 724-695-2146. Students 596.
INDUSTRY, BEAVER CO., ST. CHRISTINE, Closed. See St. Blaise, Midland.
INGRAM, ALLEGHENY CO., ASCENSION (1967) Rev. Alvin J. Adams.
Res.: 114 Berry St., 15205. Tel: 412-921-1230; Fax: 412-922-1279. Email: ascension.church1@verizon.net.
Catechesis/Religious Program—Tel: 412-922-6808. Students 83.
JEFFERSON HILLS, ALLEGHENY CO., ST. THOMAS A'BECKET (1957) Rev. Robert L. Seeman; Sr. Mary Judith Seman, S.C.N., Social Ministry.
Res.: 509 Gill Hall Rd., 15025. Tel: 412-655-2885; Fax: 412-655-0615. Email: becketst@comcast.net.
Church: 139 Gill Hall Rd., 15025.
Catechesis/Religious Program—Tel: 412-653-4322; Fax: 412-653-9979. Sr. Dolores Ann Therasse, V.S.C., D.R.E. Students 504.
Convent—Tel: 412-655-4122.
KENNEDY TOWNSHIP, ALLEGHENY CO., ST. MALACHY (1953) Rev. Michael J. Maranowski.
Res.: 343 Forest Grove Rd., Coraopolis, 15108. Tel: 412-771-5483; Fax: 412-331-7312.
School—(Grades PreSchool-8) Tel: 412-771-4545; Fax: 412-771-0922. Email: stmalachyschool@yahoo.com. Web: stmalachyschool-.home.comcast.net. Lay Teachers 10; Students 126; Preschool 24.
Catechesis/Religious Program—Tel: 412-771-7480. Students 398.
KOPPEL, BEAVER CO.
1—QUEEN OF HEAVEN (1992) [CEM] Unassigned. Consolidated from St. Monica, Wampum and St. Teresa, Koppel. Connie Reeher, Music Min.; Lou Ferrario, Parish Site Admin.
Res.: 6421 6th Ave., P.O. Box A, 16136. Tel: 724-846-5702 (Rectory); 724-846-9559 (Office); Fax: 724-846-2219. Email: qoh@zoominternet.net.
Catechesis/Religious Program—Students 60.
2—ST. TERESA, Closed. See Queen of Heaven.
LAWRENCE, WASHINGTON CO., ST. ELIZABETH, Closed. See St. Mary, Cecil.
LIBERTY BORO, ALLEGHENY CO., ST. EUGENE, Closed. See St. Mark, Port Vue.
LYNDORA, BUTLER CO.
1—ST. JOHN (1904), (Slovak), Closed. See St. Fidelis of Sigmaringen, Butler.
2—ST. STANISLAUS KOSTKA (1919), (Polish), Merged with St. Conrad, Meridian and St. John, Lyndora, to form St. Fidelis, Butler.
MCDONALD, WASHINGTON CO., ST. ALPHONSUS (1892) Rev. Walter A. Sobon.
Res.: 219 W. Lincoln Ave., 15057. Tel: 724-926-2984; Fax: 724-926-5120.
Catechesis/Religious Program—Students 132.
MCKEES ROCKS, ALLEGHENY CO.
1—SS. CYRIL AND METHODIUS, (Polish), Closed. See St. John of God.
2—ST. FRANCIS DE SALES, Closed. See St. John of God.
3—ST. JOHN OF GOD (1993) [CEM 2], Consolidated from the following churches: St. Francis de Sales, SS. Cyril & Methodius, St. Maria Goretti Chapel, St. Mark, St. Mary Help of Christians, Mother of Sorrows and St. Vincent, Pittsburgh. Revs. Louis F. Vallone; Robert J. Zajdel, Parochial Vicar; Regis J. Ryan, Parochial Vicar.
Parish Office—1011 Church Ave., 15136. Tel: 412-771-5646; Fax: 412-331-0678. Web: www.sjogparish.com.
School—3 Desiderio Way, 15136. Tel: 412-331-8501; Fax: 412-331-8500. Lay Teachers 12; Students 175.
Catechesis/Religious Program—Tel: 412-331-8573. Students 130.
4—ST. MARIA GORETTI CHAPEL, Closed. See St. John of God.
5—ST. MARK, (Slovak), Closed. See St. John of God.
6—ST. MARY HELP OF CHRISTIANS, (German), Closed. See St. John of God.
7—MOTHER OF SORROWS, (Italian), Closed. See St. John of God.
MCKEESPORT, ALLEGHENY CO.
1—HOLY TRINITY, Closed. See St. Martin de Porres.
2—ST. MARTIN DE PORRES (1993) [CEM 3], Consolidated from St. Mary, Holy Trinity, Sacred Heart and St. Peter. Rev. John B. Gizler.
Res.: 704 Market St., 15132. Tel: 412-672-9763; Fax: 412-672-2817.
School—St. Joseph Regional School, Mc Keesport, 15133. Tel: 412-678-0659; Fax: 412-678-1301. See Consolidated Schools under Institutions located in the Diocese.
Catechesis/Religious Program—Tel: 412-672-7440. Students 43.
3—ST. MARY, (German), Closed. See St. Martin de Porres.
4—ST. MARY CZESTOCHOWA (1893), (Polish), [CEM] Rev. Edward S. Litavec (Retired).
Res.: 2515 Versailles Ave., 15132. Tel: 412-672-0765; Fax: 412-672-2220. Email: stmary3@comcast.net.
Catechesis/Religious Program—Students 48.
5—ST. PATRICK (1993) [CEM], Merged with St. Denis, Versailles and St. Perpetua, McKeesport. Rev. Vincent P. Velas.
Res.: 310 32nd St., 15132. Tel: 412-673-4110; Fax: 412-678-7259. Email: stpatmck@comcast.net.
Catechesis/Religious Program—305 32nd St., 15132. Tel: 412-664-7417. Students 78.
6—ST. PERPETUA, Closed. See St. Patrick, Versailles.
7—ST. PETER, Closed. See St. Martin de Porres.
8—ST. PIUS V (1903) [CEM], Merged with St. Stephen. Rev. Stephen A. Kresak.
Res.: 2911 Versailles Ave., 15132. Tel: 412-673-8878; Fax: 412-673-8704.
Catechesis/Religious Program—Students 48.
9—SACRED HEART, (Croatian), Closed. See St. Martin de Porres.
10—ST. STEPHEN (1899), (Hungarian), Closed. See St. Pius V.
MEADOW LANDS, WASHINGTON CO., OUR LADY OF THE MIRACULOUS MEDAL (1949) [JC] Rev. John L. O'Shea.
Res.: 300 Pike St., Box 366, 15347. Tel: 724-222-1911; Fax: 724-222-5688. Email: olmm@comcast.net. Web: www.miraculousmedalchurch.org.
Catechesis/Religious Program—Tel: 724-228-9088; 724-228-8575 (CCD Activities Center); Fax: 724-228-1488. Students 147.
MERIDIAN, BUTLER CO., ST. CONRAD, Merged with St. John and St. Stanislaus Kostka, Lyndora to form St. Fidelis, Butler.
MIDLAND, BEAVER CO., ST. BLAISE (1994) Rev. Michael L. Yaksick.
Res.: 772 Ohio Ave., 15059. Tel: 724-643-4050; Fax: 724-643-6533. Email: stblaisechurch@verizon.net. Web: www.stblaise.org.
Catechesis/Religious Program—Tel: 724-643-4663. Students 150.
MILLVALE, ALLEGHENY CO.
1—ST. ANN, Closed. See Holy Spirit.
2—ST. ANTHONY, (German), Closed. See Holy Spirit.
3—HOLY SPIRIT (1994), Consolidated from St. Anthony and St. Ann. Rev. Daniel W. Whalen.
Res.: 608 Farragut St., 15209. Tel: 412-821-4424;

Fax: 412-253-4732. Email: holyspiritoffice@comcast.net.
School—100 Howard St., 15209. Tel: 412-821-4805; Fax: 412-821-4714. Email: holyspiritschool100@yahoo.com. Lay Teachers 8; Students 85.
Catechesis/Religious Program—Tel: 412-821-2099. Students 115.

4—ST. NICHOLAS, (Croatian), Closed. See the new St. Nicholas.

5—ST. NICHOLAS (1894), (Croatian), [JC 2] Rev. Daniel W. Whalen.
Administrative Center—24 Maryland Ave., 15209-2738. Tel: 412-821-3438; Fax: 412-821-8726.
Catechesis/Religious Program— Clustered with Holy Spirit Parish, Millvale. Students 10.

MONACA, BEAVER CO., ST. JOHN THE BAPTIST (1888) [CEM] Rev. John L. McKenna.
Res.: 1409 Pennsylvania Ave., 15061. Tel: 724-775-3940; Fax: 724-775-6886. Email: st.johns.church@verizon.net.
School—1501 Virginia Ave., 15061. Tel: 724-775-5774; Fax: 724-775-2997. Email: sjsmon@verizon.net. Web: www.stjohn-monaca.org. Lay Teachers 12; Students 190; Preschool 42.
Catechesis/Religious Program—Tel: 724-650-5866. Students 240.

MONONGAHELA, WASHINGTON CO.

1—ST. ANTHONY (1904), (Italian—Slovak), [CEM] Rev. Joseph E. Feltz, Admin.
Res.: 225 Park Ave., 15063-2199. Tel: 724-258-9710; Fax: 724-258-3362. Email: stanthonypadua@comcast.net.
Catechesis/Religious Program—Tel: 724-258-9233. Students 25.

2—TRANSFIGURATION (1865) [CEM 2] Rev. George F. Chortos.
Res.: 722 W. Main St., 15063. Tel: 724-258-7742; Fax: 724-258-8783. Email: transfigurationphyllis@verizon.com. Web: www.transfigurationmonongahela.parishesonline.com. See Madonna Catholic Regional School, Donora under Consolidated Schools located in the Institution section.
Catechesis/Religious Program—Students 100.

MONROEVILLE, ALLEGHENY CO.

1—ST. BERNADETTE (1955) Rev. Edward L. Yuhas; Deacon Michael W. Kelly.
Res.: 245 Azalea Dr., 15146. Tel: 412-373-0050; Fax: 412-374-8113. Email: parishoffice@stbrnadet.org. Web: www.stbrnadet.org.
School—(Grades PreK-8) Tel: 412-372-7255; Fax: 412-372-7649. Email: schooloffice@stbrnadet.org. Sisters 2; Lay Teachers 21; Students 275.
Catechesis/Religious Program—Tel: 412-373-1797. Email: mvkopper@stbrnadet.org. Students 450.

2—NORTH AMERICAN MARTYRS (1960) Rev. Joseph G. Luisi.
Res.: 2526 Haymaker Rd., 15146. Tel: 412-373-0330; Fax: 412-380-1306.
School—(Grades PreSchool-6) Tel: 412-373-0889. Lay Teachers 15; Students 99; Preschool 51.
Catechesis/Religious Program—Tel: 412-349-0942. Students 240.

MOON TOWNSHIP, ALLEGHENY CO., ST. MARGARET MARY (1956) Revs. John Ayoob; James P. Holland, Parochial Vicar.
Res.: One Parish Pl., 15108-2697. Tel: 412-264-2573; Fax: 412-264-4327. Email: contactus@stmargaretmary-moon.org. Web: st.margaretmary.org.
Catechesis/Religious Program—Tel: 412-264-9368. Email: reoffice@stmargaretmary-moon.org. Students 604.

MT. LEBANON, ALLEGHENY CO.

1—ST. BERNARD (1919) Very Rev. David J. Bonnar; Revs. Richard J. Wesoloski, Parochial Vicar; Christopher Fronk, S.J., Parochial Vicar.
Res.: 311 Washington Rd., 15216. Tel: 412-561-3300; Fax: 412-563-0211. Web: www.stbernardchurch.com.
School—(Grades PreK-8), 401 Washington Rd., 15216. Tel: 412-341-5444; Fax: 412-341-2044. Web: www.stbschool.com. Lay Teachers 24; Students 320.
Catechesis/Religious Program—401 Washington Rd., 15216. Tel: 412-561-0199. Web: stbernardchurch.com/ccd. Students 780.

2—ST. WINIFRED (Pittsburgh) (1960) Rev. Kevin J. Dominik; Deacon Joseph J. Kosko Jr.
Res.: 550 Sleepy Hollow Rd., 15228. Tel: 412-344-5010; Fax: 412-563-7279. Email: winoffice@comcast.net. Web: www.stwinifred.org.
Catechesis/Religious Program—Tel: 412-563-1414. Mary Ann Budd, Dir. Faith Formation K-6; Dianne Falvo, Dir. Music Ministries; Dana Pivik, Dir. Faith Formation 7-12. Students 285.

MUNHALL, ALLEGHENY CO.

1—ST. MARGARET, Closed. See St. Maximilian Kolbe, Homestead.

2—ST. MICHAEL, (Slovak), Closed. See St. Maximilian Kolbe, Homestead.

3—ST. RITA (1936), (Slovak), Revs. W. David Schorr; Nicholas Mastrangelo, Parochial Vicar.
Mailing Address: 219 W. Schwab Ave., 15120. Tel: 412-461-4204; Fax: 412-462-5484. Email: stritaparish@verizon.net. Web: mysite.verizon.net/stritaparish.
Res.: 1 Majka Dr., West Mifflin, 15122. Tel: 412-461-8087; Fax: 412-461-0142.
Catechesis/Religious Program—Combined with Resurrection, West Mifflin., Tel: 412-461-5787. Students 150.

4—ST. THERESE OF LISIEUX (1925) Very Rev. James G. Young; Revs. Nicholas Mastrangelo, Parochial Vicar; E. Daniel Sweeney, Parochial Vicar.
Res.: 1 St. Therese Ct., 15120-3701. Tel: 412-462-8161; Fax: 412-462-4817. Email: st.therese@sttherese.net. Web: www.st-therese.net.
School—3 St. Therese Ct., 15120. Tel: 412-462-8163; Fax: 412-462-5865. Email: sttheresemunhall@yahoo.com. Web: www.sttheresemunhall.org. Sisters of Charity 2; Lay Teachers 22; Students 325.
Catechesis/Religious Program—Students 454.

MUSE , WASHINGTON CO., HOLY ROSARY (1963) Rev. George T. DeVille.
Res.: One Orchard St., P.O. Box 447, 15350-0447. Tel: 724-745-3531; Fax: 724-745-0669.
Catechesis/Religious Program—Clyde House, D.R.E. Students 190.

NATRONA HEIGHTS, ALLEGHENY CO.

1—BLESSED SACRAMENT, Closed. See Our Lady of the Most Blessed Sacrament.

2—OUR LADY OF PERPETUAL HELP, Closed. See Our Lady of the Most Blessed Sacrament.

3—OUR LADY OF THE MOST BLESSED SACRAMENT (1992), (Slovak), Consolidated from Most Blessed Sacrament and Our Lady of Perpetual Help. Revs. Thomas A. Wagner; William P. Siple, Parochial Vicar; Deacon Patrick Wood.
Res.: 1526 Union Ave., 15065-2008. Tel: 724-226-4900; Fax: 724-224-3559. Email: olmbschurch1@verizon.net. Web: www.olmbs.org.
Catechesis/Religious Program—800 Montana Ave., Natrona Hts., 15065. Tel: 724-224-3339; Fax: 724-226-8655. Email: olmbsccd@verizon.net. Students 226.

NATRONA, ALLEGHENY CO.

1—ST. JOSEPH (1992) [CEM] [JC], Merged with St. Ladislaus and St. Mathias. Rev. Thomas A. Wagner; Deacon Patrick G. Wood.
Mailing Address: 1526 Union Ave., Natrona Heights, 15065. Tel: 724-224-1336; Fax: 724-224-3559. Email: stjosephnatrona@verizon.net.
Res.: 1283 10th Ave., Natrona Heights, 15065.
High School—800 Montana Ave., Natrona Heights, 15065. Tel: 724-224-5552; Fax: 724-224-0235. Students 145.
Catechesis/Religious Program—Tel: 724-224-3339. Email: olmbsccd@verizon.net. Clustered with Our Lady of the Most Blessed Sacrament, Natrona Heights. Students 33.

2—ST. LADISLAUS, (Polish), Closed. See St. Joseph.

3—ST. MATHIAS, Closed. See St. Joseph.

NEMACOLIN, GREENE CO., OUR LADY OF CONSOLATION (1923), (Polish), [CEM] Rev. John M. Bauer.
Res.: 408 Rte. 88, Carmichaels, 15320. Tel: 724-966-7270; Fax: 724-966-9118. Email: sthugholcpc@windstream.net.
Mission—Sacred Heart Rices Landing, Greene Co.
Mission—St. Mary Crucible, Greene Co.

NESHANNOCK, LAWRENCE CO., ST. CAMILLUS (1959) Rev. Thomas J. Lewandowski; Sr. Barbara Ann Johnston, C.S.J., Pastoral Assoc.
Res.: 314 W. Englewood Ave., New Castle, 16105-1806. Tel: 724-652-9471; Fax: 724-654-1430. Email: rectory@stcamillusparish.org.
Catechesis/Religious Program—Sr. Mary Slick, H.S.M., D.R.E. Students 392.

NEW BEDFORD, LAWRENCE CO., ST. JAMES (1844) [CEM] Rev. John W. Rebel.
Res.: P.O. Box 207, 16140. Tel: 724-964-8276; Fax: 724-964-1108. Email: stjamestheapostle@comcast.net. Web: www.stjames-church.com.
Catechesis/Religious Program—Students 126.

NEW BRIGHTON, BEAVER CO.

1—SS. CYRIL AND METHODIUS, (Slovak), Closed. See Holy Family.

2—HOLY FAMILY (1994) [CEM], Consolidated from St. Joseph and SS. Cyril and Methodius. Rev. Thomas E. Kredel; Larry Tavlarides, Music Dir.
Rectory & Office: 1851 3rd Ave., 15066. Tel: 724-847-3538; 724-847-3548; Fax: 724-847-3585. Email: hfpl8001@verizon.net.
Church: 521 7th Ave., 15066.
Catechesis/Religious Program—Tel: 724-846-9622. Joe Kralic, D.R.E. Students 131.

3—ST. JOSEPH, Closed. See Holy Family.

NEW CASTLE, LAWRENCE CO.

1—ST. JOSEPH THE WORKER (1888) [JC] Rev. Robert J. Schweitzer.
Res.: 1111 S. Cascade St., 16101. Tel: 724-658-9923 (Tel. & fax). Email: cascade1111@comcast.net. Web: www.stjosephnc.org.
Catechesis/Religious Program—Tel: 724-654-9739; Fax: 724-654-7076. Email: ladyjoe04@aol.com. Students 309.

2—ST. LUCY, (Italian), Closed. See St. Vincent de Paul.

3—MADONNA OF CZESTOCHOWA, Closed. See Mary, Mother of Hope.

4—ST. MARGARET, Closed. See St. Vincent de Paul.

5—ST. MARY, Closed. See Mary, Mother of Hope.

6—MARY, MOTHER OF HOPE (1993), (Irish—Polish), [CEM] [JC], Consolidated from St. Mary and Madonna of Czestochowa. Rev. Victor J. Molka Jr.
Res.: 124 N. Beaver St., 16101. Tel: 724-658-2564. Email: 2psecmmoh@comcast.net. Web: www.marymotherofhope.com.
Catechesis/Religious Program—Tel: 724-658-2564, Ext. 21. Students 250.

7—ST. MICHAEL, (Slovak), Closed. See St. Vincent de Paul.

8—SS. PHILIP AND JAMES, (Polish), Closed. See St. Vincent de Paul.

9—ST. VINCENT DE PAUL (1993) [CEM 2], Consolidated from the following churches in New Castle: St. Lucy, St. Michael, SS. Philip & James, St. Margaret; and Holy Cross, West Pittsburg. Rev. Steven M. Palsa; Deacon S. Daniel Kielar.
Res.: One Lucymont Dr., 16102. Tel: 724-652-5829; Fax: 724-656-0413. Email: svdppastor@verizon.net.
Catechesis/Religious Program—Students 110.

10—ST. VITUS (1901), (Italian), [JC] Rev. John D. Petrarulo, Admin. In Res., Rev. James R. Gretz.
Res.: 910 S. Mercer St., 16101. Tel: 724-652-3422; Fax: 724-652-2322.
School—915 S. Jefferson St., 16101. Tel: 724-654-9297; Fax: 724-654-9364. Lay Teachers 11; Students 139.
Catechesis/Religious Program—Tel: 724-654-9371. Students 388.

NORTH OAKLAND, BUTLER CO., ST. JOSEPH (1845) [CEM] Rev. Joseph P. Pudichery.
Res.: 864 Chicora Rd., P.O. Box 243, Chicora, 16025. Tel: 724-445-2275; Fax: 724-445-7507. Email: stj@zoominternet.net. Web: www.freewebs.com/materdolorosastjoe.
Catechesis/Religious Program—Combined with Mater Dolorosa., Tel: 724-445-3713. Students 26.

NORTH ROCHESTER, BEAVER CO., ST. PUDENTIANA, Closed. See St. Cecilia, Rochester.

O'HARA TOWNSHIP, ALLEGHENY COUNTY, ST. JOSEPH (1845) [CEM] Rev. Thomas R. Miller; Mrs. Suzanne M. Gilch, Pastoral Assoc.
Mailing Address: 342 Dorseyville Rd., 15215. Email: parishoffice@stjosephohara.com.
Res.: 330 Dorseyville Rd., 15215. Tel: 412-963-8885, Ext. 311; Fax: 412-963-1945. Email: suzanne@stjosephohara.com. Web: www.stjosephchurch.com.
Catechesis/Religious Program—342 Dorseyville Rd., 15215. Tel: 412-963-8885, Ext. 301. Email: ccd@stjosephohara.com. Students 303.

OAKDALE, ALLEGHENY CO., ST. PATRICK (1866) [CEM] Rev. Walter A. Sobon.
Res.: 7322 Noblestown Rd., 15071. Tel: 724-693-9260; Fax: 724-693-9247. Email: stpatrickparish@comcast.net. Web: www.saint-patrick-parish.com.
Catechesis/Religious Program—Tel: 724-693-8447. Email: saintpatyouth@yahoo.com. Students 78.

OAKMONT, ALLEGHENY CO., ST. IRENAEUS (1907) Rev. Frank M. Kurimsky.
Res.: 387 Maryland Ave., 15139. Tel: 412-828-3065; Fax: 412-828-1587.
School—(Grades PreSchool-8), 637 Fourth St., 15139. Tel: 412-828-8444; Fax: 412-828-8749. Sr. Carol Ann Papp, O.S.F., Prin. Lay Teachers 12; Students 125.
Catechesis/Religious Program—Tel: 412-828-9450. Students 250.

OVERBROOK, ALLEGHENY CO., ST. NORBERT (1914), (German), Rev. Mark A. Thomas.
Mailing Address: 2413 Saint Norbert St., 15234.
Res.: 3754 Brownsville Rd., 15227. Tel: 412-881-1316; 412-881-2474; Fax: 412-881-6728. Email: office@saintnorbertparish.org. Web: www.saintnorbertparish.org.
Catechesis/Religious Program—Tel: 412-881-2040. Email: ccd@saintnorbertparish.org. Students 8.

PENN HILLS, ALLEGHENY CO.

1—ST. BARTHOLOMEW (1950) Sr. Dorothy Pawlus, C.S.F.N., Parish Life Collaborator.
Res.: 111 Erhardt Dr., 15235. Tel: 412-242-3374; Fax: 412-242-1488. Email: office@stbartsparish.com. Web: www.stbartsparish.com.
School—Tel: 412-242-2511; Fax: 412-242-8317. Email: school@stbartsparish.com. Lay Teachers

13; Students 170.
Catechesis/Religious Program—Tel: 412-242-7207. Email: denise@stbartsparish.com; colleen@stbartsparish.com. Students 70.
2—ST. GERARD MAJELLA (1964) Rev. Martin F. Barkin.
Res.: 121 Dawn Dr., Verona, 15147. Tel: 412-793-3333; Fax: 412-793-4726. Email: saintgerardmajella@comcast.net.
Catechesis/Religious Program—Tel: 412-793-3959. Students 90.
3—ST. SUSANNA (1960) Rev. Martin F. Barkin.
Res.: 200 Stotler Rd., 15235-3554. Tel: 412-798-5596; Fax: 412-798-0479. Email: saintsusanna@verizon.net. Web: www.stsusannapennhills.parishesonline.com.
Catechesis/Religious Program—Tel: 412-798-3591. Email: stsusannare@verizon.net. Students 46.

PERRYSVILLE, ALLEGHENY CO., ST. TERESA OF AVILA (1867) [CEM] Revs. Robert J. Vular; Gary W. Oehmler; Deacon David R. Witter.
Res.: 1000 Avila Ct., 15237. Tel: 412-367-9001; Fax: 412-366-8415.
School—800 Avila Ct., 15237. Tel: 412-367-9001, Ext. 530; Fax: 412-364-1172. Religious 1; Lay Teachers 23; Students 228; Preschool 23.
Catechesis/Religious Program—Tel: 412-367-9001, Ext. 549; Fax: 412-548-0009. Students 321.
Convent—900 Avila Ct., 15237. Tel: 412-367-9001, Ext. 544.

PETERS TOWNSHIP, WASHINGTON CO., ST. BENEDICT THE ABBOT (1962) Revs. Samuel J. Esposito; Michael R. Ruffalo; Deacon John Layton; Dennis Gehlrlein, Pastoral Assoc.; Gregory Fincham, Dir. Music Min.
Res.: 120 Abington Dr., McMurray, 15317. Tel: 724-941-9406; Fax: 724-941-9517. Email: staff@stbenedicttheabbot.org. Web: www.stbenedicttheabbot.org.
Catechesis/Religious Program—Tel: 724-941-9587. Colette Speca, Dir. Faith Formation; Janet Roberto, Youth Min. Students 1,200.

PITCAIRN, ALLEGHENY CO., ST. MICHAEL (1895) Rev. Joseph G. Luisi.
Rectory—740 Wall Ave., 15140. Tel: 412-373-2610. Email: stmikepitcairn@verizon.net.
Church: 750 Wall Ave., 15140. Fax: 412-373-2031.
Res.: *North American Martyrs Parish*, 2526 Haymaker Rd., Monroeville, 15146. Tel: 413-373-0330.
Catechesis/Religious Program—Students 32.

PLEASANT HILLS, ALLEGHENY CO., SAINT ELIZABETH OF HUNGARY (1942) Revs. Dale E. DeNinno; Kevin F. McKnight; Deacon Joseph Compomizzi.
Res.: One Grove Pl., 15236. Tel: 412-882-8744; Fax: 412-882-8320. Email: stelizabethchurch@steliz.com. Web: www.stelizabethparish.org.
School—Tel: 412-881-2958; Fax: 412-882-0111. Web: www.steliz.com. Lay Teachers 27; Students 385.
Catechesis/Religious Program—Tel: 412-882-5023; Fax: 412-207-1647. Students 375.
Chapel of Convenience—St. David, Baldwin Boro, 15236. Tel: 412-882-8744.

PLUM, ALLEGHENY CO., ST. JANUARIUS (1946) Rev. Peter R. Pilarski.
Res.: 1450 Renton Rd., 15239. Tel: 412-793-4439; Fax: 412-793-7135. Email: stjanplum@verizon.net. Web: stjanuarius.org.
Catechesis/Religious Program—Students 118.

PORT VUE, ALLEGHENY CO.
1—ST. JOSEPH, Closed. See St. Mark.
2—ST. MARK (1993) Rev. Gerald S. Mikonis.
Administration Center—1101 Romine Ave., 15133. Tel: 412-678-6275; Fax: 412-673-1393.
St. Joseph Worship Site—1125 Romine Ave., 15133.
Res. & St. Eugene Worship Site—3210 Liberty Way, Liberty Borough, 15133. Tel: 412-678-6275.
School—St. Joseph Regional School, Tel: 412-678-0659; Fax: 412-678-1301. See Consolidated Schools under Institutions located in the Diocese.
Catechesis/Religious Program—Students 144.

PROSPECT, BUTLER CO., ST. CHRISTOPHER AT THE LAKE (1974) Rev. Matthew Tosello.
Res.: 229 N. Franklin St., 16052. Tel: 724-865-2430; Fax: 724-865-1120. Email: stchristopher@zoominternet.net. Web: christophermoraine.org.
Catechesis/Religious Program—Tel: 724-865-9840. Students 75.

RANKIN, ALLEGHENY CO., VISITATION OF THE BLESSED VIRGIN MARY, (Croatian), Closed. See Word of God, Swissvale.

RESERVE TOWNSHIP, ALLEGHENY CO., ST. ALOYSIUS (1892) Rev. Lawrence R. Smith.
3616 Mt. Troy Rd., 15212. Tel: 412-821-2951; Fax: 412-821-6480. Web: www.staloysius.us.
Res.: 1700 Harpster St., 15212. Tel: 412-231-2994; Fax: 412-231-7180.
Catechesis/Religious Program—Tel: 412-231-3002. Twinned with Most Holy Name, Pittsburgh. Students 41.

RICHEYVILLE, WASHINGTON CO., ST. AGNES (1994) Rev. John E. Forbidussi.
Res.: Box 406, 15358. Tel: 724-632-5858.
Catechesis/Religious Program—Students 96.

RICHLAND TOWNSHIP, ALLEGHENY CO., SAINT RICHARD (1992) Very Rev. Kenneth E. Oldenski.
3841 Dickey Rd., Gibsonia, 15044.
Res.: 5717 Wesleyann Dr., Gibsonia, 15044. Tel: 724-444-1971; Fax: 724-444-6001. Email: amy@saintrich.org. Web: www.saintrich.org.
Catechesis/Religious Program—Students 923.

ROBINSON TOWNSHIP, ALLEGHENY CO., HOLY TRINITY (Moon Run) (1944) Revs. Kenneth R. Keene; Barry P. O'Leary; Deacon Tim Killmeyer.
Res.: 5718 Steubenville Pike, McKees Rocks, 15136-1311. Tel: 412-787-2140; 412-787-2143; Fax: 412-787-3799. Email: htrobins@comcast.net. Web: holytrinityrobinson.org.
School—(Grades PreK-8), 5720 Steubenville Pike, Mc Kees Rocks, 15136-1311. Tel: 412-787-2656; Fax: 412-787-9487. Email: holy-trinity-school@comcast.net. Web: www.holy-trinity-school.org. Lay Teachers 18; Students 290.
Catechesis/Religious Program—Tel: 412-859-3467. Cathy Wilkinson, D.R.E.; Jason Gawaldo, Youth Min. Students 380.

ROCHESTER, BEAVER CO., ST. CECILIA (1856), (German—Italian), [CEM] Revs. Michael P. Greb, O.F.M.Cap.; Gregory J. Brown, O.F.M.Cap. In Res., Rev. William Gillum, O.F.M.Cap.
Res.: 628 Virginia Ave., 15074. Tel: 724-775-0801; Fax: 724-774-3056. Email: saintc@verizon.net. Web: www.stceciliaroch.org.
Church: 632 Virginia Ave., 15074.
Catechesis/Religious Program—633 California Ave., 15074. Tel: 724-775-2761. Students 227.
See St. Fidelis Friary under Monasteries & Residences of Priests & Brothers in the Institution section.

ROSCOE, WASHINGTON CO., ST. JOSEPH (1904) Rev. George J. Moneck.
Res.: Box 486, 15477. Tel: 724-938-2324; Fax: 724-938-2983.
Catechesis/Religious Program—Students 60.

ROSS TOWNSHIP, ALLEGHENY CO., ST. SEBASTIAN (North Hills) (1952) Revs. John R. Rushofsky; William R. Terza; John F. Naugle; Deacon Richard R. Cessar.
Res.: 311 Siebert Rd., 15237. Tel: 412-364-8999; Fax: 412-364-6330. Email: info@saintsebastianparish.org. Web: www.saintsebastianparish.org.
School—307 Siebert Rd., 15237. Fax: 412-364-5891. Email: mail@saintsebastianparish.org. Web: www.saintsebastianparish.org. Lay Teachers 30; Students 414.
Catechesis/Religious Program—Students 743.

RUSSELLTON, ALLEGHENY CO., TRANSFIGURATION (1916) [CEM] Rev. John C. Vojtek.
Res.: 15 Poma St., 15076. Tel: 724-265-1030; Fax: 724-265-1032. Email: rctransroman@aol.com.
Catechesis/Religious Program—Tel: 265-724-4860. Web: www.trccd.catholicweb.com. Students 60.

SCOTT TOWNSHIP, ALLEGHENY CO.
1—OUR LADY OF GRACE (1947) Rev. Richard A. Infante.
Res.: 310 Kane Blvd., 15243. Tel: 412-279-7070; Fax: 412-279-2385. Email: rectory@olgscott.org. Web: www.olgscott.org.
School—1734 Bower Hill Rd., 15243. Tel: 412-279-6611; Fax: 412-279-6755. Lay Teachers 25; Students 310.
Catechesis/Religious Program—1730 Bower Hill Rd., 15243. Tel: 412-276-0277; Fax: 412-276-0277. Students 340.
2—SS. SIMON AND JUDE (1955) Rev. Daniel J. Maurer. In Res., Rev. Kris D. Stubna.
Res.: 1607 Greentree Rd., 15220. Tel: 412-563-3189; Fax: 412-563-8524. Email: ssjparish@ssjpitt.org. Web: ssjparish.org.
School—1625 Greentree Rd., 15220. Tel: 412-563-1353; Fax: 412-563-8617. Lay Teachers 10; Students 85.
Catechesis/Religious Program—Tel: 412-563-1199. Students 175.

SEWICKLEY, ALLEGHENY CO., ST. JAMES (1863) [CEM] Very Rev. Daniel A. Valentine; Deacon Robert Sabatelle. In Res., Rev. Charles W. Speicher.
Res.: 200 Walnut St., 15143. Tel: 412-741-6650; Fax: 412-741-4782. Email: saintjamesparish@comcast.net. Web: www.saintjames-church.com.
School—(Grades K-8), 201 Broad St., 15143. Tel: 412-741-5540; Fax: 412-741-9038. Email: srchristysjs@yahoo.com; srdianesjs@yahoo.com. Web: www.stjamesschool.us. Gayle Salvatore, Librarian. Lay Teachers 10; Students 233; Preschool 19.
Catechesis/Religious Program—Tel: 412-741-6766. Email: stjamesreled@comcast.net. Students 450.

SHARPSBURG, ALLEGHENY CO.
1—ST. JOHN CANTIUS (1906), (Polish), Closed. See Saint Juan Diego Parish.
2—MADONNA OF JERUSALEM (1904), (Italian), Closed. See Saint Juan Diego Parish.
3—ST. MARY (1994) [CEM] Closed. See Saint Juan Diego Parish.
4—SAINT JUAN DIEGO PARISH Rev. Frank D. Almade.
201 9th St., 15215-2304. Tel: 412-784-8700; Fax: 412-781-1101. Email: saintjuandiegopgh@verizon.net. Web: www.saintjuandiegopgh.org.
Catechesis/Religious Program—Students 85.

SLIPPERY ROCK, BUTLER CO., ST. PETER (1938) [CEM] Rev. Kevin G. Poecking.
(Administration & Chapel), Res. & Parish Center: 342 Normal Ave., 16057. Tel: 724-794-2880; Fax: 724-794-1255. Email: stpeterparish@zoominternet.net.
Church: 670 S. Main St., 16057.
Catechesis/Religious Program—Tel: 724-794-5101. Kathee Gallagher, D.R.E. Students 297.
Mission—St. Anthony Church 232 Boyers Rd., Forestville, Butler Co. 16035. Tel: 724-735-2638.

SOUTH PARK, ALLEGHENY CO.
1—ST. JOAN OF ARC (1923) Rev. Phillip Pribonic.
Res.: 6414 Montour St., 15129. Tel: 412-833-2400; Fax: 412-835-1764. Web: www.mystjoan.org.
School—6470 Library Rd., 15129. Tel: 412-833-2433. Lay Teachers 13; Students 131.
Catechesis/Religious Program—Tel: 412-835-3724. Students 389.
2—NATIVITY (1905) Rev. John E. Hissrich.
Res.: 5802 Curry Rd., 15236. Tel: 412-655-3000; Fax: 412-650-4658. Email: nativitychurch@comcast.net.
Attending St. Katharine Drexel School at Nativity parish in Bethel Park.
Catechesis/Religious Program—5807 Curry Rd., 15236. Tel: 412-655-1565. Students 278.

SPRINGDALE, ALLEGHENY CO., ST. ALPHONSUS (1901) Rev. George E. Saladna.
Res.: 750 Pittsburgh St., 15144-1699. Tel: 724-274-5084; Fax: 724-274-7035. Email: stalphonsus@verizon.net. Web: www.stalphonsuschurch.com.
Catechesis/Religious Program—Tel: 724-274-2547. Students 95.

SWISSVALE, ALLEGHENY CO.
1—ST. ANSELM, Closed. See Word of God.
2—SAINT BARNABAS, (Slovak), Closed. See Word of God.
3—MADONNA DEL CASTELLO (1920), (Italian), Rev. John Lynam.
Res.: 2021 S. Braddock Ave., 15218. Tel: 412-271-5666; Fax: 412-271-2335.
Catechesis/Religious Program—Fax: 412-271-2335. Students 26.
4—WORD OF GOD (1994), (Irish—Croatian), Consolidated from the following churches: St. Anselm, St. Barnabas and Visitation of the Blessed Virgin Mary, Rankin. Rev. Frank J. Drabiska. In Res., Revs. Dozie Egbe (Nigeria); Felix Epima (Uganda).
Res.: 7446 McClure Ave., 15218. Tel: 412-241-1372; Fax: 412-241-0168. Email: wordogod@bellatlantic.net. Web: members.bellatlantic.net/~wordogod.
School—7438 McClure Ave., 15218. Tel: 412-371-8587. Sisters of Charity 2; Lay Teachers 14; Students 197.
Catechesis/Religious Program—Tel: 412-351-0670. Students 40.

TARENTUM, ALLEGHENY CO.
1—ST. CLEMENT, Closed. See Holy Martyrs.
2—HOLY MARTYRS (1992), (Slovak), [CEM] [JC 2], Consolidated from St. Clement and Sacred Heart, St. Peter. Rev. Aaron J. Kriss.
Res.: 353 W. Ninth Ave., 15084. Tel: 724-224-0770; Fax: 724-224-7070. Email: holymartyrsparish@verizon.net. Web: holymartyrsparish.org.
Catechesis/Religious Program—344 W. 9th Ave., 15084. Tel: 724-224-1234. Email: holymartyrseducation@verizon.net. Students 90.
3—SACRED HEART - ST. PETER, Closed. See Holy Martyrs.

TURTLE CREEK, ALLEGHENY CO., ST. COLMAN (1882) Rev. James E. Kunkel.
Res.: 100 Tri-Boro Ave., 15145. Tel: 412-823-2564; Fax: 412-823-6436. Email: stcolman@earthlink.net.
Catechesis/Religious Program—Tel: 412-823-9114. Students 120.

UNITY, ALLEGHENY CO., ST. JOHN THE BAPTIST (1915) [CEM] Revs. Thomas J. Galvin; John A. Geinzer.
Res.: 444 St. John St., 15239. Tel: 412-793-4511; 412-793-4580; Fax: 412-793-4311. Email: stjohnthebaptistparish@comcast.net. Web: www.stjohnthebaptistparish.net.
School—418 Unity Center Rd., 15239. Tel: 412-793-0555; Fax: 412-793-4001. Web: www.stjohnthebaptistschool.org. Lay Teachers 18; Students 220.
Catechesis/Religious Program—Tel: 412-795-6536. Email: reled@stjohnthebaptist.org. Web: www.stjohnreled.org. Students 478.

UPPER ST. CLAIR, ALLEGHENY CO.

1—ST. JOHN CAPISTRAN (1968) Rev. James J. Chepponis.
Res.: 1610 McMillan Rd., 15241. Tel: 412-221-6275; Fax: 412-257-3789. Email: sjohncap@comcast.net.
Catechesis/Religious Program—Tel: 412-221-5445. Email: sjcreled@comcast.net. Students 305.

2—ST. LOUISE DE MARILLAC (1961) Revs. Michael A. Caridi; Daniel J. Langa; Deacon William F. Strathmann Jr.; Sr. M. Philip Kwolek, C.S.S.F., Pastoral Assoc.; Kathy English, Music Min.; Mary Kay Gottermeyer, Music Min.
Res.: 320 McMurray Rd., 15241. Tel: 412-833-1010; Fax: 412-833-6624. Email: stl@stlouisedemarillac.org.
School—310 McMurray Rd., 15241. Tel: 412-835-0600; Fax: 412-835-2898. Email: kklase@stlouisedemarillac.org. Web: www.stlouiseschoolpa.org. Ken Klase, Prin. Lay Teachers 25; Students 431.
Catechesis/Religious Program—Tel: 412-835-1155; Fax: 412-833-3952. Lynn Lachut, C.R.E.; Jason Zych, Youth Min. Students 820.

VERONA, ALLEGHENY CO., ST. JOSEPH (1866) [CEM] Rev. Philip J. Przybyla.
Res.: 825 Second Ave., 15147-1498. Tel: 412-795-5114; Fax: 412-828-1236. Email: joevchurch@verizon.net.
School—Tel: 412-828-7213; Fax: 412-828-4008. Email: stjosephelementary@comcast.net. Lay Teachers 15; Students 150.
Catechesis/Religious Program—Tel: 412-828-7715. Email: stjosephreled@comcast.net. Students 81.

VERSAILLES, ALLEGHENY CO., ST. DENIS, Closed. See St. Patrick, McKeesport.

WAMPUM, LAWRENCE CO., ST. MONICA, Closed. See Queen of Heaven, Koppel.

WASHINGTON, WASHINGTON CO.

1—ST. HILARY (1919) Rev. Thomas D. O'Neil.
Res.: 320 Henderson Ave., 15301. Tel: 724-222-4087; Fax: 724-222-2130. Email: sthilary@linequest.net. Web: www.sthilaryparish.org.
Catechesis/Religious Program—340 Henderson Ave., 15301. Tel: 724-222-1381. Students 133.

2—IMMACULATE CONCEPTION (1855) [CEM 3] Revs. William P. Feeney; Joseph E. Sioli, C.O.; Donald Chortos; Nicholas A. Spirko; Sr. Margaretta Nussbaumer, C.D.P., Pastoral Assoc.
Res.: 119 W. Chestnut St., 15301. Tel: 724-225-1425; Fax: 724-229-7946. Email: ic.wash@verizon.net. Web: www.icwash.org.
School—111 W. Spruce St., 15301. Tel: 724-225-1680; Fax: 724-225-4651. Lay Teachers 21; Students 284; Preschool 52.
Catechesis/Religious Program—135 W. Chestnut St., 15301. Tel: 724-225-0382. Students 402.

WAYNESBURG, GREENE CO., ST. ANN (1839) [CEM] Rev. Richard J. Thompson.
Res.: 232 E. High St., 15370. Tel: 724-627-7568; Fax: 724-627-3735. Email: stannchurch@windstream.net.
Catechesis/Religious Program—Students 170.

WEST ALIQUIPPA, BEAVER CO., ST. JOSEPH, Closed. See St. Titus, Aliquippa.

WEST MIFFLIN, ALLEGHENY CO.

1—ST. AGNES (1867) [CEM] Rev. Joseph R. Grosko, Admin.
Res.: 622 St. Agnes Ln., 15122. Tel: 412-466-2655. Email: stagnes2@msn.com. Web: www.stagneswm.com.
School—(Grades PreSchool-8), 653 St. Agnes Ln., 15122. Tel: 412-466-6238; Fax: 412-466-2013. Sisters of the Holy Spirit 2; Lay Teachers 9; Students 134.
Catechesis/Religious Program—Students 54.
Convent—635 St. Agnes Ln., 15122. Tel: 412-466-3554.

2—HOLY SPIRIT (1963) Rev. John B. Lendvai.
Res.: 2603 Old Elizabeth Rd., 15122-2558. Tel: 412-346-0477; Fax: 412-466-4983. Email: hsrectory2603@comcast.net.
Catechesis/Religious Program—Tel: 412-346-0475; 412-346-0476 (Music Office); Fax: 412-466-3444. Email: hsccd@comcast.net. Students 240.

3—HOLY TRINITY (1901), (Slovak), [CEM] Rev. Joseph R. Grosko.
Res.: 529 Grant Ave. Ext., 15122. Tel: 412-466-6545; Fax: 412-466-6968. Email: h.trinity@verizon.net.
Catechesis/Religious Program—Combined with St. Agnes., 622 St. Agnes Ln., 15122. Tel: 412-466-6238; Fax: 412-466-2013. Students 62.

4—RESURRECTION (1936) Revs. W. David Schorr; Nicholas Mastrangelo.
Res.: 1 Majka Dr., 15122.
Catechesis/Religious Program—Combined with St. Rita., Tel: 412-461-5787. Sr. Charlotte Trogan, O.S.F., D.R.E. Students 158.

WEST PITTSBURG, LAWRENCE CO., HOLY CROSS, Closed. See St. Vincent de Paul, New Castle.

WEST SUNBURY, BUTLER CO., ST. LOUIS, Closed. See St. Alphonsus, Boyers.

WEST VIEW, ALLEGHENY CO., ST. ATHANASIUS (1905) Revs. Robert A. Norton; Kenneth E. Kezmarsky. In Res., Rev. Leroy A. DiPietro.
Res.: 7 Chalfonte Ave., 15229. Tel: 412-931-4624; Fax: 412-939-3516. Web: www.stathanasiuswv.org.
School—2 Wentworth Ave., 15229. Tel: 412-931-6633; Fax: 412-459-0104. Web: www.Familyin-God.org. Ms. Gabrielle Yingling, Prin. Lay Teachers 12; Students 79.
Catechesis/Religious Program—Tel: 412-931-3670. Students 500.

WEXFORD, ALLEGHENY CO.

1—ST. ALEXIS (1961) Rev. Paul J. Zywan.
Res.: 10090 Old Perry Hwy., 15090. Tel: 724-935-4343; Fax: 724-935-1270. Email: parish@stalexis.org. Web: www.stalexis.org.
School—(Grades PreK-8) Tel: 724-935-3940; Fax: 724-935-6070. Email: school@stalexis.org. Lay Teachers 26; Students 375.
Catechesis/Religious Program—Tel: 724-935-0877. Email: dre@stalexis.org. Joe Killian, D.R.E.; Paula Green, D.R.E. Asst. Students 350.

2—ST. ALPHONSUS (1840) [CEM] [JC] Revs. Peter P. Murphy; Sean M. Francis.
Res.: 201 Church Rd., 15090. Tel: 724-935-1151; Fax: 724-934-3877. Email: stalphonsus@zoominternet.net. Web: www.stals.org.
School—Tel: 724-935-1152; Fax: 724-935-1110. Email: stals@zoominternet.net. Sisters 1; Lay Teachers 24; Students 491; Preschool 38.
Catechesis/Religious Program—Tel: 724-935-1160; Fax: 724-934-3788. Students 304.

WHITE OAK BORO, ALLEGHENY CO., ST. ANGELA (1958) Very Rev. Stephen M. Chervenak.
Office: 1640 Fawcett Ave., 15131. Tel: 412-672-9641; Fax: 412-672-1576. Email: st.angela.merici@verizon.net.
Res.: 1732 Fawcett Ave., 15131.
School—1640R Fawcett Ave., 15131. Tel: 412-672-2360; Fax: 412-672-0880. Lay Teachers 11; Students 202.
Catechesis/Religious Program—Tel: 412-672-0913; Fax: 412-672-1576. Students 110.

WHITEHALL, ALLEGHENY CO., ST. GABRIEL OF THE SORROWFUL VIRGIN (1944) Revs. John R. Haney; Dam D. Nguyen. In Res., Revs. John E. Suhoza; Kenneth A. Sparks.
Res.: 5200 Greenridge Dr., 15236. Tel: 412-881-8115; Fax: 412-881-8117; Fax: 412-440-0160. Email: stgabeschurch@yahoo.com.
School—Tel: 412-882-3353; Fax: 412-882-2125. Lay Teachers 22; Students 405; Preschool 75.
Catechesis/Religious Program—5302 Greenridge Dr., 15236. Tel: 412-881-7950. Students 310.

WILDWOOD, ALLEGHENY CO., ST. CATHERINE OF SWEDEN (1953) Revs. Regis M. Farmer; Patrick Barkey.
Res.: 4701 Sylvan Dr., Allison Park, 15101.
Church: 2554 Wildwood Rd., P.O. Box 246, 15091. Tel: 412-486-6001; Fax: 412-486-6004. Email: info@stcatherineofsweden.org. Web: www.stcatherineofsweden.org.
Catechesis/Religious Program—Email: ccd@stcatherineofsweden.org; reledsec@stcatherineofsweden.org. Students 589.

WILKINSBURG, ALLEGHENY CO., ST. JAMES (1869) Rev. Warren W. Metzler.
Res.: 718 Franklin Ave., 15221. Tel: 412-241-1392; Fax: 412-241-6625. Email: stjameswilk@aol.com. Web: www.stjameswilkinsburg.org.
School—721 Rebecca Ave., 15221. Tel: 412-242-3515; Fax: 412-241-3199. Email: stjamesschool21@aol.com. Lay Teachers 10; Students 158; Preschool 15.
Catechesis/Religious Program—Tel: 412-242-2246; Fax: 412-241-6625. Students 23.

WILMERDING, ALLEGHENY CO.

1—ST. JUDE THE APOSTLE (1994) [CEM], Consolidated from St. Aloysius and St. Leocadia. Rev. Norbert J. Campbell.
Res.: 405 Westinghouse Ave., 15148. Tel: 412-823-8390; Fax: 412-823-8399.
Catechesis/Religious Program—Tel: 412-823-1066. Students 75.

2—ST. LEOCADIA, (Polish), Closed. See St. Jude the Apostle.

ZELIENOPLE, BUTLER CO., ST. GREGORY (1906) [CEM] Rev. Robert M. Miller.
Res.: 2 W. Beaver St., 16063. Tel: 724-452-7245; Fax: 724-452-4064. Email: stgreg.parish@zoominternet.net. Web: www.stgregzelie.org.
School—115 Pine St., 16063. Tel: 724-452-9731; Fax: 724-452-4064. Email: stgreg.school@zoominternet.net. Lay Teachers 12; Students 250.
Catechesis/Religious Program—Students 185.

Chaplains of Public Institutions

ALLEGHENY COUNTY. *Depaul Institution*, Tel: 412-924-1012. Rev. Walter G. Rydzon, M.Div. Tel: 412-381-9878.
St. Joseph House of Hospitality, Tel: 412-471-0666. Rev. John E. Suhoza. Tel: 412-881-8115.
Pittsburgh International Airport.

BEAVER COUNTY. *McGuire Memorial Home*, Tel: 724-843-3400, Ext. 1127. Rev. William Gillum, O.F.M.Cap., Dir. Pastoral Care. Tel: 724-775-0801 Home; 724-843-3400, Ext. 1127 Work. (Vacant)

Hospitals

ALLEGHENY COUNTY. *Children's Hospital*, Tel: 412-692-5325. Sr. Lisa Balcerek, C.S.J. UPMC Chaplains, Tel: 412-692-7253
St. Clair Memorial Hospital, Tel: 412-561-4900. Attended by Our Lady of Grace, Pittsburgh. Tel:412-279-7070
Heritage Valley Sewickley, Tel: 412-741-6600. Deacon Stephen M. Deskevich. Tel: 412-741-6600, Ext. 1752.
Jefferson Regional Medical Center, Tel: 412-469-5000. Rev. Robert Boyle. Tel: 724-348-7145, Judy Pasino, Pastoral Care. Tel: 412-469-5855.
Life Care Hospital of Pittsburgh, Tel: 412-247-2585. Attended by St. James, Wilkinsburg. Tel:412-241-1392
Magee-Women's Hospital, Tel: 412-647-1000. Sr. Nora Egan, C.S.J. Tel: 412-641-4525.
McKeesport UPMC, Tel: 412-664-2000. Rev. John M. Elanjileth (ROM). Tel: 412-673-5552.
Mercy Health System of Pittsburgh-Pittsburgh Mercy Hospital, Tel: 412-232-8111. Revs. Joseph Markalalonis, T.O.R., John G. Oesterle. Tel: 412-232-8198, Albert Schempp, M.I., Edward G. Stafford, T.O.R., B.A., M.Div., M.Ed. Tel: 412-232-8198.
Ohio Valley General Hospital, Tel: 412-777-6161. Attended by St. Malachy. Tel: 412-771-5483 and St. John of God. Tel: 412-771-5646
UPMC Passavant Hospital, Tel: 412-367-6700. Sr. Caritas Marshall, C.S.J. Tel: 412-367-6700. Sacramental Coordination by St. Catherine of Sweden Parish.
UPMC Shadyside Hospital, Tel: 412-623-2121. Rev. Tan Nguyen, S.V.D., Pro Tem Chap. Tel: 412-623-1692.
UPMC St. Margaret Hospital, Tel: 412-767-4672. St. Scholastica Parish & Madonna of Jerusalem Parish: Tel: 412-784-8700; Pastoral Care, Tel: 412-784-4749 & Juan Diego Parish: Tel: 412-784-8700
UPMC University of Pittsburgh Medical Center, Tel: 412-647-7560. Revs. Jude Anyaeche. Tel: 412-647-7560, John Obasi. Patient and Family Support, Tel: 412-647-7615
West Penn Allegheny Health System-Alle-Kiski Medical Center, Tel: 724-224-5100. Attended by Our Lady of the Most Blessed Sacrament, Natrona Heights. Tel: 724-226-4900
West Penn Allegheny Health System-Allegheny General, Tel: 412-359-3131. Revs. Vincent F. Kolo. Tel: 412-359-4269, Gilbert Z. Puznakoski. Tel: 412-359-4269.
West Penn Allegheny Health System-Forbes Regional, Tel: 412-858-2960. Sacramental coordination by Pastoral Vicariate Region Two.
West Penn Allegheny Health System-Suburban General Hospital. Attended by Assumption of the Blessed Virgin Mary on the Beautiful River, Bellevue. Tel:412-734-6000; 412-766-6660
West Penn Allegheny Health System-West Penn Hospital, Tel: 412-578-5000. Rev. Bartley A. Sorensen. Tel: 412-621-5679; 412-578-7229.

BEAVER COUNTY. *Heritage Valley Beaver*, Tel: 724-728-7000. Rev. William J. Schwartz. Tel: 724-775-4111.

BUTLER COUNTY. *Butler Memorial Hospital*, Tel: 724-283-6666. Attended by St. Paul Parish. Tel: 724-287-1759.

GREENE COUNTY. *Greene County Memorial*, Tel: 724-627-3101. Attended by St. Ann, Waynesburg. Tel:724-627-7568

LAWRENCE COUNTY. *Ellwood City Hospital*, Tel: 724-752-0081. Attended by Holy Redeemer Parish, Ellwood City. Tel:724-758-4441.
Jameson Health System. Mary Mother of Hope Parish, 724-658-2564, Tel: 724-658-9001.

WASHINGTON COUNTY. *Mon Valley Hospital*, Tel: 724-258-2000; 724-258-7742.
Washington Hospital, Tel: 724-225-7000. Attended by Immaculate Conception, Washington. Tel:724-225-1425
West Penn Allegheny Health System-Canonsburg Hospital, Tel: 724-745-6100. Very Rev. Gabriel Badurina, T.O.R. Tel: 724-745-6560.

Veterans Administration Hospitals

ALLEGHENY COUNTY. *VA Hospital Pittsburgh*, Tel: 412-688-6000, Ext. 6729. Tel: 412-688-6000; Tel: 1-866-482-7488 (24-Hour)
University Drive. Rev. Robert Craig, O.F.M.Cap. Tel: 412-682-6430 Home; 412-683-3000 Work.
Highland Drive. Rev. Mark W. Glasgow. Tel: 412-462-1807 Residence.

H.J. Heinz III (Aspinwall). Rev. Robert Craig, O.F.M.Cap. Tel: 412-683-3000 Work.

BUTLER COUNTY. *VA Medical Center Butler*, Tel: 800-362-8262.

Rehabilitation, Nursing and Geriatric Care Facilities

ALLEGHENY COUNTY. *Arden Courts*. Attended by Rev. Ladis Cizik '87 Tel: 412-795-3388

Arden Courts North Hills, Tel: 412-369-7887. Rev. John Walsh.

Asbury Heights, Tel: 412-341-1030. Attended by St. Bernard, Mt. Lebanon. Tel: 412-561-3300.

Baldwin Health Care, Tel: 412-885-8400. Attended by St. Elizabeth of Hungary, Pittsburgh. Tel: 412-882-8744.

Beatty Pointe Village. Attended by Rev. Ladis Cizik '87 Tel: 412-795-3388 or Tel: 412-374-9000

Beverly Manor of Monroeville, Tel: 412-856-7570. Rev. Ladis Cizik. Tel: 412-795-3388.

Canterbury Place, Tel: 412-622-9000. Attended by Our Lady of the Angels, Pittsburgh. Tel: 412-682-0929.

Cedars of Monroeville, Tel: 412-373-3900. Attended by Rev. Ladis Cizik '87 Tel: 412-795-3388

Children's Institute, St. Bede, Tel: 412-661-7222; Fax: 412-420-2400.

Collins Nursing Center. St. Bede Parish. Tel: 412-661-7222., Tel: 412-661-1740.

DT Watson Rehab Hospital, Tel: 412-741-9000. Attended by St. James, Sewickley. Tel: 412-741-6650.

Forbes Road Nursing Center, Tel: 412-665-3232. Rev. Joseph C. Beck. Tel: 412-421-5766.

Hamilton Hills Personal Care. Rev. Ladis Cizik. Tel: 412-795-3388.

Health South Hospital of Pittsburgh, Tel: 412-856-2400. Rev. Joseph C. Beck. Tel: 412-421-5766.

Healthsouth Harmarville Hospital, Tel: 412-826-4929. St. Mary of the Assumption, 412-486-4100

Heartland Health Care Center. St. Bede Parish. Tel: 412-661-7222., Tel: 412-665-2400.

Heritage Shadyside, Tel: 412-422-5100. Attended by St. Rosalia, Pittsburgh. Tel: 412-421-5766.

Independence Court of Mt. Lebanon, Tel: 412-341-4400. Attended by St. Ann, Castle Shannon. Tel: 412-531-5964; St. Thomas More, Bethel Park. Tel: 724-883-0031

Independent Court of Monroeville, Tel: 412-373-3030. Rev. Joseph C. Beck. Tel: 412-421-5766.

Kane Regional Center - Glen Hazel, Tel: 412-422-6800. Rev. Joseph C. Beck. Tel: 412-422-6839.

Kane Regional Center - McKeesport, Tel: 412-675-8600. Sr. Thomas Joseph Gaines, S.C. Tel: 412-675-8640.

Kane Regional Center - Ross, Tel: 412-369-2000. Rev. Ambrose Mouthevil. Attended by St. Sebastian. Tel: 412-364-8999.

Kane Regional Center - Scott, Tel: 412-429-3000. Rev. Richard L. Conboy, S.T.L. Tel: 412-429-3040.

Ladies of the Grand Army Republic (LGAR), Tel: 412-825-9000. Rev. Ladis Cizik. Tel: 412-795-3388.

Little Sisters of the Poor (James P. Wall Home for the Aged), Tel: 412-761-5373. Rev. Jerome A. Dixon, J.C.L. (Retired).

Longwood at Oakmont, Tel: 412-826-5917. St. Irenaeus. Tel: 412-828-3065

Manorcare Health Services, Highland Dr., 15212. Tel: 412-831-6050. Attended by St. Thomas More. Tel: 412-833-0031.

Manorcare Health Services Green Tree, Greentree Rd., 15212. Tel: 412-344-7744. Attended by SS. Simon & Jude, Tel: 412-563-3189.

Manorcare Health Services McMurray. Attended by St. Benedict the Abbot. Tel: 724-941-9406., McMurray Rd., 15212. Tel: 412-941-3080.

Manorcare Health Services Monroeville, Tel: 412-856-7071. Rev. Ladis Cizik. Tel: 412-795-3388. Tel: 412-856-7071

Manorcare Health Services North Hills, Tel: 412-369-9955. Rev. Joseph C. Beck. Tel: 412-421-5766.

Marian Manor, Inc., Tel: 412-563-6866. Rev. Regis R. Alberth. Tel: 412-563-4222, Ext. 304.

Mt. Lebanon Manor Convalescent Center, Tel: 412-257-4444. Attended by St. Thomas More. Tel: 412-833-0031.

Oakmont Nursing Center, Tel: 412-828-7300. Attended by St. Irenaeus, Oakmont. Tel: 412-828-3065

Presbyterian Seniorcare Westminister Place, Tel: 412-826-6136. Rev. Ladis Cizik. Tel: 412-795-3388. Attended by St. Irenaeus, Oakmont.

Ridgepoint, Tel: 412-653-6870. Attended by Nativity, South Park Twp. Tel: 412-655-3000.

Riverview Center for Jewish Seniors, Tel: 412-521-5900. Attended by St. Rosalia, Pittsburgh. Tel: 412-421-5766.

Seneca Hills Retirement Village. Rev. Ladis Cizik. Tel: 412-795-3388. Tel: 412-793-1700

Seneca Manor Assisted Living. Rev. Ladis Cizik. Tel: 412-795-3388. Tel: 412-798-6000

Seneca Place, Tel: 412-798-8000. Rev. Ladis Cizik. Tel: 412-795-3388. Attended by St. Bartholomew, Penn Hills. Tel: 412-242-3374.

Seneca Place. Rev. Ladis Cizik. Tel: 412-795-3388. Tel: 412-798-8000

Shadyside Nursing and Rehabilitation Center. Attended by St Bede Parish. Tel: 412-661-7222., Tel: 412-362-3500.

Southwestern Nursing and Rehabilitation Center, Tel: 412-466-0600, Ext. 5989. Attended by Holy Spirit, West Mifflin. Tel: 412-466-5048

Sunrise Assisted Living. Rev. Ladis Cizik. Tel: 412-795-3388. Tel: 412-380-2589

UPMC Rehabilitation Hospital, Tel: 412-420-2400. Attended by St. Bede, Pittsburgh. Tel: 412-661-7222.

Vincentian Collaborative System, Tel: 412-630-9980. Sr. Laverne Sihelnik, V.S.C.

Vincentian de Marillac Home. Attended by St. Raphael, Tel: 412-661-3100; 412-361-2833.

Vincentian Home, Tel: 412-366-5600. Sr. Alice Dunlap, O.S.F.

Vincentian Regency Home, Tel: 412-366-8540. Sr. Denise Hibel. Tel: 412-366-8540

Woodhaven Convalescent Center, Tel: 412-856-4770. Rev. Joseph C. Beck. Tel: 412-421-5766.

BEAVER COUNTY. *Friendship Ridge Skilled Nursing*, Tel: 724-775-7100. Rev. William J. Schwartz. Tel: 724-775-7100.

Villa St. Joseph, Tel: 724-869-6300. Rev. Philip Fink, O.F.M.Cap. Tel: 724-775-0801.

BUTLER COUNTY. *St. John Specialty Care Center*. Attended by St. Kilian Parish, Tel: 724-625-1665 or Tel: 724-625-1571.

Sunnyview Home, Tel: 724-282-1800. Attended by St. Paul Parish. Tel: 724-287-1759.

Sunrise of Cranberry. Attended by St. Kilian Parish, Tel: 724-625-1665 or Tel: 724-779-4300.

The Arbors at St. Barnabas. Attended by St. Kilian Parish, Tel: 724-625-1665 or Tel: 724-625-4000.

UPMC/Passavant Cranberry and UPMC Cranberry Place. Attended by St. Killian Parish, Tel: 724-625-1665, 724-775-5350, or Tel: 724-772-5350

Valencia Woods at St. Barnabas. Attended by St. Kilian Parish, Tel: 724-625-1665 or Tel: 724-625-4000.

Worthington of Adams. Attended by St. Kilian Parish, Tel: 724-625-1665 or Tel: 724-779-5020.

GREENE COUNTY. *Beverly Health Care*, Tel: 724-852-2020. Attended by St. Ann, Waynesburg. Tel: 724-627-7568.

Rolling Meadows, Tel: 724-627-3153. Attended by St. Ann, Waynesburg. Tel: 724-627-7568.

LAWRENCE COUNTY. *Almira Home*, Tel: 724-652-4131. Rev. Kenneth E. Myers, M.S.Ed.

Belvedere Residence, Inc., Tel: 724-924-2191. Rev. Kenneth E. Myers, M.S.Ed.

Castle Manor, Tel: 724-654-4377. Rev. Kenneth E. Myers, M.S.Ed.

Cedar Manor, Tel: 724-654-8050. Rev. Kenneth E. Myers, M.S.Ed.

Golden Hill Nursing, Inc., Tel: 724-654-7791. Rev. Kenneth E. Myers, M.S.Ed.

Haven Convalescent Home, Tel: 724-654-8833. Rev. Kenneth E. Myers, M.S.Ed.

Highland Hall Care Center, Tel: 724-658-4781. Rev. Kenneth E. Myers, M.S.Ed.

Hillview Manor, Tel: 724-658-1521. Rev. Kenneth E. Myers, M.S.Ed.

Indian Creek Nursing Home, Tel: 724-652-6340. Rev. Kenneth E. Myers, M.S.Ed.

Jack Rees Nursing and Rehabilitation Center, Tel: 724-652-3863. Rev. Kenneth E. Myers, M.S.Ed.

Majors Manor, Tel: 724-924-9568. Rev. Kenneth E. Myers, M.S.Ed.

Overlook Nursing Home, Tel: 724-946-3511. Rev. Kenneth E. Myers, M.S.Ed.

Shenango United Presbyterian Home, Tel: 724-946-3516. Rev. Kenneth E. Myers, M.S.Ed.

Silver Oak Nursing, Tel: 724-652-3863. Rev. Kenneth E. Myers, M.S.Ed.

WASHINGTON COUNTY. *Beverly South Hills*, Tel: 724-746-1300. Tel: 724-745-6560, Tel: 724-746-1300

Canon House, Tel: 724-745-7771. Tel: 724-745-6560, Tel: 724-745-7771

Charles House Home for the Aged, Tel: 724-745-6355. Tel: 724-745-0950, Tel: 724-745-6355

Greenery Nursing Home, Tel: 724-745-8000. Tel: 724-745-6560, Tel: 724-745-8000

Horizon Senior Care, Tel: 724-746-5040. Tel: 724-745-6560, Tel: 724-746-5040

Humbert Lane Health Care. Attended by Immaculate Conception, Washington., Tel: 724-228-4740.

Kade's Nursing Home. Attended by Immaculate Conception, Washington., Tel: 724-222-2148.

Pine Lawn Home, Tel: 724-746-1460. Tel: 724-746-1460

Presbyterian Senior Care, Tel: 724-222-4300. Attended by Immaculate Conception Parish, Tel: 724-228-4740.

Rest Haven Personal Care Home I, Tel: 724-745-3333.

Rest Haven Personal Care Home II, Tel: 724-746-3233.

Rest Haven Personal Care Home V, Tel: 724-746-4666. Tel: 724-746-4666

Washington County Health Center. Immaculate Conception, Washington., Tel: 724-228-5010.

Mental Health Facilities

ALLEGHENY COUNTY. *Western Psychiatric Institute & Clinic*, Tel: 412-647-3060. Attended by UPMC Chaplains. Tel: 412-647-7615.

WASHINGTON COUNTY. *Bradley Center South*, Tel: 724-746-1212; 724-746-2400. Tel: 724-746-1212

Correctional Institutions

ALLEGHENY COUNTY. *Allegheny County Jail*, Tel: 412-350-2000. Rev. G. Malcolm McDonald. Tel: 412-350-2057, Deacon Thomas O'Neill.

SCI Pittsburgh, Tel: 412-761-1955. Revs. Thomas J. Dansak, Barry P. O'Leary. Tel: 412-561-3300.

Shuman Center, Tel: 412-661-6806. Social Services. Tel: 412-665-4135.

BEAVER COUNTY. *Beaver County Jail*. Saints Peter and Paul. Tel: 724-775-4111

BUTLER COUNTY. *Butler County Jail*. St. Paul Parish (724-287-1759)

GREENE COUNTY. *State Correctional Institute at Greene*, Tel: 724-852-2902. Rev. J. Francis Frazer. Tel: 724-377-2588 Parish, Deacon James A. Kenny.

Waynesburg County Jail, Tel: 724-627-7780. St. Ann Parish (724-627-7780)

LAWRENCE COUNTY. *Lawrence County Jail*, Tel: 724-654-5384. Rev. James A. Downs. Tel: 724-667-7721.

Youth Development Center, Tel: 412-656-7300. Rev. John W. Rebel. Tel: 724-964-8276, Sr. Yvonne Dursh.

WASHINGTON COUNTY. *Washington County Jail*, Tel: 412-561-7557. Attended by Immaculate Conception, Washington. Tel: 724-225-1425.

Graduate Studies:

Revs.—

Kunz, Thomas W., Casa Santa Maria, Via dell'Umilta 30, Rome 00187 Italy.

Vaskov, Nicholas, North American College, Vatican City State 00120 Italy.

On Duty Outside the Diocese:

Rev. Msgrs.—

Kozar, John E., Pontifical Mission Societies in the U.S.A., 70 W. 36th St., 8th flr., New York, NY 10018.

Lamonde, Joseph R., 2834 Casa del Rio Ter., Jacksonville, FL 32257.

Roos, H. Jules, Centro de Obras Sociales, Apartado 473, Chimbote, Peru.

Revs.—

Bleichner, Howard P., Sulpicians, 2-1151 E. Cliff Dr., Santa Cruz, CA 95062.

Mazurek, James K., M.Div., SS. Cyril & Methodius Seminary, 3535 Indian Tr., Orchard Lake, MI 48324.

Menegay, David C., St. Louis Parish, 300 N. Chapel St., Louisville, OH 44641.

Taylor, Augustus R., Jr., 1812 W. 48th St., Los Angeles, CA 90062.

Wehner, James A., S.T.D., Pontifical College Josephinum, 7625 N. High St., Columbus, OH 43235.

Whalen, Timothy F., M.Div., Orchard Lake Schools, 3535 Indian Tr., Orchard Lake, MI 48324.

Zadroga, Clinton P., St. Vincent Archabbey, Latrobe, 15650.

Military Chaplains:

Revs.—

Brzek, Jon J., USS Dwight D. Eisenhower, Fpo, AE 09532-2830.

Fix, Donald P., PCS 559 Box 6164, Fpo, AP 96377-6164.

Glasgow, Mark W., Chap. VA Medical Center, c/o St. Maximilian Kolbe, 303 E. 10th Ave., Homestead, 15120.

Absent on Sick Leave:

Revs.—

Chortos, Donald

Czemerda, Edward M.

Jordan, John M.

Nanz, John D.

Patriquin, Garry D.

Pesanka, Nicholas A.

Rager, Patrick F.

Retired:

Rev. Msgrs.—

Findlan, Joseph G., St. John Vianney Manor, 2600 Morange Rd., 15205.

Seli, John J., Cape Hacienda #202, 6655 Ridgewood Ave., Cocoa Beach, FL 32931.

Revs.—
Bergman, Charles B., St. John Vianney Manor, 2600 Morange Rd., 15205.
Boccardi, Raymond C., 432 Beatty St., Ellwood City, 16117.
Bovard, William R., St. John Vianney Manor, 2600 Morange Rd., 15205.
Cirilli, Matthew R., 201 Heather Dr., Monroeville, 15146.
Conley, Roy H., St. John Vianney Manor, 2600 Morange Rd., 15205.
Connolly, Brian W., 3955 Bigelow Blvd., Apt. 401, 15213.
Corbett, John B., Vincentian Home, 111 Perrymont Rd., 15237.
Costello, Bernard B., Cardinal Dearden Center, 4721 Fifth Ave., 15213.
Czapinski, Richard J., 11026 Azalea Dr., 15235.
Dascenzo, Joseph J., Holy Redeemer Parish, 300 Crescent Ave., Ellwood City, 16117.
DeBlasio, Dominck A., 605 Market St., Freeport, 16229.
DeCarlo, Philip J., 801 Somerville Dr., 15243.
DeLuca, Anthony, 304 Malcolm Ct., Monroeville, 15146.
Dixon, David C., St. John Vianney Manor, 2600 Morange Rd., 15205.
Dixon, Jerome A., J.C.L., Little Sisters of the Poor, 1020 Benton Ave., 15212.
Dougherty, Eugene J., St. John Vianney Manor, 2600 Morange Rd., 15205.
Duch, Robert G., Ph.D., 411 Hickory Ct., 15238.
Elanjileth, J. Matthew, St. Pius V Parish, 2911 Versailles Ave., Mc Keesport, 15132.
Erdeljac, Frank G., M.Div., St. Vincent de Paul Parish, 1 Lucymont Dr., New Castle, 16102-1299.
Ferris, Thomas B., Little Sisters of the Poor, 1028 Benton Ave., 15212.
Fisher, Donald C., M.A., 20 Kosciusko Way, 15203.
Garvey, James W., Most Holy Name of Jesus Parish, 1700 Harpster St., 15212.
Gelati, Dario, Presso Casa Canonica Di Sustenente, Piazza Caduti, 50, Sustinente MN 46030 Italy.
Graff, Francis C., 1863 Mahan School Rd., Blairsville, 15717.
Gualtieri, Raymond A., 4940 Brightwood Rd., Apt. A102, Bethel Park, 15102.
Gutierrez, Alvin P., 3401 Rigel St., 15212.
Habe, Robert W., St. Francis of Assisi Parish, c/o 2599 Freeport Rd., 15238.
Harvey, John A., Arrowood #359, 512 N. Lewis Run Rd., West Mifflin, 15122.
Henry, Leo G., Vincentian Home, 111 Perrymont Rd., 15237.
Herrmann, Robert W., Guardian Angels Parish, 1030 Logue St., 15220.
Hoffmann, Edward, Vincentian Home, 111 Perrmont Rd., 15237.
Jackovic, George V., 124 Bennington Dr., Canonsburg, 15317.
Jones, Donald R., 202 Williamsburg Dr., Elizabeth, 15037-2442.
Jurewicz, Francis Z., 339 Valley Ave., Wall, 15148.
Keane, John J., 850 Baldwin St., Apt. 415, 15234.
Kirby, Thomas M., Sisters of the Divine Redeemer, 999 Rock Run Rd., Elizabeth, 15037.
Kohler, William F., 2611 Ventana Dr., Coraopolis, 15108.
Koser, Albert C., St. John Vianney Manor, 2600 Morange Rd., 15205.
Kuenzig, Peter A., 2727 Custer Ave., 15227.
Kurutz, Joseph V., 1317 Berryman Ave., Bethel Park, 15102.
Laboon, Joseph D., 6887 Brompton Dr., Lakeland, FL 33809.
Lachowicz, Francis B., 169 Royal Oak Dr., White Oak, 15131.
Lang, Hugh J., St. Anne Parish, 400 Hoodridge Dr., 15234.
Lauer, Eugene F., Prince of Peace Parish, 81 S. 13th St., 15203.
Le, Trieu Ngoc, c/o 517 Ap Binh An 1, Xa An Hoa, Huyen Chau Thanh - Tinh An Giang, Vietnam.
Litavec, Edward S., Sacred Heart Parish, 310 Shady Ave., 15206.
Lutz, Gerald J., St. Anthony Parish, P.O. Box 548, Ridgeland, SC 29936.
MacVeigh, Michael C., St. John Vianney Manor, 2600 Morange Rd., 15205.
Maida, Thaddeus S., 44045 Five Mile Rd., Plymouth, MI 48170.
Manion, Thomas F., Cardinal Dearden Center, 4721 Fifth Ave., 15213-2915.
Markell, John W., 938 Broadway, East Mc Keesport, 15035.
Maurer, Russell J., St. Malachy Parish, 343 Forest Grove Rd., Coraopolis, 15108-3797.
McColligan, Raymond, St Anne's Home, 685 Angela Dr., Greensburg, 15601.
McCormley, Hugh J., St. John Vianney Manor, 2600 Morange Rd., 15205.
McDermott, Michael A., 1237 Chartiers Ave., Mc Kees Rocks, 15136.
McIlvane, Donald W., 265 46th St., Apt. 1207, 15201.
McSweeney, Edward F., Cardinal Dearden Center, 4721 Fifth Ave., 15213.
Mueller, Richard J., 889 Charlamagne Blvd., Naples, FL 34112.
Murphy, Thomas R., Vincentian Home, 111 Perrymont Rd., 15237.
Nee, Thomas M., Overlook Green, 5250 Meadowgreen Dr., 15236.
O'Donnell, Thomas M., M.Div., St. Mary of Mercy, 202 Stanwix St., 15222.
O'Malley, John J., 1103 N. Highland Ave., 15206.
O'Toole, John M., 3300 Port Royale Dr. N 417, Fort Lauderdale, FL 33308.
Palko, John A., Little Sisters of the Poor, 1028 Benton Ave., 15212.
Parsons, Harry E., St. John Vianney Manor, 2600 Morange Rd., 15205.
Polak, Michael J., St. John Vianney Manor, 2600 Morange Rd., 15205.
Ragni, Richard R., Cardinal Dearden Center, 4721 Fifth Ave., 15213.
Reardon, Robert J., St. John Vianney Manor, 2600 Morange Rd., 15205.
Ritzert, William J., 954 Gameland Rd., Chicora, 16025.
Rocha, Victor J., Resurrection Parish, 1100 Creedmoor Ave., 15213-2299.
Ruggiero, James S., Vincentian Home, 111 Perrymont Rd., 15237.
Rutkowski, Theodore A., S.T.L., 2848 Darlington Rd., Beaver Falls, 15010.
Rutledge, William G., St. Mary of the Assumption Parish, 2510 Middle Rd., Glenshaw, 15116.
Savage, Paul J., S.T.L., Villa Saint Joseph, 1030 State St., Baden, 15005.
Smith, Thomas E., 658 Lake Villas Dr., Altamonte Springs, FL 32701-4909.
Szarnicki, Henry A., St. John Vianney Manor, 2600 Morange Rd., 15205.
Terdine, Richard G., Cardinal Dearden Center, 4721 Fifth Ave., 15213.
Trzeciakowski, Edward J., St. John Vianney Manor, 2600 Morange Rd., 15205.
Turner, Robert G., 3904 Main St., Apt. 2, Munhall, 15120.
Utz, Raymond M., Cardinal Dearden Center, 4721 Fifth Ave., 15213.
Vecchio, Michael J., 5775 Fernley Dr. W., Apt. 76, West Palm Beach, FL 33415.
Wichmanowski, Walter F., Vincentian Home, 111 Perrymont Rd., 15237.
Wilt, George A., St. John Vianney Manor, 2600 Morange Rd., 15205.

Permanent Deacons:
Bachner, Ralph W., Jr., St. Sylvester, Brentwood; St. Norbert, Overbrook
Bane, John J., (Retired)
Barth, Robert V., Dept. for Disabilities
Byers, Stephen J., Dept. for Religious Education
Cerenzia, Joseph A., St. Patrick, Canonsburg
Cessar, Richard R., St. Sebastian, Ross Twp.
Compomizzi, Joseph, St. Elizabeth of Hungary, Pleasant Hills
Dadowski, Francis J., St. Mary of the Assumption, Glenshaw
Deskevich, Stephen M., Sewickley Valley Hospital
DiSanto, Dale J., Pastoral Vicariate Region Two
Gaines, George W., St. Fidelis of Sigmaringen, Lyndora/Meridian
Gleason, Kenneth V., (Retired)
Grab, James R., St. Basil, Carrick
Gruseck, David J., Pastoral Vicariate Region Four
Jelinek, G. Gregory, Most Holy Name of Jesus, Troy Hill; St. Aloysius, Reserve Township
Kelly, Michael W., St. Bernadette, Monroeville
Kenny, James A., State Correctional Inst. at Greene
Kielar, S. Daniel, St. Vincent de Paul, New Castle
Killmeyer, Tim M., Dept. for Persons with Disabilities
Kosko, Joseph J., St. Winifred, Mt. Lebanon
Kriston, Louis H., (Retired)
Kuhns, Elbert A., Pastoral Vicariate Region Three
Layton, John, St. Benedict the Abbot, Peters Twp.
Leonard, James F., (Retired)
Meyer, Joseph C., Jr., (Retired)
Miles, Leon F., St. Pamphilus, Beechview
Natali, Mitchell M., St. Paul, Butler
O'Keefe, Charles L., (Retired)
O'Neill, Thomas J., Allegheny County Jail
Pikula, Stephen C., St. Martin de Porres, McKeesport
Raymond, Thomas W., Pastoral Vicariate Region Three
Sabatelle, Robert C., Saint James, Sewickley; St. Margaret Mary, Moon Township
Satter, Victor P., Dept. for Youth and Young Adult Ministry
Sheil, James M., Pastoral Vicariate Region Three
Strathmann, William F., Jr., St. Louis de Marillac, Upper Saint Clair
Sutton, Lawrence R., Our Lady of Grace, Scott Township
Very, Richard, (Retired)
Wilmer, Reynold, St. Benedict the Moor, Hill District; Epiphany, Uptown; St. Mary of Mercy, The Point/Gateway Center
Witter, David R., St. Teresa of Avila, Perrysville
Wood, Patrick G., Our Lady of the Most Blessed Sacrament, Natrona Heights; St. Joseph, Natrona

INSTITUTIONS LOCATED IN THE DIOCESE

[A] SEMINARIES, RELIGIOUS OR SCHOLASTICATES

PITTSBURGH. *Saint Paul Seminary* (1965) *College & Pre-Theology*, 2900 Noblestown Rd., 15205. Tel: 412-456-3048; Fax: 412-456-3187. Email: seminaryprog@diopitt.org. Web: www.diopitt.org. Very Revs. Dennis P. Yurochko, S.T.L., Rector; Joseph M. Mele, V.G., Ph.D., Dir. Spiritual Formation/Vice Rector; Rev. Matthew R. McClain, Dir. Vocations; Sr. Cindy Ann Kibler, S.H.S., Dir. Pastoral Formation. Priests 3; Sisters 1; Students (attending Duquesne University) 19.

[B] COLLEGES AND UNIVERSITIES

PITTSBURGH. *Carlow University* (1929) 3333 Fifth Ave., 15213. Tel: 412-578-6059; Fax: 412-578-6668. Email: admission@carlow.edu. Web: www.carlow.edu. Dr. Mary Hines, Pres.; Dr. Margaret McLaughlin, Ph.D., Vice Pres. for Academic Affairs & Provost; Elaine Misko, Librarian. Sisters of Mercy. Sisters 1; Lay Teachers 80; Total Staff 373; Total Enrollment 2,200.

Duquesne University of the Holy Spirit (1878) 600 Forbes Ave., 15282. Tel: 412-396-6000; Fax: 412-396-4334. Web: www.duq.edu. Dr. Charles J. Dougherty, Pres.; Revs. William F. Crowley, C.S.Sp. (Retired); John Fogarty; Sean M. Hogan, C.S.Sp., Exec. Vice Pres. Student Life; Sean Kealy, C.S.Sp.; John Kilcrann, C.S.Sp., Fellow for Catholic Social Thought; Raymond D. French, C.S.Sp.; James P. McCloskey, C.S.Sp., Vice Pres. Mission & Identity; Naos McCool, C.S.Sp., Asst. Dean Student Formation School of Educ.; Peter I. Osuji, Campus Min.; John A. Sawicki, C.S.Sp.; Jocelyn Gregorie, C.S.Sp.; Casimir Lawrence Nyaki, Asst. Professor, Philosophy; Eugene Uzukwu, C.S.Sp., Assoc. Prof. of Theology. The Spiritans. Priests 11; Faculty 480; Students 10,363; Total Staff 1,641.

The University is coeducational and comprises the following Colleges, Schools and Institutes:

College of Liberal Arts Tel: 412-396-5097; Fax: 412-396-4859. Dr. Christopher M. Duncan, Dean, College & Graduate School of Liberal Arts.

School of Business Administration Tel: 412-396-6238; Fax: 412-396-4764. Dr. Alan Miciak, Dean.

School of Music Tel: 412-396-6080; Fax: 412-396-5479. Dr. Edward Kocher, Dean.

School of Law Tel: 412-396-6300; Fax: 412-396-5219. Ken Gormley, Interim Dean.

School of Leadership and Professional Advancement Tel: 412-396-5600; Fax: 412-396-5072. Dr. Dorothy Bassett, Dean.

School of Education Tel: 412-396-6093; Fax: 412-396-5585. Dr. Olga Welch, Dean.

School of Nursing Tel: 412-396-6550; Fax: 412-396-6346. Dr. Eileen Zungolo, Dean.

School of Pharmacy Tel: 412-396-6380; Fax: 412-396-1810. Dr. J. Douglas Bricker, Dean, Mylan School of Pharmacy.

School of Health Sciences Tel: 412-396-6652; Fax: 412-396-5554. Dr. Gregory Frazer, Dean; Dr. David W. Seybert, Dean Bayer School of Natural & Environmental Sciences. Tel: 412-396-4900; Dr. Ralph L. Pearson, Provost & Academic Vice Pres.; Mr. Stephen Schillo, Vice Pres., Mgmt. & Business; Rev. Sean M. Hogan, C.S.Sp., Exec. Vice Pres. Student Life; Linda S. Drago, Esq., Gen. Counsel & Univ. Sec.; Dr. Laverna Saunders, Librarian.

La Roche College (1963) 9000 Babcock Blvd., 15237-5898. Tel: 412-536-1202; Fax: 412-536-1199. Email: janet.shearerlah@laroche.edu. Web: www.laroche.edu. Sr. Candace Introcaso, C.D.P., Ph.D., Pres.; Janet Dennis, Vice Pres. Devel.; Colleen Ruefle, Vice Pres. for Student Life; Rev. W. Peter Horton, M.A., M.Div., Campus Min.; Dr.

Howard Ishiyama, Vice Pres. for Academic Affairs; Dr. Rosemary McCarthy, Ph.D., Vice Pres. for Academic Affairs & Dean of Graduate Students & Adult Educ.; Kenneth Service, Vice Pres. Inst. Rels.; Robert Vogel, Vice Pres. Finance & CFO; Sr. Michele Bisbey, C.D.P., Dept. Chair Rel. Studies Philosophy; George Zaffuto, Vice Pres. Admin. Svcs.; Laverne Collins, Librarian. Sisters of Divine Providence. Priests 3; Sisters 9; Lay Teachers 184; Total Staff 311; Students 1,356.

[C] HIGH SCHOOLS, DIOCESAN

PITTSBURGH. *Bishop Canevin High School, Inc.* (1957) 2700 Morange Rd., 15205. Tel: 412-922-7400; Fax: 412-922-7403. Email: mainoffice@bishopcanevin.org. Web: www.bishopcanevin.org. Mr. Kenneth M. Sinagra, Prin.; Rev. Alvin J. Adams, Chap.; Susan Rakaczky, Librarian. Priests 1; Sisters 1; Lay Teachers 37; Students 470.

Central Catholic High School, Inc. (1927) 4720 Fifth Ave., 15213. Tel: 412-621-8189; Fax: 412-208-0555. Email: principal@pittcentralcatholic.org. Web: www.pittcentralcatholic.org. Bros. Richard Grzeskiewicz, F.S.C., Pres.; Robert Schaefer, F.S.C., Prin.; Mary Paula Kovich, Librarian. The school is a Diocesan institution under the care of the Christian Brothers. Priests 1; Brothers 9; Lay Teachers 53; Students 860; Total Staff 72.

North Catholic High School, Inc. (1939) 1400 Troy Hill Rd., 15212. Tel: 412-321-4823; Fax: 412-321-0599. Email: principal@north-catholic.org. Web: www.north-catholic.org. Mr. Michael J. Pendred II, Prin.; Mr. Frank Orga, Pres. Lay Teachers 16; Total Staff 32; Students 285.

Oakland Catholic High School, Inc. (1989) 144 N. Craig St., 15213. Tel: 412-682-6633; Fax: 412-682-2496. Email: webmaster@oaklandcath.org. Web: www.oaklandcath.org. Dr. Maureen Marsteller, Prin.; Katherine D. Freyvogel, Pres.; Mrs. Milana Galagaza Sopko, Librarian. Priests 1; Lay Teachers 49; Total Staff 65; Students 605.

BADEN. *Quigley Catholic High School, Inc.* (1967) 200 Quigley Dr., 15005. Tel: 724-869-2188; Fax: 724-869-3091. Email: office@qchs.org. Web: www.qchs.org. Dr. Madonna J. Helbling, Ph.D., Prin.; Mr. Mitchell Yanyanin, Librarian. Sisters 1; Lay Teachers 16; Students 203; Total Staff 25.

MCKEESPORT. *Serra Catholic High School, Inc.* (1961) 200 Hershey Dr., 15132. Tel: 412-751-2020; Fax: 412-751-3488. Email: 73781@diopitt.org. Web: www.serrahs.com. Timothy Chirdon, Prin.; Mrs. Wendy Seibert, Librarian. Lay Teachers 26; Students 360; Total Staff 26.

MT. LEBANON. *Seton-LaSalle Catholic High School, Inc.* (1979) 1000 McNeilly Rd., 15226. Tel: 412-561-3583; Fax: 412-561-9097. Email: schoolinfo@slshs.org. Web: www.slshs.org. Sr. Patricia Laffey, S.C., Prin.; Stephanie Schmidt, Librarian. Consolidated South Hills Catholic & Elizabeth Seton High Schools. Priests 2; Sisters 2; Lay Teachers 40; Students 511; Total Staff 42.
Under the care of Sisters of Charity. Rev. Robert J. Miller, V.F., M.A., M.Div., Chap.

NATRONA HEIGHTS. *Saint Joseph High School, Inc.*, 800 Montana Ave., 15065. Tel: 724-224-5552; Fax: 724-224-3205. Beverly K. Kaniecki, Prin.

[D] HIGH SCHOOLS, PRIVATE

PITTSBURGH. *Mt. Alvernia High School*, 146 Hawthorne Rd., 15209. Tel: 412-821-3858; Fax: 412-821-2910. Email: office@mtalvernia.com. Web: mtalvernia.com. Kimberly Minick, Prin. Sisters of St. Francis of the Neumann Communities. Lay Teachers 8; Students 100.

Vincentian Academy - Duquesne University (1932) Peebles & McKnight Rds., 15237. Tel: 412-364-1616; Fax: 412-367-5722. Email: panich@duq.edu. Web: www.vaduq.org. Sr. Camille Panich, S.C.N., Prin. Sisters of Charity of Nazareth 4; Lay Teachers 23; Students 231; Total Staff 35.

CORAOPOLIS. *Our Lady of the Sacred Heart High School* (1932) 1504 Woodcrest Ave., 15108. Tel: 412-264-5140; Fax: 412-264-4143. Email: info@olsh.org. Web: www.olsh.org. Sr. Mary Francine Horos, C.S.S.F., Prin.; Mary Patterson, Librarian; Elizabeth Santillo, Pres. Felician Sisters, C.S.S.F., State approved day high school. Sisters 2; Lay Teachers 28; Students 360; Total Staff 45.

[E] CONSOLIDATED SCHOOLS

PITTSBURGH. *Brookline Regional Catholic School*, (Grades PreK-8), (Brookline), 2690 Waddington Ave., 15226. Tel: 412-563-0858; Fax: 412-341-5610. Email: brookregcath@yahoo.com. Web: www.brcschool.com. Janet Salley Rakoczy, Prin. Serving the parishes of Our Lady of Loreto, St. Pius X and Resurrection. Lay Teachers 12; Students 153; Total Staff 12.

Cardinal Wright Regional School (1998) (Grades K-8), (North Side), 711 West Commons, 15212. Tel: 412-231-8248; Fax: 412-231-0835. Email: cwrsl@cardinalwrightregionalschool.org. Web: www.cardinalwrightregionalschool.org. Mr. Kenneth E. Macek, Prin.; Donna Harmon, Librarian. Serving the parishes of St. Aloysius, Most Holy Name of Jesus and St. Peter. Lay Teachers 9; Students 179.

Christ the Divine Teacher Catholic Academy, (Grades PreK-8), (Aspinwall), 205 Brilliant Ave., 15215. Tel: 412-781-7927; Fax: 412-781-0891. Email: cdtca@consolidated.net. Sr. Dorothy Dolak, S.C.N., Prin.; Mrs. Joann Casile, Librarian. Serving the parishes of St. Edward, St. Joseph, St. Scholastic and St. Juan Diego. Lay Teachers 13; Students 160; Total Staff 13.

St. John Neumann Regional, Catholic Elementary (1985) (Grades K-8), 250 44th St., 15201. Tel: 412-682-5096; Fax: 412-682-0811. Email: office@sjnpgh.org. Web: www.sjnpgh.org. Sr. Coletta Adelsberg, C.S.J., Prin. Serving the parishes of Our Lady of Angels, St. Matthew and St. Lawrence O'Toole. Sisters 1; Lay Teachers 8; Students 95.

BUTLER. *Butler Catholic School* (1969) 515 E. Locust St., 16001. Tel: 724-285-4276; Fax: 724-285-4896. Email: bcsoffice@butlercatholic.org. Web: www.butlercatholic.org. Sr. John Ann Mulhern, C.D.P., Prin. Serving the parishes of St. Paul, St. Michael, St. Fidelis, St. Andrew and St. Peter's, Butler. Lay Teachers 21; Students 225; Preschool 8.

DONORA. *Madonna Catholic Regional School* (1998) (Grades K-8), 1 Park Manor Rd., 15033. Tel: 724-379-5977; Fax: 724-379-7633. Email: madonnacatholicregional@earthlink.net. Web: www.madonnacatholicregional.org. Sharon Loughran Brown, Prin. Serving the parishes of St. Anthony, Mary, Mother of the Church, Our Lady of the Valley, and Transfiguration. Lay Teachers 11; Students 180; Total Staff 16.

PORT VUE. *St. Joseph Regional School*, (Grades PreK-8), 1125 Romine Ave., 15133. Tel: 412-678-0659; Fax: 412-678-1301. Email: dtima@stjoesregional.com. Web: www.stjoesregional.com. Mrs. Dianne Tima, Prin. Serving the parishes of Queen of Rosary, St. Martin de Porres, St. Mark, St. Patrick. Lay Teachers 11; Students 200; Total Staff 16.

[F] ELEMENTARY SCHOOLS, PRIVATE

PITTSBURGH. *The Campus School Of Carlow University* (1963) (Grades PreK-8), 3333 5th Ave., 15213. Tel: 412-578-6158; Fax: 412-578-8850. Email: pdcooper@carlow.edu. Web: www.campusschool.carlow.edu. Patricia D. Cooper, Dir.; Trista Mentz-Johns, Librarian. Sisters of Mercy. Sisters 1; Lay Teachers 30; Students 240; Total Staff 33.

ALLISON PARK. *Providence Heights Alpha School*, 9000 Babcock Blvd., 15101. Tel: 412-366-4455; Fax: 412-635-6317. Web: www.alphaschool.org. Sr. Paulita Kuzy, C.D.P., Prin. Sisters of Divine Providence. Sisters 2; Lay Teachers 27; Students 227.

BADEN. *Mount Gallitzin Academy Corp.*, (Grades PreK-8), 1016 State St., 15005-1399. Tel: 724-869-2505; Fax: 724-869-4932. Email: principalmga@yahoo.com. Sr. Christy Hill, C.S.J. Purpose: to engage in educational activities and the operation of educational program of the Sisters of St. Joseph. Funds, distributions, gifts, bequests, endowments, grants, and contributions from other charitable organizations and student tuitions will be used to support applicant organization's programs and ministry outreach.

[G] DEPARTMENT OF SPECIAL EDUCATION

PITTSBURGH. *DePaul School for Hearing and Speech* (1908) 6202 Alder St., 15206. Tel: 412-924-1012; Fax: 412-924-1036. Email: mjmac@depaulinst.com. Web: www.speakmiracles.org. Dennis Barrett, Ph.D., Supt.; Mary Jo McAtee, Dir. Educ. Svcs. Auditory-Oral day school for children with hearing, speech and language impairments. Sisters 1; Lay Teachers 16; Students 60.

NEW BRIGHTON. *McGuire Memorial* (1963) 2119 Mercer Rd., 15066-3437. Tel: 724-843-3400; Fax: 724-847-2004. Email: mcgm@mcguirememorial.org. Web: www.mcguirememorial.org. Residential Facility-Intermediate Care for Developmentally Challenged; Private School, Licensed Adult Training, Community Homes. Priests 1; Sisters 4; Lay Teachers 26; Lay Staff 500; Residents 81; Additional Services: Adult Training 153; Community Living Residents 55; Private Academic School 90; Bed Capacity 140; Total Assisted Annually 275.

WEXFORD. *St. Anthony School Programs*, 2000 Corporate Dr., Ste. 580, 15090. Tel: 724-940-9020. Email: lgeorge@stanthonyschoolprograms.com. Lisa George, Program Dir. Resource rooms for students with special needs in 7 elementary schools, 2 high schools and 1 Post-Secondary Program. Lay Teachers 9; Students 105; Total Staff 45.

[H] CHILD CARE INSTITUTIONS

PITTSBURGH. *Franciscan Child Day Care Center*, 1401 Hamilton Rd., 15234-2399. Tel: 412-882-5085; Fax: 412-885-7210. Email: fcdcc@osfprov.org. Web: www.osfprov.org/fcdcc.htm. Mrs. Sandra Merlo, Dir.; Sr. Barbara Zilch, O.S.F., Pres. Total Assisted 128; Total Staff 29.

Holy Family Institute (1900) 8235 Ohio River Blvd., 15202-1594. Tel: 412-766-4030; Fax: 412-766-5434. Email: schott.sandra@hfi-pgh.org. Web: www.hfi-pgh.org. Sr. Linda Yankoski, C.S.F.N., Ed.D., Pres. & CEO. Sisters of the Holy Family of Nazareth., Holy Family Institute is committed to helping children, preserving families and strengthening communities by providing a network of services including in-home counseling, residential treatment, and out-patient mental health services. Holy Family also provides special education and alternative education for grades K through 12. Volunteer opportunities are also available at Holy Family Institute. Sisters 2; Total Staff 40.

Mt. Alvernia Day Care & Learning Center, 146 Hawthorne Rd., 15209. Tel: 412-821-4302; Fax: 412-821-3318. Web: www.millvaleFranciscans.org. Sisters of St. Francis of the Neumann Communities., Provides infant, toddler, and preschool care as well as before- and after-school care for school age children, school age care on non-school days and summer. Total Assisted 200; Total Staff 40.

Providence Connections, Inc. (1994) Corporate Office, 3113 Brighton Rd., 15212-2456. Tel: 412-766-3860; Fax: 412-766-6775. Email: cmacedonia@providenceconnections.org. Web: www.providenceconnections.org. Sr. Carolyn Winschel, C.D.P., Ph.D., Exec. Dir.

Providence Family Support Center (1994) 3113 Brighton Rd., 15212-2456. Tel: 412-766-6730; Fax: 412-766-6775. Web: www.providenceconnections.org. Total Assisted 763; Total Staff 29.

Amelia House (1995) Clarion. Tel: 814-226-6682. Web: www.providenceconnections.org. Purpose: To engage in educational activities and operation of day care centers and other related services to families in need. Total Assisted 12; Total Staff 1.

Vincentian Child Development Center, 8200 McKnight Rd., 15237. Tel: 412-366-8588; Fax: 412-366-7315. Email: jparagi@vcs.org. Jill Paragi, Dir.

[I] GENERAL HOSPITALS

PITTSBURGH. *UPMC Mercy* (An affiliate of the University of Pittsburgh Medical Center), 1400 Locust St., 15219. Tel: 412-232-8111; Fax: 412-232-7380. Web: www.upmcmercy.com. Will Cook, M.H.A., Pres. Bed Capacity 535; Patients Assisted Annually 240,986; Total Staff 1,900.

[J] HOMES FOR THE AGED

PITTSBURGH. *Little Sisters of the Poor Home for the Aged* (1839) 1028 Benton Ave., 15212. Tel: 412-307-1100; Fax: 412-307-1104. Email: mspittsburgh@littlesistersofthepoor.org. Web: www.littlesistersofthepoor-pittsburgh.org. Sr. Mary Vincent Mannion, M.S., Supr. & Admin.; Rev. Jerome A. Dixon, J.C.L. (Retired). Sisters 9; Total Staff 100; Bed Capacity 88; Total Assisted Annually 100.

Marian Manor Corp. (1956) 2695 Winchester Dr., 15220-4099. Tel: 412-440-4365 (Admin.); 412-440-4343 (Nursing); Fax: 412-440-4423. Web: www.marianmanor.com. Rev. Regis R. Alberth. Sisters of the Holy Spirit 7; Total Staff 273; Total Assisted Annually 514; Residents 182; Child Day Care 72.

St. Pius X Residence, Inc. (1973) (Affiliate of Pittsburgh Mercy Health System), 2681 Waddington Ave., 15226. Tel: 412-563-5040; Fax: 412-563-3776. Barbara Irvin, Admin. Total in Residence 26; Total Staff 20.

BADEN. **Villa St. Joseph of Baden, Inc.*, 1030 State St., 15005. Tel: 724-869-6300; Fax: 724-869-6399. Email: mmurray@villastjoseph.org. Sr. Judith Maroni, C.S.J., Pres.; Ms. Mary M. Murray, N.H.A., M.P.H., Exec. Dir. Purpose: to provide a home-like environment for 120 nurshing home residents in need of skilled nursing, rehabilitation and long term intermediate care. Our mission of "competent and compassionate care" is carried out daily by our staff who focus on building relationships, while providing therapy, clinical nursing, activities, spirtual and other support in a holistic manner. Specialty services include short term rehabilitation, dementia care and home-like long term living. Beds for Patients with Dementia or Alzheimer's 30; Total Assisted Annually 250; Total Staff 200; Bed Capacity 120.

[K] REHABILITATION, NURSING AND GERIATRIC CARE FACILITIES

PITTSBURGH. *Marian Hall Home, Inc.* (1970) 934 Forest Ave., 15202-1118. Tel: 412-761-1999; Fax: 412-761-2556. Email: marian27@verizon.net. Sr. Marian Sgriccia, O.S.F., Admin. Purpose: to provide programs, facilities, and services, including, but not limited to, residential personal care, and long-term care homes for the elderly, ill, or disabled, including supportive services. Total in Residence 58; Total Assisted Annually 100; Total Staff 47.

The Community at Holy Family Manor, Inc., 301 Bellevue Rd., 15229-2194. Tel: 412-931-6996; Fax: 412-931-7255. Ransom Towsley, Pres. & CEO. Bed Capacity 59; Total Assisted Annually 713; Total Staff 140.

Vincentian de Marillac (1943) 5300 Stanton Ave., 15206. Tel: 412-361-2833; Fax: 412-361-1237. Email: mcoyne@vcs.org. Linda Schoyer, Pastoral Care; Maureen M. Coyne, B.S., M.S.W., M.P.M., L.N.H.A., Admin. Catholic, skilled nursing home. Total Staff 79; Bed Capacity 50; Total Assisted Annually 108.

Vincentian Home Inc. (1924) 111 Perrymont Rd., 15237. Tel: 412-366-5600; Fax: 412-366-1408. Web: www.vcs.org. Sr. Anne Kull, V.S.C., Admin. Sisters of Charity of Nazareth, Kentucky. Sisters 7; Total Staff 237; Bed Capacity 164; Total Assisted Annually 329; Assisted Living: Total Assisted 77; Total Staff 39.

ALLISON PARK. *Vincentian Regency* (1966) 9399 Babcock Blvd., 15101. Tel: 412-366-8540; Fax: 412-369-9789. Email: magenovich@vcs.org. Web: www.vcs.org. Sr. Mary Ann Genovich, S.C.N., Admin. Sisters of Charity of Nazareth. Bed Capacity 143; Total Assisted Annually 400; Total Staff 220.

[L] PERSONAL PRELATURES

PITTSBURGH. *Prelature of the Holy Cross and Opus Dei* (1928) Warwick House, 5090 Warwick Ter., 15213. Tel: 412-683-8448; Fax: 412-687-3806. Email: info@warwickhouse.org. Web: www.opusdei.org. Revs. Rene J. Schatteman; Charles Trullols.

[M] MONASTERIES AND RESIDENCES OF PRIESTS AND BROTHERS

PITTSBURGH. *St. Augustine Friary*, 221 36th St., 15201. Tel: 412-682-6430; Fax: 412-682-6148. Web: www.capuchin.com. Revs. Robert Craig, O.F.M.Cap., Chap., VA PGH Health Care Systems; Gervase Degenhardt, O.F.M.Cap., Chap., Sisters of St. Francis, Millvale; Francis Fugini, O.F.M.Cap., Dir. for Missions; Vernon Busch, O.F.M.Cap., Pastoral Supply; Very Rev. John Pavlik, O.F.M.Cap., Prov. Min.; Revs. Bertin Roll, O.F.M.Cap., Dir. Emeritus of Archconfraternity of Christian Mothers (Retired); Scott Seethaler, O.F.M.Cap., Preaching Ministry; DeSales Young, O.F.M.Cap.; William Henn, O.F.M.Cap., Prof. Pontifical Gregorian Univ.; Otmar Gallagher, O.F.M.Cap. (Retired); Edward Laurent, O.F.M.Cap., Pastoral Supply; Maurice Sheehan, O.F.M.Cap., Academic Dean, Holy Apostles Seminary; Jonn Pfannenstiel, O.F.M.Cap., Vicar Prov. & Communications Dir.; John J. Petrikovic, O.F.M.Cap., Vice Rector & Prefect of Studies Collegio Intern San Lorenzo Brind.; Bros. James Allman, O.F.M. Cap., Fraternal Svc.; Richard Lubomski, O.F.M.Cap., Guardian, Fraternal Svcs.; James Townsend, O.F.M.Cap., Fraternal Svcs.

In Res. Revs. Regis Schlick, O.F.M.Cap.; Victor Kriley, O.F.M.Cap., Pastoral Supply; Charles Knoll, O.F.M.Cap.; Bro. Robert Toomey, O.F.M.Cap., Exec. Sec.

Congregation of the Oratory of St. Philip Neri, The Pittsburgh Oratory, 4450 Bayard St., 15213. Tel: 412-681-3181; Fax: 412-681-2922. Email: dsa@pittsburghoratory.org. Web: www.pittsburghoratory.org. Very Rev. Drew P. Morgan, C.O., Dir. Newman Inst., Provost; Revs. David S. Abernethy, C.O., Dir. Campus Min.; Michael J. Darcy, C.O., Grad Student; Joshua Kibler, C.O., Campus Min.; Stephen Lowery, C.O., Campus Min.; Bro. Paul Werley, C.O., Novice. Total Staff 5.

St. Conrad Friary (1983) 9448 Babcock Blvd., Allison Park, 15101. Tel: 412-364-8240; Fax: 412-366-8331. Web: www.capuchin.com. Rev. Philip Fink, O.F.M.Cap., Guardian & Dir. Novices; Bro. Mark Mance, O.F.M.Cap., Vicar & Asst. Dir. Novices; Revs. Gerard O'Dempsey, O.F.M.Cap., Asst. Dir. Novices; Reynold Rynda, O.F.M.Cap.; John Gesty, O.F.M.Cap.; Roland Raible, O.F.M.Cap., Jubilarian; Christopher Rengers, O.F.M.Cap., Jubilarian (Retired); Bro. Charles O'Conner, Jubilarian. Novices 16; Total in Residence 24; Total Staff 3.

Franciscan Friars, T.O.R., Queen of Peace Friary, 5324 Carnegie St., 15201. Tel: 412-449-1020; Fax: 412-449-1035. In Res. Bro. Michael Tripka, T.O.R., Librarian; Revs. Carol Napoli, T.O.R., (Retired); Raymond Nedimyer, T.O.R. (Retired); Joseph Mankalonius, T.O.R., Hospital Chap.; Jonathan St. Andre, T.O.R., Dir. Vocations; Thomas Bourque, T.O.R., Local Min. & Dir. Planning & Mission Effectiveness.

St. John Vianney Manor, 2600 Morange Rd., 15205. Tel: 412-928-0825; 412-928-0908; Fax: 412-928-1947. Retired priests' residence. Total in Residence 23; Total Staff 8. In Res. Most Rev. William J. Winter, V.G., S.T.D. (Retired); Rev. Msgr. Joseph G. Findlan (Retired); Revs. Charles B. Bergman (Retired); William R. Bovard (Retired); Dennis J. Bradley, D.Min.; Roy H. Conley (Retired); Edward M. Czemerda; David C. Dixon (Retired), St. John Vianney Manor, 2600 Morange Rd., 15205; Eugene J. Dougherty (Retired); Joseph F. Keenan; Michael C. MacVeigh (Retired); Hugh J. McCormley (Retired); Malcolm McDonald; Robert J. Meyer; Harry E. Parsons (Retired); Nicholas A. Pesanka; Michael J. Polak (Retired); Robert J. Reardon (Retired); David E. Scharf; Henry A. Szarnicki (Retired); Edward J. Trzeciakowski (Retired); George A. Wilt (Retired); Albert C. Koser (Retired).

St. Paul of the Cross Monastery Monastery & Retreat Center., 148 Monastery Ave., S.S., 15203. Tel: 412-381-1188 (Monastery); 412-381-7676 (Retreat Center); Fax: 412-481-5049 (Monastery); 412-431-3044 (Retreat Center). Web: www.catholic-church.org/stpaulsmonastery/. Very Rev. Gerald Laba, C.P., Rector & Retreat Dir.; Revs. Donald Ware, C.P., Asst. Local Supr.; William Davin, C.P.; Timothy Fitzgerald, C.P., Auxiliary Retreat Staff; John F. McMillan, C.P.; Edwin Moran, C.P.; Daniel Sullivan, C.P.; Bro. Matthew Krawchyk, C.P.; Revs. Joseph Sedley, C.P.; Vincent Segotta, C.P.; Patrick Geinzer, C.P., Assoc. Retreat Dir.; Paul Vaeth, C.P., Aux. Retreat Staff; William Maguire, C.P., Assoc. Retreat Dir.; Jerome Vereb, C.P.; Bro. Paul Morgan, C.P. *Passionist Overseas Missions*, 5 Grandview, Ste. 107, 15211. Tel: 412-488-5090; Fax: 412-488-5093. Bro. Leo Di Fiore, C.P., Dir. Tel: 412-381-1189, Ext. 21.

Society of The Divine Word, 207 Lytton, 15213. Tel: 412-683-4030; Fax: 412-683-5033. Rev. Walter Ostrowski, S.V.D., Mission Dir. Tel: 412-683-0640. Total in Residence 4. In Res. Rev. Raymond Hober, S.V.D.; Bros. John DeBold, S.V.D.; Gerard Raker, S.V.D.

AVALON. *Holy Family Friary* (Friars Minor), The Franciscans., 232 S. Home Ave., 15202-2899. Tel: 412-761-2550; 412-761-8470; Fax: 412-761-2959. Email: holyfamilyfriary@gmail.com. Revs. David Moczulski, O.F.M.; Michael Lenz, O.F.M., Guardian; Bro. Paschal Dierks, O.F.M., (Retired); Revs. Richard Portasik, O.F.M. (Retired); Jerome J. Wolbert, O.F.M.; Bro. Felix Nowakowski, O.F.M. Friars 5.

BEAVER. *St. Fidelis Friary*, 732 East End Ave., 15009. Tel: 724-774-1242 (main); 724-774-1492 (secondary). Email: stcecilia@verizon.net. Web: www.stceciliaroch.org. Church: *St. Cecilia*, 632 Virginia Ave., Rochester, 15074. Tel: 725-775-0801; Fax: 724-774-3056. Revs. Michael P. Greb, O.F.M.Cap.; Gregory J. Brown, O.F.M.Cap. Capuchin Friars. In Res. Revs. Robert E. McCreary, O.F.M.Cap.; William Gillum, O.F.M.Cap.

BETHEL PARK. *Congregation of the Holy Spirit Province of the United States*, 6230 Brush Run Rd., 15102. Tel: 412-831-0302. Very Rev. John Fogarty, C.S.Sp., Prov. Supr.

Holy Spirit Fathers and Brothers Provincialate, 6230 Brush Run Rd., 15102. Tel: 412-831-0302; Fax: 412-831-0970. Email: csspeast@choiceonemail.com. Web: www.spiritans.org. Very Rev. John Fogarty, C.S.Sp., Prov. Supr.; Rev. Girard J. Kohler, C.S.Sp., Mission Procurator. Residents 2; Total Staff 5.

BUTLER. *St. Mary's Friary*, 821 Herman Rd., 16002. Tel: 724-282-1485; Fax: 724-285-4715. Revs. Mark Carter, O.F.M. Cap., Parochial Vicar & Guardian; John Carey, O.F.M.Cap., Replacement Ministry; DePaul Ripko, O.F.M.Cap., Replacement Ministry; Gary Stakem, O.F.M.Cap., Replacement Ministry; Ward Stakem, O.F.M.Cap.; Bro. Joseph Day, O.F.M.Cap. Capuchin Franciscan Friars, Province of St. Augustine Priests 5; Brothers 1.

[N] CONVENTS AND RESIDENCES FOR SISTERS

PITTSBURGH. *St. Benedict Monastery* (1870) Benedictine Sisters of Pontifical Jurisdiction, 4530 Perrysville Ave., 15229-2296. Tel: 412-931-2844; Fax: 412-931-8970. Email: osbpgh@osbpgh.org. Web: www.osbpgh.org. Sr. Benita DeMatters, O.S.B., Prioress. Motherhouse and Novitiate of the Benedictine Sisters in the Diocese. Sisters 56.

Benedictine Center, Inc. (1986) Tel: 412-931-6051; Fax: 412-931-6003. Sr. Benita DeMatters, O.S.B., Pres.

Ladies of Bethany (1919) 1004 Oglethorpe Ave., 15201-2151. Tel: 412-781-4022.

Other Convents:

Ladies of Bethany, 167 Golden City Rd., Saxonburg, 16056. Tel: 724-352-1361; Fax: 724-352-1361.

Motherhouse, Sisters of the Holy Spirit (S.H.S.) (Ross Township), 5246 Clarwin Ave., 15229-2208. Tel: 412-931-1917; Fax: 412-931-4324. Email: SRSHS@verizon.net. Web: www.sistersoftheholyspirit.com. Sr. M. Bridget Miller, S.H.S., Gen. Supr.; Most Rev. Paul J. Bradley, V.G., M.Div., Chap.; Rev. Robert Guay, Chap. Professed Sisters 40; Total in Community 40.

Mount Assisi Convent, Motherhouse of the School Sisters of the Third Order Regular of St. Francis United States Province, 934 Forest Ave., 15202. Tel: 412-761-6004; Fax: 412-761-0290. Email: administrationusa@verizon.net. Web: www.franciscansisters-pa.org.

Civil Law Entity: The School Sisters of the Third Order Regular of St. Francis, a Pennsylvania corporation. Sisters 95; Residents 37; Total Staff 6. In Res. Rev. Richard M. Lelonis, J.C.L., Chap.

Our Lady of Sorrows Convent of the Passionist Nuns (1910) 2715 Churchview Ave., 15227. Tel: 412-881-1155; Fax: 412-881-1091. Sr. Joyce Foga, C.P., Supr. Motherhouse and Novitiate of the Religious of the Passion. (Passionist Nuns). Professed Sisters 8; Temporary Vows 2.

Sisters of Charity of Nazareth, Saint Louise's Convent, 8200 McKnight Rd., 15237. Tel: 412-456-3129; Fax: 412-456-3197. Rev. Reginald Russo, O.F.M.Cap., Chap. (formerly VSCs)

Sisters of Mercy of the Americas - New York, Pennsylvania, Pacific West Community, Convent of Mercy, 3333 Fifth Ave., 15213. Tel: 412-578-6225; Fax: 412-578-6180. Rev. Robert J. George, Chap. Convent of Mercy Total Professed Sisters 503; Associates 394.

Sisters of St. Francis of the Providence of God, St. Francis Convent Motherhouse, 3603 McRoberts Rd., 15234-2314. Tel: 412-882-9911; Fax: 412-885-7210. Email: usa@osfprov.org. Web: www.osfprov.org. Sr. Joanne Brazinski, O.S.F., USA Prov. Min.; Rev. John E. Suhoza, Chap. Sisters 51.

Sisters of St. Francis of the Providence of God-Generalate (1922) 1401 Hamilton Rd., 15234-2364. Tel: 412-885-7211; Fax: 412-885-7215. Email: sjgardner@osfprov.org. Web: www.osfprov.org. Sr. Janet Gardner, O.S.F., General Min. Professed 120; Novices 1; Total in Community 121.

Sisters of the Holy Family of Nazareth, 285 Bellevue Rd., 15229-2195. Web: www.csfn.orgTel: 412-931-4778; Fax: 412-931-9746.

Sisters of the Holy Family of Nazareth, Holy Family Province USA Inc.

Union of Our Lady of Charity Sisters of Our Lady of Charity (1872) 4100 Vinceton St., 15214. Tel: 412-931-2299; Fax: 412-931-6044. Sr. Sheila Rooney, Local Supr. North American Union of the Sisters of Our Lady of Charity, Inc. Sisters 3.

ALLISON PARK. *Congregation of The Sisters of Divine Providence of Allegheny County* (1881) *Providence Heights Motherhouse*, 9000 Babcock Blvd., 15101-2793. Tel: 412-931-5241; Fax: 412-635-5416. Email: srmfranciscdp@hotmail.com. Web: www.divineprovidenceweb.org. Sr. Mary Francis Fletcher, C.D.P., Prov. Dir. & Pres. Motherhouse of the Sisters of Divine Providence in the Diocese (Pittsburgh); Novitiate of the Sisters of Divine Providence (Granite City, IL). In Motherhouse 81; In Province (including Puerto Rico) 258.

BADEN. *Sisters of St. Joseph* (1869) 1020 State St., 15005. Tel: 724-869-2151; 412-761-3700; Fax: 724-869-3336. Email: secofcsj@usaor.net. Web: www.stjoseph-baden.org. Sr. Mary Pellegrino, C.S.J., Congregational Moderator; Rev. David E.F. Scharf, Chap. St. Joseph Convent Motherhouse Total in Community 215; Temporary Professed 1; Residents 43.

CORAOPOLIS. *Our Lady of the Sacred Heart Convent* (1932) 1500 Woodcrest Ave., 15108. Tel: 412-264-2890; Fax: 412-264-7047. Email: cssfpa@nauticom.net. Web: www.felicianspa.org. Sr. Christopher Moore, C.S.S.F., Prov. Min.; Revs. Bernard P. Shulik, Chap.; Richard Conboy, Chap.

Provincial House of the Felician Sisters of Pennsylvania C.S.S.F. Professed 83; Total in Residence 63; Total Staff 41.

ELIZABETH. *Divine Redeemer Motherhouse* (1912) 999 Rock Run Rd., 15037-2613. Tel: 412-751-8600; Fax: 412-751-0355. Email: sisrosemarysdr@aol.com. Web: www.sistersofthedivineredeemer.org. Sr. Rosemary Horvath, S.D.R., Prov.; Rev. Thomas M. Kirby, Chap. (Retired). Motherhouse and Novitiate of the Sisters of the Divine Redeemer. Total in Community 22.

MILLVALE. *Sisters of St. Francis of the Neumann Communities, Western Pennsylvania Region, Mt. Alvernia Convent*, 146 Hawthorne Rd., 15209. Tel: 412-821-2200; Fax: 412-821-3318. Email: bich@millvalefrancans.org. Rev. Gervase Degenhardt, O.F.M.Cap., Chap. Attended by Capuchin Fathers from St. Augustine, Pittsburgh. In the Local Community: Professed Sisters 123; Associates 39; In the Regional House: Professed Sisters 72.

VILLA MARIA. *Sisters of the Humility of Mary, Inc.* (1854) *Villa Maria Community Center*, 288 Villa Dr., P.O. Box 914, 16155. Tel: 724-964-8861; Fax: 724-964-8082. Email: info@humilityofmary.org. Web: www.humilityofmary.org. Sr. Susan Schorsten, H.M., Major Supr. Professed Sisters in Congregation 178; Sisters in Residence 51; Residents 43.

[O] RETREAT HOUSES

PITTSBURGH. *Franciscan Spirit and Life Center*, 3605 McRoberts Rd., 15234-2340. Tel: 412-881-9207; Fax: 412-885-7247. Email: fslc@osfprov.org. Sisters of St. Francis of the Providence of God., Purpose: To provide a facility to individuals for retreats and spiritual programs.; Overnight accommodations for 23. Conference room and dining facility. Three hermitages available on daily, overnight or weekly basis. Total Staff 3.

Martina Spiritual Renewal Center, Inc. (1986) 5244 Clarwin Ave., 15229-2208. Tel: 412-931-9766; Fax: 412-931-1823. Email: martinaspiritual@verizon.net. Web: sistersoftheholyspirit.com. Sisters Bridget Miller, S.H.S., Pres.; Donna Smith, S.H.S., Co- Dir.; Mary Lou Witkowski, S.H.S. To provide a facility to individuals and groups for retreats and spiritual programs. Ministry of the Sisters of the Holy Spirit.

St. Paul of the Cross Retreat Center, 148 Monastery Ave., 15203. Tel: 412-381-7676; 412-381-7677; Fax: 412-431-3044. Email: stpaulrcpa@cpprov.org. Web: catholic-church.org/stpaulsretreatcenter. Rev. Patrick Geinzer, C.P., Asst. Retreat Dir.; Very Rev. Gerald Laba, C.P., Rector & Retreat Dir.; Rev. William McGuire, C.P., Assoc. Dir.; John Colaizzi, Bus. Admin.; Revs. Paul Vaeth, C.P., Aux. Retreat Team; Timothy Fitzgerald, C.P., Aux. Retreat Team. Total in Residence 3; Total Staff 25.

ALLISON PARK. *Kearns Spirituality Center* (1983) 9000 Babcock Blvd., 15101-2713. Tel: 412-366-1124; Fax: 412-635-6318. Email: kearnsscl@pghcdp.org. Web: www.divineprovidenceweb.org. Sisters Agnes Raible, C.D.P., Dir.; Mary Joan Coultas, C.D.P., Prog. Coord. Sisters of Divine Providence., Conference room for 250; overnight accommodations for 60; dining facilities for 70. Call for more information on programs offered. Total Staff 6.

BETHEL PARK. *The Spiritan Center*, 6230 Bush Run Rd., 15102. Tel: 412-835-3510; Fax: 412-835-3541. Email: spiritancenter@juno.com. Revs. Constantine J. Conan, C.S.Sp.; William F. Crowley, C.S.Sp. (Retired); Joseph L. Kelly, C.S.Sp.; Girard J. Kohler, C.S.Sp.; Norbert T. Rosso, C.S.Sp.; Thomas P. Sharkey, C.S.Sp.; William Smith, C.S.Sp.; Leonard J. Tuozzolo, C.S.Sp.; John R. Weber, C.S.Sp. Total in Residence 11; Total Staff 22.

BUTLER. *Transfiguration House of Prayer*, 295 W. Jefferson Rd., 16002. Tel: 724-352-1354. Email: mariancdp@consolidated.com. Web: www.divineprovidenceweb.org.

GIBSONIA. *Providence Villa*, 10745 Babcock Blvd., 15044-6094. Tel: 724-444-8055; Fax: 724-444-8058. Email: providencevilla@yahoo.com. Web: www.divineprovidenceweb.org. Sr. Marilyn Seidel, Dir.

[P] OFFICES FOR CAMPUS MINISTRY

PITTSBURGH. *Chaplain Services* 111 Blvd. of the Allies, 15222. Tel: 412-456-3057; Fax: 412-456-3188. Email: kwinwood@diopitt.org.

Office for Campus Ministry La Roche College, 9000 Babcock Blvd., 15237. Tel: 412-536-1050, Ext. 141; Fax: 412-536-1048. Email: hortonp1@laroche.edu. Rev. W. Peter Horton, M.A., M.Div., Dir.

Art Institute of Pittsburgh St. Mary of Mercy, Stanwix St., 15212-5296. Tel: 412-321-0711. Rev. Thomas A. Sparacino, M.Div.

La Roche College (1963) 9000 Babcock Blvd., 15237. Tel: 412-536-1050; Fax: 412-536-1048. Rev. W. Peter Horton, M.A., M.Div.

Carlow University 3333 5th Ave., 15213. Tel: 412-578-6069. Sr. Cathy Solan, R.S.M.

Carnegie-Mellon University Ryan Catholic Newman Center, 4450 Bayard St., 15213. Tel: 412-681-3181; Fax: 412-681-2922. Revs. David S. Abernethy, C.O.; Joshua Kibler, C.O.; Stephen Lowery, C.O.

Chatham College Ryan Catholic Newman Center, 4450 Bayard St., 15213. Tel: 412-681-3181; Fax: 412-681-2922. Revs. David S. Abernethy, C.O.; Joshua Kibler, C.O.; Stephen Lowery, C.O.

Community College of Allegheny County - Boyce Campus St. Bernadette Church, 5245 Azalea Dr., Monroeville, 15146. Tel: 412-373-0050; Fax: 412-374-8113. Rev. Michael W. Decewicz, V.F., M.Div.

Community College of Allegheny County - Northside Campus St. Peter Church, 720 Arch St., 15212-5296. Tel: 412-321-0711; Fax: 412-321-7807. Rev. Ralph Tajak, O.S.B.

Community College of Allegheny County - South Campus Holy Spirit Church, 2603 Old Elizabeth Rd., West Mifflin, 15122. Tel: 412-466-5048; Fax: 412-466-4983. Rev. John B. Lendvai.

Community College of Allegheny County - North Hills Campus St. Teresa of Avila, 1000 Avila Ct., 15237-2176. Tel: 412-367-9001; Fax: 412-366-8415. Rev. Robert J. Vular.

Duquesne University Campus Ministry, 15282. Tel: 412-396-6020. Mr. Matt Walsh, Dir.; Rev. Timothy Hickey, C.S.Sp.

Geneva College Campus Ministry, 289 Ridge Rd., New Brighton, 15066. Tel: 724-846-5978. Rev. James B. Farnan, Dir.

Pennsylvania State University, Beaver Campus 824 Ohio River Bend, Apt. #3, Sewickley, 15143. Tel: 724-773-3839. Mr. Richard Sealy, Dir.

Point Park College St. Mary of Mercy Church, 202 Stanwix St., 15222. Tel: 412-261-0110; Fax: 412-261-0113. Rev. Thomas A. Sparacino, M.Div.

Robert Morris College, Moon Township Campus Mr. Richard Sealy.

Robert Morris College, Downtown Pittsburgh Campus St. Benedict the Moor Church, 91 Crawford St. at Centre Ave., 15219-4394. Tel: 412-281-3141; Fax: 412-391-7151. Rev. Thomas A. Sparacino, M.Div.

University of Pittsburgh Ryan Catholic Newman Center, 4450 Bayard St., 15213. Tel: 412-681-3181; Fax: 412-681-2922. Revs. David S. Abernethy, C.O., Dir.; Joshua Kibler, C.O.; Stephen Lowery, C.O.

California University (California) St. Thomas Aquinas Church, 4th & Union Streets, California, 15419. Tel: 724-938-3204; Fax: 724-938-0434. Rev. George J. Moneck, Dir.

Westminster College St. Camillus Church, 313 W. Englewood Ave., New Castle, 16105. Tel: 724-652-9471; Fax: 724-654-1430. Rev. Thomas J. Lewandowski.

Slippery Rock University, Newman Center (Slippery Rock) 342 Normal Ave., Slippery Rock, 16057. Tel: 724-794-8459; Fax: 724-794-1150. Rev. Kevin G. Poecking, Dir.; Ms. Diane Magliocca, Campus Min.

Washington and Jefferson College (Washington) Immaculate Conception, 119 W. Chestnut St., Washington, 15301. Tel: 724-225-1425. Rev. Joseph E. Sioli, C.O.

Waynesburg College (Waynesburg) St. Ann Church, 232 E. High St., Waynesburg, 15370. Tel: 724-627-7568. Rev. Richard J. Thompson.

[Q] MISCELLANEOUS LISTINGS

PITTSBURGH. *The Capuchin Franciscan Volunteer Corps, Inc.*, 220 37th St., 15201. Tel: 412-682-6011; Fax: 412-682-0506. Email: volunteers@capuchin.com. Web: www.capuchin.com. Rev. John Pfannenstiel, O.F.M.Cap., Dir. Province of St. Augustine of the Capuchin Order., Purpose: To promote, train, supervise and support Catholic lay missions and missionaries throughout the world, especially in conjunction with the ministries and fraternities of the Capuchin Order.

Cardinal Dearden Center, 4721 5th Ave., 15213. Tel: 412-687-8022. Revs. Bernard B. Costello (Retired); John M. Jordan; Thomas F. Manion (Retired); Edward F. McSweeney (Retired); Richard R. Ragni (Retired); Richard G. Terdine (Retired); Raymond M. Utz (Retired).

Catholic Diocese of Pittsburgh Foundation, 111 Blvd. of the Allies, 15222. Tel: 412-456-3085; Fax: 412-456-3169. Email: stewardship@diopitt.org. Web: www.diopitt.org.

Catholic Employers Benefits Plan Delaware Trust, 111 Blvd. of the Allies, 15222. Tel: 412-456-3137; Fax: 412-456-3139. Email: benefits@diopitt.org. Mr. Frederick P. O'Brien, Dir.

The Catholic Historical Society of Western Pennsylvania, Mailing Address: P.O. Box 194, 15230. 108 N. Dithridge St., 15213. Tel: 412-343-0860. Email: joyccho@aol.com. Web: www.catholichistorywpa.org. Thomas White, Pres. Purpose: To promote the teaching of the Catholic Church in the United States, especially the Church in Western Pennsylvania; to recognize the growth, development and contribution of the Catholic Church by the preservation of artifacts, records and documents related to that history; to make available the results of research and study.

The Catholic Institute of Pittsburgh, PA, 111 Blvd. of the Allies, 15222. Tel: 412-456-3137; Fax: 412-456-3139. Email: fobrien@diopitt.org. Mr. Frederick P. O'Brien, CFO.

Catholic Long Term Care Network of Western Pennsylvania, Inc., 8250 Babcock Blvd., 15237. Tel: 412-630-9980. Web: www.cltcn.org. A collaborative effort of six religious communities and the Diocese of Pittsburgh. The sponsors operate four skilled nursing facilities and three assisted living-personal care homes. Sponsors: Little Sisters of the Poor, School Sisters of St. Francis, Sisters of St. Joseph, Sisters of the Holy Spirit, Sisters of St. Basil the Great, Vincentian Sisters of Charity.

Chimbote Foundation, 111 Blvd. of the Allies, 15222-1618. Tel: 412-456-3085; Fax: 412-456-3169. Email: rlengwin@diopitt.org. Web: www.diopitt.org.

Christ Child Society of Pittsburgh (1992) P.O. Box 11324, 15238-1324. Tel: 412-682-4102; Fax: 412-682-4102. Judith Kern, Pres.; Rev. Kevin G. Poecking, Spiritual Advisor. Purpose: To foster a personal love of Christ expressed in service for needy children and youths. Total Assisted 900; Volunteers 59.

Cursillo Movement-Diocese of Pittsburgh, P.O. Box 213, Wildwood, 15091. Tel: 412-221-1560. Email: pghcursillo@gmail.com. Web: www.cursillo.org/pittsburgh. Rev. Stan M. Gregorek, Spiritual Advisor; Clyde A. Werger, Lay Dir.

Elizabeth Seton Center Inc. (1985) 1900 Pioneer Ave., 15226. Tel: 412-561-8400; Fax: 412-561-8488. Email: srbarb@setoncenter.com. Web: www.setoncenter.com. Sr. Barbara Ann Boss, S.C., Pres. Care Programs for Children and Adults; Senior Citizens Center; School of Art. Sisters of Charity 12; Total Assisted 2,500; Total Staff 80.

Epiphany Association, 820 Crane Ave., 15216-3050. Tel: 412-341-7494; Fax: 412-341-7495. Email: samuto@epiphanyassociation.org. Web: www.epiphanyassociation.org. Purpose: Under the auspices of its Epiphany Academy of Formative Spirituality, the Association strives with God's help to meet the needs of parents, pastors, teachers, counselors, chaplains, and directors in pursuit of a deeper understanding of the spiritual life in accordance with the wisdom of their faith and formation traditions. Total Staff 7.

St. Francis Academy Corporation, 1401 Hamilton Rd., 15234. Tel: 412-882-9911; Fax: 412-885-7210. Email: usa@osfprov.org. Sr. Joanne Brazinski, O.S.F., Pres.

Holy Family Foundation (1992) 8235 Ohio River Blvd., Ste. 200, 15202-1594. Tel: 412-766-4030; Fax: 412-766-5434. Web: www.hfi-pgh.org. Sr. Linda Yankoski, C.S.F.N., Ed.D., Pres. & CEO. The Holy Family Foundation was incorporated in 1992 to promote & support the public charitable works & educational purposes of Holy Family Institute and any other exempt activities affiliated with Holy Family Institute.

Holy Family Social Services (1900) 8235 Ohio River Blvd., 15202. Tel: 412-766-4030; Fax: 412-766-5434. Email: mckinney.larry@hifi-pgh.org. Web: www.hfi-pgh.org. Larry McKinney, COO. Holy Family Social Services is committed to helping children, preserving families, and strengthening communities by providing a network of services including in-home counseling, residential treatment, and outpatient mental, drug, alcohol and gambling addiction counseling health services. Holy Family Social Services strives to empower children and families to lead responsible lives and develop healthy relationships built on faith, hope, and love. Sisters 2; Total Staff 159; Children 1,181; Families 8,000.

Knights of Columbus Bishop of Pittsburgh Diocese Project, P.O. Box 9691, 15226-0691. Tel: 724-422-7136 Tom Behrmann (Treasurer). Project for benefit of St. Anthony School for Programs and McGuire Memorial.

Mercy Outreach Ministries, Inc., 3333 Fifth Ave., 15213. Tel: 412-578-6202; Fax: 412-578-6180. Email: mcdonoughfx@carlow.edu. Sr. Fidelis McDonough, R.S.M., Contact Person.

Millvale Franciscans, Inc., 146 Hawthorne Rd., 15209. Tel: 412-821-2200; Fax: 412-821-3318. Email: bich@millvalefranciscan.org. Betsy Miksic, Contact Person. Sisters of St. Francis of the Neumann Communities.

Mount Assisi Academy Preschool (1980) 934 Forest Ave., 15202. Tel: 412-761-0381; Fax: 412-761-0290. Sr. Elaine Hromulak, O.S.F., Prov. Min. Sisters 2; Lay Teachers 3; Students 71.

Mount Nazareth Center, Inc. (1986) 285 Bellevue Rd., 15229-2195. Tel: 412-931-4778, Ext. 2180; Fax: 412-931-9746. Sisters of the Holy Family of Nazareth, Holy Family Province.

National Institute for Newman Studies, 211 N. Dithridge St., 15213. Tel: 412-681-4375; Fax: 412-681-4376. Email: newmanstudies@comcast.net. Web: www.newmanstudiesinstitute.org. Very Rev. Drew P. Morgan, C.O., Dir. & Contact Person; Catharine Ryan, M.A., Asst. Dir.; Jan Grice, M.A., Admin. Asst.; Damon McGraw, M.A.R., Exec. Research Fellow.

Nazareth Family Foundation (1996) 285 Bellevue Rd., 15229. Tel: 412-931-4778, Ext. 2180; Fax: 412-931-9746. Email: srcindy@juno.com. Sr. Cynthia Meyer, C.S.F.N., Pres. Purpose: To promote family life through financial support of facilities, programs, and services which enhance individual and family well-being. Total Assisted 2,000.

Nazareth Global Missions, Inc., 285 Bellevue Rd., 15229. Tel: 412-931-4778, Ext. 2180; Fax: 412-931-9746. Email: srmichelec@juno.com.

North Catholic Endowment Fund, 111 Blvd. of the Allies, 15222. Tel: 412-456-3100; Fax: 412-456-3101. Email: education@diopitt.org. Web: www.diopitt.org.

Pension Plan for the Diocese of Pittsburgh (Lay Pension Plan), 111 Blvd. of the Allies, 15222. Tel: 412-456-3137; Fax: 412-456-3139. Email: benefits@diopitt.org. Mr. Frederick P. O'Brien, Dir.

Pittsburgh Catholic Publishing Associates (1954) Purpose: To promote for Catholics and other readers an understanding of the mission and teachings of the Church and its role in the community., 135 First Ave., Ste. 200, 15222-1513. Tel: 412-471-1252; Fax: 412-471-4228. Email: info@pittsburghcatholic.org. Web: www.pittsburghcatholic.org. Mr. Robert P. Lockwood, Gen. Mgr.; Ms. Carmella A. Weismantle, Opers. Mgr.; Mr. William Cone, Editor. Total Staff 15.

Pittsburgh Mercy Health System, Inc., 3333 5th Ave., 15213. Tel: 412-578-6675; Fax: 412-697-0266. Web: www.pmhs.org. Sr. Susan Welsh, R.S.M., Pres. & CEO.

Parent company of the following subsidiaries:

Mercy Life Center Corporation/Mercy Behavioral Health Tel: 412-232-8111; Fax: 412-232-7380.

McAuley Ministries, 3333 Fifth Ave., 15213. Tel: 412-578-6225. Michele Cooper, Exec. Dir.

St. Pius X Residence, Inc. Tel: 412-232-8111; Fax: 412-232-7380.

The Portiuncula Foundation of the Sisters of Saint Francis of Millvale, Pennsylvania, 146 Hawthorne Rd., 15209. Tel: 412-821-2200; Fax: 412-821-3318. Sr. Marlene Kline, O.S.F., Exec. Dir. Sisters of St. Francis of the Neumann Communities.

Priests' Benefit Plan of the Diocese of Pittsburgh (1955) 111 Blvd. of the Allies, 15222. Tel: 412-456-3060; Fax: 412-456-3139. Email: centralaccounting@diopitt.org. Rev. Charles S. Bober, S.T.D., Chm. Purpose: To provide certain retirement and health-related benefits to eligible priests.

Procurator Assurance, Inc., c/o 111 Boulevard of the Allies, 15222. Tel: 412-456-3137; Fax: 412-456-3139. Email: insurance@diopitt.org. Mr. Frederick P. O'Brien, Dir.

Scholastic Opportunity Scholarship Program, 111 Blvd. of the Allies, 15222. Tel: 412-456-3100; Fax: 412-456-3101. Email: kstubna@diopitt.org. Web: www.diopitt.org. Rev. Kris D. Stubna, S.T.D., Contact Person.

Sisters of St. Francis of the Providence of God Ministries Corporation, 3603 McRoberts Rd., 15234-2314. Tel: 412-882-9911; Fax: 412-885-7210. Email: usa@osfprov.org. Web: www.osfprov.org. Sr. Joanne Brazinski, O.S.F., Pres. Program: Franciscan Spirit and Life Center.

**Society of Saint Vincent de Paul*, Council of Pittsburgh, 1243 N. Franklin St., 15233. Tel: 412-321-1071; Fax: 412-321-9131. Email: council@svdppitt.org. Web: www.svdppitt.org. Mark Stephen Bibro, Pres.; Fred D. Just, M.A., M.Ed., Exec. Dir. Total Assisted 82,000; Total Staff 130.

Saint Thomas More Society (1960) 600 Grant St., 44th Fl., 15219. Tel: 412-566-6994; Fax: 412-566-6099. Email: rvogliano@eckertseamans.com. Raymond C. Vogliano, Pres.

Vincentian Collaborative System, 8250 Babcock Blvd., 15237. Tel: 412-630-9980; Fax: 412-348-0186. Email: jandiorio@vcs.org. Web: www.vcs.org. Dr. JoAnne Andiorio, Ph.D., Acting CEO & Exec. Vice Pres./COO. Purpose: To provide coordination and supervision of facilities and services operating under the auspices of the Sisters of Charity of Nazareth.

Vincentian Collaborative System Charitable Foundation, 8250 Babcock Blvd., 15237. Tel: 412-548-4055; Fax: 412-348-0186.

Vincentian Collaborative System Rehabilitation Services (2000) 6000 Babcock Blvd., Ste. 1002, 15237. Tel: 412-369-5150; Fax: 412-369-5165. Email: kevans@vcs.org. Kristine Evans, B.S., B.A., M.O.T.R., System V.P. Rehabilitation.

ALLISON PARK. *Divine Providence Foundation*, 9000 Babcock Blvd., 15101. Tel: 412-635-5402; Fax: 412-635-5416. Email: maryjbeatty@hotmail.com. Sr. Mary Francis Fletcher, C.D.P., Pres. Purpose: To perform public charitable works in the area of health care and education.

Sisters of Divine Providence Charitable Trust (1985) 9000 Babcock Blvd., 15101-2793. Tel: 412-931-5241; Fax: 412-635-5416. Email: winschc@yahoo.com. Web: www.divineprovidenceweb.org. Sr. Carolyn Winschel, C.D.P., Chm.

BADEN. *The City of God Foundation*, 1020 State St., 15005. Tel: 724-869-6540; Fax: 724-869-4932. Jane Spellacy, Coord.

**Girls Hope of Pittsburgh, Inc.*, 1020 State St., 15005. Tel: 724-869-2868; Fax: 724-869-6576. Email: girlshope@bhgh.org. Sr. Sharon Costello, C.S.J., Exec. Dir. Purpose: To provide a supportive home environment and a quality education through college for girls who have potential for leadership but who because of poverty, abuse, neglect or abandonment cannot remain in their own homes. Total Assisted 22; Total Staff 10.

BETHEL PARK. *Spiritan Mission Endowment Trust*, 6230 Brush Run Rd., 15102. Tel: 412-831-0302; Fax: 412-831-0970. Email: csspeast@choiceonemail.com. Web: www.spiritans.org.

Spiritan Support Trust, 6320 Brush Run Rd., 15102. Tel: 412-831-0302; Fax: 412-831-0970. Email: csspeast@choiceonemail.com. Web: www.spiritans.org. Very Rev. John Fogarty, C.S.Sp., Prov. Supr.

CLAIRTON. *Sisters Place, Inc.* (1993) 418 Mitchell Ave., 15025. Tel: 412-233-3903; Fax: 412-233-3904. Email: info@sistersplace.org. Web: www.sistersplace.org. Edward Wodarczyk, Pres.; Sr. Mary Parks, C.S.J., Exec. Dir. Purpose: To provide housing and supportive services to women and children who are homeless. Total Staff 9; Families 27.

CRANBERRY TOWNSHIP. *Magnificat Pittsburgh*, 114 Bayberry Ln., 16066. Tel: 724-452-1150. Kay Burkot, Contact Person.

ELIZABETH. *Divine Redeemer Health Care Ministries Corp.* (1990) 999 Rock Run Rd., 15037-2613. Tel: 412-751-8600; Fax: 412-751-0355. Email: sisrosemarysdr@aol.com. Web: www.sistersofthedivineredeemer.org.

Sisters of Divine Redeemer Charitable Trust (1990) 999 Rock Run Rd., 15037-2613. Tel: 412-751-8600; Fax: 412-751-0355. Email: sisrosemarysdr@aol.com. Web: www.sistersofthedivineredeemer.org.

GREENSBURG. *Tri-Diocesan Sisters Leadership Conference*, 463 Mt. Thor Rd., 15601-1293. Tel: 724-836-0406; Fax: 724-836-8280. Email: ghartzog@scsh.org. Sisters Jeanne Marie Ulica, O.S.F., Co-Chm. Tel: 412-761-6004; Fax: 412-761-0290; Grace Hartzog, S.C., Co-Chm.

MCKEESPORT. *Auberle*, 1101 Hartman St., 15132-1500. Tel: 412-673-5856, Ext. 1310; Fax: 412-267-5275. Email: johnly@auberle.org. Web: www.auberle.org. Diane Stanoszek, Chief Program Officer; John Patrick Lydon, CEO. Purpose: To provide services to at risk children and their families. Total in Residence 123; Total Staff 275.

Auberle Development, 1101 Hartman St., Mc Keesport, 15132-1500. Tel: 412-673-5856, Ext. 1315; Fax: 412-672-7525. Email: johnly@auberle.org. Web: www.auberle.org. John Patrick Lydon, CEO; Bridget Clement, Dir. of Devel.

Intersection (1972) 115 Seventh Ave., P.O. Box 827, Mc Keesport, 15134. Tel: 412-678-6948. Email: boniheh@fyi.net. Sr. Peg O'Neill, R.S.M., Exec. Dir.

Pauline Auberle Foundation (1952) 1101 Hartman St., 15132-1500. Tel: 412-673-5856, Ext. 1310; Fax: 412-267-5275. Email: johnly@auberle.org. Web: www.auberle.org. John Patrick Lydon, CEO; Bridget Clement, Dir. of Devel. Continues mission of Pauline Auberle Foundation while providing support to Auberle through facilities and funds. Total Staff 4.

VILLA MARIA. *The Center for Learning*, Customer Service Office in Villa Maria: 2105 Evergreen Rd., P.O. Box 910, 16155. Tel: 800-767-9090; 724-964-8083; Fax: 888-767-8080. Email: mwall@centerforlearning.org. Web: www.centerforlearning.org; cflreligion.org. Melanie Wall, Pres. & CEO. Educational Publisher of values-based curriculum: Religion for Catholic schools and parishes; English/Language Arts, Social Studies and Novel/Drama Curriculum Units for all schools; Owned and operated by the Sisters of the Humility of Mary. Directed by an Ecumenical Lay Board. Administration-business office in Villa Maria.

Administrative/Editorial Office, 24600 Detroit Rd., Ste. 201, Westlake, OH 44145. Tel: 440-250-9341; Fax: 440-250-9715.

Sisters of the Humility of Mary Charitable Trust, Villa Maria Community Center, 288 Villa Dr., P.O. Box 313, 16155. Tel: 724-964-8861; Fax: 724-964-8082. Email: cmarshall@hmministry.org. Web: www.humilityofmary.org. Sr. Carolyn Marshall, H.M., Contact Person.

Villa Maria Education & Spirituality Center (1989) 16155. Tel: 724-964-8886; Fax: 724-964-8815. Email: jmerhaut@humilityofmary.org. Web: www.villaprograms.com. James R. Merhaut, Pres. & CEO. VMESC provides and promotes educational and spiritual experiences in a unique setting for people of all ages, faiths and economic status. Total Assisted 10,000; Total Staff 16.

Villa Maria Residential Services, 380 Villa Dr., P.O. Box 230, 16155. Tel: 724-964-8920, Ext. 3340; Fax: 724-964-1321. Email: kmcculloh@humilityofmary.org. Web: www.humilityofmary.org. Kathleen McCulloh, Pres. & CEO. (Villa Maria Apartments); Housing for low & moderate income for senior citizens 58 & over. Apartments 40.

RELIGIOUS INSTITUTES OF MEN REPRESENTED IN THE DIOCESE

For further details refer to the corresponding bracketed number in the Religious Institutes of Men or Women section.

[0200]—*Benedictine Monks* (St. Vincent Archabbey)—O.S.B.

[0330]—*Brothers of the Christian Schools* (Prov. of Baltimore)—F.S.C.

[0470]—*The Capuchin Friars* (Prov. of St. Augustine)—O.F.M.Cap.

[0650]—*Congregation of the Holy Spirit* (Eastern Prov.)—C.S.Sp.

[1000]—*Congregation of the Passion* (Eastern Prov.)—C.P.

[]—*Croatian Franciscans* (Croatian Commissariate)—T.O.R.

[0520]—*Franciscan Friars* (Immaculate Conception & St. John the Baptist)—O.F.M.

[0690]—*Jesuit Fathers* (Maryland Province)—S.J.

[0950]—*Oratorians*—C.O.

[]—*Society of the Brother-Servants of the Holy Spirit*—B.H.S.

[0420]—*Society of the Divine Word*—S.V.D.

[0560]—*Third Order Regular of Saint Francis* (Prov. of Sacred Heart of Jesus)—T.O.R.

RELIGIOUS INSTITUTES OF WOMEN REPRESENTED IN THE DIOCESE

[0230]—*Benedictine Sisters of Pontifical Jurisdiction*—O.S.B.

[1115]—*Dominican Sisters of Peace*—O.P.

[1170]—*Felician Sisters*—C.S.S.F.

[1190]—*Franciscan Sisters of Atonement*—S.A.

[]—*Institute of the Sisters of Mercy of the Americas* (Pittsburgh, PA)—R.S.M.

[]—*Ladies of Bethany*—L.B.

[2340]—*Little Sisters of the Poor*—L.S.P.

[2720]—*Mission Helpers of the Sacred Heart*—M.H.S.H.

[3071]—*North American Union Sisters of Our Lady of Charity*—O.L.C.

[3170]—*Religious of the Passion of Jesus Christ*—C.P.

[3430]—*Religious Teachers Filippini* (St. Lucy Filippini Prov.)—M.P.F.

[2970]—*School Sisters of Notre Dame*—S.S.N.D.

[1690]—*School Sisters of St. Francis*—O.S.F.

[0570]—*Sisters of Charity of Seton Hill, Greensburg, Pennsylvania*—S.C.

[0990]—*Sisters of Divine Providence*—C.D.P.

[1660]—*Sisters of Saint Francis of the Providence of God*—O.S.F.

[3830-13]—*Sisters of Saint Joseph*—C.S.J.

[1620]—*Sisters of St. Francis of Millvale, Pennsylvania*—O.S.F.

[1020]—*Sisters of the Divine Redeemer*—S.D.R.

[1970]—*Sisters of the Holy Family of Nazareth*—C.S.F.N.

[2040]—*Sisters of the Holy Spirit*—S.H.S.

[2110]—*Sisters of the Humility of Mary*—H.M.

[2160]—*Sisters, Servants of the Immaculate Heart of Mary*—I.H.M.

[4160]—*Vincentian Sisters of Charity*—V.S.C.

DIOCESAN CEMETERIES

PITTSBURGH. *The Catholic Cemeteries Association of the Diocese of Pittsburgh* (1952) *Central Office*, 718 Hazelwood Ave., 15217-2807. Tel: 412-521-9133; Fax: 412-521-7019. Web: www.ccapgh.org.

All Saints Catholic Cemetery & Mausoleum (Braddock Catholic), 1560 Brinton Rd., 15221-4899. Tel:

412-271-5950; Fax: 412-271-8219.

Calvary Catholic Cemetery & Mausoleum, 718 Hazelwood Ave., 15217-2807. Tel: 412-421-9959; Fax: 412-421-3670.

Christ Our Redeemer Catholic Cemetery & Mausoleum (North Side Catholic), 204 Cemetery Ln., 15237-2722. Tel: 412-931-2206; Fax: 412-931-2229.

St. Mary Catholic Cemetery, c/o Calvary Cemetery, 718 Hazelwood Ave., 15217-2807. Tel: 412-421-9959; Fax: 412-621-6439.

St. Stanislaus Catholic Cemetery & Mausoleum & St. Anthony Catholic Cemetery, 700 Soose Rd., 15209-1544. Tel: 412-821-4324; Fax: 412-821-4718.

Queen of Heaven Catholic Cemetery & Mausoleum, 2900 Washington Rd., McMurray, 15317-3278. Tel: 724-941-7601; Fax: 724-942-2550.

Resurrection Catholic Cemetery & Mausoleum, 100 Resurrection Rd., Moon Township, 15108. Tel: 724-695-2999; Fax: 724-695-3032.

Sacred Heart Catholic Cemetery and Mausoleum, 97 Sacred Heart Rd., Monongahela, 15063-9605. Tel: 724-258-2885; Fax: 724-258-2275.

Good Shepherd Catholic Cemetery & Mausoleum, 733 Patton St., Monroeville, 15146-4530. Tel: 412-824-0355; Fax: 412-823-9083.

Saint Joseph Catholic Cemetery & Mausoleum, 1443 Lincoln Hwy., North Versailles, 15137-2448. Tel: 412-823-9111; Fax: 412-823-6655.

Holy Souls Catholic Cemetery, c/o Resurrection Catholic Cemetery , 100 Resurrection Rd., Moon Township, 15108. Tel: 724-695-2999; Fax: 724-695-3032.

Our Lady of Hope Catholic Cemetery & Mausoleum, 1898 Bakerstown Rd., Tarentum, 15084. Tel: 724-224-2785; Fax: 724-224-0211.

Holy Savior Catholic Cemetery, 4629 Bakerstown Rd., Gibsonia, 15044. Tel: 724-625-3822; Fax: 724-625-3880.

Mount Carmel Catholic Cemetery & Mausoleum, 7601 Mt. Carmel Rd., Verona, 15147. Tel: 412-241-1260; Fax: 412-241-5041.

NECROLOGY

✠ McDowell, Most Rev. John B., Retired Auxiliary Bishop of Pittsburgh—Died Feb. 25, 2010
† Darkowski, Rev. Msgr. Leon S., (Retired)—Died Aug., 2009
† Blough, William G., (Retired)—Died Oct. 24, 2008
† Kohuch, Robert Andrew, (Leave of Absence)—Died July 1, 2008
† Kuenzig, Aloysius A., (Retired)—Died June 18, 2009
† Michaels, John L., (Retired)—Died July 13, 2008
† Nazimek, Francis A.—Died July 30, 2008
† Petrie, Harry F., (Retired)—Died Sept. 24, 2008
† Vanyo, Leo V., (Retired)—Died March 7, 2009

An asterisk (*) denotes an organization that has established tax-exempt status directly with the IRS and is not covered by the USCCB Group Ruling.

Diocese of Portland (In Maine)

(Dioecesis Portlandensis)

Most Reverend

RICHARD J. MALONE

Bishop of Portland; ordained priest May 20, 1972; appointed Auxiliary Bishop of Boston and Titular Bishop of Aptuca January 27, 2000; ordained March 1, 2000; appointed Bishop of Portland February 10, 2004; installed March 31, 2004. *Office: 510 Ocean Ave., Portland, ME 04103-4936. Mailing Address: P.O. Box 11559, Portland, ME 04104-7559.*

Most Reverend

JOSEPH JOHN GERRY, O.S.B.

Retired Bishop of Portland; ordained June 12, 1954; ordained Titular Bishop of Praecausa and Auxiliary Bishop of Manchester April 21, 1986; appointed Bishop of Portland December 21, 1988; installed February 21, 1989; retired February 10, 2004. *Mailing Address: St. Anselm Abbey, 100 St. Anselm Dr., Manchester, NH 03102-1310.*

ESTABLISHED JULY 29, 1853.

Square Miles 33,040.

Comprises the State of Maine.

Corporate Title: Roman Catholic Bishop of Portland, a Corporation Sole.

For the legal titles of other diocesan-related institutions, please consult Chancery.

Chancery: 510 Ocean Ave., P.O. Box 11559, Portland, ME 04104-7559. Tel: 207-773-6471; Fax: 207-773-0182.

STATISTICAL OVERVIEW

Personnel	
Bishop	1
Retired Bishops	1
Priests: Diocesan Active in Diocese	69
Priests: Diocesan Active Outside Diocese	1
Priests: Retired, Sick or Absent	86
Number of Diocesan Priests	156
Religious Priests in Diocese	32
Total Priests in Diocese	188
Extern Priests in Diocese	10
Ordinations:	
Diocesan Priests	1
Permanent Deacons in Diocese	32
Total Brothers	19
Total Sisters	318
Parishes	
Parishes	66
With Resident Pastor:	
Resident Diocesan Priests	37
Resident Religious Priests	3
Without Resident Pastor:	
Administered by Priests	26
Missions	20
New Parishes Created	6
Closed Parishes	27
Professional Ministry Personnel:	
Sisters	5
Lay Ministers	42
Welfare	
Catholic Hospitals	3
Total Assisted	557,936
Homes for the Aged	4
Total Assisted	1,026
Day Care Centers	2
Total Assisted	230
Specialized Homes	1
Total Assisted	1,031
Special Centers for Social Services	2
Total Assisted	475
Other Institutions	2
Total Assisted	4,330
Educational	
Diocesan Students in Other Seminaries	8
Total Seminarians	8
Colleges and Universities	1
Total Students	2,691
High Schools, Diocesan and Parish	1
Total Students	275
High Schools, Private	2
Total Students	733
Elementary Schools, Diocesan and Parish	12
Total Students	2,482
Elementary Schools, Private	1
Total Students	177
Catechesis/Religious Education:	
High School Students	1,031
Elementary Students	6,421
Total Students under Catholic Instruction	13,818
Teachers in the Diocese:	
Priests	4
Brothers	1
Sisters	6
Lay Teachers	282
Vital Statistics	
Receptions into the Church:	
Infant Baptism Totals	1,443
Minor Baptism Totals	122
Adult Baptism Totals	117
Received into Full Communion	122
First Communions	2,032
Confirmations	2,161
Marriages:	
Catholic	392
Interfaith	206
Total Marriages	598
Deaths	2,532
Total Catholic Population	187,306
Total Population	1,316,456

Former Bishops—Very Rev. J. COSKERY, V.G., of Baltimore, The first Bishop-Elect, declined the nomination; Rt. Revs. DAVID W. BACON, D.D., ord. Dec. 13, 1838 in Baltimore, MD; cons. Bishop of Portland April 22, 1855; died Nov. 5, 1874; JAMES AUGUSTINE HEALY, D.D., ord. June 10, 1854 in Paris, France; cons. Bishop of Portland June 2, 1875; died Aug. 5, 1900; His Eminence WILLIAM CARDINAL O'CONNELL, ord. June 8, 1884; cons. Bishop of Portland, May 19, 1901; named Coadjutor Archbishop of Boston, Feb. 8, 1906; succeeded to the See of Boston, Aug. 30, 1907; created Cardinal, Nov. 27, 1911; died April 22, 1944; Rt. Revs. LOUIS S. WALSH, D.D., ord. Dec. 23, 1882 in Rome, Italy; cons. Bishop of Portland Oct. 18, 1906; died May 12, 1924.; JOHN GREGORY MURRAY, D.D., ord. April 14, 1900 in Louvain, France; cons. Bishop of Portland April 28, 1920; transferred to the Archdiocese of St. Paul, Oct. 29, 1931; died Oct. 11, 1956; Most Revs. JOSEPH EDWARD MCCARTHY, D.D., ord. July 4, 1903; cons. Bishop of Portland Aug. 24, 1932; died Sept. 8, 1955; DANIEL JOSEPH FEENEY, D.D., LL.D., ord. May 21, 1921; appt. Titular Bishop of Sita and Auxiliary of Portland, June 22, 1946; cons. Sept. 12, 1946; Apostolic Administrator of the Diocese; appt. July 27, 1948; Coadjutor "cum jure successionis"; appt. March 4, 1952; succeeded to See, Sept. 8, 1955; died Sept. 15, 1969; PETER LEO GERETY, D.D., ord. June 29, 1939; appt. Titular Bishop of Crepedula and Coadjutor Bishop of Portland March 4, 1966; cons. June 1, 1966; appt. Apostolic Administrator, Feb. 18, 1967; succeeded to See, Sept. 15, 1969; transferred to Archdiocese of Newark, April 2, 1974; EDWARD C. O'LEARY, D.D., ord. June 15, 1946; Titular Bishop of Moglaena and Auxiliary Bishop of Portland; appt. Nov. 17, 1970; cons. Jan. 25, 1971; Apostolic Administrator; appt. June 29, 1974; ninth Bishop of Portland, Dec. 4, 1974; installed Dec. 18, 1974; resigned Sept. 27, 1988; died April 2, 2002; JOSEPH J. GERRY, O.S.B., D.D. (Retired), ord. June 12, 1954; cons. Titular Bishop of Praecausa and Auxiliary Bishop of Manchester April 21, 1986; appt. Bishop of Portland Dec. 21, 1988; installed Feb. 21, 1989; retired Feb. 10, 2004.

Vicars General—Rev. Msgrs. MICHAEL J. HENCHAL, J.C.L., V.G.; ANDREW DUBOIS, V.G.

Chancery—510 Ocean Ave., P.O. Box 11559, Portland, 04104-7559. Tel: 207-773-6471; Fax: 207-773-0182.

Office Hours: Mon.-Fri. 9-4:30 Labor Day to Memorial Day; Mon.-Thurs. 8:30-4:30, Fri. 8:30-noon Memorial Day to Labor Day. Closed Holidays. This is the address for all offices unless otherwise listed.

Moderator of the Curia—Rev. Msgr. ANDREW DUBOIS, V.G. Email: andrew.dubois@portlanddiocese.org.

Chancellor—Sr. RITA-MAE BISSONNETTE, R.S.R., J.C.L. Email: ritamae.bissonnette@portlanddiocese.org.

Vicar for Priests—Rev. PAUL A. PLANTE. Tel: 207-321-7877. Email: paul.plante@portlanddiocese.org.

Director of Communications—Ms. SUSAN Y. BERNARD. Email: sue.bernard@portlanddiocese.org.

Deans—Rev. PHILIP A. TRACY, V.F.; Very Rev. JEAN-PAUL LABRIE, V.F.

Diocesan Consultors—Rev. Msgrs. VINCENT A. TATARCZUK (Retired); J. JOSEPH FORD; RENE T. MATHIEU; MARC B. CARON, S.T.L.; ANDREW DUBOIS, V.G.; Revs. WILFRED P. LABBE; PAUL A. PLANTE; Rev. Msgrs. PAUL F. STEFANKO, J.C.L.; MICHAEL J. HENCHAL, J.C.L., V.G.

Diocesan Review Board—Mr. KEVIN GILDART; Mrs. KATHLEEN ROSSI; Ms. MELISSA CILLEY; Mr. PAUL FALCONER, Chm.; Rev. NORMAND E. CARPENTIER; Sr. MAUREEN WALLACE, R.S.M.; Mrs. EDNA CHACE; Dr. ANNE PULSIFIER. Staff: Rev. Msgr. ANDREW DUBOIS, V.G.; Sr. RITA-MAE BISSONNETTE, R.S.R., J.C.L.; Rev. Msgr. MICHAEL J. HENCHAL, J.C.L., V.G.

Diocesan Offices and Directors

Department of Pastoral and Educational Services—Mr. WILLIAM SCHULZ, Dir. Email:

bill.schulz@portlanddiocese.org.
Diocesan Office of Lifelong Faith Formation—Mr. MICHAEL LAVIGNE, Dir. Email: michael.lavigne@portlanddiocese.org.
Youth & Young Adult Ministry Coordinator—VACANT.
Retreat Coordinator—JOSEPH MAILHOT. Email: joe.mailhot@portlanddiocese.org.
Faith Formation Outreach Coordinators—JUDY MICHAUD, 46 St. Agatha Ave., Frenchville, 04745. Tel: 207-543-7731. Email: judy.michaud@portlanddiocese.org; Ms. RUTH OAKLEY. Email: ruth.oakley@portlanddiocese.org.
Catholic Schools Superintendent—Sr. ROSEMARY T. DONOHUE, S.N.D. Email: rosemary.donohue@portlanddiocese.org.
Office for Missions—Mrs. CARLEEN E. COOK, Dir.
Director of Chaplaincies—Mr. WILLIAM SCHULZ, Dir.
Latin Mass—Rev. ROBERT PARENT, Coord.
Hospital Chaplaincy—
Hispanic Ministry—Sr. PAT PORA, Dir.
Prison Ministry—
Ecumenical & Interreligious Services—Rev. RICHARD E. SENGHAS, Coord. (Retired).
Charismatic Renewal—Rev. RICHARD P. RICE, 66 Ward Circle, Brunswick, 04011-9342. Tel: 207-373-1832.
Campus Ministry—Rev. WILFRED LABBE.
Catholic Scouting—Rev. NATHAN D. MARCH, Chap., Mailing Address: Catholic Committee on Scouting, P.O. Box 1540, Lewiston, 04241-1540. Tel: 207-777-1200. Email: nathan.march@portlanddiocese.org.
Resource Center—Rev. NORMAND P. RICHARD, Coord.
Parish Planning for Evangelization—Mr. WILLIAM SCHULZ.
Department of Financial Services—Mr. DAVID P. TWOMEY JR., CPA, Dir. Email: david.twomey@portlanddiocese.org.
Parish Financial Services—Mr. PETER M. MCPARTLAND, Dir. Email: peter.mcpartland@portlanddiocese.org.
Controller—Mrs. LAURIE J. DOWNEY, CPA. Email: laurie.downey@portlanddiocese.org.
Human Resources—ELIZABETH ALLEN, Dir.
Director of Property Management—JAMES SOMMA.
Risk Management—JOHN CAVALLARO, Dir.
DICON - Diocesan Construction—GREG STONE, Supt.
Safe Environment—THOMAS MESCHINELLI, Coord.
Information Technology—MICHAEL MORE, Dir.
Department of Canonical Services—Rev. Msgr. PAUL F. STEFANKO, J.C.L.
Tribunal—
Officialis—Rev. Msgr. PAUL F. STEFANKO, J.C.L. Email: paul.stefanko@portlanddiocese.org.
Promoter of Justice—Rev. Msgr. MICHAEL J. HENCHAL, J.C.L., V.G.
Defenders of the Bond—Ms. SHANNON FOSSETT. Email: shannon.fossett@portlanddiocese.org; Mr. STEPHEN GARBITELLI, J.C.L. Email: stephen.garbitelli@portlanddiocese.org; Mr. GEORGE G. PAVLOFF, J.C.D. Email: george.pavloff@portlanddiocese.org; Sr. RITA-MAE BISSONNETTE, R.S.R., J.C.L.
Advocates—Ms. SHANNON FOSSETT; Mr. STEPHEN GARBITELLI, J.C.L.; Sr. RITA-MAE BISSONNETTE, R.S.R., J.C.L.
Notaries—Mrs. NAJLIA KERRIGAN. Email: nash.kerrigan@portlanddiocese.org; Mrs. MARY DELANEY. Email: mary.delaney@portlanddiocese.org.
Associate Judges—Rev. JOSEPH J. KOURY, J.C.D. Email: joseph.koury@portlanddiocese.org; Sr. RITA-MAE BISSONNETTE, R.S.R., J.C.L.; Rev. Msgr. MICHAEL J. HENCHAL, J.C.L., V.G.
Guardian—Rev. Msgr. ANDREW DUBOIS, V.G.
Office Coordinator—Rev. Msgr. PAUL F. STEFANKO, J.C.L.
Office of Due Process— (examination of violation of rights within the church)
Director—Ms. SHANNON FOSSETT.
Department of Administrative & Ministerial Services—Rev. Msgr. ANDREW DUBOIS, V.G.
Diocesan Office of Communications—Ms. SUSAN Y. BERNARD, Dir.
Harvest Magazine—LOIS CZENIAK, Editor.
Diocesan Office of Public Policy—Mr. MARC R. MUTTY. Email: marc.mutty@portlanddiocese.org.
Office of Professional Responsibility—Deacon JOHN S. BRENNAN, Dir. Tel: 866-829-4437 (Toll Free); 207-321-7836 (Office); Cell: 207-650-0492. Email: john.brennan@portlanddiocese.org.
Ministerial Services—Rev. Msgr. ANDREW DUBOIS, V.G., Dir.
Diaconate—Rev. Msgr. CHARLES M. MURPHY, S.T.D., V.F., Dir. (Retired).
Ministry to Priests—Rev. PAUL A. PLANTE, Vicar.
Vocations—Rev. ROBERT C. VAILLANCOURT. Email: robert.vaillancourt@portlanddiocese.org.
Seminarians—Rev. FRANK J. MURRAY.
Chancellor—Sr. RITA-MAE BISSONNETTE, R.S.R., J.C.L.
Department of Development Services—Ms. PATRICIA M. LONG, Dir. Email: patricia.long@portlanddiocese.org.
Catholic Charities Maine— Central Services: KRISTEN WELLS, Dir., Mailing Address: P.O. Box 10660, Portland, 04104-6060. Tel: 207-781-8550; Fax: 207-781-8560.
Catholic Foundation of Maine—CHRISTOPHER REILLY, Exec. Dir.
Annual Appeal—Ms. PATRICIA M. LONG, Dir. Email: patricia.long@portlanddiocese.org.
Office of Support and Assistance Ministry— (Sexual Abuse Victims) Sr. RITA-MAE BISSONNETTE, R.S.R., J.C.L., Dir. Tel: 207-321-7818; CAROLYN BLOOM, Independent Clinician. Tel: 207-782-1051. Email: c.bloom@myfairpoint.net.
Campaign for Human Development—Ms. BONITA BAGLEY, Mailing Address: P.O. Box 10660, Portland, 04104-6060. Tel: 207-781-8550; Fax: 207-781-8560. Email: bbagley@ccmaine.org.
Catholic Relief Services—Mrs. CARLEEN E. COOK. Email: carleen.cook@portlanddiocese.org.
Diocesan Priests' Benefit Plan - Trustees—Most Rev. RICHARD JOSEPH MALONE, D.D., S.T.L., Th.D., Pres.; Rev. Msgr. J. JOSEPH FORD, Chm.; Revs. CLAUDE J. ALBERT, Treas. (Retired); THOMAS M. MURPHY; ROBERT D. LARIVIERE; Rev. Msgr. ANDREW DUBOIS, V.G.; Revs. TIMOTHY J. NADEAU, Sec.; NORMAND E. CARPENTIER.
Diocesan Archivist—Sr. RITA-MAE BISSONNETTE, R.S.R., J.C.L. Contact Chancellor's Office:
Diocesan Board of Education—ROBERT SMITH, Chm.; Sr. ROSEMARY T. DONOHUE, S.N.D., Exec. Sec.; KATHLEEN MCLAUGHLIN. Members: Rev. RICHARD C. MCLAUGHLIN; Ms. MARLENE DYE; Mr. MATTHEW RANCOURT; Mrs. ANDREE TOSTEVIN; SUSAN GAJEWSKI; Ms. BARBARA ANN ARNOLDO; ROBERT CONNORS; ANNA LYONS; Sgt. JONATHAN SHAPIRO; Revs. LOUIS J. PHILLIPS; JAMES F. LAFONTAINE, S.J.; Mr. DONALD FOURNIER; Ms. DARCY COFFTA.
Diocesan Bureau of Housing—Most Rev. RICHARD JOSEPH MALONE, D.D., S.T.L., Th.D., Bishop of Portland & Pres.; Mr. DAVID P. TWOMEY JR., CPA, Treas.; THOMAS KELLY ESQ., Clerk.
Diocesan Finance Council—Most Rev. RICHARD JOSEPH MALONE, D.D., S.T.L., Th.D.; Rev. Msgrs. MICHAEL J. HENCHAL, J.C.L., V.G.; ANDREW DUBOIS, V.G.; DAVID WARREN, Vice Chm.; Mr. JOSEPH MALONE; Mr. ARTHUR BORDUAS, Chm.; MARY ARNOLD; VINCENT VERONEAU; Mr. EDWARD SNOOK; CYNTHIA NICKLESS; ROBERTSON BREED; GREGG H. GINN; GREGORY ST. ANGELO; MARK FERNANDEZ. Ex Officio Members: Sr. RITA-MAE BISSONNETTE, R.S.R., J.C.L.; Mr. DAVID P. TWOMEY JR., CPA, Finance Officer. Staff: Mrs. LAURIE J. DOWNEY, CPA; Mr. PETER M. MCPARTLAND.
Diocesan Pastoral Council—Most Rev. RICHARD JOSEPH MALONE, D.D., S.T.L., Th.D., Pres. Ex Officio: Rev. Msgr. ANDREW DUBOIS, V.G.; Sr. RITA-MAE BISSONNETTE, R.S.R., J.C.L., Chancellor; Mr. WILLIAM SCHULZ, Dir. Pastoral & Educ. Dept. Appointed Members: Mr. KEVIN BIRCH; Ms. SAIRA CLAYTON; Mrs. ELISABETH CROWLEY; Ms. KAITLYN CUNNINGHAM; Dr. DOUGLAS JORGENSEN; Mrs. WENDY JORGENSEN; Sr. ELAINE LACHANCE, S.C.I.M.; Ms. TERRI MAHER, Co Chm.; Deacon JOHN MCAULIFFE JR.; Ms. MARTHA MULDOON; Mr. MICHAEL POULIN; Sgt. JONATHAN SHAPIRO, Co Chm.; Ms. ELAINE SIPE; Deacon GEORGE STEVENS JR.; Mr. PAUL TULLY.
Diocesan Office for Worship—Rev. Msgr. MARC B. CARON, S.T.L., Dir.
General Counsel—Mr. THOMAS KELLY, Robinson Kriger & McCallum, 12 Portland Pier, P.O. Box 568, Portland, 04112-0568. Tel: 207-772-6565.
Maine Diocesan Council of Catholic Women—Most Rev. RICHARD JOSEPH MALONE, D.D., S.T.L., Th.D., Episcopal Chm.; Sr. CAROL MARTIN, P.F.M., Diocesan Moderator; Ms. KELLY DUQUETTE.
Newman Apostolate—Rev. WILFRED P. LABBE. Pastoral Associates: Revs. LAWRENCE CONLEY; THOMAS LEQUIN; Ms. BERNICE MURPHY; Ms. REBECCA HILTON; Revs. FRANK MURRAY; PAUL H. DUMAIS.
Personnel Board—Rev. JOHN R. SKEHAN; Rev. Msgr. ANDREW DUBOIS, V.G.; Rev. NORMAND E. CARPENTIER; Rev. Msgrs. J. JOSEPH FORD; RENE T. MATHIEU. Ex Officio Members: Most Rev. RICHARD JOSEPH MALONE, D.D., S.T.L., Th.D., Pres.; Rev. Msgr. MICHAEL J. HENCHAL, J.C.L., V.G., Vicar Gen.; Revs. FRANK J. MURRAY, Dir., Seminarians; PAUL A. PLANTE, Vicar for Priests.
Pontifical Association of Holy Childhood—Mrs. CARLEEN E. COOK.
Pontifical Society for the Propagation of the Faith—Mrs. CARLEEN E. COOK.
Victim Assistance Coordinator—Sr. RITA-MAE BISSONNETTE, R.S.R., J.C.L. Tel: 207-321-7819. Email: ritamae.bissonnette@portlanddiocese.org.
Independent Clinician—CAROLYN BLOOM. Tel: 207-782-1051. Email: c.bloom@myfairpoint.net.

CLERGY, PARISHES, MISSIONS AND PAROCHIAL SCHOOLS

CITY OF PORTLAND

(CUMBERLAND COUNTY)

1—CATHEDRAL OF THE IMMACULATE CONCEPTION (1853) Revs. Louis J. Phillips, Rector; Kevin Martin, Parochial Vicar; Richard D. Bertrand, S.J., Parochial Vicar; Michael J. Seavey, Parochial Vicar.
Res.: 307 Congress St., 04101-3695. Tel: 207-773-7746 (Rectory); Fax: 207-879-5547. Email: portlandcathedral@portlandcathedral.org. Web: www.portlandcathedral.org.
School—(Grades PreSchool-8), 14 Locust St., 04101-0311. Tel: 207-775-1491; Fax: 207-828-3989. Dr. Barbara Ann Arnoldo, Prin. Sisters of Mercy 1; Lay Teachers 12; Students 161.
Catechesis/Religious Program—Tel: 207-772-6597; Fax: 207-879-5547. Donna Lebel, D.R.E. Students 249.

2—ST. CHRISTOPHER'S (Peaks Island) (1923) Revs. Louis J. Phillips, Admin.; Richard D. Bertrand, S.J., Parochial Vicar; Kevin Martin, Parochial Vicar; Michael J. Seavey, Parochial Vicar.
Mailing Address: 307 Congress St., 04101-3695. Tel: 207-773-7446. Email: portlandcathedral@portlanddiocese.org. Web: www.cluster21portland.org.
Church: 15 Central Ave., Peaks Island, 04108.
Catechesis/Religious Program—
Mission— Long Island, Cumberland Co.

3—ST. DOMINIC'S, Merged with Sacred Heart, Portland to form Sacred Heart/St. Dominic's, Portland.

4—ST. JOSEPH'S (1909) Revs. Peter Kaseta, O.F.M.Cap.; Don Bosco Duquette, O.F.M.Cap.; James Hammer, O.F.M.Cap.
Res.: 673 Stevens Ave., 04103-2640. Tel: 207-797-7026; Fax: 207-797-2679. Email: sjoseph@maine.rr.com. Web: www.sjoseph.org.
School—St. Brigid School, (Grades PreSchool-8), 695 Stevens Ave., 04103-2682. Tel: 207-797-7073; Fax: 207-797-7078. Ms. Lori Ann Lee, Prin.; Sally Szemela, Librarian. St. Joseph School merged with St. Patrick School to form St. Brigid School. Lay Teachers 27; Students 328.
Catechesis/Religious Program—Tel: 207-797-9509. Pamela Fogg, D.R.E. Students 16.

5—ST. LOUIS (1915), (Polish), Revs. Louis J. Phillips, Admin.; Richard D. Bertrand, S.J., Parochial Vicar; Kevin Martin, Parochial Vicar; Michael J. Seavey, Parochial Vicar.
Mailing Address: 307 Congress St., 04101-3695. Tel: 207-773-7746; Fax: 207-879-5547. Email: portlandcathedral@portlanddiocese.org. Web: www-.stlouischurch.net. In Res., Revs. Alfred E. Irving, Chap.; Paul R. Marquis, Chap.
Res.: 279 Danforth St., 04102-3798. Web: www.stlouischurch.net.
Catechesis/Religious Program—Students 28.

6—ST. PATRICK'S (1922) Revs. James F. Lafontaine, S.J., Admin.; Robert F. Regan, S.J., Parochial Vicar; John R. d'Anjou, S.J., Parochial Vicar; James C. O'Brien, S.J., Parochial Vicar. In Res., Revs. Albin A. Andrus (Retired); Harold D. Moreshead (Retired); Normand P. Richard.
Res.: 1342 Congress St., 04102-2117. Tel: 207-772-6325; Fax: 207-772-6326.
See St. Brigid School listed under St. Joseph's, Portland.
Catechesis/Religious Program—Tel: 207-775-2185. Sandra Litcher, D.R.E. Joint program with St. Pius X, Portland. Enrollment reported under St. Pius X.

7—ST. PETER'S (1911), (Italian), Revs. Louis J. Phillips, Admin.; Richard D. Bertrand, S.J., Parochial Vicar; Kevin Martin, Parochial Vicar; Michael J. Seavey, Parochial Vicar.
Mailing Address: 307 Congress St., 04101-3695. Tel: 207-773-7746; Fax: 207-879-5547. Email: portlandcathedral@portlanddiocese.org.
Church: 72 Federal St., 04101. Tel: 207-773-0748; Fax: 207-879-0557. Web: www.stpeterschurchportland.org.
Catechesis/Religious Program—Ms. Grace Tucci Libby, P.C.L. Students 55.

8—ST. PIUS X (1962) Revs. James F. Lafontaine, S.J.; John R. d'Anjou, S.J., Parochial Vicar. In Res., Revs. James C. O'Brien, S.J.; Robert F. Regan, S.J.
Res.: 492 Ocean Ave., 04103. Tel: 207-775-3032; Fax: 207-874-7514.

Catechesis/Religious Program—Tel: 207-775-2185. Email: religioused@stpius-parish.org. Sandra Litcher, D.R.E. Students 35.

9—SACRED HEART/ST. DOMINIC (1997) Revs. Louis J. Phillips, Admin.; Richard D. Bertrand, S.J.; Kevin Martin, Parochial Vicar; Michael J. Seavey, Parochial Vicar.
Mailing Address: 307 Congress St., 04101-3695. Tel: 207-773-7746; Fax: 207-879-5547. Email: sacredh@maine.rr.com. Web: www.shsdp.com.
Church: 80 Sherman St., 04101-2290. Tel: 207-772-6182; Fax: 207-772-9615. Web: www.shsdp.org.
Catechesis/Religious Program—Students 21.

OUTSIDE THE CITY OF PORTLAND

ASHLAND, AROOSTOOK CO., ST. MARK'S, [CEM 3] Merged with Our Lady of the Lakes, Portage, St. Catherine, Washburn, Holy Rosary, Caribou, Sacred Heart, Caribou, St. Joseph, Mars Hill, St. Denis, Fort Fairfield, St. Louis, Limestone, St. Therese, Stockholm & Nativity of the Blessed Virgin Mary, Presque Isle to form Parish of the Precious Blood, Caribou.

AUBURN, ANDROSCOGGIN CO.

1—IMMACULATE HEART OF MARY PARISH (2008) Revs. Richard C. McLaughlin; Brendan G. Harnett, Parochial Vicar; Sr. Elizabeth A. Platt, C.O.C., Pastoral Assoc.; Deacon Denis Mailhot. In Res., Rev. James J. Morrison (Retired); Rev. Msgr. Andrew Dubois.
Mailing Address, Res. & Office: *Parish Center*, 24 Sacred Heart Pl., 04210-4938. Tel: 207-782-8096; 207-786-8577 (Res.); Fax: 207-782-9032.
Worship Sites:—
Sacred Heart Church—8 Sacred Heart Pl., 04210.
St. Louis Church—80 Third St., 04210.
St. Philip's Church—2365 Turner Rd., 04210.
Catechesis/Religious Program—Tel: 207-786-9045. Sandra Tardiff, D.R.E. Students 132.

2—ST. LOUIS (1902) Merged See Immaculate Heart of Mary Parish, Auburn.

3—ST. PHILIP'S (1968) Merged See Immaculate Heart of Mary Parish, Auburn.

4—SACRED HEART (1923) Merged See Immaculate Heart of Mary Parish, Auburn.

AUGUSTA, KENNEBEC CO.

1—ST. ANDREW'S (1968) Merged with St. Augustine's, Augusta, St. Mary of the Assumption, Augusta, St. Joseph's, Gardiner and St. Denis, Whitefield to form St. Michael Parish, Augusta.

2—ST. AUGUSTINE'S (1888) [CEM 2] Merged with St. Andrew's, Augusta, St. Mary of the Assumption, Augusta, St. Joseph's, Gardiner and St. Denis, Whitefield to form St. Michael Parish, Augusta.

3—ST. MARY OF THE ASSUMPTION (1834) [CEM 2] Merged with St. Andrew's Augusta, St. Augustine's, Augusta, St. Joseph's, Gardiner and St. Denis, Whitefield to form St. Michael Parish, Augusta.

4—ST. MICHAEL PARISH (2007) Revs. Francis P. Morin, Admin.; Ralph J. Boisvert, Parochial Vicar; William F. Modlin, Parochial Vicar.
Office & Mailing Address: 41 Western Ave., 04330-6324. Tel: 207-623-8823; Fax: 207-623-7574.
Res.: 1 Lincoln Ave., Gardiner, 04345-2133. Tel: 207-582-2385.
Worship Sites:—
St. Andrew Church—20 Andrew St., 04330.
St. Augustine Church—24 Washington St., 04330.
St. Mary of the Assumption Church—41 Western Ave., 04330.
St. Joseph Church—1 Lincoln St., Gardiner, 04345.
St. Stanislaus Church—Rte. 202, North Monmouth, 04265. (use summer only)
St. Leo Church—Rte. 126, Litchfield, 04350.
St. Denis Church—298 Grand Army Rd., Whitefield, 04353.
St. Francis Xavier Church—130 Rte. 133, Winthrop, 04364.
School—(Grades PreK-8), 56 Sewall St., 04330-7327. Tel: 207-623-3491; Fax: 207-623-2971. Jonathan Caron, Prin. Lay Teachers 25; Students 300.
Catechesis/Religious Program—Tel: 207-623-8823. Students 280.

BAILEYVILLE, WASHINGTON CO., ST. JAMES THE GREATER (1905) Merged See Blessed Kateri Tekakwitha Parish, Calais.

BANGOR, PENOBSCOT CO.

1—ST. JOHN'S (1856) Merged with St. Mary, Bangor, St. Joseph, Brewer, St. Teresa, Brewer, St. Matthew, Hampden & St. Gabriel, Winterport to form Saint Paul the Apostle Parish, Bangor.

2—ST. MARY (1872) Merged with St. John, Bangor, St. Joseph, Brewer, St. Teresa, Brewer, St. Matthew, Hampden & St. Gabriel, Winterport to form Saint Paul the Apostle Parish, Bangor.

3—SAINT PAUL THE APOSTLE PARISH (2009) Revs. Timothy J. Nadeau, Admin.; Seamus P. Griesbach, Parochial Vicar; Kent R. Ouellette, Parochial Vicar; Mr. Andre Vigneault, Pastoral Assoc. In Res., Revs. Roland P. Nadeau, Chap.; Apolinary Kavishe, A.J., Chap.
Office, Rectory & Mailing Address: 207 York St., 04401-5442. Tel: 207-942-6941; 207-942-9393; Fax: 207-947-5982.
Res.: 521 N. Main St., Brewer, 04412-1219. Tel: 207-989-5388; Fax: 207-989-5343.
Worship Sites:—
St. John Church—207 York St., 04401-5442.
St. Mary Church—768 Ohio St., 04401-3106.
St. Joseph Church—521 N. Main St., Brewer, 04412-1219.
St. Theresa Church—440 S. Main St., Brewer, 04412-2327.
St. Matthew Church—70 Western Ave., Hampden, 04444-1427.
St. Gabriel Church—Winterport, 04496.
See Trinity Catholic School under Prince of Peace Parish, Lewiston
School—All Saints Catholic School, (Grades K-8), P.O. Box 1749, 04401-1749. Tel: 207-947-7063; Fax: 207-942-2398. Web: allsaintsmaine.org. Marcia Diamond, Prin. St. Mary's and St. John's Campuses. Lay Teachers 26; Students 229.
School—St. Mary's Campus, (Grades PreK-2), 768 Ohio St., 04401-3165. Tel: 207-947-7063; Fax: 207-942-7356.
School—St. John's Campus, (Grades 3-8), 166 State St., 04401-5320. Tel: 207-947-0955; Fax: 207-942-2398.
Catechesis/Religious Program—Tel: 207-945-0023. Joan Winstead, D.R.E. Students 472.

BAR HARBOR, HANCOCK CO., HOLY REDEEMER (1907) [CEM] Rev. John O'Hara.
Res.: 21 Ledgelawn Ave., 04609-1303. Tel: 207-288-3535. Email: holyredeemer1@roadrunner.com. Web: www.mdicatholic.com.
Catechesis/Religious Program—Tel: 207-288-3535. Students 28.

BATH, SAGADAHOC CO.

1—ALL SAINTS PARISH Revs. Frank J. Murray, Admin.; Normand E. Carpentier, Parochial Vicar; Frederick Morse, Parochial Vicar.
Office & Mailing Address: 144 Lincoln St., 04530-2198. Tel: 207-443-3423; Fax: 207-443-5692.
Worship Sites:—
St. Mary Church—144 Lincoln St., 04530-2198.
St. Charles Church—132 McKeen St., Brunswick, 04011-2980. Tel: 207-725-2634; Fax: 207-725-4436.
St. John the Baptist Church—39 Pleasant St., Brunswick, 04011-2279.
Our Lady Queen of Peace Church—82 Atlantic Ave., Boothbay Harbor, 04538-2129. Tel: 207-633-2680; Fax: 207-633-2611.
St. Patrick Church—Academy Hill Rd., Newcastle, 04553-3473. Tel: 207-563-6038; Fax: 207-563-3218.
St. Ambrose Church—27 Kimball St., Richmond, 04357-1106. Tel: 207-737-4713; Fax: 207-737-4713.
St. Katharine Drexel Church—Harpswell, 04079.
St. Andrew—Rte. 196, Pejepscot, Topsham Co. 04086.
School—St. John's School, (Grades PreK-8), 37 Pleasant St., Brunswick, 04011-2279. Tel: 207-725-5507; Fax: 207-782-5968. Mrs. Andree Tostevin, Prin. Lay Teachers 20; Students 195.
Catechesis/Religious Program—Tel: 207-725-2624. Amy Ford, D.R.E. Students 165.

2—ST. MARY (1849) Merged with St. Charles, Brunswick; St. John the Baptist, Brunswick; Our Lady Queen of Peace, Boothbay Harbor; St. Patrick, Newcastle; St. Ambrose, Richmond; St. Katharine Drexel, Harpswell & St. Andrew, Topsham to form All Saints Parish, Bath.

BELFAST, WALDO CO., ST. FRANCIS OF ASSISI (1891) Merged with St. Mary of the Isles, Isleboro, Our Lady of Good Hope, Camden, Our Lady of Peace, North Haven, St. Bernard, Rockland & St. James, Thomaston to form Saint Brendan the Navigator Parish, Camden.

BENEDICTA, AROOSTOOK CO., ST. BENEDICT'S (1834) [CEM] Rev. Joel R. Cyr; Deacon Danny Watson.
Mailing Address: P.O. Box 27, 04733-0024. Tel: 207-365-4294; Fax: 207-365-7378.
Catechesis/Religious Program—Tel: 207-365-4269. Anna Robinson, D.R.E. Students 23.

BERWICK, YORK CO.

1—OUR LADY OF PEACE (1927) Merged with St. Michael, South Berwick to form Our Lady of the Angels, South Berwick. For inquiries for parish records contact Our Lady of the Angels.

2—OUR LADY OF THE ANGELS, Worships at Our Lady of Peace Church, Berwick. Revs. John R. Skehan; Joseph W. Cahill, Parochial Vicar; Deacon Roger M. Normand, Pastoral Assoc.
Mailing Address: P.O. Box 993, 03901-0993.
Office: 25 Saw Mill Hill, 03901. Tel: 207-698-1072; Fax: 207-698-5207. Email: berwicksangels@myfairpoint.net.
Worship Site:—
Our Lady of Peace Church—25 Saw Mill Hill, 03901.
Catechesis/Religious Program—Students 118.

BIDDEFORD, YORK CO.

1—ST. ANDRE'S (1899) [JC] Merged See Good Shepherd Parish, Saco.

2—ST. JOSEPH'S (1870) Merged See Good Shepherd Parish, Saco.

3—ST. MARY'S (1855) [CEM] Merged See Good Shepherd Parish, Saco.

BINGHAM, SOMERSET CO., ST. PETER'S (1920) Merged with St. Sebastian, Madison and Notre Dame de Lourdes, Skowhegan to form Christ the King Parish, Skowhegan.

BOOTHBAY HARBOR, LINCOLN CO., OUR LADY, QUEEN OF PEACE (1928) Merged with St. Mary, Bath; St. Charles, Brunswick; St. John the Baptist, Brunswick; St. Patrick, Newcastle; St. Ambrose, Richmond; St. Katharine Drexel, Harpswell & St. Andrew, Topsham to form All Saints Parish, Bath.

BRADLEY, PENOBSCOT CO., ST. ANN (1934) [JC] Merged See Parish of the Resurrection of the Lord, Old Town.

BREWER, PENOBSCOT CO.

1—ST. JOSEPH'S (1926) [JC] Merged with St. John, Bangor, St. Mary, Bangor, St. Teresa, Brewer, St. Matthew, Hampden & St. Gabriel, Winterport to form Saint Paul the Apostle Parish, Bangor.

2—ST. TERESA'S (1894) Merged with St. John, Bangor, St. Mary, Bangor, St. Joseph, Brewer, St. Matthew, Hampden & St. Gabriel, Winterport to form Saint Paul the Apostle Parish, Bangor.

BRIDGTON, CUMBERLAND CO., ST. JOSEPH (1971) Revs. Joseph J. Koury, Admin.; Brian D. Blanchette, Parochial Vicar.
Mailing Address: P.O. Box 310, 04009-0310.
Res.: 174 S. High St., 04009. Tel: 207-647-2334.
Church: 225 S. High St., 04009.
Catechesis/Religious Program—Tel: 207-647-8651. Students 79.
Mission—St. Elizabeth Ann Seton 857 Main St., P.O. Box 332, Fryeburg, Oxford Co. 04037-0332. Tel: 207-935-4245.

BRUNSWICK, CUMBERLAND CO.

1—ST. CHARLES (1930) Merged with St. Mary, Bath; St. John the Baptist, Brunswick; Our Lady Queen of Peace, Boothbay Harbor; St. Patrick, Newcastle; St. Ambrose, Richmond; St. Katharine Drexel, Harpswell & St. Andrew, Topsham to form All Saints Parish, Bath.

2—ST. JOHN THE BAPTIST (1877) [CEM] Merged with St. Mary, Bath; St. Charles, Brunswick; Our Lady Queen of Peace, Boothbay Harbor; St. Patrick, Newcastle; St. Ambrose, Richmond; St. Katharine Drexel, Harpswell & St. Andrew, Topsham to form All Saints Parish, Bath.

BUCKSPORT, HANCOCK CO., ST. VINCENT DE PAUL (1892) [CEM] Merged See Stella Maris Parish, Ellsworth.

CALAIS, WASHINGTON CO.

1—BLESSED KATERI TEKAKWITHA PARISH Revs. James S. Plourde, Admin.; Eugene F. Gaffey, Parochial Vicar; Sr. Janice Murphy, R.S.M., Pastoral Assoc. Tel: 207-853-2944.
Mailing Address: P.O. Box 898, 04619-0898.
Res. & Office: 31 Calais Ave., 04619. Tel: 207-454-0680; Fax: 207-454-0081.
Worship Sites:—
Immaculate Conception Church—31 Calais Ave., 04619.
St. Ann Church—Peter Dana Point Rd., Indian Twp, 04668.
St. Ann Sipayik Church—126 Bayview Dr., Perry, 04667.
St. James the Greater Church—56 Summit St., Baileyville, 04694.
St. John the Evangelist Church—39 Hersey Ln., Pembroke, 04666.
St. Joseph Church—51 Washington St., Eastport, 04631.
Catechesis/Religious Program—Tel: 207-827-2377. Students 108.

2—IMMACULATE CONCEPTION (1859) Merged See Blessed Kateri Tekakwitha Parish, Calais.

CAMDEN, KNOX CO.

1—SAINT BRENDAN THE NAVIGATOR PARISH (2009) Rev. Mark S. Reinhardt, Admin.
Res. & Office: 7 Union St., 04843-2015. Tel: 207-236-4785; Fax: 207-236-9422.
Worship Sites:—
St. Francis of Assisi Church—81 Court St., Belfast, 04915-6134.
St. Mary of the Isles—Islesboro, 04848.
Our Lady of Good Hope Church—
Our Lady of Peace Church—North Haven, 04853.
St. Bernard Church—150 Broadway, Rockland, 04841-2698.
St. James Church—Thomaston-0486.
Catechesis/Religious Program—Students 201.

2—OUR LADY OF GOOD HOPE (1967) Merged with St. Francis of Assisi, Belfast, St. Mary of the Isles, Isleboro, Our Lady of Peace, North Haven, St. Bernard, Rockland & St. James, Thomaston to form Saint Brendan the Navigator Parish, Camden.

CAPE ELIZABETH, CUMBERLAND CO., ST. BARTHOLOMEW (1968) Rev. Msgrs. Michael J. Henchal; Paul F. Stefanko, Parochial Vicar.
Res.: 150 Block Point Rd., Scarborough, 04074-4349. Church: 8 Two Lights Rd., 04107-2624. Tel: 207-799-5528; Fax: 207-799-2161. Web: www.saintbarts.com.
Catechesis/Religious Program—Students 109.

CARIBOU, AROOSTOOK CO.
1—HOLY ROSARY (1896) Merged wtih St. Mark, Ashland; Our Lady of the Lakes, Portage; St. Catherine, Washburn; Sacred Heart, Caribou; St. Joseph, Mars Hill; St. Denis, Fort Fairfield; St. Louis, Limestone; St. Therese, Stockholm & Nativity of the Blessed Virgin Mary, Presque Isle to form Parish of the Precious Blood, Caribou.
2—PARISH OF THE PRECIOUS BLOOD (2009) Very Rev. Jean-Paul Labrie; Revs. Aaron L. Damboise, Parochial Vicar; Raymond P. Morency, Parochial Vicar.
Mailing Address: P.O. Box 625, 04736-0625.
Res. & Office: 31 Calais Ave., Calais, 04619-1721. Tel: 207-454-0680; Fax: 207-454-0081.
Worship Sites:—
St. Mark's Church—Allen Farm Rd., Ashland, 04732.
Our Lady of the Lakes—Portage, 04768.
St. Catherine—Washburn, 04786.
Holy Rosary Church—31 Thomas Ave., 04736-1721.
Sacred Heart Church—1143 Van Buren Rd., 04736-3527.
St. Joseph Church—117 Main St., Mars Hill, 04758-0000.
St. Denis Church—143 Main St., Fort Fairfield, 04742-1223.
St. Louis Church—100 Main St., Limestone, 04750-1116.
St. Therese Church—Stockholm, 04783-0000.
Nativity of the Blessed Virgin Mary Church—6 Roberts St., Presque Isle, 04769-0813.
Catechesis/Religious Program—Students 92.
3—SACRED HEART (1881) Merged with St. Mark, Ashland; Our Lady of the Lakes, Portage; St. Catherine, Washburn; Holy Rosary, Caribou; St. Joseph, Mars Hill; St. Denis, Fort Fairfield; St. Louis, Limestone; St. Therese, Stockholm & Nativity of the Blessed Virgin Mary, Presque Isle to form Parish of the Precious Blood, Caribou.

DAIGLE, AROOSTOOK CO., HOLY FAMILY, Closed. For inquiries for parish records please contact St. John Vianney Parish, Fort Kent

DEXTER, PENOBSCOT CO.
1—ST. ANNE'S (1893) Merged with St. Thomas Aquinas, Dover-Foxcroft and St. Francis Xavier, Milo to form Our Lady of the Snows Parish, Dover-Foxcroft.
2—OUR LADY OF THE SNOWS PARISH (2007) Rev. Mark P. Nolette, Admin.; Deacon Frederick J. Harrigan.
Mailing Address: P.O Box 193, 04930-0193.
Office: 60 Face St., 04930. Tel: 207-924-7993; Fax: 207-924-7100. Email: olofthesnows@portlanddiocese.org. Web: www.ourladyofthesnowsme.org.
Res.: 238 Detroit St., Pittsfield, 04967. Tel: 207-487-2777.
Worship Sites:—
St. Anne Church—59 Free St., 04930.
St. Thomas Aquinas Church—45 High St., Dover Foxcroft, 04426.
Sts. Francis & Paul the Apostle Church—128 Riverside St., Milo, 04463.
Catechesis/Religious Program—Students 91.

DOVER-FOXCROFT, PISCATAQUIS CO., ST. THOMAS AQUINAS (1898) Merged with St. Anne's, Dexter and St. Francis Xavier, Milo to form Our Lady of the Snows Parish, Dover-Foxcroft.

EAGLE LAKE, AROOSTOOK CO., ST. MARY'S (1892) [CEM] Merged with St. Louis, Fort Kent, St. Charles, St. Francis and St. Joseph's, Wallagrass to form St. John Vianney Parish, Fort Kent.

EAST MILLINOCKET, PENOBSCOT CO.
1—CHRIST THE DIVINE MERCY PARISH (2007) Rev. Joel R. Cyr; Deacon Daniel Watson.
Mailing Address: P.O Box 400, 04430-0400.
Office: 56 Center St., P.O. Box 400, 04430-0400. Tel: 207-723-5902; 207-746-3333; Fax: 207-746-8188; 207-723-6395.
Res.: 58 Cedar St., 04430-1031.
Worship Sites:—
St. Peter's Church—56 Cedar St., 04430.
St. Martin of Tours Church—Colby St., Millinocket, 04462.
Catechesis/Religious Program—Julie Fiske, D.R.E. Students 45.
2—ST. PETER'S (1907) Merged with St. Martin of Tours, Millinocket to form Christ the Divine Mercy Parish, East Millinocket.

EASTPORT, WASHINGTON CO., ST. JOSEPH (1828) [JC] Merged See Blessed Kateri Tekakwitha Parish, Calais., P.O. Box 369, Baileyville, 04694-0369.

ELLSWORTH, HANCOCK CO.
1—ST. JOSEPH (1862) [CEM] Revs. Scott M. Mower, Admin.; Bruce Siket, Parochial Vicar.
Res.: 231 Main St., 04605-1613. Tel: 207-667-2342; Fax: 207-667-2043. Email: stjosephoffice@choiceonemail.com.
Catechesis/Religious Program—Students 54.
Mission—Our Lady of the Lake Green Lake, Hancock Co.
Mission—St. Margaret Winter Harbor, Hancock Co.
2—STELLA MARIS PARISH (2008) Revs. Scott M. Mower, Admin.; Bruce Siket, Parochial Vicar.
Res.: 60 Franklin St., P.O. Box S, Bucksport, 04416-1219. Tel: 207-469-3322.
Office: 231 Main St., 04605-1613. Tel: 207-667-2342; Fax: 207-667-2043.
Worship Sites:—
Our Lady of Hope Church—137 Perkins St., Castine, 04421. Tel: 207-326-8228.
St. Mary Star of the Sea—8 Granite St., Stonington, 04681. Tel: 207-367-2343.
St. Vincent de Paul—64 Franklin St., Bucksport, 04416.
Catechesis/Religious Program—Students 26.

FAIRFIELD, SOMERSET CO., IMMACULATE HEART OF MARY (1871) Merged with St. Bridget's, North Vassalboro, St. Theresa, Oakland, Parish of the Holy Spirit, Waterville, Notre Dame, Waterville, Sacred Heart, Waterville and St. John the Baptist, Winslow to form Corpus Christi Parish, Waterville.

FALMOUTH, CUMBERLAND CO., HOLY MARTYRS (1968) Rev. Msgr. J. Joseph Ford, Admin.; Deacon Dennis J. Popadak.
Office & Mailing Address: 266 Foreside Rd., 04105-1792. Tel: 207-781-4573; Fax: 207-781-3961. Email: rectory@holymartyrs.org. Web: www.holymartyrs.org.
Catechesis/Religious Program—266 Foreside Rd., 04105-1792. Tel: 207-781-2847; Fax: 207-781-3961. Students 196.

FARMINGTON, FRANKLIN CO., ST. JOSEPH'S (1885) Rev. Thomas Lequin.
Mailing Address: 133 Middle St., 04938-1598. Tel: 207-778-2778; Fax: 207-778-0268. Email: stjoefarm@myfairpoint.net.
Res.: 1 Church St., Jay, 04239-1801. Tel: 207-897-2173.
Catechesis/Religious Program—Claire Andrews, D.R.E. Students 42.

FORT FAIRFIELD, AROOSTOOK CO., ST. DENIS (1894) [CEM 2] Merged St. Mark's, Ashland; Our Lady of the Lakes, Portage; St. Catherine, Washburn; Holy Rosary, Caribou; Sacred Heart, Caribou; St. Joseph, Mars Hill; St. Louis, Limestone; St. Therese, Stockholm & Nativity of the Blessed Virgin Mary, Presque Isle to form Parish of the Precious Blood, Caribou.

FORT KENT, AROOSTOOK CO.
1—ST. JOHN VIANNEY PARISH (2007) Rev. James L. Nadeau; Joshua Houde, Pastoral Assoc.
Office & Res.: 26 E. Main St., 04743-1395. Tel: 207-834-5656; Fax: 207-834-7461. Email: stlouis@myfairpoint.net.
Worship Sites:—
St. Mary Church—3443 Aroostock Rd., Eagle Lake, 04739.
St. Louis Church—26 E. Main St., 04743.
St. Charles Church—912 Main St., St. Francis, 04774.
St. Joseph Church—7 Church St., Wallagrass, 04781.
Catechesis/Religious Program—Phyllis Pelletier, D.R.E. K-8; Carolyn Bouchard, Youth Min. 9-12. Students 428.
2—ST. LOUIS (1870) [CEM 3] Merged with St. Mary's, Eagle Lake, St. Charles, St. Francis and St. Joseph's, Wallagrass to form St. John Vianney Parish, Fort Kent.

FRENCHVILLE, AROOSTOOK CO., ST. LUCE'S (1843) [CEM] Merged with St. Joseph, Sinclair & St. Agatha, St. Agatha to form Our Lady of the Valley, St. Agatha.

GARDINER, KENNEBEC CO., ST. JOSEPH'S (1863) [CEM] Merged with St. Andrew's, Augusta, St. Augustine's, Augusta, St. Mary of the Assumption, Gardiner and St. Denis, Whitefield to form St. Michael Parish, Augusta.

GORHAM, CUMBERLAND CO., ST. ANNE (1967) Rev. Lawrence Conley.
Res.: 299 Main St., 04038-1307. Tel: 207-839-4857; Fax: 207-839-3082. Email: stannegorham@aol.com. Web: www.stannegorham.com.
Catechesis/Religious Program—Tel: 207-839-3082. Sr. Jackie Moreau, R.S.M., D.R.E. Students 169.
Mission—Our Lady of Sebago East Sebago, Cumberland Co.

GRAND ISLE, AROOSTOOK CO., ST. GERARD-MT. CARMEL (1930) [CEM] Merged with St. David's, Madawaska and St. Thomas Aquinas, Madawaska to form Notre Dame du Mont Carmel Parish, Madawaska.

GRAY, CUMBERLAND CO., ST. GREGORY (1967) Rev. Msgr. J. Joseph Ford, Admin.; Deacon Dennis J. Popadak.
Res.: 24 N. Raymond Rd., P.O. Box 345, 04039-0345. Tel: 207-657-4241. Email: stgregorychurch@main.rr.com.
Catechesis/Religious Program—Tel: 207-657-5659. Students 98.

GREENVILLE, PISCATAQUIS CO., HOLY FAMILY (1916) Very Rev. Richard C. Malo.
Office, Mailing & Res. Address: 145 Pritham Ave., P.O. Box 457, 04441-0457. Tel: 207-695-2262.
Catechesis/Religious Program—Tel: 207-695-2009. Lucy Fay, D.R.E. Students 3.
Mission—St. Joseph's [CEM] Rockwood, Somerset Co.

HALLOWELL, KENNEBEC CO., SACRED HEART (1878) Rev. George W. Hickey.
Res.: 12 Summer St., 04347-1121. Tel: 207-623-3424; Fax: 207-623-3424.
Catechesis/Religious Program—Parish Hall, 5 Summer St., 04347-1121. Tel: 207-623-3807. Karen Jones, D.R.E.; Terri Trott, D.R.E. Students 50.

HAMLIN, AROOSTOOK CO., ST. JOSEPH (1920) [CEM] Merged with St. Bruno-St. Remi, Van Buren to form Saint Peter Chanel Parish, Van Buren.

HAMPDEN, PENOBSCOT CO., ST. MATTHEW (1968) Merged with St. John, Bangor, St. Mary, Bangor, St. Joseph, Brewer, St. Teresa, Brewer & St. Gabriel, Winterport to form Saint Paul the Apostle Parish, Bangor.

HOULTON, AROOSTOOK CO., ST. MARY OF THE VISITATION (1839) Rev. David R. Raymond; Deacon Albert Burleigh.
Res.: 112 Military St., 04730-2507. Tel: 207-532-2871; Fax: 207-532-4401. Email: stmaryvisitation@portlanddiocese.org.
Catechesis/Religious Program—Tel: 207-532-0953. Students 87.

HOWLAND, PENOBSCOT CO., ST. LEO THE GREAT (1945) [CEM] Revs. Roger Cyr, O.M.I.; Leroy Landry, O.M.I., Parochial Vicar.
Mailing Address: P.O. Box 329, 04448-0329. Tel: 207-732-3495.
Rectory—18 River Rd., 04448.
Catechesis/Religious Program—Tel: 207-732-3495. Students 24.

INDIAN TOWNSHIP, WASHINGTON CO., ST. ANN (1929), (Native American), Merged See Blessed Kateri Tekakwitha Parish, Calais.

ISLAND FALLS, AROOSTOOK CO., ST. AGNES (1920) [CEM] Rev. David R. Raymond; Deacon Albert Burleigh.
Office & Mailing Address: 112 Military St., Houlton, 04730. Tel: 207-532-2871; Fax: 207-532-4401.
Church: Sewall St., 04747. Tel: 207-463-2210.
Catechesis/Religious Program—Tel: 207-528-2737. Students 10.
Mission—St. Paul 34 Katahdin St., Patten, Penobscot Co. 04765.

JACKMAN, SOMERSET CO., ST. ANTHONY (1892) [CEM] Very Rev. Richard C. Malo.
Mailing Address: P.O. Box 338, 04945-0338.
Res.: 145 Pritham Ave., Greenville, 04441. Tel: 207-695-2262.
Church: 336 Main St., 04945-5213. Tel: 207-668-2881.
Catechesis/Religious Program—Students 11.

JAY, FRANKLIN CO., ST. ROSE OF LIMA (1894) Rev. Thomas Lequin.
Office, Mailing Address & Res.: One Church St., 04239-1801. Tel: 207-897-2173; Fax: 207-897-2478. Email: saintrose@myfairpoint.net.
Catechesis/Religious Program—Tel: 207-897-2173. Students 90.

KENNEBUNK, YORK CO., ST. MARTHA'S (1909) Merged See Holy Spirit Parish, Wells.

KITTERY, YORK CO., ST. RAPHAEL'S (1916) Revs. John R. Skehan, Admin.; Joseph W. Cahill, Parochial Vicar.
Parish Center & Mailing Address: 6 Whipple Rd., 03904-1758. Tel: 207-439-0442; Fax: 207-439-0442. Email: saintraphaels@comcast.net.
Catechesis/Religious Program—Faith Formation Office Students 78.

LEWISTON, ANDROSCOGGIN CO.
1—HOLY CROSS (1923) [JC] Merged See Prince of Peach Parish, Lewiston.
2—HOLY FAMILY (1923) Merged See Prince of Peace Parish, Lewiston.
3—ST. JOSEPH'S (1857) [JC] Merged See Prince of Peace Parish, Lewiston.
4—ST. MARY'S, Closed. For inquiries for parish records contact Prince of Peace Parish, Lewiston.
5—ST. PATRICK'S (1887) [CEM] Merged See Prince of Peach Parish, Lewiston.
6—SS. PETER AND PAUL BASILICA (1870) Merged See Prince of Peace Parish, Lewiston.
7—PRINCE OF PEACE PARISH (2009) Rev. Msgr. Marc B. Caron; Revs. Nathan D. March, Parochial Vicar; Joseph E. Daniels, Parochial Vicar.

Mailing Address: P.O. Box 1540, 04241-1540. In Res., Revs. Paul M. Pare (Retired); Maurice N. Morin (Retired); Soosai Antonyian; Pichaimuthu Antonydass.
Catholic Center—16 St. Croix St., P.O. Box 1540, 04241-1540. Tel: 207-777-1200; Fax: 207-786-9223. Res.: 607 Sabattus St., 04240-4193.
Worship Sites:—
Basilica of Ss. Peter & Paul—27 Bartlett St., 04240.
Holy Cross Church—1080 Lisbon St., 04240.
Holy Family Church—607 Sabattus St., 04240.
School—Trinity Catholic School, (Grades PreK-8), Elementary Campus: 17 Baird St., 04240-5001. Tel: 207-783-9323; Fax: 207-783-9491. Junior High Campus: 396 Main St., 04240. Tel: 207-784-8811; Fax: 207-783-9522. Web: www.trinitycatholic.us. Paul Yarnevich, Prin. Sisters 1; Lay Teachers 20; Students 418.
Catechesis/Religious Program—Donald Smith, Dir. Faith Formation. Students 249.

LIMERICK, YORK CO., ST. MATTHEW (1921) Rev. Albert B. Colpitts, Admin.; Deacon Paul Lissandrello.
Res.: 19 Dora Ln., 04048-3527. Tel: 207-793-2244; Fax: 207-793-2191. Email: st.matthew19@roadrunner.com. Web: www.stmatthewlimerick.org.
Catechesis/Religious Program—Students 192.

LIMESTONE, AROOSTOOK CO., ST. LOUIS, Merged with St. Mark, Ashland; Our Lady of the Lakes, Portage; St. Catherine, Washburn; Holy Rosary, Caribou; Sacred Heart, Caribou; St. Joseph, Mars Hill; St. Denis, Fort Fairfield; St. Therese, Stockholm & Nativity of the Blessed Virgin Mary, Presque Isle to form Parish of the Precious Blood, Caribou.

LINCOLN, PENOBSCOT CO., ST. MARY (1902) Revs. Roger Cyr, O.M.I., Admin.; Myles Cyr, O.M.I., Parochial Vicar.
Res.: 164 Main St., P.O. Box 310, 04457-0310. Tel: 207-794-6333; Fax: 207-794-8044.
Catechesis/Religious Program—Students 43.
Mission—St. James Kingman, Penobscot Co.
Mission—Sacred Heart Winn, Penobscot Co.
Mission—St. Ann Danforth, Washington Co. Tel: 207-448-2959; Fax: 207-448-2959.
Mission—Guardian Angel Vanceboro, Washington Co.

LISBON FALLS, ANDROSCOGGIN CO.
1—SS. CYRIL AND METHODIUS, (Slovak), Merged with St. Anne's and Holy Family to form Holy Trinity, Lisbon Falls.
2—HOLY TRINITY (1995) [CEM 3] Rev. Lionel G. Chouinard, Admin.
Res.: 7 Highland Ave., 04252-1105.
Church & Office: 67 Frost Hill Ave., 04252-1126. Tel: 207-353-2792 (Office); Fax: 207-353-6192. Email: holytrinity@portlanddiocese.org. Web: www.portlanddiocese.org.
Catechesis/Religious Program—Students 65.

LISBON, ANDROSCOGGIN CO., ST. ANNE'S, Merged with Holy Family and SS. Cyril and Methodius to form Holy Trinity, Lisbon Falls.

LUBEC, WASHINGTON CO., SACRED HEART (1913) Merged See Saint Peter the Fisherman Parish, Machias.

LYMAN, YORK CO., ST. PHILIP (1981) [JC] Rev. James P. Brewer, Admin.
Res.: 404 Goodwins Mills Rd., 04002-5739. Tel: 207-499-2940; Fax: 207-499-7666. Email: frbrewer.stphilip@myfairpoint.net. Web: www.stphiliplyman.org.
Catechesis/Religious Program—Tel: 207-284-3736. Edith Forst, D.R.E. Students 90.

MACHIAS, WASHINGTON CO.
1—HOLY NAME OF JESUS (1828) Merged See Saint Peter the Fisherman Parish, Machias.
2—SAINT PETER THE FISHERMAN PARISH (2008) Revs. James S. Plourde, Admin.; Eugene F. Gaffey, Parochial Vicar; Deacon James J. Gillen, Business Mgr.
Mailing Address: P.O. Box 248, 04654-0248.
Office & Res.: 11 Free St., 04654. Tel: 207-733-2214.
Worship Sites:—
Holy Name of Jesus Church—10 Free St., 04654.
Sacred Heart Church—14 Hamilton St., Lubec, 04652.
St. Michael Church—Elm St., Cherryfield, 04622.
Catechesis/Religious Program—

MADAWASKA, AROOSTOOK CO.
1—ST. DAVID'S (1872) [CEM] Merged with St. Gerard-Mt. Carmel, Grand Isle and St. Thomas Aquinas, Madawaska to form Notre Dame du Mont Carmel Parish, Madawaska.
2—NOTRE DAME DU MONT CARMEL PARISH (2007) Revs. James R. Albert, Admin.; David P. Cote, Parochial Vicar; Deacon Donald R. Clavette.
Mailing Address: P.O. Box 128, 04756-0128. In Res., Rev. Msgr. Leopold G. Nicknair (Retired).
Office: 337 Thomas St., 04756. Tel: 207-728-7531; Fax: 207-728-4217.
Res.: 774 Main St., 04756. Tel: 207-728-3366.
Worship Sites:—
St. Gerard-Mt. Carmel Church—361 Main St., Grand Isle, 04746.
St. Thomas Aquinas Church—337 Thomas St., 04756.
St. David Church—774 Main St., 04756. Tel: 207-728-6472.
Catechesis/Religious Program—Tel: 207-728-7135. Ann Marie Clavette, D.R.E. Students 172.
3—ST. THOMAS AQUINAS (1929) [CEM] Merged with St Gerard-Mt. Carmel, Grand Isle and St. David's, Madawaska to form Notre Dame du Mont Carmel Parish, Madawaska.

MADISON, SOMERSET CO., ST. SEBASTIAN (1907) [CEM] Merged with St. Peter's, Bingham and Notre Dame De Lourdes to form Christ the King Parish, Skowhegan.

MARS HILL, AROOSTOOK CO., ST. JOSEPH (1927) Merged with St. Mark, Ashland; Our Lady of the Lakes, Portage; St. Catherine, Washburn; Holy Rosary, Caribou; Sacred Heart, Caribou; St. Denis, Fort Fairfield; St. Louis, Limestone; St. Therese, Stockholm & Nativity of Blessed Virgin Mary, Presque Isle to form Parish of Precious Blood, Caribou.

MECHANIC FALLS, ANDROSCOGGIN CO., OUR LADY OF RANSOM (1931) Merged See Blessed Teresa of Calcutta Parish, Norway.

MEXICO, OXFORD CO., ST. THERESA (1926) [JC] Merged See Parish of the Holy Savior, Rumford.

MILLINOCKET, PENOBSCOT CO., ST. MARTIN OF TOURS (1899) Merged with St. Peter's, East Millinocket to form Christ the Divine Mercy Parish, East Millinocket.

MILO, PISCATAQUIS CO., ST. FRANCIS XAVIER (1929) Merged with St. Anne's, Dexter and St. Thomas Aquinas, Dover-Foxcroft to form Our Lady of the Snows Parish, Dover-Foxcroft.

NEWCASTLE, LINCOLN CO., ST. PATRICK (1796) [CEM] Merged with St. Mary, Bath; St. Charles, Brunswick; St. John the Baptist, Brunswick; Our Lady Queen of Peace, Boothbay Harbor; St. Ambrose, Richmond; St. Katharine Drexel, Harpswell & St. Andrew, Topsham to form All Saints Parish, Bath.

NORTH VASSALBORO, KENNEBEC CO., ST. BRIDGET'S (1911) Merged with Immaculate Heart of Mary, Fairfield, St. Theresa, Oakland, Parish of the Holy Spirit, Waterville, Notre Dame, Waterville, Sacred Heart, Waterville and St. John the Baptist, Winslow to form Corpus Christi Parish, Waterville.

NORTHEAST HARBOR, HANCOCK CO., ST. IGNATIUS (1929) Rev. John O'Hara; Deacon Joseph LaPlante. Parish Center: 436 Seawall Rd., 04679. Tel: 207-244-0445. Email: holyredeemer@roadrunner.com. Web: www.mdicatholics.com.
Res. & Mailing Address: 21 Ledgelawn Ave., Bar Harbor, 04609-1303. Tel: 207-288-3535; Fax: 207-288-3324.
Church: 8 Lookout Way, 04679.
Catechesis/Religious Program—Joint program with Holy Redeemer Parish, Bar Harbor. Students 3.
Mission—Our Lady Star of the Sea Islesford, Hancock Co.
Mission—St. Peter's Manset, Hancock Co.

NORWAY, OXFORD CO.
1—BLESSED TERESA OF CALCUTTA PARISH (2008) Revs. Richard C. McLaughlin; Brendan G. Harnett, Parochial Vicar; Michael J. Seavey, Parochial Vicar.
Mailing Address, Office & Res.: 32 Paris St., 04268. Tel: 207-743-2606.
Worship Sites:—
Our Lady of Ransom Church—117 Elm St., Mechanic Falls, 04256.
St. Catherine of Sienna Church—32 Paris St., 04268.
St. Mary Church—276 King St., Oxford, 04270.
Catechesis/Religious Program—Sherry Turmel, D.R.E. Tel: 207-743-2213; Rose Vining, D.R.E.; Robert Rose, D.R.E. Students 102.
2—ST. CATHERINE OF SIENNA (1914) Merged See Blessed Teresa of Calcutta Parish, Norway.

OAKLAND, KENNEBEC CO., ST. THERESA (1963) Merged with Immaculate Heart of Mary, Fairfield, St. Bridget's, North Vassalboro, Parish of the Holy Spirit, Waterville, Notre Dame, Waterville, Sacred Heart, Waterville and St. John the Baptist, Winslow to form Corpus Christi Parish, Waterville.

OLD ORCHARD BEACH, YORK CO., ST. MARGARET'S (1926) Rev. David Schlaver, C.S.C. In Res., Rev. Coleman P. O'Toole.
Res.: 6 Saco Ave., P.O. Box 289, 04064-0289. Tel: 207-934-2322; Fax: 207-934-8322. Email: stmargaretoob@portlanddiocese.org. Web: www.sacobayweb.com/stmoob/index.htm.
Catechesis/Religious Program—Tel: 207-934-4232. Students 97.
Chapel—Old Orchard, St. Luke's

OLD TOWN, PENOBSCOT CO.
1—ST. ANN CHURCH, INDIAN ISLAND (1688), (Native American), Merged See Parish of the Resurrection of the Lord, Old Town.
2—HOLY FAMILY (1992) [JC] Merged See Parish of the Resurrection of the Lord, Old Town.
3—ST. JOSEPH'S, Closed. All records at Parish of the Resurrection of the Lord, Old Town.
4—ST. MARY'S, Closed. All records at Parish of the Resurrection of the Lord, Old Town.
5—PARISH OF THE RESURRECTION OF THE LORD (2009) Revs. Wilfred P. Labbe; Thomas F. Farley, Parochial Vicar.
Office & Res.: 429 Main St., 04468-1718. Tel: 207-827-4000; Fax: 207-827-2113.
Worship Sites:—
St. Ann Church—84 Main St., Bradley, 04411.
St. Ann Church—6 Down St., Indian Island, 04468.
Holy Family Church—429 Main St., 04468.
Our Lady of Wisdom Newman Center Chapel—83 College Ave., Orono, 04473.
Catechesis/Religious Program—Tel: 207-827-2377. Students 80.

OQUOSSOC, FRANKLIN CO., OUR LADY OF THE LAKES (1927) Rev. Paul A. Plante, Admin.
Mailing Address: P.O. Box 333, 04964-0333.
Res.: 43 Rangeley Ave., 04964-0333. Tel: 207-864-3795.
Catechesis/Religious Program—Students 22.
Mission—St. Luke Rangeley, Franklin Co.
Mission—St. John Stratton, Franklin Co.
Mission—Richard H. Bell Memorial Chapel Sugarloaf U.S.A., Franklin Co.

ORONO, PENOBSCOT CO.
1—ST. MARY'S (1888) [JC] Merged See Parish of the Resurrection of the Lord, Old Town.
2—OUR LADY OF WISDOM PERSONAL CAMPUS PARISH (1946) Merged See Parish of the Resurrection of the Lord, Old Town.

PERRY, WASHINGTON CO., ST. ANN (Pleasant Point) (1907), (Native American), Merged See Blessed Kateri Tekakwitha Parish, Calais.

PITTSFIELD, SOMERSET CO., ST. AGNES (1909) Rev. Mark P. Nolette, Admin.
P.O. Box 193, Dexter, 04930-0193.
Res.: 238 Detroit St., 04967. Tel: 207-487-2777. Email: cluster7@portlanddiocese.org. Web: www.ourladyofthesnowsme.org.
Office: 60 Free St., Dexter, 04930. Tel: 207-924-7104; Fax: 207-924-7993.
Church: 238 Detroit St., 04967.
Catechesis/Religious Program—Students 38.

PRESQUE ISLE, AROOSTOOK CO., NATIVITY OF B.V.M. (1895) [CEM 2] Merged with St. Mark's, Ashland; Our Lady of the Lakes, Portage; St. Catherine, Washburn; Holy Rosary, Caribou; Sacred Heart, Caribou; St. Joseph, Mars Hill; St. Denis, Fort Fairfield; St. Louis, Limestone & St. Therese to form Parish of the Precious Blood, Caribou.

RICHMOND, SAGADAHOC CO., ST. AMBROSE (1866) Merged with St. Mary, Bath; St. Charles, Brunswick; St. John the Baptist, Brunswick; Our Lady Queen of Peace, Boothbay Harbor; St. Patrick, Newcastle; St. Katharine Drexel, Harpswell & St. Andrew, Topsham to form All Saints Parish, Bath.

ROCKLAND, KNOX CO., ST. BERNARD'S (1857) [CEM 2] Merged with St. Francis of Assisi, Belfast; St. Mary of the Isles, Isleboro; Our Lady of Good Hope, Camden; Our Lady of Peace, North Haven & St. James, Thomaston to form Saint Brendan the Navigator Parish, Camden.

RUMFORD, OXFORD CO.
1—ST. ATHANASIUS-ST. JOHN (1906) [JC] Merged See Parish of the Holy Savior, Rumford.
2—PARISH OF THE HOLY SAVIOR (2008) Rev. Msgr. Andrew Dubois, Admin.; Rev. Alfred Jacques, Sacramental Min. (Retired).
Office: 126 Maine Ave., 04276-2259. Tel: 207-364-4556; Fax: 207-364-2686.
Res.: 7 Brown St., Mexico, 04257.
Worship Sites:—
St. Athanasius & St. John Church—126 Maine Ave., 04276.
Our Lady of the Snows Church—32 Paris Rd., Bethel, 04217. Tel: 207-824-2933.
School—(Grades PreK-8), 115 Maine Ave., 04276-2208. Tel: 207-364-2528. Barbara Pelletier, Prin. Lay Teachers 6; Students 54.
Catechesis/Religious Program—Mary Madigan, P.C.L. Students 88.

ST. AGATHA, AROOSTOOK CO.
1—ST. AGATHA'S (1889) Merged with St. Luce, Frenchville & St. Joseph, Sinclair to form Our Lady of the Valley, St. Agatha.
2—OUR LADY OF THE VALLEY (2006), Worships at St. Luce Church, Frenchville, St. Agatha Church, St. Agatha & St. Joseph Church, Sinclair. Rev. L. Philip Cyr.
Mailing Address: P.O. Box 10, 04772-6161.
Res.: 379 Main St., 04772-6161. Tel: 207-543-7447; Fax: 207-543-6019. Email: stajl@sjv.net.
Catechesis/Religious Program—Tel: 207-543-7366; Fax: 207-543-6193. Vicki Pelletier, D.R.E. Students 157.
Mission—St. Michael's Chapel [CEM 2] Birch Point

Rd., Madawaska, Aroostook Co. 04756.
ST. FRANCIS, AROOSTOOK CO., ST. CHARLES (1894) [CEM 4] Merged with St. Mary's, Eagle Lake, St. Louis, Fort Kent and St. Joseph's, Wallagrass to form St. John Vianney Parish, Fort Kent.
ST. JOHN, AROOSTOOK CO., ST. JOHN, Merged with St. Mary's, Eagle Lake, St. Louis, Fort Kent, St. Charles, St. Francis and St. Joseph's, Wallagrass to form St. John Vianney Parish, Fort Kent.
SABATTUS, ANDROSCOGGIN CO., OUR LADY OF THE ROSARY (1975) Rev. Lionel G. Chouinard, Admin.
Res.: 131 High St., 04280-4250. Tel: 207-375-6951; Fax: 207-375-4135. Email: olrparish@portlanddiocese.org.
Catechesis/Religious Program—Tel: 207-375-6581. Students 43.
Mission—St. Francis Greene, Androscoggin Co. Tel: 207-946-5758.
SACO, YORK CO.
1—GOOD SHEPHERD PARISH (2008) Rev. Msgr. Rene T. Mathieu, Admin.; Revs. Gregory P. Dube, Parochial Vicar; Robert L. Lupo, Parochial Vicar; Sr. Angela L. Fortier, C.S.J., Parish Life Coord.; Deacons Kevin N. Jacques; Robert M. Parenteau.
271 Main St., 04072-1510.
Pastoral Center: 41 Sullivan St., Biddeford, 04005-2618. Tel: 207-282-4812; Fax: 207-286-8679.
Bus. Office: 217 Main St., 04072-1510. Tel: 207-282-3321; Fax: 207-284-2274. Email: goodshepherd@portlanddiocese.org. Web: www.portlanddiocese.net/goodshepherd.
Res.: 43 Center St., Biddeford, 04005.
Worship Sites:—
St. Andre's Church—73 Bacon St., Biddeford, 04005.
St. Brendan Church—Lester B. Orcutt Blvd., Biddeford, 04005.
St. Joseph's Church—178 Elm St., Biddeford, 04005.
Most Holy Trinity Church—271 Main St., 04072.
School—St. James School, (Grades PreK-8), 25 Graham St., Biddeford, 04005-3297. Tel: 207-282-4084; Fax: 207-286-3693. Ms. Patricia Berthiaume, Prin. Lay Teachers 19; Students 225.
School—Notre Dame de Lourdes, (Grades PreK-8), 50 Beach St., 04072-2892. Tel: 207-283-3111; Fax: 207-286-2750. Email: ndschool@maine.rr.com. Ms. Patricia Berthiaume, Prin. Lay Teachers 10; Students 73.
Catechesis/Religious Program—Students 170.
2—MOST HOLY TRINITY (1916) Merged See Good Shepherd Parish, Saco.
3—NOTRE DAME DE LOURDES (1929) [JC] Merged See Good Shepherd Parish, Saco.
SANFORD, YORK CO.
1—HOLY FAMILY (1923) [JC] Merged with St. Ignatius Martyr, Sanford and Notre Dame, Springvale to form Saint Therese of Lisieux Parish, Sanford.
2—ST. IGNATIUS MARTYR (1892) [CEM] Merged with Holy Family, Sanford and Notre Dame, Springvale to form Saint Therese of Lisieux Parish, Sanford.
3—SAINT THERESE OF LISIEUX PARISH (2007) Rev. Robert D. Lariviere, Admin.; Gerald Coutu, Pastoral Assoc.
Worship Sites:—
Holy Family Church—66 North Ave., 04073.
St. Ignatius Martyr Church—10 St. Ignatius St., 04073.
Notre Dame Church—10 Payne St., Springvale, 04083.
Office: *Pastoral Center*, 66 North Ave., 04073-2997. Tel: 207-324-2420; Fax: 207-324-6630.
Res.: 10 Payne St., Springvale, 04083-1312. Tel: 207-324-6041.
School—St. Thomas Consolidated School, (Grades PreK-6) Tel: 207-324-5832; Fax: 207-324-2549. Web: www.saintthomassanford.org. Norman Provost, Prin. Lay Teachers 14; Students 158.
Catechesis/Religious Program—Shelly Carpenter, D.R.E. Students 134.
SCARBOROUGH, CUMBERLAND CO., ST. MAXIMILIAN KOLBE (1988) Rev. Msgrs. Michael J. Henchal; Paul F. Stefanko, Parochial Vicar.
Mailing Address: P.O. Box 57, 04070-0057.
Church, Res. & Parish Offices: 150 Black Point Rd., 04070-9349. Tel: 207-883-0334; Fax: 207-883-4246. Email: stmax@maine.rr.com. Web: www.saintmax.com.
Catechesis/Religious Program—Tel: 207-883-1742. Email: stmaxre@maine.rr.com. Kathy Sparda, D.R.E. Students 384.
SINCLAIR, AROOSTOOK CO., ST. JOSEPH (1936) [CEM] Merged with St. Luce, Frenchville & St. Agatha, St. Agatha to form Our Lady of the Valley, St. Agatha.
SKOWHEGAN, SOMERSET CO.
1—CHRIST THE KING PARISH (2007) Revs. Philip A. Tracy, Admin.; John C. Mazzei, Parochial Vicar.
P.O. Box 369, 04976-0369.
Worship Sites:—
St. Peter Church—Owens St., Bingham, 04920. Tel: 207-672-3912.
St. Sebastian Church—161 Main St., Madison, 04950. Tel: 207-696-3203.
Notre Dame Church—273 Water St., 04976.
Office & Res.: 273 Water St., 04976. Tel: 207-474-2039; Fax: 207-474-2039.
Catechesis/Religious Program—Students 75.
2—NOTRE DAME DE LOURDES (1881) [CEM] Merged with St. Peter's, Bingham and St. Sebastian, Madison to form Christ the King Parish, Skowhegan.
SOUTH BERWICK, YORK CO., ST. MICHAEL (1886) [CEM] Merged with Our Lady of Peace, Berwick to form Our Lady of the Angels, South Berwick. For inquiries for parish records contact Our Lady of the Angels.
SOUTH PORTLAND, CUMBERLAND CO.
1—CHURCH OF THE HOLY CROSS (1913) Rev. Msgrs. Michael J. Henchal; Paul F. Stefanko, Parochial Vicar.
124 Cottage Rd., 04116-3716.
Parish Office—29 Aspen Ave., 04106-5328. Tel: 207-772-7489; Fax: 207-772-7480. Web: www.hcsj.org.
Res.: 150A Blackpoint Rd., Scarborough, 04074. Tel: 207-883-1783.
School—(Grades PreK-8), 436 Broadway, 04106-2996. Tel: 207-799-6661; Fax: 207-799-8345. Web: holycrossmaine.org. Sr. Theresa Rand, R.S.M., Prin. Sisters 1; Lay Teachers 16; Students 166.
Catechesis/Religious Program—Tel: 207-773-8710; Fax: 207-772-7480. Laurie Kelly, D.R.E. Joint Program with St. John the Evangelist, South Portland. Students 62.
2—ST. JOHN THE EVANGELIST (1940) Rev. Msgrs. Michael J. Henchal; Paul F. Stefanko, Parochial Vicar.
Office: 29 Aspen Ave., 04106-5328. Tel: 207-772-7489; Fax: 207-772-7480. Web: www.hcsj.org.
Church: 611 Main St., 04106.
Catechesis/Religious Program—Joint Program with Holy Cross, South Portland., Tel: 207-773-8710; Fax: 207-772-7480. Twinned with Holy Cross, South Portland. Students 58.
SPRINGVALE, YORK CO., NOTRE DAME (1887) [CEM] Merged with Holy Family Sanford and St. Ignatius Martyr, Sanford to form Saint Therese of Lisieux Parish, Sanford.
STOCKHOLM, AROOSTOOK CO., ST. THERESE (1926) Merged with St. Mark's, Ashland; Our Lady of the Lakes, Portage; St. Catherine, Washburn; Holy Rosary, Caribou; Sacred Heart, Caribou; St. Joseph, Mars Hill; St. Denis, Fort Fairfield; St. Louis, Limestone & Nativity of the Blessed Virgin Mary to form Parish of the Precious Blood, Caribou.
STONINGTON, HANCOCK CO., ST. MARY STAR OF THE SEA (1931) Merged See Stella Maris Parish, Ellsworth.
VAN BUREN, AROOSTOOK CO.
1—ST. BRUNO - ST. REMI (1991) [CEM] Merged with St. Joseph, Hamlin to form Saint Peter Chanel Parish, Van Buren.
2—SAINT PETER CHANEL PARISH (2007) Revs. James R. Albert, Admin.; David P. Cote, Parochial Vicar.
Office: 174 Main St., 04785-1237. Tel: 207-868-2718.
Worship Sites:—
St. Joseph Church—Hamlin, 04785.
St. Bruno-St. Remi Church—174 Main St., 04785.
Catechesis/Religious Program—Students 151.
3—ST. REMI (1923) Closed. See listing for Saint Peter Chanel Parish, Van Buren.
WALLAGRASS, AROOSTOOK CO., ST. JOSEPH'S (1890) [CEM 3] Merged with St. Mary's, Eagle Lake, St. Louis, Fort Kent and St. Charles, St. Francis to form St. John Vianney Parish, Fort Kent.
WATERVILLE, KENNEBEC CO.
1—CORPUS CHRISTI PARISH (2007) Revs. Philip A. Tracy, Admin.; Daniel Baillargeon, Parochial Vicar; Paul G. Murray, Parochial Vicar; Paul G. Murray, Parochial Vicar.
Office: 70 Pleasant St., 04901-5405. Tel: 207-872-2281; Fax: 207-877-0675. Web: www.corpuschristimaine.org.
Res.: 72 Pleasant St., 04901.
Worship Sites:—
Immaculate Heart of Mary—21 High St., Fairfield, 04937.
St. Bridget Church—Main St., North Vassalboro, 04962.
Saint Theresa Church—35 Church St., Oakland, 04963.
Notre Dame Church—112 Silver St., 04901.
Sacred Heart Church—72 Pleasant St., 04901.
St. Francis de Sales Church—52 Elm St., 04901.
St. John Church—26 Monument St., Winslow, 04901.
Mission—St. Helena Belgrade Lakes, 04918. (Summers only)
School—St. John Regional Catholic School, (Grades PreK-5), 15 S. Garand St., Winslow, 04901. Tel: 207-872-7115; Fax: 207-872-2500. Mrs. Valerie Wheeler, Prin. Lay Teachers 9; Students 90.
Catechesis/Religious Program—26 Monument St., Winslow, 04901. Tel: 207-872-2373; Fax: 207-872-2264. Kimberly Suttie, Parish Life Coord. Students 184.
2—NOTRE DAME, Merged with Immaculate Heart of Mary, Fairfield, St. Bridget's, North Vassalboro, St. Theresa, Oakland, Parish of the Holy Spirit, Waterville and St. John the Baptist, Winslow to form Corpus Christi Parish, Waterville.
3—PARISH OF THE HOLY SPIRIT (1996) [JC] Merged with Immaculatge Heart of Mary, Fairfield, St. Bridget's, North Vassalboro, St. Theresa, Oakland, Notre Dame, Waterville, Sacred Heart, Waterville and St. John the Baptist, Winslow to form Corpus Christi Parish, Waterville.
4—SACRED HEART, Merged with Immaculate Heart of Mary, Fairfield, St. Bridget's, North Vassalboro, St. Theresa, Oakland, Parish of the Holy Spirit, Waterville, Notre Dame, Waterville and St. John the Baptist, Winslow to form Corpus Christi Parish, Waterville.
WELLS, YORK CO.
1—HOLY SPIRIT PARISH (2008) Rev. Thomas M. Murphy, Admin.; Deacon Darrell Blackwell.
Office & Res.: 236 Eldridge Rd., 04090-4050. Tel: 207-646-5605; Fax: 207-646-9437.
Worship Sites:—
St. Martha Church—30 Portland Rd., Kennebunk, 04043-6631. Tel: 207-985-6252; Fax: 207-985-7740.
St. Mary Church—236 Eldridge Rd., 04090-4050.
Mission—All Saints Church 45 School St., Ogunquit, 03907.
Catechesis/Religious Program—Mrs. Rosanne Smith, D.R.E. Students 376.
2—ST. MARY (1970) Merged See Holy Spirit Parish, Wells.
WESTBROOK, CUMBERLAND CO.
1—ST. ANTHONY OF PADUA PARISH (2005) Rev. Reginald R. Brissette, Admin.
Res., Office & Mailing Address: 63 Dana Ct., 04092-2912. Tel: 207-857-0490; Fax: 207-857-0494. Email: stanthonyparish@myfairpoint.net. Web: www.stanthonysparish.org.
Catechesis/Religious Program—Students 105.
2—ST. EDMUND (Prides Corner) (1975) Merged with St. Hyacinth, Westbrook and St. Mary's, Westbrook to from St. Anthony of Padua, Westbrook.
3—ST. HYACINTH (1892) [CEM] Merged with St. Edmund, Westbrook and St. Mary's, Westbrook to form St. Anthony of Padua, Westbrook.
4—ST. MARY'S (1920) [JC] Merged with St. Edmund, Westbrook and St. Hyacinth, Westbrook to form St. Anthony of Padua, Westbrook.
WHITEFIELD, LINCOLN CO., ST. DENIS (1818) [CEM] Merged with St. Andrew's, Augusta, St. Augustine's, Augusta, St. Mary of the Assumption, Augusta and St. Joseph's, Gardiner to form St. Michael Parish, Augusta.
WILTON, FRANKLIN CO., ST. MARY, Closed. All records at St. Joseph, Farmington.
WINDHAM, CUMBERLAND CO., OUR LADY OF PERPETUAL HELP (1974) Revs. Joseph J. Koury, Admin.; Brian D. Blanchette, Parochial Vicar; Deacons Peter J. Bernier; Frank Chambers.
Res.: 919 Roosevelt Tr., 04062-5641. Tel: 207-892-8288; Fax: 207-893-1072. Web: www.ourlady.com.
Catechesis/Religious Program—Students 143.
Mission—St. Raymond Chapel 584 Webbs Mill Rd., Raymond, Cumberland Co. 04071. Tel: 207-892-8288.
WINSLOW, KENNEBEC CO., ST. JOHN THE BAPTIST (1926) [JC] Merged with Immaculate Heart of Mary, Fairfield, St. Bridget's, North Vassalboro, St. Theresa, Oakland, Notre Dame, Waterville, Sacred Heart, Waterville and Parish of the Holy Spirit, Waterville to form Corpus Christi Parish, Waterville.
WINTERPORT, WALDO CO., ST. GABRIEL (1850) Merged with St. John, Bangor; St. Mary, Bangor; St. Joseph, Brewer; St. Teresa, Brewer & St. Matthew, Hampden to form Saint Paul the Apostle Parish, Bangor.
WINTHROP, KENNEBEC CO., ST. FRANCIS XAVIER (1910) [JC] Merged See St. Michael Parish, Augusta.
YARMOUTH, CUMBERLAND CO., SACRED HEART (1876) [CEM] Rev. Raymond Picard, Admin.; Cherie Piper, Pastoral Assoc.
Res.: 326 Main St., 04096-7933. Tel: 207-846-5584; Fax: 207-846-6003. Email: rectory@sheartparish.org. Web: www.sheartparish.org.
Catechesis/Religious Program—Ann Peacock, D.R.E.; Debra Gagnon, D.R.E. Students 370.
Mission—St. Jude's Freeport, Cumberland Co.
YORK HARBOR, YORK CO., ST. CHRISTOPHER-BY-THE-SEA (1947) Revs. John R. Skehan; Joseph W. Cahill, Parochial Vicar; Deacon Roger M. Normand, Pastoral Assoc.
Res.: One Lilac Ln., 03909-1020. Tel: 207-363-2111; Fax: 207-363-1586. Email: rstchris@maine.rr.com. Web: www.stchristopheryork.com.

Catechesis/Religious Program—Tel: 207-363-4177; Fax: 207-363-8934. Rose Cronin, D.R.E. Students 234.
Mission—Star of the Sea York Beach, York Co.

Chaplains of Public Institutions

PORTLAND. *St. Joseph's Manor*, Tel: 207-797-0600. Rev. Joseph R. McKenna (Retired), Sr. Judith McNamara, R.S.M., Pastoral Care.
Maine Medical Center, Tel: 207-871-0111. Revs. Alfred E. Irving, Chap., Paul R. Marquis, Chap.
Mercy Hospital, Tel: 207-879-3358. Rev. Joseph Schad, S.J., Chap., Sr. Patricia Mooney, R.S.M., Pastoral Care.

AUGUSTA. *Augusta Mental Health Institute*, Tel: 207-289-7334. Served by the staff of St. Michael Parish, Augusta.
Maine General Medical Center, Tel: 207-626-1000. Served by the staff of St. Michael Parish, Augusta.
Togus VA Medical Center, Togus. Tel: 207-623-8411, Ext. 5176. Rev. Raymond R. Lagacé, O.F.M.

BANGOR. *Eastern Maine Medical Center*, Tel: 207-943-7000. Rev. Apolinary Kavishe, A.J. Taylor Hospital, Bangor Convalescent Center,
St. Joseph's Hospital, Tel: 207-262-1798. Rev. Roland P. Nadeau, Sr. Mary Edmund, C.S.S.F., Pastoral Assoc.

BIDDEFORD. *Southern Maine Medical Center*, Tel: 207-283-3663. Served by Good Shepherd Parish, Biddleford.

LEWISTON. *Central Maine Medical Center*, Tel: 207-795-0111. Mr. Michael B. Tyne, Pastoral Care, Rev. Donald Gagne, S.M.
St. Mary's Regional Medical Center. Rev. D. Joseph Manship, Sr. Suzanne Beaudoin, S.S.Ch.
Campus Ave., P.O. Box 291, 04243-0291. Tel: 207-777-8520. Sr. Madeline Normand, P.M., Mr. Kenneth Rancort.

SOUTH PORTLAND. *Maine Youth Center*. Vacant.

WARREN. *Maine State Prison*, Thomaston. Tel: 207-828-4921. Deacon Frederick J. Harrigan.
Super Maximum Facility & Minimum Facility, Tel: 207-273-5300. Deacon Frederick J. Harrigan.

WATERVILLE. *Mid-Maine Medical Center*, Tel: 207-872-1000. Margaret Crowell, Deacon Peter Joseph.

Special or Other Diocesan Assignment:
Rev. Msgr.—
Dubois, Andrew, V.G., P.O. Box 11559, 04104-7559. Tel: 207-773-6471. Res.: St. Phillip Rectory, 2365 Turner Rd., Auburn, 04210-8437. Tel: 207-689-2281
Revs.—
Bouchard, Robert P., P.O. Box 11559, 04104-7559.
Cote, Paul E., P.O. Box 11559, 04104-7559.
Gendreau, Claude R., P.O. Box 11559, 04104-7559.
Gendreau, Michael P., P.O. Box 11559, 04104-7559.
Greenleaf, Daniel P., Theological College, 401 Michigan Ave., N.E., Washington, DC 20017-1518.
LaBree, Paul, P.O. Box 11559, 04104-7559.
Michaud, James L., P.O. Box 5296, Ellsworth, 04605-5296.
Morin, Eddy, P.O. Box 129, Saint David, 04773-0129.
Vaillancourt, Robert C., Res.: 16 SteCroix St., Lewiston, 04240.

Military Chaplains:
Rev.—
Welch, Bernard J., Brunswick Naval Station, 901 Fitch Ave., Brunswick, 04011-5000. Tel: 207-921-2223; 207-921-2231

Retired:
Rev. Msgrs.—
Begin, Raymond F., S.T.L., J.C.D., Winter, 4951 Summer Tree Rd., Venice, FL 34293-4254. Tel: 941-493-6869. Summer, 19 Northwood Dr., Windham, 04062-5306. Tel: 207-892-0771
Gleason, Paul D., Bishop Peterson House, 221 Orange St., Manchester, NH 03104-4324. Tel: 603-641-1012
Goudreau, Joseph L., 3704 2nd St., Arlington, VA 22204-1604. Tel: 703-696-3532
Lavoie, Robert G., Mt. St. Joseph Home, 7 Highwood St., #6, 04901-5740. Tel: 207-660-6096
Murphy, Charles M., S.T.D., V.F., P.O. Box 378, Kennebunkport, 04046-0378. Tel: 207-967-3788
Nicknair, Leopold G., St. David Rectory, 774 Main St., Madawaska, 04756-3103. Tel: 207-728-3366
Tatarczuk, Vincent A., P.O. Box 218, Raymond, 04071-0218. Tel: 207-655-3672
Revs.—
Albert, Claude J., 32 Portland Rd., Kennebunk, 04043-6631. Tel: 207-641-3311
Amato, Antonio, Mallview Terrace, 27A Marston St., Apt. 311, Lewiston, 04240-6171. Tel: 207-795-5095
Andrus, Albin A., St. Patrick Rectory, 1342 Congress St., 04102-2117. Tel: 207-879-0827
Arps, Joseph W., Jr., 126 Jillian Way, Glenburn, 04401-1243. Tel: 207-941-8888
Auger, Raymond D., 4675 Appletree Cir., Apt. A, Boynton Beach, FL 33436-1231. Tel: 752-561-0417
Austin, John J., Sunbury Village, 922 Ohio St., Apt. 237, Bangor, 04401-3097. Tel: 207-576-8721
Bill, J. Armand, 402A Sandpiper Dr., Fort Pierce, FL 34982-5122. Tel: 561-467-1011
Cameron, Hilary J., St. Catherine's Hall, 242 Walton St., Apt. 103, 04103-3381. Tel: 207-899-3329
Caron, Antonin R., 79 Fairlawn Ave., Lewiston, 04240-4132.
Chabot, Roger P., Winter: 123A S.W. 19th Ave., Fort Lauderdale, FL 33312. Summer: 58 Larry Dr., Monmouth, 04259. Tel: 207-513-6218
Chouinard, Marcel G., Mt. St. Joseph Home, 7 Highwood St., 04901-5739. Tel: 207-873-7653
Clogan, Paul M., P.O. Box 828428, Austin, TX 78755-8428.
Concannon, Stephen F., Our Lady Miraculous Medal, 289 Lafayette Rd., Hampton, NH 03842-2109. Tel: 603-926-2206
Connor, James E., St. Joseph Manor, Unit D, 1133 Washington Ave., 04103-3629. Tel: 207-797-0600
Coughlin, Paul E., P.O. Box 424, Springvale, 04083-0424.
Cyr, L. Chanel, St. Louis Rectory, 100 Main St., Limestone, 04750-1116. Tel: 207-325-3414
Davis, John P., 68 Webster Ave., Lewiston, 04240-6463. Tel: 207-784-6235
Dumoulin, Marcel L.
Feeney, John J., 175 A Pine St., 04102-3538. Tel: 207-780-1494
Girouard, Robert J., Winter: 10801 Bethel St., Port Richey, FL 34668-2604. Tel: 727-868-7313. Summer: 59 Libby Ave., #13, Gorham, 04038-1545. Tel: 207-839-3021
Goudreau, George W., P.O. Box 28, Rumford, 04276-0028. Tel: 207-364-7884
Gower, James M., Birch Bay Village, 27 Village Inn Rd., Apt. 222, Bar Harbor, 04609-1340. Tel: 207-288-0906
Jacques, Alfred, 137 W. Front St., Skowhegan, 04976-1165. Tel: 207-858-0362
Jacques, Donald W., Summer: 17 Lorisa Ln., Milford, NH 03055. Tel: 603-672-1981. Winter: 133 Lake Francis Dr., Lake Placid, FL 33852-6182. Tel: 863-465-3372
Knox, James, 31 Clearview Dr., Scarborough, 04074-8319. Tel: 207-883-9652
L'Heureux, Ernest L., 64 Lebonan St., Sanford, 04073-3825. Tel: 207-459-7090
Labarre, Renald D., 31 Beacon Ave., Biddeford, 04005-2917. Tel: 207-615-1378
Laplante, Laurent R., 27 Smithwheel Rd., Old Orchard Beach, 04064-1009. Tel: 207-934-5862
Lavoie, Rene G., 32 Portland Rd., Kennebunk, 04043-6631. Tel: 207-595-1985
Lebel, Maurice T., 64 Flintlock Village #64, Wells, 04090-5326. Tel: 207-641-8790
Lee, Thomas M.
Leveille, Rudolph J., 65 Juniper St., Bangor, 04401-4163. Tel: 207-942-9715
Levesque, Gerald A., 29 Patio Park Ln., Gorham, 04038-1561. Tel: 207-409-5445
Levesque, Sylvio J., 4 Choate Ln., Apt. 215, Hallowell, 04347-1469. Tel: 207-263-9231
MacDonough, Richard, S.S., St. John's Seminary, 647 Bluewater Way, Port Hueneme, CA 93041-3559.
Martel, C. James, 163 N. Parish Rd., Turner, 04282-0016. Tel: 207-225-3001
McAllister, Donald, Bishop Gendron Res., Apt. 3, 195 Dover Point Rd., Dover, NH 03820-4693. Tel: 603-742-2612
McCarthy, Richard C., St. Joseph Manor, B Wing, 1133 Washington Ave., 04103-3629. Tel: 207-797-0600
McGarrigle, Michael R., 76 Ward Cir., Brunswick, 04011-9343. Tel: 207-725-5764
McKenna, Joseph R., 100 State St., #321, 04101-3729. Tel: 207-775-1084
Moreshead, Harold D., St. Patrick Rectory, 1342 Congress St., 04102-2107. Tel: 207-828-8638
Morin, Maurice N., Holy Family Rectory, 607 Sabattus St., Lewiston, 04240-4193. Tel: 207-782-8928
Morrison, James J., Sacred Heart Rectory, P.O. Box 828, Auburn, 04212-0828.
Mulkern, Stephen M., 1258 Washington Ave., 04103-3649. Tel: 207-797-3519
Nadeau, Real J., P.O. Box 232, Moody, 04054-0232. Tel: 207-646-8709
Nadeau, Richard A., Deering Pavilion, 880 Forest Ave., Apt. 5-08, 04103-4128. Tel: 207-797-4629
Neault, Armand R., 54 Blacksmith Rd., #11, Wells, 04090-5748. Tel: 207-646-6417
Nguyen, Thanh, 115F Birchwood Dr., Apt. F, Bristol, CT 06010-2876. Tel: 860-585-6663
Nicknair, Harold W., (Winter), 5725 80th St. N., Unit #411, St. Petersburg, FL 33709-5836. Tel: 727-545-7876. (Summer), 757 Main St., #22, South Portland, 04106-5425. Tel: 207-828-8835
O'Donnell, Richard A., P.O. Box 172, Fryeburg, 04037-0172. Tel: 603-447-2021
Ouellette, Richard R., P.O. Box 154, Saint Francis, 04774-0154. Tel: 207-398-4475
Paquet, Hubert J., 46 Wentworth St., Biddeford, 04005-3153. Tel: 207-286-9674
Pare, Paul M., Holy Family Rectory, 607 Sabattus St., Lewiston, 04240-4193. Tel: 207-782-8728
Parent, Royal J., D'Youville Pavilion, 102 Campus Ave., Lewiston, 04240-6019. Tel: 207-777-4235
Patenaude, Gilbert A., 57 Oxford St., Augusta, 04330-4056. Tel: 207-622-3832
Pechillo, Arthur C., St. Francis Rectory, 130 Rte. 133, Winthrop, 04364-1356. Tel: 207-623-8823
Piselli, Costanzo J., 67 Village Green Dr., 04901-4444. Tel: 207-873-2961
Plante, Georges J., Mount St. Joseph Manor, 7 Highwood St., Apt. 9, 04901-5739. Tel: 207-873-2896
Poussard, Bertrand R., St. Joseph Manor, Unit D, 1133 Washington Ave., 04103-3629. Tel: 207-797-0600
Rice, Richard P., 66 Ward Cir., Brunswick, 04011-9342. Tel: 207-373-1832
Rokos, Richard V., 17105 Gull Blvd., Apt. 412, St. Petersburg, FL 33708. Tel: 727-394-2675
Rotunno, Anthony R., P.O. Box 183, Rockwood, 04478-0183. Tel: 207-534-8831
Roux, G. Albert, 944 Sabattus St., Lewiston, 04240-3712. Tel: 207-783-3590
Senghas, Richard E., 15 Piper Rd., Apt. J320, Scarborough, 04074-7555. Tel: 207-833-6394
Thibodeau, Clement D., 12 St. Anne Ave., Apt. C-6, Caribou, 04736-6131. Tel: 207-498-2037
Tracy, Philip Michael, 148 Breakwater Dr., #404, South Portland, 04106-1656. Tel: 207-767-6501

INSTITUTIONS LOCATED IN THE DIOCESE

[A] COLLEGES AND UNIVERSITIES

STANDISH. *Saint Joseph's College*, 278 Whites Bridge Rd., 04084-5263. Tel: 207-893-7711; Fax: 207-893-7867. Email: jlee@sjcme.edu. Web: www.sjcme.edu. Dr. Joseph Lee, Pres.; Dr. Randall Krieg, Vice Pres. for Academic Affairs & Dean of the College; Lynn Brown, Dean for Student Life; Sr. Mary George O'Toole, R.S.M., Vice Pres. for Sponsorship & Mission Integration; Deacon John McAuliffe Jr.; Philip Yauch, Vice Pres. & Chief Fin. Officer. Sisters 4; Deacons 1; Lay Professors 138; Graduate Students 853; Undergraduate Students 1,052; Undergraduate Students in Distance Education 786; Students 2,691.
Residential College Program Tel: 207-893-6641; Fax: 207-893-7861. Rachelle Davis, Dir. Library Svcs. Full-Time Enrollment 1,106; Part-Time Enrollment 1,585.

[B] HIGH SCHOOLS, REGIONAL

AUBURN. *St. Dominic Regional High School* (1941) 121 Gracelawn Rd., 04210-0452. Tel: 207-782-6911; Fax: 207-795-6439. Email: Donald.Fournier@PortlandDiocese.org. Web: www.st-dominic.net. Mr. Donald Fournier, Prin.; Peter Servidio, Librarian. Lay Teachers 24; Students 275.

[C] HIGH SCHOOLS, PRIVATE

PORTLAND. *Catherine McAuley High School* (1969) 631 Stevens Ave., 04103-2690. Tel: 207-797-3802; Fax: 207-797-3804. Email: sredwardmary@mcauleyhs.org. Sr. Edward Mary Kelleher, R.S.M., Prin.; Deidre Dupree, Librarian. Sisters of Mercy 2; Lay Teachers 27; Girls 205.
Cheverus High School (1917) 267 Ocean Ave., 04103-5798. Tel: 207-774-6238; Fax: 207-828-0207. Web: www.cheverus.org. Revs. William R. Campbell, S.J., Pres.; John A. Predmore, S.J., Mission & Identity; John H.R. Mullen, Prin. Faculty resides at St. Ignatius Residence. See separate listing for details. Priests 4; Brothers 1; Lay Teachers 45; Students 544.

[D] ELEMENTARY SCHOOLS, PRIVATE

WATERVILLE. *Mount Merici School* (1911) (Grades N-6), 152 Western Ave., 04901-5215. Tel: 207-873-3773; Fax: 207-873-6377. Email: info@mountmerici.org. Web: www.mountmerici.org. Susan H. Cote, Prin. Lay Teachers 13; Students 177.

[E] CATHOLIC CHARITIES MAINE, INC.

PORTLAND. *Catholic Charities Maine*, P.O. Box 10660, 04104-6060. 307 Congress St., 04101-3695. Tel: 207-781-8550; Fax: 207-781-8560. Web: www.ccmaine.org. Most Rev. Richard Joseph Malone, D.D., S.T.L., Th.D., Pres.; Mr. Stephen P. Letourneau, CEO; Ms. Constance Browning Jones, Human Resources Dir. Tel: 207-781-8550.

St. Elizabeth's Child Development Center, 87 High St., 04101-3811. Tel: 207-871-7444. P.O. Box 10660, 04104-6060.

St. Michael's Center, 1066 Kenduskeag Ave., Bangor, 04401-2914. Tel: 207-941-2855. Email: pvestal@ccmaine.org. Web: www.ccmaine.org. Mr. Paul K. Vestal Jr., Dir. St. Michael's Center provides Emergency Case Management and Home Based Family Services Therapy.

[F] SPECIAL RESIDENTIAL SERVICES

AUBURN. *St. Joseph Child Development Center*, c/o Catholic Charities Maine, P.O. Box 10660, 04104. Tel: 207-782-2711; Fax: 207-782-8741. Email: stjosephinfo@ccmaine.org. Ms. Michelle Cyr, Site Dir. Number Served 115.

BIDDEFORD. *St. Andre Home, Inc.*, Admin. Office, 283 Elm St., 04005-3093. Tel: 207-282-3351; Fax: 207-282-8733. Web: www.SaintAndreHome.org. Mr. Peter Fitzpatrick, Exec. Dir. Pregnant and Parenting Young Women, Adoption Services, Infant Foster Care Homes, Emergency Placement; Public Information-Education; Community Outreach Services; Residences in Biddeford, Lewiston, Bangor. Total Assisted Annually 1,031.

LEWISTON. **St. Martin de Porres Residence, Inc.*, Mailing Address: P.O. Box 7227, 04243-7227. 23 Bartlett St., 04243-7227. Tel: 207-786-4690; Fax: 207-786-8866. Email: smdporres02@aol.com. Bro. Irenee Richard, O.P., Exec. Dir.

[G] HOMES FOR THE AGED

PORTLAND. *Deering Pavilion Apartment House for Senior Citizens*, 880 Forest Ave., 04103. Tel: 207-797-8777; Fax: 207-797-8963. Email: deerpav@maine.rr.com. Web: www.deeringpavilion.com. Helen McGuinness, Exec. Dir. Apartments 200.

St. Joseph's Manor (1975) 1133 Washington Ave., 04103-3629. Tel: 207-797-0600; Fax: 207-797-4168. Web: www.saintjosephsmanor.org. Most Rev. Richard Joseph Malone, D.D., S.T.L., Th.D., Pres. Bed Capacity 165; Served 215; Total Staff 201.

AUGUSTA. *Roncalli Apartments, Inc.*, Mailing Address: P.O. Box 11559, 04104-7559. Tel: 207-773-6471, Ext. 7823. Green St., 04330. Mr. David P. Twomey Jr., CPA, Treas. Sponsored: Roman Catholic Diocese of Portland., Purpose: to provide very low and extremely low housing for the elderly in the capital city of the state.

BANGOR. *St. Xavier's Home*, P.O. Box 11559, 04104-7559. 119 Somerset St., 04401. Tel: 207-942-4815. Mr. David Twomey, Treas. & Contact Person. Units 18.

BIDDEFORD. *St. Andre Health Care & Facility*, 407 Pool St., 04005-9716. Tel: 207-282-5171; Fax: 207-282-5372. Email: aotis-higgins@standre.org. Web: standre.org. Andrea Otis-Higgins, CEO & Admin. Sponsored by Covenant Health Systems, Inc., Lexington, MA. Bed Capacity 96; Total Staff 150.

LEWISTON. **St. Marguerite d'Youville Pavilion*, 102 Campus Ave., 04240-6019. Tel: 207-777-4200; Fax: 207-777-4255. Email: dfournier@sochs.com. Web: www.stmarysmaine.com. Sr. Suzanne Beaudoin, S.S.Ch., Dir. Chaplaincy; Debra Fournier, Admin.; Rev. D. Joseph Manship, Chap.; Elizabeth Lowe, Chap. Sponsored by St. Mary's Health System. Bed Capacity 210; Total Staff 392; Total Assisted Annually 592.

St. Mary's Residence (Formerly: Maison Marcotte), 100 Campus Ave., 04240-6040. Tel: 207-786-0062; Fax: 207-777-8570. Web: www.stmarysmaine.com. Sponsored by St. Mary's Health System. Total in Residence 130.

WATERVILLE. *Mt. St. Joseph Holistic Care Community*, 7 Highwood St., 04901-5797. Tel: 207-873-0705; Fax: 207-873-6626. Email: msj@mtsj.org. Web: www.mtsj.org. Sr. Claire Labbee, C.S.J., Pastoral Care; Karen Fatz, Temp. Admin., 04901. Sisters of St. Joseph of Lyons, C.S.J. Assisted Living 27; Nursing Facility 111; Bed Capacity 138; Total Assisted Annually 165; Total Staff 250. In Res. Rev. Msgr. Robert G. Lavoie (Retired); Revs. Marcel G. Chouinard (Retired); Georges J. Plante (Retired).

Seton Village Inc., P.O. Box 11559, 04104-7559. 1 Carver St., 04901-5739. Tel: 207-873-0178; Fax: 207-873-1233. Most Rev. Richard Joseph Malone, D.D., S.T.L., Th.D., Bishop of Portland, Pres.; Mr. David P. Twomey Jr., CPA, Treas.; Mr. Harlan Cooper, Admin. Units 140; Guests 148.

[H] GENERAL HOSPITALS

PORTLAND. **Mercy Hospital*, 144 State St., 04101-3776. Tel: 207-879-3000; Fax: 207-879-3429. Web: www.mercyhospital.org. Ms. Eileen Skinner, Pres. & CEO; Rev. Joseph Schad, S.J., Chap.; Mr. James Corbett, Vice Pres. Mission Effectiveness. Lay Nurses (RN's and LPN's) 436; Bed Capacity 230; Emergency Visits 29,576; Inpatient Admissions 8,933; Outpatient Visits 254,442; Patients Assisted Annually 292,951; School of Radiology Students 20.

BANGOR. *St. Joseph Hospital*, 360 Broadway, 04401-3974. Tel: 207-262-1000; Fax: 207-262-1922. Email: sm.norberta@sjhhealth.com. Web: www.stjoeshealing.com. Sisters Barbara Theresa, C.S.S.F., Supr.; Mary Norberta, C.S.S.F., Pres. & CEO. Felician Sisters 5; Nursing Sisters 1; Lay Nurses 197; Bed Capacity 112; Total Staff 681; Patients Assisted Annually 80,184.

Pastoral Care Dept., 360 Broadway, 04401. Tel: 207-262-1798; Fax: 207-262-1922. Rev. Roland P. Nadeau; Judith Young, Dir. Pastoral Care.

BUCKSPORT. *Bridgewell, Inc.*, Box 836, 04416. Tel: 207-469-7616; Fax: 207-469-7616. Sr. Miriam Devlin, S.M.I.C., Contact Person. Health Care Research & Education.

LEWISTON. *St. Mary's Health System* (Formerly: Sisters of Charity Health System, Inc.), P.O. Box 7291, 04243-7291. Tel: 207-777-8802; Fax: 207-777-8800. Web: www.stmarysmaine.com. James E. Cassidy, Pres. & CEO. Sponsored by Covenant Health Systems, Lexington, MA.

St. Mary's Lifeline Tel: 207-777-8827; Fax: 207-777-8570. Serving 756.

St. Mary's Genesis House Tel: 207-783-7308; Fax: 207-783-1172. Residential Program for Adolescent Boys.

St. Mary's Renaissance House Tel: 207-753-5437; Fax: 207-753-5430. Residential Program for Adolescent Girls.

St. Mary's WorkMed Tel: 207-753-3080; Fax: 207-753-3088. Occupational Health Program.

St. Mary's Health Steps Tel: 207-777-8898; Fax: 207-777-3499.

St. Mary's Foundation Tel: 207-777-8863; Fax: 207-755-3380.

St. Mary's Maine Covenant Tel: 207-777-8553; Fax: 207-777-8562.

St. Mary's Take Charge Tel: 207-777-8898; Fax: 207-755-3499. Health screening programs.

St. Mary's Nutrition Center of Maine Tel: 207-513-3847; Fax: 207-782-7560. Nutrition services.

**St. Mary's Regional Medical Center* (1880) Campus Ave., P.O. Box 291, 04243-0291. Tel: 207-777-8802; Fax: 207-777-8800. Web: www.stmarysmaine.com. Lee Myles, CEO; Sisters Madeleine Normand, P.M., Chap.; Suzanne Beaudoin, S.S.Ch., Dir. & Chaplaincy Svcs.; Rev. Joseph Manship, Chap.; Kenneth Rancourt, Chap. Sponsored by St. Mary's Health System. Sisters 3; Nurses 284; LPN's 4; CNA's 113; Bed Capacity 171; Patients Assisted Annually 184,801; Total Staff 893.

Neighborhood Housing Initiative, Inc., P.O. Box 7291, 04243-7291. Tel: 207-777-8802; Fax: 207-777-8800. Web: www.stmarysmaine.com. James E. Cassidy, CEO. Sponsored by St. Mary's Health System.

[I] MONASTERIES AND RESIDENCES OF PRIESTS AND BROTHERS

PORTLAND. *St. Ignatius Residence (The Jesuits of Maine)*, 492 Ocean Ave., 04103-4936. Tel: 207-775-3032; Fax: 207-775-1229. Rev. James F. Lafontaine, S.J., Supr. Jesuit Fathers (New England Prov.). Priests 8.

ALFRED. *Notre Dame Institute*, 133 Shaker Hill Rd., P.O. Box 159, 04002-0159. Tel: 207-324-6612; Fax: 207-490-2370. Email: alfredfic@gwi.net. Bros. Jerome Lessard, F.I.C., Prov. Tel: 207-324-0067; David Denicourt, F.I.C., Supr. Tel: 207-324-6612; Rev. Theodore Letendre, F.I.C., Dir. Provincial House of Brothers of Christian Instruction. *Notre Dame Spiritual Center* Tel: 207-324-6160; Fax: 207-324-5044. Rev. Theodore Letendre, F.I.C. Tel: 207-324-1017. Brothers 14.

KENNEBUNK. *St. Anthony's Friary*, 28 Beach Ave., P.O. Box 980, Kennebunkport, 04046-0980. Tel: 207-967-2011; Fax: 207-967-5721. Email: johnbac@roadrunner.com. Web: www.framon.net. Most Rev. Paul A. Baltakis, O.F.M., Retired Bishop; Revs. Placid Barius, O.F.M., Delegate of Province; Gabriel Baltrusaitis, O.F.M.; John J. Bacevicius, O.F.M., Vicar & Pastoral Ministry; Andrew R. Bisson, O.F.M., Pastoral Ministry; Francis Giedgaudas, O.F.M.; Raimundas Bukauskas, O.F.M., Pastoral Ministry & Treasurer; Aurelijus Gricius, O.F.M., Guardian & Pastoral Ministry. Priests 8.

[J] CONVENTS AND RESIDENCES OF SISTERS

PORTLAND. *Frances Warde Convent*, 37 Capisic St., 04102-2203. Tel: 207-772-1140; Fax: 207-772-1873. Sr. Maura Murphy, R.S.M., Contact Person. Sisters 14.

Monastery of the Precious Blood (1934) 166 State St., 04101-3703. Tel: 207-774-0861; Fax: 207-774-3253. Sr. Mary Jo Divney, A.P.B., Supr. Adorers of the Precious Blood 4.

Sisters of Charity, 41 Tamarlane, 04103-4257. Tel: 207-773-8607; Fax: 207-874-6086.

Sisters of Mercy of the Americas, 84 Plymouth St., 04103-2005. Tel: 207-797-6957. Sr. Mary M. Morey, R.S.M., Contact Person. Sisters of Mercy of the Americas 2.

Sisters of Mercy of the Americas-Northeast Community, Life & Ministry Office: 605 Stevens Ave., 04103-2691. Tel: 207-797-7861; Fax: 207-797-0416. Sr. Maureen Wallace, R.S.M., Life & Ministry Admin.

ACTON. *The Sisters of the Presentation of Mary of Maine, Inc. Presentation Villa*, 246 Rte. 109, 04001. Tel: 603-669-1080. Email: tgagne@presmarynh.org. Web: www.presentationofmary.com. 495 Mammoth Rd., Manchester, NH 03104-5463. Sr. Theresa Gagne, P.M., Treas.

AUBURN. *Companions of Christ*, 503 Park Ave., 04210-8526. Tel: 207-784-5960. Email: elizabeth.platt@portlanddiocese.org. Sr. Elizabeth Platt, C.O.C., Contact Person. Sisters 2.

AUGUSTA. *St. Augustine*, 5 Kendall St., 04330. Tel: 207-622-2494; Fax: 207-261-4074. Sr. Rachel Boucher, P.M., Supr. Sisters of the Presentation of Mary. Sisters 2.

Sisters of Mercy of the Americas, 51 Sewall St., Apt. 3, 04330-7313. Tel: 207-623-4033. Sr. Theresa Conlogue, R.S.M., Contact Person.

BANGOR. *St. Joseph Convent*, 360 Broadway, 04401-3979. Tel: 207-262-1124; Fax: 207-262-1925. Email: srbarbara@sjhhealth.com. Sr. Barbara Theresa Martis, C.S.S.F., Contact Person. Felician Sisters 5.

BIDDEFORD. *St. Joseph's Convent*, 409 Pool St., 04005. Tel: 207-284-8381; Fax: 207-286-9418. Email: tbouthot@gwi.net. Sr. Theresa Bouthot, S.C.I.M., Supr. Sisters of the Immaculate Heart of Mary (Good Shepherd) 34.

Marie Fitzbach Convent, 290 Elm St., 04005. Tel: 207-282-2714. Email: fitzbach@gwi.net. Sr. Annette Nadeau, S.C.I.M., Supr. Servants of the Immaculate Heart of Mary (Good Shepherd Sisters) 6.

Marie Joseph Spiritual Center, 10 Evans Rd., 04005. Tel: 207-284-5671; Fax: 207-286-1371. Email: mariejosephcenter@yahoo.com. Web: www.mariejosephspiritual.org. Sr. Gertrude Robitaille, P.M., Supr. Sisters of the Presentation of Mary 9.

Provincial Residence, 409 Pool Rd., 04005. Tel: 207-282-4976; Fax: 207-282-7376. Email: scimpro@gwi.net. Sr. Theresa Therrien, S.C.I.M., Prov. Supr. Servants of the Immaculate Heart of Mary.

CASCO. *Community of the Resurrection A Lataste Community, Inc.*, P.O. Box 284, 04015-0284. Tel: 207-627-7184; Fax: 207-627-7184. Email: comres1@juno.com. Sr. Renata Camenzind, Supr. Total in Residence 6.

LEWISTON. *Dominican Sisters of the Roman Congregation*, Provincial Residence, 123 Dumont Ave., Apt. 1, 04240-6107. Tel: 207-782-3535; Fax: 207-782-0435. Email: moniqueb@megalink.net. Web: www.crsdop.org; www.dominicanromanusa.org. Sr. Monique Belanger, O.P., Prov. Prioress.

Holy Cross, 201 Webster St., 04240-5546. Tel: 207-782-0263. Sr. Cecile Mondor, Supr. Sisters of the Presentation of Mary 3.

OLD ORCHARD BEACH. *Sisters of Our Lady of the Holy Rosary, Regional Formation House*, 25 Portland Ave., 04064-2211. Tel: 207-934-0592. Sisters Maureen Bellerose, R.S.R., Regl. Coord.; Carole Jean Lappa, R.S.R., Formation Dir. Sisters 2.

PLEASANT POINT. *St. Ann's Convent*, P.O. Box 126, Perry, 04667-0126. Tel: 207-853-2944. Email: janicemurphy@mainline.net. Sr. Janice Murphy, R.S.M., Pastoral Assoc.

ST. AGATHA. *Our Lady of Wisdom Community*, 40 St. Agatha Housing Dr., 04772-6124. Tel: 207-543-7523; Fax: 207-543-7575. Sr. Candide Corriveau, D.W., Coord.

SABATTUS. *Dominican Sisters*, 61 Lisbon Rd., 04280-4209. Tel: 207-375-6583; Fax: 207-375-2694. Email: Lucille49@myfairpoint.net. Sr. Lucille Fournier, O.P., Prioress. Dominican Sisters of the Roman Congregation 9.

SOUTH PORTLAND. *Our Lady of Mercy Convent* (1991) 265 Cottage Rd., 04106. Tel: 207-767-5804. Email: eboyd@maine.rr.com. Sr. Carol A. LeTourneau,

R.S.M., Supr. Gen. Diocesan Sisters of Mercy of Portland 7.

WATERVILLE. *Blessed Sacrament Convent*, 101 Silver St., 04901. Tel: 207-872-7072; Fax: 207-873-2317. Email: servantsinfo@blesacrament.org. Web: www.blesacrament.org. Sr. Josephine Roney, S.S.S., Supr. Servants of the Blessed Sacrament. Sisters 8.

Ursuline Sisters, 1 Saint Angela Way, 04901-4640. Tel: 207-873-3515; Fax: 207-873-4926. Email: laurijm@verizon.net. Sr. Laurianne Michaud, O.S.U., Prioress. Ursuline Sisters 7.

WHITEFIELD. *Little Franciscans of Mary*, 298 Grand Army Rd., 04353-3419. Tel: 207-549-3945. Email: carol.martin@portlanddiocese.org. Sr. Carol Martin, P.F.M., Contact Person. Little Franciscans of Mary 2.

WINSLOW. *Provincialate of the Sisters of St. Joseph*, 93 Halifax St., 04901-6930. Tel: 207-873-4512; Fax: 207-873-1976. Email: gmdube@adelphia.net. Web: www.csjwinslowmaine.org. Sisters Gilla Dube, C.S.J., Prov. Supr.; Claire Labbee, C.S.J., Asst. Sisters in the Province 40.

[K] HERMITAGES

ELLSWORTH. *John of the Cross Monastery*, 19 Trinity Way, 04605-2800. Tel: 207-664-0026. Sr. Margaret Dorgan, D.C.M. Carmelite Sisters 2.

ST. ALBANS. *Divine Mercy Hermitage* (1995) 57 Bryant Rd., 04971-7327. Tel: 207-938-3730; Fax: 207-938-3730. Email: srmm3@yahoo.com. Sr. Margaret Mary Cuddeback.

Sky-Arch Hermitage, 47 Bryant Rd., 04971-7327. Email: sky-arch@tds.net. Sr. B. Emmanuel Bryant.

WINDSOR. *Transfiguration Hermitage*, 205 Windsor Neck Rd., 04363-3202. Tel: 207-445-8031. Email: benedicite@fairpoint.net. Web: www.transfigurationhermitage.org. Sr. Elizabeth Wagner, Contact Person. Number of Hermits 2.

[L] RETREAT HOUSES

ALFRED. *Notre Dame Retreat & Spiritual Center*, 133 Shaker Hill Rd., P.O. Box 159, 04002-0159. Tel: 207-324-6160; Fax: 207-324-5044. Email: spiritualcenter2002@yahoo.com. Rev. Theodore Letendre, F.I.C., Dir.

BIDDEFORD. *Marie Joseph Spiritual Center*, 10 Evans Rd., 04005. Tel: 207-284-5671; Fax: 207-286-1371. Email: mariejosephcenter@yahoo.com. Web: www.mariejosephspiritual.org. Sr. Gertrude Robitaille, P.M., Dir. Sisters of the Presentation of Mary. Served 3,454.

FRENCHVILLE. *Christian Life Center*, P.O. Box 128, Madawaska, 04756-0128. Tel: 207-543-6193; Fax: 207-543-6193. Email: clc4me@roadrunner.com. Web: clc4me.org. 444 US Route 1, 04745. Deacon Donald R. Clavette, Dir.

[M] NEWMAN CENTERS

PORTLAND. *University of New England-Westbrook College*

Res.: *St. Joseph Church*, 673 Stevens Ave., 04103. Tel: 207-797-7026; Fax: 207-797-2679. Revs. Peter Kaseta, O.F.M.Cap.; James Hammer, O.F.M.Cap.

University of Southern Maine Portland Campus, P.O. Box 11559, 04104-7559. Joy Geertz, Campus Min.

Gorham Campus Rev. Lawrence Conley. Tel: 207-839-4857.

BIDDEFORD. *University of New England* P.O. Box 11559, 04104-7559. Joy Geertz, Campus Min. Ministry Provided by Good Shepherd, Saco.

BRUNSWICK. *Bowdoin College* P.O. Box 11559, 04104-7559. All Saints Parish, 132 McKeen St., 04011.

Newman Center 04011. Tel: 207-576-3135.

CASTINE. *Maine Maritime Academy* 158 Franklin St., P.O. Box S, 04416. Tel: 207-469-3312. Rev. Bruce Siket, Chap.

FARMINGTON. *University of Maine at Farmington* Newman Campus Ministry, 04938. 133 Middle St., 04938. Tel: 207-778-2778; Fax: 207-778-0268. Email: stjoefarm@midmaine.com. P.O. Box 11559, 04104-7559. Rev. Thomas Lequin, Chap.

FORT KENT. *University of Maine at Fort Kent* St. John Vianney Parish, 26 E. Main St., 04743-1395. Tel: 207-834-5656; Fax: 207-834-7461. Email: stlouis@fairpoint.net. Served by personnel at St. John Vianney Parish, Fort Kent.

LEWISTON. *Bates College* 163 Wood St., 04240. Tel: 207-782-8096; Fax: 207-782-9032. Email: frmurray@aubcath.org. Web: www.bates.edu/admin/offices/chaplain. P.O. Box 11559, 04104-7559. Served by the personnel of the Lewiston Parishes.

MACHIAS. *University of Maine at Machias c/o Holy Name*, P.O. Box 248, 04654-0248. Tel: 207-255-3731. Mailing Address: P.O. Box 11559, 04104-7559. Rev. Eugene F. Gaffey.

ORONO. *University of Maine Parish of the Resurrection of the Lord*, 83 College Ave., 04473-1596. Tel: 207-866-2155; Fax: 207-866-4543. Web: www.umaine.edu/newman. Rev. Wilfred P. Labbe; Kristine B. Moody, Campus Min.; JoAnn C. Hall, Campus Min.

PRESQUE ISLE. *University of Maine at Presque Isle* P.O. Box 11559, 04104-7559.

St. Mary's Rectory 6 Roberts St., P.O. Box 813, 04769. Tel: 207-768-3671; Fax: 207-764-8644.

SOUTH PORTLAND. *Southern Maine Community College* c/o Holy Cross Parish 29 Aspen Ave., 04106-5328. Tel: 207-772-7489; Fax: 207-772-7480. Mailing Address: P.O. Box 11559, 04104-7559. Rev. Msgr. Michael J. Henchal, V.G.

STANDISH. *Saint Joseph's College* 04084-5263. Tel: 207-893-7792; Fax: 207-893-6605. Rev. Paul H. Dumais, Campus Min.; Ms. Rebecca Hilton, Campus Min. Campus Ministry Office.

WATERVILLE. *Colby College* Mayflower Hill, 04901. Tel: 207-872-2281. Email: daniel.baillargeon@portlanddiocese.org. Rev. Daniel Baillargeon, Chap., c/o Parish of the Holy Spirit, 70 Pleasant St., 04901-5405. Dean of Students Office, Colby College.

Thomas College Mid Maine Campus Ministry, 04901. Tel: 207-872-3559. Email: Daniel.Baillargeon@PortlandDiocese.org. P.O. Box 11559, 04104-7559. Rev. Daniel Baillargeon, Chap.; Bro. Rex Norris, Chap. Dean of Students Office, Colby College.

[N] MISCELLANEOUS LISTINGS

PORTLAND. **Catholic Foundation of Maine*, 510 Ocean Ave., P.O. Box 11559, 04104-7559. Tel: 207-773-6471; 207-321-7835; Fax: 207-773-0182. Email: christopher.reilly@portlanddiocese.org. Christopher Reilly, Exec. Dir. & Contact Person; Becky Owen, Admin. Asst.

St. Elizabeth's Child Development Center, 87 High St., 04101. Tel: 207-871-7444; Fax: 207-871-1178. P.O. Box 10660, 04104-6060. Total Assisted Annually 111.

Maine Catholic Radio Network Inc., Mailing Address: P.O. Box 11559, 04104-7559. Tel: 207-773-6471, Ext. 7810; Fax: 207-773-0182. Email: sue.bernard@portlanddiocese.org. 510 Ocean Ave., 04104. Sue Bernard, Contact Person.

BANGOR. *St. Michael's Center*, 1066 Kenduskeag Ave., 04401. Tel: 207-941-2855; Fax: 207-941-2835. Email: pvestal@main.org. Web: www.ccmaine.org. P.O. Box 10660, 04104-6060. Paul Vestal Jr., Dir. Functional Family Therapy and Case Management Services. Total Assisted Annually 759.

BIDDEFORD. *St. Andre Housing, Inc.*, 39 Sullivan St., 04005. Tel: 207-773-6471. Mr. David Twomey, Contact Person. Sponsored by: Roman Catholic Diocese of Portland., Purpose: to provide low income housing for the elderly in a deprived area of the state. Total Assisted Annually 35.
P.O. Box 11559, 04104-7559.

RELIGIOUS INSTITUTES OF MEN REPRESENTED IN THE DIOCESE

For further details refer to the corresponding bracketed number in the Religious Institutes of Men or Women section.

[0320]—*Brothers of Christian Instruction*—F.I.C.
[0470]—*The Capuchin Friars* (Prov. of St. Mary)—O.F.M.Cap.
[0740]—*Congregation of Marians of the Immaculate Conception (St. Stanilaus Kostka Prov.)*—M.I.C.
[0520]—*Franciscan Friars*—O.F.M.
[0690]—*Jesuit Fathers and Brothers* (New England Prov.)—S.J.
[0780]—*Marist Fathers* (Boston Prov.)—S.M.
[]—*Missionary Institute of Apostles of Jesus* (U.S.A. Zone)—A.J.
[0910]—*Oblates of Mary Immaculate* (Prov. of St. John the Baptist)—O.M.I.
[0430]—*Order of Preachers (Dominicans)* (Canadian Prov.)—O.P.
[0925]—*Society of Our Lady of the Most Holy Trinity*—S.O.L.T.

RELIGIOUS INSTITUTES OF WOMEN REPRESENTED IN THE DIOCESE

[]—*Community of the Resurrection*
[]—*Companions of Christ*—C.O.C.
[3100]—*Congregation of Our Lady of the Holy Rosary*—R.S.R.
[0960]—*Daughters of Wisdom*—D.W.
[]—*Diocesan Carmelites of Maine*—D.C.M.
[2655]—*Diocesan Sisters of Mercy*—R.S.M.
[1120]—*Dominican Sisters of the Roman Congregation*—O.P.
[1170]—*Felician Sisters*—C.S.S.F.
[1430]—*Franciscan Sisters of Our Lady of Perpetual Help*—O.S.F.
[2575]—*Institute of the Sisters of Mercy of the Americas*—R.S.M.
[2280]—*Little Franciscan of Mary*—P.F.M.
[2760]—*Missionary Sisters of the Immaculate Conception of the Mother of God*—S.M.I.C.
[3500]—*Servants of the Blessed Sacrament*—S.S.S.
[3550]—*Servants of the Immaculate Heart of Mary*—S.C.I.M.
[0610]—*Sisters of Charity of St. Hyacinthe (Grey Nuns)*—S.C.S.H.
[3000]—*Sisters of Notre Dame de Namur*—S.N.D.deN.
[3750]—*Sisters of St. Chretienne*—S.S.Ch.
[3870]—*Sisters of St. Joseph (Lyons, France)*—C.S.J.
[0150]—*Sisters of the Assumptions*—S.A.S.V.
[0110]—*The Sisters of the Precious Blood*—A.P.B.
[3310]—*Sisters of the Presentation of Mary*—P.M.
[4110]—*Ursuline Nuns (Roman Union)* (Northeastern Prov.)—O.S.U.

DIOCESAN CEMETERIES

BANGOR. *Mount Pleasant Catholic Cemetery*, 449 Ohio St., 04401. Tel: 207-947-4322; Fax: 207-947-0908. Email: cmt449ohio@aol.com. 207 York St., 04401-5442. Mr. Kenneth Hutchinson, Supt.

BIDDEFORD. *St. Joseph Cemetery*, 120 West St., P.O. Box 391, 04005. Tel: 207-282-0747. Email: stjosephscemetery@portlanddiocese.net.

LEWISTON. *St. Peter Cemetery*, 217 Switzerland Rd., 04240. Tel: 207-782-8721; Fax: 207-784-3432. Gerard J.B. Raymond, Exec. Dir.

SOUTH PORTLAND. *Calvary Cemetery*, 1461 Broadway, 04106. Tel: 207-773-5796; Fax: 207-773-5796. Email: calvarycem@maine.rr.com. Web: www.portlanddiocese.net/info.php?info_id=113. Mr. Richard Nee, Supt.

WATERVILLE. *St. Francis Catholic Cemetery*, 78 Grove St., 04901. Tel: 207-872-2770; Fax: 207-872-2770. Email: stfrancem@myfairpoint.net. Web: www.portlanddiocese.net/stfranciscemetery. P.O. Box 575, 04903-0575. Mr. Michael W. Hebert, Mgr.

NECROLOGY

† Tracy, Rev. Msgr. George E., (Retired)—Died Sept. 5, 2009
† Gorham, Peter P.—Died Sept. 14, 2009
† LeVasseur, Angelo B., Rumford, ME Parish of the Holy Savior—Died May 31, 2009
† Ouellette, Roger J., (Retired)—Died Jan. 31, 2009

An asterisk (*) denotes an organization that has established tax-exempt status directly with the IRS and is not covered by the USCCB Group Ruling.

Archdiocese of Portland in Oregon

(Archidioecesis Portlandensis in Oregon)

Most Reverend

JOHN G. VLAZNY, D.D.

Archbishop of Portland in Oregon; ordained December 20, 1961; appointed Auxiliary Bishop of Chicago and Titular Bishop of Stagno October 31, 1983; consecrated December 13, 1983; appointed Bishop of Winona May 19, 1987; installed July 29, 1987; appointed Archbishop of Portland in Oregon October 28, 1997; installed December 19, 1997.

Most Reverend

KENNETH D. STEINER, D.D.

Auxiliary Bishop of Portland in Oregon; ordained May 19, 1962; appointed Titular Bishop of Avensa and Auxiliary Bishop of Portland in Oregon December 6, 1977; ordained March 2, 1978. *Office: 2838 E. Burnside St., Portland, OR 97214.*

Square Miles 29,717.

Erected as a Vicariate-Apostolic December 1, 1843

Created Archdiocese of Oregon City, July 24, 1846; Name changed by Papal Decree to "Archdiocese of Portland in Oregon," September 26, 1928

Comprises that part of the State of Oregon lying between the summit of the Cascades and the Pacific Ocean.

For legal titles of parishes and archdiocesan institutions, consult the Archdiocesan Pastoral Center

Archdiocesan Pastoral Center: 2838 E. Burnside St., Portland, OR 97214-1895. Tel: 503-234-5334; Fax: 503-234-2545.

Web: www.archdpdx.org

Email: @archdpdx.org

STATISTICAL OVERVIEW

Personnel	
Archbishops	1
Auxiliary Bishops	1
Abbots	2
Retired Abbots	3
Priests: Diocesan Active in Diocese	97
Priests: Diocesan Active Outside Diocese	7
Priests: Diocesan in Foreign Missions	1
Priests: Retired, Sick or Absent	48
Number of Diocesan Priests	153
Religious Priests in Diocese	152
Total Priests in Diocese	305
Extern Priests in Diocese	18
Ordinations:	
Diocesan Priests	6
Religious Priests	3
Transitional Deacons	3
Permanent Deacons in Diocese	63
Total Brothers	79
Total Sisters	400
Parishes	
Parishes	124
With Resident Pastor:	
Resident Diocesan Priests	80
Resident Religious Priests	28
Without Resident Pastor:	
Administered by Priests	10
Administered by Deacons	3
Administered by Religious Women	1
Administered by Lay People	2
Missions	24
Pastoral Centers	1
Professional Ministry Personnel:	
Brothers	2
Sisters	18
Lay Ministers	155
Welfare	
Catholic Hospitals	9
Total Assisted	1,488,560
Health Care Centers	13
Total Assisted	324,986
Homes for the Aged	8
Total Assisted	2,683
Day Care Centers	4
Total Assisted	1,993
Specialized Homes	6
Total Assisted	1,094
Special Centers for Social Services	13
Total Assisted	1,072,019
Residential Care of Disabled	3
Total Assisted	8
Educational	
Seminaries, Diocesan	1
Students from This Diocese	22
Students from Other Diocese	115
Diocesan Students in Other Seminaries	18
Seminaries, Religious	1
Students Religious	29
Total Seminarians	69
Colleges and Universities	2
Total Students	5,508
High Schools, Diocesan and Parish	3
Total Students	1,408
High Schools, Private	7
Total Students	3,993
Elementary Schools, Diocesan and Parish	39
Total Students	8,407
Elementary Schools, Private	2
Total Students	453
Catechesis/Religious Education:	
High School Students	3,460
Elementary Students	14,752
Total Students under Catholic Instruction	38,050
Teachers in the Diocese:	
Priests	1
Brothers	4
Sisters	17
Lay Teachers	961
Vital Statistics	
Receptions into the Church:	
Infant Baptism Totals	5,727
Minor Baptism Totals	444
Adult Baptism Totals	363
Received into Full Communion	580
First Communions	5,073
Confirmations	2,629
Marriages:	
Catholic	671
Interfaith	289
Total Marriages	960
Deaths	1,896
Total Catholic Population	409,864
Total Population	3,269,195

Former Bishops—Most Revs. FRANCIS NORBERT BLANCHET, D.D., First Vicar Apostolic of Oregon Territory; cons. July 25, 1845, Titular Bishop of Drasa; appt. Archbishop of Oregon City, July 24, 1846 when the Vicariate was erected into an ecclesiastical province; resigned 1880; died June 18, 1883; CHARLES JOHN SEGHERS, D.D., cons. June 29, 1873; Bishop of Vancouver Island, British Columbia; coadjutor to the Archbishop of Oregon City, Dec. 10, 1880; Archbishop, Dec. 20, 1880; resigned 1884; and transferred to Vancouver Island, British Columbia; died Nov. 28, 1886; WILLIAM H. GROSS, C.Ss.R., D.D., Archbishop of Oregon City; cons. Bishop of Savannah, GA April 27, 1873; promoted by His Holiness Leo XIII Feb. 1, 1885 from Savannah to the Archiepiscopal See of Oregon City; died Nov. 14, 1898; ALEXANDER CHRISTIE, D.D., Archbishop of Oregon City; consecrated June 29, 1898, Bishop of Vancouver Island, B.C.; promoted by His Holiness Leo XIII February 12, 1899 from Vancouver Island to the Archiepiscopal See of Oregon City; died April 6, 1925; EDWARD D. HOWARD, D.D., LL.D., Titular Archbishop of Albule; ord. June 12, 1906; cons. Titular Bishop of Isauria and Auxiliary Bishop of Davenport, April 6, 1924; appt. to the See of Oregon City, April 30, 1926; asst. at the Pontifical Throne, May 2, 1939; transferred to the Titular See of Albule and as Archbishop of Portland in Oregon, Dec. 9, 1966; died Jan. 2, 1983; ROBERT JOSEPH DWYER, D.D., Ph.D., ord. June 11, 1932; cons. Bishop of Reno, Aug. 5, 1952; appt. Archbishop of Portland in Oregon, Dec. 9, 1966; resigned Jan. 22, 1974; died March 24, 1976; CORNELIUS MICHAEL POWER, D.D., J.C.D., ord. June 3, 1939; appt. Bishop of Yakima, Feb. 5, 1969; cons. May 1, 1969; appt. Archbishop of Portland in Oregon, Jan. 22, 1974; retired July 3, 1986; died May 22, 1997; WILLIAM J. LEVADA, S.T.D., ord. Dec. 20, 1961; appt. Titular Bishop of Capri and Auxiliary Bishop of Los Angeles, March 29, 1983; appt. Archbishop of Portland in Oregon, July 1, 1986; installed Sept. 21, 1986; appt. Coadjutor Archbishop of San Francisco, Aug. 17, 1995; transferred to Oct. 24, 1995; FRANCIS E. GEORGE, O.M.I., Ph.D., S.T.D., ord. Dec. 21, 1963; appt. Bishop of Yakima July 10, 1990; installed Sept. 21, 1990; appt. Archbishop of Portland in Oregon, April 29, 1996; installed May 27, 1996; appt. Archbishop of Chicago April 8, 1997; installed May 7, 1997.

Office of the Archbishop

Archdiocesan Pastoral Center—2838 E. Burnside St., Portland, 97214-1895. Tel: 503-234-5334; Fax: 503-234-2545.

Vicars and Directors

Vicar General and Moderator of the Curia—Rev. Msgr. DENNIS O'DONOVAN, Pastoral Center, 2838 E. Burnside St., Portland, 97214. Tel: 503-233-8331; Fax: 503-234-2545.

Vicar for Clergy—Rev. PATRICK BRENNAN, J.C.L.

Finance Officer—LEONARD VUYLSTEKE.

Department Directors—

Business Affairs—PAULETTE FURNESS.

Clergy—Rev. PATRICK BRENNAN, J.C.L.

Education—ROBERT MIZIA.

Chancellor/Public Services—MARY JO TULLY.

Pastoral Services—Rev. Msgr. DENNIS O'DONOVAN.

Evangelization Services—Deacon THOMAS GORNICK.

Chancellor—MARY JO TULLY.

College of Consultors—Most Revs. JOHN G. VLAZNY, D.D.; KENNETH D. STEINER, D.D.; Rev. PATRICK BRENNAN, J.C.L.; Rev. Msgr. CHARLES LIENERT; Revs. TODD MOLINARI; JOSEPH S. MCMAHON; Rev. Msgrs. GREGORY MOYS; DENNIS O'DONOVAN; Revs. JAMES NINH VAN PHAM; VINCENT TRUJILLO, O.S.B.; GEORGE WOLF.

Area Vicars—Rev. JAMES MAYO, Downtown Portland; Rev. Msgr. CHARLES LIENERT, Northeast Portland; Revs. MICHAEL EVERNDEN, C.S.P., Southeast Portland; CHARLES A. WOOD, East Portland Suburban; MICHAEL PATRICK, J.C.L., South Portland Suburban; WILLIAM C. MOISANT, West Portland Suburban; WAYNE FORBES, Beaverton Suburban; DONALD GUTMANN, Yamhill County; PETER ARTEAGA, M.Sp.S., Tualatin Valley; LUAN TRAN, Columbia County; NICHOLAS NILEMA, A.L.C.P., North Coast; WILLIAM HAMMELMAN, O.S.B., Marion County; GARY L. ZERR, Metropolitan Salem; STEVE GEER, Santiam; JOHN HENDERSON, O.F.M.Conv., Albany-Corvallis; RICHARD ROSSMAN, Metropolitan Eugene; VACANT, Middle Coast; Revs. KARL SCHRAY, South Coast; SEAN WEEKS, Southern Oregon.

Personnel Board—Rev. Msgr. CHARLES LIENERT; Revs. DONALD R. BUXMAN; MARK V. BACHMEIER; GEORGE WOLF; SEAN WEEKS. Ex Officio: Rev. PATRICK BRENNAN, J.C.L.; Rev. Msgr. DENNIS O'DONOVAN; Most Rev. JOHN G. VLAZNY.

Tribunal

Judicial Vicar—Rev. PATRICK BRENNAN, J.C.L.; LINDA WEIGEL, J.C.L., Dir. Tel: 503-233-8380.

Adjutant Judicial Vicar—Rev. KELLY VANDEHEY, J.C.L.

Judges—Revs. PATRICK BRENNAN, J.C.L.; CARL GIMPL; MICHAEL JOHNSTON; JAMES MAYO; MICHAEL PATRICK, J.C.L.; KELLY VANDEHEY, J.C.L.; PETER SMITH, J.C.L.

Defenders of the Bond—Rev. Msgr. GREGORY MOYS; Sr. MAUREEN ABBOTT, S.P.; LINDA WEIGEL, J.C.L.

Auditor— By appointment

Case Instructor—SUSAN OUFFOUE.

Notaries—MARGARET PALMER; SUSAN OUFFOUE; MARGARET NOLAN.

Advocates— Priests and pastoral ministers by appointment.

Archdiocesan Offices and Agencies

Archives—DAN HASKINS, Records Mgr. Tel: 503-233-8334. 2838 E. Burnside St., Portland, 97214-1895.

Building Commission—Most Rev. JOHN G. VLAZNY, D.D.; Rev. Msgr. DENNIS O'DONOVAN; Revs. JOSEPH HEUBERGER; LESLIE M. SIEG; JILL KIRKPATRICK; BRIAN SHEA; JIM EVANS; FRED SHIPMAN; ROBERT BOILEAU; JOSEPH GEHLEN; MICHAEL KINNE; DAVID HODGIN; PAULETTE FURNESS, Ex Officio; KEN SCOTT, Sec. Tel: 503-234-5334; SAMUEL RODRIQUEZ; Rev. PATRICK MCNAMEE.

Business Affairs—PAULETTE FURNESS, Dir., 2838 E. Burnside St., Portland, 97214-1895. Tel: 503-233-8356.

Campus Ministry—Deacon THOMAS GORNICK, Contact, 2838 E. Burnside St., Portland, 97214-1895. Tel: 503-233-8395.

Catholic Charities, Inc.—DENNIS KEENAN, Exec. Dir., 231 S.E. 12th Ave., Portland, 97214. Tel: 503-231-4866.

Catholic Deaf Ministry—Sr. LINDA ROBY, B.V.M., Dir., 2838 E. Burnside St., Portland, 97214. Tel: 503-233-8398 (V/TTY).

"Catholic Sentinel"— (Official Newspaper of the Archdiocese), Most Rev. JOHN G. VLAZNY, D.D., Publisher-in-Chief; JOHN J. LIMB, Publisher; ROBERT PFOHMAN, Editor, 5536 N.E. Hassalo St., Portland, 97213-3638. Tel: 503-281-1191. Mailing Address: P.O. Box 18030, Portland, 97218-0030.

Catholic Youth Organization/Camp Howard—Sr. KRISTA VON BORSTELL, S.S.M.O., Exec. Dir., Oregon Plaza, 825 N.E. 20th Ave., Ste. 320, Portland, 97232. Tel: 503-231-9484.

Cemeteries—Rev. Msgr. DENNIS O'DONOVAN, Dir. Tel: 503-234-5334; TIM CORBETT, Supt., Mt. Calvary Cemetery, 333 S.W. Skyline Blvd., Portland, 97221. Tel: 503-292-6621. Gethsemani Cemetery, 11666 S.E. Stevens Rd., Portland, 97266. Tel: 503-659-1350. Mount Calvary Cemetery, Eugene, 300 Mary Lane, Eugene, 97405. Tel: 541-686-8722.

Child Protection/Victim Assistance Office—CATHY SHANNON, Dir., 2838 E. Burnside St., Portland, 97214-1895. Tel: 503-416-8810 Victim Assistance; 503-233-8302 Child Protection. Email: cshannon@archdpdx.org.

Clergy Personnel—Rev. PATRICK BRENNAN, J.C.L., Vicar for Clergy, 2838 E. Burnside St., Portland, 97214-1895. Tel: 503-233-8366.

Communications—BUD BUNCE, Dir., 2838 E. Burnside St., Portland, 97214-1895. Tel: 503-233-8373.

Continuing Education for Clergy—Rev. SLIDER STEUERNOL, Dir. Board Members: Revs. ELWIN SCHWAB; RICHARD THOMPSON; STEPHEN STOBIE; RICHARD HUNEGER; ANDREW THOMAS; PATRICK BRENNAN, J.C.L., 2838 E. Burnside St., Portland, 97214-1895. Tel: 503-233-8368.

Diaconate Office—Rev. RICHARD HUNEGER, Dir.; Deacon VERN KORCHINSKI, Assoc. Dir., 2838 E. Burnside St., Portland, 97214-1895. Tel: 503-233-8368.

Ecumenical and Interreligious Affairs—Rev. RICHARD D. SIRIANNI; MARY JO TULLY, 2838 E. Burnside St., Portland, 97214. Tel: 503-233-8323.

Evangelization Services—Deacon THOMAS GORNICK, Dir., 2838 E. Burnside St., Portland, 97214-1895. Tel: 503-233-8335; MICHAL HORACE, Youth Ministry Specialist. Tel: 503-233-8310; CLAIRE WOODRUFF, Rel. Educ. Specialist. Tel: 503-233-8367.

Finance Council—Most Rev. JOHN G. VLAZNY, D.D.; Revs. PAUL PERI; THOMAS DOYLE, C.S.C.; RICHARD D. SIRIANNI; Rev. Msgr. DENNIS O'DONOVAN; DOUG WHITE; TOM EYER; PAULETTE FURNESS; DOUG TOLLEFSON; ARTHUR SCHULTE JR., Ph.D.; ROBERT BELDING; REX WARDLAW; CAMERON WILLIAMS; CAROLYN WINTER; BRIAN WILLIAMS; MICHAEL FAHEY; LEONARD VUYLSTEKE, Chm.; EDWARD HERINCKX, 2838 E. Burnside St., Portland, 97214-1895. Tel: 503-233-8359.

Financial Services—LEONARD VUYLSTEKE, Dir., 2838 E. Burnside St., Portland, 97214-1895. Tel: 503-233-8359.

Hispanic Ministries—RAUL VELAZQUEZ, Dir., 2838 E. Burnside St., Portland, 97214. Tel: 503-233-8324.

Historical Commission—MARY BETH HERKERT, Pres., 2838 E. Burnside St., Portland, 97214-1895. Tel: 503-234-5334.

Holy Childhood, Pontifical Association of—MARY JO TULLY, Dir., 2838 E. Burnside St., Portland, 97214-1895. Tel: 503-233-8323.

Human Resources—BARBARA BALTZ, Dir., 2838 E. Burnside St., Portland, 97214-1895. Tel: 503-233-8370.

Justice and Peace/Respect for Life—MATT CATO, Dir., 2838 E. Burnside St., Portland, 97214-1895. Tel: 503-233-8361; Rev. TIMOTHY MOCKAITIS, Assoc. Dir. Respect for Life Activities.

Liturgical Commission—Sr. JEREMY GALLET, S.P., Ex Officio; Revs. JAMES MAYO; JOSEPH S. MCMAHON; RICHARD RUTHERFORD, C.S.C.; Sr. LORETTA SCHAFF, O.S.F.; MARY JO TULLY; AGNES ZUEGER.

Marriage, Family Life and Aging—Deacon THOMAS GORNICK, Contact, 2838 E. Burnside St., Portland, 97214-1895. Tel: 503-233-8395.

Ministry Formation—JERILYN FELTON, Dir., 2838 E. Burnside St., Portland, 97214-1895. Tel: 503-652-7476; HEATHER WYCOFF, Mgr., Griffin Center, 11957 S.E. Fuller Rd., Milwaukie, 97222. Tel: 503-652-7476.

Mission Office—MARY JO TULLY, Dir., 2838 E. Burnside St., Portland, 97214-1895. Tel: 503-233-8323.

Oregon Catholic Conference—Most Revs. JOHN G. VLAZNY, D.D., Pres.; ROBERT F. VASA, Vice Pres.; Rev. Msgr. DENNIS O'DONOVAN, Sec. & Treas., 2838 E. Burnside St., Portland, 97214-1895. Tel: 503-234-5334.

Oregon Catholic Press—Most Rev. JOHN G. VLAZNY, D.D., Publisher-in-Chief; JOHN J. LIMB, Publisher, 5536 N.E. Hassalo St., Portland, 97213-3638. Tel: 503-281-1191. Mailing Address: P.O. Box 18030, Portland, 97218-0030.

Pastoral Services—Rev. Msgr. DENNIS O'DONOVAN, 2838 E. Burnside St., Portland, 97214-1895. Tel: 503-234-5334.

People with Disabilities—DOROTHY DESMARTEAU-COUGHLIN, Dir., 2838 E. Burnside St., Portland, 97214-1895. Tel: 503-233-8399 (V/TTY).

Pro-Life Activities— (See Justice and Peace/Respect for Life)

Project Rachel—447 N.E. 47th Ave., Ste. 100, Portland, 97213. Tel: 800-249-8074.

Propagation of the Faith, Pontifical Society for the—MARY JO TULLY, Dir., 2838 E. Burnside St., Portland, 97214-1895. Tel: 503-233-8323.

Religious Education— (See Evangelization Services)

Refugee Resettlement—CECILIA BARICEVIC, Prog. Mgr., 1910 S.E. 11th Ave., Portland, 97214. Tel: 971-222-1883.

Resource Development—DOUG TOLLEFSON, Dir., 2838 E. Burnside St., Portland, 97214-1895. Tel: 503-233-8336.

St. Mary's Home for Boys—FRANCIS MAHER, Exec. Dir., 16535 S.W. Tualatin Valley Hwy., Beaverton, 97006. Tel: 503-649-5651.

School Office—ROBERT MIZIA, Supt. Tel: 503-233-8300; Sr. ELIZABETH LARSON, O.S.B., Asst. Supt., School Personnel & Faith Formation.

Special Projects—TODD COOPER, Dir., 2838 E. Burnside St., Portland, 97214-1895. Tel: 503-233-8386.

Stewardship Office—DOUG TOLLEFSON, Dir., 2838 E. Burnside St., Portland, 97214-1895. Tel: 503-233-8336.

Vocations—Rev. KELLY VANDEHEY, J.C.L., Dir., 2838 E. Burnside St., Portland, 97214-1895. Tel: 503-233-8368.

Worship—Sr. JEREMY GALLET, S.P., Dir., 2838 E. Burnside St., Portland, 97214-1895. Tel: 503-233-8342.

Youth and Young Adult Ministry— (See Evangelization Services)

CLERGY, PARISHES, MISSIONS AND PAROCHIAL SCHOOLS

CITY OF PORTLAND

(MULTNOMAH COUNTY)

PORTLAND

1—CATHEDRAL OF THE IMMACULATE CONCEPTION (1851) Rev. George Wolf; Deacon Thomas Gornick.
Res.: 1716 N.W. Davis St., 97209. Tel: 503-228-4397; Fax: 503-242-2568. Web: www.maryscathedral.org.
School—(Grades K-8), 110 N.W. 17th Ave., 97209. Tel: 503-275-9370; Fax: 503-243-3819. Order of Servants of Mary 2; Lay Teachers 16; Students 230.
Catechesis/Religious Program—Students 50.

2—ST. AGATHA (1911) Rev. Slider Steuernol.
Office: 1430 S.E. Nehalem St., 97202. Tel: 503-236-4747; Fax: 503-236-6407. Email: stagathapdx@gmail.com. Web: www.stagatha.us.
School—(Grades PreK-8), 7960 S.E. 15th Ave., 97202. Tel: 503-234-5500; Fax: 503-232-7240. Email: sarah.lutz@stagatha.us. Web: www.stagatha.us/school. Lay Teachers 17; Students 208.

3—ALL SAINTS (1917) Rev. Richard Thompson.
Res.: 3847 N.E. Glisan, 97232. Tel: 503-232-4305; Fax: 503-238-8847. Email: parish@allsaintsportland.org. Web: www.allsaintsportland.org.
School—(Grades PreSchool-8), 601 N.E. 39th Ave., 97232. Tel: 503-236-6205; Fax: 503-236-0781. Email: office@allsaintsportland.org. Web: www.school.allsaintsportland.org. Lay Teachers 32; Students 450.
Catechesis/Religious Program—Students 157.

4—ST. ANDREW (1907) Rev. Msgr. Charles Lienert.
Res.: 806 N.E. Alberta St., 97211. Tel: 503-281-4429; Fax: 503-281-4411. Email: ouroffice@standrewchurch.com. Web: www.standrewchurch.com.
Catechesis/Religious Program—Students 50.

5—ST. ANTHONY (1917) Rev. Patrick Donoghue; Sondra Coronado, Pastoral Assoc.
Parish Office: 3720 S.E. 79th Ave., 97206. Tel: 503-771-6039; Fax: 503-772-0107. Email: stanthonyportland@archdpdx.org. Web: www.stanthonypdx.com.

6—ASCENSION (1892) Revs. Ben R. Innes, O.F.M.; William Minkel, O.F.M., Parochial Vicar; Bro. Jose Luis Nerio, O.F.M.
Mailing Address: 7507 S.E. Yamhill, 97215. Tel: 503-256-3897; Fax: 503-257-4681. Email: maryascension@qwestoffice.net. Web: ascensionpdx.org.
In Res., Revs. Matthias Tumulty, O.F.M.; Robert Beltrami, O.F.M.
Rectory—*Ascension Friary*, 404 S.E. 68th Ave., 97215. Tel: 503-253-8305.
Catechesis/Religious Program—Tel: 503-256-3897,

Ext. 21; Fax: 503-257-4681. Email: sharon-ascension@qwestoffice.net. Sharon Grigar, Pastoral Assoc.; Maria Solis, Dir. Hispanic Ministry. Students 254.

7—ASSUMPTION (1909) Closed. For inquiries for parish records contact the chancery. (Holy Cross)

8—ST. BIRGITTA (1954) Rev. Joseph Barita, A.L.C.P./O.S.S.
Church: 11820 N.W. St. Helens Rd., 97231-2319. Tel: 503-286-3929; Fax: 971-230-0546. Email: stbirgitta@msn.com. Web: stbirgitta.com.
Chapel—Portland, Chapel of Our Lady of Sinj

9—BLESSED SACRAMENT (1913) Closed. For inquiries for parish records please contact Holy Cross, Portland.

10—ST. CHARLES (1914) Rev. Elwin Schwab, Priest Moderator; Sr. Phyllis Jaszkowiak, Pastoral Admin.; Joan Winchester, Pastoral Assoc.
Parish Center—5310 N.E. 42nd, 97218. Tel: 503-281-6461; Fax: 503-281-6828. Email: stchas@stcharlespdx.org. Web: www.stcharlespdx.org.
Catechesis/Religious Program—Email: joanw@stcharlespdx.org. Students 59.

11—CHURCH OF ST. JOSEPH THE WORKER (1885) Rev. John Amsberry; Deacon Michael Caldwell.
Res.: 2310 S.E. 148th Ave., 97233. Tel: 503-761-8710; Fax: 503-761-8545. Web: www.stjosephtheworkerpdx.org.
Catechesis/Religious Program—Tel: 503-762-2704; Fax: 503-761-8545. Students 105.

12—CHURCH OF ST. MICHAEL THE ARCHANGEL (1894), (Italian), Rev. James Mayo; Deacon Charles Amsberry, Pastoral Assoc.
Res.: 424 S.W. Mill St., 97201. Tel: 503-228-8629; Fax: 503-827-7689. Email: secretary@stmichaelportland.org.

13—ST. CLARE (1913) Rev. Thomas B. Farley.
Res.: 8535 S.W. 19th Ave., 97219. Tel: 503-244-1037; Fax: 503-246-2665. Email: office@saintclarechurch.org. Web: www.saintclarechurch.org.
School—(Grades PreK-8) Tel: 503-244-7600; Fax: 503-293-2076. Lay Teachers 15; Students 231.
Catechesis/Religious Program—Email: jean@saintclarechurch.org. Students 110.

14—ST. ELIZABETH OF HUNGARY (1953) Rev. James Kolb.
Res.: 4112 S.W. Sixth Ave. Dr., 97239. Tel: 503-222-2168; Fax: 503-274-2438.
Catechesis/Religious Program—Students 4.

15—ST. FRANCIS OF ASSISI (1876) Rev. Robert Krueger, Moderator (Retired); Valerie Chapman, Pastoral Admin.
Mailing Address: 1131 S.E. Oak St., 97214. Email: stfrancis@qwest.net. Web: www.stfranpdx.catholicweb.com.
Res.: 1136 S.E. Oak St., 97214. Tel: 503-232-5880; Fax: 503-232-6449.
Catechesis/Religious Program—Students 14.

16—HOLY CROSS CATHOLIC CHURCH (1901) Rev. John Wironen, C.S.C.; Deacon Jose Gutierrez; Ana Carmina Perez, Hispanic Ministry.
Office:—5227 N. Bowdoin St., 97203. Tel: 503-289-2834; Fax: 503-283-7056. Email: office@holycrosspdx.org. Web: www.holycrosspdx.org.
School—(Grades K-8), 5241 N. Bowdoin, 97203. Tel: 503-289-3010; Fax: 503-286-5006. Sisters 2; Lay Teachers 12; Students 176.
Chapel—Christ The Teacher, University of Portland 5000 N. Willamette Blvd., 97203. Tel: 503-283-7311; Fax: 503-283-7399.
Catechesis/Religious Program—Students 130.

17—HOLY FAMILY (1931) Rev. Robert L. Barricks.
Business Office: 3732 S.E. Knapp, 97202. Tel: 503-774-1428; Fax: 503-774-1854. Email: churchlady18@comcast.net. Web: www.holyfampdx.org.
Res.: 3708 S.E. Flavel. Tel: 503-788-2051.
Church: 7525 S.E. 39th Ave., 97202.
School—(Grades PreSchool-8), 7425 S.E. 39th Ave., 97202. Tel: 503-774-8871; Fax: 503-774-8872. Email: holyfamilysch@yahoo.com. Christy Robinson, Prin. Lay Teachers 16; Students 272.
Catechesis/Religious Program—Tel: 503-774-7804 (Youth); Fax: 503-774-1854. Students 150.

18—HOLY REDEEMER (1906) Revs. John J. Dougherty, C.S.C.; J. Steele, C.S.C.; Deacon Robert Lukosh.
Church: 25 N. Rosa Parks Way, 97217. Tel: 503-285-4539; Fax: 503-285-0666. Email: holyredeemerchurch@comcast.net. Web: www.holyredeemerpdx.org.
School—(Grades K-8), 127 N. Rosa Parks Way, 97217. Tel: 503-283-5197; Fax: 503-283-9479. Sisters 5; Lay Teachers 17; Students 274.
Catechesis/Religious Program—Students 97.

19—HOLY ROSARY PARISH & DOMINICAN PRIORY (1894) Rev. Anthony M. Patalano, O.P.; Very Rev. Reginald Martin, O.P., Dir. of Rosary Confraternity & Prior. In Res., Revs. Paul A. Duffner, O.P. (Retired); Vincent Benoit, O.P.; John C. Flannery, O.P. (Retired); Thomas More J. McGreevy, O.P. (Retired); Brian T. Mullady, O.P.
Res.: 375 N.E. Clackamas St., 97232. Tel: 503-235-3163; Fax: 503-235-3551. Web: holyrosarypdx.org.
Confraternity of the Most Holy Rosary—P.O. Box 3617, 97208. Tel: 503-236-8393; Fax: 503-236-8394.
Catechesis/Religious Program—Students 191.

20—ST. IGNATIUS (1907) [JC] Revs. Christopher S. Weekly; Thomas Royce, S.J.; John Ridgway, S.J.
Res.: 3400 S.E. 43rd Ave., 97206. Tel: 503-777-1491; Fax: 503-777-3142. Email: office@stignatiusparish.org. Web: www.stignatiusparish.org.
School—(Grades K-8), 3330 S.E. 43rd St., 97206. Tel: 503-774-5533; Fax: 503-788-1134. Email: jmatcovich@stignatiusschool.org. Web: www.stignatiusschool.org. Sisters of the Holy Names of Jesus and Mary 1; Lay Teachers 16; Students 204.
Convent—Sisters of the Holy Names of Jesus and Mary, 4130 S.E. Brooklyn, 97206. Tel: 503-231-6538. Sisters 4.
Catechesis/Religious Program—Students 51.

21—IMMACULATE HEART OF MARY (1885) Rev. Nicolaus Marandu.
Res.: 2910 N. Williams Ave., 97227-1628. Tel: 503-287-3724; Fax: 503-287-5011. Email: immaculateheartportland@archdpdx.org. Web: www.immaculateheartchurch.org.

22—ST. JOHN FISHER (1959) Rev. Wayne Forbes; Scott Kolbet, Pastoral Assoc.
Res.: 7007 S.W. 46th Ave., 97219. Tel: 503-244-4945; Fax: 503-452-8570.
School—(Grades K-8) Tel: 503-246-3234; Fax: 503-246-4117. Administrators 1; Lay Teachers 17; Aides 3; Students 232.
Catechesis/Religious Program—Tel: 503-244-4945; Fax: 503-452-8570. Jeanne Moser, D.R.E. Students 52.

23—ST. JUAN DIEGO CATHOLIC CHURCH formerly St. Juan Diego Parish (2002) Rev. John Kerns; Kathy Yee, Pastoral Assoc.
Church: 1280 N.W. Saltzman Rd., 97229. Tel: 503-644-1617; Fax: 503-644-1617 (call first). Web: www.stjuandiego.org.
Catechesis/Religious Program—Bridget Becker, Dir. Faith Formation; Janette Strand, Parish Music Coord. Students 147.

24—KOREAN MARTYRS CATHOLIC CHURCH (1990), (Korean), [JC] Rev. Peter Ock Jin Cho.
Office & Church: 10930 S.E. Powell Blvd., 97266. Email: chrkor@yahoo.com.
Catechesis/Religious Program—Tel: 503-661-8468. Students 74.

25—ST. MARY MAGDALENE (1911), (The Madeleine) Rev. Michael Biewend, C.J., Admin.
Res.: 3123 N.E. 24th Ave., 97212. Tel: 503-281-5777; Fax: 503-281-0673. Web: www.themadeleine.edu.
School—(Grades K-8), 3240 N.E. 23rd Ave., 97212. Tel: 503-288-9197; Fax: 503-280-1196. Susan J. Steele, Prin. Lay Teachers 24; Students 252.
Catechesis/Religious Program—Students 150.

26—OUR LADY OF LAVANG (1999), (Vietnamese), Revs. Bartholomew Dat H. Pham, S.D.D.; Peter Khoi Anh Hoang Doan, S.D.D.; Joseph Phiet Trong Vu, C.Ss.R.; Paul Binh The Cao, S.D.D.
5404 N.E. Alameda Dr., 97213. Tel: 503-249-5892; Fax: 503-249-1776.
Catechesis/Religious Program—Students 1,300.
Mission—St. Andrew Dung-Lac 13715 S.W. Walker Rd., Beaverton, Washington Co. 97005. Tel: 503-643-9528; Fax: 503-644-8486.

27—OUR LADY OF SORROWS (1917) Rev. Ronald C. Millican; Deacon An Vu.
Res.: 5313 S.E. Knight St., 97206. Tel: 503-775-6731; Fax: 503-775-6732.
Church: 5239 S.E. Woodstock Blvd., 97206-6822.
Catechesis/Religious Program—Students 20.

28—ST. PATRICK (1885) Rev. Timothy Murphy.
Church: 1623 N.W. 19th Ave., 97209. Tel: 503-222-4086; Fax: 503-222-6642. Web: www.stpatrickspdx.org.
Catechesis/Religious Program—Tel: 360-750-4609.

29—ST. PETER (1911) Rev. David E. Zegar; Brendan Mallon, Pastoral Assoc.; Amparo Piedrahita, Hispanic Min.
Mailing Address: 8648 S.E. Foster Rd., 97266. Tel: 503-777-3321; Fax: 503-777-3351. Email: stpeterportland@archdpdx.org.
Res.: 5736 S.E. 86th St., 97266. Tel: 503-777-1026.
Catechesis/Religious Program—Tel: 503-777-3322. Students 102.

30—ST. PHILIP NERI (1912) Revs. Gerard P. Tully, C.S.P.; Michael Evernden, C.S.P.
Res.: 2408 S.E. 16th Ave., 97214. Tel: 503-231-4955; Fax: 503-736-1383. Email: info@stphilipneripdx.org. Web: www.stphilipneripdx.org.
Catechesis/Religious Program—Students 38.

31—ST. PIUS X (Cedar Mill) (1953) Rev. Craig Boly, S.J.; Deacon Robert Little.
Office: 1280 N.W. Saltzman Rd., 97229. Tel: 503-644-5264; Fax: 503-626-6540. Web: www.stpius.org/.
School—(Grades K-8), 1260 N.W. Saltzman Rd., 97229. Tel: 503-644-3244; Fax: 503-646-6568. Lay Teachers 19; Students 289.
Catechesis/Religious Program—Tel: 503-644-5264. Students 558.

32—QUEEN OF PEACE, Closed. For inquiries for parish records contact the chancery. (Holy Cross).

33—ST. RITA (1923) Rev. Patrick Brennan, Pastoral Moderator; Chris Kresek, Pastoral Admin.
Mailing Address: 10029 N.E. Prescott St., 97220. Tel: 503-252-3403; Fax: 503-256-9682.
Catechesis/Religious Program—Students 44.

34—ST. ROSE OF LIMA (1911) Rev. Peter Smith; Deacon Donald Ciffone.
Res.: 2727 N.E. 54th Ave., 97213. Tel: 503-281-5318; Fax: 503-284-8350.
School—Archbishop Howard School, (Grades PreSchool-8), 5309 N.E. Alameda St., 97213. Tel: 503-281-1912; Fax: 503-281-0554. Email: principal@archbishophoward.org. Web: www.archbishophoward.org. Donna Vandiver, Librarian. Lay Teachers 22; Students 250.
Catechesis/Religious Program—Students 33.

35—SACRED HEART (1893) Rev. Bruce Brown, Admin. (Retired).
Res.: 3910 S.E. 11th Ave., 97202. Tel: 503-231-9636; Fax: 503-231-1766. Email: sheart@att.net. Web: www.sacredheartportland.org.

36—ST. STANISLAUS (1907), (Polish), Rev. Tadeusz Rusnak, S.Ch.
Res.: 3916 N. Interstate Ave., 97227-1063. Tel: 503-281-7532; Fax: 503-281-7532. Email: stanislausparish@comcast.net. Web: www.tchr.org/portland.
Catechesis/Religious Program—Christ Our Life Students 50.

37—ST. STEPHEN (1907) Rev. Petrus B. Hoang.
Res.: 1112 S.E. 41st Ave., 97214. Tel: 503-234-5019; Fax: 503-239-5985.
Catechesis/Religious Program—Students 3.

38—ST. THERESE OF THE CHILD JESUS (1955) Rev. Roger Marcus Fernando.
Res.: 1224 N.E. 131st Pl., 97230. Tel: 503-256-5850; Fax: 503-253-3560. Email: church@sttheresor.org. Web: www.sttheresor.org.
School—(Grades PreSchool-8) Tel: 503-253-9400; Fax: 503-253-9571. Email: st.therese@comcast.net. Web: www.stthereseschool.org. Sisters of the Holy Child 1; Lay Teachers 13; Students 264.
Catechesis/Religious Program—Students 80.

39—ST. THOMAS MORE (1936) Rev. Richard D. Sirianni.
Church: 3525 S.W. Patton Rd., 97221. Tel: 503-222-2055; Fax: 503-242-1831. Email: stmparish@stmpdx.org.
School—(Grades K-8), 3521 S.W. Patton Rd., 97221. Tel: 503-222-6105; Fax: 503-227-5661. Email: stmschool@stmpdx.org. Web: www.stmpdx.org. Lay Teachers 20; Students 219.
Catechesis/Religious Program—Tel: 503-222-2055, Ext. 14; Fax: 503-242-1861. Email: stmre@yahoo.com. Students 90.

40—ST. VINCENT DE PAUL (1919), (Downtown Chapel), Rev. Robert J. Loughery, C.S.C. In Res., Rev. Ronald P. Raab, C.S.C.
Res.: 601 W. Burnside St., 97209. Tel: 503-228-0746; Fax: 503-972-1063. Web: www.downtownchapel.org.

OUTSIDE THE CITY OF PORTLAND

ALBANY, LINN CO., OUR LADY OF PERPETUAL HELP (ST. MARY) (1885) Rev. John C. Betts; Kathleen Reilly, Pastoral Assoc.
Res.: 728 Ellsworth St., S.W., 97321. Tel: 541-926-1449; Fax: 541-926-2191. Email: stmarys_albany@comcast.net. Web: www.stmarysalbany.com.
School—St. Mary, (Grades PreK-8), 815 Broadalbin St., S.W., 97321-2469. Tel: 541-928-7474; Fax: 541-926-9342. Email: stmarysch@proaxis.com. Web: www.proaxis.com/~stmarysch. Christina Meadows, Prin. Lay Teachers 12; Students 118.
Catechesis/Religious Program—Fax: 541-926-2191. Students 178.

ALOHA, WASHINGTON CO., ST. ELIZABETH ANN SETON (1982) Rev. Louis Urbanski; Deacon Jesus Espinoza, Hispanic Ministry; Ann Billings, Bookkeeper.
Res.: 3145 S.W. 192nd Ave., 97006. Tel: 503-649-9044; 503-649-6211; Fax: 503-848-2915. Email: admin@seas-aloha.org. Web: seas-aloha.org.
Catechesis/Religious Program—Tel: 503-649-9044. Email: re@seas-aloha.org. Sandi Campos, Dir. Faith Formation. Students 298.

ASHLAND, JACKSON CO., OUR LADY OF THE MOUNTAIN (1887) Rev. Sean Weeks; Deacon James McVeigh.
Res.: 987 Hillview Dr., 97520. Tel: 541-482-1146; Fax: 541-488-5174. Email: olmop@mind.net. Web: www.ourladymt.org.
Catechesis/Religious Program—Students 205.

ASTORIA, CLATSOP CO., ST. MARY, STAR OF THE SEA (1874) [JC] Rev. Kenneth Sampson.
Rectory—828 14th St., 97103.

Church: 1465 Grand Ave., 97103. Tel: 503-325-3671; Fax: 503-325-7983 (Office). Email: msteele@archdpdx.org. Web: www.stmaryastoria.org.
School—(Grades K-8) Tel: 503-325-3771. Lay Teachers 7; Students 124.
Mission—St. Francis de Sales 867 5th Ave., Hammond, Clatsop Co. 97121.
Catechesis/Religious Program—Email: keli@stmaryastoria.org. Students 24.

BANDON, COOS CO., HOLY TRINITY (1883) [CEM] Rev. Andrew Thomas.
Res.: 355 Oregon Ave., S.E., 97411. Tel: 541-347-2309; Fax: 541-347-9256. Web: www.holytrinitybandon.com.
Mission—St. John the Baptist P.O. Box 884, Port Orford, Curry Co. 97465. Tel: 541-253-6250.
Catechesis/Religious Program—Students 44.

BEAVERTON, WASHINGTON CO.

1—ST. CECILIA (1876) Revs. Patrick McNamee; Eric Michael Andersen.
Res.: 5105 S.W. Franklin Ave., 97005. Tel: 503-644-2619; Fax: 503-626-7204.
School—(Grades PreSchool-8) Tel: 503-644-2619, Ext. 1; Fax: 503-646-4217. Web: www.stcecilia.pvt.k12.or.us. Lay Teachers 17; Students 274.
Catechesis/Religious Program—Students 539.

2—HOLY TRINITY (1962) [CEM] Rev. David Gutmann.
Church: 13715 S.W. Walker Rd., 97005. Tel: 503-643-9528; Fax: 503-644-8486. Email: parish@h-t.org. Web: www.h-t.org.
School—(Grades K-8), 13755 S.W. Walker Rd., 97005. Tel: 503-644-5748; Fax: 503-643-4475. Email: holytrinity@pvt.k12.or.us. Web: www.holytrinity.pvt.k12.or.us. Lay Teachers 14; Students 242.
Catechesis/Religious Program—Students 255.

BROOKINGS, CURRY CO., STAR OF THE SEA (1923) Rev. Joseph J. Bosch; Deacon Leo H. Appel II.
Mailing Address: Box 1066, 97415. 820 Old County Rd., 97415. Tel: 541-469-2313; Fax: 541-469-9644. Email: starofsea820@nwtec.com. Web: www.starofthesea-catholicchurch.com.
Mission—St. Charles Borromeo 94323 Gauntlet, P.O. Box 529, Gold Beach, Curry Co. 97444. Tel: 541-247-2453.
Catechesis/Religious Program—Students 33.

CANBY, CLACKAMAS CO., ST. PATRICK (1882) [CEM] Rev. John Waldron.
Res.: 498 N.W. Ninth, P.O. Box 730, 97013. Tel: 503-266-9411; Fax: 503-263-2293. Email: stpatricks@canby.com. Web: www.stpatcanby.org.
Catechesis/Religious Program—488 N.W. 9th, 97013. Tel: 503-266-2401. Email: stpatrickreligiouseducation@yahoo.com. Students 235.

CENTRAL POINT, JACKSON CO., SHEPHERD OF THE VALLEY (1978) Rev. Mike Walker.
Office: 600 Beebe Rd., 97502. Tel: 541-664-1050; Fax: 541-664-9312. Email: churchoffice@shepherdcatholic.com. Web: www.shepherdcatholic.com.
Catechesis/Religious Program—Students 170.

COOS BAY, COOS CO., ST. MONICA (1888) Rev. Peter O'Brien.
Mailing Address: 357 S. 6th St., 97420.
Church: 97420. Tel: 541-267-7421; Fax: 541-267-8491. Email: stmchurch@verizon.net. Web: www-.saintmonicacoosbay.org.

COQUILLE, COOS CO., HOLY NAME (1915) Rev. John F. McGuire.
50 N. Dean St., 97423.
Catechesis/Religious Program—Students 14.
Mission—Sts. Ann and Michael 209 Second St., Myrtle Point, Coos Co. 97458. Tel: 541-396-3849.

CORNELIUS, WASHINGTON CO., ST. ALEXANDER (1881), (Hispanic), Rev. David E. Schiferl.
Mailing Address: P.O. Box 644, 97113. Tel: 503-359-0304; Fax: 503-992-8634. Email: dshiferl@msn.com.
Res.: 268 N. 17th Ave., 97113. Tel: 503-992-0133.
Catechesis/Religious Program—Students 265.

CORVALLIS, BENTON CO., ST. MARY (1861) [CEM] Revs. John Henderson, O.F.M.Conv.; Ignacio Llorente; Deacons Francis Potts; Chris Anderson; Lynette Martin, Admin. Asst.
Res.: 501 N.W. 25th St., 97330. Tel: 541-757-1988; Fax: 541-757-2788. Web: www.smcatholic.com.
Catechesis/Religious Program—Students 280.

COTTAGE GROVE, LANE CO., OUR LADY OF PERPETUAL HELP (1897) Rev. Stephen R. Ryan, O.S.M., Admin.; Deacon Kenneth E. Boone.
Res.: 1025 N. 19th St., 97424. Tel: 541-942-3420; Fax: 541-942-4712.
Mission—St. Philip Benizi 552 Holbrook, Creswell, Lane Co. 97426. P.O. Box 706, Creswell, 97426.
Catechesis/Religious Program—1025 N. 19th St., 97424. Tel: 541-942-4712. Betty Krumlauf, D.R.E. Students 94.

DALLAS, POLK CO., ST. PHILIP (1920) [JC] Rev. Michael Johnston.
Office: 825 S.W. Mill St., 97338. Tel: 503-623-2440.
Catechesis/Religious Program—Students 74.

ESTACADA, CLACKAMAS CO., ST. ALOYSIUS (1924) [JC] Rev. Patrick F. Walsh.
P.O. Box 1199, 97023.
Catechesis/Religious Program—Tel: 503-630-2416. Students 19.

EUGENE, LANE CO.

1—ST. JUDE (1969) Rev. Thomas D. Yurchak.
Office: 4330 Willamette, 97405. Tel: 541-344-1191; Fax: 541-345-6001. Email: kmorrow@st-jude.org. Web: st-jude.org.
Catechesis/Religious Program—Students 61.

2—ST. MARK (1961) Rev. Richard Rossman; Deacon Darrell Meter.
Res.: 1760 Echo Hollow Rd., 97402. Tel: 541-689-0725; Fax: 541-689-0569. Email: saintmark1760@hotmail.com. Web: www.saintmarkeugene.org.
Catechesis/Religious Program—Tel: 541-689-1054. Email: christdiva@gmail.com. Students 85.

3—ST. MARY (1887) [CEM] Revs. Mark V. Bachmeier; Mariano Regalado Escano; Deacon Thomas Altenhofen.
Church: 1062 Charnelton St., 97401. Tel: 541-342-1139; Fax: 541-334-6996. Email: info@stmaryeugene.com. Web: www.stmaryeugene.com.
Catechesis/Religious Program—Students 268.

4—ST. PAUL (1955) Rev. Stephen M. Clovis.
Res.: 1201 Satre St., 97401. Tel: 541-686-2345; Fax: 541-686-0037.
School—(Grades PreK-8) Tel: 541-344-1401; Fax: 541-344-2572. Lay Teachers 18; Students 298.
Catechesis/Religious Program—Students 67.

5—ST. PETER (1955) [JC] Rev. Richard Rossman; Deacon David Sorensen.
Res.: 1150 Maxwell Rd., 97404. Tel: 541-688-1051; Fax: 541-688-9434. Email: stpetercc@stpetereugene.org. Web: www.stpetereugene.org.
Catechesis/Religious Program—Tel: 541-689-0782. Email: stpeterff@stpetereugene.org. Paula J. Voborsky, D.R.E. Students 25.

6—ST. THOMAS MORE CHURCH formerly St. Thomas More (1915), (Catholic Campus Ministry) Rev. Daniel Rolland, O.P.; Corinne M. Lopez, D.R.E. In Res., Revs. Augustine Hilander, O.P.; David Orique, O.P.
Res.: 1386 E. 18th, 97403. Tel: 541-343-0065.
Church: 1850 Emerald St., 97403. Tel: 541-343-7021; Fax: 541-686-8028. Web: www.uonewman.org.
St. Thomas More Community—, Canonical Religious House of the Western Province.

FLORENCE, LANE CO., ST. MARY, OUR LADY OF THE DUNES (1951) Rev. David Brown.
Church: 85060 U.S. Hwy. 101 S., Box 2640, 97439. Tel: 541-997-2312; Fax: 541-902-0417. Email: stmary@oregonfast.net. Web: www.oregonfast.net/stmary.
Catechesis/Religious Program—Students 51.

FOREST GROVE, WASHINGTON CO., ST. ANTHONY (1908) [JC] Rev. Jeffrey Meeuwsen; Lani Vandehey, Pastoral Assoc. Tel: 503-357-8147; Daniel Herrera, Hispanic Ministry.
Res.: 1660 Elm St., 97116. Tel: 503-357-2989; Fax: 503-357-2217. Web: www.stanthonysforestgrove.org.
Catechesis/Religious Program—Students 236.

GERVAIS, MARION CO., SACRED HEART-ST. LOUIS (1847) [CEM] Rev. Ronald Nelson.
Office: 605 7th St., P.O. Box 236, 97026. Tel: 503-792-4231; Fax: 503-792-3749. Email: sachrt@xpressdata.net.
School—(Grades K-8), 515 7th St., 97026. Tel: 503-792-4541; Fax: 503-792-3826. Email: lashindler@gervais.com. Lucy Shindler Shawn, Prin. Lay Teachers 5; Students 59.
Catechesis/Religious Program—Students 97.

GRAND RONDE, YAMHILL CO., ST. MICHAEL (1860) Rev. Terry O'Connell; Deacon David Briedwell, Pastoral Admin.
Res.: 48520 S.W. Hebo Rd., 97347. Tel: 503-879-5480; Fax: 503-879-5480.

GRANTS PASS, JOSEPHINE CO., ST. ANNE (1896) Revs. William Holtzinger; Paschal Ezurike; Deacon Robert Chapin.
Res.: 1131 N.E. 10th St., 97526. Tel: 541-476-2240; Fax: 541-476-2194. Email: office@stannechurch.com. Web: www.stannechurch.com.
Parish Center—Tel: 541-479-4848. Email: jshibler@stannechurch.com.
School—(Grades PreK-7) Tel: 541-479-1582; Fax: 541-956-4028. Web: www.saintannecatholic-school.org. Jacqueline Henry Ross, Prin. Lay Teachers 7; Students 81.
Kelly Youth Center—Tel: 541-476-5802. Email: hmueller@stannechurch.com. Hans Mueller, Coord. Youth Min.
Catechesis/Religious Program—Tel: 541-479-4848. Email: stannereled@rio.com. Students 135.
Mission—St. Patrick of the Forest 407 W. River St., Cave Junction, Josephine Co. 97523. Tel: 541-592-3658; Fax: 541-592-3580.
Mission—Our Lady of the River Mission 3625 N. River Rd., Gold Hill, Jackson Co. 97525. Tel: 541-582-1373. Email: ourlady@qwestoffice.com.

GRESHAM, MULTNOMAH CO.

1—ST. ANNE (1957) Revs. Jose Luis Gonzalez; David Shaw.
Res.: 1015 S.E. 182nd Ave., 97233-5099. Tel: 503-665-4935; Fax: 503-661-2116.
Catechesis/Religious Program—Students 265.

2—ST. HENRY (1913) Revs. Charles E. Zach; Charles A. Wood; Deacon Del Desart.
Office: 346 N.W. First St., 97030. Tel: 503-665-9129; Fax: 503-665-8238. Email: sthenry_gresham@archdpdx.org. Web: www.sthenrygresham.org.
Catechesis/Religious Program—Students 315.

HILLSBORO, WASHINGTON CO., ST. MATTHEW (1902) [CEM] Revs. Juan Jose Gonzalez, M.Sp.S.; Peter Arteaga, M.Sp.S.; Pablo Sanchez, M.Sp.S.
Church: 475 S.E. 3rd Ave., 97123-4499. Tel: 503-648-1998; Fax: 503-648-4489. Email: parishoffice@stmatthewhillsboro.org. Web: www.stmatthewhillsboro.org.
School—(Grades K-8), 221 S.E. Walnut St., 97123. Tel: 503-648-2512; Fax: 503-648-4518. Email: pdunn@stmatthewschoolhillsboro.org. Lay Teachers 15; Students 233.
Catechesis/Religious Program—Email: mteeter@stmatthewhillsboro.org. Students 265.

INDEPENDENCE, POLK CO., ST. PATRICK CHURCH (1908) Rev. Msgr. Carl Gimpl.
Office: 1275 E St., 97351. Tel: 503-838-1242; Fax: 503-838-3856. Email: stpatrick97351@yahoo.com.
Res.: 1258 E St., 97351. Tel: 503-838-6442.
Catechesis/Religious Program—Students 201.

JORDAN, LINN CO., OUR LADY OF LOURDES (1885) [CEM] [JC 2] Rev. Kevin O'Conor, O.M.I., Moderator.
Res.: 39043 Jordan Rd., Scio, 97374. Tel: 503-394-2437; Fax: 503-394-7045.
Catechesis/Religious Program—Tel: 503-769-2050. Deanne Sumpter, D.R.E. Students 24.
Mission—St. Patrick 7th St., Lyons, Linn Co. 97358. Tel: 503-394-2603; Fax: 503-394-7045.

JUNCTION CITY, LANE CO., ST. HELEN (1916) [CEM] Rev. Thomas Michael Layton.
Res.: 1350 W. 6th Ave., 97448. Tel: 541-998-8053; Fax: 541-998-9474. Email: churchrosehelen@qwestoffice.net.
Catechesis/Religious Program—Students 55.

KEIZER, MARION CO., ST. EDWARD (1967) Rev. Gary L. Zerr.
Office: 5303 River Rd. N., 97303. Tel: 503-393-5323. Email: grace@sainteds.com. Web: www.sainteds.com.
Catechesis/Religious Program—Fax: 503-463-5439. Students 336.

LAKE OSWEGO, CLACKAMAS CO., OUR LADY OF THE LAKE (1890) [CEM] Revs. Joseph S. McMahon; Luan D. Nguyen; Deacons David Partlow; Charles Corey.
Mailing Address: 650 A Ave., 97034-2943. Tel: 503-636-7687; Fax: 503-636-9415. Email: office@ollparish.com. Web: www.ollparish.com.
School—(Grades K-8), 716 A Ave., 97034-2943. Tel: 503-636-2121; Fax: 503-635-7760. Email: jcodd@ollschool-lakeoswego.org. Web: www.ollschool-lakeoswego.org. Joan M. Codd, Prin. Lay Teachers 18; Students 219.
Catechesis/Religious Program—Tel: 503-636-7687; Fax: 503-636-9415. Email: srjan@ollparish.com. Students 315.

LEBANON, LINN CO., ST. EDWARD (1903) Rev. Paul P. Maher, O.M.I.; Deacon Richard E. Triska.
Office: 100 Main St., 97355. Tel: 541-258-5333; Fax: 541-258-2511. Email: stedwardslebanon@comcast.net.
Res.: 251 Second St., 97355.
Catechesis/Religious Program—Tel: 541-258-2224. Students 100.

LINCOLN CITY, LINCOLN CO., ST. AUGUSTINE (1925) [CEM] Rev. Amancio J. Rodrigues; Deacon William Ennis.
1139 N.W. Hwy. 101, 97367. Tel: 541-994-2216; Fax: 541-994-6554. Email: staugustinechurch@embarqmail.com.
Rectory—1139 N.W. Inlet St., 97367.
Catechesis/Religious Program—Students 23.

MCMINNVILLE, YAMHILL CO., ST. JAMES (1876) [CEM] Rev. Terry O'Connell.
Res.: 1145 N.E. First St., 97128. Tel: 503-472-5232; Fax: 503-472-4414.
School—(Grades PreK-5), 206 N. Kirby St., 97128. Tel: 503-472-2661; Fax: 503-472-5201. Lay Teachers 9; Students 107.
Catechesis/Religious Program—Students 180.
Mission—St. Martin de Porres 407 Ferry St., Dayton, Yamhill Co. 97114. Tel: 503-864-2378; Fax: 503-864-3211.

MEDFORD, JACKSON CO., SACRED HEART OF JESUS (1928) [JC] Revs. Liam Cary; Cary Ordiales Reniva.

Church: 517 W. Tenth St., 97501. Tel: 541-779-4661; Fax: 541-774-9474. Web: www.sacredheartmedford.org.
School—Sacred Heart School, (Grades PreSchool-8), 431 S. Ivy, 97501. Tel: 541-772-4105; Fax: 541-732-0633. Email: sgray@shcs.org. Web: www-.shcs.org. Shirley Gray, Prin. Lay Teachers 19; Students 258.
Mission—St. Joseph 280 N. 4th, Jacksonville, Jackson Co. 97530.
Catechesis/Religious Program—Students 389.

MILWAUKIE, CLACKAMAS CO.

1—CHRIST THE KING (1961) Rev. Donald R. Buxman; Deacon Jim Pittman.
Res.: 7414 S.E. Michael Dr., 97222. Tel: 503-659-1475, Ext. 301; Fax: 503-659-6138. Email: office@ctk.cc. Web: www.ctk.cc.
School—(Grades K-8) Tel: 503-785-2411; Fax: 503-794-9607. Email: office@ctkweb.org. Web: www.ctk-web.org. Michael Doran, Prin. Lay Teachers 15; Students 215.
Catechesis/Religious Program—Tel: 503-785-2413. Email: religiouseducation@ctk.cc. Students 164.

2—ST. JOHN THE BAPTIST (1912) Revs. Maxy D'costa, S.F.X.; Peter Fernandes, S.F.X., Parochial Vicar.
Res.: 10955 S.E. 25th, 97222. Tel: 503-654-5449; Fax: 503-653-9567. Email: parishoffice@sjbcatholicchurch.org. Web: www.sjbcatholicchurch.org.
School—(Grades PreSchool-8), 10956 S.E. 25th, 97222. Tel: 503-654-0200; Fax: 503-654-8419. Web: www.sjbcatholicschool.org. Sisters 2; Lay Teachers 17; Students 211.
Catechesis/Religious Program—Tel: 503-659-2760; Fax: 503-653-9567. Email: reoffice@qwest.net. Students 140.

MOLALLA, CLACKAMAS CO., ST. JAMES (1938) Rev. R. Ed Coleman.
Res.: 301 Frances St., 97038. Tel: 503-829-2080; Fax: 503-829-2806.
Catechesis/Religious Program—Tel: 503-829-2880. Students 124.

MONROE, BENTON CO., ST. ROSE OF LIMA (1883) [CEM] Rev. Thomas Michael Layton.
Mailing Address & Office: *c/o St. Helen*, 1350 W. 6th Ave., Junction City, 97448.
Church: 470 S. Fifth, 97456. Tel: 541-998-8053; Fax: 541-998-9474. Email: churchrosehelen@qwestoffice.net.
Catechesis/Religious Program—Students 15.

MT. ANGEL, MARION CO., ST. MARY (1881), (German), [CEM 2] Rev. Philip Waibel, O.S.B.
Res.: 575 E. College St., 97362. Tel: 503-845-2296; Fax: 503-845-2297. Web: www.stmarymtangel.org.
Catechesis/Religious Program—Tel: 503-845-4282. Email: kabaldwin@hotmail.com. Students 387.
Mission—Holy Rosary [CEM] Scotts Mills, Marion Co.

MYRTLE CREEK, DOUGLAS CO., ALL SOULS (1952) [JC] Rev. William A. Ryan, O.S.A.
Res.: 1242 N.E. Spruce St., P.O. Box 810, 97457. Tel: 541-863-3271; Fax: 541-863-6759. Email: allsoulsparish@gmail.com.
Catechesis/Religious Program—Students 18.
Mission—Holy Family 243 Marshall Ave., P.O. Box 136, Glendale, Douglas Co. 97442.

NEWBERG, YAMHILL CO., ST. PETER (1907) Rev. Donald Gutmann.
Res.: 2315 N. Main, 97132-6081. Tel: 503-538-4312; Fax: 503-538-5693. Email: stpeter.office@verizon.net.
Catechesis/Religious Program—Email: smcdougal@archdpdx.org. Stacey McDougal, C.R.E. Students 100.

NEWPORT, LINCOLN CO., SACRED HEART PARISH (1889) [JC] Rev. Brian V. Allbright.
Rectory—140 N.W. 10th St., 97365.
Church: 927 N. Coast Hwy., P.O. Box 843, 97365. Tel: 541-265-5101. Email: sacredheartchurch@charterinternet.com.
Mission—St. Mary 231 E. Logsden Rd., Siletz, Lincoln Co. 97380. Tel: 541-444-1164.
Catechesis/Religious Program—Tel: 541-265-5101. Students 146.

NORTH BEND, COOS CO., HOLY REDEEMER (1906) [JC] Rev. Karl Schray.
Res.: 2250 16th St., 97459. Tel: 541-756-6901; Fax: 541-756-3234.
Catechesis/Religious Program—Tel: 541-756-0161. Students 110.

NORTH PLAINS, WASHINGTON CO., ST. EDWARD (1913) [CEM] Most Rev. Kenneth D. Steiner.
Mailing Address: P.O. Box 507, 97133.
Church: 10990 N.W. 313th Ave., 97133. Tel: 503-647-2131 (Parish); Fax: 503-647-7527. Email: sainted@coho.net.
Catechesis/Religious Program—Tel: 503-647-2131. Students 102.

OAKRIDGE, LANE CO., ST. MICHAEL (1941) Rev. James Dowd (Retired).
Res.: 76387 Crestview St., P.O. Box 422, 97463. Tel: 541-782-3262. Email: pmorrison@archdpdx.org.
Mission—St. Henry [JC] 38925 Dexter Rd., P.O. Box 65, Dexter, Lane Co. 97431. Tel: 541-937-3033.
Catechesis/Religious Program—Students 10.

OREGON CITY, CLACKAMAS CO., ST. JOHN THE APOSTLE (1842) [CEM] Rev. Richard Huneger.
Res.: 417 Washington St., 97045. Tel: 503-742-8200; Fax: 503-742-8219. Email: churchsja@aol.com. Web: stjohn_oc.org.
School—(Grades PreSchool-8) Tel: 503-742-8230; Fax: 503-742-8239. Email: principal@sja-eagles.com. Web: sja-eagles.com. Machelle Nagel, Prin. Lay Teachers 15; Students 230.
Catechesis/Religious Program—Students 122.

OREGON CITY-REDLAND, CLACKAMAS CO., ST. PHILIP BENIZI (1969) Rev. Michael Patrick.
Res.: 18211 S. Henrici Rd., 97045. Tel: 503-631-2882; Fax: 503-631-7443. Web: www.philipbenizi.org.
Catechesis/Religious Program—Tel: 503-631-7124. Students 62.

RAINIER, COLUMBIA CO., NATIVITY B.V.M. (1909) Rev. Henry Rufo; Ron Haley, Pastoral Assoc.
Res.: 204 E. C St., P.O. Box 340, 97048. Tel: 503-556-5641. Email: nativitybvm@hotmail.com.
Catechesis/Religious Program—Students 15.
Mission—St. John the Baptist High St., Clatskanie, Columbia Co. 97016.

REEDSPORT, DOUGLAS CO., ST. JOHN THE APOSTLE (1924) Rev. David Brown.
Res. & Rectory: 12 Saint Johns Way, 97467. Tel: 541-271-5621. Email: stjohns@presys.com.
Catechesis/Religious Program—Students 5.

ROCKAWAY, TILLAMOOK CO., ST. MARY BY THE SEA (1927) [JC] Rev. Joseph Sebasty, Parish Admin.
Mailing Address: P.O. Box 390, 97136.
Church: 275 S. Pacific St., 97136. Tel: 503-355-2661 (Office); Fax: 503-355-9611.

ROSEBURG, DOUGLAS CO., ST. JOSEPH (1867) [CEM] Rev. Panneer Selvam; Deacon John H. Stenbeck.
Rectory—2425 W. Military Rd., 97470.
Church: 800 W. Stanton St., 97471. Tel: 541-673-5157; Fax: 541-672-5022.
Catechesis/Religious Program—Students 97.

ROY, WASHINGTON CO., ST. FRANCIS OF ASSISI (1908) [CEM] Rev. Philip M. Hemming.
Res.: 39135 N.W. Harrington Rd., Banks, 97106. Tel: 503-324-2231.
School—(Grades K-8), 39085 N.W. Harrington Rd., Banks, 97106. Tel: 503-324-2182; Fax: 503-324-7032. Sisters 1; Lay Teachers 5; Students 120.
Catechesis/Religious Program—Students 36.

ST. HELENS, COLUMBIA CO., ST. FREDERIC (1910) Rev. Luan Quach Tran.
Church: 175 S. 13th St., 97051. Tel: 503-397-0148; Fax: 503-366-3870. Email: stfred@comcast.net.
Catechesis/Religious Program—Tel: 503-397-0366. Students 52.

ST. LOUIS, MARION CO., ST. LOUIS, Closed. For sacramental records contact Sacred Heart-St. Louis, Gervias.

ST. PAUL, MARION CO., ST. PAUL (1839) [CEM] Rev. Msgr. Gregory Moys.
Res.: 20217 Christie St., N.E., P.O. Box 454, 97137. Tel: 503-633-4611.
School—(Grades PreK-8), 20327 Christie St., N.E., P.O. Box 188, 97137. Tel: 503-633-4622; Fax: 503-633-4624. Email: spps@stpaultel.com. Web: www.stpaulparochial.org. Mr. Charles F. Geis, Prin. Religious 1; Lay Teachers 5; Students 91.

SALEM, MARION CO.

1—ST. JOSEPH (1864) [JC] Revs. Todd Molinari; David Leo Jaspers. In Res., Rev. Antonio Gomes.
Church: 721 Chemeketa St., N.E., 97301. Tel: 503-581-1623; Fax: 503-581-7271. Email: carolyn@stjosephchurch.com. Web: stjosephchurch.com.
School—(Grades PreK-6), 373 Winter St., N.E., 97301. Tel: 503-581-2147; Fax: 503-399-7045. Email: school@stjosephchurch.com. Web: www.stjoseph.com/school. Sisters of the Holy Names of Jesus and Mary 2; Lay Teachers 6; Students 161.
Catechesis/Religious Program—Tel: 503-585-5095. Email: re@stjosephchurch.com. Students 588.

2—QUEEN OF PEACE (1963) Rev. Timothy Mockaitis; Darlene Joynt, Pastoral Asst.; Bryce Herrmann, Pastoral Assoc.
Office: P.O. Box 3016, 97302. Tel: 503-364-7202; Fax: 503-364-5882. Web: www.qpsalem.org.
School—(Grades K-6), 4227 Lone Oak Rd., S.E., 97302. Tel: 503-362-3443; Fax: 503-589-9411. Email: school@qpsalem.org. Debilyn Janota, Prin. Lay Teachers 12; Students 151.
Catechesis/Religious Program—Tel: 503-364-7202; Fax: 503-364-5882. Tricia Boyle, D.R.E. (PreK-Elementary); Martin Gay, D.R.E. (Grades 6-12); Cheri Posedel, D.R.E. (Grades 6-12). Students 256.

3—ST. VINCENT DE PAUL (1925) [JC] Rev. Joseph Heuberger; Deacon Jose Roman Mendez; Sr. Joyce Barsotti, S.S.M.O., Pastoral Assoc.; Lisa Mangers, Youth Min. (Young Adults).
Res.: 1010 Columbia St., N.E., 97301-7265. Tel: 503-363-4589; Fax: 503-363-9493. Email: stvdp@qwest.net. Web: www.stvincentsalem.org.
School—(Grades PreK-6) Tel: 503-363-8457; Fax: 503-363-1516. Email: st.vincent@comcast.net. Web: www.stvincentsalem.org. Lay Teachers 5; Students 102.
Catechesis/Religious Program—1015 Columbia St. N.E., 97301-7207. Tel: 503-363-2166; Fax: 503-363-2339. Sheila Scott, D.R.E. Students 231.

SANDY, CLACKAMAS CO., ST. MICHAEL THE ARCHANGEL (1898) Rev. Patrick F. Walsh.
Res.: 18090 S.E. Langensand Rd., 97055-9427. Tel: 503-668-4446; Fax: 503-668-4446.
Mission—St. John the Evangelist
Catechesis/Religious Program—Students 47.

SCAPPOOSE, COLUMBIA CO., ST. WENCESLAUS (1911) [CEM] Rev. James R. Stange.
Parish Office—Tel: 503-543-2110; Fax: 503-543-5159.
Res.: 51555 Old Portland Rd., 97056.
Catechesis/Religious Program—Tel: 503-543-7425; Fax: 503-543-5159. Students 114.

SCIO, LINN CO., ST. BERNARD (1912) Rev. Kevin O'Conor, O.M.I.
Mailing Address: P.O. Box 45, 97374. Tel: 503-394-2625.
38810 Cherry St., 97374. Tel: 541-258-5333.
Catechesis/Religious Program—Tel: 503-394-3732. James Brown, D.R.E. at St. Bernard; Betty Beary, D.R.E. at St. Thomas. Students 11.
Mission—St. Thomas 647 Third St., Jefferson, Marion Co. 97352. Tel: 541-327-2343.

SEASIDE, CLATSOP CO., OUR LADY OF VICTORY (1913) Rev. Nicholas Nilema, A.L.C.P./O.S.S.; Deacon Vern Korchinski.
P.O. Box 29, 97138.
Church: 120 Oceanway, 97138. Tel: 503-738-6161; Fax: 503-738-6182. Email: olvoffice@seasurf.net.
Mission—St. Peter the Fisherman, Tel: 503-436-2876.
Catechesis/Religious Program—Students 30.

SHADY COVE, JACKSON CO., OUR LADY OF FATIMA (1955) Rev. William McHugh, O.M.I.
Office & Mailing Address: P.O. Box 116, 97539.
Office: 37 Church Ln., 97539.
Church: 56 Williams Ln., 97539. Tel: 541-878-2479.
Catechesis/Religious Program—Students 27.

SHAW, MARION CO., ST. MARY - SHAW formerly St. Mary (1906) [CEM] Revs. Ben R. Innes, O.F.M.; Irudayaraj Amalanathan, Admin.
Mailing Address: P.O. Box 338, Aumsville, 97325-0338. Tel: 503-362-6159; Fax: 503-371-6435.
Res.: 9168 Silver Falls Hwy., S.E., Aumsville, 97325.
Catechesis/Religious Program—Students 42.

SHERIDAN, YAMHILL CO., GOOD SHEPHERD (1908) Rev. Terry O'Connell; Deacon David J. Briedwell, Pastoral Admin.
Mailing Address: 1145 N.E. First St., McMinnville, 97128.
Church: 127 N.E. Hill St., 97378. Tel: 503-843-2206; Fax: 503-843-2206.

SHERWOOD, WASHINGTON CO., ST. FRANCIS (1921) Rev. Thomas McCarthy, S.J.
Mailing Address & Church: 15651 S.W. Oregon St., 97140. Tel: 503-625-6185. Email: office@stfrancissherwood.org. Web: www.stfrancissherwood.org.
Res.: 22942 S.W. Pine St., 97140. Tel: 503-625-6851; Fax: 503-625-5914.
School—(Grades K-8), 15643 S.W. Oregon St., 97140. Tel: 503-625-0497; Fax: 503-625-0564. Web: www.stfrancissherwood.org. Lay Teachers 13; Students 182.
Catechesis/Religious Program—Tel: 503-625-6187; Fax: 503-625-5914. Students 194.

SILVERTON, MARION CO., ST. PAUL (1914) [CEM] Rev. William Hammelman, O.S.B.
Church: 1410 Pine St., 97381. Tel: 503-873-2044; Fax: 503-873-0304. Email: stpaulsilverton@verizon.net.
Catechesis/Religious Program—Students 190.

SPRINGFIELD, LANE CO., ST. ALICE (1947) Rev. Roy L. Antunez, S.J.
Res.: 1520 F St., 97477-4161. Tel: 541-747-7041; Fax: 541-746-5213.
Catechesis/Religious Program—Students 130.

STAYTON, MARION CO., IMMACULATE CONCEPTION (1903) [CEM] Rev. Steve Geer.
Res.: 1077 N. Sixth Ave., 97383. Tel: 503-769-2656; Fax: 503-769-5621. Web: www.immacstayton.org.
School—St. Mary, (Grades PreSchool-8), 1066 N. 6th St., 97383. Tel: 503-769-2718; Fax: 503-769-0560. Email: rick.schindler@stmarystayton.org. Web: www.stmarystayton.org. Lay Teachers 29; Students 220.
Catechesis/Religious Program—Email: gschmitt@archdpdx.org. Students 49.

SUBLIMITY, MARION CO., ST. BONIFACE (1879) [CEM] Rev. Irudayaraj Amalanathan.
Res.: 375 S.E. Church St., 97385. Tel: 503-769-5664; Fax: 503-769-4292. Email: boniface@wvi.com.
Mission—St. Catherine of Siena First & Ivy, Mill City, 97360.

Mission—St. Christopher 120 S. Detroit Ave., Detroit, 97342.

SUTHERLIN, DOUGLAS CO., ST. FRANCIS XAVIER (1957) Rev. Panneer Selvam; Deacon John H. Stenbeck.
Mailing Address: 800 Stanton St., Roseburg, 97470. Tel: 541-673-5157 (Office); Fax: 541-672-5022.

SWEET HOME, LINN CO., ST. HELEN CATHOLIC CHURCH formerly St. Helen (1953) Rev. Fred Jeffrey Anthony; Deacon Robert Malone.
Mailing Address: 600 Sixth Ave., 97386.
Res.: 815 Fifth Ave., 97386. Tel: 541-367-2530. Email: sthelenholytrinitysho@centurytel.net.
Catechesis/Religious Program—Students 18.
Mission—Holy Trinity 104 Blakely Ave., P.O. Box 145, Brownsville, Linn Co. 97327.

TIGARD, WASHINGTON CO., ST. ANTHONY (1910) [CEM] Revs. Leslie M. Sieg; Theodore R. Prentice; Deacons Art Schmidt; Mario Espinoza.
Res.: 9905 S.W. McKenzie St., 97223. Tel: 503-639-4179; Fax: 503-624-2364. Email: office@stanthonytigard.org. Web: www.stanthonytigard.org.
School—(Grades PreK-8), 12645 S.W. Pacific Hwy., 97223. Fax: 503-639-4179. Email: school@stanthonytigard.org. Karen Bolliger, Prin. Lay Teachers 25; Students 341.
Catechesis/Religious Program—Students 543.
Mission—Mission of the Atonement 7400 S.W. Scholls Ferry Rd., Beaverton, Washington Co. 97008.

TILLAMOOK, TILLAMOOK CO., SACRED HEART (1890) [CEM] Rev. Joseph Sebasty.
2411 Fifth St., 97141. Tel: 503-842-6647; Fax: 503-842-3897.
Catechesis/Religious Program—Tel: 503-842-8984. Students 115.
Mission—St. Joseph P.O. Box 9, Cloverdale, Tillamook Co. 97112. Tel: 503-392-3685.

TUALATIN, CLACKAMAS CO., RESURRECTION CATHOLIC CHURCH formerly Church of the Resurrection (1981) Rev. William C. Moisant.
Mailing Address: 21060 S.W. Stafford Rd., 97062. Tel: 503-638-1579; Fax: 503-638-8754. Email: resurrec@teleport.com. Web: www.resurrection-catholic-parish.org.
Catechesis/Religious Program—Anna Arnesen Mosey, Dir. Faith Formation. Students 330.

VENETA, LANE CO., ST. CATHERINE OF SIENA (1954) Rev. J. Michael Morrissey.
Res.: 25181 E. Broadway, P.O. Box 277, 97487. Tel: 541-935-3933; Fax: 541-935-4184. Email: st.cofsienaveneta@aol.com.
Catechesis/Religious Program—Students 34.

VERBOORT, WASHINGTON CO., VISITATION B.V.M. (1875), (Dutch), [CEM] Rev. Scott A. Vandehey.
Church: 4189 N.W. Visitation Rd., Forest Grove, 97116. Tel: 503-357-3860; Fax: 503-359-0819.
School—(Grades K-8) Tel: 503-357-6990; Fax: 503-359-0819. Email: secretary@vcskinight.org. Lay Teachers 13; Students 139.
Catechesis/Religious Program—Tel: 503-357-4190. Students 139.

VERNONIA, COLUMBIA CO., ST. MARY OF IMMACULATE CONCEPTION (1923) Rev. Luan Tran, Admin.
Church: 960 Missouri Ave., P.O. Box 312, 97064. Tel: 503-429-8841; Fax: 503-429-8841 (call first). Email: stmarys08@agalis.net.
Catechesis/Religious Program—Tel: 503-429-8092. Students 31.
Mission—Our Lady of the Woods [JC]

WALDPORT, LINCOLN CO., ST. ANTHONY (1949) Rev. Gerard Steckler, S.J., Admin.
Mailing Address: P.O. Box 770, 97394. Tel: 541-563-3246; Fax: 541-563-3734. Email: stanthony@peak.org. Web: www.pioneer.net/~stanthony. 685 N. Broadway, 97394.
Catechesis/Religious Program—Students 12.

WILSONVILLE, CLACKAMAS CO., ST. CYRIL (1926) Rev. Stephen A. Stobie.
Church: 9205 S.W. Fifth St., 97070. Tel: 503-682-2332; Fax: 503-685-9294. Email: st.cyril@verizon.net. Web: www.stcyrilparish.org.
Catechesis/Religious Program—Students 50.

WOODBURN, MARION CO., ST. LUKE (1899) [CEM] Rev. Angel A. Perez.
Office: 417 Harrison St., 97071. Tel: 503-981-5011; Fax: 503-981-5012. Email: st.luke@wbcable.net. Web: www.stlukewoodburn.com.
School—(Grades K-8), 529 Harrison St., 97071. Tel: 503-981-7441; Fax: 503-982-4697. Sisters 1; Lay Teachers 9; Students 183.
Catechesis/Religious Program—Students 375.
Mission—St. Agnes 3052 D St., Hubbard, Marion Co. 97032.

YAMHILL, YAMHILL CO., ST. JOHN (1910) Rev. David Janes, Admin.
Mailing Address: P.O. Box 580, 97148. Tel: 503-662-4291. Email: saintjohns@spiritone.com.
Catechesis/Religious Program—Students 60.

SOUTHEAST ASIAN VICARIATE
PORTLAND, MULTNOMAH CO., SOUTHEAST ASIAN VICARIATE (1982), Please refer to Our Lady of Lavang Church, Portland, OR., 5404 N.E. Alameda Dr., 97213.
Mission—St. Andrew Dung Lac 13715 S.W. Walker Rd., Beaverton, Washington Co. 97005. Tel: 503-643-9528; Fax: 503-644-8486.

Chaplains of Public Institutions

PORTLAND. *Department of Veterans' Affairs Medical Center*, 3710 S.W. U.S. Veterans' Hospital Rd., Box 1034, 97207. Tel: 503-220-8262, Ext. 57027; 503-220-8262, Ext. 57201; Fax: 503-721-1049. Rev. William E. Wickham, C.S.C.
Oregon Health Sciences University, 3181 S.W. Sam Jackson Park Rd., 97239. Tel: 503-222-2168. Rev. Jim Kolb, C.S.P. Tel: 503-222-2168.

EUGENE. *Lane County Adult Corrections*, 101 W. Fifth Ave., 97401. Tel: 541-682-2174; Fax: 541-682-2278. Sisters Margaret Graziano, S.N.J.M., Carol Lee, S.N.J.M.

NORTH BEND. *Shutter Creek Correctional Institution*, 95200 Shutters Landing Ln., 97459-0303. Tel: 541-756-6666; 541-756-6901; Fax: 541-756-6888. Rev. Karl Schray, Catholic Volunteer.

ROSEBURG. *U.S. Veterans' Administration Hospital*, 913 N.W. Garden Valley Blvd., 97470-6513. Tel: 541-440-1000, Ext. 40023. Deacon John Stenbeck.

SALEM. *Hillcrest Youth Correctional Facility*, 2450 Strong Rd., 97302. Tel: 503-986-0421; Fax: 503-986-0406. Rev. Ted Frison.
Mill Creek Correctional Facility, 5465 Turner Rd., 97301-9400. Tel: 503-378-2144. Rev. Dick Roy, Chap.
Oregon State Correctional Institution, 3405 Deer Park Dr., S.E., 97310. Tel: 503-373-0100. Vacant.
Oregon State Penitentiary, 2605 State St., 97310. Tel: 503-378-2453. Sr. Arnadene Welton Bean, S.N.J.M., Chap.
Santiam Correctional Institution, 4005 Aumsville Hwy., S.E., 97301-9112. Tel: 503-378-2144. Rev. Dick Roy, Chap.

SHERIDAN. *Federal Correctional Institution*, 27072 Ballston Rd., 97378-9601. Tel: 503-843-4442, Ext. 256. Vacant.

WHITE CITY. *U.S. Veterans Affairs Domiciliary* 97503. Tel: 541-826-2111, Ext. 3321. Felix Vistal, Chap.

WILSONVILLE. *Coffee Creek Correctional Facility*, P.O. Box 9000, 97070. Tel: 503-570-6604; Fax: 503-570-6617. Vacant.

WOODBURN. *MacLaren Youth Correctional Facility*, 2630 N. Pacific Hwy., 97071. Tel: 503-981-9531, Ext. 315; Fax: 503-982-4414. Vacant.

Special Assignment:
Revs.—
Betschart, Joseph, North American College 00120 Vatican City State.
Kueber, Michael I., Inst. dei Missionari dello Spirito Santo, Piazza S. Salvatore in Campo 57, Roma 00186 Italy.
Lange, Theodore Severin, Pontifical North American College 00120 Vatican City State.
Vuky, Michael, DeSales House, 721 Lawrence St., N.E., Washington, DC 20017.

On Duty Outside the Archdiocese:
Revs.—
Cihak, John, Villa Stritch, Via della Nocetta 63, Roma 00164 Italy.
Clark, David, Tyburn Convent, 8 Hyde Park Pl., Bayswater Rd., London W2 2LT England.
Coleman, James, Casilla 919, Santa Cruz, Bolivia.
King, Martin, 18WG/HC PSC-80, Box 22381, Apo, AP 96367.

Absent on Leave:
Revs.—
Adams, Daniel, 2150 Clinton Ave., Apt. C, Alameda, CA 94501.
Galluzzo, James, 1314 N.W. Irving, #512, 97209.
Hoang, Joseph, P.O. Box 3535, Bay City, 97107.
Junge, Heiko, 2838 E. Burnside St., 97213.
Sprauer, Michael, St. Joseph Parish, 721 Chemeketa St., N.E., Salem, 97301.

Retired:
Rev. Msgrs.—
Campbell, Francis, St. John Vianney Residence, 4525-A S.W. St. John Vianney Way, Beaverton, 97007.
Dernbach, Arthur, St. John Vianney Residence, 4630-A S.W. St. John Vianney Way, Beaverton, 97007.
Pham, James Ninh Van, 29891 S.W. Camelot St., Wilsonville, 97070.
Revs.—
Altstock, Edward, St. John Vianney Residence, 4630-C S.W. St. John Vianney Way, Beaverton, 97007.
Alvares, Augustine, 1555 S. White Rd., San Jose, CA 95127.
Baccellieri, Joseph, 13055 S.E. Stark St., #41, 97233.
Beno, Joseph, 13090 S.W. Laurmont Dr., Tigard, 97223.
Bliven, Edmond, St. John Vianney Residence, 4595-A S.W. St. John Vianney Way, Beaverton, 97007.
Borho, Charles D., Mt. Angel Towers, 1 Towers Ln., #2152, Mount Angel, 97362.
Brennan, Cathal, 14544 S.E. Brightwood Ave., Milwaukie, 97267.
Brouillard, John, 17704 N.W. Shadyfir Loop, Space 39, Beaverton, 97006.
Brown, Bruce, 6005 Skyline Dr., West Linn, 97068.
Chun, Francis, 4525-B S.W. St. John Vianney Way, Beaverton, 97007.
Cieslinski, Robert, Maryville Nursing Home, 14645 S.W. Farmington Rd., Beavertown, 97007.
Cullings, David Ronald, 638 Wimbleton Ct., Eugene, 97401.
Cunniff, Vincent, St. John Vianney Residence, 4655-D S.W. St. John Vianney Way, Beaverton, 97007.
DePra, Italo, 78 Bonita Rd., Chula Vista, CA 91911.
Dieringer, James J., P.O. Box 683, Pacific City, 97135.
Domin, John M., 14645 S.W. Farmington, Beaverton, 97007.
Dowd, James, 1875 N.E. Country Club Dr., Canby, 97013.
Durand, Donald, 62 N.W. Ava, Gresham, 97030.
Flach, Carl, J.C.L., 4655-A S.W. St. John Vianney Way, Beaverton, 97007.
Fleming, Brendan, Maryville Nursing Home, 14645 S.W. Farmington Rd., Beaverton, 97007.
Gothe, Marcus, St. John Vianney Residence, 4655-B S.W. St. John Vianney Way, Beaverton, 97007.
Hume, Kenneth, 19453 Stillmeadow Dr., Oregon City, 97045.
Hwang, Bernard, O.S.B., 19526 Lazy Creek Ln., Oregon City, 97045.
Jacobson, Gary, St. John Vianney Residence, 4595-B S.W. St. John Vianney Way, Beaverton, 97007.
Knusel, Frank, 34799 N. Honeyman Rd., Scappoose, 97056.
Krall, Jack, 1167 N.W. Wallula, #E-330, Gresham, 97030.
Krueger, Robert, 1136 S.E. Oak, 97214.
Lau, Michael, 6305 S.W. Terwilliger Blvd., 97201.
Linehan, Cornelius, 15727 N.E. Russell, #239, 97230.
McGrann, John, 1500 N.E. 15th Ave. #345, 97232.
McGreevy, Thomas More J., O.P., Holy Rosary Priory, 375 N.E. Clackamas St., 97232.
McHugh, Donald, 4525 S.W. St. John Vianney Way, Apt. C, Beaverton, 97007.
Moore, Neil, 1619 N.W. Bridgeway Ln., Beaverton, 97006.
Mosbrucker, Jacob A., 3828 N.E. 79th St., 97213.
Neuville, Joseph, Mt. Angel Towers, One Towers Lane, Box 2176, Mount Angel, 97362.
Nguyen, Joseph Hau Duc, S.E. Asian Vicariate, 5404 N.E. Alameda Dr., 97213.
Palladino, Robert J., 43330 E. Marmot Rd., Sandy, 97055.
Quintal, Gerald, 835 Sundown Dr., North Otis, 97368.
Reynolds, Daniel, St. John Vianney Residence, 4655-C S.W. St. John Vianney Way, Beaverton, 97007.
Rodakowski, Louis, Maryville Nursing Home, 14645 S.W. Farmington Rd., Beaverton, 97007.
Sassano, Rock, 71403 Fishhawk Rd., Birkenfeld, 97016.
Waddill, Dale T., 208 Madison St., Oregon City, 97045-2535.
Weber, Theodore, 14460 S.E. Sieben Creek Dr., Clackamas, 97015.

Permanent Deacons:
Altenhofen, Thomas, St. Mary, Eugene
Amsberry, Charles, St. Michael, Portland
Anderson, Chris, St. Mary, Corvallis
Appel, Leo Henry, II, Star of the Sea, Brookings
Bloudek, William, St. Francis, Sherwood
Bozulich, Martin, Holy Redeemer, North Bend
Briedwell, David, Good Shepherd, Sheridan
Brinker, Kenneth, St. Peter, Portland
Burke, Harold, Immaculate Heart, Portland
Caldwell, Michael, St. Joseph the Worker, Portland
Chapin, Robert L., Jr., St. Anne, Grants Pass
Ciffone, Donald, St. Rose, Portland
Corey, Charles, Our Lady of the Lake, Lake Oswego
Delgado, Gerald Matthew, St. John the Baptist, Milwaukie
Desart, Del, St. Henry, Gresham

Desmarais, Dennis, St. Juan Diego, Portland
Diehm, Brian, St. Thomas More, Portland
Dooley, Timothy, Holy Family, Portland
Edmonson, Brett Michael, Holy Trinity, Beaverton
Ennis, William, St. Augustine, Lincoln City
Espinoza, Jesus, St. Alexander, Cornelius
Espinoza, Marco, St. Anthony, Tigard
Giger, Gerald, St. Patrick, Canby
Gornick, Thomas, Cathedral, Portland
Gutierrez, Jose, Holy Cross, Portland
Hammes, David, St. Cecilia, Beaverton
Jacob, Ramon, St. Andrew, Portland
Korchinski, Vernard, Our Lady of Victory, Seaside
Larner, Martin, Jr., St. Joseph, Roseburg
Little, Robert, St. Pius X, Portland
Lukosh, Robert, Holy Redeemer, Portland
Luz, John, St. Paul, Eugene
Malone, Robert, St. Helen, Sweet Home
McVeigh, James G., Our Lady of the Mountain, Ashland
Mendez, Jose, St. Vincent de Paul, Salem
Morin, Edward, (Unassigned)
Page, Robert, St. Patrick, Independence
Park, William Thomas, St. Stephen, Portland
Partlow, David, Our Lady of the Lake, Lake Oswego
Philip, Donald, (Unassigned)
Pittman, James Allen, Christ the King, Milwaukie
Potts, Francis, St. Mary, Corvallis
Richardson, Bill, St. Cecilia, Beaverton
Ries, John D., (Retired)
Rilatt, John, Holy Redeemer, Portland
Rodriguez, Raul, St. James, McMinnville
Schmidt, Arthur, St. Anthony, Tigard
Seifer, Leo, St. Mary, Mount Angel
Soper, Leonard, St. Benedict Lodge, McKenzie Bridge
Sorensen, David E., St. Peter, Eugene
Stenbeck, John H., St. Joseph, Roseburg
Tabor, Stephen, Immaculate Conception, Stayton
Triska, Richard, St. Edward, Lebanon
Vandecoevering, Allen, St. Joseph, Salem
Vu, An, Our Lady of Sorrows, Portland
Wagner, Daniel, St. Ignatius, Portland
Williams, Richard, St. John the Baptist, Port Orford; Mission of Holy Trinity, Bandon

INSTITUTIONS LOCATED IN THE ARCHDIOCESE

[A] SEMINARIES AND SCHOLASTICATES

PORTLAND. *Franciscan Formation Community*, 827 N.E. Alberta, 97211. Tel: 503-287-9223. Web: www.sbfranciscans.org. Bro. Robert Rodrigues, O.F.M., Postulant Dir. Brothers 1; Postulants 5.

Jesuit Novitiate of Sheridan Orgeon, 3301 S.E. 45th Ave., 97206. Tel: 503-774-5699; Fax: 503-775-6335. Revs. Paul Fitterer, S.J., Asst. Dir. Novices & Socius; Thomas J. Lamanna, S.J., Rector & Dir. Novices. Priests 2; Novices 7.

MOUNT ANGEL. *Felix Rougier House of Studies*, 585 E. College St., 97362. Tel: 503-845-1181; Fax: 503-845-1189. P.O. Box 499, St. Benedict, 97373. Revs. Celso Marquez, M.Sp.S., Supr.; Joel Quezada, M.Sp.S., Vice Supr. Priests 2; Brothers 10.

ST. BENEDICT. *Mount Angel Seminary* 97373. Tel: 503-845-3951; Fax: 503-845-3128. Email: registrar@mtangel.edu. Rt. Rev. Peter Eberle, O.S.B., Vice-Rector & Dir. of Human Formation (Retired); Revs. Paschal Cheline, O.S.B., Vice Rector, Dir. Spiritual Life; Ezekiel Lotz, O.S.B., Academic Vice Pres.; Paul Peri, Dir. Pastoral Formation; Sr. Virginia Schroeder, S.N.J.M., Dir. of Admission; Dr. Katherine Kirsch, Ph.D., Dean Undergraduate School; Marina Keys, Registrar; Tamara Swanson-Orr, Dir. Immigration Svcs. & Office Mgr. Priests 16; Deacons 1; Brothers 1; Sisters 2; Lay Teachers 23.

Formation Directors: Rt. Rev. Peter Eberle, O.S.B. (Retired); Revs. Ralph Recker, O.S.B.; Liem Nguyen, O.S.B.; Rory Pitstick; Joel Quezada, M.Sp.S.; Terrence P. Tompkins.

[B] COLLEGES AND UNIVERSITIES

PORTLAND. **University of Portland*, 5000 N. Willamette Blvd., 97203. Tel: 503-943-7911; Fax: 503-943-7401. Email: webmaster@up.edu. Web: www.up.edu. Drew Harrington, Dir. Library. Endowed by the Congregation of Holy Cross; established 1901. Priests 9; Sisters 4; Lay Teachers 210; Adjunct Faculty 112; Students 3,706.

Executive Officers of the University: Revs. William Beauchamp, C.S.C., Pres.; Thomas Doyle, C.S.C., Exec. Vice Pres. Univ. Rels.; Bro. Donald J. Stabrowski, C.S.C., Provost; Dr. John Goldrick, Vice Pres. Student Svcs.; James Lyons, Vice Pres. Univ. Rels.; Denis Ransmeier, Financial Vice Pres.; James Ravelli, Chief Information Officer; Madeline Doll, Admin. Asst., CSC Office.

Faculty Staff: Revs. Jeffrey Allison, C.S.C.; Robert Antonelli, C.S.C.; William Beauchamp, C.S.C.; Michael T. Belinsky, C.S.C.; Gary Chamberland, C.S.C.; Thomas Doyle, C.S.C.; Charles Gordon, C.S.C.; Patrick Hannon, C.S.C.; Thomas Hosinski, C.S.C.; William Hund, C.S.C. (Retired); James Lies, C.S.C.; Charles McCoy, C.S.C.; Francis Murphy, C.S.C., Rel. Supr.; Claude Pomerleau, C.S.C.; Richard Rutherford, C.S.C.; Charles D. Sherrer, C.S.C. (Retired); Ronald Wasowski, C.S.C.; Arthur F. Wheeler, C.S.C. In Res. Revs. Richard Berg, C.S.C. (Retired); George C. Bernard, C.S.C. (Retired); John Donato, C.S.C., Assoc. Vice Pres. Student Life; James Kelly, C.S.C. (Retired); Chester Prusynski, C.S.C. (Retired); William E. Wickham, C.S.C.; John Wironen, C.S.C.; Bros. Ken Allen, C.S.C., (Retired); Fulgence Dougherty, C.S.C.; Donald J. Stabrowski, C.S.C., Provost.

Following is the Academic Structure of the University: Bro. Donald J. Stabrowski, C.S.C., Provost.

College of Arts and Sciences Tel: 503-943-7760; Fax: 503-943-7804. Rev. Stephen C. Rowan, Dean.

School of Nursing Tel: 503-943-7509; Fax: 503-943-7729. Dr. Joanne R. Warner, Interim Dean.

School of Business Administration Tel: 503-943-7224; Fax: 503-943-8041. Dr. Robin D. Anderson, Dean.

School of Engineering Tel: 503-943-7314; Fax: 503-943-7316. Dr. Zia J. Yamayee, Dean.

School of Education Tel: 503-943-7315; Fax: 503-943-8042.

Graduate School Tel: 503-943-7107. Dr. Thomas G. Greene, Dean; Drew Harrington, Dir. Tel: 503-943-7111; Fax: 503-943-7491.

MARYLHURST. *Marylhurst University*, P.O. Box 261, 97036. Tel: 503-636-8141; Fax: 503-636-9526. Email: studentinfo@marylhurst.edu. Web: www.marylhurst.edu. Judith Johansen, J.D., Pres.; Dr. David Plotkin, Provost & Contact Person; Nancy Hoover, Librarian. Sisters 4; Lay Teachers 261; Students 1,802.

[C] HIGH SCHOOLS, ARCHDIOCESAN

PORTLAND. *Central Catholic High School* (1939) (Coed), 2401 S.E. Stark St., 97214. Tel: 503-235-3138; Fax: 503-233-0073. Email: pcorrado@centralcatholichigh.org. Web: www.centralcatholichigh.org. Rev. Timothy Murphy, Pres. Emeritus; John Garrow, Prin.; Sr. Maureen Kalsch, S.S.M.O., Assoc. Prin. Academics; John Harrington, Pres.; Natalie Patterson, Librarian; Linda Wampach, Contact Person & Registrar. Priests 1; Sisters 2; Lay Teachers 56; Students 806.

EUGENE. *Marist Catholic High School* formerly Marist High School (Coed), 1900 Kingsley Rd., 97401. Tel: 541-686-2234; Fax: 541-342-6451. Email: jconroy@marisths.org. Web: www.marisths.org. Rev. David Cullings, Chap.; Jay Conroy, Prin. & Contact. Priests 1; Lay Teachers 35; Students 489.

STAYTON. *Regis Catholic High School* formerly Regis High School (1963) (Coed), 550 W. Regis St., 97383. Tel: 503-769-2159; Fax: 503-769-1706. Email: principal@regishighschool.net. Web: www.regishighschool.net. Doug Ierardi, Prin.; Jula Galvin, Librarian. Lay Teachers 12; Students 159.

Regis High School Foundation, 550 W. Regis St., 97383. Tel: 503-769-2159; Fax: 503-769-1706. Email: principal@regishighschool.net. Web: www.regishighschool.net.

[D] HIGH SCHOOLS, PRIVATE

PORTLAND. *De La Salle North Catholic High School (Coed)*, 7528 N. Fenwick Ave., 97217. Tel: 503-285-9385; Fax: 503-285-9546. Email: mpowell@delasallenorth.org. Web: www.delasallenorth.org. Matthew D. Powell, Pres./Prin.; Bro. Joe Kirk, F.S.C., Librarian. Lay Teachers 22; Brothers 2; Students 265; Sisters 1.

Jesuit High School (1956) (Coed), 9000 S.W. Beaverton-Hillsdale Hwy., 97225-2491. Tel: 503-292-2663; Fax: 503-292-0134. Email: jgladstone@jesuitportland.org. Web: www.jesuitportland.org. Mr. John J. Gladstone, Pres. & Contact Person; Mrs. Sandra Satterberg, Prin.; Mr. Paul Hogan, Academic Vice Prin.; Mr. James Naggi, Vice Prin. Admin. Svcs.; Michael J. Schwab, Vice Pres. Devel.; Mr. Chris Smart, Vice Prin. Student Life; Mrs. Shirley Poppe, Admissions Dir.; Mr. Donald Clarke, Campus Min.; Gregory Lum, Librarian. The Society of Jesus. Priests 4; Community: Priests 7; Lay Staff 120; Students 1,225.

Faculty: Rev. Joel K. Adams, S.J., J.K., Supr. In Res. Revs. Craig Boly, S.J.; Patrick J. Conroy, S.J.; William E. Hayes, S.J.; Edward P. McTighe, S.J.; Lawrence F. Robinson, S.J.; Paul Grubb, S.J.

St. Mary's Academy (1859) (Girls), 1615 S.W. Fifth Ave., 97201. Tel: 503-228-8306; Fax: 503-223-0995. Email: patb@stmaryspdx.org. Web: www.stmaryspdx.org. Patricia Barr, Prin.; Cindy Daniels, Librarian. Lay Teachers 50; Students 600.

BEAVERTON. *Valley Catholic Middle & High Schools*, (Grades 7-12), (Coed), 4275 S.W. 148th Ave., 97007. Tel: 503-644-3745; Fax: 503-646-4054. Web: www.valleycatholic.org. Mr. Ross Thomas, Prin. Sisters of St. Mary of Oregon Sisters 1; Lay Teachers 36; Students 457.

MEDFORD. *St. Mary's School*, (Grades 6-12), (Coed), 816 Black Oak Dr., 97504. Tel: 541-773-7877; Fax: 541-772-8973. Email: bspillane@smschool.us. Web: www.smschool.us. Frank Phillips, Head of School; Michelle Tresemer, Attendance & Substitute Coord.; Claircy Boggess, Librarian. Lay Teachers 44; Lay Staff 13; Students 426.

MILWAUKIE. *LaSalle Catholic College Preparatory* formerly Lasalle High School (1966) La Salle Catholic College Preparatory; (Coed), 11999 S.E. Fuller Rd., 97222. Tel: 503-659-4155; Fax: 503-659-2535. Email: tdudley@lshigh.org. Web: www.lshigh.org. Thomas R. Dudley, Prin., Admin. & Contact Person; Denise L. Jones, Pres.; Victoria McDonald, Librarian. Lay Teachers 39; Students 623.

SALEM. **Archbishop Francis Norbert Blanchet School dba Blanchet Catholic School* (1995) (Grades 6-12), 4373 Market St., N.E., 97301. Tel: 503-391-2639; Fax: 503-399-1259. Email: info@blanchetcatholicschool.com. Web: www.blanchetcatholicschool.com. Robert Weber, Prin. Lay Teachers 29; Students 400.

[E] ELEMENTARY SCHOOLS, AREA

EUGENE. *O'Hara Area Elementary Catholic School* (1889) (Grades PreSchool-8), 715 W. 18th, 97402. Tel: 541-485-5291; Fax: 541-484-9138. Web: www.oharaschool.org. Mrs. Dianne Bert, Prin.; Lynn Gori, Librarian. Comprised of students from the following parishes in Eugene: St. Jude, St. Mark, St. Mary, St. Paul, St. Peter, St. Alice and the Newman Center. Lay Teachers 31; Students 519.

[F] ELEMENTARY SCHOOLS, PRIVATE

PORTLAND. **St. Andrew Nativity School* (2000) (Grades 6-8), 4925 N.E. 9th Ave., 97211. Tel: 503-335-9600; Fax: 503-335-9494. Email: info@nativityportland.com. Web: www.nativityportland.com. Rev. Jeffrey N. McDougall, S.J., Prin.; Loretta Wiltgen, Pres. Priests 1; Lay Teachers 6; Scholastics 1; Students 58.

Franciscan Montessori Earth School/St. Francis Academy, 14750 S.E. Clinton St., 97236. Tel: 503-760-8220; Fax: 503-760-8333. Email: info@fmes.org. Web: www.fmes.org. Sr. Kathleen Ann Cieslak, F.S.E., Prin. Staffed by Franciscan Sisters of the Eucharist. Franciscan Sisters of the Eucharist 5; Lay Teachers 28; Students 289.

BEAVERTON. *Valley Catholic Elementary School*, (Grades K-6), 4440 S.W. 148th Ave., 97007. Tel: 503-626-7781; Fax: 503-626-5731. Email: sfriesen@valleycatholic.org. Web: www.valleycatholic.org. Susan Friesen, Prin. & Contact Person; Sr. Rita Watkins, S.S.M.O., Pres. Sisters of St. Mary of Oregon Sisters 2; Lay Teachers 21; Students 393.

[G] SOCIAL AND MINISTERIAL SERVICES

PORTLAND. *Catholic Charities of the Archdiocese of Portland in Oregon*, 231 S.E. 12th Ave., 97214. Tel: 503-231-4866; Fax: 503-231-4327. Email: dkeenan@catholiccharitiesoregon.org. Web: www.catholiccharitiesoregon.org. Dennis B. Keenan, M.S.W., Exec. Dir.; Richard Deml, C.P.A., CFO. CSS Group Homes 96; Resettlement Services 800; Total persons annually served by CSS 130,238.

Catholic Charities Social Service Division of Portland, 231 S.E. 12th Ave., 97214. Tel: 503-231-4866; Fax: 503-231-4327. Douglas Alles, Social Svc. Dir. Programs include: maternity and aftercare home, crisis pregnancy counseling, adoption services, mental health, case management, domestic violence intervention, parent/child development services, refugee resettlement, resident services, disaster relief, Hispanic health outreach, ministry to the elderly, Project Rachel, Immigration Legal Services, housing and social services for homeless women, anti-human trafficking, trafficking victims assistance, affordable housing for low income families and individuals, gang outreach and prevention, and Hispanic school support.

Catholic Youth Organization/Camp Howard, 825 N.E. 20th, Ste. 120, 97232-2295. Tel: 503-231-9484; Fax: 503-231-9531. Web: www.cyocamphoward.org.

Sr. Krista Von Borstel, S.S.M.O., Exec. Dir. Programs include: Youth recreation & camping.

Catholic Community Services of Lane County, 1025 G. St., Springfield, 97477. Tel: 541-345-3628; Fax: 541-744-2272. Web: www.cclc.org. Edward Monks, Exec. Dir. Programs include: Emergency shelter, utilities, and food, single mothers shelter, drug dependent mothers shelter, family shelter, young parents program, family self-sufficiency program.

Catholic Community Services of Mid-Willamette Valley and the Central Coast, 3737 Portland Rd., N.E., Salem, 97301. Tel: 503-390-2600; Fax: 503-390-6648. Web: www.ccswv.org. Jim Seymour, Exec. Dir. Programs include: Center for delinquent youth, developmentally & physically disabled group homes, shelter for displaced youth, counseling center, Hispanic mental health outreach, child abuse, parent/newborn program.

Catholic Charities In Southern Oregon, 724 S. Central Ave., Ste. 210, Medford, 97501. Tel: 541-779-0803; Fax: 541-245-5368. Programs include: Immigration legal services.

[H] CHILD DEVELOPMENT CENTERS

PORTLAND. **Providence Child Center*, 830 N.E. 47th Ave., 97213. Tel: 503-215-2400; Fax: 503-215-0660. Patricia Budo, Operations Admin.

Sisters of Providence in Oregon. Total Staff 205.

Center for Medically Fragile Children Tel: 503-215-2400; Fax: 503-215-2424. The Center for Medically Fragile Children at Providence Child Center is the only nursing facility in the Northwest providing skilled nursing care for children with complex medical needs in a residential setting. Fifty-eight beds are dedicated to children needing long-term chronic care, short-term assessment and/or respite care, and end-of-life care. Total Assisted 84.

Providence Montessori School Tel: 503-215-2400; Fax: 503-215-0660. Email: montessorischool@providence.org. Web: www.providence.org/montessori. Preschool and elementary education for children ages 3 to 7 with a broad array of developmental needs and abilities. Students 182.

Providence Wee Care Tel: 503-215-6832; Fax: 503-215-0333. Child development program for children of Providence Medical Center employees and the community, ages 6 weeks to 6 years. Developmental and age-appropriate activities support child's growth and developement. Students 116.

Providence Neurodevelopmental Center for Children Tel: 503-215-2233; Fax: 503-215-2478. Providence Neurodevelopmental Center for Children (PNCC) provides diagnostic and therapy services for children with complex developmental medical needs as well as children with developmental delays. Total Assisted 2,500.

[I] RESIDENTIAL SCHOOLS FOR YOUTHS WITH EMOTIONAL-SOCIAL PROBLEMS

BEAVERTON. *St. Mary's Home for Boys, Inc.*, 16535 S.W. Tualatin Valley Hwy., 97006. Tel: 503-649-5651; Fax: 503-649-7405. Francis Maher, Exec. Dir. & Contact Person. Residential & day treatment center for behaviorally & emotionally disturbed children. Out patient mental health services. Staff 115; Students 172.

[J] GENERAL HOSPITALS

PORTLAND. *Providence Portland Medical Center* (1941) 4805 N.E. Glisan St., 97213. Tel: 503-215-1111; 503-215-6833; Fax: 503-215-6858. Email: bruce.cwiekowski@providence.org. Web: www.providence.org. Revs. Jon Buffington (EST); Kevin T. Clarke, S.J., Chap.; Bruce Cwiekowski, Dir. Pastoral Care & Contact. Tel: 503-215-6833; Fax: 203-215-5619; Rev. John Hubbard, Presbyterian Chap.; Revs. Augustine Manyama, A.J., Chap.; Vernetta Ollison, Chap.; Barnabas Shayo, A.J., Chap.; Herbert Wheatley, Chap.; Sr. Mary Coakley, O.S.F., Chap.; Patti Fetterman, Admin. Asst.; Martha Leven, Lay Chap. (Catholic); Mary Ann Henry, Lay Chap. (Catholic); Gordon MacDonald, Chap. (Catholic); Sabine Maresco, Chap.; Jean McQuiggin, Chap. (Catholic); Andrea Partenheimer, Music Thanatologist; Barbara Stevens, Addiction Center Chap.; Sandra J. Walker, E.L.C.A., Clinical Pastoral Educ. Supvr.

Providence Health Systems, Oregon Region Priests 6; Sisters 1; Bed Capacity 483; Total Staff 3,417; Patients Assisted Annually 95,531.

Providence Medical Foundation, 4805 N.E. Glisan, 97213. Tel: 503-215-6187; Fax: 503-215-0530. Carolyn Winter, Chief Development Officer for PPMC; Kelly Buechler, Exec. Dir.

Providence St. Vincent Medical Center, 9205 S.W. Barnes Rd., 97225. Tel: 503-216-1234; Fax: 503-216-2468. Web: www.providence.org. Revs. Francis Njau, A.J., Catholic Chap.; Godfred Ocun, A.J., Catholic Chap. & Dir. Pastoral Svcs.; Antonio Ong, Catholic Chap.; Peter Siamoo, Catholic Chap.; Sr. Patricia Valentine, S.N.J.M., Catholic Chap.; Bro. Larry Eschweiler, O.H., Catholic Chap.; Barbara Blair, Protestant Child Life Specialist; Janice Burger, Admin., Providence St. Vincent Medical Center & Contact Person; Ovidiu Peter Cotuna, Protestant Chap.; Russ Danielson, Admin. Health Care Oper., Providence Health System; Charlene K. Epp, Protestant Chap.; Richard Gilbert, Protestant Chap.; Jean Keith-Altemus, Protestant Chap.; Laura A. Lamm, Music Thanatologist; Ms. Judith A. McGowan, Catholic Chap.; Ashton Roberts, Protestant Chap.; Ms. Shiela Schaeffer, Catholic Chap.; Ms. Christine Wallace, Protestant Chap.; Beth Warrick, Protestant Life Specialist.

Providence Health System., Providence Health System. Priests 3; Sisters 2; Brothers 1; Total Staff 3,820; Bed Capacity 523; Patients Assisted Annually 65,375.

**St. Vincent Medical Foundation, Portland* Tel: 503-216-2226; Fax: 503-216-4140.

EUGENE. **Sacred Heart Medical Center*, P.O. Box 10905, 97440. Tel: 541-222-7300; Fax: 541-222-2270. Web: www.peacehealth.org. 3333 Riverbend Dr., Springfield, 97477. Jill Hoggard Green, COO & Admin.; Mel Pyne, CEO, PeaceHealth OR; Robert V. Scheri, Dir. Mission Svcs, & Spiritual Care & Chap.; Revs. Daleasha Hall, Chap.; J. Noel Hickie (BAK), Priest Chap.; Ed McIndoo, Chap.; Ken Olsen, Priest Chap.; David Waggoner, Chap.; Sr. Vivian Ripp, S.N.J.M., Chap.; Ann-Marie Lemire, Chap.; Gordon Ruddick, Chap.; Micki Shirey, Chap.; Edward Harrod, Chap. Sisters of St. Joseph of Peace., Div. of Peace Health. Sisters 3; Bed Capacity 463; Total Staff 3,611; Patients Assisted Annually 148,681.

FLORENCE. *Peace Harbor Hospital*, 400 Ninth St., 97439. Tel: 541-997-8412; Fax: 541-997-2913. Email: pbyers@peachhealth.org. Web: www.peacehealth.org. James Barnhart, Regl. CEO; Sr. Noreen Terrault, C.S.J.P., Pastoral Care; Peggy Byers, Contact Person. Critical access hospital owned and operated by Peace Health, Bellevue, WA. Bed Capacity 21; Total Staff 507; Patients Assisted Annually 10,754.

MEDFORD. *Providence Medford Medical Center*, 1111 Crater Lake Ave., 97504-6225. Tel: 541-732-5000; Fax: 541-732-5872. Rev. James Clifford, O.S.A., Dir., Mission & Spiritual Care; Sisters Mary Grondin, S.P., Representative to Community Bd.; Patricia Marie Landin, S.S.M.O., Chap.

Providence Health System-Oregon dba Providence Medford Medical Center Sisters 2; Bed Capacity 168; Total Staff 1,064; Patients Assisted Annually 148,299.

**Providence Community Health Foundation, Medford* Tel: 541-732-6766; Fax: 541-772-2861. Email: jodi.barnard@providence.org. Web: www.providence.org/medford/foundation.

MILWAUKIE. **Providence Milwaukie Hospital* (1968) 10150 S.E. 32nd Ave., 97222. Tel: 503-513-8300; Fax: 503-513-8191. Email: Denise.Anderson@providence.org. Web: www.providence.org/milwaukie. Denise Anderson, Dir. Pastoral Care & Mission Integration.

Providence Health System & Service, Oregon Region. Bed Capacity 77; Total Staff 510; Patients Assisted Annually 85,333.

**Providence Milwaukie Foundation, Milwaukie* (1988) Tel: 503-513-8625; Fax: 503-513-8319. Email: Lesley.Townsend@providence.org. Lesley Townsend, Exec. Dir.

NEWBERG. *Providence Newberg Medical Center*, 1001 Providence Dr., 97132. Tel: 503-537-1555; Fax: 503-537-1800. Debbie Glass, Interim Chief Exec.; Jack R. Sumner, Dir. Finance & Contact Person. Bed Capacity 40; Total Staff 533; Patients Assisted Annually 189,071.

ROSEBURG. *Mercy Medical Center, Inc.*, 2700 Stewart Pkwy., 97471. Tel: 541-673-0611; Fax: 541-677-4830. Web: www.mercyrose.org. Kelly C. Morgan, Pres. & CEO; John S. Kasberger, Vice Pres. Fin., CFO. Tel: 541-677-2458; Marvin Gwaltney, Vice Pres., Mission Services; Rev. Cletus Osugi, Catholic Chap. Bed Capacity 174; Total Staff 1,034; Patients Assisted Annually 184,713.

Mercy Foundation, Inc., 2700 Stewart Pkwy., 97471. Tel: 541-677-4818; Fax: 541-677-4891.

Linus Oakes, Inc., 2700 Stewart Pkwy., 97471. Tel: 541-677-4800; Fax: 541-677-2106.

SEASIDE. *Providence Seaside Hospital*, 725 S. Wahanna Rd., 97138-7735. Tel: 503-717-7000; Fax: 503-717-7505. Email: mary.trudell@providence.org. Web: www.providence.org/northcoast. Krista Farnham, Admin.; Mary Trudell, Contact Person.

Sisters of Providence in Oregon. Bed Capacity 45; Total Staff 370; Patients Assisted Annually 79,127.

**Providence Seaside Hospital Foundation, Inc.* Tel: 503-717-7601; Fax: 503-717-7505.

[K] RETIREMENT AND ASSISTED LIVING

PORTLAND. **St. Anthony Village (activity of St. Anthony Village Enterprise)*, 3560 S.E. 79th Ave., 97206. Tel: 503-775-4414; Fax: 503-771-9189. Email: kmarshall@worldspark.org. Web: www.sage-fede.com. Rev. Michael Maslowsky, Pres.; Karen Marshall, Admin. & Contact Person; Cathy Walter, Leasing Coord. Assisted living facility centered around Catholic Parish. Independent, assisted living and memory care unit. Total Assisted Annually 170; Bed Capacity 126; Staff 64.

**Assumption Village (activity of St. Anthony Village Enterprise)* (2002) 9121 N. Burr Ave., 97203. Tel: 503-283-5644; Fax: 503-283-5692. Web: www.villagesage.org. Rev. Michael Maslowsky, Pres.; Rosemarie Davis, Leasing Coord.; Greg Buzzy, Admin. Retirement Village, Senior independent and assisted living, chapel with daily Mass multiple activities, gardens, intergenerational interaction with neighborhood and local social service agencies. Total Staff 36; Bed Capacity 107; Total Assisted Annually 84.

BEAVERTON. *Maryville Nursing Home*, 14645 S.W. Farmington Rd., 97007. Tel: 503-643-8626; Fax: 503-520-1435. Kathleen Parry, Admin. & Contact Person; Delores Focht, Dir. Nurses; Rev. John M. Domin, Chap. (Retired). Bed Capacity 155; Hospice Care 43; Total Assisted Annually 383; Total Staff 220.

MOUNT ANGEL. *Providence Benedictine Nursing Center*, 540 S. Main St., 97362-9532. Tel: 503-845-6841; Fax: 503-845-9229. Web: www.providence.org/benedictine. Emily Dazey, Exec. Dir.; Catherine Elia, Chap.; Rev. Aelred Yockey, O.S.B., Chap.; Rev. Dana McBrien, Interfaith Chap. Sisters of Providence Health System. Total Staff 195; Patients Assisted Annually 554.

Providence Benedictine Orchard House Tel: 503-845-2544; Fax: 503-845-2560. Personalized Living Center (ALF). Total Staff 28; Bed Capacity 50; Assisted 75.

Providence Benedictine Home Health Tel: 503-845-9226; Fax: 503-845-9880. Total Staff 46; Patients Assisted Annually 1,149.

[L] MONASTERIES AND RESIDENCES OF PRIESTS

PORTLAND. *Colombiere Community*, 3220 S.E. 43rd Ave., 97206-3104. Tel: 503-595-1930; Fax: 503-595-1929. Web: www.nwjesuits.org. Revs. Roy L. Antunez, S.J.; Peter D. Byrne, S.J., Supr.; James R. Conyard, S.J.; Richard H. Ganz, S.J.; James R. Laudwein, S.J.; Thomas Lankenau, S.J.; Patrick J. Lee, S.J., Prov.; John McBride, S.J.; Thomas McCarthy, S.J.; Jeffrey N. McDougall, S.J.; John J. Morris, S.J.; John V. Murphy, S.J.; Brad R. Reynolds, S.J.; John Ridgway, S.J.; Thomas Royce, S.J.; Gerard Steckler, S.J.; J. Patrick Stewart, S.J.; Michael A. Tyrrell, S.J.; Christopher S. Weekly; Mr. Philip P. Sutherland, S.J. Priests 19; Scholastics 1.

The Grotto, The National Sanctuary of Our Sorrowful Mother (1924) 85th and N.E. Sandy Blvd., P.O. Box 20008, 97294-0008. Tel: 503-254-7371; 503-254-7372 (Monastery); Fax: 503-254-7948. Revs. John M. Topper, O.S.M., Prior & Exec. Dir.; Robert S. Anderson, O.S.M. Priests 5; Brothers 1. In Res. Revs. Denish Ilogon-Llabore, O.S.M., Shrine Staff; Ignatius M. Kissel, O.S.M., Shrine Staff; Damian M. Kobus, O.S.M.

Holy Cross Fathers & Brothers, C.S.C. - University of Portland, 5000 N. Willamette Blvd., 97203. Tel: 503-943-8024; Fax: 503-943-7313. Email: csc@up.edu. Revs. Jeffrey Allison, C.S.C.; Robert Antonelli, C.S.C.; William Beauchamp, C.S.C.; Michael T. Belinsky, C.S.C.; Richard Berg, C.S.C. (Retired); George C. Bernard, C.S.C. (Retired); John Donato, C.S.C.; Thomas Doyle, C.S.C.; Charles Gordon, C.S.C.; Patrick Hannon, C.S.C.; Thomas Hosinski, C.S.C.; William Hund, C.S.C. (Retired); James Kelly, C.S.C. (Retired); James Lies, C.S.C.; Charles McCoy, C.S.C.; Francis Murphy, C.S.C., Supr.; Claude Pomerleau, C.S.C.; Chester Prusynski, C.S.C. (Retired); James Rigert, C.S.C. (Retired); Richard Rutherford, C.S.C.; Charles D. Sherrer, C.S.C. (Retired); Ronald Wasowski, C.S.C.; Arthur F. Wheeler, C.S.C.; William E. Wickham, C.S.C.; John Wironen, C.S.C.; Bros. Ken Allen, C.S.C., (Retired); Flugence Dougherty, C.S.C.; Donald Stabrowski, C.S.C.

Students on Scholarship from the CSC Community Revs. Francis Kule Kojo (Uganda); Davis Variath (India).

Holy Rosary Priory, 375 N.E. Clackamas St., 97232-1103. Tel: 503-235-3163; Fax: 503-235-3551. Web: www.holyrosarypdx.org. Very Rev. Reginald Martin, O.P., Prior & Dir. Rosary Confraternity; Revs. Vincent Beniot, O.P., Sub-Prior; Paul A. Duffner, O.P. (Retired); John C. Flannery, O.P. (Retired); Thomas More J. McGreevy, O.P. (Retired); Brian T.B. Mullady, O.P.; Anthony M. Patalano, O.P.

Jesuit Provincial Office (Society of Jesus, Oregon Prov.), 3215 S.E. 45th Ave., 97206. Tel: 503-226-6977; Fax: 503-228-6741. Email: oregonprov@nwjesuits.org. Web: www.nwjesuits.org. P.O. Box 86010, 97286-0010. Revs. Peter D. Byrne, S.J., Asst. Parishes & Spiritual Ministries; Thomas Lankenau, S.J., Socius, Admonitor; Stephen C. Lantry, S.J., Dir. of Vocations; Patrick J. Lee, S.J., Prov.; Michael A. Tyrrell, S.J., Treas.; Patrick J. Twohy, S.J., Dir. Rocky Mountain Mission / NW, Asst. for Native Ministries; Ms. Tina O'Brien, Dir. of Devel.; Mr. William Lockyear, CFO; Rev. Patrick J. Conroy, S.J., Asst. for Formation; Ms. Cindy Reopelle, Asst. for Secondary & Middle Schools; Asst. for Jesuit-lay Partnerships; Ms. Kathleen Marks, R.N., Asst. for Health Care; Rev. John C. Bentz, S.J., Asst. for Vocations & Internatioal Ministries. Priests 29; Novices 4.

Oregon Province Priests serving outside the U.S.: Revs. Joseph B. Danel, S.J.; Robert B. Grimm, S.J.; Dan T. Mai, S.J.; John J. McLain, S.J.; Bartholomew J. Murphy, S.J.; John J. Navone, S.J.; Bryan Viet-Hung Pham, S.J.; Gary N. Smith, S.J.; Bro. James P. Selinsky, S.J.

AMITY. *Brigittine Priory of Our Lady of Consolation - The Order of the Most Holy Savior* (1976) 23300 Walker Ln., 97101. Tel: 503-835-8080; Fax: 503-835-9662. Email: monks@brigittine.org. Web: www.brigittine.org. Bro. Bernard Ner Suguitan, O.Ss.S., Prior & Contact. Professed 8.

CORVALLIS. **Saint John Society*, 2121 N.W. Monroe, 97330. Tel: 541-753-1392; Fax: 541-753-1392. Email: corvallis@socsj.org. Web: www.socsj.org. Priests 2; Brothers 2.

LAFAYETTE. *The Cistercian (Trappist) Abbey of Our Lady of Guadalupe* (1948) P.O. Box 97, 97127. Tel: 503-852-7174; Fax: 503-852-7748. Email: community@trappistabbey.org. Rt. Rev. Peter McCarthy, O.C.S.O., Abbot; Revs. Dismas Gannon, O.C.S.O., Prior; Casey Bailey, O.C.S.O., Novice Master; Martin Cawley, O.C.S.O.; Timothy Clark, O.C.S.O.; Howard Curtis, O.C.S.O.; Joseph-Benedict Donnelly, O.C.S.O.; Francis King, O.C.S.O.; Richard Layton, O.C.S.O., Business Mgr.; Timothy Michell, O.C.S.O.; Peter Plakut, O.C.S.O.; Mark Weidner, O.C.S.O. Order of Cistercians of the Strict Observance. Solemnly Professed 30; Priests 12; Simply Professed 2; Total in Community 32.

MOUNT ANGEL. *Discalced Carmelite Friars (OCD)*, 300 Humpert Ln., 97362. Tel: 503-845-2240 Carmelite House of Studies. *Carmelite House of Studies*, P.O. Box 260, 97362. Tel: 503-845-2240 Carmelite House of Studies; Fax: 503-845-2243. Rev. Christopher LaRocca, O.C.D., Rector. Priests 2; Brothers 8.

Missionaries of the Holy Spirit, M.Sp.S., 585 E. College St., 97362. Tel: 503-845-1182; Fax: 503-845-1189. P.O. Box 499, St. Benedict, 97373. Tel: 503-845-1181; Fax: 503-845-1189. Email: msps@mspsoregon.org. Web: www.mspsoregon.org. Revs. Celso Marquez, M.Sp.S., Vice Supr.; Joel Quezada, M.Sp.S., Vice Supr. Serving the Felix Rougier House of Studies and St. Matthew Parish, Hillsboro:

MYRTLE CREEK. *Augustinian Community*, P.O. Box 810, 97457-0116. Tel: 541-863-3271; Fax: 541-863-6759. Email: frbillosa@gmail.com. Revs. James Clifford, O.S.A.; William A. Ryan, O.S.A., Regl. Supr.

ST. BENEDICT. *Mt. Angel Abbey* 97373. Tel: 503-845-3030; Fax: 503-845-3594. Email: postmaster@mtangel.edu. Web: www.mountangelabbey.org. Rt. Revs. Gregory Duerr, O.S.B., Abbot & Prior; Nathan Zodrow, O.S.B. (Retired); Peter Eberle, O.S.B. (Retired); Joseph Wood, O.S.B. (Retired); Revs. Timothy Sander, O.S.B.; Athanasius Buchholz, O.S.B.; Benedict Suing, O.S.B.; Leo Rimmele, O.S.B.; Augustine DeNoble, O.S.B.; Bede Partridge, O.S.B.; Bruno Becker, O.S.B.; Cosmas White, O.S.B.; Alexander Plasker, O.S.B.; Paschal Cheline, O.S.B.; Edmund Smith, O.S.B.; Vincent Trujillo, O.S.B.; William Hammelman, O.S.B.; Jeremy Driscoll, O.S.B.; Very Rev. Paul Thomas, O.S.B.; Revs. Philip Waibel, O.S.B.; Marius Walter, O.S.B.; Jerome Young, O.S.B.; Aelred Yockey, O.S.B.; Pius X Harding, O.S.B.; Thomas Thien Dang, O.S.B.; Vincent Liem Nguyen, O.S.B.; Michael Mee, O.S.B.; Odo Recker, O.S.B.; Ralph Recker, O.S.B.; Ezekiel Lotz, O.S.B.; Martin Grassel, O.S.B.; Joseph Nguyen, O.S.B. Priests 28; Monks in Perpetual Vows 49; Brothers 21.

[M] CONVENTS AND RESIDENCES FOR SISTERS

PORTLAND. *Convent of Sisters of Reparation of the Sacred Wounds of Jesus, Novitiate*, 2120 S.E. 24th Ave., 97214-5504. Tel: 503-236-4207; Fax: 503-236-3400. Email: repsrs@comcast.net. Web: www.reparationsisters.org. Sr. Mary of the Angels, S.R., Supr. Gen. Sisters 2; Private Vows 1; Donne Members 160.

Convent of the Good Shepherd, 562 N. Rosa Parks Way, 97217. Tel: 503-283-4931; Fax: 503-283-4933. Email: cboerboom3@msn.com. Sr. Cathleen Boerboom, Contact Person. Sisters 4.

Convent of the Society of the Holy Child Jesus, 5937 N. Denver Ave., 97217. Tel: 503-289-9975. Sisters 5.

Holy Spirit Sisters Convent (1950) 1904 S.E. Division, 97202. Tel: 503-239-0328; Fax: 503-239-0328. Email: alcssisters@aol.com. Sr. Winfrida Bonifasi Mrema, A.L.C.S., Contact Person. Sisters 7.

"Rose Hall" Reparation and Prayer Center, 2120 S.E. 24th Ave., 97214-5504. Tel: 503-236-4207; Fax: 503-236-3400. Email: mmangels@comcast.net. Web: www.reparationsisters.org. Sr. Mary of the Angels, S.R., Dir.

Sister Adorers of the Holy Cross Convent (1670) 7408 S.E. Alder, 97215. Tel: 503-254-3284; Fax: 503-255-3097. Email: mtgdlhn@yahoo.com. Sr. Mary Trinh Nguyen, M.T.G., Supr. & Contact Person.

Adorers of the Holy Cross Sisters, First foundation in the United States in 1976, founded by Bishop Pierre Lambert de la Motte. Represented in the Archdiocese of Portland in Oregon, the Diocese of Arlington, VA and the Diocese of Sacramento, CA. Sisters 29; Candidates 2.

BEAVERTON. *Convent, Franciscan Missionary Sisters of Our Lady of Sorrows* (1939) 3600 S.W. 170th Ave., 97006-5099. Tel: 503-649-7127; Fax: 503-259-9507. Email: smfc@sbcglobal.net. Web: www.olpretreat.org. Sr. Mary Francis Coleman, O.S.F., Supr. Gen., Contact Person. Sisters 12.

Sisters of St. Mary of Oregon (1886) 4440 S.W. 148th Ave., 97007. Tel: 503-644-9181; Fax: 503-646-1102. Email: srbarbarajeanl@ssmo.org. Web: www.ssmo.org. Sisters Barbara Jean Laughlin, S.S.M.O., Supr. Gen.; Michael Francine Duncan, S.S.M.O., Local Supr.; Rev. Godfred Ocun, A.J., Chap. Motherhouse of the Sisters of St. Mary of Oregon. Professed Sisters 67.

The Lovers of The Holy Cross Sisters, 7361 S.W. 175th Ter., 97007. Tel: 503-259-8767; Fax: 503-259-8767. Email: ngoan55@hotmail.com. Sr. Maria Ngoan Nguyen, Supr. Sisters 7.

BRIDAL VEIL. *Franciscan Sisters of the Eucharist Convent* (1973) *Administrative Center*, 48100 E. Columbia R. Hwy., Box 23, 97010. Tel: 503-695-2375; Fax: 503-695-2368. Email: fsebridalveil@fsecommunity.org. Web: www.fsecommunity.org. Sr. Helen Jean Brinkman, F.S.E., Supr. & Contact Person. Sisters 8.

EUGENE. *Carmel of Maria Regina* (1957) (Contemplative Order), 87609 Green Hill Rd., 97402. Tel: 541-345-8649; Fax: 541-345-4857. Sr. Elizabeth Mary, O.C.D., Prioress. Professed Sisters 8.

MARYLHURST. *Convent of the Holy Names*, P.O. Box 398, 97036. Tel: 503-675-2449; Fax: 503-675-2453. Email: meholohan@snjmuson.org. Web: www.snjmusontario.org. Sr. Jane Hibbard, S.N.J.M., Campus Coord. Provincial House of the Sisters of the Holy Names of Jesus & Mary, S.N.J.M. Sisters 163.

MT. ANGEL. *Queen of Angels Monastery* (1882) 840 S. Main St., 97362-9527. Tel: 503-845-6141; Fax: 503-845-6585. Email: qamosb@yahoo.com. Web: www.benedictine-srs.org. Sr. Donna Marie Chartraw, O.S.B., Prioress. Monastery of the Benedictine Sisters of Mt. Angel.; See separate listing for Shalom Prayer Center (retreat center) and St. Joseph Shelter (special center for social services and assistance). Sisters 39.

[N] RETREAT HOUSES

PORTLAND. *Nestucca Sanctuary*, 3301 S.E. 45th Ave., 97206-3108. Tel: 503-774-5699; Fax: 503-775-6335. Rev. Thomas J. Hamanna, S.J., Exec. Dir. Priests 1; Total Assisted Annually 2,500.

BEAVERTON. *Our Lady of Peace Retreat* (1953) 3600 S.W. 170th Ave., 97006-5099. Tel: 503-649-7127; Fax: 503-259-9507. Email: sisters@olpretreat.org. Web: www.olpretreat.org. Sr. Anne Marie Warren, O.S.F., Supr. & Contact Person. Franciscan Missionary Sisters of Our Lady of Sorrows 12.

GOLD HILL. *St. Rita's Retreat Center*, P.O. Box 310, 97525. Tel: 541-855-1333. Email: strita@rvi.net. Rev. Stephen J. Fister, Dir. & Contact Person.

MCKENZIE BRIDGE. *St. Benedict Lodge Dominican Retreat & Conference Center* (1955) 56630 N. Bank Rd., 97413-9614. Tel: 541-822-3572 (Office & Dominican Res.). Email: tfdeman@msn.com. Web: www.sblodge.org. Rev. Thomas DeMan, O.P., Chap. & Contact; Deacon Leonard Soper.

46052 McKenzie Hwy., Vida, 97488. Tel: 541-896-0284. Email: dcnlgjms@earthlink.net.

MILWAUKIE. *Franciscan Spiritual Center* (2002) *Lake Plaza South*, 6902 S.E. Lake Rd. #300, 97267. Tel: 503-794-8542; Fax: 503-794-8556. Email: info@francisspctr.com. Web: francisspctr.com. Mary Erickson, Dir.; Sisters Mary Jo Chaves, O.S.F., Spiritual Dir.; Celeste Clavel, O.S.F., Business Mgr.; Emma Holdener, O.S.F., Office Mgr. & Body-work; Mary Lonergan, O.S.F., Spiritual Dir.; Guadalupe Medina, O.S.F., Hispanic Ministry. Sisters of St. Francis of Philadelphia., Spiritual direction; day retreats; workshops and body-work. Sisters 5; Staff 9.

MT. ANGEL. *Benedictine Sisters Shalom Prayer Center*, 840 S. Main St., 97362-9527. Tel: 503-845-6773; Fax: 503-845-6585. Email: shalom@mtangel.net. Web: www.benedictine-srs.org/shalom. Sr. Dorothy Jean Beyer, O.S.B., Dir. & Contact Person. Sisters 4.

ST. BENEDICT. *Mount Angel Abbey Retreat House* 97373. Tel: 503-845-3025; Fax: 503-845-3027. Email: retreat@mtangel.edu. Web: www.mtangel.edu. Revs. Edmund Smith, O.S.B., Dir.; Vincent Trujillo, O.S.B., Guest Master.

[O] SOCIETY OF ST. VINCENT DE PAUL

PORTLAND. **Society of St. Vincent de Paul Portland Council* (1869) Portland Council, P.O. Box 42157, 97242-0157. Tel: 503-235-7837; Fax: 503-233-5581. Email: sharon@svdppdx.org. Web: svdppdx.org. 5120 S.E. Milwaukie Ave., 97202. Sharon Hills, Exec. Dir. & Contact Person. Staff 12; Total Assisted Annually 400,000.

EUGENE. *Society of St. Vincent de Paul* Archdiocesan Council., 705 S. Seneca St., P.O. Box 24608, 97402. Tel: 541-687-5820; Fax: 541-683-9423. Email: svdp@svdp.us. Web: www.svdp.us. Louise (Molly) Westling, Pres.

St. Vincent de Paul Society of Lane County, Inc. Eugene Council., 705 Seneca Rd., P.O. Box 24608, 97402. Tel: 541-687-5820; Fax: 541-683-9423. Email: info@svdp.us. Web: www.svdp.us. Louise (Molly) Westling, Pres.; Terrence R. McDonald, Exec. Dir. & Contact Person.

MEDFORD. *Society of St. Vincent de Paul* (1982) Rogue Valley District Council, P.O. Box 1663, 97501. Tel: 541-772-3828; Fax: 541-772-6886. Email: vincent@mind.net. Web: www.stvincentdepaul.info. Len Hebert, Pres. Total Assisted Annually 88,500; Volunteers 230.

SALEM. **Society of St. Vincent de Paul* (1957) Council of Mid-Willamette Valley, 3745 Portland Rd., N.E., P.O. Box 7864, 97303. Tel: 503-364-1883; Fax: 503-364-2708. Email: info@svdpsalem.org. Jerry Boschler, District Council Pres.; Mary Allen, Dir. Business & Administration. Total Assisted Annually 102,145.

SUTHERLIN. *Council of Douglas County of the Society of St. Vincent dePaul* (1997) 112 E. Central, P.O. Box 949, 97479. Tel: 541-459-3394. Email: svdp@qwest.net. Camille Hong, Pres.; Claire Crocker, Treas.

[P] NEWMAN CENTERS

PORTLAND. *Lewis & Clark College* 0615 S.W. Palatine Hill Rd., P.O. Box 171, 97219. Tel: 503-768-7080; Fax: 503-768-7084. Email: schaff@clark.edu. Web: www.lclark.edu/~newman. Sr. Loretta Schaff, O.S.F., Campus Min. Tel: 503-768-7080.

Portland State University Newman Center St. Michael Church, 424 S.W. Mill, 97201. Tel: 503-228-8629; 503-419-7473; Fax: 503-827-7689. Email: bbgr@pdx.edu. Web: www.csa.pdx.edu. Glenn Rymsza, Campus Minister.

University of Portland Campus Ministry, 5000 N. Willamette Blvd., 97203. Tel: 503-943-7131; Fax: 503-943-8567. Email: ministry@up.edu. Web: www.up.edu. Revs. Gary Chamberland, C.S.C., Dir. Campus Ministry; Michael T. Belinsky, C.S.C., Asst. Dir. Faith Formation; Vinci Paterson, Asst. Dir. Faith Formation; Maureen Briare, Assoc. Dir. for Music; Stacey Noem, Asst. Dir. for Faith Formation; Josh Noem, Asst. Dir. for Faith Formation; Theresa McCreary, Admin. Asst.

ASHLAND. *Southern Oregon University (Ashland)* , Walsh Memorial Newman Center, 1150 Ashland St., 97520. Tel: 541-482-0825; Fax: 541-488-5174. Email: olmyouthaya@gmail.com. Web: www.newmansou.com. Rev. Sean Weeks, Chap.

CORVALLIS. *Newman Center at Oregon State University (Corvallis)* Newman Center, 2127 N.W. Monroe St., 97330. Tel: 541-752-6818. Email: newmancenter@socsj.org. Web: www.osunewman.org. Revs. Lucas Laborde, Faith Formation Coord.; Ignacio Llorente, Office Dir.

Trinity Court (Student Housing) 2200 N.W. Jackson, 97330. Tel: 503-245-7899. Rev. John Henderson, O.F.M.Conv., Chap.

EUGENE. *Lane Community College* 1850 Emerald St., 97403. Tel: 541-343-7021; Fax: 541-686-8028.

University of Oregon (Eugene) Newman Center, St. Thomas More Catholic Parish, 1850 Emerald St., 97403. Tel: 541-343-7021; Fax: 541-686-8028. Web: www.uonewman.org. Rev. Daniel Rolland, O.P.; Corinne M. Lopez, Dir. Faith Formation.

FOREST GROVE. *Pacific University (Forest Grove)* (1849) 2043 College Way, 97116. Tel: 503-352-2035; Fax: 503-352-2933. James Butler, Campus Min.; Nicki Butler, Campus Minister; Deborah Francisco, Coord. Campus Min.; Rev. Jeffrey Meeuwsen, Chap.

St. Anthony Church 1660 Elm St., 97116. Tel: 503-357-8075; Fax: 503-357-2217. Email: jmeeuwsen@stanthonysforestgrove.org. Web: www.stanthonysforestgrove.org.

MARYLHURST. *Marylhurst University* 17600 Pacific Hwy., 97036. Tel: 800-634-9982; Fax: 503-636-9526. Email: campmin@marylhurst.edu. Sr. Cecilia Ranger, S.N.J.M., Univ. Min. Co-Chair; Sheila O'Connell-Roussell, Univ. Min. Co-Chair.

MCMINNVILLE. *Linfield College (McMinnville) St. James Church*, 1145 N.E. First St., 97128. Tel: 503-472-5232. Email: mdouglass@stjamesmac.com. Michael Douglas, Campus Min.

MONMOUTH. *Western Oregon University (Monmouth)* 315 N. Knox, 97361. Tel: 503-838-1242; 503-606-0113 (Campus House). Email: catholic_campus_ministry@hotmail.com. Rev. Carl Gimpl, Chap.; Lisa Silbernagel, Campus Min. Tel: 503-606-0113.

SALEM. *Willamette University (Salem) St. Joseph Church*, 721 Chemeketa St., N.E., 97301. Tel: 503-581-1623; Fax: 503-581-7271. Rev. Todd Molinari; Sarah Kresse, Youth & Young Adult Minister; Rolando Moreno, Pastoral Asst.

[Q] MISCELLANEOUS

PORTLAND. *Blanchet House of Hospitality* (1952) 340 N.W. Glisan St., 97209. Tel: 503-226-3911; Fax: 503-222-4071. Email: blanchetcntr@aol.com. Web: www.BlanchetHouse.org. Brian Ferschweiler, Exec. Dir. Tel: 503-807-4330. Served 270,000.

Brotherhood of the People of Praise, 7709 N. Denver Ave., 97217. Tel: 503-230-9999. Email: frpeter6901@yahoo.com. Rev. Peter Smith, Contact Person.

Catholic Broadcasting Northwest, Inc., KBVM-FM 88.3 (1989) P.O. Box 5888, 97228-5888. Tel: 503-285-5200; Fax: 503-285-3322. Email: info@kbvm.fm. Web: www.kbvm.fm. Tony Galati, Exec. Dir. Total Staff 7.

**The Gamelin-Oregon Association-Emilie House* (1986) 5520 N.E. Glisan, 97213-3170. Tel: 503-236-9779; Fax: 503-239-1867. Email: shannan.stickler@providence.org. Web: www.providence.org. Shannan Stickler, Dir. & Contact. Sisters of Providence., 41 apartments for the elderly and mobility impaired subsidized by the Department of Housing and Urban Development.

**Jesuit Volunteer Corps Northwest* (1956) P.O. Box 3928, 97208-3928. Tel: 503-335-8202; Fax: 503-249-1118. Email: info@jvcnorthwest.org. Web: www.jvcnorthwest.org. Jeanne Haster, Exec. Dir. & Contact Person.

St. Joseph the Worker Corporate Internship Program, Inc., 7528 N. Fenwick, 97217. Tel: 503-285-9385, Ext. 104; Fax: 503-285-9546. Email: mjacobson@delasallenorth.org. Web: www.delasallenorth.org. Michael Jacobson, Dir.

**St. Joseph the Worker Job Fund*, 605 N.W. Couch St., 97209. Tel: 503-222-5720; Fax: 503-241-7375. Email: pj@macdcenter.org. Pat Janik, Exec. Dir. & Contact Person; Marylee King, Dir. Staff 2; Total Assisted 8.

Macdonald Center and Residence, 605 N.W. Couch St., 97209. Tel: 503-222-5720, Ext. 3; Fax: 503-241-7375. Email: mk@macdcenter.org. Web: www.macdcenter.org. Pat Janik, Exec. Dir.; Marylee King, Center Dir. & Contact. Staff 40; Total People Served 1,500.

Oregon Catholic Conference (1979) 2838 E. Burnside St., 97214. Tel: 503-233-8387; Fax: 503-235-2630. Most Revs. John G. Vlazny, D.D., Pres.; Robert F. Vasa, Vice Pres.; Kenneth D. Steiner, D.D., Dir.; Rev. Msgr. Dennis O'Donovan, Sec. & Treas.

Paulist Fathers Catholic Center for Evangelization, 2408 S.E. 16th Ave., 97214. Tel: 503-231-4955, Ext. 103; Fax: 503-736-1383. Email: info@stphilipneripdx.org. Web: www.stphilipneripdx.org. Revs. Charles Brunick, C.S.P., Dir. N.W. Center Evangelization & Reconciliation; Michael Evernden, C.S.P.; Gerard P. Tully, C.S.P.; Jeanne McPherson, Offic Mgr & Dir. of Devel. Priests 2.

Sisters of the Holy Names of Jesus and Mary, Community Support Charitable Trust, P.O. Box 398, Marylhurst, 97036. Tel: 503-675-7123; Fax: 503-675-7138. Email: vcummings@snjmuson.org. Web: www.snjmusontario.org. Vicki Cummings, Contact Person & CFO.

BEAVERTON. *Our Lady of Peace Institute in Catholic Teaching*, 3600 S.W. 170th Ave., 97006. Tel: 503-649-7127; Fax: 503-259-9507. Email: sisters@olpretreat.org. Web: www.olpretreat.org. Sr. Anne Marie, O.S.F., Coord. & Contact Person. Staff 5; Students 40.

Sisters of St. Mary of Oregon Campus Schools Corporation, 4440 S.W. 148th Ave., 97007-2745. Tel: 503-644-9181; Fax: 503-646-1102. Email: srritaw@ssmo.org. 4275 S.W. 148th Ave., 97007-2745. Sr. Rita Watkins, S.S.M.O., Pres. Sisters 3; Lay Teachers 54; Students 850.

Valley Catholic Middle & High Schools (Grades 7-12), (Coed)

Valley Catholic Elementary School (Grades K-6)

Sisters of St. Mary of Oregon Little Flower Development Center, 4440 S.W. 148th Ave., 97007. Tel: 503-644-9181; Fax: 503-646-1102. Sr. Rita Watkins, S.S.M.O., Pres. Sisters 1; Lay Teachers 24; Students 197.

Sisters of St. Mary of Oregon Ministries Corporation, 4440 S.W. 148th Ave., 97007-2745. Tel: 503-644-9181; Fax: 503-646-1102. Sr. Adele Marie Altenhofen, S.S.M.O., Pres.

LAKE OSWEGO. *Holy Names Heritage Center Inc.*, 17425 Holy Names Dr., 97034. Tel: 503-607-0595; Fax: 503-607-0609. Email: tbrosseau@holynamesheritagecenter.org. Web: www.holynamesheritagecenter.org. Mailing Address: P.O. Box 398, Marylhurst, 97036. Tamra Brosseau, Dir.; Vicki Cummings, Contact Person & CFO.

**Mary's Woods at Marylhurst, Inc.*, 17400 Holy Names Dr., 97034. Tel: 503-675-2004; Fax: 503-675-2015. Email: jhansen@marywoods.com. Web: www.maryswoods.com. Sisters Mary Breiling, S.N.J.M., Pres. Bd. Dirs.; Roswitha Frawley, S.N.J.M., Mission Dir.; Ed Mawe, Exec. Dir.; Lynn Szender, Dir. Marie Rose Health Center; Sr. Joan Hansen, S.N.J.M., Dir. Admin. Svcs. Current Residency 420.

MARYLHURST. *Holy Names Sisters Foundation* (1859) c/o Development Office, P.O. Box 411, 97036. Tel: 503-675-7110; Fax: 503-675-7137. Email: acarr@snjmuson.org. Web: www.sistersoftheholynames.org/oregon. Vicki Cummings, CFO; Sisters Jane Hibbard, S.N.J.M., Pres.; Mary Breiling, S.N.J.M., Sec.; Adrianna Carr, Devel. Dir.

Sisters of the Holy Names of Jesus and Mary U.S.-Ontario Province Corporation, P.O. Box 398, 97036. Tel: 503-675-7125; Fax: 503-675-7138. Email: meholohan@snjmuson.org. Web: www.snjmusontario.org. Sisters Joan Saafeld, S.N.J.M., Provincial Supr.; Emma Bezaire, S.N.J.M., Leadership Team; Judith Mayer, S.N.J.M., Leadership Team; Jo Ann De Quattro, S.N.J.M., Leadership Team; Shirley Roberg, S.N.J.M., Vice Pres.; Mary Ellen Holohan, S.N.J.M., Treas./Sec.

MILWAUKIE. *La Salle High School Educational Foundation*, 11999 S.E. Fuller Rd., 97222. Tel: 503-353-1417; Fax: 503-496-1754. Email: mwinningham@lshigh.org. Web: www.lshigh.org. Mr. Matthew Winningham, Treas. & Contact Person.

MT. ANGEL. *Benedictine Foundation of Oregon* (1980) Box 912, 97362. Tel: 503-845-2556; Fax: 503-845-4345. Email: benfoundation@mtangel.net. Web: www.benedictine-srs.org. Steven Ritchie, Exec. Dir. & Contact Person.

Carmelite House of Studies, 300 Humpert Ln., P.O. Box 260, 97362. Tel: 503-845-2240; Fax: 503-845-2243. Revs. Christopher LaRocca, O.C.D., Rector, Student Master & Contact Person; John Melka, O.C.D. Priests 2; Seminarians 8.

St. Joseph's Shelter (1988) 925 S. Main, 97362-9527. Tel: 503-845-6147; Fax: 503-845-2815. Email: khughes@mtangel.net. Web: www.benedictine.srs.org. Karolle Hughes, Admin. & Contact Person. Special center for social services and assistance. Total Staff 9; Total People Served 290; Total Shelter Nights 14,413; Total Meals Served 17,586.

SALEM. *Salem Catholic Schools Foundation*, 643 Union St. N.E., Ste. 200, 97301. Tel: 503-371-9068; Fax: 503-362-0513. Email: kevin@mannixlawfirm.com.

ST. BENEDICT. *The Abbey Foundation of Oregon* (2002) One Abbey Dr., 97373. Tel: 503-845-3066; Fax: 503-845-3075. Web: www.mountangelabbey.org. Rev. Martin Grassel, O.S.B., Treas. & Contact Person.

RELIGIOUS INSTITUTES OF MEN REPRESENTED IN THE ARCHDIOCESE

For further details refer to the corresponding bracketed number in the Religious Institutes of Men or Women section.

[]—*Apostles of Jesus*—A.J.

[]—*Apostolic Life Community Of Priests (Holy Spirit Fathers)*—A.L.C.P.

[0140]—*The Augustinians*—O.S.A.

[0200]—*Benedictine Monks* (Mt. Angel, OR)—O.S.B.

[0895]—*Brigittine Monastery of Our Lady of Consolidation*—O.Ss.S.

[]—*Brotherhood of the People of Praise*

[0330]—*Brothers of the Christian Schools*—F.S.C.

[0350]—*Cistercians Order of the Strict Observance (Trappists)*—O.C.S.O.

[]—*Conventual Franciscans*—O.F.M.Conv

[]—*Discalced Carmelite Friars*—O.C.D.

[0520]—*Franciscan Friars* (Prov. of Santa Barbara)—O.F.M.

[0690]—*Jesuit Fathers and Brothers* (Oregon Prov.)—S.J.

[0660]—*Missionaries Of The Holy Spirit*—M.Sp.S.

[0910]—*Oblates of Mary Immaculate*—O.M.I.

[0430]—*Order of Preachers (Dominicans)* (Western Prov.)—O.P.

[1030]—*Paulist Fathers*—C.S.P.

[0610]—*Priests of the Congregation of Holy Cross*—C.S.C.

[]—*St. John Society*—S.S.J.

[1240]—*Servites* (Western Prov.)—O.S.M.

[1260]—*Society of Christ*—S.Ch.

[]—*Society of the Missionaries of St. Francis Xavier*—S.F.X.

RELIGIOUS INSTITUTES OF WOMEN REPRESENTED IN THE ARCHDIOCESE

[]—*Adrian Dominican Sisters*—O.P.

[0230]—*Benedictine Sisters of Pontifical Jurisdiction* (Mount Angel, OR)—O.S.B.

[]—*Benedictine Sisters of St. Benedict Monastery*—O.S.B.

[0420]—*Discalced Carmelite Nuns*—O.C.D.

[]—*Dominican Sisters of Caldwell, NJ*—O.P.

[1390]—*Franciscan Missionary Sisters of Our Lady of Sorrows*—O.S.F.

[]—*Holy Spirit Sisters*—A.L.C.S.

[1250]—*The Institute of the Franciscan Sisters of the Eucharist*—F.S.E.

[2575]—*Institute of the Sisters of Mercy of the Americas* (Omaha, NE)—R.S.M.

[]—*The Lovers of The Holy Cross Sisters*—T.H.C.S.

[]—*Maryknoll Missionary Sisters*—M.M.

[]—*Missionaries of the Rosary of Fatima*—M.R.F.

[]—*Oblates of Saint Martha*—O.S.M.

[]—*Religious Sisters of Mercy of Alma, Mich.*—R.S.M.

[3590]—*Servants of Mary (Servite Sisters)*—O.S.M.

[0430]—*Sisters of Charity of the Blessed Virgin Mary*—B.V.M.

[2990]—*Sisters of Notre Dame* (Denver, CO)—S.N.D.

[3350]—*Sisters of Providence* (Mother Joseph Province)—S.P.

[3360]—*Sisters of Providence of St.-Mary-of-the-Woods, IN*—S.P.

[3475]—*Sisters of Reparation of the Sacred Wounds of Jesus*—S.R.

[]—*Sisters of St. Francis* (Clinton, Iowa)—O.S.F.

[]—*Sisters of St. Dominic* (Blauvelt, NY)—O.P.

[1650]—*The Sisters of St. Francis of Philadelphia*—O.S.F.

[3890]—*Sisters of St. Joseph of Peace* (Western Prov.)—C.S.J.P.

[3960]—*Sisters of St. Mary of Oregon*—S.S.M.O.

[1830]—*The Sisters of the Good Shepherd*—R.G.S.

[1990]—*Sisters of the Holy Names of Jesus and Mary*—S.N.J.M.

[]—*Sisters Servants of the Immaculate Heart of Mary*—I.H.M.

[4060]—*Society of the Holy Child Jesus* (American Prov.)—S.H.C.J.

[4155]—*Vietnamese Adorers of the Holy Cross*—M.T.G.

ARCHDIOCESAN CEMETERIES

PORTLAND. *Gethsemani*

Mount Calvary

EUGENE. *Mount Calvary*

SALEM. *St. Barbara*

NECROLOGY

† Park, Rev. Msgr. Morton, (Retired)—Died Nov. 15, 2009

† McMahon, Joseph M., (Retired)—Died May 5, 2009

† Wraszczak, Chester, (Retired)—Died April 29, 2009

An asterisk (*) denotes an organization that has established tax-exempt status directly with the IRS and is not covered by the USCCB Group Ruling.

Diocese of Providence

(Dioecesis Providentiensis)

Most Reverend

THOMAS J. TOBIN

Bishop of Providence; ordained July 21, 1973; appointed Titular Bishop of Novica and Auxiliary Bishop of Pittsburgh, November 3, 1992; consecrated December 27, 1992; appointed Fourth Bishop of Youngstown installed February 2, 1996; appointed eighth Bishop of Providence March 31, 2005; installed May 31, 2005. *One Cathedral Sq., Providence, RI 02903-3695.*

Bishop's Office & Chancery Office: One Cathedral Square, Providence, RI 02903-3695. Tel: 401-278-4500; Fax: 401-278-4621.

Web: www.dioceseofprovidence.org

Most Reverend

ROBERT C. EVANS

Auxiliary Bishop of Providence; ordained July 2, 1973; appointed Titular Bishop of Aquae Regiae and Auxiliary Bishop of Providence October 15, 2009; consecrated December 15, 2009. *Office: One Cathedral Square, Providence, RI 02903-3695.*

Most Reverend

ROBERT E. MULVEE

Bishop Emeritus of Providence; ordained June 30, 1957; appointed Auxiliary Bishop of Manchester and Titular Bishop of Summa February 15, 1977; consecrated April 14, 1977; appointed Bishop of Wilmington February 19, 1985; installed April 11, 1985; appointed Coadjutor Bishop of Providence February 9, 1995; succeeded to See June 11, 1997; retired March 31, 2005. *Res.: 30 Fenner St., Providence, RI 02903-3603. Mailing Address: One Cathedral Sq., Providence, RI 02903-3695.* Tel: 401-278-4679; Fax: 401-278-4621.

Most Reverend

LOUIS E. GELINEAU

Bishop Emeritus of Providence; ordained June 5, 1954; appointed Bishop of Providence December 6, 1971; consecrated January 26, 1972; retired June 11, 1997. *Res.: St. Antoine Residence, 10 Rhodes Ave., North Smithfield, RI 02896.* Tel: 401-767-3500.

ESTABLISHED APRIL 16, 1872.

Square Miles 1,085.

Corporate Title: Roman Catholic Bishop of Providence, a corporation sole

Comprises the State of Rhode Island.

STATISTICAL OVERVIEW

Personnel	
Retired Archbishops	1
Bishop	1
Auxiliary Bishops	1
Retired Bishops	4
Abbots	1
Retired Abbots	2
Priests: Diocesan Active in Diocese	174
Priests: Diocesan Active Outside Diocese	6
Priests: Retired, Sick or Absent	98
Number of Diocesan Priests	278
Religious Priests in Diocese	123
Total Priests in Diocese	401
Extern Priests in Diocese	12
Ordinations:	
Diocesan Priests	3
Transitional Deacons	3
Permanent Deacons in Diocese	104
Total Brothers	83
Total Sisters	477
Parishes	
Parishes	147
With Resident Pastor:	
Resident Diocesan Priests	130
Resident Religious Priests	9
Without Resident Pastor:	
Administered by Priests	8
Missions	5
Pastoral Centers	22
New Parishes Created	3
Closed Parishes	6
Professional Ministry Personnel:	
Brothers	1
Sisters	13
Lay Ministers	103
Welfare	
Catholic Hospitals	1
Total Assisted	200,000
Health Care Centers	1
Total Assisted	240
Homes for the Aged	9
Total Assisted	44,574
Day Care Centers	2
Total Assisted	115
Specialized Homes	2
Total Assisted	182
Special Centers for Social Services	6
Total Assisted	62,300
Residential Care of Disabled	1
Total Assisted	3
Other Institutions	6
Total Assisted	90,000
Educational	
Seminaries, Diocesan	1
Students from This Diocese	9
Students from Other Diocese	13
Diocesan Students in Other Seminaries	11
Total Seminarians	20
Colleges and Universities	2
Total Students	7,689
High Schools, Diocesan and Parish	4
Total Students	2,124
High Schools, Private	8
Total Students	3,673
Elementary Schools, Diocesan and Parish	33
Total Students	7,777
Elementary Schools, Private	4
Total Students	1,456
Catechesis/Religious Education:	
High School Students	8,075
Elementary Students	23,718
Total Students under Catholic Instruction	54,532
Teachers in the Diocese:	
Priests	53
Brothers	29
Sisters	56
Lay Teachers	1,555
Vital Statistics	
Receptions into the Church:	
Infant Baptism Totals	4,030
Minor Baptism Totals	294
Adult Baptism Totals	133
Received into Full Communion	318
First Communions	4,501
Confirmations	4,345
Marriages:	
Catholic	1,107
Interfaith	192
Total Marriages	1,299
Deaths	5,164
Total Catholic Population	619,964
Total Population	1,050,788

Former Bishops—Rt. Revs. THOMAS F. HENDRICKEN, D.D., cons. first Bishop of Providence, April 28, 1872; died June 11, 1886; MATTHEW HARKINS, D.D., cons. second Bishop of Providence, April 14, 1887; died May 25, 1921; Most Revs. WILLIAM A. HICKEY, D.D., ord. Dec. 22, 1893; appt. Coadjutor Bishop of Providence, Cum jure successionis, March 10, 1919; cons. Titular Bishop of Claudiopolis, April 10, 1919; succeeded to the See of Providence, May 25, 1921; died Oct. 4, 1933; FRANCIS P. KEOUGH, D.D., cons. fourth Bishop of Providence, May 22, 1934; appt. Archbishop of Baltimore, Nov. 29, 1947; died Dec. 8, 1961; RUSSELL J. MCVINNEY, D.D., appt. May 29, 1948; cons. July 14, 1948 fifth Bishop of Providence; died Aug. 10, 1971; LOUIS E. GELINEAU, D.D., S.T.L., J.C.L. (Retired), appt. Dec. 6, 1971; cons. sixth Bishop of Providence, Jan. 26, 1972; retired June 11, 1997; ROBERT E. MULVEE (Retired), ord. June 30, 1957; appt. Auxiliary Bishop of Manchester and Titular Bishop of Summa Feb. 15, 1977; cons. April 14, 1977; appt. Bishop of Wilmington Feb. 19, 1985; installed April 11, 1985; appt. Coadjutor Bishop of Providence Feb. 9, 1995; succeeded to See June 11, 1997; retired March 31, 2005.

Vicars General—Most Rev. ROBERT C. EVANS, D.D., J.C.L.; Rev. Msgrs. PAUL D. THEROUX, S.T.B., J.C.L.; JOHN J. DARCY, M.A., J.C.L.

Episcopal Vicars and Secretaries—

Vicar for Judicial Matters—Rev. Msgr. RONALD P. SIMEONE, M.Div., J.C.L.

Secretary for Diocesan Administration—Rev. Msgr. PAUL D. THEROUX, S.T.B., J.C.L.

Secretary for Catholic Education and Evangelization—Mr. DAVID M. BEAUDOIN, D.Min.

Secretary for Ministerial Services—Rev. Msgr. JOHN J. DARCY, M.A., J.C.L.

Secretary for Planning & Financial Services—Rev. Msgr. RAYMOND B. BASTIA.

Secretary for Catholic Charities and Social Ministry—Mr. JOHN J. BARRY III.

Deans—Very Revs. WILLIAM J. LEDOUX, Deanery No. I; JOHN E. UNSWORTH, Deanery No. II; RANDOLPH G. CHEW, Deanery No. III; NORMAN W. BOURDON, Deanery No. IV; Rev. Msgrs. JACQUES L. PLANTE, Deanery No. V; BARRY R.L. CONNERTON, Deanery No. VI; Very Revs. JAMES J. VERDELOTTI, Deanery No. VII; FRANCIS P. KAYATTA, Deanery No. VIII; Rev. Msgrs. JOHN W. LOLIO, Deanery No. IX; CARLO F. MONTECALVO, Deanery No. X; Very Revs. ROBERT J. GIARDINA, Deanery No. XI; MAURICE L. BRINDAMOUR, Deanery No. XII.

Bishop's Office & Chancery Office—One Cathedral Sq., Providence, 02903-3695. Tel: 401-278-4500; Fax: 401-278-4654. Rev. MICHAEL A. COLELLO, Administrative Sec. to the Bishop.

Office Hours: Mon.-Fri. 8:30-4:30.

Vicars General—Most Rev. ROBERT C. EVANS, D.D., J.C.L. Tel: 401-278-4500; Fax: 401-278-4654; Rev. Msgrs. PAUL D. THEROUX, S.T.B., J.C.L. Tel: 401-278-4535; Fax: 401-278-4623; JOHN J. DARCY, M.A., J.C.L. Tel: 401-278-4663; Fax: 401-278-4621.

Delegate for Canonical Affairs—Rev. Msgr. WILLIAM I. VARSANYI, P.A., J.C.D. Tel: 401-278-4520.

Moderator of the Curia—Rev. Msgr. PAUL D. THEROUX, S.T.B., J.C.L. Tel: 401-278-4535; Fax: 401-278-4623.

Chancellor—Rev. Msgr. JOHN J. DARCY, M.A., J.C.L. Tel: 401-278-4663; 401-278-4518; Fax: 401-278-4621.

Vice Chancellor—Rev. TIMOTHY D. REILLY, S.T.B., J.C.L. Tel: 401-278-4567; Fax: 401-278-4621.

Diocesan Tribunal—

Judicial Vicar—Rev. Msgr. RONALD P. SIMEONE, M.Div., J.C.L. Tel: 401-278-4666; Fax: 401-278-4622.

Judges—Rev. Msgr. PAUL D. THEROUX, S.T.B., J.C.L.; Revs. JUDE O. ONUCHUKWU, J.C.D.; BRICE LEAVINS, O.F.M.; Rev. Msgr. JOHN J. DARCY, M.A., J.C.L.

Assessor and Auditor—Rev. EDWARD J. MCGOVERN (Retired).

Promoter of Justice—Rev. Msgr. WILLIAM I. VARSANYI, P.A., J.C.D.

Defenders of the Bond—Most Rev. LOUIS E. GELINEAU, D.D., S.T.L., J.C.L. (Retired); Rev. DAVID W. MASELLO, J.C.L. (part-time).

Advocate—Rev. TIMOTHY D. REILLY, S.T.B., J.C.L. (part-time).

Assessor and Counselor—Mrs. NANCY GOULD.

Notaries—Mrs. PATRICIA COSTA; Mrs. LINDA L. NASTARI.

Secretary—Rev. Msgr. RONALD P. SIMEONE, M.Div., J.C.L., Sec.

Council of Priests—One Cathedral Sq., Providence, 02903-3695. Tel: 401-278-4518.

Officers—Most Rev. THOMAS J. TOBIN, Pres.; Rev. JAMES T. RUGGIERI, Moderator; Rev. Msgr. JOHN J. DARCY, M.A., J.C.L., Sec.

Council Members—Most Rev. ROBERT C. EVANS, D.D., J.C.L.; Rev. Msgrs. GEORGE L. FRAPPIER (Retired); RAYMOND B. BASTIA; RONALD P. SIMEONE, M.Div., J.C.L.; NICHOLAS J. IACOVACCI (Retired); PAUL D. THEROUX, S.T.B., J.C.L.; Very Rev. RANDOLPH G. CHEW; Revs. STEPHEN P. AMARAL; JOSEPH D. CREEDON; ALBERT A. KENNEY, S.T.L.; RICHARD A. NARCISO; MARK A. SAURIOL; FRANK SEVOLA, O.F.M.; GILDARDO SUAREZ; RAYMOND N. SURIANI; DANIEL M. TRAINOR (Retired); MICHAEL J. WOOLLEY.

College of Consultors—Rev. Msgrs. RAYMOND B. BASTIA; JOHN J. DARCY, M.A., J.C.L.; WILLIAM J. MCCAFFREY; PAUL D. THEROUX, S.T.B., J.C.L.; Revs. JOSEPH A. ESCOBAR; ROBERT F. HAWKINS; ALBERT A. KENNEY, S.T.L.; RAYMOND N. SURIANI; DANIEL M. TRAINOR (Retired).

Finance Council—Most Rev. THOMAS J. TOBIN, Pres.; Rev. Msgrs. RAYMOND B. BASTIA; PAUL D. THEROUX, S.T.B., J.C.L.; Rev. WILLIAM P. MARQUIS, O.P.; Rev. Msgr. RICHARD D. SHEAHAN; Rev. ROBERT P. PERRON; Sr. DOROTHY SCHWARZ, S.S.D.; The Hon. LAUREEN D'AMBRA; Mr. ALMON HALL; Mr. WILLIAM WRAY; Mr. GLENN CREAMER; Mrs. VIRGINIA ROBERTS; Mrs. MARGARET RUGGIERI; Mrs. PATRICIA SMOLLEY. Staff: Mr. MICHAEL F. SABATINO, CPA; Mr. ANTHONY T. GWIAZDOWSKI.

Chief Financial Officer—Mr. MICHAEL F. SABATINO, CPA.

Diocesan Offices and Directors

Diocesan Administration—

Secretariat for Diocesan Administration—One Cathedral Sq., Providence, 02903-3695. Tel: 401-278-4535; Fax: 401-278-4623. Rev. Msgr. PAUL D. THEROUX, S.T.B., J.C.L.

Archives—Mrs. LISA A. VESPIA, Archivist, One Cathedral Sq., Providence, 02903-3695. Tel: 401-278-4522.

Censors of Books—Rev. DAVID L. STOKES; Bro. THOMAS J. WHITE, O.P.

Communications— (Legal Title: Diocesan Catholic Telecommunications Network of Rhode Island); (News Media, TV, Public Relations) Mr. MICHAEL GUILFOYLE, Dir. Communications; Ms. KAREN DAVIS, Public Affairs Mgr., One Cathedral Sq., Providence, 02903-3695. Tel: 401-278-4600; Fax: 401-278-4659.

Telecommunications— (Produces Catholic Programming, Liaison with State Interconnect and CATV Companies, ETWN Liaison) Miss SUSAN MCCARTHY. Tel: 401-278-4609.

Website Coordinator—Mrs. LAURA H. TESTA. Tel: 401-278-4602; Fax: 401-278-4659.

Education and Compliance—Lt. ROBERT N. MCCARTHY, Dir., 80 St. Mary's Dr., Cranston, 02920. Tel: 401-941-0760; Fax: 401-941-1195; 401-943-2763.

Government Liaison—Rev. BERNARD A. HEALEY, Dir., 184 Broad St., Providence, 02903-4029. Tel: 401-421-7833, Ext. 104; 401-333-1568.

Human Resources Office—Mr. WILLIAM G. MEYER III, Dir., One Cathedral Square, Providence, 02903-3695. Tel: 401-278-4584; Fax: 401-751-0049.

Newspaper— "Rhode Island Catholic", Diocesan weekly. RICK SNIZER, Editor; Rev. BERNARD A. HEALEY, Theological Consultant & Editorial Writer, 184 Broad St., Providence, 02903-4080. Tel: 401-272-1010; Fax: 401-421-8418.

Propagation of the Faith— (Legal Title: Society for the Propagation of the Faith, Diocese of Providence) Rev. Msgr. WILLIAM I. VARSANYI, P.A., J.C.D., Dir. Email: wvarsanyi@dioceseofprovidence.org; Sr. M. CAROLANNE THEROUX, R.S.M., Sec., One Cathedral Sq., Providence, 02903-3695. Tel: 401-278-4519. Email: ctheroux@dioceseofprovidence.org.

Catholic Relief Services—Rev. Msgr. WILLIAM I. VARSANYI, P.A., J.C.D. Tel: 401-278-4520. Email: wvarsanyi@dioceseofprovidence.org.

Holy Childhood Association—Rev. Msgr. WILLIAM I. VARSANYI, P.A., J.C.D. Tel: 401-278-4519. Email: wvarsanyi@dioceseofprovidence.org.

Ministerial Services—

Secretariat for Ministerial Services—Rev. Msgr. JOHN J. DARCY, M.A., J.C.L., Sec., One Cathedral Sq., Providence, 02903-3695. Tel: 401-278-4663; Fax: 401-278-4621.

Ongoing Formation of Priests—Rev. MARCEL L. TAILLON, Dir., One Cathedral Square, Providence, 02903-3695. Tel: 401-278-4516; Fax: 401-278-4515.

Priests' Personnel—Rev. Msgr. JOHN J. DARCY, M.A., J.C.L., Dir., One Cathedral Sq., Providence, 02903-3695. Tel: 401-278-4663; Fax: 401-278-4621.

Ecumenical Officer—Rev. JOHN A. KILEY, Ecumenical Officer.

Clergy Benefit Fund— (Legal Title: Our Lady, Queen of the Clergy) Rev. Msgr. JOHN J. DARCY, M.A., J.C.L., Sec.

Permanent Diaconate—Deacon PAUL J. SULLIVAN, Dir., One Cathedral Sq., Providence, 02903-3695. Tel: 401-278-4650; Fax: 401-278-4515.

Religious—Sr. JACQUELINE DICKEY, S.S.Ch., One Cathedral Sq., Providence, 02903-3695. Tel: 401-278-4633.

Council of Religious—Sr. JACQUELINE DICKEY, S.S.Ch., Coord.

Seminary of Our Lady of Providence— House of Formation for college students and pre-theologians) Revs. ALBERT A. KENNEY, S.T.L., Rector; DAVID F. GAFFNEY, M.Div., Spiritual Dir.; TIMOTHY D. REILLY, S.T.B., J.C.L., Asst. Spiritual Dir.; Dr. MICHAEL HANSEN, Dir. Human Formation, 485 Mt. Pleasant Ave., Providence, 02908. Tel: 401-331-1316; Fax: 401-521-4192. Email: mhansen@dioceseofprovidence.org.

Senior Priest Advisor—Rev. ROGER A. HOULE, Mailing Address: P.O. Box 236, North Scituate, 02857-0236. Tel: 401-647-2255.

Vocations—Rev. MICHAEL J. NAJIM, M.Div., Dir., 485 Mt. Pleasant Ave., Providence, 02908. Tel: 401-831-8011; Fax: 401-521-4192; Sr. JACQUELINE DICKEY, S.S.Ch., Assoc. Dir. Rel. Vocations, One Cathedral Sq., Providence, 02903-3695. Tel: 401-278-4633.

Secretariat for Catholic Education and Evangelization—Mr. DAVID M. BEAUDOIN, D.Min., Sec., One Cathedral Sq., Providence, 02903-3695. Tel: 401-278-4625. Email: dbeaudoin@dioceseofprovidence.org.

Black Catholic Ministry—Mrs. PATTY JANUARY, Coord.; Rev. ANDREW MCNAIR, L.C., Chap., One Cathedral Sq., Providence, 02903-3695. Tel: 401-278-4552. Email: pjanuary@dioceseofprovidence.org.

Catholic Campus Ministry—Deacon MICHAEL D. NAPOLITANO, Dir., c/o RI College Campus Ministry, RIC Donovan Dining Center, Unity Center, 600 Mt. Pleasant Ave., Providence, 02908-1991. Tel: 401-456-8168. Email: campus.ministry@ric.edu.

Catholic Schools—VACANT, Supt., One Cathedral Square, Providence, 02903-3695. Tel: 401-278-4550.

Handicapped Persons Apostolate—Rev. Msgr. GERARD O. SABOURIN, Dir., One Cathedral Sq., Providence, 02903-3695. Tel: 401-278-4630. Email: gsabourin@dioceseofprovidence.org.

Deaf and Hard of Hearing Apostolate—Rev. JOSEPH J. BRUCE, S.J., Coord., One Cathedral Sq., Providence, 02903-3695. Email: jbruce@dioceseofprovidence.org.

SPRED (Special Religious Education)—Mrs. COLLEEN TOUCHETTE, One Cathedral Sq., Providence, 02903-3695. Tel: 401-658-1174. Email: spredprov@earthlink.net.

Religious Education—Miss LISA M. GULINO, Dir., 34 Fenner St., Providence, 02903-3603. Tel: 401-278-4646. Email: lgulino@dioceseofprovidence.org.

Worship—Mrs. NANCY SMITH, Coord., One Cathedral Sq., Providence, 02903. Tel: 401-278-4586. Email: worship@dioceseofprovidence.org.

Comprehensive Youth Ministry—Miss LOUISE DUSSAULT, Dir., One Cathedral Sq., Providence, 02903-3695. Tel: 401-278-4626. Email: ldussault@dioceseofprovidence.org. Web: www.ymcyoprov.org.

Catholic Scouting-Boy Scouts, Girl Scouts, Camp Fire—Rev. ANGELO N. CARUSI, Chap. Tel: 401-278-4626; Sr. DIANE RUSSO, R.S.M., Pastoral Assoc.

Catholic Youth Organization—Tel: 401-278-4626.

Youth Summer Camp—Mother of Hope Camp, Box W, Chepachet, 02814. Tel: 401-568-3580.

Marriage Preparation and Enrichment—Deacon STEPHEN R. COTE, Coord., 34 Fenner St., Providence, 02903-3603. Tel: 401-278-4577; 401-278-4576. Email: marriage@dioceseofprovidence.org.

Social Ministry—

Secretariat for Catholic Charities and Social Ministry—Mr. JOHN J. BARRY III, Sec., 184 Broad St., Providence, 02903-4029. Tel: 401-421-7833, Ext. 105; Fax: 401-274-5450.

Community Services and Catholic Charities— (Legal Title: Diocesan Bureau of Social Services) Ms. KATHLEEN MCKEON, Supvr. & Coord., 184 Broad St., Providence, 02903-4029. Tel: 401-421-7833, Ext. 106; Fax: 401-453-6135.

AIDS Ministry—VACANT, 184 Broad St., Providence, 02903-4029. Tel: 401-421-7833, Ext. 126; Fax: 401-453-6135.

Catholic Campaign for Human Development and Catholic Charities Advocacy Fund—Mr. JOHN J. BARRY III. Tel: 401-421-7833, Ext. 104.

Chaplains of Public Institutions— Catholic Chaplaincy Team (All Correctional and Detention Institutions) Mrs. MARTHA PAONE. Tel: 401-462-5238. *Youth Correctional Training School*, VACANT. Tel: 401-462-5238.

Clearinghouse Program—Ms. KATHLEEN MCKEON. Tel: 401-421-7833, Ext. 106.

Community Advocacy—VACANT.

Hispanic Ministry—Ms. AIDA HIDALGO, Dir., 184 Broad St., Providence, 02903-4029. Tel: 401-421-7833, Ext. 133; Fax: 401-453-6135. Email: ahidalgo@dioceseofprovidence.org.

Immigration and Refugee Services—STELLA CARRERA, Coord. Tel: 401-421-7833, Ext. 129; Fax: 401-277-9027. Email: scarrera@dioceseofprovidence.org.

Interfaith Community Dire Emergency Fund/ Emergency Assistance Network—Mr. JAMES JAHNZ, Coord. Tel: 401-421-7833, Ext. 107; Fax: 401-453-6135.

Peace and Justice—VACANT. Tel: 401-421-7833, Ext. 101; Fax: 401-453-6135.

Elder Care Services— Respite Care; Friendly Visitor Mr. HECTOR MUNOZ. Tel: 401-421-7833, Ext. 112; Fax: 401-453-6135. Email: hmunoz@dioceseofprovidence.org.

Community Services and Advocacy -South County— 114 High St., Wakefield, 02879. Tel: 401-783-3149; Fax: 401-783-3149. Ms. BRENDA FAY.

Community Services and Advocacy - West Warwick Satellite—145 Washington St., West Warwick, 02893. Tel: 401-823-6211; Fax: 401-615-1410. Mrs. CHARLOTTE SANTILLI.

Community Services and Advocacy - Woonsocket Satellite—190 N. Main St., Woonsocket, 02895. Tel: 401-762-2849; Fax: 401-762-2849. Mr. RICHARD ZALEWSKI.

Life and Family Ministry— (Legal Title: Retreat House of the Immaculate Heart of Mary) *184 Broad St., Providence, 02903.* Tel: 401-421-7833; Fax: 401-331-4484.

Adoption Searches—PETER MAGNOTTA, M.S.W., L.I.C.S.W., C.C.D.P.-D. Tel: 401-421-7833, Ext. 117.

Evaluations for Maturity for Marriage—Mrs. CAROL OWENS, Elizabeth Ministry. Tel: 401-421-7833, Ext. 118.

Hispanic Parish Outreach—Mr. SILVIO CUELLAR, Coord. Tel: 401-421-7833, Ext. 120.

Project Rachel—Ms. KRISTEN CAPRONI. Tel: 401-421-7833, Ext. 119.

Rachel's Vineyard's Retreats—Ms. KRISTEN CAPRONI, Liaison. Tel: 401-421-7833, Ext. 119.

Respect Life Program—Ms. KRISTEN CAPRONI. Tel: 401-421-7833, Ext. 119; Mr. SILVIO CUELLAR. Tel: 401-421-7833, Ext. 120; Mrs. CAROL OWENS. Tel: 401-421-7833, Ext. 118 (Gabriel Project).

Project Hope/Projecto Esperanza— (Legal Title: Project Hope/Projecto Esperanza) Mr. JAMES JAHNZ, Prog. Supvr., 474 Broadway, Pawtucket, 02860. Tel: 401-728-0515; Fax: 401-728-2330.

Email: jjahnz@dioceseofprovidence.org.

St. Martin de Porres Multi-Service Center— (Legal Title: St. Martin de Porres Center) Ms. ESTHER E. PRICE, 160 Cranston St., Providence, 02907-2396. Tel: 401-274-6783; Fax: 401-274-5930.

Health Care Ministries—184 Broad St., Providence, 02903-4029. Tel: 401-421-7833, Ext. 104.

Planning and Financial Services—

Secretariat for Planning and Financial Services—Rev. Msgr. RAYMOND B. BASTIA, Vicar; Mr. MICHAEL F. SABATINO, CPA, CFO, One Cathedral Sq., Providence, 02903-3695. Tel: 401-278-4540; Fax: 401-831-1786.

Diocesan Facilities Department—Ms. CAROL ANN NELSON, Dir. Facilities; Mr. MAXIME E. GIROUARD JR., Field Project Mgr. & Environmental Engineer, One Cathedral Sq., Providence, 02903-3695. Tel: 401-278-4636; Fax: 401-278-4658; Mr. MICHAEL D. FALCONE, Field Project Mgr.; Mr. MARK PETRI, Field Project Mgr.

Cemeteries—Rev. ANTHONY W. VERDELOTTI, Dir.; Mr. ARTHUR F. LURGIO, Assoc. Dir., 80 St. Mary's Drive, Cranston, 02920. Tel: 401-944-8383.

Fiscal Office—J. TIMOTHY KOCAB, Diocesan Controller, One Cathedral Sq., Providence, 02903-3695. Tel: 401-278-4616; Fax: 401-751-6808.

Insurance Commission—Rev. Msgr. RAYMOND B. BASTIA, Chm., One Cathedral Sq., Providence, 02903-3695. Tel: 401-278-4616.

Catholic Mutual Group—Mr. GREG CARLSON, Claims & Risk Mgr., 80 St. Mary's Dr., Cranston, 02920-5200. Tel: 401-944-5375; 401-944-5379; Fax: 401-944-5380. Email: Mmurphy@catholicmutual.org.

Management Information Services—Ms. MARGARET RYAN, Dir., One Cathedral Sq., Providence, 02903-3695. Tel: 401-278-4611.

Parish Financial Assistance—Mrs. CATHERINE MESSIER, Dir.; Mr. BRIAN RICHARDS, Parish Business Analyst. Tel: 401-278-4573; Ms. KATHERINE HARRINGTON; Mrs. COLLEEN PETRECCA, One Cathedral Sq., Providence, 02903-3695. Tel: 401-278-4544.

Pastoral Planning—Ms. CONSTANCE V. THORNTON, Dir., One Cathedral Sq., Providence, 02903-3695. Tel: 401-278-4610.

Stewardship and Development— (Annual Appeal, Stewardship, Planned Giving, Major Gifts, Anchor of Hope Fund) Mr. ANTHONY T. GWIAZDOWSKI, Dir., One Cathedral Sq., Providence, 02903. Tel: 401-277-2121.

Catholic Charity Fund Appeal— (Legal Title: Catholic Charity Fund) Tel: 401-277-2121.

Catholic Foundation of R.I.— (Legal Title: Catholic Foundation of Rhode Island) Tel: 401-277-2121. ANDREA H. KRUPP, Esq., Dir.

Victim Assistance—PAULA LOUD, Dir. Office of Outreach & Prevention. Tel: 401-946-0728; Fax: 401-946-1587. Email: ploud@dioceseofprovidence.org.

CLERGY, PARISHES, MISSIONS AND PAROCHIAL SCHOOLS

CITY OF PROVIDENCE

(PROVIDENCE COUNTY)

1—CATHEDRAL OF SS. PETER AND PAUL (1837) Rev. Msgr. Anthony Mancini, Rector.
SS. Peter and Paul's Church, Providence, RI In Res., Most Rev. Robert E. Mulvee (Retired); Revs. Romano Almagno, O.F.M.; Ernest H. Berthelette; Michael A. Colello.
Res.: 30 Fenner St., 02903. Tel: 401-331-2434 (Office); Fax: 401-273-0687.
Catechesis/Religious Program—Students 2.

2—ST. ADALBERT (1902), (Polish), Rev. Marek S. Kupka.
Saint Adalbert's Church
Res.: 866 Atwells Ave., 02909-2596. Tel: 401-351-9306; Fax: 401-351-9306. Web: www.stadalberts.us.
Convent—Tel: 401-831-3336. Sisters Mary Bernice Pikul, Supr.; Janice M. Gaudette, Parish Min. Felician Sisters of St. Francis 2.
Catechesis/Religious Program—864 Atwells Ave., 02909-2596. Students 35.

3—ST. AGNES (1904) Rev. Normand J. Godin.
St. Agnes Church
Res.: 351 Branch Ave., 02904. Tel: 401-861-7265; Fax: 401-454-6839. Email: stagnesprov@cox.net.
Catechesis/Religious Program—Tel: 401-331-2547. Students 90.

4—ST. ANN (1895), (Italian), Rev. Michael J. Menna.
Saint Ann's Catholic Church of Providence, Rhode Island
Res.: 2 Russo St., 02904. Tel: 401-861-5111; Fax: 401-751-5453. Email: stann1@cox.net.
Catechesis/Religious Program—Tel: 401-862-0029. Students 40.

5—ST. ANTHONY (Olneyville) (1900) Rev. Daniel J. Sweet, Admin.
Saint Anthony's Church Corporation, Rhode Island
Res.: 549 Plainfield St., 02909. Tel: 401-943-2300; Fax: 401-943-2301. Email: stanthony549@verizon.net.
Catechesis/Religious Program—Students 70.

6—ASSUMPTION OF THE BLESSED VIRGIN MARY (1871) Rev. Gildardo Suarez (Colombia).
The Church of the Assumption, Providence, Rhode Island In Res., Rev. Robert M. Beirne (Retired).
Res.: 791 Potters Ave., 02907. Tel: 401-941-1248; Fax: 401-781-4887. Email: assumptionsouthprovidence@yahoo.com. Web: www.assumbvm.com.
Catechesis/Religious Program—Tel: 401-941-3768. Email: rel_edu.assumption@yahoo.com. Students 220.

7—ST. AUGUSTINE (1929) Rev. Msgr. Barry R.L. Connerton; Revs. Carl B. Fisette; Albert D. Ranallo Jr. (Legal title: Saint Augustine's Church, Providence, Rhode Island) In Res., Rev. Edward J. Byington (FR) (Retired).
Res.: 20 Old Rd., 02908. Tel: 401-831-3503; Fax: 401-421-9060. Email: staugprov@cox.net. Web: www.staugprov.com.
School—(Grades PreK-8), 635 Mt. Pleasant Ave., 02908. Tel: 401-831-1213; Fax: 401-831-4256. Mrs. Kathleen Morry, Prin. Sisters 1; Lay Teachers 26; Students 281.
Catechesis/Religious Program—Students 373.

8—ST. BARTHOLOMEW (1907), (Italian), Rev. Alfred P. Almonte, C.S.; Deacon Robert L. Gallo, Pastoral Assoc.
Saint Bartholomew's Church Corporation In Res., Rev. Robert E. Lacombe.
Res.: 297 Laurel Hill Ave., 02909-3897. Tel: 401-944-4466; Fax: 401-946-5866. Email: stbartholomewparish@hotmail.com.
Catechesis/Religious Program—Fax: 401-946-5866. Students 140.

9—BLESSED SACRAMENT (1888) Rev. Angelo N. Carusi; Deacon Jimmie H. Owen.
The Church of the Blessed Sacrament in Providence, Rhode Island In Res., Rev. Jose C. Cardenas Bonilla, C.S.
Res.: 239 Regent Ave., 02908. Tel: 401-751-7575; Fax: 401-621-9605. Email: blessacprov@aol.om. Web: www.blessedsacramentri.com.
School—(Grades PreK-8), 240 Regent Ave., 02908. Tel: 401-831-3993. June Spencer, Prin. Lay Teachers 22; Students 273.
Catechesis/Religious Program—Students 75.

10—ST. CASIMIR (1919), (Lithuanian), [JC] Rev. James T. Ruggieri, Admin.
Saint Casimir's Church, Providence, Rhode Island
Res.: 350 Smith St., 02908. Tel: 401-331-1051.

11—ST. CHARLES BORROMEO (1874), (French), Very Rev. Robert J. Giardina; Deacons Jose Rico, Pastoral Assoc.; Rony Lopez; Joseph Braga.
Saint Charles Borromeo Roman Catholic Church, Providence, Rhode Island In Res., Rev. Francis J. Giudice (Retired).
Res.: 178 Dexter St., 02907. Tel: 401-421-6441; Fax: 401-454-4986.
Catechesis/Religious Program—Students 44.

12—ST. EDWARD (1874) Revs. Edward S. Cardente; Nolasco Tamayo Alvarez (Colombia).
The Church of St. Joseph Geneva Rhode Island
Res.: 10 Caxton St., 02904. Tel: 401-353-3120; Fax: 401-353-5126.
Church: 997 Branch Ave., 02904. Tel: 401-331-4035. Email: stanthonynp@cox.net.
Catechesis/Religious Program—Tel: 401-353-5215. Students 51.

13—GENESIS COMMUNITY, Closed. For inquiries for parish records contact Cathedral of SS. Peter & Paul, Providence.

14—ST. HEDWIG, Closed. For inquiries for sacramental records contact St. Adalbert Parish, Providence.

15—HOLY CROSS (1949), (Italian), Rev. David C. Procaccini; Deacon John J. Natalizia.
Corporation of the Church of the Holy Cross
Res.: 18 King Philip St., 02909. Tel: 401-274-5225; Fax: 401-274-6635. Email: parishoffice@holycross.necoxmail.com.
Catechesis/Religious Program—Tel: 401-751-1144. Mrs. June Carnevale, D.R.E. Students 96.

16—HOLY GHOST (1889), (Italian), Rev. Camillo Lando, C.S.
Corporation of the Church of the Holy Ghost, Rhode Island In Res., Rev. Tarcisio Bagatin, C.S.
Res.: 472 Atwells Ave., 02909. Tel: 401-421-3551; Fax: 401-421-3557. Email: hgcri@cox.net. Web: www.geocities.com/holyghostc.
See Holy Ghost School, Providence located in the Institution section under Bread of Life Schools, Urban Catholic Schools Consortium.
Catechesis/Religious Program—Students 14.

17—HOLY NAME OF JESUS (1882), (Cape Verdean), Revs. Joseph D. Santos Jr. (Portugal); Jude O. Onuchukwu (Italy).
Church of the Holy Name of Jesus at Providence, Rhode Island In Res., Rev. John Wydeven (OAK).
Res.: 99 Camp St., 02906-1799. Tel: 401-272-4515; Fax: 401-272-4616. Email: theholyname@cox.net. Web: http://members.cox.net/holynamechurch.
Catechesis/Religious Program—Students 48.

18—IMMACULATE CONCEPTION, Closed. For inquiries for sacramental records contact St. Patrick Parish, Providence.

19—ST. JOHN, Closed. Sacramental records are located at St. Mary Church, Providence.
St. John Church of Providence Rhode Island.

20—ST. JOSEPH (Foxpoint) (1851) Rev. Msgr. Raymond B. Bastia; Sr. Mary Ellen Maytum, R.S.M., Pastoral Min.
St. Joseph's Church Providence Rhode Island In Res., Revs. Henry J. Bodah; Paul A. Charland.
Res.: 92 Hope St., 02906. Tel: 401-421-9137; Fax: 401-621-5349. Email: stjoe1851@cox.net. Web: www.saintjoesprov.org.
Catechesis/Religious Program—Students 42.

21—ST. MARON Rev. Msgr. John J. Darcy.
Church of St. Maron in Providence
Res.: One Cathedral Square, 02903-3695. Tel: 401-278-4663; Fax: 401-278-4621.

22—ST. MARY (Broadway) (1853) Revs. Frank Sevola, O.F.M.; Scott F. Brookbank, O.F.M.
St. Mary's Church Providence Rhode Island In Res., Rev. Charles J. O'Connor, O.F.M.
Res.: 538 Broadway, 02909-3329. Tel: 401-274-3434. Email: fsevola@stfrancischapel.com.
Catechesis/Religious Program—Students 75.

23—ST. MICHAEL THE ARCHANGEL (South Providence) (1859) Revs. Thomas J. Ferland; Jacques Eddy Chavannes (Haiti); Jaime A. Garcia; Deacon Juan Andres Perez.
St. Michael's Providence, Rhode Island
Res.: 239 Oxford St., 02905. Tel: 401-781-7210; Fax: 401-461-6164.
Catechesis/Religious Program—Students 335.

24—OUR LADY OF CHARITY Rev. Msgr. William I. Varsanyi.
Church of Our Lady of Charity of Providence
Res.: One Cathedral Sq., 02903-3695.

25—OUR LADY OF LOURDES (1904), (French), Rev. Brice Leavins, O.F.M., Admin.; Deacon Anthony J. Wendoloski Jr.
Church of Our Lady of Lourdes
Res.: 901 Atwells Ave., 02909. Tel: 401-272-8127; Fax: 401-861-0226.
Catechesis/Religious Program—Students 4.

26—OUR LADY OF MT. CARMEL (1921), (Italian), Rev. Raymond P. Luft.
Church of Our Lady of Mount Carmel, Providence
Res.: 12 Spruce St., 02903. Tel: 401-274-2113; Fax: 401-453-1221.
Catechesis/Religious Program—Students 31.

27—OUR LADY OF THE ROSARY (1886), (Portuguese), Revs. Joseph A. Escobar; Antonio M. Paiva, Pastor Emeritus (Retired).
Church of Our Lady of the Rosary
Res.: 463 Benefit St., 02903. Tel: 401-421-5621; Fax: 401-421-0783. Email: rosary463@aol.com.
Catechesis/Religious Program—Tel: 401-273-1685. Email: olrccd463@aol.com. Elisa Guerra Thibeault, D.R.E. Students 300.

28—ST. PATRICK (1841) Rev. James T. Ruggieri; Deacon Charles Andrade; Eduardo Birbuet, Pastoral Assoc.
St. Patrick's Church, Providence, Rhode Island
Res.: 152 Holden St., 02908. Tel: 401-421-7070; Fax: 401-751-7085. Email: stpatrickprov@yahoo.com. Web: www.stpatrick-providence.org.
School—St. Patrick Academy, (Grades 6-8), 44 Smith St., 02908. Tel: 401-421-9300; Fax: 401-421-0810. Email: steveray8@netscape.net. Web: www.stpatrick-providence.org. Mr. Stephen M. Raymond, Prin. Lay Teachers 17; Students 69.
Catechesis/Religious Program—Students 175.

29—ST. PIUS V (1918) Very Rev. Kenneth R. Letoile, O.P.; Revs. John Martin Ruiz-Mayorga, O.P.; Guy Albert Trudel, O.P.; Edward M. Gorman, O.P.
Saint Pius Church, Providence, Rhode Island In Res., Revs. John L. Sullivan, O.P.; John P. Burchill, O.P.
Res.: 55 Elmhurst Ave., 02908. Tel: 401-751-4871; Fax: 401-273-1089. Email: receptionist@stpiusvchurch.net. Web: http://stpiusvchurch.net.
School—(Grades PreK-8), 49 Elmhurst Ave., 02908. Tel: 401-421-9750; Fax: 401-455-3928. Sr. Mary Agnes Greiffendorf, O.P., Prin. Religious 4; Lay Teachers 16; Students 246.
Catechesis/Religious Program—Tel: 401-751-4871; Fax: 401-273-1089. Students 65.

Convent—30 Elmhurst Ave., 02908.
30—ST. RAYMOND (1911) Rev. Edward L. Pieroni.
Saint Raymond's Church Corporation
Res.: 2 Matilda St., 02904-1812. Tel: 401-351-4224; Fax: 401-274-3350. Email: catholichurch@straymonds.com. Web: www.straymonds.com.
Church: 1240 N. Main St., 02906. Tel: 401-351-4224; Fax: 401-274-3350.
Catechesis/Religious Program—Students 25.
31—ST. SEBASTIAN (1915) Revs. Robert W. Hayman; David L. Stokes.
Church of Saint Sebastian
Res.: 67 Cole Ave., 02906. Tel: 401-751-0196; Fax: 401-273-2753. Email: stsebastian@cox.net. Web: www.stsebastianchurch.org.
Catechesis/Religious Program—Tel: 401-272-6062. Students 84.
32—ST. TERESA OF AVILA (Olneyville) (1883) Closed. For inquiries for sacramental records contact Blessed Sacrament, Providence.
Saint Teresa's Church Providence, Rhode Island
33—ST. THOMAS (Fruit Hill) (1886) Rev. John P. Soares; Deacon Albert DePetrillo.
St. Thomas' Church of Manton Rhode Island
Res.: 65 Fruit Hill Ave., 02909-5598. Tel: 401-272-7118; Fax: 401-272-8431. Email: stthomas@cox.net.
See St. Thomas Regional School, Providence under Regional Elementary Schools located in the Institution section.
Catechesis/Religious Program—Tel: 401-272-1443; Fax: 401-272-8431. Students 122.

OUTSIDE THE CITY OF PROVIDENCE

BARRINGTON, BRISTOL CO.
1—HOLY ANGELS (1913), (Italian), Rev. Raymond J. Ferrick.
Holy Angel's Church Corporation
Res.: 341 Maple Ave., 02806. Tel: 401-245-7743; Fax: 401-245-9698.
Catechesis/Religious Program—341 Maple Ave., 02806. Tel: 401-247-1764. Students 56.
2—ST. LUKE (West Barrington) (1942) Revs. Robert F. Hawkins; Lukasz J. Willenberg.
Saint Luke's Church Corporation, Barrington
Res.: 108 Washington Rd., 02806-1133. Tel: 401-246-1212; Fax: 401-246-1301. Email: pastor@stlukesparish.com. Web: www.stlukesparish.com.
School—(Grades PreK-8), 10 Waldron Ave., 02806. Tel: 401-246-0990; Fax: 401-246-2120. Maureen Jannetta, Prin.; Nancy Brex, Librarian. Lay Teachers 21; Students 218.
Catechesis/Religious Program—110 Washington Rd., 02806. Tel: 401-246-1363. Patricia Grattan, D.R.E. (Grades 1-5); Diane Comerford, D.R.E. (Grades 6-10). Students 829.
BRISTOL, BRISTOL CO.
1—ST. ELIZABETH (1913), (Portuguese), Revs. Jared J. Costanza; Scott J. Pontes; Deacon James E. Conley.

Saint Elizabeth's Church of Bristol
Res.: 577 Wood St., 02809-2395. Tel: 401-253-8366; Fax: 401-253-7695. Email: office@saintelizabethchurch.net.
Catechesis/Religious Program—Tel: 401-253-3501. Students 436.
2—ST. MARY (1869) [CEM] Rev. Barry J. Gamache; Deacons Paul Bisbano; Bernard G. Theroux.
Saint Mary's Church, Bristol, Rhode Island
Res.: 330 Wood St., 02809. Tel: 401-253-3300; Fax: 401-253-4057. Web: www.stmarybristolri.org.
Catechesis/Religious Program—Tel: 401-253-2270. Students 203.
Mission—Our Lady of Prudence Prudence Island, Newport Co. 02872.
3—OUR LADY OF MOUNT CARMEL (1917), (Italian), [JC] Revs. Henry P. Zinno Jr.; Michael A. Sisco.
Church of Our Lady of Mount Carmel, Bristol
Res.: 141 State St., 02809. Tel: 401-253-9449; Fax: 401-253-5687. Email: hpz612@yahoo.com. Web: www.olmc-bristol.org.
School—(Grades PreK-8), 127 State St., 02809. Tel: 401-253-8455; Fax: 401-254-8234. Filippini Sisters 2; Lay Teachers 11; Students 180.
Catechesis/Religious Program—131 State St., 02809. Tel: 401-253-5052. Students 205.
BURRILLVILLE, PROVIDENCE CO.
1—ST. JOSEPH (Pascoag) (1884) Rev. Clifford J. Cabral; Deacon Anthony E. Muscatelli.
Saint Joseph's Roman Catholic Church of Pascoag, RI
Res.: 183 Sayles Ave., P.O. Box 188, Pascoag, 02859-0188. Tel: 401-568-2411; Fax: 401-568-2586.
Catechesis/Religious Program—Students 310.
2—OUR LADY OF GOOD HELP (Mapleville) (1905) Rev. Joseph A. Pescatello; Deacon Richard J. Lapierre.
Eglise de Notre Dame de Bonsecours
Res.: 1063 Victory Hwy., Mapleville, 02839. Tel: 401-568-5272; Fax: 401-568-5351. Email: pat@olgh.necoxmail.com. Web: www.ourladyofgoodhelp.org.
Catechesis/Religious Program—Ms. Patricia Ducharme, D.R.E. (Grades 1-5); Carolyn Picano, Youth Min. & D.R.E. (Grades 6-10). Students 199.
3—ST. PATRICK (Harrisville) (1854) [CEM] [JC 2] Rev. Bernard M. O'Reilly.
St. Patrick's Church, Burrillville, Rhode Island
Res.: 45 Main St., Harrisville, 02830. Tel: 401-568-5600; Fax: 401-568-7132.
Catechesis/Religious Program—Students 113.
Mission—St. Louis Chapel Old Victory Hwy., Glendale, Providence Co. 02826.
4—ST. THERESA OF THE CHILD JESUS (Nasonville) (1923) [CEM] Rev. Gerard J. Caron.
Church of Saint Teresa of the Child Jesus, Nasonville
Res.: 35 Dion Dr., Harrisville, 02830. Tel: 401-568-8280; Fax: 401-567-9238. Email: sttheresachurch3@familink.net.
Catechesis/Religious Program—Tel: 401-568-3057. Students 100.
CENTRAL FALLS, PROVIDENCE CO.
1—HOLY SPIRIT PARISH (2009) [CEM], Consolidation of the following three parishes: Holy Trinity, (Legal Title: Church of the Holy Trinity, Central Falls); Notre Dame, (Legal Title: Notre Dame Church); and St. Matthew, (Legal Title: Saint Matthew's Church of Central Falls). Revs. Timothy J. Lemlin; Andrew McNair, L.C.
Res.: 1030 Dexter St., 02863-1717. Tel: 401-726-2600; 401-725-1748; 401-723-5326; Fax: 401-722-0224. Email: the.holy.spirit.parish@gmail.com. Web: www.holyspiritcentralfalls.parishesonline.com.
Catechesis/Religious Program—Tel: 401-722-3717. Students 211.
2—HOLY TRINITY (1989) Merged See Holy Spirit Parish, Central Falls.
3—ST. JOSEPH (1906), (Polish), Rev. Dariusz J. Jonczyk.
St. Joseph's Church of Central Falls
Res.: 391 High St., 02863-3109. Tel: 401-723-5427; Fax: 401-726-5971.
Catechesis/Religious Program—Students 66.
4—ST. MATTHEW'S (1906), (French), Merged See Holy Spirit Parish, Central Falls.
5—NOTRE DAME (1873), (French), Merged See Holy Spirit Parish, Central Falls.
CHARLESTOWN, WASHINGTON CO., ST. MARY (Carolina) (1946) Rev. Paul E. Desmarais; Deacons Paul A. Theroux; John S. Shea.
Saint Mary's Church Corporation, Carolina
Res.: 437 Carolina Back Rd., P.O. Box 475, Carolina, 02812. Tel: 401-364-7214; Fax: 401-364-0182. Email: stmjparish@stmj.org. Web: www.stmj.org.
Catechesis/Religious Program—Email: marybeth@stmj.org. Students 262.
Mission—St. James 2079 Mat. School House Rd., Washington Co. 02813. Tel: 401-364-7214.
COVENTRY, KENT CO.
1—SS. JOHN AND PAUL (1955) Revs. Paul R. Grenon; Peter J. Sheehan; Peter J. D'Ambrosia, S.M.; Deacon Robert Persson.
SS. John and Paul Parish Corporation, Coventry
In Res., Rev. John J. Duggan (Ireland) (Retired).
Res.: 341 S. Main St., 02816. Tel: 401-821-5764; Fax: 401-828-5351. Email: ssjp341@stjp.necoxmail.com. Web: www.stsjohnpaulri.com.
Father John V. Doyle School—343 South Main St., 02816. Tel: 401-821-3756; Fax: 401-828-5351. Email: rido3467@ride.ri.net. Web: www.ri.net/rinet/fr_doyle. Mr. J. Robert McDermott, Prin.; Mrs. Vivian Ryan, Vice Prin. Lay Teachers 27; Students 434.
Catechesis/Religious Program—Tel: 401-821-4780; Fax: 401-828-5351. Email: annssjp@stjp.necoxmail.com. Students 1,139.
2—OUR LADY OF CZENSTOCHOWA (Quidnick) (1905), (Polish), Rev. Stephen P. Amaral.
Church of Our Lady of Czenstochowa
Res.: 445 Washington St., 02816. Tel: 401-821-7991; Fax: 401-821-8714. Email: olczenstochowa@aol.com.
Catechesis/Religious Program—Students 102.
3—ST. VINCENT DE PAUL (Anthony) (1937), (French), Rev. Michael A. Kelley. (Legal title: Church of Saint Vincent de Paul, Anthony, Rhode Island).
Res.: 6 St. Vincent de Paul St., 02816. Tel: 401-821-8719; Fax: 401-827-5071.
Catechesis/Religious Program—2 St. Vincent de Paul St., 02816. Tel: 401-828-3090. Students 120.
CRANSTON, PROVIDENCE CO.
1—ST. ANN (1858) Rev. Farrell E. McLaughlin. (Legal title: St. Anne's Church, Cranston, Rhode Island).
Res.: 1493 Cranston St., 02920. Tel: 401-942-2767; Fax: 401-942-2773. Email: stannrcchurch1@cox.net. Web: www.st-ann-parish.org.
Catechesis/Religious Program—Tel: 401-942-0655. Students 127.
2—HOLY APOSTLES (1991) Rev. Msgr. Richard D. Sheahan; Rev. Robert H. Forcier.
Holy Apostles Church, Cranston, Rhode Island
Res.: 800 Pippin Orchard Rd., 02921. Tel: 401-946-5586; Fax: 401-946-5066. Email: parishoffice@holyapostles.com. Web: www.holyapostles.com.
Catechesis/Religious Program—Students 1,218.
3—IMMACULATE CONCEPTION (Oaklawn) (1958) Rev. Ronald E. Brassard; Deacons Thomas R. Raspallo; Carmine Forlingieri; Michelle Colgan-Larney, Pastoral Assoc.
Immaculate Conception Church Corporation, Cranston
Res.: 237 Garden Hills Dr., 02920. Tel: 401-942-1854; Fax: 401-942-2897. Web: www.iccri.com.
See Immaculate Conception Catholic Regional School, Cranston under Regional Elementary Schools in the Institution section.
Catechesis/Religious Program— Barbara Prata, D.R.E.; Shawn McKay, D.R.E. Students 536.
4—ST. MARK (Garden City) (1950) Rev. Anthony W. Verdelotti.
Saint Mark's Church Corporation of Cranston In Res., Rev. Joseph F. Craddock.
Res.: 9 Garden Ct., 02920. Tel: 401-942-1616. Email: stmarkri@aol.com. Web: www.stmarkri.org.
Catechesis/Religious Program—Tel: 401-942-3231. Email: stmarkccd@aol.com. Students 252.
5—ST. MARY (Knightsville) (1925), (Italian), (Santa Maria della Civita) Very Rev. James J. Verdelotti; Rev. David G. Thurber Jr.; Deacon Armand R. Ragosta.
Saint Mary's Church, Cranston
Res.: 1525 Cranston St., 02920-5297. Tel: 401-942-1492; Fax: 401-946-2531.
School—(Grades PreK-8) Tel: 401-944-4107; Fax: 401-944-2395. Miss Lisa Lepore, Prin.; Leah Montagano, Librarian. Lay Teachers 13; Students 231.
Catechesis/Religious Program—Tel: 401-944-1323; Fax: 401-944-2461. Students 276.
6—ST. MATTHEW (Auburn) (1909) Revs. James R. Collins; Victor T. Silva.
St. Matthew's Church Corporation In Res., Rev. Chinnaiah Yerrnini.
Res.: 15 Frances Ave., 02910. Tel: 401-461-7172; Fax: 401-461-7339. Email: stmatthew@stmatthew.necoxmail.com.
Church: Elmwood & Park Ave., 02910.
School—(Grades PreK-8), 1301 Elmwood Ave., 02910. Tel: 401-941-8954; Fax: 401-781-7722. Email: stmatthew3@cox.net. Ms. Barbara C. Dwyer, Prin. Lay Teachers 15; Students 134.
Catechesis/Religious Program—Tel: 401-781-4568. Sr. Mercian Hassett, R.S.M., D.R.E. Students 240.
7—ST. PAUL (Edgewood) (1907) Revs. Francis C. Santilli; Albert P. Marcello III; Sr. Mary Ann Rossi, C.N.D., Pastoral Assoc.
Saint Paul's Church of Edgewood
Res.: One St. Paul Pl., 02905. Tel: 401-461-5734; Fax: 401-785-3613. Email: stpauledgewoodri@aol.com. Web: www.saintpaulcranston.com.
School—(Grades PreK-8), 1789 Broad St., 02905. Tel: 401-941-2030; Fax: 401-941-2084. Email: rid06826@ride.ri.net. Web: www.saintpaulschool-cranston.com. Mr. John F. Corry, Prin. Lay Teachers 15; Students 174.
Catechesis/Religious Program—Tel: 401-941-5576. Elizabeth Neubauer, D.R.E.; Julie Bradley, D.R.E. Students 230.
CUMBERLAND, PROVIDENCE CO.
1—ST. AIDAN (1962) Rev. Donald L. Depatie.
St. Aidan Church Corporation, Cumberland In Res., Rev. William F. Sears (Retired).
Res.: 1460 Diamond Hill Rd., 02864. Tel: 401-333-5897; Fax: 401-333-5078.
Catechesis/Religious Program—Tel: 401-333-9030. Students 172.
2—ST. JOAN OF ARC (Cumberland Hill) (1929) Very Rev. Norman W. Bourdon.
Saint Joan's Church, Cumberland, Rhode Island
Res.: 3357 Mendon Rd., 02864-2195. Tel: 401-658-2084; Fax: 401-658-2086. Email: joanofarc1@cox.net.
Catechesis/Religious Program—Tel: 401-658-0734. Students 505.
3—ST. JOHN BAPTIST MARY VIANNEY (Diamond Hill) (1953) Rev. Raymond C. Theroux; Deacon Paul H. Lambert.
Saint John Baptist Mary Vianney Church Corporation, Diamond Hill
Res.: 3609 Diamond Hill Rd., 02864. Tel: 401-333-6060; Fax: 401-334-4548. Email: rctheroux@verizon.net. Web: www.sjvparish.org.
Catechesis/Religious Program—3655 Diamond Hill Rd., 02864. Tel: 401-333-2347. Students 946.
4—ST. JOSEPH (Ashton) (1872) [CEM] Rev. John W. Hunt.
St. Joseph's Church, Ashton, Rhode Island
Res.: 1303 Mendon Rd., P.O. Box 7005, 02864. Tel: 401-333-4013; Fax: 401-333-4013. Email: stjosephashton@cathlicexchange.com. Web: www.stjosephashtonri.org.
Catechesis/Religious Program—Tel: 401-333-4014.

Students 205.

5—OUR LADY OF FATIMA (Valley Falls) (1953), (Portuguese), Revs. Dennis J. Kieton; Domingos M. da Cunha.
Church of Our Lady of Fatima, Valley Falls
Res.: Fatima Dr., 02864. Tel: 401-723-6719; Fax: 401-723-1698. Email: olf@olfchurch.com. Web: www.olfchurch.com.
Catechesis/Religious Program—Tel: 401-724-3454; Fax: 401-723-1698. Email: ccd@olfchurch.com. Students 290.

6—ST. PATRICK (Valley Falls) (1861) [CEM 2] Rev. Lawrence E. Toole.
St. Patrick's Church Corporation, Valley Falls, Rhode Island
Res.: 301 Broad St., 02864. Tel: 401-725-0344.
Catechesis/Religious Program—Tel: 401-725-0344. Students 70.

EAST GREENWICH, KENT CO., OUR LADY OF MERCY (1853) [CEM] Rev. Msgr. John W. Lolio; Rev. Charles R. Grondin.
Our Lady of Mercy, Greenwich, Rhode Island
Res.: 65 Third St., 02818. Tel: 401-884-4968; Fax: 401-884-1415.
Catechesis/Religious Program—Tel: 401-884-1061. Students 1,104.
Convent—Sisters of Mercy, 36 Fourth Ave., 02818. Tel: 401-884-9292.
Convent—Sisters of St. Lucy Filippini, 66 Fifth Ave., 02818. Tel: 401-886-4753.

EAST PROVIDENCE, PROVIDENCE CO.

1—ST. BRENDAN (Riverside) (1909) Very Rev. John E. Unsworth; Rev. Przemyslaw Lepak; Deacon Dominic P. DiOrio.
St. Brendan's Church
Res.: 60 Turner Ave., Riverside, 02915. Tel: 401-433-2600; Fax: 401-433-3336. Email: office@stbren.com. Web: www.stbren.com.
Catechesis/Religious Program—Tel: 401-433-2680. Tamara Primmer, D.R.E. Students 460.

2—ST. FRANCIS XAVIER (1915), (Portuguese), Rev. Msgr. Victor M. Vieira; Rev. Richard A. Narciso.
Saint Francis Xavier's Church In Res., Rev. Msgr. John J. Darcy.
Res.: 81 N. Carpenter St., 02914. Tel: 401-434-1878; Fax: 401-438-1950. Email: msgrvieira@cox.net. Web: www.sfx-ep.com.
Catechesis/Religious Program—Tel: 401-434-3153; 401-434-9421. Students 825.

3—ST. MARGARET (Rumford) (1888) Rev. Msgr. William J. McCaffrey; Deacon John F. Needham, Pastoral Assoc.
Saint Margaret's Church Corporation, East Providence Rhode Island In Res., Rev. Msgr. Paul D. Theroux.
Res.: 1098 Pawtucket Ave., Rumford, 02916. Tel: 401-438-3230; Fax: 401-438-4221. Email: office-stmargaretchurch@cox.net. Web: www.stmargaretchurch.org.
School—(Grades PreK-8), 42 Bishop Ave., Rumford, 02916. Tel: 401-434-2338; Fax: 401-431-0266. Email: jrezendes@stmargaretsch.org. Mr. John P. Rezendes, Prin. Lay Teachers 16; Students 233.
Catechesis/Religious Program—Tel: 401-435-4755. Email: sara@zapcreative.net. Ms. Sara D. Hickey, D.R.E. Students 233.

4—ST. MARTHA (1956) Rev. Douglas J. Spina; Deacon Frederick A. Young.
St. Martha's Church Corporation, East Providence In Res., Rev. Paul F. Reynolds (Retired).
Res.: 2595 Pawtucket Ave., 02914. Tel: 401-434-4060; Fax: 401-434-4849.
Catechesis/Religious Program—Tel: 401-434-7030. Students 197.

5—OUR LADY OF LORETO (1920), (Italian—Brazilian), Rev. Stanley T. Nakowicz.
Church of Our Lady of Loreto, East Providence
Res.: 346 Waterman Ave., 02914. Tel: 401-434-3535; Fax: 401-434-8204. Email: loreto5@oll.necoxmail.com.
Catechesis/Religious Program—Students 74.

6—SACRED HEART (1876) Rev. Peter S. DiTullio, S.C.
Church of the Sacred Heart
Res.: 118 Taunton Ave., 02914. Tel: 401-434-0326; Fax: 401-434-0326. Email: pdtsc@hotmail.com.
School—(Grades K-8), 56 Purchase St., 02914. Tel: 401-434-1080; Fax: 401-434-1080. Email: rid04407@ride.ri.net. Sr. Nancy McLennon, D.S.M.P., Prin. Lay Teachers 13; Students 148.
Nursery-Day Care—101 Taunton Ave., 02914. Tel: 401-434-2462. Total Staff 7; Children 75.
Catechesis/Religious Program—Students 52.

EXETER, WASHINGTON CO., BLESSED KATERI TEKAKWITHA CATHOLIC COMMUNITY (1981) Rev. Msgr. Gerard O. Sabourin, Admin.
84 Exeter Rd., 02822. Tel: 401-212-0855.
Catechesis/Religious Program—Students 51.

FOSTER, PROVIDENCE CO., ST. PAUL THE APOSTLE (1972) Rev. M.J. Bernard Dore.
St. Paul's Church Corporation, Foster
Res.: 116A Danielson Pike, 02825-1468. Tel: 401-647-3664; Fax: 401-647-3680. Email: sp10472@aol.com. Web: www.rc.net/providence/stpaul.
Catechesis/Religious Program—Mr. Fernando Botelho, D.R.E. Students 158.

GLOCESTER, PROVIDENCE CO., ST. EUGENE (Chepachet) (1956) Rev. T.J. Varghese.
St. Eugene's Church Corporation, Chepachet
Res.: 1251 Putnam Pike, P.O. Box A, Chepachet, 02814. Tel: 401-568-5102; Fax: 401-567-7847. Web: www.sainteugeneschurch.org.
Catechesis/Religious Program—Students 294.

HOPKINTON, WASHINGTON CO.

1—ST. JOSEPH (Hope Valley) (1939) Rev. Michael J. Leckie.
Saint Joseph's Church, Hope Valley
Res.: 1105 Main St., P.O. Box 388, Hope Valley, 02832. Tel: 401-539-8311. Email: stjosephhv@verizon.net. Web: www.stjosephhv.org.
Catechesis/Religious Program—Tel: 401-539-8312. Students 189.

2—OUR LADY OF VICTORY (Ashaway) (1946) Rev. James V. Farley.
Church of Our Lady of Victory, Ashaway
Res.: 169 Main St., Ashaway, 02804. Tel: 401-377-8830; Fax: 401-377-8830. Email: lmolv@yahoo.com.
Catechesis/Religious Program—Tel: 401-377-8435; Fax: 401-377-8830. Email: ggolv@yahoo.com. Students 145.

JAMESTOWN, NEWPORT CO., ST. MARK (Jamestown) (1909) [CEM] Rev. William J. O'Neill.
Saint Mark Church of Jamestown
Res.: 60 Narragansett Ave., 02835. Tel: 401-423-1421; Fax: 401-423-2067. Email: stmarkjtn@cox.net. Web: www.stmarkjtn.org.
Catechesis/Religious Program—Tel: 401-423-1518. Students 225.

JOHNSTON, PROVIDENCE CO.

1—ST. BRIGID (Thornton) (1915) Rev. Robert A. Rochon.
Saint Brigid's Church of Johnston
Res.: 1231 Plainfield, 02919. Tel: 401-944-2232; Fax: 401-944-0306. Email: stbrigidjohnston1@verizon.net. Web: www.parishesonline.com/stbrigidjohnston.
Catechesis/Religious Program—Tel: 401-946-3399. Students 96.

2—OUR LADY OF GRACE (1913), (Italian), Rev. Msgr. Carlo F. Montecalvo.
Church of Our Lady of Grace
Res.: 4 Lafayette St., 02919. Tel: 401-231-2220; Fax: 401-231-3905.
Catechesis/Religious Program—Tel: 401-231-8959. Students 147.

3—ST. ROBERT BELLARMINE (1963) Rev. John G. LaPointe; Deacon Joseph Tumminelli.
St. Robert Bellarmine Church Corporation, Johnston
Res.: 1804 Atwood Ave., 02919-3215. Tel: 401-232-5600; Fax: 401-231-5793. Email: srbp1804@aol.com. Web: www.strobertsparish.org.
Catechesis/Religious Program—Tel: 401-232-9321; Fax: 401-231-5793. Students 339.

4—ST. ROCCO (1903), (Italian), Revs. Charles Zanoni, C.S.; Mario Titotto, C.S.; Deacon Robert P. Troia.
Saint Rocco Church of Johnston In Res., Rev. Michael Tarro, C.S (Retired).
Res.: 927 Atwood Ave., 02919. Tel: 401-942-5203; Fax: 401-464-6422. Email: churchofstrocco@aol.com.
School—(Grades PreK-8), 931 Atwood Ave., 02919. Tel: 401-944-2993; Fax: 401-944-3019. Magdalen Chianese, Prin. Lay Teachers 25; Students 348.
Catechesis/Religious Program—Tel: 401-944-6040. Sr. Rose Alfieri, C.P., D.R.E. Students 220.

LINCOLN, PROVIDENCE CO.

1—ST. AMBROSE (Albion) (1905) [CEM] Rev. Bernard A. Healey; Deacon Robert McAdam.
St. Ambrose Church, Albion, Rhode Island
Res.: 191 School St., P.O. Box 67, Albion, 02802. Tel: 401-333-1568; Fax: 401-333-8941. Email: stambrosechurch@cox.net. Web: www.stambrosechurch.org.
Catechesis/Religious Program—Tel: 401-334-3735. Students 194.

2—ST. JAMES (Manville) (1874) [CEM] Rev. Richard P. Desaulniers; Deacon Gregory Horton.
Saint James Church of Manville, Rhode Island
Res.: 33 Division St., Box 60, Manville, 02838. Tel: 401-766-1558. Email: claudette@stjames.necoxmail.com.
Catechesis/Religious Program—57 Division St., Manville, 02838. Tel: 401-769-2676. Students 142.

3—ST. JUDE (Lincoln) (1946) Rev. Bernard C. Lavin; Deacon L. Bud Remillard.
St. Jude's Church, Lincoln
Res.: 301 Front St., 02865. Tel: 401-725-8140; Fax: 401-726-4946. Web: www.saintjude.us.
Catechesis/Religious Program—Tel: 401-725-8120. Sr. Mary Higgins, R.S.M., D.R.E. (Grades 1-6); Keri Carvalho, D.R.E. (Grades 7-10). Students 538.

LITTLE COMPTON, NEWPORT CO., ST. CATHERINE OF SIENA (1930) [CEM] Rev. Gerald W. Hussey.
St. Catherine's Church Corporation, Little Compton
Res.: 74 Simmons Rd., P.O. Box 208, 02837-0208. Tel: 401-635-4420; Fax: 401-635-2214. Email: gwh1178@cox.net.
Catechesis/Religious Program—Students 136.

MIDDLETOWN, NEWPORT CO., ST. LUCY (Middletown) (1952) Rev. John W. O'Brien; Deacon John E. Croy; Sr. Sheila Murphy, S.S.J., Pastoral Min.
Saint Lucy's Church Corp.
Res.: 909 W. Main Rd., 02842-6351. Tel: 401-847-6153; Fax: 401-846-1545. Email: stlucy@dioceseofprovidence.org. Web: www.stlucy.org.
Catechesis/Religious Program—Colette Savaria, Coord. Faith Formation; Emery Parillo, Adult Faith Formation. Students 186.

NARRAGANSETT, WASHINGTON CO.

1—ST. MARY, STAR OF THE SEA (Point Judith) (1960) Very Rev. Francis P. Kayatta.
St. Mary, Star of the Sea Church Corporation, Point Judith
Res.: 864 Pt. Judith Rd., 02882. Tel: 401-783-4449; Fax: 401-783-0986. Email: stmary's@dioceseofprovidence.org.
Catechesis/Religious Program—Tel: 401-789-7308; Fax: 401-783-0986. Students 225.

2—ST. THOMAS MORE (1917) Rev. Marcel L. Taillon; Deacon Paul J. Sullivan.
St. Thomas More Church, Narragansett Pier, Rhode Island
Res.: 53 Rockland St., 02882. Tel: 401-789-7682; Fax: 401-783-8646. Email: sthomasmore@cox.net. Web: www.stthomasmoreri.org.
Catechesis/Religious Program—Tel: 401-783-2113. Students 272.
Chapel—St. Veronica Chapel 1035 Boston Neck Rd., 02882.

NEW SHOREHAM, WASHINGTON CO., ST. ANDREW (Block Island) (1917) [JC] Rev. Joseph Protano Jr.
Saint Andrew's Church Corporation, Block Island
Res.: Spring St., P.O. Box 279, Block Island, 02807. Tel: 401-466-5519; Fax: 401-466-3118. Email: standrewblockisland@verizon.net.
Catechesis/Religious Program—Students 27.

NEWPORT, NEWPORT CO.

1—ST. AUGUSTIN (1911) Rev. John T. McNulty; Sr. Josephine St. Leger, S.J.C., Pastoral Assoc.
Saint Augustin's Church of Newport
Res.: 2 Eastnor Rd., 02840. Tel: 401-847-0518; Fax: 401-848-2411. Email: staugstn@intap.net.
Catechesis/Religious Program—Students 63.

2—JESUS SAVIOUR (1926), (Portuguese), Rev. Francis A. O'Loughlin; Deacons James N. Dunbar; James R. Rudnik.
Church of Jesus-Saviour, Newport
Res.: One Vernon Ave., 02840. Tel: 401-847-1267; Fax: 401-846-3375. Email: jsaviour@verizon.net. Web: www.jsaviournewportri.org.
Catechesis/Religious Program—Tel: 401-846-4095. Students 130.

3—ST. JOSEPH (1885) Rev. Raymond B. Malm.
Saint Joseph's Church of Newport, Rhode Island
Res.: 5 Mann Ave., 02840. Tel: 401-847-0065; Fax: 401-849-2195. Email: bernice@stjosephsnewport.org. Web: www.stjosephnewport.org.
Catechesis/Religious Program—Tel: 401-847-9248; Fax: 401-849-2195. Students 110.

4—ST. MARY (1826) [CEM] Rev. George B. McCarthy.

St. Mary's, Newport, Rhode Island
Res.: 12 William St., P.O. Box 547, 02840. Tel: 401-847-0475; Fax: 401-845-9497. Email: stmaryre@aol.com. Web: www.rc.net/providence/stmary.
Catechesis/Religious Program—Tel: 401-846-6057. Students 166.

NORTH KINGSTOWN, WASHINGTON CO.

1—ST. BERNARD (Wickford) (1874) [CEM] Rev. Dennis A. Reardon; Deacons Ronald DePietro; Joseph Turcotte.
St. Bernard's Roman Catholic Church of Wickford, Rhode Island
Office: St. Bernard Parish Center: 415 Tower Hill Rd., Wickford, 02852. Tel: 401-295-0387; Fax: 401-295-1713. Email: parishcenter@sbcwickford.org. Web: www.sbcwickford.org.
275 Tower Hill Rd., Wickford, 02852.
Catechesis/Religious Program—Email: sbc.gof@verizon.net. Mary Reardon, D.R.E. Students 520.

2—ST. FRANCIS DE SALES (Davisville) (1960) Revs. Bertrand L. Theroux; D. Andrew Messina.
St. Francis de Sales Church Corporation, North Kingstown
Res.: 381 School St., 02852. Tel: 401-884-2105; Fax: 401-885-4315. Email: parishoffice@saintfds.org. Web: www.saintfds.org.
Catechesis/Religious Program—Tel: 401-885-3639. Kathleen Kane, D.R.E. Students 511.

NORTH PROVIDENCE, PROVIDENCE CO.

1—ST. ANTHONY (1944), (Italian), Rev. Edward S. Cardente; Deacon Anthony Cipriano.
Saint Anthony's Church Corporation, North Providence
Res.: 5 Gibbs St., 02904. Tel: 401-353-3120; Fax: 401-353-5126. Email: stanthonynp@cox.net.
Catechesis/Religious Program—Tel: 401-353-5125. Maryann Pallotta, D.R.E. Students 389.

2—ST. LAWRENCE (Centredale) (1907) Rev. David A. Piacentini.
Saint Lawrence Church of Centredale In Res., Rev. Peter G. Young (Retired).
Res.: 624 Woonasquatucket Ave., 02911-1652. Tel: 401-231-9126; Fax: 401-231-7425.
Catechesis/Religious Program—Tel: 401-231-5255. Students 104.

3—MARY, MOTHER OF MANKIND (1967) Rev. W. Douglas Grant.
Mary, Mother of Mankind Church Corporation, North Providence In Res., Rev. Robert F. Caul (Retired).
Res.: 25 Fourth St., 02911. Tel: 401-231-3542; Fax: 401-232-0965.
Catechesis/Religious Program—Tel: 401-231-3544. Students 193.

4—PRESENTATION OF THE BLESSED VIRGIN MARY (Marieville) (1912), (French—Italian), Rev. Louis T. Natalizia; Deacon Louis A. Vani.
The Church of the Presentation of the Blessed Virgin Mary
Res.: 1081 Mineral Spring Ave., 02904. Tel: 401-722-7140; Fax: 401-722-6617. Email: pbvm1081@cox.net.
Catechesis/Religious Program—Tel: 401-722-8824; 401-722-7007 (Rel. Ed. Center). Maryann Dempsey, D.R.E. Students 102.

NORTH SMITHFIELD, PROVIDENCE CO., ST. JOHN THE EVANGELIST (Slatersville) (1872) [CEM] Rev. Raymond A. Tetreault.
St. John's Church Society, Rhode Island
Res.: 63 Church St., Box 266, Slatersville, 02876. Tel: 401-762-0946; Fax: 401-762-0944. Email: stjohn02876@yahoo.com. Web: www.stjohnslatersville.4lpi.com.
Catechesis/Religious Program—Tel: 401-762-0966. Mrs. Celeste Baillargeon, C.R.E. Students 475.

PAWTUCKET, PROVIDENCE CO.

1—ST. ANTHONY (1926), (Portuguese), Rev. Jose F. Rocha; Deacon Louis P. Serra.
Saint Anthony's Church Corporation, Pawtucket
Res.: 32 Lawn Ave., 02860. Tel: 401-723-9138; Fax: 401-725-5616. Email: stanthony32@verizon.net. Web: http://members.tripod.com/stanthonysparish.
Catechesis/Religious Program—Students 175.

2—ST. CECILIA (1910), (French), Rev. Pierre J. Plante.
Saint Cecilia's Church Corporation
Res.: 1253 Newport Ave., 02861. Tel: 401-722-1101; Fax: 401-727-3844. Email: pjvp@stcecilia.necoxmail.com. Web: www.saintcecilias.com.
School—(Grades PreK-8), 755 Central Ave., 02861. Tel: 401-723-9463; Fax: 401-722-1444. Web: www-.saintceciliaschool.com. Simone M. Kennedy, Prin. Sisters 1; Lay Teachers 25; Students 373.
Catechesis/Religious Program—Students 205.

3—ST. EDWARD (1904) Rev. Charles H. Galligan.
St. Edward's Church of Pawtucket
Office: 58 Hancock St., 02860. Tel: 401-725-7036. Email: stedwardschurch@verizon.net.
Church: 396 Weeden St., 02860.
Catechesis/Religious Program—Students 50.

4—HOLY FAMILY PARISH, PAWTUCKET (2009), Merger of the following parishes: St. Joseph, Pawtucket, est. 1873 (Legal title: St. Joseph's Church); Our Lady of Consolation, Pawtucket, est. 1895 (Legal title: Church of Our Lady of Consolation, Rhode Island); Sacred Heart of Jesus, Pawtucket, (Irish), est. 1872 (Legal title: The Church of the Sacred Heart of Jesus of Pawtucket, Rhode Island) Rev. Robert P. Perron.
Res.: 195 Walcott St., 02860. Tel: 401-724-9190; Fax: 401-724-9314. Email: leg0203@aol.com.
Catechesis/Religious Program—Students 116.

5—IMMACULATE HEART OF MARY (1979), (Cape Verdean), (An operation of Church of St. Maron in Providence) Rev. Arlindo A. Amaro, C.S.Sp., Admin.
Res.: 35 Clay St., Central Falls, 02863. Tel: 401-725-1126; Fax: 401-726-4119.
Church: 291 High St., 02860. Tel: 401-725-5456.
Catechesis/Religious Program—Students 73.

6—ST. JOHN THE BAPTIST (1884), (French), Rev. Gerald G. Harbour; Deacons Vicente Caban; Raymond M. Lagesse.
The Church of St. John the Baptist of Pawtucket Rhode Island In Res., Rev. Roman R. Manchester.
Res.: 69 Quincy Ave., 02860. Tel: 401-722-9054; Fax: 401-724-3514. Email: st.johnthebaptist@verizon.net.
Catechesis/Religious Program—Students 191.

7—ST. JOSEPH (1873) Closed. See Holy Family Parish, Pawtucket
St. Joseph's Church

8—ST. LEO THE GREAT (1916), (Irish), Rev. Giacomo Capoverdi.
Church of Saint Leo the Great in Pawtucket
Res.: 697 Central Ave., 02861. Tel: 401-722-1220; Fax: 401-726-3392. Email: greatleo@cox.net. Web: www.stleosparish.com.
Catechesis/Religious Program—Tel: 401-440-9376. Students 81.

9—ST. MARIA GORETTI (1953) Rev. Robert L. Bailey; Deacon Thomas Boutier.
St. Maria Goretti Church Corporation, Pawtucket
Res.: 165 Power Rd., 02860. Tel: 401-725-4355; Fax: 401-729-5711.
Catechesis/Religious Program—Students 225.

10—ST. MARY OF THE IMMACULATE CONCEPTION (1829) [JC] Very Rev. William J. Ledoux; Deacon C. Patrick Sheehy.
The Church of the Immaculate Conception of Pawtucket, Rhode Island
Res.: 103 Pine St., P.O. Box 518, 02862. Tel: 401-722-5425; Fax: 401-729-0341. Email: stmarypawt@cox.net.
Catechesis/Religious Program—Mrs. Madeleine Porter, D.R.E. Students 115.

11—OUR LADY OF CONSOLATION (1895) Closed. See Holy Family Parish, Pawtucket.
Church of Our Lady of Consolation Rhode Island

12—SACRED HEART OF JESUS (1872), (Irish), Closed. See Holy Family Parish, Pawtucket.
The Church of the Sacred Heart of Jesus of Pawtucket, Rhode Island

13—ST. TERESA OF THE CHILD JESUS (1929) Rev. Joseph Paquette.
Church of Saint Teresa of the Child Jesus, Pawtucket, Rhode Island In Res., Rev. John J. McElroy (Retired).
Res.: 358 Newport Ave., 02861. Tel: 401-722-4470; Fax: 401-722-2958. Email: mlombardi@stteresa.necoxmail.com. Web: www.rc.net/providence/stteresa.
School—(Grades PreK-8), 140 Woodhaven Rd., 02861. Tel: 401-726-1414; Fax: 401-722-6998. Mary Carney, Prin. Lay Teachers 19; Students 238.
Catechesis/Religious Program—Tel: 401-723-2266; 401-722-8650. Liza Roach, D.R.E. Students 218.

PORTSMOUTH, NEWPORT CO.

1—ST. ANTHONY (1901) Rev. Daniel J. Gray.
Saint Anthony's Church of Portsmouth
Res.: 2836 E. Main Rd., P.O. Box 570, 02871. Tel: 401-683-0089; Fax: 401-683-9680. Email: stanthonych@msn.com.
Catechesis/Religious Program—Tel: 401-683-3636. Students 65.

2—ST. BARNABAS (1963) Very Rev. Randolph G. Chew.
St. Barnabas Church Corporation, Portsmouth
Res.: 1697 E. Main Rd., 02871. Tel: 401-683-1343; Fax: 401-683-5065. Email: sbchurch@stbarnabas.necoxmail.com. Web: www.stbarnabasportsmouth.4lpi.com.
Catechesis/Religious Program—Tel: 401-683-3147. Email: faithformation@stbarnabas.necoxmail.com. Students 608.

SCITUATE, PROVIDENCE CO., ST. JOSEPH (North Scituate) (1940) Rev. Roger A. Houle; Deacon Paul A. Ullucci.
144 Danielson Pk., P.O. Box 236, North Scituate, 02857.
Saint Joseph's Church Corporation, North Scituate In Res., Rev. Eugene R. Lessard (Retired).
Res.: 151 Danielson Pk., P.O. Box 236, North Scituate, 02857. Tel: 401-647-2255; Fax: 401-647-2968. Email: dmc948@sj.necoxmail.com.
Catechesis/Religious Program—Tel: 401-647-2650 (D.R.E.); 401-647-2398 (Youth Min.); Fax: 401-647-2968. Mrs. Lisa Woodhead, D.R.E.; Mr. Christopher Kite, Youth Min. Students 463.

SMITHFIELD, PROVIDENCE CO.

1—ST. MICHAEL (Georgiaville) (1875) Rev. Richard A. Valentine.
St. Michael's Church, Georgiaville, Rhode Island
Res.: 80 Farnum Pike, Georgiaville, 02917. Tel: 401-231-5119; Fax: 401-231-0523. Email: info@stmikegeo.necoxmail.com. Web: www.stmichaelsmithfield.org.
Catechesis/Religious Program—Tel: 401-231-1340. Students 437.

2—ST. PHILIP (Greenville) (1852) Most Rev. Robert C. Evans; Rev. Jeremy J. Rodrigues; Deacons Harris J. Gederman; Carlo J. Sabetti.
St. Philip's Church Greenville Rhode Island
Res.: 622 Putnam Ave., Greenville, 02828-1403. Tel: 401-949-1500; Fax: 401-949-3504. Email: office@saintphilip.com. Web: www.saintphilip.com.
School—(Grades PreK-8), 618 Putnam Ave., Greenville, 02828. Tel: 401-949-1130; Fax: 401-949-1141. Email: dwalsh@stphilipschool.com. Darlene Walsh, Prin. Sisters of Mercy of the Americas 1; Lay Teachers 20; Students 266.
Catechesis/Religious Program—Tel: 401-949-0330; Fax: 401-949-5630. Email: stphilipred@yahoo.com. Marianne Jasinski, D.R.E. Students 863.

SOUTH KINGSTOWN, WASHINGTON CO.

1—CHRIST THE KING (Kingston) (1950) Rev. Joseph D. Creedon.
Christ the King Church Corporation, Kingston
Res.: 180 Old North Rd., Kingston, 02881. Tel: 401-783-7459; Fax: 401-789-3671. Email: info@ctkri.org. Web: www.ctkri.org.
Catechesis/Religious Program—Tel: 401-789-0417. Students 836.

2—ST. FRANCIS OF ASSISI (Wakefield) (1879) [CEM] Revs. Nicholas P. Smith; Gregory P. Stowe; Deacon Paul O. Iacono; Mary Ellen Battey, Music Min.; Miss Kelli McNulty, Parish Business Mgr.
Saint Francis's Church
Res.: 114 High St., Wakefield, 02879-3141. Tel: 401-783-4411; Fax: 401-783-9667. Email: saintfrancis00@aol.com. Web: http://franciswakefield.catholicweb.com.
Catechesis/Religious Program—Tel: 401-792-8684. Barbette Cullen, D.R.E.; Miss Jennifer Stefano, C.R.E. Students 520.
Chapel—St. Romuald Chapel Wakefield. 61 Atlantic Ave., Matunuck, Washington Co. 02879.

TIVERTON, NEWPORT CO.

1—ST. CHRISTOPHER (1910) Rev. Peter J. Andrews; Deacon Jesse L. Martins.
Saint Christopher's Church of Tiverton
Res.: 1554 Main Rd., 02878. Tel: 401-624-6644; Fax: 401-624-9889. Web: www.sstandctiverton.org.
Church: 1584 Main Rd., 02878.
Catechesis/Religious Program—Students 64.

2—HOLY GHOST (North Tiverton) (1913) Rev. Jay A. Finelli; Deacon Raymond E. Levesque.
Church of the Holy Ghost, North Tiverton
Res.: 311 Hooper St., 02878. Tel: 401-624-8131; Fax: 401-625-5156. Email: secretary@holyghostcc.org; pastor@holychostcc.org. Web: www.holyghostcc.org.
Catechesis/Religious Program—Tel: 401-624-3664. Email: ccd@holyghostcc.org. Students 134.

3—ST. MADELEINE SOPHIE (1948), (Portuguese), Rev. Gerald W. Hussey.
Saint Madeleine's Church Corporation of Tiverton
Res.: 35 Lake Rd., 02878. Tel: 401-624-4226; Fax: 401-624-3848.
Catechesis/Religious Program—Students 70.

4—ST. THERESA (1960) Rev. Peter J. Andrews; Deacon Jesse L. Martins.
St. Theresa's Parish Corporation, Tiverton
Res.: 265 Stafford Rd., 02878. Tel: 401-624-8746; Fax: 401-625-5384. Web: www.sstandctiverton.org.
Catechesis/Religious Program—Students 224.

WARREN, BRISTOL CO.

1—ST. ALEXANDER (1915), (Italian), [CEM] Rev. David W. Masello, Admin.
Saint Alexander's Church Corporation, Warren
Res.: 221 Main St., 02885. Tel: 401-245-6369; Fax: 401-247-5455. Email: stalex02885@aol.com.
Catechesis/Religious Program—Tel: 401-247-1764. Students 20.

2—ST. CASIMIR (1908), (Polish), [JC] Closed. For Inquiries for parish records please see St. Mary of the Bay, Warren.
Saint Casimir's Church of Warren

3—ST. JEAN BAPTISTE (1877), (French), [CEM] Rev. Peter J. Gower.
The Church of Saint Jean Baptiste of Warren Rhode Island
Res.: 645 Main St., 02885. Tel: 401-245-7000, Ext. 11; Fax: 401-245-7093. Email: stjeanwarren@aol.com. Web: www.stmaryofthebay.com.
Church: 324 Main St., 02885. Tel: 401-245-7000, Ext. 17.
Catechesis/Religious Program—Twinned with St. Mary of the Bay, Warren., Tel: 401-245-7000, Ext. 21. Students 264.

4—ST. MARY OF THE BAY (1851) [CEM] Rev. Peter J. Gower.
Church of Saint Mary of the Bay
Res. and Parish House: 645 Main St., 02885. Tel: 401-245-7000, Ext. 11; Fax: 401-245-7093. Email: stmaryofthebay@aol.com. Web: www.stmaryofthebay.com.
Catechesis/Religious Program—Tel: 401-245-7000, Ext. 21. Twinned with St. Jean Baptiste, Warren. Students 264.

5—ST. THOMAS THE APOSTLE (1952), (Portuguese), Rev. John E. Abreu; Deacon Benjamin Barboza.
Saint Thomas the Apostle Church Corporation
Res.: 500 Metacom Ave., 02885-2808. Tel: 401-245-4469; Fax: 401-245-4527. Email: stthomasap500@fullchannel.net.
Catechesis/Religious Program—Tel: 401-245-4488. Anne Furtado, C.R.E. Students 76.

WARWICK, KENT CO.

1—ST. BENEDICT (Conimicut) (1914) Rev. Roland L. Simoneau.

St. Benedict's Church, Conimicut
Res.: 135 Beach Ave., 02889. Tel: 401-737-9492; Fax: 401-739-0974. Email: stbenedictswarwick@juno.com.
Catechesis/Religious Program—70 Transit St., 02889. Tel: 401-738-2545. Students 153.

2—ST. CATHERINE (Apponaug) (1916) Rev. Richard M. Friedrichs; Deacon John F. Baker.
Saint Catherine's Roman Catholic Church of Warwick, Rhode Island In Res., Rev. Edward A. Sousa Jr.
Res.: 3252 Post Rd., 02886. Tel: 401-737-4455. Email: pastor@stcat.necoxmail.com. Web: www.stcatherineswarwick.org.
Catechesis/Religious Program—Tel: 401-737-6234; Fax: 401-736-0960. Kathleen Pesta, D.R.E.; Kelly Francoeur, D.R.E. Students 129.

3—ST. CLEMENT'S (1961) Merged with St. Rose of Lima to form St. Rose of Lima/St. Clement, Warwick. (Legal title: St. Clement Church Corporation, Warwick).

4—ST. FRANCIS OF ASSISI (Hillsgrove) (1943) Rev. John A. Kiley.
Saint Francis Church Corporation, Hillsgrove
Res.: 596 Jefferson Blvd., 02886. Tel: 401-737-5191; Fax: 401-737-1159. Email: stfrancis737@cox.net. Web: www.stfranciswarwick.com.
Catechesis/Religious Program—Students 80.
Convent—249 Chestnut St., 02888. Tel: 401-781-2464.

5—ST. GREGORY THE GREAT (Cowesett) (1961) Rev. Alfred V. Ricci; Deacon Paul F. Kirk.
St. Gregory the Great Church Corporation, Warwick In Res., Rev. David F. Ricard.
Res.: 360 Cowesett Rd., 02886. Tel: 401-884-1666; Fax: 401-884-2448. Email: info@stgregorychurchri.com. Web: www.stgregorychurchri.com.
Catechesis/Religious Program—Tel: 401-884-0797. Students 681.

6—ST. KEVIN (1956) Revs. David E. Green; Jacek Ploch.
St. Kevin's Church Corporation, Warwick
Res.: 333 Sandy Ln., 02889. Tel: 401-737-2638; Fax: 401-732-2832.
School—(Grades PreK-8), 39 Cathedral Rd., 02889. Tel: 401-737-7172; Fax: 401-738-2832. Web: www-.saintkevinschool.org. Roger R. Parent, Prin. Lay Teachers 26; Students 218.
Catechesis/Religious Program—Tel: 401-739-6309. Harriet Duffy, D.R.E. Students 538.

7—ST. PETER (Pawtuxet) (1933) Rev. Roger C. Gagne; Deacon Robert M. Morisseau.
St. Peter's Church, Warwick, Rhode Island In Res., Rev. Msgr. Nicholas J. Iacovacci (Retired).
Res.: 350 Fair St., 02888. Tel: 401-467-4895; Fax: 401-785-9282. Email: charlene0226@aol.com. Web: http://stpeterswarwick.catholicweb.com.
School—(Grades PreK-8), 120 Mayfair Rd., 02888. Tel: 401-781-9242; Fax: 401-467-5673. Mrs. Joan Sickinger, Prin. Lay Teachers 15; Students 178.
Catechesis/Religious Program—Tel: 401-461-5691. Email: dre.st.peters.warwick2@juno.com. Margaret Andreozzi, D.R.E.; Elaine Morisseau, D.R.E. Students 278.

8—ST. RITA (Oakland Beach) (1935) Rev. Bertil J. Anderson; Deacon John A. Corey.
Saint Rita's Church Corporation, Oakland Beach
Res.: 722 Oakland Beach Ave., 02889. Tel: 401-738-1800; Fax: 401-738-1806. Email: st.rita3@verizon.net.
Catechesis/Religious Program—Students 291.

9—STS. ROSE & CLEMENT (1998), Consolidation of St. Rose of Lima and St. Clement. (Legal Title: St. Clement's Church Corporation, Warwick) (Legal Title: St. Rose's Church Corporation, Warwick). Rev. Edward J. Wilson Jr.; Deacon Noel Edsall.
Res.: 171 Inman Ave., 02886-1700. Tel: 401-739-0212; Fax: 401-732-4144. Email: office@ssrc4.necoxmail.com.
School—St. Rose of Lima, (Grades PreK-8), 200 Brentwood Ave., 02886. Tel: 401-739-6937; Fax: 401-737-4632. Email: stroseoflimaschool@cox.net. Web: www.saintroseschool.com. Mrs. Jeannine N. Fuller, Prin.; Mrs. Geraldine Grant, Librarian. Lay Teachers 16; Students 240.
Catechesis/Religious Program—111 Long St., 02886. Cheryl Berube, D.R.E. Students 305.

10—ST. ROSE OF LIMA (Greenwood) (1950) Merged with St. Clement to form St. Rose of Lima/St. Clement, Warwick. (Legal title: Saint Rose's Church Corporation, Warwick).

11—ST. TIMOTHY (Hoxie) (1950) Revs. Barry M. Meehan; Michael J. McMahon; Deacon Charles McCarthy.
Saint Timothy's Church Corporation, Warwick
Res.: 1799 Warwick Ave., 02889. Tel: 401-739-9552; Fax: 401-738-2466. Email: sttim@aol.com.
Catechesis/Religious Program—Tel: 401-738-9079. Students 190.

12—ST. WILLIAM (Norwood) (1933) [CEM] Rev. Frank S. Salmani; Deacon Thomas P. O'Hara. (Legal title: Saint William Church Corporation, Norwood).
Res. & Church: 200 Pettaconsett Ave., 02888. Tel: 401-781-7226; Fax: 401-781-4177. Email: office@stwilliam.necoxmail.com.
Catechesis/Religious Program—Tel: 401-781-0343. Students 99.

WEST WARWICK, KENT CO.

1—ST. ANTHONY (Riverpoint) (1925), (Portuguese), Rev. Fernando A. Cabral (Portugal).
Saint Anthony's Church Corporation, River Point
Res.: 10 Sunset Ave., 02893. Tel: 401-821-8342. Email: stanthonyswwri@hotmail.com.
Catechesis/Religious Program—Students 146.

2—CHRIST THE KING (Centreville) (1931), (French), Rev. John C. Codega; Deacon William J. Schofield.
Church of Christ the King, West Warwick
Parish Office: 130 Legris Ave., 02893. Tel: 401-821-9228; Fax: 401-821-9228.
Res.: 120 Legris Ave., 02893.
Catechesis/Religious Program—130 Legris Ave., 02893. Ms. Christine Duggan, D.R.E.; Mr. Matthew Daley, Youth Min. Students 132.

3—ST. JAMES (1908) Merged with St. John the Baptist, West Warwick to form SS. John and James Parish, West Warwick.

4—SS. JOHN AND JAMES PARISH (2003) [CEM] Rev. Msgr. Jacques L. Plante; Deacons Paul M. Shea; Jose Farjardo.
Res.: 20 Washington St., 02893-4919. Tel: 401-821-7323; Fax: 401-826-7274. Email: ssjohnandjames@cox.net. Web: http://ssjohnjamesparish.org.
Catechesis/Religious Program— Ms. Christine Duggan, D.R.E. Students 155.

5—ST. JOHN THE BAPTIST (Arctic) (1874), (French), [CEM] Merged with St. James, West Warwick to form SS. John and James Parish, West Warwick.

6—ST. JOSEPH (Natick) (1873) Rev. Charles H. Downing; Deacon Laurence O. Gagnon.
St. Joseph's Church, Natick RI
Res.: 854 Providence St., 02893-1140. Tel: 401-821-4072; Fax: 401-821-2408. Email: downing@dioceseofprovidence.org.
School—(Grades PreK-8), 850 Wakefield St., 02893. Tel: 401-821-3450. Mr. Richard Keenan, Prin.; Karen McLaughlin, Librarian. Deacons 1; Lay Teachers 21; Students 281.
Catechesis/Religious Program—Students 165.

7—ST. MARY (Crompton) (1844) [CEM] Rev. Thomas D. O'Neill, Admin. Protem.
St. Mary's Church, Crompton Rhode Island
Res.: 70 Church St., 02893. Tel: 401-821-5555. Email: stmaryschurch1@cox.net.
Catechesis/Religious Program—Tel: 401-828-8756. Students 122.

8—OUR LADY OF GOOD COUNSEL (Phenix) (1897), (French), [CEM] Rev. Paul R. Lemoi; Deacon Raymond LaFrance.
Church of Our Lady of Good Counsel, Warwick RI
Res.: 62 Pleasant St., 02893. Tel: 401-821-6428; Fax: 401-821-2472. Email: olgc60@juno.com.
Catechesis/Religious Program—Tel: 401-822-1869. Students 71.

9—SS. PETER AND PAUL (Phenix) (1853) [CEM] Rev. Christopher M. Davenport.
SS. Peter and Paul's Church, Phoenixville, Rhode Island
Res.: 48 Highland St., 02893-5699. Tel: 401-821-2198.
Catechesis/Religious Program—Students 78.

10—SACRED HEART CHURCH (Natick) (1929), (Italian), Rev. Richard A. Bucci.
Church of the Sacred Heart, Natick RI
Res.: 820 Providence St., 02893. Tel: 401-821-4184; Fax: 401-828-8883. Email: sacredheartww@cox.net.
Catechesis/Religious Program—Students 63.

WESTERLY, WASHINGTON CO.

1—ST. CLARE (Misquamicut) (1946) Rev. Kenneth J. Suibielski; Deacons Stephen R. Cote; W. Carl LaFleur.
Saint Clare's Church Corporation, Misquamicut
Res.: 4 Saint Clare Way, Misquamicut, 02891. Tel: 401-348-8765; Fax: 401-315-5273. Email: stclareri2@cox.net.
Catechesis/Religious Program—Students 118.

2—IMMACULATE CONCEPTION (1885), (Italian), [CEM] Revs. Wilfrid G. Gregoire; Michael A. Kelley; Otoniel J. Gomez; Deacons Robert G. Alessio; John D. McGregor.
Mailing Address: P.O. Box 556, 02891-0556. Tel: 401-596-2130; Fax: 401-348-2153.
Church of the Immaculate Conception of Westerly, Rhode Island
Res.: 111 High St., 02891. Tel: 401-596-2130; Fax: 401-348-2351. Email: icc@immcon.com.
Catechesis/Religious Program—Tel: 401-596-0900; Fax: 401-348-2153. Mrs. Sharon Furman, D.R.E. (Grades 1-6); Mrs. Catherine Kimmel, D.R.E. (Grades 7-10). Students 238.

3—ST. PIUS X (1955) Rev. Raymond N. Suriani; Deacon Francis J. Valliere.
St. Pius X Parish Corporation, Westerly
Res.: 44 Elm St., 02891. Tel: 401-596-2535; Fax: 401-596-9930. Email: stpiusx@cox.net.
School—32 Elm St., 02891. Tel: 401-596-5735; Fax: 401-596-5791. Web: www.westerlystpiusxsh-cool.org. Henry Fiore Jr., Prin. Lay Teachers 17; Students 227.
Catechesis/Religious Program—Tel: 401-596-8530. Email: chrismagowan@cox.net. Christine Magowan, D.R.E. Students 130.

4—ST. VINCENT DE PAUL (Bradford) (1946) Rev. James V. Farley.
Saint Vincent's Church Corporation, Bradford
Res.: 7 Church St., P.O. Box 277, Bradford, 02808. Tel: 401-377-2289; Fax: 401-377-8830. Email: lmolv@yahoo.com.
Catechesis/Religious Program—Tel: 401-377-8435. Email: ggolv@yahoo.com. Students 135.

WOONSOCKET, PROVIDENCE CO.

1—ST. AGATHA (1953) Rev. Msgr. John C. Allard; Rev. Timothy J. Gorton; Deacon Eugene Garceau.
Saint Agatha's Church Corporation, Woonsocket In Res., Rev. John D. Dreher (Retired).
Res.: 34 Joffre Ave., 02895. Tel: 401-767-2950; Fax: 401-767-2951.
Catechesis/Religious Program—Students 121.

2—ALL SAINTS PARISH (2009) [JC], An alliance of the following three parishes: Our Lady of Victories, (French), est. 1909, (Legal title: Church of Notre Dame des Victoires); St. Aloysius, (French) est. 1902, (Legal title: Saint Aloysius Church of Woonsocket); and St. Ann, (French) est. 1890 (Legal title: St. Ann's Church Corporation of Woonsocket RI). Revs. Mark A. Sauriol; Hugo Carmona (Colombia). In Res., Rev. J.A. Roger Lacasse.
Res.: 323 Rathbun St., 02895. Tel: 401-762-1100; 401-766-0370; Fax: 401-765-6321.
Catechesis/Religious Program—Tel: 401-766-5771. Students 231.

3—ST. ALOYSIUS (1902) Merged See All Saints Parish, Woonsocket.

4—ST. ANN (1890) Merged See All Saints Parish, Woonsocket.

5—ST. ANTHONY (1924), (Italian), [JC] Rev. Msgr. Ronald P. Simeone; Deacon Bernard Archambault, (Retired).
Saint Anthony's Church, Woonsocket, RI In Res., Rev. Lionel A. Blain (Retired).
Res.: 128 Greene St., 02895. Tel: 401-766-2640; Fax: 401-766-2640. Email: saintanthonywoonsocket@verizon.net.
Catechesis/Religious Program—Students 29.

6—ST. CHARLES (1846), (Irish), [CEM] Rev. Gerald F. Finnegan, S.J.
St. Charles Borromeo's Church, Woonsocket, RI In Res., Revs. Joseph J. Bruce, S.J.; Hugo Carmona (Colombia).
Res.: 190 N. Main St., 02895-3140. Tel: 401-766-0176; Fax: 401-766-0185. Email: fr_finnegan@stcharlesborromeo.com. Web: www.stcharlesborromeo.com.
Catechesis/Religious Program—Tel: 401-766-3088. Students 19.

7—HOLY FAMILY (1902), (French), [JC] Rev. Edward G. St-Godard.
Church of the Holy Family
Res.: 414 S. Main St., 02895. Tel: 401-762-0830; Fax: 401-762-3441. Email: holyfamilyri@verizon.net.
Catechesis/Religious Program—Students 18.

8—ST. JOSEPH (East Woonsocket) (1929), (French-Canadian), Revs. Michael J. Woolley; Marcin A. Mioduszewski.
Saint Joseph's Church, Woonsocket
Res.: 1200 Mendon Rd., 02895-3999. Tel: 401-766-0626; Fax: 401-766-1632. Web: www.saintjosephwoonsocket.org.
Catechesis/Religious Program—1210 Mendon Rd., 02895. Tel: 401-766-8233. Michelle T. Barrette, D.R.E. Students 191.
Station—Woonsocket Health Center, Tel: 401-765-2100; Fax: 401-232-7275.
Station—Wyndemere Woods, Tel: 401-762-4226; Fax: 401-766-5548.

9—OUR LADY OF VICTORIES (1909) Merged See All Saints Parish, Woonsocket.

10—OUR LADY, QUEEN OF MARTYRS (1953) Very Rev. Maurice L. Brindamour; Deacon Robert A. Blais.
Our Lady, Queen of Martyrs Church Corporation, Woonsocket
Res.: 1409 Park Ave., 02895-6597. Tel: 401-762-5117; Fax: 401-765-8875. Email: parish@olqm.necoxmail.com. Web: www.olqm.info. School: See Monsignor Gadoury Regional School, Woonsocket, under The Greater Woonsocket Catholic Regional School System in the Institution section.
Catechesis/Religious Program—Tel: 401-767-2576. Students 160.

11—PRECIOUS BLOOD (1843), (French), [CEM] Rev. Msgr. John C. Allard; Rev. Timothy J. Gorton.

The Church of the Precious Blood Corporation, Woonsocket, RI In Res., Rev. Roger L. Marot (Retired).
Res.: 94 Carrington Ave., 02895. Tel: 401-762-0326; 508-883-6600 (Cemetery); Fax: 401-767-2951. Email: sapbcym6-12@cox.net.
Catechesis/Religious Program—34 Joffre Ave., 02895. Tel: 401-767-2950. Students 36.
12—SACRED HEART (1895) Rev. Ronald J. Bengford.
Church of the Sacred Heart Woonsocket, RI
Res.: 415 Olo St., 02895. Tel: 401-766-3150; Fax: 401-766-6864. Email: pathammond@cox.net. Web: www.sacredheartri.catholicweb.com.
Catechesis/Religious Program—Students 37.
13—ST. STANISLAUS (1905), (Polish), [JC] Revs. Dariusz J. Jonczyk, Admin.; Marcin A. Mioduszewski.
Saint Stanislaus Kostka Church of Woonsocket
Res.: 174 Harris Ave., 02895. Tel: 401-762-0021.
Catechesis/Religious Program—Students 45.

Chaplains of Public Institutions

PROVIDENCE. *Miriam Hospital*, 164 Summit Ave., 02906. Tel: 401-274-3700. Rev. Edward L. Pieroni.
Res.: 2 Matilda St., 02904-1812.
Rhode Island Hospital, 593 Eddy St., 02902. Tel: 401-277-4000. Revs. Jacques Eddy Chavannes (Haiti), Joseph F. Craddock, Dir. Catholic Chaplaincy, Jose Q. dos Reis, Thomas J. Ferland, Jaime A. Garcia, Chinnaiah Yerrnini, Elsa Menegozzo, Team Member.
Roger Williams Hospital, 825 Chalkstone Ave., 02908. Tel: 401-456-2000. Pastoral care provided by local parishes.
Veterans Administration Hospital, Davis Park, 02908. Tel: 401-273-7100. Rev. John L. Wydeven (OAK).
BURRILLVILLE. *Rhode Island-Zambarano State Hospital*.
. Pastoral care provided by Office of Health Ministries.
CRANSTON. *Department of Corrections*. Mrs. Martha Paone, Chaplain Coord.
c/o 184 Broad St., 02903.
Eleanor Slater Hospital. Rev. Msgr. Gerard O. Sabourin.
NEWPORT. *Newport Hospital*. Rev. Francis A. O'Loughlin.
Res.: 1 Vernon Ave., 02840. Tel: 401-847-0065.
NORTH SMITHFIELD. *St. Antoine Residence*. Most Rev. Louis E. Gelineau, D.D., S.T.L., J.C.L. (Retired).
Landmark Medical Center, Fogarty Unit. Pastoral care provided by local parishes.
PAWTUCKET. *Memorial Hospital of Rhode Island*. Pastoral care provided by local parishes.
SOUTH KINGSTOWN. *South County Hospital*. Rev. Nicholas P. Smith.
Res.: 114 High St., Wakefield, 02879-3141. Tel: 401-782-8000.
WARWICK. *Kent County Memorial Hospital*. Rev. David F. Ricard.
Res.: 41 Sandro Dr., 02886.
WESTERLY. *The Westerly Hospital*, 25 Wells St., 02891. Tel: 401-596-6000. Pastoral care provided by local parishes.
WOONSOCKET. *Landmark Medical Center, Woonsocket Unit*. Pastoral care provided by local parishes.

On Special Assignment:
Rev.—
Lopez-Bolanos, Eddy E.

On Duty Outside the Diocese:
Revs.—
Kelley, Edward J., Chap., U.S. Army
LaMontagne, Bernard L., St. Mary of Woods, IN 47876.
Marciano, Robert L., Archdiocese for Military Services
Prendiville, Edmond P., 2480 Presidental Way-Envoy 1202, West Palm Beach, FL 33401.

Graduate Studies:
Revs.—
Mahar, Christopher M., American College of Louvain, Belgium
Perri, Dean Patrick, Pontifical North American College, Rome, Italy

---

Absent on Leave:
Revs.—
Abruzzese, Joseph A.
Carpentier, Robert A.
Fisette, Kevin R.
Jimenez-Londono, Fredy A.
Petrocelli, John N.
Scagnelli, Peter J.

Retired:
Most Revs.—
Boland, Ernest B., O.P., Providence College, 02918.
Gelineau, Louis E., D.D., S.T.L., J.C.L., 10 Rhodes Ave., North Smithfield, 02896.
Mulvee, Robert E., 30 Fenner St., 02903.
Pearce, George H., S.M., D.D., 10 Rhodes Ave, N., North Smithfield, 02896.
Roque, Francis X., 255 Landsdowne Rd., Warwick, 02888.
Rev. Msgrs.—
Cavallaro, Galliano J., 10 Rhodes Ave., North Smithfield, 02896.
Dziob, Michael W., 493 Mt. Pleasant Ave., 02908.
Frappier, George L., 341 Ballou St., 02895.
Halloran, John C., 36 Coffey Ave., Narragansett, 02882.
Iacovacci, Nicholas J., 350 Fair St., Warwick, 02888.
Metsy, Norman G., 6467 Oak Shore Dr., Panama City, FL 32404.
Murray, William F., c/o Lourdes Pavilion, 311 S. Flagler Dr., Apt. 603, West Palm Beach, FL 33401-5677.
Revs.—
Allard, George L., 493 Mt. Pleasant Ave., Apt. 14, 02908.
Beaulieu, Raymond A., P.O. Box 433, Jamestown, 02835.
Behan, George P., 95 Third St., Newport, 02840.
Beirne, Gerald E., 75 Circuit Dr., Narragansett, 02882.
Beirne, Robert M., 791 Potters Ave., 02907.
Belhumeur, Roger E., 493 Mt. Pleasant Ave., Apt. 7, 02908.
Besse, Joseph A., 4000 Post Rd., Warwick, 02886.
Blain, Lionel A., 128 Greene St., 02895.
Blais, Robert L., 10 Hall St., West Warwick, 02893.
Boland, Edward F., 964 Main St., Pawtucket, 02860.
Bolton, Paul J., 85 Highland Dr., Jamestown, 02835.
Bouressa, Donald J., P.O. Box 787, Narragansett, 02882.
Brassil, Kevin J., 252 Williams St., 02906.
Cardoso, Reinaldo M., 964 Main St., Pawtucket, 02860.
Carmone, Anthony F., 18440 Cochran Blvd., Apt. 105, Port Charlotte, FL 33948.
Carty, John T., 43 Phillips Rd., East Greenwich, 02818-0472.
Caul, Robert F., 25 Fourth St., North Providence, 02911.
Champigny, Roger G., 400 Mendon Rd., North Smithfield, 02896.
Collins, Raymond F., P.O. Box 507, Saunderstown, 02874.
Courtemanche, Normand L., 58 Bouvier Ave., Manville, 02838.
Dean, Frederic D., 493 Mt. Pleasant Ave., Apt. 10, 02908-3329.
DeLellis, Francis V., 190 S. Weeden Rd., P.O. Box 28, Wakefield, 02880.
Demers, Normand J., c/o 1 Cathedral Sq., 02903.
Diogo, Louis M., 92 Hope St., 02906.
Dreher, John D., 34 Joffre Ave., 02895.
Duggan, John J. (Ireland), SS. John & Paul Rectory, 341 S. Main St., Coventry, 02816.
Duhaime, James H., 152 Elmdale Rd., North Scituate, 02857.
Dyer, Raymond E., 15 Sumner Brown Rd., Cumberland, 02864-1297.
Finerty, D. Bryan, 15323 Lime Dr., Punta Gorda, FL 33955.
Fitzgerald, Edmund H., 125 Bucklin St., Apt. 4, Pawtucket, 02861.
Freitas, Fernando P., 67 Howland Ave., East Providence, 02914.
Gibowski, Boguslaw T., 400 Sand Rd., North Haverhill, NH 03774.
Giudice, Francis J., 178 Dexter St., 02907.
Gray, John W., 505 Church Ave., Warwick, 02889.
Greaves, John G., 3 Sea Breeze Ln., Bristol, 02809.
Hamilton, James J., 73 Spring Grove Ave, Warwick, 02889.
Hazebrouck, Maurice L., c/o One Cathedral Sq., 02903.
Heaney, John F., 1 Scenic Heights Dr., Westerly, 02891.
Heaney, Joseph P., 400 Mendon Rd., North Smithfield, 02896.
Henry, Joseph P., 225 Capstan St., Jamestown, 02835.
Hogan, Ralph R., 493 Mt. Pleasant Ave., Apt. 8, 02908.
Horgan, Joseph E., 25 Leading St., Johnston, 02919.
Hynes, James P., 493 Mt. Pleasant Ave., Apt. 3, 02908.
Hynes, Joseph P., 400 Mendon Rd., Rm. 102, North Smithfield, 02896.
Iwuc, Anthony D., 493 Mt. Pleasant Ave., Apt. 6, 02908.
Johnson, Edward D., 2352 Suwanee Point Dr., Lawrenceville, GA 30043.
Kachel, Czeslaw L., 493 Mt. Pleasant Ave., 02908.
Keefe, Francis J., 493 Mt. Pleasant Ave., Apt. 15, 02908.
Keenan, Thomas L., 268 Parkview Dr., 02906.
Kehew, Donal R., 92 Hope St., Apt. 7, 02906.
Kelly, Raymond M.
Lacasse, Roger, 323 Rathbun St., 02895.
Laporte, Paul J., 218 Baxter St., Pawtucket, 02861.
Lavin, John J., 56 Boxwood Ave., Cranston, 02910.
Lessard, Eugene R., P.O. Box 236, North Scituate, 02857-0236.
LeThiez, Alphonse D., 314 Cypress Run Ct., North Port, FL 34287-3329.
Lonardo, Alfred C., P.O. Box 228, Jamestown, 02835.
Lynch, Cornelius B., 125 Bucklin St., Apt. 15, Pawtucket, 02861.
Maher, Charles E., 188 Col. John Gardner Rd., Narragansett, 02882.
Marot, Roger L., 94 Carrington Ave., 02895.
Maynard, Richard C., 400 Narragansett Pkwy., Apt. S. B4, Warwick, 02888.
McDermott, Charles B., 635 Ocean Rd., Narragansett, 02882.
McElroy, John J., 358 Newport Ave., Pawtucket, 02861.
McGeough, Jude P., 180 Franklin St., Bristol, 02809.
McGovern, Edward J., 493 Mt. Pleasant Ave., Apt. 1, 02908.
McKenna, Eugene J., 30 Blackberry Hill Dr., Wakefield, 02879.
Micarelli, Edmond C., c/o 1 Cathedral Sq., 02903.
Mongeon, Peter M. (NO), 26 Fairview Ave., Cranston, 02905.
Murphy, William F., 493 Mount Pleasant Ave., Apt. 12, 02908.
O'Hara, Francis W., 36 Eden Crest Dr., Cranston, 02920.
Oliveira, Joel D. (BO), 155 Fort St., East Providence, 02914.
Paiva, Antonio M., 463 Benefit St., 02903.
Pincince, Gerald P., 191 Hadley Rd., Sugar Hill, NH 03586.
Quinn, Charles P., 32 Lakeview Ter., Pascoag, 02859.
Rafferty, Raymond J., 493 Mt. Pleasant Ave., 02908-3329.
Randall, John F., P.O. Box 114006, North Providence, 02911.
Randall, Robert J., P.O. Box 5617, Wakefield, 02880.
Reynolds, Paul F., 2595 Pawtucket Ave., East Providence, 02914-3292.
Schenick, Joseph D., 493 Mt. Pleasant Ave., Apt. 2, 02908.
Scopa, Joseph, C.S., N. Quidnesset Rd., North Kingstown, 02852.
Sears, William F., 1460 Diamond Hill Rd., Cumberland, 02864.
Slota, Frederick V., 84 Kulas Rd., West Warwick, 02893.
Stark, Philip M., 54 Meadow Brook Ave., Cumberland, 02864. (Extern Priest)
Strumski, Matthew J., 400 Mendon Rd., Rm. 216, North Smithfield, 02896.
Susin, Angelo J., C.S., 860 N. Quidnesset Rd., North Kingstown, 02852.
Tanguay, William H., c/o One Cathedral Sq., 02903.
Tarro, Michael, C.S., 927 Atwood Ave., Johnston, 02919-6290.
Tetrault, Raymond L., 66 Appleton St., 02909.
Trainor, Daniel M., 92 Hope St., Apt. 4, 02906-2099.
Turillo, B. Samuel, 196 Lansdowne Rd., Warwick, 02888.
Walsh, Clyde J., 964 Main St., Pawtucket, 02860.
Walsh, Richard A., 309 Spring St., Newport, 02840.
Watterson, John E., 700 Shore Dr., #1108, Fall River, MA 02721.
Young, Peter G., 624 Woonasquatucket Ave., North Providence, 02911.

Permanent Deacons:
Alessio, Robert G., Immaculate Conception, Westerly
Andrade, Charles, St. Patrick, Providence
Archambault, Bernard L., (Retired)
Bacon, Normand J., (Retired)
Baker, John F., St. Catherine, Warwick
Barboza, Benjamin, St. Thomas the Apostle, Warren
Batalon, Raymond E., (Retired)
Bisbano, Paul, St. Mary, Bristol
Blais, Robert, Our Lady, Queen of Martyrs, Woonsocket
Bouchard, Thomas, Chap., Landmark Medical
Bouley, N. David, St. John, Slatersville
Boutier, Thomas F., St. Maria Goretti, Pawtucket
Braga, Joseph F., St. Charles, Providence
Caban, Vicente, St. John the Baptist, Pawtucket

Ceprano, Peter A., (Retired)
Cipriano, Anthony, St. Anthony, North Providence
Conley, James E., St. Elizabeth, Bristol
Corey, John A., Blessed Kateri Tekakwitha Catholic Community, Exeter
Cote, Stephen R., Diocesan Marriage Prep. Coord.
Croy, John E., St. Lucy, Middletown
Dadlez, Mark A., (Retired)
DePetrillo, Albert, Hopkins Manor, North Providence
DePietro, Ronald H., St. Bernard, North Kingstown
DiOrio, Dominic P., St. Brendan, Riverside
Dunbar, James N., Jesus Saviour, Newport
Edsall, Noel, SS. Rose & Clement, Warwick
Fajardo, Jose, SS. John and James, West Warwick
Forlingieri, Carmine, (Retired)
Gagnon, Laurence O., St. Joseph, West Warwick
Gallo, Robert L., St. Bartholomew, Providence
Garceau, Eugene, St. Agatha, Woonsocket
Garcia, Luis, (Leave of Absence)
Gauthier, Clovis, (Retired)
Gederman, Harris J., St. Philip, Greenville
Geoffroy, Roland R., (Leave of Absence)
Gomez, Oscar, (Leave of Absence)
Hanrahan, Charles L., (Leave of Absence)
Horton, Gregory R., St. James, Manville
Iacono, Paul O., St. Francis of Assisi, South Kingstown
Johnson, Loring F., (Retired)
Kirk, Paul, D.D.S., St. Gregory the Great, Warwick
Konold, Paul C., (Leave of Absence)
LaFleur, Norman R., (Leave of Absence)
LaFleur, W. Carl, St. Clare, Westerly
LaFrance, Raymond, (Retired)
Lagesse, Raymond M., (Retired)
Lambert, Paul H., St. John Vianney, Cumberland
Lapierre, Richard J., Our Lady of Good Help, Mapleville
Lennon, Thomas J., (Retired)
Levesque, Raymond E., (Retired)
Lopez, Pedro, Our Lady of Mt. Carmel, Providence
Lopez, Rony, St. Charles, Providence
Lucian, Robert C., (Retired)
MacLure, Robert, (Retired)
Martins, Jesse L., St. Theresa, Tiverton
Masse, Kevin P., (Leave of Absence)
Masse, Paul, (Leave of Absence)
McAdam, Robert, St. Ambrose, Lincoln
McCarthy, Charles F., St. Timothy, Warwick
McGregor, John D., Immaculate Conception, Westerly
Morisseau, Robert M., St. Peter, Warwick
Muscatelli, Anthony E., St. Joseph, Burrillville
Napolitano, Michael D., Chaplain, Rhode Island College, Providence
Natalizia, John J., Holy Cross, Providence
Needham, John F., St. Margaret, East Providence
Nicholson, Robert E., (Retired)
Nova, Leocadio, (Leave of Absence)
O'Hara, Thomas P., (Retired)
Ouellette, Lucien, (Retired)
Owen, Jimmie H., Blessed Sacrament, Providence
Pelland, Robert W., Holy Spirit, Central Falls
Perez, Juan Andres, St. Michael, Providence
Persson, Robert, SS. John & Paul, Coventry
Ragosta, Armand R., St. Mary, Cranston
Raspallo, Thomas R., Immaculate Conception, Cranston
Remillard, Lionel J., St. Jude, Lincoln
Riccio, Raymond L., Chaplain, State Hospitals
Rico, Jose, St. Charles Borromeo, Providence
Risi, Stephen M., Mary, Mother of Mankind, North Providence
Rose, Joseph, (Retired)
Rudnik, James R., Jesus Saviour, Newport
Sabetti, Carlo J., St. Philip, Greenville
Schofield, William J., Christ the King, West Warwick
Serra, Louis P., St. Anthony, Pawtucket
Shea, John S., St. Mary, Charlestown
Shea, Paul M., SS. John & James, West Warwick
Sheehy, C. Patrick, St. Mary, Pawtucket
Stone, Francis J., (Retired)
Sullivan, Paul J., St. Thomas More, Narragansett
Tanguay, Paul A., Chap., ACI, Cranston
Theroux, Bernard G., Chap., R.I. Veteran's Home
Theroux, Paul A., St. Mary, Carolina
Troia, Robert, St. Rocco's, Thornton
Tumminelli, Joseph, St. Robert Bellarmine, Johnston
Turbitt, Robert A., II, (Leave of Absence)
Turcios, Jose, Holy Ghost, Providence
Turcotte, Joseph G., St. Bernard, North Kingstown
Ullucci, Paul A., St. Joseph, Scituate
Urrico, Francis X., (Retired)
Valliere, Francis J., St. Pius X, Westerly
Vani, Louis A., Presentation of the Blessed Virgin Mary, North Providence
Walsh, James T., Holy Family, Woonsocket
Wendoloski, Anthony, Our Lady of Lourdes, Providence
Young, Frederick A., St. Martha, East Providence

INSTITUTIONS LOCATED IN THE DIOCESE

[A] SEMINARIES, DIOCESAN

PROVIDENCE. *Seminary of Our Lady of Providence*, 485 Mt. Pleasant Ave., 02908. Tel: 401-331-1316; Fax: 401-521-4192. Web: www.olpseminary.com. Revs. Albert A. Kenney, S.T.L., Rector; Michael J. Najim, M.Div., Vocation Dir.; David F. Gaffney, M.Div., Dir. of Spir. Form.; Timothy D. Reilly, S.T.B., J.C.L., Asst. Dir. Spir. Form.
Seminary of Our Lady of Providence, House of Formation for College Students and Pre-Theologians. Total Staff 6; Students 23.

[B] COLLEGES AND UNIVERSITIES

PROVIDENCE. *Providence College*, One Cunningham Sq., 02918. Tel: 401-865-1000; Fax: 401-865-2057. Email: pcadmiss@providence.edu. Web: www.providence.edu. Revs. Brian J. Shanley, O.P., Pres.; Kenneth Sicard, O.P., Exec. Vice Pres. & Treas.; Dr. Hugh V. Lena, Vice Pres. Academic Affairs & Provost; Mr. Michael V. Frazier, Vice Pres. Finance & Business/CFO; Rev. Brendan Murphy, O.P., Vice Pres. Student Affairs Admin.; Mr. Edward J. Caron, Vice Pres. College Rels.; Rev. Mark S. Nowel, O.P., Dean Undergraduate & Graduate Studies; Mr. David Wegrzyn, Vice Pres. Inst. Advancement; Revs. Michael J. Cuddy, O.P., Chap.; Joseph J. Guido, O.P., Vice Pres. Mission & Ministry; Marifrances McGinn, Vice Pres. & General Counsel; Robert Driscoll, Assoc. Vice Pres. & Athletic Dir.; Kathleen M. Alvino, Assoc. Vice Pres. Human Resources.
Providence College, Conducted by the Dominican Friars. Dominican Priests Teaching 27; Diocesan Priests Teaching 2; Sisters Teaching 2; Lay Professors 268; Undergraduate Students 3,868; Graduate Students 740; School of Continuing Educ. 495.

NEWPORT. *Salve Regina University* (1934) 100 Ochre Point Ave., 02840-4192. Tel: 401-847-6650; Fax: 401-847-0372. Email: sruadmis@salve.edu. Web: www.salve.edu. Rev. Kris M. von Maluski, Chap.; Sisters M. Therese Antone, R.S.M., Chancellor; Jane Gerety, R.S.M., Pres.; Dr. Laura O'Toole, Dean Undergraduate Studies; Dr. Dean de la Motte, Vice Pres. Academic Affairs; Dr. Leona Misto, R.S.M., Vice Pres. Mission Integration & Planning; William B. Hall, Vice Pres. Admin. & CFO; John J. Rok, Vice Pres. Student Life; Dr. Laura E. McPhie-Oliveira, Vice Pres. Enrollment Svcs.; Frederick C. Promades, Dir. Institute Research; Aida Mirante, Dir. Financial Aid; Michael Semenza, Vice Pres. Univ. Relations Advancement; Kathleen Boyd, Dir. Library Svcs.; John Quinn, Dean of Students; Thomas H. Brennan, Assoc. Vice Pres. Technology & CIO; Rev. Michael T. Malone, C.S.Sp., Assoc. Prof.; Michael N. Grandchamp, Assoc Vice Pres. Fin. & Controller; Diane F. Blanchette, Assoc. Vice Pres. Human Resources & AAO; Kristine Hendrickson, Assoc. Vice Pres. Univ. Relations & CCO; Thomas M. Sabbagh, Dean Graduate Studies & Continuing Educ.
Salve Regina University Sisters of Mercy of the Americas. Priests 2; Brothers 1; Sisters 11; Lay Teachers 109; Students: Men 889; Women 1,697.

[C] HIGH SCHOOLS, DIOCESAN

PAWTUCKET. *St. Raphael Academy*, 123 Walcott St., 02860. Tel: 401-723-8100; Fax: 401-723-8740. Web: www.saintrays.org. Rev. Daniel J. Sweet, Chap.; Mr. Michael Sweeney, Prin.
Saint Raphael Academy, Conducted by the Brothers of the Christian Schools. Priests 1; Brothers 2; Sisters 1; Lay Teachers 43; Boys 256; Girls 195.

SOUTH KINGSTOWN. *The Prout School*, 4640 Tower Hill Rd., Wakefield, 02879. Tel: 401-789-9262; Fax: 401-782-2262. Email: info@theproutschool.org. Web: www.theproutschool.org. Gary R. Delneo, Prin.; Rev. Gregory P. Stowe, Chap.
The Prout School Priests 1; Lay Teachers 47; Staff & Admin. Personnel 18; Boys 264; Girls 379.

WARWICK. *Bishop Hendricken High School* (1959) 2615 Warwick Ave., 02889. Tel: 401-739-3450; Fax: 401-732-8261. Email: hawks@hendricken.com. Web: www.hendricken.com. Joseph T. Brennan Jr., Prin.; Revs. David F. Gaffney, M.Div., Chap.; Jose Q. dos Reis, Chap. of the Brothers; Bro. Thomas R. Leto, Pres.; Priscilla Fox, Librarian.
Bishop Hendricken High School Congregation of Christian Brothers. Priests 1; Brothers 4; Sisters 1; Lay Teachers 85; Boys 940.

[D] HIGH SCHOOLS, REGIONAL

PAWTUCKET. *Bishop Francis P. Keough Regional High School* (1971) 145 Power Rd., 02860. Tel: 401-726-0335; Fax: 401-726-0336. Email: biskeo@netscape.net. Web: www.bishopkeough.org. Jeanne H. Leclerc, Prin.; Dorothy Young, Librarian. Sisters 1; Lay Teachers 12; Girls 90.

[E] HIGH SCHOOLS, PRIVATE

PROVIDENCE. *La Salle Academy*, (Grades 7-12), 612 Academy Ave., 02908. Tel: 401-351-7750; Fax: 401-444-1782. Email: dkavanagh@lasalle-academy.org. Web: www.lasalle-academy.org. Bro. Michael McKenery, F.S.C., Pres.; Mr. Donald Kavanagh, Prin.; Rev. Albert A. Kenney, S.T.L., Chap.; Carol Howard, Librarian; Roseanne Trissler, Librarian.
St. John Baptist de LaSalle Institute, Conducted by the Brothers of the Christian Schools. Priests 1; Brothers 7; Lay Teachers 116; Students 1,461; Total Staff 153.

EAST PROVIDENCE. *St. Mary Academy - Bay View, St. Mary Academy-Bayview*, 3070 Pawtucket Ave., Riverside, 02915. Tel: 401-434-0113, Ext. 156; Fax: 401-434-0335. Email: emcauliffe@smabv.org. Web: www.smabv.org. Sr. Elizabeth McAuliffe, R.S.M., Ed.D., Pres.; Ms. Colleen Gribbin, Prin.; Ms. Kathleen Gendron, Librarian. Sisters of Mercy Northeast Community. Sisters 9; Lay Teachers 68; Girls 537.

PORTSMOUTH. *Portsmouth Abbey School*, 285 Cory's Ln., 02871. Tel: 401-683-2000; Fax: 401-683-5888. Email: fathercaedmon@portsmouthabbey.org. Web: www.portsmouthabbey.org. Rt. Rev. W. Caedmon Holmes, O.S.B., Abbot; Dr. James DeVecchi, Prin.; Roberta Stevens, Librarian.
Order of St. Benedict in Portsmouth, Rhode Island Priests 10; Brothers 3; Lay Teachers 44; Students 358.

SOUTH KINGSTOWN. *Immaculate Conception Academy, Inc.*, 4780 Tower Hill Rd., Wakefield, 02879. Tel: 401-782-6200; Fax: 401-782-6209. Email: cwilders@inteducators.org. Rev. Andrew Mulcahey, L.C., Chap.; Siobhan O'Connor, Prin.; Ms. Caroline Wilders, Dir.
Overbrook, Inc. Teachers 12; Boarding School Students 70.

WARREN. *Our Lady of Fatima High School* (1965) (Grades 7-12), 360 Market St., Rte. 136, 02885. Tel: 401-245-4449; Fax: 401-245-1380. Web: www.fatimahs.org; www.findfatima.org. Sr. Mary Margaret Souza, S.S.D., Prin.; Kathleen Fanning, Librarian. Sisters of St. Dorothy. Sisters 5; Lay Teachers 16; Students 100.

WOONSOCKET. *Mount Saint Charles Academy* (1924) (Grades 7-12), 800 Logee St., 02895-5599. Tel: 401-769-0310; Fax: 401-762-2327. Email: mscpres@hotmail.com; richerh@mountsaintcharles.org. Web: mountsaintcharles.org. Herve Richer, Pres.; Edwin F. Burke, Prin.; Mrs. Amy Blanchette, Librarian.
Mount Saint Charles Academy, Inc. Brothers of the Sacred Heart. Priests 1; Brothers 10; Sisters 1; Lay Teachers 60; Students 940.

[F] ELEMENTARY SCHOOLS, PRIVATE

PROVIDENCE. *San Miguel School* (1993) 12 Carter St., 02907. Tel: 401-467-9777; Fax: 401-785-4976. Web: www.sanmiguelprov.org. Bro. Lawrence Goyette, F.S.C., Exec. Dir. Brothers 1; Lay Teachers 11; Students 62.

CUMBERLAND. *Mercymount Country Day School* (1948) 35 Wrentham Rd., 02864. Tel: 401-333-5919; Fax: 401-333-5150. Email: rido7181@ride.ri.net. Web: www.mercymount.org. Sisters Martha Mulligan, R.S.M., Prin.; Diane Russo, R.S.M., Librarian. Sisters of Mercy Northeast Community. Sisters 4; Brothers 1; Lay Teachers 28; Students 434.

EAST PROVIDENCE. *St. Mary Academy-Bay View*, (Grades PreK-8), *St. Mary Academy-Bayview*, 3070 Pawtucket Ave., Riverside, 02915. Tel: 401-434-0113, Ext. 156; Fax: 401-434-0335. Email: emcauliffe@smabv.org. Web: www.smabv.org. Mrs. Cynthia Lorincz, Prin.; Sr. Elizabeth McAuliffe, R.S.M., Ed.D., Pres.; Therese Quigley, Librarian. Sisters of Mercy Northeast Community., Day Pupils. Sisters 3; Lay Teachers 20; Students 356.

NEWPORT. *Cluny School*, (Grades PreK-8), (Day School), 75 Brenton Rd., 02840. Tel: 401-847-6043; Fax: 401-848-5678. Email: ride9678@ride.ri.net. Web: clunyschool.org. Sisters Joan Van der Zydem, S.J.L., Provincial; Luke Parker, S.J.C., Vice Provincial; Mrs. Meredith Caswell, Prin.; Sisters Ann Marie Liston, S.J.C., Sec. & Treas.; Maria Rocha, Dir.; Genevieve Marie Vigil, S.J.C., (Retired); Marilyn Brockway, Librarian.
St. Joseph of Cluny Sisters' School, Inc. Sisters 2;

Lay Teachers 6; Students 178.

PORTSMOUTH. *St. Philomena School* (1953) (Grades PreK-8), 324 Cory's Ln., 02871. Tel: 401-683-0268; Fax: 401-683-6554. Email: mainoffice@saintphilomena.org. Web: www.saintphilomena.org. Donna Bettencourt-Glavin, Prin.; Jeffrey Moniz, Vice Prin.; Jeanne Staats, Librarian. Sisters Faithful Companions of Jesus. Teaching Sisters 1; Lay Teachers 30; Students 488.

[G] REGIONAL ELEMENTARY SCHOOLS

PROVIDENCE. *St. Thomas Regional School*, (Grades K-8), 15 Edendale Ave., 02911. Tel: 401-351-0403; Fax: 401-351-0403 (call first). Email: mcdimuccio@cox.net. Mary DiMuccio, Prin. Lay Teachers 10; Students 171.

BURRILLVILLE. *Father Holland Catholic Regional Elementary School*, (Grades PreK-8), 180 Sayles Ave., Pascoag, 02859. Tel: 401-568-4589; Fax: 401-567-9069. Email: frholland@cox.net. Shawn A. Capron, Prin.; Christine Goulet, Librarian. Lay Teachers 10; Students 146.

CRANSTON. *Immaculate Conception Catholic Regional School*, (Grades PreK-8), 235 Garden Hills Dr., 02920. Tel: 401-942-7245; Fax: 401-943-5738. Email: sjennings@iccrschool.org. Web: www.iccrschool.org. Mrs. Sandra Jennings, Prin. Sisters 1; Lay Teachers 26; Students 320.

EAST GREENWICH. *Our Lady of Mercy Regional School* (1950) (Grades PreK-8), 55 Fourth Ave., 02818. Tel: 401-884-1618; Fax: 401-885-3138. Email: sjbarry@olmschool.org. Web: www.olmschool.org. Sr. Jeanne Barry, Prin.; Camille Craybas, Librarian. Priests 1; Sisters 2; Lay Teachers 25; Administrators 2; Students 433.

MIDDLETOWN. *All Saints Academy* (1971) (Grades K-8), 915 W. Main Rd., 02842. Tel: 401-848-4300; Fax: 401-848-5587. Email: rid40001@ride.ri.net. Web: allsaintsacademy.org. John T. Finnegan, Ph.D., Prin.; Bernice Whitaker, Librarian. Lay Teachers 13; Students 151.

PAWTUCKET. *Woodlawn Catholic Regional School* (1972) (Grades PreK-8), 61 Hope St., 02860. Tel: 401-723-3759; Fax: 401-722-4090. Web: www.woodlawncrs.org. Veronica Procopio, Prin. Sisters 1; Lay Teachers 8; Students 184.

WAKEFIELD. *Monsignor Matthew F. Clarke Regional School* (1967) (Grades PreK-8), 5074 Tower Hill Rd., 02880. Tel: 401-789-0860; Fax: 401-789-3164. Email: pbailey@monsignorclarkeschool.org. Web: www.monsignorclarkeschool.org. Paula F. Bailey, Prin. Lay Teachers 27; Students 430.

WARWICK. *Overbrook Academy at Our Lady of Providence Center* (Boarding School), 836 Warwick Neck Ave., 02889. Tel: 401-737-2850; Fax: 401-737-2884. Email: information@overbrookacademy.org. Web: www.overbrookacademy.org. Miss Kristina Pinero, Dir.; Rev. Edward McIlmail, L.C., Chap. Lay Teachers 16; Students 145.

[H] THE GREATER WOONSOCKET CATHOLIC REGIONAL SCHOOL SYSTEM

WOONSOCKET. *Greater Woonsocket Catholic Regional School System*, Office: *Fr. Marot CYO Center*, 77 Federal St., 02895. Mailing: P.O. Box 487, 02895-0487. Tel: 401-762-1095; Fax: 401-767-5901. Web: www.gwcrs.org. Mrs. Paula Hurteau, Admin.

Greater Woonsocket Catholic Regional School System

Member Schools

WOONSOCKET

Good Shepherd Catholic Regional School (Grades 3-8), 1210 Mendon Rd., 02895. Tel: 401-767-5906; Fax: 401-767-5905. Email: goodshepherdschool@cox.net. Web: www.gwcrs.org. Mr. Larry Poitras, Prin.; Joyce Broulliard, Librarian. Lay Teachers 16; Students 232.

Monsignor Gadoury Regional Primary School (Grades PreK-2), Three year old program, 1371 Park Ave., 02895. Tel: 401-767-5902; Fax: 401-767-5923. Email: mgprincipal@yahoo.com. Mary Chabot, Prin. Sisters 1; Lay Teachers 7; Students 157.

[I] BREAD OF LIFE SCHOOLS, URBAN CATHOLIC SCHOOLS CONSORTIUM

PROVIDENCE. *Bread of Life Schools, Urban Catholic Schools Consortium*, 155 Gordon Ave., 02905. Tel: 401-781-2370. Annmarie Bucci, Dir. Fin.

Member Schools

PROVIDENCE

Bishop McVinney Regional School (Grades PreK-8), 155 Gordon Ave., 02905. Tel: 401-781-2370; Fax: 401-785-2618. Email: bmv155@yahoo.com. Mr. Louis Hebert, Prin.; Carol Kamnski, Librarian.

Catholic Association for Regional Education Lay Teachers 10; Students 258.

The Holy Ghost School (Grades PreK-8), 35 Swiss St., 02909. Tel: 401-421-4455; Fax: 401-421-5444. Email: carolhgs@cox.net. Mrs. Carol Wood-Soltys, Prin. Lay Teachers 7; Students 160.

CENTRAL FALLS

St. Elizabeth Ann Seton Academy (1995) (Grades PreK-8), 909 Lonsdale Ave., 02863. Tel: 401-728-6230; Fax: 401-723-9532. Email: principal@setonacademyri.org. Web: www.setonacademyri.org. Mrs. Maria Rocheleau, Prin.; Therese M. Rogers, Admin. Asst. Lay Teachers 18; Students 221.

[J] CHILD CARING FACILITIES

PROVIDENCE. *Group Home for Adolescent Boys* (Whitmarsh House), 1055 N. Main St., 02904. Tel: 401-351-7230; Fax: 401-421-0198. Bro. John McHale, O.L.P., Dir. Sisters 1; Lay Teachers 5; Boys 70.

NARRAGANSETT. *Ocean Tides*, 635 Ocean Rd., 02882-1314. Tel: 401-789-1016; Fax: 401-788-0924. Email: brob@oceantides.org. Web: www.oceantides.org. Bros. Brendan Gerrity, F.S.C., Pres.; John McGann, F.S.C., Social Svcs.; John Norton, F.S.C., Court Liaison; Joseph Schafer, F.S.C., Dir. Social Svcs.; Peter Clifford, F.S.C., Admin. Asst.; Jane E. Genereux, Prin.

Ocean Tides, Inc. Brothers 5; Lay Teachers 25; Lay Staff 38; Students 112.

[K] GENERAL HOSPITALS

PROVIDENCE. *St. Joseph Health Services of Rhode Island - St. Joseph Hospital for Specialty Care* (1892) 21 Peace St., 02907. Tel: 401-456-4080; Fax: 401-456-4089. Web: www.saintjosephri.com. Mr. John M. Fogarty, Pres. & CEO; Rev. John J. Rainone, Dir. Pastoral Care; Sisters Jolly Joseph, Assoc. Chap.; Madeline Rita, Assoc. Chap.

Includes:

St. Joseph Center for Health & Human Services Tel: 401-456-4321; Fax: 401-456-4089. Dr. Abdel Hammo, M.D., Medical Dir.

NORTH PROVIDENCE. *St. Joseph Health Services of Rhode Island - Our Lady of Fatima Hospital* (1954) 200 High Service Ave., 02904. Tel: 401-456-3000; 401-456-3050; Fax: 401-456-3028; 401-456-3640. Web: www.fatimahospital.com. Mr. John M. Fogarty, Pres. & CEO; Revs. Roman R. Manchester, Chap.; John J. Rainone, Dir. Pastoral Care; Edward A. Sousa Jr., Chap.; Sr. Madeleine Guertin, Assoc. Chap.; Deacon Anthony J. Wendoloski Jr., Assoc. Chap.; Carol Ross, Acting Dir. School Nursing. Student Nurses 100; Bed Capacity 386; Patients Assisted Annually 200,000; Total Staff 1,850.

Southern New England Rehabilitation Center Tel: 401-456-4500; Fax: 401-456-4501. Web: www.sner-c.com. Jon A. Mukand, M.D., Ph.D., Medical Dir. A joint venture of St. Joseph Hospital and Rhode Island Hospital.

Corporate Care Occupational Health Services Tel: 401-456-4020; Fax: 401-456-4203. Dr. Jay Burstein, M.D., Medical Dir.

St. Joseph Center for Psychiatric Services Tel: 401-456-4437; Fax: 401-456-4078. Ronald Gobeil, D.O., Medical Dir.

St. Joseph Health Services Foundation, 200 High Service Ave., 02904. Tel: 401-456-3070. Email: obrown@saintjosephri.com. Web: www.saintjosephri-.com. Otis Brown, Vice Pres. Devel. & Public Affairs.

[L] VISITING AND NURSING OF THE SICK

PROVIDENCE. *Holy Spirit Convent*, 43 Westerly Ave., 02909. Tel: 401-946-5639. Sr. Caroline Devinez, D.H.S., Contact Person. Daughters of the Holy Spirit. Sisters 2; Visits 240; Number of Patients 2.

[M] HOMES FOR AGED

PROVIDENCE. *St. Joseph Living Center*, 153 Dean St., 02903. Tel: 401-272-3335; Fax: 401-621-8604. Diane E. Evans, R.N., B.S.N., Exec. Dir. Assisted and independent living and respite care facility, a division of St. Joseph Health Services of Rhode Island. Residents 66.

CUMBERLAND. *Mount St. Rita Health Centre* (1971) 15 Sumner Brown Rd., 02864. Tel: 401-333-6352; Fax: 401-333-1012. Email: mail@mountstrita.org. Web: www.mountstrita.org. Deborah Beards, Admin.

Mount St. Rita Health Centre Inc., Licensed Nursing Home. Residents 98; Total Staff 160.

NEWPORT. *St. Clare Home* (1909) 309 Spring St., 02840. Tel: 401-849-3204; Fax: 401-849-5780. Email: mbdaigneault@stclarehome.com. Web: stclarehome.com. Mary Beth Daigneault, Admin.; Rev. Richard A. Walsh, Chap. (Retired).

The Saint Clare Home, Nursing Facility. Daughters of the Holy Spirit 2; Lay Nurses 16; Lay Employees 52; Residents 47; Total Assisted Annually 80; Total Staff 78.

NORTH KINGSTOWN. *Scalabrini Villa* (1957) 860 N. Quidnessett Rd., 02852. Tel: 401-884-1802; Fax: 401-884-4727. Email: admin@scalabrinivilla.com. Web: www.scalabrinivilla.com. Rev. Edward J. Marino, C.S., Dir. Tel: 401-884-1802; Sr. Teresita Tauyan, F.A.S., Supr. Tel: 401-884-4594.

Scalabrini Villa Inc., Full Skilled Nursing Facility. Franciscan Apostolic Sisters 3; Residents 120; Total Staff 126; Total Assisted 43,800.

NORTH SMITHFIELD. *St. Antoine Residence* (1913) 10 Rhodes Ave., 02896. Tel: 401-767-3500; Fax: 401-769-5249. Email: wfargnoli@stantoine.net. Web: www.stantoine.net. Wendy Fargnoli, Exec. Dir.

Saint Antoine Residence Residents 260; Total Staff 415.

The Villa at Saint Antoine (2000) 400 Mendon Rd., 02896-6999. Tel: 401-767-2574; Fax: 401-767-2581. Email: wfargnoli@stantoine.net. Web: www.stantoine.net. Ms. Jean Larkin, Dir.

The Frassati Residence Total Staff 62; Total Assisted 90.

PAWTUCKET. *Jeanne Jugan Apartments*, 310 Sayles Ave., 02860. Tel: 401-723-4314; Fax: 401-723-4316. Apartments for Elderly 27; Residents 30; Total Staff 1.

Jeanne Jugan Residence, 964 Main St., 02860. Tel: 401-723-4314; Fax: 401-723-4316. Email: pwadministrator@littlesistersofthepoor.org. Rev. Msgr. William I. Varsanyi, P.A., J.C.D., Chap.

Jeanne Jugan Residence of the Little Sisters of the Poor Little Sisters of the Poor 12; Residents 100; Total Staff 86; Total Assisted 104. In Res. Revs. Edward F. Boland (Retired); Reinaldo M. Cardoso (Retired); Clyde J. Walsh (Retired).

[N] CAMPS AND COMMUNITY CENTERS

PROVIDENCE. *St. Francis Chapel & City Ministry Center*, 538 Broadway, 02909. Tel: 401-274-3434; Fax: 401-453-0034. Email: fsevola@stfrancischapel.com. Web: stfrancischapel.com. 275 Westminster St., 02903. Tel: 401-331-6510. Revs. Frank Sevola, O.F.M., Guardian & Exec. Dir.; Scott F. Brookbank, O.F.M.; Michael S. Joyce, O.F.M.; Brice Leavins, O.F.M.; Charles J. O'Connor, O.F.M., Vicar.

St. Martin de Porres Multi-Purpose Center, 160 Cranston St., 02907. Tel: 401-274-6783; Fax: 401-274-5930. Email: estherdioceseofprovidence@yahoo.com. Ms. Esther E. Price, Dir.

St. Martin de Porres Center Total under care 2,100; Total Assisted 2,500; Total Staff 13.

The McAuley Corporation dba McAuley Ministries 622 Elmwood Ave., P.O. Box 73195, 02907. Tel: 401-941-9013; Fax: 401-941-6862. Email: dwolfe@mcauleyri.org. Web: www.mcauleyri.org. Donald P. Wolfe, Exec. Dir.

The McAuley Corporation, DBA McAuley Ministries. Sisters of Mercy of the Americas Northeast Community.

McAuley Ministries - McAuley House (1975) 622 Elmwood Ave., P.O. Box 27009, 02907-3352. Tel: 401-941-9013; Fax: 401-941-6862. Web: www.mcauleyri.org. Rev. Mary Margaret Earl, Admin. Meal site assisting 10,000 homeless annually. Total Staff 5.

McAuley Ministries - McAuley Village (1990) 325 Niagara St., 02907. Tel: 401-467-3630; Fax: 401-467-2760. Web: www.mcauleyri.org. Kathryn O'Hare, Admin. Transitional Housing and Child Care assisting 23 families, 40 children in Daycare. Total Staff 20.

McAuley Ministries - The Warde-robe (1997) 1286 Broad St., Central Falls, 02863. Tel: 401-729-0405. Web: www.mcauleyri.org. Donna Benetti, Admin. Clothing and housewares for the working poor. Total Assisted Annually 10,000; Total Staff 4.

BURRILLVILLE. *Mother of Hope Camp*, Mailing Address: 1 Cathedral Sq., 02903. Tel: 401-568-3580. Email: motherofhopecamp@aol.com. Web: www.ymcyoprov.org. Box W, Chepachet, 02814. Maria Piccirilli, Dir.

Mother of Hope Camp

CRANSTON. *Rejoice in Hope Youth Center*, 804 Dyer Ave., 02920. Tel: 401-942-6571; Fax: 401-943-8686. Email: rejoiceinhope@juno.com. Pat Kane, Dir.

EAST PROVIDENCE. *Emmaus Youth Center*, 25 Metropolitan Park Dr., Riverside, 02915. Tel: 401-433-4327; Fax: 401-433-1320. Web: www.ymcyoprov.org. Pat Kane, Dir.; Phil Ricci, Admin.

WARWICK. *OLP Center, Inc.*, 836 Warwick Neck Ave., 02889. Tel: 401-739-6850; Fax: 401-738-8058. Email: info@aldrichmansion.com. Web: Aldrichmansion.com. Mrs. Paulette M. Turcotte, Dir.

OLP Center, Inc. Staff 10.

WOONSOCKET. *Fr. Marot CYO Center* (1970) 53 Federal St., P.O. Box 518, 02895-0518. Tel: 401-762-3252; Fax: 401-762-3255. Email: frmarotcyocenter@choiceonemail.com. Rev. Msgr. John C. Allard,

Chap.; Miss Fern Dery, Dir.; Mr. Roland Berard, Admin.
CYO of Northern Rhode Island, Inc.

[O] PERSONAL PRELATURES

PROVIDENCE. *Prelature of the Holy Cross and Opus Dei*, Mathewson House, 224 Bowen St., 02906. Tel: 401-272-7834; Fax: 401-272-7854. Email: info@opusdei.org. Web: www.opusdei.org. Rev. George Crafts.

[P] MONASTERIES AND RESIDENCES OF PRIESTS AND BROTHERS

PROVIDENCE. *Brothers of Our Lady of Providence* (1959) 1055 N. Main St., 02904. Tel: 401-351-7230; Fax: 401-421-0198. Bro. John McHale, O.L.P., Supr. Brothers 2.

St. Francis Friary, 214 Broadway, 02903. Tel: 401-274-3434; Fax: 401-453-0034. Email: fsevola@stfrancischapel.com. Web: stfrancischapel.com. 538 Broadway, 02909. Revs. Frank Sevola, O.F.M., Guardian & Exec. Dir.; Scott F. Brookbank, O.F.M.; Michael S. Joyce, O.F.M.; Charles J. O'Connor, O.F.M., Vicar.
St. Francis Weybosset Street Chapel, Inc. Franciscan Friars. Priests 4.

St. John Vianney Residence (1978) 493 Mt. Pleasant Ave., 02908. Tel: 401-331-9870; Fax: 401-331-5092. Rev. Edward J. McGovern, Admin. (Retired). Residence for Senior Priests. Priests 14.
Residents: Rev. Msgr. Michael W. Dziob (Retired); Revs. George L. Allard (Retired); Roger E. Belhumer (Retired); Frederic D. Dean (Retired); Ralph R. Hogan (Retired); James P. Hynes (Retired); Anthony D. Iwuc (Retired); Czeslaw L. Kachel (Retired); Francis J. Keefe (Retired); William F. Murphy (Retired); Raymond J. Rafferty (Retired); John J. Rainone; Joseph D. Schenick (Retired).

St. Pius Priory, 55 Elmhurst Ave., 02908. Tel: 401-751-4871; Fax: 401-273-1089. Very Rev. Kenneth R. Letoile, O.P.; Revs. John P. Burchill, O.P.; Edward M. Gorman, O.P., (On Military Assignment); John Martin Ruiz-Mayorga, O.P.; John L. Sullivan, O.P.; Guy Albert Trudel, O.P.
Dominican Fathers Priests 5.

St. Thomas Aquinas Priory at Providence College, 333 Eaton St., 02918-0001. Tel: 401-865-2101 (office); Fax: 401-865-2959.
Priory of St. Thomas Aquinas Dominican Friars. Bishops in Residence 1; Priests in Residence 43; Brothers in Residence 1; Priests residing outside the Priory 6.
Assigned & Residing in the Priory: Most Rev. Ernest B. Boland, O.P., Bishop Emeritus of Multan (Retired); Revs. William P. Marquis, O.P., Prior; Jon Alexander, O.P.; John E. Allard, O.P.; J. Iriarte Andujar, O.P.; Nicanor P.G. Austriaco, O.P.; Albino F. Barrera, O.P.; Peter Batts, O.P.; Thomas J. Blau, O.P.; Daniel J. Cassidy, O.P.; Edward L. Cleary, O.P.; Paul M. Conner, O.P.; Michael J. Cuddy, O.P.; G. Adrian Dabash, O.P.; James A. Driscoll, O.P.; Thomas J. Ertle, O.P.; William David Folsey, O.P.; Joseph J. Guido, O.P.; G. Nicholas Ingham, O.P.; Terence Keegan, O.P.; Bernard F. Langton, O.P.; Dominic M. Legge, O.P.; Joseph L. Lennon, O.P.; Richard A. McAlister, O.P.; Thomas P. McCreesh, O.P.; Thomas D. McGonigle, O.P.; J. Stuart McPhail, O.P.; Allen Bernard Moran, O.P.; Robert A. Morris, O.P.; David Brendan Murphy, O.P.; Edward T. Myers, O.P.; Robert D. Myett, O.P.; Mark D. Nowel, O.P.; John S. Peterson, O.P.; Jacob Petri, O.P.; R. Gabriel Pivarnik, O.P.; Matthew D. Powell, O.P.; Kevin D. Robb, O.P.; Paul E. Seaver, O.P.; Brian J. Shanley, O.P.; Kenneth Sicard, O.P.; Joseph Torchia, O.P.; John C. Vidmar, O.P.; Walter Urban Voll, O.P.
Assigned but Living Outside the Priory: Revs. Timothy F. Bellamah, O.P., (Dominican House of Studies); George L. Cochran, O.P., (Columbus, OH); James J. Davis, O.P. (Retired); Edward H. Gallagher, O.P. (Retired); Ralph T. Hall, O.P. (Retired); James Ferrer Quigley, O.P., (North American College, Rome, Italy).

BRISTOL. *St. Columban's Retirement House*, 65 Ferry Rd., Box 65, 02809. Tel: 401-253-6909; Fax: 401-253-7099. Revs. Denis Bartley, S.S.C. (Retired); John Buckley, S.S.C.; Francis P. Carroll, S.S.C., Supr.; Charles Degnan, S.S.C. (Retired); James Dwyer, S.S.C.; Howard P. Eisel, S.S.C. (Retired); Norbert F. Feld, S.S.C. (Retired); Victor Gaboury, S.S.C. (Retired); Brian Gallagher, S.S.C. (Retired); Michael Harrison, S.S.C. (Retired); John Hogan, S.S.C.; Francis Keaney, S.S.C. (Retired); John Marley, S.S.C. (Retired); Daniel McGinn, S.S.C. (Retired); Joseph McSweeney, S.S.C.; John Moran, S.S.C. (Retired); Robert O'Rourke, S.S.C. (Retired); Paul Richardson, S.S.C. (Retired); John F. Roche, S.S.C. (Retired); Alban Sueper, S.S.C. (Retired); William F. Sullivan, S.S.C.; William F. Sweeney, S.S.C.
St. Columban's Foreign Mission Society Priests 23.

BURRILLVILLE. *Brothers of the Sacred Heart Provincial House*, 685 Steere Farm Rd., Pascoag, 02859-4601. Tel: 401-568-8686; 401-568-3361; Fax: 401-568-1450. Email: NEprovincial@bshne.org. Bros. Robert Croteau, S.C., Prov. Supr. of New England Prov.; Robert T. Gagne, S.C., Accounts Mgr.; Paul J. Hebert, S.C., Exec. Asst. for Missions; Leo Labbe, S.C., Local Supr.; Willie A. Morin, S.C., Prov. Sec.; Daniel St. Jacques, S.C., Vocation Dir.
The Order of the Brothers of the Sacred Heart of New England, Inc. Brothers 26.

NARRAGANSETT. *Christian Brothers' Center*, 635 Ocean Rd., 02882. Tel: 401-789-0244; Fax: 401-783-5303. Email: jdl@cbc.necoxmail.com. Web: www.cbline.org. Rev. Charles B. McDermott, Chap. (Retired); Bros. Edmond Precourt, F.S.C., Dir.; Frederick DelAntonio, F.S.C., Dir. Finance; Mrs. Mary Yakey, Health Care Coord.
Brothers of the Christian Schools, Long Island-New England Province Brothers of the Christian Schools. Brothers 31; Brothers in the Province 70.

PORTSMOUTH. *Abbey of St. Gregory the Great* (1918) 285 Cory's Lane, 02871. Tel: 401-683-2000; Fax: 401-683-5888. Email: fathercaedmon@portsmouthabbey.org. Web: www.portsmouthabbey.org. Rt. Revs. W. Caedmon Holmes, O.S.B., Abbot; F. Mark Serna, O.S.B., Retired Abbot (Retired); Matthew Stark, O.S.B., Retired Abbot (Retired); Very Rev. R. Ambrose Wolverton, O.S.B., Prior; Revs. Julian Stead, O.S.B.; F. Philip Wilson, O.S.B.; A. Damian Kearney, O.S.B.; Michael Stafford, O.S.B.; P. Geoffrey Chase, O.S.B.; Christopher Davis, O.S.B.; T. Edmund Adams, O.S.B.; P. Paschal Scotti, O.S.B.
Order of St. Benedict in Portsmouth, Rhode Island Benedictines of the English Congregation. Abbots 3; Priests 13; Brothers 3.

WOONSOCKET. *Brothers of the Sacred Heart* (1821) 800 Logee St., 02895. Tel: 401-769-0313; Fax: 401-769-0065. Email: mscbrotherwillie@hotmail.com. Bro. Willie A. Morin, S.C., Local Supr. Brothers 6.

Brothers of the Sacred Heart (1821) 94 Carrington Ave., 02895. Bro. Ronald Champagne, S.C., Dir.

St. John's Residence, 159 Earle St., 02895. Tel: 401-766-9677. Email: bobbreault@hotmail.com. Web: www.Brothersofthesacredheart.org. Bros. Robert F. Breault, S.C., Supr. & Dir.; Alan Aubin, S.C.; Robert Croteau, S.C.; Robert T. Gagne, S.C.; Tom Greer, S.C.; Marcel Leclerc, S.C. Brothers 6.

[Q] CONVENTS AND RESIDENCES FOR SISTERS

BARRINGTON. *Monastery of Discalced Carmelites* (1930) 25 Watson Ave., 02806-4009. Tel: 401-245-3421; Fax: 401-245-6872. Email: sllbarr@juno.com. Web: home.att.net/~barringtoncarmel. Sr. Susan L. Lumb, Prioress.
Monastery of Discalced Carmelites at Nayatt, Barrington, RI Professed Sisters 14; Postulants 1.

BRISTOL. *Mt. St. Joseph Spiritual Life Center and Provincialate* formerly Mt. St. Joseph Spiritual Life Center , 13 Monkeywrench Ln., 02809-2916. Tel: 401-253-5434; Fax: 401-253-5344. Sr. Dorothy Schwarz, S.S.D., Provincial & Local Coord. Sisters of St. Dorothy. Sisters 5.

CUMBERLAND. *Sisters of Mercy of the Americas Northeast Community, Inc.* (1851) 15 Highland View Rd., 02864-1124. Tel: 401-333-6333; Fax: 401-333-6450. Email: info@mercyne.org. Sisters Ellen Kurtz, R.S.M., Pres.; Michele Aronica, R.S.M., Vice Pres.; Eileen Dooling, R.S.M, Leadership Team; Jacqueline Marie Kieslich, R.S.M., Leadership Team; Maureen McElroy, R.S.M., Leadership Team; Kathleen Turley, R.S.M., Leadership Team; Eleanor Little, R.S.M., Archivist; Susan Jenkinson, M.A., Dir. Sponsorship; Sisters Kathleen Pritty, R.S.M., Dir. Justice; Elaine Deasy, R.S.M., Dir. Vocation/Incorporation; Ann McGovern, R.S.M., Dir.Vocation/Incorporation; Dale Jarvis, R.S.M., Vocations Min.; Chloe Van Aken, Dir. Communications; Gerald Sullivan, COO.
Sisters of Mercy of the Americas Northeast Community, Inc. Sisters 794; Associates 396.
Sisters of Mercy of the Americas Northeast Community, Inc., Administrative Offices formerly Sisters of Mercy 15 Highland View Rd., 02864-1124. Tel: 401-333-2439. *Mercycrest Convent*, 125 Wrentham Rd., 02864. Tel: 401-333-5283. *Mercymount Convent*, 75 Wrentham Rd., 02864. Tel: 401-333-0158. Sisters of Mercy 3.

MIDDLETOWN. *Cluny Provincial House* (1807) 7 Restmere Ter., 02842. Tel: 401-846-4757; 401-846-4826 (Prov.); Fax: 401-846-4826 (Office). Email: clunyusa@hotmail.com. Sisters of St. Joseph of Cluny. Sisters 2,838; Sisters in Diocese 11; Sisters in Cluny Provincial of U.S.A. & Canada 27.
Provincial House Tel: 401-846-4826; Fax: 401-846-4826. Sisters Joan Van der Zyden, S.J.C., Prov. Supr.; Luke Parker, S.J.C., Vice Provincial. *St. Joseph of Cluny Convent* Tel: 401-847-3637; Fax: 401-846-4826. Sr. Joan Van der Zyden, S.J.C., Local Supr.

NEWPORT. *St. Clare Convent, Cutting Memorial*, 301 Spring St., 02840. Tel: 401-846-1025.
The Saint Clare Home Daughters of the Holy Spirit 2.

Corpus Christi Carmel, 516 Broadway, 02840. Tel: 401-847-6165. Web: www.corpuschrsticarmelite.org. Sisters Jane Francis, O.Carm.; Anna Maria, O.Carm., Regl. Supr., U.S.A. Corpus Christi Carmelite Sisters. Sisters 2.

Javouhey House (2002) 78 Carroll Ave., 02840. Tel: 401-849-5124; Fax: 253-484-7155. Email: clunyjh@cox.net. Sr. Ann Marie Liston, S.J.C., Local Coord. Sisters of St. Joseph of Cluny 5.

NORTH KINGSTOWN. *Holy Family Convent*, 1 Wright Ln., 02852. Tel: 401-294-3554. Email: theresinascully@aol.com. Web: www.passionistsisters.org. Sr. Theresina Scully, C.P., Province Leader.
Sisters of the Holy Cross and Passion, Provincial Office of the Sisters of the Cross and Passion. Sisters 3.

NORTH PROVIDENCE. *Daughters of Mary Mother of Mercy*, 2 Pope St., 02904. Tel: 401-353-8654; Fax: 401-353-5126. Sisters 3.

Franciscan Missionaries of Mary (1903) 399 Fruit Hill Ave., 02911. Tel: 401-353-5800; Fax: 401-353-2674. Email: fmmalc@aol.com. Web: www.fmmusa.org.
Franciscan Missionaries of Mary

Holy Family Community, 399 Fruit Hill Ave., 02911. Tel: 401-353-5800; Fax: 401-353-2674. Sr. Elizabeth A. Conyers, F.M.M., Supr. Sisters 13.

Our Lady, Queen of Peace, Assisted Living Community, 399 Fruit Hill Ave., 02911. Tel: 401-353-5800; Fax: 401-354-8296. Sisters Pauline Baris, F.M.M., Supr.; Pauline Williams, F.M.M., Admin. Sisters 15.

Trinity Community, Assisted Living Community, 399 Fruit Hill Ave., 02911. Tel: 401-353-5800. Sr. Agnes Begley, F.M.M., Supr. Sisters 15.

Our Lady of the Lourdes Convent, 385 Fruit Hill Ave., 02911. Tel: 401-353-6381. Sisters Rosemarie Higgins, F.M.M., Supr.; Yvette Hubert, F.M.M.; Aline Giroux, F.M.M. Sisters 5.

Bethany, (House of On-Going Formation), 397 Fruit Hill Ave., 02911. Tel: 401-353-5860. Email: bethanyfmm@verizon.net. Sr. Yvette Hubert, F.M.M., Dir.

De Chappotin Community, 399 Fruit Hill Ave., 02911. Tel: 401-353-9412; Fax: 401-353-2674. Sr. Alma Dufault, F.M.M., Supr. Sisters 5.

NORTH SMITHFIELD. *Franciscan Missionaries of Mary*, Ein Karim Community, 318 Mendon Rd., 02896. Tel: 401-766-8242; Fax: 401-766-6492. Email: karimfmm@aol.com. Sr. Joyce C. Gardella, F.M.M., Coord. Sisters 4.

SOUTH KINGSTOWN. *Congregation of the Sisters of Divine Providence Generalate* (1851) Tel: 401-782-1785; Fax: 401-782-6967.

Mother of Providence Convent, 12 Christopher St., Wakefield, 02879. Tel: 401-782-1785; Fax: 401-782-6967. Sr. Janet Folkl, C.D.P., Gen. Supr.

WEST GREENWICH. *Mary of Nazareth Novitiate*, 28 Victory Hwy., 02817. Tel: 401-392-1007; Fax: 401-392-1009. Franciscan Missionaries of Mary 5.

WOONSOCKET. *Emmanuel House*, 67 Highland St., 02895. Tel: 401-766-0525.

Franciscan Apostolic Sisters (1953) 94 Carrington Ave., 02895. Tel: 401-762-0326, Ext. 28. Email: smofas@yahoo.com; srloufas@yahoo.com. Web: www.geocities.com/franapsisters. Sr. Lourdes DeLeon, F.A.S., Local Animator. Sisters 2. 860 N. Quidnessett Rd., North Kingstown, 02852. Tel: 401-884-4594. Web: www.geocities.com/franapsisters. Sr. Lourdes DeLeon, F.A.S., Local Animator/ Regional Treas. Sisters in U.S. 15.

[R] RETREAT HOUSES

CUMBERLAND. *Mercy Lodge*, 6 Summer Brown Rd., 02864. Tel: 401-333-2801. 15 Highland View Rd., 02864-1124. Tel: 401-333-6333; Fax: 401-333-6450.

Sisters of Mercy of the Americas, Northeast Community, Inc.

NORTH PROVIDENCE. *Bethany Renewal Center*, 397 Fruit Hill Ave., 02911. Tel: 401-353-5860. Email: bethanyfmm@aol.com. Web: www.fmmusa.org. Sr. Yvette Hubert, F.M.M. Conducted by the Franciscan Missionaries of Mary.

[S] NEWMAN CENTERS

PROVIDENCE. *Brown University* Box 1931, 02912. Tel: 401-863-2344; Fax: 401-863-9359. Email: catholic@brown.edu. Web: www.brown.edu/students/Brown_Catholic. Rev. Henry J. Bodah, Chap.; Angela Howard McParland, Catholic Campus Min. Priests 1; Total Staff 2.

Johnson & Wales University Catholic Campus Ministry-CBCSI Bldg., 8 Abbott Park Place, 02903. Tel: 401-598-1830; Fax: 401-598-1171. Email: sgaumont@jwu.edu. Web: www.jwu.edu/prov/osa/spirit__cath.htm. Sandra Gaumont, Campus Min.

Rhode Island College Catholic Campus Ministry, Donovan Lower Level, 600 Mt. Pleasant Ave., 02908. Tel: 401-456-8168; Fax: 401-456-2849 (Call first). Email: campusministry@ric.edu. Web: www.ric.edu/chaplain. Deacon Michael Napolitano.

BRISTOL. *Roger Williams University* Catholic Chaplain's Office, 1 Old Ferry Rd., 02809. Tel: 401-254-3433. Rev. Michael A. Sisco.

SMITHFIELD. *Bryant University* 1150 Douglas Pk., Box 33, 02917-1284. Tel: 401-232-6045; Fax: 401-232-6362. Email: revjp@bryant.edu. Rev. Joseph A. Pescatello, Chap.

SOUTH KINGSTOWN. *University of Rhode Island Catholic Center* 90 Chapel Way, Kingston, 02881. Tel: 401-874-2324; Fax: 401-874-9099. Web: www.uricatholiccenter.org. Revs. Joseph D. Creedon; S. Matthew Glover, Chap.

[T] SECULAR INSTITUTES

GREENVILLE. *Regnum Christi*, 60 Austin Ave., 02828. Tel: 401-949-2820; Fax: 401-949-2310; 401-949-0291. Email: mtrevinousa@inteducators.org. Web: www.regnumchristi.org. Ms. Monica Trevino, Dir.

MANVILLE. *Oblate Missionaries of Mary Immaculate* (1952) P.O. Box 303, 02838. Tel: 603-362-9960; Fax: 603-362-9960. Email: pjlabbe1@juno.com. Web: www.inst.secular-ommi.com. Miss Ruth A. Valois.

[U] MISCELLANEOUS LISTINGS

PROVIDENCE. **Mandamiento Nuevo Corporation*, 184 Broad St., 02903. Tel: 401-421-7833, Ext. 104; Fax: 401-274-5450.

Miscellaneous Listings for the Diocese of Providence Mailing address for all Providence listings, Chancery Office: 1 Cathedral Sq., 02903. Tel: 401-278-4518; Fax: 401-278-4621. Email: jdarcy@dioceseofprovidence.org. Web: www.dioceseofprovidence.org. Rev. Msgr. John J. Darcy, M.A., J.C.L., Vicar General/Chancellor. For further information contact:

All Saints Catholic Community, Woonsocket, RI
Catholic Association for Regional Education
Catholic Charity Fund
Catholic Foundation of Rhode Island
Catholic Information Center of Newport
Catholic Inner City Apostolate, Inc.
Catholic Investment Trust, Inc.
Catholic Teachers' College of Providence
Charismatic Renewal, 909 Westmain Rd., Middletown, 02842-6351. Tel: 401-847-6153. Rev. John W. O'Brien.
Christ the Redeemer Academy
Cursillo Movement
200 Pettaconsett Ave., Warwick, 02888. Tel: 401-781-7226. Rev. Frank S. Salmani, Spiritual Dir.
461 Shady Valley Rd., Coventry, 02816. Tel: 401-392-1252. Edward Overton, Lay Coord.
The Church of the Immaculate Conception, North Providence
De LaSalle Academy Corporation
DiMed Corp.
Diocesan Administration Corporation Tel: 401-278-4616; Fax: 401-751-6808. J. Timothy Kocab, Diocesan Controller.
Diocesan Catholic Telecommunications Network of Rhode Island
Diocesan Plant Fund
Diocesan Service Corporation Tel: 401-278-4616; Fax: 401-751-6808.
F.A.C.E. of Rhode Island (Financial Aid for Children's Education of Rhode Island)
Father Barry CYO Center
Holy Name Society
The Holy Spirit Catholic Community, Central Falls, RI
House of the Good Shepherd of Providence
Homes for Hope Foundation
Inter-Parish Loan Fund, Inc.
LaSalle Academy
Little Sisters of the Assumption of Woonsocket
Marian Association of Northern Rhode Island
The Mercy Home and School
Mother of Hope Novitiate
Mont St. Francois of Woonsocket, RI formerly Mount St. Francois of Woonsocket, RI
Nazareth Home
New England Conference of Diocesan Directors of Religious Education
Occult Awareness Ministry
Our Lady of Peace Retreat House
Our Lady of Providence Preparatory Seminary
Our Lady, Queen of the Clergy
Parish Investment Group
Pius X Salvage Bureau
Retreat House of the Immaculate Heart of Mary
The Rhode Island Catholic Orphan Asylum (St. Aloysius Home)
Rhode Island Home for Working Boys
Roman Catholic Bishop of Providence A Corporation Sole.
St. Benedict's Hearth Corporation, East Providence.
Saint Casimir's Church of Warren
St. Dominic Savio Youth Center
Saint Francis House
Saint Hedwig's Church Corporation, Providence
St. John's Church of Providence
Saint Margaret's Home
Saint Maria Society
St. Mary Academy of the Visitation
Saint Raphael's Industrial Home and School
St. Vincent de Paul Home, Woonsocket
Saint Vincent de Paul Infant Asylum
Stella Maris Home for Convalescents
The Holy Ghost School
Vision of Hope, Inc.

BURRILLVILLE. *Father Andre Coindre Charitable Trust*, 685 Steere Farm Rd., Pascoag, 02859-4601. Tel: 401-568-3361, Ext. 3202; Fax: 401-568-1450. Email: rgagne@bshne.org. Bro. Robert Croteau, S.C., Treas. & Provincial.

CUMBERLAND. *Conference of Regional Treasurers*, 15 Highland View Rd., 02864-1124. Tel: 401-333-9145; Fax: 401-333-6450. Email: mpmurphy@mercyri.org. Sr. Marypatricia Murphy, R.S.M.

Northeast FIDES, Inc., 15 Highland View Rd., 02864-1124. Tel: 401-333-6333; Fax: 401-333-6450. Sr. Michele Aronica, R.S.M., Pres.
Northeast FIDES, Inc.

MAPLEVILLE. *Society of St. Vincent de Paul of Providence*, 525 Maureen Cir., 02839. Tel: 401-568-4709; Fax: 401-568-4709. Email: jmar10@cox.net. Web: www.svdpri.org. James Martufi, Pres., Diocesan Council of Providence.

NARRAGANSETT. *Saint Benilde Community Support Charitable Trust*, 635 Ocean Rd., 02882-1314. Tel: 401-789-0244; Fax: 401-783-5303. Email: ddetjefsc@yahoo.com. Bro. David Detje, F.S.C., Sec. & Treas.

NORTH PROVIDENCE. *Franciscan Missionaries of Mary* (1903) 399 Fruit Hill Ave., 02911. Tel: 401-353-5800; Fax: 401-354-8296. Email: almafmm@yahoo.com. Web: www.fmmusa.org.

Mission Resource Center (1988) Tel: 401-353-4470; Fax: 401-353-8779. Email: almafmm@yahoo.com. Sisters Alma Dufault, F.M.M., Dir.; Nzenzili Mboma, F.M.M.

PASCOAG. *The Charles Lwanga Charitable Trust*, 685 Steere Farm Rd., 02859-4601. Tel: 401-568-3361, Ext. 3202; Fax: 401-568-9810. Email: rgagne@bshne.org. Bro. Robert Croteau, S.C., Treasurer & Provincial.

SMITHFIELD. *LC Pastoral Services, Inc.*, 60 Austin Ave., Greenville, 02828. Tel: 401-949-2820; Fax: 401-949-2310. Rev. Jose F. Ortega, L.C., Contact Person.

Mater Ecclesiae, Inc. (1993) 60 Austin Ave., Greenville, 02828. Tel: 401-949-2820; Fax: 401-949-2310; 401-949-0291. Email: matere@ids.net. Web: www.regnumchristi.org. Luly Fernandez, Contact Person.

Vocation Action Circle, Inc., 60 Austin Ave., Greenville, 02828. Tel: 914-773-1368; Fax: 914-773-1438. Rev. Jose F. Ortega, L.C., Contact Person.

SOUTH KINGSTOWN. *Ocean Pastoral Center, Inc.*, 4780 Tower Hill Rd., Wakefield, 02879. Tel: 914-773-1368. Rev. Jose F. Ortega, L.C., Contact Person.

Overbrook, Incorporated, 4780 Tower Hill Rd., Wakefield, 02879. Tel: 914-773-1368. Rev. Jose F. Ortega, L.C., Contact Person.

WARWICK. *Hombre Nuevo (RI), Inc.* (1993) 109 Hardig Rd., 02886. Tel: 914-773-1368; Fax: 914-773-1438.

WEST WARWICK. *Tides Family Services*, 215 Washington St., 02893. Tel: 401-822-1360; Fax: 401-823-4694. Email: mail@tidesfs.org. Web: www.tidesfs.org. Bro. Michael Reis, F.S.C., CEO. Total Staff 90; Total Assisted 2,000.
Branch Offices:
Youth New Futures, 790 Broad St., 02907. Tel: 401-467-8888; Fax: 401-467-8899.
Youth New Futures, 242 Dexter St., Pawtucket, 02860. Tel: 401-724-8100; Fax: 401-724-8899.
Tides' Hispanic Outreach Project, 242 Dexter St., Pawtucket, 02860. Tel: 401-724-8201; Fax: 401-724-8899.
Outreach and Tracking Program, 242 Dexter St., Pawtucket, 02860. Tel: 401-724-8380; Fax: 401-724-8899.
Woonsocket Outreach Project, 55 Main St., Ste. 1, Woonsocket, 02895. Tel: 401-766-9320; Fax: 401-766-9324.
Learning Centers:
242 Dexter St., Pawtucket, 02860. Tel: 401-724-8060; Fax: 401-724-8899.
790 Broad St., 02907. Tel: 401-467-8228; Fax: 401-467-8899.
222 Washington St., 02893. Tel: 401-823-0157; Fax: 401-823-4694.
Youth Diversion Projects:
215 Washington St., 02893. Tel: 401-822-1360; Fax: 401-823-4694.
242 Dexter St., Pawtucket, 02860. Tel: 401-724-8380; Fax: 401-724-8899.
Preserving Families Network
242 Dexter St., Pawtucket, 02860. Tel: 401-724-8380; Fax: 401-724-8899.
55 Main St., Ste. 1, Woonsocket, 02895. Tel: 401-766-9320; Fax: 401-766-9324.
790 Broad St., 02907. Tel: 401-467-8888; Fax: 401-467-8899.
215 Washington St., 02893. Tel: 401-822-1360; Fax: 401-823-4694.

RELIGIOUS INSTITUTES OF MEN REPRESENTED IN THE DIOCESE

For further details refer to the corresponding bracketed number in the Religious Institutes of Men or Women section.

[0200]—*Benedictine Monks*—O.S.B.
[]—*Brothers of Our Lady of Providence*—O.L.P.
[0330]—*Brothers of the Christian Schools* (New England-Long Island Prov.)—F.S.C.
[1100]—*Brothers of the Sacred Heart*—S.C.
[0310]—*Congregation of Christian Brothers*—C.F.C.
[0650]—*Congregation of the Holy Spirit* (Portuguese Prov. & Irish Prov.)—C.S.SP.
[0520]—*Franciscan Friars* (Prov. of the Most Holy Name)—O.F.M.
[0730]—*Legionaires of Christ*—L.C.
[0780]—*Marist Fathers*—S.M.
[1210]—*Missionaries of St. Charles (Scalabrinians)*—C.S.
[0430]—*Order of Preachers (Dominicans)* (Prov. of St. Joseph)—O.P.
[1220]—*Servants of Charity*—S.C.
[0690]—*Society of Jesus*—S.J.
[0370]—*Society of St. Columban*—S.S.C.

RELIGIOUS INSTITUTES OF WOMEN REPRESENTED IN THE DIOCESE

[0350]—*Carmelite Sisters (Corpus Christi)*—O.Carm.
[0990]—*Congregation of Divine Providence*—C.D.P.
[]—*Daughters of Mary Mother of Mercy*—D.M.M.M.
[]—*Daughters of St. Mary of Providence*—D.S.M.P.
[0820]—*Daughters of the Holy Spirit*—D.H.S.
[0420]—*Discalced Carmelite Nuns*—O.C.D.
[1105]—*Dominican Sisters of Hope*—O.P.
[1115]—*Dominican Sisters of Peace*—O.P.
[1100]—*Dominican Sisters of the Presentation*—O.P.
[1070-05]—*Dominicans* (Amityville)—O.P.
[1070-13]—*Dominicans* (Adrian)—O.P.
[1070-15]—*Dominicans* (Blauvelt)—O.P.
[1070-07]—*Dominicans* (St. Cecilia of Nashville, TN)—O.P.
[1070-17]—*Dominicans* (de'Ricci)—O.P.
[1170]—*Felician Sisters*—C.S.S.F.
[]—*Franciscan Apostolic Sisters*—F.A.S.
[1370]—*The Franciscan Missionaries of Mary*—F.M.M.
[1180]—*Franciscan Sisters of Allegheny*—O.S.F.
[3790]—*Institute of the Sisters of St. Dorothy*—S.S.D.
[2340]—*Little Sisters of the Poor*—L.S.P.
[2470]—*Maryknoll Missionaries*—M.M.
[1360]—*Missionary Franciscan Sisters of the Immaculate Conception*—M.F.I.C.
[3230]—*Poor Handmaids of Jesus Christ*—P.H.J.C.
[3450]—*Religious of Jesus and Mary*—R.J.M.
[2070]—*Religious of the Holy Union of the Sacred Hearts*—S.U.S.C.
[4070]—*Religious of the Sacred Heart*—R.S.C.J.
[3430]—*Religious Teachers Filippini*—M.P.F.
[2970]—*School Sisters of Notre Dame*—S.S.N.D.
[2575]—*Sisters of Mercy of the Americas*—R.S.M.
[3000]—*Sisters of Notre Dame de Namur*—S.N.D.deN.
[3720]—*Sisters of Saint Anne*—S.S.A.
[3750]—*Sisters of St. Chretienne*—S.S.CH.
[0590]—*Sisters of St. Elizabeth, Convent Station*—S.C.
[3860]—*Sisters of St. Joseph of Cluny*—S.J.C.
[3830]—*Sisters of St. Joseph of Springfield*—S.S.J.
[]—*Sisters of the Adoration of the Blessed Sacrament*—S.A.B.S.
[0150]—*Sisters of the Assumption*—S.A.S.V.
[2980]—*Sisters of the Congregation of Notre Dame*—C.N.D.

[3180]—*Sisters of the Cross and Passion*—C.P.
[3310]—*Sisters of the Presentation of Mary*—P.M.
[3320]—*Sisters of the Presentation of the B.V.M.*—P.B.V.M.
[4040]—*Society of St. Ursula*—S.U.
[4048]—*Society of the Sisters, Faithful Companions of Jesus*—F.C.J.

DIOCESAN CEMETERIES

PROVIDENCE. *St. Patrick's*
BARRINGTON. *Maria Del Campo*
CRANSTON. *St. Ann's*
CUMBERLAND. *Resurrection*
EAST PROVIDENCE. *Gate of Heaven*
MIDDLETOWN. *St. Columba*
PAWTUCKET. *St. Francis*
Mount St. Mary's
WEST GREENWICH. *St. Joseph*

NECROLOGY

† Cox, Rev. Msgr. John F., (Retired)—Died March 8, 2009
† Maynard, Robert J., (Retired)—Died Feb. 8, 2009

An asterisk (*) denotes an organization that has established tax-exempt status directly with the IRS and is not covered by the USCCB Group Ruling.

Diocese of Pueblo

(Dioecesis Pueblensis)

CARITAS CHRISTI URGET NOS

Most Reverend

FERNANDO ISERN, D.D.

Bishop of Pueblo; ordained April 16, 1993; appointed Bishop of Pueblo October 15, 2009; consecrated and installed December 10, 2009. *Pastoral Center: 101 N. Greenwood, Pueblo, CO 81003.*

Catholic Pastoral Center: 101 N. Greenwood, Pueblo, CO 81003. Tel: 719-544-9861; Fax: 719-544-5202.

Web: www.dioceseofpueblo.com

Email: info@dioceseofpueblo.com

Square Miles 48,155.

Diocesan Patron: St. Therese of the Child Jesus. Secondary Patroness: Our Lady of Guadalupe.

Erected a Diocese November 15, 1941.

Comprises the 29 Counties of Alamosa, Archuleta, Baca, Bent, Conejos, Costilla, Crowley, Custer, Delta, Dolores, Fremont, Gunnison, Hinsdale, Huerfano, Kiowa, La Plata, Las Animas, Mesa, Mineral, Montezuma, Montrose, Otero, Ouray, Prowers, Pueblo, Rio Grande, Saguache, San Juan and San Miguel in the southern and western part of the State of Colorado.

For legal titles of parishes and diocesan institutions, consult the Business Office.

STATISTICAL OVERVIEW

Personnel	
Bishop	1
Retired Bishops	1
Priests: Diocesan Active in Diocese	35
Priests: Diocesan Active Outside Diocese	1
Priests: Diocesan in Foreign Missions	1
Priests: Retired, Sick or Absent	26
Number of Diocesan Priests	63
Religious Priests in Diocese	19
Total Priests in Diocese	82
Extern Priests in Diocese	2
Ordinations:	
Religious Priests	2
Transitional Deacons	1
Permanent Deacons	5
Permanent Deacons in Diocese	44
Total Brothers	2
Total Sisters	56
Parishes	
Parishes	53
With Resident Pastor:	
Resident Diocesan Priests	41
Resident Religious Priests	12
Without Resident Pastor:	
Administered by Deacons	1
Administered by Lay People	1
Missions	46
New Parishes Created	1
Professional Ministry Personnel:	
Brothers	2
Sisters	11
Lay Ministers	54
Welfare	
Catholic Hospitals	5
Total Assisted	925,000
Health Care Centers	2
Total Assisted	5,000
Homes for the Aged	1
Total Assisted	850
Special Centers for Social Services	1
Total Assisted	5,700
Educational	
Diocesan Students in Other Seminaries	4
Total Seminarians	4
Elementary Schools, Diocesan and Parish	3
Total Students	796
Elementary Schools, Private	1
Total Students	95
Catechesis/Religious Education:	
High School Students	2,280
Elementary Students	5,575
Total Students under Catholic Instruction	8,750
Teachers in the Diocese:	
Sisters	7
Lay Teachers	99
Vital Statistics	
Receptions into the Church:	
Infant Baptism Totals	1,582
Minor Baptism Totals	78
Adult Baptism Totals	205
First Communions	1,113
Confirmations	758
Marriages:	
Catholic	199
Interfaith	79
Total Marriages	278
Deaths	1,857
Total Catholic Population	98,400
Total Population	650,000

Former Bishops—Most Revs. JOSEPH CLEMENT WILLGING, D.D., First Bishop of Pueblo; ord. June 20, 1908; appt. Dec. 6, 1941; cons. Feb. 24, 1942; Assistant at Pontifical Throne, Feb. 20, 1958; died March 3, 1959; CHARLES A. BUSWELL, ord. July 9, 1939; appt. Bishop of Pueblo Aug. 8, 1959; cons. Sept. 30, 1959; installed Oct. 6, 1959; retired Sept. 18, 1979; died June 14, 2008.; ARTHUR N. TAFOYA, D.D., ord. May 12, 1962; appt. Bishop of Pueblo July 1, 1980; cons. and installed Sept. 10, 1980; retired Dec. 10, 2009.

Catholic Pastoral Center—101 N. Greenwood Ave., Pueblo, 81003. Tel: 719-544-9861; Fax: 719-544-5202. Office Hours: Mon.-Fri. 7-12 & 1-5.

Vicar General—Rev. Msgr. THOMAS M. ADRIANS, V.G.

Chancellor—Rev. Msgr. MARK A. PLEWKA, J.C.L. Tel: 719-544-9861, Ext. 162.

Diocesan Tribunal—

Judicial Vicar—Rev. Msgr. MARK A. PLEWKA, J.C.L.

Promotor Justitiae—VACANT.

Defensores Vinculi—Rev. GEORGE V. FAGAN, J.C.L.; Ms. DONI R. NEEDHAM. Tel: 719-544-9861, Ext. 161.

Judicial Expert—Rev. Msgr. MARVIN J. KAPUSHION, M.S.W., J.C.L., L.C.S.W. (Retired).

Secretarial to the Tribunal—Ms. DONI NEEDHAM. Tel: 719-544-9861, Ext. 161.

Judge—Rev. Msgr. MARK A. PLEWKA, J.C.L.

Ecclesiastical Notaries—Mrs. THERESA R. FARLEY; Ms. DONI NEEDHAM; Deacon JAKE ARELLANO.

Presbyteral Council-College of Consultors— Ex Officio: Most Rev. ARTHUR N. TAFOYA, D.D., Ex Officio; Rev. Msgrs. MARK A. PLEWKA, J.C.L., Ex Officio. Tel: 719-544-9861, Ext. 162; THOMAS M. ADRIANS, V.G., Chm.; Revs. CARLOS A. ALVAREZ, Vice Chm.; EDMUNDO VALERA, Ph.D.; DONALD P. MALIN; Rev. Msgr. MARVIN J. KAPUSHION, M.S.W., J.C.L., L.C.S.W. (Retired); Rev. NATHANAEL FOSHAGE, O.S.B.

Deans—Revs. KEVIN NOVACK; DERREK D. SCOTT, Alamosa Deanery; JAMES F. KOENIGSFELD, V.F., Durango Deanery; JOHN B. FARLEY, Grand Junction Deanery; DONALD P. MALIN; PHILLIP COURY, C.M.

Archivist—Deacon JAKE ARELLANO.

Diocesan Offices

Administrative Services—

The Bishop of Pueblo, a Corporation Sole—1001 N. Grand Ave., Pueblo, 81003. Tel: 719-544-9861, Ext. 141.

Business and Finance—Tel: 719-544-9861, Ext. 141. Mrs. BARBARA J. DUFF, Dir. Tel: 719-544-9861, Ext. 141.

Finance Advisory Council—Rev. JAMES E. KING, Chm., 611 N. 11th St., Canon City, 81212. Tel: 719-275-7549.

Stewardship—Mrs. BARBARA J. DUFF. Tel: 719-544-9861, Ext. 141.

Development—Mrs. BARBARA J. DUFF. Tel: 719-544-9861, Ext. 141.

Human Resources—Mrs. THERESA R. FARLEY, Dir. Tel: 719-544-9861, Ext. 171.

Liaison for Organizations—Sr. ANDREA VASQUEZ, O.S.B., Contact. Tel: 719-544-9861, Ext. 123.

Department of Pastoral Life—Sr. BETTY WERNER, O.P., Dir. Tel: 719-544-9861, Ext. 114.

Ministry Formation—Sr. BETTY WERNER, O.P. Tel: 719-544-9861, Ext. 114.

Superintendent of Catholic Schools—Sr. BETTY WERNER, O.P. Tel: 719-544-9861, Ext. 114.

Office of Detention Ministry—Deacon JAKE ARELLANO.

Office of Hispanic Ministry—Rev. TOMAS CARVAJAL-BASTRO.

Office of Lifelong Catechesis—Rev. MICHAEL PAPESH, Coord. Tel: 719-544-9861, Ext. 115.

Office of Worship and Spiritual Life—Rev. JOHN OZELLA, Coord. Tel: 719-544-9861, Ext. 117.

O.C.I.A. (R.C.I.A.)—Rev. MICHAEL PAPESH, Contact. Tel: 719-544-9861, Ext. 115.

Diocesan Liturgical Council—Most Rev. FERNANDO ISERN, D.D.

Office of Social Justice—Deacon JAKE ARELLANO, Coord. Tel: 719-544-9861, Ext. 151.

Evangelization—VACANT.

Vocation Office—Deacon MARCO VEGAS. Tel: 719-544-9861, Ext. 116.

Family Life & Youth—VACANT.

Web Master—Mrs. THERESA R. FARLEY. Tel: 719-544-9861, Ext. 171.

Department of Pastoral Outreach—Sr. ANDREA VASQUEZ, O.S.B., Dir. Tel: 719-544-9861, Ext. 123.

Campus Ministry—Sr. ANDREA VASQUEZ, O.S.B. Tel: 719-544-9861, Ext. 123.

Deanery Coordinator—Sr. ANDREA VASQUEZ, O.S.B., Contact. Tel: 719-544-9861, Ext. 123.

Mission Office—Sr. ANDREA VASQUEZ, O.S.B. Tel: 719-544-9861, Ext. 123.

Propagation of the Faith—Sr. ANDREA VASQUEZ, O.S.B., Contact, 1001 N. Grand Ave., Pueblo, 81003. Tel: 719-544-9861, Ext. 123.

Diocesan Newspaper— "The Chronicle of Catholic Life" Most Rev. ARTHUR N. TAFOYA, D.D., Publisher, 1001 Grand Ave., Pueblo, 81003. Tel: 719-544-9861, Ext. 151; JOANN PEARRING, Mng. Editor, 109 Pawnee Ave., Manitou Springs,

80829. Tel: 719-685-5202, Ext. 121.
Resource Library—Ms. JOYCE RIVERA, Clerk. Tel: 719-544-9861, Ext. 121.

Catholic Charities of the Diocese of Pueblo, Inc.—Mr. JOE MAHONEY, Dir., 429 W. 10th St., Ste. 101, Pueblo, 81003. Tel: 719-544-4233; Fax: 719-544-4215.
Victim Assistance Coordinator—Mr. JOE MAHONEY. Tel: 719-544-4233.
Division—Family Counseling Center, 429 W. 10th St., Ste. 101, Pueblo, 81003. Tel: 719-544-4233.

The Bishop Charles A. Buswell Trust—Most Rev. FERNANDO ISERN, D.D., 101 N. Greenwood Ave., Pueblo, 81003. Tel: 719-544-9861, Ext. 151.

Boy Scouts of America—Deacon MIKE ROVELLA, Chap., Mailing Address: 1660 Sneffles, Montrose, 81401. Tel: 970-249-3319; RIK BERGETHON, Committee Chm., 159 McNeil Rd., Pueblo, Co 81001. Tel: 719-544-1255.

Catholic Charismatic Renewal Center—Rev. DON MALIN, Mailing Address: St. Peter the Apostle, 1209 Swink Ave., Rocky Ford, 81067. Tel: 719-254-3565.

Clergy Benefit Society of the Diocese of Pueblo, Inc.—Rev. JAMES E. KING, Pres.

Diocesan Catechetical Council—Most Rev. FERNANDO ISERN, D.D., 101 N. Greenwood Ave., Pueblo, 81003. Tel: 719-544-9861, Ext. 151.

Diocesan Council of Catholic Women—Rev. RICHARD F. BECKER, Moderator, 1145 S. Aspen Rd., Pueblo, 81006. Tel: 719-544-1886.

Diocesan Pastoral Council—MICHELLE WHITNEY, 8 Towerbridge, Pueblo, 81001.

Father John Powers Memorial Basketball League, Inc.—Mr. ROBERT J. DOUGLASS, Contact Person, 144 Harvard Ave., Pueblo, 81004. Tel: 719-544-7192.

Girl Scouts of America—Mrs. LINDA ROOF, 24 Bellflower Ct., Pueblo, 81001. Tel: 719-544-6725.

Human Development Commission of the Diocese of Pueblo—Sr. ANDREA VASQUEZ, O.S.B., 101 N. Greenwood Ave., Pueblo, 81003. Tel: 719-544-9861, Ext. 110.
Catholic Campaign for Human Development—Sr. ANDREA VASQUEZ, O.S.B.

Nocturnal Adoration Society—Sr. GORGONIA PARCERO, S.S.S., 311 E. Mesa Ave., Pueblo, 81006. Tel: 719-545-PRAY.

Presbyteral Council—Most Rev. FERNANDO ISERN, D.D., Pres.; Rev. Msgr. THOMAS M. ADRIANS, V.G., Chm.; Revs. CARLOS A. ALVAREZ; EDMUNDO VALERA, Ph.D.; Rev. Msgrs. MARVIN J. KAPUSHION, M.S.W., J.C.L., L.C.S.W. (Retired); MARK A. PLEWKA, J.C.L., Sec., Ex Officio; Revs. DONALD P. MALIN; NATHANAEL FOSHAGE, O.S.B.
Standing Committees—
Clergy Assemblies—Rev. Msgr. THOMAS M. ADRIANS, V.G., Chm., 1708 Horseshoe Dr., Pueblo, 81001. Tel: 719-542-9248; Deacon STEVE LAMBERT; Rev. Msgr. LEONARD E. RACKI, Treas. (Retired).
Continuing Education and Formation—Rev. KEVIN NOVAK; Mrs. BARBARA J. DUFF, Ex Officio; Revs. CHARLES A. SENA, V.F.; DERREK D. SCOTT; Deacon HENRY WERTIN.
Personnel—Rev. Msgr. THOMAS ADRIANS, Chm.; Revs. BEN BACINO; CARLOS A. ALVAREZ; MARK T. BETTINGER; JAMES F. KOENIGSFELD, V.F.; NATHANAEL FOSHAGE, O.S.B.

**Posada Shelter*Ms. ANNE STATTELMAN, Dir., 1008 N. Grand Ave., Pueblo, 81003. Tel: 719-545-8776.

Clergy Conference of the Diocese of Pueblo—Rev. Msgr. THOMAS M. ADRIANS, V.G., 1708 Horseshoe Dr., Pueblo, 81001. Tel: 719-542-9248.

Las Hermanas de Pueblo—Mrs. ROSEANNA PADILLA, Pres., P.O. Box 4116, Pueblo, 81001. Tel: 719-544-2014.

SEARCH—Ms. SANDY HANSEN, 2 Bearclaw Ct., Pueblo, 81001. Tel: 719-542-6513; 719-320-2707. Email: sandyrose@netzero.net.

Sisters' Council—Sr. ANDREA VASQUEZ, O.S.B., 1001 N. Grand Ave., Pueblo, 81003-2948. Tel: 719-544-9861, Ext. 123.

Legion of Mary—LAURA DEISLA, 2808 W. 29th St., Pueblo, 81008. Tel: 719-543-0787.

Catechetical Ministry—Rev. MICHAEL PAPESH, Coord. Formation. Tel: 719-544-9861, Ext. 115.
Tribunal—Rev. Msgr. MARK A. PLEWKA, J.C.L. Tel: 719-544-9861, Ext. 162.
Holy Childhood, Association—Sr. ANDREA VASQUEZ, O.S.B., Contact, 1001 N. Grand Ave., Pueblo, 81003. Tel: 719-544-9861, Ext. 123.

CLERGY, PARISHES, MISSIONS AND PAROCHIAL SCHOOLS

CITY OF PUEBLO

(PUEBLO COUNTY)

1—SACRED HEART CATHEDRAL (1872) Rev. Msgr. Leonard E. Racki, Rector (Retired).
Parish Office:—414 W. 11th St., 81003. Tel: 719-544-5175; Fax: 719-586-9922. Email: shcathedral@qwest.net. Web: cathedralofthesacredheart-pueblo.com.
Catechesis/Religious Program—Margaret Ursick Leetch, C.R.E. Students 120.

2—ST. ANNE (1956) Rev. John Ozella; Deacon Michael LaConte.
Res.: 2701 E. 12th St., 81001-4708. Tel: 719-545-2644; Fax: 719-542-8089.
Catechesis/Religious Program—Marianne Ortega, C.R.E. Students 26.

3—ST. ANTHONY OF PADUA, Closed. For inquiries for parish records contact the chancery.

4—CHRIST THE KING (1957) Rev. Msgr. Thomas M. Adrians; Deacon Darrell Pagels.
1708 Horseshoe Dr., 81001. Tel: 719-542-9248; Fax: 719-545-9826.
Catechesis/Religious Program—Laura Escalera, D.R.E. Students 235.
Convent—11 MacNaughton Rd., 81001. Tel: 719-543-2465; Fax: 719-545-9826.

5—ST. FRANCIS XAVIER (1903) Rev. Uju Patrick Okeahialam, C.S.S.P., Parish Admin.; Deacons Marco Vegas; Paul Villegas.
611 Logan Ave., 81004. Tel: 719-564-1125; Fax: 719-564-1141.
Catechesis/Religious Program—Elizabeth Mestas, C.R.E. Students 145.
Mission—Our Lady of Lourdes Beulah, Pueblo Co.

6—HOLY FAMILY (1954) Rev. Heriberto Torres, C.R.; Deacon Philip Medina.
Mailing Address: 2827 Lakeview Ave., 81005. Tel: 719-564-2696; Fax: 719-564-4396.
Catechesis/Religious Program—Pam Evanoff, C.R.E. Students 252.
Mission—St. Aloysius (1936) Rye, Pueblo Co. Rev. Msgr. Marvin J. Kapushion (Retired).

7—HOLY ROSARY (1954) Revs. Kevin Novack; Jean-Marie Mondji.
Office: 2400 W. 22nd St., 81003. Tel: 719-545-7219; Fax: 719-545-7259.
Res.: 201 Lamkin St., #403, 81003. Tel: 719-545-3670.
Catechesis/Religious Program—Christine Armstrong, D.R.E. Students 13.

8—ST. JOSEPH (1960) Rev. William T. Gleeson; Deacon Peter A. Massaro. In Res., Rev. Kevin J. Bachmann, O.S.B.
Office: 1145 S. Aspen Rd., 81006. Tel: 719-544-1886; 719-543-0835; Fax: 719-544-5137.
Catechesis/Religious Program—Maria Lopez, D.R.E. Students 262.

9—ST. LEANDER (1902) Rev. Anthony A. Wojcinski; Deacon Edward Riccillo.
Office: 1402 E. Seventh St., 81001. Tel: 719-544-8411; Fax: 719-544-8202.
Catechesis/Religious Program—Jari Trujillo, C.R.E. Students 210.

10—ST. MARY HELP OF CHRISTIANS (1895) Rev. Ben Bacino; Deacon Rick Oreskey.
217 E. Mesa Ave., 81006. Tel: 719-296-8778; Fax: 719-562-1195.
Catechesis/Religious Program—Belinda Castro, C.R.E. Students 54.

11—OUR LADY OF GUADALUPE CHAPEL (1968) Closed. For inquiries for parish records please contact St. Leander, Pueblo.

12—OUR LADY OF MT. CARMEL (1901) Rev. Matthew Wertin; Deacon Steve Lumbert.
421 Clark St., 81003. Tel: 719-542-5952; Fax: 719-542-2310.
Catechesis/Religious Program—Theresa Almeda, C.R.E. Students 160.

13—OUR LADY OF THE ASSUMPTION (1949) Closed. For inquiries for parish records contact the chancery.

14—OUR LADY OF THE MEADOWS (1979) Revs. Kevin Novack; Jean-Marie Mondji; Deacon Stephen Escalera.
23 Starling Dr., 81005. Tel: 719-561-3580; Fax: 719-561-1271.
Catechesis/Religious Program—Christine Armstrong, D.R.E. Students 211.

15—ST. PATRICK (1882) Closed. For inquiries for parish records contact the chancery.

16—ST. PAUL THE APOSTLE (2009) Rev. Edward Nunez; Deacon Michael Sanchez.
1132 W. Oro Grande Dr., P.O. Box 7199, 81007.
Catechesis/Religious Program—Students 176.

17—ST. PIUS X (1955) Rev. J. William Huber; Deacon Roy Stringfellow. Call St. Pius X for information.
Parish Center—3130 Morris Ave., 81008. Tel: 719-542-4264; Fax: 719-583-8103.
Catechesis/Religious Program—142 Stardust Dr., Pueblo West, 81007. Students 95.

18—SHRINE OF ST. THERESE (1948) Rev. William "Liam" Courtney; Deacon John Wertz; Joseph Chrisman, Liturgy Dir.
300 Goodnight Ave., 81004. Tel: 719-542-1788; Fax: 719-542-2130.
Catechesis/Religious Program—Sarah Nelson, C.R.E. Students 142.

OUTSIDE THE CITY OF PUEBLO

AGUILAR, LAS ANIMAS CO., ST. ANTHONY (1875), (Spanish—Italian), [CEM] [JC] Rev. Phillip Coury, C.M.
Mailing Address: P.O. Box 577, 81020. Tel: 719-941-4124; Fax: 719-941-4124.
Catechesis/Religious Program—Amy Wilson, C.R.E. Students 24.

ALAMOSA, ALAMOSA CO., SACRED HEART (1887) Rev. Derrek D. Scott; Deacon Andres Hernandez; Mrs. Marianne Dunne, Pastoral Assoc.; Sr. Johnette Sawyer, Pastoral Assoc.
Mailing Address: 726 3rd St., P.O. Box 547, 81101. Tel: 719-589-5829 (Parish Center); Fax: 719-589-5820.
Catechesis/Religious Program—Students 276.

AVONDALE, PUEBLO CO., SACRED HEART (1960), (Spanish), Rev. William T. Gleeson.
Mailing Address: P.O. Box 279, 81022. Tel: 719-947-3092; Fax: 719-947-3082.
Catechesis/Religious Program—Students 50.

CANON CITY, FREMONT CO., ST. MICHAEL (1880) Rev. James E. King; Deacon Merle E. Runck.
611 N. 11th St., 81212. Tel: 719-275-7549; Fax: 719-275-7540. Email: stmikes@ris.net.
Catechesis/Religious Program—1016 Mystic, 81212. Tel: 719-275-3368. Students 126.

CAPULIN, CONEJOS CO., ST. JOSEPH (1912), (Hispanic), [CEM] Revs. Anthony Blount, S.O.L.T., Admin.; Baykil Williams, S.O.L.T.; Scott Giuliani, S.O.L.T.
Mailing Address: P.O. Box 40, 81124. Tel: 719-274-5304; Fax: 719-274-4454.
Catechesis/Religious Program—Sr. Mary Ann Richwald, S.O.L.T., C.R.E. Students 241.
Mission—Our Lady of the Valley 19617 S. Hwy. 285, La Jara, Conejos Co. 81140. Tel: 719-274-5647.
Mission—St. Therese of the Child Jesus 115 Main St., Manassa, Conejos Co. 81141.
Mission—St. Anthony 18900 County Rd. 28, Los Sauces, Conejos Co. 81151.
Mission—Our Lady of the Immaculate Conception 211 Blanca St., Romeo, Conejos Co. 81148.

CENTER, SAGUACHE CO., ST. FRANCIS JEROME (1951), (San Juan Catholic Community) Revs. Joseph A. Vigil, Admin.; Jose de Jesus Martinez; Deacons Donald Lamb; Jesus Ruiz.
781 Warden St., 81125. Tel: 719-754-3969; Fax: 719-754-3964. Mailing Address: P.O. Box 590, Monte Vista, 81144. Tel: 719-852-0623; Fax: 719-852-0623.
Catechesis/Religious Program—Students 102.
Mission—St. Agnes P.O. Box 590, Monte Vista, 81144.
Station—Sanctuary House Retreat Center Crestone. Tel: 719-256-4778; Fax: 719-256-4719.

CONEJOS, CONEJOS CO., OUR LADY OF GUADALUPE (1857) [CEM] Rev. Sergio Cardenas-Robles, C.R.
Mailing Address: P.O. Box 305, Antonito, 81120. Tel: 719-376-5985; Fax: 719-376-2530. 6633 Co. Rd. 13, 81129.
Catechesis/Religious Program—Renee DuPont, D.R.E.
Mission—St. Augustine 305 8th Ave., Antonito, 81120.
Mission—Sagrada Familia Antonito. 17344 Co. Rd. G, Lobatos, Conejos Co. 81120.
Mission—San Juan Nepomuceno y San Cayetano Antonito. 684 Co. Rd. B, Ortiz, Conejos Co. 81120.
Mission—San Antonio de Padua Antonito. 13148 Co. Rd. C, San Antonio, Conejos Co. 81120.
Mission—San Pedro y San Rafael Antonito. 5308 Co. Rd. 10.75, San Rafael, Conejos Co. 81120.
Mission—San Isidro Brador Las Mesitas, Conejos Co.

CORTEZ, MONTEZUMA CO., ST. MARGARET MARY (1945) Rev. Joseph Gallegos, C.R.
Mailing Address: 28 E. Montezuma, 81321. Tel: 970-565-7308 (Office); Fax: 970-565-0822.
Catechesis/Religious Program—Kevin Ketterell, D.R.E. Students 58.
Mission—St. Jude 313 N. Pine, Dove Creek, Dolores Co. 81324.

CRESTED BUTTE, GUNNISON CO., QUEEN OF ALL SAINTS (1883) Attended by St. Peter Parish, Gunnison. Rev. Steven J. Murray; Deacons Vincent Rogalski; John Stroop; Joseph W. Fitzpatrick.
303 N. Wisconsin, Gunnison, 81230.
Church: 400 W. Georgia, Gunnison, 81230. Tel: 970-641-0808; Fax: 970-641-4592.
Catechesis/Religious Program—405 Sopris. Students 50.

DEL NORTE, RIO GRANDE CO., HOLY NAME OF MARY (1879) [CEM], (San Juan Catholic Community) Revs. Joseph A. Vigil; Jose de Jesus Martinez; Deacons Donald Lamb; Jesus Ruiz.
Mailing Address: P.O. Box 590, Monte Vista, 81144. Tel: 719-852-2673; Fax: 719-852-0623. 645 Pine Ave., P.O. Box 97, 81132. Tel: 719-657-3147; Fax: 719-657-2855.
Catechesis / Religious Program—Denise Fietek, C.R.E. Students 61.
Mission—St. Francis of Assisi Los Valdeses, Rio Grande Co.
Mission—Holy Family South Fork, Rio Grande Co.
Mission—Immaculate Conception Creede, Mineral Co.

DELTA, DELTA CO., ST. MICHAEL (1911) Rev. Henry Aguwa, S.M.M.M.
Parish Office: 628 Meeker St., 81416. Tel: 970-874-3300; Fax: 970-874-4015.
Res.: 628 Meeker St., 81416. Tel: 970-874-5116.
Mission—St. Philip Benizi P.O. Box 713, Cedaredge, Delta Co. 81413. Tel: 970-856-6495.

DURANGO, LA PLATA CO.
1—ST. COLUMBA (1881) Rev. James F. Koenigsfeld; Deacon Milton Van Cleave; Mary Therese Ralph, Pastoral Assoc. & Youth Min.
1830 E. Second Ave., 81301. Tel: 970-247-0044; Fax: 970-385-5737.
School—(Grades PreK-8) Tel: 970-247-5527; Fax: 970-382-9355. Sisters of St. Dominic 2; Lay Teachers 27; Students 254.
Catechesis / Religious Program—Beth Parrott, D.R.E. Students 163.
2—SACRED HEART (1906), (Hispanic), Rev. Antonio Flores; Deacon Joseph Dunne.
254 E. Fifth Ave., 81301. Tel: 970-247-3997; Fax: 970-375-2385. Email: birdsheart@frontier.net.
Catechesis / Religious Program—Students 70.

FLORENCE, FREMONT CO., ST. BENEDICT (1895) Rev. Vincente Paz en la Casa; Deacons Larry Yatch; Michael Patterson.
622 W. Second St., 81226. Tel: 719-784-4879; Fax: 719-784-2070.
Mission—St. Patrick Rockvale, Fremont Co.

FRUITA, MESA CO., SACRED HEART (1890) Rev. Michael N. Smith, S.J.
Mailing Address: 513 E. Aspen Ave., 81521. Tel: 970-858-9605; Fax: 970-858-9605. Email: sacredheartfruita@bresnan.net. Web: sacredheartfruita.home.bresnan.net.
Catechesis / Religious Program—Noreen C. Juarez-Alexander, C.R.E. Students 75.

GARDNER, HUERFANO CO., SACRED HEART (1912) Rev. Martin Frias; Deacon John Luginbill.
Mailing Address: P.O. Box 86, Walsenburg, 81089. Tel: 719-738-1204; Fax: 719-738-1206.

GRAND JUNCTION, MESA CO.
1—IMMACULATE HEART OF MARY (1955) Rev. John B. Farley; Beverly Goodrich, Pastoral Assoc.
790 26 1/2 Rd., 81506. Tel: 970-242-6121; Fax: 970-256-0276.
Catechesis / Religious Program—Irene Fritzler, D.R.E. Students 219.
Mission—St. Ann 535 W. 1st St., Palisade, Mesa Co. 81526. Tel: 970-464-5157.
Station— Debeque.
Station— Collbran.
2—ST. JOSEPH (1884) Rev. Edmundo Valera; Carmen Fuller, Liturgy Dir.; Deacon Douglas Van Houten.
Mailing Address: 230 N. Third, 81501. Tel: 970-243-0209; Fax: 970-243-7493.
School—Holy Family School, 786 26 1/2 Rd., 81506. Tel: 970-242-6168; 970-241-1489; Fax: 970-242-4244. Ms. Ann Ashwood-Piper, Prin. Sisters 3; Lay Teachers 21; Students 365.
Catechesis / Religious Program—Sr. Rebecca Wolf, D.R.E. Students 257.

GUNNISON, GUNNISON CO., ST. PETER (1881) Rev. Steven J. Murray; Deacons Vincent Rogalski, Pastoral Assoc.; Lloyd Hawes.
Catechesis / Religious Program—400 W. Georgia Ave. Tel: 970-641-0268; Fax: 970-641-4592.
Mission—St. Rose of Lima

HOLLY, PROWERS CO., ST. FRANCES OF ROME (1920) Revs. Charlie Sena, Admin.; Albeiro Herrera-Ciro. Church: 130 S. Fifth St., P. O. Box 130, 81047. Tel: 719-537-6688. Email: stfrances@live.com.
Catechesis / Religious Program—Debra Crossland, C.R.E.; Stephanie Gonzales, C.R.E.
Mission—St. Mary Bristol, Prowers Co.

IGNACIO, LA PLATA CO., ST. IGNATIUS PARISH (1898) Rev. Doug Hunt; Deacons John O'Hare; Larry Tucker.
Mailing Address: P.O. Box 1350, 81137. Tel: 970-563-4241; Fax: 970-563-1032.
Catechesis / Religious Program—Students 36.
Mission—St. Bartholemew
Mission—SS. Peter & Rose R.R. 2, Arboles, Archuleta Co. 81137.
Station— Tiffany.

LA JUNTA, OTERO CO., OUR LADY OF GUADALUPE/ST. PATRICK (1889) Rev. Alphonsus Ihuoma; Deacon Douglas Manley.
222 Lincoln St., Box 1181, 81050. Tel: 719-384-4342; 719-384-4372; Fax: 719-384-7894.
Catechesis / Religious Program—Students 168.

LAMAR, PROWERS CO., ST. FRANCIS DE SALES-OUR LADY OF GUADALUPE (1907) Revs. Charlie Sena; Albeiro Herrera-Ciro; Deacons Allan J. Medina; Henry J. Wertin.
600 E. Parmenter St., 81052. Tel: 719-336-7759; Fax: 719-336-0291.
Catechesis / Religious Program—Tel: 719-336-7750.

LAS ANIMAS, BENT CO., ST. MARY (1910) Rev. Raymond P. Grimes (Retired).
714 Elm Ave., 81054. Tel: 719-456-0357; Fax: 719-456-1104.
Catechesis / Religious Program—Students 21.

MANCOS, MONTEZUMA CO., ST. RITA (1914) Rev. Joseph Gallegos, C.R.
Mailing Address: 28 E. Montezuma Ave., Cortez, 81321. Tel: 970-565-7308; Fax: 970-565-0822.
203 S. Main St., 81328.
Catechesis / Religious Program—Students 4.
Mission—Our Lady of Victory Church Cortez, Montezuma, Co. 81321.
Mission—Immaculate Heart of Mary Chapel Rico, Dolores Co. Tel: 970-565-7307.

MONTE VISTA, RIO GRANDE CO., ST. JOSEPH (1920), (San Juan Catholic Community) Revs. Joseph A. Vigil; Jose de Jesus Martinez; Deacons Don Lamb. Tel: 719-852-3773; Jesus Ruiz.
Mailing Address: P.O. Box 590, 81144. 425 Batterson, 81144. Tel: 719-852-4590 (Rectory #1); 719-852-0644 (Rectory #2); Fax: 719-852-0623; 719-852-2673 (Parish Hall).
Catechesis / Religious Program—Greg Kelso, C.R.E. Students 122.
Station— Lariate.
Station— Morada.
Station—Mountain Meadows Nursing Center, Tel: 719-852-5138.
Station—Colorado State Veterans Center Homelake. Tel: 719-852-5118.
Station—High Valley Manor, Tel: 719-852-5711.

MONTROSE, MONTROSE CO., ST. MARY (1906) Rev. Mark T. Bettinger; Deacons Dennis Putnam, (Retired); Michael Rovella.
Catechesis / Religious Program—Students 117.
Parish Center:—1855 St. Mary's Dr., 81401. Tel: 970-249-3319; Fax: 970-249-9088.
Mission—Our Lady of Fatima, Tel: 970-323-5146.

OURAY, OURAY CO., ST. DANIEL THE PROPHET (1883) Rev. Nathanael Foshage, O.S.B.
Mailing Address: P.O. Box 565, 81427. Tel: 970-325-4373.
Catechesis / Religious Program—Valerie Hill, D.R.E. Students 39.
Mission—St. Patrick 1005 Reece, Silverton, San Juan Co. 81433.

PAGOSA SPRINGS, ARCHULETA CO., IMMACULATE HEART OF MARY (1923), (Hispanic), [CEM] Rev. Carlos A. Alvarez; Deacons Patrick McKenzie; E. Jerome Sadler.
Mailing Address: P.O. Box 4759, 81147. Tel: 970-731-5744; Fax: 970-264-3166.
Catechesis / Religious Program—Students 113.
Mission—St. Francis Frances, Archuleta Co.
Mission—St. John Baptist Pagosa Junction, Archuleta Co.
Mission—St. James Trujillo, Archuleta Co.
Station— Chromo.

PAONIA, DELTA CO., SACRED HEART (1923) Rev. William R. Nelson.
235 N. Fork Ave., P.O. Box 988, 81428. Tel: 970-527-3214; Fax: 970-527-5468.
Catechesis / Religious Program—Students 45.
Mission—St. Margaret Mary 331 Bridge St., Hotchkiss, Delta Co. 81419. Tel: 973-872-2117.

ROCKY FORD, OTERO CO., ST. PETER (1910) Rev. Don Malin; Deacons Daniel Leetch Jr.; Terry Marinelli. 1209 Swink Ave., 81067. Tel: 719-254-3565; Fax: 719-254-3921.
Catechesis / Religious Program—Connie Fernandez, C.R.E. Students 181.
Mission—St. Joseph the Worker, Closed. Sacramental records can be found at St. Peter, Rocky Ford, 1209 Swink Ave., Rocky Ford, CO 81067-1899.
Mission—St. Peter Chapel 905 Main St., Ordway, Crowley Co. 81063. Tel: 719-267-4645.
Mission—Mary Queen of Heaven 602 7th St., P.O. Box 214, Fowler, Otero Co. 81039. Tel: 719-263-4455.

SAN LUIS, COSTILLA CO., SANGRE DE CRISTO (1881), (Hispanic), [CEM] Rev. Mauricio Cuenca-Wilson.
Res.: P.O. Box 326, 81152. Tel: 719-672-3685; 719-672-3020 (Rectory); Fax: 719-672-0300.
Catechesis / Religious Program—Students 75.
Mission—St. James Blanca, Costilla Co.
Mission—Holy Family Fort Garland, Costilla Co.
Mission—Immaculate Conception Chama, Costilla Co.
Mission—San Acacio San Acacio, Costilla Co.
Mission—SS. Peter and Paul San Pedro, Costilla Co.
Mission—St. Isidro San Isidro, Costilla Co.
Mission—St. Francis of Assisi San Francisco, Costilla Co.
Mission—Sacred Heart of Jesus Garcia, Costilla Co.

SILVERTON, SAN JUAN CO., ST. PATRICK (1883) Rev. Nathanael Foshage, O.S.B.
Mailing Address: P.O. Box 565, Ouray, 81427. Tel: 970-325-4373.

SPRINGFIELD, BACA CO., ANNUNCIATION (1932) Revs. Charlie Sena, Admin.; Albeiro Herrera-Ciro.
140 Kansas St., 81073. Tel: 719-537-6688.
Catechesis / Religious Program—Students 60.
Station— Walsh.

TELLURIDE, SAN MIGUEL CO., ST. PATRICK (1896) Rev. Nathanael Foshage, O.S.B., Supvr.; Deacon Michael Doehrman, Parish Dir.
Mailing Address: P.O. Box 398, 81435. Tel: 970-728-3387; Fax: 970-728-8029.
Mission—Our Lady of Sorrows P.O. Box 451, Nucla, Montrose Co. 81424.

TRINIDAD, LAS ANIMAS CO.
1—ST. JOSEPH, TRINIDAD AREA CATHOLIC COMMUNITY (TRINIDAD CLUSTER), Closed. For inquiries for parish records contact Most Holy Trinity, 719-846-3369.
2—MOST HOLY TRINITY, TRINIDAD AREA CATHOLIC COMMUNITY (TRINIDAD CLUSTER) (1885) [CEM] Revs. Richard F. Becker; Ogechukww Kieran Alaribe, O.S.B.; Deacon Phil Martin.
235 N. Convent St., 81082. Tel: 719-846-3369; Fax: 719-846-4856.
Catechesis / Religious Program—Bro. Henry Gonzale, D.R.E. Students 348.
Mission—St. Isidore Vigil, Las Animas Co.
Mission—St. Ignatius Segundo, Las Animas Co.
3—OUR LADY OF MT. CARMEL, TRINIDAD AREA CATHOLIC COMMUNITY (TRINIDAD CLUSTER), Closed. For inquiries for parish records contact Most Holy Trinity, 719-846-3369.

VINELAND, PUEBLO CO., ST. THERESE (1928) Rev. William T. Gleeson.
Mailing Address: 1145 S. Aspen Rd., 81006. Tel: 719-948-2410; 719-544-1886; Fax: 719-544-5137.
Catechesis / Religious Program—Maria Lopez, D.R.E. Students 10.

WALSENBURG, HUERFANO CO., ST. MARY (1896) [CEM] Rev. Martin Frias; Deacon John Luginbill; Sr. Carol Tlach, S.N.D., Pastoral Assoc.
Mailing Address: P.O. Box 86, 81089. Tel: 719-738-1204; Fax: 719-738-1206.
Catechesis / Religious Program—Students 32.
Mission—Christ the King P.O. Box 752, La Veta, Huerfano Co. 81055.
Mission—Sacred Heart P.O. Box 228, Gardner, Huerfano Co. 8104.

WESTCLIFFE, CUSTER CO., OUR LADY OF THE ASSUMPTION (1870) Rev. Vicente Paz en La Casa; Deacon Michael Patterson.
Mailing Address: P.O. Box 359, 81252. Tel: 719-783-2340.
Catechesis / Religious Program—Joan Kohler, D.R.E. Students 32.

Chaplains of Public Institutions

PUEBLO. *Colorado State Hospital*, Tel: 719-546-4434. Vacant.
St. Mary Corwin Medical Center, 1008 Minnequa Ave., 81004. Tel: 719-560-4000. Rev. Gary L. Kennedy.
Parkview Hospital. Rev. Michael C. DeSciose, 1070 Moccasin Dr., 81007.

CANON CITY. *Fremont Correctional Facility*, St. Dismas Chapel, 81212. Vacant.

CROWLEY. *Arkansas Valley Correctional Facility*. Vacant.

TRINIDAD. *State Home for the Aged*. Vacant. Administered by priests from Trinity Area Catholic Community.

On Duty Outside the Diocese:
Revs.—
Haberman, C. Robert, Asst. Professor/Dir. of Campus Min., 50 Acadia, San Rafael, CA 94901. Tel: 415-479-1249
Lopez, Ezequiel Padilla, C.R., Archdiocese of Denver
Norman, Clifford A., APO Postal #13 CP 76270 Mexico. Tel: 011-52-429-2-02-48; Fax: 011-52-429-2-00-46

Absent on Leave:
Revs.—
Bonfadini, Leo
Bouchard, Norman
Thill, Richard

Trujillo, Carlos B.
Vandenberg, James

Retired:
Rev. Msgrs.—
Delaney, Howard L., 5-A Bonnymede, 81001. Tel: 719-542-4387
Holland, George T., 2204 Wyoming Ave., 81004. Tel: 719-561-8697
Huber, Daniel R., 1648 Weatherby Ln., 81008.
Kapushion, Marvin J., M.S.W., J.C.L., L.C.S.W., 620 E. Routt, 81004. Tel: 719-545-4599
Racki, Leonard E., 31 Terrace Dr., 81001. Tel: 719-583-1988
Revs.—
Cavanagh, Michael J., Church of St. Michael, 56 Wentworth, Westwood, MA 02090. Tel: 617-326-8764
Cerwonka, Clarence J. (SY), 37 Fayette St., Binghamton, NY 13905. Tel: 607-723-5383
Corbett, Michael E., 2110 "B" Chatalet Ln., 81005. Tel: 719-566-9836
Costanzo, John J., 4947 King St., Denver, 80221. Tel: 303-477-4853
Danowski, Alexander J., 653 Country Ct., Grand Junction, 81504-5907. Tel: 970-434-7531
Gallagher, Maurice O., 1420 Murillo Ln., Boone, 81025. Tel: 719-947-9812
Grimes, Raymond P., St. Mary Parish, 652 Elm Ave., Las Animas, 81054-1738.
Kiernan, John G., 2185 Linda Ln., Grand Junction, 81501. Tel: 970-241-8035
Marcantonio, Clement, LRMC 799 CMR 402, Apo, AE 09180.
O'Flynn, John, 23 Churchill Pl., 81001.
Perez, Jesse L., 321 E. 6th St., Salida, 81201.
Pettit, Edward G. (DEN), Mesa Towers, 260 Lamar Ave., #411, 81004. Tel: 719-595-0217
Plough, James H., 711-B Fountainhead Blvd., Grand Junction, 81506. Tel: 970-255-1228
Powers, William V., 1414 E. 8th St., 81001. Tel: 719-542-1688
Quinn, Thomas J., S.J., P.O. Box 607, South Fork, 81154. Tel: 719-657-3147
Roche, Ron, 1912 Vinewood Ln., 81005. Tel: 719-565-0813
Rykowski, Jerome A., 587 Eastwood St., Grand Junction, 81504-4814. Tel: 970-243-6234
Schoening, Sylvester H., Hermitage, 1250 Mountain View Ln., P.O. Box 553, Norwood, 81423. Tel: 970-327-4346
Smigiel, Walter J., 3517 Atlantic Dr., Colorado Springs, 80910. Tel: 719-596-4294

Permanent Deacons:
Arellano, Jake, Assistant to the Bishop
Doehrman, Michael J., Parish Dir., Telluride/Nucla
Duarte, Margarito, Holy Family, Fort Garland
Dunne, Joseph, Sacred Heart, Durango
Escalera, Stephen, Our Lady of the Meadows, Pueblo
Fitzpatrick, Joseph W., Queen of All Saints, Crested Butte
Hawes, Lloyd, St. Peter, Gunnison
Hernandez, Andres, St. Margaret Mary, Cortez
LaConte, Michael, St. Anne, Pueblo
Lamb, Donald, St. Joseph, Monte Vista
Leetch, Daniel, Jr., St. Peter, Rocky Ford
Luginbill, John, St. Mary, Walsenburg
Lumbert, Steven, Mt. Carmel, Pueblo
Manley, Douglas, Our Lady of Guadalupe/St. Patrick, La Junta
Marinelli, Terry, St. Peter, Rocky Ford
Martin, Philip, Holy Trinity, Trinidad
Massaro, Peter A., St. Joseph, Pueblo
McKenzie, Patrick, Immaculate Heart of Mary, Pagosa Springs
Medina, Allan J., St. Francis de Sales/Our Lady of Guadalupe, Lamar
O'Hare, John, St. Ignatius, Ignacio & St. Bartholomew, Bayfield
Oreskey, Richard, St. Mary Help of Christians, Pueblo
Pagels, Darrell, Christ the King, Pueblo
Patterson, Michael, St. Benedict, Florence; Our Lady of the Assumption, Westcliffe
Putnam, Dennis, (Retired), St. Mary, Montrose
Reynolds, Philip, (Retired), St. Mary Help of Christians, Pueblo
Riccillo, Edward, St. Leander, Pueblo
Rodriguez, Buddy P., Sacred Heart, Avondale
Rogalski, Vincent, Queen of All Saints, Crested Butte
Rovella, Mike, St. Mary, Montrose
Ruiz, Jesus, St. Joseph, Monte Vista
Runck, Merle, St. Michael, Canon City
Sadler, Jerome, Immaculate Heart of Mary, Pagosa Springs
Sanchez, Michael, Our Lady of Mt. Carmel, Pueblo
Shafer, Jacob, Sacred Heart Cathedral
Stroop, John, Queen of All Saints, Crested Butte
Tucker, Lawrence, St. Ignatius, Ignacio
Van Cleave, Milton, Sacred Heart, Durango
Van Houten, Douglas, St. Joseph, Grand Junction
Vegas, Marco, St. Francis Xavier, Pueblo
Villegas, Paul, St. Francis, Pueblo
Wertin, Henry, St. Francis de Sales, Lamar
Wertz, John, Shrine of St. Therese, Pueblo
Yatch, Lawrence, St. Benedict, Florence

INSTITUTIONS LOCATED IN THE DIOCESE

[A] ELEMENTARY SCHOOLS, DIOCESAN

PUEBLO. *St. Therese Catholic School*, 320 Goodnight Ave., 81004. Tel: 719-561-1121; Fax: 719-561-2252. Web: www.sttherese-school.org. John Brainard, Prin. Lay Teachers 14; Total Enrollment 145.

DURANGO. *St. Columba*, (Grades PreK-8), 1801 E. 3rd Ave., 81301-5072. Tel: 970-247-5527; Fax: 970-382-9355. Email: saintc@frontier.net. Sr. Edith Marie Hauser, O.P., Prin. Sisters 2; Lay Teachers 24; Students 244.

GRAND JUNCTION. *Holy Family Catholic School*, (Grades PreK-8), 786 26 1/2 Rd., 81506. Tel: 970-242-6168; Fax: 970-242-4244. Web: holyfamily-gj.org. Ms. Ann Ashwood-Piper, Prin. Sisters 3; Lay Teachers 30; Students 413.

[B] ELEMENTARY SCHOOLS, PRIVATE

PUEBLO. *St. John Neumann Catholic Schools*, (Grades PreK-8), 2415 E. Orman Ave., 81004. Tel: 719-561-9419; Fax: 719-561-4718. Email: admissions@john-neumann.com. Web: www.john-neumann.com. Joyce Baca-Anderson, Admin. Lay Teachers 12; Students 96.

[C] GENERAL HOSPITALS

PUEBLO. *Centura Health-St. Mary-Corwin Medical Center*, 1008 Minnequa Ave., 81004. Tel: 719-557-4000; Fax: 719-557-5823. Web: www.stmarycorwin.org. Mr. Rob Ryder, CEO; Eileen Perez, Contact Person; Rev. Gary L. Kennedy, Chap.; Ms. Michele des Lauriers, Mission Integration; Sr. Darleen Maloney, O.S.F. An operating unit of Catholic Health Initiatives Colorado (an affiliate of Catholic Health Initiatives). Bed Capacity 408; Total Staff 970; Patients Assisted Annually 151,759.

CANON CITY. *Centura Health-St. Thomas More Hospital*, 1338 Phay Ave., 81212. Tel: 719-285-2000; Fax: 719-285-2016. Web: www.stthomas.org. Mrs. Diane Swagger, CEO; Rev. Tema Godwin Nnamezie, Chap. An operating unit of Catholic Health Initiatives Colorado (an affiliate of Catholic Health Initiatives). Bed Capacity 256; Patients Assisted Annually 72,252.

DURANGO. *Mercy Regional Medical Center*, 1010 Three Springs Blvd., 81301. Tel: 970-247-4311. Web: www.mercydurango.org. Kirk Dignum, Ph.D., Pres. & CEO. An operating unit of Catholic Health Initiatives Colorado (an affiliate of Catholic Health Initiatives). Beds 83; Patients Assisted Annually 239,925; Total Staff 724.
Chaplains: John Boyd, Chief Medical & Mission Officer; Diana McKenna, Contact & Dir., Mission & Spiritual Care.

GRAND JUNCTION. *Marillac Clinic, Inc.*, 2333 N. 6th St., 81501. Tel: 970-255-1782; 970-255-1799; Fax: 970-255-1711. Email: steve.hurd@stmarygj.org. Steve Hurd, Ph.D., Exec. Dir.
Sisters of Charity of Leavenworth Health System Total Staff 75; Total Assisted 38,069.
St. Mary Hospital and Medical Center, P.O. Box 1628, 81502-1628. Tel: 970-244-2273; Fax: 970-244-2891. Web: www.stmarygj.com. Email: pmontgomery@stmarygj.com. Mr. Robert W. Ladenburger, Pres. & CEO; Pat Montgomery, Exec. Asst. Sisters of Charity of Leavenworth, Kansas 10; Bed Capacity 354; Patients Assisted Annually 350,440; Total Staff 1,800.

[D] SPECIAL CARE FACILITIES

PUEBLO. *Centura Health-Villa Pueblo*, 1111 Bonforte Blvd., 81001. Tel: 719-545-5911; 303-964-2355 (Chap. Svcs.); Fax: 719-544-1354. Barbara Carochi, Exec. Dir.; Rev. Ron Kruis, Chap.; Sr. Jacki Leech, S.C., Contact Person & Dir., Senior Svc. An operating unit of Catholic Health Initiatives Colorado (an affiliate of Catholic Health Initiatives).

CANON CITY. *Centura Health-Progressive Care Center*, 1338 Phay Ave., 81212. Tel: 719-285-2540; Fax: 719-285-2256. Steven R. Lawson, Admin. An operating unit of Catholic Health Initiatives Colorado (an affiliate of Catholic Health Initiatives). Bed Capacity 116; Total Staff 98.

[E] MONASTERIES AND RESIDENCES OF PRIESTS AND BROTHERS

TRINIDAD. *Trinidad Area Catholic Community*, Rectory, 235 N. Convent St., 81082. Tel: 719-846-3360; Fax: 719-846-4856. Rev. Richard F. Becker, Supr.

[F] CONVENTS AND RESIDENCES FOR SISTERS

PUEBLO. *Servants of the Blessed Sacrament*, 311 E. Mesa Ave., 81006. Tel: 719-545-7729; Fax: 719-542-3094. Email: ssspueblo@juno.com. Web: www.blesacrament.org. Sisters 3.

[G] NEWMAN CENTERS

PUEBLO. *Campus Ministry - Diocese of Pueblo* 1001 N. Grand Ave., 81003. Tel: 719-544-9861, Ext. 123; Fax: 719-544-1220. Sr. Andrea Vasquez, O.S.B.
Adams State College (Alamosa) United Campus Ministry College Center, Rm. 329, P.O. Box 1164, Alamosa, 81102-9986. Tel: 719-587-7516. Ms. Shirley Atencio, Campus Minister.
Fort Lewis College (Durango) Fort Lewis College Center for Campus Ministry, 1830 E. 2nd Ave., Durango, 81301. Tel: 970-247-0044. Ms. Wivina Vigil, Campus Minister.
Mesa State College (Grand Junction) Newman Center, 875 Bunting, Grand Junction, 81501. Tel: 970-241-3670. Ms. Janet Johnson, Campus Min.
Western State College (Gunnison) Campus Ministry Center, 600 E. Georgia, Gunnison, 81230. Tel: 970-901-5973. Ms. Susan Searle, Campus Min.
Colorado State University - Pueblo 419 Petroleum Ave., Florence, 81226. Tel: 719-549-2089. Joyce Archuletta, Campus Min.

[H] RETREAT WORK

CRESTONE. *Spiritual Life Institute of America, Inc.*, P.O. Box 219, 81131. Tel: 719-256-4778; Fax: 719-256-4719. Email: nada@fone.net. Web: www.spirituallifeinstitute.org. Revs. Eric Hoarer, Prior; John Meoska, Ireland; Sr. Connie Bielecki, Contact. Priests 1; Brothers 1; Sisters 3.

FLORENCE. *Trinity Ranch Conference & Renewal Center, Inc.*, Mailing Address: 1061 County Rd. 290, 81226. Tel: 719-784-9701. Rev. Maurice C. Haefling, O.S.B., Vicar & Admin.

MONTROSE. *Spes in Deo Franciscan Family Retreat Center, Inc.*, 21661 Hwy. 550, 81403. Tel: 970-249-3526. Email: joyce@spesindeoretreat.com. Web: www.spesindeoretreat.com. M. Joyce Martin, Pres., Bd. of Directors.

WHITEWATER. *Whitewater Community, Inc.*, 8250 Kannah Creek Rd., 81527. Tel: 970-241-3847. Sr. Mary M. Glenn, Contact. Sisters 2.

[I] MISCELLANEOUS

PUEBLO. **Catholic Diocese of Pueblo Foundation*, 101 N. Greenwood Ave., 81003. Tel: 719-544-9861, Ext. 131; Fax: 719-544-5202. Email: ktillman@dioceseofpueblo.com. Web: www.dioceseofpueblo.com. Mrs. Kathleen Tillman, Exec. Dir.
St. Charles Community, 18 Dartmouth, 81005. Tel: 719-566-1620. Mr. Ed Sajbel, Contact Person.
Deacon Candidate Formation Council, 101 N. Greenwood Ave., 81003. Tel: 719-544-9861, Ext. 116. Email: mbettinger@dioceseofpueblo.com. Web: dioceseofpueblo.com. Deacon Marco Vegas.
Pueblo Community Soup Kitchen, Inc., 422 W. Seventh, 81003. Tel: 719-545-6540. Zola Hunyada, Dir.; Myrtle Huff, Coord.; Carolyn Manley, Coord.
S.E.T. of Pueblo, Inc. A division of Catholic Health Initiatives Colorado., 1925 E. Orman Ave., 81004. Tel: 719-557-3886; Fax: 719-557-3880. Email: cindylau@centura.org. Cindy Lau, Exec. Dir.; Sr. Jacqueline Riggio, S.C., Asst. Dir. Purpose: A ministry to low-income, disadvantaged, and underserved persons, providing wellness clinics, fitness and education for empowerment and transformation. Enroll children into federal and state healthcare programs and provide community resource referrals to clients.
SEARCH of Pueblo, 2 Bear Claw, 81001. Tel: 719-542-6513; 719-320-2707. Email: sandyrose@netzero.net. Ms. Sandy Hansen, Coord.
Serra Club of Pueblo, 5426 Stonemoor Dr., 81005. Tel: 719-566-0511. Mrs. Sally Stricca, Pres.; John Moran, Vice Pres., 23 Newpark Ln., 81001. Tel: 719-546-3843.
Sisters for Christian Community, 1081 Lynx Dr., 81007. Tel: 719-547-2416; Fax: 719-547-4401. Email: salliewatkins@juno.com. Sr. Sallie Watkins, S.F.C.C., Ph.D., Sec. & Contact.

CENTER. *Artes Del Valle (Hispanic Craft Cooperative)*, P.O. Box 627, 81125. Tel: 719-589-4769; 719-754-3191. Miss Shirley Ortega, Mgr. Artes del Valle is under the auspices of St. Francis Jerome Church, Center.

DURANGO. *Mercy Health Foundation*, 1010 Three Springs Blvd., 81301. Tel: 970-764-2804; Fax: 970-764-2809. Email: karenmidkiff@mercydurango.org. Ms. Karen Midkiff, Exec. Dir. & Contact. Affiliate of Catholic Health Initiatives.

GRAND JUNCTION. *Grand Valley Catholic Outreach*, 245 S. 1st St., 81501. Tel: 970-241-3658; Fax: 970-254-1262. Email: gvcoaid@yahoo.com. Web: www.catholicoutreach.org. Sr. Karen Bland, O.S.B., Exec. Dir.
245 S. 1st St., 81502. Tel: 970-241-3658; Fax: 970-242-3908.

Grand Valley Peace and Justice, c/o St. Joseph Church, 230 N. 3rd St., 81501. Tel: 970-243-0136; Fax: 970-243-7493. Email: gvpeace@acsol.net. Web: gvpeacejustice.net. Ms. Karen Sjoberg, Dir.

St. Mary's Hospital Foundation, 2635 N. 7th St., P.O. Box 1628, 81502-1628. Tel: 970-244-2015; Fax: 970-244-7605. Email: pennycowden@stmarygj.org. Web: www.stmarygj.org. Penny Cowden, Exec. Dir.

St. Mary's Rehabilitation Center, Inc., P.O. Box 1628, 81502.

PAGOSA SPRINGS. *Archuleta Housing Corporation*, 703 San Juan St., P.O. Box 355, 81147-0355. Tel: 970-264-2195; Fax: 970-264-4229. Email: archie@frontier.net.

RELIGIOUS INSTITUTES OF MEN REPRESENTED IN THE DIOCESE

For further details refer to the corresponding bracketed number in the Religious Institutes of Men or Women section.

[0200]—*Benedictine Monks*—O.S.B.

[]—*Congregation of the Holy Spirit*—C.S.Sp.

[1330]—*Congregation of the Mission* (Missouri Prov.)—C.M.

[0260]—*Discalced Carmelite Monks*—O.C.D.

[0690]—*Jesuit Fathers and Brothers* (Missouri Prov.)—S.J.

[]—*Society of Our Lady of the Most Holy Trinity*—S.O.L.T.

[]—*Sons of Mary Mother of Mercy*—S.M.M.M.

[1300]—*Theatine Fathers* (Rome, Italy)—C.R.

RELIGIOUS INSTITUTES OF WOMEN REPRESENTED IN THE DIOCESE

[0230]—*Benedictine Sisters of Pontifical Jurisdiction* (Chicago, IL; Covington, KY; Colorado Springs, CO; Yankton, SD)—O.S.B.

[3765]—*Capuchin Poor Clares*—O.S.C.Cap.

[1710]—*Congregation of the Third Order of St. Francis of Mary Immaculate, Joliet, IL*—O.S.F.

[0420]—*Discalced Carmelite Nuns*—O.C.D.

[1070-13]—*Dominican Sisters*—O.P.

[1115]—*Dominican Sisters of Peace*—O.P.

[2575]—*Institute of the Sisters of Mercy of the Americas*—R.S.M.

[2960]—*Notre Dame Sisters*—N.D.

[3130]—*Our Lady of Victory*—O.L.V.M.

[]—*Poor Clare Sisters*—O.S.C.Cap.

[3580]—*Servants of Mary*—O.S.M.

[3500]—*Servants of the Blessed Sacrament*—S.S.S.

[]—*Sisters for Christian Community*—S.F.C.C.

[0440]—*Sisters of Charity of Cincinnati, Ohio*—S.C.

[0480]—*Sisters of Charity of Leavenworth, Kansas*—S.C.L.

[2360]—*Sisters of Loretto At the Foot of the Cross*—S.L.

[1570]—*Sisters of St. Francis of the Holy Family*—O.S.F.

[3830-15]—*Sisters of St. Joseph*—C.S.J.

[3830-18]—*Sisters of St. Joseph*—C.S.J.

[1720]—*Sisters of the Third Order Regular of St. Francis of the Congregation of Our Lady of Lourdes*—O.S.F.

[]—*Sisters of Whitewater Community*

[4060]—*Society of the Holy Child Jesus*—S.H.C.J.

CEMETERIES, DIOCESAN AND PAROCHIAL

PUEBLO. *Gate of Heaven*
Gate of Heaven Section, Roselawn Cemetery Assoc.

AGUILAR. *St. Anthony* (St. Anthony Parish)

CAPULIN. *St. Anthony; St. Francis; St. Joseph; and Capulin* (St. Joseph Parish)

CONEJOS. *Conejos; Las Mesitas; San Antonio; Ortiz; and Labatos* (Our Lady of Guadalupe Parish)

DEL NORTE. *St. Francis of Assisi* (Holy Name of Mary Parish)

FRUITA. *Fruita Catholic* (Sacred Heart Parish)

PAGOSA SPRINGS. *St. John the Baptist; St. Andrew Avelino; St. Francis; and St. James* (Immaculate Heart of Mary Parish)

RYE. *Mount Olivet*
The Rye Mount Olivet Cemetery., (St. Daniel Mission Parish)

SAN LUIS. *San Luis; San Pedro; San Acacio; San Francisco; and Chama* (Sangre de Cristo Parish)

TRINIDAD. *Trinidad Catholic* Legal Title: Trinidad Catholic Cemetery Assoc. (Holy Trinity Parish)

WALSENBURG. *St. Mary* Legal Title: St. Mary Cemetery Association, Inc. (St. Mary Parish)

WESTCLIFFE. *Silver Cliff Assumption Catholic* (Our Lady of the Assumption Parish)

NECROLOGY

(No Deaths)

An asterisk (*) denotes an organization that has established tax-exempt status directly with the IRS and is not covered by the USCCB Group Ruling.

Diocese of Raleigh

(Dioecesis Raleighiensis)

Most Reverend

MICHAEL F. BURBIDGE, ED.D., D.D.

Bishop of Raleigh; ordained May 19, 1984; appointed Auxiliary Bishop of Philadelphia and Titular Bishop of Cluain Iraird June 21, 2002; consecrated September 5, 2002; appointed Fifth Bishop of Raleigh June 8, 2006; installed August 4, 2006. *Res.: 219 W. Edenton St., Raleigh, NC 27603. Office: 715 Nazareth St., Raleigh, NC 27606.* Tel: 919-821-9700.

Most Reverend

F. JOSEPH GOSSMAN, D.D., J.C.D.

Retired Bishop of Raleigh; ordained December 17, 1955; appointed Titular Bishop of Aguntum and Auxiliary Bishop of Baltimore July 15, 1968; ordained September 11, 1968; appointed Fourth Bishop of Raleigh April 8, 1975; installed May 19, 1975; retired June 8, 2006. *Res.: 1601 Westbridge Ct., Raleigh, NC 27606. Office: 2401 Crusader Dr., Raleigh, NC 27606.* Tel: 919-851-6218.

Catholic Center: 715 Nazareth St., Raleigh, NC 27606. Tel: 919-821-9700; Fax: 919-821-9705.

Web: www.dioceseofraleigh.org

Square Miles 31,875.

Established as Vicariate-Apostolic of North Carolina by Pope Pius IX, March 3, 1868.

Established as Diocese of Raleigh by Pope Pius XI, December 12, 1924.

Comprises the following Counties in the State of North Carolina: Alamance, Beaufort, Bertie, Bladen, Brunswick, Camden, Carteret, Caswell, Chatham, Chowan, Columbus, Craven, Cumberland, Currituck, Dare, Duplin, Durham, Edgecombe, Franklin, Gates, Granville, Greene, Halifax, Harnett, Hertford, Hoke, Hyde, Johnston, Jones, Lee, Lenoir, Martin, Moore, Nash, New Hanover, Northampton, Onslow, Orange, Pamlico, Pasquotank, Pender, Perquimans, Person, Pitt, Robeson, Sampson, Scotland, Tyrrell, Vance, Wake, Warren, Washington, Wayne and Wilson.

For legal titles of parishes and diocesan institutions, consult the Chancery.

STATISTICAL OVERVIEW

Personnel	
Bishop	1
Retired Bishops	1
Priests: Diocesan Active in Diocese	64
Priests: Retired, Sick or Absent	26
Number of Diocesan Priests	90
Religious Priests in Diocese	49
Total Priests in Diocese	139
Extern Priests in Diocese	25
Ordinations:	
Transitional Deacons	1
Permanent Deacons in Diocese	40
Total Brothers	3
Total Sisters	52
Parishes	
Parishes	78
With Resident Pastor:	
Resident Diocesan Priests	51
Resident Religious Priests	21
Without Resident Pastor:	
Administered by Priests	4
Administered by Religious Women	2
Missions	18
Pastoral Centers	5
Professional Ministry Personnel:	
Brothers	3
Sisters	21
Welfare	
Special Centers for Social Services	10
Total Assisted	42,545
Educational	
Diocesan Students in Other Seminaries	15
Total Seminarians	15
High Schools, Diocesan and Parish	1
Total Students	1,185
High Schools, Private	1
Total Students	114
Elementary Schools, Diocesan and Parish	31
Total Students	7,776
Catechesis/Religious Education:	
High School Students	4,050
Elementary Students	15,079
Total Students under Catholic Instruction	28,219
Teachers in the Diocese:	
Priests	2
Sisters	5
Lay Teachers	559
Vital Statistics	
Receptions into the Church:	
Infant Baptism Totals	5,579
Minor Baptism Totals	600
Adult Baptism Totals	176
First Communions	4,947
Confirmations	2,369
Marriages:	
Catholic	500
Interfaith	458
Total Marriages	958
Deaths	1,003
Total Catholic Population	217,225
Total Population	4,432,901

Former Bishops of Diocese—Most Revs. WILLIAM J. HAFEY, D.D., cons. June 24, 1925; transferred to the See of Scranton, PA, Oct. 2, 1937; installed Nov. 15, 1937; died May 12, 1954; EUGENE J. MCGUINNESS, D.D., cons. Dec. 21, 1937; transferred to the See of Oklahoma City and Tulsa, OK, Dec. 8, 1944; installed Jan. 10, 1945; died Dec. 27, 1957; VINCENT S. WATERS, D.D., cons. May 15, 1945; installed June 6, 1945; died Dec. 3, 1974; F. JOSEPH GOSSMAN, D.D., J.C.D. (Retired), ord. Dec. 17, 1955; appt. Titular Bishop of Aguntum and Auxiliary Bishop of Baltimore July 15, 1968; ord. Sept. 11, 1968; appt. Fourth Bishop of Raleigh April 8, 1975; installed May 19, 1975; retired Aug. 4, 2006.

Former Bishops of Vicariate-Apostolic—His Eminence JAMES CARDINAL GIBBONS, D.D., consecrated Aug. 16, 1868, Titular Bishop of Adramyttum, first Vicar-Apostolic; transferred to Richmond, VA, July 30, 1872; promoted to the See of Baltimore, Oct. 3, 1877; created Cardinal-Priest of S. Maria in Trastevere, June 7, 1886; died March 24, 1921; Most Rev. JOHN J. KEANE, consecrated Bishop of Richmond and Vicar-Apostolic of North Carolina, Aug. 25, 1878; transferred to the Titular See of Jasso, Aug. 12, 1888; elevated to the Archepiscopal Dignity with the title of Archbishop of Damascus, Jan. 9, 1897; transferred to the See of Dubuque, July 24, 1900; resigned April 3, 1911; appt. Titular Archbishop of Cios, April 28, 1911; died June 23, 1918; Rt. Revs. H. P. NORTHROP, consecrated Titular Bishop of Rosalia and Vicar-Apostolic of North Carolina, Jan. 8, 1882; transferred to Charleston, Jan. 27, 1883; died June 7, 1916; LEO HAID, O.S.B. Vicar Apostolic of North Carolina and Abbot-Ordinary of Belmont Abbey consecrated Titular Bishop of Messene, July 1, 1888; died July 24, 1924.

Office of the Bishop—715 Nazareth St., Raleigh, 27606. Tel: 919-821-9702; Fax: 919-821-9779.

Vicar General—Rev. Msgr. DAVID D. BROCKMAN, V.G., S.T.L., J.C.L., 715 Nazareth St., Raleigh, 27606. Tel: 919-821-9708.

Vicar Judicial & Chancellor—Rev. Msgr. GIRARD M. SHERBA, V.J., J.C.D., Ph.D., 2401 Crusader Dr., Raleigh, 27606-2120. Tel: 919-821-9756.

Chancery—2401 Crusader Dr., Raleigh, 27606-2120. Tel: 919-821-9756; Fax: 919-821-9779.

Chief Financial Officer/Chief Operating Officer—Mr. RUSSELL C. ELMAYAN, M.B.A., M.P.S., CFO, 715 Nazareth St., Raleigh, 27606. Tel: 919-821-9704.

Deans—Very Revs. SAMUEL JAMES BUCHHOLZ, V.F., Albemarle; MARCOS LEON-ANGULO, V.F., Cape Fear; Rev. Msgr. JEFFREY A. INGHAM, V.F., Fayetteville; Very Revs. ERNEST J. RUEDE, V.F., New Bern; JAMES F. GARNEAU, V.F., Ph.D., Newton Grove Deanery; ROBERT BENKO, O.F.M.Conv., V.F., Piedmont; JOHN J. FORBES III, V.F., Raleigh; JUSTIN KERBER, C.P., V.F., Tar River.

Diocesan Attorney—CHARLES F. POWERS III, Mailing Address: P.O. Box 10096, Raleigh, 27605-0096. Tel: 919-783-1008.

Diocesan Consultors—Rev. Msgr. DAVID D. BROCKMAN, V.G., S.T.L., J.C.L.; Very Rev. JAMES F. GARNEAU, V.F., Ph.D.; Rev. Msgr. JEFFREY A. INGHAM, V.F.; Very Rev. ERNEST J. RUEDE, V.F.; Rev. Msgrs. MICHAEL P. SHUGRUE; GIRARD M. SHERBA, V.J., J.C.D., Ph.D.; Rev. JOSEPH G. VETTER.

Diocesan Tribunal—2401 Crusader Dr., Raleigh, 27606. Tel: 919-821-9759. All rogatorial commissions should be directed to the Tribunal.

Vicar Judicial—Rev. Msgr. GIRARD M. SHERBA, V.J., J.C.D., Ph.D.

Adjutant Vicar Judicial—Rev. JOSEPH G. MULRONEY, J.C.L.

Defender of the Bond—Very Rev. STEPHEN SMITH, O.P., J.C.D.

Promoter of Justice—Rev. JOSEPH G. MULRONEY, J.C.L.

Diocesan Judges—Rev. Msgrs. THOMAS P. HADDEN (Retired); DAVID D. BROCKMAN, V.G., S.T.L., J.C.L.

Director of the Tribunal—Mrs. VIKKI NEWELL.

Notaries—Mrs. VIKKI NEWELL; Mrs. ANNE SPEICHER; Mrs. ROSEMARY DUDASH; Mrs. ANNE WOLFF.

Council of Priests—Very Revs. ROBERT BENKO, O.F.M.Conv., V.F.; SAMUEL JAMES BUCHHOLZ, V.F.; Rev. Msgr. MICHAEL G. CLAY, D.Min.; Very Revs. JOHN J. FORBES III, V.F.; JAMES F. GARNEAU, V.F.,

Ph.D.; Rev. Msgr. JEFFREY A. INGHAM, V.F.; Very Revs. JUSTIN KERBER, C.P., V.F.; MARCOS LEON-ANGULO, V.F.; Rev. JOHN E. MCGEE, O.S.F.S.; Rev. Msgr. JOHN F. O'CONNOR, V.F.; Very Rev. DANIEL D. OSCHWALD; Rev. MARK G. REAMER, O.F.M.; Very Rev. ERNEST J. RUEDE, V.F.; Rev. Msgr. MICHAEL P. SHUGRUE; Revs. PHILIP M. TIGHE; FERNANDO TORRES; JOSEPH G. VETTER. Ex Officio: Rev. Msgrs. DAVID D. BROCKMAN, V.G., S.T.L., J.C.L.; GIRARD M. SHERBA, V.J., J.C.D., Ph.D.; Very Rev. CARLOS ARCE-FLORES, V.F.; Rev. Msgr. THOMAS P. HADDEN (Retired); Very Rev. STEPHEN SMITH, O.P., J.C.D.

Council of Women Religious—Sr. BARBARA MARIE CADY, S.U.

Vicar for Priests—Very Rev. STEPHEN SMITH, O.P., J.C.D., Mailing Address: P.O. Box 12927, Raleigh, 27605. Tel: 919-833-1893; Fax: 919-833-1449.

Bishops' Delegates for Religious—Rev. Msgr. GIRARD M. SHERBA, V.J., J.C.D., Ph.D.; Sisters DAMIAN MARIE JACKSON, O.S.F., 711 Mason Rd., Durham, 27712; MARGARET GALLAGHER, I.H.M., Mailing Address: P.O. Box 934, Warrenton, 27589.

Diocesan Offices and Departments

All addresses are 715 Nazareth St., Raleigh, NC 27606 unless noted otherwise.

Business Services—Ms. KIM MCBRIDE, Dir. Tel: 919-821-9727.

Computer Services—Mr. JOHNALLAN TALLANT. Tel: 919-821-9719.

Stewardship and Institutional Advancement—Mr. MICHAEL G. PEDLEY. Tel: 919-821-9721.

Property and Construction—Mr. ARTHUR WESCHE. Tel: 919-821-9726.

Catholic Charities of the Diocese of Raleigh, Inc.—Ms. KATHLEEN WALSH, M.S.W., A.C.S.W., Dir. Tel: 919-821-9752.

Catholic Formation and Education—Dr. MICHAEL J. FEDEWA, Ed.D., Supt. Tel: 919-821-9748.

Campus Ministry—Rev. JOSEPH G. VETTER, Dir., Duke Catholic Student Center, P.O. Box 90974, Durham, 27708. Tel: 919-684-8959.

Department of Catholic Formation and Evangelization—Sr. ROSE MARIE ADAMS, I.H.M., Dir. Tel: 919-821-9746.

Office of Catechetical Formation—VACANT.

Office of Evangelization—Mr. ROBERT JONES. Tel: 919-821-9740.

Office of Lay Ministry Formation—Ms. BEATRICE CALLERY. Tel: 919-821-9715.

Office of Marriage and Family Life—Mrs. LINDA BEDO. Tel: 919-821-9753.

Youth and Young Adult Ministry—Mr. PATRICK DIENER. Tel: 919-821-9770.

Communications—Mr. FRANK MOROCK, Dir. Tel: 919-821-9732.

North Carolina Catholics Magazine—Mr. RICHARD REECE, Editor. Tel: 919-821-9736.

Web Administrator—Mrs. MICHELLE KING.

Ecumenical Commission—Rev. DAVID J. MCBRIAR, O.F.M. Tel: 919-847-8205.

Human Resources—VACANT, Dir. Tel: 919-821-9711.

Office of African Ancestry Ministry and Evangelization—Rev. Msgr. THOMAS P. HADDEN, Vicar (Retired); Mrs. LAUREN M. GREEN, Dir. Tel: 919-821-9762.

Office for Child & Youth Protection—Dr. JOHN A. PENDERGRASS, Dir. Tel: 866-535-7233.

Office of Hispanic Ministry—Very Rev. CARLOS ARCE-FLORES, V.F., Vicar; Ms. VERONICA ALVARADO, Dir. Tel: 919-821-9738.

Office of Permanent Diaconate—Very Rev. JAMES F. GARNEAU, V.F., Ph.D., Dir., P.O. Box 1145, Mount Olive, 28365. Tel: 919-658-4023.

Office for Vocations and Seminarian Formation—Rev. BERNARD E. SHLESINGER III, Dir., 226 Hillsborough St., Raleigh, 27603. Tel: 919-832-6279.

Office of Worship—Mr. GERARD T. HALL, Dir., 226 Hillsborough St., Raleigh, 27603. Tel: 919-832-6281.

Office for Peace and Justice/Respect Life—Sr. JOAN JURSKI, O.S.F., Dir. Tel: 919-821-9751.

Office of Evangelization & Catechesis—Sr. ROSE MARIE ADAMS, I.H.M. Tel: 919-821-9746.

Youth and Young Adult Ministry—Mr. PATRICK DIENER. Tel: 919-821-9770.

Adult Faith Development—Mr. ROBERT JONES. Tel: 919-821-9740.

Vicar for Hispanics—Very Rev. CARLOS ARCE-FLORES, V.F., c/o Diocese of Raleigh, Hispanic Ministry, 715 Nazareth St., Raleigh, 27606. Tel: 919-821-9738.

Vicar for African American Ancestry Ministry—Rev. Msgr. THOMAS P. HADDEN (Retired), Catholic Center, 715 Nazareth St., Raleigh, 27606. Tel: 919-821-9762.

Miscellaneous Offices—

Apostleship of the Sea—Rev. Msgr. FRANCIS R. MOESLEIN (Retired), 2106 Joslyn Dr., Morehead City, 28557-9200. Tel: 252-726-3579.

Censor Librorum—VACANT.

Engaged Encounter— Marriage Preparation and Enrichment Office *Catholic Center, 715 Nazareth St., Raleigh, 27606*. Tel: 919-821-9753.

Holy Childhood Pontifical Association—Very Rev. ROBERT J. KUS, Dir., St. Mary Catholic Church, 412 Ann St., Wilmington, 28401. Tel: 910-762-5491.

Marriage Encounter—*Catholic Center, 715 Nazareth St., Raleigh, 27606*. Tel: 919-821-9753.

Home Mission Society of the Diocese of Raleigh—Very Rev. JAMES F. GARNEAU, V.F., Ph.D., Dir., P.O. Box 1145, Mount Olive, 28365. Tel: 919-658-4023.

Pontifical Mission Societies in the United States—Very Rev. ROBERT J. KUS, Dir., St. Mary, 412 Ann St., Wilmington, 28401. Tel: 910-762-5491.

Victim Assistance Coordinator—Ms. KATHLEEN WALSH, M.S.W., A.C.S.W. Tel: 919-821-9752.

CLERGY, PARISHES, MISSIONS AND PAROCHIAL SCHOOLS

CITY OF RALEIGH

(WAKE COUNTY)

1—CATHEDRAL OF THE SACRED HEART (1834) Very Revs. Daniel D. Oschwald, Rector; Salvatore A. Busichio.
Office & Res.: 219 W. Edenton St., 27603-1724. Tel: 919-832-6030 (Office); 919-836-1790 (Res.); Fax: 919-833-4667. Web: www.sacredheartcathedral.org.
School—Tel: 919-832-4711; Fax: 919-832-8329. Web: www.cathedral-school.net. Mrs. Donna Moss, Prin. Lay Teachers 30; Students 270.
Catechesis/Religious Program—Students 441.

2—CATHOLIC STUDENT CENTER, NORTH CAROLINA STATE UNIVERSITY (1974) Mailing Address: 600 Bilyeu St., 27606. Tel: 919-833-9668; Fax: 919-833-1194.
Doggett Center at Aquinas House—600 Bilyeu St., 27606. Tel: 919-833-9668; Fax: 919-833-1194. Rev. John Alex Gonzalez, Campus Min., Asst. Vocation Dir.

3—ST. FRANCIS OF ASSISI (1982) [CEM] Revs. Mark G. Reamer, O.F.M.; David J. McBriar, O.F.M.; William E. McConville, O.F.M.; Julian Jagudilla, O.F.M.
Res.: 11401 Leesville Rd., 27613. Tel: 919-847-8205; Fax: 919-870-1790.
School—The Franciscan School, 10000 St. Francis Dr. Fax: 919-847-9558. Web: www.franciscan-school.org. Jennifer Bigelow, Prin. Lay Teachers 44; Students 691.
Early Childhood Learning Center—Nancy Bourke, Prin. Lay Teachers 25; Students 170.
Catechesis/Religious Program—Tel: 919-847-8205. Maureen Leahy, D.R.E. (Grades PreK-5, Faith Formation); Christine Miesowicz, D.R.E. (Life Long Faith Formation); Leo Moreda, D.R.E. (Middle School & High School Faith Formation). Students 1,120.

4—ST. JOSEPH (1968) Rev. Msgr. John J. Williams.
Office: 2817 Poole Rd., 27610. Tel: 919-231-6364; Fax: 919-231-9884.
Res.: 2809 Poole Rd., 27610.
Catechesis/Religious Program—Deborah Pergerson, D.R.E. Students 212.

5—ST. LUKE THE EVANGELIST (1985) Rev. Joseph G. Mulroney; Deacon Michael Sanchez.
Church & Res. Address: 12333 Bayleaf Church Rd., 27614-9165. Tel: 919-848-1533; Fax: 919-848-0662. Web: www.stluketheevangelist.org.
Catechesis/Religious Program—Tel: 919-848-3197. Students 143.

6—OUR LADY OF LOURDES (1954) [CEM] Very Rev. John J. Forbes III; Sr. Mary Agnes Ryan, I.H.M., Pastoral Assoc.; Deacons Myles J. Charlesworth; D. Thomas Mack.
Office: 2718 Overbrook Dr., 27608. Tel: 919-861-4600; Fax: 919-861-4620. Web: www.ourladyoflourdescc.org.
Tel: 919-301-8322.
School—2710 Overbrook Dr., 27608. Tel: 919-861-4610; Fax: 919-861-4630. Dr. Robert Benjamin Scripko, Prin. Sisters of Notre Dame 2; Lay Teachers 23; Students 524.
Catechesis/Religious Program—Tel: 919-861-4614. Joan Samuels Rose, D.R.E. (Min. Faith Formation); Emily West, D.R.E. (Youth Ministry). Students 222.

7—ST. RAPHAEL THE ARCHANGEL (1966) [CEM] Revs. Robert M. Hussey, S.J.; Robert Wiesenbaugh, S.J.; Michael Proterra, S.J.; Deacons Robert T. Madey; Jorge Rodriguez; Hector Velazco.
Res.: 5801 Falls of Neuse Rd., 27609. Tel: 919-865-5700; Fax: 919-865-5701.
School—St. Raphael, 5815 Fall of Neuse Rd., 27609. Tel: 919-865-5750; Fax: 919-865-5751. Mr. Barry Thomas, Prin. Students 437.
St. Raphael Catholic Early Childhood Center—Carrie Griffith, Dir. Students 184.
Catechesis/Religious Program—Jeanne Lewin, D.R.E.; Pat Foran, Youth Min. Service Coord. Students 780.

OUTSIDE THE CITY OF RALEIGH

AHOSKIE, HERTFORD CO., ST. CHARLES BORROMEO (1944) Rev. J. William Long.
Res.: P.O. Box 605, 27910. Tel: 252-332-2939.
Catechesis/Religious Program—Students 35.
Mission—St. Anne Scotland Neck, Halifax Co.

APEX, WAKE CO.

1—ST. ANDREW THE APOSTLE (1983) [CEM] Revs. David E. Fitzgerald, S.A.; Thomas Gumprecht, S.A.; Joseph Madden, O.F.M.Conv.
Res.: 304 Gentlewoods Dr., Cary, 27518. Tel: 919-303-7732. Email: standrewapex@aol.com. Web: www.saintandrew.org.
Church: 3008 Old Raleigh Rd., 27502. Tel: 919-362-0414; Fax: 919-362-5778. Email: standrewapex@aol.com. Web: www.saintandrew.org.
Catechesis/Religious Program—Tel: 919-362-0685. Katie Fortunato, D.R.E.; Theresa Reed, Youth Min.; Cheryl Koller, Music Min.; Lucille T. Wargo, Admin. Students 964.

2—ST. MARY MAGDALENE (1997) Rev. Donald F. Staib. 625 Magdala Pl., 27502. Tel: 919-657-4800; Fax: 919-657-4805. Web: www.stmm.net.
School—625 Magdala Pl., 27502. Tel: 919-657-4800; Fax: 919-657-4805. Robert Cadran, Prin. Lay Teachers 56; Students 623.
Catechesis/Religious Program—Students 817.

BURGAW, PENDER CO., ST. JOSEPH (1908) [CEM] Rev. Rafael A. Leon-Valencia.
Church & Res.: 1303 Hwy. 117 S., 28425. Tel: 910-259-2601; Fax: 910-259-7695.
Catechesis/Religious Program—Brian Wright, D.R.E., (St. Joseph); Marcia Hatcher, D.R.E., (Transfiguration). Students 24.
Mission—Transfiguration (1953) 508 E. Main St., P.O. Box 1601, Wallace, Duplin Co. 28466. Tel: 910-285-1876.

BURLINGTON, ALAMANCE CO., BLESSED SACRAMENT (1929) Very Rev. Robert Benko, O.F.M.Conv.; Revs. Paul Gabriel, O.F.M.Conv.; Jacek K. Leszczynski, O.F.M.Conv.
Mailing Address: P.O. Box 619, 27216. Tel: 336-226-8796; Fax: 336-227-2896. Web: www.blessedsacramentnc.org. In Res., Rev. Gerald Waterman, O.F.M.Conv., Campus Min.
Res.: 514 Parkview Dr., 27215. Tel: 336-222-1401.
School—515 Hillcrest Ave., 27215. Tel: 336-570-0019; Fax: 336-570-9623. Mr. Salvatore Michael Trento, Prin. Lay Teachers 23; Students 230.
Catechesis/Religious Program—Students 325.

BUTNER, GRANVILLE CO., ST. BERNADETTE (1957) Sr. Carol Loughney, I.H.M., Pastoral Admin.
Parish House & Mailing Address: 311 Eleventh St., 27509. Tel: 919-575-4744; Fax: 919-575-4744. Web: mysite.verizon.net/st_bernadette.
Church: 804 West D. St., 27509. Tel: 919-575-4744; Fax: 919-575-4744. Email: st_bernadette@verizon.net.
Catechesis/Religious Program—Students 118.

BUXTON, DARE CO., OUR LADY OF THE SEAS (1935) Rev. Robert Brown, O.S.F.S.
Mailing Address: 48478 Hwy. 12, P.O. Box 399, 27920. Tel: 252-995-6370; Fax: 252-995-6398. Email: olssecretary@aol.com. Web: www.ourladyoftheseas.org.
Catechesis/Religious Program—Students 18.

CARY, WAKE CO., ST. MICHAEL THE ARCHANGEL (1962) Rev. Msgr. John F. O'Connor; Revs. Michael R. Spurr; Joseph Kalu Oji, C.S.Sp.; Bro. Bill Martyn, S.A. In Res., Very Rev. Carlos Arce-Flores.
Res.: 804 High House Rd., 27513. Tel: 919-468-6100; Fax: 919-468-6130. Email: office@stmichaelcary.org. Web: www.stmichaelcary.org.
School—810 High House Rd., 27513. Tel: 919-468-6150; Fax: 919-468-6160. Dr. Sarah Wannemuehler, Prin.
Catechesis/Religious Program—Tel: 919-468-6120. Students 1,671.

CASTLE HAYNE, NEW HANOVER CO., ST. STANISLAUS (1914), (Polish), [CEM] Rev. Ryszard Kolodziej.
Church & Res.: 4849 Castle Hayne Rd., 28429-4849. Tel: 910-675-2336 (Office); Fax: 910-675-3116. Email: ststans4@ec.rr.com. Web: ststans-nc.org.
Catechesis/Religious Program—Students 45.

CHAPEL HILL, ORANGE CO.

1—NEWMAN CATHOLIC STUDENT CENTER, UNIVERSITY OF NORTH CAROLINA (1968) Rev. Msgr. John A. Wall

(Retired).
Res.: 218 Pittsboro St., 27516-2738. Tel: 919-929-3730; Fax: 919-929-3778.
Catechesis / Religious Program—Students 178.

2—ST. THOMAS MORE (1940) Revs. John G. Durbin; Roman A. Acero; Deacon Phil Rzewnicki; Mary Ellen McGuire, Pastoral Assoc.
Parish Offices—940 Carmichael St., 27514-4203. Tel: 919-942-1040; Fax: 919-942-6193. Web: church.st-thomasmore.org.
Res.: 301 Rossburn Way, 27516. Tel: 919-967-8485.
School—(Grades K-8), 920 Carmichael St., 27514. Tel: 919-929-1546; Fax: 919-929-1783. Web: school.st-thomasmore.org. Sr. Catherine Michael Fee, S.S.J., Prin.; Jo Williams, Librarian. Sisters 1; Lay Teachers 36; Students 415.
Catechesis / Religious Program—Tel: 919-933-1041. Jim Hynes, Elementary Faith Formation & Adult Faith Educ.; Sonia Honey, Total Youth Ministry; Georgie Clemens, Junior Youth Ministry. Students 918.

CLAYTON, JOHNSTON CO., ST. ANN (1935) Rev. Msgr. Michael G. Clay.
Church: 4057 Hwy. 70 Business W., 27520. Tel: 919-934-2084; Fax: 919-934-4639. Web: www.st-annschurch.org.
Catechesis / Religious Program—Email: faithform.stann@yahoo.com. Students 505.

CLINTON, SAMPSON CO., IMMACULATE CONCEPTION (1910) Rev. Fernando Torres.
Mailing Address: P.O. Box 859, 28329. Tel: 910-592-1384; Fax: 910-592-1384.
Catechesis / Religious Program—Sr. Maxine Tancraitor, D.R.E. Students 99.
Mission—San Juan 1710 Old U.S. Hwy. 701, Ingold, Sampson Co.

DUNN, HARNETT CO., SACRED HEART (1916) Rev. Paul M. Parkerson.
Mailing Address: P.O. Box 535, 28335. Tel: 910-891-1972; Fax: 910-891-5767. Web: www.sacredheartdunnnc.org.
Res.: 311 S. Orange Ave., 28334. Tel: 910-892-3414.
Catechesis / Religious Program—Mrs. Jan Rebman, D.R.E. Students 44.

DURHAM, DURHAM CO.

1—HOLY CROSS (1939), (African American), Rev. Raymond J. Donaldson, S.J.
Church: 2438 S. Alston Ave., 27713. Tel: 919-957-2900; Fax: 919-957-2901. Web: www.holycrossdurham.org.
Res.: 1313 Exchange Pl., 27713.
Catechesis / Religious Program—Tel: 919-425-1177. Ava Thompson, D.R.E. Students 57.

2—HOLY INFANT (1970) [CEM] Rev. Joseph T. Brennan, O.S.F.S.
Res.: 5000 Southpark Dr., 27713-9470. Tel: 919-544-7135; Fax: 919-544-1799. Email: lyndad@holyinfantchurch.org. Web: holyinfantchurch.org.
Catechesis / Religious Program—Tel: 919-544-7135, Ext. 18. Students 143.

3—IMMACULATE CONCEPTION (1906) Revs. Daniel McLellan, O.F.M.; Steve Patti, O.F.M., Parochial Vicar; William McIntyre, O.F.M., Parochial Vicar; Deacon Laurence DeCarolis.
Res.: 720 Vickers Ave., 27701. Tel: 919-667-1722; Fax: 919-682-7999. Web: www.icdurham.org.
School—Immaculata, 721 Burch Ave., 27701. Tel: 919-682-5847; Fax: 919-956-7073. Dana Corcoran, Prin. Lay Teachers 41; Students 382.
Catechesis / Religious Program—Rick Kinsey, D.R.E. Students 1,122.

4—ST. MATTHEW (1990) [CEM] Rev. Robert W. Diegelman.
Rectory—7 Timbercreek Ct., 27712. Tel: 919-471-0658; Fax: 919-479-4848.
Catechesis / Religious Program—Betsy Strauss, D.R.E.; John Toohil, Music Min. Students 100.

EDENTON, CHOWAN CO., ST. ANNE (1858) [CEM] Rev. Douglas Reed.
Mailing Address: P.O. Box 422, 27932.
Church: 207 N. Broad St., 27932. Tel: 252-482-2617; Fax: 252-482-8702.
Catechesis / Religious Program—Students 58.
Mission—All Souls 917 Main St., Columbia, Tyrrell Co. 27925.

ELIZABETH CITY, PASQUOTANK CO., HOLY FAMILY (1915) Very Rev. Samuel James Buchholz.
Mailing Address: 1453 N. Road St., 27906-1525. Tel: 252-338-2521; Fax: 252-338-4183.
Res.: 1453 N. Road St., 27909. Tel: 252-335-4419.
Catechesis / Religious Program—Sharon Lupton, D.R.E. (Grades K-5); Cathy Terranova, D.R.E. (Grades 6-12); Carl Terranova, Youth Min. Students 164.
Mission—St. Katharine Drexel 154 Maple Rd., Maple, Currituck Co. 27956. Tel: 252-453-6035.

FARMVILLE, PITT CO., ST. ELIZABETH (1931) Rev. Joseph J. Yaeger.
Mailing Address: 3447 S. Contentnea St., 27828-1686. Tel: 252-753-4367; Fax: 252-753-4400. Email: stelizabethnc@embarqmail.com. Web: www.dioceseofraleigh.org.
Catechesis / Religious Program—Rita Zalonis, C.R.E. Students 42.

FAYETTEVILLE, CUMBERLAND CO.

1—ST. ANDREW KIM (2000), (Korean), Rev. Philip Sanghyo Kim.
1401 Valencia Dr., 28303. Tel: 910-630-2316; Fax: 910-487-8737. Email: dirjdzz@hanmail.net.

2—ST. ANN (1939), (African American), Rev. Thomas Malloy, O.S.F.S.
Office: 357 N. Cool Spring St., 28301. Tel: 910-483-3216; Fax: 910-483-4185. Email: info@stanncatholicchurch.org. Web: www.stanncatholicchurch.org.
Res.: 228 Temple Ave., 28301. Tel: 910-483-5871.
School—365 N. Cool Spring St., 28301. Tel: 910-483-3902; Fax: 910-483-3195. Email: principal@stanncatholicschool.org. Web: www-.stanncatholicschool.org. N. Rene Corders, Prin. Lay Teachers 14; Students 171.
Catechesis / Religious Program—Tel: 910-488-7137; Fax: 910-483-4185. Kathy Flynn, D.R.E. Students 87.

3—ST. ELIZABETH ANN SETON (1981) Rev. Willard Rucinski, O.S.F.S.
Res.: 700 Carnegie St., 28311. Tel: 910-488-1797; Fax: 910-488-7116. Web: seachurch.net.
Catechesis / Religious Program—John Bunting, D.R.E. Students 220.

4—ST. PATRICK (1824) Rev. Msgr. Michael P. Shugrue; Rev. Michael P. Cassabon.
Mailing Address: 2844 Village Dr., 28304-3813. Tel: 910-323-2410; Fax: 910-323-3006. Email: churchoffice@stpatnc.org. Web: stpatnc.org.
Res.: 433 Holly Ln., 28305. Tel: 910-484-8253.
School—1620 Marlborough Rd., 28304. Tel: 910-323-1865; Fax: 910-484-1573. Web: stpatrickschoolnc.org. Mr. Tom Manion, Prin. Lay Teachers 20; Students 283.
Catechesis / Religious Program—Tel: 910-323-2410, Ext. 107; Fax: 910-323-3006. Margaret Blanc, D.R.E. Students 444.

FUQUAY-VARINA, WAKE CO., ST. BERNADETTE (1987) [CEM] Revs. Mark J. Betti; Francisco Javier Garcia-Gonzalez; Robert P. Staley; Deacon Anthony Meier.
Mailing Address: 1005 Wilbon Rd., 27526-9702. Tel: 919-552-8758; Fax: 919-552-1846. Email: st-bernadette@embarqmail.com. Web: st-bernadettechurch.org.
Catechesis / Religious Program—Tel: 919-552-8758. Mrs. Michele Dexter, D.R.E. Students 537.
Hispanic Office—Tel: 919-552-2922.

GARNER, WAKE CO., ST. MARY, MOTHER OF THE CHURCH (1966) Revs. Robert T. Schriber; Roger Malonda Nyimi, Parochial Vicar; Deacon Leo Tapler.
Res.: 1008 Vandora Springs Rd., 27529. Tel: 919-772-5777; 919-772-5524 (Office); Fax: 919-772-5534. Email: stmarync@bellsouth.net. Web: www.stmarygarner.org.
Catechesis / Religious Program—Tel: 919-772-5199. Email: smgfaith@bellsouth.net. Students 549.

GOLDSBORO, WAYNE CO., ST. MARY (1889) Rev. Thomas P. Norris, O.S.F.S.; Deacon Webster A. James. In Res., Rev. Paul W. Brant, S.J.
Res.: 1000 N. Jefferson Ave., 27530-3141. Tel: 919-734-5033; Fax: 919-580-0730. Email: office@saintmarygoldsboro.org. Web: www.saintmarygoldsboro.org.
School—1601 Edgerton St., 27530-3181. Tel: 919-735-1931; Fax: 919-735-1917. Email: smsprincipal@nc.rr.com. Lynn E. Magoon, Prin. Lay Teachers 17; Students 216.
Catechesis / Religious Program—Tel: 919-734-5033, Ext. 22. Email: wjames408@earthlink.net. Students 136.

GREENVILLE, PITT CO.

1—ST. GABRIEL (1936) Rev. Michael A. Butler.
Res.: 402 Trey Dr., 27834. Tel: 252-758-1504; Fax: 252-355-6128. Email: stgabriel@embarqmail.com.
Catechesis / Religious Program—Students 191.

2—ST. PETER'S (1884) Very Rev. Justin Kerber, C.P.; Rev. Edward Wolanski, C.P.
Res.: 2700 E. Fourth St., 27858. Tel: 252-757-3259; Fax: 252-752-1499. Web: www.saintpetercatholicchurch.org.
School—Tel: 252-752-3529; Fax: 252-752-7604. Web: stpeterscatholicschool.com. Ms. Page Watson, School Admin. Lay Teachers 34; Students 559.
Catechesis / Religious Program—Tel: 252-757-3259, Ext. 204. Students 410.

HAMPSTEAD, PENDER CO., ST. JUDE THE APOSTLE (1992) Rev. Terrence Collins.
Mailing Address: 18737 Hwy. 17 N., 28443. Tel: 910-270-1477; Fax: 910-270-1424.
Res.: 557 Osprey Dr., 28443. Tel: 910-270-1689; Fax: 910-270-1424.
Catechesis / Religious Program—Tel: 910-270-1477. Students 120.
Mission—St. Mary, Gate of Heaven P.O. Box 2667, Surf City, Pender Co. 28445.

HAVELOCK, CRAVEN CO., ANNUNCIATION (1953) [CEM] Rev. Gregory D. Spencer.
Mailing Address: 246 E. Main St., 28532-0720. Tel: 252-447-2112; Fax: 252-447-2113. Web: annunciationparish.org.
School—Tel: 252-447-3137; Fax: 252-447-3138. Mrs. June Pietras, Prin. Lay Teachers 14; Students 109.
Catechesis / Religious Program—Marlene Rink, D.R.E. Students 210.

HENDERSON, VANCE CO., ST. JAMES (1995) [CEM] [JC] Consolidated St. Paul and St. Catherine of Siena, Oxford merged to form St. James. Rev. William J. Upah.
Res.: 3275 Hwy. 158 Bypass, 27536. Tel: 252-438-3124; Fax: 252-438-3214.
Catechesis / Religious Program—Students 119.
Mission—St. Joseph Norlina Rd., Warrenton, Warren Co. 27589. Tel: 252-438-3124.

HILLSBOROUGH, ORANGE CO., HOLY FAMILY (1989) Rev. Thomas S. Tully.
Mailing Address: 216 Governer Burke Rd., 27278. Tel: 919-732-1030; Fax: 919-732-7852.
Rectory—2120 Rhonda Rd., 27278. Tel: 919-732-7265.
Catechesis / Religious Program—Students 174.

HOPE MILLS, CUMBERLAND CO., GOOD SHEPHERD (1981) Revs. Thanh N. Nguyen; Thomas J. Gaul, Pastor Emeritus (Retired).
Res.: 5050 Oak St., 28348. Tel: 910-425-1590; Fax: 910-423-9973. Email: gdshprd1@earthlink.net. Web: www.good-shepherd-church.org.
Catechesis / Religious Program—Tel: 910-425-5617. Janice Carnahan, D.R.E. Students 212.
Mission—St. Isidore 8569 Clinton Rd., Stedman, Cumberland Co. 28391. Tel: 910-424-2698.

JACKSONVILLE, ONSLOW CO., SHRINE OF THE INFANT OF PRAGUE, CHURCH OF THE HOLY SPIRIT (1941) Very Rev. Ernest J. Ruede; Rev. Anthony De Candia.
Mailing Address: 205 Chaney Ave., 28540. Tel: 910-347-4196; Fax: 910-347-9338. Email: iop1@ec.rr.com. Web: iopnc.org.
Res.: 330 Mildred Ave., 28540. Tel: 910-347-8881.
School—501 Bordeaux St., 28540. Tel: 910-353-1300; 910-455-0838; Fax: 910-455-0270. Myra Marks, Prin. Lay Teachers 16; Religious Male 1; Students 190.
Catechesis / Religious Program—Tel: 910-455-1296. Email: faithform@ec.rr.com. Mrs. Anne Mauthe, D.R.E. Students 345.

KINSTON, LENOIR CO., HOLY SPIRIT CATHOLIC CHURCH (1921), (African American—Hispanic), (Formerly Holy Trinity-Our Lady of the Atonement) Rev. Edward Burch.
Mailing Address: P.O. Box 1455, 28503-1455. Tel: 252-523-8898; Fax: 252-527-9495.
Res.: 137 Rae Rd., 28504. Tel: 252-523-4377.
Church: 400 Academy Heights Rd., 28504. Tel: 252-523-8898; Fax: 252-523-9495. Email: holyspirit@suddenlinkmail.com.
Catechesis / Religious Program—Pat Kaspryzk, D.R.E. Students 111.

KITTY HAWK, DARE CO., HOLY REDEEMER BY THE SEA (1937) Revs. William F. Walsh, O.S.F.S.; Edward T. Fitzpatrick, O.S.F.S.
Mailing Address: P.O. Box 510, 27949. Tel: 252-261-4700; Fax: 252-261-1405. Email: info@obxcatholicparish.org. Web: obxcatholicparish.org.
Office: 301 W. Kitty Hawk Rd., 27949.
Res.: 109 Sunrise View, 27949. Tel: 252-261-2728.
Catechesis / Religious Program—Tel: 252-261-4700; Fax: 252-261-1405. Students 111.
Mission—Holy Trinity by the Sea Catholic Nags Head, Dare Co. 27959. Tel: 252-261-1168.

LAURINBURG, SCOTLAND CO., ST. MARY (1946) [JC] Rev. JaVan Saxon.
Mailing Address: P.O. Box 1148, 28353-1148. Tel: 910-276-4468; Fax: 910-276-9519.
Catechesis / Religious Program—Students 57.

LOUISBURG, FRANKLIN CO., OUR LADY OF THE ROSARY (1999) Sr. Elizabeth Bullen, I.H.M., Pastoral Admin.
Church: 460 Fox Park Rd., 27549. Tel: 919-340-0556; Fax: 919-340-0556.
Catechesis / Religious Program—Students 85.

LUMBERTON, ROBESON CO., ST. FRANCIS DE SALES (1938) Rev. John Gillespie.
Mailing Address: 2000 Elizabethtown Rd., P.O. Box 2249, 28358. Tel: 910-739-4723; Fax: 910-739-5443.
Res.: 2000 Elizabethtown Rd., 28358.
Catechesis / Religious Program—Tel: 910-739-4713. Students 141.

MOREHEAD CITY, CARTERET CO., ST. EGBERT (1929) Rev. Douglas J. Smiley; Rev. Msgr. Francis R. Moeslein, Pastor Emeritus (Retired).
Parish Hall—1706 Evans St., 28557. Tel: 252-726-3559; Fax: 252-726-2232.
Res.: 1612 Evans St., 28557. Tel: 252-726-2535.
School—Tel: 252-726-3418; Fax: 252-727-0150. Mr. John J. Donohue, Prin. Lay Teachers 9; Students 81.

Catechesis/Religious Program—Joseph McKenzie, D.R.E. Students 90.

MOUNT OLIVE, DUPLIN CO., MARIA, REINA DE LAS AMERICAS, (Mary, Queen of the Americas) Revs. Edgar Sepulveda (Colombia). Tel: 919-429-1003; Martin Restrepo.
Mailing Address: P.O. Box 332, Kenansville, 28349.
Res.: 208 Cavenaugh St., Beulaville, 28518.
Church: 636 Whitfield Rd., 28365. Tel: 919-635-2447; Fax: 919-635-2448.
Mission—St. Teresa del Nino Jesus 206 Cavenaugh St., Beulaville, Duplin Co. 28518.

MOUNT OLIVE, WAYNE CO., ST. MARY (1916) [JC] Very Rev. James F. Garneau.
Mailing Address: P.O. Box 1145, 28365. Tel: 919-658-4023; Fax: 919-658-4023.
Catechesis/Religious Program—Students 90.

NEW BERN, CRAVEN CO., ST. PAUL (1821) [CEM] Rev. Msgr. Gerald L. Lewis, Admin. (Retired); Rev. Paul Mizener (SP); Deacon Michael A. Mahoney; Sisters Monique Dissen, I.H.M., Pastoral Assoc.; Grace Campbell, I.H.M., Pastoral Assoc.
Rectory—3108 Farrior Cir., 28562. Tel: 252-638-4436.
Church: 3005 Country Club Rd., 28562. Tel: 252-638-1984; Fax: 252-638-2144. Email: stpaul@coastalnc.us. Web: www.stpaulccnewbern.org.
School—St. Paul Catholic School, 3007 Country Club Rd., 28562. Tel: 252-633-0100; Fax: 252-633-4457. Email: specl@suddenlink.net. Web: stpaul-educationcenter.com. Monette Mahoney, Prin. Lay Teachers 11; Students 178.
Catechesis/Religious Program—Tel: 252-633-3030. Joy Harsen, D.R.E. (Elementary); Karin Coll, D.R.E. (High School). Students 148.

NEW HILL, WAKE CO., ST. HA-SANG PAUL JUNG (1988) Rev. Choong Seob Kim.
2340 New Hill Olive Chapel Rd., 27562. Tel: 919-303-6424. Web: www.tkcc.org.
Catechesis/Religious Program—Students 35.

NEWTON GROVE, SAMPSON CO., OUR LADY OF GUADALUPE (1871) [CEM] Rev. Patrick A. Keane.
Office:—P.O. Box 100, 28366. Tel: 910-594-0287; Fax: 910-594-1749. Email: olog@embarqmail.com.
Res.: 211 Irwin Dr., 28366. Tel: 910-594-0152.
Catechesis/Religious Program—Students 394.

ORIENTAL, PAMLICO CO., SAINT PETER THE FISHERMAN (2000), Mission of St. Paul, New Bern. Rev. Paul Mizener, Admin.
Res.: 5903 Asanto Domingo Ct., New Bern, 28560.
Church: 1149 White Farm Rd., 28571. Tel: 252-249-3687; Fax: 252-249-6576. Email: stpeter@always-online.com.
Catechesis/Religious Program—Students 7.

PINEHURST, MOORE CO., SACRED HEART (1919) Revs. William L. Pitts; James M. Labosky; Bill John Acosta-Escobar; Deacon August J. Mirande.
Mailing Address: P.O. Box 1768, 28370. Tel: 910-295-6550; Fax: 910-255-0299. Email: sacredheart@pinehurst.net. Web: sacredheartpinehurst.org.
Early Childhood Center—P.O. Box 5269, 28374. Tel: 910-295-3514. Jan Gatti, Dir.
Catechesis/Religious Program—Tel: 910-295-3072; Fax: 910-255-0299. Mrs. Barbara Kemple, D.R.E. Students 232.
Mission—Saint Juan Diego 6963 Hwy. 705 S., Robbins, Moore Co. 27325. Tel: 910-948-4100; Fax: 910-948-4101. Rev. Bill John Acosta-Escobar, Admin.

PLYMOUTH, WASHINGTON CO., ST. JOAN OF ARC (1959) Sr. Arcadia Rivera Gutierrez, D.S.M.G., Pastoral Admin.
Mailing Address: P.O. Box 822, 27962. Tel: 252-793-4052; Fax: 252-793-5315.
Catechesis/Religious Program—Fax: 252-793-5315. Students 46.

RAEFORD, HOKE CO., ST. ELIZABETH OF HUNGARY (1959) Sr. Jeanne Morgan, S.S.J., Pastoral Admin. P.O. Box 665, 28376-0665. Tel: 910-875-8803; Fax: 910-875-8802. Email: stelizabethofhungaryraeford@yahoo.com. Web: www.stelizabethofhungary.net.
Catechesis/Religious Program—Students 70.

RED SPRINGS, ROBESON CO., ST. ANDREW Rev. Walter Ospina.
Mailing Address: P.O. Box 649, 28377. Tel: 910-843-3440; Fax: 910-843-5700. Email: standrewrs@embarqmail.com.
Res.: 518 S. Main St., 28377. Tel: 910-843-6828.
Church: 301 Mercer Ave., 28377.
Station—Our Lady of Mount Carmel Saint Pauls, 28384.

RIEGELWOOD, COLUMBUS CO., CHRIST THE KING (1964), (Hispanic), Revs. Steven V. Carlson; Marco Antonio Gonzalez-Hernandez, Parochial Vicar.
Mailing Address: 1011 Eastwood Rd., Wilmington, 28403. Tel: 910-392-0720; Fax: 910-392-6777.
Catechesis/Religious Program—Tony Para, D.R.E. Students 10.

ROANOKE RAPIDS, HALIFAX CO., ST. JOHN THE BAPTIST (1931) [CEM] Rev. Pius S. Wekesa, Admin.
Res.: 71 Dalton Ct., 27870. Tel: 252-537-4667; Fax: 252-535-2076. Email: stjohnbaptist@embarqmail.com.
Catechesis/Religious Program—Teri Bales, D.R.E. Students 65.
Station—Immaculate Conception King St., Halifax, 27839.

ROCKY MOUNT, NASH & EDGECOMBE COS., OUR LADY OF PERPETUAL HELP (1892) Rev. Clyde Timberlake Meares.
Mailing Address: 328 Hammond St., 27804. Tel: 252-972-0452; Fax: 252-972-4780.
Res.: 501 Hammond St., 27804. Tel: 252-972-1949; Fax: 252-972-4780.
School—315 Hammond St., 27804. Tel: 252-972-1971; Fax: 252-972-7831. Mrs. Connie Urbanski, Prin. Lay Teachers 12; Students 132.
Catechesis/Religious Program—Tel: 252-972-0498. Dianne Young, D.R.E. Students 159.
Mission—Immaculate Conception 721 Virginia Ave., Nash & Edgecombe Cos. 27804.

ROXBORO, PERSON CO., STS. MARY AND EDWARD (1935) Rev. William H. Rodriguez.
Res.: 611 N. Main St., 27573-5040. Tel: 336-599-4122 (Office); Fax: 336-598-0412.
Catechesis/Religious Program—Students 106.

SANFORD, LEE CO., ST. STEPHEN THE FIRST MARTYR (1932) [CEM] Rev. Msgr. Stephen C. Worsley.
901 N. Franklin Dr., 27330.
Res.: 2402 Wicker St., 27330-7681. Tel: 919-776-1532; Fax: 919-775-1399. Email: secretaryststephen@earthlink.net. Web: www.ststephensch.net.
Catechesis/Religious Program—Students 307.

SHALLOTTE, BRUNSWICK CO., ST. BRENDAN THE NAVIGATOR (1983) [JC] Revs. Robert F. Ippolito, M.S.; Hector LaChapelle, M.S.; Deacons A. R. McGahran; Thomas Kronyak.
Mailing Address: Box 2984, 28459-9999. Tel: 910-754-8544; Fax: 910-755-6046. Email: brenavigator@atmc.net. Web: saintbrendan-shallotte.org.
Church & Office: 5101 Ocean Hwy. W., 28459.
Catechesis/Religious Program—Tel: 910-754-8544. Students 126.

SILER CITY, CHATHAM CO., ST. JULIA (1961), (Spanish), Revs. James Fukes, O.F.M.Conv.; Pedro de Oliveira, O.F.M.Conv.
Mailing Address: 210 Harold Hart Rd., 27344. Tel: 919-742-5584; Fax: 919-742-4917. Web: www.saint-julia.org. In Res., Rev. Joseph Madden, O.F.M.Conv.
Catechesis/Religious Program—Students 244.

SMITHFIELD, JOHNSTON CO., ST. ANN (1935) See new location under Clayton, NC.

SOUTHERN PINES, MOORE CO., ST. ANTHONY OF PADUA (1895) [CEM] Rev. Msgr. Jeffrey A. Ingham.
Mailing Address: P.O. Box 29, 28388-0029. Tel: 910-692-6613; Fax: 910-692-4964.
Rectory—2952 Camp Easter Rd., 28387. Tel: 910-692-9847; Fax: 910-692-4964. Email: office@st-anthony-of-padua.org. Web: www.st-anthony-of-padua.org.
School—320 N. Ashe St., 28387-0029. Tel: 910-692-6241; Fax: 910-692-2286. Email: kstepnoski@jp2catholicschool.org. Web: www.jp2catholicschool.org. Mr. Richard Kruska, Prin. Lay Teachers 14; Students 116.
Catechesis/Religious Program—Tel: 910-692-6613. Email: dwake@st-anthony-of-padua.org. Students 184.

SOUTHPORT, BRUNSWICK CO., SACRED HEART (1941) Rev. Trent L. Watts; Patricia Ciemnicki, Dir. Pastoral Svcs.
Mailing Address: 5269 Dosher Cutoff, S.E., 28461. Tel: 910-457-6173; Fax: 910-457-6421.
Res.: 213 Yaupon Dr., 28461. Tel: 910-457-0223.
Catechesis/Religious Program—Tel: 910-457-6173. Patricia Novotny, D.R.E. Students 91.

SWANSBORO, ONSLOW CO., ST. MILDRED (1947) [CEM] Rev. Donald G. Baribeau, M.S.
Res.: 616 Sabiston Dr., 28584-9674. Tel: 910-326-4370; Fax: 910-326-5589. Web: www.stmildred.info. Email: srectory@embarqmail.com.
Catechesis/Religious Program—Tel: 910-326-5589. Francine Sabisch, D.R.E. Students 196.

TARBORO, EDGECOMBE CO., ST. CATHERINE OF SIENA (1897) Rev. Frank M. Raffo.
Res.: 1004 St. David St., 27886. Tel: 252-823-3866; Fax: 252-824-0412.
Catechesis/Religious Program—Students 10.

WAKE FOREST, WAKE CO., ST. CATHERINE OF SIENA (1940) Revs. Philip M. Tighe; James C. Dull.
Church: 520 W. Holding Ave., 27587. Tel: 919-570-0070; Fax: 919-570-0071. Web: www.saintcatherinesienawf.org.
School—Lorraine Powers, Prin.
Catechesis/Religious Program—Tel: 919-570-0070, Ext. 108. Email: sgammon@saintcatherinesienawf.org. Susan Gammon, D.R.E. Students 1,194.
Early Childhood Center—Tel: 919-556-4104. Mary Jane Haga, Dir.

WASHINGTON, BEAUFORT CO., MOTHER OF MERCY (1963) Rev. M. Arturo Cabra.
Res.: 412 Crown Dr., 27889. Tel: 252-946-1792; Fax: 252-946-1399. Email: office@momchurch.org.
Church: 111 W. Ninth St., 27889. Tel: 252-946-2941.
Catechesis/Religious Program—Tel: 919-946-0769. Dana Lawson, D.R.E. Students 85.

WENDELL, WAKE CO., ST. EUGENE (1948) Revs. Joseph A. Lapauw, C.I.C.M.; Johanes Teguh Raharjo, C.I.C.M.; Deacon Willie Foggie.
Mailing Address: 608 Lions Club Rd., P.O. Box 188, 27591. Tel: 919-365-7114; Fax: 919-365-9431. Email: steugene@bellsouth.net. Web: www.steugeneparish.org.
Catechesis/Religious Program— Trish Clemmer, D.R.E. Students 300.

WHITEVILLE, COLUMBUS CO., SACRED HEART (1938) Very Rev. Marcos Leon-Angulo.
Res.: 302 N. Lee St., 28472. Tel: 910-642-3895; Fax: 910-640-1948.
Catechesis/Religious Program—Students 102.
Mission—Our Lady of the Snows 701 W. Broad St., P.O. Box 1766, Elizabethtown, Bladen Co. 28337-1766. Tel: 910-862-4998; Fax: 910-862-7298. Email: olsnw736@earthlink.net.

WILLIAMSTON, MARTIN CO., HOLY TRINITY (1951) Sr. Kieran Williams, I.H.M., Pastoral Admin.
Mailing Address: P.O. Box 894, 27892-0894. Tel: 252-792-4091; Fax: 252-792-4091.
Church: 3751 Bear Grass Rd., 27892.
Catechesis/Religious Program—Students 88.

WILMINGTON, NEW HANOVER CO.

1—IMMACULATE CONCEPTION (1925) Very Rev. John McGee, O.S.F.S.
Church: 6650 Carolina Beach Rd., 28412. Tel: 910-791-1003; Fax: 910-791-0081.
Catechesis/Religious Program—Students 286.

2—ST. MARK (1978) Revs. Steven V. Carlson; Marco Antonio Gonzalez-Hernandez; Deacon Orlando Perez.
Church & Office: 1011 Eastwood Rd., 28403. Tel: 910-392-0720, Ext. 226; Fax: 910-392-6777. Email: vicar@stmarkcatholicchurch.com. Web: www.stmarkcatholicchurch.com.
School—1013 Eastwood Rd., 28403-1905. Tel: 910-452-2800, Ext. 239; Fax: 910-332-6505. Web: www-.stmarkcatholicschool.org. Marguerite DiFulvio, Prin.
Catechesis/Religious Program—Tel: 910-392-0792, Ext. 229. Email: ffy@stmarkcatholicchurch.com. Ms. Anne Doyle, D.R.E. Students 478.
Mission—Christ the King 100 Burns Rd., Riegelwood, Columbus Co. 28456-0155.

3—ST. MARY (1912) Very Rev. Robert J. Kus.
Res.: 412 Ann St., 28401-4592. Tel: 910-762-5491; Fax: 910-762-9664. Email: secretary@thestmaryparish.org. Web: thestmaryparish.org.
School—217 S. 4th, 28401. Fax: 910-772-8034. Lay Teachers 17; Students 230.
Catechesis/Religious Program—Students 451.

WILSON, WILSON CO.

1—ST. ALPHONSUS DE LIGUORI, Closed. For sacramental records contact St. Therese, Wilson.

2—CHURCH OF ST. THERESE (1923) Revs. Gregory Lowchy; Bruce Bavinger, S.J.
Church & Office: 700 Nash St., N.E., 27893-3047. Tel: 252-237-3019; Fax: 252-237-2042. Email: wilsonsttherese@embarqmail.com.
Catechesis/Religious Program—Tel: 252-237-3019. Students 250.

WINDSOR, BERTIE CO., CATHOLIC COMMUNITY OF BERTIE & WASHINGTON COUNTIES Rev. Paul W. Brant, S.J.
Mailing Address: 403 Belmont St., P.O. Box 1394, 27983. Tel: 252-794-5086. Web: bertienccatholicweb.com.
Catechesis/Religious Program—Jeffrey Siatrez, D.R.E. Students 24.

WRIGHTSVILLE BEACH, NEW HANOVER CO., ST. THERESE (1939) Rev. Msgr. Matthew D. Hendrick; Deacon James F. Welch.
Res.: 209 S. Lumina Ave., 28480. Tel: 910-256-2471; Fax: 910-256-2459.
Catechesis/Religious Program—Students 97.

Special Assignment:

Revs.—

Labosky, James M., P.O. Box 1768, Pinehurst, 28370.

McCue, Scott E., Cardinal Gibbons High School, 1401 Edwards Mill Rd., 27607.

Shlesinger, Bernard E., III, 226 Hillsborough St., 27603. Tel: 919-832-6279

On Duty Outside the Diocese:
Rev.—
Fitzgerald, R. Martin, Chap. Major, PSC 2, Box 326, Apo, AP 96264.

Absent on Leave:
Rev.—
Davis, Thomas R. (Medical)

Retired:
Most Rev.—
Gossman, F. Joseph, D.D., J.C.D., 1601 Westbridge Ct., 27606.
Rev. Msgrs.—
Hadden, Thomas P., 2651 Mellow Field Dr., #107, 27604. Tel: 919-838-6907
Keaney, James P., 590 Central Ave., Apt. C16, Southern Pines, 28387. Tel: 910-692-9645
Leach, Phillip, 202-1835 Barclay St., Vancouver BC V6G 1K7 Canada.
Lewis, Gerald L., 3005 Country Club Rd., New Bern, 28562. Tel: 919-376-3911
Moeslein, Francis R., 2106 Joslyn Dr., Morehead City, 26557-9200. Tel: 252-726-3579
Wall, John A., Student Center, 218 Pittsboro St., Chapel Hill, 27516-2738.
Revs.—
Bryon, Paul J., 590 Central Ave., Villa A-21, Southern Pines, 28387.
Butler, James, 5758 Three Oaks Dr., 27612. Tel: 919-787-3049
Creel, Jesse, 55-15 Little Neck Pkwy., Little Neck, NY 11362.
Dash, Alan J., 6702 Rushwood Ct., Wilmington, 28405. Tel: 910-452-0547
Dorsel, John F., P.O. Box 1881, Pinehurst, 28374. Tel: 910-295-2085
Gaul, Thomas J., 5407 Gales St., Hope Mills, 28348. Tel: 910-426-3728
Ghisalberti, Giacomo G., P.O. Box 70338, Myrtle Beach, SC 29572.
Grabowski, Eugene M., 116 Sutton Dr., Cape Carteret, 28584. Tel: 252-762-3330
Keenan, Desmond R., 7901 Hinton Rd., Wake Forest, 27587.
Kelly, John R., 779 Galloway Dr., Fayetteville, 28303. Tel: 910-867-2803
Lawson, Douglas J., 1449 South Shore Dr., Southport, 28461. Tel: 910-845-2353
Maloney, Francis G., 590 Central Ave., Villa F.3, Southern Pines, 28387. Tel: 910-246-2123
Parker, Kenneth, 704 McIntosh Rd., Carthage, 28327. Tel: 910-245-4640
Perry, Francis, P.O. Box 506, La Grange, 28551.
Richardson, John L., 592 Central Dr., Villa F., Southern Pines, 28387. Tel: 910-579-8270
Shea, Robert F., 590 Central Ave., Villa F.4, Southern Pines, 28387. Tel: 910-246-0471
Turner, Richard W., P.O. Box 1039, Spring Hope, 27882. Tel: 252-475-3360
Woodhall, Jonathan A., 317-307 W. Morgan St., 27601-1471. Tel: 919-412-3388

Permanent Deacons:
Charlesworth, Myles, Our Lady of Lourdes, Raleigh
Colon, Vicente, St. Patrick, Fayetteville
Cortright, William, St. Elizabeth of Hungary, Raeford
DeCarolis, Lawrence, Immaculate Conception, Durham
Evans, Forest, Holy Family, Hillsborough
Fatica, Gerald, St. Mildred, Swansboro
Feneis, Al, St. Egbert, Morehead City
Foggie, Willie, St. Eugene, Wendell
Henriquez, Juan "Nay", St. Isidore Mission, Stedman
Hoffert, Daniel, St. Andrew the Apostle, Apex
Hubisz, John
Hunt, William, St. Paul, New Bern
James, Webster A., St. Mary, Goldsboro
Junginger, George, St. Michael, Cary
Kronyak, Thomas
Lacina, Dick, (Retired)
LaPierre, Joseph, (Unassigned)
Leahy, Michael, Holy Infant, Durham
Lewandowski, Stephen, St. Joseph, Raleigh
Mack, Tom, Holy Infant, Durham
Madey, Robert, St. Raphael, Raleigh
McGahran, Robert, St. Brendan, Shallotte
Meier, Anthony, St. Bernadette, Fuquay-Varina
Mirande, Mike, Sacred Heart, Pinehurst
Porter, Thomas, St. Anthony of Padua, Southern Pines
Price, Robert, (Unassigned)
Rodriguez, Jorge, (Unassigned)
Rzewnicki, Phil, St. Thomas More, Chapel Hill
Saez, Felix, Jr., St. James, Henderson
Sanchez, Michael, St. Luke the Evangelist, Raleigh
Schoebel, James, Ft. Bragg, Fayetteville
Snyder, Patrick, Good Shepherd, Hope Mills
Stonikinis, George, Holy Family, Elizabeth City
Tapler, Leopold, St. Mary, Garner
Velazco Bonilla, Hector, St. Raphael the Archangel, Raleigh
Waldmann, William, Immaculate Conception, Durham
Walsh, Michael, St. Ann, Clayton
Welch, James, St. Therese, Wrightsville Beach
Whitfield, Robert, St. Peter the Fisherman, Oriental
Wobser, Don, Holy Redeemer, Kitty Hawk

INSTITUTIONS LOCATED IN THE DIOCESE

[A] HIGH SCHOOLS

RALEIGH. *Cardinal Gibbons High School* (1909) 1401 Edwards Mill Rd., 27607. Tel: 919-834-1625; Fax: 919-834-9771. Email: ajay@cghsnc.org. Web: www.cghsnc.org. Mr. Jason D. Curtis, Prin.; Dale Foushee, Librarian & Media Specialist. Priests 1; Sisters 3; Lay Teachers 78; Students 1,189.

GREENVILLE. *Pope John Paul II Catholic High School*, 3250 Dickinson Ave., 27858.

[B] HIGH SCHOOLS-PRIVATE

RALEIGH. *St. Thomas More Academy*, 3109 Spring Forest Rd., 27616. Tel: 919-878-7640; Fax: 919-878-7641. Email: admissions@stmacademy.org. Web: www.stmacademy.org. Larry Henson, Headmaster. Brothers 1; Lay Teachers 14; Students 114.

[C] CHILD CARE CENTERS

RALEIGH. *St. Joseph Pre-School*, 2817 Poole Rd., 27610. Tel: 919-231-4545; Fax: 919-231-9884. Email: mshaughn@nc.rr.com. Mrs. Marjorie Shaughnessy, Dir. Students 12.

St. Raphael Catholic School and Early Childhood Center, 5815 Falls of the Neuse Rd., 27609. Tel: 919-865-5750; Fax: 919-865-5701. Mr. Barry Thomas, Prin.; Carrie Griffith, Exec. Dir. Lay Teachers 47; Students 466.

APEX. *Saint Andrew Early Childhood Center*, 3008 Old Raleigh Rd., 27502. Tel: 919-387-8656; Fax: 919-362-5778. Email: ecc@saintandrew.org. Web: www.saintandrew.org. Ann Graf, Prin. Total Staff 23; Students 150.

CARY. *St. Michael Early Childhood Center* (1983) 804 High House Rd., 27513. Tel: 919-468-6110; Fax: 919-468-6130. Email: mtoscano@stmichaelcary.org. Web: www.stmichaelcary.org. Mrs. Marianna Toscano, Dir. Total Staff 21; Students 146.

GARNER. *St. Mary Child Development Center* (1982) 1008 Vandora Springs Rd., 27529. Tel: 919-772-0009; Fax: 919-772-5534. Email: smgprek@bellsouth.net. Ms. Karen Williams, Dir. Lay Teachers 4; Total Staff 7; Students 50.

[D] GENERAL HOSPITALS

SOUTHERN PINES. *St. Joseph of the Pines*, 100 Gossman Dr., Ste. B, 28387. Tel: 910-246-3000; Fax: 910-246-3187. Web: www.sjp.org. Mr. John Capasso, Pres. & CEO.

St. Joseph of the Pines, Inc. Bed Capacity 392; Total Staff 300.

[E] CATHOLIC SOCIAL SERVICES

RALEIGH. *Catholic Charities of the Diocese of Raleigh, Inc.*, 715 Nazareth St., 27606-2187. Tel: 919-821-9750; Fax: 919-821-9712. Web: catholiccharities.dioceseofraleigh.org. Ms. Kathleen Walsh, M.S.W., A.C.S.W., Diocesan Dir. Total Staff 48; Total Assisted 42,545.

Raleigh Office, 3000 Highwoods Blvd., Ste. 128, 27604. Tel: 919-790-8533; Fax: 919-790-8836. Rick Miller-Haraway, L.C.S.W.

Cape Fear Office, 4006 Princess Pl. Dr., Wilmington, 28405. Tel: 910-251-8130; Fax: 910-251-8491.

Piedmont Office, 902 Broad St., P.O. Box 647, Durham, 27702. Tel: 919-286-1964; Fax: 919-286-4001. Susan Gilbertson, L.C.S.W.

Fayetteville Office, 590 Cedar Creek Rd. Ste. 110, Fayetteville, 28312-6097. Tel: 910-424-2020; Fax: 910-424-8435. Lisa E. Perkins, M.S.W., L.S.W.

New Bern Office, 502 Middle St., P.O. Box 826, New Bern, 28563. Tel: 252-638-2188; Fax: 252-638-2417. Linda McAlister, L.C.S.W.

Tar River Office, 204 E. Arlington Blvd., Ste. L, Greenville, 27835-8241. Tel: 252-355-5111; Fax: 252-355-1088. Betty Byrnes, L.C.S.W.

Albemarle Office, 123 Market St., Hertford, 27944. Tel: 252-426-7717; Fax: 252-426-9940. Stephanie Harrell, L.C.S.W.P.

Peace and Justice/Respect Life Office, 715 Nazareth St., 27606-2198. Tel: 919-821-9751; Fax: 919-821-9712. Sr. Joan Jurski, O.S.F.

[F] MONASTERIES AND RESIDENCE OF PRIESTS AND BROTHERS

RALEIGH. *Dominican Priory* (1994) *Dominican Priory of St. Martin de Porres*, 304 E. Park Dr., P.O. Box 12927, 27605-2927. Tel: 919-833-1893. Web: www.opraleigh.org. Very Revs. Bruce B. Schultz, O.P., Prior; Stephen Smith, O.P., J.C.D.; Revs. Richard R. Archer, O.P.; Betrand E. Ebben, O.P.; Jude Siciliano, O.P.; Paul J. Philibert, O.P.

Jesuit Community (1996) 5801 Falls of the Neuse Rd., 27609. Tel: 919-865-5700; Fax: 919-865-5701. Web: www.saintraphael.org. Priests 6.

Jesuits in Eastern North Carolina: Revs. Bruce Bavinger, S.J.; Paul W. Brant, S.J.; Raymond J. Donaldson, S.J.; Robert M. Hussey, S.J.; Michael Proterra, S.J.; Robert Wiesenbaugh, S.J.

BURLINGTON. *Conventual Franciscans, Blessed Sacrament Church*, 1236 Westbrook Ave., Elon, 27244. Tel: 336-446-6753; Fax: 336-227-2896. Email: catholic@netpath.net. Web: www.blessedsacramentnc.org. Very Rev. Robert Benko, O.F.M.Conv., V.F.; Revs. Paul Gabriel, O.F.M.Conv.; Jacek K. Leszczynski, O.F.M.Conv.; Gerald Waterman, O.F.M.Conv. Total in Residence 4.

PITTSBORO. *Our Lady of Guadalupe Friary*, P.O. Box 1638, 27312. Tel: 919-545-5600; Fax: 919-545-5650. Email: ncfriars@aol.com. Web: www.franciscanseast.org. Revs. James Fukes, O.F.M.Conv.; Pedro de Oliveira, O.F.M.Conv.; Joseph Madden, O.F.M.Conv.

[G] CONVENTS AND RESIDENCES FOR SISTERS

RALEIGH. *Congregation of the Sisters of the Holy Cross*, 2017 Quail Forest Dr., 27609. Tel: 919-876-0741.

Sisters of the Holy Cross, Inc. Sisters 3.

Additional Location: 718 Patriots Pointe Dr., Hillsborough, 27278. Tel: 919-245-1327.

Servants of the Immaculate Heart of Mary, 2912 Anderson Dr., 27608. Tel: 919-861-4640. Sisters 5.

AHOSKIE. *Sisters of St. Louis--California Region*, 409 W. Church St., 27910. Tel: 919-332-2220. Email: tmssl@yahoo.com. Web: www.St-louis-sisters.org.

CARY. *Sisters of St. Francis of Sylvania, Ohio*, 205 Twin Oaks Pl., 27511. Tel: 919-460-6218; Fax: 919-821-9705. Email: jurski@raldioc.org.

CHAPEL HILL. *Sisters, Servants of the Immaculate Heart of Mary*, 1194 Great Ridge Pkwy., 27516. Tel: 919-240-5612 (Home); 919-490-5253 (Office). Email: cgellings@aol.com. Web: ihmsisters.org.

St. Thomas More Sisters' Residence, 1232 Cranebridge Pl., 27517. Tel: 919-929-1547.

DURHAM. *Dominican Congregation of St. Catherine DeRicci* (1880) 711 Mason Rd., 27712-9229. Tel: 919-477-1285; Fax: 919-477-9485. Email: camay711@nc.rr.com. Web: www.raldio.org/avila.html.

Sisters of St. Francis of Philadelphia (1855) 711 Mason Rd., 27712-9229. Tel: 919-477-1285; Fax: 919-477-9485. Email: damian711@nc.rr.com. Web: www.raldioc.org/avila.html.

JACKSONVILLE. *Sisters of St. Ursula* (1606) 600 Windsor Cir., Apt. 206, 28546. Tel: 910-347-4196, Ext. 104; Fax: 910-347-9338. Email: bmcady@aol.com.

NEW BERN. *St. Paul Convent*, 3003 Country Club Rd., 28562. Tel: 252-637-3726. Total in Residence 2.

RAEFORD. *St. Elizabeth of Hungary Parish House* (1959) 210 W. Elwood Ave., 28376. Tel: 910-904-1251. Email: stelizabethofhungaryraeford@yahoo.com. Web: www.stelizabethofhungary.net.

TARBORO. *Congregation of St. Agnes* (1858) P.O. Box 445, 27886. Tel: 252-823-8801; Fax: 252-823-8801. Email: tcoutreach@tarboronc.com. Web: csasisters.org.

WARRENTON. *Sisters, Servants of the Immaculate Heart of Mary*, 113 Joshua Way, P.O. Box 934, 27589. Tel: 252-257-5605; Fax: 252-257-5605. Email: stjoseph@embarqmail.com.

WILLIAMSTON. *Sisters, Servants of the Immaculate Heart of Mary*, P.O. Box 894, 27892. Tel: 252-792-4091; Fax: 252-792-4091. Email: holytrinity2@suddenlink.net.

[H] RETREAT HOUSES

RALEIGH. *Madonna House* (1950) 424 Rose Ln., 27610. Tel: 919-231-4049. Email: madonnahouse@nc.rr.com. Web: www.mv.igs.net/~madonnah. Echo Lewis; Joanne Degidio; Miss Theresa Davis, Dir.

DURHAM. *Avila Retreat Center* (1980) 711 Mason Rd., 27712-9229. Tel: 919-477-1285; Fax: 919-477-9485. Email: damian711@nc.rr.com. Web: www.raldioc.org/avila.html. Sr. Damian Marie

Jackson, O.S.F., Dir. Total Staff 8; Total in Residence 2.

[I] COLLEGE CAMPUS MINISTRY CENTERS

RALEIGH. *Doggett Center for Catholic Campus Ministry at Aquinas House* North Carolina State University, 600 Bilyeu St., 27606-2152. Tel: 919-833-9668; Fax: 919-833-1194. Email: jagonza3@ncsu.edu. Web: www.ccm-raleigh.org. Rev. John Alex Gonzalez, Campus Min.

CHAPEL HILL. *Newman Catholic Student Center* University of North Carolina, 218 Pittsboro St., 27516. Tel: 919-929-3730; Fax: 919-929-3778. Web: www.newman-chapelhill.org. Rev. Msgr. John A. Wall (Retired).

DURHAM. *Newman Catholic Student Center Duke University* Box 90974, 27708-0974. Tel: 919-684-8959; Fax: 919-681-8660. Web: www.duke.edu/web/catholic/. Revs. Joseph G. Vetter, Dir.; John P. McDonagh.

North Carolina Central University Catholic Campus Ministry 525 Nelson St., 27707. Tel: 919-793-3325. Very Rev. Bruce B. Schultz, O.P., Dir., Catholic Campus Min.

ELON. *Elon University* (1889) *Catholic Campus Ministry*, Campus Box 2960, 27244-2010. Tel: 336-278-7355; Fax: 336-278-7439. Email: gwaterman@elon.edu. Web: org.elon.edu/ccm. Rev. Gerald Waterman, O.F.M.Conv., Campus Min., Res.: Blessed Sacrament Friary, 514 Parkview Dr., Burlington, 27215.

GREENVILLE. *Newman Catholic Student Center of East Carolina University* (1948) 953 E. 10th St., 27858. Tel: 252-757-1991; Fax: 252-757-1991. Email: ecunewman@hotmail.com. Web: www.clubhouse.ecu.edu/newman. Rev. William G. Quigley, C.I.C.M., Dir. Campus Min.; Ryan Downey, Assoc. Dir. Campus Min.

WILMINGTON. *Newman Catholic Student Center* (1986) *University of North Carolina at Wilmington*, UNC-W Station, P.O. Box 20044, 28407. Tel: 910-792-0507; Fax: 910-792-0507. Email: uncw.ccm@gmail.com. Web: www.newman-uncw.org. Sr. Rosemary G. McNamara, S.U., Dir. & Campus Min.

[J] MISCELLANEOUS

RALEIGH. *Catholic Housing Corporation*, 715 Nazareth St., 27606. Tel: 919-821-9704; Fax: 919-821-9705. Email: elmayan@raldioc.org.

Catholic Parish Outreach, 2013 N. Raleigh Blvd., 27604. Tel: 919-873-0245; Fax: 919-873-0260. Web: www.cporaleigh.org. Total Staff 1; Total Assisted: Avg Per Month 4,540; Total Assisted Annually 81,476.

The Clergy Retirement Plan of Diocese of Raleigh, 715 Nazareth St., 27606. Tel: 919-821-9711; Fax: 919-821-9712. Web: www.dioceseofraleigh.org.

Domicile Property, Inc., 715 Nazareth St., 27606.

Vocations Office, 226 Hillsborough St., 27603. Tel: 919-832-6280; Fax: 919-832-6284. Email: shlesinger@raldioc.org. Web: raleighvocations.org. Very Rev. Bernard (Ned) Shlesinger III, V.F., Dir.; Mr. Brad Watkins, Asst. to Vocation Dir.

NORTH TOPSAIL BEACH. *Marianist Family Ministry, Inc.* (1987) Marianist Family Ministry CFL Family Retreat Center, 2006 Wicker St., 28460. Tel: 910-328-1584. Email: cflcenter@charterinternet.com. Web: www.christianfamilyliving.org. Marilynn Shackelford, Dir. Total Staff 2.

SMITHFIELD. *Short Journey Retreat Center*, 2323 Cleveland Rd., 27577. Tel: 919-934-7463; Fax: 919-934-7464. Email: yangj@raldioc.org.

SOUTHERN PINES. *St. Joseph of the Pines Retirement Villa*, 590 Central Dr., 28387. Tel: 910-246-3001; Fax: 910-246-3016. Email: nsummers@sjp.org. Nathan Summers, Res. Support & Svcs., Pine Knoll. Total Staff 26; Total in Residence 105.

St. Joseph of the Pines, Inc., 100 Gossman Dr., Suite B, 28387. Tel: 910-246-1000; Fax: 910-246-3187. Email: kcormier@sjp.org. Web: www.sjp.org.

St. Joseph of the Pines, Inc. Long Term Care Facilities 1; Total Staff 300.

RELIGIOUS INSTITUTES OF MEN REPRESENTED IN THE DIOCESE

For further details refer to the corresponding bracketed number in the Religious Institutes of Men or Women section.

[0865]—*Congregation of Mother Coredemptrix*—C.M.C.

[0650]—*Congregation of the Holy Spirit*—C.S.Sp.

[1000]—*Congregation of the Passion*—C.P.

[0480]—*Conventual Franciscans*—O.F.M.Conv

[0520]—*Franciscan Friars*—O.F.M.

[0530]—*Franciscan Friars of the Atonement*—S.A.

[0570]—*Glenmary Home Missioners*—G.H.M.

[0690]—*Jesuit Fathers and Brothers* (Maryland & New York Provs.)—S.J.

[0720]—*The Missionaries of Our Lady of La Salette*—M.S.

[0860]—*Missionhurst Congregation of the Immaculate Heart of Mary*—C.I.C.M.

[0920]—*Oblates of St. Francis De Sales* (American Prov.)—O.S.F.S.

[0430]—*Order of Preachers (Dominicans)*—O.P.

[0760]—*Society of Mary (Marianists)*—S.M.

RELIGIOUS INSTITUTES OF WOMEN REPRESENTED IN THE DIOCESE

[]—*Adrian Dominican Sisters of the Most Holy Rosary* (Adrian, MI)—O.P.

[3710]—*Congregation of the Sisters of Saint Agnes*—C.S.A.

[3935]—*Congregation of the Sisters of St. Louis*—S.S.L.

[1920]—*Congregation of the Sisters of the Holy Cross*—C.S.C.

[]—*Daughters of St. Mary of Guadalupe* —D.S.M.G.

[0960]—*Daughters of Wisdom*—D.W.

[1070-13]—*Dominican Sisters*—O.P.

[1070-17]—*Dominican Sisters*—O.P.

[0990]—*Sisters of Divine Providence*—C.D.P.

[2520]—*Sisters of Mercy*—R.S.M.

[2990]—*Sisters of Notre Dame* (Chardon, OH)—S.N.D.

[1650]—*Sisters of St. Francis of Philadelphia*—O.S.F.

[3830]—*Sisters of St. Joseph*—S.S.J.

[3910]—*Sisters of St. Joseph of St. Mark*—S.J.S.M.

[1990]—*Sisters of the Holy Names of Jesus and Mary*—S.N.J.M.

[2150]—*Sisters, Servants of the Immaculate Heart of Mary*—I.H.M.

[2160]—*Sisters, Servants of the Immaculate Heart of Mary*—I.H.M.

[2170]—*Sisters, Servants of the Immaculate Heart of Mary*—I.H.M.

[4048]—*Society of Sisters Faithful Companions of Jesus*—F.C.J.

[4040]—*Society of St. Ursula*—S.U.

NECROLOGY

† Klaus, Joseph J., (Retired)—Died Dec. 30, 2008

† Kowal, William D., (Absent on Leave)—Died Dec. 21, 2008

† Mahoney, Edward P., (Retired)—Died Jan. 8, 2009

An asterisk (*) denotes an organization that has established tax-exempt status directly with the IRS and is not covered by the USCCB Group Ruling.

Diocese of Rapid City

(Dioecesis Rapidopolitana)

Most Reverend

BLASE J. CUPICH

Bishop of Rapid City; ordained August 16, 1975; appointed Bishop of Rapid City July 7, 1998; ordained and installed September 21, 1998.

Chancery Office: 606 Cathedral Dr., Rapid City, SD 57701. Tel: 605-343-3541; Fax: 605-348-7985.

Email: chancery@diorc.org

Square Miles 43,000.

Formerly the Diocese of Lead.

Erected August 4, 1902; See transferred to Rapid City, August 1, 1930.

Comprises the Counties of Bennett, Butte, Corson, Custer, Dewey, Fall River, Gregory, Haakon, Harding, Jackson, Jones, Lawrence, Lyman, Meade, Mellette, Pennington, Perkins, Stanley, Shannon, Todd, Tripp and Ziebach in the State of South Dakota.

For legal titles of parishes and diocesan institutions, consult the Chancery Office.

STATISTICAL OVERVIEW

Personnel	
Bishop	1
Priests: Diocesan Active in Diocese	28
Priests: Diocesan Active Outside Diocese	1
Priests: Retired, Sick or Absent	8
Number of Diocesan Priests	37
Religious Priests in Diocese	14
Total Priests in Diocese	51
Extern Priests in Diocese	2
Ordinations:	
Diocesan Priests	1
Permanent Deacons	2
Permanent Deacons in Diocese	29
Total Brothers	3
Total Sisters	43
Parishes	
Parishes	88
With Resident Pastor:	
Resident Diocesan Priests	21
Resident Religious Priests	4
Without Resident Pastor:	
Administered by Priests	62
Administered by Religious Women	1
Missions	29
Pastoral Centers	4
Professional Ministry Personnel:	
Brothers	1
Sisters	6
Lay Ministers	41
Welfare	
Health Care Centers	1
Total Assisted	15,733
Residential Care of Children	1
Total Assisted	6
Day Care Centers	1
Total Assisted	35
Specialized Homes	1
Total Assisted	7,709
Special Centers for Social Services	6
Total Assisted	21,941
Other Institutions	1
Educational	
Diocesan Students in Other Seminaries	13
Total Seminarians	13
High Schools, Diocesan and Parish	1
Total Students	247
High Schools, Private	1
Total Students	209
Elementary Schools, Diocesan and Parish	1
Total Students	568
Elementary Schools, Private	1
Total Students	345
Catechesis/Religious Education:	
High School Students	955
Elementary Students	2,434
Total Students under Catholic Instruction	4,771
Teachers in the Diocese:	
Priests	1
Sisters	1
Lay Teachers	119
Vital Statistics	
Receptions into the Church:	
Infant Baptism Totals	549
Minor Baptism Totals	54
Adult Baptism Totals	26
Received into Full Communion	81
First Communions	463
Confirmations	459
Marriages:	
Catholic	92
Interfaith	73
Total Marriages	165
Deaths	399
Total Catholic Population	25,229
Total Population	227,211

Former Bishops—Most Revs. JOHN STARIHA, D.D., cons. Oct. 28, 1902; retired March 29, 1909 and named Titular Bishop of Antipatride; died in Laibach, Austria, Nov. 28, 1915; JOSEPH F. BUSCH, D.D., cons. May 19, 1910; transferred to Saint Cloud, MN, Feb. 21, 1915; died May 31, 1953; JOHN J. LAWLER, S.T.D., cons. Titular Bishop of Greater Hermopolis and Auxiliary Bishop of St. Paul, Minnesota, May 19, 1910; transferred to the See of Lead, Jan. 29, 1916; died March 11, 1948; LEO F. DWORSCHAK, D.D., cons. Titular Bishop of Tium and Coadjutor Bishop of Rapid City "cum jure successionis," Aug. 22, 1946; transferred to Fargo, ND, April 10, 1947; WILLIAM T. MCCARTY, C.Ss.R., D.D., appt. Titular Bishop of Anaea and Delegate to the Military Vicar, Jan. 2, 1943; appt. Coadjutor Bishop of Rapid City "cum jure successionis," April 10, 1947; succeeded to March 11, 1948; retired Sept. 17, 1969; appt. Titular Bishop of Rotdon; died Sept. 14, 1972; HAROLD J. DIMMERLING, D.D., appt. Bishop of Rapid City, Sept. 17, 1969; ord. May 2, 1940; cons. Oct. 30, 1969; died Dec. 13, 1987; CHARLES J. CHAPUT, D.D., appt. Bishop of Rapid City, April 11, 1988; appt. Archbishop of Denver, Feb. 18, 1997.

Vicar General—Rev. DANIEL JUELFS, J.C.L.

Chancery Office—606 Cathedral Dr., P.O. Box 678, Rapid City, 57709. Tel: 605-343-3541; Fax: 605-348-7985. Email: chancery@diorc.org. Office Hours: Mon.-Fri. 8-5; Address all official business to this office.

Chancellor—MARGARET SIMONSON.

Diocesan Tribunal—606 Cathedral Dr., P.O. Box 678, Rapid City, 57709-0678. Tel: 605-343-3541; Fax: 605-348-7985.

Officialis—Rev. LEO HAUSMANN, J.C.L.

Diocesan Consultors—Revs. GEORGE WINZENBURG, S.J.; MICHEL MULLOY; DANIEL JUELFS, J.C.L.; STEVEN BIEGLER; BRIAN LANE; MARK MCCORMICK.

Deaneries—Revs. DAVID G. MATZKO, S.J., Rapid City; TIMOTHY S. HOAG, Spearfish; BRYAN SORENSEN, Martin; BRIAN CHRISTENSEN, Ft. Pierre; BRIAN FAWCETT, Lemmon; EDWARD G. WITT, S.J., St. Francis Mission.

Presbyteral Council—Rev. BRIAN FAWCETT, Chm.

Vicar for Retired Priests—Rev. Msgr. MICHAEL WOSTER, J.C.L.

Permanent Diaconate Program, Sioux Spiritual Center—Rev. GEORGE WINZENBURG, S.J., Dir., 20100 Center Rd., HCR 77, Box 271, Howes, 57748. Tel: 605-985-5906.

Development and Stewardship Program—ROBERT BICKETT, Dir.

Continuing Education of Clergy—Rev. KERRY PRENDIVILLE, McLaughlin.

Vocation Program—Rev. BRIAN PATRICK CHRISTENSEN, Dir., Mailing Address: P.O. Box 678, Rapid City, 57709-0678. Tel: 605-343-3541.

Diocesan Finance Manager—SUZANNE LAMBERT.

Diocesan Finance Council—Ms. VICKY COYLE; SHIRLEY STEC; DAN DUFFY; RAY SMITH; RAY HILLENBRAND; TIMOTHY FROST; Rev. BRIAN LANE; ROBERT WAGNER; FRANK SHORT; DON STUKEL; PAT BURCHILL.

Holy Childhood Pontifical Association—VERONICA VALANDRA.

Propagation of the Faith—VERONICA VALANDRA.

Catholic Relief Service—VERONICA VALANDRA, 606 Cathedral Dr., Rapid City, 57701-5498.

Native Concerns Office—VERONICA VALANDRA, Dir., 606 Cathedral Dr., Rapid City, 57701. Tel: 605-343-3541.

Director of Ongoing Formation—Rev. KERRY PRENDIVILLE, 141 Siever St., Lead, 57754-1646. Tel: 605-584-2002.

Superintendent of Schools—BARBARA HONEYCUTT.

Director of Rural Life—VACANT.

Office of Family Life—JILL SOWERS-LEGNER, Dir., 606 Cathedral Dr., P.O. Box 678, Rapid City, 57709-0678. Tel: 605-343-3541; Fax: 605-348-7985.

Family Life Sponsored Ministries—

Pro-Life Commission—SUE JIMMERSON, Chm., 606 Cathedral Dr., Rapid City, 57701.

Retreat Ministry—606 Cathedral Dr., P.O. Box 678, Rapid City, 57709-0678. Tel: 605-343-3541.

Beginning Experience, Separated, Divorced and Widowed Support Group—606 Cathedral Dr., P.O. Box 678, Rapid City, 57709-0678. Tel: 605-343-3541.

Bereavement Ministry—606 Cathedral Dr., P.O. Box 678, Rapid City, 57709-0678. Tel: 605-343-3541.

Natural Family Planning Ministry—606 Cathedral Dr., P.O. Box 678, Rapid City, 57709-0678. Tel: 605-343-3541.

Rachel's Vineyard—Mailing Address: 606 Cathedral Dr., P.O. Box 678, Rapid City, 57709-0678. Tel: 605-343-3541.

Independent Ministries—

Retrouvaille—606 Cathedral Dr., P.O. Box 678, Rapid City, 57709-0678. Tel: 605-343-3541.

Right to Life—Tel: 605-718-5215 (local contact).

Birthright—Tel: 605-343-1732.

Catholic Engaged Encounter—606 Cathedral Dr., P.O. Box 678, Rapid City, 57709-0678. Tel: 605-343-3541.

Worldwide Marriage Encounter—606 Cathedral

Dr., P.O. Box 678, Rapid City, 57709-0678. Tel: 605-343-3541.

Diocesan Office of Religious Education & Office of Faith Formation—LINDA SEVERNS, Dir., 606 Cathedral Dr., P.O. Box 678, Rapid City, 57709-0678. Tel: 605-343-3541.

Campaign for Human Development—VERONICA VALANDRA, 606 Cathedral Dr., Rapid City, 57701-5498. Tel: 605-343-3541.

Victim Assistance Coordinator—MARYANN TULLY. Tel: 605-209-3418. Email: fredoldford@hughes.net.

West River Catholic Newspaper—LAURIE HALLSTROM, Editor, 606 Cathedral Dr., Rapid City, 57701.

Catholic Youth Commission—PROVATIA POTVIN, Coord., 606 Cathedral Dr., Rapid City, 57701.

Archives—KATHY CORDES.

CLERGY, PARISHES, MISSIONS AND PAROCHIAL SCHOOLS

CITY OF RAPID CITY

(PENNINGTON COUNTY)

1—CATHEDRAL OF OUR LADY OF PERPETUAL HELP (1890) Revs. Michel Mulloy, Rector; Christopher Hathaway, F.S.S.P.; John Lule; Ed Vanorny; Tyler Dennis; Deacons Tom Lane, (Retired); George Gladfelter, (Retired); Raul Daniel; Greg Palmer. In Res., Rev. Steven Biegler.
Church: 520 Cathedral Dr., 57701-5499. Tel: 605-342-0507; Fax: 605-721-5986.
See St. Elizabeth Elementary, Middle School and St. Thomas More High School, Rapid City under Diocesan Catholic School System located in the Institution section.
Catechesis / Religious Program—Students 311.
Chapel—Immaculate Conception, Tel: 605-341-1578.
Mission—St. Michael's Hermosa, Custer Co.

2—BLESSED SACRAMENT (1947) Revs. Daniel Juelfs; Andrzej Wyrostek; Janusz Korban; Deacons Larry Kopriva; James VanLoan.
Res.: 4500 Jackson Blvd., 57702-4999. Tel: 605-342-3336; Fax: 605-341-5668. Email: bsc@blessedsacramentchurch.org. Web: www.blessedsacramentchurch.org.
Catechesis / Religious Program—Students 396.
Mission—Our Lady of Mt. Carmel Keystone, Pennington Co.
Mission—St. Rose of Lima 100 Park Ave., Hill City, Pennington Co. 57745.

3—ST. ISAAC JOGUES (1949), (Native American), Rev. David G. Matzko, S.J.; Deacons James Garnett, (Retired); Luis Usera; Marlon J. Leneaugh; Leroy DeCory, (Retired).
Res.: 221 Knollwood Dr., P.O. Box 1304, 57709-1304. Tel: 605-343-2165; Fax: 605-343-3257. Email: sij@rushmore.com.
Catechesis / Religious Program—Students 102.
Mother Butler Center—Tel: 605-343-2165; Fax: 605-343-3257. Catechetical and Social Center for Indians.
Mission—Indian Health Service, Sioux San Hospital and Pennington County Jail, Pennington Co.

4—ST. THERESE THE LITTLE FLOWER (1941) [JC], Formerly known as The Church of St. John the Evangelist. Rev. William A. Zandri; Deacons Claude Sauer, (Retired); Michael Curtin, (Retired).
Res.: 532 Adams St., 57701. Tel: 605-342-1556; Fax: 605-348-6272.
Catechesis / Religious Program—Students 153.

OUTSIDE THE CITY OF RAPID CITY

BELLE FOURCHE, BUTTE CO., ST. PAUL (1905) [JC] Revs. Timothy S. Hoag; Timothy William Castor; Deacon Ray Klein.
Res.: 855 Fifth Ave., 57717-1701. Tel: 605-723-3226; Fax: 605-723-3230. Email: stpauls@rushmore.com.
Catechesis / Religious Program—Students 81.

BISON, PERKINS CO., BLESSED SACRAMENT (1918) [JC], Served from Lemmon.
Catechesis / Religious Program—Sara Stadler, D.R.E. Students 25.

BONESTEEL, GREGORY CO., IMMACULATE CONCEPTION (1906) [CEM] Attended by St. Joseph, Gregory. Rev. Godfrey Muwanga.
Mailing Address: P.O. Box 376, 57317-0376. Tel: 605-654-2204; Fax: 605-654-2204. Email: imconsta@gwtc.net.
Res.: 414 Church Ave., Gregory, 57533. Email: stjoseph@gwtc.net.
Catechesis / Religious Program—Students 15.

BUFFALO, HARDING CO., ST. ANTHONY (1917) [CEM 2] [JC] Rev. John Heying.
Res.: 410 Allison St., P.O. Box 85, 57720-0085. Tel: 605-375-3438.
Catechesis / Religious Program—Students 30.
Mission—St. Agnes Cox, Harding Co.
Mission—St. Isidore Ralph, Harding Co.
Mission—Our Lady of the Prairie Reva, Harding Co.

BURKE, GREGORY CO., SACRED HEART (1905) [CEM 2] [JC] Attended by St. Joseph, Gregory. Rev. Godfrey Muwanga.
Res.: 414 Church Ave., Gregory, 57533.
Catechesis / Religious Program—Students 50.

CLEARFIELD, TRIPP CO., ST. BONIFACE, Closed. For inquiries for parish records contact the chancery.

COLOME, TRIPP CO., ST. ISIDORE (1909) [JC] Attended by Immaculate Conception, Winner. Rev. Msgr. Michael Woster.
Res.: P.O. Box 765, Winner, 57580. Tel: 605-842-3520; Fax: 605-842-3520. Email: parishsec@gwtc.net.
Catechesis / Religious Program—Email: dreic@gwtc.net. Students 35.

CUSTER, CUSTER CO., ST. JOHN THE BAPTIST (1911) [JC] Attended by St. Anthony's, Hot Springs. Rev. Peter Kovarik.
Res.: 449 Harney St., P.O. Box 632, 57730-0632. Tel: 605-673-4426; Fax: 605-673-4426.
Catechesis / Religious Program—Tel: 605-673-4426. Students 33.

DEADWOOD, LAWRENCE CO., ST. AMBROSE (1877) [CEM] Rev. Kerry Prendiville.
Res.: 141 S. Siever St., Lead, 57754. Tel: 605-578-1519. Email: kprendiville@rushmore.com.
Catechesis / Religious Program—

EAGLE BUTTE, DEWEY CO., ALL SAINTS (1911), (Native American), [JC] Revs. Brian Lane; Matthew Fallgren.
Res.: 138 Spruce St., P.O. Box 110, 57625-0110. Tel: 605-964-3391; Fax: 605-964-3300.
Catechesis / Religious Program—Students 49.
Mission—Immaculate Conception Bridger, Ziebach Co.
Catechesis / Religious Program—
Mission—St. Joseph Cherry Creek, Ziebach Co.
Catechesis / Religious Program—Students 3.
Mission—Sacred Heart Dupree, Ziebach Co.
Catechesis / Religious Program—Students 19.
Mission—St. Catherine Promise, Dewey Co.
Catechesis / Religious Program—Students 6.
Mission—Sacred Heart Red Scaffold, Ziebach Co.
Catechesis / Religious Program—Students 7.
Mission—St. Joseph Ridgeview, Dewey Co.
Mission—St. Luke Thunder Butte, Ziebach Co.
Mission—St. Therese White Horse, Dewey Co.
Catechesis / Religious Program—Students 11.

FAIRFAX, GREGORY CO., ST. ANTHONY'S (1904) [CEM] Attended by St. Joseph's, Gregory. Rev. Godfrey Muwanga.
Mailing Address: P.O. Box 186, 57335-0186. Tel: 605-654-2204; Fax: 605-654-2204. Email: imconsta@gwtc.net.
Catechesis / Religious Program—Students 12.

FAITH, MEADE CO., ST. JOSEPH (1917) [CEM] Rev. Marcin Stanislaw Garbacz; Deacon Larry Brown.
Res.: P.O. Box 307, 57626-0307. Tel: 605-967-2201; Fax: 605-967-2207.
Catechesis / Religious Program—Students 23.
Mission—St. Anthony Red Owl, Meade Co.
Catechesis / Religious Program—Students 5.
Mission—Our Lady of Victory Plainview, Meade Co.
Catechesis / Religious Program—
Mission—St. Joseph Mud Butte, Meade Co.
Catechesis / Religious Program—Students 8.

FORT PIERRE, STANLEY CO., ST. JOHN (1905) [JC] Rev. Brian Patrick Christensen.
Res.: 206 W. Main, P.O. Box 670, 57532-0670. Tel: 605-223-2176; Fax: 605-223-2805.
Catechesis / Religious Program—Students 72.

GREGORY, GREGORY CO., ST. JOSEPH (1905) [CEM 3] Rev. Godfrey Muwanga.
Res.: 414 Church Ave., 57533. Tel: 605-835-9290. Email: stjoseph@gwtc.net.
Catechesis / Religious Program—Mary Vale Hall, 411 Church St., 57533. Tel: 605-835-9396. Students 45.

HERMOSA, CUSTER CO., ST. MICHAEL'S, Attended by Our Lady of Perpetual Help Cathedral, Rapid City.

HILL CITY, PENNINGTON CO., ST. ROSE OF LIMA (1898) [JC] Attended by Blessed Sacrament, Rapid City. Rev. Daniel Juelfs; Deacon Frederick G. Tully.
Res.: 4500 Jackson Blvd., 57702. Tel: 605-342-3336; Fax: 605-341-5668.
Catechesis / Religious Program—Tel: 605-574-2479. Students 20.

HOT SPRINGS, FALL RIVER CO., ST. ANTHONY OF PADUA (1890) [JC] Rev. Peter Kovarik.
Res.: 501 Jennings Ave., P.O. Box 969, 57747-0969. Tel: 605-745-3393; Fax: 605-745-4303. Email: jmroe@gwtc.net.
Catechesis / Religious Program—Deacon Earl F. Witte, (Retired). Students 13.
Mission—St. James the Apostle 310 3rd Ave., P.O. Box 568, Edgemont, Fall River Co. 57735. Tel: 605-622-7801; Fax: 605-662-7801. Email: stjames@goldenwest.net.
Catechesis / Religious Program—Students 8.

KADOKA, JACKSON CO., OUR LADY OF VICTORY (1908) [JC] Attended by Our Lady of the Sacred Heart, Martin.
Catechesis / Religious Program—Lynn Herber, D.R.E. Students 21.

KENEL, CORSON CO., ASSUMPTION OF THE BLESSED VIRGIN MARY (1879), (Native American), Attended by St. Bernard, McLaughlin.
Catechesis / Religious Program—Students 23.

KENNEBEC, LYMAN CO., ST. MICHAEL'S (1906) [CEM] Attended by St. Mary, Lower Brule., Mailing Address: P.O. Box 185, Lower Brule, 57548-0185. Tel: 605-473-5335; Fax: 605-473-5453. Email: pastteam@gwtc.net.
Catechesis / Religious Program—Students 27.

KYLE, SHANNON CO., OUR LADY OF SORROWS (1910), (Native American), [CEM 2] Rev. Richard Abert, S.J. Served from Holy Rosary Mission, Pine Ridge.
Catechesis / Religious Program—Students 21.
Mission—St. John of the Cross, (Inactive), Allen, Bennett Co.
Mission—St. Stephens, (Inactive), Medicine Root, Shannon Co.

LEAD, LAWRENCE CO., ST. PATRICK'S (1878) [CEM] [JC] Rev. Kerry Prendiville.
Res.: 141 Siever St., 57754. Tel: 605-584-2002.
Catechesis / Religious Program—Students 45.

LEMMON, PERKINS CO., ST. MARY'S (1908) [JC] Rev. Brian Fawcett; Deacon Bill Dustman.
Res.: P.O. Box 210, 57638. Tel: 605-374-3767; Fax: 605-374-3768.
Catechesis / Religious Program—Sara Stadler, D.R.E. Students 66.
Mission—Sacred Heart Morristown, Corson Co.
Catechesis / Religious Program—Students 11.
Mission—Blessed Sacrament Bison, Perkins Co.
Catechesis / Religious Program—Students 25.

LOWER BRULE, LYMAN CO., ST. MARY'S (1923), (Native American), [CEM] Revs. Bernard J. Rosinski, S.C.J.; Joseph R. Dean, S.C.J.
Office: P.O. Box 185, 57548. Tel: 605-473-5335; Fax: 605-473-5453.
Catechesis / Religious Program—Students 4.

MANDERSON, SHANNON CO., ST. AGNES (1901), (Native American), [CEM] Rev. Philip Cooke, S.J.
Mailing Address: P.O. Box 88, 57756. Served by Holy Rosary Mission, Pine Ridge.
Res.: 100 Mission Dr., Pine Ridge, 57770-2100. Tel: 605-867-5491; Fax: 605-867-5874.
Catechesis / Religious Program—Students 5.
Mission—Sacred Heart, (Wounded Knee), (Inactive), P.O. Box 88, Shannon Co. 57756. Tel: 605-867-2267.

MARTIN, BENNETT CO., OUR LADY OF THE SACRED HEART (1918) [CEM] [JC] Rev. Bryan Sorensen; Deacon Calvin Clifford.
Mailing Address: P.O. Box 567, 57551. Tel: 605-685-6232. Email: martin1@gwtc.net.
Catechesis / Religious Program—Tel: 605-685-6274. Students 89.
Mission—Our Lady of Victory Kadoka

McINTOSH, CORSON CO., ST. BONAVENTURE'S (1913) [CEM] Revs. Tony Grossenburg; James Hoerter.
Res.: P.O. Box 539, McLaughlin, 57642. Tel: 605-823-4401; Fax: 605-823-2325.
Catechesis / Religious Program—Students 9.

McLAUGHLIN, CORSON CO., ST. BERNARD (1918) [CEM] Revs. Tony Grossenburg; James Hoerter.
Res.: P.O. Box 539, 57642. Tel: 605-823-4401; Fax: 605-823-2325. Email: stbern@westriv.com.
Catechesis / Religious Program—Fax: 605-823-4757. Students 21.
Mission—St. Aloysius Bullhead, Corson Co.
Catechesis / Religious Program—Students 11.
Mission—St. Bede Wakpala, Corson Co.
Catechesis / Religious Program—Students 3.
Mission—Our Lady of the Assumption Parish Kenel, Corson Co.
Catechesis / Religious Program—Students 23.

MIDLAND, HAAKON CO., ST. WILLIAM (1911) Attended by Sacred Heart, Philip., Mailing Address: P.O. Box 309, Philip, 57567. Tel: 605-859-2664; Fax: 605-859-2812.
Catechesis / Religious Program—Students 10.

MISSION, TODD CO., ST. THOMAS THE APOSTLE (1933), (Native American), [CEM] Attended by St. Francis, Mission.
Church: 150 Jefferson St., P.O. Box 151, 57555. Tel: 605-856-4618; Fax: 605-856-2273.
Catechesis / Religious Program—Tel: 605-856-2273. Gladys Bordeaux, D.R.E. Students 35.
Mission—St. Peter's P.O. Box 151, Okreek, Todd Co. 57572.

MORRISTOWN, CORSON CO., SACRED HEART (1912) [JC] Attended by St. Mary's, Lemmon., Mailing Address: P.O. Box 210, Lemmon, 57638. Tel: 605-374-3767; Fax: 605-374-3768.
Catechesis / Religious Program—Students 11.

MURDO, JONES CO., ST. MARTIN (1906) [CEM] Attended by Christ the King, Presho. Rev. Gary

Oreshoski.
Mailing Address: P.O. Box 399, Presho, 57568. Tel: 605-669-2436; Fax: 605-895-2534.
Catechesis/Religious Program—Tel: 605-895-2534. Students 2.

NEW UNDERWOOD, PENNINGTON CO., ST. JOHN THE EVANGELIST (1921) [JC] Rev. William A. Zandri. Served by St. Therese, Rapid City.
Catechesis/Religious Program—Email: sttherese@rushmore.com. Students 14.

NEWELL, BUTTE CO., ST. MARY STAR OF THE SEA (1910) Attended by St. Francis of Assisi, Sturgis, Mailing Address: 1049 Howard St., Sturgis, 57785-1999. Tel: 605-720-3579.
Catechesis/Religious Program—Students 17.

NORRIS, MELETTE CO., SACRED HEART (1955) [JC] Closed. (Inactive)

OGLALA, SHANNON CO., OUR LADY OF THE SIOUX (1916), (Native American), [CEM] Attended by Holy Rosary Mission, Pine Ridge. Sr. Connie Schmidt, S.S.N.D., Pastoral Coord.
Res.: P.O. Box 140, 57764. Tel: 605-867-5673; Fax: 605-867-1518.
Catechesis/Religious Program—Students 9.
Mission—St. Bernard, Red Shirt Table
Mission—Our Lady of Good Counsel, No Water (Drywood)

PHILIP, HAAKON CO., SACRED HEART (1907) [JC] Rev. Ron Garry.
Res.: 307 W. Elm, P.O. Box 309, 57567. Tel: 605-859-2664; Fax: 605-859-2812.
Catechesis/Religious Program—Students 93.
Mission—St. Mary Milesville, Haakon Co.

PIEDMONT-BLACK HAWK, MEADE CO., OUR LADY OF THE BLACK HILLS (1916) [JC] Rev. Mark McCormick; Deacons Walt Wilson; John Osnes.
Res.: 12365 Sturgis Rd., 57769-2007. Tel: 605-787-5168; Fax: 605-787-4106. Email: olbh@olbh.org. Web: www.olbh.org.
Catechesis/Religious Program—Students 189.

PINE RIDGE, SHANNON CO., SACRED HEART (1890), (Lakota), [JC], Attended from Holy Rosary Mission. Rev. Stephen J. Sanford, S.J.
Res.: 100 Mission Dr., 57770. Tel: 605-867-5551; Fax: 605-867-1969. Email: sacredheartpr@gwtc.net.
See Red Cloud Indian School under Holy Rosary, Pine Ridge

PORCUPINE, SHANNON CO., CHURCH OF CHRIST THE KING (1901), (Native American), [CEM] Rev. Philip Cooke, S.J. Served by Holy Rosary Mission, Pine Ridge.
Res.: 100 Mission Dr., Pine Ridge, 57770-2100. Tel: 605-867-1614; Fax: 605-867-2428.
See Red Cloud Indian School under Holy Rosary, Pine Ridge.
Catechesis/Religious Program—Students 6.
Mission—St. Paul, Sharpes Corner [CEM], (Inactive), P.O. Box 7, Shannon Co. 57772. Tel: 605-867-1614.

PRESHO, LYMAN CO., CHRIST THE KING (1906) [CEM] Rev. Gary Oreshoski.
Res.: P.O. Box 399, 57568-0399. Tel: 605-895-2534; Fax: 605-895-2534.
Catechesis/Religious Program—Students 20.
Mission—St. Anthony of Padua P.O. Box 159, Draper, Jones Co. 57531.

RELIANCE, LYMAN CO., ST. MARY'S (1911) [CEM] Attended by St. Mary's, Lower Brule., Mailing Address: P.O. Box 185, Lower Brule, 57548-0185. Tel: 605-473-5335; Fax: 605-473-5453.
Catechesis/Religious Program—Students 19.

ROSEBUD, TODD CO., ST. BRIDGET, (Native American), Rev. Timothy Manatt, S.J. Served by St. Francis Mission.
Office: P.O. Box 340, 57570. Tel: 605-747-2496.
Res.: P.O. Box 499, Saint Francis, 57572-0499. Tel: 605-747-2361; Fax: 605-747-5057.
Catechesis/Religious Program—Students 120.

ST. FRANCIS, TODD CO., ST. CHARLES BORROMEO (1886), (Native American), [CEM] Revs. John Hatcher, S.J.; Timothy Manatt, S.J.; Deacon Ben Black Bear Jr.
Res. & Office: Box 499, 57572. Tel: 605-747-2533; Fax: 605-747-5057.
Catechesis/Religious Program—Tel: 605-747-2567. Betty Young, D.R.E. Students 180.
Mission—, See listing under Indian Missions for Rosebud Reservation, St. Francis regarding details on personnel and missions.
Mission—St. Patrick Spring Creek, Todd Co.

SPEARFISH, LAWRENCE CO., ST. JOSEPH (1907) [JC] Revs. Timothy S. Hoag; Timothy William Castor.
Res.: 844 5th St., 57783-2005. Tel: 605-642-2306; Fax: 605-642-1024. Email: stjosephs@rushmore.com. Web: www.stjoseph-spearfish.com.
Catechesis/Religious Program—Students 278.

STURGIS, MEADE CO., ST. FRANCIS OF ASSISI (1840) [CEM] Rev. Arnold Kari.
Res.: 1049 Howard St., 57785-1999. Tel: 605-720-3579; Fax: 605-720-3579. Email: stfrancis@rushmore.com.
Catechesis/Religious Program—Tel: 605-720-3996. Carol Rost, D.R.E. Students 195.

TIMBER LAKE, DEWEY CO., HOLY CROSS (1910) Rev. Kevin Lee Achbach.
Res.: 506 F St., P.O. Box 70, 57656-0070. Tel: 605-865-3653. Email: achbachfr@hotmail.com.
Catechesis/Religious Program—Students 125.
Mission—St. Mary Isabel, Dewey Co.
Mission—Holy Rosary Trail City, Corson Co.

WALL, PENNINGTON CO., ST. PATRICK'S (1917) [JC] Rev. Leo Hausmann.
Res.: P.O. Box 405, 57790-0405. Tel: 605-279-2542.
Catechesis/Religious Program—Students 61.
Mission—St. Margaret Lakeside, Meade Co.
Mission—Holy Rosary Interior, Jackson Co.

WANBLEE, JACKSON CO., SAINT IGNATIUS LOYOLA (1920), (Native American), [CEM 3] [JC 5] Rev. Richard Abert, S.J.; Deacon Gerald Bush.
Res.: *Holy Rosary Mission*, 100 Mission Dr., Pine Ridge, 57770. Tel: 605-462-6170.
Catechesis/Religious Program—Students 10.
Mission—St. Henry, (Inactive), Potato Creek, Jackson Co.

WATAUGA, CORSON CO., ST. MICHAEL (1912) [CEM] Attended by St. Bernard, McLaughlin., Mailing Address: P.O. Box 539, McLaughlin, 57642. Tel: 605-823-4401; Fax: 605-823-2325.
Catechesis/Religious Program—Students 10.

WHITE RIVER, MELLETTE CO.
1—ST. IGNATIUS (1899), (Native American), [CEM] [JC] Rev. Edward G. Witt, S.J.
Res.: P.O. Box 1461, Mission, 57555-1461. Tel: 605-856-4018.
Church: P.O. Box 245, 57579-0245.
Catechesis/Religious Program—Students 10.
Mission—Our Lady of Good Counsel Wood, Melette Co. 57585. Tel: 605-452-3267.
2—SACRED HEART (1919) [JC] Rev. Edward G. Witt, S.J.
Mailing Address: 100 S. McKinley St., P.O. Box 185, 57579-0185.
Catechesis/Religious Program—Students 22.

WINNER, TRIPP CO., IMMACULATE CONCEPTION (1910) [JC] Rev. Msgr. Michael Woster.
Res.: 302 W. Fourth, P.O. Box 765, 57580. Tel: 605-842-3520; Fax: 605-842-3520.
Catechesis/Religious Program—Email: dreic@gwtc.net. Students 108.
Mission—St. Ann [JC] Keyapaha, Tripp Co.

INDIAN MISSIONS

EAGLE BUTTE, DEWEY CO., CHEYENNE RIVER RESERVATION (1911), (Native American), [CEM 8] [JC 2], Mailing Address: *All Saints*, 138 N. Spruce St., P.O. Box 110, 57625. Tel: 605-964-3391; Fax: 605-964-3300.
Catechesis/Religious Program—Students 49.

LOWER BRULE, LYMAN CO., LOWER BRULE RESERVATION (1895), (Native American), [CEM], See St. Mary's, Lower Brule for details.

PINE RIDGE, SHANNON CO., HOLY ROSARY (Pine Ridge Reservation) (1888), (Native American), Revs. Peter J. Klink, S.J.; Richard Abert, S.J., Supr.; Stephen J. Sanford, S.J.; Phillip Cooke, S.J., (Manderson & Porcupine); Dick McCaslin, S.J.
Mailing Address: 100 Mission Dr., 57770-2100. Tel: 605-867-5491. Web: www.redcloudschool.org.
School—Red Cloud Indian School, (Grades PreK-12) Tel: 605-867-5491; Fax: 605-867-1291. Mr. Nick Dressel, Prin. (High School); Jennifer Sierra, Prin. (Elementary). Sisters 2; Lay Teachers 40; High School Students 210; Elementary Students 211.
Catechesis/Religious Program—Students 554.
Mission—St. Joseph, (Inactive), Cuny Table, Shannon Co.
Mission—Our Lady of Sioux P.O. Box 140, Oglala, Shannon Co. 57764. Tel: 605-867-5673; Fax: 605-867-1518.
Mission—Our Lady of Good Counsel No Water, Shannon Co.
Mission—St. Bernard Red Shirt Table, Shannon Co.

ST. FRANCIS, TODD CO., ST. FRANCIS MISSION/ROSEBUD EDUCATIONAL SOCIETY (1886), (Native American), [CEM], St. Francis Mission and Rosebud Educational Society. Revs. John Hatcher, S.J., Supr., Mission.; Timothy Manatt, S.J.; Edward G. Witt, S.J.; Deacon Ben Black Bear Jr.
Mailing Address: P.O. Box 499, 57572-0499. Tel: 605-747-2361; Fax: 605-747-5057.
Catechesis/Religious Program—Tel: 605-747-2142. Students 450.
Mission—St. Charles, Todd Co. Tel: 605-747-2533.
Mission—St. Peter Okreek, Todd Co. Tel: 605-747-2362.
Mission—St. Patrick Spring Creek, Todd Co. Tel: 605-747-5319.
Mission—St. Agnes Box 115, Parmelee, Todd Co. 57566. Tel: 605-747-2118.
Mission—St. Bridget P.O. Box 340, Rosebud, Todd Co. 57570. Tel: 605-747-2496.
Mission—St. Ignatius Box 245, White River, Mellette Co. 57579. Tel: 605-259-3381.
Mission—Sacred Heart Box 185, White River, Mellette Co. 57579. Tel: 605-747-2362.
Mission—Our Lady of Good Counsel Wood, Mellette Co. Tel: 605-747-2362.
Mission—Sacred Heart, (Inactive)
Mission—St. Thomas Box 151, Mission, Todd Co. 57555. Tel: 605-856-4618.
Mission—St. Agnes (1927)

STANDING ROCK, CORSON CO., STANDING ROCK RESERVATION (1918) Revs. Tony Grossenburg; James Hoerter.
St. Bernard's Church: P.O. Box 539, McLaughlin, 57642. Tel: 605-823-4401; Fax: 605-823-2325.
Mission—St. Bede Wakpala, Corson Co.
Catechesis/Religious Program—Twinned with St. Aloysius, Bullhead. Students 25.
Mission—St. Aloysius Bullhead, Corson Co.
Mission—Assumption of the Blessed Virgin Mary Church Kenel, Corson Co.
Mission—St. Michael Watauga, Corson Co.

Chaplains of Public Institutions

ELLSWORTH. *Ellsworth AFB*. Rev. Jose Del Toro, 28th BW/HC, Ellsworth AFB, 57706.

On Duty Outside the Diocese:
Rev.—
Novotny, Richard

Retired:
Rev. Msgr.—
O'Connell, William, Casa Maria, 12541 N. Hwy. 79, Piedmont, 57769.
Revs.—
Baden, Robert D., 609 N. Sixth St., Ballinger, TX 76821.
Cower, D. Craig, 255 Texas St., Westhills Village F211, 57701-7356.
Dahms, Paul, 4001 Derby Ln. #319, 57701.
Deisch, Raymond J., Casa Maria, 12541 N. Hwy. 79, Piedmont, 57769.
Hight, Michael, 416 6th Ave., #3, Wall, 57790.
Scherer, Gerald N., P.O. Box 268, Hermosa, 57744-0268.
Valades, Reuben

Permanent Deacons:
Black Bear, Ben, Jr., St. Francis Mission, St. Francis
Brown, Larry, Faith
Bush, Gerald, Wanblee
Clifford, Calvin, Martin
Condon, Harold, Howes
Coy, Patrick, Sioux Spiritual Center
Curtin, Michael, (Retired), Rapid City
Daniel, Raul, Rapid City
DeCory, Leroy, (Retired), Rapid City
Dustman, Bill, Lemmon
Freece, Tom, Spearfish
Garnet, James W., (Retired), Rapid City
Gladfelter, George, Rapid City
Keller, Paul, Mobridge
Klein, Ray, Belle Fourche
Knife, Theodore, Eagle Butte
Kopriva, Larry, Rapid City
Lane, Thomas, (Retired), Rapid City
Leneaugh, Marlon, Rapid City
Orthman, Carl, Valley City, ND
Osnes, John, Piedmont
Palmer, Greg, Rapid City
Rath, Vern, (Retired), Spearfish
Sauer, Claude, (Retired), St. Therese, Rapid City
Tully, Frederick G., Hill City
Usera, Luis, Rapid City
VanLoan, James, Rapid City
Wilson, Walt, Piedmont
Witte, Earl Joseph, (Retired), St. James, Edgemont

INSTITUTIONS LOCATED IN THE DIOCESE

[A] DIOCESAN CATHOLIC SCHOOL SYSTEM

RAPID CITY. *St. Thomas More High School*, 300 Fairmont Blvd., 57701. Tel: 605-343-8484; Fax: 605-348-1315. Email: stm@rccss.net. Web: rccss.net. Wayne Sullivan, Prin.; Sidney Wang, Librarian. Priests 1; Lay Teachers 22; Students 247; Total Staff 41.
St. Elizabeth Elementary and Middle School (Grades PreSchool-8), 431 Oakland, 57701. Tel: 605-348-1477; Fax: 605-342-4367. Colleen Lecy, Prin., PreK - 5th; Keiz Shultz, Prin., 6th - 8th; Jane Holeton, Librarian. Lay Teachers 41; Students 568; Staff 63.

[B] GENERAL HOSPITALS

GREGORY. *Avera McKennan dba Avera Gregory Healthcare Center* 400 Park Ave., 57533-0400. Tel: 605-835-8394; Fax: 605-835-9422. Sponsored by Presentation of the B.V.M. of Aberdeen, SD & Benedictine Sisters of Sacred Heart Monastery, Yankton, SD. Acute Hospital Staffed Beds 25; Nursing Home Beds 43; Total Staff 118; Total Assisted 15,733.

[C] MONASTERIES AND RESIDENCES OF PRIESTS & BROTHERS

HOWES. *Kino Jesuit Community,* 20100 Center Rd., 57748-9505. Tel: 605-985-5906; Fax: 605-985-5908. Priests 5; Brothers 1. In Res. Revs. John Hatcher, S.J., Dir. of Inculturation, Supr.; Timothy Manatt, S.J.; David G. Matzko, S.J.; George Winzenburg, S.J.; Edward G. Witt, S.J.; Bro. Patrick Douglas, S.J.

LOWER BRULE. *SCJ Community House,* P.O. Box 185, 57548-0185. Tel: 605-473-5335; 605-473-5315; Fax: 605-473-5453. Email: pastteam@gwtc.net. Revs. Joseph R. Dean, S.C.J.; Bernard J. Rosinski, S.C.J. Priests 2; Total in Residence 2; Total Staff 1.

PIEDMONT. *Casa Maria Residence for Retired Priests,* 12541 N. Sturgis Rd., 57769. Tel: 605-787-4950. Email: rj@rushmore.com. Ronald Johnsen.

PINE RIDGE. *Jesuit Community of Holy Rosary Mission,* 100 Mission Dr., 57770-2100. Tel: 605-867-5491; Fax: 605-867-1291. Email: robert@redcloudschool.org. Web: www.redcloudschool.org. Revs. Richard Abert, S.J., Supr.; Phillip Cooke, S.J.; Peter J. Klink, S.J., Pastor & Pres.; Richard McCaslin, S.J.; Stephen J. Sanford, S.J.; Bros. Michael Baranek, S.J.; Bill Foster, S.J.; Michael Zimmerman, S.J.; Patrick Gilger, S.J.; Joseph Hoover, S.J. Priests 6; Brothers 3; Scholastics 2; Total in Residence 11.

[D] CONVENTS AND RESIDENCES FOR SISTERS

RAPID CITY. **Benedictine Convent of St. Martin* (1889) 1851 St. Martin Dr., 57702-9602. Tel: 605-343-8011; Fax: 605-399-2723. Email: sryvette_stmartins@knology.net. Web: www.blackhillsbenedictine.com. Sr. Yvette Mallow, O.S.B., Prioress. Motherhouse and Novitiate of the Sisters of St. Benedict. Sisters 31.

Kateri Convent (1964) 821 Farlow, 57701-0809. Tel: 605-343-6261. Tutoring in elementary schools. Oblate Sisters of the Blessed Sacrament 2.

PORCUPINE. *Our Lady of Lourdes School Convent,* P.O. Box 7, 57772-0007. Tel: 605-867-1056; Fax: 605-867-5874. Email: sistersusan@yahoo.com. School Sisters of Notre Dame.

[E] MISCELLANEOUS

RAPID CITY. *Benedictine Convent of St. Martin Retirement Trust,* 1851 St. Martin Dr., 57702-9602. Tel: 605-343-8011; Fax: 605-399-2723. Web: www.blackhillsbenedictine.com. Sr. Mary Wegher, Trustee & Contact Person.

Catholic Parish Association Contingency Fund, Inc., P.O. Box 678, 57709-0678. Tel: 605-343-3541; Fax: 605-348-7985.

Catholic Social Service, 918 5th St., 57701. Tel: 605-348-6086; Fax: 605-348-1050. Email: css@rapidnet.com. Web: www.catholic-social-services.net. James Kinyon, Dir.

Priest Retirement and Aid Association / Pension Plan Board, P.O. Box 309, Philip, 57567. Tel: 605-859-2664. Most Rev. Blase J. Cupich; Rev. Msgr. Michael Woster, J.C.L., Exec. Sec.; Revs. Kevin Lee Achbach, Recorder; Marcin Stanislaw Garbacz; Ron Garry, Pres.; Gary Oreshoski, Vice Pres.

Western South Dakota Catholic Foundation, Inc., P.O. Box 678, 57709-0678. Tel: 605-343-3541; Fax: 605-348-7985. Email: WSDCF@diorc.org.

EAGLE BUTTE. *CPT, Inc.,* P.O. Box 110, 57625-0110. Tel: 605-964-3391; Fax: 605-964-3300. Rev. Brian Lane, Dir.

Sacred Heart Center, 121 Landmark St., P.O. Box 2000, 57625-2000. Tel: 605-964-6062; Fax: 605-964-6060. Email: mdonovan@shconline.org. Web: www.shconline.org. Margaret Donovan, Exec. Dir. Total Assisted (Including Informational & Educational Outreach) 7,709; Total Staff 32.

HOWES. *The Diocese of Rapid City Mahpiya na Maka Okogna* Sioux Spiritual Center, 20100 Center Rd., 57748-7703. Tel: 605-985-5906; Fax: 605-985-5908. Email: ssc@gwtc.net. Web: puffin.creighton.edu/jesuit/ssc/. Rev. George Winzenburg, S.J., Dir. Total in Residence 1; Total Staff 6.

MANDERSON. *St. Francis Home,* P.O. Box 122, 57756-0122. Tel: 605-455-2077; Fax: 605-455-1680. Email: geraldineosf@aol.com. Sr. Geraldine Clifford, O.S.F., Min. Dir. Sisters of St. Francis Marycrest, Denver, CO., Home for abandoned and abused children (Licensed) 2-18 years of age. 6 children at a time. Personnel 3.

RELIGIOUS INSTITUTES OF MEN REPRESENTED IN THE DIOCESE

For further details refer to the corresponding bracketed number in the Religious Institutes of Men or Women section.

[1130]—*Congregation of the Priests and Brothers of the Sacred Heart*—S.C.J.

[0690]—*Jesuit Fathers and Brothers*—S.J.

[1065]—*Priestly Fraternity of St. Peter*—F.S.S.P.

RELIGIOUS INSTITUTES OF WOMEN REPRESENTED IN THE DIOCESE

[0230]—*Benedictine Sisters* (Yankton, SD)—O.S.B.

[0230]—*Benedictine Sisters of Pontifical Jurisdiction* (Rapid City, SD)—O.S.B.

[3832]—*Congregation of the Sisters of St. Joseph*—C.S.J.

[3010]—*Oblate Sisters of the Blessed Sacrament* (Marty, SD)—O.S.B.S.

[2970]—*School Sisters of Notre Dame*—S.S.N.D.

[0660]—*Sisters of Christian Charity* (Wilmette, IL)—S.C.C.

[2560]—*Sisters of Mercy*—R.S.M.

[1630]—*Sisters of St. Francis of Penance and Christian Charity* (Denver, CO)—O.S.F.

[2980]—*Sisters of the Congregation of Notre Dame* (Ridgefield, CT)—C.N.D.

[2390]—*Sisters of the Living Word*—S.L.W.

[3320]—*Sisters of the Presentation of the B.V.M.* (Aberdeen, SD; Dubuque, IA; Fargo, ND)—P.B.V.M.

NECROLOGY

† Birdsall, John M., (Retired)—Died Sept. 4, 2009

† Orians, David, (Retired)—Died Oct. 26, 2009

An asterisk (*) denotes an organization that has established tax-exempt status directly with the IRS and is not covered by the USCCB Group Ruling.

Diocese of Reno

(Dioecesis Renensis)

Most Reverend

RANDOLPH R. CALVO, D.D., J.C.D.

Bishop of Reno; ordained May 21, 1977; appointed Bishop of Reno December 23, 2005; ordained and installed February 17, 2006. *Office: 290 S. Arlington Ave., Reno, NV 89501-1713.*

Pastoral Center: 290 S. Arlington Ave., Reno, NV 89501-1713. Tel: 775-329-9274; Fax: 775-348-8619.

Web: catholicreno.org

Email: donnak@catholicreno.org

Most Reverend

PHILLIP F. STRALING, D.D.

Bishop Emeritus of Reno; ordained March 19, 1959; appointed Bishop of San Bernardino July 18, 1978; installed November 6, 1978; appointed Bishop of Reno March 21, 1995; installed June 29, 1995; retired June 21, 2005. *Office: 290 S. Arlington Ave., Reno, NV 89501-1713.*

Square Miles 70,852.

Erected as the Diocese of Reno by His Holiness Pope Pius XI March 27, 1931. Canonical Erection of the Diocese August 19, 1931; Redesignated Diocese of Reno-Las Vegas by Pope Paul VI, October 13, 1976; Reformed Diocese of Reno by His Holiness Pope John Paul II March 21, 1995.

Comprises the Counties of Carson City, Churchill, Douglas, Elko, Eureka, Humboldt, Lander, Lyon, Mineral, Pershing, Storey, and Washoe.

Patrons of the Diocese: Our Lady of the Snows (August 5); The Holy Family (Sunday in the Octave of Christmas); Established through an Apostolic brief dated August 24, 1933.

Legal Title: "The Roman Catholic Bishop of Reno and His Successors, a Corporation Sole".
For legal titles of parishes and diocesan institutions, consult the Pastoral Center.

STATISTICAL OVERVIEW

Personnel	
Bishop	1
Retired Bishops	1
Priests: Diocesan Active in Diocese	19
Priests: Retired, Sick or Absent	11
Number of Diocesan Priests	30
Religious Priests in Diocese	6
Total Priests in Diocese	36
Extern Priests in Diocese	11
Ordinations:	
Permanent Deacons	14
Permanent Deacons in Diocese	23
Total Brothers	3
Total Sisters	34
Parishes	
Parishes	28
With Resident Pastor:	
Resident Diocesan Priests	20
Resident Religious Priests	3
Without Resident Pastor:	
Administered by Priests	4
Missions	6
Professional Ministry Personnel:	
Brothers	3
Sisters	12
Lay Ministers	27
Welfare	
Catholic Hospitals	1
Total Assisted	94,486
Health Care Centers	2
Total Assisted	27,707
Day Care Centers	3
Total Assisted	268
Special Centers for Social Services	9
Total Assisted	38,000
Educational	
Diocesan Students in Other Seminaries	5
Total Seminarians	5
High Schools, Diocesan and Parish	1
Total Students	613
Elementary Schools, Diocesan and Parish	4
Total Students	1,133
Catechesis/Religious Education:	
High School Students	1,148
Elementary Students	3,730
Total Students under Catholic Instruction	6,629
Teachers in the Diocese:	
Brothers	1
Lay Teachers	135
Vital Statistics	
Receptions into the Church:	
Infant Baptism Totals	1,706
Minor Baptism Totals	62
Adult Baptism Totals	101
Received into Full Communion	371
First Communions	1,460
Confirmations	708
Marriages:	
Catholic	197
Interfaith	48
Total Marriages	245
Deaths	352
Total Catholic Population	127,749
Total Population	753,132

Former Bishops—Most Revs. THOMAS K. GORMAN, D.D., D.Sc.Hist., ord. June 23, 1917; appt. Bishop, April 24, 1931; cons. July 22, 1931; appt. Coadjutor Bishop of Dallas "cum jure successionis," Feb. 8, 1952; succeeded to the See, Aug. 19, 1954; resigned Aug. 27, 1969; died Aug. 16, 1980; ROBERT J. DWYER, D.D., Ph.D., ord. June 11, 1932; appt. May 20, 1952; cons. Aug. 5, 1952; elevated to Archiepiscopal Dignity and promoted to Portland in Oregon, Dec. 14, 1966; resigned Jan. 22, 1974; died March 24, 1976; JOSEPH GREEN, D.D., ord. July 14, 1946; appt. Titular Bishop of Trisipa and Auxiliary of Lansing, June 22, 1962; cons. Aug. 28, 1962; appt. Bishop of Reno, March 10, 1967; installed May 25, 1967; resigned Dec. 6, 1974; died Aug. 31, 1982; NORMAN F. MCFARLAND, D.D., J.C.D. (Retired), ord. June 15, 1946; appt. Titular Bishop of Bida and Auxiliary of San Francisco, June 5, 1970; ord. Bishop, Sept. 8, 1970; appt. Apostolic Admin. of Reno, Dec. 6, 1974; appt. Bishop of Reno, Feb. 10, 1976; installed March 31, 1976; appt. Bishop of Orange, Dec. 29, 1986; installed Feb. 24, 1987; retired June 30, 1998; DANIEL F. WALSH, D.D., ord. March 30, 1963; appt. Titular Bishop of Tigia and Auxiliary of San Francisco June 30, 1981; ord. Bishop, Sept. 24, 1981; appt. Bishop of Reno-Las Vegas, June 9, 1987; installed Aug. 6, 1987; appt. first Bishop of the newly established Diocese of Las Vegas, March 21, 1995; installed June 28, 1995; appt. Bishop of Santa Rosa April 11, 2000; installed May 22, 2000; PHILLIP F. STRALING, D.D., ord. March 19, 1959; appt. Bishop of San Bernardino July 18, 1978; installed Nov. 6, 1978; appt. Bishop of Reno March 21, 1995; installed June 29, 1995; retired June 21, 2005.

Bishop's Office—Most Rev. RANDOLPH ROQUE CALVO, D.D., J.C.D.

Bishop Emeritus—Most Rev. PHILLIP F. STRALING, D.D.

Secretary—DONNA KENNEDY. Tel: 775-326-9428.

Vicar General—Very Rev. CHARLES DURANTE, V.G.

Chancellor—Bro. MATTHEW CUNNINGHAM, F.S.R. Tel: 775-326-9429.

Secretary—CHRISTY PERKINS. Tel: 775-326-9410.

Tribunal—

Judicial Vicar/Officialis—Rev. JOSEPH ABRAHAM, J.C.L.

Adjutant Judicial Vicar—Rev. THOMAS FRANSISCUS, C.Ss.R., J.C.L.

Secretary/Notary—JENY HILL. Tel: 775-326-9419; PIEDAD GONZALEZ, Sec. Tel: 775-326-9411.

Promoter of Justice—Rev. GEORGE C. WOLF (Retired).

Defenders of the Bond—Revs. GEORGE C. WOLF (Retired); GARY M. LUIZ, C.PP.S., J.C.L.

Judges—Rev. ALBERT M. FOSSELMAN, J.C.L. (Retired); Rev. Msgr. STEPHEN FROST, J.C.L.; Rev. PETER ROMEO, J.C.L.

Advocates—Bro. MATTHEW CUNNINGHAM, F.S.R.; Rev. DAVID SCHUYLER, S.M., S.T.L., J.C.D.

Department of Education—

Superintendent of Catholic Schools—Mrs. KITTY BERGIN. Tel: 775-326-9430.

Diocesan School Board—Most Rev. RANDOLPH ROQUE CALVO, D.D., J.C.D.; Rev. VINCE FALLON, SS.CC.; Mrs. KITTY BERGIN; Dr. JOHN ANXO, Pres.; Dr. RANDY PANE, Vice Pres.; Ms. MAUREEN O'MARA, Sec.; Ms. BARBARA HAWN; Ms. LYNN HISTING; Ms. ELDA JUAREZ; Ms. LISA LAUGHLIN; Ms. KATHY POWER; Mr. JIM CARRICO; Mr. JIM CAVILIA.

Office of Faith Formation and Parish Pastoral Services—Co Directors: Mrs. NANCY WHIPPLE. Tel: 775-326-9431; Ms. MONIQUE JACOBS. Tel: 775-326-9439. Secretaries: LETTY ANGUIANO. Tel: 775-326-9413; BREANNA BALMUT. Tel: 775-326-9434; PAT GIANNOTTI. Tel: 775-326-9441.

Conference Associate—Sr. MAXINE LAVELL, O.S.F. Tel: 775-326-9440.

Office of Faith Formation Resource Center—BREANNA BALMUT, Admin. Tel: 775-326-9434.

Office of Safe Environment—JANE O'CONNOR. Tel: 775-326-9445.

Office of Ethnic Ministries—Mrs. MARIPAZ RAMOS, Dir. Tel: 775-326-9423; MARIA DEL ROCIO DODSON, Sec. Tel: 775-326-9415.

Archives—Bro. MATTHEW CUNNINGHAM, F.S.R., Chancellor. Tel: 775-326-9429; Sr. MAXINE LAVELL, O.S.F. Tel: 775-326-9440.

Curia—Most Rev. RANDOLPH ROQUE CALVO, D.D., J.C.D.; Bro. MATTHEW CUNNINGHAM, F.S.R.; Mrs. KITTY BERGIN; Mr. PETER VOGEL; Ms. MONIQUE JACOBS; Mr. MIKE QUILICI; Mrs. MARIPAZ RAMOS; Mrs. NANCY WHIPPLE; Mr. TIM WANNER; Rev. JOSEPH ABRAHAM, J.C.L.

Department of Stewardship and Development—Mr. MICHAEL QUILICI, Chief Devel. Officer. Tel: 775-326-9432. Secretaries: CARMEN GODOY. Tel: 775-326-9433; MARIAN HULL. Tel: 775-326-9444.

Diocesan Communications—Bro. MATTHEW CUNNINGHAM, F.S.R. Tel: 775-326-9429.

Diocesan Board of Consultors—Very Rev. CHARLES DURANTE, V.G.; Revs. THOMAS FRANSISCUS, C.Ss.R., J.C.L.; PAUL MCCOLLUM; JOSE ISSAC; ROBERT CHOREY; JORGE HERRERA; VINCE FALLON, SS.CC.; ANTHONY VERCELLONE; JOSEPH ABRAHAM, J.C.L.

Lists of Deans—Revs. DANIEL HUSSEY; ROBERT CHOREY; THOMAS FRANSISCUS, C.Ss.R., J.C.L.; ANTHONY VERCELLONE.

Finance Office—

Finance Council—Most Rev. RANDOLPH ROQUE CALVO, D.D., J.C.D.; Very Rev. CHARLES DURANTE, V.G.; Ms. VIRGINIA ZORIO; Mr. ED HOUSTON; Mr. BOB ARMSTRONG; Bro. MATTHEW CUNNINGHAM, F.S.R.; Mr. TIM WANNER; Mr. RICHARD KWAPIL; Mrs. DEBBIE GRIFFIN; Mr. DENNIS PRICE; Mr. MIKE QUILICI.

Chief Financial Officer—Mr. TIM WANNER. Tel: 775-326-9420.

Payroll and Employee Benefits Coordinator—JUDIE DAY. Tel: 775-326-9424.

Accountants and Bookkeepers—ANNA HILL. Tel: 775-326-9422; RITA SAN PAOLO-OUEILHE. Tel: 775-326-9435.

Frontier of the Faith—Mailing Address: P.O. Box 10930, Reno, 89510. Tel: 775-326-9433.

Director—Bro. MATTHEW CUNNINGHAM, F.S.R. Tel: 775-326-9429.

Missionary Co-Op—Bro. MATTHEW CUNNINGHAM, F.S.R. Tel: 775-326-9429.

"Northern Nevada Catholic" Newspaper—MAUREEN ANGEL, Editor-in-Chief, 290 S. Arlington, Ste. 200, Reno, 89501-1713. Tel: 775-329-9274; Fax: 775-348-8619. Email: nnc@gbis.com.

Ongoing Formation for Permanent Deacons—Rev. J. PATRICK FOLEY, Dir.

Our Mother of Sorrows Cemetery—2700 N. Virginia St., Reno, 89503. Tel: 775-323-0133. *Mailing Address: P.O. Box 8505, Reno, 89507.* Fax: 775-323-1229. Email: omos@catholicreno.org. SOPHIA MITCHELL, Oper. Mgr.; Sr. OFELIA ROIBAS, R.F., Counselor.

Presbyteral Council—Very Rev. CHARLES DURANTE, V.G.; Revs. THOMAS FRANSISCUS, C.Ss.R., J.C.L.; JOSE ISSAC; PAUL MCCOLLUM; ROBERT CHOREY; JORGE HERRERA; VINCE FALLON, SS.CC.; ANTHONY VERCELLONE; JOSEPH ABRAHAM, J.C.L.; Bro. MATTHEW CUNNINGHAM, F.S.R., Ex Officio & Chancellor.

Priest Personnel Board—Most Rev. RANDOLPH ROQUE CALVO, D.D., J.C.D.; Very Rev. CHARLES DURANTE, V.G.; Revs. MICHAEL MAHONE; JOSE ISACC; JOSEPH ABRAHAM, J.C.L.; Bro. MATTHEW CUNNINGHAM, F.S.R.

Detention Ministry— Carson City Area: Deacon JOE GARCIA. Tel: 775-885-2546.

Reno Area—Deacon JOSE CASTRO. Tel: 775-322-2255.

Lovelock Prison—Rev. ANTONIO QUIJANO JR., M.S. Tel: 775-273-2189.

Elko Area—SHERRY LAGIER, Chap. Tel: 775-754-6425.

Property Management—Mr. TIM WANNER.

Respect Life Commission—Rev. MARK HANIFAN; Ms. JULIANNA JERVIS; Ms. KATHLEEN ROSSI; Ms. PAT GLENN; Mr. MARK FOXWELL, Chm.; Ms. CONNIE FOXWELL; Mr. EDDIE MONTANUCCI; Ms. LINDA UGALDE, Exec. Sec.; Ms. TONI BERRY.

Seminary Board—Most Rev. RANDOLPH ROQUE CALVO, D.D., J.C.D.; Very Rev. CHARLES DURANTE, V.G.; Revs. MICHAEL MAHONE; PAUL MCCOLLUM, Dir.; MARGARET GRAHAM; Sr. MARIA AHEARN, O.C.D.

Victims' Advocates—KATHLEEN SHANE. Tel: 775-826-6555; MARILYN JANKA. Tel: 775-753-9543.

Vocations—Rev. PAUL MCCOLLUM, Dir.

Secretary—JACKIE CHAVEZ. Tel: 775-326-9426.

Life, Peace & Justice Commission—Very Rev. CHARLES DURANTE, V.G.; RUSS BERGIN; MIDGE BREEDEN; JULIE EHRMAN; ANNABELL HALL; JEFF HARDCASTLE; ELLIE HAYS; BARBARA HINSVARK; FRAN MCMILLAN; Rev. WILLIAM NADEAU; LIZ REVILLE; LISA STILLER; Sr. ROSELLI TRIA, O.P.; RITA SLOAN, Exec. Sec.

Liturgy Commission—Revs. ROBERT CHOREY; ANGELES DELEON, Chm.; Mrs. CATHY ALLARD; Mrs. GLORIA CASTELLANOS; Mrs. JEAN SOKOL, Exec. Sec.

CLERGY, PARISHES, MISSIONS AND PAROCHIAL SCHOOLS

CITY OF RENO

(WASHOE COUNTY)

1—ST. THOMAS AQUINAS CATHEDRAL (1907) Revs. Thomas Czeck, O.F.M.Conv., Rector; Masseo Gonzales, O.F.M.Conv., Parochial Vicar; Bruce Lamb, O.F.M.Conv., Parochial Vicar.
Res.: 310 W. Second St., 89503-5398. Tel: 775-329-2571; Fax: 775-329-2456.
Catechesis/Religious Program—Irma Alvardo, D.R.E. Students 26.

2—ST. ALBERT THE GREAT (1948) Revs. Mark Hanifan, Admin.; Joseph Infante, Parochial Vicar.
Res.: 3100 Coronado Dr., 89503. Tel: 775-747-0722; Fax: 775-746-3976.
School—(Grades K-8), 1255 St. Albert Dr., 89503. Tel: 775-747-3392; Fax: 775-747-6296. Email: lkane@stalbertcatholicschoolreno.org. Web: www-.stalbertcatholicschoolreno.org. Mr. Patrick Perry, Prin. Lay Teachers 15; Students 293.
St. Albert's Child Development Center—1259 St. Albert Dr., 89503. Tel: 775-747-1617; Fax: 775-746-3976. Kristen Mareno, Dir. Teachers 11; Students 90.
Catechesis/Religious Program—Beth Lujan, D.R.E. (Grades K-6); Lisa Wajda, D.R.E. (Grades 7-12). Students 294.

3—OUR LADY OF THE SNOWS (1939) Revs. Anthony Vercellone; Michael Mahone, Parochial Vicar.
Office: 1138 Wright St., 89509. Tel: 775-323-6894; Fax: 775-323-6749. Email: secretary@olsparish.com. Web: www.olsparish.com.
School—(Grades K-8), 1125 Lander St., 89509. Tel: 775-322-2773; Fax: 775-322-0827. Tim Fuetsch, Prin. Lay Teachers 11; Students 287.
Catechesis/Religious Program—Tel: 775-329-6147; Fax: 775-323-6749. Lauri-Anne Reinhart, D.R.E. Students 260.

4—OUR LADY OF WISDOM (1965) Rev. Vince Fallon, SS.CC.; Linda Wanner, Pastoral Assoc.
Mailing Address: P.O. Box 8879, 89507.
Office: 1101 N. Virginia St., 89503. Tel: 775-322-4336; Fax: 775-322-3616. Email: olwnewmancenter@gbis.com. Web: www.ladyofwisdomnewman.org.
Catechesis/Religious Program—Students 19.

5—ST. ROSE OF LIMA (1996) Revs. Larry Morrison; Cyril Apassa; Joseph Abraham, Parochial Vicar; Deacons Auguste Lemaire; Tom Cargill; Jane Lucero, Pastoral Assoc.
Mailing Address: 100 Bishop Manogue Dr., 89511. Tel: 775-851-1874; Fax: 775-851-1727. Email: srl@strosereno.com. Web: www.strosereno.com.
Catechesis/Religious Program—Terry Sheldon-Brown, D.R.E. Students 212.
Mission—Holy Spirit 1025 N. U.S. Hwy. 395, Washoe Valley, Washoe Co. 89704. Tel: 775-849-7764.

6—ST. THERESE CHURCH OF THE LITTLE FLOWER (1947) Revs. Honesto Agustin; Ariel Arias, Parochial Vicar; Deacons Robert Ruggiero; Ron Klonicke.
Office: 875 E. Plumb Ln., 89502. Tel: 775-322-2255; Fax: 775-322-0196.
Res.: 339 Urban Rd., 89509. Tel: 775-826-6579.
School—(Grades K-8), 1300 Casazza Dr., 89502. Tel: 775-323-2931; Fax: 775-323-2997. Ms. Karen Barreras, Prin.; Ms. Jennifer Sweazey, Librarian. Lay Teachers 13; Students 302.
Catechesis/Religious Program—Tel: 775-322-3415. Sr. Carol Bettencourt, S.H.F., D.R.E. Students 521.
Convent—Sisters of Mercy, 660 Casazza Dr., 89502. Tel: 775-322-5966; Fax: 775-322-5265. Sr. Elizabeth O'Neill, S.M., Contact Person. Sisters of Mercy, S.M. Sisters 2.

OUTSIDE THE CITY OF RENO

BATTLE MOUNTAIN, LANDER CO., ST. JOHN BOSCO (1940) Rev. Elberto Melendez; Deacon Dennis Cahill.
Mailing Address: P.O. Box 428, 89820.
Office: 392 S. Reese St., 89820.
Res.: 384 S. Reese St., 89820. Tel: 775-635-2576; Fax: 775-635-5729.
Catechesis/Religious Program—Tel: 775-635-2135. Yolanda Martinez, D.R.E. Students 111.
Station—Austin 113 Virginia St., Austin, Lander Co. 89310. Tel: 775-635-2576.

CARLIN, ELKO CO., SACRED HEART (1910) Deacon Craig LaGier, Admin. & Parish Life Coord.; Rev. Hermes Binlayo, S.J., Priest Supvr.
Mailing Address: P.O. Box 235, 89822.
Office: 651-3rd St., 89822. Tel: 775-754-6425; Fax: 775-754-2942.

CARSON CITY, CARSON CITY CO.

1—CORPUS CHRISTI (1949) Rev. James Setelik.
Res.: 3597 N. Sunridge Dr., 89705. Tel: 775-267-3200; Fax: 775-267-5692. Email: generaloffice@ccchurchcc.org. Web: www.ccchurchcc.org.
Catechesis/Religious Program—Email: dre@ccchurchcc.org. Raymond J. Finnegan, D.R.E. Students 50.

2—ST. TERESA OF AVILA (1858) Very Rev. Charles Durante; Rev. Edgar Villanueva, Parochial Vicar; Sr. Marie McGloin, S.A., Pastoral Assoc.; Deacons Bob Evans, Pastoral Assoc.; Gilbert Coleman.
Res.: 3000 N. Lompa Ln., 89706. Tel: 775-882-1968; Fax: 775-883-7063.
School—(Grades K-8), 567 S. Richmond Ave., 89703. Tel: 775-882-2079; Fax: 775-882-6135. Mrs. Christine Perdomo, Prin. Lay Teachers 9; Students 190.
St. Teresa Child Development Center—561 Richmond Ave., 89703. Tel: 775-283-0261; Fax: 775-283-0258. Email: jsullivan@stts.org. Ms. Jan Sullivan, Dir. Teachers 3; Students 50.
Catechesis/Religious Program—Tel: 775-882-2130. Mary Ann Randall, D.R.E. Students 650.

DAYTON, LYON CO., ST. ANN (1937) Rev. Thomas Fransiscus, C.Ss.R.; Deacon Roger Porcella.
Mailing Address: 3 Melanie Dr., P.O. Box 309, 89403. Tel: 775-246-7578; Fax: 775-246-7560.
Catechesis/Religious Program—Students 123.

ELKO, ELKO CO., ST. JOSEPH'S (1917) Revs. Daniel Hussey; Hermes Binlayo, S.J., Parochial Vicar; Deacon Cecil Gingerich.
Office: 1035 C St., 89801. Tel: 775-738-6432; Fax: 775-738-3356. Email: stjoech@ctnis.com. Web: www.elkonv.com/~stjoech/web.
Catechesis/Religious Program—Tel: 775-738-8770. Cathy Higginbotham, D.R.E. Students 467.
Mission—Our Lady of Guadalupe P.O. Box 200, Jackpot, Elko Co. 89825. Tel: 775-755-2168.

EUREKA, EUREKA CO., ST. BRENDAN'S (1872) Deacon Craig LaGier, Admin.& Parish Life Coord.; Rev. Hermes Binlayo, S.J., Priest Supvr.
Mailing Address: P.O. Box 305, 89316.
Res.: 70 N. O'Neill Ave., 89316. Tel: 775-237-5547.
Catechesis/Religious Program—Nancy Plaskett, D.R.E. Students 27.

FALLON, CHURCHILL CO., ST. PATRICK (1920) Rev. Oliver Curran; Deacons Kurt Carlson; Ronald Cherry.
Church & Mailing Address: 850 W. Fourth St., 89406. Tel: 775-423-2846; Fax: 775-423-5210. Email: patrickssandy@cccomm.net.
Catechesis/Religious Program—Students 170.

FERNLEY, LYON CO., ST. ROBERT BELLARMINE (1957) Rev. Robert Chorey; Deacon Ruben Cervantes.
Mailing Address: P.O. Box 473, 89408.
Office: 190 S. West St., 89408. Tel: 775-575-4011; Fax: 775-575-7601. Email: frbob@strobertbellarmine.org. Web: www.strobertbellarmine.org.
Catechesis/Religious Program—Sherry Hall, D.R.E. Students 114.
Mission—St. Joseph the Worker Empire, Washoe Co. 89412.

GARDNERVILLE, DOUGLAS CO., ST. GALL (1917) Revs. Paul McCollum; Jose Sobarzo, Parochial Vicar; Deacon Patrick Root.
Office & Mailing Address—1343 Centerville Rd., 89410. Tel: 775-782-2852; Fax: 775-782-2622. Email: church@stgall.org. Web: www.saintgall.org.
Catechesis/Religious Program—Tel: 775-782-3784; Fax: 775-782-3930. Laurie Barnhill, D.R.E. Students 325.

HAWTHORNE, MINERAL CO., OUR LADY OF PERPETUAL HELP (1938) Rev. Jorge Herrera.
Mailing Address: P.O. Box 850, 89415.
Office: 838 A St., 89415. Tel: 775-945-2020; Fax: 775-945-2020. Email: olph@att.net.
Res.: 794 A St., 89415.
Catechesis/Religious Program—Students 19.

INCLINE VILLAGE, WASHOE CO., ST. FRANCIS OF ASSISI (1965) Rev. William Nadeau; Deacons Donald Korson; Jose Castro.
Mailing Address: P.O. Box 4226, 89450. Tel: 775-831-0490; Fax: 775-831-2045. Email: williamomi@msn.com. Web: www.saintfrancisatincline.org.
Church: 701 St. Rte. 431 at Kelly Dr., 89450. Tel: 775-831-8184.
Catechesis/Religious Program—Students 106.

LOVELOCK, PERSHING CO., ST. JOHN THE BAPTIST (1875) Rev. Antonio Quijano Jr.
Mailing Address: P.O. Box 177, 89418-0177.
Res.: 1045 Franklin Ave, 89419-0177. Tel: 775-273-2189; Fax: 775-273-1154.
Church: 1085 Franklin Ave., 89419-0177.
Catechesis/Religious Program—Students 63.

SPARKS, WASHOE CO.

1—HOLY CROSS CATHOLIC COMMUNITY (1967) Rev. Jose Issac; Deacon Antonio Baptista.
Res.: 1299 Flora Glen Dr., 89434. Tel: 775-358-2544; Fax: 775-626-8281. Email: hccchurch@sbcglobal.net.
Catechesis/Religious Program—Chantal Hendricks, D.R.E. (Grades K-8); Veronica Crew, D.R.E. (Confirmation Family Catechesis). Students 310.

2—IMMACULATE CONCEPTION (1904) Rev. Norman A. King.
Res.: 2900 N. McCarran Blvd., 89431. Tel: 775-358-5977; Fax: 775-359-3951.
Catechesis/Religious Program—Tel: 775-358-5977. Alma Thomas, D.R.E., (Elementary); Pat Giannotti, D.R.E., (High School). Students 345.

STEAD, WASHOE CO., ST. MICHAEL'S (1967) Rev. Thomas Babu Perupayikkad.
Res.: 14075 Mt. Vida St., 89506. Tel: 775-972-7462; Fax: 775-972-9373.
Catechesis/Religious Program—Martha Flores, C.R.E. Students 178.

SUN VALLEY, WASHOE CO., ST. PETER CANISIUS (1976) Rev. Guillermo Arias.
Res.: 225 E. Fifth Ave., 89433. Tel: 775-673-6800; Fax: 775-673-2028.
Catechesis/Religious Program—Tel: 775-673-6867. Julene Cortes, D.R.E.; Dianna Adame, D.R.E. Students 300.

VIRGINIA CITY, STOREY CO., ST. MARY IN THE MOUNTAINS (1862) Rev. Tom Cronin, Admin. (Retired).
Mailing Address: P.O. Box 510, 89440.
Res.: 271 N. D St., 89440. Tel: 775-847-9099; Fax: 775-847-9098. Email: stmarysvc@earthlink.net. Web: dioceseofreno.org/mary-mountains.aspx.

WELLS, ELKO CO., ST. THOMAS AQUINAS Deacon Craig LaGier, Admin. & Parish Life Coord.; Rev. Hermes Binlayo, S.J., Priest Supvr.
Church: 619 Sixth St., P.O. Box 369, 89835. Tel: 775-752-3400; Fax: 775-752-3400.
Catechesis/Religious Program—Students 8.

WINNEMUCCA, HUMBOLDT CO., ST. PAUL (1883) Rev. Angeles DeLeon.
Mailing Address: 350 Melarkey St., 89445.
Res.: Fourth St. & Melarkey St., 89445. Tel: 775-623-2928; Fax: 775-623-6816. Email: stpaul@catholicreno.org.
Catechesis/Religious Program—Students 301.
Mission—St. Alphonsus Paradise Valley, Humboldt Co. 89426.
Mission—Sacred Heart McDermitt, Humboldt Co. 89421.

YERINGTON, LYON CO., HOLY FAMILY (1901) Rev. Jorge Herrera; Deacon Wayne Crooks.
Res.: 103 N. West St., 89447. Tel: 775-463-2882; Fax: 775-463-2162.
Catechesis/Religious Program—Jane Montalbano, D.R.E. Tel: 775-463-4258. Students 104.
Mission—St. John the Baptist Wellington. Hwy. 208, P.O. Box 258, Smith, Lyon Co. 89430. Tel: 775-465-2220; Fax: 775-465-9043.

ZEPHYR COVE, DOUGLAS CO., OUR LADY OF TAHOE (1966) Rev. Thomas Donnelly, Admin. (Retired).
Mailing Address: P.O. Box 115, 89448. 1 Elks Point Rd., 89448.
Catechesis/Religious Program—Students 8.

On Special Assignment:
Revs.—
Legerski, John, Campus Ministry, Bishop Manogue Catholic High School, 110 Bishop Manogue Dr., 89511.
Torrente, Lorenzo, Chap., Renown Medical Center, 745 Mt. Rose, 89509.
Valmonte, Arturo, Spiritual Care Svcs., St. Mary's Regional Medical Center, 235 W. Sixth St., 89520.

Retired:
Rev. Msgr.—
McFadden, Leo E., 3363 Spring Creek Cir., 89509.
Revs.—
Avella, William, 64 Jasper Ln., Dayton, 89403.
Bain, John, 2875 Idlewild Dr., 89509.
Corona, John, 1740 Lavender Ct., Minden, 89423.
DeMolen, Richard
Donnelly, Thomas, 430 Snowmass Ct., 89511.
Fosselman, Albert M., J.C.L., Double Diamond/The Meadows, 1162 Tule Dr., 89511.
Hanley, Gerald T., P.O. Box 1767, Carson City, 89702.
Hoffmann, Frank, 917 Torrence St., #20, San Diego, CA 92103.
Simpson, Robert, P.O. Box 50148, Sparks, 89435.
Wolf, George C., P.O. Box 50097, Sparks, 89435.

Permanent Deacons:
Baptista, Antonio, 6717 Magical Dr., Sparks, 89436. Tel: 775-626-2196
Cahill, Dennis, 435 W. Antelope, Battle Mountain, 89820. Tel: 775-635-0355
Cargill, Thomas, 65 Bennington Ct., 89511. Tel: 775-849-1588
Carlson, Kurt, 1888 Ryan Way, Fallon, 89406. Tel: 775-428-2055
Castro, Jose, 1586 Oxford Ave., Sparks, 89434. Tel: 775-358-8518
Cervantes, Ruben, 670 Sage Dr., Fernley, 89408. Tel: 775-575-2134
Cherry, Ronald, 428 N. Taylor St., Fallon, 89406. Tel: 775-423-7537
Coleman, Gilbert, 40 Pine View Ct., 89511. Tel: 775-852-1989
Crooks, Wayne, 103 N. West St., Yerington, 89447. Tel: 775-463-2882
Evans, Robert, 887 Thompson St., Carson City, 89703. Tel: 775-883-2341
Garcia, Joseph, 1715 Teal Dr., Carson City, 89706. Tel: 775-885-2546
Gingerich, Cecil, 158 Country Club Pkwy., Spring Creek, 89815. Tel: 775-753-5142
Gonzales, Emilio, 1185 Sage Ocean Dr., Gardnerville, 89460. Tel: 775-783-8880
Klonicke, Ron, 490 Golden Vista, 89506. Tel: 775-971-3258
Korson, Donald, 9345 Oakley St., 89521. Tel: 775-852-3650
LaGier, Craig, P.O. Box 235, Carlin, 89822. Tel: 775-754-6425
Lemaire, Auguste, 3060 Socrates Dr., 89512. Tel: 775-786-4657
McHugh, Daniel, P.O. Box 7172, #174, Stateline, 89449. Tel: 775-588-2080
Porcella, Roger, 986 Ridgeview Dr., Carson City, 89705. Tel: 775-267-5110
Root, Patrick, 3408 Long Dr., Minden, 89423. Tel: 775-267-1606
Ruggiero, Robert L., 1280 Davidson Way, 89509. Tel: 775-337-0735
Schmitt, Ron, (Leave of Absence)
Schreiner, Dennis, 3365 Lyon Ln., Carson City, 89704. Tel: 775-849-0910
Schumacher, Wendell, (Retired)
Smith, Robert, (Leave of Absence)

INSTITUTIONS LOCATED IN THE DIOCESE

[A] HIGH SCHOOLS, DIOCESAN

RENO. *Bishop Manogue Catholic High School, a Nevada non-profit corporation*, 110 Bishop Manogue Dr., 89511. Tel: 775-336-6000; Fax: 775-336-6015. Email: tim.jaureguito@bishopmanogue.org. Web: www.bishopmanogue.org. James Toner, Pres.; Tim Jaureguito, Prin.; Bruce Stewart, Vice Prin.; Rev. John Legerski, Chap.; Marcelino Ugalde, Librarian. Brothers 1; Lay Teachers 51; Students 613; Priests 1.

[B] GENERAL HOSPITALS

RENO. *Saint Mary's Foundation*, 520 W. Sixth St., 89503. Tel: 775-770-3020; Fax: 775-770-3545. Email: brent.reed@chw.edu. Brent Reed, Admin. Coord. Total Staff 6.
Saint Mary's Nell J. Redfield Health Center, 3915 Neil Rd., 89502. Tel: 775-770-3780; Fax: 775-828-7788. Laura Kennedy, Nurse Mgr. Tel: 775-770-3951. Total Assisted Annually 16,776; Total Staff 16.
Saint Mary's Regional Medical Center dba Catholic Healthcare West 235 W. Sixth St., 89520-0108. Tel: 775-770-3000; Fax: 775-770-3621. Email: gary.aldax@chw.edu. Sr. Mary Kieffer, O.P., Dir. Sponsorship. Tel: 775-770-3004. Email: mary.kieffer@chw.edu; Michael Uboldi, Pres. & CEO; Michael Johnson, Vice Pres. Community Health & Mission Integration; Rev. Arturo Valmonte; Bill Bartlett, Chap. Sisters of the Third Order of St. Dominic, Congregation of the Most Holy Name (San Rafael, CA). Sisters 3; Bed Capacity 380; Patients Assisted Annually 94,486; Total Staff 2,137.

SUN VALLEY. *Saint Mary's Nell J. Redfield Health Center at Sun Valley*, 6295 Sun Valley Blvd., 89433. Tel: 775-674-5437; Fax: 775-674-5440. Laura Kennedy, Nurse Mgr. Tel: 775-770-3951. Total Assisted Annually 10,931; Total Staff 9.

[C] DAY NURSERIES

RENO. *Holy Child Early Learning Center*, 440 Reno Ave., 89509. Tel: 775-329-2979; Fax: 775-329-8537. Email: holychild@ccsnn.org. Web: ccsnn.org/childdayhome.asp. Rebecca S. Vizina, Dir. Lay Teachers 25; Boys 73; Girls 83.

[D] MONASTERIES AND RESIDENCES FOR PRIESTS AND BROTHERS

RENO. *Brothers of Our Lady of the Holy Rosary Monastery*, 232 Sunnyside Dr., 89503-3510. Tel: 775-747-4441. Email: bros-reno@charter.net. Bros. Philip Napolitano, F.S.R.; Matthew Cunningham, F.S.R., Supr.; Edward Zuber, F.S.R. Brothers 3.

[E] CONVENTS AND RESIDENCES FOR SISTERS

RENO. *Carmelite Monastery (O.C.D.)*, 1950 La Fond Dr., 89509-3099. Tel: 775-323-3236; Fax: 775-322-1532. Email: renocarmel@carmelofreno.net. Web: www.carmelofreno.com. Sr. Susan Weber, Prioress. Discalced Carmelite Nuns 15.
St. Mary's Convent (O.P.), 411 W. Sixth St., 89503. Tel: 775-323-5196. Sr. Mary Kieffer, O.P., Dir. Sponsorship. Dominican Sisters of San Rafael. Sisters 7.
Sisters of the Holy Family, S.H.F., 6730 S. McCarran Blvd., 89509. Tel: 775-827-5370. Email: carmenb@holyfamilysisters.org. Holy Family Sisters. Sisters 2.

SPARKS. *Sisters of St. Philip Neri*, 135 Pascus Pl., 89431. Tel: 775-331-0708; Fax: 775-331-0708. Email: sistersreno@sbcglobal.net. Sr. Ofelia Roibas, R.F., Treas. Sisters 2.

[F] CAMPUS MINISTRY

RENO. *University of Nevada, Newman Community* 1101 N. Virginia St., 89503. Tel: 775-322-4336; Fax: 775-322-3616. Email: olwnewmancenter@gbis.com. Web: ladyofwisdomnewman.org. P.O. Box 8879, 89507. Rev. Vince Fallon, SS.CC. Served by Our Lady of Wisdom.

[G] CATHOLIC COMMUNITY SERVICES OF NORTHERN NEVADA

RENO. *Catholic Community Services of Northern Nevada*, P.O. Box 5099, 89513-5099. 500 E. Fourth St., 89512. Tel: 775-322-7073; Fax: 775-322-8197. Email: admin@ccsnn.org. Web: www.ccsnn.org. Mr. Peter Vogel, Dir. Tel: 775-322-7073, Ext. 241.
Adoption Meg Lee, Dir. Tel: 775-322-7073, Ext. 231.
Emergency Assistance Mary Rinden, M.S.W., Mgr. Tel: 775-322-7073, Ext. 230.
St. Vincent's Food Pantry Mary Anne Berdan, Mgr. Tel: 775-786-5266.
St. Vincent's Thrift Shop James Baker, Mgr. Tel: 775-322-9824.
Immigration Assistance Tel: 775-322-7073, Ext. 239. Leydi Cottrill, Mgr.
Holy Child Day Early Learning Center, 440 Reno Ave., 89509. Tel: 775-329-2979; Fax: 775-329-8537. Rebecca S. Vizina, Dir.
St. Vincent's Dining Room, P.O. Box 5099, 89513-5099. 325 Valley Rd., 89512. Tel: 775-329-5363. Ray Trevino, Dir.
St. Vincent's Residence, P.O. Box 5099, 89513. 395 Gould St., 89502. Tel: 775-332-2143. Tom Smith, Mgr.

[H] MISCELLANEOUS

RENO. *The Catholic Community Foundation of the Diocese of Reno*, 290 S. Arlington, Ste. 200, 89501-1713. Tel: 775-326-9420; Fax: 775-348-8619. Email: timw@catholicreno.org. Mr. Tim Wanner, CFO.
**Fertility Care Center of Reno, Inc.*, 1281 Terminal Way #114, 89502. Tel: 775-827-5111; Fax: 775-851-2114. Email: juliannajervis@att.net. Ms. Julianna Jervis, Pres.
Nevada Catholic Conference, 290 S. Arlington Ave., Ste. 200, 89501-1713. Tel: 775-326-9429; Fax: 775-348-8619.

RELIGIOUS INSTITUTES OF MEN REPRESENTED IN THE DIOCESE

For further details refer to the corresponding bracketed number in the Religious Institutes of Men or Women section.

[0960]—*Brothers of the Congregation of Our Lady of the Holy Rosary*—F.S.R.

[1140]—*Congregation of the Sacred Hearts of Jesus and Mary*—SS.CC.

[0480]—*Conventual Franciscans* (Cupertino Prov.)—O.F.M.Conv.

[0720]—*Missionaries of Our Lady of La Salette* Philippine Province—M.S.

[1070]—*Redemptorist Father* (Denver Prov.)—C.SS.R.

RELIGIOUS INSTITUTES OF WOMEN REPRESENTED IN THE DIOCESE

[0420]—*Discalced Carmelite Nuns*—O.C.D.

[1070-04]—*Dominican Sisters of San Rafael*—O.P.

[1190]—*Franciscan Sisters of the Atonement*—S.A.

[2560]—*Sisters of Mercy of Ireland* (U.S. Prov.)—R.S.M.

[]—*Sisters of St. Francis of Holy Family of Dubuque*—O.S.F.

[]—*Sisters of St. Philip Neri* (Madrid, Spain)—R.F.

[1960]—*Sisters of the Holy Family*—S.H.F.

DIOCESAN CEMETERIES

RENO. *Our Mother of Sorrows Cemetery & Mausoleum*, 2700 N. Virginia St., 89503. P.O. Box 8505, 89507. Tel: 775-323-0133; Fax: 775-323-1229. Email: omos@catholicreno.org. Sophia Mitchell, Opers. Mgr.; Sr. Ofelia Roibas, R.F., Counselor.

NECROLOGY

(No Deaths)

An asterisk (*) denotes an organization that has established tax-exempt status directly with the IRS and is not covered by the USCCB Group Ruling.

Diocese of Richmond

(Dioecesis Richmondiensis)

Most Reverend

FRANCIS X. DiLORENZO

Bishop of Richmond; ordained May 18, 1968; appointed Titular Bishop of Tigia and Auxiliary Bishop of Scranton January 26, 1988; consecrated March 8, 1988; appointed Apostolic Administrator of Honolulu October 12, 1993; succeeded to See November 29, 1994; appointed Bishop of Richmond March 31, 2004; installed May 24, 2004.

Most Reverend

WALTER F. SULLIVAN, D.D.

Bishop Emeritus of Richmond; ordained May 9, 1953; appointed Titular Bishop of Selsey and Auxiliary Bishop of Richmond October 20, 1970; consecrated December 1, 1970; appointed Apostolic Administrator of Richmond April 30, 1973; succeeded to the See, June 6, 1974; resigned September 16, 2003. *Mailing Address: 7800 Carousel Lane, Richmond, VA 23294.*

ESTABLISHED IN 1820.

Square Miles 36,711.

Comprises the State of Virginia, with the exception of the Counties of Arlington, Clarke, Culpeper, Fairfax, Fauquier, Frederick, King George, Lancaster, Loudoun, Madison, Northumberland, Orange, Page, Prince William, Rappahannock, Richmond, Shenandoah, Spottsylvania, Stafford, Warren and Westmoreland.

For legal titles of parishes and diocesan institutions, consult the Chancery Office.

Catholic Diocese of Richmond Pastoral Center: 7800 Carousel Lane, Richmond, VA 23294. Tel: 804-359-5661; Fax: 804-358-9159.

Web: www.richmonddiocese.org

Email: aedwards@richmonddiocese.org

STATISTICAL OVERVIEW

Personnel	
Bishop	1
Retired Bishops	1
Retired Abbots	1
Priests: Diocesan Active in Diocese	94
Priests: Diocesan Active Outside Diocese	2
Priests: Retired, Sick or Absent	53
Number of Diocesan Priests	149
Religious Priests in Diocese	27
Total Priests in Diocese	176
Extern Priests in Diocese	47
Ordinations:	
Diocesan Priests	1
Transitional Deacons	3
Permanent Deacons in Diocese	82
Parishes	
Parishes	146
With Resident Pastor:	
Resident Diocesan Priests	92
Resident Religious Priests	9
Without Resident Pastor:	
Administered by Priests	40
Administered by Deacons	1
Administered by Lay People	4
Missions	4
Closed Parishes	2
Professional Ministry Personnel:	
Brothers	12
Sisters	210
Lay Ministers	460
Welfare	
Catholic Hospitals	10
Total Assisted	680,000
Homes for the Aged	18
Total Assisted	2,000
Day Care Centers	2
Total Assisted	100
Specialized Homes	7
Total Assisted	11,000
Residential Care of Disabled	5
Total Assisted	2,800
Other Institutions	6
Total Assisted	30,000
Educational	
Diocesan Students in Other Seminaries	15
Total Seminarians	15
High Schools, Diocesan and Parish	5
Total Students	1,091
High Schools, Private	3
Total Students	842
Elementary Schools, Diocesan and Parish	23
Total Students	7,336
Elementary Schools, Private	2
Total Students	750
Catechesis/Religious Education:	
High School Students	5,358
Elementary Students	16,169
Total Students under Catholic Instruction	31,561
Teachers in the Diocese:	
Priests	1
Brothers	4
Sisters	16
Lay Teachers	943
Vital Statistics	
Receptions into the Church:	
Infant Baptism Totals	3,388
Minor Baptism Totals	117
Adult Baptism Totals	42
Received into Full Communion	852
First Communions	3,425
Confirmations	2,266
Marriages:	
Catholic	602
Interfaith	409
Total Marriages	1,011
Deaths	1,695
Total Catholic Population	232,456
Total Population	4,942,090

Former Bishops—Rt. Revs. PATRICK KELLY, D.D., ord. July 18, 1802; first Bishop; cons. Aug. 24, 1820; transferred to Waterford and Lismore in 1822; died Oct. 8, 1829; RICHARD V. WHELAN, D.D., ord. May 1, 1831; second Bishop; cons. March 21, 1841; transferred to Wheeling, July 23, 1850; died July 7, 1874; JOHN MCGILL, D.D., ord. June 13, 1835; cons. Nov. 10, 1850; died Jan. 14, 1872; His Eminence JAMES CARDINAL GIBBONS, D.D., ord. June 30, 1861; cons. Aug. 16, 1868; Bishop of Adramyttum, and Vicar-Apostolic of North Carolina; transferred to the See of Richmond, July 30, 1872; transferred to the See of Baltimore, Oct. 3, 1877; created Cardinal Priest of S. Maria in Trastevere, June 7, 1886; died March 24, 1921; Rt. Revs. JOHN J. KEANE, D.D., ord. July 2, 1866; cons. Aug. 25, 1878; resigned August, 1888; rector of the Catholic University, Washington, DC; transferred to Archbishopric of Dubuque, July 24, 1900; died June 27, 1918; AUGUSTINE VAN DE VYVER, D.D., ord. July 21, 1870; cons. Oct. 20, 1889; died Oct. 16, 1911; DENIS JOSEPH O'CONNELL, D.D., ord. May 26, 1877; cons. May 3, 1908; Titular Bishop of Sebaste and Auxiliary Bishop of San Francisco; appt. Bishop of Richmond, Jan. 19, 1912; resigned Jan. 15, 1926 and appt. Titular Archbishop of Marianne; died Jan. 1, 1927; Most Revs. ANDREW J. BRENNAN, D.D., ord. December 17, 1904; cons. Titular Bishop of Thapsus and Auxiliary Bishop of Scranton, April 25, 1923; appt. Bishop of Richmond, May 28, 1926; resigned April 14, 1945; appt. Titular Bishop of Telmissus; died May 23, 1956; PETER L. IRETON, D.D., ord. June 20, 1906; appt. Titular Bishop of Cime Coadjutor Bishop and Apostolic Administrator of Richmond, Aug. 3, 1935; cons. Oct. 23, 1935; named Bishop of Richmond, April 14, 1945; named Assistant at the Pontifical Throne, May 21, 1956; died April 27, 1958; JOHN J. RUSSELL, D.D., ord. July 8, 1923; appt. Bishop of Charleston, Jan. 28, 1950; cons. March 14, 1950; appt. Bishop of Richmond, July 3, 1958; retired April 3, 1973; died March 17, 1993; WALTER F. SULLIVAN, D.D. (Retired), ord. May 9, 1953; appt. Titular Bishop of Selsey and Auxiliary Bishop of Richmond Oct. 20, 1970; cons. Dec. 1, 1970; appt. Apostolic Administrator of Richmond April 30, 1973; succeeded to the See, June 6, 1974; resigned Sept. 16, 2003.

Central Administrative Offices

Unless otherwise indicated all Diocesan Offices are located at: *7800 Carousel Ln., Richmond, 23294.* Tel: 804-359-5661; Fax: 804-358-9159.

Vicar General—Rev. Msgr. THOMAS F. SHREVE, PA., J.C.L., V.G., 7800 Carousel Ln., Richmond, 23294. Tel: 804-359-5661. Regional Vicars: Rev. Msgrs. WALTER C. BARRETT, Central Vicariate. Tel: 804-222-1105; R. FRANCIS MUENCH, J.C.L., Eastern Vicariate. Tel: 804-359-5661; J. KENNETH RUSH JR., D.Min., Western Vicariate. Tel: 434-846-5245.

Bishop's Administrative Advisory Council—Rev. Msgr. THOMAS F. SHREVE, PA., J.C.L., V.G.; Mrs. DOROTHY MAHANES, Dir., Office of Human Resources; Mr. JOHN F. BARRETT, Dir. Finance; Rev. Msgr. MARK RICHARD LANE, S.T.M., D.Min., Vicar for Clergy; Mrs. ANNE C. EDWARDS.

Special Assistant and Advisor to the Bishop—Mrs. ANNE C. EDWARDS, 7800 Carousel Ln., Richmond, 23294. Tel: 804-359-5661.

Chancellor—Deacon JOHN H. THOMAS, J.D., 7800 Carousel Ln., Richmond, 23294. Tel: 804-355-9155; Fax: 804-359-2810.

Vice Chancellor—Mr. VINCENT SANSONE, S.T.L. Tel: 804-359-5661, Ext. 218.

Diocesan Tribunal Central Offices—7800 Carousel Lane, Richmond, 23294. Tel: 804-355-9155; Fax: 804-359-2810.

Judicial Vicar—Rev. Msgr. R. FRANCIS MUENCH, J.C.L.

Adjutant Judicial Vicar—Rev. MICHAEL M. DUFFY, J.C.L.

Tribunal Staff—Revs. PETER O. AKPOGHIRAN, J.C.D., Canonist; DAVID L. NOTT, Instructor.

Judges—Rev. Msgr. J. KENNETH RUSH JR., D.Min.; Revs. WAYNE BALL, J.C.L.; MICHAEL M. DUFFY, J.C.L.; KEVIN J. O'BRIEN, Ph.D.; Mr. JEFFREY STAAB, J.C.L.

Defenders of the Bond—Rev. JOSEPH FACURA, J.C.L., J.C.L.; Deacon JOHN H. THOMAS, J.D.; Mr. JOSEPH M. FITZGERALD, J.C.D., J.C.L.

Field Office—

Tidewater—5361-A Virginia Beach Blvd., Virginia Beach, 23462. Tel: 757-552-8495; Fax: 757-552-8497.

Ecclesiastical Notaries—Mrs. DENISE RYAN; CHERYL GAMBARDELLA; Mrs. KATHLEEN M. MCINTOSH; Mrs. JONICE FONTES.

Propagation of the Faith—Rev. Msgr. THOMAS F. SHREVE, PA., J.C.L., V.G., Dir.

Vicar for the Causes of Saints—Very Rev. SCOTT DUARTE.

Vicar for Clergy—Rev. Msgr. MARK RICHARD LANE, S.T.M., D.Min. Tel: 804-359-5661.

Associate Director—Deacon ROBERT D. EWAN.

Deacon Specialist—Deacon FRANK RONALD BASKIND, Ph.D.

Ethnic and Special Liturgies— Filipino, Hispanic, Korean, Vietnamese; Tridentine Latin Mass, Deaf/ Hearing Impaired. Please refer to the diocesan website for location and schedule.

Vicar for Ecumenism & Ecumenical Affairs—Rev. Msgr. RAYMOND A. BARTON.

Vicar for Vocations—Rev. MICHAEL A. RENNINGER.

Diocesan Theologians—Mr. VINCENT SANSONE, S.T.L. Tel: 804-359-5661, Ext. 218.

Director of Archives and Museum—Mr. VINCENT SANSONE, S.T.L.; Ms. COLLEEN E. YODER, Cur., Museum of Virginia Catholic History.

Office of Human Resources—Mrs. DOROTHY MAHANES, Dir.; Ms. MARYJANE M. FULLER, Asst. Dir.; Mrs. ETTA SHEPPERD, Benefits Mgr.; Mrs. SARAH L. FOGLER, H.R. Generalist.

Office of Development—Ms. CANDRA PARKER, Dir.

Office of Information Technology—Ms. JOAN PARDUE, Dir.; Ms. LYNN MOONEY, Assoc. Dir. Web Svcs. & Database Design; Mr. CHRISTOPHER G. MYERS, Assoc. Dir. Network Admin. & Support; Mr. DAN J. LIU, Asst. Dir. Network Administrative Support.

Office of Printing—Mr. NORMAN HOWARD, Dir.

Office of Pastoral Planning—Ms. ELIZABETH A. NEU, Dir.; BERNADETTE SNYDER, Research Analyst.

Office of Finance—Mr. JOHN F. BARRETT, Dir.; Mr. BERNARD K. LEISTER, Asst. Dir.; Ms. CRYSTAL LANG, Controller.

Parish & School Auditors—Mr. WILLIAM B. MURPHY; Mr. ROBERT D. BOYLE.

Parish Financial Auditor—Mrs. SARAH W. RABIN.

Diocesan Housing Corporation—Mr. MICHAEL BELLANCA, Exec. Dir.

Financial Coordinator—Mrs. SANDRA H. MOORE.

Facilities Management—Mr. JOHN W. MURPHY JR., Dir.

Office of Risk Management—Mr. KURT HICKMAN, Dir.

Office of Christian Formation—Mrs. EMILY FILIPPI, Dir.; Mrs. KATHLEEN T. MCMASTER, Assoc. Dir.; Mrs. MELANIE CODDINGTON, Southwest Region Coord.

Office of Catholic Schools—Mrs. ANNETTE PARSONS, Chief Educ. Admin.; Mrs. FRANCINE CONWAY, Supt.; Ms. MIRIAM COTTON, M.Ed., Asst. Supt.

Office of Youth Ministry—Mr. MICHAEL F. SCHOOL, Dir.

Office of Pastoral Ministry—Leadership Formation: Deacon RICHARD M. MIECH, Dir.

Office of Worship—Ms. CATHERINE COMBIER-DONOVAN, Dir.

Office of Campus and Young Adult Ministry—Mr. DAVID KAUFFMAN, Interim Dir.

Office for the Hispanic Apostolate—Mr. ERIK MANUEL GIBLIN, Dir.

Office for Black Catholics—Mrs. PAM HARRIS, Interim Coord.

Office for Catholics with Disabilities—Ms. WANETTA J. GRIGNOL, Dir.

Diocesan Councils and Organizations

Catholic Campaign for Human Development—Ms. COLLEEN P. BARRANGER.

Catholic Relief Services—Mrs. M. PATRICE SCHWERMER.

Catholic Daughters of America—State Regent: Ms. LARELLEI STELLWAG, 3118 Wynford Dr., Fairfax, 22031. Tel: 703-208-1092.

Catholic Golden Age—Mr. THOMAS MILHAUSEN, 8113 Provincetown Dr., Richmond, 23223. Tel: 804-320-1750.

"Catholic Virginian" (Diocesan Newspaper)—Mr. STEPHEN S. NEILL, Editor, 7800 Carousel Ln., Richmond, 23294. Tel: 804-359-5654; Fax: 804-359-5689; Mrs. JUDITH LINDFORS, Business Mgr. & Circulation Dir.

Council of Catholic Women—VACANT.

Catholic Women's Club—Mrs. BARBARA MCRAE, Pres., 4203 Hermitage Rd., Richmond, 23227. Tel: 804-264-9210.

Cemeteries—Rev. GEORGE E. ZAHN, Dir. Tel: 804-329-0473.

Council of Priests— See Presbyteral Council.

Catholic Charities—

Commonwealth Catholic Charities—1512 Willow Lawn Dr., Richmond, 23230-0565. Tel: 804-285-5900. Ms. JOANNE D. NATTRASS, M.B.A., B.S.N., R.N., Exec. Dir.

Office of Justice & Peace— falls under the umbrella of Commonwealth Catholic Charities and provides support and information to parishes on social justice issues within the Diocese of Richmond and global community. OJP works to form collaborative relationships with parishes to promote a comprehensive understanding of Catholic social teaching and its practical application in responsible action for the common good. OJP's focus areas include: Catholic social teaching; respect life; Haiti ministry and global solidarity; migrant ministry and domestic poverty; prison ministry and southwest Virginia ministries. *1512 Willow Lawn Dr., Richmond, 23230.* Tel: 804-285-5900 (Main Office). Email: OJPDirector@cccofva.org. Web: www.richmonddiocese.org/ojp. Regional Coordinators: Ms. COLLEEN P. BARRANGER. Tel: 804-545-5976; Mrs. M. PATRICE SCHWERMER. Tel: 804-545-5974.

Office of Migrant Ministry— falls under the umbrella of Commonwealth Catholic Charities and works with local parishes to extend the church's pastoral presence to migrant farm workers and their families particularly on the Eastern Shore and in Southside Virginia. The office networks with local agencies to meet the social service needs of migrant farm workers and advocates for social policies to protect and promote their rights. Mr. JAMES R. ALBRIGHT, Regl. Coord., Mailing Address: P.O. Box 584, Accomac, 23301. Tel: 757-787-7862.

Refugee & Immigration Services— provides a spectrum of resettlement services to over 3,000 refugees and immigrants each year, including English instruction, orientation to American schools and U.S. law, and information and referral services. RIS works with parish volunteers to resettle 600 refugees each year, providing housing, support services and employment enabling them to achieve early self-sufficiency. On a fee for service basis, RIS provides immigration counseling to low-income individuals, interpretation services and cross-cultural training. Regional offices are located at: 820 Campbell Ave., S.W., Roanoke, VA 24016. Tel. 540-342-7561; and 1615 Kecoughtan Rd., Hampton, VA 23661. Tel. 757-247-3600. Immigration counseling is also available in Harrisonburg at Blessed Sacrament Parish. Tel. 540-434-0849. *1512 Willow Lawn Dr., Ste. A, Richmond, 23230.* Tel: 804-355-4559. Mrs. MARILYN BRESLOW, Exec. Dir. *Richmond Office Director*, Ms. CAROL S. MCELHINNEY, 1512 Willow Lawn Dr. #A, Richmond, 23230. Tel: 804-355-4559. *Hampton Office Director*, Ms. KAREN SUE KURILKO, 1615 Kecoughtan Rd., Hampton, 23661. Tel: 757-247-3600. *Roanoke Office Director*, Ms. BETH LUTJEN, 1106 9th St., S.E., Roanoke, 24013. Tel: 540-342-7561.

Catholic Charities of Eastern Virginia, Inc.—5361-A Virginia Beach Blvd., Virginia Beach, 23462. Tel: 757-467-7707. Mr. DOMINICK CALGI, Dir.

Commission for Ecumenical & Interreligious Affairs—Rev. Msgr. RAYMOND A. BARTON, 712 Little Neck Rd., Virginia Beach, 23452. Tel: 757-498-7834.

Finance Council—Mr. GREGORY FRANCESKI, 513 Woodlake Rd., Virginia Beach, 23452.

Haitian Ministry Commission—Office of Justice & Peace. Tel: 804-359-5661.

Holy Childhood Association—Rev. Msgr. THOMAS F. SHREVE, PA., J.C.L., V.G.

Knights of Columbus—State Deputy: ISAIAS ALBA, 9310 Brian Run Ln., Springfield, 22153. Tel: 703-455-6010.

Nocturnal Adoration Society—Rev. JAMES KAUFFMANN, 300 N. Sheppard St., Richmond, 23220.

Diocesan Pastoral Council—Mrs. PATTY HUFFMAN.

Diocesan School Board—MICHAEL BORZA, Chm., 1805 Keeling Wood Lane, Virginia Beach, 23454.

Presbyteral Council—Rev. DONALD H. LEMAY, Chm.

Propagation of the Faith—Rev. Msgr. THOMAS F. SHREVE, PA., J.C.L., V.G.

Respect Life—VACANT.

Secular Carmelite Communities—

Community of the Holy Spirit—SUNNI COWLING, O.C.D.S., Pres., 1211 Mt. Erin Dr., Richmond, 23231.

Community of Our Lady of the Annunciation—TIRA KNIPSEL, O.C.D.S., Pres., 1288 Alanton Dr., Virginia Beach, 23454.

Lay Fraternity of St. Dominic— St. Thomas Aquinas Chapter Rev. LUKE CLARK, O.P., Supvr., 401 Alderman Rd., Charlottesville, 22903.

Serra Club of Richmond—JOHN STROTMEYER, 1000 Beveridge Rd., Richmond, 23226.

Sowers of Justice—VACANT.

Victim Assistance Coordinators—WILLIAM DEVLIN, Commonwealth Catholic Charities, 820 Campbell Ave., S.W., Roanoke, 24016. Tel: 540-344-5107; Ms. NIKI MELLO, Commonwealth Catholic Charities, P.O. Box 6565, Richmond, 23230. Tel: 804-285-5900. Catholic Charities of Eastern Virginia, Inc., 5361-A Virginia Beach Blvd., Virginia Beach, 23462. Tel: 757-467-7707; Mr. JOE NEW, Contact Person Tidewater; Catholic Charities of Eastern Virginia.

Youth Ministry Council—VACANT.

Liturgical Commission—Ms. CATHERINE COMBIER-DONOVAN.

Commission for Black Catholic—Ms. CHRISTINE THOMAS, Chm., 4700 Southmoor Rd., Richmond, 23234.

Building and Renovation Committee—Rev. Msgr. THOMAS F. SHREVE, PA., J.C.L., V.G., Chm., 11000 Smoketree Dr., Richmond, 23236.

Campus & Young Adult Ministry—Mr. ROBERT ZUPANEK, Chm., 201 High St., Farmville, 23909.

Christian Formation Commission—Mrs. TERRY COLVILLE, Chm., 8275 Meadowbridge Rd., Mechanicsville, 23116.

Diocesan Pastoral Planning Commission—Rev. CHARLES L. BREINDEL, Chm., 538 Central Blvd., Danville, 24541.

Domestic Violence Task Force—Ms. COLLEEN P. BARRANGER.

Hispanic Commission—Mr. BENNY MALAVE, Chm., 86 Meredith Way, Newport News, 23606.

Human Resources Commission—Mrs. DOROTHY MAHANES, Contact, 811 Cathedral Pl., Richmond, 23220.

Women's Commission—Ms. COLLEEN P. BARRANGER.

CLERGY, PARISHES, MISSIONS AND PAROCHIAL SCHOOLS

CITY OF RICHMOND

1—CATHEDRAL OF THE SACRED HEART (1906) [JC] Most Rev. Francis Xavier DiLorenzo; Rev. Patrick Golden, Rector; Deacons J. Brian Bergen; Marshall D. Banks.

Bishop's Office—7800 Carousel Ln., 23294. Tel: 804-359-5661; Fax: 804-358-9159.

Cathedral Office—800 S. Cathedral Pl., 23220-1569. Tel: 804-359-5651; Fax: 804-358-8043. Email: kwalters@richmondcathedral.org. Web: www.richmondcathedral.org.

Church: 18 N. Laurel, 23220.

Catechesis/Religious Program—Students 136.

2—ST. AUGUSTINE (Chesterfield Co.) (1973) Rev. Msgr. Michael S. Schmied; Deacon Eric Christopher Broughton.

Res.: 9608 Verlinda Ct., 23237. Tel: 804-778-4842.

Church: 4400 Beulah Rd., 23237. Tel: 804-275-7962; Fax: 804-271-4604. Email: staugustinechurch@hotmail.com. Web: www.staugustineparish.net.

Catechesis/Religious Program—Students 356.

3—SAINT BENEDICT (1911) [JC] Rev. James Kauffmann.

Mailing Address: 206 N. Belmont Ave., 23221.

Res.: 1129 West Ave., 23220. Tel: 804-358-2427; Fax: 804-355-5112.

Church: 300 N. Sheppard St., 23221-2407. Tel: 804-254-8810; Fax: 804-355-5112. Email: info@saintbenedictparish.org. Web:

www.saintbenedictparish.org.
School—3100 Grove Ave., 23221. Tel: 804-254-8850; Fax: 804-254-9163. Web: www.saintbenedictschool.org. Mr. Sean M. Cruess, Prin. Lay Teachers 16; Students 181.
Catechesis/Religious Program—Students 136.

4—ST. BRIDGET (Henrico Co.) (1949) Rev. Msgr. William H. Carr; Deacons John A. Arkestyn; Robert B. Giovenco.
Church: 6006 Three Chopt Rd., 23226-2730. Tel: 804-282-9511; Fax: 804-285-7227. Email: parishmail@stbridgets.org. Web: www.saintbridgetchurch.org.
School—6011 York Rd., 23226. Tel: 804-288-1994; Fax: 804-288-5730. Email: information@saintbridget.org. Web: www.saintbridget.org. Mr. Raymond E. Honeycutt, Prin. Lay Teachers 35; Students 491.
Catechesis/Religious Program—Students 472.

5—CHURCH OF THE EPIPHANY (Chesterfield Co.) (1979) Rev. Steven R. Rule; Deacons Richard M. Miech; Belardino Lupini.
Mailing Address: 11000 Smoketree Dr., 23236-3144. Tel: 804-794-0222; Fax: 804-378-2013. Email: epiphany@epiphanychurch.org. Web: www.epiphanychurch.org.
See Regional School St. Edward - Epiphany, Richmond under St. Edward, Richmond for details.
Catechesis/Religious Program—Students 761.

6—CHURCH OF THE VIETNAMESE MARTYRS (1983), (Vietnamese), Rev. Msgr. Joseph Thang Pham.
Mailing Address: 12500 Patterson Ave., 23238. Tel: 804-784-5450; Fax: 804-784-9822. Email: chathangvietnam@hotmail.com. In Res., Rev. John M. David.
Catechesis/Religious Program—Students 115.

7—ST. EDWARD THE CONFESSOR (1959) Revs. Donald H. Lemay; Kevin J. O'Brien, Parochial Vicar; Deacons James D. Greer; Thomas B. Elliott.
Res.: 10908 Ashburn Rd., 23235-2618. Tel: 804-330-0772. Email: stedward@stedwardch.org. Web: www.stedchurch.com.
Church & Mailing Address: 2700 Dolfield Dr., 23235-2618.
School—Regional School St. Edward-Epiphany, 10701 Huguenot Rd., 23235. Tel: 804-272-2881; Fax: 804-272-2904. Ms. Georgette M. Richards, Prin. Lay Teachers 23; Students 494.
Catechesis/Religious Program—Students 430.

8—ST. ELIZABETH (1923), (African American), [JC] Rev. Msgr. Walter C. Barrett, Admin.
Mailing Address: 1301 Victor St., 23222-3935. Tel: 804-329-4599; Fax: 804-321-0741. In Res., Rev. Andrew Sagayam (India).
Church: 2712 Second Ave., 23222. Fax: 804-321-0741. Email: stelizcc@verizon.net. Web: www.stelizabethcc.org.
School—All Saints, 3418 Noble Ave., 23222. Tel: 804-329-7524; Fax: 804-329-4201. Mr. Kenneth Soistman, Prin.
Catechesis/Religious Program—Students 123.

9—HOLY ROSARY (1953), (African American), Rev. Msgr. Walter C. Barrett.
Parish Office & Mailing Address: 3300 "R" St., 23223-0416. Tel: 804-222-1105; Fax: 804-226-2204. Email: holyrosarym@aol.com. Web: hrccrichmond.org.
Res.: 901 Hunters Run Dr., 23223. Tel: 804-343-7111.
Catechesis/Religious Program—Students 50.

10—ST. JOSEPH (1991) Rev. Adrian W. Harmening, O.S.B.
828 Buford Rd., 23235. Tel: 804-320-4932; Fax: 804-320-4050. Email: secretary@stjosephrichmond.org.
Catechesis/Religious Program—Students 130.

11—ST. KIM TAEGON (1986), (Korean), Rev. Matthew Un Kwang Joung.
Mailing Address: 3103 Maury St., 23224-3559. Tel: 804-232-0993; Fax: 804-232-0995.
Church: 3100 Logandale Ave., 23224.
Catechesis/Religious Program—Students 49.

12—ST. MARY (1962) Rev. Joseph Morton Biber; Sr. Pat McCarthy, s.f.c.c., Pastoral Assoc.; Deacon Frank Ronald Baskind; Rebecca Oxenreider, Parish Social Ministry; Joe Lenich, Music Min.
Mailing Address: 9505 Gayton Rd., 23229-5319. Tel: 804-740-4044; Fax: 804-740-2197. Email: parish@stmarysrichmond.org. Web: www.stmarysrichmond.org.
School—9501 Gayton Rd., 23229. Tel: 804-740-1048; Fax: 804-740-1310. Dr. Thomas D. Dertinger, Prin. Lay Teachers 38; Students 440.
Catechesis/Religious Program— John Sweet, D.R.E. & Youth Min. Students 400.

13—ST. MICHAEL (Glen Allen) (1992) Rev. Daniel O. Brady; Deacons David S. Nemetz; Andrew M. Ferguson; Curtis L. Hornstra.
Mailing Address: 4491 Springfield Rd., Glen Allen, 23060. Tel: 804-527-1037; Fax: 804-527-1039. Email: admin@saint-mikes.org. Web: www.saint-mikes.org.
Catechesis/Religious Program—Tel: 804-527-1037, Ext. 13. Email: pmundy@saint-mikes.org. Students 1,263.

14—OUR LADY OF LOURDES (Henrico Co.) (1944) [JC] Rev. Robert M. Spencer, Canonical Pastor; Deacon Robert H. Griffin, Admin.
Church: 8200 Woodman Rd., 23228-3237. Tel: 804-262-7315; Fax: 804-262-7337. Email: lourdes@ollrichva.org. Web: www.ollrichva.org.
School—8250 Woodman Rd., 23228. Tel: 804-262-1770; Fax: 804-200-6295. Email: ollofice@comcast.net. Web: www.ollschoolric.com. Lucy R. Reilley, Prin. Lay Teachers 27; Students 385.
Catechesis/Religious Program—Tel: 804-262-7317; Fax: 804-262-7337. Email: skemp@ollrichva.org. Students 278.

15—ST. PATRICK (1859) Rev. Wayne L Ball, Admin.
Mailing Address: 213 N. 25th St., 23223-7115. Tel: 804-648-0504; Fax: 804-648-5216. Email: office@saintpatrickchurchhill.org. Web: www.saintpatrickchurchhill.org. In Res., Rev. Peter O. Akpoghiran.

16—ST. PAUL (1921) [CEM] Rev. George E. Zahn.
Mailing Address: 909 Rennie Ave., 23227. Tel: 804-329-0473; 804-329-5512 (Rectory); Fax: 804-321-6454. Email: churchoffice@saintpaulscc.com. In Res., Rev. Frederick J. Feusahrens (Retired).
School—All Saints, 3418 Noble Ave., 23227. Tel: 804-329-7524; Fax: 804-321-1538. Mr. Kenneth Soistman, Prin. Lay Teachers 17; Students 123.
Catechesis/Religious Program—Students 69.

17—ST. PETER (1834) [JC] Rev. Robert A. Brownell.
Mailing Address: 800 E. Grace St., P.O. Box 933, 23219-0933. Tel: 804-643-4315; Fax: 804-783-6120. Email: stpeterchurch2@aol.com.
Res.: 4030 Forest Hill Ave., Apt. 27, 23225. Tel: 804-231-3941. Email: stpeterchurch2@aol.com.
Church: 800 E. Grace St., 23219.
Catechesis/Religious Program—Students 4.

18—SACRED HEART (1901) [JC] Rev. Shay W. Auerbach, S.J.; Deacon Mark C. Matte.
Mailing Address: 1400 Perry St., 23224-2057. In Res., Rev. G. Harry Hock, S.J.
Res.: 1409 Perry St., 23224. Tel: 804-232-2266; 804-232-8964 (Office); Fax: 804-231-9931. Email: sacred.heart.church@comast.net.
Church: 1401 Perry St., 23224.
Catechesis/Religious Program—Stephanie Robertson, C.R.E.

OUTSIDE THE CITY OF RICHMOND

ABINGDON, WASHINGTON CO., CHRIST THE KING (1983) Rev. Paul Maier; Deacon Richard Cronican.
Res. & Mailing Address: P.O. Box 1201, 24212-1201. Tel: 276-628-2941; Fax: 276-783-7282. Web: www.ctk-abingdon.org.
Church: 822 E. Main St., 24212.
Catechesis/Religious Program—Students 51.

AMELIA, WASHINGTON CO., GOOD SAMARITAN (1980) Rev. Jeffrey T. Garcia (Philippines), Admin.; Deacon Edward P. Schmidt.
Mailing Address: P.O. Box 759, 23002. Tel: 804-561-6671. Email: carolhix@tds.net.
Catechesis/Religious Program—Students 10.

AMHERST, AMHERST CO., ST. FRANCIS OF ASSISI (1995) Rev. Daniel L. Kelly.
Mailing Address: 332 S. Main St., P.O. Box 663, 24521. Tel: 434-946-2053. Email: stmarystfrancischurch@ceva.net.
Catechesis/Religious Program—Students 6.

APPOMATTOX, APPOMATTOX CO., OUR LADY OF PEACE (1982) Rev. James E. Gallagher Jr.
Mailing Address: 2938 Oakleigh Ave., P.O. Box 668, 24522-0668.
Church: Corner of Rte. 631 & Rte. 627, 24522. Tel: 434-352-0104; Fax: 434-352-0104. Email: jimg301@juno.com.
Catechesis/Religious Program—

ASHLAND, HANOVER CO., ST. ANN (1892) Rev. Christian J. Haydinger; Deacon Eugene P. Kamper.
Res.: 105 S. Snead St., 23005-1514. Tel: 804-798-5039. Email: office@stannscc.org. Web: www.stannscc.org.
Catechesis/Religious Program—Students 246.

BEDFORD, BEDFORD CO., HOLY NAME OF MARY (1874) Rev. Salvador Anonuevo; Deacon Raymond Roderique, (Retired).
Mailing Address: 1307 Oakwood St., 24523-1613. Tel: 540-586-8988; Fax: 540-587-9080.
Res.: 1531 Newton Cir., 24523. Tel: 540-586-9271. Email: hnmpastor@verizon.net. Web: holynameofmary.net.
Catechesis/Religious Program—Email: rita.zimmermann@verizon.net. Students 162.

BIG STONE GAP, WISE CO., SACRED HEART (1902) Rev. Timothy A. Drake; Deacon Barron Flanary. In Res., Rev. Leslie Schmidt, G.H.M.
Rectory—1821 Holton Ave. E., 24219-2611. Tel: 276-523-1588; Fax: 276-523-1588.
Catechesis/Religious Program—

BLACKSBURG, MONTGOMERY CO., ST. MARY (1938) Revs. Jeremiusz H. Sojka; John A. Grace, Campus Min., VA Tech.; Deacons Mike Ellerbrock; James H. Keaney.
Mailing Address: 1205 Old Mill Rd., 24060-3618. Tel: 540-552-1091; Fax: 540-953-2962. Email: officestaff@stmaryblacksburg.org. Web: www.stmarysblacksburg.org.
Res.: 1211 Old Mill Rd., 24060. Tel: 540-951-2136.
Newman Community— 203 Otey St., 24060. Tel: 540-951-0032.
Catechesis/Religious Program—Students 240.

BLACKSTONE, NOTTOWAY CO., IMMACULATE HEART OF MARY (1947) Revs. James M. Glass, O.S.B.; John S. Kloepfer, Sacramental Min. (Retired); Mrs. Therese Mansfield, Pastoral Coord.
Church & Mailing Address: 903 S. Main St., P.O. Box 266, 23824-0266. Tel: 804-292-5535; Fax: 804-292-5535. Email: tmansfield2@juno.com.
Catechesis/Religious Program—Students 22.

BRISTOL, BRISTOL CO., ST. ANNE (1903) [CEM] Rev. Timothy E. Keeney; Deacon Juan Ibarra.
Mailing Address: 350 Euclid Ave., 24201-4014. Tel: 276-669-8200 (Office Phone); Fax: 276-669-7825. Email: stannes@stannes-bristol.org. Web: www.stannes-bristol.org.
Res.: 922 Chester St., 24201. Tel: 276-466-4776.
School—(Grades PreK-8), 300 Euclid Ave., 24201. Tel: 276-669-0048; Fax: 276-669-3523. Email: sas@stannes-bristol.org. Richard Fenchak, Prin. Lay Teachers 25; Students 136.
Catechesis/Religious Program—Students 136.

BROOKNEAL, CAMPBELL CO., ST. ELIZABETH OF HUNGARY (1957) Closed. For inquiries for parish records contact the chancery.

BUCKINGHAM, BUCKINGHAM, CO., CHURCH OF THE NATIVITY (1981) [CEM] Rev. N. Alan Lipscomb.
Mailing Address: 4309 Thomas Jefferson Pkwy., Palmyra, 22963. Email: pastor@stspeterpaul.org. Web: www.saintspeterpaul.org.
Church: Rte. 60 E., 23921. Tel: 434-969-3306; Fax: 434-589-4463. Email: pastor@saintspeterpaul.org.
Catechesis/Religious Program—Students 2.

BUMPASS, LOUISA CO., IMMACULATE CONCEPTION (1876) [CEM] Rev. Michael M. Duffy; Deacons Alfonso Benet; Robert M. Esposito.
Mailing Address: P.O. Box 128, 23024-0128. Tel: 540-872-3922 (Office); 540-894-8209 (Rectory); Fax: 540-872-3726. Email: immaculate1876@earthlink.net.
Church: 1107 Fredericks Hall Rd., 23024.
Catechesis/Religious Program—Students 37.

CAPE CHARLES, NORTHAMPTON CO., ST. CHARLES BORROMEO (1886) [CEM] Rev. J. Michael Breslin; Deacon Donald Donovan.
Mailing Address: 545 Randolph Ave., 23310-3305. Tel: 757-331-1724 (Rectory); 757-331-2040 (Office); Fax: 757-331-4619. Email: saintcharles@verizon.net.
Catechesis/Religious Program—Students 61.

CAROLINE COUNTY, CAROLINE CO., ST. MARY OF THE ANNUNCIATION (1914) [CEM 2] Rev. Msgr. Walter C. Barrett; Deacon David J. Geary.
Mailing Address: P.O. Box 396, Ladysmith, 22501.
Office & Church: 10306 Ladysmith Rd., Ladysmith, 22501. Tel: 804-448-9064; Fax: 804-448-5464. Email: office@saintmarycc.org. Web: www.saintmarycc.org.
Catechesis/Religious Program—Students 62.

CHARLOTTESVILLE, ALBEMARLE CO.

1—CHURCH OF THE HOLY COMFORTER (1880) Rev. Dennis McAuliffe.
Res.: 133 Old Fifth Cir., 22902. Tel: 434-293-6867. Web: www.holycomforterparish.org.
Church: 208 E. Jefferson St., 22902-5105. Tel: 434-295-7185; Fax: 434-295-7001.
Catechesis/Religious Program—Tel: 434-295-6559. Email: tritzert@holycomforterparish.org. Students 71.
Mission—St. George's P.O. Box 9, Scottsville, Albemarle Co. 24590. Tel: 434-286-3724.

2—CHURCH OF THE INCARNATION (1976) Revs. Gregory Kandt; Edwin Montenez, Parochial Vicar; Deacons Bernard Taylor; Christopher Morash.
Office: 1465 Incarnation Dr., 22901-1716. Tel: 434-973-4381; Fax: 434-973-1757. Email: office@incarnationparish.org. Web: www.incarnationparish.org.
Res.: 2414 Commonwealth Dr., 22901. Tel: 434-978-7544.
School—Charlottesville Catholic School, 1205 Pen Park Rd., 22901. Tel: 434-964-0400; Fax: 434-964-1373. Mr. Alan Yost, Prin.
Catechesis/Religious Program—Students 582.

3—ST. THOMAS AQUINAS (1963) [JC] Revs. Luke Clark, O.P.; Gregory A. Maturi, Parochial Vicar; Deacon Frank Veraart. In Res., Rev. Augustine Thompson.
Office: Tel: 434-293-8081; 434-293-6472; Fax: 434-296-1941.
Res.: 308 Alderman Rd., 22903. Tel: 434-977-5658.
Church & Mailing Address: 401 Alderman Rd., 22903.
Catechesis/Religious Program—Email: reled@stauva.org. Students 526.

CHESAPEAKE, CHESAPEAKE CO.
1—ST. MARY (1915) Revs. Michael G. Boehling; David W. Cupps.
Church & Mailing Address: 536 Homestead Rd., 23321. Email: admin@stmarys.hrcoxmail.com.
Catechesis/Religious Program—Email: mrcbeebe@cox.net. Students 51.
2—PRINCE OF PEACE (1975) Rev. Romeo D. Jazmin.
Mailing Address: 621 Cedar Rd., 23322. Tel: 757-547-0356; 757-547-3903; Fax: 757-436-6477. Email: pop.office@popparish.org. Web: www.popparish.org.
Res.: 303 Elberon Ct., 23322. Tel: 757-547-2951.
Catechesis/Religious Program—Students 686.
3—ST. STEPHEN, MARTYR (1997) Rev. Msgr. Michael D. McCarron; Deacon Keith A. Fournier.
Mailing Address: 1544 S. Battlefield Blvd., 23322-2041. Tel: 757-421-7416; Fax: 757-421-7488. Email: ssm@ssmrcc.org. Web: ssmrcc.org.
Res.: 1117 Vineyard Dr., 23322. Tel: 757-546-9400.
Catechesis/Religious Program—Tel: 757-204-4565. Students 599.
4—ST. THERESE OF LISIEUX (1954) Rev. James E. Gordon.
Res.: 321 Saunders Dr., Portsmouth, 23701.
Church: 4137 Portsmouth Blvd., 23321-2127. Tel: 757-488-2553; Fax: 757-465-4086. Email: info@sttheresechesva.org. Web: www.sttheresechesva.org.
Catechesis/Religious Program—Students 313.

CHESTERFIELD, CHESTERFIELD CO., ST. GABRIEL (1997) Rev. Pasquale Apuzzo.
Office & Mailing Address: 8901 Winterpock Rd., 23832. Tel: 804-639-6712; Fax: 804-639-6591. Email: therese.venti@saintgabriel.org. Web: www.saintgabriel.org.
Catechesis/Religious Program—Students 318.

CHINCOTEAGUE ISLAND, ACCOMACK CO., ST. ANDREW THE APOSTLE (1965) Rev. Paschal N. Kneip, O.S.B.
Res. & Mailing Address: 6319 Mumford St., 23336. Tel: 757-336-5432; Fax: 757-336-3515. Email: standrewtheapostle1@verizon.net.
Church: 6288 Church St., 23336.
Catechesis/Religious Program—Tel: 757-336-1209. Students 27.

CHRISTIANSBURG, MONTGOMERY CO., HOLY SPIRIT CATHOLIC CHURCH (1995) Rev. John Prinelli.
355 Independence Blvd., 24068.
Church: P.O. Box 98, 24068. Tel: 540-921-3547; Fax: 540-921-3547. Email: holyspiritemail@yahoo.com.
Catechesis/Religious Program—

CLARKSVILLE, MECKLENBURG CO., ST. CATHERINE OF SIENA (1947) [CEM] Rev. John C. Kazibwe (Uganda); Deacon John E. Sadowski.
Mailing Address: P.O. Box 1537, 23927.
Res.: 810 Market St., 23927. Tel: 434-374-5040.
Church: 805 Virginia Ave., 23927. Tel: 434-374-8408; Fax: 434-374-9442. Email: saintcatherines@usa.net.
Catechesis/Religious Program—Maureen Bellissimo, D.R.E. Students 28.

CLIFTON FORGE, ALLEGHANY CO., ST. JOSEPH (1889) [CEM] Rev. Louis Benoit.
Mailing Address: 620 Jefferson Ave., 24422-1715. Tel: 540-863-5371. Email: stjoseph@ntelos.net.
Catechesis/Religious Program—Students 7.

CLINTWOOD, DICKENSON CO., ST. JOSEPH (1979) Rev. Timothy A. Drake.
Mailing Address: P.O. Box 1250, 24228-1250. Tel: 276-926-5451. Web: www.clintwoodva.catholicweb.com.
Church: 478 Clintwood Main St., 24228.
Catechesis/Religious Program—Students 4.

COLONIAL HEIGHTS, COLONIAL HEIGHTS CO., ST. ANN (1925) [CEM] Rev. Lou Ruoff.
Mailing Address: 17111 Jefferson Davis Hwy., 23834-5396. Tel: 804-526-2548; Fax: 804-526-1922. Email: saintann@verizon.net. Web: www.stanncc.com.
Res.: 2433 Aldridge Ave., 23834.
Catechesis/Religious Program—Tel: 804-526-1860. Students 522.

COLUMBIA, FLUVANNA CO., ST. JOSEPH'S/SHRINE OF ST. KATHARINE DREXEL (1884) Rev. N. Alan Lipscomb.
Mailing Address & Parish House: 28 Cameron St., P.O. Box 808, 23038-0808. Tel: 434-842-3970.
Res.: 15 Dogleg Rd., Palmyra, 22963. Tel: 804-589-5200; Fax: 434-589-4463. Email: pastor@stspeterpaul.org.
Catechesis/Religious Program—65 Community Rd., Kent Store, 23884. Tel: 434-842-3970. Mrs. Christine Evans, D.R.E. Students 16.

COVINGTON, ALLEGHANY CO., SACRED HEART (1924) Rev. Louis Benoit.
Office: 214 W. Locust St., 24426-1537. Tel: 540-962-6541.
Res.: 220 W. Locust St., 24426-1537. Email: sacredheart@ntelos.net.
Catechesis/Religious Program—Students 13.

CREWE, NOTTOWAY CO., ST. JOHN THE BAPTIST (1939) [CEM] Closed. For inquiries for parish records contact the chancery.

DANVILLE, PITTSYLVANIA CO., SACRED HEART (1878) Rev. Charles L. Breindel.
Mailing Address: 538 Central Blvd., 24541. Tel: 434-792-9456; Fax: 434-792-9463. Email: shc_adm@comcast.net. Web: www.sheartcatholic.com.
Res.: 154 College Ave., 24541. Tel: 434-792-0081.
School—540 Central Blvd., 24541. Tel: 434-793-2656; Fax: 434-793-2658. Email: sacredht@earthlink.net. Web: www.sheartschool-.com. Kimberly W. Meadows, Prin. Lay Teachers 29; Students 223.
Catechesis/Religious Program—Students 143.

DINWIDDIE, DINWIDDIE CO., ST. JOHN (1907) [CEM] Revs. John J. Wagner III; David L. Nott, Parochial Vicar; Deacon Matthew C. MacLaughlin.
Mailing Address: 7215 Squirrel Level Rd., Petersburg, 23805-7035. Tel: 804-861-0123; Fax: 804-861-0123. Email: stjohndinwiddie@verizon.net. Web: www.stjohndinwiddie.org.
Church: Squirrel Level Rd. & Flank Rd., 23805.
Catechesis/Religious Program—Students 32.

ELKTON, ROCKINGHAM CO., HOLY INFANT (1951) Rev. Alejandro P. Credo, O.S.A. (Philippines).
Mailing Address & Church: 101 W. Marshall Ave., 22827-1221. Tel: 540-298-1341. Email: infant.shepherdVA@yahoo.com. Web: www.infant-shepherd.com.
Catechesis/Religious Program—Mrs. Patricia Dobes, D.R.E. Students 19.

EMPORIA, GREENSVILLE CO., ST. RICHARD (1940) Rev. Columba A. Nnorom.
Mailing Address: P.O. Box 90, Ebony, 23845. Tel: 434-636-7782 (Rectory). Email: SPTAmail@buggs.net.
Catechesis/Religious Program—Desi Maldonado, D.R.E. Students 11.

FARMVILLE, PRINCE EDWARD CO., ST. THERESA (1939) Rev. James M. Glass, O.S.B.; Deacons Emmett R. McLane; Peter J. Menting; Mr. Robert Zupanek, Campus Min. (Longwood University & Hampden-Sydney College).
Mailing Address: 709 Buffalo St., 23901-1109.
Res.: 816 Buffalo St., 23901. Tel: 434-315-0311; 434-392-3934 (Main); Fax: 434-392-1611. Email: sttheresa@embarqmail.com.
Catechesis/Religious Program—Email: sttheresa2@embarqmail.com. Karen Balley, D.R.E. Students 87.
Longwood University—
Hampden-Sydney College—

FINCASTLE, BOTETOURT CO., CHURCH OF THE TRANSFIGURATION (1989) Rev. Stephen McNally, Admin.
Church & Mailing Address: 7624 Roanoke Rd., 24090. Tel: 540-473-2656; Fax: 540-473-2193. Email: transfigure@ntelos.net. Web: www.churchofthetransfiguration.com.
Catechesis/Religious Program—Students 90.
Mission—St. John the Evangelist (2000) 99 Second St., New Castle, Craig Co. 24127. Tel: 540-864-8686.

FORT MONROE, HAMPTON CO., ST. MARY STAR OF THE SEA (1860) Revs. Peter Sousa, C.Ss.R.; Daniel Carboy, C.Ss.R., Parochial Vicar; William Spillane, C.Ss.R., Parochial Vicar; Deacon James Wharry.
Mailing Address: 7 Frank Ln., 23651-1010. Tel: 757-722-9855; 757-722-3138; Fax: 757-726-0083. Email: stmary@starofthesea.hrcoxmail.com. Web: stmarystarofthesea.catholicweb.com.
School—St. Mary Star of the Sea, 14 N. Willard Ave., Hampton, 23663. Tel: 757-723-6358; Fax: 757-723-6544. Sr. Marie Andrea, Prin. Sisters 5; Lay Teachers 13; Students 213.
Catechesis/Religious Program—Tel: 757-722-9855. Email: drestmarys@yahoo.com. Students 31.

FRANKLIN, SOUTHAMPTON CO., ST. JUDE (1948) Rev. Charles A. Saglio.
Mailing Address: 1014 Clay St., 23851-1309. Tel: 757-569-9600; Fax: 757-569-9600 (Call First). Email: st_jude1@verizon.net. Web: mysite.verizon.net/st_jude1.
Catechesis/Religious Program—Students 65.
Mission—Infant of Prague Rte. 460, Wakefield, Southampton Co. 23888.

GATE CITY, SCOTT CO., ST. BERNARD (1956) Rev. Roland Hautz, G.H.M.
Mailing Address: 139 Linda St., 24251. Tel: 276-386-9665; Fax: 276-386-3902.
Catechesis/Religious Program—Students 5.
Mission—St. Patrick (1946)Tel: 276-386-9665.

GLOUCESTER, GLOUCESTER CO., ST. THERESE, THE LITTLE FLOWER (1939) Rev. James Cowles, Admin.
Church & Mailing Address: 6262 Main St., 23061. Tel: 804-693-5939 (Office); Fax: 804-693-4766. Email: office@stthersglo.org. Web: www.sainttheresechurch.info.
Res.: 6220 Main St., 23061.
Catechesis/Religious Program—Tel: 804-693-5939. Students 156.

HAMPTON, HAMPTON CO.
1—CATHOLIC COMMUNITY OF THE KOREAN MARTYRS (1989), (Korean), Rev. Simon Hyo-Sung Ahn; Deacon Joseph N. Riss.
Mailing Address: 2018 Bay Ave., 23661. Tel: 757-245-4485; 757-245-5513; Fax: 757-246-1277.
Catechesis/Religious Program—Students 50.
2—IMMACULATE CONCEPTION (1968) Rev. Msgr. Robert M. Perkins.
Res.: 40 Pine Cone Dr., 23669. Tel: 757-826-0050.
Church: 2150 Cunningham Dr., 23666. Tel: 757-826-0393; Fax: 757-825-0855. Email: iccc.hampton@verizon.net. Web: www.icchampton.org.
Catechesis/Religious Program—Students 152.
3—ST. JOSEPH (1955) Revs. Peter Sousa, C.Ss.R.; Daniel Carboy, C.Ss.R., Parochial Vicar; William Spillane, C.Ss.R., Parochial Vicar; Deacon Jose M. Gonzalez.
Mailing Address: 512 Buckroe Ave., P.O. Box 4126, 23664-0126.
Res.: 410 Buckroe Ave., 23664-0126. Tel: 757-851-1711.
Church: 414 Buckroe Ave., 23664-0126. Tel: 757-851-8800; Fax: 757-851-1875. Email: parishoffice@stjosephscatholicchurch.com. Web: www.stjosephscatholicchurch.com.
Catechesis/Religious Program—Students 206.
4—OUR LADY OF VIETNAM CHAPEL (1994), (Vietnamese), Rev. Joseph Phien Nguyen (Vietnam).
Mailing Address: 1806 Ashland Ave., Norfolk, 23509. Tel: 757-622-5345; 757-722-2657.
Chapel— 1307 LaSalle Ave., 23669. Fax: 757-622-4248.
5—ST. ROSE OF LIMA (1948) Rev. Simon Hyo-Sung Ahn, Admin.; Deacon Joseph N. Riss.
Mailing Address: 2114 Bay Ave., 23661. Tel: 757-245-5513; Fax: 757-245-1277. Email: strose@erols.com. Web: strosehampton.com.
Res.: 2108 Bay Ave., 23661. Tel: 757-245-6313.
Catechesis/Religious Program—Students 18.

HARRISONBURG, ROCKINGHAM CO., BLESSED SACRAMENT (1906) Rev. Thomas E. Mattingly; Deacon Fred C. La Spina, Pastoral Assoc.
Mailing Address & Church: 154 N. Main St., 22802. Tel: 540-434-4341. Web: www.bscva.com.
Res.: 843 Meadowlark Dr., 22802. Tel: 540-433-3585.
Catechesis/Religious Program—Tel: 540-434-5549. Students 473.

HIGHLAND SPRINGS, HENRICO CO., ST. JOHN THE EVANGELIST (1929) Rev. Wayne Ball.
Mailing Address: P.O. Box 190, 23075-0190. Tel: 804-737-8028; Fax: 804-328-4683. Email: office@stjohnscatholicchurch.org. Web: www.stjohnscatholicchurch.org.
Res.: 7973 Bear Grass Ln., Mechanicsville, 23111. Tel: 804-677-1854.
Church: 813 W. Nine Mile Rd., 23075.
Catechesis/Religious Program—Email: tylesane@stjohnscatholicchurch.org. Students 97.

HOPEWELL, HAMPTON CO., ST. JAMES CHURCH (1918) Rev. Frank Wiggins.
Mailing Address: 510 W. Poythress St., 23860-2508.
Res.: 102 N. Fifth Ave., 23860.
Church: 500 W. Poythress St., 23860. Tel: 804-458-9223; 804-458-9296 (Evening); Fax: 804-458-1216. Email: st.jameshopewell@verizon.net. Web: stjameshopewell.org.
Catechesis/Religious Program—Email: st.jameschristianformation@verizon.net. Students 79.

HOT SPRINGS, BATH CO., THE SHRINE OF THE SACRED HEART (1922) Rev. John McGinnity (Retired).
Mailing Address: 1499 Shady Ln., 24445-0047. Tel: 540-839-2603.
Catechesis/Religious Program—Email: shrine@tds.net. Students 3.

HURT, PITTSYLVANIA CO., ST. VICTORIA (1964) Rev. James E. Gallagher Jr.
Mailing Address: P.O. Box 640, 24563-0640. Tel: 434-324-4824. Email: stviccah@fairpoint.net.
Res.: 305 Victoria Dr., 24563. Fax: 434-324-4824.

JONESVILLE, LEE CO., CHURCH OF THE HOLY SPIRIT (1956) Rev. Timothy A. Drake; Deacon Barron Flanary.
Mailing Address: P.O. Box 923, 24263. Tel: 276-346-0269. Email: hsccjva@yahoo.com. In Res., Rev. Leslie Schmidt, G.H.M.
Church: U.S. Rte. 58 E. of Jonesville, 24263. Tel: 276-679-2336.
Catechesis/Religious Program—Students 16.

LAKE GASTON, MECKLENBERG CO., ST. PETER THE APOSTLE (1995) Rev. Columba A. Nnorom.
Church: Rte. 903, 31 Ebony Rd., Ebony, 23845. Tel: 434-636-7782; Fax: 434-636-4549. Email: sptalake@buggs.net. Web: st-peter-the-apostle.org.
Catechesis/Religious Program—Robert Walker, D.R.E. Students 2.

LEBANON, RUSSELL CO., GOOD SHEPHERD (1959) Rev. Michael J. Herbert.

Mailing Address: P.O. Box 730, 24266-0730. Tel: 276-889-1690; 276-889-0127. Email: stterese606@yahoo.com.
Church: 890 W. Main St., Ste. A, 24266.
Catechesis/Religious Program—Students 7.

LEXINGTON, ROCKBRIDGE CO., ST. PATRICK (1873) Rev. Joseph A. D'Aurora.
Office & Mailing: 221 W. Nelson St., P.O. Box 725, 24450-0725. Tel: 540-463-3533; Fax: 540-464-3790. Email: doriskstpats@embarqmail.com. Web: stpatrickslexington.com.
Res.: 225 Denny Ln., 24450-1770. Tel: 540-463-6819.
Church: 219 W. Nelson St., 24450.
Catechesis/Religious Program—Students 110.

LOVINGSTON, NELSON CO., ST. MARY (1979) Rev. Daniel L. Kelly; Deacon Richard J. Nees.
Mailing Address: 9900 Thomas Nelson Hwy., 22949-0735. Tel: 434-263-8509. Email: stmarystfrancischurch@ceva.net. Web: stmarycatholicchurch.org.
Catechesis/Religious Program—Tel: 434-263-6923. Students 35.

LYNCHBURG, CAMPBELL CO.

1—HOLY CROSS (1859) [CEM] Rev. Msgr. J. Kenneth Rush Jr.; Deacon Gordon Kenneth Cartwright.
Church & Office Address: 710 Clay St., 24504-2530. Tel: 434-846-5245; Fax: 434-846-7022. Email: hcrosshome@aol.com. Web: www.holycrosslynchburg.org.
Res.: 2000 Burnt Bridge Rd., 24503. Tel: 434-386-0220.
School—Regional School, (Grades PreK-12), 2125 Langhorne Rd., 24501. Tel: 434-847-5436. Mr. John P. Jones, Prin. Lay Teachers 45; Students 317.
Catechesis/Religious Program—Students 270.

2—ST. THOMAS MORE (1978) Rev. Richard T. Mooney; Deacon Frederick Scarletto.
3015 Roundelay Rd., 24502-2036. Tel: 434-237-5911; Fax: 434-237-8854. Email: info@stmva.com. Web: www.stmva.com.
Catechesis/Religious Program—Tel: 434-237-8852. Email: faithformation@stmva.com. Students 300.

MARION, SMYTH CO., ST. JOHN THE EVANGELIST CHURCH (1974) Rev. Paul Maier; Deacon Juan Ibarra, Hipsanic Ministry.
124 Park Blvd., 24354. Tel: 276-783-7282; Fax: 276-783-7282.
Church: 124 Park Blvd., 24354.
Catechesis/Religious Program—Students 16.

MARTINSVILLE, HENRY CO., ST. JOSEPH (1949), (Hispanic), Rev. Joseph Torretto.
Mailing Address: 2481 Spruce St., 24112. Tel: 276-638-4779; 276-638-1192; Fax: 540-638-2218. Email: stjoseph@sitestar.net. Web: www.stjoechurch.net.
Res.: 1810 Spruce St., #117, 24112. Tel: 276-632-5182.
Catechesis/Religious Program—Students 70.

MATHEWS, MATHEWS CO., CHURCH OF FRANCIS DE SALES (1983) [JC] Rev. Robert L. Cummins.
Church: 176 Lover's Ln., 23109. Fax: 804-725-5463. Email: fdschurch@msn.com. Web: churchoffrancisdesales.org.
Catechesis/Religious Program—Students 55.

MECHANICSVILLE, HANOVER CO., CHURCH OF THE REDEEMER (1976) Rev. James J. Begley Jr.; Deacons Christopher Stephen Colville; Chris Malone.
Church & Mailing Address: 8275 Meadowbridge Rd., 23116. Tel: 804-746-4911; Fax: 804-746-8657. Email: churchredeemer@churchredeemer.org. Web: www.churchredeemer.org.
Res.: 8222 N. Mayfield Ln., 23111. Tel: 804-427-6962.
Catechesis/Religious Program—Tel: 804-746-4911. Mrs. Terry Colville, D.R.E.; Mr. LeRoy Orie Jr., Youth Min.; Bernadette Harris, D.R.E. (Adult). Students 919.

MIDDLESEX, MIDDLESEX CO., CHURCH OF THE VISITATION (1983) [JC] Rev. Robert L. Cummins.
Mailing Address: P.O. Box 38, Topping, 23169-0038. Tel: 804-758-5160; Fax: 804-758-0676. Email: churchofthevisitation@va.metrocast.net. Web: www.visitationcatholicchurch.org.
Res.: 119 Club Dr., Hartfield, 23071. Tel: 804-776-0676.
Church: 8462 Puller Hwy., Topping, 23169.
Catechesis/Religious Program—Students 51.

MINERAL, LOUISA CO., ST. JUDE (1974) [CEM] Rev. Michael M. Duffy; Deacons Robert M. Esposito; Joseph J. Milkevitch; Alfonso Benet.
Mailing Address: P.O. Box 40, 23117-0040. Tel: 540-894-4266; Fax: 540-894-4993. Email: stjudemineral@verizon.net.
Church: 1937 Davis Hwy., 23117-0040.
Catechesis/Religious Program—Students 65.

MONETA, BEDFORD CO., RESURRECTION (1984) [CEM] Rev. Salvador Anonuevo; Chris Barrett, Pastoral Coord.; Joe Day, Parish Admin.
Mailing Address: 15353 Moneta Rd., 24121-9804. Tel: 540-297-5530; Fax: 540-297-6316. Email: jday@resurrectioncatholic.org. Web: www.resurrectioncatholic.org.
Catechesis/Religious Program—Students 69.

NEW CASTLE, CRAIG CO., SAINT JOHN THE EVANGELIST MISSION (1997) Rev. Stephen McNally.
99 Second St., 24127. Tel: 540-864-8686. Email: stjohncatholic@tds.net.
Catechesis/Religious Program—Students 8.

NEWPORT NEWS, NEWPORT CO.

1—ST. JEROME (1966) Rev. Joseph B. Majewski.
Mailing Address: 116 Denbigh Blvd., 23608-3333. Tel: 757-877-5021; Fax: 757-898-1437. Email: jeanieaa@stjeromennva.org. Web: www.stjeromennva.org.
Catechesis/Religious Program—Tel: 757-877-3771. Email: margie@stjeromennva.org. Students 459.

2—OUR LADY OF MOUNT CARMEL (1953) Revs. Kenneth E. Wood; Peter Tran; Deacon Bernard H. Taylor.
100 Harpersville Rd., 23601-2324. Tel: 757-595-0385; Fax: 757-599-9285. Email: jhassan@olmc.org. Web: www.olmc.org.
School—Tel: 757-596-2754; Fax: 757-596-1570. Sr. John Paul Myers, O.P., Prin. Sisters of St. Dominic 5; Lay Teachers 47; Students 549.
Catechesis/Religious Program—Tel: 757-595-0385, Ext. 119. Students 445.

3—ST. VINCENT DE PAUL (1881) Rev. Alistair McKay, C.Ss.R.
Church & Mailing Address: 230 33rd St., P.O. Box 258, 23607. Tel: 757-245-4234; Fax: 757-245-0039. Email: stvdpcc@verizon.net. Web: mysite.verizon.net/stvdpcc.
Catechesis/Religious Program—Students 61.

NORFOLK, NORFOLK CITY CO.

1—BASILICA OF ST. MARY OF THE IMMACULATE CONCEPTION (1791), (African American), [JC] Rev. Ernest Livasia Bulinda, Rector; Deacon Calvin J. Bailey.
Office & Rectory: 1000 Holt St., 23504-4201. Tel: 757-622-4487; Fax: 757-625-7969. Email: saintmary@verizon.net. Web: www.basilicaofsaintmary.org.
Church: 232 Chapel St., 23504.
Catechesis/Religious Program—Students 104.

2—BLESSED SACRAMENT (1921) [CEM] Rev. Joseph H. Metzger III.
Mailing Address: 6400 Newport Ave., 23505-4557. Tel: 757-423-8305; Fax: 757-451-3335. Email: office@blessed-sacrament.com. Web: www.blessed-sacrament.com.
Res.: 110 W. Severn Rd., 23505. Tel: 757-489-9636.
Catechesis/Religious Program—Students 200.

3—CHRIST THE KING (1949) Rev. Brian Rafferty.
Office & Mailing Address—1803 Columbia Ave., 23509-1298. Tel: 757-622-1120; 757-622-9196; Fax: 757-627-8808. Email: office@christtheking.hrcoxmail.com. Web: www.ctkparish-norfolk.org.
Res.: 1804 Ashland Ave., 23509. Tel: 757-627-1723. Email: brafferty@christtheking.hrcoxmail.com.
School—3401 Tidewater Dr., 23509. Tel: 757-625-4951; Fax: 757-623-5212. Email: info@ctkparish.org. Web: www.ctkparish.org. Mrs. Rachel Chatham, Prin. Lay Teachers 22; Students 290.
Catechesis/Religious Program—Tel: 757-625-0208. Students 155.

4—HOLY TRINITY (1921) [JC] Rev. William Daniel Beeman.
Mailing Address: 155 W. Government Ave., 23503-2905. Tel: 757-480-3433; Fax: 757-480-8749. Email: parish.office@trinitynorfolk.org. Web: www.trinitynorfolk.org.
School—154 W. Government Ave., 23503. Tel: 757-583-1873; Fax: 757-587-3677. Web: www.holytrinityschoolva.com. Ms. Deneane Nofplot, Prin. Lay Teachers 17; Students 165.
Catechesis/Religious Program—Students 139.

5—OUR LADY OF LAVANG (1991) [JC] Rev. Joseph Phien Nguyen (Vietnam), Admin.; Deacon James Wharry.
1806 Ashland Ave., 23509-1236.
Church: 409 Compostella Rd., 23509. Tel: 757-232-1424; Fax: 757-351-3648.

6—ST. PIUS X (1955) Rev. Venancio R. Balarote Jr.; Deacon Walker King.
Res.: 1615 Longdale Dr., 23518. Tel: 757-855-3297. Email: frvb@piusxparish.org. Web: www.piusxparish.org/church.
School—7800 Halprin Dr., 23518. Tel: 757-588-6171; Fax: 757-587-6580. Email: school@piusxparish.org. Web: www.piusxparish.org. Sr. Linda Taber, I.H.M., Prin. Sisters Servants of the Immaculate Heart of Mary 2; Lay Teachers 17; Students 330.
Catechesis/Religious Program—Email: sbernadette@piusxparish.org. Students 219.

7—SACRED HEART (1894) [CEM] Rev. Daniel N. Klem.
Office: 520 Graydon Ave., 23507-1711. Tel: 757-625-6763; Fax: 757-627-1965. Email: sh.church@verizon.net. Web: www.sacredheartnorfolk.org.
Catechesis/Religious Program—Students 177.

NORGE, JAMES CITY CO., ST. OLAF, PATRON OF NORWAY (1992) Rev. Peter M. Creed; Deacons Robert R. Thompson; Daniel F. Ferry.
Mailing Address: 104 Norge Ln., 23188-7229. Tel: 757-564-3819; Fax: 757-565-1099. Email: office@stolafchurch.hrcoxmail.com. Web: www.stolaf.cc.
Catechesis/Religious Program—Students 143.

NORTON, WISE CO., ST. ANTHONY (1938) Rev. Timothy A. Drake.
Mailing Address & Church: 1009 Virginia Ave., N.W., 24273-1897. Tel: 276-679-2336. Email: stanthonys3@verizon.net. Web: stanthonycatholic.org.
Catechesis/Religious Program—Students 16.
Station—University of Virginia at Wise Wise.

ONLEY, ACCOMACK CO., ST. PETER THE APOSTLE (1942) Rev. Rodrigo Mingollo.
Church & Mailing Address: 25236 Coastal Blvd., P.O. Box 860, 23418-0860. Tel: 757-787-4592; Fax: 757-787-2899. Email: stpeterapostle@verizon.net. Web: www.stpetertheapostle.com.
Catechesis/Religious Program—Students 87.

PALMYRA, FLUVANNA CO., SS. PETER & PAUL (1986) Revs. N. Alan Lipscomb; Gerald F. Musuubire, Parochial Vicar.
Mailing Address: 4309 Thomas Jefferson Pkwy., 22963-9506. Tel: 434-589-5201; Fax: 434-589-4463. Email: office@saintspeterpaul.org. Web: www.saintspeterpaul.org.
Catechesis/Religious Program—Students 157.

PEARISBURG, GILES CO., HOLY FAMILY (1965) Rev. John Prinelli.
Mailing Address: 516 Mason Court Dr., 24134-1832. Tel: 540-921-3547. Email: holyfamilyva@lycos.com.
Catechesis/Religious Program—Students 9.

PETERSBURG, PRINCE GEORGE CO., ST. JOSEPH (1842) [CEM] Rev. Esteban Eugenio Antes (RVC).
Church, Office & Mailing Address: 11 N. Market St., P.O. Box 2006, 23804-1306. Tel: 804-733-3115; Fax: 804-862-9931. Email: saintjoseph2@juno.com. Web: sjcpetersburg.com.
Res.: 19 Centre Hill Ct., 23803. Tel: 804-732-5127.
School—123 Franklin St., 23803. Tel: 804-732-3931; Fax: 804-863-2635. Sr. Margaret Mary Scally, D.C., Prin. Lay Teachers 10; Students 192.
Catechesis/Religious Program—Tel: 804-862-9977. Students 70.

POCAHONTAS, TAZEWELL CO., ST. ELIZABETH (1896) Merged with St. Mary, Richlands, St. Theresa, Tazewell & mission church of St. Joseph, Grundy to form Holy Family Parish, Tazewell.

PORTSMOUTH, PORTSMOUTH CO.

1—CHURCH OF THE HOLY ANGELS (1917) [JC] Revs. Michael G. Boehling; David W. Cupps, Parochial Vicar.
Office: 34 Afton Pkwy., 23702-2739. Tel: 757-485-2142; 757-485-2143; Fax: 757-485-3699. Email: holyangels@juno.com.
Catechesis/Religious Program—Students 59.

2—CHURCH OF THE RESURRECTION (1971) Revs. Michael G. Boehling; David W. Cupps, Parochial Vicar.
Mailing Address: 3501 Cedar Ln., 23703. Tel: 757-484-7335; Fax: 757-484-5857. Email: info@reschurch.com.
Res.: 518 High St., 23704. Tel: 757-397-7066.
Catechesis/Religious Program—Students 117.

3—ST. PAUL (1804) [CEM] [JC] Revs. Michael G. Boehling; David W. Cupps, Parochial Vicar.
Office: 518 High St., 23704-3516. Tel: 757-397-7066; Fax: 757-393-4334. Email: stpaulsptown@aol.com. Web: www.stpauls-portsmouth.org.
Church: 522 High St., 23704.
Catechesis/Religious Program—Email: mrcbeebe@cox.net. Students 170.

POWHATAN, CAMPBELL CO., ST. JOHN NEUMANN (1948) Rev. Jeffrey T. Garcia (Philippines); Deacons Edward P. Schmidt; Fulton Patrick O'Donnell.
Church: 2480 Batterson Rd., 23139-7513. Tel: 804-598-3754; 804-794-9098; Fax: 804-598-1467. Email: sjn_general@hughes.net. Web: www.sjnpowhatan.org.
Catechesis/Religious Program—Students 200.

PRINCE GEORGE COUNTY, PRINCE GEORGE CO., CHURCH OF THE SACRED HEART (1906) [CEM] Rev. Jay Wagner; Deacons Raymond K. Linden; Edward G. Hanzlik; Robert Dennis Baker; James E. Rodgers.
Mailing Address: 9300 Community Ln., Petersburg, 23805-7567. Tel: 804-732-6385; Fax: 804-732-6385. Email: sacredheart1906@verizon.net. Web: www.churchsacredheart.com.
Catechesis/Religious Program—Students 129.

QUINQUE, GREENE COUNTY, SHEPHERD OF THE HILLS (1980) Rev. Alejandro P. Credo, O.S.A. (Philippines).
Mailing Address: P.O. Box 83, 22965-0083. Tel: 434-985-3929. Email: infant.shepherdVA@yahoo.com. Web: www.infant-shepherd.com.
Church: Rte. 633, 6562 Amicus Rd., 22965-0083.

Catechesis/Religious Program—Jane Lilly, D.R.E. Students 46.

QUINTON, NEW KENT CO., ST. ELIZABETH ANN SETON (1986) Very Rev. J. Scott Duarte; Deacon William R. Hunt.
Mailing Address & Church: 2631 Pocahontas Tr., 23141-0245. Tel: 804-932-4125; Fax: 804-932-8126. Email: seascatholic@verizon.net. Web: www.seascatholicchurch.org.
Catechesis/Religious Program—Students 33.

RADFORD, MONTGOMERY CO., ST. JUDE (1967) Rev. Kenneth J. Shuping; Deacon Michael J. Ellerbrock.
Mailing Address: 1740 Tyler Rd., Christiansburg, 24073-6154. Tel: 540-639-5341; Fax: 540-639-4738. Email: stjudechurch@juno.com. Web: stjuderadfordva.org.
Res.: 1800 Tyler Rd., Christiansburg, 24073. Tel: 540-731-9541.
Catechesis/Religious Program—Students 117.

RICHLANDS, TAZEWELL CO., ST. MARY (1962) Merged with St. Theresa, Tazewell, St. Elizabeth, Pocahontas & mission church of St. Joseph, Grundy to form Holy Family, Tazewell.

ROANOKE, ROANOKE CO.

1—ST. ANDREW (1890) [JC] Rev. Msgr. Thomas G. Miller; Deacon Mark D. Allison.
Res. & Mailing Address: 631 N. Jefferson St., 24016. Email: jblanchard@standrewsroanoke.org. Web: www.standrewsroanoke.org.
Catechesis/Religious Program—Students 370.

2—ST. GERARD (1946) Rev. Rene Castillo.
809 Orange Ave., N.W., 24016-1117. Tel: 540-343-7744; Fax: 540-343-3599. Email: mail@stgerard.roacoxmail.com. Web: www.stgerard-roanoke-va.org.
Catechesis/Religious Program—Email: reled@stgerard.roacoxmail.com. Students 101.

3—OUR LADY OF NAZARETH (1914) Rev. Msgr. Joseph P. Lehman.
Mailing Address: 2505 Electric Rd., S.W., 24018-3599. Tel: 540-774-0066 (Office); 540-774-0857 (Res.); Fax: 540-774-2148. Web: www.oln-parish.org. Email: secretary@oln-parish.com.
Catechesis/Religious Program—Tel: 540-774-0773. Email: cf@oln-parish.org. Students 473.

ROCKY MOUNT, FRANKLIN CO., FRANCIS OF ASSISI (1984) Rev. Rene Castillo.
Mailing Address: 15 Glennwood Dr., 24151-2111. Tel: 540-483-9591; Fax: 540-483-5232. Email: francismom@jetbroadband.com. Web: www.francis-of-assisi.org.
Catechesis/Religious Program—Students 90.

ST. PAUL, WISE CO., ST. THERESE (1954) Rev. Michael J. Herbert.
Mailing Address: P.O. Box 56, 24283-0056. Tel: 276-762-5932; Fax: 276-762-5932. Email: stterese606@yahoo.com.
Catechesis/Religious Program—Students 6.

SALEM, PAGE CO., OUR LADY OF PERPETUAL HELP (1947) Rev. Kevin Lee Segerblom; Deacons Eric M. Surat; Stephen O'Connell.
Mailing Address: 314 Turner Rd., 24153-2399. Tel: 540-387-0491; Fax: 540-389-8237. Web: www.olphsalem.org. Email: office@olphsalem.org.
Res.: 1408 Kathryn Ln., 24153. Tel: 540-387-1020.
Catechesis/Religious Program—Email: christianformation@olphsalem.org. Students 162.

SCOTTSVILLE, ALBEMARLE CO., ST. GEORGE (1975) [CEM] Rev. Dennis McAuliffe.
Mailing Address: 7240 Scottsville Rd., P.O. Box 9, 24590-0009. Tel: 434-286-3724. Email: stgeorge604@juno.com.

SMITHFIELD, ISLE OF WIGHT CO., GOOD SHEPHERD (1984) Rev. Peter Bialkowski (Poland).
Mailing Address: P.O. Box 840, 23431-0840. Tel: 757-365-0579; Fax: 757-365-4749. Email: goodshepherd-smithfield@verizon.net. Web: goodshepherd-smithfield.org.
Church: 300 Smithfield Blvd., 23430.
Catechesis/Religious Program—Students 150.

SOUTH BOSTON, HALIFAX CO., ST. PASCHAL BAYLON (1953) [JC] Revs. John C. Kazibwe (Uganda); Nixon Negparanon (Philippines), Parochial Vicar.
Church: 800 John Randolph Blvd., 24592-2943. Tel: 434-572-2285; Fax: 434-572-1725. Email: stpaschalchurch@embarqmail.com.
Catechesis/Religious Program—Students 15.

SOUTH HILL, MECKLENBURG CO., GOOD SHEPHERD (1922) Revs. John C. Kazibwe (Uganda); Nixon Negparanon (Philippines), Parochial Vicar.
Mailing Address: P.O. Box 621, 23970-0621. Tel: 434-447-3622; Fax: 434-447-4729. Email: goodsh23970@earthlink.net.
Church: 1664 N. Mecklenburg Ave., 23970.
Catechesis/Religious Program—Students 18.

STAUNTON, AUGUSTA CO., ST. FRANCIS OF ASSISI (1844) Rev. Burt Sare (Philippines), Admin.; Alexa Shmidneiser, Pastoral Assoc.; Deacon James Kledzik.
Res.: 24401. Tel: 540-886-9121. Email: office@stfrancisparish.org. Web: www.stfrancisparish.org.
Catechesis/Religious Program—Fax: 540-885-5743. Students 196.

SUFFOLK, SUFFOLK CO., ST. MARY OF THE PRESENTATION (1927) Rev. Peter Bialkowski (Poland).
Office: 202 S. Broad St., 23434-5715. Tel: 757-539-5732; Fax: 757-538-0103. Email: stmarysuffolk@charterinternet.com. Web: www.stmarysuffolk.org.
Church: 200 S. Broad St., 23434.
Catechesis/Religious Program—Students 107.

TABB, YORK CO., BLESSED KATERI TEKAKWITHA (1986) Rev. Lawrence J. Mullaney; Mrs. Elaine Riley, Admin.
Church & Office: 3800 Big Bethel Rd., 23693-3814. Tel: 757-766-3800; Fax: 757-766-1125. Email: elaineriley@stkateri.org. Web: www.stkateri.org.
Catechesis/Religious Program—Web: www.stkateriyouth.org. Mrs. Patricia Giaccio, D.R.E. (Grades K-7); Mrs. Patricia Kovac, (Grades 8-12); Mrs. Lori Yankoski. Students 384.

TAPPAHANNOCK, ESSEX CO., ST. TIMOTHY (1972) Rev. Anthony E. Marques.
Mailing Address: 708 N. Church Ln., P.O. Box 129, 22560-0129. Web: www.sttimothysparish.org.
Church: 708 N. Church Ln., 22560. Tel: 804-443-2760; 804-443-2570; Fax: 804-443-2022. Email: sttimothychurch@verizon.net.
Catechesis/Religious Program—Students 62.

TAZEWELL, TAZEWELL CO.

1—HOLY FAMILY PARISH Rev. Gaudencio G. Pugat, S.V.D.
Church & Mailing Address: 304 Tazewell Ave., 24651. Fax: 276-988-8028. Email: theword1875@verizon.net.
Catechesis/Religious Program—Students 32.

2—ST. THERESA (1980) Merged with St. Mary, Richlands, St. Elizabeth, Pochontas & mission church of St. Joseph, Grundy to form Holy Family, Tazewell.

VIRGINIA BEACH, VIRGINIA BEACH CO., CHURCH OF THE ASCENSION (1972) [CEM] Rev. James E. Parke; Deacons Gary R. Harmeyer; Thomas E. McFeely; Michael Moro; Lisa Liedl, Business Mgr.; Diane Nestor, Music Min.
Office: 4853 Princess Anne Rd., 23462-4446. Tel: 757-495-1887; 757-495-1886; Fax: 757-495-1516. Web: www.ascensionvb.org.
Catechesis/Religious Program—Tel: 757-495-1886, Ext. 11. Thomas Esposito, Youth Min. Students 480.

VIRGINIA BEACH, VIRGINIA CO.

1—CHURCH OF THE HOLY APOSTLES (1977), (Anglican-Roman Catholic Congregation of Hampton Roads) Rev. James E. Parke.
Church: 1593 Lynnhaven Pkwy., 23453-2008. Tel: 757-427-0963; Fax: 757-427-9434. Email: apostles1@verizon.net. Web: www.ha-arc.com.
Catechesis/Religious Program—Students 15.

2—ST. GREGORY THE GREAT (1957) Revs. Mario Fulgenzi; Luke Policicchio, O.S.B.; Cristiano Aparecido Brito, O.S.B.; Carol Noona, Music Min.; Janice Sigala, Spanish Min.
Office: 5345 Virginia Beach Blvd., 23462. Tel: 757-497-8330; Fax: 757-490-1492. Email: stgregoryg@aol.com. Web: stgregoryvabeach.org.
School—5343 Virginia Beach Blvd., 23462-1896. Tel: 757-497-1811; Fax: 757-497-7005. Sr. Mary Catherine Chapman, I.H.M., Prin. Lay Teachers 50; Students 715; Religious 4.
Catechesis/Religious Program—Tel: 757-499-4494; Fax: 757-490-1492. Anne Marie Holland, D.R.E. Students 747.
Chapel—Chesapeake, St. Benedict Tridentine Chapel (1992) 521 McCosh St., Chesapeake, 23320. Tel: 757-543-0561.
Catechesis/Religious Program—Students 68.

3—HOLY FAMILY (1977) Rev. Joseph A. Slattery.
Parish Center—1279 N. Great Neck Rd., 23454-2117. Tel: 757-481-5702; 757-481-0799; Fax: 757-481-3989. Web: holyfamilyvb.org.
Catechesis/Religious Program—Students 569.

4—HOLY SPIRIT (1975) [CEM] Rev. Timothy Kuhneman; Deacon Robert J. Durel.
Office: 1396 Lynnhaven Pkwy., 23453-2710. Tel: 757-468-3600; 757-468-3601; Fax: 757-468-3342. Email: office@holyspiritvb.org. Web: www.holyspiritvb.org.
Res.: 3345 Clubhouse Rd., 23452. Tel: 757-216-2347.
Catechesis/Religious Program—Students 579.

5—ST. JOHN THE APOSTLE CHURCH (1989) Rev. Robert J. Cole (Netherlands Antilles); Deacons Joseph F. Grillo; Vernon Krajeski. In Res., Rev. Paul Gaughan (Retired). Tel: 757-426-2550.
Office, Res. & Church: 800 Los Conaes Way, 23456-6421. Tel: 757-426-2180; Fax: 757-426-6857. Email: sja.parish@cox.net. Web: www.saintjohntheapostle.org.
School—1968 Sandbridge Rd., 23456. Tel: 757-821-1100; Fax: 757-821-1047. Web: www.stjohnsandbridge.com. Joseph Badali, Prin. Staff 30; Students 204.
Catechesis/Religious Program—Tel: 757-426-2180; Fax: 757-426-6857. Email: sja.jdomingo@cox.net. Students 725.

6—ST. LUKE (1986) Rev. Silvio Kaberia (Kenya); Deacon Lawrence P. Illy, Business Mgr.
Mailing Address: 2304 Salem Rd., 23456-1215. Tel: 757-427-5776; Fax: 757-427-2260. Email: stlukecc@aol.com. Web: www.saintlukecc.com.
Catechesis/Religious Program—Tel: 757-427-5776; Fax: 757-427-2260. Students 204.

7—ST. MARK (1978) [CEM] Rev. James C. Griffin; Deacons Michael Johnson; John J. Kren.
Mailing Address: 1505 Kempsville Rd., 23464-7210. Tel: 757-479-1010; Fax: 757-479-9453. Email: secretary@stmark-parish.org. Web: www.stmark-parish.org.
Res.: 4901 Whitewood Ln., 23464. Tel: 757-467-4932.
Catechesis/Religious Program—Tel: 757-479-9897; Fax: 757-479-9453. Email: formation@stmark-parish.org. Students 456.

8—ST. MATTHEW (1924) Rev. Joseph Facura; Deacons Chris Romero; William J. Blatnik; Darrell G. Wentworth.
Office: 3314 Sandra Ln., 23464-1736. Tel: 757-420-6310; 757-420-6311; Fax: 757-420-7734. Email: st.matthews@verizon.net. Web: www.saintmatts.net.
Res.: 1020 Josephine Crescent, 23464. Tel: 757-523-1723.
School—3316 Sandra Ln., 23464. Tel: 757-420-2455; Fax: 757-420-4880. Mrs. Barbara White, Prin. Lay Teachers 36; Students 628.
Catechesis/Religious Program—Tel: 757-420-6310; Fax: 757-420-7734. Students 183.

9—ST. NICHOLAS (1963) Rev. Msgr. Raymond A. Barton.
Office & Church: 712 Little Neck Rd., 23452. Tel: 757-340-7231; Fax: 757-340-2727. Email: stnicholas@stnicholasvb.com. Web: www.stnicholasvb.com.
Res.: 3340 Old Kirkwood Dr., 23452-5807. Tel: 757-498-7834.
Catechesis/Religious Program—Students 299.

10—STAR OF THE SEA (1915) Rev. Esteban DeLeon, S.V.D.
Office: 1404 Pacific Ave., 23451-3439. Tel: 757-428-8547; Fax: 757-428-0788. Web: www.staroftheseaparish.com.
School—309 15th St., 23451. Tel: 757-428-8400; Fax: 757-428-2794. Ms. Cathryn Mary Whisman, Prin. Lay Teachers 24; Students 364.
Catechesis/Religious Program—Tel: 757-428-8547; Fax: 757-428-0788. Students 213.

WAYNESBORO, AUGUSTA CO., ST. JOHN THE EVANGELIST (1946) Rev. Rolo B. Castillo.
Mailing Address: 344 Maple Ave., 22980-4706.
Office: Tel: 540-949-6145; 540-949-6146; Fax: 540-932-8512. Web: www.stjohnevan.com.
Church: 300 Maple Ave., 22980.
Catechesis/Religious Program—Students 179.

WEST POINT, KING WILLIAM CO., OUR LADY OF THE BLESSED SACRAMENT (1918) [CEM 2] Rev. Leo J. Guarnieri, Admin.
Mailing Address: 207 W. Euclid Blvd., 23181. In Res., Rev. John Brieffies, M.S.F.
Church: 3570 King William Ave., 23181. Tel: 804-843-3125; Fax: 804-843-9158. Email: olbs@verizon.net. Web: www.catholic-church.org/olbs.
Catechesis/Religious Program—Students 65.

WILLIAMSBURG, JAMES CITY CO., ST. BEDE (1932) Revs. John Adam Abe; Arlon M. Vergara (Philippines); Deacons Dominic Cerrato; Francis Roettinger.
Res.: 4524 The Foxes, 23188. Tel: 757-220-4233.
Church & Mailing Address: 3686 Ironbound Rd., P.O. Box 5400, 23188. Tel: 757-229-3631; Fax: 757-229-7845. Email: stboffice@bedeva.org. Web: www.bedeva.org.
Catechesis/Religious Program—Students 998.

WOODLAWN, CARROLL CO., ST. JOSEPH'S (1981) Rev. Charles W. Brickner; Deacon Bruce K. Dwyer, Pastoral Assoc.
Mailing Address: 3579 Carrollton Pike, 24381-3651. Tel: 276-236-7814; Fax: 276-236-7814. Email: sjoffice@embarqmail.com.
Catechesis/Religious Program—Students 87.
Mission—Church of the Risen Lord U.S. 58 and County 625, Patrick Springs, Patrick 24133.
Catechesis/Religious Program—Students 1.
Mission—Church of All Saints Rt. 615 & Rt. 693, Floyd, Floyd Co. 24091.
Catechesis/Religious Program—Students 12.

WYTHEVILLE, WYTHE CO., ST. MARY THE MOTHER OF GOD (1845) [CEM] Rev. Charles J. Faul.
Mailing Address: P.O. Box 7, 24382-0007. Tel: 276-228-3104; Fax: 276-228-3322. Email: stmarys10@earthlink.net.
Church: 370 E. Main St., 24382.
Catechesis/Religious Program—Students 38.
Mission—St. Edward P.O. Box 1670, Pulaski, Davis Co. 24301. Tel: 276-980-6511; Fax: 276-980-6511.

Catechesis/Religious Program—Students 28.
YORKTOWN, YORK CO., ST. JOAN OF ARC (1954) Rev. Michael Joly, Admin.; Deacon Daniel F. Johnson. Office: 315 Harris Grove Ln., 23692-4014. Tel: 757-898-5570; Fax: 757-898-0737.
111 Tradewinds Dr., 23693.
Catechesis/Religious Program—Tel: 757-898-7190. Mrs. Debra Gausmann, Youth Min. Students 385.

Chaplains of Public Institutions

RICHMOND. *International Airport*. Rev. Wayne Ball, J.C.L., Chap.
McGuire VA Medical Center. Vacant. Tel: 804-343-7111.
HAMPTON. *VA Medical Center*, Chaplain Service, Bldg. 69, 23667. Tel: 757-722-9961, Ext. 3600. Rev. Donald J. Cavey.
NORFOLK. *Apostleship of the Sea*. Vacant. Tel: 757-480-3434.
PETERSBURG. *Federal Correctional Institution*. Vacant.
SALEM. *Salem VA Medical Center*, Tel: 540-982-2463. Revs. Rene Castillo, Chap., Jeremiusz H. Sojka, Chap.

Military Chaplains:
Revs.—
Caiazzo, Gregory G.
Dang, Chin Van
Huan, Joseph Van Tran
Iaucci, Thomas
McGuire, David V.

Unassigned:
Revs.—
Bostwick, John
Cowan, Steven
Kanicki, Philip A.
Smith, Russell E., S.T.D.
Trinh, Thai Z.

Retired:
Most Rev.—
Sullivan, Walter F., D.D., Bishop Emeritus of Richmond, 3203 Hawthorne Ave., 23222. Tel: 804-329-3653; 804-359-5661. Email: Bishop.Sullivan@richmonddiocese.org
Rev. Msgrs.—
Caroluzza, Thomas, 475 Water St., #203, Portsmouth, 23704. Tel: 757-425-4555. Email: caroluzza@aol.com
Frias, Santiago C., 155 W. Government Ave., Norfolk, 23503-2095. Tel: 757-480-3434. Email: fathersanti@aol.com
Michael, Chester P., 2568 Ennis Mountain Rd., Afton, 22920-5626. Tel: 540-456-6626. Email: chesterpmichael@aol.com
Pitt, William L., 3288 Page Ave., Apt. 1112, Virginia Beach, 23451. Tel: 757-481-4629. Email: paterchs@aol.com
Revs.—
Bain, Daniel, 141 Green Turtle Ln., Apt. 8, Charlottesville, 22901. Tel: 434-974-7730
Bond, B. Daniel, 8280 Woodman Rd., 23228. Tel: 804-684-5293. Email: bdaniel.bond@att.net
Carr, James V., 217 Beach 99th St., Rockaway Park, NY 11694. Email: jamesvcarr@earthlink.net
Cervantes, Leo, 664 Burgos St., Cagayan de Oro City 9000, Philippines.
Clark, Joseph L., 1016 Donation Dr., Virginia Beach, 23455. Tel: 757-464-1816. Email: rjlc@cox.net
Condon, William F., 215 N. Power Rd., Unit 132, Mesa, AZ 85205-8462. Email: wcondon@cox.net
DeSouza, Carl, 806 Longstreet Rd., Farmville, 23901. Email: rafiki_757@msn.com
Dinga, William, P.O. Box 226, Bath, ME 04530. Email: williamdinga@verizon.net
Dinges, Anthony, 3708 Canal Blvd. Apt. 5, Hays, KS 67601.
Dorgan, John J., 19 8th Ave., Southern Shores, NC 27949-3217. Tel: 252-261-9791. Email: eddiesplace@charter.net
Dorson, James E., 133 Routier Hill, Hot Springs, 24445.
Feusahrens, Frederick J., 909 Rennie Ave., 23227-4808. Email: ltlfred@aol.com
Fosnot, James, 4400 Beulah Rd., 23237. Email: jmfvausa@yahoo.com
French, Robert E., 7501-15G River Rd., Newport News, 23607. Email: ref1963@msn.com
Funk, Virgil C., 12960 S.W. Park Way, Portland, OR 97225. Tel: 503-643-3734
Gallagher, Paul V.
Gaughan, Paul, St. John's Rectory, 800 Los Conaes Way, Virginia Beach, 23456-6421. Tel: 757-426-2550
Goodman, Julian
Hamlet, Ralph, 141 Green Turtle Ln., Apt. 10, Charlottesville, 22901-2373. Tel: 434-974-1756
Hickman, J. Stephen
Ilano, Jovencio, Ph.B., M.Div., P.O. Box 341293, Arleta, CA 91334.
Kloepfer, John S., P.O. Box 1742, Clarksville, 23927. Tel: 434-374-4859. Email: tmansfield2@juno.com
Krenik, Robert L., 956 Maiden St., Apt. 4, Abingdon, 24210.
Kruc, James, P.O. Box 37116, Philadelphia, PA 19148. Tel: 302-573-3107. Email: frjkruc@comcast.net
La Fratta, William, 19 Shortwood Cir., Palmyra, 22963-2747. Tel: 434-589-0824. Email: lmfluv@gmail.com
Leonard, John E.
Malabad, Antonio R., 400 Waters Dr. #D-104, Southern Pines, NC 28387.
McEleney, Robert J., 1666 Purdum Mill Rd., Appomattox, 24522-8367. Tel: 434-352-2881. Email: robertjmceleney@yahoo.com
Moran, Edward
Murphy, Dennis
Nash, Robert, P.O. Box 1093, Deltaville, 23043-1093.
Natale, Samuel, 236 E. Market St., Long Beach, NY 11561. Email: sammymn@aol.com
Naylor, Ronald J., 100 E. Ocean View Ave., #904, Norfolk, 23503-1634. Tel: 757-587-4185. Email: revron904@cox.net
Ngo, Anthony, 12500 Patterson Ave., 23233-6411. Tel: 804-784-5450
O'Brien, William S., 751 Hillsdale Dr., Charlottesville, 22901. Tel: 757-220-4233; 757-229-3700
Pham, Thuy, 1417 Plantation Lake Cir., Chesapeake, 23320. Email: thuy2005an@yahoo.com
Quinlan, Thomas J., 4853 Princes Anne Rd., Virginia Beach, 23462. Tel: 757-333-6513. Email: tq777@cox.net
Rademacher, Robert, 100 Compton Rd., Cincinnati, OH 45215.
Ruth, Robert F., P.O. Box 258, Newport News, 23607-0258. Email: robert74@cox.net
Slowik, Joseph S.
Stickle, William, 128 Clipper Ct., Kill Devil Hills, NC 27948-9113. Tel: 252-441-4413
Teslovic, Eugene
Warren, Robert, 5517 Brookwood Rd., Crozet, 22932. Tel: 434-823-2024

Permanent Deacons:
Allison, Mark D., St. Andrew, Roanoke
Arkesteyn, John Aster, Saint Bridget, Richmond
Bailey, Calvin J., Basilica of Saint Mary of the Immaculate Conception, Norfolk
Baker, Robert Dennis, Church of the Sacred Heart, Petersburg
Banks, Marshall D., Cathedral of The Sacred Heart, Richmond
Baskind, Frank Ronald, Ph.D., St. Michael, Richmond
Benet, Alfonso, St. Jude, Mineral; Immaculate Conception
Bergen, J. Brian, Cathedral of The Sacred Heart, Richmond
Blatnik, William J., Saint Matthew, Virginia Beach
Broughton, Eric Christopher, Saint Augustine, Richmond
Cartwright, Gordon Kenneth, Holy Cross, Lynchburg
Cerrato, Dominic, St. Bede
Colville, Christopher Stephen, Church of the Redeemer, Mechanicsville
Cronican, Richard, Christ the King
Donovan, Donald, St. Charles, Cape Charles
Dowdy, Melvin, Ben Secours-St.Mary's Hospital; Cathedral of the Sacred Heart, Richmond
Durel, Robert J., Ph.D., Church of the Holy Spirit, Virginia Beach
Dwyer, Bruce K., All Saints, Floyd; Risen Lord, Woodlawn; St. Joseph, Woodlawn
Ellerbrock, Michael J., Saint Jude Catholic, Christiansburg; Our Lady Of Perpetual Help, Salem; St. Mary, Blacksburg
Elliott, Thomas B., Saint Edward the Confessor, Richmond
Esposito, Robert M., St. Jude, Mineral; Immaculate Conception
Ewan, Robert D., Pastoral Center
Ferguson, Andrew M., Saint Michael, Richmond
Ferry, Daniel, St. Olaf, Norge
Flanary, Barron, Sacred Heart, Big Stone Gap; Church of the Holy Spirit, Jonesville
Fournier, Keith A., St. Benedict, Richmond; St. Stephen Martyr
Geary, David J., St. Mary of the Anunciation
Giovenco, Robert B., Saint Bridget, Richmond
Gonzalez, Jose Miguel, St. Joseph, Hampton
Greer, James D., Saint Edward the Confessor, Richmond
Griffin, Robert H., Our Lady of Lourdes, Richmond
Grillo, Joseph F., St. Paul, Virginia Beach; St. John the Apostle, Virginia Beach
Hanzlik, Edward G., Church of the Sacred Heart, Petersburg
Harmeyer, Gary R., Church of the Ascension, Virginia Beach
Hornstra, Curtis L., Saint Michael, Richmond
Hunt, William R., St. Elizabeth Ann Seton
Ibarra, Juan, St. Anne's Catholic Church; St. John, Marion
Illy, Lawrence P., Saint Luke, Virginia Beach
Johnson, Daniel F., Saint Joan of Arc, Yorktown
Johnson, Michael, St. Mark
Kamper, Eugene P., Saint Ann, Ashland
King, Walker P., St. Pius X, Norfolk
Kledzik, James, St. Francis of Assisi, Staunton
Krajeski, Vernon, St. John the Apostle, Virginia Beach
Kren, John J., Saint Mark, Virginia Beach
LaSpina, Fred C., Blessed Sacrament Church, Harrisonburg
Linden, Raymond K., Church of the Sacred Heart, Prince George County
Lupini, Belardino, Church of the Epiphany
MacLaughlin, Matthew C., Saint John, Petersburg
Mahefky, Paul, St. Benedict, Richmond
Malone, Christopher M., Church of the Redeemer, Mechanicsville
Mammi, Nicholas, All Saints, Woodlawn; Risen Lord; St. Joseph
Matte, Mark C., Sacred Heart, Richmond
Mavrelli, Louis A., (Retired)
McFeely, Thomas E., Church of the Ascension, Virginia Beach
McLane, Emmett R., St. Theresa, Farmville
Menting, Peter J., St. Theresa, Farmville
Miech, Richard, Pastoral Center Staff, Church of the Epiphany
Milkevitch, Joseph J., Immaculate Conception; St. Jude
Morash, Christopher, Incarnation, Charlottesville
Moro, Michael, Church of the Ascension, Virginia Beach
Mullen, Thomas, U of R Campus Ministry
Nees, Richard J., Saint Mary, Lovingston
Nemetz, David S., St. Michael, Richmond
O'Connell, Stephen, Our Lady Of Perpetual Help, Salem
O'Donnell, Fulton Patrick, St. John Neumann
Riss, Joseph N., St. Rose of Lima, Hampton
Roderique, Raymond, Holy Name of Mary
Rodgers, James E., Church of the Sacred Heart
Roettinger, Francis, St. Bede, Williamsburg
Romero, Crisanto D., St. Matthew, Virginia Beach
Sadowski, John E., St. Catherine of Siena, Clarksville
Scarletto, Frederick, St. Thomas More, Lynchburg
Schmidt, Edward P., St. John Neumann, Powhatan; Good Samaritan, Amelia
Surat, Eric M., Our Lady of Perpetual Help, Salem
Taylor, Bernard H., Incarnation, Charlottesville
Taylor, Bernard F., Our Lady of Mt. Carmel, Newport News
Thomas, John H., J.D.
Thompson, Robert R., St. Olaf, Norge
Torres-Lisboa, Patricio, (Assigned Outside the Diocese)
Wentworth, Darrell G., Saint Matthew, Virginia Beach
Wharry, James, St. Mary Star of the Sea, Fort Monroe; Our Lady of Lavang

INSTITUTIONS LOCATED IN THE DIOCESE

[A] HIGH SCHOOLS, DIOCESAN

DANVILLE. *Sacred Heart School* (1953) (Grades PreK-9), 540 Central Blvd., 24541. Tel: 434-793-2656; Fax: 434-793-2658. Email: sacredht@earthlink.net. Web: www.sheartschool.com. Kimberly W. Meadows, Prin.; Barbara Hopkins, Librarian. Lay Teachers 20; Total Staff 34; Total Enrollment 223.

LYNCHBURG. *Holy Cross Regional School* (1879) (Grades PreK-12), 2125 Langhorne Rd., 24501. Tel: 434-847-5436; 434-847-5464; Fax: 434-847-4156. Email: office@hcrs-va.org. Web: www.hcrs-va.org. Mr. William S. Coursey, Headmaster. Lay Teachers 30; Students 158.

NEWPORT NEWS. *Peninsula Catholic High School*, (Grades 8-12), 600 Harpersville Rd., 23601. Tel: 757-596-7247; Fax: 757-591-9718. Web: www.peninsulacatholic.com. Francine Gagne, Ed.D., Pres.; Janine C. Franklin, Prin.; Anne Catron, Librarian. Lay Teachers 30; Total Staff 13; Students 310.

ROANOKE. *Roanoke Catholic School,* (Grades PreK-12), 621 N. Jefferson St., 24016-1416. Tel: 540-982-3532; Fax: 540-345-0785. Email: info@roanokecatholic.com. Web: www.roanokecatholic.com. Ray-Eric Correia, Pres.; Susan R. Thompson, Prin. (Lower School); John K. Finnerty, Prin. (Upper School). Lay Teachers 47; Students 459.

VIRGINIA BEACH. *Bishop Sullivan Catholic High School,* 4552 Princess Anne Rd., 23462. Tel: 757-467-2881; Fax: 757-467-0284. Email: info@chsvb.org. Web: www.chsvb.org. Mr. Dennis W. Price, Prin.; Mrs. Eileen Hodermarsky, Librarian. Deacons 1; Lay Teachers 33; Students 451.

[B] HIGH SCHOOLS, PRIVATE

RICHMOND. *Benedictine High School* (1911) 304 N. Sheppard St., 23221. Tel: 804-342-1300; Fax: 804-355-2407. Email: info@benedictinehighschool.org. Web: www.benedictinehighschool.org. Rev. Gregory Gresko, O.S.B., Headmaster; Sally Boykin, Librarian. A Military High School in the Charge of the Benedictine Monks. Priests 3; Lay Teachers 34; Students 279.

Saint Gertrude High School (1922) 3215 Stuart Ave., 23221. Tel: 804-358-9114; Fax: 804-355-5682. Email: sghs@saintgertrude.org. Web: www.saintgertrude.org. Mrs. Susan Walker, Pres.; Mrs. Barbara Filler, Prin. Benedictine Sisters 2; Lay Teachers 29; Students 283.

WILLIAMSBURG. *Walsingham Academy Upper School,* (Grades 8-12), 1100 Jamestown Rd., 23185. Tel: 757-229-6026; Fax: 757-259-1401. Email: pbender@walsingham.org. Web: www.walsingham.org. Peter Bender, Prin.; Anne Massey, Librarian. Private Day School for Boys and Girls. Lay Teachers 32; Administrators 7; Students 315.

[C] ELEMENTARY SCHOOLS, DIOCESAN

RICHMOND. *All Saints Catholic School,* (Grades PreK-8), 3418 Noble Ave., 23222. Tel: 804-329-7524; Fax: 804-329-4201. Email: allsaintsric@juno.com. Web: www.allsaintsric.com. Mr. Kenneth W. Soistman, Prin.; Ms. Gloria J. Smith, Librarian. Lay Teachers 15; Total Staff 27; Total Enrollment 123.

St. Benedict School (1919) (Grades K-8), 3100 Grove Ave., 23221. Tel: 804-254-8850; Fax: 804-254-9163. Email: principal@saintbenedictschool.org. Web: www.SaintBenedictSchool.org. Mr. Sean M. Cruess, Prin.; Lori Sturtevant, Librarian. Teachers 16; Total Staff 25; Total Enrollment 181.

St. Bridget School, (Grades K-8), 6011 York Rd., 23226. Tel: 804-288-1994; Fax: 804-288-5730. Email: information@saintbridget.org. Web: www.saintbridget.org. Mr. Raymond E. Honeycutt, Prin.; Mrs. Nancy Downing, Librarian. Priests 1; Lay Teachers 33; Total Enrollment 472; Total Staff 59.

St. Edward/Epiphany School (1961) (Grades PreK-8), 10701 W. Huguenot Rd., 23235. Tel: 804-272-2881; Fax: 804-327-0788. Email: office@seeschool.com. Web: www.seeschool.com. Ms. Georgette M. Richards, Prin.; Helen Lorenz, Librarian. Lay Teachers 45; Total Enrollment 430.

St. Mary's Catholic School (1965) (Grades N-8), 9501 Gayton Rd., 23229. Tel: 804-740-1048; Fax: 804-740-1310. Email: tdertinger@saintmary.org. Web: www.saintmary.org. Dr. Thomas D. Dertinger, Prin.; Mrs. Kelly Taylor, Librarian. Lay Teachers 32; Students 440.

BLACKSBURG. *St. Mary's Little Angels Preschool* (1988) 706 Harding Ave., N.E., 24060-3618. Tel: 540-951-0916; Fax: 540-953-2962. Lesley Lafon, Dir. (Ages 3 to 5 years). Lay Teachers 9; Students 70.

BRISTOL. *St. Anne Catholic School,* (Grades PreK-8), 300 Euclid Ave., 24201. Tel: 276-669-0048; Fax: 276-669-3523. Email: sas@stannes-bristol.org. Web: www.stannes-bristol.org. Richard Fenchak, Ed.D., Prin.; Mrs. Patricia Johnson, Asst. Prin. Lay Teachers 19; Total Staff 28; Total Enrollment 136.

CHARLOTTESVILLE. *Charlottesville Catholic Elementary School,* (Grades PreK-8), 1205 Pen Park Rd., 22901. Tel: 434-964-0400; Fax: 434-964-1373. Email: info.ccs@cvillecatholic.org. Web: www.cvillecatholic.com. Mr. Alan Yost, Prin.; Pam Beard, Librarian; Carolyn Hexter, Librarian. Lay Teachers 26; Aides 6; Students 366.

HAMPTON. *St. Mary Star of the Sea,* (Grades PreK-8), 14 N. Willard Ave., 23663. Tel: 757-723-6358; Fax: 757-723-6544. Email: admin@SaintMaryStaroftheSea.com. Web: www.SaintMaryStaroftheSea.com. Sr. Mary Amata, O.P., Prin.; Mrs. Sandra Stearns, Librarian. Sisters 4; Lay Teachers 18; Total Staff 31; Total Enrollment 201.

NEWPORT NEWS. *Our Lady of Mt Carmel* (1954) (Grades PreK-8), 52 Harpersville Rd., 23601. Tel: 757-596-2754; Fax: 757-596-1570. Email: olmcadmissions2754@cavtel.net. Web: www.olmc-school.com. Sr. John Paul, O.P., Prin.; Mrs. Melissa Small, Librarian. Sisters 5; Lay Teachers 36; Total Staff 59; Total Enrollment 430.

NORFOLK. *Christ the King,* (Grades PreK-8), 3401 Tidewater Dr., 23509. Tel: 757-625-4951; Fax: 757-623-5212. Email: info@ctkparish.org. Web: www.ctkparish.org. Mrs. Rachael Chatham, Prin.; Carrie Srodulski, Librarian. Priests 1; Lay Teachers 23; Total Staff 32; Total Enrollment 296.

Holy Trinity School, (Grades PreK-8), 154 W. Government Ave., 23503. Tel: 757-583-1873; Fax: 757-587-3677. Email: dnofplot@HolyTrinitySchoolVA.com. Web: www.HolyTrinitySchoolVA.com. Ms. Deneane Nofplot, Prin.; Ellen Mazzanti, Librarian. Lay Teachers 16; Total Staff 31; Total Enrollment 140.

St. Pius X School, (Grades PreK-8), 7800 Halprin Dr., 23518. Tel: 757-588-6171; Fax: 757-587-6580. Email: lbarrett@piusxparish.org. Web: www.stpiusxschoolva.org. Sr. Linda Taber, I.H.M., Prin.; Ms. Katherine Oliver, Technology Teacher. Sisters 2; Lay Teachers 26; Total Staff 38; Total Enrollment 312.

PETERSBURG. *St. Joseph School,* (Grades PreK-8), 123 Franklin St., 23803. Tel: 804-732-3931; Fax: 804-732-6479. Email: school@saintjosephschool.com. Web: www.saintjosephschool.com. Diane Young, Prin.; Teresa Fisher, Librarian. Sisters 2; Lay Teachers 12; Total Staff 25; Total Enrollment 122.

PORTSMOUTH. *Portsmouth Catholic Regional,* 2301 Oregon Ave., 23701. Tel: 757-488-6744; Fax: 757-465-8833. Email: office@pces.hrcoxmail.com; principal@pces.hrcoxmail.com. Web: www.pces.info. Mrs. Mary Ellen Paul, Prin.; Mr. Franklin Baker, Librarian. Lay Teachers 16; Total Staff 29; Total Enrollment 148.

POWHATAN. *Blessed Sacrament Huguenot* (1998) (Grades PreK-12), 2501 Academy Rd., 23139. Tel: 804-598-4211; Fax: 804-598-1053. Email: jfortune@bshknights.org. Web: www.BlessedSacramentHuguenot.com. Mr. Joseph J. Oley Jr., Prin.; Mr. Mike Henderson, Asst. Prin.; Mrs. Jennifer Sylvester, Librarian. Lay Teachers 46; Students 363.

RICHMOND, HENRICO. *Our Lady of Lourdes School,* (Grades PreK-8), 8250 Woodman Rd., 23228. Tel: 804-262-1770; Fax: 804-200-6295. Email: ollofice@comcast.net. Web: www.ollschoolric.com. Lucy R. Reilley, Prin. Total Staff 35; Total Enrollment 385.

VIRGINIA BEACH. *St. Gregory the Great School* (1964) (Grades PreK-8), 5343 Virginia Beach Blvd., 23462. Tel: 757-497-1811; Fax: 757-497-7005. Email: podonne@stgregory.pvt.k12.va.us. Web: www.stgregory.pvt.k12va.us. Sr. Mary Catherine Chapman, I.H.M., Ed.D., Prin.; Mrs. Sandy Batkin, Librarian. Priests 3; Sisters 4; Teachers 44; Total Staff 70; Total Enrollment 673.

St. John the Apostle Catholic School (2002) (Grades PreK-8), 1968 Sandbridge Rd., 23456. Tel: 757-821-1100; Fax: 757-821-1047. Web: www.stjohnsandbridge.org. Joseph Badali, Prin. Lay Teachers 17; Total Enrollment 239; Total Staff 12.

St. Matthew School, (Grades PreK-8), 3316 Sandra Ln., 23464. Tel: 757-420-2455; Fax: 757-420-4880. Email: office@smsvb.net. Web: www.smsvb.net. Mrs. Barbara White, Prin.; Mrs. Ziegenfuss, Librarian. Lay Teachers 35; Total Enrollment 535; Total Staff 67.

Star of the Sea School (1958) (Grades PreK-8), 309 15th St., 23451. Tel: 757-428-8400; Fax: 757-428-2794. Email: adelaide.grandfield@sosschool.org. Web: www.sosschool.org. Dr. Catherine Whisman, Prin.; Sarah Coles, Librarian. Lay Teachers 24; Total Staff 16; Total Enrollment 292.

[D] ELEMENTARY SCHOOLS, PRIVATE

NORFOLK. **Barry Robinson Schools of Norfolk* (2001) P.O. Box 1180, 23501. Tel: 757-440-5500. Charles V. McPhillips, Pres.

St. Patrick Catholic School, (Grades PreK-8), 1000 Bolling Ave., 23508. Tel: 757-440-5500; Fax: 757-440-5200. Email: info@stpcs.org. Web: www.stpcs.org. Mr. Stephen Hammond, Prin.; Mrs. Elizabeth Woodard, Librarian. Lay Teachers 25.

WILLIAMSBURG. *Walsingham Academy* (1947) (Grades PreK-12), 1100 Jamestown Rd., 23185. Tel: 757-229-2642 (Elementary); 757-229-6026 (Secondary); Fax: 757-259-4679. Email: walsingham@aol.com. Web: www.walsingham.org. Sisters Mary Jeanne Oesterle, R.S.M., Pres. Tel: 757-229-2642; Rose Morris, R.S.M, Rel. Coord., Lower School; Peter Bender, Prin., Upper School; Margaret Hineycutt, Prin., Lower School. Day School for Boys and Girls. Sisters 2; Lay Teachers 96; Students 760.

[E] GENERAL HOSPITALS

RICHMOND. *Bon Secours Richmond Health System,* 5801 Bremo Rd., 23226. Tel: 804-281-8330; Fax: 804-288-1908. Email: Teri_Dizon@bshsi.org. Web: www.bonsecours.com. Peter Bernard, CEO. Sisters of Bon Secours. Sisters 2; Bed Capacity 850; Total Staff 5,375; Inpatients 48,096; Outpatients 390,123.

Bon Secours-Richmond Health Care Foundation, 5875 Bremo Rd., Ste. 710, 23226. Tel: 804-287-7700; Fax: 804-287-7316. Terry Mohr, CEO.

Bon Secours-Richmond Community Hospital, 1500 N. 28th St., 23233. Tel: 804-225-1701; Fax: 804-225-1725. Michael D. Robinson, CEO. Bed Capacity 104; Total Staff 308; Inpatients 3,202; Outpatients 44,864.

St. Mary's Hospital Toni R. Ardabell, CEO. Sisters 2; Bed Capacity 391; Total Staff 2,361; Inpatients 22,544; Outpatients 135,769.

Bon Secours Memorial Regional Medical Center, 8260 Atlee Rd., Mechanicsville, 23116. Tel: 804-764-6000; Fax: 804-764-6420. Michael D. Robinson, CEO. Bed Capacity 225; Inpatients 13,429; Outpatients 133,875; Total Staff 1,698.

MIDLOTHIAN. *St. Francis Medical Center (Bon Secours Richmond Health System),* 13700 St. Francis Blvd., Ste. 100, 23114. Tel: 804-594-7400. Mark M. Gordon, Exec. Vice Pres. & Admin. Bed Capacity 130; Total Assisted Annually (Inpatient) 8,921; Total Assisted Annually (Outpatient) 75,615; Total Staff 1,009.

NEWPORT NEWS. *Mary Immaculate Hospital* (1952) 2 Bernardine Dr., 23602-4499. Tel: 757-886-6600; Fax: 757-886-6751. Web: www.bonsecourshamptonroads.com. Patricia Lee Robertson, Exec. Vice Pres. & Admin. Tel: 757-886-6768; Fax: 757-886-6751; Sr. Bernard Marie Magill, O.S.F., M.S., N.A.C.C., Dir. Pastoral Care Dept. The Bernardine Sisters of the Third Order of St. Francis 9; Bed Capacity 110; Inpatients 7,522; Outpatients 88,160; Total Staff 6,773.

Bernardine Franciscan Sisters Foundation, Inc., 2 Bernardine Dr., 23602. Tel: 757-886-6025; Fax: 757-886-6881. Rev. Lee Guarnieri, Priest Chap.

NORFOLK. *Bon Secours De Paul Medical Center, Inc.,* 150 Kingsley Ln., 23505. Tel: 757-889-5000; Fax: 757-889-5837. Web: bonsecourshamptonroads.com. Daniel Duggan, Exec. Vice Pres. & Admin.

Bon Secours DePaul Medical Center

Bon Secours DePaul Health Foundation

Bon Secours Bayley Properties Sisters of Bon Secours., Clinic is connected with hospital. Staff 836; Bed Capacity 110; Inpatients 7,522; Outpatients 88,160.

PORTSMOUTH. *Bon Secours Hampton Roads Health Systems, Inc.,* 3636 High St., 23707-3236. Michael K. Kerner, CEO.

Bon Secours Maryview Medical Center, 3636 High St., 23707. Tel: 757-398-2200; Fax: 757-398-2359. Web: www.bonsecourshamptonroads.com. Michael K. Kerner, Exec. Vice Pres./Admin.; Richard Chasse, Dir. Pastoral Care; Rita Hickey, Vice Pres. Mission; Rev. Pantaleon O. Manalo, Chap.

Maryview Hospital Sisters of Bon Secours. Bed Capacity 346; Inpatients 1,400; Outpatients 187,915; Total Staff 1,569.

Maryview Behavioral Medicine Center, 3636 High St., 23707. Tel: 757-398-2361; Fax: 757-398-2396. Web: www.BonSecoursHamptonRoads.com. Carol Taaffe, Admin. Bed Capacity 54; Patients Assisted Annually 2,700; Total Staff 65.

[F] ORPHANAGES AND INFANT HOMES

NORFOLK. *St. Mary's Home for Disabled Children,* 6171 Kempsville Cir., 23502. Tel: 757-622-2208; Fax: 757-627-5314. Email: tmaryshome@hamptonroads.com. Web: www.saintmaryshome.org. William C. Giermak, CEO; Terry Lyle, Prin. Long-term care for multiply handicapped children birth to twenty-one years old. Daughters of Wisdom 1; Bed Capacity 92; Lay Teachers 8; Total Staff 247.

[G] CHILD LEARNING CENTERS

RICHMOND. *Sacred Heart Center, Inc.,* 1400 Perry St., 23224. Tel: 804-230-4399; Fax: 804-231-7247. Email: melissa_canaday@shcrichmond.org. Melissa F. Canaday, Exec. Dir. Neighboring Communities Day Care, After School Care, Adult Education, Social Services.

NORFOLK. *Christ the King Early Childhood Learning Center,* 3401 Tidewater Dr., 23509. Tel: 757-625-4951; Fax: 757-623-5212. Email: jmislan@ctkparish.org. Mrs. Jan Mislan, Asst. Prin.; Mrs. Rachael Chatham, Prin.; Ms. Dawn Lindey, Librarian. Lay Teachers 3; Early Childhood 70; School-Age Extended Care 75.

VIRGINIA BEACH. *Holy Family Day School*, 1279 N. Great Neck Rd., 23454-2117. Tel: 757-481-1180; Fax: 757-481-3989. Email: dayschoolprincipal@holyfamilyvb.org. Web: www.holyfamilyvb.org. Cynthia Girard, Prin.; Colleen Oates, Bookkeeper. Lay Teachers 1.

[H] HOMES FOR THE AGED

RICHMOND. *St. Francis Home, Inc.*, 2511 Wise St., 23225-3952. Tel: 804-231-1043; Fax: 804-231-1065. Email: bgrow@saintfrancishome.com. Mr. David Cran, Dir. Bed Capacity 105; Total Assisted Annually 140; Total Staff 62.

St. Joseph's Home for the Aged (1874) 1503 Michaels Rd., 23229. Tel: 804-288-6245; Fax: 804-288-8906. Email: msrichlsp@earthlink.net. Sr. Marcel Joseph McCanless, L.S.P., Supr. Attended by Rev. Leo Gagnon Little Sisters of the Poor 11; Guests 96; Total Assisted Annually 120; Total Staff 110.

St. Mary Wood's (1986) 1257 Marywood Ln., 23229. Tel: 804-741-8624; Fax: 804-740-7912. Email: stmw@mindsprings.com. Web: stmaryswoods.com. Randy Scott, Admin. Units 118; Independent Units 54; Total Staff 56; Total Assisted 64.

Marywood Apartments, 1261 Marywood Ln., 23229. Tel: 804-740-5567; Fax: 804-740-9016. Email: marywood1@verizon.net. Patricia Scott, Senior Mgr. Residents 129; Total Staff 7.

Our Lady of Hope Health Center, Inc., 13700 N. Gayton Rd., 23233. Tel: 804-360-1960; Fax: 804-364-0737. Email: brichard@ourladyofhope.com. Web: www.ourladyofhope.com. Becky Richard, Admin. Residents 133; Nursing Home Residents 60; Total Assisted Annually 77; Total Staff 150.

CHARLOTTESVILLE. *Our Lady of Peace*, 751 Hillsdale Dr., 22901. Tel: 434-973-1155; Fax: 434-973-3397. Sara Warden, Exec. Dir. Nursing Bed Capacity 30; Independent Units 32; Assisted Units 94; Total Occupancy 167; Total Staff 125.

HAMPTON. *Seton Manor*, 215 Marcella Rd., 23666. Tel: 757-827-6512; Fax: 757-827-0132. Email: manager@setonmanor.hrcoxmail.com. Pam Jensen, Mgr. Residents 112; Total Staff 5.

LYNCHBURG. *McGurk House Apartments*, 2425 Tate Springs Rd., 24501. Tel: 434-846-2425; Fax: 434-847-5046. Email: mcgurkhouse@lynchburg.net. Hannah Herward, Dir. Independent Living for adults 62 yrs. or older, or mobility impaired. Apartments 88; Total Staff 5.

NEWPORT NEWS. *St. Francis Nursing Center*, 4 Ridgewood Pkwy., 23602. Tel: 757-886-6500; Fax: 757-886-6539. Web: www.bshsihr.com. Tim Short, Admin. Tel: 757-886-6500. Beds 115; Total Assisted 1,582; Total Assisted Annually 108; Total Staff 118.

NORFOLK. *Madonna Home*, 814 W. 37th St., 23508. Tel: 757-623-6662; Fax: 757-623-4966. Charlene Davis, Dir. Total Staff 6; Residents 16; Total Assisted Annually 16.

ROANOKE. *Our Lady of the Valley Retirement Community*, 650 N. Jefferson St., 24016. Tel: 540-345-5111; Fax: 540-985-6561. Web: www.OurLadyoftheValley.com. Ryan J. Koeniger, Admin. Assisted Living Units 86; Skilled Nursing Facility Beds 70.

SUFFOLK. *Bon Secours-Maryview Nursing Care*, 4775 Bridge Rd., 23435. Tel: 757-686-0488; Fax: 757-686-8211. Diana L. Jarrett, Admin. Bed Capacity 120.

Martha W. Davis Cancer Center
Maryview Employee Assistance Program
Maryview MedCare Centers (Urgent Care)
Maryview Wellspring Home Health Agency
Maryview Hospice Program

VIRGINIA BEACH. *Marian Manor* (1988) 5345 Marian Ln., 23462. Tel: 757-456-5018; Fax: 757-497-7561. Web: www.marian-manor.com. Desiree Mitchell, Admin. Units 117; Total Assisted Annually 135; Total Staff 90.

Our Lady of Perpetual Help Health Center, Inc., 4560 Princess Anne Rd., 23462-7905. Tel: 757-495-4211; Fax: 757-495-7366. Email: 1oryn@ourladyperpetualhelp.com. Web: www.OurLadyPerpetualHelp.com. Bed Capacity 123; Total Assisted Annually 123; Total Staff 158.

Russell House, 900 First Colonial Rd., 23454. Tel: 757-481-0770; Fax: 757-496-0859. Email: russellhouse@erols.com. Eleanor Olsen, Admin. Total Staff 6; Units 119; Residents 126.

Sullivan House, Inc., 2033 General Booth Blvd., 23454. Tel: 757-563-9955; Fax: 757-563-2992. Email: sullivan.house@worldnet.att.net. Cecile Shelton, Mgr. 198 units for very low income elderly.

The Sullivan House, 2033 General Booth Blvd., 23454. Tel: 757-437-0220. Mrs. Joanne Lindauer, Admin.

[I] SERVICES FOR THE DISABLED

LYNCHBURG. *Nott Homes, Inc.*, 3009-3011 Roundelay Rd., 24502. Tel: 434-239-0722; Fax: 434-239-1042. Mrs. Helen Smith, Residential Mgr. Residents 8; Bed Capacity 8; Total Staff 19.

VIRGINIA BEACH. *Assisi House*, 3700 Big Ben Rd., 23452. Tel: 757-431-8522; Fax: 757-431-9776. Email: fpatroll@verizon.net.

[J] SPECIALIZED SERVICES

RICHMOND. *Commonwealth Catholic Charities* (1923) 1512 Willow Lawn Dr., 23230-0565. Tel: 804-285-5900; Fax: 804-285-9130. Email: agency@cccofva.org. Web: www.cccofva.org. Ms. Joanne D. Nattrass, M.B.A., B.S.N., R.N., Exec. Dir.
Satellite Offices:
918 Harris St., Charlottesville, 22903. Tel: 800-974-4494.
Commonwealth Catholic Charities, 541 Luck Ave., Roanoke, 24016. Tel: 540-344-5107; Fax: 540-342-3307.
1024 Park Ave., N.W., Norton, 24273. Tel: 276-679-0967; Fax: 276-679-2719. Total Assisted 24,000.

VIRGINIA BEACH. *Catholic Charities of Eastern Virginia, Inc.*, 5361-A Virginia Beach Blvd., 23462. Tel: 757-456-2366; Fax: 757-456-2367. Email: help@cceva.org. Web: www.cceva.org. Dominick R. Calgi, Exec. Dir.
Branch Offices:
4855 Princess Anne Rd., 23462. Tel: 757-467-7707; Fax: 757-495-3206.
1802 Ashland Ave., Norfolk, 23509. Tel: 757-533-5217; Fax: 757-533-9562.
3804 Poplar Hill Rd., Ste. A, Chesapeake, 23321. Tel: 757-484-0703; Fax: 757-484-1096.
12829 Jefferson Ave., Ste. 101, Newport News, 23608. Tel: 757-875-0060; Fax: 757-877-7883.
1315 Jamestown Rd., Ste. 202, Williamsburg, 23185. Tel: 757-253-2847; Fax: 757-253-1296. Total Assisted 12,142.
510 N. Main St., Franklin, 23851. Tel: 757-562-6222; Fax: 757-562-3930.
General Delivery, Belle Haven, 23306. Tel: 757-442-6211; Fax: 757-442-6211.
Other Offices:
Catholic Charities Outreach Center, 5361-A Virginia Beach Blvd., 23462. Tel: 757-490-4931; Fax: 757-456-2367.

[K] MONASTERIES AND RESIDENCES OF PRIESTS AND BROTHERS

RICHMOND. *Mary Mother of the Church Abbey*, 12829 River Rd., 23238-7206. Tel: 804-784-3508; Fax: 804-784-2214. Email: gregorygresko3@gmail.com. Web: www.richmondmonks.org. Revs. Donald F. Scales, O.S.B., Prior; Adrian W. Harmening, O.S.B., Procurator; Theophile W. Brown, O.S.B.; Joseph M. Lukyamuzi, O.S.B.; James M. Glass, O.S.B.; Theophile W. Brown, O.S.B.; Mark Purcell, O.S.B.; Gregory Gresko, O.S.B., Prior Admin.; Bros. David Owen, O.S.B.; Jeffery Williams, O.S.B.; Robert Nguyen, O.S.B.; John Mary Lugemwa, O.S.B.; Vincent McDermott, O.S.B.; Paul Leuthard, O.S.B. Benedictine Monks. Priests 9; Brothers 6.

WEST POINT. *Missionaries of the Holy Family, General Mission Office-M.S.F., Inc.*, 260 W. Euclid Blvd., P.O. Box 918, 23181. Tel: 804-843-2622; Fax: 804-843-3182. Email: msfinc2@aol.com. Rev. John Brieffies, M.S.F., Pres. & Dir. Priests 1; Total Staff 3; Total Assisted 400.

[L] CONVENTS AND RESIDENCES FOR SISTERS

RICHMOND. *Benedictine Sisters of Virginia, Saint Gertrude Convent*, 6826 Monument Ave., 23226. Tel: 804-282-4136. Web: osbva.org. Email: vocations@osbva.org. Sisters Andrea Verchuck, O.S.B., Convent Coord.; Vicki Ix, O.S.B.; Charlotte Lange, O.S.B. Sisters 3.

Comboni Missionary Sisters, Provincial House, 1307 Lakeside Ave., 23228-4710. Tel: 804-266-2975; 804-262-8827; Fax: 804-264-2906. Email: cmsusaprov@verizon.net. Web: www.combonisrs.com. Sr. Maria de la Luz Aguilera, C.M.S., Prov. Sisters 23.

BARHAMSVILLE. *Bethlehem Monastery of the Poor Clare Nuns*, 5500 Holly Fork Rd., 23011. Tel: 757-566-1684; Fax: 757-566-1697. Email: mtstfrancis@megasurf.net. Web: www.poor-clares.org. Sr. Mary Clare, P.C.C., Abbess. Observing the Primitive Rule of St. Clare, Constitutions of the Poor Clare Federation of Mary Immaculate (strictly cloistered, solemn vows). Solemnly Professed 13.

CLINTWOOD. *Sisters of the Holy Cross, Inc.*, P.O. Box 835, 24228. Tel: 276-926-4328.

CROZET. *Our Lady of the Angels Monastery* (1987) *Cistercian Nuns of the Strict Observance (Virginia)*, 3365 Monastery Dr., 22932. Tel: 434-823-1452; Fax: 434-823-6379. Email: community@olamonastery.org. Web: www.olamonastery.org. Sr. Marion Rissetto, O.C.S.O., Prioress. Professed 10.

NEWPORT NEWS. *Bernardine Sisters of the Third Order of St. Francis*, 6E Ridgewood Pkwy., 23602. Tel: 757-886-6395; Fax: 757-886-6751. Web: www.bfranciscan.org. Sisters 9.

NORFOLK. *Sisters Servants of the Immaculate Heart of Mary* (1845)
St. Pius X Convent, 7813 Halprin Dr., 23518. Tel: 757-587-8657 (Home); 757-588-6171 (School); Fax: 757-587-6580. Email: piusihmva@aol.com (Home). Web: piusxparish.org. Sr. Brenda Query, I.H.M., Supr. Sisters 5.

PETERSBURG. *Daughters of Charity of St. Vincent de Paul* (1633) St. Joseph Convent, 127 Franklin St., 23803-3307. Tel: 804-732-8501. Email: petersburgstjoe@doc.org. Web: www.thedaughtersofcharity.org. Sr. Patricia Nee, D.C., Local Supr. Sisters 5.

PORTSMOUTH. *Sisters of Bon Secours* (1824) 412 West Rd., 23707. Tel: 757-397-3869. Email: rita_thomas@bshsi.com. Sr. Rita Thomas, M.S.N., Pres.

ROCKVILLE. *Monastery of the Visitation Monte Maria*, 12221 Bienvenue Rd., 23146. Tel: 804-749-4885; Fax: 804-749-8606. Email: info@visitmontemaria.com. Web: www.visitmontemaria.com. Sr. Mary Emmanuel Stahl, V.H.M., Supr. Visitation Sisters 13.

VIRGINIA BEACH. *Sisters Servants of I.H.M.*, St. Gregory the Great, 5349 Virginia Beach Blvd., 23462. Tel: 757-497-7517; Fax: 757-497-7005. Email: smaryihm@stgregory.pvt.k12.va.us; stgregsihms@aol.com Convent. Sr. Mary Catherine Chapman, I.H.M., Ed.D., Supr./Prin.

WILLIAMSBURG. *Sisters of Mercy, Walsingham Academy*, 1100 Jamestown Rd., P.O. Box 8702, 23187-8702. Tel: 757-229-2642; 757-220-8735; Fax: 757-259-1401. Web: www.walsingham. Sisters Mary Jeanne Oesterle, R.S.M., Pres.; Berenice Eltz, Coord.; Jean A. Burns, C.S.J., Treas.; Rose Morris, R.S.M, Religion Coord. Sisters 4.

[M] RETREAT HOUSES

RICHMOND. *Benedictine Retreat and Conference Center*, Mary Mother of the Church Abbey, 12829 River Rd., 23233. Tel: 804-784-3508; Fax: 804-784-2214. Email: retreat_director@richmondmonks.org. Web: www.richmondmonks.org. Bro. Jeffery Williams, O.S.B.

ABINGDON. *Jubilee House Retreat Center*, 822 E. Main St., 24210-4415. Tel: 276-619-0919; Fax: 276-739-7753. Email: info@jubileeretreat.com. Web: www.jubileeretreat.com.

HAMPTON. *Holy Family Retreat*, 1414 N. Mallory St., P.O. Box 3151, 23663. Tel: 757-722-3997; Fax: 757-723-2478. Email: holyfretreat@aol.com. Web: www.holyfamilyretreat.com. Very Rev. John Smyth, C.Ss.R., Supr. & Dir.; Revs. James Geiger, C.Ss.R., Asst. Retreat Dir.; Alistair McKay, C.Ss.R.; Bro. Darrell Cevasco, C.Ss.R., Admin. & Asst. Dir. In Res. Rev. Anthony Morris, C.Ss.R.

LYNCHBURG. *Tabor Retreat Center*, 2125 Langhorne Rd., 24501. Tel: 434-846-6475; Fax: 434-846-3047. Email: taborretreat@verizon.net. Web: www.taborretreat.com. Deacon Gordon Kenneth Cartwright.

MONTPELIER. *Shalom House*, P.O. Box 196, 23192. Tel: 804-883-6149; Fax: 804-883-5298. Mary E. Alexander, Dir.

ROANOKE. *Madonna House*, 828 Campbell Ave., S.W., 24016. Tel: 540-343-8464. Email: combermere@madonnahouse.org. Web: www.madonnahouse.org. Patricia Lawton, Dir.

SMITHFIELD. *The Well* (1987) 18047 Quiet Way, 23430. Tel: 757-255-2366. Email: staff@thewellretreatcenter.org. Web: www.thewellretreatcenter.org.

[N] MISCELLANEOUS

RICHMOND. *The Catholic Foundation of the Diocese of Richmond* (1998) 811 Cathedral Pl., 23220. Tel: 804-359-5661; Fax: 804-358-9159. Ms. Candra Parker, Contact Person.

St. Francis Home of Richmond Foundation, Ltd., 2511 Wise St., 23224. Tel: 804-231-1043; Fax: 804-231-1065. Mr. David Cran, Dir. Provides grants to subsidize cost of care for aged, infirm and disabled residents of limited means.

Shroud of Turin Center, Mary Mother of the Church Abbey, 12829 River Rd., 23233. Tel: 804-784-3366; Fax: 804-784-3431. Email: shroud@erols.com. Bryan Walsh, Dir. Provides educational services and conducts historical research into the Shroud of Turin.

CHARLOTTESVILLE. *Saint Anselm Institute for Catholic Thought* (2001) P.O. Box 6432, 22906-6432. Tel: 434-924-0952; Fax: 434-243-5590. Email: info@stanselminstitute.org. Web:

www.stanselminstitute.org. Joseph E. Davis.

PORTSMOUTH. *Catholic Elementary Education Foundation of Hampton Roads*, 2301 Oregon Ave., 23701. Tel: 757-488-6744; Fax: 757-465-8833. Email: sec@pces.hrcoxmail.com. Mr. Edward P. Williams, Prin.

ROANOKE. *Catholic Historical Society of the Roanoke Valley* (Museum & Religious Goods), 400 W. Campbell Ave., S.W., 24016-3627. Tel: 540-982-0152; Fax: 540-982-0152. John Wagner, Pres.; Vernon E. Jolley, Vice Pres.; Loretta Jolley, Sec.; Margaret Cochener, Treas.

St. Francis House, Inc. (1973) P.O. Box 2215, 24009. Tel: 540-345-9090; Fax: 540-345-9090. Email: feedthepoor@cox.net. Eileen Stone, Dir. Food Distribution & Social Svcs.

VIRGINIA BEACH. *Catholic Charities of Eastern Virginia Foundation*, 5361-A Virginia Beach Blvd., 23462. Tel: 757-456-2366; Fax: 757-456-2367. Web: www.cceva.org. Katherine Kitterman, Exec. Dir.

San Lorenzo Spiritual Center, 4556 Indian River Rd., 23456. Tel: 757-471-8949; Fax: 757-424-1313.

RELIGIOUS INSTITUTES OF MEN REPRESENTED IN THE DIOCESE

For further details refer to the corresponding bracketed number in the Religious Institutes of Men or Women section.

[0200]—*Benedictine Monks* (Latrobe, PA)—O.S.B.
[1350]—*Brothers of St. Francis Xavier*—C.F.X.
[0630]—*Congregation of the Missionaries of the Holy Family*—M.S.F.
[0570]—*The Glenmary Home Missioners*—Glmy.
[0690]—*Jesuits Fathers and Brothers*—S.J.
[0430]—*Order of Preachers (Dominicans)* (Province of St. Joseph)—O.P.
[1070]—*Redemptorist Fathers* (Baltimore Prov.)—C.SS.R.

RELIGIOUS INSTITUTES OF WOMEN REPRESENTED IN THE DIOCESE

[0230]—*Benedictine Sisters of Pontifical Jurisdiction*—O.S.B.
[1810]—*Bernardine Sisters of the Third Order of St. Francis*—O.S.F.
[0670]—*Cistercian Nuns of the Strict Observance*—O.C.S.O.
[0690]—*Comboni Missionary Sisters*—C.M.S.
[0270]—*Congregation of Bon Secours*—C.B.S.
[1070-09]—*Congregation of St. Catherine of Siena, Racine*—O.P.
[1070-07]—*Congregation of St. Cecelia, Nashville*—O.P.
[1070-13]—*Congregation of the Most Holy Rosary, Adrian*—O.P.
[1920]—*Congregation of the Sisters of the Holy Cross*—C.S.C.
[0760]—*Daughters of Charity of St. Vincent de Paul*—D.C.
[0820]—*Daughters of the Holy Spirit*—D.H.S.
[0960]—*Daughters of Wisdom*—D.W.
[1180]—*The Franciscan Sisters*—O.S.F.
[1840]—*Grey Nuns of the Sacred Heart*—G.N.S.H.
[2575]—*Institute of the Sisters of Mercy of the Americas*—R.S.M.
[2340]—*Little Sisters of the Poor*—L.S.P.
[2490]—*Medical Mission Sisters*—S.C.M.M.
[2490]—*Medical Mission Sisters*—M.M.S.
[2480]—*Medical Missionaries of Mary*—M.M.M.
[2790]—*Missionary Servants of the Most Blessed Trinity*—M.S.B.T.
[3760]—*Order of St. Clare*—P.C.C.
[3640]—*Poor Servants of the Mother of God*—S.M.G.
[3465]—*Religious of the Sacred Heart of Mary* (Eastern American Prov.)—R.S.H.M
[2970]—*School Sisters of Notre Dame*—S.S.N.D.
[1070-03]—*Sinsinawa Dominican Congregation of the Most Holy Rosary*—O.P.
[]—*Sisters for Christian Community*—S.F.C.C.
[0500]—*Sisters of Charity of Nazareth*—S.C.N.
[0590]—*Sisters of Charity of St. Elizabeth, Convent Station*—S.C.
[0990]—*Sisters of Divine Providence* (Our Lady of Divine Providence Prov.)—C.D.P.
[2990]—*Sisters of Notre Dame*—S.N.D.
[3000]—*Sisters of Notre Dame de Namur*—S.N.D.deN.
[1530]—*Sisters of St. Francis of the Congregation of Our Lady of Lourdes, Sylvania, Ohio*—O.S.F.
[3840]—*Sisters of St. Joseph of Carondelet*—C.S.J.
[2980]—*Sisters of the Congregation of Notre Dame*—C.N.D.
[1990]—*Sisters of the Holy Names of Jesus and Mary*—S.N.J.M.
[2110]—*Sisters of the Humility of Mary*—H.M.
[2170]—*Sisters, Servants of the Immaculate Heart of Mary* (Immaculata, PA)—I.H.M.
[4130]—*Ursuline Sisters of the Congregation of Tildonk, Belgium*—O.S.U.
[4190]—*Visitation Nuns*—V.H.M.

DIOCESAN CEMETERIES

RICHMOND. *Holy Cross*, First Ave. & Daniels St., 23222. Tel: 804-321-5936.

Mount Calvary, 1400 S. Randolph St., 23220. Tel: 804-355-5277.

LYNCHBURG. *Holy Cross*, 710 Clay St., 24504. Tel: 434-846-5245; Fax: 434-846-7022.

NORFOLK. *St. Mary's Catholic Cemetery*, 3000 Church St., 23504. Tel: 757-627-2874; Fax: 757-627-0369.

PETERSBURG. *Sacred Heart Cemetery Corporation*, 9300 Community Ln., 23805. Tel: 804-733-0081. Email: 5k3b2g@comcast.net.

PORTSMOUTH. *St. Paul's Cemetery Portsmouth Catholic Cemetery Commission*, P.O. Box 155, 23705. Tel: 757-488-1723. 2701 Elm Ave., 23705.

ROANOKE. *St. Andrew Diocesan Cemetery*, 3601 Salem Tpke., N.W., P.O. Box 6616, 24017. Tel: 540-342-9180; Fax: 540-342-9180. Email: standrewscemetery@juno.com.

NECROLOGY

† Boddie, John D., Topping, VA Church of the Visitation; Mathews, VA Church of Francis de Sales—Died May 19, 2009
† Fisher, Charles M., Richmond, VA Our Lady of Lourdes—Died Jan. 9, 2009
† Hanna, Don Michael, (Retired)—Died Nov. 15, 2009
† Ridgell, John E., (Retired)—Died March 1, 2009
† Rodrigues, Anthony, (Retired)—Died Oct. 11, 2009

An asterisk (*) denotes an organization that has established tax-exempt status directly with the IRS and is not covered by the USCCB Group Ruling.

Diocese of Rochester

(Dioecesis Roffensis)

Most Reverend

MATTHEW H. CLARK, D.D.

Bishop of Rochester; ordained December 19, 1962; appointed Bishop of Rochester April 23, 1979; consecrated May 27, 1979; installed June 26, 1979. *Res.: 1150 Buffalo Rd., Rochester, NY 14624.*

Pastoral Center: 1150 Buffalo Rd., Rochester, NY 14624-1890. Tel: 585-328-3210; 800-388-7177; Fax: 585-328-3149.

Web: www.dor.org

ESTABLISHED MARCH 3, 1868.

Square Miles 7,107.

Comprises the Counties of Cayuga, Chemung, Livingston, Monroe, Ontario, Schuyler, Seneca, Steuben, Tioga, Tompkins, Wayne and Yates in the State of New York.

Legal Title of Diocese: The Diocese of Rochester. For legal titles of parishes and diocesan institutions, consult the Pastoral Center.

STATISTICAL OVERVIEW

Personnel	
Bishop	1
Abbots	2
Retired Abbots	2
Priests: Diocesan Active in Diocese	102
Priests: Diocesan Active Outside Diocese	7
Priests: Retired, Sick or Absent	76
Number of Diocesan Priests	185
Religious Priests in Diocese	46
Total Priests in Diocese	231
Extern Priests in Diocese	25
Ordinations:	
Diocesan Priests	1
Religious Priests	1
Permanent Deacons	6
Permanent Deacons in Diocese	127
Total Brothers	29
Total Sisters	481
Parishes	
Parishes	124
With Resident Pastor:	
Resident Diocesan Priests	72
Resident Religious Priests	3
Without Resident Pastor:	
Administered by Priests	25
Administered by Deacons	6
Administered by Religious Women	8
Administered by Lay People	10
Missions	4
New Parishes Created	3
Closed Parishes	8
Professional Ministry Personnel:	
Brothers	1
Sisters	68
Lay Ministers	273
Welfare	
Catholic Hospitals	2
Total Assisted	250,000
Health Care Centers	2
Total Assisted	1,200
Homes for the Aged	4
Total Assisted	1,600
Day Care Centers	1
Total Assisted	180
Specialized Homes	8
Total Assisted	620
Special Centers for Social Services	76
Total Assisted	845,000
Residential Care of Disabled	10
Total Assisted	102
Educational	
Diocesan Students in Other Seminaries	5
Total Seminarians	5
High Schools, Diocesan and Parish	1
Total Students	95
High Schools, Private	6
Total Students	3,308
Elementary Schools, Diocesan and Parish	24
Total Students	5,159
Elementary Schools, Private	3
Total Students	418
Catechesis/Religious Education:	
High School Students	5,260
Elementary Students	17,578
Total Students under Catholic Instruction	31,823
Teachers in the Diocese:	
Priests	7
Sisters	26
Lay Teachers	798
Vital Statistics	
Receptions into the Church:	
Infant Baptism Totals	2,579
Minor Baptism Totals	499
Adult Baptism Totals	197
Received into Full Communion	292
First Communions	2,797
Confirmations	2,579
Marriages:	
Catholic	721
Interfaith	328
Total Marriages	1,049
Deaths	3,509
Total Catholic Population	309,773
Total Population	1,485,097

Former Bishops—Rt. Rev. BERNARD J. MCQUAID, D.D., ord. Jan. 16, 1848; appt. March 31, 1868; cons. July 12, 1868; died Jan. 18, 1909; Most Revs. THOMAS F. HICKEY, D.D., ord. March 25, 1884; cons. May 24, 1905; succeeded to the See, Jan. 18, 1909; appt. assistant at the Pontifical Throne, May 4, 1925; made Archbishop of the Titular See of Viminacium, Oct. 30, 1928; died Dec. 10, 1940; JOHN FRANCIS O'HERN, D.D., ord. Feb. 17, 1901; appt. Bishop of Rochester, Jan. 4, 1929; cons. March 19, 1929; died May 22, 1933; His Eminence EDWARD CARDINAL MOONEY, D.D., appt. Papal Delegate to India Jan. 1, 1926; cons. Jan. 31, 1926; appt. Apostolic Delegate to Japan Jan. 1, 1931; appt. Bishop of Rochester Jan. 1, 1933; installed Bishop of Rochester Oct. 12, 1933; transferred to Detroit, May 26, 1937; installed Archbishop of Detroit, Aug. 3, 1937; created Cardinal, Feb. 18, 1946; died Oct. 25, 1958; Most Revs. JAMES E. KEARNEY, D.D., ord. Sept. 19, 1908; appt. Bishop of Salt Lake, Utah, July 1, 1932; cons. Oct. 28, 1932; transferred to Rochester, July 31, 1937; installed Nov. 11, 1937; retired Oct. 26, 1966; died Jan. 12, 1977; FULTON J. SHEEN, D.D., ord. Sept. 30, 1919; appt. Titular Bishop of Cesariana and Auxiliary of New York, May 28, 1951; cons. June 11, 1951; appt. to Rochester, Oct. 26, 1966; installed Dec. 15, 1966; resigned Oct. 15, 1969; appt. Titular Archbishop of Newport; died Dec. 9, 1979; JOSEPH L. HOGAN, S.T.D., D.D., ord. June 6, 1942; appt. to Rochester, Oct. 15, 1969; cons. and installed Nov. 28, 1969; retired Nov. 28, 1978; died Aug. 27, 2000.

Pastoral Center Administration

Pastoral Center—1150 Buffalo Rd., Rochester, 14624-1890. Tel: 585-328-3210; 800-388-7177 (Toll Free within Diocese); Fax: 585-328-3149. Web: www.dor.org.

Vicars General—Very Rev. JOSEPH A. HART, S.T.D., V.G.; Rev. JOHN M. MULLIGAN, V.G. (Retired).

Moderator of the Pastoral Center—Very Rev. JOSEPH A. HART, S.T.D., V.G.

Chancellor—Rev. DANIEL J. CONDON, J.C.L.

Judicial Vicar—Rev. LOUIS A. SIRIANNI, J.C.L.

Vice Chancellor and Administrator of the Bishop's Office—Sr. MARY ANN BINSACK, R.S.M.

Secretary to the Bishop—Mrs. MARY MOORHOUSE.

Office of the Chancellor and Department of Legal Services

Chancellor and Director of the Department of Legal Services—Rev. DANIEL J. CONDON, J.C.L.

Judicial Vicar—Rev. LOUIS A. SIRIANNI, J.C.L.

Vice Chancellor—Sr. MARY ANN BINSACK, R.S.M.

Administrative Assistant—Ms. BARBARA FULLE.

Diocesan Archives—Sr. CONNIE DERBY, R.S.M., Dir. Archival Svcs. Email: archives@dor.org.

Censores Librorum—Very Rev. JOSEPH A. HART, S.T.D., V.G.; Rev. WILLIAM F. LAIRD, J.C.L.; Rev. Msgr. WILLIAM H. SHANNON (Retired); Revs. WILLIAM E. GRAF, D.Min. (Retired); JOSEPH W. MARCOUX, S.T.L.

Conciliation Board—Rev. LANCE M. GONYO.

Information Technology—Mr. THOMAS VEEDER, Dir.; Mr. DAVID KILPATRICK, Network Admin. Computer Coordinators: Mr. MARK DARLING; Mr. RICHARD BRAXTON; Mr. FRED STRINGER; Mr. KIM FAY; Ms. RENATA PARKS; Mrs. JOYCE CROOKS, Technical Support Specialist; Mr. RICHARD HARRINGTON. Catholic Charities Computer Associates: Ms. LISA ZELAZNY; Mr. MICHAEL DABRAMO; Mr. SHAWN MLECZYNSKI.

Tribunal—

Director—EMMETT G. WELLS, J.D., J.C.L.

Judges—Revs. LOUIS A. SIRIANNI, J.C.L., Judicial Vicar; R. RICHARD BRICKLER, Adjutant Judicial Vicar; Ms. RENEE LISS-SIRACO, J.C.L.; Revs. JOHN A. LYNCH (Retired); KEVIN E. MCKENNA, J.C.D.; JOHN M. MULLIGAN, V.G. (Retired); T. PIUS PATHMARAJAH, J.C.L.; Mr. EMMETT G. WELLS, J.D., J.C.L.

Defender of the Bond—Rev. Msgr. GERARD KRIEG, J.C.L. (Retired).

Staff—Ms. MARY ELLEN GOVERTS, Case Instructor, Advocate & Notary; Rev. WILLIAM E. GRAF, D.Min., Expert (Retired); Miss ANDREA IMBURGIA, Admin. Asst. & Notary; Deacons JAMES STEIGER, Auditor; RICHARD SCHULER, Auditor; Ms. ROSANNE WARNER, Case Instructor, Advocate & Notary.

Consultative Bodies

Bishop's Stewardship Council—Most Rev. MATTHEW HARVEY CLARK, D.D., Pres.; Ms. BARBARA KELLEY, Chm.

College of Consultors—Rev. DANIEL J. CONDON, J.C.L., Contact.

Priest Consultors—Most Rev. MATTHEW HARVEY CLARK, D.D.; Very Rev. JOSEPH A. HART, S.T.D., V.G.; Revs. JOHN M. MULLIGAN, V.G. (Retired); MICHAEL CONBOY; DANIEL J. CONDON, J.C.L.; KEVIN E. MCKENNA, J.C.D.; ROBERT J. SCHRADER; ROBERT J. KENNEDY; WILLIAM F. LAIRD, J.C.L.

Priests' Council—Rev. ROBERT J. SCHRADER, Chm.

Regional Coordinator—Sr. MARY ANN BINSACK, R.S.M., Liaison.

Catholic Charities—

Catholic Charities of the Diocese of Rochester—1150 Buffalo Rd., Rochester, 14624. Tel: 585-328-3210. JACK BALINSKY, Diocesan Dir.; ANDREW HISLOP, Chm. Bd. Directors, (Refer to Catholic Charities section under Institutions Located in the Diocese for further listings).

Diocesan Newspapers "Catholic Courier"— "El Mensajero Catolico" Tel: 585-529-9530; 800-600-3628. KAREN FRANZ, Gen. Mgr. & Editor.

Board of Directors—Most Rev. MATTHEW HARVEY CLARK, D.D., Pres.; Very Rev. JOSEPH A. HART, S.T.D., V.G., Vicar Gen. & Vice Pres.; Rev. DANIEL J. CONDON, J.C.L., Sec.; MARY AMATO; DONNA DEDEE; SCOTT BENJAMIN; KARLEE BOLAKOS; THOMAS FLYNN; JOANNE GORDON; WILLIAM H. KEDLEY, Treas.; MARY HOLLERON; MYRTLE FONTENETTE; Rev. EDWARD L. PALUMBOS; GEORGE A. PARK JR.; JAMES REDMOND; CAROLINE RIBY; GLORIBEL ARBELLO PARK; Rev. ROBERT J. SCHRADER; LISA FLEMING; DOLORES PASTO-ZIOBRO.

Faith Development Ministry—

Department of Catholic Schools—ANNE WILLKENS LEACH, Supt. Schools. Assistant Superintendents: Sr. MARGARET MANCUSO, S.S.J., Curriculum & Instruction; Mrs. ANN FRANK, Coord. Assessment & Professional Growth; KATHLEEN GRAY, Business Mgr.; RICHARD J. LONG, Dir. Human Resources for Catholic Schools.

Department of Evangelization and Catechesis—Ms. MARIBETH MANCINI, Dir.

AV Resource Librarian—Sr. CONNIE DERBY, R.S.M.

Director of Young Adult and Campus Ministry—Ms. SHANNON LOUGHLIN.

Coordinator of Youth Ministry—SUE VERSLUYS.

Coordinator for Family & Catechist Formation—JONATHAN SCHOTT.

Coordinator for Evangelization and Sacramental Catechesis—MARY DUNDAS.

CYO Administrator—GERI PIETRZAK.

Office of Stewardship and Communications—Mr. DOUG MANDELARO.

Associate Directors of Stewardship and Communications—Mr. MARK J. CLARK; Mr. DAVID KELLY.

Administrative Assistant—LYNN TRELLY.

Department of Financial Services—

Chief Financial Officer—Ms. LISA M. PASSERO.

Administrative Assistant—VACANT.

Director of Financial Services—Ms. MARY ZIARNIAK.

Buildings and Properties—Mr. ERIC PATCHKE, Mgr.

Controller—KATHLEEN M. MOORE.

Human Resources—Ms MARY F. BAUER, Dir.; Ms. JEAN WOOD, Admin. Asst.

Benefits Administration—Ms. PATRICIA HOSKING, Coord.; Ms. AMY IRISH, Dir. Benefits Planning & Pension Admin.

Clergy Services—Mrs. SANDRA GROCKI, Coord.

Deacon Personnel—Deacon DAVID A. PALMA, Dir. & Contact, Deacon Personnel Board.

Department of Management and Staff Relations—Mrs. BARBARA PEDEVILLE, Dir.

Department of Priest Personnel—Rev. MICHAEL CONBOY, Dir.

Department of Human Resources for Catholic Schools—RICHARD J. LONG, Dir.

Ministry to Priests—Rev. WILLIAM E. GRAF, D.Min., Coord. (Retired), 63 Mason Rd., Fairport, 14450. Tel: 585-223-5500. Email: graf@dor.org.

Newly Ordained Priests—Revs. PETER C. CLIFFORD; DANIEL TORMEY (Retired).

Pension Committee (Lay and Priests)—Very Rev. JOSEPH A. HART, S.T.D., V.G.; Revs. DANIEL J. CONDON, J.C.L.; MICHAEL F. CONBOY; THOMAS H. WHEELAND; Ms. PAULA DOLAN; Ms MARY F. BAUER; Ms. AMY IRISH; Ms. LISA M. PASSERO; JAMES GOULD.

Priests' Personnel Board—Rev. MICHAEL F. CONBOY, Chm.

Priests' Sabbatical Committee—Rev. GEORGE P. HEYMAN.

Office of Seminarians—Rev. JAMES A. SCHWARTZ, Dir., St. Joseph, 43 Gebhardt Rd., Penfield, 14526.

Office of Vocations—Revs. MICHAEL CONBOY, Dir., Becket Hall, 2617 East Ave., Rochester, 14610. Tel: 585-461-2890. Email: fconboy@dor.org; TIMOTHY E. HORAN, Dir.

Office of Vocations Awareness—Ms CAROL DADY, Coord. Vocations Awareness. Tel: 585-328-3210.

Vicar for Religious—Rev. DANIEL J. CONDON, J.C.L.

Parish Support Ministries—Tel: 585-328-3228, Ext. 1337.

Director—Mr. BERNARD GRIZARD.

Secretary—DIANA COLLINS.

Office of Liturgy—VACANT.

Liturgical Commission—NANCY VERONESI, Chm.

Office of Pastoral Planning—Mr. BERNARD GRIZARD, Dir. Liaisons: Ms. KAREN RINEFIERD; Ms. DEBORAH HOUSEL; DIANA COLLINS, Administrative Asst.

Ministry Offices—

Multicultural Services—Mr. BERNARD GRIZARD, Dir.

Office of Health Care Ministry—Deacon JOHN BRASLEY, Coord.

Office of Migrant Ministry—Rev. JESUS FLORES, Coord.

Office of Spanish Apostolate—Bro. JUAN LOZADA ROCA, C.S.J.E., Coord.

Urban Subsidy Program—Bro. JUAN LOZADA ROCA, C.S.J.E., Coord.

Office of Ecumenical and Interreligious Services—Deacon JOHN BRASLEY, Coord.

Jail Ministry Coordinator—Deacon JOHN BRASLEY.

Diocesan Missions—

The Society for the Propagation of the Faith—Rev. ROBERT C. BRADLER, Dir. (Retired), 1150 Buffalo Rd., Rochester, 14624. Tel: 585-436-9200.

World and Diocesan Missions/Mission Awareness—Sr. JANET KORN, R.S.M., Coord.; JOSEPHINE C. CONLON, Sec. & Bookkeeper.

Specialized Ministries—

Bishop Sheen Ecumenical Housing Foundation—935 East Ave., Ste. 300, Rochester, 14607. Tel: 585-461-4263; Fax: 585-461-5177. Email: sheen@rochester.rr.com. Web: sheenhousing.org. ALLYNN SMITH, Exec. Dir.; ROSEANNE HENNESSEY, Pres. Bd. Directors, Subsidiary: Bloomfield Meadows, Inc.

Clergy Relief Society—Rev. THOMAS H. WHEELAND, Holy Cross Church, 4492 Lake Ave., Rochester, 14617. Tel: 585-663-2244.

Diocesan Building Commission—Mr. ERIC PATCHKE, Contact.

Diocesan Women's Commission—Ms. SHANNON LOUGHLIN, Diocesan Liaison. Leadership Team: BETTE RAE SIMMONS; MARY KATE DRISCOLL.

Holy Sepulchre Cemetery—Mr. JAMES WEISBECK, Dir. & Asst. Treas., 2461 Lake Ave., Rochester, 14612. Tel: 585-458-4110.

Victim Assistance Coordinator—Mrs. BARBARA PEDEVILLE. Tel: 585-328-3228, Ext. 1215. Email: pedeville@dor.org.

CLERGY, PARISHES, MISSIONS AND PAROCHIAL SCHOOLS

METROPOLITAN ROCHESTER

(MONROE COUNTY)

1—SACRED HEART CATHEDRAL (1910) Revs. Kevin E. McKenna; Edison Tayag, Parochial Vicar; Deacons Lynn W. Kershner; John Giugno. In Res., Most Rev. Matthew Harvey Clark; Rev. John M. Mulligan, Senior Priest (Retired).
The Cathedral Community—, (Holy Rosary, Most Precious Blood, Sacred Heart Cathedral), 296 Flower City Pk., 14615. Tel: 585-254-3221; Fax: 585-254-8970.
See Sacred Heart Cathedral School, Rochester under Monroe County School System located in the Institution section.
Catechesis/Religious Program—Ms. Marianne Himmelsbach, D.R.E. Students 49.
Convent—287 Flower City Pk., 14615. Tel: 716-254-5048.

2—ST. AMBROSE (1921) Merged with St. James, Rochester & St. John the Evangelist, Rochester to form Peace of Christ Roman Catholic Parish of Rochester, NY.

3—ST. ANDREW (1914) Merged with Church of the Annunciation, Rochester to form Light of Christ Roman Catholic Parish, Rochester.

4—ST. ANNE (1930) [CEM] Sr. Joan Sobala, S.S.J., Pastoral Admin.; Rev. Gary L. Tyman, Sacramental Min. In Res., Revs. Dennis Bonsignore; John A. Lynch (Retired).
Res.: 1600 Mt. Hope Ave., 14620-4598. Tel: 585-271-3260; Fax: 585-271-7160.
Catechesis/Religious Program—Students 47.

5—ST. ANTHONY OF PADUA (1906), (Italian—Vietnamese), Closed. For inquiries for parish records, contact Holy Apostles Church, Rochester, NY.

6—ST. AUGUSTINE (1898) Closed. For inquiries for parish records contact St. Monica, Rochester.

7—BLESSED SACRAMENT (1902) Rev. Robert J. Kennedy.
Parish—534 Oxford St., 14607.
Res. & Mailing Address: 259 Rutgers St., 14607. Tel: 585-271-7240; Fax: 585-442-7517.
Catechesis/Religious Program—Students 62.
Convent—247 Rutgers St., 14607. Tel: 585-271-7736.

8—ST. BONIFACE (1860), (German), [CEM] Rev. R. Richard Brickler.
Res.: 330 Gregory St., 14620. Tel: 585-473-4271; Fax: 585-256-0868.
Catechesis/Religious Program—Students 39.

9—ST. BRIDGET (1854) Rev. Paul Gitau, Parochial Admin.
Church: 14 Mark St., 14605. Tel: 585-454-4236; Fax: 585-454-0835.
Catechesis/Religious Program—Students 62.

10—ST. CECILIA (1949) [CEM] Rev. William B. Leone, Parochial Admin.; Deacon Walter E. Toot Jr. In Res., Revs. Peter Abas; Walter F. Cushing (Retired).
Res.: 2732 Culver Rd., 14622. Tel: 585-467-4286; Fax: 585-544-8889.
Catechesis/Religious Program—Ann G. Kubiak, D.R.E. Students 139.

11—ST. CHARLES BORROMEO (1925) Revs. John A. Firpo; Mark Alan Brewer, Parochial Vicar. In Res., Rev. Thomas R. Statt (Retired).
Res.: 3003 Dewey Ave., 14616. Tel: 585-663-3230; Fax: 585-663-8055.
Catechesis/Religious Program—Tel: 585-663-8000; Fax: 585-663-8055. Students 220.

12—CHRIST THE KING (1955) Revs. Norman C. Tanck, C.S.B.; Joseph A. Trovato, C.S.B., Parochial Vicar; Morgan Rice, C.S.B.; Peter Abas, Parochial Vicar. In Res., Rev. Peter J. Etlinger, C.S.B.
Res.: 445 Kings Hwy. S., 14617. Tel: 585-266-1288; Fax: 585-266-1074.
See Christ the King School, Rochester under Monroe County School System located in the Institution section.
Catechesis/Religious Program—Tel: 585-388-1146. Mrs. Mary Ann Obark, D.R.E. Lay Teachers 88; Students 426.

13—CHURCH OF THE ANNUNCIATION (1917), (Italian), Merged with St. Andrew, Rochester to form Light of Christ Roman Catholic Parish, Rochester.

14—EMMANUEL CHURCH OF THE DEAF OF THE DIOCESE OF ROCHESTER (1981) Rev. Raymond H. Fleming; Deacon Patrick A. Graybill.
Parish—75 Ernestine St., 14619.
Res.: 34 St. Monica St., 14619. Tel: 585-235-3244; 585-235-1812.

15—ST. FRANCIS ASSISI (1929) Closed. For inquiries for parish records, please contact: Holy Apostles, 7 Austin St., Rochester, NY 14606; Tel: 585-254-7171; Fax: 585-254-5813; Email: rholyapo@dor.org.

16—ST. FRANCIS XAVIER, Merged in 2008 with Corpus Christi and Our Lady of Mt. Carmel to form Our Lady of the Americas. All inquiries should be directed to the listed address: 80 Prince St., Rochester, NY 14605

17—ST. GEORGE (1907), (Lithuanian), Rev. Dominic F. Mockevicius, Parochial Admin. (Retired).
Res.: 545 Hudson Ave., 14605. Tel: 585-232-4111.

18—GUARDIAN ANGELS (1960) Rev. Gerald Appleby, Sacramental Min.; Deacon Emmanuel Asis; Barbara Swiecki, Pastoral Admin.
Res.: 2061 E. Henrietta Rd., 14623-3999. Tel: 585-334-1412; Fax: 585-334-7145.

19—ST. HELEN (1940), Includes Vietnamese Community. Revs. Malachy Nwosu, Parochial Admin.; Cao Xuan Cahn, Parochial Vicar.
Res.: 310 Hinchey Rd., 14624. Tel: 585-235-1210; Fax: 585-235-8018.
Catechesis/Religious Program—Students 88.

20—HOLY APOSTLES (1884) Rev. Anthony P. Mugavero; Deacons John Crego; Salvador Otero; Nemesio Martinez Vellon.
Parish—530 Lyell Ave., 14606.
Res.: 7 Austin St., 14606. Tel: 585-254-7170; Fax: 585-254-5813.

21—HOLY CROSS (1873) Revs. Thomas H. Wheeland; Frederick F. Eisemann (Retired); John Reif, Parochial Vicar (Retired); Deacon Ed Giblin.
Res.: 4492 Lake Ave., 14612. Tel: 585-663-2244; Fax: 585-865-5379.
Catechesis/Religious Program—Tel: 585-621-8133. Mary Toot, D.R.E. Students 252.
Convent—4490 Lake Ave., 14612. Tel: 716-663-5351.

22—HOLY FAMILY (1864), (German), Merged with Holy Apostles, Rochester. For inquiries for parish records contact Holy Apostles, Rochester.

23—HOLY GHOST (1875) [CEM] Rev. Thomas F. Nellis; Deacon David Cadregari. In Res., Rev. Timothy Brown.
Res.: 220 Coldwater Rd., 14624. Tel: 585-247-3535; Fax: 585-247-4223.

Catechesis/Religious Program—Tel: 585-426-1289. Students 150.

24—HOLY NAME OF JESUS (1964) Rev. John F. Gagnier; Deacon Joseph Placious.
Res.: 15 St. Martin's Way, 14616. Tel: 585-621-4040; Fax: 585-621-6343; 585-621-1339.
Catechesis/Religious Program—Tel: 585-621-6343. Students 79.

25—HOLY REDEEMER-ST. FRANCIS XAVIER (1867-1888), Merged with Our Lady of Mt. Carmel and Our Lady of the Americas of Rochester, NY., Mailing Address: *Our Lady of the Americas*, 80 Prince St., 14605.

26—HOLY ROSARY (1889) Merged with Most Precious Blood & Sacred Heart Cathedral, Rochester to form Sacred Heart Cathedral. For inquiries for parish records contact Sacred Heart Cathedral, Rochester.

27—IMMACULATE CONCEPTION (1849) Rev. Paul Gitau, Parochial Admin.
Office:—445 Frederick Douglass St., 14608. Tel: 585-325-3893; Fax: 585-325-2082.

28—ST. JAMES (1949) Merged with St. Ambrose, Rochester & St. John the Evangelist, Rochester to form Peace of Christ Roman Catholic Parish of Rochester, NY.

29—ST. JOHN THE EVANGELIST (1914) Merged with St. Ambrose, Rochester & St. James, Rochester to form Peace of Christ Roman Catholic Parish of Rochester, NY.
See separate listing under Monroe County School System in the Institution section.

30—ST. JOHN THE EVANGELIST (1865) Revs. John V. Forni; T. Pius Pathmarajah; Deacon Paul Virgilio.
Res.: 2400 Ridge Rd., W., 14626. Tel: 585-225-8980; Fax: 585-723-9825.
Catechesis/Religious Program—Tel: 585-225-4200. Rose Battisto, D.R.E. Students 101.

31—ST. JOSEPH (1836) Closed. For inquiries for parish records contact Our Lady of Victory.

32—ST. JUDE THE APOSTLE (1968) Rev. Michael J. Schramel; Deacon Patrick M. Shanley.
Res.: 4100 Lyell Rd., 14606. Tel: 585-247-4322; Fax: 585-429-5111.
Catechesis/Religious Program—Tel: 585-247-5275. Students 159.

33—ST. LAWRENCE (1959) Revs. Frank J. Falletta; Donald J. Haycock, C.S.C.; Thomas O'Brien, S.J., Parochial Vicar; Deacon James L. Chatterton.
Res.: 1000 N. Greece Rd., 14626. Tel: 585-723-1350; Fax: 585-723-1361.
See St. Lawrence School, Rochester under Monroe County School System located in the Institution section.
Catechesis/Religious Program—Tel: 585-225-7320. Mrs. Jamie O'Mara, D.R.E. Students 504.

34—LIGHT OF CHRIST ROMAN CATHOLIC PARISH, Formed by the merger of St. Andrews & Annunciation. Rev. Michael A. Mayer; Deacon Robert Meyer. 923 Portland Ave., 14621. Tel: 585-342-8686; Fax: 585-342-8686.
Catechesis/Religious Program—Karen Fox Riordan, D.R.E. Students 18.

35—ST. LUCY (1912) Closed. For inquiries for parish records contact Immaculate Conception Church.

36—ST. MARGARET MARY (1929) Rev. Timothy E. Horan. In Res., Revs. Peter T. Bayer; John Rosse (Retired); Thomas M. Erdle (Retired).
Res.: 401 Rogers Pkwy., 14617. Tel: 585-342-2100; Fax: 585-467-7694.
Catechesis/Religious Program—Tel: 585-342-7114; Fax: 585-266-9322. Students 426.

37—ST. MARK (1964) Rev. Louis A. Sirianni; Deacon Frank Pettrone. In Res., Rev. Frederick Bush (Retired).
Res.: 54 Kuhn Rd., 14612. Tel: 585-225-3710; Fax: 585-227-6824.
Catechesis/Religious Program—Tel: 585-227-6824; Fax: 585-225-8910. Students 312.

38—ST. MARY (1834) Rev. William Donnelly, Sacramental Min.; Anne-Marie Brogan, Pastoral Assoc.
Res.: 15 St. Mary's Pl., 14607. Tel: 585-232-7142; Fax: 585-232-6289.
Catechesis/Religious Program—Students 98.

39—ST. MICHAEL (1872), (German—Hispanic), Rev. Laurence C. Tracy, Sacramental Min.; Deacons Daniel Hurley, Pastoral Admin.; Jorge Malave; Jose Berrios.
Office & Res.: 124 Evergreen St., 14605-1016. Tel: 585-325-4040; Fax: 585-325-5771.
Church: 869 N. Clinton Ave., 14605-1196.
Catechesis/Religious Program—Students 77.

40—ST. MONICA (1898) Rev. Raymond H. Fleming; Deacon Robert Burke. Cluster of Our Lady of Good Counsel, St. Augustine & Ss. Peter and Paul. Consolidated with St. Monica.
Office: 34 Monica St., 14611. Tel: 585-235-3340; Fax: 585-235-8315.

41—MOST PRECIOUS BLOOD (1930), (Italian), Merged with Holy Rosary & Sacred Heart Cathedral, Rochester to form Sacred Heart Cathedral. For inquiries for parish records contact Sacred Heart Cathedral, Rochester.

42—OUR LADY OF GOOD COUNSEL (1928) Closed. for inquiries for parish records contact St. Monica, Rochester.

43—OUR LADY OF LOURDES (1928) Rev. Gary L. Tyman, Sacramental Min.; Sr. Joan Sobala, S.S.J., Pastoral Admin.
Res.: 150 Varinna Dr., 14618. Tel: 585-473-9656; Fax: 585-271-6472.
Catechesis/Religious Program—Tel: 585-244-2361. Students 84.

44—OUR LADY OF MERCY (1957) Rev. John F. Gagnier, Parochial Admin.; Deacon Dick Lombard.
Res.: 36 Armstrong Rd., 14616. Tel: 585-865-0775; Fax: 585-865-9403.
Catechesis/Religious Program—Tel: 585-865-2917; Fax: 585-865-9403.

45—OUR LADY OF MOUNT CARMEL (1909), Clustered with Holy Redeemer-St. Francis Xavier & Corpus Christi to form Our Lady of the Americas of Rochester, NY. For inquiries for parish records contact Our Lady of the Americas of Rochester, NY.
St. Martin's Soup Kitchen—Tel: 716-325-6500.

46—OUR LADY OF PERPETUAL HELP (1905) Rev. Laurence C. Tracy, Sacramental Min.; Deacons Daniel Hurley, Pastoral Admin.; John Brasley; Jorge Malave; Jose Berrios. In Res., Rev. Laurence C. Tracy.
Res.: 1089 Joseph Ave., 14621. Tel: 585-467-2725; Fax: 585-467-6841.
Catechesis/Religious Program—Students 8.

47—OUR LADY OF THE AMERICAS OF ROCHESTER, NY (1888), Clustered with Holy Redeemer-St. Francis Xavier Church and Our Lady of Mt. Carmel Church. Rev. Vincent P. Panepinto; Deacons Carlos Vargas; Bienvenido DeJesus; Kenneth A. Scarciotta.
Mailing Address: 34 Teresa St., 14605.
Office: 80 Prince St., 14605. Tel: 585-287-5161; Fax: 585-482-1260.
Church: 864 Main St. E., 14605.
Catechesis/Religious Program—Tel: 585-232-3032; Fax: 585-262-3576. Students 199.

48—OUR LADY OF VICTORY-ST. JOSEPH (1848) Rev. Ronald A. Antinarelli, K.C.H.S.
Res.: 210 Pleasant St., 14604. Tel: 585-454-2244; Fax: 585-454-2246.

49—OUR LADY QUEEN OF PEACE (1960) Very Rev. Joseph A. Hart, Sacramental Min.; Rev. Bernard Dan, Sacramental Min.; Margaret Ostromecki, Pastoral Admin. In Res., Rev. John T. Walsh (Retired).
Parish—601 Edgewood Ave., 14618-4329.
Res.: 18 Viennawood Dr., 14618. Tel: 585-244-3010 (Office); Fax: 585-242-7733 (Office).
Catechesis/Religious Program—Students 81.

50—OUR MOTHER OF SORROWS (1829), (Irish), [CEM] Rev. Alexander H. Bradshaw; Deacon Thomas Kluchko. In Res., Revs. Edwin Metzger (Retired); Winfried Kellner (Retired).
Res.: 5000 Mt. Read Blvd., 14612. Tel: 585-663-5432; Fax: 585-663-7683.
School—(Grades K-8) Mr. Samuel Zalacca, Prin. See separate listing under Monroe County School System in the Institution section.
Catechesis/Religious Program—Tel: 585-621-3495. Students 243.

51—ST. PATRICK (1832) Closed. (Old Cathedral). Records can be obtained from Holy Apostles, 7 Austin St., Rochester, NY 14608. Tel: 585-254-5813.

52—PEACE OF CHRIST ROMAN CATHOLIC PARISH OF ROCHESTER, NY Revs. Robert J. Schrader; Robert Thomas Werth, Parochial Vicar; Brian Kumar Carpenter, Parochial Vicar.
Mailing Address: 25 Empire Blvd., 14609. Tel: 585-288-5000; Fax: 585-654-7658. Email: rpeace@dor.org. Web: www.peaceofchristparish.org.
Res.: 549 Humboldt St., 14610. Tel: 585-482-4210.
Catechesis/Religious Program—Students 65.

53—SS. PETER AND PAUL (1843) Closed. for inquiries for parish records contact St. Monica, Rochester.

54—ST. PHILIP NERI (1929), (Italian), Closed. For inquiries for parish records, refer to Light of Christ, 923 Portland Ave., Rochester, NY 14621. Tel: 585-342-8686.

55—ST. PIUS TENTH (1954) [CEM] William Rabjohn, Pastoral Admin.; Rev. Timothy Brown.
Mailing Address: 3010 Chili Ave., 14624.
Res.: 3032 Chili Ave., 14624. Tel: 585-247-2566 (Office); Fax: 585-247-8848.
See St. Pius X School, Rochester under Monroe County School System located in the Institution section.
Catechesis/Religious Program—3000 Chili Ave., 14624. Tel: 585-247-5269; Fax: 585-247-7409; 585-247-5746. Students 207.

56—ST. SALOME (1925) Revs. Norman C. Tanck, C.S.B.; Richard J. Beligotti, Parochial Vicar; Joseph A. Trovato, C.S.B., Parochial Vicar; Morgan Rice, C.S.B., Parochial Vicar; Deacon Laurence Feasel.
Res.: 4282 Culver Rd., 14622. Tel: 585-323-1160; Fax: 585-544-4810.
Catechesis/Religious Program—Annette Truby, D.R.E. Students 33.

57—ST. STANISLAUS (1890), (Polish), Rev. Adam Ogorzaly; Deacon James Witulski. In Res., Rev. Brian Cool.
Res. & Mailing: 34 St. Stanislaus St., 14621. Tel: 585-467-3068; Fax: 585-467-3072.
Church: 1124 Hudson Ave., 14621.
Catechesis/Religious Program—919 Norton St., 14621. Tel: 585-544-2614. Students 42.

58—ST. THEODORE (1924) Rev. Stephen Kraus; Deacon Angelo Coccia. In Res., Revs. Paul J. Freemesser (Retired); Walter J. Plominski.
Res.: 168 Spencerport Rd., 14606. Tel: 585-429-6811; Fax: 585-429-7726.
Catechesis/Religious Program—Tel: 585-429-5650. Students 267.

59—ST. THERESA (1927), (Polish), Closed. For inquiries for parish records contact St. Stanislaus, Rochester.

60—ST. THOMAS MORE (1953) Very Rev. Joseph A. Hart, Sacramental Min.; Rev. Bernard Dan, Sacramental Min.; Margaret Ostromecki, Pastoral Admin.; Deacon H. Wilson Johnson. In Res., Rev. Michael Conboy.
Res.: 2617 East Ave., 14610. Tel: 585-381-4200; Fax: 585-381-6327.
Catechesis/Religious Program—Tel: 585-381-0470. Students 76.

61—ST. THOMAS THE APOSTLE (1922) Revs. Norman C. Tanck, C.S.B.; Peter Abas, Parochial Vicar; Joseph A. Trovato, C.S.B., Parochial Vicar; Morgan Rice, C.S.B., Parochial Vicar; Deacons Thomas H. Beck; Laurence Feasel.
Res.: 4536 St. Paul Blvd., 14617. Tel: 585-342-2323; Fax: 585-342-0356.
Catechesis/Religious Program—Tel: 585-342-1704. Students 111.

OUTSIDE METROPOLITAN ROCHESTER

ADDISON, STEUBEN CO., ST. CATHERINE OF SIENA (1854) [CEM] Rev. Patrick L. Connor, Parochial Admin.
Res.: P.O. Box 153, Bradford, 14815. Tel: 607-583-4290.
Church: 51 Maple St., 14801.
Catechesis/Religious Program—Tel: 607-359-2550. Students 53.

APALACHIN, TIOGA CO., ST. MARGARET MARY (1955) Merged with St. Francis, Catatonk; St. John the Evangelist, Newark Valley; St. Pius the Tenth, Van Etten; and St. James, Waverly to form Blessed Trinity, Owego.

AUBURN, CAYUGA CO.

1—ST. ALOYSIUS, Closed. For inquiries for parish records please see Holy Family, Auburn.

2—ST. ALPHONSUS (1853), (German), [JC] Rev. Louis A. Vasile; Deacon Gregg Lawson.
Parish—85 E. Genesee St., 13021.
Mailing & Res.: 10 S. Lewis St., 13021. Tel: 315-252-7261; Fax: 315-252-7262.
See St. Joseph's School (Auburn), Auburn under Schools Outside Monroe County located in the Institution section.
Catechesis/Religious Program—Tel: 315-253-6147. Marie Venaglia, D.R.E. Students 202.

3—ST. FRANCIS OF ASSISI (1907), (Italian), [JC] Deacon Gary R. DiLallo, Pastoral Admin.; Revs. Michael Brown, Sacramental Min.; Richard Murphy, Sacramental Min.
Res.: 299 Clark St., 13021. Tel: 315-252-7593; Fax: 315-252-2447.
Catechesis/Religious Program—Tel: 315-252-5132. Students 65.

4—HOLY FAMILY (1834) Rev. Dennis Shaw, Parochial Admin. In Res., Rev. Ronald E. Gaesser (Retired).
Parish—85 North St., 13021. Tel: 315-252-9576; Fax: 315-255-1506.
School—St. Joseph's School, Tel: 315-253-8327; Fax: 315-253-2401.
Catechesis/Religious Program—Tel: 315-252-9578; 315-258-9317; Fax: 315-255-1506. Students 100.

5—ST. HYACINTH (1905), (Polish), [JC] Revs. Michael Brown, Sacramental Min.; Richard Murphy, Sacramental Min. In Res., Revs. Michael R. Brown; Felicjan Sierotowicz.
Church & Res.: 61 Pulaski St., 13021. Tel: 315-252-7297; Fax: 315-252-2447.
Church Office: 299 Clark St., 13021.
School—St. Joseph School, Tel: 315-253-8327. A consolidation of the following parishes: Holy Family; Sacred Heart; St. Alphonsus; and St. Hyacinth.
Catechesis/Religious Program—Tel: 315-252-5132. Students 96.

6—ST. MARY (1868), (Irish), Rev. Frank E. Lioi.
Res.: 15 Clark St., 13021. Tel: 315-252-9545; Fax: 315-252-9546.
School—St. Joseph's, Tel: 315-253-8357. Also serving the parishes of Auburn.

Catechesis/Religious Program—90 Melrose Rd., 13021. Tel: 315-252-3439. Students 72.

7—SACRED HEART (1955) [JC] Sr. Chris J. Treichel, O.S.F., Pastoral Admin.; Deacon Nicholas Valvo; Revs. Michael Brown, Sacramental Min.; Felicjan Sierotowicz, Sacramental Min.
Res.: 90 Melrose Rd., 13021. Tel: 315-252-7271; Fax: 315-255-0716.
School—St. Joseph School, 89 E. Genesee St., 13021. Tel: 315-253-8327; Fax: 315-253-2401. Kathleen A. Coye, Prin. A consolidation of the following parishes: Holy Family; Sacred Heart; and St. Alphonsus.
Catechesis/Religious Program—Tel: 315-253-3439. Students 177.
Mission—St. Ann (1912) Main St., Owasco, Cayuga Co. 13021. Tel: 315-252-7271.

AURORA, CAYUGA CO.

1—GOOD SHEPHERD CATHOLIC COMMUNITY, [CEM] Rev. Richard J. Shatzel.
Mailing Address: P.O. Box 296, 13026-0296. Tel: 315-364-7197; Fax: 315-364-7197.
Catechesis/Religious Program—

2—ST. PATRICK (1858) Closed. For inquiries for parish records contact Good Shepherd Catholic Community, Aurora.

AVON, LIVINGSTON CO., ST. AGNES (1866) [CEM] Sr. Karen Dietz, S.S.J., Pastoral Admin.; Rev. Michael Upson, Sacramental Min.; Deacon Edward Mathis.
Res.: 108 Prospect St., 14414. Tel: 585-226-2100; Fax: 585-226-6436.
School—(Grades PreK-6), For detailed school information please see Category Schools outside Monroe located in the Institution section.
Catechesis/Religious Program—Tel: 585-226-3232. Michael Drexler, D.R.E. Students 115.

BATH, STEUBEN CO., ST. MARY (1860) [CEM] Deacon David LaFortune, Pastoral Admin.; Rev. James P. Jaeger, Sacramental Min.; Deacon Edward Wight.
Res.: 32 E. Morris St., 14810. Tel: 607-776-3327; Fax: 607-776-3409.
Catechesis/Religious Program—36 E. Morris St., 14810. Tel: 607-776-4767; Fax: 607-776-3409. Students 55.

BRADFORD, STEUBEN CO., ST. STANISLAUS (1922), (Polish), Revs. Patrick L. Connor, Parochial Admin.; Francis J. Erb, Sacramental Min. (Retired); Deacon Daniel Troy Williams.
Mailing Address: 51 Maple St., Addison, 14801.
Res.: Main St., P.O. Box 153, 14815-0153. Tel: 607-359-2115; Fax: 607-359-2121.
Catechesis/Religious Program—Students 48.
Mission—St. Joseph (1870) P.O. Box 153, Campbell, Steuben Co. 14815-0153.

BROCKPORT, MONROE CO., NATIVITY OF THE BLESSED VIRGIN MARY (1848) [CEM] Rev. Peter Enyan-Boadu.
Res.: 152 Main St., 14420-1972. Tel: 585-637-4500; Fax: 585-637-4232.
Catechesis/Religious Program—Tel: 585-637-8490. Joan Tannous, D.R.E. Students 91.

CALEDONIA, LIVINGSTON CO., ST. COLUMBA (1885) [CEM] Rev. William McGrath; Deacon David Paluskiewicz.
Res.: 198 North St., 14423. Tel: 585-538-2126.
Catechesis/Religious Program—Students 123.
Mission—St. Patrick (1854) Church St., Mumford, Monroe Co. 14511.

CANANDAIGUA, ONTARIO CO., ST. MARY (1844) [CEM] Revs. Thomas P. Mull; William G. Darling, Parochial Vicar; Dominic Nyamai Munini, Sacramental Min.
Res.: 95 N. Main St., Canadaigua, 14424. Tel: 585-394-1220; Fax: 585-396-3230.
See St. Mary (Canandaigua), Canandaigua under Finger Lakes & Southern Tier Schools located in the Institution section.
Catechesis/Religious Program—16 Gibson St., 14424. Tel: 585-394-4590. Students 243.

CANISTEO, STEUBEN CO., ST. JOACHIM (1880) Closed. See Our Lady of the Valley, Hornell.

CATO, CAYUGA CO., ST. PATRICK (1875) Merged with St. Joseph, Weedsport and St. John, Port Byron to form Our Lady of the Snow, Weedsport.

CAYUGA, CAYUGA CO., ST. JOSEPH (1870) Closed. For inquiries for parish records contact Good Shepherd Catholic Community, Aurora.

CHURCHVILLE, MONROE CO., ST. VINCENT DE PAUL (1869) [CEM] Rev. Theodore J. Auble; Charlotte M. Bruney, Pastoral Admin.
Res.: 11 N. Main St., P.O. Box 609, 14428. Tel: 716-293-1400; Fax: 716-293-0531.
Catechesis/Religious Program—Tel: 585-293-1180. Students 100.

CLIFTON SPRINGS, ONTARIO CO.

1—ST. FELIX (1856) Clustered with St. Francis, Phelps to form St. Felix/St. Francis Parish Cluster, Clifton Springs.

2—ST. FELIX/ST. FRANCIS PARISH CLUSTER (1992) [CEM 2] Rev. Donald J. Curtiss; Deacon Robert Cyrana.
Office:—12 Hibbard Ave., 14432. Tel: 315-548-5331 (St. Francis); 315-462-2961 (St. Felix); Fax: 315-462-3608.
Catechesis/Religious Program—Students 54.

CLYDE, WAYNE CO., ST. JOHN THE EVANGELIST (1852), (Italian), [CEM] Sr. Diane Dennie, S.S.J., Pastoral Admin.; Deacon Gregory Kiley; Rev. Joseph W. Marcoux, Sacramental Min.
Res.: 114 Sodus St., 14433. Tel: 315-923-3941; Fax: 315-923-3941.
Catechesis/Religious Program—Students 53.
Mission—St. Patrick (1875) Grand Ave., Savannah, Wayne Co. 13146. Tel: 315-365-3244.

COHOCTON, STEUBEN CO.

1—HOLY FAMILY CATHOLIC COMMUNITY, Merger of St. Mary's, Dansville; St. Joseph's, Wayland; Sacred Heart of Jesus, Perkinsville; and St. Pius V, Cohocton. Church: 35 Maple Ave., Cohocton.

2—ST. PIUS V (1861), (German), Consolidated with St. Joseph's, Wayland; St. Mary's Danville; and Sacred Heart of Jesus, Perkinsville to form Holy Family Catholic Community, Cohocton.

CORNING, STEUBEN CO.

1—ALL SAINTS Revs. Boniface Ewah (Nigeria), Sacramental Min.; Lewis E. Brown, Sacramental Min. (Retired); Deacon Dean Condon, Pastoral Admin.
Mailing Address: 222 Dodge Ave., 14830. Tel: 607-936-4689; Fax: 607-936-0222.
Rectory—15 E. High St., Painted Post, 14870. Tel: 607-962-0422.
School— For detailed school information please see Category Schools outside Monroe located in the Institution section.
Catechesis/Religious Program—Arlene Goodman, D.R.E. Students 263.

2—ST. MARY (1848) Closed. For inquiries for parish records contact All Saints, Corning.

3—ST. PATRICK (1903) Closed. For inquiries for parish records contact All Saints, Corning.

4—ST. VINCENT DE PAUL (1913) Closed. For inquiries for parish records contact All Saints, Corning.

DANSVILLE, LIVINGSTON CO., ST. MARY (1845) Consolidated with St. Joseph's, Wayland; St. Pius V, Cohocton; and Sacred Heart of Jesus, Perkinsville to form Holy Family Catholic Community, Cohocton.

DRYDEN, TOMPKINS CO., HOLY CROSS (1962) Rev. Scott Kubinski.
Parish—375 S. George Rd., Freeville, 13068. Tel: 607-844-8314; Fax: 607-844-8358.
Catechesis/Religious Program—Barbara Ivers, D.R.E. Students 75.

EAST BAY, WAYNE CO., ST. JOHN FISHER (1935) Closed. All inquiries for mission records can be made at Blessed Trinity, Wolcott.

EAST BLOOMFIELD, ONTARIO CO., ST. BRIDGET (1850) [CEM] Revs. Thomas P. Mull; William G. Darling, Parochial Vicar; Dominic Nyamai Munini, Sacramental Min.; Deacon Claude Lester.
Mailing Address: P.O. Box 248, 14443.
Res.: 15 Church St., 14443. Tel: 585-657-7626; Fax: 585-657-5349.
Catechesis/Religious Program—Students 31.

EAST ROCHESTER, MONROE CO., ST. JEROME (1905) Rev. Steven W. Lape. In Res., Rev. William Endres.
Res.: 207 S. Garfield St., 14445. Tel: 585-586-3231; Fax: 585-586-0537.
Catechesis/Religious Program—206 West Ave., 14445. Tel: 585-586-1625. Students 141.

ELMIRA HEIGHTS, CHEMUNG CO., ST. CHARLES BORROMEO (1904) Merged with Our Lady of Lourdes, Elmira & St. Casimir, Elmira to form Christ the Redeemer, Elmira.

ELMIRA, CHEMUNG CO.

1—ST. ANTHONY (1908), (Italian), Merged with St. Patrick, Elmira & Sts. Peter & Paul Catholic Parish, Elmira to form Blessed Sacrament Roman Catholic Church of Elmira, NY.

2—BLESSED SACRAMENT ROMAN CATHOLIC CHURCH OF ELMIRA, NY Revs. Richard T. Farrell; Thomas O'Brien, S.J.; Deacon George Welch.
Mailing Address: 604 Park Pl., 14901. Tel: 607-733-0300; Fax: 607-733-3606. Email: eeastsid@dor.org. Web: www.elmirablessedsacrament.org.
School—Holy Family Catholic Schools, Tel: 607-737-0536. Serving the parishes in Elmira. See St. Mary, St. Casimer, and Our Lady of Lourdes for details.
Catechesis/Religious Program—Students 159.

3—ST. CASIMIR (1890), (Polish), Merged with Our Lady of Lourdes, Elmira & St. Charles Borromeo, Elmira Heights to form Christ the Redeemer, Elmira.

4—ST. CECILIA OF EASTSIDE CATHOLIC PARISH (1904) Closed. For inquiries for parish records contact Blessed Sacrament, Elmira.

5—CHRIST THE REDEEMER Rev. Jeremiah P. Moynihan; Deacon Alberto Pacete.
Parish—304 Demarest Pkwy., 14905.
Res.: 120 Fairmont Rd., 14905. Tel: 607-732-6261; Fax: 607-732-7256.
See Holy Family Intermediate, Elmira under Schools Outside Monroe County located in the Institution section.
Catechesis/Religious Program—Tel: 607-734-0727. Students 146.

6—ST. JOHN THE BAPTIST OF EASTSIDE CATHOLIC PARISH (1866), (German), Closed. For sacramental records contact Blessed Sacrament , Elmira.

7—ST. MARY (1873), (Irish), [CEM] Revs. John A. DeSocio; Jeffrey Tunnicliff, Parochial Vicar. In Res., Rev. Robert C. MacNamara (Retired).
Res.: 224 Franklin St., 14904. Tel: 607-734-6254; Fax: 607-733-8890.
See Holy Family Primary, Elmira under Schools Outside Monroe County located in the Institution section.
Catechesis/Religious Program—Tel: 607-734-5220; Fax: 607-733-8890. Students 92.

8—OUR LADY OF LOURDES (1940) Merged with St. Charles Borromeo, Elmira Heights & St. Casimir, Elmira to form Christ the Redeemer, Elmira.

9—ST. PATRICK (1871), (Irish), Merged with St. Anthony, Elmira & Sts. Peter & Paul Catholic Parish, Elmira to form Blessed Sacrament Roman Catholic Church of Elmira, NY.

10—STS. PETER AND PAUL CATHOLIC PARISH (1848) Merged with St. Anthony, Elmira & St. Patrick, Elmira to form Blessed Sacrament Roman Catholic Church of Elmira, NY.

FAIRPORT, MONROE CO.

1—ASSUMPTION OF THE BLESSED VIRGIN MARY (1866) [CEM] Revs. Edward L. Palumbos; Robert L. Beligotti, Parochial Vicar; John Loncle, Parochial Vicar; Deacons Ronald J. Tocci; Stephen Carroll; Robert Corsaro.
Res.: 20 East Ave., 14450. Tel: 585-388-0040; Fax: 585-388-0248.
Catechesis/Religious Program—Assumption School of Religion, Tel: 585-223-0525; Fax: 585-223-5253. Students 825.

2—CHURCH OF THE RESURRECTION (1973) Rev. George P. Heyman, Sacramental Min.; Sr. Joan Cawley, S.S.J., Pastoral Admin.
Res.: 52 Mason Rd., 14450. Tel: 585-223-6686; Fax: 585-223-6958.
Church: 63 Mason Rd., 14450. Tel: 585-223-5500; Fax: 585-223-6958.
Catechesis/Religious Program—Students 226.

3—ST. JOHN OF ROCHESTER (1962) Rev. Peter C. Clifford; Deacon Thomas J. Cleary. In Res., Rev. Michael C. Hogan (Retired).
Ministry Bldg.—8 Wickford Way, 14450. Tel: 585-248-5993; Fax: 585-387-0517.
Rectory—18 Wickford Way, 14450.
Catechesis/Religious Program—Tel: 585-248-8850. Students 668.

FLEMING, CAYUGA CO., ST. ISAAC JOGUES (1946) Closed. For sacramental records contact Good Shepherd Catholic Community, Aurora, NY.

GENESEO, LIVINGSTON CO.

1—ST. LUKE THE EVANGELIST ROMAN CATHOLIC CHURCH SOCIETY OF LIVINGSTON COUNTY (1854) [CEM] Michael Sauter, Pastoral Admin.; Rev. Edward J. Dillon, Parochial Vicar (Retired); Deacon George Spezzano.
Office: 13 North St., 14454. Tel: 585-243-1100; Fax: 585-243-0240.
Catechesis/Religious Program—Cathy Meyer, D.R.E. Students 216.

2—ST. MARY, Merged with Holy Angels, Nunda, St. Patrick, Mt. Morris & St. Thomas Aquinas, Leicester & St. Mary, Retsof to form St. Luke the Evangelist Roman Catholic Church Society of Livingston County.

GENEVA, ONTARIO CO.

1—ST. FRANCIS DE SALES (1835) [CEM] [JC 2] Merged with St. Stephen, Geneva to form Our Lady of Peace Roman Catholic Church of Geneva, NY.

2—OUR LADY OF PEACE ROMAN CATHOLIC CHURCH OF GENEVA, NY Revs. Paul J. Tomasso; William Coffas, Parochial Vicar.
Mailing Address: 130 Exchange St., 14456. Tel: 315-789-0930; Fax: 315-781-1985. Email: gourladyofpeace@dor.org. Web: www.genevarc.org.
School—St. Francis DeSales/St. Stephen School, (Grades K-8), 17 Elmwood Ave., 14456. Tel: 315-789-1828; Fax: 315-789-9179. Email: sfssdcs@dor.org. Mrs. Elaine Morrow, Prin.

3—ST. STEPHEN (1904) [JC] Merged with St. Francis de Sales, Geneve, NY to form Our Lady of Peace Roman Catholic Church of Geneva, NY.

GROTON, TOMPKINS CO., ST. ANTHONY (1873) [CEM] Rev. Scott Kubinski; Deacon George Kozak.
Res.: 312 Locke Rd., R.D. 2, 13073. Tel: 607-898-5135; Fax: 607-898-7608.
Catechesis/Religious Program—Students 62.

HAMLIN, MONROE CO., ST. ELIZABETH ANN SETON (1982) Rev. William V. Spilly; Deacon Christopher Fisher.
Mailing Address: P.O. Box 149, 14464.
Res.: 1634 Lake Rd., P.O. Box 149, 14464. Tel: 585-964-8560; Fax: 585-964-3352.

Catechesis/Religious Program—Tel: 716-964-3352. Students 86.

HAMMONDSPORT, STEUBEN CO., ST. GABRIEL (1845) [JC] Rev. James P. Jaeger, Sacramental Min.; Maureen O'Neill, Pastoral Admin.
Res.: 78 Shethar St., 14840. Tel: 607-569-3501; Fax: 607-569-3226.
Catechesis/Religious Program—Fax: 607-569-3501. Students 42.

HENRIETTA, MONROE CO., CHURCH OF THE GOOD SHEPHERD (1911) [CEM] Nancy DeRycke, Pastoral Admin.; Rev. Augustine Chumo; Deacon Tony Caruso.
Res.: 3318 E. Henrietta Rd., 14467. Tel: 585-334-3518; Fax: 585-334-6015.
See Good Shepherd School, Henrietta under Monroe County School System located in the Institution section.
Catechesis/Religious Program—Tel: 585-334-3023. Margaret Churnetski, D.R.E. Students 281.

HILTON, MONROE CO., ST. LEO (1884) Rev. Joseph R. Catanise; Deacon William Lenhart.
Res.: 167 Lake Ave., 14468. Tel: 585-392-2710, Ext. 2; Fax: 585-392-9254.
Catechesis/Religious Program—Tel: 585-392-2710, Ext. 3. Students 28.

HONEOYE FALLS, MONROE CO., ST. PAUL OF THE CROSS (1870) [CEM] Rev. Lawrence A. Gross; Deacon Gregory Emerton.
Res.: 37 Monroe St., 14472. Tel: 585-624-1443; Fax: 585-624-5169.
Catechesis/Religious Program—Students 86.

HONEOYE, ONTARIO CO., ST. MARY, OUR LADY OF THE HILLS (1868) [CEM] Rev. John H. Hayes; Deacon Roger Loomis.
Parish—8961 Main St., P.O. Box 725, 14471.
Res.: Rte. 20A, Box 725, 14471. Tel: 585-229-5007.
Catechesis/Religious Program—Students 44.

HORNELL, STEUBEN CO.
1—ST. ANN (1849) [CEM] [JC 2], See Our Lady of the Valley, Hornell.
See St. Ann, Hornell under Schools Outside Monroe County located in the Institution section.
2—ST. IGNATIUS LOYOLA (1931), See Our Lady of the Valley, Hornell.
3—OUR LADY OF THE VALLEY (2004), Merger of St. Ann's, Hornell; St. Joachim, Canisteo; St. Ignatius Loyola, Hornell; St. Mary's, Rexville. Rev. Peter Anglaaere; Deacon Robert W. McCormick.
Mailing Address: 27 Erie Ave., 14843. Tel: 607-324-5811; Fax: 607-324-0116. Email: ourladyofthevalley@dor.org. In Res., Revs. Robert Kanka (Retired); Paul Schnacky (Retired).
See St. Ann, Hornell under Schools Outside Monroe County located in the Institution section.

HORSEHEADS, CHEMUNG CO., ST. MARY OUR MOTHER (1866) [CEM] Rev. Christopher E. Linsler. In Res., Rev. Casimir Mahimbo (Tanzania).
Res.: 816 W. Broad St., 14845. Tel: 607-739-3817; Fax: 607-739-5628.
See St. Mary Our Mother (Horseheads), Horseheads under Schools Outside Monroe County located in the Institution section.
Catechesis/Religious Program—Tel: 607-739-8214. Students 351.

INTERLAKEN, SENECA CO., ST. FRANCIS SOLANUS (1875) Rev. Bartholomew Minson, O.F.M.Cap.
Mailing Address: *c/o Holy Cross Church*, P.O. Box 337, Ovid, 14521.
Office: P.O. Box 337, Ovid, 14521-0337. Tel: 607-869-2261; Fax: 607-869-9825.
St. Fidelis Friary: 7790 County Rd. 153, 14847. Tel: 607-532-4432; Fax: 607-532-9271.
Church: 3660 Orchard St., 14847. Tel: 607-869-2261; Fax: 607-869-9825.

ITHACA, TOMPKINS CO.
1—ST. CATHERINE OF SIENA (1960) Rev. Martin Kuusangnayir.
Res.: 302 St. Catherine Cir., 14850. Tel: 607-257-2493; Fax: 607-257-5901.
Catechesis/Religious Program—Students 73.
2—IMMACULATE CONCEPTION (1848) [CEM 2] Rev. Leo J. Reinhardt.
Res.: 113 N. Geneva St., 14850. Tel: 607-273-6121; Fax: 607-273-0185.
See Immaculate Conception, Ithaca under Schools Outside Monroe County located in the Institution section.
Catechesis/Religious Program—Tel: 607-273-0303. Students 47.

KING FERRY, CAYUGA CO., OUR LADY OF THE LAKE, KING FERRY (1868) Closed. For inquiries for parish records contact Good Shepherd Catholic Community, Aurora.

LANSING, ALL SAINTS (1913) Rev. Scott Kubinski; Deacon George Kozak.
Res.: 347 Ridge Rd., 14882. Tel: 607-533-7344.
Catechesis/Religious Program—Students 140.

LEICESTER, LIVINGSTON CO., ST. THOMAS AQUINAS (1897) Merged with Holy Angels, Nunda, St. Lucy, Retsof, St. Mary, Geneseo & St. Patrick, Mt. Morris to form St. Luke the Evangelist Roman Catholic Church Society of Livingston County, Geneseo.

LIMA, LIVINGSTON CO., ST. ROSE (1848) [CEM] Rev. Lawrence F. Gross; Deacon Gregory Emerton.
Mailing Address: P.O. Box 8A, 14485.
Res.: 7553 Corby Rd., Honeoye Falls, 14472.
Church: 1985 Lake Ave., 14485.
Catechesis/Religious Program—Tel: 585-624-1005; Fax: 585-582-2663. Students 33.

LIVONIA CENTER, LIVINGSTON CO., ST. MICHAEL (1848) Closed. For inquiries for parish records contact St. Mary's, Honeoye.

LIVONIA, LIVINGSTON CO.
1—ST. JOSEPH (1911) Closed. For inquiries for parish records contact St. Matthew Catholic Church Society, Livonia.
2—ST. MATTHEW CATHOLIC CHURCH SOCIETY, [CEM] Merged with St. William, Conesus and St. Joseph, Livonia. Rev. John H. Hayes.
Mailing Address: P.O. Box 77, 14487. Tel: 585-346-3815; Fax: 585-346-9445.
Catechesis/Religious Program—41 Spring St., 14487. Tel: 585-346-2500; Fax: 585-346-9440. Students 69.

LYONS, WAYNE CO., ST. MICHAEL (1852), (Italian), Clustered with St. John the Evangelist, Clyde and Mission St. Patrick, Savannah. Sr. Dianne Dennie, S.S.J., Pastoral Admin.; Rev. Joseph W. Marcoux, Sacramental Min.
Res.: 3 Holley St., 14489-1505. Tel: 315-946-4182; Fax: 315-946-4736.
Catechesis/Religious Program—Students 17.

MACEDON, WAYNE CO., ST. PATRICK (1883) [CEM] Rev. William F. Laird.
Res.: 52 Main St., 14502. Tel: 315-986-5671; Fax: 315-986-4398.
Catechesis/Religious Program—Tel: 315-986-2021. Students 170.

MARION, WAYNE CO., ST. GREGORY (1914), Clustered with St. Anne, Palmyra. Rev. William F. Laird.
Mailing Address: 136 Church St., Palmyra, 14522. Tel: 315-597-4571.
Church: 3806 Union St., 14505. Tel: 315-926-4323.
Catechesis/Religious Program—Students 34.

MENDON, MONROE CO., ST. CATHERINE OF SIENA (1902) Rev. Robert Scott Bourcy; Deacon Philip Yawman.
Res.: 26 Mendon-Ionia Rd., 14506. Tel: 585-624-4990; Fax: 585-624-4996.
Catechesis/Religious Program—Students 349.
Convent—15 Mendon-Ionia Rd., 14506. Tel: 716-624-1538.

MONTEZUMA, CAYUGA CO., ST. MICHAEL (1865) Closed. For inquiries for parish records contact Our Lady of the Snows, Weedsport.

MORAVIA, CAYUGA CO., ST. PATRICK (1872) Closed. For inquiries for parish records contact Good Shepherd Catholic Community, Aurora.

MOUNT MORRIS, LIVINGSTON CO., ST. PATRICK (1869) [CEM] Merged with Holy Angels, Nunda, St. Mary, Geneseo, St. Thomas Aquinas, Leicester & St. Mary, Retsof to form St. Luke the Evangelist Roman Catholic Church Society of Livingston County, Geneseo.

NAPLES, ONTARIO CO., OUR LADY OF THE LAKES CATHOLIC COMMUNITY, (St. Januarius & Our Lady of the Grapes Shrine, Naples and St. Patrick's, Prattsburg) Revs. Robert P. Ring; John Orenge Omboga; George Wiant, Sacramental Min. (Retired); Deacon Edward Sergeant.
Rectory & Mailing Address: 210 Keuka St., Penn Yan, 14527. Tel: 585-374-2414; Fax: 585-374-2415.
Church: 180 N. Main St., 14512.
Catechesis/Religious Program—Students 31.

NEWARK VALLEY, TIOGA CO., ST. JOHN THE EVANGELIST (1880) Merged with St. Francis of Assisi, Catatonk; St. Margaret Mary, Apalachin; St. Pius the Tenth, Van Etten and St. James, Waverly to form Blessed Trinity, Owego.

NEWARK, WAYNE CO., ST. MICHAEL (1863) Rev. Felix Dalimpuo.
Res.: 401 Main St., 14513. Tel: 315-331-6753; Fax: 315-331-2925.
See St. Michael (Newark), Newark under Schools Outside Monroe County located in the Institution section.
Catechesis/Religious Program—Tel: 315-331-3408. Students 205.

NORTH CHILI, MONROE CO., ST. CHRISTOPHER (1968) Rev. Robert Gaudio; Deacon John Cunningham.
Res.: 3350 Union St., P.O. Box 399, 14514. Tel: 585-594-1400.
Catechesis/Religious Program—Tel: 585-594-1441. Students 190.

NUNDA, LIVINGSTON CO., HOLY ANGELS (1854) Merged with St. Patrick, Mt. Morris, St. Mary, Geneseo, St. Thomas Aquinas, Leicester & St. Lucy, Retsof to form St. Luke the Evangelist Roman Catholic Church Society of Livingston County, Geneseo.

ODESSA, SCHUYLER CO., ST. BENEDICT (1965) Rev. Paul Bonacci, Admin.; Deacons Daniel Pavlina; Rick Roy.
Mailing Address: c/o St. Mary's of the Lake, P.O. Box 289, Watkins Glen, 14891.
Res.: 1101 1/2 Tenth St., Watkins Glen, 14891. Tel: 607-535-2786; Fax: 607-535-2990.
Church: Speedway, 14869. Tel: 607-594-2226.
Catechesis/Religious Program—Students 2.

ONTARIO, WAYNE CO.
1—ST. MARY OF THE LAKE (1869) [CEM] Merged with Epiphany, Sodus to form St. Maximilian Kolbe, Ontario.
2—ST. MAXIMILIAN KOLBE Rev. Symon Peter Ntaiyia; Deacon James B. Nail.
Res.: 5823 Walworth Rd., P.O. Box 499, 14519. Tel: 315-524-2611; Fax: 607-524-8353.
Catechesis/Religious Program—5823 Walworth Rd., 14519. Tel: 315-524-7421. Students 76.

OVID, SENECA CO., HOLY CROSS (1849) [CEM] Rev. Bartholomew Minson, O.F.M.Cap.
7231 Main St., P.O. Box 337, 14521-0337.
St. Fidelis Friary: 7790 County Rd. 153, Interlaken, 14847. Tel: 607-869-2261; Fax: 607-869-9825.
Catechesis/Religious Program—Students 25.

OWEGO, TIOGA CO.
1—BLESSED TRINITY (2003) Revs. William A. Moorby; John Yaw Afoakwah; Thomas H. Watts, Pastor Emeritus (Retired); Deacon Michael Donovan.
Mailing Address: *Blessed Trinity and St. Patrick Parishes*, 300 Main St., 13827. Tel: 607-687-1068; 607-625-3192 (Rectory); Fax: 607-687-8122. Email: blessedtrinity@dor.org.
Res.: 1110 Pennsylvania Ave., Apalachin, 13732.
2—ST. PATRICK (1842) [CEM] Revs. William A. Moorby; Thomas H. Watts, Pastor Emeritus (Retired); John Yaw Afoakwah; Deacon Michael Donovan.
Mailing Address: 300 Main St., 13827. Tel: 607-687-1068; Fax: 607-687-8122.
Res.: 1110 Pennsylvania Ave., Apalachin, 13732. Tel: 607-625-3192.
Catechesis/Religious Program—Students 188.

PAINTED POST, STEUBEN CO., IMMACULATE HEART OF MARY (1952) Closed. For inquiries for parish records contact All Saints, Corning.

PALMYRA, WAYNE CO., ST. ANNE (1850) [CEM] Rev. William F. Laird.
Res.: 136 Church St., 14522. Tel: 315-597-5252; Fax: 315-597-4571.
Catechesis/Religious Program—Tel: 315-926-4323; Fax: 315-597-5252. Elaine Doyle, D.R.E. Students 30.

PENFIELD, MONROE CO.
1—HOLY SPIRIT (1965) Revs. P. Frederick Helfrich; Gerard J. McMahon (Retired); Deacon Brian Mahoney.
Parish Address—1355 Hatch Rd., Webster, 14580. Tel: 585-671-5520; Fax: 585-671-7262.
Catechesis/Religious Program—Tel: 585-671-5680. Students 93.
2—ST. JOSEPH (1860) [CEM] Revs. James A. Schwartz; James E. Boyle (Retired); Deacons Don Germano; Duncan Harris. In Res., Revs. Robert G. Kreckel (Retired); William Amann (Retired).
Parish—43 Gebhardt Rd., 14526.
Res.: 35 Gebhardt Rd., 14526. Tel: 585-586-8089; Fax: 585-586-0674.
See St. Joseph School, Penfield under Monroe County School System located in the Institution section.
Catechesis/Religious Program—Patrick B. Fox, D.R.E. Students 623.

PENN YAN, YATES CO., ST. MICHAEL (1850) [CEM 2] Revs. Bob Ring; John Orenge Omboga, Parochial Vicar; Deacon Claude Curtin.
Mailing Address: 210 Keuka St., 14527.
Res.: 312 Liberty St., 14527. Tel: 315-536-7459; Fax: 315-536-3817.
See St. Michael (Penn Yan), Penn Yan under Schools Outside Monroe County located in the Institution section.
Catechesis/Religious Program—210 Keuka St., 14527. Tel: 315-536-3794. Mary Tyrrell, D.R.E. Students 40.
Mission—St. Andrew (1877) Union St., Dundee, Yates Co. 14837.

PERKINSVILLE, STEUBEN CO., SACRED HEART OF JESUS, Consolidated with St. Joseph's, Wayland; St. Mary's, Dansville; and St. Pius V, Cohocton to form Holy Catholic Community, Cohocton.

PHELPS, ONTARIO CO., ST. FRANCIS (1869) Merged with St. Felix, Clifton Springs to form St. Felix/St. Francis Parish Cluster, Clifton Springs.

PITTSFORD, MONROE CO.
1—CHURCH OF THE TRANSFIGURATION (1983) Rev. Michael Bausch; Deacons Michael Piehler; Anthony Sciolino.
50 W. Bloomfield Rd., 14534. Tel: 585-248-2427; Fax: 585-385-9870.
Catechesis/Religious Program—Tel: 585-248-2467; Fax: 585-248-3922. Students 594.

2—ST. LOUIS (1911) Rev. Kevin P. Murphy; Deacon John Payne.
64 S. Main St., 14534. In Res., Rev. Msgr. Gerard C. Krieg (Retired), (Senior Priest); Revs. Raymond Booth (Retired), (Senior Priest); Albert L. Delmonte (Retired).
Res.: 60 S. Main St., 14534. Tel: 585-586-5675; Fax: 585-387-9888.
See St. Louis School, Pittsford under Monroe County School System located in the Institution section.
Saint's Place—46 S. Main St., 14534. Tel: 585-385-6860. Email: saintlady@stlouischurch.org. Web: www.saintsplace.org. Colleen Knauf, Dir.
Catechesis/Religious Program—64 S. Main St., 14534. Tel: 585-381-4455; Fax: 585-387-9888. Students 437.

RED CREEK, WAYNE CO., ST. THOMAS THE APOSTLE (1882) [CEM] Merged with St. Mary Magdalen, Wolcott & St. Jude Chapel, Fair Haven to form Catholic Community of the Blessed Trinity. For inquiries for parish records contact Blessed Trinity, Wolcott.

REXVILLE, STEUBEN CO., ST. MARY (1845), (Irish), [CEM 4], See Our Lady of the Valley, Hornell.

RUSH, MONROE CO., ST. JOSEPH (1863) Rev. James E. Hewes, Parochial Admin.
Res.: 1209 Rush West Rush Rd., 14543-0320. Tel: 585-533-1719.
Catechesis/Religious Program—Fax: 585-533-1790. Students 218.

SCIPIO CENTER, CAYUGA CO., ST. BERNARD (1867) Closed. For inquiries for parish records contact Good Shepherd Catholic Community, Aurora.

SCOTTSVILLE, MONROE CO., ST. MARY OF THE ASSUMPTION (1853) [CEM] Rev. William Endres; Irene Goodwin, Pastoral Admin.
Res.: 99 Main St., P.O. Box 23, 14546. Tel: 585-889-3100; Fax: 585-889-7806.
Catechesis/Religious Program—Tel: 585-889-8440; Fax: 585-889-7806. Students 91.

SENECA FALLS, SENECA CO., ST. PATRICK (1831) [CEM] Rev. James Fennessy; Deacon Robert Cyrana.
Mailing Address: 25 Center St., Waterloo, 13165.
Res.: 97 W. Bayard St., 13148. Tel: 315-568-5203; Fax: 315-568-6609.
Catechesis/Religious Program—81 W. Bayard St., 13148. Tel: 315-568-2573. Students 156.

SHORTSVILLE, ONTARIO CO., ST. DOMINIC (1885) [CEM] Rev. Donald J. Curtiss.
Mailing Address: 12 Hibbard Ave., Clifton Springs, 14432. Tel: 315-462-2961; Fax: 315-462-3608.
Church: 6 Canandaigua St., 14548.
Catechesis/Religious Program—Students 42.

SODUS, WAYNE CO., EPIPHANY (1922) Merged with St. Mary of the Lake, Ontario to form St. Maximilian Kolbe, Ontario.

SPENCERPORT, MONROE CO., ST. JOHN THE EVANGELIST (1867) [CEM] Rev. Lance M. Gonyo; Deacon Thomas Driscoll. In Res., Revs. Pius S. Wekesa; Daniel F. Holland (Retired).
Parish—55 Martha St., 14559.
Res.: 60 Martha St., 14559. Tel: 585-352-5481; Fax: 585-352-3759.
Catechesis/Religious Program—Tel: 585-352-0225; 585-352-7468 (Youth Min.); Fax: 585-352-3759. Shirley Curatolo, D.R.E. Students 211.

STANLEY, ONTARIO CO., ST. THERESA (1875) [CEM] Revs. Bob Ring; John Orenge Omboga; Deacon John Erb.
Mailing Address: c/o St. Michael's, 210 Keuka St., Penn Yan, 14527. Tel: 585-526-5566; Fax: 585-526-5566. Main St., 14561.
Res.: 312 Liberty St., Penn Yan, 14527. Tel: 315-536-7459; Fax: 315-536-6964.
Catechesis/Religious Program—Students 31.
Mission—St. Mary (1869) Gilbert St., Rushville, Ontario Co. 14561.

TRUMANSBURG, TOMPKINS CO., ST. JAMES THE APOSTLE (1857) [CEM] Rev. John Tokaz, O.F.M.Cap.
Res.: 17 Whig St., P.O. Box 709, 14886. Tel: 607-387-6781; Fax: 607-387-3763.
Catechesis/Religious Program—Students 44.

UNION SPRINGS, CAYUGA CO., ST. MICHAEL'S (1851) Closed. For inquiries for parish records contact Good Shepherd Catholic Community, Aurora.

VAN ETTEN, CHEMUNG CO., ST. PIUS THE TENTH (1954) Merged with St. Francis, Catatonk; St. Margaret Mary, Apalachin; St. John the Evangelist, Newark Valley; and St. James, Waverly to form Blessed Trinity, Owego., Mailing Address: *Blessed Trinity*, 300 Main St., Owego, 13827.

VICTOR, ONTARIO CO., ST. PATRICK (1856), (Irish), [CEM] Rev. Timothy L. Niven; Deacon Peter Niche.
Res.: 115 Maple Ave., 14564. Tel: 585-924-7111; Fax: 585-742-3296.
Catechesis/Religious Program—115 Maple Ave., 14564. Tel: 585-924-2800. Students 438.

WATERLOO, SENECA CO., ST. MARY (1868) [CEM] Rev. James Fennessy.
25 Center St., 13165.
Res.: 35 Center St., 13165. Tel: 315-539-2944; Fax: 315-539-8841.
Catechesis/Religious Program—Tel: 315-539-8146. Lena Shipley, D.R.E. Students 163.

WATKINS GLEN, SCHUYLER CO., ST. MARY OF THE LAKE (1846), (Irish—Italian), [CEM 2] Rev. Paul Bonacci, Admin.; Deacons Daniel Pavlina; George (Rick) Roy.
Parish—905 N. Decatur St., P.O. Box 289, 14891.
Res.: 110 1/2 Tenth St., 14891. Tel: 607-535-2786; Fax: 607-535-2990.
Parish Center—10th St., 14891.
Catechesis/Religious Program—Tel: 607-535-2786, Ext. 12.

WAVERLY, TIOGA CO., ST. JAMES (1881) [CEM] Merged with St. Francis of Assisi, Catatonk; St. Margaret Mary, Apalachin; St. John the Evangelist, Newark Valley and St. Pius the Tenth, Van Etten to form Blessed Trinity, Owego.

WAYLAND, STEUBEN CO.
1—HOLY FAMILY CATHOLIC COMMUNITY Revs. Stephen Karani; Michael Twardzik; Deacons Dan Slattery; Thomas Driscoll.
Mailing Address: 206 Fremont St., 14572-1298. Tel: 585-728-2228; Fax: 585-728-2232.
Rectory—St. Mary's, 40 Elizabeth St., Dansville, 14437. Tel: 585-335-2700.
Catechesis/Religious Program—Students 150.
2—ST. JOSEPH'S (1881), (German), Consolidated with St. Pius V, Cohocton; St. Mary's, Dansville; and Sacred Heart of Jesus, Perkinsville to form Holy Family Catholic Community, Cohocton.

WEBSTER, MONROE CO.
1—HOLY TRINITY (1861) [CEM] Rev. William C. Michatek; Deacon Raymond Mielcarek.
Res.: 1460 Ridge Rd., 14580. Tel: 585-265-0391; Fax: 585-265-1627.
Catechesis/Religious Program—Tel: 585-265-4750. Students 315.
2—ST. PAUL (1967) Rev. Stanley Kacprzak; Deacon Mark Robbins.
Res.: 783 Hard Rd., 14580. Tel: 585-671-2112; Fax: 585-787-8907.
Catechesis/Religious Program—Tel: 585-671-2110. Linda Pepe, D.R.E. Students 285.
3—ST. RITA (1950) Revs. Charles J. Latus; Hoan Dinh, Parochial Vicar; Deacon John McDermott.
Res.: 1008 Maple Dr., 14580. Tel: 585-671-1100; Fax: 585-671-5446.
See St. Rita School, Webster under Monroe County School System located in the Institution section.
Catechesis/Religious Program—Tel: 585-671-2079. Students 450.

WEEDSPORT, CAYUGA CO.
1—ST. JOHN (1865) Merged with St. Joseph, Weedsport and St. Patrick, Cato to form Our Lady of the Snow, Weedsport.
2—ST. JOSEPH (1854) [CEM] Merged with St. John, Port Byron and St. Patrick, Cato to form Our Lady of the Snow, Weedsport.
3—OUR LADY OF THE SNOW (2005) Rev. John Gathenya, Parochial Admin.
Mailing Address: 2667 Hamilton St., 13166. Tel: 315-834-6266; Fax: 315-834-6278. Email: wstjosep@dor.org.

WOLCOTT, WAYNE CO.
1—CATHOLIC COMMUNITY OF THE BLESSED TRINITY OF WOLCOTT, NY (2006) Rev. Joseph P. McCaffrey.
11956 Washington St., 14590-1133. Tel: 315-594-9430; Fax: 315-594-9430. 2006 consolidation of St. Thomas the Apostle, Red Creek; St. Mary Magdalene, Wolcott and St. Jude Chapel, Fair Haven.
2—ST. MARY MAGDALENE (1940) Merged with St. Thomas the Apostle, Red Creek & St. Jude Chapel, Fair Haven to form Catholic Community of the Blessed Trinity of Wolcott, NY.

Chaplains of Public Institutions

ITHACA. *Cornell University*, G-22 Anabel Taylor Hall, 14853. Rev. Daniel T. McMullin, Dir.

Health Care Facilities

ROCHESTER. *St. Ann's Home/Heritage*. Rev. Peter T. Bayer, Dir. Spiritual Care.
1500 Portland Ave., 14621. Tel: 585-697-6446. Sheila Kinsky, Pastoral Care Coord. Tel: 585-697-6447, Sr. Livia Ruocco, Pastoral Care Coord. Tel: 585-697-6448.
Highland Hospital. Rev. Dennis Bonsignore, Chap.
1000 South Ave., 14620. Tel: 585-341-6890.
Monroe Community Hospital. Rev. Dennis Bonsignore, Sr. Mary Doran, S.S.J., Co-Chap.
435 E. Henrietta Rd., 14620. Tel: 585-760-6164.
Park Ridge Hospital/Unity Health System, 1555 Long Pond Rd., 14626. Tel: 585-723-7969. Jeanne Marie Jongen, Chap. Tel: 585-723-7969, Carl Coloney, Chap. Tel: 585-723-7318, Megan Hoose, Chap. Tel: 585-723-7967.
Rochester General Hospital/Via Health. Sr. Margaret Kunder, S.S.J., Chap.
1425 Portland Ave., 14621. Tel: 585-922-5121.
Strong Health System. Revs. William Endres, Dennis Bonsignore.
601 Elmwood Ave., 14642. Tel: 585-275-2187.
Unity Health System, St. Mary's Genesee St. Campus, 14651. Rev. Walter J. Plominski, Sacramental Min., Suzanne Shady, Chap. Tel: 585-368-3268.
89 Genesee St., 14611. Tel: 585-328-3268.

AUBURN. *Mercy Health and Rehabilitation Center*. Stephen Ash, Admin. Cayuga Co.
3 St. Anthony St., 13021. Tel: 315-253-0351; Fax: 315-258-3904. Rev. Felicjan Sierotowicz, Chap.

BATH. *Soldiers' Home and Veterans' Hospital*, Tel: 607-664-4402, Ext. 1382.

CANANDAIGUA. *Veteran's Hospital*, Tel: 585-394-2000, Ext. 3052. Revs. Martin D. Smith-Sourcier, Chap., William Cosgrove (Retired).

HORNELL. *St. James Mercy Hospital*. Ms. Astuti Bijlefeld, Chap., Deacon Robert W. McCormick. Steuben Co.
411 Canisteo St., 14843. Tel: 607-324-8153.

State Facilities

ROCHESTER. *Finger Lakes DDSO - Rochester Site*, 620 Westfall Rd., 14620. Tel: 585-461-8676. Deacon Edward Sergeant.
Rochester Psychiatric Center, 1111 Elmwood Ave., 14620. Tel: 585-473-3230. Deacon Brian McNulty, Chap.

AUBURN. *Auburn Correctional Facility*, 135 State St., P.O. Box 618, 13021. Tel: 315-253-8401, Ext. 4321. Rev. Michael R. Brown, Chap., Deacon John Tomandl.

ELMIRA. *Elmira Correctional Facility, Center and Camp Monterey*, P.O. Box 500, 14902. Tel: 607-734-3901. Rev. Richard T. Farrell, Deacon Michael R. McGuire.
Elmira Psychiatric Center, 100 Washington St., 14901. Tel: 607-737-4991. Deacon Michael Mangione, Chap.

GENESEO. *Finger Lakes DDSO - Geneseo Site*, 3 Park St., 14454-1217. Tel: 585-243-6405. Deacon Edward Sergeant.

INDUSTRY. *State Agricultural & Industrial School, Div. of Youth* 14474. Tel: 585-533-2600. Deacon Owen Bowers.

MORAVIA. *Cayuga Correctional*, P.O. Box 1150, 13118. Tel: 315-497-1110, Ext. 4000. Rev. Felicjan Sierotowicz, Sacramental Min., Maureen Collins.

NEWARK. *Finger Lakes DDSO - Newark Site*, 703 E. Maple Ave., 14513. Tel: 315-331-1700. Deacon Edward Sergeant.

PINE CITY. *Southport Correctional Facility*, P.O. Box 2000, 14871-2000. Tel: 607-737-0850. Rev. Richard T. Farrell, Chap., Mrs. Theresa Stanley, Chap.

RED CREEK. *Butler Correctional Facility*, P.O. Box 388, 13143. Tel: 315-754-8001. Rev. Felicjan Sierotowicz, Chap.

ROMULUS. *Five Points Correctional Facility*, State Rte. 96, 14541. Tel: 607-869-5111. Rev. P. Paul Brennan, Deacon Gregory Kiley, Chap.

SONYEA. *Livingston Correctional Facility and Seneca Correctional Facility*, Rt. 36, P.O. Box 49, 14556. Tel: 585-658-3710. Rev. Michael R. Brown, Deacons Nemesio Martinez Vellon, Paul Clement.

SONYEA. *Groveland Correctional Facility*, 7000 Sonyea Rd., P.O. Box 50, 14556. Tel: 585-658-2871, Ext. 4807. Rev. Michael R. Brown, Deacon Paul Clement.

WILLARD. *Drug Treatment Center*, 7116 County Rd. 132, P.O. Box 303, 14588-0303. Tel: 607-869-5500, Ext. 4800. Rev. P. Paul Brennan.

County Jail Chaplains

ROCHESTER. *Livingston County Jail*.
4 Court St., Geneseo, 14454. Tel: 585-243-1100.
Monroe County Jail. Rev. Robert Thomas Werth, Sr. Judith Greene, S.S.J., Chap., Deacon Salvador Otero.
Tompkins County Jail. Vacant.
Yates County Jail. Vacant.

On Duty Outside the Diocese:
Revs.—
Bartollotta, Victor W., Jr., 6231 St. Moritz Ave., Dallas, TX 75214.
Curran, Charles E., 4125 Woodcreek Dr., Dallas, TX 75220.
Fleming, Terence K. (SP), Roper/St. Francis Healthcare, 125 Doughty St., Ste. 760, Charleston, SC 29403.
Valenti, Thomas J., Church of St. John the Baptist, 670 Yonkers Ave., Yonkers, 10704.
Van Durme, Patrick, S.T.L., 10100 Lee Rd., Ft. Jackson, SC 29207.

Military Chaplains:
Revs.—
Van Durme, Patrick, S.T.L., Chap., USACHCS, CH-BOLC 08-002, 10100 Lee Rd., Ft. Jackson, SC 29207. U.S. Army

Zygadlo, Mitchell, Chap. Capt., United States Air Force, PSC 9 Box 2912, Apo, AE 09123.

Unassigned:
Rev.—
Celso, B. Thomas, 163 Patterson St., Newark, 14513.

Absent on Leave:
Revs.—
Chase, Lee P., S.T.L.
DeBellis, Peter
Della Pietra, Douglas
Manning, Charles T.
Walczak, Melvin

Retired:
Rev. Msgrs.—
Krieg, Gerard C., J.C.L., St. Louis Rectory, 64 S. Main St., Pittsford, 14534.
Shannon, William H., Sisters of St. Joseph, 150 French Rd., 14618.
Revs.—
Amann, William, St. Joseph Rectory, 43 Gebhardt Rd., Penfield, 14526.
Ammering, Bruce F., Sisters of St. Joseph, 150 French Rd., 14618.
Appelby, Gerald J., 130 Southland Dr., 14623.
Barrett, William, 15 Washington St., Mayville, 14757.
Billotte, Philip J., 777 Germania Rd., P.O. Box 135, Frenchville, PA 16836.
Booth, Raymond, 60 S. Main St., Pittsford, 14534.
Boyle, James E., St. Joseph Rectory, 43 Gebhardt Rd., Penfield, 14526.
Bradler, Robert C., 269 Garford Rd., 14622.
Brennan, Paul P., 345 Waters Edge, Auburn, 13021.
Burke, James C., 2123 S.E. 5th Ter., Cape Coral, FL 33990.
Bush, Frederick, St. Mark's Rectory, 54 Kuhn Rd., 14612.
Calimeri, Anthony F., P.O. Box 24, Phelps, 14532.
Connor, Gerald T., McAuley Residence, 1437 Blossom Rd., 14610.
Cosgrove, William, 295 Chestnut Ridge Rd., 14624.
Cushing, Walter F., St. Cecilia's Rectory, 2732 Culver Rd., 14622.
Deckman, Peter
Delmonte, Albert L., St. Louis Rectory, 60 S. Main St., Pittsford, 14534.
Dillon, Edward J., St. Luke the Evangelist, 13 North St., Geneseo, 14454.
Dillon, John D.
Dollen, Bernard, 4477 Buffalo Rd., North Chili, 14514.
Donovan, Robert, McAuley Residence, 1437 Blossom Rd., 14610. Tel: 716-342-8686
Doyle, James, Chapel Oaks #1110, 1550 Portland Ave., 14621.
Eisemann, Frederick F., 151 Sheppler St., 14612.
Erb, Francis J., P.O. Box 96, Painted Post, 14870.
Erdle, Thomas M., St. Margaret Mary Rectory, 401 Rogers Pkwy., 14617.
Falcone, Sebastian, McAuley Residence, 1437 Blossom Rd., 14610.
Fratts, Ralph J., 113 Genesee St., New Hartford, 13413.
Freemesser, Paul J., St. Theodore Rectory, 168 Spencerport Rd., 14606.
Gaesser, Ronald E., Holy Family Rectory, 85 North St., Auburn, 13021.
Glogowski, John J., 11899 Lake Rd., P.O. Box 418, Lyndonville, 14098.
Golden, Edward, 965 Cherry Ridge Blvd., Webster, 14580.
Gordinier, William J., Sisters of St. Joseph, 150 French Rd., 14610.
Graf, William, 681 High St., Victor, 14564.
Hafner, Gerard, 10452 Clairmont Cir. E., Tamarac, FL 33321-7840.
Hoctor, Thomas D., 3110 Brierfield Rd., Alpharetta, GA 30004.
Hogan, Michael C., St. John of Rochester Rectory, 8 Wickford Way, Fairport, 14450. Tel: 716-248-5993
Holland, Daniel F., St. John the Evangelist Rectory, 55 Martha St., Spencerport, 14559.
Kanka, Robert, St. Ann's Rectory, 343 Canisteo St., Hornell, 14843. Tel: 607-324-0410
Kellner, Winfried, Our Mother of Sorrows Rectory, 5000 Mt. Read Blvd., 14612.
Kiggins, Roy, St. Patrick Rectory, 97 W. Bayard St., Seneca Falls, 13148.
Kreckel, Robert G., St. Joseph's Rectory, 35 Gebhardt Rd., 14626.
Lawlor, James F., St. Thomas More Rectory, 2617 East Ave., 14610.
Lynch, John A., St. Anne Rectory, 1600 Mt. Hope Ave., 14620.
MacNamara, Robert C., St. Mary Rectory, 224 Franklin St., Elmira, 14904.
Mans, Leo J., 30 A. Fulton Dr., New Oxford, PA 17350.
McDonald, Elmer J., 6145 Sun Blvd., #505B, St. Petersburg, FL 33715.
McMahon, Gerald J., 1355 Hatch Rd., Webster, 14580.
Meng, Robert A., 7 Harwood Ln., East Rochester, 14445.
Metzger, Edwin, Mother of Sorrows Rectory, 5000 Mt. Read Blvd., 14612.
Mockevicius, Dominic F., 1156 Plank Rd., Webster, 14580.
Morgan, John A., St. Mary Magdalen Rectory, 2532 Ventura Blvd., Camarillo, CA 93010.
Mulligan, John M., V.G., The Cathedral Community, 296 Flower City Park, 14615.
Murphy, David M., 45 Smith Ave., Newton, MA 02165.
Murphy, Richard M., Chiropractic College, Box 800, Seneca Falls, 13148-0800.
O'Connell, Richard C., McAuley Residence, 1437 Blossom Rd., 14610.
O'Connor, John L., 3351 James Rd., Keuka Park, 14478.
Phillips, John, 8 Wickford Way, Fairport, 14450.
Reif, John, Holy Cross Rectory, 4492 Lake Ave., 14612.
Rosse, John, 401 Rogers Pkwy., 14616.
Sasso, Joseph M., 8112 Oatka Tr., LeRoy, 14482.
Schifferli, Jerome F., 45 Washington St., Apt. 2, Box 311, Livonia, 14487.
Schnacky, Paul, St. Ann's Rectory, 343 Canisteo St., Hornell, 14843.
Smith, Robert, 9306 Blind Sodus Bay Rd., Red Creek, 13143.
Statt, Thomas R., P.O. Box 752, Honeoye, 14471.
Sundholm, Conrad, 3465 Treetop Cir., Spring Hill, FL 34606.
Tormey, Daniel, 48 Holiday Harbour, Canandaigua, 14424.
Ventura, Gennaro J., 8247 Dutch Hollow Rd., Wayland, 14572.
Vogt, Otto J., Sisters of St. Joseph Motherhouse, 150 French Rd., 14618.
Wainwright, Walter L., 1502 Maple Ave., Elmira, 14904.
Walsh, John T., M.Div., 18 Viennawood Dr., 14618.
Watts, Thomas H., 126 Washington St., Sayre, PA 18840.
Weis, Eugene R., 1759 W. Schwartz Blvd., Lady Lake, FL 32159-6126.
Wiant, George, 5782 County Rd. 33, Canandaigua, 14424.
Zenkel, Edward B., 4218 East Lake Rd., Livonia, 14487.

Permanent Deacons:
Abballe, Dominic, (Retired)
Almeter, Robert C., Diocese of Syracuse; (Leave of Absence)
Aman, Leo, (Retired)
Antenucci, John, Outside of Diocese; (Leave of Absence)
Arnold, Kenneth, Irondequoit Senior Ministries
Asis, Emmanuel, Guardian Angels, Henrietta
Baker, William, (Leave of Absence)
Beck, Thomas, Christ the King, St. Salome & St. Thomas the Apostle, Rochester
Behe, Thomas, R.I.T. Catholic Community
Berrios, Jose, Parish Support Ministries & Our Lady of the Angels, Rochester
Birx, Charles, Diocese of Richmond
Bowers, Owen F., (Retired)
Brasley, John, Parish Support Ministries & Our Lady of the Angels, Rochester
Burke, Robert, St. Monica, Rochester
Cadregari, David, Holy Ghost, Gates
Carges, Kevin, St. Patrick, Macedon; St. Anne, Palmyra; St. Gregory, Marion
Carra, James, St. Joseph, Rush
Carroll, Stephen, Church of the Assumption, Fairport
Caruso, Anthony, Good Shepherd, Henrietta
Casey, Lawrence B., Diocese of Atlanta
Cass, K. Thomas, Archdiocese of NY
Chatterton, James, St. Lawrence, Rochester
Cleary, Thomas J., (Retired)
Clement, Paul F., Groveland Correctional Facility, Sonyea; St. Luke the Evangelist, Geneseo
Coccia, Angelo, St. Theodore & St. Francis House, Rochester
Coffey, William, Ministry to Deacons
Colomaio, Robert, St. Gabriel, Hammondsport; Catholic Charities of Steuben County
Condon, Dean, All Saints, Corning
Corsaro, Robert, Church of the Assumption, Fairport
Crego, John, City West Parishes, Rochester
Cunningham, John, St. Christopher, North Chili
Curtin, Claude, Our Lady of the Lakes, Penn Yan
Cyrana, Robert, St. Patrick's Church Seneca Falls, NY
Dardess, George, Parish Support Ministry
Datz, Ramon, (Retired)
Defendorf, Ray, St. Mary's Church Bath, NY
Dejesus, Benny, Parish Support Ministries; Our Lady of the Americas
DiLallo, Gary R., Blessed Trinity & St. Patrick, Owego
Donahue, Dennis, Good Shepherd Catholic Community, Aurora
Donovan, Michael, Blessed Trinity/St. Patrick, Owego; Lourdes Hospice, Tioga Co.
Dougherty, William P., (Retired)
Douglas, Stanley, (Retired)
Doyle, Gregory J., (Retired)
Driscoll, Thomas, Holy Family Catholic Community, Wayland
Ecker, Thomas R., Bethany House, Rochester; St. Jerome's, East Rochester
Edwards, Eugene L., Jr., (Retired)
Emerton, Gregory, St. Paul of the Cross, Honeoye Falls; St. Rose, Lima
Erb, John, Our Lady of the Lakes Catholic Community, Penn Yan
Feasel, Laurence, St. Salome's; St. Thomas the Apostle & Christ the King, Irondequoit; Rochester Gen. Hospital
Federowicz, Joseph F., (Retired)
Fisher, Christopher, St. Elizabeth Ann Seton, Hamlin
Fitch, James E., (Retired)
Germano, Donald, St. Joseph, Penfield
Giblin, Edward, Holy Cross Church, Rochester
Giugno, John M., The Cathedral Community, Rochester
Graff, Stephen, Diocese of Syracuse
Graybill, Patrick A., Emmanuel Church of the Deaf
Haber, Francis, (Retired)
Hankey, James D., All Saints Parish, Corning
Harris, Duncan, St. Joseph, Penfield
Henry, Murray, (Leave of Absence)
Hoerner, Gerard A., (Outside the Diocese)
Holmes, John, Jr., Diocese of St. Augustine
Hudzinski, David, St. Anne/Our Lady of Lourdes, Rochester
Hurley, Daniel R., Our Lady of the Angels, Rochester
Jewell, Thomas, St. John Fisher College, Rochester
Johnson, H. Wilson, St. Thomas More & Our Lady Queen of Peace, Brighton
Kershner, Lynn W., The Cathedral Community, Rochester
Kester, Leo A., (Retired)
Kiley, Gregory, St. John the Evangelist, Clyde; Five Points Correctional Facility, Romulus
Kinsky, Daniel M., St. John of Rochester, Fairport
Kluchko, Thomas J., Our Mother of Sorrows, Greece (Rochester)
Kohlmeier, Charles P., (On Leave of Absence)
Kohlmeier, Edward, Blessed Trinity Community, Fairhaven/Wolcott/Red Creek
Kozak, George, Holy Cross, Freeville; St. Anthony, Groton; All Saints, Lansing
LaFortune, David, Schuyler Community, Watkins Glen
Lawson, Gregg K., St. Alphonsus, Auburn
Lebron, Juan, (Outside the Diocese)
Lenhart, William, St. Leo, Hilton
Lester, Claude E., St. Mary's, Canandaigua
Lohouse, Dennis, St. Pius X, Chili
Lombard, Richard J., Our Lady of Mercy Church, Greece
Loomis, Roger, St. Mary's, Honeoye
Mahany, Richard E., (Retired)
Mahoney, Brian, Holy Spirit, Webster
Mahoney, I. Michael, (Diocese of Raleigh)
Malave, Jorge, Parish Support Ministries; Our Lady of the Angels, Rochester
Mangione, Michael, Elmira Psychiatric Hospital
Mathis, Edward, St. Agnes, Avon
Maune, William D., (Retired), Diocese of Chicago
McCormick, Robert W., St. James Mercy Hospital, Hornell; Our Lady of the Valley, Hornell
McDermott, John, St. Rita's, Webster
McGuire, Michael R., Elmira Correctional Facility
McNulty, Brian J., Rochester Psychiatric Center
Mercadel, Anthony J., (Retired)
Mercado, Conrado, (Outside the Diocese)
Meyer, Robert, Light of Christ, Rochester
Mielcarek, Raymond, Holy Trinity, Webster
Morin, Kenneth, (Outside the Diocese)
Nail, James B., Catholic Community of Western Wayne County; St. Maximilian, Kolbe, Ontario
Nelson, John, Diocese of Rockford
Niche, Peter, St. Patrick's Victor
Otera, Salvador, Holy Apostles Church; Parish Support Ministries;
Pacete, Alberto, Elmira Correctional Facility; Christ the Redeemer, Elmira
Palma, David, Dir. Deacon Personnel & Deacon

Formation, Pastoral Center
Paluskiewicz, David L., St. Columba/St. Patrick, Caledonia/Mumford
Pavlina, Daniel, Catholic Community of Schuyler County
Payne, John F. X., St. Louis, Pittsford
Pettrone, Frank, St. Mark, Rochester
Piehler, Michael J., Transfiguration, Pittsford
Placious, Joseph, Holy Name of Jesus, Rochester
Robbins, Mark, St. Paul, Webster
Rodriguez, Agenol, Diocese of Orlando
Roy, George, Schuyler Catholic Community
Rutan, Warren, (Retired)
Scarciotta, Kenneth A., (Retired)
Schmitz, William F., (Retired)
Schrader, Robert, (Retired)
Schrage, Thomas, (On Leave of Absence)
Schuler, Richard, Tribunal-Pastoral Center
Sciolino, Anthony, Transfiguration, Pittsford
Sergeant, Edward R., Our Lady of the Lakes Catholic Community, Penn Yan
Shanley, Patrick M., St. Jude Church, Rochester
Skerrett, Jerry, Migrant Ministries, Parish Support Ministries
Slattery, Daniel P., Holy Family Catholic Comm., Southern Livingston & Northern Steuben
Smith, Edward A., St. Felix, Clifton Springs; St. Francis, Phelps; St. Dominic, Shortsville
Spezzano, George, St. Luke the Evangelist, Geneseo
Squilla, David, St. John the Evangelist, Spencerport
Steiger, James P., Tribunal-Pastoral Center
Stowell, Robert, Our Lady of the Lakes, Penn Yan
Stratton, W. Craig, Catholic Newman Community, U. of R.; Catholic Chaplaincy U. of R. Medical Center
Sullivan, Timothy, Extern - Catholic Charities of Wayne Co.
Tocci, Ronald J., Rochester General Hospital, Rochester
Tomandl, John D., Auburn Correctional
Toot, Walter, St. Cecilia, Irondequoit
Valvo, Nicholas, Sacred Heart, Auburn
Van Etten, Laurence A., Newman Center, S.U.N.Y Brockport
Vargas, Carlos H., Parish Support Ministries; Our Lady of the Americas
Vellon, Nemesio Martinez, Livingston Correctional Facility, Sonyea; Holy Apostles, Rochester; Parish Support Ministries
Verkon, Ronald, Diocese of Scranton
Virgilio, Paul, St. John the Evangelist, Greece
Welch, George J., St. Joseph's Hospital; Blessed Sacrament, Elmira
Wight, Edward, St. Mary's, Bath
Williams, Daniel, St. Stanislaus, Bradford; St. Joseph, Campbell & Steuben County Catholic Charities
Wilson, Albro C., Jr., (Diocese of Phoenix)
Witulski, James, St. Stanislaus Kostka, Rochester
Yawman, Philip, St. Catherine of Siena, Mendon

INSTITUTIONS LOCATED IN THE DIOCESE

[A] GRADUATE SCHOOL OF THEOLOGY

ROCHESTER. *St. Bernard's School of Theology & Ministry*, 120 French Rd., 14618. Tel: 585-271-3657; Fax: 585-271-2045. Email: lbarton@stbernards.edu. Web: www.stbernards.edu. Dr. Patricia A. Schoelles, S.S.J., Pres.; Sr. Katherine Hanley, C.S.J., Dean at Albany; Rev. George Heyman, Dir. Community Education; Ms. Mary Muggleton, Dir. Business Affairs; Dr. Devadasan Premnath, Dean; Ellen Morningstar, Registrar; Rev. Sebastian Falcone (Retired); Sheila Smyth, Librarian. Priests 1; Sisters 2; Lay Teachers 3; Total Staff 14; Total Enrollment 192.

[B] HIGH SCHOOLS

ROCHESTER. *The Aquinas Institute* (1902) 1127 Dewey Ave., 14613-9989. Tel: 585-254-2020; Fax: 585-254-7401. Email: jknapp@aquinasinstitute.com. Web: www.aquinasinstitute.com. Michael Daley, Pres.; Dennis Sadler, Prin.; Sandy Stevens, Librarian. Lay Teachers 62; Students 887.

Bishop Kearney High School (Coed), 125 Kings Hwy., 14617-5596. Tel: 585-342-4000; Fax: 585-342-4694. Email: principal@bkhs.org. Web: www.bkhs.org. Donna Dedee, Pres.; Julie Locey, Prin.; Andrew Smagin, Vice Prin. Curriculum Instruction; Sharon Kowalski, Athletic Dir.; Fred Tillinghast, Dean Students; Anne Rehor, Librarian. Sponsored by the Congregation of Christian Brothers in association with the School Sisters of Notre Dame, Wilton Province. Sisters 1; Lay Teachers 35; Students 535.

McQuaid Jesuit High School (1954) 1800 S. Clinton Ave., 14618. Tel: 585-473-1130; Fax: 585-256-6171. Email: jesuitres@mcquaid.org. Web: www.mcquaid.org. Revs. Brian Frain, S.J., Supr.; James J. Fischer, S.J., Chancellor; William Hobbs, Pres.; Revs. John P. Carriero, S.J.; Joseph DeMaio, O.Carm.; Jack Healy, O.Carm.; Richard D. Hunt, S.J.; Lawrence J. Wroblewski, S.J.; Kimberly Hanna, Librarian; Rev. James K. Coughlin, S.J., Prin. Jesuit Fathers. Priests 1; Lay Teachers 64; Students 846.

Nazareth Schools The Hall' The Academy (1871) 1001 Lake Ave., 14613. Tel: 585-647-8733; Fax: 585-647-8737. Web: nazarethschools.org. Sr. Patricia Carroll, S.S.J., Pres.; James Karg, Prin. (Grades 5-12); Diana Duell, Prin. (Grades PreK-4). Sisters of St. Joseph 7; Lay Teachers 61; Students 595.

Our Lady of Mercy High School, (Grades 7-12), 1437 Blossom Rd., 14610. Tel: 585-288-7120; Fax: 585-288-7966. Web: www.mercyhs.com. Mr. Terry Quinn, Prin.; Kimberly Rouleau, Librarian. Sisters of Mercy 3; Lay Teachers 52; Students 650.

ELMIRA. *Notre Dame High School* (1955) 1400 Maple Ave., 14904. Tel: 607-734-2267; Fax: 607-737-8903. Email: kellyn@notredamehighschool.com. Web: www.notredamehighschool.com. Sr. Mary Walter Hickey, R.S.M., Pres.; Rev. Vincent McDonough, S.J., Chap. Priests 1; Sisters of Mercy 4; Lay Teachers 27; Students 222.

GENEVA. *De Sales High School* (Incorporated under the laws of the State of New York), 90 Pulteney St., 14456. Tel: 315-789-5111; Fax: 315-789-8230. Email: mainoffice@desaleshs.org. Web: www.desaleshs.org. Gerald Macaluso, Prin.; Jack Howard, Librarian. Lay Teachers 11; Students 95.

[C] MONROE COUNTY CATHOLIC SCHOOLS

ROCHESTER. *Monroe County Catholic Schools*, 1150 Buffalo Rd., 14624. Tel: 585-328-3210; Fax: 585-328-3149. Email: charris@dor.org. Web: www.dor.org. Carmetha A Harris, Contact. Sisters 6; Lay Teachers 235; Students 3,446.

Junior High Schools:

Siena Catholic Academy (Grades 7-8), 2617 East Ave., 14610-3111. Tel: 585-381-1220; Fax: 585-381-1223. Email: scadcs@dor.org. Timothy E. Leahy, Prin.

Elementary Schools:

Christ the King School (Grades PreK-6), 445 Kings Hwy. S., 14617-4138. Tel: 585-467-8730; Fax: 585-467-5392. Email: ctkdcs@dor.org. Sr. Kathleen Lurz, S.S.J., Prin.

Cathedral School at Holy Rosary (Grades PreK-6), 420 Lexington Ave., 14613-1997. Tel: 585-254-8180; Fax: 585-254-4604. Email: cshrdcs@dor.org. Kathleen Dougherty, Prin.

Mother of Sorrows School (Grades K-8), 1777 Latta Rd., 14612-3731. Tel: 585-663-1100; Fax: 585-663-5552. Email: mosdcs@dor.org. Mr. Samuel Zalacca, Prin.

St. John Neumann School (Grades PreK-6), 31 Empire Blvd., 14609-4335. Tel: 585-288-0580; Fax: 585-288-2612. Email: sjndcs@dor.org. Marie L. Arcuri, Prin.

St. Joseph School (Grades PreK-6), 39 Gebhardt Rd., Penfield, 14526-1398. Tel: 585-586-6968; Fax: 585-586-4619. Email: sjpendcs@dor.org. Sr. Christina Marie Luczynski, C.S.S.F., Prin.

St. Lawrence School (Grades K-6), 1000 N. Greece Rd., 14626-1098. Tel: 585-225-3870; Fax: 585-225-1336. Email: slawrdcs@dor.org. Susan Sak, Prin.

St. Louis School (Grades PreK-6), 11 Rand Pl., Pittsford, 14534-2084. Tel: 585-586-5200; Fax: 585-586-4561. Email: slsdcs@dor.org. Ms. Kathleen Carroll, Prin.

St. Pius X School (Grades PreK-6), 3000 Chili Ave., 14624-4598. Tel: 585-247-5650; Fax: 585-247-7409. Email: spxdcs@dor.org. Stephen Oberst, Prin.

St. Rita School (Grades PreK-6), 1008 Maple Dr., Webster, 14580-1726. Tel: 585-671-3132; Fax: 585-671-4562. Email: sritadcs@dor.org. Sr. Katherine Ann Rappl, R.S.M., Prin.

Seton Catholic School (Grades PreK-6), 165 Rhinecliff Dr., 14618-1525. Tel: 585-473-6604; Fax: 585-473-3347. Email: setondcs@dor.org. Martin Swenson, Prin.

[D] FINGER LAKES AND SOUTHERN TIER SCHOOLS

AUBURN. *St. Joseph School (Auburn)*, (Grades PreK-8), 89 E. Genesee St., 13021-4161. Tel: 315-253-8327; Fax: 315-253-2401. Web: schools.dor.org/stjoauburn. Kathleen A. Coye, Prin.; Jeri Jerris, Librarian. Lay Teachers 11; Students 173; Preschool 36.

AVON. *St. Agnes*, (Grades PreK-6), 60 Park Pl., 14414-1053. Tel: 585-226-8500; Fax: 585-226-8500 (call first). Email: sagnesdcs@dor.org. Dr. Gerald E. Benjamin, Prin. Lay Teachers 8; Students 123; Preschool 35.

CANANDAIGUA. *St. Mary School (Canandaigua)*, (Grades PreK-8), 16 E. Gibson St., 14424-1310. Tel: 585-394-4300; Fax: 585-394-3954. Email: smcdcs@dor.org. Web: www.stmaryscanandaigua.org. Ms. Ann Marie Deutsch, Prin.; Christine Pohorence, Librarian. Lay Teachers 18; Students 202.

CORNING. *All Saints Academy*, (Grades PreK-8), 158 State St., 14830-2594. Tel: 607-936-9234; Fax: 607-936-1797. Email: asadcs@dor.org. Web: schools.dor.org/allsaints. Rose Ann Ewanyk, Prin.; Aurella Dean, Librarian. Lay Teachers 13; Aides 2; Students 129; Preschool 8.

ELMIRA. *Holy Family Elementary*, (Grades N-3), 421 Fulton St., 14904-1709. Tel: 607-732-3588; Fax: 607-732-1850. Email: hfpdcs@dor.org. Web: www.schools.dor.org/holyfamilypri. M. Bernadette McClelland, Prin.; Roberta Considine, Information Technology Coord. Lay Teachers 17; Students 144; Preschool 35.

Holy Family Middle School (1971) (Grades 7-8), 1010 Davis St., 14901-1013. Tel: 607-734-0336; Fax: 607-734-4977. Email: hfjhdcs@dor.org. Web: schools.org/holyfamilyjh. Elizabeth Berliner, Prin.; William Giancoli, Librarian. Lay Teachers 11; Students 98.

GENEVA. *St. Francis Desales/St. Stephen*, (Grades PreK-8), 17 Elmwood Ave., 14456-2299. Tel: 315-789-1828; Fax: 315-789-9179. Email: sfssdcs@dor.org. Web: www.catholicschoolsfl.org. Mrs. Elaine Morrow, Prin.; Valerie Venuti, Librarian. Lay Teachers 13; Students 130; Preschool 4.

HORNELL. *St. Ann* (1863) (Grades PreK-8), 27 Erie Ave., 14843-1909. Tel: 607-324-0733; Fax: 607-324-0985. Email: sanndcs@dor.org. Web: www.stannhornell.org. Lisa M. Dirlam, Prin. Lay Teachers 7; Students 86; Preschool 32.

HORSEHEADS. *St. Mary Our Mother (Horseheads)* (1959) (Grades PreK-6), 811 Westlake St., 14845-2099. Tel: 607-739-9157; Fax: 607-739-2532. Email: smomdcs@dor.org. Marilyn Zinn, Prin.; Karen Solometo, Librarian. Lay Teachers 12; Students 98; Preschool 10.

ITHACA. *Immaculate Conception*, (Grades PreK-8), 320 W. Buffalo St., 14850-4193. Tel: 607-273-2707; Fax: 607-272-8456. Email: icdcs@dor.org. Web: schools.dor.org/ic. Diana M. Oravec, Prin. Lay Teachers 12; Students 106; Preschool 36.

NEWARK. *St. Michael (Newark)*, (Grades PreK-8), 320 S. Main St., 14513-1721. Tel: 315-331-2297; Fax: 315-331-2299. Email: smndcs@dor.org. Mrs. Pauline DeCann, Prin. Lay Teachers 13; Students 120; Preschool 19.

OWEGO. *St. Patrick School*, (Grades PreSchool-5), 309 Front St., 13827. Fax: 607-687-4305. Email: spodcs@dor.org. Web: www.stpatrickowego.org. Paula Smith, Prin.; Linda Williams, Librarian. Lay Teachers 7; Students 61; Preschool 25.

PENN YAN. *St. Michael (Penn Yan)* (1884) (Grades PreK-5), 214 Keuka St., 14527-1143. Tel: 315-536-6112; Fax: 315-536-6112. Email: smpydcs@dor.org. Web: stmichaelpennyan.org. David M. Paddock, Prin.; Gloria Long, Librarian. Lay Teachers 7; Students 114; Preschool 13.

[E] HOMES FOR AGED

ROCHESTER. *St. Ann's Home for the Aged*, 1500 Portland Ave., 14621. Tel: 585-697-6000; Fax: 585-342-9585. Email: info@stannscommunity.com. Web: www.stannscommunity.com. Betty Mullin-DiProsa, Pres. & CEO; Rev. Peter T. Bayer, Dir. of Pastoral Care; Sr. Livia Ann Ruocco, R.S.M., Pastoral Care Coord.; Sheila Kinsky, Pastoral Care Coord. Residents 388.

St. Ann's Nursing Home Co., Inc. (The Heritage), 1450 Portland Ave., 14621. Tel: 585-697-6000; Fax: 585-342-9585. Email: info@stannscommunity.com. Web: www.stannscommunity.com. Betty Mullin-Di Prosa, Pres. & CEO; Rev. Peter T. Bayer, Dir. Pastoral Care; Sr. Livia Ann Ruocco, R.S.M., Pastoral Care Coord.; Sheila Kinsky, Pastoral Care Coord. Residents 203.

Chapel Oaks:, 1550 Portland Ave., 14621. Tel: 585-342-3052; Fax: 585-338-3453. Email: info@stannscommunity.com. Web: www.stannscommunity.org. Betty Mullin-DiProsa, Pres. & CEO; Rev. Peter T. Bayer, Dir. of Pastoral Care; Sr. Livia Ann Ruocco, R.S.M., Pastoral Care Coord.; Sheila Kinsky, Pastoral Care Coord.

[F] SPECIALTY HOUSING

ROCHESTER. *Providence Housing Development Corporation*, 1136 Buffalo Rd., 14624. Tel: 585-328-3228, Ext. 1393; Fax: 585-529-9525. Email: mmccullough@dor.org. Web: www.providencehousing.org. Monica C.

McCullough, Exec. Dir.; Jack Balinsky, Pres. Bd. of Directors; Minchin G. Lewis, Chief Operating Officer; Helen Bianchi, Dir. Asset Mgmt.; Mary Jo Carbonaro, Shelter Plus Care, Dir.; Lisa Alcott, Home Ownership, Dir.; Lori A. Foster, Mktg. & Fundraising Dir.; Fran Haywood, Dir. Finance. Mission Statement: To strengthen families & communities by creating & providing access to quality affordable housing enriched by the availability of supportive services. Providence, a not-for-profit corporation affiliated with Catholic Charities of the Diocese of Rochester, develops, finances, & manages housing for individuals & families in the 12 counties of the Diocese of Rochester.

Providence Atwood Park Housing Development Fund Company, Inc., 1136 Buffalo Rd., 14624. Tel: 585-328-3210; 585-529-9525. Email: mmccullough@dor.org. Web: www.providencehousing.org. Monica C. McCullough, Pres.

Providence Lyons Housing Development Fund Company, Inc., 1136 Buffalo Rd., 14624. Tel: 585-328-3228, Ext. 1434; Fax: 585-529-9525. Web: www.providencehousing.org. Paul Pickering, Pres.; Monica C. McCullough, Sec.

Providence Northstar Housing Development Fund Company, Inc., 1136 Buffalo Rd., 14624. Tel: 585-328-3228, Ext. 1434; Fax: 585-529-9525. Email: mmccullough@dor.org. Web: www.providencehousing.org. Monica C. McCullough, Pres.

Providence Yates Housing Development Fund Company, Inc., 1136 Buffalo Rd., 14624. Tel: 585-328-3228, Ext. 1434; Fax: 585-529-9525. Email: mmccullough@dor.org. Web: www.providencehousing.org. Paul Pickering, Pres.; Monica C. McCullough, Sec.

[G] CAMPS

LIVONIA. *Camp Stella Maris*, 4395 E. Lake Rd., 14487. Tel: 585-346-2243; Fax: 585-346-6921. Email: info@campstellamaris.org. Web: campstellamaris.org. Dan Dey, Bd. Pres. Purpose: Residential camping under Catholic auspices, for boys and girls (ages 7-14) of all faiths. Encampment period: Eight weeks during summer (June/July/August). Rental of facility available September-June for family/youth development retreats. ACA accredited.; Day Camp Center for boys and girls (ages 5-12). Encampment period: Eight weeks during June/July/August in conjunction with resident camp. Adventure-Based Learning Experience (ABLE) high and low challenge ropes courses ideal for building trust, confidence, cooperation, teamwork, self-esteem, communication, and leadership skills. Total Staff 8; Summer/Seasonal 140.

Conesus Lake, 4395 E. Lake Rd., 14487. Tel: 585-346-2243; Fax: 585-346-6921. John Quinlivan, Exec. Dir.

[H] GENERAL HOSPITALS

AUBURN. *Mercy Health & Rehabilitation Center Nursing Home Co., Inc.* (1972) 3 St. Anthony St., 13021. Tel: 315-253-0351. Web: www.mercyrehab.net. Sr. Frances Ann Thom, Dir. Mission Svcs. & Spiritual Care; Rev. Felicjan Sierotowicz, Chap.; Stephen Ash, Admin. Sisters of the Third Franciscan Order. Nursing Facility Beds 297.

ELMIRA. **St. Joseph's Health System, Inc.*, 555 E. St. Josephs Blvd., P.O. Box 1512, 14902-1512. Tel: 607-733-6541, Ext. 264; Fax: 607-737-7837. Web: www.stjosephs.org. Sr. Marie Castagnaro, S.S.J., Pres. & Contact.

St. Joseph's Hospital (1908) 555 E. St. Josephs Blvd., 14901. Tel: 607-733-6541; Fax: 607-737-7837. Email: mcastagnaro@stjosephs.org. Web: www.stjosephs.org. Sr. Marie Castagnaro, S.S.J., Pres. & CEO. Skilled Nursing Facility. Total Staff 959; Bed Capacity 224; Skilled Nursing Facility 71; Patients Assisted Annually 110,000.

St. Joseph's Hospital Foundation, Inc., 555 E.St. Josephs Blvd., 14901. Tel: 607-737-7004; Fax: 607-271-3418. Email: dsullivan@stjosephs.org. David P. Sullivan, Pres.

HORNELL. *St. James Mercy Health System*, 411 Canisteo St., 14843. Tel: 607-324-8000; Fax: 607-324-8115. Email: mlarowe@sjmh.org. Web: www.stjamesmercy.org. Mary LaRowe, Pres. & CEO. Total Staff 916; Bed Capacity 297; Patients Assisted Annually 226,739.

[I] CATHOLIC CHARITIES

ROCHESTER. *Catholic Charities of the Diocese of Rochester, Inc.*, 1150 Buffalo Rd., 14624. Tel: 585-328-3210; Fax: 585-529-9534. Email: balinsky@dor.org. Web: www.dor.org/charities/index.htm. Jack Balinsky, Diocesan Dir.; Andrew Hislop, Chm. Bd. of Dir.; Jann K. Armantrout, Life Issues Coord.; Ruth Putnam Marchetti, Justice & Peace Coord. for Wayne & Finger Lakes Counties.

Regional Diocesan Administration Tel: 607-734-9847; Fax: 607-734-3764. Anthony T. Barbaro, Assoc. Diocesan Dir. Tel: 607-734-9784; Fax: 607-734-3764; Lee Randall, Dir. Fin. Svcs. Tel: 607-734-9784; Fax: 607-733-3614; Donna L. Rieker, H.R. Dir. Tel: 607-734-9784, Ext. 165; Fax: 607-734-3764; Barbara Poling, Sr. H.R. Dir.

Regional Offices:

Catholic Charities Community Services, 1945 E. Ridge Rd., Ste. 24, 14622. Tel: 585-339-9800; Fax: 585-339-9377. Paul Pickering, Exec. Dir.; Ed Starowicz, Chm. Bd. of Directors; Barbara Poling, Human Resources Dir.; Tracy Boff, AIDS Svcs. Dir.; Kathleen Termine, Devel. Disabilities Svcs. Dir.; Anne Sawyko, Devel. Dir.; Penny Coon, Quality Compliance Dir.; Tracy McNett, Traumatic Brain Injury Dir.

Catholic Family Center, 87 N. Clinton Ave., 14604. Tel: 585-546-7220; Fax: 585-546-6396. Carolyn A. Portanova, Pres. & CEO; John M. Pennell, CFO; Carl Hatch, Vice Pres. Gov't. & Community Affairs; Anthony Adams, Chm. Bd. of Dir.; Carol DeMoulin, Sr. Vice Pres. Devel. & Mktg.; Chris Gullo, Senior Vice Pres. Strategic Planning & Prog. Svcs.

Departments of Catholic Family Center:

Aging & Adult Services Tel: 585-232-1840; Fax: 585-454-6286. Mary Kanerva, Dept. Dir.

Children, Youth and Family Services Tel: 585-262-7115; Fax: 585-325-3867. Anne Eichas, Dir.

Employee Assistance & Counseling Tel: 585-262-7029; Fax: 585-262-7091. Tina Simson, Dir.

Homeless & Housing Services Tel: 585-423-9590; Fax: 585-262-7006. Lisa Lewis, Dir.

Intensive Psychiatric Rehabilitation Tel: 585-232-1840; Fax: 585-232-8419. Cheryl Steele, Interim Dir.

Mental Health Tel: 585-262-7034; Fax: 585-423-2201. Peter Roche, Interim Dir.

Office of Social Policy & Research Tel: 585-262-7021; Fax: 585-546-2042. Marvin Mich, Dir.

Refugee Immigration Employment Services Tel: 585-262-7082; Fax: 585-262-7084. Mr. Ben Murphy, Dir.

Restart Substance Abuse Services Tel: 585-262-7052; Fax: 585-546-2042. Betty Mandly, Dir. Residential Svcs.; Cathy Saresky, Dir. Outpatient Svcs.

Fund Development & Community Relations Tel: 585-262-7020; Fax: 585-262-7166. Mel Carpino, Dir.

Catholic Charities of the Finger Lakes Tel: 315-789-2235; Fax: 315-789-5785. (Serving Yates, Ontario, Seneca, and Cayuga Counties)

Main Office:, 94 Exchange St., Geneva, 14456-2235. Tel: 315-789-2686; Fax: 315-789-5785. Ellen Wayne, Exec. Dir.; Ruth Putnam Marchetti, Dir. Parish Svcs.; L. Trojnor, Dir. Cayuga County Office; Robert Kernan, Bd. Chm. (Satellite Office at: 134 E. Genesee St., Auburn, NY 13021. Tel: 312-262-0018)

Catholic Charities of Wayne County, 1141 E. Union St., Newark, 14513. Tel: 315-331-4867; Fax: 315-331-4918. Carmen Pagano, Bd. Chm.; Timothy Sullivan, Exec. Dir.

College Bound A. Mulberger, Contact Person.

Community Outreach P. Mares, Contact Person.

Early Intervention I. Rojas, Contact Person.

General Counseling I. Rojas, Contact Person.

Justice & Peace/Parish Social Ministry Support R. Putnam-Marchetti, Contact Person.

LaCasa Transitional Housing P. Mares, Contact Person.

PINS Diversion and Counseling S. VanLiew, Contact Person.

Wolcott Clothing Center C. Guyette-Vienna, Contact Person.

Catholic Charities of Chemung/Schuyler, 215 E. Church St., Elmira, 14901. Tel: 607-734-9784; Fax: 607-734-6588. Bridget Steed, Exec. Dir.; Marie Finnerty, Bd. Chm.; Kathy Dubel, Dir., Justice & Peace. Tel: 607-734-9784, Ext. 135; K. Applin, Dir., Residential Svcs.; E. Topping, Dir., Agency Youth Svcs.; L. Waters, Devel.; M. McInerny, Contact Person, Property Dept.

Second Place East Homeless Services/Shelter S. Fritz, Dir. Emergency Svcs.

Homeless Intervention Program Samaritan Center T. Parker, Dir., Samaritan Center.

First Time Homebuyer J. Galvin, Contact Person.

Schuyler Services P. Marx, Contact Person.

Catholic Charities of Steuben, 23 Liberty St., Bath, 14810. Tel: 607-734-8085; Fax: 607-776-4092. Laura Opelt, Exec. Dir.; Robert Turissini, Bd. Chm.; Robert Colomino, (Justice & Peace).

Turning Point D. Cherry, Contact Person.

Substance Abuse Services, Prevention and Education J. Bassage, Contact Person.

Catholic Charities of Tompkins/Tioga, 324 W. Buffalo St., Ithaca, 14850. Mary Berens, Bd. Chm.; Christine Sanchirico, Exec. Dir.

Justice and Peace, Tompkins L. Nowinski, Contact Person.

Justice and Peace, Tioga K. Dubel, Contact Person.

Family Empowerment Services T. Miller, Contact Person.

Samaritan Center M. Brichaceko, Contact Person.

Immigrant Support Services S. Chaffe, Contact Person.

Tioga Outreach A. Klopf, Contact Person.

Food Bank of the Southern Tier, 945 County Rt. 64, Elmira, 14903. Natasha Thompson, Exec. Dir.; Mary Pat Dolan, Bd. Chm.

Catholic Charities of Livingston County, 34 E. State St., Mt. Morris, 14510. Tel: 716-658-4466; Fax: 585-658-2513. Joseph Dimino, Exec. Dir.

Departments: Tina Brooks, Rural Outreach; Christa Barrows, Faith in Action; Susan Bell, Youth Mentoring Program; Bridgit Hurley, Parish Social Ministry; Tabitha Brewster, Budget & Mgmt. Emergency Housing; Michelle Dourie, Community of Caring; M. O'Hearn, Hispanic Outreach; C. Tinney, SSI Case Mgmt.; Pamela Kingsley, Prog. Devel.; Mary Ann Thompson, Connections; Matthew Gaynor, Bd. Chm.

Catholic Charities of the Southern Tier, 215 E. Church St., Elmira, 14901. Tel: 607-734-9784; Fax: 607-734-6588.

Kinship Family and Youth Services, 2 Bethesda Dr., Ste. 10, Hornell, 14843. Tel: 607-324-0909; Fax: 607-324-0983. Joseph Weider, Exec. Dir.; Barbara Fairbanks, Pres. Bd. of Dir.

In-Home Family Preservation S.H.A.P.E. M. Duff, Contact Person.

Healthy Families M. Duff, Contact Person.

Foster Care L. Galatio, Contact Person.

Alcoholism Services K. Robards-Smith, Contact Person.

[J] MONASTERIES AND RESIDENCES OF PRIESTS AND BROTHERS

ROCHESTER. *Basilian Residence*, 3497 East Ave., 14618. Tel: 585-586-4600; Fax: 585-385-6383. Revs. Joseph M. Lanzalaco, C.S.B., Supr.; T. Paul Broadhurst, C.S.B.; Albert W. Cylwicki, C.S.B.; Leo A. Hetzler, C.S.B., Councilor; John R. Lee, C.S.B.; Thomas M. Miller, C.S.B.; John C. Murray, C.S.B.; John A. Poluikis, C.S.B.; Donald J. Lococo, C.S.B., Councilor.

Priests of the Region Serving Elsewhere: Revs. William J. Sheehan, C.S.B., Collegio San Clemente, Via Labicana, 95, 00184, Rome, Italy; Jim Stenberg, Graduate Studies, Syracuse University; George Kosicki, C.S.B., c/o Companions of Christ the Lamb, P.O. Box 12, Paradise, MI 49768. Tel: 906-492-3647; J. Gareth Poupore, C.S.B., 16 Village Trail, Honeoye Falls, 14472.

Becket Hall, 2617 East Ave., 14610. Tel: 585-647-6657. Email: beckethall@dor.org. Web: www.dor.org. Rev. Michael F. Conboy, Dir. Residence for Pre-Theologate candidates.

Missionaries of the Precious Blood (1815) 1261 Highland Ave., 14620-1873. Tel: 585-461-0318; Fax: 585-461-0318. Email: jcolacino@sjfc.edu. Rev. John A. Colacino, C.PP.S. Tel: 716-461-2750.

Whitefriars Priory, 625 Colebrook Dr., 14617. Tel: 585-266-2560. Revs. Joseph DeMaio, O.Carm.; Jack Healy, O.Carm., Prior & Treas.; Matthew Temple, O.Carm. Total in Residence 3.

INTERLAKEN. *St. Fidelis Friary* (1951) 7790 County Rd. 153, 14847. Tel: 607-532-4423; Fax: 607-532-9271. Rev. Bartholomew Minson, O.F.M.Cap., Vicar; Bros. Antonine Lizama, O.F.M.Cap.; Carmine Funaro, O.F.M.Cap.; Revs. John Tokaz, O.F.M.Cap., Guardian; Eugene O'Hara, O.F.M.Cap. Capuchin Friars-Province of St. Mary (Order of Friars Minor Capuchin). Priests 3; Brothers 2.

PIFFARD. *Abbey of the Genesee* (1951) 3258 River Rd., 14533. Tel: 585-243-0660. Email: community@geneseeabbey.org. Web: www.geneseeabbey.org. Rt. Revs. John Denburger, O.C.S.O., Abbot; John Eudes Bamberger, O.C.S.O., Retired Abbot (Retired); Revs. Eugene Chung, O.C.S.O.; Francis R. Steger, O.C.S.O.; Marcellus R. Earl, O.C.S.O.; Raymond J. Fournier, O.C.S.O.; Jerome J. Machar, O.C.S.O.; Robert O. Moore, O.C.S.O.; Stephen Muller, O.C.S.O.; Justin R. Sheehan, O.C.S.O.; Gerard D'Souza, O.C.S.O.; Aelred W. Wentz, O.C.S.O. The Order of Cistercians of the Strict Observance (Trappists). Professed Monks 33; Priests 13; Total in Community (Piffard) 33.

Absent on Leave: Rev. Michael M. Hayden, O.C.S.O.

PINE CITY. *Mount Saviour Monastery* (1950) 231 Monastery Rd., 14871-9787. Tel: 607-734-1688; Fax: 607-734-1689. Email: info@msaviour.org. Web: www.msaviour.org. Rev. James Cronin, O.S.B. Professed Monks 9; Professed Priests 2; Total in Community 11.

[K] CONVENTS AND RESIDENCES FOR SISTERS

ROCHESTER. *Sisters of Mercy of the Americas - New York, Pennsylvania, Pacific West Community*, 1437 Blossom Rd., 14610. Tel: 585-288-2710; Fax: 585-288-2756. Email: nhoff@mercynyppaw.org. Web: www.sistersofmercy.org. Sr. Nancy Hoff, R.S.M, Pres.; Rev. Peter Abas, Chap. Professed Sisters & Perpetual Vows 503; Associates 490.

Sisters St. Joseph of Rochester (1854) 150 French Rd., 14618-3822. Tel: 585-641-8100; Fax: 585-641-8524. Email: cong@ssjrochester.org. Web: www.ssjrochester.org. Sr. Mary Louise Mitchell, S.S.J., Congregational Pres.; Rev. Msgr. William H. Shannon, Chap. (Retired); Rev. Bruce F. Ammering, Chap. (Retired). Sisters of St. Joseph of Rochester, Inc. Priests 8; Professed Sisters in Community 278; Total Assisted 56; Total Staff 120.

Spirit House, Inc. (1981) 72 Dorvid Rd., 14617. Tel: 585-544-5698; Fax: 585-266-2611. Email: spirithouse1@juno.com. Web: www.wounded-in-spirit.com. Sr. Mary Ann Ayers, R.S.M., Dir.

ELMIRA. *Monastery of Mary the Queen, Dominican Nuns*, 1310 W. Church St., 14905. Tel: 607-734-9506; Fax: 607-734-1452. Email: mmtqblog@gmail.com. Web: http://monasteryofmarythequeen.op.org. Sr. Miriam Scheel, O.P., Prioress. Solemn Vows 13.

PITTSFORD. *Monastery of Our Lady and St. Joseph Carmelite Monastery*, 1931 W. Jefferson Rd., 14534-1041. Tel: 585-427-7094; Fax: 585-427-8141. Sr. Therese Marie of Jesus Crucified, O.C.D., Prioress. Discalced Carmelite Nuns. Professed Nuns with Solemn Vows 13.

[L] RETREAT HOUSES

ROCHESTER. *Mercy Prayer Center* (1978) 65 Highland Ave., 14620. Tel: 585-473-6893; Fax: 585-473-6414. Email: info@mercyprayercenter.org. Web: www.mercyprayercenter.org. Sponsored by Sisters of Mercy, New York, Pennsylvania, Pacific West Community. Total in Residence 2; Total Staff 7.

CANANDAIGUA. *Notre Dame Retreat House* (1967) 5151 Foster Rd., Box 342, 14424. Tel: 585-394-5700; Fax: 585-394-9215. Web: ndretreat.org. Revs. Michael Sergi, Rector; Thomas Barrett, C.Ss.R.; Paul A. Miller, C.Ss.R.

[M] CAMPUS MINISTRY

ROCHESTER. *Campus Ministry* Pastoral Center, 1150 Buffalo Rd., 14624. Tel: 585-328-3210; Fax: 585-328-3149. Email: loughlin@dor.org. Ms. Shannon Loughlin, Dir. of Young Adult & Campus Ministry.

Catholic Newman Community at the University of Rochester Interfaith Chapel, 320 Wilson Blvd., 14627. Tel: 585-275-4321; Fax: 585-506-0203. Rev. Brian Cool, Dir.; Deacon W. Craig Stratton, Medical Center Outreach; Nathan Drahms, Campus Min.; Sr. Jacqulyn Reichart, R.S.M., Campus Min.

Eastman School of Music Catholic Students Organization Tel: 585-275-4321; Fax: 585-506-0203. Rev. Brian Cool, Contact Person.

Nazareth College of Rochester 4245 East Ave., 14618. Tel: 585-389-2308; Fax: 585-389-2300. Jamie Fazio, Campus Min.

Newman (Catholic Campus) Parish, RIT/NTID Interfaith Center, 40 Lomb Memorial Dr., 14623. Tel: 585-475-5172; Fax: 585-475-5485. Email: rdhcpm@rit.edu. Web: www.rit.edu/~newman/. Rev. Richard D. Hunt, S.J., Dir.; Deacon Thomas Behe.

St. John Fisher College 3690 East Ave., 14618. Tel: 585-385-8368; Fax: 585-385-8129. Rev. Joseph M. Lanzalaco, C.S.B., Dir., Campus Min. Tel: 585-385-8368.

State University College at Brockport, the Newman Oratory of Brockport 101 Kenyon St., Brockport, 14420. Tel: 585-637-5036; Fax: 585-637-7866. Email: campusminister1@aol.com. Margot Van Etten, Dir. of Campus Ministry; Rev. Matthew Kawiak, Sacramental Min.; Deacon Lawrence Van Etten, Pastoral Min.

State University College at Geneseo (Geneseo), Newman Catholic Community at the Interfaith Center 11 Franklin St., Geneseo, 14454. Tel: 585-243-1460. Email: sauter@geneseo.edu. Mike Sauter, Dir.; Rev. Edward J. Dillon, Sacramental Min. (Retired).

The Cornell Catholic Community, Inc. (Ithaca) Cornell University, G-22 Anabel Taylor Hall, Ithaca, 14853. Tel: 607-255-4228; Fax: 607-255-7793. Email: catholic@cornell.edu. Rev. Daniel T. McMullin, Dir. & Chap.; Sr. Donna Fannon, M.H.S.H., Campus Min.; Rev. Robert Smith, Chap. (Retired).

The Catholic Community of Ithaca College 100 Muller Chapel, Ithaca College, 953 Danby Rd., Ithaca, 14850. Tel: 607-274-3103; Fax: 607-274-1901. Rev. Carsten Martensen, S.J., Dir.; Lee Imbriano, Campus Min.

Elmira College One Park Place, Elmira, 14901. Tel: 607-732-1994. Rev. Walter L. Wainwright, Contact Person (Retired).

Hobart and William Smith College c/o Our Lady of Peace, 130 Exchange St., Geneva, 14456. Tel: 315-789-0930. Rev. Paul J. Tomasso. Tel: 315-789-0930. Roman Catholic Community.

Keuka College c/o St. Michael's Church 312 Liberty St., Penn Yan, 14527. Tel: 315-536-7459; Fax: 315-536-6964. Rev. Robert P. Ring, Our Lady of the Lakes.

Roberts Wesleyan College c/o St. Christopher Church 2301 Westside Dr., North Chili, 14514. Tel: 585-595-1400. Rev. Robert Gaudio.

Wells College, c/o Good Shepherd Catholic Community Main St., P.O. Box 296, Aurora, 13026-0296. Tel: 315-364-7197. Rev. Richard J. Shatzel.

Cayuga Community College P.O. Box 1000, Auburn, 13021.

New York Chiropractic College c/o St. Hyacinth, 63 Pulaski St., Auburn, 13021. Tel: 315-252-7297 (Rectory); 315-568-3124 (College); Fax: 315-568-4893. Rev. Richard M. Murphy (Retired). Priests 15; Total Staff 31; Total Assisted 120,721.

[N] MISCELLANEOUS LISTINGS

ROCHESTER. *Apostleship of Prayer*, Diocesan Pastoral Center, 1150 Buffalo Rd., 14624. Tel: 716-328-3210. Rev. Thomas P. Mull.

Archivist (Diocese of Rochester Archives), 1150 Buffalo Rd., 14624. Tel: 585-328-3210, Ext. 1204; Fax: 585-328-3149. Email: archive@dor.org. Sr. Connie Derby, R.S.M., Dir. of Archives and Records.

Catholic Committee on Scouting, 1150 Buffalo Rd., 14624. Tel: 585-328-3210; Fax: 585-328-3149. Email: versluys@dor.org. Web: www.dor.org. Rev. William McGrath; Sue Versluys, Contact Person.

Catholic Gay & Lesbian Family Ministry, c/o 91 New Wickham Dr., Penfield, 14526. Tel: 585-388-6973. Ms. Karen Rinefierd, Diocesan Liaison.

Cistercian Publications, Inc., Abbey of the Genesee, 3258 River Rd., Piffard, 14533. Tel: 585-243-0660. Email: frbrendan@newmelleray.org. Web: www.spencerabbey.org/cistpub. Rev. Brendan Freeman, O.C.S.O., Pres.; Bro. Patrick Hart, Assoc. Editor.

Communis Fund of the Diocese of Rochester, Inc., 1150 Buffalo Rd., 14624. Tel: 585-328-3228, Ext. 1269.

Daystar For Medically Fragile Infants, Inc., 47 Lochnavar Pkwy., Pittsford, 14534. Tel: 585-385-6287; Fax: 585-383-0033. Web: daystarssj.org. Sr. Eileen Daly, S.S.J., Councilor.

DOR Holding, Inc., 1150 Buffalo Rd., 14624. Tel: 585-328-3228, Ext. 1269; Fax: 585-328-4142.

Dunn Tower Apartments, Inc. (1976) 100 Dunn Tower Dr., 14606. Tel: 585-429-5520; Fax: 585-429-9720. Email: dt1@dunntower.com. Web: www.dunntower.com. Housing for Seniors. Total Staff 6; Total in Residence 192.

Family Rosary For Peace, Inc. (1950) 7 Austin St., 14606. Tel: 585-254-7170; Fax: 585-254-5813. Email: rholyapo@dor.org. Rev. Paul J. Tomasso, Dir.; Dolores Mary Brien, Sec.

Holy Childhood Association, 1150 Buffalo Rd., 14624. Tel: 585-436-9200; Fax: 585-529-9501. Email: jconlon@dor.org. Web: www.dor.org/missions. Rev. Robert C. Bradler, Dir. (Retired).

St. Joseph's House of Hospitality, 402 South Ave., 14620. Tel: 585-232-3262. Email: cathwork@frontiernet.net. Mailing Address: P.O. Box 31049, 14603. Tel: 585-232-3262. Services provide soup kitchen, personal assistance to the needy, emergency men's housing and social justice advocacy. Total Staff 5; Total Assisted 120.

Magnificat - Rochester, 199 Meadowdale Dr., P.O. Box 24787, 14624. Tel: 585-436-1284. Kathleen Murty, Treas. & Contact.

Marriage Encounter Apostolate (Worldwide), 132 Clay Ave., 14613. Tel: 585-719-9848. Email: jbrasley@dor.org. Web: www.wwme.org. Rev. John Murray, C.S.B.; Deacon John Brasley, Contact Person; Belinda Brasley, Contact Person. Priests 2; Total Staff 18.

Mercy Outreach Center, Inc. (1977) 142 Webster Ave., 14609. Tel: 585-288-2634; Fax: 585-288-0252. Web: www.mercyoutreachcenter.org. Jodi M. Cammilleri, Exec. Dir. Health and dental services for the uninsured and advocacy.

Mercy Residential Services (1980) 198 Oriole St., 14613-1923. Tel: 585-254-2175; Fax: 585-254-2229. Email: info@mercyresidential.org. Web: www.mercyresidential.org. Susan B. Aiello, Exec. Dir. & Pres. Supportive Housing for Single Mothers and their Children. Total Staff 17; Families Assisted 90.

Nativity Preparatory Academy Associates of Rochester Inc, 15 Whalin St., 14620. Tel: 585-271-1630; Fax: 585-271-1633. Email: nativityrocny@aol.com. Web: www.nativityrochester.org. School: 15 Whalin St., 14620. William M. Carpenter, Bd. Chm. & Contact.

Notre Dame Learning Center, Inc., P.O. Box 77175, 14617. Tel: 585-254-5110. Email: ndlc@frontiernet.net. Web: www.ndlcenter.org. 71 Pkwy., 14608. Sr. Joan Doyle, S.S.N.D., Treas. Ministry for children by providing educational opportunities in literacy, reading & math to enable them to reach the fullness of their potential & become successful & productive citizens.

St. Peter's Kitchen, Inc, 681 Brown St., P.O. Box 11031, 14611. Tel: 585-235-6511. Email: stpeterskitchen@dor.org. Candice Johnson, Pres.; Tom Zamiara, Vice Pres.; Deacon Ed Giblin, Sec.; Patricia Lorenzen, Prog. Dir. Provide nutritious lunches to men, women, and children in need. In addition there is a clothing closet.

Providence Housing Development Corporation (1994) 1136 Buffalo Rd., 14624. Tel: 585-328-3228, Ext. 1393; Fax: 585-529-9525. Email: mmccullough@dor.org. Web: www.providencehousing.org. Programs offered: Property Management, Shelter & Care for the Homeless, First-time Homebuyers and Housing Information, Credit Repair, Housing Development and Housing Consultation. Units Developed 780; Units Managed 550.

Rochester Catholic Worker Bethany House (1978) 111 Joseph Ave., 14611. Tel: 585-454-4197; Fax: 585-454-4197 *51. Email: rbethan1@rochester.rr.com. Donna Ecker, Contact Person. Total Staff 4.

Sisters of Saint Joseph of Rochester Charitable Trust, c/o Thomas Nientimp, Presiding Trustee, 150 French Rd., 14618. Tel: 585-641-8166; Fax: 585-641-8525. Alicia Pender, Contact Person.

Sisters of Saint Joseph of Rochester Ministry Foundation, Inc. (2004) 150 French Rd., 14618-3822. Tel: 585-641-8124; Fax: 585-641-8524. Web: www.ssjrochester.org. Sr. Barbara Staropoli, S.S.J.

St. Theodore's Apartment Housing Development Fund Co., Inc. (Dunn Tower II Apts.) (1980) 200 Dunn Tower Dr., 14606. Tel: 585-429-6840; Fax: 585-247-3723. Email: dt2@dunntower.com. Web: www.dunntower.com.

CORNING. *Anawim Community Center*, 122 E. First St., 14830. Tel: 607-936-4965; Fax: 607-936-0207. Email: oxford@anawim.com. Web: www.anawim.com. Revs. Daniel Healy (Philippines), Dir.; Richard M. Rusk, Missions & Vocations Dir. Priests 2; Total in Residence 4; Total Staff 10.

FAIRPORT. *Catholic Charismatic Renewal*, 48 South Ave., 14450. Tel: 585-475-8494. Email: don.germano@gmail.com. Deacon Donald Germano, Diocesan Liaison.

GENEVA. *DeSales Institution Foundation Inc.*, 90 Pulteney St., 14456. Tel: 315-789-5111; Fax: 315-789-8230. Web: www.desaleshs.org.

OWEGO. *Owego -Tioga Rural Ministry* (1978) 143 North Ave., 13827. Tel: 607-697-3021; Fax: 607-687-3033. Email: sphilrsm@stny.rr.com. Sr. Phyllis McGuire, R.S.M., Exec. Dir. This ministry serves as a food pantry and an emergency outreach to the poor and elderly of the county. Total Staff 3; Total Assisted 2,496.

SENECA FALLS. *Patrician Fund Trust*, 25 Center St., Waterloo, 13165. Tel: 315-651-4349; Fax: 315-539-8841. Email: sstpatri@dor.org. Web: www.senecafallsonline.com/stpats/. Sean Anglim.

SPENCERPORT. *Rochester Comitium*, 1522 Nine Mile Point Rd., Penfield, 14526. Tel: 716-266-8087. Ms. Marcy Leonardo, Pres.

RELIGIOUS INSTITUTES OF MEN REPRESENTED IN THE DIOCESE

For further details refer to the corresponding bracketed number in the Religious Institutes of Men or Women section.

[0170]—*Basilian Fathers*—C.S.B.

[0200]—*Benedictine Monks*—O.S.B.

[0470]—*The Capuchin Friars* (Province of St. Mary)—O.F.M.Cap.

[0270]—*Carmelite Fathers and Brothers*—O.Carm.

[0350]—*Cistercians Order of the Strict Observance (Trappists)*—O.C.S.O.

[0310]—*Congregation of Christian Brothers* (Eastern Prov.)—C.F.C.

[1140]—*Congregation of the Sacred Hearts of Jesus and Mary*—SS.CC.

[0480]—*Conventual Franciscans* (Buffalo & Immaculate Conception Provinces)—O.F.M.Conv.

[0520]—*Franciscan Friars* (Assumption B.V.M. Prov.)—O.F.M.

[0690]—*Jesuit Fathers and Brothers* (New York Province)—S.J.

[0610]—*Priests of the Congregation of Holy Cross*—C.S.C.

[1070]—*Redemptorist Fathers* (Baltimore Province)—C.SS.R.

[0760]—*Society of Mary (Marianists)*—S.M.

[1060]—*Society of the Precious Blood*—C.PP.S.
[0560]—*Third Order Regular of Saint Francis*—T.O.R.

RELIGIOUS INSTITUTES OF WOMEN REPRESENTED IN THE DIOCESE

[3110]—*Congregation of Our Lady of the Retreat in the Cenacle*—R.C.
[0760]—*Daughters of Charity of St. Vincent de Paul*—D.C.
[0420]—*Discalced Carmelite Nuns*—O.C.D.
[1050]—*Dominican Contemplative Nuns*—O.P.
[1070-13]—*Dominican Sisters (Adrian, MI)*—O.P.
[1070-05]—*Dominican Sisters (Amityville, NY)*—O.P.
[]—*Franciscan Sisters of Allegheny, New York*—O.S.F.
[2575]—*Institute of the Sisters of Mercy of the Americas* (Rochester, NY)—R.S.M.
[2470]—*Maryknoll Sisters of St. Dominic*—M.M.
[]—*Misioneras Guadalupanas del Espiritu Santo*
[3430]—*Religious Teachers Filippini*—M.P.F.
[2970]—*School Sisters of Notre Dame*—S.S.N.D.
[3950]—*Sisters of Saint Mary of Namur*—S.S.M.N.
[1800]—*Sisters of St. Francis of the Third Order Regular (Williamsville, New York)*—O.S.F.
[3840]—*Sisters of St. Joseph of Carondolet*—C.S.J.
[3830-14]—*Sisters of St. Joseph (Rochester)*—S.S.J.
[3730]—*Sisters of the Order of St. Basil the Great*—O.S.B.M.
[1490]—*Sisters of the Third Franciscan Order*—O.S.F.
[3620]—*Sisters, Servants of Mary Immaculate*—S.S.M.I.
[2160]—*Sisters, Servants of the Immaculate Heart of Mary*—I.H.M.
[4120-04]—*Ursuline Sisters of Cleveland*—O.S.U.

DIOCESAN CEMETERIES

ROCHESTER. *Holy Sepulchre*, 2461 Lake Ave., 14612. Tel: 585-458-4110; Fax: 585-458-3059. Web: www.holysepulchre.org. Email: jim@holysepulchre.org.

REGIONAL CEMETERIES

AUBURN. *St. Joseph's*
CORNING. *St. Mary*
ELMIRA. *SS. Peter and Paul's*
GENEVA. *St. Mary's and St. Patrick's*

NECROLOGY

† D'Aurizio, Joseph F., (Retired)—Died Sept. 5, 2009
† Mahler, Michael J., Ithaca, NY St. Catherine of Siena—Died June 29, 2009
† McNamara, Robert F., (Retired)—Died May 22, 2009
† Miller, Neil R., (Retired)—Died Dec. 27, 2009
† O'Connor, Gerald T., (Retired)—Died Nov. 20, 2009

An asterisk (*) denotes an organization that has established tax-exempt status directly with the IRS and is not covered by the USCCB Group Ruling.

Diocese of Rockford

(Dioecesis Rockfordiensis)

Most Reverend

THOMAS G. DORAN

Bishop of Rockford; ordained December 20, 1961; appointed Bishop of Rockford April 19, 1994; consecrated and installed June 24, 1994. *Res.: P.O. Box 7044, Rockford, IL 61125.*

Diocesan Chancery: 555 Colman Center Dr., P.O. Box 7044, Rockford, IL 61125. Tel: 815-399-4300; Fax: 815-399-5266.

Web: www.rockforddiocese.org

Email: chancery99@aol.com

Most Reverend

ARTHUR J. O'NEILL, D.D., V.G.

Retired Bishop of Rockford; ordained March 27, 1943; appointed Bishop of Rockford August 19, 1968; consecrated and installed October 11, 1968; retired April 19, 1994. *Res.: 3330 Maria Linden Dr., Rockford, IL 61114.* Tel: 815-877-7416.

ESTABLISHED SEPTEMBER 23, 1908.

Square Miles 6,457.

Comprises Jo Daviess, Stephenson, Winnebago, Boone, McHenry, Carroll, Ogle, DeKalb, Kane, Whiteside and Lee Counties in the State of Illinois.

For legal titles of parishes and diocesan institutions, consult the Chancery Office.

STATISTICAL OVERVIEW

Personnel	
Bishop	1
Retired Bishops	2
Abbots	1
Retired Abbots	2
Priests: Diocesan Active in Diocese	145
Priests: Diocesan Active Outside Diocese	9
Priests: Diocesan in Foreign Missions	1
Priests: Retired, Sick or Absent	48
Number of Diocesan Priests	203
Religious Priests in Diocese	42
Total Priests in Diocese	245
Extern Priests in Diocese	11
Ordinations:	
Diocesan Priests	2
Transitional Deacons	4
Permanent Deacons in Diocese	136
Total Brothers	11
Total Sisters	120
Parishes	
Parishes	105
With Resident Pastor:	
Resident Diocesan Priests	85
Resident Religious Priests	8
Without Resident Pastor:	
Administered by Priests	12
Administered by Deacons	1
Professional Ministry Personnel:	
Lay Ministers	7
Welfare	
Catholic Hospitals	3
Total Assisted	562,134
Health Care Centers	17
Total Assisted	231,610
Homes for the Aged	7
Total Assisted	3,261
Day Care Centers	1
Total Assisted	33
Special Centers for Social Services	12
Total Assisted	24,025
Educational	
Diocesan Students in Other Seminaries	23
Total Seminarians	23
High Schools, Diocesan and Parish	6
Total Students	3,190
High Schools, Private	2
Total Students	962
Elementary Schools, Diocesan and Parish	41
Total Students	10,580
Catechesis/Religious Education:	
High School Students	7,118
Elementary Students	25,312
Total Students under Catholic Instruction	47,185
Teachers in the Diocese:	
Priests	32
Brothers	9
Sisters	14
Lay Teachers	1,370
Vital Statistics	
Receptions into the Church:	
Infant Baptism Totals	6,016
Minor Baptism Totals	134
Adult Baptism Totals	203
Received into Full Communion	333
First Communions	6,845
Confirmations	3,959
Marriages:	
Catholic	743
Interfaith	298
Total Marriages	1,041
Deaths	2,036
Total Catholic Population	451,509
Total Population	1,850,609

Former Bishops—Most Revs. PETER J. MULDOON, D.D., ord. Dec. 18, 1886; cons. Titular Bishop of Tamassus and Auxiliary Bishop of Chicago, July 25, 1901; appt. Bishop of Rockford, Sept. 28, 1908; made Assistant to the Pontifical Throne, June 8, 1921; died Oct. 8, 1927; EDWARD F. HOBAN, S.T.D., ord. July 11, 1903; cons. Titular Bishop of Colonia and Auxiliary Bishop of Chicago, Dec. 21, 1921; appt. Bishop of Rockford, Feb. 10, 1928; appt. Assistant at the Pontifical Throne, Nov. 25, 1937; appt. Titular Bishop of Listra and Coadjutor Bishop of Cleveland, Nov. 16, 1942; succeeded to the See of Cleveland, Nov. 2, 1945; died Sept. 22, 1966; JOHN J. BOYLAN, D.D., Ph.D., ord. July 28, 1915; appt. Nov. 21, 1942; cons. Feb. 17, 1943; died July 19, 1953; RAYMOND P. HILLINGER, D.D., ord. April 2, 1932; appt. Nov. 3, 1953; cons. Dec. 29, 1953; appt. Titular Bishop of Derbe and Auxiliary Bishop of Chicago, June 27, 1956; died Nov. 13, 1971; Rt. Rev. DONALD M. CARROLL, D.D., ord. April 7, 1934; appt. June 27, 1956; resigned Sept. 25, 1956; died Jan. 3, 2002; Most Revs. LORAS T. LANE, D.D., ord. March 19, 1937; appt. Titular Bishop of Bencenna and Auxiliary of Dubuque, May 29, 1951; cons. Aug. 20, 1951; appt. to Rockford, Oct. 11, 1956; died July 22, 1968; ARTHUR J. O'NEILL, D.D., V.G., ord. March 27, 1943; appt. Bishop of Rockford Aug. 19, 1968; cons. and installed Oct. 11, 1968; retired April 19, 1994.

Diocesan Chancery—555 Colman Center Dr., P.O. Box 7044, Rockford, 61125. Tel: 815-399-4300; Fax: 815-399-5266. Address all official business to this office. Office Hours: Mon.-Fri. 8:30-12, 1-4:30.

Vicars General—Most Rev. ARTHUR J. O'NEILL, D.D., V.G.; Rev. Msgrs. THOMAS C. BRADY, P.A., V.G., Ph.D. (Retired); DAVID D. KAGAN, V.G., J.C.L.; GLENN L. NELSON, J.C.L., Christ the Teacher Parish, 512 Normal Rd., DeKalb, 60115. Tel: 815-787-7770; Fax: 815-758-2053.

Moderator of the Curia—Rev. Msgr. DAVID D. KAGAN, V.G., J.C.L.

Vicar for Clergy and Religious—Rev. Msgr. ERIC R. BARR, S.T.L.

Parish Services and Directors—Mr. FRANK VONCH, Dir. Social Svcs., 555 Colman Center Dr., P.O. Box 7044, Rockford, 61125; VACANT, Asst. Dir. Social Svcs., 102 S. Madison, Rockford, 61104; Rev. JOHN A. SLAMPAK, Dir. Pastoral Svcs., Blessed Sacrament Church, 801 Oak St., North Aurora, 60542; LORRIE GRAMER, Asst. Dir. Pastoral Svcs., Bishop Lane Retreat Center, 7708 E. McGregor Rd., Rockford, 61102; Sr. PATRICIA DOWNEY, O.P., Dir. Educational Svcs., Catholic Education Office, 555 Colman Center Dr., P.O. Box 7044, Rockford, 61125; Mr. JOHN MCGRATH, Asst. Dir. Educational Svcs., Catholic Education Office, 555 Colman Center Dr., P.O. Box 7044, Rockford, 61125; Dr. WAYNE LENELL, CPA, Ph.D., Dir. Financial & Admin. Svcs., 555 Colman Center Dr., P.O. Box 7044, Rockford, 61125; Mrs. JODI RIPPON, Asst. Dir. Financial & Admin. Svcs., 555 Colman Center Dr., P.O. Box 7044, Rockford, 61125.

Chancellor—Rev. Msgr. GLENN L. NELSON, J.C.L.

Vice Chancellor—Rev. MARTINS EMEH, J.C.L.

Bishop's Secretary for Retired Priests—Rev. Msgr. DANIEL J. DEUTSCH, V.F.

Secretary to the Bishop & Diocesan Master of Ceremonies—Rev. MATTHEW BERGSCHNEIDER.

Diocesan Tribunal—555 Colman Center Dr., P.O. Box 7044, Rockford, 61125. Tel: 815-399-4300; Fax: 815-399-4861. Address all official business to this office.

Judicial Vicar—Rev. Msgr. MICHAEL A. KURZ, J.C.L.

Adjunct Judical Vicar—Rev. Msgr. ARQUIMEDES VALLEJO, J.C.D.

Secretary for Administrative Processes—Rev. Msgr. ROBERT J. SWEENEY.

Promoter of Justice—Rev. Msgr. ARQUIMEDES VALLEJO, J.C.D.
Defenders of the Bond—Rev. Msgrs. ARQUIMEDES VALLEJO, J.C.D.; MICHAEL A. HACK, J.C.D.
Pro Synodal Judges—Rev. Msgrs. RAYMOND J. WAHL, P.A., J.C.D. (Retired); DAVID D. KAGAN, V.G., J.C.L.; THOMAS L. DZIELAK, V.F.; WILLIAM H. SCHWARTZ, P.A., S.T.L.; GERALD P. KOBBEMAN; Rev. FRANCIS E. MCDONNELL (Retired).
Advocates—Sisters MARGARET ANNE FLOTO, O.S.F.; NADINE MEYER, S.S.N.D.
Experts—Rev. Msgr. THOMAS J. MONAHAN, Ph.D. (Retired); Mr. MICHAEL M. KAGAN, M.A.
Notaries—Mrs. DENISE GEORGE; Mrs. DONNA HAYES.
Diocesan Consultors—Rev. Msgrs. THOMAS C. BRADY, P.A., V.G., Ph.D. (Retired); DAVID D. KAGAN, V.G., J.C.L.; DANIEL J. HERMES; ERIC R. BARR, S.T.L.; WILLIAM MCDONNELL, V.F.; JOHN J. MITCHELL (Retired); RAYMOND J. WAHL, P.A., J.C.D. (Retired); DANIEL J. DEUTSCH, V.F.; Revs. DONALD M. AHLES; STEPHEN ST. JULES; STEPHEN J. KNOX, S.T.L.; GEOFFREY D. WIRTH.
Deans—Rev. Msgrs. DANIEL J. DEUTSCH, V.F., Aurora Deanery; GLENN L. NELSON, J.C.L., DeKalb Deanery; JOSEPH B. LINSTER, Elgin Deanery; P. WILLIAM MCDONNELL, Freeport Deanery; JAMES W. MCLOUGHLIN, McHenry County Deanery; GERALD P. KOBBEMAN, Rockford Deanery; THOMAS L. DZIELAK, V.F., Sterling Deanery.

Diocesan Offices and Directors

Accounting and Data Processing Office—DAN O'MALLEY, Dir. Accounting; BOB WHITE, Dir. Information Technology; LORI KUEHNE, Office Mgr., Mailing Address: P.O. Box 7044, Rockford, 61125. Tel: 815-399-4300; Fax: 815-399-5657.
Catholic Campaign for Human Development—555 Colman Center Dr., P.O. Box 7044, Rockford, 61125. Tel: 815-399-4300; Fax: 815-399-6303.
Catholic Charismatic Renewal Services—Mr. RON BERGMAN, Diocesan Liaison, 1910 Bracknel Blvd., Rockford, 61103. Tel: 815-654-4111.
Catholic Office of the Deaf—Rev. Msgr. GLENN L. NELSON, J.C.L., Dir., Christ the Teacher Parish, 512 Normal Rd., Dekalb, 60115. Tel: 815-787-7770 (Voice); 815-962-2994 (TTY); Fax: 815-758-2053.
Catholic Relief Services—Mr. THOMAS MCKENNA, 555 Colman Center Dr., P.O. Box 7044, Rockford, 61125. Tel: 815-399-4300; Fax: 815-399-6303.
Catholic Social Services—Mr. FRANK VONCH, Dir., Mailing Address: P.O. Box 7044, Rockford, 61125. Tel: 815-399-4300; Fax: 815-399-6303.
Cemeteries—Rev. Msgr. THOMAS C. BRADY, P.A., V.G., Ph.D., Exec. Dir. (Retired); Dr. WAYNE LENELL, CPA, Ph.D., Admin.; CAROL GIAMBALVO, Dir., 8616 W. State St., Winnebago, 61088. Tel: 815-965-1450; Fax: 815-965-9632.
Censores Librorum—Rev. Msgr. CHARLES W. MCNAMEE, P.A., J.C.L. (Retired); Rev. FRANCIS E. MCDONNELL (Retired).
Charities—Mr. FRANK VONCH, Acting Dir., Offices: 102 S. Madison, Rockford, 61104. Tel: 815-965-0623; Fax: 815-965-0628. 1700 N. Farnsworth Ave., Ste. 18, Aurora, 60505. 1315 Pleasant St., DeKalb, 60115. 566 Dundee Ave., Elgin, 60120. 1231 S. Walnut Ave., Freeport, 61032. 706 West St., Galena, 61036. 5215 W. Bull Valley Rd., McHenry, 60050. 801 W. 11th St., Sterling, 61081. 360 S. Division #3, Harvard, 60033.
Satellite Office—554 S. Main St., 2nd Fl., Belvidere, 61008.
Clergy Relief Society, Priests' Retirement Committee—Rev. Msgr. DANIEL J. DEUTSCH, V.F., Exec. Sec., 2300 Main St., Batavia, 60510. Tel: 630-879-4750; Fax: 630-879-9502.
Communications—Ms. PENNY WIEGERT, Dir., 555 Colman Center Dr., P.O. Box 7044, Rockford, 61125. Tel: 815-399-4300; Fax: 815-399-6225.
Conciliation and Arbitration Council—Mrs. ELLEN LYNCH HARRISON, Exec. Sec., 555 Colman Center Dr., P.O. Box 7044, Rockford, 61125. Tel: 815-399-4300; Fax: 815-399-6168.
Council of Catholic Women, Diocesan—Rev. Msgr. THOMAS L. DZIELAK, V.F., Moderator, 708 10th Ave., Rock Falls, 61071. Tel: 815-625-4508; JEANETTE GAWRONSKI, 11530 Wagon Lane, Roscoe, 61073. Tel: 815-623-8559.
Cursillo Movement—Rev. ROBERT N. SHERRY, Dir., 5211 W. Bull Valley Rd., McHenry, 60050. Tel: 815-385-5673.
Development Office—Mr. DAVID HOUGAN, Dir., 555 Colman Center Dr., P.O. Box 7044, Rockford, 61125. Tel: 815-399-4300; Fax: 815-399-5657.
Divine Worship, Office for— (and RCIA Resources)--Rev. JOSEPH P. NAILL, Dir., 3500 Washington St., McHenry, IL 60050. Tel: 815-385-0025; Fax: 815-385-0861.
Ecumenism, Office of—Rev. Msgr. THOMAS L. DZIELAK, V.F., 708 Tenth Ave., Rock Falls, 61071. Tel: 815-625-4508; Fax: 815-625-1569.
Education—Sr. PATRICIA DOWNEY, O.P., Supt. Schools; Mr. JOHN MCGRATH, Dir., Rel. Educ. & Formation, 555 Colman Center Dr., P.O. Box 7044, Rockford, 61125. Tel: 815-399-4300; Fax: 815-399-6278.
Ethicist for Health Care Issues, Diocesan—Rev. Msgr. TIMOTHY L. DOHERTY, Ph.D., S.T.L., 555 Colman Center Dr., P.O. Box 7044, Rockford, 61125. Tel: 815-399-4300; Fax: 815-399-6303.
Family Life—LORRIE GRAMER, Dir., 7708 E. McGregor Rd., Rockford, 61102. Tel: 815-965-5011; Fax: 815-965-5811.
Finance and Administration—Dr. WAYNE LENELL, CPA, Ph.D., Dir. Fin. & Admin. Svcs., 555 Colman Center Dr., P.O. Box 7044, Rockford, 61125. Tel: 815-399-4300; Fax: 815-399-5591.
Hispanic Ministry Offices—Rev. Msgr. ARQUIMEDES VALLEJO, J.C.D., 555 Colman Center Dr., P.O. Box 7044, Rockford, 61125. Tel: 815-399-4300; Fax: 815-399-6303. Offices for Diocese Aurora Deanery: Centro Cristo Rey, 115 State St., Aurora, 60505. DeKalb Deanery: Centro Cuerpo de Cristo, 308 Fisk Ave., Dekalb, 60115. Elgin Deanery: Centro Jesus Resucitado, 90 N. Kennedy Dr., Carpentersville, 60110. Freeport Deanery: Centro Jesus Galileo, 21 Burr Oaks Dr., E., Stockton, 61085. McHenry Deanery: St. Thomas the Apostle, 272 King St., Crystal Lake, 60014. Rockford Deanery: P.O. Box 7044, Rockford, 61125. Sterling Deanery: Centro TU C.A.S.A., 202 W. Sixth St., Sterling, 61081.
Holy Childhood Association—Sr. PATRICIA DOWNEY, O.P., Dir., 555 Colman Center Dr., P.O. Box 7044, Rockford, 61125. Tel: 815-399-4300; Fax: 815-399-6278.
Immigration Services—Mrs. JEANNE LINDBERG, Dir., 1505 S. Main St., Rockford, 61102. Tel: 815-399-1709; Fax: 815-399-1731.
Investment and Loan—Dr. WAYNE LENELL, CPA, Ph.D., 555 Colman Center Dr., P.O. Box 7044, Rockford, 61125. Tel: 815-399-4300; Fax: 815-399-5591.
Liturgical Commission, Diocesan—Rev. JOSEPH P. NAILL, Chm., St. Patrick, 3500 Washington St., McHenry, 60050. Tel: 815-385-0025.
Ministry Formation, Office of—Mr. JOHN MCGRATH, Dir., 555 Colman Center Dr., P.O. Box 7044, Rockford, 61125. Tel: 815-399-4300; Fax: 815-399-6278.
Ministry to Priests Program—Rev. Msgr. ERIC R. BARR, S.T.L., Vicar, Clergy Sabbaticals and Diocesan Priests' Retreats, 555 Colman Center Dr., P.O. Box 7044, Rockford, 61125. Tel: 815-399-4300; Fax: 815-399-5962.
Newman-Campus Ministry—Rev. Msgr. GLENN L. NELSON, J.C.L., 512 Normal Rd., DeKalb, 60115. Tel: 815-787-7770; Fax: 815-758-2053.
Newspaper— "The Observer" Ms. PENNY WIEGERT, Mng. Editor; Rev. Msgr. DAVID D. KAGAN, V.G., J.C.L., Assoc. Publisher, 555 Colman Center Dr., P.O. Box 7044, Rockford, 61125. Tel: 815-399-4300; Fax: 815-399-6225.
Permanent Diaconate Program Diocesan—Rev. Msgr. WILLIAM H. SCHWARTZ, P.A., S.T.L., Dir., 555 Colman Center, P.O. Box 7044, Rockford, 61125. Tel: 815-399-4300; Fax: 815-399-6303.
Priests' Eucharistic League—Rev. Msgr. THOMAS J. MONAHAN, Ph.D. (Retired), 4295 Ahlstrand Dr., Rockford, 61101. Tel: 815-282-9972.
Priest Personnel—Rev. Msgr. ERIC R. BARR, S.T.L., Vicar, Clergy and Religious, 555 Colman Center Dr., P.O. Box 7044, Rockford, 61125. Tel: 815-399-4300; Fax: 815-399-5962.
Pro-Life Activities, Office of—Mrs. PATRICIA BAINBRIDGE, Dir., 555 Colman Center Dr., P.O. Box 7044, Rockford, 61125. Tel: 815-877-LIFE; Fax: 815-282-5086.
Propagation of the Faith—Rev. Msgr. ROBERT J. SWEENEY, Dir., 555 Colman Center Dr., P.O. Box 7044, Rockford, 61125. Tel: 815-399-4300; Fax: 815-399-4861.
Property Management Office—Mr. BRIAN HEINKEL, Mailing Address: P.O. Box 7044, Rockford, 61125. Tel: 815-399-4300; Fax: 815-399-5657.
Research and Planning—Dr. MICHAEL CIESLAK, Ph.D., Dir., 555 Colman Center Dr., P.O. Box 7044, Rockford, 61125. Tel: 815-399-4300; Fax: 815-399-6225.
Rural Life Conference—Mr. THOMAS MCKENNA, Dir., 555 Colman Center Dr., P.O. Box 7044, Rockford, 61125. Tel: 815-399-4300; Fax: 815-399-6303.
Scouts—Rev. MATTHEW MCMORROW, 4000 St. Francis Dr., Rockford, 61103. Tel: 815-877-0531; Fax: 815-877-2544.
Diocesan Administration Offices—Mrs. GWEN LASHOCK, Bldg. Mgr., 555 Colman Center Dr., P.O. Box 7044, Rockford, 61125. Tel: 815-399-4300; Fax: 815-399-6303.
Unemployment Insurance Office—JUDITH A. CROSS, Mgr., Mailing Address: P.O. Box 7044, Rockford, 61125. Tel: 815-399-4300; Fax: 815-399-5657.
Victim Assistance Coordinator—JOHN MCCOY, M.S.W. Tel: 815-962-9347. Email: chancery99@aol.com.
Vocations—Revs. MICHAEL G. LAVAN, Dir.; JOHN P. LOVELL, Asst. Dir., 555 Colman Center Dr., P.O. Box 7044, Rockford, 61125. Tel: 815-399-4300; Fax: 815-399-6085.

CLERGY, PARISHES, MISSIONS AND PAROCHIAL SCHOOLS

CITY OF ROCKFORD

(WINNEBAGO COUNTY)

1—ST. PETER CATHEDRAL (1922) Very Rev. Kenneth P. Wasilewski, S.T.L., Rector; Rev. Kevin M. Butler, Parochial Vicar; Deacons Charles Cooper; Martin Czerniewski; Randy Fast; Robert Mitchison.
Res.: 1243 N. Church St., 61103. Tel: 815-965-2765; Fax: 815-965-0743.
School—(Grades PreK-8), 1231 N. Court St., 61103. Tel: 815-963-3620; Fax: 815-963-0551. Ms. Cori Gendron, Prin.; Cindy Buffo, Librarian. Lay Teachers 16; Students 285.
Catechesis/Religious Program—Mr. William Easton, D.R.E. Students 113.

2—ST. ANTHONY OF PADUA (1909), (Italian), Revs. Anthony Labedis, O.F.M.Conv.; John Grigus, O.F.M.Conv.
Res.: 1010 Ferguson St., 61102. Tel: 815-965-2761; Fax: 815-968-2798. Email: sainttonys@aol.com. Web: stanthonyrockford.com.
Catechesis/Religious Program—Tel: 815-965-3448. Email: sttonysdre@aol.com. Students 139.

3—ST. BERNADETTE (1957) Revs. Kenneth Stachyra; Joel Lopez; Deacon Richard Gerdeman; Mary Trapani, Business Mgr.; Ms. Joan Wagner, Liturgy & Music Dir. In Res., Rev. Msgr. Philip E. O'Neil (Retired); Rev. Pierre G. Polycarpe.
Res.: 2400 Bell Ave., 61103. Tel: 815-968-0904; Fax: 815-987-9476. Web: www.stbernadette.info.
Church: Rockton Ave. & Bell Ave., 61103. Tel: 815-968-0904; Fax: 815-987-9476.
School—2300 Bell Ave., 61103. Tel: 815-968-2288; Fax: 815-987-9453. Mrs. Elizabeth Heitkamp, Prin. Lay Teachers 13; Students 149.
Catechesis/Religious Program—2300 Bell Ave., 61103. Tel: 815-962-7345. Mrs. Judy Rossato, D.R.E. Students 50.

4—ST. EDWARD (1929) Revs. Michael G. Black; Anthony Pantyra; Deacon Lambert Verstynen.
Parish Office—3004 11th St., 61109. Tel: 815-229-0282; Fax: 815-229-8912. Web: www.stedwardrockford.org.
Res.: 3026 11th St., 61109. Tel: 815-398-1249.
School—3020 S. 11th St., 61109. Tel: 815-398-2631; Fax: 815-398-3134. Ms. Margo Shifo, Prin. Lay Teachers 14; Students 207.
Catechesis/Religious Program—Tel: 815-229-8914. Sandra Dettori, D.R.E. Students 587.

5—HOLY FAMILY (1963) Rev. Msgr. Thomas E. Bales; Revs. David Vogel; Randy Fronek; Deacons William Bronzi; Robert Sweeney; Michael Cristoforo.
4401 Highcrest Rd., 61107. Tel: 815-398-4280; Fax: 815-398-4287. Web: www.holyfamilyrockford.org.
School—4407 Highcrest Rd., 61107. Tel: 815-398-5331; Fax: 815-398-5902. Web: www.holyfamilyrockford.org. Mr. Anthony Smerko, Prin. Lay Teachers 28; Students 534.
Catechesis/Religious Program—Tel: 815-397-9395; Fax: 815-398-4287. Joellen Lansing, D.R.E. Students 309.

6—ST. JAMES (1853) [JC] Rev. Dean E. Russell; Deacons Ronald Magee; William Dean.
Res.: 428 N. Second St., 61107. Tel: 815-962-1214; Fax: 815-962-1236.
School—(Grades K-8), 409 N. First St., 61107. Tel: 815-962-8515. Mr. Michael Kagan, Prin. Lay Teachers 16; Students 255.
Catechesis/Religious Program—Tel: 815-962-5588. Students 92.

7—ST. MARY ORATORY (1997) Rev. Brian Bovee.
Res.: 517 Elm St., 61102. Tel: 815-965-5971; Fax: 815-965-6029. Email: stmaryrockford@institute-christ-king.org. Web: www.institute-christ-king.org.

8—ST. PATRICK (1919) [JC] Rev. Ricardo Hernandez; Deacon Frank Barone.
Res.: 2505 School St., 61101. Tel: 815-965-9539; Fax: 815-965-0086. Email: stpatrickchurchh@tds.net.
Catechesis/Religious Program—Students 197.

9—SS. PETER AND PAUL (1911), (Hispanic), Rev. Zbigniew Zajchowski, O.F.M.Conv. (Poland).
Res.: 617 Lincoln Ave., 61102. Tel: 815-962-7171; Fax: 815-962-5184. Email: zzajchowski@yahoo.com.

Catechesis/Religious Program—Fax: 815-962-5184. Students 210.

10—ST. RITA (1914) Rev. Msgr. Gerald P. Kobbeman; Rev. Matthew J. Camaioni; Deacon William Dall. In Res., Rev. Msgr. Michael A. Kurz; Rev. Michael G. Lavan.
Res.: 6254 Valley Knoll Dr., 61109-1898. Tel: 815-398-0853; Fax: 815-397-7499. Email: kbehrense@stritarockford.org. Web: www.stritarockford.org.
School—6284 Valley Knoll Dr., 61109-1898. Tel: 815-398-3466; Fax: 815-398-6104. Email: school@stritarockford.org. Patrick Flanagan, Prin. Lay Teachers 14; Students 271.
Catechesis/Religious Program—Tel: 815-398-6483; Fax: 815-397-7499. Doug Colloton, C.R.E.; Paul Vogrine, Coord.Youth Ministry. Students 155.

11—ST. STANISLAUS KOSTKA (1912), (Polish), Rev. Peter Sarnicki, O.F.M.Conv.; Bro. Henryk Lukawski, O.F.M.Conv.; Deacon James Hudzinski.
Res.: 201 Buckbee St., 61104. Tel: 815-965-3913; Fax: 815-965-3915. Email: margaretb@st-stanislaus.org. Web: www.st-stanislaus.org.
Catechesis/Religious Program—Students 68.

OUTSIDE THE CITY OF ROCKFORD

ALBANY, WHITESIDE CO., ST. PATRICK (1948) Rev. David M. Austin.
Hwy. 84, 61230. Tel: 815-589-3542; 815-589-4915. Email: icsecretary@mchsi.com. Mailing Address: 703 12th Ave., Fulton, 61252.
Catechesis/Religious Program—Students 3.

ALGONQUIN, MCHENRY CO., ST. MARGARET MARY (1954) Revs. Michael J. Tierney; Edward Staniukiewicz, O.F.M.Conv.; Slawomir Zimodro; Darek Barna; Deacons Howard Fischer; Simon Grossmayer; Patrick Maher; Donald Miller; Michael LeRoy.
Parish Office—111 S. Hubbard St., 60102. Tel: 847-658-7625; Fax: 847-658-7882. Web: www.saintmargaretmary.org.
School—(Grades PreK-8), 119 S. Hubbard St., 60102. Tel: 847-658-5313; Fax: 847-854-0501. Mrs. Susan Snyder, Prin. Lay Teachers 24; Students 478.
Catechesis/Religious Program—Jr. High/H.S. R.E. Prog.: 113 S. Hubbard St., 60102. Tel: 847-658-7881; Fax: 847-658-2378. Email: teresa@saintmargaretmary.org. Elementary R.E. Prog.: 119 S. Hubbard St., 60102. Tel: 847-658-9339; Fax: 847-854-0501. Email: enelson@saintmargaretmary.org. Mrs. Ellie Nelson, D.R.E.; Mrs. Teresa Chiappone, D.R.E. (Junior High & High School). Students 926.

AMBOY, LEE CO., ST. PATRICK (1857) [CEM] Revs. Carl E. Beekman; Cyprian Thoguru; Deacon Kevin Prunty.
Res.: 32 N. Jones Ave., 61310. Tel: 815-857-2315; Fax: 815-857-3485. Email: office@stpatrickamboy.org. Web: stpatrickamboy.org.
Catechesis/Religious Program—Web: www.st-patrickamboy.org. Students 146.

APPLE RIVER, JO DAVIESS CO., ST. JOSEPH (1868) [CEM] Rev. Max J. Striedl, Parochial Admin.
Mailing Address: c/o *St. Ann*, 608 E. Railroad St., P.O. Box 665, Warren, 61087. Tel: 815-745-2312; Fax: 815-745-2312. Email: parishes@catholic.org. Church: 107 Webster St., 61001. Tel: 815-745-2312; Fax: 815-745-2312.
Catechesis/Religious Program— Twinned with St. Ann, Warren. Students 20.

AURORA, KANE CO.

1—ANNUNCIATION OF THE BLESSED VIRGIN MARY (1875) [CEM] Rev. George R. Glover, O.S.B.; Deacons Harold Poss; Michael Giblin.
Res.: 1820 Church Rd., 60505. Tel: 630-851-1436; Fax: 630-851-2435. Email: mario26@msn.com.
School—1840 Church Rd., 60505. Tel: 630-851-4300; Fax: 630-851-4316. Karen Wollwert, Prin. Lay Teachers 24; Students 247.
Catechesis/Religious Program—Tel: 630-851-4300. Students 177.

2—HOLY ANGELS (1892) Rev. Msgr. Martin G. Heinz; Rev. Marianna Ery; Deacons Tim White; Tom Hawksworth.
Mailing Address: 180 S. Russell Ave., 60506.
Res.: 720 Hardin Ave., 60506-4997. Tel: 630-897-1194; Fax: 630-897-1370.
School—720 Kensington Pl., 60506. Tel: 630-897-3613; Fax: 630-897-8233. Mr. Norb Rozanski, Prin. Lay Teachers 27; Students 607.
Catechesis/Religious Program—Tel: 630-897-1194, Ext. 26. Email: releducation@holy-angels.org. Students 184.

3—ST. JOSEPH (1899) [CEM] Rev. Jerome L. Leake; Deacon Norbert Szudarski, Pastoral Assoc.
Mailing Address: 722 High St., P.O. Box 4395, 60507. In Res., Rev. Msgr. Robert J. Willhite (Retired).
Res.: 405 St. Joseph Ave., 60505. Tel: 630-844-3780; Fax: 630-844-1338. Email: stjoe722@sbcglobal.net. Web: www.stjosephaurora.4lpi.com.
School—706 High St., 60505. Tel: 630-844-3781; Fax: 630-844-3656. Miss Marie Bockhaus, Prin. Lay Teachers 16; Students 182.
Catechesis/Religious Program—Tel: 630-844-3782. Students 60.

4—ST. MARY (1851), (Irish), [CEM] Rev. Timothy Piasecki; Deacon William Rees.
Res.: 430 E. Downer Pl., 60505-3475. Tel: 630-892-0480; Fax: 630-892-8664.
Catechesis/Religious Program—Aurora Deanery Center for Religious Education, 432 E. Downer Pl., 60505. Tel: 630-859-3922; Fax: 630-859-9637. Email: auroraareacenter@sbcglobal.net; stmary432@yahoo.com. Students 148.

5—ST. NICHOLAS (1862), (Hispanic), [CEM] Revs. Andres Salinas, Parochial Admin.; Luis Alfredo Rios.
Res. & Mailing Address: 308 High St., 60505. Tel: 630-898-8707; Fax: 630-585-6423. Email: stnicholascatholicaurora@yahoo.com.
Catechesis/Religious Program—Tel: 630-898-8707; Fax: 630-585-6423. Sr. Herlinda Rodriguez, M.R.F., D.R.E. Students 540.

6—OUR LADY OF GOOD COUNSEL (1909) Rev. David R. Engbarth; Deacons Carlos Navarro; Ray Weaver.
Res.: 620 S. Fifth St., 60505. Tel: 630-851-1100; Fax: 630-851-4069. Email: olgcchurch@aol.com. Web: www.ourladyofgoodcounsel.net.
School—601 Talma St., 60505. Tel: 630-851-4400; Fax: 630-851-8220. Mr. Elden Stockey, Prin. Students 241.
Catechesis/Religious Program—Tel: 630-851-1100; Fax: 630-851-4069. Students 322.

7—ST. PETER (1929) Rev. Antoni Kretowicz (Poland); Deacon Carlos Navarro.
Res.: 925 Sard Ave., 60506. Tel: 630-896-6816; Fax: 630-896-2534. Email: st.peterchurch@comcast.net. Web: www.saintpetersl.org.
School—915 Sard Ave., 60506. Tel: 630-892-1283; Fax: 630-892-4836. Sr. Ann Brummel, O.P., Prin. Sisters 4; Lay Teachers 10; Students 134.
Catechesis/Religious Program—Students 60.

8—ST. RITA OF CASCIA (1927) Revs. Cesar C. Pajarillo; Louis Busemeyer, S.J.
Res.: 750 W. Old Indian Trail Rd., 60506. Tel: 630-892-5918; Fax: 630-892-6273. Web: www.saint-rita.org/church.
School—770 W. Old Indian Trail Rd., 60506. Tel: 630-892-0020; Fax: 630-892-4236. Ms. Elizabeth Faxon, Prin. Lay Teachers 17; Students 262.
Catechesis/Religious Program—Tel: 630-892-9507. Sr. Rita Mary Phalen, O.S.F., D.R.E. Students 617.

9—SACRED HEART (1861), (Hispanic), [CEM] Rev. Msgr. Arquimedes Vallejo; Rev. Jorge H. Loaiza; Deacons Richard Groom; Jose Falcon.
Res.: 771 Fulton St., 60505. Tel: 630-898-4165; Fax: 630-898-3940.
Catechesis/Religious Program—771 Fulton St., 60505. Tel: 630-499-4023; Fax: 630-898-3940. Cecilia Gutierres, C.R.E. Students 220.

10—ST. THERESE OF JESUS (1925) Rev. Michael I. Miller, M.S.C.; Deacons Bruce M. Watermann; Julio Rosado.
Res.: 271 N. Farnsworth Ave., 60505. Tel: 630-898-5422; Fax: 630-898-5327. Email: stthereseaurora@sbcglobal.net. Web: www.sttheresaaurora.41pi.com.
School—255 N. Farnsworth Ave., 60505. Tel: 630-898-0620; Fax: 630-898-3087. Mr. William O'Dea, Prin. Lay Teachers 7; Students 90.
Catechesis/Religious Program—Tel: 630-898-5422; Fax: 630-898-5327. Students 589.

BATAVIA, KANE CO., HOLY CROSS (1871) [JC] Rev. Msgr. Daniel J. Deutsch; Revs. Paul J. Fasano; John R. Evans; Deacons Raymond J. Martin; Larry Motyka; William L. Jacobson, Business Mgr.; Karen A. Mc Quillan, Early Teen Minister.
2300 Main St., 60510-7625. Tel: 630-879-4750; Fax: 630-879-9502. Email: staff@holycross-batavia.org. Web: www.holycross-batavia.org.
Rectory—
School—Tel: 630-593-5290; Fax: 630-593-5289. Tricia H. Weis, Prin. Students 317.
Catechesis/Religious Program—(2008)Tel: 630-879-4751. Patricia A. Roatch, Children's Minister; Jennifer A. Haviland, Early Teen Youth Minister; Patrick B. Haviland, H.S. Youth Minister. Students 1,335.

BELVIDERE, BOONE CO., ST. JAMES (1886) [CEM] Revs. Brian A. Geary; Diego Ospina; Deacon James D. Olson.
Office: 535 Caswell St., 61008. Tel: 815-547-6397; Fax: 815-547-0607. Web: stjamesbelvidere.org.
Res.: 514 Caswell St., 61008. Tel: 815-547-6397.
School—320 Logan Ave., 61008. Tel: 815-547-7633; Fax: 815-544-2294. Mr. Gregory Wilhelm, Prin. Lay Teachers 14; Students 169.
Catechesis/Religious Program—Tel: 815-544-3698. Judith Cadie, D.R.E. Students 700.

BYRON, OGLE CO., ST. MARY (1895) [CEM] Rev. Sylvester Nnaso.
P.O. Box 1070, 61010. Tel: 815-234-7431; Fax: 815-234-2133.
Catechesis/Religious Program—Joetta Hass, C.R.E.; Beth Hildreth, C.R.E. Students 291.

CARPENTERSVILLE, KANE CO., ST. MONICA (1957), (Hispanic), Revs. Ariel Valencia; Rafael Laiton; Josue Lara; Deacons John Bach; J. Michael Frazier; Dennis Garber; Policarpo Jimenez.
Res.: 90 N. Kennedy Dr., 60110-1695. Tel: 847-428-2646; Fax: 847-428-1021. Email: saintmonica@sbcglobal.net.
Catechesis/Religious Program—Tel: 847-428-7562. Mary Helin, D.R.E. Students 884.

CARY, MCHENRY CO., SS. PETER & PAUL (1904) Revs. Stephen St. Jules; John Gow; Deacons Howard Ganschow II; Michael Boyce.
Res.: 410 N. First St., 60013. Tel: 847-516-2636; Fax: 847-639-3474. Email: info@ssppcary.org. Web: www.peterpaulchurchcary.org.
School—416 N. First St., 60013. Tel: 847-639-3041; Fax: 847-639-5329. Email: dstrzelinski@ssppcary.org. Sr. Katrina Lamkin, O.P., Prin. Dominican Sisters 1; Lay Teachers 25; Students 493.
Catechesis/Religious Program—Tel: 847-639-0414; Fax: 847-639-5329. Email: tzbylut@ssppcary.org. Terri Zbylut, D.R.E. Students 1,295.

CRYSTAL LAKE, MCHENRY CO.

1—ST. ELIZABETH ANN SETON (1978) Revs. Brian D. Grady; Bruce J. Ludeke; Tricia Westhoven, Business Mgr.
Office: 1023 McHenry Ave., 60014. Tel: 815-459-3033; Fax: 815-459-3040. Email: parish.office@elizabethannseton.org. Web: www.elizabethannseton.org.
Res.: 991 McHenry Ave., 60014. Tel: 815-788-0062.
Catechesis/Religious Program—Tel: 815-459-3096; Fax: 815-459-3040. Vicky Serio, C.R.E.; Craig Fiedler, Youth Min. Students 965.

2—ST. THOMAS THE APOSTLE (1881) Rev. Msgr. Daniel J. Hermes; Revs. Akan S. Simon; Rafael Tunarosa; Timothy J. Barr.
Res.: 200 Washington St., 60014. Tel: 815-455-5407; Fax: 815-455-2733.
Pastoral Center—272 King St., 60014. Tel: 815-455-5400; Fax: 815-455-2733.
School—(Grades PreK-8), 265 King St., 60014. Tel: 815-459-0496; Fax: 815-459-0591. Mrs. Deanne Roy, Prin. Lay Teachers 31; Students 409.
Catechesis/Religious Program—Tel: 815-455-9787. Janet Kayser, D.R.E. Students 1,265.

DEKALB, DEKALB CO.

1—CHRIST THE TEACHER, UNIVERSITY PARISH OF NORTHERN ILLINOIS UNIVERSITY (1963) Rev. Msgr. Glenn L. Nelson, Dir.; Revs. Alejandro del Toro; Godwin Asuquo; Deacon James Dombek.
Office: 512 Normal Rd., 60115. Tel: 815-787-7770; Fax: 815-758-2053. Email: parishoffice@newmanniu.org. Web: www.newmanniu.org.
Catechesis/Religious Program—Email: clehman@newmanniu.org. Web: www.newmanniu.org. Mrs. Cheryl Lehman, D.R.E. Students 342.

2—ST. MARY (1861) [CEM] Revs. Kenneth J. Anderson (CHI); Victor H. Alcazar; Saul E. Cruz. In Res., Rev. Anthony Vu Khac Long; Deacon Stephen Puscas.
Office: 302 Fisk Ave., 60115. Tel: 815-758-5432; Fax: 815-758-2487. Email: mail@stmarydekalb.org. Web: www.stmarydekalb.org.
Res.: 321 Pine St., 60115. Tel: 815-748-5654.
School—210 Gurler Rd., 60115. Tel: 815-756-7905; Fax: 815-758-1459. Patricia Weis, Prin. Lay Teachers 18; Students 242.
Catechesis/Religious Program—Tel: 815-758-8504. Students 202.

DIXON, LEE CO.

1—ST. ANNE (1928) Rev. Michael E. Morrissey, Admin.
Res.: 1104 N. Brinton Ave., 61021. Tel: 815-288-3131; Fax: 815-288-3139.
School—(Grades PreK-8), 1112 N. Brinton Ave., 61021. Tel: 815-288-5619; Fax: 815-288-5820. Sr. Marcianne Bzdon, S.S.N.D., Prin. Lay Teachers 15; Students 104.
Catechesis/Religious Program—Tel: 815-288-3131; Fax: 815-288-3139. Students 82.
Convent—926 N. Brinton Ave., 61021.

2—ST. PATRICK (1854) Rev. James R. Keenan; Deacons Sam Berard; Terry Wagner.
Office: 612 S. Highland, 61021. Tel: 815-284-7719; Fax: 815-284-4758. Email: stpatdixon@essexl.com. Web: www.stpatrickdixon.org.
School—St. Mary Elementary & Junior High, (Grades PreK-8), 704 S. Peoria Ave., 61021. Tel: 815-284-6986; Fax: 815-284-6905. Email: st_marysschool@comcast.net. Web: www.stmarysdixon.org. Mrs. Jean Spohn, Prin. Lay Teachers 14; Students 195.
Catechesis/Religious Program—Tel: 815-284-2867; Fax: 815-284-4758. Mrs. Maureen Fischbach, D.R.E. Students 60.

DUNDEE, KANE CO., ST. CATHERINE OF SIENA (1912) Rev. Msgr. Timothy L. Doherty; Deacons William Whitehead Jr.; Steven Fox; Hank Schmalen.
Office: 845 W. Main St., 60118. Tel: 847-426-2217; Fax: 847-426-1130.
School—(Grades PreK-8) Tel: 847-426-4808; Fax: 847-426-0437. Renee Link, Prin. Lay Teachers 19; Students 263.
Catechesis/Religious Program—Roberta Bellock, D.R.E. Students 782.
Mission—St. Mary [CEM] c/o 845 W. Main St., West Dundee, Kane Co. 60118. Tel: 847-836-8315.

DURAND, WINNEBAGO CO., ST. MARY (1862), (Irish), [CEM 2] Rev. Msgr. Eric R. Barr.
Mailing Address: 606 W. Main St., 61024. Tel: 815-248-2490; Fax: 815-248-9100.
Catechesis/Religious Program—Students 153.
Mission—St. Patrick [CEM] Irish Grove Rd., Stephenson Co.

EAST DUBUQUE, JO DAVIESS CO., ST. MARY (1868) [JC] Rev. James W. Parker.
Res.: 170 Montgomery Ave., 61025. Tel: 815-747-3221; Fax: 815-747-3212. Email: stmaryeastdubuque@yahoo.com. Web: www.stmaryedbq.org.
School—701 Rte. 35 N., 61025. Tel: 815-747-3010; Fax: 815-747-6188. Web: www.stmary-ed.org. Mrs. Wendi Kletecka, Prin. Lay Teachers 5; Students 67.
Catechesis/Religious Program—Daisy Bauman, C.R.E. Students 66.

ELBURN, KANE CO., ST. GALL (1870), (Irish), [CEM] Rev. Karl P. Ganss.
Res.: 120 W. Shannon, 60119. Tel: 630-365-6030; Fax: 630-365-5483. Email: parishoffice@stgall.com. Web: www.stgall.com.
Catechesis/Religious Program—Tel: 630-365-9166; Fax: 630-365-9166. Students 353.

ELGIN, KANE CO.

1—ST. JOSEPH (1887), (German—Spanish), Revs. John Earl; Leonardo Maldonado; Ruben Herrera; Deacons John Sauceda; Armando Martinez.
Res.: 272 Division St., 60120. Tel: 847-931-2800; Fax: 847-931-2810.
School—274 Division St., 60120. Tel: 847-931-2804; Fax: 847-931-2811. Janine M. Bolchazy, Prin. Lay Teachers 13; Students 176.
Catechesis/Religious Program—Tel: 847-931-2808. Students 939.

2—ST. LAURENCE (1929) Rev. Joseph F. Kulak.
Office: 565 Standish St., 60123. Tel: 847-468-6900; Fax: 847-468-6904.
Res.: 226 Orchard St., 60123. Tel: 847-468-6105.
School—(Grades PreK-8), 572 Standish St., 60123. Tel: 847-468-6100; Fax: 847-468-6104. Mrs. Phyllis Jensen, Prin. Lay Teachers 14; Students 207.
Catechesis/Religious Program—Tel: 847-468-6900; Fax: 847-468-6104. Students 172.

3—ST. MARY (1851) Revs. Edward J. Seisser; Lisandro Cristancho; Matthew DeBlock; Deacon Henry Orlik.
Parish Office—397 Fulton St., 60120. Tel: 847-888-2828; Fax: 847-888-2883. Web: www.stmaryelgin.com.
Res.: 390 Fulton St., 60120. Tel: 847-888-0502.
School—(Grades K-8), 103 S. Gifford St., 60120. Tel: 847-695-6609; Fax: 847-695-6623. Mrs. Mary Beth Mitchell, Prin. Lay Teachers 11; Students 207.
Catechesis/Religious Program—Tel: 847-888-2718; Fax: 847-888-2883. Deacon Henry Orlik, D.R.E. Students 327.

4—ST. THOMAS MORE (1959) [JC] Revs. Geoffrey D. Wirth; Arturo O. Mallari; Deacons Jack Roder; Robert Plazewski; Gregory Stevens. In Res., Rev. Andrew J. Plesa (Retired).
Office: 215 Thomas More Dr., 60123. Tel: 847-888-1682; Fax: 847-888-3198.
School—1625 W. Highland Ave., 60123. Tel: 847-742-3959; Fax: 847-931-1066. Ms. Margaret Fabrizius, Prin. Lay Teachers 17; Students 234.
Catechesis/Religious Program—Tel: 847-888-4887. Mr. Ron Becker, D.R.E. Students 62.

ELIZABETH, JO DAVIESS CO., ST. MARY (1886) [CEM] Rev. Leonardo M. Jacob.
Res.: 112 E. Washington St., Box 246, 61028. Tel: 815-858-3422; Fax: 815-858-2622. Email: st_mary@jcwifi.com. Web: www.stmarysch.org.
Catechesis/Religious Program— Patricia Brown, C.R.E. Students 25.

FREEPORT, STEPHENSON CO.

1—ST. CATHERINE, Closed. For inquiries for parish records contact the chancery.

2—ST. JOSEPH (1862), (German), [CEM] Rev. Howard C. Barch Jr.
Res.: 229 W. Washington Pl., 61032. Tel: 815-232-8271; Fax: 815-235-4690. Email: stjosephfreeport@comcast.net.
School—Aquin Elementary School, 202 W. Pleasant St., 61032. Tel: 815-232-6416. Mrs. Kathy Runte, Prin.; Mrs. Diane Potts, Admin. & Prin. Lay Teachers 7; Students 196.
Catechesis/Religious Program—Tel: 815-235-4324. Students 77.

3—ST. MARY (1846) [CEM] Rev. Howard C. Barch Jr.; Deacon Gary Klocke.
Office: 704 S. State Ave., 61032. Tel: 815-235-7544; Fax: 815-233-0005.
Res.: 704 S. State Ave., 61032.
Catechesis/Religious Program— (Freeport Catholic School System) Students 40.

4—ST. THOMAS AQUINAS (1921) Rev. Msgr. P. William McDonnell; Rev. Manuel Recera; Deacons H. Donald Brunette; Richard Dinneen; Vincent Drees; Stephen Pospischil.
Res.: 1400 Kiwanis Dr., 61032. Tel: 815-232-3225; Fax: 815-232-3231. Email: stthomas9@verizon.net. Web: www.stthomas-freeport.com.
Catechesis/Religious Program—Tel: 815-232-3225; Fax: 815-232-3231. Marie Dinneen, C.R.E.; Julie Dorsey, C.R.E. Students 64.

FULTON, WHITESIDE CO., IMMACULATE CONCEPTION (1863) Rev. David M. Austin.
Res.: 703 12th Ave., 61252. Tel: 815-589-3542; Fax: 815-589-4915. Email: ICSecretary@mchsi.com.
Catechesis/Religious Program—Students 41.

GALENA, JO DAVIESS CO.

1—ST. MARY (1850), (German), [CEM] Revs. Christopher J. Kuhn; Stanislaw Kos.
Res.: 406 Franklin St., 61036. Tel: 815-777-0134; Fax: 815-776-0138.
Catechesis/Religious Program—Tel: 815-777-2219. Patricia Schuler, D.R.E. Students 95.

2—ST. MICHAEL (1832), (Irish), [CEM] Rev. Christopher J. Kuhn.
Res.: 227 S. Bench St., 61036. Tel: 815-777-2053; Fax: 815-777-1193.
Catechesis/Religious Program— Cindy Kocol, D.R.E. Students 86.

GENEVA, KANE CO., ST. PETER (1911) [JC] Revs. Martins Emeh; Dennis M. Morrissy; Deacons Michael Zibrun; Michael Sullivan.
Office: 1891 Kaneville Rd., 60134. Tel: 630-232-0124; Fax: 630-232-9262. Email: writetostpeter@stpetergeneva.org. Web: www.stpeterchurch.com.
Res.: 1771 Kaneville Rd., 60134. Tel: 630-208-1625.
School—(Grades PreK-8), 1881 Kaneville Rd., 60134. Tel: 630-232-0476; Fax: 630-208-5681. Mrs. Roseann Feldmann, Prin. Lay Teachers 25; Students 510.
Catechesis/Religious Program— Mr. John N. Lamperis, D.R.E. Students 1,373.

GENOA, DEKALB CO., ST. CATHERINE OF GENOA (1912) [CEM] Rev. Timothy J. Seigel.
Res.: 350 S. Stott St., 60135. Tel: 815-784-2355; Fax: 815-784-2045. Web: www.st-catherine-genoa.org.
Catechesis/Religious Program—Email: alaisa340@atcyber.net. Alaisa Emmens, C.R.E. Students 266.

GILBERTS, KANE CO., ST. MARY'S MISSION OF GILBERTS, [CEM] Rev. Msgr. Timothy L. Doherty; Deacons William Whitehead Jr.; Steven Fox; Hank Schmalen.
Mailing Address: 845 W. Main St., Dundee, 60118. 10 Matteson Rd., 60136.

HAMPSHIRE, KANE CO., ST. CHARLES BORROMEO (1878) [CEM] Rev. Joseph P. Nicolosi.
Res.: 297 E. Jefferson Ave., 60140-7646. Tel: 847-683-2391; Fax: 847-683-2396. Email: parishoffice@scbparish.org. Web: www.scbparish.org.
School—(Grades PreK-8), 288 E. Jefferson Ave., 60140. Tel: 847-683-3450; Fax: 847-683-3209. Email: scbschool@scbparish.org. Kel Kissamis, Prin. Lay Teachers 13; Students 126.
Catechesis/Religious Program—297 E. Jefferson Ave., 60140. Tel: 847-683-1536. Email: CVincent@scbparish.org. Mrs. Cynthia Vincent, D.R.E. Students 255.

HANOVER, JO DAVIESS CO., ST. JOHN THE EVANGELIST (1925) [JC] Rev. Leonardo M. Jacob.
Res.: 103 Savanna Rd., 61041. Tel: 815-591-2258; Fax: 815-591-3533. Email: st_john@jcwifi.com. Web: www.stjohnsch.org.
Catechesis/Religious Program—Tel: 815-591-2258. Students 20.

HARMON, LEE CO., ST. FLANNEN (1898), (Irish), [CEM] Revs. Carl E. Beekman; Cyprian Thoguru.
Res.: 32 N. Jones Ave., Amboy, 61310. Tel: 815-857-2670; Fax: 815-857-3485. Web: www.stpatrickamboy.org/office.
Catechesis/Religious Program—Tel: 815-857-2670; Fax: 815-857-3485.

HARTLAND, MCHENRY CO., ST. PATRICK (1837) [CEM] Rev. Msgr. Aaron R. Brodeski; Deacons Arthur Holt; Joseph Kayser.
Parish Office—15012 St. Patrick Rd., Woodstock, 60098. Tel: 815-338-7883; Fax: 815-338-5570.
Catechesis/Religious Program—Tel: 815-338-5570. Students 34.

HARVARD, MCHENRY CO., ST. JOSEPH (1866) [CEM] Rev. Paul C. White; Deacons Anthony Koss; Phillip Emmert.
Res.: 206 E. Front St., 60033. Tel: 815-943-6406; Fax: 815-943-1604. Email: pmc@stjoeharvard.org.
School—(Grades PreK-8), 201 N. Division St., 60033. Tel: 815-943-6933; Fax: 815-943-0549. Email: principal@stjoeharvard.org. Mr. Michael J. Shukis, Prin. Lay Teachers 7; Students 97.
Catechesis/Religious Program—Tel: 815-943-1644; Fax: 815-943-1604. Amber Emmert, D.R.E. Students 124.

HUNTLEY, MCHENRY CO., ST. MARY (1873) [CEM] Revs. Stephen J. Knox; David Reese; W. Scott DuVall; Deacons Thomas W. O'Brien; Armand Ferrini; Anthony Schubert; John A. McPhee; Louis Farinella; George Coltman; Mr. Thomas O'Brien, Pastoral Assoc.
Res. & Mailing Address: 10307 Dundee Rd., 60142. Tel: 847-669-3137; Fax: 847-669-3138. Web: www.stmaryhuntley.org.
Catechesis/Religious Program—Students 1,396.

JOHNSBURG, MCHENRY CO., ST. JOHN THE BAPTIST (1841) [CEM] Rev. Jacek Junak, C.R.; Deacon Jerry Giessinger.
Res.: 2302 W. Church St., 60051. Tel: 815-385-1477; Fax: 815-363-3333.
School—(Grades PreK-8), 2304 W. Church St., 60051. Tel: 815-385-3959; Fax: 815-363-3337. Pamela Dvonch, Prin. Sisters 1; Lay Teachers 12; Students 186.
Catechesis/Religious Program—Tel: 815-385-4870. Kim Schaefer, D.R.E. Students 381.

LEE, LEE CO., ST. JAMES (1878) [CEM 2] Rev. Bonaventure Okoro (Nigeria).
221 W. Kirke Gate, P.O. Box 100, 60530.
Res.: 321 S. Viking Vie, 60530. Tel: 815-824-2004; 815-824-2053 (Office); Fax: 815-824-2043 (Office). Email: saint.jameslee@verizon.net.
Catechesis/Religious Program—Tel: 815-824-2053. Students 53.

LENA, STEPHENSON CO., ST. JOSEPH (1870) [CEM] Rev. Max J. Striedl Jr., Parochial Admin.
Res.: 410 W. Lena St., 61048. Tel: 815-369-2810; Fax: 815-369-9137. Email: stjoes@aeroine.net.
Catechesis/Religious Program—Tel: 815-369-2810. Louise Kloepping, D.R.E. Students 71.

LOVES PARK, WINNEBAGO CO., ST. BRIDGET (1946) Revs. Burt H. Absalon; John P. Lovell; Deacon Philip Abel. In Res., Rev. Msgr. Arquimedes Vallejo.
Res.: 600 Clifford Ave., 61111. Tel: 815-633-6311; Fax: 815-633-6314.
School—(Grades K-8), 604 Clifford Ave., 61111. Tel: 815-633-8255; Fax: 815-633-5847. Web: www.saint-bridget.org. Mr. David Hawkinson, Prin. Religious 1; Lay Teachers 22; Students 383.
Catechesis/Religious Program—Tel: 815-633-4006. Students 386.

MAPLE PARK, DEKALB CO., ST. MARY (1850) [CEM 2] Rev. Joachim B. Tyrtania (Poland).
Res.: 123 S. County Line Rd., 60151-8024. Tel: 815-827-3218.
Novak Center—211 S. County Line Rd., 60151-8024. Tel: 815-827-3205; Fax: 815-827-3062.
Catechesis/Religious Program—Tel: 815-827-3205; Fax: 815-827-3062. Students 105.

MARENGO, MCHENRY CO., SACRED HEART (1902) [CEM] Rev. Richard M. Russo; Deacons Robert Anchor; John O'Leary.
Res.: 323 N. Taylor St., 60152. Tel: 815-568-7878; Fax: 815-568-7929. Email: sacredheart7929@sbcglobal.net. Web: www.sacredheartmarengo.4lpi.com.
Catechesis/Religious Program—Tel: 815-568-6230; Fax: 815-568-7929. Robert Olsen, D.R.E.; Brenda Ramus, C.R.E. Students 286.

MAYTOWN, LEE CO., ST. PATRICK (1840) [CEM] [JC 2] Revs. Carl E. Beekman; Cyprian Thoguru.
Res.: 32 N. Jones Ave., Amboy, 61310. Tel: 815-857-2670; Fax: 815-857-3485. Web: www.stpatrickamboy.org/office.
Catechesis/Religious Program—

MCHENRY, MCHENRY CO.

1—CHURCH OF HOLY APOSTLES (1989) [CEM] Revs. Robert N. Sherry; Oscar Cortes; Deacon Joseph Phelan.
Church: 5211 W. Bull Valley Rd., 60050. Tel: 815-385-5673; Fax: 815-385-6045. Email: hapostles@thechurchofholyapostles.org. Web: www.thechurchofholyapostles.org.
Catechesis/Religious Program—Tel: 815-385-4273. Jeanne Fraser, D.R.E. Students 687.

2—ST. MARY (1894), (German), [CEM] Rev. Robert A. Balog.
Res.: 1401 N. Richmond Rd., 60050. Tel: 815-385-0024; Fax: 815-385-7809. Email: stmarylady@aol.com.
School—Montini-Middle Grades, 1405 N. Richmond Rd., 60050. Tel: 815-385-1022; Fax: 815-363-7536. Mrs. Sheila Murphy, Prin. Consolidated with St. Patrick and Church of Holy Apostles. Lay Teachers 17; Students 246.
Catechesis/Religious Program—1407 N. Richmond

Rd., 60050. Tel: 815-385-2135. Deacon Tom O'Brien, D.R.E. Students 66.

3—St. Patrick (1840), (Irish), [CEM 2] Revs. Joseph P. Naill; Arogyaswamy Lakkineni.
Res.: 3500 W. Washington St., 60050. Tel: 815-385-3101; Fax: 815-385-0861. Email: parishoffice@stpatrickmchenry.org. Web: www.stpatrickmchenry.org.
School—Montini Primary Center, Tel: 815-385-5380; Fax: 815-385-5017. Mrs. Sheila Murphy, Prin.; Mrs. Marilyn Knapp, Asst. Prin. Lay Teachers 30; Students 517.
Catechesis/Religious Program—Tel: 815-385-2959; Fax: 815-385-0861. Students 212.

Menominee, Jo Daviess Co., Nativity of the Blessed Virgin Mary (1864), (German), [CEM] Rev. James W. Parker.
Res.: 170 Montgomery Ave, East Dubuque, 61025. Fax: 815-747-3212. Email: office@nativity-bvm.com. Web: www.nativity-bvm.com.
Church: 15406 W. Creek Valley Rd., East Dubuque, 61025. Tel: 815-747-3670; Fax: 815-747-2050.
School—Email: principal@nativity-bvm.com. Diane Makovec, Prin. Lay Teachers 5; Students 31.
Catechesis/Religious Program—Email: reled@nativity-bvm.com. Students 23.

Morrison, Whiteside Co., St. Mary (1904) Rev. William R. Antillon.
Office: 13320 Garden Plain Rd., 61270. Tel: 815-772-3095 (Rectory); 815-772-4890 (Church Office); Fax: 815-772-4890. Email: stmarymor@frontiernet.net.
Res.: 611 Greenwood Dr., 61270. Tel: 815-772-3095; Fax: 815-772-4890. Email: william_antillon@yahoo.com.
Catechesis/Religious Program—Tel: 815-772-4890. Students 51.

Mount Carroll, Carroll Co., SS. John and Catherine (1923) Attended by Savanna. Rev. Dennis D. Atto.
Res.: 314 S. Main St., P.O. Box 193, 61053. Tel: 815-244-1835 (Church); Fax: 815-244-1835. Email: jccatholic@grics.net. Web: www.ssjohncatherinech.org.
Catechesis/Religious Program—Fax: 815-244-1835. Students 37.

North Aurora, Kane Co., Blessed Sacrament Catholic Church (1970) Rev. John A. Slampak.
Res.: 801 Oak St., 60542-1063. Tel: 630-897-1029; Fax: 630-897-1062. Email: blesacra@sbcglobal.net. Web: http://blessedsacrament-na.org.
Catechesis/Religious Program—Tel: 630-897-4396. Sr. Rose Marie Weber, O.S.F., D.R.E. Students 271.

Oregon, Ogle Co., St. Mary (1885) [CEM] Rev. Richard R. Kramer.
Res. & Rectory: 303 N. 4th St., 61061. Tel: 815-732-2234; Fax: 815-732-6332. Email: st.marys.rectory@comcast.net. Web: www.st-mary-parish.com.
Catechesis/Religious Program—Tel: 815-732-7383; 815-973-5602; Fax: 815-732-4742. Students 78.

Pecatonica, Winnebago Co., St. Mary (1872), (Irish—German), [CEM] Rev. Msgr. Robert J. Sweeney; Deacons Warren LaMont; Michael Giambalvo.
Res.: 126 W. Fifth St., P.O. Box 656, 61063. Tel: 815-239-1271.
Catechesis/Religious Program—Students 96.

Polo, Ogle Co., St. Mary's (1854) [CEM] [JC] Rev. Brian A. Olsen.
Res.: 211 N. Franklin Ave., 61064. Tel: 815-946-2535; Fax: 815-946-9025. Email: shoj@frontiernet.net.
Catechesis/Religious Program—Tel: 815-493-6227; Fax: 815-946-9025. Students 60.

Prophetstown, Whiteside Co., St. Catherine (1917) Rev. Zdzislaw F. Wawryszuk.
Res.: 308 E. Third St., 61277. Tel: 815-537-2077; Fax: 815-537-2077. Email: stcatherine@mchsi.com.
Catechesis/Religious Program—Tel: 815-537-2626. Brigette Young, D.R.E. Students 26.
Mission—St. Ambrose [JC] P.O Box 746, Erie, Whiteside Co. 61250. Tel: 309-659-2781 (Tuesdays Only); 815-537-2077.
Catechesis/Religious Program—Students 50.

Richmond, McHenry Co., St. Joseph (1899), (German), [CEM] Rev. Msgr. James W. McLoughlin; Deacons Albert Dietz; Gregory Duffey.
Res.: 10519 Main St., 60071. Tel: 815-678-7421; Fax: 815-678-6961. Email: saintjosephchurch@gmail.com.
Catechesis/Religious Program—Tel: 815-678-4720. Laura Wisinski, C.R.E. Students 113.

Rochelle, Ogle Co., St. Patrick (1868) [CEM] Revs. Steven J. Lange; William Vallejo.
Res.: 250 Kelley Dr., 61068. Tel: 815-562-2370; Fax: 815-562-5250. Email: stpats@rochelle.net. Web: www.stpatricks.rochelle.net.
Catechesis/Religious Program—Tel: 815-561-0079. Kalah Williams, D.R.E. Students 302.

Rock Falls, Whiteside Co., St. Andrew (1950) [JC] Rev. Msgr. Thomas L. Dzielak; Rev. Louis F. Tosto.
Res.: 708 10th Ave., 61071. Tel: 815-625-4508; Fax: 815-625-1569. Email: standrews.church@comcast.net.
School—(Grades PreK-8), 701 11th Ave., 61071. Tel: 815-625-1456; Fax: 815-625-1724. Email: standrewsgrad@comcast.net. Mr. Philip D. Bellini, Prin. Lay Teachers 10; Students 200.
Catechesis/Religious Program—Tel: 815-625-4508. Students 49.

St. Charles, Kane Co.

1—St. John Neumann (1977) Revs. Richard A. Rosinski; Andrew Skrobutt; Deacons Tom Elms; Paul Iwanski; Ronald Williams.
Res.: 2900 E. Main St., 60174. Tel: 630-377-2797; Fax: 630-377-2834.
Catechesis/Religious Program—Tel: 630-377-2803. Jan Donovan, D.R.E.; William Crow, H.S. Youth Min.; Joe Weyers, Jr. High Youth Min. Students 1,469.

2—St. Patrick (1851) Rev. Msgr. Joseph B. Linster; Revs. Moises Apostol; Nicholas T. Federspiel.
Res. & Church Address: 6N487 Crane Rd., Saint Charles, 60175. Tel: 630-338-8000; Fax: 630-338-8008.
School—118 N. Fifth St., Saint Charles, 60174. Tel: 630-584-6367; Fax: 630-584-9759. Mr. Joseph Battisto, Prin. Sisters 3; Lay Teachers 29; Students 530.
Catechesis/Religious Program—211 N. 4th St., 60174. Tel: 630-513-2247. Sr. Joelyn Hayes, D.R.E.; Patrice Spirou, D.R.E.; Jerome Ryndak, D.R.E. Students 2,005.

Sandwich, DeKalb Co., St. Paul (1925) [CEM] Rev. Andrew C. Hougan.
Office: 110 N. Eddy St., 60548. Tel: 815-786-9266; Fax: 815-786-2977. Email: stpaulssandwich@aol.com.
Parish Center: 340 Arnold Rd., 60548. Tel: 815-786-8964.
Rectory—505 W. Lisbon St., 60548.
Catechesis/Religious Program—Tel: 815-786-2004. Students 190.

Savanna, Carroll Co., St. John the Baptist (1884) [CEM] Rev. Dennis D. Atto.
Res.: 318 Chicago Ave., 61074. Tel: 815-273-3961; Fax: 815-273-3503. Email: stjohnbaptistch@mchsi.com. Web: www.stjohnbaptistch.org.
Catechesis/Religious Program—Students 35.

Scales Mound, Jo Daviess Co., Holy Trinity (1863) [CEM 2] Revs. Christopher J. Kuhn; Stanislaw Kos.
Res.: 406 Franklin St., Galena, 61036.
Rectory & Church: 302 Franklin St., 61075. Email: holytrinity@jcwifi.com. Web: www.holytrinitych.us.
Catechesis/Religious Program—Tel: 815-845-2347. Carol Bilgri, C.R.E. Students 53.

Shannon, Carroll Co., St. Wendelin (1870) [CEM] Rev. Michael J. Bolger.
18 S. Linn St., P.O. Box 23, 61078. Tel: 815-864-2548 (Church); Fax: 815-864-2729.
Catechesis/Religious Program—Students 35.

Somonauk, DeKalb Co., St. John the Baptist (1865) [CEM] Rev. Thomas E. Brantman.
Res.: 320 S. Depot St., Box 276, 60552. Tel: 815-498-2010; Fax: 815-498-2770. Email: stjbsom@mchsi.com.
Catechesis/Religious Program—Tel: 815-498-2627. Students 226.

South Beloit, Winnebago Co., St. Peter (1909) Revs. Jerome P. Koutnik; Robert J. McClellan; Deacons Peter Calgaro; Michael Ryan.
Res.: 620 Blackhawk Blvd., 61080. Tel: 815-389-2024; Fax: 815-389-2274. Email: jkoutnik@rockforddiocese.org. Web: www.stpeterrcparish.org.
School—320 Elmwood Ave., 61080. Tel: 815-389-3193; Fax: 815-389-3476. Email: saintpeterprincipal@yahoo.com. Mr. John Fitzsimmons, Prin. Lay Teachers 14; Students 114.
Catechesis/Religious Program—Tel: 815-389-9091. Jeanne Pulkrabek, D.R.E. Students 300.
Mission—Church of the Holy Spirit P.O. Box 478, Roscoe, Winnebago Co. 61073. Tel: 815-623-6930; Fax: 815-623-1890.
Catechesis/Religious Program—Fax: 815-623-1890. Email: religioused@charter.net. Kate Elliott, D.R.E. Students 64.

Spring Grove, McHenry Co., St. Peter (1900), (German), [CEM] Rev. Msgr. Joseph F. Jarmoluk.
Church: 2118 Main St., P.O. Box 129, 60081. Tel: 815-675-2288; Fax: 815-675-6774.
Catechesis/Religious Program—Tel: 815-675-2576. Students 171.

Sterling, Whiteside Co.

1—St. Mary (1898) [CEM] Revs. Donald M. Ahles; Jesus Dominguez; Deacons John Kellen; James Lopez; Jane Olson, Pastoral Assoc.
Res.: 600 Ave. B, 61081. Tel: 815-625-0640; Fax: 815-625-1684.
School—6 W. Sixth St., 61081. Tel: 815-625-2253; Fax: 815-625-8942. Web: www.smsterling.org. Mrs. Rebecca Schmitt. Lay Teachers 20; Students 262.
Catechesis/Religious Program—6 W. 6th St., 61081. Tel: 815-625-6688; Fax: 815-625-8942. Students 251.

2—Sacred Heart (1870), (German), [CEM] Rev. David C. Finn, Parochial Admin.; Deacons Ronald Szakatits; Larry Zitkus.
Res.: 2224 Avenue J, 61081. Tel: 815-625-0631; 815-625-1134; Fax: 815-625-1138. Web: www.sacredheartparish.net.
Catechesis/Religious Program—Tel: 815-625-4385; Fax: 815-625-1138. Students 135.

Stockton, Jo Daviess Co., Holy Cross (1893), (German), [CEM] Rev. Dean M. Smith.
223 E. Front Ave., 61085.
Res.: 216 E. Benton Ave., 61085. Tel: 815-947-2545; Fax: 815-947-3705. Email: holycross7@verizon.net.
Catechesis/Religious Program—Students 75.

Sublette, Lee Co., Our Lady of Perpetual Help (1860) [CEM] Rev. Max Lasrado.
Mailing Address: Box 80, 61367. Tel: 815-849-5412; Fax: 815-849-5412.
Church: 101 Locust St., 61367.
Catechesis/Religious Program—Students 35.

Sugar Grove, Kane Co., St. Katharine Drexel Parish (2008) Rev. Robert W. Jones.
264 Main St., P.O. Box 1189, 60554. Tel: 630-466-0303; Fax: 630-466-0333. Email: stephanie@stkatharinedrexel-sugargrove.org. Web: www.stkatharinedrexel-sugargrove.org.
Catechesis/Religious Program—Mrs. Pat Weis, D.R.E. Students 160.

Sycamore, De Kalb Co., St. Mary (1885) [CEM] Rev. Frank John Timar, M.S.C.; Deacon Lee Deatherage.
Res.: 244 Waterman St., 60178. Tel: 815-895-3275; Fax: 815-899-7890. Email: churchofstmary@stmarysycamore.com. Web: www.stmarysycamore.com.
School—(Grades PreK-8), 222 Waterman St., 60178. Tel: 815-895-5215; Fax: 815-895-5295. Email: stmarys@tbcnet.com. Mr. Ross Bubolz, Prin. Lay Teachers 18; Students 236.
Catechesis/Religious Program—322 Waterman St., 60178. Tel: 815-895-3726; Fax: 815-895-4561. Students 403.

Tampico, Whiteside Co., St. Mary (1875) [CEM] Rev. Msgr. Thomas L. Dzielak; Deacon William Lemmer.
Res.: 105 Benton St., P.O. Box 159, 61283. Tel: 815-438-5425; Fax: 815-438-5425. Email: heartofmary@thewisp.net. Web: www.saintmarytampico.org.
Catechesis/Religious Program—Students 29.

Virgil, Kane Co., SS. Peter and Paul (1909) [CEM] Rev. Perfecto L. Vasquez; Deacon Jim Newhouse.
Res.: 5 N. 939 Meredith Rd., 60151. Tel: 630-365-6618; Fax: 630-365-6659. Email: ssppvirgil@aol.com. Web: www.ssppvirgil.com.
Catechesis/Religious Program—Students 76.

Walton, Lee Co., St. Mary (1913) [JC] Revs. Carl E. Beekman; Cyprian Thoguru.
Res.: 32 N. Jones Ave., Amboy, 61310. Tel: 815-857-2670; Fax: 815-857-3485.
Catechesis/Religious Program—

Warren, Jo Daviess Co., St. Ann (1914) [CEM] Rev. Max J. Striedl, Parochial Admin.
608 E. Railroad St., P.O. Box 665, 61087.
Res.: 410 W. Lena St., Lena, 61048. Tel: 815-369-2810; Fax: 815-369-9137. Email: stjoes@aeroinc.net.
Catechesis/Religious Program—Students 43.

West Brooklyn, Lee Co., St. Mary (1889) [CEM] Rev. Max Lasrado.
Mailing Address: 758 3rd. St., P.O. Box 80, 61378. Tel: 815-628-3901; Fax: 815-628-3901.
Catechesis/Religious Program—Fax: 815-849-5412. Students 35.

Wonder Lake, McHenry Co., Christ the King (1949) [CEM] Rev. Steven M. Sabo.
Res.: 5006 E. Wonder Lake Rd., 60097. Tel: 815-653-2561; Fax: 815-653-9401. Email: ctksecretary@comcast.net.
Catechesis/Religious Program—Tel: 815-653-2581. Mrs. Karen Verr, C.R.E. Students 75.

Woodstock, McHenry Co.

1—St. Mary (1853) [CEM] Rev. Msgr. Aaron R. Brodeski; Rev. Lorenzo Gonzalez; Deacons Louis Barone; Hans Rokus; Jim Devona.
Res.: 312 Lincoln Ave., 60098. Tel: 815-338-3377; Fax: 815-338-3497.
School—313 Tryon St., 60098. Tel: 815-338-3598; Fax: 815-338-3408. Diane Vida, Prin. Lay Teachers 20; Students 333.
Catechesis/Religious Program—Tel: 815-338-3413; Fax: 815-334-4391. Mrs. Diane O'Donnell, D.R.E. Students 379.

2—Resurrection (1978) Rev. Stephen Glab, C.R.
Mailing Address: 2918 S. Country Club Rd., 60098. Tel: 815-338-7330; Fax: 815-338-7365. Email: office.rcc@hughes.net. Web: www.resurrectionparish.catholicweb.com.

Catechesis/Religious Program—Nancy Neumeister, D.R.E. Students 89.

Chaplains of Public Institutions

ELGIN. *Elgin State Hospital*, 750 S. State St., 60123. Vacant.

MOOSEHEART. *School of the Loyal Order of Moose*, 301 Fifth Ave., 60539. Vacant.

ST. CHARLES. *Illinois State Youth Center*, Chapel of the Immaculate Conception, 60175. Records kept at St. Patrick, St. Charles.

Special Assignment:
Rev. Msgrs.—
Barr, Eric R., S.T.L., Vicar for Clergy & Religious, 555 Colman Center Dr., P.O. Box 7044, 61125. Tel: 815-399-4300
Doherty, Timothy L., Ph.D., S.T.L., Diocesan Ethicist
Kagan, David D., V.G., J.C.L., Vicar Gen., Moderator of the Curia, 555 Colman Center Dr., 61125. Tel: 815-399-4300
Kurz, Michael A., J.C.L., Judicial Vicar, 555 Colman Center Dr., P.O. Box 7044, 61125. Tel: 815-399-4300
Nelson, Glenn L., J.C.L., Vicar Gen. & Chancellor, 555 Colman Center Dr., P.O. Box 7044, 61125. Tel: 815-399-4300
Schwartz, William H., P.A., S.T.L., Diocesan Dir. of Permanent Deacons
Sweeney, Robert J., Propagation of the Faith, Tribunal, P.O. Box 7044, 61125. Tel: 815-399-4300
Vallejo, Arquimedes, J.C.D., Episcopal Vicar for Hispanic Ministry Tribunal, 555 Colman Center Dr., P.O. Box 7044, 61125. Tel: 815-399-4300
Revs.—
Bergschneider, Matthew, Sec. to the Bishop & Diocesan Master of Ceremonies
Birungyi, George, St. Joseph Hospital, Elgin
Camacho, Robert, Hispanic Ministry, Freeport Deanery
Cruz, Saul E., Hispanic Ministry, 302 Fisk Ave., DeKalb, 60115. Tel: 815-758-5432
Doyle, Thomas J., Asst. Principal, Marion CC High School, Woodstock
Emeh, Martins, J.C.L., Vice Chancellor
Etheredge, F. William, Supt., Aurora CC High School, Aurora
Finn, David C., Acting Prin., Newman High School, Sterling
Fuller, Michael J.K., S.T.D., Mundelein, IL
Lavan, Michael G., Vocations Dir.
Lipinski, Paul M., Acting Principal, Boylan CC High School, Rockford
Long, Anthony Vu Khac, Vietnamese Catholic Ministry, St. Mary Parish, 321 Pine St., DeKalb, 60115.
Lovell, John P., Asst. Vocations Dir.
McMorrow, Matthew, Asst. Prin.; Dir. of Rel. Ed., Boylan CC High School, Rockford (Diocesan Scout Chap.)
Naill, Joseph P. Office of Divine Worship
Peck, David A., Superintendent, St. Edward CC High School, Elgin
Polycarpe, Pierre G., Chap., St. Anthony Hospital, Rockford
Stringini, John L., Chap. (Retired), Provena Cor Mariae Center, Rockford
Wentink, William R., Chaplain St. Anthony Hospital, St. Anthony Hospital, 5666 E. State St., 61108.

Active Outside the Diocese:
Revs.—
Donahugh, Donald E., Port Arthur, TX
Falcone, Emilio (Retired), United States Air Force
Garrity, Robert M., Ave Maria University, Naples, FL
Kaim, Phillip, United States Air Force
Schuessler, William R., Missions, Peru

Retired:
Rev. Msgrs.—
Brady, Thomas C., P.A., V.G., Ph.D., 16 Country Club Beach, 61103. Tel: 815-654-1274
Clausen, William J., 747 Tulip Ln., 61107.
Dempsey, Thomas J., 13750 White Oak Rd., Huntley, 60142. Tel: 847-659-9395
Hoffman, Robert B., 271 Trent Dr., Batavia, 60510.
McNamee, Charles W., P.A., J.C.L., Unit 15, 4718 Covey Ridge Ct., Loves Park, 61111. Tel: 815-639-9690
Mitchell, John J., 250 Spring Cove Dr., Elgin, 60123. Tel: 847-741-3888
Monahan, Thomas J., Ph.D., 4295 Ahlstrand Dr, 61103. Tel: 815-282-9972
O'Neil, Philip E., 2323 Rockton Ave., 61103. Tel: 815-962-7806
Wahl, Raymond J., P.A., J.C.D., Cor Mariae Center, 3330 Maria Linden Dr., 61114.
Willhite, Robert J., P.O. Box 4395, Aurora, 60507. Tel: 630-844-3780
Revs.—
Beauvais, David E., P.O. Box 94, Rock City, 61070.
Becker, Anthony J., Oak Ridge Manor, 124 Liberty Ct., Dixon, 61021.
Budden, William A., 4878 Ashelford Dr., Byron, 61010.
Burr, Thomas E., 401 Inverrary #17, Rockport, TX 78382.
Cahill, John W., 13351 Red Alder Ave., Huntley, 60142.
Clapsaddle, Harlan, P.O. Box 7044, 61125.
Collins, William P., Luther Center, 111 W. State St., Apt. 1303, 61101. Tel: 815-963-6997
DeSalvo, Donald D., 15519 Crystal Acres Dr., Somonauk, 60552.
Echevia, Les Suberi, 987 Stonefield Ln, 61108.
Gillespie, Edward F., 6152 Wingate Dr., Lisle, 60532. Tel: 630-960-4838
Guagliardo, Salvatore J., Siena on Brendenwood, 4444 Brendenwood Rd., 61107. Tel: 815-394-1962
Hanrahan, John A., 7937 Brixham Rd, 61107.
Heraty, John T., 11936 Tuliptree Ln, Huntley, 60142.
Hiller, Everett J., 2520 W. Council Hill Rd., Scales Mound, 61075.
Hughes, Edward R., 5455 N. Sheridan Rd., 60640.
Jackson, Robert, Cor Mariae Center, 3330 Maria Linden Dr., 61114. Tel: 815-282-5452
Jones, Ronald A., P.O. Box 7044, 61125.
Kaiser, Joseph W., Cor Mariae Center, 3330 Maria Linden Dr., 61114. Tel: 815-877-7416
Knott, William P., 15528 W. Sky Hawk Dr., Sun City West, AZ 85375. Tel: 623-214-2520
Kraemer, John A., 6033 A Sheridan Rd., Apt. 32J, Chicago, 60660. Tel: 773-561-9857
Lewandowski, Theodore V., N1829 William Dr., Waupaca, WI 54981. Tel: 715-256-9268
Librandi, Michael A., 6419 Columbine Blvd., 61108. Tel: 815-289-1833
Lutz, Joseph L., 136 Lakeside Dr., Apt. 716, 60174. Tel: 630-989-1110
McDonnell, Francis E., 1801 Ave. G, Sterling, 61081. Tel: 815-626-0771
McKitrick, James V., N.1555 Shadow Ln., Fontana, WI 53125. Tel: 262-275-6711
Mullane, Bernard J., P.O. Box 1403, Williams Bay, WI 53191. Tel: 262-245-5592
Neumann, Aloysius J., 5225 N. Bernard St., Chicago, 60625. Tel: 773-220-9980
Neville, Harold, Mohan Health Care Center, 2340 Airport Dr., Columbus, OH 43219.
Paddock, Richard W., 1284 Oakleaf Ct., Aurora, 60506. Tel: 630-907-1663
Peterson, William F., 147 Shadowood Dr., Martinez, GA 30907. Tel: 706-860-4738
Plesa, Andrew J., 215 Thomas More Dr., Elgin, 60123. Tel: 847-888-1682
Ratazak, Bernard A., Cor Mariae Center, 3330 Maria Linden Dr., 61114. Tel: 815-877-7416
Rudden, Matthew T., 6102 Garrett Ln., 61107. Tel: 815-226-3605
Shindelar, Vincent J., Cor Mariae Center, 3330 Maria Linden Dr., 61114.
Stringini, John L., Cor Mariae Center, 3330 Maria Linden Dr., 61114. Tel: 815-877-7416
Tranel, Daniel D., 8615 N. Tranel Rd., East Dubuque, 61025. Tel: 815-747-3792
Urbaniak, Lawrence M., 4210 W. Marshall Ave., Phoenix, AZ 85019.
Vlasz, Melvyn J., Cor Mariae Center, 3330 Maria Linden Dr., 61114. Tel: 815-986-7518

Permanent Deacons:
Abel, Philip, St. Bridget, Loves Park
Anchor, Robert, Sacred Heart, Marengo
Bach, John, St. Monica, Carpentersville
Barone, Frank, St. Patrick, Rockford
Barone, Louis, St. Mary, Woodstock
Berard, Samuel, St. Patrick, Dixon
Bondi, Allen, St. Thomas the Apostle, Crystal Lake
Boyce, Michael, SS. Peter & Paul, Cary
Bracken, Robert, (Retired)
Brandenburg, Robert, (Retired)
Bronzi, William, Holy Family, Rockford
Brunette, Donald J., St. Thomas Aquinas, Freeport
Calgaro, Peter, St. Peter, South Beloit; Church of the Holy Spirit, Roscoe
Callahan, Donald J., (Retired)
Chaplin, Mark, St. Gall, Elburn
Ciochon, Thaddeus, (Retired)
Coltman, George, St. Mary, Huntley
Cooper, Charles, St. Peter Cathedral, Rockford
Cristoforo, Michael, Holy Family, Rockford
Czerniewski, Martin, St. Peter Cathedral, Rockford
Dall, William, St. Rita, Rockford
Dean, William, St. James, Rockford
Deatherage, Lee, St. Mary, Sycamore
Demming, Robert
Devona, James, St. Mary, Woodstock
Dietz, Albert, St. Joseph, Richmond
Dinneen, Richard, St. Thomas Aquinas, Freeport
Dombek, James, Christ the Teacher, DeKalb
Drees, Vincent, St. Thomas Aquinas, Freeport
Duffey, Gregory, St. Joseph, Richmond
Ekstrom, Richard
Elms, Thomas, St. John Neumann, St. Charles
Emmert, Phillip, St. Joseph, Harvard
Falcón, Jose, Sacred Heart, Aurora
Farinella, Louis, St. Mary, Huntley
Fast, Randy, St. Peter Cathedral, Rockford
Felix, Ignacio, St. Rita of Cascia, Aurora
Ferrini, Armand, St. Mary, Huntley
Fischer, Howard, St. Margaret Mary, Algonquin
Fox, Steven, St. Catherine of Siena, Dundee
Frazier, J. Michael, St. Monica, Carpentersville
Freund, Walter, (Retired)
Gagnon, Charles, St. Elizabeth Ann Seton, Crystal Lake
Ganshow, Howard, SS. Peter & Paul, Cary
Garber, Dennis, St. Monica, Carpentersville
Gartland, William, St. Patrick, St. Charles
Geinosky, Larry
Gerdeman, Richard, St. Bernadette, Rockford
Giambalvo, Michael, St. Mary, Pecatonica
Giblin, Michael, Annunciation B.V.M., Aurora
Giessinger, Jerry, St. John the Baptist, Johnsburg
Goetz, Daniel
Graw, Ronald, St. Patrick, Rockford
Groom, Richard, Sacred Heart, Aurora
Grossmayer, Simon, St. Margaret Mary, Algonquin
Hainchek, Alex J., (Retired)
Hawksworth, Thomas, Holy Angels, Aurora
Hetzel, Martin, St. John Neumann, St. Charles
Holt, Arthur, St. Patrick, Hartland
Hudzinski, James, St. Stanislaus, Rockford
Iwanski, Paul, St. John Neumann, St. Charles
Jimenez, Policarpo, St. Monica, Carpentersville
Johnson, William, St. Patrick, St. Charles
Kayser, Joseph, St. Patrick, Hartland
Kellen, John, St. Mary, Sterling
Klocke, Gary, St. Mary, Freeport
Kocol, Theodore, St. Mary, Galena
Koss, Anthony, St. Joseph, Harvard
Kulpin, John, (Retired)
LaMont, Warren R., St. Mary, Pecatonica
Lemmer, William, St. Mary, Tampico
LeRoy, Michael, St. Margaret Mary, Algonquin
Lopez, James, St. Mary, Sterling
Magee, Ronald, St. James, Rockford
Maher, Patrick, St. Margaret Mary, Algonquin
Martin, Raymond J., Holy Cross, Batavia
Martin, Richard, St. Rita of Cascia, Aurora
Martinez, Armando, St. Joseph, Elgin
McNealy, Ken
McPhee, John, St. Mary, Huntley
Milano, Robert, St. Anne, Dixon
Miller, Donald, St. Margaret Mary, Algonquin
Mitchison, Robert, Cathedral of St. Peter, Rockford
Morrison, Edward, St. Thomas the Apostle, Crystal Lake
Motyka, Larry, Annunciation, Aurora
Moynihan, Patrick
Mulcahey, Richard, St. Mary, Durand
Navarro, Carlos, St. Peter, Aurora; Our Lady of Good Counsel, Aurora
Nelson, John, St. Charles Borromeo, Hampshire
Newhouse, James, SS. Peter & Paul, Virgil
O'Brien, Thomas, St. Mary, Huntley
O'Leary, Jack, Sacred Heart, Marengo
Olson, James D., St. James, Belvidere
Orlik, Henry, St. Mary, Elgin
Petit, Thomas, St. Rita of Cascia, Aurora
Phelan, Joseph, Church of Holy Apostles, McHenry
Plazewski, Robert, St. Thomas More, Elgin
Porter, John, (Retired)
Pospischil, Steven, St. Thomas Aquinas, Freeport
Poss, Harold, Annunciation of the B.V.M., Aurora
Prunty, Kevin, St. Patrick, Amboy
Puscas, Stephen, St. Mary, DeKalb
Raz, Mark, Christ the King, Wonder Lake
Real, Robert, St. Laurence, Elgin
Rees, William, St. Mary, Aurora
Roder, John, St. Thomas More, Elgin
Rokus, Hans, St. Mary, Woodstock
Rosado, Julio, St. Therese of Jesus, Aurora
Ryan, Michael, St. Peter, South Beloit
Sauceda, John, (Retired)
Schmalen, Hank, St. Catherine of Siena, Dundee
Schubert, Anthony, St. Mary, Huntley
Sims, Fred, St. Patrick, St. Charles
Skrade, Fred, (Retired)
Smith, Daniel
Smits, Robert
Statter, Ralph, St. Thomas, Crystal Lake
Stevens, Greg, St. Thomas More, Elgin
Sullivan, Michael, St. Peter, Geneva
Swearingen, Alvin, St. Mary, Morrison
Sweeney, Robert, Holy Family, Rockford
Szakatits, Ronald, Sacred Heart, Sterling

Szudarski, Norbert, St. Joseph, Aurora
Urban, Gregory, St. Mary, Maple Park
Valesano, James J., (Retired)
Verstynen, Lambert, St. Edward, Rockford
Wagner, Terrence, St. Patrick, Dixon
Watermann, Bruce, St. Therese, Aurora; St. Nicholas, Aurora
Weaver, Raymond, Our Lady of Good Counsel, Aurora
Welch, Thomas
White, Thomas, Holy Angels, Aurora
Whitehead, William, Jr., St. Catherine of Siena, Dundee
Wilbricht, David, (Retired)
Williams, Ronald, St. John Neumann, St. Charles
Woeste, James
Zibrun, Michael, St. Peter, Geneva
Zitkus, Lawrence, Sacred Heart, Sterling

INSTITUTIONS LOCATED IN THE DIOCESE

[A] SEMINARIES, RELIGIOUS OR SCHOLASTICATES

AURORA. *Marmion Abbey* (1933) 850 Butterfield Rd., 60502. Tel: 630-897-7215; Fax: 630-897-0393. Email: vbataille@marmion.org. Web: www.marmion.org. Rt. Rev. Vincent De Paul Bataille, O.S.B., Abbot; Very Rev. Basil Yender, O.S.B., Prior; Rt. Rev. David J. Cyr, O.S.B. Priests 28; Brothers 11.

[B] HIGH SCHOOLS, DIOCESAN

ROCKFORD. *Boylan Central Catholic High School*, 4000 St. Francis Dr., 61103. Tel: 815-877-0531; Fax: 815-877-2544. Email: boylan@boylan.org. Web: www.boylan.org. Revs. Paul M. Lipinski, Acting Prin.; Matthew McMorrow, Asst. Prin. & D.R.E.; Mr. Dan Appino, Guidance Dir.; Mrs. Mary Gavan, Asst. Prin.; Mr. Dennis Hiemenz, Asst. Prin., Academic Affairs; Jerry Kerrigan, Asst. Prin., Student Affairs; Mr. William C. Thumm, Dean of Students; Mrs. Denise Ethum, Librarian. Priests 6; Lay Teachers 86; Students 1,202.

AURORA. *Aurora Central Catholic High School*, 1255 N. Edgelawn Dr., 60506. Tel: 630-907-0095; Fax: 630-907-1076. Email: fetheredge@auroracentral.com. Web: www.auroracentral.com. Rev. F. William Etheredge, Prin. & Supt.; Mr. Mark Krebs, Asst. Prin. Priests 5; School Sisters of St. Francis 1; Lay Teachers 40; Students 527.

ELGIN. *St. Edward Central Catholic High School*, 335 Locust St., 60123. Tel: 847-741-7535; Fax: 847-695-4682. Email: stedward@stedhs.org. Web: www.stedhs.org. Rev. David A. Peck, Supt. & Prin.; Mr. Rich Thomas, Asst. Prin. & Dean; Mrs. Susan Doherty, Librarian. Priests 6; Lay Teachers 32; Students 408.

FREEPORT. *Aquin Central Catholic High School*, 1419 S. Galena Ave., 61032. Tel: 815-235-3154; Fax: 815-235-3185. Email: superintendent@aquinschools.org. Web: www.aquinschools.org. Mrs. Kathleen Runte, Prin.; Rev. Michael J. Bolger, Asst. Prin. & Chm. Religious Studies Dept.; Mrs. Connie Gogel, Librarian. Priests 1; Lay Teachers 17; Students 153.

STERLING. *Newman Central Catholic High School* (1915) 1101 W. 23rd St., 61081-9002. Tel: 815-625-0500; Fax: 815-625-8444. Email: ffinn@newmancchs.org. Web: www.newmancchs.org. Rev. David C. Finn, Prin. & Supt.; Kristine Schauff, Librarian. Priests 1; Lay Teachers 23; Students 246.

WOODSTOCK. *Marian Central Catholic High School* (1959) 1001 McHenry Ave., 60098. Tel: 815-338-4220; Fax: 815-338-4253. Email: tlanders@marian.com. Web: www.marian.com. Mr. Thomas E. Landers, Supt. & Prin.; Rev. Msgr. Aaron R. Brodeski, Spiritual Dir.; Mrs. Mary Ann Martinez, Devel. Dir.; Mr. Charles Maveus, Dean of Students; Rev. Thomas J. Doyle, Asst. Prin.; Mr. Charles Rakers, Dir. Academics & Personnel. Priests 7; Lay Teachers 49; Students 735.

[C] HIGH SCHOOLS, PRIVATE

AURORA. *Marmion Academy*, 1000 Butterfield Rd., 60502. Tel: 630-897-6936; Fax: 630-897-7086. Email: jmilroy@marmion.org. Web: www.marmion.org. Rt. Rev. Vincent De Paul Bataille, O.S.B., Abbot & Pres., 850 Butterfield Rd., 60504. Tel: 630-897-1881; Fax: 630-897-0393. Email: vbataille@marmion.org. Web: www.marmion.org; Mr. John K. Milroy, Headmaster; Rev. Mario Pedi, O.S.B., Librarian. Day School for Boys. Benedictines 13; Lay Teachers 34; Students 486.

Rosary High School (1962) 901 N. Edgelawn Ave., 60506. Tel: 630-896-0831; Fax: 630-896-8372. Email: spbop@rosaryhs.com. Web: www.rosaryhs.com. Sr. Patricia Burke, O.P., Prin. Sisters of St. Dominic 5; Lay Teachers 38; Girls 483.

[D] GENERAL HOSPITALS

ROCKFORD. *Saint Anthony College of Nursing* (1915) 5658 E. State St., 61108. Tel: 815-395-5091; Fax: 815-395-2275. Email: Terriburch@sacn.edu. Web: www.sacn.edu. Terese A. Burch, Ph.D., R.N., Pres. Dean. Faculty 25; Undergraduate Students 173; Graduate Students 29; Staff 12.

Saint Anthony Medical Center, 5666 E. State St., 61108. Tel: 815-226-2000; Fax: 815-395-5449. Web: www.osfhealthcare.org. Mailing Address: 1175 St. Francis Ln., East Peoria, 61611. Mr. David Schertz, Pres. & CEO; Rev. William R. Wentink, Chap. & Dir. of Pastoral Care. Sisters of the Third Order of St. Francis 2; Bed Capacity 254; Patients Assisted Annually 371,727; Total Staff 2,461.

AURORA. *Provena Mercy Medical Center*, 1325 N. Highland Ave., 60506. Tel: 630-859-2222. Web: www.provenamercy.com. James D. Witt, M.B.A., FACHE, R.N., Pres & CEO; Edward J. Hunter, Regl. Vice Pres. Mission Svcs.

Provena Hospitals dba Provena Mercy Medical Center. Bed Capacity 299; Patients Assisted Annually 209,326; Total Staff 1,167.

Center for Diabetic Wellness, 1325 N. Highland Ave., 60506. Tel: 630-897-4000; Fax: 630-897-9032.

Health Institute, 1975 Melissa Ln., 60505. Tel: 630-907-1129; Fax: 630-907-1354.

ELGIN. *Provena Saint Joseph Hospital* (1902) 77 N. Airlite St., 60123. Tel: 847-695-3200; Fax: 847-931-5550. Email: edward.hunter@provena.org. Web: www.provena.org. Mr. William A. Brown, System Sr. Vice Pres., Pres & CEO; Edward J. Hunter, Regl. Vice Pres. Mission Svcs.; Rev. George Birungyi.

Provena Hospitals dba Provena Saint Joseph Hospital. Sisters 4; Bed Capacity 193; Patients Assisted Annually 210,367; Total Staff 1,209.

Provena Saint Joseph Hospital MedCare, 2250 W. Algonquin Rd., Lake in the Hills. Tel: 847-854-5511; Fax: 847-854-5531.

Provena Family Care, Huntley, 12155 Regency Sq. Pkwy., Huntley, 60142. Tel: 847-515-2100; Fax: 847-515-2328.

Provena Family Care, Carpentersville, 2201 Randall Rd., Carpentersville, 60110. Tel: 847-844-7800; Fax: 847-783-0628.

Provena Family Care, Hampshire, 895 S. State St., Ste. 201, Hampshire, 60140. Tel: 847-683-7099; Fax: 847-683-7104.

[E] SCHOOLS FOR EXCEPTIONAL ADOLESCENTS AND ADULTS

FREEPORT. *Provena St. Vincent's Community Living Facility and Supported Living Arrangement*, 659 E. Jefferson St., 61032. Tel: 815-232-6181; Fax: 815-232-6143. Ms. Diane Cushman, Prog. Dir. Patients Assisted Annually 40.

[F] HOMES FOR AGED AND ADULT DAY CARE CENTERS

ROCKFORD. *St. Anne Place*, 4444 Brendenwood Rd., 61107. Tel: 815-399-6167; Fax: 815-399-6169. Email: kathleen.balsara@provena.org. Web: www.stanneplace.org. Kathleen Balsara, Exec. Dir. Owned by the Rockford Diocese, managed by Provena Senior Services. Total Staff 40; Total in Residence 120; Apartment Capacity 105.

Provena Cor Mariae Center, 3330 Maria Linden Dr., 61114. Tel: 815-877-7416; Fax: 815-877-4299. Web: www.provenacormariae.com. Teresa Wester-Peters, Admin.; Rev. John L. Stringini, Chap. (Retired).

Provena Senior Services dba Provena Cor Mariae Center. Bed Capacity 162; Total Assisted Annually 500; Total Staff 179.

Provena St. Anne Center, 4405 Highcrest Rd., 61107. Tel: 815-229-1999; Fax: 815-229-1560. Email: janelle.chadwick@provena.org. Web: www.provena.org. Janelle Chadwick, Admin.; Sr. Marie Ange Marcotte, Dir. Pastoral Care.

Provena Senior Services dba Provena St. Anne Center. Bed Capacity 179; Total Assisted Annually 990; Total Staff 230.

AURORA. *Provena Fox Knoll*, 421 N. Lake St., 60506. Tel: 630-844-0380; Fax: 630-844-0702. Web: www.provena.org/foxknoll. Carol Ricken, Exec. Dir.

Provena Senior Services dba Provena Fox Knoll. Total Staff 69; Total in Residence 165; Independent Living 88; Assisted Living 77.

Provena McAuley Manor (1985) 400 W. Sullivan Rd., 60506. Tel: 630-859-3700; Fax: 630-264-1862. Web: www.provena.org/mcauley. Sr. Peg Barrett, R.S.M., Dir. Pastoral Care. Bed Capacity 87; Total Staff 110; Total Assisted Annually 550.

Batavia

Assisi Homes-Batavia Apartments, Inc. (1993) 1259 E. Wilson St., Batavia, 60510. Tel: 630-879-3117; Fax: 630-879-0665. Web: www.wfhealthcare.org. Susan M. Dillberg, Contact. Housing Units 290; Residents 619; Staff 9.

ELGIN. *Provena Home Health, Inc. dba Provena Home Care* 799 S. McLean Blvd, 60123. Tel: 847-931-5553; Fax: 847-622-2055. Thomas F. Nehring, Contact Person.

FREEPORT. *Provena St. Joseph Adult Day Center*, 659 E. Jefferson St., 61032. Tel: 815-266-8067; Fax: 815-266-8001. Email: sharon.batten@provenahealth.org. Ms. Sharon Batten, Dir. Total Staff 10; Total Assisted Annually 55.

Provena St. Joseph Center, 659 E. Jefferson St., 61032. Tel: 815-232-6181; Fax: 815-232-6143. Sr. Mary Waters, Dir. Pastoral Care; Ms. Theresa Parsek, Admin.

Provena Senior Services dba Provena St. Joseph Center. Sisters 1; Aged Residents 120; Total Staff 150.

GENEVA. *Provena Geneva Care Center*, 1101 E. State St., 60134. Tel: 630-232-7544; Fax: 630-232-4409. Email: dawn.furman@provena.org. Web: www.provena.org/genevacare. Dawn Renee Furman, B.S.N., L.N.H.A., Admin.; Elena Haas, Dir. Pastoral Care.

Provena Senior Services dba Provena Geneva Care Center. Bed Capacity 107; Total Staff 100; Total Assisted Annually 200.

ST. CHARLES. *Provena Pine View Care Center*, 611 Allen Ln., 60174. Tel: 630-377-2211; Fax: 630-377-4352. Email: mary.wright@provena.org. Web: provena.org. Sr. Maureen Becker, Dir. Pastoral Care; Mary Wright, Admin.

Provena Senior Services dba Provena Pine View Care Center. Bed Capacity 120; Total Staff 140; Residents 98; Total Assisted Annually 375.

[G] MONASTERIES AND RESIDENCES OF PRIESTS AND BROTHERS

AURORA. *Marmion Abbey* (1933) 850 Butterfield Rd., 60502. Tel: 630-897-7215; Fax: 630-897-0393. Email: vbataille@marmion.org. Web: www.marmion.org. Rt. Revs. Vincent De Paul Bataille, O.S.B., Abbot; Gerald Benkert, O.S.B., Abbot Emeritus (Retired); David J. Cyr, O.S.B., Abbot Emeritus; Very Revs. John Brahill, O.S.B.; Basil Yender, O.S.B., Prior; Revs. Thomas Bailey, O.S.B.; Michael Burrows, O.S.B.; Rene Otzoy Colaj, O.S.B.; Damien Daprai, O.S.B.; Aaron Devett, O.S.B.; Patrick Gillmeyer, O.S.B.; George R. Glover, O.S.B.; Orlando Perez Gomez, O.S.B.; Philip Kremer, O.S.B.; Juan Francisco Peren Mux, O.S.B.; Gregory Obee, O.S.B. (Retired); David Palmatier, O.S.B.; Mario Pedi, O.S.B.; Frederick Peterson, O.S.B.; Christian Pusateri, O.S.B.; Cristobal Coche Quic, O.S.B.; Charles Reichenbacher, O.S.B.; Joel Rippinger, O.S.B.; Nathanael Roberts, O.S.B.; Bernard Schaefer, O.S.B.; Bede Stocker, O.S.B. (Retired); Kenneth Theisen, O.S.B.; Paul Weberg, O.S.B.

Marmion. Priests 28; Brothers 11.

Missionaries of the Sacred Heart Community (1854) 305 S. Lake St., P.O. Box 270, 60507. Tel: 630-892-2371; Fax: 630-892-1678. Email: provincial@misacor-usa.org. Web: www.misacor-usa.org. Revs. Peter E. Campbell, M.S.C.; Philip DeRea, M.S.C.; Michael I. Miller, M.S.C.; Bro. Daniel Rakow, M.S.C.; Revs. John Schweikert, M.S.C.; Frank John Timar, M.S.C.; Norbert B. Weber, M.S.C.; Bros. Steve Boland, M.S.C.; Nicholas Lanese, M.S.C.; James Miller, M.S.C., Prov. Treas.; Warren Perrotto, M.S.C.; John Peralta, M.S.C.; Joseph Tesar, M.S.C. Provincial Administrative Office of the Missionaries of the Sacred Heart. Priests 11; Brothers 5.

Priests and Brothers of the Province Serving Elsewhere In Papua, New Guinea; In Issoudun, France:

In Chicago, IL Rev. Joseph Gleixner, M.S.C., Asst. Treas.; Very Rev. Joseph Jablonski, M.S.C.; Revs. Moo-Chan Benedict Ko, M.S.C.; Hugo Leon Londono, M.S.C.; Jean-Marie Ndour, M.S.C., Student in Residence; Andrew Torma, M.S.C., Vocation Dir.; Bro. Frank Natale, M.S.C.

In Pennsylvania Very Rev. Raymond Diesbourg, M.S.C., Prov. Supr.; Bro. George Farkas, M.S.C.

In Bogota, Columbia: Very Rev. Dario Moreno, M.S.C.; Revs. German Barona, M.S.C.; Tito Medina, M.S.C.; Hector Mejia, M.S.C.; Very Rev. Luis Alfonso Segura, M.S.C., Formation-Pre-novitiate Dir.; Bros. Jesus Benavides, M.S.C.; Favio Castro, M.S.C.; Guillermo Cuaran, M.S.C.; Deacon Eduard Riascos, M.S.C.; Bros. Juan Contreras Romero,

M.S.C.; William Andres Tamayo, M.S.C.; Fabier Antonio Vargas, M.S.C.

In Rome, Italy: Very Rev. Mark McDonald, M.S.C., Supr. Gen.

In Papua New Guinea: Rev. Leon Weisenberger, M.S.C., Local Supr.

MCHENRY. *Villa Desiderata Retreat House*, 3015 N. Bayview Ln., 60051-9641. Tel: 815-385-2264. Bro. Patrick T. Drohan, C.S.V., Facilities Mgr.

[H] CONVENTS AND RESIDENCES FOR SISTERS

ROCKFORD. *The Poor Clares of Rockford* (1916) Corpus Christi Monastery, 2111 S. Main St., 61102-3591. Tel: 815-963-7343; Fax: 815-963-7369. Web: www.poorclares.org/rockford/. Sr. Mary Regina Dice, P.C.C., Abbess. Poor Clare Colettines. Cloistered Sisters 19; Extern Sisters 1.

BATAVIA. *Holy Heart of Mary Novitiate*, 717 N. Batavia Ave., 60510. Tel: 630-879-1296; Fax: 630-879-7831. Email: evelynbv@sbcglobal.net. Web: www.sscm-usa.org. Sr. Evelyn Varboncoeur, S.S.C.M., Supr. & Formation Dir. Servants of the Holy Heart of Mary. Professed Sisters 7.

FREEPORT. *Congregation of the Sisters of the Immaculate Heart of Mary, Mother of Christ-Nigeria* (1937) 1209 S. Walnut St., 61032. Tel: 815-297-8287; Fax: 815-297-1786. Sisters 4.

[I] COMMUNITY SERVICES

ROCKFORD. *St. Elizabeth Catholic Community Center* (1911) 1536 S. Main St., 61102. Tel: 815-969-6526; Fax: 815-969-0541. Email: saintel911@ccrfd.org. Web: www.stelizabeth-rockford.org. Karen Carlson, Dir. Educ. & Social Svcs. Total Staff 17; Total Assisted Annually 17,015.

AURORA. *Public Action to Deliver Shelter, Inc. (PADS)*, 659 S. River St., 60506. Tel: 630-897-2165; Fax: 630-801-9759. Email: info@hesedhouse.org. Web: www.hesedhouse.org. Ryan J. Dowd, M.P.A., J.D., Exec. Dir. Ecumenical advocacy, overnight and transitional shelters and daytime drop-in center for homeless persons. Total Assisted 47,491.

[J] RETREAT HOUSES

ROCKFORD. *Bishop Lane Retreat Center* (1966) 7708 E. McGregor Rd., 61102. Tel: 815-965-5011; Fax: 815-965-5811. Email: lorrie@dpsrfd.org. Web: www.blrc.dpsrfd.org. Lorrie Gramer, Dir.; Don Gramer, Asst. Dir.

[K] FOUNDATIONS

ROCKFORD. *Boylan Educational Foundation, Inc.* (1980) 4000 St. Francis Dr., 61103. Tel: 815-877-8008; Fax: 815-877-2544. Email: boylan@boylan.org. Web: www.boylan.org.

The Catholic Foundation for the People of the Diocese of Rockford, 555 Colman Center Dr., P.O. Box 7044, 61125-7044. Tel: 815-399-4300; Fax: 815-399-5657. Email: gurban@rockforddiocese.org. Web: www.foundationrockford.org. Mr. Gregory Urban, Exec. Dir.

AURORA. *Aurora Catholic Education Foundation* (1973) P.O. Box 234, 60507. Tel: 630-898-2998; Fax: 630-898-2998.

CRYSTAL LAKE. *St. Thomas the Apostle School Foundation, Inc.*, 272 King St., 60014. Tel: 815-455-5400; Fax: 815-455-2733.

DEKALB. *Newman Center of Northern Illinois University Educational Program*, 512 Normal Rd., 60115. Tel: 815-787-7770; Fax: 815-758-2053. Email: parishoffice@newmanniu.org. Web: www.newmanniu.org.

Newman Center of Northern Illinois University Educational Program and Development Fund, Inc. Total Staff 9.

ELGIN. *St. Edward Central Catholic High School Education Foundation*, 335 Locust St., 60123. Tel: 847-741-7535; Fax: 847-695-4682. Email: Stedward@stedhs.org. Web: www.stedhs.org. Joseph Liss, Foundation Chm.

FREEPORT. *Education Through the 90's Foundation*, 1419 S. Galena Ave., 61032. Tel: 815-235-3154; Fax: 815-235-3185. Email: superintendent@aquinschools.org. Web: www.aquinschools.org. The foundation provides financial support for the Aquin Catholic School System.

Freeport Catholic Education Foundation, 1419 S. Galena Ave., 61032. Tel: 815-235-3154; Fax: 815-235-3185. Email: superintendent@aquinschools.org. Web: www.aquinschools.org. The foundation provides financial support for the Aquin Catholic School System.

STERLING. *Sauk Valley Catholic Education Foundation*, 1101 St. Mary's Rd., 61081. Tel: 815-626-5570; Fax: 815-626-5570. Email: ckromm@whitesideeroe.org. Web: www.whitesideroe.org.

Sauk Valley Area Religious Education Center, 1101 St. Mary Rd., 61081. Tel: 815-626-5570; Fax: 815-626-5570.

SYCAMORE. *St. Mary's Educational Foundation, Ltd.* (1981) 244 Waterman St., 60178. Tel: 815-895-3275, Ext. 707; Fax: 815-899-7890. Email: fjtimar@stmarysycamore.com. Web: www.stmarysycamore.com. Rev. Frank John Timar, M.S.C.

[L] NEWMAN CENTERS

DEKALB. *Newman Foundation for Catholic Students of Northern Illinois University* 512 Normal Rd., 60115. Tel: 815-787-7770; Fax: 815-758-2053. Email: parishoffice@newmanniu.org. Web: www.newmanniu.org. Rev. Msgr. Glenn L. Nelson, J.C.L., Dir. Campus Ministries; Revs. Alejandro del Toro, S.T.L., Assoc. Campus Ministries; Godwin Asuquo, Assoc. Campus Ministries; Leslie Venere, Dir. Music; Denise Sanders, Campus Min./ Dir. H.S. Youth Min.

[M] MISCELLANEOUS

ROCKFORD. *Catholic Office of the Deaf*, 555 Colman Center Dr., P.O. Box 7044, 61125. Tel: 815-399-4300 (Voice); 815-399-8184 (TTY); Fax: 815-399-5266. Email: RockfordHI@aol.com. Web: http://DeafApostolateRockfordDiocese.weebly.com.

Vineyard Books, Gifts & Church Supplies, Highcrest Centre, 1638 N. Alpine Rd., 61107. Tel: 815-398-4030; Fax: 815-398-8477; 800-587-9777. Email: customercare@catholicfamilygifts.com. Web: www.catholicfamilygifts.com; www.catholicbiblestore.com. Chris Weickert, Mgr. Total Staff 9.

AURORA. **Dominican Literacy Center, Aurora* (1993) 260 Vermont Ave., 60505-3100. Tel: 630-898-4636; Fax: 630-898-4636. Email: domlitctr@sbcglobal.net. Web: www.dominicanliteracycenter.org. Sr. Kathleen Ryan, Dir.

The J. Chevalier Charitable Trust, Old Second National Bank, Trustee, 37 S. River St., 60506-4172. Tel: 630-906-5478; Fax: 630-892-0170. Email: sbeach@02bancorp.com. Web: www.02bancorp.com. Stewart A. Beach, C.F.A., Sr. Vice Pres.

HAVARD. *Magnificat, A Ministry to Catholic Women*, 905 Dewey St., Harvard, 60033. Tel: 815-546-5063.

ST. CHARLES. *Cultivation Ministries* (1990) P.O. Box 662, 60174. Tel: 630-513-8222; Fax: 630-549-3031. Email: info@cultivationministries.com. Web: www.cultivationministries.com. Frank Mercadante, Exec. Dir. To cultivate team-based, comprehensive and disciple-making Catholic youth ministries by training, resourcing and supporting adult and student leaders.

Queen of Americas Guild, 345 Kautz Rd., P.O. Box 851, 60174. Tel: 630-584-1822; Fax: 630-587-2200. Email: staff@queenoftheamericasguild.org. Web: www.queenoftheamericasguild.org. Most Revs. Raymond L. Burke, D.D., J.C.D., Dir.; Joseph J. Madera, M.Sp.S., D.D., Episcopal Moderator; Sr. Christa Marie, F.S.G.M., Sec.; Mr. Stephen Banaszak, Vice Pres.; Mr. Frank Smoczynski, Pres.; Beverly Smoczynski, Treas. & Dir.

Board of Directors: Revs. George M. Hastrich; Christopher Rengers, O.F.M.Cap.; Mrs. Ruth Sloan.

SAVANNA. *Mercy Homecare/Hospice*, 1121 N. 5th St., 61074. Tel: 815-273-2628; Fax: 815-273-7025. Email: nocj@mercyhealth.com. Web: www.mercyclinton.com. Joan Noe, B.S.N., M.B.A., Vice Pres. Prof. Srvcs., Admin; Sharon Meister, R.N., M.S.N., Dir.; Donna Oliver, CEO. Sponsor: Trinity Health of Novi, Michigan, Catholic Health Ministries.

STERLING. *St. Vincent DePaul Society*, Tel: 815-625-0311; Fax: 815-625-1684. Email: dblum.61081@yahoo.com. Total Staff 12; Total Assisted 3,289.

St. Mary's Conference, 600 Ave. B, 61081. Tel: 815-625-0640; Fax: 815-625-1684.

STOCKTON. *Christ in the Wilderness* (1980) 7500 S. Randecker Rd., 61085-8922. Tel: 815-947-2476; Fax: 815-947-2476. Email: citw@dishmail.net. Web: www.citwretreat.com. Sr. Julia Marie Bathon, O.S.F., Dir., Center of Solitude and Prayer.

SYCAMORE. **Lighthouse Catholic Media NFP*, 303 E. State St., 60178. Tel: 847-488-0333; Fax: 815-895-0333. Email: tim@lighthousecatholicmedia.org. Web: www.lighthousecatholicmedia.org. Tim Truckenbrod, Vice Pres. Mktg. & Opers.

RELIGIOUS INSTITUTES OF MEN REPRESENTED IN THE DIOCESE

For further details refer to the corresponding bracketed number in the Religious Institutes of Men or Women section.

[0200]—*Benedictine Monks* (Marmion Abbey, Aurora)—O.S.B.

[1320]—*Clerics of St. Viator*—C.S.V.

[1080]—*Congregation of the Resurrection* (Chicago Prov.)—C.R.

[0480]—*Conventual Franciscans* (St. Bonaventure Province)—O.F.M.Conv

[]—*Institute of Christ the King Sovereign Priest (Provincial House-Italy)*

[1110]—*Missionaries of the Sacred Heart* (U.S. Province)—M.S.C.

[0690]—*Society of Jesus*—S.J.

RELIGIOUS INSTITUTES OF WOMEN REPRESENTED IN THE DIOCESE

[0350]—*Carmelite Sisters (Corpus Christi)*—O.Carm.

[2100]—*Congregation of the Humility of Mary*—C.H.M.

[1920]—*Congregation of the Sisters of the Holy Cross*—C.S.C.

[1710]—*Congregation of the Third Order of St. Francis of Mary Immaculate*—O.S.F.

[]—*Daughters of Mary Help of Christians Salesian Sisters of St. John Bosco*—F.M.A.

[1070-03]—*Dominican Sisters*—O.P.

[1070-10]—*Dominican Sisters*—O.P.

[1070-13]—*Dominican Sisters*—O.P.

[1430]—*Franciscan Sisters of Our Lady of Perpetual Help*—O.S.F.

[1450]—*Franciscan Sisters of the Sacred Heart*—O.S.F.

[]—*Missionaries of the Rosary of Fatima*—M.R.F.

[]—*Passionist Sisters*—C.F.P.

[3760]—*Poor Clare Colettines*—P.C.C.

[2970]—*School Sisters of Notre Dame*—S.S.N.D.

[1680]—*School Sisters of St. Francis*—O.S.F.

[3520]—*Servants of the Holy Heart of Mary*—S.S.C.M.

[0430]—*Sisters of Charity of the Blessed Virgin Mary*—B.V.M.

[2360]—*Sisters of Loretto at the Foot of the Cross*—S.L.

[2575]—*Sisters of Mercy of the Americas* (Chicago, IL)—R.S.M.

[]—*Sisters of St. Francis* (Clinton, IA)—O.S.F.

[1570]—*Sisters of St. Francis of the Holy Family*—O.S.F.

[3930]—*Sisters of St. Joseph of the Third Order of St. Francis*—S.S.J.-T.O.S.F.

[2183]—*Sisters of the Immaculate Heart of Mary Mother of Christ, Nigeria*—I. H. M.

[1770]—*Sisters of the Third Order of St. Francis* (Peoria, Illinois)—O.S.F.

DIOCESAN CEMETERIES

ROCKFORD. *Calvary-St. Mary's/St. James*

AURORA. *Mount Olivet*

BATAVIA. *Geneva-St. Charles Resurrection*

ELGIN. *Mount Hope*

WINNEBAGO. *Calvary*

NECROLOGY

† London, Lawrence, (Retired)—Died Nov. 1, 2009

An asterisk (*) denotes an organization that has established tax-exempt status directly with the IRS and is not covered by the USCCB Group Ruling.

Diocese of Rockville Centre

(Dioecesis Petropolitana In Insula Longa)

Most Reverend

JAMES J. DALY

Retired Auxiliary Bishop of Rockville Centre; ordained May 22, 1948; appointed Titular Bishop of Castra Nova and Auxiliary to the Bishop of Rockville Centre February 28, 1977; ordained May 9, 1977; retired July 1, 1996.

Most Reverend

EMIL A. WCELA

Retired Auxiliary Bishop of Rockville Centre; ordained June 2, 1956; appointed Titular Bishop of Filaca and Auxiliary Bishop of Rockville Centre October 21, 1988; ordained December 13, 1988; retired April 3, 2007. *Church of St. John the Evangelist, 546 St. John's Pl., Riverhead, NY 11901.* Tel: 631-727-2030.

Most Reverend

JOHN C. DUNNE, D.D.

Auxiliary Bishop of Rockville Centre; ordained June 1, 1963; appointed Titular Bishop of Abercorn and Auxiliary Bishop of Rockville Centre October 21, 1988; ordained December 13, 1988. *Central Vicariate - Diocese of Rockville Centre, P.O. Box 39, Farmingdale, NY 11735-0039.* Tel: 516-249-1700.

Most Reverend

WILLIAM FRANCIS MURPHY, S.T.D., L.H.D.

Bishop of Rockville Centre; ordained December 16, 1964; appointed Auxiliary Bishop to the Archbishop of Boston and Titular Bishop of Saia Maggiore, November 21, 1995; consecrated December 27, 1995; appointed Fourth Bishop of Rockville Centre, June 26, 2001; installed September 5, 2001. *Mailing Address: Diocesan Pastoral Center, P.O. Box 9023, Rockville Centre, NY 11571-9023.* Email: bishopsoffice@drvc.org.

Pastoral Center: P.O. Box 9023, Rockville Centre, NY 11571-9023. Tel: 516-678-5800; Fax: 516-764-3316.

Web: drvc.org

Most Reverend

PAUL H. WALSH

Auxiliary Bishop of Rockville Centre; ordained June 9, 1966; appointed Titular Bishop of Abthugni and Auxiliary Bishop of Rockville Centre April 3, 2003; ordained May 29, 2003. *Western Vicariate - Diocese of Rockville Centre, P.O. Box 933, Roosevelt, NY 11575-0933.* Tel: 516-867-6341.

Most Reverend

PETER A. LIBASCI

Auxiliary Bishop of Rockville Centre; ordained April 1, 1978; appointed Titular Bishop of Satafis and Auxiliary Bishop of Rockville Centre April 3, 2007; ordained June 1, 2007. *Mailing Address: Eastern Vicariate, P.O. Box 5046, Southampton, NY 11969.* Tel: 631-727-5376.

ESTABLISHED APRIL 6, 1957.

Square Miles 1,222.

The Roman Catholic Diocese of Rockville Centre, New York.

Comprises the Counties of Nassau and Suffolk (excepting Fishers Island) in the State of New York.

For legal titles of parishes and diocesan institutions, consult the Chancery Office.

STATISTICAL OVERVIEW

Personnel	
Bishop	1
Auxiliary Bishops	3
Retired Bishops	2
Priests: Diocesan Active in Diocese	226
Priests: Diocesan Active Outside Diocese	10
Priests: Diocesan in Foreign Missions	1
Priests: Retired, Sick or Absent	129
Number of Diocesan Priests	366
Religious Priests in Diocese	30
Total Priests in Diocese	396
Extern Priests in Diocese	128
Ordinations:	
Diocesan Priests	4
Transitional Deacons	4
Permanent Deacons	9
Permanent Deacons in Diocese	265
Total Brothers	80
Total Sisters	1,131
Parishes	
Parishes	133
With Resident Pastor:	
Resident Diocesan Priests	130
Resident Religious Priests	3
Missions	1
Professional Ministry Personnel:	
Brothers	8
Sisters	90
Lay Ministers	447
Welfare	
Catholic Hospitals	5
Total Assisted	593,750
Health Care Centers	3
Total Assisted	31,040
Homes for the Aged	3
Total Assisted	2,268
Residential Care of Children	3
Total Assisted	340
Specialized Homes	9
Total Assisted	1,977
Special Centers for Social Services	31
Total Assisted	41,002
Residential Care of Disabled	20
Total Assisted	213
Other Institutions	115
Total Assisted	104,150
Educational	
Seminaries, Diocesan	1
Students from This Diocese	12
Students from Other Diocese	28
Diocesan Students in Other Seminaries	2
Total Seminarians	14
Colleges and Universities	1
Total Students	3,500
High Schools, Diocesan and Parish	5
Total Students	4,827
High Schools, Private	5
Total Students	7,749
Elementary Schools, Diocesan and Parish	53
Total Students	18,624
Elementary Schools, Private	4
Total Students	1,418
Non-residential Schools for the Disabled	1
Total Students	70
Catechesis/Religious Education:	
High School Students	2,698
Elementary Students	107,584
Total Students under Catholic Instruction	146,484
Teachers in the Diocese:	
Priests	14
Brothers	50
Sisters	57
Lay Teachers	1,851
Vital Statistics	
Receptions into the Church:	
Infant Baptism Totals	17,174
Adult Baptism Totals	601
Received into Full Communion	429
First Communions	18,506
Confirmations	18,131
Marriages:	
Catholic	3,186
Interfaith	770
Total Marriages	3,956
Deaths	12,026
Total Catholic Population	1,521,842
Total Population	3,513,536

Former Bishops—Most Revs. WALTER P. KELLENBERG, D.D., first Bishop of Rockville Centre; ord. June 2, 1928; appt. Titular Bishop of Joannina and Auxiliary Bishop of New York, Aug. 25, 1953; cons. Oct. 5, 1953; appt. Bishop of Ogdensburg, Jan. 19, 1954; appt. first Bishop of Rockville Centre, April 16, 1957; installed May 27, 1957; retired May 3, 1976; died Jan. 11, 1986; JOHN R. MCGANN, D.D., second Bishop of Rockville Centre; ord. June 3, 1950; appt. Titular Bishop of Morosbisdus and Auxiliary to the Bishop of Rockville Centre, Nov. 12, 1970; cons. Jan. 7, 1971; appt. second Bishop of Rockville Centre, May 3, 1976; installed June 24, 1976; retired Jan. 4, 2000; died Jan. 29, 2002; JAMES T. MCHUGH, S.T.D., third Bishop of Rockville Centre; ord. May 25, 1957; appt. Titular Bishop of Morosbisdo and Auxiliary Bishop of Newark, Nov. 20, 1987; cons. Jan. 25, 1988; appt. Bishop of Camden, May 13, 1989; installed June 20, 1989; appt. Coadjutor Bishop of Rockville Centre, Dec. 7, 1998; installed Feb. 22, 1999; succeeded to the See, Jan. 4, 2000; died Dec. 10, 2000.

Diocesan Bishop—Most Rev. WILLIAM FRANCIS MURPHY, S.T.D., L.H.D.

Auxiliary Bishops—Most Revs. EMIL A. WCELA, D.D., Emeritus; PAUL H. WALSH, D.D.; JOHN C. DUNNE, D.D.; PETER A. LIBASCI, D.D.; JAMES J. DALY, D.D., Emeritus.

Secretary to the Bishop—Rev. Msgr. ROBERT O. MORRISSEY, M.Div., J.C.D. Tel: 516-678-5800, Ext. 402; Fax: 516-678-3138. Email: rmorrissey@drvc.org.

Vicar General and Moderator of the Curia—Rev. Msgr. ROBERT J. BRENNAN, P.O. Box 9023, Rockville Centre, 11571-9023. Tel: 516-678-5800, Ext. 622. Email: rbrennan@drvc.org.

Vicar General—Rt. Rev. Msgr. JOHN A. ALESANDRO, P.A., J.C.D., Church of St. Ignatius Loyola, 129 Broadway, Hicksville, 11801. Tel: 516-931-0056.

Episcopal Vicars—Western Vicariate: Most Rev. PAUL H. WALSH, D.D., P.O. Box 933, Roosevelt, 11575-0933. Tel: 516-867-6340; Fax: 516-867-6341. Email: phwalsh@drvc.org. Central Vicariate: Most Rev. JOHN C. DUNNE, D.D., Mailing Address: P.O. Box 39, Farmingdale, 11735-0039. Tel: 516-249-1700; Fax: 516-249-1701. Email: dunnejc@worldnet.att.net. Eastern Vicariate: Most Rev. PETER A. LIBASCI, D.D., Mailing Address: P.O. Box 5046, Southampton, 11969. Tel: 631-727-5376. Email: plibasci@drvc.org.

Chancery Office—

Chancellor—Sr. KATHLEEN SCHAETZLE, C.S.J. Tel: 516-678-5800, Ext. 583. Email: chancellor@drvc.org.

Vice Chancellors—Sr. LUCY BLYSKAL, C.S.J., J.C.D. Email: dueprocess@drvc.org; Rev. Msgr. ROBERT O. MORRISSEY, M.Div., J.C.D. Email: rmorrissey@drvc.org.

Cabinet—

Secretary for Administration—Mr. CHARLES TRUNZ

III. Tel: 516-678-5800, Ext. 225. Email: ctrunz@drvc.org.

Secretary for Communications—Mr. SEAN P. DOLAN. Tel: 516-678-5800, Ext. 625. Email: rvcinfo@drvc.org.

Secretary for Education—Sr. JOANNE CALLAHAN, O.S.U. Tel: 516-678-5800, Ext. 548. Email: jcallahan@drvc.org.

Secretary for Faith Formation—Sr. MARY ALICE PIIL, C.S.J., Ph.D. Tel: 516-678-5800, Ext. 512. Email: mapiil@drvc.org.

Secretary for Ministerial Personnel—Rev. Msgr. BRIAN J. MCNAMARA. Tel: 516-678-5800, Ext. 585. Email: bmcnamara@drvc.org.

Secretary for New Evangelization—Bro. JAMES MCVEIGH, O.S.F. Tel: 516-678-5800, Ext. 309. Email: jmcreigh@drvc.org.

Secretary for Social Services—LAURA CASSELL. Tel: 516-733-7013. Email: cassell.laura@catholiccharities.cc.

Secretary for Institutional Advancement—ENES CARNESECCA. Tel: 516-379-5210, Ext. 226. Email: ecarnesecca@drvc.org.

Secretary to the Bishop—Rev. Msgr. ROBERT O. MORRISSEY, M.Div., J.C.D. Tel: 516-678-5800, Ext. 402. Email: rmorrissey@drvc.org.

Chancellor—Sr. KATHLEEN SCHAETZLE, C.S.J. Tel: 516-678-5800, Ext. 583. Email: chancellor@drvc.org.

Vicar General—Rev. Msgr. ROBERT J. BRENNAN. Tel: 516-678-5800, Ext. 622. Email: rbrennan@drvc.org.

Censors of Books—Rt. Rev. Msgr. JOHN A. ALESANDRO, P.A., J.C.D.; Rev. CHARLES CACCAVALE, S.T.L., S.T.D.; Rev. Msgrs. FRANCIS X. GLIMM, S.T.L. (Retired); GEORGE P. GRAHAM, J.C.D., Ph.D. (Retired); ROBERT O. MORRISSEY, M.Div., J.C.D.; FRANCIS J. SCHNEIDER, M.Div., J.C.D.; Revs. ROBERT J. SMITH, S.T.L., S.T.D.; PETER I. VACCARI, S.T.L.

Diocesan Tribunal—P.O. Box 9023, Rockville Centre, 11571-9023. Tel: 516-678-5800; Fax: 516-594-1548.

Judicial Vicar—Rev. Msgr. JAMES F. PEREDA, M.Div., M.A., J.C.D. Tel: 516-678-5800, Ext. 566. Email: jpereda@drvc.org.

Adjutant Judicial Vicar—Rev. THOMAS V. ARNAO, M.Div., J.C.D. Tel: 516-678-5800, Ext. 558.

Defenders of the Bond—Rt. Rev. Msgr. CHARLES A. GUARINO, P.A., M.A., M.Div., J.C.D.; Rev. ANTONIO S. PASCUAL, J.C.L. (Retired).

Promoter of Justice—Rt. Rev. Msgr. CHARLES A. GUARINO, P.A., M.A., M.Div., J.C.D.

Administrative Judge for Interdiocesan Tribunal and Secretary of the Tribunal—Deacon THOMAS B. RICH, J.C.L., D.Min. Tel: 516-678-5800, Ext. 559.

Judges for Interdiocesan Tribunal—Rev. Msgr. RICHARD C. BAUHOFF, J.C.D., Ph.D.; Sr. LUCY BLYSKAL, C.S.J., J.C.D.; Rev. Msgrs. THOMAS D. CANDREVA, S.T.L., J.C.D. (Retired); GEORGE P. GRAHAM, J.C.D., Ph.D. (Retired); DOMENICK T. GRAZIADIO, M.A.; RICHARD P. KOPINSKI, M.S., M.A.; FRANCIS S. MIDURA, M.Div., M.Ch.A.; THOMAS E. MOLLOY; ROBERT O. MORRISSEY, M.Div., J.C.D.; JOHN C. NOSSER, M.S., M.Div. (Retired); Rev. JOHN J. TUTONE, M.Div., J.C.D.

Notaries—Sr. RUTH BORGERSEN, R.S.M., M.A.; Mrs. CAROL GATZ; Mrs. HELEN HOWE; Mrs. TONI TUZZOLINO; Mrs. NANNO E. HAYES.

In-Take Secretary—Mrs. NANNO E. HAYES. Tel: 516-678-5800, Ext. 571.

Medical Experts—SIMEON RYAN, Ph.D.; MARY W. HOULIHAN, Ph.D.; Sr. THOMAS MORE FAHEY, R.G.S., Psy.D.

Coordinator of Post-Annulment Counseling Program—Mrs. BARBARA BUTLER, M.A., L.M.F.T. Tel: 631-754-9765.

Procurator & Advocates—Sr. AGNES CLAUDIA ALLEN, C.S.J.; Deacon GEOFFREY ANISANSEL; Mrs. LORRAINE ANISANSEL; Mrs. TERRI BLAKENEY; Mrs. MARIAN BOPP; Rev. WILLIAM G. BRESLAWSKI; Ms. NOREEN BRITTENHAM; Mrs. BARBARA BUTLER, M.A., L.M.F.T.; Sr. HELEN BYRNE, C.S.J.; Deacons FRANCISCO CALES; JAMES CARROLL; TONY CEDRONE; Mrs. MARCY CHAPUISAT; Ms. MAUREEN COLLINS; Mrs. DOLORES CONNORS; Sr. MIRIAM HONORA CORR, C.S.J.; Rev. THOMAS C. COSTA; Deacon FRANK COVE; Sr. EILEEN CURLEY, R.S.M.; Deacon ANTHONY CUSEO; Dr. JOAN B. DORR; Ms. ANITA DOS SANTOS; Rev. LAWRENCE T. DUNCKLEE; Mrs. VALERIE DUNNE; Deacon THOMAS J. EVRARD; Rev. ERIC R. FASANO; Deacon ANDREW GARGIULO; Sr. KATHLEEN GEANEY, R.S.M.; Deacon RONALD J. GILLETTE; Mr. JOHN E. GLYNN; Rev. THOMAS HAGGERTY; Mrs. NANNO E. HAYES; Dr. JOANNE HEANY-HUNTER; Sr. FRANCENE HORAN, R.S.M.; Mr. RICHARD HUMINSKI; Ms. DENISE KANCLER; Rev. WALTER F. KEDJIERSKI; Sisters BONNIE KELLY, C.S.J.; JANE LYONS, C.I.J.; Rev. JAMES P. MANNION JR.; Rev. Msgr. JAMES M. MCDONALD; Rev. MARTIN MCGEOUGH, C.M.; Mr. STEVE MCGIFF; Deacon JAMES MCQUADE; Ms. ANN MESSINA; Rev. JOSEPH A. MIRRO; Sr. MADELINE MOORE, R.S.M.; Mr. CHRISTOPHER J. MURANO; Deacons CHARLES MUSCARNERA; MONTFORD D. NAYLER; Rev. CHRISTOPHER NOWAK, O.S.A.; Deacon JOHN O'CONNOR; Mrs. MARY ANN O'CONNOR; Deacon THOMAS O'CONNOR; Dr. MARY O'GRADY; Ms. ROSEMARY PADALA; Ms. DIANA PADILLA; Deacon PHIL PAOLICELLI; Mr. JOSEPH PARADISE; Ms. EILEEN PHILLIPS; Mr. JOHN P. REALI; Deacon GEORGE REICH; Mrs. LINDA REICH; Ms. VILMA RIVERA; Rev. ROBERT ROMEO; Ms. CARMEN RONCAL; Ms. JANE SMITH; Deacons NEIL SQUITIERI; JOHN SULLIVAN; Sisters KATHLEEN T. SULLIVAN, C.S.J.; EUGENIA M. TRAVERS, O.P.; Rev. Msgr. EDMOND J. TRENCH (Retired); Sr. PATRICIA TURLEY, C.S.J.; Ms. JULIE VAN NOSTRAND; Rev. MICHAEL A. VETRANO; Sr. ELLEN ZAK, C.S.F.N.; Revs. KENNETH M. ZACH; ANDRZEJ ZGLEJSZEWSKI.

Senate of Priests (Presbyteral Council/College of Consultors)—Most Revs. JOHN C. DUNNE, D.D.; PAUL H. WALSH, D.D.; PETER A. LIBASCI, D.D.; Rev. Msgr. ROBERT J. BRENNAN; Rt. Rev. Msgr. JOHN A. ALESANDRO, P.A., J.C.D.; Revs. WILLIAM G. BRESLAWSKI; PETER DEVARAJ, S.A.C.; Rev. Msgrs. PETER J. PFLOMM; DENNIS M. REGAN; Rev. ROBERT J. CLERKIN; Rev. Msgr. JOSEPH DEGROCCO; Rev. ROBERT KUZNIK; Rev. Msgr. ROBERT O. MORRISSEY, M.Div., J.C.D., Exec. Sec.; Rev. STEVEN CAMP; Rev. Msgr. THOMAS L. SPADARO; Revs. FRANCIS PIZZARELLI, S.M.M.; GERARD GENTLEMAN; PAUL RAHILLY; Rev. Msgr. FRANCIS J. SCHNEIDER, M.Div., J.C.D.; Revs. ROBERT J. SMITH, S.T.L., S.T.D.; GONZALO OAJACA-LOPEZ; MICHAEL A. VETRANO; THOMAS COOGAN; Rev. Msgr. BRENDAN P. RIORDAN.

Deans—Rockville Centre Deanery: Rev. Msgr. FRANK J. CALDWELL, C.S.W. North Hempstead Deanery: Rev. Msgr. JOHN J. MCCANN. Oyster Bay Deanery: Rev. THOMAS C. COSTA. Belmont Deanery: Rev. Msgr. THOMAS J. HAROLD. Hicksville Deanery: Rev. GERARD A. RINGENBACK, M.S.Ed., M.A. Five Towns Deanery: Rev. JOHN J. TUTONE, M.Div., J.C.D. Seaford Deanery: Rev. Msgr. PETER J. PFLOMM. Huntington Deanery: Rev. Msgr. T. PETER RYAN. Smithaven Deanery: Rev. Msgr. JAMES M. MCNAMARA. Babylon Deanery: Rev. Msgr. CHRISTOPHER J. HELLER. Islip Deanery: Rev. THOMAS COOGAN. North Brookhaven Deanery: Rev. Msgr. WILLIAM A. HANSON. South Brookhaven Deanery: Rev. EDWARD R. D'ANDREA, M.Div. Peconic Deanery: Rev. JOSEPH MIRRO.

Diocesan Offices

Pastoral Center—P.O. Box 9023, Rockville Centre, 11571-9023. Tel: 516-678-5800; Fax: 516-764-3316.

Director of Administration—Mr. CHARLES TRUNZ III. Tel: 516-678-5800, Ext. 225. Email: ctrunz@drvc.org; Ms. ELLEN CARAVELLA, Internal Auditor. Tel: 516-678-5800, Ext. 291. Email: ecaravella@drvc.org.

Archives—Mrs. JEAN LYNCH, Archivist, Seminary of the Immaculate Conception, 440 W. Neck Rd., Huntington, 11743. Tel: 631-423-0483; Fax: 631-423-7922. Email: archives@drvc.org.

Institutional Advancement—ENES CARNESECCA. Tel: 516-379-5210, Ext. 226. Email: ecarnesecca@drvc.org.

Catholic Ministries Appeal—Mailing Address: P.O. Box 4000, Rockville Centre, 11571. Tel: 516-379-5210, Ext. 210; Fax: 516-379-5043. Email: catholicministries@drvc.org.

Parish Stewardship—200 W. Centennial Ave., Ste. 202, Roosevelt, 11575. Tel: 516-379-4055; Fax: 516-379-3234. Email: stewardship@prodigy.net. Web: www.stewardshipli.org.

Religious & Priest Retirement Fund—Tel: 516-379-5210, Ext. 210; Fax: 516-379-5043. Email: catholicministries@drvc.org.

Catholic Charities—LAURA A. CASSELL, Exec. Dir., 90 Cherry Ln., Hicksville, 11801. Tel: 516-733-7013 See separate listing below.

Cemeteries—Mr. NEAL S. BARLIN, Dir., Mailing Address: Catholic Cemeteries, Diocese of Rockville Centre, P.O. Box 182, Westbury, 11590. Tel: 516-334-7990; Fax: 516-334-4383. Email: director@holyroodcemetery.org. Web: www.holyroodcemetery.org; Holy Rood Cemetery, 111 Old Country Rd., Box 182, Westbury, 11590-0182. Tel: 516-334-7990; Fax: 516-334-4383. Holy Sepulchre Cemetery, 3442 Rte. 112, Coram, 11727. Tel: 631-732-3460; Fax: 631-732-3476. Queen of All Saints Cemetery, 115 Wheeler Rd., Central Islip, 11722. Tel: 631-234-8297; Fax: 631-234-8632.

Chaplains (Uniformed)—

Chaplain of the Nassau County Firemen's Association—Rev. KEVIN M. SMITH, St. Francis de Sales, Patchogue.

Chaplains of the Nassau County Police Department—Rt. Rev. Msgr. JOHN A. ALESANDRO, P.A., J.C.D., St. Dominick, Oyster Bay; Rev. JOSEPH D'ANGELO; Rev. Msgr. THOMAS J. HARTMAN.

Chaplains of the Suffolk County Police Department—Rev. Msgr. JAMES M. KISSANE, St. John of God, Central Islip; Rev. BRUCE J. POWERS, St. Patrick, Bay Shore.

Consultation Service for Religious Personnel—Sr. MILDRED SCHUBERT, S.C., Exec. Dir., Mailing Address: P.O. Box 467, Rockville Centre, 11571. Tel: 516-678-2135.

Deacons—Deacons JAMES MURPHY, Dir. Deacon Personnel, Seminary of the Immaculate Conception, Office of Deacons, 440 W. Neck Rd., Huntington, 11743. Tel: 631-424-8360, Ext. 177; Fax: 631-424-8361. Email: jmurphy@drvc.org; THOMAS W. CONNOLLY, Dir. Diaconate Formation. Tel: 631-424-8360, Ext. 178. Email: tconnolly@drvc.org.

Due Process (Conciliation-Arbitration)—Sr. LUCY BLYSKAL, C.S.J., J.C.D., Admin., St. Joseph Renewal Center, 1725 Brentwood Rd., Brentwood, 11717-5587. Tel: 631-273-1187, Ext. 32; Fax: 631-273-1451. Email: dueprocess@drvc.org.

Ecumenical & Interreligious Affairs—Rev. Msgr. DONALD M. BECKMANN, Dir. Tel: 516-678-5800, Ext. 613; Fax: 516-763-1078.

Education—Sr. JOANNE CALLAHAN, O.S.U., Supt. Tel: 516-678-5800, Ext. 548; Fax: 516-678-7362. Email: education@edrvc.org; Dr. JOANNE O'BRIEN, M.A., M.Ed., Ed.D., Assoc. Supt. Tel: 516-678-5800, Ext. 546; Sisters LORRAINE MCDONALD, O.P., M.S., P.D., Asst. Supt. Elementary Schools. Tel: 516-678-5800, Ext. 545; KATHLEEN EGAN, C.S.J., M.A., Asst. Supt. Public Policy & Govt. Programs. Tel: 516-678-5800, Ext. 555; BIAGIO ARPINO, Asst. Supt. Personnel. Tel: 516-678-5800, Ext. 553; Sisters CATHERINE STARE, S.C., M.S., M.A., Asst. Supt. Curriculum & Testing. Tel: 516-678-5800, Ext. 550; ANTOINETTE DE AVEIRO, O.P., M.S., Asst. Supt. Early Childhood Programs. Tel: 516-678-5800, Ext. 277; NORMA WHITLEY, Asst. Supt. Technology. Tel: 516-678-5800, Ext. 404.

Faith Formation—Sr. MARY ALICE PIIL, C.S.J., Ph.D., Dir. Tel: 516-678-5800, Ext. 512; Fax: 516-536-3473. Email: mapiil@drvc.org; ESTELLE PECK, Assoc. Dir. Adult Faith Formation. Tel: 516-678-5800, Ext. 200; Fax: 516-536-3473. Email: epeck@drvc.org; LAURA RIVAS, Assoc. Dir. Children & Youth Formation. Tel: 516-678-5800, Ext. 506; Fax: 516-536-3473. Email: lrivas@drvc.org; KATHLEEN LOGAN, Dir. Family Ministry. Tel: 516-678-5800, Ext. 202; Fax: 516-536-3473. Email: klogan@drvc.org; JOHN ROMANOWSKY, Assoc. Dir. Media Technology. Tel: 516-678-5800, Ext. 210; Fax: 516-536-3473. Email: jromanowsky@drvc.org.

Financial Affairs—

Parish Administrator—Mr. KEVIN T. MURPHY. Tel: 516-678-5800, Ext. 543; Fax: 516-536-6554. Email: ktmurphy@drvc.org.

Controller—JOSEPH YOUNG. Tel: 516-678-5800, Ext. 234. Email: jyoung@drvc.org.

Procurement Officer—MARTIN DWONARSKI. Tel: 516-678-5800, Ext. 205. Email: mdwonarski@drvc.org.

Education Finance Officer—THOMAS DOODIAN. Tel: 516-678-5800, Ext. 522. Email: tdoodian@drvc.org.

General Counsel—THOMAS RENKER. Tel: 516-678-5800, Ext. 241. Email: trenker@drvc.org.

Information Technology Officer—SCOTT CASTELLANO. Tel: 516-678-5800, Ext. 409. Email: scastellano@drvc.org.

Facilities and Risk Management—Mr. WILLIAM G. CHAPIN, Dir. Tel: 516-678-5800, Ext. 261; Fax: 516-763-2606. Email: wgchapin@drvc.org.

Human Resources—JOHN COUGHLIN. Tel: 516-678-5800, Ext. 639; Fax: 516-678-9566. Email: jcoughlin@drvc.org.

Treasury Operations—Ms. MAUREEN SCADUTO, Dir. Tel: 516-678-5800, Ext. 526; Fax: 516-536-6554. Email: mtscaduto@drvc.org.

Health Care Apostolate—Catholic Health Services of Long Island, 992 N. Village Ave., Rockville Centre, 11570. Tel: 516-705-3700. Mr. JAMES HARDEN, Dir. Catholic Health Svcs.; Mrs. CATHY B. GRANDJEAN, 1010 Rte. 112, Port Jefferson Station, 11776. Tel: 631-474-5663; Fax: 631-331-0586 For individual hospitals and other healthcare institutions see separate listings below.

Office of Public Information—Mr. SEAN P. DOLAN, Dir. Tel: 516-678-5800, Ext. 625; Fax: 516-594-0984. Email: rvcinfo@drvc.org.

Migration Office—Ms. CARMEN MAQUILAN, Dir. Immigrant Svcs. Catholic Charities, 143 Schleigel Blvd., Amityville, 11701. Tel: 631-789-5210; Fax: 631-789-5245.

Ministry to Senior Priests—Rev. Msgr. THOMAS F. MULVANERTY; Bro. PATRICK MURPHY, St. Pius X Residence, 555 Albany Ave., Amityville, 11701.

Office of New Evangelization—Bro. JAMES MCVEIGH, O.S.F. Tel: 516-678-5800, Ext. 309. Email: jmcveigh@drvc.org.

Catholics of African Ancestry—DARCEL WHITTEN-WILAMOWSKI. Tel: 516-678-5800, Ext. 239.

Campus Ministry—VACANT. Tel: 516-678-5800, Ext. 614.

Haitian-American Apostolate—Rev. EDDY JULIEN. Tel: 516-678-5800, Ext. 233. Email: ejulien@drvc.org.

Hispanic Ministry—Rev. Msgr. PABLO M. RODRIQUEZ, Vicar for Hispanics. Tel: 516-489-3675; Deacon FRANCISCO CALES, Coord. Tel: 516-678-5800, Ext. 618.

Hispanic Apostolate of the South Fork—168 Hill St., Southampton, 11968. Tel: 631-283-4379; Fax: 631-204-0817. Revs. STEPHEN M. GROZIO, C.M.; MARTIN MCGEOUGH, C.M.; ARNULFO JARA, C.M.; Sr. BREIGE LAVERY, R.S.M.

Mission Office— Society for the Propagation of the Faith, Holy Childhood Association, Catholic Relief Services, Diocesan Mission in the Dominican Republic, American Home Missions, Secretariat for Latin America. Rev. JOSEPH MCCABE, M.M. Tel: 516-678-5800, Ext. 513.

Youth and Young Adult Ministry—VACANT. Tel: 516-678-5800, Ext. 616. Email: youth@drvc.org.

Renewal Apostolate—Dr. JOHN PALMER. Tel: 516-678-5800, Ext. 408. Email: jpalmer@drvc.org.

Newspaper - "The Long Island Catholic"— (published by the Catholic Press Association of the Diocese of Rockville Centre, Inc.) *200 W. Centennial Ave., Ste. 201, P.O. Box 9000, Roosevelt, 11575.* Tel: 516-594-1000; Fax: 516-594-1092. Web: www.licatholic.org. Email: editor@licatholic.org (editorial); adstlic@licatholic.org (advertisements). RICHARD HINSHAW, Editor.

Office for the Protection of Children & Young People—EILEEN PUGLISI, Dir. Tel: 516-678-5800, Ext. 573; Fax: 516-887-1584. Email: epuglisi@drvc.org.

Clergy Personnel—Rev. Msgr. BRIAN J. MCNAMARA. Tel: 516-678-5800, Ext. 585; Fax: 516-764-3467. Email: bmcnamara@drvc.org.

Priestly Life and Ministry—Rev. Msgr. JAMES P. SWIADER, Seminary of the Immaculate Conception, 440 W. Neck Rd., Huntington, 11743. Tel: 631-423-0483.

Priests' Personnel Assignment Board—Most Revs. JOHN C. DUNNE, D.D.; PAUL H. WALSH, D.D.; PETER A. LIBASCI, D.D.; Rev. Msgrs. ROBERT J. BRENNAN; BRIAN J. MCNAMARA; Rev. WILLIAM G. BRESLAWSKI; Rev. Msgr. THOMAS J. HAROLD; Rev. JOHN V. O'FARRELL; Rev. Msgr. PETER J. PFLOMM; Revs. PATRICK J. WHITNEY; ROBERT J. SMITH, S.T.L., S.T.D.; Mrs. PATRICIA FERGUS, Sec.

Priests' Personnel Policy Board—Rev. Msgr. BRIAN J. MCNAMARA; Rev. BRIAN INGRAM; Rev. Msgrs. THOMAS F. MULVANERTY; FRANCIS J. SCHNEIDER, M.Div., J.C.D.; Rev. ANTHONY M. STANGANELLI; Rev. Msgr. JAMES P. SWIADER.

Priests' Retirement Board—Most Rev. JOHN C. DUNNE, D.D., Ex Officio; Rev. Msgrs. BRIAN J. MCNAMARA; THOMAS F. MULVANERTY, Sec. & Ex Officio; RICHARD C. BAUHOFF, J.C.D., Ph.D.; Rev. ROBERT J. CLERKIN; Rev. Msgrs. GEORGE P. GRAHAM, J.C.D., Ph.D. (Retired); JOHN P. MARTIN (Retired); Revs. DONALD F. DIEDERICH, J.C.D. (Retired); PETER C. DOOLEY; Rt. Rev. Msgr. EMMET FAGAN.

Prison Ministry and Criminal Justice Affairs—26 S. Saxon Ave., Bay Shore, 11706-8920. Tel: 631-969-0837; Fax: 631-666-5073. Bro. JACK MOYLAN, O.S.F., D.Min., Dir.; SUZANNE D. JONES, Coord. Ministerial Svcs.

Nassau County Correctional Center—100 Carman Ave., East Meadow, 11554-1146. Tel: 516-572-4145; 516-572-3622. Chaplains: Rev. RALPH FERRO; Sr. DOLORES CASTELLANO, C.I.J.; Deacon JOHN H. MCGONIGLE; Sr. VIRGINIA WATERS, F.S.P.; Deacon MANUEL RAMOS.

Nassau County Juvenile Detention Center—61 Carman Ave., Westbury, 11590. Tel: 516-571-9153. Sr. DOLORES CASTELLANO, C.I.J.; Bro. JACK MOYLAN, O.S.F., D.Min., Chap.

Suffolk County Correctional Facility—100 Center Dr., Riverhead, 11901. Tel: 631-852-2294; 631-852-2728. Chaplains: Sr. MICHELLE BREMER, C.S.F.N.; Deacon CHRIS VIGLIOTTA.

Suffolk County Minimum Security Facility—Mailing Address: P.O. Box 69, Yaphank, 11980. Tel: 631-852-4713. Chaplains: Deacons MIGUEL ROMERO; CHRIS VIGLIOTTA; Sr. MICHELLE BREMER, C.S.F.N.

Religious—Vicar for Religious: Bro. JAMES MCVEIGH, O.S.F. Tel: 516-678-5800, Ext. 588. Email: jmcveigh@drvc.org; Sr. MARY WALSH, C.S.J. Tel: 516-678-5800, Ext. 589. Email: mwalsh@drvc.org.

Respect Life—Rev. Msgr. FRANCIS J. MANISCALCO, Dir., 200 W. Centennial Ave., Roosevelt, 11575. Tel: 516-379-8292, Ext. 224; Fax: 516-379-0041.

Television (Telecare/TV 29)—1200 Glenn Curtiss Blvd., Uniondale, 11553. Tel: 516-538-8700; Fax: 516-489-9701. Email: info@telecaretv.org. Rev. Msgr. JAMES C. VLAUN.

Victim Assistance Coordinator—EILEEN PUGLISI. Tel: 516-678-5800, Ext. 573. Email: epuglisi@drvc.org.

Vocations—Rev. BRIAN P. BARR, Dir., Vocation Office, 440 W. Neck Rd., Huntington, 11743. Tel: 631-242-9888; Fax: 631-242-9889. Email: vocations@drvc.org. Web: www.drvc.org/vocations.

Worship—Rev. ANDRZEJ ZGLEJSZEWSKI, Dir. Tel: 516-678-5800, Ext. 503; Sr. SHEILA BROWNE, R.S.M., Coord. Tel: 516-678-5800, Ext. 231. Email: worship@drvc.org.

Diocesan Organizations

Apostleship of Prayer—Rev. Msgr. JAMES M. MCDONALD, Dir., 35 N. Service Rd., Dix Hills, 11746. Tel: 631-499-8520; Fax: 631-499-1530.

Catholic Accountants' Guild—Miss MARY R. GOELLER, Contact Person, 155 Garfield Ave., Mineola, 11501. Tel: 516-746-1223.

Catholic Lawyer's Guild—Rev. Msgr. GEORGE P. GRAHAM, J.C.D., Ph.D., Chap. (Retired), 3100 Hempstead Turnpike, Levittown, 11756. Tel: 516-579-5304.

Catholic Youth Organization of Nassau and Suffolk—Ms. MARGARET JOHNSON, Dir.; Rev. GERARD A. RINGENBACK, M.S.Ed., M.A., 20 E. Cherry St., Hicksville, 11801.

Nocturnal Adoration Society—Rev. Msgr. JAMES M. MCDONALD, Dir., 35 N. Service Rd., Dix Hills, 11746. Tel: 631-499-8520; Fax: 631-499-1530.

Legion of Mary—Rev. Msgr. JAMES M. MCDONALD, Dir., 35 N. Service Rd., Dix Hills, 11746. Tel: 631-499-8520; Fax: 631-499-1530.

Society of St. Vincent de Paul—JAMES T. DILTS, Exec. Dir., 249 Broadway, Bethpage, 11714. Tel: 516-822-3132; Fax: 516-822-2728.

CLERGY, PARISHES, MISSIONS AND PAROCHIAL SCHOOLS

VILLAGE OF ROCKVILLE CENTRE

(NASSAU COUNTY)

1—ST. AGNES CATHEDRAL (1894) Rev. Msgr. William E. Koenig, Rector; Revs. German Villabon, O.S.A.; John D. McCarthy; Deacons Thomas McDaid; Donald Stamm. In Res., Rt. Rev. Msgr. James P. Kelly, Rector Emeritus (Retired); Rev. Msgr. Robert J. Brennan; Revs. Francis Oranefo; Andrzej Zglejszewski (Poland).
Res.: 29 Quealy Pl., 11570. Tel: 516-766-0205; Fax: 516-763-0745. Email: parishoffice@stagnescathedral.org. Web: www.stagnescathedral.org.
School—70 Clinton Ave., 11570. Tel: 516-678-5550; Fax: 516-678-0437. Sr. Kathleen Carlin, Co-Prin.; Helen Newman, Co-Prin. Sisters of St. Dominic 1; Lay Teachers 47; Students 852.
Catechesis/Religious Program—Tel: 516-678-2306. Mrs. Donna Eschenauer, D.R.E. Students 1,351.

2—CAMPUS PARISH OF LONG ISLAND (1972) Rev. Brian P. Barr, Admin. & Dir.
P.O. Box 9023, 11571. Tel: 516-678-5800, Ext. 614; Fax: 516-763-1078.
For details, please refer to Campus Ministries and Newman Centers under the Institution section.

OUTSIDE VILLAGE OF ROCKVILLE CENTRE

AMITYVILLE, SUFFOLK CO., ST. MARTIN OF TOURS (1897) Rev. Richard T. Stelter; Deacons John Sheehan; Michael Aprile; Richard Ferri.
Res.: 37 Union Ave., 11701. Tel: 631-264-0124; Fax: 631-264-0139. Email: martours@optonline.net.
School—41 Union Ave., 11701. Tel: 631-264-7166; Fax: 631-264-0136. Web: smtschool.org. Sisters of St. Joseph 1; Lay Teachers 24; Students 392.
Catechesis/Religious Program—Tel: 631-691-1617. Students 199.

BABYLON, SUFFOLK CO., ST. JOSEPH (1877) [CEM] Rev. Msgr. Christopher J. Heller; Revs. Joseph V. Arevalo; Seth N. Arwo-Dogu; Francis A. Samuel, O.C.I.; Deacons Michael J. Leyden; John F. Sullivan; Barry P. Croce; George F. Nealis; Geoffrey R. Anisanel.
Res.: 39 N. Carll Ave., 11702-2701. Tel: 631-669-0068; Fax: 631-669-9175. Email: parishoffice@stjosephsbabylon.org. Web: www.stjosephsbabylon.org.
Catechesis/Religious Program—Tel: 631-587-4717. Mrs. Lee Ann Abseck, D.R.E. Students 1,272.
Mission— Oak Beach, Suffolk Co. 11702. (Summer)
Mission— West Gilgo Beach, Suffolk Co. 11702. (Summer)

BALDWIN, NASSAU CO., ST. CHRISTOPHER (1915) Revs. Steven Camp; Robert A. Holz; Deacons Charles Muscarnera; Anthony Banno; James Carroll. In Res., Rev. Anthony Madu.
Res.: 11 Gale Ave., 11510-3202. Tel: 516-223-0723; Fax: 516-867-5678. Email: info@stchris.com. Web: www.stchris.com.
School—15 Pershing Blvd., 11510. Tel: 516-223-4404; Fax: 516-223-1409. Anne Lederer, Prin. Lay Teachers 24; Students 383.
Catechesis/Religious Program—Tel: 516-223-5813; Fax: 516-223-5609. Mrs. Gail Milne, D.R.E.; Joan Defendini, D.R.E. (Adult); James Montalbano, Music Dir. Students 872.

BAY SHORE, SUFFOLK CO., ST. PATRICK'S (1883) [CEM] Revs. Thomas M. Coogan; Cyril Obi Bayim (Nigeria); Harold J. Noviello; Deacons Joseph Peralta; Frank Keach. In Res., Rev. Michael Holzmann, Chap.
Res.: 9 N. Clinton Ave., 11706. Tel: 631-665-4911; Fax: 631-665-8388.
School—Tel: 631-665-0569; Fax: 631-968-6007. Web: www.spsbayshore.org. Mrs. Roseann Petruccio, Prin. Lay Teachers 22; Students 427.
Catechesis/Religious Program—Tel: 631-665-4914; Fax: 631-665-9009. Students 1,301.

BAYVILLE, NASSAU CO., ST. GERTRUDE'S (1959) Rev. Stephen J. Brigandi.
Res.: 28 School St., 11709. Tel: 516-628-1113; Fax: 516-628-9032.
School—*Pre School*, Tel: 516-628-3710. Students 30.
Catechesis/Religious Program—Tel: 516-628-2432; Fax: 516-628-0224. Students 328.

BELLMORE, NASSAU CO., ST. BARNABAS THE APOSTLE (1912) Revs. Peter C. Dooley; Charles Omotu (Nigeria); Valentine D. Rebello (India); Deacons Bernard Sherlock; Thomas Coleman; Richard Iandoli.
Res.: 2320 Bedford Ave., 11710. Tel: 516-785-0054; Fax: 516-221-7789. Web: www.stbarnabasny.org.
See St. Elizabeth Ann Seton Regional School, Bellmore under Regional Schools located in the Institution section.
Catechesis/Religious Program—Tel: 516-785-0130. Email: stbarnabasocf@yahoo.com. Students 1,900.

BELLPORT, SUFFOLK CO., MARY IMMACULATE (1905) Rev. Gennaro J. DiSpigno.
Res.: 16 Brown's Ln., 11713. Tel: 631-286-0154; Fax: 631-286-2937. Email: pastormib@aol.com. Web: maryimmaculatechurch.net.
See Holy Angels Regional School, Patchogue under Regional Schools located in the Institution section.
Catechesis/Religious Program—Tel: 631-286-3504; Fax: 631-286-2937. Students 440.

BETHPAGE, NASSAU CO., ST. MARTIN OF TOURS (1923) Revs. John Tizio, C.Ss.R.; Henry Sattler, C.Ss.R.; James Szobonya, C.Ss.R; Deacons James A. Biggin; Eugene Capobianco; Thomas Hennessy.
Res.: 40 Seaman Ave., 11714. Tel: 516-931-0818; Fax: 516-931-0559.
See St. John Baptist de LaSalle Regional School, Farmingdale under Regional Schools located in the Institution section.
Catechesis/Religious Program—220 Central Ave., 11714. Tel: 516-822-9768; Fax: 516-932-8454. Barbara Pinnola, D.R.E.; Patricia Ryan, C.R.E.; Laura Leigh Agnese, C.R.E. Students 1,400.

BLUE POINT, SUFFOLK CO., OUR LADY OF THE SNOW (1917) Rev. Edward R. D'Andrea; Sr. Noreen Cleary, S.C., Pastoral Assoc.; Deacons Robert Gronenthal; Steve Kramer; Frank Hartmann. In Res., Rev. Diarmuid F. McGann (Retired).
Res.: 175 Blue Point Ave., 11715. Tel: 631-363-6385; Fax: 631-363-7394. Email: olsbp@aol.com. Web: www.ourladyofthesnowbluepoint.e-paluch.com.
See Prince of Peace Regional School, Sayville under Regional Schools located in the Institution section.
Catechesis/Religious Program—Tel: 631-363-6394. Students 1,056.

BOHEMIA, SUFFOLK CO., ST. JOHN NEPOMUCENE (1919) [CEM] Revs. James L. Wood; Kevin W. Gruber; Sr. Phyllis Esposito, C.S.J., Pastoral Assoc.; Deacons James Bohuslaw; Anthony Cusumano; George Reich; Roger Mott.
Res.: 1140 Locust Ave., 11716. Tel: 631-589-0540; Fax: 631-244-8086. Email: stjohnep@optonline.net. Web: mychurchandtown.com.
See Prince of Peace Regional School, Sayville under Regional Schools located in the Institution section.
Catechesis/Religious Program—1150 Locust Ave., 11716. Tel: 631-567-1765. Mrs. Cathy Roberts, D.R.E. Students 1,663.

BRENTWOOD, SUFFOLK CO.

1—ST. ANNE'S (1895) Revs. Francis M. Nelson; Eden Jean Baptiste; Gonzalo Oajaca-Lopez; Deacons Terence A. Rasanen; Thomas R. Samson; John E. Walters; Miguel Romero.
Res.: 88 Second Ave., 11717. Tel: 631-273-8113; Fax: 631-436-7914. Web: www.stannesbrentwoodny.org.

See Our Lady of Providence Regional School, Central Islip under Regional Schools located in the Institution section.
Catechesis/Religious Program—Tel: 631-231-7344. Students 640.

2—ST. LUKE (1965), (Hispanic), [JC] Rev. Msgr. Thomas E. Molloy; Rev. Carlos Prieto (Venezuela); Deacons Richard A. Luken; Wenceslao Rivera, (Retired).
Res.: 266 Wicks Rd., 11717. Tel: 631-273-1110; Fax: 631-951-2779.
See Our Lady of Providence Regional School, Central Islip under Regional Schools located in the Institution section.
Catechesis/Religious Program—Tel: 631-273-4333. Students 40.

BRIDGEHAMPTON, SUFFOLK CO., QUEEN OF THE MOST HOLY ROSARY (1922) Rev. Peter Devaraj, S.A.C.
See Stella Maris Regional School, Sag Harbor under Regional Schools located in the Institution section.
Catechesis/Religious Program—P.O. Box 3035, 11932. Tel: 631-537-0156. Helen McDowell, D.R.E. Students 20.

BROOKVILLE, NASSAU CO., ST. PAUL THE APOSTLE (1962) Rev. Robert J. Clerkin.
Res.: 2534 Cedar Swamp Rd., Rte. 107, 11545. Tel: 516-935-1880; Fax: 516-938-3683. Email: stpaulbrookville@aol.com. Web: www.stpaulsbrookville.com.
Catechesis/Religious Program—Tel: 516-938-4531. Sr. Regina Kraft, O.P., D.R.E.; Bro. Joseph Bellizzi, S.M., D.R.E. Students 471.

CARLE PLACE, NASSAU CO., CHURCH OF OUR LADY OF HOPE (1987) Rev. Msgr. Richard C. Bauhoff; Deacons John T. Hickey; Thomas B. Rich; Raymond J. Tirelli; Patrick J. Dunphy; Raymond J. Henderson, Music Min.
Church: 534 Broadway, 11514-1712. Tel: 516-334-6288; Fax: 516-997-4622.
School—St. Brigid/ Our Lady of Hope Regional School, 101 Maple Ave., Westbury, 11590. Tel: 516-333-0580; Fax: 516-333-0590.
Catechesis/Religious Program—Tel: 516-334-4781. Donna Manley, D.R.E. Students 529.

CEDARHURST, NASSAU CO., ST. JOACHIM (1894) Rev. Paul Rahilly; Deacons Frank J. Bono; Charles R. Goldburg.
Res.: 614 Central Ave., 11516. Tel: 516-569-1845; Fax: 516-569-0117. Email: joachimrcc@yahoo.com.
Catechesis/Religious Program—Tel: 516-569-2290. Students 80.

CENTER MORICHES, SUFFOLK CO., ST. JOHN THE EVANGELIST (1898) Revs. Joseph C. Coschignano; John J. Corcoran, Pastor Emeritus (Retired); Robert J. Kline; Deacons Galvin Murphy; Chris Vigliotta.
Res.: 25 Ocean Ave., 11934. Tel: 631-878-0009; Fax: 631-874-2466. Email: stjohnch@optonline.net.
See Our Lady, Queen of the Apostles Regional School, Center Moriches under Regional Schools located in the Institution section.
Catechesis/Religious Program—Tel: 631-878-4141. Students 2,050.

CENTEREACH, SUFFOLK CO., ASSUMPTION OF THE BLESSED VIRGIN MARY (1955) Rev. Msgr. Joseph K. Curley; Rev. Charles N. Srion; Deacon Michael Montelione.
Res.: 20 Chestnut St., 11720. Tel: 631-585-8760; Fax: 631-585-3601. Email: assumption@optonline.net. Web: www.mychurchandtown.com.
Catechesis/Religious Program—Tel: 631-588-6408. Email: jflynnabvm@optonline.net. Mrs. Jeanne Flynn, D.R.E. Students 1,309.

CENTERPORT, SUFFOLK CO., OUR LADY QUEEN OF MARTYRS (1966) Rev. Msgr. T. Peter Ryan; Sr. Eileen Corcoran, O.P., Pastoral Assoc.; Deacons Christopher Sisinni; Richard Bilella.
Res.: 53 Prospect Rd., 11721. Tel: 631-757-8184; Fax: 631-262-0155. Email: rectory@olqmparish.org. Web: www.olqmparish.org.
See Trinity Regional School, East Northport under Regional Schools located in the Institution section.
Catechesis/Religious Program—Tel: 631-757-0720; Fax: 631-757-3512. Email: olqmre@optonline.net. Margaret Dritto, D.R.E.; Marilyn Borghard, Parish Social Ministry. Students 1,178.

CENTRAL ISLIP, SUFFOLK CO., ST. JOHN OF GOD (1904) [CEM] Rev. Msgr. James M. Kissane; Rev. Humberto E. Contreras (Colombia); Sisters Agnes Claudia Allen, C.S.J., Pastoral Assoc. (Spanish Apostolate); Valerie Scholl, C.S.J., Pastoral Assoc. Admin.; Deacons Ronald J. Gillette, Pastoral Assoc.; Frank Gariboldi, Pastoral Assoc.
Res.: 84 Carleton Ave., 11722. Tel: 631-234-6535; Fax: 631-234-7474. Email: sjogno1@aol.com. Web: stjohnofgodparish.org.
See Our Lady of Providence Regional School, Central Islip under Regional Schools located in the Institution section.
Catechesis/Religious Program—Tel: 631-234-4040. Email: sjogre@verizon.net. Maggie Martin, D.R.E. Students 630.
Parish Outreach—Tel: 631-234-1884. Marjorie Banegas, Dir.
Convent—Sisters of St. Joseph, 330 St. John St., 11722. Tel: 631-234-6533. Email: nunsnine@aol.com.

COMMACK, SUFFOLK CO., CHRIST THE KING (1959) Revs. Joseph V. Davanzo; Brian McQuade; Deacons Joseph Marfoglio; Louis Anetrella; Christopher Ferraro, Pastoral Assoc.
Res.: 2 Indian Head Rd., 11725. Tel: 631-864-1623; Fax: 631-864-8891. Email: parishoffice@ctkrcc.org. Web: ctkrcc.org.
See Holy Family Regional School, Commack under Regional Schools located in the Institution section.
Catechesis/Religious Program—Tel: 631-864-3696; Fax: 631-864-1623. Mrs. Margaret Marconi, D.R.E. Students 1,913.

COPIAGUE, SUFFOLK CO., OUR LADY OF THE ASSUMPTION (1928) Revs. Joseph J. Nixon; Piotr Rozek; Camillo Lugo (Colombia); Deacon Philip Mills Jr.
Res.: 1 Molloy St., 11726. Tel: 631-842-5211; 631-842-5476; Fax: 631-789-5326. Email: assumptioncopia@optonline.net.
Catechesis/Religious Program—Tel: 631-842-3545. Ruth Durago, D.R.E. Students 575.

CORAM, SUFFOLK CO., ST. FRANCES CABRINI (1953) Rev. Donald M. Baier; Deacons Carmen L. Pagrotta; Monte Naylor Jr.
Res.: 134 Middle County Rd., 11727. Tel: 631-732-8445; Fax: 631-732-8978. Email: coramcab@aol.com. Web: www.buoy.com/~sfc.
See Holy Angels Regional School, Patchogue under Regional Schools located in the Institution section.
Catechesis/Religious Program—Tel: 631-698-3149. Eugene Johann, C.R.E. Students 599.

CUTCHOGUE, SUFFOLK CO.

1—OUR LADY OF OSTRABRAMA (1909), (Polish), [JC] Rev. Marian Bicz.
Res.: 3000 Depot Ln., Box 997, 11935. Tel: 631-734-6446; Fax: 631-734-4117.
School—North Fork Regional Catholic School, Cutchogue, Tel: 631-734-5166. See Regional Schools under Institutions Located in the Diocese.
Catechesis/Religious Program—Students 36.

2—SACRED HEART (1901) [CEM] Rev. Joseph W. Staudt; Sr. Anne Lynch, R.S.M., Pastoral Assoc.; Deacon Jeffrey Sykes.
Res.: 27905 Main Rd., P.O. Box 926, 11935-0926. Tel: 631-734-6722; Fax: 631-734-7906.
See Our Lady of Mercy Regional School, Cutchogue under Regional Schools located in the Institution section.
Catechesis/Religious Program—Tel: 631-734-2568. Sr. Ann Lynch, D.R.E. Students 380.
Mission—Our Lady of Good Counsel Main Rd., Mattituck, Suffolk Co. 11952.

DAVIS PARK, FIRE ISLAND SUFFOLK CO., MOST PRECIOUS BLOOD (1962), (Summer Mission) Rev. Francis Pizzarelli, S.M.M.
Mailing Address: P.O. Box 358, Port Jefferson, 11777. Tel: 631-928-2377; Fax: 631-473-5210.
Res.: Spindrift Walk, Fire Island, 11728. Tel: 631-597-6525.

DEER PARK, SUFFOLK CO., SS. CYRIL AND METHODIUS (1956) Rev. Msgr. Francis X. Gaeta; Revs. Caetano F. Costa (India); Lee R. Descoteaux; Francis D. Sang (Vietnam); Richard F. Kammerer; Deacons John F. Fitzpatrick; Charles F. Huber. In Res., Rev. Msgr. Thaddeus Rooney (Retired).
Res.: 125 Half Hollow Rd., 11729-4288. Tel: 631-667-4044; Fax: 631-667-6237.
School—Tel: 631-667-6229; Fax: 631-667-0093. Dr. Jennifer Gallagher, Prin. Lay Teachers 21; Students 264; Preschool 36.
Catechesis/Religious Program—Tel: 631-667-6264; Fax: 631-667-7767. Virginia Conzo, D.R.E. Students 1,819.

DIX HILLS, SUFFOLK CO., ST. MATTHEW (1965) Revs. John J. McCartney; Lawrence A. Chadwick; Raymond Akpunonu; Robert Kayser (Retired); Deacons James M. McQuade; James Hanly; Carmine DeStefano; Luis Roberto Polanco.
Res.: 35 N. Service Rd., 11746. Tel: 631-499-8520; Fax: 631-499-1530. Email: pastor@smrcc.org. Web: smrcc.org.
See Holy Family Regional School, Commack under Regional Schools located in the Institution section.
Catechesis/Religious Program—Tel: 631-499-8521. Mary Donaldson, D.R.E. Students 1,806.

EAST HAMPTON, SUFFOLK CO., MOST HOLY TRINITY (1894) [CEM] Rev. Msgr. Donald M. Hanson, Pastor.
Res.: 57 Buell Ln., 11937. Fax: 631-907-1619. Email: pastor@mht-eh.org. Web: mht-eh.org.
Business: 79 Buell Ln., 11937. Tel: 631-324-0134; Fax: 631-329-3552. Email: kbyrnes@mht-eh.org.
See Stella Maris Regional School, Sag Harbor under Regional Schools located in the Institution section.
Catechesis/Religious Program—44 Meadow Way, 11937. Tel: 631-324-0134, Ext. 730. Email: slieder@mht-eh.org. Suzanne Lieder, D.R.E. Students 279.
Mission—St. Peter the Apostle Main St., Amagansett, Suffolk Co. 11930.

EAST ISLIP, SUFFOLK CO., ST. MARY'S (1898) Rev. Donald E. Babinski; Rev. Msgr. Peter A. Chiara, Pastor Emeritus (Retired); Revs. Hugh D. Cannon; Janusz Mocarski; Sr. Pat Tippen, Pastoral Assoc.
Res.: 20 Harrison Ave., 11730. Tel: 631-581-4266; Fax: 631-581-0112. Email: tvanburen@stmaryseastislip.org. Web: www.stmaryseastislip.org.
School—16 Harrison Ave., 11730. Tel: 631-581-4266, Ext. 5; Fax: 631-581-7509. Biagio Arpino, Prin. Lay Teachers 33; Students 456.
Catechesis/Religious Program—Email: cmoule@stmaryseastislip.org. Students 1,500.

EAST MEADOW, NASSAU CO., ST. RAPHAEL (1941) Revs. Thomas Haggerty; Antony Asir; Joseph Lobo; Deacons Angelo D'Aversa; Victor R. Costa; Joan Heaney-Hunter, Pastoral Assoc.; Dr. Kathleen Andersen, Pastoral Assoc.; Sr. Judy Fay, C.S.J., Parish Social Ministry; Diane Lawlor, Business Mgr.
Res.: 600 Newbridge Rd., 11554. Tel: 516-785-0236; Fax: 516-783-9578. Web: www.straphaelparish.org.
See St. Elizabeth Ann Seton Regional School, Bellmore under Regional Schools located in the Institution section.
Catechesis/Religious Program—Tel: 516-221-9096; Fax: 516-221-9084. Email: raphaelreo@hotmail.com. Mrs. Helen Giordano, Dir. Faith Formation. Students 1,168.

EAST NORTHPORT, SUFFOLK CO., ST. ANTHONY OF PADUA (1951) Rev. Msgr. John R. Dreasen; Revs. Frank M. Grieco; James Calledo (Philippines); Rev. Msgr. John R. Dreasen; Deacon Robert Braun.
Res.: 20 Cheshire Pl., 11731-2591. Tel: 631-261-1077; Fax: 631-757-0572. Email: pastor@saintanthonyofpadua.org. Web: www.saintanthonyofpadua.org.
See Trinity Regional School, East Northport under Regional Schools located in the Institution section.
Catechesis/Religious Program—Tel: 631-261-1306. Mrs. Judith Corbellini, D.R.E.; Mrs. Eileen Schlee, D.R.E.; Mrs. Patricia Seibert, D.R.E. Students 2,033.

EAST PATCHOGUE, SUFFOLK CO., ST. JOSEPH THE WORKER (1955) Revs. John Mellitt, O.F.M.Cap.; Robert Phelps, O.F.M.Cap.; Deacon Albert Pickford. In Res., Rev. William H. Winters, O.F.M.Cap.
Church: 510 Narragansett Ave., 11772. Tel: 631-286-9133; Fax: 631-286-9145. Email: sjw1956@hotmail.com. Web: www.stjosephtheworkerep.net.
See Holy Angels Regional School, Patchogue under Regional Schools located in the Institution section.
Catechesis/Religious Program—Tel: 631-286-2550; Fax: 631-286-9145. Mrs. Mary Mensch, D.R.E. Students 550.

EAST ROCKAWAY, NASSAU CO., ST. RAYMOND'S (1909) Rev. Msgrs. William W. Jablonski; William V. Singleton, Pastor Emeritus (Retired); Revs. John Poku (Ghana); Francis X. Eisele; Deacons Richard W. LaRossa, Pastoral Assoc.; Robert C. Campbell; Thomas W. Connolly; Guy Donza, Pastoral Assoc.
Res.: 263 Atlantic Ave., 11518. Tel: 516-593-5000; Fax: 516-887-0554. Email: strayrcc@optonline.net. Web: www.saintraymonds.org.
School—Tel: 516-593-9010; Fax: 516-593-0986. Sr. Ruthanne Gypalo, I.H.M., Prin. Sisters, Servants of the Immaculate Heart of Mary 4; Lay Teachers 23; Students 364.
Catechesis/Religious Program—Tel: 516-593-9075. Email: econtaldisrre@optonline.net. Mrs. Evelyn Contaldi, C.R.E. Students 697.

ELMONT, NASSAU CO.

1—ST. BONIFACE (1852) [CEM] Revs. William J. Gomes; Eddy Julien; Gabriel Miah; Sr. Evelyn Lamoureux, D.W., Human Svcs.; Deacons William Mildeberger; Dominique Silien. In Res., Rev. George Punti (Retired).
Res.: 631 Elmont Rd., 11003. Tel: 516-354-0715; Fax: 516-354-0446.
Catechesis/Religious Program—Tel: 516-437-7112. Nancy Cosgrove, D.R.E. Students 565.

2—ST. VINCENT DE PAUL (1951) Revs. James F. Drew; Joseph Nedumankuzhiyil (India); Deacon John McGowan; Ms. Mary Alice Burchell, Coord. Pastoral Svcs. In Res., Rev. Richard R. Viladesau.
Res.: 1500 dePaul St., 11003. Tel: 516-352-2127; Fax: 516-216-5350. Email: svdp1500@optonline.net.
Catechesis/Religious Program—1510 dePaul St., 11003. Tel: 516-352-2265. Email: svreled@optonline.net. Students 200.

FARMINGDALE, NASSAU CO., ST. KILIAN (1896) Rev. Msgr. Michael P. Flynn; Revs. Augustine Fernando (India); Lennard Sabio (Philippines); Stanislaw Wadowski (Poland); Deacons Frank D. Barone;

Lucio Cotone; Francis P. Marino; George Owen; Mark Wetzel; Frank Shanley, Business Mgr. In Res., Most Rev. John C. Dunne.
Res.: 485 Conklin St., 11735. Tel: 516-249-0127; Fax: 516-249-7131. Email: info@stkilian.com. Web: www.stkilian.com.
See St. John Baptist de LaSalle Regional School, Farmingdale under Regional Schools located in the Institution section.
Catechesis/Religious Program—Tel: 516-694-0633; Fax: 516-454-8612. Mr. Jon Lindstrom, D.R.E.; Mr. Paul C. Phinney, Music Dir. Students 1,623.
Parish Social Ministry/Outreach—Tel: 516-756-9656. Lisa Molluso, Dir.

FARMINGVILLE, SUFFOLK CO., CHURCH OF THE RESURRECTION (1988) Rev. Malcolm J. Burns; Deacon James DiGiovanna.
Church: 50 Granny Rd., 11738. Tel: 631-696-0232; Fax: 631-696-0271. Email: info@resurrectionrcchurch.org. Web: resurrectionrcchurch.org.
Catechesis/Religious Program—Tel: 631-696-0270, Ext. 25. Email: religioused@resurrectionrcchurch.org. Rosemarie Hayman, D.R.E. Students 936.

FLORAL PARK, NASSAU CO.

1—ST. HEDWIG'S (1902), (Polish), Rev. Msgr. Edward Wawerski.
Res.: One Depan Ave., 11001. Tel: 516-354-0042; Fax: 516-327-2458. Email: sthedwig@optonline.net.
Catechesis/Religious Program—Students 72.

2—OUR LADY OF VICTORY (1921) Rev. John V. O'Farrell; Rev. Msgr. Charles J. Nosser, Pastor Emeritus (Retired); Revs. Walter F. Kedjierski; Bruno Dekrem; Deacon Lawrence P. Mulligan; Jane Parrinelli, Business Mgr.; Eileen Tracy, Youth Min.; Donald Lefante, Dir. Music Ministry & Liturgy.
Res.: 2 Floral Pkwy., 11001-3198. Tel: 516-354-0482; 516-354-0479; Fax: 516-354-7450.
School—2 Bellmore St., 11001. Tel: 516-352-4466; 516-354-2150; Fax: 516-352-2998. Margaret M. Augello, Prin. Lay Teachers 25; Students 457.
Catechesis/Religious Program—Tel: 516-352-0510. Ellen Fox, D.R.E. Students 975.

FRANKLIN SQUARE, NASSAU CO., ST. CATHERINE OF SIENNA (1913) Rev. Msgr. Richard M. Figliozzi; Revs. William D. O'Rourke; Edward M. Sheridan; Dennis Whelan; Johnny Mendonca; Deacons John Fodale; Joseph Benincasa; Francisco Gonzalez.
Res.: 33 New Hyde Park Rd., 11010. Tel: 516-352-0146; Fax: 516-326-7427. Web: siennacenter.org.
School—990 Holzheimer St., 11010. Tel: 516-437-2733; Fax: 516-437-6073. Web: scsschool.org. Ms. Cecelia Rando, Prin. Lay Teachers 13; Students 265.
Catechesis/Religious Program—Tel: 516-354-4554. Felicia Navarro, Faith Formation Coord. Students 1,500.

FREEPORT, NASSAU CO., OUR HOLY REDEEMER (1903) Revs. Douglas R. Arcoleo; Nestor Watin (Philippines); Deacons Francisco Cales; Bruce A. Burnham; Cristobal Sanchez, Pastoral Assoc. In Res., Rev. Benet Uwasomba (Nigeria), Hospital Chap.
Res.: 37 S. Ocean Ave., 11520. Tel: 516-378-0665; Fax: 516-546-1416. Email: ohr1903@aol.com. Web: ohrfreeport.org.
Catechesis/Religious Program—87 Pine St., 11520. Tel: 516-546-1057; Fax: 516-546-0526. Email: reled3@aol.com. Joanne Stuhlinger, C.R.E. Students 487.

GARDEN CITY, NASSAU CO.

1—ST. ANNE (1929) Rev. Msgr. John D. Gilmartin; Rev. Rudy Pesongco; Deacons George Browne; James J. O'Brien.
Res.: 35 Dartmouth St., 11530. Tel: 516-352-5904; Fax: 516-352-1360. Web: www.stannesgc.org.
School—25 Dartmouth St., 11530. Tel: 516-352-1205; Fax: 516-352-5969. Dr. William O'Sullivan, Prin. Lay Teachers 28; Students 518.
Catechesis/Religious Program—Tel: 516-488-1032; Fax: 516-352-1360. Kate Kern, D.R.E. Students 1,117.

2—ST. JOSEPH'S (1901) Revs. Joseph M. Schlafer; Gregory Breen; Deacon John J. McKenna; Joseph Cangialosi, Dir. Music & Liturgy; Sr. Louise Cullen, R.S.M., Dir. Stewardship. In Res., Rev. Msgrs. Charles A. Guarino; Brian J. McNamara.
Res.: 130 Fifth St., 11530. Tel: 516-747-3535; Fax: 516-746-0719.
School—450 Franklin Ave., 11530. Tel: 516-747-2730; Fax: 516-747-2854. Dr. Eileen Kilbride, Prin.; Ms. Florence Puff, Asst. Prin.; Regina A. Cioffi, Asst. Prin.; Sr. Virginia Maguire, O.P., Dir. Human Svcs. Lay Teachers 25; Students 320.
Catechesis/Religious Program—Tel: 516-741-7787; Fax: 516-741-5049. Susan Mirabella, D.R.E. Students 1,438.

GLEN COVE, NASSAU CO.

1—ST. PATRICK'S (1856) [CEM] Revs. Thomas C. Costa; Rolando Ticllasuca, M.R.S.M. (Peru); Martin L. Klein; Mr. Cantalicio Gamarra, Spanish Min.; Deacons Frank Borchardt; Alfredo Mora; Michael Devenney, Business Mgr.; Juan Guilfu; Frances Howlett, Music Min.
Res.: 235 Glen St., 11542. Tel: 516-676-0276; Fax: 516-674-9137. Email: stpatshill@aol.com. Web: www.stpatrickshill.com.
For Hispanic Ministry—Tel: 516-759-6039.
See All Saints Regional Catholic School, Glen Cove under Regional Schools located in the Institution section.
Catechesis/Religious Program—Tel: 516-671-7223. Sr. Teresa Raftery, I.H.M., D.R.E. Students 403.
Convent—Sisters of St. Joseph, 16 Pearsall St., 11542. Tel: 516-671-3963. (Brentwood Congregation) Sisters 2.

2—ST. ROCCO (1937), (Italian), Rev. Aaron T. Vellaramparampil.
Res.: 18 Third St., 11542. Tel: 516-676-2482; Fax: 516-676-2117. Email: stroccochurch@netzero.org. Web: www.saintrocco.org.
See All Saints Regional Catholic School, Glen Cove under Regional Schools located in the Institution section.
Catechesis/Religious Program—Students 293.

GLEN HEAD, NASSAU CO., ST. HYACINTH (1909), (Polish), Rev. Msgr. Richard P. Kopinski; Revs. Ryszard Ficek; Joseph P. Kozlowski, Pastor Emeritus (Retired).
Res.: 319 Cedar Swamp Rd., 11545. Tel: 516-676-0361; Fax: 516-674-4728.
See All Saints Regional Catholic School, Glen Cove under Regional Schools located in the Institution section.
Catechesis/Religious Program—Tel: 516-676-0361, Ext. 123. Miss Eileen Meserole, D.R.E. Students 225.

GREAT NECK, NASSAU CO., ST. ALOYSIUS (1876), (Hispanic—Korean), Rev. Msgr. Brendan P. Riordan; Rev. Basil C. Colasito (Philippines) (Retired), Hispanic Ministry. In Res., Rev. Msgr. Alan J. Placa.
Res.: 592 Middle Neck Rd., 11023. Tel: 516-482-2770; Fax: 516-829-3504. Email: saintals592@aol.com.
Catechesis/Religious Program—Tel: 516-482-5660; Fax: 516-829-4054. Students 364.

GREENLAWN, SUFFOLK CO., ST. FRANCIS OF ASSISI (1966) Rev. Peter Kaczmarek; Rev. Msgr. Robert J. Batule; Deacon Allan Longo.
Res.: 29 Northgate Dr., 11740. Tel: 631-757-7435; Fax: 631-757-0469.
See Trinity Regional School, East Northport under Regional Schools located in the Institution section.
Catechesis/Religious Program—Tel: 631-754-6436. Mrs. Theresa DeMayo, D.R.E. Students 547.

GREENPORT, SUFFOLK CO., ST. AGNES (1886), (Hispanic), [CEM] Rev. Thomas P. Murray.
Res.: 523 Front St., 11944. Tel: 631-477-0048; Fax: 631-477-8519. Email: rectory@optonline.net. Web: stagnesgpt.org.
See Our Lady of Mercy Regional School, Cutchogue under Regional Schools located in the Institution section.
Catechesis/Religious Program—Tel: 631-477-1422. Students 205.

HAMPTON BAYS, SUFFOLK CO., ST. ROSALIE'S (1901) Rev. Msgr. Dennis M. Regan; Revs. Sabbas Rodrigues; Joy Varkey; Deacons Christopher Ervin, Pastoral Assoc.; Robert Mongillo, Pastoral Assoc. & Business Mgr.
Res.: 31 Montauk Hwy., 11946. Tel: 631-728-9461; Fax: 631-728-2559. Web: www.saintrosalie.com.
See Our Lady of the Hamptons Regional School, Southampton under Regional Schools located in the Institution section.
Catechesis/Religious Program— Eileen McPhelin, D.R.E. Students 546.
Mission— 31 Montauk Hwy., East Quogue, Suffolk Co. 11946.

HAUPPAUGE, SUFFOLK CO., ST. THOMAS MORE (1967) Rev. Msgr. Francis S. Midura; Joan Dorr, Pastoral Assoc.; Deacon Robert Weisz.
Res.: 115 Kings Hwy., 11788-4221. Tel: 631-234-5551; Fax: 631-234-6412. Email: stm73@live.com.
See Holy Family Regional School, Commack under Regional Schools located in the Institution section.
Catechesis/Religious Program—119 Kings Hwy., 11788. Tel: 631-234-0397; Fax: 631-234-1199. Mrs. Mary Ellen Carroll, D.R.E.; Mrs. Patricia Chapin, D.R.E. Students 1,475.

HEMPSTEAD, NASSAU CO.

1—ST. JOHN CHRYSOSTOM MALANKARA MISSION (1999) Rev. Louis Charuvila Pathenveedu (India), Admin.
115 Greenwich St., 11550. Tel: 516-775-1779; Fax: 516-216-5350.

2—ST. LADISLAUS (1915), (Polish), Rev. Msgr. Edward Wawerski; Rev. Piotr Wasek. In Res., Rev. John Siebor (Retired).
Res.: 18 Richardson Pl., 11550. Tel: 516-489-0368; Fax: 516-292-9193. Email: edwawer@aol.com.
See St. Martin de Porres Regional School, Uniondale under Regional Schools located in the Institution section.
Catechesis/Religious Program—John Pitrowski, D.R.E. Students 8.

3—OUR LADY OF LORETTO (1870) Rev. Msgr. Pablo M. Rodriguez; Revs. Fruto Rosales; Gerardo Bengochea, S.J.; Sr. Winifred Cunniff, S.C., Pastoral Assoc.; Deacons Jose Roa; Juan Perez; Mrs. Rosemary Viola.
Res.: 104 Greenwich St., 11550. Tel: 516-489-3675; Fax: 516-485-8371.
See St. Martin de Porres Regional School, Uniondale under Regional Schools located in the Institution section.
Catechesis/Religious Program—Tel: 516-483-3643. Esperanza Robinson, D.R.E. Students 322.

HEWLETT, NASSAU CO., ST. JOSEPH'S (1872) Rev. Thomas Moriarty Jr.; Deacons Thomas Costello; Daniel Otton. In Res., Revs. Thomas V. Arnao; John Hein (Vietnam) (Retired).
Res.: 1346 Broadway, 11557. Tel: 516-374-0290; Fax: 516-374-2598. Email: joehewlett@aol.com. Web: saintjoseph-hewlett.org.
Catechesis/Religious Program—1355 Noel Ave., 11557. Tel: 516-569-6080; Fax: 516-374-3664. Elizabeth McCaffrey, D.R.E. Students 405.

HICKSVILLE, NASSAU CO.

1—HOLY FAMILY (1951), (Irish—Italian), Revs. Gerard J. Gentleman; Henry W. Reid; Deacons Joseph G. McNicholas; John H. McGonigle; Ronald Land, Music Dir.; Ms. Donna Grosso, Business Mgr.
17 Fordham Ave., 11801. In Res., Revs. Sebastian Owusa-Mensah; R. Michael Reid.
Res.: 5 Fordham Ave., 11801. Tel: 516-938-3846; Fax: 516-938-6241.
School—Holy Family School, 25 Fordham Ave., 11801. Fax: 516-938-5041. Email: phillin@hfsli.org. Web: hfsli.org. Mr. Vincent Albrecht, Prin. Lay Teachers 19; Students 296.
Catechesis/Religious Program—Fax: 516-938-3875. Mrs. Cathy Weiss, D.R.E. Students 500.
Outreach—Email: outreach@holyfamilyparishny.org. Janice Manaskie, Dir.; Maureen Szigethy, Dir.

2—ST. IGNATIUS LOYOLA (1859) Rev. Msgr. Donald T. Bennett; Rev. Jose Quilcate (Peru); Rev. Msgr. Edward L. Tarrant, Pastor Emeritus (Retired); Mrs. Rosemary Cassese, Pastoral Asst.; Deacon George A. Mais Jr.; Ms. Jennifer Toohey, Music Min.
129 Broadway, 11801. Tel: 516-931-0056; Fax: 516-939-0852. Email: stignatius1859@aol.com. Web: st-ignatius-parish.org.
School—30 E. Cherry St., 11801. Tel: 516-931-0831; Fax: 516-933-6528. Web: www.stignatiushicksville-.org. Sisters Mary Ann Noonan, R.S.M., Prin.; Mary F. O'Donnell, O.P., Co-Prin. Lay Teachers 18; Students 225.
Catechesis/Religious Program—Tel: 516-935-6873. Mary Jane Mastrodomenico, D.R.E. Students 499.

3—OUR LADY OF MERCY (1953) Revs. Robert Y. Blyman; Richard F. Kammerer; Thomas P. Tuite Jr.; Rev. Msgr. James E. Boesel (Retired).
Res.: 500 S. Oyster Bay Rd., 11801. Tel: 516-931-4351; Fax: 516-433-8702. Email: therectory@olmrcc.org. Web: www.ourladyofmercy.org.
School—Tel: 516-433-7040; Fax: 516-433-8286. Email: jdeegan@olmercy.drvc.org. Sr. Mary Joanne Deegan, R.S.M., Prin. Sisters of Mercy 5; Lay Teachers 28; Students 484.
Catechesis/Religious Program—Tel: 516-681-1228; Fax: 516-681-1527. Email: religioused@olmrcc.org. Joanne Kolasa, D.R.E. Students 816.

HOLBROOK, SUFFOLK CO., GOOD SHEPHERD (1970) Rev. Msgr. Thomas L. Spadaro; Revs. Francis Lasrado; Babu Michael; Deacons Robert Hernandez; Thomas O'Connor; Edward Tappin; John Newhall; Mary E. Rieger, Business Mgr.
Res.: 1370 Grundy Ave., 11741. Tel: 631-588-7689; Fax: 631-588-7603. Web: www.goodshepherdonline.com.
See Prince of Peace Regional School, Sayville under Regional Schools located in the Institution section.
Catechesis/Religious Program—Tel: 631-981-3889. Sisters Lillian Delorme, O.P., D.R.E.; Ellen Zak, C.S.F.N., D.R.E.; Jeanne Cook, D.R.E. Students 1,037.

HUNTINGTON STATION, SUFFOLK CO., ST. HUGH OF LINCOLN (1913) Rev. Msgr. Joseph P. Granata; Rev. Michael J. Bartholomew; Deacons Edward W. Billia; Vito B. Taranto; Thomas Reilly; Luis Giraldo.
Res.: 21 E. Ninth St., 11746. Tel: 631-427-0638; Fax: 631-427-1319. Email: rectory@sthugh.org. Web: sthugh.org.
Parish Center—1450 New York Ave., 11746.
See Trinity Regional School, East Northport under Regional Schools located in the Institution section.
Catechesis/Religious Program—Tel: 631-271-6081. Mrs. Florence Johnson, D.R.E. Students 710.

HUNTINGTON, SUFFOLK CO., ST. PATRICK'S (1849) [CEM] Rev. Msgr. John F. Bennett; Revs. Adrian

McHugh, Parochial Vicar; Thomas P. Tuite Jr., Parochial Vicar; Deacon William Casey; Alan Jones, Business Mgr. In Res., Revs. Thomas Edamattan (India); Ned Mattimoe, S.J.
Res.: 400 Main St., 11743-3208. Tel: 631-385-3311; Fax: 631-673-4102. Web: www.stpatrickchurchhunt.org.
School—360 Main St., 11743-3298. Tel: 631-673-5325; Fax: 631-673-4609. Sr. Maureen McDade, Prin.; Mrs. Jean Grasso, Asst. Prin. Sisters 1; Lay Teachers 34; Students 738.
Catechesis/Religious Program—Tel: 631-673-5323. Miss Jill Rowbo, C.R.E. Students 1,493.

INWOOD, NASSAU CO., OUR LADY OF GOOD COUNSEL (1910) Rev. Lawrence T. Duncklee; Deacon George Bruck.
Res.: 68 Wanser Ave., 11096. Tel: 516-239-0953; Fax: 516-239-0386.
Catechesis/Religious Program—Tel: 516-239-0662. Sr. Kathryn Slevin, C.S.J., D.R.E. Students 40.

ISLAND PARK, NASSAU CO., SACRED HEART (1938) Rev. John J. Tutone.
Res.: 282 Long Beach Rd., 11558. Tel: 516-432-0655; Fax: 516-897-7567.
Catechesis/Religious Program—Tel: 516-431-7877. Mrs. Carmel Caracciolo, D.R.E. Students 255.

ISLIP TERRACE, SUFFOLK CO., ST. PETER THE APOSTLE (1962) Rev. Anthony Iaconis. In Res., Rev. Christopher Okoli (Nigeria).
Res.: 94 Valley Stream St., 11752. Tel: 631-277-9448. Email: stpeters@spec.net.
See Our Lady of Providence Regional School, Central Islip under Regional Schools located in the Institution section.
Catechesis/Religious Program—92 Valley Stream St., 11752. Tel: 631-650-0950. Mrs. Eileen C. Will, D.R.E. Students 400.

KINGS PARK, SUFFOLK CO., ST. JOSEPH'S (1888) Revs. Seán J. Gann; Francis P. Vattakudiyil; Paul J. Mijas (Poland); Deacons John E. Trodden; Roy Smith. In Res., Rev. Msgr. Alexander F. Manly (Retired).
Parish Center—59 Church St., 11754. Tel: 631-269-6635; Fax: 631-269-7508.
See Holy Family Regional School, Commack under Regional Schools located in the Institution section.
Catechesis/Religious Program—Tel: 631-269-4383. Students 2,020.

LAKE RONKONKOMA, SUFFOLK CO., ST. ELIZABETH ANN SETON (1988) Rev. Msgr. Daniel A. Picciano; Deacons Joseph Maffeo; John Grebe; Michele Hahn, Pastoral Assoc.; Lori Marando, Business Mgr.
Res.: 59 Frances Blvd., Holtsville, 11742.
Church: 800 Portion Rd., 11779. Tel: 631-737-4388; Fax: 631-737-4389. Email: steas@optonline.net. Web: www.steas.org.
Catechesis/Religious Program—800 Portion Rd., 11779. Tel: 631-737-8915. Email: marydvdre@optonline.net. Mrs. Mary DellaVecchia, D.R.E. Students 1,182.

LEVITTOWN, NASSAU CO., ST. BERNARD (1948) Revs. Gerard A. Ringenback; Christopher M. Costigan; Deacon John Blakeney. In Res., Rev. Msgr. George P. Graham (Retired); Rev. Cyprian Osuegbu (Nigeria).
Res.: 3100 Hempstead Tpke., 11756. Tel: 516-731-4220; Fax: 516-731-4355. Email: stbrnd@optonline.net. Web: www.stbernardslevittown.org.
Catechesis/Religious Program—Tel: 516-731-8511; Fax: 516-731-7860. Students 1,305.

LINDENHURST, SUFFOLK CO., OUR LADY OF PERPETUAL HELP (1871) Rev. Anthony M. Trapani; Rev. Msgr. Daniel S. Hamilton, Pastor Emeritus (Retired); Revs. James T. Stachacz; Moise Aime (Haiti); Robert J. Kline; Stanislaw Wadowski (Poland); Deacon Frank A. Odin.
Res.: 210 S. Wellwood Ave., 11757-4989. Tel: 631-226-7725; Fax: 631-225-9597. Email: olphlindenhurst@gmail.com. Web: www.olphlindenhurst.org.
School—240 S. Wellwood Ave., 11757. Tel: 631-226-0208; Fax: 631-226-4221. Lay Teachers 23; Students 358.
Catechesis/Religious Program—Tel: 631-226-2384. Email: dcastellano@olphlindenhurst.org. Diana Castellano, Coord. Prog. Admin. Students 1,440.

LONG BEACH, NASSAU CO.

1—ST. IGNATIUS MARTYR (1926) Rev. Msgr. Donald M. Beckmann; Rev. Joseph Paul Fernando. In Res., Rev. Msgr. Edward A. Sweeny.
Res.: 721 W. Broadway, 11561. Tel: 516-432-0045; Fax: 516-432-6848. Email: saintignatiusmar@yahoo.com. Web: home.catholicweb.com/stignatiusmartyr/index.cfm.
See Long Beach Regional Catholic School, Long Beach under Regional Schools located in the Institution section.
Catechesis/Religious Program—Tel: 516-432-6788. Pam Shannon, D.R.E. Students 32.
Parish Social Ministry/Outreach—Tel: 516-432-4899. Frances Alkire Barden, Dir.; Sr. Diane Morgan, O.P., Pastoral Assoc.; Deacon Phillip J. Newton.

2—ST. MARY OF THE ISLE (1915) Revs. Christopher Nowak, O.S.A.; Thomas E. Donohoe (Retired); Deacons John P. Dunlop; Nelson Daza; Sr. Frances Monuszko, O.P., Pastoral Assoc. & Dir. St. Mary of the Isle Community Center.
Res.: 315 E. Walnut St., 11561. Tel: 516-432-0157; Fax: 516-897-0566. Email: stmarylb@gmail.com.
See Long Beach Regional Catholic School, Long Beach under Regional Schools located in the Institution section.
Catechesis/Religious Program—Tel: 516-432-1320. Maryann Specht, D.R.E. Students 335.

LYNBROOK, NASSAU CO., OUR LADY OF PEACE (1941) Rev. William G. Breslawski; Deacons Aniello Squitieri; Anthony M. Cedrone; Thomas J. Evrard; Kevin McCormack; Sr. JoAnn Bonauro, S.C., Pastoral Assoc.
Res.: 25 Fowler Ave., 11563. Tel: 516-599-6414; Fax: 516-596-1847. Email: olprcc@olplynbrook.com.
School—21 Flower Ave., 11563. Tel: 516-593-4884; Fax: 516-593-9861. Email: olpschool@optonline.net. Sisters of Mercy 1; Lay Teachers 19; Students 300.
Catechesis/Religious Program—Tel: 516-593-5150. Email: srgracem@olplynbrook.com. Students 613.

MALVERNE, NASSAU CO., OUR LADY OF LOURDES (1926) Rev. Frank J. Parisi; Deacon Francis X Cove. In Res., Revs. Richard R. Donovan (Retired); John F. Wymes, M.M. (Retired); Chux Okochi.
Res.: 65 Wright Ave., 11565. Tel: 516-599-1269; Fax: 516-887-9517. Email: ollmalvchurch@aol.com.
School—76 Park Blvd., 11565. Tel: 516-599-7328; Fax: 516-599-3813. Mary Carmel Murphy, Prin. Lay Teachers 18; Students 280.
Catechesis/Religious Program—Tel: 516-599-7222; Fax: 516-599-2256. Miss Mary Lasar, D.R.E. Students 410.

MANHASSET, NASSAU CO., ST. MARY'S (1853) Rev. Msgrs. John J. McCann; John J. Skelly, Pastor Emeritus (Retired); Rev. Allan Sikorski; Deacons Charles Kammerer; Frank Bice.
Res.: 1300 Northern Blvd., 11030. Tel: 516-627-0385; Fax: 516-627-6070. Email: information@stmary.ws. Web: stmary.ws.
School—St. Mary's Elementary School, 1340 Northern Blvd., 11030. Tel: 516-627-0184; Fax: 516-627-3795. Web: www.stmary11030.org. (Elementary) Lay Teachers 32; Students 470.
High School—St. Mary's High School, (Coed), 51 Clapham Ave., 11030. Tel: 516-627-2711; Fax: 516-627-3209. Web: www.stmary.ws/highschool. Dominican Sisters 1; Marist Brothers 1; Lay Teachers 57; Students 950.
Catechesis/Religious Program—Tel: 516-627-4028; Fax: 516-627-5543. Students 1,105.

MANORHAVEN, NASSAU CO., OUR LADY OF FATIMA (1948) Rev. Steven J. Peterson; Deacon Arthur Candido; Sr. Kathy Somerville, O.P., Parish Social Ministry; Mrs. Gloria Robledc, Spanish Apostolate Coord.; Barbara Minerud, Business Mgr. In Res., Rev. Andrew P. Connolly (Retired).
Res.: 6 Cottonwood Rd., Port Washington, 11050. Tel: 516-767-0781; Fax: 516-767-2981.
Catechesis/Religious Program—Tel: 516-944-8322. Sr. Gerri O'Neil, O.P., D.R.E. Students 140.

MANORVILLE, SUFFOLK CO., STS. PETER & PAUL (1912) Rev. Bruce J. Powers; Deacon Robert Dejewski.
Res.: 781 Wading River Rd., P.O. Box 207, 11949. Tel: 631-369-1273; Fax: 631-369-7141. Email: pmc207@optonline.net. Web: www.saintspeterandpaul.org.
Catechesis/Religious Program—Tel: 631-208-1978. Students 547.

MASSAPEQUA PARK, NASSAU CO., OUR LADY OF LOURDES (1955) Rev. Msgr. James P. Lisante; Revs. Gregory Heinlein; Edward M. Seagriff; Deacon Domenick Valdaro. In Res., Rev. Robert E. Mason (Retired).
Res.: 855 Carmans Rd., 11762. Tel: 516-541-3270; Fax: 516-797-9851. Email: ollmpk@aol.com. Web: www.ollmp.org.
School—Tel: 516-798-7926. Lay Teachers 17; Students 264.
Catechesis/Religious Program—379 Linden St., 11762. Tel: 516-799-5179. Students 457.

MASSAPEQUA, NASSAU CO., ST. ROSE OF LIMA (1952) Revs. Kenneth Zach; Aloysius Pakianather (Sri Lanka); Paul Vezhaparambil (India); Lachlan T. Cameron; Deacons Thomas J. Forbes; Frank J. Flood; Francis B. McGuinness; Dennis R. O'Connor. In Res., Rev. Msgr. Daniel J. Hurley, Pastor Emeritus.
Res.: 2 Bayview Ave., 11758-7299. Tel: 516-798-4992; Fax: 516-795-7836. Email: michelez@stroseoflimaparish.org. Web: www.stroseoflimaparish.org.
School—4704 Merrick Rd., 11758. Tel: 516-541-1546; Fax: 516-797-0351. Web: www.stroseoflimaparish.org/school. Sr. Kathleen Gallina, Prin. Sisters of St. Dominic 1; Lay Teachers 24; Students 494.
Catechesis/Religious Program—Tel: 516-541-1712. Email: religioused@stroseoflimaparish.org. Students 2,800.

MASTIC BEACH, SUFFOLK CO., ST. JUDE (1949) Revs. Gregory Yacyshyn; Todd C. Saccoccia; Deacons Thomas Gillen; Kenneth Geoghan; Mark Herrmann; Joseph Simeone. In Res., Rev. Msgr. John T. Heinlein.
Res.: 89 Overlook Dr., 11951. Tel: 631-281-5743; Fax: 631-395-5786. Email: rectory@stjudemb.org. Web: stjudemb.org.
See Our Lady, Queen of the Apostles Regional School, Center Moriches under Regional Schools located in the Institution section.
Catechesis/Religious Program—Tel: 631-281-2835. Theresa Amorese, D.R.E. Students 1,500.
Parish Human Services Center—89 Overlook Dr., 11951. Tel: 631-281-5634.

MEDFORD, SUFFOLK CO., ST. SYLVESTER (1948) Rev. Edward J. Kealey; Deacons George J. Riegger; Frank Rivera; John McNally, Music Min.
Res.: 68 Ohio Ave., 11763. Tel: 631-475-4506; Fax: 631-475-1057. Email: mainoffice@stsylvesterli.org. Web: www.stsylvesterli.org.
See Holy Angels Regional School, Patchogue under Regional Schools located in the Institution section.
Catechesis/Religious Program—Tel: 631-475-8191. Frances McMahon, D.R.E.; Denise Monaco, D.R.E. Students 1,600.

MELVILLE, SUFFOLK CO., ST. ELIZABETH (1962) Rev. Msgr. Francis J. Schneider; Deacons Joseph Mercolino; John Failla.
Res.: 181 Wolf Hill Rd., 11747. Tel: 631-271-4455; Fax: 631-271-1415.
Church: 175 Wolf Hill Rd., 11747. Email: certer@stelizabeth.org. Web: www.stelizabeth.org.
See Trinity Regional School, East Northport under Regional Schools located in the Institution section.
Catechesis/Religious Program—Students 794.

MERRICK, NASSAU CO., CURÉ OF ARS (1926) Revs. Charles N. Mangano; Zachary Callahan (Retired); Josep Augustine Kadungamparambil (India).
Res.: 2323 Merrick Ave., 11566. Tel: 516-623-1400; Fax: 516-623-1107. Web: www.cureofarschurch.net.
See St. Elizabeth Ann Seton Regional School, Bellmore under Regional Schools located in the Institution section.
Catechesis/Religious Program—Tel: 516-623-1400, Ext. 101. Students 1,013.

MINEOLA, NASSAU CO., CORPUS CHRISTI (1901), (Spanish—Portuguese), Revs. Robert Coyle; Tomaz Gomide; Gabriel Miah; Deacons John C. Reinhart; Brian J. Mannix. In Res., Rev. Msgrs. Edward L. Tarrant (Retired); Eugene F. Murphy (Retired); Revs. Ethel Anarado (Nigeria), Hospital Chap.; Polycarp Nnajiofor (Nigeria), Hospital Chap.
Res.: 155 Garfield Ave., 11501. Tel: 516-746-1223; Fax: 516-294-5311.
School—(Grades N-8), 120 Searing Ave., 11501. Tel: 516-746-2966; Fax: 516-739-3363. Mrs. Susan Anaischik, Prin. Sisters of St. Dominic 2; Lay Teachers 16; Students 183.
Catechesis/Religious Program—Tel: 516-294-0631; Fax: 516-294-0352. Mrs. Ursula Bordonaro, D.R.E. Students 552.

MONTAUK, SUFFOLK CO., ST. THERESE OF LISIEUX (1950) Rev. Michael J. Rieder.
Res.: 55 S. Etna Ave., P.O. Box 5027, 11954. Tel: 631-668-2200; Fax: 631-668-2384.
See Stella Maris Regional School, Sag Harbor under Regional Schools located in the Institution section.
Day Care/Nursery School—Tel: 631-668-5353. (3 & 4 years old) Children 43.
Catechesis/Religious Program—Tel: 631-668-2460. Students 163.

NESCONSET, SUFFOLK CO., CHURCH OF THE HOLY CROSS (1988) Rev. James McNamara; Deacons Gerard K. Steffens, Pastoral Min.; Owen E. Farley Jr., Pastoral Min.; Mrs. Judith Pickel, Pastoral Assoc.
95 Old Nichols Rd., 11767.
Res.: 85 Old Nichols Rd., 11767. Tel: 631-979-2386; Fax: 631-265-2229. Email: pothc@aol.com; pothc@optonline.net. Web: www.pothc.org.
Catechesis/Religious Program—Tel: 631-265-2200, Ext. 12. Email: hcreled@optonline.net. Mrs. Mary Schultz, D.R.E. Students 1,700.

NEW HYDE PARK, NASSAU CO.

1—HOLY SPIRIT (1893) Rev. Joseph E. Nohs. In Res., Rev. Ralph Ferro; Deacon Richard Garcia; Rev. Lachlan T. Cameron.
Res.: 16 S. Sixth St., 11040. Tel: 516-354-0359; Fax: 516-354-2611 (Rectory). Email: holyspchurch@aol.com. Web: www.holyspiritchurch.com.
Catechesis/Religious Program—13 S. 6th St., 11040. Tel: 516-354-2363. Students 540.

2—NOTRE DAME (1941) Rev. William T. Slater; Rev. Msgr. Romualdo Sosing; Deacon Peter DiGiuseppe,

Pastoral Assoc.; Sr. Margaret Ann Hartigan, R.S.M., Pastoral Assoc. In Res., Rev. John Denniston.
Res.: 45 Mayfair Rd., 11040. Tel: 516-352-7203; Fax: 516-326-7988.
School—25 Mayfair Rd., 11040. Tel: 516-354-5618; Fax: 516-354-5373. Mrs. Margaret Moss, Prin. Sisters of St. Dominic (Amityville) 1; Lay Teachers 28; Students 419.
Catechesis/Religious Program—25 Mayfair Rd., 11040. Tel: 516-437-5604. Sr. Mary Jane Coleman, R.S.M., D.R.E. Students 1,002.

NORTH MERRICK, NASSAU CO., SACRED HEART (1952) Rev. Thomas G. Gallagher; Rev. Msgr. James A. Brassil (Retired); Rev. Joseph D'Angelo.
Mailing Address: 720 Merrick Ave., 11566. Tel: 516-379-1356; Fax: 516-379-1610. Email: sacredheartnmerrick@hotmail.com. Web: www.hearttoheartparish.org.
Res.: 1918 Old Mill Rd., 11566. Tel: 516-377-6061.
School—730 Merrick Ave., 11566. Tel: 516-378-5797; Fax: 516-378-5797. Kerry Kahn, Prin. Sisters of St. Joseph 1; Lay Teachers 20; Students 207.
Catechesis/Religious Program—Tel: 516-868-9406. Mrs. Cecelia Lerro, D.R.E. Students 1,100.

NORTHPORT, SUFFOLK CO., ST. PHILIP NERI (1894) [CEM] Rev. Peter J. Garry; Deacon John F. Burkart; Sr. Grace Vagnini, C.S.J., Pastoral Assoc. In Res., Rev. Msgr. Thomas J. Colgan (Retired); Rev. Peter Francis, O.F.M.
Office: 15 Prospect Ave., 11768. Tel: 631-261-2485; Fax: 631-261-2701.
Res.: 344 Main St., 11768. Fax: 631-261-7420.
See Trinity Regional School, East Northport under Regional Schools located in the Institution section.
Catechesis/Religious Program—Tel: 631-261-2485; Fax: 631-261-2701. Kathleen Reid, Dir. Adult Faith Formation; Patricia Merenda, D.R.E.(Levels 1-4); Carol Arote, D.R.E. (Levels 5-8). Students 1,003.

OCEAN BEACH, (FIRE ISLAND) SUFFOLK CO., OUR LADY OF THE MAGNIFICAT (1921) Rev. Msgr. John C. Nosser (Retired).
Mailing Address: P.O. Box 445, 11770. Tel: 631-583-5868.
Catechesis/Religious Program—

OCEANSIDE, NASSAU CO., ST. ANTHONY (1927) Rev. D. James French, S.J.; Rev. Msgr. Conrad R. Dietz (Retired); Revs. Pierce A. Brennan, S.J.; Patrick J. Sullivan, S.J.; Deacons James W. Flannery; James O'Neill; John O'Connor; Anna Maria Sirianni, Parish Outreach Coord. Tel: 516-764-9257.
Res.: 110 Anchor Ave., 11572. Tel: 516-764-0048; Fax: 516-282-2525. Email: saoffice3@aol.com. Web: stanthonyoceanside.org.
Catechesis/Religious Program—Tel: 516-282-2520. Lucy Vavosa, D.R.E.

OYSTER BAY, NASSAU CO., ST. DOMINIC'S (1894) Rev. Kevin M. Smith; Rev. Msgr. Romualdo Sosing; Rev. Dariusz Koszyk.
Res.: 93 Anstice St., 11771. Tel: 516-922-4488; Fax: 516-922-9491. Email: parishoff@stdoms.org. Web: stdoms.org.
School—35 School St., 11771. Tel: 516-922-4233; Fax: 516-624-7613. Email: sdes@stdoms.org. Sisters of the Immaculate Heart of Mary 2; Lay Teachers 14; Students 224.
High School—110 Antice St., 11771. Tel: 516-922-4888; Fax: 516-922-5794. Email: sdhs@stdoms.org. Lay Teachers 31; Students 420.
Catechesis/Religious Program—Tel: 516-922-7788. Email: religioused@stdoms.org. Students 927.

PATCHOGUE, SUFFOLK CO.

1—ST. FRANCIS DE SALES (1888) [CEM] Rev. John J. McGratty; Deacons Martin McIndoe; Francisco Diaz-Granados; Mrs. Anne Boyce, Pastoral Assoc.; Lourdes Taglialatela, Outreach Coord.
Res.: 7 Amity St., 11772. Tel: 631-475-0161; Fax: 631-475-1481.
See Holy Angels Regional School, Patchogue under Regional Schools located in the Institution section.
Catechesis/Religious Program—Tel: 631-289-4339. Email: sanfraninpatch@hotmail.com. Elaine Heschl, D.R.E. Students 431.

2—OUR LADY OF MT. CARMEL (1925), (Italian), Rev. Michael J. Torpey; Deacon Joseph Mystkowski; Christine Erhart, Business Mgr.
Res.: 495 New North Ocean Ave., 11772. Tel: 631-475-4739; Fax: 631-447-1030. Web: www.ourladyofmtcarmelofpatchogue.org.
See Holy Angels Regional School, Patchogue under Regional Schools located in the Institution section.
Catechesis/Religious Program—Tel: 631-289-7327. Students 670.

PLAINVIEW, NASSAU CO., ST. PIUS X (1955) Rev. Msgr. Domenick T. Graziadio; Linda Curro, Pastoral Assoc.
Res.: One St. Pius Ct., 11803. Tel: 516-938-3956; Fax: 516-433-6138. Email: spxrecty@optonline.net.
See St. John Baptist de LaSalle Regional School, Farmingdale under Regional Schools located in the Institution section.
Catechesis/Religious Program—Tel: 516-822-8348; Fax: 516-938-0001. Students 390.

POINT LOOKOUT, NASSAU CO., OUR LADY OF THE MIRACULOUS MEDAL (1937), (Irish), Rev. Patrick J. Callan. In Res., Rev. Thomas E. Donohoe (Retired).
Res.: 75 Parkside Dr., P.O. Box 20, 11569. Tel: 516-431-2772; Fax: 516-432-8669. Email: olmmc@optonline.net. Web: olmmc.com.
See Long Beach Regional Catholic School, Long Beach under Regional Schools located in the Institution section.
Catechesis/Religious Program—Tel: 516-432-8074. Email: reled@optonline.net. Students 65.

PORT JEFFERSON STATION, SUFFOLK CO.

1—ST. GERARD MAJELLA (1968) Rev. Msgr. William A. Hanson; Deacon Vincent Beckles.
Res.: 300 Terryville Rd., 11776. Tel: 631-473-2900; Fax: 631-473-0015. Web: www.stgmajella.org.
See Our Lady of the Wisdom Regional School, Port Jefferson under Regional Schools located in the Institution section.
Catechesis/Religious Program—Tel: 631-928-2550. Fran Bursztyn, D.R.E. Students 1,430.

2—INFANT JESUS (1903) Revs. Charles Romano; Paul Dolan; Deacons William J. Powers; Richard E. Waldmann; Robert A. Kruse. In Res., Revs. Samuel Aririatu; Martin Bancroft.
Res.: 110 Myrtle Ave., 11777. Tel: 631-473-0165; Fax: 631-331-8094. Web: www.infantjesus.org.
See Our Lady of the Wisdom Regional School, Port Jefferson under Regional Schools located in the Institution section.
Catechesis/Religious Program—Tel: 631-928-0447; Fax: 631-928-2370. Ms. Maryanne Trezza, D.R.E. Students 1,466.

PORT WASHINGTON, NASSAU CO., ST. PETER OF ALCANTARA (1901) Rev. Patrick J. Whitney; Rev. Msgr. Walter E. Simmons, Pastor Emeritus (Retired); Deacon Frank G. D'Angelo.
Res.: 1327 Port Washington Blvd., 11050. Tel: 516-883-6675; Fax: 516-944-7461.
School—Tel: 516-944-3772; Fax: 516-767-8075. Sean O'Connell, Prin. Lay Teachers 28; Students 330.
Catechesis/Religious Program—Tel: 516-883-5584; Fax: 516-767-6194. Students 735.
Convent—Sisters, Servants of the Immaculate Heart of Mary (Scranton, PA), 1317 Port Washington Blvd., 11050. Tel: 516-767-1282.

RIVERHEAD, SUFFOLK CO.

1—ST. ISIDORE'S (1903), (Polish), [CEM] Revs. Robert Kuznik; Ryszard Ficek.
Res.: 622 Pulaski St., 11901. Tel: 631-727-2114; Fax: 631-369-3566. Email: sisidore@optonline.net.
School—515 Marcy Ave., 11901. Tel: 631-727-1650; Fax: 631-727-3945. Email: sljsis@aol.com. Sr. Linda Joseph Chichi, C.S.F.N., Prin. Sisters of the Holy Family of Nazareth 1; Lay Teachers 17; Students 275.
Catechesis/Religious Program—Students 100.

2—ST. JOHN THE EVANGELIST (1861) [CEM] Rev. Thomas W. Coby. In Res., Most Rev. Emil A. Wcela; Deacon John Lovett.
Res.: 546 St. John's Pl., 11901. Tel: 631-727-2030; Fax: 631-369-5228. Email: stjohnriverhead@aol.com.
Catechesis/Religious Program—Tel: 631-727-6774. Students 321.

ROCKY POINT, SUFFOLK CO., ST. ANTHONY OF PADUA (1948) Rev. Richard P. Hoerning; Sr. Josephine Olimpieri, C.S.J., Pastoral Assoc.
Res.: 614 Rte. 25A, 11778. Tel: 631-744-2609; Fax: 631-744-5782. Email: stasrp@optonline.net. Web: www.starockypoint.com.
Catechesis/Religious Program—Tel: 631-821-0872. Sr. Phylis O'Dowd, O.P., D.R.E. Students 1,657.

RONKONKOMA, SUFFOLK CO., ST. JOSEPH'S (1910) Revs. Michael T. Maffeo; Rene Tapel; Juniper J. Thomas; Peter T. Liu (Retired); Michael Boyle; Deacons James Altonji; Michael J. DeBellis; Joseph Dougherty, (Retired); Joseph Califano; Michael Devenney; William Dobbins; Frank Dell'Aglio.
Res.: 45 Church St., 11779-3300. Tel: 631-588-8456; Fax: 631-471-2569. Email: info@stjoronk.org. Web: stjoronk.org.
School—25 Church St., 11779. Tel: 631-588-4760; Fax: 631-588-0543. Email: school@stjoronk.org. Leona Arpino, Prin. Lay Teachers 19; Students 254.
Catechesis/Religious Program—35 Church St., 11779. Tel: 631-981-1805; Fax: 631-588-6140. Email: reled@stjoronk.org. Sr. Anne Marie Dean, C.S.J., D.R.E. Students 1,085.

ROOSEVELT, NASSAU CO., QUEEN OF THE MOST HOLY ROSARY (1919) Revs. Joseph Baidoo; Gabriel Muteru (Kenya) (NY); Deacons Clinton Lewis; Thomas Jackson; Mrs. Elena A. Powers, Music Min. In Res., Most Rev. Paul H. Walsh.
Res.: 196 W. Centennial Ave., 11575. Tel: 516-378-1315; Fax: 516-378-5754. Email: qmhr@optonline.net.
Catechesis/Religious Program—200 W. Centennial Ave., 11575. Tel: 516-623-1391; Fax: 516-378-5754. Email: cherylwhite@optonline.net. Cheryl White, D.R.E. Students 98.

ROSLYN, NASSAU CO., ST. MARY'S (1871) Rev. Richard A. Nilsson; Deacon Edward M. Case.
Res.: 110 Bryant Ave., 11576. Tel: 516-621-2222; Fax: 516-621-7892.
See All Saints Regional Catholic School, Glen Cove under Regional Schools located in the Institution section.
Catechesis/Religious Program—Tel: 516-621-6798. Nora Toal, C.R.E. Students 450.

ST. JAMES, SUFFOLK CO., SS. PHILIP AND JAMES (1907) Revs. Anthony M. Stanganelli; Edward H. Koch, Parochial Vicor; Deacons Kenneth Maher; Robert Heschl, (Retired); John Keenan; Gerard Reda; Ronald Blasius. In Res., Rev. James L. Maltese, Hospital Chap.
Res.: 1 Carow Pl., 11780. Tel: 631-584-5454; Fax: 631-862-9675. Email: info@sspj.org. Web: www.sspj.org.
School—(Grades PreK-8), 11780. Tel: 631-584-7896; Fax: 631-584-3258. Web: sspjschool.net. Mr. Anthony Giordano, Prin. Lay Teachers 20; Students 380.
Catechesis/Religious Program—Tel: 631-584-3204. Students 1,950.

SAG HARBOR, SUFFOLK CO., ST. ANDREW'S (1859) [CEM] Rev. Peter Devaraj, S.A.C., Admin. In Res., Rev. Andrew P. Blake, Pastor Emeritus (Retired).
Res.: 122 Division St, 11963-3154. Tel: 631-725-0123; Fax: 631-725-3310.
See Stella Maris Regional School, Sag Harbor under Regional Schools located in the Institution section.
Catechesis/Religious Program—Tel: 631-725-0123, Ext. 22. Students 80.

SALTAIRE, SUFFOLK CO., OUR LADY STAR OF THE SEA, MISSION CHAPEL, (Summer Mission) Rev. Richard R. Viladesau, Admin.
Res.: 1500 de Paul St., Elmont, 11003. Tel: 516-352-2127.
Church: 300 Pilot Walk, 11706. Tel: 631-583-7613.

SAYVILLE, SUFFOLK CO., ST. LAWRENCE THE MARTYR (1895) [CEM] Rev. Nicholas J. Figliola; Rev. Msgr. John T. Heinlein; Deacon Patrick LaBella.
Res.: 27 Handsome Ave., 11782. Tel: 631-589-0042; 631-589-8135; 631-589-3887; Fax: 631-589-5318. Email: stlawsay@aol.com. Web: stlawrencesayville.org.
See Prince of Peace Regional School, Sayville under Regional Schools located in the Institution section.
Catechesis/Religious Program—Tel: 631-589-3160. Mrs. Maria Davidson, D.R.E. Students 1,275.

SEA CLIFF, NASSAU CO., ST. BONIFACE MARTYR (1898) Rev. Robert A. Romeo; Deacons Tom Fox; Theodore Kolakowski; Eileen Krieb, Business Mgr.; Jeff Schrieider, Music Dir. In Res., Rev. Frederick Kutubebi, Hospital Chap. (Glen Cove Hospital).
Rectory, Office & Parish Center: 145 Glen Ave., 11579. Tel: 516-676-0676; Fax: 516-674-6742. Email: stbon.church@verizon.net. Web: saintboniface.org.
Res.: 220 Carpenter Ave., 11579.
See All Saints Regional Catholic School, Glen Cove under Regional Schools located in the Institution section.
Catechesis/Religious Program—Tel: 516-671-0418. Email: stbon.ccd@verizon.net. Karen Croce, D.R.E. Students 360.

SEAFORD, NASSAU CO.

1—ST. JAMES (1951) Revs. Robert S. Hewes; Vincent Schifano; Khoa T. Le; Deacons James G. Beirne; Richard Brunner; John J. Lynch; Allan J. Helmbrecht, Business Mgr.; Jane Lawson, Music Min.
Res.: 80 Hicksville Rd., 11783. Tel: 516-731-3710; Fax: 516-731-4828. Email: stjamesrcchurch@aol.com.
See St. John Baptist de LaSalle Regional School, Farmingdale under Regional Schools located in the Institution section.
Catechesis/Religious Program—Tel: 516-796-2979; Fax: 516-731-4828. Marianne Mirkow, Co-Coord. Rel. Educ.; Julie Lebeck, Co-Coord. Rel. Educ. Students 1,648.

2—MARIA REGINA (1954) Rev. Msgr. Peter J. Pflomm; Revs. Allan Arnaud; Innocent Mbaegbu; Deacons Gerald F. Whitfield; Andrew Gargiulo; John R. Nuzzi; Paul Neuhedel.
Res.: 3945 Jerusalem Ave., 11783. Tel: 516-798-2415; Fax: 516-798-7493.
School—4045 Jerusalem Ave., 11783. Tel: 516-541-1229; Fax: 516-541-1235. Mrs. Denise Carlin Seck, Prin.; Mrs. MaryAlice Doherty, Asst. Prin. Lay Teachers 28; Students 470.
Catechesis/Religious Program—3945 Jerusalem Ave., 11783. Tel: 516-541-0921; Fax: 516-795-2510. Carol Tannehill, D.R.E. Students 1,617.

3—ST. WILLIAM THE ABBOT (1928) Rev. Robert L. Hayden; Rev. Msgr. Thomas G. Leavey, Pastor Emeritus (Retired); Revs. Paul F. Butler; Bala Rathinam; Deacons Thomas Buchenberger; John Lynch. In Res., Rev. Richard R. Viladesau.
Res.: 2000 Jackson Ave., 11783. Tel: 516-785-1266; Fax: 516-785-4824. Email:

information@stwilliam.org. Web: www.stwilliam.org.
School—2001 Jackson Ave., 11783. Tel: 516-785-6784; Fax: 516-785-2752. Email: aguardino@stwilliamtheabbot.net. Web: www.stwilliamtheabbot.net. Mrs. Anna Guardino, Prin. Lay Teachers 27; Students 602.
Catechesis/Religious Program—Tel: 516-679-9558; Fax: 516-679-1649. Email: reled@stwilliam.org. Mrs. Georgette Levesque, D.R.E.; Mrs. Mary Calabrese, D.R.E. Students 1,466.

SELDEN, SUFFOLK CO., ST. MARGARET OF SCOTLAND (1948) Revs. Christopher J. Aridas; Joseph Alenchery (India); Deacons William E. Kogler; Biagio Muratore; Phil Paolicelli; Joseph Scollan; Barbara Mahon, Admin.
Web: saintmargaret.com.
Res.: 81 College Rd., 11784. Tel: 631-732-3131; Fax: 631-732-8827.
See Holy Angels Regional School, Patchogue under Regional Schools located in the Institution section.
Catechesis/Religious Program—Tel: 631-698-0798. Marilynne Schaefer, C.R.E.; Sharon Orabona, C.R.E.; Eileen Lord, C.R.E.; Tina Muller, C.R.E.; Marianne Hordt, Youth Min. Students 1,020.

SETAUKET, SUFFOLK CO., ST. JAMES (1949) [CEM] Revs. Robert J. Smith; James P. Mannion Jr. In Res., Rev. John J. Fitzgerald (Retired).
Res.: 429 Rte. 25-A, 11733. Tel: 631-941-4141; Fax: 631-751-6607.
See Our Lady of the Wisdom Regional School, Port Jefferson under Regional Schools located in the Institution section.
Catechesis/Religious Program—Tel: 631-751-7287. Louise DiCarlo, D.R.E. Students 1,361.

SHELTER ISLAND, SUFFOLK CO., OUR LADY OF THE ISLE (1907) [CEM] Revs. Thomas Murray, Admin.; Peter DeSanctis.
Shelter Island Heights, Box 3027, Shelter Island Heights, 11965. Tel: 631-749-0001; Fax: 631-749-4218. Email: oliheights@aol.com.
See Stella Maris Regional School, Sag Harbor under Regional Schools located in the Institution section.
Catechesis/Religious Program—Students 10.

SHOREHAM, SUFFOLK CO., ST. MARK (1973) Rev. Theodore J. Howard; Rev. Msgr. Ivan Gonzalez; Rev. Frank Gnanasegaram (Sri Lanka); Deacon Patrick Gerace.
Res.: 105 Randall Rd., 11786. Tel: 631-744-2800; Fax: 631-821-1628. Email: stmarksrcc@aol.com.
Catechesis/Religious Program—Tel: 631-821-0550. Email: ridglynn@aol.com. Mrs. Lynn Fein, D.R.E. Students 1,194.

SMITHTOWN, SUFFOLK CO., ST. PATRICK (1952), (Irish—Italian), [CEM] Rev. Msgr. Ellsworth R. Walden; Revs. Patrick M. Riegger; Desmond Chilagorom. In Res., Revs. Frederick Hill; Anselm Okeke.
Res.: 280 E. Main St., 11787. Tel: 631-265-2271; Fax: 631-863-1586. Email: stpats333@aol.com.
School—284 E. Main St., 11787. Tel: 631-724-0285; Fax: 631-265-4841. Web: www.sps-smithtown.org. Mrs. Eileen Sadicario, Prin. Sisters of St. Joseph 1; Lay Teachers 26; Students 529.
Catechesis/Religious Program—Tel: 631-724-7454; Fax: 631-265-1250. Email: stpatsrfc@optonline.net. Mrs. Elaina Kedjierski, D.R.E. (Levels 1-4); Peggy Soviero, D.R.E. (Levels 5-8). Students 1,700.

SOUND BEACH, SUFFOLK CO., ST. LOUIS DE MONTFORT (1971) Rev. Charles E. Papa; Rev. Msgr. John A. McGuire, Pastor Emeritus (Retired); Deacons Joseph T. Bartolotto, Pastoral Assoc.; Gary F. Swane.
75 New York Ave., 11789-2506. Tel: 631-744-8566; Fax: 631-744-8611. Email: tkretz@sldmrc.org.
See Our Lady of the Wisdom Regional School, Port Jefferson under Regional Schools located in the Institution section.
Catechesis/Religious Program—Tel: 631-744-9515; Fax: 631-821-6089. Email: jmcnamara@sldmrc.org. Mr. John McNamara, D.R.E. Students 2,248.

SOUTHAMPTON, SUFFOLK CO.

1—OUR LADY OF POLAND (1918), (Polish), Rev. Stanley Kondeja; Deacon James Ashe.
Res.: 35 Maple St., 11968. Tel: 631-283-0667; Fax: 631-287-4146.
See Our Lady of the Hamptons Regional School, Southampton under Regional Schools located in the Institution section.
Catechesis/Religious Program—Tel: 631-283-5230; Fax: 631-283-5230. Students 320.

2—SACRED HEARTS OF JESUS AND MARY (1896) [CEM] Rev. Jeffrey J. Madley; Rev. Msgr. Edmond J. Trench, Pastor Emeritus (Retired); Deacon John P. Moran.
Res.: 168 Hill St., 11968. Tel: 631-283-0097; Fax: 631-283-3836.
See Our Lady of the Hamptons Regional School, Southampton under Regional Schools located in the Institution section.
Catechesis/Religious Program—Tel: 631-283-0508. Students 410.

SOUTHOLD, SUFFOLK CO., ST. PATRICK'S (1865) [CEM] Rev. George J. Michell.
Res.: Main Rd., P.O. Box 1117, 11971-1401. Tel: 631-765-3442; Fax: 631-765-9631. Email: saintpat@optonline.net.
See Our Lady of Mercy Regional School, Cutchogue under Regional Schools located in the Institution section.
Catechesis/Religious Program—Tel: 631-765-2338. Students 290.

SYOSSET, NASSAU CO., ST. EDWARD CONFESSOR (1952) Rev. Thomas M. Fusco; Sr. Jacqueline Walsh, R.S.M., Pastoral Assoc. Tel: 516-921-8030, Ext. 134; Deacons James Murphy; Thomas F. Reilly Jr.; Raymond P. D'Alessio.
Res.: 205 Jackson Ave., 11791-4218. Tel: 516-921-8030; Fax: 516-921-4549. Web: www.st-edwards.org.
School—2 Teibrook Ave., 11791. Tel: 516-921-7767; Fax: 516-496-0001. Mrs. Joanne Fitzgerald, Prin. Lay Teachers 17; Students 232.
Catechesis/Religious Program—Tel: 516-921-8030, Ext. 126 (Grades 1-5); 516-921-8030, Ext. 124 (Grades 6-8). Pamela Sanders, D.R.E.; Sr. Anne Carron, R.S.M., Dir. Parish Social Ministry. Students 1,103.

UNIONDALE, NASSAU CO., ST. MARTHA (1949) Rev. Msgr. Frank J. Caldwell, C.S.W.; Most Rev. Alfonso Cabezas, C.M.; Rev. John Madigan, O.P.; Sr. Elizabeth Myles, C.S.J., Pastoral Assoc.
Tel: 516-481-2550, Ext. 40 (Pastor's Office); 516-292-1603 (Parish Outreach).
Res.: 546 Greengrove Ave., 11553. Tel: 516-481-2550; Fax: 516-564-4552. Email: saintmartha@dellmail.com. Web: www.saintmartha.org.
See St. Martin de Porres Marianist School, Uniondale under Elementary Schools, Private located in the Institution section.
Catechesis/Religious Program—Tel: 516-481-2550, Ext. 343. Sr. Eileen Curley, R.S.M., D.R.E.; Mrs. Marlene Jean-Baptiste, Dir. Parish Social Ministry. Students 252.

VALLEY STREAM, NASSAU CO.

1—BLESSED SACRAMENT (1950) Rev. Peter Dugandzic; Deacon John F. Coughlin.
Res.: 201 N. Central Ave., 11580. Tel: 516-568-1027; Fax: 516-872-1499.
School—50 Rose Ave., 11580. Tel: 516-825-7334; Fax: 516-825-4376. Ms. Mary Earvolino, Prin. Lay Teachers 18; Students 235.
Catechesis/Religious Program—Tel: 516-561-1407. Eileen McEnaney, D.R.E. Students 350.

2—HOLY NAME OF MARY (1902) Rev. Msgr. Thomas J. Harold; Revs. Theodore J. LeTure, Pastor Emeritus (Retired); Robert W. Ketcham; Deacons James O'Hara; Clyde Ruggieri; Richard F. Raad. In Res., Rev. Msgr. Edward J. Donnelly (Retired).
Res.: 55 E. Jamaica Ave., 11580. Tel: 516-825-1450; Fax: 516-568-1906. Email: holynamemary@aol.com. Web: www.hnom.org.
School—90 S. Grove St., 11580. Tel: 516-825-4009; Fax: 516-825-2710. Richard A. Mc Mahon, Prin. Lay Teachers 18; Students 288.
Catechesis/Religious Program—90 S. Grove St., 11580. Tel: 516-825-1810; Fax: 516-256-0724. Sr. Emily Masse, O.P., D.R.E. Students 818.
Religious Education—Fax: 516-825-5092. Sr. Margie Kelly, C.S.J., Dir.; Kevin Faughey, Music Min.; Rosemary Pettei, Dir. Family Ministry.

WADING RIVER, SUFFOLK CO., ST. JOHN BAPTIST (1922) Rev. John J. Barrett; Sr. Sheila Molloy, O.S.U., Pastoral Assoc.; Deacons Frederick Finter; Gregory Senholzi; Vincent Pozzolano.
Res.: 1488 North Country Rd., 11792. Tel: 631-929-4339; Fax: 631-929-6961.
Catechesis/Religious Program—Students 713.

WANTAGH, NASSAU CO., ST. FRANCES DE CHANTAL (1952) Revs. Gregory J. Cappuccino; Lito D. Amande; Antonio S. Pascual (Retired); Francisco Gius Garcia (Philippines); Sr. Jocelyn Panzetta, C.I.J.; Deacons Robert O'Donovan; Joseph Torres. In Res., Rev. Msgr. John J. Rowan (Retired).
Res.: 1309 Wantagh Ave., 11793. Tel: 516-785-2333; Fax: 516-826-7645. Web: www.stjanefrances.com.
See St. Elizabeth Ann Seton Regional School, Bellmore under Regional Schools located in the Institution section.
Catechesis/Religious Program—Tel: 516-785-2333, Ext. 205. Ellen Lafonte, D.R.E.; Donna Mugno, Admin. Students 2,228.

WEST BABYLON, SUFFOLK CO., OUR LADY OF GRACE (1963) Rev. Msgr. Vincent Rush; Revs. Gilbert D. Lap; Eugenio Solera (Philippines); Deacons Irwin Saffran; William Austin; Brian Miller.
Res.: 666 Albin Ave., 11704. Tel: 631-587-5185; Fax: 631-587-1427. Email: ologrhowace@ourladyofgrace.net. Web: ourladyofgrace.net.
Catechesis/Religious Program—700 Albin Ave., 11704. Tel: 631-661-9353. Mrs. Barbara McGrellis, D.R.E.; Mrs. Susan Martin, D.R.E. Students 1,685.

WEST HEMPSTEAD, NASSAU CO., ST. THOMAS, THE APOSTLE (1931) Rev. Msgr. Francis J. Maniscalco; Revs. Noel Effiong, M.S.P. (Nigeria); Fernando Egargo; Deacons John E. Ford; Edward Cunningham; Jacques Philippeaux; Anthony S. D'Auria.
Res.: 24 Westminster Rd., 11552. Tel: 516-489-8585; Fax: 516-292-2651. Email: stthomasap@optonline.net. Web: stthomasapostle.org.
School—12 Westminster Rd., 11552. Tel: 516-481-9310; Fax: 516-481-8769. Mrs. Christina Teisch, Prin. Sisters 2; Lay Teachers 28; Students 466.
Catechesis/Religious Program—Tel: 516-538-7460. Mrs. Mary Ann Pellegrino, D.R.E.; Eileen Minutoli, Asst. D.R.E. Students 602.
Mission—Chapel 876 Hempstead Ave., Nassau Co. 11552. Tel: 516-483-4091.

WEST ISLIP, SUFFOLK CO., OUR LADY OF LOURDES (1956) Revs. Michael A. Vetrano; Robert C. Scheckenback; Stanislaus Chukwube; Deacons Stephen M. Behar; John Teufel; John DeGuardi; Jack Meehan.
Res.: 455 Hunter Ave., 11795. Tel: 631-661-3224; Fax: 631-661-7143.
School—44 Toomey Rd., 11795. Tel: 631-587-7200; Fax: 631-587-4531. Regina A. Cioffi, Prin. Lay Teachers 18; Students 355.
Catechesis/Religious Program—Tel: 631-661-5440; Fax: 631-661-3606. Sisters Diane Liona, D.R.E.; Nancy Campkin, D.R.E. Students 2,600.

WESTBURY, NASSAU CO., ST. BRIGID (1850) Rev. Msgr. Ralph Sommer; Revs. Ronel Charelus, S.M.M.; John Derasmo; Jaime Calderon; Deacons Manuel J. Ramos; Michael Metzdorff; James Morris; Frank Pesce. In Res., Rev. Jim Hannon.
Res.: 75 Post Ave., 11590. Tel: 516-334-0021; Fax: 516-334-0082. Email: parish@saintbrigid.net. Web: www.saintbrigid.net.
School—St. Brigid/ Our Lady of Hope Regional School, 101 Maple Ave., 11590. Tel: 516-333-0580; Fax: 516-333-0590. Paul P. Clagnaz, Prin. School Sisters of Notre Dame 1; Lay Teachers 20; Students 294.
Catechesis/Religious Program—101 Maple Ave., 11590. Tel: 516-333-9434. Sr. Ann Horn, O.P., D.R.E.; Socorro Moreno, D.R.E.; Meg Westfall, D.R.E. Students 850.

WESTHAMPTON BEACH, SUFFOLK CO., IMMACULATE CONCEPTION (1891) Rev. Joseph A. Mirro; Deacon Joseph Byrne; Virginia Mattera, Pastoral Assoc.
Res.: 580 Main Rd., 11978. Tel: 631-288-1423; Fax: 631-288-5498.
See Our Lady, Queen of the Apostles Regional School, Center Moriches under Regional Schools located in the Institution section.
Catechesis/Religious Program—Tel: 631-288-4188; Fax: 631-288-8215. Virginia Mattera, D.R.E. Students 575.

WILLISTON PARK, NASSAU CO., ST. AIDAN'S CHURCH (1928) Rev. Msgrs. James M. McDonald; Robert J. Kirwin, Pastor Emeritus (Retired); Revs. Thomas W. Tassone; Kevin J. Dillon; Deacons Francis J. Love; Salvatore Villani; Robert S. O'Donovan, Business Mgr.; Joseph F. Connelly. In Res., Rev. Msgr. James C. Vlaun.
Res.: 505 Willis Ave., 11596. Tel: 516-746-6585; Fax: 516-746-6055.
School—(Grades N-3), 525 Willis Ave., 11596. Tel: 516-746-6585, Ext. 202; Fax: 516-746-8817. Mrs. Patti Serrano, Librarian.
School—(Grades 4-8), 510 Willis Ave., 11596. Tel: 518-747-6585, Ext. 302; Fax: 516-746-3086. Eileen Oliver, Prin.; Marie-Elaine Galenskas, Asst. Prin. Lay Teachers 28; Students 551.
Catechesis/Religious Program—Tel: 516-746-6585, Ext. 404. Mr. James F. Corrigan, D.R.E. Students 1,260.

WOODBURY, NASSAU CO., HOLY NAME OF JESUS (1962) Revs. Lawrence B. Rafferty; Yong Don Ju (Korea, South), (Spiritual Leader Korean Catholic Apostolate).
Res.: 690 Woodbury Rd., 11797-2504. Tel: 516-921-2334; Fax: 516-682-8161. Email: frrafferty@hnjchurch.net. Web: www.hnjchurch.net.
Catechesis/Religious Program—Students 146.

WYANDANCH, SUFFOLK CO., OUR LADY OF THE MIRACULOUS MEDAL (1932) Rev. William F. Brisotti; Deacons Donald Zirkel; Jules Gagnon.
Res.: 1434 Straight Path, 11798. Tel: 631-643-7568; Fax: 631-643-5935.
Gerald Ryan Outreach Center, Inc.—Tel: 631-643-7591. Noelle Campbell, Dir.; Naycha Florival, Religious Education & Youth Ministry. Tel: 631-643-3364.
Catechesis/Religious Program—Tel: 631-643-3364. Students 240.

Chaplains of Public Institutions

ROCKVILLE CENTRE. *Mercy Medical Center*, 1000 N. Village Ave., 11570. Tel: 516-705-2525. Revs. Anthony Madu, Francis Oranefo, Sisters Mary

Alice Aschenbach, C.I.J., Chap., Vice Pres., Pastoral Care, Mary Ellen Eichmann, Chap., Norma Jean Lokcinski, C.I.J., Chap., Eileen Vassallo, Chap.

Good Shepherd Hospice (Nassau), 245 Old Country Rd., Melville, 11747. Tel: 631-465-6300. Rev. Robert Dawley, Chap., Deacon Michael Metzdorff, Dir. Pastoral Care, Sisters Mary Alice Duggin, O.S.U., Chap., Lorraine Leibold, O.P., Chap., Joyce Osgood, O.P., Chap., Pauline T. Lavelle, Chap.

AMITYVILLE. *South Oaks Psychiatric Hospital*, Sunrise Hwy., 11701. Tel: 631-264-4000. Rev. Robert A. Hyatt (Retired).

BAY SHORE. *Southside Hospital*, Montauk Hwy., 11706. Tel: 631-968-3000. Revs. Peter J. McCrann, S.M.M., Christopher Okoli (Nigeria).

BETHPAGE. *New Island Hospital, New Island Hospital*, 4295 Hempstead Tpke., 11714. Tel: 631-520-0222. Rev. Hilary Ezenwa.

EAST MEADOW. *Nassau County Police Department*. Rev. Msgr. John A. Alesandro, Rev. Joseph D'Angelo, Rev. Msgr. Thomas J. Hartman.

Nassau County, Fire Chiefs, Council of. Rev. Kevin M. Smith.

Nassau University Medical Center, 2201 Hempstead Tpke., 11554. Tel: 516-572-3195; 516-572-6069. Sr. Maureen Chase, Dir. Pastoral Care, Revs. Cyprian Osuegbu (Nigeria), Sebastian Owusa-Mensah.

GLEN COVE. *North Shore University Hospital at Glen Cove*, Tel: 516-674-7300. Rev. Frederick Kutubebi.

HUNTINGTON. *Huntington Hospital*, 270 Park Ave., 11743. Tel: 631-351-2000. Rev. Thomas Edamattan (India), Deacon Edward Billia.

LONG BEACH. *Long Beach Memorial Medical Center*, 455 E. Bay Dr., 11561. Rev. Joseph Paul Fernando, Chap.

MANHASSET. *North Shore Univ. Hospital*, 1554 Community Dr., 11030. Tel: 516-562-0100. Revs. Antony Xavier, Benet Uwusomba, Jon Overvold, Dir.

North Hills Hospital, Tel: 516-562-4713.

MELVILLE. *Long Island Developmental Center*, Box 788, 11747. Tel: 516-385-2700. Rev. Malachy Flaherty, O.F.M.Cap.

MINEOLA. *Winthrop Hospital*, First St., 11501. Tel: 516-663-0333. Revs. Polycarp Nnajiofor (Nigeria), Ethel Anarado (Nigeria).

Corpus Christi, 155 Garfield Ave., 11501-2583. Tel: 516-746-1223.

NESCONSET. *Nesconset Nursing Home* 11767. Tel: 516-361-8800. Vacant.

NORTHPORT. *Veteran's Administration Hospital* 1176. Tel: 631-261-4400, Ext. 7194. Revs. John Malone, David Lazar Mani.

OCEANSIDE. *South Nassau Communities Hospital*, Tel: 516-763-2030. Rev. Jerome Francis Ackah, Deacon Charles Muscarnera.

PATCHOGUE. *Brookhaven Hospice*, Tel: 631-687-2960. Deacon Bob Gronenthal, Elaine Kotlowski.

Brookhaven Memorial Hospital, 100 Hospital Rd., 11772. Tel: 631-654-7100. Rev. John Attakruh, James Maloney.

PLAINVIEW. *North Shore Hospital at Plainview*, 888 Old Country Rd., 11083. Tel: 516-681-8900. Rev. Jose Simon Palliparambil.

St. Pius X: 1 St. Pius Ct., 11803-4023. Tel: 516-938-3959.

PORT JEFFERSON. *St. Charles Hospital, Port Jefferson, New York* 11777. Tel: 631-474-6411. Revs. Samuel Aririatu (Nigeria) (NY), Charles Oppong (Ghana), Deacon Joseph Scollan, Sisters Josefita Rodriguez, O.P., Dir., Pastoral Care, Edith Menegus, O.S.U., Chap.

Maryhaven Center of Hope 11777. Tel: 631-474-3400. Sisters Maryaline Zierle, O.P., Cathy Smith, O.P.

Mather Memorial Hospital 11777. Tel: 631-473-1320, Ext. 4007. Rev. Martin Bancroft.

ROCKVILLE CENTRE. *Catholic Health Services of Long Island*, 992 N. Village Ave., 11570. Tel: 516-705-3700; 631-474-5663. Mary T. O'Neill, Vice Pres. for Spiritual Care & Pastoral Educ., Mrs. Cathy B. Grandjean, Dir. Chaplaincy.

ROSLYN. *St. Francis Hospital* 11576. Revs. Emmanuel Okeiyi, John B. Ephraim, Sisters Minda Castrillo, F.M.M., Elisa Fernando, F.M.M., Mari Garesche, Pauline Gilmore, F.M.M., Dir., Pastoral Care, Thresi Kalloorthottiyil, Claire MacDonald, O.P., Ms. Mary Toole, Mary Ellen Beneivenga, Patricia Tarpinian.

SAYVILLE. *Good Samaritan Nursing Home*. 11782. Tel: 631-244-2400. Sr. Doris Marie Deane, S.C., Chap.

SMITHTOWN. *St. Catherine of Siena Hospital* 11787. Tel: 631-360-2000. Sr. Patricia McDonnell, O.P., Dir., Revs. Frederick Hill, Mark Applewhite, Anselm Okeke, Theresa Maynard, Chap.

280 E. Main St., 11787. Tel: 631-862-3000; 631-979-1292.

STONY BROOK. *L.I. State Veterans' Home*, Tel: 631-444-8737. Rev. Peter O'Rourke.

Stony Brook University Hospital, SUNY at Stony Brook, 11790. Tel: 631-444-8157. Revs. Steve Unger, Dir. Pastoral Care, James L. Maltese, (on call weekends), Patrick Chudi Okafor, Thomas Aidoo, Patrick Okafor, (M T W on-call), Sr. Lynn Queck, Chap., Mrs. Anne Coulehan, Chap.

UNIONDALE. *Holly Patterson Geriatric Center*, 875 Jerusalem Ave., 11553. Tel: 516-572-1500. Rev. R. Michael Reid.

Res.: *Holy Family*, Hicksville, 11801. Tel: 516-938-3846.

VALLEY STREAM. *Franklin Medical Center Hospital* 11580. Tel: 516-256-6000. Revs. James Barnum, Augustine Okochi, Kathryn Martino, Chap.

Our Lady of Peace, 25 Fowler Ave., Lynbrook, 11563. Tel: 516-399-6414.

WEST BRENTWOOD. *Pilgrim Psychiatric Center*, P.O. Box A, 11717. Tel: 631-761-2828. Rev. Lawrence J. O'Leary (Retired), Sr. Mary Summerville, C.S.J.

WEST ISLIP. *Consolation Nursing Home* 11795. Tel: 631-587-1600. Rev. William R. Logan, Rabbi Kathleen Novick, Deacon Robert Raines, Mrs. Theresa McNally, Chap., Mrs. Peggy Nixdorf, Dir., Pastoral Care, Mrs. Sandra Smith, Chap., Ms. Alycia Zawol, Chap.

Good Samaritan Hospital Medical Center 11795. Tel: 631-376-3000. Revs. Jerome Madumelu, Cletus Nwaogwugwu, Paul Nwobi, Sisters Mona Garrett, D.W., Jean Agnes Geraghty, O.P., Rosemary Jermusryk, O.P., Ellen Moore, O.P., Gertrude O'Brien, D.W., Ann Marie Pierce, O.P., Mary Ann Bonner, Chap., Carmen Springer, Chap., Kevin Stolz, Chap.

Catholic Home Care, 15 Park Ave., Hauppauge, 11749. Tel: 631-929-8200. Mr. Charles Zeiss, Kevin Danaher, Linda Smith, Alex Daszewski.

Prison Ministry

BAY SHORE. *Office of Prison Ministry and Criminal Justice Affairs*, 26 S. Saxon Ave., 11706-8920. Tel: 631-969-0837; Fax: 631-666-5073. Bro. Jack Moylan, O.S.F., D. Min., Dir., Suzanne D. Jones, Coord. of Ministerial Svcs.

EAST MEADOW. *Nassau County Correctional Center*, 100 Carman Ave., 11554-1146. Tel: 516-572-4145. Rev. Ralph Ferro, Sisters Dolores Castellano, C.I.J., Virginia Waters, F.S.P., Deacons John H. McGonigle, Manuel Ramos.

RIVERHEAD. *Suffolk County Correctional Facility*, 100 Center Dr., 11901. Tel: 631-852-2294; 631-852-2728. Sr. Michelle Bremer, C.S.F.N., Deacon Chris Vigliotta.

WESTBURY. *Nassau County Juvenile Detention Center*, 61 Carman Ave., 11590. Tel: 516-571-9153. Bro. Jack Moylan, O.S.F., D.Min., Sr. Dolores Castellano, C.I.J.

YAPHANK. *Suffolk County Minimum Security Facility*, P.O. Box 69, 11980. Tel: 631-852-4713. Sr. Michelle Bremer, C.S.F.N., Deacons Miguel Romero, Chris Vigliotta.

Academic Leave:
Rev. Msgr.—
Batule, Robert J.
Revs.—
Dugandzic, Peter, S.T.D.
Rannazzisi, Gregory, Via Del Gianicolo 14 00120 Vatican City State.
Zientarski, Nicholas A.

Leave of Absence:
Revs.—
Donnelly, Stephen H.
Hannafin, Steven J.
Kennedy, Glenn
Pietrowski, Stephen J.
Rogers, Paul E.
White, John

Serving Outside the Diocese:
Rev. Msgrs.—
Boccafola, Kenneth
Cervini, John
Revs.—
Atkins, James
Coyle, Robert
Denniston, John
Grace, Patrick
Morris, Stephen
Rowan, Mark P.
Viladesau, Richard R., S.T.D.

Medical Leave:
Rev. Msgr.—
Hayde, Ronald
Revs.—
Bie, Paul R.
Johnston, Jeffrey
Lubrano, Robert

Unassigned:
Rev. Msgr.—
Placa, Alan J.
Revs.—
Allen, Peter
Ditta, Angelo J.
Saloy, Thomas
Sheridan, Daniel
Twomey, Gerald S.

Retired:
Most Revs.—
Daly, James, Diocese of Rockville Centre, P.O. Box 9023, 11571-9023.
Wcela, Emil, Church of St. John the Evangelist, 546 St. John's Pl., Riverhead, 11901.
Rev. Msgrs.—
Ballweg, Lawrence F., 220 Main Blvd. 1C, Boynton Beach, FL 33435.
Boesel, James E., Church of Our Lady of Mercy, 500 S. Oyster Bay Rd., Hicksville, 11801.
Brassil, James A., Church of the Sacred Heart, 720 Merrick Ave., North Merrick, 11566.
Candreva, Thomas D., S.T.L., J.C.D., 560 West Broadway #4R, Long Beach, 11561.
Chiara, Peter A., St. Mary, 20 Harrison Ave., East Islip, 11730-2314.
Colgan, Thomas J., St. Philip Neri, 15 Prospect Ave., Northport, 11768.
Donnelly, Edward J., 10 Gotham Walk, Breezy Point, 11697.
Fagan, Robert Emmet, M.S.W., Sem. of the Immaculate Conception, 440 W. Neck Rd., Huntington, 11743.
Gill, William J., Sacred Hearts of Jesus & Mary, 168 Hill St., Southampton, 11968.
Glimm, Francis X., S.T.L., St. Joseph Guest House, 350 Cuba Hill Rd., Huntington, 11743-4896.
Graham, George P., J.C.D., Ph.D., St. Bernard, 3100 Hempstead Tpke., Levittown, 11756.
Hamilton, Daniel S., Church of Our Lady of Perpetual Help, 210 S. Wellwood Ave., Lindenhurst, 11757.
Kane, Thomas S., 4384 Bowspirit Ct. 2D, Fort Myers, FL 33919.
Kirwin, Robert J., St. Aidan, 505 Willis Ave., Williston Park, 11596-1786.
Leavey, Thomas G., St. William the Abbot, 2000 Jackson Ave., Seaford, 11783-2688.
Manly, Alexander F., St. Joseph, 59 Church St., Kings Park, 11754.
Martin, John P., 37 N. Bayview Rd., Southampton, 11968.
McGuire, John A., St. Louis de Montfort, 75 New York Ave., Sound Beach, 11789-0810.
Murphy, Eugene F., Church of Corpus Christi, 155 Garfield Ave., Mineola, 11501.
Nosser, Charles J., Church of Our Lady of Victory, 2 Floral Parkway, Floral Park, 11001.
Nosser, John C., M.S., M.Div., Church of Our Lady of the Magnificat, P.O. Box 445, Ocean Beach, 11770.
Ribaudo, Charles A., 20 Suncrest Dr., Dix Hills, 11746.
Rooney, Thaddeus, Ss. Cyril & Methodius, 125 Half Hollow Rd., Deer Park, 11795-4288.
Rowan, John J., P.O. Box 1142, Southold, 11971.
Saccacio, Robert J., 3102 Bludds Dr. S., Baiting Hollow, 11933.
Savastano, Anthony J., St. Pius X Residence, 1220 Front St., Uniondale, 11553.
Simmons, Walter E., St. Peter of Alcantara, 1327 Port Washington Blvd., Port Washington, 11050-3096.
Singleton, William V., St. Raymond, 263 Atlantic Ave., East Rockaway, 11518-1117.
Skelly, John J., P.O. Box 5217, Rocky Point, 11778.
Tarrant, Edward L., Corpus Christi, 155 Garfield Ave., Mineola, 11501.
Trench, Edmond J., P.O. Box 1503, East Quogue, 11942.
Revs.—
Alarcon, Felix, 207 Oxford House, 21267 Gertrude Ave., Port Charlotte, FL 33952.
Anderson, Arthur C., 245 Alphano Rd., Great Meadows, NJ 07838.
Benack, Henry I., St. Patrick, 235 Glen St., Glen Cove, 11542-3091.
Blake, Andrew P., St. Andrew, 122 Division St., Sag Harbor, 11963-3154.
Bogert, James, 721 S.W. Lake Court #104, Boynton Beach, FL 33426.
Buckley, Harold P., St. Rose of Lima, Two Bayview Ave., Massapequa, 11758-7299.
Callahan, Zachary, Church of Cure of Ars, 2323 Merrick Ave., Merrick, 11566.
Carmody, James P., 26 Panorama Dr., Binghamton, 13901.
Colasito, Basil C. (Philippines), Church of St. Aloysius, 592 Middle Neck Rd., Great Neck, 11023.

Collins, Edwin J., 24065 Martin Dr., Brooksville, FL 34601.
Connolly, Andrew P., St. Francis de Sales, 7 Amity St., P.O. Box 71, Patchogue, 11772.
Corali, Serafino A., St. Pius X Residence, 1220 Front St., Uniondale, 11553-2097.
Corcoran, John J., St. John the Evangelist, 25 Ocean Ave., Center Moriches, 11934.
D'Souza, Claude J., Church of St. Luke, 2892 S. Congress Ave., Palm Springs, FL 33461.
Dahm, Paul J., 176 Montauk Hwy., Southampton, 11968.
Dailey, William, St. Pius X Residence, 1220 Front St., Uniondale, 11553.
De Vita, James C., 4760-A Greentree Way, Boynton Beach, FL 33436.
Delaney, William I., Maria Regina Residence, 1725 Brentwood Rd., Brentwood, 11717.
Diederich, Donald F., J.C.D., Founders Village Apt. 18 B, 2555 Youngs Ave., Southold, 11971.
Dineros, Santiago A., Church of St. Pius X, One St. Pius X Ct., Plainview, 11803.
Donohoe, Thomas E., Church of St. Mary of the Isle, 315 E. Walnut St., Long Beach, 11561.
Donovan, Richard R., Our Lady of Lourdes, 65 Wright Ave., Malverne, 11565.
Drab, John P., 24 Pheasant Rd., Noyac, 11963-2908.
Driscoll, Paul G., 16 Croyden Rd., Mineola, 11501.
Fernando, Simon, Suwinda Dummalademoya, Wennappuwa, Sri Lanka.
Filmanski, Francis E., Cypress Club Condominiums, 145 Cypress Club Dr., Apt. 509, Pompano Beach, FL 33060.
Fitzgerald, John J., Church of St. James, 429 Route 25A, East Setauket, 11733.
Gallagher, William G., 9949 Shore Rd., Brooklyn, 11209.
Gartner, Charles A., Our Lady of Mercy, 500 S. Oyster Bay Rd., Hicksville, 11801-3570.
Giuntini, Robert J., St. Joseph Guest House, 350 Cuba Hill Rd., Huntington, 11743.
Hagan, Vincent J., Bloomsfield Station, P.O. Box 18 PE Canada.
Hall, Martin J., M.A., St. Bernard, 3100 Hempstead Tpke., Levittown, 11756-1339.
Hannon, James J., Church of St. Brigid, 75 Post Ave., Westbury, 11590.
Heenan, Michael F., 2021 Bonisle Cir., Palm Beach Gardens, FL 33418.
Hein, John (Vietnam), Church of St. Joseph, 1346 Broadway, Hewlett, 11557.
Henry, John P., St. Ignatius, P.O. Box 1306, Tarpon Springs, FL 34688.
Hyatt, Robert A., 298 Elton St., Riverhead, 11901.
Kayser, Robert, Manor Park, 215 Carll's Path, Apt. 4C, Deer Park, 11729.
Kohli, Charles F., St. Joseph Guest House, 350 Cuba Hill Rd., Huntington, 11743.
Kottaram, Mathew, Kottarathil House, Grace Hill, Upper Coonoor, Tamilnadu 643102 India.
Kozlowski, Joseph P., St. Hyacinth, 319 Cedar Swamp Rd., Glen Head, 11545-2296.
LeTure, Theodore J., 2443 S.W. Sansome Ln., Port St. Lucie, FL 34953.
Liu, Peter T., 2886 Fernley Dr. E. #75, West Palm Beach, FL 33417.
Maloney, Thomas P., Church of St. Joseph, 39 N. Carll Ave., Babylon, 11702.
Mason, Robert E., Church of Our Lady of Lourdes, 855 Carmans Rd., Massapequa Park, 11762.
McCabe, John H., St. Pius X Residence, 1220 Front St., Uniondale, 11553.
McCarthy, Thomas, 215 W. Santa Barbara Rd., Lindenhurst, 11757.
McCarthy, William E., M.M., St. Teresa's Residence, P.O. Box 321, Maryknoll, 10545.
McComiskey, Joseph C., 137 Brookside Dr., Smithtown, 11787.
McGann, Diarmuid F., Church of Our Lady of the Snow, 175 Blue Point Ave., Blue Point, 11715.
McMullen, Francis R., 14415 Capt. John Smith Dr., Accokeek, MD 20607.
Minturn, Joseph, 107 Colonial Pkwy., Manhasset, 11030.
Murphy, William T., 288 Court House Rd., Franklin Square, 11010.
Murray, John P., 51 Fox Blvd., Massapequa, 11758.
Newman, Louis I., St. Columba's Rectory, 3327 Glencolum Dr., San Diego, CA 92123.
Nieva, Constantino S., St. Pius X Residence, 1220 Front St., Uniondale, 11553.
Niewczas, Taddeus, 84 Berry St. Apt. 1L, Brooklyn, 11211.
Nuss, Francis B., Church of St. Matthew, 35 N. Service Rd., Dix Hills, 11746.
O'Leary, Lawrence J., Maria Regina Residence, 1725 Brentwood Rd., Brentwood, 11717.
Pascual, Antonio S., J.C.L., Church of St. Francis de Chantal, 1309 Wantaugh Ave., Wantagh, 11793.
Pedzik, Vitalis B., 7-8 State St., New York, 10004.
Punti, George, St. Boniface, 631 Elmont Road, Elmont, 11003-4028.
Rudnicki, Wladyslaw, Church of Our Lady of Ostrabrama, Box 997 Depot Ln., Cutchogue, 11935.
Sheehan, Augustine J., 85 Richmond Blvd. 1A, Ronkonkoma, 11779.
Sheridan, Denis J., St. Pius X Residence, 1220 Front St., Uniondale, 11553-2097.
Siebor, John, Church of St. Ladislaus, 18 Richardson Pl., Hempstead, 11550.
Smith, Robert S., 108 Iriquois Rd., Ithaca, 14850.
Swiatocha, Bruno, 34 Country Club Dr., Shallotte, NC 28470.
Traynor, John J., 25 Pitch Pine Pl., Medford, 11763.
Weerasinghe, Felix M. (Sri Lanka), 52 Alles Rd., Negombo, Sri Lanka.
Whelan, John F., 413 Marcellus Rd., Mineola, 11501.
Wilutis, John P., St. Pius X Residence, 1220 Front St., Uniondale, 11553-2097.
Wodziak, Michael, c/o Mrs. R. Sircovics, 1148 5th Ave., Berwick, PA 18603.

Rt. Rev. Msgr.—
Kelly, James P., St. Agnes Cathedral, 29 Quealy Pl., 11570.

Permanent Deacons:
Abrahams, Vincent, St. Patrick, Smithtown
Altonji, James F., St. Joseph, Ronkonkoma
Anetrella, Louis, Christ the King, Commack
Anisansel, Geoffrey, St. Joseph, Babylon
Aprile, Michael, St. Martin of Tours, Amityville
Ashe, James C., Our Lady of Poland, Southampton
Audia, John, Pastoral Min. for the Deaf
Austin, William, Our Lady of Grace, West Babylon
Banno, Anthony, St. Christopher, Baldwin
Barone, Frank D., St. Kilian, Farmingdale
Bartolotto, Joseph T., St. Louis De Montfort, Sound Beach
Beckles, Vincent, St. Gerard Majella, Port Jefferson Station
Bedell, Paul, Campus Ministry
Behar, Stephen, Mary Immaculate, Bellport
Beirne, James G., St. James, Seaford
Bellevue, Hernst, St. Martha, Uniondale
Benincasa, Joseph, St. Catherine of Sienna, Franklin Square
Bice, Frank, St. Mary, Manhasset
Biggin, James A., St. Martin of Tours, Bethpage
Bilella, Richard, Our Lady Queen of Martyrs, Centerport
Billia, Edward W., St. Hugh of Lincoln, Huntington Station
Blakeney, John, St. Bernard, Levittown
Blasius, Ronald, Ss. Philip & James, St. James
Bohuslaw, James, St. John Nepomucene, Bohemia
Bono, Frank J., St. Joachim, Cedarhurst
Bonocore, Michael, St. Isadore, Riverhead
Borchardt, Frank, St. Patrick, Glen Cove
Braun, Robert G., St. Anthony of Padua, East Northport
Browne, George J., St. Anne, Garden City
Bruck, George P., Our Lady of Good Counsel, Inwood
Brunner, Richard, St. James, Seaford
Buchenberger, Thomas E., St. William the Abbot, Seaford
Burkart, John F., St. Philip Neri, Northport
Burnham, Bruce A., Our Holy Redeemer, Freeport
Byrne, Joseph, Immaculate Conception, Westhampton Beach
Cales, Francisco, Our Holy Redeemer, Freeport
Califano, Joseph, St. Joseph, Ronkonkoma
Cameron, Lachlan, Holy Spirit, New Hyde Park
Campbell, David, St. Gertrude, Bayville
Campbell, Robert, St. Raymond, East Rockaway
Candido, Arthur, Our Lady of Fatima, Manorhaven
Cantave, Jean, St. Francis of Assisi, Greenlawn
Capobianco, Eugene, St. Martin of Tours, Bethpage
Carroll, James P., St. Christopher, Baldwin
Case, Edward M., St. Mary, Roslyn
Casey, William, St. Patrick, Huntington
Cedrone, Anthony M., Our Lady of Peace, Lynbrook
Cepeda, Jose A., Our Lady of Assumption, Copiague
Chamberlain, Anthony J., St. Anthony, Rocky Point
Choi, Stephen Gil Soo, St. Aloysius, Great Neck
Coleman, Thomas, St. Barnabas the Apostle, Bellmore
Connelly, Joseph F., St. Aidan, Williston Park
Connolly, Thomas, St. Raymond, East Rockaway
Costa, Victor R., St. Raphael, East Meadow
Costello, Thomas P., St. Joseph, Hewlett
Cotone, Louis, St. Kilian, Farmingdale
Coughlin, John F., Blessed Sacrament, Valley Stream
Cove, Francis K., Our Lady of Lourdes, Malverne
Croce, Barry, St. Joseph, Babylon
Cunningham, Edward F., St. Thomas the Apostle, West Hempstead
Cusumano, Anthony P., St. John Nepomucene, Bohemia
D'Alessio, Raymond P., St. Edward Confessor, Syosset
D'Angelo, Frank G., St. Peter of Alcantara, Port Washington
D'Auria, Anthony S., St. Thomas the Apostle, West Hempstead
D'Averse, Angelo D., St. Raphael, East Meadow
Daza, H. Nelson, St. Mary of the Isle, Long Beach
DeBellis, Michael J., St. Joseph, Ronkonkoma
DeGuardi, John P., Our Lady of Lourdes, West Islip
Dejewski, Robert, Ss. Peter & Paul, Manorville
Dell'Aglio, Frank, St. Joseph, Ronkonkoma
DeStefano, Carmine E., St. Matthew, Dix Hills
Devenney, Michael L., St. Joseph, Ronkonkoma
Diaz, Juan, St. Anne, Brentwood
Diaz-Granados, Francisco, St. Francis de Sales, Patchogue
DiGiovanna, James R., Resurrection, Farmingville
DiGiuseppe, Peter A., Notre Dame, New Hyde Park
Dobbins, William, St. Joseph, Ronkonkoma
Donza, Gaetano, St. Raymond, East Rockaway
Dougherty, Joseph M., St. Joseph, Ronkonkoma
Dunphy, Patrick J., Our Lady of Hope, Carle Place
Ervin, Christopher, St. Rosalie, Hampton Bays
Evrard, Thomas J., Our Lady of Peace, Lynbrook
Failla, John, St. Elizabeth, Melville
Farley, Owen, Holy Cross, Nesconset
Faulkenberry, Lawrence, Church of the Most Holy Trinity, East Hampton
Ferreiro, Douglas, Holy Spirit, New Hyde Park
Ferri, Richard, St. Martin of Tours, Amityville
Finter, Frederick E., St. John the Baptist, Wading River
Fitzpatrick, John F., Ss. Cyril and Methodius, Deer Park
Flannery, James W., St. Anthony, Oceanside
Flood, Frank J., St. Rose of Lima, Massapequa
Fodale, John E., St. Catherine of Siena, Franklin Square
Forbes, Thomas J., St. Rose of Lima, Massapequa
Ford, John E., St. Thomas the Apostle, West Hempstead
Fox, Thomas, St. Boniface Martyr, Sea Cliff
Gagnon, Jules O. A., Our Lady of the Miraculaous Medal, Wyandanch
Gargiulo, Andrew T., Maria Regina, Seaford
Gariboldi, Frank, St. John of God, Central Islip
Geoghan, Kenneth, St. Jude, Mastic Beach
Gerace, Patrick C., St. Mark, Shoreham
Gillen, Thomas J., St. Jude's, Mastic Beach
Gillette, Ronald J., St. John of God, Central Islip
Giraldo, Luis D., St. Hugh of Lincoln, Huntington Station
Goldburg, Charles R., St. Joachim, Cederhurst
Gonzalez, Francisco, St. Catherine of Sienna, Franklin Square
Graff, Charles, Our Lady of Grace, West Babylon
Graviano, Anthony, Our Lady of Mount Carmel, Patchogue
Grebe, John, St. Elizabeth Ann Seton, Lake Ronkonkoma
Gronenthal, Robert W., Our Lady of Snow, Blue Point
Guilfu, Juan, St. Patrick, Glen Cove
Hanly, James, St. Matthew, Dix Hills
Hartmann, Frank C., Our Lady of the Snow, Blue Point
Hennessy, Thomas R., St. Martin of Tours, Bethpage
Hernandez, Robert, Good Shepherd, Holbrook
Herrmann, Mark, St. Jude, Mastic Beach
Heschl, Robert J., Sts. Philip & James, St. James
Hickey, John, Our Lady of Hope, Carle Place
Huber, Charles F., SS. Cyril & Methodius, Deer Park
Iandoli, Richard, St. Barnabas the Apostle, Bellmore
Jackson, Thomas H., Queen of the Most Holy Rosary, Roosevelt
Kammerer, Charles, St. Mary, Manhasset
Keach, Frank, St. Patrick, Bay Shore
Keenan, John, Sts. Philip & James, St. James
Kogler, William E., St. Margaret of Scotland, Selden
Kolakowski, Theodore, St. Boniface Martyr, Sea Cliff
Kramer, Steven L., Our Lady of the Snow, Blue Point
Kruse, Robert A., Infant Jesus, Port Jefferson
LaBella, Patrick, St. Lawrence the Martyr, Sayville
LaRossa, Richard W., St. Raymond, East Rockaway
Lewis, Clinton, Queen of the Most Holy Rosary, Roosevelt
Leyden, Michael J., St. Joseph, Babylon
Logan, George, Most Holy Trinity, East Hampton
Logsdon, Patrick B., Anthony House, Roosevelt
Longo, Allan D., St. Francis of Assisi, Greenlawn
Love, Francis J., St. Aidan, Williston Park
Lucie, Thomas, Our Lady of Lourdes, West Islip

Luken, Richard A., St. Luke, Brentwood
Lynch, John, St. William the Abbot, Seaford
Lyon, Robert, Mary Immaculate, Bellport
Maffeo, Joseph R., St. Elizabeth Ann Seton, Lake Ronkonkoma
Maggipinto, Anthony V., SS. Philip and James, St. James
Maher, Kenneth, SS. Philip & James, St. James
Mais, George A., Jr., St. Ignatius Loyola, Hicksville
Mannix, Brian, Corpus Christi, Mineola
Marfoglio, Joseph, Christ the King, Commack
Marino, Francis, St. Kilian, Farmingdale
McCormack, Kevin, Our Lady of Peace, Lynbrook
McDaid, Thomas P., St. Agnes, Rockville Centre
McGauvran, John W., Queen of the Most Holy Rosary, Bridgehampton
McGonigle, John H., Holy Family, Hicksville
McGowan, John, Our Lady of Mercy, Hicksville
McGuinness, Francis B., St. Rose of Lima, Massapequa
McIndoe, Martin B., St. Francis de Sales, Patchogue
McKenna, John J., St. Joseph, Garden City
McKenna, Michael A., St. Boniface, Elmont
McLaughlin, James, St. Anthony of Padua, Rocky Point
McNicholas, Joseph G., Holy Family, Hicksville
McQuade, James J., St. Matthew, Dix Hills
Meehan, John J., Our Lady of Lourdes, West Islip
Mercolino, Joseph T., St. Elizabeth, Melville
Metzdorff, Michael C., St. Brigid, Westbury
Mildeberger, William, St. Boniface, Elmont
Miller, Brian, Our Lady of Grace, West Babylon
Mills, Philip, Jr., Our Lady of the Assumption, Copiague
Mongillo, Robert, St. Rosalie, Hampton Bays
Montelione, Michael, Assumption of BVM, Centereach
Mora, Alfredo, St. Patrick, Glen Cove
Moran, John, Sacred Hearts of Jesus and Mary, Southampton
Morris, James P., St. Brigid, Westbury
Mott, Roger P., St. John Nepomucene, Bohemia
Mulligan, Lawrence P., Our Lady of Victory, Floral Park
Murano, James A., Ss. Cyril & Methodius, Deer Park
Muratore, Biagio V., St. Margaret of Scotland, Selden
Murphy, Galvin C., St. John the Evangelist, Center Moriches
Murphy, James, St. Edward the Confessor, Syosset
Muscarnera, Charles, St. Christopher, Baldwin
Mystkowski, Joseph J., Our Lady of Mt. Carmel, Patchogue
Naylor, Montford D., St. Francis Cabrini, Coram
Nealis, George F., St. Joseph, Babylon
Neuhedel, Paul, Maria Regina, Seaford
Newhall, John, Good Shepherd, Holbrook
Newton, Philip, St. Ignatius Martyr, Long Beach
Nuzzi, John, Maria Regina, Seaford
O'Brien, James J., St. Anne, Garden City
O'Connor, Dennis R., St. Rose of Lima, Massapequa
O'Connor, John, St. Anthony, Oceanside
O'Connor, Thomas F., Good Shepherd, Holbrook
O'Donovan, Robert S., St. Frances de Chantal, Wantagh
O'Hara, James, Holy Name of Mary, Valley Stream
O'Neill, James, St. Anthony, Oceanside
Odin, Frank A., Our Lady of Perpetual Help, Lindenhurst
Otton, Daniel, St. Joseph, Hewlett
Owen, George, St. Kilian, Farmingdale
Owens, Thomas F., St. James, Setauket
Padula, Wayne, St. James, Setauket
Pagnotta, Carmen, St. Frances Cabrini, Coram
Paolicelli, Philip, St. Margaret of Scotland, Selden
Pellegrino, Joseph C., St. Christopher, Baldwin
Peralta, Joseph F., St. Patrick, Bay Shore
Perez, Juan, Our Lady of Loretto, Hempstead
Pesce, Frank V., St. Brigid, Westbury
Pettorino, John C., SS. Peter and Paul, Manorville
Philppeaux, Jacques, St. Thomas the Apostle, West Hempstead
Pickford, Albert, St. Joseph the Worker, East Patchogue
Polanco, Luis Roberto, St. Matthew, Dix Hills
Powers, William J., Infant Jesus, Port Jefferson
Pozzolano, Vincent, St. John the Baptist, Wading River
Quinn, Thomas J., St. Rose of Lima, Massapequa
Quinones, Fernando J., St. Francis de Sales, Patchogue
Raad, Richard, Holy Name of Mary, Valley Stream
Ramos, Manuel J., St. Brigid, Westbury
Rasanen, Terence A., St. Anne, Brentwood
Reda, Gerard, Ss. Philip & James, St. James
Reich, George F., St. John Nepomucene, Bohemia
Reilly, Thomas, St. Edward the Confessor, Syosset
Reilly, Thomas J., St. Hugh of Lincoln, Huntington Station
Reinhart, John C., Corpus Christi, Mineola
Rich, Thomas B., J.C.L., D.Min., Our Lady of Hope, Carle Place
Rieger, John, Our Lady Queen of Martyrs, Centerport
Riegger, George J., St. Sylvester, Medford
Rivera, Franklin, St. Sylvester, Medford
Rivera, Wenceslao, St. Luke, Brentwood
Roa, Jose, Our Lady of Loretto, Hempstead
Romero, Miguel A., St. Anne, Brentwood
Ruggieri, Clyde, Holy Name of Mary, Valley Stream
Saffran, Irwin, Our Lady of Grace, West Babylon
Samson, Thomas R., St. Anne, Brentwood
Sanchez, Cristobal, Our Holy Redeemer, Freeport
Sandberg, Louis C., Queen of the Most Holy Rosary Church, Roosevelt
Sanfilippo, Carl, St. Andrew, Sag Harbor
Schultz, Peter F., St. John the Evangelist, Riverhead
Scollan, Joseph M., St. Margaret of Scotland, Selden
Senholzi, Gregory B., St. John the Baptist, Wading River
Sheehan, John W., St. Martin of Tours, Amityville
Sherlock, Bernard F., St. Barnabas Apostle, Bellmore
Silien, Dominique, St. Boniface, Elmont
Simeone, Joseph, St. Jude, Mastic Beach
Sisinni, Christopher, Our Lady Queen of Martyrs, Centerport
Smith, Douglas, Our Lady of Perpetual Help, Lindenhurst
Smith, Roy, St. Joseph, Kings Park
Squiteri, Aniello, Our Lady of Peace, Lynbrook
Stamm, Donald, St. Agnes Cathedral, Rockville Centre
Steffens, Gerard K., Holy Cross, Nesconset
Sullivan, John F., St. Joseph, Babylon
Sullivan, Kenneth R., St. Martha, Uniondale
Swane, Gary, St. Louis de Montfort, Sound Beach
Sykes, Jeffrey, Church of the Sacred Heart, Cutchogue
Tappin, Edward, Church of the Good Shepherd, Holbrook
Taranto, Vito, St. Hugh, Huntington Station
Teufel, John G., Our Lady of Lourdes, West Islip
Tirelli, Raymond J., Our Lady of Hope, Carle Place
Torres, Joseph, St. Frances de Chantal, Wantagh
Trodden, John E., St. Joseph, Kings Park
Valdaro, Domenick, Our Lady Lourdes, Massapequa Park
Valdes, Jesus, St. Dominic, Oyster Bay
Vigliotta, Crescenzo T., St. John the Evangelist, Center Moriches
Villani, Salvatore B., St. Aidan, Williston Park
Waldmann, Richard E., Infant Jesus, Port Jefferson
Walters, John, St. Anne, Brentwood
Weisz, Robert D., St. Thomas More, Hauppauge
Wetzel, Edward V., St. Kilian, Farmingdale
Whitfield, Gerald F., Maria Regina, Seaford
Zirkel, Don, Our Lady of the Miraculous Medal, Wyandanch

INSTITUTIONS LOCATED IN THE DIOCESE

[A] SEMINARIES, DIOCESAN

HUNTINGTON. *Diocesan Seminary of the Immaculate Conception*, 440 West Neck Rd., 11743. Tel: 631-423-0483; Fax: 631-423-2346. Email: info@icseminary.edu. Most Rev. William Francis Murphy, S.T.D., L.H.D., Chm., Bd. of Governors; Rev. Msgrs. James M. McDonald, Rector; Charles R. Fink, Dir. Spiritual Formation; Sr. Mary Louise Brink, S.C., Ph.D., Academic Dean; Rev. Msgr. James P. Swiader, Dir. Pastoral Formation & Dean of Seminarians; Elyse B. Hayes, M.L.S., Library Dir.; Dennis J. Schlosser, Dir. Finance & Operations; Ms. Kathryn Zahner, Registrar; Rev. Patrick J. Griffin, C.M., Prof. of Scripture; Katherine M. Hayes, Ph.D., Prof. of Scripture; Revs. Gerard H. Luttenberger, C.M., Prof. of Systematic Theology; Peter I. Vaccari, S.T.L., Assoc. Prof. of Church History; Richard G. Henning, M.A., M.Div., Assoc. Prof. of Scripture; Michael Hoonhout, Ph.D., Assoc. Prof. of Systematic Theology; Rev. Charles Caccavale, S.T.L., S.T.D., Assoc. Prof. of Moral Theology. Priests 8; Sisters 1; Lay Professors 2; Support Lay Staff 25; Seminarians 40; M.A. Students 132.

[B] COLLEGES AND UNIVERSITIES

ROCKVILLE CENTRE. *Molloy College* (1955) 1000 Hempstead Ave., P.O. Box 5002, 11571-5002. Tel: 516-678-5000; 888-466-5569; Fax: 516-678-7295. Web: www.molloy.edu. Drew Bogner, Ph.D., Pres.; Linda Albanese, Vice Pres. for Enrollment Management; Valerie Collins, Ph.D., Vice Pres. Academic Affairs & Dean Faculty; Sr. Dorothy Anne Fitzgibbons, O.P., Ed.D., Vice Pres. for Mission; Robert Houlihan, Vice Pres. Student Affairs; Michael McGovern, Vice Pres. Finance & Treas.; Edward J. Thompson, Vice Pres. for Advancement; Robert Paterson, Ph.D., Vice Pres. Information Technology, Planning & Research; Rev. John A. Madigan, O.P., M.A., Chap. Priests 4; Chaplains 1; Sisters of St. Dominic (Amityville Community) 22; Lay Teachers 499; Students 4,025.

[C] HIGH SCHOOLS, DIOCESAN

NASSAU COUNTY

HICKSVILLE
Holy Trinity Diocesan High School (1966) 98 Cherry Ln., 11801. Tel: 516-433-2900; Fax: 516-433-2827. Email: hths98@holytrinityhs.echalk.com. Web: www.holytrinityhs.org. Mr. Gene Fennell, Prin. Tel: 516-433-2900, Ext. 140; Rev. Joseph Fitzgerald, M.Div., Chap. Sisters 3; Lay Teachers 94; Students 1,410. In Res. Revs. Brian Barr; Irinel Racos.

SUFFOLK COUNTY

RIVERHEAD
McGann Mercy High School, 1225 Ostrander Ave., 11901. Tel: 631-727-5900; Fax: 631-727-8483; 631-369-7328. Web: www.mcgann-mercy.org. Dr. Steven F. Cheeseman, Prin.; Mrs. Lisa Navarra, Asst. Prin.; Mr. Charles Bender, Dean of Students. Directed by the Diocese of Rockville Centre/Sisters of Mercy., (Coed) Sisters of Mercy (Brooklyn) 2; Other Sisters 1; Lay Teachers 35; Students 495.

WEST ISLIP
St. John the Baptist, 1170 Montauk Hwy., 11795. Tel: 631-587-8000; Fax: 631-587-8996. Web: www.stjohnsdhs.org. Walter D. Lace, Prin.; Rev. Michael Holzmann, Chap. Priests 1; Sisters 3; Lay Teachers 113; Students 1,736.

[D] HIGH SCHOOLS, PRIVATE

HEMPSTEAD. *Sacred Heart Academy* College preparatory-girls, 47 Cathedral Ave., 11550. Tel: 516-483-7383; Fax: 516-483-1016. Email: sha@sacredheartacademyhempstead.org. Web: www.sacredheartacademyhempstead.org. Sisters Jeanne Marie Ross, C.S.J., Pres.; Joanne Forker, C.S.J., Prin.; Regina Foge, Librarian. Sisters 6; Lay Teachers 69; Students 897.

MINEOLA. *Chaminade High School (Boys)* (1930) Directed by the Society of Mary (Marianists), 340 Jackson Ave., 11501. Tel: 516-742-5555; Fax: 516-742-1989. Email: flyers@chaminade-hs.org. Web: www.chaminade-hs.org. Rev. James C. Williams, S.M., Pres.; Bro. Joseph D. Bellizzi, S.M., Prin.; Mr. Salvatore Trentacoste, Asst. Prin.; Mr. Daniel Petruccio, Dir. of Guidance; Bro. Thomas J. Cleary, S.M., Dean of Students; Mr. Michael Ingrassia, Dir. Student Svcs.; Rev. Garrett J. Long, S.M., Chap.; Bro. Peter H. Heiskell, S.M., Dir. of Apostolic Action. Priests 3; Brothers 18; Lay Teachers 55; Students 1,700.

SOUTH HUNTINGTON. *St. Anthony's High School* (1933) College Prep., 275 Wolf Hill Rd., 11747-1394. Tel: 631-271-2020; Fax: 631-547-6820. Email: administration@stanthonyshs.org. Web: www.stanthonyshs.org. Bro. Gary Cregan, O.S.F., Prin. Directed by the Franciscan Brothers of Brooklyn. Priests 1; Brothers 18; Permanent Deacons 1; Intercommunity Sisters 7; Lay Teachers 108; Students 2,400.

SYOSSET. *Our Lady of Mercy Academy* Girls-day students., 815 Convent Rd., 11791-3895. Tel: 516-921-1047; Fax: 516-921-3634. Email: olma1@yahoo.com. Web: www.olma.org. Sr. Helen Lyons, R.S.M., Co-Prin.; Mrs. Joan Gordon, Co-Prin.; Mrs. Sheila Wilson, Librarian. Directed by the Sisters of Mercy/Mid-Atlantic Community. Sisters of Mercy 3; Sisters of St. Joseph 1; Sisters of St. Dominic 1; Sisters of St. Ursula 1; Lay Teachers 49; Students 525.

UNIONDALE. *Kellenberg Memorial High School* (1987) 1400 Glenn Curtiss Blvd., 11553. Tel: 516-292-0200; Fax: 516-292-0877. Email: brokenneth@kellenberg.org. Web: www.kellenberg.org. Rev. Philip K. Eichner, S.M., Pres.; Bro. Kenneth M. Hoagland, S.M., Prin.; Rev. Albert Bertoni, S.M., Asst. Prin. Guidance; Ms. Maria Korzekwinski, Asst. Prin. Latin School; Bro. Roger Poletti, S.M., Asst. Prin. Activities; Rev. Thomas A. Cardone, S.M., Chap.; Mrs. Marina Trentacoste, Dean of Students; Mr. John McCutcheon, Dean of Men; Bro. Richard Hughes, S.M., Dir. Apostolic Activities; Mr. Edward Solosky, Athletic Dir.; Mr. John Krumm, Supvr. of Building Maintenance & Landscaping; Bro. Donald Nussbaum, S.M., Suprv. New Construction, Vehicles; Mr. Jim Payne, Supvr. Cleaning Maintenance; Mrs. Catherine Zabrouski, Financial Supvr.; Bro. David

Bruner, S.M., Librarian. Directed by the Society of Mary. Priests 4; Brothers 10; Lay Teachers 109; Students 2,581.

[E] REGIONAL SCHOOLS

BELLMORE. *St. Elizabeth Ann Seton Regional School* Tel: 516-785-5709; Fax: 516-785-4468. Email: lag@seas.edrvc.org. Supported by the following parishes: St. Barnabas, Bellmore; St. Raphael, East Meadow; Cure of Ars, Merrick; St. Frances de Chantal, Wantagh. Lay Teachers 29; Students 341.

Bellmore Campus, 2341 Washington Ave., 11710. Tel: 516-785-5709; Fax: 516-785-4468. Leeann Graziose, Prin. Sisters 1; Lay Teachers 31; Students 450.

Wantagh Campus, 1309 Wantagh Ave., Wantagh, 11793. Tel: 516-826-3882; Fax: 516-679-2082. N-K Early Childhood Center Lay Teachers 4; Students 145.

CENTER MORICHES. *Our Lady, Queen of Apostles Regional School*, 2 St. Johns Pl., 11934. Tel: 631-878-1033; Fax: 631-878-1059. Email: sreileen@olqa.edruc.org. Sr. Eileen Martin, S.C., Prin. Supported by the following parishes: St. John Evangelist, Center Moriches; St. Jude, Mastic Beach; Immaculate Conception, Westhampton Beach; Ss. Peter & Paul, Manorville. Sisters 2; Lay Teachers 19; Students 294.

CENTRAL ISLIP. *Our Lady of Providence Regional School* (1992) 82 Carleton Ave., 11722. Tel: 631-234-6324; Fax: 631-234-6360. Email: provcsj@aol.com. Web: www.olprov.org. Jo Ann DiNardo, Prin.; Lorena Fitzpatrick, School Sec. Supported by the following parishes: St. Anne, Brentwood; St. Luke, Brentwood; St. John of God, Central Islip; St. Peter the Apostle, Islip Terrace. Sisters 1; Lay Teachers 21; Students 270.

COMMACK. *Holy Family Regional School*, Indian Head Rd., P.O. Box 729, 11725. Tel: 631-543-0202; Fax: 631-543-2818. Email: hfrs@aol.com. Mrs. Constance Jenkins, Prin.; Sr. Dorothy Sconzo, Librarian. Supported by the following parishes: Christ the King, Commack; St. Matthew, Dix Hills; St. Thomas More, Hauppauge; St. Joseph, Kings Park. Sisters 4; Lay Teachers 17; Students 340.

CUTCHOGUE. *Our Lady of Mercy Regional School*, 27685 Main Rd., P.O. Box 970, 11935. Tel: 631-734-5166; Fax: 631-734-4266. Email: olm@olmregional.org; ldelgenio@olmregional.org. Web: www.olmregional.org. Mrs. Lorraine Del Genio, Prin. Supported by the following parishes: Sacred Heart, Cutchogue; Our Lady of Ostrabrama, Cutchogue; St. Agnes, Greenport; and St. Patrick, Southold. Lay Teachers 11; Students 141.

EAST NORTHPORT. *Trinity Regional School*, 1025 Fifth Ave., 11731. Tel: 631-261-5130; Fax: 631-266-5345. Email: tregion@optonline.net. Web: trinityregional.com. Ms. Jeanne Morcone, Prin.; Mrs. Patricia Ayers, Asst. Prin.; Mrs. Mary Ellen McFaul, Librarian. Supported by the following parishes: Our Lady Queen of Martyrs, Centerport; St. Anthony of Padua, East Northport; St. Francis of Assisi, Greenlawn; St. Hugh of Lincoln, Huntington Station; St. Elizabeth, Melville; St. Philip Neri, Northport. Sisters 1; Lay Teachers 32; Students 600.

Satellite campuses exist at:

175 Wolf Hill Rd., Melville, 11747-1340. Tel: 631-549-7450; Fax: 631-549-7464. Email: tregion@optonline.net. Web: trinityregional.com.

364 Main St., Northport, 11768. Tel: 631-261-8520; Fax: 631-261-8560. Email: tregion@optonline.net. Web: trinityregional.com.

FARMINGDALE. *St. John Baptist de LaSalle Regional School*, (Grades N-8) Tel: 516-694-3610; Fax: 516-694-7296. Email: jbaptisoffice@optionline.net. Ms. Christine Bendish, Prin.; Eileen Navagh, Librarian. Supported by the following parishes: St. Martin of Tours, Bethpage; St. Kilian, Farmingdale; St. Pius X, Plainview; St. James, Seaford. Lay Teachers 16; Students 222.

GLEN COVE. *All Saints Regional Catholic School*, 12 Pearsall Ave., 11542-3052. Tel: 516-676-0762; Fax: 516-676-0660. Web: www.asrcatholic.com. Supported by the following parishes: St. Boniface, Sea Cliff; St. Hyacinth, Glen Head; St. Mary, Roslyn; St. Patrick, Glen Cove; St. Rocco, Glen Cove. Lay Teachers 26; Students 434.

Primary Campus (Grades N-PreSchool), 319 Cedar Swamp Rd., Glen Head, 11545-2298. Tel: 516-671-4247; Fax: 516-671-4247.

Upper Campus (Grades K-8), 12 Pearsall Ave., 11542-3052. Tel: 516-676-0762; Fax: 516-676-0660. James W. Thompson, Prin.; Theresa A. Kemp, Librarian.

LONG BEACH. *Long Beach Catholic Regional School*, (Grades PreK-8), 735 W. Broadway, 11561. Tel: 516-432-8900; Fax: 516-432-3841. Email: lbcatholic@aol.com. Web: lbcrs.org. Mrs. Veronica Danca, Prin. Supported by the following parishes: St. Ignatius, Long Beach; St. Mary of the Isle, Long Beach, and Our Lady of the Miraculous Medal, Point Lookout. Sisters 2; Lay Teachers 25; Students 500.

PATCHOGUE. *Holy Angels Regional School* (1923) (Grades K-8), Division St., 11772. Tel: 631-475-0422; Fax: 631-475-2036. Email: smelise@optonline.net. Web: www.holyangelsregional.org. Sr. Elise Bier, R.S.M., Prin. Supported by the following parishes: Mary Immaculate, Bellport; St. Frances Cabrini, Coram; St. Joseph the Worker, E. Patchogue; St. Sylvester, Medford; Our Lady of Mount Carmel, Patchogue; St. Frances de Sales, Patchogue, and St. Margaret of Scotland, Selden. Sisters 3; Lay Teachers 19; Students 380.

PORT JEFFERSON. *Our Lady of Wisdom Regional School*, 114-116 Myrtle Ave., 11777. Tel: 631-473-1211; Fax: 631-473-1064. Email: ninaed@optonline.net. Web: www.ourladyofwisdom.com. Dorothy Onysko, Prin. Supported by the following parishes: Infant Jesus, Port Jefferson; St. Louis de Montfort, Sound Beach; St. James, Setauket; St. Gerard Majella, Port Jefferson Station. Lay Teachers 14; Students 225; Total Staff 25.

SAG HARBOR. *Stella Maris Regional School*, 135 Division St., 11963. Tel: 631-725-2525; Fax: 631-725-0568. Email: stellamarisrs@yahoo.com. Web: www.StellaMarisSchool.org. Ms. Jane Peters, Prin.; Joanne Brady, Librarian. Supported by the following parishes: St. Therese of Lisieux, Montauk; Most Holy Trinity, East Hampton; St. Andrew, Sag Harbor; Queen of the Most Holy Rosary, Bridgehampton; Our Lady of the Isle, Shelter Island. Sisters 2; Lay Teachers 17; Students 220.

SAYVILLE. *Prince of Peace Regional Catholic School* (1992) (Grades N-8), 200 Main St., 11782. Tel: 631-589-3426; Fax: 631-589-4523. Web: www.poprcs.org. Jane F. Harrigan, Prin.; Mrs. Patricia Fried, Librarian. Supported by the following parishes: Our Lady of Snow, Blue Point; St. John Nepomucene, Bohemia; Good Shepherd, Holbrook; St. Lawrence, Sayville. Lay Teachers 20; Students 240.

SOUTHAMPTON. *Our Lady of the Hamptons Regional School*, (Grades PreK-8), 160 N. Main St., 11968. Tel: 631-283-9140; Fax: 631-287-3958. Email: sks@hamptons.com. Web: www.olh.org. Nursery and PreK.; Supported by the following parishes: St. Rosalie, Hampton Bays; Our Lady of Poland, Southampton, and Sacred Hearts Jesus Mary, Southampton.

31 Montauk Hwy., Hampton Bays, 11946. Tel: 631-723-3740; Fax: 631-728-2559. Sisters Kathryn Schlueter, C.S.J., Prin.; Virginia Crowley, C.S.J., Asst. Prin.; Linda Robins, Librarian. Sisters 2; Lay Teachers 26; Students 376.

[F] ELEMENTARY SCHOOLS, PRIVATE

FREEPORT. *The De La Salle School* (2001) 87 Pine St., 11520-3615. Tel: 516-379-8660; Fax: 516-379-8806. Email: DeLaSalleLI@hotmail.com. Web: www.delasalleschool.org. Bro. Thomas P. Casey, F.S.C., Exec. Dir.; Kevin Rall, Dean Student Life; Kathleen Boniello, Dean Academics. Brothers 1; Lay Teachers 6; Total Enrollment 61.

MANHASSET. *Our Lady of Grace Montessori School and Center*, (Grades N-2), 29 Shelter Rock Rd., 11030. Tel: 516-365-9832; Fax: 516-365-9329. Sr. Kelly Quinn, Prin. Sisters, Servants of the Immaculate Heart of Mary 3; Lay Teachers 18; Students 213.

OLD WESTBURY. *Holy Child Academy*, (Grades N-8), 25 Store Hill Rd., 11568. Tel: 516-626-9300; Fax: 516-626-7914. Email: cbowen@holychildacademy.org. Web: www.holychildacademy.org. Mr. Michael O'Donoghue, Head of School; Palma Gartland, Asst. to Head; Gail Walker, Dir. Curriculum & Professional Devel.; Chris Cannon, Dean Middle School. Lay Teachers 50; Students 250.

UNIONDALE. *St. Martin de Porres Marianist School* (2004) 530 Hempstead Blvd., 11553. Tel: 516-481-3303; Fax: 516-483-4138. Web: www.stmartinmarianist.org. Bro. Kenneth M. Hoagland, S.M., Prin.; Mr. John Holian, Headmaster; Mrs. Andrea Nordquist, Asst. Prin.; Bro. James W. Conway, S.M., Dir. Student Svcs. Brothers 2; Sisters 1; Lay Teachers 20; Students 460.

[G] SPECIALIZED CHILD CARE AGENCIES

NESCONSET. *Cleary Deaf Child Center, Inc.* (1925) 301 Smithtown Blvd., 11767. Tel: 631-588-0530 (Voice and TTY); Fax: 631-588-0016. Email: kenm@clearyschool.org. Web: www.clearyschool.org. Mr. Kenneth Morseon, Supt. Directed by Catholic Charities., Day School (Infants thru 21 years). Students 85.

SYOSSET. *MercyFirst* (1894) 525 Convent Rd., 11791-3864. Tel: 516-921-0808; Fax: 516-921-4542. Email: gmccaffery@mercyfirst.org. Web: www.mercyfirst.org. Gerard McCaffery, CEO. Under the sponsorship of the Sisters of Mercy., Residential services provided in campus and group home settings, including diagnostic/group emergency foster care, non secure detention, hard to place (JD and clinically intensive), abuse treatment and prevention, mother/child, and OMH programs.; Foster Boarding Home/Adoption, Aftercare and Prevention Services programs provide services in Nassau, Queens and Brooklyn. Bed Capacity 193; Total Assisted 3,891; Total Staff 615.

WADING RIVER. *Little Flower Children & Family Services of New York* (1929) 2450 N. Wading River Rd., 11792-1402. Tel: 631-929-6200; Fax: 631-929-6121. Web: www.LittleFlowerNY.org. Sr. Rita Wasilewski, C.S.F.N., Supr.; Grace G. Lo Grande, Exec. Dir. & CEO; Kevin Kundmueller, CFO. Sisters of the Holy Family of Nazareth., Affiliated with the Diocese of Brooklyn. Foster care, adoption & post-adoption svcs., intermediate care facilities, residential treatment center, Special Act school district, family day care, family care for MR/DD clients, foster homes for teen mothers & their babies. Therapeutic foster boarding homes. Eldercare Solutions: Counseling for employees of client organizations. Bed Capacity 141; Total Assisted 2,600; Total Staff 525.

[H] CATHOLIC CHARITIES

HICKSVILLE. *Catholic Charities*, 90 Cherry Ln., 11801-6299. Tel: 516-733-7000; Fax: 516-733-7099. Web: www.catholiccharities.cc. Laura A. Cassell, CEO. Tel: 516-733-7013; Paul Engelhart, Chief Oper. Officer. Tel: 516-733-7012; Fax: 516-733-7099; Robert J. Manfredi, Dir., IT. Tel: 516-733-7003; Fax: 516-733-7098; John Gonta, Dir., Purchasing & Facilities. Tel: 516-733-7090; Fax: 516-733-7099; Anthony Mullen, Chief Community Svcs. Officer.

Human Resources, 90 Cherry Lane, 11801-6299. Tel: 516-733-7005; Fax: 516-733-7038. Edward Moore, Dir., Human Resources. Tel: 516-733-7005; Fax: 516-733-7038.

Finance, 90 Cherry Ln., 11801-6299. Tel: 516-733-7015; Fax: 516-733-7099. Edwin M. Kennedy, CFO; Richard Balcom, Dir. Finance.

Mental Health Residences, 333 N. Main St., Freeport, 11520. Tel: 516-634-0012; Fax: 516-634-0017. Howard G. Duff, Prog. Dir., Mental Health Progs.

Regina Maternity Services/Mentoring Tel: 516-223-7888; Fax: 516-223-2752. Kathleen Ryan, Dir. Maternity Svcs.

Regina Maternity Services Corporation, 90 Cherry Ln., 11801.

Chemical Dependency Services, 155 Indian Head Rd., Commack, 11725. Tel: 631-543-6200; Fax: 631-543-6203.

Outpatient Clinics:

Talbot House Alcohol Crisis Center, 30-C Carlough Rd., Bohemia, 11716. Tel: 631-589-4144; Fax: 631-589-3281. Kathleen Ayers-Lanzillotta, Dir., Chemical Dependency Svcs.

Mental Health Programs, 333 N. Main St., Freeport, 11520. Tel: 516-634-0012, Ext. 126; Fax: 516-634-0017. Howard G. Duff, Dir., Mental Health Svcs.

Dental Services Program, 333 N. Main St., Freeport, 11520. Tel: 516-623-4420; Fax: 516-623-1313. Dr. Fabiola Milford, Dental Dir.

Housing Services (1980) 90 Cherry Ln., 11801-6299. Tel: 516-733-7076; Fax: 516-733-7098. Jay Korth, Dir. Housing & Legal Affairs.

Commodity Supplemental Food Program, 66 N. 19th St., Wyandanch, 11798. Tel: 631-491-4166; Fax: 631-491-4950.

Health Services:

Office for Persons with Disabilities, 147 Schleigel Blvd., Amityville, 11701. Tel: 631-789-5218; Fax: 631-789-3844.

Residential Services, 147 Schleigel Blvd., Amityville, 11701. Tel: 631-665-3434; Fax: 631-665-3586. Diane Ammirati, Dir. Disability Svcs.

Bi-County Alliance of Senior Clubs Tel: 516-733-7051; Fax: 516-733-7099.

Sr. Services Case Management, 201 Debevoise Ave., Roosevelt, 11575. Tel: 516-348-8010; Fax: 516-546-0502.

Senior Services, 90 Cherry Ln., 11801. Tel: 516-733-7071; Fax: 516-733-7098. Eileen Verity, Dir., Senior Svcs.

Immigrant Services, 143 Schleigel Blvd., Amityville, 11701. Tel: 631-789-5210; Fax: 631-789-5245. Carmen Maquilon, Dir., Immigrant Svcs.

Parish Social Ministry, 90 Cherry Ln., 11801. Tel: 516-733-7059; Fax: 516-733-7098. Jan Jamroz, Prog. Dir., Parish Social Min. Tel: 516-733-7084.

Central Intake & Referral Developers Tel: 516-733-7045; Fax: 516-733-7098.

Development and Communications, 90 Cherry Ln.,

11801. Tel: 516-733-7042; Fax: 516-733-7098. Scott A. Stepp, Dir. Devel. & Communications. Tel: 516-733-7042.
Catholic Charities Health Systems Corp. of the Diocese of Rockville Centre, Inc.
Catholic Charities Support Corp.

[I] CATHOLIC HEALTHCARE APOSTOLATE NASSAU COUNTY

ROCKVILLE CENTRE
Catholic Health Services of Long Island dba Catholic Health System of Long Island, Inc. 992 N. Village Ave., 11570. Tel: 516-705-3700; Fax: 516-705-3730. Web: www.chsli.org.
Catholic Healthcare Network of Long Island, 992 N. Village Ave., 11570. Tel: 516-705-3700; Fax: 516-705-3730. Mr. James Harden, Pres. & CEO; Richard J.J. Sullivan Jr., Bd. Chair; Sr. Elaine Callahan, Vice Chair; Thomas F. Christman, Treas.; Terence G. Daly, Senior Vice Pres. Finance & Chief Fin. Officer; Joel Yohai, M.D., Senior Vice Pres. Medical Affairs & CMO; Patricia Garofalo Esq., J.D., Senior Vice Pres. & Gen. Counsel.
Hospitals:
St. Charles Hospital and Rehabilitation Center, 200 Belle Terre Rd., Port Jefferson, 11777. Tel: 631-474-6600; Fax: 631-474-6884. William E. Allison, Pres. & CEO; James O'Connor, Exec. Vice Pres.
Catholic Charities Health Systems, 90 Cherry Ln., Hicksville, 11801.
Mercy Medical Center, 1000 N. Village Ave., 11570. Tel: 516-705-1401; Fax: 516-705-1406. Alan D. Guerci, M.D., Pres. & CEO; Nancy Simmons, Exec. Vice Pres.
St. Francis Hospital, 100 Port Washington Blvd., Roslyn, 11576. Tel: 516-629-2445; Fax: 516-629-2448. Alan D. Guerci, M.D., Pres. & CEO; Akram Boutros, M.D., Exec. Vice Pres. & Chief Admin. Officer.
St. Catherine of Siena Medical Center, 50 Rte. 25A, Smithtown, 11787. Tel: 631-862-3000; Fax: 631-862-3105. William E. Allison, Pres. & CEO; Sharon Kennish, Exec. Dir. & Chief Admin. Officer.
Good Samaritan Hospital Medical Center, 1000 Montauk Hwy., West Islip, 11795. Tel: 631-376-4001; Fax: 631-376-4208. William E. Allison, Pres. & CEO; Charles Bove, Senior Vice Pres. & Chief Admin. Officer.
Nursing Homes and Sub-Acute Care:
Good Shepherd Hospice Foundation, Inc., 4747-20 Nesconset Hwy., Port Jefferson Station, 11776.
Long Term Care Facilities:
Good Samaritan Nursing Home, 101 Elm St., Sayville, 11782. Tel: 631-244-2400; Fax: 631-244-2405. Jennifer James, Admin. Operating under the license of Good Samaritan Hospital Medical Center
St. Catherine of Siena Nursing Home, 52 Rte. 25A, Smithtown, 11787. Tel: 631-862-3900; Fax: 631-862-3983. Michael Quartararo, Sr. Admin. Operating under the license of St. Catherine of Siena Medical Center.
Our Lady of Consolation Geriatric Care Center dba Our Lady of Consolation Nursing and Rehabilitative Care Center 111 Beach Dr., West Islip, 11795. Tel: 631-587-1600; Fax: 631-587-5960. Dennis J. Verzi, Pres. & CEO.
Hospice and Palliative Care Services:
Good Shepherd Hospice, 4747-20 Nesconset Hwy., Port Jefferson Station, 11776. Tel: 631-474-5500; Fax: 631-474-2568. Marianne Gillan, Pres. & CEO.
Nursing Sisters Home Care, Inc. dba Catholic Home Care 15 Park Ave., Ste. 200, Bay Shore, 11706. Tel: 631-969-8200; Fax: 631-224-8678. Mary Ellen Polit, Pres. & CEO.
Behavioral/Developmentary Disabled Programs:
Maryhaven Center of Hope, Inc., 51 Terryville Rd., Port Jefferson Station, 11776. Tel: 631-474-4120; Fax: 631-474-4110. Lewis Grossman, Pres. & CEO.
Adult Day Services (over age 18): Participants develop skills necessary to obtain employment within an array of community-based options, or within the agency's work center.; Participants receive assistance with learning skills necessary for independent living.; Individuals receive intensive therapeutic services along with increased community integration.
Vocational Training/Supported Work/Sheltered Center formerly Vocational Training/Supported Work/Sheltered Workshop Tel: 631-924-5900; Fax: 631-924-2464.
Day Habilitation Tel: 631-474-4100; Fax: 631-474-4156.
Adult Residential Services: The agency operates a variety of housing alternatives within community-based settings.; Individuals still living at home receive assistance in accessing needed support services.
Adult Residences Tel: 631-474-4100; Fax: 631-474-9014.
Mental Health Services: Staff offer individuals assistance with accessing supports and services, advocacy and individual follow-up.; These day programs work to develop individual skills to improve a person's living, working, learning, and social situations.
Personalized Recovery Oriented Services for People with Psychiatric Disabilities (PROS East & West) formerly Continuing Day Treatment/Intensive Psychiatric Rehabilitation Treatment Tel: 631-727-4044; Fax: 631-727-6531.
Children Services (Ages 5-21): Progressive educational programming for children with developmental disabilities. The school is committed to the IEP diploma recipient and has a specialization in autism.; Provides 24-hour programming for students requiring greater support than can be provided at home.
Maryhaven School Tel: 631-474-3400; Fax: 631-474-4181.
Children's Residences Tel: 631-474-3400; Fax: 631-474-4181.
Maryhaven School Corporation, 51 Terryville Rd., Port Jefferson Station, 11776. Tel: 631-474-4120; Fax: 631-474-4110. Robin Dwyer.
**Maryhaven Transportation Services, Inc.*, 51 Terryville Rd., Port Jefferson Station, 11776. Tel: 631-474-4120; Fax: 631-474-4110. Alice Stanek.
Miscellaneous Entities:
CHS Services, Inc., 992 N. Village Ave., 11570. Tel: 516-705-2900; Fax: 516-705-1997. 245 Old Country Rd., Melville, 11747. Tel: 631-465-6000; Fax: 631-465-6500. Mr. James Harden, Pres.
Catholic Charities Support Corporation, 90 Cherry Ln., Hicksville, 11801.
Riverhead Hostel Holding Corp., 51 Terryville Rd., Port Jefferson Station, 11776. Tel: 631-474-4120; Fax: 631-474-4110.
Suffolk Hearing & Speech Center, Inc., 369 E. Main St., East Islip, 11730. Tel: 631-376-4001; Fax: 631-376-4208. A diagnostic and treatment center.
The Samaritan Corporation, 1000 Montauk Hwy., West Islip, 11795. Tel: 631-376-4001; Fax: 631-376-4208.
St. Charles Corporation, 200 Belle Terre Rd., Port Jefferson, 11777. Tel: 631-474-6600; Fax: 631-474-6884.
CHS Home Support Services, 15 Power Dr., Hauppauge, 11788. Tel: 631-940-3390; Fax: 631-940-3405. Robert Schwarz, Dir.
The St. Francis Research and Educational Corporation, 100 Port Washington Blvd., Roslyn, 11576. Tel: 516-629-2445; Fax: 516-629-2448.
The St. Francis-Mercy Corporation, 100 Port Washington Blvd., Roslyn, 11576. Tel: 516-629-2445; Fax: 516-629-2448.
Siena Village, Inc., 2000 Bishop's Rd., Smithtown, 11787. Tel: 631-360-6000; Fax: 631-360-6006. Kim Parbst, Admin. A low income housing program.
**Wisdom Gardens Housing Development Fund Company, Inc., c/o Maryhaven Center of Hope*, 51 Terryville Rd., Port Jefferson Station, 11776. Tel: 631-474-4120; Fax: 631-474-4110.
The Maryhaven Center of Hope Foundation, 51 Terryville Rd., Port Jefferson Station, 11776. Tel: 631-474-4120; Fax: 631-474-4110. Lewis Grossman, Pres. & CEO.
Siena Retirement Community Realty, LLC, 50 Rte. 25A, Smithtown, 11787. Tel: 631-862-3100; Fax: 631-862-3105.

[J] RESIDENCES FOR AGED

AMITYVILLE. *Dominican Village, Inc.*, 565 Albany Ave., 11701. Tel: 631-842-6091; Fax: 631-842-6131. Email: dv@dominicanvillage.org. Kenneth Ruthinoski, Pres. & CEO; Sisters Mary Casey, Vice Pres. Operations; Elizabeth Stringer, O.P., Vice Pres. Environment. Housing Units 266; Total Assisted 66; Total Staff 130.

HUNTINGTON. *St. Joseph's Guest Home for the Aged, Inc.*, 350 Cuba Hill Rd., 11743. Tel: 631-368-9528; Fax: 931-266-1015. Email: sjgh350@yahoo.com. Web: www.missionarysistersofstbenedict.org. Sr. M. Joachima Mystkowska, O.S.B., Admin. Missionary Sisters of St. Benedict. Bed Capacity 45; Total Assisted Annually 40; Total Staff 21. In Res. Rev. Msgr. Francis X. Glimm, S.T.L. (Retired); Rev. Robert J. Giuntini (Retired).

[K] SOCIETY OF ST. VINCENT DE PAUL

BETHPAGE. **Society of St. Vincent de Paul-Central Council* (1833) 249 Broadway, 11714. Tel: 516-822-3132; Fax: 516-822-2728. Email: jdilts@svdprvc.org. Web: svdprvc.org. Rev. Msgr. Patrick J. Armshaw, Spiritual Dir.; Paul Hodernarsky, Pres.; James T. Dilts, Exec. Dir. & COO. Total Assisted 215,515; Volunteers 1,143; Total Staff 93.

[L] HOME HEALTH SERVICES

HAMPTON BAYS. *Dominican Sisters Family Health Service*, 103-6 W. Montauk Hwy., 11946. Tel: 631-728-0181; Fax: 631-723-0866. Email: pash@dsfhs.org. Web: www.dsfhs.org. Pamella Ash, B.S.N., M.A., Admin. Suffolk Offices.
360 Montauk Hwy., P.O. Box 678, Wainscott, 11975. Tel: 631-537-6759; Fax: 631-537-7187. Web: www.dsfhs.org.
1729A N. Ocean Ave., Medford, 11763. Tel: 631-207-1170; Fax: 631-207-0149. Web: www.dsfhs.org.
DSFHS Special Programs, P.O. Box 1028, 11946. Tel: 631-728-0937; Fax: 631-728-7162. Web: www.dsfhs.org.

[M] MONASTERIES AND RESIDENCES OF PRIESTS AND BROTHERS

AMITYVILLE. *St. Pius X Residence*, 565 Albany Ave., 11701. Tel: 631-608-2622; Fax: 631-608-2624. Revs. Peter A. Allen; Brian J. Brinker; Angelo J. Ditta; Rev. Msgr. Thomas F. Mulvanerty, Vicar for Senior Priests; Rev. Gerald S. Twomey; Bro. Patrick Murphy, O.S.F., Pastoral Assoc. for Senior Priests In Res. Rev. Msgr. John J. Skelly (Retired); Revs. Serafino A. Corali (Retired); John H. McCabe (Retired); Rev. Msgr. Thomas F. Mulvanerty; Revs. Denis J. Sheridan (Retired); John P. Wilutis (Retired); William Dailey (Retired); Rev. Msgrs. Thaddeus Rooney (Retired); Anthony J. Savastano (Retired); Revs. Charles A. Gartner (Retired); Francis B. Nuss (Retired); Robert Kayser (Retired); Rev. Msgr. Thomas J. Hartman; Rev. Martin J. Hall, M.A. (Retired).

BAY SHORE. *Montfort Missionaries*, 26 S. Saxon Ave., 11706. Tel: 631-666-7500; Fax: 631-665-4349. Email: PRETRE@worldnet.att.net. Revs. Roger M. Charest, S.M.M. (Retired); Everett Brown, S.M.M.; James Manning, S.M.M.; J. Patrick Gaffney, S.M.M., Preaching Team; George J. Werner, S.M.M., Supr., Preaching Team; William M. Dilgen, S.M.M. (Retired); Francis Pizzarelli, S.M.M., Hope House Ministry; Peter J. McCrann, S.M.M., Hospital Chap.; Theodore Murphy, S.M.M. (Retired); Bro. Christopher Golla, S.M.M., Hospital Chap. Montfort Spiritual Center and Headquarters of "Montfort Publications" Priests 8; Brothers 1. *Montfort Missionaries - Retreat Center* (1928) 26 S. Saxon Ave., 11706. Tel: 631-666-7500; Fax: 631-666-4349.

GLEN COVE. *St. Josaphat's Monastery, Novitiate and Retreat House*, East Beach Dr., 11542. Tel: 516-671-0545; Fax: 516-676-7465. Email: sjmosbm@hotmail.com. Revs. Athanasius B. Pekar, O.S.B.M.; Taras Prokopiw, O.S.B.M.; Roberto (Tarcisio) Lucavei, O.S.B.M., Provincial Treas.; Theodosius (Roman) Ilnicki, O.S.B.M., Provincial Sec.; Bro. Eleuterio Choma, O.S.B.M. Basilian Fathers.
Manorville
Shrine of Our Lady of the Island, 258 Eastport Manor Rd., Manorville, 11949. Tel: 631-325-0661; Fax: 631-325-5592. Web: ourladyoftheisland.org. Rev. Roy Tvrdik, S.M.M., Dir.

MINEOLA. *Provincial Residence and Novitiate*, 240 Emory Rd., 11501. Tel: 516-742-5555; Fax: 516-742-1989. Email: tcleary@chaminade-hs.org. Bro. Thomas J. Cleary, S.M., Prov. & Asst. for Educ.; Revs. Garrett J. Long, S.M., Asst. Prov. & Asst. Rel. Life; Thomas A. Cardone, S.M., Councilor; Bros. James W. Conway, S.M., Asst. Temporalities; Timothy S. Driscoll, S.M., Councilor. Society of Mary (Marianists). In Res. Rev. Ernest P. Lorfanfant, S.M.

OYSTER BAY. *Vincentian Community*, 104 Anstice St., 11771. Tel: 516-922-3494; Fax: 516-922-5715. Email: vinchouse@aol.com. Rev. Gerard H. Luttenberger, C.M., Supr., Formation Dir.; Most Rev. Alfonso Cabezas, C.M.; Revs. Gregory J. Semeniuk, C.M, Asst. Supr., Treas.; Orlando Cardona, C.M.; Patrick Sean Flanagan, C.M.

[N] CONVENTS AND RESIDENCES FOR SISTERS

ROCKVILLE CENTRE. *Congregation of the Infant Jesus* (1905) 984 N. Village Ave., 11570. Tel: 516-823-3808; Fax: 516-594-0412. Email: bsdownes@yahoo.com. Web: www.cijnssp.org. Congregation of the Infant Jesus (Nursing Sisters of the Sick Poor). Professed Sisters 51.

AMITYVILLE. *Queen of the Rosary, Motherhouse* (1853) 555 Albany Ave., 11701-1197. Tel: 631-842-6000; Fax: 631-842-0240. Email: prioress@amityop.org. Web: www.amityvilleop.org. Sisters Mary Hughes, O.P., Prioress; Jane Creighton, O.P., Admin.; Rev. Sam Natale, Chap.
Sisters of the Order of St. Dominic
Amityville Dominican Sisters, Inc. Sisters of St. Dominic. Total in Residence 103.

BAY SHORE. *New Jerusalem*, 106 N. Penataquit Ave., 11706-6939. Tel: 631-968-8859. Sisters 5.

BLUE POINT. *St. Ursula Center*, 186 Middle Rd., 11715. Tel: 631-363-2422; Fax: 631-363-0319. Email: kobrien@tildonkursuline.org. Web: www.ursulinesofbluepoint.org. Kathleen O'Brien, Admin. Ursuline Sisters, Congregation of Tildonk.

BRENTWOOD. *Saint Joseph Convent* (1856) Motherhouse, 1725 Brentwood Rd., 11717. Tel:

631-273-4531; Fax: 631-273-1451. Email: rooney@csjbrentwood.org. Web: www.brentwoodcsj.org. Sisters Jean Amore, C.S.J., Pres.; Helen Rooney, C.S.J., Gen. Sec.; Joanne Feulner, C.S.J., Gen. Treas.; Virginia Dowd, C.S.J., Community Archivist. Sisters of Saint Joseph Generalate. Sisters 661.

Saint Joseph Novitiate, 1725 Brentwood Rd., 11717. Tel: 631-273-1187; Fax: 631-273-1451. Web: www.brentwoodcsj.org. Sr. Mary Walsh, C.S.J., Coord.

Maria Regina Residence, Inc. Sisters of St. Joseph, 1725 Brentwood Rd., Bldg. 1, 11717-5589. Tel: 631-299-3000; Fax: 631-952-2378. Email: mrr2007@mariareginaresidence.org. Web: www.mariareginaresidence.org.

FRANKLIN SQUARE. *Spiritual Life Center*, 1031 Mosefan St., 11010. Tel: 516-328-7438. Email: kmurphyop@optonline.net. Sr. Kathleen Murphy, O.P., Dir. Sisters of St. Dominic. Sisters 2.

HAMPTON BAYS. *St. Joseph's Villa Retreat and Renewal Center*, 81 Lynn Ave., 11946. Tel: 631-728-6074; Fax: 631-273-1451. Email: stjosephvilla@optonline.net. Web: www.csjbrentwoodny.org. Sisters of St. Joseph 2.

HUNTINGTON. *Missionary Sisters of St. Benedict*, 350 Cuba Hill Rd., 11743. Tel: 631-368-9528; Fax: 631-266-1015. Email: mssb350@yahoo.com. Web: www.missionarysistersofstbenedict.org. Sr. M. Matea Mirecka, O.S.B., Supr. Sisters 21.

ISLIP. *Daughters of Wisdom (Administration)*, 385 Ocean Ave., 11751. Tel: 631-277-2660; Fax: 631-277-3274. Email: jrohan@daughtersofwisdom.org. Web: www.daughtersofwisdom.org. Sr. Ann Gray, D.W., Prov. Administration Offices. Sisters 4.

OCEANSIDE. *St. Anthony's Parish House*, 111 Anchor Ave., 11572. Tel: 516-536-3308. Email: oceansideop@verizon.net. Sr. Margaret Sammon, O.P., Contact Person. Sisters of St. Dominic 3.

POINT LOOKOUT. *St. Clare Convent-Franciscan Sisters of Allegany*, 104 Ocean Blvd., 11569. Tel: 718-842-2615; 347-963-4552. Sr. Catherine Moran, O.S.F., Contact Person.

St. Elizabeth Convent-Franciscan Sisters of Allegany, 29 Ocean Blvd., 11569. Tel: 718-842-2615; 347-963-4552. Sr. Catherine Moran, O.S.F., Contact Person.

RONKONKOMA. *Religious of Our Lady of the Retreat in the Cenacle*, 310 Cenacle Rd., 11779-0430. Tel: 631-588-8366; Fax: 631-580-2050. Web: www.cenaclesisters.org.

Cenacle Retreat House Tel: 631-588-8366; Fax: 631-580-2050. Sr. Mary Jane Laffan, Supr.

St. Therese Couderc Community, 312 Cenacle Rd., 11779-2203. Tel: 631-588-8366; Fax: 631-580-2050. Sr. Mary Jane Laffan, Supr.

Maude Adams House, 310 Cencale Rd., 11779. Tel: 631-588-8366; Fax: 631-738-9511. Sr. Mary Spratt, Contact.

Cenacle Sisters at Brentwood (Maria Regina Convent) Tel: 631-273-4500. Sr. Mary Walsh, C.S.J., Contact Person. Sisters 4.

ROOSEVELT. *Oblate Sisters of the Most Holy Redeemer, Mother of Good Counsel Home*, 290 Babylon Tpke., P.O. Box 329, 11575-0329. Tel: 516-223-1013; Fax: 516-223-4254. Email: ossr290@earthlink.net. Sr. Matilde Murillo, O.SS.R., Dir. Mother of Good Counsel Home is a group home for pregnant and parenting teenage mothers and their infants.

SOUND BEACH. *Our Lady of Perpetual Help Convent*, 49 Convent Dr., 11789. Tel: 631-744-2477; Fax: 631-744-2515. Email: sbeachdirector@aol.com. Donna Appleby, Dir. Daughters of Wisdom 23.

[O] RETREAT HOUSES

CENTERPORT. *St. Francis Center, Inc.* (1961) 105 Prospect Rd., P.O. Box 301, 11721. Tel: 631-261-5730; Fax: 631-754-4204. Email: alverniacenterportny@gmail.com. Web: www.alvernia.org. Directed by Franciscan Bros. of Brooklyn.

MANHASSET. *St. Ignatius Retreat House, Inisfada*, 251 Searingtown Rd., 11030. Tel: 516-621-8300; Fax: 516-521-7201. Email: inisfada@inisfada.net. Web: www.inisfada.net. Revs. Damian O. Halligan, S.J.; William P. Walsh, S.J.; Marc J. Roselli, S.J. The Society of Jesus. Sisters 1; Total Staff 4.

PATCHOGUE. *St. Joseph's Prayer Center*, 312 Maple Ave., 11772. Tel: 631-730-6210; Fax: 631-730-6210. Email: stjoepc@optonline.net. Craig W. Nurnberger, Dir.; Rev. James J. Wheeler, S.J., Apostolic Dir. Priests 2; Total Assisted 500; Total Staff 10.

RONKONKOMA. *Cenacle Retreat Center*, 310 Cenacle Rd., P.O. Box 4005, 11779-0430. Tel: 631-588-8366; Fax: 631-738-9511. Email: retreat@cenaclesisters.org. Web: www.cenaclesisters.org. Sr. Mary Spratt, Dir. Ministry. Religious of the Cenacle. Ministry Staff 9.

SAG HARBOR. *Cormaria Retreat House* (1949) P.O. Box 1993, 11963. Tel: 631-725-4206; Fax: 631-725-1837. Email: cormaria@aol.com. Web: www.cormaria.org. Sr. Ann Thaddeus Marino, R.S.H.M., Retreat Dir. Directed by the Religious of the Sacred Heart of Mary. Religious of the Sacred Heart of Mary 6; Total Staff 12.

SHELTER ISLAND HEIGHTS. *St. Gabriel's Spiritual Center for Youth*, P.O. Box 3015/64 Burns Rd., 11965. Tel: 631-749-0850; Fax: 631-749-3154. Web: www.saintgabes.org. Rev. Vincent Youngberg, C.P., Retreat Dir. A youth retreat ministry directed by the Passionists. Retreats available for youth, women, men and married couples.

[P] MISCELLANEOUS

ROCKVILLE CENTRE. **Ecclesia Assurance Company*, P.O. Box 9023, 11571.

Mission Assistance Corporation, P.O. Box 9023, 11571. Tel: 516-678-5800. Mr. Kevin T. Murphy, Diocesan Admin.

**Tomorrow's Hope Foundation, Inc.*, P.O. Box 9023, 11571. Tel: 516-678-5800. Ms. Maureen Scaduto, Treas.

Unitas Investment Fund Inc., P.O. Box 9023, 11571-9023. Tel: 516-678-5800. Mr. Kevin T. Murphy, Diocesan Admin.

AMITYVILLE. *Amityville Dominican Sisters, Inc.*, 555 Albany Ave., 11701. Tel: 631-842-6000; Fax: 631-842-0240. Email: prioress@amityop.org. Web: www.amityvilleop.org. Sisters Mary Hughes, O.P., Pres.; Elaine Jahrsdoerfer, O.P., Vice Pres.; Theresa A. Gallagher, O.P., Sec. & Treas.

Benincasa Family Services, Inc., 555 Albany Ave., 11701. Tel: 631-842-6000, Ext. 351; Fax: 631-842-1596. Email: mkbenin555@aol.com. Sr. Margaret A. Krajci, O.P., Contact.

Dominican Sisters Community Support Corp., 555 Albany Ave., 11701. Tel: 631-842-6000; Fax: 631-842-0240. Email: prioress@amityop.org. Web: www.amityvilleop.org. Sisters Mary Hughes, O.P., Pres.; Elaine Jahrsdoerfer, O.P., Vice Pres.; Theresa A. Gallagher, O.P., Sec. & Treas.

Sisters of the Order of St. Dominic, 555 Albany Ave., 11701. Tel: 631-842-6000, Ext. 212; Fax: 631-842-0240. Web: www.amityvilleop.org. Sr. Mary Hughes, O.P., Prioress.

BAY SHORE. *Pronto of Long Island, Inc.*, 128 Pine Aire Dr., 11706. Tel: 631-231-8290; Fax: 631-231-8390. Email: prontoli@optonline.net. Web: www.prontoli.org. Vivian Hart, Exec. Dir.

BRENTWOOD. *Congregation of the Sisters of St. Joseph (1856) Charitable Trust*, Brentwood Rd., 11717-5587. Tel: 631-273-1187; Fax: 631-273-1345. Web: www.brentwoodcsj.org. Sr. Joanne Feulner, C.S.J., Treas.

CSJ Learning Connection for Adult Education, Inc., 1725 Brentwood Rd., 11717. Tel: 631-951-4783; Fax: 631-951-0642. Email: CSJTLC@optonline.net. Sr. Kathleen Carberry, C.S.J., Dir.

Sisters of Saint Joseph Lay Employee Pension Plan Charitable Trust, 1725 Brentwood Rd., 11717. Tel: 631-273-1187; Fax: 631-273-1451. Web: www.brentwoodcsj.org. Sr. Joanne Feulner, C.S.J., Trustee.

CENTERPORT. *Mt. Alvernia, Inc.* (1888) 105 Prospect Rd., P.O. Box 301, 11721. Tel: 631-261-5730; Fax: 631-754-4204. Email: alverniacenterportny@gmail.com. Web: www.alvernia.org. Directed by the Franciscan Brothers.

Camp Alvernia Tel: 631-261-5730; Fax: 631-754-4204. Email: info@campalvernia.org. Web: www-.campalvernia.org. Directed by the Franciscan Brothers.

Mt. Alvernia Center for Retreats Tel: 631-261-5730; Fax: 631-754-4204. Email: alverniacenterportny@gmail.com. Web: www.alvernia.org. Directed by the Franciscan Brothers.

FARMINGVILLE. *Religious Computer Systems* (1982) P.O. Box 508, 11738-0508. Tel: 631-732-7270; Fax: 631-732-6591. Email: rcsjane@cs.com. Web: www.rcswebsite.org. Sr. Jane Muller, O.P. Social Security and computer services for Religious institutions under sponsorship of the Amityville Dominicans

HAMPTON BAYS. *Centro Corazon de Maria, Inc.*, 31 Montauk Hwy. E., 11946. Tel: 631-728-5558; Fax: 631-728-5559.

ISLIP. *Wisdom Charitable Trust*, 385 Ocean Ave., 11751. Tel: 631-277-2660; Fax: 631-277-3274. Email: anngray@daughtersofwisdom.org. Web: www.daughtersofwisdom.org.

NEW HYDE PARK. *Sisters of the Imitation of Christ United States Mission, Inc.*, 1653 Highland Ave., 11040.

OAKDALE. *Saint John Baptist De La Salle of New York, Inc.*, P.O. Box 538, 11769. Tel: 401-789-0244; Fax: 401-783-5303. Email: eprecourt@cbc.necoxmail.com. Bro. Edmond Precourt, F.S.C., Provincial.

ROOSEVELT. *Friends of Mother of Good Counsel Home, Inc.*, 290 Babylon Tpke., 11575. Tel: 516-223-1013; Fax: 516-223-4254. Email: ossr290@earthlink.net. Sr. Matilde Murillo, O.SS.R., Dir. Bed Capacity 6; Total Assisted Annually 12; Total Staff 3.

Syosset

**Emmaus House Foundation, Inc. dba Harvest Houses* 235 Cold Spring Rd., Syosset, 11791. Sr. Jeanne A. Brendel, O.P., Contact Person.

UNIONDALE. *TELECARE of the Diocese of Rockville Centre*, 1200 Glenn Curtiss Blvd., 11553. Tel: 516-538-8700; Fax: 516-489-9701. Email: info@telecaretv.org. Web: www.telecaretv.org. Rev. Msgr. James C. Vlaun, Pres. & CEO.

WESTBURY. *Sisters, Lovers of the Holy Cross, Inc.* (1993) 43 Crown Ln, 11590. Tel: 516-333-9464; Fax: 516-333-9464. Email: sr.theresa@worldnet.att.net.

St. Theresa Convent, 43 Crown Ln., 11590. Tel: 516-333-9464; Fax: 516-333-9464. Email: sr.theresa@worldnet.att.net. Sr. Theresa Nguyen, L.H.C., Pres.

WYANDANCH. *Gerald J. Ryan Outreach Center, Inc.*, 1434 Straight Path, 11798. Tel: 631-643-7591; Fax: 631-643-1871. Email: ryanouthreach@optonline.net. Edda Nieves, Hispanic Ministry Coord./Asst. to Dir.; Ivonne Taveras, Support Svcs. Total Assisted 20,150; Volunteers 35; Total Staff 4.

The Opening Word Program, Inc. (1991) 1434 Straight Path, 11798. Tel: 631-643-0541; Fax: 631-643-0541. Email: opword@optonline.net. Sisters Mary Ryan, O.P., Treas.; Leonore Toscano, O.P., Exec. Dir.; Mary Hughes, O.P., Chairperson. Directed by the Sisters of St. Dominic.

RELIGIOUS INSTITUTES OF MEN REPRESENTED IN THE DIOCESE

For further details refer to the corresponding bracketed number in the Religious Institutes of Men or Women section.

[0330]—*Brothers of the Christian Schools*—C.F.C.
[0470]—*The Capuchin Friars* (St. Mary Prov.)—O.F.M.Cap.
[1330]—*Congregation of the Mission-Vincentians* (Eastern Prov.)—C.M.
[1000]—*Congregation of the Passion* (Prov. of St. Paul of the Cross)—C.P.
[0490]—*Franciscan Brothers of Brooklyn*—O.S.F.
[0690]—*Jesuit Fathers and Brothers* (NY Prov.)—S.J.
[0770]—*The Marist Brothers*—F.M.S.
[0800]—*Maryknoll*—M.M.
[0720]—*Missionaries of Our Lady of La Salette*—M.S.
[0870]—*Montfort Missionaries*—S.M.M.
[0430]—*Order of Preachers-Dominicans*—O.P.
[1070]—*Redemptorist Fathers*—C.SS.R.
[0760]—*Society of Mary* (Provs. of NY; Meribah)—S.M.

RELIGIOUS INSTITUTES OF WOMEN REPRESENTED IN THE DIOCESE

[]—*Congregation of Notre Dame*—C.N.D.
[3110]—*Congregation of Our Lady of the Retreat in the Cenacle*—R.C.
[2240]—*Congregation of the Infant Jesus*—C.I.J.
[]—*Daughters of Mary* (Haiti)—F.de M.
[0960]—*Daughters of Wisdom*—D.W.
[1070-05]—*Dominican Sisters* (Amityville)—O.P.
[1070-15]—*Dominican Sisters* (Blauvelt)—O.P.
[1070-16]—*Dominican Sisters* (Hope)—O.P.
[1070-11]—*Dominican Sisters* (Sparkill)—O.P.
[1370]—*Franciscan Missionaries of Mary*—F.M.M.
[1180]—*Franciscan Sisters of Allegany, New York*—O.S.F.
[1425]—*Franciscan Sisters of Peace*—F.S.P.
[1840]—*Grey Nuns of the Sacred Heart*—G.N.S.H.
[2070]—*Holy Union Sisters*—S.U.S.C.
[2575]—*Institute of the Sisters of Mercy of the Americas* (Mid-Atlantic Community)—R.S.M.
[]—*Maryknoll Sisters*—M.M.
[0210]—*Missionary Benedictine Sisters*—O.S.B.
[]—*Missionary Servants of the Most Blessed Trinity*—M.S.B.T.
[3030]—*Oblate Sisters of M.H. Redeemer*—O.SS.R.
[3465]—*Religious of the Sacred Heart of Mary*—R.S.H.M.
[2970]—*School Sisters of Notre Dame*—S.S.N.D.
[0640]—*Sisters of Charity of St. Vincent de Paul* (Halifax)—S.C.
[0650]—*Sisters of Charity of St. Vincent de Paul, of New York*—S.C.
[0430]—*Sisters of Charity of the Blessed Virgin Mary*—B.V.M.
[2990]—*Sisters of Notre Dame de Namur*—S.N.D.
[3000]—*Sisters of Notre Dame de Namur* (Baltimore & Base Communities Provinces)—S.N.D.deN.
[3830-05]—*Sisters of St. Joseph* (Brentwood, NY)—C.S.J.
[3840]—*Sisters of St. Joseph of Carondelet* (Province

of Albany)—C.S.J.

[3830-11]—*Sisters of St. Joseph of Nazareth*—S.S.J.

[3180]—*Sisters of the Cross and the Passion*—C.P.

[1830]—*Sisters of the Good Shepherd*—R.G.S.

[1970]—*Sisters of the Holy Family of Nazareth*—C.S.F.N.

[]—*Sisters of the Imitation of Christ*—S.I.C.

[2392]—*Sisters, Lovers of the Holy Cross* (Brookville, N.Y.)—L.H.C.

[2160]—*Sisters, Servants of the Immaculate Heart of Mary*—I.H.M.

[4130]—*Ursuline Sisters of the Congregation of Tildonk, Belgium*—O.S.U.

DIOCESAN CEMETERIES

CENTRAL ISLIP. *Queen of All Saints*, 115 Wheeler Rd., 11722. Tel: 631-234-8297.

CORAM. *Holy Sepulchre*, 3442 Rte. 112, 11727. Tel: 631-732-3460.

WESTBURY. *Holy Rood*, 111 Old Country Rd., Box 182, 11590. Tel: 516-334-7990.

NECROLOGY

† McCarren, Rev. Msgr. Edgar, (Retired)—Died Jan. 13, 2009

† Casey, Francis M., (Retired)—Died March 13, 2009

† Dolan, James J., (Retired)—Died May 23, 2009

† Dower, Douglas, West Islip, NY Good Samaritan Hospital Medical Center—Died Oct. 15, 2009

† Duvelsdorf, Peter L., (Retired)—Died June 13, 2009

† Hourihane, Francis, (Retired)—Died Oct. 23, 2009

† Nirrengarten, Andrew G., (Retired)—Died Jan. 25, 2009

† Sullivan, Edward G., (Retired)—Died Oct. 6, 2009

An asterisk (*) denotes an organization that has established tax-exempt status directly with the IRS and is not covered by the USCCB Group Ruling.

Diocese of Sacramento

(Dioecesis Sacramentensis)

Most Reverend

JAIME SOTO, D.D., M.S.W.

Bishop of Sacramento; ordained June 12, 1982; appointed Auxiliary Bishop of Orange and named Titular Bishop of Segia March 23, 2000; installed May 31, 2000; appointed Coadjutor Bishop of Sacramento October 11, 2007; installed November 18, 2007; Succeeded to the See November 30, 2008. *Diocesan Pastoral Center: Office of the Bishop, 2110 Broadway, Sacramento, CA 95818-2541.* Tel: 916-733-0203; Fax: 916-733-0215.

Diocesan Pastoral Center: 2110 Broadway, Sacramento, CA 95818-2541. Tel: 916-733-0100; Fax: 916-733-0195.

Web: www.diocese-sacramento.org

Most Reverend

WILLIAM K. WEIGAND, D.D.

Retired Bishop of Sacramento; ordained May 25, 1963; appointed Bishop of Salt Lake City September 3, 1980; ordained and installed November 17, 1980; appointed Bishop of Sacramento November 30, 1993; installed January 27, 1994; retired November 30, 2008. *Diocesan Pastoral Center, Office of the Bishop: 2110 Broadway, Sacramento, CA 95818-2541.* Tel: 916-733-0202; Fax: 916-733-0215.

Most Reverend

FRANCIS A. QUINN, D.D., ED.D.

Retired Bishop of Sacramento; ordained June 15, 1946; appointed Titular Bishop of Numana and Auxiliary Bishop of San Francisco April 28, 1978; Episcopal ordination June 29, 1978; appointed Bishop of Sacramento December 18, 1979; retired November 30, 1993. *Office: 2110 Broadway, Sacramento, CA 95818-2541.* Tel: 916-733-0200.

Square Miles 42,597.

Erected by His Holiness, Leo XIII, May 28, 1886.

Comprises the Counties of Amador, Butte, Colusa, El Dorado, Glenn, Lassen, Modoc, Nevada, Placer, Plumas, Sacramento, Shasta, Sierra, Siskiyou, Solano, Sutter, Tehama, Trinity, Yolo and Yuba in the State of California.

Co-Patrons of Diocese: St. Patrick; Our Lady of Guadalupe.

Legal Title: "Roman Catholic Bishop of Sacramento, A Corporation Sole."
For legal titles of parishes and diocesan institutions, consult the Diocesan Pastoral Center.

STATISTICAL OVERVIEW

Personnel	
Bishop	1
Retired Bishops	2
Abbots	1
Retired Abbots	2
Priests: Diocesan Active in Diocese	107
Priests: Diocesan Active Outside Diocese	4
Priests: Retired, Sick or Absent	59
Number of Diocesan Priests	170
Religious Priests in Diocese	82
Total Priests in Diocese	252
Extern Priests in Diocese	38
Ordinations:	
Diocesan Priests	2
Religious Priests	1
Transitional Deacons	3
Permanent Deacons in Diocese	148
Total Brothers	22
Total Sisters	161
Parishes	
Parishes	104
With Resident Pastor:	
Resident Diocesan Priests	75
Resident Religious Priests	5
Without Resident Pastor:	
Administered by Priests	24
Missions	40
Pastoral Centers	5
New Parishes Created	1
Professional Ministry Personnel:	
Brothers	1
Sisters	20
Lay Ministers	104
Welfare	
Catholic Hospitals	6
Total Assisted	646,111
Homes for the Aged	1
Total Assisted	130
Specialized Homes	1
Total Assisted	169
Special Centers for Social Services	11
Total Assisted	269,007
Educational	
Diocesan Students in Other Seminaries	39
Total Seminarians	39
Colleges and Universities	1
Total Students	118
High Schools, Diocesan and Parish	3
Total Students	603
High Schools, Private	3
Total Students	2,409
Elementary Schools, Diocesan and Parish	41
Total Students	9,429
Elementary Schools, Private	1
Total Students	28
Catechesis/Religious Education:	
High School Students	2,779
Elementary Students	21,452
Total Students under Catholic Instruction	36,857
Teachers in the Diocese:	
Priests	5
Scholastics	2
Brothers	2
Sisters	10
Lay Teachers	761
Vital Statistics	
Receptions into the Church:	
Infant Baptism Totals	9,632
Minor Baptism Totals	462
Adult Baptism Totals	410
Received into Full Communion	630
First Communions	7,098
Confirmations	5,013
Marriages:	
Catholic	1,052
Interfaith	211
Total Marriages	1,263
Deaths	2,810
Total Catholic Population	980,650
Total Population	3,533,652

Former Bishops—Rt. Revs. EUGENE O'CONNELL, D.D., ord. May 21, 1842; cons. Titular Bishop of Flaviopolis and appt. Vicar Apostolic of Marysville, Feb. 3, 1861; appt. First Bishop of Grass Valley, March 22, 1868; resigned March 17, 1884 and appt. Titular Bishop of Joppa; died Dec. 4, 1891; PATRICK MANOGUE, D.D., ord. Dec. 21, 1861; cons. Titular Bishop of Ceremos, Coadjutor to Bishop O'Connell of Grass Valley, Jan. 16, 1881; succeeded to the See of Grass Valley on Bishop O'Connell's resignation, March 17, 1884; became the first Bishop of Sacramento, May 1886; died Feb. 27, 1895; THOMAS GRACE, D.D., cons. June 16, 1896; died Dec. 27, 1921; PATRICK J. KEANE, D.D., ord. June 20, 1895; cons. Bishop of Samaria, Dec. 14, 1920; appt. to See of Sacramento, March 17, 1922; died Sept. 1, 1928; Most Revs. ROBERT J. ARMSTRONG, D.D., Litt.D., ord. Dec. 10, 1910; cons. March 12, 1929; died Jan. 14, 1957; JOSEPH T. MCGUCKEN, D.D., S.T.D., LL.D., ord. Jan. 16, 1928; cons. Titular Bishop of Sanavo and Auxiliary Bishop of Los Angeles, March 19, 1941; Coadjutor Bishop of Sacramento, Oct. 26, 1955; succeeded to Jan. 14, 1957, as Bishop of Sacramento; promoted to the See of San Francisco, Feb. 21, 1962; died Oct. 6, 1983; ALDEN J. BELL, D.D., M.S.S.W., ord. May 14, 1932; appt. Titular Bishop of Rhodopolis and Auxiliary Bishop of Los Angeles, April 18, 1956; cons. June 4, 1956; appt. Bishop of Sacramento, March 30, 1962; retired March 15, 1979; died Aug. 28, 1982; JOHN S. CUMMINS, D.D., ord. Jan. 24, 1953; appt. Titular Bishop of Lambesi and Auxiliary Bishop of Sacramento, Feb. 26, 1974; cons. May 26, 1974; appt. Bishop of Oakland, May 3, 1977; FRANCIS A. QUINN, D.D., Ed.D., ord. June 15, 1946; appt. Titular Bishop of Numana and Auxiliary Bishop of San Francisco, April 28, 1978; Episcopal Ordination, June 29, 1978; appt. Bishop of Sacramento, Dec. 18, 1979; retired Nov. 30, 1993; ALPHONSE GALLEGOS, O.A.R., D.D., ord. May 24, 1958; appt. Titular Bishop of Sassabe and Auxiliary Bishop of Sacramento, Sept. 1, 1981; cons. Nov. 4, 1981; died Oct. 6, 1991; WILLIAM K. WEIGAND, D.D., ord. May 25, 1963; appt. Bishop of Salt Lake City Sept. 3, 1980; ord. and installed Nov. 17, 1980; appt. Bishop of Sacramento Nov. 30, 1993; installed Jan. 27, 1994; retired Nov. 30, 2008.

Moderator of the Curia—Rev. Msgr. JAMES MURPHY. Tel: 916-733-0200; Fax: 916-733-0215.

Vicar General—Rev. Msgr. JAMES MURPHY. Tel: 916-733-0216; Fax: 916-733-0215.

Director of Finance—Mr. THOMAS J. MCNAMARA. Tel: 916-733-0277; Fax: 916-733-0295.

Director of Pastoral Services—KATHY CONNER. Tel: 916-733-0204; Fax: 916-733-0215.

Vicar Episcopal for Clergy—Rev. MICHAEL J. HEBDA. Tel: 916-733-0216; Fax: 916-733-0215.

Director of Hispanic Institute and Director Permanent Diaconate—Sr. PAULINA HURTADO, O.P. Tel: 916-733-0244; Fax: 916-733-0224.

Director of Social Services—Rev. MICHAEL F. KIERNAN. Tel: 916-733-0253; Fax: 916-733-0224.

Chancellor—KATHY CONNER. Tel: 916-733-0204; Fax: 916-733-0215.

Vice Chancellor and Secretary to the Bishop—Rev. TIMOTHY NONDORF.

Coordinator for Retired Priests—Rev. RONAN P. BRENNAN (Retired). Tel: 530-887-8842.

Delegate for Deacons—Deacon LOU DEL GAUDIO, 2110 Broadway, Sacramento, 95818-2541. Tel: 916-733-0256; Fax: 916-733-0224.

Vicars Forane—Rev. MATHEW M. MARANKULAM, (Shasta); Rev. Msgr. JAMES C. KIDDER, (Gold Country); Revs. AMBROSE UGWUEGBU, (Mother Lode); MERVIN P. CONCEPCION, (Siskiyou); LAWRENCE J. BECK, (Ridge); LINO O. OTERO, L.C., (Southern Suburbs); JOSEPH XUAN HUONG NGUYEN, (Sutter Buttes); BLAISE R. BERG, S.T.D., Alternate, (Sutter Buttes); POLYCARPO (POL) R. GUMAPO, (West Placer); LORETTO B. ROJAS, (Yolo); DANIEL A. LOONEY, (Solano); MICHAEL F. KIERNAN, (City); GERALD H. ROBINSON, S.J., (American River).

Diocesan Tribunal— Please direct all requests to the Tribunal. *2110 Broadway, Sacramento, 95818-2541.* Tel: 916-733-0225; Fax: 916-733-0224.

Judicial Vicar—Very Rev. MARK R. RICHARDS, J.C.L.

Adjutant Judicial Vicar—Rev. SANTIAGO RAUDES, J.C.L.

Judges—Rev. JOSEPH HUYEN NGUYEN, J.C.L.; LYNDA ROBITAILLE, J.C.D.; Rev. DAVID L. DEIBEL, J.D., J.C.L.

Promoter of Justice—VACANT.

Defenders of the Bond—Rev. Msgr. ROBERT P. WALTON; DEBORAH A. BARTON, J.C.L.

Approved Advocates—SUSAN BOONE; CAROL LEE; GAYLA PONCE.

Notaries—CAROL LEE; GAYLA PONCE; LUCI GUADARRRAMA; YVETTE ESPINOZA.

College of Consultors—Rev. Msgr. JAMES F. CHURCH; Revs. JOHN HEALY; MICHAEL F. KIERNAN; FRANCISCO VELASQUEZ; ROY DONER; LEON JUCHNIEWICZ; Very Rev. MARK R. RICHARDS, J.C.L.; Rev. Msgr. ROBERT P. WALTON.

Diocesan Offices and Directors

AIDS, Ministry to—Rev. JOHN HEALY, Coord., Mercy General Hospital, 4001 J St., Sacramento, 95819. Tel: 916-453-4753.

Alcoholism Advisory Board—Rev. THOMAS J. MAGUIRE (Retired). Tel: 916-985-2561, Ext. 4206.

Archives—Rev. WILLIAM F. BREAULT, S.J., Archivist, 2110 Broadway, Sacramento, 95818-2541. Tel: 916-733-0299; 916-480-2165.

Black Catholic Council—CHARLENE HARRIS, Office: 2110 Broadway, Sacramento, 95818-2541. Tel: 916-733-0160; 916-227-2288; Fax: 916-733-0195.

Building Committee— Direct inquiries to: Mr. THOMAS J. MCNAMARA, Staff, Diocesan Pastoral Center, 2110 Broadway, Sacramento, 95818-2541. Tel: 916-733-0277; Fax: 916-733-0295.

Department of Evangelization and Catechesis—STEPHEN PATTON, Dir. & Respect Life/NFP Coord.; STEPHEN MATUSZAK, Assoc. Dir. Catechesis; CARSON WEBER, Assoc. Dir. New Media Evangelization & Catechesis; Deacon ANTONIO RAMIREZ, Coord., Spanish Catechesis; Sr. VIRGINIA ALCALA, S.C.J.C., Asst. Hispanic Catechesis; DEBBIE ANDERSON, Project Rachel Coord. Coordinators Deaf Ministry: Mrs. MARGARET WALRATH; STANLEY SIMONET; KEVIN STASZKOW, Assoc. Dir. Youth & Young Adult.

Evangelization and Catechetical Commission—Rev. LORETO ROJAS JR., Chm.; Sr. KATHERINE DOYLE, R.S.M.; STEPHEN PATTON; Dr. HOLLY PETERSON; Sr. MAURA POWER, R.S.M.; Deacon ANTONIO RAMIREZ; CARSON WEBER.

Department of Social Services—Rev. MICHAEL F. KIERNAN, Vicar, 2110 Broadway, Sacramento, 95818. Tel; 916-733-0253; Fax: 916-733-0224; LORI ROSENE, Dir. Pendola Center; KATHLEEN BARBER, Admin. Camp Recreation.

Catholic Charities of Sacramento, Inc.—Rev. MICHAEL F. KIERNAN, Exec. Dir., 2110 Broadway, Sacramento, 95818. Tel: 916-733-0253; Fax: 916-733-0224.

Cemeteries—Mr. PHILIP NIEDERBERGER, Dir., 2110 Broadway, Sacramento, 95818. Tel: 916-733-0247; Fax: 916-733-0224.

Communications and Media—BOB DUNNING. Tel: 916-733-0168; Fax: 916-733-0195.

Presbyteral Council—Rev. MICHAEL F. KIERNAN. Tel: 530-673-1573; Most Rev. JAIME SOTO; Revs. JEREMY P. LEATHERBY; REY BERSABAL; STEPHEN M. BORLANG; Very Rev. MARK R. RICHARDS, J.C.L.; Revs. THOMAS A. BLAND; FRANCISCO J. HERNANDEZ-GOMEZ; LINO O. OTERO, L.C.; Rev. Msgr. JAMES T. MURPHY; Revs. MATHEW M. MARANKULAM; STEVEN EUGENE FOPPIANO; JOHN P. SULLIVAN (Retired); MICHAEL HEBDA, Direct all correspondence to: 2110 Broadway, Sacramento, 95818-2541.

Development—MICHAEL HALLORAN, Diocesan Dir., 2110 Broadway, Sacramento, 95818-2541. Tel: 916-733-0266; Fax: 916-733-0295.

Diocesan Pastoral Council— Please direct all inquiries to: KATHY CONNER, Chancellor. Tel: 916-733-0204.

Diocese of Sacramento Priests' Pension Trust—Most Rev. JAIME SOTO, Plan Sponsor. Please direct all inquiries to: Rev. Msgr. MURROUGH C. WALLACE (Retired), St. Theresa Church, 1041 Lyons Ave., South Lake Tahoe, 96150. Tel: 530-544-3533; Fax: 916-544-4662.

Divorced and Separated, Ministry to—Direct inquiries to: Catholic Evangelization & Catechesis, 2110 Broadway, Sacramento, 95818-2541. Tel: 916-733-0123; Fax: 916-733-0195.

Due Process— Direct inquiries to: Very Rev. MARK R. RICHARDS, J.C.L., 2110 Broadway, Sacramento, 95818-2541. Tel: 916-733-0225; Fax: 916-733-0224.

Eastern Catholic Churches—VACANT.

"Ecclesia Dei" Community (Latin Mass)—Rev. MATTHEW MCNEELY, F.S.S.P., Mailing Address: 5461 44th St., Sacramento, 95820. Tel: 916-455-5114; Fax: 916-455-1018.

Ecumenical & Interreligious Affairs—Rev. MICHAEL F. KIERNAN, 2110 Broadway, Sacramento, 95818-2541. Tel: 916-733-0253; Fax: 916-733-0224.

Finance Council—Members: Rev. Msgr. T. BRENDAN O'SULLIVAN (Retired); ROBERT GRANUCCI, Esq.; ANNE HECK LONG; Mr. MICHAEL PROFUMO; Very Rev. MARK R. RICHARDS, J.C.L.; SUSAN GODWIN; Rev. F. IGNATIUS HARAN (Retired); Mr. LON BURFORD. Ex Officio: Rev. Msgr. JAMES MURPHY; Mr. THOMAS J. MCNAMARA, Chancery Office, 2110 Broadway, Sacramento, 95818-2541. Tel: 916-733-0277.

Investment Review Committee— Direct inquiries to: Mr. THOMAS J. MCNAMARA, 2110 Broadway, Sacramento, 95818-2541. Tel: 916-733-0277; Fax: 916-733-0295.

Finance Office—Mr. THOMAS J. MCNAMARA, Dir., 2110 Broadway, Sacramento, 95818-2541. Tel: 916-733-0277; Fax: 916-733-0295.

Hispanic Apostolate—Deacon GERMAN TORO, 2110 Broadway, Sacramento, 95818-2541. Tel: 916-733-0177; Fax: 916-733-0195.

Holy Childhood Association—2110 Broadway, Sacramento, 95818-2541. Tel: 916-733-0110; Fax: 916-733-0120.

Hospitals, Diocesan Liaison for Catholic—Rev. JOHN J. HEALY, Mercy General Hospital, 4001 J St., Sacramento, 95819. Tel: 916-453-4753.

Lay Personnel—KAREN FILIPICH, Mgr., 2110 Broadway, Sacramento, 95818-2541. Tel: 916-733-0240; Fax: 916-733-0295.

Marriage Preparation—STEPHEN PATTON, Dir., Evangelization & Catechesis, 2110 Broadway, Sacramento, 95818-2541. Tel: 916-733-0123.

Newspapers— "Catholic Herald" and "El Heraldo Catolico" Ms. JULIE SLY, Editor, 2110 Broadway, Sacramento, 95818. Tel: 916-733-0170.

Ongoing Education of Clergy—Rev. MICHAEL J. HEBDA, Vicar Episcopal for Clergy, 2110 Broadway, Sacramento, 95818. Tel: 916-733-0216.

Permanent Diaconate Office—Sr. PAULINA HURTADO, O.P., Dir. Delegate for Deacons: Deacon LOU DEL GAUDIO, Office, 2110 Broadway, Sacramento, 95818-2541. Tel: 916-733-0244.

Priests' Personnel Board, Diocesan—Please direct all inquiries to: Priest Personnel, Office of the Bishop, 2110 Broadway, Sacramento, 95818. Tel: 916-733-0216. Revs. DANIEL A. LOONEY, Chm.; RODOLFO D. LLAMAS; THOMAS A. BLAND; EDUINO T. SILVEIRA; LEON JUCHNIEWICZ; Rev. Msgr. JAMES C. KIDDER; Revs. JOHN K. HANNAN (Retired); CHARLES KELLY; Rev. Msgr. ROBERT P. WALTON, Chm.; Revs. LIAM MACCARTHY; BENEDICT DELEON; TIMOTHY NONDORF.

Propagation of the Faith—Rev. Msgr. JAMES F. CHURCH, Dir., 2110 Broadway, Sacramento, 95818-2541. Tel: 916-733-0200; Fax: 916-733-0215.

Properties Committee— Please direct all inquiries to: Mr. THOMAS J. MCNAMARA, Staff, 2110 Broadway, Sacramento, 95818-2541. Tel: 916-733-0277.

Radio and Television— See Communications and Media

Research and Planning—VACANT.

Respect Life/NFP—STEPHEN PATTON, Diocesan Coord., Catholic Evangelization & Catechesis, 2110 Broadway, Sacramento, 95818-2541. Tel: 916-733-0123.

Schools—Mr. DOMINIC PUGLISI, Interim Supt., 2110 Broadway, Sacramento, 95818-2541. Tel: 916-733-0110; Fax: 916-733-0120.

Pastoral Care Coordinator—CATHI FISHER. Tel: 916-733-0142.

Safe Environment Coordinator—MARY HASTINGS. Tel: 916-733-0227.

Theological Commission—Very Rev. MARK R. RICHARDS, J.C.L., Chm. Tel: 916-733-0200; Rev. BLAISE R. BERG, S.T.D.; Sr. PAULINA HURTADO, O.P.; STEPHEN MATUSZAK; Rev. LORETO ROJAS JR.

Vocations—Rev. CHARLES KELLY.

Worship, Office of—Mrs. SANDRA HOLLAND, Dir., 2110 Broadway, Sacramento, 95818. Tel: 916-733-0221; Fax: 916-733-0295.

Lay Organizations—

Beginning Experience—MARIE ALFUSO, Contact, Mailing Address: P.O. Box 161761, Sacramento, 95816. Tel: 916-835-2282. Web: www.sacramentobe.org. Email: besacramento@yahoo.com.

Catholic Alumni Club—VACANT, Mailing Address: P.O. Box 1777, Carmichael, 95609-1777. Tel: 916-962-6107.

Catholic Daughters of the Americas—

Court Sacramento #172— St. Paul Parish, Florin FRANCIS B. GOMEZ, Regent, 6940 Mirador Way, Sacramento, 95828. Tel: 916-421-0300.

Court Our Lady of the Visitation #1890— St. Philomene Parish, Sacramento VALERIE K. MUNOZ, 5069 Pasadena Ave., Sacramento, 95841.

Court St. Felicitas #1939— St. Lawrence Parish, North Highlands PAT KORF, Regent, 6255 Stagecoach Dr., Sacramento, 95842. Tel: 916-331-4255.

Court Our Lady of Wisdom #2392— St. John Vianney Parish, Rancho Cordova JOAN DUBOIS, Regent, 8313 Pillares Dr., Sacramento, 95827. Tel: 916-363-2847.

Charismatic Renewal—Rev. Msgr. ANDREW V. COFFEY, Diocesan Liaison (Retired); Deacon JERRY PAULY, Assoc. Diocesan Liaison. Tel: 916-452-6866.

Cursillo Movement—Office: 2110 Broadway, Sacramento, 95818-2541. Tel: 916-733-0181.

Daughters of Isabella—KIMBERLY PEREZ, Regent, Mailing Address: P.O. Box 276, Galt, 95632. Tel: 209-745-1389.

Diocesan Council of Catholic Women—Rev. Msgr. EDWARD J. KAVANAGH, Moderator (Retired); DEE TASSINARI, Pres., 6628 Oak Branch Ct., Citrus Heights, 95621. Tel: 916-729-7684.

Italian Catholic Federation—LYNDA COOK, District Pres., Mailing Address: P.O. Box 1780, Sutter Creek, 95685. Tel: 209-267-9235.

Knights of Peter Claver and Ladies Auxiliary—PHILLIP MOSEBY, Grand Knight, Council #175, 6391 Weatherford Way, Sacramento, 95823. Tel: 916-224-7186; LENA N. HALL, Ladies Auxiliary Area Deputy, 559 Rivergate Way, Sacramento, 95831. Tel: 916-392-2796.

Knights of Columbus—JOHN NORWOOD, Northern California Chapter Pres., 1523 Pine Valley Circle, Roseville, 95661. Tel: 916-783-0453.

Legion of Mary—Rev. ALDRIN BASARTE, 1040 39th St., Sacramento, 95816. Tel: 916-452-4136; HOPE HARRINGTON, Pres., 1056 44th St., Sacramento, 95819. Tel: 916-456-1015.

Marriage Encounter Worldwide—Coordinators: EDDY HOOD; ABBY HOOD. Tel: 707-451-9871. Additional Contacts: PAT SWEENEY; DIANE SWEENEY. Tel: 707-447-4481; 866-825-2046. Email: pndsweeney@aol.com. Web: www.lovemoredeeply.org. Hispanic Coordinators: ABEL CARDENAS; YUYU CARDENAS. Tel: 916-606-7849. Web: www.wwme.org.

Scouting, Diocesan Catholic Committee on—Very Rev. MARK R. RICHARDS, J.C.L., Chap., 2110 Broadway, Sacramento, 95818. Tel: 916-733-0200; KEVIN STASZKOW, Contact. Tel: 916-733-0152; Fax: 916-733-0195.

Secular Franciscan Order—

Little Portion Fraternity—KATHLEEN MOLARO, SFO Regl. Sec. Tel: 530-272-1416.

Sacramento-St. Francis of Assisi Parish— Fraternidad De San Juan (Spanish) VACANT.

Secular Order of Discalced Carmelites—JUDY CARLSON, 7056 Rushwood Dr., El Dorado Hills, 95762. Tel: 916-933-6163.

Serra Club of Sacramento—ROBERT LEACH, 2161 Tenstone Loop, Roseville, 95747. Tel: 916-797-0830. Email: rcl1939@gmail.com.

Young Ladies Institute—MARILYN WALTER, Mailing Address: 2605 Zinfandel Dr., Rancho Cordova, 95670. Tel: 916-638-7905; Fax: 916-635-4381.

St. Thomas More Society—HERB BOLZ, Pres. Tel: 530-848-7252. Email: stms.sacramento@yahoo.com. Web: www.sacstms.org.

CLERGY, PARISHES, MISSIONS AND PAROCHIAL SCHOOLS

CITY OF SACRAMENTO

(SACRAMENTO COUNTY)

1—CATHEDRAL OF THE BLESSED SACRAMENT (1889) Most Rev. Jaime Soto; Rev. Michael F. Kiernan, Rector; Deacons Don De Haven; Raul Leon; Jorge Usi. Catechetical Center Cathedral Parish Hall conducted by parish CCD and Daughters of Charity of Canossa. In Res., Rev. Msgr. James Murphy; Very Rev. Mark R. Richards.
Church: 1017 Eleventh St., 95814. Tel: 916-444-3071; Fax: 916-443-2749. Email: blessed@cathedralsacramento.org. Web: www.cathedralsacramento.org.
Catechesis/Religious Program—1949 North Ave., 95838. Tel: 916-444-5364; 916-925-4001; Fax: 916-925-8897. Email: jenny@cathedralsacramento.org. Sr. Jenny Aldeghi, D.R.E. Students 512.

2—ALL HALLOWS (1942) Revs. Oscar Gomez-Medina; Walter Borkowski, Parochial Vicar; Deacons Gilberto Miranda; Tou Moua; Orin Rovito.
Res.: 5500 13th Ave., 95820. Tel: 916-456-7206; Fax: 916-456-7325.
Church: 5501 13th Ave., 95820.
School—John Paul II, (Grades PreSchool-8), 5700 13th Ave., 95820. Tel: 916-457-5621; Fax: 916-736-0204. Web: www.johnpauliischool.com. Fran Wise, Prin. Lay Teachers 13; Students 264.
Catechesis/Religious Program— Twinned with St. Peter Parish, Sacramento. Students 299.

3—ST. ANNE (1961) Rev. Luis Ido Urrego (Colombia); Deacons Pedro Manriquez, (Retired); Alani Vivi.
Res.: 7724 24th St., 95832. Tel: 916-422-8380; Fax: 916-422-7538.
Catechesis/Religious Program—Tel: 916-422-2419. Students 185.

4—ST. ANTHONY (1974) Rev. John E. Boll; Rev. Msgr. T. Brendan O'Sullivan, Pastor Emeritus (Retired); Deacons James Healy; Richard Koppes; Michael Crowley. In Res., Rev. Michael J. Hebda.
Res.: 660 Florin Rd., 95831. Tel: 916-428-5678; Fax: 916-428-0312. Email: office@stanthony-sacramento.org. Web: stanthony-sacramento.org.
Catechesis/Religious Program—Tel: 916-392-6362. Students 318.

5—ST. CHARLES BORROMEO (1960), (Spanish), Revs. Desmond T. O'Reilly, Parochial Admin.; Edward Pepka, Parochial Vicar; Eugenio Lopez-Restrepo, Parochial Vicar.
Res.: 7584 Center Pkwy., 95823. Tel: 916-421-5177; Fax: 916-392-4831.
School—7580 Center Pkwy., 95823. Tel: 916-421-6189; Fax: 916-421-3954. Susan Jaftok, Prin. Lay Teachers 10; Students 226.
Catechesis/Religious Program—Tel: 916-421-1063; 916-421-7174. Students 757.

6—DIVINE MERCY (2005) Rev. Cesar R. Ageas.
2175 Burberry Way, 95835. Tel: 916-285-9031. Email: divinemercy.parish@sbcglobal.net. Web: www.divinemercynatomas.org.
Catechesis/Religious Program—Sr. Dolores Brophy, R.V.M., D.R.E. Students 215.

7—ST. ELIZABETH (1909), (Portuguese), Revs. Giancarlo Mittempergher, C.S.S. (Italy); Antonio dos Santos, C.S.S. (Brazil), Parochial Vicar.
Res.: 1817 12th St., 95811-6508. Tel: 916-442-2333; Fax: 916-498-0676. Email: stelizportugal@gmail.com. Web: www.stelizabethsac.org.

8—ST. FRANCIS OF ASSISI (1894) Rev. Anthony Garibaldi, O.F.M.; Sr. Margaret Chambers, O.M.C., Pastoral Assoc.; Bro. James Swan, O.F.M., Music Dir.
1066 26th St., 95816. Tel: 916-443-8084; Fax: 916-443-7356. Email: info@stfrancisparish.com. Web: www.stfrancisparish.com. In Res., Rev. Larry Dunphy, O.F.M.; Bros. John Summers, O.F.M.; Mark Schroeder, O.F.M.
School—2500 K St., 95816. Tel: 916-442-5494; Fax: 916-442-1390. Web: www.stfranciselem.org. Mrs. Laurie Power, Prin. Lay Teachers 15; Students 300.
Catechesis/Religious Program—Students 134.
Parish Children's Faith Formation Program—Tel: 916-443-8084, Ext. 112. Email: georgies@stfrancisparish.com. Georgie Saydak, Dir. Youth Faith Formation. Students 134.

9—HOLY SPIRIT (1940) Revs. Albert O'Connor; Charles Brady, Pastor Emeritus (Retired).
Res.: 3159 Land Park Dr., 95818. Tel: 916-443-5442; Fax: 916-446-9015. Email: holyspiritlandpark@sbcglobal.net. Web: www.holyspiritparishsac.org.
School—3920 W. Land Park Dr., 95822. Tel: 916-448-5663; Fax: 916-444-9631. Marilee Bellotti, Prin. Lay Teachers 17; Students 299.
Catechesis/Religious Program—Tel: 916-448-8257. Students 61.
Convent—Sisters of Mercy (Auburn, CA), Tel: 916-448-3578.

10—ST. IGNATIUS OF LOYOLA (1954) Revs. Michael E. Moynahan, S.J.; Thomas G. Piquado, S.J., Parochial Vicar; Arthur J. Wehr, S.J., Parochial Vicar; Deacon Jackson Gualco.
Res.: P.O. Box 254647, 95865-4647. Tel: 916-482-6060; Fax: 916-972-8037.
School—3245 Arden Way, 95825. Tel: 916-488-3907; Fax: 916-488-0569. Patricia Lane, Prin. Lay Teachers 15; Students 347.
Catechesis/Religious Program—Tel: 916-482-9666, Ext. 238; Fax: 916-482-4869. Fatima Avila-Ohlsen, D.R.E. Students 195.
Ignatian Institute for Family Life—Tel: 916-482-9666, Ext. 205.

11—IMMACULATE CONCEPTION (1909) Rev. Santiago Raudes; Deacon Gerald Pauly, Parish Steward. In Res., Revs. William Feeser; Patrick J. Lee (Retired).
Parish Office—3263 First Ave., 95817. Tel: 916-452-6866; Fax: 916-452-3879. Email: info@icparishsac.com. Web: icparishsac.com.
Catechesis/Religious Program—Students 168.

12—ST. JEONG-HAE ELIZABETH (1993), (Korean), [CEM] Rev. Chundo Her (Korea, North).
Res.: 9354 Kiefer Blvd., 95826. Tel: 916-368-9204; Fax: 916-368-8304. Web: www.sackcc.net.
Catechesis/Religious Program—

13—ST. JOSEPH'S (1924) Rev. Francisco Velazquez; Sr. Rose Ereba, H.H.C.J., Parish Min.; Deacon Henry Garcia.
Res.: 1717 El Monte Ave., 95815. Tel: 916-925-3584; Fax: 916-925-1045. Web: saintjosephsacramento.org.
School—(Grades PreSchool-8), 1718 El Monte Ave., 95815. Tel: 916-925-1465; Fax: 916-925-0963. Mrs. Patricia Peterson, Prin. Filipino Sisters Religious of the Virgin Mary 3; Lay Teachers 6; Students 150.
Catechesis/Religious Program—Tel: 916-925-3485, Ext. 24. Sr. Soledad Castillo, H.R.F., D.R.E. (Spanish); Irene Ogbonna, D.R.E. Students 343.

14—ST. MARIA GORETTI (2007) Revs. Terry Fulton; Daniel Ray, L.C., Vice Pres. for Mission & Chap.; Deacon Raymond Helgeson.
8998 Robins Rd., 95829. Email: pastor@smgcc.info. Web: www.saintmariagoretti.net.
Catechesis/Religious Program—Students 70.

15—ST. MARY (1906) Revs. James Narithookil, C.M.I.; Francis Chirackal, C.M.I., Parochial Vicar; Deacons George Kriske; Lou Del Gaudio.
Res.: 1333 58th St., 95819. Tel: 916-452-0296; Fax: 916-452-3908. Web: www.stmarys-sacramento.com.
School—1351 58th St., 95819. Tel: 916-452-1100; Fax: 916-453-2750. Web: www.saintmaryschool-.com. Laura Allen, Prin. Tel: 916-452-1100, Ext. 11. Lay Teachers 19; Aides 7; Students 364.
Catechesis/Religious Program—Tel: 916-452-0296, Ext. 25. Email: jfgisla_sms@yahoo.com. Students 50.

16—OUR LADY OF GUADALUPE SHRINE (1958), (Hispanic), Revs. Lino O. Otero, L.C.; Octavio Ventura, L.C., Parochial Vicar; Jose Helio Cantu, L.C., Parochial Vicar.
Mailing Address: 711 T St., 95811. In Res., Revs. Robert Presutti, L.C.; Jason Clark, L.C.; Jeffrey Bowker, L.C.
Res.: 1909 7th St., 95811. Tel: 916-442-3211; Fax: 916-442-3679.
Catechesis/Religious Program—Tel: 916-446-3500. Students 370.

17—OUR LADY OF LOURDES (1957) Revs. Mieczyslaw "Mitch" Maleszyk, Parochial Admin.; Anthony Traynor, Pastor Emeritus (Retired).
Res.: 1951 North Ave., 95838. Tel: 916-925-5313; Fax: 916-922-0625. Email: ourladyoflourdes@comcast.net.
Catechesis/Religious Program—Tel: 916-925-4001. Students 110.
Convent—Daughters of Charity of Canossa, 1949 North Ave., 95838. Tel: 916-925-4001; Fax: 916-925-8897. Email: fdcc_sac@yahoo.com.

18—ST. PAUL (1958) Revs. Vicente Teneza; Hippolytu Njoku, Parochial Vicar; Deacon Charles Morrison.
Res.: 7200 Gardner Ave., P.O. Box 292280, 95829. Tel: 916-381-5200; Fax: 916-381-0332. Email: stpaulsflorin@aol.com. Web: www.stpaul-florin.org.
Catechesis/Religious Program—Students 420.

19—ST. PETER (1955) Revs. Oscar Gomez-Medina; Walter Borkowski; Deacons Gilberto Miranda; Tou Moua; Orin Rovito.
Mailing Address: *All Hallows Church*, 5500 13th Ave., 95820.
Church: 6210 McMahon Dr., 95824. Tel: 916-456-7206; Fax: 916-456-7325.
Catechesis/Religious Program— Combined with All Hallows, Sacramento
Convent—Sisters Servants of the Blessed Sacrament (Guadalajara, Mexico), 5929 61st St., 95824. Tel: 916-457-0182.

20—ST. PHILOMENE (1948) Revs. Eduino T. Silveira; John K. Hannan, Pastor Emeritus (Retired); Deacon Charles Cheever; Eduardo Arnouil, Hispanic Ministry; Alan Nissila, Music Dir.
Res.: 2428 Bell St., 95825. Tel: 916-481-6757; Fax: 916-481-1603. Web: www.stphilomene.com.
School—2320 El Camino Ave., 95821. Tel: 916-489-1506; Fax: 916-489-2642. Email: dmosbrucker@stphilomene.org. Web: www.stphilomene.org. Debra Mosbrucker, Prin. Lay Teachers 11; Students 173.
Catechesis/Religious Program— Jane Rocha, Dir. Faith Formation. Students 250.

21—PRESENTATION OF THE BLESSED VIRGIN MARY (1961) Revs. Jeremy P. Leatherby; Paul Ricks, Parochial Vicar. In Res., Rev. Troy David Powers.
Res.: 4123 Robertson Ave., 95821. Tel: 916-481-7441; Fax: 916-481-2841. Email: barbara@presentationparish.org. Web: www.presentationparish.org.
School—3100 Norris Ave., 95821. Tel: 916-482-0351; Fax: 916-482-0377. Lay Teachers 13; Students 160.
Parish Center—3110 Norris Ave., 95821. Tel: 916-482-8883.
Catechesis/Religious Program—Tel: 916-482-8883. Students 128.

22—ST. ROBERT (1955) Rev. Kieran M. McMahon.
Res.: 2243 Irvin Way, 95822. Tel: 916-451-1475, Ext. 10; Fax: 916-451-0534. Email: churchst.robert@comcast.net.
School—2251 Irvin Way, 95822. Tel: 916-452-2111; Fax: 916-452-5765. Brian James, Prin. Lay Teachers 14; Students 277.
Catechesis/Religious Program—Tel: 916-454-1747. Students 34.

23—ST. ROSE (1942) Rev. Msgrs. James F. Church, Parochial Admin.; Edward J. Kavanagh, Pastor Emeritus (Retired); Rev. Jesus E. Montoya, Parochial Vicar.
Res.: Oak Park Station, P.O. Box 5037, 95817. Tel: 916-421-1414; Fax: 916-421-0460.
School—St. Patrick, 5945 Franklin Blvd., 9582. Tel: 916-421-4963; Fax: 916-421-3849. John Rieschick, Prin. Lay Teachers 14; Students 161.
Catechesis/Religious Program—Tel: 916-392-5679. Students 674.

24—SACRED HEART OF JESUS (1926) Rev. Msgr. Robert P. Walton; Rev. Felipe Paraguya (Philippines); Deacons Gilbert Parra; William Riehl.
Res.: 1040 39th St., 95816. Tel: 916-452-4136; Fax: 916-457-9361.
School—Sacred Heart, 3933 I St., 95816. Tel: 916-456-1576; Fax: 916-456-4773. Theresa Sparks, Prin. Lay Teachers 13; Students 287.
Catechesis/Religious Program—Tel: 916-454-3640. Kristin Hansen, D.R.E. Students 45.

25—ST. STEPHEN THE FIRST MARTYR PARISH (2002), (Tridentine Latin Mass) Revs. John Lyons, D.M.V., Parochial Vicar; Matthew McNeely, F.S.S.P., Parochial Admin.; Michael Stinson, F.S.S.P., Parochial Vicar.
5461-44th St., 95820. Tel: 916-455-5114; Fax: 916-455-1018. Email: stephenproto@yahoo.com. Web: www.sacfssp.com.
Catechesis/Religious Program—Tel: 916-455-5114; Fax: 916-455-1018. Students 28.

26—VIETNAMESE MARTYRS CHURCH (1976), (Vietnamese), Revs. Philip B. Tran, C.M.C., Rector; Charles Pham, C.M.C., Asst. Rector; Deacons Anthony Huy Nguyen; Tien Nam Nguyen; An Binh Nguyen.
Res.: 8191 Florin Rd., 95828. Tel: 916-383-4276; Fax: 916-383-4276.
Church: 8181 Florin Rd., 95828.
Catechesis/Religious Program—Students 500.

OUTSIDE THE CITY OF SACRAMENTO

ALTURAS, MODOC CO., SACRED HEART (1883) Rev. Bernardin Mugabowakigeri.
Res.: 507 E. Fourth St., 96101-3406. Tel: 530-233-2119; Fax: 530-233-2575.
Catechesis/Religious Program—Students 15.
Mission—St. James Bonner St. & Garfield St., Cedarville, Modoc Co. 96104.

ANDERSON, SHASTA CO., SACRED HEART (1949) Rev. Mathew M. Marankulam; Deacons Michael Evans; Anthony Short; Rich Valles.
Res.: 3141 St. Stephen's Dr., 96007. Tel: 530-365-8573; Fax: 530-365-9544. Email: info@sacredheartparish.com. Web: sacredheartparish.com.
School—(Grades PreK-8), 3167 St. Stephen's Dr., 96007. Tel: 530-365-1429; Fax: 530-365-3039. Larry Butcher, Prin. Lay Teachers 6; Students 115.
Catechesis/Religious Program—Students 48.
Mission—St. Anne 2nd St. & Main St., Cottonwood, Shasta Co. 96022.

AUBURN, PLACER CO.

1—ST. JOSEPH (1861) [CEM] Revs. Brian Atienza; Arthur Najera Jr., Parochial Vicar; Deacons Richard Cadanesso; Jose Revelo; Mike Young.

Res.: 1162 Lincoln Way, 95603. Tel: 530-885-2956; Fax: 530-823-6676. Email: stjosephparish@auburncatholic.com. Web: www.auburncatholic.com.
School—11610 Atwood Rd., 95603. Tel: 530-885-4490; Fax: 530-885-0182. Mira Wordelman, Prin. Lay Teachers 15; Students 249.
Catechesis/Religious Program— Katie Prust, D.R.E. Students 65.
Mission—St. Joseph of Foresthill (1994) 22200 Foresthill Rd., Foresthill, Placer Co. 95631.
Station— Forest Hill.

2—ST. TERESA OF AVILA PARISH Revs. Michael A. Carroll; Arthur Najera Jr., Parochial Vicar.
11600 Atwood Rd., 95603. Email: info@stteresaauburn.com. Web: stteresaauburn.com.
Catechesis/Religious Program—Judy Jones, C.R.E. Students 198.

BENICIA, SOLANO CO., ST. DOMINIC (1854) [CEM] Revs. Mark Padrez, O.P., Parish Admin.; Michael Hurley, O.P., Parochial Vicar; Patrick O'Neil, O.P., Dominican Supr.; Deacons Ed Lazarek, (Retired); John Flanagan, (Retired); Juvencio Vela.
Mailing Address: P.O. Box 756, 94510-0756. In Res., Revs. Anthony Cordeiro, O.P. (Retired); Victor Cavalli, O.P. (Retired).
Res. & Church: 475 E. I St., 94510-3427. Tel: 707-747-7220; Fax: 707-745-5642.
School—935 E. 5th St., 94510-3427. Tel: 707-745-1266; Fax: 707-745-1841. Theresa Cullen, Prin. Lay Teachers 22; Students 366.
Catechesis/Religious Program—Students 669.

BURNEY, SHASTA CO., ST. FRANCIS OF ASSISI (1948) Rev. Efren Fergus Garcia Flores.
Mailing Address: 37464 Juniper Ave., P.O. Drawer 160, 96013.
Res. & Church: 37464 Juniper Ave., 96013. Tel: 530-335-2372; Fax: 530-335-2306. Web: www.stfrancisburney.org.
Catechesis/Religious Program—Tel: 530-294-5290. Students 29.
Mission—St. Stephen Hwy. 299, Bieber, Lassen Co. 96009. Students 16.
Mission—Our Lady of the Valley 43434 Main St., Fall River Mills, Shasta Co. 96028. Tel: 530-336-6212. Students 22.

CARMICHAEL, SACRAMENTO CO.

1—ST. JOHN THE EVANGELIST (1960) Revs. Thomas A. Bland; Roland B. Ramirez, Parochial Vicar; Deacons James Weeks, (Retired); Floyd Shields, (Retired); Lawrence Niekamp. In Res., Rev. Alban Uba, S.M.M.M. (Nigeria).
Res.: 5751 Locust Ave., 95608. Tel: 916-483-8454; Fax: 916-481-8326. Email: office@sjecarmichael.org. Web: www.sjecarmichael.org.
School—5701 Locust Ave., 95608. Tel: 916-481-8845; Fax: 916-481-1319. Web: www.stjohnev.com. Mrs. Nancy Conroy. Lay Teachers 13; Students 268.
Catechesis/Religious Program—Tel: 916-483-4628. Sr. Hannah O'Donoghue, D.R.E. Students 165.

2—OUR LADY OF THE ASSUMPTION (1952) Rev. Brendan McKeefry; Deacon Michael Tateishi.
Res.: 5057 Cottage Way, 95608. Tel: 916-481-5115; Fax: 916-481-4026. Email: parish@ourlady-sacto.org. Web: www.ourlady-sacto.org.
School—2141 Walnut Ave., 95608. Tel: 916-489-8958; Fax: 916-489-3237. Robert Love, Prin. Lay Teachers 15; Students 293.
Catechesis/Religious Program—Tel: 916-488-4626. Kimberly Sax, C.R.E. Students 180.
Convent—Ladies of Loretto (Toronto, Canada), Tel: 916-488-8188.
Convent—5055 Cottage Way, 95608. Tel: 916-488-8188.

CHICO, BUTTE CO.

1—ST. JOHN THE BAPTIST (1878) Revs. Blaise R. Berg; Christopher Frazer, Parochial Vicar; Deacons Jesus Padilla Campos; Stephen Schwartz. In Res., Rev. Hector Montoya.
Res.: 435 Chestnut St., 95928. Tel: 530-343-8741; Fax: 530-345-8602. Email: stjohn33@sbcglobal.net. Web: www.stjohnthebaptistchico.org.
School—Notre Dame Elementary School, (Grades K-8), 435 Hazel St., 95928. Tel: 530-342-2502; Fax: 530-342-6292. Web: www.ndschico.org. Mr. Michael Garcia, Prin. Lay Teachers 13; Students 202.
Catechesis/Religious Program—Students 365.
Mission—St. James [JC] P.O. Box 562, Durham, Butte Co. 95938.

2—OUR DIVINE SAVIOR (1967) Rev. Joel S. Genabia, Parochial Admin.
Office: 566 E. Lassen Ave., 95973. Tel: 530-343-4248; Fax: 530-343-3538. Email: ourdivines@yahoo.com.
Catechesis/Religious Program—Students 250.

CITRUS HEIGHTS, SACRAMENTO CO., HOLY FAMILY (1949) Revs. Polycarpo (Pol) R. Gumapo, Parochial Admin.; Ruel Z. Mesa, Parochial Vicar.
Res.: 7817 Old Auburn Rd., 95610. Tel: 916-723-2494; Fax: 916-723-0199. Email: holyfamilychurch@surewest.net. Web: www.holyfamilych.org.
School—Tel: 916-722-7788; Fax: 916-722-5297. Sr. Arlene Connelly, I.B.V.M., Pres.; Mr. Charles Suarez, Prin. Lay Teachers 19; Students 366.
Preschool—Tel: 916-722-4620; Fax: 916-722-4509. Lucy Eberhardt, Preschool Dir. Tel: 916-722-4620. Lay Teachers 7; Students 45.
Catechesis/Religious Program—Tel: 916-726-7217. Bonnie Johnson, D.R.E. Students 371.

CLARKSBURG, YOLO CO., ST. JOSEPH (1893) Rev. Daniel Madigan.
Res. & Church Address: 32890 S. River Rd., 95612. Tel: 916-665-1132; Fax: 916-665-9264.
Catechesis/Religious Program—Students 56.

COLFAX, PLACER CO., ST. DOMINIC (1929) [CEM] Revs. Ambrose Ugwuegbu (Nigeria), Parochial Admin.; William P. Kinane, Pastor Emeritus (Retired).
Mailing Address: 58 E. Oak St., P.O. Box 752, 95713.
Res. & Church: 58 E. Oak St., 95713. Tel: 530-346-2286; Fax: 530-346-8122.
Catechesis/Religious Program—Tel: 530-389-2553; Cell: 530-906-0302; Fax: 530-389-2653. Students 75.

COLUSA, COLUSA CO., OUR LADY OF LOURDES (1870) Revs. Roy Doner; Julian Medina, Parochial Vicar; Deacon Miguel Fernandez.
Parish Office: 745 Ware Ave., 95932. Tel: 530-458-4170; Fax: 530-458-8728. Web: ourladyoflourdes-colusa.org.
Church: 345 Oak St., 95932.
School—(Grades PreK-8), 741 Ware Ave., 95932. Tel: 530-458-8208; Fax: 530-458-8657. Mrs. Barbara Genera, Prin. Lay Teachers 6; Students 118.
Catechesis/Religious Program—Students 135.
Mission—St. Joseph 1st St. & Center St., Princeton, Colusa Co. 95970.
Station—Our Lady of Sorrows [CEM] [JC] Sycamore.

CORNING, TEHAMA CO., IMMACULATE CONCEPTION (1946) [JC] Rev. Juan Manuel Ponce.
Res.: 814 Solano St., 96021. Tel: 530-824-5879; Fax: 530-824-6534.
Catechesis/Religious Program—Tel: 530-824-4989. Students 80.
Mission—St. Stanislaus 4th St. & D St., Tehama, Tehama Co. 96090.

DAVIS, YOLO CO., ST. JAMES (1912) [JC] Rev. Loreto Rojas Jr.; Deacons Paul Taloff, (Retired); Sam Colenzo; Clark Goecker; Joe O'Donnell.
1275 B St., 95616. Tel: 530-756-3636; Fax: 530-756-5342. Web: stjamesdavis.org. In Res., Rev. Msgr. Andrew V. Coffey, Pastor Emeritus (Retired); Revs. Philip J. Wells; Innocent Subiza (Rowanda).
School—1215 B St., 95616. Tel: 530-756-3946; Fax: 530-753-9765. Web: www.sjsdavis.com. David Perry, Prin. Lay Teachers 17; Students 299.
Catechesis/Religious Program—Tel: 530-756-3636, Ext. 208. Linda O'Hara, D.R.E. Students 448.
Newman Center— 514 C St., 95616. Tel: 530-753-7393; Fax: 530-753-2794.

DIXON, SOLANO CO., ST. PETER (1877) Revs. Carlos Farfan, P.E.S. (Peru), Parochial Admin.; Eduardo W. Mendoza, P.E.S., Parochial Vicar; Deacons Robert H. Ikelman; John King; Felix Lupercio.
105 S. 2nd St., 95620.
Res.: 1015 Folsom Downs Cr., 95620. Tel: 707-678-9424; Fax: 707-678-9432.
Catechesis/Religious Program—Students 380.

DOWNIEVILLE, SIERRA CO., IMMACULATE CONCEPTION (1853) [CEM] [JC] Revs. Sylvester Kwiatkowski; Cecilio Tupasi (Philippines), Parochial Vicar.
Mailing Address: P.O. Box 302, 95936.
Office & Church: Church Street, 95936. Tel: 530-289-3102.
Mission—St. John 10047 Flume St., North San Juan, Nevada Co. 95960.

DUNSMUIR, SISKIYOU CO., ST. JOHN THE EVANGELIST (1899) [JC] Rev. Michael Canny.
Church: 5603 Shasta Ave., 96025. Fax: 530-235-4759.
Catechesis/Religious Program—Tel: 530-235-4705; Fax: 530-235-4759. Twinned with St. Anthony, Mt. Shasta. Students 6.

EL DORADO HILLS, EL DORADO CO., HOLY TRINITY (1992) Rev. Msgr. James C. Kidder; Susie Hahn, Pastoral Assoc.; Deacons Neil Zachary; Robert T. Shauger; James Hopp. In Res., Rev. P. Colm O'Kelly (Retired).
Church: 3111 Tierra de Dios Dr., 95762-8008. Tel: 530-677-3234; Fax: 530-677-3570. Email: holytrinity@holytrinityparish.org. Web: www.holytrinityparish.org.
School—3115 Tierra de Dios Dr., 95762-8008. Tel: 530-677-3591; Fax: 530-350-3032. Email: htschool@holytrinityparish.org. Web: www.holytrinityparish.org/school. Mrs. Trisha Uhrhammer, Prin.
Catechesis/Religious Program—Tel: 530-677-3234, Ext. 133. Students 274.

ELK GROVE, SACRAMENTO CO.

1—GOOD SHEPHERD CATHOLIC CHURCH (1993) Revs. Alfredo L. Tamayo; Francis Stevenson, Parochial Vicar.
9539 Racquet Ct., 95758.
Res.: 6808 Kilconnell Dr., 95758. Tel: 916-684-5722; Fax: 916-684-4472. Email: goodshepherdchurch@frontiernet.net.
School—St. Elizabeth Ann Seton Elementary School, Tel: 916-684-7903; Fax: 916-691-4064. Trina Koontz, Prin. Students 318.
Catechesis/Religious Program—Tel: 916-683-2963, Ext. 30. Students 900.

2—ST. JOSEPH (1962) Revs. Rodolfo D. Llamas; Bony Arackal, Parochial Vicar; Deacons Antonio Ramires; Dennis Merino.
Res.: 9961 Elk Grove-Florin Rd., 95624. Tel: 916-685-3681; Fax: 916-685-7254. Web: www.stjoseph-elkgrove.net.
Catechesis/Religious Program—Tel: 916-685-5636. Students 822.
Mission— 14673 Cantova Way, Rancho Murieta, Sacramento Co. 95683. Tel: 916-354-2403.

FAIR OAKS, SACRAMENTO CO., ST. MEL (1948) Revs. Liam P. McSweeney; George Snyder, Parochial Vicar; Deacons David Lehman; Anthony Pescetti.
Res. & Church: 4745 Pennsylvania Ave., P.O. Box 1180, 95628. Tel: 916-967-1229; Fax: 916-967-5659. Web: www.stmelchurch.org.
School—Tel: 916-967-2814; Fax: 916-967-0705. Web: www.stmelschool.org. Janet Nagel, Prin. Lay Teachers 13; Students 260.
Catechesis/Religious Program—Tel: 916-966-4314. Students 181.
Convent—P.O. Box 1180, 95628. Tel: 916-967-9504.

FAIRFIELD, SOLANO CO.

1—HOLY SPIRIT (1950) Revs. Michael Downey; Julito R. Orpilla, Parochial Vicar; Orlando Gomez, Parochial Vicar.
Mailing Address: P.O. Box X, 94533.
Res. & Church: 1050 N. Texas St., 94533. Tel: 707-425-3138; Fax: 707-425-2029. Email: hschurch3138@aol.com. Web: www.holyspiritfairfield.com.
School—(Grades K-8) Tel: 707-422-5016; Fax: 707-422-0874. Sr. Elizabeth Curtis, C.H.F., Prin.; Bonnie Hiris, Librarian. Sisters 3; Lay Teachers 17; Students 342.
Catechesis/Religious Program—Tel: 707-425-9042. Suselia Hernandez, D.R.E. Students 733.
Convent—Sisters of the Holy Faith (Dublin, Ireland), Tel: 707-425-3572.

2—OUR LADY OF MOUNT CARMEL, (1979), (Carmelite Fathers) Rev. David A. Fontaine, O.Carm.; Deacon Phil Verba.
Parish Office—Tel: 707-422-7767; Fax: 707-422-7946.
Res. & Church: 2700 Dover Ave., 94533. Tel: 707-426-3639.
Catechesis/Religious Program—Tel: 707-422-2814. Students 232.

FOLSOM, SACRAMENTO CO., ST. JOHN THE BAPTIST (1857) [CEM] Revs. Rey Bersabal; F. Ignatius Haran, Pastor Emeritus (Retired); Arbel Cabasagan, Parochial Vicar; Deacon Dominic Kim.
307 Montrose Dr., 95630. Tel: 916-985-2065; Fax: 916-985-7579. Email: office@stjohnsfolsom.org. Web: stjohnsfolsom.org. In Res., Rev. Thomas J. Maguire (Retired).
Res.: 107 Joseph Way, 95630. Tel: 916-351-1939.
School—St. John's-Notre Dame, Tel: 916-985-4129; Fax: 916-985-7958. Web: sjnds.com. Sue Halfman, Prin. Lay Teachers 18; Students 321.
Catechesis/Religious Program—Tel: 916-985-7338. Email: re@stjohnsfolsom.org. Students 848.
Station—Folsom State Prison P.O. Box W, Represa, 95671. Tel: 916-985-2561; Fax: 916-351-3070. Deacon William Goeke, Chap.
Station—California State Prison P.O. Box 29, 95671. Tel: 916-985-8610; Fax: 916-985-6425.

FORT JONES, SISKIYOU CO., SACRED HEART (1921) [CEM] Revs. Aldrin Basarte; Bernard Tape.
Res.: 101 Carlock St., P.O. Box 126, 96032-0126. Tel: 530-468-2605; Fax: 530-468-5577.
Catechesis/Religious Program—Students 25.
Mission—St. Mary's Etna. 386 Center St., Etna, Siskiyou Co. 96027.
Mission—All Saints 1321 Indian Creek Rd., Happy Camp, Siskiyou Co. 96093. Tel: 530-493-2657.
Mission—St. Joseph Etna. Sawyer's Bar Rd., Sawyer's Bar, Siskiyou Co. 96027.

GALT, SACRAMENTO CO., ST. CHRISTOPHER (1885) Rev. Robert A. Copsey.
Mailing Address: 950 S. Lincoln Way, 95632.
Res.: P.O. Box 276, 95632. Tel: 209-745-1389; Fax: 209-744-2183. Email: mpolanco_1@sbcglobal.net. Web: www.st-christopherchurch.com. Students 415.
Catechesis/Religious Program—Tel: 209-745-1389, Ext. 304.

GRASS VALLEY, NEVADA CO., ST. PATRICK (1855) [CEM] Revs. Sylvester Kwiatkowski; Nicholas Phelan, Pastor Emeritus (Retired); Cecilio Tupasi

(Philippines), Parochial Vicar; Deacons James Chatigny; Brian Moore.
Res.: 235 Chapel St., 95945. Tel: 530-273-2347; Fax: 530-272-9681.
School—Mt. St. Mary's, Tel: 530-273-4694; Fax: 530-273-1724. Edee Wood, Prin. Religious 1; Lay Teachers 9; Students 115.
Catechesis/Religious Program—Tel: 530-273-2336. Students 165.

GRIDLEY, BUTTE CO., SACRED HEART (1926) Rev. Miguel Silva.
Res. & Church: 1560 Hazel St., 95948. Tel: 530-846-2140; Fax: 530-846-5077. Email: sacredheartgridley@sbcglobal.net.
Catechesis/Religious Program—Students 244.
Mission—Our Lady of Guadalupe 9660 Broadway, Live Oak, Sutter Co. 95953.

IONE, AMADOR CO., SACRED HEART OF JESUS (1932) [JC] Revs. Thomas L. Seabridge; Thomas Relihan, Pastor Emeritus (Retired); Geraldo J. Ranin, Parochial Vicar.
20 Relihan Dr., P.O. Box 4, 95640.
Rectory—170 New York Ranch Rd., P.O. Box 4, Jackson, 95642. Tel: 209-223-2145.
Catechesis/Religious Program—Students 45.
Mission—Preston California Youth Facility, Ione 201 Waterman Rd., Amador Co. 95640. Tel: 209-274-4771, Ext. 250. Deacon Ned Quigley.
Mission—Mule Creek State Prison P.O. Box 409099, Amador Co. 95640. Tel: 209-274-4911. Rev. Diogo Baptista.

ISLETON, SACRAMENTO CO., ST. THERESE'S (1953) Rev. Andrew A. Koziczuk.
Res.: 100 4th St., P.O. Box 697, 95641. Tel: 916-777-6871; Fax: 916-777-6871.
Church: 4th St. & Jackson Blvd., 95641.
Catechesis/Religious Program—Students 52.

JACKSON, AMADOR CO., ST. PATRICK'S (1864) [CEM 2] Revs. Thomas L. Seabridge; Geraldo J. Ranin, Parochial Vicar; Jeannine Crew, Pastoral Assoc.; Deacons William Thompson, (Retired); Gary Evans; Jaime Garcia.
115 Court St., 95642.
Res.: 170 New York Ranch Rd., 95642. Tel: 209-223-2145; Fax: 209-223-2548. Email: stpat@stpatparish.org. Web: stpatparish.org.
Catechesis/Religious Program—Students 110.
Mission—Our Lady of the Pines Pioneer. 26750 Tiger Creek Rd., Buckhorn, Amador Co. 95666. Tel: 209-295-4909.
Mission—St. Bernard Plug-Emigrant St., Volcano, Amador Co. 95689.

KNIGHTS LANDING, YOLO CO., ST. PAUL (1949) [CEM] Rev. Joseph Huyen Van Nquyen, Parochial Admin.; Deacons Antonio Gonzalez; Hermenegildo Valera.
Res.: 222 Sycamore Way, P.O. Box 176, 95645. Tel: 530-735-6478; Fax: 530-735-9498. Email: parishofstpaul@yahoo.com.
Catechetical Center—6th St. & Locust St., 95645.
Catechesis/Religious Program—Students 95.
Mission—St. Agnes 9865 Main St., Zamora, Yolo Co. 95645.

LINCOLN, PLACER CO., ST. JOSEPH (1892) [CEM] [JC] Revs. Eric Lofgren; Fernando Meza, Parochial Vicar; Deacons Jesus Rodriguez; Roberto Ruiz.
Res.: 280 Oak Tree Ln., 95648. Tel: 916-645-2102; Fax: 916-645-1422.
Catechesis/Religious Program—Tel: 916-645-7754; Fax: 916-645-2144. Students 480.
Mission—St. Boniface 1028 Marcum Rd., Nicolaus, Sutter Co. 95659. Tel: 916-656-2368.
Mission—St. Daniel 214 Main St., Wheatland, Yuba Co. 95692. Tel: 916-633-0344.
Shrine—Our Lady of Guadalupe 3rd St. & K St., 95648.

LOOMIS, PLACER CO., ST. JOSEPH MARELLO (2004) Rev. Arnold Ortiz, O.S.J.; Deacon Dennis Gorsuch.
Mailing Address: P.O. Box 547, 95650.
Church: 6530 Wells Ave., 95650. Tel: 916-652-5001; Fax: 916-652-0202. Email: frarnold@osjoseph.org; sjmarelloparish@yahoo.com. Web: stjosephmarello.org.
Catechesis/Religious Program—Cyndee Reed, D.R.E. (Grades 1-5); Mary Maguire, Youth Min. (Grades 6-12). Students 400.

MARYSVILLE, YUBA CO., ST. JOSEPH (1852) [CEM] Revs. Joseph Huong; Julian Medina, Parochial Vicar; Deacons Jesus Munoz; David Perez.
Office & Mailing Address: 223 Eighth St., 95901. Email: stjoseph115@sbcglobal.net.
Res.: 319 Seventh St., 95901. Tel: 530-742-6461; Fax: 530-742-0346.
Catechesis/Religious Program—Students 557.
Mission—Sacred Heart Church P.O. Box 208, Dobbins, Yuba Co. 95953.

MAXWELL, COLUSA CO., SACRED HEART (1881) Revs. Derek R. P. LaBranch, Admin.; John J. Myles, Pastor Emeritus (Retired).
P.O. Box 1327, Williams, 95987. Tel: 530-473-2432. Email: sh_maxwell@yahoo.com. Web: www.sacredheart-maxwell.org.
Church: 45 Elm St., 95955. Tel: 530-438-2532.
Office: 627 8th St., Williams, 95987.
Mission—Holy Cross 408 Laurel St., Arbuckle, Colusa Co. 95912.
Mission—Annunciation 617 8th St., Williams, Colusa Co. 95987.
Mission—St. Mary of the Mountain 2nd St. & Geary St., Stonyford, Colusa Co. 95979.
Catechesis/Religious Program—Students 370.

MCCLOUD, SISKIYOU CO., ST. JOSEPH (1933) [JC] Rev. Aldrin Basarte.
Church & Mailing Address: 213 Colombero Dr., P.O. Box 518, 96057. Tel: 530-842-4874; Fax: 530-842-7076.
Res.: 314 4th St., Yreka, 96097. Tel: 530-842-3842.
Catechesis/Religious Program—Students 40.

MOUNT SHASTA, SISKIYOU CO., ST. ANTHONY (1954) Rev. Michael Canny.
Res. & Church: 507 Pine St., 96067. Tel: 530-926-4477; Fax: 530-926-4234. Email: stanthonyshasta@sbcglobal.net.
Catechesis/Religious Program—Tel: 530-926-3061. Students 36.

NEVADA CITY, NEVADA CO., ST. CANICE (1851) [CEM] Revs. Sylvester Kwiatkowski; Cecilio Tupasi (Philippines), Parochial Vicar.
Res.: 317 Washington St., 95959. Tel: 530-265-2049; Fax: 530-265-3697. Email: stcanice@sbcglobal.net.
Church: 316 Washington St., 95959.
Catechesis/Religious Program—Students 30.

NORTH HIGHLANDS, SACRAMENTO CO., ST. LAWRENCE THE MARTYR (1955) Rev. Enrique Alvarez; Deacon Donald Galli.
Res.: 4325 Don Julio Blvd., 95660. Tel: 916-332-4777; Fax: 916-332-8325. Web: saintlawrencechurch.org.
Catechesis/Religious Program—Tel: 916-332-4777. Email: jean@saintlawrencechurch.org. Students 377.

ORANGEVALE, SACRAMENTO CO., DIVINE SAVIOR (1987) Rev. Roman Mueller, S.D.S.
Mailing Address: 9079 Greenback Ln., 95662-4703. Tel: 916-989-7400; Fax: 916-989-7410. Web: www.divinesavior.com. In Res., Rev. Dennis Thiessen, S.D.S.
Res.: 8680 Hickory Leaf Pl., 95662-3444. Tel: 916-989-5425.
Catechesis/Religious Program—Email: sharon@divinesavior.com. Students 247.

ORLAND, GLENN CO., ST. DOMINIC (1919) Rev. Hernando Gomez Amaya (Colombia).
Mailing Address: Box 816, 95963.
Res. & Church: 822 A St., 95963. Tel: 530-865-4550; Fax: 530-865-8451. Email: dominicorland@yahoo.com.
Catechesis/Religious Program—Students 337.
Mission—St. Mary 400 Los Robles, Hamilton City, Glenn Co. 95951.

OROVILLE, BUTTE CO., ST. THOMAS THE APOSTLE (1857) Rev. Rolan Pabellan; Deacons Emmett Pogne; Jesus Venegas; Tom O'Connell.
Res.: 1330 Bird St., 95965. Tel: 530-533-0262; Fax: 530-533-1148.
Rectory—
School—1380 Bird St., 95965. Tel: 530-534-6969; Fax: 530-534-9374. Joani Briggs, Prin. Lay Teachers 7; Students 74.
Catechesis/Religious Program—Students 40.

PARADISE, BUTTE CO., ST. THOMAS MORE (1949) Rev. Steven Eugene Foppiano.
Res.: 767 Elliott Rd., 95969. Tel: 530-877-4501; Fax: 530-877-5633. Web: www.stmparadise.com.
Catechesis/Religious Program—Tel: 530-514-3892. Students 100.

PLACERVILLE, EL DORADO CO., ST. PATRICK'S (1852) Revs. John Cantwell; Walter Tabios; Deacons Stan S. Rudger; Manuel Ocon.
Res.: 3109 Sacramento St., 95667. Tel: 530-622-0373; Fax: 530-621-7770.
Catechesis/Religious Program—3090 Benham St., 95667. Tel: 530-622-7692. Email: spcff@sbcglobal.net. Students 261.
Mission—St. James 2831 Harkness St., Georgetown, El Dorado Co. 95634. Tel: 530-333-9432.
St. Patrick Ladies Society—
St. Patrick Aid Ministry (S.P.A.M.)—
Mother Teresa Maternity Home—
The Upper Room— Providing hot meals to those in need.
St. James Society—2831 Harkness St., Georgetown, 95634.

PORTOLA, PLUMAS CO., HOLY FAMILY (1929) Revs. Renier C. Siva, Parochial Admin.; James B. Walsh, Pastor Emeritus (Retired).
Res. & Church: 108 Taylor Ave., 96122. Tel: 530-832-5006; Fax: 530-832-5520. Email: hfport@sbcglobal.net.
Catechesis/Religious Program—Students 79.
Mission—Holy Rosary 614 4th St., Loyalton, Sierra Co. 96118.

QUINCY, PLUMAS CO., ST. JOHN (1947) [JC 6] Revs. Lawrence J. Beck, Parochial Admin.; Mario Valmorida, Parochial Vicar.
Mailing Address: P.O. Box 510, 95971.
Res. & Church: Hwy. 70 W, 170 Lawrence St., 95971. Tel: 530-283-0890; Fax: 530-283-4204.
Catechesis/Religious Program—Students 50.
Mission—St. Anthony 209 Jesse St., Greenville, Plumas Co. 95947. Tel: 530-284-6882.

RANCHO CORDOVA, SACRAMENTO CO., ST. JOHN VIANNEY (1958) Revs. Martin J. Moroney; Bernard Tape, Parochial Vicar; Deacons Walter Little; David Robinson.
Res.: 10497 Coloma Rd., 95670. Tel: 916-362-1385; Fax: 916-361-8102.
School—10499 Coloma Rd., 95670. Tel: 916-363-4610; Fax: 916-363-3243. Julia Boen, Prin. Lay Teachers 11; Students 240.
Catechesis/Religious Program—Tel: 916-362-3827; 916-368-9410 (Spanish). Students 430.

RED BLUFF, TEHAMA CO., SACRED HEART (1867) [JC] Rev. Joyle Martinez; Deacon Jack Bullen.
Parish Hall—2355 Monroe St., 96080. Tel: 530-527-1351; Fax: 530-529-2586. Email: sacredheartrb@hotmail.com.
School—2255 Monroe St., 96080. Tel: 530-527-6727; Fax: 530-527-5026. Email: sacredheart@sacredheartparishschool.org. Web: sacredheartparishschool.org. Ms. Teresa Sobieralski, Prin. Lay Teachers 10; Students 104.
Catechesis/Religious Program—Students 111.

REDDING, SHASTA CO.
1—ST. JOSEPH (1907) [CEM] Revs. Benedict DeLeon; John M. Lawrence, Parochial Vicar; Deacons David Gasman; Frank Lopez; Michael Mangas.
Res.: 2040 Walnut Ave., 96001. Tel: 530-243-3463; Fax: 530-243-7999. Email: stjoeparish@sbcglobal.net.
School—2460 Gold St., 96001. Tel: 530-243-2302; Fax: 530-243-2747. Lay Teachers 10; Students 131.
Catechesis/Religious Program—Students 60.
Mission—St. Michael 3440 Shasta Dam Blvd., Shasta Lake City, Shasta Co. 96019.
2—OUR LADY OF MERCY (1980) Revs. Jonathan B. Molina; Uriel Ojeda, Parochial Vicar.
Office: 2600 Shasta View Dr., 96002. Tel: 530-222-3424; Fax: 530-221-5717. Web: ourladyofmercyparish.org.
Catechesis/Religious Program—Tel: 530-222-3424, Ext. 12. Email: jodiephillips@sbcglobal.net. Students 144.
Mission—Mary Queen of Peace 30725 Shingletown Ridge Rd., Shingletown, Shasta Co. 96088. Tel: 530-474-1870.

RIO VISTA, SOLANO CO., ST. JOSEPH (1885) [CEM 2] Revs. Manuel B. Soria; William K. Walsh, Pastor Emeritus (Retired).
130 S. 4th St., 94571. Tel: 707-374-2155; 707-374-2672; 707-374-2607 (Parish Hall); Fax: 707-374-5071. Email: stjosephoffice@frontiernet.net.
Catechesis/Religious Program—Students 50.

ROCKLIN, PLACER CO., SS. PETER AND PAUL (1981) Revs. Stanley Poltorak; Glenn Giovanni Jaron, Parochial Vicar.
Res. & Church: 4450 Granite Dr., P.O. Box 824, 95677. Tel: 916-624-5827; Fax: 916-624-5924. Email: linblin@sbcglobal.net. Web: sspeter-paul.net.
Catechesis/Religious Program—Tel: 916-624-5827, Ext. 210; Fax: 916-624-9125. Students 1,122.

ROSEVILLE, PLACER CO.
1—ST. CLARE (1992) [JC] Rev. Liam MacCarthy; Deacons Carl Kube; Richard Driggs.
Res.: 1950 Junction Blvd., 95747. Tel: 916-772-4717; Fax: 916-772-4152. Email: stclare@surewest.net. Web: www.stclare-church.org.
Catechesis/Religious Program—(Faith Formation) 470.
2—ST. ROSE OF LIMA (1907), (Mexican), Revs. Michael O'Reilly; Michael C. McKeon, Pastor Emeritus (Retired); Juan Perez, Parochial Vicar; Joshy Mathew, C.M.I., Parochial Vicar; Deacons Peter M. Silott; Mark Van Hook. In Res., Rev. Michael J. Cormack, Pastor Emeritus (Retired).
Res.: 615 Vine Ave., 95678. Tel: 916-783-5211; Fax: 916-783-5212.
School—633 Vine Ave., 95678. Tel: 916-782-1161; Fax: 916-782-7862. Suzanne Smolley, Prin. Sisters 1; Lay Teachers 14; Students 293.
Catechesis/Religious Program—Tel: 916-786-0650. Kelly Risse, Life Teen Dir.; Dona Gentile, D.R.E.; Frida Callejas, D.R.E. (Spanish). Students 690.

SOUTH LAKE TAHOE, EL DORADO CO., ST. THERESA (1951) Rev. Jeronimo Marcelo, Parochial Admin.; Rev. Msgr. Murrough C. Wallace, Pastor Emeritus (Retired); Rev. John J. Grace, Pastor Emeritus (Retired).
Res.: 1041 Lyons Ave., 96150. Tel: 530-544-3533; Fax: 530-544-4662. Email: sttheresa@sbcglobal.net. Web: www.sttheresachurch.org.
School—1081 Lyons Ave., 96150. Tel: 530-544-8944; Fax: 530-544-8909. Danette Winslow, Prin. Lay Teachers 11; Students 107; Preschool 30.

Catechesis/Religious Program—Tel: 530-544-4788; Fax: 530-544-8909. Students 192.
Mission—Our Lady of the Sierra Camp Sacramento, El Dorado Co.

SUSANVILLE, LASSEN CO., SACRED HEART (1912) Rev. Patrick J. Henry.
Mailing Address: P.O. Box 430, 96130.
Res. & Church: 120 N. Union St., 96130-3935. Tel: 530-257-3230; Fax: 530-257-9213. Email: sacredheartssv@yahoo.com.
Catechesis/Religious Program—Msgr. Moran Hall, 140 N. Weatherlow St., 96130-3935. Tel: 530-257-8008 (local calls only). Students 50.
Station— Herlong.

SUTTER CREEK, AMADOR CO., IMMACULATE CONCEPTION (1864) [CEM 4] Revs. Thomas L. Seabridge; Ronan P. Brennan, Pastor Emeritus (Retired); Geraldo J. Ranin, Parochial Vicar; Deacon Ed Pogue.
125 Amelia St., P.O. Box 127, 95685. Tel: 209-267-5602; Fax: 209-267-1278. Email: office@suttercreekparish.com.
Catechesis/Religious Program—Spanish St. & Amelia St., 95685. Students 62.
Mission—St. Mary of the Mountains 18765 Church St., Plymouth, Amador Co. 95669.

TAHOE CITY, PLACER CO., CORPUS CHRISTI (1961) Rev. Robert E. Brooks.
Mailing Address: P.O. Box 1878, 96145.
Church & Res.: 905 W. Lake Blvd., 96145. Tel: 530-583-4409; Fax: 530-583-1408. Email: secretary@corpuschristi-tahoe.org. Web: www.corpuschristi-tahoe.org.
Catechesis/Religious Program—Tel: 530-581-4637. Email: education@corpuschristi-tahoe.org. Students 25.
Mission—Queen of the Snows 1550 Squaw Valley Rd., Olympic Valley, Placer Co. 96146.
Station—Marie Sluchak Community Park Pine & Wilson Sts., Tahoma.

TRUCKEE, NEVADA CO., ASSUMPTION OF THE BLESSED VIRGIN MARY (1870) Rev. Matthew Blank; Deacon Ray Craig.
Mailing Address: P.O. Box 34014, 96160.
Res. & Church: 10124 E. St., 96160. Tel: 530-587-3595; Fax: 530-582-8648. Email: info@assumptiontruckee.com. Web: assumptiontruckee.com.
Catechesis/Religious Program—Students 295.
Mission—Our Lady of the Lake 8363 Steelhead, Kings Beach, Placer Co. 96143.

TULELAKE, SISKIYOU CO., HOLY CROSS (1949) Rev. Mervin P. Concepcion, Admin.
Mailing Address: P.O. Box 266, 96134.
Church: 765 First St., P.O. Box 266, 96134. Tel: 530-667-2727.
Catechesis/Religious Program—Students 47.
Mission—Our Lady of Good Counsel W. 3rd St., Dorris, Siskiyou Co. 96023.

VACAVILLE, SOLANO CO.

1—ST. JOSEPH (1992) [JC] Revs. Daniel A. Looney; Vincent P. O'Reilly, Pastor Emeritus; Jacob Antonio Caceres, Parochial Vicar.
Res.: 1791 Marshall Rd., 95687. Tel: 707-447-2354; Fax: 707-447-9322. Web: www.stjoseph-vacaville.org.
School—Notre Dame, 1781 Marshall Rd., 95687. Tel: 707-447-1460; Fax: 707-447-1498. Lay Teachers 15; Students 275.
Catechesis/Religious Program—Students 226.

2—ST. MARY (1947) Revs. Humberto Gomez; Michael McFadden, Pastor Emeritus; John Tran E. Nguyen, Parochial Vicar; Deacon Domingo Cabrera, (Retired).
Res.: 350 Stinson Ave., 95688. Tel: 707-448-2390; Fax: 707-448-2818. Email: st.maryschurch@sbcglobal.net. Web: www.stmarysvacaville.com.
Catechesis/Religious Program—Tel: 707-446-1881. Students 270.

VALLEJO, SOLANO CO.

1—ST. BASIL (1941) Revs. Leon Juchniewicz; Giovanni Gamas, Parochial Vicar; Deacons Mike Urick; Errol Kissinger.
Parish Office: 1225 Tuolamne St., 94590. Tel: 707-644-5251; Fax: 707-644-1423. Web: stbasilvallejo.org.
Res.: 1200 Tuolumne St., 94590.
School—1230 Nebraska St., 94590. Tel: 707-642-7629; Fax: 707-642-8635. Mr. Neil Orlina, Prin. Lay Teachers 24; Students 329; Preschool 140.
Catechesis/Religious Program—Tel: 707-644-8309. Students 324.

2—ST. CATHERINE OF SIENA (1964) [CEM] Revs. Jesus T. Soriano; Michael Olszewski (Poland), Parochial Vicar; Deacons Pete Lobo; Rudy David; Bobby Peregrino.
Res. & Mailing Address: 3450 Tennessee St., 94591. Tel: 707-553-1355; Fax: 707-557-6896.
School—(Grades K-8), 3460 Tennessee St., 94591. Tel: 707-643-6691; Fax: 707-647-4441. Linda Mazzei, Prin. Lay Teachers 19; Students 288.
Catechesis/Religious Program—Tel: 707-647-4445. Students 291.

3—ST. VINCENT FERRER (1855) Revs. Stephen M. Borlang; Isnardo Serrano Rodriguez, Parochial Vicar.
Office & Res.: 816 Santa Clara St., 94590. Tel: 707-644-8396; Fax: 707-644-1330. Email: resource@stvincentferrer.org; fund@stvincentferrer.org. Web: www.stvincentferrer.org. In Res., Revs. Ronan B. Rances (LA); Luis V. Resma.
School—420 Florida St., 94590. Tel: 707-642-4311; Fax: 707-642-1329. Web: svfsvallejo.org. Tom Yurkovic, Prin. Lay Teachers 19; Students 364.
Catechesis/Religious Program—Tel: 707-643-0188. Email: ccd@stvincentferrer.org. Students 133.

WALNUT GROVE, SACRAMENTO CO., ST. ANTHONY (1931) Rev. Andrew A. Koziczuk.
Res. & Church: 14012 Walnut Ave., P.O. Box 436, 95690. Tel: 916-776-1330.
Catechesis/Religious Program— St. Anthony Parish Hall, Walnut Grove. Students 120.

WEAVERVILLE, TRINITY CO., ST. PATRICK (1853) [CEM] Rev. Perlito De la Cruz.
Res.: P.O. Box 1219, 96093-1219. Tel: 530-623-4383; Fax: 530-623-4383.
Church: 102 Church St., 96093.
Catechesis/Religious Program—Students 8.
Mission—Holy Trinity Hayfork, Trinity Co.
Mission—St. Gilbert Lewiston, Trinity Co.

WEED, SISKIYOU CO., HOLY FAMILY (1933) Rev. Mervin P. Concepcion, Parish Admin.
Res.: 1051 N. Davis Ave., 96094. Tel: 530-938-2076; 530-938-4334 (Office); Fax: 530-938-3837.
Catechesis/Religious Program—Tel: 530-459-5124. Students 50.

WEST SACRAMENTO, YOLO CO.

1—HOLY CROSS (1913) Revs. Giancarlo Mittempergher, C.S.S. (Italy); Antonio dos Santos, C.S.S. (Brazil), Parochial Vicar.
Res.: 1321 Anna St., 95605. Tel: 916-371-1211; Fax: 916-371-9277. Email: holycrossws@gmail.com.
School—800 Todhunter Ave., 95605. Tel: 916-371-1313; Fax: 916-371-4193. Email: hcsinformation@yahoo.com. Web: www.holycross.ws. Mrs. Mollie Lashinsky, Prin. Sisters 1; Lay Teachers 5; Students 109.
Catechesis/Religious Program—Tel: 916-371-5884. Students 321.
Convent—Sisters of Mercy (Auburn, CA), Tel: 916-371-1931; 916-933-0971.

2—OUR LADY OF GRACE (1949) Rev. Nicholas Ho.
Res.: 911 Park Blvd., 95691. Tel: 916-371-4814. Email: olgoffice@wavecable.com.
School—1990 Linden Rd., 95691. Tel: 916-371-9416; Fax: 916-371-1319. Mr. Joshua Rucker, Prin. Lay Teachers 12; Students 248.
Catechesis/Religious Program—Fax: 916-371-4816. Students 62.

WESTWOOD, LASSEN CO., OUR LADY OF THE SNOWS (1929) Revs. Lawrence J. Beck; Mario Valmorida, Parochial Vicar.
Res.: 307 Fifth St., P.O. Box 905, 96137. Tel: 530-256-3344; Fax: 530-256-2572. Email: ourladyofthesnows@frontiernet.net.
Church: 425 Cedar St., 96137.
Catechesis/Religious Program—Students 11.
Mission—Christ the King 534 Melissa St., Chester, Plumas Co. 96020.

WILLOWS, GLENN CO., ST. MONICA (1877) [CEM] Rev. Maurice O'Brien.
Res.: 1129 W. Wood St., 95988. Tel: 530-934-3314.
Catechesis/Religious Program—Tel: 530-934-3293. Students 140.
School—Catechetical School, 1151 W. Wood St., 95988. Tel: 530-934-5916; Fax: 530-934-3205. Students 161.

WINTERS, YOLO CO., ST. ANTHONY (1913) [JC] Rev. Michael McFadden; Deacon Alejandro Arroyo.
Mailing Address: 511 Main St., 95694.
Res.: 303 Main St., 95694. Tel: 530-795-2230; Fax: 530-795-5470.
Church: 301 Main St., 95694.
Catechesis/Religious Program—Kathy Long, Coord. Faith Formation. Students 250.
Mission—St. Martin 25633 Grafton Rd., Esparto, Yolo Co. 95627. Tel: 530-787-3750.

WOODLAND, YOLO CO., HOLY ROSARY (1870) [CEM] Revs. Terry Fulton; Francisco Leon, Parochial Vicar; Heriberto Serrano, Parochial Vicar; Deacons Edward Kull; Gonzalo Chavez; Antonio Fernandez; Jose Luis Collazo.
Mailing Address: 503 California St., 95695. Tel: 530-662-2805.
Parish Pastoral Center: 503 California St., 95695. Fax: 530-662-0796. Email: parish@holyrosary.com. Web: www.holyrosary.com.
(Corner of Walnut & Court Sts.), Church: 301 Walnut St., 95695.
School—505 California St., 95695. Tel: 530-662-3494; Fax: 530-668-2442. Email: office@hrsaints.com. Web: www.hrsaints.com. Marianne Cates, Prin. Lay Teachers 12; Students 224.
Catechesis/Religious Program—575 California St., 95695. Tel: 530-662-5394 (English); Fax: 530-662-1310. Darcy McGraw, Coord. (English); Ana Elizabeth Contreras, Coord. (Spanish). Tel: 530-662-2894. (English) 168; (Spanish) 475.
Mission—Our Lady of Guadalupe 36670 Sacramento St., Yolo, Yolo Co. 95697. (Not in service)

YREKA, SISKIYOU CO., ST. JOSEPH (1855) Revs. Aldrin Basarte; Dariusz Malczuk (Poland), Parochial Vicar.
Res.: 314 Fourth St., 96097. Tel: 530-842-3842; Fax: 530-842-7076.
Catechetical Center—310 Fourth St., 96097. Tel: 530-842-4874.
Catechesis/Religious Program—Tel: 530-842-4874. Students 37.
Mission—Immaculate Conception Hawkinsville, Siskiyou Co.

YUBA CITY, SUTTER CO., ST. ISIDORE (1952) Revs. Francisco J. Hernandez-Gomez; Martin Ramat, Parochial Vicar.
Res.: 222 Clark Ave., 95991. Tel: 530-673-1573; Fax: 530-673-2512.
School—200 Clark Ave., 95991. Tel: 530-673-2217; Fax: 530-673-3673. Mrs. Karen McDonald, Prin. Lay Teachers 11; Students 212.
Catechesis/Religious Program—Tel: 530-673-1573, Ext. 221. Students 638.

Chaplains of Public Institutions

SACRAMENTO. *Mule Creek State Prison*.
P.O. Box 409099, Ione, 95640. Tel: 209-274-4911. Rev. Diogo Baptista.
Sacramento International Airport. Rev. Cesar R. Ageas.
Sacramento Juvenile Hall, 9601 Kiefer Blvd., 95827. Tel: 916-875-5083. Vacant, Youth Chap. & Contact Person. Tel: 916-489-3394.
Sutter General Hospital, 2801 L St., 95816. Rev. James P. Sheets.
Sutter Memorial Hospital, 52nd & F Sts., 95819. Tel: 916-454-3333. Rev. James P. Sheets.
University of California, Davis Medical Center, 2315 Stockton Blvd., 95817. Tel: 916-453-2011. Revs. Paul Ricks, Hippolytus Njoku, S.M.M.M. (Nigeria).

ELK GROVE. *Rio Consumnes Correctional Center*, 12500 Bruceville Rd, 95758. Tel: 916-684-2001. Vacant.

FOLSOM. *California State Prison*, Tel: 916-985-8610, Ext. 6025.
P.O. Box 29, Represa, 95671. Deacon Dennis Merino.
Folsom State Prison.
P.O. Box 71, Represa, 95671. Tel: 916-985-2561, Ext. 4206. Rev. Polycarp Ndugbu (Nigeria).

IONE. *Preston California Youth Facility* 95640. Tel: 209-274-8250. Deacon Adolfo Rivera, Chap.

SUSANVILLE. *California Correctional Center*, P.O. Box 790, 96130. Tel: 530-257-2181, Ext. 1180. Rev. Anthony B. Warnakula, C.H.S.P.
High Desert State Prison, P.O. Box 750, 96130. Tel: 916-251-5100, Ext. 6722. Vacant.

VACAVILLE. *California Medical Facility*, P.O. Box 2000, 95688. Tel: 707-448-6841, Ext. 2976. Rev. Godwin Xavier, Chap.
California State Prison, Solano, P.O. Box 4000, 95696. Tel: 707-451-0182, Ext. 5474. Vacant. (Vacant)

Special Assignment:
Revs.—
Ageas, Cesar R., Chap. to Airport, Divine Mercy Parish, 2231 Club Center Dr., 95835. Tel: 916-285-9031
dos Santos, Antonio, C.S.S. (Brazil), Chap. to Port of West Sacramento, Holy Cross Parish, 1321 Anna St., West Sacramento, 95605. Tel: 916-371-1211
Mittempergher, Giancarlo, C.S.S. (Italy), Chap. to Port of West Sacramento, Holy Cross Parish, 1321 Anna St., West Sacramento, 95605. Tel: 916-371-1211
Ternullo, Joseph P., Chap. to Sheriff Deputies & Firefighters, St. Lawrence, 4325 Don Julio Blvd., North Highlands, 95660. Tel: 916-442-2333

On Duty Outside the Diocese:
Revs.—
Brown, Avram E., North American College, Vatican City
Juan, Vincent R., Catholic University of America, Washington D.C.
Lacre, Cormac, Diocese of Antipolo, Philippines
Rata, Jovito, Holy Trinity Parish, Philippines

Absent on Leave:
Revs.—
Bosque, Peter J.
Brusato, Martin
Nguyen, Charles
Powers, Troy David
Ternullo, Joseph P.

Valenzuela, Luciano

Retired and in Senior Ministry:
Rev. Msgrs.—
Coffey, Andrew V., 200 West 14th St., Davis, 95616.
Kavanagh, Edward J., c/o St. Rose Parish, P.O. Box 5037 - Oak Park Station, 95817.
Mennis, James F., 1601 Ocean Dr. S. #203, Jacksonville, FL 32250.
O'Neill, Patrick J., 14 Lexington Rd., Annandale, NJ 08801.
O'Sullivan, T. Brendan, 84 Shore Line Cir., 95831.
Schons, Gerard, c/o St. Rose Parish, P.O. Box 5037 - Oak Park Station, 95817.
Terra, Russell G., 2040 Walnut Ave., Redding, 96001.
Wallace, Murrough C., P.O. Box 612043, South Lake Tahoe, 96150.
Revs.—
Batch, Thomas A., 9000 Lankin Rd., Live Oak, 95953.
Brady, Charles, 33 Miranda Ct., 95822.
Brennan, Ronan P., 6600 VanMaren Ln., #12A, Citrus Heights, 95621.
Canterbury, Keith E., P.O. Box 2663, Weaverville, 96093.
Carrigan, Thomas C., Clarabricken House, Kilkenny, Co. Clifden Ireland.
Casey, Daniel, P.O. Box 5006 Fair Oaks, CA
Cormack, Michael J., 6600 VanMaren Ln., #2B, Citrus Heights, 95621.
Delahunty, Thomas P., 3247 Sandhurst Ct., Cameron Park, 95682.
Dermody, Thomas, P.O. Box 1151, Brawley, 92227.
Dinelli, William J., Christian Brothers H. S., 4315 Martin Luther King Jr. Blvd., 95820.
Duggan, Nicholas, 6600 VanMaren Ln. #2A, Citrus Heights, 95621.
Grace, John J., 3035 Berkeley Ave., South Lake Tahoe, 96150.
Hall, Rodney, 6600 Van Maren Ln., #3B, Citrus Heights, 95621.
Hall, Sidney, Mercy McMahon Terrace, 3865 J St., 95816.
Hannan, John K., 6600 VanMaren Ln., #5B, Citrus Heights, 95621.
Haran, F. Ignatius, 105 Joseph Way, Folsom, 95630.
Hold, William, 873 Colombine Way, Central Pointe, OR 97502.
Kinane, William P., 6600 Van Maren Ln., #4B, Citrus Heights, 95621.
Lee, Patrick J., c/o Immaculate Conception, 3263 1st Ave., 95817.
Lenehan, Vincent, 8 Glenburren Park, Co. Galway, Ireland.
Macdonald, Colin, 6600 Van Maren Ln. #12-B, Citrus Heights, 95621.
Maguire, Thomas J., 418 Coventry Ct., Folsom, 95630.
McKeon, Michael C., 8020 Walerga Rd., #1162, Antelope, 95843.
McKnight, James, 9 MaLinmore Mews, Dublin Rd., Down BT3585A Ireland.
Myles, John J., Whitegate Keel - Castlemaine, Co. Kerry, Ireland.
O'Hara, Edward, Lisryan, Longford, Granard Ireland.
O'Kelly, P. Colm, 3109 Tierra de Dios, El Dorado Hills, 95762-8008.
O'Leary, Sean, Bunowen Rd., Louisburgh, Co. Mayo Ireland.
O'Rafferty, Patrick, 6600 VanMaren Ln., #3A, Citrus Heights, 95621.
O'Reilly, Aidan, Virginia, Co. Cavan Ireland.
Phelan, Nicholas, Mercy McMahon Terrace, 3865 J St., #107, 95816.
Ramos, Cipriano, 6600 Van Maren Ln., #4A, Citrus Heights, 95621.
Relihan, Thomas, c/o Sacred Heart of Jesus Parish, P.O. Box 4, Ione, 95640.
Ryan, Lawrence A., Campus Commons, 22 Cadilac Dr., Apt. 136, 95825.
Schloeder, Paul, 2640 3rd Ave., 95818.
Storan, William, P.O. Box 1675, Paradise, 95967.
Sullivan, John P., c/o Holy Family Parish, 7817 Old Auburn Rd., Citrus Heights, 95610.
Traynor, Anthony, 6212 Rebel Cir., Citrus Heights, 95621-4720.
Walsh, James B., 14 Castle Demesne, Tralee, Kerry Ireland.
Walsh, William K., 50 River Rd., #30, Rio Vista, 94571.
Wdowiak, Boleslaw, 2404 Ruby Ct., Rocklin, 95677.

Permanent Deacons:
Arroyo, Alejandro, (Retired), St. Anthony, Winters
Astesana, Carlos, (Retired), Immaculate Conception, Downieville
Bullen, Jack, Sacred Heart, Red Bluff; St. Dominic, Orland
Burke, Keith, (Retired)
Burkett, James, Our Divine Savior Parish, Chico
Cabrera, Domingo, (Retired), Divine Mercy, Sacramento
Cadenasso, Richard, St. Joseph, Auburn
Chatigny, James, (Retired), St. Patrick, Grass Valley
Chavez, Gonzalo, Holy Rosary, Woodland
Cheever, Charles, St. Philomene, Sacramento
Colenzo, Sam, St. James, Davis
Collazo, Jose Luis, Holy Rosary, Woodland
Conley, Roger, (Unassigned)
Craig, Ray, Assumption, Truckee
Cronk, Dennis, St. John the Baptist, Folsom
Crowley, Michael, St. Anthony, Sacramento
David, Rudy, St. Catherine of Siena, Vallejo
DeHaven, Donald, (Retired), Cathedral, Sacramento
Del Gaudio, Lou, St. Mary, Sacramento
Donovan, Michael, (Retired), All Hallows, Sacramento
Driggs, Richard, St. Clare, Roseville
Dufault, Duane, St. Joseph, McCloud; St. Joseph, Yreka
Elias, Raymond, Holy Spirit, Fairfield
Enos, Richard, (Retired), St. Joseph, Yreka
Evans, Gary, St. Patrick, Jackson
Evans, Michael, Sacred Heart, Anderson
Fernandez, Antonio, (Retired), Holy Rosary, Woodland
Fernandez, Miguel, Our Lady of Lourdes, Colusa
Flanagan, John, (Retired), St. Dominic, Benicia
Ford, David, St. Teresa of Avila, Auburn
Galli, Donald, St. Lawrence, N. Highlands
Garcia, Henry, (Retired), St. Joseph, Sacramento
Garcia, Jaime, St. Patrick, Jackson
Gasman, David H., (Retired), St. Joseph, Redding
Godinez, Rafael, (Retired), St. Joseph, Elk Grove
Goecker, Clark, St. James, Davis; Newman Center, Davis
Goeke, William, St. John the Baptist, Jackson
Gonzalez, Antonio, St. Paul, Knights Landing
Gorsuch, Dennis, St. Joseph Marello, Granite Bay
Gualco, Jack, St. Ignatius of Loyola, Sacramento
Haproff, David, SS. Peter & Paul, Rocklin
Healy, James, (Retired), St. Anthony's, Sacramento
Helgeson, Raymond, St. Maria Goretti, Elk Grove
Hemenway, Raymond, Our Lady of Mercy, Redding
Henning, Patrick, St. Mel, Fair Oaks
Hernandez, Jesus, (Unassigned)
Holt, Mark, Holy Family, Citrus Heights
Hopp, James, Holy Trinity, El Dorado Hills
Ikelman, Robert, St. Peter, Dixon
Imrisek, Paul, (Retired), St. Joseph, Elk Grove
Iredale, Michael, St. Charles, Sacramento
Kearns, Patrick, Our Lady of Mercy, Redding
Kim, Dominic, St. John the Baptist, Folsom
King, John, St. Mary, Vacaville
Kissinger, Errol, St. Basil, Vallejo
Klimecki, Lawrence, Presentation, Sacramento
Koppes, Richard, St. Anthony, Sacramento
Kriske, George, (Retired), St. Mary's, Sacramento
Kube, Carl, St. Clare, Roseville
Kull, Edward, Holy Rosary, Woodland
Layne, Everett H., (Retired), Our Lady of Mercy, Redding
Lazarek, Edward, (Retired), St. Dominic, Benicia
Lehman, David, St. Mel, Fair Oaks
Leon, Raul, Cathedral of the Blessed Sacrament
Link, Robert, (Unassigned)
Little, Walter, St. John Vianney, Rancho Cordova
Lobo, Pete, St. Catherine of Siena, Vallejo
Lopez, Frank, St. Joseph, Redding; St. Michael Mission, Shasta
Lupercio, Felix, St. Peter, Dixon
Madero, Alejandro, St. Vincent Ferrer, Vallejo
Mangas, Michael, St. Joseph, Redding
Mangoba, Leo, (Retired), St. Vincent Ferrer, Vallejo
Manriquez, Pedro, (Retired), St. Anne, Sacramento
Marchese, Charles, Jr., (Retired), Divine Savior, Orangevale
McFadden, James, Divine Savior, Orangevale
Merino, Dennis, St. Joseph, Elk Grove
Meucci, James, (Retired), Holy Trinity, El Dorado Hills
Miranda, Gilberto, All Hallows, Sacramento; St. Peter, Sacramento
Moore, Brian, (Retired), St. Patrick, Grass Valley
Morales, Rick, Divine Mercy, Sacramento
Morgado, Edwin, Teresa of Avila, Auburn
Morrison, Charles, St. Paul, Sacramento
Moua, Tou, St. Peter, Sacramento; All Hallows, Sacramento
Munoz, Jesus, St. Joseph, Marysville
Nguyen, An Binh, Vietnamese Catholic Martyrs, Sacramento
Nguyen, Anthony, Vietnamese Catholic Martyrs, Sacramento
Nguyen, Tien Nam, Vietnamese Martyrs, Sacramento
Niekamp, Lawrence, St. John the Evangelist, Carmichael
O'Connell, Tom, St. Thomas the Apostle, Oroville
O'Donnell, Joseph, St. James, Davis
Ocon, Manuel, St. Patrick, Placerville
Padilla, Jesus, St. John the Baptist, Chico
Parra, Gilbert, Sacred Heart, Sacramento
Pauly, Gerald, Immaculate Conception, Sacramento
Peregrino, Bobby, St. Catherine of Siena, Vallejo
Perez, David, (Retired), St. Joseph's, Marysville
Pescetti, Anthony, St. Mel, Fair Oaks
Pierre, Allen, (Retired), St. Joseph, Elk Grove
Pogue, Edwin, (Retired), Immaculate Conception, Sutter Creek
Pogue, Emmett, St. Thomas the Apostle, Oroville
Quigley, Ned, St. Joseph, Elk Grove
Ramirez, Antonio, St. Paul, Sacramento
Ramirez, Jose, (Unassigned)
Ramirez, Preciliano, St.Anne, Sacramento; St. Robert, Sacramento
Revelo, Jose, St. Joseph, Auburn; Holy Family, Citrus Heights
Rey, Rafael, St. Vincent Ferrer, Vallejo
Reyna, Pedro, Sacred Heart, Maxwell
Rico, Benito, St. Dominic, Orland
Riehl, William, (Retired), Sacred Heart, Sacramento
Rivera, Adolfo, (Unassigned)
Robinson, David, St. John Vianney, Rancho Cordova
Rodriguez, Jesus, St. Joseph, Lincoln
Rojo, Ruben, St. Isidore, Yuba City
Rovito, Orin, St. Peter/All Hallows, Sacramento
Rudger, Stanley, St. Patrick, Placerville
Ruiz, Roberto, St. Joseph, Lincoln
Schirmer, Erik, Sacred Heart, Susanville
Schwartz, Steve, St. John the Baptist, Chico
Shauger, Robert T., Holy Trinity, El Dorado Hills
Sheldon, Lawrence, (Retired), (Unassigned)
Shields, Floyd, (Retired), St. John the Evangelist, Carmichael
Short, Anthony, (Retired), Sacred Heart, Anderson
Silott, Peter, (Retired), St. Rose of Lima, Roseville
Smith, Colby, Sacred Heart, Susanville
Smith, Edward, Good Shepherd, Elk Grove
Sousa, William, Good Shepherd, Elk Grove
Symkowick, Joseph, Newman Catholic Community, Sacramento
Taloff, Paul, (Retired), St. James, Davis
Tateishi, Michael, Our Lady of the Assumption, Carmichael
Thompson, William, (Retired), St. Patrick, Jackson
Tokuno, Doug, Sacred Heart, Gridley
Toro, German, Hispanic Ministry for the Diocese, Sacramento
Urick, Michael, St. Basil, Vallejo
Usi, Jorge, Cathedral of the Blessed Sacrament, Sacramento
Valles, Rich, Sacred Heart, Anderson
Van Hook, Mark, St. Rose of Lima, Roseville
Varela, Hermengildo, St. Paul Church, Knights Landing
Vela, Juvencio, St. Dominic, Benecia
Venegas, Jesus, St. Thomas, Oroville
Verba, Phil, Jr., Our Lady of Mt. Carmel, Fairfield
Vignery, Eldon, St. Isidore, Yuba City
Vivi, Alani, St. Anne, Sacramento
Weeks, James, (Retired), St. John the Evangelist, Carmichael
Ya, Jacques, All Hallows, Sacramento
Yang, Gnia, All Hallows, Sacramento
Young, Michael, (Retired), St. Joseph, Auburn
Zachary, Neil, Holy Trinity, El Dorado Hills
Zellmer, Gary, St. Thomas More, Paradise

INSTITUTIONS LOCATED IN THE DIOCESE

[A] SEMINARY, RELIGIOUS

LOOMIS. *Mount St. Joseph Novitiate and Seminary* (1964) 6530 Wells Ave., P.O. Box 547, 95650. Tel: 916-652-6336; Fax: 916-652-0620. Email: fphil@osjoseph.org. Web: www.osjoseph.org. Revs. Philip Massetti, O.S.J., Rector; Arnold Ortiz, O.S.J.; Bro. Mathew Chipp, O.S.J. Novitiate of Oblates of St. Joseph. Priests 2; Brothers 1.

VINA. *Abbey of New Clairvaux, Trappist Seminary* (1955) 26240 7th St., P.O. Box 80, 96092. Tel: 530-839-2161; Fax: 530-839-2332. Email: pmschwan@newclairvaux.org. Web: www.newclairvaux.org. Rev. Paul Mark Schwan, O.C.S.O., Abbot. Priests 8; Brothers 12; Novices 1; Postulants 1. In Res. Rt. Revs. Thomas X. Davis, O.C.S.O., J.C.L.,

Abbot Emeritus; Bernard Johnson, O.S.C.O., J.C.L., Abbot Emeritus; Revs. Anthony R. Bellesorte, O.C.S.O.; Lawrence A. Glaser, O.C.S.O.; Paul Jerome Konkler, O.C.S.O.; Harold K. Meyer, O.C.S.O.; Mark Scott, O.C.S.O., S.S.L., Prof. of Scripture; Bro. Placid Morris, Librarian.

[B] COLLEGES AND UNIVERSITIES

SACRAMENTO. *University of Sacramento*, 1531 I St., 95814. Tel: 916-443-4760; Fax: 916-443-4765. Email: info@universityofsacramento.org. Web: www.universityofsacramento.org. Revs. Robert Presutti, L.C., Ph.D., Pres.; Declan Murphy, Ph.D., M.B.A., Dean, College of Business Admin.; Ray Helgeson, M.A., Dir. Academic Progs, College of Educ. Founded by the Legionaries of Christ. Priests 2; Lay Staff 4; Total Enrollment 118; Faculty 15.

[C] HIGH SCHOOLS, DIOCESAN

SACRAMENTO. *St. Francis High School* (Girls), 5900 Elvas Ave., 95819. Tel: 916-452-3461; Fax: 916-452-1591. Email: sfhsinfo@stfrancishs.org. Web: www.stfrancishs.org. Marion L. Bishop, Pres.; Patrick O'Neill, Prin.; Judy Walker, Librarian. Lay Teachers & Staff 130; Girls 1,137.

RED BLUFF. *Mercy Catholic High School*, 233 Riverside Way, 96080. Tel: 530-527-8313; Fax: 530-527-3058. Email: mercy@mercy-high.org. Web: www.mercy-high.org. Cheryl Ramirez, Prin. Lay Teachers 10; Students 93.

VALLEJO. *St. Patrick-St. Vincent High School*, 1500 Benicia Rd., 94591. Tel: 707-644-4425; Fax: 707-644-3107. Email: meryan@spsv.org. Web: www.spsv.org. Mary Ellen Ryan, Prin.; Alexa Stoneman, Librarian. Lay Teachers 47; Students 603.

[D] HIGH SCHOOLS, PRIVATE

SACRAMENTO. *Christian Brothers High School of Sacramento, Inc.* (1876) 4315 Martin Luther King Jr. Blvd., 95820. Tel: 916-733-3600; Fax: 916-733-3624. Web: www.cbhs-sacramento.org. Lorcan P. Barnes, Pres.; Mr. Raymond Burnell, Prin. Brothers 3; Lay Teachers 70; Students 1,070.

Cristo Rey High School, 6200 McMahon Dr., 95824-3153. Tel: 916-733-2660; Fax: 916-739-1310. Web: www.cristoreynetwork.org. Joseph M. Peggi, Prin. Sisters 2; Lay Teachers 13.

Jesuit High School (1963) P.O. Box 254647, 95865-4647. 1200 Jacob Ln., Carmichael, 95608-6024. Tel: 916-482-6060; Fax: 916-482-2310. Email: gilsonm@jhssac.org. Web: www.jhssac.org. Revs. Gregory R. Bonfiglio, S.J., Pres.; Michael C. Gilson, S.J., Supr.; Francis G. Hernandez, S.J.; David F. Klein, S.J.; Kevin A. Leidich, S.J.; Charles R. Olsen, S.J.; William K. Stolz, S.J.; Dennis Thiessen, S.D.S.; Bro. Justin DeChance, S.J.; Ms. Brianna Latko, Prin.; Mrs. Heidi Bleckmann, Librarian; Mr. Phillip Ganir, S.J.; Mr. Julian Climaco, S.J. (Boys) Jesuit Priests 7; Religious 1; Brothers 1; Scholastics 2; Lay Teachers 75; Boys 1,070.

[E] ELEMENTARY SCHOOLS

ELK GROVE. *St. Elizabeth Ann Seton Elementary* (1999) 9539 Racquet Ct., 95758. Tel: 916-684-7903; Fax: 916-691-4064. Email: office@stelizabetheg.org. Web: www.stelizabetheg.org. Trina Koontz, Prin. Lay Teachers 13; Students 317; Total Staff 36.

[F] DAY NURSERY AND CHILD CARE HOMES

SACRAMENTO. *St. Patrick Children's Home, Inc.*, 5945 Franklin Blvd., 95824. Tel: 916-733-0253; Fax: 916-733-0224. Email: mkiernan@diocese-sacramento.org. Web: www.saintpatricks.net. Rev. Michael F. Kiernan, Exec. Dir.

Two Residential Group Homes for Girls Ages 12-18: State funded for low income families-12 children ages 2-5. Private care: non-state funded. Kamiko Lucas, Dir. Res. Treatment & Foster Care & Adoptions. Tel: 916-421-1620, Ext. 214; Fax: 916-421-3729.

Lemon Hill, 5036 Lemon Hill Ave., 95824. Tel: 916-421-1620, Ext. 214; Fax: 916-421-3729.

McMahon, 8529 Florin Rd., 95828. Tel: 916-421-1620, Ext. 214; Fax: 916-421-3729.

St. Patrick's Foster Care Program/Adoption Tel: 916-421-1620, Ext. 230; Fax: 916-421-8773. Email: cbelle@sphsac.org. (Ages 0-17) 21; Total Assisted 29.

[G] HOMES FOR SENIOR CITIZENS

SACRAMENTO. *Mercy-McMahon Terrace*, 3865 J St., 95816. Tel: 916-733-6510; Fax: 916-733-6515. Email: mmtcook@comcast.net. Web: www.mercymcmahonterrace.org. Jim Cook, Admin. Mercy Senior Housing, Inc. Licensed Units 118; Total Assisted Annually 135; Total Staff 60.

[H] GENERAL HOSPITALS

SACRAMENTO. *Mercy General Hospital, a DBA of Catholic Healthcare West* (1897) 4001 J St., 95819. Tel: 916-453-4545; Fax: 916-453-4587. Web: www.mercygeneral.org. Denny Powell, Pres. Sponsored by Sisters of Mercy of the Americas West Midwest Community. Sisters of Mercy 7; Patients Assisted Annually 147,640; Beds 342; Total Staff 2,100.

CARMICHAEL. *Mercy San Juan Medical Center, a DBA of Catholic Healthcare West* (1967) 6501 Coyle Ave., 95608. Tel: 916-537-5000; Fax: 916-537-5111. Web: www.mercysanjuan.org. Brian Ivie, Pres. Sponsored by Sisters of Mercy of the Americas West Midwest Community. Sisters of Mercy 5; Beds 260; Patients Assisted Annually 171,848; Total Staff 2,139.

FOLSOM. *Mercy Hospital of Folsom, a DBA of Catholic Healthcare West* (1962) 1650 Creekside Dr., 95630. Tel: 916-983-7400; Fax: 916-983-7406. Web: www.mercyfolsom.org. Don Hudson, Pres. Sponsored by Sisters of Mercy of the Americas West Midwest Community. Sisters of Mercy 2; Bed Capacity 85; Total Staff 622; Patients Assisted Annually 56,168.

MT. SHASTA. *Mercy Medical Center Mt. Shasta, a DBA of Catholic Healthcare West* (1938) 914 Pine St., 96067. Tel: 530-926-6111; Fax: 530-926-0517. Web: www.mercy.org. Kenneth Platou, Interim Pres. Sponsored by Auburn Regional Community of the Sisters of Mercy. Sisters 1; Bed Capacity 80; Patients Assisted Annually 46,631; Total Staff 334.

RED BLUFF. *St. Elizabeth Community Hospital, a DBA of Catholic Healthcare West* (1906) 2550 Sr. Mary Columba Dr., 96080-4397. Tel: 530-529-8000; Fax: 530-529-8009. Web: www.mercy.org. Jon Halfhide, Pres. Sponsored by Sisters of Mercy of the Americas West Midwest Community. Sisters 1; Bed Capacity 76; Patients Assisted Annually 71,520; Total Staff 471.

REDDING. *Mercy Medical Center Redding, a DBA of Catholic Healthcare West* (1944) 2175 Rosaline Ave., 96001. Tel: 530-225-6000; Fax: 530-225-6125. Web: www.mercy.org. Jon Halfhide, Interim Pres. Sponsored by Sisters of Mercy of the Americas West Midwest Community. Sisters of Mercy 1; Beds 273; Patients Assisted Annually 152,304; Total Staff 1,694.

[I] MONASTERIES AND RESIDENCES OF PRIESTS AND BROTHERS

CARMICHAEL. *Sacramento Jesuit Community* (1963) 1200 Jacob Ln., 95608. Tel: 916-482-6060; Fax: 916-972-8037. Email: mgilson@calprov.org. Web: www.jhssac.org. Revs. Gregory R. Bonfiglio, S.J.; William F. Breault, S.J.; Michael C. Gilson, S.J., Supr. Email: mgilson@calprov.org; Francis G. Hernandez, S.J.; David F. Klein, S.J.; Kevin A. Leidich, S.J.; Michael E. Moynahan, S.J.; Charles R. Olsen, S.J.; Thomas G. Piquado, S.J. Email: tpiquado@calprov.org; Gerald H. Robinson, S.J. Email: grobinson@calprov.org; William K. Stolz, S.J.; George V. Wanser, S.J.; Arthur J. Wehr, S.J. Email: awehr@calprov.org; Bro. Justin DeChance, S.J.; Mr. Phillip Ganir, S.J.; Mr. Julian Climaco, S.J. (California Prov., Los Gatos) Priests 13; Brothers 1; Scholastics 2.

CITRUS HEIGHTS. *Christ the King Retreat*, 6520 Van Maren Ln., 95621. Tel: 916-723-5162; Fax: 916-723-6368. Email: christtheking@passionist.org. Web: www.passionist.org. Revs. San Juan Alfonso, C.P.; David Colhour, C.P.; Richard L. Parks, C.P.; George Stanfield, C.P.; Bro. Kurt Wernert, C.P. The Passionists (Chicago, IL)., A community residence for the Passionist priests and brothers who conduct missions and retreats. Priests 4; Brothers 1.

VINA. *Abbey of New Clairvaux, Trappist*, 26240 7th St., P.O. Box 80, 96092. Tel: 530-839-2161; Fax: 530-839-2332. Email: txdavis@maxinet.com. Web: www.newclairvaux.org. Rev. Paul Mark Schwan, O.C.S.O., Abbot; Rt. Revs. Thomas X. Davis, O.C.S.O., J.C.L., Abbot Emeritus; Bernard Johnson, O.S.C.O., J.C.L., Abbot Emeritus; Revs. Harold K. Meyer, O.C.S.O.; Lawrence A. Glaser, O.C.S.O.; Paul Jerome Konkler, O.C.S.O.; Anthony R. Bellesorte, O.C.S.O.; Rt. Rev. Mark A. Scott, O.C.S.O. Cistercian Abbey, Cistercians of the Strict Observance. Priests 8; Professed Brothers 13; Postulants 1; Novices 1.

WALNUT GROVE. *Monastery of Chau Son Sacramento*, 14080 Leary Rd., P.O. Box 99, 95690. Tel: 916-766-1356; Fax: 916-776-1921. Email: chausonus@gmail.com. Revs. Dominic Hung Tran, Prior; Francis Xavier Phan Bao Luyen; Mark Kieu Thai Hoc; Vincent Nguyen Dinh Hau, Cantor; Bro. Leo Nguyen Van Tien.

[J] CONVENTS AND RESIDENCES FOR SISTERS

SACRAMENTO. *Canossian Daughters of Charity* (1808) Our Lady of Lourdes Convent, 1949 North Ave., 95838. Tel: 916-925-4001; Fax: 916-925-8897. Email: fdcc_sac@yahoo.com. Web: www.fdcc.org. Sisters 4.

Religious of the Virgin Mary, 8804 El Verano Ave., 95626-0444. Tel: 916-992-6318. Sisters 6.

Sister Servants of the Blessed Sacrament (1904, Congregation); (1971, Community) 5929 61st St., 95824. Tel: 916-457-0182; Fax: 916-453-8950. Email: sisterleonor@yahoo.com. Sisters 4.

Sisters Catechists of Jesus Crucified (1962) Ave Maria House, 1123 W St., 95818. Tel: 916-443-7626; Fax: 916-442-1748. Email: hermanascjc@aol.com. Sisters 5.

Sisters of the Holy Rosary of Fatima (1952) 1708 U St., 95818. Tel: 916-442-8646; Fax: 916-733-0195. Email: vicentalemus@sbcglobal.net. Sisters 2.

AUBURN. *Sisters of Mercy of the Americas West Midwest Community, Inc.*, 535 Sacramento St., 95603-5699. Tel: 530-887-2000; Fax: 530-887-0789. Email: info@mercywmw.org. Web: www.mercywestmidwest.org. Sisters Norita Cooney, R.S.M., Pres.; Judith Frikker, R.S.M., Substitute for Pres.; Sheila Megley, R.S.M., Treas.; Judith Cannon, R.S.M., Sec.; Kathy Thornton, R.S.M., Leadership Team; Michelle Gorman, R.S.M., Leadership Team; Kim Kinsel, Community Oper. Officer; Carol Kelley, Community Fin. Officer; Sandy Goetzinger-Comer, Dir. Communications. As of July 1, 2008 the Sisters of Mercy of the Americas Regional Communities of Auburn, CA; Burlingame, CA; Cedar Rapids, IA; Chicago, IL; Detroit, MI and Omaha, NE, merged to create Sisters of Mercy of the Americas West Midwest Community, Inc. Sisters 810; Associates 565.

CARMICHAEL. *Religious of the Institute of the Blessed Virgin Mary*, Assumption Convent, 5055 Cottage Way, 95608. Tel: 916-488-8188; Fax: 916-722-5297. Sisters 3.

Other Locations: *Religious of the Institute of the Blessed Virgin Mary*, 3606 Chadsworth Way, 95821. Tel: 916-485-6384; Fax: 916-485-6385. Sisters 2. *Religious of the Institute of the Blessed Virgin Mary*, 9190 Sebastiani Way, 95829. Tel: 916-681-2016; Fax: 916-739-1178. Sisters 1. *Religious of the Institute of the Blessed Virgin Mary*, 3632 Ardmore Rd., 95821. Tel: 916-489-8931. Sisters 1.

FAIRFIELD. *Sisters of the Holy Faith* (1867) Holy Spirit Convent, 1050 N. Texas St., 94533. Tel: 707-425-3572. Email: ecurtis@diocese-sacramento.org. Web: www.hsschool.org. Sisters 3.

GEORGETOWN. *Discalced Carmelite Nuns* (1935) P.O. Box 4210, 95634. Tel: 530-333-1617; Fax: 530-333-1617. Web: www.carmelitemonastery.com. Carmel of the Holy Family and Saint Therese. Sisters 15.

[K] RETREAT HOUSES

SACRAMENTO. *Pendola Center*, 2110 Broadway, 95818-2541. Tel: 916-736-0141; 916-733-0127; Fax: 916-733-0195. Email: camppendola@diocese-sacramento.org. Web: www.pendola.org. Center located in Sierra-Nevada foothills near Camptonville. Summer camp for boys and girls 6-16. Available for teenage and young adult retreats, school midweek retreats, field trips. Contact: Dir. of Pendola Center.

APPLEGATE. *Our Lady of the Oaks Villa*, P.O. Box 128, 95703. Tel: 530-878-2776; Fax: 530-878-1615. Email: appvillia@pacbell.net. Rev. Gerald H. Robinson, S.J., Dir. Tel: 916-482-9666; Bro. James Sanders, S.J., Asst. Dir. Tel: 916-482-6060; Ronald W. Weingart, Resident Mgr. Tel: 530-878-2776. Available for retreats and conferences from September 1 to May 15.

AUBURN. *Mercy Center Auburn*, 535 Sacramento St., 95603-5699. Tel: 530-887-2019; Fax: 530-887-1154. Email: info@mercycenter.org. Web: www.mercycenter.org. A ministry of the Sisters of Mercy of the Americas West Midwest Community.

CITRUS HEIGHTS. *Christ the King Passionist Retreat Center*, 6520 Van Maren Ln., 95621. Tel: 916-725-4720; Fax: 916-725-4812. Email: christtheking@passionist.org. Web: www.passionist.org/christtheking/. Bro. Kurt Wernert, C.P., Retreat Dir.; Rev. David Colhour, C.P., Retreat Team; Sr. Marcella Fabing, C.S.J., Assoc. Dir.; Loretta Pehanich, Dir. Devel. & Public Rels.; Mr. Joseph Sebastian, Admin.

Christ the King Institute for Counseling & Spiritual Direction, 6520 Van Maren Ln., 95621. Tel: 916-783-9005; Fax: 916-723-6368. Elizabeth Evans, M.A., Dir.

[L] CAMPUS MINISTRIES AND NEWMAN CENTERS

CHICO. *Newman Catholic Community at Sacramento State University aka The Newman Club of Sacramento* (1967) Mailing Address: 5900 Newman Ct., 95819-2610. Tel: 916-454-4188; Fax: 916-454-4180. Email: kawasakim@sacnewman.org. Web: www.sacnewman.org. Rev. George Wanser, S.J., Dir.; Sr. Kathryn Camacho, S.N.D.deN., Pastoral Assoc.; Maggie Kawasaki-Murray, M.A., Campus Min.; Ms. Mary Ann Williams, Business Mgr. (St. Thomas Aquinas Newman Center).

Newman Catholic Student Community @ Davis 514 C St., Davis, 95616. Tel: 530-753-7393; Fax: 530-753-2794. Web: www.davisnewman.org. Deacon Clark Goecker, Dir.; Rev. Innocent Subiza (Rowanda), Chap.; Ellie Wright, Admin. Asst.

St. Thomas Aquinas Newman Center @ Chico 346 Cherry St., 95928. Tel: 530-342-5182; Fax: 530-342-3016. Email: newmancenterchico@yahoo.com. Web: www.chiconewman.org. Rev. Blaise R. Berg, S.T.D., Dir.

[M] CATHOLIC SOCIAL WELFARE ACTIVITIES

SACRAMENTO. *Catholic Charities of Sacramento, Inc.*, 2110 Broadway, 95818. Tel: 916-733-0253; Fax: 916-733-0224. Email: mkiernan@diocese-sacramento.org. Rev. Michael F. Kiernan, Chm. Bd. of Directors & Exec. Dir.

Member Agencies of Catholic Charities of Sacramento, Inc.:

Catholic Social Service of Sacramento, 5890 Newman Ct., 95819-2608. Tel: 916-452-7481; Fax: 916-736-0282. Web: www.csssac.org. Rev. Michael F. Kiernan, Chm. Bd. of Dir.; Kurt Chismark, Exec. Dir. Total Staff 9; Total Assisted 675.

Northern Valley Catholic Social Service, 2400 Washington Ave., Redding, 96001. Tel: 530-241-0552; Fax: 530-247-3354. David Gasman, Chm. Bd. of Directors; Don Chapman, Interim Exec. Dir. Total Staff 152; Total Served 16,798.

Catholic Social Service of Solano County, 125 Corporate Pl., Ste. A, Vallejo, 94590. Tel: 707-644-8909; Fax: 707-644-6314. Email: admin@csssolano.org. Web: www.csssolano.org. Ellen McBride, Chm. Bd. of Directors; Kurt Chismark, Exec. Dir. Total Staff 12; Total Assisted 5,500.

Subsidiaries of Catholic Charities of Sacramento:

Sacramento Food Bank and Family Services, 3333 Third Ave., 95817. Tel: 916-456-1980; Fax: 916-451-5920. Charles Sylva, Chm. Bd. of Directors; Blake Young, Exec. Dir. Total Staff 31; Total Served 56,104.

Administrative Project of Catholic Charities of Sacramento:

Mother Teresa Maternity Home, 3109 Sacramento St., Placerville, 95667. Tel: 530-295-8006. Barbara Goyette, Chm. Bd. of Directors. Total Staff 9; Total Served 169.

Cathedral Neighborhood Senior Center, 711 J St., 95814. Tel: 916-442-9014; Fax: 916-442-2438. Elizabeth White, Prog. Dir. Total Staff 2; Total Assisted 10,000.

Centro Guadalupe, 730 S St., 95814. Tel: 916-443-5367; Fax: 916-443-5845. Elizabeth White, Prog. Dir. Total Staff 2; Total Assisted 5,000.

Mercy Education Resource Center, 6007 Folsom Blvd. #200, 95819. Tel: 916-737-6026; Fax: 916-737-6507. Email: terry@mercyeducation.org. Web: www.mercyeducation.org. Sponsored by the Sisters of Mercy West Midwest Community., Provides marriage counseling and individual counseling, psycho-educational assessment for learning disabilities, school counseling, school resource teachers and instructional services, English language services for adults. Total Staff 36; Total Assisted 3,800.

Society of St. Vincent de Paul, Sacramento District Council, Thrift Store: 2275 Watt Ave., 95825. Tel: 916-972-1212; Fax: 916-972-1242. Email: jhallissy@svdp-sacramento.org. Web: svdp-sacramento.org. Office: 608 University Ave., 95825. John P. Hallissy, Pres.

Society St. Vincent de Paul, Sacramento District Council. Tel: 916-649-2214; Fax: 916-649-9241. Email: jhallissy@svdp-sacramento.org. Total Assisted 136,000; Total Staff 12.

AUBURN. *Grand Council, Catholic Ladies Relief Society of the Diocese of Sacramento*, 215 Terrace St., 95603. Tel: 530-823-3767. Mary Collins, Grand Pres.; Rev. Michael F. Kiernan, Grand Chap.

ROSEVILLE. *Society of St. Vincent DePaul* (1983) 503 Giuseppe Ct. #8, 95678. Tel: 916-781-3303 (Dining Room/Office. Hours: 10am-3pm M-F); 916-781-3368 (Thrift Store. Hours: 10am-4pm, M-Sat.); 916-781-3335 (Food Locker. Hours: 9am-11:30am, Tues-Sat.); Fax: 916-781-8105 (Office Fax). Mr. Tom Stanko, Pres. Emergency Services, Clothing Vouchers, Food Assistance, Dining Room, Thrift Store, Mail Service, SSI Payee, 15 transitional housing units etc. Also free medical clinic on Wednesday mornings 8:30 a.m. to 11:00 a.m. Provide triage and urgent care; no longitudinal care. Total Assisted 24,130.

VALLEJO. *Society of St. Vincent de Paul*, 1225 Tuolumne St., 94590. Tel: 707-644-0376; Fax: 707-644-1423. Benedict Archer, Pres. Total Assisted 3,000.

[N] YOUTH AND YOUNG ADULT MINISTRIES

SACRAMENTO. *Catholic Committee on Scouting*, 2110 Broadway, 95818. Tel: 916-733-0123; Fax: 916-733-0224. Email: mrichards@diocese-sacramento.org. Web: www.oharanetworks.com/dccs.htm. Very Rev. Mark R. Richards, J.C.L., Diocesan Chap.

Department of Evangelization & Catechesis, 2110 Broadway, 95818. Tel: 916-733-0123; Fax: 916-733-0195. Web: www.diocese-sacramento.org. Steve Patton, Dir.; Stephen Matuszak, S.T.L., Assoc. Dir., Catechesis; Carson Weber, Assoc. Dir. New Media Evangelization & Outreach; Deacon Antonio Ramirez, Coord. Spanish Catechesis; Mrs. Margaret Walrath, Coord. Deaf Ministry; Stanley Simonet, Deaf Ministry Worker; Steve Patton, Respect Life Coord.; Debbie Anderson, Project Rachel Coord.; Sr. Virginia Alcala, S.C.J.C., Hispanic Catechesis; Kevin Staszkow, Assoc. Dir., Youth & Young Adults.

[O] MISCELLANEOUS

SACRAMENTO. *California Catholic Conference* (1971) 1119 K St., 95814. Tel: 916-443-4851; Fax: 916-443-5629. Web: www.cacatholic.org. Most Revs. Stephen E. Blaire, D.D., Pres.; Daniel F. Walsh, D.D., Vice Pres.; Gerald E. Wilkerson, D.D., V.G., Sec. & Treas.; Mr. Edward "Ned" E. Dolejsi, Exec. Dir.; Carol Hogan, Dir. Pastoral Projects & Communication; Debbie McDermott, Exec. Asst./Assoc. Dir. Restorative Justice CA Catholic Conference; Mrs. Linda Wanner, Assoc. Dir. Governmental Relations; Stephen J. Pehanich, Senior Dir. Advocacy & Educ. CA Catholic Conference; Ginger Silvera, Assoc. Lobbyist; Barbara Caselli, Office Mgr.

Catholic Charities of California, Inc. (1987) 1119 K St., 2nd Fl., 95814. Tel: 916-313-4005; Fax: 916-443-4731. Email: smlahey@catholiccharitiesca.org. Web: www.catholiccharitiesca.org. Shannon M. Lahey, Exec. Dir.; Greg Kepferle, Pres.; Solomon Belette, Vice Pres.; Catherine Manfredo, Sec. & Treas.

The Catholic Foundation of the Diocese of Sacramento, Inc., P.O. Box 189656, 95818-9656. Tel: 916-733-0277; Fax: 916-733-0295. Mr. Larry Garcia Esq., Pres.

The Manogue Perpetual Endowment Foundation, Inc., P.O. Box 188066, 95818. Tel: 916-733-0277; Fax: 916-733-0295. Mr. Lon Burford, Pres.

Mercy Senior Housing, Inc. dba Mercy McMahon Terrace (1919) 3865 J St., 95816. Tel: 916-733-6510; Fax: 916-733-6515.

The Parochial Fund, Inc., P.O. Box 189666, 95818. Tel: 916-733-0277; Fax: 916-733-0295. Rev. F. Ignatius Haran, Pres. (Retired).

PAX Ministerio Foundation Trust Fund, 2110 Broadway, 95818. Tel: 916-733-0245. Web: www.diocese-sacramento.org. Sr. Paula Hurtado, O.P., Dir.

The Preserving Our Past, Building Our Future Foundation of Northern California, Inc., P.O. Box 188617, 95818. Tel: 916-733-0277; Fax: 916-733-0295. Mr. David Krotine Esq., Pres.

Sacramento Catholic Forum (2002) P.O. Box 254848, 95865-4848. Tel: 916-930-1144. Web: www.saccatholicforum.org.

**Stanford Settlement* (1936) 450 W. El Camino Ave., 95833-2299. Tel: 916-927-1303; Fax: 916-922-1694. Email: srjfelion@sbcglobal.net. Web: www.stanfordsettlement.org. Sr. Jeanne Felion, S.S.S., Exec. Dir. Total Assisted Annually 8,000.

LOOMIS. *Dominican Sisters of Mary, Mother of the Eucharist - Loomis*, 5820 Rocklin Rd., 95650. Tel: 734-994-7437. Email: sjdr@sistersofmary.org. Sr. John Dominic Rasmussen, Treas.

**IHR Educational Broadcasting*, 3256 Penryn Rd., Ste. 100, 95633. Tel: 866-774-3278. Douglas Sherman, Pres.; Lori Brown, Contact Person.

Spiritus Sanctus Enrichment, 5820 Rocklin Rd., 95650. Tel: 734-994-7437. Email: sjdr@sistersofmary.org. Sr. John Dominic Rasmussen, Treas. Sponsored by Dominican Sisters of Mary, Mother of the Eucharist - Loomis.

RANCHO CORDOVA. *Catholic Healthcare West - Sacramento Office*, 3400 Data Dr., 95670. Tel: 916-851-2000; Fax: 916-851-2727. Web: www.chwhealth.org/sacramento.

Corporate Headquarters, Catholic Healthcare West, 185 Berry St., Ste. 300, San Francisco, 94107. Tel: 415-438-5500; Fax: 415-438-5726.

Mercy Foundation (1954) 3400 Data Dr., 95670. Tel: 916-851-2700; Fax: 916-851-2724. Email: mercyfoundationsac@chw.edu. Web: www.supportmercyfoundation.org. Sr. Bridget McCarthy, R.S.M., Pres.; Alison Sadler, Chief Operating Officer.

WOODLAND. *Sociedad Guadalupana de Woodland*, Mailing Address: P.O. Box 1173, 95776. 920 North St., 95695. Tel: 530-662-4025. Email: ncampiz@cal.net. Ms. Luz Elena Campiz, Pres.

RELIGIOUS INSTITUTES OF MEN REPRESENTED IN THE DIOCESE

For further details refer to the corresponding bracketed number in the Religious Institutes of Men or Women section.

[]—*Augustinian Assumptionist Fathers*—A.A.
[0330]—*Brothers of the Christian Schools* (Napa, CA)—F.S.C.
[0270]—*Carmelite Fathers & Brothers* (Barrington, IL)—O.Carm.
[0350]—*Cistercians Order of the Strict Observance-Trappists* (Rome, Italy)—O.C.S.O.
[0370]—*Columban Fathers*—S.S.C.
[]—*Congregation of Mother Coredemptrix*—C.M.C.
[1000]—*Congregation of the Passion* (Chicago, IL)—C.P.
[]—*Crusade of the Holy Spirit*
[0520]—*Franciscan Friars* (Prov. of St. Barbara)—O.F.M.
[]—*Franciscan Order of the Atonement*—S.A.
[]—*Hermits of the Most Blessed Virgin Mary of Mt. Carmel*—H.O.C.
[0690]—*Jesuit Fathers and Brothers* (California Prov., Los Gatos, CA)—S.J.
[0730]—*Legionaries of Christ*—L.C.
[0930]—*Oblates of St. Joseph* (Santa Cruz, CA)—O.S.J.
[]—*Oratorians* (Colombia)
[0950]—*Oratorians*—C.O.
[0430]—*Order of Preachers-Dominicans*—O.P.
[1065]—*Priestly Fraternity of St. Peter*—F.S.S.P.
[1200]—*Society of the Divine Savior* (Milwaukee, WI)—S.D.S.
[]—*Society of the Divine Word*—S.V.D.

RELIGIOUS INSTITUTES OF WOMEN REPRESENTED IN THE DIOCESE

[1940]—*Congregation of the Sisters of the Holy Faith*—C.H.F.
[0730]—*Daughters of Charity of Canossa* (Rome, Italy)—Fd.CC.
[]—*Daughters of Divine Love*
[0820]—*Daughters of the Holy Spirit* (Putnam, CT)—D.H.S.
[0420]—*Discalced Carmelite Nuns*—O.C.D.
[1070-03]—*Dominican Sisters* (Sinsinawa, WI)—O.P.
[1070-04]—*Dominican Sisters* (San Rafael, CA)—O.P.
[]—*Dominican Sisters of Charity of the Presentation of the Blessed Virgin Mary*—O.P.
[]—*Dominican Sisters of Mary, Mother of the Eucharist - Loomis* (Ann Arbor, MI)
[]—*Handmaids of the Holy Child Jesus*—H.H.C.J.
[2370]—*Institute of the Blessed Virgin Mary (Loretto Sisters)*—I.B.V.M.
[2575]—*Institute of the Sisters of Mercy of the Americas*—R.S.M.
[]—*Religious of the Virgin Mary* (Quezon City, Philippines)—R.V.M.
[3499]—*Sister Servants of the Blessed Sacrament*—S.S.B.S.
[]—*Sisters Catechists of Jesus Crucified* (Mexico)—S.J.C.
[]—*Sisters of Mercy* (Omaha)—R.S.M.
[]—*Sisters of Mercy of Cashel* (U.S. Province)—R.S.M.
[4080]—*Sisters of Social Service of Los Angeles, Inc.*—S.S.S.
[1630]—*Sisters of St. Francis of Penance and Christian Charity* (Redwood City, CA)—O.S.F.
[]—*Sisters of St. Joseph of Carondelet*—C.S.J.
[1960]—*Sisters of the Holy Family* (San Jose, CA)—S.H.F.
[]—*Sisters of the Holy Rosary of Fatima* (Salvatierra, Mexico)—H.R.F.
[3680]—*Sisters of the Sacred Hearts of Jesus and Mary* (Essex)—S.H.J.M.
[4110]—*Ursuline Nuns of the Congregation of Paris*—O.S.U.
[]—*Visitation Sisters of Alleppey*—S.V.C.

DIOCESAN CEMETERIES

SACRAMENTO. *St. Joseph Catholic Cemetery*, 2615 21st St., 95818. Tel: 916-452-4831; Fax: 916-452-1364.

St. Mary's Catholic Cemetery & Mausoleum, 6700

21st Ave., 95820-5981. Tel: 916-452-4831; Fax: 916-452-1364.

CITRUS HEIGHTS. *Calvary Catholic Cemetery & Mausoleum*, 7101 Verner Ave., 95841. Tel: 916-726-1232; Fax: 916-726-4821.

COLUSA. *Holy Cross Catholic Cemetery*, 745 Ware Ave., 95932. Tel: 530-458-4170; Fax: 530-458-8728.

FAIRFIELD. *St. Alphonsus Catholic Cemetery*, 1801 Union Ave., 94533. Tel: 707-425-3111; Fax: 707-425-2029.

GRASS VALLEY. *St. Patrick Catholic Cemetery*, Rough & Ready Hwy., 95945. Tel: 530-271-5947; Fax: 530-477-2072.

RANCHO MURIETA. *St. Vincent DePaul Catholic Cemetery*, Jackson Hwy., 95683. Tel: 916-452-4831; Fax: 916-452-1364.

RIO VISTA. *St. Joseph Catholic Cemetery*, 130 S. 4th St., 94571. Tel: 707-374-2155; Fax: 707-374-5071.

VALLEJO. *All Souls Catholic Cemetery & Mausoleum*, 550 Glen Cove Rd., 94591. Tel: 707-644-5209; Fax: 707-554-4091.

St. Vincent, 550 Glen Cove Rd., 94591. Tel: 707-644-5209; Fax: 707-554-4091.

WOODLAND. *St. Joseph Catholic Cemetery & Mausoleum*, 503 California St., 95695. Tel: 530-662-8645; Fax: 530-662-0796.

NECROLOGY

† Mistretta, Rev. Msgr. Vito F., Citrus Heights, CA Holy Family—Died Oct. 13, 2009

† McGrath, Patrick, (Retired)—Died July 12, 2009

† O'Callaghan, Matthias J., Willows, CA St. Monica—Died April 9, 2009

An asterisk (*) denotes an organization that has established tax-exempt status directly with the IRS and is not covered by the USCCB Group Ruling.

Diocese of Saginaw

(Dioecesis Saginavensis)

Most Reverend

JOSEPH R. CISTONE

Bishop of Saginaw; ordained May 17, 1975; appointed Titular Bishop of Casae Medianae and Auxiliary Bishop of Philadelphia; ordained July 28, 2004; appointed Bishop of Saginaw May 20, 2009; installed July 28, 2009.

Established February 26, 1938.

Square Miles 6,955.

Comprises the following Counties in the State of Michigan: Arenac, Bay, Clare, Gladwin, Gratiot, Huron, Isabella, Midland, Saginaw, Sanilac and Tuscola.

For legal titles of parishes and diocesan institutions, consult the Chancery Office.

Chancery: 5800 Weiss St., Saginaw, MI 48603-2762. Tel: 989-799-7910; Fax: 989-797-6670.

Web: www.saginaw.org

STATISTICAL OVERVIEW

Personnel	
Bishop	1
Priests: Diocesan Active in Diocese	55
Priests: Diocesan Active Outside Diocese	3
Priests: Retired, Sick or Absent	35
Number of Diocesan Priests	93
Religious Priests in Diocese	7
Total Priests in Diocese	100
Extern Priests in Diocese	8
Ordinations:	
Diocesan Priests	3
Transitional Deacons	2
Permanent Deacons in Diocese	15
Total Sisters	94
Parishes	
Parishes	106
With Resident Pastor:	
Resident Diocesan Priests	56
Resident Religious Priests	5
Without Resident Pastor:	
Administered by Priests	20
Administered by Deacons	7
Administered by Religious Women	12
Administered by Lay People	6
Professional Ministry Personnel:	
Sisters	24
Lay Ministers	26
Welfare	
Catholic Hospitals	1
Total Assisted	318,460
Health Care Centers	1
Total Assisted	1,294
Homes for the Aged	1
Total Assisted	140
Residential Care of Children	3
Total Assisted	177
Day Care Centers	11
Total Assisted	357
Specialized Homes	3
Total Assisted	165
Special Centers for Social Services	5
Total Assisted	7,544
Other Institutions	3
Total Assisted	13,972
Educational	
Diocesan Students in Other Seminaries	12
Total Seminarians	12
High Schools, Diocesan and Parish	3
Total Students	660
Elementary Schools, Diocesan and Parish	22
Total Students	2,856
Catechesis/Religious Education:	
High School Students	1,036
Elementary Students	6,501
Total Students under Catholic Instruction	11,065
Teachers in the Diocese:	
Priests	1
Lay Teachers	265
Vital Statistics	
Receptions into the Church:	
Infant Baptism Totals	1,122
Minor Baptism Totals	105
Adult Baptism Totals	80
Received into Full Communion	309
First Communions	1,237
Confirmations	1,593
Marriages:	
Catholic	303
Interfaith	180
Total Marriages	483
Deaths	1,566
Total Catholic Population	110,563
Total Population	708,764

Former Bishops—Most Revs. William F. Murphy, J.C.L., LL.D., S.T.D., ord. June 13, 1908; appt. first Bishop of Saginaw, March 17, 1938; cons. May 17, 1938; died Feb. 7, 1950; Stephen S. Woznicki, D.D., second Bishop; ord. Dec. 22, 1917; appt. Titular Bishop of Pelte and Auxiliary Bishop of Detroit, Dec. 13, 1937; cons. Jan. 25, 1938; transferred to Saginaw, March 28, 1950; Assistant at the Pontifical Throne, Dec. 22, 1967; resigned and transferred to the Titular See of Tiava, Oct. 30, 1968; died Dec. 10, 1968; Francis F. Reh, S.T.L., J.C.D., third Bishop; ord. Dec. 8, 1935; appt. Bishop of Charleston, June 4, 1962; cons. June 29, 1962; transferred to the Titular See of Macrinna in Maurentania; Rector Pontifical North American College in Rome, Sept. 5, 1964; transferred to Saginaw, Dec. 18, 1968; installed Feb. 26, 1969; retired April 29, 1980; died Nov. 14, 1994; Kenneth E. Untener, ord. June 1, 1963; ord. and installed as Bishop of Saginaw Nov. 24, 1980; died March 27, 2004.; Robert J. Carlson, ord. May 22, 1970; appt. Titular Bishop of Aviocala and Auxiliary Bishop of Saint Paul and Minneapolis Nov. 22, 1983; cons. Jan. 11, 1984; appt. Coadjutor Bishop of Sioux Falls Jan. 13, 1994; Succeeded to the See March 21, 1995; appt. Bishop of Saginaw Dec. 29, 2004; installed Feb. 24, 2005; appt. Archbishop of St. Louis April 21, 2009.

Vicar General—Rev. Thomas J. McNamara.

Vicar for Priests—Rev. Ronald F. Wagner, 5800 Weiss St., Saginaw, 48603. Tel: 989-797-6649.

Episcopal Vicars—

Territorial Vicars—Revs. Robert Pare; William J. Gruden; Richard Bokinskie; John F. Cotter; James M. Fitzpatrick; Peter J. Gaspeny; William Rutkowski; Randy J. Kelly.

Hispanic Ministries Director—Maria Cepeda. Tel: 989-797-6604.

Delegate for Religious—Sr. Janet Fulgenzi, O.P., Ph.D., 5800 Weiss St., Saginaw, 48603-2799. Tel: 989-799-7910.

Chancery—5800 Weiss St., Saginaw, 48603-2799. Tel: 989-799-7910; Fax: 989-797-6670.

Chancellor—Sr. Mary Judith O'Brien, R.S.M., J.D., J.C.D.

Director of Human Resources—Connie Huiskens Wojda.

Administrative Assistant to the Bishop—Karen Schultz.

Financial and Business Operations—

Chief Financial Officer—Brian Buckingham. Tel: 989-797-6688.

Director of Accounting Services—Nancy Schultz. Tel: 989-797-6642.

Accounting Assistant—Josephine Mendoza. Tel: 989-797-6629.

Catholic Cemeteries—Kenneth Groya, Dir.

Diocesan Finance Council—Shelley Storer, Chm.

Diocesan Building Commission—Dan Kozakiewicz, Chm., 5800 Weiss St., Saginaw, 48603-2799. Tel: 989-799-7910.

Diocesan Investment Committee—Michael T. Gavin, Chm.

Inter-Parish Deposit & Loan—Robert Wolak, Chm.

Catholic Services Appeal—Amy Nietling, 5800 Weiss St., Saginaw, 48603-2799. Tel: 989-799-7910.

Tribunal—5800 Weiss St., Saginaw, 48603-2799. Tel: 989-799-7910.

Judicial Vicar—Rev. Robert J. DeLand.

Tribunal Coordinator—Heidi Krupp, J.C.L.

Defenders of the Bond—Sr. Victoria Vondenberger, R.S.M., J.C.L.

Judges—Rev. Robert J. DeLand; Sr. Mary Judith O'Brien, R.S.M., J.D., J.C.D.; Rev. Richard M. Filary, J.C.L.; Heidi Krupp, J.C.L.

Promoter of Justice—Rev. Michael Bradley.

Notary—Chris Wolak.

Diocesan Presbyteral Council—Rev. Peter J. Gaspeny, Chm., 1503 Kosciuszko Ave., Bay City, 48708-8027. Tel: 989-893-6421.

Clergy Personnel Board—Rev. William Taylor, Chm. (Retired), 1525 S. Washington, Saginaw, 48601-2895. Tel: 989-755-8020.

Diocesan Council of Catholic Women—Rita Faith Maher, Pres., 3028 McGill St., Marlette, 48453; Rev. Craig L. Albrecht, Moderator, 4195 Midland St., Box 99, Merrill, 48637-0099.

Office of Communication—Erin Looby Carlson; Matt Treadwell, 5800 Weiss St., Saginaw, 48603-2799. Tel: 989-797-6666.

Mission Office—Sr. Margo Tafoya, M.S.Sp., Dir. for Missions, 5800 Weiss St., Saginaw, 48603-2799. Tel: 989-797-6633.

Education/Formation—Joan M. LaPointe, Coord. Lay Formation. Tel: 989-797-6609; Dr. Ed Hogan, Dir. Deacon Formation & Diocesan Theologian; Sr. Yvonne Mary Loucks, R.S.M., Catholic Identity & Mission; Mr. Mark Graveline, Assoc. Dir. Youth Ministry & Vocations; Patricia D. Preston, Sec.

Bay Area Catholic Schools—Rev. William Rutkowski, Vicar; Michael J. Knoff, Dir., 607 E. South Union, Bay City, 48706. Tel: 989-894-8777.

Saginaw Area Catholic Schools—Irene Hensinger, Dir., 5802 Weiss St., Saginaw, 48603. Tel: 989-797-6632; Fax: 989-399-2257.

Ecumenism Ministry—Rev. JAMES R. CARLSON, 5800 Weiss St., Saginaw, 48603. Tel: 989-790-5086.

Ministry to Charismatic Renewal—MARGE FOBEAR, Dir., Charismatic Renewal Center, 1110 State St., Bay City, 48706. Tel: 989-684-4640.

Ministry to Priests—Rev. RONALD F. WAGNER, Vicar for Priests. Tel: 989-797-6649.

Roman Catholic Diocese of Saginaw Catholic School Foundation—5800 Weiss St., Saginaw, 48603-2799. Tel: 989-797-6679. VACANT.

Roman Catholic Diocese of Saginaw Inter-Parish Endowment Fund—5800 Weiss St., Saginaw, 48603-2799. Tel: 989-797-6683. ANNETTE M. O'BRIEN, Dir. Office of Stewardship & Planned Giving.

Office of Church Ministries—Dr. ED HOGAN, Dir.

Office of Christian Service—TERRI GRIERSON, Dir.; SANDY BUZA, Outreach Worker: Vic. 1, 2, 8, 11 & Respect Life Coord.

Marriage and Family Coordinator—MARY ANN CHERRY.

Coordinator of Multicultural Ministry—NATALIE MARZONIE.

Office of Liturgy—Sr. CHRISTINE GRETKA, C.S.J., Assoc. Liturgical Music; ELIZABETH GRZEMKOWSKI, Mgr., 5800 Weiss St., Saginaw, 48603-2799. Tel: 989-797-6664.

Organizations and Services—

Diocese of Saginaw Priests' Retirement Association—Rev. ROBERT J. MEISSNER, 2956 E. North Union Rd., Bay City, 48706-9246. Tel: 989-684-1170.

Conciliation-Arbitration—ANN M. SCHULTE, Conciliation Clerk, 5800 Weiss, Saginaw, 48603.

Holy Childhood Association—Sr. MARGO TAFOYA, M.S.Sp., 5800 Weiss St., Saginaw, 48603-2799.

Director of Development—DAN MCKUNE.

Office of Stewardship and Planned Giving—ANNETTE O'BRIEN, 5800 Weiss St., Saginaw, 48603-2799. Tel: 989-797-6679.

Victim Assistance Coordinator—Sr. JANET FULGENZI, O.P., Ph.D. Tel: 989-797-6682. Email: janet@dioceseofsaginaw.org.

CLERGY, PARISHES, MISSIONS AND PAROCHIAL SCHOOLS

CITY OF SAGINAW

(SAGINAW COUNTY)

1—CATHEDRAL OF MARY THE ASSUMPTION formerly St. Mary Cathedral (1853) Rev. Thomas J. McNamara, Rector; Most Rev. Joseph R. Cistone.
Res.: 615 Hoyt Ave., 48607. Tel: 989-752-8119; Fax: 989-752-2165.
Convent—Our Lady of the Assumption Convent Religious Sisters of Mercy Sisters 4.
Catechesis/Religious Program—
St. Mary Cathedral Parish Inter-Parish Endowment Fund

2—ST. ANDREW Rev. Ronald F. Wagner.
Res.: 612 N. Michigan Ave., 48602. Tel: 989-754-0487; Fax: 989-754-0308.
Catechesis/Religious Program—

3—ST. ANTHONY OF PADUA, [JC] Rev. Francis Voris, O.F.M.Cap.
Res.: 3680 S. Washington Rd., 48601. Tel: 989-752-1971; Fax: 989-752-1441.
Catechesis/Religious Program—Students 53.

4—SS. CASIMIR & ST. GEORGE formerly St. Casimir/St. George [JC] Rev. Reginaldo Salcedo, Admin.
Res.: 2122 S. Jefferson Ave., 48601. Tel: 989-752-6648; Fax: 989-752-6691.
Catechesis/Religious Program—Students 19.

5—ST. GEORGE, [JC] Merged with St. Casimir, Saginaw to form SS. Casimir & St. George, Saginaw.

6—ST. HELEN, [JC] Rev. Emmett L. Marceau; Joyce DeKarske, Pastoral Assoc.
Res.: 2445 N. Charles St., 48602. Tel: 989-793-0618; Fax: 989-793-5487.
School—(Grades PreSchool-8), 2415 N. Charles St., 48602. Nico Beer, Prin. Lay Teachers 10; Students 107.
Catechesis/Religious Program—Students 58.

7—HOLY FAMILY, [CEM] Rev. Ronald F. Wagner, Sacramental Min.; Deacon Roger Pasionek, Pastoral Admin.
Res.: 1525 S. Washington Ave., 48601. Tel: 989-755-8020; Fax: 989-755-7193.
Catechesis/Religious Program—

8—HOLY ROSARY, Closed. For inquiries for parish records contact SS. Simon and Jude Parish, Saginaw.

9—ST. JOHN VIANNEY Rev. James R. Carlson.
Church: 6400 McCarty Rd., 48603. Tel: 989-790-5086; Fax: 989-790-1681.
Catechesis/Religious Program—Kathy Bronz, D.R.E.; Jim Rapin, Youth Min. Students 185.

10—ST. JOSEPH Rev. Daniel Anholzer, O.F.M.Cap.
Res.: 936 N. Sixth Ave., 48601. Tel: 989-755-7561; Fax: 989-755-1090.
Catechesis/Religious Program—Students 75.

11—OUR LADY HELP OF CHRISTIANS, Closed. For inquiries for parish records contact SS. Simon and Jude Parish, Saginaw.

12—OUR LADY OF MOUNT CARMEL, Closed. For inquiries for parish records contact SS. Simon and Jude Parish, Saginaw.

13—SS. PETER AND PAUL Rev. John R. Johnson; Catalina Echeverri, Pastoral Assoc.
Res.: 4735 W. Michigan Ave., 48638. Tel: 989-799-5448; Fax: 989-799-1495.
School—(Grades PreSchool-8) Tel: 989-799-9006. Sr. Kathleen Stafford, D.C., Prin. Lay Teachers 6; Students 79; Religious 1.
Catechesis/Religious Program—Students 44.
SS. Peter & Paul Catholic School Foundation Endowment Fund

14—ST. RITA, Closed. For inquiries for parish records contact SS. Simon & Jude Parish, Saginaw.

15—SACRED HEART, Closed. For inquiries for parish records contact SS. Simon and Jude Parish, Saginaw.

16—SS. SIMON AND JUDE Rev. John Mancini, O.S.F.S.
Res.: 2395 S. Outer Dr., 48601. Tel: 989-752-7424; Fax: 989-752-0216.
Catechesis/Religious Program—Students 12.

17—ST. STEPHEN Rev. James Heller; Audrey Ann Wilson, Pastoral Assoc. In Res., Rev. William Taylor (Retired).
Res.: 2711 Mackinaw St., 48602. Tel: 989-799-2334; Fax: 989-793-3611.
School—(Grades Day Care-8) Tel: 989-793-2811; Fax: 989-793-8463. Dave Szymanowski, Prin. Lay Teachers 21; Students 305.
Catechesis/Religious Program—Sharon Wahl, D.R.E. Students 85.
St. Stephen Catholic School Foundation Endowment Fund

18—ST. THOMAS AQUINAS, [JC] Revs. Randy J. Kelly; Jose Parra.
Res.: 5376 State Rd., 48603. Tel: 989-799-2460; Fax: 989-799-0207.
School—Bernardine Sisters of Third Order of St. Francis, (Grades PreSchool-8) Sr. Ann de Guise, O.S.F., Prin. (Farmington, MI) Sisters 1; Lay Teachers 25; Students 402.
Catechesis/Religious Program—Jennifer Giddings, Youth Min.; Dana Dugan, D.R.E. Students 116.
St. Thomas Aquinas Catholic School Foundation Endowment Fund

OUTSIDE THE CITY OF SAGINAW

ALBEE, SAGINAW CO., ST. MARY Rev. Todd Arnberg.
Res.: 5661 Fergus Rd., Rte. 2, St. Charles, 48655. Tel: 989-770-4453; Fax: 989-770-5111.
Catechesis/Religious Program—Joy Tanner, D.R.E. Students 42.

ALMA, GRATIOT CO., ST. MARY Rev. Kevin Maksym; Deacon John J. Cremin, Pastoral Assoc.
Res.: 510 N. Prospect Ave., 48801. Tel: 989-463-5370; Fax: 989-463-1369.
School—(Grades PreSchool-6), 220 W. Downie St., 48801. Tel: 989-463-4579. Lisa Seeley, Prin. Lay Teachers 11; Students 112.
Catechesis/Religious Program—Marilyn Lorenz, D.R.E.; Linda Goodman, Youth Min.; Kathleen Cranna, Youth Min. Students 70.

ARGYLE, SANILAC CO., ST. JOSEPH, [CEM] Rev. Joseph M. Griffin.
Res.: 4960 N. Ubly Rd., 48410. Tel: 989-658-8145; Fax: 989-658-8105.
Mission—St. Ignatius Frieburg, Sanilac Co.
Catechesis/Religious Program—Edith Izydorek, D.R.E. Students 38.

AUGRES, ARENAC CO., ST. MARK Rev. James E. Falsey.
Res.: 415 S. Court St., 48703. Tel: 989-876-7925; Fax: 989-876-7778.
Catechesis/Religious Program—Nancy LaLonde, D.R.E. Students 9.

AUBURN, BAY CO., ST. ANTHONY/ST. JOSEPH, Operates jointly with St. Anthony, Fisherville. Rev. Thomas E. Sutton.
Res.: 84 W. Midland Rd., 48611. Tel: 989-662-6861; Fax: 989-662-0064.
Church: 4699 S. 11 Mile Rd., Auburn, Fisherville, 48611.
School—Area School, (Grades PreSchool-5) Terri Duch, Prin. Students 77; Lay Teachers 6.
School—Auburn Area Catholic, Early Childhood Center, (Grades PreSchool-5), 1492 W. Midland Rd., 48611. Tel: 989-662-6481; Fax: 989-662-3391. Tia Hahn, Prin.
Catechesis/Religious Program—Kellie Deming, D.R.E.; Michelle Butterfield, Youth Min. Students 149.

BAD AXE, HURON CO., SACRED HEART, [CEM] Rev. Robert J. Howe; Jan Rapson, Pastoral Assoc.
Res.: 311 Whitelam St., 48413. Tel: 989-269-7729; Fax: 989-269-4010.
Catechesis/Religious Program—Mickey Gavitt, D.R.E.; Jeff Cantrell, Youth Min. Students 137.

BANNISTER, GRATIOT CO., ST. CYRIL Rev. Wolfgang Streichardt.
Res.: 517 E. Main St., 48807. Tel: 989-862-5270; Fax: 989-862-4534.
Catechesis/Religious Program—Students 65.

BAY CITY, BAY CO.

1—ST. BONIFACE Rev. Dale A. Orlik; Mary Jo Bourdon, Admin.
Res.: 510 N. Lincoln St., 48708. Tel: 989-893-4851; Fax: 989-893-1781.
Catechesis/Religious Program—Diane Seidel, D.R.E. Students 116.
St. Boniface Parish Inter-Parish Endowment Fund

2—ST. HEDWIG Rev. Kevin Kerbawy, Sacramental Min.; Sr. Joann Plumpe, O.P., Pastoral Admin.
Res.: 1504 S. Kiesel St., 48706. Tel: 989-893-1072; Fax: 989-893-4710.
Catechesis/Religious Program—Phyllis Madziar, D.R.E. Students 34.

3—HOLY TRINITY Revs. Robert S. Gohm; Kevin Kerbawy; Nancy Ruh, Pastoral Min.
Res.: 1008 S. Wenona St., 48706. Tel: 989-893-4073; Fax: 989-893-7087.
School—(Grades PreSchool-5) Tel: 989-892-3018. Terrie DeWaele, Prin. Lay Teachers 7; Students 81.
Catechesis/Religious Program—Mary Dierich, D.R.E. Students 163.
Holy Trinity Parish Inter-Parish Endowment Fund

4—ST. HYACINTH, [CEM] Rev. Edward J. Konieczka; Deacon Lee Stilwell, Pastoral Assoc.
Res.: 1515 Cass Ave., 48708. Tel: 989-895-5581; Fax: 989-895-5583.
Catechesis/Religious Program—Susana Roznowski, D.R.E. Students 70.
Convent—912 S. Farragut St., 48708.

5—ST. JAMES (1983) [CEM] Rev. Robert J. DeLand; Deacon George Keller.
Res.: 710 Columbus Ave., 48708. Tel: 989-893-4693; Fax: 989-893-1504.
School—(Grades PreK-5) Tel: 989-892-4371. Sr. Julie Gatza, S.C., Prin. Sisters of Charity of Cincinnati 2; Lay Teachers 9; Students 138.
Catechesis/Religious Program—Students 58.
Convent—200 S. Farragut St., 48708.

6—ST. JOSEPH Revs. Patrick C. O'Connor, Sacramental Min.; Dale A. Orlik, Sacramental Min.; Sisters Gail Addis, I.H.M., Pastoral Admin.; JoAnne Witucki, I.H.M., Pastoral Assoc.
Res.: 1005 Third St., 48708. Tel: 989-895-5783; Fax: 989-895-8837.
Catechesis/Religious Program—Ruth Neitzel, D.R.E. Students 53.

7—ST. MARIA GORETTI Sr. Virginia Scally, S.N.D.deN., Pastoral Admin.; Rev. George J. Serour, Sacramental Min. (Retired).
Res.: 2872 N. Euclid Ave., 48706. Tel: 989-684-1523; Fax: 989-684-8286.
Catechesis/Religious Program—Barbara Walkley, D.R.E.; Debbie Stanolis, Youth Min.; Joe Stanolis, Youth Min. Students 62.

8—ST. MARY OF THE ASSUMPTION Rev. Craig L. Albrecht.
Res.: 607 E. S. Union St., 48706. Tel: 989-892-6031; Fax: 989-892-4005.
Catechesis/Religious Program—Students 69.
St. Mary Parish Inter-Parish Endowment Fund

9—OUR LADY OF GUADALUPE Rev. Reginaldo Salcedo, Sacramental Min.; Maria Cepeda, Pastoral Admin.
Res.: 1619 Broadway, 48708. Tel: 989-894-0661; Fax: 989-894-0771.
Catechesis/Religious Program—Josefina Ramirez, D.R.E. Students 4.

10—OUR LADY OF THE VISITATION Rev. Stephen Fillion.
Res.: 1106 State St., 48706. Tel: 989-684-5184; Fax: 989-684-5189.
Catechesis/Religious Program—Gerald Hegenauer, D.R.E. Students 4.

11—ST. STANISLAUS KOSTKA Revs. William Rutkowski; Daniel E. Roa; Sr. Beatrice M. Plamondon, C.S.S.F., Pastoral Ministry; Linda Studniarz, Pastoral Ministry.
Res.: 1503 Kosciuszko Ave., 48708. Tel: 989-893-6421; Fax: 989-893-3985.
School—(Grades PreK-5) Christine Szatkowski, Prin. Lay Teachers 5; Students 68.
Catechesis/Religious Program—Jan Musinski, D.R.E. Students 98.

12—ST. VINCENT DE PAUL Rev. Robert J. Meissner; Cathy Converse, Pastoral Min.
Res.: 2956 E. North Union Rd., 48706. Tel: 989-684-1203; Fax: 989-684-4925.
Catechesis/Religious Program—Chris Platko, D.R.E. Students 77.

BEAL CITY, ISABELLA CO., ST. JOSEPH THE WORKER, [CEM] Rev. Thomas J. McNamara.
Res.: 2163 N. Winn Rd., Mount Pleasant, 48858. Tel: 989-644-2041; Fax: 989-644-2026.
School—(Grades 1-6) Tel: 989-644-3970. Mrs. Mary Hauck, Prin. Lay Teachers 8; Students 131.
Catechesis/Religious Program—Barbara Schafer, D.R.E.; Josette Lorence, Youth Min. Students 71.

BEAVER, BAY CO., ST. VALENTINE, [CEM] Rev. Jerzy Dobosz, Admin.; Deacon Michael Arnold, Pastoral Assoc.
Res.: 999 S. 9 Mile Rd., Kawkawlin, 48631. Tel: 989-662-6843; Fax: 989-662-0152.
School—(Grades K-6), 1010 S. 9 Mile Rd., Kawkawlin, 48631. Tel: 989-662-6964; Fax: 989-662-0152. James Fielbrandt, Prin. Lay Teachers 3; Students 26.

BIRCH RUN, SAGINAW CO., SACRED HEART Rev. John S. Sarge; Noreen Harkins, Pastoral Assoc.
Res.: 12157 Church St., 48415. Tel: 989-624-9098; Fax: 989-624-9427.
Catechesis/Religious Program—Ginger Scheffler, D.R.E.; Janet Scheffler, Youth Min. Students 68.

BRIDGEPORT, SAGINAW CO.
1—ASSUMPTION OF THE BLESSED VIRGIN MARY Rev. John S. Sarge.
Res.: 7877 Bell Rd., P.O. Box 602, 48722. Tel: 989-777-1200; Fax: 989-777-6280.
Catechesis/Religious Program—Dave Fackler, D.R.E.; Janet Scheffler, Youth Min. Students 99.
2—ST. CHRISTOPHER Rev. John Mancini, O.S.F.S., Sacramental Min.; Sr. Ellen Rinke, I.H.M., Pastoral Admin.
Res.: 3945 Williamson Rd., 48601. Tel: 989-777-2091; Fax: 989-777-9691.
Catechesis/Religious Program—Karen Smith, C.R.E. Students 50.

CARO, TUSCOLA CO., SACRED HEART, [CEM] Rev. Dennis H. Kucharczyk.
Res.: 140 Atwood St., 48723. Tel: 989-673-2346; Fax: 989-673-5669.
Catechesis/Religious Program—Lisa Bednarski, D.R.E.; Karen Cody; Ann Reinelt. Students 143.

CARROLLTON, SAGINAW CO.
1—ST. JOHN THE BAPTIST Rev. Ronald J. Dombrowski, Sacramental Min.; Sr. Christine Gretka, S.S.J., Pastoral Admin.
Res.: 3160 Carla Dr., 48604. Tel: 989-753-5103; Fax: 989-753-4943.
Catechesis/Religious Program—Students 35.
2—ST. JOSAPHAT Rev. Ronald J. Dombrowski.
Res.: 469 Shattuck Rd., 48604. Tel: 989-753-2497; Fax: 989-753-2498.
Catechesis/Religious Program—Sr. Janet Pewoski, C.S.J., D.R.E. Students 11.

CASEVILLE, HURON CO., ST. ROCH Rev. Robert Pare.
Res.: 6253 Main St., P.O. Box 1238, 48725. Tel: 989-856-4933; Fax: 989-856-2861.
Catechesis/Religious Program—Elizabeth Weisenbach, C.R.E. Students 37.

CASS CITY, TUSCOLA CO., ST. PANCRATIUS Rev. Donald J. Eppenbrock, Sacramental Min. (Retired); Sr. Maria Dina Puddu, M.C., Pastoral Admin.
Res.: 4292 S. Seeger St., 48726. Tel: 989-872-3336; Fax: 989-872-1852.
Catechesis/Religious Program—Mary Shantz, D.R.E. Students 76.

CHESANING, SAGINAW CO., OUR LADY OF PERPETUAL HELP, [CEM] Rev. Richard Bokinskie; Diane Hunderford, Pastoral Assoc.
Res.: 404 S. Wood, 48616. Tel: 989-845-6894; Fax: 989-845-7787.
School—(Grades PreK-6), 802 Lockwood St., 48616. Lay Teachers 7; Students 41.
Catechesis/Religious Program—Students 99.

CLARE, CLARE CO., ST. CECILIA, [CEM] Rev. Patrick M. Jankowiak.
Res.: 106 E. Wheaton Ave., 48617. Tel: 989-386-9862; Fax: 989-386-3550.
School—(Grades PreSchool-6) Lay Teachers 7; Students 70.
Catechesis/Religious Program—Ann Strick, D.R.E. Students 40.
St. Cecilia Catholic School Foundation Endowment Fund

COLEMAN, MIDLAND CO., ST. PHILIP NERI Sr. Mary Ellen McDonald, O.P., Admin.; Rev. Raymond Moeggenberg, Sacramental Min. (Retired); Deacon Frank Alex.
Res.: 5199 W. Shaffer Rd., P.O. Box 512, 48618. Tel: 989-465-1768; Fax: 989-465-6311.
Catechesis/Religious Program—Judie Klimkiewicz, D.R.E. Students 24.
Mission—*St. Anne* Edenville, Gladwin Co.
Catechesis/Religious Program—Students 52.

CROSWELL, SANILAC CO., ST. PATRICK, [CEM] Rev. Christopher M. Coman, Admin.
Mailing Address: P.O. Box 399, Lexington, 48450.
Res.: 105 W. Sanborn Ave., 48422-1353. Tel: 810-679-3849; Fax: 810-679-3903.
Catechesis/Religious Program—Christina Lowry, D.R.E. Students 65.

ESSEXVILLE, BAY CO., ST. JOHN THE EVANGELIST Rev. Patrick C. O'Connor; Kathy Madziar, Pastoral Min.
Res.: 614 Pine St., 48732. Tel: 989-894-2701; Fax: 989-895-5558.
School—(Grades PreSchool-5), 619 Main St., 48732. Sue Grzegorczyk, Prin. Lay Teachers 6; Students 78.
Catechesis/Religious Program—Rose Yagiel, D.R.E.; Catherine Treadwell, Youth Min. Students 172.

FISHERVILLE, BAY CO., ST. ANTHONY/ST. JOSEPH, [CEM], See St. Anthony/St. Joseph, Auburn.

FRANKENMUTH, SAGINAW CO., BLESSED TRINITY Rev. Robert H. Byrne; Sr. Patricia Radomski, S.J., Pastoral Min.; Senior Deacon Larry Masserang.
Res.: 958 E. Tuscola St., 48734. Tel: 989-652-3259; Fax: 989-652-2206.
Catechesis/Religious Program—Carol Fox, D.R.E. Students 312.

FREELAND, SAGINAW CO., ST. AGNES Rev. Lawrence M. Pashak; Sr. Anne La Haie, R.S.M., Pastoral Min.
Res.: 300 Johnson St., 48623. Tel: 989-695-5652; Fax: 989-695-6275.
Catechesis/Religious Program—Laurie Finney, Youth Min. Students 227.

GAGETOWN, TUSCOLA CO., ST. AGATHA Sr. Dorothy Ann Blasko, O.P., Pastoral Admin.; Rev. Donald J. Eppenbrock, Sacramental Min. (Retired).
Res.: 4618 South St., Box 139, 48735. Tel: 989-665-9966; Fax: 989-665-9966.
Catechesis/Religious Program—Students 16.

GLADWIN, GLADWIN CO., SACRED HEART Rev. John F. Cotter.
Res.: 300 N. Silverleaf St., 48624. Tel: 989-426-7154; Fax: 989-426-0896.
School—(Grades PreK-8), 330 N. Silverleaf St., 48624. Tel: 989-426-8574. Joanne Sievewright, Prin. Lay Teachers 5; Students 37.
Catechesis/Religious Program—Students 55.

HARBOR BEACH, HURON CO., OUR LADY OF LAKE HURON, [CEM] Rev. William Spencer.
Res.: 412 S. First St., 48441. Tel: 989-479-3393; Fax: 989-479-3335.
School—(Grades PreK-8), 222 Court St., 48441. Tel: 989-479-3427. David Mausolf, Prin. Lay Teachers 9; Students 101.
Catechesis/Religious Program—Jean Winkel, D.R.E. Students 25.
Convent—406 S. First St., 48441.

HARRISON, CLARE CO., ST. ATHANASIUS Rev. Noel Rudy, Sacramental Min. (Retired); Sr. Jean T. Baumann, O.S.F., Pastoral Admin.
Res.: 310 S. Broad St., P.O. Box 528, 48625. Tel: 989-539-6232; Fax: 989-539-0129.
Catechesis/Religious Program—Students 22.

HELENA, HURON CO., ST. ANTHONY, [CEM] Rev. William Spencer.
Church: 8233 Helena Rd., Harbor Beach, 48441.
Catechesis/Religious Program—Students 36.

HEMLOCK, SAGINAW CO., ST. MARY, [CEM] Rev. Steven M. Gavit.
Res.: 151 St. Mary's Dr., 48626. Tel: 989-642-5606; Fax: 989-642-5240.
St. Mary Center—245 St. Mary's Dr., 48626.
Catechesis/Religious Program—Sheila Bugbee, D.R.E.; Wally Rohn, D.R.E. Students 67.

ITHACA, GRATIOT CO., ST. PAUL THE APOSTLE Carol Hale, Pastoral Admin.
Res.: 121 N. Union St., 48847. Tel: 989-875-2852; Fax: 989-875-7027.
Catechesis/Religious Program—Teresa Davaloz Cervantes, D.R.E. Students 57.
Mission—*St. Martin De Porres* Perrinton, Gratiot Co.
Catechesis/Religious Program—Students 38.

KAWKAWLIN, BAY CO., SACRED HEART Rev. Jerzy Dobosz, Admin.
Res.: 2510 Fraser Rd., 48631. Tel: 989-684-1402; Fax: 989-684-0038.
Catechesis/Religious Program—Leoma Bujalski, D.R.E.; Jeffrey Buczek, Youth Dir. Students 128.

KINDE, HURON CO., ST. MARY-ST. EDWARD Rev. Mieczyslaw Oniskiewicz; Sr. Judy O'Brien, I.H.M., Pastoral Min.
Office: 5083 Park St., 48445.
Res.: 1709 Moeller Rd., P.O. Box 68, 48445. Tel: 989-874-4744; Fax: 989-874-4744.
Catechesis/Religious Program—Sr. Judy O'Brien, I.H.M., D.R.E. Students 121.

LEXINGTON, SANILAC CO., ST. DENIS, [CEM] Rev. Christopher M. Coman, Admin.
Res.: 5366 Main St., P.O. Box 399, 48450. Tel: 810-359-5400; Fax: 810-359-5833.
Catechesis/Religious Program—Sr. John Marie Charniga, O.P., D.R.E.; Matthew Tonge, Youth Min. Students 39.

LINWOOD, BAY CO., ST. ANNE Rev. Jerzy Dobosz.
Res.: 315 W. Center St., 48634. Tel: 989-697-4443; Fax: 989-697-3630.
School—(Grades PreK-6) Tel: 989-697-3100. John Gravlin, Prin. Lay Teachers 5; Students 62.
Catechesis/Religious Program—Luann Hugo, Youth Min. Students 45.

MAPLE GROVE, SAGINAW CO., ST. MICHAEL, [CEM] Rev. T.J. Fleming.
Res.: 18994 Lincoln Rd., New Lothrop, 48460. Tel: 989-845-7011; Fax: 989-845-4729.
Catechesis/Religious Program—Students 326.

MARLETTE, SANILAC CO., ST. ELIZABETH Rev. Andrzej Boroch.
Res.: 6785 Marlette St., 48453. Tel: 989-635-7581; Fax: 989-635-5808.
Catechesis/Religious Program—Roxann Ross, D.R.E.; Rick Tanis, Youth Min. Students 60.

MAYVILLE, TUSCOLA CO., ST. JOSEPH Sr. Riccardina Silvestri, M.C., Pastoral Admin.
315 W. Ohmer Rd., 48744. Tel: 989-843-6565; Fax: 989-683-2556. Mailing Address: 1951 Kingston Rd., Deford, 48729.
Catechesis/Religious Program—Students 47.

MERRILL, SAGINAW CO., SACRED HEART, [CEM] Rev. Prentice Tipton Jr., Admin.
Res.: 419 S. Midland St., P.O. Box 99, 48637. Tel: 989-643-5366; Fax: 989-643-7710.
Catechesis/Religious Program—Students 78.

MIDLAND, MIDLAND CO.
1—ASSUMPTION OF THE BLESSED VIRGIN MARY Rev. Richard M. Filary.
Res.: 3516 E. Monroe Rd., 48642. Tel: 989-631-4447; Fax: 989-835-9722.
Catechesis/Religious Program—Betty Zeestraten, D.R.E.; Maria Christie, D.R.E.; Sr. Mary Lou Owczarzak, M.S.Sp., Youth Min. Students 156.
2—BLESSED SACRAMENT Rev. Peter J. Gaspeny; Deacon Michael Jankowiak.
Res.: 3109 Swede Ave., 48642. Tel: 989-835-6777; Fax: 989-835-2451.
School—(Grades PreSchool-5) Lee Ann Berg, Prin. Lay Teachers 8; Students 175.
Catechesis/Religious Program—Janet Martyn, Dir., Faith Formation; Lauree Birchmeier, Youth Min. Students 602.
Blessed Sacrament Parish Inter-Parish Endowment Fund
3—ST. BRIGID Rev. Nicholas F. Coffaro, Sacramental Min.; Deacon Aloysius J. Oliver, Pastoral Admin.
Res.: 207 Ashman St., 48642. Tel: 989-835-7121; Fax: 989-835-9141.
School—(Grades K-7), 130 W. Larkin St., 48640-6579. Tel: 989-835-9481; Fax: 989-835-9141. Maureen Becker, Prin. Lay Teachers 13; Students 143.
Catechesis/Religious Program—Paula Dachsteiner, Youth Min. Students 143.

MOUNT PLEASANT, ISABELLA CO.
1—ST. MARY UNIVERSITY PARISH Rev. William Prospero, S.J.; Jeremy Priest, Pastoral Assoc.
Res.: 1405 S. Washington St., 48858. Tel: 989-773-3931; Fax: 989-772-2745.
Catechesis/Religious Program—
St. Mary University Parish Inter-Parish Endowment Fund
2—SACRED HEART, [CEM] Revs. Loren M. Kalinowski; David John Jenuwine; Deacon Larry Fussman.
Res.: 302 S. Kinney Ave., 48858. Tel: 989-772-1385; Fax: 989-773-9118.
School—(Grades PreK-12), 200 S. Franklin St., 48858. Dennis Starnes, Prin. Lay Teachers 21; Students 317.
High School—*Sacred Heart Academy*, (Grades 7-12), 316 E. Michigan Ave., 48858. Tel: 989-772-1457. Dennis Starnes, Prin. Priests 1; Lay Teachers 12; Students 144.
Catechesis/Religious Program—Mary Gagnon, D.R.E. Students 145.

MUNGER, BAY CO., ST. NORBERT Rev. William J. Gruden; Sr. Tereska Wozniak, O.P., Pastoral Assoc.
Res.: 126 W. Munger Rd., 48747. Tel: 989-659-2193; Fax: 989-659-3417.
Catechesis/Religious Program—Mary Anne Adams, D.R.E.; Judy Lauria, Youth Min. Students 47.

OAKLEY, SAGINAW CO., ST. MICHAEL, [CEM] Rev. Richard Bokinskie, Sacramental Min.
Res.: 509 Parshall St., P.O. Box 75, 48649. Tel: 989-845-3545; Fax: 989-845-5499.
Catechesis/Religious Program—Students 42.

PALMS, SANILAC CO., ST. PATRICK Rev. Peter Nwokoye, Admin.
Res.: 1801 Palms Rd., 48465. Tel: 810-376-4853; Fax: 810-376-4853.
Catechesis/Religious Program—Students 10.

PARISVILLE, HURON CO., ST. MARY Rev. Peter Nwokoye.
Res.: 4190 Parisville Rd., P.O. Box 55, Ruth, 48470. Tel: 989-864-3523; Fax: 989-864-3164.
Catechesis/Religious Program—Brenda Plester, D.R.E. Students 43.

PIGEON, HURON CO., ST. FRANCIS BORGIA, [CEM] Rev. John Weis, Admin.
Res.: 25 Moeller St., 48755. Tel: 989-453-2151; Fax: 989-453-2090.
Catechesis/Religious Program—Linda Oeschger, D.R.E. Students 46.

PINCONNING, BAY CO.
1—ST. MARY, [CEM] Rev. Joseph K. Miller.
Res.: 739 W. Cody-Estey Rd., 48650. Tel: 989-879-5596; Fax: 989-879-6151.
Catechesis/Religious Program—Terry Stevens, D.R.E. Students 57.
Station—St. Agnes, (Closed), 216 E. Fifth St., 48650.
2—ST. MICHAEL Rev. Joseph K. Miller; Deacon Ralph Brisson, Pastoral Admin.
Res.: 225 S. Jennings St., 48650. Tel: 989-879-2141; Fax: 989-879-6633.
School—(Grades PreK-8) Tel: 989-879-3063. Annette Charchan, Prin. Lay Teachers 7; Students 110.
Catechesis/Religious Program—Students 42.
St. Michael Catholic School Foundation Endowment Fund

PINNEBOG, HURON CO., ST. FELIX, [CEM] Rev. Robert Pare.
Res.: 2515 Limerick Rd., Kinde, 48445. Tel: 989-874-5833; Fax: 989-874-6534.
Catechesis/Religious Program—Cynthia Tait, Youth Min. Students 30.

PORT AUSTIN, HURON CO., ST. MICHAEL, [CEM] Rev. Andrew D. Booms.
Res.: 8637 Garfield, P.O. Box 355, 48467. Tel: 989-738-7521; Fax: 989-738-5886.
Parish Center—8661 Independence Ave., P.O. Box 350, 48467.
Catechesis/Religious Program—Students 37.

PORT SANILAC, SANILAC CO., ST. MARY, [CEM] Rev. Paul Bala.
Res.: 7066 W. Main St., P.O. Box 467, 48469. Tel: 810-622-9904; Fax: 810-622-7953.
Catechesis/Religious Program—Maureen O'Mara, D.R.E. Students 40.
Mission—St. John Chrysostom Forestville, Sanilac Co.

RAPSON, HURON CO., ST. JOSEPH, [CEM] Rev. Robert J. Howe.
Res.: 3455 Rapson Rd., Bad Axe, 48413. Tel: 989-269-8084; Fax: 989-269-8084.
Catechesis/Religious Program—Students 28.
Mission—Most Holy Trinity [CEM] Smiths Corners, Huron Co.
Catechesis/Religious Program—Students 13.

REESE, TUSCOLA CO., ST. ELIZABETH, [CEM] Rev. William J. Gruden; Sr. Tereska Wozniak, O.P., Pastoral Assoc.
Res.: 12835 E. Washington Rd., P.O. Box 392, 48757. Tel: 989-868-4081; Fax: 989-868-0060.
School—(Grades PreSchool-8) Tel: 989-868-4108. M. Gabriela Marguery Costoya, Prin. Lay Teachers 5; Students 81.
Catechesis/Religious Program—Louis Pierce, D.R.E. Students 39.

ROSEBUSH, ISABELLA CO., ST. HENRY/ ST. CHARLES, [CEM] Lynn Trudell, Pastoral Admin.; Rev. Donald E. Henkes (MEM), Sacramental Min.
Res.: 4079 E. Vernon Rd., 48878. Tel: 989-433-2229; Fax: 989-433-5440.
Catechesis/Religious Program—Erin Zimmer, D.R.E. Students 40.

RUTH, HURON CO., SS. PETER AND PAUL, [CEM] Rev. Peter Nwokoye.
Res.: 7115 E. Atwater Dr., P.O. Box 55, 48470. Tel: 989-864-3649; Fax: 989-864-8600.
Catechesis/Religious Program—Students 38.

RYAN, MIDLAND CO., ST. PATRICK, [CEM] Rev. Prentice Tipton Jr.
Res.: 4708 S. Meridian Rd., Merrill, 48637. Tel: 989-643-5652; Fax: 989-643-5505.
Catechesis/Religious Program—Students 163.

ST. CHARLES, SAGINAW CO., IMMACULATE CONCEPTION, [CEM] Rev. Todd Arnberg.
Res.: 708 Sanderson St., 48655. Tel: 989-865-9460; Fax: 989-865-6690.
Catechesis/Religious Program—Joy Tanner, D.R.E. Students 58.

ST. LOUIS, GRATIOT CO., ST. JOSEPH Rev. Kevin Maksym.
Office: 605 S. Franklin St., 48880. Tel: 989-681-5080; Fax: 989-681-2887.
Catechesis/Religious Program—Kathy Fairchild, D.R.E.; Linda Goodman, Youth Min. Students 31.

SANDUSKY, SANILAC CO., ST. JOSEPH Rev. Charles Hammond.
Res.: 511 N. Sandusky Rd., P.O. Box 249, 48471. Tel: 810-648-2968; Fax: 810-648-2968.
Catechesis/Religious Program—Christina Lowry, D.R.E. Students 64.
Mission—St. John [CEM] Peck, Sanilac Co.
Catechesis/Religious Program—

SANFORD, MIDLAND CO., ST. AGNES Rev. Daniel Fox, O.F.M.Cap.; Deacon Edward Kebblish.
Res.: 2500 N.W. River Rd., 48657. Tel: 989-687-5657; Fax: 989-687-2450.
Catechesis/Religious Program—Laura Schelbert, D.R.E. Students 131.

SEBEWAING, HURON CO., HOLY FAMILY, [CEM] Rev. John Weis.
Res.: 8370 Unionville Rd., 48759. Tel: 989-883-2746; Fax: 989-883-2810.
Catechesis/Religious Program—Patty Burgett, D.R.E. Students 41.

SHEPHERD, ISABELLA CO., ST. VINCENT DE PAUL, [CEM] Sr. Patricia Warbritton, C.S.J., Pastoral Admin.; Rev. Frederick J. Kawka, Sacramental Min. (Retired); Deacon John Wilberding.
Res.: 168 Wright, 48883. Tel: 989-828-5720; Fax: 989-828-4652.
Catechesis/Religious Program—Karon Van Antwerp Latham, Dir. Faith Formation. Students 51.
Mission—St. Leo [CEM] Winn, Isabella Co.
Catechesis/Religious Program—
Mission—St. Patrick Irishtown, Gratiot Co.
Catechesis/Religious Program—Kathy Duffy, D.R.E. Students 41.

SHIELDS, SAGINAW CO., HOLY SPIRIT Rev. David L. Parsch; Sr. Marie Markel, I.H.M., Pastoral Assoc.
Res.: 1035 N. River Rd., 48609. Tel: 989-781-2457; Fax: 989-781-5518.
Catechesis/Religious Program—Sandy Des Jardins, D.R.E.; Melissa Shields, Youth Min. Students 242.

STANDISH, ARENAC CO., RESURRECTION OF THE LORD, [CEM] Rev. James M. Fitzpatrick.
Res.: W. 423 Cedar St., P.O. Box 306, 48658-0306. Tel: 989-846-9545; Fax: 989-846-9566.
Catechesis/Religious Program—Students 53.
Mission—St. Joseph Alger, Arenac Co. 48610.

UBLY, HURON CO.
1—ST. COLUMBKILLE, [CEM] Rev. Joseph M. Griffin.
Res.: 4470 N. Washington St., 48475. Tel: 989-658-8824; Fax: 989-658-2088.
Church: 3031 McAlpine Rd., Sheridan Twp.
Catechesis/Religious Program—Students 40.
2—ST. JOHN THE EVANGELIST, [CEM] Rev. Joseph M. Griffin.
Res.: 4470 N. Washington St., 48475. Tel: 989-658-8824; Fax: 989-658-2088.
Catechesis/Religious Program—Audean Vatter, D.R.E. Students 128.

VASSAR, TUSCOLA CO., ST. FRANCES XAVIER CABRINI Philip Krill, Pastoral Admin.
Res.: 334 Division St., 48768. Tel: 989-823-2911; Fax: 989-823-2999.
Mission—St. Bernard Millington, Tuscola Co. Closed.
Catechesis/Religious Program—Students 29.

WILMOT, TUSCOLA CO., ST. MICHAEL, [CEM] Sr. Riccardina Silvestri, M.C., Pastoral Admin.
Res.: 1951 Kingston Rd., Deford, 48729. Tel: 989-683-2475; Fax: 989-683-2556.
Catechesis/Religious Program—Students 29.

ZILWAUKEE, SAGINAW CO., ST. MATTHEW Rev. Ronald J. Dombrowski, Sacramental Min.; Sr. Janet Pewoski, C.S.J., Pastoral Admin.
Res.: 511 W. Cornell St., 48604. Tel: 989-755-7336; Fax: 989-755-4228.
Catechesis/Religious Program—Students 47.

Chaplains of Public Institutions

BAY CITY. *Bay Medical Center and Bay Osteopathic Hospital*, 1201 S. Erie, 48706. Vacant.

Outside the Diocese:
Revs.—
Cabrera, Jose, Casa Santa Maria, Via dell'Umilta 30, Rome 00187 Italy.
Friske, Joseph P. (Retired), Burgermeister-Keller Strasse, Munich 81829 Germany.
Heames, Denis M., Casa Santa Maria, Via dell'Umilta 30, Rome 00187 Italy.
Mullet, John, 1200 Seventh Ave., Saint Petersburg, FL 33705.

Retired:
Revs.—
Balwinski, Gerald E.
Boucher, Edward F.
Ederer, John A.
Eppenbrock, Donald J.
Favara, Joseph F.
Frego, Max
Friske, Joseph P.
Gavit, James F., J.C.D.
Janowicz, Barney J.
Jozwiak, Richard
Kawka, Frederick J.
Klimas, George H.
Kowalczyk, Thomas M.
LeFleur, R. Keith
Loos, Frederick C.
Maher, Michael L.
Moeggenberg, Raymond
Pilarski, Chester J.
Ratajczak, Richard C.
Roach, Joseph W., S.A.G.
Rudy, Noel
Schabel, Joseph A.
Serour, George J.
Shine, Robert W.
Sierminski, Vernon
Sikorski, Harold R.
Skornia, Bernard L.
Spleet, Julius A.
Surman, Stanley
Taylor, William R.
Thome, John J.
Vaughn, Mason
Welna, Floyd
Wolf, Michael H.
Yaroch, Kenneth E.

Permanent Deacons:
Alex, Frank, St. Anne, Edenville; & St. Philip Neri, Coleman
Arnold, Michael, St. Valentine Church, Beaver
Brisson, Ralph, St. Michael, Pinconning
Cremin, John J., St. Mary, Alma
Fussman, Lawrence, Sacred Heart Church, Mount Pleasant
Hudson, Francis W., St. Brigid, Midland
Jankowiak, Michael, Blessed Sacrament, Midland
Kebblish, Edward, St. Agnes, Sanford
Keller, George, St. James, Bay City
Masserang, Lawrence, Blessed Trinity, Frankenmuth
Oliver, Aloysius J., St. Brigid, Midland
Pasionek, Roger, Holy Family, Saginaw
Stilwell, Lee, St. Hyacinth, Bay City
Wilberding, John, St. Vincent de Paul, Shepherd

INSTITUTIONS LOCATED IN THE DIOCESE

[A] HIGH SCHOOLS, INTER-PAROCHIAL

SAGINAW. *Nouvel Catholic Central High School* (1984) 2555 Wieneke Rd., 48603. Tel: 989-791-4330; Fax: 989-797-6603. Email: pfallon@sacschools.org. Web: www.sacschools.org. Paul D. Fallon, Prin.; Kathy Myles, Campus Min.; Sue Schell, Librarian. Lay Teachers 36; Students 362.
Nouvel Catholic Central Educational Foundation Endowment Fund

BAY CITY. *All Saints Central Catholic Middle and High School*, 217 S. Monroe St., 48708. Tel: 989-892-2533; Fax: 989-892-7188. Web: www.bayareacatholicschools.org. John Hoving, Prin.; Brian Campbell, Asst. Prin.; Laura Tacey, Librarian. Lay Teachers 15; Students 270.

[B] ELEMENTARY SCHOOLS

AUBURN. *Auburn Area Catholic Schools*, (Grades PreK-5), East Campus: W. 114 Midland Rd., 48611. Tel: 989-662-6431; Fax: 989-662-3391. Email: aacs@vsol.com. Web: www.auburnac.org. Terri Duch, Prin. Lay Teachers 6; Students 77.

[C] CHILDREN'S HOMES

SAGINAW. *Holy Cross Children's Services*, 925 N. River Rd., 48609. Tel: 989-781-2780; Fax: 989-781-5422. Sharon Berkobien, L.M.S.W., Regl. Dir. Residential and community-based treatment programs for troubled youth and families with facilities located throughout the state of Michigan, under the auspices of the Brothers of the Holy Cross at Notre Dame. Includes Specialized Foster Care, Supervised Independent Living and In-Home Treatment. Youths 300.
Queen of Angels Center, 3400 S. Washington, 48601. Tel: 989-755-1971; Fax: 989-755-2780.

[D] GENERAL HOSPITALS

SAGINAW. *St. Mary's of Michigan Medical Center*, 800 S. Washington Ave., 48601-2524. John Graham, CEO; Rev. Thai Hung Nguyen, Chap. Daughters of Charity of St. Vincent de Paul, East Central Province, Evansville, IN. Bed Capacity 268; Patients Assisted Annually 318,460.
Field Neurosciences Institute, 800 S. Washington Ave., 48601-2524.

[E] HOMES FOR AGED

SAGINAW. *St. Francis Home of Saginaw* (1953) 915 N. River Rd., 48609. Tel: 989-781-3150; Fax: 989-781-3791. Total Staff 145; Residents 100.

[F] FAMILY SERVICE

SAGINAW. *Catholic Family Service of the Diocese of Saginaw*, Administrative Center: 5800 Weiss St., 48603-2799. Tel: 989-797-6638; Fax: 989-797-7436. Web: www.cfssite.org. Thomas Conklin, L.M.S.W., Exec. Dir.

Adoption Center: 915 Columbus Ave., Bay City, 48708-6690. Tel: 989-892-2504; Fax: 989-892-1923.

Counseling Centers:

Bay City:

915 Columbus Ave., Bay City, 48708. Tel: 989-892-2504; Fax: 989-892-1923.

Mt. Pleasant:

210 Court St., Mount Pleasant, 48858. Tel: 989-773-9328; Fax: 989-773-9803.

Saginaw:

710 N. Michigan Ave., 48602-4372. Tel: 989-753-8336; Fax: 989-753-2582.

[G] CONVENTS AND RESIDENCES FOR SISTERS

SAGINAW. *Franciscan Poor Clare Nuns, O.S.C.* (1991) 4875 Shattuck Rd., 48603-2962. Tel: 989-797-0593. Email: sisters@srsclare.org. Web: www.srsclare.com. Sr. Dianne Doughty, O.S.C., Abbess. Solemnly Professed 4.

Motherhouse and Novitiate of the Mission Sisters of the Holy Spirit (1932) 1030 N. River Rd., 48609. Tel: 989-781-0934. Sr. Margo Tafoya, M.S.Sp., Pres. Sisters 7.

ALMA. *Motherhouse and Novitiate of the Religious Sisters of Mercy* (1973) 1965 Michigan Ave., 48801. Tel: 989-463-6035; Fax: 989-463-5811. Web: www.rsmofalma.org. Sisters Mary Quentin Sheridan, R.S.M., Supr. Gen.; Mary McGreevy, R.S.M., Vicar Gen. Sisters 25.

[H] CATHOLIC EDUCATION ENDOWMENT FUNDS

SAGINAW. *Roman Catholic Diocese of Saginaw Catholic School Foundation*, 5800 Weiss St., 48603-2799. Tel: 989-797-6679. Annette M. O'Brien, Contact Person.

MIDLAND. *The James Cardinal Hickey Educational Endowment Fund for St. Brigid Catholic School*, 207 Ashman St., 48640-6579. Tel: 989-835-7121; Fax: 989-835-9141. Deacon Aloysius J. Oliver, Pastoral Admin.

[I] MISCELLANEOUS LISTINGS

SAGINAW. **Catholic Community Foundation of Mid-Michigan*, P.O. Box 6883, 48608-6883. Tel: 989-797-6683.

**The Catholic Weekly*, 1520 Court St., P.O. Box 1405, 48605-1405. Tel: 989-793-7661; Fax: 989-793-7663. Email: catholicweekly@sbcglobal.net.

Holy Spirit Sisters Charitable Trust (1988) 1030 N. River Rd., 48609. Tel: 989-781-0934. Sr. Margo Tafoya, M.S.Sp., Pres.

**Little Books of the Diocese of Saginaw, Inc.*, 5800 Weiss St., 48603-2799. Tel: 989-797-6653; Fax: 989-797-6606. Leona Jones, Operations Mgr.; Cathy Haven, Editor.

St. Mary's of Michigan Medical Center, 800 S. Washington Ave., 48601.

**Partnership Center*, 122 S. Hamilton St., 48602-2013. Tel: 989-249-4290. Phil Ropp, Dir.

**St. Robert Bellarmine Trust*, 5800 Weiss St., 48603. Tel: 989-797-6642.

Roman Catholic Diocese of Saginaw Inter-Parish Endowment Fund, 5800 Weiss St., 48603-2799. Tel: 989-797-6683. Annette M. O'Brien, Dir., Office of Stewardship & Planned Giving.

ALMA. *Saint Joseph Corporation*, 1965 Michigan Ave., 48801. Tel: 989-463-6035; Fax: 989-463-5811. Sr. Jane Firestone, R.S.M., Pres.

**Sacred Heart Mercy Health Care Center* (1981) 2025 W. Cheesman Rd., 48801. Tel: 989-463-3451; Fax: 989-463-1534. Email: spgshm@charterinternet.com. Web: www.sacredheartmercy.org. Sr. Mary Patricia Glowski, R.S.M., Admin.

BAY CITY. *Society of St. Vincent de Paul, Bay County Council*, 523 Michigan Ave., 48708. Tel: 989-893-5772. Email: bcsvdp@mail.speednetllc.com. Mr. Paul Dombrowski, Pres. Member Conferences: Bay City-Holy Trinity, St. Hyacinth, St. James, St. Joseph's, St. Mary, Visitation, St. Vincent de Paul; Essexville-St. John.

RELIGIOUS INSTITUTES OF MEN REPRESENTED IN THE DIOCESE

For further details refer to the corresponding bracketed number in the Religious Institutes of Men or Women section.

[0470]—*The Capuchin Friars* (St. Joseph Prov.)—O.F.M.Cap.

[0920]—*Oblates of St. Francis De Sales*—O.S.F.S.

[0690]—*Society of Jesus*—S.J.

RELIGIOUS INSTITUTES OF WOMEN REPRESENTED IN THE DIOCESE

[1810]—*Bernadine Sisters of Third Order of St. Francis*—O.S.F.

[1150]—*Congregation of St. Joseph*—C.S.J.

[3832]—*Congregation of the Sisters of St. Joseph*—C.S.J.

[0720]—*Consolata Missionary Sisters*—M.C.

[0760]—*Daughters of Charity of St. Vincent de Paul* (Evansville)—D.C.

[1070-03]—*Dominican Sisters* (Sinsinawa, WI)—O.P.

[1070-13]—*Dominican Sisters* (Adrian, MI)—O.P.

[1070-26]—*Dominican Sisters* (Oxford, MI)—O.P.

[1070-14]—*Dominican Sisters* (Grand Rapids)—O.P.

[1115]—*Dominican Sisters of Peace*—O.P.

[1170]—*Felician Sisters*—C.S.S.F.

[]—*Franciscan Poor Clare Nuns*—O.S.C.

[2740]—*Mission Sisters of the Holy Spirit*—M.S.Sp.

[2790]—*Missionary Servants of the Most Blessed Trinity*—M.S.B.T.

[3760]—*Order of St. Clare*—O.S.C.

[2519]—*Religious Sisters of Mercy of Alma, Michigan*—R.S.M.

[3560]—*Servants of Jesus*—S.J.

[0440]—*Sisters of Charity of Cincinnati, Ohio*—S.C.

[2575]—*Sisters of Mercy of the Americas* (Detroit, MI)—R.S.M.

[3000]—*Sisters of Notre Dame de Namur* (Boston, MA; Cincinnati, OH)—S.N.D.deN.

[1570]—*Sisters of St. Francis of the Holy Family* (Dubuque, IA)—O.S.F.

[3260]—*Sisters of the Precious Blood (Dayton, Ohio)*—C.PP.S.

[2150]—*Sisters, Servants of the Immaculate Heart of Mary* (Monroe)—I.H.M.

DIOCESAN CEMETERIES

SAGINAW. *St. Andrew's, Mt. Olivet & Calvary*

BAY CITY. *St. Patrick's, Calvary & St. Stanislaus*

LINWOOD. *St. Anne*

MIDLAND. *Calvary*

NECROLOGY

† Eickholt, Henry C., (Retired)—Died July 27, 2009

† Ganley, Charles, (Retired)—Died Dec. 11, 2008

† LeMarre, Theodore E., (Retired)—Died June 16, 2009

† Ryan, Joseph, (Retired)—Died April 20, 2009

An asterisk (*) denotes an organization that has established tax-exempt status directly with the IRS and is not covered by the USCCB Group Ruling.

Diocese of St. Augustine

(Dioecesis Sancti Augustini)

Most Reverend

VICTOR BENITO GALEONE

Bishop of St. Augustine; ordained December 18, 1960; appointed Bishop of St. Augustine June 26, 2001; ordained August 21, 2001. *Office: 11625 Old St. Augustine Rd., Jacksonville, FL 32258.*

LOVE · JOY · PEACE

Catholic Center: 11625 Old St. Augustine Rd., Jacksonville, FL 32258. Tel: 904-262-3200; Fax: 904-262-0698.

Web: www.dosafl.com

Square Miles 11,032.

Florida, east of the Apalachicola River, was erected by Pope Pius IX into a Vicariate-Apostolic in the year 1857, and in 1870 into the Diocese of St. Augustine.

Comprises all of the northeastern Counties of the State of Florida including Alachua, Baker, Bradford, Clay, Columbia, Dixie, Duval, Flagler, Gilchrist, Hamilton, Lafayette, Levy, Nassau, Putnam, St. Johns, Suwannee and Union Counties.

For legal titles of parishes and diocesan institutions, consult the Catholic Center.

STATISTICAL OVERVIEW

Personnel	
Bishop	1
Retired Bishops	1
Priests: Diocesan Active in Diocese	70
Priests: Diocesan Active Outside Diocese	2
Priests: Retired, Sick or Absent	32
Number of Diocesan Priests	104
Religious Priests in Diocese	15
Total Priests in Diocese	119
Extern Priests in Diocese	29
Ordinations:	
Transitional Deacons	1
Permanent Deacons in Diocese	62
Total Brothers	1
Total Sisters	100
Parishes	
Parishes	52
With Resident Pastor:	
Resident Diocesan Priests	47
Resident Religious Priests	5
Without Resident Pastor:	
Administered by Priests	2
Missions	8
New Parishes Created	1
Welfare	
Catholic Hospitals	1
Total Assisted	164,059
Homes for the Aged	2
Total Assisted	43,836
Special Centers for Social Services	9
Total Assisted	82,200
Residential Care of Disabled	4
Total Assisted	20
Other Institutions	5
Total Assisted	326
Educational	
Diocesan Students in Other Seminaries	7
Total Seminarians	7
High Schools, Diocesan and Parish	4
Total Students	2,448
Elementary Schools, Diocesan and Parish	27
Total Students	8,111
Non-residential Schools for the Disabled	1
Total Students	119
Catechesis/Religious Education:	
High School Students	1,013
Elementary Students	8,465
Total Students under Catholic Instruction	20,163
Teachers in the Diocese:	
Priests	1
Scholastics	2
Sisters	14
Lay Teachers	655
Vital Statistics	
Receptions into the Church:	
Infant Baptism Totals	2,191
Minor Baptism Totals	149
Adult Baptism Totals	192
Received into Full Communion	591
First Communions	2,652
Confirmations	2,055
Marriages:	
Catholic	353
Interfaith	219
Total Marriages	572
Deaths	1,121
Total Catholic Population	171,000
Total Population	1,966,314

Former Bishops—Most Revs. AUGUSTIN VEROT, S.S., D.D., cons. April 25, 1858; Vicar-Apostolic of Florida; translated to the See of Savannah in July, 1861; appt. Bishop of St. Augustine March, 1870; died June 10, 1876; JOHN MOORE, D.D., cons. May 13, 1877; died July 30, 1901; WILLIAM JOHN KENNY, D.D., ord. Jan. 15, 1879; cons. May 18, 1902; died Oct. 23, 1913; M. J. CURLEY, D.D., cons. June 30, 1914; promoted to See of Baltimore Aug. 10, 1921; died May 16, 1947; PATRICK BARRY, D.D., ord. June 9, 1895; appt. Feb. 22, 1922; cons. May 3, 1922; died Aug. 13, 1940; JOSEPH P. HURLEY, D.D., ord. May 25, 1919; appt. Aug. 16, 1940; cons. Oct. 6, 1940; Received Personal title of Archbishop Aug. 18, 1950; died Oct. 30, 1967; PAUL F. TANNER, D.D., ord. May 30, 1931; appt. Titular Bishop of Lamasba, Oct. 18, 1965; appt. Bishop of Saint Augustine, Feb. 21, 1968; retired April 21, 1979; Remained as Administrator to Dec. 4, 1979; died July 29, 1994; JOHN J. SNYDER, D.D. (Retired), ord. June 9, 1951; appt. Titular Bishop of Forlimpopuli Dec. 19, 1972; cons. Feb. 2, 1973; appt. Bishop of St. Augustine Oct. 2, 1979; installed Dec. 5, 1979; retired Dec. 12, 2000; remained as Administrator to Aug. 21, 2001.

Catholic Center—11625 Old St. Augustine Rd., Jacksonville, 32258. Tel: 904-262-3200; Fax: 904-262-0698. Office Hours: Mon.-Fri. 9-4:30.

Vicar General—Rev. WILLIAM A. KELLY, V.G., V.F.

Chancellor—Rev. MICHAEL P. MORGAN, J.D., J.C.L.

Secretary to the Bishop—NANCY ELLIS.

Secretary to the Chancellor—JUDY T. PINSON.

Fiscal Office—Ms. CATHERINE MACINA, CPA, Chief Fiscal Officer.

Diocesan Tribunal—11625 Old St. Augustine Rd., Jacksonville, 32258. Tel: 904-262-3200. Rev. CAESAR RUSSO, M.A., J.C.L., S.T.L.

Judicial Vicar—Rev. TIMOTHY M. LINDENFELSER, J.C.L.

Associate Judges—Rev. Msgr. DANIEL B. LOGAN; Rev. MICHAEL P. MORGAN, J.D., J.C.L.; KAREN KIGHT, J.C.L.

Defenders of the Bond—Revs. CAESAR RUSSO, M.A., J.C.L., S.T.L.; PETER AKIN-OTIKO.

Promoter of Justice—Rev. RALPH L. BESENDORFER, J.C.D.; MARY C. SLEEPER, Administrative Asst.

Diocesan Consultors—Rev. DANIEL CODY; Rev. Msgr. VINCENT J. HAUT, V.G., M.S.W.; Revs. WILLIAM A. KELLY, V.G., V.F.; JOSE J. KULATHINAL, C.M.I.; MICHAEL P. MORGAN, J.D., J.C.L.; THANH T. NGUYEN; MICHAEL PENDERGRAFT; MICHAEL S. WILLIAMS.

Diocesan Pastoral Council—RAY MAKOWSKI, Chm., Diocese of St. Augustine Catholic Center, 11625 Old St. Augustine Rd., Jacksonville, 32258. Tel: 904-262-3200; Fax: 904-262-0698.

Presbyteral Council—Most Rev. VICTOR GALEONE, Pres.; Revs. THANH T. NGUYEN; ROBERT TRUJILLO; MICHAEL S. WILLIAMS, Vice Chm.; MICHAEL P. MORGAN, J.D., J.C.L., Treas.; JOSE J. KULATHINAL, C.M.I.; TIMOTHY R. LOZIER; FREDERICK R. PARKE, Chm.; WILLIAM A. KELLY, V.G., V.F.; JHON GUARNIZO; TIMOTHY S. CUSICK; MICHAEL PENDERGRAFT, Sec.; DANIEL CODY; Rev. Msgr. VINCENT HAUT, V.G., M.S.W.

Deans—Revs. THOMAS S. WILLIS, St. Augustine Deanery; ROLAND M. JULIEN, V.F., Gainesville Deanery; JOSE J. KULATHINAL, C.M.I., North Jacksonville Deanery; WILLIAM A. KELLY, V.G., V.F., South Jacksonville Deanery.

Building Commission—Most Rev. VICTOR GALEONE, Chm.; Rev. MICHAEL P. MORGAN, J.D., J.C.L., Chancellor; Rev. Msgr. DANIEL B. LOGAN; Revs. MICHAEL J. LARKIN; WILLIAM A. KELLY, V.G., V.F.; Ms. CATHERINE MACINA, CPA, Fiscal Mgr.; Mr. JOHN BOTTARO; Mr. JAY DEMETREE; Mr. CHARLES DAVID, Dir. Planning, Construction & Mgmt.

Catholic Foundation of Diocese of St. Augustine—VACANT, Exec. Dir.; Most Rev. VICTOR GALEONE, Pres.

Finance Committee—Rev. WILLIAM A. KELLY, V.G., V.F., Chm., 11625 Old St. Augustine Rd., Jacksonville, 32258. Tel: 904-262-3200.

Insurance Committee, Diocesan—Mr. RON GINDER, Chm., 11625 Old St. Augustine Rd., Jacksonville, 32258. Tel: 904-262-3200.

Diocesan Offices and Directors

Apostleship of the Sea—Deacon GJET BAJRAKTARI, Providence Center, 134 E. Church St., Jacksonville, 32202-3130. Tel: 904-356-3104.

Archives of Diocese—Sr. CATHERINE BITZER, S.S.J., Archivist, Mailing Address: P.O. Box 3506, Saint Augustine, 32085. Tel: 904-823-8707.

Multicultural Ministry—134 E. Church St., Jacksonville, 32202. Tel: 904-353-3243. Rev. MICHAEL P. MORGAN, J.D., J.C.L., Dir.; Ms. ALBA M. OROZCO, Hispanic Ministry Coord. Tel: 904-854-0669; Revs. JHON GUARNIZO, Moderator; JAMES R. BODDIE JR., Moderator.

Diocesan Schools and Social Action Appeal—Rev. EDWARD K. ROONEY, Dir., 1606 Blanding Blvd., Middleburg, 32068. Tel: 904-282-0439.

Christian Formation—ERIN MCGEEVER, Dir., 11625 Old St. Augustine Rd., Jacksonville, 32258. Tel: 904-262-3200.

Catholic Burse Endowment Fund, Inc.— (Education of Priests), *11625 Old St. Augustine Rd., Jacksonville, 32258.* Tel: 904-262-3200.

Catholic Charities Bureau, Inc.—Mr. WILLIAM C. BEITZ, Exec. Dir., 134 E. Church St., Jacksonville, 32202. Tel: 904-262-3200 See separate listing for more details.

Catholic Relief Services—Mr. WILLIAM C. BEITZ, Dir., 134 E. Church St., Jacksonville, 32202. Tel: 904-262-3200.

Catholic Women, Council of—Rev. LUKE MCLOUGHLIN, Spiritual Moderator, St. Matthew Church, 1773 Blanding Blvd., Jacksonville, 32210. Tel: 904-388-8698.

Charismatic Renewal—VACANT, Liaison; KATHERINE A. PERNINI, Sec., Mailing Address: P.O. Box 13888, Gainesville, 32604. Tel: 352-371-2185.

Civil Institutions—Rev. JOSE MANIYANGAT, Mailing Address: St. Mary Parish, P.O. Box 1120, Macclenny, 32063. Tel: 904-259-6414.

Communications Commission—ART MARSHALL, Chm., 11625 Old St. Augustine Rd., Jacksonville, 32258. Tel: 904-262-3200.

Communications, Office of—KATHLEEN BAGG, Dir., 11624 Old St. Augustine Rd., Jacksonville, 32258. Tel: 904-262-3200.

Continuing Education for Priests—Deacon ROBERT DELUCA, Dir., 12366 Brady Place Blvd., Jacksonville, 32223. Tel: 904-880-2692.

Cursillos de Cristiandad—Rev. Msgr. VINCENT J. HAUT, V.G., M.S.W., Diocesan Spiritual Dir., Blessed Trinity Parish, 10472 Beach Blvd., Jacksonville, 32246. Tel: 904-641-1414; Rev. TIMOTHY R. LOZIER, Asst. Diocesan Spiritual Dir., Most Holy Redeemer, 8523 Normany Blvd., Jacksonville, 32221. Tel: 904-786-1192; Mr. PETER LASHER, Rgnl. Coord. Tel: 904-910-6646. Email: petelasher@earthlink.net; PETE ROYAL, Lay Leader. Tel: 904-707-6625.

Disabilities, Ministry of Persons with—TRISHA KEE, Dir., Mailing Address: Providence Center, 134 E. Church St., Jacksonville, 32202-3130. Tel: 904-356-0810; Fax: 904-358-7302.

Ecumenism and Interfaith—Rev. MICHAEL P. MORGAN, J.D., J.C.L., Chm., 11625 Old St. Augustine Rd., Jacksonville, 32258. Tel: 904-262-3200.

Educational Services—PATRICIA H. BRONSARD, M.S., M.A., Supt. Schools, 11625 Old St. Augustine Rd., Jacksonville, 32258. Tel: 904-262-3200.

Family Life, Diocesan Center for—VACANT, Dir.; Rev. DANIEL CODY, Consultant, 11625 Old St. Augustine Rd., Jacksonville, 32258. Tel: 904-262-3200. Regional Office: St. Vincent's Health System. Tel: 904-308-7474.

Farmworker Services Program—Ms. OLGA LARA-MOSER, Dir., 234 S. Summit St., Crescent City, 32112. Tel: 386-698-4234.

Florida Catholic Conference—D. MICHAEL MCCARRON, Ph.D., Exec. Dir., 201 W. Park Ave., Tallahassee, 32301-7715. Tel: 850-222-3803.

Holy Childhood Association, The—Deacon BRYAN OTT, Dir., 107A 15th St., Saint Augustine, 32080. Tel: 904-461-5762.

Holy Name Societies—VACANT.

Diocesan Investment Committee—Rev. WILLIAM A. KELLY, V.G., V.F., Chm.

Justice and Peace Commission—Mr. WILLIAM J. TIERNEY, Chm., 11625 Old. St. Augustine Rd., Jacksonville, 32258. Tel: 904-262-3200.

Legalization—Mrs. JULIA CASTRO, Dir., Providence Center, 134 E. Church St., Rm. D-21, Jacksonville, 32202. Tel: 904-354-5904; Fax: 904-356-2092.

Legion of Mary—Rev. JOSE MANIYANGAT, Spiritual Dir., Mailing Address: P.O. Box 1120, Macclenny, 32063. Tel: 904-259-6414.

Office of Liturgy—Rev. THOMAS S. WILLIS, Dir., 11625 Old St. Augustine Rd., Jacksonville, 32258. Tel: 904-262-3200.

Priests' Spirituality Committee—Rev. JOHN M. PHILLIPS, 747 N.W. 43rd St., Gainesville, 32607. Tel: 352-376-5405.

Propagation of the Faith—Deacon BRYAN OTT, Dir., 107A 15th St., Saint Augustine, 32080. Tel: 904-461-5762.

Refugee Resettlement—JOHN FITZGERALD, Dir., Providence Center, 134 E. Church St., Jacksonville, 32202-3130. Tel: 904-354-3416.

Respect Life Activities—LORRAINE ALLAIRE, Respect Life Coord.; Rev. THOMAS S. WILLIS, Spiritual Moderator, 2577 Park St., Jacksonville, 32204. Tel: 904-308-7474.

Rural Life Director—Rev. MICHAEL PENDERGRAFT, Mailing Address: 1905 S.W. Epiphany Court, Lake City, 32025. Tel: 386-752-4470.

Scouts—Revs. JAMES R. BODDIE JR., Chap.; EDWARD W. MURPHY, Asst. Chap., Mailing Address: 11625 Old St. Augustine Rd., Jacksonville, 32258. Tel: 904-262-3200.

Seminarians—Rev. REMIGIUSZ BLASZKOWSKI, Dir., 11625 Old St. Augustine Rd., Jacksonville, 32258. Tel: 904-262-3200.

Vicar for Priests—Rev. DONAL P. SULLIVAN, V.F., 7190 Hwy. 17 S., Green Cove Springs, 32043. Tel: 904-262-3200.

Vicar for Deacons—Deacon HENRY ZMUDA, 258 S.W. 132nd Terr., Newberry, 32669.

Episcopal Delegate for Religious—Sr. MAUREEN KELLEY, O.P., 1649 Kinglsey Ave., Orange Park, 32073. Tel: 904-262-3200.

Vicar for Senior Priests—Rev. Msgr. EUGENE C. KOHLS, P.A., J.C.D. (Retired), 5201 Atlantic Blvd., #228, Jacksonville, 32207. Tel: 904-348-3983.

Victim Assistance Coordinator—JUDY PINSON. Tel: 904-262-3200. Email: jpinson@dosafl.com.

Vocations—Revs. REMIGIUSZ BLASZKOWSKI, Dir.; DAVID RUCHINSKI, Assoc. Dir., 11625 Old St. Augustine Rd., Jacksonville, 32258. Tel: 904-262-3200.

Youth and Young Adult Ministry—11625 Old St. Augustine Rd., Jacksonville, 32258. Tel: 904-262-3200; Fax: 904-262-0698. ERIN MCGEEVER, Dir.

CLERGY, PARISHES, MISSIONS AND PAROCHIAL SCHOOLS

CITY OF ST. AUGUSTINE

(ST. JOHN'S COUNTY)

1—CATHEDRAL - BASILICA OF ST. AUGUSTINE (1565) [CEM] [JC] Revs. Thomas S. Willis; Andy Blaszkowski, Parochial Vicar; Edward Booth; Deacon John Pelletier.
Res.: 35 Treasury St., 32084. Tel: 904-824-2806; Fax: 904-824-0761. Email: cathparish@gmail.com. Web: www.thefirstparish.org.
School—Cathedral Parish School, (Grades K-8), 259 St. George St., 32084. Tel: 904-824-2861; Fax: 904-829-2059. Email: mrogero@cathedralparishschool.org. Web: www.cathedralparishschool.org. Mrs. Janet Morton, Prin. Lay Teachers 25; Students 349.
Cathedral Parish Early Education Center—10 Sebastian Ave., 32084. Tel: 904-829-2933; Fax: 904-829-9339. Email: valleycpeec@aol.com. Web: www.cpeec.org. Jill Valley, Dir. (Preschool with Before and After School Care) Lay Teachers 14; Students 92.
Catechesis/Religious Program—Tel: 904-824-2806, Ext. 335. Email: cathedralcfp@gmail.com. Matthew Weiler, D.R.E. Students 67.
Mission—Prince of Peace San Marco Ave., St. Johns Co. 32084.
Mission—St. Benedict the Moor Martin Luther King Ave., St. Johns Co. 32084.

2—ST. ANASTASIA (1988) Rev. D. Terrence Morgan; Deacons Bob Lucian; Ron Gagne; Paul Pettie; George Murati; Ken Baechel; William Joyce; Bryan Ott.
Mailing Address: 5205 A1A S., 32080-8006. Email: stanastasiacc@aol.com. Web: stanastasiacc.org.
Res.: 5319 Fifth St., 32080. Tel: 904-471-5364 (Office); Fax: 904-471-7448.
Catechesis/Religious Program—Email: stanastaciaccdre@aol.com. Sr. Marilyn Dingman, S.S.J., D.R.E. Students 190.

3—MISSION OF NOMBRE DE DIOS AND SHRINE OF OUR LADY OF LA LECHE (1565) [JC] Eric P. Johnson, Dir.
Office: 27 Ocean Ave., 32084. Tel: 904-824-2809; Fax: 904-829-0819. Email: shrine@missionandshrine.org. Web: www.missionandshrine.org.

4—OUR LADY OF GOOD COUNSEL (2008) Rev. Guy Noonan.
5950 State Rd. 16, 32092. Tel: 904-824-8688. Web: www.ourladyofgoodcounsel-church.org.
Church: 5005 Church Rd., 32092-0459. Fax: 904-824-5110. Email: olgcoffice@bellsouth.net.
Catechesis/Religious Program—Tony Mouzon, D.R.E. Students 150.

5—SAN SEBASTIAN (1968) Revs. Thomas P. Walsh; Marek Dzien, Parochial Vicar; Deacon James Swanson.
Res.: 1112 State Rd. 16, 32084. Tel: 904-824-6625; Fax: 904-829-0459. Web: sansebastiancatholicchurch.com.
Catechesis/Religious Program—Students 150.

OUTSIDE THE CITY OF ST. AUGUSTINE

ATLANTIC BEACH, DUVAL CO., ST. JOHN THE BAPTIST (1967) Rev. Mark S. Waters.
Mailing Address: P.O. Drawer 330005, 32233. Tel: 904-246-6014; Fax: 904-246-1219.
Catechesis/Religious Program—Carole Fuchs, D.R.E. Students 149.

BRANFORD, SUWANNEE CO., SAN JUAN MISSION (1976) Rev. Sebastian K. George, C.M.I.
Mailing Address: P.O. Box 949, 32008. Tel: 386-935-2632; Fax: 386-935-4050. Email: sanjuancruz@live.com. Web: sanjuanmission.org.
Catechesis/Religious Program—Students 46.

BUNNELL, FLAGLER CO., ST. STEPHEN (1957) Rev. James May. Mission Church for St. Elizabeth Ann Seton.
Res.: 2400 E. Hwy. 100, 32110. Tel: 904-445-2246; Fax: 904-445-7808.
Catechesis/Religious Program— Twinned with St. Elizabeth Ann Seton, Palm Coast.

CALLAHAN, NASSAU CO., OUR LADY OF CONSOLATION (1974) Rev. Ralph L. Besendorfer.
Res.: 541668 U.S. Hwy. One, P.O. Box 692, 32011. Tel: 904-879-3662.
Catechesis/Religious Program—Sandy Wilfong, D.R.E. Students 59.

CHIEFLAND, LEVY CO., ST. JOHN THE EVANGELIST (1981), (Hispanic), Rev. Joseph McDonnell.
Mailing Address: P.O. Box 863, 32644.
Res.: 4050 N.W. Alternate 27, 32626. Tel: 352-493-1561 (Rectory); 352-493-9723 (Office); Fax: 352-493-9724 (Office). Email: stjhc@bellsouth.net.
Catechesis/Religious Program—Students 61.
Mission—Holy Cross 18278 S.E. Hwy. 19, Cross City, 32628. Tel: 352-498-5671.

CRESCENT CITY, PUTNAM CO., ST. JOHN THE BAPTIST (1906) [CEM] [JC] Rev. Jhon Guarnizo.
Res.: 2725 Hwy. 17, P.O. Box 908, 32112. Tel: 386-698-2055; Fax: 386-698-4146. Email: stjohnbcc@windstream.net. Web: stjohnbaptistcatholicchurch.com.
Catechesis/Religious Program—Students 163.

ELKTON, ST. JOHN CO., ST. AMBROSE (1875), (Minorcan), [CEM] Rev. Timothy M. Lindenfelser; Deacon Ed Wolff.
Res.: 6070 Church Rd., 32033. Tel: 904-692-1366; Fax: 904-692-1136. Email: choffice1@windstream.net. Web: www.saintambrose-church.org.
Catechesis/Religious Program—Email: olgcsareledu@windstream.net. Students 12.

FERNANDINA BEACH, AMELIA ISLAND NASSAU CO., ST. MICHAEL'S (1872) [JC] Rev. Brian Eburn; Sr. Bridie Ryan, R.S.M., Pastoral Assoc.
Res.: 505 Broome St., 32034. Tel: 904-261-3472; Fax: 904-321-1901. Email: smjdean@bellsouth.net. Web: www.stmichaelscatholic.com.
School—St. Michael's Academy, (Grades PreK-8), 228 N. 4th St., 32034. Tel: 904-321-2102; Fax: 904-321-2330. Deborah Suddarth, Prin.; Colleen Hodge, Librarian. Students 178.
Catechesis/Religious Program—Students 216.

FLAGLER BEACH, FLAGLER CO., SANTA MARIA DEL MAR (1970) Rev. Alberto Esposito; Deacon Michael Moody.
Res.: 915 N. Central Ave., P.O. Box 130, 32136. Tel: 386-439-2791; Fax: 386-439-1362. Web: www.smdm-fb.org.
Catechesis/Religious Program—Students 323.

FLEMING ISLAND, CLAY CO., SACRED HEART (1954) [CEM] Revs. Donal Sullivan; Rene Robert, Parochial Vicar.
7190 Hwy. 17 S., 32003. Tel: 904-284-3811; Fax: 904-529-8845. Email: shbulletin3811@bellsouth.net. Web: www.sacredheartgcs.org.
Res.: 1065 Live Oak Ln., 32003. Tel: 904-284-2169.
Catechesis/Religious Program—Tel: 904-284-9983. Kristin Michler-Belleza, C.R.E. (Elementary); Sandra Curtis, C.R.E. (High School). Students 662.

GAINESVILLE, ALACHUA CO.

1—ST. AUGUSTINE (1923), (Student Center) Revs. John D. Gillespie; David Ruchinski, Parochial Vicar. In Res., Revs. Jose L. Mesa, S.J. (Dominican Republic); Anthony M. Eseke.
Res.: 1738 W. University Ave., P.O. Box 13888, 32604. Tel: 352-372-3533; Fax: 352-378-9010.
Catechesis/Religious Program—Thomas Rinkoski, Dir. Family Faith & Youth Min. Students 65.

2—HOLY FAITH (1973) Revs. John M. Phillips; Emmanuel J. Pazhayapurackal, C.M.I. (India).
Res.: 747 N.W. 43 St., 32607. Tel: 352-376-5405; Fax: 352-375-7568. Web: holyfaithchurch.org.
Catechesis/Religious Program—Tel: 352-376-5405; Fax: 352-375-7568. Dr. Charlotte Chadik, D.R.E. Students 137.

3—ST. PATRICK CHURCH (1887) Revs. Roland M. Julien; Dung Quang Bui, Parochial Vicar; Deacons Richard Dugan; Jack Raymond. In Res., Revs. Robert J. McDermott; Alan Bower.
Res.: 500 N.E. 16th Ave., 32601. Tel: 352-372-4641; Fax: 352-376-0575. Email: stpatchurch@bellsouth.net. Web: www.saintpatricksparish.org.
Catechesis/Religious Program—Tel: 352-376-9878, Ext. 60. Diane St. Onge, D.R.E. Students 46.
Mission—St. Philip Neri 1908 Hwy. 301 S., Hawthorne, Alachua Co. 32640. Tel: 352-481-3353.

4—QUEEN OF PEACE (1987) [JC] Revs. Jeffrey A. McGowan; Kazimierz Ligeza; Deacon Bo Turner.

Church: 10900 S.W. 24th Ave., 32607. Tel: 352-332-6279; Fax: 352-331-7347. Email: office@queenofpeaceparish.org. Web: www.queenofpeaceparish.org.
School—Tel: 352-332-8808. Web: www.queenofpeaceacademy.org. Sr. Nancy Elder, I.H.M., Prin. Sisters 2; Lay Teachers 41; Students 358.
Catechesis/Religious Program—Tel: 352-332-6279, Ext. 17. Sr. Beatrice Caulson, I.H.M., D.R.E. Students 470.

HIGH SPRINGS, ALACHUA CO., ST. MADELEINE SOPHIE PARISH (1925) Rev. Sebastian K. George, C.M.I.
Mailing Address: 17155 N.W. US Hwy. 441, 32643. Tel: 386-454-2358; Fax: 386-454-4985. Email: stmadeleinecc@windstream.net. Web: www.stmadeleinecatholicchurch.com.
Catechesis/Religious Program—Students 43.
Mission—San Juan 304 S.E. Plant St., P.O. Box 949, Branford, Suwannee Co. 32008. Tel: 386-935-2632; Fax: 386-935-4050.

INTERLACHEN, PUTNAM CO., ST. JOHN (1968) [JC] Rev. Robert L. Napier.
Res.: P.O. Box 207, 32148. Tel: 386-684-2528; Fax: 386-684-3819. Email: sjcc1200@aol.com.
Catechesis/Religious Program—Students 18.

JACKSONVILLE BEACH, DUVAL CO., ST. PAUL'S (1930) Revs. William A. Kelly; Tomykkutty Velliydathupathlil; Jose Kallukalam (India), Parochial Vicar; Deacon Tom Hughes.
Res.: 224 N. Fifth St., 32250. Tel: 904-249-2600; Fax: 904-249-3635.
School—Tel: 904-249-5934; Fax: 904-241-2911. Mrs. Katherine Boice, Prin. Lay Teachers 3; Students 592.
Catechesis/Religious Program—Tel: 904-249-2660; Fax: 904-249-8085. Mary Coleman, D.R.E. Students 523.
Mission—St. Peter 960 Girvin Rd., Duval Co. 32225.

JACKSONVILLE, DUVAL CO.

1—ASSUMPTION (South Jacksonville) (1913) Revs. Frederick R. Parke; Lam Nguyen, Parochial Vicar; Anthony G. Sebra, Parochial Vicar.
Res.: 2403 Atlantic Blvd., 32207. Tel: 904-398-1963; Fax: 904-398-6115. Email: assumptionchurch@cxp.com. Web: www.assumptioncatholicchurch.org.
School—2431 Atlantic Blvd., 32207. Tel: 904-398-1774; Fax: 904-398-6712. Angela Fuller, Prin. Lay Teachers 33; Students 475.
Catechesis/Religious Program—Sr. Therese Ryan, D.R.E. Students 116.

2—BLESSED TRINITY (1957) Rev. Msgr. Vincent J. Haut; Rev. Andrzej Mitera, Parochial Vicar.
Res.: 10472 Beach Blvd., 32246. Tel: 904-641-1414; Fax: 904-641-8171. Email: btcc@bellsouth.net. Web: www.btccjax.com.
School—(Grades PreK-8) Tel: 904-641-6458; Fax: 904-645-3762. Email: btschool@comcast.net. Web: www.blessedtrinitycatholicschool.org. Marie Davis, Prin. Students 241.
Catechesis/Religious Program—Tel: 904-646-4320. Email: prep@blessedtrinitycatholicschool.org. Mrs. Aixa Feliciano, D.R.E. Students 185.

3—CHRIST THE KING (1954) Rev. Thanh T. Nguyen; Deacon David MacNamara, Pastor Emeritus; Rev. Steven Zehler, Parochial Vicar; Deacon James Scott.
Res.: 742 Arlington Rd. N., 32211. Tel: 904-724-0080; Fax: 904-724-3340. Web: www.ctkcatholic.com.
School—6822 Larkin Rd., 32211. Tel: 904-724-2954; Fax: 904-721-8004. Email: ctks@ctks.org. Stephanie Chinault, Prin. Lay Teachers 23; Teacher Aides 3; Students 320.
Catechesis/Religious Program—Tel: 904-724-9617; Fax: 904-721-8585. Lucille Guzzone, D.R.E. & Dir. Students 134.

4—CHURCH OF THE CRUCIFIXION (1974), (African American), Revs. Callistus Onwere (Nigeria); Michael R. Houle.
Mailing Address & Rectory: 3183 W. Edgewood Ave., 32209-2209. Tel: 904-765-5284; Fax: 904-765-1680. Email: crucifixion@comcast.net.
Catechesis/Religious Program—6739 Alaro Rd., 32209. Tel: 904-765-2851. Beatrice Gilliard, D.R.E. Students 11.

5—ST. EPHREM SYRIAC ANTIOCHIAN CATHOLIC CHURCH (1986) Rev. Selwan Sulaiman Taponi.
Church: 4650 Kernan Blvd. S, 32224. Tel: 904-998-7800; Fax: 904-997-9656.

6—ST. FRANCIS CHOE CHAPEL (1997), (Korean), Rev. Gi Weon Choi.
Res.: 8051 Rampart Rd., 32244. Tel: 904-573-1833; Fax: 904-519-1004.
Catechesis/Religious Program—Students 7.

7—HOLY FAMILY (1974) Rev. Gregory J. Fay. In Res., Rev. Msgr. Mortimer Danaher (Retired); Rev. John Reynolds.
Office: 9800 Baymeadows Rd., 32256. Tel: 904-641-5838; Fax: 904-641-9704. Email: admin@holyfamilyjax.org. Web: www.holyfamilyjax.org.
School—9800-3 Baymeadows Rd., 32256. Tel: 904-645-9875; Fax: 904-899-6060. Rosemary Nowotny, Prin. Lay Teachers 28; Students 435.
Catechesis/Religious Program—Mellissa Motsett, D.R.E. Students 215.

8—HOLY ROSARY (1921) Revs. Callistus Onwere (Nigeria); Michael R. Houle.
Res.: 2110 Blue Ave., 32209. Tel: 904-764-3241; Fax: 904-765-4995.
Church: 683 Linwood Ave., 32206. Email: holyrosaryjax@comcast.net.
School—Sisters of Notre Dame, Tel: 904-764-9032; 904-765-6522; Fax: 904-765-9486. Sr. Dianne Rumschlag, S.N.D., Prin. (Toledo Prov.) Sisters 6; Lay Teachers 12; Students 190.
Catechesis/Religious Program—Students 18.

9—HOLY SPIRIT (1966) Rev. Ananda Prasad Maddineni, M.S.F.S.
Res.: 11665 Fort Caroline Rd., 32225. Tel: 904-641-7244; Fax: 904-641-7266. Email: info@holyspiritchurchjax.org. Web: holyspiritchurchjax.org.
School—(Grades PreK-8) Tel: 904-642-9165; Fax: 904-642-1047. Web: www.hscatholicschool.com. John Luciano, Prin.; Karen Galas, Librarian. Lay Teachers 17; Students 284.
Catechesis/Religious Program—Email: judy40plus@bellsouth.net. Judy Altmiller, D.R.E. Students 284.

10—IMMACULATE CONCEPTION (1854) [CEM] [JC] Revs. Antonio Leon; Warren Keene; Edward W. Murphy; Deacon Robert DeLuca.
Res.: 121 E. Duval St., 32202. Tel: 904-359-0331; Fax: 904-356-8133.
Catechesis/Religious Program—Students 52.

11—ST. JOSEPH'S (1883) [CEM] Revs. Daniel Cody; Anthony Bonela, M.S.F.S. (India). In Res., Rev. Bernie Ahern.
Res.: 11730 Old St. Augustine Rd., 32258-2002. Tel: 904-268-5422; Fax: 904-292-0248.
School—11600 Old St. Augustine Rd., 32258. Tel: 904-268-6688; Fax: 904-268-8989. Mrs. Rhonda Rose, Prin. Lay Teachers 31; Students 548.
Catechesis/Religious Program—Tel: 904-880-6404; Fax: 904-880-1559. Dodi Flora, D.R.E. Students 752.

12—MARY QUEEN OF HEAVEN (1988) Rev. Denis O'Shaughnessy, Admin.
Res.: 9401 Staples Mill Dr., 32244. Tel: 904-647-7641; 904-777-3168 (Office); Fax: 904-777-6772. Email: mqoh@att.net. Web: maryqueenofheaven.org.
Catechesis/Religious Program—Tel: 904-777-3168. Students 70.

13—ST. MATTHEW'S (Lake Shore) (1949) Revs. Luke McLoughlin; Peter Akin-Otiko, Parochial Vicar.
Res.: 1773 Blanding Blvd., 32210. Tel: 904-388-8698; Fax: 904-384-1233. Email: stmatthews@stmatthewsjax.com. Web: www.stmatthewsjax.com.
School—Tel: 904-387-4401; Fax: 904-388-4404. Email: stmatthewsoffice@comcast.net. Web: www-.stmatthewscs.org. Mrs. Cathy Tuerk, Prin. Lay Teachers 18; Students 293.
Catechesis/Religious Program—Tel: 904-388-1207. Email: onieshine@aol.com. Onie Lee, D.R.E. Students 130.

14—MOST HOLY REDEEMER (1962) Rev. Timothy R. Lozier.
Res.: 8523 Normandy Blvd., 32221-6701. Tel: 904-786-1192; Fax: 904-786-4224. Email: mhrjax@mhrjax.org. Web: www.mhrjax.org.
Catechesis/Religious Program—Sharon Tomore, D.R.E. Students 108.

15—OUR LADY OF THE ANGELS (1917) [CEM] Closed. Records moved to St. Paul's Parish, 2609 Park St., Jacksonville.

16—ST. PATRICK (1959) Rev. Jose J. Kulathinal, C.M.I. (India).
Res.: 1429 Broward Rd., 32218. Tel: 904-768-2593; Fax: 904-768-2251. Email: frjose@stpatrickjax.org. Web: stpatrickjax.org.
School—(Grades PreK-8) Tel: 904-768-6323; Fax: 904-768-2144. Sr. Carmel O'Callahan, R.S.M., Prin. Lay Teachers 13; Students 193.
Catechesis/Religious Program—Students 100.

17—ST. PAUL'S (1923) Rev. Jan A. Ligeza.
Res.: 2609 Park St., 32204. Tel: 904-387-2554; Fax: 904-388-6871. Email: stpaulsriverside@hotmail.com.
School—Tel: 904-387-2841; Fax: 904-387-1781. Mrs. Jo-Ann Leskanic, Prin. Lay Teachers 18; Students 225.
Catechesis/Religious Program—Students 40.

18—ST. PIUS THE FIFTH (1919), (African American), Revs. Callistus Onwere (Nigeria); Michael R. Houle.
Res.: 2110 Blue Ave., 32209. Tel: 904-354-1501; Fax: 904-354-7240.
School—1470 W. 13th St., 32209. Tel: 904-354-2613; Fax: 904-356-4522. Email: stpiusvjax@aol.com. Web: www.edline.net/pages/st--pius_school. Sr. Elise Kennedy, S.S.J., Prin. Sisters 2; Lay Teachers 12; Students 174.
Catechesis/Religious Program—Tel: 904-354-1501; Fax: 904-354-7240. Students 31.

19—PRINCE OF PEACE (1970) Rev. Michael J. Larkin.
Res.: 6320 Bennett Rd., 32216. Tel: 904-733-6860; Fax: 904-367-0215.
Catechesis/Religious Program—Tel: 904-733-6011; Fax: 904-367-0215. Email: theresalcurtis@bellsouth.net. Web: www.princeofpeacecatholicchurch.net. Students 74.

20—RESURRECTION (1959) Rev. Jason Trull; Deacon Stan Grenn.
Res.: 3383 University Blvd. N., 32277-2483. Tel: 904-744-0833; Fax: 904-744-7235. Web: www.respar.net.
School—5710 Jack Rd., 32277. Tel: 904-744-1266; Fax: 904-744-5800. Patricia Sevilla, Prin. Lay Teachers 16; Students 200.
Catechesis/Religious Program—Tel: 904-744-0833; Fax: 904-744-7235. Patrick Goin, D.R.E. Students 110.

21—SACRED HEART (1959) Revs. Victor Z. Narivelil, C.M.I. (India); Slawomir Bielasiewicz, Parochial Vicar; Deacons Stephen Turner; Edgardo SanAgustin; Jeffrey P. Burgess. In Res., Rev. Michael P. Morgan.
Res.: 5752 Blanding Blvd., 32244. Tel: 904-771-2152; Fax: 904-573-8816.
School—Tel: 904-771-5800; Fax: 904-771-5323. Marybeth O'Neill, Prin. Lay Teachers 34; Students 525.
Catechesis/Religious Program—Tel: 904-771-5800, Ext. 23; Fax: 904-771-5323. Santa Cochran, C.R.E. Students 179.

22—SAN JOSE (1959) Revs. James Moss; Heriberto Vergara, Parochial Vicar.
Mailing Address: 3619 Toledo Rd., 32217.
School—Tel: 904-733-2510; Fax: 904-731-7169. Mrs. Jan Magiera, Prin. Lay Teachers 30; Students 495.
Catechesis/Religious Program—Tel: 904-733-1630, Ext. 18; Fax: 904-731-4335. Email: dre@sjcatholic.org. Sr. Ambrose Cruise, R.S.M., D.R.E. Students 211; Spanish Students 41.

KEYSTONE HEIGHTS, CLAY CO., ST. WILLIAM (1948) [JC] Rev. Michael S. Williams.
210 Peach St., P.O. Box 721, 32656.
Res.: P.O. Box 721, 32656. Tel: 352-473-4136; Fax: 352-473-4119. Email: stwilliamcatholi@bellsouth.net.
Catechesis/Religious Program—Tel: 352-473-4223. Students 65.

KORONA, FLAGLER CO., ST. MARY (1914) [CEM] Rev. Slawomir S. Podsiedlik, O.C.D.
Mailing Address: 89 St. Mary's Pl., Bunnell, 32110-1537. Tel: 386-437-5098. Email: stmarysfl@bellsouth.net. Web: www.stmaryccfl.org.
Res.: 141 Carmelite Dr., Bunnell, 32110. Tel: 386-437-2910; Fax: 386-437-5125. Email: carmelitefathers@aol.com.
Catechesis/Religious Program—Michael Aversa, D.R.E. Students 10.

LAKE CITY, COLUMBIA CO., EPIPHANY (1965) Revs. Michael Pendergraft; Dennis (Dan) Nelson, Parochial Vicar.
Res.: 1905 SW Epiphany Ct., 32025. Tel: 386-752-4470; Fax: 386-752-4652. Email: epiphanycatholic@bellsouth.net.
School—Tel: 386-752-2320; Fax: 386-752-2364. Email: epiphanyeagles@yahoo.com. Web: epiphanycatholiclakecity.com. Mrs. Rita Klenk, Prin. Lay Teachers 13; Students 115.
Catechesis/Religious Program—Students 77.

LIVE OAK, SUWANNEE CO., ST. FRANCIS XAVIER (1979) Rev. Richard Perko.
Res.: 928 E. Howard St., P.O. Box 1179, 32064. Tel: 386-364-1108; Fax: 386-364-1836. Email: stfx@windstream.net.
Catechesis/Religious Program—Tel: 386-330-2736. Sherri Ortega, D.R.E. Students 99.
Mission—St. Therese of the Child Jesus P.O. Box 890, Jasper, Hamilton Co. 32052. Tel: 386-364-1108.

MACCLENNY, BAKER CO., ST. MARY'S (1960) [JC] Rev. Jose Maniyangat.
Res.: 894 Jacqueline Cir., P.O. Box 1120, 32063. Tel: 904-259-6414; Fax: 904-259-9712. Web: www.stmarymacclenny.com.
Catechesis/Religious Program—Clare Tillis, D.R.E.; Bryan Hobbs, D.R.E. Students 39.
Chaplaincy— Northeast Florida State Hospital, Macclenny; Union Correctional Institute, Raiford; and Florida State Prison, Starke.

MIDDLEBURG, CLAY CO., ST. LUKE (1982) Rev. Edward K. Rooney.
1606 Blanding Blvd., 32068. Email: office@stlukesparish.org. Web: www.stlukesparish.org.
Res.: 3205 Bear Run Blvd., Orange Park, 32065. Tel: 904-272-5946; Fax: 904-291-9711.
Catechesis/Religious Program—Blair Gaynes, D.R.E. Students 420.

ORANGE PARK, CLAY CO., ST. CATHERINE'S (1877) Revs. James R. Boddie Jr.; Robert Trujillo, Parochial Vicar; Rafal Mazurowski, Parochial Vicar.
Res.: 1649 Kingsley Ave., 32073. Tel: 904-264-0577; Fax: 904-264-7999. Email: parish@stcatherinesiena.com. Web: www.stcatherinesiena.com.
Catechesis/Religious Program—Tel: 904-264-2470. Vincent Reilly, Dir. Faith Formation. Students 481.
Mission—Moosehaven Chapel 1700 Park Ave., Clay Co. 32073. Tel: 904-278-1210.

PALATKA, PUTNAM CO., ST. MONICA (1858) [CEM] Rev. Ignatius J. Plathanam, C.M.I. (India).
114 S. 4th St., 32177.
Office:—210 S. 4th St., 32177. Tel: 386-325-9777; Fax: 386-329-1960. Email: stmonicacatholic@bellsouth.net. Web: www.stmonicacatholicchurch.com.
Catechesis/Religious Program— Tracy McKeown, D.R.E. Students 44.

PALM COAST, FLAGER CO., ST. ELIZABETH ANN SETON (1978) [CEM] Revs. James May; Timothy Cusick, S.S., Parochial Vicar; Christopher Liguori, Parochial Vicar; Deacons Perlito (Tom) Alayu, Pastoral Min.; James Casapulla, Pastoral Min.; Doug Nullet, Pastoral Assoc.
Res.: 4600 Belle Terre Pkwy., 32164. Tel: 386-445-2246; Fax: 386-445-7808. Email: motherseton@bestnetpc.com. Web: www.stelizabethannseton.org.
Catechesis/Religious Program—Eileen Daley, D.R.E. Students 408.

PONTE VEDRA BEACH, ST. JOHN CO., OUR LADY STAR OF THE SEA (1972) Rev. Msgr. Daniel B. Logan; Revs. Remigiusz Blaszkowski, Parochial Vicar; Glenn S. Charest, Parochial Vicar; Deacons Anthony Marini, (Retired); Daniel Scrone.
Mailing Address: 545 Hwy. A1A N., 32082. Tel: 904-285-2698; Fax: 904-285-2502. Email: office@olsspvb.org. Web: www.olsspvb.org.
Preschool—Tel: 904-285-2698, Ext. 2; Fax: 904-273-9740. Email: lsdirector@olsspvb.org. Chris Saliba, Dir.
School—Palmer Catholic Academy, 4889 Palm Valley Rd., 32082. Tel: 904-543-8515; Fax: 904-543-8750. Web: www.palmercatholic.org. Mrs. Linda Earp, Prin.
Catechesis/Religious Program—Tel: 904-285-2698, Ext. 5; Fax: 904-273-0590. Email: dre@olsspvb.org. Dina Voutour, D.R.E. Students 584.

ST. AUGUSTINE SHORES, ST. JOHN CO., CORPUS CHRISTI (1975) [CEM] Rev. William C. Mooney.
Res.: P.O. Box 3064, 32085. Tel: 904-797-4842; Fax: 904-797-2746.
Catechesis/Religious Program—Students 78.

ST. JOHN, ST. JOHN CO., SAN JUAN DEL RIO (1977) Revs. John H. Tetlow; Anthony Ike; Lawrence Mulinda; Deacons Lawrence Geinosky; Jeff C. Silvernale.
Res.: 1718 State Rd., No. 13, 32259. Tel: 904-287-0519 (Office); Fax: 904-287-1504. Web: www.sjdrparish.org.
School—1714 State Rd. 13, 32259. Tel: 904-287-8081; Fax: 904-287-4574. Lay Teachers 28; Students 354.
Catechesis/Religious Program—Tel: 904-287-2801. Students 786.

STARKE, BRADFORD CO., ST. EDWARD (1941) Rev. Conrad Cowart.
Res.: 441 N. Temple Ave., 32091-3207. Tel: 904-964-6155; Fax: 904-964-1411. Email: stedsecretary@yahoo.com. Web: www.stedward.com.
Catechesis/Religious Program—Web: www.stedstarke.com. Students 15.

WILLISTON, LEVY CO., HOLY FAMILY (1970) Rev. Rodolfo Godinez.
Res.: 17353 N.E. 27 A, 32696. Tel: 352-528-2893; Fax: 352-528-6002. Email: holyfamilycathch@earthlink.net. Web: www.holyfamilywilliston.com.
Catechesis/Religious Program—Email: dre.holyfamily@earthlink.net. Students 55.
Mission—St. Anthony the Abbot P.O. Box 1070, Inglis, Levy Co. 34449. Tel: 352-447-4573; Fax: 352-447-4573.

Special Assignment:
Rev. Msgr.—
Brennan, Keith R., J.C.D., Rector, St. Vincent de Paul Seminary, 10701 S. Military Tr., Boynton Beach, 33436. Tel: 904-262-3200; Fax: 904-262-0698
Revs.—
Gagan, Philip R., Pastoral Care/St. Vincent's Medical Center, 1800 Barrs St., 32254.
Houle, Michael R., M.A., M.Ed., M.Div., Pres., Bishop Kenny High School, P.O. Box 5544, 32247.
McDermott, Robert, Chap., Prison Ministry, Shands Hospital, 500 N. East 16th Ave., Gainesville, 32601.
Palazzolo, Anthony P., 101 Marsh Cove Ln., Ponte Vedra Beach, 32082. Tel: 904-280-5422 Diocese of Mandeville, Jamaica
Young, Dennis M., V.A. Medical Center, 1601 S.W. Archer Rd., Gainesville, 32608-1197.

On Duty Outside the Diocese:
Rev.—
O'Neal, James E., Active Duty U.S. Army Chaplain Corps

Unassigned:
Rev.—
Camarda, Ronald A.

Absent or Sick Leave:
Revs.—
Brandstrup, Christian
Brault, Gilles
Buchmelter, Brendan
Cody, Thomas
Fisher, Roe
Kerr, Robert
Morse, Michael
Oliver, John
Pollard, John L.
Thompson, Michael
Whitehead, Joseph

Retired:
Rev. Msgrs.—
Conesa, Diego
Danaher, Mortimer, 7843 Fawn Oaks Ct., 32256.
Dux, John H., 311 Ayers Cir., Summerville, SC 29485.
Heslin, James J., P.O. Box 16552, 32245.
Kohls, Eugene C., P.A., J.C.D., 5201 Atlantic Blvd., #228, 32207.
Lenihan, John J., 102 Hammock Circle, 32095.
Revs.—
Colasurdo, Peter, 3800 Michael's Landing E., 32224.
Ducci, Alex, Poste Italiane BG Centro, C.P. 127, 24100 Bergamo, Italy.
Finlay, Joseph F.
Florez, Luis, 2201 Glencoe Dr., Orange Park, 32073.
Haryasz, Francis S., 244 St. Thomas St., 32095.
Hochheim, William A., Casa San Pedro, 1714 State Rd. 13 Ste. 6, 32259.
Maniangat, Joseph
Meehan, Joseph
Moore, Frederick Thomas
Notarpole, Joseph
O'Flynn, Seamus
Revilla, Francisco, Suecia 100-3-3B, 28022 Madrid, Spain.
Shashy, Daniel, 671 D'Orleans Ct., 32211.
Sullivan, Thomas K.
Walsh, Flannan J.

INSTITUTIONS LOCATED IN THE DIOCESE

[A] DIOCESAN SCHOOLS

ST. AUGUSTINE. *St. Joseph's Academy, Inc.*, 155 State Rd. 207, 32084. Tel: 904-824-0431; Fax: 904-826-4477. Web: www.sjaweb.org. Rev. Michael Houle, Pres.; Michael Heubeck, Prin.; Sr. Suzan Foster, S.S.J., Vice Prin.; Mr. Michael Maloney, Athletic Dir. & Dean of Students. Day School. Priests 1; Sisters 2; Lay Teachers 24; Students 305.

GAINESVILLE. *St. Francis High School, Inc.*, 4100 N.W. 115 Ter., 32606. Tel: 352-376-6545; Fax: 352-248-0418. Email: info@sfchs.org. Web: www.sfchs.org. Ernest D. Herrington Jr., Prin.; Theresa D. Cartell, Librarian. Sisters 2; Lay Teachers 21; Students 263.

JACKSONVILLE. *Bishop John Snyder High School, Inc.*, 5001 Samaritan Way, 32221. Tel: 904-771-1029; Fax: 904-908-8988. Email: davidyazdiya@bishopsnyder.org. Web: www.bishopsnyder.org. Deacon David Yazdiya, Prin. Lay Teachers 33; Students 524; Total Staff 50.
Bishop Kenny High School, Inc. (1952) 1055 Kingman Ave., P.O. Box 5544, 32247. Tel: 904-398-7545; Fax: 904-398-5728. Rev. Michael R. Houle, M.A., M.Ed., M.Div., Pres.; Mr. Todd Orlando, M.Ed., Prin.; Robert West, M.Ed., Vice Prin. & Athletic Dir.; Mrs. Mary DeSalvo, M.Ed., Vice Prin.; Dave Williams, M.Ed., Dean of Students. Priests 1; Sisters 1; Lay Teachers 93; Students 1,400.
Guardian Catholic Schools, Inc., 4920 Brentwood Ave., 32206. Tel: 904-765-1920; Fax: 904-765-8155. Shariffa A. Spicer, Exec. Dir.; Lori Rush, Admin. Asst. This alliance includes the following schools:
Holy Rosary Catholic School (Grades PreK-8), 4920 Brentwood Ave., 32206. Tel: 904-765-6522; Fax: 904-765-9486. Email: drumschlag@cxp.com. Sr. Dianne Rumschlag, S.N.D., Prin.; April Rice, Librarian/Media Specialist. Sisters 5; Lay Teachers 14.
St. Pius Catholic School Campus (Grades PreK-8), 1470 W. 13th St., 32209. Tel: 904-354-2613; Fax: 904-356-4522. Email: kennede@aol.com. Web: www.edline.net/pages/st__pius_school. Sr. Elise Kennedy, S.S.J., Prin.; Michele Rademacher, Librarian. Sisters 2; Lay Teachers 14.

[B] ELEMENTARY SCHOOLS, INTERPAROCHIAL

GAINESVILLE. *St. Patrick School*, 550 N.E. 16th Ave., 32601. Tel: 352-376-9878; Fax: 352-371-6177. Email: stpatrickschool@bellsouth.net. Web: www.stpatrickschoolgnv.org. J. Mark Akerman, Prin. Interparish school composed of students from St. Patrick, Holy Faith & St. Augustine, Gainesville. Lay Teachers 25; Students 347.

MIDDLEBURG. *Annunciation School* (1993) (Grades PreK-8), 1610 Blanding Blvd., 32068. Tel: 904-282-0504; Fax: 904-282-6808. Email: saltieri@annunciationcatholic.org. Web: www.annunciationcatholic.org. Mrs. Susan Altieri, Prin.; Vicki Cowman, Librarian. Interparish school composed of students from Sacred Heart, Green Cove Springs; St. Catherine's, Orange Park; and St. Luke, Middleburg. Lay Teachers 25; Students 414.

[C] CATHOLIC CHARITIES

ST. AUGUSTINE. *Catholic Charities Bureau St. Augustine Regional Office*, 225 W. King St., P.O. Box 543, 32085. Tel: 904-829-6300; Fax: 904-829-0494. Email: info@ccbstaug.org. Web: ccbstaug.org. Rebecca Stringer, COO.

GAINESVILLE. *Catholic Charities Regional Office*, 1717 N.E. 9th St., 32609. Tel: 352-372-0294; Fax: 352-371-3157. Email: coo@catholiccharitiesgainesville.org. Web: www.catholiccharitiesgainesville.org. Karen M. Slevin, Exec. Dir. & COO. Emergency services, counseling, respite care, and adoptions.

JACKSONVILLE. *Catholic Charities Bureau, Inc.*, 134 E. Church St., 32202. Tel: 904-899-5500; Fax: 904-899-5510. Web: www.ccbjax.org. Mr. William C. Beitz, Diocesan Dir. Tel: 904-262-3200.
Catholic Charities Regional Office (1945) 134 E. Church St., 32202. Tel: 904-354-4846, Ext. 233; Fax: 904-354-4718. Email: lhickey@ccbjax.org. Web: www.ccbjax.org. Laura M. Hickey, COO. Provides counseling services for substance abuse, marriage, families, & maternity. Also, emergency financial assistance for housing/utilities, food pantry, adoption programs, & financial assistance for housing opportunities for persons with AIDS, and refugee resettlement.

LAKE CITY. *Catholic Charities Regional Office*, 258 N.W. Burke Ave., 32055. Tel: 386-754-5325; Fax: 386-754-5325. Email: cclc@bellsouth.net. Suzanne Edwards, Exec. Dir.

[D] SPECIAL APOSTOLATES

ST. AUGUSTINE. *Religious Education for Catholic Deaf and Blind*, 30 Ocean Ave., 32084-2813. Tel: 904-825-4272 (Voice/TDD); Fax: 904-825-4348. Email: religiouseduc90@bellsouth.net. Web: www.catholicdeaf.org. Florida School for the Deaf and Blind. Total Staff 5.

JACKSONVILLE. *L'Arche Harbor House* (1985) 700 Arlington Rd. N., 32211. Tel: 904-721-5992; Fax: 904-721-7143. Email: communityleader@bellsouth.net. Web: larchejacksonville.org. Amy Finn-Schultz, Exec. Dir. & Community Leader. A residential community for adults with developmental disabilities and those who choose to share life with them (assistants). We also have an adult day program called the Rainbow Workshop. Bed Capacity 20; Total Assisted Annually 30; Total Staff 25.
Morning Star School (1956) 725 Mickler Rd., 32211. Tel: 904-721-2144; Fax: 904-721-1040. Email: jmbarnes23@bellsouth.net. Web: www.morningstar-jax.org. Jean Barnes, Prin. A school for exceptional children. Lay Teachers 16; Students 118.

[E] GENERAL HOSPITALS

JACKSONVILLE. *St. Luke's - St. Vincent's HealthCare, Inc. dba St. Luke's Hospital* 4201 Belfort Rd., 32216. Tel: 904-308-4025; 907-308-7300; Fax: 904-308-4072 2. Web: www.stlukesjax.com. Laurie Teppert, Sr. Vice Pres. & Gen. Counsel. Bed

Capacity 313; Total Assisted Annually 32,500; Total Staff 500.

St. Vincent's Health System, Inc., 1 Shircliff Way, 32204. Tel: 904-308-8446; 904-308-7300; Fax: 904-308-2947. Scott A. Whalen, Ph.D., Pres. & CEO. Statistics are reported under St. Vincent's Medical Center, Inc. Bed Capacity 528.

St. Vincent's Medical Center, Inc., One Shircliff Way, P.O. Box 2982, 32203. Tel: 904-308-7300; Fax: 904-308-7326. Web: www.jaxhealth.com. Daughters of Charity of St. Vincent de Paul., Member St. Vincent's Health System, Inc. Nurses 936; Total Staff 2,908; Bed Capacity 528; Bassinets 30; Outpatients 135,500; Inpatients 28,559.

St. Vincent's Foundation, Inc. Tel: 904-308-7306; Fax: 904-308-7573.

St. Vincent's Ambulatory Care, Inc. Tel: 904-308-2110; Fax: 904-396-3646.

St. Catherine Laboure Manor, Inc. Tel: 904-308-4702; Fax: 904-308-2987.

[F] HOMES FOR AGING

JACKSONVILLE. *All Saints Catholic Nursing Home & Rehabilitation Center, Inc.*, 5888 Blanding Blvd., 32244. Tel: 904-772-1220; Fax: 904-772-6334. Email: blee@allsaintsnursing.org. Web: www.allsaintsnursing.org. Connie O'Donnell, Admin. Physical Therapy, Speech Therapy, Occupational Therapy Available, Respite Services, Medicare, Medicaid Accepted, VA, inpatient & outpatient rehabilitative services provided. Total Assisted 42,373; Bed Capacity 120; Total Staff 167.

Casa San Pedro, 365 Marywood Dr., St. Johns, 32259. Tel: 904-230-2562; Fax: 904-230-2563. Email: csanpedr@bellsouth.net. Web: www.marywoodcenter.org. Mary Ruth Mustonen.

St. Catherine Laboure Manor, 1750 Stockton St., 32204. Tel: 904-308-4700; Fax: 904-308-2987. Email: mgartlan@jaxhealth.com. Web: www.stvincentshealth.com. Long term health care Skilled Nursing Facility. Bed Capacity 240; Sisters 3; Total Staff 239; Patients Assisted Annually 1,194.

[G] CATHOLIC CHARITIES OFFICE OF HOUSING

JACKSONVILLE. *Jacksonville, Family Housing Management Co.* (1986) 134 E. Church St., 32202. Tel: 904-632-1255; Fax: 904-632-2135. Email: aballard@ccbjax.org. Alma C. Ballard, Exec. Dir.

Jacksonville, Office of Housing Development, 134 E. Church St., 32202. Tel: 904-632-1255; Fax: 904-632-2135. Alma C. Ballard, Exec. Dir.

Hurley Manor Apartments (1984) 3333-35 University Blvd. N., 32277. Tel: 904-744-6022; Fax: 904-744-6037. Email: hurleymanorapt@bellsouth.net. Alton W. Yates, Pres.; Franceli Gimenez, Mgr. Parent Co., Catholic Charities Housing Association of Jacksonville, Inc.

Barry Manor Apartments (1984) 1000 Husson Ave., Palatka, 32177. Tel: 386-328-5137; Fax: 386-328-5138. Email: bishop1@atlantic.net. June Henley, Pres.; Marilyn Canup, Mgr. Parent Co., Palatka Retirement Villas, Inc.

Providence Center, 134 E. Church St., 32202. Tel: 904-632-1255; Fax: 904-632-2135.

San Jose Manor I (1991) 3630 Galicia Rd., 32217. Tel: 904-739-0555; Fax: 904-739-0559. Email: sjm@sanjosemanor.comcastbiz.net. Alton W. Yates, Pres.; Kathleen Garrett, Mgr. (Parent Company: Housing Association of the Diocese of St. Augustine.)

San Jose Manor II (2000) 3622 Galicia Rd., 32217. Tel: 904-739-0555; Fax: 904-739-0559. Email: sjm@sanjosemanor.comcastbiz.net. John Connolly, Pres.; Kathleen Garrett, Mgr. (Parent Company: San Jose Catholic Housing Assoc., Inc.)

[H] MONASTERIES AND RESIDENCES OF PRIESTS AND BROTHERS

BUNNELL. *Discalced Carmelite Fathers of Florida*, 141 Carmelite Dr., 32110. Tel: 386-437-2910; Fax: 386-437-5125. Email: carmelitefathers@aol.com. Revs. Joseph F. Zawada, O.C.D.; Arthur Chojda, O.C.D.; Slawomir S. Podsiedlik, O.C.D., Prior; Bro. Anthony Gemmato, O.C.D. Total Staff 4.

[I] CONVENTS AND RESIDENCES FOR SISTERS

ST. AUGUSTINE. *Motherhouse of the Sisters of St. Joseph of St. Augustine, Florida*, 241 St. George St., P.O. Box 3506, 32085. Tel: 904-824-1752; Fax: 904-826-0949. Email: ssjfl@bellsouth.net. Web: ssjfl.org. Sr. Ann Kuhn, S.S.J., Gen. Supr. Professed Sisters 75.

The Sisters of St. Joseph Continuing Community Support Trust Fund. Tel: 904-824-1752; Fax: 904-826-0949.

Sisters of St. Francis Xavier Inc., 2585 Oak St., 32204. Tel: 904-308-8980; Fax: 904-308-7713. Email: beatrice_lashi@yahoo.com. Sr. Beatrice Khawnyi, Contact Person.

[J] RETREAT HOUSES

JACKSONVILLE. *Marywood Center for Spirituality and Ministry*, 235 Marywood Dr., St. Johns, 32259. Tel: 904-287-2525; Fax: 904-287-9738. Email: info@marywoodcenter.org. Web: www.marywoodcenter.org. Mr. Charles David, Admin.; Ginger Eddy, Prog. Coord. Total Staff 15.

[K] NEWMAN CENTERS

ST. AUGUSTINE. *Flagler College Newman Center* c/o Cathedral of St. Augustine, 35 Treasury St., 32084. Tel: 904-461-5795. Email: ccfis@juno.com. Rev. Thomas S. Willis.

[L] MISCELLANEOUS

ST. AUGUSTINE. *St. Augustine House of Prayer & Evangelization Center*, 34 Ocean Ave., 32084. Tel: 904-824-4831.

Sisters of St. Joseph's Architectural Stained Glass, 2745 Industry Center Rd., #6, 32084. Tel: 904-669-5388. Email: liteart@aol.com. Web: www.ssjstainedglass.com. Sr. Diane Couture, S.S.J., Dir.

GAINESVILLE. *The Center for the Study of the Passion of Christ and the Holy Shroud*, 1738 W. University, 32603. Tel: 352-372-3533. Mrs. Gerry DeGraff, Exec. Sec.

Spirit Radio of North Florida, Inc., 500 N.E. 16th Ave., 32601. Tel: 352-372-2191; Fax: 352-376-0575. Email: rolandjulien@hotmail.com. Web: www.spirit-radio.org. Rev. Roland M. Julien, V.F.

JACKSONVILLE. **Association of St. Lawrence Communita Cenacold America Inc.*, 1050 Talleyrand Ave., 32206. Albino Aragno, Exec. Dir.

DSA Land, Inc., 11625 Old St. Augustine Rd., 32258.

Florida Catholic Heritage Museum, Inc., 11625 Old St. Augustine Rd., 32258. Tel: 904-262-3200.

Office for the Maryknoll Fathers & Brothers, 3619 Toledo Rd., 32217. Tel: 904-739-1112. Deacon Larry Hart.

RELIGIOUS INSTITUTES OF MEN REPRESENTED IN THE DIOCESE

For further details refer to the corresponding bracketed number in the Religious Institutes of Men or Women section.

[0275]—*Carmelites of Mary Immaculate*—C.M.I.
[0260]—*Discalced Carmelite Friars*—O.C.D.
[0650]—*Holy Ghost Fathers*—C.S.Sp.
[0690]—*Jesuit Fathers and Brothers*—S.J.
[]—*Marist Brothers*—F.M.S.
[0920]—*Oblates of St. Francis de Sales*—M.S.F.S.

RELIGIOUS INSTITUTES OF WOMEN REPRESENTED IN THE DIOCESE

[]—*Carmelite Sisters*—O.Carm.
[0685]—*Claretian Missionary Sisters*—R.M.I.
[3110]—*Congregation of Our Lady of Retreat in the Cenacle*—R.C.
[0760]—*Daughters of Charity of St. Vincent de Paul* (Eastern Prov.)—D.C.
[1070-13]—*Dominican Sisters*—O.P.
[2170]—*Servants of the Immaculate Heart of Mary*—I.H.M.
[]—*Servants Sisters of the Home of the Mother*—S.S.H.M.
[]—*Sisters for Christian Community*—S.F.C.C.
[]—*Sisters of Mercy of Ireland*—R.S.M.
[2575]—*Sisters of Mercy of the Americas*—R.S.M.
[2990]—*Sisters of Notre Dame* (Toledo Prov.)—S.N.D.
[]—*Sisters of St. Francis Xavier*—S.F.X.
[3900]—*Sisters of St. Joseph of St. Augustine, FL*—S.S.J.
[]—*Trinitarian Handmaids of the Divine Word*—T.H.D.W.

DIOCESAN CEMETERIES

ST. AUGUSTINE. *St. Augustine Diocesan Cemeteries* Operates San Lorenzo Cemetery in St. Augustine and St. Mary Cemetery in Bunnell., 1635 U.S. 1 S., 32084. Tel: 904-824-6680; Fax: 904-824-3845. Email: srnicole@nflcemeteries.org. Rev. Timothy M. Lindenfelser, J.C.L., Dir.; Sr. Nicole Cayer, S.S.J., Dir. Family Svcs. Priests 1; Total Staff 4.

NECROLOGY

(No Deaths)

An asterisk (*) denotes an organization that has established tax-exempt status directly with the IRS and is not covered by the USCCB Group Ruling.

Diocese of St. Cloud

(Dioecesis S. Clodoaldi)

Most Reverend

JOHN F. KINNEY, D.D., J.C.D.

Bishop of St. Cloud; ordained February 2, 1963; appointed Titular Bishop of Caorle and Auxiliary Bishop of St. Paul and Minneapolis November 16, 1976; consecrated January 25, 1977; appointed Bishop of Bismarck June 28, 1982; installed August 23, 1982; appointed Bishop of St. Cloud May 9, 1995; installed July 6, 1995. *Office: 214 Third Ave. S., P.O. Box 1248, St. Cloud, MN 56302-1248.* Tel: 320-251-2340.

Chancery: 214 Third Ave. S., P.O. Box 1248, St. Cloud, MN 56302. Tel: 320-251-2340; Fax: 320-251-0470.

Web: www.stcdio.org

Square Miles 12,251.

Corporate Title: "The Diocese of St. Cloud."

Erected as the Vicariate of Northern Minnesota, February 12, 1875.

Created as the Diocese of St. Cloud, September 22, 1889.

Comprises the Counties of Stearns, Sherburne, Benton, Morrison, Mille Lacs, Kanabec, Isanti, Pope, Stevens, Traverse, Grant, Douglas, Wilkin, Otter Tail, Todd and Wadena in the State of Minnesota.

For legal titles of parishes and diocesan institutions, consult the Chancery Office.

STATISTICAL OVERVIEW

Personnel	
Bishop	1
Abbots	1
Retired Abbots	1
Priests: Diocesan Active in Diocese	62
Priests: Retired, Sick or Absent	49
Number of Diocesan Priests	111
Religious Priests in Diocese	103
Total Priests in Diocese	214
Extern Priests in Diocese	6
Ordinations:	
Diocesan Priests	1
Transitional Deacons	3
Permanent Deacons in Diocese	48
Total Brothers	56
Total Sisters	464
Parishes	
Parishes	135
With Resident Pastor:	
Resident Diocesan Priests	55
Resident Religious Priests	10
Without Resident Pastor:	
Administered by Priests	70
Closed Parishes	1
Professional Ministry Personnel:	
Sisters	10
Lay Ministers	86
Welfare	
Catholic Hospitals	4
Total Assisted	310,748
Homes for the Aged	12
Total Assisted	1,084
Residential Care of Children	1
Total Assisted	392
Special Centers for Social Services	60
Total Assisted	46,476
Residential Care of Disabled	8
Total Assisted	56
Other Institutions	11
Total Assisted	727
Educational	
Diocesan Students in Other Seminaries	20
Seminaries, Religious	1
Total Seminarians	20
Colleges and Universities	2
Total Students	4,127
High Schools, Diocesan and Parish	1
Total Students	654
High Schools, Private	1
Total Students	328
Elementary Schools, Diocesan and Parish	31
Total Students	4,658
Catechesis/Religious Education:	
High School Students	5,199
Elementary Students	11,290
Total Students under Catholic Instruction	26,276
Teachers in the Diocese:	
Priests	9
Brothers	10
Sisters	15
Lay Teachers	760
Vital Statistics	
Receptions into the Church:	
Infant Baptism Totals	2,101
Adult Baptism Totals	71
Received into Full Communion	206
First Communions	2,103
Confirmations	1,818
Marriages:	
Catholic	534
Interfaith	223
Total Marriages	757
Deaths	1,391
Total Catholic Population	142,576
Total Population	558,890

Former Bishops—Rt. Revs. RUPERT SEIDENBUSCH, O.S.B., D.D., ord. June 22, 1853; cons. Bishop of Halia, Vicar-Apostolic of Northern Minnesota, May 30, 1875; resigned Nov. 15, 1888; died June 2, 1895; OTTO ZARDETTI, D.D., ord. Aug. 21, 1870; cons. Oct. 20, 1889; transferred to Bucharest, Romania, and raised to the Archiepiscopal Dignity, Feb. 23, 1894; died May 9, 1902; MARTIN MARTY, O.S.B., D.D., ord. Sept. 14, 1856; cons. Bishop of Tiberias, Feb. 1, 1880; Bishop of Sioux Falls, 1889; transferred to St. Cloud, Jan. 21, 1895; died Sept. 19, 1896; JAMES TROBEC, D.D., ord. Sept. 8, 1865; cons. Bishop of St. Cloud, Sept. 21, 1897; resigned April 15, 1914; appt. Titular Bishop of Lycopolis; died Dec. 14, 1921; Most Revs. JOSEPH F. BUSCH, D.D., ord. July 28, 1889; appt. Bishop of Lead, S. D., April 9, 1910; cons. May 19, 1910; transferred to See of St. Cloud, Jan. 19, 1915; died May 31, 1953; PETER W. BARTHOLOME, D.D., ord. June 12, 1917; appt. Titular Bishop of Lete and Coadjutor Bishop of St. Cloud "cum jure successionis", Dec. 6, 1941; cons. March 3, 1942; succeeded to See May 31, 1953; appt. Assistant at the Pontifical Throne July 23, 1954; resigned Jan. 31, 1968; died June 17, 1982; GEORGE H. SPELTZ, D.D., Ph.D., ord. June 2, 1940; appt. Auxiliary Bishop of Winona and Titular Bishop of Claneus February 13, 1963; cons. March 25, 1963; appt. Coadjutor of St. Cloud April 4, 1966; succeeded Jan. 31, 1968; resigned Jan. 13, 1987; died Feb. 1, 2004; JEROME HANUS, O.S.B., D.D., ord. July 30, 1966; appt. Bishop of St. Cloud, July 6, 1987; ord. and installed Aug. 24, 1987; appt. Coadjutor Archbishop of Dubuque, IA, Aug. 23, 1994.

Chancery—214 Third Ave. S., P.O. Box 1248, St. Cloud, 56302. Tel: 320-251-2340; 320-259-5227 (after hours); Fax: 320-251-0470. Office Hours: Mon.-Fri. 8:30-12 & 1-4:30.

Vicar General—Rev. MARVIN ENNEKING, J.C.L.

Chancellor—Rev. ROBERT ROLFES, J.C.L.

Vice Chancellor—CATHERINE M. COGHLAN.

Assistant Chancellor—Sr. MARY MANDERNACH, O.S.B.

Diocesan Tribunal—305 Seventh Ave. N., St. Cloud, 56303. All marriage cases are to be directed to: The Tribunal, Box 576, St. Cloud, 56302. Tel: 320-251-6557.

Judicial Vicar—Rev. VIRGIL A. HELMIN, J.C.L.

Adjutant Judicial Vicar—Rev. ROBERT C. HARREN, J.C.L.

Promoter Justitiae—Rev. ROBERT HARREN, J.C.L.

Defensor Vinculi—Revs. NICHOLAS LANDSBERGER, S.T.L.; GREGORY LIESER (Retired); ROBERT ROLFES, J.C.L.; THOMAS OLSON; ROGER KLASSEN, O.S.B.; Deacon JOHN SALCHERT.

Judges—Revs. MARVIN ENNEKING, J.C.L.; ROBERT C. HARREN, J.C.L.; THERESA A. WYBURN, J.C.L.; Deacon DONALD TZINSKI, J.C.L.

Notaries—Revs. VIRGIL A. HELMIN, J.C.L.; ROBERT ROLFES, J.C.L.; THERESA A. WYBURN, J.C.L.; Deacon DONALD TZINSKI, J.C.L.; KARRIE MOLLNER; JENNA VAVRA.

Advocates—Revs. JOSEPH KORF; MARK INNOCENTI; Mrs. DOLORES SALCHERT.

Marriage Counseling—Caritas Family Services, 911 18th St. N., St. Cloud, 56303. Tel: 320-650-1660.

Diocesan Consultors—Revs. KEVIN ANDERSON; TIMOTHY BALTES; THOMAS BECKER; LAUREN GERMANN; MARVIN ENNEKING, J.C.L.; MARK STANG; WILLIAM VOS (Retired); STANLEY WIESER.

Deans—Revs. STEVEN BINSFELD, Alexandria/Morris; STEPHEN BEAUCLAIR, O.S.B., Cold Spring; DONALD WAGNER, Fergus Falls/Wadena; JOSEPH KORF, Foley/Princeton; KENNETH BRENNY, Little Falls (Retired); THOMAS BECKER, Melrose/Sauk Centre; GREGORY LIESER, St. Cloud (Retired).

Diocesan Corporate Board—Most Rev. JOHN F. KINNEY, D.D., J.C.D., Pres.; Revs. MARVIN ENNEKING, J.C.L., Vice Pres.; ROBERT ROLFES, J.C.L., Sec.; JOSEPH KORF; LAUREN GERMANN.

Diocesan Finance Council—Most Rev. JOHN FRANCIS KINNEY, D.D., J.C.D.; JOSEPH SPANIOL, Finance Officer; Revs. MARVIN ENNEKING, J.C.L.; RONALD WEYRENS; Sr. ARDELLA KVAMME, O.S.B.; MERVIN CIHLAR; Mr. PETER FUCHSTEINER; MARY KESKE; Mr. JAMES MEGEL; Mr. PAUL PFANNENSTEIN; Mr. RAYMOND SCHULTE; NANCY WHITNEY.

Due Process Service—THERESA A. WYBURN, J.C.L., 305 7th Ave. N., P.O. Box 576, St. Cloud, 56302.

Presbyteral Council—Revs. KEVIN ANDERSON; MARK INNOCENTI; TIMOTHY BALTES, Chm.; ALFRED STANGL (Retired); PETER VANDERWEYST; JOSEPH HERZING; MARVIN ENNEKING, J.C.L.; JEFFREY D. ETHEN; JOSEPH FEDERS, O.S.B.; GREGORY PAFFEL; LAUREN GERMANN; MARK STANG, Address correspondence to: Assumption Church, Box 287, Morris, 56267.

Pastoral Council—PATRICIA LOXTERCAMP, Exec. Sec.; Revs. ANTHONY KROLL (Retired); GREGORY POSER, O.S.C.; JOSE BRACAMONTE; Deacon FREDERICK ST. JEAN; PEGGY KOSCIELNIAK; PHYLLIS DUERR; EUGENE FISCHER; CONNIE GRAFF; MARILYNE MORISETTE; ERICA ZABINSKI; IRENE SCHMIDT; NICHOLAS LAHR; Sr. ALICE IMDIEKE, O.S.B.; Mrs. MAYULI BALES; LINDA CHRISTEN.

Diocesan Offices and Programs

Archives—LOUISE THEISEN, Archivist. Tel: 320-251-2340. Email: ltheisen@gw.stcdio.org.

Boy Scouts—Rev. LEROY SCHEIERL, Dir., 16921 County Rd. 7, N.W., Brandon, 56315.

Catholic Campaign for Human Development—KATHY LANGER, 911 18th St. N., P.O. Box 2390, St. Cloud, 56302. Tel: 320-229-6020.

Campus Ministry—Rev. ANTHONY OELRICH, S.T.L., Newman Center, 396 First Ave. S., St. Cloud, 56301.

Catholic Charities—Mr. STEVEN BRESNAHAN, Exec. Dir., 911 18th St. N., P.O. Box 2390, St. Cloud, 56302. Tel: 320-650-1550; Fax: 320-650-1528 Senior Services (Central Minnesota Foster Grandparent Program, Senior Dining); Caritas Family Services (Adoption, Counseling, Emergency Services -Food- Clothing-Financial, Financial Counseling, La Cruz Community Liaison; Life Transition Services, Caritas Mental Health Clinic, Pregnancy Counseling, Legal Immigration Services); Housing Services (Housing Management Services and Transitional Housing); Residential and Day Services (Bethany Home, Adult Foster Care for Handicapped Individuals, Day Programs, Support and Advocacy for Independent Living, Transitional Housing for Youth, Young Learners, Hope Community Support, Intensive Treatment Unit, Mother Teresa Home, St. Anne's Home, St. Cloud Children's Home, St. Elizabeth Residential Care, St. Francis Home, St. Luke's Home, St. Michael's Home, Semi-Independent Living Services, Waivered Services for Mental Retardation and Related Conditions, St. Margaret's Home), Social Concerns. Web: www.ccstcloud.org.

Catholic Foundation of the Diocese of St. Cloud—GEORGE SJOGREN, Exec. Dir., 305 7th Ave. N., St. Cloud, 56303. Tel: 320-258-0390.

Catholic Relief Services—Rev. WILLIAM VOS, Dir. (Retired), Mailing Address: 11 Eighth Ave. S., St. Cloud, 56301. Tel: 320-251-1100; Fax: 320-251-2061.

Catholic Women, Council of—Rev. GREGORY LIESER, Moderator (Retired), Mailing Address: 308 3rd Ave. S., Sauk Rapids, 56379. Tel: 320-250-6390; IRENE SCHMIDT, 9246 County Rd. 17, Rice, 56367. Tel: 320-393-2472.

Cemeteries Assumption-Calvary—2341 Roosevelt Rd., St. Cloud, 56301. Tel: 320-251-5511.

Censores Librorum—Revs. PAUL ZYLLA (Retired); ROBERT C. HARREN, J.C.L.; Sr. RENEE DOMEIER, O.S.B.

Clerical Aid Association—Most Rev. JOHN FRANCIS KINNEY, D.D., J.C.D., Pres.; Rev. ROBERT ROLFES, J.C.L., Sec. Directors: Revs. MARVIN ENNEKING, J.C.L.; VIRGIL R. BRAUN; NICHOLAS LANDSBERGER, S.T.L.; PETER K. KIRCHNER JR.; THOMAS KNOBLACH, Ph.D.; LAURN VIRNIG; ROBERT LANDSBERGER (Retired), Address Mail to: The Chancery, P.O. Box 1248, St. Cloud, 56302.

Communications Office— (Radio, Television, Public Information), REBECCA KUROWSKI, Dir., Pastoral Center, Diocese of St. Cloud, 305 N. Seventh Ave., St. Cloud, 56303. Tel: 320-251-0558.

Continuing Formation of Priests—Rev. ANTHONY OELRICH, S.T.L., 305 7th Ave. N., Saint Cloud, 56303. Tel: 320-251-8335.

Development Office—GEORGE SJOGREN, Dir. Devel., 305 7th Ave. N., Ste. 105, St. Cloud, 56303. Tel: 320-258-0390.

Diocesan Education Council—Rev. LAUREN GERMANN; Deacon MARK BARDER; Sr. ALICE IMDIEKE, O.S.B.; LINDA KAISER; BRENDA KRESKY; DAN HOLLENHORST; KATHY LANGER; SCOTT FRIELER; ROBERT DOYLE; KATERI MANCINI; KENT SCHMITZ; Mrs. MAYULI BALES; TIMOTHY WELCH.

Office of Catholic Education Ministries—LINDA KAISER, Dir.; DAN HOLLENHORST, School Consultant; VACANT, Consultant for Disabilities & Catechist Formation; TIMOTHY WELCH, Consultant, Educational Technology; KENT SCHMITZ, Consultant for Youth Ministry & Rel. Educ.; BRENDA KRESKY, Consultant for Adult Faith Formation & Ministry Formation Prog.; JULIE TSCHIDA, Receptionist/Sec., Address all correspondence to: Catholic Education Ministries, Pastoral Center, Diocese of St. Cloud, 305 Seventh Ave., N., St. Cloud, 56303. Tel: 320-251-0111.

Diocesan Commission on Ecumenical and Interreligious Affairs—Rev. GERALD DALSETH, Chm., Address all correspondence to: P.O. Box 428, Pierz, 56364-0428.

Diocesan Planning Council—JANE MARRIN, Dir.; Revs. MICHAEL KELLOGG, Chm.; VINCENT LIESER; EUGENE DOYLE; MEINRAD DINDORF, O.S.B.; Ms. RITA CLASEMANN; PATRICIA LOXTERCAMP; Sisters JEAN SCHWARTZ, O.S.B.; CLARA STANG, O.S.F.; Mr. STEVEN BRESNAHAN.

Diocesan Priests Pension Plan Trustees—Most Rev. JOHN FRANCIS KINNEY, D.D., J.C.D.; Revs. MARVIN ENNEKING, J.C.L.; THOMAS OLSON; VIRGIL A. HELMIN, J.C.L.; JAMES DAVID HAHN; GERALD MISCHKE (Retired); STANLEY WIESER; RICHARD LEISEN (Retired); ROBERT ROLFES, J.C.L.

Director of Retired Priests—Rev. ROBERT ROLFES, J.C.L.

Health Ministry—Rev. THOMAS KNOBLACH, Ph.D., Consultant for Healthcare Ethics; KATHLEEN THEISEN, Coord. Parish Health.

Holy Childhood Association—Rev. WILLIAM VOS, Dir. (Retired), 11 Eighth Ave., S., St. Cloud, 56301.

Koinonia Program of Central Minnesota—Rev. DAVID MACIEJ, Mailing Address: P.O. Box 38, Lastrup, 56344.

Legion of Decency—Rev. ROBERT ROLFES, J.C.L., Mailing Address: P.O. Box 1248, St. Cloud, 56302.

Legion of Mary—Rev. RAYMOND STEFFES, O.S.C., Crosier Monastery, Onamia, 56359.

Multicultural Ministry—Rev. JOSE BRACAMONTE, Coord. Hispanic Ministry.

Office of Marriage and Family—CHRISTINE CODDEN, Dir., 305 N. 7th Ave., Ste. 100, St. Cloud, 56303. Tel: 320-252-4721; Fax: 320-258-7658.

Newspaper "St. Cloud Visitor"—Pastoral Center, Diocese of St. Cloud, 305 N. Seventh Ave., Box 1068, St. Cloud, 56302. Tel: 320-251-3022. JOE TOWALSKI, Editor.

Office of Diaconate—Deacon MARK BARDER, Dir., 305 7th Ave. N., Ste. 100, Saint Cloud, 56303. Tel: 320-203-0554; Fax: 320-258-7658; Rev. BERNARD GRUENES, Vicar for Permanent Deacons, Church of St. Michael, 1036 County Rd. 4, Saint Cloud, 56303; Deacon STEVEN DUPAY, Pres. Diaconal Community, 305 Seventh Ave. N., St. Cloud, 56303. Tel: 612-252-4721.

Personnel Committee—Revs. VINCENT LIESER, Dir.; MARVIN ENNEKING, J.C.L.; RALPH ZIMMERMAN; JOSEPH HERZING; DONALD WAGNER; ROGER KLASSEN, O.S.B.; Deacon DAVID LINDMEIER; JANE MARRIN, Mailing Address: 211 S. 5th Ave. E., Melrose, 56352.

Propagation of the Faith—ROSEANNE FISCHER, Dir., 11 Eighth Ave. S., St. Cloud, 56301. Tel: 320-251-1100; Fax: 320-251-2061.

Rural Life Program—KATHY LANGER, 911 18th St. N., P.O. Box 2390, Saint Cloud, 56302. Tel: 320-229-6020.

TEC (Central Minnesota TEC) (Together Encountering Christ)—MICHAEL LENTZ, Coord., Mailing Address: P.O. Box 500, Onamia, 56359. Tel: 320-532-3103.

Victim Assistance Coordinator—ROXANNE STORMS. Tel: 320-248-1563.

Vocations—Rev. GREGORY MASTEY, Dir., 305 Seventh Ave. N., Ste. 100, St. Cloud, 56303-3633. Tel: 320-251-5001; Fax: 320-258-7658. Email: gmastey@gw.stcdio.org.

Worship, Office of—ANITA FISCHER, Dir., Pastoral Center, Diocese of St. Cloud, 305 N. Seventh Ave., St. Cloud, 56303. Tel: 320-255-9068.

CLERGY, PARISHES, MISSIONS AND PAROCHIAL SCHOOLS

CITY OF ST. CLOUD

(BENTON, STEARNS, SHERBURNE COUNTIES)

1—ST. MARY'S CATHEDRAL OF ST. CLOUD, [JC] Revs. Anthony Oelrich, Rector; Aaron J. Kuhn; Deacon Leo Kosiba. In Res., Rev. Gerald Mischke (Retired).
Res.: 25 Eighth Ave. S., 56301-4279. Tel: 320-251-1840; Fax: 320-251-1840 (Press 6 after menu). Email: cathedral@stmarystcloud.org.
School-See St. Augustine's/St. Mary's Cathedral, St. Cloud under St. Augustine, St. Cloud for details.
Catechesis/Religious Program—Lisa Neu, D.R.E. Students 56.

2—ST. ANTHONY OF PADUA (1920) Revs. Thomas Knoblach; Jimmy Joseph, V.C.
Office: 2405 1st St. N., 56303. Tel: 320-251-5966; Fax: 320-251-0664.
School-See St. Elizabeth Ann Seton School, St. Cloud under Inter-Parochial Schools located in the Institution section.
Catechesis/Religious Program—2410 1st. St. N., 56303. Virginia Duschner, D.R.E. Students 166.

3—ST. AUGUSTINE (1919) Revs. Anthony Oelrich; Aaron J. Kuhn; Deacon Richard Scheierl.
Office: 442 Second St., S.E., 56304. Tel: 320-251-8335; Fax: 320-529-3231. Email: info@staugs.com. Res.: 25 8th Ave. S., Saint Cloud, 56301. Tel: 320-251-1840.
School—St. Augustine's/St. Mary's Cathedral, (Grades PreK-6), Day Care, Tel: 320-251-2376; Fax: 320-529-3222. Pat Lindeman, Prin.; Juliana Elchert, Librarian. Lay Teachers 12; Students 127.
Catechesis/Religious Program—Tel: 320-252-6042; Fax: 320-529-3236. Lisa Neu, D.R.E. Students 144.

4—CHRIST CHURCH (1964) Revs. Anthony Oelrich; Aaron J. Kuhn.
Office: 396 First Ave. S., 56301. Tel: 320-251-3260; Fax: 320-252-3930.
Catechesis/Religious Program—Students 145.

5—HOLY ANGELS, Closed. For inquiries for parish records contact St. Mary's Cathedral, St. Cloud.

6—HOLY SPIRIT (1952) [JC] Revs. Thomas Knoblach; Jimmy Joseph, V.C.; Deacon Vernon Schmitz; Sr. Diane Hunker, C.S.J., Pastoral Assoc.
Office: 2405 Walden Way, 56301. Tel: 320-251-3764; Fax: 320-252-5143. Email: hspirit@charterinternet.com. Web: holyspirit-stcloud.com.
School-See St. Elizabeth Ann Seton School, St. Cloud under Inter-Parochial Schools located in the Institution section.
Catechesis/Religious Program—Ginny Duschner, D.R.E. Students 175.

7—ST. JOHN CANTIUS Revs. Thomas Knoblach; Jimmy Joseph, V.C.; Deacon Fred Reker.
Office: 1515 Third St. N., 56303. Tel: 320-251-4455; Fax: 320-240-1238. Email: stjohncantius@charter.net.
Catechesis/Religious Program—Ginny Duschner, D.R.E. Students 71.

8—ST. MICHAEL (1970) [CEM] Revs. Bernard Gruenes; George Michael, V.C.; Deacon Todd Warren.
Res.: 1036 Co. Rd. 4, 56303. Tel: 320-251-6923; Fax: 320-202-1104.
School-See Sts. Peter & Paul & Michael, St. Cloud under Inter-Parochial Schools located in the Institution section.
Catechesis/Religious Program—Students 183.

9—ST. PAUL (1946) [JC] Rev. Alan Wielinski; Deacon David Lindmeier.
Office: 1125 11th Ave. N., 56303. Tel: 320-251-4831; Fax: 320-251-2648. Email: general@churchofstpaul.org.
School-See Sts. Peter & Paul & Michael, St. Cloud under Inter-Parochial Schools located in the Institution section.
Catechesis/Religious Program—Geralyn Nathe Evans, D.R.E. Students 95.

10—ST. PETER (1947) [JC] Rev. Alan Wielinski; Deacon William Ritchie.
Office: 930 31st Ave. N., 56303. Tel: 320-252-2113; Fax: 320-529-0796. Email: stpeters@charterinternet.com.
School-See Sts. Peter & Paul & Michael, St. Cloud under Inter-Parochial Schools located in the Institution section.
Catechesis/Religious Program—Tel: 320-253-5768. Laura Mullin, D.R.E. Students 126.

OUTSIDE THE CITY OF ST. CLOUD

ALBANY, STEARNS CO., SEVEN DOLORS (1868) [CEM] Very Rev. Michael Naughton, O.S.B.
Res.: P.O. Box 277, 56307. Tel: 320-845-2705. Email: 7dolors@albanytel.com.
School—Holy Family, (Grades K-6) Tel: 320-845-2011; Fax: 320-845-7380. Email: hfamily@albanytel.com. Bonnie Massmann, Prin. Lay Teachers 9; Students 136.
Catechesis/Religious Program—Tel: 320-845-4335. Sr. Alice Imdieke, O.S.B., D.R.E. Students 341.

ALEXANDRIA, DOUGLAS CO., ST. MARY'S (1882) [CEM] Rev. Steven Binsfeld.
Office: 420 Irving St., P.O. Box 669, 56308. Tel: 320-763-5781; Fax: 320-763-4833. Email: stmary@stmaryalexandria.org.
School—(Grades K-6) Tel: 320-763-5861; Fax: 320-763-7992. Email: stmaryss@stmaryalexandria.org. Troy Sladek, Prin.; Jeanne Nelsen, Librarian. Lay Teachers 15; Students 199.
Catechesis/Religious Program—Tel: 320-763-9202. Email: stmreled@stmaryalexandria.org. Students 512.

AVON, STEARNS CO., ST. BENEDICT'S, [CEM] Rev. Blane Wasnie, O.S.B.
Church: P.O. Box 98, 56310. Tel: 320-356-7121; Fax: 320-356-9203.
Catechesis/Religious Program—Clarey McInerny, Coord. Faith Formation. Students 288.

BATTLE LAKE, OTTER TAIL CO., OUR LADY OF THE LAKE (1953) [CEM] Revs. Gregory Paffel; LeRoy Schik.
Res.: 407 Lake Ave. N., P.O. Box 671, 56515. Tel: 218-864-5619; Fax: 218-864-5747.
Catechesis/Religious Program—Students 110.

BECKER, SHERBUNE CO., IMMACULATE CONCEPTION (1918) [CEM] Rev. Eugene Doyle.
Res.: 12100 Sherburne Ave., Box 426, 55308. Tel: 763-261-4242; Fax: 763-261-2242. Email: genedoyle@izoom.net.
Catechesis/Religious Program—Sr. Julie Schleper, O.S.B., D.R.E. Students 378.

BELGRADE, STEARNS CO., ST. FRANCIS DE SALES (1890) [CEM] Rev. Jeffrey D. Ethen.
Office: 541 Martin Ave., P.O. Box 69, 56312. Tel: 320-254-8218; Fax: 320-254-8218.
Catechesis/Religious Program—JoAnn Braegelman, D.R.E. Students 75.

BELLE PRAIRIE, MORRISON CO., HOLY FAMILY (1852) [CEM] Revs. Nicholas Landsberger; Mark Innocenti; Deacon Bruce Geyer.
Office: 18777 Riverwood Dr., Little Falls, 56345. Tel: 320-632-5720. Email: holyfam@fallsnet.com.
Catechesis/Religious Program—Tel: 320-632-5754. Cindy Loidolt, D.R.E. Students 106.

BELLE RIVER, DOUGLAS CO., ST. NICHOLAS (1871) [CEM] Rev. David Jeffrey Petron; Deacon Stanley Hennen.
Res.: P.O. Box F, Osakis, 56360.
Catechesis/Religious Program—Tel: 320-852-7041. Tonya Beulke, D.R.E. Students 57.

BERTHA, TODD CO., ST. JOSEPH (1914) [CEM] Rev. Daniel Walz.
Res.: P.O. Box 158, 56437-0158. Tel: 218-924-2605; Fax: 218-924-2144. Email: stjoseph_bertha@yahoo.com.
Catechesis/Religious Program—Tel: 218-924-2144. Stephanie Heinze, D.R.E. Students 56.

BIG LAKE, SHERBURNE CO., OUR LADY OF THE LAKE (1958) [CEM] Rev. Eugene Doyle; Deacon Steven Dupay, Parish Life Coord.
Res.: 440 Lake St. N., Box 100, 55309. Tel: 763-263-2863; Fax: 763-263-3187. Email: parish@ourladybiglake.org.
Catechesis/Religious Program—Students 386.

BLUEGRASS, WADENA CO., ST. HUBERT (1908) [CEM] Rev. Scott Wittkop.
Res.: 20 Brown St. N., P.O. Box C, Verndale, 56481. Tel: 218-445-5786; Fax: 218-445-5087.
Catechesis/Religious Program—23764 U.S. Hwy. 71, Sebeka, 56477. Tel: 218-631-1836; 218-631-1711. Vera Malone, D.R.E. Students 79.

BLUFFTON, OTTER TAIL CO., ST. JOHN THE BAPTIST (1902) [CEM] Rev. Donald Wagner.
Res.: 310 Main St., P.O. Box 36, 56518. Tel: 218-385-2608; Fax: 218-385-2808.
Catechesis/Religious Program—Students 121.

BOWLUS, MORRISON CO., ST. STANISLAUS KOSTKA, [CEM] Revs. Michael Kellogg; Gregory Ombok.
Office: P.O. Box 8, 56314. Tel: 320-584-5313; Fax: 320-584-8231.
Catechesis/Religious Program—Sandy Fussy, D.R.E. Students 49.

BRAHAM, ISANTI CO., ST. PETER & PAUL (1986) [CEM] Rev. Kevin Anderson; Deacon Thomas Pinataro, Parish Life Coord.
Res.: 1050 Southview Ave., P.O. Box 483, 55006. Tel: 320-396-3105. Email: stspeter_paulchurch@yahoo.com.
Catechesis/Religious Program—Students 150.

BRANDON, DOUGLAS CO., CHURCH OF ST. ANN, [CEM] Rev. LeRoy Scheierl. In Res., Rev. Eugene Lemm (Retired).
Res.: P.O. Box 256, 56315. Tel: 320-834-5095. Email: stanns@gctel.com.
Catechesis/Religious Program— Marilyn Kelly, D.R.E. Students 62.

BRECKENRIDGE, WILKIN CO., ST. MARY OF THE PRESENTATION (1898) [CEM 2] Rev. Kenneth Popp.
Res.: 221 Fourth St. N., 56520-1496. Tel: 218-643-5173; Fax: 218-643-1881.
School—(Grades PreK-8) Tel: 218-643-5443. Linda Johnson, Prin. Lay Teachers 11; Students 102.
Catechesis/Religious Program—Students 149.

BRENNYVILLE, BENTON CO., ST. ELIZABETH OF HUNGARY (1927) [CEM] Rev. Antonio Marfori.
Res.: 16426 125th Ave., N.E., Foley, 56329. Tel: 320-355-2454; Fax: 320-355-2819.
Catechesis/Religious Program—Tel: 320-387-3332. Students 39.

BROOTEN, STEARNS CO., ST. DONATUS (1911) [CEM] Rev. Jeffrey D. Ethen.
Office: 301 Eastern Ave. S., P.O. Box 159, 56316. Tel: 320-346-2431; Fax: 320-346-2431. Email: stdonatus@tds.net.
Catechesis/Religious Program—Tel: 320-346-2431. Audrey Radermacher, C.R.E. Students 54.

BROWERVILLE, TODD CO., CHRIST THE KING (1978) [CEM] Rev. Ralph Zimmerman; Deacon Mark Zenner.
Res.: 720 Main St. N., P.O. Box 83, 56438. Tel: 320-594-2291. Email: ctkparish_school@embarqmail.com.
School—(Grades PreK-6) Tel: 320-594-6114; Fax: 320-594-6313. Paula Becker, Prin. Lay Teachers 4; Students 49.
Catechesis/Religious Program—Beverly Geraets, D.R.E. Tel: 320-594-2441. Students 155.

BROWN'S VALLEY, TRAVERSE CO., ST. ANTHONY'S (1896) [CEM] Rev. Joseph Vandeberg.
Church: 122 2nd St. S., Box 359, 56219. Tel: 320-695-2621.
Catechesis/Religious Program—Students 54.

BUCKMAN, MORRISON CO., ST. MICHAEL'S, [CEM] Rev. Gerald Dalseth; Deacon Guy Beck.
Res.: P.O. Box 428, Pierz, 56364. Tel: 320-468-6033; Fax: 320-468-2296.
Catechesis/Religious Program—Tel: 320-468-2640. Students 125.

BUTLER, OTTER TAIL CO., HOLY CROSS (1910) [CEM] Rev. Joseph Herzing.
54216 County Hwy. 148, Menahga, 56464.
Res.: 234 - 2nd Ave. S.W., Perham, 56573. Tel: 218-346-4240.
Catechesis/Religious Program—Mary Peeters, D.R.E.; Glenda Hofland, D.R.E. Students 55.

CAMBRIDGE, ISANTI CO., CHRIST THE KING, [CEM] Rev. James David Hahn; Deacon Eugene Kramer.
Res.: 230 Fern St. N., 55008-1094. Tel: 763-689-1221; Fax: 763-689-8950.
Catechesis/Religious Program—Tel: 763-689-3728. Students 127.

CHOKIO, STEVENS CO., ST. MARY'S (1897) [CEM] Revs. Timothy Baltes; Peter VanderWeyst.
Res.: P.O. Box 187, 56221. Tel: 320-324-2680; Fax: 320-324-2732. Email: stmarych@fedtel.net.
Catechesis/Religious Program—Anita Marty, D.R.E. Students 57.

CLARISSA, TODD CO., ST. JOSEPH (1896) [CEM] Rev. Ralph Zimmerman; Deacon Mark Zenner.
Res.: Box 83, Browerville, 56438. Tel: 320-594-2291; Fax: 320-594-6313.
Office & Mailing Address: 105 John St. S., P.O. Box 5, 56440. Tel: 218-756-2205; Fax: 218-756-2203. Email: stjoschu@eaglevalleytel.net.
Catechesis/Religious Program—Tel: 218-756-3614. Eileen Uhlenkamp, D.R.E. Students 46.

CLEAR LAKE, SHERBURNE CO., ST. MARCUS (1888) [CEM] Rev. Virgil A. Helmin.
Res.: 8701 Main Ave., P.O. Box 237, 55319. Tel: 320-743-2481; Fax: 320-743-3346. Email: stmarcus@frontiernet.net.
Catechesis/Religious Program—Tel: 320-743-3346. Melissa Fox, D.R.E. Students 143.

COLD SPRING, STEARNS CO., ST. BONIFACE (1878) [CEM] Rev. Cletus Connors, O.S.B.; Deacon Lawrence Sell.
Res.: 501 Main St., 56320. Tel: 320-685-3280; Fax: 320-685-7792.
School—(Grades PreSchool-6) Tel: 320-685-3541. Sr. Sharon Waldoch, S.S.N.D., Prin. Lay Teachers 15; Students 266.
Catechesis/Religious Program—Tel: 320-685-8222, Ext. 103. Karen Neu, D.R.E. Students 448.

COLLEGEVILLE, STEARNS CO., ST. JOHN THE BAPTIST (1875) [JC] Rev. Eugene J. McGlothlin, O.S.B.; Deacon Michael Keable.
Res.: 14241 Fruit Farm Rd., P.O. Box 6366, 56321. Tel: 320-363-2765. Email: emcglothin@csbsju.edu.
Catechesis/Religious Program—Julie Ortloff, D.R.E. Students 72.

DENT, OTTER TAIL CO., SACRED HEART (1921) [CEM] Rev. Daniel Walz.
Res.: 36963 State Hwy. 108, 56528. Tel: 218-758-2700; Fax: 218-758-3861. Email: sacredheart@arvig.net.
Catechesis/Religious Program—Joe Sazama, D.R.E.; Diane Sazama, D.R.E. Students 70.

DONNELLY, STEVENS CO., ST. THERESIA, Closed. For inquiries for parish records contact St. Charles, Herman.

DUELM, BENTON CO., ST. LAWRENCE'S, [CEM] Rev. Bernard Kahlhamer.
Res.: 10915 Duelm Rd., N.E., Foley, 56329. Tel: 320-968-7502; Fax: 320-968-7252.
Catechesis/Religious Program—Tel: 320-968-6595. Betty Pundsack, D.R.E. Students 210.

DUMONT, TRAVERSE CO., ST. PETER'S, Closed. For inquiries for Parish Records contact: Ave Maria, Wheaton. Mailing address: 201 9th St. S., Wheaton, MN 56296.

EDEN VALLEY, STEARNS CO., THE CHURCH OF THE ASSUMPTION (1892) [CEM 2] Rev. Virgil R. Braun.
Res.: P.O. Box 9, 55329. Tel: 320-453-2788.
Catechesis/Religious Program—Tel: 320-453-7388. Rose Fink, D.R.E.; Sherri Lego, D.R.E. Students 176.

ELBOW LAKE, GRANT CO., ST. OLAF, [CEM] Rev. Arlie Sowada; Deacon Joseph Wood.
Res.: 518 E. Division St., 56531. Tel: 218-685-4318.
Catechesis/Religious Program—Students 60.

ELIZABETH, OTTER TAIL CO., ST. ELIZABETH, [CEM] Rev. Stanley Wieser.
Res.: 706 W. Pleasant Ave., 56533. Tel: 218-736-5230.
Catechesis/Religious Program—Tel: 218-739-1140. Jan Dumas, D.R.E. Students 18.

ELK RIVER, SHERBURNE CO., THE CHURCH OF ST. ANDREW (1890) [CEM] Revs. Joseph Korf; Omar Guanchez; Deacon Frederick St. Jean.
Res.: 566 Fourth St., 55330. Tel: 763-441-1483; Fax: 763-441-1485.
School—(Grades K-6), 428 Irving Ave., 55330. Tel: 763-441-2216; Fax: 763-441-1146. Kari Staples, Prin. Sisters 1; Lay Teachers 16; Students 240.
Catechesis/Religious Program—Tel: 763-441-3202. Students 1,592.

ELMDALE, MORRISON CO., ST. EDWARD'S, [CEM] Revs. Michael Kellogg, Admin.; Gregory Ombok.
P.O. Box 8, Bowlus, 56314. Tel: 320-584-5313; Fax: 320-584-8231.
Catechesis/Religious Program—308 S. Main St., Upsala, 56384. Tel: 320-573-2132. Students 52.

ELROSA, STEARNS CO., SS. PETER AND PAUL (1891) [CEM] Rev. Jeffrey D. Ethen.
Res.: 302 State St., P.O. Box 95, 56325. Tel: 320-697-5541; Fax: 320-254-3239.
Catechesis/Religious Program—Tel: 320-254-8218; Fax: 320-254-8218. Jo Braegelman, D.R.E. Students 74.

FARMING, STEARNS CO., ST. CATHERINE'S (1879) [CEM] Rev. Corwin Collins, O.S.B.; Deacon Gerald Theis.
Res.: 26966 County Rd. 23, Richmond, 56368. Tel: 320-548-3550.
Catechesis/Religious Program—Tel: 320-597-3033. Mary Brinkman, D.R.E. Students 36.

FERGUS FALLS, OTTER TAIL CO., OUR LADY OF VICTORY (1881) [CEM] Revs. Gregory Paffel; LeRoy Schik.
Office & Mailing Address: 207 N. Vine St., 56537. Tel: 218-736-2429.
Res.: 407 Lake Ave. N., P.O. Box 671, Battle Lake, 56515. Tel: 218-736-7988; Fax: 218-736-4407. Email: olv@prtel.com.
School—(Grades PreSchool-6), 426 W. Cavour Ave., 56537. Tel: 208-736-6661; Fax: 218-736-6931. Sandy Carpenter, Prin.; Sue Herder, Librarian. Lay Teachers 9; Students 122.
Catechesis/Religious Program—Tel: 218-736-6837. Becky Pyle, D.R.E.; Chastity Soupir, D.R.E. Students 240.

FLENSBURG, MORRISON CO., SACRED HEART, [CEM 2] Rev. Leo Moenkedick.
Mailing Address: 9406 Church Cir., Little Falls, 56345. Tel: 320-632-6930; Fax: 320-632-5644.
Catechesis/Religious Program—Sheila Gardner, D.R.E. Students 30.

FOLEY, BENTON CO., ST. JOHN'S, [CEM] Rev. Robert Kieffer.
Office: 621 Dewey St., P.O. Box 337, 56329. Tel: 320-968-7913.
Res.: 310 Murphy St., Box 242, 56329. Tel: 320-968-7143.
School—St. John's Area School, (Grades PreSchool-6), P.O. Box 368, 56329. Tel: 320-968-7972; Fax: 320-968-9956. Mary Sabin, Prin.; Michelle Buettner, Librarian. Lay Teachers 8; Students 117.
Catechesis/Religious Program—Fax: 320-968-4424. Sheila Matteson, D.R.E.; Andrea Rahm, D.R.E.; Shannon Schmit, D.R.E. & Youth Min. Students 176.

FORESTON, MILLE LACS CO., ST. LOUIS BERTRAND, [CEM] Rev. James H. Remmerswaal, O.S.C.
Res.: 187 First St. S., P.O. Box 128, 56330. Tel: 320-294-5460; Fax: 320-294-5588. Email: stlouis@jetup.net.
Catechesis/Religious Program—Students 85.

FOXHOME, WILKIN CO., ST. JOSEPH, Closed. For inquiries for parish records contact St. Mary of the Presentation, Breckenridge.

FREEPORT, STEARNS CO., SACRED HEART (1881) [CEM] Rev. Roger Klassen, O.S.B.; Deacon Richard Scherping.
Res.: 106 - 3rd Ave., N.E., P.O. Box 155, 56331-9017. Tel: 320-836-2143; Fax: 320-836-2142. Email: triparish@albanytel.com.
School—(Grades PreSchool-6), 303 2nd St. N.E., P.O. Box 39, 56331. Tel: 320-836-2591; Fax: 320-836-2514. Email: shs@albanytel.com. Kathy Well, Prin. Lay Teachers 6; Students 72.
Catechesis/Religious Program—Students 87.

GILMAN, BENTON CO., SS. PETER AND PAUL (1872) [CEM] Rev. Antonio Marfori.
Res.: P.O. Box 86, 56333. Tel: 320-387-2255; Fax: 320-355-2819.
See St. John's School, Foley under Inter-Parochial Schools located in the Institution section.
Catechesis/Religious Program—Tel: 320-387-3332. Students 94.

GLENWOOD, POPE CO., SACRED HEART (1903) [CEM 2] Rev. Peter K. Kirchner Jr.; Deacon Frank Schmainda.
Office: P.O. Box 128, 56334. Email: sheartchurch@gmail.com.
Res.: 105 Franklin St. N., 56334. Tel: 320-634-3813.
Catechesis/Religious Program—Tel: 320-634-4828. Diane Mrnak, D.R.E. Students 153.

GREENWALD, STEARNS CO., ST. ANDREW'S (1924) [CEM] Rev. Thomas Becker.
Res.: P.O. Box 120, 56335. Tel: 320-987-3160; Fax: 320-987-3306. Email: stjohn1@meltel.net.
School—(Grades K-2) Tel: 320-987-3133. Mr. Jeri Bachel, Prin. Lay Teachers 2; Students 28.
Catechesis/Religious Program—Tel: 320-352-2783. Ruth Klaphake, D.R.E. Students 16.

GREY EAGLE, TODD CO., ST. JOSEPH'S, [CEM 2] Revs. Mark Willenbring; Ronald Dockendorf.

Res.: 118 Minnesota St., P.O Box 366, 56336. Tel: 320-285-2545; Fax: 320-285-5255.
Catechesis/Religious Program—Students 108.

HARDING, MORRISON CO., HOLY CROSS (1904) [CEM] Rev. David Maciej.
Mailing Address: 29482 243rd St, Pierz, 56364.
Res.: 28520 Church St., P.O. Box 38, Lastrup, 56344. Tel: 320-468-2111.
Catechesis/Religious Program—Students 81.

HENNING, OTTER TAIL CO., CHURCH OF ST. EDWARD OF HENNING (1945) [CEM] Rev. Daniel Walz.
Res.: 201 Douglas Ave., 56551. Tel: 218-583-2490.
Catechesis/Religious Program—Lyn Andrews, D.R.E. Students 55.

HERMAN, GRANT CO., ST. CHARLES (1913) [CEM] Revs. Timothy Baltes; Peter VanderWeyst.
Res.: P.O. Box 187, Chokio, 56221. Tel: 320-677-2433; Fax: 320-324-2732. Email: stmarych@fedtel.net.
Catechesis/Religious Program—Katy Blume, D.R.E. Students 28.

HILLMAN, MORRISON CO., ST. RITA'S (1920) [CEM] Revs. Jude Verley, O.S.C.; Jerome Schik, O.S.C.; Gregory Poser, O.S.C.
Mailing Address: 16691 371st Ave., 56338. Tel: 320-277-3807. Email: strita@brainerd.net.
Catechesis/Religious Program—Wendy Tretter, Faith Formation Coord.; Carol Wacker, Faith Formation Coord. Students 46.

HOLDINGFORD, STEARNS CO.
1—ST. HEDWIG'S, [CEM] Rev. Mark Stang.
Res.: P.O. Box 308, 56340. Tel: 320-746-2231; Fax: 320-746-2449. Email: fivepoffice@yahoo.com.
Catechesis/Religious Program—Students 59.
2—ST. MARY'S (1883) [CEM] Rev. Mark Stang.
Res.: P.O. Box 308, 56340. Tel: 320-746-2231; Fax: 320-746-2449. Email: fivepoffice@yahoo.com.
Catechesis/Religious Program—Students 114.

ISANTI, ISANTI CO., ST. ELIZABETH ANN SETON (1976) Rev. Jose Edayadiyil, V.C. (India), Parochial Admin.
Office: 207 County Rd. 23 N.W., 55040. Tel: 763-444-4035; Fax: 763-444-6019.
Res.: 109 Fifth Ave. S., 55040. Tel: 763-444-5226; Fax: 763-444-5226. Email: annseton76@yahoo.co.in.
Catechesis/Religious Program—Mary Mack, D.R.E. Students 200.

JACOB'S PRAIRIE WAKEFIELD TOWNSHIP, STEARNS CO., ST. JAMES, [CEM] Rev. Julius Beckermann, O.S.B.
Res.: 25042 County Rd. 2, Cold Spring, 56320. Tel: 320-685-3479.
Catechesis/Religious Program—Students 27.

KENSINGTON, GRANT CO., OUR LADY OF THE RUNESTONE, [CEM] Rev. Roger Thoennes.
Res.: 25890 110th St., Lowry, 56349-4580. Tel: 320-283-5273; Fax: 320-283-5253.
Catechesis/Religious Program—Students 52.

KENT, WILKIN CO., ST. THOMAS, [CEM] Rev. Kenneth Popp.
P.O. Box 23, 56553. Tel: 218-557-8312.
Catechesis/Religious Program—Christi Hopping, D.R.E. Students 29.

KIMBALL, STEARNS CO., CHURCH OF SAINT ANNE (1919) [CEM] Rev. Thomas Olson.
Res.: 441 Hazel Ave. E., P.O. Box 99, 55353. Tel: 320-398-2229; 320-398-2211 (Office); Fax: 320-398-3860 (Office). Email: sannekim@meltel.net.
Catechesis/Religious Program—Students 130.

LAKE HENRY, STEARNS CO., ST. MARGARET'S, [CEM] Rev. Glenn A. Krystosek; Deacon James Schulzetenberg. In Res., Rev. Walter Bednark (Retired).
Office: 505 Burr St., Paynesville, 56362. Tel: 320-243-4413; Fax: 320-243-4443.
Catechesis/Religious Program—JoAnn Weidner, D.R.E. Students 60.

LAKE RENO, POPE CO., ST. JOHN NEPOMUK, [CEM] Rev. Roger Thoennes.
Res.: 25890 110th St., Lowry, 56349-4580. Tel: 320-283-5273; Fax: 320-283-5253.
Catechesis/Religious Program—Students 44.

LASTRUP, MORRISON CO., ST. JOHN NEPOMUK (1900) [CEM] Rev. David Maciej, Canonical Admin.
Res.: 28520 Church St., P.O. Box 38, 56344. Tel: 320-468-2111.
Catechesis/Religious Program—Students 94.

LITTLE FALLS, MORRISON CO.
1—ST. MARY, [CEM 3] Rev. Nicholas Landsberger; Deacon Bruce Geyer.
Res.: 305 Fourth St., S.E., 56345. Tel: 320-632-5640; Fax: 320-632-6002. Email: office@stmaryslf.org.
See Mary of Lourdes Elementary and Middle School, Little Falls under Inter-Parochial Schools located in the Institution section.
Catechesis/Religious Program—Tel: 320-632-3911. Brenda Przybilla, D.R.E. Students 219.
2—OUR LADY OF LOURDES, [CEM] Revs. Mark Innocenti; Skariajohnus Cherunilath, V.C.; Deacons Bruce Geyer; Gerald Snyder.
Res.: 208 W. Broadway, 56345. Tel: 320-632-8243; Fax: 320-616-2129.
See Mary of Lourdes Elementary and Middle School, Little Falls under Inter-Parochial Schools located in the Institution section.
Catechesis/Religious Program—Tel: 320-616-9689. Linda Benson, D.R.E. Students 322.

LONG PRAIRIE, TODD CO., ST. MARY OF MT. CARMEL (1868) [CEM] [JC] Rev. Richard Walz.
Res.: 409 Central Ave., 56347. Tel: 320-732-2635; Fax: 320-732-0950. Email: stmarylp@embarqmail.com.
School—(Grades PreK-6), Day Care, 425 Central Ave. S, 56347. Tel: 320-732-3478; Fax: 320-732-8023. Email: lpstmarys@embarqmail.com. Brenda Guggelberger, Prin. Lay Teachers 8; Students 99.
Catechesis/Religious Program—410 - 1st Ave. S., 56347. Tel: 320-732-6590; Fax: 320-732-0950. Email: smrock@embarqmail.com. Mrs. Tami Westerberg, D.R.E. Students 276.

LUXEMBURG, STEARNS CO., ST. WENDELIN'S (1859) [CEM] Rev. Marvin Enneking.
Office: 22714 State Hwy. 15, 56301. Tel: 320-251-6944. Email: stwencc@mq.com.
School—(Grades PreK-6) Tel: 320-251-9175; Fax: 320-654-9030. Email: stwend@citescape.com. Lynn Rasmussen, Prin. Sisters 1; Lay Teachers 6; Students 61.
Catechesis/Religious Program—Students 93.

MAINE, OTTER TAIL CO., CHURCH OF SAINT JAMES AT MAINE, [CEM] Revs. Gregory Paffel; LeRoy Schik.
Res.: 32009 County Hwy. 74, Underwood, 56586. Tel: 218-495-2184; Fax: 218-495-2185.
Catechesis/Religious Program—Students 52.

MAYHEW LAKE, BENTON CO., ANNUNCIATION (1896) [CEM] Rev. Timothy Wenzel.
Res.: 9965 Mayhew Lake Rd., N.E., Sauk Rapids, 56379. Tel: 320-252-1729; Fax: 320-252-1729. Email: annunciation@cloudnet.com.
Catechesis/Religious Program—Tel: 320-259-4941. Shirley Scapanski, D.R.E. Students 160.

MEIRE GROVE, STEARNS CO., ST. JOHN'S (1858) [CEM] Rev. Thomas Becker.
Res.: P.O. Box 120, Greenwald, 56335. Tel: 320-987-3160; Fax: 320-987-3306. Email: stjohn1@meltel.net.
School—(Grades 3-6) Tel: 320-987-3491. Mr. Jeri Bachel, Prin. Lay Teachers 2; Students 37.
Catechesis/Religious Program—Tel: 320-352-2783. Ruth Klaphake, D.R.E. Students 34.

MELROSE, STEARNS CO., ST. MARY'S (1958) [CEM 2] Rev. Vincent Lieser; Deacon Ernest Kociemba.
Res.: 211 S. Fifth Ave. E., 56352-1427. Tel: 320-256-4207; Fax: 320-256-4208. Email: stmarys@stmarysmelrose.com.
School—(Grades PreSchool-6), 320 S. 5th E., 56352. Tel: 320-256-4257. Email: sms@meltel.net. Robert Doyle, Prin.; Autumn Nelson, Librarian & Media Specialist. Lay Teachers 9; Students 142.
Catechesis/Religious Program—Tel: 320-256-4258. Debra Duclos, D.R.E. Students 355.

MENAHGA, WADENA CO., THE CHURCH OF THE ASSUMPTION OF OUR LADY OF MENAHGA (1953) [CEM 4] Rev. Scott Wittkop.
Church: 113 Aspen Ave., 56464.
Res.: P.O. Box C, Verndale, 56481. Tel: 218-445-5786; Fax: 218-445-5087.
Catechesis/Religious Program—Kathy Olson, D.R.E. Students 17.

MILACA, MILLE LACS CO., ST. MARY'S (1954) [CEM] Rev. James H. Remmerswaal, O.S.C.
Res.: 625 3rd Ave., S.E., 56353. Tel: 320-983-3255; Fax: 320-983-6564. Email: stmary.milaca@frontiernet.net.
Catechesis/Religious Program—Students 127.

MILLERVILLE, DOUGLAS CO., SEVEN DOLORS (1870) [CEM] Rev. LeRoy Scheierl.
Res.: 16921 County Rd. 7, N.W., Brandon, 56315. Tel: 320-876-2240.
Catechesis/Religious Program—Tel: 320-834-7889. Beverly Hanson, D.R.E. Students 36.

MORA, KANABEC CO., ST. MARY'S (1895) [CEM] Rev. Eugene Doyle, Canonical Pastor; Ms. Rita Clasemann, Parish Life Coord.
Res.: 201 Forest Ave. E., 55051. Tel: 320-679-1593; Fax: 320-679-6896.
Catechesis/Religious Program—Sue Grabowski, D.R.E. Students 202.

MORAN, TODD CO., ST. ISIDORE, [CEM] Closed. For inquiries for parish records contact Christ the King, Browerville.

MORRILL, MORRISON CO., ST. JOSEPH'S (1914) [CEM] Rev. Antonio Marfori.
Res.: 16454 125th Ave., N.E., Foley, 56329. Tel: 320-355-2454; Fax: 320-355-2819.
Catechesis/Religious Program—Students 100.

MORRIS, STEVENS CO., ASSUMPTION OF THE BLESSED VIRGIN MARY, [CEM] Revs. Timothy Baltes; Peter VanderWeyst.
Res.: 207 E. Third, Box 287, 56267. Tel: 320-589-3003; Fax: 320-589-1822. Email: assump@info-link.net.
School—(Grades K-6) Tel: 320-589-1704; Fax: 320-589-1703. Jennifer Grammond, Prin. Lay Teachers 7; Students 83.
Catechesis/Religious Program—Lorna Lauringer, C.R.E. Students 123.

MOTLEY, MORRISON CO., ST. MICHAEL'S, [JC] Rev. Ronald Schmelzer; Deacon John Wolak.
Mailing Address: P.O. Box 177, Staples, 56479. Tel: 218-894-2291. Email: sheart@arvig.net.
Catechesis/Religious Program—Tel: 218-352-6782. Students 108.

NEW MUNICH, STEARNS CO., IMMACULATE CONCEPTION (1857) [CEM] Rev. Roger Klassen, O.S.B.; Deacon Richard Scherping.
Res.: 106 3rd Ave., N.E., P.O. Box 155, Freeport, 56331. Tel: 320-836-2143; Fax: 320-836-2142. Email: triparish@albanytel.com.
Church: 650 Main St., P.O. Box 131, 56356-9028.
Catechesis/Religious Program—Rita Revermann, D.R.E. Students 115.

NORTH PRAIRIE, MORRISON CO., HOLY CROSS (1876) [CEM] Rev. Laurn Virnig.
Res.: P.O. Box 258, Royalton, 56373. Tel: 320-584-5484; Fax: 320-584-0028.
Catechesis/Religious Program—Students 31.

OGILVIE, KANABEC CO., ST. KATHRYN'S (1947) [CEM] Rev. Eugene Doyle, Canonical Pastor; Ms. Rita Clasemann, Parish Life Coord.
Res.: 201 Forest Ave. E., Mora, 55051. Tel: 320-679-1593; Fax: 320-679-6896. Email: ritac@stmarysmora.org.
Catechesis/Religious Program—Students 61.

ONAMIA, MILLE LACS CO., THE CHURCH OF THE HOLY CROSS OF ONAMIA (1910) [CEM] Revs. Jude Verley, O.S.C.; Jerome Schik, O.S.C.; Gregory Poser, O.S.C.
Res.: *Crosier Priory of the Holy Cross*, P.O. Box 500, 56359. Tel: 320-532-3122; Fax: 320-532-5222.
Catechesis/Religious Program—Students 51.

OPOLE, STEARNS CO., OUR LADY OF MT. CARMEL (1887) [CEM] Rev. Mark Stang.
Res.: *St. Mary's Rectory*, P.O. Box 308, Holdingford, 56340. Tel: 320-746-2231; Fax: 320-746-2449. Email: fivepoffice@yahoo.com.
Catechesis/Religious Program—Students 115.

OSAKIS, DOUGLAS CO., IMMACULATE CONCEPTION (1899) [CEM] Rev. David Jeffrey Petron; Deacon Stanley Hennen.
Res.: 316 Third Ave. W., P.O. Box F, 56360. Tel: 320-859-2390. Email: iccosakis@arvig.net.
School—*St. Agnes*, (Grades PreSchool-6) Tel: 320-859-2130; Fax: 320-859-5850. Tammy Boushek, Prin.; Rosalie Kreemer, Librarian. Lay Teachers 6; Students 64.
Catechesis/Religious Program—Shelly Ferris, D.R.E. Students 130.

PADUA, STEARNS CO., CHURCH OF ST. ANTHONY OF PADUA, Closed. For inquiries for parish records contact St. Donatus Church, Brooten.

PARKERS PRAIRIE, OTTER TAIL CO., CHURCH OF ST. WILLIAM (1951) [CEM] Rev. LeRoy Scheierl.
Res.: 209 W. Soo St., P.O. Box 339, 56361.
Catechesis/Religious Program—Students 86.

PAYNESVILLE, STEARNS CO., ST. LOUIS (1899) [CEM] Rev. Glenn A. Krystosek; Deacon James Schulzetenberg.
Res.: 505 Burr St., 56362. Tel: 320-243-4413; Fax: 320-243-4443. Email: frglenn@clearwire.net.
Catechesis/Religious Program—Shelby Vaske, D.R.E. Students 282.

PEARL LAKE, STEARNS CO., HOLY CROSS (1897) [CEM] Rev. Jerome Nordick; Deacon Andrew Kunkel.
Res.: P.O. Box 7, Rockville, 56369. Tel: 320-223-1685; Fax: 320-398-7873. Email: holycros@netlinkcom.com.
School—(Grades PreK-6), Day Care, Tel: 320-398-7885; Fax: 320-398-7873. Anna Moran, Prin.; Lorraine Gregory, Librarian. Lay Teachers 5; Students 65.
Catechesis/Religious Program—Twinned with Rockville. Students 29.

PELICAN RAPIDS, OTTER TAIL CO., ST. LEONARD'S (1951) [CEM] Rev. Stanley Wieser; Deacon Joseph Hilber.
Res.: P.O. Box 378, 56572. Tel: 218-863-5161.
Catechesis/Religious Program—Ann Bergquist, D.R.E. Students 65.

PERHAM, OTTER TAIL CO.
1—ST. HENRY'S (1875) [CEM] Rev. Joseph Herzing.
Res.: 234 2nd Ave S.W., 56573. Tel: 218-346-4240; Fax: 218-346-4235. Email: sthenry@arvig.net.
School—*St. Henry Area School*, (Grades K-6), 253 2nd St. S.W., 56573. Tel: 218-346-6190; Fax: 218-346-6190. Email: sthenryschool@arvig.net. Jason Smith, Prin. Lay Teachers 8; Students 94.
Catechesis/Religious Program—Tel: 218-346-7030. Students 147.
2—ST. STANISLAUS (1895) [CEM] Closed. For inquiries for parish records contact St. Henry, Perham.

PIERZ, MORRISON CO., ST. JOSEPH'S, [CEM] Rev. Gerald Dalseth; Deacon Guy Beck.
Res.: 68 Main St., P.O. Box 428, 56364. Tel: 320-468-6033; Fax: 320-468-2296.

See Holy Trinity School, Pierz under Inter-Parochial Schools located in the Institution section.
Catechesis/Religious Program—P.O. Box 205, 56364. Tel: 320-468-2640. Students 198.

PRINCETON, MILLE LACS CO., ST. EDWARD'S (1898) [CEM] Rev. Kevin Anderson; Deacon Mark Barder.
Office: 807 - 7th Ave. S., 55371.
Res.: Box 152, Zimmerman, 55398. Tel: 763-631-9208.
Catechesis/Religious Program—Nancy Patten, D.R.E. Students 514.

RANDALL, MORRISON CO., ST. JAMES, [CEM] Rev. Leo Moenkedick.
Mailing Address: P.O. Box 225, 56475.
Catechesis/Religious Program—Students 98.

RICE, BENTON CO., IMMACULATE CONCEPTION (1885) [CEM] Rev. Timothy Wenzel.
Office: 130 First Ave., N.E., P.O. Box 189, 56367. Tel: 320-393-2725; Fax: 320-393-7507.
Catechesis/Religious Program—Tel: 320-393-2826. Pat Spence, D.R.E. Students 140.

RICHMOND, STEARNS CO., SS. PETER AND PAUL (1856) [CEM] Rev. Stephen Beauclair, O.S.B.
Res.: 56 - 1st St. N.E., P.O. Box 69, 56368. Tel: 320-597-2575; Fax: 320-597-5231. Email: pbruno1856@aol.com.
Church: 110 Central Ave. N., 56368.
School—(Grades K-6), 111 Central Ave. N., 56368. Tel: 320-597-2565; Fax: 320-597-4385. Email: jwalz@warpdriveonline.com. Jacqueline Walz, Prin. & Librarian. Lay Teachers 7; Students 108.
Catechesis/Religious Program—Tel: 320-597-3720. Teri Krowka-Ansberry, D.R.E. Students 190.

ROCKVILLE, STEARNS CO., MARY OF THE IMMACULATE CONCEPTION (1911) [CEM] Rev. Jerome Nordick.
Res.: 113 Broadway, P.O. Box 7, 56369. Tel: 320-251-7801. Email: micchurch@mywdo.com.
Catechesis/Religious Program—Students 137.

ROSCOE, STEARNS CO., ST. AGNES, [CEM] Rev. Glenn A. Krystosek; Deacon James Schulzetenberg. In Res., Rev. Leo Leisen (Retired).
Office: 505 Burr St., Paynesville, 56362. Tel: 320-243-4413; Fax: 320-243-4443. Email: frglenn@clearwire.net.
Catechesis/Religious Program—Students 22.

ROYALTON, MORRISON CO., HOLY TRINITY (1897) [CEM] Rev. Laurn Virnig.
Res.: P.O. Box 258, 56373. Tel: 320-584-5484; Fax: 320-584-0028. Email: htrinity@fallsnet.com.
Catechesis/Religious Program—Students 190.

RUSH LAKE, OTTER TAIL CO., ST. LAWRENCE (1886) [CEM] Rev. Daniel Walz.
Res.: 46404 County Hwy. 14, Perham, 56573. Tel: 218-346-7729; Fax: 218-346-5946.
Catechesis/Religious Program—Students 52.

ST. ANNA, STEARNS CO., IMMACULATE CONCEPTION, [CEM] Rev. Mark Stang.
Res.: *St. Mary's Rectory*, P.O. Box 308, Holdingford, 56340. Tel: 320-746-2231; Fax: 320-746-2449. Email: fivepoffice@yahoo.com.
Catechesis/Religious Program—Students 89.

ST. ANTHONY, STEARNS CO., ST. ANTHONY'S (1874) [CEM] Very Rev. Michael Naughton, O.S.B.
Res.: 24326 Trobec St., Albany, 56307. Tel: 320-845-2416; Fax: 320-845-2414.
Catechesis/Religious Program—Marlene Ramacher, D.R.E. Students 49.

ST. AUGUSTA, STEARNS CO., ST. MARY HELP OF CHRISTIANS (1856) [CEM] Rev. Robert Rolfes.
Res.: 24588 County Rd. 7, 56301. Tel: 320-252-1799; Fax: 320-252-1992.
School—(Grades K-6) Tel: 320-251-3937; Fax: 320-251-3937. Bonnie Van Heel, Prin.; Shelly Gohmann, Librarian. Lay Teachers 10; Students 127.
Catechesis/Religious Program—Jan Minke, D.R.E. Students 234.

ST. FRANCIS, STEARNS CO., ST. FRANCIS OF ASSISI, [CEM] Revs. Michael Kellogg; Gregory Ombok, Parochial Vicar.
Res.: P.O. Box 8, Bowlus, 56314. Tel: 320-584-5313.
Church: 44055 State Hwy. 238, Freeport, 56331. Tel: 320-573-2203; Fax: 320-573-2205.
Catechesis/Religious Program—Jane Keepers, D.R.E. Students 61.

ST. JOSEPH, STEARNS CO., ST. JOSEPH'S (1856) [CEM] Rev. Joseph Feders, O.S.B.; Deacon Thomas A. Murray.
Res.: 12 W. Minnesota St., 56374. Tel: 320-363-7505; Fax: 320-363-0710. Email: parish@churchstjoseph.org.
School—(Grades PreSchool-6), Day Care, Tel: 320-363-7769; Fax: 320-363-7760. Email: principal@churchstjoseph.org. Carl Terhaar, Prin. Lay Teachers 10; Students 125.
Catechesis/Religious Program—Students 251.

ST. MARTIN, STEARNS CO., ST. MARTIN (1858) [CEM] Rev. Corwin Collins, O.S.B.; Deacon Gerald Theis.
Res.: 119 Maine St., Box 290, 56376. Tel: 320-548-3550.
Catechesis/Religious Program—Tel: 320-548-3209. Joan Rothstein, D.R.E. Students 69.

ST. NICHOLAS, STEARNS CO., ST. NICHOLAS (1857) [CEM] Rev. Thomas Olson.
Res.: 441 Hazel Ave. E., Kimball, 55353. Tel: 320-398-2229.
Catechesis/Religious Program—Students 41.

ST. ROSA, STEARNS CO., ST. ROSE OF LIMA (1898) [CEM] Rev. Roger Klassen, O.S.B.; Deacon Richard Scherping. In Res., Rev. Arthur Hoppe (Retired).
Res.: 106-3rd Ave. N.E., Freeport, 56331. Tel: 320-836-2143; Fax: 320-836-2142. Email: triparish@albanytel.com.
Catechesis/Religious Program—Mary Kimman, D.R.E. Students 117.

ST. STEPHEN, STEARNS CO., ST. STEPHEN'S, [CEM] Rev. Robert C. Harren.
Res.: 103 Central Ave. S., 56375. Tel: 320-251-1520.
Catechesis/Religious Program—Tel: 320-251-5066. Andrew Case, D.R.E. Students 191.

ST. WENDEL, STEARNS CO., ST. COLUMBKILLE'S, [CEM] Rev. Mark Stang. In Res., Rev. Robert Landsberger (Retired).
Rectory—St. Mary's, P.O. Box 308, Holdingford, 56340. Tel: 320-746-2231; Fax: 320-746-2449. Email: fivepoffice@yahoo.com.
Catechesis/Religious Program—Students 85.

SARTELL, STEARNS CO., ST. FRANCIS XAVIER (1948) [CEM] Rev. Lauren Germann; Deacons Stephen Pareja; Stephen Yanish.
Res.: 219 - 2nd St. N., P.O. Box 150, 56377. Tel: 320-252-1363; Fax: 320-259-7090.
School—(Grades PreSchool-6) Tel: 320-252-9940. Email: lwilfahrt@stfrancis.sartell.org. Linda Wilfahrt, Prin. Lay Teachers 12; Students 150.
Catechesis/Religious Program—Tel: 320-252-8761. Students 646.

SAUK CENTRE, STEARNS CO.

1—OUR LADY OF THE ANGELS, [CEM] Rev. James Statz; Deacon Lawrence Kaas.
Res.: 211 S. 7th St., 56378-1505. Tel: 320-352-3502; Fax: 320-351-3502. Email: angels@mainstreetcom.com.
Catechesis/Religious Program—Tel: 320-352-5580. Students 120.

2—ST. PAUL'S (1870) [CEM] Rev. Todd Schneider; Deacons Thomas McFadden; Lawrence Kaas.
Res.: 304 Sinclair Lewis Ave., 56378. Tel: 320-352-2196; Fax: 320-351-8475. Email: stpaulschurch@mainstreetcom.com.
See Holy Family School, Sauk Centre under Inter-Parochial Schools located in the Institution section.
Catechesis/Religious Program—220 S. Birch, 56378. Tel: 320-352-5580. Students 185.

SAUK RAPIDS, BENTON CO.

1—ST. PATRICK, [CEM] Rev. Bernard Kahlhamer.
Res.: 7286 Duelm Rd., N.E., 56379. Tel: 320-252-2069.

2—SACRED HEART (1919) [CEM] Rev. Ronald Weyrens.
Mailing Address: 2875 - 10th Ave. N.E., 56379. Tel: 320-251-8115; Fax: 320-252-0710. Email: parish@sacredheartsaukrapids.org.
School—(Grades K-6), Day Care, 324 Third Ave. S., 56379. Tel: 320-251-2854; Fax: 320-251-0705. Email: shs@charterinternet.com. Erin Hatlestad, Prin.; Ruth Steffes, Librarian. Lay Teachers 10; Students 170.
Catechesis/Religious Program—Joan Krause, D.R.E. Students 352.

SEDAN, POPE CO., IMMACULATE CONCEPTION, Closed. For inquiries for parish records contact Sacred Heart, Glenwood.

SOBIESKI, MORRISON CO., ST. STANISLAUS (1884) [CEM] Rev. Leo Moenkedick.
Res.: 9406 Church Cir., Little Falls, 56345-9803. Tel: 320-632-6930; Fax: 320-632-5644. Email: ststans@littlefalls.net.
Catechesis/Religious Program—Students 41.

SPRING HILL, STEARNS CO., ST. MICHAEL'S (1857) [CEM] Rev. Thomas Becker. In Res., Rev. Richard McGuire (Retired).
Res.: 211 2nd Ave. N., P.O. Box 120, Greenwald, 56335. Tel: 320-987-3160.
Catechesis/Religious Program—Tel: 320-987-3192. Hortense Walz, D.R.E. Students 63.

STAPLES, TODD CO., SACRED HEART, [JC] Rev. Ronald Schmelzer; Deacon John Wolak.
Res.: 310 Fourth St., N.E., Box 177, 56479. Tel: 218-894-2296; Fax: 218-894-2296. Email: sheart@arvig.net.
School—Sacred Heart Area School, (Grades PreSchool-6), 324 - 4th St. N.E., 56479. Tel: 218-894-2077. James Opelia, Prin. Lay Teachers 8; Students 105.
Catechesis/Religious Program—Tel: 218-894-1095. Students 94.

SWANVILLE, MORRISON CO., ST. JOHN THE BAPTIST, [CEM] Revs. Mark Willenbring; Ronald Dockendorf.
Res.: P.O. Box 366, Grey Eagle, 56336. Tel: 320-285-2545; Fax: 320-547-2578.
Catechesis/Religious Program—P.O. Box 68, 56382. Tel: 320-547-2920. Students 153.

TINTAH, TRAVERSE CO., ST. GALL (1881) [CEM] Rev. Arlie Sowada; Deacon Joseph Wood.
Res.: 110 Minnesota Ave., P.O. Box 127, 56583. Tel: 218-369-2188. Email: stgull@runestone.net.
Catechesis/Religious Program—Students 13.

UPSALA, MORRISON CO., ST. MARY, [CEM] Revs. Michael Kellogg; Gregory Ombok.
Res.: P.O. Box 8, Bowlus, 56314. Tel: 320-584-5313; Fax: 320-584-8231.
Catechesis/Religious Program—Students 74.

URBANK, OTTER TAIL CO., SACRED HEART (1902) [CEM] Rev. LeRoy Scheierl.
Res.: 60 Central Ave. N., Parkers Prairie, 56361. Tel: 218-267-2661.
Catechesis/Religious Program—Students 27.

VERNDALE, WADENA CO., ST. FREDERICK (1910) [CEM] Rev. Scott Wittkop.
Res.: 20 Brown St. N., P.O. Box C, 56481. Tel: 218-445-5786; Fax: 218-445-5087.
Catechesis/Religious Program—23764 U.S. Hwy. 71, Sebeka, 56477. Tel: 218-631-1771; Fax: 218-445-5280. Vera Malone, D.R.E. Students 60.

VILLARD, POPE CO., ST. BARTHOLOMEW'S (1883) [CEM] Rev. Peter K. Kirchner Jr.
105 N. Franklin, Glenwood, 56334. Tel: 320-634-3813; Fax: 320-634-0590.
Office: P.O. Box 128, Glenwood, 56334.
Catechesis/Religious Program—Leonard Heidelberger, D.R.E. Students 20.

VINELAND, MILLE LACS CO., ST. THERESE, LITTLE FLOWER INDIAN MISSION, [CEM] [JC] Revs. Jerome Schik, O.S.C.; Jude Verley, O.S.C.; Gregory Poser, O.S.C.
Mailing Address: *Crosier Priory of the Holy Cross*, P.O. Box 500, Onamia, 56359. Tel: 320-532-3601; Fax: 320-532-5222.
Catechesis/Religious Program—Students 2.

WADENA, WADENA CO., ST. ANN'S (1895) [CEM] Rev. Donald Wagner.
Res.: 514 First St., S.E., 56482. Tel: 218-631-1593; Fax: 218-631-7149.
School—(Grades PreSchool-6) Tel: 218-631-2631; Fax: 218-632-5612. Eileen Weber, Prin.; Ronnie Lee, Librarian. Lay Teachers 4; Students 40.
Catechesis/Religious Program—Students 99.

WAHKON, MILLE LACS CO., SACRED HEART, [CEM] Revs. Jude Verley, O.S.C.; Jerome Schik, O.S.C.; Gregory Poser, O.S.C.
Mailing Address: P.O. Box 68, 56386.
Catechesis/Religious Program—Tel: 320-495-3324. Lola Larson, D.R.E. Students 33.

WAITE PARK, STEARNS CO., ST. JOSEPH'S (1916) [CEM] Revs. Bernard Gruenes; George Michael, V.C.; Deacon Joseph Kresky.
Office: 106 7th Ave. N., 56387. Tel: 320-251-5231; Fax: 320-251-3010. Email: stjosephwp@charterinternet.com.
School—(Grades PreSchool-6), Day Care & Nursery, 108 7th Ave. N., 56387. Tel: 320-251-4741, Ext. 1; Fax: 320-230-2161. Kathy Cziok, Prin. Lay Teachers 9; Students 124.
Catechesis/Religious Program—Students 68.

WARD SPRINGS, TODD CO., ST. BERNARD'S, Closed. For inquiries for parish records contact St. Joseph, Grey Eagle.

WEST UNION, TODD CO., ST. ALEXIUS, [CEM] Rev. James Statz.
Res.: 211 S. 7th St., Sauk Centre, 56378. Tel: 320-352-3502.
Catechesis/Religious Program—Box 4A, 56389. Tel: 320-352-2563; Fax: 320-352-2930. Students 26.

WHEATON, TRAVERSE CO., AVE MARIA, [JC] Rev. Joseph Vandeberg.
Res.: 201 Ninth St. S., 56296. Tel: 320-563-4421.
Catechesis/Religious Program—Barb Tauber, D.R.E. Students 118.

ZIMMERMAN, SHERBURNE CO., ST. PIUS X, [CEM] Rev. Kevin Anderson; Deacon Mark Barder.
Res.: Box 152, 55398. Tel: 763-856-4401; Fax: 763-856-4401.
Catechesis/Religious Program—Tel: 763-856-2400. Noreen Olson, D.R.E. Students 202.

Chaplains of Public Institutions

ST. CLOUD. *Minnesota State Reformatory for Men.* Vacant.
U.S. Veteran's Hospital 56301.

CAMBRIDGE. *Cambridge State School and Hospital* 55008. Vacant.

FERGUS FALLS. *State Hospital Chapel* 56537. Vacant.

Special Assignment:
Revs.—
Belland, David
Caskey, John
Holmes, Albert
Ostendorf, Mark
Trussel, Christopher

Retired:
Most Rev.—
Sowada, Alphonse, O.S.C., 308 3rd Ave. S., Sauk Rapids, 56379.
Rev. Msgr.—
Taufen, Daniel J., S.T.L., 308-3rd Ave. S., #105, Sauk Rapids, 56379.
Revs.—
Bednark, Walter, 23189 State Hwy. 4, Paynesville, 56362.
Brenny, Kenneth, P.O. Box 608, Buckman, 56317.
Donnay, Raymond, 808 Ann Marie Cir., # 701, Little Falls, 56345.
Eccleston, John, 1810 Minnesota Blvd., S.E., Saint Cloud, 56304.
Fehrenbacher, Henry, 371-7th Ave. #2404, New York, NY 10001.
Folsom, Paul, 39880 Crane Lake Dr., Battle Lake, 56515.
Haupt, Lloyd, 929 Brenda Lee Dr., 56303.
Hoppe, Arthur, 28905 County Rd. 17, Freeport, 56331.
Kalkman, Richard, 23 Diaz Ave., San Francisco, CA 94132.
Kleinschmidt, Sylvester, 412 First St. S., Apt. 1, Sauk Centre, 56378.
Kraemer, Edwin, 828 Village Ave., Sartell, 56377.
Kroll, Anthony, 308-3rd Ave. S., #203, Sauk Rapids, 56379.
Landsberger, Robert, 12536 County Rd. 4, Avon, 56310.
Leisen, Leo, 100 Lillie Ave., Roscoe, 56371.
Leisen, Richard, 308-3rd Ave. S., #107, Sauk Rapids, 56379.
Lemm, Eugene, P.O. Box 256, Brandon, 56315.
Lieser, Gregory, 308 3rd Ave. S., Sauk Rapids, 56379.
Ludwig, Alexander, 1423 Melvina Ln., Alexandria, 56308.
Majerus, Daniel, 6007 Royal Breeze, San Antonio, TX 78239.
Marthaler, Andrew, 750 Railroade Ave., Apt. 132, Sauk Centre, 56378.
Maus, Le Roy, 11367 Phoenix Dr., #75, Yuma, AZ 85367.
McGuire, Richard, 102 St. Michael Ave. N., Melrose, 56352.
Mischke, Gerald, 25-8th Ave. S., Saint Cloud, 56301.
Otto, Leo, 12372 92nd Ave., Box 118, Little Falls, 56345.
Pavelis, Harold, Box 88, Concord, CA 94522.
Poncelet, Frank, 20 S. Freemont St., #608, Prairie Du Chien, WI 53821.
Quade, Alvin, P.O. Box 225, Randall, 56475.
Riedemann, Kenneth, 21398 Alcott Ln., Sauk Centre, 56378.
Rieder, Donald, 21-16 Ave., Saint Joseph, 56374.
Riley, Patrick, 3034 Fulton Cir., Clearwater, 55320.
Schefers, Eberhard, 702-2nd St., N.E., Saint Joseph, 56374.
Schmitt, Silverius, 5290-175th St., N.W., Royalton, 56373.
Schwieters, Severin, 1980 15th Ave. S.E. #12, 56304.
Slominski, Leon, 822 10th Ave. N. #4, Sartell, 56377.
Snyers, Peter, 520-1st St. N.E., Sartell, 56377.
Stangl, Alfred, 210 3rd St. S. #303, Saint Cloud, 56301.
Thielman, Kenneth, Park View Center, 125 N. Fifth Ave. W., Melrose, 56352.
Thoennes, James, P.O. Box 1248, Saint Cloud, 56302.
Tomasiewicz, Frank, 27240 Lakewood Dr., N.W., Isanti, 55040.
Torborg, Elmer, 615 1st St. N., #110, Cold Spring, 56320.
Vogel, Arthur, 617 Pinecone Rd., Apt. 308, Sartell, 56377.
Vos, William, 1664 Payton Ct., N.E., Sauk Rapids, 56379.
Wey, Richard, 89 Greenstone Ln., Waite Park, 56387.
Zimmer, Nicholas, Elmhurst Commons, 400 3rd St., S.W., Apt. 211, Braham, 55006.
Zylla, Paul, 1615-15th Ave., S.E. #251, 56304.

Permanent Deacons:
Adams, Cecil, (Retired)
Anderberg, George, (Retired)
Barder, Mark, St. Edward, Princeton; St. Pius X, Zimmerman
Beck, Guy, St. Michael, Buckman; St. Joseph, Pierz
Bobertz, Charles
Clack, James
Curry, Dirck
Dupay, Steven, Our Lady of the Lake, Big Lake
Fromm, Jeffrey, 5 Parish Cluster, Holdingford
Geyer, Bruce, Our Lady of Lourdes, Little Falls; Holy Family, Belle Prairie
Hennen, Stanley, St. Nicholas, Belle River; Immaculate Conception, Osakis
Hilber, Joseph, St. Leonard's, Pelican Rapids; St. Elizabeth, Elizabeth
Kaas, Lawrence, Our Lady of the Angels, Sauk Centre
Kampa, Charles, Our Lady of Victory, Fergus Falls
Keable, Michael, St. John Baptist, Collegeville
Kedrowski, Kirk
Kociemba, Ernest, St. Mary, Melrose
Kosiba, Leo, St. Mary, St. Cloud
Kramer, Eugene, Christ the King, Cambridge
Krebs, Brian
Kresky, Joseph, St. Joseph, Waite Park
Kunkel, Andrew, Holy Cross, Pearl Lake
Lindmeier, David, St. Paul, St. Cloud
Maltzen, Bruce
McFadden, Thomas, St. Paul's Sauk Centre
Midas, Richard, (Retired)
Murray, Thomas A., St. Joseph, St. Joseph.
Nord, Carl
Pareja, Stephen, St. Francis, Sartell
Pinataro, Thomas, Sts. Peter & Paul, Braham
Reker, Fred, St. John Cantius, St. Cloud
Ritchie, William, St. Peter, St. Cloud
Roth, Jerome, (Retired)
Salchert, John, (Retired)
Scheierl, Richard, St. Augustine, St. Cloud
Scherping, Richard, Sacred Heart, Freeport; Immaculate Conception, New Munich; St. Rose, St. Rosa
Schmainda, Frank, Sacred Heart, Glenwood
Schmitz, Vernon, Holy Spirit, St. Cloud
Schulzetenberg, James, St. Margaret, Lake Henry; St. Louis, Paynesville; St. Agnes, Roscoe
Schwarzbauer, Jerome, (Retired)
Scott, John W., (Retired)
Sell, Lawrence, St. Boniface, Cold Spring
Shaffer, Robert
Snyder, Gerald, Our Lady of Lourdes, Little Falls
St. Jean, Fred, St. Andrew, Elk River
Steele, Gregory J.
Theis, Gerald, St. Catherine's, Farming; St. Martin, St. Martin
Tzinski, Donald, J.C.L., (Diocesan Tribunal)
Warren, Todd, St. Michael, St. Cloud
Wolak, John, Sacred Heart, Staples; St. Michael, Motley
Wood, Joseph, St. Olaf, Elbow Lake; St. Gall, Tintah
Yanish, Stephen, St. Francis, Sartell
Zenner, Mark, Christ the King, Browerville; St. Joseph, Clarissa

INSTITUTIONS LOCATED IN THE DIOCESE

[A] SEMINARIES, RELIGIOUS OR SCHOLASTICATES

COLLEGEVILLE. *St. John's School of Theology and Seminary*, P.O. Box 7288, 56321. Tel: 320-363-2100; Fax: 320-363-3145. Web: www.csbsju.edu/sot. Rev. Michael Patella, O.S.B., Rector; Dr. William Cahoy, Dean; Sr. Stephanie Weisgrram, O.S.B., Librarian.

St. John's School of Theology and Seminary Priests 4; Sisters 1; Lay Teachers 9; Students 113.

[B] COLLEGES AND UNIVERSITIES

COLLEGEVILLE. *Saint John's University* (1857) (Men), Box 2000, 56321-2000. Tel: 320-363-2011; Fax: 320-363-2504. Email: rknuesel@csbsju.edu. Web: www.csbsju.edu. Rt. Rev. John Klassen, O.S.B., Ph.D., Abbot & Chancellor. Sponsored by the Collegeville Benedictine Monks as a division of the corporate Order of Saint Benedict, Collegeville, MN.; Sponsored Programs: The Hill Museum and Manuscript Library and Saint John's Pottery Studio and The Liturgical Press; The Graduate School of Theology (Coed)/Saint John's Seminary (Men): M.A. in Theology, Liturgical Studies, Liturgical Music, Pastoral Ministry and a Master of Divinity. The Undergraduate College of Liberal Arts and Sciences (Men), in full coordinate academic relation with the College of Saint Benedict, St. Joseph (Women), offers forty departments, ten pre-professional and ten special academic programs. Priests 7; Brothers 10; Sisters 3; Lay Teachers 168; Students 2,021.

Officers Group: Bro. Benedict Leuthner, O.S.B., Corp. Treas.; Rev. Robert Koopmann, O.S.B., Pres.; Dr. William Cahoy, Dean, School of Theology; Mr. Rob Culligan, Vice Pres., Institutional Advancement; Rev. Douglas Mullin, O.S.B., Vice Pres., Student Devel.; Rita Knuesel, Provost Academic Affairs; Jon McGee, Vice Pres. Planning & Public Affairs.

Administrative Group: Rt. Rev. John Klassen, O.S.B., Ph.D., Abbot & Chancellor; Revs. Timothy Backous, O.S.B., Headmaster, Prep School; Jerome Tupa, O.S.B., Dir. Campus Ministry; Columba Stewart, O.S.B., Exec. Dir. Hill Museum & Manuscript Library; Bro. David Klingeman, O.S.B., Archivist; Scott Richardson, The Michael Blecker Professorship; Dr. David Bennetts, Dir. Summer Academic Prog.; Margrette Newhouse, The John & Elizabeth Myers Chair in Mgmt.; Mr. Richard Bresnahan, Potter, Saint John's Pottery Studio; Barry Cytron, Rabbi, The Jay Phillips Center for Jewish-Christian Learning; Patti Epsky, Exec. Asst. to the Pres.; Dr. Bernard Evans, The Butler Family's Virgil Michel Ecumenical Chair in Rural Social Ministries; Dr. Daniel Rush Finn, The William & Virginia Clemens Chair in Economics & the Liberal Arts; Ms. Julie Gruska, Registrar; Dr. Nicholas P. Hayes, Univ. Chair in Critical Thinking; Mr. Gregory Hoye, Exec. Dir. Communications & Mktg.; Kathy Parker, Dir. Libraries and Media; Mr. James Koenig, Dir. Information Technology Svcs.; Mr. Michael Connolly, Dean of Campus Life; Bernadette W. Suwareh, Dir. Intercultural Center; Mr. Stuart Perry, Dir. Financial Aid; Carol Abell, Dir. Human Resources; Mr. John Young, Assoc. Vice Pres. Devel.

ST. JOSEPH. *College of Saint Benedict* (1913) (Women), 37 College Ave. S., 56374-2099. Tel: 320-363-5011; Fax: 320-363-5136. Email: rknuesel@csbsju.edu. Web: www.csbsju.edu.

College of Saint Benedict Sisters of the Order of Saint Benedict., Affiliation: Roman Catholic, established for the undergraduate education of women by the Sisters of the Order of Saint Benedict.; Partnership: The College of Saint Benedict is a private, nationally recognized women's, residential, liberal arts, Catholic, Benedictine college, located in St. Joseph, MN joined in a coeducational mission with Saint John's University for men. As the only Catholic all women's Baccalaureate I college, Saint Benedict's is unique in its commitment to gender specific education within a coeducational environment. Sisters 10; Faculty 172; Administrators 162; Students 2,106.

Officers Group: Mary Geller, Vice Pres. Student Devel.; MaryAnn Baenninger, Pres.; Joseph Des Jardins, Assoc. Provost & Academic Dean; Stuart Lang, Vice Pres. Institutional Advancement; Susan Palmer, Vice Pres. of Finance & Admin.; Rita Knuesel, Provost, Academic Affairs.

Administrative Group: Jason Kelly, Dir. of Academic Advising/Asst. Dean; Mike Durbin, Dir. Athletic Media Rels.; Jim Schumann, Exec. Dir. Facilities, Security & Safety; Mary Geller, Vice Pres. of Student Devel.; Ms. Julie Gruska, Registrar; Mary Harlander-Locke, Assoc. Dir. Career Svcs.; Jane Haugen, Exec. Dir. Fin. Aid; Carol Howe-Veenstra, Dir. Athletics; Greg Hoye, Exec. Dir. Communication & Mktg. Svc.; Kathy Parker, Dir. Libraries & Media; Mr. James Koenig, Dir., Information Technology Svc.; Jon McGee, Vice Pres. Planning & Public Affairs; Michael Hemmesch, Dir. SJU Media Rels.; Jody Terhaar, Dean of Students; Carol Abell, Dir. Human Resources.

[C] HIGH SCHOOLS, DIOCESAN

ST. CLOUD. *Cathedral High and John XXIII Middle School*, (Grades 7-12), P.O. Box 1579, 56302. Tel: 320-251-3421; Fax: 320-253-5576. Email: mmullin@chsj23.org. Mr. Michael Mullin, Pres.; Ms. Lynn Grewing, Prin.; Rev. Christopher Trussel; Barb Bestick, Librarian. Priests 1; Sisters 1; Lay Teachers 46; Students 654.

Cathedral High School Education Foundation, P.O. Box 1579, 56302. Tel: 320-251-3421; Fax: 320-253-5576.

[D] HIGH SCHOOLS, PRIVATE

COLLEGEVILLE. *St. John's Preparatory School*, (Grades 7-12), College Preparatory., 1857 Water Tower Rd., P.O. Box 4000, 56321. Tel: 320-363-3315; Fax: 320-363-3513. Email: tbackous@csbsju.edu. Web: www.sjprep.net. Rev. Timothy Backous, O.S.B., Headmaster; Kathryn Kockler, Prin.; Cindy Peterson, Librarian. Priests 1; Lay Teachers 38; Students 328.

[E] INTER-PAROCHIAL SCHOOLS

ST. CLOUD. *St. Elizabeth Ann Seton School*, (Grades K-6), 1615 Eleventh Ave. S., 56301. Tel: 320-251-1988; Fax: 320-229-2149. Email: ttroness@stelizabethannseton.net. Tom Troness, Prin.; Kaye Sauer, Librarian. Consolidation of schools of the following parishes: Holy Spirit, St. Anthony and St. John Cantius, St. Cloud. Lay Teachers 13; Students 169.

Sts. Peter, Paul and Michael School, (Grades K-4), Primary: 925 30th Ave. N., 56303. Tel: 320-251-4737; Fax: 320-253-7110. Email: sppm945@charterinternet.com. Sharon Bichler, Prin.; Amy O'Neal, Librarian. Consolidation of the following parishes: St. Michael; St. Paul; St. Peter, St. Cloud. Lay Teachers 20; Students 250.

Preschool, 1036 County Rd. 4, 56303. Tel: 320-251-6923. Lay Teachers 1; Students 33.

Middle (Grades 5-8), 1215 N. 11th Ave., 56303. Tel: 320-251-5295; Fax: 320-251-7014. Email: sppmmiddle@charterinternet.com. Mary Cheryl Opatz, Asst. Prin.; Mary Kiefer, Librarian. Lay Teachers 13; Students 156.

FOLEY. *St. John's Area School*, (Grades PreK-6), 215 7th Ave. S., P.O. Box 368, 56329. Tel: 320-968-7972; Fax: 320-968-9956. Email: sjasfm@cloudnet.com. Web: www.cloudnet.com~sjasfm. Mary Sabin, Prin.; Michelle Buettner, Librarian. Consolidation of the following parishes: St. John's, Foley; St. Lawrence, Duelm; St. Elizabeth, Brennyville; St. Joseph, Morrill; SS. Peter and Paul, Gilman; St. Louis, Foreston; St. Patrick of Minden Township Lay Teachers 8; Students 108.

LITTLE FALLS. *Mary of Lourdes School*, (Grades PreK-4), Primary: 307 Fourth St., S.E., 56345. Tel: 320-632-5408; Fax: 320-632-5409. Email: pschieffert@molschool.org. Web: www.molschool.org. Paul Schieffert, Prin.; Julie Barton, Librarian. Consolidation of following parishes: St. Mary and Our Lady of Lourdes, Little Falls Lay Teachers 14; Students 157; Preschool Students 30.

Middle: (Grades 5-8), 205 N.W. Third St., 56345. Tel: 320-632-6742; Fax: 320-632-3556. Email: mhbecker@molschool.org. Maria Heymans-Becker, Prin.; Katie Schumann, Librarian. Lay Teachers 9; Students 145.

PIERZ. *Holy Trinity School*, (Grades PreK-6), 80 Edward St. S., Box 427, 56364. Tel: 320-468-6446; Fax: 320-468-6446. Email: dmm@holytrinitypierz.org. Web: holytrinitypierz.org. Debra Meyer-Myrum, Prin.; Kristi Schmidbauer, Librarian. Consolidation of the following parishes: St. Michael's, Buckman; Holy Cross, Harding; St. John Nepomuk, Lastrup; St. Joseph, Pierz. Lay Teachers 12; Students 180.

SAUK CENTRE. *Holy Family School*, (Grades K-6), 231 Sinclair Lewis Ave., 56378. Tel: 320-352-6535; Fax: 320-352-6537. Email: hfs@isd743.k12.mn.us. Web: www.rc.net/stcloud/hfs. Lynn Peterson, Prin.; Patty Dirkes, Librarian. Consolidation of the following parishes: St. Paul's and Our Lady of the Angels, Sauk Centre. Lay Teachers 17; Students 224.

[F] HOMES FOR EMOTIONALLY DISTURBED AND HANDICAPPED

ST. CLOUD. *St. Cloud Children's Home of the Diocese of St. Cloud*, 1726 Seventh Ave. S., 56301. Tel: 320-650-1500; Fax: 320-650-1508. Mr. Steven P. Bresnahan, Exec. Dir.; John Krueger, Dir. Residential Svcs. Children 78.

St. Elizabeth Home Contact John Krueger at Catholic Charities, 306 15th Ave. N., 56303. Tel: 320-240-3350. Email: jkrueger@gw.stcdio.org. Mr. Steven P. Bresnahan, Exec. Dir.; John Krueger, Dir. Residential Day Svcs. Board and Lodging Home for Functionally Impaired Adults. Residents 18.

LaPaz Community Inc., Catholic Charities Housing Services, 530 S. 16th St., 56301. Mailing Address: 157 Roosevelt Rd., Ste. 200, 56301. Mr. Steven P. Bresnahan, Exec. Dir.; Harvey Schmitt, Dir. Housing Svcs. Residents 36.

COLD SPRING. *St. Anne's Home* Contact Catholic Charities, 103 10th Ave. N., 56320. Tel: 320-685-7898; Fax: 320-685-9819. Mr. Steven P. Bresnahan, Exec Dir.; John Krueger, Dir. Residential Day Svcs. Supervised Living Situation for Persons with Developmental Disabilities. Residents 4.

Bethany Home Contact John Krueger at Catholic Charities, 13 Eighth Ave. S., 56320. Tel: 320-685-7899; Fax: 320-685-9808. Email: jkrueger@gw.stcdio.org. Mr. Steven P. Bresnahan, Exec Dir.; John Krueger, Dir. Residential Day Svcs. Supervised Living Situation for Persons with Developmental Disabilities. Residents 4.

St. Luke's Home Contact Catholic Charities, 411 Eighth Ave. N., 56320. Tel: 320-685-7750. Mr. Steven P. Bresnahan, Exec. Dir.; John Krueger, Dir. Residential Svcs. Adults with mild to moderate developmental disabilities. Residents 4.

Mother Teresa Home Contact Catholic Charities, 101 Tenth Ave., 56320. Tel: 320-685-8626; Fax: 320-685-8626. Mr. Steven P. Bresnahan, Exec. Dir.; John Krueger, Dir. Residential Day Svcs. Supervised Living Situation for Persons with Developmental Disabilities. Residents 4.

FERGUS FALLS. *Catholic Charities Intensive Treatment Unit*, 1010 Maryland Ln., 56537. Tel: 218-739-9325; Fax: 218-739-2242. Mr. Steven Bresnahan, Exec. Dir.; John Krueger, Dir. Residential Day Svcs. Capacity 16; Total Served 33.

LITTLE FALLS. *St. Camillus Place*, 1100 S.E. Fourth St., 56345. Tel: 320-632-1212; Fax: 320-632-1383. Lisa Thielman, Dir.; Barbara A. Miller, Admin.; Bea Britz, Chap. Bed Capacity 14.

PAYNESVILLE. *Adult Foster Care for Handicapped Individuals*, 1790 W. Mill St., 56362. Tel: 320-243-3750; Fax: 320-243-3718. John Krueger, Dir. Catholic Charities Residential & Day Svcs. Bed Capacity 4.

WAITE PARK. *St. Francis Home*, P.O. Box 326, 56387. Tel: 320-251-7630; Fax: 320-240-8097. Mr. Steven P. Bresnahan, Exec. Dir.; John Krueger, Dir. Residential Day Svcs. Supervised Living Situation for Persons with Developmental Disabilities. Residents 4.

[G] GENERAL HOSPITALS

ST. CLOUD. *St. Cloud Hospital*, 1406 Sixth Ave. N., 56303. Tel: 320-251-2700; Fax: 320-255-5711. Web: www.stcloudhospital.com. Craig Broman, Pres.; Bret Reuter, Dir. Mission and Spiritual Care; Rev. Roger Botz, O.S.B., Chap. Sisters of St. Benedict 3; Bed Capacity 489; Bassinets 40; Patients Assisted Annually 240,451.

ALBANY. *Albany Area Hospital* (1969) 300 Third Ave., 56307. Tel: 320-845-2121; Fax: 320-845-6127. Web: www.albanyareahospital.com. Nick Brander, Admin.; Deborah Robinson, Chap. Bed Capacity 16; Patients Assisted Annually 10,000.

BRECKENRIDGE. *St. Francis Medical Center* (1899) 2400 St. Francis Dr., 56520. Tel: 218-643-3000; Fax: 218-643-0850. Email: davidnelson@catholichealth.net. Web: www.sfcare.org. David Nelson, Pres.; Ann Trebsch, Vice Pres. Mission; Rev. Kenneth Popp, Chap. Bed Capacity 25; Patients Assisted Annually 26,000.

LITTLE FALLS. *St. Gabriel's Hospital*, 815 S.E. Second St., 56345. Tel: 320-632-5441; Fax: 320-632-1190. Carl P. Vaagenes, Pres. & CEO; Bea Britz, Chap. Licensed Beds 25; Bassinets 10; Patients Assisted Annually 34,297.

[H] HOMES FOR AGED

ST. CLOUD. *St. Benedict's Senior Community* (1978) 1810 Minnesota Blvd., S.E., 56304. Tel: 320-252-0010; Fax: 320-654-2351. Linda Doerr, Exec. Dir.; Sr. Susan Rudolph, O.S.B., Dir. of Pastoral Care & Lay Ecclesial Health Care Min.; Rev. Meinrad Dindorf, O.S.B., Chap. Corporate Division of the St. Cloud Hospital. Operated under the auspices of the local Catholic Church of St. Cloud.; Care Center managed by St. Benedict's Senior Community. A division of the St. Cloud Hospital. Operated under the auspices of the local Catholic Church of St. Cloud. Residents 178; Short Stay Units - Beds 44.

Benedict Village: 2000 15th Ave., S.E., 56304. Tel: 320-252-4380; Fax: 320-654-2351. Linda Doerr, Exec. Dir.; Robin Theis, Admin., Housing and Community Svcs.; Debra Galvez, Asst. Lay Ecclesial Min., Health Care Ministry. Managed by St. Benedict's Senior Community. A Division of the St. Cloud Hospital. Operated under the auspices of the local Catholic Church of St. Cloud. Residents 115.

Benedict Homes (4), 1342 Minnesota Blvd., S.E., 56304. Tel: 320-252-0010. Residential Homes for residents with Alzheimers. All Benedict Homes are managed by St. Benedict's Senior Community. A division of the St. Cloud Hospital. Operated under the auspices of the local Catholic Church of St. Cloud. Residents 24.

Benedict Court, 1980 15th Ave., S.E., 56304. Tel: 320-252-0010; Fax: 320-654-2351. Linda Doerr, Exec. Dir.; Robin Theis, Admin., Housing and Community Svcs. 39 assisted living apartments; Managed by St. Benedict's Senior Community. A Division of the St. Cloud Hospital. Operated under the auspices of the local Catholic Church of St. Cloud. Residents 40.

Benet Place, 1420 Minnesota Blvd., S.E., 56304. Tel: 320-252-2557; Fax: 320-654-2351. Subsidized apartments with supportive services for older adults only. Managed by St. Benedict's Senior Community. Tenants 40.

Benet Place South, 1975 15th Ave., S.E., 56304. Tel: 320-529-8700; Fax: 320-654-2351. Tenants 36.

ALBANY. *Mother of Mercy Campus of Care*, Box 676, 56307. Tel: 320-845-2195; Fax: 320-845-7092. Email: jhoefs@momnursinghome.com. John J. Hoefs, Admin. & CEO. Guests 188.

BRECKENRIDGE. *Appletree Court* (1998) 601 Oak St., 56520. Tel: 218-643-0407; Fax: 218-643-0850. Email: jolyndohman@catholichealth.net. Web: sfcare.org. David Nelson, CEO. Residents 20.

St. Francis Home, 2400 St. Francis Dr., 56520. Tel: 218-643-3000; Fax: 218-643-0850. Web: www.sfcare.org. David Nelson, CEO; Rev. Kenneth Popp, Chap. Residents 120.

COLD SPRING. *Assumption Court*, 615 First St. N., 56320. Tel: 320-685-4110; Fax: 320-685-7044. Jan Luthens, Admin.; Rev. Julius Beckermann, O.S.B., Chap. Apartments 59.

Assumption Home (1963) 715 First St. N., 56320. Tel: 320-685-3693; Fax: 320-685-7044. Email: janl@assumption.com. Jan Luthens, Admin.; Rev. Julius Beckermann, O.S.B. Residents 80.

John Paul Apartments, 200 Eighth Ave. N., 56320. Tel: 320-685-4429; Fax: 320-685-7044. Email: jpa@cloudnet.com. Jan Luthens, Admin.; Rev. Julius Beckermann, O.S.B., Chap. Pioneer Housing Development, Inc. Apartments 61.

LITTLE FALLS. *Alverna Apartments*, 300 Eighth Ave., S.E., 56345. Tel: 320-631-5030; Fax: 320-631-5680. Bea Britz, Chap.; Judy Venske, Mgr. (An Affiliate of Catholic Health Initiatives.) Residents 60.

MORRIS. *West Wind Village*, 1001 Scott Ave., 56267. Tel: 320-589-1133; Fax: 320-589-7955. Email: solson@wwv.sfhs.org. Deacon Joseph Wood, Pastoral Care. Guests 104.

PARKERS PRAIRIE. *St. William's Living Center* (1963) P.O. Box 30, 56361. Tel: 218-338-4671; Fax: 218-338-5917. Email: pbaer@midwestinfo.net. Paul Baer, Admin. Bed Capacity 93.

[I] MONASTERIES AND RESIDENCES OF PRIESTS AND BROTHERS

COLLEGEVILLE. *Holy Cross Trust*, 31802 County Rd. 159, 56321.

St. John's Abbey, of the Order of St. Benedict and St. John's University, School of Theology, Seminary, Preparatory School and Novitiate., 31802 Co. Rd. 159, P.O. Box 2015, 56321-2015. Tel: 320-363-2011; Fax: 320-363-2504. Web: www.sja.osb.org. Rt. Rev. John Klassen, O.S.B., Ph.D., Abbot & Chancellor; Very Revs. Thomas Andert, O.S.B., Prior; Paul Richards, O.S.B., Subprior & Dir. Formation; Revs. Knute Anderson, O.S.B.; Alexander Andrews, O.S.B.; Timothy Backous, O.S.B., Pres. St. John's Preparatory School; Stephen Beauclair, O.S.B.; Nickolas Becker, O.S.B.; Julius Beckermann, O.S.B.; Luigi Bertocchi, O.S.B.; Michael Bik, O.S.B.; Burton Blums, O.S.B.; Roger Botz, O.S.B.; Allan Bouley, O.S.B.; Fintan Bromenshenkel, O.S.B.; Jerome Coller, O.S.B.; Corwin Collins, O.S.B.; Cletus Connors, O.S.B.; Alberic Culhane, O.S.B.; Meinrad Dindorf, O.S.B.; Ian Dommer, O.S.B.; Daniel Durken, O.S.B.; John Patrick Earls, O.S.B.; Richard Eckroth, O.S.B.; Geoffrey Fecht, O.S.B.; Joseph Feders, O.S.B.; Jonathan Fischer, O.S.B.; Thomas Gillespie, O.S.B.; Nathanael Hauser, O.S.B.; Henry Bryan Hays, O.S.B.; Francis Hoefgen, O.S.B., (Leave of Absence); Eric Hollas, O.S.B.; Roger Kasprick, O.S.B.; Timothy Kelly, O.S.B.; Chrysostom Kim, O.S.B.; Roger Klassen, O.S.B.; Robert Koopmann, O.S.B.; John Kulas, O.S.B.; Michael Kwatera, O.S.B.; Dale Launderville, O.S.B.; Donald LeMay, O.S.B.; Jonathan Licari, O.S.B., Subprior; Matthew Luft, O.S.B; Brennan Maiers, O.S.B.; Luke Mancuso, O.S.B.; Paul Marx, O.S.B.; J. Patrick McDarby, O.S.B.; Finian McDonald, O.S.B.; Kilian McDonnell, O.S.B.; Eugene J. McGlothlin, O.S.B.; Rene McGraw, O.S.B.; Gregory Miller, O.S.B.; Dunstan Moorse, O.S.B.; Florian Muggli, O.S.B.; Douglas Mullin, O.S.B.; Very Rev. Michael Naughton, O.S.B.; Revs. Michael Patella, O.S.B.; Raymond Pedrizetti, O.S.B.; Robert Pierson, O.S.B.; Martin Rath, O.S.B.; James Reichert, O.S.B.; Stanley Roche, O.S.B.; Anthony Ruff, O.S.B.; Dominic Ruiz, O.S.B.; William Schipper, O.S.B.; Julian Schmiesing, O.S.B.; Kevin Seasoltz, O.S.B.; Mathias Spier, O.S.B.; Luke Steiner, O.S.B.; Columba Stewart, O.S.B., HMML Dir.; Edwin Stueber, O.S.B.; Don Talafous, O.S.B.; Allen Tarlton, O.S.B.; Donald Tauscher, O.S.B.; Gordon Tavis, O.S.B.; Mark Thamert, O.S.B.; Wilfred Theisen, O.S.B.; Hilary Thimmesh, O.S.B.; Simeon J. Thole, O.S.B.; Thomas Thole, O.S.B.; Jerome Tupa, O.S.B., Univ. Chap.; Blane Wasnie, O.S.B.; Arnold Weber, O.S.B.; Magnus Wenninger, O.S.B.; Hugh Witzmann, O.S.B.; George Wolf, O.S.B. Priests within Diocese 78; Priests Elsewhere 20; Brothers 46.

On Special Assignments: Revs. Joel Kelly, O.S.B.; Barnabas Laubach, O.S.B., St. Bernardine Hospital, 2101 N. Waterman Ave., San Bernardino, CA 92404. Tel: 909-883-8711; Very Rev. Roman Paur, O.S.B., Prior; Revs. Francisco Schulte, O.S.B.; Daniel Ward, O.S.B., 2613 Woodege Rd., Silver Spring, MD 20906. Tel: 301-933-0447; Fax: 301-589-2897; Cyprian Weaver, O.S.B.

Priests of the Abbey Serving Abroad: Revs. Cyril Gorman, O.S.B.; Peter Kawamura, O.S.B., Holy Trinity Benedictine Monastery, 3110 Fujimi-Fujimi Machi, Nagano Ken 399-0211 Japan. Tel: 011-81-266-62-8770; Fax: 011-81-266-62-8765; Kieran Nolan, O.S.B., Holy Trinity Benedictine Monastery,

3110 Fujimi-Fujimi Machi, Nagano Ken 399-0211 Japan. Tel: 011-81-266-62-8770; Fax: 011-81-266-62-8765; William Skudlarek, O.S.B.; Mel Taylor, O.S.B., St. Augustine Monastery, Box N-3940, Nassau, Bahamas. Tel: 242-364-1331; Fax: 242-364-8929; Very Rev. Thomas Wahl, O.S.B., Prior, Holy Trinity Benedictine Monastery, 3110 Fujimi-Fujimi Machi, Nagano Ken 399-0211 Japan. Tel: 011-81-266-62-8770; Fax: 011-81-266-62-8765; Rev. Edward Vebelun, O.S.B., Holy Trinity Benedictine Monastery, 3110 Fujimi-Fujimi Machi, Nagano Ken 399-0211 Japan. Tel: 011-81-266-62-8770; Fax: 011-81-266-62-8765.

ONAMIA. *Crosier Priory* (1922) *Crosier Priory of the Holy Cross*, 104 Crosier Dr. N., P.O. Box 500, 56359. Tel: 320-532-3103; Fax: 320-532-5222. Email: info@crosier.org. Web: www.crosier.org. Very Rev. Kermit Holl, O.S.C., Prior; Revs. Joseph Brennan, O.S.C.; John J. Fleischhacker, O.S.C.; David Gallus, O.S.C.; Edward Greiwe, O.S.C.; Clement N. Gustin, O.S.C.; John Hawkins, O.S.C.; Richard John, O.S.C.; Charles Kunkel, O.S.C.; Ernest Martello, O.S.C.; Bernard Mischke, O.S.C.; James Moeglein, O.S.C.; Kenneth Opat, O.S.C.; Eugene D. Plaisted, O.S.C.; Gregory Poser, O.S.C.; Adrian Piotrowski, O.S.C.; James H. Remmerswaal, O.S.C.; Jerry Schik, O.S.C.; Oscar Schoenberg, O.S.C.; Raymond Steffes, O.S.C.; Jude Verley, O.S.C.

Crosier Fathers of Onamia, The National Shrine of St. Odilia is sponsored and maintained by the Crosier Fathers of Onamia Priests in Residence 21; Priests Elsewhere 4; Brothers in Residence 10. Priests Elsewhere: Revs. Joseph Bruemmer, O.S.C.; Joseph Cain, O.S.C.; James Cashman, O.S.C.; Joseph Fichtner, O.S.C.

[J] CONVENTS AND RESIDENCES FOR SISTERS

LITTLE FALLS. *St. Francis Convent* (1891) 116 Eighth Ave., S.E., 56345. Tel: 320-632-2981; Fax: 320-632-6313. Email: info@fslf.org. Web: www.fslf.org. Sr. Mary C. Obowa, Community Min. Motherhouse of Franciscan Sisters of Little Falls, MN. Sisters 62; Total in Community 172.

Franciscan Life Center Sr. Bernice Rieland, O.S.F., Contact Person.

ST. JOSEPH. *St. Benedict's Monastery* (1857) 104 Chapel Ln., 56374-0220. Tel: 320-363-7100; Fax: 320-363-7130. Email: jbraun@csbsju.edu. Web: www.sbm.osb.org. Sisters Nancy Bauer, O.S.B., J.C.D., Prioress; Elaine Schroeder, O.S.B., Coord. Eucharistic Presiders. Motherhouse and Formation House for Sisters of the Order of Saint Benedict. Sisters 150; Total in Community 270.

SAUK RAPIDS. *St. Clare's Monastery* (1923) Major Papal Cloister, 421 4th St. S., 56379. Tel: 320-251-3556; Fax: 320-203-7052. Sr. Mary Matthew, O.S.C., Abbess. Franciscan Poor Clare Nuns. Cloistered Nuns: Solemn Professed 17; Simple Professed 1; Extern Sisters: Perpetual Professed 2.

[K] RETREAT HOUSES

ST. FRANCIS. *Pacem in Terris Center for Spirituality*, Mailing Address: *Hermitage Retreats*, P.O. Box 418, 55070. Tel: 763-444-6408; Fax: 763-444-9649. Email: alain@paceminterris.org. Shirley Wanchena, Dir.

[L] NEWMAN CENTERS

ST. CLOUD. *Newman Center, Inc.* 396 First Ave. S., 56301. Tel: 320-251-3260; Fax: 320-252-3930. Email: newmancenter@charterinternet.com. Web: scsucatholicorg. Rev. Anthony Oelrich, S.T.L., Admin.

MORRIS. *Newman Catholic Student Center* 306 E. Fourth St., 56267. Tel: 320-589-1947. Email: newman@hometownsolutions.net. Web: www.mrs.umn.edu/~catholic. Scott Crumb, Dir. Campus Ministry.

[M] MISCELLANEOUS

ST. CLOUD. *Affordable Community Housing, Inc.*, P.O. Box 2390, 56303. Tel: 320-229-4576. Harvey Schmitt, Dir. Housing; Mr. Steven P. Bresnahan, Exec. Dir.

Carmelite Hermits of Adoration, Inc. (1986) 1810 Minnesota Blvd. S.E., 56304. Tel: 320-252-0010. Sr. Imelda, Prioress. Sisters 2.

Central Minnesota Residents Encountering Christ (1998) 6667 County Rd. 91 SE, 56304. Tel: 320-251-0098. Email: ccarolt@yahoo.com. Carol Tembreull, Prog. Coord.

Domus Transitional Housing, 17 S. 19 1/2 Ave., 56301. Mr. Steven P. Bresnahan, Exec. Dir.; Harvey Schmitt, Contact Person.

Key Row Community, Inc., 157 Roosevelt Rd., Ste. 200, 56301. Tel: 320-229-4576. 700-709 S. 14th St., 56301. Mr. Steven P. Bresnahan, Exec. Dir.; Harvey Schmitt, Contact Person. Providing low-cost housing to elderly and families in Morris and St. Cloud.

BROWNS VALLEY. **Browns Valley Health Center*, 114 Jefferson St. S., 56219. Tel: 320-695-2165; Fax: 320-695-2166. Email: cward@bvhc.sfhs.org. Capacity 41.

Valley Vista Apartments of Browns Valley Inc., 317 S.W. 2nd Ave., 56219. Saint Cloud, 56301.

CAMBRIDGE. *Benedictine Care Centers*, 1995 E. Rum River Dr. S., 55008. Tel: 763-689-1162; Fax: 763-689-1197. Dale M. Thompson, Pres. & CEO.

Benedictine Health Dimensions, Inc., 1995 E. Rum River Dr., S., 55008. Tel: 763-689-1162; Fax: 763-689-1197. Email: webmaster@bhshealth.org. Web: www.bhshealth.org. Dale M. Thompson, Pres. & CEO.

LITTLE FALLS. *Franciscan Sisters of Little Falls, MN Charitable Trust*, 116 Eighth Ave., S.E., 56345. Tel: 320-632-2981; Fax: 320-632-6313. Email: info@fslf.org. Web: www.fslf.org.

Key Row Little Falls, Inc., 905 N.E. 6th Ave., 56345. 157 Roosevelt Rd., Ste. 200, Saint Cloud, 56301. Harvey Schmitt, Dir. Housing & Contact Person.

MELROSE. *Rose Mill Apartments, LLC*, 157 Roosevelt Rd., Ste. 200, 56301. 407 E. 5th St. N., 56352. Mr. Steven P. Bresnahan, Exec. Dir.; Harvey Schmitt, Dir. Housing Svcs.

MILACA. *Key Row Milaca, Inc.*, 410 N.W. 4th Ave., 56353. Tel: 320-229-4576; Fax: 320-253-7464. 157 Roosevelt Rd., Ste. 200, Saint Cloud, 56301. Harvey Schmitt, Dir. Housing & Contact Person.

MORRIS. *St. Francis Health Services* (1984) 801 Nevada, Ste. 100, 56267. Tel: 320-589-2004; Fax: 320-589-1270. Email: lhoffman@sfhs.org. Web: www.sfhs.org.

Prairie Community Services (1987) 801 Nevada Ave., P.O. Box 468, 56267. Tel: 320-589-3077; Fax: 320-589-2543. Web: www.pcs.sfhs.org.

Key Row Community, Inc., 151 Sunnyslope Rd., Bldgs. 301, 306, 311, 318, 324, 56267. Tel: 320-589-4661; Fax: 320-589-4661.

ONAMIA. *National Shrine of St. Odilia Crosier Priory of the Holy Cross*, P.O. Box 500, 56359-0500. Tel: 320-532-3103; Fax: 320-532-5222. Email: info@crosiers.org. Web: www.crosiers.org. Bro. Albert Becker, O.S.C., Contact Person & Dir. Devel. Sponsored and maintained by The Crosiers of Onamia.

RICHMOND. *Maple Apartments of Richmond , Inc.*, 488 1st St., N.E., 56368. Tel: 320-229-4576; Fax: 320-253-7464. 157 Roosevelt Rd., Ste. 200, Saint Cloud, 56301. Mr. Steven P. Bresnahan, Exec. Dir.; Harvey Schmitt, Dir. Housing Svcs.

ST. JOSEPH. *Monastic Interreligious Dialogue*, St. Benedict's Monastery, 104 Chapel Ln., 56374-2020. Tel: 320-363-7187; Fax: 320-363-7173. Email: khoward@csbsju.edu. Web: www.monasticdialog.org. Sr. Katherine Howard, O.S.B., Contact Person.

St. Joseph's Apartment, Inc., 410 W. Minnesota St., 56374. 157 Roosevelt Rd., Ste. 200, 56301. Mr. Steven P. Bresnahan, Exec. Dir.; Harvey Schmitt, Dir. Housing Svcs.

SAUK CENTRE. *Sauk Centre Apts.*, 157 Roosevelt Rd., Ste. 200, 56301. 217 Railroad Ave. Ct., 56378. Mr. Steven P. Bresnahan, Exec. Dir.; Harvey Schmitt, Dir. Housing Svcs. & Contact Person.

RELIGIOUS INSTITUTES OF MEN REPRESENTED IN THE DIOCESE

For further details refer to the corresponding bracketed number in the Religious Institutes of Men or Women section.

[0200]—*Benedictine Monks* (Collegeville, MN)—O.S.B.

[0400]—*Canons Regular of the Order of the Holy Cross* (Province of St. Odilia)—O.S.C.

RELIGIOUS INSTITUTES OF WOMEN REPRESENTED IN THE DIOCESE

[0230]—*Benedictine Sisters of Pontifical Jurisdiction*—O.S.B.

[1920]—*Congregation of the Sisters of the Holy Cross*—C.S.C.

[1310]—*Franciscan Sisters of Little Falls, Minnesota*—O.S.F.

[3760]—*Order of St. Clare*—O.S.C.

[2970]—*School Sisters of Notre Dame* (Northwestern Prov.)—S.S.N.D.

[1710]—*Sisters of St. Francis of Mary Immaculate*—O.S.F.

NECROLOGY

† Belair, Eugene, (Retired)—Died June 18, 2009

† Heid, Richard J., Brandon, MN Church of St. Ann—Died Feb. 1, 2009

An asterisk (*) denotes an organization that has established tax-exempt status directly with the IRS and is not covered by the USCCB Group Ruling.

Archdiocese of St. Louis

(Archidioecesis S. Ludovici)

Most Reverend

ROBERT JAMES CARLSON

Archbishop of St. Louis; ordained May 22, 1970; appointed Titular Bishop of Aviocala and Auxiliary Bishop of Saint Paul and Minneapolis November 22, 1983; consecrated January 11, 1984; appointed Coadjutor Bishop of Sioux Falls January 13, 1994; Succeeded to the See March 21, 1995; appointed Bishop of Saginaw December 29, 2004; installed February 24, 2005; appointed Archbishop of St. Louis April 21, 2009; installed June 10, 2009. *Office: 4445 Lindell Blvd., St. Louis, MO 63108-2497.*

Most Reverend

ROBERT J. HERMANN, D.D.

Auxiliary Bishop of St. Louis; ordained March 30, 1963; appointed Auxiliary Bishop of St. Louis October 16, 2002; ordained December 12, 2002. *Office: 20 Archbishop May Dr., St. Louis, MO 63119.*

4445 Lindell Blvd., St. Louis, MO 63108-2497. Tel: 314-633-2222; Fax: 314-633-2333.

Web: www.archstl.org

Email: communication@archstl.org

Square Miles 5,968.

Diocese July 18, 1826; Archdiocese July 20, 1847.

Comprises that portion of the State of Missouri bounded on the north by the northern line of the County of Lincoln; on the west by the western lines of the Counties of Lincoln, Warren, Franklin and Washington; on the south by the southern lines of the Counties of Washington, St. Francois and Perry; on the east by the Mississippi River.

Heavenly Patrons--Saint Louis, King, Saint Vincent de Paul and Saint Rose Philippine Duchesne.

For legal titles of parishes and archdiocesan institutions, consult the Catholic Center.

STATISTICAL OVERVIEW

Personnel	
Archbishops	1
Auxiliary Bishops	1
Abbots	1
Retired Abbots	2
Priests: Diocesan Active in Diocese	261
Priests: Diocesan Active Outside Diocese	11
Priests: Diocesan in Foreign Missions	3
Priests: Retired, Sick or Absent	98
Number of Diocesan Priests	373
Religious Priests in Diocese	358
Total Priests in Diocese	731
Extern Priests in Diocese	18
Ordinations:	
Diocesan Priests	4
Religious Priests	1
Transitional Deacons	9
Permanent Deacons	11
Permanent Deacons in Diocese	274
Total Brothers	130
Total Sisters	1,426
Parishes	
Parishes	190
With Resident Pastor:	
Resident Diocesan Priests	160
Resident Religious Priests	21
Without Resident Pastor:	
Administered by Priests	9
Closed Parishes	1
Welfare	
Catholic Hospitals	12
Total Assisted	1,790,768
Homes for the Aged	41
Total Assisted	28,920
Residential Care of Children	3
Total Assisted	1,706
Day Care Centers	8
Total Assisted	26,416
Specialized Homes	7
Total Assisted	2,120
Special Centers for Social Services	8
Total Assisted	10,500
Educational	
Seminaries, Diocesan	2
Students from This Diocese	51
Students from Other Diocese	62
Diocesan Students in Other Seminaries	6
Seminaries, Religious	2
Students Religious	47
Total Seminarians	104
Colleges and Universities	2
Total Students	15,534
High Schools, Diocesan and Parish	12
Total Students	4,933
High Schools, Private	16
Total Students	8,564
Elementary Schools, Diocesan and Parish	108
Total Students	30,162
Elementary Schools, Private	9
Total Students	1,868
Non-residential Schools for the Disabled	4
Total Students	179
Catechesis/Religious Education:	
High School Students	132
Elementary Students	22,324
Total Students under Catholic Instruction	83,800
Teachers in the Diocese:	
Priests	46
Brothers	21
Sisters	87
Lay Teachers	3,925
Vital Statistics	
Receptions into the Church:	
Infant Baptism Totals	5,711
Minor Baptism Totals	277
Adult Baptism Totals	323
Received into Full Communion	497
First Communions	6,619
Confirmations	6,723
Marriages:	
Catholic	1,454
Interfaith	618
Total Marriages	2,072
Deaths	4,110
Total Catholic Population	531,770
Total Population	2,232,379

Former Bishops—Most Revs. LOUIS WILLIAM VALENTINE DUBOURG, Archbishop of the Cardinalatial See of Besancon; ord. 1788; cons. in Rome, Sept. 24, 1815, Bishop of Louisiana, Upper and Lower, took his first residential seat in St. Louis, Jan. 6, 1818. On July 18, 1826, the Diocese of Louisiana was divided and the Sees of St. Louis and New Orleans erected. Bishop DuBourg having resigned the See of Louisiana, was transferred to the Diocese of Montauban in France, Aug. 13, 1826, and made Archbishop of the Cardinalatial See of Besancon, Feb. 15, 1833, where he died Dec. 12 of the same year; JOSEPH ROSATI, C.M., Bishop of St. Louis; born Jan. 12, 1789 in Lazio, Italy; ord. Feb. 10, 1811; cons. Bishop of the Titular See of Tenagra and constituted Coadjutor of Bishop DuBourg of Louisiana at Donaldsville, LA, March 25, 1824. When the See of Louisiana was divided Bishop Rosati was made Bishop of St. Louis and Administrator of New Orleans. He died while on business in Rome on Sept. 25, 1843; PETER RICHARD KENRICK, D.D., Archbishop of St. Louis; born Aug. 17, 1806 in Dublin, Ireland; ord. March 6, 1832; cons. Nov. 30, 1841, Bishop of Drasa and Coadjutor to Bishop of St. Louis; Succeeded as Bishop Sept. 25, 1843; appt. Archbishop of St. Louis July 12, 1847; retired May 21, 1895; died March 4, 1896; JOHN JOSEPH KAIN, D.D., Archbishop of St. Louis; born May 31, 1841 in Martinsburg, Virginia; ord. July 2, 1866; cons. Bishop of Wheeling, WV on May 23, 1875; Titular Archbishop of Oxyrynchia and Coadjutor "cum jure successionis" of Archbishop of St. Louis, 1893; Administrator of Archdiocese of St. Louis, Dec. 14, 1893; created Archbishop of St. Louis on May 21, 1895; died Oct. 13, 1903; His Eminence JOHN CARDINAL GLENNON, D.D., Archbishop of St. Louis; born June 14, 1862; ord. Dec. 20, 1884; appt. Titular Bishop of Pinara and Coadjutor to the Bishop of Kansas City, March 14, 1896; cons. June 29, 1896; transferred to St. Louis, April 27, 1903, as Coadjutor to the Archbishop of St. Louis "cum jure successionis"; Archbishop of St. Louis, Oct. 13, 1903; Pallium received May 14, 1905; Assistant at the Pontifical Throne, June 21, 1921; created Cardinal Priest, Feb. 18, 1946; died March 9, 1946; JOSEPH CARDINAL RITTER, D.D., Archbishop of St. Louis; born July 20, 1892; ord. May 30, 1917; appt. Titular Bishop of Hippo, Feb. 3, 1933 and Auxiliary Bishop of Indianapolis; cons. March 28, 1933; appt. Archbishop of

Indianapolis, Nov. 11, 1944; appt. Archbishop of St. Louis, July 20, 1946 assistant at the Pontifical Throne, Oct. 5, 1956; created Cardinal, Priest Jan. 16, 1961; died June 10, 1967; JOHN JOSEPH CARDINAL CARBERRY, D.D., S.T.D., J.C.D., Ph.D., Archbishop of St. Louis; born July 31, 1904 in Brooklyn, New York; ord. July 28, 1929; appt. Titular Bishop of Elis and Coadjutor of Lafayette in Indiana, May 3, 1956; cons. July 25, 1956; Succeeded to See, Nov. 20, 1957; transferred to Columbus, Jan. 16, 1965; appt. Archbishop of St. Louis, Feb. 17, 1968; installed March 25, 1968; created Cardinal, April 28, 1969; retired July 31, 1979; died June 17, 1998; Most Rev. JOHN L. MAY, D.D., Archbishop of St. Louis; born March 31, 1922 in Evanston, Illinois; ord. May 3, 1947; appt. Auxiliary Bishop of Chicago, June 21, 1967; cons. Aug. 24, 1967; transferred to Mobile, Oct. 8, 1969; installed as Bishop of Mobile, Dec. 10, 1969; appt. Archbishop of St. Louis, Jan. 29, 1980; installed March 25, 1980; resigned Dec. 9, 1992; died March 24, 1994; His Eminence JUSTIN CARDINAL RIGALI, J.C.D., Archbishop of St. Louis; born April 19, 1935; ord. April 25, 1961; appt. Titular Archbishop of Bolsena, June 8, 1985; cons. Sept. 14, 1985; appointed Archbishop of St. Louis, Jan. 25, 1994; installed March 15, 1994; Pallium received June 29, 1994; transferred to Archdiocese of Philadelphia, July 15, 2003; created Cardinal, Sept. 28, 2003; installed as Archbishop of Philadelphia, Oct. 7, 2003; Most Rev. RAYMOND L. BURKE, D.D., J.C.D., born June 30, 1948 in Richland Center, Wisconsin; ord. June 29, 1975; appt. to the Residential See of La Crosse Dec. 10, 1994; cons. Jan. 6, 1995; installed as Eighth Bishop of La Crosse Feb. 22, 1995; appt. Archbishop of St. Louis Dec. 2, 2003; installed Jan. 26, 2004; appt. Prefect of the Apostolic Signatura June 27, 2008.

The Catholic Center—4445 Lindell Blvd., St. Louis, 63108-2497. Tel: 314-633-2222; Fax: 314-633-2333. Office Hours: Mon.-Fri. 8:30-4.

Archdiocesan Administrator—Most Rev. ROBERT J. HERMANN, D.D.

Moderator of the Curia—Rev. Msgr. VERNON E. GARDIN, Ph.D.

Office of Child and Youth Protection—Deacon PHILIP R. HENGEN, 20 Archbishop May Dr., St. Louis, 63119. Tel: 314-792-7704.

Chancellor—Ms. NANCY J. WERNER, 20 Archbishop May Dr., St. Louis, 63119. Tel: 314-633-2273; Fax: 314-633-2304.

Chancellor for Canonical Affairs—Rev. Msgr. JEROME D. BILLING, S.T.L., J.C.L., 20 Archbishop May Dr., St. Louis, 63119. Tel: 314-633-2261; Fax: 314-633-2306.

Vice Chancellor for Special Projects—Mrs. JENNIFER STANARD.

Master of Ceremonies—Rev. BRIAN R. FISCHER.

Archdiocesan Master of Ceremonies—Rev. KEVIN M. SCHROEDER.

Metropolitan Tribunal—20 Archbishop May Dr., St. Louis, 63119. Tel: 314-633-2280; Fax: 314-633-2301.

Judicial Vicar—Rev. Msgr. JOHN B. SHAMLEFFER, J.C.L., M.C.L., M.A., M.Div.

Adjutant Judicial Vicar—VACANT.

Defender of the Bond—Rev. Msgr. JEROME D. BILLING, S.T.L., J.C.L.

Judges—Revs. DENNIS M. DOYLE, J.C.L.; NICHOLAS E. KASTENHOLZ, J.C.L.; Deacon J. GERARD QUINN.

Promoter of Justice—Rev. Msgr. JEROME D. BILLING, S.T.L., J.C.L.

Notaries—Mrs. ANN MERTEN; Mrs. PATRICIA LANASA.

Missouri Appellate Tribunal—20 Archbishop May Dr., St. Louis, 63119. Tel: 314-792-7167.

Judicial Vicar—Rev. Msgr. MARK S. RIVITUSO, J.C.L., M.C.L., M.A., M.Div.

Archdiocesan Consultors—Most Rev. ROBERT J. HERMANN, D.D.; Rev. Msgrs. JOHN B. SHAMLEFFER, J.C.L., M.C.L., M.A., M.Div.; JOHN J. LEYKAM, V.F.; VERNON E. GARDIN, Ph.D.; JOHN J. BRENNELL; MICHAEL DIECKMANN; Rev. JOHN M. SEPER.

Deaneries/Deans—Rev. Msgrs. MARK C. ULLRICH, M.Div., M.S.W., V.F., North City - St. Louis; MICHAEL E. TUREK, V.F., South City - St. Louis; A. JOHN SCHULER, V.F., Northeast County; Rev. CHARLES E. BURGOON, Northwest County; Very Revs. THOMAS M. MOLINI, M.A., V.F., Southwest County; GARY M. GEBELEIN, V.F., Southeast County; PATRICK J. CHRISTOPHER, V.F., Festus; Rev. Msgrs. GREGORY L. SCHMIDT, V.F., St. Charles; MATTHEW M. MITAS, Washington; Very Rev. ANTHONY A. DATTILO, V.F., Ste. Genevieve.

Chief Financial Officer—Deacon C. FRANK CHAUVIN.

Chief Administrative Officer—Dr. DAVID MUECKL, Ph.D.

Archdiocesan Offices and Directors

Archdiocesan Archives—Rev. Msgr. JEROME D. BILLING, S.T.L., J.C.L., Chancellor for Canonical Affairs; AUDREY POWDERLY-NEWCOMER, Archivist, 20 Archbishop May Dr., St. Louis, 63119. Tel: 314-792-7020; Fax: 314-792-7029.

Catholic Family Counseling—Dr. JERRY L. MARKS, D.S.W., L.C.S.W., Exec. Dir., 9200 Watson Rd., G101, Saint Louis, 63126. Tel: 314-544-3800; Fax: 314-843-0552 See MISCELLANEOUS section for more information.

Catholic Family Tuition—20 Archbishop May Dr., St. Louis, 63119.

Annual Catholic Appeal—Mr. FRANK COGNATA JR., Chief Devel. Officer; BRIAN NIEBRUGGE, Dir., 20 Archbishop May Dr., St. Louis, 63119. Tel: 314-792-7680; Fax: 314-792-7699. See MISCELLANEOUS section for more information.

Catholic Relief Services—Mrs. JENNIFER STANARD, 20 Archbishop May Dr., St. Louis, 63119. Tel: 314-633-2212.

Catholic Cemeteries of St. Louis—Rev. Msgr. DENNIS M. DELANEY, Dir., 5239 W. Florissant Ave., Saint Louis, 63115. Tel: 314-381-1313 See CEMETERIES section for more information.

Central Purchasing—Mr. DARREL KALBFLEISCH, Dir., 20 Archbishop May Dr., St. Louis, 63119. Tel: 314-792-7065; Fax: 314-792-7019.

Charismatic Renewal—Rev. Msgr. EDMUND O. GRIESEDIECK, Dir. (Retired), 10909 St. Henry Lane, Saint Ann, 63074. Tel: 314-427-7786.

Finance Office—20 Archbishop May Dr., St. Louis, 63119-5738. Tel: 314-792-7100.

Catholic Charities—Rev. Msgr. MARK C. ULLRICH, M.Div., M.S.W., V.F., Pres., 4532 Lindell Blvd., St. Louis, 63108. Tel: 314-367-5500; Fax: 314-367-2982. Web: www.ccstl.org. See MISCELLANEOUS section for more information.

Cardinal Ritter Senior Services—Sr. SUZANNE WESLEY, C.S.J., COO, 7601 Watson Rd., St. Louis, 63119. Tel: 314-961-8000; Fax: 314-961-1934. Email: swesley@ccstl.org. See SERVICES FOR THE ELDERLY section for more information.

Archdiocesan Deaf Ministry—Rev. VICTOR A. BARNHART, Dir., 7530 Natural Bridge Rd., Normandy, 63121. Teletype: 314-727-2747 See MISCELLANEOUS section for more information.

Archdiocesan Data Center—Mr. GERALD F. LAWLER, Dir. Mgmt. Information Systems, 20 Archbishop May Dr., St. Louis, 63119. Tel: 314-792-7570; Fax: 314-792-7579.

Office for Ecumenical & Interreligious Affairs—LAWRENCE J. WELCH, Ph.D., Acting Dir., 20 Archbishop May Dr., St. Louis, 63119. Tel: 314-792-7060; Fax: 314-792-7164.

Office of Consecrated Life—Rev. Msgr. EDWARD M. RICE, 20 Archbishop May Dr., St. Louis, 63119. Tel: 314-792-7250.

Fleur de Lis—20 Archbishop May Dr., St. Louis, 63119.

Archdiocesan Office of Worship—Rev. Msgr. WILLIAM W. MCCUMBER, 20 Archbishop May Dr., St. Louis, 63119. Tel: 314-792-7230; Fax: 314-792-7019.

Archdiocesan Commission for Sacred Liturgy—Sr. CATHY DOHERTY, S.S.N.D., Chm.

Archdiocesan Commission for Sacred Music—Mr. JEFF BUSH, Chm.

Archdiocesan Commission for Sacred Art and Architecture—Mr. ROBERT BARRINGER, Chm.

Council of Catholic Youth—Rev. Msgr. JOHN J. BORCIC, Exec. Dir., 20 Archbishop May Dr., St. Louis, 63119. Tel: 314-633-2511; Fax: 314-792-7619.

Holy Childhood, Pontifical Association—Rev. Msgr. FRANCIS X. BLOOD, Dir., 20 Archbishop May Dr., St. Louis, 63119. Tel: 314-792-7655; Fax: 314-792-7669.

Holy Name Society—Mr. NICK PFISTER, Archdiocesan Pres., Mailing Address: Holy Name Society, P.O. Box 190435, St. Louis, 63119-6435. Tel: 314-428-9073.

Human Resources—Mr. KEVIN J. LOOS, Mng. Dir., 20 Archbishop May Dr., St. Louis, 63119. Tel: 314-792-7542.

Latin American Apostolate, Archdiocese of St. Louis—Rev. Msgr. FRANCIS X. BLOOD, Dir., 20 Archbishop May Dr., St. Louis, 63119. Tel: 314-792-7655; Fax: 314-792-7669.

The Legion of Mary—336 E. Ripa Ave., Saint Louis, 63125. Spiritual Directors: Revs. DAVID L. WICHLAN; EDWARD J. HILGEMAN (Retired).

Pan y Amor—Rev. Msgr. FRANCIS X. BLOOD, Dir., 20 Archbishop May Dr., St. Louis, 63119. Tel: 314-792-7655; Fax: 314-792-7669.

Archdiocesan Newspaper "The St. Louis Review"—Rev. Msgr. JOSEPH D. PINS, Theological Consultant; Ms. ANNE STEFFENS, Chief Communications Officer; TEAK PHILLIPS, Editor, 20 Archbishop May Dr., St. Louis, 63119. Tel: 314-792-7500; Fax: 314-792-7534.

Pastoral Planning, Office of—Deacon DANIEL H. HENROID, Dir., 20 Archbishop May Dr., St. Louis, 63119. Tel: 314-633-2237; Fax: 314-633-2312.

Archdiocesan Office of Stewardship & Development—Mr. FRANK J. COGNATA JR., Chief Devel. Officer, 20 Archbishop May Dr., St. Louis, 63119-5004. Tel: 314-792-7210.

Archdiocesan Planned Giving and Endowment Council— See MISCELLANEOUS section for more information.

Priests' Mutual Benefit/Risk Management—BOB RYAN, Dir.; Mr. FRED J. HUMMEL, Admin., 20 Archbishop May Dr., St. Louis, 63119. Tel: 314-792-7200; Fax: 314-792-7209.

Priests' Purgatorial Society—Rev. Msgr. JEROME D. BILLING, S.T.L., J.C.L., Pres.

Respect Life Apostolate—Mrs. BETH LAUVER, Dir., 20 Archbishop May Dr., St. Louis, 63119. Tel: 314-792-7555; Fax: 314-792-7569.

Project Rachel—20 Archbishop May Dr., St. Louis, 63119.

Regina Cleri—Ms. NANCY BRYANT, Admin., 10 Archbishop May Dr., St. Louis, 63119. Tel: 314-968-2240; Fax: 314-968-1049.

Society for the Propagation of the Faith—Rev. Msgr. FRANCIS X. BLOOD, Dir., 20 Archbishop May Dr., St. Louis, 63119. Tel: 314-792-7655; Fax: 314-792-7669.

Building and Real Estate—THOMAS W. RICHTER, P.E., Dir., 20 Archbishop May Dr., Saint Louis, 63119.

Today and Tomorrow Education Foundation—20 Archbishop May Dr., St. Louis, 63119. Tel: 314-792-7620; Fax: 314-792-7629.

Criminal Justice Ministry—Rev. J. EDWARD VOGLER, Chap., 4127 Forest Park Ave., Saint Louis, 63108. Tel: 314-241-8062; Fax: 314-531-6712.

Office of Communications—Ms. ANNE STEFFENS, Dir.; Ms. ELIZABETH WESTHOFF, Asst. Dir., 20 Archbishop May Dr., St. Louis, 63119. Tel: 314-792-7632; Fax: 314-792-7639.

Society of St. Vincent de Paul, Council of St. Louis—Rev. JAMES CORMACK, C.M., Spiritual Advisor; Mr. RONALD F. GUZ, Pres., 4127 Forest Park Ave., St. Louis, 63108. Tel: 314-521-2183; Fax: 314-531-6712 See MISCELLANEOUS section for more information.

Society of St. Vincent de Paul, Council of the United States--(Territory: United States)—JOSEPH D. FLANNIGAN, Natl. Pres.; ROGER T. PLAYWIN, Natl. Exec. Dir., 58 Progress Pkwy., St. Louis, 63043-3706. Tel: 314-576-3993; Fax: 314-576-6755 See MISCELLANEOUS section for more information.

Schools/Catholic Education Office—Mr. GEORGE HENRY, Supt., 4445 Lindell Blvd., Saint Louis, 63108. Tel: 314-792-7300; Fax: 314-792-7399 See SCHOOLS section for more information.

St. Louis Roman Catholic Theological Seminaries, Inc.—Rev. Msgr. JEROME D. BILLING, S.T.L., J.C.L., Sec., 20 Archbishop May Dr., St. Louis, 63119. Tel: 314-633-2261.

Kenrick-Glennon Seminary— (St. Louis Roman Catholic Theological Seminary-Kenrick School of Theology) Rev. Msgr. TED L. WOJCICKI, Ed.D., Pres. & Rector.

Cardinal Glennon College—Rev. Msgr. TIMOTHY P. CRONIN, Rector, 5200 Glennon Dr., St. Louis, 63119. Tel: 314-792-6100; Fax: 314-792-6500 See SEMINARIES section for more information.

Office of Vocations—Rev. Msgr. EDWARD M. RICE, Dir., 5200 Glennon Dr., St. Louis, 63119. Tel: 314-792-6460; Fax: 314-792-6502.

Archdiocesan Council of Priests—Revs. JEFFREY G. VOMUND, Chm.; WILLIAM G. KEMPF, Sec.

Office of Priests' Personnel and Continuing Formation of Priests—Rev. Msgr. RICHARD E. HANNEKE, Dir., 20 Archbishop May Dr., St. Louis, 63119. Tel: 314-792-7550; Fax: 314-792-7554.

Archdiocesan Office of Urban and Community Affairs—Rev. Msgr. SALVATORE E. POLIZZI, Dir.; LOUIS G. BERRA, Consultor, 6052 Waterman, St. Louis, 63112. Tel: 314-721-6340; Fax: 314-721-1656.

Archdiocesan Office of the Permanent Diaconate—Rev. MICHAEL J. WITT, Dir.; Rev. Msgr. JOHN J. BORCIC, Spiritual Dir. Formation; Deacon CHRISTOPHER M. AST, Assoc. Dir., Deacon Formation; Ms. SUE CURRAN, Sec., 20 Archbishop May Dr., St. Louis, 63119. Tel: 314-633-2530; Fax: 314-633-2539.

Office of Apostolic Services—Mrs. SUSAN EDWARDS, Exec. Dir., 20 Archbishop May Dr., St. Louis, 63119-5738. Tel: 314-792-7180; Fax: 314-792-7199.

Blessed John XXIII Center—8300 Morganford Rd., St. Louis, 63123-6815. Tel: 314-633-2600; Fax: 314-633-2529.

Cardinal Rigali Center—VACANT, Bldg. Admin., 20 Archbishop May Dr., St. Louis, 63119. Tel: 314-792-7000; Fax: 314-792-7019.

Office of Youth Ministry—Rev. Msgr. JOHN J. BORCIC, Exec. Dir.; Rev. BRIAN R. FISCHER, Part-Time Dir.

Victim Assistance Coordinator—Mrs. CAROL BRESCIA.

CLERGY, PARISHES, MISSIONS AND PAROCHIAL SCHOOLS

CITY OF ST. LOUIS

ST. LOUIS COUNTY

1—CATHEDRAL BASILICA OF SAINT LOUIS (1896) Rev. Msgr. Joseph D. Pins, Rector; Rev. Kevin M. Schroeder.
4431 Lindell Blvd., 63108. Email: parish@cathedralstl.org. Web: www.cathedralstl.org. In Res., Most Rev. Robert J. Hermann, Auxiliary Bishop; Rev. Msgr. Mark C. Ullrich.
School—(Grades PreSchool-8) Tel: 314-373-8250; Fax: 314-373-8289. Michel Wendell, Prin. Lay Teachers 10; Students 136.

2—ST. AGATHA PARISH, POLISH ROMAN CATHOLIC CHURCH (1871), (Polish), Rev. Czeslaw Litak.
Mailing Address: 3239 S. Ninth St., 63118. Tel: 314-772-1603; Fax: 314-772-3979. Email: parishoffice@polishchurchstlouis.org. Web: www.polishchurchstlouis.org.

3—ST. ALBAN ROE (1980) Rev. Msgr. Gregory R. Mikesch; Rev. Gerald Blessing; Deacons Mark A. Guilford; Norman Nuelle. In Res., Rev. Msgr. William A. Drennan (Retired).
Res.: 2001 Shepard Rd., Wildwood, 63038. Tel: 636-458-2977; Fax: 636-405-1276. Web: www.stalbanroe.org/site.
School—2005 Shepard Rd., Wildwood, 63038. Tel: 636-458-6084. Mary Chrapek, Prin. Religious 3; Lay Teachers 23; Students 519.
Catechesis/Religious Program—Tel: 636-458-2460; Fax: 636-405-3026. Email: slowery@stalbanroe.org. Sarah Lowery, C.R.E. Students 717.

4—ALL SAINTS (1901) Rev. Kenneth A. Brown, Admin.
Res.: 6403 Clemens Ave., University City, 63130. Tel: 314-721-6403; Fax: 314-659-9799. Email: all_saintschurch@sbcglobal.net.
Catechesis/Religious Program—Students 12.

5—ALL SOULS (1906) Rev. Robert W. Burkemper; Deacons Arnold Krieger, (Retired); Samuel Lee.
Res.: 9550 Tennyson Ave., Overland, 63114. Tel: 314-427-0442; Fax: 314-427-3872.
Catechesis/Religious Program—Students 63.
Convent—9600 Tennyson Ave., Overland, 63114. Tel: 314-427-3413.

6—ST. ALOYSIUS (SPANISH LAKE) (1871) Closed. For inquiries regarding sacramental records, contact the Archdiocesan Archives, 20 Archbishop May Dr., Saint Louis, MO 63119.

7—ST. ALOYSIUS GONZAGA (1892) Closed. For inquiries regarding sacramental records, contact the Archdiocesan Archives, 20 Archbishop May Dr., Saint Louis, MO 63119.

8—ST. ALPHONSUS LIGUORI (1867) Rev. Matthew S. Bonk, C.Ss.R.; Bro. Terrence Burke, C.Ss.R. In Res., Revs. David Polek, C.Ss.R.; Kyle Fisher, C.Ss.R.
Res.: 1118 N. Grand Blvd., 63106. Tel: 314-533-0304; Fax: 314-533-4260.
Catechesis/Religious Program—Ms. Donna Lane, D.R.E.

9—ST. AMBROSE (1903) Rev. Msgr. Vincent R. Bommarito; Rev. William J. Kester; Deacons John J. Stoverink; Daniel J. Tracy Sr.
Res.: 5130 Wilson Ave., 63110. Tel: 314-771-1228; Fax: 314-771-0454.
School—(Grades K-8), 5110 Wilson Ave., 63110. Tel: 314-772-1437; Fax: 314-771-4560. Sr. Carol Sansone, A.S.C.J., Prin. Sisters (Apostles of the Sacred Heart of Jesus) 4; Lay Teachers 22; Students 300.
Catechesis/Religious Program—Tel: 314-771-5298. Students 332.

10—ST. ANDREW (1905) Rev. Victor A. Barnhart; Deacon C. Allen Boedeker.
Res.: 309 Hoffmeister Ave., 63125-1609. Tel: 314-631-0691; Fax: 314-631-0692.
Catechesis/Religious Program—Mrs. Mary Boedeker, D.R.E. Students 58.
Convent—Sisters of Notre Dame, 232 Hoffmeister Ave., 63125. Tel: 314-631-2010.

11—ST. ANDREW KIM (2001), (Korean), Rev. Park Chi Young, Admin.
Church: 8665 Olive Blvd., University City, 63132. Tel: 314-993-1277; Fax: 314-993-2031.

12—ST. ANGELA MERICI (1962) Revs. Thomas G. Keller; Antony Tekkoliekal, O.S.B.Silv.; Deacons Matthew E. Duban; Ronald S. Le Fors.
Res.: 14005 Davey Dr., Florissant, 63034. Tel: 314-838-6565; Fax: 314-838-6566.
School—(Grades K-8), 3860 N. Hwy. 67, Florissant, 63034. Tel: 314-831-8012. Lay Teachers 17; Students 256.

13—ST. ANN (1856) [CEM] Rev. William G. Kempf.
Res.: 7530 Natural Bridge Rd., Normandy, 63121. Tel: 314-385-5090; Fax: 314-385-6527.
School—(Grades K-8), 7532 Natural Bridge, Normandy, 63121. Tel: 314-381-0113; Fax: 314-381-1367. Mary Reichenbach, Prin. Lay Teachers 13; Students 196.
Catechesis/Religious Program—Teresa Robison-Mullins, D.R.E.

14—ST. ANN, MOTHER B.V.M., Closed. For inquiries regarding sacramental records, contact the Archdiocesan Archives, 20 Archbishop May Dr., Saint Louis, MO 63119.

15—ANNUNCIATION (1950) Rev. Mark A. Dolan.
Res.: 12 W. Glendale Rd., Webster Groves, 63119. Tel: 314-962-5955; Fax: 314-961-0643. Email: annunciationchurch@sbcglobal.net. Web: www.goannunciation.com.
School—(Grades K-8), 16 W. Glendale, Webster Groves, 63119. Tel: 314-961-7712; Fax: 314-961-2157. Mrs. Catherine Davis, Prin. Lay Teachers 15; Students 136.
Catechesis/Religious Program—Email: lanzafameb@charter.net. Students 130.

16—ST. ANSELM (1966) Revs. Gerard Garrigan, O.S.B.; R. Benedict Allin, O.S.B.; Deacons Steven H. Wohlert, Pastoral Assoc.; Charles Durban.
Res.: 530 S. Mason Rd., 63141. Tel: 314-878-2120; Fax: 314-878-2199. Email: parishoffice299@att.net. Web: www.stanselmstl.org.
Catechesis/Religious Program—Students 302.

17—ST. ANTHONY OF PADUA (1863) Revs. James A. Lause, O.F.M.; Richard Jeske, O.F.M.; Bro. Thomas Smith, O.F.M., Pastoral Assoc.; Lisa Sieve, Bookkeeper.
Res.: 3140 Meramec St., 63118. Tel: 314-353-7470; Fax: 314-655-0573.
Catechesis/Religious Program—Tel: 314-655-0552. Students 32.

18—ASCENSION (1923) Rev. Msgr. Dennis R. Stehly; Rev. Brian E. Hecktor; Deacons C. Frank Chauvin; Robert Keeney; John Marino. In Res., Rev. Matthew O'Toole.
Res.: 230 Santa Maria Dr., Chesterfield, 63005. Tel: 636-532-3304; Fax: 636-532-3518. Web: ascensionchesterfield.org.
Preschool—Ascension Early Childhood Center, 238 Santa Maria Dr., Chesterfield, 63005. Tel: 636-532-3375.
School—(Grades K-8), 238 Santa Maria Dr., Chesterfield, 63005. Tel: 636-532-1151; Fax: 636-532-6502. Mrs. Cathie Wayland, Prin. Lay Teachers 34; Students 464.
Catechesis/Religious Program—Tel: 636-532-1136. Students 636.

19—ASCENSION-ST. PAUL (1995) Closed. For inquiries for sacramental records contact the Archdiocesan Archives, 20 Archbishop May Dr., St. Louis, MO 63119.

20—ASSUMPTION (1839) [CEM] Revs. John M. Seper; John J. Ghio.
Res.: 4725 Mattis Rd., 63128. Tel: 314-487-7970; Fax: 314-892-5513. Web: www.assumptionstl.org.
School—(Grades K-8) Tel: 314-487-6520; Fax: 314-487-3598. Email: hastenc@assumptionstl.org. Lay Teachers 22; Students 330.
Catechesis/Religious Program—Tel: 314-487-7970, Ext. 1218. Evelyn Tucker, C.R.E. (Adult); Donna Koppy, C.R.E. (Children). Students 200.

21—ST. AUGUSTINE (1992) [JC], Consolidation of St. Barbara, St. Rose of Lima, St. Edward, St. Mark, and Notre Dame de Lourdes (Wellston). Rev. Msgr. Robert J. Gettinger.
1371 Hamilton Ave., 63112. Tel: 314-385-1934; Fax: 314-385-2949.
Catechesis/Religious Program—Students 214.

22—ST. BARBARA, Closed. For inquiries regarding sacramental records, contact the Archdiocesan Archives, 20 Archbishop May Dr., Saint Louis, MO 63119.

23—ST. BARTHOLOMEW (HAZELWOOD) (1959) Closed. For inquiries regarding sacramental records, contact the Archdiocesan Archives, 20 Archbishop May Dr., Saint Louis, MO 63119.

24—BASILICA OF ST. LOUIS, KING OF FRANCE (1770) Rev. Msgr. Jerome D. Billing; Rev. Richard J. Quirk.
Res.: 209 Walnut St., 63102. Tel: 314-231-3250; Fax: 314-231-4280.

25—ST. BERNADETTE (1947) Rev. Gary J. Faust; Deacon Michael Buckley.
Res.: 68 Sherman Rd., Lemay, 63125. Tel: 314-892-6882; Fax: 314-892-7716. Email: stbrect@mindspring.com.
Catechesis/Religious Program—Tel: 314-892-8379. Students 21.

26—ST. BLAISE (MARYLAND HEIGHTS) (1961) Closed. For inquiries regarding sacramental records, contact the Archdiocesan Archives, 20 Archbishop May Dr., Saint Louis, MO 63119.

27—BLESSED TERESA OF CALCUTTA (2005) Revs. Robert T. Rosebrough; Timothy R. Cook; Deacons Charles R. Davanzo; Ralph Hayes; Allen F. Love.
Mailing Address: 1050 Smith Ave., Ferguson, 63135. Tel: 314-524-0500; Fax: 314-524-0744.
School—150 N. Elizabeth, Ferguson, 63135. Tel: 314-522-3888; Fax: 314-595-9274. Jennifer Stursman, Prin.
Catechesis/Religious Program—Debbie Davisson, P.S.R. Dir. Students 45.

28—ST. BONIFACE (1859) Closed. For inquiries regarding sacramental records, contact the Archdiocesan Archives, 20 Archbishop May Dr., Saint Louis, MO 63119.

29—ST. BRIDGET OF ERIN (1853) Closed. For inquiries regarding sacramental records, contact the Archdiocesan Archives, 20 Archbishop May Dr., Saint Louis, MO 63119.

30—ST. CASIMIR (HATHAWAY MANOR), Closed. For inquiries regarding sacramental records, contact the Archdiocesan Archives, 20 Archbishop May Dr., Saint Louis, MO 63119.

31—ST. CATHERINE LABOURE (1953) Revs. James B. Cormack, C.M.; Ignatius M. Melito, C.M.; Deacon George Tichacek.
Res.: 9740 Sappington Rd., 63128. Tel: 314-843-3245; Fax: 314-843-3196. Web: www.sclparish.org.
School—(Grades K-8), 9750 Sappington Rd., 63128. Tel: 314-843-2819; Fax: 314-843-7687. Mrs. Peggy Visconti, Prin. Lay Teachers 27; Students 513.
Catechesis/Religious Program—Tel: 314-843-2996. Peggy Brinkmann, D.R.E. Students 243.

32—ST. CATHERINE OF ALEXANDRIA (RIVERVIEW GARDENS) (1921) Closed. For inquiries regarding sacramental records, contact the Archdiocesan Archives, 20 Archbishop May Dr., Saint Louis, MO 63119.

33—ST. CATHERINE OF SIENA (PAGEDALE) (1909) Closed. For inquiries regarding sacramental records, contact the Archdiocesan Archives, 20 Archbishop May Dr., Saint Louis, MO 63119.

34—ST. CECILIA (1906), (Hispanic), Revs. William F. Vatterott; Carlos R. Roman.
Res.: 5418 Louisiana Ave., 63111. Tel: 314-351-1318; Fax: 314-351-3372.
Church: Eiler & Alaska Ave., 63111.
School—(Grades K-8), 906 Eichelberger Ave., 63111. Tel: 314-353-2455; Fax: 314-353-2411. Jim Ford, Prin. Lay Teachers 12; Students 169.
Catechesis/Religious Program—Edgar Ramirez, D.R.E. Students 136.

35—CHRIST THE KING (1927) Rev. Timothy M. Foley; Deacon E. Ray Kiely. In Res., Rev. John Jay Hughes (Retired).
Res.: 7316 Balson Ave., University City, 63130. Tel: 314-721-8737; Fax: 314-721-8738.
School—(Grades PreK-8), 7324 Balson Ave., University City, 63130. Tel: 314-725-5855; Fax: 314-725-5981. Mrs. Susan E. Hooker, Prin. Lay Teachers 15; Students 211.

36—CHRIST, PRINCE OF PEACE (1971) Rev. Charles Barthel; Deacon Joseph M. Kennedy. In Res., Rev. Robert L. Corbett (Retired).
Res.: 415 Weidman Rd., Manchester, 63011. Tel: 636-391-1307; Fax: 636-391-1319. Email: nzoia@christprinceofpeace.com. Web: www.christprinceofpeace.com.
School—(Grades K-8), 417 Weidman Rd., Manchester, 63011. Tel: 636-394-6840; Fax: 636-394-3860. Email: ceinig@christprinceofpeace.com. Web: www.cpopschool.com. Mrs. Chris Einig, Prin. Lay Teachers 29; Students 367.
Catechesis/Religious Program—Tel: 636-391-1560. Email: caliperti@christprinceofpeace.com. Students 162.

37—ST. CHRISTOPHER (FLORISSANT) (1967) Closed. For inquiries regarding sacramental records, contact the Archdiocesan Archives, 20 Archbishop May Dr., Saint Louis, MO 63119.

38—CHURCH OF THE ANNUNZIATA (1929) Rev. Msgr. John J. Leykam; Rev. John A. Ditenhafer (Retired); Deacons Thomas J. Gottlieb; John B. Wainscott.
Res.: 9305 Clayton Rd., Ladue, 63124. Tel: 314-993-4422; Fax: 314-994-7877.
Catechesis/Religious Program—Students 135.

39—ST. CLARE OF ASSISI (1963) Rev. Msgr. Kevin G. Callahan; Revs. Timothy J. Henderson; Patrick J. Driscoll; Deacons Dennis K. Stovall; W. Alan Whitson.
Res.: 15642 Clayton Rd., Ellisville, 63011. Tel: 636-394-7307; Fax: 636-394-6264. Email: assisi@swbell.net. Web: saintclareofassisi.org.
School—(Grades K-8), 15668 Clayton Rd., Ellisville, 63011. Tel: 636-227-8654; Fax: 636-394-0359. Mrs.

Marie Sinnett, Prin. Lay Teachers 24; Students 438.
Catechesis/Religious Program—Tel: 636-394-4368; Fax: 636-591-0024. Mrs. Jerrie Coughlin, C.R.E. Students 342.

40—ST. CLEMENT (1952) Rev. Msgr. James E. Pieper; Revs. Nicholas J. Muenks; John J. O'Brien; Deacon Richard Vehige.
Res.: 1510 Bopp Rd., 63131. Tel: 314-965-0709; Fax: 314-965-1486. Email: saintclementrectory@yahoo.com.
School—(Grades K-8), 1508 Bopp Rd., 63131. Tel: 314-822-1903; Fax: 314-822-8371. Jean Grana, Prin. Lay Teachers 36; Students 328.
Catechesis/Religious Program— Mary Alice Helmsing, D.R.E. Students 160.

41—CORPUS CHRISTI (JENNINGS) (1915) Closed. For inquiries regarding sacramental records, contact the Archdiocesan Archives, 20 Archbishop May Dr., Saint Louis, MO 63119.

42—ST. CRONAN (1878) Rev. Gerald J. Kleba.
Res.: 1203 S. Boyle Ave., 63110. Tel: 314-289-9545; Fax: 314-256-9350.
Catechesis/Religious Program—Tel: 314-371-3200. Students 65.

43—CURE' OF ARS (1966) Rev. Msgr. Mark S. Rivituso; Deacons Patrick G. Monahan; Theodore J. Rodis.
Res.: 670 S. Laclede Station Rd., 63119. Tel: 314-962-5883; Fax: 314-968-3554.

44—ST. DISMAS (FLORISSANT) (1956) Closed. For inquiries regarding sacramental records, contact the Archdiocesan Archives, 20 Archbishop May Dr., Saint Louis, MO 63119.

45—ST. DOMINIC SAVIO (1956) Rev. John S. Siefert; Deacons James L. Murphy; John W. Beckmann. In Res., Rev. Michael J. Lydon.
Res.: 6120 Pebble Hill Dr., Affton, 63123. Tel: 314-353-7629; Fax: 314-481-2908.
Church: 7748 MacKenzie Rd., Affton, 63123.
School—(Grades PreK-8) Tel: 314-832-4161; Fax: 314-352-6331. Kathy Wisemann, Prin. Lay Teachers 16; Students 326.
Catechesis/Religious Program—Students 81.

46—ST. EDWARD (1893) Closed. For inquiries regarding sacramental records, contact the Archdiocesan Archives, 20 Archbishop May Dr., Saint Louis, MO 63119.

47—ST. ELIZABETH OF HUNGARY (1956) Rev. Gregory Lockwood, Admin.; Deacons Robert Snyder; William G. Meister. In Res., Rev. John P. Comer (Retired).
Res.: 1420 S. Sappington Rd., Crestwood, 63126. Tel: 314-968-0760; Fax: 314-968-8023.
Catechesis/Religious Program—Tel: 314-963-8868. Students 54.
Convent—1406 S. Sappington Rd., Crestwood, 63126. Tel: 314-961-2630.

48—ST. ELIZABETH, MOTHER OF JOHN THE BAPTIST (1891), (African American), Rev. Jeffrey G. Vomund; Deacon Charles M. Allen. In Res., Rev. Arthur J. Cavitt, O.P.
Res.: 4330 Shreve Ave., 63115. Tel: 314-381-4145; Fax: 314-381-2212.
School—*St. Louis Catholic Academy*, 4720 Carter Ave., 63115. Tel: 314-389-0401; Fax: 314-389-7042. Mr. Mere Smith, Prin. Religious 1; Lay Teachers 12; Students 200.

49—EPIPHANY OF OUR LORD (1911) Rev. Thomas C. Miller; Deacon James E. Tetreault.
Res.: 6596 Smiley Ave., 63139. Tel: 314-781-1199; Fax: 314-645-8760. Web: epiphanyarchstl.org.
School—Tel: 314-781-5626; Fax: 314-645-7166. Sharon Morgenthaler, Prin. Lay Teachers 13; Students 125.
Catechesis/Religious Program—Students 6.
Convent—6580 Smiley Ave., 63139. Tel: 314-647-3610.

50—ST. FERDINAND (1788) Rev. Msgr. A. John Schuler; Revs. William J. Baier; Joseph S. Post; Deacons Joseph C. Kroutil; Peter E. Gounis.
Res.: 1765 Charbonier Rd., Florissant, 63031. Tel: 314-837-3165; Fax: 314-837-5799. Email: stferd@juno.com. Web: stferdinand.org.
School—(Grades K-8), 1735 Charbonier Rd., Florissant, 63031. Tel: 314-921-2201; Fax: 314-921-2253. Ursuline Sisters of the Roman Union 1; Lay Teachers 15; Students 289.
Catechesis/Religious Program—Tel: 314-831-2919. Students 131.

51—ST. FRANCES XAVIER CABRINI (JENNINGS) (1965) Closed. For inquiries regarding sacramental records, contact the Archdiocesan Archives, 20 Archbishop May Dr., Saint Louis, MO 63119.

52—ST. FRANCIS OF ASSISI (1927) Very Rev. Gary M. Gebelein; Rev. Christopher J. Dunlap; Deacons George R. Fink; William Sinak; Alan Ecker.
Res.: 4556 Telegraph Rd., 63129. Tel: 314-487-5736; Fax: 314-487-3701. Email: sfaparish@sbcglobal.net. Web: sfastl.org.
School—(Grades K-8), 4550 Telegraph Rd., 63129. Fax: 314-416-7118. Email: sfaschool@sbcglobal.net. Web: sfaschool-stlouis.org. Mr. Gregory Sturgill, Prin. Lay Teachers 21; Students 375.
Catechesis/Religious Program—Tel: 314-487-5736, Ext. 125. Students 187.

53—ST. FRANCIS XAVIER (1841), (College) Revs. Richard O. Buhler, S.J.; James J. Costello, S.J.
3628 Lindell Blvd., 63108. Tel: 314-977-7300; Fax: 314-977-7315. Email: church@slu.edu.
Catechesis/Religious Program—Tel: 314-977-7302. Students 150.

54—ST. GABRIEL THE ARCHANGEL (1934) Revs. Robert J. Samson; Bernard J. Schloemer (Retired); Deacons James Volansky; David J. Willis.
Res.: 6303 Nottingham Ave., 63109. Tel: 314-353-6303; Fax: 314-353-7704.
School—4711 Tamm Ave., 63109. Tel: 314-353-1229; Fax: 314-353-6737. Lay Teachers 39; Students 520.
Catechesis/Religious Program—Students 835.

55—ST. GEORGE (1915) Rev. Thomas M. Robertson; Deacons Roy E. Schulze; Robert Penberthy.
Res.: 4980 Heege Rd., 63123. Tel: 314-352-3544; Fax: 314-832-6916.
School—Consolidated with St. Dominic Savio, St. Louis, MO.

56—ST. GERARD MAJELLA (1955) Very Rev. Thomas M. Molini; Rev. Thomas C. Bryon; Deacons Timothy Dolan; Donald Denham; Leslie Walrath, Pastoral Assoc.
Res.: 1969 Dougherty Ferry Rd., Kirkwood, 63122. Tel: 314-965-3985; Fax: 314-965-7650.
School—(Grades K-8), 2005 Dougherty Ferry Rd., Kirkwood, 63122. Tel: 314-822-8844; Fax: 314-822-8588. Dr. Jane Koberlein, Prin. Lay Teachers 28; Students 348.
Catechesis/Religious Program—Students 274.

57—GOOD SHEPHERD (FERGUSON) (1958) Closed. For inquiries regarding sacramental records, contact the Archdiocesan Archives, 20 Archbishop May Dr., Saint Louis, MO 63119.

58—ST. GREGORY (ST. ANN) (1942) Closed. For inquiries regarding sacramental records, contact the Archdiocesan Archives, 20 Archbishop May Dr., Saint Louis, MO 63119.

59—SAINT GREGORY THE GREAT AND SAINT AUGUSTINE OF CANTERBURY ORATORY (2007) Rev. Bede Price, O.S.B.
530 S. Mason Rd., Creve Coeur, 63141.
Catechesis/Religious Program—Marilyn Lonigro, D.R.E. Students 36.

60—ST. HEDWIG (1904) Closed. For inquiries regarding sacramental records, contact the Archdiocesan Archives, 20 Archbishop May Dr., Saint Louis, MO 63119.

61—HOLY ANGELS (KINLOCH) (1931), (African American), Closed. For inquiries regarding sacramental records, contact the Archdiocesan Archives, 20 Archbishop May Dr., Saint Louis, MO 63119.

62—HOLY FAMILY (1898) Closed. For inquiries regarding sacramental records, contact the Archdiocesan Archives, 20 Archbishop May Dr., Saint Louis, MO 63119.

63—HOLY GHOST (BERKELEY) (1923) Closed. For inquiries regarding sacramental records, contact the Archdiocesan Archives, 20 Archbishop May Dr., Saint Louis, MO 63119.

64—HOLY GUARDIAN ANGELS (1866) Closed. For inquiries regarding sacramental records, contact the Archdiocesan Archives, 20 Archbishop May Dr., Saint Louis, MO 63119.

65—HOLY INFANT (1954) Rev. Msgr. Thomas J. Dempsey; Revs. Mark S. Ebert; Timothy L. Bannes; Deacons Kenneth C. Clemens Jr.; William J. Krull.
Res.: 627 Dennison Dr., Ballwin, 63021. Tel: 636-227-7440; Fax: 636-227-4548. Email: rectoryoffice@holyinfantballwin.org. Web: www.holyinfantballwin.org.
School—(Grades K-8) Tel: 636-227-0802; Fax: 636-227-9184. Email: schooloffice@holyinfantschool.org. Web: www.holyinfantschool.org. Sr. Rosario Delaney, R.S.M., Prin. Sisters of Mercy (Meath Mercy Generalate, Ireland) 2; Lay Teachers 41; Students 760.
Catechesis/Religious Program—Email: psroffice@holyinfantballwin.org. Students 550.
Convent—239 Nancy Pl., Ballwin, 63021. Tel: 636-391-1528.

66—HOLY INNOCENTS (1893) Closed. For inquiries regarding sacramental records, contact the Archdiocesan Archives, 20 Archbishop May Dr., Saint Louis, MO 63119.

67—HOLY NAME OF JESUS (2005) Rev. Michael L. Henning; Deacon George Watson.
Mailing Address: 10235 Ashbrook Dr., 63137. Tel: 314-868-2310; Fax: 314-868-3919. Email: parishoffice10235@sbcglobal.net. Web: www.archstl.org/parishes/502.shtml.
School—*Christ, Light of the Nations*, (Grades PreK-8) Tel: 314-741-0400; Fax: 314-653-2531. Email: sr_mary@christlightofthenations.com. Web: www.christlightofthenations.com.
Catechesis/Religious Program—Students 267.

68—HOLY REDEEMER (1886) Rev. Michael G. Murphy; Deacons John P. Flanigan Jr.; Leonard Sisul. In Res., Rev. Eugene R. Sinz (Retired); Rev. Msgr. Edward M. Rice.
Res.: 17 Joy Ave., Webster Groves, 63119. Tel: 314-962-0038; Fax: 314-962-2084. Web: www.holyr.org.
School—(Grades K-8), 341 E. Lockwood, Webster Groves, 63119. Tel: 314-962-8989; Fax: 314-962-3560. Wayne Schiefelbein, Prin. Lay Teachers 16; Students 239.
Catechesis/Religious Program—Tel: 314-962-2043. Email: cre@holyr.org. Patricia Maloney, C.R.E. Students 170.

69—HOLY SPIRIT (2004), St. Blaise closed and merged with St. Lawrence, and formed Holy Spirit. Revs. Richard J. Bockskopf; Matthew D. Barnard; Deacons Jacob W. Dorhauer; Eugene Naumann; Charles Georges.
Res.: 3130 Parkwood Ln., Maryland Heights, 63043. Tel: 314-739-0230; Fax: 314-739-0237. Web: www.holyspiritstl.org.
School—(Grades K-8) Tel: 314-739-1934; Fax: 314-739-7703. Sisters 1; Lay Teachers 15; Students 167.
Catechesis/Religious Program— Ree Gerdes, D.R.E. Students 237.

70—HOLY TRINITY (2002) Revs. Paul J. Niemann; Michael J. Houser; Deacons William F. Priesmeyer; David Bolderson; Kevin Carroll.
Res.: 3500 St. Luke Ln., St. Ann, 63074. Tel: 314-733-1463; Fax: 314-395-1326.
School—(Grades K-8), 10901 St. Henry Ln., St. Ann, 63074. Tel: 314-426-8966; Fax: 314-428-7084. Margaret Ahle, Prin. Students 209.
Catechesis/Religious Program—Students 360.

71—IMMACOLATA (1945) Rev. Msgr. Walter M. Whited; Deacons Joseph LaMartina; David Osmack. In Res., Rev. Msgr. Vernon E. Gardin.
Church: 8900 Clayton Rd., Richmond Heights, 63117. Tel: 314-991-5700; Fax: 314-991-5700.
School—(Grades K-8), 8910 Clayton Rd., Richmond Heights, 63117. Tel: 314-991-5700, Ext. 302; Fax: 314-991-9354. Web: www.immacolata.org. Mr. Salvatore Latragna, Prin. Lay Teachers 22; Students 266.
Catechesis/Religious Program—Tel: 314-991-5700, Ext. 303. Students 85.

72—IMMACULATE CONCEPTION (1904) [JC] Rev. James C. Gray; Deacons Clyde McEntire; Lawrence L. Clark.
Res.: 2934 Marshall Ave., Maplewood, 63143. Tel: 314-645-3307; Fax: 314-645-0672. Email: icmplwd@sbcglobal.net.
Catechesis/Religious Program—Tel: 314-644-6787. Students 50.

73—IMMACULATE CONCEPTION-ST. HENRY (1865) Closed. For inquiries regarding sacramental records, contact the Archdiocesan Archives, 20 Archbishop May Dr., Saint Louis, MO 63119.

74—IMMACULATE HEART OF MARY (1951) Revs. Edward F. Ramatowski, Admin.; Brad Modde.
Res.: 4092 Blow St., 63116. Tel: 314-481-7543; Fax: 314-481-6316.
School—(Grades PreK-8), 4070 Blow St., 63116. Tel: 314-832-1678; Fax: 314-832-1627. Web: www.ihm4070.org. Mr. Richard Danzeisen, Prin. Lay Teachers 20; Students 253.

75—INCARNATE WORD (1965) Revs. G. Timothy Vowels; Gerald T. Nienhaus; James M. Sullivan, Senior Assoc.; Deacons James Russell; Larry Stallings.
Res.: 13416 Olive Blvd., Chesterfield, 63017. Tel: 314-576-5366; Fax: 314-576-2046. Web: www.incarnate-word.org.
School—(Grades K-8) Tel: 314-576-5366, Ext. 11. C. Michael Welling, Prin. Lay Teachers 23; Students 460.
Catechesis/Religious Program—Tel: 314-576-5366, Ext. 26. John Valenti, D.R.E. Students 325.

76—ST. JAMES THE GREATER (1860), (Irish), Rev. John J. Johnson.
Res.: 6401 Wade Ave., 63139. Tel: 314-645-0167; Fax: 314-645-0168.
School—(Grades K-8), 1360 Tamm Ave., 63139. Tel: 314-647-5244; Fax: 314-647-8237. Ms. Karen Battaglia, Prin. Lay Teachers 14; Students 135.
Catechesis/Religious Program—Students 151.

77—ST. JEROME (BISSELL HILLS) (1952) Closed. For inquiries regarding sacramental records, contact the Archdiocesan Archives, 20 Archbishop May Dr., Saint Louis, MO 63119.

78—ST. JOAN OF ARC (1941) Rev. Msgr. Michael E. Turek; Rev. Nicholas W. Smith; Deacon Daniel H. Henroid. In Res., Rev. Theodore J. Brunnert (Retired).
Res.: 5800 Oleatha St., 63139. Tel: 314-832-2838; Fax: 314-352-9350.
School—Tel: 314-752-4171; Fax: 314-351-8562. Mrs. Debra Dalay, Prin. Lay Teachers 13; Students 220.

79—STS. JOHN AND JAMES (FERGUSON) (1882) Closed. For inquiries regarding sacramental records, contact the Archdiocesan Archives, 20 Archbishop May Dr., Saint Louis, MO 63119.

80—ST. JOHN BOSCO (1972) Rev. Gerard R. Welsch.
Res.: 12934 Marine Ave., Maryland Heights, 63146. Tel: 314-434-1312; Fax: 314-514-0478.
Catechesis/Religious Program—Tel: 314-878-6492. Students 126.

81—ST. JOHN NEPOMUK CHAPEL (1854) Rev. Paul J. Spielman.
Res.: 1625 S. 11th St., 63104. Tel: 314-231-0141; Fax: 314-231-0141.

82—ST. JOHN THE APOSTLE AND EVANGELIST (1847) Rev. Msgr. Dennis M. Delaney.
Res.: 15 Plaza Sq., 63103. Tel: 314-421-3467; Fax: 314-588-9544.
Catechesis/Religious Program—Students 3.

83—ST. JOHN THE BAPTIST (1914) Revs. Richard J. Rath; Leo J. Spezia.
4200 Delor St., 63116. Tel: 314-353-1255; Fax: 314-752-3154. Email: sjb4200@sbcglobal.net.
School—5021 Adkins, 63116. Tel: 314-481-6654; Fax: 314-481-3179. Religious Sisters 4; Lay Teachers 17; Students 275.
Catechesis/Religious Program—4170 Delor, 63116. Tel: 314-773-3070; Fax: 314-773-3070. Students 120.

84—ST. JOSEPH (1904), (Croatian), Rev. Joseph M. Abramovic, O.F.M.
Res.: 2112 S. 12th St., 63104. Tel: 314-771-0958; Fax: 314-771-0958.
Catechesis/Religious Program—Students 39.

85—ST. JOSEPH (1865) [CEM] Revs. Thomas J. Santen; Binu E. Kuriachen, M.S.F.S.; Robert J. Menner.
Res.: 567 St. Joseph Ln., Manchester, 63021. Tel: 636-227-5247; Fax: 636-391-8393. Email: info@stjoemanchester.org. Web: stjoemanchester.org.
School—(Grades PreK-8), 555 St. Joseph Ln., Manchester, 63021. Tel: 636-391-1253; Fax: 636-391-1462. Jeannie Dandino, Prin. Lay Teachers 29; Students 383.
Catechesis/Religious Program—Tel: 636-391-1404. Students 495.

86—ST. JOSEPH (1842) Rev. Msgr. John B. Shamleffer; Rev. Thomas J. Schaab, Senior Assoc.; Deacons Albert Williams; Delfin S. Leonardo.
Res.: 106 N. Meramec Ave., Clayton, 63105. Tel: 314-726-1221; Fax: 314-721-5110. Email: pat_stj@hotmail.com. Web: www.stjosephclayton.org.
Catechesis/Religious Program—Tel: 314-727-9059; Fax: 314-727-2271. Mrs. Terri Venneman, D.R.E. Students 193.

87—ST. JUDE (1953) Rev. Joseph L. Parisi.
Res.: 2218 N. Warson Rd., Overland, 63114. Tel: 314-428-2262; Fax: 314-890-2257.
Catechesis/Religious Program—Students 21.

88—ST. JUSTIN MARTYR (1964) Revs. Joseph A. Weber; John L. Mayer, Senior Assoc.; Deacon Christian H. Winkelmann.
Res.: 11910 Eddie and Park Rd., Sunset Hills, 63126. Tel: 314-843-8482; Fax: 314-843-8507.
School—(Grades K-8), 11914 Eddie and Park Rd., 63126. Tel: 314-843-6447; Fax: 314-843-9257. Mrs. Beth Bartolotta, Prin. Lay Teachers 16; Students 194.
Catechesis/Religious Program—Tel: 314-843-8482, Ext. 3. Elizabeth D. Balbo-Ryan, D.R.E. Students 90.

89—ST. KEVIN (ST. ANN) (1953), (Irish), Closed. For inquiries regarding sacramental records, contact the Archdiocesan Archives, 20 Archbishop May Dr., Saint Louis, MO 63119.

90—ST. LAWRENCE THE MARTYR (BRIDGETON) (1960) Closed. For inquiries regarding sacramental records, contact the Archdiocesan Archives, 20 Archbishop May Dr., Saint Louis, MO 63119.

91—ST. LIBORIUS (1856) Closed. For inquiries regarding sacramental records, contact the Archdiocesan Archives, 20 Archbishop May Dr., Saint Louis, MO 63119.

92—LITTLE FLOWER (1925) Rev. Lawrence A. Herzog; Deacon William G. Weiss.
1264 Arch Terrace, Richmond Heights, 63117. Email: littleflower@little-flower-parish.org. Web: www.little-flower-parish.org.
School—(Grades PreK-8), 1275 Boland Pl., Richmond Heights, 63117. Tel: 314-781-4995; Fax: 314-781-9177. Robert Baird, Prin. Lay Teachers 15; Students 176.

93—ST. LOUISE DE MARILLAC (JENNINGS) (1935) Closed. For inquiries regarding sacramental records, contact the Archdiocesan Archives, 20 Archbishop May Dr., Saint Louis, MO 63119.

94—ST. LUCY (JENNINGS) (1957) Closed. For inquiries regarding sacramental records, contact the Archdiocesan Archives, 20 Archbishop May Dr., Saint Louis, MO. 63119.

95—ST. LUKE THE EVANGELIST (1914) Rev. Msgr. William W. McCumber.
Res.: 7230 Dale Ave., 63117. Tel: 314-644-2144; Fax: 314-644-4624.

96—ST. MARGARET MARY ALACOQUE (1962) Rev. Msgrs. Norbert A. Ernst; Joseph F. Classen; Rev. William Leach; Deacons Andrew Daus; Robert Orr.
4900 Ringer Rd., 63129. Fax: 314-487-4475. Web: www.smmaparish.org.
Res.: 5056 Faust Ct., 63129. Tel: 314-487-2522.
School—(Grades K-8) Tel: 314-487-1666. Lay Teachers 35; Students 544.
Catechesis/Religious Program—Students 250.

97—ST. MARGARET OF SCOTLAND (1899) Rev. Thomas W. Wyrsch.
Res.: 3854 Flad Ave., 63110. Tel: 314-776-0363; Fax: 314-776-0364. Web: www.stmargaretstl.org.
School—(Grades PreK-8), 3964 Castleman, 63110. Tel: 314-776-7837; Fax: 314-776-7955. Web: smos-school.org. Lay Teachers 23; Students 274.

98—ST. MARK (2003) Rev. Msgr. Patrick K. Hambrough; Rev. Thomas M. Pastorius.
8300 Morganford Rd., 63123. Tel: 314-743-8600; Fax: 314-743-8619. Web: www.stmarkstl.com. In Res., Rev. Msgr. Charles Forst (Retired).
Rectory—4230 Ripa Ave., 63125. Tel: 314-743-8620.
School—4220 Ripa Ave., 63125. Tel: 314-743-8640; Fax: 314-743-8690. Students 210.
Catechesis/Religious Program—Students 320.

99—ST. MARK, EVANGELIST (PAGE & ACADEMY) (1893) Closed. For inquiries regarding sacramental records, contact the Archdiocesan Archives, 20 Archbishop May Dr., Saint Louis, MO 63119.

100—ST. MARTIN DE PORRES (1962) Revs. Ferdinand J. Wesloh; Robert L. Szydlowski, Senior Assoc.; Deacon David Pacino.
Res.: 615 Dunn Rd., Hazelwood, 63042-1799. Tel: 314-895-1100; Fax: 314-895-5992.
Knobbe House—627 Undercliff, Hazelwood, 63042.
Catechesis/Religious Program—Students 94.

101—ST. MARTIN OF TOURS (1939) Rev. Charles F. Ferrara; Deacons Edward Fronick; Phillip Warren. In Res., Rev. Msgr. James J. Ramacciotti.
Res.: 610 W. Ripa Ave., Lemay, 63125. Tel: 314-544-5664; Fax: 314-631-3118.
Catechesis/Religious Program—Students 25.

102—ST. MARY (BRIDGETON) (1852) Closed. For inquiries regarding sacramental records, contact the Archdiocesan Archives, 20 Archbishop May Dr., Saint Louis, MO 63119.

103—STS. MARY AND JOSEPH CHAPEL (1821) Rev. Ronald J. Hopmeir, Chap.
Res.: 6304 Minnesota Ave., 63111. Tel: 314-481-6304; Fax: 314-481-6337.
Catechesis/Religious Program—Students 2.

104—ST. MARY MAGDALEN (1919) Rev. Msgr. John J. Borcic; Rev. Edward R. Goldian, S.J.; Deacon Joseph Iovanna.
Res.: 4924 Bancroft Ave., 63109. Tel: 314-352-2111; Fax: 314-481-7661.
School—St. Katharine Drexel, (Grades K-8) Tel: 314-353-1451; Fax: 314-351-8464.
Catechesis/Religious Program—Southside Regional Parish School of Religion, 4170 Delor, 63116. Tel: 314-773-3070. Students 70.

105—ST. MARY MAGDALEN (1912) Rev. Msgr. C. Eugene Morris; Deacons Leroy Martin; Edward Grotpeter.
Res.: 2618 Brentwood Blvd., Brentwood, 63144. Tel: 314-961-8400; Fax: 314-961-7019.
School—8762 Magdalen Ave., Brentwood, 63144. Tel: 314-961-0149; Fax: 314-961-7208. Email: smmsch@stmmlab.com. Web: stmmlab.com. Marlise Albert, Prin. Lay Teachers 16; Students 157.
Catechesis/Religious Program—Students 100.

106—ST. MARY OF VICTORIES (1843), (Hungarian), Rev. Paul J. Spielman.
Res.: 744 S. 3rd St., 63102. Tel: 314-231-8101.

107—MARY, MOTHER OF THE CHURCH (1971) Rev. Msgr. James T. Telthorst; Rev. James J. Byrnes; Deacons Richard Coffman; Richard Bub.
Res.: 5901 Kerth Rd., 63128. Tel: 314-894-1373; Fax: 314-894-3801.
Catechesis/Religious Program— Ed Lewandowski, D.R.E. Students 288.

108—MARY, QUEEN OF PEACE (1922) Very Rev. Gerald A. Meier; Rev. Msgr. Richard J. Lubeley, Senior Priest (Retired).
Res.: 676 W. Lockwood Blvd., Webster Groves, 63119. Tel: 314-962-2311; Fax: 314-968-9885.
School—(Grades K-8), 680 W. Lockwood Ave., Webster Groves, 63119. Tel: 314-961-2891; Fax: 314-961-7469. Dr. Jerry Kettenbach, Prin. Lay Teachers 34; Students 586.
Catechesis/Religious Program— Sr. Charlotte Flarlong, D.R.E. Students 89.

109—MARY, QUEEN OF THE UNIVERSE (1955) Closed. For inquiries regarding sacramental records, contact the Archdiocesan Archives, 20 Archbishop May Dr., Saint Louis, MO 63119.

110—ST. MATTHEW, APOSTLE (1893), (African American), [CEM] Rev. Mark D. McKenzie, S.J. In Res., Revs. Jeffrey D. Harrison, S.J.; William J. Hutchison, S.J.
Res.: 2715 N. Sarah St., 63113. Tel: 314-531-6443; Fax: 314-533-7318. Email: stmatthews@sbcglobal.net. Web: www.st-matthew-church.org.
Catechesis/Religious Program—Students 43.

111—ST. MATTHIAS (1959) Rev. Dennis R. Port; Deacon Joseph Hercules.
Res.: 796 Buckley Rd., 63125. Tel: 314-892-5109; Fax: 314-892-0629. Email: st.matthias@sbcglobal.net.
Catechesis/Religious Program—Students 84.

112—ST. MICHAEL (1895) Rev. Dennis J. Doyle.
Res.: 7622 Sutherland Ave., Shrewsbury, 63119. Tel: 314-647-5611; Fax: 314-781-9211. Email: stmikeshrewsbury@sbcglobal.net. Web: www.stmike.org.
School—(Grades K-8), 7630 Sutherland Ave., 63119. Tel: 314-647-7159; Fax: 314-644-1433. Lay Teachers 12; Students 131.
Catechesis/Religious Program—Students 67.

113—ST. MONICA (1872) [CEM] Rev. Msgr. Dennis E. Doerhoff; Rev. Michael L. Donald, Senior Assoc.; Deacons Robert Birkenmaier; Millard R. Miller; James P. Martin.
Res.: 12136 Olive Blvd., Creve Coeur, 63141-6629. Tel: 314-434-4211; Fax: 314-434-5978.
School—(Grades K-8), 12132 Olive Blvd., Creve Coeur, 63141-6698. Tel: 314-434-2173; Fax: 314-434-7689. Mrs. Kathy Hunt, Prin. Lay Teachers 25; Students 285.
Catechesis/Religious Program—Tel: 314-205-9276. Email: mdoerr@stmonicastl.org. Students 85.

114—MOST BLESSED SACRAMENT (1907) Closed. For inquiries regarding sacramental records, contact the Archdiocesan Archives, 20 Archbishop May Dr., Saint Louis, MO 63119.

115—MOST HOLY NAME OF JESUS (EAST GRAND) (1875) Closed. For inquiries regarding sacramental records, contact the Archdiocesan Archives, 20 Archbishop May Dr., Saint Louis, MO 63119.

116—MOST HOLY ROSARY (1891) Closed. For inquiries regarding sacramental records, contact the Archdiocesan Archives, 20 Archbishop May Dr., Saint Louis, MO 63119.

117—MOST HOLY TRINITY (1848) Rev. Richard H. Creason; Sr. Janice Munier, S.S.N.D., Pastoral Assoc.
Res.: 3519 N. Fourteenth St., 63107-3796. Tel: 314-241-9165; Fax: 314-436-9291.
School—(Grades K-8), 1435 Mallinckrodt St., 63107-3796. Tel: 314-231-9014; Fax: 314-436-9291. Carol Werner, Prin. Lay Teachers 6; Students 104.
Catechesis/Religious Program—Students 80.
Convent—Tel: 314-621-6835.

118—MOST PRECIOUS BLOOD (LEMAY) (1961) Closed. For inquiries regarding sacramental records, contact the Archdiocesan Archives, 20 Archbishop May Dr., Saint Louis, MO 63119.

119—ST. NICHOLAS (1865) Rev. Urey P. Mark, S.V.D.; Deacon Stanley Peterson. In Res., Bro. Larry Camilleri, S.V.D.
Res.: 701 N. 18th St., 63103. Tel: 314-231-2860; Fax: 314-241-9823. Email: stnickcatholic@yahoo.com. Web: snrcc.org.
School—Central Catholic/St. Nicholas School, (Grades PreK-8), 1805 Lucas St., 63103. Tel: 314-421-1822. Lay Teachers 40; Students 300.
Catechesis/Religious Program—Students 9.

120—ST. NORBERT (1965) Revs. James M. Mitulski; Eric F. Olsen; Deacon William H. Twellman. In Res., Rev. Msgr. Richard A. Buchheit (Retired).
Res.: 16455 New Halls Ferry Rd., Florissant, 63031. Tel: 314-831-3874; Fax: 314-830-3586. Email: secretary@saintnorbert.com. Web: www.saintnorbert.com.
School—(Grades K-8), 16475 New Halls Ferry Rd., Florissant, 63031. Tel: 314-839-0948; Fax: 314-839-3053. Email: stnlabl@stnorbert.com. Mrs. Pam Gilbert, Prin. Lay Teachers 25; Students 342.
Catechesis/Religious Program—Web: home.catholicweb.com/stnpsr. Students 82.

121—NORTH AMERICAN MARTYRS (FLORISSANT) (1955) Closed. For inquiries regarding sacramental records, contact the Archdiocesan Archives, 20 Archbishop May Dr., Saint Louis, MO 63119.

122—NOTRE DAME DE LOURDES (WELLSTON) (1902) Closed. For inquiries regarding sacramental records, contact the Archdiocesan Archives, 20 Archbishop May Dr., Saint Louis, MO 63119.

123—ORATORY OF ST. FRANCIS DE SALES (2005), (Roman Missal of 1962) Revs. Michael K. Wiener, Rector; Jason Apple. Administered by the Institute of Christ the King Sovereign Priest Extraordinary form of the Roman Rite.
Res.: 2653 Ohio Ave., 63118. Tel: 314-771-3100; Fax: 314-771-3295. Email: sfds@institute-christ-king.org. Web: www.institute-christ-king.org.

124—OUR LADY OF FATIMA (FLORISSANT) (1950) Closed. For inquiries regarding sacramental records, contact the Archdiocesan Archives, 20 Archbishop

May Dr., Saint Louis, MO 63119.

125—OUR LADY OF GOOD COUNSEL (BELLEFONTAINE NEIGHBORS) (1951) Closed. For inquiries regarding sacramental records, contact the Archdiocesan Archives, 20 Archbishop May Dr., Saint Louis, MO 63119.

126—OUR LADY OF GUADALUPE (1954), (Hispanic), Revs. John Paul Hopping, Admin.; Dick Vogt, S.J.; Sr. Cathy Doherty, S.S.N.D., Pastoral Assoc.
Res.: 17 Hawkesbury Dr., 63121. Tel: 314-522-9264; Fax: 314-522-8461.
School—(Grades K-8), 1115 S. Florissant Rd., Ferguson, 63121. Tel: 314-524-1948. Peggy O'Brien, Prin. Lay Teachers 10; Students 175.
Catechesis/Religious Program—Students 52.

127—OUR LADY OF LORETTO (SPANISH LAKE) (1959) Closed. For inquiries regarding sacramental records, contact the Archdiocesan Archives, 20 Archbishop May Dr., Saint Louis, MO 63119.

128—OUR LADY OF LOURDES (1916) Rev. Msgrs. Edward J. Sudekum; Norbert J. Dietz (Retired); Deacon Albert X. Vaughn. In Res., Rev. Nicholas E. Kastenholz.
Res.: 7148 Forsyth Blvd., University City, 63105. Tel: 314-726-6200; 314-726-6201; Fax: 314-726-1602. Email: rectory@ucitylourdes.org. Web: www.ucitylourdes.org.
School—(Grades K-8), 7157 Northmoor Dr., University City, 63105. Tel: 314-726-3352; Fax: 314-726-0503. Lay Teachers 24; Students 258.

129—OUR LADY OF MERCY (HAZELWOOD) (1964) Closed. For inquiries regarding sacramental records, contact the Archdiocesan Archives, 20 Archbishop May Dr., Saint Louis, MO 63119.

130—OUR LADY OF MOUNT CARMEL (1872) Closed. For inquiries regarding sacramental records, contact the Archdiocesan Archives, 20 Archbishop May Dr., Saint Louis, MO 63119.

131—OUR LADY OF PERPETUAL HELP (1873) Closed. For inquiries regarding sacramental records, contact the Archdiocesan Archives, 20 Archbishop May Dr., Saint Louis, MO 63119.

132—OUR LADY OF PROVIDENCE (1954) Rev. David E. Rauch; Deacon David Amelotti. In Res., Rev. Msgr. Francis X. Blood.
Res.: 8866 Pardee Rd., 63123. Tel: 314-843-3570; Fax: 314-843-8033. Email: ladyprov@charter.net. Web: www.olpstl.com.
School—(Grades K-8), 8874 Pardee Rd., 63123. Tel: 314-842-2073; Fax: 314-842-2406. Ms. Clare Ortmeier, Prin. Lay Teachers 14; Students 149.
Catechesis/Religious Program—Students 54.

133—OUR LADY OF SORROWS (1907) Rev. Peter M. Blake; Deacons Robert Wertz; Ed Auer; Daniel Skillman. In Res., Rev. Joy Thachil, S.A.C.
Res.: 5020 Rhodes Ave., 63109. Tel: 314-351-1600; Fax: 314-351-1602. Email: olsorrows@sbcglobal.net. Web: www.olsorrows.org.
School—*St. Katharine Drexel*, 5831 S. Kingshighway Blvd., 63109. Tel: 314-353-1451; Fax: 314-351-8464. Lay Teachers 30; Students 242.
Catechesis/Religious Program—Students 242.

134—OUR LADY OF THE HOLY CROSS (1864) Rev. Donald L. Buhr; Deacons Donald Driscoll; J. Gerard Quinn.
Res.: 8115 Church Rd., 63147. Tel: 314-381-0323; Fax: 314-381-4828.

135—OUR LADY OF THE PILLAR (1938) Revs. James M. Tobin, S.M.; William R. Wightman, S.M.; Gerald R. Hammel, S.M.; Deacon James R. Powers.
Res.: 401 S. Lindbergh Blvd., 63131. Tel: 314-993-2280; Fax: 314-993-6462.
School—(Grades K-8), 403 S. Lindbergh Blvd., 63131. Tel: 314-993-3353; Fax: 314-993-2172. Franciscan Sisters of Our Lady of Perpetual Help 1; Lay Teachers 22; Students 172.
Catechesis/Religious Program—Students 105.

136—OUR LADY OF THE PRESENTATION (1915) Rev. Robert T. Evans.
Res.: 8860 Tudor Ave., Overland, 63114. Tel: 314-427-0486; Fax: 314-423-3020.

137—OUR LADY OF THE ROSARY (2005) Rev. Thomas Haley.
Mailing Address: 11725 Bellefontaine Rd., 63138. Tel: 314-741-7700; Fax: 314-653-0910. Email: shartig@sbcglobal.net. Web: www.archstl.org.
School—*Christ Light of the Nations*, 1650 Redman Rd., 63138. Tel: 314-741-0400; Fax: 314-653-2531. Email: st_mary@christlightofthenations.com. Web: www.christlightofthenations.com. Sr. Mary Lawrence, S.S.N.D., Prin. Lay Teachers 15; Students 209.
Catechesis/Religious Program—Sr. Nancy Becker, S.S.N.D., D.R.E.

138—ST. PATRICK (1981) Closed. For inquiries for parish records contact the chancery.

139—ST. PATRICK (UNIVERSITY CITY) (1940) Closed. For inquiries regarding sacramental records, contact the Archdiocesan Archives, 20 Archbishop May Dr., Saint Louis, MO 63119.

140—ST. PAUL (1878) [CEM] Rev. Msgr. Michael Dieckmann; Revs. Sebastian Mundackal, O.S.B.; Vincent Nyman; Deacons John Weatherholt; Paul Crafts.
Res.: 15 Forest Knoll, Fenton, 63026-3105. Tel: 636-343-1234; Fax: 636-343-4809. Web: www.stpaulfenton.org.
School—(Grades K-8), 465 New Smizer Mill Rd., Fenton, 63026. Tel: 636-343-4333; Fax: 636-343-1769. Web: www.stpaulfenton.org/school. Lay Teachers 28; Students 370.
Catechesis/Religious Program—Students 435.

141—ST. PAUL THE APOSTLE, Merged to form Ascension-St. Paul, Normandy.

142—ST. PETER (1832) [CEM] Rev. Msgr. John M. Costello; Rev. Michael J. Esswein; Deacons Richard L. Renard; John W. Komotos.
Res.: 243 W. Argonne Dr., Kirkwood, 63122. Tel: 314-966-8600; Fax: 314-966-5721.
School—(Grades K-8), 215 N. Clay St., Kirkwood, 63122. Tel: 314-821-0460. Lay Teachers 29; Students 495.
Catechesis/Religious Program—Tel: 314-822-1347. Linda Doyle, C.R.E.; Jan Hartman, C.R.E. Students 359.

143—STS. PETER AND PAUL (1849) Rev. Bruce H. Forman; Deacons Thomas Gorski; Dennis Chitwood.
Res.: 1919 S. 7th St., 63104. Tel: 314-231-9923; Fax: 314-231-7464.

144—ST. PIUS V (1905) Rev. John Rogers Vien; Deacons Walter W. Christ; Thomas A. Buhr; Sisters Paulette Weindel, C.PP.S., Pastoral Assoc.; Dorothy Ann Katke, C.PP.S., Pastoral Assoc.; Mary Henry, C.C.V.I., Pastoral Assoc.
Res.: 3310 S. Grand Blvd., 63118. Tel: 314-772-1525; Fax: 314-772-5615. Web: www.stpiusv.org.
See St. Frances Cabrini Academy, St. Louis under St. Wenceslaus, St. Louis for details.

145—ST. PIUS X (GLASGOW VILLAGE) (1954) Closed. For inquiries regarding sacramental records, contact the Archdiocesan Archives, 20 Archbishop May Dr., Saint Louis, MO 63119.

146—QUEEN OF ALL SAINTS (1972) Rev. Msgr. Joseph M. Simon; Rev. Eric J. Kunz; Deacons Richard Schellhase; Joseph Wingbermuehle.
Res.: 6603 Christopher Dr., 63129. Tel: 314-846-8207; Fax: 314-846-0636.
School—(Grades K-8), 6611 Christopher Dr., 63129. Tel: 314-846-0506; Fax: 314-846-4939. Dr. Catherine Johns, Prin. Students 469.
Catechesis/Religious Program—Tel: 314-846-8126. Ms. Carrie Sallwasser, C.R.E. Students 373.

147—ST. RAPHAEL THE ARCHANGEL (1950) Rev. Msgr. Henry J. Breier; Deacons Gerald Geiser; Roger Kreitler. In Res., Rev. Richard H. Suren (Retired).
Res.: 6047 Bishops Pl., 63109. Tel: 314-352-8100; Fax: 314-353-6603.
School—(Grades K-8), 6000 Jamieson, 63109. Tel: 314-352-9474; Fax: 314-352-7285. Margaret Kenny, Prin. Lay Teachers 13; Students 157.
Catechesis/Religious Program—Students 175.

148—RESURRECTION OF OUR LORD (1930), (Vietnamese), Revs. Dominic Nguyen, S.V.D.; Binh Thanh Nguyen, S.V.D.
3900 Meramec St., 63116. Tel: 314-832-7023; Fax: 314-832-7024.
Catechesis/Religious Program—Students 60.

149—ST. RICHARD (1963) Rev. Charles E. Burgoon; Deacons John A. Bischof; Jerry N. McGuire. In Res., Rev. John P. Kennehan.
Res.: 11223 Schuetz Rd., 63146. Tel: 314-432-6224; Fax: 314-432-6030.
School—(Grades K-8), 11211 Schuetz Rd., 63146. Tel: 314-872-3152; Fax: 314-872-0931. Miss Julie Smith, Prin. Lay Teachers 14; Students 112.

150—ST. RITA (1919) Rev. David L. Wichlan; Deacon Louis J. Reynoso.
Res.: 8240 Washington St., 63114. Tel: 314-428-4845; Fax: 314-428-4845.
Catechesis/Religious Program—Students 2.

151—ST. ROCH (1911) Rev. Msgr. Salvatore E. Polizzi; Rev. Robert T. McDermott.
Res.: 6052 Waterman Blvd., 63112. Tel: 314-721-6340; Fax: 314-721-1656. Web: strochparish.com.
School—(Grades K-8), 6040 Waterman Blvd., 63112. Tel: 314-721-2595. Gloria Openlander, Prin. Lay Teachers 13; Students 204.

152—ST. ROSE OF LIMA (1884) Closed. For inquiries regarding sacramental records, contact the Archdiocesan Archives, 20 Archbishop May Dr., Saint Louis, MO 63119.

153—ST. ROSE PHILIPPINE DUCHESNE Revs. Carl J. Scheble; Joseph Rajpaul Sundararaj.
Mailing Address: 2650 Parker Rd., Florissant, 63033. Tel: 314-837-3410; Fax: 314-837-6628. Web: www.strpdparish.org.
School—3500 St. Catherine, Florissant, 63033. Tel: 314-921-3023; Fax: 314-921-3025. Students 317.
Catechesis/Religious Program—Marie Carter, D.R.E. Students 70.

154—ST. SABINA (1960) Rev. Joseph W. Banden; Deacons Harold A. Strauss; Gerard M. Lauterwasser. In Res., Rev. Eugene P. Brennan (Retired).
Res.: 1365 Harkee Dr., Florissant, 63031. Tel: 314-837-1365; Fax: 314-837-7680.
School—1625 Swallow Dr., Florissant, 63031. Tel: 314-837-6524; Fax: 314-837-3162. Sr. Joan Galli, C.S.J., Prin. Sisters 2; Lay Teachers 15; Students 137.
Catechesis/Religious Program—Tel: 314-837-0146. Students 145.

155—SACRED HEART (1889) Revs. Richard J. Schilli; Lijo Kallarackal, O.S.B.Silv.; Deacon Thomas L. Eultgen.
Res.: 350 E. Fourth St., Eureka, 63025. Tel: 636-938-5048; Fax: 636-587-2736. Web: www.sacredhearteureka.org.
School—(Grades K-8) Tel: 636-938-4602; Fax: 636-938-5802. Monica Wilson, Prin. Lay Teachers 13; Students 220.
Catechesis/Religious Program—Tel: 636-938-9507. Students 365.

156—SACRED HEART (1866) Revs. Edward J. Stanger; Robert Dorhauer; Deacon Bruce A. Burkhard.
Res.: 751 N. Jefferson St., Florissant, 63031. Tel: 314-837-3757; Fax: 314-837-8897. Email: rectory@mostsacredheartchurch.org.
School—(Grades K-8), 501 St. Louis St., Florissant, 63031. Tel: 314-831-3372. Lois Vollmer, Prin. Lay Teachers 22; Students 317.
Catechesis/Religious Program—Tel: 314-837-3757, Ext. 221. Students 68.

157—SACRED HEART (1903) [CEM] Revs. Denny M. Schaab; Mark A. Chrismer; Sr. Cathy Vetter, C.C.V.I., Pastoral Assoc.; Deacons Dave Lemoine; Thomas E. Forster; Charles R. Snyder. In Res., Rev. Robert J. Suit.
Res.: 17 Ann Ave., Valley Park, 63088. Tel: 636-225-5268; Fax: 636-225-6969.
School—(Grades PreK-8), 12 Ann Ave., Valley Park, 63088. Tel: 636-225-3824; Fax: 636-225-8941. Joan Wojciechowski, Prin. Lay Teachers 27; Students 408.
Catechesis/Religious Program—Students 585.

158—ST. SEBASTIAN (GLEN OWEN), Closed. For inquiries regarding sacramental records, contact the Archdiocesan Archives, 20 Archbishop May Dr., Saint Louis, MO 63119.

159—SEVEN HOLY FOUNDERS (1927) Revs. Donald Siple, O.S.M.; Albert Susai Pragasam, O.S.M.; Bro. Arnaldo Sanchez, O.S.M., Pastoral Assoc.; Deacons Charles Lombardo; Joel Lechner, O.S.M.
Office: 6820 Aliceton Ave., Affton, 63123. Tel: 314-638-3938; Fax: 314-638-0613. Web: www.foundersaffton.org.
Church: 6741 Rock Hill Rd., 63123. Tel: 314-631-3938.
School—(Grades K-8), 6737 Rock Hill Rd., 63123. Tel: 314-631-8149; Fax: 314-631-8442. Web: www-.shfschool.org. Mr. Richard Danzeisen, Prin. Lay Teachers 16; Students 252.
Catechesis/Religious Program—Students 148.

160—SHRINE OF ST. JOSEPH (1844) Rev. Dale P. Wunderlich, Rector.
Res.: 1220 N. 11th St., 63106. Tel: 314-231-9407; Fax: 314-231-0802. Web: www.shrineofstjoseph.org.

161—ST. SIMON OF CYRENE (1993) Closed. For inquiries regarding sacramental records, contact the Archdiocesan Archives, 20 Archbishop May Dr., Saint Louis, MO 63119.

162—ST. SIMON THE APOSTLE (1959) Revs. Erich A. Fechner; Albert A. Mattler; Deacons David Camden; Paul F. Stackle. In Res., Rev. Mitchell S. Doyen.
Res.: 11011 Mueller Rd., 63123. Tel: 314-842-3848; Fax: 314-842-9829. Email: stsimon@sbcglobal.net. Web: archstl.org/parishes/282.shtml.
Preschool—11015 Mueller Rd., 63123. Tel: 314-842-3435; Fax: 314-842-4935. Email: simonsaysecc@sbcglobal.net. Web: www.simonsaysecc.com.
School—(Grades K-8), 11019 Mueller Rd., 63123. Tel: 314-842-0181; Fax: 314-849-6355. Email: mtalleur@stsimonschool.org. Web: www.stsimonschool.org. Lay Teachers 24; Students 372.
Catechesis/Religious Program—Students 140.

163—STE. GENEVIEVE DU BOIS (1956) Rev. Daniel E. Mosley; Rev. Msgr. John M. Unger; Deacons Donald Heitert, (Retired); J. Michael Buckley.
Res.: 1575 N. Woodlawn Ave., Warson Woods, 63122. Tel: 314-966-3780; Fax: 314-966-4687. Email: stegan@sbcglobal.net. Web: www.catholic-forum.com/churches/015stgenevieve/.
School—(Grades K-8) Tel: 314-821-4245; Fax: 314-822-4881. Mrs. Claudia Dougherty, Prin. Lay Teachers 13; Students 163.
Catechesis/Religious Program—Students 90.

164—ST. STEPHEN, PROTOMARTYR (1926) Rev. Ronald J. Hopmeir; Deacon Richard Stevens. In Res., Rev. Msgr. Richard E. Hanneke.

Res.: 3949 Wilmington Ave., 63116. Tel: 314-481-1133; Fax: 314-481-6036.
School—(Grades K-8), 3923 Wilmington Ave., 63116. Tel: 314-752-4700; Fax: 314-752-5165. Meghan Bohac, Prin. Lay Teachers 15; Students 178.
Catechesis/Religious Program—Students 7.

165—STS. TERESA AND BRIDGET (2003) Revs. Gary Meier; Cajetan Ihewulezi, C.SS.P.
3636 N. Market, 63113. Tel: 314-371-1190; Fax: 314-531-1047. Email: pastor@ststb.org. Web: www.ststb.org.

166—ST. TERESA OF AVILA (1865) Closed. For inquiries regarding sacramental records, contact Sts. Teresa & Bridget Church, 3636 N. Market St., Saint Louis, MO 63113.

167—ST. THOMAS MORE (BEL-RIDGE) (1955) Closed. For inquiries regarding sacramental records, contact the Archdiocesan Archives, 20 Archbishop May Dr., Saint Louis, MO 63119.

168—ST. THOMAS OF AQUIN (1882) Closed. For inquiries regarding sacramental records, contact the Archdiocesan Archives, 20 Archbishop May Dr., Saint Louis, MO 63119.

169—ST. THOMAS THE APOSTLE (FLORISSANT) (1960) Closed. For inquiries regarding sacramental records, contact the Archdiocesan Archives, 20 Archbishop May Dr., Saint Louis, MO 63119.

170—ST. TIMOTHY (1958) Closed. For inquiries regarding sacramental records, contact the Archdiocesan Archives, 20 Archbishop May Dr., Saint Louis, MO 63119.

171—TRANSFIGURATION (FLORISSANT) (1965) Closed. For inquiries regarding sacramental records, contact the Archdiocesan Archives, 20 Archbishop May Dr., Saint Louis, MO 63119.

172—ST. VINCENT DE PAUL (1841) Rev. Paul Otto Schneebeck, C.M.; Mr. Dennis Wells, Pastoral Assoc.
Res.: 1408 S. Tenth St., 63104. Tel: 314-231-9328; Fax: 314-621-2232. Email: mail@stvstl.org. Web: www.stvstl.org.
Catechesis/Religious Program—Email: lmertz@stvstl.org. Linda Mertz, D.R.E. Students 30.

173—VISITATION-ST. ANN'S SHRINE (1881) Rev. J. Edward Vogler.
Res.: 4515 Evans Ave., 63113. Tel: 314-535-8804; Fax: 314-531-8486. Email: vizstann@netzero.net. Web: www.vizstann.greatnow.com.

174—ST. WENCESLAUS (1895) Revs. James E. Wuerth, M.S.F.; John C. Lombardi, M.S.F.; Bro. John T. Griffin, M.S.F.; Deacon George W. Miller. In Res., Rev. R. Francois Rakotovoavy, M.S.F.
Res.: 3014 Oregon Ave., 63118-1498. Tel: 314-865-1020; Fax: 314-664-8260.
Catechesis/Religious Program—St. Frances Cabrini Academy, 3022 Oregon Ave., 63118. Tel: 314-776-0883; Fax: 314-776-4912. Students 135.

175—ST. WILLIAM (WOODSON TERRACE) (1953) Closed. For inquiries regarding sacramental records, contact the Archdiocesan Archives, 20 Archbishop May Dr., Saint Louis, MO 63119.

CHURCHES OUTSIDE ST. LOUIS CITY AND ST. LOUIS COUNTY

APPLE CREEK, PERRY CO., ST. JOSEPH (1828) [CEM] [JC 2] Very Rev. Anthony A. Dattilo.
Res.: 138 St. Joseph Ln., 63775. Tel: 573-788-2330; Fax: 573-788-2351.
Catechesis/Religious Program—Tel: 573-547-5246. Students 40.

ARNOLD, JEFFERSON CO.

1—ST. DAVID (1963) Rev. Jeffrey A. Maassen; Deacons Thomas G. Politte; Diosdado Maranan.
Res.: 2334 Tenbrook Rd., 63010. Tel: 636-296-7823; Fax: 636-296-8717. Email: stdavid@swbell.com.
See Holy Child School, Arnold under Immaculate Conception, Arnold for details.
Catechesis/Religious Program—Students 175.

2—IMMACULATE CONCEPTION (1840) [CEM] Revs. Mark Whitman, Admin.; John G. Dempsey; Deacons Steven M. Schisler; Bradford M. Buchek.
Res.: 2300 Church Rd., 63010. Tel: 636-321-0002; Fax: 636-287-9035; 636-321-0004.
School—Holy Child School, (Grades K-8), Consolidated with St. David, Arnold., Fax: 636-296-5639. Dr. Robert Cowell, Prin. Lay Teachers 12; Students 162.
Catechesis/Religious Program—Tel: 636-321-0002, Ext. 23. Mary Winkelmann, D.R.E. Students 287.

AUGUSTA, ST. CHARLES CO., IMMACULATE CONCEPTION (1851) [CEM] Rev. Edward L. Heim.
Res.: 5912 Hwy. 94 S., 63332. Tel: 636-482-4455; Fax: 636-228-4529. Email: icaugustamo@hotmail.com. Web: www.rc.net/stlouis/immac.
Catechesis/Religious Program—Students 20.

BELGIQUE, PERRY CO., NATIVITY OF THE BLESSED VIRGIN MARY, Closed. For inquiries regarding sacramental records, contact the Archdiocesan Archives, 20 Archbishop May Dr., Saint Louis, MO 63119.

BERGER, ST. PAUL (1853), (German), [CEM] Rev. John C. Deken.
Res.: 603 Miller St., New Haven, 63068. Tel: 573-237-3372; Fax: 573-237-3372.
Catechesis/Religious Program—Students 7.

BIEHLE, PERRY CO., ST. MAURUS (1870) [CEM] [JC] Very Rev. Anthony A. Dattilo.
Res.: 10198 Hwy. B, Perryville, 63775. Tel: 573-788-2330; 573-547-5246; Fax: 573-788-2351.
Catechesis/Religious Program—Students 45.

BLOOMSDALE, STE. GENEVIEVE CO., ST. AGNES (1835) [CEM] Rev. Clark B. Maes; Deacon James Basler.
Res.: 40 St. Agnes Dr., P.O. Box 124, 63627. Tel: 573-483-2555; Fax: 573-483-9497. Email: stagnes@brick.net.
School—(Grades PreK-8) Tel: 573-483-2506. Patricia A. Kirk, Prin. Sisters of the Most Precious Blood (O'Fallon, MO) 1; Lay Teachers 11; Students 183.
Catechesis/Religious Program—Students 23.

BONNE TERRE, ST. FRANCOIS CO., ST. JOSEPH'S (1872) [CEM] Rev. John H. Schneider.
Res.: 15 St. Joseph St., 63628. Tel: 573-358-2112; Fax: 573-358-4233.
School—(Grades K-6) Tel: 573-358-5947. Lay Teachers 4; Students 29.
Catechesis/Religious Program—Students 38.
Mission—St. Anne 5425 Brickey Rd., P.O. Box 307, French Village, St. Francois Co. 63036. Tel: 573-358-2112.

BREWER, PERRY CO., CHRIST THE SAVIOR (1907) [CEM] Rev. R. William Rhinehart, C.M.
Res.: 57 Shady Ln., Perryville, 63775. Tel: 573-547-2677; Fax: 573-547-7556. Email: christthesavior57@yahoo.com.
Catechesis/Religious Program—Students 38.

CATAWISSA, FRANKLIN CO., ST. JAMES (1913) [CEM] Rev. Mark S. Bozada.
Res.: 1107 Summit Dr., 63015. Tel: 636-451-4685; Fax: 636-742-4820. Email: simarparr@aol.com.
Mission—St. Patrick [CEM] Hwy. NN & Rock Church Rd., Armagh, Franklin Co. 63015. Tel: 636-257-2227.

CLOVER BOTTOM, FRANKLIN CO., ST. ANN (1883) [CEM] Rev. Richard V. Coerver, Admin.
Res.: 7851 Hwy. YY, Washington, 63090-4050. Tel: 636-239-3222; Fax: 636-390-2849. Email: stann@yhti.net. Web: www.stannschurch.yhti.net.
Catechesis/Religious Program—Students 38.

COFFMAN, STE. GENEVIEVE CO., ST. CATHERINE OF ALEXANDRIA (1929) [CEM] [JC] Attended by River Aux Vases Rev. F. Joseph Reilly.
Res.: 18411 RAV Church Rd., Ste. Genevieve, 63670. Tel: 573-883-2923; Fax: 573-883-9605.
Catechesis/Religious Program—Students 1.

CONCORD HILL, WARREN CO., ST. IGNATIUS LOYOLA (1857) [CEM 3] Rev. Finbarr Dowling, O.S.B.; Deacon Paul J. Hector.
Res.: 19127 Mill Rd., Marthasville, 63357-1439. Tel: 636-932-4445; Fax: 636-932-4032.
School—691 Mill Rd., 63357. Tel: 636-932-4444; Fax: 636-932-4479. Email: office@saintignatius.net. Jennifer Fregalette, Prin. Lay Teachers 5; Students 69.

COTTLEVILLE, ST. CHARLES CO., ST. JOSEPH (1873) [CEM] Rev. Msgr. James P. Callahan; Revs. Christopher M. Martin; Rodger P. Fleming; Sr. Mary Pezold, C.C.V.I., Pastoral Assoc.; Deacons Michael Piva; Eugene Schaeffer III; Glennon Schultheis; Mrs. Judy Powers, Pastoral Assoc.
Res.: 1355 Motherhead Rd., St. Charles, 63304. Tel: 636-441-0055; Fax: 636-926-7341. Email: parish@stjoecot.org.
School—(Grades K-8), 1351 Motherhead Rd., St. Charles, 63304. Fax: 636-441-9932. Email: info@stjoecot.org. Web: www.stjoecot.org. Sr. Maria Christi, O.P., Prin.; Mr. Daniel Mullenschlader, Asst. Prin.; Mrs. Lesa Keeven, Asst. Prin. Lay Teachers 43; Students 932.
Catechesis/Religious Program—Tel: 636-441-0055, Ext. 300; Fax: 636-926-7341. Mrs. Laura Weinzirl, C.R.E. Tel: 636-441-0055, Ext. 300. Students 1,060.
Convent—1353 Motherhead Rd., St. Charles, 63304. Tel: 636-244-2257.

CRYSTAL CITY, JEFFERSON CO., SACRED HEART (1881) [CEM] Rev. Joseph E. Wormek, Admin.; Deacon Gerard G. Stoverink.
Res.: 555 Bailey Rd., 63019-1798. Tel: 636-937-4662; Fax: 636-931-5507. Email: sh324cc@sbcglobal.net.
Catechesis/Religious Program—Tel: 636-937-5298. Students 148.

DARDENNE PRAIRIE, ST. CHARLES CO., IMMACULATE CONCEPTION (1880) [CEM] Revs. Robert J. Reiker; Stephen P. Giljum; John I. Caffe; Deacons Don Schiffman; Russ Butler; Ernie Rohaly; Paul Bast.
Res.: 7701 Hwy. N., 63368. Tel: 636-561-6611; Fax: 636-561-3883. Email: parishoffice@icdparish.org. Web: www.icdparish.org.
School—(Grades K-8) Tel: 636-561-4450. Web: www.icdschool.org. Lay Teachers 35; Students 770.
Catechesis/Religious Program—Tel: 636-561-1974. Email: psr@icdparish.org. Students 1,220.

DE SOTO, JEFFERSON CO., ST. ROSE OF LIMA (1885) [CEM] Rev. Alexander R. Anderson; Deacon Edward J. Boyer.
Res.: 504 S. Third St., 63020. Tel: 636-337-2212; Fax: 636-337-2394.
School—(Grades K-8) Tel: 636-586-3594; 636-337-7855. Imogene Renick, Prin. Lay Teachers 8; Students 71.
Catechesis/Religious Program—Students 127.

DUTZOW, WARREN CO., ST. VINCENT DE PAUL (1856) [CEM] Rev. Eugene G. Robertson.
Res.: 13497 S. Hwy. 94, Marthasville, 63357. Tel: 636-433-2678; Fax: 636-433-2924.
School—13495 S. State Hwy. 94, Marthasville, 63357. Tel: 636-433-2466. Sisters 1; Lay Teachers 5; Students 72.
Catechesis/Religious Program—Students 6.

ELSBERRY, LINCOLN CO., SACRED HEART (1905) Rev. Raymond D. Hager.
Res.: 714 Lincoln St., 63343. Tel: 573-898-2202; Fax: 573-898-2652.
Catechesis/Religious Program—Students 87.

FARMINGTON, ST. FRANCOIS CO., ST. JOSEPH (1890) [JC 2] Revs. Rickey J. Valleroy; James W. Dyer; Deacon Albin A. Gegg.
Res.: 10 N. Long St., 63640. Tel: 573-756-4250; Fax: 573-756-6938. Web: www.stjosephfarmington.com.
School—(Grades K-8), 501 Ste. Genevieve Ave., 63640. Tel: 573-756-6312; Fax: 573-756-0738. Web: www.stjosephhornets.com. Students 113.
Catechesis/Religious Program—Students 94.

FESTUS, JEFFERSON CO., OUR LADY (1956) Rev. John V. Kerber; Sr. Pat Murray, O.S.F., Pastoral Assoc.
Res.: 1550 St. Mary Ln., 63028-1543. Tel: 636-937-5513; 636-931-4702 (toll-free); Fax: 636-933-2230. Email: olchurch@sbcglobal.net. Web: www.ourladyfestus.org.
School—(Grades K-8), 1599 St. Mary Ln., 63028-1557. Tel: 636-937-5008. Email: ourladyschool@sbcglobal.net. Lay Teachers 20; Students 287.
Catechesis/Religious Program—Students 171.

FLINT HILL, ST. CHARLES CO., ST. THEODORE (1883) [CEM] Rev. Gary L. Vollmer; Deacons Patrick Rankin; Thomas N. Rothermich.
Res.: 5051 Hwy. P, P.O. Box 246, 63346. Tel: 636-332-9269; Fax: 636-639-1385. Email: sttheodore.church@centurytel.net.
School—5059 Hwy. P, Wentzville, 63385. Tel: 636-332-9269, Ext. 4; Fax: 636-327-5115. Email: sttheodore.school@centurytel.net. Lay Teachers 13; Students 204.
Catechesis/Religious Program—Students 20.

GILDEHAUS, FRANKLIN CO., ST. JOHN THE BAPTIST (1839) [CEM] Rev. Msgr. Jeffrey N. Knight.
Res.: 5567 Gildehaus Rd., Villa Ridge, 63089. Tel: 636-583-2488; Fax: 636-583-6114. Email: stjohnsgild@yhti.net.
School—(Grades PreSchool-8) Tel: 636-583-2392. Barbara Danner, Prin. Lay Teachers 16; Students 141.
Catechesis/Religious Program—Students 59.

HAWK POINT, LINCOLN CO., ST. MARY (1919) [CEM 2] Rev. Francis F. Koeninger.
Res.: P.O. Box 205, 63349. Tel: 636-338-4331; Fax: 636-338-4007.
Catechesis/Religious Program—Fax: 636-338-4331. Students 30.

HERCULANEUM, JEFFERSON CO., CHURCH OF THE ASSUMPTION OF B.V.M. (1916) [CEM] Rev. Robert V. Fleiter; Deacon Steven D. Baugh.
Res.: 329 Station St., 63048-1328. Tel: 636-475-5305.
Catechesis/Religious Program—Students 8.

HIGH RIDGE, JEFFERSON CO., ST. ANTHONY OF PADUA (1944) Rev. Kevin J. Mahoney.
Res.: 3009 High Ridge Blvd., 63049. Tel: 636-677-4868; Fax: 636-677-4868. Email: rusalynesahr@att.net. Web: www.stanthonyhr.org.
Catechesis/Religious Program—Students 91.

HILLSBORO, JEFFERSON CO., CHURCH OF THE GOOD SHEPHERD (1934) [CEM] Rev. Christopher F. Holtmann; Deacons Kenneth A. Henning; Paul A. Martin.
Res.: 703 Third St., 63050-4342. Tel: 636-789-3356; Fax: 636-789-9986. Email: goodshepherd@juno.com. Web: mygoodshepherd.com.
School—(Grades PreK-8), 701 Third St., 63050. Tel: 636-797-2300; Fax: 636-797-2300. Mrs. Julie Connors, Prin. Lay Teachers 10; Students 85.
Catechesis/Religious Program—Students 116.

HOUSE SPRINGS, JEFFERSON CO., OUR LADY, QUEEN OF PEACE (1961) [CEM 2] Very Rev. Patrick J. Christopher; Rev. James T. Beighlie, C.M.; Deacons Thomas Gerling; Paul Turek. In Res., Rev. Donald F. Molitor (Retired).
Res.: 4696 Notre Dame Ln., 63051. Tel: 636-671-3062; Fax: 636-671-0003.
School—(Grades K-8), 4675 Notre Dame Ln.,

63051. Tel: 636-671-0247; Fax: 636-671-0418. Mrs. Debbi Clark, Admin. Sisters 1; Lay Teachers 15; Students 226.
Catechesis / Religious Program—Students 175.

IMPERIAL, JEFFERSON CO.

1—ST. JOHN (1869) [CEM] Rev. Steven P. Robeson; Deacons Norbert Gawedzinski; Charles Ryder; Lawrence Nava.
Res.: 4525 Old Hwy. 21, 63052. Tel: 636-296-8061; Fax: 636-296-8067.
Catechesis / Religious Program—Students 122.

2—ST. JOSEPH (1905) [CEM] Revs. John J. Brennell; Edward G. Nemeth; Deacons Roland Kaiser; Brian T. Selsor.
Res.: 6020 Old Antonia Rd., 63052-0968. Tel: 636-464-1013; Fax: 636-461-0411.
School—(Grades K-8), 6024 Old Antonia Rd., 63052. Tel: 636-464-9027; Fax: 636-464-3574. Mary Ellen Smith, Prin. Students 317.
Catechesis / Religious Program—Students 340.

JOSEPHVILLE, ST. CHARLES CO., ST. JOSEPH (1852) [CEM] Rev. Larry T. Huber; Deacon Fielding Harrison.
Res.: 1390 Josephville Rd., Wentzville, 63385. Tel: 636-332-6676; Fax: 636-332-8648.
School—(Grades PreK-8), 1410 Josephville Rd., Wentzville, 63385. Tel: 636-332-5672. Dwight Elmore, Prin. Lay Teachers 8; Students 101.
Catechesis / Religious Program—Bassy Clayton, D.R.E. Students 20.

KRAKOW, FRANKLIN CO., ST. GERTRUDE (1845) [CEM] Rev. Richard V. Coerver; Deacon Charles Gildehaus. In Res., Rev. Bernard J. Wilkins (Retired).
Res.: 6535 Hwy. YY, Washington, 63090. Tel: 636-239-4216; Fax: 636-239-3590. Email: stger@charter.net. Web: www.stgertrudekrakow.org.
School—(Grades K-8), 6520 Hwy. YY, Washington, 63090. Tel: 636-239-2347; Fax: 636-239-3550. Email: stgertrude@primary.net. Mike Newbanks, Prin. Lay Teachers 21; Students 278.
Catechesis / Religious Program—Students 89.

LAKE ST. LOUIS, ST. CHARLES CO., SAINT GIANNA (2006) Rev. Timothy P. Elliott.
Res.: 331 Charity Dr., Lake Saint Louis, 63367. Tel: 636-332-0531; Fax: 636-561-1299.

LAWRENCETON, STE. GENEVIEVE CO., ST. LAWRENCE (1872) [CEM] Attended by St. Agnes Rectory. Rev. Clark B. Maes.
8055 State Rt. Y, P.O. Box 124, Bloomsdale, 63627. Tel: 573-483-2555; Fax: 573-483-9497.
Catechesis / Religious Program—Students 13.

LUEBBERING, FRANKLIN CO., ST. FRANCIS OF ASSISI (1874) [CEM] Rev. John B. McEntee.
Res.: 1000 Luebbering Rd., Lonedell, 63060-3100. Tel: 636-629-1717; Fax: 636-629-8408.
Catechesis / Religious Program—Students 62.

MILLWOOD, LINCOLN CO., ST. ALPHONSUS (1850) [CEM] Rev. Charles P. Tichacek, Admin.
Res.: 29 St. Alphonsus Rd., Silex, 63377. Tel: 573-384-6223; Fax: 573-384-5981.
School—Tel: 573-384-5305. Lay Teachers 5; Students 59.
Catechesis / Religious Program—Students 40.

NEIER, FRANKLIN CO., ST. JOSEPH (1881) [CEM] Rev. Kevin V. Schmittgens.
Res.: 2401 Neier Rd., Union, 63084. Tel: 636-583-2806; Fax: 636-583-0627.
Catechesis / Religious Program—Students 61.

NEW HAVEN, FRANKLIN CO., ASSUMPTION (1892) [CEM] Rev. John C. Deken.
Res.: 603 Miller St., 63068. Tel: 573-237-3372; Fax: 573-237-3372.
Catechesis / Religious Program—Students 107.

NEW MELLE, ST. CHARLES CO., IMMACULATE HEART OF MARY (1945) [CEM] Rev. Richard L. Stoltz; Deacons Lonnie Weishaar; Christopher M. Ast.
Res.: 8 W. Hwy. D, Box 100, 63365-0100. Tel: 636-398-5270; Fax: 636-398-5577. Web: www.ihm-newmelle.org.
Catechesis / Religious Program— Mr. Shawn Mueller, D.R.E. Students 198.

O'FALLON, ST. CHARLES CO.

1—ASSUMPTION (1871) [CEM] Revs. Joseph G. Kempf; Ronald J. Rubbelke; James D. Theby; Deacons Fred Volansky; Howard Vanbooven. In Res., Rev. Eugene F. Bendel (Retired).
Res.: 403 N. Main St., 63366. Tel: 636-240-3721; Fax: 636-240-3722. Web: www.asumptionbvm.org.
School—(Grades K-8), 203 W. Third St., 63366. Tel: 636-240-4474. Lay Teachers 22; Students 450.
Catechesis / Religious Program—Tel: 636-240-1020. Students 546.

2—ST. BARNABAS (1961) Rev. Msgr. Daniel M. Hogan.
Res.: 1400 N. Main St., 63366. Tel: 636-240-4556; Fax: 636-978-3358.
Catechesis / Religious Program—Tel: 636-281-3211. Students 50.

OLD MINES, WASHINGTON CO., ST. JOACHIM (1723) [CEM 3] Rev. Theodore X. Pieper.
Res.: 10120 Crest Rd., Cadet, 63630. Tel: 573-438-6181; Fax: 573-438-3685. Email: stjoachimparish@hotmail.com. Web: stjoachimchurch.com.
School—Tel: 573-438-3973; Fax: 573-438-3161. Email: stjoachimschool_63630@yahoo.com. Web: stjoachimschool.com. Joyce Politte, Prin. Lay Teachers 6; Students 73.
Catechesis / Religious Program—Students 25.

OLD MONROE, LINCOLN CO., IMMACULATE CONCEPTION (1867) [CEM] Rev. Msgr. Gregory L. Schmidt; Deacon Anthony Trautman.
Res.: 110 Maryknoll Rd., 63369. Tel: 636-661-5002; Fax: 636-661-5002.
School—120 Maryknoll Rd., 63369. Tel: 636-661-5156. Susan Schutz, Prin. Sisters of the Third Order Regular of St. Francis (Oldenburg, IN) 1; Lay Teachers 12; Students 210.
Catechesis / Religious Program—Students 45.
Convent—122 Maryknoll Rd., 63369. Tel: 636-665-5086.

OZORA, STE. GENEVIEVE CO., SACRED HEART (1898) [CEM] Rev. James W. Schaefer.
Res.: 17742 State Rte. N., St. Mary, 63673. Tel: 573-543-2209; Fax: 573-543-5576.
School—17740 State Rte. N., Saint Mary, 63673. Tel: 573-543-2997. Sr. Agnes Keena, B.V.M., Prin. Sisters of Charity 1; Lay Teachers 2; Students 22.
Catechesis / Religious Program—Students 18.

PACIFIC, FRANKLIN CO., ST. BRIDGET CHURCH (1841) [CEM 2] Rev. John A. Keenoy; Deacon Michael E. Suden. In Res., Rev. Martin J. Mulvihill.
Res.: 111 W. Union St., 63069. Tel: 636-271-3993; Fax: 636-257-6265.
School—Tel: 636-257-4533; Fax: 636-257-2504. Lay Teachers 10; Students 145.
Catechesis / Religious Program—Students 85.

PARK HILLS, ST. FRANCOIS CO., IMMACULATE CONCEPTION (1903) [CEM] [JC] Rev. James R. French; Deacon Michael D. Burch.
Res.: 1020 W. Main St., Box 66, 63601-0066. Tel: 573-431-2427; Fax: 573-431-4060.
Catechesis / Religious Program—Students 42.
Mission—St. John (1879) [CEM] [JC] Maple St. & Walnut St., Bismarck, St. Francois Co. 63624.

PERRYVILLE, PERRY CO., ST. VINCENT DE PAUL (1817) [CEM 4] Revs. Joseph S. Williams, C.M.; Milton F. Ryan, C.M.
Res.: 1000 Rosati Court, 63775. Tel: 573-547-4591; Fax: 573-547-4145.
Parish Center—1010 Rosati Ct., 63775.
School—(Grades K-8) Tel: 573-547-6503. Elaine Blair, Prin. Lay Teachers 23; Students 369.
High School—Tel: 573-547-2560. Lisa Best, Prin. Lay Teachers 20; Students 163.
Catechesis / Religious Program—Parish School of Religion Email: ldauster@svdepaul.org. Students 244.
Mission—St. Joseph 1701 W. St. Joseph, Highland, Perry Co. 63775. Tel: 314-547-4591.
Mission—St. James c/o St. Vincent De Paul Parish, Crosstown, Perry Co. 63775.

PORT HUDSON, FRANKLIN CO., HOLY FAMILY (1872) [CEM] Rev. James J. Foster.
Res.: 124 Holy Family Church Rd., New Haven, 63068. Tel: 573-459-6441; Fax: 573-459-2257.
Catechesis / Religious Program—Tel: 573-459-6594; 573-764-3292. Students 30.
Mission—St. Gerald 124 Holy Family Church Rd., New Haven, Franklin Co. 63068.

PORTAGE DES SIOUX, ST. CHARLES CO., ST. FRANCIS OF ASSISI (1799), (French—German), [CEM 2] Rev. Robert L. Banken; Deacon Robert Klostermann.
Res.: 1355 Farnham St., P.O. Box 129, 63373. Tel: 636-899-0906; Fax: 636-899-0909.
Mission—Immaculate Conception 14060 Hwy. 94 N., P.O. Box 129, St. Charles Co. 63373.

POTOSI, WASHINGTON CO., ST. JAMES (1829) [CEM 2] Rev. Joseph J. Welschmeyer.
Res.: 201 N. Missouri Ave., 63664. Tel: 573-438-4686; 888-868-8188 (toll-free); Fax: 573-438-2100.
Catechesis / Religious Program—Students 68.

RICHWOODS, WASHINGTON CO., ST. STEPHEN (1841) [CEM] Rev. Robert C. Liss.
Res.: 11514 Hwy. A, P.O. Box 233, 63071-2561. Tel: 573-678-2207; 573-678-2203 (Hall); Fax: 573-678-2380.

RIVER AUX VASES, STE. GENEVIEVE CO., SS. PHILIP AND JAMES (1840) [CEM] Rev. F. Joseph Reilly.
Res.: 18411 RAV Church Rd., Ste. Genevieve, 63670. Tel: 573-883-2923; Fax: 573-883-9605.
Catechesis / Religious Program—Students 32.

ST. CHARLES, ST. CHARLES CO.

1—ST. CHARLES BORROMEO (1792) Rev. John H. Reiker; Rev. Msgr. Donald C. Schramm.
Res.: 601 N. 4th St., 63301. Tel: 636-946-6370; 636-946-1893; Fax: 636-946-5598. Web: borromeoparish.com.
School—(Grades K-8), 431 Decatur, 63301. Tel: 636-946-2713; Fax: 636-946-3096. Web: borromeoschool.com. Sisters of Notre Dame 1; Lay Teachers 23; Students 365.
Catechesis / Religious Program—Tel: 636-946-2916. Students 160.

2—ST. CLETUS (1965) Revs. James J. Benz; Terry J. Borgerding; Deacons Frank Olmsted; Mark McCarthy; Kenneth M. Potzman.
Res.: 2705 Zumbehl Rd., 63301. Tel: 636-946-6327; Fax: 636-946-6466.
School—2721 Zumbehl Rd., 63301. Tel: 636-946-7756; Fax: 636-946-6526. Lay Teachers 21; Students 289.
Catechesis / Religious Program—Tel: 636-946-5936. Students 152.

3—ST. ELIZABETH ANN SETON (1975) Rev. Msgr. Robert P. Jovanovic; Rev. David P. Skillman; Deacons Gerald Hurlbert; Richard Tadlock. In Res., Rev. Msgr. Edward W. Reilly (Retired).
Res.: 2 Seton Ct., 63303. Tel: 636-946-6717; Fax: 636-946-9263. Web: setonscene.org.
School—Tel: 636-946-6716; Fax: 636-946-2670. Lay Teachers 21; Students 272.
Catechesis / Religious Program—Tel: 636-669-6706. Web: www.setonscene.org. Nancy Burian, D.R.E. Students 269.

4—STS. JOACHIM AND ANN (1981) Revs. John A. Brockland; Noah A. Waldman; James L. Gahan; Deacons Timothy Schulte; Paul Antor.
Mailing Address: 4112 McClay Rd., 63304. Tel: 636-441-7503; Fax: 636-441-6574.
School—(Grades K-8), 4110 McClay Rd., 63304-7915. Tel: 636-441-4835; Fax: 636-441-9534. Mrs. Debbie Pecher, Prin. Lay Teachers 24; Students 355.
Catechesis / Religious Program—Tel: 314-926-0021. Students 400.

5—ST. PETER (1850) [CEM] Revs. Stephen F. Bauer; Frederick A. Meyer; Deacon John Schiffer. In Res., Rev. Msgr. Raymond A. Hampe.
Res.: 324 S. Third St., 63301-3413. Tel: 636-946-6641; Fax: 636-946-9789.
School—201 First Capitol Dr., 63301. Tel: 636-947-9669. Lay Teachers 15; Students 176.
Catechesis / Religious Program—Students 63.

6—ST. ROBERT BELLARMINE (1964) Rev. Patrick Ryan; Deacons Joseph C. Meiergerd; Phillip King.
Res.: 1424 First Capitol Dr. S., 63303. Tel: 636-946-6799; Fax: 636-946-0380. Email: strsecretary@sbcglobal.net.
School—St. Elizabeth / St. Robert Regional School, Tel: 636-946-6716; Fax: 636-946-2670. Email: sesr@seton.scene.org. Web: www.setonscene.org.
Catechesis / Religious Program—Tel: 636-946-6461. Email: carolbreckle@charternet.com. Students 78.

ST. CLAIR, FRANKLIN CO., ST. CLARE (1916) [CEM] Rev. Robert Knight.
Res.: 165 E. Springfield St., 63077. Tel: 636-629-0315; Fax: 636-629-2327.
School—Tel: 636-629-0413. Lay Teachers 8; Students 82.
Catechesis / Religious Program—Students 60.

ST. MARY, STE. GENEVIEVE CO., IMMACULATE CONCEPTION (1869) [CEM] Rev. Richard C. Kasznel.
Res.: 481 Immaculate Conception Dr., 63673. Tel: 573-543-2536; Fax: 573-543-2536.

ST. PAUL, ST. CHARLES CO., ST. PAUL (1850) [CEM] Rev. Msgr. John J. Hickel; Deacons James J. Litteken; Martin G. Towey.
Res.: 1223 Church Rd., 63366. Tel: 636-978-1900, Ext. 240 (Rectory); 636-978-1900, Ext. 221 (Parish Center Offices); Fax: 636-980-2722 (Parish Center Offices).
School—1235 Church Rd., 63366. Tel: 636-978-1944; Fax: 636-272-4469. Lay Teachers 16; Students 221.
Catechesis / Religious Program—Tel: 636-978-1900, Ext. 222. Students 155.

ST. PETERS, ST. CHARLES CO., ALL SAINTS (1815) [CEM] Revs. Donald R. Wester; Philip G. Krahman; Robert C. Lane; Deacons Gerald Knobbe; Gary Meyerkord.
Res.: 7 McMenamy Rd., 63376. Tel: 636-397-1440; Fax: 636-397-1421. Email: asparish@allsaints-stpeters.org. Web: www.allsaints-stpeters.org.
School—5 McMenamy Rd., Saint Peters, 63376. Tel: 636-397-1477; Fax: 636-970-3735. Rae Ann Kielty, Prin. Religious Teachers 1; Lay Teachers 24; Students 344.
Catechesis / Religious Program—Tel: 636-397-6995. Ms. Marya Pohlmeier, D.R.E. Students 333.

SERENO, PERRY CO., OUR LADY OF VICTORY (1908) [JC] Rev. R. William Rhinehart, C.M.
Res.: 172 PCR 920, Perryville, 63775. Tel: 573-547-6812; Fax: 573-547-1427.
Catechesis / Religious Program—Students 50.

SILVER LAKE, PERRY CO., ST. ROSE OF LIMA (1885) [CEM] Rev. Joseph S. Williams, C.M.
Res.: 1010 Rosati Ct., Perryville, 63775. Tel: 573-547-4591; Fax: 573-547-4145.

STE. GENEVIEVE, STE. GENEVIEVE CO., STE. GENEVIEVE (1759) [CEM] Revs. Dennis C. Schmidt; Gregory S. Klump.
Res.: 49 Du Bourg Pl., 63670. Tel: 573-883-2731; Fax: 573-883-2907.

School—40 N. Fourth St., 63670. Tel: 573-883-2403; Fax: 573-883-7413. Lay Teachers 21; Students 252.
High School—Valle High School, Tel: 573-883-7496; Fax: 573-883-9142. Lay Teachers 17; Students 132.
Catechesis/Religious Program—Students 54.

SULLIVAN, FRANKLIN CO.

1—ST. ANTHONY (1891) [CEM] Rev. Paul E. Telken.
Res.: 201 W. Springfield Ave., 63080. Tel: 573-468-6101; Fax: 573-468-8584.
School—119 W. Springfield Ave., 63080. Tel: 573-468-4423. Joann Kuchler, S.F.C.C., Prin. Lay Teachers 9; Students 90.
Catechesis/Religious Program—Students 50.

2—CHURCH OF THE HOLY MARTYRS OF JAPAN (1879) [CEM 2] Rev. John Patrick Day, C.P., Admin.
Church: 8244 Hwy. AE, 63080-3229. Tel: 573-627-3378; Fax: 573-627-3387.
Catechesis/Religious Program—Students 45.

TIFF, WASHINGTON CO., ST. JOSEPH (1905) [CEM] Rev. Theodore X. Pieper, Admin.
Res.: 10120 Crest Rd., Cadet, 63630. Tel: 573-438-6181; Fax: 573-438-3685.

TROY, LINCOLN CO., SACRED HEART (1891) [CEM] Rev. Thomas Wissler; Sr. Mary Ann Fisher, C.S.J., Pastoral Min.
Res.: 100 Thompson Dr., 63379. Tel: 636-528-8219; Fax: 636-528-3983. Email: tlwsheart@lincoln.mo.us. Web: sacredhearttroy.org.
School—110 Thompson Dr., 63379. Tel: 636-528-6684; Fax: 636-528-3923. Sr. Jeannette Fennewald, S.S.N.D., Prin. Lay Teachers 13; Students 298.
Catechesis/Religious Program—Students 300.

UNION, FRANKLIN CO., IMMACULATE CONCEPTION (1866) [CEM] Rev. Msgr. Matthew M. Mitas; Deacon Gerald H. Becker.
Res.: 100 N. Washington Ave., 63084. Tel: 636-583-5144; Fax: 636-583-7784.
School—6 W. State St., 63084. Tel: 636-583-2641; Fax: 636-583-3073. Sisters 1; Lay Teachers 21; Students 352.
Catechesis/Religious Program—Students 109.
Convent—111 N. Washington Ave., 63084. Tel: 636-583-2188.

VILLA RIDGE, FRANKLIN CO., ST. MARY OF PERPETUAL HELP (1905) [CEM] Rev. Mark S. Bozada.
Res.: 1587 Hwy. AM, 63089. Tel: 636-451-4685; Fax: 636-742-4820. Email: stmarparr@aol.com.
Catechesis/Religious Program—811 American Inn Rd., 63089. Tel: 636-742-2460. Carolyn Henneken, D.R.E.

WARRENTON, WARREN CO., HOLY ROSARY (1868) [CEM] Rev. William C. Thess; Deacon Ray Burle; Mrs. Carol Ditto, Pastoral Assoc.
Res.: 724 E. Booneslick Rd., 63383. Tel: 636-456-3698, Ext. 1; Fax: 636-456-5560. Email: holyrosary724@earthlink.net. Web: www.holyrosarywarrenton.com.
School—716 Booneslick Rd., 63383. Tel: 636-456-3698, Ext. 2; Fax: 636-456-6181. Email: archstl369@centurytel.net. Web: www.holyrosary-warrenton.net. Mr. Michael Etter, Prin. Permanent Deacons 1; Lay Teachers 12; Students 107.
Catechesis/Religious Program—Students 80.

WASHINGTON, FRANKLIN CO.

1—ST. FRANCIS BORGIA (1834) [CEM] Revs. Andrew J. Sigmund; John W. Mayo; Deacon Leon Noelker.
115 Cedar St., 63090. Email: sfbparish@sfbparish.org. Web: www.sfbparish.org.
Res.: 311 W. 2nd St., 63090. Tel: 636-239-6701; Fax: 636-239-9499.
School—225 Cedar St., 63090. Tel: 636-239-2590; Fax: 636-239-3501. Lay Teachers 28; Students 320.
Catechesis/Religious Program—Students 99.

2—OUR LADY OF LOURDES (1958) Rev. Michael P. Boehm, Admin.; Deacon Richard J. Boland.
Res.: 1014 Madison Ave., 63090-4806. Tel: 636-239-3520; Fax: 636-239-7682. Email: lourdes1014@yahoo.com. Web: ollwashingtonmo.com.
School—950 Madison Ave., 63090. Tel: 636-239-5292; Fax: 636-239-7682. Lay Teachers 13; Students 196.
Catechesis/Religious Program—Students 103.

WEINGARTEN, STE. GENEVIEVE CO., OUR LADY, HELP OF CHRISTIANS (1872) [CEM] Rev. William Wigand.
Res.: 13370 Hwy. 32, Ste. Genevieve, 63670-9402. Tel: 573-883-3796; Fax: 573-883-8871. Email: olhc@isp.com.
Catechesis/Religious Program—Students 31.

WENTZVILLE, ST. CHARLES CO., ST. PATRICK (1905) [CEM] [JC] Rev. Msgr. Patrick J. O'Laughlin; Revs. Donald A. Glastetter; Frank A. D'Amico; Deacon Bernard A. Buckman.
Res.: 405 S. Church St., 63385. Tel: 636-332-9225; Fax: 636-332-6998.
School—701 Church St., 63385. Tel: 636-332-9913; Fax: 636-332-4877. Diane Kelly, Prin. Lay Teachers 22; Students 471.
Catechesis/Religious Program—Tel: 636-332-9036; Fax: 636-332-4877. Students 362.

ZELL, STE. GENEVIEVE CO., ST. JOSEPH (1845) [CEM] Rev. Msgr. James E. Hanson.
Res.: 11824 Zell Rd., Ste. Genevieve, 63670. Tel: 573-883-3481; Fax: 573-883-7829. Email: stjozell@isp.com.
School—Tel: 573-883-5097. Adorers of the Blood of Christ (Ruma, IL) 2; Lay Teachers 4; Students 42.
Catechesis/Religious Program—Students 112.

Chaplains of Public Institutions

ST. LOUIS. *St. Anthony's Medical Center*, Tel: 314-525-1000. Vacant.
Barnes - Jewish Hospital. Rev. James C. Gray. Tel: 314-747-3000.
Christian Hospital Northeast-Northwest, 11133 Dunn Rd., 63136. Tel: 314-653-5000 (Northeast); 314-953-6000 (Northwest). Vacant.
DePaul Health Center. Rev. Lawrence F. Asma, C.M.
St. John's Mercy Medical Center, Tel: 314-569-6000. Rev. John P. Kennehan.
Lambert - St. Louis International Airport. Rev. Eugene P. Brennan (Retired), Deacon Arnold Krieger. Tel: 314-427-8787.
St. Mary's Health Center, Tel: 314-768-8000. Vacant.

ST. CHARLES. *St. Joseph Health Center*, Tel: 636-946-6641. Rev. Msgr. Raymond A. Hampe. Tel: 636-947-5000.

WASHINGTON. *St. John's Mercy Hospital*, Tel: 636-239-8000. Rev. Timothy J. Toohey.

Special Assignment:
Rev. Msgr.—
Lyons, William J., S.T.L., North American College, Rome, Faculty
Revs.—
Aten, Robert L., Heart of Mary Hermitage, Lesterville. Tel: 573-648-2467
Bene, Philip J., J.C.D., 25 E. 39th St., New York, NY 10016.
Chochol, Ronald C., Chap., Mother of Good Counsel Home, 6825 Natural Bridge Rd., St. Louis, 63121.
Fischer, Brian R., Master of Ceremonies
Heil, John P., S.S.D., Catholic University, 620 Michigan Ave. N.E., DC 20069.
Nord, Aaron P., Casa Santa Maria, Via dell'Umilta 30, Rome 00187 Italy.
O'Connor, Andrew
Teater, Kristian C., Casa Santa Maria, via dell' Umilta, 30, Rome 00187 Italy.

On Duty Outside the Archdiocese:
Revs.—
Blattner, Joseph H., Moyle Springs, ID
Hauck, Herbert C., Carefree, AZ
Hayden, Patrick T., La Paz, Bolivia
Koch, Donald J. (Retired), Boca Raton, FL
Kopfensteiner, Thomas R., Foxfield, CO
Kovalcin, John A., Las Vegas, NV
Manning, Robert C., Colorado Springs
Means, David A., Anchorage, AK
Mesa, Luis, Colombia
Michler, James R., La Paz, Bolivia.

Military Chaplains:
Rev. Msgr.—
Butler, Michael T.
Revs.—
Breig, Gary R.
Kirchhoefer, Thomas A.

On Medical Leave:
Revs.—
Edwards, James T. (Retired)
Heier, Vincent A.
Sandweg, Michael J., Ph.D.
Wetmore, John J.

On Leave of Absence:
Revs.—
Doherty, Glennon C.
Hederman, Kevin F.
Zacheis, Dennis B.
Zinser, Robert E.

Retired:
Rev. Msgrs.—
Anthony, Paul G., Regina Cleri, 10 Archbishop May Dr., St. Louis, 63119.
Baker, Joseph W., 3200 Southern Aire Place, St. Louis, 63125.
Buchheit, Jerome J., 3293 Old County Rd., DeSoto, 63020.
Buchheit, Richard A., St. Norbert, 16455 New Halls Ferry Rd., Florissant, 63031.
Dietz, Norbert J., 7148 Forsyth, St. Louis, 63105.
Drennan, William A., St. Alban Roe Church, 2001 Shephard Rd., Wildwood, 63038.
Eichor, Edward C., M.A., Pope John Paul II Residence for Priests, St. Agnes Home, 10341 Manchester Rd., St. Louis, 63122.
Forst, Charles J., Saint Mark, 4230 Ripa, St. Louis, 63125.
Granich, Bernard E., Regina Cleri, 10 Archbishop May Dr., St. Louis, 63119.
Griesedieck, Edmund O., Kenrick-Glennon Seminary, 5200 Glennon Dr., St. Louis, 63119.
Kennedy, John J., Regina Cleri, 10 Archbishop May Dr., St. Louis, 63119.
Lubeley, Richard J., 676 W. Lockwood Blvd., St. Louis, 63119.
McCarthy, Robert, St. Agnes Home, 10341 Manchester Rd., St. Louis, 63122.
Meyer, Louis F., 4908 Sutherland, St. Louis, 63109.
Overman, Robert F., 4917 Ravenswood Dr. Apt. 357, San Antonio, TX 78227.
Ratermann, David A., Regina Cleri, 10 Archbishop May Dr., St. Louis, 63119.
Rau, Donald E., Regina Cleri, 10 Archbishop May Dr., St. Louis, 63119.
Reilly, Edward W., St. Elizabeth Ann Seton, 2 Seton Ct., St. Charles, 63303.
Ronquest, John T., Regina Cleri, 10 Archbishop May Dr., St. Louis, 63119.
Schneider, Nicholas A., 6333 S. Rosebury Ave. 2W, Clayton, 63105.
Wilkerson, Jerome F., Ph.D., Pope John Paul II Residence for Priests, St. Agnes Home, 10341 Manchester Rd., 63122.
Woracek, Thomas J., Regina Cleri, 10 Archbishop May Dr., St. Louis, 63119.
Revs.—
Ahrens, William B., Alexian Brothers, 4624 Lansdowne, St. Louis, 63116.
Althoff, Arthur J., Regina Cleri, 10 Archbishop May Dr., St. Louis, 63119.
Argent, Robert W., Regina Cleri, 10 Archbishop May Dr., St. Louis, 63119.
Begley, Thomas M., 404 W. Adams, Apt. A, 63122.
Bendel, Eugene F., Assumption, 403 N. Main St., O'Fallon, 63366.
Blomberg, John F., Regina Cleri, 10 Archbishop May Dr., St. Louis, 63119.
Boisaubin, Robert D., Regina Cleri, 10 Archbishop May Dr., St. Louis, 63119.
Brennan, Eugene P., St. Sabina, 1365 Harkee Dr., Florissant, 63031.
Brennan, George P., 300 N. Fourth St., #501, St. Louis, 63102.
Britt, William J., Regina Cleri, 10 Archbishop May Dr., St. Louis, 63119.
Brunnert, Theodore J., St. Joan of Arc Church, 5800 Oleatha Ave., 63139.
Burghoff, Theodore H., Mother of Good Counsel Home, 6825 Natural Bridge Rd., St. Louis, 63121.
Comer, John P., Regina Cleri, 10 Archbishop May Dr., St. Louis, 63119.
Corbett, Robert L., Christ, Prince of Peace Church, 415 Weidman Rd., Manchester, 63011.
Dalton, Donald T., 116 Hancock Ct., Festus, 63028.
Danter, Albert F., St. Agnes Home, 10341 Manchester Rd., Kirkwood, 63122.
Ditenhafer, John A., Annunziata Church, 9305 Clayton Rd., St. Louis, 63124.
Edwards, James T.
Everding, Richard F., Regina Cleri, 10 Archbishop May Dr., St. Louis, 63119.
Fitzgibbon, Edmond J., Regina Cleri, 10 Archbishop May Dr., St. Louis, 63119.
Forst, Aloysius A., 4141 Germania, Apt. 2B, St. Louis, 63116.
Galovich, George, 100 Aldergate #8, Bonne Terre, 63628.
Geoghegan, John F., Regina Cleri, 10 Archbishop May Dr., St. Louis, 63119.
Halleman, John L., Pope John Paul II Residence for Priests, St. Agnes Home, 10341 Manchester Rd., St. Louis, 63122.
Heimos, Robert L., P.O. Box 85, Gray Summit, 63039.
Heman, Richard J., 9405 Pancho Dr., St. Louis, 63123.
Hilgeman, Edward J., 8728 Magdalen Ave., St. Louis, 63144.
Hughes, John Jay, Christ the King Church, 7316 Balson Ave., University City, 63130.
Julius, James A., 29 Pecan Dr., Long Beach, MS 39560.
Kersgieter, Paul J., Mother of Good Counsel Home, 6825 Natural Bridge Rd., 63121.
Knoll, Urban H., 629 S. Fourth St., St. Charles, 63301.
Koch, Donald J.
Lampert, Robert E., 680 E. Basse Rd., Apt. 426, San Antonio, TX 78209.
Leibrecht, Robert G., Regina Cleri, 10 Archbishop May Dr., St. Louis, 63119.
Lewis, Leo T., 73 Kings Rd., Evergreen, CO 80439.

Mannion, Martin K., Regina Cleri, 10 Archbishop May Dr., St. Louis, 63119.
Marshall, James C., The Arbors at Mount Carmel, 720 Jackson St. Apt. 2, St. Charles, 63301.
Marshall, Robert A., St. Agnes Home, 10341 Manchester Rd., St. Louis, 63122.
Mersinger, Norbert A., Regina Cleri, 10 Archbishop May Dr., St. Louis, 63119.
Molitor, Donald F., 478 Vass Creek Rd., Union, 63084.
Monahan, Joseph R., Regina Cleri, 10 Archbishop May Dr., St. Louis, 63119.
Murphy, James E., 16 Tournament Tee Dr., O'Fallon, 63366.
Novak, David A., Regina Cleri, 10 Archbishop May Dr., St. Louis, 63119.
Oge, Raymond J., 12134 Lakewood Dr., Sainte Genevieve, 63670.
Rodis, James, 4840 Germania, St. Louis, 63116.
Roedig, Robert L., Regina Cleri, 10 Archbishop May Dr., St. Louis, 63119.
Ruff, Charles R., Regina Cleri, 10 Archbishop May Dr., St. Louis, 63119.
Ryan, Joseph J., Aston Gardens, 249 Courtyards Blvd., Apt. 104, Sun City Center, FL 33573.
Schloemer, Bernard J., St. Gabriel the Archangel, 6303 Nottingham Ave., St. Louis, 63109.
Selzer, Eugene P., St. Matthias, 796 Buckley Rd., St. Louis, 63125.
Sullivan, David C., St. Agnes Home, 10341 Manchester, St. Louis, 63122.
Suren, Richard H., 6047 Bishops Pl., St. Louis, 63109.
Thomas, David T., 4445 Lindell Blvd., 63108.
Utrup, Eugene E., 867 Fairway Dr., Union, 63084.
Voelker, Harold H., Regina Cleri, 10 Archbishop May Dr., St. Louis, 63119.
Walter, David A., Regina Cleri, 10 Archbishop May Dr., St. Louis, 63119.
Wilkins, Bernard J., St. Gertrude, 6535 Hwy. YY, 63090.
Winzerling, James L., 12685 Dorsett Rd., #228, Maryland Heights, 63043.
Wolf, Joseph B., 347 Autumn Creek (D), Valley Park, 63088.
Zinzer, Walter W., 3605 Hidden Rd., #B-4, San Antonio, TX 78217.

Permanent Deacons:
Allen, Charles M., St. Elizabeth, Mother of John the Baptist, St. Louis
Amelotti, David, Our Lady of Providence, Grantwood
Ast, Christopher M., Immaculate Heart of Mary, New Melle
Auer, Edward J., (Retired)
Bachista, Ronald J., (Retired)
Bansbach, Paul, (Retired)
Basler, James H., St. Agnes, Bloomsdale
Bast, Paul, Immaculate Conception, Dardenne Prairie
Baugh, Steven D., Assumption, Herculaneum
Becker, Gerald H., Immaculate Conception, Union
Beckmann, John W., St. Dominic Savio, Affton
Beirne, Edward R., (Temporary Leave of Absence)
Bernsen, Albert B., (Retired)
Birkenmaier, Robert G., St. Monica, Creve Coeur
Bischof, John A., St. Richard, Creve Coeur
Boedeker, C. Allen, St. Andrew, Lemay
Boland, Richard J., Our Lady of Lourdes, Washington
Bolderson, David A., (Temporary Leave of Absence)
Boyer, Edward J., St. Rose of Lima, DeSoto
Broyles, Jimmy D., St. Agnes Home, Kirkwood
Bub, Richard F., (Retired)
Buchek, Bradford M., Immaculate Conception, Arnold
Buckley, James Mike, Ste. Genevieve Du Bois, Warson Woods
Buckley, Michael L., St. Bernadette, Lemay
Buckman, Bernard A., St. Patrick, Wentzville
Buhr, Thomas A., (Retired)
Burch, Michael D., Immaculate Conception, Park Hills
Burkard, Bruce A., Sacred Heart, Florissant
Burkemper, Thomas B., (Retired)
Burle, Raymond J., Jr., Holy Rosary, Warrenton
Burton, James L., (Retired)
Butler, James R., Immaculate Conception, Dardenne Prairie
Camden, David M., St. Simon the Apostle, Green Park
Carroll, Kevin, Holy Trinity, St. Ann
Casseau, William U., (Retired)
Chauvin, C. Frank, Ascension, Chesterfield
Chavaux, Paul H., (Retired)
Chitwood, Dennis M., Sts. Peter and Paul, St. Louis
Christ, Walter W., (Retired)
Clark, Lawrence L., Immaculate Conception, Maplewood
Clemens, Kenneth C., Jr., Holy Infant, Ballwin
Coffman, Richard W., Mary, Mother of the Church, Mattese
Conley, Allen M., (Retired)
Coppage, Michael J., Jr., (Leave of Absence)
Crafts, R. Paul, St. Paul, Fenton
Craska, Paul D., St. John Bosco, Creve Coeur
Curtin, John A., (Temporary Leave of Absence)
Czarnecki, Eugene J., (Retired)
Damato, Larry, (Retired)
Danna, Frank, (Retired)
Darin, John, St. Vincent de Paul, Perryville
Daus, Andrew C., St. Margaret Mary Alacoque, Oakville
Davanzo, Charles R., Blessed Teresa of Calcutta, Ferguson
Dehler, Thomas F., (Retired)
Denham, Donald C., St. Gerard Majella, Kirkwood
Dickerson, Raymond A., (Retired)
Dingman, Edwin H., (Retired)
Dodson, Fred, (Retired)
Dolan, Timothy C., St. Gerard Majella, Kirkwood
Donnelly, Daniel R., St. Joseph, Manchester
Dorhauer, Jacob W., (Retired)
Driscoll, Donald L., Our Lady of the Holy Cross, St. Louis
Duban, Matthew E., St. Angela Merici, Florissant
Dubbs, Harvey, St. Clare, St. Clair
Durban, Charles, St. Anselm, Creve Coeur
Ecker, Alan E., St. Francis of Assisi, Oakville
Ehrhard, Herbert L., (Retired)
Esswein, Leo F., (Temporary Leave of Absence)
Eultgen, Thomas L., Most Sacred Heart, Eureka
Falbo, Anthony, St. Gianna, Lake St. Louis
Farley, Robert G., Assumption, Mattese
Felber, David A., St. Norbert, Florissant
Fink, George Russ, St. Francis of Assisi, Oakville
Flanigan, John P., Jr., Holy Redeemer, Webster Groves
Follen, Dale J., St. Joseph, Manchester
Forster, Thomas E., Sacred Heart, Valley Park
Fronick, Edward C., St. Martin of Tours, Lemay
Gawedzinkski, Norbert L., St. John, Imperial
Gearon, William A., (Retired)
Gegg, Albin A., St. Joseph, Farmington
Geiser, Gerald J., St. Raphael the Archangel, St. Louis
Georges, Charles W., Holy Spirit, Maryland Heights
Gerling, Thomas J., Our Lady, Queen of Peace, House Springs
Gettemeier, Herbert B., (Retired)
Gildehaus, Charles R., St. Gertrude, Krakow
Gorski, Thomas, Sts. Peter and Paul, St. Louis
Gottlieb, Thomas J., Church of the Annunziata, Ladue
Gounis, Peter E., St. Ferdinand, Florissant
Griffard, James M., Sacred Heart, Florissant
Groner, H. Wayne, Assumption, New Haven; St. Paul, Berger
Grotpeter, Edward R., St. Mary Magdalen, Brentwood
Guilford, Mark A., St. Alban Roe, Wildwood
Gunsaullus, Roland J., (Retired)
Haefner, Joseph Tom, St. Anthony, Sullivan
Haehnel, Fred M., St. Charles Borromeo, St. Charles, MO
Hanses, Eugene J., (Retired)
Harpring, David I., Our Lady of the Rosary, Spanish Lake
Harrison, R. Fielding, (Retired)
Hayes, Ralph, Blessed Teresa of Calcutta, Ferguson
Hecktor, Paul J., St. Ignatius, Concord Hill
Heitert, Donald C., (Retired)
Hengen, Philip R., Washington University, Newman Center
Henning, Kenneth A., Church of the Good Shepherd, Hillsboro
Henroid, Daniel H., St. Joan of Arc, St. Louis
Hercules, Joseph E., St. Matthias, Lemay
Holmes, Charles E., (Retired)
Holtmeyer, Gilbert C., (Retired)
Hurlbert, Gerald R., St. Elizabeth Ann Seton, St. Charles
Iovanna, Joseph, St. Mary Magdalen, St. Louis
Janson, Norman F., (Retired)
Johnson, Leslie A., (Retired)
Johnson, William P., St. Rose Philippine Duchesne, Florissant
Kaiser, Roland, St. Joseph, Imperial
Keeney, Robert J., Ascension, Chesterfield
Kelly, Lawrence C., St. Francis of Assisi, Oakville
Kennedy, Joseph M., Christ, Prince of Peace, Manchester
Kenney, T. Michael, III, (Retired)
Kiely, Edward Ray, Christ the King, University City
King, Philip, St. Robert Bellarmine, St. Charles
Klintz, Donald, Our Lady, Festus
Klostermann, Robert A., Sr., St. Francis of Assisi, Portage des Sioux
Knobbe, Gerald E., All Saints, St. Peters
Komotos, John W., St. Peter, Kirkwood
Kreitler, Roger A., St. Raphael the Archangel, St. Louis
Krieger, Arnold F., Airport Chaplaincy
Kroutil, Joseph C., St. Ferdinand, Florissant
Krull, William J., (Retired)
La Martina, Joseph A., Immacolata, Richmond Heights
Lauterwasser, Gerard M., St. Sabina, Florissant
Le Fors, Ronald S., St. Angela Merici, Flourissant
Lechner, Joel, O.S.M., Seven Holy Founders, Affton
Lee, Samuel, All Souls, Overland
Lemoine, David E., Sacred Heart, Valley Park
Leonardo, Delfin S., St. Joseph, Clayton; Chap., St. John's Mercy Hospital
Litteken, James J., St. Paul, St. Paul
Lombardo, Charles W., Seven Holy Founders, Affton
Long, James
Love, Allen F., Blessed Teresa of Calcutta, Ferguson
Macauley, Edward C., (Retired)
Maranan, Diosdado L., St. David, Arnold
Marino, John, Ascension, Chesterfield
Martin, James P., St. Monica, Creve Coeur
Martin, Leroy A., Jr., St. Mary Magdalen, Brentwood
Martin, Paul A., Church of the Good Shepherd, Hillsboro
Maxwell, Perez E., (Leave of Absence)
Mayo, Robert J., II, St. Rose Philippine Duchesne, Florissant
McCarthy, Mark J., St. Cletus, St. Charles
McElroy, Donald L., St. Charles Borromeo, St. Charles
McEntire, Clyde W., Immaculate Conception, Maplewood
McGuire, Jerry N., St. Richard, Creve Coeur
McKee, Paul R., Ph.D., (Retired)
McKenna, William J., (Retired)
Meere, John F., Ste. Genevieve, Ste. Genevieve
Meiergerd, Joseph C., St. Robert Bellarmine, St. Charles
Meister, William G., St. Elizabeth of Hungary, Crestwood
Menard, Louis A., (Retired)
Meyerkord, Gary A., All Saints, St. Peters
Miller, George W., St. Wenceslaus, St. Louis
Miller, George A., St. Joseph, Manchester
Miller, Millard Ray, St. Monica, Creve Coeur; Cardinal Glennon Children's Hospital
Monahan, Patrick G., Cure of Ars, Shrewsbury
Moore, Richard R., Saint Gianna, Lake St. Louis
Mroczkowski, Raymond V., (Retired)
Mueller, Frederick J., (Retired)
Mulvihill, Thomas O., Mary, Queen of Peace, Webster Groves
Murphey, James W., Jr., Immaculate Heart of Mary, St. Louis
Murphy, James L., St. Dominic Savio, Affton
Murphy, Thomas P., (Retired)
Murphy, Thomas O., (Retired)
Murray, Stephen L., (Retired)
Naumann, Eugene J., Holy Spirit, Maryland Heights
Nava, Lawrence, St. John, Imperial
Nesbitt, Frank E., (Temporary Leave of Absence)
Nicolai, Michael A., St. James the Greater, St. Louis
Noelker, Leon R., St. Francis Borgia, Washington
Nuelle, Norman C., St. Alban Roe, Wildwood
Olmsted, Francis J., St. Cletus, St. Charles; Asst., DeSmet Jesuit High School
Orr, Robert J., St. Margaret Mary Alacoque, Oakville
Osmack, David, Immacolata, Richmond Heights
Pacino, David, St. Martin De Porres, Hazelwood
Penberthy, Robert S., St. George, Gardenville
Peterson, Stanley M., Jr., St. Nicholas, St. Louis
Pimmel, Terrance, St. Joan of Arc, St. Louis
Piva, Michael J., St. Joseph, Cottleville
Politte, Glennon P., Sr., (Retired)
Politte, Stephen A., (Retired)
Politte, Thomas J., St. David, Arnold
Porterfield, Paul D., (Retired)
Potzman, Kenneth M., St. John's Mercy Hospital, St. Cletus, St. Charles
Powers, James R., Ph.D., Our Lady of the Pillar, Saint Louis
Powers, Robert J., (Retired)
Prideaux, Frank W., (Retired)
Priesmeyer, William F., Jr., Holy Trinity, St. Ann
Prives, Gerald J., (Retired)
Quinn, J. Gerard, Judge, Missouri Appellate Tribunal; Our Lady of the Holy Cross, St. Louis
Quistorff, Richard, St. Patrick, Wentzville
Rankin, Patrick J., St. Theodore, Flint Hill
Renard, Richard L., St. Peter, Kirkwood
Reynoso, Louis J., St. Rita, Vinita Park
Riegel, Robert C., (Retired)
Roberson, Robert L., (Retired)
Rodis, Theodore J., Cure of Ars, Shrewsbury

Rohaly, Ernest G., Immaculate Conception, Dardenne Prairie
Rothermich, Thomas N., St. Theodore, Flint Hill
Ruegg, Walter J., (Retired)
Russell, James W., St. Martin of Tours, Lemay
Ryder, Charles T., St. John's Mercy Medical Center; St. John, Imperial
Schaeffer, Eugene W., III, St. Joseph, Cottleville
Schellhase, Richard H., Queen of All Saints, Oakville
Schiffer, John, St. Peter, St. Charles
Schiffman, Donald J., (Retired)
Schisler, Steven M., Immaculate Conception, Arnold
Schmitt, Donald J., (Retired)
Schnable, Robert H., (Retired)
Schulte, Edwin, (Retired)
Schultheis, Glennon J., St. Joseph, Cottleville; St. Joseph's Health Center
Schultz, Timothy, Sts. Joachim and Ann, St. Charles
Schulze, Roy E., St. George, Gardenville
Selsor, Brian T., St. Joseph, Imperial
Shannon, John R., (Retired)
Shelby, Richard L., (Retired)
Sinak, William S., De Greeff Hospice House; St. Francis of Assisi, Oakville
Sisul, Leonard A., Holy Redeemer, Webster Groves
Skillman, Daniel, Our Lady of Sorrows, St. Louis
Smith, Randall G., St. John the Baptist, Gildehaus
Snyder, Charles R., St. John's Mercy Medical Center; Sacred Heart, Valley Park
Snyder, Robert J., St. Elizabeth of Hungary, Crestwood
Stackle, Paul F., St. Simon the Apostle, Green Park
Stallings, Larry J., Incarnate Word, Chesterfield
Stevens, Richard L., St. Anthony of Padua, High Ridge
Stigall, Donald R., Mary, Queen of Peace, Webster Groves
Stovall, Dennis K., St. Clare of Assisi, Ellisville
Stoverink, Gerard G., Sacred Heart, Crystal City
Stoverink, John J., St. Ambrose, St. Louis
Strauss, Harold A., St. Sabina, Florissant
Streckfuss, Joseph C., (Retired)
Suden, Michael E., D.D.S., St. Bridget, Pacific
Sulze, Joseph W., (Retired)
Sutton, Ronald L., (Retired)
Tadlock, Richard, St. Elizabeth Ann Seton, St. Charles
Tetreault, James E., Epiphany of Our Lord, St. Louis
Tichacek, George A., St. Catherine Laboure, Sappington
Towey, Martin G., Ph.D., St. Paul, St. Paul
Tracy, Daniel J., St. Ambrose, St. Louis
Trautman, Anthony G., Immaculate Conception, Old Monroe
Turek, Paul J., Sr., Our Lady, Queen of Peace, House Springs
Twellman, William H., St. Norbert, Florissant
Van Booven, Howard J., Assumption, O'Fallon; Unity Health Hospice
Vaughn, Albert X., Our Lady of Lourdes, University City
Vehige, Richard J., St. Clement of Rome, Des Peres
Volansky, Fred N., Assumption, O'Fallon
Volansky, James M., St. Gabriel the Archangel, St. Louis
Wainscott, John B., Church of the Annunziata, Ladue
Walbridge, William F., (Retired)
Warren, Phillip C., St. Martin of Tours, Lemay
Watson, George H., Holy Name of Jesus, Bissel Hills
Weatherholt, H. John, St. Paul, Fenton
Weishaar, Lonnie G., Immaculate Heart of Mary, New Melle
Weiss, William G., Little Flower, Richmond Heights
Werner, Norman B., (Retired)
Wertz, Robert E., Our Lady of Sorrows, St. Louis
White, Otis D., (Retired)
Whitson, Alan W., St. Clare of Assisi, Ellisville
Willbrand, Thomas J., (Retired)
Williams, Albert C., St. Joseph, Clayton
Willis, David J., St. Gabriel the Archangel, St. Louis
Wingbermuehle, Joseph, Queen of All Saints, Oakville
Winkelmann, Christian H., St. Justin Martyr, Sunset Hills
Wohlert, Steven H., St. Anselm, Creve Coeur
Wussler, Donald A., (Retired)

INSTITUTIONS LOCATED IN THE ARCHDIOCESE

[A] SEMINARIES, ARCHDIOCESAN

ST. LOUIS. *Kenrick-Glennon Seminary* (1818) (St. Louis Roman Catholic Theological Seminary), Tel: 314-792-6100; Fax: 314-792-6500. Email: wojcicki@kenrick.edu. Web: www.kenrick.edu.

Kenrick School of Theology, 5200 Glennon Dr., 63119. Tel: 314-792-6100; Fax: 314-792-6500. Web: www.kenrick.edu. Revs. Thomas McDermott, O.P., Asst. Prof. Spirituality; John M. Hunthausen, S.J., Spiritual Dir.; Gregory Lockwood, Mariology; Donald E. Henke, Assoc. Academic Dean, Moral Theology; Rev. Msgr. Ted L. Wojcicki, Ed.D., Pres. - Rector; Rev. Edward J. Richard, M.S., Vice Rector & Dean Students; Rev. Msgr. Edmund O. Griesedieck, Assist. Spiritual Dir. (Retired); Rev. Lawrence C. Brennan, S.T.D., Vice Rector, Academic Dean; Rev. Msgr. James J. Ramacciotti, Canon Law; Revs. Michael J. Witt, Ph.D., Assoc. Prof. Church History; Dennis M. Doyle, J.C.L., Spiritual Dir./Confessor; Kristian C. Teater, Asst.Prof. Spiritual Theology; Paul J. Rothschild, Assoc. Dean Students; Randy Soto, S.Th.D., Prof. New Testament Scripture; Sr. Catherine Marie Stewart, S.D.S.H., Rel. Educ.; Dr. Daniel Van Slyke, Assoc. Prof. Church History; John Cleary, Dir. of Devel.; Dr. Susanne M. Harvath, Ph.D., Prof. Pastoral Counseling; Mary Beth Wittry, Dir. of Music; Dr. John L. Gresham, Assoc. Prof. Systematic Theology; Lucius Hernandez, M.A., Latin & Spanish; Dr. Andrew J. Sopko, Ph.D., Dir. of Library; Dr. Sebastian Mahfood, Assoc. Prof. Intercultural Studies; Dr. Lawrence J. Welch, Ph.D., Prof. Systematic Theology. Priests 15; Students 90; St. Louis Students 32; Permanent Staff: Priests 15; Lay Staff 10.

Cardinal Glennon College, 5200 Glennon Dr., 63119. Tel: 314-792-6100; Fax: 314-792-6500. Rev. Msgr. Timothy P. Cronin, Rector; Rev. Dennis M. Doyle, J.C.L.; Dr. Randall Colton, Asst. Prof. Philosophy/Assoc. Academic Dean; Dr. John Doyle, Distinguished Prof. Philosophy; Dr. Ryan Madison, Asst. Prof. Philosophy. Priests 9; Sisters 1; Lay Teachers 3; Students 23; St. Louis Students 19; Permanent Staff: Priests 3; Sisters 1; Lay Teachers 3; Kansas City in Kansas 2; Springfield-Cape Girardeau 1; Colorado Springs 1.

[B] SEMINARIES, RELIGIOUS, OR SCHOLASTICATES

ST. LOUIS. *Aquinas Institute of Theology*, 23 S. Spring St., 63108. Tel: 314-256-8800; Fax: 314-256-8888. Email: info@ai.edu. Web: www.ai.edu. Revs. Richard A. Peddicord, O.P., Pres.; Gregory J. Heille, O.P., Vice Pres. & Academic Dean; Thomas Barbarak, Dir. Mktg & Communications; David Werthmann, Dir. Admissions; Barbara Maynard, Dir. Inst. Advancement; Brad Buchek, Dir. Finance; Janel Esker, Registrar. Priests 9; Sisters 6; Lay Faculty & Admin Staff 9.

Faculty: Revs. Seán Martin; Harry M. Byrne, O.P.; George R. Boudreau, O.P.; Michael R. Carey, O.P.; Daniel Harris; Dominic Holtz, O.P.; Jose Santiago, O.P.; Sisters Jean deBlois, C.S.J.; Maribeth Howell, O.P.; Colleen Mary Mallon, O.P.; Carla Mae Streeter, O.P.; Catherine Vincie, R.S.H.M.; Patricia Walter, O.P.; Kathleen Tehan, Librarian; Ann Garrido; Marian Love; Celeste Mueller; Michael Porterfield; Carolyn Wright.

St. John Neumann House (1986) Redemptorist College Seminary Residence, 3737 Washington Blvd., 63108. Tel: 314-531-2777; Fax: 314-531-5726. Web: www.redemptorists-denver.org. Revs. Patrick A. Keyes, C.Ss.R., Formation Dir., Supr.; Richard Schiblin, C.Ss.R. (Retired); Anthony Nguyen, C.Ss.R., Formation Dir.; Larry Sanders, C.Ss.R., Vocation Dir.; Peter Tenchai Getsurin, C.Ss.R.; Bros. Marvin Mamman, C.Ss.R., Treas.; Juan Carlos Garcia, C.Ss.R. Brothers 2; Priests 6; Seminarians 7.

Faculty: Rev. Daniel E. Harris, C.M.; Ann Garrido; Ken Homan, Ph.D.

[C] COLLEGES AND UNIVERSITIES

ST. LOUIS. *Fontbonne University* (1923) 6800 Wydown Blvd., 63105. Tel: 314-862-3456; Fax: 314-889-1451. Email: mjohnson@fontbonne.edu. Web: www.fontbonne.edu. Dennis C. Golden, Ed.D., Pres. Sisters 6; Lay Teachers 67; Students 2,827.

Saint Louis University (1818) Corporate Title: Saint Louis University, 221 N. Grand Blvd., Rm. 417, 63103-2097. Tel: 314-977-2222; Fax: 314-977-3874. Email: admitme@slu.edu. Web: www.slu.edu. Mr. John Pruellage, Chm. Bd. of Trustees; Rev. Lawrence H. Biondi, S.J., Pres.; Manoj Patankar, Ph.D., Interim Provost. Priests 37; Brothers 1; Sisters 5; Lay Teachers 1,634; Total Staff 3,667; Total Enrollment 12,309.

Vice Presidents: Robert Woodruff, Vice Pres. & CFO; Mr. Thomas W. Keefe, Vice Pres. Univ. Advancement; Kathleen T. Brady, Vice Pres. Facilities Mgmt. & Civic Affairs; William R. Kauffman, J.D., Vice Pres. & General Counsel; Kenneth Fleischmann, J.D., Vice Pres. Human Resource Mgmt.; Kent Porterfield, Vice Pres. Student Devel.; Tim Brooks, Vice Pres., Chief Info. Officer; Rev. Frank Reale, S.J., Vice Pres. Mission & Ministry; Ray Tait, Vice Pres. Provost Research.

Deans:

Allied Health Professions, Doisy School of Tel: 314-977-8501; Fax: 314-977-4344. Charlotte Brasic Royeen, Ph.D., Dean.

Arts and Sciences, College of Tel: 314-977-2244; Fax: 314-977-3649. Donald Brennan, Ph.D., Dean.

John Cook School of Business Tel: 314-977-3833; Fax: 314-977-3497. Ellen F. Harshman, J.D., Ph.D., Dean.

Graduate School Tel: 314-977-2244; Fax: 314-977-3943. Donald G. Brennan, Ph.D., Dean.

Law, School of Tel: 314-977-8172; Fax: 314-977-3333. Jeffrey E. Lewis, J.D., Dean.

Medicine, School of Tel: 314-977-9801; Fax: 314-977-9899. Philip Alderson, M.D., Vice Pres. Health Svcs.

Nursing, School of Tel: 314-977-8910; Fax: 314-977-8949. Teri A. Murray, Ph.D., R.N., Dean.

Parks College of Engineering, Aviation and Technology Tel: 314-977-8631; Fax: 314-977-8403. Manoj Patankar, Ph.D., Dean.

Philosophy and Letters, College of Tel: 314-977-2701; Fax: 314-977-7211. Rev. Michael D. Barber, S.J., Dean.

Professional Studies, School of Tel: 314-977-3349; Fax: 314-977-2333. Marla Berg-Weger, Ph.D., L.C.S.W., Dean.

Public Health, School of Tel: 314-977-8188; Fax: 314-977-8150. Homer Schmitz, Ph.D., Interim Dean.

College of Education and Public Service Tel: 314-977-2749; Fax: 314-977-3290. John Watzke, Ph.D., Dean.

Academic Advising and Support Tel: 314-977-2369; Fax: 314-977-1424. Tom McGinnis, Ph.D., Dir.

Pius XII Memorial Library Tel: 314-977-3580; Fax: 314-977-3108. Gail Staines, Ph.D., Asst. Provost Univ. Libraries.

Student Educational Services Tel: 314-977-2930; Fax: 314-977-3315. Elizabeth Callahan, J.D., Assoc. Vice Pres. Enrollment & Academic Svcs.

Madrid Spain Campus Tel: 314-977-8177; Fax: 314-977-1445. Rev. Frank Reale, S.J., Rector.

Other Jesuits Associated with the University: Revs. R. Bentley Anderson, S.J.; James H. Baker, S.J.; Michael D. Barber, S.J.; Lawrence H. Biondi, S.J.; Paul J. Coutinho, S.J.; Anthony C. Daly, S.J.; Denis E. Daly, S.J.; Terrence E. Dempsey, S.J.; Everett A. Diederich, S.J., Center for Liturgy; John B. Foley, S.J.; Michael D. French, S.J.; James F. Goeke, S.J.; W. Charles Heiser, S.J.; John J. Kavanaugh, S.J.; Thomas E. J. Kelly, S.J.; Edwin Lisson, S.J.; Michael K. May, S.J.; David V. Meconi, S.J.; John J. Mueller, S.J.; William P. O'Brien, S.J.; Claude N. Pavur, S.J.; Robert L. Poirier, S.J.; Patrick T. Quinn, S.J.; Frank Reale, S.J.; Albert C. Rotola, S.J.; Mr. Michael D. Rozier, S.J.; Revs. Stephen A. Schoenig, S.J.; James A. Sebesta, S.J.; Gary G. Seibert, S.J.; Paul V. Stark, S.J.; David J. Suwalsky, S.J.; James V. Veltrie, S.J.; James K. Voiss, S.J.; Bro. William R. Rehg, S.J.

Pastoral Care Dept. of Saint Louis University Hospital: Sr. Sheila Hammond, R.S.C.J., Pastoral Care Dir.

[D] RELIGIOUS EDUCATION

ST. LOUIS. *Paul VI Institute of Catechetical and Pastoral Studies*, 20 Archbishop May Dr., 63119. Tel: 314-633-2550; Fax: 314-633-2559. Email: paul6@archstl.org. Web: www.archstl.org/paul6. Revs. Edward J. Richard, M.S., Dir.; Donald E. Henke, Assoc. Dir.; Dr. John L. Gresham, Curriculum & Technology Coord.; Sr. Catherine Marie Stewart, S.D.S.H., Coord. of Sacramental/Catechetical Retreats; Mary L. Beier, Registrar - Business Mgr.; Marisol D. Pfaff, Admin. Asst.- Online Course System Admin.; Dr. Shawn McCauley Welch, Assoc. Dean. Priests 4; Sisters 4; Lay Teachers 11; Total Enrollment 951.

[E] HIGH SCHOOLS, ARCHDIOCESAN

ST. LOUIS. *Bishop DuBourg High School* (1950) 5850 Eichelberger St., 63109. Tel: 314-832-3030; Fax: 314-832-0529. Email: cdandridge@bishopdubourg.org. Web: www.bishopdubourg.org. Mr. Kermit V. Boschert, Pres.; Ms. Bridget Timoney, Prin. A Co-Educational School Staffed by Diocesan Priests, Religious and Lay Teachers. Priests 1; Deacons 1; Lay Teachers 55; Students 665.

Cardinal Ritter College Prep, 701 N. Spring, 63108. Tel: 314-446-5500; Fax: 314-446-5570. Email: chall@archstl.org. Web: info.csd.org/ritter.htm. Leon Henderson, Pres.; Mrs. Carmele U. Hall,

Prin.; Christine Turland, Librarian. Co-Educational High School Staffed by Religious and Laity. Priests 1; Sisters 1; Lay Teachers 35; Students 400.

Saint Mary's High School (1931) 4701 S. Grand Blvd., 63111. Tel: 314-481-8400; Fax: 314-481-3670. Email: mainoffice@stmaryshs.com. Web: www.stmaryshs.com. Rev. Mitchell S. Doyen, Pres.; Mr. Kevin Hacker, B.A., M.Ed., Prin.; Jake Parent, Librarian. For Boys, Staffed by Brothers of Mary and Archdiocesan Priests. Priests 2; Sisters 1; Lay Teachers 33; Total Enrollment 390.

Rosati-Kain High School (1911) 4389 Lindell Blvd., 63108-2701. Tel: 314-533-8513; Fax: 314-533-1618. Email: rkoffice@rosati-kain.org. Web: www.rosati-kain.org. Sr. Joan Andert, S.S.N.D., Pres.; Mrs. Judy Mohan, Assoc. Prin.; Susan Faron, Librarian. Conducted for Girls by the Archdiocese of St. Louis, the Sisters of St. Joseph and the School Sisters of Notre Dame. Sisters 2; Lay Teachers 32; Girls 388.

Trinity Catholic High School (2002) 1720 Redman Ave., 63138. Tel: 314-741-1333; Fax: 314-741-1335. Email: office@trinitycatholichighschool.org. Web: www.trinitycatholichighschool.org. Ms. Nancy Lydon, Prin.; Mrs. Gail Hoffmann, Librarian. Priests 1; Sisters 1; Lay Teachers 32; Students 427.

FESTUS. *St. Pius X High School*, 1030 St. Pius Dr., 63028. Tel: 636-937-3695; 636-931-7488; Fax: 636-931-7487. Email: lancer@stpius.com. Web: stpius.com. Mrs. Karen De Costy, Prin. A Co-Educational High School Conducted by Diocesan Priests and Lay Faculty. Priests 2; Lay Teachers 21; Students 260.

MANCHESTER. *John F. Kennedy Catholic High School* (1968) 500 Woods Mill Rd., 63011. Tel: 636-227-5900; Fax: 636-227-0298. Email: admin@kennedycatholic.net. Web: www.kennedycatholic.net. Christine A. Bolesta, Pres.; Mary Hey, Prin.; Shelagh Fant, Librarian. A Co-Educational High School Staffed by Lay Faculty. Priests 1; Lay Teachers 30; Students 365.

O'FALLON. *St. Dominic High School* (1962) 31 St. Dominic Dr., 63366. Tel: 636-240-8303; Fax: 636-240-9884. Email: mainoffice@stdominichs.org. Web: www.stdominichs.org. Sr. Mary H. Bender, S.S.N.D., Pres.; Cathy Fetter, Prin.; Mary Fridley, Librarian. A Co-Educational High School Conducted by Diocesan Priests laymen and laywomen. Priests 1; Sisters 1; Lay Teachers 55; Students 736.

ST. CHARLES. *Duchesne High School*, 2550 Elm St., 63301-1494. Tel: 636-946-6767; Fax: 636-946-6267. Email: tgravemann@duchesne-hs.com. Web: www.duchesne-hs.org. Terry W. Gravemann, Pres.; Mrs. Nancy Repking, Prin.; Rev. James L. Gahan, Campus Min.; Ms. Sharon Ziegler, Librarian. A Co-Educational College Prep High School Conducted by Archdiocesan Priests and Catholic Lay Staff. Under the Auspices of the Catholic Education Office and the Archdiocese of St. Louis. Priests 1; Lay Teachers 49; Students 545.

WASHINGTON. *St. Francis Borgia Regional High School* (1982) 1000 Borgia Dr., 63090. Tel: 636-239-7871; Fax: 636-239-1198. Email: mtraffas@borgia.com. Web: www.borgia.com. Marilyn Traffas, Admin.; Mr. George Wingbermuehle, Prin.; Rebecca Price, Librarian. A Co-Educational High School Staffed by Diocesan Priests and dedicated lay faculty. Priests 1; Sisters 1; Lay Teachers 41; Students 545.

[F] HIGH SCHOOLS, PRIVATE

ST. LOUIS. *Christian Brothers College High School (C.B.C.)* (1850) 1850 De La Salle Dr., 63141. Tel: 314-985-6100; Fax: 314-985-6115. Email: admin@cbchs.org. Web: www.cbchs.org. Rev. Matthew L. O'Toole, Chap.; Mr. Michael F. England, Pres.; Bro. David Poos, F.S.C., Prin.; Charlotte Hanselman, Librarian. Priests 1; Brothers 4; Lay Teachers 80; Students 1,020.

Cor Jesu Academy (1956) 10230 Gravois Rd., 63123. Tel: 314-842-1546; Fax: 314-842-6061. Email: principal@corjesu.org. Web: www.corjesu.org. Sisters Barbara Thomas, A.S.C.J., Pres.; Kathleen Mary Coonan, A.S.C.J., Prin. Apostles of the Sacred Heart. Sisters 6; Lay Teachers 51; Students 580.

De Smet Jesuit High School, 233 N. New Ballas Rd., 63141. Tel: 314-567-3500; Fax: 314-567-1519. Web: www.desmet.org. Dr. Gregory A. Densberger, Ph.D., Prin.; Rev. Walter T. Sidney, S.J., Pres. Priests 5; Sisters 2; Scholastics 2; Brothers 1; Lay Teachers 86; Students 1,103.

St. Elizabeth Academy (1882) 3401 Arsenal St., 63118. Tel: 314-771-5134; Fax: 314-771-3528. Email: ccheak@stelizabethacademy.org. Web: stelizabethacademy.org. Christina R. Cheak, Prin.; Head of School. Sisters of the Most Precious Blood. Sisters 3; Lay Teachers 25; Students 215.

Incarnate Word Academy (1932) 2788 Normandy Dr., 63121. Tel: 314-725-5850; Fax: 314-725-2308. Email: rmikolas@iwacademy.org. Web: www.iwacademy.org. Randy Berzon-Mikolas, Ph.D.; Mary T. Maguire, Prin.; Julie Hamilton, Librarian; Sr. Eileen O'Keeffe, C.C.V.I., Mission Integration. Sisters of Charity of Incarnate Word of San Antonio. Lay Teachers 40; Support Staff 14; Students 500.

St. Joseph's Academy (1840) 2307 S. Lindbergh Blvd., 63131. Tel: 314-965-7205; Fax: 314-965-9114. Email: pdunphy@stjosephacademy.org. Web: www.stjosephacademy.org. Sr. Pat Dunphy, C.S.J., Prin. Religious 9; Sisters of St. Joseph of Carondelet 7; Lay Teachers 63; Girls 643.

St. Louis University High School, George H. Backer Memorial, 4970 Oakland Ave., 63110. Tel: 314-531-0330; Fax: 314-534-3441. Web: www.sluh.org. Revs. Thomas W. Cummings, S.J.; Carl J. Heumann, S.J., Supr.; Michael A. Marchlewski, S.J.; James G. Knapp, S.J., Supr.; Ralph D. Houlihan, S.J.; John Lan Tran, S.J. Priests 6; Administrators 6; Lay Teachers 92; Students 1,068.

Notre Dame High School (1934) 320 E. Ripa Ave., 63125. Tel: 314-544-1015; Fax: 314-544-8003. Email: emmem@ndhs.net. Web: www.ndhs.net. Sr. Michelle Emmerich, S.S.N.D., Ed.D., Prin.; Amanda Meehan, Librarian. Sisters 8; Lay Teachers 32; Girls 320.

CREVE COEUR. *Chaminade College Preparatory School Inc.*, 425 S. Lindbergh Blvd., 63131-2799. Tel: 314-993-4400; Fax: 314-993-4403. Email: archstl851@impresso.com. Web: www.chaminademo.com. Rev. Ralph A. Siefert, S.M., Pres.; Dr. Louis Peters, Prin.; James Zolnowski, Librarian. Society of Mary., Residents and Day Students. Priests 2; Brothers 1; Sisters 1; Lay Teachers 62; Students 513.

St. Louis Priory School, 500 S. Mason Rd., 63141-8500. Tel: 314-434-3690; Fax: 314-576-7088. Web: www.priory.org. Very Rev. J. Gregory Mohrman, O.S.B., Prior; Rev. Michael Brunner, O.S.B., Headmaster; Very Rev. M. Paul Kidner, O.S.B.; Revs. Ambrose Bennett, O.S.B.; Bede Price, O.S.B.; Augustine Wetta, O.S.B.; D. Ralph Wright, O.S.B.; Mrs. Maralea K. Gangloff, Librarian. Priests 7; Brothers 7; Lay Teachers 44; Students (9-12) 258; Students (7-8) 166.

FRONTENAC. *Villa Duchesne/Oak Hill* (1929) 801 S. Spoede Rd., 63131. Tel: 314-432-2021; Fax: 314-432-0199. Email: vdoh@vdoh.org. Web: www.vdoh.org. Dr. Patty Fagin, Prin. (7-12); Deborah Steurer, Prin. (PreK-6); Sr. Lucie Nordmann, Head of School. Religious of the Sacred Heart., (Girls: PreK-12; Boys: PreK-6) Sisters 5; Lay Teachers 110; High School Students (7-12) 450; Elementary School Students (PreK-6) 310.

KIRKWOOD. *St. John Vianney High School* (1960) 1311 S. Kirkwood Rd., 63122. Tel: 314-965-4853; Fax: 314-965-1950. Email: lkeller@vianney.com. Web: www.vianney.com. Mr. Michael Loyet, Pres.; Mr. Lawrence D. Keller, Prin.; Mr. Gerard Stevison, Librarian. Conducted for Boys by the Society of Mary (Marianists). Brothers 2; Lay Teachers 47; Students 605.

Ursuline Academy (1848) 341 S. Sappington Rd., 63122. Tel: 314-984-2800; Fax: 314-966-3795. Email: treichardt@ursulinestl.org. Web: www.ursulinestl.org. Dr. Tina Reichardt, Pres.; Sr. Mary Ann Dooling, O.S.U., Prin.; Bernyce Christiansen, Librarian. Ursuline Nuns of the Roman Union. Sisters 4; Lay Teachers 47; Students 645.

TOWN AND COUNTRY. *Visitation Academy* (1833) 3020 N. Ballas Rd., 63131. Tel: 314-625-9100; Fax: 314-432-7210. Web: www.visitationacademy.org. Mrs. Rosalie Henry, Head of School; Mrs. Mary Ellen Schraeder, Upper School Prin. (Grades 7-12); Mrs. Margaret Karl, Lower School Prin. (PK-6). Sisters in the Monastery 13; Lay Teachers 74; Students 420.

WEBSTER GROVES. *Nerinx Hall High School* (1924) 530 E. Lockwood, 63119. Tel: 314-968-1505; Fax: 314-968-0604. Email: broche@nerinxhs.org. Web: www.nerinxhs.org. Sr. Barbara Roche, S.L., Pres.; Mrs. Jane W. Kosash, Prin.; Mrs. Angela F. Zinkl, Assoc. Prin.; Carol Ann K. Winkler, Librarian. Sisters of Loretto at the Foot of the Cross 3; Religious 3; Lay Teachers 61; Students 633.

[G] ELEMENTARY SCHOOLS, PRIVATE

ST. LOUIS. **De La Salle Middle School*, 4145 Kennerly Ave., 63113. Tel: 314-531-9820; Fax: 314-531-4820. Corey M. Quinn, Pres.; Mr. Phil Pusateri, Prin. Lay Teachers 7; Students 54.

Loyola Academy of St. Louis (1994) 3851 Washington Blvd., 63108. Tel: 314-531-9091; Fax: 314-531-3603. Email: eclark@loyolaacademy.org. Web: www.loyolaacademy.org. M. H. Eric Clark, Pres. & Prin. Religious 1; Lay Teachers 7; Students 70.

Marian Middle School (1999) 4130 Wyoming, 63116. Tel: 314-771-7674; Fax: 314-771-7679. Email: mhermann@mms-stl.org. Web: www.mms-stl.org. Maureen A. Herrmann, Dir.; Ms. Christy Leming, Prin. Lay Teachers 7; Students 75.

CREVE COEUR. *Chaminade College Preparatory*, (Grades 6-12), 425 S. Lindbergh Blvd., 63131. Tel: 314-993-4400; Fax: 314-993-4403. Email: archstl851@impresso.com. Web: www.chaminademo.com. Rev. Ralph A. Siefert, S.M., Pres.; Mr. Michael T. Bander, Prin.; James Zolnowski, Librarian. Society of Mary., (Middle School), Residents and Day Students (Boys) Priests 2; Brothers 1; Sisters 1; Lay Teachers 26; Students 275.

FESTUS. *Ursuline Learning Center*, 201 Brierton Ln., 63028. Tel: 636-937-3344. Sr. Madonna O'Hara, O.S.U., Contact Person.

FRONTENAC. *Villa Duchesne* (1929) (Grades 7-12), (Girls), 801 S. Spoede Rd., St. Louis, 63131-2699. Tel: 314-432-2021; Fax: 314-432-7713. Email: pfaginc@vdoh.org. Web: www.vdoh.org. Mrs. Margaret Karl, Prin. (PreK-6); Dr. Patty Fagin, Prin. (7-12; Jack Rizzo, Head of School. Sisters 2; Lay Teachers 45; Girls 310.

ST. CHARLES. *Academy of the Sacred Heart* (1818) (Coed), 619 N. 2nd St., 63301. Tel: 636-946-6127; Fax: 636-949-6659. Email: mglavin@ash1818.org. Web: www.ash1818.org. Sr. Maureen Glavin, Head of School; Mrs. Kathy Hopper, Prin. Upper School; Mrs. Marcia Renken, Prin. Lower School. Sisters 6; Lay Teachers 51; Students 590.

TOWN AND COUNTRY. *Visitation Academy* (1833) (Grades PreK-12), 3020 N. Ballas Rd., 63131. Tel: 314-625-9100; Fax: 314-432-5355. Email: swilliams@visitationacademy.org. Web: www.visitationacademy.org. Mrs. Rosalie Henry, Head of School; Mrs. Margaret Karl, Prin. (PreK-6); Mrs. Mary Ellen Schraeder, Prin. (Grades 7-12). Visitation Sisters 1; Lay Teachers 65; Students 195.

[H] DEPARTMENT OF SPECIAL EDUCATION

ST. LOUIS. *Department of Special Education* (1950) 20 Archbishop May Dr., 63119. Tel: 314-792-7320; Fax: 314-792-7325. Email: ktichy@archstl.org. Dr. Karen Tichy, Assoc. Supt.; Rev. Msgr. Vernon E. Gardin, Ph.D., Spiritual Advisor. Special Education Ungraded classrooms at Ascension, Chesterfield; St. John the Baptist and Seven Holy Founders. Special Education Schools at Annunziata and the Academy at St. Rose Philippine Duchesne. Special Education Day Care, Preschool and Early Intervention Services at St. Mary's-North-South. Special Education Program for children with autism and developmental delays at St. Gemma Center. Special Education services for high school students with disabilities at partner Catholic high schools through St. Joseph's special services. Special religious education classes for children and adults with developmental disabilities or major learning disabilities. Psycho-Educational Testing Service. Administrative office for above programs and services. Total Staff 78; Total Number of Students Served 320.

St. Mary's Special Services (1952) 1724 Redman Ave., 63138. Tel: 314-653-2591; Fax: 314-653-6811. Web: www.special-education.org. Rev. Msgr. Vernon E. Gardin, Ph.D., Exec. Dir.

St. Mary's Special School for Exceptional Children, Early Intervention therapies and child care for preschool children (ages 6 weeks-5 years) developmentally disabled in a normalized mainstream setting (capacity 100); Inclusionary early childhood education for children ages 3-6 years (capacity 20). Lay Staff 29; Clients 150.

CHESTERFIELD. *St. Joseph Institute for the Deaf*, 1809 Clarkson Rd., 63017-5065. Tel: 636-532-3211 (Voice/TTY); Fax: 636-532-4560. Web: www.sjid.org. Deborah S. Wilson, Pres. School for the Deaf; Auditory-oral day school for hearing-impaired children from birth-8th grade. Early intervention therapy for children 0-5; pre- & elementary school offering intense speech & academic prog. Sisters 5; Lay Teachers 30; Personnel 50; Therapists 7; Students 65.

[I] SERVICES FOR THE ELDERLY

ST. LOUIS. *Cardinal Carberry Senior Living Center*, 7601 Watson Rd., 63119. Tel: 314-961-8000; Fax: 314-961-1934. Email: swesley@ccstl.org. Web: www.cardinalcarberry.org; www.ccstl.org/crss. Sr. Suzanne Wesley, C.S.J., CEO.

Cardinal Ritter Senior Services, 7601 Watson Rd., 63119. Tel: 314-961-8000; Fax: 314-961-1934. Email: swesley@ccstl.org. Web: www.cardinalrittersenior services.org. Sr. Suzanne

Wesley, C.S.J., CEO.

Cardinal Ritter Senior Services, Catholic Charities network of agencies provides social services, in home services, residences, adult day care, employment and volunteer services for the elderly. Total Staff 645; Total Housing Units 2,047; Total Clients Served 28,600.

Cardinal Ritter Senior Services - Adult Day Program, 7663 Watson Rd., 63119. Tel: 314-962-7501; Fax: 314-962-7140. Web: www.cardinalrittersseniorservices.org.

Cardinal Ritter Senior Services Residential Services, Inc., 7601 Watson Rd., 63119. Tel: 314-961-8000; Fax: 314-961-4850. Web: www.cardinalritterseniorservices.org. Sr. Suzanne Wesley, C.S.J., CEO. Provides housing mgmt., housing & assisted living facilities for the elderly.

St. Robert Adult Day Program, 1424 First Capitol Dr. S., St. Charles, 63303. Tel: 636-916-3709; Fax: 636-916-3732.

Alexian Court Apartments, 2636 Chippewa St., 63118. Tel: 314-771-5604; Fax: 314-771-7629. Web: www.alexianbrothers.net.

Alexian Brothers Services, Inc., Sponsored by Alexian Brothers of Missouri, Inc., Managed by National Church Residency.

St. John Neumann Apartments, Inc., St. John Neumann Apartments, Inc., 8424 Lucas & Hunt Rd., 63136. Tel: 314-385-0707; Fax: 314-385-5299. Web: www.cardinalritterseniorservices.org.

St. Joseph Apartments, Inc., 7677 Watson Rd., 63119. Tel: 314-962-0969; Fax: 314-962-1393. Web: www.cardinalritterseniorservices.org.

St. Patrick Apartments, Inc., 555 Bluff Parks Dr., 63031. Tel: 314-839-3212; Fax: 314-839-7537. Web: www.cardinalritterseniorservices.org.

St. Patrick's Apartments II, Inc., 583 Bluff Parks Dr., Florissant, 63031. Tel: 314-837-4101; Fax: 314-837-4389. Web: www.cardinalritterseniorservices.org.

Holy Infant Apartments, Inc., 7663 Watson Rd., 63119. Tel: 314-962-7878; Fax: 314-962-1393. Web: www.cardinalritterseniorservices.org.

St. Agnes Apartments, Inc., 2840 Wisconsin, 63118. Tel: 314-664-1255; Fax: 314-664-1192. Web: www.cardinalritterseniorservices.org.

Santa Maria Apartments, 12565 Santa Maria Ct., Hazelwood, 63042. Tel: 314-739-7220; Fax: 314-739-2950.

Pope John Paul II Apartments, Inc., 6325 Waterways Dr., 63033. Tel: 314-653-0400, Ext. 294; Fax: 314-653-2840. Web: www.cardinalritterseniorservices.org.

St. Ann Assisted Living, 10441 International Plaza Dr., St. Ann, 63074. Tel: 314-423-0600; Fax: 314-423-4842. Web: www.cardinalritterseniorservices.org.

St. Elizabeth Hall, 325 N. Newstead, 63108. Tel: 314-652-9525; Fax: 314-652-8879. Web: www.cardinalritterseniorservices.org.

Du Bourg House, 5890 Eichelberger, 63109. Tel: 314-752-1901; Fax: 314-752-0572. Web: www.cardinalritterseniorservices.org.

Cardinal Carberry Senior Living Center Tel: 314-961-8000; Fax: 314-961-1934. Sr. Suzanne Wesley, C.S.J., CEO.

Our Lady of Life Apartments, Inc., 7655 Watson Rd., 63119. Tel: 314-968-9447; Fax: 314-968-1758. Web: www.cardinalritterseniorservices.org.

Mother of Perpetual Help Residence, Inc., Mother of Perpetual Help Residence, Inc., 7609 Watson Rd., 63119. Tel: 314-918-2260; Fax: 314-961-3061. Web: www.cardinalritterseniorservices.org.

Mary, Queen and Mother Center, 7601 Watson Rd., 63119. Tel: 314-961-8000; Fax: 314-961-1548. Web: www.cardinalritterseniorservices.org.

Holy Angels Apartments I, Inc., 3455 DePaul Ln., Bridgeton, 63044. Tel: 314-298-9505; Fax: 314-298-2414. Web: www.cardinalritterseniorservices.org.

Holy Angels Apartments II, Inc., 3499 DePaul Ln., Bridgeton, 63044. Tel: 314-291-1345; Fax: 314-291-2851. Web: www.cardinalritterseniorservices.org.

St. Clare of Assisi Senior Village, Inc., 409 Warrenton Village Dr., Warrenton, 63383. Tel: 314-298-9505; Fax: 314-298-2414. Web: www.cardinalritterseniorservices.org.

St. William Apartments I, Inc., 1979 Hanley Rd., Dardenne Prairie, 63368. Tel: 636-379-9990.

St. William Apartments II, Inc., 1983 Hanley Rd., Dardenne Prairie, 63368. Tel: 636-379-9990.

Corporate Action for the Care of the Elderly, Inc., 4330 Olive St., 63108. Tel: 314-533-4770; Fax: 314-533-3226. Sr. Cathy Vetter, C.C.V.I., Pres. Association Composed of Representatives of 14 Religious Communities. Grants offered to assist those who work with the elderly.

St. Elizabeth Adult Day Care Center (1981) 3401 Arsenal St., 63118. Tel: 314-772-5107; Fax: 314-772-3674. Email: sjamiller@juno.com. Web: www.seadcc.org. Sr. John Antonio Miller, C.PP.S., Admin. Conducted by the Sisters of the Most Precious Blood to Provide Day Care for the Elderly and Handicapped.

St. Elizabeth Adult Day Care Center of Florissant (1994) 1831 N. New Florissant Rd., Florissant, 63033. Tel: 314-838-5005; Fax: 314-838-5005.

St. Elizabeth Adult Day Care Center of Overland (1997) 2543 Hood, Overland, 63114. Tel: 314-890-0005; Fax: 314-890-0005. Web: www.seadcc.org.

St. Elizabeth Arnold Adult Day Care Center, 2000 El Lago, Arnold, 63010. Tel: 636-461-0730; Fax: 636-461-0730. Web: www.seadcc.org.

St. Elizabeth Adult Day Care Center - Mapaville, 3825 Plass, Box 105, Mapaville, 63065. Tel: 636-931-7498; Fax: 636-931-7498. Web: www.seadcc.org.

St. Elizabeth Adult Day Care Center - Olivette, 9723 Grandview, Olivette, 63132. Tel: 314-994-9165; Fax: 314-994-9165. Web: www.seadcc.org.

St. Elizabeth Adult Day Care Center - Lemay, 317 Hoffmeister, Lemay, 63125. Tel: 314-638-8850; Fax: 314-638-8850. Web: www.seadcc.org.

St. Elizabeth Adult Day Care Center - Ste. Genevieve, 765 Market St., Sainte Genevieve, 63670. Tel: 573-883-7603; Fax: 573-883-7603. Web: www.seadcc.org.

[J] GENERAL HOSPITALS

ST. LOUIS. *St. Anthony's Medical Center* (1900) 10010 Kennerly Rd., 63128. Tel: 314-525-1000; Fax: 314-525-4485. Email: sandra-straub@samcstl.org. Web: www.stanthonysmedcenter.com. Sr. Monica Marie Laws, O.F.M., Dir. Mission Integration; Revs. Nathan McNally, O.F.M., Chap. (Retired); William Cardy, O.F.M., Chap. Licensed Beds 767; Operating Beds 554; Total Staff 3,846; Full-Time Employees 3,105; Patients Assisted Annually 528,372.

SSM St. Mary's Health Center (1924) 6420 Clayton Rd., 63117. Tel: 314-768-8000; Fax: 314-768-8011. Email: rob_shelton@ssmhc.com. Web: www.stmarys-stlouis.com. William M. Jennings, Pres. Member of SSM Health Care Bed Capacity 585; Total Staff 1,960; Patients Assisted Annually 189,445.

BRIDGETON. *SSM De Paul Health Center Foundation* (1828) 12303 De Paul Dr., 63044. Tel: 314-344-6000; Fax: 314-344-6172. Email: patrice_komoroski@ssmhc.com. Web: www.ssmdepaul.com. Pat Komoroski, Pres.; David Fitzgerald, Pastoral Care; Revs. David Boyle, Chap.; Raphael Paul, Chap.; Charlene Raitt, Chap.; Rev. Glenn Reitz, Chap.; Teresa Roberson-Mullins, Chap.; Rev. Michael Southcombe, Chap. Member of SSM Health Care.

SSM DePaul Health Center (Operating) Excluding Nursery 478; (Licensed) Excluding Nursery 478; Sisters 3; Patients Assisted Annually 179,727; Staff 2,171.

St. Vincent Division, 12303 De Paul Dr., 63044. Tel: 314-344-7135. Pre-Adolescent, Adolescent, Adult & Gero Psychiatric Care and Chemical Dependency. Operating 98; Licensed 98.

CREVE COEUR. *St. John's Mercy Medical Center,* 615 S. New Ballas Rd., 63141. Tel: 314-251-6000; Fax: 314-251-4168. Web: www.stjohnsmercy.org. Denny DeNarvaez, Pres. & CEO; Rev. John P. Kennehan, Chap.; Deacon Ken Potzman, Chap. Conducted by the Sisters of Mercy of the Americas-St. Louis Region., (See Branch Unit under Washington, MO). Sisters 3; Nurses 2,000; Bed Capacity 979; Skilled Nursing 120; Total Staff 5,800.

FENTON. *SSM St. Clare Health Center* (1954) 1015 Bowles Ave., 63026. Tel: 636-496-2500; Fax: 636-496-4901. Sherry Hausmann, Pres. Member of SSM Health Care. Sisters 1; Bed Capacity 154; Total Nurses 471; Total Staff 1,017; Total Assisted Annually 77,788.

SSM St. Clare Health Center Foundation, 1015 Bowles Ave., 63026. Tel: 636-496-2515; Fax: 636-496-4901. Email: rachel_covington@ssmhc.com. Web: www.ssmstclare.com.

LAKE ST. LOUIS. *SSM St. Joseph Hospital West,* 100 Medical Plaza, Lake Saint Louis, 63367. Tel: 314-625-5200; Fax: 636-755-3876. Web: www.ssmstjoseph.com. Drew Rector, Pres.; Sisters Donna Olson, Pastoral Care; Charlotte Lehman, Pastoral Care. Member of SSM Health Care. Bed Capacity 122; Total Staff 800; Patients Assisted Annually 106,487.

ST. CHARLES. *SSM St. Joseph Health Center,* 300 First Capitol Dr., 63301. Tel: 314-947-5000; Fax: 314-947-5090. Web: www.ssmstjoseph.com. Gaspare Calvaruso, Pres.; David Fitzgerald, Dir. Pastoral Care; Rev. Msgr. Raymond A. Hampe. Member of SSM Health Care. Sisters 3; Bed Capacity 352; Total Staff 1,569; Patients Assisted Annually 119,196.

WASHINGTON. *St. John's Mercy Hospital* (1926) 901 E. 5th St., 63090. Tel: 636-239-8000; Fax: 636-569-6733. Web: www.stjohnsmercy.org/sjmh. Terry McLain, Pres.; Mary Salois, Mgr. Pastoral Svcs.; Rev. Timothy J. Toohey, Chap.; Sr. Michaelanne Estoup, R.S.M., (Retired); Rev. Tom Haller, Chap. (Protestant); Melba Peters, Chap., Parish Nurse; Deacon Harvey Dubbs, Chap. (See Listing Under Creve Coeur, MO). Bed Capacity 187; Total Staff 790; Total Assisted Annually 18,990.

WENTZVILLE. *SSM St. Joseph Health Center - Wentzville,* 500 Medical Dr., 63385. Tel: 636-327-1000; Fax: 636-327-1110. Web: www.ssmstjoseph.com. Gaspare Calvaruso, Pres.; David Fitzgerald, Contact Person. (Member: SSM Health Care) 74; Total Staff 204; Patients Assisted Annually 28,320.

[K] SPECIAL HOSPITALS

ST. LOUIS. *SSM Cardinal Glennon Children's Medical Center* (1956) 1465 S. Grand Blvd., 63104. Tel: 314-577-5610; Fax: 314-268-6468. Email: sherlyn_hailstone@ssmhc.com. Web: www.cardinalglennon.com. Member of SSM Health Care. Sisters 4; Bed Capacity (for Children) 190; Total Staff 1,821; Patients Assisted Annually 150,978.

CREVE COEUR. *SSM Rehab,* 10101 Woodfield Ln., Ste. 100, Exec. Offices, 63132. Tel: 314-768-5300; Fax: 314-768-5355. Web: www.ssmrehab.com. Victoria Horst, Exec. Vice Pres. Rehab. Opers. Member of SSM Health Care; For rehabilitation of pediatrics, adolescents and adults. Bed Capacity: SSM St. Mary's Health Center, St. Louis 80; SSM St. Joseph Health Center, St. Charles 20; Outpatient Locations 24.

[L] PROTECTIVE INSTITUTIONS

Day Care Centers

ST. LOUIS

Guardian Angel Settlement Association, P.O. Box 2055, 63158-0055. Tel: 314-231-3188; Fax: 314-231-8126. Email: efmurphy@guardianangelsettlement.org. Web: www.guardianangelsettlement.org. Rev. Edward F. Murphy, C.M., Exec. Dir. Founded by the Daughters of Charity of St. Vincent de Paul., Child Care Services and Social Services. Priests 2; Total Staff 55; Total Assisted Annually 26,123.

DeSales Child Care Center, 2652 Iowa, 63118. Tel: 314-771-6417; Fax: 314-231-8126.

Gabriel Child Care Center, 818 Cass Ave., 63106. Tel: 314-621-2898; Fax: 314-231-8126.

Guardian Angel at Hosea House, 2635 Gravois Ave., 63118. Tel: 314-773-9027; Fax: 314-773-6140.

Peace for Kids, 4415 Maryland, 63108. Tel: 314-531-0511, Ext. 104; Fax: 314-531-2954. Email: meversgerd@ccstl.org. Constance S. Neumann, Exec. Dir.; Mary Ann Eversgerd, Dir. A child development center including daycare ages 6 weeks to 6 years and counseling for ages 6-12. Counseling available. Licensed by the City of St. Louis, State of MO and accredited by COA. Students 42.

Sacred Heart Villa (1940) 2108 Macklind Ave., 63110. Tel: 314-771-2224; Fax: 314-771-1262. Web: sacredheartvilla.org. Sr. John Catherine Coleman, A.S.C.J., Dir. & Prin. Conducted by the Apostles of the Sacred Heart of Jesus., Full-Time Care From 6:30-5:30 for children 3-5 years old. Total Assisted 120; Total Staff 26.

IMPERIAL

Queen of Apostles Center (1989) 800 Montebello Camp Rd., 63052. Tel: 636-464-0163; Fax: 636-464-0163. Email: rbuttice@yahoo.com. Days of Recollection, conferences and private weekend retreats; children's spirituality classes, spiritual direction. Apostles of the Sacred Heart of Jesus 5; Total Staff 4.

KIRKWOOD

Carmelite Child Development Center, 1111 N. Woodlawn Ave., 63122. Tel: 314-822-0058; Fax: 314-822-3573. Email: vocations@carmelitedcj.org. Web: www.carmelitedcj.org. Ann Cunningham, Dir. Operated by the Carmelite Sisters of the Divine Heart of Jesus. Provides child development, child care and services. Full Day 106; Total Staff 15.

[M] HOMES FOR CHILDREN

ST. LOUIS. *Boys Hope/Girls Hope of St. Louis, Inc.,* 755 S. New Ballas Rd., Ste. 120, 63141. Tel: 314-692-7477; Fax: 314-692-7810. Email: hopestlouis@bhgh.org. Web: www.hopestlouis.org. Michael E. Howard, Exec. Dir. Residential Care for Adolescent Boys and Girls, Troubled by Family Disruptions, who are Capable of College Preparatory High School Work. Ages 10-18. Total Assisted Annually 25; Total Staff 11.

FLORISSANT. *Child Center - Marygrove* (1849) 2705 Mullanphy Ln., 63031. Tel: 314-837-1702; Fax: 314-830-6263. Email: hnegri@ccstl.org. Web: www.marygroveonline.org. Sr. Rita Downey, CEO. Owned and operated under the auspices of Catholic Charities; Residential treatment for emotionally disturbed males and females (ages 6-21). Special education, therapy and medical services. Overnight emergency care: and crisis nursery males and females (Birth-21). Transitional Services, Apartments, Sequoia House and Drury House. Male and Female (ages 17-21). Bed Capacity 132; Total Staff 201; Total Assisted 624.

NORMANDY. *St. Vincent Home for Children* (1850) 7401 Florissant Rd., 63121. Tel: 314-261-6011; Fax: 314-385-1467. Email: lataylor@saintvincenthome.org. Web: www.saintvincenthome.org. Lee Ann Taylor, Exec. Dir.; Jill Kelsey, Dir. Educ./Prin.

The German St. Vincent Orphan Association, Chapel of the Sacred Heart. Lay Teachers 7; Teacher Assistants 7; Therapists 6; Interventionists 5; Children 112; Child Care 34; Total Staff 99; Total Assisted 1,057.

[N] HOMES FOR AGED

ST. LOUIS. *Alexian Brothers Lansdowne Village* (1988) 4624 Lansdowne, 63116. Tel: 314-351-6888; Fax: 314-351-5825. Web: ablv.org. Tony Altobella, Admin. Bed Capacity 180; Total Assisted Annually 157; Total Staff 160.

Alexian Brothers Sherbrooke Village (1991) 4005 Ripa Ave., 63125. Tel: 314-544-1111; Fax: 314-544-5134. Email: mroth@alexianbrothers.net. Web: alexianbrothers.net. C. Michael Roth, Pres. Total in Residence (Assisted Living) 44; Total Assisted (Nursing Care) 120; Total Assisted Annually 590; Total Staff 206.

Little Sisters of the Poor, Home for the Aged (1869) 3225 N. Florissant Ave., 63107. Tel: 314-421-6022; Fax: 314-436-9069. Sr. Mary Sylvia Karl, L.S.P., Supr.; Rev. James Beegan, M.S.F., Chap. Sisters 13; Residents 116; Total Assisted 125; Total Staff 119.

Mary, Queen and Mother Center, 7601 Watson Rd., 63119. Tel: 314-961-8000; Fax: 314-961-3580. Email: kledbetter@ccstl.org. Web: www.ccstl.org/crss. Cindy Woods, Admin. Skilled Nursing Facility.; A part of Cardinal Carberry Living Center Bed Capacity 230; Total Staff 255; Total Assisted Annually 630.

Mother of Good Counsel Home (1932) 6825 Natural Bridge Rd., (St. Louis Co.), 63121. Tel: 314-383-4765; Fax: 314-383-7256. Email: administration@mogch.org. Web: mogch.org. Sr. M. Mikela Meidl, Admin. Conducted by Sisters of St. Francis of the Martyr St. George., Skilled Nursing Facility for Men and Women. Sisters 12; Residents 70; Total Staff 100.

Mother of Perpetual Help Residence, 7609 Watson Rd., 63119. Tel: 314-918-2260; Fax: 314-961-3061. Email: swesley@ccstl.org. Web: cardinalcarberry.org; www.ccstl.org/crss. Sr. Suzanne Wesley, C.S.J., CEO; Bonnie Sue Hugo, Admin. A part of Cardinal Ritter Senior Services Total Assisted 106; Total Staff 52.

Nazareth Living Center, 2 Nazareth Ln., 63129. Tel: 314-487-3950; Fax: 314-487-8001. Email: lwesthoff@nlccsj.com. Web: www.nazarethlivingcenter.com. Lola J. Westhoff, CEO & Admin.; Julie Sivawan, Dir. Assisted Living; Betty Fuller, Dir. Mission & Pastoral Care. Sisters of St. Joseph of Carondelet and General Public & Benedictine Health System., Residential and Skilled Nursing Care Facility. Total Assisted 290; Total Staff 330.

Our Lady of Life Apartments, Inc., 7655 Watson Rd., 63119. Tel: 314-968-9447; Fax: 314-968-1758. Web: www.csstl.org/crss. A part of Cardinal Ritter Senior Services. Total Independent Living Apartments 207; Total Staff 41.

Regina Cleri Residence (1959) 10 Archbishop May Dr., 63119. Tel: 314-968-2240; Fax: 314-968-1049. Email: reginacleri@earthlink.net. Ms. Nancy Bryant, Admin. A Residence for Retired Diocesan Priests of the Archdiocese of St. Louis. Conducted by the Archdiocese of St. Louis. Sisters of the Most Precious Blood (O'Fallon, MO) 2; Franciscan Sisters of Our Lady of Perpetual Help 2; Priests 37; Total Staff 26; Total Assisted Annually 45.

EUREKA. *St. Joseph Hill Infirmary, Inc. dba St. Joseph Hill Infirmary* P.O. Box 550, 63025. Tel: 636-587-3661; Fax: 636-938-6398. Bro. Bernardo Trosa, O.S.F., Admin. A skilled nursing facility conducted by the Franciscan Missionary Brothers of the Sacred Heart of Jesus. Brothers 8; Residents 126; Total Assisted 120; Total Staff 55.

Price Memorial, Forby Rd., P.O. Box 476, 63025. Tel: 636-587-3200; Fax: 636-938-5266. Email: pricesnf@mindspring.com. Bro. John A. Spila, O.S.F., Admin. A skilled nursing facility conducted by the Franciscan Missionary Brothers of St. Joseph's Hill Infirmary. Brothers 3; Residents 120.

KIRKWOOD. *St. Agnes Home for the Elderly*, 10341 Manchester Rd., 63122. Tel: 314-965-7616; Fax: 314-965-3179. Web: www.stagneshome.com. Dianne Strutynski, Admin.; Rev. James B. Wilke, Chap.

Carmelite Sisters of the Divine Heart of Jesus of Missouri Sisters 16; Bed Capacity 150; Total Staff 124; Total Assisted Annually 124.

[O] MONASTERIES AND RESIDENCES OF PRIESTS AND BROTHERS

ST. LOUIS. *The Abbey of St. Mary and St. Louis* (1955) 500 S. Mason Rd., 63141-8500. Tel: 314-434-3690; Fax: 314-434-0795. Web: www.priory.org. Rt. Revs. Thomas Frerking, O.S.B., Abbot; J. Luke Rigby, O.S.B. (Retired); Very Revs. Timothy Horner, O.S.B.; J. Gregory Mohrman, O.S.B., Prior; M. Paul Kidner, O.S.B.; Revs. D. Ralph Wright, O.S.B.; R. Benedict Allin, O.S.B.; P. Finbarr Dowling, O.S.B.; J. Laurence Kriegshauser, O.S.B.; Gerard Garrigan, O.S.B.; Dominic Lenk, O.S.B.; Bede Price, O.S.B.; Augustine Wetta, O.S.B.; Ambrose Bennett, O.S.B.; Michael Brunner, O.S.B., Headmaster. Benedictines of the English Congregation. Priests 15; Brother Monks 14; Total Staff 29.

Bellarmine House of Studies, 3737 Westminster Pl., 63108-3407. Tel: 314-652-8862; Fax: 314-535-4597. Revs. Timothy M. McMahan, S.J., Rector; James F. Goeke, S.J., Treas.; Frank Reale, S.J.; David J. Suwalsky, S.J., Min.; James M. Short, S.J.; Bro. William R. Rehg, S.J. Jesuit Residence for Students in the College of Philosophy and Letters of St. Louis University. Priests 5; Brothers 1; Students 20; Total Staff 6.

Congregation of the Resurrection, Seminary House, 4252 W. Pine Blvd., 63108. Very Rev. Michael Danek, C.R., Prov. Supr.

De Smet Jesuit High School Community, 330 Emerson Rd., 63141. Tel: 314-567-3500; Fax: 314-567-1519. Email: jcraig@desmet.org. Revs. John V. Craig, S.J., Supr.; John J. Bergin, S.J.; Robert E. Bosken, S.J.; Michael H. Durso, S.J.; Walter T. Sidney, S.J.; Bro. Donald E. Lee, S.J.; Mr. Vincent A. Giacabazi, S.J.; Mr. Ronald R. O'Dwyer, S.J. Priests 5; Brothers 1; Scholastics 2; Jesuits 8.

St. Dominic Priory, 3601 Lindell Blvd., 63108. Tel: 314-633-4400; Fax: 314-256-8888. Web: www.op.org/stlouis. Revs. Donald Goergen, O.P., Ph.D., S.T.M., Prior; Aaron Arce, O.P.; Benedict M. Ashley, O.P.; Vincent W. Bryce, O.P.; David L. Delich, O.P., Syndic; Jay M. Harrington, O.P.; Dominic Holtz, O.P., Vicar; Thomas McDermott, O.P., Subprior; James R. Motl, O.P.; Jose Santiago, O.P.; Scott Steinkerchner, O.P.; David Wright, O.P. Priests 12; Student Brothers 22; Total in Residence 34.

Dominican Community of St. Louis (1982) St. Louis Bertrand Priory - Province of St. Albert the Great., 97 Waterman Pl., 63112-1820. Tel: 314-361-4445; Fax: 314-256-8888. Revs. Charles E. Bouchard, O.P., Prior; Alfred A. Lopez, O.P.; Gregory J. Heille, O.P., Business Mgr.; Charles E. Bouchard, O.P., Subprior; Richard A. Peddicord, O.P.; Michael R. Carey, O.P. Priests 5.

Franciscan Friary of St. Anthony of Padua (Franciscan Province of the Sacred Heart-Provincial Headquarters), 3140 Meramec St., 63118-4339. Tel: 314-353-7470; Fax: 314-353-0935. Email: provoff@aol.com. Web: www.thefriars.org. Bros. Patrick Darnell, O.F.M., Household Staff; Patrick Hanrahan, O.F.M.; Herman Joseph James, (Retired); Christopher Lambert, O.F.M., Province Sec.; Joseph Rogenski, Dir. Franciscan Missionary Union, Holy Land Commissariat & Sec. for Missionary Evangelization; Revs. Andrew Lewandowski, O.F.M., Chap. for Franciscan Sisters of Mary, Charismatic Ministry; John Rausch, O.F.M., Fraternal Svc.; Nathan McNally, O.F.M. (Retired); Bros. Damian Pfeifer, O.F.M., Maintenance; David Schulte, O.F.M., Maintenance; William Schulte, O.F.M., St. Anthony Health Care, Bread for the Poor & Franciscan Charities; Revs. Alois Gabrus, Health Care; William Cardy, O.F.M., Chap. St. Anthony's Hosp.; Bernardine Hahn, Chap. Poor Clares; Edwin Albers, O.F.M., Supply Ministry; Edmund Mundwiller, O.F.M., Contemplative & Visual Ministry, 3140 Meramec St., 63118-4399. Tel: 314-353-7470; Bro. Donald Lachowicz, O.F.M., Dir., Stone by Stone Project; Revs. Damien Dougherty, O.F.M., Permanent Diaconate Office; Joseph B. Hagen, O.F.M.; James Lause, O.F.M.; Michael Grawe, O.F.M., Supply Ministry; Richard Jeske, O.F.M., Sr. Assoc.; Thomas Nairn, O.F.M., Sr. Ethicist Catholic Health Assoc. of the US; Friars Daniel Piasecki, O.F.M., Fraternal Svc.; Charles Reid, O.F.M., Franciscan Connection & Stone by Stone Project; Javier Ruiz E. Cadena, O.F.M., Franciscan Connection & Prison Ministry; Rev. William Spencer, O.F.M.; Bro. Thom Smith, O.F.M., Pastoral Assoc.

The Franciscan Friars of the State of Missouri, Co-sponsor of The Franciscan Action Network Priests 16; Brothers 10.

Military Chaplains: Rev. Richard Bendorf, O.F.M., Georgia.

Friars of Sacred Heart Province Serving Abroad: Bro. Jeffery Haller, O.F.M., Foreign Experts Building, Fraternite Franciscaine, 1, rue Charrin, Villeurbanne 69100 France. Tel: 33-4-78547621; Revs. Jesus Aguirre-Garza, O.F.M., Eglise Catholique, Rue El Iman Ali, Marrakech-Gueliz 40000 Morocco. Tel: 212-0-44-43-05-85; Kenneth Capalbo, O.F.M., Teaching in Vietnam; Joseph Tan Doan Nguyen, O.F.M., Teaching in Vietnam, c/o Franciscan Missionary Office, 3140 Meraec St., 63118; Michael Perry, O.F.M., Gen. Vicar O.F.M. Order Serving in Rome, Italy.

Friars Attached to the Province but Residing Elsewhere: Friar Jack Hardesty, O.F.M., Fraternal Svc.; Revs. Eric Kahn, O.F.M. (Retired); Leon Reuter, O.F.M., St. Joseph, 125 E. Broadway, Shelbyville, IN 46176. Tel: 317-398-8227; Theodosius A. Schelich, O.F.M., Chap. St. Francis Hospital, 1215 E. Union, Litchfield, IL 62056.

Ignatius House (1990) 4517 W. Pine Blvd., 63108-2191. Tel: 314-361-6145; Fax: 314-758-7185. Email: dfleming@jesuits-mis.org. Web: www.jesuits-mis.org. Revs. David L. Fleming, S.J., Supr.; Edward K. Burger, S.J., Pastoral Min.; Daniel C. O'Connell, S.J., Writer; Paul C. Pilgram, S.J., Aide in Province Offices; John D. Arnold, S.J., Asst. Treas. Total in Residence 5.

Jesuit Community Corporation at Saint Louis University - Jesuit Hall, 3601 Lindell Blvd., 63108-3393. Tel: 314-633-4400; Fax: 314-633-4404. Email: rghuse@gmail.com. Revs. Ralph G. Huse, S.J., Rector; R. Bentley Anderson, S.J.; James H. Baker, S.J.; Peter W. Bayhi, S.J.; Lawrence H. Biondi, S.J.; Richard F. Bocklage, S.J.; Francis C. Brennan, S.J.; Joseph E. Brown, S.J.; Richard O. Buhler, S.J.; J. Richard Burtschi, S.J.; John J. Callahan, S.J.; Thomas Joseph Casey, S.J.; Francis X. Cleary, S.J.; Richard Comboy, S.J.; J. David Corrigan, S.J.; James. J. Costello, S.J.; Robert T. Costello, S.J.; Richard F. Costigan, S.J.; Paul J. Coutinho, S.J., Prof.; Donald M. Cunningham, S.J.; Anthony C. Daly, S.J.; Denis E. Daly, S.J.; Carl A. Dehne, S.J.; Michael V. Delaney, S.J.; Terrence E. Dempsey, S.J.; Thomas F. Denzer, S.J.; Everett A. Diederich, S.J.; James J. Dougherty, S.J.; William B. Faherty, S.J.; Philip C. Fischer, S.J.; John B. Foley, S.J.; Michael D. French, S.J.; Chester E. Gaiter, S.J.; Eugene E. Grollmes, S.J.; Francis J. Guentner, S.J.; Garth L. Hallett, S.J.; W. Charles Heiser, S.J.; Thomas J. Hogan, S.J.; John M. Hunthausen, S.J.; Ralph G. Huse, S.J.; John F. Kavanaugh, S.J.; Thomas E. J. Kelly, S.J.; Muthumbi wa Kimani, S.J.; David L. Koesterer, S.J.; Leonard E. Kraus, S.J.; Philip D. Kraus, S.J.; Gerhardt B. Lehmkuhl, S.J.; Edwin Lisson, S.J.; Edward L. Maginnis, S.J.; L. Gene Martens, S.J.; Michael K. May, S.J.; John L. McCarthy, S.J.; Frederick G. McLeod, S.J.; David V. Meconi, S.J., Prof.; Thomas J. Melancon, S.J., Dir. Fusz Pavilion; John F. Montag, S.J.; John J. Mueller, S.J.; Francis J. Murphy, S.J.; Walter G. Nesbit, S.J.; William P. O'Brien, S.J.; Martin D. O'Keefe, S.J.; James M. O'Leary, S.J.; John W. Padberg, S.J.; Claude N. Pavur, S.J.; Frank L. Pedrotti, S.J.; Patrick T. Quinn, S.J.; Ralph C. Renner, S.J.; Albert C. Rotola, S.J.; James A. Sebesta, S.J.; Anthony J. Short, S.J.; Robert A. Simms, S.J.; John F. Snyder, S.J.; Paul V. Stark, S.J.; Rene C. Tacastacas, S.J.; John P. Teeling, S.J.; William S. Udick, S.J.; John G. Valenta; James V. Veltrie, S.J.; Richard J. Vogt, S.J.; Ralph E. Vonderhaar, S.J.; J. Patrick Walsh, S.J.; James P. Walsh, S.J.; Raymond L. Windle, S.J.; Robert F. Weiss, S.J.; Bros. Robert L. Aug, S.J.; Herbert A. Bussen, S.J.; Robert C. Snyder; Henry E. Welch, S.J. Priests 77; Brothers 4.

The Jesuits of the Missouri Province, 4511 W. Pine Blvd., 63108-2191. Tel: 314-361-7765; Fax: 314-758-7164. Email: moprov@jesuits-mis.org. Web: www.jesuits-mis.org. Revs. Douglas W. Marcouiller, S.J., Provincial; Michael G. Harter, S.J., Socius; David J. Suwalsky, S.J.; Mr. Thom Digman, Dir. Advancement; Rev. John F. Armstrong, S.J., Asst. for Formation; Mr. Sean Agniel, Asst. for Social Ministries; Revs. Louis J. McCabe, S.J., Asst. for Vocations & Planning; Richard O. Buhler, S.J., Asst. for Pastoral & Spiritual Ministries; L. Gene Martens, S.J., Assoc. Dir. Devel.; Mr. Art Zinselmeyer, Asst. for Secondary & Pre-Secondary Educ.; David P. Miros, Ph.D., Archivist; Revs. William B. Faherty, S.J., Archivist Emeritus; Robert F. Weiss, S.J., Delegate for Higher Educ. Missouri Province of the Society of Jesus. Priests 204; Students in Major Seminary 19; Novices 6; Brothers 16.

Sacred Heart Jesuit Community, 3900 Westminster Pl., 63108-3902. Revs. John F. Armstrong, S.J.; Michael G. Harter, S.J.; Douglas W. Marcouiller, S.J.; Louis J. McCabe, S.J.; Ronald A. Mercier;

William P. O'Brien, S.J.; Steven A. Schoenig.

Lazarist Residence, 13245 Tesson Ferry Rd., 63128-3888. Tel: 314-843-0108; Fax: 314-849-1267. Revs. John F. Clark, C.M., M.A.; Joseph E. Begue, C.M.; George S. Busieka, C.M.; Martin J. Culligan, C.M. (Retired); Ray Van Dorpe, C.M.; Jeffrey H. Harvey, C.M.; Michael P. Joyce, C.M.; Richard L. Lause, C.M.; Very Rev. James E. Swift, C.M.; Revs. Ignatius M. Melito, C.M.; Francis H. Agnew, C.M.; Lawrence F. Asma, C.M.; Robert J. Brockland, C.M.; Daniel E. Harris, C.M.; Thomas R. Hinni, C.M.; Daniel R. Thiess; Bro. David W. Berning. Priests 16.

Leo Brown Jesuit Community, 3550 Russell Blvd., 63104. Tel: 314-771-5884; Fax: 314-771-6953. Email: poirierb@jesuits-mis.org. Revs. Robert L. Poirier, S.J., Supr.; Michael D. Barber, S.J.; Roger de la Rosa, S.J.; Peter Lah, S.J.; Gary G. Seibert, S.J.; James K. Voiss, S.J.; Thomas M. Rochford, S.J.; Mr. Michael D. Rozier, S.J. Priests 6; Total in Residence 7.

St. Louis University High School Jesuit Community, #3 Lawn Pl., 63110. Tel: 314-652-5425; Fax: 314-652-7028. Web: sluh.org. Revs. Thomas W. Cummings, S.J., Supr.; Ralph D. Houlihan, S.J.; James G. Knapp, S.J.; Michael A. Marchlewski, S.J.; Carl J. Heumann, S.J.; John Lan Tran, S.J. Priests 5.

Marianist Community, P.O. Box 718, Eureka, 63025. Tel: 636-938-5470; Fax: 636-938-3493. Email: mcmrcc@aol.com. Revs. Jose Ramirez, S.M.; Eugene Sweeney, S.M. (Retired); Bros. James Droste, S.M., Dir.; Joseph Markel, S.M.; Robert Massa, S.M.; Irwin Wachtel, S.M. Priests 2; Brothers 5.

Marianists, Province of the United States (Society of Mary), 4425 W. Pine, 63108-2301. Tel: 314-533-1207; Fax: 314-533-0778. Email: sglodek@sm-usa.org. Web: www.marianist.com. Bros. Stephen Glodek, S.M., Prov.; Joseph Markel, S.M., Asst. Temporalities, Councilor; Edward Brink, S.M., Asst. Education, Councilor; Revs. James Fitz, S.M., Asst. Prov.; Joseph Lackner, S.M., Councilor; George Cerniglia, S.M., Asst. Religious Life, Councilor. Total Staff 28.

Priests of the Province on Special Assignment: Revs. John L. Bakle, S.M., St. Agatha Rectory, 2777 E. Livinstone Ave., Columbus, OH 43209-3039. Tel: 416-237-4689; Jorge de Silva, S.M., 461 Monterey Ave., Los Gatos, CA 95030-5302. Tel: 408-395-1816; Bro. William Campbell, S.M.; Revs. Raymond J. Kacirk, S.M., 25149 Hanover St., Dearborn Heights, MI 48125-1831. Tel: 313-292-0629; James F. Kunes, S.M., 4649 Country Ln., Apt. D, Saint Ann, 63074-1254. Tel: 314-428-7990; Joseph Lynch, S.M.; John A. Melloh, S.M., 1922 Churchill Dr., South Bend, IN 46617-2213. Tel: 574-287-2263; William Meyer, S.M., 109 Oblate Dr., San Antonio, TX 78216-6613. Tel: 201-349-9928; Bro. Robert Moriarty, S.M.; Revs. Francis Nakagawa, S.M., 1184 Bishop St., Honolulu, HI 96813-2857. Tel: 808-536-7036; David Paul, S.M.; Patrick Philbin, S.M., 7734 Santiago Canyon Rd., Orange, CA 92869-1829. Tel: 714-633-2698; Bros. Lawrence Scrivani, S.M.; Edwin Shiras, S.M.; Joseph Spehar, S.M.; Fred Stovall, S.M.; Rev. Paul Donoghue, S.M., 363 Ocean Dr. W., Shippan Pt., Stamford, CT 06902-8222. Tel: 203-324-7889.

Priests of the Province Serving Outside the USA: Revs. Neville O'Donohue, S.M., St. Colmba's, Church Ave., Ballybrack, Dublin Ireland. Tel: 011-353-1285-8301; Fax: 011-353-1235-2789; Michael R. Reaume, S.M., St. Colmba's, Church Ave., Ballybrack, Dublin Ireland. Tel: 011-353-1285-8301; Fax: 011-353-1235-2789; Bros. James Contadino, S.M., St. Colmba's, Church Ave., Ballybrack, Dublin Ireland. Tel: 011-353-1285-8301; Fax: 011-353-1235-2789; Gerard McAuley, S.M., Dir., St. Colmba's, Church Ave., Ballybrack, Dublin Ireland. Tel: 011-353-1285-8301; Fax: 011-353-1235-2789; Fred Rech, S.M., St. Colmba's, Church Ave., Ballybrack, Dublin Ireland. Tel: 011-353-1285-8301; Fax: 011-353-1235-2789; Timothy Phillips, S.M., (Rome, Italy); Edward Violett, S.M., (Rome, Italy).

Priests of the Province Serving in the Missions: Bros. Ralph Doorack, S.M. (Peru), Peru; David Herbold, S.M. (Japan), Japan; Revs. Anthony G. Jansen, S.M., Marianist Community, P.O. Box 32494, Lusaka 10101 Zambia. Tel: 011-260-124-07-45; Fax: 011-260-124-07-45; Richard A. Loehrlein, S.M., Chaminade Marianist Community, P.O. Box 100, Karonga, Malawi. Tel: 011-265-1-362334; Michael F. Nartker, S.M., Marianist Novitiate, P.O. Box 210, Limuru 00217 Kenya. Tel: 011-254-066-73158; Martin A. Solma, S.M., Bro. Vincent House, 00603 Lavington, P.O. Box 25156, Nairobi, Kenya. Tel: 011-254-20-3873149; William Christensen, S.M.

Marycliff Marianist Community, 4000 Hwy. 109, Box 718, Eureka, 63025-0178. Tel: 636-938-5470; Fax: 636-938-3493. Bros. James Droste, S.M., Dir.; Joseph Markel, S.M.; Irwin Wachtel, S.M.; Revs. Jose Ramirez, S.M.; Eugene Sweeney, S.M. (Retired). Priests 2; Brothers 3. *Chaminade Community*, 17 Chaminade Dr., 63141-8421. Tel: 314-997-4336; Fax: 314-997-4762. Rev. Oscar Vasquez, S.M.; Bros. James Eppy; Louis Pinckert, Dir. Priests 1; Brothers 3. *Maryland Avenue Marianist Community*, 4528 Maryland Ave., 63108. Tel: 314-367-0390. Bros. Joseph Grieshaber, S.M.; Francis Heyer; James Maus; Robert Resing, S.M.; Kenneth Straubinger; Revs. James Fitz, S.M.; Martin A. Solma, S.M.; Robert Osborne, S.M.; Alvin McMenamy, S.M. Priests 4; Brothers 5. *Marianist Community, Our Lady of the Pillar Parish*, 401 S. Lindbergh Blvd., 63131-2729. Tel: 314-993-2282; Fax: 314-993-6462. Rev. James M. Tobin, S.M., Dir.; Bro. William O'Leary, S.M.; Revs. Gerald Hammel, S.M.; William R. Wightman, S.M. Priests 3; Brothers 1. *Marianist Community*, 4314 Lindell Blvd., 63108. Tel: 314-533-3047. Rev. George Cerniglia, S.M.; Bros. Stephen Glodek, S.M.; Jack Ventura, S.M.; Rev. Joseph Lackner, S.M. Brothers 2; Priests 2. *Cure of Ars Marianist Community*, 1311 S. Kirkwood Rd., 63122-7299. Tel: 314-965-0727; Fax: 314-835-1342. Revs. Timothy Kenney, S.M.; Joseph Uvietta, S.M.; Bro. Chester Burnog, S.M.; Rev. J. Donald Cahill, S.M. (Retired); Bros. Walter Ebbesmeyer, S.M.; Kenneth Jung; Melvin Meyer, S.M.; Richard Middleton, S.M.; Leonard Rudy, S.M.; Leo Slay, S.M. Priests 3; Brothers 7. *Marybrook Marianist Community*, 4707 Westminster Pl., 63108-1805. Tel: 314-367-2204. Bros. Edward Brink, S.M.; Charles J. Johnson, S.M.; Brian Zampier, S.M., Dir.; Rev. Ralph A. Siefert, S.M. Priests 1; Brothers 3.

St. Matthew Jesuit Community, 2715 N. Sarah St., 63113-2940. Tel: 314-531-6443; Fax: 314-533-7318. Email: stmatthews@sbcglobal.net. Web: www.st-matthew-church.org. Revs. Mark D. McKenzie, S.J., Pastor & Supr.; Peter P. Saengthien, S.J.; William J. Hutchison, S.J. Priests 3.

Missionaries of LaSalette, Province of Mary, Mother of the Americas, 4650 S. Broadway, 63111-1398. Tel: 314-353-5000; Fax: 314-353-4582. Web: www.lasalette.org. Rev. Dennis J. Meyer, M.S., Local Supr.

Missionaries of La Salette Corp. of Missouri LaSalette Spirituality Center Tel: 314-353-5000; Fax: 314-353-4582. Kathleen Crawford, Dir.; Revs. James R. Dunphy, M.S.; Edward Richard, M.S.; Bro. Luke D. Bauer, Oblate; Revs. John Nuelle, M.S.; Richard Lavoie, M.S.; Bro. Roman Wilbers, M.S. *La Salette Novitiate*, 4650 S. Broadway, 63111-1398. Tel: 314-353-5000. Rev. Dennis J. Meyer, M.S., Novitiate Dir. *North American La Salette Mission Center*, 4650 S. Broadway, 63111-1398. Tel: 314-352-0064; Fax: 314-352-3737. Email: lsmc2@charter.net. Web: www.lsmc.org. Rev. John Nuelle, M.S., Dir.

North American La Salette Mission Center

Redemptorist Fathers (1867) 1118 N. Grand Blvd., 63106. Tel: 314-533-0304; Fax: 314-533-4260. Email: the-rock@saintly.com. Web: www.stalphonsusrock.org. Total Staff 6. In Res. Revs. Joseph The Pham, C.Ss.R.; David Polek, C.Ss.R.; Kyle Fisher, C.Ss.R.; Matthew S. Bonk, C.Ss.R.; Bro. Terrence Burke, C.Ss.R.; Deacon Richard W. Fischer, C.Ss.R.

Vincentian Residence, 2904 Arsenal St., 63118. Tel: 314-773-7633; Fax: 314-773-0882. Revs. Romain G. Morales, C.M., Supr.; Edward F. Murphy, C.M.; Daniel A. Ricci, C.M.; David G. Nations, C.M.; William Hartenbach, C.M.; Thomas E. Esselman, C.M.; Bro. David P. Goodman, C.M. Priests 5; Brothers 1.

Attached But Not In Residence: Revs. Lawrence F. Asma, C.M.; James Beighlie; P. Vincent Aherne, C.M., Carlsbad, CA; Philip M. Floersh, C.M., Tucson, AZ.

Vincentian Residence, 2912 Arsenal St., 63118. Tel: 314-771-1869; Fax: 314-771-2410. Bro. David Nations, C.M.; Rev. Thomas E. Esselman, C.M.

White House Retreat Jesuit Community (1922) 7410 Christopher Dr., 63129-5799. Tel: 314-846-2575; Fax: 314-293-0931. Email: whretreat@whretreat.org. Web: www.whretreat.org. (1922) Office: 7410 Christopher Dr., 63129-5799. Tel: 314-533-8903; 800-643-1003; Fax: 314-533-8428. Email: reservations@whretreat.org. Revs. James J. Burshek, S.J., Dir. & Supr.; Richard E. Hadel, S.J., Assoc. Dir.; Edward C. O'Brien, S.J., Assoc. Dir.; Eugene C. Renard, S.J., Assoc. Dir.; Leonard E. Kraus, S.J., Assoc. Dir.; Bro. John Fava, S.J., Assoc. Dir.

DARDENNE PRAIRIE. *Franciscan Brothers of the Holy Cross St. Charles Friary*, 12 Dardenne Woods Ct., 63368. Tel: 636-561-0589. Email: bdavids61@aol.com. Web: www.franciscanbrothers.net. Bros. David Sarnecki, F.F.S.C., Supr.; Luke Morin, F.F.S.C., Asst. Supr.; Raphael Kreikemeier, F.F.S.C.

DITTMER. *Servants of the Paraclete* (1947) St. Michael's Community, 6476 Eime Rd., 63023. Tel: 636-274-5226; Fax: 636-274-1430. Email: paulsp1000@yahoo.com. Web: www.theservants.org. Rev. Raymond Gunzel, s.P.; Very Rev. Liam Hoare, s.P. *Vianney Renewal Center* (1989) 6476 Eime Rd., 63023. Tel: 636-274-5226; Fax: 636-274-1430.

EARTH CITY. *Congregation of the Mission Western Province (Vincentians)*, 13663 Rider Tr. N., 63045-1512. Tel: 314-344-1184; Fax: 314-344-2989. Email: cmstlouis@vincentian.org. Web: www.vincentian.org. Revs. Perry Henry, C.M., Prov.; Mark S. Pranaitis, C.M., Asst. Prov.; Mr. Thomas Beck, Treas.

EUREKA. *Franciscan Brothers House of Studies*, Forby Rd., P.O. Box 129, 63025. Tel: 636-938-5539. Bro. John A. Spila, O.S.F., Dir. House of Studies of Franciscan Missionary Brothers of the Sacred Heart of Jesus. Total in Residence 2; Total Staff 1.

HIGH RIDGE. *Society of Our Mother of Peace* (1966) Sons of Our Mother of Peace, Mary the Font Solitude, 6150 Antire Rd., 63049-2135. Tel: 636-677-3235; Fax: 636-677-6284. Email: marythefont@yahoo.com. Rev. Placid Guste, S.M.P., Supr. Gen. Priests 3; Brothers 2; Total in Residence 5; Total Staff 3.

LIGUORI. *Alphonsian Foundation*, One Liguori Dr., 63057-9999. Tel: 636-223-1455; Fax: 636-223-1394. Email: foundation@alfonsiana.edu. Web: www.alfonsiana.edu. Rev. John C. Vargas, C.Ss.R., Exec. Dir. Purpose: to provide public relations and financial support for the Alphonsian Academy of Moral Theology in Rome.

St. Clement Health Care Center (1988) 300 Liguori Dr., 63057. Tel: 636-464-3666; Fax: 636-464-4717. Revs. Theodore L. Lawson, C.Ss.R., Rector & Dir.; Joseph R. Armshaw, C.Ss.R. (Retired); Albert C. Babin, C.Ss.R.; Charles C. Bueche, C.Ss.R. (Retired); William Emmett Collins, C.Ss.R. (Retired); Edward Cosgrove, C.Ss.R.; Paul A. Farrell, C.Ss.R.; Roderick Garvey, C.Ss.R. (Retired); Joseph M. Greenwell, C.Ss.R (Retired); William F. Hogan, C.Ss.R.; Bruno V. Lischwe, C.Ss.R.; Henry McKeever, C.Ss.R. (Retired); Francis A. Novak, C.Ss.R. (Retired); James J. Nugent, C.Ss.R. (Retired); Joseph Nuttman, C.Ss.R. (Retired); Eugene M. Oates, C.Ss.R. (Retired); James Patterson, C.Ss.R. (Retired); Gerard J. Pecht, C.Ss.R. (Retired); Michael P. Quinn, C.Ss.R.; Mark Scheffler, C.Ss.R., Asst. Dir.; Anthony P. Slane, C.Ss.R. (Retired); Earl J. Toups, C.Ss.R.; Bros. Raymond Bowersox, C.Ss.R., (Retired); James Burke, C.Ss.R., (Retired); Andrew J. Lawson, C.Ss.R., (Retired); Thomas C. Sanhuber, C.Ss.R., (Retired); Michael Schnittker, C.Ss.R., (Retired); Martin Temple, C.Ss.R., (Retired). The Redemptorists. Total in Residence 35; Total Staff 2.

Liguori Mission House/Redemptorists, Ten Liguori Dr., 63057. Tel: 636-464-6999; Fax: 636-464-6765. Email: vkarls@liguorimissionhouse.org. Revs. James Gleason; Victor Karls, C.Ss.R., Supr.; Andrew Meiners, C.Ss.R., Vicar; Thomas Danielsen, C.Ss.R.; William H. Broker, C.Ss.R.; Joseph Butz, C.Ss.R.; Joseph M. Curalli, C.Ss.R.; Albert J. Castellino, C.Ss.R.; Donnell Kirchner, C.Ss.R.; John Phelps, C.Ss.R.; Gilbert Enderle, C.Ss.R.; Peter Scharitz, C.Ss.R.; Bros. Paul Yasenak, C.Ss.R.; Robert T. Ruffing, C.Ss.R.; Marvin Hamann, C.Ss.R. Priests 11; Brothers 3.

PACIFIC. *Franciscan Missionary Brothers of the Sacred Heart of Jesus*, 265 St. Joseph Rd., 63069. Tel: 636-587-3661; Fax: 636-938-4960. Web: www.franciscancaring.org. Bro. John Spils, O.S.F., Dir. Gen. Generalate of Franciscan Missionary Brothers of the Sacred Heart of Jesus., Apostolate: Price Memorial Nursing Home and St. Joseph's Hill Infirmary/Black Madonna Shrine, Adult Boarding Facility at Camilus Hall Boarding Home, Merkle Knipprath Nursing home, Joliet Diocese and Countryside Villas Retirement Center, Clifton, IL 60927. Professed Brothers 9.

PERRYVILLE. *Congregation of the Mission*, St. Mary's Seminary, 63775-1599. Tel: 573-547-6533; Fax: 573-547-2204. Revs. Alphonse X. Hoernig, C.M.; Louis J. Derbes, C.M.; Oscar Lukefahr, C.M.; Edward J. Mullin, C.M.; Edward Hartrick Sullivan, C.M.; John A. Cantore, C.M.; Jerome Fortenberry, C.M.; Thomas A. Grace, C.M.; Thomas J. Meik, C.M.; Charles E. Prost, C.M.; Arthur L. Trapp, C.M.; Robert E. Lamy, C.M.; Felipe J. Martinez, C.M.; Raymond J. Ross, C.M.; John F. Gagnepain, C.M.; Bros. Harvey Goertz, C.M.; Richard A. Hermann, C.M.; Mark Howard Argus, C.M.; Revs. Patrick J. Keeley, C.M.; Richard O'Brien, C.M.; James G. Ward, C.M.; Bros. Paul P. Joseph, C.M.; John Mangogna, C.M.; Matthew J. Teel, C.M.; Richard Zoellner, C.M. U.S. Motherhouse of the Congregation of the

Mission (Vincentian Fathers, Prov. of the Midwest). Fathers 20; Professed Brothers 7; Total Staff 5.

ROCKY MOUNT. *Contemplative Heart of Mary Hermitage*, 20542 Echo Valley Rd., 65072. Tel: 573-557-2119. Rev. Robert L. Aten.

[P] PERSONAL PRELATURES

KIRKWOOD. *Prelature of the Holy Cross and Opus Dei*, Wespine Study Center, 100 E. Essex Ave., 63122. Tel: 314-821-1608; Fax: 314-821-4722. Email: info@wespine.org. Web: www.opusdei.org. Revs. Michael E. Giesler; John J. Alvarez.

[Q] CONVENTS AND RESIDENCES FOR SISTERS

ST. LOUIS. *Adorers of the Blood of Christ, United States Region*, 4233 Sulphur Ave., 63109. Tel: 314-351-6294; Fax: 314-351-6789. Email: kenileyd@adorers.org. Web: www.adorers.org. Sr. Jan Renz, A.S.C., Regl. Leader.

Carmel of St. Joseph (1863) 9150 Clayton Rd., 63124-1898. Tel: 314-993-4394; Fax: 314-993-5039. Email: stlouiscarmel@sbcglobal.net. Sr. Mary Joseph, O.C.D., Prioress. Discalced Carmelites., Chapel of the Precious Blood. Professed 9; Extern Sisters 1.

Carmelite Religious of Trivandrum, 4172 Delor, 63116. Sr. Vivienne Gemma Mendonca, C.C.R., Contact Person.

Congregation of Mary, Queen, 3811 Westminster Pl., 63108. Tel: 314-371-1294. Email: vocation@trinhvuong.org. Web: www.trinhvuong.org. Sr. Irene Dinh, C.M.R., Local Supr.

Daughters of Mary, Mother of Israel's Hope, 4950 Heege Rd., 63123. Tel: 314-352-5683; Fax: 314-352-5683.

Daughters of Our Mother of Peace (1966) 8307 Madison Ave., 63114-6225. Tel: 314-426-7725. Email: smpconvent@yahoo.com. Sr. Maryjoy Lambert, S.M.P., Supr. Sisters 3.

Daughters of St. Paul Convent, 9804 Watson Rd., 63126. Tel: 314-965-6935; Fax: 314-984-8431. Email: stlouis@pauline.org. Web: www.pauline.org. Sisters 6.

Eucharistic Missionaries of St. Theresa, 12934 Marine Ave., 63146. Tel: 314-434-1312.

Franciscan Sisters of Mary Administration (1872) 1100 Bellevue Ave., 63117-1826. Tel: 314-768-1824; Fax: 314-768-1880. Email: rdowling@fsmonline.org. Web: www.fsmonline.org. Sr. Rose Mary Dowling, F.S.M., Pres.; Rev. Andrew Lewandowski, O.F.M., Chap. Offices of the Franciscan Sisters of Mary & Convent. Professed Sisters in Archdiocese 42; In Residence 59.

Franciscan Sisters of Mary Novitiate (1872) 1100 Bellevue Ave., 63117-1826. Tel: 314-768-1828; Fax: 314-768-1880. Email: sschwartz@fsmonline.org. Web: www.fsmonline.org.

Franciscan Sisters of Our Lady of Perpetual Help (1901) 335 S. Kirkwood Rd., 63122. Tel: 314-965-3700; Fax: 314-965-3710. Email: rms@fsolph.org. Web: www.franciscansisters-olph.org. Sr. Regina Marie Strassburger, O.S.F., Supr. Gen. Motherhouse and Novitiate of Franciscan Sisters of Our Lady of Perpetual Help. Total in Community 100; Total Staff 5.

Heart of Mary Center, 6220 Westway Pl., 63109-3417. Tel: 314-752-4459. Email: chanelatwellspring@sbcglobal.net. Web: www.dhmna.org. Sr. Nancy Fell, D.H.M., Supr. Daughters of the Heart of Mary 4.

St. Joseph's Convent of Mercy, 611 S. New Ballas Rd., 63141. Tel: 314-569-6800; Fax: 314-215-1920. Email: cacallahan@rsm-stl.org. Sr. Carol Ann Callahan, R.S.M., Coord. Sisters of Mercy of the Americas. Sisters 45.

St. Joseph's Provincial House (1836) 6400 Minnesota Ave., 63111-2899. Tel: 314-481-8800; Fax: 314-481-2366. Email: pclune@csjsl.org. Web: www.csjsl.org. Sisters Helen Flemington, C.S.J., Province Leadership Team; Patricia Giljum, C.S.J., Province Leadership Team; Marion Renkens, C.S.J., Admin. Prov. House of the Sisters of St. Joseph of Carondelet. Sisters in Province 387; In Archdiocese 256.

Loretto Center, 590 E. Lockwood, 63119-3217. Tel: 314-968-1887; Fax: 314-968-4887. Sisters 23; Total Staff 16.

Marillac Provincial House (1910) 4328 Westminster, 63108-2624. Tel: 314-533-3004. Email: mwalz@dcwcp.org. Web: www.daughters-of-charity.org. Daughters of Charity of St. Vincent de Paul., Provincial House for Daughters of Charity.

Marillac Provincial Offices, 4330 Olive St., 63108-2622. Tel: 314-533-4770, Ext. 230; Fax: 314-533-3226. Email: choelscher@dcwcp.org. Web: www.daughters-of-charity.org. Sr. Mary Walz, D.C., Visitatrix; Rev. John F. Clark, C.M., M.A., Provincial Dir. Sisters in Archdiocese 65.

Missionaries of Charity, 3629 Cottage Ave., 63113-3539. Tel: 314-533-2777. Sr. M. Marcella, M.C., Regl. Supr. Missionaries of Charity also in: Peoria, IL; Chicago, IL; Detroit, MI; Memphis, TN; Dallas, TX; Little Rock, AR; Baton Rouge, LA; Lafayette, LA; Jenkins, KY; Atlanta, GA; Charlotte, NC; Gary, IN; Indianapolis, IN., Houston, TX; Minneapolis, MN. Sisters 7; Total Assisted Annually 19,669.

Monastery of St. Clare of the Immaculate Conception, 200 Marycrest Dr., 63129-4813. Tel: 314-846-2618. Sr. Mary Leo Hoffman, O.S.C., Abbess. Poor Clare Nuns. Cloistered Nuns 9.

Mount Grace Convent and Chapel of Perpetual Adoration, 1438 E. Warne Ave., 63107. Tel: 314-381-2654; Fax: 314-381-6756. Email: mountgrace@sbcglobal.net. Web: www.mountgraceconvent.org. P.O. Box 16459, 63125. Tel: 314-381-2654; Fax: 314-381-6756. Sr. Mary Catherine, S.Sp.S.deA.P., Supr. Sister Servants of the Holy Spirit of Perpetual Adoration (Generalate, Bad Driburg, Germany)Attended by Divine Word Fathers. Sisters 24.

1438 E. Warne Ave., 63107-6756. Tel: 314-381-2654; Fax: 314-381-6756.

1446 E. Warne Ave., 63107. Tel: 314-381-0219; Fax: 314-381-8521. Sisters 24.

Provincial House, Society of the Sacred Heart-United States Province, 4120 Forest Park Ave., 63108. Tel: 314-652-1500; Fax: 314-534-6800. Email: provincialhouse@rscj.org. Web: www.rscj.org. Sr. Paula Toner, R.S.C.J., Prov. Province Corporations: California Province of the Society of the Sacred Heart, Inc.; Ladies of the Sacred Heart of St. Louis, Missouri; Society of the Sacred Heart, Chicago Province, Inc.; Religious of the Sacred Heart, Washington Province, Inc.; Religious of the Sacred Heart, New York Province, Inc.; Religious of the Sacred Heart in Massachusetts, Inc. Sisters in Archdiocese 30.

Salesian Missionaries of Mary Immaculate, 798 Buckley Rd., 63125. Tel: 314-416-1778. Sr. Elsy Joyce, S.M.M.I., Supr.

School Sisters of Notre Dame (1895) Sancta Maria in Ripa, 320 E. Ripa Ave., 63125-2897. Tel: 314-544-0455; Fax: 314-544-6754. Email: abonvie@ssnd-sl.org. Web: www.ssnd.org. Sr. Joan Markus, S.S.N.D., Prov. Leader; Rev. Charles C. Deister, Chap. Motherhouse of the School Sisters of Notre Dame, St. Louis Province. Sisters in Diocese 303.

Interprovincial Novitiate for School Sisters of Notre Dame (1982) 320 E. Ripa, 63125. Tel: 314-633-7082; Fax: 314-633-7077.

Liturgical Fabric Arts (1983) Tel: 314-544-0455; 314-633-7030; Fax: 314-544-6754. Email: josephinessnd@yahoo.com. Web: www.liturgicalfabricarts.com.

Maria Center (1980) Tel: 314-544-6757; 314-633-7050; Fax: 314-633-7052. Email: mariacenter@ssnd-sl.org.

Resource Development (1991) Tel: 314-631-3530; Fax: 314-633-7056. Email: ssndrdo@ssnd-sl.org. Web: www.ssnd-sl.org.

Sisters of Good Shepherd Province of Mid North America (1999) 7654 Natural Bridge Rd., 63121. Tel: 314-381-3400; Fax: 314-381-7102. Email: bbeasley@gspmna.org. Web: goodshepherdsisters.org. Sr. Mary Catherine Massei, R.G.S., Prov.

Sisters of the Good Shepherd Candidate House, 4116 W. Pine Blvd., 63108. Email: cmcquaid@gspmna.org. Web: www.goodshepherdsisters.org. Sr. Mary Carolyn McQuaid, R.G.S., Contact Person.

Sisters of the Good Shepherd Formation House, 4317 Forest Park Ave., 63108. Tel: 314-533-0834; Fax: 314-652-2305. Email: virginiagordon@sbcglobal.net. Sr. Virginia Gordon, Contact Person. Professed Sisters 2.

Sisters of Mercy of the Americas, Regional Community of St. Louis, 2039 N. Geyer Rd., 63131-3399. Tel: 314-966-4313; Fax: 314-909-4600. Email: jarvin@corp.mercy.net. Web: www.sistersofmercy.org. Sr. Jane Mary Hotstream, R.S.M., Regl. Pres. Regional Sisters in Archdiocese 82.

Convent Corporations:

Sisters of Mercy of the St. Louis Regional Community, Inc. Tel: 314-966-4313; Fax: 314-909-4600.

Other: Mercy Center, Conference Retreat Ministry Tel: 314-966-4686; Fax: 314-909-4631.

Health Institutions:

Sisters of Mercy Health System (1986) Tel: 314-579-6100; Fax: 314-628-3732.

Sisters of St. Francis of the Martyr St. George Tel: 314-383-4765; Fax: 314-383-7256. Web: mogch.org.

Mother of Good Counsel Home, 6825 Natural Bridge Rd., 63121. Tel: 314-383-4765; Fax: 314-383-7256. Sisters 12.

Sisters of the Good Shepherd (1835) 7654 Natural Bridge Rd., 63121. Tel: 314-381-3400; Fax: 314-382-5294. Email: mckirst@gspmna.org. Web: www.goodshepherdsisters.org. Sr. Mary Charlotte Kirst, R.G.S., Contact Person. Sisters 12; Total Staff 10.

Sisters of the Good Shepherd Generalate, 7654 Natural Bridge Rd., 63121. Sr. Mary Carolyn McQuaid, R.G.S., Contact Person.

Society of Helpers (Paris 1856) (St. Louis 1903) 2800 Olive St., Apt 12K, 63103. Tel: 314-535-2622. Email: httngr@peoplepc.com. Web: www.helpers.org. Sr. Patricia A. Hottinger, S.H., Contact.

Society of the Helpers of the Holy Souls., Spiritual Direction, Parish Weeks of Guided Prayer, Secretarial work, Visiting homebound and frail elders.

3817 McDonald Ave., 63116. Tel: 314-776-6917. Email: m.funge@worldnett.att.net.

BRIDGETON. *Incarnate Word Sisters* (1869) 3393 McKelvey Rd., Apt. 326, 63044. Tel: 314-387-3326. Email: mseeker314@aol.com. Web: www.ccrtsantonio.org. Sisters Bette Bluhm, C.C.V.I., Prov. Coord.; Mary Ann Seeker, C.C.V.I., Contact (Retired). Sisters 24.

Sisters of Divine Providence, 3415 Bridgeland Dr., 63044. Tel: 314-209-9181; Fax: 314-209-9207. Email: cdpfrancis@hotmail.com. Web: www.divineprovidenceweb.org. Sr. Mary Francis Fletcher, C.D.P., Prov.

Sisters of Divine Providence of Missouri

Sisters of Divine Providence of Missouri Charitable Trust Providence Ministry Corporation. Sisters 35.

CHESTERFIELD. *Missionary Sisters of St. Peter Claver* (1894) 667 Woods Mill Rd. S., P.O. Box 6067, 63006-6067. Tel: 314-469-4932; Fax: 314-469-0869. Email: Chesclaver@usfamily.net. Sr. Genevieve Kudlik, Delegate. Sisters 4.

ELLISVILLE. *Passionist Nuns Monastery* (1948) 15700 Clayton Rd., 63011-2300. Tel: 636-527-6867. Sr. Mary Salvador, C.P., Supr. Cloistered Contemplatives. Professed Religious 10.

FLORISSANT. *Contemplative Sisters of the Good Shepherd* (1859) 2711 Mullanphy Ln., 63031. Tel: 314-837-1719; Fax: 314-837-5925. Email: cgsflo@mindspring.com. Web: www.archstl.org. Sr. Sharon Rose Authorson, C.G.S., Supr. Sisters 4.

Pallottine Missionary Sisters-Queen of Apostles Province (Rome 1838) (U.S. 1912) 15270 Old Halls Ferry Rd., 63034-1611. Tel: 314-837-7100; 314-838-5129; Fax: 314-837-1041. Email: srgail@sbcglobal.net. Web: www.pallottinespirit.org. Sr. Gail Borgmeyer, S.A.C., Prov. Provincialate, novitiate & renewal center of the Missionary Sisters of the Catholic Apostolate. Sisters at Provincial House 5; Total Staff 17.

FRONTENAC. *Congregational Office of the Sisters of St. Joseph of Carondelet*, 2311 S. Lindbergh Blvd., 63131. Tel: 314-966-4048; Fax: 314-966-5041. Email: congctrcsj@attglobal.net. Web: www.csjcarondelet.org. Sisters Laura Bufano, C.S.J., Congregational Leadership Team; Francine Costello, C.S.J., Congregational Leadership Team; Susan Hames, C.S.J., Congregational Leadership Team; Catherine McNamee, C.S.J., Congregational Leadership Team; Elizabeth Ney, C.S.J., M.S.W., Congregational Leadership Team; Pam Harding, C.S.J., Admin. Asst. Sisters 5.

Religious of the Sacred Heart Convent (1929) Villa Duchesne, 801 S. Spoede Rd., 63131. Tel: 314-432-2021; Fax: 314-432-7713. Email: nghio@rscj.org. Sisters 3.

HIGH RIDGE. *Society of Our Mother of Peace, Daughters of Our Mother of Peace* (1966) Mary the Font Solitude, 6150 Antire Rd., 63049-2135. Tel: 636-677-3235; Fax: 636-677-5284. Email: marythefont@yahoo.com. Web: our-mother-of-peace.org. Sisters Mary Perpetua Spranger, S.M.P., Local Supr.; Anne Marie DeFord, S.M.P., Treas. & Sec. Total in Residence 6.

KIRKWOOD. *Carmelite Sisters of the Divine Heart of Jesus Provincial House and Novitiate* (1891) 10341 Manchester Rd., 63122. Tel: 314-965-7616; Fax: 314-822-3154. Email: vocations@carmelitedcj.org. Web: carmelitedcj.org. Sr. Mary Joseph Heisler, Prov. Superior. The Sisters own and operate two nursing homes and one day care center in their Province. Final Professed 14; Junior Professed 4; Novices 2; Postulants 1.

Ursuline Provincialate, 353 S. Sappington Rd., 63122. Tel: 314-821-6884; Fax: 314-821-6888. Email: ursulines@osucentral.org. Web: www.osucentral.org. Sr. Diane Fulgenzi, O.S.U., Prov. Prioress. Central Province of the Ursuline Nuns of the Roman Union. Sisters: In Province 125; In the Archdiocese 27.

Other Locations: *Ursuline Sisters*, 500 Clemens Dr., Florissant, 63033. Tel: 314-839-2803; Fax: 314-839-1533. Sisters 4.

Ursuline Sisters, 5821 Sutherland, 63109. Tel: 314-353-5745. Sisters 6.

Ursuline Sisters, 801 Fairdale Ave., St. Louis, 63119. Tel: 314-968-9591. Sisters 3.

LIGUORI. *Monastery of St. Alphonsus* (1960) 200 Liguori Dr., 63057-9999. Tel: 636-464-1093; Fax: 636-464-9446; 636-464-1073. Email: rednun@redemptoristinenuns.org; prayerrequest@redemptoristinenuns.org. Web: www.redemptoristinenuns.org. Sisters Janice Marie Klein, O.Ss.R., Prioress; Mary Supawadee Khamsamran, Solemn Professed; Weena Suttinavin, Solemn Professed. Order of the Most Holy Redeemer (Redemptoristine Nuns). Professed 14.

NORMANDY. *Convent of the Immaculate Heart*, 7626 Natural Bridge Rd., 63121. Tel: 314-383-0300; Fax: 314-383-0337. Email: rgsmarie@hotmail.com. Web: www.goodshepherdsisters.org. A residence for aged & infirm Good Shepherd Sisters of the Mid-North America Prov. Total Staff 40; Total in Residence 25.

O'FALLON. *St. Mary's Institute of O'Fallon*, 204 N. Main St., 63366-2299. Tel: 636-240-6010; Fax: 636-272-5031. Email: mwhited@cpps-ofallon.org. Web: www.cpps-ofallon.org. Sr. Mary Whited, C.PP.S., Supr. Gen. Motherhouse of the Sisters of the Most Precious Blood., Chapel of St. Joseph. Sisters in Archdiocese 136.

ST. CHARLES. *Franciscan Sisters of Mary* (1872) 320 Jackson St., 63301-3496. Tel: 636-255-0194; Fax: 636-947-5090. Email: inez_kennedy@ssmhc.com.

Religious of the Sacred Heart (1800) 301 Decatur St., 63301-2089. Tel: 636-946-7276; Fax: 636-949-6659. Email: mmmunch@rscj.org. Sisters 2; Religious 2.

Religious of the Sacred Heart-Regis, 221 Decatur St., 63301. Tel: 636-946-6456; Fax: 636-949-6659. Email: mbusch@rscj.org. Sisters 4.

ST. LOUIS COUNTY. *Religious of the Sacred Heart*, 13644 Conway Rd., 63141. Tel: 314-434-7687. Email: hpadberg@rscj.org. Sisters 2.

Religious of the Sacred Heart, 541 S. Mason Rd., 63141-8550. Tel: 314-878-6705. Email: lnordmann@rscj.org. Web: www.rscj.org. Sisters 6.

TOWN AND COUNTRY. *Monastery of the Visitation, St. Louis*, 3020 N. Ballas Rd., 63131. Tel: 314-625-9260; Fax: 314-432-5354. Email: srvharonik@visitationacademy.org. Web: www.visitationmonastery.org/stlouis. Sr. M. Veronica Haronik, V.H.M., Supr. Residence of Visitation Nuns Teaching or Living at the Monastery of the Visitation. Sisters 14.

[R] HOMES FOR MEN AND WOMEN

ST. LOUIS. *Cathedral Tower*, 325 N. Newstead Ave., 63108. Tel: 314-367-5500, Ext. 121; Fax: 314-361-5099. Email: tgorski@ccstl.org. Web: www.ccstl.org. Building which houses several agencies of Catholic Charities: Queen of Peace Center; St. Elizabeth Hall; and Peace for Kids, Inc. Residents 150.

Father Dempsey's Hotel, Inc., 3427 Washington Ave., 63103. Tel: 314-535-7221; Fax: 314-535-7289. Email: maboussie@archstl.org. Martie Aboussie, Exec. Dir. Total Staff 4; Total in Residence 50.

Father Jim's Home, 3427 Washington Ave., 63103. Tel: 314-535-7221; Fax: 314-535-7289. Email: maboussie@archstl.org. Martie Aboussie, Exec. Dir. Total Staff 4; Total in Residence 50.

St. Martha's Hall, P.O. Box 4950, 63108. Tel: 314-533-1313; Fax: 314-533-2035. Email: stmarthashall@sbcglobal.net. Web: www.saintmarthas.org; www.ccstl.org. Michelle Schiller-Baker, Dir. Provides Shelter, Advocacy and Support to Abused Women & their Children. Capacity 24; Total Staff 14; Total Assisted Annually 300.

St. Philippine Home (1996) 1015 Goodfellow Blvd., 63112. Tel: 314-454-1012; Fax: 314-367-7455. Email: cneumann@ccstl.org. Constance S. Neumann, Exec. Dir. Transitional housing for drug affected homeless city women and their children. Bed Capacity 33; Outpatients 20; Total Assisted Annually 96; Total Staff 12.

Queen of Peace Center (1985) 325 N. Newstead Ave., 63108. Tel: 314-531-0511; Fax: 314-531-1458. Email: cneumann@ccstl.org. Constance S. Neumann, Exec. Dir. Comprehensive residential and outpatient behavioral healthcare for addicted women and their children. Specialty in pregnant women, trauma and dually diagnosed. Permanent and transitional housing programs. Licensed by the Department of Mental Health Division of Alcohol and Drug Abuse. Accredited by COA Council on Accreditation. Vouchers 244; Total Staff 93; Total Assisted Annually 1,312.

Rosati Center, 4220-24 N. Grand Ave., 63107. Tel: 314-534-6624; Fax: 314-535-4394. Permanent supportive housing for former homeless single adults. Managed by St. Patrick Center. Total Assisted 30; Studio Apartments 26; Total Staff 8.

Rosati Group Home, Inc., 4218 N. Grand Blvd., 63107. Tel: 314-534-6624; Fax: 314-535-4394. Email: nboland@stpatrickcenter.org. Web: stpatrickcenter.org. Greg Vogelweid, Admin. Group Home for homeless mentally ill adults. Managed by St. Patrick Center. Total Assisted 140; Total Staff 10.

NORMANDY. *Maria Droste Residence* (1979) 7660 Natural Bridge Rd., 63121. Tel: 314-383-5553; Fax: 314-382-1325. Web: goodshepherdsisters.org. Sisters of the Good Shepherd., For Women in Need. Capacity 10; Total Assisted 70; Total Staff 6.

[S] RETREAT HOUSES

ST. LOUIS. *Mercy Center*, 2039 N. Geyer Rd., 63131. Tel: 314-966-4686; Fax: 314-909-4631. Email: mkaletta@corp.mercy.net. Mary Ann Kaletta, Admin. Operated by the Sisters of Mercy of the Americas, Province St. Louis., Conference and Renewal Ministry.

Mercy Conference and Retreat Center, Sisters of Mercy of the Americas, 2039 N. Geyer Rd., 63131. Tel: 314-966-4686; Fax: 314-909-4631. Sr. Miriam Nolan, R.S.M., Contact Person.

White House Retreat (1922) 7400 Christopher Dr., 63129. Tel: 314-533-8903; Fax: 314-533-8428; Tel: 800-643-1003. Email: whretreat@whretreat.org. Web: www.whretreat.org.

Retreat House (1922) 7400 Christopher Dr., 63129. Tel: 314-846-2575; Fax: 314-293-0931. Revs. James J. Burshek, S.J., Dir.; Richard E. Hadel, S.J., Assoc. Dir.; Eugene C. Renard, S.J., Assoc. Dir.; Edward C. O'Brien, S.J., Assoc. Dir.; Leonard E. Kraus, S.J., Assoc. Dir.; Bro. John Fava, S.J., Assoc. Dir. Total in Residence 6; Total Staff 6.

DITTMER. *Il Ritiro-The Little Retreat* (1981) 7935 St. Francis Ln., P.O. Box 38, 63023. Tel: 636-274-0554 (Toll Free from St. Louis); Fax: 636-274-2380. Email: gpeter@nightowl.net. Revs. Bertin Miller, O.F.M., Exec. Dir.; Michael Crosby, O.F.M., Dir.; Dismas Bonner, O.F.M.; Bros. Patrick Kendrick, O.F.M.; Michael Jennrich, O.F.M.; Pio Jackson, O.F.M. Operated by the Franciscan Friars. Priests 5; Brothers 1; Total in Residence 6; Total Staff 8.

Vianney Renewal Center (1988) 6476 Eime Rd., P.O. Box 130, 63023. Tel: 636-274-5226; Fax: 636-274-1430. Web: www.theservants.org. Very Rev. Liam Hoare, s.P., Paraclete Dir.; Rev. Philip Taylor, s.P., Prog. Dir.; Dr. Rob Furey, Ph.D., Clinical Dir. Operated by the Servants of the Paraclete. Total in Residence 21; Total Staff 17.

EUREKA. *Marianist Retreat & Conference Center* (1967) P.O. Box 718, 63025-0718. Tel: 636-938-5390; Fax: 636-938-3493. Email: macmrcc@aol.com. Web: www.mretreat.org. Sr. Paulette Patritti, O.P., Dir.; Revs. Jose Ramirez, S.M.; Eugene Sweeney, S.M. (Retired). Conducted by the Society of Mary., Center for Formation and Growth in the Christian Life. Total in Residence 8; Total Staff 22.

FLORISSANT. *Pallottine Renewal Center* (1969) 15270 Old Halls Ferry Rd., 63034. Tel: 314-837-7100; Fax: 314-837-1041. Email: Pall4@juno.com. Web: www.pallottinerenewal.org. Sr. Elizabeth Monsanto, Dir. Pallottine Missionary Sisters, Queen of Apostles Province. Total in Residence 7; Total Staff 17.

HIGH RIDGE. *Society of Our Mother of Peace at Mary the Font Solitude* (1966) 6150 Antire Rd., 63049-2135. Tel: 636-677-3235; Fax: 636-677-5284. Email: marythefont@yahoo.com. Web: marythefont.org. Sisters Mary Perpetua Spranger, S.M.P., Local Supr.; Anne Marie DeFord, S.M.P., Treas.; Rev. Placid Guste, S.M.P.

PEVELY. *Vision of Peace Ministries* (1977) Abbey Ln., P.O. Box 69, 63070. Tel: 636-475-3697; Fax: 636-475-3697. Email: visofpeace@juno.com. Mrs. Jane Guenther, Treas. Total in Residence 1; Total Staff 1.

WILDWOOD. *La Salle Institute - Retreat and Conference Center* (1886) 2101 Rue De La Salle, 63038-2299. Tel: 636-938-5374; Fax: 636-587-9792. Email: Cblasalle@sbcglobal.net.

Christian Brothers (De La Salle) (1886) Tel: 636-938-6142; Fax: 636-587-9792. Bro. Bill Brynda, Community Dir.; Mr. Michael Sawicki, Pres.; Gerri Schroeder, Retreat Coord. Community 6; Total in Residence 6; Total Staff 11.

[T] NEWMAN CENTERS

ST. LOUIS. *University of Missouri, St. Louis, Catholic Newman Center* (1965) 8200 Natural Bridge Rd., 63121. Tel: 314-385-3455; Fax: 314-385-1523. Email: cnc@cncumsl.org. Web: www.cncumsl.org. Rev. William G. Kempf, Dir.

Washington University Newman Centers, Washington University Newman Chapel, 6352 Forsyth Blvd., 63105-2269. Tel: 314-935-9191, Ext. 213; Fax: 314-727-6053. Email: braun@washucsc.org. Web: www.washucsc.org. Rev. Gary G. Braun, Archdiocesan Dir. of Campus Ministries. Total in Residence 1; Total Staff 15.

[U] ASSOCIATIONS OF THE FAITHFUL

ST. LOUIS. *Oblates of Wisdom Study Center*, P. O. Box 13230, 63157. Tel: 314-621-2055. Email: jfmccarthy1@bcglobal.net. Rev. Msgr. John F. McCarthy, Dir.

[V] MISCELLANEOUS

ST. LOUIS. *Alexian Brothers of Missouri, Inc.* (1984) *Alexian Brothers (Residence)*, 3900 S. Grand, 63118. Tel: 314-771-5800; Fax: 314-771-7830.

Alexian Brothers of St. Louis, Inc. (1972) *Alexian Brothers (Residence)*, 3910 Ohio, 63118. Tel: 314-865-2224; Fax: 314-865-2664.

Alexian Brothers Services, Inc., 3900 S. Grand, 63118.

Almost Home (1993) 3200 St. Vincent Ave., 63104-1336. Tel: 314-771-4663; Fax: 314-865-4692. Email: smukhtiar@almosthomestl.org. Web: www.almosthomestl.org. Sheroo Mukhtiar, Exec. Dir. Transitional living program for teenage mothers and their children who are homeless. Members and Children 40; Total Staff 20.

American Academy of FertilityCare Professionals, 11700 Studt Ave., Ste. C, 63141. Tel: 314-991-0327; Fax: 314-692-8097. Email: diane.daly@mercy.net. Web: aafcp.org. Mrs. Diane Daly.

The Angela Foundation for Ursuline Education, 341 S. Sappington Rd., 63122. Tel: 314-966-7725.

Anna Trust, 6400 Minnesota Ave., 63111. Tel: 314-481-8800; Fax: 314-481-2366. A Charitable Trust Fund Established to Support the Religious and Charitable Purposes of the Sisters of St. Joseph of Carondelet, St. Louis Province.

Annual Catholic Appeal, 20 Archbishop May Dr., 63119. Tel: 314-792-7680; Fax: 314-792-7229. Email: niebruggeb@archstl.org. Web: www.archstl.org. Brian Niebrugge, Dir., Annual Catholic Appeal. Staff 5.

Archdiocesan Planned Giving & Endowment Council, 4445 Lindell Blvd., 63108. Tel: 314-633-2222; Fax: 314-633-2333. Web: www.archstl.org. Mr. Frank J. Cognata Jr., Chief Devel. Officer; Mrs. Jeanne Rudolph, Co-Planned Giving Assoc.; Ms. April Esenwah, Co-Planned Giving Assoc.; Mr. Jonathan W. Igoe, Chm.; Mr. George T. Bidleman Jr.; Mr. William A. Drennan; David Fairchild; Ms. Rosemary Fairhead; Mr. Daniel Gunn; Most Rev. Robert Hermann; Mr. William Jochens; Ms. Marie Kenyon, J.D.; Mr. Raymond S. Kreienkamp; Mr. Joseph McAuliffe; Mr. Carl Markus; Mr. Michael F. Niemann; Mr. William P. O'Connor; Mrs. Jill M. Palmquist; Mrs. Carolyn Parmer; Mr. Gregory Reynders; Mr. Mark Riordan; Ms. Sharon Sanders; Mr. James Schaller; Mr. Dan Shasserre; Mr. Robert M. Ventimiglia; Mr. Michael Weisbrod.

Archdiocesan Stewardship Education Committee, 20 Archbishop May Dr., 63119. Tel: 314-792-7215; Fax: 314-792-7229. Email: erschen@arstl.org. Web: www.archstl.org/stewardship. Mr. Frank J. Cognata Jr., Chief Devel. Officer; Susan Erschen, Dir. Stewardship Education; Mr. Thom Digman; Matthew Mayer; Beth Moritz; Don Lapoint; Mary Reichenbach; Deacon Thomas Forster; Revs. James J. Benz; Christopher M. Martin; Rev. Msgr. Gregory R. Mikesch; Rev. John Siefert; Rev. Msgr. Joseph M. Simon; Rev. William Vatterot.

ASC Health, 4233 Sulphur Ave., 63109. Tel: 314-351-6294.

Ascension Health, 4600 Edmundson Rd., 63134. Tel: 314-733-8000; Fax: 314-733-8013. Email: atersigni@ascensionhealth.org. Web: www.ascensionhealth.org. Anthony R. Tersigni, Pres. & C.E.O. Co-sponsored by four of the United States Provinces of the Daughters of Charity: Northeast Prov., Albany, NY; Southeast Prov., Emmitsburg, MD; East Central Prov., Evansville, IN; West Central Prov., St. Louis, MO and by the Congregation of St. Joseph and the Congregation of the Sisters of St. Joseph of Carondelet.

Ascension Health-IS, Inc., 4600 Edmundson Rd., 63134. Tel: 314-733-8000; Fax: 314-733-8013. Email: atersigni@ascensionhealth.org. Web: www.ascensionhealth.org. Anthony R. Tersigni, Pres. & CEO.

Aware, Inc. (1973) St. Anthony's Medical Center, 10016 Kennerly Rd., 63128. Tel: 314-525-1622. Karen Molner, Pres.

Birthright, 2206 S. Brentwood Blvd., 63144. Tel: 314-962-5300; Fax: 314-962-7606. Web: www.birthrightstlouis.org. Ruth A. Bradberry, Admin. Dir. Total Assisted 5,679; Total Staff 25.

Branch Offices:

6680 Chippewa, 63109. Tel: 314-962-3653; Fax: 314-351-4531.

3435-C Bridgeland, Bridgeton, 63044. Tel: 314-298-0945; Fax: 314-298-0813.

205 N. 5th St., St. Charles, 63301. Tel: 636-724-1200; Fax: 636-946-0447.
625 N. Euclid, 63108. Tel: 636-946-4900; Fax: 314-361-0129.
800 N. Tucker Blvd., 63101. Tel: 636-916-4300; Fax: 314-588-1179.
Cardinal Glennon Children's Foundation, 1465 S. Grand Blvd., 63104. Tel: 314-577-5605; Fax: 314-268-6416. Email: info@glennon.org. Web: www.glennon.org. Member of SSM Health Care
The Caroline Trust (1991) 320 E. Ripa Ave., 63125-2897. Tel: 314-633-7021; Fax: 314-633-7057. Email: lindajansen@ssnd-sl.org. Supports the Religious and Charitable Purposes of the School Sisters of Notre Dame and Provides Support for the Aged, Infirm and Disabled Sisters of the Province.
Carondelet Health System, Inc., 4600 Edmundson Rd., 63134. Tel: 314-733-8000; Fax: 314-733-8013. Email: atersigni@ascensionhealth.org. Anthony R. Tersigni, Pres. & CEO.
Catholic Charities Foundation, 4532 Lindell Blvd., 63108. Tel: 314-367-5500; Fax: 314-367-2982. Email: tmulhearn@ccstl.org. Web: www.ccstl.org. A Charitable Fund Established to Support the Activities of Catholic Charities.
Catholic Charities Housing Resource Center, 800 N. Tucker Blvd., 63101. Tel: 314-802-5440; Fax: 314-802-5408. Email: cchrc@ccstl.org. Web: www.ccstl.org. Karen Wallensak, Dir. A Program of Catholic Charities helping homeless and near-homeless people achieve stability in safe, affordable housing. Total Staff 34; Total Assisted Annually 16,010.
Catholic Charities Parish Social Ministry, 4532 Lindell Blvd., 63108. Tel: 314-367-5500, Ext. 155; Fax: 314-361-5099. Email: rohde@ccstl.org. Web: www.ccstl.org. Recruitment and placement of volunteers serving the agencies and programs of Catholic Charities Federation.
Catholic Charities Service Agency, 4532 Lindell Blvd., 63108-2497.
Catholic Charities Information and Referral Services (Dial Help), 4532 Lindell, 63108. Tel: 314-371-4357 (314-371-HELP).
Catholic Charities Refugee Services, 2840 Wisconsin Ave., 63118-1632. Tel: 314-771-2570; Fax: 314-771-6406. Mary Carroll, Resettlement Dir.
Catholic Charities Southside Center (Vietnamese and Hispanic Programs), 5880 Christy, 63116. Tel: 314-773-6100; 314-664-8990. Courtney Prentis, Dir.
Hispanic Programs Tel: 314-773-6100.
Vietnamese Programs Tel: 314-664-8990.
Catholic Charities Father Tolton Center, 1018 Baden, 63147. Tel: 314-385-3445; Fax: 314-385-4479. Monica Anderson, Dir.
Catholic Charities Jefferson County Center, 110 N. Brierton Ln. at N. 2nd, Crystal City, 63019-1720. Tel: 636-931-5859; Fax: 636-933-5148. P.O. Box 668, Festus, 63028-0668. Loretta Kelly, Dir.
Catholic Charities Midtown Center (Including Friends of Moms Program), 1202 S. Boyle Ave., 63110-3814. Tel: 314-534-1180; Fax: 314-534-3727. John Pachak, Dir.
Catholic Charities St. Charles Area Center, 255 Spencer Rd., #202, St. Peters, 63376-1632. Tel: 636-498-2273; Fax: 636-498-0390. Gerry Mazzuca, Dir.
Catholic Charities St. Jane Center, 7005 Ascension Dr., 63121-3427. Tel: 314-383-6539; Fax: 314-383-6591. Jamie Saunders, Dir.
Catholic Deaf Ministry, 7530 Natural Bridge Rd., 63121. Tel: 314-727-2747 (TTY). Email: vbarnhart@archstl.org. Provides Services for Deaf and Hearing Impaired Persons.
Catholic Family Services (1992) 9200 Watson Rd., G101, 63126. Tel: 314-544-3800; 800-652-8055; Fax: 314-843-0552. Dr. Jerry L. Marks, D.S.W., L.C.S.W., Exec. Dir. Provides residential and social services, professional counseling and health care access to families and communities. Staff 54; Total Assisted Annually 12,599.
Locations:
Catholic Family Service, 255 Spencer Rd., Ste. 202, St. Peters, 63376. Tel: 636-498-2273, Ext. 10; 877-498-2271; Fax: 636-498-0390.
Catholic Family Services South Office, 9200 Watson Rd., G101, 63126-1528. Tel: 314-544-3800; Fax: 314-843-0552.
Catholic Family Services Schools Partnership Program, 9200 Watson Rd, G101, 63126-1528. Tel: 314-544-3800; Fax: 314-843-0552.
Language Access Metro Project (LAMP), 8050 Watson, Ste. 340, 63119. Tel: 314-842-0062; Fax: 314-842-1303. Nicole Lopresti, Dir.
Fatherhood Initiative/Places for Fathers, 1911 N. Taylor Ave., 63113-2601. Tel: 314-535-0017; Fax: 314-535-3155.
Catholic Family Services West County Office, 498 Woods Mill Rd., Manchester, 63011-4144. Tel: 636-391-9966; Fax: 636-394-4678.
Family Wellness Program, 100 W. Main St., Union, 63084-1363. Tel: 636-583-1800; 800-583-8355; Fax: 636-583-0836.
Catholic Family Services Northwest Office, 1385 Harkee Rd., Florissant, 63031. Tel: 314-831-1533; Fax: 314-831-1391.
The Catholic Health Association of the United States, 4455 Woodson Rd., 63134-3797. Tel: 314-427-2500; Fax: 314-427-0029. Web: www.chausa.org. Sr. Carol Keehan, D.C., Pres. & CEO. Established June 24, 1915. Total Staff 70.
Catholic High School Association, Cardinal Rigali Center, Ste. 2110, 20 Archbishop May Dr., 63119-5738. Tel: 314-792-7300; Fax: 314-792-7399. Email: stlsupt@archstl.org. Web: www.archstl.org/education/. Mr. George Henry, Supt.
Catholic Education Office, Cardinal Rigali Center, Ste. 2110, 20 Archbishop May Dr., 63119-5738. Tel: 314-792-7300; Fax: 314-792-7399. Email: stlsupt@archstl.org. Web: www.archstl.org/education/. Mr. George Henry, Supt.
Catholic Kolping Society of America, 4035 Keokuk St., 63116. Tel: 314-776-5312. Noreen G. Nutt, Treas.
Catholic Legal Assistance Ministry, 321 N. Spring, 63108. Tel: 314-977-3993; Fax: 314-977-3334. Email: kenyonm@slu.edu. Ms. Marie Kenyon, J.D., Dir. A Program of Catholic Charities providing legal advocacy and representation in civil matters and immigration for low-income clients.
Catholic Office of Disability Ministry (1980) 20 Archbishop May Dr., 63119. Tel: 314-792-7150; 314-792-7158 (TDD); Fax: 314-792-7199. Email: dministry@archstl.org. Web: www.archstl.org.
Central Bureau of the C.C.V.A., 3835 Westminster Pl., 63108-3472. Tel: 314-371-1653; Fax: 314-371-0889. Email: centbur@sbcglobal.net. Web: www.socialjusticereview.org. Rev. Edward Krause, C.S.C., Dir. & Editor of the Social Justice Review.
St. Charles Lwanga Center (1978) 4746 Carter Ave., Ste. 100, 63115-2238. Tel: 314-367-7929; Fax: 314-367-4134. Email: info@lwangacenter.org. Web: www.archstl.org/lwangacenter/. Jane Wexler Brown, Exec. Dir. A spiritual formation Center for leadership in the African American Catholic Community, in the Archdiocese of St. Louis. The Center collaborates with other Christians throughout the United States and provides leadership training for junior high and teenage youth and adult laity. In conjunction with our service to 10 sponsoring parishes, we conduct workshops on the Sacrament of Confirmation, evangelization, coping with grief and loss, marriage preparation, marriage enrichment, days of reflection, pastoral care and retreats. Total Staff 6.
Chiara Corporation (1995) 1100 Bellevue Ave., 63117-1826. Tel: 314-768-1817; Fax: 314-768-1803. Email: joshaughnessy@fsmonline.org. Mr. John O'Shaughnessy, Contact Person. Ministries that promote, enhance and provide for the spiritual, religious, physical or mental well-being of members of society in accordance with the religious and charitable purposes of the Franciscan Sisters of Mary.
Collaborative Dominican Novitiate, 4928 Washington Blvd., 63108-1621. Tel: 314-454-0664; Fax: 314-454-3849. Email: kelsner@spdom.org. Katherine Elsner, Contact Person; Patricia Hanvey, O.P., Contact Person.
**Covenant House Missouri*, 2727 N. Kingshighway Blvd., 63113.
CSJ Ministries, 6400 Minnesota Ave., 63111. Tel: 314-481-8800; Fax: 314-481-2366.
Daughters of Charity Foundation (1996) c/o *Ascension Health*, 4600 Edmundson Rd., 63134. Tel: 314-802-2060; Fax: 314-802-2051. Email: jimpicciche@ascensionhealth.org. Web: www.daughtersofcharityfdn.org. Joseph R. Impicciche, Sr. Vice Pres. & Gen. Counsel.
Daughters of Charity Foundation of St. Louis (1995) 231 S. Bemiston, Ste. 735, 63105. Tel: 314-802-2060; Fax: 314-802-2051. Web: www.daughtersofcharityfdn.org. Email: jkuester@docfdn.org. Sr. Joan Kuester, D.C., Exec. Dir.
Daughters of Charity National Health System, Inc., 4600 Edmundson Rd., 63134. Tel: 314-733-8000; Fax: 314-733-8013. Email: atersigni@ascensionhealth.org. Anthony R. Tersigni, Pres. & CEO.
Dismas House of St. Louis, 5025 Cote Brilliante Ave., 63113. Tel: 314-361-2802; Fax: 314-367-0604. John R. Flatley, Exec. Dir. Total in Residence 170; Total Staff 60.
Equestrian Order of the Holy Sepulchre of Jerusalem, 2870 S. Lindbergh Blvd., 63131. Tel: 314-984-5077; Fax: 314-984-9390. Email: nardance@aol.com. Nancy Ross, Sec.
St. Francis de Sales Association (Paris 1872) (St. Louis 1950) 9328 Pine Ave., 63144. Tel: 314-963-9603. Email: ann.wiedl@sbcglobal.net. Ann Doody Wiedl, Councilor for U.S.A. A call to the laity to live their individual vocation in the spirit of Jesus, using the writings of St. Francis de Sales as a means to see and do God's will and grow in holiness.; Private Universal Association of the Faithful.
The Franciscan Connection (1991) 2903 Cherokee St., 63118. Tel: 314-773-8485; Fax: 314-773-8573. Email: franciscanconnection@thefriars.org. Web: www.franciscanconnection.org. Rev. Lawrence M. Nickels, O.F.M., Exec. Dir.
Franklin County Catholic Church Real Estate Corporation (1834) 20 Archbishop May Dr., 63119. Tel: 314-633-2222; Fax: 314-633-2333. Rev. Msgr. Jerome D. Billing, S.T.L., J.C.L., Contact Person.
Good Shepherd Children & Family Services, 1340 Partridge Ave., 63130. Tel: 314-854-5700; Fax: 314-854-5747. Email: goodshepinfo@ccstl.org. Peggy Slater, Exec. Dir. A Catholic Charities agency merging the services of Catholic Services for Children & Youth, Father Dunne's Newsboys' Home, Marian Hall Agencies, St. Joseph's Home and Family Support Services, and Villa Maria Center. Provides child welfare services including the foster care, adoption, expectant parent counseling, advocacy and residential services.
Good Shepherd Mission Development Corporation, 7654 Natural Bridge Rd., 63121. Sr. Mary Carolyn McQuaid, R.G.S., Contact Person.
Good Shepherd Programs, Inc. (1979) 7654 Natural Bridge Rd., 63121. Tel: 314-381-3400; Fax: 314-382-1325. Web: goodshepherdsisters.org. Operates the Maria Droste Residence. Total Staff 6; Total Assisted 70.
Hispanic Ministry of the Archdiocese of St. Louis (1995) 20 Archbishop May Dr., 63119. Tel: 314-792-7890; Fax: 314-792-7898.
Incarnate Word Foundation, Missouri (1997) 5257 Shaw Ave., Ste. 309, 63110. Tel: 314-773-5100; Fax: 314-773-5102. Email: info@iwfdn.org. Web: www.incarnatewordfund.com. Bridget M. Flood, Exec. Dir.
Institute for Theological Encounter with Science & Technology (ITEST), 20 Archbishop May Dr., 63119. Tel: 314-792-7220. Email: mariannepost@archstl.org. Web: www.faithscience.org. Sr. Marianne Postiglione, R.S.M., Assoc. Dir.
Institute of Jesuit Sources (1961) 3601 Lindell Blvd., 63108. Tel: 314-633-4622; Fax: 314-633-4623. Email: ijs@jesuitsources.com. Web: www.jesuitsources.com. Rev. John W. Padberg, S.J., Dir. Priests 5; Total Staff 7.
Intercommunity Housing Association (1993) 1049 N. Clay, Ste. 300, Kirkwood, 63122. Tel: 314-965-4700. Email: donald.schneiber@sbcglobal.net. Web: www.intercommunityhousing.org. Provides safe, affordable housing & supportive svcs. for economically disadvantaged & working poor families in St. Louis; operates Pillar Place Apartments, Compton Place Apartments.
Jefferson County Catholic Church Real Estate Corporation, 4445 Lindell Blvd., 63108. Tel: 314-633-2222; Fax: 314-633-2333. Rev. Msgr. Jerome D. Billing, S.T.L., J.C.L., Contact Person.
The Jesuits of the Missouri Province, Office of Advancement, 4511 W. Pine Blvd., 63108-2191. Tel: 314-361-7765; Fax: 314-758-7163. Email: advancement@jesuits-mis.org. Web: www.jesuits-mis.org. Mr. Thom Digman, Dir.; Revs. L. Gene Martens, S.J., Assoc. Dir.; Robert F. Weiss, S.J., Assoc. Dir.; James M. Short, S.J., Assoc. Dir.
The Jesuits of the Missouri Province
Ladies of Charity of St. Catherine Laboure, 12160 Leelaine Dr., 63126. Susan Tumminia, Pres. Affiliate with Ladies of Charity of the United States & the Assoc. of Intl. Charities of St. Vincent de Paul.
Ladies of Charity of St. Vincent-Guardian Angel, Tel: 314-231-9328; Fax: 314-621-2232. Email: stvstl@swbell.net. Affiliate with Ladies of Charity of the United States & the Assoc. of Intl. Charities of St. Vincent de Paul.
St. Vincent's Church: 1408 S. Tenth St., 63104. Tel: 314-231-9328; Fax: 314-621-2232.
Ladies of Charity Service Center, 7500 Natural Bridge Rd., 63121. Tel: 314-383-4207; Fax: 314-383-0605. Rosemary Fischer, Pres.
Ladies of Charity Service Center, Ladies of Charity Service Center; Thrift Store & Food Pantry. Total Staff 25; Total Assisted 1,065.
Lincoln County Church Real Estate Corporation, 20 Archbishop May Dr., 63119. Tel: 314-633-2222; Fax: 314-633-2333. Rev. Msgr. Jerome D. Billing, S.T.L., J.C.L., Contact Person.
The St. Louis Archdiocesan Fund, 20 Archbishop May Dr., Shrewsbury, 63119-5738. Tel: 314-792-7129. Email: dfairchi@archstl.org. David Fairchild, Finance Mgr.

St. Louis Area Women Religious Collaborative Ministries (1998) 4330 Olive St., 63108. Tel: 314-770-2627; Fax: 314-533-3226. Email: etpproject@aol.com. Sr. M. Philip Agnew, D.C., Contact Person. Includes English Tutoring Project for Immigrant/Refugee Children and Intercommunity Environmental Council.

St. Louis Catholic Charismatic Renewal, 10909 St. Henry Ln., St. Ann, 63074. Tel: 314-427-7786; Fax: 314-427-7789. Email: janeguenther@archstl.org. Web: www.stlrenewal.org. Rev. Msgr. Edmund O. Griesedieck, Dir. (Retired); Mrs. Jane Guenther, Coord.

Abiding Bible Companion (2001) Tel: 314-725-6527.

Healing & Deliverance Ministry

Magnificat Tel: 314-427-7786; Fax: 314-427-7789.

Tree House Healing Ministry Tel: 314-427-7768; Fax: 314-427-7768.

Theotokos Ministry, 4311 S. Compton, 63111. Tel: 314-351-6061. Center with books & tapes, prayer time, ministry times, retreats for parishes, leaders training, small faith groups, conferences, special events & days of renewal.

Two Alike Tel: 314-427-7786; Fax: 314-427-7789.

St. Louis County Catholic Church Real Estate Corporation, 20 Archbishop May Dr., 63119. Tel: 314-633-2222; Fax: 314-633-2333. Rev. Msgr. Jerome D. Billing, S.T.L., J.C.L., Contact Person.

Mary and Joseph Trust, 1100 Bellevue Ave., 63117-1826. Tel: 314-768-1817; Fax: 314-768-1803. Email: joshaughnessy@fsmonline.org.

Mary Queen Charitable Trust Fund, La Salette Missionaries, 4650 South Broadway, 63111. Tel: 314-353-5000.

Mercy Foundation for Health Innovation (2003) 14528 S. Outer Forty, Ste. 100, Chesterfield, 63017. Tel: 314-579-6100; Fax: 314-628-3732. Email: bbartoo@corp.mercy.net. Mr. Bruce Bartoo, Pres.

Mercy Investment Services, Inc., 2039 N. Geyer Rd., 63131.

Midwest Coalition for Responsible Investment, 6400 Minnesota Ave., 63111.

Missionaries of the Holy Family Retirement Trust Fund, 3014 Oregon Ave., 63118. Tel: 314-577-6300; Fax: 314-577-6301.

National Catholic Ministry to the Bereaved, P.O. Box 16353, 63125-0353. Tel: 314-638-2638; Fax: 314-638-2639. Email: NCMBereave@aol.com. Web: www.griefwork.org. Sr. Mary Ann Wachtel, S.F.C.C., Exec. Dir.; John Cherek, Pres. N.C.M.B. offers pastoral and spiritual support to the bereaved, caregivers, agencies, dioceses, congregations, and parishes through education and resources for the development of grief support groups and a training program & manual for ministers of consolation. Total Staff 1; Total Assisted 12,000.

National Christian Life Community of the United States of America (CLC) (1540) 3601 Lindell Blvd., Rm. 202 (Jesuit Hall), 63108-3393. Tel: 314-633-4628; Fax: 314-633-4404. Web: www.clc-usa.org. Ann Marie Brennan, Pres. Founded c. 1540 & approved 1584, a public, intl. assn. of the Faithful of Pontifical Right which builds small Faith-Communities for mission & svc. to the church. It uses the Spiritual Exercises of Saint Ignatius of Loyola as its specific source & characteristic instrument for its spirituality. Membership equally open to primarily catholic christian men, women, youth & young adults, clergy, brothers & sisters.

Network of Sacred Heart Schools, Inc., 700 N. Third St., St. Charles, 63301. Tel: 636-724-7003; Fax: 636-724-4049. Email: nshoffice@sofie.org. Web: www.sofie.org. Madeleine Ortman, Dir.

Notre Dame Ministry Corporation (1994) 320 Ripa Ave., 63125. Tel: 314-544-0455; Fax: 314-544-6754. Mr. Michael Reilly, Pres.; Mrs. Niki Stilwell, Vice Pres.; Mr. Dan Strieker, Treas.; Mr. Bernard Huger, Legal Counsel, Asst. Sec.; Sr. Jean Schmid, S.S.N.D., Recording Sec. Includes: Notre Dame High School, Notre Dame Preschool.

Our Lady's Inn (1981) 4223 S. Compton, 63111. Tel: 314-351-4590; Fax: 314-351-2119. Email: glee@ourladysinn.org. Web: www.ourladysinn.org. 3607 Hwy. D., Defiance, 63341. Tel: 636-398-5375; Fax: 636-398-5376. Gloria Lee, Contact Person. Residential shelters for pregnant women who have no home, who are being abused, who have no one who cares, and/or who are being pressured to abort their baby. We provide living facilities, food, clothing, counseling, vocational guidance and followup care. Total Assisted 650; Total Staff 40. 3607 Hwy. D, Defiance, 63341. Tel: 636-398-5375; Fax: 636-398-5376.

St. Patrick Center (1983) 800 N. Tucker, 63101. Tel: 314-802-0700; Fax: 314-802-1981. Email: gvogelweid@stpatrickcenter.org. Web: stpatrickcenter.org. Located in downtown St. Louis, St. Patrick Center provides opportunities for self-sufficiency and dignity to persons who are homeless or at risk of becoming homeless. Individuals achieve permanent, positive changes in their lives through education, affordable housing, sound mental health, employment and financial stability. Total Assisted 8,000; Total Staff 125.

Pauline Books and Media, 9804 Watson Rd., 63126. Tel: 314-965-3512; 314-965-5273; Fax: 314-821-8401. Email: stlouis@pauline.org. Web: www.pauline.org. Daughters of St. Paul.

Pelletier Trust, a Charitable Trust of the Sisters of the Good Shepherd (1990) 63121. Tel: 314-381-3400; Fax: 314-381-6449.

Perpetual Help Retirement Corporation (2002) 335 S. Kirkwood Rd., 63122. Tel: 314-965-3700; Fax: 314-965-3710. Email: srmaryanne@fsolph.org. Web: www.franciscansisters-olph.org. Established by the Franciscan Sisters of Our Lady of Perpetual Help to Support the Religious and Charitable Purposes of the Franciscan Sisters of Our Lady of Perpetual Help.

Perry County Catholic Church Real Estate Corporation, 20 Archbishop May Dr., 63119. Tel: 314-633-2222; Fax: 314-633-2333. Rev. Msgr. Jerome D. Billing, S.T.L., J.C.L., Contact Person.

Redemptorists of Mattese (1989) 1118 N. Grand Blvd., 63106. Tel: 314-533-0304; Fax: 314-533-4260. Bro. Terrence Burke, C.Ss.R.

Review for Religious, 3601 Lindell Blvd., 63108. Tel: 314-633-4610; Fax: 314-633-4611. Email: review@slu.edu. Web: www.reviewforreligious.org. Rev. David L. Fleming, S.J., Editor. Total Staff 5.

Rosati Center, 4220 N. Grand Ave., 63107.

The Sarah Community, 1100 Bellevue Ave., 63117-1826. Tel: 314-768-1817; Fax: 314-768-1803. Email: joshaughnessy@fsmonline.org. Purpose: provides retirement housing and services to members of religious congregations and laity. Operates the following: Anna House, a skilled nursing facility; Veronica House, a residential care facility; Naomi House, an independent living facility.

The Sarah Community Foundation, 1100 Bellevue Ave., 63117-1826. Tel: 314-768-1817; Fax: 314-768-1803. Email: joshaughnessy@fsmonline.org. Mr. John O'Shaughnessy, Contact Person.

Seton Institute, Ascension Health, 4600 Edmundson Rd., P.O. Box 45998, 63164. Tel: 314-733-8286; Fax: 314-733-8013. Email: jimpicciche@ascensionhealth.org. Web: www.setoninstitute.org. Joseph R. Impicciche, Senior Vice Pres. & Gen. Counsel, Ascension Health.

Sisters of the Good Shepherd Province of Mid-North America Foundation (2001) 7654 Natural Bridge Rd., 63121. Tel: 314-381-3400; Fax: 314-381-7102. Email: cmcquaid@gspmna.org. Web: goodshepherdsisters.org. Sr. Mary Carolyn McQuaid, R.G.S.

Society Devoted to the Sacred Heart, 9600 Tennyson Ave., 63114. Tel: 314-429-0526; Fax: 314-429-0794. Email: sdshstl@juno.com. Web: www.sacredheartsisters.com.

Society of St. Vincent de Paul, Council of St. Louis (1845) 100 N. Jefferson Ave., 63103. Tel: 877-238-3228; 314-881-6000; Fax: 314-531-6712. Email: info@svdpstl.org. Web: www.servingthepoor.com. Lay-based volunteer organization which provides both direct aid and program services to all eleven counties of the Archdiocese. Affiliated with 142 parishes; Car donation program which provides cars to those in need; Serves the incarcerated, their families, and victims through a three-fold approach of direct service, public education, and advocacy for systemic change within the judicial and corrections systems; Provides referrals for people seeking work, for those addicted to drugs or alcohol, and for those with emotional problems; Archdiocesan outreach program targeting hunger and utility relief, administered by the Society of St. Vincent de Paul; Provides household resources to members attempting to help needy individuals. Offers low-cost items for sale to the public. Proceeds benefit agency programs and services. Total Assisted 259,021; Total Staff 45; Volunteer Members 2,800.

Vinnie's Auto, 4127 Forest Park Ave., 63108-2808. Tel: 800-240-4225; Fax: 314-531-6712. Email: info@svdpstl.org. Web: www.servingthepoor.org.

Criminal Justice Ministry, 100 N. Jefferson Ave., 63103. Tel: 314-652-8062; Fax: 314-531-6712. Email: info@svdpstl.org. Web: www.servingthepoor.org.

Food and Fuel for Life, 100 N. Jefferson Ave., 63103. Tel: 877-238-3228; 314-881-6000; Fax: 314-531-6712. Email: info@svdpstl.org. Web: www.servingthepoor.org. Mr. Ronald F. Guz, Pres.

St. Vincent de Paul Thrift Store, 4127 Forest Park Ave., 63108. Tel: 314-881-6013; Fax: 314-531-6712. Email: info@svdpstl.org. Provides household resources to members helping needy individuals. Offers low-cost items for sale to the public. Proceeds benefit agency programs and services.

St. Vincent de Paul Thrift Store, 1071 Regency Pkwy., St. Charles, 63303. Tel: 636-946-1700.

**Society of St. Vincent de Paul, National Administration Services, Inc.*, 58 Progress Pkwy., 63043-3706. Tel: 314-576-3993; Fax: 314-573-6755. Email: usacouncil@svdpusa.org. Web: www.svdpusa.org. Roger T. Playwin, Natl. Exec. Dir.; Terry Wilson, Bd. Chair.

**Society of St. Vincent DePaul, Council of the United States* (1845) 58 Progress Pkwy., 63043-3706. Tel: 314-576-3993; Fax: 314-576-6755. Email: usacouncil@svdpusa.org. Web: www.svdpusa.org. Joseph D. Flannigan, National Pres.; Roger T. Playwin, National Exec. Dir.; Most Rev. John Quinn, Natl. Episcopal Advisor.

SSM Health Businesses, 477 N. Lindbergh, 63141. Tel: 314-994-7800; Fax: 314-994-7900. Email: june_pickett@ssmhc.com. Member of SSM Health Care.

SSM Health Care Corporation, 477 N. Lindbergh, 63141. Tel: 314-994-7800; Fax: 314-994-7782. Email: june_pickett@ssmhc.com. Member of SSM Health Care.

SSM Health Care Portfolio Management Company, 447 N. Lindbergh Blvd., 63141. Tel: 314-994-7800; Fax: 314-994-7900. Email: june_pickett@ssmhc.com. Member of SSM Health Care

SSM Health Care St. Louis, 1173 Corporate Lake Dr., 63132. Tel: 314-989-2000; Fax: 314-989-2400. Web: www.ssmhealth.com. Email: judy_gartland@ssmhc.com. Member of SSM Health Care.

SSM Hospice and Home Care Foundation, 10143 Paget Dr., 63132. Tel: 314-989-2545; Fax: 314-989-2903. Greg Hewitt, Foundation Dir.

SSM St. Mary's Health Center Foundation, 6420 Clayton Rd., 63117. Tel: 314-768-8741; Fax: 314-768-7124. Email: lindsey_fortner@ssmhc.com. Web: www.stmarys-stlouis.com. Member of SSM Health Care.

SSM Regional Health Services, 477 N. Lindbergh Blvd., 63141. Tel: 314-994-7800; Fax: 314-994-7900. Email: june_pickett@ssmhc.com. Member of SSM Health Care.

St. Charles County Catholic Church Real Estate Corporation, 20 Archbishop May Dr., 63119. Tel: 314-633-2222; Fax: 636-633-2333. Rev. Msgr. Jerome D. Billing, S.T.L., J.C.L., Contact Person.

St. Francois County Catholic Church Real Estate Corporation, 20 Archbishop May Dr., 63119. Tel: 314-633-2222; Fax: 314-633-2333. Rev. Msgr. Jerome D. Billing, S.T.L., J.C.L., Contact Person.

St. Louis City Catholic Church Real Estate Corporation, 20 Archbishop May Dr., 63119. Tel: 314-633-2222; Fax: 314-633-2333. Rev. Msgr. Jerome D. Billing, S.T.L., J.C.L., Contact Person.

Ste. Genevieve County Catholic Church Real Estate Corporation, 20 Archbishop May Dr., 63119. Tel: 314-633-2222; Fax: 314-633-2333. Rev. Msgr. Jerome D. Billing, S.T.L., J.C.L., Contact Person. Priests 1.

Theology Digest, 3800 Lindell Blvd., 63156-0907. Tel: 314-977-3410; Fax: 314-977-3704. Email: thdigest@slu.edu. Total Staff 3.

Ursuline Sisters Trust Fund, 353 S. Sappington Rd., 63122. Tel: 314-821-6884; Fax: 314-821-6888. Web: www.osucentral.org. Sr. Virginia Cirone, O.S.U.

The Vincentian Press Religious Supply, 1405 S. Ninth St., 63104. Tel: 314-421-2834; Fax: 314-421-0684. Rev. Joseph E. Begue, C.M., Dir. Total Staff 2.

Warren County Catholic Church Real Estate Corporation, 20 Archbishop May Dr., 63119. Tel: 314-633-2222; Fax: 314-633-2333. Rev. Msgr. Jerome D. Billing, S.T.L., J.C.L., Contact Person.

Washington County Catholic Church Real Estate Corporation (1821) 20 Archbishop May Dr., 63119. Tel: 314-633-2222; Fax: 314-633-2333. Rev. Msgr. Jerome D. Billing, S.T.L., J.C.L., Contact Person.

We & God Spirituality Center, 3601 Lindell Blvd., Ste. 617, 63108. Tel: 314-633-4630; Fax: 314-633-4404. Email: wgsc@weandgod.org. Web: www.weandgod.org.

**Women for Faith and Family* (1984) P.O. Box 300411, 63130. Tel: 314-863-8385; Fax: 314-863-5858. Email: editor@wf-f.org. Web: www.wf-f.org. Mrs. Helen Hull Hitchcock, Pres.

Young Catholic Musicians, 1919 S. 7th St., 63104. Tel: 314-962-9260; Fax: 314-231-7464. Email: revycm@charter.net. Mary Smith, Contact Person.

BRIDGETON. *Boys Hope Girls Hope*, 12120 Bridgeton Square Dr., 63044. Tel: 314-298-1250; Fax: 314-298-1251. Email: hope@bhgh.org. Web: www.boyshopegirlshope.org. Paul A. Minorini, Pres. & CEO. A College Prepatory Residential Child Care Agency Serving Abandoned, Abused and Neglected Children. Founded in 1977; With affiliated programs in: Baton Rouge; Chicago; Cincinnati; Denver; Detroit; Nevada; New Orleans; New York; Northeast Ohio; Orange County, CA; Phoenix; Pittsburgh; St. Louis; San

Francisco, Baltimore, Kansas City. Total Staff 130; Total Assisted 500.

Providence Ministry Corporation (1998) 3415 Bridgeland Dr., 63044. Tel: 314-209-9181; Fax: 314-209-9207. Email: cdpfrancis@hotmail.com. Web: www.divineprovidenceweb.org. Sr. Mary Francis Fletcher, C.D.P., Prov.

Sisters of Divine Providence, 3415 Bridgeland Dr., 63044. Tel: 314-209-9181; Fax: 314-209-9207. Email: cdpfrancis@hotmail.com. Web: www.divineprovidenceweb.org. Sr. Jacklyn Pritchard, C.D.P., Contact Person.

SSM De Paul Health Center, 12303 De Paul Dr., 63044.

SSM DePaul Health Center Foundation, 12303 DePaul Dr., 63044. Tel: 314-344-7003; Fax: 314-344-6172. Email: valerie_stricker@ssmhc.com. Web: www.ssmdepaulfoundation.org. Member of SSM Health Care.

CADET. *Rural Parish Workers of Christ the King* (1942) 15540 Cannon Mines Rd., 63630. Tel: 636-586-5171; Fax: 636-586-5918. Email: rpwck@sbcglobal.net. Web: rpwck.com. Miss Natalie Villmer, Gen. Dir. A Secular Institute of the Archdiocese of St. Louis. Workers 5; Total Assisted 2,500; Total in Residence 4; Total Staff 6.

CHESTERFIELD. *Gateway Academy Incorporated*, 17815 Wild Horse Creek Rd., 63005. Tel: 914-773-1368. Email: jortega@legionaries.org. Web: www.gatewayacademy.org. Rev. Jose Felix Ortega, L.C., Sec. & Treas.

Saint Louis LaSalle Leadership, Inc. (1996) 645 Clovertrail Dr., 63017-2612. Tel: 314-434-8789; Fax: 314-434-8789. Email: stl3i@aol.com. Waldemar E. Bode, Pres.; Gregory M. Gantz, Vice Pres.; John J. Hall, Sec.; Staunton E. Boudreau, Treas.

McAuley Portfolio Management Company, 14528 S. Outer 40, Ste. 100, 63017. Tel: 314-628-3676; Fax: 314-628-3732. Email: philip.wheeler@mercy.net. Mr. Philip Wheeler Sr., Vice Pres. & Gen. Counsel.

MHM Support Services, 14528 S. Outer Forty, Ste. 100, 63017. Tel: 314-579-6100. Mr. Philip Wheeler Sr., Vice Pres. & Gen. Counsel.

Sisters of Mercy Health System, 14528 S. Outer Forty, Ste. 100, 63017. Tel: 314-579-6100; Fax: 314-628-3732. Email: rfrye@corp.mercy.net. Web: www.mercy.net. John Sullivan, Pres.

CREVE COEUR. *SSM Rehab Foundation* (1991) 10101 Woodfield Ln., Ste. 100, Exec. Offices, 63132. Tel: 314-989-2439; Fax: 314-989-2401. Email: stacy_conway@ssmhc.com. Web: www.ssmrehab.com. Member of SSM Health Care.

DARDENNE PRAIRIE. *St. William Apartments II, Inc.*, 1983 Hadley Rd., 63368. Tel: 314-484-0763.

DITTMER. *Our Lady of Victory Charitable Foundation*, 6476 Eime Rd., 63023. Tel: 636-274-5226; Fax: 636-274-1430.

Servants of the Paraclete Missouri Generalate Corporation, 6476 Eime Rd., 63023. Tel: 636-274-5226; Fax: 636-274-1430. Very Rev. Liam Hoare, s.P., Dir.

EARTH CITY. *Congregation of the Mission International Fund*, 13663 Rider Tr. N., 63045-1512. Tel: 314-344-1184; Fax: 314-344-2989.

Ladies of Charity of the United States of America (1960) 13663 Rider Trail, N., 63045. Tel: 314-344-1184, Ext. 102; Fax: 314-344-2989. Email: lcstlouis@aol.com. Web: www.famvin.org/lcusa. Albe McGurk, Pres. 2009-2010. LCUSA continues, expands, and improves the charitable works of the local associations of the LCUSA, which number 70.

Lazarist Trust Fund, 13663 Rider Tr. N., 63045-1512. Tel: 314-344-1184; Fax: 314-344-2989.

FESTUS. *TEC Conference (Teens Encounter Christ)*, 114 S. 2nd St., 63028. Ronald Reiter, Exec. Dir.

FLORISSANT. *Child Center Foundation* (1947) 2705 Mullanphy Ln., 63031. Tel: 314-837-1702; Fax: 314-830-6263. Email: rdowney@ccstl.org. Mr. Timothy Drury, Pres., Bd. of Directors. Child Center Foundation provides financial support to the Child Center - Marygrove, a residential and day treatment facility serving severely emotionally disturbed children and their families.

Pope John Paul II Apartments, Inc., 6325 Waterways Dr., 63033. Tel: 314-653-0400; Fax: 314-653-2840. Email: bperrone@ccstl.org. Web: www.ccstl.org/cri/independent.html. Purpose: to provide facilities and services specifically designed to meet the physical, social, spiritual and psychological needs of elderly persons.

KIRKWOOD. *Ursuline Provincialate Foundation, Central Province of the United States*, 353 Sappington Rd., 63122.

LIGUORI. *Redemptorist Fathers dba Liguori Publications* One Liguori Dr., 63057. Tel: 636-464-2500; Fax: 636-464-8449. Email: mkessler@liguori.org. Web: www.liguori.org. Rev. Mathew Kessler, C.Ss.R., Pres. & Publisher.

O'FALLON. *Centers for Professional and Pastoral Services*, 204 N. Main St., 63366-2299. Tel: 636-240-6010; Fax: 636-272-5031. Email: fraia@cpps-ofallon.org. Sisters Fran Raia, C.PP.S., Admin.; Mary Whited, C.PP.S. Sponsored by Sisters of the Most Precious Blood of O'Fallon, MO. Centers 1; Total Assisted 300; Total Staff 2.

Charitable Trust, Sisters of the Most Precious Blood of O'Fallon, MO, 204 N. Main St., 63366-2299. Tel: 636-240-6010; Fax: 636-272-5031. Email: cschnyder@cpps-ofallon.org. Web: www.cpps-ofallon.org. Trust fund for support of retired Sisters of the Most Precious Blood.

St. Dominic Endowment Fund, St. Dominic High School, 31 St. Dominic Dr., 63366. Tel: 314-240-8303; Fax: 314-240-9884. Email: mainoffice@stdominichs.org. Web: www.stdominichs.org. Sr. Mary H. Bender, S.S.N.D., Treas.

PACIFIC. *Providence Trust*, Our Lady of the Angels Monastery, 265 St. Joseph Rd., 63069. Fax: 636-938-4960. Web: www.franciscancaring.org. Purpose: To support the religious and charitable purposes of the Franciscan Missionary Brothers of the Sacred Heart.

PERRYVILLE. *Association of the Miraculous Medal* (1918) 1811 W. Saint Joseph St., 63775. Tel: 573-547-8343; Fax: 573-547-1389. Email: ammfather@amm.org. Web: www.amm.org. Rev. James G. Ward, C.M., Pres.

Catholic Home Study Service, P.O. Box 363, 63775. Tel: 573-547-4084. Email: chss@ldd.net. Web: www.amm.org/chss.htm. Rev. Oscar Lukefahr, C.M., Dir. Priests 1; Total Staff 5; Total Assisted 14,000.

Offers free correspondence courses on the Catholic Faith.

Ladies of Charity of St. Vincent de Paul Parish, 1010 Rosati Ct., 63775. Tel: 573-547-4591; Fax: 573-547-4145. Email: svdepaul@svdepaul.org. Marilyn R. Schumer, Pres. Affiliate with Ladies of Charity of the United States & the Assoc. of Intl. Charities of St. Vincent de Paul. Total Assisted 4,067.

St. Vincent De Paul Educational Foundation, 1010 A Rosati Ct., 63775. Tel: 573-547-4591; Fax: 573-547-4145. Email: svdepaul@svdepaul.org. Web: www.svdepaul.org. Rev. Joseph S. Williams, C.M., Moderator. Develops, Promotes and Sustains Catholic Education in Perry County.

ST. CHARLES. *Academy of the Sacred Heart of St. Charles, Missouri Endowment Trust Fund* (1818) 619 N. 2nd St., 63301. Tel: 636-946-5632; Fax: 636-949-6659. Email: mglavin@ash1818.org. Web: www.ash1818.org.

Duchesne High School Endowment Fund Inc., 2550 Elm St., 63301. Tel: 636-946-6767; Fax: 636-946-6267. Email: tgravemann@duchesne-hs.org. Web: www.duchesne-hs.org. Terry W. Gravemann, Pres. Receives Bequests and Gifts from Various Donors for the Express Purpose of Aiding and Benefitting Duchesne High School, St. Charles, and by Investment and Use of Such Bequests and Gifts and Income therefrom Aids and Benefits the High School in Fulfilling its Educational Purposes.

Sts. Joachim and Ann Care Service, 4116 McClay Rd., 63304. Tel: 636-441-1302; Fax: 636-229-4684. Email: mmahon@jacares.org. Web: jacares.org. Miriam Mahan, Exec. Dir.

Saint William Apartments, Inc., 1967 Hanley Rd., 63366.

SSM St. Joseph Foundation, 300 First Capitol Dr., 63301. Tel: 314-947-5612; Fax: 636-947-5676. Web: www.ssmstjoseph.com. Member of SSM Health Care.

Warrenton Senior Village, Inc., Hwy. U & Woolf Rd., Warrenton, 63383.

WILDWOOD. *Gateway Educational Foundation, Inc.*, 19015 Fox Lake Rd., 63069. Tel: 914-773-1368; Fax: 914-773-1438. Rev. Jose Felix Ortega, L.C., Sec. & Treas.

RELIGIOUS INSTITUTES OF MEN REPRESENTED IN THE ARCHDIOCESE

For further details refer to the corresponding bracketed number in the Religious Institutes of Men or Women section.

[0120]—*Alexian Brothers* (Chicago)—C.F.A.
[0140]—*The Augustinians. (Prov. of Our Mother of Good Counsel)*—O.S.A.
[0200]—*Benedictine Monks. (English, Swiss American Congregation)*—O.S.B.
[]—*Brothers of St. Charles Lwanga*—B.S.C.L.
[0330]—*Brothers of the Christian Schools. (St. Louis Prov.)*—F.S.C.
[]—*Canons Regular of the New Jerusalem* (Chesterfield, MO)—C.R.N.J.
[0470]—*The Capuchin Friars* (Kansas City, MO)—O.F.M.Cap.
[1330]—*Congregation of the Mission (Midwest Prov.)*—C.M.
[0630]—*Congregation of the Missionaries of the Holy Family* (Europe)—M.S.F.
[1000]—*Congregation of the Passion (Eastern Prov. of Holy Cross)*—C.P.
[1000]—*Congregation of the Passion (Western Prov. of Holy Cross)*—C.P.
[1130]—*Congregation of the Priests of the Sacred Heart*—S.C.J.
[1080]—*Congregation of the Resurrection* (Rome, Italy)—C.R.
[0480]—*Conventual Franciscans. (Our Lady of Consolation Prov.)*—O.F.M.Conv.
[]—*Franciscan Brothers of the Holy Cross*—F.F.S.C.
[0520]—*Franciscan Friars. (Croatian Franciscan Commissariat, Sacred Heart Prov.)*—O.F.M.
[0540]—*Franciscan Missionary Brothers of the Sacred Heart of Jesus* (Eureka, MO)—O.S.F.
[0690]—*Jesuit Fathers and Brothers* (Missouri Prov.)—S.J.
[0730]—*Legionaries of Christ*—L.C.
[0800]—*Maryknoll*—M.M.
[0720]—*The Missionaries of Our Lady of La Salette*—M.S.
[0870]—*Monfort Missionaries*—S.M.M.
[0430]—*Order of Preachers*—O.P.
[0610]—*Priests of the Congregation of Holy Cross*—C.S.C.
[1070]—*Redemptorist Fathers* (Denver Prov.)—C.SS.R.
[1230]—*Servants of the Paraclete*—s.P.
[1240]—*Servites* (Chicago)—O.S.M.
[0760]—*Society of Mary* (St. Louis Prov.)—S.M.
[0975]—*Society of Our Lady of the Most Holy Trinity*—S.O.L.T.
[0420]—*Society of the Divine Word* (Northern Prov.)—S.V.D.
[]—*Sons of Our Mother*—S.M.P.

RELIGIOUS INSTITUTES OF WOMEN REPRESENTED IN THE ARCHDIOCESE

[0100]—*Adorers of the Blood of Christ* (U.S. Prov.)—A.S.C.
[0130]—*Apostles of the Sacred Heart of Jesus*—A.S.C.J.
[0360]—*Carmelite Sisters of the Divine Heart of Jesus* (Carmel)—D.C.J.
[3110]—*Congregation of Our Lady of the Retreat in the Cenacle*—R.C.
[]—*Congregation of Our Lady of the Rosary*
[]—*Congregation of Our Lady of the Sacred Heart*
[]—*Congregation of St. Catherine of Siena*
[]—*Congregation of the Most Holy Rosary*
[0460]—*Congregation of the Sisters of Charity of the Incarnate Word*—C.C.V.I.
[1730]—*Congregation of the Third order of St. Francis Oldenburg, IN*—O.S.F.
[1830]—*Contemplatives of the Good Shepherd*—C.G.S.
[0760]—*Daughters of Charity of St. Vincent de Paul*—D.C.
[]—*Daughters of Our Mother of Peace*—S.M.P.
[0810]—*Daughters of the Heart of Mary*—D.H.M.
[0420]—*Discalced Carmelite Nuns*—O.C.D.
[1070-19]—*Dominican Sisters* (of Houston, TX)—O.P.
[]—*Eucharist Missionaries of St. Theresa*—M.E.S.T.
[1370]—*Franciscan Missionaries of Mary*—F.M.M.
[1310]—*Franciscan Sisters of Little Falls, Minnesota*—O.S.F.
[1415]—*Franciscan Sisters of Mary*—F.S.M.
[1430]—*Franciscan Sisters of Our Lady of Perpetual Help*—O.S.F.
[]—*Franciscan Sisters, Daughters of the Sacred Hearts of Jesus and Mary*
[2340]—*Little Sisters of the Poor*—L.S.P.
[2490]—*Medical Mission Sisters*—M.M.S.
[2710]—*Missionaries of Charity*—M.C.
[0390]—*Missionary Carmelites of St. Teresa*—C.M.S.T.
[3990]—*Missionary Sisters of St. Peter Claver*—S.S.P.C.
[3760]—*Order of St. Clare*—O.S.C.
[2010]—*Order of the Most Holy Redeemer*—O.SS.R.
[0950]—*Pius Society Daughters of St. Paul*—F.S.P.
[3170]—*Religious of the Passion of Jesus Christ*—C.P.
[3465]—*Religious of the Sacred Heart of Mary*—R.S.H.M.
[2970]—*School Sisters of Notre Dame*—S.S.N.D.
[]—*Sinsinawa Dominican Congregation of the Most Holy Rosary*
[0430]—*Sisters of Charity of the Blessed Virgin Mary*—B.V.M.
[0460]—*Sisters of Charity of the Incarnate Word* (San Antonio, TX)—C.C.V.I.
[0660]—*Sisters of Christian Charity*—S.C.C.
[0990]—*Sisters of Divine Providence*—C.D.P.

[2360]—*Sisters of Loretto at the Foot of the Cross* (St. Louis Prov.)—S.L.

[2570]—*Sisters of Mercy*—R.S.M.

[2580]—*Sisters of Mercy of the Americas*—R.S.M.

[1540]—*Sisters of Saint Francis, Clinton, Iowa*—O.S.F.

[1600]—*Sisters of St. Francis of the Martyr St. George*—F.S.G.M.

[3830]—*Sisters of St. Joseph*—C.S.J.

[1830]—*Sisters of the Good Shepherd*—R.G.S.-C.G.

[3270]—*Sisters of the Most Precious Blood* (O'Fallon, MO)—C.PP.S.

[3150]—*Sisters of the Pallottine Missionary Society*—S.A.C.

[3540]—*Sisters Servants of the Holy Spirit of Perpetual Adoration*—S.Sp.S.deA.

[2150]—*Sisters, Servants of the Immaculate Heart of Mary*—I.H.M.

[1890]—*Society of Helpers of the Holy Souls*—S.H.

[4070]—*Society of the Sacred Heart*—R.S.C.J.

[4110]—*Ursuline Nuns*—O.S.U.

[4190]—*Visitation Nuns*—V.H.M.

ARCHDIOCESAN CEMETERIES

ST. LOUIS. *Calvary*, Business Office: 5239 W. Florissant Ave., 63115. Tel: 314-381-1313; Fax: 314-381-3218.
Location:
Calvary Cemetery, 5239 W. Florissant Ave., 63115.
Sacred Heart Cemetery, Graham Rd., Florissant, 63033.
Saint Ferdinand Cemetery, Graham Rd., Hazelwood, 63042.
Saint Mary Cemetery, 5200 Fee Fee Rd., Hazelwood, 63042.
Saint Peter Cemetery, Geyer at W. Monroe Ave., Kirkwood, 63122.
Cemetery of Our Lady, Lake St. Louis Blvd. & Orf Rd., Lake St. Louis, 63366.
Saint Charles Borromeo Cemetery, Randolph St., St. Charles, 63301.
Ste. Philippine Cemetiere, 4057 Towers Rd., St. Charles, 63304.

Resurrection, Business Office: 6901 Mackenzie Rd., 63123. Tel: 314-352-5300.
Location:
Resurrection Cemetery, 6901 Mackenzie Rd., 63123.
Saints Peter and Paul Cemetery, 7030 Gravois Ave., 63116.
Saint Vincent Cemetery, 1488 Romaine Creek Rd., Fenton, 63026.
Holy Cross Cemetery, 16200 Manchester Rd., Ellisville, 63011.
Mount Olive Cemetery, 3906 Mt. Olive Rd., Lemay, 63125.
Ascension Cemetery, 5563 Country Club Rd., Washington, 63090.

NECROLOGY

† Glynn, Rev. Msgr. Gerard N., (Retired)—Died Feb. 4, 2009
† Good, Rev. Msgr. Clarence P., (Retired)—Died May 21, 2009
† Hartnett, Rev. Msgr. James R., (Retired)—Died March 29, 2009
† O'Connell, Rev. Msgr. James P., (Retired)—Died Dec. 24, 2008
† Albert, Xavier, (Retired)—Died April 9, 2009
† Gambon, John A., (Retired)—Died July 7, 2009
† Krings, James A., St. Louis, MO St. Joseph—Died June 27, 2009
† Matyas, Francis B., (Retired)—Died Jan. 21, 2009

An asterisk (*) denotes an organization that has established tax-exempt status directly with the IRS and is not covered by the USCCB Group Ruling.

Archdiocese of St. Paul and Minneapolis

(Archidioecesis Paulopolitana et Minneapolitana)

Most Reverend

JOHN C. NIENSTEDT, S.T.D., D.D.

Archbishop of Saint Paul and Minneapolis; ordained July 27, 1974; appointed Auxiliary Bishop of Detroit June 12, 1996; episcopal ordination July 9, 1996; appointed Bishop of New Ulm June 12, 2001; installed August 6, 2001; appointed Coadjutor Archbishop of Saint Paul and Minneapolis April 24, 2007; succeeded to the See May 2, 2008. *Office: 226 Summit Ave., St. Paul, MN 55102*. Tel: 651-291-4511; Fax: 651-291-4549.

Most Reverend

HARRY J. FLYNN, D.D.

Archbishop Emeritus of Saint Paul and Minneapolis; ordained May 28, 1960; appointed Coadjutor of Lafayette April 19, 1986; episcopal ordination June 24, 1986; appointed Bishop of Lafayette May 13, 1989; appointed Coadjutor Archbishop of Saint Paul and Minneapolis February 22, 1994; succeeded to the See September 8, 1995; retired May 2, 2008. *Office: 226 Summit Ave., St. Paul, MN 55102*. Tel: 651-291-4420; Fax: 651-291-4549.

Chancery: 226 Summit Ave., St. Paul, MN 55102. Tel: 651-291-4400; Fax: 651-290-1629.

Web: www.archspm.org

Email: archcom@archspm

Most Reverend

LEE ANTHONY PICHÉ

Auxiliary Bishop of Saint Paul and Minneapolis; ordained May 26, 1984; appointed Auxiliary Bishop of Saint Paul and Minneapolis and Titular Bishop of Tamata May 27, 2009; episcopal ordination June 29, 2009. *Office: 226 Summit Ave., St. Paul, MN 55102*. Tel: 651-291-4521; Fax: 651-290-1637. Email: bishop piche@archspm.org.

Square Miles 6,187.

Diocese Established, July 19, 1850. Archdiocese Established, May 4, 1888.

Comprises the following twelve Counties of the State of Minnesota: Ramsey, Hennepin, Anoka, Carver, Chisago, Dakota, Goodhue, Le Sueur, Rice, Scott, Washington and Wright.

Corporate Title: The Archdiocese of Saint Paul and Minneapolis.

For legal titles of parishes and archdiocesan institutions, consult the Chancery.

STATISTICAL OVERVIEW

Personnel	
Archbishops	1
Retired Archbishops	1
Auxiliary Bishops	1
Priests: Diocesan Active in Diocese	224
Priests: Diocesan Active Outside Diocese	6
Priests: Diocesan in Foreign Missions	2
Priests: Retired, Sick or Absent	108
Number of Diocesan Priests	340
Religious Priests in Diocese	96
Total Priests in Diocese	436
Extern Priests in Diocese	33
Ordinations:	
Diocesan Priests	3
Transitional Deacons	7
Permanent Deacons	7
Permanent Deacons in Diocese	215
Total Brothers	34
Total Sisters	722
Parishes	
Parishes	219
With Resident Pastor:	
Resident Diocesan Priests	213
Resident Religious Priests	6
Missions	5
Pastoral Centers	4
Professional Ministry Personnel:	
Brothers	2
Sisters	49
Lay Ministers	467
Welfare	
Catholic Hospitals	4
Total Assisted	228,000
Health Care Centers	8
Total Assisted	30,000
Homes for the Aged	7
Total Assisted	1,600
Residential Care of Children	2
Total Assisted	1,000
Day Care Centers	2
Total Assisted	150
Specialized Homes	4
Total Assisted	1,250
Special Centers for Social Services	17
Total Assisted	5,200
Residential Care of Disabled	4
Total Assisted	1,050
Other Institutions	5
Total Assisted	13,000
Educational	
Seminaries, Diocesan	2
Students from This Diocese	67
Students from Other Diocese	173
Diocesan Students in Other Seminaries	1
Seminaries, Religious	1
Total Seminarians	68
Colleges and Universities	3
Total Students	17,000
High Schools, Diocesan and Parish	10
Total Students	8,000
High Schools, Private	4
Total Students	600
Elementary Schools, Diocesan and Parish	91
Total Students	30,000
Elementary Schools, Private	3
Total Students	500
Catechesis/Religious Education:	
High School Students	16,500
Elementary Students	40,000
Total Students under Catholic Instruction	112,668
Teachers in the Diocese:	
Priests	41
Brothers	9
Sisters	115
Lay Teachers	500
Vital Statistics	
Receptions into the Church:	
Infant Baptism Totals	8,755
Minor Baptism Totals	304
Adult Baptism Totals	293
Received into Full Communion	1,285
First Communions	9,425
Confirmations	7,849
Marriages:	
Catholic	1,433
Interfaith	796
Total Marriages	2,229
Deaths	4,502
Total Catholic Population	650,000
Total Population	3,000,000

Former Bishops—Rt. Rev. JOSEPH CRETIN, D.D., cons. Jan. 26, 1851; died Feb. 22, 1857; Most Revs. THOMAS L. GRACE, O.P., D.D., cons. July 24, 1859; resigned July 31, 1884; named Titular Bishop of Menith, and later, Titular Archbishop of Siunia; died Feb. 22, 1897; JOHN IRELAND, D.D., cons. Dec. 21, 1861; Bishop of Maronea, and Coadjutor to; died Sept. 25, 1918; THOMAS L. GRACE, O.P., D.D., succeeded to the See of St. Paul, July 31, 1884; appt. Archbishop, May 15, 1888; died Sept. 25, 1918; AUSTIN DOWLING, D.D., Archbishop of St. Paul; ord. June 24, 1891; appt. Bishop of Des Moines, Iowa, Jan. 31, 1912; cons. April 25, 1912; Nominated Archbishop of St. Paul, Feb. 1, 1919; died Nov. 29, 1930; JOHN GREGORY MURRAY, S.T.D., ord. April 14, 1900; appt. Titular Bishop of Flavias, Auxiliary to the Bishop of Hartford, Nov. 15, 1919; cons. April 28, 1920; transferred to the Diocese of Portland, May 29, 1925; appt. Archbishop of St. Paul, Oct. 29, 1931; died Oct. 11, 1956; WILLIAM O. BRADY, D.D., Archbishop of St. Paul; ord. Dec. 21, 1923; appt. Bishop of Sioux Falls, June 10, 1939; cons. Aug. 24, 1939; appt. Titular Archbishop of Selymbria and Coadjutor "cum jure successionis" of St. Paul, June 16, 1956; succeeded to See, Oct. 11, 1956; died Oct. 1, 1961; LEO C. BYRNE, D.D. Coadjutor Archbishop "cum jure successionis" of Saint Paul and Minneapolis ord. June 10, 1933; appt. titular Bishop of Sabidia and Auxiliary of St. Louis, May 21, 1954; cons. June 29, 1954; transferred to Wichita, "cum jure successionis" 1961; appt. Apostolic Administrator of Wichita, Feb. 25, 1963; promoted to St. Paul and Minneapolis, Aug. 2, 1967; died Oct. 21, 1974; LEO BINZ, D.D., ord. March 15, 1924; appt. Titular Bishop of Pinara and Coadjutor Bishop of Winona, Nov. 21, 1942; cons. Dec. 21, 1942; Titular Archbishop of Silyum and Coadjutor to the Archbishop of Dubuque "cum jure successionis," Oct. 15, 1949; Archbishop of Dubuque, Dec. 2, 1954; appt. Archbishop of Saint Paul, Dec. 16, 1961; resigned May 21, 1975; died Oct. 9, 1979; JOHN R. ROACH, D.D., Archbishop of St. Paul and Minneapolis; ord. June 8, 1946; appt. Titular Bishop of Cenae and Auxiliary Bishop of St. Paul and Minneapolis, July 12, 1971; cons. Sept. 8, 1971; appt. Archbishop of St. Paul and Minneapolis, May 21, 1975; resigned Sept. 8, 1995; died July 11, 2003; HARRY J. FLYNN, D.D., ord. May 28, 1960; appt. Coadjutor of Lafayette April 19, 1986; cons. June 24, 1986; appt. Bishop of Lafayette May 13, 1989; appt. Coadjutor Archbishop of Saint Paul and Minneapolis Feb. 22, 1994; appt. Archbishop of Saint Paul and

Minneapolis Sept. 8, 1995; retired May 2, 2008.

Chancery—226 Summit Ave., St. Paul, 55102. Tel: 651-291-4400; Fax: 651-290-1629. Office Hours: Mon.-Fri. 9-5

Office of the Archbishop—Most Rev. JOHN C. NIENSTEDT; Ms. DEB THIELEN, Administrative Asst. to the Archbishop. Tel: 651-291-4511; Fax: 651-290-1637. Email: thielend@archspm.org; Mr. THOMAS SCHULZETENBERG, Administrative Chancellor, 226 Summit Ave., St. Paul, 55102. Tel: 651-290-1644. Email: schulzetenbergt@archspm.org.

Office of the Auxiliary Bishop, Episcopal Vicar and Vicar General—Most Rev. LEE ANTHONY PICHE. Email: bishoppiche@archspm.org; Ms. LORNA ANDERSON, Administrative Asst. to the Auxiliary Bishop, 226 Summit Ave., St. Paul, 55102. Tel: 651-291-4521. Email: andersonl@archspm.org.

Office of Vicar General and Moderator of the Curia—Very Rev. PETER A. LAIRD, M.A., M.Div., Vicar Gen. & Moderator of the Curia. Email: vicargeneral@archspm.org; Ms. LAURIE WOHLERS, Administrative Asst. to the Vicar Gen., 226 Summit Ave., St. Paul, 55102. Tel: 651-291-4430; Fax: 651-290-1629. Email: wholersl@archspm.org.

Presbyteral Council—

Executive Director—Rev. THOMAS J. WALKER, J.D., Saint Ambrose of Woodbury, 4125 Woodbury Dr., Woodbury, 55129-9627. Secretary: Rev. MICHAEL F. ANDERSON, Church of St. Bernard, 1160 Woodbridge St., St. Paul, 55117-4491. Treasurer: VACANT.

Deanery 1—Rev. RALPH TALBOT, Church of St. Jude of the Lake, 700 Mahtomedi Ave., Mahtomedi, 55115.

Deanery 2—Rev. PATRICK J. HIPWELL, Church of the Nativity, 1900 Wellesley Ave., St. Paul, 55105.

Deanery 3—Rev. MICHAEL F. ANDERSON, Church of St. Bernard, 1160 Woodbridge St., St. Paul, 55117-4491.

Deanery 4—Rev. ROBERT H. HART, Church of Transfiguration, 6133 15th St. N., Oakdale, 55128.

Deanery 5—VACANT.

Deanery 6—Rev. JAY K. KYTHE, Mailing Address: Church of Saint Pius V, P.O. Box 367, Cannon Falls, 55009-9294.

Deanery 7—Rev. TROY D. PRZYBILLA, Mailing Address: Church of the Immaculate Conception, P.O. Box 169, Lonsdale, 55046-0169.

Deanery 8—Rev. WILLIAM A. MURTAUGH, Church of St. Thomas Becket, 4455 S. Robert Trail, Eagan, 55123.

Deanery 9—Rev. THEODORE C. CAMPBELL, Church of The Good Shepherd, 145 Jersey Ave. S., Golden Valley, 55426.

Deanery 10—Rev. ROBERT L. WHITE, Church of St. Victoria, 8228 Victoria Dr., Victoria, 55386-9692.

Deanery 11—Rev. MICHAEL L. RUDOLPH, St. Thomas the Apostle, 20000 County Rd. 10, Corcoran, 55340-9501.

Deanery 12—Rev. MICHAEL VAN SLOUN, Church of St. Stephen, 525 Jackson St., Anoka, 55303-2353. Tel: 763-712-7449.

Deanery 13—Rev. PATRICK JOHNSON, C.S.P., Church of St. Lawrence, 1203 5th St., S.E., Minneapolis, 55414-2030.

Deanery 14—Rev. PAUL C. TREACY, Our Lady of Peace, 5425 11th Ave. S., Minneapolis, 55417-2505. Tel: 612-824-3455.

Deanery 15—Rev. ANTHONY G. VANDERLOOP, Church of Saint Peter, 6730 Nicollet Ave. S., Richfield, 55423.

Deanery 16— (Academic) VACANT.

Deanery 17— (Specialized) Rev. STEPHEN J. LACANNE, M.Div., N.A.C.C., St. Joseph Hospital, 45 10th St. E., St. Paul, 55101-2222.

Deanery 18— (Retired) Revs. FRANCIS A. POULIOT, Leo C. Byrne Residence #230, 60 S. Mississippi River Blvd., St. Paul, 55105-1052; FRANCIS R. KITTOCK (Retired), Leo C. Byrne Residence #228, 60 S. Mississippi River Blvd., St. Paul, 55105-1052.

Appointees—Revs. CORY J. ROHLFING, Church of the Most Holy Redeemer, 206 Vine Ave. W., Montgomery, 56069-1063; PETER J. WILLIAMS, Church of the Maternity of the Blessed Virgin Mary, 1414 Dale St. N., St. Paul, 55117; JOHN P. FLOEDER, St. Stephen, 525 Jackson St., Anoka, 55303-2353.

Ex Officio—Most Revs. JOHN C. NIENSTEDT, S.T.D., D.D.; LEE ANTHONY PICHE; Very Rev. PETER A. LAIRD, M.A., M.Div., 226 Summit Ave., St. Paul, 55102.

Archdiocesan Finance Council (AFC)—Mr. BRIAN WENGER, Chm.; Deacon WILLIAM HEIMAN; Rev. MARK A. HUBERTY; Mr. STEWART W. LAIRD; Mr. MARK MISUKANIS; Deacon ROBERT SCHNELL; Mr. FLIP SPANIER; Ms. KATHLEEN WERTHMANN; Most Revs. JOHN C. NIENSTEDT, S.T.D., D.D., Archbishop; LEE ANTHONY PICHE, Auxiliary Bishop; Very Rev. PETER A. LAIRD, Vicar Gen. & Moderator of the Curia; Mr. JOHN BIERBAUM, CFO; Ms. LISA GIEFER, Staff Support, 226 Summit Ave., St. Paul, 55102.

College of Consultors—Revs. DANIEL F. GRIFFITH, St. Peter, 2600 Margaret St. N., North Saint Paul, 55109-2361; ROBERT H. HART, Church of Transfiguration, 6133 15th St. N., Oakdale, 55128; PATRICK J. HIPWELL, Church of the Nativity, 1900 Wellesley Ave., St. Paul, 55105; Very Rev. PETER A. LAIRD, 226 Summit Ave., St. Paul, 55102; Revs. JAMES M. PERKL, St. Elizabeth Ann Seton, 2035 15th St. W., Hastings, 55033-9294; THOMAS H. SIEG, St. Michael, 16311 Duluth Ave., S.E., Prior Lake, 55372-2423; PETER J. WILLIAMS, Church of the Maternity of the Blessed Virgin Mary, 1414 Dale St. N., St. Paul, 55117; THOMAS KUNNEL, T.O.R., Church of the Immaculate Conception, 4030 Jackson St., N.E., Columbia Heights, 55421-2929; RALPH TALBOT, Church of St. Jude of the Lake, 700 Mahtomedi Ave., Mahtomedi, 55115-1673; THOMAS J. WALKER, J.D., Saint Ambrose of Woodbury, 4125 Woodbury Dr., Woodbury, 55129-9627; FRANCIS R. KITTOCK (Retired), Leo C. Byrne Residence #228, 60 S. Mississippi River Blvd., St. Paul, 55105-1052.

Archdiocesan Curia

Chancellor for Civil Affairs—Mr. ANDREW J. EISENZIMMER, J.D., 226 Summit Ave., St. Paul, 55102. Tel: 651-291-4405; Fax: 651-290-1629. Email: eisenzimmera@archspm.org.

Chancellor for Canonical Affairs—Ms. JENNIFER HASELBERGER, J.C.L., Ph.D., 226 Summit Ave., St. Paul, 55102. Tel: 651-291-4437; Fax: 651-290-1629. Email: haselbergerj@archspm.org.

Vice Chancellor—Mr. SEAN MCDONOUGH, 226 Summit Ave., St. Paul, 55102. Tel: 651-291-4406; Fax: 651-290-1629. Email: mcdonoughs@archspm.org.

Protection of Children and Youth Initiative—Ms. RITA BEATTY, Coord., 328 Kellogg Blvd. W., St. Paul 55102. Tel: 651-251-7742; Fax: 651-290-1629. Email: beattyr@archspm.org.

Delegate for Religious—Ms. JENNIFER HASELBERGER, J.C.L., Ph.D., 226 Summit Ave., St. Paul, 55102. Tel: 651-291-4437; Fax: 651-290-1629. Web: www.archspm.org/vicar.

Office of Conciliation—Ms. JENNIFER HASELBERGER, J.C.L., Ph.D., 226 Summit Ave., St. Paul, 55102. Tel: 651-291-4437; Fax: 651-290-1629. Web: www.archspm.org/conciliation.

Archives—Mr. STEVEN T. GRANGER, Archivist. Tel: 651-291-4485. Email: archives@archspm.org; Ms. THERESA HARTNETT, Archives/Records Asst., 226 Summit Ave., St. Paul, 55102. Tel: 651-291-4486. Email: hartnettt@archspm.org.

Records—Ms. SUSAN STEPKA, Mgr., 226 Summit Ave., St. Paul, 55102. Tel: 651-291-4481. Email: stepkas@archspm.org.

Administration and Financial Services—Mr. JOHN BIERBAUM, Dir. Tel: 651-291-4400. Email: bierbaumj@archspm.org; Mr. SCOTT J. DOMEIER, Asst. Controller, 226 Summit Ave., St. Paul, 55102. Tel: 651-290-1641. Email: domeiers@archspm.org.

Benefits/Human Resources—Ms. NATALIE MCKLIGET, 226 Summit Ave., St. Paul, 55102. Tel: 651-291-4426. Email: mckligetn@archspm.org.

Schools - Christian Formation—Ms. MARTHA FRAUENHEIM, M.Ed., Dir., 328 Kellogg Blvd. W., St. Paul, 55102. Tel: 651-291-4498. Web: www.archspmschools.org.

Office of Marriage, Family, & Life—Ms. KATHLEEN M. LAIRD, 328 Kellogg Blvd. W., St. Paul, 55102. Tel: 651-291-4438. Web: www.archspm.org/family.

Worship—Revs. JOHN PAUL ERICKSON, Dir.; ANDREW H. COZZENS, S.T.D., Assoc. Dir.; Ms. LAURINDA IRWIN, Administrative Asst., 226 Summit Ave., St. Paul, 55102. Tel: 651-251-7727; Fax: 651-290-1629. Email: irwinl@archspm.org. Web: www.archspm.org/worship.

Development and Stewardship—Mr. JAMES J. FENNELL, Dir., 328 Kellogg Blvd. W., St. Paul, 55102. Tel: 651-290-1649. Web: www.archspm.org/developmentoffice.

Communications—Mr. DENNIS B. MCGRATH, Dir., 226 Summit Ave., St. Paul, 55102. Tel: 651-291-4412. Email: mcgrathd@archspm.org.

Parish Services Team—Mr. JIM LUNDHOLM-EADES, Dir., 328 Kellogg Blvd. W., St. Paul, 55102. Tel: 651-291-4512. Email: lundholmeadesj@archspm.org.

Catholic Charities—Mr. PAUL MARTODAM, CEO, 1200 2nd Ave., S., Minneapolis, 55403. Tel: 612-664-8527. Web: www.cctwincities.org.

Common Bond Communities—Mr. PAUL FATE, Pres. & CEO, 328 Kellogg Blvd. W., St. Paul, 55102. Tel: 651-291-1750; Fax: 651-291-1003. Web: www.commonbond.org.

Catholic Senior Services—Mr. DANIEL GANNON, Pres., 328 Kellogg Blvd. W., St. Paul, 55102. Tel: 651-500-4380. Email: gannond@archspm.org.

Ecumenical and Interreligious Affairs—Rev. ERICH RUTTEN, University of St. Thomas, 2115 Summit Ave., Mail #5028, St. Paul, 55105-1096. Tel: 651-962-6560. Email: erutten@stthomas.edu.

Center for Mission—Deacon MICKEY FRIESEN, Dir., 328 Kellogg Blvd. W., St. Paul, 55102. Tel: 651-291-4445. Web: www.centerformission.org.

Priestly Life and Ministry—Rev. EUGENE W. TIFFANY, Dir., 226 Summit Ave., St. Paul, 55102. Tel: 651-251-7721. Email: tiffanye@archspm.org.

Clergy Personnel and Diaconate—Deacon RUSSELL SHUPE, Dir., 226 Summit Ave., St. Paul, 55102. Tel: 651-291-4428. Email: shuper@archspm.org.

Clergy Review Board—Mr. ANDREW J. EISENZIMMER, J.D., 226 Summit Ave., St. Paul, 55102. Tel: 651-291-4405.

The Saint Paul Seminary School of Divinity—Rev. Msgr. ALOYSIUS R. CALLAGHAN, S.T.L., J.C.D., Rector-Vice Pres., 2260 Summit Ave., St. Paul, 55105. Tel: 651-962-5050. Web: www.stthomas.edu/spssod.

Saint John Vianney Seminary—Rev. WILLIAM J. BAER, Rector-Pres., 2115 Summit Ave., St. Paul, 55105. Tel: 651-962-6825. Web: www.vianney.net.

Vocations—Rev. PETER J. WILLIAMS, 2260 Summit Ave., St. Paul, 55105. Tel: 651-962-6892. Email: stpaulpriest@10000vocations.org.

"Catholic Spirit"— (Newspaper) Most Rev. JOHN C. NIENSTEDT, S.T.D., D.D., Publisher; Mr. ROBERT ZYSKOWSKI, Assoc. Publisher, 244 Dayton Ave., St. Paul, 55102. Tel: 651-291-4453. Web: www.thecatholicspirit.com.

Office for Safe Environment—Rev. KEVIN M. MCDONOUGH, Delegate, 226 Summit Ave., St. Paul, 55102. Tel: 651-646-1797. Email: mcdonoughk@archspm.org.

Promotion of Ministerial Standards—Mr. TIM ROURKE, Dir., 226 Summit Ave., St. Paul, 55102.

Victim Assistance—Ms. GRETA SAWYER, Dir., 328 Kellogg Blvd. W., St. Paul, 55102. Tel: 651-291-4497. Email: sawyerg@archspm.org.

Catholic Cemeteries—Mr. JOHN CHEREK, Dir., 2105 Lexington Ave. S., Mendota Heights, 55120. Tel: 651-228-9991; Fax: 651-228-9995. Web: www.catholic-cemeteries.org.

Censores Librorum—Revs. GEORGE A. WELZBACHER, Church of St. John of St. Paul, 977 5th St., St. Paul, 55106. Tel: 651-771-3690; Fax: 651-771-7919; DAVID W. SMITH; MARK B. DOSH; Very Rev. JOSEPH R. JOHNSON; Dr. DON J. BRIEL; Dr. CATHERINE CORY; Rev. J. MICHAEL BYRON, S.T.D.; Dr. CHRISTOPHER THOMPSON.

Metropolitan Tribunal—

Judicial Vicar—Very Rev. CHRISTOPHER J. BEAUDET, J.C.L., 328 Kellogg Blvd. W., St. Paul, 55102-1997. Tel: 651-291-4466; Fax: 651-291-4467. Email: tribunal@archspm.org. Web: www.archspm.org/tribunal.

Archdiocesan Council on Catholic Women—Rev. DAVID W. KOHNER, Moderator; Ms. THERESA CERMAK, Pres., 328 Kellogg Blvd. W., St. Paul, 55102. Tel: 651-291-4545. Web: www.accwarchspm.org.

Hispanic Ministry—Rev. KEVIN M. MCDONOUGH, Chap.; SAGRADO CORAZON DE JESUS, 3800 Pleasant Ave., S., Minneapolis, 55409. Tel: 612-874-7169.

Archbishop's Commission on Bio-Medical Ethics—Very Rev. PETER A. LAIRD, M.A., M.Div., Vicar Gen. & Moderator of the Curia, 226 Summit Ave., St. Paul, 55102. Tel: 651-291-4430; Fax: 651-290-1629. Email: vicargeneral@archspm.org.

Commission for Black Catholics—Rev. KEVIN M. MCDONOUGH, J.C.D., Church of St. Peter Claver, 375 N. Oxford, St. Paul, 55102. Tel: 651-646-1797; Fax: 651-647-5394.

Office for the Deaf—Deacon MICHAEL POWERS, Dir., 701 Fillmore St., N.E., Minneapolis, 55413. Web: www.archspm.org/deaf.

Office of Indian Ministry—Ms. CHRISTINE ROY, Prog. Dir., 3045 Park Ave. S., Minneapolis, 55407. Tel: 612-824-7606. Email: royc@archspm.org.

Office of Social Justice—Ms. KATHLEEN TOMLIN, Admin., 328 Kellogg Blvd. W., St. Paul, 55102. Tel: 651-291-4537. Web: www.osjspm.org.

Propagation of the Faith—Deacon MICKEY FRIESEN, Dir., 328 W. Kellogg Blvd., St. Paul, 55102. Tel: 651-222-6566.

CLERGY, PARISHES, MISSIONS AND PAROCHIAL SCHOOLS

METROPOLITAN ST. PAUL

(RAMSEY COUNTY)

1—CATHEDRAL OF SAINT PAUL (1850) Very Rev. Joseph R. Johnson, Rector; Rev. Michael C. Kaluza; Deacons James Meyer; Russell Shupe; Phil Stewart.
Res.: 239 Selby Ave., 55102. Tel: 651-228-1766; Fax: 651-228-9942. Email: info@cathedralsaintpaul.org. Web: www.cathedralsaintpaul.org.
Catechesis/Religious Program—Students 63.

2—ST. ADALBERT (1881), (Vietnamese—Polish), Rev. Minh Vu. In Res., Rev. Thomas Tam (Vietnam).
Office & Res.: 265 Charles Ave., 55103. Tel: 651-228-9002; Fax: 651-225-0902. Email: stadalbert@comcast.net.
Catechesis/Religious Program—Students 175.

3—ST. AGNES (1887), (Austrian), Revs. John L. Ubel; John Paul Erickson; Deacons Harold Hughesdon; Bernard Pedersen; Nathan Allen.
Office & Res.: 548 Lafond Ave., 55103. Tel: 651-952-8888; Fax: 651-925-8808. Email: rectory@stagnes.net. Web: www.stagnes.net.
School—(Grades K-12), 530 Lafond Ave., 55103. Tel: 651-925-8700; Fax: 651-228-1158. Web: stagnesschools.org. Rev. John L. Ubel, Head of Schools (K-12); Mr. James Morehead, Prin. K-12. Sisters of Charity of Our Lady, Mother of the Church 3; Lay Teachers 31; Students 450.
Catechesis/Religious Program—Students 41.

4—ST. ANDREW (1895) Rev. Mark R. Juettner.
Office & Res.: 1051 Como Ave., 55103. Tel: 651-488-6775; Fax: 651-488-4461. Email: standrewoffice@usfamily.net.
See Maternity of Mary/St. Andrew School, St. Paul under Elementary Schools, Consolidated, Parochial located in the Institution section.
Catechesis/Religious Program—Tel: 651-489-8827; Fax: 651-488-4055. Recorded with Maternity of Mary, St. Paul. Students 7.

5—ST. ANDREW KIM (1990), (Korean), [JC] Rev. Raymond Won.
Church & Office: 1850 Mississippi River Blvd. S., 55116. Tel: 651-644-1605; Fax: 651-846-4842. Email: mr.korean.catholic@gmail.com.
Catechesis/Religious Program—Fax: 651-644-4908. Students 62.

6—ASSUMPTION (1856), (German), Revs. John M. Malone; Stephen R. O'Gara; Deacon Jerome Ciresi.
Church & Office: 51 W. Seventh St., 55102. Tel: 651-224-7536; Fax: 651-224-8514. Web: www.assumptionsp.org.
Catechesis/Religious Program—261 E. 8th St., 55101. Tel: 651-222-2619. Students 42.

7—BLESSED SACRAMENT (1916) Rev. Curtis C. Wehmeyer; Deacon Jeremiah Saladin; Deborah Phillips, Business Admin.
Office: 1801 La Crosse Ave., 55119. Tel: 651-735-3707; Fax: 651-578-1125.
Catechesis/Religious Program—Students 156.

8—ST. CASIMIR (1892) Rev. Joseph Ferraioli, O.M.I. In Res., Rev. Harry Winter, O.M.I.
Church & Office: 934 E. Geranium Ave., 55106. Tel: 651-774-0365; Fax: 651-774-0508. Email: rectory0365@msn.com. Web: www.stcasimirchurch.org.
Catechesis/Religious Program—Tel: 651-774-0365, Ext. 101. Email: suevanyo@stcasimirchurch.org. Students 54.

9—ST. CECILIA (1912) Rev. J. Michael Byron.
Church & Office: 2357 Bayless Pl., 55114. Tel: 651-644-4502; Fax: 651-647-1445. Email: info@stceciliaspm.org. Web: www.stceciliaspm.org.
Catechesis/Religious Program—Students 83.

10—CHURCH OF ST. BERNARD (1890), (German), Rev. Michael F. Anderson.
Mailing Address: 1160 Woodbridge St., 55117-4491. Tel: 651-488-6733; Fax: 651-489-9203. Email: kserva@churchofstbernard-stp.org. Web: www.stbernardstpaul.org.
Church & Office: 1167 Rice St., 55117. Tel: 651-488-6733.
School—(Grades 9-12), 170 W. Rose Ave., 55117-4437. Tel: 651-489-1338; Fax: 651-488-9466. Web: www.saintbernards-school.org. Jennifer Cassidy, Pres. & Prin. (9-12); Sue Flaherty, Librarian. Lay Teachers 25; Students 200.
Catechesis/Religious Program—Students 35.

11—CHURCH OF LUMEN CHRISTI, (Merger of St. Therese, St. Gregory and St. Leo in 2004.) Rev. Paul F. Feela.
Office: 2055 Bohland Ave., 55116. Tel: 651-698-5581; Fax: 651-698-9526. Web: www.lumenchristicc.org.
See Highland Catholic School, St. Paul under Elementary Schools, Consolidated, Parochial located in the Institution section.
Catechesis/Religious Program—Lynn Johnson, D.R.E. Students 57.

12—ST. COLUMBA (1914), (Irish), Rev. Hoang D. Nguyen; Deacon Thomas Stiles.
Office: 1327 Lafond Ave., 55104. Tel: 651-645-9179; Fax: 651-645-9170. Web: www.stcolumba.org.
Catechesis/Religious Program—Students 90.

13—ST. FRANCIS DE SALES (1884), (German), Revs. Juan Miguel Betancourt, S.E.M.V.; Luis Curbelo, S.E.M.V.; Luis Mendez, S.E.M.V.; Deacon Steven Maier.
Office: 650 Palace Ave., 55102-3593. Tel: 651-228-1169; Fax: 651-224-7744.
496 View St., Saint Paul, 55102.
School—St. Francis-St. James United School, (Grades K-8), 486 View St., 55102. Tel: 651-228-1167; Fax: 651-228-0169. Lay Teachers 11; Students 75.
Catechesis/Religious Program—Shared program with St. James. Students 14.

14—ST. GREGORY THE GREAT (1951) Merged See Lumen Christi Catholic Community, St. Paul for records.

15—HOLY CHILDHOOD (1946) Rev. James G. Wolnik.
Office: 1435 Midway Pkwy., 55108. Tel: 651-644-7495. Web: www.holychildhoodparish.org.
School—(Grades K-8), 1435 Midway Pkwy., 55108. Tel: 651-644-2791; Fax: 651-917-8797. Chuck Wollmering, Prin. Lay Teachers 12; Students 90.
Catechesis/Religious Program—Tel: 651-644-5645. Rev. James G. Wolnik, D.R.E. Students 8.

16—HOLY SPIRIT (1936) Rev. Daniel C. Haugan.
Office: 515 S. Albert St., Saint Paul, 55116. Tel: 651-698-3353; Fax: 651-698-1605. Web: www.holy-spirit.org.
School—(Grades K-8) Dr. Mary Adrian, Prin. Lay Teachers 22; Students 276.
Catechesis/Religious Program—Tel: 651-698-3353; Fax: 651-698-1605. Christopher Menzhuber, Dir. Faith Formation. Students 40.

17—THE IMMACULATE HEART OF MARY (1949) Merged with St. Luke, St. Paul to form St. Thomas More, St. Paul.

18—ST. JAMES (1887) Revs. Juan Miguel Betancourt, S.E.M.V.; Luis Curbelo, S.E.M.V.; Luis Mendez, S.E.M.V.; Deacon Steven Maier.
Office: 496 View St., 55102. Web: www.sf-sj.org.
See St. Francis-St. James United School, St. Paul under St. Francis De Sales, St. Paul for details.
Catechesis/Religious Program—See St. Francis, St. Paul for details., Tel: 651-228-1169; Fax: 651-224-7744. Students 34.

19—ST. JOHN OF ST. PAUL (1886) Rev. George A. Welzbacher; Deacon Terrence Schneider.
Office: 977 E. Fifth St., 55106. Tel: 651-771-3690; Fax: 651-771-7919. Email: stjohns@stjstp.org. Web: www.stjstp.org.

20—ST. LEO (1945) Merged See Lumen Christi Catholic Community, St. Paul for records.

21—ST. LOUIS KING OF FRANCE (1868), (French), Revs. Paul F. Morrissey, S.M.; Joseph Hurtuk, S.M.; Paul M. Cabrita, S.M.
Office: 506 Cedar St., 55101-2280. Tel: 651-224-3379; Fax: 651-224-0017. Email: stlouischurch@comcast.net.
Catechesis/Religious Program—See St. Mary's, St. Paul.

22—ST. LUKE (1888) Merged with Immaculate Heart of Mary, St. Paul to form St. Thomas More, St. Paul.

23—ST. MARK (1889) Rev. Humberto Palomino, P.E.S.; Bros. Adam Keiji Tokashiki, P.E.S.; Alvaro Perez, P.E.S.
Office: 2001 Dayton Ave., 55104. Tel: 651-645-5717; Fax: 651-644-0011. Email: stmarkstpaul@yahoo.com. Web: www.saintmark-mn.org.
School—(Grades K-8), 1983 Dayton Ave., 55104. Tel: 651-644-3380; Fax: 651-644-1923. Lay Teachers 24; Students 293.
Catechesis/Religious Program—Students 65.

24—ST. MARY (1865) Rev. Biju Mathew, C.F.I.C. In Res., Revs. Anthony Scaria, C.F.I.C.; Benny Mekkat, C.F.I.C.
Office: 261 E. 8th St., 55101. Tel: 651-222-2619; Fax: 651-224-1190. Email: stmoff@usfamily.net. Web: www.stmarystpaul.parishesonline.com.
Catechesis/Religious Program—Students 21.

25—MATERNITY OF THE BLESSED VIRGIN (1949) Revs. Peter J. Williams; Francis A. Pouliot; Deacons Dennis Chlebeck; Francis Asenbrenner.
Office: 1414 N. Dale St., 55117. Tel: 651-489-8825; Fax: 651-488-4055. Email: info@maternityofmarychurch.org. Web: www.maternityofmarychurch.org.
See Maternity of Mary/St. Andrew School, St. Paul under Elementary Schools, Consolidated, Parochial located in the Institution section.
Catechesis/Religious Program—Tel: 651-489-8825; Fax: 651-488-4055. Nicole Bettini, C.R.E. & Youth Ministry. Students 85.

26—ST. MATTHEW (1886), (German), Rev. Stephen J. Adrian; Deacon John Murphy.
Office: 490 Hall Ave., 55107. Tel: 651-224-9793.
Church: 510 Hall Ave, 55107. Tel: 651-224-9793; Fax: 651-228-9448.
Res.: 909 Delaware Ave., Saint Paul, 55118. Tel: 651-224-1037; Fax: 651-292-0925.
School—(Grades K-8), 497 Humboldt Ave., 55107. Tel: 651-224-6912. Lay Teachers 14; Students 192.
Catechesis/Religious Program—Students 95.

27—THE NATIVITY OF OUR LORD (1922) Revs. Patrick J. Hipwell; John J. Bauer, Parochial Vicar.
Office:—1900 Wellesley Ave., 55105. Tel: 651-696-5401; Fax: 651-696-5458. Email: info@nativity-mn.org. Web: www.nativity-mn.org.
School—(Grades K-8), 1900 Stanford Ave., 55105. Tel: 651-699-1311; Fax: 651-696-5420. Mrs. Margo Weiberg, Prin.; Ms. Kate Wollan, Prin. Lay Teachers 43; Students 785.
Catechesis/Religious Program—Tel: 651-696-5454; Fax: 651-696-5458. Students 105.

28—OUR LADY OF GUADALUPE (1931), (Hispanic), Rev. Kevin T. Kenney; Deacon Martin Jaques.
Center: 401 Concord Street, 55107. Tel: 651-228-0506; Fax: 651-224-5162.
Res.: 397 Robie St., Saint Paul, 55107.
Catechesis/Religious Program—Students 471.

29—ST. PASCAL BAYLON (1946) Rev. J. Anthony Andrade; Deacon Richard Pashby.
Office: 1757 Conway St., 55106. Tel: 651-774-1585; Fax: 651-774-9152. Email: church@stpascals.org. Web: www.stpascalbaylon.com.
School—(Grades K-8) Tel: 651-776-0092. Lay Teachers 16; Students 222.
Catechesis/Religious Program—Students 90.

30—ST. PATRICK (1884), (Irish), Rev. Jerome B. Hackenmueller.
Office: 1095 De Soto St., 55130. Tel: 651-774-8675; Fax: 651-774-9106.
Catechesis/Religious Program—Tel: 651-776-7686. Students 140.

31—ST. PETER CLAVER (1892), (African American), Rev. Kevin M. McDonough; Deacon Fred L. Johnson.
Office: 375 N. Oxford St., 55104. Tel: 651-646-1797; Fax: 651-647-5341. Email: mcdonoughk@archspm.org. Web: www.stpc.org.
School—(Grades K-8), 1060 W. Central Ave., Saint Paul, 55104. Josie Johnson, Prin.; Helen Stassen, Librarian. Lay Teachers 12; Students 142.
Catechesis/Religious Program—Students 169.

32—SACRED HEART (1881) Rev. Eugene Michel, O.F.M.; Deacon Wayne Wittman. In Res., Bro. Robert Gross, O.F.M.
Office: 840 E. Sixth St., 55106. Tel: 651-776-2741; Fax: 651-776-2759. Email: sucod@qwest.net.
Catechesis/Religious Program—Students 115.

33—ST. STANISLAUS (1872), (Czech), Rev. John C. Clay.
Office: 398 Superior St., 55102. Tel: 651-292-0303. Web: www.ststans.org.
Catechesis/Religious Program—395 Superior St., 55102. Tel: 651-292-1913. Students 95.

34—ST. THERESE (1926) Merged See Lumen Christi Catholic Community, St. Paul for records.

35—ST. THOMAS MORE Rev. Joseph E. Weiss, S.J.; Deacons Thomas Dzik; David Ingwell.
1079 Summit Ave., 55105-2243. Tel: 651-227-7669; Fax: 651-227-0847.
School—St. Thomas More Catholic School, (Grades K-8), 1065 Summit Ave., 55105. Tel: 651-224-4836; Fax: 651-224-0097. Email: dwitucki@morecommunity.org. Web: www.morecommunity.org. Patrick Lofton, Prin.; Hagdis Tschunko, Librarian. Sisters 1; Lay Teachers 25; Students 352; Total Staff 39.
Catechesis/Religious Program—Email: mzetvas@luke-acts.org. Students 132.

36—ST. THOMAS THE APOSTLE (1954) Rev. Curtis C. Wehmeyer; Deacons Richard Moore; Jeremiah Saladin.
Office: 2119 Stillwater Ave., 55119. Tel: 651-738-0677; Fax: 651-738-6492. Web: www.stthomasap.org.
Catechesis/Religious Program—Students 100.

37—ST. VINCENT DE PAUL (1888) [CEM] Rev. Michael C. Kaluza; Very Rev. Joseph R. Johnson; Deacon Naokao Yang.
Center: 651 Virginia St., 55103. Tel: 651-488-6737; Fax: 651-228-9942.
Res.: 239 Selby Ave., Saint Paul, 55102.
Catechesis/Religious Program—Students 71.

OUTSIDE METROPOLITAN ST. PAUL

COTTAGE GROVE, WASHINGTON CO., CHURCH OF ST. RITA (1966) Rev. William Deziel, O.S.C.; Deacons Jack Nicklay; Steve Koop.
8694 80th St. S., 55016. Tel: 651-459-4596; Fax: 651-459-5364. Email: stritas@saintritas.org. Web: www.saintritas.org.
Catechesis/Religious Program—Students 522.

LITTLE CANADA, RAMSEY CO., ST. JOHN OF LITTLE CANADA (1851) [CEM] Rev. David W. Kohner; Suzanne Laddusire, Dir. Pastoral Ministry.

Office: 380 Little Canada Rd., 55117. Tel: 651-484-2708; Fax: 651-484-0567. Email: info@stjohnoflc.org. Web: www.stjohnsoflc.org.
School—(Grades PreK-8), 2621 McMenemy St., 55117. Tel: 651-484-3038; Fax: 651-481-1355. Mary Kay Rowan, Prin. Lay Teachers 21; Students 225.
Catechesis/Religious Program—Tel: 651-484-0048; Fax: 651-288-3233. Jean Conant Winter, D.R.E. Students 212.

MAHTOMEDI, WASHINGTON CO., ST. JUDE OF THE LAKE (1939) Rev. Ralph W. Talbot Jr.
Office: 700 Mahtomedi Ave., 55115. Tel: 651-426-3245; Fax: 651-653-3554. Web: www.stjudeofthelake.org.
School—(Grades K-8), 600 Mahtomedi Ave., 55115. Tel: 651-426-2562; Fax: 651-653-3662. Sally Hermes, Prin. Lay Teachers 21; Students 220.
Catechesis/Religious Program—Students 403.

MAPLEWOOD, RAMSEY CO.

1—HOLY REDEEMER/SAINT PETER (1880), (Italian), Merged See St. Peter, North St. Paul.

2—ST. JEROME (1940) Rev. Cletus Basekela.
1894 McMenemy Rd., 55117.
Church & Office: 380 Roselawn Ave. E., 55117. Tel: 651-771-1209; Fax: 651-771-3623. Email: mahles@stjerome-church.org. Web: www.stjeromechurch.org.
School—(Grades PreK-8), 384 E. Roselawn Ave., 55117. Tel: 651-771-8494; Fax: 651-771-3466. Patti Eckert, Librarian. Sisters 2; Lay Teachers 14; Students 141.
Catechesis/Religious Program—Students 58.

3—PRESENTATION OF THE BLESSED VIRGIN MARY (1946) Rev. Mark A. Huberty; Deacon James Saumweber.
Office: 1725 Kennard St., 55109. Tel: 651-777-8116; Fax: 651-777-8743. Web: www.presentationofmary.org.
School—(Grades K-8), 1695 Kennard St., 55109. Tel: 651-777-5877; Fax: 651-777-8283. Lay Teachers 13; Students 180.
Catechesis/Religious Program—Fax: 651-777-8743. Students 172.

MENDOTA, DAKOTA CO., ST. PETER (1840), (Native American—French), [CEM] Rev. Joseph G. Gallatin.
Mailing Address & Office: P.O. Box 50679, 55150. Tel: 651-452-4550; Fax: 651-456-0646. Email: church@stpetersmendota.org. Web: www.stpetersmendota.org.
Center: 1405 Hwy. 13, 55150.
See Faithful Shepherd Catholic School, Eagan under Elementary Schools, Consolidated, Parochial located in the Institution section.
Catechesis/Religious Program—Tel: 651-452-4550; Fax: 651-456-0646. Kathy Raible, D.R.E. Students 188.

NEW BRIGHTON, RAMSEY CO., ST. JOHN THE BAPTIST (1906), (Polish), [CEM] Revs. Michael C. Skluzacek; Michael Johnson, Parochial Vicar; Deacons Thomas Quayle; Rodney Palmer; Peter D'Heilly.
Office: 835 2nd Ave., N.W., 55112. Tel: 651-633-8333; Fax: 651-633-7404. Email: stjohnnyb@pclink.com. Web: www.stjohnnyb.com.
Res.: 812 1st Ave., N.W., 55112.
School—(Grades K-8), 845 2nd Ave., N.W., 55112. Tel: 651-633-1522. Lay Teachers 25; Students 388.
Catechesis/Religious Program—Tel: 651-633-1540; Fax: 651-633-7404. Students 453.

NORTH ST. PAUL, RAMSEY CO., ST. PETER (1888) [CEM] Rev. Daniel F. Griffith; Deacon Robert Bisciglia.
2600 N. Margaret St., North Saint Paul, 55109. Tel: 651-777-8304; Fax: 651-777-0497.
School—(Grades PreK-8) Lay Teachers 26; Students 356.
Catechesis/Religious Program—Tel: 651-777-1231. Students 241.

OAKDALE, WASHINGTON CO.

1—GUARDIAN ANGELS (1885) [CEM] Rev. William F. Martin; Sr. Dorothy Mrock, O.S.F.; Deacon Terry Beer.
Office: 8260 4th St. N., 55128. Tel: 651-738-2223; Fax: 651-738-2453. Email: ga@guardian-angels.org. Web: www.guardian-angels.org.
Preschool—Email: sdwuznik@guardian-angels.org. Lay Teachers 8; Students 120.
Catechesis/Religious Program—Students 550.

2—TRANSFIGURATION (1939) Rev. Robert H. Hart; Deacon Glenn Skuta.
Office: 6133 15th St. N., 55128. Tel: 651-738-2646; Fax: 651-501-2230. Web: www.tranny.org.
Res.: 2633 Harvester Ave. N., Maplewood, 55119.
School—(Grades K-8), 6135 15th St. N., 55128. Tel: 651-501-2220; Fax: 651-501-2258. Ted Zarembski, Prin. Lay Teachers 23; Students 377.
Catechesis/Religious Program—Students 473.

ROSEVILLE, RAMSEY CO.

1—CORPUS CHRISTI (1939) Rev. Francis L. Fried; Deacon Michael Humbert.
Office: 2131 Fairview Ave, N., 55113-5499. Tel: 651-639-8888; Fax: 651-639-8288. Email: corpus@mninter.net. Web: www.churchofcorpuschristi.org.
Catechesis/Religious Program—Students 209.

2—ST. ROSE OF LIMA (1939) Rev. Robert J. Fitzpatrick; Deacon Donald Hamilton.
Office: 2048 N. Hamline Ave., 55113. Tel: 651-645-9389; Fax: 651-646-4187. Web: saintroseoflima.net.
School—(Grades PreSchool-8), 2072 Hamline Ave. N., 55113. Tel: 651-646-3832; Fax: 651-647-6437. Greg Pizzolato, Prin. Sisters 1; Lay Teachers 29; Students 281.
Catechesis/Religious Program—Tel: 651-646-8029; Fax: 651-646-4187. Deb McPherson, D.R.E. Students 147.

SHOREVIEW, RAMSEY CO., ST. ODILIA (1960) Revs. Phillip J. Rask; Nels H. Gjengdahl; Deacons Ramon Garcia De Gollardo; John Flood; John Crowley; Ifeangi John Ochiagha.
3495 N. Victoria St., 55126. Tel: 651-484-6681; Fax: 651-484-0780. Web: www.stodilia.org.
School—(Grades K-8) Tel: 651-484-3364; Fax: 651-415-3395. Mr. Robert Grose, Prin.; Molly Conway, Librarian. Lay Teachers 33; Students 552.
Catechesis/Religious Program—3510 Vivian Ave., 55126. Tel: 651-484-2777. Sr. Penny Dunn, O.S.F., D.R.E. Students 749.

WEST ST. PAUL, DAKOTA CO.

1—ST. JOSEPH (1942) Revs. Michael Creagan; Joseph Fink; Deacon Jerry Scherkenbach.
Office: 1154 Seminole Ave., 55118. Tel: 651-457-2781; Fax: 651-451-1272. Web: www.churchofstjoseph.org.
School—(Grades PreSchool-8), 1138 Seminole Ave., 55118. Tel: 651-457-8550; Fax: 651-457-0780. Web: www.stjosephwsp.org. Sally McNamera, Librarian. Lay Teachers 51; Students 640.
Catechesis/Religious Program—Tel: 651-457-8841. Duane Bower, D.R.E. Students 124.

2—ST. MICHAEL (1868) Rev. Kenneth L. O'Hotto.
Church & Office: 337 E. Hurley Ave., 55118. Tel: 651-457-2334; Fax: 651-451-1668.
School—(Grades K-8), 335 Hurley Ave., E., 55118. Tel: 651-457-2510; Fax: 651-457-5049. Sisters 1; Lay Teachers 11; Students 93.
Catechesis/Religious Program—Tel: 651-457-0172. Students 45.

WHITE BEAR LAKE, RAMSEY CO.

1—ST. MARY OF THE LAKE (1881) [CEM] Rev. Rodger Bauman. In Res., Rev. Roger P. Pierre.
Office: 4690 Bald Eagle Ave., 55110. Tel: 651-429-7771; Fax: 651-429-9539. Email: contactus@stmarys-wbl.org. Web: www.stmarys-wbl.org.
School—(Grades PreK-8), 4690 Bald Eagle Ave., 55110. Lay Teachers 24; Students 350.
Catechesis/Religious Program—Tel: 651-429-8001. Helen Welter, D.R.E.; Karlene Feidt, D.R.E. Students 284.

2—ST. PIUS X (1954) Rev. John J. Mitchell; Deacon Thomas L. Semlak.
Mailing Address: 3878 Highland Ave., 55110. Tel: 651-429-5337; Fax: 651-429-5339. Email: parish@stpiusx-wbl.org. Web: www.stpiusx-wbl.org. In Res., Rev. Cory Belden.
School—(Grades PreSchool-8) Tel: 651-429-9359; Fax: 651-429-9359. Email: kgroettum@spxhf-wbl.org. Web: www.spxhf-wbl.org. K. Groettum, Prin.; M. Lindley, Librarian. Lay Teachers 21; Students 220.
Catechesis/Religious Program—Tel: 651-762-3634. Email: sgutowski@stpiusx-wbl.org. Students 225.

WOODBURY, WASHINGTON CO., SAINT AMBROSE OF WOODBURY (1998) Revs. Thomas J. Walker; Brian T. Lynch; Deacon Rip Riordan.
Office: 4125 Woodbury Dr., 55129-9627. Tel: 651-714-1058; Fax: 651-714-9257.
School—(Grades K-8) Tel: 651-768-3000. Lay Teachers 43; Students 586.
Catechesis/Religious Program—Tel: 651-768-3011. Students 1,721.

METROPOLITAN MINNEAPOLIS

(HENNEPIN COUNTY)

1—ST. ALBERT THE GREAT (1935) Rev. Joseph P. Gillespie, O.P. In Res., Revs. C.A. Kilroy, O.P.; Joseph E. Bidwill, O.P.; James A. Spahn, O.P.; Paul Johnson, O.P.; Brian Walker, O.P.; Bro. Kevin W. Carroll, O.P.
Office: 2836-33rd Ave. S., 55406. Tel: 612-724-3643; Fax: 612-722-9726. Email: info@saintalberthegreat.org. Web: www.saintalberthegreat.org.
Res.: 2833 32nd Ave. S., 55406. Tel: 612-724-3644; Fax: 612-724-5057.
Catechesis/Religious Program—Students 23.

2—ALL SAINTS (1916), (Polish), Rev. Patrick Johnson, C.S.P.
Res.: 435 4th St., N.E., 55413. Tel: 612-379-4996.
See Pope John Paul II Catholic School, Minneapolis under Elementary Schools, Consolidated, Parochial located in the Institution section.
Catechesis/Religious Program—See St. Boniface, Minneapolis for details., Tel: 612-379-2761; Fax: 612-676-1532.

3—ST. ANNE (1884) Closed. See Church of St. Anne-St. Joseph Hien.

4—ANNUNCIATION (1922) Rev. James R. Himmelsbach; Deacon Joseph Damiani.
Office: 509 W. 54th St., 55419-1818. Tel: 612-824-0787; Fax: 612-824-8232. Web: www.annunciation.org.
School—(Grades K-8), 525 W. 54th St., 55419-1818. Tel: 612-823-4394; Fax: 612-824-0998. Lay Teachers 25; Students 436.
Catechesis/Religious Program—Tel: 612-824-9993, Ext. 260. Students 85.

5—ST. ANTHONY OF PADUA (1849) Rev. Glen T. Jenson; Deacon John Belian.
Office: 804 Second St., N.E., 55413. Tel: 612-379-2324; Fax: 612-379-2325. Email: stanthonychrch@msn.com. Web: www.stanthony-paduampls.org.
See Pope John Paul II Catholic School, Minneapolis under Elementary Schools, Consolidated, Parochial located in the Institution section.
Catechesis/Religious Program—See St. Boniface, Minneapolis for details.

6—ASCENSION (1890) Rev. Michael O'Connell.
Office: 1723 Bryant Ave. N., 55411. Tel: 612-529-9684; Fax: 612-529-7618.
School—(Grades K-8), 1726 Dupont Ave. N., 55411. Tel: 612-521-3609; Fax: 612-522-3862. Lay Teachers 20; Students 265.
Catechesis/Religious Program—Tel: 612-521-7454; Fax: 612-529-3343. Students 148.

7—ST. AUSTIN (1937), (Polish), Rev. George Kallumkalkudy, C.M.I., Parochial Admin.
Church & Office: 4050 Upton Ave. N., 55412. Tel: 612-529-9561; Fax: 612-529-8787. Email: sacc-christy@qwest.net. Web: www.staustincc.org.
Catechesis/Religious Program— Consolidated records at Our Lady of Victory, 5155 Emerson Ave. N., Minneapolis, MN, 55430 Students 10.

8—THE BASILICA OF ST. MARY CO-CATHEDRAL (1907) Rev. John M. Bauer; Deacons Del Ferguson; Roger Carlson.
Mailing Address: P.O. Box 50010, 55405-0010.
Office: 88 N. 17th St., 55403-1295. Tel: 612-333-1381; Fax: 612-333-7230. Email: bsm@mary.org. Web: www.mary.org.
Catechesis/Religious Program—Tel: 612-317-3473. Students 296.

9—ST. BONIFACE (1858), (German), Rev. John F. Brandes, Parochial Admin. (Retired). In Res., Rev. James T. Livingston.
Office, Church & Res.: 629 Second St., N.E., 55413. Tel: 612-379-2761; Fax: 612-676-1532. Email: boniface1858@usfamily.net. Web: www.stboniface-minneapolis.org.
See Pope John Paul II Catholic School, Minneapolis under Elementary Schools, Consolidated, Parochial located in the Institution section.
Catechesis/Religious Program—This is a shared program with St. Clement, All Saints, St. Hedwig, St. Anthony, Sts Cyril & Methoduis, Minneapolis., Tel: 612-379-2451. Students 100.

10—ST. BRIDGET (1915) Very Rev. Anthony M. Criscitelli, T.O.R.; Deacon Richard Heineman. In Res., Revs. Patrick Foley, T.O.R.; Jude Perera, T.O.R.; Vajira Silva, T.O.R.
Office: 3811 Emerson Ave. N., 55412. Tel: 612-529-7779; Fax: 612-529-8451. Email: sbrigid2@juno.com.
Catechesis/Religious Program—555 Emerson Ave., North Minneapolis, 55430. Tel: 612-521-7454. Students 21.

11—ST. CHARLES BORROMEO (1938) Revs. Paul A. LaFontaine; John D. Meyer; Deacon Stephen Najarian.
Church, Office & Res.: 2739 Stinson Blvd., St. Anthony, 55418-3124. Tel: 612-781-6529; Fax: 612-787-1170.
School—(Grades K-8), 2727 Stinson Blvd., St. Anthony, 55418-3124. Tel: 612-781-2643; Fax: 612-787-1110. Lay Teachers 22; Students 297.
Catechesis/Religious Program—Students 125.

12—CHRIST THE KING (1938) [JC] Rev. Dale J. Korogi.
Church & Office: 5029 Zenith Ave. S., 55410. Tel: 612-920-5030; Fax: 612-920-1179. Web: www.ctkmpls.org.
School—Carondelet Catholic School, (Grades K-8) Tel: 612-927-8673; 612-920-9075; Fax: 612-927-7426. Cooperative program with St. Thomas the Apostle, Minneapolis. Religious 2; Lay Teachers 36; Students 460.
Catechesis/Religious Program—Students 103.

13—CHURCH OF GICHIWAA KATERI (2008) Rev. James C. Notebaart; Deacon Joseph Damiani.
Church & Office: 3045 Park Ave., 55407-1517. Tel: 612-824-7606; Fax: 612-824-7616. Email: indianministry@archspm.org.

14—CHURCH OF ST. ANNE - ST. JOSEPH HIEN (1884/1987) Revs. Hilary Khanh, C.M.C.; John Busco Pham V. Tai, C.M.C.

Office: 2627 Queen Ave. N., 55411. Tel: 612-529-0503; Fax: 612-529-5860.
Catechesis/Religious Program— Recorded at St. Mary's, Minneapolis

15—ST. CLEMENT (1902) Rev. Earl C. Simonson.
Res.: 911 24th Ave., N.E., 55418. Tel: 612-789-3533.
See Pope John Paul II Catholic School, Minneapolis under Elementary Schools, Consolidated, Parochial located in the Institution section.
Catechesis/Religious Program—Combined with St. Boniface, Minneapolis. Records at St. Boniface.

16—SS. CYRIL & METHODIUS (1891), (Slovak—Hispanic), Rev. Edison Galarza, O.C.C.S.S.; Deacon Clarence Shallbetter.
Res.: 1315 2nd St., N.E., 55413-1905. Tel: 612-379-9736. Email: cyrill890@aol.com.
Catechesis/Religious Program—

17—ST. FRANCES CABRINI (1946) Rev. Leo J. Tibesar; Marie Rossa, Admin.; Deacon Mickey Friesen.
Office: 1500 Franklin Ave., S.E., 55414-3697. Tel: 612-339-3023; Fax: 612-339-0734. Email: office@cabrinimn.org. Web: www.cabrinimn.org.
Catechesis/Religious Program—Students 62.

18—ST. HEDWIG (1914), (Polish), Revs. Glen T. Jenson; Donald Schwalm (Retired); Deacon John Belian.
Office: 129 29th Ave., N.E., 55418. Tel: 612-789-4830; Fax: 612-789-1985.
See Pope John Paul II Catholic School, Minneapolis under Elementary Schools, Consolidated, Parochial located in the Institution section.
Catechesis/Religious Program—Combined program with St. Boniface. See St. Boniface, Minneapolis for details.

19—ST. HELENA (1913) Rev. Richard R. Villano.
3204 E. 43rd St., 55406. Tel: 612-729-7344.
Office: 3204 33rd Ave. S., 55406. Tel: 612-729-2252; Fax: 612-724-8695.
School—(Grades K-8), 3200 E. 44th St., 55406. Tel: 612-729-9301. Nancy Rivers, Librarian. Lay Teachers 9; Students 199.
Catechesis/Religious Program—Tel: 612-729-7321. Students 30.

20—HOLY CROSS (1886), (Polish), Revs. Glen T. Jenson; Waldemar Matusiak, S.Ch.; Deacon John Belian.
Office: 1621 University Ave., N.E., 55413. Tel: 612-789-7238; Fax: 612-789-5769. Web: ourholycross.com.
See Pope John Paul II Catholic School, Minneapolis under Elementary Schools, Consolidated, Parochial located in the Institution section.
Catechesis/Religious Program—Tel: 612-789-9168. Students 102.

21—HOLY NAME (1916) Rev. Leo J. Schneider.
Office: 3637 11th Ave. S., 55407. Tel: 612-724-5465; Fax: 612-724-5466. Web: www.churchoftheholyname.org.
See Risen Christ Catholic School, Minneapolis under Elementary Schools, Consolidated, Parochial located in the Institution section.
Catechesis/Religious Program—Students 48.

22—HOLY ROSARY (1878), (Hispanic), Rev. Jose M. Santiago, O.P.; Sr. Margaret McGuirk, Admin.
Office: 2424 18th Ave. S., 55404. Tel: 612-724-3651; Fax: 612-728-8944.
See Risen Christ Catholic School, Minneapolis under Elementary Schools, Consolidated, Parochial located in the Institution section.
Catechesis/Religious Program—Students 285.
Convent—1614 E. 24th St., 55404. Tel: 612-724-2620. Dominican Sisters (Sinsinawa, WI) 6.

23—CHURCH OF THE INCARNATION (1909) Rev. Robert Monaghan.
Office: 3817 Pleasant Ave., 55409-1296. Tel: 612-822-2101; Fax: 612-822-7928.
See Risen Christ Catholic School, Minneapolis under Elementary Schools, Consolidated, Parochial located in the Institution section.

24—ST. JOAN OF ARC (1946) Revs. James R. DeBruycker; James Cassidy.
Office: 4537 3rd Ave. S., 55419. Tel: 612-823-8205; Fax: 612-825-7028.
Catechesis/Religious Program—Kathy Itzin, D.R.E. Students 606.

25—ST. JOSEPH HIEN (1987), (Vietnamese), [JC] Closed. See Church of St. Anne-St. Joseph Hien, Minneapolis.

26—ST. LAWRENCE-NEWMAN CENTER (1887) Rev. Patrick Johnson, C.S.P.; Deacon Paul Carlson. In Res., Revs. Robert J. O'Donnell; Richard Chilson, C.S.P., Hospital Chap.; James Brucz, C.S.P.
Church & Office: 1203 5th St., S.E., 55414. Tel: 612-331-7941; Fax: 612-378-1771. Email: parish@umncatholic.org. Web: www.umncatholic.org.
Catechesis/Religious Program—Students 28.

27—ST. LEONARD OF PORT MAURICE (1941), (African American), Rev. Joseph Ayeridaga Atadana, Pastoral Admin.; Deacon Steve Boatwright.
Church & Office: 3949 Clinton Ave. S., 55409. Tel: 612-825-5811; Fax: 612-825-5811. Email: slpm3949@msn.com.

28—ST. OLAF (1941) [JC] Revs. Mark L. Pavlik; Michael A. Souber.
Office: 215 S. 8th St., 55402. Tel: 612-332-7471; Fax: 612-332-3412. Web: www.saintolaf.org.

29—OUR LADY OF LOURDES (1877), (French-Canadian), Rev. Charles L. Froehle; Deacon Mike Wurdock.
Office: One Lourdes Pl., 55414. Tel: 612-379-2259; Fax: 612-379-0165. Email: info@ourladyoflourdesmn.com. Web: www.ourladyoflourdesmn.com.
Catechesis/Religious Program—Students 60.

30—OUR LADY OF MOUNT CARMEL (1938), (Italian), Deacon Michael D. Powers; Margery E. Powers, Parish Life Admin.
Church & Office: 701 Fillmore St., N.E., 55413. Tel: 612-623-4019; Fax: 612-331-3407. Email: olmc@olmcpls.org. Web: www.olmmpls.org.
See Pope John Paul II Catholic School, Minneapolis under Elementary Schools, Consolidated, Parochial located in the Institution section.

31—OUR LADY OF PEACE (1991) Rev. Paul C. Treacy; Deacon Paul Tatone.
Office & Church: 5426 12th Ave., S., 55417. Tel: 612-824-3455; Fax: 612-823-5102. Email: ourladyofpeace@olpmn.org. Web: www.olpmn.org.
School—(Grades K-8), 5435 11th Ave. S., 55417. Tel: 612-823-8253; Fax: 612-824-7328. Lay Teachers 18; Students 197.
Catechesis/Religious Program—Students 151.

32—OUR LADY OF PERPETUAL HELP, Closed. For inquiries for parish records contact the chancery.

33—OUR LADY OF VICTORY (1945) Rev. Terrence M. Hayes.
Office: 5155 Emerson Ave. N., 55430. Tel: 612-529-7788; Fax: 612-529-3343.
Church: 52nd and Fremont Aves., 55430.
Catechesis/Religious Program—Tel: 612-521-7454. Students 34.

34—ST. PHILIP (1906) [CEM] Rev. Jules Omba Omalanga.
Church & Office: 2507 Bryant Ave. N., 55411. Tel: 612-529-3125; Fax: 612-287-9133. Web: www.churchofstphilip.org.
Catechesis/Religious Program—Students 30.

35—ST. STEPHEN (1885) Rev. Joseph A. Williams; Deacon Luis Rubi.
Parish Center—2211 Clinton Ave., 55404. Tel: 612-874-0311; Fax: 612-874-0313. Email: mail@ststevensmpls.org. Web: www.ststephensmpls.org.
See Risen Christ Catholic School, Minneapolis under Elementary Schools, Consolidated, Parochial located in the Institution section.
Catechesis/Religious Program—Students 75.

36—ST. THOMAS THE APOSTLE (1908) Rev. Harold J. Tasto.
Office: 2914 W. 44th St., 55410. Tel: 612-922-0041; Fax: 612-922-1921. Email: info@sta-mpls.org. Web: www.sta-mpls.org.
School—Carondelet Catholic School, (Grades K-8), 2900 W. 44th St., 55410. Tel: 612-920-9075; Fax: 612-927-7426. Web: carondeletcatholicschool.com. Combined program with Christ the King, Minneapolis.; See Christ the King for details.
Catechesis/Religious Program—Students 412.

37—VISITATION (1946) Rev. Thomas F. O'Brien.
Church & Office: 4530 Lyndale Ave. S., 55419. Tel: 612-822-3139; Fax: 612-824-3515. Email: visichurch@aol.com. Web: www.visitationchurch.com.
Catechesis/Religious Program—Students 4.

OUTSIDE METROPOLITAN MINNEAPOLIS

BLAINE, ANOKA CO., ST. TIMOTHY'S (1943) Rev. Charles A. Brambilla; Deacons Don Hamilton; Gary Schneider.
Office: 707 89th Ave., N.E., 55434. Tel: 763-784-1329; Fax: 763-784-0652. Email: info@churchofsttimothy.com. Web: www.churchofsttimothy.com.
Catechesis/Religious Program—Students 557.

BLOOMINGTON, HENNEPIN CO.

1—ST. BONAVENTURE (1959) Revs. Bernard Zajdel, O.F.M.Conv.; Robert St. Martin, O.F.M.Conv.; Deacons Jack Herzog; Jon DeLuney. In Res., Rev. Thomas Merrill, O.F.M.Conv.
Office: 901 E. 90th St., 55420. Tel: 952-854-4733; Fax: 952-851-9690. Email: office@saintbonaventure.org. Web: www.saintbonaventure.org.
Catechesis/Religious Program—Tel: 952-854-4753. Email: faithformation@saintbonaventure.org. Students 172.

2—ST. EDWARD (1967) Rev. Michael Tegeder.
Office: 9401 Nesbitt Ave. S., 55437. Tel: 952-835-7101; Fax: 952-835-0156. Email: receptionist@stedwardchurch.org. Web: www.StEdwardsChurch.org.
Catechesis/Religious Program—Students 502.

3—NATIVITY OF THE BLESSED VIRGIN MARY (1949) Rev. Stephen D. Ulrick; Deacon James McLaughlin.
Office: 9900 Lyndale Ave. S., 55420-4733. Tel: 952-881-8671; Fax: 952-881-8692. Email: nativity@nativitybloomington.org.
School—(Grades K-8), 9901 Bloomington Fwy., 55420. Tel: 952-881-8160; Fax: 952-881-3032. Barbara Castagna, Prin. Lay Teachers 21; Students 305.
Catechesis/Religious Program—Karl Hemmesch, D.R.E. Students 180.

BROOKLYN CENTER, HENNEPIN CO., ST. ALPHONSUS (1959) Revs. Patrick Grile, C.Ss.R.; Martin Stillmock, C.Ss.R.; Joseph Stenger, C.Ss.R.; William Bueche, C.Ss.R.; Wil Lowery, C.Ss.R.; Brian Johnson, C.Ss.R.; Brian Gilles, C.Ss.R.; Thomas Pham, C.Ss.R.; Deacons David Holst; John Winkelman.
Office: 7025 Halifax Ave. N., 55429. Tel: 763-561-5100; Fax: 763-561-0336. Email: parishoffice@stalsmn.org. Web: www.stalsmn.org.
School—(Grades K-8), 7031 Halifax Ave., N., 55429. Tel: 763-561-5101; Fax: 763-503-3368. Lay Teachers 16; Students 230.
Catechesis/Religious Program—4111 71st Ave. N., 55429. Tel: 763-503-3340 (D.R.E.); Fax: 763-560-8634. Barbara Walhood, D.R.E. Students 471.

BROOKLYN PARK, HENNEPIN CO.

1—ST. GERARD MAJELLA (1970) Very Rev. Giles A. Schinelli, T.O.R.; Rev. Terrence Smith, T.O.R.
Office: 9600 Regent Ave. N., 55443. Tel: 763-424-8770; Fax: 763-424-4327. Web: www.st-gerard.org.
Catechesis/Religious Program—Tel: 763-424-8600; Fax: 763-424-4327. Students 515.

2—ST. VINCENT DE PAUL (1855), (French), [CEM] Revs. John Long; Chue Vang; Deacon Sean Curtan; Margaret Schauer, Pastoral Min.; Okey Anyanwu, Pastoral Min.
Office: 9100 93rd Ave. N., 55445-1407. Tel: 763-425-2210; Fax: 763-425-7898.
School—(Grades K-8) Tel: 763-425-3970; Fax: 763-425-2674. Lay Teachers 28; Students 439.
Catechesis/Religious Program—Charles Pratt, D.R.E.; Renee Paske, D.R.E. (Elementary Coord.); Molly Schors, Youth Min.; Kathleen Pomerleau, D.R.E., (Preschool Coord.); Sandra Wheeler, D.R.E., (Junior High School Coord.). Students 1,037.

BURNSVILLE, DAKOTA CO.

1—CHURCH OF THE RISEN SAVIOR (1970) Revs. Tim Wozniak; James Gorman; Marilyn Lyden, Admin.
Office: 1501 E. County Rd. 42, 55306. Tel: 952-431-5222; Fax: 952-431-5221. Web: www.risensavior.org.
Catechesis/Religious Program—Denise Lutz, D.R.E. Students 661.

2—MARY, MOTHER OF THE CHURCH (1965) Rev. James C. Zappa Jr.; Deacon Rob Warhol; Kay Craighead, Admin.
Office: 3333 Cliff Rd., 55337. Tel: 952-890-0045; Fax: 952-890-0789.
Catechesis/Religious Program—Students 532.

COLUMBIA HEIGHTS, ANOKA CO., IMMACULATE CONCEPTION (1923) Rev. Thomas Kunnel, T.O.R. (India); Deacon Larry Palkert.
Office: 4030 Jackson St., N.E., 55421. Tel: 763-788-9062; Fax: 763-788-0202. Email: icchurch@immac-church.org. Web: www.immac-church.org.
School—(Grades K-8), 4030 Jackson St., N.E., 55421. Tel: 763-788-9065; Fax: 763-788-9066. Email: ischool@immac-church.org. Sisters of St. Francis 1; Lay Teachers 16; Students 213.
Catechesis/Religious Program—Students 78.

COON RAPIDS, ANOKA CO., CHURCH OF THE EPIPHANY (1964) [CEM] Revs. Dennis Zehrem; Dennis J. Backer; Shane A. Campbell; Deacon Bruce Maltzen; Michael Lentz, Admin. In Res., Rev. Peter Yakubu Ali.
Office: 1900 111th Ave., N.W., 55433. Tel: 763-755-1020; Fax: 763-862-4303. Web: www.epiphanymn.org.
School—(Grades K-8), 11001 Hanson Blvd. N.W., 55433. Tel: 763-754-1750; Fax: 763-862-4350. Jane Carroll, Prin. Lay Teachers 38; Students 542.
Catechesis/Religious Program—Tel: 763-862-4331; Fax: 763-862-4354. Students 899.

CRYSTAL, HENNEPIN CO., ST. RAPHAEL (1951) Revs. Richard Hogan; James Herrmann, O.S.C.; Deacon Bruce Bowman.
Office: 7301 Bass Lake Rd., 55428. Tel: 763-537-8401; Fax: 763-537-4878. Web: www.srsmn.org.
School—(Grades PreSchool-8) Tel: 763-504-9450; Fax: 763-504-9460. Sisters 2; Lay Teachers 15; Students 204.
Catechesis/Religious Program—Tel: 763-537-8401, Ext. 211; Fax: 763-537-4878. Paulette Schatz, D.R.E. Students 231.

EAGAN, DAKOTA CO.

1—ST. JOHN NEUMANN (1977) Revs. Charles V. Lachowitzer; Steven B. Hoffman; Deacons Richard Klish; Richard Stevens.
Office: 4030 Pilot Knob Rd., 55122. Tel: 651-454-2079; Fax: 651-454-0860. Web: www.sjn.org.
See Faithful Shepherd Catholic School under Elementary Schools, Consolidated, Parochial located in the Institution section.
Catechesis/Religious Program—Judy

Doonan-Twohy, D.R.E. (Grades K-5). Students 1,380.

2—ST. THOMAS BECKET (1989) Rev. William A. Murtaugh; Deacon Bob Kelly.
Office: 4455 S. Robert Tr., 55123. Tel: 651-683-9808 (Parish Center); Fax: 651-683-0361. Email: parish@st.thomasbecket.org. Web: www.st.thomasbecket.org.
See Faithful Shepherd Catholic School under Elementary Schools, Consolidated, Parochial located in the Institution section.
Catechesis/Religious Program—Students 697.

EDEN PRAIRIE, HENNEPIN CO., PAX CHRISTI (1981) Rev. Patrick A. Kennedy; Deacon Al Schroeder; Sue Kelley, Parish Dir.
Office: 12100 Pioneer Tr., 55347-4208. Tel: 952-941-3150; Fax: 952-941-7942. Email: pax@paxchristi.com. Web: www.paxchristi.com.
Catechesis/Religious Program—Fax: 952-941-7942. Students 996.

EDINA, HENNEPIN CO.

1—OUR LADY OF GRACE (1946) Revs. Robert M. Schwartz; Matthew Ehmke; Deacon Anthony Pasko.
5071 Eden Ave., 55436. Tel: 952-929-3317; Fax: 952-929-4612.
Church: 5051 Eden Ave., 55436. Web: www.olgparish.org.
School—(Grades K-8) Tel: 952-929-5463; Fax: 952-929-8170. Web: www.olgschool.net. Lay Teachers 55; Students 674.
Catechesis/Religious Program—Patrick Miller, Youth Min. Students 583.

2—ST. PATRICK (1857) Rev. Gregory T. Welch.
Office: 6908 St. Patrick's Ln., 55439. Tel: 952-941-3164; Fax: 952-941-7371. Email: office@stpatrick-edina.org. Web: www.stpatrick-edina.org.
Catechesis/Religious Program—Patricia Brady, D.R.E.; Cheryl Wood, D.R.E.; Brenda McLennan, D.R.E. Students 612.

FRIDLEY, ANOKA CO., ST. WILLIAM (1963) Rev. Joseph Whalen; Deacon Jim Wagner.
Parish Center—6120 5th St., N.E., 55432. Tel: 763-571-5600; Fax: 763-571-6924.
Catechesis/Religious Program—Students 98.

GOLDEN VALLEY, HENNEPIN CO.

1—GOOD SHEPHERD (1946) [JC] Rev. Theodore C. Campbell.
Office: 145 Jersey Ave. S., 55426. Tel: 763-544-0416; Fax: 763-544-9896. Email: info@goodshepherdgv.org. Web: www.goodshepherdgv.org.
School—(Grades K-6) Tel: 763-545-4285; Fax: 763-545-1896. Email: contact@gsgvschool.org. Web: www.gsgvschool.org. Lay Teachers 21; Students 330.
Catechesis/Religious Program—Tel: 763-544-0416; Fax: 763-544-0416. Students 60.

2—ST. MARGARET MARY (1946) Rev. Paul Moudry.
Office: 2323 Zenith Ave., N., 55422. Tel: 763-588-9466; Fax: 763-588-0040. Email: info@smm-gv.org. Web: www.smm-gv.org.
See St. Elizabeth Seton School under Elementary Schools, Consolidated, Parochial located in the Institution section.
Catechesis/Religious Program—Students 54.

HAM LAKE, ANOKA CO., CHURCH OF SAINT PAUL (1981) Rev. Jon Vander Ploeg.
Office: 1740 Bunker Lake Blvd., N.E., 55304. Tel: 763-757-6910; Fax: 763-757-6920. Email: contact@churchofsaintpaul.com. Web: www.churchofsaintpaul.com.
Catechesis/Religious Program—Tel: 763-757-1148. Sean Lavell, D.R.E. Students 638.

LINO LAKES, ANOKA CO., ST. JOSEPH (1891) [CEM] Rev. Mark J. Underdahl; Deacon Thomas A. Konkel.
Office: 171 Elm St., 55014. Tel: 651-784-3015; Fax: 651-784-3699. Email: office@saintjosephparish.org. Web: www.saintjosephparish.org.
Catechesis/Religious Program—Denise Walsh, Coord. Confirmation & Middleschool Faith Formation; Jean Longendyke, D.R.E.; Chris Sauter, D.R.E.; Steve Robach, D.R.E.; Kathy Indihar, Sacramental Dir. Students 800.

NEW HOPE, HENNEPIN CO., ST. JOSEPH (1858) [CEM] Rev. Terry Rassmussen; Deacon Robert Bramwell; Donna Kranz, Bookkeeper.
Church: 8701 36th Ave. N., 55427. Tel: 763-544-3352; Fax: 763-544-3435. Web: www.stjosephparish.com.
Res.: 13015 Rockford Rd., Plymouth, 55441. Tel: 763-559-0318.
Parish Center & Office—Tel: 763-544-3352; Fax: 763-544-3435.
Catechesis/Religious Program—Mary Greving, D.R.E., (Catechetics). Tel: 763-544-3352, Ext. 111; Phil Arellano, D.R.E. Tel: 763-544-3352, Ext. 138 (High School); Larry Thomas, D.R.E. Tel: 763-544-3352, Ext. 139 (Middle School). Students 435.

PLYMOUTH, HENNEPIN CO., ST. MARY OF THE LAKE (1935) Rev. Curtis F. Lybarger.
Office: 105 Forestview Ln. N., 55441. Tel: 763-545-1443; Fax: 763-797-0996. Web: www.stmaryofthelakeply.org.
Catechesis/Religious Program—Students 201.

RICHFIELD, HENNEPIN CO.

1—THE CHURCH OF THE ASSUMPTION (1876) Rev. Thomas Merrill, O.F.M.Conv.; Deacon Robert Smith.
Office: 305 E. 77th St., 55423. Tel: 612-866-5019; Fax: 612-866-5274.
School—Blessed Trinity Nicollet & Penn Campus, (Grades PreK-8) Tel: 612-869-5200 (Nicollet); 612-866-6906 (Penn); Fax: 612-869-0277; 612-767-2191. Email: doylek@btcsmn.org. Web: www.btcsmn.org. Lay Teachers 22; Students 352.
Catechesis/Religious Program—Students 195.

2—ST. PETER (1943) Rev. Tony VanderLoop; Deacon Mark Johanns.
Office: 6730 Nicollet Ave. S., 55423. Tel: 612-866-5089; Fax: 612-866-5080. Email: ann@btcsmn.org. Web: www.stpetersrichfield.org.
School—Blessed Trinity Nicollet & Penn Campuses, (Grades PreK-8), 6720 Nicollet Ave. S., 55423. Tel: 612-869-5200; Fax: 612-767-2191. Email: karrs@btcsmn.org. Web: www.btcsmn.org. Jackie Spano, Librarian. Consolidation of Assumption, St. Peter & St. Richard.
Catechesis/Religious Program—Students 370.

3—ST. RICHARD (1952) Rev. Thomas Krenik; Deacon Bob Schnell.
Office:—7540 Penn Ave. S., 55423. Tel: 612-869-2426; Fax: 612-869-0277. Email: secretary@strichards.com. Web: www.strichards.com.
School—Blessed Trinity Catholic School, (Grades PreK-8) Tel: 612-866-6906; Fax: 612-866-5274. Email: kerrs@btcsmn.org. Web: www.btcsmn.org. Jackie Spano, Librarian. Consolidation of Assumption, St. Peter & St. Richard. Lay Teachers 32; Students 420.
Catechesis/Religious Program—Students 150.

ROBBINSDALE, HENNEPIN CO., SACRED HEART (1910) Rev. Bryan J. B. Pedersen; Deacon James Ramsey.
Office: 4087 W. Broadway, 55422. Tel: 763-537-4561; Fax: 763-537-5426. Email: sacredheartrobbinsdale@yahoo.com. Web: www.sacredheartrobbinsdale.org.
Res.: 4510 40-1/2 Ave. N., 55422.
School—(Grades PreSchool-8), 4050 Hubbard Ave., N., 55422. Tel: 763-537-1329; Fax: 763-537-1486. Web: www.sacredheartschoolrobbinsdale.org. Lay Teachers 19; Students 277.
Catechesis/Religious Program—Cyrilene Brouillard, D.R.E. Students 138.

ST. LOUIS PARK, HENNEPIN CO.

1—HOLY FAMILY (1926) Rev. Thomas W. Dufner.
Office: 5900 W. Lake St., 55416. Tel: 952-929-0113; Fax: 952-915-1474. Web: www.hfcmn.org.
Catechesis/Religious Program—Students 125.

2—MOST HOLY TRINITY (1943) Rev. Brian J. Fier; Deacon James DeShane; Sherri Schroeder, Parish Admin.
Parish Center—4017 Utica Ave., 55416. Tel: 952-926-7516; Fax: 952-922-6069. Web: www.mostholytrinity.org.
Church: 3946 Wooddale Ave., 55416.
Catechesis/Religious Program—Tel: 952-926-7516, Ext. 201. Students 60.

OUTSIDE TWIN-CITY METROPOLITAN AREA

ALBERTVILLE, WRIGHT CO., ST. ALBERT (1902) [CEM] Rev. Xavier Thelakkatt (India); Deacon John Wallin.
Mailing Address: P.O. Box 127, 55301. Tel: 763-497-2474; Fax: 763-497-7678. Email: stalbertmn@embarqmail.com. Web: www.stalbertschurch.org.
Office: 11400 57th St. N.E., 55301-0127.
Catechesis/Religious Program—P.O. Box 67, 55301. Tel: 763-497-3782. Students 247.

ANNANDALE, WRIGHT CO., ST. IGNATIUS (1882) [CEM] Rev. Victor Valencia.
Mailing Address: P.O. Box 126, 55302. Tel: 320-274-8828; Fax: 320-274-3961.
Office: 35 Birch St., E., 55302-0126. Web: www.stignatiusmc.com.
Catechesis/Religious Program—Tel: 320-274-8828, Ext. 24; Fax: 320-274-3961. Students 207.

ANOKA, ANOKA CO., ST. STEPHEN (1856) [CEM] Revs. Michael Van Sloun; Bennet Tran; John P. Floeder; Deacons Peter Bednarczyk; Dominic Ehrmantraut; Charles Waugh.
Office:—525 Jackson St., 55303. Tel: 763-421-2471; Fax: 763-421-4230. Web: www.ststephenchurch.org.
School—(Grades PreSchool-8), 506 Jackson St., 55303. Tel: 763-421-3236; Fax: 763-712-7433. Lay Teachers 22; Students 470.
Catechesis/Religious Program—Students 957.

BAYPORT, WASHINGTON CO., ST. CHARLES (1943) [CEM] [JC] Rev. Randal J. Kasel; Deacon Roger B. Carlson.
Office: 409 N. 3rd St., 55003. Tel: 651-439-4511; Fax: 651-430-9717. Email: parishoffice@stcharlesbayport.org. Web: www.stcharlesbayport.org.
See St. Croix Catholic School, Stillwater under Elementary Schools, Consolidated, Parochial located in the Institution section.
Catechesis/Religious Program—Tel: 651-439-7142; Fax: 651-439-7705. Web: www.scuff.org. Students 34.

BELLE CREEK, GOODHUE CO., ST. COLUMBKILL (1860), (Irish), [JC] Rev. Bruce Peterson; Deacon Paul Tschann.
Office: 36483 Co. 47 Blvd., Goodhue, 55027. Tel: 651-258-4307.
Catechesis/Religious Program—Combined program with Holy Trinity. Students 139.
Mission—Holy Trinity 308 4th St. N., Goodhue, Goodhue Co. 55027. Tel: 651-923-4472.

BELLE PLAINE, SCOTT CO., OUR LADY OF THE PRAIRIE (1972) [CEM 2] Rev. James Jong-Seong Kim; Deacon Robert Raleigh.
Office: 215 N. Chestnut St., 56011. Tel: 952-873-6564; Fax: 952-873-6717.
School—(Grades K-6) Lay Teachers 6; Students 35.
Catechesis/Religious Program—Patrick Schroers, D.R.E. Students 138.

BELLECHESTER, GOODHUE CO., ST. MARY (1859), (Luxembourgian), [CEM] Rev. Bruce Peterson, Admin.
Church & Office: 223 Chester Ave., 55027. Tel: 651-923-4305.
Catechesis/Religious Program—Students 41.

BUFFALO, WRIGHT CO., ST. FRANCIS XAVIER (1888) [CEM 2] Rev. David R. Hennen; Deacon Sherman H. Otto.
Parish Office—223 - 19th Street N.W., 55313-5042. Tel: 763-684-0075; Fax: 763-684-4711. Web: www.stfxb.org.
School—(Grades K-8), 219 19th St., N.W., 55313-5042. Tel: 763-684-0075, Ext. 200. Kim Zumbusch, Prin.; Pat Miller, Librarian. Lay Teachers 19; Students 208.
Catechesis/Religious Program—Tel: 763-684-0075, Ext. 105. Tim Stanoch, D.R.E. Students 470.

CANNON FALLS, GOODHUE CO., ST. PIUS V (1856) [CEM] Rev. Jay K. Kythe.
Office: 410 W. Colvill Ave., P.O. Box 367, 55009-0367. Tel: 507-263-2578; Fax: 507-263-8005. Email: stpiusvcf@fronteirnet.net. Web: stpiusvcf.org.
Catechesis/Religious Program—Tel: 507-263-4800 (Faith Formation Office); 507-263-4680 (Grades 7-12); Fax: 507-263-8005. Students 251.

CARVER, CARVER CO., ST. NICHOLAS (1868) [CEM 2] Rev. Thomas Joseph.
Office: 412 W. Fourth St., Box 133, 55315. Tel: 952-448-2345; Fax: 952-368-0502.
Catechesis/Religious Program—Tel: 952-448-6181. Students 85.

CEDAR LAKE, SCOTT CO., ST. PATRICK OF CEDAR LAKE TOWNSHIP (1856) [CEM] Rev. Orlando G. Tatel.
Office: 24425 Old Hwy. 13 Blvd., Cedar Lake Twp., Jordan, 55352. Tel: 952-492-6276; Fax: 952-492-6290.
Catechesis/Religious Program—Tel: 952-492-6290. Students 92.
Mission—St. Catherine of Spring Lake Township (1865) [CEM] 24425 Old Hwy. 13 Blvd., Jordan, Scott Co. 55352. Tel: 952-447-2180.

CEDAR, ANOKA CO., ST. PATRICK (1894), (Irish), [CEM] Rev. David Blume; Deacon George Stahl.
Office: 19921 Nightingale St., N.W., Oak Grove, 55011-9204. Tel: 763-753-2011; Fax: 763-753-9803. Email: stpats@st-patricks.org. Web: www.st-patricks.org.
Catechesis/Religious Program—Students 884.

CENTERVILLE, ANOKA CO., ST. GENEVIEVE (1854) [CEM] Rev. Thomas P. Fitzgerald; Deacon Daniel D. Kirchoffner.
Office: 7087 Goiffon Rd., 55038. Tel: 651-429-7937; Fax: 651-653-0071. Email: stgens@usfamily.net. Web: www.stgen.org.
Catechesis/Religious Program—Tel: 612-426-1818. Students 260.

CHANHASSEN, CARVER CO., ST. HUBERT (1865), (German), [CEM] Revs. Michael J. Krenik; Paul A. Kammen; Deacons Timothy Helmeke; Jim McDonald.
Office: 8201 Main St., 55317. Tel: 952-934-9106; Fax: 952-934-8209. Web: www.sthubert.org.
School—(Grades K-8) Tel: 952-934-6003; Fax: 952-906-1229. Connie Klingelhutz, Librarian. Lay Teachers 41; Students 690.
Catechesis/Religious Program—Students 990.

CHASKA, CARVER CO., GUARDIAN ANGELS (1858) [CEM] Rev. Paul Jarvis; Deacon Gregg Sroder.
Office: 215 W. 2nd St., 55318. Tel: 952-227-4000; Fax: 952-227-4051. Web: www.gachaska.org.
School—(Grades K-8) Tel: 952-227-4010; Fax: 952-227-4050. Lay Teachers 18; Students 190.
Catechesis/Religious Program—Tel: 952-227-4007. Students 295.

CLEARWATER, WRIGHT CO., ST. LUKE (1870) [CEM] Rev. Jacob Yali (Nigeria); Deacon Peter G. Bellavance.
Church, Office & Mailing Address: 17545 Huber Ave. N.W., 55320-0249. Tel: 320-558-2124; Fax: 320-558-2875.

Catechesis/Religious Program—Students 105.

CLEVELAND, LE SUEUR CO., CHURCH OF THE NATIVITY OF THE BLESSED VIRGIN MARY (1865), (Irish—German), [CEM] Unassigned.Mailing Address: P.O. Box 187, 56017-0187. Tel: 507-243-3166; Fax: 507-243-3849.
Church & Office: 200 W. Main, 56017.
Catechesis/Religious Program—Students 75.

COATES, DAKOTA CO., ST. AGATHA (1870) [CEM] Rev. Richard J. Mahoney (Retired).
Office: 3700 160th St. E., Rosemount, 55068. Tel: 651-689-0660; Fax: 651-696-1972.
Catechesis/Religious Program—Students 28.

COLOGNE, CARVER CO., ST. BERNARD (1859) [CEM] Rev. Martin Shallbetter.
Church & Office: 212 Church St. E., 55322. Tel: 952-466-2031; Fax: 952-466-3319. Email: parishinfo@st-bernard-cologne.org. Web: www.st-bernard-cologne.org.
School—(Grades PreSchool-6), 300 Church St. E., 55322. Tel: 952-466-5917. Email: schoolinfo@st-bernard-cologne.org. Religious 2; Lay Teachers 5; Students 41.
Catechesis/Religious Program—Students 40.
Convent—Franciscan Clarist Congregation, 214 Church St., 55320. Tel: 952-466-5620.

CORCORAN, HENNEPIN CO., ST. THOMAS THE APOSTLE (1896) [CEM 4] [JC 4] Rev. Michael L. Rudolph.
Office: 20,000 County Rd. 10, Hamel, 55340. Tel: 763-420-2385; Fax: 763-420-4710. Email: office@churchofstthomas.org. Web: www.churchofstthomas.org.
Catechesis/Religious Program—Pamela Dombek, D.R.E. (Grades PreK-10). Students 278.

DAYTON, HENNEPIN CO., ST. JOHN THE BAPTIST (1862), (French-Canadian), [CEM 2] Revs. Xavier Thelakkatt (India); John T. Wallin.
P.O. Box 201, 55327. Email: sjbchurch@yahoo.com. Web: www.stjohnsdayton.org.
Office: 18380 Columbus St., 55327. Tel: 763-428-2828; Fax: 763-428-6462.
Catechesis/Religious Program—Students 113.

DEEPHAVEN, HENNEPIN CO., ST. THERESE (1946) Rev. Douglas E. Dandurand; Deacon Joseph Smith.
Office: 18323 Minnetonka Blvd., 55391. Tel: 952-473-4422; Fax: 952-261-0585. Email: parish@st-therese.org. Web: www.st-therese.org.
School—(Grades K-8), 18325 Minnetonka Blvd., 55391. Tel: 952-473-4355; Fax: 952-261-0630. Laura Porter-Jones, Prin. Sisters 4; Lay Teachers 20; Students 203.
Catechesis/Religious Program—Lauri Becker, D.R.E. Students 528.

DELANO, WRIGHT CO.

1—ST. JOSEPH (1902), (Polish), [CEM] Rev. Christopher T. Wenthe; Deacons Joseph Kittok; Michael Dewitte.
Church: 401 N. River St., P.O. Box 470, 55328-0470. Tel: 763-972-2077; Fax: 763-972-6177. Web: www.delanocatholic.com.
School—St. Peter School, (Grades K-6), Combined with St. Peter's parish., Tel: 763-972-2528; Fax: 763-972-6177.
Catechesis/Religious Program— Clustered with St. Peter, Delano.; Records at St. Peter, Delano.

2—ST. MARY OF CZESTOCHOWA (1884), (Polish), [CEM] Rev. Thomas J. Balluff.
Office & Res.: 1867 95th St., S.E., 55328. Tel: 952-955-1139. Web: www.stboniface-stmary.org.
Catechesis/Religious Program—Tel: 952-955-1180. Students 36.

3—ST. PETER (1865), (German), [CEM 2] Rev. Christopher T. Wenthe; Deacons Michael Dewitte; Joseph Kittok.
Offices: 204 S. River St., P.O. Box 470, 55328. Tel: 763-972-2077; Fax: 763-972-6177. Email: dcc@delanocatholic.com. Web: www.delanocatholic.com.
School—St. Peter, (Grades K-6) Tel: 763-972-2528; Fax: 763-972-2528. Combined with St. Joseph, Delano, MN Lay Teachers 8; Students 85.
Catechesis/Religious Program—235 S. 2nd St., 55328. Tel: 763-972-2976; Fax: 763-972-6177. Jane Speckel, C.R.E. Clustered with St. Joseph, Delano. Students 279.

ELYSIAN, LE SUEUR CO., ST. ANDREW (1894) Rev. Michael W. Ince, Admin.
Church: Box 261, 56028. Tel: 507-267-4928; Fax: 507-362-4339.
Catechesis/Religious Program—Students 50.

EXCELSIOR, HENNEPIN CO., ST. JOHN THE BAPTIST (1903) [CEM] Rev. Mark B. Dosh.
Office: 680 Mill St., 55331-3243. Tel: 952-474-8868; Fax: 952-474-5962. Email: ctheis@stjohns.org. Web: www.stjohns-excelsior.org.
School—(Grades PreK-8) Tel: 952-474-5812; Fax: 952-401-8778. Email: kchapman@stjohns-excelsior.org. Lay Teachers 14; Students 149.
Catechesis/Religious Program—Email: mgibson@stjohns-excelsior.org. Students 139.

FARIBAULT, RICE CO.

1—DIVINE MERCY CATHOLIC CHURCH (2002) [CEM 2] Revs. J. Kevin Finnegan; Fernando Ortega; Deacons R. Daniel Wesley; Steven Moses.
Office: 4 Second Ave., S.W., 55021-6029. Tel: 507-334-2266; Fax: 507-334-3895. Web: www.divinemercycatholics.org.
Church: 139 Mercy Dr., 55021.
See Divine Mercy Catholic School of Faribault, Faribault under Elementary Schools, Consolidated, Parochial located in the Institution section.
Catechesis/Religious Program—Tel: 507-334-2266, Ext. 20. Email: stvoh@divinemercycatholics.org. Students 398.

2—IMMACULATE CONCEPTION (1856) Merged with Sacred Heart and St. Lawrence, Faribault to form Divine Mercy Catholic Church, Faribault.

3—ST. LAWRENCE (1869), (German), Merged with Sacred Heart and Immaculate Conception, Faribault to form Divine Mercy Catholic Church, Faribault.

4—SACRED HEART, (French—German), Merged with St. Lawrence and Immaculate Conception, Faribault to form Divine Mercy Catholic Church, Faribault.

5—SACRED HEART - ST. LAWRENCE OF FARIBAULT, Merged with Immaculate Conception, Faribault to form Divine Mercy Catholic Church, Faribault.

FARMINGTON, DAKOTA CO., ST. MICHAEL (1854) [CEM] Rev. Dennis Thompson.
Church and Center: 22120 Denmark Ave., 55024. Tel: 651-463-3360; Fax: 651-463-2339. Email: info@stmichael-farmington.org. Web: www.stmichael-farmington.org.
Catechesis/Religious Program—Students 570.

FOREST LAKE, WASHINGTON CO., ST. PETER (1904) [CEM] Revs. Donald E. DeGrood; Mark J. Joppa; Deacons Gary Houle; Ralph L'Allier; Terrence Moravec.
Office: 1250 S. Shore Dr., 55025. Tel: 651-982-2200; Fax: 651-982-2220. Web: www.stpeterfl.org.
School—(Grades K-6) Tel: 651-982-2215; Fax: 651-982-2230. Web: www.schools.stpeterfl.org. Ann Laird, Prin. Lay Teachers 20; Students 352.
Catechesis/Religious Program—Tel: 651-982-2235. Susan Fast, D.R.E. Students 712.

HAMEL, HENNEPIN CO., ST. ANNE (1879) [CEM] Rev. Kevin P. Magner.
Office: 200 Hamel Rd., Box 256, 55340-0256. Tel: 763-478-6644; Fax: 763-478-9141. Email: office@saintannehamel.org. Web: www.saintannehamel.org.
Catechesis/Religious Program—Students 123.

HAMPTON, DAKOTA CO., ST. MATHIAS (1900) [CEM] Rev. Stan P. Mader.
Office: 23315 Northfield Blvd., 55031. Tel: 651-437-9030; Fax: 651-437-3427. Email: parishoffice@stmathias.com. Web: www.stmathias.com.
School—(Grades PreK-5), 23335 Northfield Blvd., 55031. Tel: 651-437-5282; Fax: 651-437-5848. Email: connie@stmathias.com. Lay Teachers 3; Students 38.
Catechesis/Religious Program—Tel: 651-480-1795. Students 95.

HANCOCK TOWNSHIP, CARVER CO., ASSUMPTION, Closed. For inquiries for parish records contact the chancery.

HASSAN TOWNSHIP, HENNEPIN CO., ST. WALBURGA (1857) Closed. For inquiries for parish records please see Mary Queen of Peace, Rogers.

HASTINGS, DAKOTA CO., ST. ELIZABETH ANN SETON (1987) [CEM] [JC] Revs. James M. Perkl; Allan Paul Eilen, Parochial Vicar; Abraham George Kochupurackel, C.M.I.
Office: 2035 W. Fifteenth St., 55033. Tel: 651-437-4254; Fax: 651-438-2948. Web: www.seasparish.org.
School—(Grades PreSchool-8), 600 Tyler St., 55033. Tel: 651-437-3098; Fax: 651-438-3377. Rita Humbert, Prin. Lay Teachers 21; Students 298; Preschool 54.
Catechesis/Religious Program—Tel: 651-437-9191. Students 590.

HAZELWOOD, RICE CO., ANNUNCIATION OF THE B.V.M. (1863) [CEM] Rev. Thomas Rayar.
Office: 4996 Hazelwood Ave., Northfield, 55057-4255. Tel: 952-652-2625; Fax: 952-652-2625.
Catechesis/Religious Program—Students 65.

HEIDELBERG, LE SUEUR CO., ST. SCHOLASTICA (1856), (German—Czech), [CEM] Rev. Kevin I. Clinton.
Office: 31525 181st Ave., New Prague, 56071. Tel: 952-758-3225; Fax: 952-758-2960.
Catechesis/Religious Program—Students 21.

HOPKINS, HENNEPIN CO.

1—ST. JOHN THE EVANGELIST (1950) Rev. James C. Liekhus; Deacons Darrel Branch; Juan Duran; James Murphy.
Office: 6 Interlachen Rd., 55343. Tel: 952-935-5536; Fax: 952-938-2724. Email: receptionistchurch@stjohnhopkins.org. Web: www.stjohnshopkins.org.
School—(Grades K-6), 1503 Boyce St., 55343. Tel: 952-935-7782. Email: tnelson@stjohnhopkins.org. Lay Teachers 12; Students 164.
Catechesis/Religious Program—Students 78.

2—ST. JOSEPH'S (1922) [CEM] Rev. Gerald Dvorak; Deacon Francis J. Tangney.
Office: 1310 Main St., 55343. Tel: 952-935-0111; Fax: 952-935-4539. Email: parishoffice@stjoeshopkins.org. Web: www.stjoeshopkins.org.
Catechesis/Religious Program—Tel: 952-935-7004; 952-935-5059. Email: dirreligioused@stjoeshopkins.org; elemreligioused@stjoeshopkins.org. Students 104.

HUGO, WASHINGTON CO., ST. JOHN THE BAPTIST (1902), (French), [CEM] Rev. Jonathan P. Shelley.
Office: 14383 N. Forest Blvd., 55038. Tel: 651-429-9170; Fax: 651-429-3190. Email: cpaslawski@stjohn-hugo.com. Web: www.stjohnhugo.org.
Catechesis/Religious Program—Tel: 651-762-4676. Theresa Moore, C.R.E.; Deb Seelig, C.R.E. Students 130.

INVER GROVE HEIGHTS, DAKOTA CO., CHURCH OF ST. PATRICK (1856), (Irish), [CEM] Rev. Sebastien Bakatu.
Office: 3535 72nd St. E., 55076. Tel: 651-455-6624; Fax: 651-455-8984. Email: tlevi@churchofstpatrick.com. Web: www.churchofstpatrick.com.
Catechesis/Religious Program—Students 370.

JORDAN, SCOTT CO., ST. JOHN THE BAPTIST (1858) [CEM] [JC] Rev. Timothy J. Yanta.
Office: 313 E. 2nd St., 55352. Tel: 952-492-2640; Fax: 952-492-5683. Web: www.stjohnthebaptistjordan.org.
School—(Grades PreSchool-6), 215 Broadway St. N., 55352. Tel: 952-492-2030; Fax: 952-492-3211. Email: bonita.jungels@stjohynschool/jordan.org. Sue Colling, Librarian. Lay Teachers 13; Students 125.
Catechesis/Religious Program—Tel: 952-492-5827. Email: cburnell@frontiernet.net. Cate Bunnell, D.R.E. Students 34.

KENYON, GOODHUE CO., ST. MICHAEL (1944) [CEM] Revs. Kevin Finnegan; Fernando Ortega; Deacon Newell McGee.
Church & Office: 108 Bullis St., 55946. Tel: 507-789-6120; Fax: 507-789-6120 (Call first.).
Res.: 4 2nd Ave. S.W., Faribault, 55021. Tel: 507-334-2266.
Catechesis/Religious Program—Students 56.

KILKENNY, LE SUEUR CO., ST. CANICE (1858), (Irish), [CEM] Revs. Cory J. Rohlfing; David Barrett.
Church & Office: 183 W. Maple St. W., Box 37, 56052. Tel: 507-595-2561. Email: stcanice@frontiernet.net.
Catechesis/Religious Program—Students 31.

LAKE ST. CROIX BEACH, WASHINGTON CO., ST. FRANCIS OF ASSISI (1938) Rev. Jerome F. Keiser.
Church & Office: 16770 13th St., 55043. Tel: 651-436-7817; Fax: 651-436-6524. Email: sfa55043@aol.com. Web: www.catholic-church.org/st-francis.
Catechesis/Religious Program—Email: faithformationsf@aol.com. Students 280.

LAKEVILLE, DAKOTA CO., ALL SAINTS (1877) [CEM] Revs. Thomas Wilson; Douglas Ebert, Parochial Vicar; Deacons James Marschall; George Nugent.
Church & Office: 19795 Holyoke Ave., 55044. Tel: 952-469-4481; Fax: 952-469-5752. Web: www.allsaintschurch.com.
School—(Grades K-8) Tel: 952-469-3332; Fax: 952-469-4484. Jan Heuman, Prin. Lay Teachers 25; Students 350.
Catechesis/Religious Program—Tel: 952-469-6461. Students 1,153.

LE CENTER, LE SUEUR CO., ST. MARY (1899) [CEM] Rev. Christopher Shofner.
Church & Office: 165 N. Waterville Ave., 56057. Tel: 507-357-4838; Fax: 507-357-4838. Email: joso@frontiernet.net; lafram@frontiernet.net.
Catechesis/Religious Program—Tel: 507-357-6633. Students 247.

LE SUEUR, LE SUEUR CO., ST. ANNE (1852) [CEM 2] Rev. George J. Grafsky.
Res.: 217 N. 3rd St., 56058. Tel: 507-665-2047.
Church & Office: 503 N. 4th St., 56058. Tel: 507-665-3811; Fax: 507-665-3811.
School—(Grades K-5) Tel: 507-665-2489; Fax: 507-665-6186. Lay Teachers 5; Students 52.
Catechesis/Religious Program—Tel: 507-665-2995. Barbara Irlander, D.R.E. Students 52.

LEXINGTON, LE SUEUR CO., ST. JOSEPH (1903), (Polish), [CEM] Rev. Kevin I. Clinton.
Church & Office: 31525 181st Ave., New Prague, 56071. Tel: 952-758-3325.

LINDSTROM, CHISAGO CO., ST. BRIDGET OF SWEDEN (1948) Rev. Mark H. Wehmann.
Mailing Address: P.O. Box 754, 55045. Email: stbridgets@frontiernet.net.
Church & Office: 13060 Lake Blvd., 55045. Tel: 651-257-2474; Fax: 651-257-1498. Web: www.stbridgetofsweden.org.

Catechesis/Religious Program—Tel: 651-257-0694. Students 319.

LONG LAKE, HENNEPIN CO., ST. GEORGE (1917) [CEM] Rev. Ralph Huar.
Mailing Address: 133 N. Brown Rd., 55356-9560. Tel: 952-473-1247; Fax: 952-404-0129.
Church & Office: Tel: 952-476-0170; Fax: 952-404-0129. Email: stgeorge@msn.com. Web: www.stgeorgelonglake.org.
Catechesis/Religious Program—Students 46.

LONSDALE, RICE CO., IMMACULATE CONCEPTION (1903) [CEM 2] Rev. Troy D. Przybilla.
Office & Mailing Address: P.O. Box 169, 55046-0169. Tel: 507-744-2829. Email: icparish@means.net.
See Holy Cross LNMV Catholic School, Lonsdale under Elementary Schools, Consolidated, Parochial located in the Institution section.
Catechesis/Religious Program—Students 117.

LORETTO, HENNEPIN CO., SS. PETER AND PAUL (1867) [CEM] Rev. John Gallas; Deacon Darrel Courrier.
Mailing Address: P.O. Box 96, 55357. Tel: 763-479-0535; Fax: 763-479-4383.
Church & Office: 145 Railway St., E., 55357. Web: www.cspap.org.
School—(Grades PreSchool-8), 150 Railway St., E., 55357. Tel: 763-479-0540, Ext. 21; Fax: 763-479-4046. Lay Teachers 15; Students 104.
Catechesis/Religious Program—Tel: 763-479-2810. Students 108.

MAPLE GROVE, HENNEPIN CO., ST. JOSEPH THE WORKER (1870) Revs. Michael Sullivan; Donald J. Piche; Deacon Kevin O'Connor.
Church & Office: 7180 Hemlock Ln., 55369-5597. Tel: 763-425-6505; Fax: 763-425-6587. Web: www.sjtw.net.
Catechesis/Religious Program—Tel: 763-425-9801, Ext. 230. Ruth Fleming, D.R.E. Students 975.

MAPLE LAKE, WRIGHT CO., ST. TIMOTHY (1882) [CEM 3] Rev. Michael J. Izen; Deacons Ron Freeman; Michael Medley.
Church & Office: 8 Oak Ave., N., 55358. Tel: 320-963-3726; Fax: 320-963-2008. Web: www.churchofsttimothy.org.
School—(Grades K-6) Tel: 320-963-3417; Fax: 320-963-8804. Lay Teachers 10; Students 109.
Catechesis/Religious Program—Students 220.

MARYSBURG, LESUEUR CO., IMMACULATE CONCEPTION OF MARYSBURG (1857) [CEM] Rev. Edwin Savandra.
Church & Office: 27528 Patrick St., Madison Lake, 56063. Tel: 507-243-3166.
Catechesis/Religious Program—Fax: 507-243-3849. Students 35.

MARYSTOWN, SCOTT CO., ST. MARY OF THE PURIFICATION (1855), (German), [CEM] Rev. Peter C. Wittman.
15850 Marystown Rd., Shakopee, 55379-9341. Tel: 952-445-3469; Fax: 952-403-9330. Email: stmarysmarystown@comcast.net. Web: www.stmarypurification.org.
Parish Center:—Tel: 952-445-2647; Fax: 952-403-9330.
See Shakopee Area Catholic School, Shakopee under Elementary Schools, Consolidated, Parochial located in the Institution section.
Catechesis/Religious Program—Shakopee Area Religious Education (SARE), 2700 17th Ave. W., Shakopee, 55379. Tel: 952-445-3387, Ext. 145; Fax: 952-445-7256. Students 45.

MIESVILLE, DAKOTA CO., ST. JOSEPH (1873), (German—Irish), [CEM] Rev. Jay K. Kythe.
Office: 23955 Nicolai Ave. E., 55033-9650. Tel: 651-437-3526; Fax: 651-437-3506. Email: stjosephm@embarqmail.com.
Catechesis/Religious Program—Students 165.

MINNETONKA, HENNEPIN CO., IMMACULATE HEART OF MARY (1946) Rev. David T. Ostrowski.
Church & Office: 13505 Excelsior Blvd., 55345-4999. Tel: 952-935-1432; Fax: 952-935-0474.
Catechesis/Religious Program—Tel: 952-935-7077. Students 175.

MONTGOMERY, LE SUEUR CO., MOST HOLY REDEEMER (1881) [CEM 2] Rev. Cory J. Rohlfing.
Church & Office: 206 Vine Ave. W., 56069. Tel: 507-364-7981; Fax: 507-364-8660. Email: hredeemer@frontiernet.net. Web: www.hredeemerparish.org.
School—(Grades PreSchool-8), 205 Vine Ave., W., 56069. Tel: 507-364-7383; Fax: 507-364-5964. Email: mymgmurop@frontiernet.net. Sisters of Dominican 1; Lay Teachers 9; Students 94.
Catechesis/Religious Program—Students 121.
Mission—St. Canice Kilkenny, Le Sueur Co. 56052. Tel: 507-595-2561. Email: stcanice@frontiernet.net.

MONTICELLO, WRIGHT CO., ST. HENRY (1904) [CEM] Rev. Timothy C. Rudolphi; Deacon Mark Barder.
Office:—1001 E. 7th St., 55362. Tel: 763-295-2402; Fax: 763-295-6333.
Catechesis/Religious Program—Tel: 763-271-3079. Students 550.

MOUND, HENNEPIN CO., OUR LADY OF THE LAKE (1909) [CEM] Rev. Abraham George Kochupurackel, C.M.I.; Deacon Russell Kocemba.
Church & Office: 2385 Commerce Blvd., 55364. Tel: 952-472-1284; Fax: 952-472-1216. Web: ourladyofthelake.com.
Preschool—Tel: 952-472-1284, Ext. 142; Fax: 952-472-9152. Email: mrosenberg@oll.pvt.k12.mn.us. Students 70.
School—(Grades PreK-8) Tel: 952-472-1284, Ext. 151. Ellen Feuling, Prin. Lay Teachers 15; Students 205.
Catechesis/Religious Program—Tel: 952-472-1284, Ext. 144; Fax: 952-472-1216. Scott Brazil, D.R.E.; Bryan Bush, Youth & Adult Educ. Students 245.

NEW MARKET, SCOTT CO., ST. NICHOLAS (1893), (German), [CEM] Rev. James F. Adams.
Church & Office: 51 Church St., P.O. Box 9, Elko/New Market, 55020. Tel: 952-461-2403; Fax: 952-461-2423.
See Holy Cross LNMV Catholic School, Lonsdale under Elementary Schools, Consolidated, Parochial located in the Institution section.
Catechesis/Religious Program—Students 148.

NEW PRAGUE, SCOTT CO., ST. WENCESLAUS (1857) [CEM] Rev. Kevin I. Clinton; Deacon Robert Wagner.
Church & Office: 215 Main St. E., 56071-1837. Tel: 952-758-3225; Fax: 952-758-2960. Web: www.saintwenceslaus.org.
School—(Grades K-8), 227 Main St. E., 56071. Tel: 952-758-3133; Fax: 952-758-2958. Kimberly Doyle, Prin. Lay Teachers 21; Students 282.
Catechesis/Religious Program—Tel: 952-758-2276. Jennifer Schneider, D.R.E. Students 458.

NEW TRIER, DAKOTA CO., ST. MARY (1856) [CEM] Rev. Stan P. Mader.
Church & Office: 8433 239th St. E., Hampton, 55031. Fax: 651-437-5546.
Catechesis/Religious Program—Students 30.

NORTH BRANCH, CHISAGO CO., ST. GREGORY THE GREAT (1874) [CEM] Rev. Mark Shane Wasinger; Deacon Michael Martin Jr.
Church & Office: 38725 Forest Blvd., P.O. Box 609, 55056. Tel: 651-674-4056; 651-674-4272 (Rectory); Fax: 651-277-4563. Email: info@stgregorynb.org. Web: www.stgregorynb.org.
Catechesis/Religious Program—Tel: 651-277-4563. Students 280.

NORTHFIELD, RICE CO., ST. DOMINIC (1869) [CEM] Rev. Dennis Dempsey; Deacon Len Gruber.
Office & Mailing Address: 216 N. Spring St., 55057-1431. Tel: 507-645-8816; Fax: 507-645-8818. Email: secretary@churchofstdominic.org. Web: www.churchofstdominic.org.
Res.: 116 N. Linden St., 55057. Tel: 507-663-0154.
School—(Grades K-8) Tel: 507-650-0680; Fax: 507-645-8818. Kim Bobert, Librarian. Lay Teachers 14; Students 169.
Catechesis/Religious Program—Students 267.

NORWOOD, CARVER CO., ASCENSION (1859), (German), [CEM 2] Rev. Martin Shallbetter.
Church & Office: 323 Reform St., N., 55368. Tel: 952-467-3351. Web: www.ascensionnye.org.
Catechesis/Religious Program—Students 170.

PINE ISLAND, GOODHUE CO., ST. MICHAEL (1878) [CEM] Rev. Timothy E. Dolan.
Church & Office: 451 5th St., S.W., 55963. Fax: 507-356-2080. Email: ckunz@pitel.net. Web: www.stmichaels-pineisland.4lpi.com.
Catechesis/Religious Program—Tel: 507-356-4280. Students 92.

PRIOR LAKE, SCOTT CO., ST. MICHAEL (1912) [CEM 2] Rev. Thomas H. Sieg; Deacon Richard Roy.
Office: 16311 Duluth Ave., S.E., 55372. Tel: 952-447-2491; Fax: 952-447-2489. Email: info@stmichael-pl.org. Web: www.stmichael-pl.org.
School—(Grades PreSchool-8), 16280 Duluth Ave., S.E., 55372. Tel: 952-447-2124; Fax: 952-447-2132 (Primary); 952-447-2348 (Middle School). Email: haycraft@saintmpl.org. Lay Teachers 30; Students 487.
Catechesis/Religious Program—Tel: 612-447-2486; Fax: 612-447-2489. Janel Boegeman, D.R.E. (Elementary); Gina Tupy, D.R.E. (Senior High); Melissa Carlson, Dir. Faith Formation; Laura Shupe, Dir. Adult & Family Ministries. Students 707.

RAMSEY, ANOKA CO., ST. KATHARINE DREXEL (2004) Rev. Paul A. Jaroszeski; Deacon Randy Bauer; Sisters Dianne Perry, S.S.N.D., Pastoral Assoc.; Bridget Waldorf, S.S.N.D., Youth Min.; Marc Stockert, Liturgy Dir.
Office & Church: 7101 143rd Ave., N.W., Ste. G, 55303. Tel: 763-323-4424; Fax: 763-323-7040. Email: info@stkdcc.org. Web: www.stkdcc.org.
Catechesis/Religious Program—Students 177.

RED WING, GOODHUE CO., CHURCH OF ST. JOSEPH (1865) [CEM] Rev. Thomas M. Kommers.
Church & Office: 426 8th St., 55066. Tel: 651-388-1133; Fax: 651-388-5294.
School—St. Joseph School, (Grades PreSchool-5), 469 12th St., 55066. Tel: 651-388-9493; Fax: 651-385-0769. Lori Ann Myers, Prin. Lay Teachers 7; Students 70.
Catechesis/Religious Program—Tel: 651-388-6000. Debby Bradley, D.R.E. Students 250.

ROGERS, HENNEPIN CO.
1—ST. MARTIN (1912) Closed. For inquiries for parish records contact the chancery.
2—THE CATHOLIC CHURCH OF MARY QUEEN OF PEACE, Merged in Jan. 2003. Rev. Mark D. Moriarty.
Church & Office: 21304 Church Ave., 55374. Tel: 763-428-2585. Email: mqpchurchoffice@yahoo.com.
School—(Grades PreSchool-8), 21201 Church Ave., 55374. Tel: 763-428-2355; Fax: 763-428-2062. Web: www.mqpcatholicschool.org. Lay Teachers 12; Students 136.
Catechesis/Religious Program—Students 411.

ROSEMOUNT, DAKOTA CO., ST. JOSEPH (1865) [CEM 2] Rev. Thomas F. Hill, O.F.M.Cap.
Church & Office: 13900 Biscayne Ave., 55068. Tel: 651-423-4402; Fax: 651-423-6616. Web: www.stjosephcommunity.org.
Res.: 13889 Blanca Court, 55068.
School—(Grades K-8) Tel: 651-423-1658. Sisters 1; Lay Teachers 12; Students 220.
Catechesis/Religious Program—Esther Jaeger, D.R.E., (Elementary School); Bridget Samson, D.R.E., (High School). Students 678.

RUSH CITY, CHISAGO CO., SACRED HEART (1870) [CEM] Revs. Ralph Talbot; Cory Belden, Sacramental Min.
Mailing Address: P.O. Box 45, 55069. Email: sacredheart@g.com. Web: www.sacredheartrushcity.org.
Church & Office: 415 W 5th St., 55069. Tel: 320-358-4370; Fax: 320-358-4452.
Catechesis/Religious Program—Students 89.

ST. BENEDICT, SCOTT CO., ST. BENEDICT, (German), [CEM] [JC] Rev. Elgar Bockenfeld, O.F.M.
Res.: 20087 Hub Dr., New Prague, 56071. Tel: 952-738-4642.
Catechesis/Religious Program—Combined with St. John the Evangelist.

ST. BONIFACIUS, HENNEPIN CO., ST. BONIFACE (1859), (German), [CEM] Rev. Thomas J. Balluff.
Church & Office: 4025 Main St., P.O. Box 68, 55375. Tel: 952-446-1054; Fax: 952-446-1158. Email: stbonifaceoffice@mchsi.com. Web: www.stboniface-stmary.org.
Catechesis/Religious Program—8801 Wildwood Ave., P.O. Box 276, 55375. Tel: 952-446-1224. Students 49.

ST. HENRY, LE SUEUR CO., CHURCH OF ST. HENRY (1859) [CEM] Rev. Christopher Shofner.
165 N. Waterville, Le Center, 56057. Tel: 507-357-4838.
Catechesis/Religious Program—Combined with St. Mary, Le Center.

ST. MICHAEL, WRIGHT CO., ST. MICHAEL (1857) [CEM 2] Revs. Peter M. Richards; Gregory E. Abbott; Deacons Maynard Warne; Greg Steele; Donald Becker.
Church & Office: 11300 Frankfort Pkwy. N.E., 55376. Tel: 763-497-2745; Fax: 763-497-5273. Web: www.stmcatholicchurch.org.
School—(Grades K-6), 14 Main St. N., Saint Michael, 55376. Tel: 763-497-3887; Fax: 763-497-9159. Jenny Haller, Prin. Lay Teachers 22; Students 324.
Catechesis/Religious Program—Carol Freeman, D.R.E.; Kathy Pope, D.R.E. Students 694.

ST. PAUL PARK, WASHINGTON CO., ST. THOMAS AQUINAS (1884) [CEM] Rev. Gregory L. Esty; Deacon James T. Price.
Church & Office: 920 Holley Ave., 55071. Tel: 651-459-2131; Fax: 651-459-8765.
Catechesis/Religious Program—Fax: 651-459-8756. Students 145.

ST. THOMAS, LE SUEUR CO., ST. THOMAS (1858), (Irish), [CEM] Rev. Kevin I. Clinton.
Church & Office: 31525 181st Ave., New Prague, 56071. Tel: 952-758-3325; Fax: 952-758-2960.
Catechesis/Religious Program—

SAVAGE, SCOTT CO., ST. JOHN THE BAPTIST (1854) [CEM] Rev. Michael Tix; Deacons Bob Durham; Jerry Little.
Church & Office: 4625 W. 125th St., 55378-1357. Tel: 952-890-9465; Fax: 952-890-3006. Web: www.stjohns-savage.org.
School—(Grades PreK-8), 12508 Lynn Ave. S., 55378. Tel: 952-890-6604; Fax: 952-890-9481. Jean Algren, Librarian. Lay Teachers 35; Students 750.
Catechesis/Religious Program—Tel: 952-890-9434; Fax: 952-890-9481. Lori Taormina, Youth Min.; Andi Little, D.R.E.; Jan Jirik, C.R.E. (Grades 7-9). Students 641.

SHAKOPEE, SCOTT CO.
1—CHURCH OF ST. MARY (1865), (Irish), [CEM] [JC] Rev. Peter C. Wittman.
Office: 2700 17th Ave. E., 55379. Tel: 952-445-1319; Fax: 952-445-0511.
Church: 535 S. Lewis St., 55379.
See Shakopee Area Catholic School, Shakopee under Elementary Schools, Consolidated, Parochial located in the Institution section.

Catechesis/Religious Program—Shakopee Area Religious Education, 2700 17th Ave. W., 55379. Tel: 952-445-3387. This is a consolidation of three parish programs. Students 128.

2—ST. MARK (1856), (German), [JC 2] Rev. Timothy L. Norris; Deacon James Pufahl. In Res., Rev. Thomas Boedy, S.J.
Church & Office: 350 S. Atwood St., 55379-1238. Tel: 952-445-1229; Fax: 952-445-9639. Email: stmarkshakopee@usfamily.net. Web: www.stmarkshakopee.com.
See Shakopee Area Catholic School, Shakopee under Elementary Schools, Consolidated, Parochial located in the Institution section.
Catechesis/Religious Program—2700 17th Ave. E., 55379. Tel: 952-445-3387; Fax: 952-445-7256. Web: www.sacsschools.org. Students 243.

SHIELDSVILLE, RICE CO., ST. PATRICK (1856), (Irish–Czech), [CEM] Revs. Kevin Finnegan; Fernando Ortega; Deacon Steven Moses.
Church & Office: 7525 Dodd Rd., 55021. Tel: 507-334-6002; Fax: 507-334-1960. Email: spshieldsville@quest.net.
Catechesis/Religious Program—Students 63.

SOUTH ST. PAUL, DAKOTA CO.

1—ST. AUGUSTINE (1896) Revs. John P. Echert; Robert J. Grabner.
Church & Office: 747 6th Ave. S, 55075. Tel: 651-451-1212; Fax: 651-455-7600.
Catechesis/Religious Program—Tel: 651-451-0685. Students 62.

2—HOLY TRINITY (1918), (Polish), Rev. John P. Echert.
Church & Office: 749 6th Ave. S., 55075. Tel: 651-455-1228; 651-455-1302 (Office); Fax: 651-455-7600.
School—(Grades K-8), 745 6th Ave. S., 55075. Tel: 651-455-8557; Fax: 651-455-9696. Lay Teachers 14; Students 158.
Catechesis/Religious Program—Tel: 651-455-6004; Fax: 651-455-7600. Students 107.

3—ST. JOHN VIANNEY (1946) [CEM] Rev. Terry P. Beeson.
Church & Office: 789 17th Ave. N., 55075. Tel: 651-451-1863; Fax: 651-451-1864. Email: sjvssp@comcast.net. Web: www.sjvssp.org.
School—(Grades K-8), 1815 Bromley St., 55075. Tel: 651-451-8395. Lay Teachers 16; Students 140.
Catechesis/Religious Program—Students 178.

STILLWATER, WASHINGTON CO.

1—ST. MARY (1865), (German), [JC] Rev. Michael J. Miller; Deacon Mark Skala. In Res., Rev. Robert L. Valit (Retired).
Church, Office & Res.: 423 S. Fifth St., 55082. Tel: 651-439-1270; Fax: 651-439-7045. Email: liz@stmarysstillwater.org. Web: www.stmarysstillwater.org.
See St. Croix Catholic School, Stillwater under Elementary Schools, Consolidated, Parochial located in the Institution section.
Catechesis/Religious Program—Tel: 651-439-7142. Students 651.

2—ST. MICHAEL (1853) [JC] Rev. Michael J. Miller; Deacons Roger Carlson; Guy Glover; Mark Skala. In Res., Revs. John G. Donahue (Retired); Robert L. Valit (Retired).
Church & Office: 611 S. Third St., 55082-4908. Tel: 651-439-4400; Fax: 651-430-3271. Email: info@costm.org. Web: www.stillwatercatholics.org.
See St. Croix Catholic School, Stillwater under Elementary Schools, Consolidated, Parochial located in the Institution section.
Catechesis/Religious Program—218 E. Willard St., 55082. Tel: 651-351-3175; Fax: 651-379-1279. Students 473.

TAYLORS FALLS, CHISAGO CO., ST. JOSEPH'S (1873) [CEM] [JC] Rev. Daniel J. Bodin.
Church & Office: Box 234, 55084. Tel: 651-465-7345; Fax: 651-465-6683. Email: sjtaylorsfalls@yahoo.com. Web: www.stjosephtaylorsfalls.org.
Catechesis/Religious Program—Students 109.
Mission—*St. Francis Xavier* Shafer, Chisago Co. 55074. Web: www.stfrancisfranconia.org.

UNION HILL, LE SUEUR CO., ST. JOHN THE EVANGELIST, [CEM] Rev. Elgar Bockenfeld, O.F.M.
Church & Office: 20087 Hub Dr., New Prague, 56071. Tel: 952-758-4642.
Catechesis/Religious Program—Combined with St. Benedict, New Prague. Students 150.

VERMILLION, DAKOTA CO., ST. JOHN THE BAPTIST (1881) [CEM] Rev. Stan P. Mader.
Church & Office: 106 W. Main St., 55085. Tel: 651-437-5652; Fax: 651-437-5652.
School—(Grades PreSchool-5), 111 W. Main St., 55085. Tel: 651-437-2644; Fax: 651-437-9006. Email: stjohnscverm@bevcomm.net. Web: www.stjohnvermillion.com. Franciscan Clarist Sisters 3; Lay Teachers 6; Students 124.
Catechesis/Religious Program—Email: stjohnsc@bevcomm.net. Students 75.

VESELI, RICE CO., MOST HOLY TRINITY (1874), (Czech), [CEM 2] Rev. John G. Lapensky.
Church & Office: 9845 Main St., 55046. Tel: 507-744-2823; Fax: 507-744-2823.
See Holy Cross LNMV Catholic School, Lonsdale under Elementary Schools, Consolidated, Parochial located in the Institution section.
Catechesis/Religious Program—Students 66.

VICTORIA, CARVER CO., ST. VICTORIA (1856), (German), [CEM] Rev. Robert L. White; Deacon Ray Ortman.
Church & Office: 8228 Victoria Dr., 55386. Tel: 952-443-2661; Fax: 952-443-3866. Web: www.stvictoria.net.
Catechesis/Religious Program—Tel: 952-443-3536. Students 487.

WACONIA, CARVER CO., ST. JOSEPH (1859) [CEM] Rev. Lawrence R. Blake; Deacon Timothy Harrer.
Church & Office: 41 E. 1st St., 55387. Tel: 952-442-2384 (Office); Fax: 952-442-3719. Web: www.stjosephwaconia.org. Email: churchoffice@stjosephwaconia.org.
School—(Grades PreSchool-8) Tel: 952-442-4500. Email: schooloffice@stjosephwaconia.org. Lay Teachers 21; Students 280.
Catechesis/Religious Program—Students 396.

WATERTOWN, CARVER CO., IMMACULATE CONCEPTION (1863), (German–Irish), [CEM] Rev. Frank J. Wampach.
Church & Office: 109 Angel Ave., N.W., P.O. Box 548, 55388. Tel: 952-955-1458; Fax: 952-955-1777.
Catechesis/Religious Program—109 Angel Ave., N.W., 55388. Tel: 952-955-1777; Fax: 952-955-1777. Jessica Soden, D.R.E. Students 280.

WATERVILLE, LE SUEUR CO., HOLY TRINITY (1892) [CEM] Rev. Michael W. Ince.
Church & Office: 506 Common St., 56096. Tel: 507-362-4311; Fax: 507-362-4339. Email: holyt7@frontiernet.net.
Catechesis/Religious Program—Tel: 507-362-8396. Students 80.

WAVERLY, WRIGHT CO., ST. MARY (1884) [CEM] [JC 3] Rev. Timothy D. Cloutier.
Mailing Address: P.O. Box 278, 55390. Tel: 763-658-4319; Fax: 763-658-3519.
Church & Office: 607 Maple Ave., 55390. Email: stmarys-waverly@live.com.
Catechesis/Religious Program—Tel: 763-658-4118. Students 213.

WAYZATA, HENNEPIN CO.

1—ST. BARTHOLOMEW (1916) Rev. Michael A. Reding; Deacon Richard P. Witucki.
Office & Church: 630 E. Wayzata Blvd., 55391-1743. Tel: 952-473-6601; Fax: 952-473-0980. Email: stbarts@st-barts.org. Web: www.st-barts.org.
School—(Grades PreK-6) Tel: 952-473-6189; Fax: 952-745-4598. Corrine Rudnick, Librarian. Lay Teachers 15; Students 242.
Catechesis/Religious Program—Students 312.

2—HOLY NAME OF JESUS (1865) [CEM] Revs. Timothy Morin; Joseph-Quoc T. Vuong; Deacons Joe Wierschem; Terry Schneider; Sam Catapano; Dennis Hanson.
Church & Office: 155 County Rd., 24, 55391. Fax: 763-745-3488. Email: info@hnoj.org. Web: www.hnoj.org.
School—(Grades K-6) Tel: 763-473-3675; Fax: 763-745-3499. Lay Teachers 27; Students 344.
Catechesis/Religious Program—Tel: 763-473-7901. Students 875.

ZUMBROTA, GOODHUE CO., ST. PAUL (1900) [CEM] [JC] Rev. Timothy E. Dolan.
Office & Mailing Address: 749 S. Main St., 55992-1608. Tel: 507-732-5324; Fax: 507-732-5327. Email: stpauls@hcinet.net. Web: www.stpaul-zumbrota.4Lpi.com.
Catechesis/Religious Program—Students 85.

Chaplains of Public Institutions

ST. PAUL. *HealthEast, Inc. & HealthEast Hospice*. Rev. Stephen J. LaCanne, M.Div., N.A.C.C., Contact Person.
St. Joseph's Hospital, Tel: 651-232-3611 (Spiritual Care Dept.). Revs. Stephen J. LaCanne, M.Div., N.A.C.C., Dir. Spiritual Care, Jonathan Fischer, O.S.B.
Ramsey County Correctional Facilities. Rev. Antony Skaria, C.F.I.C.
Regions Medical Center. Revs. Ronald Harrer, O.M.I., Antony Skaria, C.F.I.C.
United Children's Hospital. Rev. Michael G. Monogue.
United Hospitals, Inc. Rev. Michael G. Monogue.

MINNEAPOLIS. *Abbot-Northwestern Hospital*, 3617 38th Ave. S., 55066. Rev. John Hofstede.
Fairview University Medical Center. Revs. Joseph Whalen, Richard Chilson, C.S.P.
Hennepin County Courts.
Hennepin County Medical Center, 2421 Third Ave. S., 55404. Rev. Benny Mekkatt Varghese, C.F.I.C.
Minneapolis Children's Hospital, 3617 38th Ave. S., 55406. Rev. John Hofstede.
Veterans Administration Medical Center. Rev. Damien Schill.

EDINA. *Fairview-Southdale Hospital*. Rev. Jerry Fehn, (On Military Leave).

COON RAPIDS. *Mercy Hospital*. Rev. Peter Yakubu.

FARIBAULT. *Faribault State School and Hospital*. Attended by Immaculate Conception Parish.

GOLDEN VALLEY. *North Memorial Hospital*. Rev. James T. Livingston.

HASTINGS. *Regina Medical Center*. Rev. Robert J. Altier.

LINO LAKES. *Minnesota Correctional Facility*. Vacant. 1121 E. 46th St., 55407.

MAPLEWOOD. *St. John's Hospital*, 1575 Beam Ave., 55109. Rev. Leo J. Schneider. (Lutheran)

SHAKOPEE. *Women's State Reformatory*. Vacant.

ST. LOUIS PARK. *Methodist Hospital*. Rev. Jerry Fehn, (On Military Leave).

STILLWATER. *Minnesota State Prison*. Vacant.

Special Assignment:
Revs.—
Estrem, John, (On Leave), Catholic Charities
Hubbard, Lawrence E., Hispanic Ministry
Lepak, Roy C. (Retired), Hermit, Cotton, MN
Maus, Mark T., Chancery Pro Tem
Notebaart, James C., (Retired), Office of Indian Ministry
Smith, James D., Chancery Pro Tem
Snyder, Larry J., Catholic Charities, U.S.A.
Walsh, Harry A., Chancery Pro Tem

On Duty Outside the Archdiocese:
Revs.—
O'Connell, Marvin R. (Retired), University of Notre Dame, IN
Schaffer, Gregory J., El Buen Pastor Parroquia San Francisco de Asis, Apartado 22, Puerto Ordaz, Estado Bolivar 8015 Venezuela.

Military Chaplains:
Revs.—
Fehn, Jerome W.
Magnuson, Sean R.
Thiesen, Eugene

Graduate Studies:
Revs.—
Burns, James P., Waltham, MA.
Carl, Scott M., St. Paul Seminary - School of Divinity
Pish, Robert, Washington D.C.

Retired:
Rev. Msgrs.—
Baumgaertner, William L., 60 S. Mississippi River Blvd., #16, 55105.
Boxleitner, J. Jerome, 1001 E. 46th St., 55407.
Kneal, Ellsworth, 2260 Summit Ave., 55105.
Lavin, James M., 2115 Summit Ave., 55105.
Sankovitz, John P., 60 S. Mississippi River Blvd., 55105.
Srnec, Stanley J., 60 S. Mississippi River Blvd., 55105.
Revs.—
Abbott, Eugene J., 1241 Edgcumbe Rd., 55105.
Beckman, Martin A., P.O. Box 1751, Minnetonka, 55345.
Berg, Richard V., 60 S. Mississippi River Blvd., Apt. 319, 55105.
Blais, Melvin J., 26 W. 10th St., Apt. 1305, 55102.
Brandes, John F., 629-2nd St. N.E., 55413-1905.
Bury, Harold J., 60 S. Mississippi River Blvd., Apt. 318, 55105.
Carroll, Roger, 60 S. Mississippi River Blvd., Apt. 317, 55105.
Clubb, Ronald E., S.T.P., 4300 W. River Pkwy., 55406.
Colon, Vincent A., 2350 Springside Dr., Maplewood, 55119.
Dahlheimer, Ronald W.
Dobihal, Robert F., 60 S. Mississippi River Blvd., Apt. 119, 55116.
Doffing, Gordon M., 5820 E. Marlin St., Mesa, AZ 85215.
Dolan, Leo A.
Donahue, John G.
Endres, Gilbert J., 652 Ellsworth Rd., Lot #197, Mesa, AZ 85208.
Erlander, Michael
Fitzpatrick, John P., 642 Monn Ave., Vadnais Heights, 55127.
Fleming, Martin M.P., 383 Portland Ave., 55102.
Forliti, John E.
Friberg, Daniel, 2021 Wentworth, South St. Paul, 55075.
Gamber, William K., 133 S. Mill St., #205, Fergus Falls.
Gannon, Joseph T., 60 S. Mississippi River Blvd., Apt. 309, 55105.

Grieman, Gerald G., 264 Ashurst Dr., Phoenix, AZ.
Gutierrez, Jose, 60 S. Mississippi River Blvd., 55105.
Hamel, Robert F., 225 Frank St., 55106.
Holl, James E., 86 Wilkin St., 55102.
Huntstiger, Thomas, 625 Oaks Dr., Apt. 204, Pompano Beach, FL 33069.
Janski, Jerome J., 10419 El Captain Cir., Sun City, AZ 85351.
Jenniges, Leonard J., 18760 City Hwy 17, Sanborn, 56083.
Jude, Robert J., 660 Park St. E., #231, Annandale, 55302.
Keane, Robert E., 5921 14th Ave. S., 55417.
Keefe, Gerald E., 1310 Main St., Hopkins, 55343.
Keller, Lawrence E.
Kennedy, Michael J.
Kenney, William J., 1690 McKnight Ln., Maplewood, 55109.
Kittock, Francis R., 60 S. Mississippi River Blvd., Apt. 228, 55102.
Kivel, Joseph G.
Klaers, Marvin J., 8433 239th St. E., Hampton, 55031.
Klein, Bernard C., 86 Wilkin St., #203, 55102.
Kovalik, George J.
LaVan, Kenneth G., 1657 Granada N., Apt. 105, Oakdale, 55128.
Lepak, Roy C., 8830 Strand Lake Rd. N., Cotton, 55724.
Ludescher, Kenneth F.
Mahon, Ambrose J., 1010 Coventry Pl., Edina, 55435.
Mahoney, Richard J., 60 S. Mississippi River Blvd., Apt. 315, 55105.
Mertz, Frederick A.
Moorman, Raymond J., 3220 S. Yosemite Ave. S., St. Louis Park, 55416.
Moudry, Richard P., 11113 Hyland Ter., Eden Prairie, 55344.
Namie, James B., 4010 Galt Ocean Dr., Apt. #1203, Fort Lauderdale, FL.
Nolan, Timothy F.
Nygaard, Robert C.
O'Connell, Marvin R., 15625 Hearthstone Dr., Mishawaka, IN 46545.
Parkos, John F.
Pierre, Kenneth J., 894 Hoyt Ave., 55117.
Power, J. Timothy
Reidy, James E., 60 S. Mississippi River Blvd., Apt. 124, 55105.
Riley, John F., 60 S. Mississippi River Blvd., 55105.
Roach, Francis J., 2132 Bard Ct., P.O. Box 1064, Faribault, 55021.
Schoenberger, James T., 60 S. Mississippi River Blvd., Apt. 312, 55105.
Siebenaler, John M.
Siebenaler, Leonard, 325 Hillcrest Dr., St. Michael, 55376.
Siebenaler, Martin, Farm St., Hastings, 55033.
Sipe, Robert J.
Skluzacek, Richard F., (Inactive)
Slusser, Michael S., Bryne Residence
Stromberg, James S., 60 S. Mississippi River Blvd., 55105.
Valit, Robert L., 423 5th St., 55082.
Whittier, William O., St. Mary of the Lake, 2801 Flag Ave. No., New Hope, 55427.
Wolter, Richard J., 60 S. Mississippi River Blvd., Apt. 117, 55105.

Permanent Deacons:
Asenbrenner, Francis, Maternity of Mary, St. Paul
Babcock, George H., (Retired)
Backmann, Howard, (On Leave)
Barrett, Ervin F., (Retired)
Barrett, Thomas F., (Retired)
Baskfield, James F., Diocese of Duluth
Beck, William E., (Retired)
Becker, Donald L., St. Michael, St. Michael
Bednarczyk, Peter, St. Stephen, Anoka
Beer, Terry, Guardian Angels
Belian, John, St. Anthony, St. Hedwig & Holy Cross, Minneapolis; Health East-St. Joseph Hospital
Bellavance, Peter G., St. Luke, Clearwater
Berghoff, William J., (Retired)
Bernard, Charles V., (Retired)
Bisek, Jerome H., On Leave of Absence
Blissenbach, Gerald, (Retired)
Boatwright, Stephen, St. Leonard, Minneapolis
Boisclair, A. Richard, On Leave of Absence
Bramwell, Robert, St. Joseph, New Hope
Brown, Fredrick L., (Retired)
Campbell, Kevin A., On Leave of Absence
Carlson, Paul, St. Lawrence, Minneapolis
Carlson, Roger B., Michaels, Stillwater
Catapano, Salvatore, Holy Name of Jesus
Chlebeck, Dennis, Maternity of Mary, St. Paul
Christensen, Harlan L., On Leave of Absence
Ciresi, Jerome D., Assumption, St. Paul
Clasen, James
Coleman, Thomas F., Medical Leave
Courrier, Darrel, Ss. Peter & Paul, Loretto
Crowley, John, St. Odelia
Curtan, Sean, St. Vincent de Paul, Brooklyn Park
D'Heilly, Peter, (Retired)
Damiani, Joseph, Annunication, Minneapolis; Office of Indian Ministry
DeFrank, Frank, Chicago
DeLuney, Jon, St. Bonaventure, Bloomington
DeShane, James, Most Holy Trinity
Devine, Gerald L., Calix Ministry
Dewitte, Michael, Delano Catholic Community, Delano
Dolan, Thomas E., (Retired)
Dols, Bernard R., (Retired)
Dornfeld, Willard, (Retired)
Dzik, Thomas W., St. Thomas More
Ehrmantraut, Dominic, St. Stephen, Anoka and St. Walburga, Fletcher
Erpenbach, William L., (Retired)
Evans, Patrick, St. Joseph, Red Wing
Falvey, William E., (Retired)
Feffer, Edward F., (Retired)
Ferguson, Delmar F., (Retired)
Fidler, Donald, Marion Center, St. Paul
Flood, John J., (Retired)
Frederick, Joseph J., On Leave of Absence
Freeman, Ronald, St. Timothy, Maple Lake
Friesen, Michael, St. Francis Cabrini, Minneapolis
Garcia Degollado, Ramon, Hispanic Ministry-St. Odilia, Shoreview; St. Stephen, Anoka
Getz, Ronald L., (Retired)
Glover, Guy, St. Michael/St. Mary, Stillwater
Gregory, Gabriel, (Retired)
Gruber, Leonard L., St. Dominic, Northfield
Hamilton, Don, St. Rose of Lima, Roseville; St. Timothy, Blaine
Hanson, Dennis, Holy Name, Wayzata
Harrer, Timothy, St. Joseph, Waconia
Haselhuhn, Walter, (Retired)
Hathaway, Donald F., (Retired)
Heidenreich, Michael, Diocese of Las Vegas, NV
Heiman, William, St. Mary, Shakopee; St. Mary of the Purification, Shakopee
Heineman, Richard, St. Bridget
Helmeke, Timothy, St. Hubert, Chanhassen
Hepp, James E., (Retired)
Herzog, Jack, St. Bonaventure, Bloomington
Hoffman, Gary, St. John the Baptist, Jordan
Holst, David, St. Alphonsus, Brooklyn Park, MN
Houle, Gary J., St. Peter, Forest Lake
Huber, James, On Leave of Absence
Huberty, Peter J., (Retired)
Hughesdon, Harold, St. Agnes, St. Paul
Huibregtse, David, (Retired)
Humbert, Michael, Corpus Christi, Roseville
Ingwell, David, St. Thomas More, St. Paul
Janes, Edward, (Retired)
Jaques, Martin, Our Lady of Guadalupe
Jents, Kevin, (Retired)
Johanns, Mark, St. Peter, Richfield
Johnson, Fred, St. Peter Claver, St. Paul
Kasbohm, Thomas F., (Retired)
Kelly, Robert, St. Thomas Becket
Kenney, Joseph G., (Retired)
Keyes, Thomas, St. John's Hospital, Maplewood
Kirchoffner, Daniel D., St. Genevieve, Centerville
Kittok, Joseph, Delano Catholic Community
Klish, Richard, St. John Neumann, Eagan
Kocemba, Russell, Our Lady of the Lake, Moundo
Konkel, Thomas A., St. Joseph, Lino Lakes
Koop, Steven E., St. Rita, Cottage Grove
Kuebler, Myon, On Loan
L'Allier, Ralph, St. Peter, Forest Lake
Langlois, Thomas, (Retired)
Laqui, Marciano I., On Loan
Lee, Joseph Chang, National Korean Evangelization
Little, Gerald, St. John the Baptist
Lo, Va Thai, (Retired)
Maier, Steven, St. Francis de Sales; St. James, St. Paul
Maltzen, Bruce, Epiphany, Coon Rapids - incardinating
Mangan, John T., (Retired)
Mann, George A., (Retired)
Marshall, James, All Saints, Lakeville
Martin, Michael, Jr., St. Gregory, North Branch; MN Correctional Facility, Rush City
Masla, John, (Retired)
McDonald, James F., St. Hubert, Chanhassen
McGee, Newell, St. Michael, Pine Island; MN Correctional Facility, Faribault
McLaughlin, James, Nativity, Bloomington
McPherson, Joseph T., (Retired)
Medley, Michael, St. Timothy Maple Lake
Medlicott, James V., (Retired)
Meyer, James, Cathedral of St. Paul, St. Paul
Michaud, Thomas P., (Retired)
Moore, Richard, St. Thomas the Apostle
Moravec, Terry, St. Peter, Forest Lake
Moses, Steven, Divine Mercy Catholic, Fairbault
Murphy, John W., Jr., St. John's, Hopkins
Murphy, John L., St. Matthew, St. Paul
Najarian, Stephen, St. Charles Borromeo, Minneapolis
Nelson, Ronald, On Loan
Neumann, Dennis J., (Retired)
Nicklay, John, St. Rita, Cottage Grove
Nowak, David, On Leave of Absence
Nugent, George J., All Saints, Lakeville
O'Connor, Kevin, St. Joseph, Maple Grove
O'Connor, Robert, (Retired)
Ochiagha, Ifeangi John, St. Odilia, Shoreview
Ortman, Raymond, St. Victoria
Otto, Sherman H., St. Francis Xavier, Buffalo
Palkert, Lawrence, Immaculate Conception, Columbia Heights
Palmer, Rodney, St. John the Baptist, New Brighton
Pashby, Richard E., St. Pascal, St. Paul
Pasko, Anthony, Our Lady of Grace, Edina
Pederson, Bernard A., St. Agnes, St. Paul
Pendergast, Donald, (Retired)
Powers, Michael, Our Lady of Mt. Carmel, Minneapolis
Pufahl, James, St. Mark's, Shakopee
Quayle, Thomas, St. John the Baptist, New Brighton
Rajcich, G. Michael, On Leave of Absence
Raleigh, Robert, Our Lady of the Prairie, Belle Plaine; Minnesota Correctional Facility
Ramsey, James, Ph.D., Sacred Heart, Robbinsdale
Reed, John A., Diocese of Duluth
Rinkenberger, Donald, (Retired)
Riordan, Ripperton W., St. Ambrose, Woodbury
Rollings, Virgil, (Retired)
Roy, Richard, St. Michael, Prior Lake
Rubi, Luis, St. Stephen, Minneapolis; Hennepin County Home School
Rudolphi, Byron W., Jr., (Retired)
Saladin, Jeremiah, Blessed Sacrament & St. Thomas, St. Paul
Saumweber, James, Presentation, Maplewood
Scherer, Terrance P., On Leave of Absence
Schmitz, Joseph, (Retired)
Schneider, Frank J., (Retired)
Schneider, Gary, St. Timothy, Blaine; Unity Hospital, Fridley; Mercy Hospital, Coon Rapids
Schneider, Terrence, Holy Name of Jesus, Wayzata
Schnell, Robert, St. Richard's, Richfield
Schramer, Joseph J., (Retired)
Schroeder, Allan, (Retired)
Schroeder, Alphonse, Pax Christi, Eden Prairie
Seaton, James B., (Retired)
Semlak, Thomas L., St. Pius X, White Bear Lake
Shallbetter, Clarence, Sts. Cyril & Methodius
Shambour, Leonard, (Retired)
Shoberg, Mylo, On Leave of Absence
Shupe, Russell, Cathedral, St. Paul
Skala, Mark, St. Michael's, Stillwater
Skuta, Glenn, Transfiguration, Annadale
Smith, James, (Retired)
Smith, Joseph, St. Therese, Deephaven
Smith, Robert B., Assumption, Richfield
Sroder, Gregory, Guardian Angels, Chaska
Stahl, George, St. Peter, Oak Grove
Stevens, Richard, St. John Neuman, Eagan
Stewart, Phillip, Cathedral of St. Paul, St. Paul
Stiles, Thomas G., St. Columba, St. Paul
Stipe, Bruce, Leave of Absence
Straub, Art, On Leave of Absence
Stromen, Sherman, (Retired)
Swirtz, Lawrence, (Retired)
Tangney, Francis J., (Retired)
Tatone, Paul M., Our Lady of Peace, Minneapolis
Thell, Frank J., On Leave of Absence
Thoennes, Michael, On Leave of Absence
Thornton, James, (Retired)
Tift, J. Neil, On Loan
Timmerman, Dale, (Retired)
Tschann, Paul, Holy Trinity, Goodhue
Umphress, William G., (Retired)
Urbanski, Roger G., (Retired)
Valdez, Carl R., Sagrado Corazon de Jesus, Minneapolis
Wagner, James M., St. William's, Fridley
Wagner, Robert C., St. Wenceslaus, New Prague
Walker, Lawrence, (On Loan)
Wallin, John, St. Albert, Albertville; St. John, Dayton
Warhol, Robert W., Mary, Mother of the Church, Burnsville
Warne, Maynard E., St. Michael, St. Michael
Waugh, Charles, St. Stephen, Anoka
Weiland, John D., Immaculate Heart of Mary, Minnetonka
Wesley, R. Daniel, (Retired)
Wierschem, Joseph G., Holy Name, Medina
Wilkenson, Del, Leave of Absence

Winkelman, John W., St. Alphonsus, Brooklyn Center
Winn, Michael, (Retired)
Winninger, Thomas, St. Olaf, Minneapolis
Wittman, Wayne C., Sacred Heart, St. Paul
Witucki, Richard P., St. Bartholomew, Wayzata
Woznick, Greg, St. Henry, Monticello
Wright, Scott, St. Mark & St. Paul
Wurdock, Mike, Our Lady of Lourdes
Yaeger, Loren, (Retired)
Yang, Naokao, St. Vincent de Paul, St. Paul
Yekaldo, Fred, (Retired)
Zinda, Timothy, St. Paul's, Ham Lake; Ramsey County Corrections

INSTITUTIONS LOCATED IN THE ARCHDIOCESE

[A] SEMINARIES, ARCHDIOCESAN

ST. PAUL. *St. John Vianney Seminary*, 2115 Summit Ave., #5024, 55105. Tel: 651-962-6825; Fax: 651-962-6835. Email: sjv@stthomas.edu. Web: www.vianney.net. Rev. William J. Baer, Rector & Pres. Deacons 1; Priests 7; Students 152; Total Staff 6.

Spiritual Directors & Counselors: Rev. Msgr. Michael Becker; Revs. John Acrea; Albert P. Backmann; Paul Gitter; Rolf R. Tollefson; Mr. John Daniewicz, Dir. Academic Formation.

The Saint Paul Seminary (1894) School of Divinity of the University of St. Thomas, 2260 Summit Ave., 55105. Tel: 651-962-5050; Fax: 651-962-5790. Email: blac7536@stthomas.edu. Web: www.stthomas.edu/sod. Rev. Msgr. Aloysius R. Callaghan, S.T.L., J.C.D., Rector & Vice Pres.; Revs. Jerome M. Dittberner, S.T.D.; Andrew H. Cozzens, S.T.D.; J. Michael Byron, S.T.D.; Thomas Margevicius, S.T.L., Dir., Worship; Thomas Fisch, Ph.D.; Kenneth D. Synder, Ph.D.; Charlotte Berres, Ph.D., Assoc. Dir. Pastoral Formation; David Jenkins, D.Mus., Dir. Liturgical Music; Sisters Paul Therese Saiko, S.S.N.D., M.A.; Katarina Schuth, O.S.F., Ph.D.; Very Rev. Peter A. Laird, M.A., M.Div., Vice Rector; Mr. N. Curtis LeMay, Librarian; Very Rev. Christopher J. Beaudet, J.C.L.; Revs. Scott M. Carl; Jeffrey H. Huard, Dir., Spiritual Formation; John A. Klockeman, Assoc.Dir. Spiritual Formation; Christopher Thompson, Ph.D., Academic Dean; Rev. Robert H. Pish, Dean of Men; Stephen A. Hipp, S.T.D.; Deborah Savage, Ph.D.; Christian D. Washburn, Ph.D.; Rev. Juan Miguel Betancourt, S.E.M.V.

The Saint Paul Seminary M.Div./Seminarians 76; School of Divinity 77; Priests 12; Sisters 3; Lay Staff 8; Total Staff 23; Students 153.

[B] SEMINARIES, RELIGIOUS, OR SCHOLASTICATES

ST. PAUL. *Jesuit Novitiate*, 1035 Summit Ave., 55105-3034. Tel: 651-224-5593; Fax: 651-224-4734. Email: sjstpaul@aol.com. Rev. Matthew L. Linn, S.J., Retreat Dir. (House is closed for 2009-2010 school year) Priests 1; Total Staff 1.

[C] COLLEGES AND UNIVERSITIES

ST. PAUL. *St. Catherine University* (1905) 2004 Randolph Ave., 55105. Tel: 651-690-6000; Fax: 651-690-8752. Email: admissions@stkate.edu. Web: www.stkate.edu. Andrea J. Lee, Ph.D., IHM Vice Pres.; Tammy McGee, Finance & Admin.; Marjorie Mathison Hance, Vice Pres., External Rels.; Colleen Hegranes, Sr. Vice Pres.; Alan Silva, Ph.D., Dean of Arts & Sciences, School of Humanities A&S; Alice Swan, Dean Henrietta Schnoll School of Health; Brian Bruess, Ph.D., Vice Pres. Enrollment Mgmt. & Dean Student Affairs; Carol Johnson, Librarian. Sisters of St. Joseph of Carondelet 5; Lay Teachers 307; Total Staff 415; Students 5,277.

University of St. Thomas (1885) 2115 Summit Ave., 55105. Tel: 651-962-5000; 651-962-6626; Fax: 651-962-6504. Web: www.stthomas.edu. Rev. Dennis J. Dease, Pres.; Susan Huber, Interim Exec. Vice Pres. & Chief Academic Officer; Dr. Susan Alexander, Exec. Advisor to the Pres; Dr. Marisa Kelly, Dean of the College of Arts & Sciences; Dr. Angeline Barreta-Herman, Assoc. Vice Pres. Academic Affairs; Dr. Joseph Kreitzer, Assoc. Vice Pres. Academic Affairs; Jane W. Canney, Vice Pres. Students Affairs; Rev. John M. Malone, Vice Pres. for Mission; Mr. Quentin J. Hietpas, Senior Vice Pres. External Affairs Emeritus; Dr. Mark Dienhart, Exec. Vice Pres. & Chief Oper. Officer; Christopher Puto, Ph.D., Dean College of Business; Ms. Karen Lange, Dean of Student Life; Dr. Donald Weinkauf, Dean, School of Engrg.; Dr. Samuel Levy, Vice Pres. Information Resources & Technologies; Mr. Doug Hennes, Vice Pres. Univ. & Govt. Rels.; Mr. Thomas Mengler, Dean School of Law; Rev. Msgr. Aloysius R. Callaghan, S.T.L., J.C.D., Vice Pres. & Rector of St. Paul Seminary School of Divinity; Dr. Christopher Thompson, Dean St. Paul Seminary School of Divinity; Dr. Bruce Kramer, Interim Dean School of Education; Dr. Barbara Shank, Dean School of Social Work; Rev. Msgrs. William L. Baumgaertner, Prof. Emeritus, School of Divinity (Retired); James D. Habiger, Campus Ministry; James M. Lavin, Alumni Affairs (Retired); Revs. William J. Baer, Rector, St. John Vianney Seminary; J. Michael Byron, S.T.D., Asst. Prof. of Systematic Theology, School of Divinity; Andrew H. Cozzens, S.T.D., Instructor, Sacramental Theology; Jerome M. Dittberner, S.T.D., Prof. Dogmatic Theology; Erich Rutten, Dir. Campus Ministry; Jan Michael Joncas, Assoc. Prof. Theology, Catholic Studies; Very Rev. Peter A. Laird, M.A., M.Div., Asst. Prof., Moral Theology; Revs. James R. Motl, O.P., Ph.D., Assoc. Prof. Emeritus Homiletics (Retired); Thomas Margevicius, Instructor, Sacramental Theology & Liturgy Dir. of Worship; Steven J. McMichael, Asst. Prof. Theology; James E. Reidy (Retired), English Dept.; John F. Riley, Theology Dept. (Retired); Michael J. Keating, Asst. Prof. Catholic Studies; Hugo L. Montero, Campus Ministry, Instructor Theology; David W. Smith, Prof. Theology; James S. Stromberg, Philosophy Dept. (Retired); Martin L. Warren (England), Asst. Prof. English; Dwight Reginald Whitt, O.P., Prof. Law; Jean Pierre Bongila, Asst. Prof., Leadership, Policy & Admin.; John Acrea, Spiritual Dir., St. John Vianney Seminary; Deacon William Heiman, Vice Pres., Devel., St. John Vianney Seminary; Very Rev. Christopher J. Beaudet, J.C.L., Instructor, Canon Law; Revs. John Klockeman, Formator Spiritual Dir., St. John Vianney Seminary; Rolf R. Tollefson, Formator Spiritual Dir., St. John Vianney Seminary; Albert P. Backmann, St. John Vianney Seminary; Rev. Msgr. Michael Becker, St. John Vianney Seminary; Revs. Paul Gitter, St. John Vianney Seminary; James P. Burns, Grad. School Prof. Psychology; Scott M. Carl, School of Divinity; Jeff Huard, School of Divinity; Robert Pish, School of Divinity; Peter J. Williams, School of Divinity; Michael Erlander (Retired). Priests 15; Sisters 1; Lay Teachers 862; Students 10,851; Total Faculty & Staff 1,972.

MINNEAPOLIS. *St. Catherine University (Minneapolis)*, 601 25th Ave. S., 55454. Tel: 651-690-7702; Fax: 651-690-7849. Web: www.stkate.edu. Alice Swan, Interim Dean; Andrea Lee, IHM Pres.; Cindy Graham, Librarian. Coed Health Occupation Human Service and Continuing Education Programs. Sisters 1; Total Staff 75; Lay Teachers 100; Students 1,160.

[D] HIGH SCHOOLS, ARCHDIOCESAN

ST. PAUL. *The Saint Thomas Academy* (Boys), 949 Mendota Heights Rd., Mendota Heights, 55120-1496. Dr. Thomas B. Mich, B.A., M.A., Ph.D., Headmaster; Mr. Michael Byrne, Asst. Headmaster; Ann Girres, Librarian. Lay Teachers 62; Total Staff 80; Students 690.

[E] HIGH SCHOOLS, PRIVATE

ST. PAUL. *Cretin-Derham Hall*, 550 S. Albert St., 55116. Tel: 651-690-2443; Fax: 651-696-3394. Email: rengler@c-dh.org. Web: www.c-dh.org. Richard Engler, Pres. & Prin.; Kathleen Roy, Librarian. Co-Sponsors: Brothers of the Christian Schools and Sisters of St. Joseph of Carondelet. Brothers 3; Lay Teachers 88; Students 1,322; Total Staff 168.

MINNEAPOLIS. *Cristo Rey Jesuit High School - Twin Cities*, 2924 - 4th Ave. S, 55408. Tel: 612-545-9700. Rev. David Haschka, S.J., Pres.; Dr. Kristine Melloy, Prin. Priests 1; Sisters 2; Lay Teachers 17; Students 750; Total Staff 29.

DeLaSalle High School, Christian Brothers, One DeLaSalle Dr., 55401. Tel: 612-676-7600; Fax: 612-676-7691. Email: principal@delasalle.com. Web: www.delasalle.com. Bro. Michael Collins, F.S.C., Pres.; Barry C. Lieske, Prin. Brothers 3; Sisters 1; Lay Teachers 36; Students 660.

Totino-Grace High School, 1350 Gardena Ave., N.E., Fridley, 55432-5899. Tel: 763-571-9116; Fax: 763-571-9118. Email: michels@totinograce.org. Web: www.totinograce.org. Bro. Milton Barker, F.S.C., Pres.; Julie Michels, Prin.; Christie Burke, Librarian. Brothers 1; Lay Teachers 63; Students 920; Total Staff 130.

FARIBAULT. *Bethlehem Academy*, (Grades 7-12), 55021. Tel: 507-334-3948; Fax: 507-334-3949. Email: rthibault@bacards.pvt.k12.mn.us. Web: www.bacards.pvt.k12.mn.us. Ron Thibault, Prin. Lay Teachers 24; Students 255; Total Staff 38.

MAPLEWOOD. *Hill-Murray School*, (Grades 7-12), 2625 Larpenteur Ave. E., 55109-5098. Tel: 651-777-1376; Fax: 651-748-2444. Email: jpeschges@hill-murray.org. Web: www.hill-murray.org. Joseph M. Peschges, Pres.; Susan Paul, Prin.; Jane Rolnick, Librarian. Lay Teachers 74; Students 910; Total Staff 120.

MENDOTA HEIGHTS. *Convent of the Visitation School* (1873) (Grades PreK-12), 2455 Visitation Dr., 55120. Tel: 651-683-1700; Fax: 651-454-7144. Email: phealy@vischool.org. Web: www.visitation.net. Dr. Dawn Nichols, Head of School; Katie Owens, Dir. Admissions; Michelle Mechtel, Prin. Lower School; Curt Zander, Prin. Middle School; Renee Genereux, Prin. Upper School; Tracy Joyce, Librarian Lower School; Harriet Spira, Librarian Middle & Upper School. Grades P-6 are co-ed classes. Day School for Girls grades 7-12. Sisters 2; Lay Teachers 48; Total Faculty 50; Students 570; Total Staff 69.

RICHFIELD. *Academy of Holy Angels*, 6600 Nicollet Ave. S., 55423-2498. Tel: 612-798-2600; Fax: 612-798-2610. Email: jreilly@academyofholyangels.org. Web: www.academyofholyangels.org. Dr. Jill M. Reilly, Pres.; Heidi Foley, Prin.; Sheila Brennan, Media Dir. Priests 1; Lay Teachers 58; Students 764; Total Staff 154; Faculty 59.

ST. LOUIS PARK. *Benilde-St. Margaret's School* (1907) 2501 Hwy. 100 S., 55416. Tel: 952-927-4176; Fax: 952-920-8889. Web: www.bsm-online.org. Dr. Bob Tift, Pres.; Dr. Sue Skinner, Prin.; Mary Andersen, Asst. Prin.; Lynn Bottge, Librarian. Priests 1; Sisters 1; Lay Teachers 100; Students 1,203; Total Staff 142.

VICTORIA. *Holy Family Catholic High School* (2000) 8101 Kochia Ln., 55386. Tel: 952-443-4659; Fax: 952-443-1822. Email: communications@hfchs.org. Web: www.hfchs.org. Barbara Burke, Chm.; Scott Lutz, Vice Chm.; Mike Zunwinkle, Sec.; Jim Hamburge, Pres.; Kathleen Brown, Prin.; Ann Carstens, Librarian. Lay Teachers 49; Students 595; Total Staff 69.

[F] ELEMENTARY SCHOOLS, PRIVATE

MINNEAPOLIS. **San Miguel Middle School of Minneapolis* (2000) (Grades 6-8), 3800 Pleasant Ave. S., 55409-1229. Tel: 612-870-1109; Fax: 612-870-1224. Email: sanmiguel-mpls@hutman.net. Web: www.sanmiguel-mpls.org. Sr. Mary Willette, S.S.N.D., Prin.; Benjamin Murray, Pres. Sisters 1; Lay Teachers 8; Students 60; Total Staff 14.

[G] ELEMENTARY SCHOOLS, CONSOLIDATED, PAROCHIAL

ST. PAUL. *Highland Catholic School*, (Grades K-8), 2017 Bohland Ave., 55116. Tel: 651-690-2477; Fax: 651-699-1869. Email: jschmidt@highlandcatholic.org. Web: www.highlandcatholic.org. Jane Schmidt, Prin.; Helen Stasson, Librarian. Serving the parishes of Lumen Christi Catholic Community. Lay Teachers 30; Students 415; Total Staff 52.

Maternity of Mary/St. Andrew School (1953) (Grades PreSchool-8), 592 Arlington Ave. W., 55117. Tel: 651-489-1459; Fax: 651-489-3560. Email: principal@mnsaschool.org. Web: www.mmsaschool.org. Melissa Dan, Prin.; Beth Timmerman, Librarian. Serving the parishes of Maternity of Mary and St. Andrew. Sisters 1; Lay Teachers 18; Students 275; Total Staff 25.

MINNEAPOLIS. *Pope John Paul II Catholic School*, (Grades K-8), 1630 Fourth St, N.E., 55413. Tel: 612-789-8851; Fax: 612-789-8773. Web: www.popejohnpaul2school.org. Debra King, Prin. Serving the parishes of St. Cyril & Methodius, Holy Cross, St. Anthony, All Saints, Our Lady of Lourdes, St. Hedwig, St. Clement, St. Boniface, St. Maron, Our Lady of Mt. Carmel and St. Lawrence. Lay Teachers 8; Students 90; Total Staff 19.

Risen Christ Catholic School (1993) (Grades K-8), 1120 E. 37th St., 55407. Tel: 612-822-5329; Fax: 612-729-2336. Email: hdahlman@risenchristschool.org. Web: risenchristschool.org. Helen Dahlman, Pres.; Liz Ramsey, Prin.; Fran Russcione Murnane, Dir. Devel. Founded by the parishes of Holy Name, Holy Rosary, Incarnation, St. Albert the Great and St. Stephen. Lay Teachers 20; Students 321; Total Staff 38.

EAGAN. *Faithful Shepherd Catholic School*, (Grades K-8), 3355 Columbia Dr., 55121. Tel: 651-406-4747; Fax: 651-406-4743. Email: info@fscsmn.org. Web: www.fscsmn.org. Revs. Joseph G. Gallatin; Charles V. Lachowitzer, Canonical Admin.; William A. Murtaugh; John Boone, Prin.; Molly Conway, Librarian. Serving the parishes of St. Peter, St. John Neumann and St. Thomas Becket. Lay Teachers 35; Total Staff 55; Total Enrollment 540.

FARIBAULT. *Divine Mercy Catholic School*, (Grades PreK-6), 15 S.W. Third Ave., 55021. Tel: 507-334-7706; Fax: 507-332-2669. Email: bseidel@divinemercycatholics.org. Web: www.divinemercycatholics.org. Mr. Robert Seidel, Prin. Serving the parish of Divine Mercy Catholic Church. Lay Teachers 20; Students 329; Total Staff 34.

HASTINGS. *St. Elizabeth Ann Seton School*, (Grades PreK-8), 600 Tyler St., 55033. Tel: 651-437-3098; Fax: 651-438-3377. Web: http://schoolweb.seasparish.org. Rita Humbert, Prin. Lay Teachers 25; Students 299; Total Staff 41.

St. Elizabeth Ann Seton Early Childhood Campus, 2035 15th St. W., 55033. Tel: 651-438-3223.

RICHFIELD. *Blessed Trinity Catholic School of Richfield, Minnesota* (1994) (Grades PreK-8), 6720 Nicollet Ave., 55423. Tel: 612-866-5200; Fax: 612-767-2191. Email: kerrs@btcsmn.org. Web: www.btcsmn.org. Sue Kerr, Prin. Serving the parishes of Assumption, St. Peter's and St. Richard's. Lay Teachers 21; Students 370; Total Staff 48.

SHAKOPEE. *Shakopee Area Catholic Education Consolidation, Inc.* (1895) (Grades PreK-8), 2700 17th Ave. E., 55379. Tel: 952-445-3387; Fax: 952-445-7256. Email: dlee@sacsschools.org. Web: www.sacsschools.org. Diane M. Lee, CEC Admin.; Scott Breimhorst, Prin.; Joellen Marx, Dean; Sandy Greening, Librarian. Serving the parishes of St. Mark, St. Mary, St. Mary of the Purification. Lay Teachers 45; Students 850; Total Staff 83.

STILLWATER. *St. Croix Catholic School*, (Grades PreSchool-8), 621 S. Third St., 55082. Tel: 651-439-5581; Fax: 651-439-8360. Email: cepperly@stccs.com. Web: www.stcroixcatholic.com. Rev. Michael J. Miller, Canonical Admin.; Cressy Epperly, Prin.; Jenny Koenning, Librarian. Serving the parishes of St. Charles, Bayport; St. Mary, Stillwater; St. Michael, Stillwater. Sisters 4; Lay Teachers 25; Students 450; Total Staff 34.

WEBSTER. *Holy Cross Catholic School*, (Grades PreSchool-8), 6100 37th St. W., 55088. Tel: 952-652-6100; Fax: 952-652-6102. Email: lisar@holycrossschool.net. Web: www.holycrossschool.net. Lisa Reicherlt, Prin. Serving the parishes of Lonsdale, New Market and Veseli. Lay Teachers 15; Students 220; Total Staff 30.

[H] GENERAL HOSPITALS

ST. PAUL. **HealthEast St. Joseph's Hospital* (1853) 45 W. 10th St., 55102. Tel: 651-232-4144; Fax: 651-232-3518. Email: sjcriger@healtheast.org. Sara Criger, CEO & Vice Pres.; Revs. Stephen J. LaCanne, M.Div., N.A.C.C., Dir., Spiritual Care. Tel: 651-232-3060; Fax: 651-232-4155; Jonathan Fischer, O.S.B. Priests 2; Bed Capacity 401; Lay Staff 1,216; Total Staff 1,600; Total Assisted 13,936.

HASTINGS. *Regina Medical Center*, 1175 Nininger Rd., 55033. Tel: 651-480-4100; Fax: 651-480-4212. Email: kochendorferp@reginamedical.org. Web: www.reginamedical.org. Mark D. Wilson, CEO; Rev. Robert J. Altier, Chap.; Sr. LaVonne Schackman; Mary Salm, Dir. Pastoral Care; Joanne Peters, Contact. A part of Regina Healthcare. Other Sister Personnel 1; Patients Assisted Annually 46,255; Total Staff 463; Bed Capacity 57.

NEW PRAGUE. *Queen of Peace Hospital* (1952) 301 Second St., N.E., 56071. Tel: 952-758-4431; Fax: 952-758-2166. Email: info@qofp.org. Web: www.queenofpeacehospital.com. Mary Klimp, CEO & Admin.; Mary Jean Horstmann, Chap.; Marla Mayer, Public Rels. Dir. Sisters 2; Nurses 97; Bed Capacity 25; Patients Assisted Annually 51,683; Lay Staff 382; Total Staff 384.

SHAKOPEE. *St. Francis Regional Medical Center* (1938) 1455 St. Francis Ave., 55379-3380. Tel: 952-428-2002; Fax: 952-428-2656. Email: diana.robertson@allina.com. Web: www.stfrancis-shakopee.com. Mike Baumgartner, M.S.A., CEO & Pres.; Diana Robertson, Chap. & Mgr. Spiritual Care Dept. Sponsored by Sisters of St. Benedict, Duluth, MN. Nurses 272; Bed Capacity 93; Patients Assisted Annually 117,218; Total Staff 809.

[I] SPECIAL HOSPITALS AND SANATORIA FOR INVALIDS

ST. PAUL. *Our Lady of Good Counsel Home* (1941) 2076 St. Anthony Ave., 55104-5096. Tel: 651-646-2797; Fax: 651-646-7884. Web: www.ourladyhome.org; www.franciscancare.org. Franciscan Health Community Nursing Sisters 2; Bed Capacity 40; Patients Assisted Annually 173; Total Staff 40.

[J] HOMES FOR AGED

ST. PAUL. *Bethany Convent for Retired Sisters*, 1870 Randolph, 55105. Tel: 651-696-2500; Fax: 651-696-2501. Email: bcarlson@csjstpaul.org. Sisters Lillian Waldera, C.S.J., M.A., Community Living Coord.; George Ann Bohl, C.S.J., B.A., Asst. Community Living Coord.; Kevin Bopp, C.S.J., Assoc. Community Living Coord. Sisters of St. Joseph of Carondelet, St. Paul Province. Bed Capacity 160; Lay Staff 120; Total in Residence 100.

Franciscan Health Community (1936) 1925 Norfolk Ave., 55116. Tel: 651-696-8400; Fax: 651-696-8404. Email: ceo@fhcare.org. , Web: www.franciscancare.org. Joseph Stanislav, Pres. & CEO. Aged Residents 298; Bed Capacity 310; Total Assisted Annually 521; Total Staff 170.

Good Shepherd Care Center, Inc., 324 Johnson Pkwy., 55106. Tel: 651-774-4000; Fax: 651-774-9641. Mary Roy, Admin. & CEO; Shuji Moriichi, Chap. Bed Capacity 126; Patients Assisted Annually 350; Lay Staff 184; Total Staff 185; Clergy 1.

Holy Family Residence, 330 Exchange St. S., 55102. Tel: 651-227-0336; Fax: 651-227-7321. Email: msstpaul@littlesistersofthepoor.org. Web: www.littlesistersofthepoor.org. Sr. Theresa Robertson, Supr., Admin. & Pres. Little Sisters of the Poor 13; Aged Residents 72; Apartments 32; Bed Capacity 74; Total Staff (All Facilities) 106; Total Assisted Annually 116.

MINNEAPOLIS. *Benedictine Health Center of Minneapolis*, 618 E. 17th St, 55404. Tel: 612-879-2800. Mr. David Brennan, Admin. & CEO.

HASTINGS. *Regina Retirement Center*, 1175 Nininger Rd., 55033. Tel: 651-480-4100; Fax: 651-480-4212. Email: kochendorferp@reginamedical.org. Web: www.reginamedical.org. Rev. Robert J. Altier, Resident Chap. Total Assisted Annually 303; Total Staff 159; Bed Capacity 190.

Regina Medical Center Tel: 651-480-4100; Fax: 651-480-4212. A part of Regina Healthcare. Number under care 181; Nursing Care 61; Assisted Living 129; Total Staff 159.

SHAKOPEE. *St. Gertrude's Health and Rehabilitation Center*, 1850 Sarazin St., 55379. Tel: 952-233-4400; Fax: 952-233-4476. Lee Larson, Admin.; Bill Wermerskirchen, Chairperson; Kevin Rymanowski, Treas. Bed Capacity 115; Total Staff 183; Total Assisted Annually 26,500.

The Gardens at St. Gertrudes Assisted Living

[K] MONASTERIES AND RESIDENCES OF PRIESTS AND BROTHERS

ST. PAUL. *Congregation of the Sons of the Immaculate Conception*, 261 8th St. E., 55101. Tel: 651-222-2619; Fax: 651-224-1190. Revs. Biju Mathew, C.F.I.C., Supr. & Pastor; Antony Skaria, C.F.I.C., Chap.; Benny Mekkatt Varghese, C.F.I.C., Chap.

Franciscan Brothers of Peace, Queen of Peace Friary, 1289 Lafond Ave., 55104-2035. Tel: 651-646-8586; Fax: 651-646-9083. Web: www.brothersofpeace.org. Bros. Paul O'Donnell, F.B.P., Guardian Overall; Anthony Sweere, F.B.P.; Conrad Richardson, F.B.P., Vocation Dir.; Joseph Katzmarek, F.B.P., QPF House Guardian, Vicar; John Mary Kaspari, F.B.P.; Pio King, F.B.P.; Maximilian Connolly, F.B.P., Novice; James Voeller, F.B.P.; Seraphim Wirth, F.B.P.

Oblate Residence, 104 N. Mississippi River Blvd., 55104-2374. Tel: 651-645-3560; Fax: 651-645-3704. Bro. Anthony Szklarski, O.M.I., Dir. of House In Res. Revs. Robert Allie, O.M.I.; Ronald Harrer, O.M.I.; Joseph Menker, O.M.I.; Robert Morin, O.M.I.; John E. Pilaczynski, O.M.I.

MINNEAPOLIS. *St. Albert the Great Priory*, 2833 32nd Ave. S., 55406. Tel: 612-724-3644; Fax: 612-724-5057. Email: dommpls@comcast.net. Order of Preachers (Dominicans). Province of St. Albert the Great. Total in Residence 6.

St. Bridget Friary, 3811 Emerson Ave. N., 55412-2038. Tel: 612-588-9078; Fax: 612-529-8451. Web: www.franciscanfriarstor.com. Bros. John Kerr, T.O.R., Pastoral Min., St. Bridget Parish; David Liedl, T.O.R., Formation Dir., Local Min., Prov. Councilor; Rev. Patrick Foley, T.O.R., Vocation Dir.; Bro. Jeffrey Wilson, T.O.R. Third Order Regular of St. Francis, Province of the Immaculate Conception. Priests 1; Brothers 3.

St. Gerard Friary (1990) 9600 Regent Ave. N., Brooklyn Park, 55443-1499. Tel: 763-425-7659. Very Rev. Giles A. Schinelli, T.O.R., S.T.B., B.A., M.A.S.T.; Rev. Terrence Smith, T.O.R.

Paulist Fathers, 1203 5th St., S.E., 55414. Tel: 612-331-7941; Fax: 612-378-1771. Email: parish@umncatholic.org. Web: www.umncatholic.org. Revs. Patrick Johnson, C.S.P., Pastor & Dir.; James Brucz, C.S.P.; Robert J. O'Donnell; Richard Chilson, C.S.P. Total in Residence 4.

BLOOMINGTON. *Maryknoll Fathers and Brothers, Catholic Foreign Mission Society of America* (1911) P.O. Box 20626, 55420. Tel: 952-884-1024; Fax: 952-884-1371. Email: minneapolis@maryknoll.org. Web: www.maryknoll.org. Mr. Gregory Darr, Dir.; Rev. Edward M. Doughtery, Supr. Gen.; Bette Jane Baxter.

BROOKLYN CENTER. *Redemptorist Fathers of Hennepin County*, 7025 Halifax Ave. N., 55429-1394. Tel: 763-561-5100; Fax: 763-561-0336. Rev. William Bueche, C.Ss.R., Religious Supr.

LAKE ELMO. *Carmelite Hermitage of the Blessed Virgin Mary* (1987) 8249 De Montreville Tr. N., 55042-9545. Tel: 651-779-7351; Fax: 651-779-7351. Email: carmelus@earthlink.net. Web: www.decorcarmeli.com. Revs. Patrick Peter Peach, O.Carm.; John M. Burns, O.Carm., Prior; Joseph V. Vaccaro, O.Carm. Carmel of the Blessed Virgin Mary. Priests 3; Brothers 4.

[L] CONVENTS AND RESIDENCES FOR SISTERS

ST. PAUL. *Contemplative Sisters of the Good Shepherd*, 5104 Hodgson Rd., 55126-1229. Tel: 651-482-5240; Fax: 651-482-5242. Email: cgsstpaul@usfamily.net. Sr. Beverly Hedgecoth, Coord. Sisters 11.

Convent of the Good Shepherd, 5100 Hodgson Rd., 55126-1297. Tel: 651-484-0221; Fax: 651-486-1611. Email: vocations@goodshepherdsisters.org. Web: www.goodshepherdsisters.org. Sr. Bernadette Faulhaber, R.G.S., Coord. Sisters of the Good Shepherd 26. *Contemplative Sisters of the Good Shepherd*, 5104 Hodgson Rd., 55126-1229. Tel: 651-482-5240; Fax: 651-486-1600. Sisters 4.

Franciscan Sisters of St. Paul (1863) Franciscan Regional Center, 1388 Prior Ave. S., 55116. Tel: 651-690-1501; Fax: 651-690-2509. Email: spfranci@askmotherrose.org. Web: www.askmotherrose.org. Sr. Mary Lucy Scheffler, O.S.F., Regl. Dir. Sisters 10.

St. Mary's Mission House (1894) 265 Century Ave., 55125. Tel: 651-738-9704; Fax: 651-738-9704. Email: sspcdelegateoffice@usfamily.net. Web: www.clavermissionarysisters.org. Sr. Maria Moryl, S.S.P.C., Supr. Missionary Sisters of St. Peter Claver. Sisters 7.

Monastery of the Visitation (1873) 2455 Visitation Dr., Mendota Heights, 55120. Tel: 651-683-1700; Fax: 651-454-0602. Sisters Mary Denise Villaume, V.H.M., Supr.; Brigid Marie Keefe, Sec. Visitation Nuns 9.

St. Paul's Monastery, 2675 Benet Rd., 55109-5097. Tel: 651-777-8181; Fax: 651-777-4442. Email: lucia@stpaulsmonastery.org. Web: www.osb.org/spm. Sisters Lucia Schwickerath, D.S.B., Prioress; Annette Esboldt, D.S.B., Subprioress. Benedictine Sisters of Pontifical Jurisdiction. Sisters 52.

Sisters of St. Joseph of Carondelet (1851) 1884 Randolph Ave., 55105-1700. Tel: 651-690-7000; Fax: 651-690-7039. Web: www.csjstpaul.org. Sisters of Province 285; Total Staff 186.

Province Leadership Team: Carondelet Center; St. Joseph School of Music; Editorial Development Associates; Good Ground Press; Vineyard; St. Mary's Health Clinics; Youth & Family Center, Inc.; Sisters of St. Joseph of Carondelet Ministries Foundation, St. Paul Province; Learning in Style; Women at the Well; Adult Literacy; The College of St. Catherine; Minnesota Center for Health Care Ethics; Wisdom Ways: A Resource Center for Spirituality; St. Joseph Worker Program; Sarah's, an Oasis for Women; Celeste's Dream; Dwelling in the Woods; C.S.J. Ministry Collaborative. Sisters Katherine Rossini, C.S.J.; Margaret Gillespie, C.S.J.; Jean Wincek, C.S.J.

MINNEAPOLIS. *St. Clare's Monastery of the Infant Jesus*, 8650 Russell Ave. S., 55431-1998. Tel: 952-881-4766. Email: fgosc@juno.com. Web: www.poorclareminneapolis.org. Sr. Frances Getchell, O.S.C., Abbess. Franciscan Poor Clare Nuns. Professed Nuns 11.

Visitation Monastery of Minneapolis, 1527 Fremont Ave. N., 55411. Tel: 612-521-6113; Fax: 612-521-4020. Email: vmonastery@aol.com. Web: www.visitationmonasteryminneapolis.org. Sr. Karen Mohan, V.H.M., Supr. Sisters 7.

DEEPHAVEN. *Franciscan Clarist Congregation, F.C.C.*, Vimala Province, Convent of St. Therese House, 17931 Minnetonka Blvd., 55391-3322. Tel: 952-473-4771. Email: srtresamargret@yahoo.com. Sr. Tresa Margret, Prin. & Regl. Supr. Total in Residence 12.

LAKE ELMO. *Carmel of Our Lady of Divine Providence* (1952) 8251 De Montreville Tr. N., 55042-9547. Tel: 651-777-3882. Sr. Marie of the Incarnation, O.C.D., Prioress; Rev. John M. Burns, O.Carm., Chap. Discalced Carmelite Nuns. Professed 12; Novices 1.

[M] SECULAR INSTITUTES

ST. PAUL. *Missionaries of the Kingship of Christ*, 8951 Thomas Ln., Woodbury, 55125. Tel: 651-501-3640. Email: woodburyjane@aol.com. Web:

www.simrc.org. Secular Institute of Pontifical Right for women and men founded in Italy in 1919.

[N] RETREAT HOUSES AND CENTERS OF SPIRITUALITY

ST. PAUL. *Benedictine Center - St. Paul's Monastery*, 2675 E. Larpenteur Ave., 55109. Tel: 651-777-7251; Fax: 651-773-5124. Email: benedictinecenter@stpaulsmonastery.org. Web: www.stpaulsmonastery.org. Victor Klimoski, Dir. Total Staff 5.

Loyola, 389 N. Oxford St., 55104. Tel: 651-641-0008; Fax: 651-641-0554. Email: loyolasrr.@comcast.net. Web: www.loyolaspiritualitycenter.org. Tom Allen, Spiritual Dir.; David Rothstein, Spiritual Dir.; Sheila Laughton, Spiritual Dir.; Barbara Leonard, Spiritual Dir.; Kay VanderVort, M.A., Spiritual Dir.; Sisters Joanne Dehmer, S.S.N.D., M.A., Spiritual Dir.; Elizabeth Kerwin, C.S.J., Spiritual Dir. Total Staff 8.

Maryhill (1790) 1988 Summit Ave., 55105. Tel: 651-696-2970; Fax: 651-696-1190. Email: maryhill1988@aol.com. Web: www.dhmna.org. Daughters of the Heart of Mary 6; Total in Residence 1; Total Staff 1.

BUFFALO. *Christ the King Retreat Center* (1952) 621 First Ave. S., 55313. Tel: 763-682-1394; Fax: 763-682-3453. Email: christtheking@kingshouse.com. Web: www.kingshouse.com. Revs. Aloysius Svobodny, O.M.I.; Raymond R. Kirtz, O.M.I.; Louis Studer, O.M.I., Dir.; James Deegan, O.M.I.; Raymond A. Prybis, O.M.I., Bus. Mgr.; Lon Konold, O.M.I.; Gari Ruttenberg, O.M.I.; Bro. Daniel Bozek, O.M.I. Priests 7; Brothers 1; Total in Residence 8; Lay Staff 31; Total Staff 39.

FRONTENAC. *Villa Maria Retreat and Conference Center*, 29847 County 2 Blvd., 55026. Tel: 651-345-4582; Fax: 651-345-3457. Email: villamaria_retreats@yahoo.com. Web: villamariaretreats.org. Sr. Rose Elsbernd, F.S.P.A., Dir. Total Served Annually 4,598.

LAKE ELMO. *Jesuit Retreat House* (1948) 8243 Demontreville Tr. N., 55042-9546. Tel: 651-777-1311; Fax: 651-777-1312. Revs. Edward S. Sthokal, S.J., Asst.; Patrick M. McCorkell, S.J., Office Dir. Total in Residence 2; Total Staff 10.

MARINE ON ST. CROIX. *Christian Brothers Retreat Center*, 15525 St. Croix Tr. N., 55047. Tel: 651-433-2486; Fax: 651-433-5755. Email: dunrovin@dunrovin.org. Web: www.dunrovin.org. Jerome Meeds, Pres. Total in Residence 6; Total Staff 2; Total Assisted 65.

PRIOR LAKE. *Franciscan Retreats* (1956) 16385 Saint Francis Ln., 55372. Tel: 952-447-2182; Fax: 952-447-2170. Email: director@franciscanretreats.net. Web: www.franciscanretreats.net. Revs. Steven McMichael, O.F.M.Conv., Guardian; James Van Dorn, O.F.M.Conv., Assoc. Dir.; Howard Hansen, O.F.M.Conv., Staff; Bro. Bob Roddy, O.F.M.Conv., Retreat Dir. Priests 3; Brothers 1; Lay Staff 6; Staff 9; People Served 1,700.

[O] HOMES FOR DISABLED

ST. PAUL. *Our House of Minnesota, Inc. I* (1975) 1846 Dayton Ave., 55104. Tel: 651-644-6650; Fax: 651-646-1104. Bed Capacity 6; Staff 19; Mentally Handicapped Adults 6; Total Assisted 6.
Office: Tel: 615-646-1104; Fax: 615-646-1104. Dennis Holman, Admin.

Our House of Minnesota, Inc. II (1975) 1846 Portland, 55104. Tel: 651-644-2411; Fax: 651-646-1104. Bed Capacity 6; Staff 19; Mentally Handicapped Adults 6; Total Assisted Annually 6.
Office: Tel: 615-646-1104; Fax: 615-646-1104. Dennis Holman, Admin.

WEST ST. PAUL. *Guild Incorporated* (1990) 130 S. Wabasha St., Ste. 90, Saint Paul, 55107. Tel: 651-450-2220; Fax: 651-450-2221. Email: info@guildincorporated.org. Web: www.guildincorporated.org. Formed by the Guild of Catholic Women. Guild Incorporated provides an array of recovery oriented behavioral health & human services for individuals with serious and persistent mental illness. Total Assisted Annually 1,420; Total Staff 121.

[P] ASSOCIATIONS OF THE FAITHFUL

ST. PAUL. *The Companions of Christ* (1992) 2137 Marshall Ave., 55104. Tel: 651-642-5933. Email: contact@companionsofchrist.org. Web: www.CompanionsOfChrist.org. Rev. Jon Vander Ploeg, Supr. Total in Residence 11.

Franciscan Brothers of Peace, Queen of Peace Friary, 1289 Lafond Ave., 55104-2035. Tel: 651-646-8586; Fax: 651-646-9083. Email: franciscan@brothersofpeace.org. Web: www.brothersofpeace.org. Bros. Paul O'Donnell, F.B.P., Guardian Overall; Anthony Sweere, F.B.P.; Joseph Katzmarek, F.B.P., Vicar; Conrad Richardson, F.B.P., Vocation Dir.; James Voeller, F.B.P.; John Mary Kaspari, F.B.P.; Pio King, F.B.P.; Seraphim Wirth, F.B.P.; Maximilian Connolly, F.B.P. Total in Residence 8; Total Staff 1.

WEST ST. PAUL. *Community of Christ the Redeemer*, 110 Crusader Ave. W., 55118. Tel: 651-451-6114; Fax: 651-453-0810. Email: info@ccredeemer.org. Web: www.ccredeemer.org. Dr. James C. Kolar, Pres.

[Q] CAMPS AND COMMUNITY CENTERS

MCGREGOR. *Catholic Youth Camps, Inc.*, Administrative Offices: 2131 Fairview Ave. N., #200, Roseville, 55113. Tel: 651-636-1645. Email: office@cycamp.org. Web: www.cycamp.org. Camp location: 19590 520th Ln., 55760. Tel: 218-426-3383; Fax: 218-426-4675. Natalie King, Exec. Dir.; Rev. Robert C. Nygaard, Pres., Bd. Dirs. (Retired); John Breon, Chm. & Vice Pres., Bd. Dirs. Total Assisted 650; Total Staff 20.

[R] NEWMAN CENTERS

MINNEAPOLIS. *Newman Center at St. Lawrence* 1203 5th St., S.E., 55414. Tel: 612-331-7941; Fax: 612-378-1771. Email: parish@umncatholic.org. Web: www.umncatholic.org. Revs. Patrick Johnson, C.S.P.; James Brucz, C.S.P.; Robert J. O'Donnell. Total Staff 3.

[S] MISCELLANEOUS LISTINGS

ST. PAUL. **Catholic Community Foundation*, One Water St. W., Ste. 200, Saint Paul, 55107. Tel: 651-389-0300; Fax: 651-389-0650. Email: info@ccf-mn.org. Web: www.catholiccommunityfoundation.org. Dr. Marilou Eldred, Pres.

Christian Brothers Youth Home (1983) 1540 Lincoln Ave., 55105. Tel: 651-699-0736. Bro. Michael Lee Anderson, F.S.C., Dir.; Mr. Bob Paradise, Pres. Brothers 1; Bed Capacity 5; Total Assisted 4; Total Staff 1.

Friends of Catholic Urban Schools (FOCUS), 375 N. Oxford St., 55104. Tel: 651-646-1797; Fax: 651-647-1797. Web: www.focustwincities.org. Thomas McCarver, Dir.

Growing in Faith Capital Campaign, 226 Summit Ave., 55102. Tel: 651-290-1610; Fax: 651-290-1609.

St. Mary's Health Clinics (1992) 1884 Randolph Ave., 55105-1700. Tel: 651-690-7020; Fax: 651-690-7075. Email: bdickie@stmarysclinics.org. Web: www.stmaryshealthclinics.org. Barbara L. Dickie, Exec. Dir. Neighborhbood Clinics 9; Park Nicollet Clinics 11; Patients Assisted Annually 11,417; Total Staff 8; Lay Staff 6; Sisters 2.

Minnesota Catholic Conference, 475 University Ave. W., Ste. B, 55103. Tel: 651-227-8777; Fax: 651-227-2675. Email: info@mncc.org. Web: www.mncc.org. Christopher Leifeld, Exec. Dir.; Dr. Peter A. Noll, Dir. Educ.; Alexandra Fitzsimmons Esq., Policy Dir. The M.C.C. is a Minnesota Corporation, the purpose of which is to promote the general welfare of the people of the State of Minnesota. All Catholic Bishops of the State of Minnesota constitute Ex Officio the Board of Directors. Total Staff 5.

**Minnesota Catholic Education Association*, 475 University Ave., 55103-1996. Tel: 651-227-8777; Fax: 651-227-2675. Email: pnoll@mncc.org. Web: www.mncc.org. Dr. Peter Noll, Exec. Dir.

Nativity of Our Lord Endowment Fund, 1900 Wellesley Ave., 55105. Tel: 651-696-5401; Fax: 651-696-5458. Email: info@nativity-mn.org. Web: www.nativity-mn.org. Laura Barr, Admin. Total Assisted 5,000; Total Staff (Finance Council) 7.

Oblate Media and Communication Corporation, 104 N. Mississippi River Blvd., 55104. Tel: 651-645-3560. Rev. Louis Lougen, Pres. Oblates of Mary Immaculate, U.S. Province.

Sisters of St. Joseph of Carondelet Ministries Foundation, St. Paul Province, 1884 Randolph Ave., 55105. Tel: 651-690-7026; Fax: 651-690-7039. Email: ioneill@csjstpaul.org. Web: www.ministriesfoundation.com. Sr. Irene O'Neill, C.S.J., Exec. Dir.

WomanWell, 1784 La Crosse Ave., 55119-4808. Tel: 651-739-7953; Fax: 651-739-7475. Email: seeking@WomanWell.org. Web: www.womanwell.org. Sr. Delmarie Gibney, F.S.P.A., Dir. Sisters 2; Bed Capacity 14; Lay Staff 2; Total Staff 4; Total Assisted 3,000.

MINNEAPOLIS. *Catholic Eldercare, Inc.* (1982) 817 Main St., N.E., 55413. Tel: 612-379-1370; Fax: 612-362-2486. Email: mshasky@catholiceldercare.org. Web: www.catholiceldercare.org. Dan Johnson, Pres. & CEO. Total Assisted 439; Total Staff 350.

Skilled Nursing Facility Tel: 612-379-1370; Fax: 612-379-2486. Web: www.catholiceldercare.org. Sisters 5; Bed Capacity 150; Lay Staff 220; Total Staff 225; Total Assisted 375.

Main Street Lodge Assisted Living, 909 Main St., N.E., 55413. Tel: 612-362-2450; Fax: 612-362-2449. Web: www.catholiceldercare.org. Units 50; Lay Staff 20; Total Staff 20; Total Assisted 64.

Catholic Eldercare By Day Tel: 612-362-2405; Fax: 612-362-2401. Web: www.catholiceldercare.org. Assisted 80; Lay Staff 16; Staff 10.

Catholic Eldercare, Inc., 1101 on Main Apartments, 1101 Main St., NE, 55413. Tel: 612-378-8814; Fax: 612-378-4725. Web: www.1101onmain.com. Units 45.

River Village East Assisted Living, 2919 Randolph St. N.E., 55418. Tel: 612-605-2500; Fax: 612-605-2404. Web: www.catholiceldercare.org. Units 71; Staff 25; Total Assisted 80.

Cristo Rey Corporate Internship Program - Twin Cities, 2924 - 4th Ave. S., 55408. Tel: 612-545-9703. Stephen J. Schulz, Exec. Dir.; Rev. David Haschka, S.J., Pres.

The Islander Foundation, 1 De La Salle Dr., 55401. Tel: 612-676-7603. David Medernach, Treas.

Queen Anne Communities, 2627 Queen Ave., 55411. Tel: 612-529-0503; Fax: 612-529-5860. Rev. Khanh Hai Nguyen, Pres.

Safe Place for Newborns, Office: 120 S. 6th St., Ste. 1150, 55402. Tel: 612-317-2895; 877-440-2229 24/7 Crisis Line; Fax: 612-317-2899. Email: safeplace@safeplacefornewborns.com. Web: www.safeplacefornewborns.com. P.O. Box 16550, Saint Paul, 55116. Laure L. Krupp, Exec. Dir.

Sagrado Corazon de Jesus, 2645 1st Ave., S., 55408. Tel: 612-874-7169; Fax: 612-870-0408. Email: sagradocorazonl@msn.net. Rev. Lawrence E. Hubbard, Pres.; Bradley Capouch, Vice Pres.; Hugo Artola, Sec.; Armando Blas Garcia, Treas.

Society of St. Vincent De Paul, Archdiocesan Council, 2939 12th Ave., S., 55407. Tel: 612-722-7882; Fax: 612-722-0667. Ed Koerner, Dir.

Twin Cities Catholic Alumni Club (1958) P.O. Box 581321, 55458-1321. Tel: 651-603-1412. Carl Berstrom, Club Pres. Members 75.

Youth and Family Center Inc. (1986) 4405 E. Lake St., 55406. Tel: 612-722-9612. Sisters Martha Merriman, C.S.J., Dir.; Betty Wurm, C.S.J., Dir. Counseling Center. Total Assisted 35; Total Staff 2.

HASTINGS. *Regina Foundation*, 1175 Nininger Rd., 55033. Tel: 651-480-4104; Fax: 651-480-4212. Email: kochendorferp@reginamedical.org. Web: www.reginamedical.org. Mark D. Wilson, Pres. & CEO; Pam Kochendorfer, Corp. Sec.

Regina Healthcare, Inc., 1175 Nininger Rd., 55033. Tel: 651-480-4104; Fax: 651-480-4212. Email: kochendorferp@reginamedical.org. Web: www.reginamedical.org. Mr. Stewart W. Laird, Pres./Chair; Pam Kochendorfer, Corp. Sec.

INVER GROVE HEIGHTS. *Catholic Finance Corporation* (2000) 5826 Blackshire Path, 55076. Tel: 651-389-1070; Fax: 651-389-1071. Email: info@catholicfinance.org. Web: www.catholicfinance.org. Michael P. Schaefer, Exec. Dir.; Amanda Ellefson, Mgr. Office Operations.

MAPLEWOOD. *The Hill-Murray Foundation*, 2625 Larpenteur Ave., E., 55109. Tel: 651-777-1376. Joseph M. Peschges, Pres.

Maple Tree: Monastery Childcare Center, 2625 Benet Rd., 55109. Tel: 651-770-0766. Email: jschlauch2@aol.com. Sisters Carol Rennie, O.S.B., Prioress - St. Paul Monastery; Jeron Osterfeld, Bd. Pres. Religious 4; Lay Staff 3; Bd. Members 7; Total Assisted 74; Total Staff 23.

To Encounter Christ of the Archdiocese of St. Paul-Minneapolis, Minnesota, Inc., (Twin Cities TEC): 1725 Kennard St., Ste. 201, 55109. Tel: 651-281-0085; Fax: 866-600-2748. Email: retreats@twincitiestec.org. Web: www.twincitiestec.org. Lisa Vang, Admin.; Angela Hunstiger, Devel. Officer; Nate Lamasgt, Prog. Dir. Total Assisted 2,500; Total Staff 3.

NEW PRAGUE. *First Avenue Properties of New Prague*, 215 Main St. E, 56071. Tel: 952-758-3920. David B. Bruzek, Pres.

OSSEO. *Benedictine Senior Living at Steeple Pointe*, 625 Central Ave., 55369. Tel: 763-425-4440; Fax: 763-391-0747. Email: bobbie.guidry@bhshealth.org. Roberta Guidry, Resident Svcs. Admin. Bedrooms 59; Lay Staff 37; Total Assisted 100.

SCANDIA. *The Brothers and Sisters of Penance of St. Francis*, 20939 Quadrant Ave. N., 55073. Tel: 651-433-2753. Bruce A. Fahey, Admin.; Michele L. Fahey, Admin.

STILLWATER. *St. Croix Valley Faith Formation*, 218 E. Willard St., 55082. Tel: 651-379-1274. Bob Collett, Interim Dir.

WEST ST. PAUL. *NET Ministries, Inc.*, 110 Crusader Ave. W., 55118-4427. Tel: 651-450-6833; Fax: 651-450-9984. Email: ministry@netusa.org. Web: www.netusa.org. Mr. Mark Berchem, Exec. Dir. Total Staff 30.

Saint Paul's Outreach, Inc., 110 Crusader Ave., W., 55118. Tel: 651-451-6114; Fax: 651-453-0810. Email: info@spoweb.org. Web: www.spoweb.org. Mr. Gordon C. DeMarais, Exec. Dir.; Very Rev. Peter A. Laird, M.A., M.Div., Bd. Pres.

RELIGIOUS INSTITUTES OF MEN REPRESENTED IN THE ARCHDIOCESE

For further details refer to the corresponding bracketed number in the Religious Institutes of Men or Women section.

[0200]—*Benedictine Monks* (St. John's Abbey)—O.S.B.
[0330]—*Brothers of the Christian Schools* (Midwest Prov.)—F.S.C.
[0470]—*The Capuchin Fathers* (Prov. of St. Joseph)—O.F.M.Cap.
[0270]—*Carmelite Fathers and Brothers*—O.Carm.
[]—*Carmelite Hermitage of the Blessed Virgin Mary*—O.Carm.
[]—*Carmelites of Mary Immaculate* (Sacred Heart Province); (Kerala, India)—C.M.I.
[]—*Congregation of the Mother Co-Redemptrix* (Carthage, MO)—C.M.C.
[]—*Congregation of the Sons of the Immaculate Conception* (Woodbridge, Ontario)—C.F.I.C.
[0480]—*Conventual Franciscans* (Prov. of Our Lady of Consolation)—O.F.M.Conv.
[0520]—*Franciscan Friars* (St. Louis); (Prov. of Sacred Heart)—O.F.M.
[0690]—*Jesuit Fathers and Brothers* (Wisconsin Prov.)—S.J.
[0780]—*Marist Fathers* (American Prov.)—S.M.
[0800]—*Maryknoll*—M.M.
[]—*Misioneros Oblatos de los Sagrados Corazones* (Ecuador)—O.C.C.S.S.
[]—*Oblates of Mary Immaculate* (Washington, DC)—O.M.I.
[]—*Order of Preachers* (Province of Poland)—O.P.
[0430]—*Order of Preachers (Dominicans)* (Prov. of St. Albert the Great)—O.P.
[1030]—*Paulist Fathers*—C.S.P.
[]—*Pro Ecclesia Sancta* (Peru)—P.E.S.
[1070]—*Redemptorist Fathers* (St. Louis Prov.)—C.SS.R.
[]—*Servants of the Holy Eucharist of the Blessed Virgin Mary* (Puerto Rico)—S.E.M.V.
[]—*Society of Christ* (Lombard, IL)—S.CH.
[1060]—*Society of the Precious Blood* (Cincinnati Prov.)—C.PP.S.
[0560]—*Third Order Regular of St. Francis* (Prov. of the Immaculate Conception)—T.O.R.
[]—*Vincentian Congregation* (India)—V.C.

RELIGIOUS INSTITUTES OF WOMEN REPRESENTED IN THE ARCHDIOCESE

[0230]—*Benedictine Sisters of Pontifical Jurisdiction* St. Paul, St. Joseph, Duluth, MN; Watertown, SD)—O.S.B.
[]—*Congregation of Our Lady of Sion* (Toronto, ON)—N.D.S.
[3710]—*Congregation of the Sisters of St. Agnes*—C.S.A.
[3832]—*Congregation of the Sisters of St. Joseph* (Created from merger of several C.S.J. Provinces)—C.S.J.
[1780]—*Congregation of the Sisters of the Third Order of St. Francis of Perpetual Adoration* (Eastern Region)—F.S.P.A.
[]—*Contemplative Sisters of the Good Shepherd*—C.G.S.
[0810]—*Daughters of the Heart of Mary*—D.H.M.
[0420]—*Discalced Carmelite Nuns*—O.C.D.
[1070-03]—*Dominican Sisters*—O.P.
[]—*Dominican Sisters Congregation of St. Cecilia* (Nashville, TN)
[]—*Franciscan Clarist Congregation* (Deephaven, MN)—F.C.C.
[1310]—*Franciscan Sisters of Little Falls, Minnesota*—O.S.F.
[1485]—*Franciscan Sisters of St. Paul, MN*—O.S.F.
[]—*Guadalupan Sisters* (Congregacion de Hermanas de La Salle); (Mexico)—H.G.S.
[]—*Immaculate Heart of Mary Mother of Christ* (Nigeria)—I.H.M.
[2575]—*Institute of the Sisters of Mercy of the Americas* (West/Midwest Community; Omaha, NE)—R.S.M.
[2340]—*Little Sisters of the Poor*—L.S.P.
[3990]—*Missionary Sisters of St. Peter Claver*—S.S.P.C.
[3760]—*Order of St. Clare*—O.S.C.
[2970]—*School Sisters of Notre Dame*—S.S.N.D.
[1680]—*Schools Sisters of St. Francis*—O.S.F.
[3590]—*Servants of Mary (Servite Sisters)*—O.S.M.
[]—*Sisters of Charity of our Lady, Mother of the Church* (Baltic, CT)—S.C.M.C.
[0520]—*Sisters of Charity of Our Lady, Mother of Mercy*—S.C.M.M.
[0430]—*Sisters of Charity of the Blessed Virgin Mary*—B.V.M.
[]—*Sisters of Providence of St. Mary-of-the-Woods* (Indiana)—S.P.
[1705]—*The Sisters of St. Francis of Assisi* (Democratic Republic of Congo)—S.S.F.A.T.
[1530]—*Sisters of St. Francis of the Congregation of Our Lady of Lourdes, Sylvania, Ohio*—O.S.F.
[1570]—*Sisters of St. Francis of the Holy Family* (Dubuque, IA)—O.S.F.
[3840]—*Sisters of St. Joseph of Carondelet*—C.S.J.
[3930]—*Sisters of St. Joseph of the Third Order of St. Francis*—S.S.J.-T.O.S.F.
[1830]—*The Sisters of the Good Shepherd*—R.G.S.
[]—*Sisters of the Living Word* (Arlington Heights, IL)—S.L.W.
[3320]—*Sisters of the Presentation of the B.V.M.* (Dubuque, IA; Aberdeen, SD)—P.B.V.M.
[1720]—*Sisters of the Third Order Regular of St. Francis of the Congregation of Our Lady of Lourdes* (Rochester, MN)—O.S.F.
[2150]—*Sisters, Servants of the Immaculate Heart of Mary* (Monroe, MI)—I.H.M.
[4110]—*Ursuline Nuns (Roman Union)*—O.S.U.
[4190]—*Visitation Nuns*—V.H.M.

ARCHDIOCESAN CEMETERIES

ST. PAUL. *Calvery*
The Catholic Cemeteries, 2105 Lexington Ave., S., Mendota Heights, 55120. Tel: 651-228-9991; Fax: 651-228-9995. Web: www.catholic-cemeteries.org. John Chevek, Dir.; Sharon Albertson, Dir.; Sr. Fran Donnelly, B.V.M., Dir.

MINNEAPOLIS. *St. Anthony & St. Mary*

MENDOTA HEIGHTS. *Resurrection*

NEW HOPE. *Assumption & Gethsemane*

PARISH CEMETERIES

SHAKOPEE. *Catholic Cemeteries of Shakapee, Minnesota, Inc.*, 350 S. Atwood St., 55379. Tel: 952-445-1229; Fax: 952-445-9639. A corporation formed by the Church of St. Mark and the Church of St. Mary, both of Shakopee, to consolidate separate cemeteries.

NECROLOGY

† Hessian, Rev. Msgr. Patrick J., (Retired)—Died 2009
† Murphy, Rev. Msgr. Terrance J., (Retired)—Died 2009
† Boller, Robert J., (Retired)—Died Nov. 9, 2009
† Conroy, Thomas J., (Retired)—Died March 12, 2009
† Grzeskowiak, Edward S., (Retired)—Died March 24, 2009
† Kubat, Alphonse M., (Retired)—Died 2009
† Vakoc, Timothy H.—Died June 20, 2009

An asterisk (*) denotes an organization that has established tax-exempt status directly with the IRS and is not covered by the USCCB Group Ruling.

Diocese of St. Petersburg

(Dioecesis Sancti Petri in Florida)

Most Reverend

ROBERT N. LYNCH

Fourth Bishop of St. Petersburg; ordained May 13, 1978; appointed Fourth Bishop of St. Petersburg December 5, 1995; consecrated and installed January 26, 1996. *Office: P.O. Box 40200, St. Petersburg, FL 33743-0200.*

PRO AMICIS SUIS

Pastoral Center: P.O. Box 40200, St. Petersburg, FL 33743-0200. Tel: 727-344-1611; Fax: 727-345-2143.

Web: www.dioceseofstpete.org

Email: communicate@dosp.org

ESTABLISHED JUNE 17, 1968.

Square Miles 3,177.

Comprises the Counties of Citrus, Hernando, Hillsborough, Pasco and Pinellas in the State of Florida.

For legal titles of parishes and diocesan institutions, consult the Pastoral Center.

STATISTICAL OVERVIEW

Personnel	
Bishop	1
Retired Bishops	1
Abbots	1
Priests: Diocesan Active in Diocese	91
Priests: Diocesan Active Outside Diocese	5
Priests: Diocesan in Foreign Missions	2
Priests: Retired, Sick or Absent	51
Number of Diocesan Priests	149
Religious Priests in Diocese	116
Total Priests in Diocese	265
Extern Priests in Diocese	75
Ordinations:	
Diocesan Priests	2
Transitional Deacons	2
Permanent Deacons	60
Permanent Deacons in Diocese	118
Total Brothers	52
Total Sisters	210
Parishes	
Parishes	75
With Resident Pastor:	
Resident Diocesan Priests	63
Resident Religious Priests	12
Missions	6
Professional Ministry Personnel:	
Brothers	1
Sisters	60
Welfare	
Catholic Hospitals	2
Total Assisted	300,000
Health Care Centers	7
Total Assisted	35,000
Homes for the Aged	10
Total Assisted	830
Day Care Centers	16
Total Assisted	1,350
Specialized Homes	5
Total Assisted	139
Special Centers for Social Services	65
Total Assisted	25,000
Educational	
Diocesan Students in Other Seminaries	29
Total Seminarians	29
Colleges and Universities	1
Total Students	14,339
High Schools, Diocesan and Parish	4
Total Students	1,997
High Schools, Private	2
Total Students	1,000
Elementary Schools, Diocesan and Parish	26
Total Students	7,726
Elementary Schools, Private	2
Total Students	941
Non-residential Schools for the Disabled	2
Total Students	102
Catechesis/Religious Education:	
High School Students	2,094
Elementary Students	17,765
Total Students under Catholic Instruction	45,993
Teachers in the Diocese:	
Priests	2
Brothers	10
Sisters	22
Lay Teachers	829
Vital Statistics	
Receptions into the Church:	
Infant Baptism Totals	4,902
Minor Baptism Totals	724
Received into Full Communion	506
First Communions	5,206
Confirmations	3,983
Marriages:	
Catholic	764
Interfaith	373
Total Marriages	1,137
Deaths	4,002
Total Catholic Population	424,951
Total Population	2,875,177

Former Bishops—Most Revs. CHARLES B. MCLAUGHLIN, D.D., ord. June 6, 1941; appt. Titular Bishop of Risinium and Auxiliary of Raleigh, Jan. 13, 1964; appt. First Bishop of St. Petersburg, May 8, 1968; installed June 17, 1968; died in Office, Dec. 14, 1978; W. THOMAS LARKIN, D.D. (Retired), ord. May 15, 1947; Second Bishop of St. Petersburg; appt. April 24, 1979; ord. Bishop, May 27, 1979; installed June 28, 1979; retired Nov. 28, 1988; died Nov. 4, 2006.; JOHN C. FAVALORA, D.D., S.T.L., Third Bishop of St. Petersburg; ord. Dec. 20, 1961; appt. Bishop of Alexandria, June 16, 1986; ord. and installed July 29, 1986; appt. Third Bishop of St. Petersburg, March 7, 1989; installed May 16, 1989; installed Third Archbishop of Miami, Dec. 20, 1994.

Diocesan Offices

Pastoral Center—6363 Ninth Ave. N., St. Petersburg, 33710. Tel: 727-344-1611; Fax: 727-345-2143. *Mailing Address: P.O. Box 40200, St. Petersburg, 33743-0200.*

Tribunal—905 S. Prospect Ave., Clearwater, 33756. Tel: 727-446-2326; 727-442-8884; Fax: 727-446-4287.

WBVM 90.5 FM, Inc.—Mailing Address: P.O. Box 18081, Tampa, 33679. Tel: 813-289-8040.

Office of the Bishop

Office of the Bishop—Most Rev. ROBERT N. LYNCH; Mrs. ANGELICA "VIVI" IGLESIAS, Exec. Sec. to Bishop Lynch & Very Rev. Robert Morris, V.G.

Diocesan Curia

Vicar General—Very Rev. ROBERT F. MORRIS, V.G.

Moderator of the Curia—Very Rev. ROBERT F. MORRIS, V.G.

Chancellor—Mrs. JOAN G. MORGAN, Chancellor & Notary; Mrs. MARIA T. GONZALEZ, Exec. Sec.; Mrs. LISA MOBLEY, Archivist & Notary.

Vice Chancellor—Deacon ERIC WELL, J.C.L.

Victim Assistance Coordinator—Ms. MARTI ZEITZ, M.A., 1213 16th St. N., St. Petersburg, 33705. Tel: 866-407-4505 (Toll Free). Email: mzeitz@ccdosp.org.

Secretary for Administration—Mrs. ELIZABETH DEPTULA; Mrs. ANGELICA "VIVI" IGLESIAS, Exec. Sec. & Special Project Coord.

Secretary for Priest Personnel—Rev. LEONARD PIOTROWSKI.

Secretary of Christian Formation—Very Rev. ROBERT F. MORRIS, V.G.

Secretary of Christian Service and Formation—Mr. FRANK V. MURPHY III.

The Tribunal—

Judicial Vicar—Rev. RONALD AUBIN, J.C.L.

Coordinator of Tribunal Services—Mr. DAVID RIDENOUR, J.D., J.C.L.

Tribunal Staff—

Judges—Rev. Msgr. ROBERT C. GIBBONS, J.C.L.; Revs. RONALD AUBIN, J.C.L.; WILLIAM J. SWENGROS, J.C.D.; Deacon ERIC WELLS, J.C.L.; Rev. JOSEPH L. WATERS, J.C.L.; Mr. DAVID RIDENOUR, J.D., J.C.L.

Promoter of Justice—Rev. Msgr. DACIAN DEE, J.C.D. (Retired).

Defender of the Bond—Rev. Msgr. DACIAN DEE, J.C.D. (Retired).

Auditor—KAZ MIELCAREK, Ph.D.

Notaries—Mrs. MARY SUE OLIVER; Ms. ANA RIVERA.

Administrative Assistant and Receptionist—KIM PACANA.

College of Consultors—Very Rev. ROBERT F. MORRIS, V.G.; Rev. Msgrs. ROBERT C. GIBBONS, J.C.L.; BRENDAN MULDOON; ANTON DECHERING; Rev. RONALD AUBIN, J.C.L.; Rev. Msgr. COLMAN M. COOKE, V.F., Ph.D.; Very Revs. RICHARD JANKOWSKI, V.F.; THOMAS MORGAN, V.F.; Rev. LEONARD PIOTROWSKI; Very Revs. ARTHUR PROULX, V.F.; MICHAEL SUSZYNSKI, V.F.; Rev. JOHN TAPP.

Vocations Office—Rev. LEONARD PLAZEWSKI, Dir. Vocations; Mrs. HEIDI VARLEY, Sec.

Permanent Diaconate Office—Rev. RALPH J. ARGENTINO, Dir.; Deacons JAMES GREVENITES, Asst. Dir.; JOHN ALVAREZ, Dir. Formation; PETER ANDRE, Supervision of Practicums; Mrs. SUE HUERTAS, Administrative Asst.

Vicar for Religious—Sisters GERMAINE BEVANS, O.S.B., Dir.; EUGENE MARIE SCHNEIDER, O.S.F., Sec.

Department of Christian Formation

Department of Christian Formation—Very Rev. ROBERT F. MORR.

Sea, Apostleship of the—

Tampa Port Ministry-Seafarers Center—1912 Eastport Dr., Tampa, 33610. Tel: 813-234-8693; Fax: 813-238-5060. Deacon MAXIMO MONTAYRE, Chap.

Charismatic Renewal—

English—DOTTIE VINSON, Dir. Tel: 813-961-3675. Email: tandyvinson@msn.com.

Spanish Speaking Spiritual Moderator—Rev. Msgr. ANTONIO DIEZ, 6819 Krycul Ave., P.O. Box 418, Riverview, 33568. Tel: 813-677-2175; MARIA RODRIGUEZ, Pres., Commission, 17306 Hubers Ct., Odessa, 33556. Email: bythespiritonly@aol.com.

Cursillo, English—Rev. ANGELUS MIGLIORE, T.O.R., Spiritual Advisor. Cursillo, Spiritual Advisors: Rev. ANGELUS MIGLIORE, T.O.R., St. Patrick Parish, 4518 S. Manhattan Ave., Tampa, 33611. Tel: 813-839-5337; Deacon ROBERT "BOB" ANDERSON, Asst. Spiritual Dir., St. Frances Xavier Cabrini Parish. Tel: 352-683-9666; FRANK MALICK, Lay Dir. Tel: 727-784-9803.

Cursillo, Spanish—Rev. RAFAEL E. MARTOS, Spiritual Advisor, St. Clement. Tel: 813-759-2721; NYDIA VIZCARRONDO, Directora Laica. Tel: 727-942-6606.

Ecumenical and Inter-Religious Affairs—Rev. Msgr. J. BERNARD CAVERLY, St. Raphael Church, 1376 Snell Isle Blvd., N.E., St. Petersburg, 33704. Tel: 727-821-7989.

Lay Pastoral Ministry Institute—Sr. MARLENE WEIDENBORNER, Dir.; DALE BROWN, Coord. Ministries; ELAINE THELAN, Coord. Mentors.

Multicultural Ministry—Sr. PAT HALEY, S.C.N., Asst. Dir.; Mrs. PIEDAD ARISTIZABAL, Sec.

Our Lady of Good Counsel Camp—Very Rev. JAMES B. JOHNSON, V.F., Dir., 8888 E. Gobbler Dr., Floral City, 34436. Tel: 352-726-2198. Email: goodcounselcamp@aol.com.

Propagation of the Faith—Rev. PAUL KOCHU, Dir.; Mrs. CAROLYN MARHEFKA, Sec.

Worship, Office of—Rev. JOHN TAPP, Sec. Worship; Mr. DOUGLAS REATINI, Dir.; Ms. KATHY PROEFKE, Assoc. Dir.

Evangelization and Lifelong Faith Formation—Mr. BRIAN A. LEMOI, Dir.; Mrs. KATHY FILIPPELLI, Assoc. Dir. Catechist Certification; Mrs. DIANE KLEDZIK, Assoc. Dir. Adult Faith Formation; Mrs. ANNA MARIE WRIGHT, Assoc. Dir. Youth & Young Adult Ministry.

Scouting Office, Girls—Rev. Msgr. ANTON DECHERING, Dir., 1600 54th Ave. S., St. Petersburg, 33712. Tel: 727-867-3663; JOSEPHINE MAESTAS, Diocesan Chair. Tel: 813-748-3043.

Scouting Office, Boys—Rev. TIMOTHY CUMMINGS, Diocesan Chap. Tel: 727-733-8305; Mr. MICHAEL KOSIBA, Diocesan Chm. Tel: 813-839-4644; Mr. MACK ZEWALK, Vice Chm. Tel: 813-620-9112.

Department of Christian Service

Secretary of Christian Service—Mr. FRANK V. MURPHY III; Mrs. ANGELICA "VIVI" IGLESIAS, Exec. Sec.

Communications Office—Mr. FRANK V. MURPHY III, Dir.; Mr. WALTER PRUCHNIK, Web Editor; Mrs. MARIA T. GONZALEZ, Sec.

Diocesan Radio - WBVM 90.5 FM—Mr. JOHN MORRIS, Station Mgr., Mailing Address: P.O. Box 18081, Tampa, 33679. Tel: 813-289-8040; 800-223-9286 (800-223-WBVM); Fax: 813-282-3580.

Prison and Jail Ministry—Deacon PETER ANDRE, Dir.; Mrs. HEIDI SUMNER, Sec. Tel: 727-344-1611, Ext. 414; 727-344-1611, Ext. 415.

Catholic Schools Office—Dr. JOHN CUMMINGS, Ed.D., Supt.; Mrs. HELEN S. MARSTON, M.S., Assoc. Supt. for Administrative Svcs.; Mrs. KAY RIZZO, MAT, CAS, Assoc. Supt. for Curriculum and Instruction; Mr. CHRISTOPHER WIAND, M.Ed., Assoc. Supt.; Mr. ADAM JENKINS, Admin. Power School.

Life Ministry—Mrs. SABRINA BURTON-SCHULTZ, Dir. Tel: 727-344-1611, Ext. 325.

Father William F. Balfe Memorial Library—Located at: Bishop McLaughlin High School, 13651 Hays Rd., Spring Hill, 34610.

Parish Ministry Support—Mr. PETER BURNS, Dir. Tel: 727-344-1611, Ext. 325.

Department of Administration

Department of Administration—Mrs. ELIZABETH DEPTULA, Sec. for Admin.; Mr. PAUL A. WARD JR., Exec. Dir., Finance Office.

Calvary Catholic Cemetery and Miserere Guild—Rev. Msgr. NORMAN BALTHAZAR, Dir. Cemeteries.

Finance and Accounting—Mr. PAUL A. WARD JR., Exec. Dir.; Ms. LISA CAMPBELL, Controller; Mr. MICHAEL AKERS, Dir. Parish & School Accounting; Mrs. CAROL PILARSKI, Technology Coord.

Diocesan Finance Council—Rev. JOSEPH A. PELLEGRINO; Very Rev. RICHARD JANKOWSKI, V.F.; Mr. NEIL J. RAUENHORST; Mr. ROBERT S. FISHER; Mr. MICHAEL CARRERE; Mr. GREG KIELER; Mr. EMIL MARQUARDT; Ms. RETIA MCADORY; Mrs. NANCY RIDENOUR; Mr. JOSEPH WHITE; Mrs. ELIZABETH DEPTULA; Mr. FRANK V. MURPHY III; Mr. GERALD P. GIGLIA.

Insurance and Risk Management—Mr. RICARDO OSORIO, Dir.; Ms. VALERIE KELLERMAN, Admin. Asst.

Real Estate and Plannning—Mr. STEVE B. ZIENTEK, Real Estate Planning Mgr.

Information Technology—Mr. MARK MOFFITT, Dir.; Ms. CHRISTINE DANDARAW, Training Coord.; Mr. SCOTT SHARLOW, Computer Tech. & Network Admin.; Mr. RAY MILLER, Enterprise Information Analyst.

Office of Construction Management—Mr. RICK KOLHOFF, Exec. Dir.; Mr. BRIAN LAVERTY, Project Mgr.; Mrs. LISA BAGGETT, Admin. Coord.; Mrs. KATHLEEN FIXTER, Sec.

Human Resources—Mr. CHRIS RAJK, Exec. Dir.; Mr. ANDRE GLAUDE, Safe Environment Mgr.; Mrs. JOYCE VELENO, Admin. Asst.; Mrs. MONITA BONCZEK, Coord. Employee Benefits; Mrs. CHARLOTTE MYERS, Payroll Mgr.

Internal Services Administration—Ms. MARY SHEALY, Dir.

Office of Stewardship and Development—VACANT. Parish Resource Specialists: Mrs. ANGELINA KARPINSKI; Ms. JEANNE SMITH.

The Catholic Foundation—VACANT, Dir.; Mrs. TERRI RICK, Sec.

Pastoral Offices and Consultative Bodies to the Diocesan Curia

Presbyteral Council—

Executive Committee—Most Rev. ROBERT N. LYNCH, Pres.; Very Rev. ROBERT F. MORRIS, V.G.; Revs. JOSEPH A. PELLEGRINO, Chm.; JOHN TAPP, Vice Chm.

Vicars Forane—Very Revs. DENNIS E. HUGHES, V.F., Pasco; JOHN A. D'ANTONIO, V.F., Upper Pinellas; RICHARD JANKOWSKI, V.F., Hernando; ARTHUR PROULX, V.F., East Hillsborough; THOMAS MORGAN, V.F., West Hillsborough; JAMES B. JOHNSON, V.F., Citrus; JOSEPH WATERS, V.F., Lower Pinellas.

Elected Pastors—Rev. Msgr. ROBERT C. GIBBONS, J.C.L.; Revs. JOSEPH A. PELLEGRINO; ROBERT CADRECHA; KENNETH MALLEY; JOHN TAPP; PAUL PECCHIE.

Elected Parochial Vicars—Revs. TIMOTHY CUMMINGS; CARL J. MELCHIOR JR.; JOSEPH MUSCO; LEONARD PLAZEWSKI; THOMAS SPILLETT; ROBERT WISEMAN, C.S.C.

Appointed Members—Revs. CARLOS ROJAS; ANDREW J. REITZ, O.F.M.

Personnel Board—Rev. ERIC HUNTER; Very Rev. JAMES B. JOHNSON, V.F.; Rev. JOSEPH A. PELLEGRINO; Very Rev. ROBERT F. MORRIS, V.G.; Revs. LEONARD PLAZEWSKI; KENNETH MALLEY; LEONARD PIOTROWSKI.

Incardination Committee—Very Revs. JOHN A. D'ANTONIO, V.F.; DENNIS E. HUGHES, V.F.; Rev. Msgr. PATRICK IRWIN; Rev. ALAN WEBER. Ex Officio: Very Rev. ROBERT F. MORRIS, V.G.; Rev. LEONARD PIOTROWSKI.

Diocesan Legal Counsel— DiVito & Higham, P.A. Mr. JOSEPH A. DIVITO; FREDERICK A. HIGHAM JR., 4514 Central Ave., St. Petersburg, 33711-1041. Tel: 727-321-1201; Fax: 727-321-5181.

Diocesan Pastoral Council—Mr. FRED DOBBINS, Chm. Tel: 813-224-2498.

Diocesan Review Board—Mrs. SUE BRETT, Chm. Tel: 727-384-0730; Fax: 727-344-4060.

Organizations Serving the Diocese

Pension Plan For Employees of the Entities of the Diocese of St. Petersburg—

Pension Plan Administrator—Gabriel, Roeder, Smith & Co., One E. Broward Blvd., Ste. 505, Fort Lauderdale, 33301-1872. Tel: 954-527-1616; Fax: 954-525-0083.

Catholic Charities, Diocese of St. Petersburg, Inc.—

Central Services—1213 16th St., N., St. Petersburg, 33705. Tel: 727-893-1314; Fax: 727-893-1307. Web: www.ccdosp.org. Mr. FRANK V. MURPHY III, Pres.; SHEILA LOPEZ, COO.

Pious Foundations

Catholic Education Foundation, Inc.—6363 Ninth Ave. N., St. Petersburg, 33710. Tel: 727-344-1611. *Mailing Address: P.O. Box 40200, St. Petersburg, 33743-0200.*

Emmaus Foundation, Inc.—dba Catholic Foundation of the Diocese of St. Petersburg 6363 Ninth Ave. N., St. Petersburg, 33710. Tel: 727-344-1611. *Mailing Address: P.O. Box 40200, St. Petersburg, 33743-0200.*

Organizations of the Catholic Faithful

Catholic Daughters of America—Ms. GRACE DICAIRANO, Natl. Regent, Manasquan, NJ; Ms. DAHLIA PEREZ, State Regent. Tel: 813-876-7100. National Office. Tel: 212-877-3041.

Diocesan Council of Catholic Women—Rev. JOHN MCEVOY, Diocesan Moderator. Tel: 727-526-5783.

Family of St. Jerome, "Familian Sancti Hieronymi"—Mr. JAN G. HALISKY, P.A., Praeses Generalis, 507 S. Prospect Ave., Clearwater, 33756.

Knights of Columbus—Rev. PAUL HERVEY, Diocesan Chap. (Retired). Tel: 813-634-2328.

Knights of Peter Claver— St. Peter Claver, Tampa Council #379 Grand Knight CONRAD JOHNSON. Tel: 813-835-0529. Web: kofpc.org (National); kpc379.org (Local).

Knights of Peter Claver Ladies Auxiliary— St. Peter Claver, Tampa Court #379 Grand Lady YVONNE NELLUM. Tel: 813-681-3010. Web: kofpc.org (National); kpc379.org (Local).

Society of St. Vincent de Paul—

Central Council of St. Petersburg Diocese—7021 Bougenville Dr., Port Richey, 34668. Tel: 727-868-8160. RAYMOND W. WATSON, Pres.; Mr. MARVIN ROPERT, Exec. Dir. Tel: 813-839-9325.

Hernando Citrus St. Vincent de Paul Society District Council—Mr. RON LEGER. Tel: 352-688-1511.

West Hillsborough District Council—Mr. KENT MILLER.

East Hillsborough District Council—Ms. MARY KAY LEE. Tel: 813-649-0903.

Pasco District Council—Ms. PAT DWYER. Tel: 813-944-0447.

Lower Pinellas District Council—Mr. ROBERT KUBECK, Pres. Tel: 727-823-2516.

Upper Pinellas District Council—PATRICK FARMER. Tel: 727-442-5306.

CLERGY, PARISHES, MISSIONS AND PAROCHIAL SCHOOLS

CITY OF ST. PETERSBURG

(PINELLAS COUNTY)

ST. PETERSBURG

1—CATHEDRAL OF ST. JUDE THE APOSTLE (1950) Very Rev. Joseph Waters, Rector; Rev. Wayne C. Genereux, O.de.M. In Res., Very Rev. Robert F. Morris; Rev. Leonard Plazewski.

Res.: 5815 Fifth Ave. N., Saint Petersburg, 33710. Tel: 727-347-9702; Fax: 727-343-8370.

School—(Grades PreSchool-8) Tel: 727-347-8622; Fax: 727-343-0305. Thomas Predergast, Prin. Lay Teachers 31; Students 432.

Catechesis/Religious Program—Tel: 727-347-9702; Fax: 727-343-8370. Students 237.

2—BLESSED TRINITY (1960) Rev. Msgr. Anton Dechering; Rev. J. Frederick McGuire (CIN); Sr. Jean Barrett, O.S.F., Pastoral Assoc.; Deacon Lionel Roberts; Dr. Jonathan Wright, Music Dir.; Robert Dudley, Contemporary Choir Dir.

Res.: 1600 54th Ave. S., 33712. Tel: 727-867-3663; Fax: 727-864-2679.

See St. Paul Interparochial School, St. Petersburg under Elementary Schools, Interparochial located in the Institution section.

Catechesis/Religious Program—Tel: 727-867-3663; Fax: 727-864-2679. Mrs. Sonya Adkins, D.R.E.; Ellen Voegele, Youth Min. Students 62.

3—HOLY CROSS (1965) Revs. Paul Kochu; Raphael Kilumanga; Deacons Richard Nagle Jr.; Lowell Hecht.

Res.: 7851 54th Ave. N., 33709. Tel: 727-546-3315; 727-541-2242; Fax: 727-547-2005.

Catechesis/Religious Program—Tel: 727-547-2004; Fax: 727-547-2005. Students 192.

4—HOLY FAMILY (1956) Revs. John Tapp; Paul Mangiafico; Deacons Michael Columbus; Peter Andre, Admin.

Res.: 200 78th Ave., N.E., 33702-4416. Tel: 727-526-5783; Fax: 727-521-2545. Email: holyfamily33702@yahoo.com. Web: www.holyfamilystpete.com.

School—(Grades PreSchool-8), 250 78th Ave., N.E., 33702-4416. Tel: 727-526-8194; Fax: 727-527-6567. Web: www.holyfamily-school.com; www.holyfamily-school.com. Sr. Florence Ann Marino, I.H.M., Prin.; Mrs. Mary Karbowsky, Librarian. Sisters 1; Lay Teachers 21; Students 266.

Catechesis/Religious Program—Tel: 727-526-5783, Ext. 21; Fax: 727-521-2545. George Pioli, D.R.E. (Adult & Elementary); Linda Johnston, Dir. Faith Formation. Students 289.

5—ST. JOSEPH (1926) Rev. Timothy H. Sherwood.

Mailing Address: 2025-22 Ave. S., 33712. Tel: 727-822-2153; Fax: 727-823-5820. Email: stjosephstpete@tampabay.rr.com. Web: stjosephstpete.org.

Preschool—Immaculate Conception, 2100 26 Ave. S., 33712. Tel: 727-822-2156; Fax: 727-553-9133. Lay Teachers 18; Students 142.

Catechesis/Religious Program—Students 20.

6—ST. MARY OUR LADY OF GRACE (1921) Revs. Cletus M. Watson, T.O.R.; Brian J. Miller, T.O.R.; Julio Rivero, T.O.R.

Res.: 515 Fourth St. S., 33701. Tel: 727-896-2191; Fax: 727-895-6279. Email: info@stmaryolg.org. Web: www.stmaryolg.org.

Catechesis/Religious Program—Students 11.

7—ST. PAUL (1929) Rev. Msgr. Robert C. Gibbons; Rev. Babu Gangolu, S.A.C.
Res.: 1800 12th St. N., 33704. Tel: 727-822-3481; Fax: 727-822-1754. Web: stpaulstpete.com.
See St. Paul Catholic School, St. Petersburg under Elementary Schools, Interparochial located in the Institution section.
See St. Paul Children's Center under Pre Schools and Day Care Centers located in the Institution section.
Catechesis/Religious Program—Tel: 727-822-3481; Fax: 727-822-1754. Students 74.
Mission—The Mercy of God Polish Mission 1358 20th Ave. N., Pinellas Co. 33704. Tel: 727-823-6997; Fax: 727-821-8242. Rev. Janusz Burzawa (Poland).

8—ST. RAPHAEL (1961) Rev. Msgr. J. Bernard Caverly; Rev. Thomas Spillett. In Res., Rev. Jose G. Gonzalez (Retired).
Res.: 1376 Snell Isle Blvd., N.E., 33704. Tel: 727-821-7989; Fax: 727-896-9619. Web: www.st-raphaels.com.
School—(Grades PreK-8) Tel: 727-821-9663; Fax: 727-502-9594. Web: www.straphaelschool.net. Ms. Valerie Wostbrock, Prin.; Jane Venzke, Librarian. Lay Teachers 25; Students 210.
Catechesis/Religious Program—Tel: 727-821-0155. Lynn Edmonds, D.R.E. Students 265.

9—TRANSFIGURATION (1959) Rev. Msgr. Avelino R. Garcia.
Church: 4000 43rd St. N., 33714. Tel: 727-525-0262; Fax: 727-526-7794. Email: parishadmin@transfigparish.org. Web: transfigparish.org.
Transfiguration Early Childhood Center—, (Ages 2-5), *Lower Pinellas Deanery*, 4300 43rd St., N., Saint Petersburg, 33714. Tel: 727-527-2880. Ms. Amy Lounsbury, Dir.
Catechesis/Religious Program—Email: religioused@transfigparish.org. Sue Sharlow, D.R.E. Students 124.

OUTSIDE THE CITY OF ST. PETERSBURG

BEVERLY HILLS, CITRUS CO., OUR LADY OF GRACE (1966) Rev. Msgr. Austin Mullen; Rev. Francis Muteesasira Lubowa; Deacon John Moniz.
Res.: 6 Roosevelt Blvd., 34465. Tel: 352-746-2144; Fax: 352-746-6892. Email: olgbh@earthlink.net. Web: www.ourladyofgracefl.catholicweb.com.
See Pope John Paul II, Lecanto under Elementary Schools, Interparochial located in the Institution section.
Catechesis/Religious Program—Tel: 352-746-2144; Fax: 352-746-6892. Clara Makoid, D.R.E. Students 87.

BRANDON, HILLSBOROUGH CO., CHURCH OF THE NATIVITY (1960) [JC] Very Rev. Arthur J. Proulx; Rev. Msgr. James C. Lara, Pastor Emeritus (Retired); Revs. Philip Dac Clement; Thomas Shea, C.S.C.; Deacons Mark Taylor; Luis Zayas. In Res., Rev. Msgr. John A. Cippel (Retired).
Church: 705 E. Brandon Blvd., 33511. Tel: 813-681-4608; Fax: 813-653-9482. Web: www.nativitycatholicchurch.org.
Res.: 805 Westbrook, 33511. Tel: 813-684-0256.
School—(Grades PreK-8) Tel: 813-689-3395; Fax: 813-681-5406. Web: www.nativitycatholicschool.org. Dr. Bernadette Kunnen, Prin. Lay Teachers 33; Students 750.
Catechesis/Religious Program—Tel: 813-689-9101; Fax: 813-684-1880. Vicki Hawkins, D.R.E. Students 874.

BROOKSVILLE, HERNANDO CO., ST. ANTHONY THE ABBOT (1892) Rev. Craig Morley; Deacons Manuel Carreiro; Michael Ruffner.
Res.: 20428 Cortez Blvd., 34601-5601. Tel: 352-796-2096; Fax: 352-796-7144. Email: parishoffice@stantchurch.org. Web: www.stantchurch.org.
See Notre Dame Interparochial School, Spring Hill under Elementary Schools, Interparochial located in the Institution section.
Catechesis/Religious Program—Tel: 352-796-2096; Fax: 352-796-7144. Email: faithformation@stantchurch.org. Sr. Jean Little, R.S.M., Dir. Faith Formation. Students 160.

CITRUS SPRINGS, CITRUS CO., ST. ELIZABETH ANN SETON (1976) Rev. Eric Peters; Rev. Msgr. George Cummings, Pastor Emeritus (Retired).
Office & Mailing Address: 1460 W. St. Elizabeth Pl., 34434. Tel: 352-489-4889; Fax: 352-489-4770. Email: steas@tampabay.rr.com. Web: stelizabeth-citrussprings.parishesonline.com.
See Pope John Paul II, Lecanto under Elementary Schools, Interparochial located in the Institution section.
Catechesis/Religious Program—Tel: 352-489-4889. Students 108.

CLEARWATER, PINELLAS CO.

1—ALL SAINTS (1987) Rev. Callist N. Nyambo; Deacon Jack Lyons.
Office: 2801 Curlew Rd., 33761. Tel: 727-789-1025; Fax: 727-784-8025. Email: allsaintsclearwater@verizon.net. Web: allsaints-northpinellas.org.
See Guardian Angels Interparochial School, Clearwater under Elementary Schools, Interparochial located in the Institution section.
Catechesis/Religious Program—Tel: 727-789-1025; Fax: 727-784-8025. Students 101.

2—ST. BRENDAN (1978) Rev. Eric Hunter; Rev. Msgrs. Michael F. Devine, Pastor Emeritus (Retired); Edward Mulligan, Pastor Emeritus (Retired); Deacon James Grevenites.
Res.: 245 Dory Passage, 33767. Tel: 727-443-5485; Fax: 727-442-5896. Email: stbrendan@tampabay.rr.com. Web: www.stbrendan-catholic.org.
See St. Cecelia Interparochial School, Clearwater under Elementary Schools, Interparochial located in the Institution section.
Catechesis/Religious Program—Students 40.

3—ST. CATHERINE OF SIENA (1976) Revs. Kenneth Malley; Carl J. Melchior Jr.; Sisters Kathleen Beatty, S.S.J., Pastoral Assoc.; Marie Cella, S.S.J., Pastoral Assoc.; Deacon Barry Wallace.
Res.: 1955 S. Belcher Rd., 33764. Tel: 727-531-7721; Fax: 727-531-7723. Web: www.scosparish.org.
See St. Cecelia Interparochial School, Clearwater under Elementary Schools, Interparochial located in the Institution section.
Catechesis/Religious Program—Tel: 727-531-7721; Fax: 727-531-7723. Carla Lamont, D.R.E. Students 173.

4—ST. CECELIA (1924) Rev. Msgrs. Patrick Irwin; Aiden Foynes, Pastor Emeritus (Retired); Rev. Gilberto Quintero; Deacon Peter Andre.
Office: 820 Jasmine Way, 33756. Tel: 727-447-3494; Fax: 727-442-4810. Email: office@stceceliachurch.org. Web: www.stceceliachurch.org.
See St. Cecelia Interparochial School, Clearwater under Elementary Schools, Interparochial located in the Institution section.
Catechesis/Religious Program—Email: dre@stceceliachurch.org. Mary Russell, D.R.E. Students 290.
Convent—1305 Franklin St., 33756. Tel: 727-447-3331.

5—LIGHT OF CHRIST (1966) Rev. Jacob Monteleone; Deacon James Hassett.
Res.: 2176 Marilyn St., 33765. Tel: 727-441-4545; Fax: 727-441-8771. Email: locchurch@ij.net.
See St. Cecelia Interparochial School, Clearwater under Elementary Schools, Interparochial located in the Institution section.
Pre-School—Tel: 727-442-4797; Fax: 727-441-8771. Mrs. Rebecca Daschbach, Dir. Lay Teachers 8; Students 80.
Catechesis/Religious Program—Tel: 727-442-7081. Ruth Appel, C.R.E. Students 223.

6—ST. MICHAEL THE ARCHANGEL (1981) Revs. Gregg Tottle; Ted Costello; Sisters Therese Carolan, Pastoral Assoc.; Therese Dugan, S.N.D., Pastoral Assoc.
2281 State Rd. 580, 33763. Tel: 727-797-2375; Fax: 727-791-8287. Email: smaclw@verizon.net.
Catechesis/Religious Program—Mrs. Katie White, D.R.E. Students 232.

CRYSTAL RIVER, CITRUS CO., ST. BENEDICT (1953) Rev. Ryszard Stradomski; Deacon James Pullar.
Mailing Address: 455 S. Suncoast Blvd., 34429. Tel: 352-795-4478; 352-795-4479; Fax: 352-795-3801. Email: stbens@tampabay.rr.com. Web: stbenedict-crystalriver.org.
See Pope John Paul II, Lecanto under Elementary Schools, Interparochial located in the Institution section.
Catechesis/Religious Program—Tel: 352-795-4479; Fax: 352-795-3108. Students 62.
Daystar—6751 W. Gulf to Lake Hwy., 34429.

DADE CITY, PASCO CO.

1—ST. RITA (1912), (Hispanic), Revs. Daniel R. Kayajan, C.S.C.; William Persia, C.S.C.
Office & Mailing Address: 14404 14th St., 33523. Tel: 352-567-2894; Fax: 352-567-2777. Web: www.stritaparish.org.
See St. Anthony Interparochial School, San Antonio under Elementary Schools, Interparochial located in the Institution section.
Catechesis/Religious Program—Sisters Silvia Vivas, M.D.M.L., D.R.E.; Martha Flores, M.D.M.L., D.R.E. Students 434.

2—SACRED HEART (1888) [CEM] Rev. John C. Murphy; Deacon William Connors.
Res.: 32145 St. Joe Rd., 33525. Tel: 352-588-3641; Fax: 352-588-5299. Email: shcdadecity@embarqmail.com.
See St. Anthony Interparochial School, San Antonio under Elementary Schools, Interparochial located in the Institution section.
Catechesis/Religious Program—Tel: 352-588-3641; Fax: 352-588-5299. Students 96.
Sacred Heart Child Care Center—32245 St. Joe Rd., 33525. Tel: 352-588-4060; Fax: 352-588-4871. Email: shecctw@embarqmail.com. Mrs. Toni Watkins.

DUNEDIN, PINELLAS CO., OUR LADY OF LOURDES (1958) Revs. Gary Dowsey, Parish Admin.; Timothy Cummings.
Res.: 750 San Salvador Dr., 34698. Tel: 727-733-3606; Fax: 727-733-8305. Email: ourlady@gate.net. Web: ourladydunedin.org.
School—730 San Salvador Dr., 34698. Tel: 727-733-3776; Fax: 727-733-3776. Kathy Bogataj, Prin.; Tracy Maclean, Librarian. Lay Teachers 17; Students 228.
Catechesis/Religious Program—Tel: 813-733-0872; Fax: 813-733-8305. Email: faithformation@ourladydunedin.org. Americo Menendez, D.R.E. & Youth Min. Students 379.

GULFPORT, PINELLAS CO., MOST HOLY NAME OF JESUS (1960) Rev. Vladimir Dziadek, Parochial Admin. Pro Tem; Deacon Glenn Pickart; Eileen Plasse, Business Mgr.
Res.: 5800 15th Ave. S., 33707. Tel: 727-347-9989; Fax: 727-343-6420. Email: parishoffice@mostholyname.org. Web: mostholyname.org.
Most Holy Name of Jesus Early Childhood Center—Lower Pinellas Deanery, 1508 59th St., S., Saint Petersburg, 33707. Tel: 727-347-1774; Fax: 727-381-7225. Email: ceveland@mostholyname.org. Ms. Carrie Eveland, Dir. Lay Teachers 4; Students 40.
School—Preschool, Tel: 727-347-1774; Fax: 727-381-7225. Ms. Carrie Eveland, Dir. Lay Teachers 4; Students 40.
Catechesis/Religious Program—Email: dre@mostholyname.orgTel: 727-347-9989; Fax: 727-343-6420. Fran Marinari, D.R.E.; Colleen Lockamy, Youth Min. Students 105.
Mission—St. Casimir Lithuanian Mission Office: 555 68th Ave., St. Pete Beach, Pinellas Co. 33706. Tel: 727-367-2408; 727-368-0523 (English). Rev. Bernardas Talaisis, O.F.M.

HOLIDAY, PASCO CO., ST. VINCENT DE PAUL (1969) Revs. Michael Arkins, S.S.S.; Thomas Fitzgerald, S.S.S.; Deacons Frank Longo; Gerard White.
Res.: 4843 Mile Stretch Dr., P.O. Box 3865, 34690. Tel: 727-938-1974; Fax: 727-938-1975. Web: svdp4843.org.
See Bishop Larkin Interparochial School, Port Richey under Elementary Schools, Interparochial located in the Institution section.
Catechesis/Religious Program—Tel: 727-938-1001. Email: svdpfaithformation@yahoo.com. Jane Etzel, D.R.E. Students 136.

HOMOSASSA, CITRUS CO., ST. THOMAS THE APOSTLE (1987) Rev. Ronald Marecki; Deacons Sam Hunt; David Varner; Susan Pistone, Office Admin.
Church: 7040 S. Suncoast Blvd., 34446. Tel: 352-628-7000; Fax: 352-628-4723. Web: home.catholicweb.com/sthomashomosassa.
Res.: 18 Beverly Ct., 34446. Tel: 352-503-6260.
See Pope John Paul II, Lecanto under Elementary Schools, Interparochial located in the Institution section.
Catechesis/Religious Program—Email: reled60@embarqmail.com. Sharon Bassing, D.R.E. Students 55.

HUDSON, PASCO CO., ST. MICHAEL THE ARCHANGEL (1971) Revs. Henry J. Riffle; Seamus Collins, O.P.; James Ruhlin; Deacon Robert Simpson.
Res.: 8014 State Rd. #52, 34667. Tel: 727-868-5276; Fax: 727-862-9187. Email: office@saintmichaelchurch.org. Web: www.saintmichaelchurch.org.
Catechesis/Religious Program—Tel: 727-819-5131. Mary Alber, Dir. Faith Formation. Students 310.

INDIAN ROCKS BEACH, PINELLAS CO., ST. JEROME (1956) Rev. Msgr. Brendan Muldoon; Rev. Robert Wiseman, C.S.C.; Sr. Lucia Brady, O.S.C., Pastoral Assoc.; Thomas Kurt, Dir. Music Min.
Mailing Address: P.O. Box 100, 33785. Email: sjcc@tampabay.rr.com. Web: stjeromeonline.org.
Res.: 10895 Hamlin Blvd., Largo, 33774. Tel: 727-595-4610; Fax: 727-596-6792.
Early Childhood Center—Tel: 727-596-9491; Fax: 727-596-8953. Denise Roach, Dir.
Catechesis/Religious Program—Tel: 727-595-3100. Web: stjeromeonline.org. Tamara Gildea, D.R.E. Students 230.

INVERNESS, CITRUS CO., OUR LADY OF FATIMA (1955) Very Rev. James B. Johnson; Rev. Charles Leke; Deacons Eric Makoid; Steve Kurylowicz.
Mailing Address: 550 U.S. Hwy. 41 S., 34450. Tel: 352-726-1670; Fax: 352-344-8384. Web: home.catholicweb.com/ladyofatima.
Res.: 518 Desota Ave., 34450. Tel: 352-726-1670.
See Pope John Paul II, Lecanto under Elementary Schools, Interparochial located in the Institution section.
Catechesis/Religious Program—Rebecca Pound, D.R.E.; Annette Tremante, D.R.E. Students 222.

LAND O'LAKES, PASCO CO., OUR LADY OF THE ROSARY (1952) Revs. Ronald Aubin; Jose Tejada; Diego A. Ossamora; Deacons Augustin Ortiz; Eric Wells; William T. Ditewig; Jose Salorzano.
P.O. Box 1229, 34639. Email: office@ladyrosary.org. Web: www.ladyrosary.org.
Res.: 2348 Collier Pkwy., Land O Lakes, 34639. Tel: 813-949-4565; Fax: 813-948-1981. Email: office@ladyrosary.org. Web: ladyrosary.org.
See Most Holy Redeemer Interparochial School, Tampa under Elementary Schools, Interparochial located in the Institution section.
Catechesis/Religious Program—Tel: 813-949-2699; Fax: 813-948-1981. Email: religioused@ladyrosary.org. Constance Whittington, C.R.E. Students 1,049.

LARGO, PINELLAS CO.
1—ST. MATTHEW (1985) Rev. Patrick M. Rebel; Deacons Bernard Braun; Anthony Kijonka.
Mailing Address: P.O. Box 10097, 33773-0097. Email: info@stmat.org. Web: www.stmat.org.
Office: 9111 90th Ave. N., 33777. Tel: 727-393-1288; Fax: 727-398-2683.
Catechesis/Religious Program—Tel: 727-398-6618, Ext. 207. Regina Dougherty, D.R.E. Students 102.
Mission—Holy Martyrs of Vietnam 9099 90th Ave. N., Pinellas Co. 33777. Tel: 727-397-7906. Rev. Joseph Thai Tran.
2—ST. PATRICK (1958) Revs. Paul Pecchie; Claudius Mpuya; Deacons Richard Brady; Ken Spaulding.
Res.: 2121 16th Ave., S.W., 33770. Tel: 727-584-2318; Fax: 727-586-5413. Email: stpat2000@aol.com. Web: www.stpatrick-largo.com.
School—1501 Trotter Rd., 33770. Tel: 727-581-4865; Fax: 727-581-7842. Sr. Veronica Visceglia, S.S.N.D., Prin. Lay Teachers 17; Students 188.
Catechesis/Religious Program—Joseph Blum, D.R.E.; Sr. Kathleen Luger, D.R.E. Students 102.

LECANTO, CITRUS CO., ST. SCHOLASTICA CHURCH (1987) Rev. Michael R. Smith; Deacons Terrence E. Knox; Stephen Sablone; Richard Meyer.
Res. & Church: 4301 W. Homosassa Trail, 34461. Tel: 352-746-9422; Fax: 352-746-2335. Web: stscholastica.org.
See Pope John Paul II, Lecanto under Elementary Schools, Interparochial located in the Institution section.
Catechesis/Religious Program—Tel: 352-746-9422; Fax: 352-746-2335. Maria Chadburg, D.R.E. Students 151.

LUTZ, HILLSBOROUGH CO., ST. TIMOTHY (1985) Revs. Patrick Kennedy; Sojan Punakkattu; Deacons Peter Burns; Jerry L. Crall.
Res.: 17512 Lakeshore Rd., 33558-4802. Fax: 813-961-9429. Email: parishmanager@sainttims.org. Web: www.sainttims.org.
See Most Holy Redeemer Interparochial School, Tampa under Elementary Schools, Interparochial located in the Institution section.
Catechesis/Religious Program—Tel: 813-961-1716. Judy Anderson, Youth Min.; Jean Gadoury, Dir. Faith Formation. Students 800.

MASARYKTOWN, PASCO CO., ST. MARY, OUR LADY OF SORROWS (1931) Rev. James A. Bucaria.
Mailing Address: P.O. Box 9250, 34604. Tel: 352-796-2792; Fax: 352-544-0398. Email: sacerdos@bellsouth.net. Web: www.saintmaryols.com.
See Notre Dame Interparochial School, Spring Hill under Elementary Schools, Interparochial located in the Institution section.
Catechesis/Religious Program—Mary Ann Martin, D.R.E. Students 14.

NEW PORT RICHEY, PASCO CO.
1—OUR LADY QUEEN OF PEACE (1913) Revs. Jairo L. Atehortua, C.M.; Sebastian Earthedath, M.S.T.; Joseph Kalarickal, M.S.T.; Joseph A. Pastick (Retired); Deacons Roger F. Lind; Juan Valentin.
Res.: 5340 High St., 34652. Tel: 727-849-7521; Fax: 727-849-4814. Email: office@ladyqueenofpeace.org. Web: ladyqueenofpeace.org.
See Bishop Larkin Interparochial School, Port Richey under Elementary Schools, Interparochial located in the Institution section.
Catechesis/Religious Program—Tel: 727-842-9396; Fax: 727-841-6601. Patricia A. Mahoney, D.R.E. Students 273.
2—ST. THOMAS AQUINAS (1980) Revs. Michael Lydon; George Varkey, M.S.T.
Res.: 8320 Old C.R. #54, 34653-6415. Tel: 727-372-8600; Fax: 727-376-7204. Email: sta@stanpr.org. Web: www.stanpr.org.
St. Thomas Early Childhood Development Center—Tel: 727-376-2330; Fax: 727-372-5712. Email: staecc@aol.com.
See Bishop Larkin Interparochial School, Port Richey under Elementary Schools, Interparochial located in the Institution section.
Catechesis/Religious Program—Fax: 727-372-5712. Email: toservechurch@yahoo.com. Philip Coit, D.R.E. Students 390.

PALM HARBOR, PINELLAS CO., ST. LUKE THE EVANGELIST (1985) Very Rev. John A. D'Antonio; Rev. Msgr. Cesar Petilla; Sr. Bridget Mulligan, O.S.C., Pastoral Assoc.; Deacons James Blaney, Pastoral Assoc.; Joe Reid, Pastoral Assoc.
Res.: 2757 Alderman Rd., 34684. Tel: 727-786-3648; Fax: 727-789-9556. Email: stluke1@verizon.net. Web: www.stlukepalmharbor.org.
St. Luke Early Childhood Center—Tel: 727-787-2914; Fax: 727-786-8648. Email: stlecc@gte.net.
See Guardian Angels Interparochial School, Clearwater under Elementary Schools, Interparochial located in the Institution section.
Catechesis/Religious Program—Tel: 727-787-2845; Fax: 727-786-8648. Rosemary Mandery, D.R.E. Students 271.

PINELLAS PARK, PINELLAS CO., SACRED HEART (1910) Revs. Anthony Coppola; Tom Tobin; Deacons L. Roger Cartier; John Buckley.
Church: 7809 46th Way, 33781. Tel: 727-541-4447; Fax: 727-541-2073. Email: office@sacredheartcatholic.org.
School—7951 46th Way N., 33781. Tel: 727-544-1106; Fax: 727-548-9606. Mr. Andy Shannon, Prin. Religious 1; Lay Teachers 16; Students 178.
Catechesis/Religious Program—Email: religiouseducation@sacredheartcatholic.org. Marion Gawlowicz, D.R.E. Students 96.

PLANT CITY, HILLSBOROUGH CO., ST. CLEMENT (1912) Revs. Thomas Anastasia; Rafael E. Martos; Carlos Rojas; Deacons Manuel Santiago; Neil Legner.
Church & Mailing Address: 1104 N. Alexander St., 33563. Tel: 813-752-8251; Fax: 813-759-2721; 813-764-8019. Email: info@stclementpc.org. Web: www.stclementpc.org.
St. Clement Early Childhood Center—, (Ages 3-5), Tel: 813-754-1237. Maureen Ringley, Dir.
Catechesis/Religious Program—Steven Surrenay, C.R.E. Students 483.

PORT RICHEY, PASCO CO., ST. JAMES THE APOSTLE (1984) Rev. Michael Robert Cormier; Deacon Daniel McCarthy.
Res.: 8400 Monarch Dr., 34668. Tel: 727-869-3130; Fax: 727-869-8886.
See Bishop Larkin Interparochial School, Port Richey under Elementary Schools, Interparochial located in the Institution section.
Catechesis/Religious Program—Email: faith.formation@stjamesportrichey.org. Barbara Ferreris, D.R.E. Students 212.

RIDGE MANOR, HERNANDO CO., ST. ANNE (1960) Rev. John S. Hays; Deacon Robert Mintz.
4142 Treiman Blvd., Hwy. 301, 33523. Email: stanne@embarqmail.com.
Res.: 35135 Whispering Oaks Blvd., 33523. Tel: 352-583-2550; Fax: 352-583-0300.
Catechesis/Religious Program—Sr. Patricia Saunders, O.P., D.R.E. Students 6.

RIVERVIEW, HILLSBOROUGH CO., RESURRECTION (1983) Rev. Msgr. Antonio Diez.
Mailing Address: P.O. Box 418, 33568.
Res.: 6819 Krycul Ave., 33578. Tel: 813-677-2175; Fax: 813-671-7844.
Resurrection Early Childhood Center—, (Ages 3-4), Tel: 813-672-0077. Ivonne Roldan-Cortes, Dir.
Catechesis/Religious Program—Tina Ver Pault, D.R.E. Students 225.

RUSKIN, HILLSBOROUGH CO., ST. ANNE (1956) Revs. John McEvoy; Nelson Restrepo, O.D.C.; Deacon Dale Bacik.
Office: 106 11th Ave., N.E., 33570-3625. Tel: 813-645-1714; Fax: 813-645-5570. Email: office@saintanneruskin.org. Web: www.saintanneruskin.org.
Catechesis/Religious Program—Email: offices@saintanneruskin.org. Mrs. Cindy Cyman, Dir. Faith Formation; Mrs. Kathy Nason, Dir. Faith Formation; Ms. Lorna Carter, Min. & Volunteer Coord. Students 562.

ST. PETE BEACH, PINELLAS CO., ST. JOHN VIANNEY (1939) Revs. John Blum; Allan Tupa; Deacon Joseph Grote. In Res., Rev. Peter Foley.
Church: 445 82nd Ave., 33706. Tel: 727-360-1147; Fax: 727-367-4418 (Office).
School—500 84th Ave., 33706. Tel: 727-360-1113; Fax: 727-367-8734. Email: nsebok@sjvcc.org. Web: www.sjvcs.org. Dr. Kristy Swol, Prin. Lay Teachers 25; Students 201.
Catechesis/Religious Program—Tel: 727-360-1147, Ext. 101; Fax: 727-367-4418. Students 80.

SAFETY HARBOR, PINELLAS CO., ESPIRITU SANTO (1960) Revs. Robert J. Schneider; J. Glenn Diaz; Sr. Paulamarie Lacy, S.N.D., Dir. Liturgical Ministries; Deacons Vincent Alterio, Parish Admin.; Dominic P. Friscia.
Office: 2405 Philippe Pkwy., 34695. Tel: 727-726-8477; Fax: 727-799-2062. Web: www.espiritusanto.cc.
See Espiritu Santo Catholic School, Safety Harbor under Elementary Schools, Interparochial located in the Institution section.
Catechesis/Religious Program—Tel: 727-812-4656; Fax: 727-812-4658. Students 662.

SAN ANTONIO, PASCO CO., ST. ANTHONY OF PADUA (1883) [CEM] Rev. Edwin Palka; Deacons Michael Arno; Irvin Lau.
Res.: 32832 St. Anthony Way, P.O. Box 875, 33576. Tel: 352-588-3081; Fax: 352-588-5070. Email: stanthony@3oaks.com.
See St. Anthony Interparochial School, San Antonio under Elementary Schools, Interparochial located in the Institution section.
Catechesis/Religious Program—Tel: 352-588-3081; Fax: 352-588-5070. Mrs. Sandra Lau, Music Min. Students 142.

SEFFNER, HILLSBOROUGH CO., ST. FRANCIS OF ASSISI (1987) Revs. Christopher Fitzgerald, I.C.; Michael O'Neill, I.C.; Deacons Jerome Thomas; Richard Beaudry.
Res.: 4450 C.R. 579, 33584. Tel: 813-681-9115; Fax: 813-689-4148.
Catechesis/Religious Program—Students 260.

SEMINOLE, PINELLAS CO.
1—BLESSED SACRAMENT (1959) Revs. James Gordon, I.C.; G. Richard Pilger, I.C.
Res.: 11565 66th Ave. N., 33772. Tel: 727-391-4661. Email: sinbuster2@yahoo.com.
School—11501 66th Ave. N., 33772. Tel: 727-391-4660; Fax: 727-391-5638. Web: www.bsschool.org. Cindy Yevich, Prin. Lay Teachers 18; Students 177.
Catechesis/Religious Program—Tel: 727-391-4661; Fax: 727-391-5638. Students 176.
2—ST. JUSTIN MARTYR (1987) Rev. Michael T. O'Brien.
Mailing Address: 10851 Ridge Rd., 33778. Web: www.stjustinmartyr.net.
Catechesis/Religious Program—Tel: 727-397-3312, Ext. 307; Fax: 727-392-6653. Walt Smith, D.R.E. Students 99.

SPRING HILL, HERNANDO CO.
1—ST. FRANCES XAVIER CABRINI (1980) Very Rev. Richard Jankowski; Revs. Krzysztof Gazdowicz; Edward Wal; Deacon James Leonard.
Mailing Address: 5030 Mariner Blvd., 34609. Tel: 352-683-9666; Fax: 352-688-2660. Email: frontdesk@stfrances.org. Web: www.stfrances.org.
In Res., Rev. Andrew Beaudoin, S.S.S.; Deacons Roland Desjardins; Edward Lyczak; Gregorio Lugo; Edward Smith; Robert "Bob" Anderson.
See Notre Dame Interparochial School, Spring Hill under Elementary Schools, Interparochial located in the Institution section.
Catechesis/Religious Program—Tel: 352-686-9954, Ext. 201. Sherri Collinsworth, D.R.E. Students 931.
2—SAINT JOAN OF ARC (1988) Rev. Raymond F. O'Neill; Deacon Lee Hinderscheid.
Res.: 13485 Spring Hill Dr., 34609. Tel: 352-688-0663; Fax: 352-686-7937. Email: jchrchca@campabay.rr.com. Web: home.catholiweb.com/stjoanspringhill.fl.
See Notre Dame Interparochial School, Spring Hill under Elementary Schools, Interparochial located in the Institution section.
Catechesis/Religious Program—Tel: 352-688-0663; Fax: 352-686-7937. Donna Greco, D.R.E. Students 304.
3—ST. THERESA (1969) Revs. James McAteer, I.C.; Edward Wal, Spanish Ministry; Deacons Abraham Rosa; Jose Rios; James McMahon.
Res.: 1107 Commercial Way, 34606. Tel: 352-683-2849; Fax: 352-683-3437. Email: sttheresa.office@bellsouth.net.
See Notre Dame Interparochial School, Spring Hill under Elementary Schools, Interparochial located in the Institution section.
Catechesis/Religious Program—Dorothy Siegrist, D.R.E. Students 213.

SUN CITY CENTER, HILLSBOROUGH CO., PRINCE OF PEACE (1970) Revs. Joel Kovanis; Augustine Mailadiyil; Deacon Angelo Pignataro; Maureen Vilcheck, Business Mgr.
Mailing Address: 702 Valley Forge Blvd., 33573-5353. Tel: 813-634-2328; Fax: 813-633-6670. Web: www.popcc.org.
Res.: 1002 Fordham Dr., 33573. Tel: 813-634-2328.
Catechesis/Religious Program—Email: pat@popcc.org. Students 68.
Mission—Our Lady of Guadalupe Mission (1989) 16650 U.S. 301 S., Wimauma, Hillsborough 33598. Tel: 813-633-2384; Fax: 813-642-9047. Rev. Demetrio Lorden.

TAMPA, HILLSBOROUGH CO.
1—BLESSED SACRAMENT (1959) Rev. Kazimierz Domek.
Res.: 1205 Windermere Way, 33619-4601. Tel: 813-626-2984; Fax: 813-626-2842. Email: office@blessedsacramentcatholic.org.
Church: 7001 12th Ave. S., 33619-4601.
Catechesis/Religious Program—Students 80.
2—CHRIST THE KING (1941) Rev. Msgr. Desmond Daly; Revs. Ralph J. Argentino; Rufino Gepiga.
Res.: 821 S. Dale Mabry Hwy., 33609. Tel: 813-876-5841; Fax: 813-873-2426. Web: www.ctk-tampa.org.

School—3809 Morrison Ave., 33629. Tel: 813-876-8770; Fax: 813-879-0315. Web: www.cks-school.org. Gerard Carrier, Prin. Lay Teachers 40; Students 474.
Catechesis/Religious Program—Tel: 813-870-2509. William W. Woodward, D.R.E. Students 415.

3—Epiphany of Our Lord (1963) Revs. Ignatius Tuoc; Pierre A Dorvil, S.M.M.; Deacon Maximo E. Montayre.
Mailing Address: P.O. Box 11246, 33680. Tel: 813-234-8693; Fax: 813-238-5060. Email: epiphany-tampa@yahoo.com.
Res.: 2510 E. Hanna Ave., 33610. Tel: 813-234-8693; Fax: 813-238-5060.
Catechesis/Religious Program—Tel: 813-238-1751. Students 75.
Mission—St. Joseph Vietnamese Mission 2510 E. Hanna Ave., Hillsborough Co. 33610. Tel: 813-238-8693.
Mission—Immaculate Conception Haitian Catholic Mission 2510 E. Hanna Ave., Hillsborough Co. 33610. Tel: 813-234-8693; Fax: 813-238-5060.

4—Incarnation (1962) Very Rev. Michael Suszynski; Revs. Eugeniusz Gancarz; Jose George; Deacons Frank Julian; Joseph Krzanowski; Pablo Maldonado.
Res.: 5124 Gateway Dr., 33615. Tel: 813-885-7861; Fax: 813-884-3624. Email: irenemartz@tampabay.rr.com. Web: icctampa.org.
School—5111 Webb Rd., 33615. Tel: 813-884-4502; Fax: 813-885-3734. Email: icsmood@icstampa.org. Web: icstampa.org. Mrs. Carolyn Goslee, Prin. Lay Teachers 31; Students 398.
Catechesis/Religious Program—(Grades PreK-5) Tel: 813-887-5110. Janet Foxenberger, D.R.E. Students 781.

5—St. Joseph (1896) Rev. Felix Sanchez.
Mailing Address: P.O. Box 4298, 33677. Email: stjoecctpa@tampabay.rr.com.
Res.: 3012 Cherry St., 33607. Tel: 813-877-5729; Fax: 813-877-5720.
School—St. Joseph Catholic School, (Grades 3-8) Tel: 813-879-7720; Fax: 813-873-0804. Web: www-.stjosephcatholicschooltampa.org. Sr. Lou Ann Fautauzza, F.M.A., Prin.; Mrs. Maria Kremsrieter, Librarian. Daughters of Mary Help of Christians (Paterson, NJ) 4; Lay Teachers 15; Students 201.
Catechesis/Religious Program—Students 167.

6—St. Lawrence (1959) Very Rev. Thomas Morgan; Rev. Msgr. Laurence E. Higgins, Pastor Emeritus (Retired); Rev. Peter K. Bwayo, A.J.; Deacons Gregory Lambert; Julio Vazquez. In Res., Rev. Edward C. Keating, O.F.M. (Retired).
Res. and Mailing: 5225 N. Himes Ave., 33614. Tel: 813-875-4040; Fax: 813-876-0491. Email: office@stlawrence.org. Web: www.stlawrence.org.
School—Tel: 813-879-5090; Fax: 813-879-6886. Therese Hernandez, Prin. Lay Teachers 40; Students 563.
Catechesis/Religious Program—Tel: 813-875-4040, Ext. 206; Fax: 813-876-0491. Students 220.

7—St. Mark the Evangelist (1996) Rev. David DeJulio.
Church: 9724 Cross Creek Blvd., 33647-2594. Tel: 813-907-7746, Ext. 307; Fax: 813-907-7556. Email: frdavid@stmarktampa.org. Web: www.stmarktampa.org.
Catechesis/Religious Program—Tel: 813-907-7746, Ext. 308; Fax: 813-907-7556. Email: faithformation@stmarktampa.org. Mrs. Sandra Bonilla, D.R.E. Students 895.

8—St. Mary (1966) Revs. Jude Vera; Ramon Hernandez; Deacons John Iadanza; Frank Urrico; Sr. Nancy Christopher, O.S.F., Pastoral Assoc.
Church: 15520 North Blvd., 33613. Tel: 813-961-1061; Fax: 813-961-3782. Email: office@stmarytampa.org. Web: www.stmarytampa.org.
Res.: 604 Shellcracker Ct., 33613.
See Most Holy Redeemer Interparochial School, Tampa under Elementary Schools, Interparochial located in the Institution section.
Catechesis/Religious Program—Tel: 813-963-2079; Fax: 813-968-7218. Students 272.
Mission—Santa Maria 14004 N. 15th St., 33613-3554. Tel: 813-910-3575.

9—Mary Help of Christians (1966) Revs. Bruce Craig, S.D.B.; Dominic Dong Kyr Yeom, S.D.B.; Deacon Edmond Anctil.
Tel: 813-626-7588; Fax: 813-626-5882. Email: goodshepherd6410@aol.com; mhcparishtampa@gmail.com.
Res.: 6400 E. Chelsea St., 33610.
Catechesis/Religious Program—Tel: 813-626-9991 (Sundays). Students 42.

10—Most Holy Redeemer (1937) Revs. John C. Aurilia, O.F.M.Cap.; Alfonso D. Pagliara, O.F.M-.Cap.; Edward Henning, O.F.M.Cap.; Peter Nicosia, O.F.M.Cap.; Bro. Miguel Ramirez, O.F.M.Cap.
Res.: 10110 Central Ave., N., 33612-7402. Tel: 813-933-2859; Fax: 813-932-6153. Email: mhroffice@aol.com.
See Most Holy Redeemer Interparochial School, Tampa under Elementary Schools, Interparochial located in the Institution section.
Catechesis/Religious Program—Students 92.

11—Our Lady of Perpetual Help (1890), (Hispanic—Haitian), [JC] Rev. Thomas A. Stokes, S.M.
Res.: 1711 11th Ave., 33605. Tel: 813-248-5701; Fax: 813-241-4128.
Catechesis/Religious Program—Students 63.

12—St. Patrick (1958) [JC] Revs. Angelus Migliore, T.O.R.; Stanley Holland, T.O.R., Parochial Vicar; Mr. Francis (Buzz) Bruno, Operations Mgr.
Parish Office—4518 S. Manhattan Ave., 33611. Tel: 813-839-5337; Fax: 813-831-2778. Web: www.stpatricktampa.org.
Catechesis/Religious Program—Tel: 813-839-4958. Students 80.

13—St. Paul (1963) Revs. Leonard Piotrowski; Joseph Musco; Jose Colina; Deacons Greg Kovalesky, Pastoral Assoc.; John Alvarez; Ron Rojas; Winston McDonald.
Mailing Address: 12708 N. Dale Mabry, 33618. Tel: 813-961-3023; Fax: 813-962-8780. Web: www.stpaul-church.com.
See Most Holy Redeemer Interparochial School, Tampa under Elementary Schools, Interparochial located in the Institution section.
Catechesis/Religious Program—Tel: 813-264-3309; Fax: 813-962-8780. Sue Sferra, D.R.E. Students 830.

14—St. Peter Claver (1893), (African American), Rev. Hugh Chikawe; Deacon William Mahood.
1203 N. Nebraska Ave., 33602-3044. Tel: 813-223-7098. Email: stpeterclaver@gmail.com. Web: spc.catholicweb.com.
Res.: 3708 N. 12th St., 33603. Tel: 813-425-4840; Fax: 813-223-6520.
School—(Grades PreK-8), 1401 Grovernor St., 33602-3044. Tel: 813-224-0865; Fax: 813-223-1982. Sr. Maria Goretti Babatunde, Prin. Lay Teachers 14; Students 90.
Catechesis/Religious Program—Students 20.

15—Sacred Heart (1860) Revs. Andrew J. Reitz, O.F.M.; Sean O'Brien, O.F.M.; George C. Corrigan, O.F.M.
Mailing Address: P.O. Box 1524, 33601. Tel: 813-229-1595; Fax: 813-221-2350. Web: sacredheartfla.org.
School—3515 N. Florida Ave., 33603. Tel: 813-229-0618; Fax: 813-223-7667. Mrs. Margaret Ruiz Carus, Prin. Lay Teachers 16; Students 145.
Catechesis/Religious Program—Students 110.

Tarpon Springs, Pinellas Co., St. Ignatius of Antioch (1889) Revs. Joseph A. Pellegrino; Mathew Moothasseril; Kevin Molloy; Deacons Samuel Moschetto; John Edgerton.
Mailing Address: P.O. Box 1306, 34688-1306. Email: kcreamer@ignatius.net. Web: st.ignatius.net. In Res., Rev. John P. Henry (RVC) (Retired).
Res.: 715 E. Orange St., 34689. Tel: 727-937-4050; Fax: 727-943-0676. Email: kcreamer@ignatius.net. Web: st.ignatius.net.
See Guardian Angels Interparochial School, Clearwater under Elementary Schools, Interparochial located in the Institution section.
St. Ignatius Early Childhood Center— (1984)Tel: 727-937-4050, Ext. 225; Fax: 727-722-9000. Web: stignatiusecc.org. Nancy Gorby, Dir.
Catechesis/Religious Program—Tel: 727-937-4050, Ext. 223; Fax: 727-942-2331. Matthew Moothasseril, Dir. Faith Formation. Students 702.

Temple Terrace, Hillsborough Co., Corpus Christi (1958) Revs. Robert Cadrecha; Erwin Belgica.
Mailing Address: 9715 N. 56th St., 33617. Tel: 813-988-1593; Fax: 813-985-3583. Web: www.spiritualhome.org.
School—Tel: 813-988-1722; Fax: 813-989-2665. Web: www.corpuschristicatholicschool.org. Carmen Caltigirone, Prin. Lay Teachers 16; Students 227.
Catechesis/Religious Program—Lily Hughson, D.R.E. Students 433.

Trinity, Pasco, Co.
St. Peter the Apostle Catholic Church in Trinity, Inc.— (2008) 10710 S.R. 54, Ste. 101, 34655. Tel: 727-264-8968; Fax: 727-264-8969. Email: dhughes54@tampabay.rr.com. Very Rev. Dennis E. Hughes.

Valrico, Hillsborough Co., St. Stephen (1987) Revs. William J. Swengros; Michael Juran; Deacons Daniel Gratkowski; Richard Zeitler. In Res., Rev. Msgr. John Scully (Retired).
Church: 5049 Bell Shoals Rd., 33594. Tel: 813-689-4900; Fax: 813-689-7492. Web: www.ststephencatholic.org.
Catechesis/Religious Program—10424 St. Stephen Cir., Riverview, 33569. Tel: 813-671-4434; Fax: 813-671-2994. Nancy Slade, D.R.E. Students 1,330.

Zephyrhills, Pasco Co., St. Joseph Catholic Church (1912) Revs. George Rozycki; Mathew K. Abraham, A.L.C.P.; Theobold Weria, A.L.C.P.; Deacon Neil Huiskens; Mrs. Theresa H. Miner, Business Admin. Email: thminer@stjoezhills.org.
Church: 5316 11th St., 33542. Tel: 813-782-2813; Fax: 813-788-1036. Email: info@stjoezhills.org. Web: home.catholicweb.com/stjosephzhills/.
See St. Anthony Interparochial School, San Antonio under Elementary Schools, Interparochial located in the Institution section.
Catechesis/Religious Program—Tel: 813-788-2510. Sr. Kathleen Lyons, S.N.D., D.R.E. Students 100.

On Duty Outside the Diocese:
Revs.—
Lamp, Edward
McDonagh, Donat Michael
Mizener, Paul
Morris, Michael J.
Muhr, Michael
Scott, Philip
Toups, David
Young, Robert

Retired:
Rev. Msgrs.—
Bumpus, Harold
Cippel, John A.
Cooke, Colman, V.F.
Cummings, George
Dee, Dacian, J.C.D.
Devine, Michael F.
DuBois, William
Earner, Thomas
Foynes, Aiden
Higgins, Laurence E., P.A.
Lara, James C.
McCahon, Joseph F.
Mulligan, Edward
Neff, John
Scully, John
Revs.—
Colgan, John
Cottrell, James
Dauss, Francis
Dionne, Francis
Donlan, Robert
Estibalez, Inocencio
Gonzalez, Jose G.
Goudreau, Paul
Hervey, Paul
Kane, John
Kearney, William
Lawlor, Brendan
Lettre, Raymond
Mahony, John
Morton, Vincent, V.F.
Villemaire, Arthur

Permanent Deacons:
Alterio, Vincent
Alvarez, John
Anctil, Edmond
Anderson, Kenneth
Anderson, Robert "Bob"
Andre, Peter
Arno, Michael
Bacik, Dale
Beaudry, Richard
Bevvino, Frank, On Duty Outside of Diocese
Blaney, James
Brady, Richard
Braun, Bernard
Buckley, John J.
Burns, Peter
Cardona, David
Carreiro, Manuel
Cartier, Roger L.
Columbus, Michael
Connelly, Bartley
Connors, William
Crall, Jerry
Desjardins, Roland
Dever, Raymond
Diaz, William
Ditewig, William T., Ph.D.
Dunphy, Melvin
Edgerton, John
Evans, Forrest, On Duty Outside the Diocese
Fahrendorf, Ted
Fox, John
Friscia, Dominic
Garcia, Luis
Gibson, James
Gould, Stanley, On Duty Outside of Diocese
Gratkowski, Daniel
Grevenites, James
Grote, Joseph
Hassett, James
Hecht, Lowell
Hinderscheid, Lee

Hooks, James
Huiskens, Nell
Hunt, Samuel
Iadanza, John
Julian, Frank
Kennedy, James, (Brooklyn)
Keough, James J.
Kijonka, Anthony
Knox, Terrence
Koppenaal, John, On Duty Outside of Diocese
Kovalesky, Gregory
Krzanowski, Joseph
Kunder, Frederick
Kurylowicz, Stephen
Lambert, Gregory
Lamothe, Allan
Lau, Irvin
Legner, Neil
Leonard, James
Lesieur, David
Lind, Roger F.
Longo, Frank
Lugo, Gregorio
Lyczak, Edward
Lyons, John
Mahood, William
Makoid, Eric, (Philadelphia)
Maldonado, Pablo
McCarthy, Daniel E.
McDonald, Winston
McGory, Gerald
McMahon, James
Meyer, Richard
Minary, James
Mintz, Robert
Moniz, John
Montayre, Maximo
Moronta, Jose
Moschetto, Samuel
Nagle, Richard, Jr.
Nova, Leocadio
Orth, Kevin
Ortiz, Augustin
Paine, Scott
Pickart, Glenn
Pignataro, Angelo
Polcari, Joseph
Postadan, Romulo, (Newark)
Pullar, James
Quiles, Rafael
Reid, Joseph
Rios, Jose
Roberts, Lionel
Rodriguez, Manuel
Rojas, Ronald
Rosa, Abraham
Ruffner, Michael
Sablone, Stephen
Santiago, Manuel
Shiel, Thomas
Simpson, Robert C.
Sirrianna, David
Smith, Edward
Snyder, Dennis
Solomon, Michael
Solorzano, Jose
Sparks, Robert, (Toronto, Canada)
Spaulding, Ken, (Lansing)
Stahl, Raymond
Stout, Crispin
Taylor, Mark, M.D.
Thomas, Jerome
Torres, Eusebio
Urrico, Frank
Valentin, Juan E.
Vance, Ronald
Varner, David
Vasquez, Julio
Wallace, Barry
Wells, Eric, J.C.L.
White, Gerard
Zayas, Luis
Zeitler, Richard

INSTITUTIONS LOCATED IN THE DIOCESE

[A] COLLEGES

SAINT LEO. *Saint Leo University, Office of Assessment and Institutional Research*, MC 2004, P.O. Box 6665, St. Leo, 33574-6665. Tel: 352-588-8200; 352-588-8331; Fax: 352-588-8885. Email: stephen.brown@saintleo.edu. Web: www.saintleo.edu. Dr. Arthur F. Kirk Jr., Pres.; Rev. Stephan Brown, S.V.D., Dir. of Univ. Ministry. Email: stephan.brown@saintleo.edu; Ms. Linda Taggart, Dir., Center for Catholic-Jewish Studies; Rev. Anthony Kissel, Ph.D., S.T.D., Dept. Chm. Philosophy & Religion; Sr. Mary Dorothy Neuhofer, O.S.B., Prof. & Archivist; Rev. Michael Cooper, S.J., S.T.D., Asst. Prof. Religion; Deacon William T. Ditewig, Ph.D., Dir. Graduate Theology Program.

Saint Leo University, Inc.

Saint Leo University Educational Fund, Inc., An Independent and Catholic Coeducational Liberal Arts University Priests 3; Sisters 1; Lay Teachers 145; Total Enrollment 14,339.

[B] HIGH SCHOOLS, DIOCESAN

ST. PETERSBURG. *St. Petersburg Catholic High School, Inc.*, 6333 Ninth Ave. N., 33710. Tel: 727-344-4065; Fax: 727-343-9311. Email: info@spchs.org. Web: spchs.org. Rev. Michael Conway, S.D.B., Pres.; Bro. Gerald D. Meegan, S.D.B., Prin.; Mrs. Kathleen King, Asst. Prin.; Ms. Lori Wright, Media Center Coord.; Mr. Tod Creneti, Asst. Dir. Athletics; John McMahon, Dean of Students; Mr. Stephen McEntegart, Coord. of Youth Ministry; Mr. John Gerdes, Athletic Dir.; Ms. Lori Wright, Librarian. Salesians of St. John Bosco (New Rochelle, NY) 4; Sisters of the Third Franciscan Order (Syracuse, NY) 1; Lay Teachers 33; Students 551.

CLEARWATER. *Clearwater Central Catholic High School, Inc* (1962) 2750 Haines Bayshore Rd., 33760. Tel: 727-531-1449; Fax: 727-535-7034. Email: jdeputy@ccchs.org. Web: www.ccchs.org. John Venturella, Pres.; James Deputy, Prin.; Cyndi Kibby, Media Specialist; Karen Johnson, Media Specialist. Lay Teachers 35; Students 535.

SPRING HILL. *Bishop McLaughlin Catholic High School, Inc* (2003) 13651 Hays Rd., 34610. Tel: 727-857-2600; Fax: 727-857-2610. Email: rmckendrick@bmchs.com. Web: bmchs.com. Sarah M. Regan, Prin.; Linda Haynie, Media Specialist. Lay Teachers 25; Students 257.

TAMPA. *Tampa Catholic High School, Inc* (1962) 4630 N. Rome Ave., 33603. Tel: 813-870-0860; Fax: 813-877-9136. Email: contactperson@tampacatholic.org. Web: www.tampacatholic.org. Mr. Thomas Reidy, Prin. Congregation of Christian Brothers (New Rochelle, NY) 3; Sisters 1; Lay Teachers 56; Students 704.

[C] HIGH SCHOOLS, PRIVATE

TAMPA. *Academy of the Holy Names High School* (1881) 3319 Bayshore Blvd., 33629. Tel: 813-839-5371; Fax: 813-839-1486. Email: webmaster@holynamestpa.org. Web: www.holynamestpa.org. Dr. Harry Purpur, Pres.; Ms. Penelope Jennings, Prin. High School; Ms. Darcy Devrnja, Prin. Elementary; Mrs. Emily Swigger, Dir. Media Svcs.

Academy of the Holy Names of Florida, Inc. Sisters of the Holy Name of Jesus and Mary (U.S. Ontario Province) 5; Lay Teachers 90; Students 314.

Jesuit High School, 4701 N. Himes Ave., 33614. Tel: 813-877-5344; Fax: 813-872-1853. Web: www.jesuittampa.org. Revs. Douglas Hypolite, S.J., Rector; Richard C. Hermes (S.J.), Chap. & Pres.; Joseph Sabin, Prin.; Ted Beil, Librarian.

Jesuit High School of Tampa, Inc., FKA St. Louis Catholic, Benevolent and Educational Association, Inc.

Jesuit High School Foundation, Inc. Priests 3; Scholastics 3; Sisters 1; Lay Teachers 50; Students 687.

[D] ELEMENTARY SCHOOLS, INTERPAROCHIAL

ST. PETERSBURG. *St. Paul School* (Early Childhood Care Program-K-8), 1900 12th St. N., 33704. Tel: 727-823-6144; Fax: 727-896-0609. Email: efulham@sp1930.org. Web: www.sp1930.org. Elizabeth Fulham, Prin.; Sr. Joan Carberry, Asst. Prin. & Librarian. Serving Blessed Trinity and St. Paul. Sisters 2; Lay Teachers 21; Students 330.

CLEARWATER. *St. Cecelia Interparochial School*, (Grades PreK-8), 1350 Court St., 33756. Tel: 727-461-1200; Fax: 727-446-9140. Email: scsoffice@st-cecelia.org. Web: www.st-cecelia.org. Ms. Mary Beth Scanlon, Prin.; Barbara Bailey, Librarian; Sheila Dale, Contact Person & Admin. Asst. Serving Light of Christ, St. Brendan, St. Catherine of Siena and St. Cecelia. Lay Teachers 37; Students 448.

Guardian Angels Catholic School, (Grades K-8), 2270 Evans Rd., 33763. Tel: 727-799-6724; Fax: 727-724-9018. Email: cmalinski@gacsfl.com. Web: www.gacsfl.com. Cindy Malinski, Prin. & Contact Person; Bridget Carey, Librarian. Serving All Saints, St. Ignatius, St. Luke and St. Michael the Archangel. Sisters 1; Lay Teachers 28; Students 331.

LECANTO. *Pope John Paul II Catholic School*, 4341 W. Homosassa Tr., 34461. Tel: 352-746-2020; Fax: 352-746-3448. Email: lwhitaker@pjp2.net. Web: www.pjp2.net. Dr. Lou Whitaker, Prin.; Lisa Nalepa, Admin. Coord. & Contact Person; Heather Austin, Librarian. Serving Our Lady of Fatima, Our Lady of Grace, St. Benedict, St. Elizabeth Ann Seton, St. Scholastica and St. Thomas the Apostle. Lay Teachers 20; Students 196.

PINELLAS PARK. *Sacred Heart Interparochial School*, (Grades PreK-8), 7951 46th Way N., 33781. Tel: 727-544-1106; Fax: 727-541-2073. Email: principal@sacredheartcatholic.org. Mr. Andy Shannon, Prin. Religious 1; Lay Teachers 16; Students 178.

PORT RICHEY. *Bishop Larkin Interparochial School*, (Grades PreK-8), 8408 Monarch Dr., 34668. Tel: 727-862-6981; Fax: 727-869-9893. Email: office@bishoplarkin.org. Sr. Regina Ozuzu, H.H.C.J., Prin.; Mary S. Barzelay, Librarian. Serving Our Lady Queen of Peace, St. James, St. Michael the Archangel, St. Thomas Aquinas, St. Vincent de Paul and St. Peter the Apostle. Lay Teachers 14; Sisters 3; Students 242.

RIVERVIEW. *St. Stephen Catholic School* (2001) 3-6, Extended Day; 3 yrs. to 8th grade, 10424 Saint Stephen Cir., 33569. Tel: 813-741-9203; Fax: 813-741-9622. Email: tjackson@ststephencatholic.org. Web: www.ststephencatholicschool.org. Therese Jackson, Prin. Lay Teachers 25; Students 408.

SAFETY HARBOR. *Espiritu Santo Catholic School* (2001) (Grades PreK-8), Formerly Espiritu Santo Early Childhood Center., 2405A Philippe Pkwy., 34695-2047. Tel: 727-812-4650; Fax: 727-812-4658. Email: mpenn@escschool.org. Margaret Penn, Prin. Lay Teachers 30; Students 487.

SAN ANTONIO. *St. Anthony Interparochial Catholic School* (1884) (Grades K-8), 32902 Saint Anthony Way, P.O. Box 847, 33576-0847. Tel: 352-588-3041; Fax: 352-588-3142. Email: srbailey@saswarriors.org. Web: www.teacherclasspage.com/1814. Sr. Roberta Bailey, O.S.B., Prin.; Mrs. Betty Will, Librarian. Serving Sacred Heart, St. Anthony, St. Joseph and St. Rita, St. Mark's, St. Anne's, St. Anthony, Brooksville. Sisters 1; Lay Teachers 13; Students 156.

SPRING HILL. *Notre Dame Catholic School*, (Grades PreK-8), 1095 Commercial Way, 34606. Tel: 352-683-0755; Fax: 352-683-3924. Email: notredame@ndischool.org. Web: www.ndischool.org. Sisters Eileen Marie Woodbury, F.S.S.E., Prin.; Alice Ottapurackal, F.S.S.E., Asst. Prin.; Patricia Cameron, Librarian. Serving St. Anne, St. Anthony, St. Frances Xavier Cabrini, St. Joan of Arc, St. Mary and St. Theresa. Sisters 2; Lay Teachers 14; Students 175.

TAMPA. *Most Holy Redeemer Interparochial School* (1954) (Grades K-8), 302 E. Linebaugh Ave., 33612. Tel: 813-933-4750; Fax: 813-933-3181. Email: office@mhr-tampa.org. Web: www.mhr-tampa.org. Fred Coffaro, Prin.; Dr. Jo Ann Quinn, Asst. Prin.; Mary Anderson, Librarian. Serving Most Holy Redeemer, Our Lady of the Rosary, St. Mary, St. Paul, St. Timothy and St. Mark. Lay Teachers 24; Students 275.

[E] ELEMENTARY SCHOOLS, PRIVATE

TAMPA. *Academy of the Holy Names* (1881) (Grades PreK-12), 3319 Bayshore Blvd., 33629. Tel: 813-839-5371; Fax: 813-837-5710. Email: webmaster@holynamestpa.org. Web: www.holynamestpa.org. Ms. Jacqueline Landry, Pres.; Ms. Darcy Devrnja, Prin. Elementary School; Ms. Penelope Jennings, Prin. High School; Ms. Emily Swiger, Dir. Media Svcs.

Academy of the Holy Names of Florida, Inc.

Academy of the Holy Names Foundation, Inc. Sisters of the Holy Names of Jesus and Mary (U.S.-Ontario Provinces) 5; Lay Teachers 90; Students 860.

Villa Madonna School, (Grades PreK-8), (Early Childhood Care Program-3-8), 315 W. Columbus Dr., 33602. Tel: 813-229-1322; Fax: 813-223-4812. Email: hgodin24@villamadonnaschool.com. Web: www.villamadonna.org; villamadonnaschool.com. Sr. Helene Godin, F.M.A., Prin. & Contact; Mrs. Vicki Fabiano, Librarian.

Salesian Sisters of Tampa, Inc. Daughters of Mary Help of Christians 4; Lay Teachers 32; Students 473.

[F] PRESCHOOLS AND DAY CARE CENTERS

ST. PETERSBURG. *Immaculate Conception Early Childhood Center* (1970) Ages 2-5, Extended Care., Lower Pinellas Deanery, 2100 26th Ave. S., 33712. Tel: 727-822-2156; Fax: 727-553-9133. Email: icrita@tampabay.rr.com. Roberta Bell, Dir. & Contact Person; Rev. Timothy H. Sherwood. Lay Teachers 18; Children 142; Total Staff 25.

St Paul Children's Center, 1800 12th St. N., 33704. Tel: 727-822-3481; Fax: 727-822-1754. Email: laura@stpaulstpete.com. Laura Seyss, Dir. 2 months through 2 yrs.

CLEARWATER. *Light of Christ (Early Childhood Center)* (1985) Ages 2-5, Extended Care., Upper Pinellas Deanery, 2176 Marilyn St., 33765. Tel: 727-442-4797; Fax: 727-441-8771. Email: locecc@ij.net. Mrs. Rebecca Daschbach, Preschool Dir. Lay Teachers 13; Students 78.

Little Nazareth Early Childhood Center Ages 3-4., Upper Pinellas Deanery, 820 Jasmine Way, 33756. Tel: 727-447-3494; Fax: 727-442-4810. Email: nazareth@stceceliachurch.org. Web: www.stceceliachurch.org. Mrs. Sandra A. Barbeau, Dir.; Rev. Msgr. Patrick Irwin. Lay Teachers 1; Children 21.

DADE CITY. *Sacred Heart Early Childhood Center* Infant-PreK, Extended Care., Pasco Deanery, 32245 Saint Joe Rd., 33525. Tel: 352-588-4060; Fax: 352-588-4871. Email: shecctw@embargmail.com. Mrs. Toni Watkins, Dir. & Admin. Lay Teachers 28; Children 180.

LAND O'LAKES. *Our Lady of the Rosary Early Childhood Center - Mary's House - ECC*, 2348 Collier Pkwy., P.O. Box 1229, Land O Lakes, 34639. Tel: 813-949-4565. Corrine Ertl, Admin.; Rev. Ronald Aubin, J.C.L. Lay Teachers 8; Students 163.

LARGO. *St. Jerome Early Childhood Center* (1990) Ages 2-4., 10895 Hamlin Blvd., 33774. Tel: 727-596-9491; Fax: 727-596-8953. Email: sjecc@tampabay.rr.com. Web: stjeromeonline.org/ecc. Denise Roach, Dir.; Rev. Msgr. Brendan Muldoon. Lay Teachers 5; Total Staff 12; Children 75.

LUTZ. *St. Timothy Catholic Early Childhood Learning Center*, 17512 Lakeshore Rd., 33558. Tel: 813-960-4857; Fax: 813-961-9429. Email: daisy.cintron@sainttims.org. Web: www.sainttims.org. Ms. Daisy Cintron, M.Ed., Dir.; Rev. Paddy Kennedy. Lay Teachers 7; Students 110.

NEW PORT RICHEY. *St. Thomas Aquinas Early Childhood Center*, 8320 Old CR 54, 34653. Tel: 727-376-2330; Fax: 727-376-2330. Email: staecc@aol.com. Mrs. Cindy McKallip, Dir.; Rev. Michael Lydon; Pamela Bruno, Sec. Lay Teachers 5; Assistants 5; Children 100.

PALM HARBOR. *St. Luke Early Childhood Center* Ages 2-4, Extended Care., 2757 Alderman Rd., 34684. Tel: 727-787-2914; Fax: 727-786-8648. Email: stlecc@verizon.net. Bonnie Faucher, Dir.; Very Rev. John A. D'Antonio, V.F. Lay Teachers 3; Children 141.

TAMPA. *St. Paul Child Enrichment* (1981) Ages 3-4., 12708 N. Dale Mabry Hwy., 33618-2802. Tel: 813-264-3314; Fax: 813-962-8780. Email: jruddy@stpaulchurch.com. Mrs. Joanne Ruddy, Dir.; Rev. Leonard Piotrowski. Lay Teachers 14; Children 120.

TARPON SPRINGS. *St. Ignatius Early Childhood Center* Ages 2-5., 725 E. Orange St., 34689-1306. Tel: 727-937-5427; Fax: 727-722-9000. Email: ngorby@ignatius.net. Web: www.siecc.net. Nancy Gorby, Dir.; Rev. Joseph A. Pellegrino. Teachers 14; Children 120.

[G] SCHOOLS FOR EXCEPTIONAL CHILDREN

PINELLAS PARK. *Morning Star Catholic School - Pinellas Park, Inc.* (1969) 4661 80th Ave. N., 33781. Tel: 813-544-6036; Fax: 813-546-9058. Email: mschool2@tampabay.rr.com. Web: www.morningstarschool.org. Ms. Mary Lou Giacobbe, Prin. Lay Teachers 7; Students 55.

TAMPA. *Morning Star Catholic School - Tampa, Inc.* (1958) 210 E. Linebaugh Ave., 33612. Tel: 813-935-0232; Fax: 813-932-2321; Fax: 813-932-2321. Email: edaly@tampa-morningstar.org. Web: www.tampa-morningstar.org. Eileen Daly, Prin.; Leslie Maggio, Librarian. Lay Teachers 11; Students 66.

[H] SCHOOLS FOR THEOLOGICAL AND SPIRITUAL TRAINING

ST. PETERSBURG. *Father William F. Balfe Memorial Library*, 1365 Hays Rd., Spring Hill, 34610. Very Rev. Robert Morris, V.G., Exec. Dir. Diocesan Library

CLEARWATER. *The Cenacle of Our Lady of Divine Providence* School of Spirituality., 702 S. Bayview Ave., 33759. Tel: 727-724-9505; Fax: 727-724-9421. Email: cenacleofourlady@aol.com. Web: www.divineprovidence.org. Ronald W. Novotny, S.T.L., Ph.D., Dir. & Contact Person. Lay Teachers 2; Total Staff 9; Total Enrollment 125.

[I] CATHOLIC CHARITIES

ST. PETERSBURG. *Catholic Charities, Diocese of St. Petersburg, Inc.* Tel: 727-893-1313; Fax: 727-893-1307. Email: catholic.charities@ccdosp.org. Web: www.ccdosp.org. Mr. Frank V. Murphy III, Pres.; Sheila Lopez, Chief Operating Officer. Personnel 95.

Jeff Forbes Center - Administrative Offices, 1213 16th St. N., 33705. Tel: 727-893-1313; Fax: 727-893-1307. Email: catholiccharities@ccdosp.org. Web: www.ccdosp.org.

Services Provided Life Ministry: Elder: Respite Programs for Caregivers of Memory Loss Clients, Parish based Volunteer Support. Family Services: Family Support & Case Management, Life Skills Education, Counseling, Resettlement & Immigration Assistance, Mobile Medical Unit for Farm Workers, Pregnancy & Parenting Support.; Shelter Ministry: HIV Services: Permanent & Transitional Housing & Voucher Program.Farm Worker Services: Full Service for Migrant Farm Workers including 122 apartments. Homeless Services: Prevention, Housing Counseling, Respite, Emergency, Permanent & Transitional Housing. Elder: HUD 202 Very Low-Income Senior Housing, HUD 202 Service Co-ordination. Affordable Housing: Homebuyer Education & Housing Counseling & Foreclosure Prevention.Email: catholic.charities@cdosp.org. Web: www.ccdosp.org.

Catholic Charities Community Development Corp., 1213 16th St. N., 33705. Tel: 727-893-1313; Fax: 727-893-1307. Email: cccdc@ccdosp.org. Web: www.ccdosp.org. Mr. Frank V. Murphy III, Pres.

[J] GENERAL HOSPITALS

ST. PETERSBURG. *St. Anthony's Hospital, Inc.*, 1200 7th Ave. N., 33705. Tel: 727-825-1103; Fax: 727-825-1223. Web: www.stanthonys.com. Email: john.mullet@baycare.org. Rev. John Mullet, M.Div., M.A., Dir. Pastoral Care; Rev. Al Hall, Chap. (Baptist); Sr. Susan McGillicudy, O.S.F., Foundation.

St. Anthony's Hospital, Inc.

St. Anthony's Ancillary Services, Inc.

St. Anthony's Professional Buildings and Services, Inc.

St. Anthony's Health Care Foundation, Inc. Franciscan Sisters of Allegany.

TAMPA. *St. Joseph's Hospital, Inc* (1934) 3001 W. Martin Luther King Blvd., 33607. Tel: 813-870-4020; Fax: 813-870-4639. Email: sisterpat.shirley@baycare.org. Web: www.sjbhealth.org. P.O. Box 4227, 33677. Tel: 813-870-4000; Fax: 813-870-4639. Revs. Kenneth Gerth, M.C.C.J., Chap.; Carmen Caban, Chap.; Marilyn Cummings, Chap.; George Francis, Chap.; Sabrina Mc Gavock, Chap.; John Aransi, Chap.; Denis Kitenge (Congo), Chap.; Tina Imperato, Chap.; Gail Radu, Chap.; Revs. Bernard Smith, Chap.; George Maliekal, Chap.; Molly Mary Darnet, Chap.; Bev Shives, Chap.; Jan Hoyt, Pastoral Care Educ.

St. Joseph's Hospital, Inc.

St. Joseph's Ancillary Services, Inc.

St. Joseph's Community Care, Inc.

St. Joseph's Enterprises, Inc.

St. Joseph's Health Care Center, Inc.

St. Joseph's Hospital of Tampa Foundation, Inc.

St. Joseph's Specialty Services, Inc.

John Knox Village of Tampa Bay, Inc.

Franciscan Properties, Inc.

San Damiano Enterprises, Inc. Franciscan Sisters of Allegany. Inpatient Admissions 41,954; Emergency Room Visits 111,415; Outpatient Visits 151,594; Pastoral Care Volunteers 18; Eucharistic Ministers 70; Bed Capacity 889; Physicians 1,200; Total Assisted Annually 122,438; Total Staff 3,441.

[K] RETIREMENT AND HEALTH CARE CENTERS

ST. PETERSBURG. *Bon Secours St. Petersburg Home Care Services Inc.*, 11001 Roosevelt Blvd, Ste. 1000, Saint Petersburg, 33716. Tel: 727-577-7990; Fax: 727-576-6138. Email: janet_keller@bshsi.com. Web: www.bonsecoursstpete.org. Karen Reich, Exec. Vice Pres. Sisters of Bon Secours, (Serves Pinellas & Pasco Counties)

**Bon Secours-Maria Manor Nursing Care Center, Inc.*, 10300 Fourth St. N., 33716. Tel: 727-576-1025; Fax: 727-576-1447. Email: janet_ford@bshsi.org. Web: www.bonsecourstpete.org. Karen Reich, Exec. Vice Pres.; Janet Keller, Admin. Sisters of Bon Secours. Bed Capacity 274; Residents Year Round 260; Total Assisted Annually 360; Total Staff 400.

CLEARWATER. *La Clinica Guadalupana, Inc.* (1995) 1000 Lakeview Rd., Unit 4, 33756. Tel: 727-461-7730; Fax: 727-462-8117. Dr. Jay E. Carpenter, M.D., Pres. Total Assisted Annually 3,000; Staff 1.

[L] RETIREMENT HOUSING

ST. PETERSBURG. *Blessed Trinity Housing, Inc. dba Trinity House* 5701 16th St. S., 33705. Tel: 727-865-7590; Fax: 727-867-1701. Email: managertrinityhouse@verizon.net. Nanci Huffer, Mgr. Residents 76; Total Staff 5.

St. Clement Housing, Inc., 6363 9th Ave., N., P.O. Box 40200, 33743-0200. Rev. Thomas Anastasia, Contact Person.

Holy Cross Housing dba Casa Santa Cruz 7825 54th Ave. N., 33709. Tel: 727-541-2631; Fax: 727-547-6741. Email: fguerra@ccdosp.org. Mr. Joseph A. DiVito, Registered Agent. Total Staff 5; Total in Residence 76.

CLEARWATER. *St. Michael's Housing, Inc. dba Casa Miguel* (1984) 2285 State Rd. #580, 33763. Tel: 727-797-8551. Email: glungaro@ccdosp.org. Mrs. JoAnn Lungaro, Admin. Independent Living. Total Staff 5; Residents 82.

HUDSON. *Bethlehem Housing, Inc. dba Bethlehem House* 8010 State Rd. 52, 34667. Tel: 727-819-2861; Fax: 727-869-2781. Email: bethlehem.house@verizon.net. Virginia Seamster, Mgr. Residents 60; Total Staff 3.

TAMPA. *Blessed Sacrament Housing, Inc. dba Blessed Sacrament Manor* 6801 12th Ave. S., 33619. Tel: 813-620-0221; Fax: 813-620-0473. Email: cgallo@ccdosp.org. Mr. Frank Murphy, Pres. Clients 74; Total Staff 2.

Christ the King Housing, Inc. dba Kings Arms 4125 N. Lincoln Ave., 33607. Tel: 813-873-0234; Fax: 813-871-2061. Email: k.arms@verizon.net. Jesus Arias, Mgr. Total Staff 4; Total in Residence 90.

Christ the King Housing, Inc. dba Kings Manor 2946 W. Columbus Dr., 33607. Tel: 813-875-0139; Fax: 813-876-2182. Email: kingsmanor.km@verizon.net. Betsy Rowen, Admin. Residents 110; Total Staff 5.

Epiphany Housing of Tampa, Inc. dba Epiphany Arms 2508 E. Hanna Ave., 33610. Tel: 813-232-2693; Fax: 813-232-2984. Email: epiparms@aol.com. Total Staff 12; Residents 80.

St. Lawrence Housing, Inc., 5225 N. Himes Ave., 33614-6623. Tel: 813-875-4040; Fax: 813-876-0491. Very Rev. Thomas Morgan, V.F., Pres.

St. Lawrence Housing II, Inc., c/o 5225 N. Himes Ave., 33614. Tel: 813-875-4040; Fax: 813-876-0491. Very Rev. Thomas Morgan, V.F.

St. Patrick's Housing Corporation dba Patrician Arms 4516 S. Manhattan Ave., 33611. Tel: 813-835-8227; Fax: 813-835-7918. Email: blendstrom@ccdosp.org. Total Staff 6; Total in Residence 85.

St. Patrick's Housing Corporation II, 4516 S. Manhattan Ave., 33611. Tel: 727-430-1767.

[M] SENIOR CENTERS

LARGO. *Bethlehem Centre, Inc.*, 10895 Hamlin Blvd., 34644. Tel: 727-596-9394; Fax: 727-596-6792. Lois Wisuri, Dir. & Contact. Senior Center offering programs in Fitness, Exercise, Social, Educational, Music, Art, Computers, and Religious Nature on Tuesday, Wednesday, and Friday. Hot luncheon is available on Tuesday and Friday (Oct.-April). Total Staff 1; Total Assisted Per Week 100.

[N] MONASTERIES AND RESIDENCES OF PRIESTS AND BROTHERS

ST. PETERSBURG. *St. Anthony Friary* Franciscan Residence and Retirement Community., 357 Second St. N., 33701. Tel: 727-822-7917; Fax: 727-821-8067. Email: saf102@tampabay.rr.com. Revs. Roy Gasnick, O.F.M.; Cornelius Conti, O.F.M.; Mario Di Lella, O.F.M.; Gerald M. Dolan, O.F.M.; Louis V. Iasiello, O.F.M.; Venant Lalonde, O.F.M.; Miguel A. Loredo, O.F.M.; John J. Marino, O.F.M.; Venard Murphy, O.F.M.; James F. Toal, O.F.M., Guardian; Bros. Paul J. Chelus, O.F.M.; Michael Madden, O.F.M.; Valerian Vaverchack, O.F.M. Total in Residence 26; Total Staff 7.

Full-time Active Ministry: Revs. Thomas K. Murphy, O.F.M.; William Bried, O.F.M.; John Anglin, O.F.M.; Martin Bednar, O.F.M.; Roderic Petrie, O.F.M.; Bro. John Capozzi, O.F.M., Vicar.

Retirement Community: Revs. James Jones, O.F.M. (Retired); Guy Morgan, O.F.M. (Retired); Alexis P. Morris, O.F.M. (Retired); Alexius J. Mulrenan, O.F.M. (Retired); Emeric Szlezak, O.F.M. (Retired); Edward J. Dillon, O.F.M. (Retired); Roch A. Coogan, O.F.M. (Retired).

Missionaries of Africa (1868) 5757 Seventh Ave. N., 33710. Tel: 727-343-1001; Fax: 727-343-4395. Email: mafr.fl2@verizon.net. Revs. Richard Archambault, M.Afr., Office Coord.; Joseph E. Hebert, M.Afr., Coord.; John J. Braun, M.Afr.; Roger Bisson, M.Afr.; Youville Labonte, M.Afr.; Joseph Kay, M.Afr.; Joseph Sys, M.Afr.; Bros. Charles Feldmann, M.Afr.; Vernon Zachman, M.Afr. Priests 7; Brothers 2.

St. Peter Nolasco Residence (1984) 5650 Seventh Ave. N., 33710-7112. Tel: 727-345-4766; Fax: 727-347-5345. Email: wayne@orderofmercy.org. Revs. Wayne C. Genereux, O.de.M., Local Supr.; Oscar Kozyra, O.de.M.; Michael E. Perry, O.de.M.

Fathers of Our Lady of Mercy, Inc. Total Staff 4; Total in Residence 4.

CLEARWATER BEACH. *St. Paul Friary*, 50 Somerset St., 33767-1543. Tel: 727-443-7351; Fax: 727-462-0150. Rev. Edmund Ansaloni, O.F.M., Vicar; Bros. Kenneth Ghastin, O.F.M.; Mark Brown, O.F.M.

PINELLAS PARK. *Priests of the Sacred Heart*, 6701 82nd Ave. N., 33781. Tel: 727-541-2661; Fax: 727-547-0408. Revs. Thomas Burns, S.C.J.; Frank Burshnick, S.C.J.; Joseph Doscher, S.C.J. (Retired); Ralph Intranuovo, S.C.J.; Steve Pujdak, S.C.J., House Treas.; Gregory Speck, S.C.J., Assoc. Coord.; Leonard Tadyszak, S.C.J. (Retired); Raymond Vega, S.C.J. (Retired); Charles Yost, S.C.J. (Retired); Bros. Benedict Humpfer, S.C.J., Coord.; Gabriel Kersting, S.C.J., (Retired); Timothy Murphy, S.C.J., (Retired). Total Staff 2; Total in Residence 11.

ST. LEO. *St. Leo Abbey* (1889) P.O. Box 2350, 33574. Tel: 352-588-8624; Fax: 352-588-5217. Web: www.saintleoabbey.org. Rt. Rev. Isaac Camacho, O.S.B., Abbot; Revs. Damian DuQuesnay, O.S.B.; James Hoge, O.S.B.; Andrew Metzger, O.S.B.; Paul Romfh, O.S.B.; David Steinwachs, O.S.B., Prior; Robert Velten, O.S.B. Priests 9; Brothers 13; Internal Oblates 1; Novices & Juniors 1.

ST. PETE BEACH. *Franciscan Friary*, 555 - 68th Ave., 33706. Tel: 727-367-2408. Rev. Bernardas Talaisis, O.F.M.

SEMINOLE. *Capuchin Franciscan Residence*, 7171 128th St. N., 33776. Tel: 727-397-0011; Fax: 727-392-7183. Web: www.capuchin.org. Rev. Gregory Reisert, O.F.M.Cap., Admin.

[O] CONVENTS AND RESIDENCES FOR SISTERS

ST. PETERSBURG. *St. Anthony Hospital Convent*, 631 11th St. N., 33705-1409. Tel: 727-825-1142; 727-825-1602 Sr. Flynn; Fax: 727-825-1490. Email: marfln@juno.com. Sr. Marita Flynn, O.S.F., Contact & Local Min. Franciscan Sisters of Allegany (Allegany, NY). Total in Residence 6.

ST. LEO. *Holy Name Monastery* (1889) 33201 State Hwy. 52, 33574-2450. Tel: 352-588-8320; Fax: 352-588-8319. Email: holyname@saintleo.edu. Web: www.floridabenedictines.com. P.O. Box 2450, 33574-2450. Sr. Mary Clare Neuhofer, O.S.B., Prioress.

Benedictine Sisters of Florida, Motherhouse and Novitiate of the Benedictine Sisters of Florida. Professed Sisters 18.

TAMPA. *St. Clare Convent*, Franciscan Sisters of Allegany, Attn: Brenda Johnson: 2924 W. Curtis St., 33614-7102. Tel: 813-870-4272; Fax: 813-414-9074. Franciscan Sisters of Allegany (Allegany, NY).

St. Elizabeth Convent, 3000 N. Perry Ave., 33603-5345. Tel: 813-229-1978; 813-229-2229; Fax: 813-228-9066. Email: st.e3000@juno.com. Web: www.alleganyfranciscans.org. Franciscan Sisters of Allegany. Total Staff 3; Total in Residence 14.

Franciscan Convent, 3006 Perry Ave., 33603-5345. Tel: 813-229-2492; Fax: 813-228-0748. Email: cmcahill4@verizon.net. Franciscan Sisters of Allegany. Total in Residence 4.

Surfside Condos - Franciscan Sisters of Allegany, NY, 15462 Gulf Blvd., #1003, Madeira Beach, 33708. Tel: 727-898-9501. Email: berose@ij.net.

Villa Madonna Convent, 2611 N. Massachusetts Ave., 33602. Tel: 813-229-1322, Ext. 393; Fax: 813-223-4812. Email: kkeraitis@villamadonnaschool.com. Web: www.villamadonnaschool.com. Daughters of Mary Help of Christians (Haledon, NJ). Total Staff 4; Total in Residence 4.

[P] RETREAT CENTERS

CLEARWATER. *Retreat Ministry of the Marian Servants of Divine Providence*, 702 S. Bayview Ave., 33759. Tel: 727-799-4003; Fax: 727-724-9421. Email: msretreats@aol.com. Web: www.divineprovidence.org. Adrienne Novotny, Contact Person.

LUTZ. *Bethany Center, Inc.*, 18150 Bethany Center Dr., 33558. Tel: 813-960-6300; Fax: 813-960-6303. Web: www.bethanycenterfl.org. Rev. John B. Lipscomb, Spiritual Dir.

SAINT LEO. *Saint Leo Abbey Retreat Center* (1975) 33601 State Rd. 52, P.O. Box 2350, 33574-2350. Tel: 352-588-8184; Fax: 352-588-5217. Email: donna.cooper@saintleo.edu. Web: www.saintleoabbey.org. Bro. Jacob Tippett, Guest Master. Total Staff 4.

TAMPA. *Franciscan Center, Retreat House*, 3010 N. Perry Ave., 33603-5345. Tel: 813-229-2695; Fax: 813-228-0748. Email: cmcahill4@verizon.net. Web: www.franciscancentertampa.org. Sr. Catherine Cahill, O.S.F., Dir.; Christina Strain, Admin.; Maureen R. Connors, Ph.D., Co-Dir. Progs.; Carol Mitchell, Ph.D., Co-Dir. Progs.; Karen Davies, Admin. Asst.; Ellen Hochschwender, Dir. Public Rels. Franciscan Sisters of Allegany. Total Staff 12.

Salesian Society of Florida, Inc. dba Mary Help of Christians Center (1928) 6400 E. Chelsea St., 33610-5628. Tel: 813-626-6191; Fax: 813-621-5251. Email: ddonovan@mhctampa.org. Web: www.mhctampa.org. Revs. Michael Chubirko, S.D.B.; Bruce Craig, S.D.B.; Dennis Donovan, S.D.B., Dir.; John Masiello, S.D.B.; Paul Chuong Nguyen, S.D.B.; Bro. David Tieney, S.D.B.; Rev. Dominic Dong Kyr Yeom, S.D.B.; Bros. Joseph Ackroyd, S.D.B.; Kevin Connolly, S.D.B.; David Iovacchini, S.D.B.; George Marquis, S.D.B.; John Zito, S.D.B.

[Q] PRIVATE ASSOCIATIONS OF THE CHRISTIAN FAITHFUL

CLEARWATER. *Community of the Marian Servants of Divine Providence* (1981) 711 S. Bayview Ave., 33759. Tel: 727-797-7412; Fax: 727-726-1631. Email: marianservants@juno.com. Web: www.divineprovidence.org. Diane F. Brown, Dir.

Our Lady of Divine Providence House of Prayer Tel: 727-797-7412; Fax: 727-726-1631. Email: marianservant@juno.com.

[R] SUMMER CAMPS

ST. PETERSBURG. *Our Lady of Good Counsel Camp* (1948) 8888 E. Gobbler Dr., Floral City, 34436. Tel: 352-726-2198; Fax: 352-726-3212. Email: goodcounselcamp@aol.com. Web: goodcounselcamp.catholicweb.com. Very Rev. James B. Johnson, V.F., Dir.

Our Lady of Fatima Church: 550 U.S. Hwy. 41 S., Inverness, 34450. Tel: 352-726-1910; Fax: 352-344-8384. Very Rev. James B. Johnson, V.F., Pastor.

[S] CAMPUS MINISTRY

ST. PETERSBURG. *Eckerd College - Catholic Campus Ministry* c/o 5650 7th Ave. N., 33710-7112. Tel: 727-864-8470; Fax: 727-864-8040. Rev. Oscar Kozyra, O.de.M., Chap. Total in Residence 1.

TAMPA. *Catholic Student Center, University of South Florida* (1967) 13005 N. 50th St., Temple Terrace, 33617-1022. Tel: 813-988-3727; Fax: 813-988-3727. Email: director@catholicusf.org. Web: www.catholicusf.org. Rev. Alan Weber, Dir.

University of Tampa - Catholic Student Organization c/o Sacred Heart Catholic Church, P.O. Box 1524, 33601. Tel: 813-229-1595; Fax: 813-221-2350.

[T] MISCELLANEOUS

ST. PETERSBURG. *Catholic Charities Community Dev. Corp.*, 1213 16th St. N., 33705. Tel: 727-893-1313; Fax: 727-893-1307. Web: www.ccdosp.org. Mr. Frank V. Murphy III, Pres.

Catholic Charities Housing, Inc., 1213 16th St. N., 33705. Tel: 727-893-1314, Ext. 202; Fax: 727-893-1307. Email: housing@ccdosp.org. Web: www.ccdosp.org. Mr. Frank V. Murphy III, Pres.

Magnificat Inc., Lower Pinellas Deanery Chapter of the Diocese of St. Petersburg, Florida, 4401 14th St. NE, 33702. Tel: 727-526-3969. Email: abdiaco@aol.com.

Marian Servants of the Holy Spirit, Inc., 6363 9th Ave. N., P.O. Box 40200, 33710. Tel: 727-344-1611; Fax: 727-345-3086. Email: dmcd1050@hotmail.com. Rev. Donat Michael McDonagh, Pres.

Partners with Haiti, Inc., 1800 12th St., N., Saint Petersburg, 33704. Tel: 727-822-3481; Fax: 727-822-1754. Rev. Msgr. Robert C. Gibbons, J.C.L.

Pastoral Center, 6363 9th Ave N., 33710. For detailed information on the following listings contact the Chancery Office.

Allegany Community Out Reach Grant Fund, Inc.
Catholic Charities Housing, Inc.
Catholic Education Foundation, Inc.
Catholic Media Ministry, Inc.
Christopher Assurance, Inc.
The Congregation of the Sisters of St. Clare (Florida), Inc., 625 Court St. 2nd Fl., Clearwater, 33756.
Allegany Franciscan Ministries, Inc.
Regis Manor, Inc.
WBVM, 90.5 FM, Inc., Clearwater.
Catholic Charities Community Development, Corp.
Catholic Charities Foundation of Tampa Bay, Inc.
The Greater Tampa Catholic Lawyers Guild, Inc., P.O. Box 1816, Tampa, 33601.
Franciscan Center of Tampa, FL, Inc., 3010 Perry Ave., Tampa, 33603. Tel: 813-229-2695; Fax: 813-228-0748.
Savings and Loan Trust
Employee Benefit Trust
The Salesian Society of St. Petersburg, Inc., 6470 13th Ave., N., 33710. Tel: 727-374-0224. Rev. Dennis Donovan, S.D.B., Contact Person.

BELLAIR. *Mantle of Mary, Inc.*, 845 Indian Rocks Rd., Belleair, 33756. Tel: 727-446-0939. Email: info@mantleofmercy.co; info@mantlepublishing.com. Web: www.mantlepublishing.com. Carol Marquardt, Pres., Founder.

CLEARWATER. *Allegany Franciscan Ministries, Inc.* (1997) 33290 U.S. Hwy 19, #269, 34684. Tel: 727-507-9668; Fax: 727-507-8557. Email: eboyle@afmfl.org. Web: www.afmfl.org. Total Staff 7.

OLDSMAR. **Living His Life Abundantly International, Inc.*, 325 Scarlet Blvd., 34677-3019. Tel: 813-854-1518; 800-558-5452; Fax: 813-891-1267. Email: info@lhla.org. Web: www.lhla.org. Johnnette S. Benkovic, Pres.

TAMPA. **Help Brings Hope for Haiti, Inc.*Email: bbyars1@verizon.net.

VALRICO. **Knanya Catholic Congress of Central Florida, Inc.*, 2620 Washington, 33594. Tel: 813-681-6189; Fax: 813-230-8031. Email: jillikal@aol.com.

RELIGIOUS INSTITUTES OF MEN REPRESENTED IN THE DIOCESE

For further details refer to the corresponding bracketed number in the Religious Institutes of Men or Women section.

[]—*Apostles of Jesus*—A.J.
[0380]—*Comboni Missionaries of the Sacred Heart* (Verona)—M.C.C.J.
[0310]—*Congregation of Christian Brothers* (New Rochelle, NY)—C.F.C.
[0220]—*Congregation of the Blessed Sacrament* (Cleveland, OH)—S.S.S.
[1330]—*Congregation of the Missions* (Madrid, Spain)—C.M.
[0520]—*Franciscan Friars* (New York, NY; Dublin, Ireland)—O.F.M.
[]—*Franciscan Province of Our Lady of Guadalupe*—O.F.M
[]—*Holy Spirit Fathers*—A.L.C.P.
[0300]—*Institute of Charity* (Peoria, IL)—I.C.
[0780]—*Marist Brothers* (New York, NY)—F.M.S.
[0780]—*Marist Fathers* (Washington, D.C.)—S.M.
[0800]—*Maryknoll Brothers*—M.M.
[0850]—*Missionaries of Africa* (Washington, DC)—M.Afr.
[0380]—*Missionary Society of St. Thomas the Apostle*—M.S.T.
[0870]—*Montford Missionaries*—SMM
[0350]—*Order of Cistercians of the Strict Observance* Spencer, MA—O.C.S.O.
[0470]—*Order of Friar Minor Capuchin* (White Plains, NY; Union City, NJ)—O.F.M.Cap.
[0970]—*Order of Our Lady of Mercy* (Cleveland, OH)—O.deM.
[0430]—*Order of Preachers (Dominicans)* (Dublin, Ireland)—O.P.
[0200]—*Order of St. Benedict* (St. Leo, FL)—O.S.B.
[0610]—*Priests of the Congregation of the Holy Cross* (Bridgeport, CT)—C.S.C.
[1130]—*Sacred Heart Fathers and Brothers* (Hales Corner, WI)—S.C.J.
[1190]—*Salesians of St. John Bosco* (New Rochelle, NY)—S.D.B.
[]—*Scarboro Foreign Missions* (Scarboro, Ontario, Canada)—S.F.M.
[0690]—*Society of Jesus* (New Orleans, LA; Chicago, IL; Boston, MA)—S.J.
[0990]—*Society of the Catholic Apostolate*—S.A.C.
[0420]—*Society of the Divine Word* (Waukegen, IL.)—S.V.D.
[0560]—*Third Order Regular of Saint Francis* (Pittsburgh, PA; Etlers, PA)—T.O.R.

RELIGIOUS INSTITUTES OF WOMEN REPRESENTED IN THE DIOCESE

[]—*African Benedictine Sisters of St. Agnes*
[0230]—*Benedictine Sisters of Florida* (St. Leo, FL)—O.S.B.
[1010]—*Congregation of Divine Providence* (San Antonio, TX)—C.D.P.
[3110]—*Congregation of Our Lady of Retreat in the Cenacle* (Lake Ronkonkoma, NY)—R.C.
[0850]—*Daughters of Mary Help of Christians* (Haledon, NJ)—F.M.A.
[0960]—*Daughters of Wisdom* (Islip, NY)—D.W.
[1070-13]—*Dominican Sisters* (Adrian, MI)—O.P.
[1070-11]—*Dominican Sisters of Our Lady of the Rosary* (Sparkill, NY)—O.P.
[1370]—*Franciscan Missionaries of Mary* (Bronx, NY)—F.M.M.
[1180]—*Franciscan Sisters of Allegany, New York*—O.S.F.
[1430]—*Franciscan Sisters of Our Lady of Perpetual Help* (St. Louis, MO)—O.S.F.
[1460]—*Franciscan Sisters of St. Elizabeth* (Parsippany, NJ)—F.S.S.E.
[3760]—*Fransiscan Poor Clare* (New Orleans, LA)—O.S.C.

[1260]—*Handmaids of the Holy Child Jesus* (Nigeria)—H.H.C.J.

[]—*Hermanas Franciscanas deLa Imaculada*—H.F.I.

[]—*Hermit: Consecrated Virgin* (St. Petersburg, FL)—HER.C.V.

[2577]—*Institute of the Sisters of Mercy of the Americas* (Cumberland, RI)—R.S.M.

[2420]—*Marist Missionary Sisters (Missionary Sisters of the Society of Mary)*—S.M.S.M.

[2490]—*Medical Mission Sisters* (Philadelphia, PA)—M.M.S.

[]—*Missionaries of Our Lady of Light*—M.D.M.L.

[D]—*Our Lady of Kilimanjaro* (Tanzania, Africa)—C.D.N.K.

[3760P]—*Poor Clare Sisters* (Evansville, IN)—O.S.C.

[2970]—*School Sisters of Notre Dame* (Baltimore, MD; Chicago, IL; Wilton Prov.)—S.S.N.D.

[1680]—*School Sisters of St. Francis* (Milwaukee, WI)—S.S.S.F.

[3590]—*Servants of Mary (Servite Sisters)* (Ladysmith, WI)—O.S.M.

[1070-03]—*Sinsinawa Dominicans* (Sinsinawa, WI)—O.P.

[0440]—*Sisters of Charity of Cincinnati* (Mt. St. Joseph, OH)—S.C.

[0500]—*Sisters of Charity of Nazareth* (Nazareth, KY)—S.C.N.

[0590]—*Sisters of Charity of Saint Elizabeth* (Convent Station, NJ)—S.C.

[2575]—*Sisters of Mercy of The Americas* (Chicago, IL; Buffalo, NY)—R.S.M.

[2990]—*Sisters of Notre Dame* (Chardon, OH)—S.N.D.

[3360]—*Sisters of Providence* (St. Mary of the Woods, IN)—S.P.

[1490]—*Sisters of Saint Francis of the Neuman Communities* (Syracuse)—O.S.F.

[3893]—*Sisters of Saint Joseph of Chestnut Hill, Philadelphia*—S.S.J.

[]—*Sisters of St. Anne Bangalore*—S.A.B.

[3730]—*Sisters of St. Basil the Great* (Uniontown, PA)—O.S.B.M.

[0230]—*Sisters of St. Benedict of Beech Grove, IN*—O.S.B.

[3750]—*Sisters of St. Chretienne* (Wrentham, MA)—S.S.Ch.

[3770]—*Sisters of St. Clare* (Dublin, Ireland)—O.S.C.

[1710]—*Sisters of St. Francis of Mary Immaculate* (Joliet, IL)—O.S.F.

[1630]—*Sisters of St. Francis of Penance and Christian Charity* (Stella Niagara, NY)—O.S.F.

[1570]—*Sisters of St. Francis of the Holy Family* (Dubuque, IA)—O.S.F.

[3900]—*Sisters of St. Joseph* (St. Augustine, FL)—S.S.J.

[3893]—*Sisters of St. Joseph* (Chestnut Hill, PA)—S.S.J.

[3930]—*Sisters of St. Joseph, Third Order of St. Francis*—S.S.J.-T.O.S.F.

[]—*Sisters of St. Michael the Archangel* (Toronto, Canada)—S.S.M.A.

[1920]—*Sisters of the Holy Cross* (Notre Dame, IN)—C.S.C.

[1930]—*Sisters of the Holy Cross* (Montreal, Quebec, Canada)—C.S.C.

[1990]—*Sisters of the Holy Names of Jesus and Mary* (Albany, NY)—S.N.J.M.

[2160]—*Sisters, Servants of the Immaculate Heart of Mary* (Scranton, PA)—I.H.M.

[4190]—*Visitation of Holy Mary* (Wheeling, WV)—V.H.M.

DIOCESAN CEMETERIES

CLEARWATER. *Miserere Guild, Inc. dba Calvary Catholic Cemetery* 5233 118th Ave. N., 33760. Tel: 727-572-4355; Fax: 727-592-9241. Rev. Msgr. Norman Balthazar, Dir.

ST. PETERSBURG. *Holy Cross Catholic Cemetery, Inc.*, 6363 Ninth Ave. N., 33713.

NECROLOGY

† Bolger, Rev. Msgr. John F., St. Petersburg, FL Transfiguration—Died 2009

† Trainor, Rev. Msgr. Patrick, St. Pete Beach, FL St. John Vianney—Died Feb. 7, 2009

† Dambrauskas, Stephen, (Retired)—Died Dec. 30, 2009

† Lagan, Hugh, (Retired)—Died June 25, 2009

An asterisk (*) denotes an organization that has established tax-exempt status directly with the IRS and is not covered by the USCCB Group Ruling.

Diocese of Salina

(Dioecesis Salinensis)

Most Reverend

PAUL S. COAKLEY, S.T.L., D.D.

Bishop of Salina; ordained May 21, 1983; appointed Bishop of Salina October 21, 2004; ordained and installed December 28, 2004. *Mailing Address: P.O. Box 980, Salina, KS 67402-0980.*

Chancery Office: 103 N. Ninth, P.O. Box 980, Salina, KS 67402-0980. Tel: 785-827-8746; Fax: 785-827-6133.

Email: chancery@salinadiocese.org

Most Reverend

GEORGE K. FITZSIMONS, D.D.

Retired Bishop of Salina; ordained March 18, 1961; appointed Titular Bishop of Pertusa and Auxiliary Bishop of Kansas City-St. Joseph May 27, 1975; Episcopal ordination July 3, 1975; appointed Bishop of Salina March 22, 1984; installed May 29, 1984; retired October 21, 2004. *Mailing Address: P.O. Box 980, Salina, KS 67402-0980.*

Square Miles 26,685.

Formerly Diocese of Concordia.

Established August 2, 1887.

See transferred to Salina December 23, 1944.

(New boundaries established by Apostolic Letters dated July 1, 1897).

Bounded on the west by Colorado, on the north by Nebraska, on the east by the east lines of Washington, Riley, Geary and Dickinson Counties, and on the south by the south lines of Dickinson, Saline, Ellsworth, Russell, Ellis, Trego, Gove, Logan and Wallace Counties in the State of Kansas.

For legal titles of parishes and diocesan institutions, consult the Chancery Office.

STATISTICAL OVERVIEW

Personnel	
Bishop	1
Retired Bishops	1
Priests: Diocesan Active in Diocese	38
Priests: Retired, Sick or Absent	22
Number of Diocesan Priests	60
Religious Priests in Diocese	16
Total Priests in Diocese	76
Extern Priests in Diocese	7
Ordinations:	
Diocesan Priests	1
Transitional Deacons	2
Permanent Deacons	7
Permanent Deacons in Diocese	7
Total Brothers	1
Total Sisters	151
Parishes	
Parishes	86
With Resident Pastor:	
Resident Diocesan Priests	29
Resident Religious Priests	6
Without Resident Pastor:	
Administered by Priests	40
Administered by Religious Women	1
Administered by Lay People	5
Closed Parishes	2
Welfare	
Homes for the Aged	5
Total Assisted	412
Educational	
Diocesan Students in Other Seminaries	14
Total Seminarians	14
High Schools, Diocesan and Parish	4
Total Students	375
High Schools, Private	1
Total Students	225
Elementary Schools, Diocesan and Parish	11
Total Students	1,756
Catechesis/Religious Education:	
High School Students	1,646
Elementary Students	4,171
Total Students under Catholic Instruction	8,187
Teachers in the Diocese:	
Priests	3
Sisters	2
Lay Teachers	230
Vital Statistics	
Receptions into the Church:	
Infant Baptism Totals	875
Minor Baptism Totals	37
Adult Baptism Totals	76
Received into Full Communion	149
First Communions	759
Confirmations	840
Marriages:	
Catholic	190
Interfaith	178
Total Marriages	368
Deaths	630
Total Catholic Population	46,255
Total Population	315,983

Former Bishops—Rt. Revs. RICHARD SCANNELL, D.D., cons. in Nashville, Tenn., Nov. 30, 1887; transferred to Omaha, Jan. 30, 1891; died Jan. 8, 1916; JOHN J. HENNESSY, D.D. Apostolic Administrator, 1891-98, Bishop of Wichita; THADDEUS BUTLER, D.D., Bishop-elect; died July 17, 1897; JOHN F. CUNNINGHAM, D.D., cons. Sept. 21, 1898; died June 23, 1919; Most Revs. FRANCIS J. TIEF, D.D., cons. March 30, 1921; retired and appointed Titular Bishop of Nisa, June 11, 1938; died Sept. 22, 1965; FRANK A. THILL, D.D., cons. Oct. 28, 1938; transferred to Salina, Dec. 23, 1944; died May 21, 1957; FREDERICK W. FREKING, D.D., J.C.D., cons. Nov. 30, 1957; transferred to LaCrosse, Dec. 30, 1964; CYRIL J. VOGEL, D.D., ord. Bishop, June 17, 1965; died Oct. 4, 1979; DANIEL W. KUCERA, O.S.B., Ph.D., D.D., ord. May 26, 1949; appt. Titular Bishop of Natchez and Auxiliary Bishop of Joliet, June 6, 1977; cons. July 21, 1977; appt. Bishop of Salina, March 11, 1980; installed May 7, 1980; transferred to Archbishop of Archdiocese of Dubuque, Feb. 23, 1984; retired Oct. 16, 1995; GEORGE K. FITZSIMONS, D.D. (Retired), ord. March 18, 1961; appt. Titular Bishop of Pertusa and Auxiliary Bishop of Kansas City-St. Joseph May 27, 1975; Episcopal ord. July 3, 1975; appt. Bishop of Salina March 22, 1984; installed May 29, 1984; retired Oct. 21, 2004.

Chancery Office—103 N. Ninth, P.O. Box 980, Salina, 67402-0980. Tel: 785-827-8746; Fax: 785-827-6133.

Vicars General—Rev. RANDALL WEBER, J.C.L., V.G., Res.: 118 N. 9th, Salina, 67401; Rev. Msgr. JAMES E. HAKE, J.C.L., V.G., Mailing Address: P.O. Box 327, Lincoln, 67455-0327.

Moderator of the Curia—Rev. RANDALL WEBER, J.C.L., V.G., Res.: 118 N. 9th, Salina, 67401.

Chancellor—Rev. BARRY BRINKMAN, J.C.L., Mailing Address: P.O. Box 980, Salina, 67402-0980.

Diocesan Finance Officer—Rev. JEROME L. MORGAN; JENNIFER HOOD, Asst. Finance Officer & Business Mgr., Mailing Address: P.O. Box 980, Salina, 67402-0980.

Diocesan Tribunal—103 N. Ninth, P.O. Box 980, Salina, 67402-0980. Tel: 785-827-8746; Fax: 785-827-6133.

Judicial Vicar-Officialis—Rev. KENNETH P. LOHRMEYER, J.C.L.

Associate Judges—Revs. KENNETH P. LOHRMEYER, J.C.L.; BARRY BRINKMAN, J.C.L.

Defender of the Bond—Rev. Msgr. JAMES E. HAKE, J.C.L., V.G.

Auditor-Notary—SUSAN OTTLEY.

Promoter of Justice and Guardian—Rev. DANIEL L. SCHEETZ, J.C.L.

Procurator and Advocate—Rev. RANDALL WEBER, J.C.L., V.G.

Diocesan Finance Council—Most Rev. PAUL S. COAKLEY, S.T.L., D.D.; Rev. JEROME L. MORGAN; BILL BECKMEYER; DONALD P. DIEDERICH; JOHN GRAHAM; JENNIFER HOOD; ROBERT SCHMIDT; JAN MARKS; CHUCK HEIDRICK; JOHN O. FARMER; STEVE BROWN; Mr. SHAWN D. CRAWFORD, Ph.D.

College of Consultors—Most Rev. PAUL S. COAKLEY, S.T.L., D.D.; Rev. Msgr. JAMES E. HAKE, J.C.L., V.G.; Revs. ALLEN SCHEER; JARETT KONRADE; NORBERT DLABAL; JEROME L. MORGAN; KERRY NINEMIRE; JOSEPH KIEFFER; CHARLES STEIER; RANDALL WEBER, J.C.L., V.G.

Vicariate Representatives—Revs. NORBERT DLABAL, Western Vicariate; DARYL OLMSTEAD, West Central Vicariate; KERRY NINEMIRE, East Central Vicariate; MARK WESELY, East Vicariate.

Council of Priests—Most Rev. PAUL S. COAKLEY, S.T.L., D.D.; Revs. MARK WESELY; ALLEN SCHEER, Member At-Large; MICHAEL ELANJIMATTATHIL, C.M.I.; CHARLES STEIER, Member At-Large; Rev. Msgr. JAMES E. HAKE, J.C.L., V.G.; Revs. JARETT KONRADE; JEROME L. MORGAN, Ex Officio Member; CARLOS RUIZ-SANTOS; KERRY NINEMIRE; RANDALL WEBER, J.C.L., V.G., Ex Officio Member; DARYL OLMSTEAD; NORBERT DLABAL; JOSEPH KIEFFER; LARRY GRENNAN.

Personnel Board—Most Rev. PAUL S. COAKLEY, S.T.L., D.D.; Revs. NORBERT DLABAL; LARRY GRENNAN, Chm.; CHARLES STEIER; JEROME L. MORGAN; KEVIN WEBER; Rev. Msgr. JAMES E. HAKE, J.C.L., V.G., Ex Officio; Revs. BARRY BRINKMAN, J.C.L., Chancellor, Ex Officio; RANDALL WEBER, J.C.L., V.G., Ex Officio.

Office of Priestly Vocations—Most Rev. PAUL S. COAKLEY, S.T.L., D.D.; Rev. JARETT KONRADE, Dir.

Diocesan Offices and Directors

Art and Architecture Commission—Rev. JEROME L. MORGAN, Chm.; Rev. Msgr. JAMES E. HAKE, J.C.L.,

V.G., Vice Chm.; Revs. FRANK COADY; DONALD D. ZIMMERMAN; KEVIN WEBER; RANDALL WEBER, J.C.L., V.G.; Mr. CHARLES BOSTER; JENNIFER HOOD.

Priests' Continuing Formation Committee—Revs. KERRY NINEMIRE, Chm.; FRANK COADY; BENJAMIN SAW; JARETT KONRADE. Ex Officio: Rev. Msgr. JAMES E. HAKE, J.C.L., V.G.; Rev. RANDALL WEBER, J.C.L., V.G.

Catholic Charities Board—Dr. KAREN S. HAUSER, Ed.D., CEO; LARRY TRIPLETT; Revs. DONALD D. ZIMMERMAN; DANA CLARK; NORMAN KELLY; KATIE PLATTEN; Mr. SHAWN D. CRAWFORD, Ph.D., Advisor; DAVID KRELLER, Vice Pres.; GINGER THULL, Sec.; GERALD HUNTER, Pres.; LEON BOOR, Treas.; MARY JO BOOR; VICTOR LYCZAK; MARY LYCZAK; Most Rev. PAUL S. COAKLEY, S.T.L., D.D., Ex Officio.

Catholic Charities of Salina, Inc.—Dr. KAREN S. HAUSER, Ed.D., CEO; JOSEPHINE HERNANDEZ, L.S.C.S.W., Adoption & Counseling; CARLISLE BERGQUIST, M.A., L.C.M.F.T., Counseling; YVONNE SAUBER, Finance Officer, 425 W. Iron, P.O. Box 1366, Salina, 67401. Tel: 785-825-0208; 888-468-6909; Fax: 785-826-9708. Email: ccharsal@salhelp.org. Web: www.catholiccharitiessalina.org.

Family Life—REG KONRADE, Co Dir.; JAN KONRADE, Co Dir.; SHEILA MARCOTTE, Exec. Sec.

Immigration—MARIA TORRES, Immigration Consultant; MARIBEL PANUCO, Hispanic Svcs. Coord.; BLANCA BANDA, Immigration & Hispanic Prog. Asst.; MIDELIS DEL REAL, Immigration & Hispanic Svcs. Sec.

Catholic Charities Outreach Office - Hays—JOAN PERKINS, Office Mgr.; JANET RUSSELL, L.S.C.S.W., Adoption & Counseling; Rev. WILLIAM J. SURMEIER, PsyD., L.C.P.C., Counseling, 2707 Vine, #17, P.O. Box 811, Hays, 67601. Tel: 785-625-2644; 877-625-2644; Fax: 785-625-6497. Email: cchaysof@sbcglobal.net.

Catholic Charities Outreach Office - Manhattan—TERESA HERNANDEZ, Adoption & Counseling, 323 Poyntz, Ste. 102, Manhattan, 66502. Tel: 785-323-0644. Email: ccmanhattan@flinthills.com.

Catholic Charities - Colby—VACANT, Counseling, 350 S. Range, Ste. 2, Colby, 67701. Tel: 785-426-3426.

Catholic Charities - Concordia—J. HUSCH HATHORNE, L.S.C.S.W., Adoption & Counseling, 520 Washington, Ste. D, Concordia, 66901. Tel: 785-243-4167. Email: hathorneh@sbcglobal.net.

Catholic Community Annual Appeal—Mailing Address: P.O. Box 980, Salina, 67402-0980. Fax: 785-827-6133.

Office of Catholic Formation—Sr. BARBARA ELLEN APACELLER, C.S.J., Dir., 103 N. Ninth, P.O. Box 825, Salina, 67402. Tel: 785-827-8746; Fax: 785-827-6133.

Coordinator of Office of Catholic Formation—Sr. BARBARA ELLEN APACELLER, C.S.J. Email: barbcsj@salinadiocese.org.

Director of Religious Education—Sr. BARBARA ELLEN APACELLER, C.S.J. Email: barbcsj@salinadiocese.org.

Superintendent of Schools—Dr. NICK COMPAGNONE. Email: ministry@salinadiocese.org. Web: www.salinadiocese.com.

Consultant for Religious Education & Media—(Grades K-8), PEGGY HERBERT. Email: avlibrary@salinadiocese.org.

Consultant for Religious Education— (Grades 9-12), Sr. BARBARA ELLEN APACELLER, C.S.J.

Director Adult Faith Formation—Rev. FRANK COADY. Email: liturgy@salinadiocese.org.

Office of Deacons—Rev. FRANK COADY, Dir., Mailing Address: P.O. Box 980, Salina, 67402. Email: liturgy@salinadiocese.org.

Audiovisual—PEGGY HEBERT. Email: avlibrary@salinadiocese.org.

Catholic Youth Organization and Youth Ministry—Sr. BARBARA ELLEN APACELLER, C.S.J., Mailing Address: P.O. Box 980, Salina, 67402.

Office of Communications—Rev. BARRY BRINKMAN, J.C.L., Mailing Address: P.O. Box 980, Salina, 67402.

Cursillo—Rev. DAMIAN RICHARDS, Spiritual Dir., St. Boniface Church, Box 87, Tipton, 67485. Tel: 785-373-4455. Contact Persons: DAVID STUDER; LORETTA A. STUDER, 203 Blaine, Atwood, 67730. Tel: 785-626-3109.

Holy Childhood, Pontifical Association—Rev. STEVEN HEINA, Dir., Mailing Address: P.O. Box 980, Salina, 67402.

Office of Liturgy—Rev. FRANK COADY, Dir., Mailing Address: P.O. Box 980, Salina, 67402. Tel: 785-827-8746; Fax: 785-827-6133. Email: liturgy@salinadiocese.org.

Newspaper— The Register of the Roman Catholic Diocese of Salina, Inc. DOUG WELLER, Editor; JENNIFER HOOD, Business Mgr. Email: newspaper1@salinadiocese.org; Mailing Address: P.O. Box 1038, Salina, 67402.

Propagation of the Faith—Rev. STEVE HEINA, Dir., Mailing Address: P.O. Box 980, Salina, 67402. Tel: 785-827-8746.

Rural Life Conference—Rev. ALLEN SCHEER, Dir., Mailing Address: Sacred Heart Cathedral, 118 N. 9th, Salina, 67401. Tel: 785-823-7221; Fax: 785-820-8063. Email: rurallifecommission@hotmail.com.

Salina Diocesan Clergy Health and Retirement Association, Inc.—Board of Trustees: Most Rev. PAUL S. COAKLEY, S.T.L., D.D., Pres., 103 N. Ninth, P.O. Box 980, Salina, 67402-0980; Revs. LARRY LETOURNEAU; NORBERT DLABAL; LOREN J. WERTH (Retired); KEVIN WEBER; DONALD F. PFANNENSTIEL; Mr. SHAWN D. CRAWFORD, Ph.D. Ex Officio: Revs. JEROME L. MORGAN; BARRY BRINKMAN, J.C.L.; RANDALL WEBER, J.C.L., V.G.; JENNIFER HOOD.

Salina Diocesan Council of Catholic Women (S.D.CC.W.)—Rev. DAMIAN RICHARDS, Moderator, St. Boniface, Box 87, Tipton, 67485.

Boy Scouts—Rev. JARETT KONRADE, 230 E. Cloud, Salina, 67401.

Girl Scouts—Sr. BARBARA ELLEN, C.S.J., Dir., Mailing Address: P.O. Box 825, Salina, 67402-0825.

Office of Priestly Vocations—Rev. JARETT KONRADE, Dir.

Lay Review Board-Diocesan Committee Regarding Alleged Cases of Child Sexual Abuse—Rev. BARRY BRINKMAN, J.C.L.; Mrs. JOYCE RATCLIFF, Chm.; Mrs. NANCY MAIN; Dr. GEORGE JERKOVICH; Mrs. ANNE KRESIN, Victim Assistance Coord.; Mrs. MONICA WOOLSONCROFT; Mr. GUY STEIER. Consultors: Revs. JEROME L. MORGAN; WILLIAM J. SURMEIER, PsyD., L.C.P.C.; Rev. Msgr. JAMES E. HAKE, J.C.L., V.G., Ex Officio Member; Rev. RANDALL WEBER, J.C.L., V.G.

Victim Assistance Coordinator—Mrs. ANNE KRESIN, P.O. Box 2984, Salina, 67402. Tel: 785-825-0865. Email: reportabuse@salinadiocese.org.

Respect Life—

Moderator—Rev. HENRY BAXA, St. Andrew's Church, 311 S. Buckeye, Box 429, Abilene, 67410. Tel: 785-263-1570. Email: frhenry@eaglecom.net. Coordinators: Mr. GIL OTTER; Mrs. CAROL OTTER, 509 N. 1st St., Norton, 67654. Tel: 785-877-5423. Email: caotter@ruraltel.net.

Office of Development—Mr. SHAWN D. CRAWFORD, Ph.D., Dir., Chancery Office: P.O. Box 980, Salina, 67402-0980. Email: development@salinadiocese.org.

Office of Hispanic Ministry—Rev. CARLOS RUIZ-SANTOS, Moderator.

Office of Ecumenical and Interreligious Affairs—Rev. RANDALL WEBER, J.C.L., V.G., Dir.

Office of Information Technology—Mr. JEFF EASTER, Dir.

CLERGY, PARISHES, MISSIONS AND PAROCHIAL SCHOOLS

CITY OF SALINA

(SALINE COUNTY)

1—SACRED HEART CATHEDRAL PARISH (1876) [JC] Revs. Allen Scheer, Rector; Carlos Ruiz-Santos; Sisters Carmella Thibault, C.S.J., Pastoral Assoc.; Carolyn Juenemann, C.S.J., Pastoral Assoc. In Res., Revs. Jarett Konrade; Randall Weber.
Church: 118 N. Ninth St., 67401. Tel: 785-823-7221; Fax: 785-820-8063.
Catechesis/Religious Program—Sherry Headlee, D.R.E. Students 335.

2—ST. ELIZABETH ANN SETON PARISH (1982) [JC] Rev. Frank Coady, Priest Supvr.; Sr. Rose Walters, C.S.A., Parish Life Coord.
Res.: 1000 Burr Oak Ln., 67401. Tel: 785-825-5282; Fax: 785-825-1140. Email: stelizabethsalina@ruraltel.net. Web: www.stelizabethsalina.com.
Rectory—1061 Burr Oak Ln., 67401.
Catechesis/Religious Program—Melanie Melander, D.R.E.; Lucy Larson, D.R.E. Students 180.

3—ST. MARY QUEEN OF THE UNIVERSE PARISH (1959) [JC] Revs. Kerry Ninemire; Nicholas Parker (NSH), Parochial Vicar.
Res.: 230 E. Cloud St., 67401. Tel: 785-827-5575; Fax: 785-827-8997.
Rectory—324 Albert, 67401.
School—(Grades PreK-6), 304 E. Cloud St., 67401. Tel: 785-827-4200; Fax: 785-827-7765. Dr. Nick Compagnone, Prin. Lay Teachers 32; Students 405.
Catechesis/Religious Program—Nancy Sherffius, D.R.E. Students 220.

OUTSIDE THE CITY OF SALINA

ABILENE, DICKINSON CO., ST. ANDREW PARISH (1874) [CEM] Rev. Henry Baxa.
Rectory—201 S.W. 4th. Tel: 785-263-7094.
Church: 311 S. Buckeye Ave., P.O. Box 429, 67410. Tel: 785-263-1570; Fax: 785-263-3570.
School—(Grades PreK-5) Tel: 785-263-2453. Christina Bacon, Prin. Lay Teachers 5; Students 80.
Catechesis/Religious Program—Tel: 785-263-1570. Joanna Picking, C.R.E. Students 111.

ANGELUS, SHERIDAN CO., ST. PAUL PARISH (1887), (German), [CEM] Attended by St. Joseph Parish, Oakley. Rev. Michael Elanjimattathil, C.M.I. (India).
Mailing Address: *c/o St. Joseph Parish*, 625 Freeman Ave., Oakley, 67748. Email: stpauls@st-tel.net. Church: Tel: 785-824-3221; Fax: 785-824-3215.
Catechesis/Religious Program—Students 36.

ANTONINO, ELLIS CO., OUR LADY HELP OF CHRISTIANS PARISH (1905) Attended by St. Joseph, Hays. Rev. Earl Befort, O.F.M.Cap.
Mailing Address: *c/o St. Joseph Parish*, 215 W. 13th, Hays, 67601. Tel: 785-628-9214; Fax: 785-625-7394.

ATWOOD, RAWLINS CO., SACRED HEART PARISH (1879) [CEM] [JC 3] Rev. Stephen Folorunso.
Res.: 508 N. Railroad Ave., 67730. Tel: 785-626-3335; Fax: 785-626-3431. Email: church508@yahoo.com.
Catechesis/Religious Program—Loretta A. Studer, Office Mgr./D.R.E. Students 70.

AURORA, CLOUD CO., ST. PETER PARISH (1880) [CEM] [JC] Attended by St. John the Baptist Parish, Clyde. Rev. Larry Letourneau.
P.O. Box 9, 67417.
Catechesis/Religious Program—Students 5.

BEARDSLEY, RAWLINS CO., ST. JOHN NEPOMUCENE PARISH (1910), (Slovak), [CEM] Rev. Stephen Folorunso.
Mailing Address: *c/o Sacred Heart Parish*, 508 N. Railroad Ave., Atwood, 67730. Tel: 785-626-3335; Fax: 785-626-3431.
Church: Atwood, 67730.
Catechesis/Religious Program—Students 25.

BELLEVILLE, REPUBLIC CO., ST. EDWARD PARISH (1901) [CEM] Rev. Barry Brinkman, Parochial Admin.
Res.: 1827 Q St., P.O. Box 99, 66935. Tel: 785-527-5559. Email: stedward6810@sbcglobal.net.
Catechesis/Religious Program—Sacred Hearts Center, 1813 Q St., 66935. Tel: 785-527-5819. Steve Heiman, D.R.E. Students 70.

BELOIT, MITCHELL CO., ST. JOHN THE BAPTIST PARISH (1869) [CEM] Rev. Joseph Kieffer.
Office: 622 E. Main, 67420. Email: sjparish@nckcn.com. Web: www.nckcn.com/homepage/stjohns/parish.htm.
Res.: 701 E. Court St., 67420. Tel: 785-738-2851; Fax: 785-738-3410.
School—(Grades PreK-5) Tel: 785-738-3941; Fax: 785-738-3703. Web: gostj.com. Lay Teachers 10; Students 79.
High School—(Grades 6-12) Tel: 785-738-2942; Fax: 785-738-4462. Martin Hesting, Prin. (K-12). Lay Teachers 11; Students 63.
Catechesis/Religious Program— Andrew Niewald, D.R.E. Students 97.

BIRD CITY, CHEYENNE CO., ST. JOSEPH PARISH (1911) [JC] Attended by St. Francis Parish, St. Francis. Rev. Roger K. Meitl.
Mailing Address: *c/o St. Francis Parish*, 625 River St., P.O. Box 1170, St. Francis, 67756. Tel: 785-332-2680.
Church: 67731.
Catechesis/Religious Program—Rose Hengen, D.R.E. Students 16.

BROOKVILLE, SALINE CO., ST. JOSEPH PARISH (1884) [CEM] Attended by St. Patrick Parish, Lincoln. Rev. Msgr. James E. Hake.
Mailing Address: *c/o St. Patrick Parish*, 206 N. 5th, P.O. Box 327, Lincoln, 67455. Tel: 785-524-4823.
Church: 67425.
Catechesis/Religious Program—Students 14.

CATHARINE, ELLIS CO., ST. CATHERINE PARISH (1892), (German), [CEM 2] Rev. Earl Befort, O.F.M.Cap., Priest Supvr.; Glenda Schuetz, Parish Life Coord.
Mailing Address: 1681 St. Joseph St., P.O. Box 18, 67627-0018. Tel: 785-625-5091; Fax: 785-625-5091. Email: stonehill@ruraltel.net.
Catechesis/Religious Program—Ann Schmidt, C.R.E. Students 9.

CAWKER CITY, MITCHELL CO., SAINTS PETER AND PAUL PARISH (1878), (German), [CEM] Attended by St. Boniface Parish, Tipton. Rev. Damian Richards.
c/o St. Boniface Parish, 308 Gambrinus, P.O. Box 87, Tipton, 67485-0087.
Church: Tel: 785-781-4319; 785-373-4455.
Catechesis/Religious Program—1202 Holly, 67430. Tel: 785-781-4835. Deanne Winkel, D.R.E. Students 27.

CHAPMAN, DICKINSON CO., ST. MICHAEL PARISH (1883) [CEM] Rev. Henry Baxa, Priest Supvr.; Marita Campbell, Parish Life Coord.
Res.: 210 E. 6th St., P.O. Box 217, 67431-0217. Tel: 785-922-6509. Email: smichael-chapman@sbcglobal.net. Web: smchapmanparish.org.
Catechesis/Religious Program—Tel: 785-922-6509. Laurie McLaughlin, D.R.E. Students 50.

CLAY CENTER, CLAY CO., SAINTS PETER AND PAUL PARISH (1879) [CEM] Rev. Lawrence E. Grennan.
Res.: 730 Court St., 67432. Tel: 785-632-5011; Fax: 785-632-3914. Email: sspp@eaglecom.net. Web: www.claycentercatholics.parishesonline.com.
Catechesis/Religious Program—Tel: 785-632-3204. Cyndy Schwensen, D.R.E. Students 111.

CLIFTON, WASHINGTON CO., ST. MARY PARISH, (French—German), [CEM] Attended by St. John the Baptist Parish, Clyde. Rev. Larry Letourneau.
Mailing Address: *c/o St. John the Baptist*, 204 N. High, Clyde, 66938. Tel: 785-446-3474. Email: stjohn@nckcn.com.
Catechesis/Religious Program—Tel: 785-348-5404. Therese Leiszler, D.R.E. Students 51.

CLYDE, CLOUD CO., ST. JOHN THE BAPTIST PARISH (1880), (French—German), [CEM] Rev. Larry Letourneau; Brenda Koch, Pastoral Asst.
Res.: 204 N. High, 66938. Tel: 785-446-3474. Email: stjohn@nckcn.com.
Catechesis/Religious Program—Nicole Francis, C.R.E. Students 90.

COLBY, THOMAS CO., SACRED HEART PARISH (1886) [CEM] Rev. Dana Clark.
Res.: 585 N. French Ave., 67701. Tel: 785-462-2179. Web: www.sacredheartcolby.com.
School—(Grades PreK-5) Tel: 785-460-2813; Fax: 785-460-9688. Mr. David Evert, Prin. Lay Teachers 10; Students 141.
Catechesis/Religious Program—Fax: 785-460-6613. Students 128.

COLLYER, TREGO CO., ST. MICHAEL PARISH (1893), (German), [CEM] [JC] Attended by Christ the King Parish, WaKeeney, Mailing Address: Ainsie Ave., Box 174, 67631.
Catechesis/Religious Program—Edna Mader, D.R.E. Students 4.

CONCORDIA, CLOUD CO., OUR LADY OF PERPETUAL HELP PARISH (1887), (French), [CEM 2] Rev. Barry Brinkman.
Office: 307 E. Fifth, P.O. Box 608, 66901. Tel: 785-243-1099; Fax: 785-243-1939.
Res.: 420 Kansas, P.O. Box 608, 66901. Tel: 785-243-4658. Email: conolph@yahoo.com. Web: www.concordiacatholicchurch.com.
Catechesis/Religious Program—Tel: 785-243-1410. Laura Jo Meyer, D.R.E. Students 211.

CUBA, REPUBLIC CO., ST. ISIDORE PARISH (1873), (Czech), [CEM] Attended by St. Edward Parish, Belleville. Rev. Barry Brinkman, Parochial Admin.
Mailing Address: *c/o St. Edward Parish*, P.O. Box 99, Belleville, 66935.
Catechesis/Religious Program—

DAMAR, ROOKS CO., ST. JOSEPH PARISH (1912), (French), [CEM] Attended by Immaculate Heart of Mary Parish, Hill City. Rev. Henry Saw Lone.
Mailing Address: 100 N. Main, P.O. Box 68, 67632. Tel: 785-839-4343.
Catechesis/Religious Program—Tel: 785-737-4341. Monte Keller, D.R.E. Students 41.

DELPHOS, OTTAWA CO., ST. PAUL PARISH, [CEM] Merged Canonically merged with Immaculate Conception Parish, Minneapolis. Rev. Kenneth P. Lohrmeyer.
Res.: 216 Cherry St., Box 167, Minneapolis, 67467. Tel: 785-392-2079.

DORRANCE, RUSSELL CO., ST. JOSEPH PARISH (1902), (German—Irish), [CEM] Attended by St. Wenceslaus Parish, Wilson. Rev. James Hoover.
Mailing Address: *c/o St. Wenceslaus Parish*, P.O. Box 528, Wilson, 67490. Tel: 785-658-3361.

DOWNS, OSBORNE CO., ST. MARY PARISH (1903) Attended by St. Aloysius Gonzaga Parish, Osborne. Rev. Alexander Cho.
Mailing Address: *c/o St. Aloysius Gonzaga Parish*, P.O. Box 267, Osborne, 67473-0267.
Church: 1312 Prentiss, 67437. Tel: 785-454-3551.
Catechesis/Religious Program—Students 23.

ELLIS, ELLIS CO., ST. MARY PARISH (1870) [CEM] Rev. Curtis Carlson, O.F.M.Cap.; Sr. Doris M. Flax, C.S.J., Pastoral Assoc.
703 Monroe, 67637-2231.
Church: 603 Monroe, 67637. Tel: 785-726-4696. Email: stmary@gbta.net. Web: www.stmarysofellis.org/church.
School—(Grades K-6), 605 Monroe St., 67637. Tel: 785-726-3185; Fax: 785-726-3166. James Moeder, Prin.; Pamela Newton, Librarian. Lay Teachers 11; Students 63.
Catechesis/Religious Program—Amy Rohr, C.R.E. Students 74.

ELLSWORTH, ELLSWORTH CO., ST. BERNARD PARISH (1909) Rev. Steve Heina.
Res.: 911 Kansas St., 67439. Tel: 785-472-3136; Fax: 785-472-3593. Email: stbernards@att.net.
Catechesis/Religious Program—Students 66.

ELMO, DICKINSON CO., ST. COLUMBA PARISH, [CEM] Attended by St. John the Evangelist Parish, Herington. Rev. Mark Wesely.
c/o St. John the Evangelist Parish, 712 N. Broadway, Herington, 67449. Tel: 785-258-2013.
Catechesis/Religious Program—

ESBON, JEWELL CO., SACRED HEART PARISH (1887) [CEM] Attended by St. Theresa Parish, Mankato. Rev. George Chalbhagam, C.M.I. (India).
Mailing Address: *c/o St. Theresa Parish*, P.O. Box 265, Mankato, 66956. Fax: 785-378-3913.
Church: Tel: 785-378-3939. Email: stheresa@nckcn.com.
Catechesis/Religious Program—Students 15.

FORT RILEY, GEARY CO., FORT RILEY CATHOLIC COMMUNITY, Attended by Archdiocese for the Military Services. Rev. Orlando R. Fuller, Chap.
Chapel—Morris Hill Chapel Bldg 5315, 66442.

GLASCO, CLOUD CO., ST. MARY PARISH (1878) [CEM] Attended by St. Patrick Parish, Lincoln. Rev. Kenneth Lohrmeyer, Parochial Admin.
Mailing Address: *c/o Immaculate Conception*, P.O. Box 167, Minneapolis, 67467. Tel: 785-392-2079.
Church: 301 E. First St., P.O. Box 554, 67445.
Catechesis/Religious Program—Peggy Forshee, D.R.E.

GOODLAND, SHERMAN CO., OUR LADY OF PERPETUAL HELP PARISH (1887) Rev. Norbert Dlabal; Sr. Barbara Berthiaume, C.S.J., Pastoral Assoc.
Church: 307 W. 13th, 67735. Tel: 785-890-7205; Fax: 785-890-7205.
Catechesis/Religious Program—Sr. Clara Ann Fluech, D.R.E. (Grade School). Students 113.

GORHAM, RUSSELL CO., ST. MARY HELP OF CHRISTIANS PARISH (1894) [CEM] Rev. William J. Surmeier.
Res.: 135 - 3rd St., Box 135, 67640. Tel: 785-637-5241. Email: st_marys@gorhamtel.com.
Catechesis/Religious Program—Tonya Murphy, D.R.E.; Pam Nowak, D.R.E. Students 17.

GRAINFIELD, GOVE CO., ST. AGNES PARISH (1910), (German), [JC] Attended by Sacred Heart Parish, Park. Rev. James Maruthukunnel, C.M.I.
Mailing Address: *c/o Sacred Heart Parish*, P.O. Box 78, Park, 67751-0078. Tel: 785-673-4684.
Catechesis/Religious Program—Jerri Palmquist, D.R.E. Students 45.

GREENLEAF, WASHINGTON CO., SACRED HEART PARISH (1890) [CEM] Attended by St. John the Baptist, Hanover. Rev. David Metz.
Mailing Address: *c/o St. John the Baptist*, 114 S. Church St., P.O. Box 395, Hanover, 66945. Tel: 785-337-2342.
Catechesis/Religious Program—Sherri McGatlin, D.R.E. Students 20.

GRINNELL, GOVE CO., IMMACULATE CONCEPTION OF THE BLESSED VIRIGIN MARY PARISH (1896), (German), [CEM] Attended by Sacred Heart, Park. Rev. James Maruthukunnel, C.M.I.
Church & Mailing Address: 308 Monroe, P.O. Box 69, 67738. Fax: 785-824-3215.
Catechesis/Religious Program—Tel: 785-824-3221. Joyce Baalman, C.R.E. Students 27.

GYPSUM, SALINE CO., ST. PATRICK PARISH, Attended by Immaculate Conception of the Blessed Mary Parish, Solomon. Rev. John Wolesky, Priest Supvr.; Daylene Tracy, Parish Life Coord.
c/o Immaculate Conception of the Blessed Virgin Mary Parish, 3599 N. Field Rd., P.O. Box 337, Solomon, 67480-0337.
Catechesis/Religious Program—Carol Craver, D.R.E. Students 10.

HANOVER, WASHINGTON CO., ST. JOHN THE BAPTIST PARISH (1868), (Bohemian), [CEM] Rev. David Metz.
Res.: 114 S. Church St., Box 395, 66945. Tel: 785-337-2342.
School—Tel: 785-337-2368. Timothy Rundle, Prin. Lay Teachers 7; Students 95.
Catechesis/Religious Program—Students 50.

HAYS, ELLIS CO.

1—IMMACULATE HEART OF MARY PARISH (1967) [JC] Revs. Kevin Weber; Joshua Werth, Parochial Vicar.
Res.: 1805 Vine, 67601. Tel: 785-625-7339; Fax: 785-625-7643. Web: www.ihm-church.com.
Catechesis/Religious Program—Rick Binder, Youth Dir.; Annette Hammeke, D.R.E. Students 383.

2—ST. JOSEPH PARISH (1876) [JC] Revs. Gilmary Tallman, O.F.M.Cap., Priest Supvr.; Canice Froelich, O.F.M.Cap.; Deacon Mark Roberti; Jane Vanek, Parish Life Coord.
Res.: 210 W. 13th St., P.O. Drawer 1000, 67601. Tel: 785-625-7356; Fax: 785-625-7394. Email: stjoseph@eaglecom.net. Web: www.stj-church.com.
See Holy Family Grade School, Hays under Grade Schools, Inter-Parochial located in the Institution section.
See Thomas More Prep Marian High School, Hays under High Schools Inter-Parochial located in the Institution section.
Catechesis/Religious Program—Martha A. Brungardt, D.R.E. Students 94.

3—ST. NICHOLAS OF MYRA PARISH (1983) Rev. Daryl Olmstead.
Office & Mailing Address: 2901 E. 13th, 67601. Tel: 785-628-1446; Fax: 785-623-4207.
Catechesis/Religious Program— Kathy Volker, C.R.E. Students 157.

HERINGTON, DICKINSON CO., ST. JOHN THE EVANGELIST PARISH, [CEM] Rev. Mark Wesely.
Res.: 712 N. Broadway, 67449. Tel: 785-258-2013.
Catechesis/Religious Program—Kathleen Walter, D.R.E.; Annetta Vasholtz, Dir. Youth Ministry. Students 78.

HERNDON, RAWLINS CO., ASSUMPTION OF MARY PARISH (1880), (German), [CEM] Attended by Sacred Heart Parish, Atwood. Rev. Stephen Folorunso.
Mailing Address: *c/o Sacred Heart Parish*, 508 N. Railroad Ave., Atwood, 67730. Tel: 785-626-3335; Fax: 785-626-3431.
Church: P.O. Box 247, 67739.
Catechesis/Religious Program—Students 21.

HILL CITY, GRAHAM CO., IMMACULATE HEART OF MARY PARISH (1958) Rev. Henry Saw Lone.
Res.: 110 N. 10th Ave., 67642. Tel: 785-421-2535. Email: ihmhc@ruraltel.net.
Catechesis/Religious Program—Tel: 785-421-2819. Joyce Tauber, D.R.E. Students 71.
Mission—St. Joseph Parish 107 N. Oak, Damar, Rooks Co. 67632. Tel: 785-839-4343. Email: sjdamar@ruraltel.net.

HOLYROOD, ELLSWORTH CO., ST. MARY PARISH (1886) Attended by St. Wenceslaus Parish, Wilson. Rev. James Hoover.
Mailing Address: *c/o St. Wenceslaus Parish*, Box 528, Wilson, 67490. Tel: 785-658-3361.
Catechesis/Religious Program—Students 27.

HOPE, DICKINSON CO., ST. PHILLIP PARISH, Attended by St. John Parish, Herington. Rev. Mark Wesely.
Mailing Address: *c/o St. John Parish*, 712 N. Broadway, Herington, 67449. Tel: 785-258-2013.
Church: 67451. Tel: 785-366-7353.
Catechesis/Religious Program—Students 17.

HOXIE, SHERIDAN CO., ST. FRANCES CABRINI PARISH (1948) [CEM] Rev. B. Thomas Mangat, C.M.I. (India).
Res.: 924 N. 17th, Box 38, 67740. Tel: 785-675-3300; Fax: 785-675-2235. Email: sfrances@ruraltel.net.
Catechesis/Religious Program—Verlene Feldt, D.R.E. Twinned with St. Martin's, Seguin, Hoxie, KS. Students 79.

JAMESTOWN, CLOUD CO., ST. MARY'S (1873) Closed. For sacramental records contact Our Lady of Perpetual Help, Concordia.

JUNCTION CITY, GEARY CO., ST. FRANCIS XAVIER PARISH (1867) [CEM] Rev. Aloysius Brungardt.
Res.: 218 N. Washington, P.O. Box 399, 66441. Tel: 785-238-2998; Fax: 785-238-4731.
School—(Grades PreK-12), 200 N. Washington St., 66441. Tel: 785-238-2841; Fax: 785-238-5021. Web: www.saintxrams.org. Lori Balderrama, Co-Prin. (Elementary and High School); Rhonda Millard, Co-Prin. (Elementary and High School). Lay Teachers 12; Students 160.
High School—Lay Teachers 10; Students 27.
Catechesis/Religious Program—Tel: 785-238-2841; Fax: 785-238-5021. Students 156.

KANOPOLIS, ELLSWORTH CO., ST. IGNATIUS LOYOLA PARISH (1947), (Mexican), [JC] Attended by St. Bernard Parish, Ellsworth. Rev. Steve Heina.
Mailing Address: *c/o St. Bernard Parish*, 911 Kansas, Ellsworth, 67439. Tel: 785-472-3136.
Church: Tel: 785-472-4628.
Catechesis/Religious Program—127 N. Missouri, 67454. Students 23.

LEOVILLE, DECATUR CO., IMMACULATE CONCEPTION OF THE BLESSED VIRGIN MARY PARISH (1885) [CEM] Attended by Sacred Heart Parish, Oberlin. Rev. Mark Berland.
c/o Sacred Heart Parish, 210 E. Washington, Oberlin, 67749. Tel: 785-475-3103.
Catechesis/Religious Program—Stephanie Ritter, D.R.E. Students 47.

LINCOLN, LINCOLN CO., ST. PATRICK PARISH (1870) [CEM 2] Rev. Msgr. James E. Hake.
Res.: 206 N. Fifth, Box 327, 67455. Tel: 785-524-4823.
Catechesis/Religious Program—Tel: 785-524-3043. Dora Schroeder, D.R.E. Students 68.

LOGAN, PHILLIPS CO., ST. JOHN PARISH (1878) [CEM] Attended by Saints Philip & James Parish, Philipsburg. Rev. Benjamin Saw (Burma).
Mailing Address: P.O. Box 128, 67646. Tel: 785-689-4299. Email: stjohn1@ruraltel.net.
Catechesis/Religious Program—Tel: 785-689-4299. Terra Brown, D.R.E. Students 30.

MANHATTAN, RILEY CO.
1—ST. ISIDORE CATHOLIC STUDENT CENTER PARISH (1963) Rev. Keith Weber.
Res.: 711 Denison Ave., 66502. Tel: 785-539-7496; Fax: 785-539-0220. Email: stisidores@stisidores.com. Web: www.stisidores.com.
2—SEVEN DOLORS OF THE BLESSED VIRGIN MARY PARISH (1880) Revs. Joseph Popelka; Francisco Montoya, Parochial Vicar.
Res.: 731 Pierre St., 66502. Tel: 785-565-5000; Fax: 785-565-5003. Email: seven_dolors@sbcglobal.net. Web: www.sevendolors.com.
Rectory—624 Pierre St., 66502.
Catechesis/Religious Program—Rosie Rundell, D.R.E.; Sharon Runyan, D.R.E. & Dir. Youth Ministry. Students 130.
3—ST. THOMAS MORE PARISH (1981) Rev. Donald D. Zimmerman; Wayne Talbot, Pastoral Assoc.
Church Office: 2900 Kimball Ave., 66502. Tel: 785-776-5151; Fax: 785-776-5219. Email: stm@interkan.net. Web: stm.manhattanks.org.
Catechesis/Religious Program— Sherry Watts, D.R.E.; Mark Ellner, D.R.E.; Monique McCollough, D.R.E.; Beryl Adams, Youth Min. Students 387.

MANKATO, JEWELL CO., ST. THERESA PARISH (1949) [CEM] Rev. George Chalbhagam, C.M.I. (India).
Res.: 422 N. Commercial, Box 265, 66956-0265. Tel: 785-378-3939; Fax: 785-378-3913. Email: stheresa@nckcn.com.
Catechesis/Religious Program—Students 28.

MILTONVALE, CLOUD CO., ST. ANTHONY PARISH (1910) Attended by Saints Peter and Paul Parish, Clay Center. Rev. Lawrence E. Grennan.
Mailing Address: *c/o Saints Peter and Paul Parish*, 730 Court St., Clay Center, 67432. Tel: 785-632-5011; Fax: 785-632-3914.
Church: Tel: 785-427-2263.

MINNEAPOLIS, OTTAWA CO., IMMACULATE CONCEPTION OF THE BLESSED VIRGIN MARY PARISH, Merged St. Paul Parish, Delphos. Canonically merged with St. Paul Parish, Delphos. Rev. Kenneth P. Lohrmeyer.
Res.: 216 Cherry St., Box 167, 67467. Tel: 785-392-2079 (Parish House); 785-392-2013 (Church Hall).
Catechesis/Religious Program—Students 48.

MORROWVILLE, WASHINGTON CO., SAINTS PETER AND PAUL PARISH (1887) [CEM] Merged Canonically merged with St. Augustine's Parish, Washington. Rev. David Metz.
c/o St. Augustine Parish, 410 B St., Washington, 66968. Tel: 785-325-2346.

MUNDEN, REPUBLIC CO., ST. GEORGE PARISH (1887), (Czech), [CEM] Attended by St. Edward Parish, Belleville. Rev. Barry Brinkman, Parochial Admin.
Mailing Address: *c/o St. Edward Parish*, P.O. Box 99, Belleville, 66935.
Catechesis/Religious Program—Steve Heiman, D.R.E. Students 8.

MUNJOR, ELLIS CO., ST. FRANCIS OF ASSISI PARISH (1876) [CEM] Rev. Daryl Olmstead; Mrs. Lilly Binder, Pastoral Assoc.
Church: 883 Moscow, 67601. Tel: 785-625-5314. Email: st_francis_church@hotmail.com.
Catechesis/Religious Program—Wendy Richmeier, C.R.E. Students 23.

NEW ALMELO, NORTON CO., ST. JOSEPH PARISH (1874) [CEM] Attended by St. Francis of Assisi Parish, Norton. Rev. Vincent Thu Laing.
Res. & Mailing Address: 28035 St. John St., 67645-9742. Tel: 785-567-4875; Fax: 785-567-4261.
Catechesis/Religious Program—Gayle James, D.R.E. Students 28.

NORTON, NORTON CO., ST. FRANCIS OF ASSISI PARISH (1878) Rev. Vincent Thu Laing.
Res.: 108 S. Wabash, Box 148, 67654. Tel: 785-877-2234; Fax: 785-874-4096. Email: stfranci@ruraltel.net.
Catechesis/Religious Program—Pam Engelbert, D.R.E. Students 106.
Mission—St. Joseph's Church 28035 St. John St., New Almelo, Norton Co. 67652. Tel: 785-567-4875. Email: stjosephcc@ruraltel.net.

OAKLEY, LOGAN CO., ST. JOSEPH PARISH (1890) [CEM] Rev. Michael Elanjimattathil, C.M.I. (India); Maranda Bussen, Pastoral Assoc.
Res.: 625 Freeman Ave., 67748. Tel: 785-671-3828; Fax: 785-671-3828. Email: sjsadmin@st-tel.net. Web: www.sjoakley.org.
School—(Grades K-5), 725 Freeman Ave., 67748. Tel: 785-671-4451; Fax: 785-671-3919. Kimberly Shirley, Prin.; Gayle Bremenkamp, Librarian. Priests 1; Lay Teachers 8; Students 61.
Catechesis/Religious Program—St. Joseph Parish Annex Brad Hemmert, D.R.E.; Bradley Joseph, D.R.E. Students 90.

OBERLIN, DECATUR CO., SACRED HEART PARISH (1888) [JC] Rev. Mark Berland.
Res.: 210 E. Washington, 67749. Tel: 785-475-3103.
Catechesis/Religious Program—Megan Carter, D.R.E.; Jennifer Juenemann, D.R.E. Students 47.

OGDEN, RILEY CO., ST. PATRICK PARISH (1859) [CEM] Attended by Seven Dolors of the Blessed Virgin Mary Parish, Manhattan. Revs. Joseph Popelka; Francisco Montoya, Parochial Vicar; Deacon John Bloomfield.
Mailing Address: *c/o Seven Dolors of the Blessed Virgin Mary Parish*, 731 Pierre, Manhattan, 66502.
In Res., Most Rev. George K. Fitzsimons, Bishop Emeritus (Retired).
Res.: P.O. Box A, 66517. Tel: 785-565-5090.

OSBORNE, OSBORNE CO., ST. ALOYSIUS GONZAGA PARISH (1881) [CEM] Rev. Alexander Cho.
Res.: Box 267, 67473. Tel: 785-346-5582. Email: stal@ruraltel.net.
Catechesis/Religious Program—Brenda Henke, D.R.E. Students 51.
Mission—St. Mary's 1312 Prentice, Downs, Osborne Co. 67437. Tel: 785-454-3551.

PARK, GOVE CO., SACRED HEART PARISH (1898), (German), [CEM] Rev. James Maruthukunnel, C.M.I.
Res.: 202 S. Cottonwood, P.O. Box 78, 67751. Tel: 785-673-4684; Fax: 785-673-4248. Email: shcpark@ruraltel.net.
Catechesis/Religious Program—Tel: 785-673-4329. Donna Garrett, D.R.E. Tel: 785-673-4315. Students 49.

PFEIFER, ELLIS CO., HOLY CROSS, Closed. For sacramental records contact St. Fidelis, Victoria.

PHILLIPSBURG, PHILLIPS CO., SAINTS PHILIP AND JAMES PARISH (1875) Rev. Benjamin Saw (Burma).
Res.: 690 S. 7th, 67661. Tel: 785-543-5577; 785-543-5367. Email: sspjchurch@sbcglobal.net.
Catechesis/Religious Program—Patricia Dusin, D.R.E. Students 86.
Mission—St. John the Evangelist Logan, Phillips Co. Tel: 785-689-4299.

PLAINVILLE, ROOKS CO., SACRED HEART PARISH (1890) [CEM] Rev. Galen Long.
Church: 206 N. Washington, P.O. Box 100, 67663. Tel: 785-434-4658; Fax: 785-434-2480. Email: sacredheartchurch@ruraltel.net. Web: sacredheartplainville.org.
School—Tel: 785-434-2157. Carol Parker, Prin. Lay Teachers 7; Students 57.
Catechesis/Religious Program—Students 112.

RUSSELL, RUSSELL CO., ST. MARY QUEEN OF ANGELS PARISH formerly St. Mary Queen of the Angels Parish (1886) [CEM] Rev. Charles Steier.
Church: 415 S. Windsor St., 67665.
Rectory—Rectory Office & Mailing Address: 28 N. Kansas St., 67665. Tel: 785-483-2871; Fax: 785-483-2871 (Call First).
Catechesis/Religious Program—Tel: 785-483-2871. Bonita Ney, D.R.E. Students 139.

ST. FRANCIS, CHEYENNE CO., ST. FRANCIS OF ASSISI PARISH (1912), (German), [JC] Rev. Roger K. Meitl.
Res.: 625 S. River St., P.O. Box 1170, 67756. Tel: 785-332-2680.
Catechesis/Religious Program—Myra Douthit, D.R.E. Students 28.
Mission—St. Joseph's 203 N. Bird, Bird City, Cheyenne Co. 67731. Tel: 785-734-2287.

SCHOENCHEN, ELLIS CO., ST. ANTHONY PARISH (1877) [CEM] Attended by St. Joseph Parish, Hays. Rev. Earl Befort, O.F.M.Cap.
Res.: 215 W. 13th, Hays, 67601. Tel: 785-628-9214; Fax: 785-625-7394.

SEGUIN, SHERIDAN CO., ST. MARTIN PARISH (1910) [CEM] Attended by St. Frances Cabrini Parish, Hoxie. Religious education twinned with St. Francis Cabrini, Hoxie, KS. Rev. B. Thomas Mangat, C.M.I. (India).
Mailing Address: *c/o St. Francis Cabrini Parish*, 924 N. 17th St., P.O. Box 38, Hoxie, 67740. Tel: 785-675-3300.

SELDEN, SHERIDAN CO., SACRED HEART PARISH (1906) [CEM] Rev. Mark Berland.
Res.: 205 S. Missouri, P.O. Box 57, 67757. Tel: 785-386-4496.
Catechesis/Religious Program—Dolores Juenemann, D.R.E. Students 33.

SHARON SPRINGS, WALLACE CO., HOLY GHOST PARISH (1907), (German), Attended by Our Lady of Perpetual Help Parish, Goodland. Rev. Norbert Dlabal.
Mailing Address: *c/o Our Lady of Perpetual Help Parish*, 307 W. 13th, Goodland, 67735.
Res.: 403 N. Main St., 67758. Tel: 785-852-4984.
Catechesis/Religious Program—Sr. Clara Ann Fluech, D.R.E. (Grade & High School). Students 70.

SMITH CENTER , SMITH CO., ST. MARY PARISH (1959) Attended by St. Theresa Parish, Mankato. Rev. George Chalbhagam, C.M.I. (India).
403 W. Hwy. 6, Box 263, 66967. Tel: 785-282-6888.
Catechesis/Religious Program—Mrs. Stacey Rempe, D.R.E. Students 43.

SOLOMON, DICKINSON CO., IMMACULATE CONCEPTION OF THE BLESSED VIRGIN MARY PARISH (1886) [CEM] Rev. John Wolesky, Priest Supvr.; Daylene Tracy, Parish Life Coord.
Res.: 3599 N. Field Rd., P.O. Box 337, 67480. Tel: 785-655-2221; Fax: 785-655-2221.
Catechesis/Religious Program—Kim Kuhn, D.R.E. Students 34.
Mission—St. Patricks Gypsum, Saline Co. 67448.

STOCKTON, ROOKS CO., ST. THOMAS PARISH (1878), (German), [CEM] Attended by Sacred Heart Parish, Plainville. Rev. Galen Long.
Mailing Address: *c/o Sacred Heart Parish*, 206 N. Washington, P.O. Box 100, Plainville, 67663-0100.
Res.: 722 Main, 67669. Tel: 785-425-6656. Web: sacredheartplainville.org.
Catechesis/Religious Program—Joanie Bellerive, C.R.E. Students 53.

TIPTON, MITCHELL CO., ST. BONIFACE PARISH (1874) [CEM] Rev. Damian Richards.
Res.: 308 Gambrinus, P.O. Box 87, 67485. Tel: 785-373-4455.
High School—Tel: 785-373-5635. Gary Hake, Prin. Priests 1; Lay Teachers 6; Students 35.
Catechesis/Religious Program—Lori Schmitt, D.R.E. Students 45.
Mission—SS. Peter & Paul 1202 Holly, P.O. Box 25, Cawker City, Mitchell Co. 67430.

VICTORIA, ELLIS CO., ST. FIDELIS PARISH (1876), (German—Russian), [CEM] Rev. Michael Scully, O.F.M.Cap.
Church Office: 601 10th St., 67671. Tel: 785-735-2777; Fax: 785-735-2779.
Res.: 900 Cathedral Ave., 67671. Tel: 785-735-2777; 785-735-9456; Fax: 785-735-9455. Email: fidelis@ruraltel.net. Web: www.stfidelischurch.com.
Catechesis/Religious Program—Tel: 785-735-9244; Fax: 785-735-2779. Email: sfreled@ruraltel.net. Shirley Brungardt, D.R.E. Students 201.

VINCENT, ELLIS CO., ST. BONIFACE PARISH (1904), (German—Russian), [CEM] Attended by St. Fidelis Parish, Victoria. Rev. Michael Scully, O.F.M-.Cap.
c/o St. Fidelis Parish, 601 10th St., Victoria, 67671. Tel: 785-735-2777; 785-735-9456; Fax: 785-735-2779.
Catechesis/Religious Program—Students 23.

WAKEENEY, TREGO CO., CHRIST THE KING PARISH (1933) [CEM] Rev. Donald F. Pfannenstiel.
Res.: 412 N. Ninth St., 67672. Tel: 785-743-2330.
Catechesis/Religious Program—Tel: 785-743-2339. Verna Flax, D.R.E. Students 120.
Mission—St. Michael c/o 412 N. 9th, Wa Keeney, Trego Co. 67672.

WALKER, ELLIS CO., ST. ANN PARISH (1904), (German—Russian), [CEM] Attended by St. Fidelis Parish, Victoria. Rev. Michael Scully, O.F.M-.Cap.
Mailing Address: *c/o St. Fidelis Parish*, 601 10th St., Victoria, 67671. Tel: 785-735-2777; Fax: 785-735-2779.
Catechesis/Religious Program— Attended by St. Fidelis, Victoria. Students 5.

WASHINGTON, WASHINGTON CO., ST. AUGUSTINE PARISH (1946) [JC] Revs. David Metz; James Hoover, Priest Supvr.; Sr. Marilyn Wall, C.S.J., Parish Life Coord.
Res.: 410 B St., 66968. Tel: 785-325-2346; Fax: 785-325-3147.
Catechesis/Religious Program—Twinned with SS. Peter & Paul, Morrowville, Washington, KS., and Sacred Heart, Greenleaf. Cristi Gilliam, C.R.E. Students 76.

WILSON, ELLSWORTH CO., ST. WENCESLAUS PARISH (1882), (Slovak), [CEM] Rev. James Hoover.
Res.: P.O. Box 528, 67490. Tel: 785-658-3361; Fax: 785-658-3364. Email: swchurch@wtciweb.com.
Catechesis/Religious Program—Tel: 785-658-2341. Students 46.
Mission—St. Joseph P.O. Box 528, Dorrance, Russell Co. 67490.
Mission—St. Mary Parish Holyrood, Ellsworth Co. 67450.

Retired:
Most Rev.—
Fitzsimons, George K., P.O. Box 980, 67402-0980.
Rev. Msgr.—
Weber, John George, Smokey Hill Rehabilitation Center, 1007 Johnstown, Room 411, 67401.
Revs.—
Aschenbrenner, Ralph, Priests Retirement Center, 6900 E. 45th St., N., Apt. B3, Bel Aire, 67226.
Colucci, Bennett, 900 Cathedral Ave., Victoria, 67671-9782.
Dallen, James, W. 818 21st Ave., Spokane, WA 99203.
Gibson, Beryl, 501 3rd St., Phillipsburg, 67661.
Grennan, James, 403 Barton St., Russell, 67665.
Hough, Roger, 1902 W. 139th St., Leawood, 66224-4567. Tel: 785-346-5582
Kieffer, Merlin, 618 Pierre, Manhattan, 66502.
Kramer, Carl, St. John's Inc., 701 7th St., Victoria, 67671.

Long, Melvin, P.O. Box 4350, Palm Springs, CA 92263-4350.
Lutgen, Richard, 1121 Village, Concordia, 66901.
Mattas, Louis, Assisted Living Center, 6550 E. 45th St. N., Apt. 108, Bel Aire, 67226.
McCarthy, Donald, 1203 Holly, Cawker City, 67430.
Metro, LeRoy, 137 N. 9th, 67401.
Moeder, August L., 217 Grant, P.O. Box 74, Quinter, 67752.
Moeder, John, 1414 N. Kuney St., P.O. Box 265, Abilene, 67410.
Pierce, Larry E., P.O. Box 237, Oakley, 67748.
Scheetz, Daniel, J.C.L., P.O. Box 224, Kanopolis, 67454.
Scheetz, Joseph, 510 Easter Ave., WaKeeney, 67672.
Torrez, Basil, P.O. Box 214, Collyer, 67631.
Walsh, John E., Sheridan County Health Complex, 826 18th St., P.O. Box 167, Hoxie, 67740.
Werth, Alvin, 501 W. 37th, #11, Hays, 67601.
Werth, Loren J., 1725 Winne Dr., Manhattan, 66502.

INSTITUTIONS LOCATED IN THE DIOCESE

[A] HIGH SCHOOLS, INTER-PAROCHIAL

SALINA. *Sacred Heart Junior-Senior High School* (1908) 234 E. Cloud, 67401. Tel: 785-827-4422; Fax: 785-827-8648. Email: heart@sacredheartknights.org. Web: www.sacredheartknights.org. John Krajicek, Prin.; Rev. Nicholas Parker (NSH), Chap.; Susan Goodman, Librarian. Sisters 1; Lay Teachers 25; Students 250.

HAYS. *Thomas More Prep-Marian* (1908) 1701 Hall, 67601. Tel: 785-625-6577; Fax: 785-625-3912. Email: dewitt@tmp-m.org. Web: www.tmp-m.org. Rev. Fred Gatschet; William DeWitt, Prin.
Thomas More Prep-Marian High Inc., Four-year Catholic High School, with college preparatory programs conducted by the local Catholic parishes; residency programs for boys and girls; special program for candidates for Priesthood and Religious Life. Priests 2; Lay Teachers 30; Students 225; Total Staff 30.
Endowment Foundation of Thomas More Prep-Marian, Inc. Galen Romme, Pres.
Thomas More Prep-Marian Alumni Assoc., 1701 Hall, 67601. Rev. Earl Befort, O.F.M.Cap., Pres.

[B] GRADE SCHOOLS, INTER-PAROCHIAL

HAYS. *Holy Family Elementary Grade School*, (Grades PreSchool-6), 1800 Milner, 67601-3796. Tel: 785-625-3131; Fax: 785-625-2098. Email: jsimon@hfehays.org. Web: www.hfehays.org. Jana Simon, Prin. Lay Teachers 22; Students 356.

MAHATTAN. *Manhattan Catholic Schools*, (Grades PreK-8), 306 S. Juliette Ave., Manhattan, 66502-6297. Tel: 785-565-5050; Fax: 785-565-5055. Email: lroggenkamp@mcscardinals.org. Web: www.mcscardinals.org. Linda R. Roggenkamp, Prin.; Linda Fetters, Librarian. Lay Teachers 24; Students 259.

[C] HOMES FOR AGED

HAYS. *St. John's Inc.*, 2403 Canterbury, 67601. Tel: 785-625-0077; Fax: 785-625-4760. Web: www.via-christi.org. David Karlin, CEO.
St. John's Victoria, 701 Seventh St., Victoria, 67671. Tel: 785-735-2208; Fax: 785-735-2270. Email: david_karlin@via-christi.org. Web: www.via-christi.org. Rev. Harvey Dinkel, O.F.M.Cap., M.A., M.S., Chap.; Laura Sadeghi, Pastoral Care; David Karlin, CEO. Total Staff 100; Skilled Nursing Beds 90.
St. John's Assisted Living, 2225 Canterbury, 67601. Tel: 785-628-8742; Fax: 785-625-3973. Email: david_karlin@via-christi.org. Web: www.via-christi.org. Theresa Thomas, Exec. Dir.; Sr. Vivian Kleinsorge, C.S.A. Assisted Living Units 57; Total Staff 34.
St. John's Hays, 2401 Canterbury, 67601. Tel: 785-628-3241; Fax: 785-628-3310. Joe Hess, Chairperson; Renee Davison, Exec. Dir; Rev. Harvey Dinkel, O.F.M.Cap., M.A., M.S., Chap.; Sr. Mary Ann Schippers, C.S.A., B.S., B.Ed., Pastoral Care. Total Staff 84; Skilled Nursing Beds 60.

MANHATTAN. *St. Joseph Village, Inc.* (1990) Owned & operated by the Via Christi Health System of Wichita., 2800 Willow Grove, 66502. Tel: 785-539-7671; Fax: 785-539-9125. Email: dfrihart@via.christi.org. Web: www.via-christi.org/stjosephvillage. Total Staff 165; Skilled Nursing 96; Assisted Living 40; Independent Living 8.

[D] MONASTERIES AND RESIDENCES OF PRIESTS AND BROTHERS

HAYS. *St. Joseph's Friary* (1876) 215 W. 13th St., 67601. Tel: 785-628-9214; Fax: 785-625-7394. Revs. Gilmary Tallman, O.F.M.Cap.; Earl Befort, O.F.M.Cap.; Curtis Carlson, O.F.M.Cap.; Didacus Dunn, O.F.M.Cap.; Canice Froelich, O.F.M.Cap. Priests 3; Total Assisted 794; Total Staff 5.

VICTORIA. *St. Fidelis Friary* 67671. Tel: 785-735-9456; Fax: 785-735-9455. Revs. Michael Scully, O.F.M.Cap.; Gregory Beyer, O.F.M.Cap.; Harvey Dinkel, O.F.M.Cap., M.A., M.S.; Bennett Collucci, O.F.M.Cap.; Thaddeus J. Posey, O.F.M.Cap.; Simon Conrad, O.F.M.Cap.; Bro. Joseph McGlynn, O.F.M.Cap. Total in Residence 5.

[E] CONVENTS AND RESIDENCES FOR SISTERS

CONCORDIA. *Nazareth Convent & Academy Corporation Sisters of St. Joseph of Concordia, Administration Offices*, 215 Court St., P.O. Box 279, 66901. Tel: 785-243-2149; Fax: 785-243-4741. Email: csjcenter@sbcglobal.net. Web: www.csjkansas.org. Sr. Marcia Allen, C.S.J., Pres., Nazareth Motherhouse for the Sisters of St. Joseph; Contact Person; Rev. John Schlaf, Chap. Professed Sisters 151; Total in Community 151.

[F] RETREAT CENTERS

CONCORDIA. *Manna House of Prayer*, 323 E. Fifth St., Box 675, 66901. Tel: 785-243-4428; Fax: 785-243-4321. Email: mannahse@mannahouse.org. Web: www.mannahouse.org. Sr. Betty Suther, C.S.J., Admin. Total Staff 10; Total in Residence 7.

VICTORIA. *Capuchin Center for Spiritual Life*, 900 Cathedral Ave., 67671. Tel: 785-735-9393; Fax: 785-735-9455. Email: ccsl@ruraltel.net. Rev. Michael Scully, O.F.M.Cap.

[G] CAMPUS MINISTRY

HAYS. *Comeau Catholic Campus Center* Office: 506 W. Sixth, 67601. Tel: 785-625-7396. Email: comeauccc@yahoo.com. Rev. Fred Gatschet, Chap. Total Staff 2.

MANHATTAN. *St. Isidore's Catholic Student Center* , Kansas State University., 711 Denison Ave., 66502. Tel: 785-539-7496. Email: stisidores@stisidores.com. Web: www.stisidores.com. Total Staff 4; Total in Residence 1. In Res. Rev. Keith Weber, Chap.

[H] MISCELLANEOUS

SALINA. *St. Joseph Annex, Inc.*, 401 W. Iron, P.O. Box 980, 67401. Tel: 785-827-8746; Fax: 785-827-6133. Rev. Jerome L. Morgan.
Marymount Memorial Educational Trust Fund, P.O. Box 980, 67402-0980. Tel: 785-827-8746; Fax: 785-827-6133. Email: chancery@salinadiocese.org. Most Rev. Paul S. Coakley, S.T.L., D.D., Trustee.
The Register of the Roman Catholic Diocese of Salina, Inc., 103 N. Ninth St., P.O. Box 980, 67402-0980.
Roman Catholic Diocese of Salina Deposit and Loan Inc., 103 N. Ninth St., P.O. Box 980, 67401. Tel: 785-827-8746; Fax: 785-827-6133. Email: chancery@salinadiocese.org.
Roman Catholic Diocese of Salina St. Joseph Fund, Inc., P.O. Box 980, 67402-0980.
Sacred Heart Junior-Senior Endowment Fund, Inc., 234 E. Cloud, 67401-6436. Tel: 785-825-4011; Fax: 785-827-8648. Email: melissaa@sacredheartknights.org. Web: www.sacredheartknights.org. Melissa Anderson, Special Events Coord.
Salina Catholic Diocese Education Endowment, Inc., 103 N. Ninth St., P.O. Box 980, 67402-0980. Tel: 785-827-8746; Fax: 785-827-6133. Email: chancery@salinadiocese.org.
Salina Catholic Diocese Gift & Annuity Fund, Inc., 103 N. Ninth St., P.O. Box 980, 67402-0980. Tel: 785-827-8746; Fax: 785-827-6133. Email: chancery@salinadiocese.org.
Salina Catholic Diocese Seminary Burses, Inc., 103 N. Ninth St., P.O. Box 980, 67402-0980. Tel: 785-827-8746; Fax: 785-827-6133. Email: chancery@salinadiocese.org.
Salina Diocesan Clergy Health and Retirement Association, Inc., Diocese of Salina, P.O. Box 980, 67402-0980. Tel: 785-827-8746; Fax: 785-827-6133. Most Rev. Paul S. Coakley, S.T.L., D.D., Pres.
The Serra Club of Salina, Kansas, 103 N. Ninth, P.O. Box 980, 67402-0980.

RELIGIOUS INSTITUTES OF MEN REPRESENTED IN THE DIOCESE

For further details refer to the corresponding bracketed number in the Religious Institutes of Men or Women section.

[0470]—*The Capuchin Friars* (Province of Mid-America)—O.F.M.Cap.

[0275]—*Carmelites of Mary Immaculate* (Provincial House - Kerala, India)—C.M.I.

RELIGIOUS INSTITUTES OF WOMEN REPRESENTED IN THE DIOCESE

[3710]—*Congregation of the Sisters of Saint Agnes*—C.S.A.

[3832]—*Congregation of the Sisters of St. Joseph*—C.S.J.

[1115]—*Dominican Sisters of Peace*—O.P.

[]—*Missionaries of the Eucharistic Heart of Christ the King*

[3830-15]—*Sisters of St. Joseph*—C.S.J.

NECROLOGY

† Kieffer, Henry, (Retired)—Died Jan. 10, 2009
† Lahey, John, (Retired)—Died Nov. 3, 2008

An asterisk (*) denotes an organization that has established tax-exempt status directly with the IRS and is not covered by the USCCB Group Ruling.

Diocese of Salt Lake City

(Dioecesis Civitatis Lacus Salsi)

Most Reverend

JOHN C. WESTER

Bishop of Salt Lake City; ordained May 15, 1976; appointed Bishop of Salt Lake City January 8, 2007; installed March 14, 2007. *Office: 27 C St., Salt Lake City, UT 84103-2397.* Tel: 801-328-8641, Ext. 304; Fax: 801-328-0324.

Diocesan Offices and Organizations: 27 C St., Salt Lake City, UT 84103-2397. Tel: 801-328-8641; Fax: 801-328-9680.

Web: www.dioslc.org

ESTABLISHED AS A VICARIATE-APOSTOLIC ON NOV. 23, 1886.

Square Miles 84,990.

Erected a Diocese on January 27, 1891.

Originally comprised all Utah and the Counties of Eureka, Lander, Lincoln, White Pine, Nye, Elko and Clark in the State of Nevada. By Apostolic Constitution dated March 27, 1931, the Nevada section was separated from the Salt Lake Diocese and incorporated in the Reno Diocese. The name was changed to Diocese of Salt Lake City on March 31, 1951.

Comprises the State of Utah.

Patron of the Diocese of Salt Lake City: St. Mary Magdalene.

For legal titles of parishes and diocesan institutions, consult the Chancery Office.

STATISTICAL OVERVIEW

Personnel	
Bishop	1
Abbots	1
Retired Abbots	2
Priests: Diocesan Active in Diocese	40
Priests: Diocesan Active Outside Diocese	1
Priests: Retired, Sick or Absent	12
Number of Diocesan Priests	53
Religious Priests in Diocese	24
Total Priests in Diocese	77
Extern Priests in Diocese	10
Ordinations:	
Transitional Deacons	2
Permanent Deacons in Diocese	80
Total Brothers	10
Total Sisters	40
Parishes	
Parishes	48
With Resident Pastor:	
Resident Diocesan Priests	36
Resident Religious Priests	8
Without Resident Pastor:	
Administered by Priests	1
Administered by Deacons	1
Administered by Lay People	2
Missions	19
Professional Ministry Personnel:	
Brothers	1
Sisters	6
Lay Ministers	90
Welfare	
Homes for the Aged	1
Total Assisted	1,100
Day Care Centers	4
Total Assisted	485
Special Centers for Social Services	3
Total Assisted	47,500
Educational	
Diocesan Students in Other Seminaries	12
Seminaries, Religious	1
Total Seminarians	12
High Schools, Diocesan and Parish	3
Total Students	1,713
Elementary Schools, Diocesan and Parish	13
Total Students	3,862
Catechesis/Religious Education:	
High School Students	1,745
Elementary Students	7,825
Total Students under Catholic Instruction	15,157
Teachers in the Diocese:	
Priests	1
Sisters	2
Lay Teachers	313
Vital Statistics	
Receptions into the Church:	
Infant Baptism Totals	4,108
Minor Baptism Totals	255
Adult Baptism Totals	326
Received into Full Communion	724
First Communions	3,161
Confirmations	1,880
Marriages:	
Catholic	330
Interfaith	122
Total Marriages	452
Deaths	551
Total Catholic Population	250,000
Total Population	2,736,424

Former Bishops—Rt. Revs. LAWRENCE SCANLAN, D.D., ord. June 24, 1868; appt. Vicar-Apostolic of Utah, Jan. 25, 1887; cons. Titular Bishop of Larandum, June 29, 1887; named first Bishop of Salt Lake, Jan. 30, 1891; died May 10, 1915; JOSEPH S. GLASS, C.M., D.D., LL.D., ord. Aug. 15, 1897; cons. Aug. 24, 1915; died Jan. 26, 1926; JOHN J. MITTY, D.D., ord. Dec. 22, 1906; cons. Sept. 8, 1926; made Coadjutor Archbishop of San Francisco, cum jure successionis, Feb. 4, 1932; Titular Archbishop of Egina; succeeded to the See, March 5, 1935; died Oct. 15, 1961; Most Revs. JAMES E. KEARNEY, D.D., ord. Sept. 19, 1908; appt. July 4, 1932; cons. Oct. 28, 1932; appt. Bishop of Rochester, July 31, 1937; installed Nov. 11, 1937; died Jan. 12, 1977; LEO J. STECK, D.D., ord. June 8, 1924; appt. Auxiliary Bishop of Salt Lake, March 3, 1948; cons. Titular Bishop of Ilium, May 20, 1948; died June 19, 1950; DUANE G. HUNT, D.D., LL.D., ord. June 27, 1920; appt. Aug. 6, 1937; cons. Oct. 28, 1937; appt. assistant at the Pontifical Throne; appt. May 25, 1946; died March 31, 1960; JOSEPH LENNOX FEDERAL, D.D., ord. Dec. 8, 1934; appt. Auxiliary Bishop of Salt Lake City, Feb. 5, 1951; cons. April 11, 1951; made Coadjutor Bishop of Salt Lake City, May 8, 1958; succeeded to the See, March 31, 1960; retired April 22, 1980; died Aug. 31, 2000; WILLIAM KEITH WEIGAND, D.D., ord. May 25, 1963; appt. Sept. 3, 1980; ord. Bishop, Nov. 17, 1980; transferred to the See of Sacramento; installed Jan. 27, 1994; GEORGE H. NIEDERAUER, Ph.D., ord. April 30, 1962; appt. Bishop of Salt Lake City Nov. 3, 1994; ord. Jan. 25, 1995; appt. Archbishop of San Francisco Dec. 15, 2005; installed Feb. 15, 2006.

Diocesan Pastoral Center—27 C St., Salt Lake City, 84103-2397. Tel: 801-328-8641; Fax: 801-328-9680.

Office of the Bishop—SHIRLEY MARES, Exec. Asst. Tel: 801-328-8641, Ext. 304; Fax: 801-328-0324.

Vicar General and Moderator of the Curia—Rev. Msgr. J. TERRENCE FITZGERALD, P.A. Tel: 801-328-8641.

Chancellor—Deacon SILVIO MAYO. Tel: 801-328-8641, Ext. 315.

Vice Chancellor—Rev. LANGES J. SILVA, J.C.D. Tel: 801-328-8641, Ext. 312.

Diocesan Offices

Apostleship of Prayer—Rev. Msgr. MATTHEW O. WIXTED, Dir. (Retired).

Archives—GARY TOPPING, Ph.D., Dir. Tel: 801-328-8641, Ext. 346.

Campus Ministry—MATTHEW BOERKE.

Catholic Community Services—ROBERT C. STEINER; BRADFORD R. DRAKE, Exec. Dir., 745 E. 300 S., Salt Lake City, 84102. Tel: 801-977-9119, Ext. 1215; Fax: 801-977-8227.

Catholic Foundation of Utah—ARMANDO LUJAN, Pres.; JENNIFER L. CARROLL, Exec. Dir. Tel: 801-328-8641, Ext. 306.

Catholic Relief Services—Deacon SILVIO MAYO. Tel: 801-328-8641, Ext. 315.

Catholic Schools Offices—Sr. CATHERINE KAMPHAUS, C.S.C., Supt. Tel: 801-328-8641, Ext. 330; PAM PERRI, Sec. Tel: 801-328-8641, Ext. 329.

Cemetery--Mount Calvary—CURTIS ROSENTRETER, Dir. Tel: 801-355-2476; Fax: 801-328-3294; OLIVIA SAGASTUME, Sec.

Chancery—Deacon SILVIO MAYO, Chancellor. Tel: 801-328-8641, Ext. 315; DEBRA ALIRES, Sec. Tel: 801-328-8641, Ext. 317.

College of Consultors—Rev. Msgrs. J. TERRENCE FITZGERALD, P.A.; ROBERT R. SERVATIUS; ROBERT J. BUSSEN; TERENCE M. MOORE, Ph.D.; JOSEPH M. MAYO; COLIN F. BIRCUMSHAW; Revs. HERNANDO DIAZ; FRANCISCO PIRES; JAVIER G. VIRGEN.

Communications Media Office—COLLEEN GUDREAU. Tel: 801-328-8641, Ext. 344.

Deans—Rev. Msgrs. COLIN F. BIRCUMSHAW, Salt Lake Deanery; MICHAEL J. WINTERER, Southwestern Deanery; Revs. MARTIN DIAZ, Wasatch Deanery; DONALD E. HOPE, Eastern Deanery; KENNETH L. VIALPANDO, Northern Deanery.

Continuing Diaconate Formation—Deacon FORREST GRAY, Dir. Tel: 801-328-8641, Ext. 327.

Diaconate Training—VACANT, Dir.

Diocesan Development Drive—SHANNON LEE, Dir. Tel: 801-328-8641, Ext. 328.

Diocesan Office for Persons with Disabilities—DOLORES LOPEZ. Tel: 801-328-8641, Ext. 333.

Diocesan Pastoral Council—JULIANA BOERIO-GOATES, Ph.D., Pres.; COLLEEN GUDREAU, Staff Liaison.

Ecumenical Commission—Rev. Msgrs. VICTOR G. BONNELL; JOSEPH M. MAYO; Rev. LANGES J. SILVA, J.C.D.

Engaged Encounter—FRANK PEDROZA; JOANNA PEDROZA. Tel: 801-486-9828.

Family Life-Natural Family Planning—VEOLA MARTINEZ-BURCHETT. Tel: 801-328-8641, Ext. 324.

Finance Council—Most Rev. JOHN C. WESTER; Rev. Msgr. COLIN F. BIRCUMSHAW; Rev. FRANCISCO PIRES; MARY KAY GRIFFIN, CPA; O. YOGI GILLILAND; DAVE SIMPSON; KATHY BROWN ROBERTS, Esq.; MICHAEL LEE; NANCY ESSARY; Ms. JOAN LOFFREDO, CPA, Staff Liaison; LANDELL FROERER; GEORGE BEATON.

Finance Office—Ms. JOAN LOFFREDO, CPA, CFO. Tel: 801-328-8641, Ext. 309; DEBRA CANDELARIA, Sec. Tel: 801-328-8641, Ext. 310.

Government Liaison—DEE ROWLAND. Tel: 801-328-8641, Ext. 336.

Hispanic Ministry—MARIA-CRUZ GRAY, Dir. Tel: 801-328-8641, Ext. 361; SANDRA MAXWELL, Sec. Tel: 801-328-8641, Ext. 332.

Hispanic Affairs—Rev. JAVIER G. VIRGEN, Episcopal Vicar. Tel: 801-328-8641, Ext. 358; Deacon RICARDO ARIAS, Asst. Tel: 801-328-8641, Ext. 398.

Holy Childhood Association—Deacon SILVIO MAYO, Dir. Tel: 801-328-8641, Ext. 315.

Liturgy Office—TIMOTHY JOHNSTON, Dir. Tel: 801-328-8641, Ext. 321; RUTH DILLON, Sec. Tel: 801-328-8641, Ext. 322.

Liturgical Commission—Rev. Msgr. COLIN F. BIRCUMSHAW, Chm. Tel: 801-487-1000.

Correctional Institution Ministry—Rev. JAMES E. BLAINE, Dir. Utah State Prison, Mailing Address: P.O. Box 142, American Fork, 84003. Tel: 801-756-7771; ILLA WRIGHT, Coord. Ministry for Salt Lake Valley Detention Center, Decker Lake, Wasatch Youth Center and Adult Detention Complex 3357 Enterada Ave., West Valley City, 84119. Tel: 801-969-5617; Rev. RICHARD T. SHERMAN Central Utah Correctional Facility, Gunnison, UT.Tel: 435-896-5593.

Board For Formation of Priests— Clergy Continuing Education, Most Rev. JOHN C. WESTER; Rev. Msgr. J. TERRENCE FITZGERALD, P.A.; Rev. JAVIER G. VIRGEN, Chm. Team: Revs. MARTIN DIAZ; OSCAR MARTINEZ; FRANCISCO PIRES; KENNETH L. VIALPANDO; ANDRZEJ SKRZYPIEC; SAMUEL DINSDALE.

Native American Ministry—DOLORES LOPEZ. Tel: 801-328-8641, Ext. 333.

Newspaper— "Intermountain Catholic" MARIE MISCHEL, Editor. Tel: 801-328-8641, Ext. 340; CHRIS YOUNG, Staff Writer. Tel: 801-328-8641, Ext. 341; ARTHUR HEREDIA, Business Mgr. Tel: 801-328-8641, Ext. 356; LAURICE LAKE, Advertising Rep. & Mktg. Dir. Tel: 801-328-8641, Ext. 339; DAVID COLE, Staff Writer, Web Master & Information Svcs. Tel: 801-328-8641, Ext. 342.

Peace and Justice Commission—DEE ROWLAND, Dir. Tel: 801-328-8641, Ext. 336.

Presbyteral Council—Rev. Msgr. TERENCE M. MOORE, Ph.D., Pres.; Revs. DONALD E. HOPE, Vice Pres.; SAMUEL DINSDALE, Sec.

Priests' Mutual Benefit Society (Retirement)—Board of Directors: Most Rev. JOHN C. WESTER, Chm.; Rev. Msgrs. J. TERRENCE FITZGERALD, P.A., Pres.; ROBERT J. BUSSEN; JOSEPH M. MAYO; TERENCE M. MOORE, Ph.D.; ROBERT R. SERVATIUS; Rev. FRANCISCO PIRES; Ms. JOAN LOFFREDO, CPA.

Priests' Personnel Board—Most Rev. JOHN C. WESTER; Rev. Msgrs. J. TERRENCE FITZGERALD, P.A.; ROBERT J. BUSSEN; COLIN F. BIRCUMSHAW; Revs. JAVIER G. VIRGEN; LANGES J. SILVA, J.C.D.; ROBERT T. MORIARITY; KENNETH L. VIALPANDO.

Real Estate Office—MICHAEL LEE, Dir. Tel: 801-328-8641, Ext. 364.

Religious Education—SUSAN NORTHWAY, Dir. Tel: 801-328-8641, Ext. 326.

Sisters' Council—Executive Team: Sisters GENEVRA ROLF, C.S.C., Vicar Rel. Women; MARTHA ANN NORWOOD, C.S.C., Pres.; MARY ZENZEN, O.S.B., Vice Pres.; CECILIA VAN ZANDT, D.C., Treas.; KARLA MCKINNIE, C.S.C., Sec.

Society for the Propagation of the Faith—Deacon SILVIO MAYO, Dir. Tel: 801-328-8641, Ext. 315.

Pastoral Operations—MICHAEL LEE, Dir. Tel: 801-328-8641, Ext. 364.

Special Needs Program Scholarship Assistance—Sisters STELLA MARIE ZAHNER, D.C. Tel: 801-328-8641, Ext. 334; GERMAINE SARRAZIN, D.C. Tel: 801-328-8641, Ext. 357; CECILIA VAN ZANDT, D.C., Sec. Tel: 801-328-8641, Ext. 334.

Tribunal—

Judicial Vicar—Rev. LANGES J. SILVA, J.C.D. Tel: 801-328-8641, Ext. 312.

Secretary and Notary—VIOLA SMITH. Tel: 801-328-8641, Ext. 316.

Promoter of Justice—Rev. Msgr. COLIN F. BIRCUMSHAW.

Defenders of the Bond—Rev. Msgrs. ROBERT R. SERVATIUS; J. TERRENCE FITZGERALD, P.A.; JOSEPH M. MAYO.

Judges—Revs. LANGES J. SILVA, J.C.D.; DAVID H. SCHULYER, S.M.; Mr. ROBERT J. FLUMMERFELT, J.C.L.

Victim Assistance Coordinator and Safe Environment—COLLEEN GUDREAU. Tel: 801-328-8641, Ext. 344. Email: colleengudreau@dioslc.org.

Vocation Office—Rev. Msgr. COLIN F. BIRCUMSHAW, Dir. Tel: 801-328-8641, Ext. 358; Rev. JAVIER G. VIRGEN. Tel: 801-328-8641, Ext. 358; Deacon RICARDO ARIES, Sec. Tel: 801-328-8641, Ext. 398.

Youth and Young Adult Ministry—MATTHEW BOERKE, Dir. Tel: 801-328-8641, Ext. 313.

CLERGY, PARISHES, MISSIONS AND PAROCHIAL SCHOOLS

SALT LAKE CITY

(SALT LAKE COUNTY)

1—CATHEDRAL OF THE MADELEINE LLC 202 (1866) Rev. Msgr. Joseph M. Mayo; Revs. Gregory A. Glenn, Pastoral Admin.; Omar Ontiveros; Deacons Lynn R. Johnson; Silvio Mayo; Scott Dodge. In Res., Rev. Langes J. Silva.
Res.: 331 E. S. Temple St., 84111. Tel: 801-328-8941; Fax: 801-364-6504.
School—Madeleine Choir School, 205 E. 1st Ave., 84103. Tel: 801-323-9850; Fax: 801-323-0581. Christina Vierra McGill, Prin. Priests 1; Lay Teachers 19; Students 232.
Catechesis/Religious Program—Fax: 801-364-6504. Students 140.
Good Samaritan Program—Laurel Dokos Griffith, Prog. Dir. Number Served 135,000.

2—SAINT AMBROSE LLC 214 (1948) Revs. Andrzej Skrzypiec; Lourduraj Gregory Gally, Parochial Vicar; Deacons John Bash; George Reade.
Res.: 2315 Redondo Ave., 84108. Tel: 801-485-5610; Fax: 801-484-3642. Email: paroff@xmission.com. Web: www.stambroseslc.com.
School—J. E. Cosgriff Memorial School, (Grades PreK-8), 2335 Redondo Ave., 84108. Tel: 801-486-3197; Fax: 801-484-8270. Mrs. Elizabeth Hunt, Prin. Lay Teachers 20; Preschool 50; Students 340.
Catechesis/Religious Program—Tel: 801-485-9324; Fax: 801-484-1065. Students 155.

3—SAINT ANN LLC 215 (1917) Rev. Msgr. Colin F. Bircumshaw; Deacon Mansueto Flaim.
Res.: 2119 S. 400 E., 84115-2872. Tel: 801-487-1000; Fax: 801-487-1416.
School—(Grades PreSchool-8), 430 E. 2100 S., 84105. Tel: 801-486-0741; Fax: 801-486-0742. Kathleen McMahon, Prin.; Mary T. Sena, Librarian. Lay Teachers 18; Students 285.
Catechesis/Religious Program—Tel: 801-261-5943; Fax: 801-261-5903 (Call first). Email: slavole9@msn.com. Students 86.

4—SAINT CATHERINE OF SIENA LLC 218 (1981) Revs. Peter Rogers, O.P.; Peter Do, O.P.
Res.: 170 S. University, 84102. Tel: 801-359-6066; Fax: 801-359-4547.
Catechesis/Religious Program—Students 104.

5—OUR LADY OF GUADALUPE LLC 208 (1944), (Hispanic), Rev. Michael R. Sciumbato; Deacon Mario A. Rodriguez.
Res.: 672 Redondo Ave., 84105. Fax: 801-359-2678.
Church: 715 W. 3rd N., 84116. Tel: 801-364-2019.
Catechesis/Religious Program—Monica Miramontes, C.R.E. Students 606.

6—OUR LADY OF LOURDES LLC 211 (1913) [CEM] Rev. J. J. Schwall; Deacon Lowell Palm.
Res.: 1085 E. 700 S. St., 84102. Tel: 801-322-3330; Fax: 801-363-6007.
School—(Grades PreK-8), 1065 E. 700 S. St., 84102. Tel: 801-364-5624; Fax: 801-364-0925. Louise Herman, Prin. Lay Teachers 13; Students 237.
Catechesis/Religious Program—Tel: 801-322-3330; Fax: 801-363-6007. Students 9.

7—OUR LADY OF PERPETUAL HELP LLC 261 (1994), (Vietnamese), (Vietnamese Parish) Rev. Dominic Thuy Dang Ha.
Mailing Address: P.O. Box 18306, 84118-0306. Tel: 801-968-8981.
Church & Res.: 5415 S. 4360 W., 84118. Tel: 801-968-8981.
Catechesis/Religious Program—Students 180.

8—SAINT PATRICK LLC 257 (1892) Rev. Samuel Dinsdale; Deacon Sefo A. Manu.
Res.: 1058 W. 400 S., 84104-1261. Tel: 801-596-7233; Fax: 801-363-3743.
Catechesis/Religious Program—Students 105.

9—SACRED HEART LLC 210 (1917) Rev. Eugenio Yarce.
Res.: 948 S. 2nd East St., 84111. Tel: 801-363-8632; Fax: 801-363-1539. Email: sacredheart.slc@hotmail.com.
Catechesis/Religious Program—174 E. 900 S., 84111. Students 449.

10—SAINT THOMAS MORE CATHOLIC CHURCH LLC 248 (1981) Revs. David L. Van Massenhove; Paul J. McCarthy, S.J.; Deacon Steven W. Kirts. In Res., Rev. Anastasius Iwuoha.
Res. & Parish Center: 3015 E. Creek Rd., Sandy, 84093-6575. Tel: 801-942-5285 (Office); 801-942-7678 (Rectory); Fax: 801-942-5287. Email: stm@stmore.com. Web: www.stmore.com.
Catechesis/Religious Program—Tel: 801-942-5285. Students 272.

11—SAINT VINCENT DE PAUL LLC 250 (1925) Rev. Msgr. M. Francis Mannion; Deacons John Kranz; David Osman.
Res.: 1375 E. Spring Ln., 84117. Tel: 801-272-9216; Fax: 801-273-1156.
School—(Grades PreK-8), 1385 E. Spring Ln., 84117. Tel: 801-277-6702; Fax: 801-424-0450. Mark Longe, Prin. Lay Teachers 28; Students 299.
Catechesis/Religious Program—Tel: 801-527-2037. Students 142.

SUBURBAN SALT LAKE CITY

1—BLESSED SACRAMENT LLC 201 (1972) Rev. Msgr. Robert R. Servatius; Deacons Russell Langner; Marcel Soklaski; Sharon Jackson, Pastoral Assoc.
Res.: 9757 S. 1700 E., Sandy, 84092. Tel: 801-571-5517 (Office); 801-576-1644 (Rectory); Fax: 801-676-0900. Web: blessedsacramentsandy.parishesonline.com.
School—(Grades PreSchool-8), 1745 E. 9800 S., Sandy, 84092. Tel: 801-572-5311; Fax: 801-572-0251. Email: tnielsen@blessedsacschool.org. Web: www.blessedsacschool.org. Mrs. Judy Julian, Prin.; Mr. John Nuttall, Librarian. Lay Teachers 21; Students 286.
Catechesis/Religious Program—1745 E. 9800 S., Sandy, 84092. Tel: 801-571-2071. Email: rloflin@blessedsacschool.org. Robin Loflin, D.R.E. Students 113.
Station—Our Lady of the Snows Alta. Tel: 801-742-2889.

2—SAINT FRANCIS XAVIER LLC 222 (1955) Revs. Robert T. Moriarty; Eleazar Silva; Deacon Rubel J. Salaz.
Res.: P.O. Box 18631, Kearns, 84118. Tel: 801-968-2123; Fax: 801-966-1639.
See St. Francis Xavier Regional School, Kearns under Elementary Schools, Regional located in the Institution section.
Catechesis/Religious Program—Tel: 801-968-2123, Ext. 413. Students 825.

3—IMMACULATE CONCEPTION LLC 206 (1890) Rev. Dennis Ruane, Sacramental Min.
Res.: 112 W. State Hwy., P.O. Box 151, Copperton, 84006. Tel: 801-569-2706.

4—SAINT JOSEPH THE WORKER LLC 232 (1964) Rev. Patrick F. Carley, Admin.
Res.: 7405 S. Redwood Rd., P.O. Box 98, West Jordan, 84084. Tel: 801-255-8902; Fax: 801-255-5003. Email: office@stjoseph-wj.org. Web: www.stjoseph-wj.org.
Catechesis/Religious Program—Tel: 801-561-4062; Fax: 801-561-4062. Students 160.

5—SAINT JUDE (1975), (Maronite), [CEM] Rev. Msgr. William Bonczewski.
Res.: 4893 Wasatch St., Murray, 84107. Tel: 801-268-2820. Email: stjudechurch@stinger.net.
Catechesis/Religious Program—Fax: 801-268-4404. Students 30.

6—SAINT MARTIN DE PORRES LLC 236 (1982) Rev. Jan Bednarz.
Mailing Address: 4976 Valois Cir., Taylorsville, 84118. Tel: 801-968-2369.
Church: 4914 S. 2200 W., Taylorsville, 84118.
Catechesis/Religious Program—Students 48.

7—OUR LADY OF LOURDES LLC 209 (1916) [CEM] Rev. John Norman; Deacon Billy Martin.
Res.: 2840 S. 9000 W., P.O. Box 38, Magna, 84044. Tel: 801-508-1598; Fax: 801-250-7027.
Catechesis/Religious Program—8585 W. 3010 S., Magna, 84044. Tel: 801-250-6052. Students 129.

8—SAINTS PETER AND PAUL LLC 243 (1972) Revs. Stanislaw Herba; Jose Alberto Barrera, Pastoral Assoc.; Dennis Reily, O.P., Pastoral Assoc.; Deacons Eugene Farrell; Hector Mota.
Mailing Address: 3560 W. 3650 S., West Valley City, 84119.
Res.: 3580 W. 3650 S., West Valley City, 84119.
Catechesis/Religious Program—Tel: 801-966-5111, Ext. 202; Fax: 801-966-2114. Students 185.

9—SAINT THERESE OF THE CHILD JESUS LLC 246 (1925), (Spanish), Revs. Martin Diaz, Admin.; Denis Reilly, O.P., Parochial Vicar; Deacons Stanley L. Stott; Meliton Sanchez.
Office: 7832 S. Allen St., Midvale, 84047. Tel: 801-255-3721; Fax: 801-255-4516. Email: stthereses@yahoo.com. Web: www.stthererse.org.
Res.: 7860 S. Allen St., Midvale, 84047. Tel: 801-561-6015. 612 Lennox St., Midvale, 84047. Tel: 801-568-3650.
Catechesis/Religious Program—Tel: 801-561-2495. Students 500.

OUTSIDE SALT LAKE CITY

AMERICAN FORK, UTAH CO., SAINT PETER LLC 242 (1969) Rev. James E. Blaine.
634 N. 600 E., 84003. Email: stpeters6@yahoo.com. Web: www.stpetersamericanfork.parishesonline.com.
Catechesis/Religious Program—Tel: 801-756-2747. Students 175.

Station—Eagle Mountain
BOUNTIFUL, DAVIS CO., SAINT OLAF LLC 239 (1944) Rev. Msgr. Rudolph A. Daz; Deacons Dan Essary; Manuel Trujillo.
Res.: 276 E. 1700 S., 84010. Tel: 801-295-3621; Fax: 801-295-8261.
School—(Grades K-8), 1793 S. Orchard Dr., 84010. Tel: 801-295-5341; Fax: 801-295-5915. Lay Teachers 13; Students 148.
Catechesis/Religious Program—Students 116.
BRIGHAM CITY, BOX ELDER CO., SAINT HENRY LLC 225 (1950) Rev. Patrick Reuse, S.J.
Res.: 380 S. 2nd E., P.O. Box 872, 84302. Tel: 435-723-2941; Fax: 435-723-1215. Email: sthenrys@comast.net.
Catechesis/Religious Program—Tel: 435-723-1215. Students 154.
Mission—Santa Ana 760 W. 600 N., Tremonton, Box Elder Co. 84337.
CEDAR CITY, IRON CO., CHRIST THE KING LLC 203 (1934) [JC] Rev. Msgr. Michael J. Winterer; Rev. Oscar Martinez; Deacon Denny Davies; Sr. Yvonne Hatt, C.S.C.
Res.: 690 S. Cove Dr., 84720. Tel: 435-586-8298; Fax: 435-865-5960.
Catechesis/Religious Program—Students 153.
Mission—St. Gertrude 690 S. Cove Dr., Iron Co. 84720.
Mission—St. Sylvester Escalante, Garfield Co. 84726.
Station—St. Dominic
Station— Duck Creek Village, Kane Co. 84762.
CENTRAL VALLEY, SEVIER CO., SAINT ELIZABETH LLC 220 (1947) Rev. Richard T. Sherman.
Mailing Address: 815 N. SR 110, 84754.
Res.: 76 S. 200 W., Richfield, 84701. Tel: 435-896-8734; Fax: 435-896-8734.
Catechesis/Religious Program—Students 120.
Mission—St. Anthony of the Desert North on Sandcreek Rd., Torrey, Wayne Co. 84775. Tel: 435-425-3319.
Mission—St. Jude 160 E. Center St., Ephraim, Sanpete Co. 84627. Tel: 435-283-6242.
Mission—San Juan Diego Mission 25 W. Center St., Gunnison, Sanpete Co. 84634.
Station—Central Utah Correctional Facility [JC] Gunnison. Tel: 801-528-6000; Fax: 801-528-6259.
DRAPER, SALT LAKE CO., SAINT JOHN THE BAPTIST LLC 252 (1999) Rev. Msgr. Terence M. Moore; Deacon Paul Graham.
300 E. 11800 S., 84020. Tel: 801-984-7101; Fax: 801-984-7114.
School—Tel: 801-984-7100; Fax: 801-984-7122.
Catechesis/Religious Program—Tel: 801-984-7101; Fax: 801-984-7114. Students 464.
EAST CARBON, CARBON CO., GOOD SHEPHERD LLC 204 (1947) Rev. Donald E. Hope, Pastoral Admin.
Res.: P.O. Box 99, 84520. Tel: 435-888-3306.
Catechesis/Religious Program—Students 20.
Mission—St. Michael 140 N. Long St., Green River, Emery Co. 84525. Tel: 435-637-1846.
EUREKA, JUAB CO., SAINT PATRICK LLC 257 (1885) Rev. Joseph S. Rooney, S.J.
Res.: P.O. Box 387, Payson, 84651. Tel: 801-465-4782. Email: sanandres@qwestoffice.net.
Catechesis/Religious Program—Students 1.
HELPER, CARBON CO., SAINT ANTHONY OF PADUA CATHOLIC CHURCH LLC 216 (1944) [JC] Rev. Edward Metzger, O.F.M.
Res.: 5 S. Main, 84526-1533. Tel: 435-472-5661; Fax: 435-472-3235; 435-472-5661. Email: santhony@emerytelcom.net. Web: www.stanthony-helper.org.
Catechesis/Religious Program—Tel: 435-472-8367; Fax: 435-472-8367. Students 55.
HUNTSVILLE, WEBER CO., SAINT FLORENCE CATHOLIC COMMUNITY LLC 254 (1990) Rev. Charles T. Cummins, Admin.
Mailing Address: 514-24th St., Ogden, 84401-1594. Tel: 801-399-9531.
Church: 6461 E. Hwy. 39, 84317. Tel: 801-745-5673.
Catechesis/Religious Program—Students 34.
KANAB, KANE CO., SAINT CHRISTOPHER LLC 219 (1953) Deacon Denny Davies, Pastoral Admin.
Res.: 39 W. 200 S., 84741. Tel: 435-644-3414 (Office).
Catechesis/Religious Program—
LAYTON, DAVIS CO., SAINT ROSE OF LIMA LLC 245 (1948) Rev. Msgr. Victor G. Bonnell; Rev. Jose Alexis Davila; Deacons Willis Bassett; Robert J. Quintana, (Retired); John C. Weis.
Mailing Address: P.O. Box 557, 84041. 210 S. Chapel St., 84041. Tel: 801-544-4269; Fax: 801-593-0808.
Res.: 321 Whitesides St., 84041. Tel: 801-546-2541. Email: stroseoflimacatl@qwestoffice.net. Web: www.stroseoflimacatholic.net.
Catechesis/Religious Program—Tel: 801-544-5425. Students 343.
LOGAN, CACHE CO., SAINT THOMAS AQUINAS LLC 247 (1941) Rev. Clarence J. Sandoval; Deacon Jim Miller.
Res.: 573 E. 2050 N., North Logan, 84341. Tel: 435-753-6724.
Church: 725 S. 250 E., Hyde Park, 84318. Tel: 435-752-1478; Fax: 435-792-3792. Email: newman@cc.usu.edu. Web: www.stthomaslogan.org.
Catechesis/Religious Program—Tel: 435-752-1478. Students 399.
Mission—Utah State University St. Jerome Newman Center, 795 N. 800 E., Cache Co. 84321. Tel: 435-753-7670.
MILFORD, BEAVER CO., SAINT BRIDGET LLC 217 (1948) Michael Lee, Admin.; Rev. Marco T. Lopez, Sacramental Min.
Res.: 210 S. 1st W., P.O. Box 785, 84751. Tel: 435-387-2732.
Catechesis/Religious Program—Students 20.
Mission—St. John Bosco P.O. Box 924, Delta, Millard Co. 84624. Tel: 435-864-3710.
Mission—Holy Family P.O. Box 292, Fillmore, Millard Co. 84631.
MOAB, GRAND CO., SAINT PIUS X LLC 244 (1955) Rev. William F. Wheaton.
Res.: 122 W. 400 N., P.O. Box 357, 84532. Tel: 435-259-5211; Fax: 435-259-3984. Email: piusx@frontiernet.net.
Catechesis/Religious Program—Students 25.
Mission—Sacred Heart Hwy. 46/Main, LaSal, San Juan Co. 84530. Tel: 435-686-2255.
MONTICELLO, SAN JUAN CO., SAINT JOSEPH LLC 229 (1935) [JC] Rev. William F. Wheaton.
Res. & Mailing Address: 365 S. Main, P.O. Box 518, 84535. Tel: 435-587-2322.
Catechesis/Religious Program—Students 45.
Station— Blanding.
OGDEN, WEBER CO.
1—HOLY FAMILY LLC 205 (1979) Rev. Patrick H. Elliott.
Res. & Office: 1100 E. 5550 S., 84403. Tel: 801-479-1112; Fax: 801-479-1126. Web: holyfamilycatholicchurch.org.
Catechesis/Religious Program—Students 97.
2—SAINT JAMES THE JUST LLC 226 (1966) Rev. Erik J. Richtsteig; Deacons Herschel Hester; Robert W. Bambrick.
Res.: 495 N. Harrison Blvd., 84404. Tel: 801-782-5393; Fax: 801-782-9559.
Catechesis/Religious Program—Tel: 801-782-7372; Fax: 801-479-4909. Email: stjames_dre@comcast.net. Students 197.
3—SAINT JOSEPH LLC 230 (1875) Revs. Kenneth L. Vialpando; Martin Picos; Charles T. Cummins; Deacons John Conniff; Anthony J. Lopez.
Res.: 514 24th St., 84401. Tel: 801-399-5627; Fax: 801-399-5918.
See St. Joseph Regional School, Ogden under Elementary Schools, Regional located in the Institution section.
Catechesis/Religious Program—Tel: 801-621-3602. Students 508.
Mission—St. Florence 6481 E. Hwy. 39, Huntsville, Weber Co. 84317. Tel: 801-745-5673.
4—SAINT MARY LLC 237 (1957) Revs. Martin I. Rock, S.J.; Leo P. Prengaman, S.J.; Deacons Jack Clark; Steve Neveraski.
Mailing Address: 4050 S. 3900 W., West Haven, 84401. Tel: 801-621-7961; Fax: 801-394-1244.
Catechesis/Religious Program—Tel: 801-621-2274. Students 302.
OREM, UTAH CO., ST. FRANCIS OF ASSISI LLC 221 (1892) [CEM] Revs. David J. Bittmenn; Jose Gregorio Rausseo Gomez, Parochial Vicar.
Mailing Address: 65 E. 500 N., 84057-4030. Email: oremstfrancis@lycos.com.
Res.: 1661 N. 500 E., 84057-4030. Tel: 801-221-1307.
Catechesis/Religious Program—Tel: 801-221-0750, Ext. 16; Fax: 801-221-0759. Students 500.
Mission—Mission San Isidro Elberta, Utah Co. 84626.
PARK CITY, SUMMIT CO., SAINT MARY OF THE ASSUMPTION LLC 238 (1881) Rev. Msgr. Robert J. Bussen; Rev. Marco T. Lopez; Deacon Tom Tosti.
Res.: 1505 W. White Pine Canyon Rd., 84060. Tel: 435-649-9676; Fax: 435-658-0067. Web: www.stmarysparkcity.com.
Catechesis/Religious Program—Students 500.
Mission—St. Lawrence 1st West Center, Heber City, Wasatch Co. 84032. Tel: 435-654-4035; Fax: 435-654-4035.
PAYSON, UTAH CO., SAN ANDRES LLC 212 (1986) Rev. Joseph S. Rooney, S.J.
Church & Mailing Address: 315 E. 100 N., P.O. Box 387, 84651. Fax: 801-465-7729. Email: sanandres@qwestoffice.net.
Catechesis/Religious Program—Students 71.
PRICE, CARBON CO., NOTRE DAME DE LOURDES LLC 207 (1918) Rev. Donald E. Hope.
185 N. Carbon Ave., 84501.
Res.: 205 N. Carbon Ave., 84501. Tel: 435-636-8124; Fax: 435-637-6338. Web: www.notredamechurch.com.
Catechesis/Religious Program—Tel: 435-637-6338; 435-630-0815. Students 130.
Mission—San Rafael 1716 S. Hwy. 10, Huntington, Emery Co. 84528. Tel: 435-687-2116; Fax: 435-384-3215.
RIVERTON, SALT LAKE CO., SAINT ANDREW CATHOLIC CHURCH LLC 233 (2006) Rev. Francisco Pires.
11835 S. 3600 W., 84065. Tel: 801-984-7500; Fax: 801-254-1142. Email: standrew@catholicweb.com. Web: www.standrewriverton.com.
Catechesis/Religious Program—Students 198.
ROOSEVELT, DUCHESNE CO., SAINT HELEN LLC 224 (1940) [CEM] Rev. Albert Kileo, A.L.C.P.
Res.: 433 E. 200 N., P.O. Box 415, 84066. Tel: 435-722-2975; Fax: 435-722-0525.
Catechesis/Religious Program—Tel: 435-722-0525. Students 24.
Mission—Holy Spirit Duchesne, Duchesne Co.
Mission—Blessed Kateri Tekakwitha Fort Duchesne, Uintah Co. Tel: 435-722-4734.
ST. GEORGE, WASHINGTON CO., ST. GEORGE LLC 223 (1955) Revs. Gustavo Vidal; Raynato Rodillas, Parochial Vicar; Deacons Rigoberto Aquirre; Jack Gorman; Rogaciano Tellez; Mark A. Bourget Sr.; Willie Folkes.
Mailing Address: 259 W. 200 N., P.O. Box 188, 84771. Tel: 435-688-1948 (Church); 435-673-2604 (Office); Fax: 435-688-2704. Email: st_george_catholic@hotmail.com. Web: www.saintgeorgecatholics.com.
Res.: 289 W. 200 N., 84770. Tel: 435-673-7354.
Catechesis/Religious Program—Bishop Scanlan Bldg., 157 N. 200 W. Tel: 435-673-6701; Fax: 435-688-2704. Students 534.
Mission—San Pablo Beryl, Iron Co. 84714.
Station—Zion National Park, Tel: 435-772-3256. (Lodge)
Station—Saint Paul Catholic Center 171 S. Main, Hurricane, 84737. Tel: 435-635-9186. 1st & 3rd Sun.
TOOELE, TOOELE CO., ST. MARGUERITE LLC 235 (1910) Rev. Hernando Diaz; Deacon Rick Huffman.
Res.: 15 S. 7th St., 84074. Tel: 435-882-3860; Fax: 435-882-3866. Email: stmarg@qwestoffice.net.
School—(Grades PreK-6) Tel: 435-882-0081. Web: stmargschool.org. Marcella Burden, Prin.
Catechesis/Religious Program—Students 286.
VERNAL, UINTAH CO., SAINT JAMES THE GREATER LLC 227 (1923) [JC] Revs. Albert Kileo, A.L.C.P.; Beda Msaki, A.L.C.P.
Res.: 138 N. 100 West St., 84078. Tel: 435-789-3016; Fax: 435-789-5774.
Catechesis/Religious Program—Tel: 435-789-3034. Students 99.
WENDOVER, TOOELE CO., SAN FELIPE LLC 251 (2000), (Spanish), Rev. German Umaña, Admin.
Res.: 606 E. Aria Blvd., P.O. Box 1270, 84083. Tel: 435-665-2339.
Catechesis/Religious Program—Students 330.

Chaplains of Public Institutions

SALT LAKE CITY. *Adult Detention Complex*, Tel: 801-743-5500.
County Youth Detention Center, Tel: 801-261-2060.
Decker Lake Youth Detention Center, Tel: 801-954-9200. Illa Wright. Tel: 801-969-5617.
Veterans Administration Hospital, 500 Foothill Dr., 84113. Tel: 801-582-1565. Rev. Lourduraj Gregory Gally.
Wasatch Youth Center, Tel: 801-265-5860.
DRAPER. *Utah State Prison*, P.O. Box 142, American Fork, 84003. Tel: 801-576-7827. Rev. James E. Blaine. Tel: 801-576-7485.
GUNNISON. *Central Utah Correctional Facility*, Tel: 435-528-6000. Rev. Richard T. Sherman. Tel: 435-896-5539.

On Duty Outside the Diocese:
Rev.—
Gaeta, David R., 1225 E. Bennington St., Boston, MA 02128.

Retired:
Rev. Msgrs.—
Davich, George
Pellegrino, Francis B.
Pollock, Robert C.
Sweeney, Lawrence P.
Wixted, Matthew O.
Revs.—
Culleton, Thomas
Curnutte, William G.
Fogarty, James
Govorchin, Vincent
Hart, John B.
Janda, James A.
Rodriguez, Reyes G.
Semple, James

Permanent Deacons:
Aquirre, Rigoberto, St. George, St. George
Arias, Ricardo, Office of Hispanic Affairs
Bambrick, Robert W., St. James, Ogden
Bash, John, St. Ambrose, Salt Lake City
Bassett, Willis, St. Rose of Lima, Layton
Biediger, Douglas C., St. Francis Xavier, Kearns
Bourget, Mark A., Sr., St. George, St. George
Bulson, Michael E., St. Andrew, Riverton
Clark, Jack, St. Mary, West Haven
Conniff, John, St. Joseph, Ogden
Cormier, Joe H., (Out of Diocese)
Corrao, Thomas P., St. Pius X, Moab
Cummings, Owen, Mount Angel Seminary, Oregon
Davies, Denny, Christ the King, Cedar City
Dillon, Dale R., St. John the Baptist, Draper & St. Peter, American Fork
Dodge, Scott, Cathedral, Salt Lake City
Espinoza, Sunday S., St. Joseph the Worker, West Jordan
Essary, Dan, St. Olaf, Bountiful
Farrell, Eugene, Sts. Peter and Paul, West Valley
Flaim, Mansueto, St. Ann, Salt Lake City
Folkes, Willie, St. George, St. George
Garcia, James D., (Retired)
Glodowski, Robert J., (On Duty Outside the Diocese)
Gorman, Jack, St.George, St. George
Graham, Paul, St. John the Baptist, Draper
Gray, Forrest, Diaconate Dir.
Hardy, Robert H., St. Mary of the Assumption, Park City
Hester, Herschel, St. James, Ogden
Huber, Roger, (On Duty Outside the Diocese)
Huffman, Rick, Sts. Peter & Paul, West Valley City
Hunnel, Dwayne A., St. Henry, Brigham City
Januszewski, William A., (On Duty Outside the Diocese)
Johansson, Otto, Christus St. Joseph Villa, Salt Lake City
Johnson, Lynn R., Cathedral, Salt Lake City
Keyser, John, St. Catherine of Siena, Salt Lake City
Kirts, Steven W., St. Thomas More, Sandy
Klein, Richard H., St. Pius X, Moab
Kranz, John, St. Vincent de Paul, Murray
Langner, Russell, Blessed Sacrament, Sandy
Lopez, Anthony J., St. Joseph, Ogden
Manu, Sefo A., St. Patrick, Salt Lake City
Martin, Billy, Our Lady of Lourdes, Magna
Mayo, Silvio, Chancellor, Cathedral of the Madeleine, Salt Lake
McElfresh, James L., (Retired)
Merino, Reynaldo Q., (On Duty Outside the Diocese)
Meyersick, Karl E., St. Henry, Brigham City
Miller, James P., St. Thomas Aquinas, Hyde Park
Moreno, Honorio, St. Joseph, Ogden
Mota, Hector, St. Peter & Paul, Grange
Murphy, Kenneth W., St. Mary, West Haven
Neveraski, Steve, St. Mary, Ogden
Norrell, Keith W., St. Joseph, Ogden
O'Brien, John P., (Retired)
Osman, David, St. Vincent de Paul, Murray
Palm, Lowell, Our Lady of Lourdes, Salt Lake City
Petersen, Drew M., Jr., Cathedral of the Madeleine, Salt Lake City
Quintana, Robert J., (Retired)
Reade, George, St. Ambrose, Salt Lake City
Rodgers, Thomas A., Christ Prince of Peace, Hill AFB
Rodriguez, Mario A., Our Lady of Guadalupe, Salt Lake City
Ruiz, Moises, St. Francis of Assisi, Orem
Salaz, Rubel J., St. Francis Xavier, Kearns
Sanchez, Mel J., St. Theresa, Midvale
Sluga, George J., St. Peter & Paul, West Valley City
Smith, Douglas B., Holy Family, Ogden; St. Joseph Catholic High School, Ogden
Soklaski, Marcel, Blessed Sacrament, Sandy
Solak, Mark E., St. Thomas More, Sandy
Solorzano, Armando, Cathedral of the Medeleine, Salt Lake City
Spencer, Noel, (On Duty Outside the Diocese)
Stewart, Thomas J., (On Duty Outside the Diocese)
Stott, Stanley L., St. Therese, Midvale
Tellez, Rogaciano, St. George, St. George
Thaeler, John S., Holy Family, Ogden
Toro, German A., Sacramento, CA
Tosti, Tom, St. Mary, Park City
Trudell, William J., Christ the King, Cedar City
Trujillo, Manuel, St. Olaf, Bountiful
Velez, Manuel, St. Marguerite, Tooele
Waiss, Terrance, St. Florence Mission, Huntsville
Weis, John C., St. Rose of Lima, Layton

INSTITUTIONS LOCATED IN THE DIOCESE

[A] SEMINARIES, RELIGIOUS, OR SCHOLASTICATES

HUNTSVILLE. *Abbey of Our Lady of the Holy Trinity*, 1250 S. 9500 E., 84317. Tel: 801-745-3784; Fax: 801-745-6430. Email: hta@xmission.com. Web: www.xmission.com/~hta. Rev. Charles J. Cummings, O.C.S.O., Novice Master. Priests 10; Brothers 8; Oblates 1.

[B] HIGH SCHOOLS, DIOCESAN

SALT LAKE CITY. *Judge Memorial Catholic High School* (1921) 650 S. 1100 E., 84102. Tel: 801-363-8895; Fax: 801-236-2923. Web: www.judgememorial.com. J. Richard Bartman, Prin.; Linda Bult, Librarian. Day School. (Coed) Lay Teachers 63; Students 747; Total Staff 96.

DRAPER. *Juan Diego Catholic High School* (1999) 300 E. 11800 S., 84020. Tel: 801-984-7650; Fax: 801-984-7601. Email: drgaleycolosimo@skaggscatholiccenter.org. Web: www.jdchs.org. Dr. Gabriel Colosimo, Prin.; Jan Duane, Librarian. Faculty 60; Total Staff 75; Total Enrollment 790.

OGDEN. *St. Joseph Catholic High School*, 1790 Lake St., 84401. Tel: 801-394-1515; Fax: 801-394-6428. Email: hscampusoffice@stjosephutah.com. Web: www.stjosephutah.com. Norman Allred, Prin.; Terri Sousa, Librarian. Lay Teachers 22; Total Staff 29; Students 193.

[C] ELEMENTARY SCHOOLS, REGIONAL

KEARNS. *St. Francis Xavier Regional School*, (Grades PreSchool-8), 4501 W. 5215 S., 84118. Tel: 801-966-1571; Fax: 801-966-1639. Email: preeder@stfrancisxavier.org. Web: stfrancisxavierschool.org. Rev. Robert T. Moriarity, Pastor; Patrick Reeder, Prin.; Mrs. Kathleen Kilby, Librarian. Lay Teachers 17; Students 278.

OGDEN. *St. Joseph Catholic Elementary School* (1877) (Grades PreSchool-8), 2980 Quincy Ave., 84403. Tel: 801-393-6051; Fax: 801-393-6086. Email: lklos@stjosephutah.com. Web: www.stjosephutah.com/es. Rev. Kenneth L. Vialpando; Armando Venegas, Prin.; Paige Laubacher, Librarian. Lay Teachers 29; Total Staff 48; Students 423.

[D] FOUNDATIONS

SALT LAKE CITY. *Catholic Foundation of Utah* (1984) 27 C St., 84103. Tel: 801-328-8641, Ext. 306; Fax: 801-355-5904. Email: jennifer.carroll@dioslc.org. Web: www.catholicfoundationofutah.org. Jennifer L. Carroll, Exec. Dir.; Armando Lujan, Pres.

OGDEN. *St. Benedict's Foundation* (1994) 6000 S., 1075 E., 84405-4945. Tel: 801-479-1800; Fax: 801-479-4997. Email: stbenedictsfd@mbmutah.org. Web: www.mbmutah.org. Yvonne Coiner, Exec. Dir.; Gary Francis, Chm. Bd. Dir.

[E] HOMES FOR AGED

SALT LAKE CITY. *Christus Health Utah dba Christus St. Joseph Villa* 451 Bishop Federal Ave., 84115. Tel: 801-487-7557; Fax: 801-487-1112. Web: www.stjosephvilla.com. Rev. Anastasius Iwuoha, Chap. Total Assisted 1,050; Total Staff 320; Bed Capacity 340.

CHRISTUS St. Joseph Villa, 451 Bishop Federal Ln., 84115-2295. Tel: 801-487-7557; Fax: 801-487-1112. Email: stjosephvilla@christussjv.org. Web: www.stjosephvilla.com. Galen K. Ewer, Pres. & CEO. Operated by CHRISTUS Health. Residents 300; Total in Residence 340; Total Assisted 1,100; Total Staff 320.

[F] MONASTERIES AND RESIDENCES OF PRIESTS AND BROTHERS

HUNTSVILLE. *Abbey of Our Lady of the Holy Trinity of the Order of Cistercians* (1947) 1250 S. 9500 E., 84317. Tel: 801-745-3784; Fax: 801-745-6430. Email: hta@xmission.com. Web: www.xmission.com/~hta. Revs. Alan Hohl, O.C.S.O.; David Altman, O.C.S.O., Abbot; Patrick Boyle, O.C.S.O.; Charles J. Cummings, O.C.S.O., Novice Master; Leander Dosch, O.C.S.O.; Malachy Flaherty, O.C.S.O.; Joseph Schroer, O.C.S.O.; Baldwin Shea, O.C.S.O.; Emmanuel Spillane, O.C.S.O.

Abbey of Our Lady of the Holy Trinity of the Order of Cistercians of the Strict Observance Priests 10; Brothers 8; Oblates 1; Total in Community 19. Residing Elsewhere: Rev. Gregory Santos, O.C.S.O.

[G] CONVENTS, MONASTERIES AND RESIDENCES FOR SISTERS

SALT LAKE CITY. **Carmel of the Immaculate Heart of Mary Monastery* (1952) 5714 Holladay Blvd., 84121. Tel: 801-277-6075; Fax: 801-277-4263. Email: carmelsl@xmission.com. Web: www.carmelslc.org. Sr. Maureen Goodwin, O.C.D., Prioress. Professed Cloistered Sisters 7; Professed Out-Sisters 1.

St. Joseph Villa Convent (1866) 451 Bishop Federal Ln., 84115-2295. Tel: 801-466-0047; Fax: 801-468-6851. Email: incarnateword@utahweb.com. Congregation of Sisters of Charity of the Incarnate Word 3.

Our Lady of Lourdes Convent, 675 S. 1100 E., 84102. Tel: 801-583-1204. Sisters of the Holy Cross 3.

DRAPER. *Congregation of the Sisters of the Holy Cross, Vivian Skaggs Armstrong Convent* (1998) 554 E. 11800 S., 84020. Tel: 801-501-8349; Fax: 801-984-7342. Email: celinedounies@sjbelementary.org; karlamckinnie@standrewut.org.
Sisters of the Holy Cross, Inc. Sisters 3.

MURRAY. *Sisters of the Holy Cross Convent*, 1238 W. Bullion St., 84123. Tel: 801-313-9611.
Sisters of the Holy Cross, Inc. Sisters 2.

OGDEN. *Mount Benedict Monastery* (1994) 6000 S. 1075 E., 84405-4945. Tel: 801-479-6030; Fax: 801-479-4997. Email: mbmutah@mbmutah.org. Web: www.mbmutah.org. Sisters of St. Benedict 8.

PARK CITY. *Congregation of the Sisters of the Holy Cross*, 3221 Homestead Rd., 84098. Tel: 435-655-7980.
Sisters of the Holy Cross, Inc. Sisters 2.

WEST JORDAN. *St. Joseph the Worker Convent* (1982) 7405 S. Redwood Rd., 84084-4004. Tel: 801-561-4090.

[H] NEWMAN CENTERS

SALT LAKE CITY. *University of Utah, Newman Center* , (St. Catherine of Siena University Parish), 170 S. University, 84102. Tel: 801-359-6066; Fax: 801-359-4547. Web: www.unewman.org. Revs. Peter J. Rogers, O.P.; Peter Do, O.P. Total Students in Residence 7; Total Staff 3.

EPHRAIM. *St. Jude Catholic Center* 160 E. Center, 84627. Tel: 435-896-8527. Rev. Richard T. Sherman.

OGDEN. *Weber State University, Newman Center* 3738 Custer Ave., 84403. Tel: 801-399-9531. Rev. Charles T. Cummins, Dir. Total in Residence 1; Total Staff 1.

[I] CATHOLIC SOCIAL SERVICES

SALT LAKE CITY. *Catholic Community Services*, 745 E. 300 S., 84102. Tel: 801-977-9119; Fax: 801-977-8227; 801-977-9224. Web: www.ccsutah.org. Robert C. Steiner, Board Pres.; Bradford R. Drake, Exec. Dir. Total Assisted 400,000; Meals served at the St. Vincent de Paul Center 253,396; Total Staff 70.

Catholic Community Services Joyce Hansen Hall Food Bank & Social Services, 2504 F. Ave., Ogden, 84401. Tel: 801-394-5944; Fax: 801-621-8468. Mailing Address: P.O. Box 869, Ogden, 84402.

CCS-Treatment Program for Women, 745 E. 300 S., 84102. Tel: 801-977-9119; Fax: 801-977-8227.

CCS-St. Mary's Treatment Program for Men, 745 E. 300 S., 84102. Tel: 801-328-1894; Fax: 801-328-1895. Residential Substance Abuse Treatment for Adult Males.

CCS-St. Vincent de Paul Resource Center, 745 E. 300 S., 84102. Tel: 801-363-7710; Fax: 801-595-8532.

Bishop Weigand Resource Center, 745 E. 300 S., 84102. Tel: 801-363-7710; Fax: 801-595-8532.

CCS-Immigration and Refugee Resettlement, 745 E. 300 S., 84102. Tel: 801-977-9119; Fax: 801-977-9224.

Holy Cross Ministries, 860 E. 4500 S., Ste. 204, 84107. Tel: 801-261-3440; Fax: 801-261-3390. Email: sbrennan@hcmutah.org. Web: www.holycrossministries.org. Sr. Suzanne Brennan, C.S.C. Outreach Program, English as a Second Language (ESL), Seniors, Children, Women, Legal Assistance for Immigration, Bi-Lingual Counseling, Parish Health, Afterschool Summer Programs. Total Staff 35; Total Assisted Annually 7,500.

[J] MISCELLANEOUS

SALT LAKE CITY. *Catholic Diocese of Salt Lake City Capital Development Corporation*, 27 C St., 84103.

Catholic Diocese of Salt Lake City Real Estate Corporation, 27 C St., 84103.

Mercy Housing Utah, Inc. (2002) 67 N. B St., 84103. Tel: 801-521-3183; Fax: 801-521-3093. Email: arowland@mercyhousing.org. Web: www.mercyhousing.org. Amy Rowland, Regl. Housing Dir.

Ministries of the Catholic Diocese of Salt Lake City LLC, 27 C St., 84103.

DRAPER. *Skaggs Catholic Center LLC*, 300 E. 11800 S., 84020.

RELIGIOUS INSTITUTES OF MEN REPRESENTED IN THE DIOCESE

For further details refer to the corresponding bracketed number in the Religious Institutes of Men or Women section.

[]—*Apostolic Life Community Priests in the Opus Spiritus Sanctu*—A.L.C.P.

[0220]—*Congregation of the Blessed Sacrament*—S.S.S.

[0520]—*Franciscan Friars*—O.F.M.

[0690]—*Jesuit Fathers* (California Prov.)—S.J.

[0690]—*Jesuit Fathers* (NY Prov.)—S.J.

[0350]—*Order of Cistercians of the Strict Observance (Trappists)*—O.C.S.O.

[0430]—*Order of Preachers (Dominicans)* (Western Province)—O.P.

[0420]—*Society of the Divine Word*—S.V.D.

RELIGIOUS INSTITUTES OF WOMEN REPRESENTED IN THE DIOCESE

[0230]—*Benedictine Sisters of Pontifical Jurisdiction*—O.S.B.

[0470]—*Congregation of the Sisters of Charity of the Incarnate Word, Houston, Texas*—C.C.V.I.

[1920]—*Congregation of the Sisters of the Holy Cross*—C.S.C.

[0760]—*Daughters of Charity of St. Vincent de Paul* (Province of the West)—D.C.

[0420]—*Discalced Carmelite Nuns*—O.C.D.

[]—*Franciscan Missionaries of Jesus Crucified*—F.M.J.C.

[1190]—*Franciscan Sisters of the Atonement*—S.A.

[3130]—*Our Lady of Victory Missionary Sisters*—O.L.V.M.

[]—*Sisters for Christian Community*—S.F.C.C.

DIOCESAN CEMETERIES

SALT LAKE CITY. *Mount Calvary Catholic*, Office, 275 U St., 84103. Tel: 801-355-2476. Curtis Rosentreter, Dir.

NECROLOGY

† Kenny, Rev. Msgr. James T., (Retired)—Died May 31, 2009

† Fischer, Louis A., (Retired)—Died Feb. 6, 2009

† Flegge, William—Died April 4, 2009

An asterisk (*) denotes an organization that has established tax-exempt status directly with the IRS and is not covered by the USCCB Group Ruling.

Diocese of San Angelo

(Dioecesis Angeliana)

Most Reverend
MICHAEL D. PFEIFER, O.M.I.

Bishop of San Angelo; ordained December 21, 1964; consecrated and installed Bishop of San Angelo July 26, 1985. *Res.: P.O. Box 1829, San Angelo, TX 76902.*

ESTABLISHED OCTOBER 16, 1961.

Square Miles 37,433.

Comprises 29 Counties in the State of Texas as follows: Andrews, Brown, Callahan, Coke, Coleman, Concho, Crane, Crockett, Ector, Glasscock, Howard, Irion, Kimble, McCulloch, Martin, Menard, Midland, Mitchell, Nolan, Pecos, Reagan, Runnels, Schleicher, Sterling, Sutton, Taylor, Terrell, Tom Green and Upton.

For legal title of parishes and diocesan institutions, consult the Chancery Office.

The Chancery: P.O. Box 1829, San Angelo, TX 76902. Tel: 325-651-7500; Fax: 325-651-6688.

Web: www.san-angelo-diocese.org

Email: mdpomi@aol.com

STATISTICAL OVERVIEW

Personnel	
Bishop	1
Priests: Diocesan Active in Diocese	44
Priests: Diocesan Active Outside Diocese	3
Priests: Retired, Sick or Absent	5
Number of Diocesan Priests	52
Religious Priests in Diocese	9
Total Priests in Diocese	61
Permanent Deacons in Diocese	61
Total Sisters	17
Parishes	
Parishes	47
With Resident Pastor:	
Resident Diocesan Priests	38
Resident Religious Priests	5
Without Resident Pastor:	
Administered by Priests	11
Administered by Deacons	2
Missions	22
Professional Ministry Personnel:	
Sisters	17
Lay Ministers	14
Educational	
Diocesan Students in Other Seminaries	17
Total Seminarians	17
Elementary Schools, Diocesan and Parish	3
Total Students	764
Catechesis/Religious Education:	
High School Students	4,324
Elementary Students	8,362
Total Students under Catholic Instruction	13,467
Teachers in the Diocese:	
Sisters	1
Lay Teachers	51
Vital Statistics	
Receptions into the Church:	
Infant Baptism Totals	1,795
Minor Baptism Totals	117
Adult Baptism Totals	176
Received into Full Communion	239
First Communions	1,581
Confirmations	1,303
Marriages:	
Catholic	277
Interfaith	96
Total Marriages	373
Deaths	609
Total Catholic Population	84,520
Total Population	792,891

Former Bishops—Most Revs. THOMAS J. DRURY, D.D., LL.D., ord. June 2, 1935; appt. Oct. 16, 1961; cons. and installed Jan. 24, 1962; transferred to Corpus Christi, July 19, 1965; died July 22, 1992; THOMAS TSCHOEPE, D.D., ord. May 30, 1943; appt. Bishop Jan. 12, 1966; cons. March 9, 1966; transferred to Dallas, Aug. 27, 1969; died Jan. 24, 2009; STEPHEN A. LEVEN, D.D., ord. June 10, 1928; cons. Feb. 8, 1956, Auxiliary of San Antonio; appt. to San Angelo Oct. 22, 1969; retired April 16, 1979; died June 28, 1983; JOSEPH A. FIORENZA, ord. May 29, 1954; appt. Sept. 4, 1979; ord. and installed Oct. 25, 1979; transferred to Galveston-Houston, Dec. 18, 1984.

Vicar General—Rev. Msgr. LARRY J. DROLL, B.A., M.A., J.C.L.

Chancery Office—804 Ford, San Angelo, 76905. Tel: 325-651-7500; Fax: 325-651-6688. *Mailing Address: Box 1829, San Angelo, 76902.* Office Hours: Mon.-Fri. 9-5.

Chancellor—Mr. MICHAEL WYSE.

Diocesan Tribunal—Mailing Address: P.O. Box 1829, San Angelo, 76902.

Judicial Vicar—Rev. TOM BARLEY, M.S.W., M.B.A., M.Div., J.C.L., Mailing Address: P.O. Box 1829, San Angelo, 76902.

Judges—Rev. Msgr. MAURICE VOITY, S.T.L., S.T.M.; Mr. TOM BURKE, S.T.B., M.C.L., J.C.L., Tribunal Judge.

Promoter Justitiae—Rev. Msgr. JAMES A. PLAGENS, S.T.B., M.A.

Defensores Vinculi—Rev. Msgr. LARRY J. DROLL, B.A., M.A., J.C.L.; Revs. CHARLES C. GREENWELL, Ed.D.; MARK WOODRUFF, B.A.

Diocesan Consultors—Rev. Msgr. LARRY J. DROLL, B.A., M.A., J.C.L.; Revs. HUBERT WADE; BARRY L. MCLEAN; MARK MILLER, C.PP.S.; Rev. Msgr. FREDERICK NAWARSKAS; Rev. TOM BARLEY, M.S.W., M.B.A., M.Div., J.C.L.

Priests' Personnel Board—Rev. Msgr. LARRY J. DROLL, B.A., M.A., J.C.L., Chm.; Rev. BERNARD L. GULLY; Rev. Msgr. FREDERICK NAWARSKAS; Rev. TOM BARLEY, M.S.W., M.B.A., M.Div., J.C.L.; Mr. MICHAEL WYSE, Ex Officio.

Presbyteral Council—Rev. TOM BARLEY, M.S.W., M.B.A., M.Div., J.C.L.; Rev. Msgr. LARRY J. DROLL, B.A., M.A., J.C.L.; Mr. MICHAEL WYSE; Revs. HUBERT WADE, Chm.; BERNARD L. GULLY; THOMAS MANIMALA; BARRY L. MCLEAN; SANTIAGO D. UDAYAR, Ed.D.; MARK MILLER, C.PP.S.; Rev. Msgr. FREDERICK NAWARSKAS.

Vicar for Women Religious—Sr. MALACHY GRIFFIN, O.P.

Diocesan Offices and Directors

Diocesan Finance Officer—REGINA BODIFORD.

Director of Seminarians—Rev. HUBERT WADE.

Campaign for Human Development—Mr. MICHAEL WYSE.

Catholic Relief Services—MICHAEL R. WYSE.

Catholic University, Friends of—VACANT.

Communications Office—Mr. JIMMY PATTERSON.

Continuing Education of the Clergy—Rev. BARRY L. MCLEAN.

Cursillos de Cristiandad—Rev. BERNARD L. GULLY.

Deans—Revs. TOM BARLEY, M.S.W., M.B.A., M.Div., J.C.L., San Angelo Deanery; BERNARD L. GULLY, Midland-Odessa Deanery; Rev. Msgr. FREDERICK NAWARSKAS, Abilene Deanery.

Diocesan Liturgical Commission—Rev. EDWARD T. DE LEON, O.M.I.

Holy Childhood, Pontifical Association—Miss MARY SUE BREWER.

Pastor Review Board—Rev. Msgr. FREDERICK NAWARSKAS.

Newspaper— "West Texas Angelus" Mr. JIMMY PATTERSON, Editor.

Office of Education and Formation—Sr. HILDA MAROTTA, O.S.F.

Permanent Deacon Director—Deacon TIM GRAHAM.

Prison Ministry Coordinator—Sr. ESTELA TOVAR, C.D.P.

Permanent Deacon Formation—Deacon TIM GRAHAM.

Pro-Life—Mr. JERRY MICHAEL PETERS.

Priests' Pension Plan—Rev. Msgr. LARRY J. DROLL, B.A., M.A., J.C.L. Board of Directors: Rev. HUBERT WADE, Chm.; Rev. Msgrs. LARRY J. DROLL, B.A., M.A., J.C.L., Sec.; MAURICE VOITY, S.T.L., S.T.M.; Rev. BARRY L. MCLEAN; Rev. Msgr. FREDERICK NAWARSKAS.

Propagation of the Faith—Mr. MICHAEL WYSE.

Rural Life—Deacon CHARLIE EVANS, Dir.

Schools—Sr. ELIZABETH ANN SWARTZ, S.S.N.D., Supt.

Victim Assistance Coordinator—Mrs. LORI HINES. Tel: 325-651-7500.

Vocations—Rev. BARRY L. MCLEAN, Dir.

CLERGY, PARISHES, MISSIONS AND PAROCHIAL SCHOOLS

CITY OF SAN ANGELO

(TOM GREEN COUNTY)

1—CATHEDRAL OF THE SACRED HEART (1884) Rev. Msgr. Maurice Voity, Rector. In Res., Rev. Tom Barley.

Office: 19 S. Oakes St., 76903-5929. Tel: 325-658-6567; Fax: 325-659-0588. Email: shcsanangelo@hotmail.com.

School—Angelo Catholic School, Sacred Heart Campus, (Grades 2-6) Tel: 325-655-3325; Fax: 325-655-1286. Mrs. Lucy Thomas, Prin. Lay Teachers 13; Students 116.

Catechesis/Religious Program—Mr. Steve Zimmerman, C.R.E. Students 264.

Sacred Heart Cathedral-Parish Educational Endowment Fund, Inc.—Tel: 915-658-6567.

2—HOLY ANGELS (1961) Rev. Charles C. Greenwell; Deacon Harry J. Pelto Sr.

Parish Office: 2202 Rutgers Ave., 76904. Tel: 325-949-3308; 325-944-8967; Fax: 325-944-8967.
Church: 2309 A & M Ave., 76904.
School—Angelo Catholic School, (Grades PreK-1), 2315 A & M Ave., 76904. Tel: 325-949-1747; Fax: 325-942-1547. Mrs. Lucy Thomas, Prin. Holy Angels Campus Lay Teachers 7; Students 55.
Catechesis/Religious Program—Tel: 325-942-8192; Fax: 325-944-3633. Mrs. Lori Hines, D.R.E., (Grades PreK-12). Students 220.

3—ST. JOSEPH (1942), (Hispanic), Rev. Rodney White; Deacon Ray Ramirez.
Res.: 301 W. 17th, 76903. Tel: 325-653-5006; Fax: 325-659-2795.
Catechesis/Religious Program—Students 391.

4—ST. MARGARET (1967) Rev. Joseph Choutapalli (India).
Office: 2619 Era St., 76905. Tel: 325-651-4633; Fax: 325-651-4366.
Catechesis/Religious Program—Patricia Pilger, C.R.E. (Elementary). Tel: 325-450-5330; Michael Scammel, C.R.E. (High School); Susan Reddy, C.R.E. (CYM). Students 26.

5—ST. MARY'S (1930), (Hispanic), Rev. David Herrera; Deacons Roy Ibarra; Mario Torres.
Res.: 7 West Ave. N., 76903. Tel: 325-655-6278; Fax: 325-655-1524. Email: saintmarychurch.office@verizon.net.
Catechesis/Religious Program—Tel: 325-665-1976; Fax: 325-665-1524. Minnie Ibarra, C.R.E. Students 713.

OUTSIDE THE CITY OF SAN ANGELO

ABILENE, TAYLOR CO.

1—ST. FRANCIS OF ASSISI (1906), (Hispanic), Rev. George Thirumangalam, C.M.I.; Deacon Jose Sanchez, (Retired).
Office: 826 Cottonwood St., 79601. Tel: 325-672-6695; Fax: 325-670-0129. Email: saintfrancisabilene@yahoo.com. Web: stfrancis-abilene.org.
Catechesis/Religious Program—Marc P. Main, C.R.E. Students 181.

2—HOLY FAMILY (1976) Rev. Msgr. Frederick Nawarskas; Deacons Paul Klein; Gerald Schwalb; Michael Kenny; Charles Lambert.
Res.: 5410 Buffalo Gap Rd., P.O. Box 5970, 79606. Tel: 325-692-1820; Fax: 325-698-5131. Email: mail@holyfamilyabilene.org. Web: www.holyfamilyabilene.org.
Catechesis/Religious Program—Sr. Helen Louise Rivas, C.D.P., D.R.E.; Mrs. Penny Pope, Coord. Youth Min. Students 578.

3—SACRED HEART (1891) Rev. Robert Bush; Deacon Arturo Casarez.
Res.: 837 Jeanette St., 79602-2410. Tel: 325-677-7951; Fax: 325-677-7710.
Catechesis/Religious Program—Tel: 325-673-0697. Gina Martinez, C.R.E. Students 253.
Mission—Sts. Joachim and Ann [CEM] N. 1st St. & Cherry St., Clyde, Callahan Co. 79510. Deacon Peter Ballaro.
Oratory—Sacred Heart Perpetual Adoration Chapel 1541 S. 8th St., 79602.

4—ST. VINCENT PALLOTTI (1963), (Mexican-American), Rev. Terence V. Brenon.
Res.: 2525 Westview Dr., 79603-2138. Tel: 325-672-1794 (Office); Fax: 325-672-8780. Email: office@stvincent-pallotti.org. Web: www.stvincent-pallotti.org.
Catechesis/Religious Program—Students 306.
Mission—Our Mother of Mercy 1300 S. Locust, P.O. Box 206, Merkel, Taylor Co. 79536. Tel: 325-928-5239; Fax: 325-928-3739.

ANDREWS, ANDREWS CO., OUR LADY OF LOURDES (1958) Rev. Joey Faylona.
Res.: 201 N.E. Ave. K, 79714. Tel: 432-523-4215; Fax: 432-523-5070. Email: ollandrews@valornet.com.
Catechesis/Religious Program—Marilyn Heman, D.R.E. Students 329.

BALLINGER, RUNNELS CO., ST. MARY STAR OF THE SEA (1885) Rev. Hubert Wade; Deacon Henry Martinez.
Res.: 608 N. 6th St., 76821-4836. Tel: 325-365-2687; Fax: 325-365-9986.
Catechesis/Religious Program—Caroline Toliver, D.R.E. Students 194.
Mission—St. James 215 N. Washington, Bronte, Coke Co. 76933.
Mission—Our Lady of Guadalupe 601 W. 10th, Robert Lee, Coke Co. 76945.

BIG LAKE, REAGAN CO., ST. MARGARET OF CORTONA (1949), (Hispanic), [JC] Rev. Isidore Ochiabuto, Pastoral Admin.
Res.: 107 E. 1st. St., 76932. Tel: 325-884-2645; Fax: 325-884-3070.
Church & Office: 100 N. Mississippi St., 76932.
Catechesis/Religious Program—Lori Torres, C.R.E.; Sandra Huerta, C.R.E.; Loriza Hernandez, C.R.E.; Mercy Navarez, C.R.E. Students 130.
Mission—St. Thomas 110 Hwy. 67, Rankin, 79778.
Mission—St. Francis 500 S. Blanton, Iraan, Pecos Co. 79744.

BIG SPRING, HOWARD CO.

1—HOLY TRINITY PARISH Revs. Bernard L. Gully; Ariel R. Lagunilla, Parochial Vicar.
Res.: 610 S. Main St., P.O. Box 951, 79721. Tel: 432-714-4930; Fax: 432-714-4932. Email: htcch@crcom.net.
Catechesis/Religious Program—Tel: 432-263-0648. Richard Light, D.R.E.; Elaine Martinesz, C.R.E.; Adrian Saldivar, C.R.E.; Mrs. Christine Sparks, C.R.E. Students 450.

2—IMMACULATE HEART OF MARY (1961) Consolidated with St. Thomas and Sacred Heart, Big Spring to form Holy Trinity Parish, Big Spring.

3—SACRED HEART (1948), (Hispanic), Consolidated with St. Thomas and Immaculate Heart of Mary, Big Spring to form Holy Trinity Parish, Big Spring.

4—ST. THOMAS (1887), (Hispanic), Consolidated with Sacred Heart and Immaculate Heart of Mary, Big Spring to form Holy Trinity Parish, Big Spring.

BRADY, MCCULLOCH CO., ST. PATRICK'S (1876) [JC] Rev. Hilary A. Ihedioha.
Rectory—201 S. Pecan St., 76825. Tel: 325-597-2324; Fax: 325-597-2991. Web: www.stpatrickbradytx.com.
Catechesis/Religious Program—Mary Gutierrez, C.R.E. (K-5); Tina Selvera, C.R.E. (6-12). Students 150.
Mission—St. Francis Xavier Melvin, McCullogh Co.

BROWNWOOD, BROWN CO., ST. MARY'S (1896), (Hispanic), [JC] Rev. Serafin P. Avenido Jr. (Philippines); Deacons John Specht; William Brady.
Office: 1101 Booker St., 76801. Email: stmarys@pgrb.com.
Res.: 1105 Main Ave., 76801. Tel: 325-646-7455; Fax: 325-646-6643.
Catechesis/Religious Program— Leslie Redfern, C.R.E. Students 271.

CARLSBAD, TOM GREEN CO., ST. THERESE OF THE CHILD JESUS (1957) Rev. Joseph Choutapalli (India).
Mailing Address: P.O. Box 416, 76934-0416. Tel: 325-465-8062; Fax: 325-465-4472.
Catechesis/Religious Program—Students 16.
Station—San Angelo State School for the Mentally Retarded, Tel: 915-465-4391.

COLEMAN, COLEMAN CO., SACRED HEART (1892), (Anglo—Hispanic), Rev. Romanus Arinze Akamike (Nigeria).
Mailing Address: 303 E. College, 76834. Tel: 325-625-5773; Fax: 325-625-3320. Email: scrdhrt@web-access.net. Web: www.web-access.net/~scrdhrt.
Catechesis/Religious Program—201 San Saba, 76834. Fax: 325-625-3320. Students 100.

COLORADO CITY, MITCHELL CO., ST. ANN'S (1943), (Hispanic), [JC] Rev. Michael Udegbunam (Nigeria).
Res.: 107 E. 21st St., 79512. Tel: 325-728-3252; Fax: 325-728-3266. Email: ann-joseph@att.net.
Catechesis/Religious Program—Tel: 325-728-5865. Students 128.
Mission—St. Joseph (1924) 403 S. Hinson, Loraine, Mitchell Co. 79532.

CRANE, CRANE CO., GOOD SHEPHERD (1943) Rev. Laurent Mvondo; Deacons Julio Carrasco; Apolonio Gutierrez; Felix Segura.
Res.: 1109 S. Virginia St., P.O. Box 1294, 79731. Tel: 432-558-7497. Email: abmvondo@yahoo.com.
Church & Mailing Address: 810 S. Virginia St., P.O. Box 1294, 79731. Tel: 432-558-2718; Fax: 432-558-7917. Email: gcatholic@att.net.
Catechesis/Religious Program— Teresa Figueroa, C.R.E. Students 242.
Mission—St. Isidore 4614 S. Frank, Coyanosa, Pecos Co. Tel: 432-652-8216; Fax: 432-652-3875.
Mission—Our Lady of Lourdes 103 Merrill Ave., Imperial, Pecos Co.

EDEN, CONCHO CO., ST. CHARLES (1927), (Mexican—German), [JC] Rev. Joseph Ogbonna; Deacons Leroy Beach; Joe Lopez.
P.O. Box 575, 76837.
Res.: 802 S. Main, P.O. Box 575, 76837. Tel: 325-869-8311; Fax: 325-869-5396.
Rectory—
Catechesis/Religious Program—Tel: 325-869-2891. Students 26.
Mission—Our Lady of Guadalupe P.O. Box 123, Millersview, Concho C. 76862. Tel: 915-483-5426.

ELDORADO, SCHLEICHER CO., OUR LADY OF GUADALUPE (1924), (Hispanic), [CEM] [JC] Rev. Joseph Vathalloor, C.M.I.; Deacons Michael Kahlig; Victor Belman.
Res.: P.O. Box 211, 76936. Tel: 325-853-2663; Fax: 325-853-3638.
Catechesis/Religious Program—Tel: 325-853-3366. Sylvia Belman, C.R.E.; Rosie Diaz, D.R.E. Students 75.
Mission—Immaculate Conception P.O. Box 36, Knickerbocker, Tom Green Co. 76939. Tel: 325-944-2820.
Mission—St. Peter's 324 N. Commerce, P.O. Box 471, Mertzon, Irion Co. 76941. Tel: 325-835-2000. Deacon Michael Kahlig.

FORT STOCKTON, PECOS CO.

1—ST. AGNES (1953), (Hispanic), [CEM] [JC] Revs. Thomas Manimala; Maxim Fernandez, Parochial Vicar; Deacon Reuben Reyes, RCIA Coord.; Alicia Salcido, Bookkeeper.
Mailing Address: 4094 N. Hwy. 18, P.O. Box 1487, 79735. Tel: 432-336-2724; Fax: 432-336-6950.
Catechesis/Religious Program—Tel: 432-336-3192. Sr. Virginia Isabel Tadeo, O.N.D., D.R.E.; Lillian Subia, C.R.E.; Arabella Granado, C.R.E.; Arcelina Contreras, C.R.E.; Maria Gomez, C.R.E. Students 435.

2—ST. JOSEPH'S (1875), (Hispanic), [CEM] [JC] Revs. Thomas Manimala; Maxim Fernandez, Parochial Vicar; Deacons Cosme Ureta Jr.; Reuben Reyes.
Mailing Address: P.O. Box 1488, 79735.
Res.: 113 S. Sage, 79735. Tel: 432-336-5027; Fax: 432-336-6668.
Res.: 403 S. Main, 79735. Tel: 432-336-2440.
Catechesis/Religious Program—Tel: 432-336-3192. Sr. Virginia Isabel Tadeo, O.N.D., D.R.E.; Maria Gomez, C.R.E.; Lillian Subia, C.R.E.; Arabella Granado, C.R.E. Students 435.
Mission—St. James 209 E. Hackberry, P.O. Box 526, Sanderson, 79848. Tel: 432-345-2354; Fax: 432-345-2354.

JUNCTION, KIMBLE CO., ST. THERESA OF THE CHILD JESUS (1959) [JC] Rev. Knick Knickerbocker, Sacramental Priest, P.O. Box 129, London, 76854; Deacon James T. Graham, Pastoral Coord.
Res.: South 7th & Oak St., P.O. Box 486, 76849. Tel: 325-446-3393; Fax: 325-446-4803. Email: st.theresachurch@verizon.net.
Catechesis/Religious Program—Students 43.

MCCAMEY, UPTON CO., SACRED HEART (1935) Rev. Laurent Mvondo; Deacons Julio Carrasco; Felix Segura; Apolonio Gutierrez.
Res.: 710 Burleson St., Box 1320, 79752. Tel: 432-652-8216; Fax: 432-652-3875. Email: blm@apex2000.net.
Catechesis/Religious Program—Tel: 432-652-8810. Students 125.

MENARD, MENARD CO., SACRED HEART (1873) [JC] Deacon James T. Graham, Pastoral Coord.; Rev. Knick Knickerbocker.
Res.: 609 Ellis, P.O. Box 788, 76859. Tel: 325-396-4906; Fax: 325-396-2076. Email: sacredheartchurch1@verizon.net.
Catechesis/Religious Program—Tel: 325-396-4906; Fax: 325-396-2076. Students 24.
Mission—St. Theresa Church 114 S. 7th St. & Oak St., Junction, Kimble Co. 76849. Tel: 325-446-3393; Fax: 325-446-4803. Email: stheresa@ktc.com.

MIDLAND, MIDLAND CO.

1—ST. ANN'S (1896) Rev. Msgrs. Larry J. Droll; James A. Plagens, Senior Priest; Rev. Emilio Sosa; Steve Pepper, Business Mgr.
Mailing Address: 1906 W. Texas Ave., 79701-6564. Tel: 432-682-6303; Fax: 432-684-4528. Web: www.st-anns.us.
Res.: 1910 W. Indiana Ave., 79701-6951. Tel: 432-682-3218.
School—(Grades PreK-8), 2000 W. Texas Ave., 79701. Tel: 432-684-4563; Fax: 432-687-2468. Ms. Joan Wilmes, Prin.; Mrs. Stephanie Dworsky, Librarian. Lay Teachers 26; Students 360.
Catechesis/Religious Program—Tel: 432-682-6304. Carol Ann Hunt, D.R.E.; Leonor Spencer, C.R.E.; Alison Pope, Youth Min. Students 413.

2—OUR LADY OF GUADALUPE (1960), (Hispanic), Rev. Edward T. de Leon, O.M.I.; Deacons Jesse Guajardo; Victor Lopez; Ignacio Villa; Benjamin Vigil.
P.O. Box 7, 79702.
Res.: 1401 E. Garden Ln., P.O. Box 7, 79702. Tel: 432-682-2581; Fax: 432-682-9364. Email: guadalupe@olgmidland.com. Web: www.olgmidland.com.
Catechesis/Religious Program—Tel: 432-683-8908. Sr. Isabelita Lucero, O.N.D., D.R.E. (Elem.); Crissy Renteria, D.R.E. (Jr. High & High School); Sarah Gonzalez, Youth Min. Students 357.

3—OUR LADY OF SAN JUAN DE LOS LAGOS (1984), (Hispanic), Rev. Frank Chavez.
Res.: 1008 W. New Jersey, 79701. Tel: 432-570-0952; Fax: 432-687-5082. Email: ourladyofsanjuan@sbcglobal.net.
Catechesis/Religious Program—Tel: 432-620-9546. Elidia Padilla, D.R.E. Students 242.

4—ST. STEPHEN'S (1982) Rev. Msgr. James P. Bridges; Revs. Gilbert Rodriguez; Quirino Cornejo; Deacons Robert Leibrecht; Fidel Saldivar; Dennis Robson, Pastoral Assoc.
Res. & Mailing Address: 4601 Neely Ave., 79707. Tel: 432-520-7394; Fax: 432-520-7395. Email: d.robson@att.net. Web: www.ststephenmidland.org.
Rectory—2410 Wydewood, 79707.
Catechesis/Religious Program—Students 878.

MILES, RUNNELS CO., ST. THOMAS (1962) [JC] Unassigned.
Res.: P.O. Box 306, 76861. Tel: 325-468-3171; Fax: 325-468-2146. Email: st.thomas_miles@wcc.net.

Catechesis/Religious Program—Tel: 915-468-2665. Students 80.

ODESSA, ECTOR CO.

1—ST. ANTHONY (1948), (Hispanic), Revs. Joseph H. Uecker, C.PP.S.; Mark Miller, C.PP.S.; Deacons Bonifacio Rodriguez; Alex Sosa; Flavio Franco; Paul Hinojos.
1321 W. Monahans St., 79763.
Office: 907 S. Dixie Blvd., 79761. Tel: 432-337-2213; Fax: 432-333-3631. Email: jucpps@sbcglobal.net.
Catechesis/Religious Program—Tel: 915-337-0241. Sisters Regina C. Javier, O.N.D., D.R.E.; Esperanza Razura, A.S.C., Dir. Adult Formation. Students 380.

2—ST. ELIZABETH ANN SETON (1982) Revs. Mark Woodruff; Chinnapparaj Mariasavary, Parochial Vicar; Blas Campos Jr., Bus. Manager; Victoria Detiveaux, Sec.
Office: 7601 N. Grandview Ave., 79765-3401. Tel: 432-367-4657; Fax: 432-367-0700. Email: seas@nts-online.net. Web: seas-odessa.com.
Catechesis/Religious Program—Tel: 432-367-4668. Maria Isela Carrasco, C.R.E. (Elementary). Students 650.
Mission—Our Lady of San Juan 901 E. Hillmont, Ector Co. 79765. Tel: 432-362-2017; Fax: 432-362-2017.
Catechesis/Religious Program—Delfina M. Hernandez, C.R.E.; JoAnn Acosta, Sec. Students 75.

3—HOLY REDEEMER (1961), (Hispanic), Revs. Bernardito Getigan; Nilo Nalugon (Philippines); Deacons Ignacio Cisneros; Antonio Gonzales.
Res.: 2633 Conover, 79763. Tel: 432-580-4295; Fax: 432-332-6631. Email: hrcc@clearwire.net.
Catechesis/Religious Program—Tel: 432-332-9231. Anita T. Diaz, C.R.E.; Steven D. Rojo, C.R.E. Students 800.

4—ST. JOSEPH (1948), (Hispanic), Revs. Joseph H. Uecker, C.PP.S.; Mark Miller, C.PP.S.; Deacons Flavio Franco; Paul Hinojos; Bonifacio Rodriguez; Alex Sosa.
Res.: 1321 W. Monahans, 79763. Tel: 432-337-1093; Fax: 432-333-3631. Email: jucpps@sbcglobal.net.
Catechesis/Religious Program—Tel: 432-334-6478. Sisters Regina C. Javier, O.N.D., D.R.E.; Esperanza Razura, A.S.C., Dir. Adult Formation. Students 571.
Mission—St. Martin de Porres 2821 E. Hammett, Ector Co. 79766. Tel: 432-337-2213.

5—ST. MARY'S (1938) [CEM] Rev. Santiago D. Udayar.
Res.: 612 E. 18th St., 79761. Tel: 432-332-5334; Fax: 432-332-1844.
School—(Grades PreK-6), 1703 N. Adams, 79761. Tel: 432-337-6052; Fax: 432-337-6052. Web: stmarysknights.com. Josie Mediano, Prin.; Delma Balerio, Librarian. Sisters 1; Lay Teachers 16; Students 233.
Catechesis/Religious Program—Tel: 432-332-1154. Rose Mendez, C.R.E. (K-5); Monica Ramirez, C.R.E. (6-12). Students 449.

OLFEN, RUNNELS CO., ST. BONIFACE (1901) [CEM] Rev. Bhaskar Morugudi (India).
Res.: 1118 CR 234, P.O. Box 96, Rowena, 76875-0096. Tel: 325-442-2893. Email: sntboniface@yahoo.com.
Church: 1118 County Rd. 234, Rowena, 76875. Tel: 325-442-2893; Fax: 325-442-2893.
Catechesis/Religious Program—Students 30.

OZONA, CROCKETT CO., OUR LADY OF PERPETUAL HELP (1929), (Hispanic), Rev. Felix Okeke.
Res.: 227 Martinez St., P.O. Box 1069, 76943. Tel: 325-392-3353; Fax: 325-392-3720.
Catechesis/Religious Program—Siliva Coy, C.R.E. (Elementary); Adrian Tijerina, C.R.E. (High School); Lilia Tijerina, C.R.E. (High School); Michelle Ramos, C.R.E. (Jr. High); Rita Vasquez, Sec. Students 144.
Mission—Good Shepherd Sheffield, Pecos Co.

ROWENA, RUNNELS CO., ST. JOSEPH'S (1906), (German—Czech), [CEM] Unassigned.
Res.: 501 Bennie St., P.O. Box 96, 76875. Tel: 325-442-3521; Fax: 325-442-4602. Email: stjosephcatholic@verizon.net. Web: www.stjosephrowenatx.com.
Catechesis/Religious Program—Charles Frerich, D.R.E. Students 90.

ST. LAWRENCE, GLASSCOCK CO., ST. LAWRENCE (1948), (German), [CEM] Rev. Francis Njoku (Africa).
Res.: 2400 FM 2401, Garden City, 79739. Tel: 432-397-2300; Fax: 432-397-2777.
Catechesis/Religious Program—Tel: 432-397-2777. Linda Jones, D.R.E. Students 150.
Mission—St. Thomas Midkiff, Upton Co. Tel: 432-535-2266.
Mission—St. Paschal Baylona P.O. Box 271, Sterling City, Sterling Co. 76951-0271.

SANDERSON, TERRELL CO., ST. JAMES (1916), (Hispanic), Rev. Thomas Manimala.
Res.: 209 E. Hackberry, 79848. Tel: 432-345-2354; Fax: 432-345-2354.
Catechesis/Religious Program— Diana Escamilla, D.R.E. Students 36.

SONORA, SUTTON CO., ST. ANN'S (1927), (Hispanic), Rev. Lionel Fernando.
Office: 311 W. Plum St., P.O. Box 1397, 76950-1397. Tel: 325-387-2278; Fax: 915-387-2797. Email: stannsec@verizon.net.
Res.: 105 Oakwood, Box 1397, 76950. Tel: 325-387-5966.
Catechesis/Religious Program—Students 225.

STANTON, MARTIN CO., ST. JOSEPH'S (1881), (Mexican-American), Deacons Ernie Sanchez, (Retired); Mike Medina; Clemente Villa, Pastoral Coord.
Res.: 405 N. Convent St., P.O. Box 846, 79782-0846. Tel: 432-756-3743; Fax: 432-756-3756. Email: clemby1@yahoo.com.
Catechesis/Religious Program—Tel: 432-756-3743. Students 159.
Mission—St. Isidore [CEM] Lenorah, Martin Co.
Catechesis/Religious Program—Students 27.

SWEETWATER, NOLAN CO.

1—HOLY FAMILY (1885), (Hispanic), Rev. Michael Rodriguez; Deacon W. W. Butler.
Mailing Address: P.O. Box 847, 79556.
Res.: 507 Crane St., 79556. Tel: 325-235-2694; Fax: 325-235-3483.
Catechesis/Religious Program—Tel: 915-235-3529. Gloria Wilson, C.R.E. Students 71.

2—IMMACULATE HEART OF MARY (1962), (Hispanic), Rev. Michael Rodriguez; Deacon W. W. Butler.
511 W. Alabama, 79556.
Res.: 507 Crane St., 79556. Tel: 915-235-3318 (Office); Fax: 915-235-0258.
Catechesis/Religious Program—Students 212.
Mission—St. Albert the Great 205 Laurel St., Roscoe, Nolan Co. 79545.

WALL, TOM GREEN CO., ST. AMBROSE (1941) [CEM] Rev. Mario Ortiz.
Res.: 8602 Loop 570, P.O. Box 228, 76957. Tel: 325-651-7551; Fax: 325-651-6605. Email: saint_ambrose@zipnet.us. Web: www.saint-ambrose.org.
Catechesis/Religious Program—Dolores Gully, C.R.E.; Kathy Braden, C.R.E.; Sharon Morris, C.R.E.; Berni Halfmann, C.R.E.; Sylvia Chappa, C.R.E. Students 305.
Mission—Holy Family 18370 Bledsoe Rd., Mereta, Tom Green Co. 76940. Tel: 325-468-3101.

WINTERS, RUNNELS CO., OUR LADY OF MT. CARMEL (1962), (Hispanic), Rev. Romanus Arinze Akamike (Nigeria).
Res.: 119 W. College, 79567. Tel: 325-754-4626; Fax: 325-754-4015.
Catechesis/Religious Program—Tel: 325-754-5436; 325-754-5011. Marianne Woffenden, D.R.E.; Rene Woffenden, Youth Dir. Students 57.

Military Chaplains:
Revs.—
Covos, Ruben
Hicks, Steven, 74822 Twilight Dr., Twentynine Palms, CA 92277.

Retired:
Rev. Msgrs.—
Frey, Francis, 7523 Ralick Ct., Spring, 77379. Tel: 281-251-0815
Zientek, Benedict, P.O. Box 2447, Brenham, 77834.
Revs.—
Gallagher, Raymond, 1352 Ford Rd., Lyndhurst, OH 44124.
Kennelly, Stephen (Ireland), Lislaughtin, Ballylongford, Co. Kerry, Ireland.
Regan, Richard J., 1001 Society Hill Blvd., Cherry Hill, NJ 08003. Tel: 432-264-2936

Permanent Deacons:
Arguello, Juan, Sacred Heart, Big Spring
Ballaro, Peter, Sts. Joachim & Ann Mission, Clyde
Beach, Leroy, Our Lady of Guadalupe, Millersview
Belman, Victor, Our Lady of Guadalupe, Eldorado
Brady, Bill, St. Mary, Brownwood
Butler, Bill, Holy Family, Sweetwater
Camacho, Isaac, Holy Family, Abilene
Carrasco, Julio, Good Shepherd, Crane
Casarez, Art, Sacred Heart, Abillene
Cisneros, Ignacio, Holy Redeemer, Odessa
Crochet, Larry, Austin
Esparza, Jose, Our Lady of Lourdes, Imperial
Evans, Charlie, St. Patrick, Brady
Fernandez, Abel, Our Lady of Grace, Goodfellow AFB
Franco, Flabio, St. Joseph, Odessa
Giovannitti, Thomas, (On Duty Outside the Diocese)
Gonzales, Antonio, Holy Redeemer, Odessa
Graham, Tim, St. Theresa, Junction
Guajardo, Jesse, Our Lady of Guadalupe, Midland
Gutierrez, Apolonio, Good Shepherd, Crane
Hernandez, Andres, St. Agnes, Ft. Stockton
Hinojos, Paul, St. Joseph, Odessa
Ibarra, Roy, St. Mary, San Angelo
Kahlig, Michael, St. Peter, Mertzon
Kenny, Mike, Holy Family, Abilene
Klein, Paul, Holy Family, Abilene
Lambert, Charles, Holy Family, Abilene
LaMonica, Michael, Our Lady of San Juan, Midland
Leibrecht, Robert, St. Stephen, Midland
Lopez, Joseph, St. Philip's, Eola
Lopez, Victor, Our Lady of Guadalupe, Midland
Luevano, Manuel, St. Elizabeth, Odessa
Martinez, Enrique, St. James, Bronte
Medina, Mike, St. Joseph, Stanton
Neff, Alan, St. Elizabeth Ann Seton, Odessa
Ortiz, Jesse, St. Mary, Odessa
Pelto, Harry J., Sr., Holy Angels, San Angelo
Pena, Daniel, (On Duty Outside the Diocese)
Perez, Alex, Our Lady of San Juan, Midland
Primera, Salvador, St. Elizabeth Ann Seton, Midland
Ramirez, Reinaldo, St. Joseph, San Angelo
Reyes, Reuben, St. Joseph's, Fort Stockton; St. Agnes, Fort Stockton
Rodriguez, Bonfacio (Barney), St. Anthony's, Odessa
Saldivar, Fidel, St. Stephen, Midland
Sanchez, Ernie, St. Joseph, Stanton
Sanchez, Pedro, St. Francis, Abilene
Schwalb, Gerald, Holy Family, Abilene
Segura, Felix, Good Shepherd, Crane
Smith, Raymond, (On Duty Outside the Diocese)
Sosa, Alex, St. Anthony, Odessa
Sotelo, Sador, Our Lady of San Juan, Midland
Specht, John, St. Mary, Brownwood
Torres, Mario, St. Mary, San Angelo
Trevino, Jerry, Sacred Heart, San Angelo
Ureta, Cosme, St. Joseph, Fort Stockton
Villa, Clemente, Jr., St. Joseph, Stanton
Villa, Ignacio, Our Lady of San Juan, Midland
Yanez, Horacio, St. Thomas, Big Spring

INSTITUTIONS LOCATED IN THE DIOCESE

[A] MONASTERIES AND RESIDENCES OF PRIESTS & BROTHERS

CHRISTOVAL. *Hermits of the Blessed Virgin Mary of Mount Carmel* (1991) P.O. Box 337, 76935-0337. Tel: 325-896-2249; Fax: 325-896-2265. Email: stellamaris@carmelitehermits.org. Web: www.CarmeliteHermits.org. Rev. Fabian Maria Rosette, O.Carm., Prior. Mt. Carmel Hermitage Hermits 6.

[B] CONVENTS AND RESIDENCES FOR SISTERS

SAN ANGELO. *School Sisters of St. Francis*, 110 Creswiod, 76905. Tel: 325-651-2403. Sr. Hilda Marotta, O.S.F., Contact Person.

ABILENE. *Congregation of Divine Providence*, P.O. Box 5970, 79608. Tel: 325-698-2367; Fax: 325-698-5131.

CHRISTOVAL. *Carmelite Nuns of the Ancient Observance* (1989) *Monastery of Our Lady of Grace*, 6202 CO Rd. 339, 76935-3023. Tel: 325-853-1722; Fax: 325-853-1722. Email: desertcarmel@carmelnet.org. Web: carmelnet.org/christoval/christoval.htm. Sr. Mary Grace Erl, O.Carm., Vicar Prioress.

MIDLAND. *Oblates of Notre Dame* (1991) 1400 Garden Ln., 79701. Tel: 432-684-8318; Fax: 432-336-5027. Sr. Isabelita Lucero, O.N.D., D.R.E. (Elementary, High School & Adult Faith Formation).

ODESSA. *Oblates of Notre Dame*, 907 S. Dixie Blvd., 79761. Tel: 432-337-2213; Fax: 432-333-3631. Email: rcjond@sbcglobal.net.

[C] ST. VINCENT DE PAUL SOCIETY

SAN ANGELO. *Catholic Outreach Services*, 410 N. Chadbourne, 76903. Tel: 915-658-4124; Fax: 915-481-0315. Email: cos.margie@verizon.net. Thrift Store Social Services. Total Assisted Annually 5,000; Total Staff 30.

ABILENE. *St. Vincent De Paul Society*, 1241 Walnut, 79601. Tel: 915-677-6871. Total Assisted 12,000; Total Staff 4.

St. Vincent De Paul Thrift Store

BIG SPRING. *St. Vincent De Paul Society* Food Distribution., 1009 Hearn, 79720. Tel: 432-267-4124; Fax: 432-267-7844. Email: ihmch@crcom.net. Families 1,280; People 2,296.

MIDLAND. *St. Vincent De Paul Society* (1985) 1906 W. Texas Ave., 79701. Tel: 432-682-6303. Priests 3.

ODESSA. *Catholic Charities Community Services Odessa, Inc.*, 606 W. 10th, 79761. Tel: 432-332-1387; 432-332-2398. Faye Rodriguez, Dir.

STANTON. *St. Vincent De Paul Society*, P.O. Box 846, 79782. Tel: 432-756-3743; Fax: 432-756-3756. Deacon Clemente Villa Jr., Pastoral Coord.

[D] CAMPUS MINISTRY

SAN ANGELO. *Catholic Newman Center* 2451 Dena Dr., 76904. Tel: 325-949-8033. Email: newman@wcc.net. Sr. Marie Malachy Griffin, O.P., Campus Min. Total Staff 1.

[E] MISCELLANEOUS

SAN ANGELO. *Christ the King Retreat Center*, 802 Ford, 76905. Tel: 325-651-5352; 325-651-5358; Fax: 325-651-5667. Email: ckrc@zipnet.us. Total Staff 20.

RELIGIOUS INSTITUTES OF MEN REPRESENTED IN THE DIOCESE

For further details refer to the corresponding bracketed number in the Religious Institutes of Men or Women section.

[0910]—*Oblates of Mary Immaculate* (Southern American Prov.)—O.M.I.

[]—*Order of Preachers (Dominicans)* (Philippines)—O.P.

[1060]—*Society of the Precious Blood* (Kansas City Prov.)—C.PP.S.

RELIGIOUS INSTITUTES OF WOMEN REPRESENTED IN THE DIOCESE

[0320]—*Carmelite Nuns of the Ancient Observance*—O.Carm.

[1010]—*Congregation of Divine Providence of San Antonio, Texas*—C.D.P.

[1070-03]—*Dominican Sisters, Sinsinawa*—O.P.

[2960]—*Oblates of Notre Dame*—O.N.D.

[]—*Oblates of Notre Dame* (Midland, TX)

[]—*Oblates of Notre Dame, Philippines*

[1680]—*School Sisters of St. Francis*—S.S.S.F.

[0990]—*Sisters of Divine Providence*—C.D.P.

[1570]—*Sisters of St. Francis of the Holy Family*—O.S.F.

NECROLOGY

† Moeller, Louis, (Retired)—Died Dec. 29, 2008

An asterisk (*) denotes an organization that has established tax-exempt status directly with the IRS and is not covered by the USCCB Group Ruling.

Archdiocese of San Antonio

(Archidioecesis Sancti Antonii)

Most Reverend

OSCAR CANTÚ

Auxiliary Bishop of San Antonio; ordained May 21, 1994; appointed Auxiliary Bishop of San Antonio and Titular Bishop of Dardanus April 10, 2008; ordained June 2, 2008. *Pastoral Center: P.O. Box 28410, San Antonio, TX 78228-0410.* Tel: 210-734-2620; Fax: 210-734-0708. Email: oscar.cantu@archsa.org.

Most Reverend

PATRICK F. FLORES, D.D.

Retired Archbishop of San Antonio; ordained May 26, 1956; appointed Titular Bishop of Italica and Auxiliary of San Antonio March 18, 1970; consecrated May 5, 1970; appointed Bishop of El Paso April 4, 1978; installed May 29, 1978; promoted Archiepiscopal See of San Antonio August 28, 1979; installed October 13, 1979; Pallium conferred May 25, 1982; retired December 29, 2004. *Res.: Padua Place, 80 Peter Baque Rd., San Antonio, TX 78209.* Tel: 210-826-7721.

(VACANT SEE)

Pastoral Center: 2718 W. Woodlawn Ave., P.O. Box 28410, San Antonio, TX 78228-0410. Tel: 210-734-2620; Fax: 210-734-0231.

Web: www.archdiosa.org

Email: administrator@archdiosa.org

Most Reverend

BERNARD F. POPP, D.D.

Retired Auxiliary Bishop of San Antonio; ordained February 24, 1943; appointed Titular Bishop of Capsus and Auxiliary Bishop of San Antonio June 7, 1983; consecrated July 25, 1983; retired March 23, 1993. *Res.: Padua Place, 80 Peter Baque Rd., San Antonio, TX 78209.* Tel: 210-826-7721.

Most Reverend

THOMAS J. FLANAGAN, D.D.

Retired Auxiliary Bishop of San Antonio; ordained June 10, 1956; appointed Auxiliary Bishop of San Antonio and Titular Bishop of Bavagaliana January 15, 1998; consecrated February 16, 1998; retired December 15, 2005. *Res.: Oblate Madonna House, 5722 Blanco Rd., San Antonio, TX 78216-6615.* Tel: 210-734-2620; 210-734-1610. *Mailing Address: P.O. Box 28410, San Antonio, TX 78228-0410.*

ESTABLISHED AUGUST 28, 1874.

Square Miles 23,180.

Created an Archbishopric, August 3, 1926.

The San Antonio Archdiocese comprises Atascosa, Bandera, Bexar, Comal, Edwards, Frio, Gillespie, Gonzales, Guadalupe, Karnes, Kendall, Kerr, Kinney, McMullen (that part of McMullen County north of the Nueces River), Medina, Real, Uvalde, Val Verde and Wilson.

For legal titles of parishes and archdiocesan institutions, consult the Pastoral Center.

STATISTICAL OVERVIEW

Personnel	
Retired Archbishops	1
Auxiliary Bishops	1
Retired Bishops	3
Priests: Diocesan Active in Diocese	102
Priests: Diocesan Active Outside Diocese	4
Priests: Retired, Sick or Absent	44
Number of Diocesan Priests	150
Religious Priests in Diocese	205
Total Priests in Diocese	355
Extern Priests in Diocese	46
Ordinations:	
Diocesan Priests	9
Religious Priests	1
Transitional Deacons	1
Permanent Deacons	3
Permanent Deacons in Diocese	352
Total Brothers	86
Total Sisters	726
Parishes	
Parishes	139
With Resident Pastor:	
Resident Diocesan Priests	93
Resident Religious Priests	46
Without Resident Pastor:	
Administered by Priests	5
Missions	34
Professional Ministry Personnel:	
Brothers	6
Sisters	27
Lay Ministers	170
Welfare	
Catholic Hospitals	6
Total Assisted	400,000
Health Care Centers	5
Total Assisted	37,800
Homes for the Aged	9
Total Assisted	698
Residential Care of Children	3
Total Assisted	989
Day Care Centers	9
Total Assisted	983
Specialized Homes	4
Total Assisted	2,998
Special Centers for Social Services	9
Total Assisted	12,828
Other Institutions	1
Total Assisted	80
Educational	
Seminaries, Diocesan	1
Students from This Diocese	24
Students from Other Diocese	58
Diocesan Students in Other Seminaries	2
Seminaries, Religious	4
Students Religious	25
Total Seminarians	51
Colleges and Universities	5
Total Students	13,994
High Schools, Diocesan and Parish	5
Total Students	1,127
High Schools, Private	6
Total Students	2,584
Elementary Schools, Diocesan and Parish	31
Total Students	8,026
Elementary Schools, Private	6
Total Students	1,730
Catechesis/Religious Education:	
High School Students	11,361
Elementary Students	32,315
Total Students under Catholic Instruction	71,188
Teachers in the Diocese:	
Priests	26
Brothers	24
Sisters	62
Lay Teachers	1,573
Vital Statistics	
Receptions into the Church:	
Infant Baptism Totals	9,980
Minor Baptism Totals	801
Adult Baptism Totals	426
Received into Full Communion	701
First Communions	9,162
Confirmations	5,846
Marriages:	
Catholic	1,643
Interfaith	321
Total Marriages	1,964
Deaths	4,530
Total Catholic Population	702,547
Total Population	2,315,988

Former Bishops—Rt. Revs. ANTHONY DOMINIC PELLICER, D.D., ord. Aug. 15, 1850; cons. Dec. 8, 1874; died April 14, 1880; JOHN C. NERAZ, D.D., ord. Feb. 19, 1854; cons. May 8, 1881; died Nov. 15, 1894; JOHN ANTHONY FOREST, D.D., ord. April 12, 1863; cons. Oct. 28, 1895; died March 11, 1911; Most Revs. JOHN W. SHAW, D.D., Coadjutor Bishop of San Antonio; appt. Feb. 7, 1910; cons. Titular Bishop of Castabala, April 14, 1910; succeeded to the See of San Antonio, March 11, 1911; made assistant at the Pontifical Throne, Sept., 1916; promoted to the See of New Orleans, Jan. 25, 1918; died Nov. 2, 1934; ARTHUR JEROME DROSSAERTS, D.D., LL.D., Bishop of San Antonio; appt. July 18, 1918; cons. Dec. 8, 1918; named Archbishop, Aug. 3, 1926; assistant at the Pontifical Throne, Aug. 19, 1934; died Sept. 8, 1940; ROBERT E. LUCEY, S.T.D., Bishop of Amarillo; appt. Feb. 10, 1934; cons. May 1, 1934; promoted to the Archiepiscopal See of San Antonio, Jan. 23, 1941; retired June 4, 1969; died Aug. 1, 1977; FRANCIS J. FUREY, Titular Bishop of Temnus and Auxiliary of Philadelphia; appt. Aug. 24, 1960; cons. Dec. 22, 1960; promoted to Coadjutor and Apostolic Administrator "sede plena" of San Diego, July 25, 1963; succeeded March 6, 1966; promoted to Archiepiscopal See of San Antonio, June 4, 1969; Pallium conferred, Dec. 15, 1969; died April 23, 1979; PATRICK F. FLORES, D.D. (Retired), ord. May 26, 1956; appt. Titular Bishop of Italica and Auxiliary of San Antonio March 18, 1970; cons. May 5, 1970; appt. Bishop of El Paso April 4, 1978; installed May 29, 1978; promoted Archiepiscopal See of San Antonio Aug. 28, 1979; installed Oct. 13, 1979; retired Dec. 29, 2004; JOSE H. GOMEZ, S.T.D., ord. Aug. 15, 1978; appt. Auxiliary Bishop of Denver and Titular See of Belali Jan. 23, 2001; ord. March 26, 2001; appt. Archbishop of San Antonio Dec. 29, 2004; installed Feb. 15, 2005; Pallium conferred June 29, 2005; appt. Coadjutor Archbishop of Los Angeles April 6, 2010.

Vicars General—Most Revs. THOMAS J. FLANAGAN, D.D., V.G.; OSCAR CANTÚ, D.D., S.T.L., S.T.D., V.G., Mailing Address: P.O. Box 28410, San Antonio, 78228-0410. Tel: 210-734-2620; Fax: 210-734-1670.

Office of Victim Assistance and Safe Environment—Mr. STEVE MARTINEZ, L.C.S.W., L.S.O.T.P., Dir. Email: smartinez@archsa.org; TRACIE B. ENRIQUEZ, M.B.A., C.P.M., Assoc. Dir. Email: tracie.enriquez@archsa.org; NORMA ALVARADO, Admin. Asst., St. Paul Community Center, 120 Donaldson, San Antonio, 78228. Tel:

210-734-7786; 877-700-1888 (Toll Free). Email: ovase@archsa.org.

Moderator of the Curia & Director of Administration—Rev. MARTIN J. LEOPOLD. Tel: 210-734-1674.

Pastoral Center—2718 W. Woodlawn Ave., P.O. Box 28410, San Antonio, 78228-0410. Tel: 210-734-2620; Fax: 210-734-0231. Office Hours: Mon.-Fri. 8:30-5.

Chancellor—Rev. Msgr. TERENCE NOLAN, J.C.L. Tel: 210-734-1676.

Archives—Bro. EDWARD J. LOCH, S.M., Archivist, Mailing Address: P.O. Box 28410, San Antonio, 78228-0410. Tel: 210-734-2620; 210-734-1609. Email: eloch@archsa.org.

Baptismal Records Office—Mrs. MARGARET PEREZ, Mailing Address: P.O. Box 28410, San Antonio, 78228-0410. Tel: 210-734-2620; 210-734-1647. Email: mperez@archsa.org.

Administrative Assistant to the Archbishop—Rev. MARTIN J. LEOPOLD. Tel: 210-734-1674. Email: mleopold@archsa.org.

Office of the Archbishop—Secretaries to the Archbishop: JOSIE G. PEREZ. Tel: 210-734-1664. Email: jperez@archsa.org; LUCIANE URBAN, 2718 W. Woodlawn Ave., P.O. Box 28410, San Antonio, 78228-0410. Tel: 210-734-2620; 210-734-1665; Fax: 210-734-0708. Email: lurban@archsa.org.

College of Consultors—Most Revs. BERNARD F. POPP, D.D. (Retired); THOMAS J. FLANAGAN, D.D., V.G.; OSCAR CANTÚ, D.D., S.T.L., S.T.D., V.G.; Rev. Msgrs. LAWRENCE J. STUEBBEN (Retired); TERENCE NOLAN, J.C.L.; THOMAS MURPHY (Retired); CARLOS DAVALOS, V.F.; JAMES JANISH; FRANCISZEK KURZAJ; MICHAEL BOULETTE, V.F.; Rev. DAVID GARCIA.

Deans—In Metropolitan Area: Very Rev. Msgr. MICHAEL YARBROUGH, V.U., North; Very Revs. KEVIN FAUSZ, C.M., V.U., Central; JAIME A. DIAZ, O.P., V.U., Northwest; EDUARDO D. MORALES, V.U., Northeast; FIDELE C. DIKETE, V.U., Western; LENIN NAFFATE, V.U., Southwest; JOHN J. FLANAGAN, V.U., Southeast; Very Rev. Msgr. PATRICK RAGSDALE, V.U., North Central. In Rural Area: Very Rev. GREGORY SAWICKI, S.D.S., V.F., Floresville; Rev. Msgr. MICHAEL BOULETTE, V.F., Fredericksburg; Very Revs. WALLIS STILES, V.F., Hondo; GILBERTO VALLEJO, V.F., Pleasanton; GREGORY J. NEVLUD, V.F., Seguin; JAMES FISCHLER, C.I.C.M., V.F., Uvalde.

Vicar for Clergy—Rev. TONY VILANO, Pastoral Center. Tel: 210-734-2620, Ext. 1672. Email: tony.vilano@archsa.org.

Vicar for Retired Priests—Rev. Msgr. JOHN WAGNER (Retired), Casa De Padres, 8520 Cross Mountain Trail #202, San Antonio, 78255. Tel: 210-698-0175.

Archdiocesan Presbyteral Council—Most Revs. BERNARD F. POPP, D.D. (Retired); THOMAS J. FLANAGAN, D.D., V.G.; OSCAR CANTÚ, D.D., S.T.L., S.T.D., V.G.; Rev. Msgrs. TERENCE NOLAN, J.C.L.; JOHN WAGNER (Retired); Very Rev. Msgr. MICHAEL YARBROUGH, V.U., Chm.; Very Revs. KEVIN FAUSZ, C.M., V.U.; JAIME A. DIAZ, O.P., V.U.; EDUARDO D. MORALES, V.U.; GREGORY J. NEVLUD, V.F.; JOHN J. FLANAGAN, V.U.; Revs. MARTIN J. LEOPOLD; TONY VILANO; Very Revs. FIDELE C. DIKETE, V.U.; GREGORY SAWICKI, S.D.S., V.F.; Very Rev. Msgr. PATRICK RAGSDALE, V.U.; Very Revs. WALLIS STILES, V.F.; GILBERTO VALLEJO, V.F.; LENIN NAFFATE, V.U.; Rev. Msgrs. MICHAEL BOULETTE, V.F.; CARLOS DAVALOS, V.F., At Large; JAMES JANISH, At Large; FRANCISZEK KURZAJ, At Large; Very Rev. JAMES FISCHLER, C.I.C.M., V.F.; Rev. DAVID GARCIA, At Large.

Women's Commission—Mrs. CHRIS ALDERETE, Chm., 1602 Hillcrest Dr., E., San Antonio, 78228.

Archdiocesan Tribunal—Mailing Address: P.O. Box 28410, San Antonio, 78228-0410. Tel: 210-734-2620, Ext. 1135; 210-734-1696.

Judicial Vicar—Rev. Msgr. TERENCE NOLAN, J.C.L.

Assistant Director—Ms. MARGARITA M. GONZALEZ.

Judges—Rev. Msgrs. TERENCE NOLAN, J.C.L.; JAMES HENKE; JAMES JANISH; Rev. EMMET CAROLAN; Rev. Msgr. JOSEPH LOPEZ.

Defenders of the Bond—Rev. Msgr. KEVIN E. RYAN; Rev. PAUL CLEARY; Rev. Msgr. THOMAS MURPHY (Retired).

Promoter Justitiae—Rev. JOHN M. MAKOTHAKAT, Ph.D., S.T.D., J.C.D. (Retired).

Approved Advocates—Mrs. ADRIANA FERRARO SEAWRIGHT; Sr. MARY DOLORES DOYLE, C.C.V.I.

Notaries—Ms. MARGARITA M. GONZALEZ; Ms. SYLVIA FALCON; Ms. THERESA VALLEJO; Mrs. LORETTA REYES; Mrs. ROSE MCGUIRE; Mrs. IRENE KING.

Interdiocesan Appellate Court—Mailing Address: P.O. Box 28410, San Antonio, 78228-0410. Tel: 210-736-9444; 210-734-2620, Ext. 1147; 210-734-1608.

Moderator—VACANT.

Judicial Vicar—Rev. WARREN A. BROWN III, O.M.I., J.C.D.

Adjutant Judicial Vicar—Rev. Msgr. LESLIE A. VANCE, J.C.L.

Judges—Rev. Msgr. ALBERT HUBERTUS (Retired); Revs. DAVID MARIA A. JAEGER, O.F.M., J.C.D.; JOHN M. MAKOTHAKAT, Ph.D., S.T.D., J.C.D. (Retired).

Defenders of the Bond—Revs. ANH Q. TRAN, J.C.L.; JAMES A. KOTARA; MATTHEW C. IWUJI, J.C.D.; TIMOTHY A. GOLLOB; RENE ANGEL, J.C.L.; RICHARD B. WILLIAMS, O.P., J.D.; EDWARD RODEN-LUCERO, J.C.L.; MICHAEL P. COLWELL, J.C.L.; Mr. CARLOS VENEGAS, J.C.L.; Sr. MARGARET A. RAMSDEN, S.F.C.C., J.C.L.; Ms. DENISE J. DOYLE, J.C.D., Ph.D.; Ms. LAURA L. LEFAVE, J.C.L.

Notaries—Mrs. LUANN HARTNETT; Mrs. DONNA MILLS.

Due Process: Councils of Conciliation and Arbitration—Chancery Office, 2718 W. Woodlawn Ave., San Antonio, 78228-5195. Tel: 210-734-2620.

Diocesan Administration

Administrative Services Department—Rev. MARTIN J. LEOPOLD, Dir., Mailing Address: P.O. Box 28410, San Antonio, 78228-0410. Tel: 210-734-2620; 210-734-1674.

Archdiocesan Chief Financial Officer—Mr. RUBEN HINOJOSA, Mailing Address: P.O. Box 28410, San Antonio, 78228-0410. Tel: 210-734-2620; 210-734-1916; Fax: 210-734-2774.

Archdiocesan Controller—Mrs. DELIA THOMAS, Mailing Address: 2718 W. Woodlawn, San Antonio, 78228. Tel: 210-734-2620; 210-734-1677; Fax: 210-734-2774. Email: dthomas@archsa.org.

Archdiocesan Office of Stewardship and Development—VACANT, Dir., Mailing Address: P.O. Box 28410, San Antonio, 78228-0410. Tel: 210-734-2620; 210-734-1604; Fax: 210-734-0231.

Office of Construction, Real Estate and Facilities Management—ROBERT B. HOLBROOK, Mgr., Mailing Address: 2718 W. Woodlawn, San Antonio, 78228. Tel: 210-438-8138. Email: robert.holbrook@archsa.org.

Office of Risk Management—Mr. HAL HENRY, Dir., Mailing Address: 2718 W. Woodlawn, San Antonio, 78228. Tel: 210-431-3465; 800-831-9107 (Toll Free); Fax: 210-431-7742.

Archdiocesan Finance Council—ELIZANDRO DE LOS SANTOS; Ms. LISA SIMS; Ms. RACHEL BENAVIDES; Mr. BRUCE HAAN; Ms. DIXIE BROWN; Ms. GAIL DERESZEWSKI, Chm.; Mr. RAY STRAUCH; Ms. PAMELA C. SMITH; Mr. MEL SHRADER; Ms. JENNIFER ROTHE; Mr. EDWARD ADAM; Mr. ALTON PETSCH.

Archdiocesan Debt Review Committee—Mr. RICHARD IDAR; Mrs. DELIA THOMAS, Chm.; Mr. LOUIS SANCHEZ; Mrs. NANCY DOUCETTE.

Building Board—Mr. ROBERT ZEPEDA; Mr. COSMO F. GUIDO, Chm.; Mr. JIM RODRIGUEZ; Mr. DAN CERNA; Mr. STEVE PERSYN; Mr. BENNETT R. FEINSILBER.

Lay Pension Plan Committee—Mr. CHRIS MCGUIRE; Mr. ROBERT CARLSON; Mrs. DELIA THOMAS; Mrs. VICTORIA ESPARZA; Rev. MARTIN J. LEOPOLD; Mr. RUBEN HINOJOSA, Mailing Address: P.O. Box 28410, San Antonio, 78228-0410. Tel: 210-734-2620; 210-734-1633.

Archdiocesan Cemeteries Office—Mr. RUBEN HINOJOSA; Mr. ROBERT CORNEJO, Exec. Dir., 746 Castroville Rd., San Antonio, 78207. Tel: 210-432-2303.

Information Technology—Mailing Address: 2718 W. Woodlawn, San Antonio, 78228. Mr. ARTURO DE LOS SANTOS. Tel: 210-734-2620, Ext. 1183; ALFONSO REBELLOSO. Tel: 210-734-2620, Ext. 1188; DAN SMITH. Tel: 210-734-2620, Ext. 1183.

Pension Office—JEANETTE GARCIA. Tel: 210-734-2620, Ext. 1140.

Human Resources—Mrs. VICTORIA ESPARZA, Mailing Address: 2718 W. Woodlawn, San Antonio, 78228. Tel: 210-734-2620, Ext. 1324.

Annual Appeal, Grants—LUCY HERRERA, Mailing Address: 2718 W. Woodlawn, San Antonio, 78228. Tel: 210-734-2620, Ext. 1223.

Catholic Community Foundation—Mr. JEFF JUNG, Pres. Tel: 210-734-2620, Ext. 1241; Mr. ED BENNINGER. Tel: 210-734-2620, Ext. 1189.

Parish and School Accounting—Mrs. CHANA FINCH. Tel: 210-734-2620, Ext. 1245.

Mail Room—MARIA HINJOSA. Tel: 210-734-2620; 210-734-1631; Fax: 210-734-0231.

Print Service Center—Mr. CHUCK FLOYD. Tel: 210-734-2620, Ext. 1501.

Department of Educational Services—Sr. THERESE SAN MIGUEL, O.S.F., Dir., Mailing Address: P.O. Box 28410, San Antonio, 78228-0410. Tel: 210-734-2620, Ext. 1201.

Archdiocesan Catechetical-Religious Education Center—Mrs. RITA T. MINKLEY, Dir., Mailing Address: P.O. Box 28410, San Antonio, 78228-0410. Tel: 210-734-2620. Email: rminkley@archdiosa.org.

Office of Catholic Youth and Young Adult Ministry—Mr. MICHAEL LOFLIN, Dir., Mailing Address: P.O. Box 28410, San Antonio, 78228-0410. Tel: 210-734-2620.

Catholic Committee on Scouting (Boys)—Mr. RICH MAZZARA, Assoc. Dir., 2718 W. Woodlawn, San Antonio, 78228. Tel: 210-734-2620, Ext. 1115.

Catholic Committee on Girl Scouting—Mrs. BARBARA COVERTINO, Assoc. Dir., 2718 W. Woodlawn, San Antonio, 78228. Tel: 210-734-2620, Ext. 1157.

Catholic Campus Ministry (Newman Apostolate)—For Information Contact: . Tel: 210-734-2620, Ext. 1201. *Catholic Student Center, San Antonio College, 312 W. Courtland, San Antonio, 78212. St. Anthony Catholic Student Center at U.T.S.A., 14523 Roadrunner Way, San Antonio, 78249. St. Philip College. Palo Alto College, 1405 W. Villaret Blvd., San Antonio, 78224.* SAC, UTSA, UTSA Downtown, Texas A&M Extension, Northwest Vista, Texas Lutheran University, Schreiner University, Kerrville, Trinity, UT Health Science Center, S.W. Texas Junior College-Uvalde.

Catholic Campus Ministry Center—Palo Alto College, 1405 W. Villaret Blvd., San Antonio, 78224.

The Pontifical Mission Societies - Missions Awareness Office— (Holy Childhood Pontifical Assn.; Propagation of the Faith). MARY WISNIEWSKI, Dir., Mailing Address: P.O. Box 28410, San Antonio, 78228-0410. Tel: 210-734-2620.

Office of Worship—Rev. HELIODORO LUCATERO, Dir., Mailing Address: P.O. Box 28410, San Antonio, 78228-0410. Tel: 210-734-2620, Ext. 1203; 210-734-1912.

Young Adult Ministry—VACANT, Coord., Mailing Address: P.O. Box 28140, San Antonio, 78228-0410. Tel: 210-734-1651.

Department of Catholic Schools—

Superintendent—Ms. PATRICIA DAVIS, Mailing Address: P.O. Box 28410, San Antonio, 78228-0410. Tel: 210-734-2620; 210-734-1657. Web: sacatholicschools.org. Email: patricia.davis@archsa.org.

Associate Superintendent for Professional Development, Recruitment—Mrs. JOANN GAWLIK.

Associate Superintendent for Curriculum and Government Programs—BEVERLY LEJESKI.

Director of School Finance—Mr. DAVID NIXON.

Department of Formation—Mr. MARCO ROMAN, Dir., Mailing Address: P.O. Box 28410, San Antonio, 78228-0410. Tel: 210-734-2620; 210-734-1911. Email: marco.roman@archsa.org.

Office of Marriage and Family Life/N.F.P.—Mr. JAKE SAMOUR, Dir., Mailing Address: P.O. Box 28140, San Antonio, 78228-0410. Tel: 210-734-2620; 210-734-1648. Email: jake.samour@archsa.org.

Office for Evangelization—Miss MARTHA FERNANDEZ-SARDINA, Dir., Mailing Address: P.O. Box 28410, San Antonio, 78228. Tel: 210-734-2620; 210-734-1668. Email: mfernandez-sardina@archsa.org.

Office of Christian Initiation—Mr. MARCO ROMAN, Dir., Mailing Address: P.O. Box 28410, San Antonio, 78228-0410. Tel: 210-734-1911. Email: marco.roman@archsa.org.

Office of Life, Justice and Peace—Mr. RICK DOUCETTE, Assoc. Dir., Mailing Address: P.O. Box 28410, San Antonio, 78228-0410. Tel: 210-734-1655. Email: rdoucette@archsa.org.

Campaign for Human Development—VACANT.

Department of Clergy and Consecrated Life—Rev. TONY VILANO, Dir. & Vicar for Clergy, Mailing Address: P.O. Box 28410, San Antonio, 78228-0410. Tel: 210-734-2620; 210-734-1672.

Priests Personnel Board—Most Revs. OSCAR CANTÚ, D.D., S.T.L., S.T.D., V.G.; THOMAS J. FLANAGAN, D.D., V.G., Dir.; BERNARD F. POPP, D.D. (Retired); Rev. MARTIN J. LEOPOLD; Very Rev. Msgr. MICHAEL YARBROUGH, V.U.; Very Revs. KEVIN FAUZ, C.M., V.U.; JAIME A. DIAZ, O.P., V.U.; EDUARDO D. MORALES, V.U.; FIDELE C. DIKETE, V.U.; LENIN NAFFATE, V.U.; JOHN J. FLANAGAN, V.U.; Very Rev. Msgr. PATRICK RAGSDALE, V.U.; Very Rev. GREGORY SAWICKI, S.D.S., V.F.; Rev. Msgr. MICHAEL BOULETTE, V.F.; Very Revs. WALLIS STILES, V.F.; GILBERTO VALLEJO, V.F.; GREGORY J. NEVLUD, V.F.; JAMES FISCHLER, C.I.C.M., V.F.

Permanent Diaconate Program—Rev. JAMES RUTKOWSKI, S.T.L., Dir., 2718 W. Woodlawn, San Antonio, 78228. Tel: 210-734-2620; Fax: 210-734-0231.

Vocation Office—Revs. ARTURO CEPEDA, S.T.D., Dir.; JONATHAN W. FELUX, Asst. Dir.; Sr. JANE MARIE GAWLICK, C.S.S.F., Assoc. Dir., 2600 W. Woodlawn Ave., San Antonio, 78228-5196. Tel: 210-735-0553.

Office for Religious—Sr. MARY TERESA CULLEN, C.S.B., Dir., Mailing Address: P.O. Box 28410, San Antonio, 78228-0410. Tel: 210-734-2620; 210-734-1907.

Ecumenical Relations—Rev. MARTIN J. LEOPOLD.

Vicar for Retired Priests—Rev. Msgr. JOHN WAGNER

(Retired), Casa De Padres, 8520 Cross Mountain Trail, San Antonio, 78255. Tel: 210-698-8682.

Department of Assumption-St. John's Seminary—Rev. LAWRENCE J. CHRISTIAN, Rector & Pres., 2600 W. Woodlawn, San Antonio, 78228-5196. Tel: 210-734-5137.

Vice Rector—Rev. ARTURO CEPEDA, S.T.D.

Business Office—Mrs. SALLY ELIZONDO-RIPPY, Gen. Mgr.

Development Coordinator—Mrs. NELDA WOHL.

Department of Communications—Deacon PAT RODGERS, Dir., 2718 W. Woodlawn, San Antonio, 78228. Tel: 210-734-1610; Fax: 210-734-2939. Email: pat.rodgers@archsa.org; CYNTHIA CASTILLO, Administrative Asst. Tel: 210-734-1988. Email: cynthia.castillo@archsa.org.

Catholic Television of San Antonio (CTSA), Channel 15—Deacon PAT RODGERS, 2718 W. Woodlawn, San Antonio, 78228. Tel: 210-734-2620, Ext. 1109; 210-734-1610; Fax: 210-734-2939.

Today's Catholic Newspaper—Mr. JORDAN MC MORROUGH, Editor, 2718 W. Woodlawn, San Antonio, 78228. Tel: 210-734-2620; Fax: 210-734-2939.

Department of Social and Community Services—Mr. STEVE SALDANA, Dir., 202 W. French, San Antonio, 78212. Tel: 210-222-1294; Fax: 210-227-0217.

Catholic Counseling and Consultation Center—Mr. HOWARD KRAVITZ, O.P.A., M.A., N.C.C., L.P.C.S., Mng. Dir., 1844 Lockhill-Selma Rd., Ste. 101, San Antonio, 78216. Tel: 210-377-1133; Fax: 210-377-1230.

Deaf and Hard of Hearing Ministry—Rev. THOMAS COUGHLIN, O.P.Miss., Dir., Dominican Missionaries for the Deaf Apostolate, 143 Honeysuckle Ln., San Antonio, 78213. Tel: 210-627-6303. Office: San Francesco di Paola, 205 Piazza Italia, San Antonio, 78207. Tel: 210-227-0548.

Ministry to Persons with Disabilities—Sr. JO-MICHELE SIERRA, S.S.C.J., 7112 Hagy Circle, San Antonio, 78216. Tel: 210-872-8794.

Bexar County Detention Ministries—Sr. TERESA CARTER, C.S.B. Tel: 210-299-4540; Rev. CARL SCHINDLER, C.Ss.R.; Bro. CHARLES FUCIK, C.Ss.R., 503 San Pedro, San Antonio, 78212. Tel: 210-299-4540; Sr. KATHLEEN EGGERING, S.S.N.D., Juvenile Detention, Cindi Kreir Correctional Center, 3621 Farm Rd., San Antonio, 78223. Tel: 210-335-1754.

St. Peter and Joseph's Home— (See Protective Institutions)

Seton Home— (See Protective Institutions)

Health Ministry Committee—Mrs. PAT SAMMIS. Tel: 210-302-2266.

Catholic Charities, Archdiocese of San Antonio, Inc.—Mr. STEVEN SALDANA, Pres., 202 W. French, San Antonio, 78212-5818. Tel: 210-222-1294; Fax: 210-227-0217.

Refugee Services—PAULA WALKER, 202 W. French, San Antonio, 78212-5818. Tel: 210-222-1294; Fax: 210-242-3174.

Immigration Services—LINDA BRANDMILLER, 2903 W. Salinas St., San Antonio, 78207. Tel: 210-433-3256; Fax: 210-433-0851.

Diocesan Offices And Directors

Archdiocesan Council of Catholic Women—MARGARET TRACY, 7145 Webwood Way, San Antonio, 78250. Tel: 210-647-8728; Rev. WILLIAM MCNAMARA, Spiritual Moderator, Mailing Address: P.O. Box 248, Elmendorf, 78112-0248. Tel: 210-635-8539.

Catholic Center for Charismatic Renewal—Most Rev. THOMAS J. FLANAGAN, D.D., V.G., Dir., Liaison; ROSBEL HERNANDEZ, 1707 S. Flores, San Antonio, 78204. Tel: 210-226-7545; Fax: 210-212-9330. Email: info@cccr.net.

Catholic Lawyers Guild—Rev. Msgr. TERENCE NOLAN, J.C.L., Spiritual Moderator, Mailing Address: P.O. Box 28410, San Antonio, 78228-0410. Tel: 210-734-2620.

Catholic Physicians Guild—Rev. JOHN A. LEIES, S.M., S.T.D.; MIGUEL BEDOLLA, M.D., Ph.D., Pres., 520 Fordham Ln., San Antonio, 78228. Tel: 210-436-3227.

Censores Librorum—VACANT.

Movimiento de Apostolado Familiar & Marriage Encounter (Rural)—Rev. JOSEPH G. RASKY, S.M., 1403 N. St. Marys, San Antonio, 78215. Tel: 210-225-1360.

Movimiento Familiar Cristano (Urban)—Presidents: MANUEL GUERRA; CRUCITA GUERRA, 117 Stonewall, San Antonio, 78214. Tel: 210-924-1890. Email: mguerra45@juno.com.

Black Catholic Apostolate—Mrs. CAROL WHITE, 1819 Nevada, San Antonio, 78203. Tel: 210-532-5358.

Cursillo Movement (Spanish)—VACANT, Spiritual Advisor; RUDY RAMIREZ, Lay Dir., 602 Urban Loop, San Antonio, 78207. Tel: 210-492-8788.

Cursillos of Christianity of the Archdiocese of San Antonio—Rev. EINER OCHOA, Spiritual Advisor; ANN J. HALL, Dir.; VERONICA TREVINO, Treas., Mailing Address: P.O. Box 5152, San Antonio, 78201. Tel: 210-492-8788.

Ecumenical Affairs—Rev. MARTIN J. LEOPOLD.

Holy Childhood, Pontifical Association—MARY WISNIEWSKI, Mailing Address: P.O. Box 28410, San Antonio, 78228-0410. Tel: 210-734-2620; 210-734-1913.

Holy Name Society—Mr. EDWARD GONZALEZ, 6283 Apple Valley, San Antonio, 78242. Tel: 210-673-4590.

Pre-Seminary Program—Rev. ARTURO CEPEDA, S.T.D., Dir., Assumption Seminary, 2600 W. Woodlawn, San Antonio, 78228-5196. Tel: 210-735-0553.

Priests Eucharistic League—Most Rev. THOMAS J. FLANAGAN, D.D., V.G., Dir., Mailing Address: P.O. Box 28410, San Antonio, 78228-0410. Tel: 210-734-2620.

Propagation of the Faith—MARY WISNIEWSKI, Mailing Address: P.O. Box 28410, San Antonio, 78228-0410.

Retreats, Men—Rev. ROCKY GRIMARD, O.M.I., Dir., Oblate Renewal Center, 127 Oblate Dr., San Antonio, 78216. Tel: 210-349-4173.

Respect Life Program—Mr. RICK DOUCETTE, Mailing Address: Office of Life, Justice and Peace, P.O. Box 28410, San Antonio, 78228-0410. Tel: 210-734-2620; 210-734-1655.

CLERGY, PARISHES, MISSIONS AND PAROCHIAL SCHOOLS

CITY OF SAN ANTONIO

1—CATHEDRAL OF SAN FERNANDO (1731), (Hispanic), Revs. Tony Vilano, Rector; Steven Gamez, Parochial Vicar; Jose Ramon Perez-Martinez; Deacons Albert Garza, (Retired); Doroteo E. Pedroza; Pedro Garza.
Res. & Mailing Address: 231 W. Commerce, 78205. Tel: 210-227-1297; Fax: 210-271-0149.
Catechesis/Religious Program—Students 90.
Mission—San Francesco di Paola (Italian) 205 Piazza Italia, Bexar Co. 78207. Tel: 210-227-0548; Fax: 210-226-5086. P.O. Box 7783, 78207-7783. Rev. Anton Quang Dinh Van, Admin.

2—ST. AGNES (1923), (Hispanic), Rev. Einer Ochoa.
Office: 814 Ruiz St., 78207. Tel: 210-227-8258; Fax: 210-212-7757.
Res.: 804 Ruiz St., 78207.
Catechesis/Religious Program—Yolanda Vargas, D.R.E. Students 288.

3—ST. ALPHONSUS (1925), (Hispanic), Rev. Mario Castro Martinez, O.F.M.Conv.; Sr. Adele Massaro, Pastoral Assoc.; Deacons Trinidad Gutierrez; Roy Y. Muñoz Jr.
Res.: 2004 Chihuahua St., 78207. Tel: 210-433-9365; Fax: 210-433-9365.
Catechesis/Religious Program—Tel: 210-432-3176. Students 66.

4—ST. ANN (1912), (Hispanic), Revs. John Restrepo, O.P.; Luis Roberto Aguilar, O.P.; Andrew K. Kolzow, O.P.; Wayne A. Cavalier, O.P. In Res., Revs. Victor LaRoche, O.P.; John Markey, O.P.
Res.: 210 St. Ann St., 78201. Tel: 210-734-6687; 210-734-6688; Fax: 210-738-1755.
Catechesis/Religious Program—Tel: 210-734-6687, Ext. 112. Sr. Blanca Hinojosa, H.C.G., D.R.E. Students 250.

5—ST. ANTHONY MARY CLARET (1988) Rev. Jan Klak; Deacons Jesse C. Galvan; Angel Arredondo; Charles King; Jerome P. Kozar.
Res.: 6150 Roft Rd., 78253. Tel: 210-688-9033; Fax: 210-688-3575. Email: saclaret@saclaret.com.
Catechesis/Religious Program—Catherine Prochko, D.R.E. Students 980.

6—ST. ANTHONY OF PADUA (1957) Rev. Kevin Shananhan, M.S.C.; Deacons Gilbert Wiessler; William I. Simmonds; Hipolito Huerta; Joe Borrego.
Res.: 102 Lorenz Rd., 78209. Tel: 210-824-1743; Fax: 210-824-3283. Email: secretary@stanthonydepadua.org.
Catechesis/Religious Program—Students 421.

7—BASILICA OF THE NATIONAL SHRINE OF THE LITTLE FLOWER, OUR LADY OF MT. CARMEL AND ST. THERESE PARISH (1926), (Hispanic), Discalced Carmelite Fathers. Revs. Luis Gerardo Belmonte, O.C.D.; James A. Curiel, O.C.D.; Jenaro De la Cruz, O.C.D.; Henry Bordeaux, O.C.D.; Deacons Antonio G. Rodriguez; Jimmy Garza.
Office & Mailing Address: 824 Kentucky Ave., 78201. Tel: 210-735-9126; Fax: 210-735-1389.
Res.: 906 Kentucky Ave., 78201-6097. Tel: 210-735-9127; Fax: 210-738-0818.
School—(Grades PreK-8), 905 Kentucky Ave., 78201. Tel: 210-732-9207; Fax: 210-732-3214. Web: www.littleflowerschool.net. Rita Graves, Prin.; Cecilia Garibay, Librarian. Sisters of the Holy Spirit 2; Sisters 1; Lay Teachers 17; Students 296.
Catechesis/Religious Program—Tel: 210-734-4893. Mr. Rafael Savcedo, D.R.E. Students 296.

8—ST. BENEDICT (1958), (Polish—Hispanic), Rev. Edward Bernal; Deacons Charles Lammons; James Raso.
Res.: 4535 Lord Rd., 78220. Tel: 210-648-0123; Fax: 210-648-1722.
School—(Grades PreK-6) Tel: 210-648-1611. Ms. Susan Gonzales, Prin. Religious 1; Lay Teachers 5; Students 61.
Catechesis/Religious Program—Tel: 210-648-4632. Students 101.

9—BLESSED SACRAMENT (1956) Rev. John O'Donoghue; Deacons Joe Fertitta; Joseph Jorgensen; Frank Martinez.
Office: 600 Oblate Dr., 78216. Tel: 210-824-7231; Fax: 210-824-4293.
School—(Grades K-8) Tel: 210-824-3381; Fax: 210-826-6146. Mr. Michael Fierro, Prin. Lay Teachers 23; Students 241; Day Care 123.
Catechesis/Religious Program—Students 200.

10—ST. BONAVENTURE (1959), (Hispanic), Rev. Raymond Schuster; Deacons Fidel Hinojosa; Amador Gonzalez; Luis L. Arredondo.
Res.: 1918 Palo Alto Rd., 78211. Tel: 210-922-1685; Fax: 210-922-7821.
Catechesis/Religious Program—Tel: 210-922-1882. Mrs. Diane Guerra, D.R.E. Students 618.

11—ST. BRIGID (1972) Rev. Msgr. Leslie A. Vance; Rev. Jonathan W. Felux; Deacons Thomas Billimek; Pasquale M. Benigno, (Retired); Patrick F. Frisina; Paul Heye; Juan Espinosa; Harold DeCuir; Donald V. Bradley Jr.; Ernest Roy Amo.
Res.: 6907 Kitchener St., 78240. Tel: 210-696-0896; Fax: 210-696-7319.
Catechesis/Religious Program—Renee Kuntz, D.R.E. Students 532.

12—ST. CECILIA (1919), (Hispanic), Rev. Ruben Garcia, O.C.D.; Deacons Ricardo Villarreal; Richard Hobbs.
Res.: 125 W. Whittier St., 78210-2897. Tel: 210-533-7109; Fax: 210-532-2599.
School—(Grades PreK-8) Tel: 210-534-2711; Fax: 210-533-8284. Mrs. Mary I. Crow, Prin.; Sr. Theresa Naughton, Librarian. Sisters 4; Lay Teachers 11; Students 177.
Catechesis/Religious Program—Tel: 210-532-1994. Mrs. Limba Reyes, D.R.E. Students 96.
Mission—Purisima Concepcion 807 Mission Rd., Bexar Co. 78210. Rev. James Rutkowski; Deacon Raymond F. Jiminez.

13—CHRIST THE KING (1928), (Hispanic), Rev. Lawrence Mattingly, O.F.M.Conv.; Laura Cardenas, Admin.; Martha Martinez, Asst. Bookkeeper.
Res.: 2623 Perez St., 78207. Tel: 210-433-6301; Fax: 210-435-2736.
Catechesis/Religious Program—Tel: 210-433-3640. Lily Landeros, D.R.E. Students 153.

14—ST. CLARE (1959), (Hispanic), Rev. Msgr. Lambert S. Bily; Deacon Gilbert M. Maldonado.
Res.: 7701 Somerset Rd., 78211. Tel: 210-924-5252.
Catechesis/Religious Program—Tel: 210-922-6458. Maria Delores M. Marek, D.R.E. Students 118.

15—DIVINE PROVIDENCE (1981), (Hispanic), Rev. Jean-Marie Mvumbi Phongo, C.I.C.M. (Congo); Deacons Juan G. Martinez, (Retired); Ricardo DeLaGarza.
Church: 5667 Old Pearsall Rd., 78242-2335. Tel: 210-623-3970; Fax: 210-623-3978.
Catechesis/Religious Program—Tel: 210-623-3971. Diana Garza-Valdez, D.R.E. Students 409.

16—ST. DOMINIC (1971) Rev. Eric Ritter; Deacons Bert Stewart; Ree Stockton; Scott Imburgia.
Res.: 5919 Ingram Rd., 78228. Tel: 210-435-6211; Fax: 210-435-1732.
Catechesis/Religious Program—Sr. Dympna Clark, S.H.Sp., D.R.E. Students 354.

17—ST. ELIZABETH ANN SETON (1961) Rev. Msgr. Conor McGrath.
Res.: 8500 Cross Mountain Tr., 78255. Tel: 210-698-1941; Fax: 210-698-1983.
Catechesis/Religious Program—Dina S. Elva, Co-ord. Faith Formation. Students 459.

18—ST. FRANCIS OF ASSISI (1980) Rev. Msgr. James Henke; Sr. Rose Kruppa, C.D.P., Pastoral Assoc.; Deacons Tom Franklin; Brian Clayton; Jim H. Hewson.
Office & Mailing Address: 4201 De Zavala Rd., 78249-2000. Tel: 210-492-4600; Fax: 210-492-8128.
Res.: 14107 Red Mulberry Woods, 78249. Tel: 210-493-8571.
Catechesis/Religious Program—Anthony Deosdade, D.R.E. Students 585.

19—ST. GABRIEL (1958), (Hispanic), Rev. Richard Pena.
Res.: 747 S.W. 39th St., 78237. Tel: 210-433-3689; Fax: 210-433-0546.
Catechesis/Religious Program—Tel: 210-433-3354.

Virginia Ibarra, D.R.E.; Clarisa Jean Enriquez, D.R.E. Students 203.

20—ST. GERARD MAJELLA (1911) Rev. James E. Shea, C.Ss.R.; Deacon Jose L. Ocampo; Rick McLaughlin, Music Dir. In Res., Revs. Francis Han Pham, C.Ss.R.; Monroe Perrier, C.Ss.R., Supr.; John Farnik, C.Ss.R.; Alton Carr, C.Ss.R.
Res.: 1523 Iowa St., 78203. Tel: 210-533-0161 (Church Office); Fax: 210-533-0558.
Catechesis/Religious Program—Students 107.

21—ST. GREGORY'S (1955) Rev. Msgr. Michael B. O'Gorman (Ireland); Sr. M. Carmel O'Callaghan, P.B.V.M., Pastoral Assoc.; Robert Martinez, Pastoral Assoc.; Deacon Fred Campos Jr.
Res.: 700 Dewhurst, 78213. Tel: 210-342-5271; Fax: 210-342-0542.
School—(Grades PreK-8) Tel: 210-342-0281; Fax: 210-308-7177. Martha Gomez, Prin.; Joyce Greenlee, Librarian. Lay Teachers 37; Students 571.
Catechesis/Religious Program—Tel: 210-342-3826. Gloria Silva, D.R.E. Students 332.

22—ST. HELENA (1974) Rev. Msgr. Leo M. Dolan; Deacons Leonard Stancombe; Paul Gustowski; Laura Yzaguirre, Pastoral Assoc.
Office: 14714 Edgemont, 78247. Tel: 210-653-3316; Fax: 210-653-2702.
Res.: 14527 Angora, 78247. Tel: 210-653-3850.
Catechesis/Religious Program—Tel: 210-653-3316; Fax: 210-653-2702. Corrie Solis, D.R.E. Students 640.

23—ST. HENRY (1904), (Hispanic), Rev. Msgr. Emil J. Wesselsky; Deacon Ruben Peter Olivares.
Res.: 1619 S. Flores St., 78204. Tel: 210-225-6877; Fax: 210-212-5802.
Catechesis/Religious Program—Tel: 210-227-1585. Sr. Virginia Clara Ruiz, H.C.G., D.R.E. Students 372.

24—HOLY FAMILY (1963), (Hispanic), Rev. Emmet Carolan; Deacons Manuel Carranza; Pedro Castillo.
Res.: 152 Florencia, 78228-5899. Tel: 210-433-8216; Fax: 210-433-0090.
Catechesis/Religious Program—Tel: 210-433-3006. Sr. Lelia Martinez, D.R.E.; Ester Mango, C.R.E. Students 186.

25—HOLY NAME (1961), (Polish—Hispanic), Rev. Arkadiusz Szyda; Deacon Reynaldo Hinojosa Sr.
Res.: 3814 Nash Blvd., 78223. Tel: 210-333-5020; Fax: 210-333-5021.
School—(Grades PreK-8) Tel: 210-333-7356; Fax: 210-333-7642. Mr. Chad Mills, Prin. Lay Teachers 14; Students 262.
Catechesis/Religious Program—Tel: 210-333-5020; Fax: 210-333-5021. Cathy Kelley, D.R.E. Students 400.

26—HOLY REDEEMER (1901), (African American), [CEM] Very Rev. Kevin Fausz, C.M.
Res.: 1819 Nevada, 78203. Tel: 210-532-5358.
Catechesis/Religious Program—Students 67.

27—HOLY ROSARY (1948), (Hispanic), Rev. Christian A. Janson, S.M.; Bro. Richard Schrader, S.M., Pastoral Assoc.; Deacons Felipe Barajas; Richard B. Salazar.
Res.: 159 Camino Santa Maria, 78228. Tel: 210-433-3241; Fax: 210-433-2133.
Catechesis/Religious Program—Debi Garza, C.R.E. Students 205.

28—HOLY SPIRIT (1964) Revs. Carlos B. Velazquez; Edwin Vigil; Deacons Jesse Greer; Patrick Cunningham; William Peche; Evan Wittig; Pat Keene, Pastoral Assoc.
Res.: 758 W. Ramsey Rd., 78216. Tel: 210-341-1395; Fax: 210-341-8438.
School—(Grades PreK-8), 770 W. Ramsey Rd., 78216. Tel: 210-349-1169; Fax: 210-349-1247. Sandy Galvan, Prin. Lay Teachers 49; Students 470.
Catechesis/Religious Program—Tel: 210-341-1397; Fax: 210-341-2287. Students 828.

29—HOLY TRINITY (1987) Most Rev. Oscar Cantú; Rev. Alex Pereida, Parochial Vicar; Deacons Jerry Micek; Chris Laskowski; Guy LoTruco.
Res.: 20523 Huebner Rd., 78258-3915. Tel: 210-497-4200; Fax: 210-497-4285.
Catechesis/Religious Program—Tel: 210-497-4145; Fax: 210-497-3041. Kristen Casas, C.R.E.; Eric Dietel, Asst.C.R.E. Students 1,263.

30—IMMACULATE CONCEPTION (1933), (Hispanic), Rev. William Collins, M.S.C.; Deacons Jose Hernandez; Marcos Criado.
Res.: 314 Merida St., 78207. Tel: 210-225-2986; Fax: 210-225-2987.
Catechesis/Religious Program—Herlinda Barrentos, D.R.E. Students 114.

31—IMMACULATE HEART OF MARY (1912), (Hispanic), Revs. Alberto M. Ruiz, C.M.F.; Ignacio A. Blanco, C.M.F.; Deacons Jorge Bonilla-Valentin; Alfonso Cervantes. In Res., Revs. Stephen K. Sherwood, C.M.F.; Luis Dussan, C.M.F. (Retired); Bro. Richard Suttle, C.M.F.
Res.: 617 S. Santa Rosa Blvd., 78204. Tel: 210-226-8268; 210-472-2160 (Res.); Fax: 210-226-2412.
Catechesis/Religious Program—Tel: 210-224-8829. Alfonso Cervantes, D.R.E. Students 130.

32—ST. JAMES THE APOSTLE (1954), (Hispanic), Revs. Plutarco Belanggoy, C.I.C.M.; Archie Tacay, C.I.C.M., Parochial Vicar; Deacons Jesse P. Alcala; Ernest Huizar; Charlie Von Allmen; Onofre Toscano, Pastoral Assoc.
Res.: 907 W. Theo Ave., 78225. Tel: 210-922-2136; Fax: 210-923-0940.
School—(Grades PreK-8) Tel: 210-924-1201; Fax: 210-924-0201. Sr. Mary Link, F.M.A., Prin. Daughters of Mary Help of Christians 4; Lay Teachers 15; Students 233.
Catechesis/Religious Program—Tel: 210-922-4061. Mary Toscano, D.R.E. Students 549.

33—ST. JOHN BERCHMANS (1910), (Hispanic), Rev. Rudy T. Carrola Jr.; Deacons Jose G. Diaz; Francisco Sandoval; Jesus Rodriguez.
Res.: 1147 Cupples Rd., 78226. Tel: 210-434-3247; Fax: 210-432-0431.
School—Tel: 210-433-0411; Fax: 210-433-2335. Mrs. Beverly Abbott, Prin. (PreK 3-8) Lay Teachers 25; Students 370.
Catechesis/Religious Program—Tel: 210-433-2121; Fax: 210-432-0431. Marta Lucia Garcia, C.R.E. Students 211.

34—ST. JOHN NEUMANN (1977) Rev. Octavio Muguerza, Admin. Pro-Tem.
Mailing Address: 6680 Crestway Dr., 78239. Tel: 210-654-1643; Fax: 210-654-8031.
Catechesis/Religious Program—Tel: 210-654-3707. Students 311.

35—ST. JOHN THE EVANGELIST (1956) Rev. Stuart Juleen.
Office: 4603 St. John's Way, 78212. Tel: 210-738-2201; Fax: 210-738-0599.
Catechesis/Religious Program—Mrs. Kelly Aguilar, D.R.E. Students 125.

36—ST. JOSEPH (Downtown) (1868) [CEM] Revs. Mario Marzocchi, S.S.S.; Robert Lussier, S.S.S.
Res.: 623 E. Commerce St., 78205. Tel: 210-227-0126; Fax: 210-227-7690.
Catechesis/Religious Program—Students 44.

37—ST. JOSEPH (South San) (1935), (Hispanic), Very Rev. Lenin Naffate (Mexico); Rev. Tu T. Nguyen; Deacon Genaro Herrera.
Res.: 535 New Laredo Hwy., 78211-1900. Tel: 210-924-4383; Fax: 210-928-9020. Email: church@stjosephsouthsan.org.
Catechesis/Religious Program—Tel: 210-924-4383. Students 250.

38—ST. JUDE (1954), (Hispanic), Rev. Roney M. Cardoso, O.S.A.; Deacons Sylvester Ortega; Bartolo Ramos.
Res.: 130 S. San Augustine Ave., 78237. Tel: 210-432-8044; Fax: 210-432-1760.
Catechesis/Religious Program—Tel: 210-438-0392; Fax: 210-433-3959. Students 368.
Mission—Santa Maria Goretti, Bexar Co.

39—ST. LAWRENCE (1959), (Hispanic), Rev. Florencio Rodriguez, T.O.R.; Deacons Alois Keller, (Retired); Ernesto Leal, (Retired); Arturo Garcia; Richard Gonzales; Ricardo Medina.
Res.: 236 E. Petaluma, 78221. Tel: 210-924-4401; Fax: 210-924-4075.
Catechesis/Religious Program—Tel: 210-924-6470. Alcia J. Ortiz, D.R.E. Students 538.

40—ST. LEO (1919), (Hispanic), Rev. Frank Macias; Deacons Alvino Pacheco, Pastoral Assoc.; Gerald Gonzalez; Tom Torrez; Lupe Sielski, Pastoral Assoc.
Office: 4401 S. Flores, 78214. Tel: 210-533-9108; Fax: 210-533-0643. Email: stleochurch@sbcglobal.net.
Res.: 148 Hafer, 78214.
School—(Grades PreK-8), 119 Octavia Pl., 78214. Tel: 210-532-3166; Fax: 210-532-5997. Carol Johnson, Prin.; Sr. Phellipa Wall, Librarian. Lay Teachers 11; Students 158.
Catechesis/Religious Program—Teresa Sanchez, D.R.E.; Diana Rodriguez, Youth Min. Students 356.

41—ST. LEONARD'S (1966), (Hispanic), Revs. David Gutierrez, T.O.R. (Mexico); Juan Carlos Bello, T.O.R.; Deacons Carlos Salinas, (Retired); Rey Ybarra.
Res.: 8510 S. Zarzamora, 78224-2099. Tel: 210-924-6000; Fax: 210-924-5552.
Catechesis/Religious Program—Tel: 210-924-6000, Ext. 19. Students 333.

42—ST. LUKE (1959) Revs. James P. Barlow; Fernando E. Rodriguez.
Office: 4603 Manitou, 78228-1889. Tel: 210-433-2777; Fax: 210-433-2778.
Res.: 6014 Horizon, 78228. Tel: 210-436-9777.
School—(Grades PreK-8) Tel: 210-434-2011; Fax: 210-432-2419. Marcella Salazar, Prin.; Ms. Mindy Davis, Librarian. Lay Teachers 34; Students 561.
Catechesis/Religious Program—Rick Olivarez, C.R.E.; Ileana Schneegans, Faith Formation Dir. Students 555.

43—ST. MARGARET MARY (1955), (Hispanic), Rev. Norman Ermis; Deacons Gerardo Mechler; Zeke Moczygemba; Jose Almanza; Wilfred Lamm, (Retired); Gabriel J. Rosas; Francisco Lafuente. In Res., Rev. David Garcia.
Res.: 1314 Fair Ave., 78223. Tel: 210-532-6309; Fax: 210-532-6333. Email: stmargaretmary@yahoo.com.
School—1202 Fair Ave., 78223. Tel: 210-534-6137; Fax: 210-534-2225. Mr. Ramon Guerra, Prin. (PreK 3-8) Felician Sisters 2; Lay Teachers 12; Students 171.
Catechesis/Religious Program— Lucia Reyes, Faith Formation Dir. Students 365.
Mission—St. Catherine 2202 Hicks, Bexar Co. 78210.

44—ST. MARK THE EVANGELIST (1976) Rev. Msgr. Kevin E. Ryan; Dorothea G. Hamlin, Pastoral Admin.; Catherine Lopez, Pastoral Assoc.; Deacons Steven Marques; Gilbert S. Hernandez.
Res.: 1602 Thousand Oaks Dr., 78232-2398. Tel: 210-494-1606; 210-494-1607; Fax: 210-494-4957.
Catechesis/Religious Program—Tel: 210-494-7434. Theresa Crow, D.R.E. (Elem.); Cindy Hamilton, D.R.E. (High School); Shane Hamilton, D.R.E. (High School). Students 997.

45—ST. MARTIN DE PORRES (1964), (Hispanic), Rev. Gilbert Obin, C.I.C.M.; Deacons Jose Menchaca; Anthony Patlan; Benito Resendiz; Jesus Lucio Jr.
Res.: 1730 Dahlgreen Ave., 78237. Tel: 210-432-5203; Fax: 210-436-1187.
Catechesis/Religious Program—Tel: 210-436-2071. Students 328.

46—ST. MARY (1852) [CEM] Rev. John J. Gordon, O.M.I.
Res.: 202 N. St. Mary's St., 78205. Tel: 210-226-8381; Fax: 210-226-8440.

47—ST. MARY MAGDALEN (1940), (Hispanic), Revs. Joseph Mary Marshall, S.M.; Will Combs; Deacon Gerald Campa. In Res., Revs. George T. Montague, S.M.; Robert E. Hogan.
Office: 1710 Clower St., 78201. Tel: 210-735-5269; Fax: 210-738-0698.
Res.: 1701 Alametos St., 78201. Tel: 210-734-6727.
School—(Grades PreK-8) Tel: 210-735-1381; Fax: 210-735-2406. Roberta Guajardo, Prin. Brothers 1; Sisters 2; Lay Teachers 11; Students 219.
Catechesis/Religious Program—Tel: 210-735-5284. Linda Froboese, D.R.E. Students 652.

48—ST. MATTHEW'S (1968) Very Rev. Msgr. Michael Yarbrough; Revs. James L. Empereur, S.J., Parochial Vicar; Valentine Gallegos Jr., Parochial Vicar; Deacons Tom Fox; Wilbur Hoelschler; Norman Kutschenreuter; Keith Werner, (Retired); Ernesto Garza, (Retired); Anton Svatek, (Retired); James Exparza; Rafael Lara; Pedro Luz Cuellar; Gabriel N. Mendiola; Michael F. Nealis; Roberto Rios; Anthony Rivera.
Res.: 10703 Wurzbach Rd., 78230. Tel: 210-478-5000; Fax: 210-696-8858.
School—(Grades PreK-8) Tel: 210-478-5099; Fax: 210-696-7624. Alvin Caro, Prin.; Diane Michaud, Librarian. Lay Teachers 60; Students 728.
Catechesis/Religious Program—Fax: 210-696-8858. Sr. Therese Gleitz, D.R.E. Students 1,084.

49—ST. MICHAEL (1866), (Hispanic), [CEM] Rev. Heliodoro Lucatero, Admin.
Res.: 418 Indiana, 78210. Tel: 210-532-3707; Fax: 210-532-3707.
Catechesis/Religious Program—Augustin Solis, D.R.E. Students 68.

50—OUR LADY OF GOOD COUNSEL (1952), (Hispanic), Very Rev. Fidele C. Dikete.
Res.: 1204 Castroville Rd., 78237. Tel: 210-432-0873; Fax: 210-432-7576.
Catechesis/Religious Program—Tel: 210-432-6430. Students 136.

51—OUR LADY OF GRACE (1938) Rev. Msgr. Lawrence Walsh; Rev. Martin J. Leopold, Parochial Vicar; Deacons Reynaldo Q. Merino; Frank Gallardo.
Res.: 223 E. Summit Ave., 78212. Tel: 210-734-7285; Fax: 210-734-8334.
Catechesis/Religious Program—Students 172.

52—OUR LADY OF GUADALUPE (1911), (Hispanic), Revs. Ronald Gonzales, S.J.; Martin L. Elsner, S.J., Parochial Vicar; James Marshall, S.J.; Bro. Alexander Gussio, S.J.; Deacons Robert Galvan; Carlos Sandoval; Ruben Felan; David Zamora.
Res.: 1321 El Paso St., 78207. Tel: 210-226-4064; Fax: 210-226-4973.
Catechesis/Religious Program—R. Lee Thielen, D.R.E. Students 89.

53—OUR LADY OF PERPETUAL HELP (1913), (Hispanic), Rev. Daniel Cisneros.
Res.: 618 S. Grimes St., 78203. Tel: 210-532-7031; Fax: 201-532-7031.
Catechesis/Religious Program—Tel: 210-534-7193. Students 242.

54—OUR LADY OF SORROWS (1915), (Hispanic), Rev. Thaddeus Tabak, S.D.S.; Deacon Jesse Fraga. In Res., Rev. Marian Piekarczyk, S.D.S., Dir. Polish Catholic Mission & Army Chap.
Res.: 3107 N. St. Mary's St., 78212. Tel: 210-732-6295; 210-736-6719 (Polish); Fax: 210-732-9249.
Catechesis/Religious Program—Students 92.

55—OUR LADY OF THE ANGELS (1947), (Hispanic), Rev. James Hynes (Peru); Deacons Albert Ramirez; Jose F. Moreno.
Res.: 1214 Stonewall St., 78211. Tel: 210-924-6591; Fax: 210-924-6593.
Catechesis/Religious Program—Tel: 210-924-8046. Alicia Q. Gutierrez, D.R.E. Students 180.

56—OUR LADY OF THE ATONEMENT CATHOLIC CHURCH (1983), (A Personal Parish for the Anglican Use). Rev. Christopher G. Phillips; Deacons James P. Orr, Business Mgr.; Michael D'Agostino; Mr. Edmund G. Murray, Music Dir.; Mrs. Chalon Murray, Asst. Dir. Music.
Res.: 8015 Shady Hollow Ln., 78255. Tel: 210-695-3332.
Church: 15415 Red Robin Rd., 78255. Tel: 210-695-2944; Fax: 210-695-9679.
School—The Atonement Academy, (Grades PreK-12) Tel: 210-695-2240. Mr. Ralph Johnson, Prin.; Mrs. Deborah Divis, Librarian. Priests 1; Religious 1; Lay Teachers 36; Students 491.
Catechesis/Religious Program—Deacon James P. Orr, D.R.E. Students 40.
Convent—The Poor Clares of Perpetual Adoration, Tel: 210-621-5560. Sr. Grace Marie, Supr. Sisters 5.

57—ST. PATRICK (1895), (Hispanic), Rev. Andre K. Bakajika, C.I.C.M.; Deacons Jose A. Suniga; Juan Jose Delgado.
Res.: 1114 Willow St., 78208. Tel: 210-226-5223; Fax: 210-227-8616.
Catechesis/Religious Program—Students 119.

58—ST. PAUL (1954), (Hispanic), Rev. Msgr. Franciszek Kurzaj; Deacons Daniel Muriada; Agustin Arismendez; Pedro Patlan; Albert Sanchez.
Res.: 350 Sutton Dr., 78228-3199. Tel: 210-733-7152; Fax: 210-733-0929.
School—(Grades K-8), 307 John Adams, 78228. Tel: 210-732-2741; Fax: 210-732-7702. Mrs. Sandra Sanchez, Prin. Lay Teachers 28; Students 259.
Ministry & Service Office—1201 Donaldson, 78228. Tel: 210-732-8735; Fax: 210-732-6279. Deacon Pedro Patlan, Coord.
Community Center—Tel: 210-736-0055; Fax: 210-738-9600. Mary Davila, Dir.
Learning Center—Tel: 210-738-8715; Fax: 210-738-8403. Marisa Morales, Dir. (Daycare) Children 99.
Catechesis/Religious Program—Yolanda Gutierrez, D.R.E. Students 214.

59—ST. PETER PRINCE OF THE APOSTLES (1923) Very Rev. Eduardo D. Morales; Becky Finley, Admin.; Deacons John Dunn, (Retired); Richard De Hoyos.
Office & Res.: 111 Barilla Pl., 78209. Tel: 210-822-3367; Fax: 210-828-5826.
School—112 Marcia Pl., 78209. Tel: 210-824-3171; Fax: 210-822-4504. Ann Lauder, Prin. (PreK 3-8) Lay Teachers 33; Students 365.
Catechesis/Religious Program—Tel: 210-822-1605. Alma Small, D.R.E. Students 245.

60—ST. PHILIP OF JESUS (1914), (Hispanic), Rev. Michael DeGerolami; Deacons Jose Sanchez; Gilbert C. De La Portilla.
Res.: 131 Bank St., 78204. Tel: 210-226-5024; Fax: 210-226-9005.
School—(Grades PreK-8), 134 E. Lambert St., 78204. Tel: 210-222-2872; Fax: 210-229-1829. Graciela Luna, Prin.; Rosario Ramon, Librarian. Lay Teachers 15; Aides 4; Students 161.
Catechesis/Religious Program—Tel: 210-225-6622. Mary Lou Martinez, D.R.E. Students 216.

61—ST. PIUS X (1957) Revs. Francis McHugh (Ireland); Gonzalo E. Meza; Deacon Eugene Townsend, (Retired).
Office: 3303 Urban Crest, 78209. Tel: 210-824-0139; Fax: 210-829-5125.
School—(Grades PreK-8), 7734 Robin Rest Dr., 78209. Tel: 210-824-6431; Fax: 210-824-7454. Dr. Richard Arndt, Prin.; Kathy Gray, Librarian. Lay Teachers 26; Students 266.
Catechesis/Religious Program—Humberto Hernandez, Youth Min. Students 290.

62—PRINCE OF PEACE (1980) Rev. Msgr. Patrick Cronin; Deacons Agripino Sanabria; Art Marin; Robert G. Correa; Louis P. Bernal; Heriberto "Eddie" Limas; Wayne Archer.
Res.: 7893 N. Grissom Rd., 78251. Tel: 210-681-8330; Fax: 210-681-2286.
Catechesis/Religious Program—Tel: 210-681-5063. Students 1,204.

63—RESURRECTION OF THE LORD (1981) Rev. Msgr. Adolfo Valdivia; Deacons Thomas Swift, (Retired); Richard Gomez; George Salazar Sr.; Jose Angel Martinez.
Office & Mailing Address: 7990 W. Military Dr., 78227. Tel: 210-675-1470; Fax: 210-675-8203.
Res.: 7151 Cypress Grove, 78227.
Catechesis/Religious Program—Students 470.

64—ST. ROSE OF LIMA (1981) Rev. Msgr. Juan Alfaro; Revs. Virgil Elizondo; Martin Garcia; Deacons Rey Jasso; Antonio Lira; Chester Ostaszewski; Robert Espinosa.
Res.: 9883 Marbach Rd., 78245. Tel: 210-675-1920; Fax: 210-675-6067.
Catechesis/Religious Program—Students 1,400.

65—SACRED HEART (1899), (Hispanic), Rev. Walter O. D'heedene, C.I.C.M. (Belgium); Deacons Valentin Gallegos; Rudy Rodriguez.
Res.: 2114 W. Houston St., 78207-3496. Tel: 210-227-5059; Fax: 210-227-6209. Email: sacredheartsa@hotmail.com.
Catechesis/Religious Program—Tel: 210-227-9763. Sr. Juanita Ramirez, M.J.M.J., D.R.E. Students 266.

66—SAN FRANCISCO DE LA ESPADA (1731), (Hispanic), Revs. Herbert Jones, O.F.M.; Lawrence Brummer, O.F.M.
Res.: 10040 Espada Rd., 78214. Tel: 210-627-2064; Fax: 210-627-2059.
Catechesis/Religious Program—Tel: 210-627-2962. Students 73.
Mission—St. Frances Cabrini 1606 San Casimiro, Bexar Co. 78214.

67—SAN JOSE Y SAN MIGUEL (1720), (Hispanic), Revs. J. Antonio Posadas, O.F.M.; Nicholas Baxter, O.F.M.; Deacons Santiago Rodriguez; Frank J. "Chip" Perry III; Mike R. Munoz. In Res., Revs. Charles Gunti, O.F.M.; Edward Boren, O.F.M.
Res.: 701 E. Pyron Ave., 78214. Tel: 210-922-0543; Fax: 210-932-2271.
Catechesis/Religious Program—Tel: 210-923-8681. Joyce Broussard, D.R.E. Students 200.

68—SAN JUAN CAPISTRANO (1731), (Hispanic), Rev. James Gerard Galvin (Ireland), Admin. Pro-Tem.
Mailing Address: P.O. Box 14308, 78214-0308.
Res.: 9101 Graf Rd., 78214.
Church: 78214. Tel: 210-534-3161; Fax: 210-534-2426.
Catechesis/Religious Program—Students 99.
Mission—St. Ann Southton, Bexar Co.

69—SAN JUAN DE LOS LAGOS SHRINE (1952), (Hispanic), Rev. Arthur Flores, O.M.I.; Deacons Albert Salinas; Robert Cruz.
Res.: 3231 El Paso St., 78207. Tel: 210-433-9722; Fax: 210-433-9526.
Catechesis/Religious Program—Tel: 210-433-2411. Students 235.

70—SANTO NINO DE CEBU (1993), (Filipino), Revs. Martin Parayno, O.S.B. (Philippines); Anthony Maria Mendoza, O.S.B.; Deacons Arsenio Reyes Jr.; Wallace Daniel Kearns; Mrs. Belma De la Cruz, Parish Council Chair. Tel: 830-426-8984.
Mailing Address: 5655 Rigsby Ave., 78222. Tel: 210-648-1705; Fax: 210-648-5365.
Catechesis/Religious Program—Students 97.

71—SHRINE OF ST. PADRE PIO OF PIETRELCINA (2001) Very Rev. Msgr. Patrick Ragsdale; Deacons Ed Bozek; Kevin Kanter.
Mailing Address: PMB 611, 20770 Hwy 281 N., Ste. 108, 78258-7500. Tel: 210-481-2576; Fax: 210-481-5107; Cell: 210-317-1729.
Catechesis/Religious Program—Teresa Hinojosa, D.R.E. Students 584.
Shrine—Shrine of St. Padre Pio 3843 Bulverde Pkwy., 78259. Tel: 210-497-6101; Fax: 210-497-2956.

72—ST. STEPHEN (1965), (Hispanic), Rev. Luis Ruiz.
Res.: 2127 S. Zarzamora St., 78207. Tel: 210-224-8474; Fax: 210-224-8474.
Catechesis/Religious Program—Tel: 210-224-7116. Beatrice Martinez, C.R.E. Students 48.

73—ST. THOMAS MORE (1964) Rev. James A. Kotara; Deacons Jerome Ciarrocchi, (Retired); Paul Charron; Roberto Rosas; Timothy M. Tate Sr.
Res.: 4411 Moana, 78218. Tel: 210-655-5070; Fax: 210-655-8446.
School—(Grades PreK-8), 4427 Moana, 78218. Tel: 210-655-2882; Fax: 210-655-9603. Mr. William D. Smith, Prin. Lay Teachers 12; Students 150.
Catechesis/Religious Program—Tel: 210-654-6824. Students 235.

74—ST. TIMOTHY'S (1953), (Hispanic), Rev. Edward Boren, O.F.M., Admin.; Deacons Rudy Medrano; Antonio Caballero.
Res.: 1515 Saltillo St., 78207. Tel: 210-434-2391; Fax: 210-434-4828.
Catechesis/Religious Program—Maria Del Refugio Rodriquez, D.R.E. Students 120.

75—VIETNAMESE MARTYRS CATHOLIC CENTER (1976) Rev. Francis Han Pham, C.Ss.R.
Center—1240 Holbrook, 78218. Tel: 210-646-0726; Fax: 210-646-0726.
Catechesis/Religious Program—Students 80.

76—ST. VINCENT DE PAUL (1961) Rev. Agustin Estrada-Fernandez, Admin.; Sr. Katrina Ruane, S.H.Sp., Pastoral Assoc.; Deacon Leobardo Longoria.
Res.: 4222 S.W. Loop 410, 78227-4495. Tel: 210-674-1200; Fax: 210-674-1640.
Catechesis/Religious Program—Tel: 210-674-4291. Lucille O'Barr, C.R.E. Students 394.

OUTSIDE THE CITY OF SAN ANTONIO

BANDERA, BANDERA CO., ST. STANISLAUS (1855), (Polish), [CEM] [JC] Rev. Stanislaw Oleksy, S.D.S.; Deacon Robert J. Stein.
Res.: Box 757, 78003-0757. Tel: 830-460-4712; Fax: 830-796-7641.
Catechesis/Religious Program—Tel: 830-796-3573. Elouise Mangold, C.R.E. Students 205.
Mission—St. Victor's Chapel 10514 Park Rd. 37, Lakehills, Bandera Co. 78063. Tel: 830-751-2557.

BOERNE, KENDALL CO., ST. PETER THE APOSTLE (1866), (German), Rev. Anthony O. Cummins; Deacons Paul Rayburg; James Stenstrom; Mary Ann Hawn, Pastoral Assoc.
Mailing Address: 202 W. Kronkosky St., 78006. Tel: 830-816-2233; Fax: 830-249-6175.
Catechesis/Religious Program—Julia Cortez, D.R.E.; Laura Balderama Contreras, D.R.E.; Jeanette Belter, D.R.E.; Michelle Pechacek, D.R.E. Students 605.

BRACKETTVILLE, KINNEY CO., ST. MARY MAGDALEN (1875) [CEM] Rev. Pius Ezeigbo; Deacons James Bader; Joseph E. Goebel.
Res.: Box 95, 78832. Tel: 830-563-2487; Fax: 830-563-3088.
Catechesis/Religious Program—Students 130.
Mission—St. Blaise Spofford Junction, Kinney Co.

CANYON LAKE, COMAL CO., ST. THOMAS THE APOSTLE (1967) Rev. Msgr. Marvin G. Doerfler; Deacon Paul Hunsucker.
Res.: 180 St. Thomas Dr., 78133-4131. Tel: 830-964-3497; Fax: 830-964-2574.
Catechesis/Religious Program—Rosemary Burkhardt, D.R.E./C.R.E.; Christine Hanly, Youth Min. Students 96.

CASTROVILLE, MEDINA CO., ST. LOUIS (1844), (Alsatian), [CEM] Rev. James Conway; Deacons Gene Ebner; Archibald Henson; George White, (Retired).
Res.: 610 Madrid, 78009. Tel: 830-931-2826; Fax: 830-931-9016.
School—(Grades PreK-5) Tel: 830-931-3544; Fax: 830-931-0155. Dr. Joe Ramos, Prin. Lay Teachers 14; Students 169.
Catechesis/Religious Program—Tel: 830-931-2556; Fax: 830-931-2826. Deborah Ruiz, D.R.E. Students 420.
Mission—St. Francis of Assisi (Medina Lake Chapel) Mico, Medina Co.

CESTOHOWA, KARNES CO., NATIVITY OF THE BLESSED VIRGIN MARY (1873), (Polish), [CEM] Rev. Andrzej Waszczenko, S.D.S.
Res.: 300 FM 3191 Cestohowa, Falls City, 78113. Tel: 830-745-2633; Fax: 830-745-9004.
Catechesis/Religious Program—Students 34.

CHARLOTTE, ATASCOSA CO., ST. ROSE OF LIMA (1909), (Hispanic), Rev. Horacio Florez-Coicedo, Admin.
Mailing Address: P.O. Box 69, 78011. Tel: 830-277-1242; Fax: 830-274-1700.
Catechesis/Religious Program—Tel: 830-274-1841. Rosa Juarez, D.R.E. Students 100.
Mission—St. Joseph 703 Congress St., P.O. Box 297, Tilden, McMullen Co. 78072. Tel: 361-274-3374.

COMFORT, KENDALL CO., SACRED HEART (1949) Rev. James Cashin.
Mailing Address: P.O. Box 599, 78013-0599. Tel: 830-995-3708.
Church: 510 Broadway, 78013. Tel: 830-995-3708; Fax: 830-995-2952.
Res.: 104 Daniel St., 78013. Tel: 830-995-3501.
Catechesis/Religious Program—Students 173.

CONVERSE, BEXAR CO., ST. MONICA (1959) Revs. Dennis Arechiga; Mauricio Lopez; Deacon Donald Lauer.
Res.: 501 North St., P.O. Box 1209, 78109. Tel: 210-658-3816; Fax: 210-566-3821.
School—(Grades Day Care-8) Tel: 210-658-6701; Fax: 210-658-6945. Joann Wood, Prin.; Margaret Fischer, Librarian. Lay Teachers 22; Students 511; Day Care 224.
Catechesis/Religious Program—Tel: 210-658-7920. Janice Van Slambrouck, D.R.E. Students 782.

D'HANIS, MEDINA CO., HOLY CROSS (1847), (Hispanic), [CEM] Very Rev. Wallis Stiles.
Res.: P.O. Box 426, 78850. Tel: 830-363-7268; Fax: 830-363-7269 (Call before faxing).
Catechesis/Religious Program—Students 109.
Mission—Immaculate Heart of Mary Yancey, Medina Co.

DEL RIO, VAL VERDE CO.

1—ST. JOSEPH'S (1927) [CEM] Rev. Jesus Camacho; Deacons Filomeno Salazar, (Retired); Efrain Santana; Raymundo Mendoza; Ronnie Van Dyke, (Retired).
Res.: 510 Wernett St., P.O. Box 1429, 78841-1429. Tel: 830-775-4753; Fax: 830-774-7128.
Catechesis/Religious Program—Tel: 830-775-5200. Esther G. Cardenas, D.R.E.; Mr. Evaristo Patino, D.R.E.; Mrs. Blanca Patino, D.R.E. Students 657.

2—OUR LADY OF GUADALUPE (1906), (Hispanic), Revs. Jaime Renteria-Torres, M.N.M.; Javier Uribe Guzman, M.N.M.; Deacons Elieser Hernandez; Adrian Falcon; Juan Padilla.
Office: 505 Cuellar St., 78840.
Res.: 509 Garza St., 78840. Tel: 830-775-3713; Fax:

830-775-9161.
Catechesis/Religious Program—Tel: 830-775-2178. Students 317.
Mission—San Juan Diego Chapel 523 Jeffery Dr., V V Park Estates, Valverde Co. 78840.
3—SACRED HEART (1895) [CEM] Very Rev. James Fischler, C.I.C.M.; Deacons John C. Graf; Robert C. Kusenberger; David B. Scarbo; Roger Rodriguez.
Mailing Address: P.O. Box 1503, 78841-1503.
Office: 307 E. Losoya, 78840. Tel: 830-775-2143; Fax: 830-775-9902.
Res.: 411 Spring St., 78840. Tel: 830-775-4240.
School—(Grades PreK-8), 209 E. Greenwood, 78840. Tel: 830-775-3274; Fax: 830-774-2800. Mrs. Aurora Guerra, Prin. Lay Teachers 21; Students 231.
Catechesis/Religious Program—Sr. Luisita Iglesias, O.N.D., D.R.E. Students 198.
Mission—Mary, Queen of the Universe Comstock, Valverde Co.
DEVINE, MEDINA CO., ST. JOSEPH'S (1897) [CEM] Rev. Alejandro Del Bosque, L.C., Admin. Pro-Tem.
Res.: 108 S. Washington Dr., 78016. Tel: 830-663-2244; Fax: 830-665-4400 (Call before faxing).
Catechesis/Religious Program—Students 225.
Mission—St. Augustine Moore, Frio Co. 78057.
Mission—Our Lady of Mt. Carmel Bigfoot, Frio Co. 78005.
DILLEY, FRIO CO., ST. JOSEPH'S (1899), (Hispanic), Rev. Jose A. Villanueva; Deacons Bernard Carroll; Salvador Tijerina.
Res.: 114 E. Frio, P.O. Box N, 78017. Tel: 830-965-1926; 830-965-2080 (Office); Fax: 830-965-2080 (Call first).
Catechesis/Religious Program—Steve Lozano, D.R.E. Students 115.
Mission—St. Mary, Frio Co.
ELMENDORF, BEXAR CO., ST. ANTHONY (1896) [CEM] Rev. William McNamara; Deacons John K. Miller; Robert Thayer.
Mailing Address: P.O. Box 248, 78112.
Res.: 16505 Killowatt Rd., 78112. Tel: 210-635-8539; Fax: 210-635-8644.
Catechesis/Religious Program—Tel: 210-635-8570. Catherine Halbardier, D.R.E. Students 180.
Mission—Our Lady of Perpetual Help [CEM] Saspamco, Bexar Co.
FALLS CITY, KARNES CO., HOLY TRINITY (1902), (Polish), [CEM] Very Rev. Gregory Sawicki, S.D.S. (Poland); Deacon Stanley Kolodzie, (Retired).
Mailing Address: Box 158, 78113. Tel: 830-254-3539; Fax: 830-254-3530.
Res.: 211 W. Meyer St., 78113.
Catechesis/Religious Program—Amy Dzuik, D.R.E. Students 112.
FLORESVILLE, WILSON CO., SACRED HEART (1882) [CEM] Rev. Phillip D. Henning; Deacons Scott Donaho; Doroteo Chavarria; Ralph E. Guerra.
Res.: 1009 Trail St., 78114. Tel: 830-393-6117; 830-216-7706 (Metro); Fax: 830-393-9071.
School—(Grades K-5) Tel: 830-393-2117; Fax: 830-393-6968. Ms. Kimberly Patek, Prin.; Margie Pruski, Librarian. Lay Teachers 8; Students 60.
Catechesis/Religious Program—Students 422.
FREDERICKSBURG, GILLESPIE CO., ST. MARY'S (1846), (German), [CEM] Rev. Msgr. Enda McKenna; Deacons Gregorio Martinez Jr.; Francisco De La Torre; Patrick Klein; James Bacon, (Retired); Ken Knopp, (Retired).
Res.: 306 W. San Antonio St., 78624. Tel: 830-997-9523; Fax: 830-997-1037.
School—(Grades PreK-8) Tel: 830-997-3914; Fax: 830-997-2382. Billy Pahl, Prin.; Theresa Walch, Librarian. Lay Teachers 25; Students 310.
Catechesis/Religious Program—Tel: 830-997-9523; Fax: 830-997-1037. Students 334.
Mission—Our Lady of Guadalupe, Gillespie Co.
GONZALES, GONZALES CO., ST. JAMES (1885) [CEM] Rev. Paul A. Raaz; Deacons Alfonso Moreno; Terrence Brennan.
Res.: 417 N. College St., 78629. Tel: 830-672-2945; Fax: 830-672-1058.
Catechesis/Religious Program—Tel: 830-672-6291. Mrs. Patricia Brennan, D.R.E. Students 478.
Mission—Sacred Heart 426 St. John, Gonzales Co. 78629. Rev. Paul A. Raaz.
Mission—St. Patrick U.S. Hwy. 90 A, Waelder, Gonzales Co. 78959.
Station—Texan Nursing and Rehab, Tel: 830-672-2867.
Station—Hill Country Nursing and Rehab, Tel: 830-672-2887.
HARPER, GILLESPIE CO., ST. ANTHONY'S (1908) [CEM] Rev. Paul E. Grala, S.O.L.T.; Deacons Curtis Klein; Denis Link.
Mailing Address: P.O. Box 309, 78631. Tel: 830-864-4026; Fax: 830-997-9691.
Res.: 163 N. Third St., 78631.
Catechesis/Religious Program—Students 60.
HELOTES, BEXAR CO., OUR LADY OF GUADALUPE (1942) [CEM] Rev. Msgr. Carlos Davalos; Revs. Henry Clay Hunt III; Cesar Betancourt; Deacons Timothy Houlihan; Daniel D. Quaderer; William Thornberry; Joaqiun Varela; Peter Gutierrez; Anthony Ludolph; Ernest G. Zepeda; Larry Edwards; Laura Garcia Brill, Pastoral Assoc.
Res.: 13715 Riggs Rd., 78023. Tel: 210-695-8791; Fax: 210-695-9957.
Catechesis/Religious Program—Danna Peaks, D.R.E.; Sara Weir, Youth Min. (Middle School); John Lopez, Youth Min.; Nancy Baize, Youth Min. (Elementary). Students 525.
HOBSON, KARNES CO., ST. BONIFACE (1901), (German—Polish), [CEM] Very Rev. Gregory Sawicki, S.D.S. (Poland); Rev. Gabriel Kamienski, S.D.S.
Res.: 358 CR 220, 78117. Tel: 830-780-3559.
Catechesis/Religious Program—Students 47.
HONDO, MEDINA CO., ST. JOHN THE EVANGELIST (1892) [CEM] Rev. Kenneth M. Dakin; Deacons Richard Edminson; John Schoellman; Vangie Pimentel, Admin.
Mailing Address: 2102 Ave. J, 78861. Tel: 830-426-3260; Fax: 830-426-3339.
Catechesis/Religious Program—Tel: 830-741-2513. Sylvia Fernandez, D.R.E.; Laura Leyendecker, C.R.E. Students 448.
JOURDANTON, ATASCOSA CO., ST. MATTHEW'S (1912) [CEM] Rev. Kazimierz Oleksy, S.D.S.; Deacon Eusebio Guevara.
Mailing Address: P.O. Box 670, 78206.
Res.: 1608 Campbell Ave., 78206. Tel: 830-769-3687; Fax: 830-769-2861.
Catechesis/Religious Program—Students 140.
Mission—St. Ignatius 101 W. Ave. F, Christine, Atascosa Co. 78012.
KARNES CITY, KARNES CO., ST. CORNELIUS (1917) Revs. Stanislaw P. Marciniak; Mariusz Lazarek.
Res.: 605 E. Calvert St., 78118. Tel: 830-780-3947; Fax: 830-780-3948.
Catechesis/Religious Program—Tel: 830-780-3949. Vivian Janysek, D.R.E.; Maggie Ybarra, D.R.E. Students 186.
Mission—St. Elizabeth Fashing, Atascosa Co.
KENEDY, KARNES CO., OUR LADY QUEEN OF PEACE (1959) [CEM] Rev. Norbert H. Herman (Poland).
Mailing Address: P.O. Box 89, 78119.
Res.: One Notre Dame Pl., 78119. Tel: 830-583-2417; Fax: 830-583-2410.
Catechesis/Religious Program—Tel: 830-583-2247. Ms. Diana Martinez, C.R.E. Students 84.
KERRVILLE, KERR CO., NOTRE DAME (1889) Revs. Michael Peinemann; John Reidman (SFS); Alberto Colin; Deacons Daniel Arriaga; Charles Domingues; Juan A. Martinez; Sonny Kaufield.
Mailing Address: 909 Main St., 78028.
Res.: 959 Main St., 78028. Tel: 830-257-5961; Fax: 830-895-9771.
School—(Grades PreK-8), 907 Main St., 78028. Tel: 830-257-6707; Fax: 830-792-4370. Ms. Sandra Trujillo-Garcia, Prin. Lay Teachers 21; Students 132.
Catechesis/Religious Program—Tel: 830-896-4233. Students 550.
KIRBY, BEXAR CO., ST. JOAN OF ARC (1971) Rev. Francisco Puente; Deacons John Buchanan, (Retired); Robert Galan Jr.; Gilbert P. Rivera; John X. Huttinger; Wilfredo (Todd) Dapilmoto.
Res.: 2829 Ackermann Rd., 78219-2100. Tel: 210-661-5277; Fax: 210-661-5735.
Catechesis/Religious Program—Tel: 210-661-2220. Mrs. Paulette Petron, D.R.E. Students 373.
KOSCIUSZKO, WILSON CO., ST. ANN'S (1898), (Polish), [CEM] Rev. Andrew Waszczenko.
Res.: 8161 FM 541-E, Stockdale, 78160-6554. Tel: 830-745-2541; Fax: 830-745-2434.
Catechesis/Religious Program—Students 43.
LA VERNIA, WILSON CO., ST. ANN (1917) [CEM] Rev. Stanislaw Fiuk (Poland); Deacons Israel Bocanegra; Wesley Rist.
Res.: 14151 U.S. Hwy. 87 W., 78121. Tel: 830-779-3131; Fax: 830-779-1749.
Catechesis/Religious Program—Tel: 830-253-8124. Marie Gerlich, D.R.E. Students 278.
LACOSTE, MEDINA CO., OUR LADY OF GRACE (1911) [CEM] Rev. Paul Cleary; Deacon Joseph C. Boland.
Mailing address: P.O. Box 39, 78039.
Res.: 15825 Bexar St., 78039. Tel: 830-985-3357 (Office); 830-985-3346 (Rectory); Fax: 830-985-3400.
Catechesis/Religious Program—Tel: 830-985-3355. Mr. Jesse Mendoza, D.R.E. Students 195.
Mission—St. John Vianney 12703 Cinco de Mayo, Bexar Co. 78252. Tel: 210-677-0954.
LOSOYA, BEXAR CO., EL CARMEN CATHOLIC CHURCH (1813), (Hispanic), [CEM], (Our Lady of Mt. Carmel) Rev. Carl R. Maurer.
Res.: 18555 Leal Rd. (Losoya), 78221. Tel: 210-626-2333; Fax: 210-626-1874.
Catechesis/Religious Program—Maria Celia Aldrich, C.R.E. Students 157.
LYTLE, ATASCOSA CO., ST. ANDREW (1904) [CEM] Rev. Romeo D. Olivares, C.I.C.M.
Res.: P.O. Box 326, 78052. Tel: 830-709-4287 (Rectory/Res.); 830-709-9896 (Office); Fax: 830-709-0069.
Catechesis/Religious Program—Students 242.
Mission—St. John Bosco Natalia, Medina Co.
Mission—Immaculate Conception P.O. Box 326, Coal Mine, Atascosa Co. 78052.
MACDONA, BEXAR CO., OUR LADY QUEEN OF HEAVEN (1994), (Hispanic), Rev. Msgr. James Janish.
Mailing Address: P.O. Box 94, 78054-0094. Tel: 210-622-3282.
Res.: 11150 Macdona-LaCoste Rd., Atascosa, 78002. Tel: 210-622-9477; Fax: 210-622-0877.
Catechesis/Religious Program—Betty Arredondo, D.R.E. Students 156.
MARTINEZ, BEXAR CO., ST. JEROME (1925) [CEM] Very Rev. John J. Flanagan.
Res.: 7955 Real Rd., 78263. Tel: 210-648-2694; Fax: 210-648-3690.
Catechesis/Religious Program—Tel: 210-260-3489. Sandra Dorsey, D.R.E. Students 238.
NEW BRAUNFELS, COMAL CO.
1—HOLY FAMILY (1964) Revs. Ignatius Himawan, M.S.F.; Mario Galindo, M.S.F.; Victor Garcia, Parish Mgr.
Res.: 245 S. Hidalgo, 78130. Tel: 830-609-5320; Fax: 830-609-5322.
Catechesis/Religious Program—Tel: 210-608-9615. Angie Kiesling, Rel. Coord. Students 308.
2—OUR LADY OF PERPETUAL HELP (1926) Rev. Eugene Ronan, M.S.F.; Deacon Ralph Brock.
Res.: 138 W. Austin St., 78130. Tel: 830-625-3534; Fax: 830-625-3566.
Catechesis/Religious Program—Tel: 830-629-4506. Sr. Mary Louise, C.R.E. Students 175.
Mission—St. John 210 House St., Comal Co. 78130.
3—SS. PETER AND PAUL (1845) [CEM 2] Rev. Anthony Pesek; Deacons Fred Fey; Ben Wehman; Frank Fikac; William Schroeder; Robert Gorman; Beck E. Knox; Rusty W. Brandt; John Schwartze.
Res.: 386 N. Castell St., 78130. Tel: 830-625-4531; Fax: 830-606-5461.
School—(Grades PreK-8), 198 W. Bridge St., 78130. Tel: 830-625-4531, Ext. 3; Fax: 830-606-6916. John T. Pelicano, Prin.; Kathy Foegelle, Librarian. Lay Teachers 21; Students 267.
Catechesis/Religious Program—386 N. Castell, 78130. Tel: 830-625-4531, Ext. 201. Bill Smith, D.R.E. Students 1,025.
Mission—St. Joseph Comal, Comal Co.
NIXON, GONZALES CO., ST. JOSEPH'S (1915) [CEM] Rev. Alfonso Gioppato, O.M.I.; Deacon John Moreno.
Res.: 207 S. Washington Ave., 78140-2920. Tel: 830-582-1127.
Catechesis/Religious Program—Students 98.
PANNA MARIA, KARNES CO., IMMACULATE CONCEPTION OF THE BLESSED VIRGIN MARY (1854), (Polish), [CEM] Rev. Mariusz Lazarek.
Res.: P.O. Box 9, 78144. Tel: 830-780-2748; Fax: 830-780-2334.
Catechesis/Religious Program—Tel: 830-745-2021. Students 55.
Mission—St. Helena Helena, Karnes Co.
PEARSALL, FRIO CO., IMMACULATE HEART OF MARY (1891) [CEM] [JC] Rev. Andrew Kafara (Poland); Deacon Marcus Salazar.
Res.: 422 W. Brazos, P.O. Box AK, 78061. Tel: 830-334-2382; Fax: 830-334-4046.
Catechesis/Religious Program—Tel: 210-334-4879. Marcus Salazar, D.R.E.; Elda Carrizales, D.R.E. Students 412.
PLEASANTON, ATASCOSA CO.
1—ST. ANDREW (1913), (Hispanic), [CEM] [JC 3] Very Rev. Gilberto Vallejo; Rev. Jesus Gerardo Anguiano; Deacon Bennie Garcia Jr.
Res.: 626 Market St., 78064-2747. Tel: 830-569-3356; 830-281-4902 (Metro); Fax: 830-569-1158.
Catechesis/Religious Program—Sr. Bonnie McHugh, D.R.E. Students 451.
Mission—Sacred Heart Campbell and St. Francis St., Campbellton, Atascosa Co. 78008.
2—ST. LUKE-LOIRE (1859) Rev. Stefan Wiera; Deacon Jose Guadalupe Trevino.
Res.: 3930 FM 536, 78064. Tel: 830-393-6021; Fax: 830-216-4286.
Catechesis/Religious Program—Students 45.
Mission—Our Lady of Guadalupe [CEM] [JC 2] 170 Hackberry St., Leming, Loire Co. 78050.
POTEET, ATASCOSA CO., ST. PHILIP BENIZI (1897), (Hispanic), [CEM] Rev. Sady Nelson Santana.
Res.: P.O. Box 348, 78065. Tel: 830-742-3796; 210-276-8260 (Metro); Fax: 830-742-8853.
Catechesis/Religious Program—Rudy Gonzales, D.R.E. Students 130.
POTH, WILSON CO., BLESSED SACRAMENT (1910) [CEM] Rev. Grzegorz Szewczyk, S.D.S. (Poland); Deacon Alan Crosby.
Mailing Address: P.O. Box 339, 78147.
Res.: 488 W. Westmeyer, 78147. Tel: 830-484-3302; Fax: 830-484-2903.
Catechesis/Religious Program—Tel: 830-484-3303.

Students 281.

ROCKSPRINGS, EDWARDS CO., SACRED HEART OF MARY (1900), (Hispanic), [JC] Rev. Marco Lino Rodriguez-Toloza (Colombia), Admin.
Res.: P.O. Box 887, 78880. Tel: 830-683-2165; Fax: 830-683-6165.
Catechesis/Religious Program—
Mission—St. Mary Magdalen P.O. Box 610, Camp Wood, Real Co. 78833. Tel: 830-597-5165.
Mission—St. Raymond of Pennafort P.O. Box 989, Leakey, Real Co. 78873. Tel: 830-232-5852. Deacons Ruben Navarro; Warren Seymour.

RUNGE, KARNES CO., ST. ANTHONY'S (1901), (Polish), [CEM 2] Rev. Norbert H. Herman (Poland), Admin.
Mailing Address: P.O. Box 188, 78151.
Res.: 101 W. Arenoso St., 78151. Tel: 830-239-4146.
Catechesis/Religious Program—Pablo Nunez, C.R.E. Students 72.

ST. HEDWIG, BEXAR CO., ANNUNCIATION OF THE BLESSED VIRGIN MARY (1855), (Polish), [CEM] Rev. Boleslaw Zadora, S.D.S.
Res.: P.O. Box 100, 78152. Tel: 210-667-1232; Fax: 210-667-9088.
Catechesis/Religious Program—Students 224.

SABINAL, UVALDE CO., ST. PATRICK'S (1884) [CEM] Rev. Antonio X. Hernandez.
Res.: Box 117, 78881. Tel: 830-988-2255.
Catechesis/Religious Program—Students 58.
Mission—St. Joseph Knippa, Uvalde Co.
Mission—St. Mary Vanderpool, Bandera Co.

SCHERTZ, GUADALUPE CO., CHURCH OF THE GOOD SHEPHERD (1972) Very Rev. Gregory J. Nevlud; Rev. Msgr. Roger P. Robbins, Parochial Vicar; Kathy Wilkes, Admin.; Deacons John J. Gorman; Paul La Combe, (Retired); George Vick Jr., (Retired); Harvey Balcer; Elmer Fernandez.
Res.: P.O. Box 929, 78154. Tel: 210-658-4350; Fax: 210-658-7051.
Catechesis/Religious Program—Tel: 210-658-6188. Mrs. Geri Grimm, D.R.E.; Mrs. Jean Smith, D.R.E. Students 400.
Mission—Immaculate Conception Santa Clara and Klein, Marion, Guadalupe Co. 78124. Tel: 210-420-8122.

SEGUIN, GUADALUPE CO.

1—ST. JAMES (1873) [CEM] Rev. Msgr. Dennis Darilek; Bruce Peterson, Pastoral Admin.
Res.: 510 S. Camp St., 78155. Tel: 830-379-1796; Fax: 830-379-1797.
School—(Grades PreK-8), 507 S. Camp St., 78155. Tel: 830-379-2878; Fax: 830-379-2878. Deanna Sanchez, Prin. Lay Teachers 15; Students 200.
Catechesis/Religious Program—Tel: 830-379-7689. Antonia Hernandez, D.R.E.; Catherine Castaneda, Youth Min. Students 124.

2—OUR LADY OF GUADALUPE (1908), (Hispanic), [CEM] Revs. David Tonary, M.S.F.; Jack Kilburg, M.S.F.; Tomasz Grabara, M.S.F. (Poland); Deacon Nick Carillo; Bro. Rolland Kapsner, M.S.F.
Res.: 409 W. Krezdorn, 78155-4429. Tel: 830-379-4338; Fax: 830-303-1002.
Catechesis/Religious Program—Tel: 830-379-2818. Glenda Moreno, D.R.E. Students 557.
Mission—St. Joseph 2858 Redwood Rd., Redwood, Guadalupe Co. 78666.

SELMA, BEXAR CO., OUR LADY OF PERPETUAL HELP (1897), (German), [CEM] Revs. Jose Luis De La Rosa; James K. Seiwert; Deacons Clifford Friesenhahn; Edward F. Courtney; Louis Heimer; Jacques Abat.
Res.: 16075 N. Evans Rd., 78154-3824. Tel: 210-651-6913; Fax: 210-651-5272.
School—(Grades PreK-8) Tel: 210-651-6811; Fax: 210-651-5516. Ms. Jacqueline S. Palermo, Prin.; Christine Martinez, Librarian. Lay Teachers 38; Students 429.
Catechesis/Religious Program—Vilma Vasquez De Torres, D.R.E.; Suzy Krisak, D.R.E. Students 814.

SMILEY, GONZALES CO., ST. PHILIP BENIZI (1963), (Hispanic), Rev. Alfonso Gioppato, O.M.I.; Deacons Frank Rojas, Pastoral Admin. (Retired); John J. Moreno.
Res.: P.O. Box 32, 78159-0032. Tel: 830-587-6258.
Catechesis/Religious Program—Students 45.

SOMERSET, BEXAR CO., ST. MARY'S (1920), (Hispanic), [CEM] Rev. Edward Pavlicek Jr.; Deacon Robert Cruz.
Mailing Address: Box 295, 78069.
Res.: 19711 N. Dixon St., 78069. Tel: 830-701-3123.
Catechesis/Religious Program—Mrs. Sylvia Cruz, D.R.E. Students 205.

SPRING BRANCH, COMAL CO. (HONEY CREEK), ST. JOSEPH (1876) [CEM] Rev. Jimmy David Drennan; Deacons James Legendre, (Retired); Ken Nickel.
Res.: 25781 Hwy. 46 W., 78070-3613. Tel: 830-980-2268; Fax: 830-980-3184.
Catechesis/Religious Program—Kim Barton, D.R.E. Students 581.

STOCKDALE, WILSON CO., ST. MARY (1895) [CEM] Rev. Dennis Jarzombek; Deacons Jack Karam; Benjamin Gimenez.
Box 535, 78160.
Res.: 1201 W. St. Mary St., 78160. Tel: 830-996-3415; Fax: 830-996-3415.
Catechesis/Religious Program—Students 76.

STONEWALL, GILLESPIE CO., ST. FRANCIS XAVIER (1945), (German—Hispanic), [CEM] Rev. James A. Harnan, M.S.C.
Res.: 400 St. Francis St., P.O. Box 209, 78671-3717. Tel: 830-644-2368; Fax: 830-644-2068.
Catechesis/Religious Program—Students 44.

UVALDE, UVALDE CO., SACRED HEART (1883), (Hispanic), [CEM] Rev. Wieslaw Iwaniec; Deacons Hector V. Garcia; Antonio Hinojosa; Fortunato Hinojosa, (Retired); Gilbert Salazar; Daniel A. Ibarra; Federico Flores.
Res.: 408 Fort Clark St., 78801. Tel: 830-278-3448; Fax: 830-278-2835.
School—(Grades PreK-6) Tel: 830-278-2661; Fax: 830-279-0634. David Emrich, Prin.; Ms. Quiroga, Librarian. Lay Teachers 11; Students 132.
Catechesis/Religious Program—Tel: 830-278-4846. Linda Milam, D.R.E. Students 998.

VON ORMY, BEXAR CO.

1—ST. PETER THE FISHERMAN (1990), (Hispanic), Rev. Miguel Arango-Medina (Colombia); Deacons Richard Wells; Ernesto Bravo.
Office: 17534 N. State Hwy. 16, 78073. Tel: 830-276-8778; 830-276-4985 (Res.); Fax: 830-276-8778.
Catechesis/Religious Program—Students 109.

2—SACRED HEART (1935), (Hispanic), Rev. Msgr. James Janish; Deacons Carlos Rodriguez; Larry Contreras.
Mailing Address: P.O. Box 722, 78073-0722. Tel: 210-622-3457.
Res.: P.O. Box 94, Macdona, 78054-0094. Tel: 210-622-9477.
Catechesis/Religious Program—Anna Padilla, D.R.E. Students 141.

KOREAN APOSTOLATE

BOERNE, KENDALL CO., KOREAN MARTYRS CATHOLIC CHURCH (1982), (Korean), Rev. James Song.
Res.: 7655 Curres Creek, 78015. Tel: 210-698-3877.

OLD SPANISH MISSIONS

SAN ANTONIO, BEXAR CO., OLD SPANISH MISSIONS *aka Las Misiones* Rev. David Garcia.
Mailing Address: *c/o Catholic Chancery*, P.O. Box 28410, 78228.
Purisima Concepcion—807 Mission Rd., 78210. Rev. James Rutkowski.
San Francisco de la Espada—10040 Espada Rd., 78214.
San Juan Capistrano—9101 Graf Rd., 78214.
San Jose—701 E. Pyron Rd., 78214.

Chaplains of Public Institutions

SAN ANTONIO. *Audie Murphy VA Hospital*, 7400 Merton Minter Blvd., 78229. Tel: 210-617-5308. Rev. Donald Kloster.
Baptist Memorial Hospital, 111 Dallas St., 78205. Tel: 210-222-8431. Mrs. Pat Sammis.
Brooke Army Medical Center, Tel: 210-916-1105; 210-916-2172; Fax: 210-916-1169. Rev. James E. Schellenberg, D.Min. Tel: 210-916-4141 (After 4:30 pm & weekends).
Res.: 3851 Roger Brooke Blvd., Bldg. 3600, Fort Sam Houston, 78234. Tel: 210-916-4141 (After 4:30pm & Weekends).
St. Luke's Baptist Hospital; University Hospital, 4502 Medical Dr., 78229. Tel: 210-680-2635 (Res.). Rev. Nicholas Brown, S.C.J.
Methodist Hospital, 7700 Floyd Curl, 78229. Tel: 210-692-4030. Revs. Marian Piekarczyk, S.D.S., Joseph Determan, O.P.
San Antonio State Hospital, 6711 S. New Braunfels, 78223. Tel: 210-532-8811. Vacant.
Santa Rosa Hospital System, 519 W. Houston, 78207. Tel: 210-704-2021. Revs. Guillermo Casipong, C.I.C.M., Roy Quioque, C.I.C.M., Mr. Richard Woodley.
Southwest General Hospital, Tel: 210-921-2000. Deacon Leon Mueller.

KERRVILLE. *Veterans' Administration Hospital*, Tel: 830-896-2020. Sr. Jane McKenzie, O.S.F.

Special Assignment:
Revs.—
Dymowski, Thomas H., O.SS.T., Chap., Incarnate Word University, Trinitarian House, 401 Squires Row, 78213-2529.
Foster, John Mary, F.J., 1346-A Hueco Springs LP, New Braunfels, 78132. Tel: 830-629-5042
Pillari, Moses de Jesus, 1346-A Hueco Springs Loop, New Braunfels, 78132. Tel: 830-629-5042

On Duty Outside the Archdiocese:
Revs.—
Mannion, P. John (Retired), Ireland
Martinez, Manuel, Providence Memorial Hospital, Dept. Spiritual Care, 2001 N. Oregon St., El Paso, 79902.
Pogorelc, Anthony J., S.S., Washington, DC.

Military Chaplains:
Revs.—
Eke, Rafael E. (Nigeria), U.S. Army
Gonzalez, George G., Chap. Major, 4707 Winged Foot Way, Columbus, GA 31909.
Hernandez, Alfred Ricardo, Col. Catholic Chap., 9028 Privilege Point, Converse, 78109. Tel: 210-566-3523
Nee, Eugene O., PSC 50 Box 667, APO, AE 09494.
Tellez, Jairo A., Major, U.S.A.F., Air Police CMR 480, Box 3029, APO, AE 09128.

On Sabbatical:
Revs.—
Horan, Mike
Maxwell, Palmer

On Leave:
Revs.—
Duran, Jorge
Hernandez, Antonio X.
Kammerer, James
Ruiz, Enrique
Sandoval, Luis
Sieczynski, Jerzey

Retired:
Most Revs.—
Flores, Patrick F., D.D., 80 Peter Baque Rd., 78209. Tel: 210-826-7721
Flanagan, Thomas J., D.D., Oblate Madonna House, 5722 Blanco Rd., 78216-6615.
Popp, Bernard F., D.D., 8520 Cross Mountain Tr., #1001, 78255. Tel: 210-698-5524
Yanta, John W., D.D., 5015 Bayonne, 78228.
Rev. Msgrs.—
Brosnan, Dermot, 2006 Steves Ave., 78210. Tel: 210-534-7426
Brosnan, Liam P., 2006 Steves Ave., 78210. Tel: 210-534-7426
Fater, Douglas, 619 Birdsong S., 78258.
Fecher, Vincent, 8520 Cross Mountain Tr., #302, 78255. Tel: 210-698-3923
Flanagan, Patrick J., 3843 Barrington #204A, 78217. Tel: 210-599-4900
French, Thomas A., 4707 Broadway, 78209. Tel: 210-822-0385
Garcia, Raymond, 80 Peter Baque Rd., 78209. Tel: 210-826-7721
Goertz, Alois J., 8520 Cross Mountain Tr., #100, 78255. Tel: 210-698-9067
Hubertus, Albert, 8520 Cross Mountain Tr., #4, 78255. Tel: 210-698-8682
Marron, Patrick L., P.O. Box 206, Fischer, 78623-9998.
Martinez, Leo, 8520 Cross Mountain Tr., #1101, 78255. Tel: 210-698-9875
Matocha, John L., 4130 S. Alemeda St., Corpus Christi, 78411-1529.
Murphy, Thomas, Casa de Padres, 8520 Cross Mountain Tr., 78255.
O'Callaghan, Eugene
Palmer, Thomas, 2717 N. Flores, #26, 78202.
Petsch, Joseph, Casa de Padres, 8520 Cross Mountain Tr., #702, 78255. Tel: 210-698-7055
Rihn, Roy, 8520 Cross Mountain Tr., #301, 78255. Tel: 210-698-0287
Smith, Sherrill, Padua Place, 80 Peter Baque Rd., 78209. Tel: 210-826-7721
Stuebben, Lawrence J., Casa de Padres, 8520 Cross Mountain Tr., 78255. Tel: 210-288-0988
Wagner, John A., 8520 Cross Mountain Tr., #202, 78255. Tel: 210-698-1332
Revs.—
Avau, Felix A., C.I.C.M., P.O. Box 1824, Poteet, 78065. Tel: 210-225-0150
Baistra, Jorge, 442 Ceralvo, 78207-7732.
Benonis, Richard (PH), HC33, Box 850, Barksdale, 77828-9706.
De La Garza, Joseph, 1138 Plateau Ridge, New Braunfels, 78132-2114. Tel: 830-694-4228
Dillane, Maurice, Ireland
Ebarb, Walter, 18866 Stoneoak Pkwy., Ste. 103-64, 78258.
Haby, Gerald, S.M., 1403 N. St. Mary's St., 78215.
Heitkamp, Samuel, 764 Fredricksburg Rd., New Braunfels, 78130-6014.
Hoelscher, James, Padua House, 80 Peter Baque Rd., 78209. Tel: 210-826-7721
Johnston, Robert F., 837 Village Sq., Palm Springs, CA 92262. Tel: 760-322-3236
Kaczkowski, Conrad J., S.M., Ph.D., 5903 Babcock Rd., #1606, 78240. Tel: 210-475-3588
Lampert, Robert E., 680 E. Basse Rd., 78209.
Makothakat, John M., Ph.D., S.T.D., J.C.D., 285 Oblate Dr., 78216. Tel: 210-341-1366
Mannion, Patrick J., , Galway Ireland.
Martin, Harry

McKenna, Peter, 123 Trillium, 78213. Tel: 210-366-2188
Mushalla, Walter, P.O. Box 467, Somerset, 78069.
O'Callaghan, Patrick, 630 W. Woodlawn Ave., 78202. Tel: 210-736-3177
Paniagua, Pablo, 80 Peter Baque Rd., 78209. Tel: 210-826-7721
Rubaj, Leon, Casa de Padres, 8520 Cross Mountain Tr., 78255.
Uribe-Guzman, Francisco J., Our Lady of Guadalupe, 505 Cueller St., Del Rio, 78840.
Verboomen, Willy, C.I.C.M., Padua Place, 80 Peter Baque Rd., #11, 78209.
Zumaya, David, Mexico

Permanent Deacons:
Abat, Jacques, Our Lady of Perpetual Help, Selma
Alcala, Jesse, St. James, San Antonio
Almanza, Jose M., St. Margaret Mary, San Antonio
Alvarado, Thomas, (Retired)
Amo, Ernest Roy, St. Brigid, San Antonio
Archer, Wayne, Prince of Peace, San Antonio
Arismendez, Agustin, St. Paul, San Antonio
Arredondo, Luis L., St. Bonaventure, San Antonio
Arriaga, Dan, Notre Dame, Kerrville
Bacon, James, St. Mary's, Fredericksburg
Bader, James W., St. Mary Magdalen, Brackettville
Baker, Robert L., Colonial Beach, VA
Balcer, Harvey J., Good Shepherd, Schertz
Barajas, Felipe, Holy Rosary, San Antonio
Behling, James, St. Stanislaus, Bandera
Beinke, George, St. James, Seguin
Bellg, Bruce, (Unassigned)
Benavides, Myron, St. Philip of Jesus, San Antonio
Benigno, Pasquale, St. Brigid, San Antonio
Berg, Jim, (Unassigned)
Bernal, Louis P., Prince of Peace, San Antonio
Billimek, Thomas E., St. Brigid, San Antonio
Bocanegra, Israel, St. Ann, La Vernia
Boland, Joseph C., Our Lady of Grace, La Coste
Bonilla-Valentin, Jorge, Immaculate Heart of Mary, San Antonio
Borrego, Joe T., St. Anthony of Padua, San Antonio
Bowlin, William R., (Unassigned)
Bozek, Edwin J., Jr., St. Francis Assisi, Mico
Bradley, Donald V., St. Brigid, San Antonio
Brandt, Rusty W., SS. Peter & Paul, New Braunfels
Bravo, Ernesto G., St. Peter the Fisherman, Von Ormy
Brennan, Terrence, St. James, Gonzales
Brock, Ralph, Our Lady of Perpetual Help, New Braunfels
Brumley, Denson C., St. Leonard, San Antonio
Buchanan, John, (Retired)
Caballero, Antonio, St. Timothy, San Antonio
Caldwell, Robert M., Jr., San Francisco de Paola, San Antonio
Callaway, George, Jr., (Retired)
Camero, A. C., Our Lady of Guadalupe & Jail Ministry, San Antonio
Campa, Gerard, St. Mary Magdalen, San Antonio
Campos, Fred, Jr., St. Gregory the Great, San Antonio
Carranza, Manuel G., Jr., Holy Family, San Antonio
Carrillo, Nick L., Our Lady of Guadalupe, Seguin
Carrizales, Manuel, Immaculate Heart of Mary, Pearsall
Carroll, Bernard, St. Joseph, Dilley
Casanova, Ismael G., St. Margaret Mary, San Antonio
Castellano, Frank V., St. Gabriel, San Antonio
Castillo, Pedro C., Holy Family, San Antonio
Cena, Librado, St. John Berchmans, San Antonio
Cervantes, Alfonso, Immaculate Heart of Mary, San Antonio
Charron, Paul, St. Thomas More, San Antonio
Chavarria, Doroteo, Sacred Heart, Floresville
Chavez, Hugo V., St. Luke, San Antonio
Ciarrochi, Jerome, (Retired)
Clancey, Patrick, The Patrician Movement, San Antonio
Clayton, Brian J., St. Francis of Assisi, San Antonio
Colley, Earl M., St. Monica, Converse, TX
Contreras, Larry, Holy Spirit, McAllen
Correa, Robert G., Prince of Peace, San Antonio
Courtney, Edward F., Our Lady of Perpetual Help, Selma, TX
Criado, Marcos, Immaculate Conception, San Antonio
Crosby, Alan, Blessed Sacrament, Poth
Cruz, Robert, San Juan de los Lagos, San Antonio
Cruz, Roberto, St. Mary's, Somerset
Cuellar, Pedro Luz, St. Matthew, San Antonio
Cunningham, W. Patrick, Holy Spirit, San Antonio
D'Agostino, Michael, St. Helena, San Antonio
Dapilmoto, Wilfredo M., St. Joan of Arc, Kirby
De Hoyos, Richard, St. Peter Prince, San Antonio
De La Portilla, Gilbert C., St. Philip, San Antonio
DeCuir, Harold, Sacred Heart Cathedral, San Angelo
DeLaGarza, Gustavo, (On Leave)
DeLaGarza, Ricardo, Divine Providence, San Antonio
DeLeon, Joseph L., (Diocese of Harrisburg, PA)
Delgado, Juan Jose, St. Patrick, San Antonio
Diaz, Jose G., St. John Berchmans, San Antonio
Dillard, Henry, (On Leave)
Dirksen, Kenneth, Sacred Heart, Uvalde
Domingues, Charles, Notre Dame, Kerrville
Donaho, Scott, Jr., Sacred Heart, Floresville
Donias, Justo, (Unassigned)
Ebner, Eugene, St. Louis, Castroville
Edminson, Richard, St. John Evangelist, Hondo
Edwards, Larry, Our Lady of Guadalupe, Helotes
Elliot, Robert R., St. James, Seguin
Enriquez, Marcos, (On Leave)
Espinosa, Jose R., (On Leave)
Espinosa, Juan, St. Brigid, San Antonio
Espinosa, Robert, St. Rose of Lima, San Antonio
Estrada, Melchor, (Unassigned)
Exparza, James, St. Matthew, San Antonio
Falcon, Adrian, Our Lady of Guadalupe, Del Rio
Felan, Ruben, Our Lady of Guadalupe, San Antonio
Fernandez, Elmer, Good Shepherd, Schertz
Fertitta, J. V., Sr., Blessed Sacrament, San Antonio
Fey, Fred, Sts. Peter & Paul, New Braunfels
Fikac, Frank J., Sts. Peter & Paul, New Braunfels
Flores, Federico, Sacred Heart, Uvalde
Fox, Thomas J., St. Matthew's, San Antonio
Fraga, Jesse, Our Lady of Sorrows, San Antonio
Franklin, Thomas M., St. Francis of Assisi, San Antonio
Friesenhahn, Clifford, Our Lady of Perpetual Help, Selma
Frisina, Patrick, St. Brigid, San Antonio
Galan, Robert, Jr., St. Joan of Arc, Kirby
Gallardo, Frank, Our Lady of Grace, San Antonio
Gallegos, Valentine, Sacred Heart, San Antonio
Galvan, Jesse C., St. Anthony Mary Claret, San Antonio
Galvan, Robert, (Unassigned)
Garcia, Arturo, St. Lawrence, San Antonio
Garcia, Bennie, St. Andrew, Pleasanton
Garcia, Hector, Sacred Heart, Uvalde
Garcia, Julio, III, San Fernando Cathedral, San Antonio
Garza, Albert G., (Retired)
Garza, Ernesto, St. Matthew, San Antonio
Garza, Jimmy, Our Lady of Mt. Carmel, San Antonio
Garza, Lionel, Jr., (Retired)
Garza, Pedro F., San Fernando Cathedral, San Antonio
Garza, Robert M., St. Luke, San Antonio
Gimenez, Benjamin, St. Mary's, Stockdale
Goebel, Joseph E., St. Mary Magdalen, Brackettville
Gomez, Gaspar, St. Monica, Converse
Gomez, Richard, Resurrection of the Lord, San Antonio
Gonzalez, Amador, St. Bonaventure
Gonzalez, Gerald, St. Leo, San Antonio
Gonzalez, Richard, St. Luke, San Antonio
Gordon, Ralph, (Unassigned)
Gorman, John J., Good Shepherd, Schertz
Gorman, Robert, SS. Peter & Paul, New Braunfels
Gorton, Everett D., (Retired)
Graf, John E., (Retired)
Greer, Jesse R., Church of the Holy Spirit, San Antonio
Guerra, Ralph E., Sacred Heart, Floresville
Guevara, Eusebio, St. Matthew's, Jourdanton
Gustowski, Paul, St. Helena's, San Antonio
Gutierrez, Pedro, Our Lady of Guadalupe, Helotes
Gutierrez, Ramon, (On Leave)
Gutierrez, Trinidad, St. Alphonsus, San Antonio
Hansbauer, Eugene, St. Luke, San Antonio
Heimer, Louis H., Our Lady of Perpetual Help, Selma
Henson, Archibald, St. Louis, Castroville
Herbert, David L., Sacred Heart, Von Ormy
Hernandez, Elieser, Our Lady of Guadalupe, Del Rio
Hernandez, Gilbert S., St. Mark the Evangelist, San Antonio
Hernandez, Jose D., St. Lawrence, San Antonio
Herrera, Genaro M., St. Joseph's (South San), San Antonio
Herrera, Ramon, (On Leave)
Hewson, Jim H., St. Francis Assisi, San Antonio
Heye, Paul F., St. Brigid, San Antonio
Hinojosa, Antonio, Sacred Heart, Uvalde
Hinojosa, Fidel, St. Bonaventure, San Antonio
Hinojosa, Fortunato, (Retired)
Hinojosa, Reynaldo G., Sr., Our Lady of the Atonement, San Antonio
Hobbs, John R., St. Cecilia, San Antonio
Hoelscher, Wilbur L., St. Matthew's, San Antonio
Holmstrom, Joseph, (Retired)
Houle, Thomas W., Prince of Peace, San Antonio
Houlihan, Timothy, Our Lady of Guadalupe, Helotes, TX
Huerta, Hipolito, St. Anthony of Padua, San Antonio
Huizar, Ernest, St. James, San Antonio
Hunsucker, Paul, St. Thomas the Apostle, Canyon Lake
Huttinger, John X., St. Joan of Arc, Kirby
Ibarra, Daniel A., Sacred Heart, Uvalde
Imburgia, Scott, St. Dominic, San Antonio
Jasso, Reynaldo, St. Rose of Lima, San Antonio
Jiminez, Raymond F., Mission Concepcion, San Antonio
Jorgensen, J. D., Blessed Sacrament, San Antonio
Kanter, Kevin, St. Padre Pio of Pietrelcina, San Antonio
Karam, Jack, St. Mary's, Stockdale
Kattengell, Leon E., (On Leave)
Kaufold, Harold "Sonny", Notre Dame, Kerrville
Kearns, W. Daniel, St. Benedict, San Antonio
Keller, Alois, Jr., (Retired)
King, Charles D., St. Anthony Mary Claret, San Antonio
Klein, Curtis, St. Anthony, Harper
Klein, Patrick, St. Mary, Fredricksburg
Knopp, Kenneth P., (Retired)
Knox, Beck E., SS. Peter & Paul, New Braunfels
Kolodzie, Stanley, (Retired)
Kozar, Jerome P., St. Anthony Mary Claret, San Antonio
Krupa, Joseph, (On Leave)
Kusenberger, Robert, Sacred Heart, Del Rio
Kutschenreuter, Norman, St. Matthew's, San Antonio
La Combe, Paul B., (Retired)
Lafuente, Francisco, St. Margaret Mary, San Antonio
Lamm, Wilfred, (Retired)
Lammons, Charles, St. Benedict, San Antonio
Lara, Rafael, St. Matthew, San Antonio
Laskowski, Norbert C., Holy Trinity, San Antonio
Lauer, Donald E., (Retired)
Leal, Ernesto T., (Retired)
Legendre, James F., St. Joseph, Honey Creek, Spring Branch
Lewis, Brian Anthony, St. Vincent de Paul, San Antonio
Limas, Heriberto "Eddie", Prince of Peace, San Antonio
Limones, Manuel R., St. Joseph, Del Rio
Link, John Dennis, St. Anthony, Harper
Lira, Antonio, St. Rose of Lima, San Antonio
Lira, Rodolfo, Toledo, OH
Longoria, Leobardo, (Retired)
LoTurco, Guy S., Holy Trinity, San Antonio
Lucio, Jesus, Jr., St. Martin de Porres, San Antonio
Ludolph, Anthony, Our Lady of Guadalupe, Helotes
Maldonado, Gilbert M., St. Clare, San Antonio
Marin, Arturo, Prince of Peace, San Antonio
Marques, Steven J., St. Mark the Evangelist, San Antonio
Martinez, Frank, Blessed Sacrament, San Antonio
Martinez, John, (Unassigned)
Martinez, Jose Angel, Resurrection, San Antonio
Martinez, Juan A., Notre Dame, Kerrville
Martinez, Juan G., (Retired)
Mechler, Gerardo A., St. Margaret Mary, San Antonio
Medina, Ricardo, St. Lawrence, San Antonio
Medrano, Rudy C., St. Timothy, San Antonio
Menchaca, Jose, St. Martin De Porres, San Antonio
Mendez, Ernest, SS. Peter and Paul, New Braunfels
Mendiola, Gabriel, St. Matthew, San Antonio
Mendoza, Raymundo V., St. Joseph, Del Rio
Merino, Reynaldo Q., Our Lady of Grace, San Antonio
Meyers, Joseph L., (Retired)
Micek, Jerome, Holy Trinity, San Antonio
Michel, John A., St. Pius X, San Antonio
Miller, John K., St. Anthony, Elmendorf
Miller, Mark C., Indianapolis, IN
Miller, Myles, (Diocese of Fort Worth)
Miller, Paul, (Retired)
Moczygemba, Zafirin, St. Margaret Mary, San Antonio
Morales, Cayetano, Our Lady of Perpetual Help, New Braunfels
Moreno, Alfonso, Sacred Heart, Gonzales
Moreno, Florencio, Jr., St. Clare, San Antonio
Moreno, John J., St. Philip's, Smiley & Nixon
Moreno, Jose F., Our Lady of Angels, San Antonio
Mueller, Leon, (Retired)
Munoz, Mike R., Mission San Jose, San Antonio
Munoz, Roy Y., St. Alphonsus, San Antonio
Muraida, Daniel, St. Paul's, San Antonio
Navarro, Ruben W., St. Raymond Pennafort, Leakey
Nealis, Michael F., St. Matthew, San Antonio
Nelson, Robert W., (Retired)
Neville, Richard F., Jr., Randolph, A.F.B., San Antonio

Nichols, Jackey Don, St. Luke, San Antonio
Nickel, Kenneth F., St. Joseph, Honey Creek & Spring Branch
Novian, Donald, (On Leave)
Ocampo, Jose L., St. Gerard, San Antonio
Olivares, Jesse, (Unassigned)
Olivares, Peter, St. Henry, San Antonio
Orr, James, Our Lady of Atonement, San Antonio
Ortega, Sylvester, St. Jude, San Antonio
Ostaszewski, Chester R., St. Rose of Lima, San Antonio
Pacheco, Alvino, St. Leo, San Antonio
Padilla, Juan R., O.L., Guadalupe, Del Rio
Patlan, Antonio, St. Martin de Porres, San Antonio
Patlan, Pedro, St. Paul, San Antonio
Peche, William, Holy Spirit, San Antonio
Pedroza, Doroteo E., San Fernando, San Antonio
Perez, Julio T., (Diocese of Fort Worth)
Perez, Miguel, Jr., St. Joseph, Devine
Perez, Oscar, Mission San Francisco de la Espada, San Antonio
Perry, Frank J. "Chip", III, San Jose Mission, San Antonio
Pope, Charles F., Sr., St. Clare, San Antonio
Pratt, Gilbert, (Retired)
Prevott, Raymond, (Retired)
Quaderer, Daniel D., Our Lady of Guadalupe, Helotes
Ramirez, Albert, Our Lady of Angels, San Antonio
Ramirez, Victor, (Retired)
Ramos, Bartolo, St. Jude, San Antonio
Raso, James, St. John Berchmans, San Antonio
Rayburg, Paul M., St. Peter, Boerne
Resendiz, Benito, St. Martin de Porres, San Antonio
Reyes, Arsenio, Jr., Santo Nino de Cebu, San Antonio
Riojas, Francisco, St. Philip, Smiley & Nixon
Rios, Roberto, St. Matthew, San Antonio
Rist, Wesley Raymond, St. Ann, La Vernia
Rivera, Anthony, St. Matthew, San Antonio
Rivera, Gilbert, St. Joan of Arc, Kirby
Rodriguez, Antonio G., Basilica of Little Flower, San Antonio
Rodriguez, Carlos, Sacred Heart, Von Ormy
Rodriguez, Jesus, St. John Berchmans, San Antonio
Rodriguez, Roger, Sacred Heart, Del Rio, TX
Rodriguez, Rudolph, Sacred Heart, San Antonio
Rodriguez, Santiago, San Jose Mission, San Antonio
Rosas, Gabriel J., St. Margaret Mary, San Antonio
Rosas, Roberto, St. Thomas More, San Antonio
Ruiz, Roberto R., Espada Mission, San Antonio
Salazar, Filomeno, St. Joseph, Del Rio
Salazar, George, Sr., Resurrection of the Lord, San Antonio
Salazar, Gilberto, Sacred Heart, Uvalde
Salazar, Marcus, Immaculate Heart of Mary, Pearsall
Salazar, Richard B., Holy Rosary, San Antonio
Salinas, Alberto, San Juan DeLos Lagos, San Antonio
Salinas, Carlos, (Retired)
Sanabria, Agripino, Prince of Peace, San Antonio
Sanchez, Albert, St. Paul, San Antonio
Sanchez, Jose H., St. Philip of Jesus, San Antonio
Sandoval, Carlos, Our Lady of Guadalupe, San Antonio
Sandoval, Jose F., St. John Berchmans, San Antonio
Santana, Efrain, St. Joseph, Del Rio
Scarbo, David B., Sacred Heart, Del Rio
Schoellman, John J., St. John Evangelist, Hondo
Schroeder, William, SS. Peter and Paul, New Braunfels
Schwartze, John, SS. Peter & Paul, New Braunfels
Sekinger, Eugene E., Holy Spirit, San Antonio
Seymour, Warren V., (Retired)
Shoemake, William, (Diocese of Austin)
Simmonds, William I., St. Anthony of Padua, San Antonio
Stancombe, Leonard, St. Helena, San Antonio
Stein, Robert J., St. Stanislaus, Bandera
Stenstrom, James, St. Peter the Apostle, Boerne
Stewart, Wilbert, St. Dominic, San Antonio
Stockton, Ree, St. Dominic, San Antonio
Stokes, Leslie, (Diocese of Phoenix)
Suniga, Jose A., St. Patrick, San Antonio
Svatek, Anton, (Retired)
Swift, Thomas N., (Retired)
Tamez, Javier, (On Leave)
Tate, Timothy M., Sr., St. Thomas More, San Antonio
Telfer, James, (On Leave)
Terry, Frank, (Retired)
Thayer, Robert, St. Anthony, Elmendorf
Thornberry, William, Our Lady of Guadalupe, Helotes
Tijerina, Salvador, St. Joseph, Dilley
Torres, George R., St. Joseph, Devine
Torres, Thomas, San Jose Mission, San Antonio
Townsend, Eugene, St. Pius X, San Antonio
Trevino, Jimmie, St. Dominic, San Antonio
Trevino, Jose S., St. Luke Loire, Pleasanton
Trujillo, Jose M., (Diocese of Austin)
Uriegas, Gonzalo, (Retired)
Valdez, Oscar J., St. Luke, San Antonio
Van Dyke, Ronnie, St. Joseph, Del Rio
Varela, JoaQuin, Our Lady of Guadalupe, Helotes
Vasquez, Eleodoro, San Juan de Los Lagos, San Antonio
Vick, George, Jr., Good Shepherd, Schertz
Villanueva, Luis, St. Joseph, Devine
Villareal, Ricardo, St. Cecilia, San Antonio
Von Allmen, Charles, St. James, San Antonio
Wasniewski, Michael S., (Unassigned)
Wehman, Ben, Sts. Peter and Paul, New Braunfels
Weissler, Gilbert, (Retired)
Wells, Richard, St. Peter The Fisherman, Von Ormy
Werner, Keith N., (Retired)
White, George, (Retired)
Wittig, Evan, Holy Spirit, San Antonio
Ybarra, Hermengildo Rey, St. Leonard, San Antonio
Ybarra, Raymond, Holy Family, New Braunfels
Zamora, David, Our Lady of Guadalupe, San Antonio
Zapata, Thomas, (On Leave)
Zepeda, Ernest G., Our Lady of Guadalupe, Helotes

INSTITUTIONS LOCATED IN THE ARCHDIOCESE

[A] SEMINARIES, ARCHDIOCESAN

SAN ANTONIO. *Assumption Seminary aka Assumption-St. John's Seminary* 2600 W. Woodlawn Ave., P.O. Box 28240, 78228. Tel: 210-734-5137; Fax: 210-734-2324. Web: www.assumptionseminary.org. Revs. Lawrence J. Christian, Rector, Devel. & Admin.; Arturo Cepeda, S.T.D., Vice Rector; Jeffrey Pehl, Formation Faculty Coord. & Dean of Men; John Collet, O.M.I., Spiritual Dir.; Victor Carillo, Vice Rector for Collegians; Jaime Robledo, Liturgy Dir.; James S. Tucker, S.S., Dir. Spirituality; Mrs. Amy Zuberbueler, Dir. Music; Sr. Carmen Terese Lazo, M.C.D.P., Dir. Multicultural Formation; Rev. Msgr. Joseph A. Lopez, Pastoral Formation; Chris Stravitsch, M.A., Dir. Collegians & Admissions; Revs. Arnold Ibarra, Formation Faculty; Rafael Ramirez, Formation Faculty.

The Seminary of the Assumption of the Blessed Virgin Mary-St. John of San Antonio, TX Priests 9; Sisters 2; Seminarians 82; Domestic Dept.: Josephine Sisters (Mexico City, Mexico) 14; Lay Staff 3.

Diaconate Program, Pastoral Center, P.O. Box 28410, 78228-0410. Tel: 210-734-2620; Fax: 210-734-0231. Email: diacprog@swbell.net. Rev. James Rutkowski, S.T.L., Dir.

[B] SEMINARIES, RELIGIOUS OR SCHOLASTICATES

SAN ANTONIO. *Congregation of Holy Cross - Formation Community* (1989) Bro. Charles Andersen Residence, 320 Brahan Blvd., 78215-1020. Tel: 210-223-9117. Bro. Jerome Donnelly, C.S.C., Dir. Brothers 6.

Dominican Missionaries for the Deaf Apostolate House of Studies, 143 Honeysuckle Ln., 78213-2527. Tel: 210-627-6303. Web: dominicanmissionaries.org. Rev. Thomas Coughlin, O.P.Miss., Prior Gen.; Bro. Adam Zawadzki, O.P.Miss., Subprior. Seminarians 5; Postulants 3.

George Sexton House of Studies (Theology), 314 E. King's Hwy., 78212. Tel: 210-735-7318; Fax: 210-734-3150. Revs. John Staak, O.M.I.; Raul Salas, O.M.I. Missionary Oblates of Mary Immaculate, United States Province. Scholastic Brothers 13.

MSF Formation Community, 104 Cas-Hills Dr., 78213-3322. Tel: 210-344-9145; Fax: 210-344-9146. Web: www.catholic-forum.com/msf. Rev. James Wasser, M.S.F., Dir. of Formation. Brothers 1; Candidates 3.

San Antonio de Padua Friary (Franciscan Friars), 318 Oblate Dr., 78216-6632. Tel: 210-377-2518. Email: charlieofm@aol.com. Web: www.olgofm.org. Revs. Charlie Martinez, O.F.M., Supr.; Jack Clark Robinson, O.F.M., Dir. Formation. Priests 2; Brothers 1; Seminarians 4.

San Damiano Friary, Prenovitiate House of Formation, 1104 Kentucky Ave., 78201. Tel: 210-734-4962. Revs. Gerard Herman, O.F.M.Conv.; Phillip G. Ley, O.F.M.Conv.; Camillus Gott, O.F.M.Conv., Guardian & Dir. House of Formation; Lawrence Mattingly, O.F.M.Conv.; Gary W. Johnson, O.F.M.Conv.; Bros. Paul Clark, O.F.M.Conv.; Timothy Unser, O.F.M.Conv. Conventual Franciscan Friars. Pre-Novitiates 3; Professed 4.

[C] COLLEGES AND UNIVERSITIES

SAN ANTONIO. *St. Mary's University of San Antonio, Texas* (1852) One Camino Santa Maria, 78228-8572. Tel: 210-436-3722; Fax: 210-431-2226; 210-431-6864 (Alumni Relations). Email: ccotrell@stmarytx.edu. Web: www.stmarytx.edu. Dr. Charles Cotrell, Pres.; Rev. Rudy Vela, S.M., Vice Pres. Mission & Identity; Dr. Andre Hampton, J.D., Interim Vice Pres. Academic Affairs; Rebeckah J. Day, Vice Pres. Admin. & Finance; Ms. Katherine Sisoian, Vice Pres. Student Devel.; Suzanne Petrusch, Vice Pres. Enrollment Mgmt.; Dr. Janet Dizinno, Dean School of Humanities & Social Sciences; Thomas B. Gavin, Vice Pres. Univ. Advancement; Dr. Tanja Singh, Ph.D., Interim Dean, Bill Greehey School of Business; Dr. Winston Erevelles, Ph.D., Dean School of Science, Engineering and Technology; Dr. Henry Flores, Dean Graduate School; Mr. Charles Cantu, Dean School of Law; Chad Bridwell, Dir. Admissions; Dr. H. Palmer Hall, Dir. Louis J. Blume Academic Library; Sr. Gretchen Trautman, F.M.I., Marianist Leadership; Robert Hu, Dir. Law Library; Dr. Grace Walle, F.M.I., Chap. Law School; Revs. Norbert C. Brockman, S.M.; Conrad J. Kaczkowski, S.M., Ph.D. (Retired); John A. Leies, S.M., S.T.D.; George T. Montague, S.M.; W. Franz Schorp, S.M.; Richard Wosman, S.M.; Charles Stander, S.M. Conducted by the Society of Mary., (Coed) Priests 11; Brothers 10; Sisters 1; Lay Teachers 340; Students 3,882.

The Mexican American Catholic College (1972) 3115 W. Ashby Pl., 78228-5104. Tel: 210-732-2156; 886-893-6222; Fax: 210-732-9072. Web: www.maccsa.org. Most Rev. Michael D. Pfeifer, O.M.I., Chm.; Arturo Chavez, Ph.D., Pres. & CEO. The Mexican American Catholic College (MACC)'s mission is to empower and educate leaders for service in a culturally diverse Church and society by offering a bi-literate, multicultural formation program that can lead to a BA and MA degree in Pastoral Ministry. MACC offers a holistic program that integrates the four elements of ministry formation — the human, spiritual, intellectual and pastoral dimensions; MACC has been a leader in higher education since 1972, providing excellent courses that are accepted for credit by many accredited institutions. The Continuing Education courses and workshops continue to prepare leaders for service in Hispanic and Multicultural communities; The Mexican American Catholic College sponsors a Ministry Formation Program with Hispanic Ministry for the 21st Century, Hispanic Pastoral Ministry, and Language Studies which is accredited by the United States Conference of Catholic Bishops Commission on Certification and Accreditation, 3211 S. Lake Dr., Ste. 317, St. Francis, WI 53235 (414-486-0139). Religious 2; Lay Teachers 17; Staff 19.

Oblate School of Theology (1903) (Coed) (Graduate Theology), 285 Oblate Dr., 78216-6693. Tel: 210-341-1366; Fax: 210-341-4519. Email: info@ost.edu. Web: www.ost.edu. Rev. Ronald Rolheiser, O.M.I., Pres.; Sr. Elaine Brothers, O.S.F., Ph.D., Vice Pres. Academic Affairs & Dean; Mrs. Rose A. Marden, M.T.S., M.Div., Continuing Educ. Dean; Mr. James Oberhausen, Dir. Admissions, Registrar; Mr. Morris Lim, Dir. Facilities; Mr. Rene Espinosa, Vice Pres. Finance & Human Resources; Ms. Elva Barba, Admin. Asst. Pres. Conducted by the Missionary Oblates of Mary Immaculate. Priests 19; Sisters 6; Brothers 1; Lay Professors 8; Students 254.

Faculty: Revs. Warren A. Brown III, O.M.I., J.C.D., Exec. Vice Pres.; Ken Hannon, O.M.I., Ph.D.; David Kalert, O.M.I., S.T.L., Ph.L., M.S.Ed., Vice Pres. Inst. Advancement; Jan Piotr Klak, Ph.L., S.T.L.; Rev. Msgr. Joseph A. Lopez; Revs. John M. Makothakat, Ph.D., S.T.D., J.C.D. (Retired); Ray John Marek, O.M.I., D.Min.; William J. Meyer, S.M., D.Min., Dir. Ministry to Ministers. Tel: 210-349-9928; Francis Kelly Nemeck, O.M.I., S.S.D.; Leopoldo G. Perez, O.M.I., S.T.D., M.Div., Co-Dir. M. Div. Prog.; Joseph LaBelle, O.M.I., S.T.D., Dir. M.A. Sp. Prog.; Stephen K. Sherwood, C.M.F., S.T.D.; James S. Tucker, S.S.; Rocky Grimard, O.M.I., Dir. Opers.; Robert E. Wright, O.M.I., Ph.D., Co-Dir. M. Div. Prog.; Ronald W. Young, O.M.I., S.T.D.; Sisters Maria Cimperman, O.S.U., Ph.D.; Sarah Ann Sharkey, O.P., Ph.D.; Ms. Bonnie Le Melle Abadie, Dir. Lay Ministry; Mrs. Rita Velasquez, Asst. Dir. Lay Ministry; Mrs. Sally T. Gomez-Jung, M.T.S., M.A., Dir. T.F.E.; Sisters Susan Pontz, S.S.C.M., IT Dir.; Laura Gonzalez,

S.S.C.J., Asst. Dir. Ministry to Ministers; Dr. Ronald Quillo, Th.D., Dir. M.A.(TH) Prog.; Dr. Ed Alcott; Rev. J. Edward Owens, O.SS.T., Asst. Dir. D. Min. Prog.; Dr. Scott Woodward; Dr. Greg Zuschlag, Ph.D.; Sr. Linda Gibler, O.P., Assoc. Academic Dean.

Our Lady of the Lake University, 411 S.W. 24th, 78207-4689. Tel: 210-434-6711; Fax: 210-438-9496. Email: pollt@lake.ollusa.edu. Web: www.ollusa.edu. Dr. Tessa Martinez Pollack, Ph.D., Pres.; David C. Estes, Ph.D., Exec. Vice Pres.; Gloria Urrabazo, Vice Pres. Mission & Ministry; Allen R. Klaus, B.B.A., Vice Pres. Finance & Facilities; Michael E. Acosta, Ph.D., Vice Pres. Enrollment; Paul T. Kettering, Vice Pres. Inst. Advancement; Mrs. Susan Schleicher, Chief of Staff; Helen J. Streubert, Ed.D., Vice Pres. Academic Affairs; Judith Larson, Librarian. Sponsored by Congregation of Divine Providence. Sisters 5; Lay Teachers 120; Students 2,642.

Campus Ministry Team: Dr. Peter Zoskafos, Ph.D., Dir.

The United Colleges of San Antonio (A Consortium of Catholic Colleges in San Antonio), 285 Oblate Dr., 78216. Tel: 210-341-1366; Fax: 210-341-4519. Rev. Ronald Rolheiser, O.M.I.; Charles L. Cotrell, Ph.D.; Dr. Louis Agnese Jr., Ph.D.; Dr. Tessa Martinez Pollack, Ph.D.

University of the Incarnate Word, 4301 Broadway, 78209. Tel: 210-829-6000; Fax: 210-829-3901. Email: douge@uiwtx.edu. Web: www.uiw.edu. Dr. Louis J. Agnese Jr., Ph.D., Pres.; Sr. Kathleen Coughlin, C.C.V.I., Vice Pres. Inst. Advancement; Douglas B. Endsley, M.B.A., C.P.A., Vice Pres. Fin. & Technology; Dr. David Jurenovich, Ph.D., Vice Pres. Enrollment & Statistical Svcs.; Kevin B. Vichcales, Ph.D., Dean Graduate Studies & Research; Dr. Patricia Watkins, Ph.D., Vice Pres. Intl. Programs; Dr. Denise Doyle, Ph.D., Provost; Dr. Renee Moore, Ph.D., Dean Campus Life; Andrea Cyterski, Dean of Enrollment; Robert Kunczt, Dir. Human Resources; Dr. Shawn Daly, Ph.D., Dean Business Admin.; Dr. Arcelia Johnson-Fannin, Ph.D., Dean Pharmacy; Elizabeth F. Villarreal, Dir. Campus Min.; Sr. Eilish Ryan, Th.D., Dir. Pastoral Institute; Dr. Bobbye Fry, Ed.D., Registrar; Dr. Robert Connelly, Ph.D., Dean Humanities, Arts & Social Sciences; Dr. Glenn E. James, Ph.D., Dean Math, Science & Engineering; Dr. Kathleen Light, Ph.D., Dean Nursing & Health Professionals; Dr. Cheryl Anderson, Dir. Library Svcs.; Edith Cogdell, C.P.A., Comptroller; Dr. Cyndi Wilson Porter, Vice Pres. Extended Programs; Vincent Porter, Dean, School for Extended Studies; Rita Russ, Dean, Virtual Univ.; Dr. Hani Ghazi Birry, Dean of Optometry; Dan Ochoa, Dean, Univ. Preparatory Programs. Priests 1; Charity of the Incarnate Word 4; Lay Faculty 213; Students 7,166.

[D] HIGH SCHOOLS, ARCHDIOCESAN

SAN ANTONIO. *Antonian College Preparatory High School*, 6425 West Ave., 78213. Tel: 210-344-9265; Fax: 210-344-9267. Email: gsaenz@Antonian.org. Web: Antonian.org. Mr. Gilbert L. Saenz, Prin.; Rev. John G. Castro, O.M.I.; Marlene Graham, Librarian. (Coed) Priests 1; Deacons 1; Lay Teachers 50; Students 733.

St. Gerard Catholic High School, (Grades 8-12), 521 S. New Braunfels Ave., 78203. Tel: 210-533-8061; Fax: 210-533-3697. Email: royals1927@gmail.com. Web: www.stgerardsa.org. Very Rev. Kevin Fauz, C.M., V.U., Admin.; Maurice Abadie, Dir. Devel. & Alumni; Andrea Johnson, Prin.; Maria Villanueva, Librarian. Sisters 3; Lay Teachers 11; Students 114.

[E] HIGH SCHOOLS, REGIONAL

KERRVILLE. *Our Lady of the Hills Regional Catholic High School* (2002) 575 Peterson Farm Rd., 78028. Tel: 830-895-0501; Fax: 830-895-3470. Email: olh@ktc.com. Web: www.ourladyofthehills.org. Mr. Barry J. Neuburger, M.Ed., M.B.A., Prin.; Mary McWithey, Librarian. Lay Teachers 17; Total Enrollment 97.

NEW BRAUNFELS. *John Paul II High School*, 6720 FM 482, 78132. Andrew Iliff, Prin. Staff 10; Students 33.

[F] HIGH SCHOOLS, PRIVATE

SAN ANTONIO. *St. Anthony Catholic High School*, 3200 McCullough Ave., 78212-3099. Tel: 210-832-5600; 210-832-5603; Fax: 210-832-5615. Email: elgalind@uiwtx.edu. Web: www.sachs.org. Henry Galindo, Prin.; Rev. Henry Walker, O.M.I., S.T.L.; Douglas B. Endsley, M.B.A., C.P.A., Vice Pres. Business & Finance; Amanda Briggs Brack, Librarian. Priests 1; Sisters 1; Lay Teachers 31; Students 440.

Central Catholic High School, 1403 N. St. Mary's St., 78215-1785. Tel: 210-225-6794; Fax: 210-227-9353. Email: admissions@cchs-satx.org. Web: www.cchs-satx.org. Bro. Peter Pontolillo, S.M., Pres.; Mr. Edward Ybarra, Prin.; Revs. Donald Cowie, S.M.; Patrick McDaid, S.M. Priests 2; Brothers 9; Deacons 1; Lay Teachers 36; Students 526.

Healy Murphy Center, Inc., 618 Live Oak St., 78202. Tel: 210-223-2944; Fax: 210-224-1033. Email: dwatson@healymurphy.org. Douglas J. Watson, Exec. Dir. Day School for High School Students. Provides an alternative to the Regular School System. Sisters 3; Lay Teachers 17; Counselors 2; Nurses 1; On Campus Clinic: Nurses 1; Students 300; Childhood Development Department: Ages 6 wks - 5 yrs 110.

Holy Cross of San Antonio, (Grades 6-12), 426 N. San Felipe, 78228. Tel: 210-433-9395; Fax: 210-433-1666. Email: SAHCMAN@hotmail.com. Web: www.holycross-sa.org. Bro. Stanley Culotta, C.S.C., Pres.; Mr. Angel Cedillo, Prin.; Ms. Mary Huebscher, Librarian. Brothers of Holy Cross. Brothers 2; Lay Teachers 27; Students 415.

Incarnate Word High School, 727 E. Hildebrand Ave., 78212-2598. Tel: 210-829-3100; Fax: 210-829-3120. Web: www.incarnatewordhs.org. B.J. Nelsen, Prin.; Michiko Tonegawa, Librarian. Sisters 3; Brothers 1; Lay Teachers 41; Students 553.

Providence Catholic School, (Grades 6-12), 1215 N. St. Mary's St., 78215-1737. Tel: 210-224-6651; Fax: 210-224-6214. Email: abristol@providencehs.net. Web: www.providencehs.net. Anne Bristol, Pres.; Sr. Antoinette Billeaud, C.D.P., High School Prin.; Charlene Ibrom, Prep School Prin.; Stella Gonzalez, Librarian. Sisters 3; Lay Teachers 35; Students 350.

[G] ELEMENTARY SCHOOLS, PRIVATE

SAN ANTONIO. *St. Anthony's School*, (Grades PreK-8), 205 W. Huisache St., 78212. Tel: 210-732-8801; Fax: 210-732-5968. Email: kennedy@stanthonysa.org. Web: www.stanthonysa.org. John P. Kennedy, Ed.D., Prin.; Rev. Patrick Guidon, O.M.I.; Laurie Packard, M.L.S., Librarian. Priests 1; Sisters 1; Lay Teachers 40; Students 423.

St. John Bosco School (1944) (Grades K-8), 5630 W. Commerce St., 78237. Tel: 210-432-8011; Fax: 866-214-8083. Email: fmasuojbc@aol.com. Sr. Rosann Ruiz, F.M.A., Pres.; Mrs. Roxanne LeBlanc, Prin.; Linda Gonzalez, Librarian. Institute of the Daughters of Mary Help of Christians (Salesian Sisters of St. John Bosco)., Day School. Sisters 8; Lay Teachers 14; Students 305.

Mount Sacred Heart School, Inc., (Grades PreK-8), 619 Mount Sacred Heart Rd., 78216. Tel: 210-342-6711; Fax: 210-342-4032. Email: mcasto@msheagles.com. Web: www.mountsacredheart.com. Ms. Maria V. Casto, Prin.; Shantel Ramirez, Librarian. Sisters 5; Lay Teachers 28; Students 428.

**Rolling Hills Academy, Inc.* (1996) (Grades PreK-8), 21240 Gathering Oak, 78260. Tel: 210-497-0323; Fax: 210-497-5192. Email: info@rhacademy.org. Sergio Teran, Prin.; Revs. Thomas Salazar, L.C.; Javier Fayos, L.C.; Carmel Chapline, Librarian. Lay Teachers 21; Students 199.

PLEASANTON. *Our Lady of Grace*, 626 Market St., 78064. Margie Coleman, Prin. Staff 4; Students 34.

[H] GENERAL HOSPITALS

SAN ANTONIO. *Christus Santa Rosa Children's Hospital*, 333 N. Santa Rosa Blvd., 78207. Tel: 210-704-2011; Fax: 210-704-3632. Email: marcy.doderer@christushealth.org. Web: www.christussantarosa.org. Marcela Doderer, Regl. Vice Pres. & Admin. Owned and operated by Christus, Santa Rosa Health Care Corp. Licensed Beds 275; Total Staff 750; Patients Assisted Annually 160,000.

Christus Santa Rosa Health Care Corporation, 333 N. Santa Rosa Blvd., 78207. Tel: 210-704-2011; Fax: 210-704-3632. Web: www.christussantarosa.org. Don A. Beeler, Pres. & CEO; Rosario Perez, Mission, Integration, Outreach; Rich Woodley, Dir. Pastoral Ministry; Revs. Guillermo Casipong, C.I.C.M.; Roy Quioque, C.I.C.M.; Victor LaRoche, O.P. Health related activities Priests 3; Sisters 3; Staff 4,300; Bed Capacity 1,128; Patients Assisted Annually 400,000.

Christus Santa Rosa Hospital-City Centre, 333 N. Santa Rosa Blvd., 78207. Tel: 210-704-2011; Fax: 210-704-3632. Web: www.christussantarosa.org. Michael McBride, Regl. Vice Pres. & Admin. Owned and operated by Christus, Santa Rosa Health Care Corp. Licensed Beds 393; Patients Assisted Annually 69,000; Total Staff 1,135.

Christus Santa Rosa Hospital, Westover Hills Owned & operated by Christus Santa Rosa Health Care Corp., 11212 Hwy. 151, 78251. Tel: 210-703-8000. Bed Capacity 150; Staff 350.

Christus Santa Rosa Hospital-Medical Center, 2827 Babcock Rd., 78229. Tel: 210-705-6300; Fax: 210-705-6094. Email: Michael.McBride@ChristusHealth.org. Web: www.christussantarosa.org. Michael McBride, Regl. Vice Pres. & Admin. Bed Capacity 143; Staff 560; Patients Assisted Annually 39,000.

Christus Santa Rosa Rehabilitation Hospital (Part of CRSH - Medical Center), 2827 Babcock, 78229. Tel: 210-705-6100; Fax: 210-705-6028. Owned and operated by Christus Health, Santa Rosa Health Care Corp. Bed Capacity 35; Staff 120; Patients Assisted Annually 9,300.

San Fernando Health Care Centre of San Antonio, 2718 W. Woodlawn, 78228. Tel: 210-734-2620. Rev. Martin J. Leopold, Contact Person.

NEW BRAUNFELS. *Christus Santa Rosa Hospital-New Braunfels*, 600 N. Union Ave., 78130. Tel: 830-606-9111. Web: www.christussantarosa.org. Jim Wesson, Regl. Vice Pres. & Admin. Owned and operated by Christus, Santa Rosa Health Care Corp. Licensed Beds 132; Patients Assisted Annually 83,000; Total Staff 680.

[I] PROTECTIVE INSTITUTIONS

SAN ANTONIO. *Father Flanagan's Boys' Town of San Antonio*, 503 Urban Loop, 78204. Tel: 210-271-1010; Fax: 210-271-3333. Email: cook@boystown.org. Web: www.boystown.org. Ms. Janie Cook, Pres. Total Staff 41; Bed Capacity 49; Children Under Care 511.

Residential Center, 8400, 8401, 8402, 8405, 8406 Flanagan St., 78249. Tel: 210-271-1010; Fax: 210-271-3333. (For Children under 18) Staff 24; Bed Capacity 30; Children Served 63.

Family Preservation Services, 503 Urban Loop, 78204. Tel: 210-271-1010; Fax: 210-271-3333. Staff 17; Families Assisted 241.

St. Peter & St. Joseph Childrens' Home (1891) 919 Mission Rd., 78210. Tel: 210-533-1203; Fax: 210-533-6199. Web: www.stpjhome.org. James Castro, Exec. Dir. House Parent Staff 80; Administrative & Support Staff 36; Bed Capacity 139; Children Under Care (Ages Infant-17) 90; Total Assisted 400.

Seton Home, 1115 Mission Rd., 78210. Tel: 210-533-3504; Fax: 210-533-3467. Email: margretstarkey@setonhomesa.org. Web: www.setonhomesa.org. Margret Starkey, Exec. Dir. Bed Capacity 80; Total Assisted 168; Total Staff 52.

Visitation House Ministries, 945 W. Huisache, 78201. Tel: 210-735-6910; Fax: 210-738-8794. Web: www.vhmin.org. Sr. Cynthia Stacy, C.C.V.I., Dir. Operated by the Sisters of Charity of the Incarnate Word of San Antonio, TX., A nonprofit corporation chartered under the laws of the State of Texas; Provides a two year transitional housing program for homeless women and children, and training for women. Total Assisted 48; Staff 5; Capacity 20.

BOERNE. *Childrens' Inn*, 216 W. Highland Dr., 78006. Tel: 830-249-9456; Fax: 830-249-3327. Email: children@gvtc.com. Sr. Kathleen Kean, S.S.J., Co-Dir.; Marilyn Haider, Co-Dir. Provides foster care for children with special needs in a holistic setting. Total Assisted 7.

[J] DAY CARE CENTERS AND KINDERGARTENS

SAN ANTONIO. *St. Anthony Day Care Learning Center; Infant and Toddler Center*, 1707 Centennial Blvd., 78211. Tel: 210-924-4443; Fax: 210-924-4469. Email: salc@satx.rr.com. Sisters Mary Ann Domagalski, M.S.S.A., Admin.; Lucelia Sanchez, M.S.S.A., Dir. Sisters 2; Lay Staff 22; Children 140.

Blessed Sacrament Academy, (Grades Day Care-PreSchool), 1135 Mission Rd., 78210. Tel: 210-532-4731; Fax: 210-534-2882. Email: odilia@sbcglobal.net. Web: netnuns.com; blessedsacramentacademy.net. Sr. M. Odilia Korenek, I.W.B.S., Exec. Dir.

Child Development Center Tel: 210-532-5363; Fax: 210-532-2149. Carol Silva, Dir. Sisters of the Incarnate Word and Blessed Sacrament 1; Lay Teachers 29; Students 185; Support Staff 16.

Blessed Sacrament Learning Center, 227 Keller St., 78204. Tel: 210-223-5013; Fax: 210-444-0779. Email: teresitap@sbcglobal.net. Sr. Rita Pinedo, H.M.S.S., Dir. Mercedarian Sisters of the Blessed Sacrament. Sisters 2; Children 15.

Carmelite Learning Center, 2006 Martin Luther King Dr., 78203. Tel: 210-533-0651; Fax: 210-533-3910. Email: smf3964@yahoo.com. Sr. Maria Faustina, D.C.J., Dir. Attended from St. Patrick's Church. Carmelite Sisters of the Divine Heart of Jesus 3; Lay Staff 8; Day Care 80.

Immaculate Conception Kindergarten and Nursery, 2407 W. Travis St., 78207. Tel: 210-226-3934; Fax:

210-226-3934. Sr. Maria Del Carmen Sanchez, A.P.G., Dir. Sisters 4; Lay Staff 10; Kindergarten & Nursery Children 52.

[K] HOMES FOR AGED

SAN ANTONIO. *Casa De Padres*, 8520 Cross Mountain Tr. #100, 78255. Tel: 210-698-0175; Fax: 210-698-5138. Email: jengberg@gvtc.com. Mrs. Jeannine Engberg, Dir. Tel: 210-698-0175; 830-981-9192; Rev. Msgrs. Alois J. Goertz (Retired). Tel: 210-698-9067 No. 402; Roy Rihn (Retired). Tel: 210-698-0287 No. 301; Vincent Fecher (Retired). Tel: 210-698-3923 No. 302; Albert Hubertus (Retired). Tel: 210-698-8682 No. 1101; Joseph Petsch (Retired). Tel: 210-698-7055 No. 702; Leo Martinez (Retired). Tel: 210-698-9875 No. 1002; John Wagner (Retired). Tel: 210-698-1332 No. 202; Lawrence Steuben (Retired). Tel: 210-288-0988 No. 201; Rev. Michael McManus (Retired), No. 1102; Rev. Msgr. Thomas Murphy (Retired), No. 1301; Rev. Leon B. Rubaj (Retired), No. 1202. Home for retired Priests of San Antonio. In Res. Rev. Msgr. Terence Nolan, J.C.L. Tel: 201-698-0349 No. 701.

St. Francis Nursing Home and Boarding Home for the Aged, 630 W. Woodlawn, 78212. Tel: 210-736-3177; Fax: 210-738-2221. Sisters Helen Haladyna, S.O.L.S., Pres. of Corp.; Agnes Bochenek, S.O.L.S., Admin. Seraphic Sisters of Our Lady of Sorrows., Home for the Aged and Convalescents. Sisters 11; Bed Capacity 143; Total Staff 150; Total Assisted 155.

**Franciscan Communities Villa de San Antonio*, 8103 N. Hollow, 78240. Tel: 210-558-7600; Fax: 210-881-2092. Email: joannmatyas@franciscancommunities.com. Web: www.franciscancommunities.com. Joann Matyas, Exec. Dir.; Amanda Bryan, Mgr. Admin. Svcs. Total Apartments 138; Staff 80; Assisted Living 55.

Incarnate Word Retirement Community, 4707 Broadway, 78209. Tel: 210-829-7561; Fax: 210-828-0020. Email: sftxnc@aol.com. Web: www.IwRetire.org. Mr. Steven E. Fuller, Exec. Dir.; Rev. Msgr. Thomas A. French, Chap. (Retired). For lay persons also. Total in Residence 265; Staff 220; Bed Capacity 299.

Marianist Residence: Skilled Nursing, 520 Fordham Ln., 78228-4821. Tel: 210-436-3771 (Nurses' Station); Fax: 210-431-4240. Email: lkaehler@stmarytx.edu. Bros. Lester Kaehler, S.M., Dir.; James Jaeckle, S.M., Sub Dir., Health Care Oper.; Revs. Paul Ryan, S.M. Tel: 210-436-3766; Herbert Pieper, S.M. Tel: 210-436-3773; August Biehl, S.M.; Joseph A. Tarrillion, S.M., D.Min.; Richard O'Shaughnessy, S.M.; Adolf Windish, S.M.; Michael Barber, S.M. Home for Infirm Marianist Brothers and Priests. Infirm Priests 7; Infirm Brothers 8; Total Assisted 29; Total Staff 43.

McCullough Hall Nursing Center, Inc. (1992) (Incorporated 2003) 603 S.W. 24th St., 78207-4696. Tel: 210-435-7711; Fax: 210-433-6600. Email: mmcgannon@mchall.org. Mary "Mimi" McGannon, B.S., M.A., Admin. Bed Capacity 51; Staff 52; Total Assisted 51.

Oblate Madonna Residence, 5722 Blanco Rd., 78216. Tel: 210-341-2350; Fax: 210-340-3732. Email: roblatemadonna@satx.rr.com. Revs. Michael Levy, O.M.I., Dir.; Charles Banks, O.M.I.; Richard Beck, O.M.I.; Rolland Bennett, O.M.I.; Charles Borgers, O.M.I.; Ronald Carignan, O.M.I.; Edward Cunningham, O.M.I.; William Dubuisson, O.M.I.; Leo Gauvin, O.M.I.; Jose Gago, O.M.I.; Jan Heemrood, O.M.I., S.S.L.; Richard A. Houlahan, O.M.I.; Henri Janssen, O.M.I.; Donald J. Joyce, O.M.I., M.Div.; Adolph Kaler, O.M.I.; Charles Krzewinski, O.M.I., Supr.; Alfred Lavoie, O.M.I.; John Mahoney, O.M.I.; John McGrath, O.M.I.; Clarence Menard, O.M.I.; James Miller, O.M.I.; Galeb Mokarzel, O.M.I.; Francis Pfeifer, O.M.I.; George Protopapas, O.M.I.; Charles Sellars, O.M.I.; Richard Sheehan, O.M.I.; John Sokolski, O.M.I.; Francis Montalbano, O.M.I.; Robert Vreteau, O.M.I.; Gerald Weber, O.M.I.; Andrew Wueste, O.M.I.; Bros. Benjamin Juarez, O.M.I.; Valmond LeClerc, O.M.I. Missionary Oblates of Mary Immaculate., Home for retired Priests and Brothers. Bishops 1; Priests 27; Brothers 3; Total Staff 33; Assisted Living 10; Bed Capacity 38. In Res. Most Rev. Thomas J. Flanagan, D.D., V.G.

Padua Place, 80 Peter Baque Rd., 78209. Tel: 210-826-7721; Fax: 210-824-4554. Email: paduaplace@missionaryservants.org. Sr. Rose Mary Martinez, M.S.S.A., Admin. Home for infirm and retired Priests and Brothers. Priests 13; Bed Capacity 17; Total Assisted Annually 17. In Res. Most Revs. Patrick F. Flores, D.D.; Bernard F. Popp, D.D. (Retired); Rev. Msgrs. Ramon V. Garcia; Sherrill Smith (Retired); Revs. Robert Bradley (CC) (Retired); John P. Buzga (E) (Retired); James Hoelscher (Retired); Francis Nelan, M.S.C.; Pablo Paniagua (Retired); Willy Verboomen, C.I.C.M. (Retired); Charles Zeyen, M.S.F.

KENEDY. *John Paul II Nursing Home*, 209 S. 3rd St., P.O. Box 359, 78119. Tel: 830-583-9841; Fax: 830-583-9458. Krystiana Sadlo, Admin. Seraphic Sisters of Our Lady of Sorrows 5; Residents 64; Independent Living 13; Total Staff 75.

[L] MONASTERIES AND RESIDENCES OF PRIESTS AND BROTHERS

SAN ANTONIO. *Casa Maria Marianist Community*, St. Mary's University, One Camino Santa Maria, #18, 78228-8518. Tel: 210-436-3066; Fax: 210-431-4216. Rev. Timothy Dwyer, S.M. Tel: 210-436-3242; Bros. Timothy Pieprzyca, S.M. Tel: 210-436-3513; Michael Sullivan, S.M. Tel: 210-436-3258; Dennis Bautista, S.M. Tel: 210-436-3775; Roberto Rivera, S.M. Tel: 210-431-2269; Brian Halderman, S.M., Dir. Tel: 210-436-3239; Bob Jones, S.M. Aspirants 2.

Casa Pasionista Guadalupe, 700 Waverly, 78201-6138. Tel: 210-736-5228; Fax: 210-737-6549. Email: clementecp@cs.com. Web: www.passionist.org. Rev. Clemente Barron, C.P.

Casa San Juan Marianist Community, 1701 Alametos, 78201. Tel: 210-734-6727; Fax: 210-738-0698. Email: GMontague@stmarytx.edu. Revs. George T. Montague, S.M., Dir.; Joseph Mary Marshall, S.M.

Central Catholic Marianist Community, 1403 N. St. Mary's St., 78215-1785. Tel: 210-225-1112; Fax: 210-227-9353. Email: jimburk@cchs-satx.org. Revs. Donald Cowie, S.M.; Joseph G. Rasky, S.M.; Gerald Haby, S.M. (Retired); Bro. James Burkholder, Dir. Priests 3; Brothers 4.

De Mazenod House (Faculty Residence), 7707 Madonna Dr., 78216. Tel: 210-349-8572; Fax: 210-349-8572. Revs. Warren A. Brown III, O.M.I., J.C.D., Supr.; Ken Hannon, O.M.I., Ph.D.; Ray John Marek, O.M.I., D.Min.; Joseph LaBelle, O.M.I., S.T.D.; David Kalert, O.M.I., S.T.L., Ph.L., M.S.Ed.; Henry Walker, O.M.I., S.T.L. Missionary Oblates of Mary Immaculate. Priests 6.

Discalced Carmelite Fathers of San Antonio, 906 Kentucky Ave., 78201-6097. Tel: 210-735-9127; Fax: 210-738-0818. Web: www.littleflowerbasilica.org. Bro. Joseph Le, O.C.D., Supr.; Revs. Luis G. Belmonte Luna, O.C.D.; James A. Curiel, O.C.D.; Jenaro De la Cruz, O.C.D.; Henry Bordeaux, O.C.D.; Juan Evangelista de Maria Inmaculada, O.C.D. Priests 4.

Dominican Priory of San Juan Macias, 210 St. Ann St., 78201-6357. Tel: 210-732-9526; 210-734-6688. Email: st-ann@juno.com. Revs. Andrew K. Kolzow, O.P., Prior; John J. Restropo, O.P.; Wayne Cavalier, O.P.; Joseph Determan, O.P., 5622 Evers Rd., #3501, 78238. Tel: 210-680-2806; Luis Roberto Aguilar, O.P.; Victor LaRoche, O.P.; John J. Markey, O.P. Priests 7.

Holy Cross Community, 426 N. San Felipe St., 78228. Tel: 210-434-9100; Fax: 210-433-1666. Email: SAHCMAN@hotmail.com. Web: www.holycross-sa.org. Rev. Lawrence A. LeVasseur, C.S.C.; Bro. Stanley Culotta, C.S.C., Dir. Priests 1; Brothers 4. *Bro. Charles Andersen Residence*, 320 Brahan Blvd., 78215. Tel: 210-223-9117; Fax: 210-223-2081. Bro. Jerome Donnelly, C.S.C., Dir. Brothers 6.

Holy Rosary Marianist Community, 159 Camino Santa Maria, 78228-4997. Tel: 210-433-6137; Fax: 210-433-2133. Email: cjanson@swbell.net. Rev. Christian A. Janson, S.M.; Bros. Richard Schrader, S.M.; Richard Thompson, S.M., Dir.; Ralph Newman, S.M.

Hospital Ministry House, 6111 Walking Gait, 78240. Tel: 210-437-0147. Rev. Nicholas Brown, S.C.J.

Joseph Gerard House, 222 Oblate Dr., 78216. Tel: 210-377-3462. Rev. Robert E. Wright, O.M.I., Ph.D. Tel: 210-348-0545.

Ligustrum Marianist Community, 253 W. Ligustrum Dr., 78228-4020. Tel: 210-433-9114; Fax: 210-433-9124. Email: rvela3@stmarytx.edu. Bro. Thomas Suda, S.M., Dir.; Revs. Rudy Vela, S.M.; Bernard Lee, S.M.

Marianist Residence, St. Mary's University, 520 Fordham Ave., 78228-4821. Tel: 210-436-3744; Fax: 210-436-3747. Email: lkaehler@stmarytx.edu. Bro. Lester Kaehler, S.M., Dir. Tel: 210-436-3745; Revs. John A. Leies, S.M., S.T.D. Tel: 210-436-3227; W. Franz Schorp, S.M. Tel: 210-431-2259. Priests 2; Brothers 13.

Marianist Vocation Ministry, One Camino Santa Maria, 78228-8556. Tel: 210-431-2193; Fax: 210-436-3724. Email: gtrautman@sm-usa.org. Web: marianist.com/vocations. Sr. Gretchen Trautman, F.M.I., Dir.

Missionaries of the Sacred Heart Sectional Headquarters of the Irish Province for California and Southern States., 123 W. Laurel St., 78212-4667. Tel: 210-226-5514; Fax: 210-226-5725. Email: magnoliamsc@sbcglobal.net. Revs. William Collins, M.S.C., Supr.; James Dudley, M.S.C.; James A. Harnan, M.S.C.; Jeremiah McCarthy, M.S.C.; Michael O'Brien, M.S.C.; Patrick O'Connor, M.S.C.; Patrick O'Shea, M.S.C.; Stephen White, M.S.C. *Religious Activities Office*, 3700 N. Capitol St. N.W., Washington, DC 20317. Tel: 202-882-1888.

Missionary Oblates of Mary Immaculate, Southwest Area Office, 327 Oblate Dr., 78216-6602. Tel: 210-349-1475; Fax: 210-349-7411. Email: swarea@omiusa.org. Web: www.omiusa.org. Revs. Warren A. Brown III, O.M.I., J.C.D., Regl. Councilor. Tel: 210-342-3492; Thomas Ovalle, O.M.I., Southwest Area Councilor. *Oblate Vocation Office*, 327 Oblate Dr., 78216-6602. Tel: 210-349-1475; 800-358-4394; Fax: 210-349-7411. Email: vocations@omiusa.org. Rev. Charles Banks, O.M.I., Province Vicar for Vocations. 214 Oblate Dr., 78216-6630. Revs. Hugo Van Den Bussche, O.M.I. Tel: 210-348-9045; John G. Castro, O.M.I. 218 Oblate Dr., 78216-6630. Rev. Ronald Rolheiser, O.M.I. Tel: 210-342-3492; Bro. Paul Hoemeke, O.M.I. 222 Oblate Dr., 78216. Rev. Robert E. Wright, O.M.I., Ph.D. Tel: 210-377-3462.

Missionhurst C.I.C.M. Residence, 1746 Donaldson, 78228. Revs. Francis Loos, C.I.C.M. Tel: 210-432-6062; Roy Milton Quiogue, C.I.C.M. Tel: 210-704-2849.

Oblate Benson Residence (Southwest Area), 334 W. Kings Hwy., 78212. Tel: 210-732-5162; Fax: 210-732-6143. Revs. Pat Guldon, O.M.I. Tel: 210-732-8024; Thomas Ovalle, O.M.I. Tel: 210-732-8771; Leo Perez, O.M.I. Tel: 210-735-5906; David Tarlizzo, O.M.I. Missionary Oblates of Mary Immaculate - Southwest Area. Priests 3.

Redemptorists of Texas-San Antonio #1, 1617 Iowa St., 78203. Tel: 210-313-6669; Fax: 210-533-0558. Email: monper@satx.rr.com. Revs. Monroe Perrier, C.Ss.R., Supr., 1523 Iowa St., 78203; Robert A. Ruhnke, C.Ss.R. Fax: 210-534-1280; Carl Schindler, C.Ss.R.; Francis Han Pham, C.Ss.R., 1523 Iowa St., 78203; John Farnik, C.Ss.R., 1523 Iowa St., 78203; Alton Carr, C.Ss.R., 1523 Iowa St., 78203; James E. Shea, C.Ss.R.; Nghia Cao, C.Ss.R.; Bro. Charles Fucik, C.Ss.R. (Province of Denver)

San Damiano Friary, 1104 Kentucky Ave., 78201. Tel: 210-734-4962. Revs. Phillip G. Ley, O.F.M.Conv.; Camillus Gott, O.F.M.Conv., Guardian; Gerald Herman, O.F.M.Conv.; Lawrence Mattingly, O.F.M.Conv.; Gary W. Johnson, O.F.M.Conv.; Bros. Paul Clark, O.F.M.Conv.; Tim Unser, O.F.M.Conv. Conventual Franciscan Friars.

Trinitarian Residence, 302 Oblate Dr., 78216. Tel: 210-465-7283. Rev. J. Edward Owens, O.SS.T.

Woodlawn Marianist Community, 3303 W. Woodlawn Ave., 78228. Tel: 210-436-0182; Fax: 210-436-0188. Email: rwosmansm@wosman.com. Revs. Norbert C. Brockman, S.M.; Charles Stander, S.M.; Patrick McDaid, S.M.; Richard Wosman, S.M. Priests 2; Brothers 4.

FALLS CITY. *Salvatorian Fathers Community of Texas*, 211 W. Meyer St., P.O. Box 158, 78113. Tel: 830-254-3539; Fax: 830-254-3530. Revs. Gregory Sawicki, S.D.S., Supr.; Grzegorz Szewczyk, S.D.S. (Poland); Stanislaw Oleksy, S.D.S.; Krzystof Bugno, S.D.S.; Eugeniusz Grytner, S.D.S.; Gabriel Kamienski, S.D.S.; Josef Musiol, S.D.S.; Kazimierz Oleksy, S.D.S.; Andrzej Waszczenko, S.D.S.; Thaddeus Tabak, S.D.S.; Dariusz Ziebowicz, S.D.S.

[M] CONVENTS AND RESIDENCES FOR SISTERS

SAN ANTONIO. *St. Anthony Convent*, 100 Peter Baque Rd., 78209. Tel: 210-824-4553; Fax: 210-824-4554. Web: missionaryservants.org. Sr. Mary Ann Domagalski, M.S.S.A., Supr. Motherhouse and Novitiate of the Missionary Servants of St. Anthony; St. Anthony Retreat Center; St. Anthony Learning Center; Padua Place. Sisters 3.

Blessed Sacrament Convent, 227 Keller St., 78204. Tel: 210-223-5013; Fax: 210-444-0779. Email: teresitap@sbcglobal.net. Sr. Teresita Paz, H.M.S.S., Supr. Mercedarian Sisters of the Blessed Sacrament. Sisters 13.

Blessed Sacrament and Incarnate Word Convent, 1135 Mission Rd., 78210. Tel: 210-534-8005; Fax: 210-534-2882. Email: odilia@sbcglobal.net. Sr. M. Odilia Korenek, I.W.B.S., Supr. Sisters of the Incarnate Word and Blessed Sacrament. Sisters 9.

St. Brigid's Convent, 5118 Loma Linda Dr., 78201. Tel: 210-733-0701; 210-738-1721; Fax: 210-785-2820. Email: brigidines@sbcglobal.net. Web: www.brigidine.org.au. Sr. Anne Drea, C.S.B., Regl. Coord. Regional House.; Address matters connected with congregation to the Regl. Coord. Sisters 15.

Carmelite Convent, 2006 Martin Luther King Dr., 78203. Tel: 210-533-0651; Fax: 210-533-3910. Email: smf3694@yahoo.com. Sr. M. Faustina, D.C.J., Supr. Carmelite Sisters of the Divine Heart of Jesus. Sisters 5.

Convent of the Sisters of the Holy Spirit and Mary Immaculate, 300 Yucca St., 78203. Tel: 210-533-5149; Fax: 210-533-3434. Email: holyspirit@shsp.org. Web: www.shsp.org. Sr. Miriam Mitchell, S.H.Sp., Gen. Supr. Motherhouse of the Sisters of the Holy Spirit and Mary Immaculate. Sisters 46.

Cordi-Marian Missionary Sisters, Cordi-Marian Villa, 11624 FM 471, #501, 78253. Tel: 210-798-8220; 210-688-3099; Fax: 210-798-8225. Email: mcormprov@aol.com. Web: cordi-marian.org. Sisters M. Teresa Cruz, M.C.M., Prov. Supr.; Christine Romo, M.C.M., Local Supr.; Celina Martin, M.C.M., Retreat Center; Rev. Christopher Udeani, C.M.F., Chap. Convent, Provincial House, Retirement and Retreat Center. Sisters 34.

Cordi-Marian Missionary Sisters Convent (1921) 2902 Morales St., 78207. Tel: 210-433-5064; Fax: 210-433-5064; 210-835-5003. Email: mcmalicia@aol.com. Sisters Alicia Macias, M.C.M., Supr. & Formation Provider; Oralia Anzola, M.C.M.; Ofelia Cervantez, M.C.M. Sisters 3; Novices 3.

Daughters of Charity Convent, 7603 Somerset Rd., 78211. Tel: 210-927-2795. Sr. Lucretia Burns, D.C., Supr. Daughters of Charity of St. Vincent de Paul. Sisters 4.

Eucharistic Franciscan Missionary Sisters, 558 Cumberland, 78204. Tel: 210-224-7993. Sr. Maria Flora Ramirez, M.E.F., Supr. Sisters 4.

Generalate of the Congregation of Divine Providence, 515 S.W. 24th St., 78207. Tel: 210-434-1866; Fax: 210-568-1050. Email: generalate@cdptexas.org. Web: www.cdptexas.org. Sr. Jane Ann Slater, Supr. Gen. Sisters 5.

Sophia Women's Learning Center Ida Ayala, Dir.

Mobile Ministry Sr. Bernadette Bezner, C.D.P., Dir. Sisters 2.

Hermanas Catequistas Guadalupanas Convent, 4110 S. Flores St., 78214. Tel: 210-532-9344; Fax: 210-532-9344. Sr. Teresa O. Rodriguez, H.C.G., Supr. Sisters 7.

Hermanas Josefinas, 2622 W. Summit Ave., 78228. Tel: 210-737-0584; Fax: 210-737-0584. Sr. Crispina Paraguirre, Regl. Delegate.

Casa Santa Maria de Guadalupe, 2622 W. Summit Ave., 78228. Tel: 210-737-0584; Fax: 210-737-0584. Sisters 4.

Communidad de la Asuncion, 3203 W. Ashby Pl., 78228. Tel: 210-734-0039. Sisters 10.

Casa San Jose (Retired Sisters), 402 John Adams Dr., 78228. Tel: 210-732-1973. Sisters 12.

Incarnate Word Generalate (1869) 4503 Broadway, 78209-6297. Tel: 210-828-2224; Fax: 210-828-9741. Email: yolanda.tarango@amormeus.org. Web: www.amormeus.org. Sr. Yolanda Tarango, C.C.V.I., Gen. Supr. General Administration of the Congregation of Sisters of Charity of the Incarnate Word. Total in Congregation 377; Total in U.S. Province 192.

Headwaters Coalition (San Antonio Headwaters Coalition, Inc.), 4503 Broadway, 78209. Tel: 210-828-2224; Fax: 210-828-9741. Web: www.headwaterscoalition.org. Lacey Halstead, Exec. Dir.

Womens Global Connection, 4106 Bretton Ridge, 78217. Tel: 210-653-7492. Email: dorthy.ettling@sbcglobal.net. Web: www.womensglobalconnection.org. Sr. Dorthy Ettlinger, C.C.V.I., Dir.

Incarnate Word Retirement Community, U.S. Province, 4707 Broadway, 78209-6215. Tel: 210-829-7561 (Retirement Center); Fax: 210-828-0020. Email: steve.fuller@iwretire.org. Web: www.iwretire.org. Mr. Steven Fuller, CEO; Thelma Martinez, Admin. Extended Care; Sr. Margaret Kelly, Asst. Coord. Extended Care; Alma Cosme, Dir.Community Relations; Rev. Msgr. Thomas A. French (Retired). Total in Residence 265.

Institute of the Daughters of Mary Help of Christians, Province of Mary Immaculate, 6019 Buena Vista St., 78237-1700. Tel: 210-432-0089; 210-432-0090; Fax: 210-432-4016. Email: sneavesfma@yahoo.com. Web: www.salesiansisterswest.org. Sr. Sandra Neaves, F.M.A., Prov. Supr. Salesian Sisters of St. John Bosco.

St. James Convent, 402 Nunes, 78225. Tel: 210-533-9659; Fax: 210-924-0201. Email: fmasuojames@gmail.com. Sr. Mary Link, F.M.A., Supr. Daughters of Mary Help of Christians (Salesian Sisters of St. John Bosco). Sisters 5.

St. John Bosco Convent, 5630 W. Commerce St., 78237. Tel: 210-432-8011; Fax: 866-214-8083. Email: fmasuojbc@stjohnbosco-satx.org. Sr. Rosann Ruiz, F.M.A., Supr. Daughters of Mary Help of Christians. Sisters 10.

St. Joseph's Convent - S.S.N.D. House of Formation, 2372 W. Southcross, 78211-1898. Tel: 210-923-2364; Fax: 210-924-2229. Email: dsiebenmorgen@yahoo.com. Sr. Dolores Marie Siebenmorgen, Coord. Sisters 4; Postulants 1.

Marianist Sisters Residence, 235 Ligustrum Dr., 78228. Tel: 210-433-5501; Fax: 210-433-0300. Email: EscobarFMI@yahoo.com. Web: www.marianistsisters.org. Sisters Evangeline Escobar, F.M.I., Prov.; Lavon Kampf, F.M.I., Dir. of Sisters. Centralhouse of the Congregation of the Daughters of Mary Immaculate. Marianist Sisters, (Community Dayton, OH). Sisters 16.

McCullough Hall Nursing Center, Inc., 603 S.W. 24th St., 78207-4696. Tel: 210-435-7711; Fax: 210-433-6600. Mary "Mimi" McGannon, B.S., M.A., Admin. Sisters 50.

Missionary Catechists of Divine Providence Central House and Admin. Offices, St. Andrew's Convent, 2318 Castroville Rd., 78237. Tel: 210-432-0113; Fax: 210-432-1709. Email: mainoffice-mcdp@yahoo.com. Sr. Mary Louise Barba, M.C.D.P., Supr. Gen. Sisters 41.

Missionary Sisters of Our Lady of Perpetual Help (M.P.S.), 427 Rigsby, 78210. Tel: 210-532-3546; Fax: 210-532-3546. Sr. Isaura Flores, M.P.S., Contact Person. Sisters 4.

Monastery of the Discalced Carmelite Nuns, 6301 Culebra & St. Joseph Way, 78238-4909. Tel: 210-680-1834; Fax: 210-680-3106. Email: saocdnun21@sbcglobal.net. Web: www.carmelsanantonio.org. Sr. Therese Leonard, O.C.D., Prioress. Sisters 7.

Our Lady of the Lake Convent Center, 515 S.W. 24th St., 78207. Tel: 210-434-1866; Fax: 210-431-9965. Sisters of Divine Providence., Home for retired Sisters of Divine Providence. Professed Sisters 56.

O.L.L. Convent Home for retired Sisters of Divine Providence Sisters Frances Lorene Lange, C.D.P., Coord.; Cathy Parent, C.D.P., Coord.; Ann Regina Ross, C.D.P., Coord.; Madeline Zimmerer, C.D.P., Coord.

Our Lady of Victory Missionary Sisters, 2101 Vera Cruz, Apt. 113, 78207-6727. Tel: 210-433-3296. Sr. M. Adele Massaro, O.L.V.M.

Presentation Convent, 8931 Callaghan Rd., 78230-4570. Tel: 210-342-2503; Fax: 210-349-4772. Email: pbvmsat@juno.com. Sr. Therese Gleitz, P.B.V.M., Supr. Residence of the Community of the Union of the Sisters of the Presentation of the B.V.M. Sisters 14.

Provincial Offices of the Sisters of the Sacred Heart of Jesus of St. Jacut, 11931 Radium St., 78216-2714. Tel: 210-344-7203; Fax: 210-341-0721. Email: cecie1@juno.com. Sr. Cecilia Rodriguez, S.S.C.J., Prov. Sisters 41.

Convent: St. Joseph Community, 1014 Spent Wing, 78213. Tel: 210-375-2914. Sisters 3. 818 Firefly, 78216. Tel: 210-349-6689. Sisters 4.

Convent: Sacred Heart Convent, 7112 Hagy Cir., 78216. Tel: 210-340-0249. Sisters 5.

Convent: Holy Spirit Convent, 10802 Silhouette Dr., 78216. Sisters 7.

Convent: Casa Ste. Emile, 302 Harriet Dr., 78216. Tel: 210-822-9844. Sisters 5.

Convent: Santa Maria Community, 10803 Silhouette Dr., 78216. Tel: 210-340-1872. Sisters 5.

Convent: Beth Rachamim Community, 1203 Viewridge, 78213. Tel: 210-308-0257. Sisters 5.

Religious of Mary Immaculate Convent, 719 Augusta St., 78215. Tel: 210-226-0025; Fax: 210-226-3305. Email: villamarmi@yahoo.com. Web: www.religiosasdemariainmaculada.org. Sr. Martha Ochoa, R.M.I., Local Supr. Religious of Mary Immaculate Sisters. Sisters 8.

School Sisters of Notre Dame, 3415 W. Woodlawn, 78228. Tel: 210-435-3234; Fax: 210-434-6635. Sr. Ann Semel, S.S.N.D., Correspondent. Sisters 4.

Seraphic Sisters of Our Lady of Sorrows Convent, 621 W. Woodlawn Ave., 78212. Tel: 210-734-3364. Sr. Inez Smietana, S.O.L., Supr. Sisters 7.

The Sisters of Perpetual Adoration Convent, 2403 W. Travis St., 78207. Tel: 210-227-5546; Fax: 210-226-3934. Sr. Maria Concepcion Quesada-Aguirre, A.P.G., Supr. Sisters 9.

Sisters of the Incarnate Word and Blessed Sacrament, 811 Jackson Keller #2, 78216. Tel: 210-979-8650. Sr. Mary Theresa Fritz, I.W.B.S., Supr. Sisters of the Incarnate Word and Blessed Sacrament.

St. Teresa's Convent, 138 Fair Ave., 78223-1014. Tel: 210-533-5330; Fax: 210-533-2532. Email: ameliastj@aol.com. Web: www.teresians.org. Sr. Amelia Ibarra, S.T.J., Coord. Society of St. Teresa of Jesus 10.

Ursuline Residence, 3810 Portsmouth Dr., 78223. Tel: 210-333-2907; Fax: 210-333-2907. Sr. Diane Fulgenzi, O.S.U., Prioress. Sisters 2.

Ursuline Convent, 3807 South Port, 78223. Tel: 210-333-4213; 210-333-2907. Sisters 2.

BOERNE. *St. Scholastica Monastery*, 416 W. Highland, 78006. Tel: 830-249-2645; 830-816-8504; Fax: 830-249-1365. Email: benstrs@ktc.com. Web: www.boernebenedictines.com. Sr. Bernadine Reyes, O.S.B., Prioress. Congregation of Benedictine Sisters, Monastery, and Novitiate. Sisters 17.

UVALDE. *Society of St. Teresa of Jesus* (Teresian Sisters), 466 Encino, 78801. Tel: 830-278-6724; Fax: 830-278-5170. Email: stjsendin@yahoo.com. Web: teresians.org. Sr. Angeles Sendin, S.T.J., Coord. Sisters 3.

[N] RETREAT HOUSES

SAN ANTONIO. *Oblate Renewal Center*, Mailing Address: 5700 Blanco Rd., 78216-6615. Tel: 210-349-4173; Fax: 210-349-4281. Email: orc@ost.edu. Web: www.ost.edu/oblate_renewal_center.htm. Revs. Rocky Grimard, O.M.I., M.Div., MTh., Dir.; William E. Zapalac, O.M.I.; Sisters Theresa O'Toole, S.H.Sp.; Susan Hazenski, SS.C.M., Hospitality Dir.

BOERNE. *Omega Retreat Center* (1982) 216 W. Highland Dr., 78006. Tel: 830-816-8470 (San Antonio); 830-249-3894 (Boerne); Fax: 830-249-3327. Email: omegactr@gvtc.com. Web: www.boernebenedictines.com. Mr. Andrew Anderson, Dir.

CASTROVILLE. *Moye Retreat Center*, 600 London, 78009. Tel: 830-931-2233; Fax: 830-931-2227. Web: www.moyecenter.org. Email: moyecenter@cdptexas.org. Linda Follis, Exec. Dir. Under the direction of the Sisters of Divine Providence., Center for Retreats, Renewal, and Conferences. Sisters 2.

[O] CATHOLIC CHARITABLE ORGANIZATIONS AND CLINICS

SAN ANTONIO. *Catholic Charities, Archdiocese of San Antonio* Crisis intervention/emergency assistance; pregnancy/parenting education and support services; transitional housing for homeless, pregnant women; mental health services; senior volunteer services; guardianship services; money management services; immigration and refugee services; pre-certification services for victims of human trafficking; community voicemail program; military family relief services; community center providing social services; Doula services; summer fan for seniors program; volunteer income tax assistance.

Administration, 202 W. French Pl., 78212. Tel: 210-222-1294; Fax: 210-227-0217. Email: info@ccaosa.org. Web: www.ccaosa.org. Mr. Steve Saldana, Pres. & CEO.

Office: 202 W. French, 78212. Tel: 210-222-1294; Fax: 210-227-0217.

Immigration Services and Crisis Intervention Programs, 2903 W. Salinas St., 78207. Tel: 210-433-3256; Fax: 210-433-0851.

Refugee Services, 202 W. French, 78212. Tel: 210-222-1294; Fax: 210-242-3174.

Guadalupe Home for Homeless Pregnant Women, 1223 S. Trinity St., 78207. Tel: 210-476-0707; Fax: 210-224-7388.

San Antonio Birth Doulas, 1223 S. Trinity, 78207. Tel: 210-222-0988; Fax: 210-223-3980. Email: doulas@ccaosa.org.

Catholic Counseling and Consultation Center, 7711 Madonna, 78216. Tel: 210-377-1133; Fax: 210-377-1230. Rev. James Rutkowski, S.T.L., Clinical Dir. See Curia Section - Department of Social & Community Services.

Guadalupe Community Center, 1801 W. Durango, 78207. Tel: 210-226-6178; Fax: 210-226-9188.

Daughters of Charity Services of San Antonio, 7607 Somerset Rd., 78211. Tel: 210-334-2300; Fax: 210-922-0332. Email: larry.mejia@dcssa.org. Web: www.dcssa.org. Mr. Larry Mejia, Pres. & CEO, Daughters of Charity Svcs.

This corporation operates centers at four locations:

De Paul Family Center, 7607 Somerset, 78211. Tel: 210-334-2311; Fax: 210-922-0332. Sisters 7.

El Carmen Wellness Center, 18555-1 Leal Rd., 78221. Tel: 210-626-1745; Fax: 210-626-1849. Sisters 4.

La Mision Family Health Care, 19780 U.S. Hwy. 281 S., 78221. Tel: 210-626-0600; Fax: 210-626-1174.

DePaul-Wesley Children's Center, 1201 Lenard St., 78211. Tel: 210-334-2390; Fax: 210-924-1879.

[P] NEWMAN CENTERS

SAN ANTONIO. *Catholic Campus Ministry* 2718 W. Woodlawn, 78228. Tel: 210-734-2620. Archdiocesan Campus Ministry.

St. Anthony Catholic Student Center at U.T.S.A. 1604 Campus 14523 Roadrunner Way, 78249. Tel: 210-699-9594; Fax: 210-699-9572.

[Q] FOUNDATIONS, ENDOWMENTS AND TRUSTS

SAN ANTONIO. *The Archbishop Charity Fund*, Mailing Address: P.O. Box 28410, 78228. Tel: 210-734-2620; Fax: 210-734-0708.

Archbishop Flores Charity Fund, Mailing Address: P.O. Box 28410, 78228. Tel: 210-734-2620; Fax: 210-734-0708.

Archdiocesan Designated Catholic Schools Endowment Fund, 2718 W. Woodlawn, 78228. Tel: 210-734-2620.

Archdiocesan Endowment Fund, Mailing Address: P.O. Box 28410, 78228-0410. Tel: 210-734-2620; Fax: 210-734-0708. Most Rev. Jose H. Gomez, S.T.D.

Archdiocese of San Antonio Endowment Fund for Parishes, School and Ministries, 2718 W. Woodlawn, 78228. Tel: 210-734-2620. Rev. Msgr. Lawrence J. Stuebben (Retired).

Assumption Seminary Endowment Fund, Mailing Address: P.O. Box 28410, 78228-0410. Tel: 210-734-2620; Fax: 210-734-0708. Most Rev. Jose H. Gomez, S.T.D.

Casa de Padres Endowment Fund, Mailing Address: P.O. Box 28410, 78228-0410. Tel: 210-734-2620; Fax: 210-734-0708. Most Rev. Jose H. Gomez, S.T.D.

The Catholic Community Foundation for the Roman Catholic Church of the Archdiocese of San Antonio, 2718 W. Woodlawn Ave., 78228. Tel: 210-734-1910. Mr. Jeff Jung, Vice Pres.

Friends of Santa Rosa Foundation dba Friends of Christus Santa Rosa Foundation 333 N. Santa Rosa Blvd., 78207. Tel: 210-704-2541; Fax: 210-704-2384. Web: www.christussantarosa.org. Linda O'Brien, Vice Pres. & Chief Devel. Office.

Historical Centre Foundation (2000)Mailing Address: P.O. Box 831-078, 78283-1078. Tel: 210-576-1365; Fax: 210-576-1367. Email: hcfed@sfcathedral.org. Web: www.sfcathedral.org. Amelia G. Nieto, C.F.R.E. Exec. Dir.; Rev. Tony Vilana.

Holy Spirit Sisters' Trust, 300 Yucca St., 78203. Tel: 210-533-8142; Fax: 210-533-3434. Email: holyspirit@shsp.org. Sr. Miriam Mitchell, S.H.Sp., Pres. Sisters of the Holy Spirit.

Mary Jane Ihle Clark Endowment Fund for Ministry to Persons with Disabilities, 2718 W. Woodlawn, 78228. Tel: 210-734-2620. Rev. Msgr. Lawrence J. Stuebben (Retired).

National Foundation for Mexican-American Vocations, 2600 W. Woodlawn, 78228. Tel: 210-735-0553; Fax: 210-734-4942. Web: savocations.org. Rev. Arturo Cepeda, S.T.D., Vocation Office. A nonprofit organization to financially help Mexican American Seminarians.

Providence Trust, 515 S.W. 24th St., 78207. Tel: 210-434-1866; Fax: 210-431-9965. Sisters Ramona Bezner, C.D.P., Trustee; Ann Petrus, C.D.P., Trustee; Anita Brenk, C.D.P., Trustee. Congregation of Divine Providence, Inc. Charitable Trust.

San Antonio Catholic Worker Community Housing Trust of 1992, 622 Nolan St., 78202. Tel: 210-533-5149. Email: veronicacahill@hotmail.com. Sr. Veronica Cahill, S.H.Sp., Contact Person.

Seton Home Endowment Fund, Mailing Address: P.O. Box 28410, 78228-0410. Tel: 210-734-2620; Fax: 210-734-0708. Most Rev. Jose H. Gomez, S.T.D.

BOERNE. *Benedictine Sisters Charitable Trust One*, 416 W. Highland Dr., 78006. Tel: 210-219-5514; Fax: 210-348-6745. Email: srmika@texas.net. Sr. Susan Mika, O.S.B., Trustee.

Benedictine Sisters Charitable Trust Two, 416 W. Highland, 78006. Tel: 830-816-8504; Fax: 830-249-1365. Sr. Sylvia Ahr, O.S.B., Trustee.

[R] SHRINES

SAN ANTONIO. *Basilica of the National Shrine of the Little Flower* 1715 N. Zarzamora, 78201. Tel: 210-735-9127; Fax: 210-738-0818. Web: www.littleflowerbasilica.org. Mailing Address: 824 Kentucky Ave., 78201.

Oblate Lourdes Grotto Shrine of the Southwest, Tepeyac de San Antonio 5712 Blanco Rd., 78216. Tel: 210-342-9864; Fax: 210-342-7144. Email: omsa@oblatemissions.org. Web: www.oblatemissions.org. Revs. Saturnino Lajo, O.M.I., Ministries Dir.; Leopoldo G. Perez, O.M.I., S.T.D., M.Div., Grotto Dir.

Our Lady of Czestochowa Grotto Shrine and Convent, 138 Beethoven St., 78210. Tel: 210-337-8193 (Convent). Sr. Elza Lyszczarz, S.O.L.S., Supr.; Rev. Louis V. LeDoux (LAF), Chap. Seraphic Franciscan Sisters of Our Lady of Sorrows. Sisters 5.

[S] MISCELLANEOUS

SAN ANTONIO. *Acts Missions, c/o Oblate School of Theology*, 285 Oblate Dr., 78216. Tel: 210-342-1077; Fax: 866-541-9261. Email: acts@ost.edu. Web: www.actsmissions.org. Mr. Tom Peterson, Exec. Dir.

**The Alexander House Apostolate*, 1343 Alpine Pond, 78260. P.O. Box 59-2107, 78259-2107. Tel: 210-858-6195. Email: info@thealexanderhouse.org. Web: www.thealexanderhouse.org. Gregory Alexander, Co-Founder & Dir.; Julie Alexander, Co-Founder & Dir.

Archdiocesan Union of Holy Name Societies, 6283 Apple Valley, 78242. Tel: 210-673-4590.

Benitia Family Center, 4650 Eldridge Ave., 78237-2600. Tel: 210-433-9300; Fax: 210-432-6739. Email: benitia@benitia.org. Web: www.benitia.org. Vacant, Dir.

Brothers of the Beloved Disciple A private association of the faithful., 1701 Alametos, 78201. Tel: 210-734-6727; Fax: 210-738-0698. Email: GMontague@stmarytx.edu. Web: www.brothersofthebeloveddisciple.org. Revs. George T. Montague, S.M.; Robert E. Hogan, B.B.D., M.A., B.B.D.; Joseph Mary Marshall; William H. Combs, B.B.D.

Catholic Association of Latino Leaders, Inc., Pastoral Center - Archdiocese of San Antonio, 2718 W. Woodlawn Ave., 78228. Tel: 210-734-1653; Fax: 210-734-0708. Web: www.call-usa.org. Robert Aguirre, Dir. & Treas.

Catholic Cemeteries of the Archdiocese of San Antonio, 1735 Cupples Rd., 78237. Tel: 210-438-8134. Mr. Robert Cornejo, Gen. Mgr.

Catholic Physicians Guild, c/o Christus Santa Rosa City Centre, 333 N. Santa Rosa St., 78207. Tel: 210-704-2805; Fax: 210-705-6556.

Catholic Television of San Antonio, P.O. Box 28410, 78228-0410. Tel: 210-734-1610; Fax: 210-734-2939. Email: pat.rogers@archsa.org. 2718 W. Woodlawn, 78228.

Christus Continuing Care dba Christus Homecare 4241 Woodcock Dr., Ste. A-100, 78228. Email: patrick.carrier@ChristusHealth.org. Web: www.christushomecare.org.

Christus Santa Rosa Family Health Center, 333 N. Santa Rosa, 78207. Tel: 210-704-2535; Fax: 210-704-2545. Email: todd.thames@christushealth.org. Web: www.christussantarosa.org. Dr. Todd Thames, M.D., Dir. Family Health Ctr.
2829 Babcock Rd. #236 C, 78229.

Cordi-Marian Education Center (2003) 2910 Morales St., 78207. Tel: 210-433-5064; Fax: 210-798-8225. Email: mjaime@cordi-marian.org. Sr. Matilda Jaime, M.C.M., B.A., Dir.

Daughters of Mary Help Development Office, 6019 Buena Vista St., 78237-1700. Tel: 210-431-4999; Fax: 210-431-5944. Email: sswdevelopment@sbcglobal.net. Web: salesiansisterswest.org. Nanette Dion, Dir. Promotes the apostolic works of both the Daughters of Mary Help of Christians (Salesian Sisters) and VIDES-USA (Volunteers International for Development, Education, and Service).

Deaf Ministry of San Antonio, 205 Piazza Italia, 78207-7783. Tel: 210-227-1879; 866-322-9448 (Direct Video Phone); Fax: 210-226-5086. Email: pat.deafministry@satx.rr.com. Mailing Address: P.O. Box 7783, 78207-7783. Rev. Thomas Coughlin, O.P.Miss., Dir.; Mrs. Patricia Gawlik.

Eucharistic Adoration of San Antonio, Inc., Mailing Address: P.O. Box 691006, 78269-1006. Tel: 210-558-8802; Cell: 210-724-5842; Fax: 512-366-9787. Email: adore24@aol.com; sanctusangelicus@yahoo.com. Web: www.adore24.org. Mary Therese Corcoran, Pres. & Exec. Dir.

Federation of Catholic Parent Teacher Clubs of the Archdiocese of San Antonio, c/o Catholic Schools Office, 2718 W. Woodlawn, 78228. Tel: 210-734-2620. Web: www.archdiosa.org. Terry Edgington, Pres.

Focolare Movement, Mailing Address: P.O. Box 15726, 78212. Tel: 210-341-8445; Fax: 210-341-4160. Email: southwest@focolare.us. Web: www.focolare.org. (Work of Mary) (Men and Women), Founded in Trent, Italy, in 1943. International Headquarters is in Rome.

Women's Branch, Texas, 10714 Mt. Tipton, 78213. Tel: 210-341-8445; Fax: 210-341-4160. Isabel C. Furtado, Dir.

Men's Branch, Texas, 9315 Overton Rd., 78217. Tel: 210-590-8812; Fax: 210-590-8921. Mr. Claudio Amato, Dir.

Friends of the Patrician Movement, 222 E. Mitchell St., 78210. Tel: 210-532-3126; Fax: 210-534-3779. Email: pclancey@thepm-sa.org. Deacon Patrick Clancey, Exec. Dir.

**La Promesa Foundation aka Guadalupe Radio Network* 1406 E. Garden Ln., Midland, 79701. Tel: 432-682-1485; Fax: 432-682-5230. Web: www.grnonline.com.

Ladies of Charity of El Carmen, 18555 Leal Rd., 78221. Tel: 210-626-1745. Marina A. Bello, Admin.

Madonna Neighborhood Center, 1906 Castroville Rd., 78237. Tel: 210-432-2374; Fax: 210-432-2389. Email: normafunari@flash.net. Norma J. Funari, Dir. Casework, Day Care, After School Care, Social Services, Adult & Youth Socialization Programs. Emergency Food Pantry, Clothing, Furniture, Counseling, Noon Meal, Summer Recreation, Case Management, Sports.

Marian Center of San Antonio, Mailing Address: P.O. Box 831001, 78283-1001. Tel: 210-225-6279; Fax: 210-225-0044. Email: mariancenterofsa@hotmail.com. Ms. Therese H. Palacios, Pres.

Marian Community of Reconciliation Associations of Consecrated Life, 2715 Marlborough Dr., 78230. Tel: 210-541-0635. Email: mcrsanantonio@fraternasusa.org. Web: www.fraternas.org. Luciane Urban, Supr.

Mary Help Network (ADMA), 6019 Buena Vista St., 78237. Tel: 210-373-9532; 512-320-1913. Email: v.adma@vides.us. Sr. Mary Gloria Mar, F.M.A., Dir.

MCSP, Inc. dba Youth Sports, Inc. 2718 W. Woodlawn, 78228. Tel: 210-734-1944; Fax: 210-734-2774. James Trimboli, Special Projects Mgr.

Merced Housing Texas, 212 W. Laurel St., 78212. Tel: 210-281-0234; Fax: 210-281-0238. Email: merced@mercedhousingtexas.org. Web: www.mercedhousingtexas.org. Susan R. Sheeran, Pres. Founded by a consortium of religious orders to provide quality, affordable, service enriched housing for the economically poor, to strengthen families and promote healthy communities.

St. Monica's Guild (1929) 6515 Broadway, 78209. Tel: 210-828-9266; Fax: 210-824-6110. Email: mcbarron@worldnet.att.net. Mrs. Celeste Barron, Contact Person. A social, civic, and charitable group.

Oblate Missions, 323 Oblate Dr., 78216-6629. Tel: 210-736-1685; Fax: 210-736-1314. Email: omsa@oblatemissions.org. Web: www.oblatemissions.org. Mailing Address: P.O. Box 659432, 78265-9432. Revs. Thomas Ovalle, O.M.I., Chap.; Saturnino Lajo, O.M.I., Spanish Consultant.

Office of Youth Ministry, Mailing Address: 2718 W. Woodlawn, 78228. Tel: 210-734-1625; Fax: 210-734-0231. Email: oym@archsa.org. Web: www.archsa.org/oym. Mr. Michael Loflin, Exec. Dir.

Parents Academy, 1135 Mission Rd., 78210. Tel: 210-532-0894; Fax: 210-532-6698. Sr. M. Odilia Korenek, I.W.B.S., Dir. & Supr.; Katherine Lozano, Prin. Sisters 1; Lay Teachers 3; Support Staff 9; Students 500.

The Patrician Movement, 222 E. Mitchell St., 78210. Tel: 210-532-3126; Fax: 210-534-3779. Email: pclancey@thepm-sa.org.
Field Offices: A nonprofit corporation chartered under the laws of the State of Texas.; Provides comprehensive, Residential and Outpatient Substance Abuse Treatment Services. Accredited by the Joint Commission on Accreditation of Healthcare Organizations. Licensed by the Texas Commission on Alcohol and Drug Abuse.
1249 S. St. Mary St., 78210. Tel: 210-534-4029; Fax: 210-534-4835.
278 E. Mitchell, 78210. Tel: 210-533-2507.
215 Claudia, 78210. Tel: 210-533-0226; Fax: 210-533-8847. Deacon Patrick M. Clancey, Ed.D., Exec. Dir. & Contact Person.
222 E. Mitchell, 78210. Tel: 210-532-3126; Fax: 210-534-3779. Total Assisted 2,732.

Pilgrim Center of Hope - Evangelization Center (1993) 7680 Joe Newton, 78251. Tel: 210-521-3377; Fax: 210-521-0288. Email: trust@catholic.org. Web: www.pilgrimcenterofhope.org. Deacon Tom Fox, Dir.; Mrs. Mary Jane Fox, Dir.

Polish American Priest Association (P.A.P.A.), 5035 Bernadine, 78220. Tel: 210-648-1991. Rev. Eric Orzech, Pres.

Project Rachel of San Antonio, 9862 Lorene Ln., Ste. 108, 78216. Tel: 210-342-4673; 210-722-4213 (Spanish); (800) 651-HOPE; Fax: 210-341-1572. Email: rachel@anewchoice.org. Web: www.anewchoice.org; www.projectrachelsanantonio.org. Mary Ann Parks, Dir. Total Assisted 814.

Religious of Mary Immaculate (Pontifical), Villa Maria, 719 Augusta St., 78215. Tel: 210-226-0025; Fax: 210-223-8163. Email: villamarmi@yahoo.com. Web: www.religiosasdemariainmaculada.org. Sr. Martha Ochoa, Local Supr. Apostolic Work: Counseling & guidance of young women of good moral conduct of any race or religion. Sisters 8; Girls 70.

San Antonio Community Law Center, 322 W. Woodlawn Ave., 78212. Tel: 210-271-9595; Fax: 210-734-4410. Email: SACommunityLawCenter@netzero.net. Bro. William Dooling, C.S.C., Attorney; Ms. Denise Rodriguez, Attorney. Provides legal assistance to the working poor, children, and underserved.

San Antonio Inter-Community Finance Office, 11931 Radium Dr., 78216. Tel: 210-341-8884; Fax: 210-341-0721. Email: kmoylan@saifo.com. Kimberly Moylan, Accounting Business Office Mgr.

San Antonio Rolling Hills, Inc., 21240 Gathering Oak, 78260. Tel: 210-497-0323; Fax: 210-497-5192. Rev. Thomas Salazar, L.C., Contact Person.

Servants of Jesus and Mary, S.A., 5734 Quail Canyon, 78249. Tel: 210-691-0684. Web: www.servantsofjesusandmary.ning.com. Milagros Abellera, Pres.

Socially Responsible Investment Coalition, Mailing Address: P.O. Box 90238, 78209. Tel: 210-344-6778. Email: info@sric-south.org. Web: www.sric-south.org. Sr. Susan Mika, O.S.B., Exec. Dir.

The Southside Consortium of Catholic Schools, Inc., 119 Octavia, 78214. Tel: 210-532-3166; Fax: 210-532-5997. Email: cjohnson@archdiosa.org. Carol Johnson, Chm.

Teleton Navideno, 2903 W. Salinas, 78207. Tel: 210-433-3256; Fax: 210-433-0851. Email: egeffre@ccaosa.org. Ms. Ester Geffre, Dir. Christmas Telethon-Branch of Catholic Charities Archdiocese of San Antonio, Inc.

Today's Catholic Newspaper, Mailing Address: P.O. Box 28410, 78228-0410. 2718 W. Woodlawn Ave., 78228. Tel: 210-734-2620; Fax: 210-734-2939. Email: tcpaper@archsa.org. Web: www.satodayscatholic.org. Most Rev. Jose H. Gomez, S.T.D., Publisher; Mr. Jordan B. McMorrough, Editor. Official Catholic newspaper of the Archdiocese of San Antonio.

The World Apostolate of Fatima, 719 Wayside, 78213. Tel: 210-344-9810.

BOERNE. *Benedictine Ministries Corporation*, 416 Highland Dr., 78006. Tel: 830-428-0000; Fax: 830-249-7064. Email: smbbmc@gvtc.net. Web: www.boernebenedictines.com. Sr. Michael Brandt, O.S.B., Exec. Dir.

INGRAM. *St. Peter Upon the Water, A Center For Spiritual Direction and Formation*, Mailing Address: P.O. Box 509, 78025-0509. Email: michael.boulette@archsa.orgTel: 830-367-5959; Fax: 830-367-3774. 234 Indian Creek Rd., 78025. Rev. Msgr. Michael Boulette, V.F., Dir.

MOUNTAIN HOME. *Tecaboca - A Marianist Center For Spiritual Renewal*, 5045 Junction Hwy. 27, 78058. Tel: 830-866-3425; Fax: 830-866-3781. Email: office@tecaboca.com. Web: www.tecaboca.com. Operated by the Society of Mary, Province of the U.S.A., Texas Catholic Boy's Camp (mid-June to mid-August).

RELIGIOUS INSTITUTES OF MEN REPRESENTED IN THE ARCHDIOCESE

For further details refer to the corresponding bracketed number in the Religious Institutes of Men or Women section.

[0140]—*The Augustinians* (Prov. of Castile)—O.S.A.
[0200]—*Benedictine Monks*—O.S.B.
[0600]—*Brothers of the Congregation of Holy Cross*—C.S.C.
[0360]—*Claretian Missionaries* (Western Prov.)—C.M.F.
[0310]—*Congregation of Christian Brothers*—C.F.C.
[0220]—*Congregation of the Blessed Sacrament*—S.S.S.
[1330]—*Congregation of the Mission*—C.M.
[0630]—*Congregation of the Missionaries of the Holy Family*—M.S.F.
[1000]—*Congregation of the Passion*—C.P.
[1130]—*Congregation of the Priests of the Sacred Heart*—S.C.J.
[0480]—*Conventual Franciscans*—O.F.M.Conv.
[0260]—*Discalced Carmelite Fathers*—O.C.D.
[]—*Dominican Missionaries*—O.P.Miss.
[0520]—*Franciscan Friars* (Sacred Heart Prov.; Our Lady of Guadalupe Prov.)—O.F.M.
[0690]—*Jesuit Fathers and Brothers* (New Orleans Prov.)—S.J.
[0730]—*Legionaries of Christ*—L.C.
[]—*Missionaries of the Nativity of Mary* (Mexico)—M.N.M.
[1110]—*Missionaries of the Sacred Heart*—M.S.C.
[0860]—*Missionhurst Congregation of the Immaculate Heart of Mary*—C.I.C.M.
[0910]—*Oblates of Mary Immaculate*—O.M.I.
[0430]—*Order of Preachers (Dominican)* (New Orleans Prov.)—O.P.
[1310]—*Order of The Holy Trinity*—O.SS.T.
[0610]—*Priests of the Congregation of Holy Cross*—C.S.C.
[1070]—*Redemptorist Fathers*—C.SS.R.
[0760]—*Society of Mary (Marianists)*—S.M.
[0975]—*Society of Our Lady of the Most Holy Trinity*—S.O.L.T.
[1290]—*Society of St. Sulphice*—S.S.
[1200]—*Society of the Divine Savior*—S.D.S.
[0560]—*Third Order Regular of St. Francis*—T.O.R.

RELIGIOUS INSTITUTES OF WOMEN REPRESENTED IN THE ARCHDIOCESE

[0100]—*Adorers of the Blood of Christ*—A.S.C.
[0230]—*Benedictine Sisters of the Pontifical Jurisdiction*—O.S.B.
[1810]—*Bernardine Sisters of the Third Order of St. Francis*—O.S.F.
[]—*Caritas Christi*—C.C.
[]—*Carmelitas del Sagrado Corazon*—O.C.D.
[0360]—*Carmelite Sisters of the Divine Heart of Jesus*—Carmel.D.C.J.
[0460]—*Congregation of Sisters of Charity of the Incarnate Word*—C.C.V.I.
[3735]—*Congregation of St. Brigid*—C.S.B.
[0870]—*Congregation of the Daughters of Mary Immaculate (Marianist Sisters)*—F.M.I.
[2200]—*Congregation of the Incarnate Word and Blessed Sacrament*—I.W.B.S.
[0725]—*Cordi-Marian Sisters*—M.C.M.
[0760]—*Daughters of Charity of St. Vincent de Paul*—D.C.
[0850]—*Daughters of Mary Help of Christians*—F.M.A.
[0420]—*Discalced Carmelite Nuns*—O.C.D.
[1070-19]—*Dominican Sisters*—O.P.
[1115]—*Dominican Sisters of Peace*—O.P.
[1150]—*Eucharistic Franciscan Missionary Sisters*—M.E.F.
[1170]—*Felician Sisters*—C.S.S.F.
[1900]—*Hermanas Catequistas Guadalupanas*—H.C.G.
[1910]—*Hermanas Josefinas*—H.J.
[2590]—*Hermanas Mercedarias Del Santisimo Sacramento*—H.M.S.S.
[]—*Marian Community of Reconciliation*—M.C.R.
[2470]—*Maryknoll*—M.M.
[]—*Misionarios Del Nino De Salud*—M.N.J.S.
[2770]—*Missionaries of Jesus, Mary and Joseph*—M.J.M.J.
[2690]—*Missionary Catechists of Divine Providence, San Antonio, Texas*—M.C.D.P.
[2890]—*Missionary Servants of St. Anthony*—M.S.S.A.
[]—*Missionary Sisters of Mary Immaculate*—M.S.M.I.
[]—*Missionary Sisters of Our Lady of Perpetual Help*—M.P.S.
[]—*Oblate Missionaries of Mary Immaculate*—O.M.M.I.
[]—*Oblates of Notre Dame* (Phillipines)—O.N.D.
[3130]—*Our Lady of Victory Missionary Sisters*—O.L.V.M.
[]—*Pax Christi Institute*—P.C.I.
[]—*Poor Clares of Perpetual Adoration*—P.C.P.A.
[3460]—*Religious of Mary Immaculate*—R.M.I.
[2540]—*Religious Sisters of Mercy*—R.S.M.
[2970]—*School Sisters of Notre Dame*—S.S.N.D.
[1690]—*School Sisters of the Third Order of St. Francis*—O.S.F.
[]—*Seraphic Franciscan Sisters of Our Lady of Sorrows* (Poland)—O.L.S.
[]—*Sisters for Christian Community*—S.F.C.C.
[1010]—*Sisters of Divine Providence of San Antonio, Texas*—C.D.P.
[3195]—*Sisters of Perpetual Adoration*—A.P.G.
[]—*Sisters of St. Cyril and Methodius*—S.S.C.M.
[1640]—*Sisters of St. Francis of Perpetual Adoration*
[1570]—*Sisters of St. Francis of the Holy Family*—O.S.F.
[3840]—*Sisters of St. Joseph of Carondolet*—C.S.J.
[1960]—*Sisters of the Holy Family*—S.H.F.
[2050]—*Sisters of the Holy Spirit and Mary Immaculate*—S.H.Sp.
[3320]—*Sisters of the Presentation of the B.V.M.*—P.B.V.M.
[3670]—*Sisters of the Sacred Heart of Jesus*—S.S.C.J.
[2150]—*Sisters, Servants of the Immaculate Heart of Mary*—I.H.M.
[4020]—*Society of St. Theresa of Jesus*—S.T.J.
[4110]—*Ursuline Nuns (Roman Union)*—O.S.U.

ARCHDIOCESAN CEMETERIES

SAN ANTONIO. *Holy Cross*, 17501 Nacogdoches, 78218. Tel: 210-651-6011. Mailing Address: 1735 Cupples Rd., 78237.

San Fernando No. 1, 1100 S. Colorado, 78207. Tel: 210-432-2303. Mailing Address: 1735 Cupples Rd., 78237.

San Fernando No. 2, 746 Castroville Rd., 78237. Tel: 210-432-2303. Mailing Address: 1735 Cupples Rd., 78237.

San Fernando No. 3 (Roselawn), 2500 Frio City Rd., 78226. Tel: 210-432-2364. Mailing Address: 1735 Cupples Rd., 78237.

PRIVATE RELIGIOUS ORDER CEMETERY

SAN ANTONIO. *Resurrection*, 11624 FM 471 #501, 78253. Tel: 210-798-8220; Fax: 210-798-8225. Email: resurrection@cordi-marian.org. Richard Ruiz, Gen. Mgr.

NECROLOGY

† Sicilia, Rev. Msgr. Pablo, (Retired)—Died Aug. 24, 2009
† Carrillo, Victor M., San Antonio, TX Assumption Seminary—Died Nov. 18, 2009
† Garrett, Sean, (On Duty Outside the Archdiocese)—Died Dec. 11, 2008
† Kelly, John Edward, San Antonio, TX San Francesco di Paola—Died Jan. 18, 2009

An asterisk (*) denotes an organization that has established tax-exempt status directly with the IRS and is not covered by the USCCB Group Ruling.

Diocese of San Bernardino

Most Reverend

GERALD R. BARNES

Bishop of San Bernardino; ordained December 20, 1975; appointed Titular Bishop of Montefiascone and Auxiliary of San Bernardino January 27, 1992; succeeded to the See, December 28, 1995; installed as Second Bishop of San Bernardino March 12, 1996. *Office: 1201 E. Highland Ave., San Bernardino, CA 92404-4641.*

Diocesan Pastoral Center: 1201 E. Highland Ave., San Bernardino, CA 92404-4641. Tel: 909-475-5300; Fax: 909-475-5155.

Web: www.sbdiocese.org

Email: sbdiocese@sbdiocese.org

Most Reverend

RUTILIO DEL RIEGO

Auxiliary Bishop of San Bernardino; ordained June 5, 1965; appointed Titular Bishop of Daimlaig and Auxiliary Bishop of San Bernardino July 26, 2005; ordained September 20, 2005. *Office: 1201 E. Highland Ave., San Bernardino, CA 92404-4641.*

ESTABLISHED NOVEMBER 6, 1978.

Square Miles 27,293.

Comprises the Counties of San Bernardino and Riverside.

Legal Titles:
The Roman Catholic Bishop of San Bernardino, a Corporation Sole (Churches, Rectories, Halls, Catechetical Centers, etc.).
Diocese of San Bernardino Education and Welfare Corporation (Schools, Convents, Newman Facilities, etc.).
Catholic Charities of San Bernardino/Riverside.
St. Bernardine Plaza.
La Paz Dev. Corp. (Senior Citizens Housing).
Caritas Telecommunications, A California Nonprofit Corporation.
Diocesan Development Fund, Inc.
Blessed Junipero Serra House of Formation, Inc.
Diocese of San Bernardino Land Development Corporation.
Blessed Kateri Tekakwitha Fund.
Diocesan Cemetery Corporation.

STATISTICAL OVERVIEW

Personnel	
Bishop	1
Auxiliary Bishops	1
Priests: Diocesan Active in Diocese	60
Priests: Diocesan Active Outside Diocese	2
Priests: Retired, Sick or Absent	50
Number of Diocesan Priests	112
Religious Priests in Diocese	123
Total Priests in Diocese	235
Extern Priests in Diocese	36
Ordinations:	
Diocesan Priests	2
Transitional Deacons	2
Permanent Deacons	5
Permanent Deacons in Diocese	108
Total Brothers	19
Total Sisters	156
Parishes	
Parishes	93
With Resident Pastor:	
Resident Diocesan Priests	34
Resident Religious Priests	28
Without Resident Pastor:	
Administered by Priests	18
Administered by Deacons	2
Administered by Religious Women	4
Administered by Lay People	6
Missions	11
Professional Ministry Personnel:	
Brothers	1
Sisters	11
Lay Ministers	141
Welfare	
Catholic Hospitals	2
Total Assisted	203,618
Health Care Centers	1
Total Assisted	1,200
Homes for the Aged	1
Total Assisted	150
Special Centers for Social Services	15
Total Assisted	46,601
Educational	
Seminaries, Diocesan	1
Students from This Diocese	17
Diocesan Students in Other Seminaries	19
Total Seminarians	36
High Schools, Diocesan and Parish	2
Total Students	854
High Schools, Private	1
Total Students	340
Elementary Schools, Diocesan and Parish	27
Total Students	5,886
Elementary Schools, Private	1
Total Students	460
Catechesis/Religious Education:	
High School Students	7,890
Elementary Students	25,674
Total Students under Catholic Instruction	41,140
Teachers in the Diocese:	
Priests	3
Sisters	11
Lay Teachers	310
Vital Statistics	
Receptions into the Church:	
Infant Baptism Totals	10,746
Adult Baptism Totals	926
Received into Full Communion	892
First Communions	14,950
Confirmations	6,936
Marriages:	
Catholic	1,434
Interfaith	274
Total Marriages	1,708
Deaths	2,525
Total Catholic Population	1,167,208
Total Population	4,168,603

Former Bishop—Most Rev. PHILLIP F. STRALING, D.D., ord. March 19, 1959; appt. Bishop of San Bernardino July 18, 1978; cons. Nov. 16, 1978; transferred to See of Reno, June 29, 1995.

Diocesan Pastoral Center—1201 E. Highland Ave., San Bernardino, 92404-4641. Tel: 909-475-5300; Fax: 909-475-5155. Office Hours: Mon.-Fri. 8:30-4:30.

All correspondence should be addressed to the Diocesan Pastoral Center unless otherwise noted.

Office of the Bishop—Email: bishopsoffice@sbdiocese.org.

Senior Office Administrator to the Bishop—EDNA PRECIADO. Tel: 909-475-5113; Fax: 909-475-5109. Email: epreciado@sbdiocese.org.

Administrator to the Office of Auxiliary Bishop—MARTHA DE JIMENEZ. Tel: 909-475-5117; Fax: 909-475-5109. Email: mdejimenez@sbdiocese.org.

Episcopal Master of Ceremonies/Special Assistant to the Bishop—Mr. RICHARD C. HERBST. Tel: 909-475-5124; Fax: 909-475-5109. Email: rherbst@sbdiocese.org.

Office of Episcopal Vicars—Riverside Episcopal Region: Most Rev. RUTILIO J. DEL RIEGO, D.D., V.G. Riverside Pastoral Region: Very Rev. Msgr. THOMAS M. WALLACE, E.V. San Bernardino Pastoral Region: Very Rev. ROMEO N. SELECCION, M.S., E.V.

Administrative Assistant to the Episcopal Vicars—CYNTHIA ORTEGA. Tel: 909-475-5107; Fax: 909-475-5109. Email: cortega@sbdiocese.org.

Vicars Forane—Hemet: Very Rev. THOMAS J. BURDICK, V.F. Tel: 951-325-7707. High Desert: Very Rev. MICHAEL LAMA, V.F. Tel: 760-246-7083. Low Desert: Very Rev. ELISEO LUCAS, V.F. Tel: 760-396-2717. Riverside: Very Rev. BENJAMIN E. ALFORQUE, M.S.C., V.F. Tel: 951-689-8921. San Bernardino: Very Rev. ROBERT L. MILLER, V.F. Tel: 909-475-5459. West End: Very Rev. PATRICK J. O'HAGAN, SS.CC., V.F. Tel: 909-465-5503.

Chief Financial Officer—Ms. MARYROSE WALLACE. Tel: 909-475-5150; Fax: 909-475-5457.

Legal Counsel—WILFRID C. LEMANN, Fullerton, Lemann, Schaefer and Dominick LLP, 215 N. "D" St., San Bernardino, 92401-1701. Tel: 909-889-3691; Fax: 909-888-5119.

Office of Canonical Services (Tribunal)—Tel: 909-475-5320; Fax: 909-475-5330. Email: canonicalservices@sbdiocese.org.

Judicial Vicar—Very Rev. DAVID ANDEL, J.C.L., J.V. Email: dandel@sbdiocese.

Director—Mr. STEPHEN H. OSBORN, J.D., J.C.L. Email: sosborn@sbdiocese.org.

Defender of the Bond—Rev. Msgr. ROBERT E. LAWRENCE, J.C.L. (Retired).

Promoter of Justice—Mr. STEPHEN H. OSBORN, J.D., J.C.L. Email: sosborn@sbdiocese.org.

Judges—Rev. Msgr. DONALD S. WEBBER, J.C.L. (Retired); Very Rev. DAVID ANDEL, J.C.L., J.V.; Rev. Msgr. PHILIP A. BEHAN, J.C.L.; Rev. GEORGE GONZALES (Retired); Deacon SCOTT HUNSICKER, J.C.L.; Mr. STEPHEN H. OSBORN, J.D., J.C.L.; Ms. MARLA V. PRUNEDA, J.C.L.

Canonical Administrative Assistant—GINA GRADIAS-PENMAN. Email: ggradias@sbdiocese.org.

Canonical Auditor/Consultant—VACANT.

Diocesan Notaries—GINA GRADIAS-PENMAN. Email: ggradias@sbdiocese.org; IRENE MARTINEZ. Email: imartinez@sbdiocese.org.

Assessor—VACANT.

Office of Worship—Tel: 909-475-5335; Fax: 909-475-5334. Email: worship@sbdiocese.org. Sr. MARILU COVANI, S.P., Dir. Tel: 909-475-5336. Email: mcovani@sbdiocese.org.

Bishop's Advisory Boards, Commissions and Committees

College of Consultors—Most Revs. GERALD R. BARNES, D.D.; RUTILIO J. DEL RIEGO, D.D., V.G.; Very Rev. Msgr. GERARD M. LOPEZ, S.T.L., V.G.; Very Rev. ROMEO N. SELECCION, M.S., E.V.; Very Rev. Msgr. THOMAS M. WALLACE, E.V.; Very Revs. BENJAMIN E. ALFORQUE, M.S.C., V.F.; DAVID ANDEL, J.C.L., J.V.; JACK BARKER, V.F., K.C.H.S.; MICHAEL LAMA, V.F.; Rev. JAMES MCLAUGHLIN; Very Rev. PATRICK J. O'HAGAN, SS.CC., V.F.

Diocesan Curia—Most Revs. GERALD R. BARNES, D.D.; RUTILIO J. DEL RIEGO, D.D., V.G.; Very Rev. Msgrs. GERARD M. LOPEZ, S.T.L., V.G.; THOMAS M. WALLACE, E.V.; Very Rev. ROMEO N. SELECCION, M.S., E.V.; Ms. THERESA D. MONTMINY; Deacon F. MICHAEL JELLEY; Sr. SARA M. KANE, C.S.J.; JEANETTE ARNQUIST; MARIA ESCHEVERRIA; Mr. THEODORE FURLOW; Mr. STEPHEN H. OSBORN, J.D., J.C.L.; MARYROSE WALLACE; Mr. JOHN H. ANDREWS, B.A.

Presbyteral Council—Most Rev. GERALD R. BARNES, D.D., Pres. Ex Officio Member: Most Rev. RUTILIO J. DEL RIEGO, D.D., V.G., Auxiliary Bishop; Very Rev. Msgrs. GERARD M. LOPEZ, S.T.L., V.G.; THOMAS M. WALLACE, E.V.; Very Rev. ROMEO N. SELECCION, M.S., E.V. Officers: Rev. DAVID T. FITZGERALD, s.P., Chm.; Very Rev. ELISEO LUCAS, V.F.; Rev. MARK E. KOTLARCZYK, Sec. & Treas. Appointed Members: Very Revs. BENJAMIN E. ALFORQUE, M.S.C., V.F.; THOMAS J. BURDICK, V.F.; MICHAEL LAMA, V.F.; ROBERT L. MILLER, V.F.; PATRICK J. O'HAGAN, SS.CC., V.F. Elected Members: Revs. CIRO LIBANATI; HOWARD A. LINCOLN; GEORGE M. MATANIC, O.P.; ALAN JENKINS, S.V.D.; ANTHONY C. DAO, O.P.; EDMUND GOMEZ; EDMOND "NED" G. O'DONNELL; JAMES OROPEL; DENNIS L. LEGASPI; JOHN F. WAGNER.

Finance Council—MARYROSE WALLACE, CFO. Tel: 909-475-5150; Fax: 909-475-5457; DON CAVAZOS, Chm.

Council for Consecrated Life—Most Rev. GERALD R. BARNES, D.D.; Very Rev. PATRICK J. O'HAGAN, SS.CC., V.F.; Rev. ANTONIO G. ABUAN-GAONA, M.S.; Sisters MARY FRANCES COLEMAN, R.S.M.; FELIPA GONZALEZ, F.S.J.; CAROL HALLMEYER, S.N.J.M.; THERESA PHAN, L.H.C.; MARY ANN SCHEPERS, O.S.B.; MAYELA ORTEGA, H.C.J.S.; CATHY WHITE, S.P.; Bro. STEPHEN PARDY, S.V.D.

Ministerial Personnel and Placement Board—Ex Officio: Most Revs. GERALD R. BARNES, D.D.; RUTILIO J. DEL RIEGO, D.D., V.G.; Very Rev. Msgr. GERARD M. LOPEZ, S.T.L., V.G. Elected Members: Rev. ARTURO J. MANZON-BALAGAT; JOYCE DRAKE; Deacon STEPHEN SEREMBE; Revs. EDMUND GOMEZ; MARK C. LANDER; Ms. KIRSTEN R. THORSTAD; Very Rev. ROMEO N. SELECCION, M.S.; Revs. PATRICK V. KIRSCH; CHARLES A. PATRON; Very Rev. Msgr. THOMAS M. WALLACE, E.V.

Commission on the Status of Women in Church and Society—URSULA HINKSON, Chm., 1201 E. Highland Ave., San Bernardino, 92404-4641. Tel: 909-475-5153.

Commission for Ministry with Families of Gay and Lesbian Catholics—Rev. DAVID T. FITZGERALD, s.P., Chm., Our Lady of the Assumption, 796 W. 48th St., San Bernardino, 92407. Tel: 909-882-2931.

Diocesan Building Committee—Tel: 909-475-5310. Email: building@sbdiocese.org. Rev. TIM KEPPEL, C.R., Chm.

Diocesan Review Committee—Very Rev. Msgr. GERARD M. LOPEZ, S.T.L., V.G.

Ecumenical Office—Rev. GREGORY ELDER, Chm., St. Adelaide Church, 27457 E. Baseline St., Highland, 92346. Tel: 909-862-8669.

Office of the Vicar General/Moderator of the Curia—Very Rev. Msgr. GERARD M. LOPEZ, S.T.L., V.G. Tel: 909-475-5120; Fax: 909-475-5109. Email: glopez@sbdiocese.org.

Office Administrator to the Vicar General—YOLANDA LEAR. Tel: 909-475-5123; Fax: 909-475-5109. Email: ylear@sbdiocese.org.

Coordinator of Victim Assistance Ministry—Sr. ROSALINE O'CONNOR, R.S.M. Tel: 909-855-2296; Fax: 909-475-5109. Email: roconnor@sbdiocese.org.

Office of the Chancellor—Ms. THERESA D. MONTMINY. Tel: 909-475-5100; Fax: 909-475-5109. Email: officeofthechancellor@sbdiocese.org.

Administrator to the Office of Chancellor—LILIANA B. MENDEZ-CHAVEZ. Tel: 909-475-5104; Fax: 909-475-5109. Email: lmendez-chavez@sbdiocese.org.

Archives/Records Management—PETER BRADLEY, Archivist. Tel: 909-475-5399; Fax: 909-475-5109. Email: pbradley@sbdiocese.org.

Development Office—Tel: 909-475-5460; Fax: 909-475-5155. Email: development@sbdiocese.org. RICHARD MERCADO, Dir. Tel: 909-475-5461. Email: rmercado@sbdiocese.org.

Office of Human Resources—Tel: 909-475-5170; Fax: 909-475-5189. Email: humanresources@sbdiocese.org. VIRGINIA TURNER, Dir. Tel: 909-475-5172. Email: vturner@sbdiocese.org.

Diocesan Office of Child and Youth Development—Tel: 909-475-5125; Fax: 909-475-5126. Sr. CATHY WHITE, S.P., Dir. Tel: 909-475-5127; Fax: 909-475-5126. Email: cwhite@sbdiocese.org.

Vice Chancellor, Apostolic and Ethnic Affairs—MARIA ECHEVERRIA. Tel: 909-475-5140; Fax: 909-475-5343. Email: mecheverria@sbdiocese.org.

Administrative Secretary to the Vice Chancellor—MIRYAM CACHU. Tel: 909-475-5140; Fax: 909-475-5343.

Vice Chancellor, Ecclesial Services—Deacon F. MICHAEL JELLEY. Tel: 909-475-5119; Fax: 909-475-5164. Email: mjelley@sbdiocese.org.

Administrative Assistant to the Vice Chancellor—NORMA VERDUGO. Tel: 909-475-5160; Fax: 909-475-5164.

Diocesan Departments

Department of Catholic Communications—Tel: 909-475-5420; Fax: 909-475-5357. Mr. JOHN H. ANDREWS, B.A., Dept. Dir.

Information Services—Tel: 909-475-5400; Fax: 909-475-5357. Email: informationservices@sbdiocese.org. DALE JONASSON, M.S., Office Dir. Tel: 909-475-5401. Email: djonasson@sbdiocese.org; ALFRED VELASQUEZ, Oper. Mgr. Tel: 909-475-5405. Email: avelasquez@sbdiocese.org.

Media Relations—Mr. JOHN H. ANDREWS, B.A., Dept. Dir. Tel: 909-475-5420; Fax: 909-475-5357.

Caritas Telecommunications—Tel: 909-475-5350; Fax: 909-475-5357. Email: caritas@sbdiocese.org. Mr. JOHN H. ANDREWS, B.A., Dept. Dir. Tel: 909-475-5420; Fax: 909-475-5357.

Department of Community Services—JEANETTE ARNQUIST, Dept. Dir. Tel: 909-475-5478; Fax: 909-475-5473.

Office of Social Concerns—Tel: 909-475-5465; Fax: 909-475-5473. JEANETTE ARNQUIST, Office Dir. Tel: 909-475-5478. Email: jarnquist@sbdiocese.org.

Office of Restorative Justice—Tel: 909-475-5474; Fax: 909-475-5473. Sr. SUE REIF, O.S.F., Dir.

Catholic Campaign for Human Development—Mr. VERNE SCHWEIGER, Dir. Tel: 909-475-5468; Fax: 909-475-5473. Email: vschweiger@sbdiocese.org.

Pro Life Catholic Ministries—Tel: 909-475-5350; Fax: 909-475-5473. MARIE WIDMANN, Office Dir. Tel: 909-475-5351.

Department of Ecclesial Services—Tel: 909-475-5160; Fax: 909-475-5164. Deacon F. MICHAEL JELLEY, Vice Chancellor & Dept. Dir. Tel: 909-475-5119; Fax: 909-475-5109. Email: mjelley@sbdiocese.org.

Office of Continuing Formation of Priests—Very Rev. ROBERT L. MILLER, V.F., Dir. Tel: 909-475-5455. Email: rmiller@sbdiocese.org.

Office of the Vicar for Clergy—Tel: 909-475-5459; Fax: 909-475-5343. Rev. DAVID T. FITZGERALD, s.P., Chm.

Office of Vicar for Retired Priests—VACANT.

Office for Consecrated Life—Tel: 909-475-5345; Fax: 909-475-5343. Email: religious@sbdiocese.org. Sr. MARY FRANCES COLEMAN, R.S.M., Office Dir. Tel: 909-475-5342; Fax: 909-475-5343.

Office of Permanent Diaconate Formation—Tel: 909-475-5163; Fax: 909-475-5343. Email: diaconate@sbdiocese.org. Deacon EDWARD CLARK, Dir. Tel: 909-475-5162; Fax: 909-475-5343. Email: eclark@sbdiocese.org.

Office of Seminarians—Rev. JOSE A. SANZ, D.L.P., Office Dir., 12725 Oriole Ave., Grand Terrace, 92313. Tel: 909-783-0260; Fax: 909-783-0223.

Office of Vocations—Tel: 909-783-1305; Fax: 909-783-0223. Email: vocations@sbdiocese.org. Sr. SARAH SHREWSBURY, O.S.C., Office Dir.; Rev. JEROME OCHETTI, Assoc. Dir.

Blessed Junipero Serra House of Formation—12725 Oriole Ave., Grand Terrace, 92313. Tel: 909-783-0260; Fax: 909-783-0223. Revs. JOSE A. SANZ, D.L.P., Rector; JUAN L. GARCIA, D.L.P., Spiritual Dir.

Department of Educational Services—Tel: 909-475-5450; Fax: 909-475-5155. Email: educationalservices@sbdiocese.org. Sr. SARA M. KANE, C.S.J., Dept. Dir. Tel: 909-475-5340. Email: skane@sbdiocese.org; MARCELLA RUIZ, Dept. Office Admin. Tel: 909-475-5450. Email: mruiz@sbdiocese.org.

Office of Charismatic Renewal—1201 E. Highland Ave., San Bernardino, 92404-4641. Tel: 909-475-5365; Fax: 909-475-5369. Email: crc@sbdiocese.org. MARINA CARRION, Office Dir. Tel: 909-475-5366. Email: mcarrion@sbdiocese.org.

Ministry Formation Institute—Tel: 909-475-5375; Fax: 909-475-5379. Email: mfi@sbdiocese.org. Web: mfi.sbdiocese.cc. JOYCE DRAKE, Dir. Tel: 909-475-5381. Email: jdrake@sbdiocese.org.

Ministry With Youth Office—1201 E. Highland Ave., San Bernardino, 92404-4641. Tel: 909-475-5165; Fax: 909-475-5398. Email: ministrywithyouth@sbdiocese.org. KATHERINE JA-EUN CHO, Dir. Tel: 909-475-5166; Cell: 909-938-5405. Email: kcho@sbdiocese.org.

Office of Campus Ministry—LUZ LARA, Campus Min. Tel: 909-475-5451; Fax: 909-475-5155.

Office of Catholic Schools—Tel: 909-475-5437; Fax: 909-475-5477. Email: catholicschools@sbdiocese.org. PATRICIA VESELY, Supt.

Office of Catechetical Ministry—Tel: 909-475-5452. MARIA COVARRUBIAS, Office Dir. Email: mcovarrubias@sbdiocese.org.

Office of Small Faith Communities—Tel: 909-475-5195; Fax: 909-475-5155. Email: smallfaithcommunities@sbdiocese.org. STEVE VALENZUELA, Office Dir. Tel: 909-475-5197. Email: svalenzuela@sbdiocese.org.

Department of Financial Affairs—Tel: 909-475-5150; Fax: 909-475-5156. Email: financialaffairs@sbdiocese.org. MARYROSE WALLACE, CFO & Dept. Dir. Email: mrwallace@sbdiocese.org.

Accounting Services—Tel: 909-475-5480; Fax: 909-475-5489. Email: accounting@sbdiocese.org. PEGGY KOSTER, Office Dir. Tel: 909-475-5482. Email: pkoster@sbdiocese.org.

Catholic Mutual Insurance Group—2724 N. Waterman Ave., Ste. J, San Bernardino, 92404. Tel: 909-886-6001; Fax: 909-883-9311. Email: wanchales@catholicmutual.org. TAMAR BRINKERHOFF, Claims & Risk Mgr. Email: tbrinkerhoff@catholicmutual.org.

Office of Payroll Services—Tel: 909-475-5188; Fax: 909-475-5183. Email: payroll@sbdiocese.org. TRANG PHAM, Office Dir. Tel: 909-475-5182; Fax: 909-475-5183. Email: tpham@sbdiocese.org.

Office of Parish Assistance—Tel: 909-475-5490; Fax: 909-475-5307. Email: parishassistance@sbdiocese.org. Web: www.sbdiocese.org/parish-assistance.htm. CAROLINE BEATTY, Dir. Tel: 909-475-5492. Email: cbearry@sbdiocese.org.

Department of Pastoral and Ethnic Ministries—MARIA ECHEVERRIA, Vice Chancellor & Dir. Tel: 909-475-5141; Fax: 909-475-5109. Email: mecheverria@sbdiocese.org.

Commission and Assembly for Catholics of African Descent—1201 E. Highland Ave., San Bernardino, 92404-4641. Tel: 909-475-5194; Fax: 909-475-5155. Mr. CARL JONES, Pres.

Asian-Pacific Islander Ministry—Tel: 909-475-5348; Fax: 909-475-5364. Sr. THERESA PHAN, L.H.C., Dir. Email: tphan@sbdiocese.org.

The following ministries can be contacted through the Office of Asian/Pacific Islander Ministry:

Chamorro Ministry—

Filipino Ministry—

Indonesian Ministry—

Korean Ministry—

Nigerian Igbo Ministry—

Vietnamese Ministry—

Tongan Ministry—

The Ministry of Hispanic Affairs—Tel: 909-475-5362; Fax: 909-475-5364. Email: hispanicaffairs@sbdiocese.org. Web: hispanicaffairs.sbdiocese.cc. PETRA ALEXANDER, Dir. Tel: 909-475-5363. Email: palexander@sbdiocese.org.

Native American Ministry—Rev. EARL HENLEY, M.S.C., Chap. & Pastor, 23600 Soboba Rd., P.O. Box 1027, San Jacinto, 92581. Tel: 951-654-2086; Fax: 951-654-2086 (Call First).

Mission Office of the Diocese of San Bernardino—Mailing Address: P.O. Box 1416, San Bernardino, 92402-1416. Tel: 909-475-5130; Fax: 909-475-5135. Email: mission@sbdiocese.org. Web: missions.sbdiocese.cc. Rev. RENO AIARDI, I.M.C., Dir. Tel: 909-475-5131. Email: raiardi@sbdiocese.org.

Marriage Ministry— Please contact the office of Maria Echeverria, Vice Chancellor for all Marriage Ministries.

Engaged Encounter (English)—

Engaged Encounter (Spanish)—

Marriage Encounter (English)—

Marriage Encounter (Spanish)—

Marriage Enrichment—

Retrouvaille Coordinators—

Apostolic Organizations in the Diocese— Please contact the office of Maria Echeverria, Vice Chancellor for all lay organizations.

Catholic Committee on Scouting—

Catholic Daughters of America—

Council of Catholic Women—

Couples for Christ—

Cursillo—
English Movement—
Filipino Movement—
Korean Movement—
Spanish Movement—
Vietnamese Movement—
El Shaddai—
Equestrian Order of Holy Sepulchre of Jerusalem—
Escuela de Evangelizacion Nazareth (E.D.E.N.)—
Fellowship for Catholic Christian Women (FCCW)—
Italian Catholic Federation—
Jovenes Para Cristo—
Knights of Columbus—
Knights of Malta—
Knights of Peter Claver—
Ladies Auxiliary, Knights of Peter Claver—
Magnificat—
Movimiento Familiar Cristoano—
Serra International—
Society of St. Vincent de Paul—
Talleres de Oracion y Vida—
World Apostolate of Fatima (Blue Army)-San Bernardino Division—

Department of Planning—Tel: 909-475-5146; Fax: 909-475-5144. Email: pastoralplanning@sbdiocese.org. Mr. TED FURLOW, Dept. Dir. Tel: 909-475-5147; Fax: 909-475-5144. Email: tfurlow@sbdiocese.org.

Office of Construction and Real Estate—Tel: 909-475-5310; Fax: 909-475-5319. Email: ocre@sbdiocese.org. JUDY A. JUAREZ-FLORES, Opers. Mgr. Tel: 909-475-5313. Email: jjuareaflores@sbdiocese.org.

Office of Pastoral Planning—Tel: 909-475-5146; Fax: 909-475-5109. Email: pastoralplanning@sbdiocese.org. Web: www.futureofhope.org. Mr. TED FURLOW, Office Dir. Tel: 909-475-5147; Fax: 909-475-5744. Email: tfurlow@sbdiocese.org.

Office of Safety and Emergency Preparedness—Mr. GERALD WHITE, Coord. Tel: 909-475-5171. Email: jwhite@sbdiocese.org. Web: safety.sbdiocese.cc.

CLERGY, PARISHES, MISSIONS AND PAROCHIAL SCHOOLS

CITY OF SAN BERNARDINO

(SAN BERNARDINO COUNTY)

1—OUR LADY OF THE ROSARY CATHEDRAL (1927) Revs. Alan Jenkins, S.V.D.; Pavol Sochulak, S.V.D., Parochial Vicar; Deacon Michael Jelley.
Office, Church & Mailing Address: 265 W. 25th St., 92405-3799. Tel: 909-883-8991; Fax: 909-882-2061. Email: olrosary.sb@sbdiocese.org. Web: http://ourladyoftherosarycathedral.catholicweb.com. Church: 2525 Arrowhead Ave., 92405-3799.
School—Holy Rosary Academy, (Grades K-8), 2620 Arrowhead Ave., 92405. Tel: 909-886-1088; Fax: 909-475-5263. Ms. Cheryll Austin, Prin. Lay Teachers 8; Students 139.
Catechesis/Religious Program—Ms. Monica Havins, D.R.E. Students 55.

2—ST. ANTHONY (1948) Rev. Stephen Ayisu, S.V.D.; Deacons Nelson Glass; Mario Gutierrez.
Office: 1640 Western Ave., 92411-1300. Tel: 909-887-3810; Fax: 909-880-0982. Email: stanthony.sb@sbdiocese.org.
School—St. Anthony School, (Grades K-8), 1510 W. 16th St., 92411. Tel: 909-887-5413; Fax: 909-887-9908. Ms. Lori K. Campbell, Prin. Religious Teachers 1; Lay Teachers 10; Students 172.
Catechesis/Religious Program—Tel: 909-887-3210. Wilma Cochrane, D.R.E.; Amparo Martinez, C.R.E. (Spanish). Students 448.

3—ST. BERNARDINE (1862) Rev. Leonard DePasquale, I.M.C., Admin.
Office: 531 N. F. St., 92410-3109. Tel: 909-884-0104; Fax: 909-885-4634. Email: stbernardine.sb@sbdiocese.org.
Catechesis/Religious Program—Ms. Mary Schmidt, C.R.E. (English). Students 327.

4—OUR LADY OF GUADALUPE (1925), (Hispanic), Revs. Eliseo Hernandez, C.O.R.C.; Francisco Martin Alanis, C.O.R.C., Parochial Vicar; Deacon Dan Taylor.
Office: 1430 W. 5th St., 92411. Tel: 909-888-0044; Fax: 909-888-4428. Email: olg.sb@sbdiocese.org.
Catechesis/Religious Program—Ms. Andrea Garcia, D.R.E. (Spanish); Ms. Olga Saenz, D.R.E. (English).

5—OUR LADY OF HOPE CATHOLIC COMMUNITY, INC. (2006) Very Rev. Romeo N. Seleccion, M.S., Priest Mod.; Revs. Eduardo Aguirre; Joseph Chuc Tran, M.M.; Sr. Maureen Chicoine, R.S.C.J., Pastoral Coord.; Deacon Nam Bui.
Mailing Address: P.O. Box 3860, 92413-3860.
Office: 6885 Del Rosa Ave., 92404. Tel: 909-884-6375; Fax: 909-884-8976. Email: ourladyofhope.sb@sbdiocese.org.
Del Rosa Avenue Worship Site—6885 Del Rosa Ave., 92404.
Valencia Avenue Worship Site—1000 Valencia Ave., 92410. Tel: 909-885-0948.
Catechesis/Religious Program—Ms. Luz Hernandez, C.R.E. - Valencia; Ms. Laura Aguilar, C.R.E. - Del Rosa; Sr. Mary Tin Nguyen, L.H.C., C.R.E. - Del Rosa (Vietnamese).

6—OUR LADY OF THE ASSUMPTION (1954) Revs. David T. Fitzgerald, s.P., Admin.; Luis Guido, Parochial Vicar; Deacon Daniel O'Camb.
Office: 796 W. 48th St., 92407-3594. Tel: 909-882-2931; Fax: 909-883-4851. Email: olassumption.sb@sbdiocese.org.
School—Our Lady of the Assumption School, (Grades K-8) Tel: 909-881-2416. Ms. Sue Long, Prin. Lay Teachers 11; Students 197.
Catechesis/Religious Program—Sr. Maura Redington, R.S.M., D.R.E. Students 413.

OUTSIDE THE CITY OF SAN BERNARDINO

ADELANTO, SAN BERNARDINO CO., CHRIST THE GOOD SHEPHERD (1962) Very Rev. Michael Lama.
Mailing Address: P.O. Box 577, 92301-0577.
Office: 17900 Jonathan St., 92301-1731. Tel: 760-246-7083; Fax: 760-246-4603. Email: christthegoodshepherd.adelanto@sbdiocese.org.
Catechesis/Religious Program— Ms. Armida Romero, D.R.E. Students 260.

ALTA LOMA, SAN BERNARDINO CO., ST. PETER & ST. PAUL (1970) Rev. Patrick V. Kirsch; Deacon Donnie Geaga. In Res., Rev. Cletus Imo (Nigeria).
Office: 9135 Banyan St., 91737-2338. Tel: 909-987-9312; Fax: 909-890-9404. Email: stpeterstpaul.altaloma@sbdiocese.org. Web: www.stpeterstpaul.com.
School—St. Peter and St. Paul School, (Preschool), Tel: 909-987-7908; Fax: 909-987-6779. Ms. Patricia Ferrer, Prin. Lay Teachers 2; Students 96.
Catechesis/Religious Program—Tel: 909-980-9423. Ms. Araceli Esparza, D.R.E.

ANZA, RIVERSIDE CO., SACRED HEART (1988) Rev. Hilary Fischer, M.S.C., Admin.
Mailing Address: P.O. Box 390118, 92539-0118.
Office: 56250 Hwy. 371, 92539. Tel: 951-763-5636; Fax: 951-763-0236. Email: sacredheart.anza@sbdiocese.org.
Catechesis/Religious Program— Ms. Oralia Ortiz, D.R.E. Students 49.

APPLE VALLEY, SAN BERNARDINO CO., OUR LADY OF THE DESERT (1974) Revs. Antonio G. Abuan, M.S.; Arlan G. Intal, M.S., Parochial Vicar.
Office: 18386 Corwin Rd., 92307-2328. Tel: 760-242-4427; Fax: 760-242-1195. Email: oldesert.applevalley@sbdiocese.org. Web: ourladyofthedesert92307.parishworld.net.
Catechesis/Religious Program—Tel: 760-242-5819. Ms. Susan Janowicz, D.R.E. Students 359.

BARSTOW, SAN BERNARDINO CO., ST. JOSEPH (1914) Revs. Charles A. Patron; Erik L. Esparza, Parochial Vicar; Deacon Margo Saenz.
Office: 505 E. Mountain View Ave., 92311-2924. Tel: 760-256-6818; Fax: 760-256-8307. Email: stjoseph.barstow@sbdiocese.org.
Catechesis/Religious Program—Mr. John Salazar, D.R.E. Students 582.
Mission—Our Lady of the Desert 57457 Hwy. 127, Baker, San Bernardino Co. 92309. Tel: 760-733-4308.

BEAUMONT, RIVERSIDE CO., BLESSED KATERI TAKAKWITHA CATHOLIC COMMUNITY, INC. (2006) Revs. Trong Joseph Nguyen, S.V.D.; Jesus Zamarripa, S.V.D., Parochial Vicar; Deacons Mark Hodnick; Armando Luevano.
Mailing Address: P.O. Box 155, 92223-0155.
Office: 1234 Palm Ave., 92223. Tel: 951-845-2849; Fax: 951-849-8698. Email: blessedkateritekakwitha.banning@sbdiocese.org.
Catechesis/Religious Program—Tel: 951-849-1897. Ms. Vivian Roppelt, D.R.E.; Ms. Bernadette Hironimus, C.R.E. - (Banning); Mr. Rolando Rosales, C.R.E. - (Beaumont). Students 450.

BIG BEAR LAKE, SAN BERNARDINO CO., ST. JOSEPH (1931) [JC] Rev. Michael Krelovich; Deacon Ralph Partida Jr.
Mailing Address: P.O. Box 1709, 92315-1709.
Office: 42242 N. Shore Dr., 92315-1709. Tel: 909-866-3030; Fax: 909-866-5087. Email: stjoseph.bigbear@sbdiocese.org.
Catechesis/Religious Program—Tel: 909-938-1781. Ms. Patricia Hodges, D.R.E. Students 55.

BLOOMINGTON, SAN BERNARDINO CO., ST. CHARLES BORROMEO (1939), (Hispanic), Rev. Richard A. Humphrys.
Mailing Address: P.O. Box 248, 92316-0248.
Office: 11342 Spruce Ave., 92316-3400. Tel: 909-877-0792; Fax: 909-877-4304. Email: stcharlesborromeo.bloomington@sbdiocese.org.
Catechesis/Religious Program—Tel: 909-421-1494. Ms. Socorro Olivas, D.R.E.

BLYTHE, RIVERSIDE CO., ST. JOAN OF ARC (1920) Rev. Henry Licznerski, C.R., Admin.; Deacon Hikyung H.K. Han.
Office: 875 E. Chanslorway, 92225. Tel: 760-922-3261; Fax: 760-922-5279. Email: stjoanofarc.blythe@sbdiocese.org.
Catechesis/Religious Program—Tel: 760-922-8934.

CATHEDRAL CITY, RIVERSIDE CO., ST. LOUIS (1948) Revs. Michael N. Maher, SS.CC.; Omar Martinez, O.P., Parochial Vicar.
Office: 68633 C St., 92234-1817. Tel: 760-328-2398; Fax: 760-770-4598. Email: stlouis.cathedralcity@sbdiocese.org.
Catechesis/Religious Program— Raquel Nunez, D.R.E. Students 512.

CHINO HILLS, SAN BERNARDINO CO., ST. PAUL THE APOSTLE (1986) Very Rev. Patrick J. O'Hagan, SS.CC.; Deacon Pat Martinez.
Office: 14085 Peyton Dr., 91709-1610. Tel: 909-465-5503; Fax: 909-465-1683. Email: stpaultheapostle.chinohills@sbdiocese.org. Web: www.stpacc.org.
School—St. Paul the Apostle Little Tots, (Grades PreSchool) Ms. Christina Stutzman, Prin. Lay Teachers 4; Students 31.
Catechesis/Religious Program—Ms. Lori Muñiz, D.R.E.; Concha Ebbit, C.R.E. (Spanish); Mr. Jeanie Kiefer, C.R.E. (English). Students 2,451.

CHINO, SAN BERNARDINO CO.

1—ST. MARGARET MARY (1947) [JC] Revs. Peter Bosque, Admin.; Rafael Garces-Solis (Mexico), Parochial Vicar.
Office: 12686 Central Ave., 91710. Tel: 909-627-8466; Fax: 909-627-8049. Email: stmargaretmary@sbdiocese.org.
School—St. Margaret Mary School, (Grades PreK-8), 12664 Central Ave., 91710. Tel: 909-591-8419; Fax: 909-591-6960. Web: www.stmargaretmary-school.org. Ms. Joan Blank, Prin. Religious 1; Lay Teachers 15; Students 276.
Catechesis/Religious Program—Tel: 909-591-7408. Ms. Nancy Keegan, D.R.E. Students 683.

2—OUR LADY OF GUADALUPE (1902), (Hispanic), [JC] Rev. Robert Guerrero, Admin.; Deacon Anthony Brenes-Rios.
Office: 5048 D St., 91710. Tel: 909-591-9402; Fax: 909-591-9404. Email: olg.chino@sbdiocese.org.
Catechesis/Religious Program—Tel: 909-628-3615. Mr. Rolando Rosales, D.R.E.

COACHELLA, RIVERSIDE CO., OUR LADY OF SOLEDAD (1923), (Hispanic), Revs. Bruce K. Cecil, C.S.C.; John S. Connor, C.S.C., Parochial Vicar; Deacons Miguel Badena; Jose Israel Garcia; Sergio Vazquez. In Res., Rev. Jaime Irwin, C.S.C.
Office: 52-525 Oasis Palm Ave., 92236-3047. Tel: 760-398-5577, Ext. 21; Fax: 760-398-1783. Email: olsoledad.coachella@sbdiocese.org.
Catechesis/Religious Program—Ms. Virginia Hoy, D.R.E.; Ms. Virginia Luna, D.R.E. Students 80.
Mission—San Felipe de Jesus 67-305 Hwy. 86, Thermal, Riverside Co. 92274.
Mission—Sacred Heart of Mary & Jesus Torres-Martinez Indian Reservation, Thermal, Riverside Co. 92274.

COLTON, SAN BERNARDINO CO.

1—IMMACULATE CONCEPTION (1943) [CEM 2] [JC] Revs. Joseph Quattropane, O.F.M.Cap., Admin.; Abel E. Balbi, Parochial Vicar; Deacon Robert Amadore. In Res., Rev. Michael Fredericks.
Office: 1106 N. La Cadena Dr., 92324. Tel: 909-825-5110; Fax: 909-825-0912. Email: immaculateconception.colton@sbdiocese.org.
Catechesis/Religious Program—Tel: 909-825-4685. Lorenzo Rangel, D.R.E.

2—SAN SALVADOR (1852), (Hispanic), Revs. Joseph Quattropane, O.F.M.Cap., Admin.; Abel E. Balbi, Parochial Vicar; Deacon Robert Amadore.
Mailing Address: 178 W. K St., 92324-3446.
Office: 169 W. K St., 92324. Tel: 909-825-3481; Fax: 909-825-4473. Email: sansalvador.colton@sbdiocese.org. Web: www.coltoncatholic.net.
Catechesis/Religious Program—Lorenzo Rangel, D.R.E. Students 125.

CORONA, RIVERSIDE CO.

1—CORPUS CHRISTI (1994) Rev. Gerald C. De Luney.
Office: 3760 McKinley St., 92879-1956. Tel: 951-272-9043; Fax: 951-272-6821. Email: corpuschristi.corona@sbdiocese.org.
Catechesis/Religious Program—Tel: 951-272-9043, Ext. 11. Ms. Maria V. Sell, D.R.E. Students 970.

2—ST. EDWARD (1896) Revs. Jose Varela, C.O.R.C.; Josué Arellano-Reynoso, C.O.R.C., Parochial Vicar; Jorge Luis Rodriguez, C.O.R.C., Parochial Vicar; Ikechukwu Eliseus Uju (Nigeria), Parochial Vicar; Deacon Paul Von Ins.
Mailing Address: 605 W. 5th St., 92882-2155.
Office & Church: 417 W. Grand Blvd., 92882-2199. Tel: 951-549-6000, Ext. 200; Fax: 951-549-6009.

Email: stedwards.corona@sbdiocese.org. Web: http://stedward92882.parishworld.net.
School—St. Edward School, (Grades PreK-8), 500 S. Merrill St., 92882. Tel: 951-737-2530; Fax: 951-737-1074. Mrs. Leilani Lister, Prin. Lay Teachers 22; Students 392.
Catechesis/Religious Program—Tel: 951-549-6000, Ext. 203. Ms. Irinea Arrizon, D.R.E.

3—ST. MARY MAGDALENE (1989) Revs. Vincent Au, C.M.C.; Ignatius Kinh Hai Duong Nguyen, C.M.C., Parochial Vicar.
Office: 8540 Weirick Rd., 92883-4995. Tel: 951-277-1801; Fax: 951-277-2513. Email: stmarymagdalene@sbcglobal.net. Web: www.smmcorona.com.
Catechesis/Religious Program—Cathy Townsend, D.R.E.; Lourdes Chumacero, C.R.E. (Spanish). Students 265.

4—ST. MATTHEW (1973) Revs. Neil Fuller, S.V.D.; Ky Ngoc Dinh, S.V.D., Parochial Vicar.
Office: 2140 W. Ontario Ave., 92882-5651. Tel: 951-737-1621; Fax: 951-737-9715. Email: stmatthew.corona@sbdiocese.org. Web: www.stmatthewcorona.com.
Catechesis/Religious Program—Isaura Cera, D.R.E. Students 971.

CRESTLINE, SAN BERNARDINO CO., ST. FRANCES XAVIER CABRINI (1946) Rev. Tom Burns, M.S.C., Admin.
Mailing Address: P.O. Box 3817, 92325-3817.
Office: 23079 Crest Forest Dr., 92325-3817. Tel: 909-338-2303; Fax: 909-338-2383. Email: stfrancesxaviercabrini.crestline@sbdiocese.org. Web: www.stfrancesxaviercabrini.org.
Catechesis/Religious Program—Doreen Kenedy, D.R.E. Students 318.

DESERT HOT SPRINGS, RIVERSIDE CO., ST. ELIZABETH OF HUNGARY (1946) Rev. Dennis L. Legaspi; Deacon Gerald Campbell.
Office: 66-700 Pierson Blvd., 92240-3740. Tel: 760-329-8794; Fax: 760-329-6760. Email: stelizabethofhungary.deserthotsprings@sbdiocese.org. Web: stelizabethofhungarydhs.catholicweb.com.
Catechesis/Religious Program—Tel: 760-251-9268. Yvonne Bacchus, D.R.E. Students 360.

FONTANA, SAN BERNARDINO CO.

1—BLESSED JOHN XXIII CATHOLIC COMMUNITY, INC. (2006) Revs. Leonard Kryzwda, C.R.; Marcelo de Jesumaria, C.R., Parochial Vicar; James M. Gibson, C.R., Parochial Vicar; Deacon Abel Zamora. In Res., Revs. Humphrey Ruszel, C.R. (Retired); Henry Ruszel, C.R. (Retired); Casmir T. Tadla, C.R. (Retired); Patrick A. Brennan, O.S.A.
Office: 7650 Tamarind Ave., 92336. Tel: 909-822-4732; Fax: 909-822-0620. Email: blessedjohnxxiii.fontana@sbdiocese.org.
School—Resurrection Academy, (Grades PreSchool-8), 17434 Miller Ave., 92336. Tel: 909-822-4431; Fax: 909-822-0617. Email: resurrection.ocs@sbdiocese.org. Madeleine Thomas, Prin. Lay Teachers 13; Students 209.
Catechesis/Religious Program—Tel: 909-822-4040. Mrs. Lupe Huerta, D.R.E. Students 376.

2—ST. GEORGE (1954) Rev. Gerardo Mendoza; Deacon Manuel Olivas.
Office: 17895 San Bernardino Ave., 92335-6155. Tel: 909-877-1531; Fax: 909-877-6531. Email: stgeorge.fontana@sbdiocese.org.
Catechesis/Religious Program—Tel: 909-877-3935. Maria Ramirez, D.R.E. Students 346.

3—ST. JOSEPH (1930) Revs. Luc Nghi Tran, Admin.; John Gunningham, Parochial Vicar; Deacon Michael Juback.
Office: 17080 Arrow Blvd., 92335-3807. Tel: 909-822-0566; Fax: 909-829-1739. Email: stjoseph.fontana@sbdiocese.org.
Catechesis/Religious Program—Tel: 909-822-3411. Ms. Patricia Velazquez, D.R.E. Students 390.

4—ST. MARY (1939) Rev. Gerard O'Shaughnessy, S.S.C.
Mailing Address: 16548 Jurupa Ave., 92337-7452.
In Res., Revs. Brendan O'Sullivan, S.S.C.; Bernard E. Toal, S.S.C. (Retired).
Office: 16550 Jurupa Ave., 92337-7452. Tel: 909-822-5670, Ext. 0; Fax: 909-357-4688. Email: stmary.fontana@sbdiocese.org.
Catechesis/Religious Program—Tel: 909-822-5670, Ext. 222. Julian Ochoa, D.R.E. Students 140.

FRENCH VALLEY, RIVERSIDE CO., BLESSED TERESA OF CALCUTTA CATHOLIC COMMUNITY, INC. (2006) Very Rev. Thomas J. Burdick; Deacon Manuel Robles.
Office & Mailing Address: 31579 Vinters Pointe Ct., 92596. Tel: 951-325-7707; Fax: 951-325-2306. Email: blessedteresaofcalcutta.winchester@sbdiocese.org.
Catechesis/Religious Program—Students 231.

GRAND TERRACE, SAN BERNARDINO CO., CHRIST THE REDEEMER (1981) Very Rev. Romeo N. Seleccion, M.S., Priest Mod.; Sr. Deanna M. O'Neill, O.S.B., Pastoral Coord.; Rev. Jose G. Jaramillo, M.G., Chap., San Bernardino Region Korean Community.
Office: 12745 Oriole Ave., 92313-6133. Tel: 909-783-3811; Fax: 909-783-4689. Email: christtheredeemer.grandterrace@sbdiocese.org.
Catechesis/Religious Program—Tel: 909-783-3800. Kay Kendal, D.R.E. Students 170.

GUASTI, SAN BERNARDINO CO., SAN SECONDO D'ASTI (1926), (Italian), Rev. Louis N. Marx.
Mailing Address: P.O. Box 1056, 91743-1056.
Office: 250 N. Turner Ave., 91743. Tel: 909-390-0011; Fax: 909-390-9919. Email: sansecondodasti.guasti@sbdiocese.org. Web: www.sansecondodasti.com.
Catechesis/Religious Program—Tel: 909-390-6364. Thomas Edgington, D.R.E. Students 142.

HEMET, RIVERSIDE CO.

1—HOLY SPIRIT (1991) Very Rev. Msgr. Thomas M. Wallace, Priest Moderator; Rev. Jeremiah Holland, SS.CC., Priest Min.; Deacon Fernando Vera; Ms. Joyce Fritchel, Pastoral Coord.
Mailing Address: P.O. Box 5268, 92544.
Office: 26340 Soboba St., 92544. Tel: 909-927-8544; Fax: 909-927-8546. Email: holyspirit.hemet@sbdiocese.org. Web: www.holyspirithemet.org.
Catechesis/Religious Program—Ms. Vilma Cuevas, C.R.E. Students 217.

2—OUR LADY OF THE VALLEY (1946) Revs. Phillip R. Howard, C.S.Sp.; Barnabas S. Kileu, C.S.Sp., Parochial Vicar; Joseph L. Deniger, C.S.Sp., Parochial Vicar; Wayne Epperley, C.S.Sp., Parochial Vicar.
Office: 780 S. State St., 92543-7163. Tel: 951-929-6131; Fax: 951-929-8009. Email: olvhemet@sbdiocese.org.
Catechesis/Religious Program—Tel: 951-658-7436. Mr. Gustavo Lermus, D.R.E. Students 561.

HESPERIA, SAN BERNARDINO CO., HOLY FAMILY (1963) Revs. Santos L. Ortega; John Fahnestock, M.S.C., Parochial Vicar; Rigoberto Sanchez-Maya, Parochial Vicar; Deacons Santo Aguilera; Scott Hunsicker.
Office: 9974 I Ave., 92345. Tel: 760-244-9180; Fax: 760-244-1959. Email: holyfamily.hesperia@sbdiocese.org.
Catechesis/Religious Program—Tel: 760-244-5423. Ms. Rose Esparza, D.R.E.; Mercedes Sandoval, C.R.E. (Spanish); Ms. Laura Goodman, C.R.E. (English). Students 861.

HIGHLAND, SAN BERNARDINO CO., ST. ADELAIDE (1956) Rev. Pierre L. Deglaire, C.S.Sp.; Deacon Joe Acosta. In Res., Rev. Jose G. Jaramillo, M.G.
Office: 27457 E. Baseline, 92346-3206. Tel: 909-862-8669; Fax: 909-862-1603. Email: stadelaide.highland@sbdiocese.org.
School—St. Adelaide School, (Grades K-8), 27487 E. Base Line Rd., 92346. Tel: 909-862-5851; Fax: 909-862-2877. Mr. Greg Blanco, Prin. Lay Teachers 12; Students 158.
Catechesis/Religious Program—Tel: 909-862-8184. Ms. Nadine Scharnoff-Morales, D.R.E. Students 440.
Mission—St. John Bosco 28991 Merris St., East Highlands, San Bernardino Co. 92346. Tel: 909-425-0931.

IDYLLWILD, RIVERSIDE CO., QUEEN OF ANGELS (1942) Rev. Charles E. Miller.
Mailing Address: P.O. Box 1106, 92549-1106.
Office: 54525 N. Circle Dr., 92549-1106. Tel: 951-659-2708; Fax: 951-659-0208. Email: queenofangels.idyllwild@sbdiocese.org.
Catechesis/Religious Program—Ms. Linda Quijada, D.R.E. Students 49.

INDIO, RIVERSIDE CO., OUR LADY OF PERPETUAL HELP (1937) Very Rev. Msgr. Thomas M. Wallace, Priest Mod.; Laura Lopez, Pastoral Coord.; Revs. Miguel Corona, M.Sp.S., Priest Min.; Franklin Cubas-Ramirez, S.M., Priest Min.; Deacon Brijido Rodriguez.
Mailing Address: 45299 Deglet Noor St., 92201.
Office: 82-450 Bliss St., 92201. Tel: 760-347-3507; Fax: 760-347-8367. Email: olph.indio@sbdiocese.org.
School—Our Lady of Perpetual Help School, (Grades PreK-8), 82-470 Bliss St., 92201. Tel: 760-347-3786; Fax: 760-347-7207. Ms. Diane Arias, Prin. Lay Teachers 12; Students 224.
Catechesis/Religious Program—Tel: 760-347-0594. Margaret Rivera, D.R.E. Students 379.

JOSHUA TREE, SAN BERNARDINO CO., ST. CHRISTOPHER OF THE DESERT (1961) [JC] Rev. G. Ignatius Rasquinha; Deacon Glen Miller.
Mailing Address: 61350 Wahl Ter., 92252-2768.
Office: 61261 Sunburst Dr., 92252-2768. Tel: 760-366-8710; Fax: 760-366-2960. Email: stchristopherofthedesert.joshuatree@sbdiocese.org.
Catechesis/Religious Program—Combined with St. Mary of the Valley, Yucca Valley.

LA QUINTA, RIVERSIDE CO., ST. FRANCIS OF ASSISI (1974) Revs. James McLaughlin; Tong Ba Nguyen, Parochial Vicar; Deacon Pablo Benavides.
Office: 47-225 Washington St., 92253. Tel: 760-564-1255; Fax: 760-564-0763. Email: stfrancisofassisi.laquinta@sbdiocese.org. Web: www.stfrancislq.org.
Catechesis/Religious Program—Tel: 760-564-1255, Ext. 208. Lupita Jimenez, C.R.E. Students 467.

LAKE ARROWHEAD, SAN BERNARDINO CO., OUR LADY OF THE LAKE (1938) [CEM] Rev. Leonard Kryzwda, C.R.
Mailing Address: P.O. Box 1929, 92352-1929.
Office: 27627 Rim of the World Dr., 92352. Tel: 909-337-2333; Fax: 909-337-5041. Email: ollake.lakearrowhead@sbdiocese.org.
Catechesis/Religious Program—Tel: 909-337-2333, Ext. 140. Gia Brown, D.R.E. Students 278.

LENWOOD, SAN BERNARDINO CO., ST. PHILIP NERI (1979) [JC] Rev. Charles A. Patron.
Mailing Address: 505 E. Mountain View St., Barstow, 92311.
Office & Church: 25333 Third St., 92311. Tel: 760-253-5412; Fax: 760-253-3191. Email: stphilipneri.barstow@sbdiocese.org.
Catechesis/Religious Program—Mr. John Salazar, D.R.E. Twinned with St. Joseph, Barstow.

LOMA LINDA, SAN BERNARDINO CO., ST. JOSEPH THE WORKER (1944) Rev. Ignatius Rodrigues; Deacons William Shalhoub; Victor Barrion.
Office: 10816 Mt. View Ave., 92354. Tel: 909-796-2605; Fax: 909-796-0755. Email: stjosephtheworker.lomalinda@sbdiocese.org.
Catechesis/Religious Program—Tel: 909-796-4308; Fax: 909-796-4308. Cary Santiago, D.R.E. Students 167.

LUCERNE VALLEY, SAN BERNARDINO CO., ST. PAUL (1963) Revs. Antonio G. Abuan, M.S.; Arlan G. Intal, M.S., Parochial Vicar.
Mailing Address: P.O. Box 588, 92356.
8973 Mesa Rd., 92356. Tel: 760-248-7410; Fax: 760-248-2559. Email: stpaul.lucernevalley@sbdiocese.org.
Catechesis/Religious Program—Betty Curnett, D.R.E. Students 50.

MECCA, RIVERSIDE CO., SANCTUARY OF OUR LADY OF GUADALUPE (1964), (Hispanic), Very Rev. Eliseo Lucas, Admin.; Deacon Miguel Badena.
Mailing Address: P.O. Box 218, 92254.
Office: 65-100 Dale Kiler Rd., 92254. Tel: 760-396-2717, Ext. 110; Fax: 760-396-0047. Email: olgshrine.mecca@sbdiocese.org.
Catechesis/Religious Program—Tel: 760-396-2717, Ext. 112. Ms. Maribel Lopez, C.R.E.

MONTCLAIR, SAN BERNARDINO CO., OUR LADY OF LOURDES (1955) Revs. Anthony C. Dao, O.P., Admin.; Mark Bertelli, Parochial Vicar; Deacon Donald Norris.
Office: 10191 Central Ave., 91763-3801. Tel: 909-626-7278; Fax: 909-626-0562. Email: ollourdes.montclair@sbdiocese.org.
School—Our Lady of Lourdes School, (Grades K-8), 5303 Orchard St., 91763. Tel: 909-621-4418; Fax: 909-625-5034. Sr. Fidelma Lyne, P.B.V.M., Prin. Sisters of the Presentation 2; Lay Teachers 13; Students 205.
Catechesis/Religious Program—Tel: 909-626-0318. Sr. Angela Callanan, P.B.V.M., D.R.E. Students 754.

MORENO VALLEY, RIVERSIDE CO.

1—ST. CHRISTOPHER (1957) Revs. Joven T. Junio, M.S.; Miguel R. Ceja, Parochial Vicar; Frederick A. Costales, M.S., Parochial Vicar; Arnel Macabio, M.S., Parochial Vicar; Deacon Carlos Morales. In Res., Rev. Enrique C. Lapuebla Jr., M.S.
Office: 25075 Cottonwood Ave., 92553-0397. Tel: 951-924-1968, Ext. 101; Fax: 951-247-6477. Email: stchristopher.morenovalley@sbdiocese.org.
School—St. Christopher Preschool, (Grades Pre-School) Tel: 951-924-1968. Email: stchristopher.ocs@sbdiocese.org. Rebecca Reynoso, Prin. Lay Teachers 1; Students 36.
Catechesis/Religious Program— Ms. Teresita Felix, D.R.E. (Spanish); Ms. Jessica Mejia-Lara, C.R.E. (English). Students 1,479.

2—ST. PATRICK (1989) Very Rev. Msgr. Thomas M. Wallace, Priest Moderator; Deacons Richard Heames, Pastoral Coord.; Austin Kilbourn.
Office: 10915 Pigeon Pass Rd., 92557. Tel: 951-485-6673; Fax: 909-485-3834. Email: stpatrick.morenovalley@sbdiocese.org. Web: stpatrick92557.parishworld.net.
Catechesis/Religious Program—Tel: 951-485-6673, Ext. 113. Chris Robbins, D.R.E.; Ms. Graciela Gutierrez, C.R.E. (Spanish). Students 964.

MURRIETA, RIVERSIDE CO., ST. MARTHA (1992) Very Rev. Jack D. Barker; Rev. Gregory Elder, Parochial Vicar; Deacons Patrick Necerato; Fred Von Voigt.
Office: 37200 Whitewood Rd., 92563-5040. Tel: 951-698-8180; Fax: 951-698-7353. Email: stmartha.murrieta@sbdiocese.org.
Catechesis/Religious Program—Tel: 951-698-1528; Fax: 951-698-5546. Annette Wester, D.R.E. Students 1,084.

NEEDLES, SAN BERNARDINO CO., ST. ANN (1887) [JC 2] Rev. Amaro Saumell III.
Mailing Address: P.O. Box 190, 92363-0190.
Office: 218 D St., 92363. Tel: 760-326-2721; Fax: 760-326-3068. Email: stann.needles@sbdiocese.org.

Web: http://home.catholicweb.com/saintann catholicchurch.
Catechesis/Religious Program—Elaine Blake, D.R.E.

NORCO, RIVERSIDE CO.

1—ST. ANDREW KIM KOREAN COMMUNITY (1989) Rev. Young Seung J. Han; Deacons Paul Ahan; John Kim.
Office: 4110 Corona Ave., 92860. Tel: 951-372-9932; Fax: 951-340-1947. Email: stkimdaekonandrew.norco@sbdiocese.org.
Catechesis/Religious Program—Ms. Scholastica Hong, D.R.E. Students 92.

2—ST. MEL (1959) Revs. Declan Fogarty, O.S.A., Admin.; Emmanuel Ukaegbu-Onuoha, Parochial Vicar; Deacon Joe Vela.
Mailing Address: P.O. Box 700, 92860-0700.
Office: 4140 Corona Ave., 92860. Tel: 951-737-7144; Fax: 951-735-8332. Email: stmel.norco@sbdiocese.org.
Catechesis/Religious Program—Tel: 951-737-8140. Emily Guilherme, D.R.E. Students 669.

ONTARIO, SAN BERNARDINO CO.

1—ST. ELIZABETH ANN SETON (1980) Revs. John S. Vieira; Augustine I. Obasi, Parochial Vicar.
Office: 2713 S. Grove Ave., 91761-6931. Tel: 909-947-2956, Ext. 15; Fax: 909-923-2946. Email: stelizabethannseton.ontario@sbdiocese.org. Web: www.seascc-ont.org.
Catechesis/Religious Program—Tel: 909-947-2956, Ext. 27. Ms. Armida Duran, D.R.E.

2—ST. GEORGE (1905) [CEM] [JC] Revs. Michael L. Sturn; Fabian Reynalte, Parochial Vicar; Deacon Chris Carroll. In Res., Rev. Msgr. Timothy F. Lawlor (Retired).
Office: 505 N. Palm Ave., 91762. Tel: 909-983-2637, Ext. 101; Fax: 909-395-9707. Email: stgeorge.ontario@sbdiocese.org.
School—St. George School, (Grades PreK-8), 322 W. D St., 91762. Tel: 909-984-9123; Fax: 909-984-0921. Peter Horton, Prin. Lay Teachers 13; Students 258.
Catechesis/Religious Program—Tel: 909-460-1578. Ms. Katherine Martinez, D.R.E. (English); Sr. Mary Faith Tin, L.H.C., D.R.E. (Vietnamese). Students 224.

3—OUR LADY OF GUADALUPE (1948), (Hispanic), Revs. Alex Castillo; Pedro Garcia-Sanchez, O.F.M., Parochial Vicar.
Office: 710 S. Sultana Ave., 91761-2554. Tel: 909-986-6154; Fax: 909-984-1541. Email: olg.ontario@sbdiocese.org.
Catechesis/Religious Program—Tel: 909-983-2904. Maria Elana Puga, D.R.E. Students 684.

PALM DESERT, RIVERSIDE CO.

1—CHRIST OF THE DESERT (1928), (Newman Center) Rev. Howard A. Lincoln.
Office: 73441 Fred Waring Dr., 92260-2286. Tel: 760-346-0089; Fax: 760-340-2245. Email: christofthedesert.pd@sbdiocese.org. Web: www.sacredheartpalmdesert.com.
Catechesis/Religious Program—Combined with Sacred Heart, Palm Desert.

2—SACRED HEART (1956) Rev. Howard A. Lincoln; Deacon Fernando Heredia.
Office: 43-775 Deep Canyon Rd., 92260-3164. Tel: 760-346-6502; Fax: 760-773-4873. Email: sacredheart.pd@sbdiocese.org. Web: www.sacredheartpalmdesert.com.
School—Sacred Heart School, (Grades PreK-8) Tel: 760-346-3513; Fax: 760-773-0673. Alan Bruzzio, Prin. Religious Teachers 1; Lay Teachers 25; Students 575.
Catechesis/Religious Program—Tel: 760-346-6502. Ms. Silvia Ramirez, D.R.E. Students 387.

PALM SPRINGS, RIVERSIDE CO.

1—OUR LADY OF GUADALUPE (1912), (Cahuilla Indian), Rev. John P. Kavcak, M.S.C.
Mailing Address: P.O. Box 1947, 92263-1947.
204 S. Calle El Segundo, 92263-1947. Tel: 760-325-5809; Fax: 760-325-9031. Email: olg.palmsprings@sbdiocese.org. Web: ourladyofguadalupe92263.parishworld.net.

2—OUR LADY OF SOLITUDE (1928), (Hispanic), [JC] Revs. John P. Kavcak, M.S.C.; David K. Foxen, M.S.C., Parochial Vicar; Deacon John Skora.
Office: 151 W. Alejo Rd., 92262-5666. Tel: 760-325-3816; Fax: 760-325-5316. Email: olsolitude.ps@sbdiocese.org. Web: ourladyofsolitude92262.parishworld.net.
Catechesis/Religious Program—Ms. Maria Torres, D.R.E. (Spanish). Students 294.

3—ST. THERESA (1948) Rev. Msgr. Philip A. Behan.
Office: 2800 E. Ramon Rd., 92264-7996. Tel: 760-323-2669; Fax: 760-322-8581. Email: sttheresa.ps@sbdiocese.org. Web: www.sttheresaps.com.
School—St. Theresa School, (Grades K-8), 455 S. Compadre, 92262-7996. Tel: 760-327-4919; Fax: 760-327-4429. Email: sttheresa.ocs@sbdiocese.org. Web: www.stsps.org. Cheryl Corey, Prin. Lay Teachers 20; Students 370.
Catechesis/Religious Program—Tel: 760-323-4351 (English). Ms. Catherine Knox, D.R.E.; Ms. Jacqueline Macias, C.R.E. Students 272.

PERRIS, RIVERSIDE CO., ST. JAMES (1907) Revs. Edmund Gomez; Minh Nguyen, Parochial Vicar.
Office: 269 W. Third St., 92570-2073. Tel: 951-657-2380; Fax: 951-943-7290. Email: stjamesperris@sbdiocese.org. Web: stjames92570.googlepages.com.
School—St. James School, (Grades K-8), 250 W. Third St., 92570-2005. Tel: 951-657-5226; Fax: 951-657-1793. Email: stjames.ocs@sbdiocese.org. Sr. Sylvia Parkes, R.S.M., Prin. Religious Teachers 1; Lay Teachers 11; Students 170.
Catechesis/Religious Program—Tel: 951-940-5219; Fax: 951-940-5192. Cecelia Fornelli, D.R.E. Students 1,342.
Convent—230 W. B St., 92570. Tel: 951-657-4050.

PHELAN, SAN BERNARDINO CO., BLESSED JUNIPERO SERRA CHURCH (1989) Rev. Frank T. Dicristina.
Mailing Address: P.O. Box 292570, 92329-2570.
Office: 8820 Sheep Creek Rd., 92371. Tel: 760-868-4342; Fax: 760-868-4342. Email: blessedjuniperoserra.phelan@sbdiocese.org. Web: www.blessedjuniperoserra.org.
Catechesis/Religious Program—Tel: 760-868-4342, Ext. 42. Rita Evens, D.R.E. Students 222.

RANCHO CUCAMONGA, SAN BERNARDINO CO.

1—OUR LADY OF MOUNT CARMEL (1905) Very Rev. Romeo N. Seleccion, M.S., Priest Moderator; Deacon Luis Sanchez; Ms. Josefina Herrera, Pastoral Coord.
Office: 10079 Eighth St., 91730. Tel: 909-987-2717, Ext. 20; Fax: 909-987-3818. Email: olmtcarmel.rc@sbdiocese.org.
Catechesis/Religious Program—Tel: 909-987-2717, Ext. 21. Ms. Esthela Garcia, D.R.E. Students 330.

2—SACRED HEART (1953) Very Rev. Romeo N. Seleccion, M.S., Priest Moderator; Revs. Cristobal Subosa, F.I.M., Priest Min.; Henry M. Sseriiso, I.M.C., Priest Min.; Benedict C. Nwachukwu-Udaku (Nigeria), Priest Min.; Deacons Roberto Cardenas; Edward Clark; Patrick Necerato; Dr. Peter Newburn, Pastoral Coord. In Res., Rev. Edward J. Molumby, S.T.
Office: 12704 Foothill Blvd., 91739-9795. Tel: 909-899-1049, Ext. 110; Fax: 909-899-3229. Email: sacredheart.rc@sbdiocese.org. Web: www.sacredheartrc.org.
School—Sacred Heart School, (Grades K-8), 12676 Foothill Blvd., 91739. Tel: 909-899-1049; Fax: 909-899-0413. Ms. Trenna Meins, Prin. Lay Teachers 13; Students 260.
Catechesis/Religious Program—Students 792.

REDLANDS, SAN BERNARDINO CO., THE HOLY NAME OF JESUS CATHOLIC COMMUNITY, INC. (2006) Very Rev. Romeo N. Seleccion, M.S., Priest Moderator; Revs. Celestine Mbanu, Priest Min.; Adalberto Jeronimo-Garcia, C.O.R.C., Priest Min.; Sr. Mary Garascia, C.P.P.S., Pastoral Coord.; Deacons Bill Keough; Frank Enderle.
Office: 115 W. Olive Ave., 92373-5245. Tel: 909-793-2469; Fax: 909-335-1719. Email: theholynameofjesus.redlands@sbdiocese.org. Web: www.theholynameofjesus.org.
Columbia Street Worship Site—1214 Columbia St., 92373-5245.
Olive Avenue Worship Site—115 W. Olilve Ave., 92374.
School—Sacred Heart Academy, (Grades K-8), 215 S. Eureka St., 92373. Tel: 909-792-3958; Fax: 909-792-7292. Sr. Linda Nicholson, C.S.J., Prin. Religious Teachers 1; Lay Teachers 14; Students 253.
Catechesis/Religious Program—Tel: 909-798-4167; Fax: 909-335-1719. Ms. Miriam Padilla, D.R.E. Students 565.

RIALTO, SAN BERNARDINO CO., ST. CATHERINE OF SIENA (1949) Revs. Stephen C. Porter; Arturo S. Gomez, C.M.F., Parochial Vicar; Deacons Gonzalo Sotelo; Eric Vilchis.
Office: 339 N. Sycamore Ave., 92376-5943. Tel: 909-875-1360, Ext. 100; Fax: 909-875-2822. Email: stcatherineofsiena.rialto@sbdiocese.org. Web: stcatherineofsiena92376.parishworld.net.
School—St. Catherine of Siena School, (Grades PreSchool-8), 335 N. Sycamore Ave., 92376. Tel: 909-875-7821; Fax: 909-875-7948. Enrique Landin, Prin. Lay Teachers 9; Students 176.
Catechesis/Religious Program—Tel: 909-875-1360, Ext. 122. Ms. Terry Moriarty, D.R.E. Students 860.

RIVERSIDE, RIVERSIDE CO.

1—ST. ANDREW NEWMAN CENTER (1971), Serving Riverside Community College & University of California at Riverside. Revs. George M. Matanic, O.P.; Thomas Cassian Lewinski, O.P., Parochial Vicar.
Office: 105 W. Big Springs Rd., 92507-4737. Tel: 909-682-8751; Fax: 909-682-3513. Email: newman.riv@sbdiocese.org. Web: newmancenter92507.parishworld.net.
Catechesis/Religious Program—Tel: 951-682-8751, Ext. 13. Frances Hodgkinson, D.R.E. Students 130.

2—ST. ANTHONY OF PADUA (1923) Rev. Adrian Ochoa-Lugo, O.de.M., Admin.; Deacon Carlos Rosado.
Office: 3074 Madison St., 92504-4478. Tel: 951-352-8393; Fax: 951-352-8816. Email: stanthony.riv@sbdiocese.org.
Catechesis/Religious Program—Tel: 951-785-4908. Ms. Lily Gonzalez, D.R.E. Students 320.

3—ST. CATHERINE OF ALEXANDRIA (1946) Rev. Generoso Sabio, M.S.C.; Very Rev. Benjamin E. Alforque, M.S.C., Parochial Vicar; Deacons John DeGano; Donald Tillitson. In Res., Revs. Adrianus Budhi, M.S.C.; Nicholas B. Gito, M.S.C.
Office & Mailing Address: *(Ministry Center)*, 7005 Brockton Ave., 92506. Tel: 951-781-9855; Fax: 951-683-4114. Email: stcatherineofalexandria.riv@sbdiocese.org. Web: www.stcofa.org.
Church: 3680 Arlington Ave., 92506.
School—Sr. Catherine of Alexandria School, (Grades PreK-8), 7025 Brockton Ave., 92506. Tel: 951-684-1091; Fax: 951-684-4936. Rick Howick, Prin. Religious Teachers 1; Lay Teachers 16; Students 320.
Catechesis/Religious Program—Tel: 951-781-9855, Ext. 25; Fax: 951-781-3061. Ms. Olivia Garcia, D.R.E. Students 667.

4—ST. FRANCIS DE SALES (1886) [JC] Revs. Reno Aiardi, I.M.C., Admin.; Louis Abdoo, I.M.C., Parochial Vicar.
Office: 4268 Lime St., 92501-3868. Tel: 951-686-4004; Fax: 951-686-3948. Email: stfrancisdesales.riv@sbdiocese.org.
School—St. Francis de Sales School, (Grades PreSchool-8), 4205 Mulberry St., 92501. Tel: 951-683-5083; Fax: 951-683-0249. Mrs. Elaine Roy, Prin. Religious Teachers 1; Lay Teachers 11; Students 274.
Catechesis/Religious Program—Tel: 951-534-0929. Ms. Toni Bastian, D.R.E. (English); Ms. Consuelo Grajeda, D.R.E. (Spanish). Students 229.

5—ST. JOHN THE EVANGELIST (1956) Revs. Genaro Zavala, M.S.P.; Leonel Vega-Medina, M.S.P., Parochial Vicar.
Office: 3980 Opal St., 92509-7297. Tel: 951-684-6864; Fax: 909-684-3115. Email: stjohntheevangelist.riv@sbdiocese.org.
Catechesis/Religious Program—Tel: 909-686-5181. Lorraine Pittman, D.R.E. Students 571.
Mission—Our Lady of Guadalupe 2518 Hall Ave., Riverside Co. 92509. Tel: 909-788-1464.

6—OUR LADY OF GUADALUPE SHRINE (1929), (Hispanic), Rev. Alfonso Duran-Ortega, O.de M.
Office: 2858 Ninth St., 92507-4957. Tel: 951-684-0279; Fax: 951-684-0390. Email: olgshrine.riv@sbdiocese.org.
Catechesis/Religious Program—Tel: 951-683-1123. Maria Elena Alba.

7—OUR LADY OF PERPETUAL HELP (1955) Most Rev. Rutilio J. del Riego, Priest Moderator; Revs. Nicholas J. Barille, S.T., Priest Min.; Thoai "Aloysius" Ngoc Tran, C.M.C., Parochial Vicar; Charles E. Piatt, S.T., Priest Minister; Deacons Nam Bui; Ysidro Gurrola; Dr. Sara Elder, Pastoral Coord. In Res., Rev. Joseph Cornely, S.T.
Office: 5250 Central Ave., 92504-1825. Tel: 951-689-8921, Ext. 20; Fax: 951-689-3619. Email: olph.riv@sbdiocese.org. Web: http://olphriv.wordpress.com/.
School—Our Lady of Perpetual Help School, (Grades PreK-8), 6866 Streeter Ave., 92504-2299. Tel: 951-689-2125; Fax: 951-689-9354. Ms. Laurie Moore, Prin.; Maria Lopez, Librarian. Lay Teachers 11; Students 236.
Catechesis/Religious Program—Tel: 909-689-9821, Ext. 23. Ms. Mary Fisher, C.R.E. (English); Ms. Eva Jaimes, C.R.E. (Spanish); Sr. Hang Le, C.R.E. (Vietnamese). Students 741.

8—QUEEN OF ANGELS (1949) Revs. Miguel Ruiz, S.V.D.; Deebar Yonas, S.V.D., Parochial Vicar; Deacon James Neufell.
Office: 4824 Jones Ave., 92505-1432. Tel: 951-689-3674, Ext. 101; Fax: 951-687-6146. Email: queenofangelsriv@sbdiocese.org. Web: http://qofar.e-paluch.com/.
Catechesis/Religious Program—Tel: 951-687-3674, Ext. 121. Mariana Flores, D.R.E. Students 668.

9—SACRED HEART (1945) [JC] Rev. Martin S. Rodriguez, C.O.R.C., Admin.; Deacon John Barna.
Office: 9935 Mission Blvd., 92509. Tel: 951-685-5058; Fax: 951-354-7402. Email: sacredheart.riv@sbdiocese.org. Web: www.sacredheartriv.com.
Catechesis/Religious Program—Tel: 951-685-8510. Maria Ornales, D.R.E. Students 884.

10—ST. THOMAS THE APOSTLE (1903) Rev. Joseph F. Felker; Deacon Paul Myers.
Office: 3774 Jackson St., 92503-4359. Tel: 951-689-1131; Fax: 909-354-7402. Email: stthomastheapostel.riv@sbdiocese.org. Web:

www.stthomasriverside.com.
School—St. Thomas the Apostle School, (Grades K-8), 9136 Magnolia Ave., 92503. Tel: 951-689-1981; Fax: 951-689-1985. Cathy Thompson, Prin. Lay Teachers 13; Students 238.
Catechesis / Religious Program—Tel: 951-689-7980. Francesca Cover, D.R.E. Students 12.

RUNNING SPRINGS, SAN BERNARDINO CO., ST. ANNE IN THE MOUNTAINS (1963) Rev. Leonard Kryzwda, C.R.
Mailing Address: P.O. Box 2400, 92382-2400.
Office: 30480 Fredalba Rd., 92382. Tel: 909-867-2832; Fax: 909-867-2832. Email: stanne.runningsprings@sbdiocese.org.
Catechesis / Religious Program—Combined with Our Lady of the Lake, Lake Arrowhead.

SAN JACINTO, RIVERSIDE CO., ST. ANTHONY (1890) Rev. Cristobal Subosa, F.I.M., Admin.
Office: 630 S. Santa Fe Ave., 92583-4012. Tel: 951-654-7911; Fax: 951-654-2309. Email: stanthony.sjc@sbdiocese.org.
School—St. Hyacinth Academy, (Grades K-8), 275 S. Victoria Ave., 92583. Tel: 951-654-2013; Fax: 951-654-5644. Ladonna Lambert, Prin. Religious Teachers 2; Lay Teachers 13; Students 281.
Catechesis / Religious Program—Elizabeth Cortez, D.R.E.; Sr. Nina Achacoso, C.R.E. (English); Ana Melgar, C.R.E. (Spanish). Students 530.

SOBOBA INDIAN RESERVATION, RIVERSIDE CO., ST. JOSEPH MISSION (1888), (Native American), [CEM] Rev. Earl Henley, M.S.C.
Mailing Address: *Soboda Indian Reservation*, P.O. Box 1027, San Jacinto, 92581-1027.
Office: 23600 Soboba Rd., San Jacinto, 92583. Tel: 951-654-2086; Fax: 951-654-2086. Email: stjoseph.sanjacinto@sbdiocese.org.
Catechesis / Religious Program—Students 90.
Chapel—Our Lady of the Snows Chapel Cahuilla Indian Reservation, Cahuilla.
Chapel—St. Theresa Chapel Santa Rosa Indian Reservation, Santa Rosa. Tel: 909-659-2708.
Chapel—St. Mary Chapel Morongo Indian Reservation (11231 Mission Rd.), Banning, 92220.
Mission—El Senor de la Misericordia 87-217 Kokell Ave., Thermal, Riverside Co. 92274.
Chapel—St. Michael Chapel Pechanga Indian Reservation, Temecula, 92592.

SUN CITY, RIVERSIDE CO., ST. VINCENT FERRER (1965) [JC] Rev. Antonio Das Neves.
Office: 27931 Murrieta Rd., 92586-2320. Tel: 951-679-4531; Fax: 951-679-7521. Email: stvincentferrer@sbdiocese.org. Web: stvincentferrer92586.parishworld.net.
Catechesis / Religious Program—Tel: 951-672-4019. Mary Wedeking, D.R.E. Students 599.

TEMECULA, RIVERSIDE CO., ST. CATHERINE OF ALEXANDRIA (1979) Revs. John F. Wagner; Manuel Cardoza, Parochial Vicar; Deacons John Barth; Jose Ibarra; James Kincaid; Dennis Malkowski; Robert Phillips.
Office: 41875 C St., 92592-3029. Tel: 951-676-4403; Fax: 951-695-6659. Email: stcatherineofalexandria.temecula@sbdiocese.org. Web: stcatherineofalexandria92592.parishworld.net.
Catechesis / Religious Program—Tel: 951-695-6656. Letha Heylmun, D.R.E. Students 1,057.

TRONA, SAN BERNARDINO CO., ST. MADELEINE SOPHIE BARAT (1936) Rev. Charles A. Patron. All sacramental records located at St. Joseph, Barstow.
Office & Mailing Address: 505 E. Mountain View Rd., Barstow, 92311. Tel: 760-256-6818; Fax: 760-256-8307. Email: stmadeleinesophiebarat.trona@sbdiocese.org; stjoseph.barstow@sbdiocese.com.
Church: 83395 Trona Rd., 93562.
Catechesis / Religious Program—Mr. John Salazar, D.R.E. Students 7.

TWENTYNINE PALMS, SAN BERNARDINO CO., BLESSED SACRAMENT (1940) Rev. Gerald Vidad, Admin.; Deacon John Stanley.
Office: 6785 Sage Ave., 92277-9227. Tel: 760-367-3343; Fax: 760-367-0543. Email: blessedsacrament.29palms@sbdiocese.org.
Catechesis / Religious Program—Laurette Hill, D.R.E. Students 105.

UPLAND, SAN BERNARDINO CO.
1—ST. ANTHONY (1974) Very Rev. Romeo N. Seleccion, M.S., Priest Moderator; Rev. Patrick A. Brennan, O.S.A., Priest Min.; Deacons Robert Beidle; Stephen Serembe, Pastoral Coord.
Mailing Address: P.O. Box 608, 91785.
Office: 2110 N. San Antonio Ave., 91784. Tel: 909-958-2803; Fax: 909-982-8643. Email: st.anthony1@netscape.com.
Catechesis / Religious Program—Christina Moore, D.R.E. Students 448.
2—ST. JOSEPH (1922) [JC] Revs. Jerome Ochetti, Admin.; Scott Nguyen, Parochial Vicar; Oscar Reynoso, Parochial Vicar; Deacon Greg Moore.
Office: 877 N. Campus Ave., 91786-3930. Tel: 909-981-8110; Fax: 909-982-8991 1. Email: stjoseph.upland@sbdiocese.org. Web: www.stjosephupland.org.
School—St. Joseph School, (Grades PreSchool-8), 905 N. Campus Ave., 91786. Tel: 909-920-5185; Fax: 909-920-5190. Sr. Mary Kelly, P.B.V.M., Prin. Religious Teachers 2; Lay Teachers 12; Students 335.
Catechesis / Religious Program—Tel: 909-981-8110, Ext. 29. Debbi Aud, D.R.E. Students 437.
Convent—Sisters of the Presentation of the Blessed Virgin Mary (P.B.V.M.), 925 N. Campus Ave., 91786. Tel: 909-982-2686.

VICTORVILLE, SAN BERNARDINO CO.
1—HOLY INNOCENTS (1991) Revs. Mark C. Lander; James Oropel, Parochial Vicar; Deacons William Shellem; Marcial Ampuero.
Office: 13230 El Evado Rd., 92392. Tel: 760-955-6010; Fax: 760-955-2100. Email: holyinnocents.victorville@sbdiocese.org. Web: holyinnocents92392.parishworld.net.
Catechesis / Religious Program—Tel: 769-955-2100. Eileen Dutch, D.R.E. Students 309.
2—ST. JOAN OF ARC (1922) Rev. Ciro Libanati; Deacon Manual Gomez.
Office: 15512 Sixth St., 92395-3209. Tel: 760-245-7674; Fax: 760-245-7077. Email: stjoanofarc.victorville@sbdiocese.org.
Catechesis / Religious Program—Tel: 760-245-4904. Ms. Alicia Lombardo, C.R.E.

WILDOMAR, RIVERSIDE CO., ST. FRANCES OF ROME (1887) [JC] Rev. Mark E. Kotlarczyk; Deacons Rigoberto Ruano; Joseph Franco.
Office: 21591 Lemon St., 92595-8410. Tel: 951-674-6881, Ext. 222; Fax: 951-674-6443. Email: sfrancesofrome.wildomar@sbdiocese.org.
School—St. Frances of Rome Preschool, Tel: 951-471-5144; Fax: 951-471-5154. Catherine Beck, Prin. Lay Teachers 1; Students 34.
Catechesis / Religious Program—Tel: 951-674-6881, Ext. 224. Sr. Angelita Bacleon, M.S.M., D.R.E.

WRIGHTWOOD, SAN BERNARDINO CO., OUR LADY OF THE SNOWS (1946) Rev. Frank T. Dicristina.
Mailing Address: 8820 Sheep Creek Rd., Phelan, 92371-8988.
Office: 975 Lark, 92397. Tel: 760-868-4342; Fax: 760-868-2171. Email: olsnows.wrightwood@sbdiocese.org. Web: www.our-lady-of-the-snows.org.
Catechesis / Religious Program—Tel: 760-868-4342, Ext. 42. Rita Evans, D.R.E. Students 45.

YUCAIPA, SAN BERNARDINO CO., ST. FRANCES XAVIER CABRINI (1948) Very Revs. Romeo N. Seleccion, M.S., Priest Moderator; David Andel; Ms. Kirsten R. Thorstad, Pastoral Coord.; Deacons Peter S. Bond; Daniel D. Hudec.
Office: 12687 California St., 92399-4405. Tel: 909-797-2533; Fax: 909-790-5803. Email: stfrancesxaviercabrini.yucaipa@sbdiocese.org. Web: www.stfrancesxcabrinichurch.org.
Catechesis / Religious Program—Linda Ornelas, D.R.E. Students 318.

YUCCA VALLEY, SAN BERNARDINO CO., ST. MARY OF THE VALLEY (1953) Very Rev. Msgr. Thomas M. Wallace, Priest Moderator; Sr. Sara Michael King, C.S.J., Pastoral Coord.
Office: 7495 Church St., 92284-3247. Tel: 760-365-2287, Ext. 221; Fax: 760-369-0622. Email: stmaryofthevalley.yuccavalley@sbdiocese.org. Web: www.saintmaryofthevalley.org.
Catechesis / Religious Program—Tel: 760-365-2287. Sr. Sara Michael King, C.S.J., D.R.E. Students 161.

Chaplains of Public Institutions

SAN BERNARDINO. *St. Bernardine Medical Center*. 2101 N. Waterman Ave., 92404. Tel: 909-883-8711; Fax: 909-881-4546. Rev. Msgr. Antonio Sudario (Philippines).
Patton State Hospital, 3102 E. Highland Ave., Patton, 92369. Tel: 909-425-7429. Rev. Edmond "Ned" G. O'Donnell.
San Bernardino Community Hospital. 805 Medical Center Dr., 92411. Tel: 909-887-6333. Rev. Arul Pragasam Irudayaraj, S.V.D.

APPLE VALLEY. *St. Mary Medical Center*, 18300 Hwy. 18, 92307-0404. Tel: 760-242-2311. Rev. Gerald Onuoha, Chap.

BLYTHE. *Ironwood State Prison*, 19005 Wileys Well Rd., P.O. Box 1968, 92226. Tel: 760-921-3000. Rev. Ron Rusk.

CHINO. *California Institute for Men*, P.O. Box 128, 91710. Tel: 909-782-7455. Rev. Michael Bucaro.

COLTON. *Arrowhead Regional Medical Center*, 400 N. Pepper, 92324. Tel: 909-580-1000. Rev. Miguel A. Urrea.

CORONA. *California Institute for Women*, 16756 Chino-Corona Rd., Frontera, 91720. Tel: 909-597-1771. Vacant.

FONTANA. *Kaiser Permanente Hospital*, 9961 Sierra Ave., 92335. Tel: 909-829-5850. Rev. Javier Gonzales-Cabrera.

LOMA LINDA. *Loma Linda Community Hospital*, 2533 Barton Rd., 92354. Tel: 909-224-0800. Rev. Msgr. Cesar E. Encinares (Philippines), Rev. Stanley I. Onwuegbule.
Loma Linda U.M.C. East Campus, Barton Rd. and Anderson St., 92354. Tel: 909-796-7311, Ext. 4367. Rev. Msgr. Cesar E. Encinares (Philippines), Rev. Stanley I. Onwuegbule.

MORENA VALLEY. *Riverside County Regional Medical Center*, 56520 Cactus Ave., 92555. Tel: 951-486-4334. Rev. Enrique Canavelar LaPuebla, M.S.

NORCO. *California Rehabilitation Center*, Western & Fifth Sts., P.O. Box 1841, 91760. Tel: 909-737-2683, Ext. 4305. Vacant.

RIVERSIDE. *Riverside Community Hospital*, 4445 Magnolia Ave., 92501. Tel: 909-788-3000. Rev. Adrianus Budhi, M.S.C.

Special or Other Diocesan Assignment:
Very Rev. Msgrs.—
Lopez, Gerard M., S.T.L., V.G., Moderator of the Curia, Dir. Priest Personnel, & Vicar Gen.
Wallace, Thomas M., E.V., Episcopal Vicar
Rev. Msgrs.—
Lawrence, Robert E., J.C.L., Defender of the Bond (Retired)
Webber, Donald S., J.C.L., Judge, Canonical Services (Retired)
Very Revs.—
Andel, David, J.C.L., J.V., Judicial Vicar
Miller, Robert L., V.F., Dir. Continuing Priest Formation
Seleccion, Romeo N., M.S., E.V., Episcopal Vicar
Revs.—
Airdi, Reno, I.M.C., Dir. Missions
Barry, Michael, SS.CC., Mary's Mercy Center
Garcia, Juan L., D.L.P., Spiritual Dir., Blessed Junipero Serra House
Henley, Earl, M.S.C., Chap., St. Joseph Indian Mission
Jaramillo, Jose G., M.G., San Bernardino Region Korean Chap.
Lewinski, Thomas Cassian, O.P., Assoc. Dir. St. Andrew Newman Center
Nguyen, Matthias Huy Chuong, C.M.C., Chap., Shrine of the Presentation
Ochetti, Jerome, Assoc. Vocations Dir.
Partida, Rafael A., Special Works
Sanz, Jose A., D.L.P., Rector, Blessed Junipero Serra House

On Duty Outside the Diocese:
Revs.—
Lowe, Frank E.
Partida, Rafael A.

On Sabbatical:
Revs.—
Bertelli, Mark
Borba, Joseph

On Leave of Absence:
Revs.—
Granillo, Paul C., J.C.L.
Hindman, John
Jenkins, Kenneth F.
Manzon-Balagat, Arturo J.

Retired:
Rev. Msgrs.—
Andreatta, Tullio, 2245 Fort Stockton Rd., San Diego, 92103.
Battle, Lawrence, 73450 Country Club Dr. #190, Palm Desert, 92260.
Corciulo, Cosimo, 316 Mount Shasta Dr., Norco, 92860.
Lawlor, Timothy F., St. George Church, 505 N. Palm Ave., Ontario, 91762.
Lawrence, Robert E., J.C.L., 1300 Cypress Point Dr., Banning, 92220.
Ryan, John, 934 N. Dearborn, Redlands, 92374.
Webber, Donald S., J.C.L., 26634 Amhurst Ct., Sun City, 92586.
Revs.—
Baseford, Paul, 485 Foxenwood Dr., Santa Maria, 92355.
Benjamin, John J., 19184 Palo Verde Dr., Apple Valley, 92308.
Brinn, Adrian J., 6086 Pebble Beach, Banning, 92220.
Buchanan, Robert E., 1201 E. Highland Ave., 92404.
Cardoza, Edward, 21267 George Brown, 92518.
Casey, Donald A., 546 Reliance Ave., Henderson, NV 89015-9690.
Chavez, Arturo, 26071 St. Mary, Sun City, 92586.
Cima, Jose, 23505 Evening Snow, Moreno Valley, 92557.
Connor, Vincent, 23277 San Canyon Circle, Corona, 92883.

Devine, Charles F., P.O. Box 3021, Idyllwild, 92549.
DiLeo, Anthony, 43981 Northgate, Temecula, 92592.
Domas, John R., 5801 Sun Lake Blvd. Apt. 205, Banning, 92220.
Donat, Robert J., 5412 Calle de Arboles, Torrance, 90505.
Erickson, Robert J., P.O. Box 460, Rim Forest, 92378.
Gaglia, Fred R., 3250 W. 46th Ave., Denver, CO 80211.
Ganahl, James A., 801 Magnolia Ave., Corona, 92879.
Gillespie, Thomas, 1100 E. Ocean Blvd. #2, Long Beach, 90802.
Gonzales, George, c/o Vina de Lestonnac Ministry Center, 39300 De Portola Rd., Temecula, 92592.
Gorman, John, Nazareth House, 6333 Rancho Mission Rd., San Diego, 92108.
Grajek, Lawrence, P.O. Box 2077, Big Bear City, 92314.
Guillen-Santoyo, Patricio, 2002 S. Magnolia Ave., Ontario, 91762.
Kiefer, William J., 27920 Niagara Ct., Sun City, 92586.
Kopec, Chester C., O.P., 4320 Columbia Ave., 92501.
Kurilec, Robert E., 7743 Grundy St., Pensacola, FL 32507.
Leahy, Maurice J., St. Barnabas Church, Chicago, IL 60643.
Marcotte, William, 2699 Maryknoll Dr., Colfon, 92324.
McGuiness, Edward J., 4667 Braemar Pl. #210, 92513.
McGuinness, Gerard J., 4667 Braemar Pl., #224, 92513.
McNally, Michael R., P.O. Box 3802, 92413.
O'Day, Michael, Nazareth House, 6333 Rancho Mission Rd., San Diego, 92108.
O'Donnell, Edmond G., P.O. Box 1405, Upland, 91786.
Rogan, Brian, 819 Sherwood St., Redlands, 92373.
Schultz, Charles F., Jr., S.T.D., 31 Jasmine Creek Dr., Corona Del Mar, 92625.
Speno, Eugene, 43-129 Rutledge Way, Palm Desert, 92260.
Tomkins, Robert J., 5800 Hamner Ave., #349, Mira Loma, 91752.
Walters, Vincent, 4647 Braemar Pl. #26, 92501-3040.

Permanent Deacons:
Acosta, Joseph, (Retired)
Aguilera, Santo, Hesperia
Ahan, Paul, Norco
Alaniz, Frank, (Retired)
Amadore, Robert, Colton
Ampuero, Marcial, Victorville
Badena, Miguel, Coachella
Barna, John, Riverside
Barrion, Victor, Loma Linda
Bassford, Rick, Crestline
Beidle, Robert, Upland
Bellinder, Michael, Redlands
Benavides, Pablo, La Quinta
Bond, Peter S., Yucaipa
Brannick, Tom, (Retired)
Bui, Nam, San Bernardino
Burgett, Donald, (Retired)
Burris, Bud, (Retired)
Campbell, Gerald, Desert Hot Springs
Cardenas, Roberto, Rancho Cucamonga
Carroll, Chris, Ontario
Castanon, Leonard, Colton
Clark, Ed, Rancho Cucamonga
Clinton, Jack, (Retired), Upland
Cover, Richard, (Retired)
DeGano, John, Riverside
Enderle, Frank, Redlands
Fausto, John
Filipek, Marlin, (Retired)
Franco, Joseph, Wildomar
Garcia, Jose Israel, Coachella
Geaga, Donnie, Alta Loma
Glass, Nelson, San Bernardino
Gonzalez, Victor, Coachell
Gurrola, Ysidro, Riverside
Gutierrez, Mario, San Bernardino
Han, Hikyung H.K., Blythe
Henke, Jack, (Retired)
Heredia, Fernando, Palm Desert
Hodnick, Mark, Beaumont
Hoy, Wayne, (Retired)
Hudec, Daniel D., Yucaipa
Hunsicker, Scott, J.C.L., Hesperia
Ibarra, Jose, Temecula
Jelley, Michael, San Bernardino
Juback, Michael, Fontana
Keough, Bill, (Retired)
Kilbourn, Austin, Moreno Valley
Kim, John, M.D., Norco
Kincaid, James, Temecula
Luevano, Armando, Beaumont
Malkowski, Dennis, Temecula
Martinez, Pat, Chino Hills
Miller, Glenn, Joshua Tree
Mirci, Philip, (Inactive)
Moore, Greg, Upland
Morales, Carlos, Moreno Valley
Necerato, Patrick, Murrieta
Neufell, James, Riverside
Norris, Donald, Montclair
O'Camb, Daniel, San Bernardino
Olivas, Manuel, Fontana
Partida, Ralph, Jr., Big Bear
Phillips, Robert, Temecula
Quilliam, Larry
Rehaume, Ronald J., (Retired), Sun City
Rodriguez, Brijido, Indio
Rosado, Carlos, Riverside
Ruano, Rigoberto, Wildomar
Saenz, Margo, Barstow
Salinas, Arcadio, Jr., (Retired)
Sanchez, Luis, Rancho Cucamonga
Sepulveda, Ralph, (Retired), San Bernardino
Serembe, Stephen, San Bernardino
Shalhoub, William J., Loma Linda
Shellem, William, Victorville
Simoni, Frank, (Retired)
Skora, John, Palm Springs
Sotelo, Gonzalo, Rialto
Taylor, Daniel, San Bernardino
Tillitson, Donald, Riverside
Uribe, Ricardo, Moreno Valley
Vasquez, Sergio, Coachella
Vela, Joe, Norco
Vera, Fernando, Hemet
Vilchis, Eric, Rialto
Von Ins, Paul, Corona
Ybarra, Rudy, (Retired), Riverside
Zamora, Abel, Fontana

INSTITUTIONS LOCATED IN THE DIOCESE

[A] SEMINARIES, RELIGIOUS OR SCHOLASTICATES

GRAND TERRACE. *Blessed Junipero Serra House of Formation* (1985) 12725 Oriole Ave., 92313. Tel: 909-783-0260; Fax: 909-783-0223. Revs. Juan L. Garcia, D.L.P., Spiritual Dir.; Jose A. Sanz, D.L.P., Rector. Priests 2; Sisters 2; Seminarians 15; Lay Persons 1.

[B] HIGH SCHOOLS, DIOCESAN

SAN BERNARDINO. *Aquinas High School* (Coed), 2772 N. Sterling Ave., 92404. Tel: 909-886-4659; Fax: 909-886-7717. Email: Aquinas@Aquinashs.net. Web: www.aquinashs.net. Mr. Francis Herdlein, Prin.; Mr. Daryl Sequeira, Pres. Priests 1; Sisters 1; Lay Teachers 32; Students 338.

RIVERSIDE. *Notre Dame High School* (Coed), 7085 Brockton Ave., 92506. Tel: 951-275-5896; Fax: 951-781-9020. Email: jsalley@ndhsriverside.org. Web: ndhsriverside.org. Dr. Jo Dean Salley, Prin.; Mrs. Lydia Dashkovitz, Librarian. Sisters 2; Priests 1; Lay Teachers 30; Students 515.

[C] HIGH SCHOOLS, PRIVATE

PALM DESERT. **Xavier College Preparatory High School*, 34-200 Cook St., 92211. Tel: 760-601-3900; Fax: 760-601-3901. Email: calling@xavierprep.org. Web: xavierprep.org. Mr. Chris Alling, Prin. Lay Teachers 25; Students 340.

[D] ELEMENTARY SCHOOLS, PRIVATE

TEMECULA. *Saint Jeanne Lestonnac School*, (Grades PreSchool-8), 32650 Avenida Lestonnac, 92592. Tel: 951-587-2505; Fax: 951-587-2515. Email: sjdls@sjdls.com. Web: www.sjdls.com. Sr. Esperanza Flores, O.D.N., Prin.; Ms. Kristen Mora, Prin. Sisters 4; Staff 50; Students 460.

[E] HOMES FOR SENIOR CITIZENS

SAN BERNARDINO. *St. Bernardine Plaza*, 550 W. Fifth St., 92401. Tel: 909-888-0153; Fax: 909-381-1589. Email: stbern2@la.twcbc.com. Dee Moyes, Resident Mgr. Total Staff 5; Units 150.

PALM DESERT. *La Paz Villas*, 43555 Deep Canyon Rd., 92211. Mailing Address: *Sacred Heart Parish*, 43775 Deep Canyon Rd., 92211. Tel: 760-346-6502; Fax: 760-773-4873. Email: dpelletier@sacredheartpalmdesert.com. Dorothy Pelletier, Contact Person. Units 6.

[F] GENERAL HOSPITALS AND CLINICS

SAN BERNARDINO. *St. Bernardine Medical Center* a dba of Catholic Healthcare West, 2101 N. Waterman Ave., 92404. Tel: 909-883-8711; Fax: 909-881-4531. Email: sbmcf@chw.edu. Web: www.stbernardinemedctr.org. Steve Barron, Pres. & CEO. Bed Capacity 463; Total Assisted Annually 102,618; Total Staff 1,592.

St. Bernardine Medical Center Foundation, 2101 N. Waterman Ave., 92404. Tel: 909-883-8711. Patricia A. Davis, Pres. Foundation.

APPLE VALLEY. *St. Mary Medical Center*, 18300 Hwy. 18, 92307. Tel: 760-242-2311; Fax: 760-242-2994. Web: stmaryapplevalley.com. John Perring-Mulligan, Ph.D., Vice Pres., Mission Integration. Bed Capacity 186; Total Assisted Annually 150,000; Total Staff 1,532.

St. Joseph Health System, Orange. Tel: 714-347-7500. Employed Catholic Priest Chaplain 2; Sisters 2; Brothers 1; Bed Capacity 186.

St. Mary Medical Center Auxiliary Tel: 760-242-2311; Fax: 760-242-9750.

St. Mary Hospital Foundation Tel: 760-242-2311; Fax: 760-242-9750. Bed Capacity 186; Patients Assisted Annually 110,000; Total Staff 1,550.

Sisters of St. Joseph, 18810 Munsee Rd., 92307. Tel: 760-242-7644. (Residence for sisters missioned to the hospital, owned by the hospital).

[G] ALCOHOL AND DRUG REHABILITATION CENTERS

VICTORVILLE. *St. John of God Health Care Services*, 13333 Palmdale Rd., P.O. Box 2457, 92393. Tel: 760-241-4917; Fax: 760-241-8911. Email: admin@sjghcs.org. Sponsored by the Brothers of St. John of God., Alcohol & Drug Rehabilitation Program. Brothers 1; Total Staff 29; Bed Capacity 77; Patients Assisted Annually 1,200.

[H] CATHOLIC SOCIAL SERVICE ORGANIZATIONS

SAN BERNARDINO. *Catholic Charities San Bernardino/ Riverside, Administration Office*, 1450 N. D St., 92405. Tel: 909-388-1239; Fax: 909-384-1130. Email: infor@ccsbriv.org. Web: www.ccsbriv.org. Ken F. Sawa, M.S.W., L.C.S.W., CEO, Exec. Vice Pres.; Beverly Earl, Dir. Family & Community Svcs., San Bernadino Co.; Belinda Marquez, Dir. Family & Community Svcs., Riverside Co.

Counseling Services, 1265 La Cadena Dr., Ste. 4, Colton, 92324. Tel: 909-370-1293; Fax: 909-370-4679. Gary McMane, M.S.W., Dir. Counseling Svcs.; James Billings, Ph.D., Assoc. Dir. Counseling Svcs.

**Mary's Mercy Center, Inc.*, 641 Roberds Ave., P.O. Box 7563, 92411. Tel: 909-889-2558; Fax: 909-386-7704. Email: mmcinc@msn.com. Web: marysmercycenter.org. Adrienne Schubert, Vice Pres.

INDIO. **Martha's Village & Kitchen, Inc.*, 83-791 Date Ave., 92201. Tel: 760-347-4741; Fax: 760-347-9551. Email: gloria.gomez@neighbor.org. Web: www.marthasvillage.org. Gloria Gomez, Contact Person & Founder. A member of Father Joe's Villages. Total Staff 92.

[I] MONASTERIES AND RESIDENCES OF PRIESTS AND BROTHERS

APPLE VALLEY. *Hospitaller Brothers of St. John of God, O.H.*, P.O. Box 1664, 92307. Tel: 760-242-6560. Bros. Anthony Scully, O.H., Prior; Peter Gelfer, O.H.; Eric Hoffer, O.H.; Paul Hanson, O.H.; Ignatius Sudal, O.H. Brothers 6.

Missionaries of Our Lady of La Salette. MS, 18386 Corwin Rd., 92307. Tel: 760-242-4427; Fax: 760-242-1195. Revs. Antonio G. Abuan-Gaona, M.S.; Arlan G. Intal, M.S.

CHINO HILLS. *Congregation of the Sacred Hearts of Jesus & Mary, SS.CC.*, Western U.S. Province, St. Paul the Apostle Rectory, 14085 Peyton Dr., 91709. Tel: 909-465-5503; Fax: 909-465-1683. Very Rev. Patrick J. O'Hagan, SS.CC., V.F., Pastor; Revs. Michael Barry, SS.CC.; Pat Crowley, SS.CC.; Peter K. Dennis, SS.CC.; Michael J. Gilsenan, SS.CC., Parochial Vicar; Jeremiah Holland, SS.CC.

COACHELLA. *Congregation of Holy Cross*, 52-525 Oasis Palm Dr., 92236. Tel: 760-398-5577; Fax: 760-398-1783. Web: www.soledad-coachella.org. Revs. Bruce K. Cecil, C.S.C.; John S. Connor, C.S.C., Parochial Vicar; Jaime Irwin, C.S.C.; Peter Pacini, C.S.C.

CORONA. *Confraternity of Operarios Del Reino De Cristo, C.O.R.C.*, 610 Msgr. Thompson Cir., 92882. Tel: 951-549-6000; Fax: 951-549-6009. Revs. Pedro Enrique Amezcua (Mexico), Regl. Dir.; Josue Arellano, C.O.R.C.; Eliseo Hernandez, C.O.R.C.; Jorge Luis Rodriguez, C.O.R.C.; Martin S. Rodriguez, C.O.R.C.; Jose Varela, C.O.R.C.

Congregation of the Mother Co-Redemptrix, C.M.C., 1775 S. Main St., 91720-4961. Tel: 909-737-4125;

951-340-9880; Fax: 951-479-0002. Email: corona@dongcong.net. Web: www.medangcom.net. Revs. Ignatius Kinh Hai Duong Nguyen, C.M.C., Dir.; Aloysius Thoai Ngoc Tran, C.M.C.; Luke M. Binh Dinh Do, C.M.C.; John Vu Cao, C.M.C.; Vincent Au, C.M.C. Shrine of Presentation (Den Thanh Duc Me Dang Con).

FONTANA. *Congregation of the Resurrection, CR*, 7650 Tamarind St., 92336. Tel: 909-822-4732; Fax: 909-822-0620. Revs. Marcelo de Jesumaria, C.R.; James M. Gibson, C.R.; Timothy F. Keppel, C.R.; Richard McGee, C.R. (Retired); Humphrey Ruszel, C.R. (Retired); Henry Ruszel, C.R. (Retired); Casmir T. Tadla, C.R. (Retired). P.O. Box 1929, Lake Arrowhead, 92359. Tel: 909-337-2333; Fax: 909-337-5041. Rev. Leonard Krzywda, C.R. 875 E. Chanslorway, Blythe, 92225. Tel: 760-922-3261; Fax: 760-922-5279. Rev. Henry Licznerski, C.R.

GRAND TERRACE. *Diocesan Laborer Priests, DLP, Blessed Juniper Serra House of Formation*, 12725 Oriole Ave., 92313. Tel: 909-783-0260; Fax: 909-783-0223. Revs. Jose A. Sanz, D.L.P., Dir. of Seminarians; Juan L. Garcia, D.L.P., Spiritual Dir.

HEMET. *Congregation of the Holy Spirit*, Casa Laval Retirement Community, 309 E. Whitter Ave., P.O. Box 3509, 92546-3509. Tel: 951-658-2241; Fax: 909-765-3137. Email: spiritan@pc.net. Web: www.spiritan.org. Revs. George Healy, C.S.Sp., Acting Supr. (Retired); Joseph B. Gaglioni, C.S.Sp. (Retired); Francis Kichak, C.S.Sp. (Retired); Albert McKnight, C.S.Sp. (Retired).

LUCERNE VALLEY. *The Cistercian Congregation of the Holy Family, St. Joseph Monastery*, 21010 Lucerne Valley Cutoff, P.O. Box 960, 92356-0960. Tel: 714-625-9466. Email: saintjoseph.ocist@yahoo.com. Rev. M. Anthony Hanh Si Pham, O.Cist., Supr.; Rt. Rev. M. John Lam Dinh Vuong, O.Cist., Abbot (Retired); Revs. M. Justin Cong Huu Ho, O.Cist.; M. Timothy Qui Van Than, O.Cist.; Bros. M. Peter-Binh Quynh Dang Pham, O.Cist.; M. Matthew-Gam Phong Hoai Nguyen, O.Cist.; M. Francis of Assisi Phu Quoc Nguyen, O.Cist.

MORENO VALLEY. *Missionaries of Our Lady of La Salette, MS*, 25075 Cottonwood Ave., 92553. Tel: 951-924-1968; Fax: 951-247-6477. Very Rev. Romeo N. Seleccion, M.S.; Revs. Enrique C. Lapuebla Jr., M.S.; Frederick A. Costales, M.S.; Joven T. Junio, M.S.; Arnel Macabio, M.S.

REDLANDS. *Discalced Carmelites, OCD*, P.O. Box 446, 92373. Tel: 909-792-1047; Fax: 909-798-3497. Email: elcarmelo@juno.com. Web: www.elcarmelo.org. Revs. Charles Garrity, O.C.D., Supr.; Matthew Williams, O.C.D., Prov.; Thomas Koller, O.C.D.; Jorge Zakowicz, O.C.D.; Bro. Boniface Scheerer, O.C.D.

RIVERSIDE. *Divine Word Seminary, Western Province - Society of the Divine Word, S.V.D.*, 11316 Cypress Ave., 92505. Tel: 951-689-4858; Fax: 951-785-0327. Email: dwrc05@cs.com. Revs. Briccio Tamoro, S.V.D., Provincial Supr.; Jose Rodriguez Goopio, S.V.D., Rector; William J. Caffrey, S.V.D.; Herman Manuel, S.V.D.; John P. McHenry, S.V.D.; John A. Neissen, S.V.D.; Donald O'Connor, S.V.D.; Ponciano Ramos, S.V.D.; Emilio Reyes, S.V.D., Dir., Retreat Center; Paul Lester Schmidt, S.V.D.; Joseph P. Scott, S.V.D.; Sony Sebastian, S.V.D.; John Tran, S.V.D.; Bros. Bernard Dorade, S.V.D.; Andrew Hotchkiss, S.V.D.; Steve Kerekes, S.V.D.; Vinh Trinh, S.V.D.; Daniel Yunck, S.V.D.

St. Vincent Ferrer House Dominican Priests and Brothers, Western Province, OP, 872 Spruce St., 92507. Tel: 951-784-0160. Revs. Lawrence Farrell, O.P.; Thomas Cassian Lewinski, O.P.; George M. Matanic, O.P. Dominicans.

[J] CONVENTS AND RESIDENCES FOR SISTERS

SAN BERNARDINO. *Daughters of St. Joseph of California, F.S.J.*, 6677 Del Rosa Ave., 92404. Tel: 909-888-4877; Fax: 909-888-4387. Email: daughtersjoseph@aol.com. Sisters Pilar Soto, F.S.J., Major Supr.; Ma. Cristina Garza Longoria, Supr. Sisters 5.

APPLE VALLEY. *Sisters of St. Joseph of Orange, C.S.J.O*, 18810 Munsee Rd., 92307. Tel: 760-242-7644. Sisters 2.

BIG BEAR LAKE. *Society Devoted to the Sacred Heart, S.D.S.H.*, 896 Cienega Rd., P.O. Box 1795, 92315. Tel: 909-866-5696; Fax: 909-866-5650. Email: shrcbb@msn.com. Sisters 5.

CALIMESA. *Missionary Sisters of the Immaculate Conception* (SMIC), 1271 Nugget Ct., 92320. Fax: 909-795-8128. Email: judinefran@aol.com. Sisters Judine Jacobs, S.M.I.C., OB-GYN Nurse Practitioner; Frances Karovic, S.M.I.C., Coord., Parish Health Ministry at Blessed Kateri Tekakwitha Church. Sisters (Madonna of Desert Community) 2.

GRAND TERRACE. *Sisters of St. Benedict, Holy Spirit Monastery*, 22791 Pico St., 92313-5725. Tel: 909-783-4446; Fax: 909-783-3525. Email: hsmonastery@prodigy.net. Web: www.holyspiritmonastery.org. Sr. Mary Ann Schepers, O.S.B., Prioress. Sisters 6.

REDLANDS. *Sisters of Mercy, U.S. Province, U. S. Province, Provincial House*, 1075 Bermuda Dr., 92374. Tel: 909-798-4747; Fax: 909-798-5300. Email: roconnor-sm@sbdiocese.org. Web: www.sistersofmercy.ie. Sr. Rosaline O'Connor, R.S.M., Prov. Total in Residence 4; Total in U.S. Province 84.

TEMECULA. *Congregation of Kkottongnae Sisters of Jesus* (CKSJ), 37885 Hwy. 79 S., 92592. Tel: 951-302-3400; Fax: 951-302-3400. Email: tmclkkot@hotmail.com.

Sisters of the Company of Mary Our Lady, Convent, 32650 Avenida Lestonnac, 92592. Tel: 951-587-2504; Fax: 951-587-2515. Email: hruvalcaba@sjdls.com. Web: www.sjdls.com. Sr. Henrietta Ruvalcaba, O.D.N., Admin./Teacher. Sisters 4.

Vina de Lestonnac Ministry Center-Convent, 39300 De Portola Rd., 92592. Tel: 951-302-2800; Fax: 951-491-0686. Email: vinaodn@verizon.net. Web: www.companyofmary.us. Total in Residence 12.

[K] DIOCESAN CORPORATIONS

SAN BERNARDINO. *Blessed Junipero Serra House of Formation, Inc.*, 1201 E. Highland Ave., 92404. Tel: 909-475-5150; Fax: 909-475-5156. Email: mrwallace@sbdiocese.org. Ms. MaryRose Wallace, CFO.

The Catholic Foundation, 1201 E. Highland Ave., 92404. Tel: 909-475-5150; Fax: 909-475-5156. Email: mrwallace@sbdiocese.org. Ms. MaryRose Wallace, CFO.

Diocesan Development Fund, Inc., 1201 E. Highland Ave., 92404. Tel: 909-475-5150; Fax: 909-475-5156. Email: mrwallace@sbdiocese.org. Ms. MaryRose Wallace, CFO.

Diocese of San Bernardino Cemetery Corp., Inc., 1201 E. Highland Ave., 92404. Tel: 909-475-5150; Fax: 909-457-5156. Email: cemeteries@sbdiocese.org. Ms. MaryRose Wallace, CFO.

Diocese of San Bernardino Education & Welfare Corporation, 1201 E. Highland Ave., 92404-4641. Tel: 909-475-5150; Fax: 909-457-5156. Email: mrwallace@sbdiocese.org. Ms. MaryRose Wallace, CFO.

Diocese of San Bernardino Land Development Corporation, 1201 E. Highland Ave., 92404. Tel: 909-475-5150; Fax: 909-475-5156. Email: mrwallace@sbdiocese.org. Ms. MaryRose Wallace, CFO.

SAN JACINTO. *Kateri Tekakwitha Fund*, P.O. Box 302, 92581-0302. Tel: 951-654-2086; Fax: 951-654-2086. Sr. Marianna Torrano, R.S.C.J., Sec. & CFO.

[L] CAMPS & RETREATS

BIG BEAR LAKE. *Sacred Heart Retreat Camp*, 896 Cienega Rd., P.O. Box 1795, 92315. Tel: 909-866-5696; Fax: 909-866-5650. Email: shrcbb@msn.com. Web: www.sacredheartsisters.com/sacredheartretreatcamp/. Total in Residence 5; Total Staff 12.

REDLANDS. *El Carmelo Retreat House*, 926 E. Highland Ave., P.O. Box 446, 92373. Tel: 909-792-1047; Fax: 909-798-3497. Email: elcarmelo@juno.com. Web: www.elcarmelo.org. Revs. Charles Garrity, O.C.D., Supr.; Thomas Koller, O.C.D.; Bro. Boniface Scheerer, O.C.D. Priests 3; Sisters 4; Total in Residence 7; Total Staff 6.

RIVERSIDE. *Divine Word - Seminary - Divine Word Retreat Center*, 11316 Cypress Ave., 92505. Tel: 951-689-2961; Fax: 909-785-0327. Email: aishmiel@yahoo.com.

RUNNING SPRINGS. *St. Anne in the Mountains Retreat Center*, P.O. Box 2400, 92382. Tel: 909-867-2832; Fax: 909-867-2832. Email: stanneinthemountains@verizon.net. Web: www.mountaincatholic.org. Terri MacDonald, Contact Person.

TEMECULA. *Vina de Lestonnac Ministry Center - Retreat*, 39300 De Portoal Rd., 92592. Tel: 951-302-5571; Fax: 951-302-2830.

Lestonnac Chalet, 24719 San Moritz Dr., Crestline, 92325. Tel: 909-338-1525; Fax: 714-835-0648.

[M] NEWMAN CENTERS

SAN BERNARDINO. *California State University Newman Center* 1201 E. Highland Ave., 92494. Tel: 909-537-7337; Fax: 909-475-5457; Cell: 909-816-6393. Email: lgonzalez@sbdiocese.org. Web: RCNMinistry.catholicweb.com. Luz Gonzalez.

RIVERSIDE. *St. Andrew Newman Center* 105 W. Big Springs Rd., 92507. Tel: 951-682-8751; Fax: 951-682-3513. Email: catholicucr@earthlink.net; newmancenter92507@parishworld.net. Revs. George M. Matanic, O.P., Dir.; Thomas Cassian Lewinski, O.P., Assoc. Dir. Serving Riverside Community College and University of California at Riverside.

[N] MISCELLANEOUS

SAN BERNARDINO. **Caritas Telecommunications*, 1201 E. Highland Ave., 92404. Tel: 909-475-5107; Fax: 909-475-5109. Email: jandrews@sbdiocese.org. Web: www.sbdiocese.org. Mr. John H. Andrews, B.A., Dir.

Ministerio Biblico Verbo Divino (MBVD), Mailing Address: P.O. Box 1610, 92402. 555 N. E St., 92401. Tel: 909-383-1610; Fax: 909-383-4987. Web: www.verbodivino.org. Rev. Joseph Scott, Pres. & Contact Person.

**Wordnet, Inc.*, 532 N. "D" St., 92401-1304. Tel: 909-383-4333; Fax: 909-383-4347. Email: exdir@wordnet.tv. Web: wordnet.tv. Rev. Michael Manning, S.V.D., Pres.; Sr. Patricia Phillips, S.H.C.J., Exec. Dir.; Rev. Sony Sebastian, S.V.D., Exec. Producer; Bro. Stephen Pardy, S.V.D., Devel. Dir.; Sr. Jeanne Harris, O.P., Communications Dir.; Miranda Emde, Dir. Mktg. Brothers 1; Priests 2; Lay Staff 3; Sisters 2.

[O] CLOSED OR MERGED PARISHES

ALBERHILL. *Blessed Sacrament Parish* Closed 1965. For sacramental records, contact Diocesan Archives.

AMBOY. *St. Raymond Parish* Closed 1970. For sacramental records, contact Diocesan Archives.

BANNING. *Precious Blood* (1890) Closed 2006. For sacramental records, contact Blessed Kateri Tekakwitha, Tel: 951-849-2434.

BEAUMONT. *Sacred Heart Parish* Closed 1965. For sacramental records, contact Blessed Kateri Tekakwitha, Tel: 951-849-2434.

San Gorgonio (1908) Closed 2006. For sacramental records, contact Blessed Kateri Tekakwitha, Tel: 951-849-2434.

EAGLE MOUNTAIN. *St. Augustine* Closed 2001. For sacramental records, contact Diocesan Archives.

FONTANA. *Church of the Resurrection* (1953) Closed 2006. For sacramental records, contact Blessed John XXIII, Tel: 909-822-4732.

HIGHGROVE. *Our Lady of Guadalupe* Closed 1981. For sacramental records, contact Christ the Redeemer, Tel: 909-475-5399.

LUDLOW. *St. Michael Parish* Closed 1962. For sacramental records, contact Diocesan Archives.

ORO GRANDE. *St. Cecilia Parish* Closed 1975. For sacramental records, contact St. Joan of Arc, Victorville, Tel: 760-245-7674.

REDLANDS. *St. Mary* (1941) Closed 2006. For sacramental records, contact The Holy Name of Jesus, Tel: 909-793-2469.

Sacred Heart (1894) Closed 2006. For sacramental records, contact The Holy Name of Jesus, Tel: 909-793-2469.

RIALTO. *St. Thomas More* (1961) Closed 2006. For sacramental records, contact Blessed John XXIII, Tel: 909-822-4732.

RIVERSIDE. *St. Ignatius Parish* Closed 1972. For sacramental records, contact Our Lady of Guadalupe Shrine, Tel: 951-684-0279.

SAN BERNARDINO. *St. Anne* (1938) Closed 2006. For sacramental records, contact Our Lady of Hope, Tel: 909-884-6375.

Christ the King (1934) Closed 2006. For sacramental records, contact Our Lady of Hope, Tel: 909-884-6375.

Our Lady of Fatima (1952) Closed 2006. For sacramental records, contact Our Lady of Hope, Tel: 909-884-6375.

St. Theresa Parish Closed 1992. For sacramental records, contact Diocesan Archives.

THOUSAND PALMS. *St. Philip the Apostle* (1991) Closed 2007. For sacramental records, contact Diocesan Archives.

RELIGIOUS INSTITUTUES OF MEN REPRESENTED IN THE DIOCESE

For further details refer to the corresponding bracketed number in the Religious Institutes of Men or Women section.

[0140]—*Augustinians*—O.S.A.

[]—*Byzantine Brothers of St. Francis*—B.B.S.F.

[0470]—*Capuchin Franciscan Friars*—O.F.M.Cap.

[0340]—*Cistercian Fathers*—O.Cist.

[0360]—*Claretian Missionaries (Western Province)*—C.M.F.

[]—*Confraternity of Operarios del Reino de Cristo*—C.O.R.C.

[0533]—*Congregation of Franciscan Friars of the Immaculate*—F.I.

[0610]—*Congregation of Holy Cross*—C.S.C.

[]—*Congregation of Kkottongnae Brothers of Jesus*—C.K.B.J.

[]—*Congregation of Mother Coredemptrix*—C.M.C.

[0650]—*Congregation of the Holy Spirit*—C.S.Sp.
[1080]—*Congregation of the Resurrection*—C.R.
[1140]—*Congregation of the Sacred Hearts of Jesus and Mary* (Western Prov.)—SS.CC.
[0390]—*Consolata Missionaries*—I.M.C.
[]—*Diocesan Laborer Priests*—D.L.P.
[0260]—*Discalced Carmelite Friars* (Western Prov.)—O.C.D.
[0520]—*Franciscan Friars*—O.F.M.
[]—*Guadalupe Missioners*—M.G.
[0670]—*Hospitaller Brothers of St. John of God*—O.H.
[0780]—*Marist Fathers*—S.M.
[0800]—*Maryknoll*—M.M.
[]—*Misioneros Servidores de la Palabra*—M.S.P.
[0720]—*Missionaries of Our Lady of La Salette*—M.S.
[1110]—*Missionaries of the Sacred Heart*—M.S.C.
[]—*Missionaries of the Sacred Heart* (Philippines)—M.S.C.
[0840]—*Missionary Servants of the Most Holy Trinity*—S.T.
[0520]—*National Fraternity of the Secular Franciscan Order, U.S.A.*
[0340]—*Order of Cistercians*—O.Cist.
[0970]—*Order of Our Lady of Mercy*—O.de.M.
[0430]—*Order of Preachers (Dominican)* (Southern Province)—O.P.
[0430]—*Order of Preachers (Dominican)*—O.P.
[0430]—*Order of Preachers (Dominican)* (Western Province)—O.P.
[0200]—*Order of St. Benedict* (MN)—O.S.B.
[1230]—*Servants of the Paraclete*—s.P.
[0370]—*Society of St. Columbian*—S.S.C.
[0420]—*Society of the Divine Word* (Western Prov.)—S.V.D.

RELIGIOUS INSTITUTES OF WOMEN REPRESENTED IN THE DIOCESE

[0230]—*Benedictine Sisters of Pontifical Jurisdiction* (Grand Terrace, CA)—O.S.B.
[2020]—*Community of the Holy Spirit*—C.H.S.
[]—*Congregation of Kkottongnae Sisters of Jesus*—C.K.S.J.
[3260]—*Congregation of Sisters of the Precious Blood*—C.PP.S.
[]—*Congregation of the Sacred Heart*—S.H.
[2549]—*Congregation of the Sisters of Mercy* (U.S. Prov.)—R.S.M.
[3935]—*Congregation of the Sisters of St. Louis, Juilly-Monaghan*—S.S.L.
[0790]—*Daughters of Divine Charity* (Staten Island)—F.D.C.
[0790]—*Daughters of Divine Charity* (Akron, OH)—F.D.C.
[0880]—*Daughters of Mary and Joseph*—D.M.J.
[]—*Daughters of Mary Mother of Mercy*—D.M.M.M.
[1070-13]—*Dominican Sisters* (Adrian)—O.P.
[1070-19]—*Dominican Sisters* (Houston)—O.P.
[1070-30]—*Dominican Sisters* (Oakford, South Africa)—O.P.
[1070-15]—*Dominican Sisters* (Blauvelt)—O.P.
[1070-12]—*Dominican Sisters of Mission San Jose*—O.P.
[]—*Esclavas De La Inmaculata Nina*—E.I.N.
[]—*Franciscan Sisters of the Heart of Jesus* Pakistan—C.J.H.
[]—*Hermanas del Corazon de Jesus Sacramentado*—H.C.J.S.
[]—*Hermanas Evangelizadoras Eucharisticas de los Pobres*—E.E.P.
[2390]—*Lovers of the Holy Cross*—L.H.C.
[2420]—*Marist Missionary Sisters*—S.M.S.M.
[]—*Misioneras Servidoras de la Palabra* Mexico—M.S.P.
[2800]—*Missionaries of the Sacred Heart of Jesus (Hiltrup)*—M.S.C.
[]—*Missionary Sisters of Mary*—M.S.M.
[2760]—*Missionary Sisters of the Immaculate Conception of the Mother of God*—S.M.I.C.
[]—*Oblates of Santa Marta*—O.S.M.
[3130]—*Our Lady of Victory Missionary Sisters*—O.L.V.M.
[0930]—*Religious Daughters of St. Joseph*—F.S.J.
[4070]—*Religious of the Sacred Heart*—R.S.C.J.
[3465]—*Religious of the Sacred Heart of Mary*—R.S.H.M.
[1680]—*School Sisters of St. Francis*—O.S.F.
[]—*Sisters for Christian Community*—S.F.C.C.
[0430]—*Sisters of Charity of the Blessed Virgin Mary*—B.V.M.
[]—*Sisters of Charity of the Incarnate Word*—C.C.V.I.
[1070-30]—*Sisters of St. Dominic* (Oakford, So. Africa)—O.P.
[3360]—*Sisters of Providence of St. Mary of-the-Woods*—S.P.
[1540]—*Sisters of Saint Francis* Clinton, Iowa—O.S.F.
[3770]—*Sisters of St. Clare*—O.S.C.
[1650]—*The Sisters of St. Francis of Philadelphia*—O.S.F.
[3840]—*Sisters of St. Joseph of Carondolet*—C.S.J.
[3830-03]—*Sisters of St. Joseph of Orange*—C.S.J.
[3890]—*Sisters of St. Joseph of Peace*—C.S.J.P.
[0700]—*Sisters of the Company of Mary Our Lady*—O.D.N.
[1990]—*Sisters of the Holy Names of Jesus and Mary*—S.N.J.M.
[]—*Sisters of the Korean Martyrs*—S.K.M.
[1720]—*Sisters of the Third Order Regular of St. Francis of the Congregation of Our Lady of Lourdes* (Rochester)—O.S.F.
[4050]—*Society Devoted to the Sacred Heart*—S.D.S.H.
[4060]—*Society of the Holy Child*—S.H.C.J.
[3320]—*Union of Sisters of the Presentation of the B.V.M.*—P.B.V.M.

DIOCESAN CEMETERIES

SAN BERNARDINO. *Our Lady Queen of Peace Catholic Cemetery*, Mailing Address: 1201 E. Highland Ave., 92404-4641. Tel: 909-475-5122; Fax: 909-475-5109. 3510 Washington St., Colton, 92324. Tel: 909-796-9351.

NECROLOGY

† Chavez, Rev. Msgr. Adolphus, (Retired)—Died Dec. 28, 2008
† Connolly, Rev. Msgr. Edward J., San Bernardino, CA Diocesan Pastoral Center—Died March 4, 2009
† Ngo, Joseph Trong, (Retired)—Died July 11, 2009

An asterisk (*) denotes an organization that has established tax-exempt status directly with the IRS and is not covered by the USCCB Group Ruling.

Diocese of San Diego

(Dioecesis Sancti Didaci)

Most Reverend

ROBERT H. BROM, D.D.

Bishop of San Diego; ordained December 18, 1963; appointed Bishop of Duluth March 25, 1983; consecrated and installed May 23, 1983; appointed Coadjutor Bishop of San Diego April 22, 1989; appointed Bishop of San Diego July 10, 1990. *Office: P.O. Box 85728, San Diego, CA 92186-5728.* Tel: 858-490-8200.

Pastoral Center: P.O. Box 85728, San Diego, CA 92186-5728. Tel: 858-490-8200; Fax: 858-490-8272.

Web: www.diocese-sdiego.org

Email: scallaha@diocese-sdiego.org

ESTABLISHED JULY 11, 1936.

Square Miles 8,852.

Comprises the Counties of Imperial and San Diego in the State of California.

Legal Titles: The Roman Catholic Bishop of San Diego, a Corporation Sole--(Churches, Rectories, Halls, Catechetical Centers, etc.) Diocese of San Diego.
For legal titles of parishes and diocesan institutions, consult the Diocesan Office.

STATISTICAL OVERVIEW

Personnel	
Bishop	1
Abbots	1
Priests: Diocesan Active in Diocese	110
Priests: Diocesan Active Outside Diocese	3
Priests: Retired, Sick or Absent	65
Number of Diocesan Priests	178
Religious Priests in Diocese	87
Total Priests in Diocese	265
Extern Priests in Diocese	77
Ordinations:	
Transitional Deacons	3
Permanent Deacons	7
Permanent Deacons in Diocese	137
Total Brothers	23
Total Sisters	271
Parishes	
Parishes	99
With Resident Pastor:	
Resident Diocesan Priests	87
Resident Religious Priests	10
Without Resident Pastor:	
Administered by Priests	1
Administered by Lay People	1
Missions	15
Professional Ministry Personnel:	
Brothers	23
Sisters	271
Welfare	
Catholic Hospitals	2
Total Assisted	37,000
Homes for the Aged	3
Total Assisted	269
Residential Care of Children	1
Total Assisted	200
Day Care Centers	1
Total Assisted	400
Specialized Homes	6
Total Assisted	83,020
Special Centers for Social Services	2
Total Assisted	179,520
Residential Care of Disabled	1
Total Assisted	70
Educational	
Diocesan Students in Other Seminaries	5
Students Religious	2
Total Seminarians	7
Colleges and Universities	2
Total Students	7,826
High Schools, Diocesan and Parish	3
Total Students	2,719
High Schools, Private	2
Total Students	1,477
Elementary Schools, Diocesan and Parish	44
Total Students	12,019
Elementary Schools, Private	3
Total Students	934
Non-residential Schools for the Disabled	1
Total Students	274
Catechesis/Religious Education:	
High School Students	8,399
Elementary Students	25,926
Total Students under Catholic Instruction	59,581
Teachers in the Diocese:	
Priests	3
Brothers	1
Sisters	30
Lay Teachers	1,117
Vital Statistics	
Receptions into the Church:	
Infant Baptism Totals	10,301
Minor Baptism Totals	591
Adult Baptism Totals	356
Received into Full Communion	253
First Communions	8,464
Confirmations	5,919
Marriages:	
Catholic	1,512
Interfaith	353
Total Marriages	1,865
Deaths	2,712
Total Catholic Population	981,211
Total Population	3,118,990

Former Bishops—Most Revs. CHARLES F. BUDDY, D.D., S.T.D., Ph.D., ord. Sept. 19, 1914; appt. First Bishop of San Diego, Oct. 31, 1936; cons. Dec. 21, 1936; named Asst. at Pontifical Throne, Jan. 12, 1964; died March 6, 1966; FRANCIS J. FUREY, D.D., Ph.D., LL.D., ord. March 15, 1930; appt. Auxiliary Bishop of Philadelphia, Aug. 24, 1960; cons. Dec. 22, 1960; succeeded to the See of San Diego, March 6, 1966; translated to Archbishop of San Antonio, June 4, 1969; died April 23, 1979; LEO T. MAHER, D.D., Bishop of San Diego; ord. Dec. 18, 1943; First Bishop of Santa Rosa; appt. Feb. 21, 1962; cons. April 5, 1962; translated to San Diego, Aug. 27, 1969; retired July 10, 1990; died Feb. 23, 1991.

Pastoral Center—3888 Paducah Dr., San Diego, 92117. Mailing Address: P.O. Box 85728, San Diego, 92186-5728. Tel: 858-490-8200; Fax: 858-490-8272. Office Hours: Mon.-Fri. 8:30-4:30.

Vicar General—Very Rev. Msgr. STEVEN F. CALLAHAN, J.C.L. Tel: 858-490-8310.

Chancellor—RODRIGO VALDIVIA, J.C.L. Tel: 858-490-8310.

Assistant to the Bishop—Rev. ANTHONY SAROKI.

Judicial Vicar—Very Rev. EDWARD P. MCNULTY, J.C.L.

Diocesan Tribunal

Adjutant Judicial Vicar—Very Rev. Msgr. STEVEN F. CALLAHAN, J.C.L.

Promoter of Justice—Rev. DAVID N. CROISETIERE.

Defenders of the Bond—KELLY BEAURIVAGE, J.C.D.; Rev. Msgr. DANIEL J. DILLABOUGH.

Diocesan Judges—RODRIGO VALDIVIA, J.C.L.; Rev. Msgr. MARK A. CAMPBELL, J.C.L.

Tribunal Auditors—Deacons RAYMOND ARNOLD; ROBERT FITZMORRIS.

Notaries—CONNIE NOEL; LETICIA MENDOZA.

Diocesan Offices and Directors

Archivist—Contact: Chancellor's Office. Tel: 858-490-8208.

Catholic Charities—Sr. RAYMONDA DUVALL, C.H.S., Exec. Dir., 349 Cedar St., San Diego, 92101. Tel: 619-231-2828.

Cemetery Committee—Very Rev. Msgr. DENNIS MIKULANIS, Dir., Holy Cross Cemetery, 4470 Hilltop Dr., San Diego, 92102. Tel: 619-264-3127.

Censores Librorum—Very Rev. Msgr. RICHARD DUNCANSON, S.T.D.; BERNADEANE CARR, S.T.L.

Child and Youth Protection—RODRIGO VALDIVIA, J.C.L. Tel: 858-490-8310.

Civil Affairs—MARIA C. ROBERTS, Esq. Tel: 858-490-8277.

Spiritual Direction for Candidates and Priests—Rev. WILLIAM DILLARD. Tel: 619-291-5042.

Computer Services—RENE NG. Tel: 858-490-8329.

Construction Services—DANIEL RANCOURT, Dir. Tel: 858-490-8215.

Ecumenical and Interreligious Affairs—Very Rev. Msgr. DENNIS MIKULANIS, Vicar, 17252 Bernardo Center Dr., Rancho Bernardo, 92128-2086. Tel: 858-487-4314.

Education—

Evangelization & Catechetical Ministry—MARYJO WAGGONER, Dir. Tel: 858-490-8232.

Institute for Adult Education and Formation for Ministry—BERNADEANE CARR, S.T.L., Dir. Tel: 858-490-8212.

Schools—STEVAN LAAPERI, Dir. Tel: 858-490-8240; Sr. BREEGE BOYLE, S.S.L., Assoc. Dir. Tel: 858-490-8240; PATRICIA BANNON, Assoc. Dir. Tel: 858-490-8244.

Media Center—Tel: 858-490-8230.

Youth Ministry—GERARDO ROJAS, Dir. Tel: 858-490-8260.

Young Adult Ministry—CARRIE GIEBEL, Dir. Tel: 858-490-8261.

Facilities and Related Services—RODRIGO VALDIVIA, J.C.L., Dir. Tel: 858-490-8301.

Finance—Mr. GERARD A. WILLS, Finance Officer. Tel: 858-490-8316; SHIRLEY PAJANOR, Controller. Tel: 858-490-8207.

Human Resources—Deacon DANIEL POWERS, Dir. Tel: 858-490-8282.

Liturgy and Spirituality—Rev. EARL EGGLESTON, Dir. Tel: 858-490-8290.

Marriage and Family Life—MARGARET SKIANO, Dir. Tel: 858-490-8295.

Missions—Rev. JOSEPH MILLER, S.V.D., Dir.; Sr. EVA RODRIGUEZ, Assoc. Dir. Tel: 858-490-8250.

Cultural Diversity—RODRIGO VALDIVIA, J.C.L., Dir. Tel: 858-490-8306.

Parish Administration—Deacon DANIEL POWERS, Dir. Tel: 858-490-8284.

Permanent Diaconate—Sr. CARLOTTA DI LORENZO, C.S.J., Dir.; JOSE ERNESTO GONZALEZ, Assoc. Tel: 858-490-8239.

Priests—Rev. MICHAEL MURPHY, Dir., 655 C Ave., Coronado, 92118-3167. Tel: 619-437-4846; Fax: 619-437-1572.

Priestly Formation -- St. Francis Center—Rev. MATTHEW D. SPAHR, Dir. Tel: 619-291-7446; Fax: 619-291-7011.

Social Ministry—KENT PETERS, Dir. Tel: 858-490-8324; Deacon JAMES WALSH, Asst. Dir. Tel: 858-490-8375; LINDA ARREOLA, Asst. Dir. Tel: 858-490-8323.

"Southern Cross"--(Diocesan Newspaper)—Rev. CHARLES FULD, Editor. Tel: 858-490-8279.

Spiritual Direction for Candidates and Priests—Rev. WILLIAM DILLARD, Dir. Tel: 619-291-5042.

Priestly Vocations—Rev. ANTHONY SAROKI, Dir. Tel: 619-291-7446.

Women Religious—Sr. JEANETTE LUCINIO, S.P., Dir. Tel: 858-490-8289.

Vocations—Sr. AURORA LOPEZ-ORNELAS, S.J.S., Dir. Tel: 858-490-8346.

Advisory Bodies

Clergy Personnel Board—Very Rev. Msgr. STEVEN F. CALLAHAN, J.C.L., Chm. Tel: 858-490-8310; Very Rev. EDWARD P. MCNULTY, J.C.L.; Revs. MICHAEL PHAM; JAMES POULSEN; RONALD J. BUCHMILLER; MICHAEL A. CUNNANE; PETER ESCALANTE; PETER MCGUINE; PATRICK J. MURPHY.

College of Consultors—Rev. Msgrs. DANIEL J. DILLABOUGH; HENRY F. FAWCETT (Retired); Very Rev. Msgr. STEVEN F. CALLAHAN, J.C.L.; Rev. MATTHEW D. SPAHR; Very Rev. BRUCE ORSBORN.

Diocesan Pastoral Council—Most Rev. ROBERT H. BROM, D.D., Ex Officio.

Finance Council—Most Rev. ROBERT H. BROM, D.D., Chm.; Mr. FRED BARANOWSKI; Mr. THOMAS BLAKE; Very Rev. Msgr. STEVEN F. CALLAHAN, J.C.L.; Dr. CONSTANCE CARROLL; Mrs. SUSAN CARTER; Mr. DEAN DWYER; Mr. MICHAEL EYER; Mr. MICHAEL MAHER; Mr. TIMOTHY MEISSNER; Deacon FRANK MERCARDANTE; Ms. LORI HOUSE; Mr. BRIAN RILEY; Rev. ANTHONY SAROKI; Mr. LAWRENCE SHEA; Mr. MICHAEL WEST.

Presbyteral Council—Most Rev. ROBERT H. BROM, D.D.; Rev. JOHN PROCTOR JR., Special Works; Very Rev. Msgr. STEVEN F. CALLAHAN, J.C.L.; Rev. RONALD J. BUCHMILLER, El Cajon Deanery; Very Rev. BRUCE J. ORSBORN; Revs. MICHAEL MURPHY; MATTHEW D. SPAHR; WILLIAM M. PETRUSKA, Military Liaison; Very Rev. EDDIE RUIZ, El Centro Deanery; Revs. ANTHONY SAROKI, Exec. Sec.; JAMES BAHASH; Rev. Msgrs. MARK A. CAMPBELL, J.C.L.; DANIEL J. DILLABOUGH; Revs. MANUEL EDIZA; PETER ESCALANTE; Rev. Msgr. HENRY F. FAWCETT (Retired); Revs. STEVEN LARION; RAYMOND G. O'DONNELL; MICHAEL RATAJCZAK.

Vicars Forane—Very Rev. BRUCE J. ORSBORN, Cathedral; Very Rev. Msgrs. EDWARD BROCKHAUS, El Cajon; LAWRENCE M. PURCELL, Oceanside; Very Revs. EDDIE RUIZ, El Centro; JOHN P. DOLAN, South Bay; Very Rev. Msgrs. RICHARD DUNCANSON, S.T.D., Mission; DENNIS MIKULANIS, Escondido.

Miscellaneous

Apostleship of the Sea—Deacon SAM MARTINEZ. Tel: 619-702-4703; Rev. JAMES BOYD, Chap. Tel: 858-292-1822.

Hispanic Charismatic Renewal Center (Carismatica Hispana)—JOSE MACIAS, Coord. Tel: 619-423-2474.

Cursillo—Spiritual Advisors: Deacon CHARLES FRICE; PATRICK O'BRIEN, Lay Dir.

Filipino—LUZ MONTEMAYER, Lay Dir.; Rev. DIONISIO MACALINTAL, Spiritual Advisor; Deacon SAM MARTINEZ, Assoc. Spiritual Advisor. Tel: 619-267-0074.

Hispanic—RICARDO DE ROSARIOS, Pres. Secretariat. Tel: 619-656-1132; Rev. ANDRES RIVERO, O.F.M., Spiritual Advisor. Tel: 619-232-6681.

Vietnamese—Rev. DOAN VAN LAI, Spiritual Dir.; VINCENT KY DINH, Lay Dir. Tel: 858-697-2320.

Holy Childhood Association—Sr. EVA LUCIA RODRIGUEZ, Assoc. Dir., Mailing Address: P.O. Box 82386, San Diego, 92138-2386. Tel: 858-490-8250.

Propagation of the Faith—Rev. JOSEPH MILLER, S.V.D., Dir., Mailing Address: P.O. Box 82386, San Diego, 92186-2386. Tel: 858-490-8250.

Victim Assistance Coordinator—Very Rev. Msgr. STEVEN F. CALLAHAN, J.C.L. Tel: 858-490-8310.

CLERGY, PARISHES, MISSIONS AND PAROCHIAL SCHOOLS

CITY OF SAN DIEGO

(SAN DIEGO COUNTY)

1—ST. JOSEPH CATHEDRAL (1874) Rev. Peter Escalante. In Res., Rev. William Ortman (Retired); Rev. Msgr. Edward F. Lyng (Retired).
Res.: 1535 Third Ave., 92101-3192. Tel: 619-239-0229; Fax: 619-239-3788.
Catechesis/Religious Program—Students 65.

2—ST. AGNES (1908) Very Rev. Edward P. McNulty.
Res.: 1140 Evergreen St., 92106. Tel: 619-223-2200; Fax: 619-223-7568.
Catechesis/Religious Program—Tel: 619-223-9748; Fax: 619-223-4725. Students 118.

3—ST. ANNE (2008) Revs. Carl Gismondi, F.S.S.P.; Federico Masutti, F.S.S.P.
621 Sicard St., 92113. Tel: 619-239-8253.

4—ASCENSION (1980) Rev. Anthony Saroki; Deacon Jim Scull.
Res.: 5335 La Cuenta Dr., 92124-1524. Tel: 858-268-7188.
Catechesis/Religious Program—Tel: 858-279-1023. Students 196.

5—BLESSED SACRAMENT (1938) Very Rev. Bruce J. Orsborn; Rev. Bernardo Ranoa (Philippines); Deacons A. Anthony Albers; Herbert Kelsey. In Res., Revs. Jerry Hamperzonian; James Burson, C.J.M.
Res.: 4540 El Cerrito Dr., 92115. Tel: 619-582-5722; Fax: 619-582-2505. Email: jyin@blessedsacrament-sd.org. Web: www.blessedsacrament-sd.org.
School—(Grades PreK-8), 4551 56th St., 92115. Tel: 619-582-3862; Fax: 619-265-9310. Ms. Theodora Furtado, Prin. Lay Teachers 20; Students 273.
Catechesis/Religious Program—Tel: 619-582-4633. Students 55.
Mission—SDSU Newman Center 5855 Hardy Ave., San Diego Co. 92115. Tel: 619-583-9181; Fax: 619-583-8925.

6—ST. BRIGID (1940) Very Rev. Msgr. Steven F. Callahan; Rev. Msgr. Sean Murray, Pastor Emeritus (Retired); Rev. Steven Larion; Deacon Michael Daniels; Sr. Josephine Breen, R.S.M., Pastoral Assoc.
Church & Res.: 4735 Cass St., 92109-2698. Tel: 858-483-3030; Fax: 858-483-7131.
Catechesis/Religious Program—Tel: 858-483-3032. Sr. Hilda McDonagh, R.S.M., D.R.E.; Erika Toraya, C.R.E. Tel: 858-483-8905; Grant Milbrand, Youth Min. Tel: 858-459-1732; Carrie Giebel, Young Adult Min. Tel: 858-483-3416. Students 224.

7—ST. CATHERINE LABOURE (1964) Rev. Msgr. Patrick J. Mullarkey.
Mailing Address: 4124 Mt. Abraham Ave., 92111.
Res.: 4038 Mt. Abraham Ave., 92111. Tel: 858-277-3133; Fax: 858-277-9181. Email: stcl@sbcglobal.net.
Catechesis/Religious Program—Tel: 858-279-0587; Fax: 858-277-9181. Sandra Welch, D.R.E. Students 193.

8—ST. CHARLES (1946) Revs. George Decasa; Arnold Tadena; Deacons Howard Mick Dennison; Ken Montoya; Sam Martinez, (Retired).
Res.: 990 Saturn Blvd., 92154. Tel: 619-423-0242; Fax: 619-423-1966. Web: www.saintcharles.org.
School—(Grades K-8), 929 18th St., 92154. Tel: 619-423-3701; Fax: 619-423-5331. Mr. Steve Stutz, Prin.; Sr. Elizabeth Wekall, Librarian. Sisters of Mercy 1; Lay Teachers 13; Students 237.
Catechesis/Religious Program—Tel: 619-575-2240. Students 608.

9—ST. CHARLES BORROMEO (1946) Rev. William A. Kernan; Deacon Richard Sanderville.
Res.: 2802 Cadiz St., 92110-4813. Tel: 619-225-8157; Fax: 619-225-2288. Web: www.stcharlesborromeo.us.
School—(Grades K-8) Tel: 619-223-8271; Fax: 619-223-2695. Thomas Mamara, Prin. Lay Teachers 12; Students 168.
School—Preschool, Tel: 619-758-0903. Karen Snedden, Dir. Lay Teachers 2; Students 33.
Catechesis/Religious Program—Students 85.

10—CHRIST THE KING (1938) Rev. Tommie Jennings; Deacon Harry Guess Jr.
Church: 29 N. 32nd St., 92102. Tel: 619-231-8906; Fax: 619-238-7060. Email: ctksango@sbcglobal.net.
Catechesis/Religious Program—Students 198.

11—ST. COLUMBA (1955) Rev. Mario Elias. In Res., Rev. Chol-Min Ahn.
Res.: 3327 Glencolum Dr., 92123. Tel: 858-277-3863; Fax: 858-277-3883. Web: www.stcolumbasandiego.com.
School—(Grades PreK-8) Tel: 858-279-1882; Fax: 858-279-1653. Mrs. Geraldine Nau, Prin. Lay Teachers 16; Students 249.
Catechesis/Religious Program—Tel: 858-277-3861. Students 175.

12—ST. DIDACUS (1926) Rev. Michael Sinor; Deacon Peter Nguyen.
Church: 4772 Felton St., 92116. Tel: 619-284-3472; Fax: 619-284-3484. Email: stdidacusparish@pacbell.net. Web: www.stdidacus.com.
School—(Grades PreSchool-8), 4630 34th St., 92116. Tel: 619-284-8730; Fax: 619-284-1764. Mrs. Elizabeth LaCosta, Prin.; Celeste Dueber, Librarian. Lay Teachers 14; Students 274.
Catechesis/Religious Program— Elena Platas, D.R.E. Students 256.

13—GOOD SHEPHERD (1970) Revs. Michael Robinson; Joseph Freeman; Phien Van Pham; Deacons Magno Carpizo; Jaime Aquino. In Res., Rev. Richard Huston (Retired).
Res.: 8200 Gold Coast Dr., 92126-3699. Tel: 858-271-0207; Fax: 858-271-0748.
School—(Grades K-8), 8180 Gold Coast Dr., 92126. Tel: 858-693-1522; Fax: 858-271-3439. Email: gsoffice@san.rr.com. Web: www.gscs-online.org. Mrs. Chris Corpora, Prin. Lay Teachers 14; Students 262.
Catechesis/Religious Program—Tel: 858-271-8769. Lay Teachers 65; Students 1,053.

14—ST. GREGORY THE GREAT (1985) Rev. Nicholas P. Clavin; Deacons L. Ferris Bell, (Retired); Ronald H. Diem.
Mailing Address: 11451 Blue Cypress Dr., 92131. Tel: 858-653-3540; Fax: 858-653-3550. Email: information@stgg.org. Web: www.saintgregorythegreat.org.
School—St. Gregory the Great School, (Grades K-4), 15315 Stonebridge Pkwy., 92131. Tel: 858-397-1290. Maeve O'Connell, Prin. Lay Teachers 4; Students 60.
Catechesis/Religious Program—Tel: 858-653-3594. Lay Teachers 5; Students 1,185.

15—HOLY FAMILY (1942) Rev. Michael Pham; Deacon Frank Santoyo.
Res.: 1957 Coolidge St., 92111-7098. Tel: 858-277-0404; Fax: 858-279-6414. Email: hfchurch@san.rr.com. Web: holyfamilysd.org.
School—(Grades PreSchool-8) Tel: 858-277-0222; Fax: 858-277-0224. Email: hschool1@san.rr.com. Mr. Daniel O'Neal, Prin. Lay Teachers 14; Students 175.
Catechesis/Religious Program—Tel: 858-268-0557. Students 185.

16—HOLY SPIRIT (1952) Rev. Msgr. Roger A. Lechner; Rev. Doan Van Lai; Deacon Marvin Threatt. In Res., Rev. Lawrence Agi.
Res.: 2725-55th St., 92105-5094. Tel: 619-262-2435; Fax: 619-262-8718. Web: www.holyspiritsd.org.
Catechesis/Religious Program—Tel: 619-263-9307. Students 720.

17—THE IMMACULATA CHURCH USD CAMPUS (1958) Rev. Matthew D. Spahr.
St. Francis Center: 1667 Santa Paula Dr., 92111. Tel: 619-291-7446; Fax: 619-291-7011. Web: www.theimmaculata.org.
Catechesis/Religious Program—Tel: 619-574-5702; Fax: 619-574-5703. Students 139.

18—IMMACULATE CONCEPTION (1849) [CEM] Rev. Msgr. Mark A. Campbell; Deacon Robert H. Fitzmorris. In Res., Rev. Msgr. Thomas Prendergast (Retired).
Res.: 2540 San Diego Ave., 92110-2840. Tel: 619-295-4148; Fax: 619-297-6916. Web: www.ic-sandiego.org.
Catechesis/Religious Program—Tel: 619-295-4148, Ext. 12. Students 43.

19—ST. JEROME (1985) Rev. James Bahash; Deacon Raul Hernandez.
Office: 2515 Beyer Blvd., 92154-1502. Tel: 619-423-0405; Fax: 619-423-9363.
Catechesis/Religious Program—Tel: 619-423-5302. Veronica Arce, D.R.E. Students 232.

20—ST. JOHN THE EVANGELIST (1913) Rev. William Dillard; Deacon Robert Booth. In Res., Rev. Tommie Jennings.
Res.: 1638 Polk Ave., 92103. Tel: 619-291-1660; Fax: 619-291-4597. Email: sjesd@sbcglobal.net. Web: www.sje-sd.e-paluch.com.
Catechesis/Religious Program—Students 32.

21—ST. JUDE (1946) [CEM] Revs. Pedro Rivera; Emmet L. Farrell; Hignio Garcia; Deacons Manuel Nunez; Manuel Rodriguez.
Res.: 1407 41st St., 92113. Tel: 619-264-2195; Fax: 619-264-8528. Web: www.stjudesd.com.
School—(Grades PreSchool-8), 1228 S. 38th St., 92113. Tel: 619-264-3154; Fax: 619-264-8050. Web: www.stjudeacademy.com. Yolanda Minton, Prin.; Barbara Weber, Librarian. Lay Teachers 13; Students 250.
St. Jude's Child Care and Development Center—3751 Boston Ave., 92113. Tel: 619-264-8256; Fax: 619-264-2793.
St. Jude's Senior Nutrition Program—Tel: 619-264-4771; Fax: 619-264-0797.
Catechesis/Religious Program—Tel: 619-264-4795. Rosa Murguia, D.R.E. Students 857.

22—ST. MARY MAGDALENE (1953) Rev. Stephen P. McCall; Rev. Msgr. John A. Dickie, Pastor Emeritus (Retired). In Res., Rev. Anthony C. May (Retired).

Church: 1945 Illion St., 92110. Tel: 619-276-1041; Fax: 619-276-0144.
School—(Grades PreK-8) Tel: 619-276-6545; Fax: 619-276-5359. Donna Wittouck, Prin. Lay Teachers 30; Students 569.
Catechesis/Religious Program—Tel: 619-276-1248. Mrs. Margaret Mansur, D.R.E. Students 145.

23—ST. MAXIMILIAN KOLBE MISSION (1971), (Polish), Rev. Jerszy Frydrych, S.Ch.
1735 Grand Ave., 92109.
Res.: 8585 La Mesa Blvd., La Mesa, 91941. Tel: 858-272-7655; Fax: 619-668-0028.
Catechesis/Religious Program—Tel: 619-668-0485. Students 35.

24—ST. MICHAEL (1957) Revs. Manuel Ediza; Oscar Banzon; Deacon Carl Shelton.
Church: 2643 Homedale St., 92139. Tel: 619-470-1977; Fax: 619-470-6357.
Preschool—6285 Seascape Dr. Tel: 619-472-5437; Fax: 619-470-5231.
School—(Grades PreSchool-8), 2637 Homedale St., 92139. Tel: 619-470-4880; Fax: 619-267-9397. Mrs. Evelyn Urbitzando, Prin.; Diana Gonsalves, Librarian. Lay Teachers 14; Students 171.
Catechesis/Religious Program—Tel: 619-470-2291; Fax: 619-267-9397. Ms. Barbara Kearns, D.R.E. Students 487.

25—MISSION BASILICA SAN DIEGO DE ALCALA (1769), (California's First Mission) Rev. Msgr. Richard F. Duncanson; Rev. William A. Springer; Deacons H. William Vasquez Jr.; Ernest Grosso.
Res.: 10818 San Diego Mission Rd., 92108-2429. Tel: 619-283-7319; Fax: 619-283-7762. Email: pastor@missionsandiego.com. Web: www.missionsandiego.com.
Catechesis/Religious Program—Tel: 619-624-0900; Fax: 619-624-0019. Students 210.

26—OUR LADY OF ANGELS (1906) Rev. Earl Eggleston.
Res.: 656 24th St., 92102-2911. Tel: 619-239-1231; Fax: 619-234-5520. Email: ourladyofangels@cox.net.
Catechesis/Religious Program—Evangely Alianyan, D.R.E. Students 397.

27—OUR LADY OF GUADALUPE (1919) Revs. Robert Fambrini, S.J.; James I. Rasura, S.J.; William Ameche, S.J.
Res.: 1770 Kearny Ave., 92113-1128. Tel: 619-233-3838; Fax: 619-233-3252.
School—Our Lady's School, 650 24th St., 92102. Tel: 619-233-8888; Fax: 619-501-2951. Peter Hickey, Prin. Please see Our Lady's School under Our Lady of the Angels. Lay Teachers 16; Students 231.
Catechesis/Religious Program—Tel: 619-233-3838; Fax: 619-233-3252. Students 525.

28—OUR LADY OF MT. CARMEL (1976) Rev. Patrick J. Murphy; Rev. Msgr. Henry F. Fawcett, Pastor Emeritus (Retired); Deacons Noel Rivera; Manny Porciuncula; Juan Faus; Robert Holgren.
Res.: 13541 Stoney Creek Rd., 92129. Tel: 858-566-3550; 858-484-1070; Fax: 858-484-6157. Email: ourlady@olmc-sandiego.org. Web: www.olmc-sandiego.org.
Catechesis/Religious Program—Students 667.

29—OUR LADY OF REFUGE (1977) Rev. David N. Croisetiere.
Res.: 4226 Jewell St., 92109. Tel: 858-274-9670; Fax: 858-274-7486.
Catechesis/Religious Program—Tel: 858-274-2959. Vicky Jimenez, D.R.E. Students 85.

30—OUR LADY OF THE ROSARY (1925), (Italian), Revs. Steven M. Grancini, C.R.S.P.; Louis M. Solcia, C.R.S.P.; Joseph Tabigue, C.R.S.P.
Res.: 1659 Columbia St., 92101. Tel: 619-234-4820; Fax: 619-234-3559. Web: www.olrsd.org.
Catechesis/Religious Program—Tel: 619-234-4820; Fax: 619-234-3445. Esther Leuzzi, D.R.E. Students 172.

31—OUR LADY OF THE SACRED HEART (1911) Revs. Duong Nguyen, S.V.D.; Walter Miller, S.V.D. In Res., Rev. Raymundus Wea, S.V.D.
Church: 4177 Marlborough Ave., 92105-1412. Tel: 619-280-0515; Fax: 619-280-0517. Email: ourladyofsacred@hotmail.com.
School—(Grades PreK-8), 4106 42nd St., 92105. Tel: 619-284-1715; Fax: 619-284-8332. Ms. Christine Haddad, Prin. Lay Teachers 14; Students 220.
Catechesis/Religious Program—Tel: 619-283-9262. Ms. Ada Padilla, D.R.E. Students 502.

32—OUR MOTHER OF CONFIDENCE (1964) Rev. Msgr. Donal C. Sheahan; Deacons William Klopchin; Arnold Hess; Sr. Angela Therse Merami, Pastoral Assoc.
Church: 3131 Governor Dr., 92122. Tel: 858-453-0222; Fax: 858-453-2547. Email: omcchurch@san.rr.com. Web: www.omoc.org.
Catechesis/Religious Program—Tel: 858-453-3554. Ian Mascarenhas, D.R.E. Students 265.

33—ST. PATRICK (1921) Rev. Thomas G. Verber, O.S.A.; Deacon Fernando Lopez-Castillo, O.S.A.
Parish Center Office: 3014 Capps St., 92104.
Church: 3585 30th St., 92104. Tel: 619-295-2157; Fax: 619-688-1225.
School—(Grades K-8) Tel: 619-297-1314; Fax: 619-297-3346. Mr. Daniel O'Neal, Prin. Lay Teachers 13; Students 152.
Catechesis/Religious Program—Students 306.
Chapel—St. Augustine 3266 Nutmeg St., 92104. Tel: 619-282-2028; Fax: 619-282-2233. Jim Horne, Prin.

34—ST. RITA (1941) Rev. Armando P. Escurel; Rev. Msgr. W. Francis Pattison; Rev. Joseph Viet Hoang.
Church: 5124 Churchward St., 92114-3797. Tel: 619-264-3165; Fax: 619-264-2907.
School—(Grades PreK-8), 5165 Imperial Ave., 92114. Tel: 619-264-0109. Rosemary Watson, Prin. Lay Teachers 14; Students 230.
Catechesis/Religious Program—Tel: 619-264-4399. Sr. Margaret Castro, D.R.E. Students 338.

35—SACRED HEART (1911) Rev. Ronald Hebert; Deacon Giles Schmitt.
Church: 4776 Saratoga Ave., 92107-9990. Tel: 619-224-2746; Fax: 619-224-0459. Web: www.sacredheartob.org.
School—(Grades K-8), 4895 Saratoga Ave., 92107. Tel: 619-222-7252; Fax: 619-222-2836. Web: www.s-h-a.org. Mr. Jeff Saavedra, Prin. Lay Teachers 10; Students 150.
Catechesis/Religious Program—Tel: 619-223-4594. Cathleen Hornsby, D.R.E. Students 66.

36—SAN RAFAEL (1974) Very Rev. Msgr. Dennis Mikulanis; Rev. Msgr. Lloyd Bourgeois, Pastor Emeritus (Retired); Deacons Leonard Vaillancourt, Pastoral Assoc.; Ward Thompson; Bernard Yeatts.
Church: 17252 Bernardo Center, 92128. Tel: 858-487-4314; Fax: 858-487-1498. Email: office@sanrafaelparish.org. Web: www.sanrafael-sandiego.e-paluch.com.
Catechesis/Religious Program—Tel: 858-487-0491. Sisters Laura Abat, O.S.F., D.R.E.; Michele McQueeney, O.S.F., D.R.E. Students 582.

37—ST. THERESE (1956) Rev. Msgr. Frederick J. Florek; Rev. William Stevenson; Deacons Robert Ekhaml; Michael Maria.
Res.: 6016 Camino Rico, 92120-3099. Tel: 619-582-3716; Fax: 619-582-2535. Web: www.stthereseparish.org.
School—St. Therese Academy, (Grades PreSchool-8), 6046 Camino Rico, 92120. Tel: 619-583-6270; Fax: 619-583-5721. Mark Sperrazzo, Prin.; Sr. Damien Peters, F.D.C., Librarian. Sisters 4; Lay Teachers 16; Students 321.
Catechesis/Religious Program—Tel: 619-582-2585. Dorothy Hulburt, D.R.E. Students 219.

38—ST. THERESE OF CARMEL (1985) Very Rev. Nicholas Dempsey; Deacon John Fanelle.
Church: 4355 Del Mar Trails Rd., 92130-2296. Tel: 858-481-3232; Fax: 858-481-3289. Web: www.sttheresecarmel.org. Email: parishoffice@sttheresecarmel.org.
Catechesis/Religious Program—Tel: 858-481-4061. Jessica Firsching, Coord. Faith Formation; Cort Peters, D.R.E.; Tony Krzmarzick, Youth Ministry. Students 75.

39—ST. VINCENT DE PAUL (1910) Rev. Msgr. Dennis R. Clark, Admin.
Church: 4077 Ibis St., 92103-1899. Tel: 619-299-3881; Fax: 619-299-9509. Web: www.vincentcatholic.org.
School—(Grades K-8) Tel: 619-296-2222; Fax: 619-296-2763. Web: www.svscatholic.org. Sr. Kathleen Walsh, R.S.M., Prin. Sisters of Mercy 2; Lay Teachers 13; Students 220.
Catechesis/Religious Program—Tel: 619-299-3880. Students 71.

OUTSIDE THE CITY OF SAN DIEGO

ALPINE, SAN DIEGO CO., QUEEN OF ANGELS (1950) Rev. Chris Kintanar; Deacon John A. Snyder.
2569 Victoria Dr., 91901-3662. Tel: 619-445-2145; Fax: 619-445-9682. Email: parish@queenofangels.org. Web: www.queenofangels.org.
Catechesis/Religious Program—Students 215.

BONITA, SAN DIEGO CO., CORPUS CHRISTI (1984) Rev. Patrick J. Mulcahy; Deacons James H. Hitch; Guillermo Jiron; Wil Hollowell.
Mailing Address: P.O. Box 1349, 91908-1349.
Church: 450 Corral Canyon Rd., 91902-4072. Tel: 619-482-3954; Fax: 619-482-7236. Web: www.corpuschristicatholic.org.
Catechesis/Religious Program—Tel: 619-482-3953; Fax: 619-482-7236. Michael Wickham, D.R.E. Students 1,075.

BORREGO SPRINGS, SAN DIEGO CO., ST. RICHARD (1954) [CEM] Rev. Victor Maristela.
Res.: 611 Church Ln., P.O. Box 1128, 92004-1128. Tel: 760-767-5701; Fax: 760-748-0215.
Catechesis/Religious Program—Students 43.
Mission— Frontage Rd., off Hwy. 86 at S22, Salton City, Imperial Co. 92275.

BRAWLEY, IMPERIAL CO.

1—ST. MARGARET MARY (1934) Rev. Jose Luis Muro.
Res.: 620 S. Cesar Chavez St., 92227. Tel: 760-344-3571; Fax: 760-344-3598. Email: smmbrawley@yahoo.com.
Catechesis/Religious Program—Tel: 760-344-6515; Fax: 760-344-7598. Students 310.

2—OUR LADY OF PERPETUAL HELP (1956) Rev. Jorge Moreno.
Res.: 1250 B St., P.O. Box 1283, 92227. Tel: 760-344-2226; Fax: 760-344-1557.
Catechesis/Religious Program—Tel: 760-344-5787; 760-344-1557. Julia Garcia, D.R.E. Students 132.

3—SACRED HEART (1908) Rev. Reynoldo Roque; Deacon Donald L. Spinney.
Church: 402 S. Imperial Ave., 92227. Tel: 760-344-3171; Fax: 760-344-3174.
School—(Grades PreK-8), 428 S. Imperial Ave., 92227. Tel: 760-344-2662; Fax: 760-344-1910. Mrs. Yvonne Burns, Prin. Lay Teachers 8; Students 77.
Catechesis/Religious Program—Carol Sassie, C.R.E.; Alicia Rangel, C.R.E. Students 88.

CALEXICO, IMPERIAL CO., OUR LADY OF GUADALUPE (1907), (Mexican), Rev. Gerardo Fernandez; Deacon Refugio Gonzalez.
Res.: 124 E. Fifth St., 92231. Tel: 760-357-1822; Fax: 760-357-0115.
School—Our Lady of Guadalupe Academy, (Grades PreSchool-8), 535 Rockwood Ave., 92231. Tel: 760-357-1986; Fax: 760-357-3282. Sr. Maria Elvia Gonzalez, S.J.S., Prin.; Silvia Chavarin, Librarian. Lay Teachers 23; Students 497.
Catechesis/Religious Program— Gloria Wong, C.R.E. Students 421.

CALIPATRIA, IMPERIAL CO., ST. PATRICK (1919) Rev. Amador Lopez, O.M.I.; Deacon Michael Heidenreich.
Res.: 133 E. Church St., P.O. Box 238, 92233. Tel: 760-348-2733; Fax: 760-348-7070.
Catechesis/Religious Program—Tel: 760-348-2454. Students 203.
Mission—Immaculate Heart of Mary P.O. Box 238, 92233. 19 Sixth St., Niland, 92257. Tel: 760-359-0464.

CARLSBAD, SAN DIEGO CO.

1—ST. ELIZABETH SETON (1977) Rev. Donald E. Coleman; Deacons Henry Chia; Dale Fickes.
Res.: 6628 Santa Isabel St., 92009-5148. Tel: 760-438-3393; Fax: 760-438-7739. Web: www.stelizabeth-seton.org.
Catechesis/Religious Program—Tel: 760-438-3438. Email: reled-ses@stelizabeth-seton.org. Larry Broding, D.R.E. Students 786.

2—ST. PATRICK (1943) Revs. William F. Rowland, C.J.M.; Ricardo Chinchilla, C.J.M.; Deacons Michael Frazee; Gerald McClellan Jr.; Edward Moser.
Church: 3821 Adams St., 92008-0249. Tel: 760-729-2866; Fax: 760-434-3325. Web: www.stpatrickcarlsbad.com.
School—(Grades K-8), 3820 Pio Pico, 92008. Tel: 760-729-1333; Fax: 760-729-4643. Web: www.stpaddys.org. Mary Beth Lents, Prin.; Denise Coates, Prin.; Annette Broome, Librarian. Lay Teachers 26; Students 464.
Catechesis/Religious Program—Tel: 760-729-8442. Students 726.

CAMPO, SAN DIEGO CO., ST. ADELAIDE OF BURGUNDY PARISH Rev. Ignatius Dibeashi.
1347 Dewey Pl., P.O. Box 369, 91906. Tel: 619-478-1017.
Catechesis/Religious Program—Students 18.
Mission—St. Mary Magdalene 44686 Calexico Ave., Jacumba, San Diego Co. 91934.

CHULA VISTA, SAN DIEGO CO.

1—MATER DEI (2004) Rev. Jovencio D. Ricafort.
P.O. Box 212047, 91921. Tel: 619-656-3735. Email: parish@materdeicv.org. Web: www.materdeicv.org.
Catechesis/Religious Program—Tel: 619-656-3740; Fax: 619-656-2939. Email: rep@materdeicv.org. Students 625.

2—MOST PRECIOUS BLOOD (1957) Revs. Paul Nourie, O.M.I.; Patrick Thompson, O.M.I.; Deacons Daniel Parra; Rolando Bongatt; Ruben Pelina.
Church: 1245 4th Ave., 91911-3012. Tel: 619-422-2100; Fax: 619-422-1375. Email: churchmpb@attglobal.net. Web: www.preciousbloodchurch.com.
Catechesis/Religious Program—Tel: 619-422-2159. Sr. Camille Crabbe, C.V.I., D.R.E. Students 572.

3—OUR LADY OF GUADALUPE (1945) Rev. Peter Navarra; Deacon Margarito Lozoya.
Church: 345 Anita St., 91911-4198. Tel: 619-422-3977; Fax: 619-422-1056.
Catechesis/Religious Program—Tel: 619-422-1887. Students 312.

4—ST. PIUS X (1955) Rev. Luke Jauregui; Rev. Msgr. Donald R. Kulleck, Pastor Emeritus (Retired); Rev. Edwin Tutor; Deacons Glenn Vecchitto; Daniel Prado; Peter Johnson.
Church: 1120 Cuyamaca Ave., 91911-3506. Tel: 619-420-9193; Fax: 619-420-9353. Email: office@saintpiusx.org. Web: www.saintpiusx.org.
School—(Grades K-8), 37 E. Emerson, 91911. Tel: 619-422-2015; Fax: 619-422-0048. Eileen Hanson, Prin. Lay Teachers 13; Students 286.
Catechesis/Religious Program—Tel: 619-420-9193

ext. 104/105; Fax: 619-427-0015. Dora Castenada, D.R.E. Students 472.

5—ST. ROSE OF LIMA (1913) Very Rev. John P. Dolan; Rev. Alexander Aquino; Deacons Gerardo Marquez; Gregory Smyth; Charles Frice. In Res., Rev. Mario Vesga (Retired).
Church: 293 H St., 91910-4703. Tel: 619-427-0230; Fax: 619-427-5786.
School—(Grades K-8), 473 Third Ave., 91910. Tel: 619-422-1121; Fax: 619-422-8007. Web: www-.strosecv.com. Mrs. Maria Tollefson, Prin. Religious 1; Lay Teachers 12; Students 315.
Catechesis/Religious Program—Tel: 619-426-6717. Sisters Patricia Weldon, D.R.E.; Joan King, O.S.B., D.R.E. Students 655.

CORONADO, SAN DIEGO CO., SACRED HEART (1897) Rev. Michael F. Murphy; Deacons Robert E. Griffin Jr.; Kevin Murray; Frank Osgood.
655 C Ave., 92118-2229. Tel: 619-435-3167; Fax: 619-437-1572. Web: www.sacredheartcor.org. In Res., Rev. Msgr. Jeremiah O'Sullivan, Pastor Emeritus (Retired).
Res.: 672 B Ave., 92118-2229. Tel: 619-435-3167; Fax: 619-437-1572.
School—(Grades K-8), 706 C Ave., 92118. Tel: 619-437-4431; Fax: 619-437-1473. Web: www.sacredheartcoronado.org. Mr. Peter Harris, Prin. Lay Teachers 9; Students 239.
Catechesis/Religious Program—Tel: 619-435-3167, Ext. 302. Students 258.

DESCANSO, SAN DIEGO CO., OUR LADY OF LIGHT (1935) Rev. Gerald F. Palcheck.
Res.: 9136 Riverside Dr., P.O. Box 219, 91916. Tel: 619-445-3620; Fax: 619-445-3620.
Catechesis/Religious Program—Eleanor Denton, D.R.E. Students 22.

EL CAJON, SAN DIEGO CO.

1—HOLY TRINITY (1903) Revs. Brian Hayes; Nemesio Sungcad; Deacon Louis Rocha.
Church: 405 Ballard St., 92019-2123. Tel: 619-444-9425; Fax: 619-444-9426. Web: www.holytrinityelcajon.org.
School—(Grades PreK-8) Tel: 619-444-7529; Fax: 619-444-3721. Web: holytrinityschool.mswin.net. Francine Wright, Prin. Lay Teachers 18; Students 307.
Catechesis/Religious Program—Email: admin@holytrinityelcajon.org. Students 256.

2—ST. KIERAN (1958) Rev. Ben Davison; Deacon D. Frank Reilly.
Office: 1510 Greenfield Dr., 92021-3511. Tel: 619-588-6881; Fax: 619-588-5274. Email: secretary@stkierans.sdcoxmail.com. Web: www.stkierans.org.
School—(Grades PreSchool-8), 1347 Camillo Way, 92021. Tel: 619-588-6398; Fax: 619-588-6382. Mr. Peter Harris, Prin. Sisters 2; Lay Teachers 9; Students 149.
Catechesis/Religious Program—Students 62.

3—ST. LOUISE DE MARILLAC (1944) Rev. Justin Langille.
Church: 2005 Crest Dr., 92021-4309. Tel: 619-444-3076; Fax: 619-440-1325.
Catechesis/Religious Program—Students 12.

4—ST. LUKE (1985) Rev. Ronald Cochran; Deacon Dennie C. Nickell.
Church: 1980 Hillsdale Rd., 92019. Tel: 619-442-1697; Fax: 619-442-2293. Email: parishoffice@thechurchofstluke.org. Web: www.thechurchofstluke.org.
Catechesis/Religious Program—Tel: 619-442-2515. Cindy Stiso, D.R.E. (K-5); Jane Alfano, D.R.E. (6-12). Students 202.

5—OUR LADY OF GRACE (1954) Revs. Michael J. Gallagher; Lucas Thumma; Sr. Alyce Waters, Pastoral Assoc.; Deacons George Shea; Raymond Arnold, (Retired); William Korty; Ron Allen. In Res., Rev. Omer LeBlanc, C.J.M.
Church: 2766 Navajo Rd., 92020-2183. Tel: 619-469-0133; Fax: 619-469-0575. Web: www.olg-church.org.
School—(Grades K-8) Tel: 619-466-0055; Fax: 619-466-8994. Web: www.olg.org. Mrs. Therese Martin, Prin. Lay Teachers 17; Students 301.
Catechesis/Religious Program—Tel: 619-466-5656. Students 364.

EL CENTRO, IMPERIAL CO.

1—ST. MARY (1907) [JC] Rev. Edward Horning.
Church: 795 LaBrucherie, 92243. Tel: 760-352-4211; Fax: 760-352-7397.
School—(Grades PreSchool-8) Tel: 760-352-7285; Fax: 760-352-9727. Sr. Juanita Pereyra, S.J.S., Prin. Sister Servants of the Blessed Sacrament 2; Lay Teachers 16; Students 214.
Catechesis/Religious Program—Tel: 760-353-8260 (K-8); 760-353-7280 (9-12). Students 276.

2—OUR LADY OF GUADALUPE (1946), (Mexican), Revs. Ruben Valenzuela; Jose Alfredo Moreno; Deacon Domingo Enriquez.
Church: 153 E. Brighton Ave., 92243. Tel: 760-352-5535; Fax: 760-352-8003.
Catechesis/Religious Program—Tel: 760-352-5554. Sr. Flavia Arellano, C.V.I., D.R.E.; Blanca Barela, Youth Min. Students 516.
Mission—Sacred Heart 40 E. Main, Heber, Imperial Co. 92249.

ENCINITAS, SAN DIEGO CO., ST. JOHN THE EVANGELIST (1946) Revs. Brian Corcoran; Marcelino Bandico.
Church: 1001 Encinitas Blvd., 92024-2828. Tel: 760-753-6254; Fax: 760-753-7118. Email: admin@stjohnencinitas.org.
School—(Grades PreSchool-8), 1003 Encinitas Blvd., 92024. Tel: 760-944-8227; Fax: 760-944-8939. Barbara Picco, Prin. Lay Teachers 33; Students 574.
Catechesis/Religious Program—Tel: 760-436-0664. Students 732.

ESCONDIDO, SAN DIEGO CO.

1—CHURCH OF ST. TIMOTHY (1985) Rev. Fernando Ramirez; Deacons J. Michael Early; John Depner.
Church and Administration Center: 2960 Canyon Rd., 92025-7402. Tel: 760-489-1200; Fax: 760-489-2731. Web: www.sttimothychurch.com.
Catechesis/Religious Program—Tel: 760-489-0482. Christopher O'Donnell, D.R.E. Students 219.

2—CHURCH OF THE RESURRECTION (1970) [JC] Revs. Kenneth Del Priore; Eduardo Bernardino; Deacons Mitch Rennix; Edwin Gonzales Montoya; Michael Partida; Christine Whitten, Pastoral Assoc.
Church: 1445 Conway Dr., 92027. Tel: 760-747-2322; Fax: 760-747-7079. Web: www.resurrectionchurch.org.
Catechesis/Religious Program— Debbie Nehring, C.R.E. Tel: 760-747-2322. Students 662.
Comunidad Hispana—

3—ST. MARY (1890) Revs. Richard L. Perozich; Burt Boudoin; Deacons Lawrence Michaels; Amador Duran; James Kostick.
Church: 1160 S. Broadway Ave., 92025-5815. Tel: 760-745-1611; Fax: 760-745-1238. Email: pastor@stmary.sdcoxmail.com.
School—(Grades PreSchool-8) Tel: 760-743-3431; Fax: 760-743-6808. Web: www.stmesc.org. Mrs. Cynthia Ashbury, Prin. Lay Teachers 15; Students 314.
Catechesis/Religious Program—130 E. 13th Ave., 92025. Tel: 760-745-8255; Fax: 760-745-8337. Sharon Twilliger, D.R.E. Students 1,422.

FALLBROOK, SAN DIEGO CO., ST. PETER (1946) Revs. Ramon Marrufo; Manuel Villarreal.
Church: 450 S. Stage Coach Ln., 92028. Tel: 760-728-7034; Fax: 760-723-4050. Web: www.stpeterscc.org.
School—St. Peter's Catholic School, (Grades PreK-8) Tel: 760-728-6961; Fax: 760-723-8973. Ms. Anne Lewis, Prin. Lay Teachers 11; Students 130.
Catechesis/Religious Program—Students 633.

HOLTVILLE, IMPERIAL CO., ST. JOSEPH (1911) Very Rev. Eddie Ruiz.
Church: 560 Maple Ave., 92250. Tel: 760-356-2147; Fax: 760-356-1985. Email: saint_josephchurch@yahoo.com.
Catechesis/Religious Program—Tel: 760-356-5738. Rocio Ramirez, D.R.E. Students 263.

IMPERIAL, IMPERIAL CO., ST. ANTHONY OF PADUA (1948) Rev. David Sereno, Admin.
Church: 210 W. Seventh St., 92251. Tel: 760-355-1347; Fax: 760-355-1226. Web: www.stanparish.org.
Catechesis/Religious Program—Tel: 760-355-1304. Maria Fugett, C.R.E. Students 324.

JACUMBA, SAN DIEGO CO., ST. MARY MAGDALENE (1947) See separate listing. A mission of St. Adelaide of Burgundy, Campo.

JAMUL, SAN DIEGO CO., ST. PIUS X (1956) Rev. Scott A. Burnia; Deacons John Trumble; John Turcich.
Res.: 14107 Lyons Valley Rd., P.O. Box 369, 91935-0369. Tel: 619-669-0085; Fax: 619-669-0087.
Catechesis/Religious Program—Tel: 619-669-0086. Students 69.

JULIAN, SAN DIEGO CO., ST. ELIZABETH OF HUNGARY (1949) Rev. Cecilio Moraga.
Res.: 2814 B St., P.O. Box 366, 92036-0366. Tel: 760-765-0613; Fax: 760-765-0552.
Catechesis/Religious Program—Students 35.

LA JOLLA, SAN DIEGO CO.

1—ALL HALLOWS (1959) Rev. Raymond G. O'Donnell; Deacon Joseph Wood.
Res.: 6602 La Jolla Scenic Dr. S., 92037-5799. Tel: 858-459-2975; Fax: 858-459-9712. Web: www.allhallows.com.
School—(Grades K-8), 2390 Nautilus, 92037. Tel: 858-459-6074; Fax: 858-459-4602. Ms. Michaele Durant, Prin. Lay Teachers 21; Students 236.
Catechesis/Religious Program—Karen Downs, D.R.E. Students 105.

2—MARY, STAR OF THE SEA (1906) Rev. James Rafferty.
Office: 7669 Girard Ave., 92037.
Church: 7713 Girard Ave., 92037-4480. Tel: 858-454-2631; Fax: 858-454-5968. Email: marystarofthesea@san.rr.com.
School—Stella Maris Academy, (Grades K-8), 7654 Herschel Ave., 92037. Tel: 858-454-2461; Fax: 858-454-4913. Web: www.stellamarisacademy.org. Patricia Lowell, Prin. Lay Teachers 15; Students 225.
Catechesis/Religious Program—Tel: 858-551-8359. Donna Widmer, D.R.E.; Martin Magana, D.R.E. Students 230.

LA MESA, SAN DIEGO CO., ST. MARTIN OF TOURS (1921) Rev. James Poulsen. In Res., Rev. Msgr. Patrick J. O'Neill (Retired).
Res.: 7710 El Cajon Blvd., 91941. Tel: 619-465-5334; Fax: 619-465-7297. Email: stmartinch@juno.com. Web: www.stmartinoftours.org.
School—(Grades PreSchool-8), 7708 El Cajon Blvd., 91941. Tel: 619-466-3241; Fax: 619-466-0285. Web: www.stmartinacademy.org. Antoinette Dimuzio, Prin. Lay Teachers 18; Students 257.
Catechesis/Religious Program—Tel: 619-698-8434. Christine Davis, D.R.E. Students 107.

LAKESIDE, SAN DIEGO CO.

1—BLESSED KATERI TEKAKWITHA (1982) [CEM] [JC 3] Rev. Michael X Tran, Chap.; Deacon Bill Clarke; Edward Nolan, Pastoral Coord.
Res.: 1054 Barona Rd., 92040-1502. Tel: 619-443-3412; Fax: 619-443-3018. Email: bktparish@aol.com.
Catechesis/Religious Program—Tel: 619-445-8333. Josephine Whaley, D.R.E. Students 103.
Mission—Assumption of BVM
Mission—Nativity of BVM Alpine, San Diego Co.
Mission—Immaculate Conception of BVM El Cajon, San Diego Co.

2—OUR LADY OF PERPETUAL HELP (1947) Revs. Ronald J. Buchmiller; Joseph Khuyen Van Lai; Deacon Dennis O'Neil.
Res.: 13208 Lakeshore Dr., 92040. Tel: 619-443-1412; Fax: 619-443-1733. Email: rectory@olphchurch.org. Web: www.olphchurch.org.
School—(Grades K-8) Tel: 619-443-1440; Fax: 619-443-1714. Web: olphcatholicschool.com. Dr. Colleen Mauricio, Prin.; Pat Garcia, Librarian. St. Joseph of Carondelet Sisters 1; Lay Teachers 12; Students 140.
Catechesis/Religious Program—Tel: 619-443-1477. Sr. Frances Michele, D.R.E. (Adult Educ.). Students 240.

LEMON GROVE, SAN DIEGO CO., ST. JOHN OF THE CROSS (1939) Very Rev. Msgr. Edward Brockhaus; Revs. Richard Brown; Ruben Fuentes, O.F.M.; Deacons Juan Francisco Santoyo; Martin Villafana; James Robert.
Res.: 8086 Broadway, 91945-2598. Tel: 619-466-3209; Fax: 619-466-9276. Web: www.stjohncross.org.
School—(Grades K-8), 8175 Lemon Grove Way, 91945. Tel: 619-466-8624; Fax: 619-466-3732. Web: www.stjohncross.org/sindex.htm. Sr. Marilupe Mier Y Teran, H.M.S.S., Prin. Lay Teachers 32; Students 624.
Catechesis/Religious Program—Tel: 619-461-2681. Karen Dey, D.R.E. Students 706.
Convent—8171 Lemon Grove Way, 91945. Tel: 619-460-4271. Sisters of Mercy of the Blessed Sacrament 5.

NATIONAL CITY, SAN DIEGO CO.

1—ST. ANTHONY OF PADUA (1910), (Mexican), Rev. Jose Edmundo Zarate-Suarez; Deacons Joe Arismendez; Braulio Gutierrez.
410 W. 18th St., 91950. Email: stanthonyofpadua@sbcglobal.net.
Res.: 1816 Harding Ave., 91950. Tel: 619-477-4520; Fax: 619-477-8708.
Catechesis/Religious Program—Martha Mendoza, D.R.E. Students 285.

2—ST. MARY (1926) Rev. Dionisio Macalintal.
Mailing Address: 426 E. Seventh St., 91950-2322.
Res.: 1310 L Ave., 91950-4811. Tel: 619-474-1501; Fax: 619-474-1502.
Catechesis/Religious Program—Tel: 619-474-5777; Fax: 619-474-5777. Rev. Pilar Bernal Ignacio, D.R.E. Students 281.

NILAND, IMPERIAL CO., IMMACULATE HEART OF MARY, See separate listing. No longer a parish; now a mission of St. Patrick, Calipatria.

OCEANSIDE, SAN DIEGO CO.

1—ST. MARGARET (1977) Rev. Cavana Wallace.
Res.: 4300 Oceanside Blvd., 92056-2999. Tel: 760-941-5560; Fax: 760-941-1857. Web: www.oceanside4christ.net.
Catechesis/Religious Program—Max Pawlowski, D.R.E. Students 243.

2—ST. MARY, STAR OF THE SEA (1937) Rev. Michael Diaz.
Res.: 609 Pier View Way, 92054-2861. Tel: 760-722-1688; Fax: 760-722-2653. Web: www.stmarystars.org.
School—(Grades PreSchool-8), 515 Wisconsin Ave., 92054. Tel: 760-722-7259; Fax: 760-722-0862. Alan J. Hicks, Prin. Lay Teachers 20; Students 370.
Catechesis/Religious Program—Students 380.

3—MISSION SAN LUIS REY (1798) Revs. Charles Talley, O.F.M.; Raul Alejos, O.F.M.; Adrian Peelo, O.F.M.

Res.: 4070 Mission Ave., 92057-6497. Tel: 760-757-3250; Fax: 760-757-3299. Web: www.sanluisreyparish.org.
Catechesis/Religious Program—Tel: 760-757-3250, Ext. 334. Students 672.

4—ST. THOMAS MORE (1985) Rev. Michael Ratajczak; Deacon Thomas A. Goeltz.
Church & Mailing Address: 1450 S. Melrose Dr., 92056. Tel: 760-758-4100; Fax: 760-758-4165.
Res.: 4703 Majorca Way, 92056.
Catechesis/Religious Program—Students 235.

PALA, SAN DIEGO CO., MISSION SAN ANTONIO DE PALA (1816) Rev. Reynaldo Manahan; Deacon Dan Powers.
Res.: 3015 Mission Rd., P.O. Box 70, 92059-0070. Tel: 760-742-3317; Fax: 760-742-3040. Web: www.missionsanantonio.org.
Catechesis/Religious Program—Tel: 760-742-1600. Students 157.
Chapel—Rincon Indian Reservation, St. Bartholomew
Chapel—La Jolla Indian Reservation, Our Lady of Refuge
Chapel—Pauma Indian Reservation, St. James

POWAY, SAN DIEGO CO.

1—ST. GABRIEL (1973) Rev. Michael Froidurot; Deacon Robert Troy. In Res., Rev. Harold Tindall (Retired).
Church: 13734 Twin Peaks Rd., 92064. Tel: 858-748-5348; Fax: 858-748-5764. Email: office@saintgabrielschurch.com. Web: www.saintgabrielschurch.com.
Catechesis/Religious Program—Tel: 858-748-7475. Mary Romag, D.R.E. Students 466.

2—ST. MICHAEL (1959) Rev. Msgrs. Neal T. Dolan; Joseph L. Finnerty, Pastor Emeritus (Retired); Rev. Melchisedech Monreal (Philippines); Deacon Ralph Skiano.
Church: 15546 Pomerado Rd., 92064-2404. Tel: 858-487-4755; Fax: 858-487-5937. Web: www.stmichaelschurch-poway.org.
School—(Grades PreSchool-8), 15542 Pomerado Rd., 92064. Tel: 858-485-1303; Fax: 858-485-5059. Kathleen Mock, Prin. Clergy 1; Sisters of Mercy of Sligo 1; Lay Teachers 35; Students 557.
Catechesis/Religious Program—Tel: 858-485-1392; 858-487-0473. M.J. Heggeness, D.R.E. Students 765.

RAMONA, SAN DIEGO CO., IMMACULATE HEART OF MARY (1947) Rev. Andres Ramos, Admin.; Deacon Lou Rocha.
Church: 537 E St., 92065. Tel: 760-789-0583; Fax: 760-789-3875. Email: ihmramona@parishmail.com. Web: www.ihmramona.parishesonline.com.
Catechesis/Religious Program—Tel: 760-789-6151. Students 247.

RANCHO SANTA FE, SAN DIEGO CO., CHURCH OF THE NATIVITY (1985) Very Rev. Msgr. Lawrence M. Purcell.
Mailing Address: P.O. Box 8770, 92067-8770. Web: www.nativitycatholic.org.
Church: 6309 El Apajo Rd., 92067. Tel: 858-756-1911; Fax: 858-756-9562. Email: lmpurcell@nativitycatholic.org.
School—(Grades K-8), 6309 El Apajo Rd., P.O. Box 9180, 92067. Tel: 858-756-6763; Fax: 858-756-9128. Email: office@nativitycatholic.org. Mrs. Margaret Heveron, Prin. Students 175.
Catechesis/Religious Program— Mrs. Patti Smiley, D.R.E.; Mike James, Youth Min. Students 288.

SAN MARCOS, SAN DIEGO CO., ST. MARK (1963) [CEM] Revs. George Dunkley; Alfred Heyrosa; Deacons Frank Mercardante; Dennis Sullivan; David Bennett; Agustin Castro.
Church: 1147 W. Discovery St., 92078-1313. Tel: 760-744-1540; Fax: 760-744-3828. Email: office@stmarksrcc.org.
Catechesis/Religious Program—Tel: 760-744-1130. Students 1,200.
Mission— 568 Deer Springs Rd., San Diego Co. 92069.

SAN YSIDRO, SAN DIEGO CO., OUR LADY OF MT. CARMEL (1927) Revs. Jose Castillo; Jose Whittingham; Deacons Jose Luis Medina; Raul Gonzalez.
Church: 2020 Alaquinas Dr., 92173-2107. Tel: 619-428-1415; Fax: 619-428-5626.
School—(Grades K-8) Tel: 619-428-2091; Fax: 619-428-8324. Sr. Ana Rosa Aceves, Prin.; Ma. Eugenia Villareal, Librarian. Sisters of the Most Blessed Sacrament 6; Lay Teachers 33; Students 306.
Catechesis/Religious Program—109 Seaward Ave., 92173. Tel: 619-428-3686. Students 503.

SANTA YSABEL, SAN DIEGO CO., SANTA YSABEL INDIAN MISSION (1818) [CEM] Rev. Dennis O'Connor.
Res.: 23013 Hwy. 79, P.O. Box 129, 92070-1010. Tel: 760-765-0810; Fax: 760-765-3494.
Mission—St. Francis of Assisi Hwy. 79 & Stage Rd., Warner Springs, San Diego Co. 92086.
Catechesis/Religious Program—Students 22.

SANTEE, SAN DIEGO CO., GUARDIAN ANGELS (1962) Rev. Michael A. Cunnane; Deacons Louis Principe; Richard Melrose. In Res., Rev. Kevin P. Casey, S.J.
Church: 9310 Dalehurst Rd., 92071-1010. Tel: 619-448-1213; Fax: 619-448-2980. Email: par.sec@cox.net. Web: www.guardianangelssantee.org.
Catechesis/Religious Program—9310 Dalehurst, 92071. Tel: 619-448-1213, Ext. 312. Sr. Mary Potter, R.S.M., D.R.E. Students 302.

SOLANA BEACH, SAN DIEGO CO., ST. JAMES (1911) Revs. John Howard, C.J.M.; A. Ernesto Torres, C.J.M.; Deacons Joseph R. Santen; Peter Hodsdon; Albert P. Graff. In Res., Rev. Gerard Lecomte, C.J.M.
Office: 625 S. Nardo Ave., 92075-2398. Tel: 858-755-2545; Fax: 858-755-3824.
School—St. James Academy, (Grades K-8), 623 S. Nardo Ave., 92075. Tel: 858-755-1777; Fax: 858-755-3124. Kathy Dunn, Prin. Lay Teachers 13; Students 266.
Catechesis/Religious Program—Tel: 858-755-2545, Ext. 106; Fax: 858-755-3845. Robert Kidd, D.R.E.; Lee Santen, D.R.E. Students 250.
Mission—St. Leo 936 Genevieve, San Diego Co. 92075. Tel: 858-481-6788; Fax: 858-481-5832. Sr. Zita Toto, O.L.C., Coord.
Catechesis/Religious Program—Vicente Leal, D.R.E. (Spanish). Students 399.

SPRING VALLEY, SAN DIEGO CO., SANTA SOPHIA (1956) Rev. Peter McGuine; Deacon Michael Maria. In Res., Rev. Masilamony Devadhason.
Res.: 9800 San Juan St., 91977. Tel: 619-463-6629; Fax: 619-463-8101. Web: www.santasophia.org.
School—(Grades PreSchool-8) Tel: 619-463-0488; Fax: 619-668-5469. Lay Teachers 14; Aides 8; Students 290.
Catechesis/Religious Program—Tel: 619-463-6011; Fax: 619-668-5458. Bernadette Padlo, D.R.E. Students 263.

VALLEY CENTER, SAN DIEGO CO., ST. STEPHEN (1981) Rev. Elmer Mandac, Admin.; Deacons Charles Embury; Gilbert Salinas.
Church: 31020 Cole Grade Rd., P.O. Box 1015, 92082-1015. Tel: 760-749-3324; Fax: 760-749-6684.
Catechesis/Religious Program—Tel: 760-749-3352; Fax: 760-749-6608. Ellen MacPhee, D.R.E. Students 410.

VISTA, SAN DIEGO CO., ST. FRANCIS OF ASSISI (1941) Revs. Edward Kaicher; Peter Vu Lam; Agustin Opalalic; Deacons Loi Hoang; Ronald Arnold; Pedro Enciso; Miguel Enriquez; Robert Mueller. In Res., Rev. Bernard A. Rapp (Retired).
Church: 525 W. Vista Way, 92083-5974. Tel: 760-945-8000; Fax: 760-945-8036. Email: info@stfrancis-vista.org. Web: www.stfrancis-vista.org.
School—(Grades PreSchool-8) Tel: 760-630-7960; Fax: 760-726-2910. Email: info@sfs-vista.org. Web: www.sfs-vista.org. Linda McCotter, Prin. Lay Teachers 19; Students 289.
Catechesis/Religious Program—Tel: 760-945-8010. Susan Ferraris, D.R.E. Students 1,550.

WESTMORLAND, IMPERIAL CO., ST. JOSEPH (1939), Administered by St. Anthony of Padua, Imperial., Mailing Address: P.O. Box 627, 92281. Tel: 760-351-1961; Fax: 760-344-3721.
Res.: 300 N. Center St., 92281.
Catechesis/Religious Program—Students 25.

WINTERHAVEN, IMPERIAL CO., ST. THOMAS (INDIAN MISSION) (1780) Rev. Duncan W. Monohan.
Res.: 350 Picacho Rd., P.O. Box 1176, 92283-1176. Tel: 760-572-0283.
Catechesis/Religious Program—Students 25.

Eastern Catholic Churches

EL CAJON, SAN DIEGO CO., ST. PETER CATHEDRAL (1973), (Chaldean Eastern Catholic) Most Rev. Sarhad Y. Jammo; Rev. Michael J. Bazzi; Rev. Msgr. Polis Khammi; Rev. Andrew Younan.
Res.: 1627 Jamacha Way, 92019. Tel: 619-579-7913; 619-588-9921; Fax: 619-588-8281.
Catechesis/Religious Program—Khelood Allos, D.R.E. Students 710.
Convent—Chaldean Sisters, 1591 Jamacha Way, 92019. Tel: 619-447-4842.

LA MESA, SAN DIEGO CO., OUR LADY OF PERPETUAL HELP (1960), (Ukrainian Catholic) Rev. James Bankston.
4400 Palm Ave., 91941. Tel: 619-697-5085; Fax: 619-697-7374.
Catechesis/Religious Program—Students 8.

Chaplains of Public Institutions
Hospitals

SAN DIEGO. *Alvarado Hospital*, Tel: 619-287-3270. Rev. Masilamony Devadhason, Chap.
Children's Hospital, Tel: 858-541-3475. Rev. Raymundus Wea, S.V.D.
Kaiser Permanente Medical Center, Tel: 619-528-5188. Rev. Masilamony Devadhason.
Scripps Hospital, Tel: 858-457-4123. Rev. Thomas Thompson, Chap.
Scripps Mercy Hospital, Tel: 619-260-7020. Revs. Lawrence Agi, James Schorr, Chap.
Sharp Grossmont Hospital, Tel: 619-465-0711. Rev. Masilamony Devadhason.
Sharp Memorial Hospital, Tel: 858-541-3475. Rev. Raymundus Wea, S.V.D.
UCSD Medical Center, Tel: 619-543-6737. Rev. David Leon, Chap.

CHULA VISTA. *Scripps Mercy Hospital*, 435 H St., 91910. Tel: 619-691-7251; Fax: 619-691-7522. Web: www.scrippshealth.org. Sr. JoCeal Young, R.S.M., Dir. Mission Integration, Mark Weber, Chap. Bed Capacity 183; Total Staff 872; Patients Assisted Annually 9,592.
Sharp Chula Vista Medical Center, East 752 Medical Center Ct., 91910. Tel: 619-421-6110. Vacant.

LA JOLLA. *Thornton Hospital*. Rev. Thomas Thompson, Chap. Tel: 858-657-7000.
Veterans Administration Hospital, Tel: 858-552-8585. Revs. Jerry Hamperzonian, Chap. Tel: 858-552-8585, Ext. 421, B. Jeffrey Blangiardi, S.J.

OCEANSIDE. *Tri City Hospital*, 4002 Vista Way, 92049. Tel: 760-724-8411. Rev. Peter Vu Lam, Chap.

Retirement Homes

SAN DIEGO. *Nazareth House*, 6333 Rancho Mission Rd., 92108. Tel: 619-563-0480. Rev. David Leon, Chap.

LA MESA. *Little Flower Haven*, 8585 La Mesa Blvd., 91941. Tel: 619-466-3163. Rev. Philip Bronk, S.T. Tel: 619-466-3163.

Detention Ministries

SAN DIEGO. *East Mesa Detention Facility*, 446 Alta Rd., 92158. Tel: 619-661-2669. Doris Argoud, Chap. Tel: 619-423-0567.
Geo West Regional Detention Facility. Contact: Office for Social Ministry, (858) 490-8375., Tel: 619-232-9221.
George F. Bailey Detention Facility. Contact: Office for Social Ministry, Tel: 858-490-8375, Tel: 619-661-2620.
Kearny Mesa Juvenile Detention Facility. Contact: Office for Social Ministry, (858) 490-8375., Tel: 858-694-4500.
Metropolitan Correction Center, Tel: 619-232-4311. Rev. Edgar Serrano, Chap. Tel: 619-232-4311, Ext. 1463.
R.J. Donovan Correctional Facility. Rev. Romeo Supnet, O.S.A. Tel: 619-661-6500, Ext. 6632.
San Diego Central Jail, Tel: 619-615-2737. Tom Erpelding, Chap. Tel: 619-696-6526.
San Diego Correction Facility, Federal. Contact: Office for Social Ministry, Tel: (858) 490-8375., Tel: 619-661-9119.

BRAWLEY. *Calipatria State Prison*, Tel: 760-348-7000. Deacon Michael Heidenreich. Tel: 769-348-7000, Ext. 6339.

CHULA VISTA. *South Bay Detention Facility*. Contact: Office for Social Ministry, Tel: (858) 490-8375., Tel: 619-691-4810. Vacant.

EL CENTRO. *El Centro Juvenile Hall*, 324 Applestill Rd., 92243. Refugio Hernandez. Tel: 760-622-8898.
Imperial County Jail, 328 Applestill Rd., 92243. Tel: 760-339-6369. Refugio Hernandez. Tel: 760-339-6367.

IMPERIAL. *Centinela State Prison*, Tel: 760-337-7900. Rev. Luis Valenciano. Tel: 760-337-7900, Ext. 6372.

SANTEE. *Las Colinas Women's Detention Facility*, 9000 Cottonwood Rd., 92071. Frances Dickey, Chap. Tel: 858-486-3038.

VISTA. *Vista Detention Facility*, 325 Melrose Dr., Ste. 200, 92083. Jim Hamilton, Chap. Tel: 760-757-9865.

State Conservation Camps

SAN DIEGO. *Rainbow Conservation Camp*, 8215 Rainbow Heights Rd., Fallbrook, 92028. Tel: 760-728-7034. Cliff Sumrall, Chap. Tel: 760-451-5095.

Ports

SAN DIEGO. *Port of San Diego*, 1760 Water St., 92101. Tel: 619-702-4703. Deacon Sam Martinez, Rev. James Boyd, Chap. Tel: 858-292-1822.
San Diego Airport, 2802 Cadiz St., 92110-4813. Tel: 619-225-8157. Rev. William A. Kernan.

On Duty Outside the Diocese:
Revs.—
Stanonik, Anthony
White, Robert

Military Chaplains:
Rev.—
Merris, Christopher

Unassigned:
Revs.—
Dunn, Stephen
Foley, Patrick
Rodriguez, Henry, Jr.

Retired:
Most Rev.—
Chavez, Gilbert E., D.D.

Rev. Msgrs.—
Bolger, William
Bourgeois, Lloyd
Chylewski, Anthony
Coughlan, Michael J.
Creighton, Edward
Cuddihy, William
Dickie, John A.
Elliott, William
Fawcett, Henry F.
Finnerty, Joseph L.
Fox, Patrick
Giesing, Anthony
Hanley, Andrew W.
Harnett, Timothy
Kirk, Raymond
Kulleck, Donald R.
Lyng, Edward F.
Moloney, Alphonsus
Murray, Sean
O'Donoghue, James P.
O'Neill, Patrick J.
O'Sullivan, Jeremiah
Portman, John R.
Prendergast, Thomas
Shipley, William
Vidra, Thomas
Revs.—
Byrne, George
Caldwell, James V.
Chase, Maurice
Collier, Joseph
Fischer, Eugene
Flynn, Edward R.
Fuld, Charles L.
Gold, William
Holland, Kilian
Huston, Richard
Lucev, John
May, Anthony C.
McGray, James
Mooney, William
Nesbitt, John B.
Ortiz, Michael
Ortman, William
Palmitessa, Paul
Penko, Francis
Quinn, John T.
Rapp, Bernard A.
Roll, David H.
Ryland, Raymond
Salada, Urbano
Salca, Louis
Sheslo, Charles
Smith, Aquinas
Sostrich, John L.
Thompson, J. Noel
Tindall, Harold
Vesga, Mario

Permanent Deacons:
Albers, A. Anthony, Blessed Sacrament, San Diego
Allen, Ronald, Our Lady of Grace, El Cajon
Amicone, Nicholas, Springville, CA
Aquino, Jaime, Good Shepherd, San Diego
Arias, Luciano, (Retired), El Centro
Arismendez, Joe, St. Anthony of Padua, National City
Arnold, Raymond, Our Lady of Grace, El Cajon
Arnold, Ronald, St. Francis of Assisi, Vista
Beatty, Lewis, St. Mary Star of the Sea, Oceanside
Beiner, Robert, St. John the Evangelist, Encinitas
Bell, L. Ferris, (Retired), San Diego
Bennet, David, St. Mark, San Marcos
Bongatt, Rolando, Most Precious Blood, Chula Vista
Booth, Robert, St. John the Evangelist, San Diego
Bucon, Mark, Mary Star of the Sea, La Jolla
Carpizo, Magno, Good Shepherd, San Diego
Casabosch, Miguel, Mission, TX
Castro, Agustin, Resurrection, Escondido
Chia, Henry, (Retired), Carlsbad
Clarke, William G., Blessed Kateri Tekakwitha, Lakeside
Collins, Michael, Nampa, ID
Cooper, James, Morro Bay, CA
Corrao, Jack P., (Retired), San Diego
Daniels, Michael, St. Brigid, San Diego
Davidson, Paul, Oceanside
Dean, Bennett, Sioux Falls, SD
Delano, Joseph, (Retired), Chula Vista
Dennison, Howard Mick, St. Charles, San Diego
Depner, John, St. Timothy, Escondido
DePozo, Daniel, Henderson, NV
Diem, Ronald H., St. Gregory the Great, San Diego
Donarski, Conrad, Camp Pendleton, Oceanside
Dube, Leo, (Retired), San Diego
Duran, Amador, St. Mary, Escondido
Early, John Michael, St. Timothy, Escondido
Ekhaml, Robert T., St. Therese, San Diego
Ellis, John A., Baker, LA
Embury, Charles, St. Stephen, Valley Center
Enciso, Pedro, St. Francis of Assisi, Vista
Enriquez, Domingo, Our Lady of Guadalupe, El Centro
Enriquez, Miguel, St. Francis of Assisi, Vista
Fanelle, John, St. Therese of Carmel, San Diego
Faus, Juan, Our Lady of Mt. Carmel, San Diego
Fickes, Dale, St. Elizabeth Seton, Carlsbad
Finn, Kenneth, (Retired), Escondido
Fitzmorris, Robert H., Immaculate Conception, San Diego
Frazee, Michael, St. Patrick, Carlsbad
Frice, Charles, St. Rose of Lima, Chula Vista
Gasparovic, Anthony L., (Retired), Lakeside
Goeltz, Thomas A., St. Thomas More, Oceanside
Gonzalez, Raul, Our Lady of Mt. Carmel, San Ysidro
Gonzalez, Refugio, Our Lady of Guadalupe, Calexico
Graff, Albert P., (Retired), La Jolla
Griffin, Robert E., Jr., Sacred Heart, Coronado
Grosso, Ernest, Mission San Diego de Alcala, San Diego
Guess, Harry, Jr., Christ the King, San Diego
Gullotta, Daniel, Lakeside, MT
Gutierrez, Braulio, St. Anthony of Padua, National City
Hardick, Richard, St. Augustine High School, San Diego
Heindenreich, Michael, St. Patrick, Calipatria
Hernandez, Raul, St. Jerome, San Diego
Hess, Arnold, (Retired), San Diego
Hitch, James, Corpus Christi, Bonita
Hoang, Loi, St. Francis of Assisi, Vista
Hodsdon, Peter, St. James, Solana Beach
Holgren, Robert, Our Lady of Mt. Carmel, San Diego
Hollowell, Christopher Wil, Corpus Christi, Bonita
Hunt, Samuel, Homosassa, FL
Jansing, Richard, (Retired), Stevens Pt., WI
Jiron, Guillermo, Corpus Christi, Bonita
Johnson, Peter, St. Pius X, Chula Vista
Keeley, James, St. Catherine Laboure, San Diego
Kelsey, Herbert, Blessed Sacrament, San Diego
Klopchin, William, Our Mother of Confidence, San Diego
Korty, William, Our Lady of Grace, El Cajon
Kostick, James, St. Mary, Escondido
Kutler, Harold, (Retired), Oceanside
Leach, David, (Retired), Carlsbad
Lewandowski, Daniel, (Retired), Spring Valley
Lopez-Castillo, Fernando, O.S.A., St. Patrick, San Diego
Lozoya, Margarito, Our Lady of Guadalupe, Chula Vista
Mackey, Robert, (Retired), Anaheim Hills, CA
Magana, Gustavo, San Diego
Maria, Michael, St. Therese, San Diego
Marquez, Gerardo, St. Rose of Lima, Chula Vista
Martinez, Seodello A., (Retired), San Diego
Mather, Richard, (Retired), Oceanside
McClellan, Gerald, Jr., St. Patrick, Carlsbad
McDaniel, Alvin, Hemet, CA
Medina, Jose Luis, Our Lady of Mt. Carmel, San Ysidro
Melrose, Richard, Guardian Angels, Santee
Mercardante, Frank, St. Mark, San Marcos
Michaels, Larry, St. Mary, Escondido
Miller, James, Logan, UT
Montoya, Edwin Gonzales, Resurrection, Escondido
Montoya, Kenneth, St. Charles, San Diego
Moser, Edward, St. Patrick, Carlsbad
Mueller, Robert, St. Francis of Assisi, Vista
Murray, Kevin, Sacred Heart, Coronado
Nguyen, Peter, St. Didacus, San Diego
Nickell, Dennie, St. Luke, El Cajon
Nunez, Manuel, St. Jude Shrine of the West, San Diego
O'Neil, Dennis, Our Lady of Perpetual Help, Lakeside
O'Riordan, Stephen, Our Lady of the Rosary, San Diego
Osgood, Franklin B., Sacred Heart, Coronado
Parra, Daniel, Most Precious Blood, Chula Vista
Partida, Michael, Resurrection, Escondido
Paulicivic, George, Sr., Warren, OH
Pelina, Ruben, Most Precious Blood, Chula Vista
Phelps, John, (Retired), Santee
Pollock, William, (Retired), San Diego
Porciuncula, Manuel, Our Lady of Mt. Carmel, San Diego
Powers, Daniel, Mission San Antonio de Pala, Pala
Prado, Daniel, St. Pius X, Chula Vista
Principe, Louis, (Retired), Lakeside
Reilly, Frank, St. Kieran, El Cajon
Rennix, Mitchell, Resurrection, Escondido
Rivera, Noel, Our Lady of Mt. Carmel, San Diego
Robbins, Ralph, (Retired), San Marcos
Robert, James, St. John of the Cross, Lemon Grove
Robles, Manuel, Winchester, CA
Rocha, Louis, Holy Trinity, El Cajon
Rodriguez, Manuel, St. Jude Shrine of the West, San Diego
Roy, James, Sahuarita, AZ
Salinas, Gilbert, St. Stephen, Valley Center
Sanderville, Richard, St. Charles Borromeo, San Diego
Santen, Joseph R., St. James, Solana Beach
Santiago, Nicholas M., Tucson, AZ
Santoyo, Juan Francisco, St. John of the Cross, Lemon Grove
Schmitt, Giles V., (Retired), San Diego
Scull, James, Ascension, San Diego
Shea, George, (Retired), El Cajon
Shelton, Carl, St. Michael, San Diego
Shockley, Gordon E., San Antonio, TX
Skiano, Ralph, St. Michael, Poway
Skupnik, Raymond, Seal Beach, CA
Smyth, Gregory, St. Rose of Lima, Chula Vista
Snyder, John A., Queen of Angels, Alpine
Spinney, Donald L., Sacred Heart, Brawley
Stanley, James, St. John of the Cross, Lemon Grove
Sullivan, Dennis, St. Mark, San Marcos
Thompson, Ward, San Rafael, San Diego
Threatt, Marvin, Holy Spirit, San Diego
Treadwell, Timothy, St. Martin of Tours, La Mesa
Troy, Robert, St. Gabriel, Poway
Trumble, John, St. Pius X, Jamul
Turcich, John, St. Pius X, Jamul
Vaillancourt, Leonard, San Rafael, San Diego
Vargas, Jim, Mary Star of the Sea, La Jolla
Vasquez, H. William, Jr., Mission San Diego de Alcala, San Diego
Vecchitto, Glenn, St. Pius X, Chula Vista
Villafana, Martin, St. John of the Cross, Lemon Grove
Vivio, William, Phoenix, AZ
Walling, Robert K., (Retired), Bend, OR
Walsh, James, Nativity, San Diego
Warren, David, St. Peter, Fallbrook
Wood, Joseph, (Retired), La Jolla
Woznicki, Walter, (Retired), La Mesa
Yeatts, Bernard, San Rafael, San Diego

INSTITUTIONS LOCATED IN THE DIOCESE

[A] SEMINARIES, DIOCESAN

SAN DIEGO. *St. Francis De Sales Center*, 1667 Santa Paula Dr., 92111. Tel: 619-291-7446; Fax: 619-291-7011. Email: eceliceo@diocese-sdiego.org. Web: www.diocese-sdiego.org. Revs. William Dillard, Spiritual Dir. Candidates for Priest; Matthew D. Spahr, Dir. of Priestly Formations; Anthony Saroki, Dir. of Vocations. For priests and priestly formation. Priests 3; Students 7.

[B] COLLEGES AND UNIVERSITIES

SAN DIEGO. **John Paul the Great Catholic University*, 10174 Old Grove Rd., Ste. 200, 92131. Tel: 858-653-6740; Fax: 858-653-3791. Email: info@jpcatholic.com. Web: www.jpcatholic.com. Derry (Jeremiah) Connolly, Ph.D., Pres.; Dominic Iocco, Provost; Sara Harold, Librarian.

University of San Diego (1949) 5998 Alcala Park, 92110-2492. Tel: 619-260-4600. Web: www.sandiego.edu. Dr. Mary E. Lyons, Pres.; Dr. Julie H. Sullivan, Vice Pres. & Provost; Rev. Msgr. Daniel J. Dillabough, Vice Pres. Mission & Ministry; Ms. Carmen M. Vazquez, Vice Pres. Student Affairs; Dr. Mary Boyd, Dean College of Arts & Sciences; Dr. David Pyke, Dean School of Business Admin.; Dr. Paula Cordeiro, Dean School of Leadership & Education Sciences; Kevin Cole, Dean School of Law; Dr. Sally B. Hardin, Dean Hahn School of Nursing & Health Science; Dr. Timothy O'Malley, Vice Pres. Univ. Rels. Priests 2; Sisters 3; Lay Teachers 365; Total University Full-Time Faculty 369; Law Students 1,112; Undergraduate Students 5,111; Graduate Students 1,461.

University Ministers: Michael Lovette-Colyer, Dir. Univ., Min.; Robert Gilmore, Assoc. Univ. Min.; Amy Gualtieri, Sacristan; Mary Kruer, Assoc. Univ. Min.; Kelly Czajka, Assoc. Univ. Min.; Maria Toretto-Coaughan, Assoc. Univ. Min.; Sr. Regin Shin, Assoc. Univ. Min.; Rev. Owen Mullen, Univ. Chap.; Mark Peters, Asst. Dir. Univ. Min.; Sr. Virginia Rodee, R.S.C.J., Asst. Vice Pres. for Mission; Annette Walsh, Assoc. Univ. Min.; Rev. Michael White, C.S.Sp., Univ. Chap.

Faculty: Revs. William Headley, Admin.; Dennis Krouse; Norbert Rigali, S.J.; Saba Shofany; Ron Pachence (Retired); Michael White, C.S.Sp.; Sisters Mary Hotz; Terri Monroe, R.S.C.J.; Anice Callahan, R.S.C.J.; Maria Pascuzzi, C.S.J.

Msgr. John Portman Chair of Roman Catholic Systematic Theology Tel: 619-260-7844; Fax: 619-260-2260. Web: www.sandiego.edu/theo.

Center for Catholic Thought and Culture Sr. Maria Pascuzzi, C.S.J., Dir. Tel: 619-260-7936.

Center for the Study of Latino/Latina Catholicism Tel: 619-260-4525; Fax: 619-260-2260. Web: www.sandiego.edu/theo/latino-cath. Dr. Orlando Espin, Dir.

Center for Christian Spirituality Tel: 619-260-4784; Fax: 619-260-7905. Sr. Barbara Quinn, R.S.C.J., Dir.

Pastoral Care and Counseling Program Tel: 619-260-4784; Fax: 619-260-7905.

Values Institute Tel: 619-260-4705; Fax: 619-260-7950. Web: www.sandiego.edu/values. Dr. Larry Hinman, Dir.

[C] HIGH SCHOOLS, PRIVATE

SAN DIEGO. *Academy of Our Lady of Peace* (1882) 4860 Oregon St., 92116. Tel: 619-297-2266; Fax: 619-297-2473. Email: aolpadmin@excite.com. Web: www.aolp.org. Sr. Dolores Anchondo, C.S.J., Prin.; Deanna Buhr, Librarian. (Girls) Sisters of St. Joseph of Carondelet 4; Lay Teachers 46; Students 740.

St. Augustine High School (1922) 3266 Nutmeg St., 92104-5199. Tel: 619-282-2184; Fax: 619-282-1203. Email: kevenson@sahs.org. Web: www.sahs.org. James Horne, Prin.; Edwin Hearn, Pres.; Revs. Robert W. Gavotto, O.S.A., Chap. Campus Ministry; Alvin Paligutan, O.S.A.; Deacon Richard Hardick; Craig da Luz, Librarian. Conducted by The Augustinians., (Boys); (For information concerning the monastery see separate listing under Monasteries). Priests 2; Deacons 1; Lay Teachers 48; Students 722.

SAN MARCOS. *Saint Joseph Academy* (Co-Ed), 500 Las Flores Dr., 92078. Tel: 760-305-8505; Fax: 760-305-8466; 760-305-8466. Web: www.saintjosephacademy.org. Carol Kewell, Prin.

[D] HIGH SCHOOLS, DIOCESAN

SAN DIEGO. *Cathedral Catholic High School*, 5555 Del Mar Heights Rd., 92130. Tel: 858-523-4000; Fax: 858-523-4073. Web: www.cathedralcatholic.org. Mr. James Tschann, Pres.; Mr. Michael Deely, Prin.; Ms. Pat Prather, Librarian. Sisters 1; Lay Teachers 96; Students 1,743.

CALEXICO. *Vincent Memorial High*, 525 W. Sheridan, 92231. Tel: 760-357-3461; Fax: 760-357-0902. Email: vmchs@aol.com. Web: vmchs.com. Sisters Lilia M. Barba, S.J.S., Prin.; Lilia Vega, Librarian. (Coed). Conducted by Sisters Servants of the Blessed Sacrament. Sisters 3; Lay Teachers 14; Students 244.

CHULA VISTA. *Mater Dei Catholic High School*, 1615 Mater Dei Dr., 91913. Tel: 619-423-2121; Fax: 619-423-6910. Email: kchudy@materdeicatholic.org. Web: www.materdeicatholic.org. Mr. George E. Milke, Prin.; Mr. Thomas Clayton Beecher, Pres. (Coed) Lay Teachers 47; Students 732.

[E] ELEMENTARY SCHOOLS PRIVATE

SAN DIEGO. *Nazareth School*, (Grades PreSchool-8), 10728 San Diego Mission Rd., 92108. Tel: 619-641-7987; Fax: 619-280-4652. Dr. Colleen Mauricio, Prin.; Mrs. Nora Smyth, Librarian. Sisters 1; Lay Teachers 21.

Notre Dame Academy, (Grades PreSchool-8), 4345 Del Mar Trails Rd., 92130. Tel: 858-509-2300; Fax: 858-509-5915. Web: www.ndacademy.com. Sr. Marie Pascale, U.S.S.C., Prin. Sisters 3; Lay Teachers 34; Students 371.

SAN MARCOS. *St. Joseph Academy*, (Grades K-8), (Co-Ed), 500 Las Flores Dr., 92078. Tel: 760-305-8505; Fax: 760-305-8466. Web: www.saintjosephacademy.org. Carol Kewell, Prin.

[F] SPECIAL SCHOOLS

SAN DIEGO. *Mater Dei Language Academy/Juan Diego Adult Center*, 938 18th St., 92154. Tel: 619-621-5711. Email: storrez@mariancatholic.org. Sylvia Torrez, Dir.

EL CAJON. *St. Madeleine Sophie's Center for Adults with Developmental Disorders*, 2119 E. Madison Ave., 92019-1111. Tel: 619-442-5129; Fax: 619-442-2590. Email: dturner@stmsc.org. Web: www.stmsc.org. Debra Turner Emerson, Exec. Dir. Lay Teachers 110; Enrollment 300.

OCEANSIDE. *Old Mission Montessori School*, (Grades PreK-8), 4070 Mission Ave., 92057. Tel: 760-757-3232; Fax: 760-721-0305. Email: office@omms.org. Wanda King, Prin.; Elisabeth Bush, Librarian. Lay Teachers 18.

[G] PROTECTIVE INSTITUTIONS

SPRING VALLEY. *Noah Homes* (1983) 12526 Campo Rd., 91978. Tel: 619-660-6200; Fax: 619-660-1481. Email: m.nocon@noahhomes.org. Web: www.noahhomes.org. Molly Nocon, Chief Exec. Dir. Total Assisted Annually 70; Total Staff 60.

[H] HOSPITALS

SAN DIEGO. *Scripps Mercy Hospital* (1890) 4077 Fifth Ave., 92103. Tel: 619-294-8111; Fax: 619-686-3530. Web: www.scrippshealth.org. Tom Gammiere, CEO; Sr. JoCeal Young, R.S.M., Dir. Mission Integration; Revs. James Schorr; Lawrence Agi; Michael Harkay, Chap.; Ann Albrecht, Chap.; Sr. Mary Gallagher, R.S.M., Chap. Mgr.; Rev. Gerald Swanson, Chap. (Baptist). Bed Capacity 519; Total Staff 2,000; Patients Assisted Annually 21,214.

Scripps Mercy Chula Vista, 435 H St., Chula Vista, 91910. Tel: 619-691-7000. Rev. Mark Weber, B.C.C.; Sr. Pauline Dibb, C.S.Sp., Chap. Bed Capacity 700; Staff 3,075; Patients Assisted Annually 208,176.

[I] HOMES FOR SENIOR CITIZENS

SAN DIEGO. *Cathedral Plaza*, 1551 Third Ave., 92101. Tel: 619-234-0093; Fax: 619-234-5168. Bobbi Pentchev, Resident Mgr.; John Adams, Supvr. Maintenance.

Cathedral Plaza Development Corp., A California Nonprofit Corporation Apartments 222; In Residence 253; Total Staff 6; Total Assisted 172.

Guadalupe Plaza, 4142 42nd St., 92105. Tel: 619-584-2414; Fax: 619-584-2886. Marie Creveling, Resident Mgr.

Guadalupe Plaza Development Corp., A California Nonprofit Corporation Apartments 126; In Residence 142.

St. John's Plaza, 8150 Broadway, Lemon Grove, 91945. Tel: 619-466-5354; Fax: 619-466-6643. Email: stjohnsplaza@sjp.sdcoxmail.com. Jeanne DeFlorio, Resident Mgr.

Calexico Plaza Development Corp., A California Nonprofit Corporation Residences 99; Total in Residence 97; Total Staff 2.

Nazareth House Retirement Home, 6333 Rancho Mission Rd., 92108. Tel: 619-563-0480; Fax: 619-624-9215. Email: mbrodyca@lycos.com. Sr. Margaret Spence, C.S.N., Admin.; Rev. David Leon, Chap. Retired Priests Residential and Assisted Living Capacity 139; Priests 20; Sisters of Nazareth of San Diego 8.

LA MESA. *Little Flower Haven*, 8585 La Mesa Blvd., 91942. Tel: 619-466-3163; Fax: 619-466-9642. Email: littleflwrhaven@yahoo.com. Sr. M. Luz Divina Carmel, D.C.J., Supr.; Rev. Philip Bronk, S.T., Chap. Total Staff 34; Aged Residents 54; Bed Capacity 60.

[J] MONASTERIES AND RESIDENCES OF PRIESTS AND BROTHERS

SAN DIEGO. *Augustinian Community* (1922) 3266 Nutmeg St., 92104. Tel: 619-282-2028; Fax: 619-282-2233. Revs. Jerome F. Bevilacqua, O.S.A.; Robert W. Gavotto, O.S.A., Chap.; James E. Hannan, O.S.A.; Patrick J. Keane, O.S.A.; John D. Keller, O.S.A., Prior; Alvin Paligutan, O.S.A.; John P. Pejza, O.S.A.; Anthony J. Wasko, O.S.A (Retired); Harry M. Neely, O.S.A.; Thomas G. Verber, O.S.A., St. Patrick's Parish, 3585 30th St., 92104-4196. Tel: 619-295-2157; Fax: 619-688-1225; Bro. Fernando L. Castillo. *Augustinian Provincialate* (1981) 1605 28th St., 92102-1417. Tel: 619-235-0247; Fax: 619-231-2814. Very Rev. Gary Sanders, O.S.A., Prov.

Austin House (1981) 1605 28th St., 92102-1417. Tel: 619-233-9141. Deacon Richard Hardick. Total in Residence 1. *Office of the Provincial* Tel: 619-235-0247; Fax: 619-231-2814. Email: osa-west@sbcglobal.net. Web: www.osa-west.org. Very Rev. Gary Sanders, O.S.A., Prior Prov. Tel: 619-235-0247; Fax: 619-231-2814.

Monica House - Augustinian Community, 1621 28th St., 92102-1417. Tel: 619-338-9268. Very Rev. Gary Sanders, O.S.A. Total in Residence 2.

BOULEVARD. *Holy Trinity Hermitage-Augustinian Community*, 1371 Tierra del Sol Rd., 91905-9694. Tel: 619-766-4101. *Provincial Office*, 1605 28th St., 92102-1417. Tel: 619-235-0247; Fax: 619-231-2814. A contemplative retreat setting that only accommodates 8 people.

OCEANSIDE. *Mission San Luis Rey* (1798) 4050 Mission Ave., 92057-6402. Tel: 760-757-3651; Fax: 760-757-4613. Email: james@sanluisrey.org. Web: www.sanluisrey.org. Bro. Maurice Peltier, O.F.M., (Retired); Revs. Mel Bucher, O.F.M. (Retired); Thomas Herbst, O.F.M.; Andres Rivero, O.F.M.; Raul Alejos, O.F.M.; Laurence Dolan, O.F.M., Guardian; Philip Garcia, O.F.M.; Bros. James Lockman, O.F.M., Exec. Dir.; Stephen Gillis, O.F.M.; Kelly Cullen, O.F.M., Retreat Center Dir. Franciscan Friars. Priests 6; Brothers 5.

Prince of Peace Abbey, 650 Benet Hill, 92058-1253. Tel: 760-967-4200; Fax: 760-967-8711. Email: princeabby@aol.com. Web: www.princeofpeaceabbey.org. Rt. Rev. Charles Wright, O.S.B., Abbot; Revs. Sharbel Ewen, O.S.B., Prior; Alexis Foyo, O.S.B.; Basil Mattingly, O.S.B.; Herbert Palmer, O.S.B.; Stephanos Pedrano, O.S.B.; Bros. Peter Aslin, O.S.B.; Timothy Balk, O.S.B., Bro. Oblate; Joseph Black, O.S.B.; Anselm Clark, O.S.B.; Blaise Heuke, O.S.B.; Benedict Menezes, O.S.B.; Raphael Meyer, O.S.B.; Michel Pham, O.S.B., Cleric; Mario Quizon, O.S.B.; Daniel Sokol, O.S.B.; Meinrad Taylor, O.S.B.; David Cobos, O.S.B.; Paul Farrelly, O.S.B., Cleric; Noel Greenawalt, O.S.B.; Philip Poutous, O.S.B.; Gabriel Stern, O.S.B.; Emmanuel Tran, O.S.B.; Damien Evangelista, O.S.B. Benedictine Fathers. Priests 5; Brothers 18; Clerics 2; Oblates 1.

[K] CONVENTS AND RESIDENCES FOR SISTERS

SAN DIEGO. *Carmelite Monastery of San Diego, California* (Discalced); Cloistered Contemplative Nuns, 5158 Hawley Blvd., 92116-1934. Tel: 619-280-5425; Fax: 619-280-3775. Email: carmelsd@sbcglobal.net. Web: www.carmelsandiego.com. Sr. Yvonne Hanke, O.C.D., Prioress. Sisters 14; Junior Professed 1.

Congregation of the Sisters of Nazareth, 6330 Rancho Mission Rd., 92108. Tel: 619-563-0480; Fax: 619-624-9215. Email: mbrodyca@lycos.com. Sisters 9.

Daughters of Divine Charity, 6036 Camino Rico, 92120. Tel: 619-287-1320. Sisters 3.

Daughters of St. Paul (1915) 5945 Balboa Ave., 92111. Tel: 858-565-9181; Fax: 858-565-9295. Sr. Frances Obrovac, F.S.P., Contact Person.

Dominican Sisters of Adrian, 640 Camino de la Reina #1117, 92117. Tel: 619-255-4238. Email: kclausen2@cox.net. Sisters 6.

Maryknoll Sisters, 4070 Kansas St. #312, 92104. Tel: 619-283-5678. Sisters 4.

Missionaries of Charity (1950) 3877 Boston Ave., 92113-3218. Tel: 619-263-9566. Sr. Maria Fatima, Major Supr. Sisters 7.

Religious of Jesus and Mary, 1318 Pequena St., 92154. Tel: 619-690-0242; Fax: 619-690-0257. Email: rosy1510@aol.com. Sr. Rosemary Nicholson, R.J.M., Regl. Supr. Sisters 4.

Religious of Jesus and Mary, 1510 Third Ave., 92101. Tel: 619-234-0556. Email: rosy1510@aol.com. Sisters 4.

School Sisters of Notre Dame, 1997 Magdalene Way, 92110. Tel: 619-276-5830. Email: jweisma1@san.rr.com. Sisters 4.

Sisters of Loretto (1812) 440 San Antonio Ave. #6, 92106. Tel: 619-224-2341.

Sisters of Mercy of the Americas (West-Midwest), 4123 Fifth Ave., #15, 92103. Tel: 619-296-4272. Sisters 11.

Sisters of Mercy US Province (1831) 10726 Caminito Cascara, 92108. Tel: 619-284-1027; Fax: 619-284-1027. Email: smjobreen@att.net. Sisters 11.

Sisters of Social Service, 3525 Third Ave., 92103-4908. Tel: 619-295-1896. Sisters 4.

Sisters of St. Joseph Brentwood, NY, 2115 Clematis St., 92105. Tel: 619-528-1531.

Sisters of St. Joseph of Carondelet, 4860 Oregon St., 92116. Tel: 619-295-2887; Fax: 619-297-2473. Email: danchondo@aolp.org. Sisters 17.

Sisters of St. Joseph of Peace, 2880 Caulfield Dr., 92154. Tel: 619-423-7360. Sisters 3.

Sisters of St. Louis, 5824 Kantor Ct., 92122. Tel: 858-490-8240. Email: bboyle@diocese-sdiego.org. Web: www.st-louis-sisters.org.

Sisters of the Precious Blood (1833) 4202 58th St., 92115. Tel: 619-229-1817. Email: kelliecpps@live.com. Sisters 2.

Society of the Holy Child Jesus, 6243 Caminito Telmo, 92111. Tel: 619-231-7788. Sisters 7.

BONITA. *Sister Servants of the Blessed Sacrament* (1904) 3173 Winnetka Dr., 91902. Tel: 619-267-0720; Fax: 619-267-0920. Email: sup@sjsusprovince.sdcoxmail.com. Sr. Maria Paz Uribe, S.J.S., Provincial Supr. Sisters 12.

CALEXICO. *Sister Servants of the Blessed Sacrament*, 536 Rockwood, 92231. Tel: 760-357-1046; Fax: 760-357-3282. Email: sjsclx@aol.com. Sisters 23.

CARLSBAD. *Sisters de L'Union-Chretienne de Saint Chammound*, 3109 La Costa Ave., 92009. Tel: 858-509-2300. Sr. Marie Pascale Clisson, U.C.S.C., Contact Person. Sisters 3.

CHULA VISTA. *Benedictine Sisters of Glendora* (1956) 236 Alvarado, 91910-3610. Tel: 619-422-3610; Fax: 619-427-5786. Email: jokingosb@strosecv.com. Sisters 2.

Franciscan Missionaries of Our Lady of Peace (1941) 575 E. St. #20, 91910. Tel: 619-691-9008; Fax: 619-425-7514. Email: marumfp@hotmail.com. Sisters 2.

Medical Mission Sisters (Western Office), 3270 Holly Way, 91910. Tel: 619-426-5561; Fax: 619-426-5561. Web: www.medicalmissionsisters.org.

Society of Catholic Medical Missionaries, Inc. 3270 Holly Way, 91910-3217. Tel: 619-426-5561. Sisters 2. 2250 Tampa Ave., #1, El Cajon, 92020. Tel: 619-466-7100. 8150 Broadway, Lemon Grove, 91945. Tel: 619-462-3888; 619-464-8221; 619-697-7331. Sisters 3.

Religious of the Incarnate Word (1625) 153 Rainier Ct., 91911. Tel: 619-420-0231; Fax: 619-691-5939. Email: ccrabbe@hotmail.com. Sisters (Chula Vista) 5; Sisters (El Centro) 3.

EL CENTRO. *Our Lady of Victory Missionary Sisters*, 142 E. Octillo Dr., 92243. Tel: 760-352-1263. Sisters 4.

Religious of the Incarnate Word, 102 W. Holt, 92243-2730. Tel: 760-353-4146; Fax: 760-353-1261. Sisters 10.

FALLBROOK. *Hermanas del Corazon de Jesus Sacramentado*, 133 Alvarado Ct., 92028. Tel: 760-645-3372; Fax: 760-645-3372. Email: hcjsfbrk@aol.com. Sisters 4.

LA MESA. *Carmelite Sisters of the Divine Heart of Jesus*, 8585 La Mesa Blvd., 91941. Tel: 619-466-3163; Fax: 619-462-8261. Sisters Mary Alice Prieto, Local Supr. Tel: 619-466-3163; Fax: 619-466-9642; M. Carmela, Contact Person. Sisters 14; Novices 4.

LEMON GROVE. *Mercedarian Sisters of the Blessed Sacrament*, 8171 Lemon Grove Way, 91945. Tel: 619-460-4271; Fax: 619-460-1060. Email: smarilup@stjohncross.org. Sisters 4.

PALA. *Sisters of St. Francis (Philadelphia)* (1855) P.O. Box M, 92059. Tel: 760-742-3317; Fax: 760-742-3040. Sisters 2.

SAN MARCOS. *Daughters of Mary and Joseph* (1817) 1545 Via Brisa del Lago, 92069. Tel: 760-744-6578; Fax: 760-744-3828. Email: ballygoughlan@aol.com.

SAN YSIDRO. *Dominican Sisters, Tacoma WA*, 1879 Via Las Tonadas, 92173. Tel: 619-428-1629. Sisters 4.

Medical Missionaries of Mary, P.O. Box 431134, 92143-1134. Tel: 619-690-9237; Fax: 619-428-9551. Web: www.mmmusa.org.

Sisters Servants of the Blessed Sacrament, 333 W. Park Ave., 92173. Tel: 619-207-0333; Fax: 619-428-8324. Email: sanysidrosjs@yahoo.com.mx. Sisters 7.

SPRING VALLEY. *Community of the Holy Spirit* (1970) 275 S. Worthington St., 91977. Tel: 619-434-8529. Email: jwagenbrenner@cox.net. Sr. Joanne Wagenbrenner, C.H.S., M.A., M.S., Gen. Coord. Sisters 7.

Sisters of St. Joseph of Orange, 10771 Del Rio Rd., 91978. Tel: 619-670-9663; Fax: 619-670-6554. Sisters 4.

VISTA. *Sisters of St. Clare (O.S.C.)*, 1171 Via Santa Paulo, 92081. Tel: 760-295-0611; Fax: 760-945-8036. Email: srmadfitz@yahoo.com.

[L] SOCIAL SERVICES

SAN DIEGO. *Catholic Charities*, 349 Cedar St., 92101. Tel: 619-231-2828; Fax: 619-234-2272. Email: srmduvall@ccdsd.org. Web: www.ccdsd.org. Sr. RayMonda DuVall, C.H.S., Exec. Dir.; Dr. Robert Moser, Deputy Dir. Counseling Services.; Homeless Women's Services.

Emergency Services (Main Office) Tel: 619-231-2828; Fax: 619-234-2272.

Clinical Services Tel: 619-231-2828; Fax: 619-234-2272. Patricia Petterson, Ph.D., Dir.

Pregnancy and Adoption Tel: 619-231-2828; Fax: 619-234-2272. Patricia Petterson, Ph.D., Dir.

Immigrant Services--San Diego Tel: 619-287-9454; Fax: 619-234-2272. Dede Hollowell, Dir.

La Posada de Guadalupe de Carlsbad Tel: 760-929-2322; Fax: 760-929-8712. Eduardo Presciado, Dir.

El Centro--Imperial Valley Services, 250 W. Orange, El Centro, 92243. Tel: 760-353-6822; Fax: 760-353-0120.

House of Hope--El Centro Tel: 760-352-1182; Fax: 760-352-5492.

Our Lady of Guadalupe Shelter Tel: 760-357-0894; Fax: 760-357-0895.

Rachel's Women's Center--San Diego, 92101. Tel: 619-236-9074.

The Tomorrow Project Tel: 619-230-1151. Martha Ransom, Dir.

Joan of Arc Residence, 1510 Third Ave., 92101. Tel: 619-239-2663. Email: rosy1510@aol.com. Sr. Rosemary Nicholson, R.J.M., Admin. Residence for Employed Young Women and College Students 21-60 Years. Religious 4; Permanent Residents 60; Capacity 71.

**Mexican American Neighbor Organization* (1962) P.O. Box 81635, 92138. Tel: 619-298-5859; Fax: 888-221-7609. Email: info@manosandiego.org. Total Assisted 200; Total Staff 15.

**S.V.D.P. Management Inc.*, 3350 E St., 92102. Tel: 619-446-2100; Fax: 619-446-2129. Web: fatherjoesvillages.org. Rev. Msgr. Joseph A. Carroll, Pres. Owns and manages the property for St. Vincent de Paul Village, Inc.; Fr. Joe's Villages; Martha's Village & Kitchen in Indio, CA, Toussaint Youth Villages in San Diego, and Natl. Aids Foundation. Total Staff 85.

**St. Vincent de Paul Village* (1950) 3350 E St., 92102-3332. Tel: 619-446-2100; Fax: 619-446-2129. Web: www.neighbor.org. Rev. Msgr. Joseph A. Carroll, Pres. Total Staff 400; Total Assisted Annually 162,540.

Joan Kroc Homeless Center (1987) 1501 Imperial Ave., 92101. Tel: 619-446-2100; Fax: 619-446-2129. Web: www.neighbor.org. Mary Case, Vice Pres. Housing for families & single women (326).

Bishop Maher Men's Center (1989) 1501 Imperial Ave., 92101. Tel: 619-446-2100; Fax: 619-446-2129. Web: www.neighbor.org. Single men's center - 150 residents.

National Aids Foundation dba Josue Homes 3350 E St., 92102. Tel: 619-466-4827; Fax: 619-446-2129. Web: www.neighbor.org. Housing for persons with AIDS (38).

Paul Mirabile Center--Mirabile Housing Inc. (1994) 1501 Imperial Ave., 92101. Tel: 619-446-2100; Fax: 619-446-2129. Emergency housing for 270 men & 80 women; free dining room (4000 meals daily).

Toussaint Academy of Arts & Sciences, 1404-5th St., 92101. Tel: 619-687-1080, Ext. 3399; Fax: 619-446-2129. Web: www.neighbor.org. Residential for 35 homeless teens.

Thrift Stores (1950) 815 33rd St., 92102. Tel: 619-446-2711; Fax: 619-446-2129. Keith MacKay, Vice Pres.

Rancho San Vincente, Campo. Tel: 619-446-2701; Fax: 619-446-2129. Web: www.neighbor.org. Rev. Msgr. Joseph A. Carroll, Devel. Dir.

Village Place, 32-17th St., 92101. Tel: 619-446-2100; Fax: 619-446-2129. 54 units - low to moderate income apartments.

3350 E St., 92102. Tel: 619-687-1315; Fax: 619-687-1010.

Villa Harvey Mandel, 72-17th St., 92101. Tel: 619-446-2100; Fax: 619-446-2129. 95 units - Low to moderate income apts.

Padre Luis Jayme International Outreach, 3350 E St., 92101. Tel: 619-446-2100; Fax: 619-446-2129. Providing assistance to colonias, prison ministries and orphanages; earthquakes and flood relief in Mexico. Total Assisted Annually 6,450; Staff 4.

[M] RETREATS

SAN DIEGO. *Spiritual Ministry Center* (1987) 4822 Del Mar Ave., 92107-3407. Tel: 619-224-9444; Fax: 619-224-1082. Email: spiritmin@rscj.org. Web: www.spiritmin.org.

Whispering Winds Catholic Conference Center (1978) 8186 Commercial St., La Mesa, 91942-2926. Tel: 619-464-1479; Fax: 619-464-4491. Email: office@whisperingwinds.org. Web: www.whisperingwinds.org. Facility: 17606 Harrison Park Rd., Julian, 92036. Don Kojis, Co-Founder/Community Rels. Purpose: Serve over 7,000 guests each year for 6th grade camp, retreats, family camp, Confirmation, RCIA, family reunions, leadership training and parish meetings.

DESCANSO. *Camp Oliver*, P.O. Box 206, 91916. Tel: 619-445-5945; Fax: 619-445-3326. Email: director@campoliver.com. Web: www.campoliver.com. Annie Korn, Exec. Dir. Summer Resident Camp for Girls & Boys, ages 6-16. Owned by Sisters of Social Service. (June-Aug.; Available Sept.-June for rental groups).

OCEANSIDE. *Mission San Luis Rey Retreat*, 4050 Mission Ave., 92057-6402. Tel: 760-757-3659; Fax: 760-757-8025. Email: slretreat@sanluisrey.org. Web: www.sanluisrey.org. Bro. Kelly Cullen, O.F.M., Retreat Center Dir.

Prince of Peace Retreat Center, 650 Benet Hill Rd., 92058-1253. Tel: 442-967-4200; 442-967-4200, Ext. 248; Fax: 442-967-8711. Email: princeabby@aol.com. Web: www.princeofpeaceabbey.org. Bro. Benedict Menezes, O.S.B., Guest Master. Benedictine Fathers-Benet Hill. Priests 6; Brothers 20.

[N] NEWMAN CENTERS

SAN DIEGO. *Newman Center - SDSU* 5855 Hardy Ave., 92115. Tel: 619-583-9181; Fax: 619-583-8925. Email: office@sdsucatholic.org. Very Rev. Bruce J. Orsborn, Dir.; Mr. Michael McIntyre, Asst. Dir.; Rev. Edgar Serrano, Asst. Dir.

University of California at San Diego (Campus Ministry) 4321 Eastgate Mall, 92121-2102. Tel: 858-452-1957 (Office); Fax: 858-452-1985. Email: cathcom@ucsd.edu. Web: www.cathcom-ucsd.org. Revs. John Paul Forte, O.P., Dir.; Joseph Sergott, O.P., Assoc. Dir.

[O] MISCELLANEOUS

SAN DIEGO. *Catholic Committee on Scouting*, 3350 E St., 92102. Tel: 619-446-2116; Fax: 619-446-2129. Rev. Msgr. Joseph A. Carroll, Scout Chap.; Mike McNelly, Chm.; Jim Freed, Coord. Tel: 619-687-1024.

Catholic Secondary Education - Diocese of San Diego, Incorporated (2003) P.O. Box 85728, 92186. Tel: 858-490-8301; Fax: 858-490-8272.

Christ Child Society, 4212 Swift Ave., 92104. Tel: 619-523-1375. Rev. Anton Kollar, O.Carm., Spiritual Advisor; Marie Nopper, Pres.

Magnificat (Central) San Diego Chapter, 5592 Gala Ave., 92120. Tel: 619-583-3389. Rev. Louis M. Solcia, C.R.S.P., Spiritual Advisor; Barbara Faucher, Coord.

Mercy Hospital Foundation, San Diego, 4077 Fifth Ave., 92103. Tel: 619-686-3836; Fax: 619-293-0095. Email: braunwarth.mary@scrippshealth.org. Web: www.scrippsfoundation.org. Mary Braunwarth, Exec. Dir.; Karen Stone, Exec. Vice Pres.

Nazareth School of San Diego, Inc., 10728 San Diego Mission Rd., 92108. Tel: 619-641-7987; Fax: 619-280-4652.

Pauline Books & Media, 5945 Balboa Ave., 92111. Tel: 858-565-9181; Fax: 858-565-9295. Email: sandiego@pauline.org. Web: www.pauline.org. Sr. Frances Obrovac, F.S.P., Supvr. Daughters of St. Paul. Sisters 2.

The Sisters of Nazareth of San Diego Real Estate Holdings, Inc., 6333 Rancho Mission Rd., 92108. Tel: 619-563-0480; Fax: 619-624-9215.

**Spirit Ministries*, 2725 - 55th St., 92105. Tel: 619-262-9685; Fax: 619-262-8718. Email: spiritministries@cox.net. Rev. Jerry Bevilacqua, O.S.A., Spiritual Dir.; Sarah I. McTimmonds, Admin. Asst.

EL CAJON. **Catholic Answers, Inc.*, 2020 Gillespie Way, 92020. Tel: 619-387-7200; Fax: 619-387-0042. Email: publications@catholic.com. Web: www.catholic.com. Karl Keating, Pres.

Kraemer Endowment Foundation, Inc. (1992) 2119 E. Madison Ave., 92019-1111. Tel: 619-844-0211; Fax: 619-236-9710. Email: cynkatia@aol.com. Web: www.stmsc.org.

ENCINITAS. **Catholic Exchange* (2001) P.O. Box 231820, 92023. Tel: 760-635-1122; Fax: 760-635-1132. Email: info@catholicexchange.com. Web: www.catholicexchange.com.

ESCONDIDO. **Benedictus*, 8975-76 Lawrence Welk Dr., 92026. Tel: 760-751-8541; Fax: 760-751-8505. Email: bendictus1@aol.com. Web: www.stdismas.org. Deacon Kenneth J. Finn, Contact Person.

PALA. *Pala Rey Camp*, 10779 Pala Rd., 92059.

SAN YSIDRO. *The Mother Teresa of Calcutta Center*, 524 W. Calle Primera, Ste. 1005N, 92173. Tel: 619-662-1484; Fax: 619-662-1268. Web: www.motherteresa.org.

VALLEY CENTER. *North County Magnificat*, 13747 Little Pond Rd., 92082. Tel: 760-749-3457. Rev. Frank Nouza, Chap.; Rosemary Geiger, Coord.

RELIGIOUS INSTITUTES OF MEN REPRESENTED IN THE DIOCESE

For further details refer to the corresponding bracketed number in the Religious Institutes of Men or Women section.

[0140]—*The Augustinians*—O.S.A.
[0200]—*Benedictine Monks*—O.S.B.
[0270]—*Carmelite Fathers*—O.Carm.
[0160]—*Clerics Regular of St. Paul*—C.R.S.P.
[0450]—*Congregation of Jesus and Mary*—C.J.M.
[0520]—*Franciscan Friars*—O.F.M.
[0650]—*Holy Ghost Fathers*—C.S.Sp.
[0690]—*Jesuit Fathers and Brothers*—S.J.
[]—*Miles Christi*—M.C.
[]—*Missionaries of Charity Fathers*—M.C.
[0840]—*Missionary Servants of the Most Holy Trinity*—S.T.
[0910]—*Oblates of Mary Immaculate*—O.M.I.
[0430]—*Order of Preachers (Dominicans)*—O.P.
[1030]—*Paulist Fathers*—C.S.P.
[1065]—*Priestly Fraternity of St. Peter*—F.S.S.P.
[1260]—*Society of Christ*—S.Ch.
[0370]—*Society of St. Columban*
[0420]—*Society of the Divine Word*—S.V.D.

RELIGIOUS INSTITUTES OF WOMEN REPRESENTED IN THE DIOCESE

[0230]—*Benedictine Sisters of Pontifical Jurisdiction* (Glendora, CA; St. Joseph, MN)—O.S.B.
[0360]—*Carmelite Sisters of the Divine Heart of Jesus*—Carmel.D.C.
[2020]—*Community of the Holy Spirit*—C.H.S.
[3242]—*Congregation of the Sisters of Nazareth*—C.S.N.
[0790]—*Daughters of Divine Charity*—F.D.C.
[0880]—*Daughters of Mary and Joseph*—D.M.J.
[0420]—*Discalced Carmelite Nuns*—O.C.D.
[1070-03]—*Dominican Sisters*—O.P.
[1070-13]—*Dominican Sisters*—O.P.

[1070-20]—*Dominican Sisters*—O.P.
[1070-11]—*Dominican Sisters*—O.P.
[]—*Franciscan Missionaries of Our Lady of Peace*—M.F.P.
[1845]—*Guadalupan Missionaries of the Holy Spirit*—M.G.Sp.S.
[]—*Hermanas del Corazon de Jesus Sacramentado*—H.C.J.S.
[]—*Immaculate Heart Community*—I.H.M.
[2470]—*Maryknoll Sisters of St. Dominic*—M.M.
[2490]—*Medical Mission Sisters*—M.M.S.
[2480]—*Medical Missionaries of Mary*—M.M.M.
[2590]—*Mercedarian Sisters of the Blessed Sacrament*—H.M.S.S.
[2710]—*Missionaries of Charity*—M.C.
[]—*Missionary Sisters of the Society of Mary*—S.M.S.M.
[3070]—*North American Unions of Sisters of Our Lady of Charity*—N.A.U.-O.L.C.
[3130]—*Our Lady of Victory Missionary Sisters*—O.L.V.M.
[0950]—*Pious Society Daughters of St. Paul*—F.S.P.
[3450]—*Religious of Jesus and Mary*—R.J.M.
[3449]—*Religious of the Incarnate Word*—C.V.I.
[2970]—*School Sisters of Notre Dame*—S.S.N.D.
[0520]—*Sisters of Charity of Our Lady, Mother of Mercy*—S.C.M.M.
[0430]—*Sisters of Charity of the Blessed Virgin Mary*—B.V.M.
[2360]—*Sisters of Loretto At the Foot of the Cross*—S.L.
[2549]—*Sisters of Mercy of Ireland & U.S. Province*—R.S.M.
[2575]—*Sisters of Mercy of The Americas* (West-Midwest)—R.S.M.
[]—*Sisters of Providence*—S.P.
[1540]—*Sisters of Saint Francis, Clinton, Iowa*—O.S.F.
[4080]—*Sisters of Social Service of Los Angeles, Inc.*—S.S.S.
[3770]—*Sisters of St. Clare*—O.S.C.
[1705]—*The Sisters of St. Francis of Assisi*—O.S.F.
[1650]—*Sisters of St. Francis of Philadelphia*—O.S.F.
[3830-03]—*Sisters of St. Joseph* (Orange)—C.S.J.
[3830-05]—*Sisters of St. Joseph* (Brentwood, NY)—C.S.J.
[3840]—*Sisters of St. Joseph of Carondelet* (Los Angeles, CA; St. Louis, MO)—C.S.J.
[3890]—*Sisters of St. Joseph of Peace* (Bellevue, WA)—C.S.J.P.
[3935]—*Sisters of St. Louis*—S.S.L.
[1960]—*Sisters of the Holy Family*—S.H.F.
[3260]—*Sisters of the Precious Blood (Dayton, Ohio)*—C.PP.S.
[3499]—*Sisters Servants of the Blessed Sacrament*—S.J.S.
[4060]—*Society of the Holy Child Jesus*—S.H.C.J.
[4070]—*Society of the Sacred Heart*—R.S.C.J.

DIOCESAN CEMETERIES

PALA INDIAN MISSIONS. 6 separate Indian burial grounds.

SAN LUIS REY. *Mission San Luis Rey*

SANTA YSABEL INDIAN MISSIONS. 15 separate Indian burial grounds.

NECROLOGY

† Aldasoro, Rev. Msgr. Francisco, (Retired)—Died Sept. 9, 2009
† McDermott, Rev. Msgr. Thomas J., (Retired)—Died Nov. 5, 2008
† Twarog, Theodore S., (Retired)—Died Dec. 31, 2008

An asterisk (*) denotes an organization that has established tax-exempt status directly with the IRS and is not covered by the USCCB Group Ruling.

Archdiocese of San Francisco

(Archidioecesis Sancti Francisci)

Most Reverend

GEORGE H. NIEDERAUER

Archbishop of San Francisco; ordained April 30, 1962; appointed Bishop of Salt Lake City November 3, 1994; Episcopal ordination January 25, 1995; appointed Archbishop of San Francisco December 15, 2005; installed as Archbishop February 15, 2006. *Office: One Peter Yorke Way, San Francisco, CA 94109-6602.*

The Chancery Office: One Peter Yorke Way, San Francisco, CA 94109-6602. Tel: 415-614-5500; Fax: 415-614-5555.

Web: www.sfarchdiocese.org

Email: info@sfarchdiocese.org

Most Reverend

IGNATIUS WANG, J.C.D.

Retired Auxiliary Bishop of San Francisco; ordained July 4, 1959; appointed Titular Bishop of Sitipa and Auxiliary Bishop of San Francisco December 13, 2002; installed January 30, 2003; retired May 16, 2009. *Office: One Peter Yorke Way, San Francisco, CA 94109-6602.*

Most Reverend

WILLIAM J. JUSTICE

Auxiliary Bishop of San Francisco; ordained May 17, 1968; appointed Titular Bishop of Mathara in Proconsulari and Auxiliary Bishop of San Francisco April 10, 2008; ordained May 28, 2008. *Office: One Peter Yorke Way, San Francisco, CA 94109-6602.*

His Eminence

WILLIAM J. LEVADA, S.T.D.

Prefect, Congregation for the Doctrine of the Faith; Archbishop Emeritus of San Francisco; ordained December 20, 1961; appointed Titular Bishop of Capri and Auxiliary Bishop of Los Angeles March 29, 1983; Episcopal ordination May 12, 1983; appointed Archbishop of Portland in Oregon July 1, 1986; installed as Archbishop of Portland in Oregon September 21, 1986; appointed Coadjutor Archbishop of San Francisco August 17, 1995; succeeded to See December 27, 1995; appointed Prefect of the Congregation for the Doctrine of the Faith May 13, 2005; departed San Francisco August 15, 2005; Created Cardinal March 24, 2006. *Office: Congregazione perla Dottrina della Fede, Palazzo del S. Uffizio, Vatican City State 00120.*

Most Reverend

JOHN R. QUINN

Archbishop Emeritus of San Francisco; ordained July 19, 1953; appointed Auxiliary Bishop of San Diego and Titular Bishop of Thisiduo October 21, 1967; Episcopal ordination December 12, 1967; transferred to Oklahoma City and Tulsa November 18, 1971; appointed as Archbishop of the Archdiocese of Oklahoma City on February 6, 1973; appointed Archbishop of San Francisco February 22, 1977; installed as Archbishop of San Francisco April 26, 1977; resigned December 27, 1995. *Res.: 2140 Santa Cruz Ave., A103, Menlo Park, CA 94025.* Tel: 650-233-8280; Fax: 650-233-8286. *Office: 1100 Woodside Rd., Redwood City, CA 94061.* Tel: 650-780-9078.

ESTABLISHED JULY 29, 1853.

Square Miles 1,012.

Code Address: Roman, San Francisco.

Comprises the Counties of San Francisco, San Mateo and Marin in the State of California.

Patrons of the Archdiocese of San Francisco: St. Francis of Assisi, October 4; St. Patrick, March 17.

Legal Title: The Roman Catholic Archbishop of San Francisco, a Corporation Sole.
For legal titles of parishes and archdiocesan institutions, consult the Chancery Office.

STATISTICAL OVERVIEW

Personnel	
Archbishops	1
Retired Archbishops	1
Auxiliary Bishops	1
Retired Bishops	2
Priests: Diocesan Active in Diocese	115
Priests: Diocesan Active Outside Diocese	7
Priests: Diocesan in Foreign Missions	1
Priests: Retired, Sick or Absent	81
Number of Diocesan Priests	204
Religious Priests in Diocese	163
Total Priests in Diocese	367
Extern Priests in Diocese	75
Ordinations:	
Diocesan Priests	3
Religious Priests	2
Transitional Deacons	6
Permanent Deacons in Diocese	79
Total Brothers	38
Total Sisters	744
Parishes	
Parishes	90
With Resident Pastor:	
Resident Diocesan Priests	77
Resident Religious Priests	13
Without Resident Pastor:	
Administered by Priests	1
Missions	11
Pastoral Centers	21
Professional Ministry Personnel:	
Brothers	6
Sisters	34
Lay Ministers	87
Welfare	
Catholic Hospitals	3
Total Assisted	568,365
Health Care Centers	4
Total Assisted	288,408
Homes for the Aged	6
Total Assisted	3,400
Residential Care of Children	2
Total Assisted	500
Day Care Centers	2
Total Assisted	300
Specialized Homes	19
Total Assisted	5,700
Special Centers for Social Services	21
Total Assisted	16,432
Residential Care of Disabled	8
Total Assisted	500
Other Institutions	4
Total Assisted	1,500
Educational	
Seminaries, Diocesan	1
Students from This Diocese	12
Students from Other Diocese	82
Diocesan Students in Other Seminaries	5
Seminaries, Religious	1
Students Religious	3
Total Seminarians	20
Colleges and Universities	3
Total Students	12,627
High Schools, Diocesan and Parish	4
Total Students	3,543
High Schools, Private	10
Total Students	4,551
Elementary Schools, Diocesan and Parish	54
Total Students	15,051
Elementary Schools, Private	9
Total Students	2,041
Catechesis/Religious Education:	
High School Students	1,764
Elementary Students	10,283
Total Students under Catholic Instruction	49,880
Teachers in the Diocese:	
Priests	8
Brothers	8
Sisters	49
Lay Teachers	1,643
Vital Statistics	
Receptions into the Church:	
Infant Baptism Totals	6,341
Minor Baptism Totals	309
Adult Baptism Totals	289
Received into Full Communion	551
First Communions	4,940
Confirmations	3,682
Marriages:	
Catholic	811
Interfaith	249
Total Marriages	1,060
Deaths	2,275
Total Catholic Population	444,008
Total Population	1,850,035

Former Bishops—Rt. Rev. FRANCISCO GARCIA DIEGO Y MORENO, O.F.M., ord. 1808; cons. Bishop of both Californias, Oct. 4, 1840; died in Santa Barbara, April 30, 1846; Most Revs. JOSEPH SADOC ALEMANY, O.P., D.D., cons. Bishop of Monterey, June 30, 1850; appt. first Archbishop of San Francisco, July 29, 1853; resigned and appt. Titular Archbishop of Pelusio, Dec. 28, 1884; died in Valencia, Spain, April 14, 1888; PATRICK WILLIAM RIORDAN, D.D., cons. Titular Archbishop of Cabasa and appt. Coadjutor Archbishop of San Francisco cum jure successionis Sept. 16, 1883; succeeded to Dec. 28, 1884; died in San Francisco, Dec. 27, 1914; GEORGE MONTGOMERY, D.D., cons. Titular Bishop of Tmui and appt. Coadjutor

Bishop of Monterey and Los Angeles cum jure successionis April 8, 1894; succeeded to May 6, 1896; appt. Titular Archbishop of Osimo and Coadjutor Archbishop of San Francisco cum jure successionis March 27, 1903; died in San Francisco, Jan. 10, 1907; EDWARD J. HANNA, D.D., cons. Titular Bishop of Titopolis and appt. Auxiliary Bishop of San Francisco Dec. 4, 1912; appt. Archbishop of San Francisco, June 1, 1915; resigned and appt. Titular Archbishop of Gortyna, March 2, 1935; died July 10, 1944; JOHN JOSEPH MITTY, D.D., cons. Bishop of Salt Lake City, June 21, 1926; appt. Coadjutor Archbishop of San Francisco cum jure successionis, Jan. 29, 1932; succeeded to March 2, 1935; died Oct. 15, 1961; JOSEPH T. MCGUCKEN, S.T.D., appt. Auxiliary of Los Angeles, Feb. 4, 1941; cons. Titular Bishop of Sanavo March 19, 1941; appt. Coadjutor Bishop of Sacramento cum jure successionis, Oct. 26, 1955; succeeded to Jan. 14, 1957; appt. Archbishop of San Francisco, Feb. 21, 1962; appt. Assistant at the Pontifical Throne, March 19, 1966; retired Feb. 22, 1977; died Oct. 26, 1983; JOHN R. QUINN, D.D. (Retired), appt. Auxiliary Bishop of San Diego, Oct. 21, 1967; cons. Titular Bishop of Thisiduo, Dec. 12, 1967; transferred to Oklahoma City and Tulsa, Nov. 18, 1971; appt. Archbishop of the Archdiocese of Oklahoma City, Feb. 6, 1973; appt. Archbishop of San Francisco, April 26, 1977; resigned Dec. 27, 1995; WILLIAM J. LEVADA, S.T.D., ord. Dec. 20, 1961; appt. Titular Bishop of Capri and Auxiliary Bishop of Los Angeles March 29, 1983; Episcopal ord. May 12, 1983; appt. Archbishop of Portland in Oregon July 1, 1986; installed as Archbishop of Portland in Oregon Sept. 21, 1986; appt. Coadjutor Archbishop of San Francisco Aug. 17, 1995; succeeded to See Dec. 27, 1995; appt. Prefect of Doctrine of the Faith May 13, 2005; created Cardinal March 24, 2006.

Chancery and Pastoral Center—One Peter Yorke Way, San Francisco, 94109-6602. Tel: 415-614-5500; Fax: 415-614-5555. Open Mon.-Fri. All applications for dispensations, faculties, etc., and all correspondence should be addressed: Chancery and Pastoral Center.

Office of the Archbishop—

*Archbishop—*Most Rev. GEORGE H. NIEDERAUER, D.D., Ph.D.

*Executive Assistant to the Archbishop—*LAUREL MILLER. Tel: 415-614-5605; Fax: 415-614-5601.

*Auxiliary Bishop, Vicar General & Vicar for Clergy—*Most Rev. WILLIAM J. JUSTICE, V.G. Tel: 415-614-5611; Fax: 415-614-5613.

*Manager, Office of the Auxiliary Bishop, Office of the Vicar for Clergy—*ANNABELLE C.A. GROH. Tel: 415-614-5612; Fax: 415-614-5613. Email: groha@sfarchdiocese.org. Administrative Assistants: KATYA ALCARAZ. Tel: 415-614-5614. Email: alcarazk@sfarchdiocese.org; GERALDINE BURBANK. Tel: 415-614-5679.

*Office of the Permanent Diaconate—*Deacon LEON KORTENKAMP. Tel: 415-614-5531; Fax: 415-614-5555.

*Office of Diaconate Formation—*Deacon ED CUNNINGHAM. Tel: 415-614-5615; Fax: 415-614-5568.

*Office of Vocations—*Rev. THOMAS A. DALY, Dir. Tel: 415-614-5683.

*Episcopal Vicar for the Spanish Speaking—*Rev. Msgr. JOSE RODRIGUEZ. Tel: 415-614-5591.

*Episcopal Vicar for Filipinos—*Rev. Msgr. FLORO B. ARCAMO. Tel: 415-751-0450.

*Office for Women Religious—*Sr. ROSINA CONROTTO, P.B.V.M., Dir. Tel: 415-614-5535.

*Chancellor—*Very Rev. C. MICHAEL PADAZINSKI, J.C.D. Tel: 415-614-5619; Fax: 415-614-5696.

*College of Consultors—*Most Revs. GEORGE H. NIEDERAUER, D.D., Ph.D.; WILLIAM J. JUSTICE, V.G.; Rev. THOMAS A. DALY; Rev. Msgrs. MICHAEL D. HARRIMAN; ROBERT W. MCELROY; Very Rev. C. MICHAEL PADAZINSKI, J.C.D.; Rev. Msgrs. JOSE A. RODRIGUEZ; HARRY G. SCHLITT; Revs. JAMES T. TARANTINO; EUGENE D. TUNGOL.

*Deans—*Revs. RAYMUND REYES, Deanery 1; CHARITO E. SUAN, Deanery 2; JOHN J. TALESFORE, Deanery 3; RENE J. ITUBE, Deanery 4; MARIO P. FARANA, Deanery 5; THOMAS A. DALY, Deanery 6; PAUL J. ROSSI, Deanery 7; RENE R. RAMOSO, Deanery 8; Very Rev. C. MICHAEL PADAZINSKI, J.C.D., Deanery 9; Revs. ANTHONY E. MCGUIRE, Deanery 10; JAMES H. MACDONALD, Deanery 11.

*Council of Priests—*Rev. MARIO P. FARANA, Chm.

*Archdiocesan Pastoral Council—*Sr. DEE MYERS, B.V.M., Pres.

*Censor Librorum—*Rev. Msgr. WARREN HOLLERAN, S.T.D.

*Apostleship of the Sea—*Rev. Msgr. MICHAEL D. HARRIMAN, Chap.

*Moderator of the Curia and Vicar for Administration—*Rev. Msgr. HARRY G. SCHLITT.

*Administrative Assistant—*TERA ENGLISH. Tel: 415-614-5589.

*Director of the Office for the Protection of Children and Youth—*Deacon JOHN H. NORRIS. Tel: 415-614-5504; Fax: 415-614-5658.

*Victim Assistance Coordinator—*BARBARA ELORDI. Tel: 415-614-5506; Fax: 415-614-5658. Email: elordib@sfarchdiocese.org.

*Director of Finance/Chief Finance Officer—*Mr. RICHARD P. HANNON. Tel: 415-614-5510.

*Office of Development—*Mr. MICHAEL O'LEARY, Dir. Tel: 415-614-5582; Mr. ROBERT DALTON, Assoc. Dir. Tel: 415-614-5581.

*Development Associate—*FLORIAN ROMERO. Tel: 415-614-5537.

*Archdiocesan Legal Office—*Mr. JACK M. HAMMEL, Esq.; Mr. LARRY JANNUZZI, Esq. Legal Secretary: KATYA ALCARAZ. Tel: 415-614-5623.

*Office of the Propagation of the Faith—*GENEVIEVE ELIZONDO, Dir. Tel: 415-614-5673.

*Holy Childhood Association Coordinator—*Rev. MANUEL J. MEJIA, M.M.

*Office of Real Estate and Administrative Services—*KATIE HALEY, Dir.; MYRA CASTELLON HAGGERTY, Administrative Asst.; JOSE LEON, Facilities Mgr.; JEFFREY WESTBROOK, I.T. Mgr.

*Office of Human Resources—*Mr. CARL FEIL, Dir. Tel: 415-614-5541; Mr. PATRICK SCHMIDT, Assoc. Dir. Tel: 415-614-5538; Mr. TOM HOFFMAN, Benefits Mgr. Tel: 415-614-5539; SUZANNE NAZARIO, Human Resources Coord. Tel: 415-614-5540.

*Catholic Cemeteries—*KATHERINE ATKINSON, Mailing Address: P.O. Box 1577, Colma, 94014. Tel: 650-756-2060; Fax: 650-757-0752. Email: keatkinson@holycrosscemeteries.com.

*Archdiocesan Archives—*Deacon JEFFREY BURNS, Ph.D., Dir. Tel: 650-328-6502.

*Office of Ecumenism and Interreligious Affairs—*VACANT.

Metropolitan Tribunal and Office of Canonical Affairs—

San Francisco Metropolitan Tribunal—One Peter Yorke Way, San Francisco, 94109-6602. Tel: 415-614-5690; Fax: 415-614-5696.

*Judicial Vicar and Director—*Very Rev. C. MICHAEL PADAZINSKI, J.C.D.

*Promoter of Justice—*Rev. THUAN V. HOANG, J.C.L.

*Defenders of the Bond—*Revs. THUAN V. HOANG, J.C.L.; STEPHEN A. MERIWETHER, J.C.L.; DIANE L. BARR, J.C.D.

*Judges—*ROBERT J.B. FLUMMERFELT, J.C.L.; ROBERT W. GRAFFIO, J.C.L.; KRYSTYNA AMBORSKI, J.C.D.

*Tribunal Auditors—*JOANN NORRIS; REINA PARADA; JAN SCHACHERN.

*Notaries and Secretaries to the Tribunal—*REINA A. PARADA; TWYLA POWERS; CAROL KUMAGAI.

*Archbishop's Cabinet—*Most Revs. GEORGE H. NIEDERAUER, D.D., Ph.D.; WILLIAM J. JUSTICE, V.G.; Rev. Msgrs. HARRY G. SCHLITT; JOSE A. RODRIGUEZ; Very Rev. C. MICHAEL PADAZINSKI, J.C.D.; Deacon JOHN H. NORRIS; Ms. MAUREEN HUNTINGTON; MAURICE E. HEALY.

*Department of Pastoral Ministry—*Deacon JOHN H. NORRIS, Dir. Tel: 415-614-5504; Fax: 415-614-5658. Email: norrisj@sfarchdiocese.org.

*Hispanic Coordinator—*Mrs. CECILIA ARIAS-RIVAS. Tel: 415-614-5573.

*Office of Evangelization—*MARY JANSEN. Tel: 415-614-5596; Fax: 415-614-5658.

*Office of Ethnic Ministries—*Sr. MARIA HSU, Fd.CC., Dir. Tel: 415-614-5575. Email: hsum@sfarchdiocese.org; ELLA TSANG, Administrative Asst. Tel: 415-614-5574.

*African American Ministry—*Rev. KENNETH M. WESTRAY, St. Isabella Church, 1 Trinity Way, San Rafael, 94903. Tel: 415-479-1560.

*Chinese Ministry—*Sr. MARIA HSU, Fd.CC. Tel: 415-614-5575. Email: hsum@sfarchdiocese.org.

*Japanese Mission—*Rev. ERIC FREED, St. Benedict Parish, 1801 Octavia St., San Francisco, 94109. Tel: 415-567-9855.

*Arab-American Catholic Ministry—*Rev. Msgr. LABIB KOBTI, St. Thomas More Church, 1300 Junipero Serra Blvd., San Francisco, 94132. Tel: 415-452-9634.

*Polish, Croatian, Slovenian Mission—*Rev. TADEUSZ WINNICKI, S.Ch., Nativity Church, 245 Linden St., San Francisco, 94102. Tel: 415-252-5799. Email: twinnicki@tchr.org.

*Korean Catholic Ministry—*Rev. VINCENT KANG GUN-LEE, St. Michael Korean Church, 32 Broad St., San Francisco, 94112. Tel: 415-333-1194; Fax: 415-333-1196.

*Tongan Ministry—*Rev. SIONE LAINA KATOA, St. Timothy Church, 1515 Dolan Ave., San Mateo, 94401. Tel: 650-342-2470; Fax: 650-342-8156.

*Vietnamese Catholic Ministry—*Rev. TE VAN NGUYEN, St. Brendan Church, 29 Rockaway Ave., San Francisco, 94127. Tel: 415-681-4225.

*Brazilian Ministry—*Rev. Msgr. LABIB KOBTI, St. Thomas More Church. Tel: 415-452-9634.

*Burmese Ministry—*ELIZABETH LAW. Email: tinpe@hotmail.com.

*Filipino Ministry—*Rev. Msgr. FLORO B. ARCAMO, Star of the Sea Church, 4420 Geary Blvd., San Francisco, 94118. Tel: 415-751-0450.

*Hispanic & Haitian Ministry—*Rev. Msgr. JOSE A. RODRIGUEZ. Tel: 415-614-5591; Mrs. CECILIA ARIAS-RIVAS. Tel: 415-614-5573.

*Irish Ministry—*Rev. BRENDAN MCBRIDE, Coord., St. Philip the Apostle Parish, 725 Diamond St., San Francisco, 94114. Tel: 415-282-0104.

*Italian Ministry—*Rev. Msgr. BRUNO PESCHIERA, Coord. Catholic Ministry, 101 W. Avalon Dr., Pacifica, 94044. Tel: 650-355-8377; CONSTANCE MERTES, 1550 44th Ave., San Francisco, 94122. Tel: 415-759-1422.

*Native American Ministry—*SACHEEN LITTLEFEATHER, Coord., San Francisco Kateri Tekawitha Prayer Circle, P.O. Box 150346, San Rafael, 94915. Tel: 415-485-5950.

*Igbo Nigerian Ministry—*Rev. CHARLES ONUBUGO, St. Anthony of Padua Church, 3215 Cesar Chavez St., San Francisco, 94110. Tel: 415-647-2704.

*Samoan Ministry—*JOANNA ILAOA, Contact, Mailing Address: 17 Cypress Lane, Daly City, 94014. Tel: 415-859-9511; 415-646-5756. Email: joanna_ilaoa@yahoo.com; MAYA SUISALA. Tel: 415-647-4368; 415-705-2000, Ext. 215. Email: maya.suisala@ssa.gov.

*Office of Religious Education and Youth Ministry—*Sr. CELESTE ARBUCKLE, S.S.S., Dir. Tel: 415-614-5652; JANET FORTUNA, Coord. Special Needs. Tel: 415-614-5655; Sr. GRACIELA MARTINEZ, O.S.F., Assoc. Dir. Hispanic Ministry & Rel. Educ. Tel: 415-614-5653; Ms. ANELITA REYES, Assoc. Dir. Catechetical Ministries. Tel: 415-614-5651; VIVIAN CLAUSING, Assoc. Dir. Youth Ministry & Catechetics. Tel: 415-614-5654.

*Ministry of Consolation—*BARBARA ELORDI. Tel: 415-614-5506; Fax: 415-614-5658. Email: elordib@sfarchdiocese.org.

*Office of Young Adult and Campus Ministry—*MARY JANSEN, Dir. Tel: 415-614-5596; Fax: 415-614-5658. Email: jansenm@sfarchdiocese.org.

*Office of Worship—*PATRICK VALLEZ-KELLY, Dir. Tel: 415-614-5586. Email: vallezkellyp@sfarchdiocese.org.

*Department of Catholic Schools—*Ms. MAUREEN HUNTINGTON, Supt.; ANNETTE BROWN, Asst. Supt. Planning & Finance; BRET E. ALLEN, Assoc. Supt. Educational & Professional Leadership; Sr. MARIANNE VIANI, S.N.J.M., Assoc. Supt. Curriculum/School Improvement; Mrs. JANET SUZIO, Asst. Supt. Faith Formation & Rel. Instruction.

*Archdiocesan Board of Education—*Most Rev. GEORGE H. NIEDERAUER, D.D., Ph.D.; Dr. BRUCE COVILLE; Ms. CATHY CARROLL; Mrs. JOAN HIGGINS; Deacon JAMES SHEA; Mrs. CYLYN CRUZ-MONTERO; Mr. PAUL NANCE; Mrs. EVALYNNA HO; Mr. JOE HOUK; Mrs. MAUREEN LUNDY; Dr. MARIA MANUEL; Ms. ANNE KEARNEY; Rev. VINCENT RIENER; Dr. FRANCIS YU; Mr. KENNETH J. WILLERS, Chm.; Rev. KENNETH M. WEARE; Mr. FRED TOTAH, Vice Chm.

The Roman Catholic Welfare Corporation of San Francisco— (dissolved April 1, 2008)

*Department of Communications and Outreach—*MAURICE E. HEALY, Dir.

*Archdiocesan Publication: "Catholic San Francisco"—*Most Rev. GEORGE H. NIEDERAUER, D.D., Ph.D., Publisher; MAURICE E. HEALY, Exec. Dir.

*Office of Public Policy and Social Concerns—*Tel: 415-614-5572. Web: www.sflifeandjustice.org. GEORGE WESOLEK, Dir. Tel: 415-614-5571; Fax: 415-614-5568. Email: wesolekg@sfarchdiocese.org.

*Administrative Assistant—*PATRICIA RIBEIRO. Tel: 415-614-5570. Email: ribeirop@sfarchdiocese.org.

*Restorative Justice and Catholic Campaign for Human Development—*GEORGE WESOLEK, Dir. Tel: 415-614-5571. Email: wesolekg@sfarchdiocese.org.

*Catholic Campaign for Human Development—*Parish Outreach Organizer: MONICA M. LANDEROS, Assoc. Dir. Tel: 415-614-5570. Email: scannellm@sfarchdiocese.org.

*Respect Life—*VICKI EVANS, Prog. Coord. Tel: 415-614-5533. Email: evansv@sfarchdiocese.org.

Project Rachel— (Post Abortion Counseling) MARY ANN SCHWAB. Tel: 415-717-6428.

*Project Gabriel—*FREDI D'ALESSIO, Prog. Coord. Email: sfgabrielproject@gmail.com.

CLERGY, PARISHES, MISSIONS AND PAROCHIAL SCHOOLS

CITY OF SAN FRANCISCO

(SAN FRANCISCO COUNTY)

1—CATHEDRAL OF ST. MARY (ASSUMPTION) (1891) Revs. John J. Talesfore; Lawrence J. Finegan; Francisco J. Gamez; Deacons Peter I. Boulware; R. Christoph Sandoval. In Res., Most Rev. William J. Justice.
Cathedral Office—1111 Gough St., 94109. Tel: 415-567-2020; Fax: 415-567-2040. Web: www.stmarycathedralsf.org.
Catechesis/Religious Program—Students 60.

2—ST. AGNES (1893) Rev. Raymond Allender. In Res., Revs. Frank C. Buckley, S.J.; Donald B. Sharp, S.J.; Mr. Dario Gonzalez, S.J., Scholastic.
Res.: 1025 Masonic Ave., 94117. Tel: 415-487-8560; Fax: 415-487-8575. Web: www.saintagnessf.com.

3—ALL HALLOWS CHAPEL OF OUR LADY OF LOURDES (1886) Closed. For sacramental records please contact Our Lady of Lourdes, San Francisco.
Chapel—Our Lady of Lourdes

4—ST. ANNE (1904) Revs. Raymund Reyes; Marvin P. Felipe, S.D.B. (Philippines); Deacon John Dupre. In Res., Revs. John J. Cloherty (Retired); Francisco Bagadiong (Retired); Rev. Msgr. Juan Alarcon (Retired).
Res.: 850 Judah St., 94122. Tel: 415-665-1600; Fax: 415-665-1603. Web: www.stanne-sf.org.
School—1320 14th Ave., 94122. Tel: 415-664-7977; Fax: 415-661-6904. Web: www.stanne.com. Thomas C. White, Prin. Sisters 3; Lay Teachers 22; Students 450.
Catechesis/Religious Program—Tel: 415-665-1600, Ext. 38; Fax: 415-665-1603. Students 43.

5—ST. ANTHONY OF PADUA (1893) Revs. Gabriel Flores; Victorio Balagapo. In Res., Revs. Guglielmo Lauriola, O.F.M.; Charles Onubugo.
Res.: 3215 Cesar Chavez St., 94110. Tel: 415-647-2704; Fax: 415-647-7282. Email: sanantonio1893@yahoo.com.
Chapel—Immaculate Conception Chapel 3255 Folsom St., 94110. Tel: 415-824-1762; Fax: 415-824-0129.
School—St. Anthony-Immaculate Conception, (Grades K-8), 299 Precita Ave., 94110. Tel: 415-648-2008; Fax: 415-648-1825. Mr. Dennis Ruggiero, Prin. Lay Teachers 5; Students 135.
Catechesis/Religious Program—Tel: 415-641-2704; Fax: 415-647-7286. Students 70.

6—ST. BENEDICT PARISH AT ST. FRANCIS XAVIER CHURCH (1913), (Japanese), (Founded 1962 for Deaf and Hearing Impaired). Rev. Paul Zirimenya, Chap. In Res., Rev. Ghislain C. Bazikila.
Res.: 1801 Octavia, 94109. Tel: 415-567-9855; 415-567-0438 (TDD); 866-896-0968 (Video Phone); Fax: 415-567-0916. Email: info@sfdeafcatholics.org. Web: www.sfdeafcatholics.org.
Catechesis/Religious Program—Students 12.

7—ST. BONIFACE (1860), (German), Revs. John S. Hardin, O.F.M.; Jorge Hernandez, O.F.M.; Armando Lopez, O.F.M.; Thomas B. West, O.F.M.; John Luat Nguyen, O.F.M.; Finian McGuinn, O.F.M. In Res., Revs. Hoang T. Trinh, O.F.M.; Stephen Tan Nguyen, O.F.M.; Richard P. Purcell, O.F.M.; Bros. Peter Boegel, O.F.M.; John Kiesler, O.F.M.; Robert Brady, O.F.M.; Diadacus Clavel, O.F.M.; Rami M. Fodda, O.F.M.
Res.: 133 Golden Gate Ave., 94102. Tel: 415-863-0111; Fax: 415-863-7602. Email: info@saintbonifacesf.org. Web: www.stbonifacesf.org.
Catechesis/Religious Program—Students 225.

8—ST. BRENDAN (1929) Revs. Daniel Nascimento; Michael F. Quinn; Te Van Nguyen; Sr. Necy Guan, Fd.CC., Pastoral Assoc.
Res.: 29 Rockaway Ave., 94127. Tel: 415-681-4225; Fax: 415-681-3976. Email: navigator@stbrendanparish.org. Web: www.stbrendanparish.org.
School—(Grades K-8), 940 Laguna Honda Blvd., 94127-1239. Tel: 415-731-2665; Fax: 415-731-7207. Email: sbs@stbrendansf.com. Web: www.stbrendansf.com. Mrs. Carol Grewal, Prin.; Jan Donovan, Asst. Prin.; Ruth Nelson, Librarian. Lay Teachers 23; Students 327.
Catechesis/Religious Program—Tel: 415-664-8481. Sr. Catherine Cappello, Fd.CC., Adult Faith Formation. Students 5.

9—ST. BRIGID (1863) Closed. For sacramental records please contact St. Vincent de Paul, San Francisco.

10—ST. CECILIA (1917) Rev. Msgr. Michael D. Harriman; Revs. Lodovico Joseph Landi; Daniel T. Keohane. In Res., Rev. Msgr. Maurice M. McCormick (Retired).
Res.: 2555 17th Ave., 94116. Tel: 415-664-8481; Fax: 415-661-2957.
School—660 Vicente St., 94116. Tel: 415-731-8400; Fax: 415-731-5686. Email: office@stceciliaschool.org. Web: www.stceciliaschool.org. Sr. Marilyn Miller, S.N.J.M., Prin. Sisters of the Holy Names of Jesus and Mary 4; Lay Teachers 24; Students 590.
Catechesis/Religious Program—Students 85.

11—ST. CHARLES BORROMEO (1887) Revs. Moises Agudo; Manuel D. Igrobay. In Res., Rev. John Wadeson.
Res.: 713 S. Van Ness Ave., 94110. Tel: 415-824-1700; Fax: 415-824-0844. Email: sancarlosborromeo@sbcglobal.net.
School—3250 18th St., 94110. Tel: 415-861-7652; Fax: 415-861-0221. Mr. Daniel Dean, Prin. Dominican Sisters of the Most Holy Rosary (Philippines) 6; Lay Teachers 10; Students 315.
Catechesis/Religious Program—Students 219.

12—CHURCH OF THE EPIPHANY (1914) Revs. Eugene D. Tungol; Shouraiah Pudota (India); Deacons Ding Viray; Ramon Zamora. In Res., Rev. Rolando A. Caverte (Retired).
Res.: 827 Vienna St., 94112. Tel: 415-333-7630; Fax: 415-333-1803. Web: www.epiphanysf.com.
School—600 Italy Ave., 94112. Tel: 415-337-4030; Fax: 415-337-8583. Web: www.epiphanysf.org. Diane Elkins, Prin. Sisters 1; Lay Teachers 23; Students 630.
Catechesis/Religious Program—Tel: 415-333-7630, Ext. 15; Fax: 415-333-1801. Students 203.

13—CORPUS CHRISTI (1898) Revs. Ramon M. Zarate, S.D.B.; Aloysius J. Pestun, S.D.B.; Jose Lucero, S.D.B.; Edward Liptak, S.D.B.
Res.: 62 Santa Rosa Ave., 94112. Tel: 415-585-2991; Fax: 415-230-5450.
School—75 Francis St., 94112. Tel: 415-587-7014; Fax: 415-587-1575. Sr. Martina Ponce, F.M.A., Prin. Salesian Sisters of St. John Bosco (Daughters of Mary Help of Christians) 6; Lay Teachers 12; Students 198.
Catechesis/Religious Program—Tel: 415-585-3240. Sr. Maria Luong, F.M.A., D.R.E. Students 125.

14—ST. DOMINIC (1873) Revs. Xavier M. Lavagetto, O.P.; Garry J. Cappleman, O.P.; Edward Scanlon, O.P.; Francis Goode, O.P.; Paschal D. Salisbury, O.P.; Deacons Fred Swanson, (Retired); Charles McNeil; Michael F. Curran. In Res., Revs. Felix F. Cassidy, O.P.; Anthony R. Rosevear, O.P., Novice Master; Martin de Porres Walsh, O.P.; Anselm Ramelow, O.P.; Bro. Gregory R. Lira, O.P.
Res.: 2390 Bush St., 94115. Tel: 415-567-7824; Fax: 415-567-1608. Email: info@stdominics.org. Web: www.stdominics.org.
Catechesis/Religious Program—Students 80.

15—ST. EDWARD (1916) Closed. For sacramental records please contact St. Dominic, San Francisco.

16—ST. ELIZABETH (1912) Revs. Charito E. Suan; Elias M. Salomon.
Res.: 449 Holyoke Ave., 94134. Tel: 415-468-0820; Fax: 415-468-1457.
School—450 Somerset St., 94134. Tel: 415-468-3247; Fax: 415-468-1804. Gene Dabdoub, Prin. Lay Teachers 7; Students 134.
Catechesis/Religious Program—Tel: 415-468-0423. Students 70.

17—ST. EMYDIUS (1913) Rev. William J. Brady. In Res., Rev. David M. Pettingill (Retired).
Res.: 286 Ashton Ave., 94112. Tel: 415-587-7066; Fax: 415-587-6690. Email: stemydius@sbcglobal.net.
Catechesis/Religious Program—

18—ST. FINN BARR (1926) [CEM] Revs. Jose M. Corral; Ernesto E. Espina, C.M. (Australia).
Res.: 415 Edna St., 94112. Tel: 415-333-3627; Fax: 415-333-4090. Email: stfinnbarr@yahoo.com.
School—419 Hearst Ave., 94112. Tel: 415-333-1800; Fax: 415-452-0177. Web: www.stfinnbarr.org. Tom Dooher, Prin. Lay Teachers 10; Students 213.
Catechesis/Religious Program—Students 44.

19—ST. FRANCIS OF ASSISI, NATIONAL SHRINE (1849) 610 Vallejo St., 94133. Tel: 415-983-0405; Fax: 415-983-0407. Email: shrinesf@flash.net.

20—ST. GABRIEL (1941) Revs. Thomas M. Hamilton; Michael J. Konopik; Deacon Thomas Reardon. In Res., Revs. P. Gerard O'Rourke (Retired); Paul Zirimenya.
Res.: 2535 40th Ave., 94116. Tel: 415-731-6161; Fax: 415-731-1270. Web: www.rc.net/sanfrancisco/stgabriel.
School—2550 41st Ave., 94116. Tel: 415-566-0314; Fax: 415-566-3223. Email: office@stgabrielsf.com. Web: www.stgabrielsf.com. Sr. M. Pauline Borghello, R.S.M., Prin. Lay Teachers 24; Students 511.
Catechesis/Religious Program—Students 160.

21—HOLY CROSS (1887), (Korean), Closed. For inquiries for parish records contact the chancery.

22—HOLY FAMILY CHINESE MISSION *aka St. Mary's Chinese Catholic Center--1903)* (1921), (Chinese), Rev. Daniel E. McCotter, C.S.P.; Deacon Simon Tsui, Pastoral Assoc. & Teahouse Ministry; Ms. Lisa Tom French, Exec. Dir. St. Mary's Capital Campaign.
Res.: 660 California St., 94108. Tel: 415-288-3835; Fax: 415-929-4698. Email: danielcsp@aol.com. Web: stmaryschinese.org.
School—St. Mary Chinese Day School, 910 Broadway, 94133. Tel: 415-929-4690; Fax: 415-929-4699. Web: www.stmaryschinese.org. Nancy Fiebelkorn, Prin.; Evelyn Hall, Librarian. Sisters 2; Lay Teachers 15; Students 110.
School—Chinese Language School, 910 Broadway, 94133. Tel: 415-929-4694. Stephen Woon Wah Tang, Prin. - St. Mary's Language School; Bill Cheng, Vice Prin. Teachers 14; Elementary Students 300; High School Students 10.
Holy Family Association—Tel: 415-929-4696; Fax: 415-929-4698. Juliana Chung, Chair.
Catechesis/Religious Program—Tel: 415-929-4690. Cynthia Fong, D.R.E. Students 8.

23—HOLY NAME OF JESUS (1925) Revs. Arnold Zamora; Nicasio G. Paloso. In Res., Most Rev. Ignatius C. Wang; Deacon Michael Doherty.
Res.: 3240 Lawton St., 94122. Tel: 415-664-8590; Fax: 415-664-9007. Email: hnparishsecretary@gmail.com. Web: holyname-sf.org.
School—1560 40th Ave., 94122. Tel: 415-731-4077; Fax: 415-731-3328. Email: office@holynameschool.com. Web: www.holynamesf.com. Judy Cosmos, Prin. Sisters 1; Lay Teachers 14; Students 360.
Catechesis/Religious Program—Students 75.

24—ST. IGNATIUS (1855) Revs. Charles R. Gagan, S.J.; Albert A. Grosskopf, S.J.; James R. Blaettler, S.J.; John A. Coleman.
Res.: 650 Parker Ave., 94118. Tel: 415-422-2188; Fax: 415-387-1867. Web: www.stignatiussf.org.
Catechesis/Religious Program—Tel: 415-422-2195. Email: faloon@usfca.edu. Web: www.stignatiussf.org (click Parish Programs). Dan Faloon, D.R.E. Students 238.

25—ST. JAMES (1888) Rev. Jerome P. Foley. In Res., Rev. Walter E. Jenkins.
Res.: 1086 Guerrero St., 94110. Tel: 415-824-4232; Fax: 415-824-0605. Email: stjmscath@aol.com.
School—321 Fair Oaks St., 94110. Tel: 415-647-8972; Fax: 415-647-0166. Web: www.saintjamessf.org. Sr. Mary S. Vasquez, O.P., Prin. Lay Teachers 11; Students 177.
Catechesis/Religious Program—Tel: 415-824-4233. Students 74.
Mission—Dominican Sisters of Mission San Jose 1212 Guerrero St., San Francisco Co. 94110. Tel: 415-648-7460.

26—ST. JOHN OF GOD (1967) Revs. Raymund M. Reyes, Admin.; Methodius S. Kiwale, A.L.C.P.
Res. & Church: 1290 Fifth Ave., 94122. Tel: 415-566-5610; Fax: 415-566-5073. Email: StJohnofGod-SF@sbcglobal.net. Web: www.sjog.net.
Catechesis/Religious Program—Tel: 415-637-7935. Email: suecoll@pacbell.net. Students 32.

27—ST. JOHN THE EVANGELIST (1893) Rev. Msgr. Jose A. Rodriguez; Rev. Benildo M. Pilande (Philippines). In Res., Rev. Msgr. John F. Rodriguez (Retired).
Res.: 19 St. Mary's Ave., 94112-1098. Tel: 415-334-4646; Fax: 415-334-0891.
Parish Center—98 Bosworth St., 94112. Tel: 415-334-4646; Fax: 415-334-0891. Email: stjohn_the_evangelist@yahoo.com.
School—925 Chenery St., 94131. Tel: 415-584-8383; Fax: 415-584-8359. Web: www.stjohnseagle.com. Mr. Kenneth J. Willers, Prin. Lay Teachers 11; Students 263.
Catechesis/Religious Program—Tel: 415-334-4646, Ext. 15. Ms. Maria Figueroa, D.R.E. Students 83.

28—ST. JOSEPH (1861) Closed. For sacramental records please contact St. Patrick, San Francisco.

29—ST. KEVIN (1922) Rev. Ulysses L. D'Aquila.
Res.: 704 Cortland Ave., 94110. Tel: 415-648-5751; Fax: 415-648-4441.
Catechesis/Religious Program—Tel: 415-282-0277. Students 73.

30—ST. MICHAEL KOREAN CATHOLIC CHURCH (1898), (Korean), Revs. Vincent Kang Gun-Lee; Yong-Kyu Lee; Vimal Kishmore, S.J., Youth Min.
Res.: 32 Broad St., 94112. Tel: 415-333-1194; Fax: 415-333-1196. Email: stmichael_info@yahoo.com. Web: www.sfstmichael.org.
Catechesis/Religious Program—Email: stmichael_info@yahoo.com. Students 43.

31—MISSION DOLORES BASILICA (1776) [CEM], (San Francisco de Asis), Revs. Arturo L. Albano; Luello N. Palacpac (Philippines). In Res., Deacon Vicente Cervantes.
Res.: 3321 16th St., 94114. Tel: 415-621-8203; Fax: 415-621-2294. Email: parish@missiondolores.org.
School—3371 16th St., 94114. Tel: 415-861-7673; Fax: 415-861-7620. Ms. Andreina Gualco, Prin. Lay Teachers 9; Students 182.
Catechesis/Religious Program—Maria Rosales-Uribe, D.R.E. Students 50.

32—ST. MONICA (1911) Rev. John L. Greene. In Res., Rev. Msgr. Fred A. Bitanga (Retired); Rev. Lawrence Gould, S.A.C.

Res.: 470 24th Ave., 94121. Tel: 415-751-5275; Fax: 415-751-0440. Email: monicarectory@sbcglobal.net. *School*—5950 Geary Blvd., 94121. Tel: 415-751-9564; Fax: 415-751-0781. Email: office@stmonicasf.org. Web: stmonicasf.org. Lay Teachers 11; Students 153.

Catechesis/Religious Program— Joint program with Star of the Sea

33—MOST HOLY REDEEMER (1900) Rev. Stephen A. Meriwether. In Res., Rev. William W. Young (Retired).

Res.: 100 Diamond St., 94114-2414. Tel: 415-863-6259; Fax: 415-552-8786. Email: mhr-admin@mhr.org. Web: www.mhr.org.

Catechesis/Religious Program—

34—NATIVITY (1902), (Polish—Croatian), Rev. Tadeusz Winnicki, S.Ch.

Res.: 245 Linden St., 94102. Tel: 415-252-5799; Fax: 415-252-5799.

Catechesis/Religious Program—

35—NOTRE DAME DES VICTOIRES (1856), (French), Revs. Rene Iturbe, S.M.; Etienne Siffert, S.M.; Dennis Steik, S.M., Parochial Vicar.

Res.: 566 Bush St., 94108. Tel: 415-397-0113; Fax: 415-397-3217. Email: ndveglise@ndvsf.org. Web: ndvsf.org.

School—(Grades K-8), 659 Pine St., 94108. Tel: 415-421-0069; Fax: 415-421-1440. Email: office@ndvsf.org. Mary K. Ghisolfo, Prin. Lay Teachers 21; Students 277.

Catechesis/Religious Program—Tel: 415-397-0113; Fax: 415-397-3217. Email: ndveglise@ndvsf.org. Students 25.

36—OLD ST. MARY'S CATHEDRAL (1854) Revs. Charles R. Kullmann, C.S.P.; Peter G. Shea, C.S.P.; Bartholomew K. Landry, C.S.P. In Res., Revs. Thomas J. Dove, C.S.P. (Retired); George R. Fitzgerald, C.S.P.; James W. Donovan, C.S.P.; Daniel E. McCotter, C.S.P.; Vincent P. Manalo, C.S.P.; Thomas F. Foley; Terrance Ryan.

Res.: 660 California St., 94108. Tel: 415-288-3800; Fax: 415-288-3838. Web: www.oldsaintmarys.org.

37—OUR LADY OF FATIMA BYZANTINE CATHOLIC CHURCH (1954) Rev. Eugene M. Ludwig, O.F.M-.Cap.; Deacon Kyrril Bruce E. Pagacz.

Res.: 101 20th Ave., 94121-1398. Tel: 415-752-2052. Web: www.byzantinecatholic.org.

38—OUR LADY OF GUADALUPE, Closed. For sacramental records please contact SS. Peter and Paul, San Francisco.

39—OUR LADY OF LOURDES (1942) Rev. Daniel E. Carter.

Res.: 1715 Oakdale Ave., 94124. Tel: 415-285-3377; Fax: 415-285-2191. Email: ollsanfran@aol.com.

Catechesis/Religious Program— Joint program with St. Paul of the Shipwreck. Students 47.

Mission—All Hallows Chapel 1440 Newhall St., San Francisco Co. 94124. Tel: 415-285-3377; Fax: 415-285-2191. Email: ollsanfran@aol.com.

40—ST. PATRICK (1851) Revs. Eduardo Dura; Calixto A. Pablo.

Res.: 756 Mission St., 94103. Tel: 415-421-3730; Fax: 415-512-9730.

41—ST. PAUL (1880) Rev. Mario P. Farana. In Res., Rev. Don D. Flickinger.

Res.: 221 Valley St., 94131. Tel: 415-648-7538; Fax: 415-648-4740.

St. Paul Littlest Angel Pre-School—Tel: 415-824-5437; Fax: 415-824-5430. Ms. Peg Kayser, Prin. Students 42.

School—St. Paul, 1690 Church St., 94131. Tel: 415-648-2055; Fax: 415-648-1920. Arleen Guaraglia, Prin. Lay Teachers 9; Students 235.

Catechesis/Religious Program—Tel: 415-826-4484. Dorothy Vigna, D.R.E. Students 102.

Convent—Novitiate of the Missionaries of Charity, 312 29th St., 94131. Tel: 415-647-1889.

42—ST. PAUL OF THE SHIPWRECK (1915) Rev. Paul Gawlowski, O.F.M.Conv.; Bros. Mark Folger, O.F.M-.Conv.; George Cherrie, O.F.M.Conv.; Deacon Larry Chatmon.

Mailing Address: 1122 Jamestown Ave., 94124.

Res.: 3350 Jennings St., 94124. Tel: 415-468-3434; Fax: 415-468-1400. Email: spswoffice@aol.com. Web: www.stpauloftheshipwreck.org.

Catechesis/Religious Program—Students 62.

43—ST. PETER (1867) Revs. J. Manuel Estrada; Marlon M. Verduzco-Peregrino (Mexico); Deacon David Gamarra. In Res., Rev. John T. Jimenez.

Res.: 1200 Florida St., 94110. Tel: 415-282-1652; Fax: 415-282-6097.

School—1266 Florida St., 94110. Tel: 415-647-8662; Fax: 415-647-4618. Vicki Butler, Prin. Sisters 3; Lay Teachers 13; Students 387.

Catechesis/Religious Program—Tel: 415-282-1176. Students 363.

44—SS. PETER AND PAUL (1884), (Italian), Revs. John Itzaina, S.D.B.; Salvatore H. Giacomini, S.D.B.; Andrew Ping Yee Ng, S.D.B.; Harold Danielson, S.D.B. In Res., Revs. Austin Conterno, S.D.B.; Paul Maniscalco, S.D.B. (Retired); Mario A. Rosso, S.D.B.; Armand Oliveri, S.D.B.; Bro. Ernest Martiniez, S.D.B.

Res.: 666 Filbert St., 94133. Tel: 415-421-0809; Fax: 415-421-0217. Email: gibbons@stspeterpaul.san-francisco.ca.us. Web: www.stspeterpaul.san-francisco.ca.us/church.

School—632 Filbert St., 94133. Tel: 415-421-5219; Fax: 415-421-1831. Dr. Lisa Haris, Prin. Salesian Sisters 4; Lay Teachers 12; Students 246.

Catechesis/Religious Program—Bro. Thien Nguyen, S.D.B., Coord. Youth Min. Students 50.

45—ST. PHILIP THE APOSTLE (1910) Rev. Anthony La Torre; Rio Stefanus, Business Mgr. In Res., Rev. Brendan McBride (Ireland).

Res.: 725 Diamond St., 94114. Tel: 415-282-0141; Fax: 415-282-8962. Email: saintphilip@sbcglobal.net.

School—665 Elizabeth St., 94114. Tel: 415-824-8467; Fax: 415-282-5746. Email: reverett@saintphilipschool.com. Web: www.saintphilipschool.com. Remy Everett, Prin. Lay Teachers 14; Students 220.

Catechesis/Religious Program—Students 6.

46—SACRED HEART (1885) Closed. For inquiries for parish records contact the chancery.

47—STAR OF THE SEA (1894) Rev. Msgr. Floro B. Arcamo; Revs. Elmer Magat; Clifford A. Martin. In Res., Rev. Msgr. John R. Pernia (Retired); Revs. Benedict Chang (Retired); Martin R. Muruli.

Res.: 4420 Geary Blvd., 94118. Tel: 415-751-0450; Fax: 415-386-5651. Email: starparish@sbcglobal.net. Web: www.staroftheseachurchsf.com.

School—360 Ninth Ave., 94118. Tel: 415-221-8558; Fax: 415-221-7118. Web: www.staroftheseа.com. Terrence Hanley, Prin. Lay Teachers 19; Students 224.

Catechesis/Religious Program—Tel: 415-713-5624. Students 49.

48—ST. STEPHEN (1950) Rev. Joseph R. Walsh; Deacons Gary West; Dan Rosen. In Res., Revs. Leonard J. Calegari (Retired); Edward K. Murray.

Office: 451 Eucalyptus Dr., 94132. Tel: 415-681-2444; Fax: 415-681-7843. Email: info@saintstephensf.org. Web: www.saintstephensf.org.

Res.: 601 Eucalyptus Dr., 94132. Tel: 415-681-2707.

School—401 Eucalyptus Dr., 94132. Tel: 415-664-8331; Fax: 415-242-5608. Web: ststephenschools-f.org. Mrs. Sharon McCarthy Allen, Prin. Lay Teachers 19; Students 315.

Catechesis/Religious Program—Thu-Ha Rae, D.R.E. Students 42.

49—ST. TERESA (1880) Rev. Paul Warren; Deacon Charles Allen Jr.; Sr. Maureen O'Brien, B.V.M., Pastoral Assoc.

Res.: 390 Missouri St., 94107. Tel: 415-285-5272; Fax: 415-285-8510. Email: info@stteresasf.org. Web: stteresasf.org.

Catechesis/Religious Program—Students 24.

50—ST. THOMAS MORE (1950) Rev. Msgr. Labib Kobti; Rev. Andrew R. Johnson; Deacon Khaled Abu-Alshaer.

Res.: 1300 Junipero Serra Blvd., 94132. Tel: 415-452-9634; Fax: 415-452-9653. Email: stmchurch2002@aol.com. Web: www.stmchurch.com.

Catechesis/Religious Program—Students 15.

51—ST. THOMAS THE APOSTLE (1922) Rev. Daniel J. Maguire. In Res., Rev. Francis P. Filice (Retired).

Res.: 3835 Balboa St., 94121. Tel: 415-387-5545; Fax: 415-221-0868. Email: stthomasapostlechurchsf@gmail.com.

School—3801 Balboa St., 94121. Tel: 415-221-2711; Fax: 415-221-8611. Judy Borelli, Prin. Lay Teachers 23; Students 265.

Catechesis/Religious Program—Sr. Noreen O'Connor, C.S.F., D.R.E. Students 25.

52—ST. VINCENT DE PAUL (1901) Revs. John K. Ring; J. Michael Strange, S.S.

Res.: 2320 Green St., 94123. Tel: 415-922-1010; Fax: 415-922-7203. Web: svdpsf.org.

School—2350 Green St., 94123. Tel: 415-346-5505; Fax: 415-346-0970. Web: www.svdpsf.org. Ms. Barbara Harvey, Prin. Lay Teachers 35; Students 250.

53—VISITACION, CHURCH OF THE (1907) Revs. Rafael Antonio de Avila y Romero; Thuan V. Hoang.

Res.: 655 Sunnydale Ave., 94134. Tel: 415-494-5517; Fax: 415-494-5513. Email: pastor@visitacionchurch.org. Web: www.visitacionchurch.org.

School—Our Lady of the Visitacion, 785 Sunnydale Ave., 94134. Tel: 415-239-7840; Fax: 415-239-2559. Sr. Louise Camous, Prin. Daughters of Charity of St. Vincent de Paul 4; Lay Teachers 14; Students 112.

Catechesis/Religious Program—Tel: 415-595-1670. Moises Pelayo, D.R.E. Students 200.

Mission—Our Lady of Guadalupe 285 Alvarado St., Brisbane, San Mateo Co. 94005. Tel: 415-467-9727.

OUTSIDE THE CITY OF SAN FRANCISCO

BELMONT, SAN MATEO CO.

1—IMMACULATE HEART OF MARY (1947) Revs. Stephen H. Howell; Arsenio G. Cirera (Philippines); Deacons Steven Hackett; Henry Jacquemet. In Res.,

Res.: 1040 Alameda de las Pulgas, 94002. Tel: 650-593-6157; Fax: 650-593-1665. Email: office@ihmbelmont.org. Web: ihmbelmont.org.

School—1000 Alameda de las Pulgas, 94002. Tel: 650-593-4265; Fax: 650-593-4342. Email: ihmschool@ihmschoolbelmont.com. Web: www.ihm-schoolbelmont.com. Sandra Larragoiti, Prin. Lay Teachers 12; Students 287.

Catechesis/Religious Program—Mrs. Dede Waters-Masters, D.R.E. Students 304.

2—ST. MARK (1965) Rev. Al Furtado, C.S.Sp. In Res., Rev. Edward A. Bohnert.

Res.: 325 Marine View Ave., 94002. Tel: 650-591-5937; Fax: 650-591-7645. Email: st_markschurch@yahoo.com. Web: www.saintmarks.us.

Catechesis/Religious Program—Email: st_markschurch@yahoo.com. Students 81.

BURLINGAME, SAN MATEO CO.

1—ST. CATHERINE OF SIENA (1908) Revs. John A. Ryan; Edward S. Inyanwachi (Nigeria); Deacon Roy Twitty. In Res., Revs. Frank K. Murray (Retired); James W. Livingstone.

Res.: 1310 Bayswater Ave., 94010. Tel: 650-344-6884; Fax: 650-344-1022. Email: parishoffice@stcsiena.org. Web: www.stcsiena.org.

School—1300 Bayswater Ave., 94010. Tel: 650-344-7176; Fax: 650-344-7426. Email: office@stcatherineofsiena.net. Web: www.stcos.com. Sr. Antonella Manca, M.S.C., Prin. Missionary Sisters of the "Sacro Costato" 4; Lay Teachers 16; Students 288.

Catechesis/Religious Program—Email: silvia@stcsiena.org. Students 119.

2—OUR LADY OF ANGELS (1926) Revs. Michael Mahoney, O.F.M.Cap.; Flavian Welstead, O.F.M-.Cap.; Brian McKenna, O.F.M.Cap.; Michael James O'Shea, O.F.M.; Sr. Patricia Hunter, S.N.J.M., Pastoral Assoc. In Res., Rev. Eugene M. Ludwig, O.F.M.Cap.

Res.: 1721 Hillside Dr., 94010. Tel: 650-347-7768; Fax: 650-347-3550. Email: parishoffice@olaparish.org. Web: www.olaparish.org.

School—1328 Cabrillo Ave., 94010. Tel: 650-343-9200; Fax: 650-343-5260. Patricia Bordin, Asst. Prin.; Judy O'Rourke, Asst. Prin.; Teresita Santiago, Youth Min. & Dir. Confirmation. Tel: 650-343-5809. Lay Teachers 20; Religious Teachers 1; Students 313.

Preschool—1341 Cortez Ave., 94010. Tel: 650-343-3115. Lysette Cukor, Dir.; Daniel Martin, Site Supvr. Lay Teachers 7; Students 61.

Catechesis/Religious Program—Tel: 650-347-3671. Mrs. Kathryn Jones, D.R.E. Students 385.

COLMA, SAN MATEO CO., HOLY ANGELS (1914) Revs. Manuel Curso; Jose Pelagio A. Padit (Philippines); Deacons Lernito Prudenciado; Juan Ruiz.

Res.: 107 San Pedro Rd., 94014. Tel: 650-755-0478; Fax: 650-755-7653. Email: holyangels755@hotmail.com. Web: www.holyangelschurchcolma.com.

School—20 Reiner St., 94014. Tel: 650-755-0220; Fax: 650-755-0258. Email: holyangls@aol.com. Web: www.holyangelscolma.com. Sisters 6; Lay Teachers 12; Students 239.

Catechesis/Religious Program—Tel: 650-992-5539. Email: holyangelsccd@hotmail.com. Sr. Anita Torres, P.B.V.M., C.R.E. Students 248.

DALY CITY, SAN MATEO CO.

1—ST. ANDREW (1968), (Filipino), Revs. Alex L. Legaspi; Dominador Corrales (Philippines).

Church: 1571 Southgate Ave., 94015. Tel: 650-756-3223; Fax: 650-756-0251.

Rectory—One Ridgefield Ave., 94015. Tel: 650-756-3222; Fax: 650-756-0251.

Catechesis/Religious Program—Tel: 650-991-2937. Michele Bussey, D.R.E. Students 275.

2—OUR LADY OF MERCY (Westlake) (1954) Revs. William E. Brown; T. Noel G. Laput, C.M. (Philippines); Deacon Michael J. Ghiorso. In Res., Rev. Joseph Palathingal (India), Chap.

Res.: One Elmwood Dr., 94015. Tel: 650-755-2727; Fax: 650-755-6704. Web: www.olmcath.org.

School—7 Elmwood Dr., 94015. Tel: 650-756-3395; Fax: 650-756-5872. Web: www.olmbulldogs.org. Alex Endo, Prin.; Sr. Virgie Barcelona, R.V.M., Pastoral Assoc. Lay Teachers 28; Students 478.

Catechesis/Religious Program—Tel: 650-992-5769; Fax: 650-756-3457. Web: www.olmcath.org. Sr. Fe P. Bigwas, R.V.M., D.R.E. Students 191.

Convent—Religious of the Virgin Mary, Our Lady of Mercy, 15 Elmwood Dr., 94015. Tel: 650-992-5769; Fax: 650-756-3457. Email: bigwasfe@yahoo.com. In Res., Sisters Ma Nicolina Estevez, R.V.M.; Auxencia Bitangjol, R.V.M.

3—OUR LADY OF PERPETUAL HELP (1925) Revs. Antonio G. Petilla; Dwight Dennis G. Barlaan (Philippines); Deacon William Bruening. In Res., Rev. Aquino Padilla (Retired).

Res.: 60 Wellington Ave., 94014. Tel: 650-755-9786;

Fax: 650-756-2268. Email: info@olph.com. Web: www.olpcath.com.
School—80 Wellington Ave., 94014. Tel: 650-755-4438; Fax: 650-755-7366. William Kovacich, Prin. Religious 1; Lay Teachers 18; Students 230.
Catechesis/Religious Program—Tel: 650-755-4010. Email: dnsgb@yahoo.com. Students 243.

EAST PALO ALTO, SAN MATEO CO., ST. FRANCIS OF ASSISI (1951) Rev. Lawrence C. Goode; Deacons Louis Dixon; Benjamin Koloamatangi. In Res., Revs. Robert P. Cipriano (Retired); John R. Coleman (Retired).
Res.: 1425 Bay Rd., 94303. Tel: 650-322-2152; Fax: 650-322-7319. Email: sfofassisi@sbcglobal.net.
Catechesis/Religious Program—Tel: 650-325-6236; Fax: 650-322-7319. Students 500.

FAIRFAX, MARIN CO., ST. RITA (1930) Rev. Kenneth M. Weare; Deacons Peter Kehrlein; William Turrentine; Noele Kostelic, Pastoral Assoc.
Res.: 100 Marinda Dr., 94930. Tel: 415-456-4815; Fax: 415-456-3677. Email: saintritafairfax@att.net.
School—102 Marinda Dr., 94930. Tel: 415-456-1003; Fax: 415-456-7946. Web: www.strita.edu. Mrs. Carol Arritola, Prin. Lay Teachers 12; Students 151.
Catechesis/Religious Program—Email: nkostelic@sbcglobal.net. Students 55.

FOSTER CITY, SAN MATEO CO., ST. LUKE (1970) Rev. Jonathan Paala; Deacons Mar Tano; Paul Lucia.
1111 Beach Park Blvd., 94404. Web: www.saintlukefc.org.
Res.: 1388 Halibut St., 94404. Tel: 650-345-6660; Fax: 650-345-8167. Web: www.saintlukefc.org.
Catechesis/Religious Program—Tel: 650-574-9191; Fax: 650-573-7409. Students 261.

HALF MOON BAY, SAN MATEO CO., OUR LADY OF THE PILLAR (1868) [CEM] Revs. Domingo Orimaco; Erick E. Arauz; Deacons John McGhee; Virgil Capetti.
Res.: 400 Church St., 94019. Tel: 650-726-4674; Fax: 650-726-0980. Email: info@ourladyofthepillar.org. Web: www.ourladyofthepillar.org.
Catechesis/Religious Program—Tel: 650-726-5587. Students 900.
Mission—St. Anthony [CEM]
Mission—Our Lady of Refuge 146 Sears Ranch Rd., La Honda, San Mateo Co. 94060. Tel: 650-747-9555; Fax: 650-747-0419.

KENTFIELD, MARIN CO., ST. SEBASTIAN (1951) Revs. Mark V. Taheny; Paul E. Perry.
Res.: 373 Bon Air Rd., 94904. Tel: 415-461-0704; Fax: 415-461-2018.
Catechesis/Religious Program—Students 73.

LAGUNITAS, MARIN CO., ST. CECILIA (1937) Rev. Cyril O'Sullivan.
Mailing Address: Box 289, 94938. Email: stcecilia.lagunitas@yahoo.com. Web: www.stcecilia-lagunitas.org.
Rectory—450 West Cintura Ave., 94938. Tel: 415-488-9799; Fax: 415-488-9809. Web: www.stcecilia-lagunitas.org.
Catechesis/Religious Program—Students 27.
Mission—St. Mary (1867) Town Square, Nicasio, Marin Co. 94946. Tel: 415-488-9799; Fax: 415-488-9809. Email: stmary.nicasio@yahoo.com. Web: stmary-nicasio.org.

LARKSPUR, MARIN CO., ST. PATRICK (1915) Revs. Paul Arnoult; Augusto E. Villote.
Res.: 114 King St., 94939. Tel: 415-924-0600; Fax: 415-924-3617.
School—120 King St., 94939. Tel: 415-924-0501; Fax: 415-924-3544. Linda Kinkade, Prin. Lay Teachers 15; Students 233.
Catechesis/Religious Program—Tel: 415-924-3719. Students 157.

MENLO PARK, SAN MATEO CO.

1—ST. ANTHONY (1951) Revs. Fabio E. Medina; Fernando Rogelio Velasco; Alberto R. Cuevas.
Res.: 3500 Middlefield Rd., 94025. Tel: 650-366-4692; Fax: 650-366-4135. Email: santonio@catholic.org.
Catechesis/Religious Program—Tel: 650-365-6071. Asusena Chavez, D.R.E. Students 587.
Mission—San Jose Obrero 400 Heller St., Redwood City, San Mateo Co. 94063.

2—THE CHURCH OF THE NATIVITY (1877) Rev. Msgr. Steven D. Otellini; Revs. Clement A. Davenport, Pastor Emeritus (Retired); Rolando De la Rosa (Philippines); Deacon Dominick Peloso.
Res.: 210 Oak Grove Ave., 94025. Tel: 650-323-7914; Fax: 650-323-3231. Email: nativityparish@sbcglobal.net. Web: www.nativitymenlo.org.
School—1250 Laurel St., 94025. Tel: 650-325-7304; Fax: 650-325-3841. Email: info@nativityschool.com. Web: www.nativityschool.com. Lay Teachers 15; Students 275.
Catechesis/Religious Program—Tel: 650-327-2319. Sr. Merlynn Martin, C.S.J., D.R.E. Sisters 1; Students 106.

3—ST. DENIS (1853; Restored 1961) Rev. Jose Shaji (India); Sr. Mary De Chantal, R.S.M., Pastoral Assoc.
Res.: 2250 Avy Ave., 94025. Tel: 650-854-5976; Fax: 650-854-3754. Web: www.stdenisparish.org.
Mission—Our Lady of the Wayside (1902) 930 Portola Rd., Portola Valley, San Mateo Co. 94028. Tel: 650-851-5085; Fax: 650-851-1019. In Res., Rev. Thomas D. Moran (Retired).
Catechesis/Religious Program—Tel: 650-854-1081. Rosemary Lyon, D.R.E. Students 225.

4—ST. RAYMOND (1950) Revs. William Myers; James H. Morris.
Office: 1100 Santa Cruz Ave., 94025. Tel: 650-323-1755; Fax: 650-323-3206.
Res.: 1231 Arbor Rd., 94025.
School—1211 Arbor Rd., 94025. Tel: 650-322-2312; Fax: 650-322-2910. Sr. Ann Bernard O'Shea, C.S.J., Prin. Sisters 6; Lay Teachers 17; Students 245.
Catechesis/Religious Program—Kristen Quinlan, D.R.E. Students 90.

MILL VALLEY, MARIN CO., OUR LADY OF MT. CARMEL (1910) Rev. Patrick T. Michaels; Mr. Michael L. Morison, Pastoral Assoc.
Res.: 3 Oakdale Ave., 94941. Tel: 415-388-4190; Fax: 415-388-4197. Email: staff@olmcmv.org. Web: www.olmcmv.org.
Catechesis/Religious Program—17 Buena Vista, 94941. Tel: 415-388-1008; Fax: 415-388-4297. Email: olmcmv@gmail.com. Students 220.

MILLBRAE, SAN MATEO CO., ST. DUNSTAN (1940) Revs. Diarmid Casey, C.S.Sp.; Joseph Glynn, C.S.Sp.; Patrick Donovan, C.S.Sp.; James L. Livingstone.
Res.: 1133 Broadway, 94030. Tel: 650-697-4730; 650-697-4736; Fax: 650-697-5203. Email: secretary@saintdunstanchurch.org. Web: www.saintdunstanchurch.org.
School—1150 Magnolia Ave., 94030. Tel: 650-697-8119; Fax: 650-697-9295. Bruce Colville, Prin. Lay Teachers 14; Students 287.
Catechesis/Religious Program—Tel: 650-697-7451. Sherre Leone, D.R.E. Students 170.

NOVATO, MARIN CO.

1—ST. ANTHONY OF PADUA (1968) Revs. Toan X. Nguyen; William H. Thornton; Deacons Joseph Brumbaugh; Joseph Borg, (Retired); Barbara DeBarros, Youth Min. & Coord. Confirmation. In Res., Rev. Edward Phelan (Retired).
Res.: 1000 Cambridge St., 94947. Tel: 415-883-2177; Fax: 415-883-4049.
Catechesis/Religious Program—Tel: 415-883-9000. Email: religious-education@saint-anthonys.com. Judith Ann Ross, C.R.E. (Grades 1-6). Students 359.

2—OUR LADY OF LORETTO (1892) Revs. William H. McCain; William C. Nicholas; Patrick Reeder; Sr. Jeanette Lombardi, O.S.U., Pastoral Assoc.
Res.: 1806 Novato Blvd., 94947. Tel: 415-897-2171; Fax: 415-897-8251. Email: erin@ollnovato.org. Web: www.ollnovato.org.
School—1811 Virginia Ave., 94945. Tel: 415-892-8621; Fax: 415-892-9631. Ms. Susan Maino, Prin. Lay Teachers 10; Students 231.
Catechesis/Religious Program—Tel: 415-897-6714. Mary Furnanz, D.R.E.; Victoria Birnberg, D.R.E.; Perrin G. Brady-Cheney, Youth Min. Students 240.

OLEMA, MARIN CO., SACRED HEART (1867) [CEM] Rev. John O'Neill.
Mailing Address: P.O. Box 70, 94950. Tel: 415-663-1139; Fax: 415-663-9660.
Res.: 10189 State Route # 1, 94950.
Catechesis/Religious Program—Students 45.
Mission—St. Mary Magdalene 16 Horseshoe Hill, Bolinas, Marin Co. 94924.

PACIFICA, SAN MATEO CO.

1—GOOD SHEPHERD (1951) Rev. Piers M. Lahey; Sr. Carol Fleitz, S.N.J.M., Pastoral Assoc.; Deacons Emmanual R. Santillan; Ben Salvan; James H. Haug.
Res.: 901 Oceana Blvd., 94044. Tel: 650-355-2593; Fax: 650-355-1832. Email: good.shepherd.pac@sbcglobal.net. Web: gschurchca.org.
School—909 Oceana Blvd., 94044. Tel: 650-359-4544; Fax: 650-359-4558. Email: goodsheppac@hotmail.com. Patricia Volan, Prin. Lay Teachers 15; Students 215.
Catechesis/Religious Program—Tel: 650-355-4214; Fax: 650-355-1832. Email: gsrel@sbcglobal.net. Mr. Kenneth Schwend, D.R.E. Students 108.

2—ST. PETER (1956) Rev. Mark G. Mazza; Deacon Peter Solan.
Res.: 700 Oddstad Blvd., 94044. Tel: 650-359-6313; Fax: 650-359-2262. Email: stpeterpacifica@comcast.net. Web: www.stpeterspacifica.org.
Catechesis/Religious Program—Tel: 650-359-5000. Mrs. Elizabeth Neopolitan, D.R.E.; Mrs. Lauren Bergesen, D.R.E. (High School). Students 240.

PORTOLA VALLEY, SAN MATEO CO., OUR LADY OF THE WAYSIDE (1941) See separate listing. See St. Denis, Menlo Park. Rev. Thomas D. Moran (Retired).

REDWOOD CITY, SAN MATEO CO.

1—ST. MATTHIAS (1961) Rev. John F. Glogowski; Deacon George A. Salinger.
Res.: 1685 Cordilleras Rd., 94062. Tel: 650-366-9544; Fax: 650-366-4817. Web: www.stmatthiasparish.org.
St. Matthias Preschool—533 Canyon Rd., 94062. Tel: 650-367-1320; Fax: 650-366-1049. Web: www-.stmatthiasparish.org. Students 90.
Catechesis/Religious Program—Email: cff@stmatthiasparish.org. Students 160.

2—OUR LADY OF MOUNT CARMEL (1887) Revs. John A. Balleza; Paulinus M. Mangesho, A.L.C.P. (Tanzania), Parochial Vicar; Deacon Thomas J. Boyle.
Res.: 347 Grand St., 94062.
Parish Center—300 Fulton St., 94062. Tel: 650-366-3802; Fax: 650-366-1421. Email: parish@mountcarmel.org. Web: www.mountcarmel.org.
School—301 Grand St., 94062. Tel: 650-366-6127; Fax: 650-366-0902. Lay Teachers 16; Students 282.
Catechesis/Religious Program—Tel: 650-368-8237. Students 280.

3—ST. PIUS (1951) Revs. James H. MacDonald; Honesto Gile Jr. In Res., Revs. Kevin Kennedy; Gerald D. Coleman, S.S.
Res.: 1100 Woodside Rd., 94061. Tel: 650-361-1411; Fax: 650-369-3641. Email: parish@pius.org. Web: www.pius.org.
School—Tel: 650-368-8327; Fax: 650-368-7031. Email: administration@stpiusschool.org. Web: stpiusschool.org. Rita Carroll, Prin. Lay Teachers 14; Students 299.
Catechesis/Religious Program—Fax: 650-369-3641. Email: maria@pius.org. Web: www.pius.org. Maria Cornell, C.R.E. Students 152.

ROSS, MARIN CO., ST. ANSELM (1907) Revs. Cornelius J. Healy; Warlito F. Namo; Deacons Bernard O'Halloran; Edward Cunningham.
Mailing Address: P.O. Box 1061, 94957. In Res., Rev. Peter McDonald, Pastor Emeritus (Retired).
Res.: 97 Shady Ln. & Bolinas Ave., P.O. Box 1061, 94957-1061. Tel: 415-453-2342; Fax: 415-453-8713. Email: st.anselm@att.net. Web: www.saintanselm.org.
School—40 Belle Ave., San Anselmo, 94960. Tel: 415-454-8667; Fax: 415-454-4730. Email: stanselmsschool@comcast.net. Web: stanselmschool-.com. Odile Steel, Prin. Lay Teachers 22; Students 270.
Catechesis/Religious Program—Tel: 415-453-2342. Tom Kavanaugh, D.R.E. Students 236.

SAN BRUNO, SAN MATEO CO.

1—ST. BRUNO (1912) Revs. Michael Brillantes (Philippines); Santos Rodriguez; Deacons Ramon De La Rosa; Joseph Lavulo.
Res.: 555 San Bruno Ave. W., 94066. Tel: 650-588-2121; Fax: 650-588-6087. Web: saintbrunos.org.
Catechesis/Religious Program—Tel: 650-588-2121, Ext. 14. Kacey Carey, D.R.E. (Spanish). Students 327.

2—ST. ROBERT (1958) Revs. Roberto A. Andrey; William Paul O'Dell; Deacons Rusty Duffey; John Meyer. In Res., Rev. Vincent D. Ring (Retired).
Res.: 1380 Crystal Springs Rd., 94066. Tel: 650-589-2800; Fax: 650-588-3628. Web: www.saintroberts.org.
School—345 Oak Ave., 94066. Tel: 650-583-5065; Fax: 650-583-1418. Yvonne Olcomendy, Prin. Lay Teachers 14; Students 314.
Catechesis/Religious Program—Tel: 650-588-0477. Students 334.

SAN CARLOS, SAN MATEO CO., ST. CHARLES (1928) Revs. David A. Ghiorso; John J. Sakowski; Deacon Michael Murphy.
Res.: 880 Tamarack Ave., 94070. Tel: 650-591-7349; Fax: 650-637-1968. Email: st.charleschurch@sbcglobal.net. Web: www.stcharlesparish.org.
School—850 Tamarack Ave., 94070. Tel: 650-593-1629; Fax: 650-593-9723. Email: stcharlesschoolsc@stcharlesschoolsc.org. Web: stcharlesschoolsc.org. Maureen Grazioli, Prin. Lay Teachers 15; Students 298.
Catechesis/Religious Program—Nancy Farrant, D.R.E. Students 297.

SAN MATEO, SAN MATEO CO.

1—ST. BARTHOLOMEW (1955) Revs. Michael J. Healy; Teodoro P. Magapayo (Philippines); Deacon John Sequeira.
Res.: 300 Alameda de las Pulgas, 94402. Tel: 650-347-0701; Fax: 650-347-2429. Email: stbarts@barts.org. Web: www.barts.org.
Catechesis/Religious Program—Joanne Ferretti, D.R.E. Students 360.

2—ST. GREGORY (1941) Rev. Msgr. Robert W. McElroy; Revs. Joseph Hung Pham; Vincent "Mark" Reburiano; Deacons Fred Iskander; Stephen Fox. In Res., Rev. Msgr. Edward P. McTaggart (Retired); Rev. Joseph A. Bradley (Retired).
Res.: 2715 Hacienda St., 94403. Tel: 650-345-8506; Fax: 650-345-9329.

School—2701 Hacienda St., 94403. Tel: 650-573-0111; Fax: 650-573-6548. Lorraine Welch Paul, Prin. Lay Teachers 15; Students 322.
Catechesis/Religious Program—2715 Hacienda St., 94403. Tel: 650-574-8716. Students 418.

3—ST. MATTHEW (1863) Revs. Anthony E. McGuire; William J. Ahlbach; Juan M. Lopez; Dominic Savio Lee; Deacons James Shea; Rafeal Brown.
Res.: One Notre Dame Ave., 94402. Tel: 650-344-7622; Fax: 650-344-4830. Web: www.stmatthew-parish.org.
School—910 S. El Camino Real, 94402. Tel: 650-343-1373; Fax: 650-343-2046. Email: info@stmatthewcath.org. Web: www.stmatthew-cath.org. Mrs. Beverly Viotti, Prin. Lay Teachers 21; Students 605.
Catechesis/Religious Program—Students 427.

4—ST. TIMOTHY (1954) Revs. Francis Mark P. Garbo; Peter D. Balili, S.T.D.; Sione Laina Katoa (Tonga); Deacons Angel Aguilar; Nicolas Rodriguez; Faiva Po'oi.
Res.: 1515 Dolan Ave., 94401. Tel: 650-342-2468; Fax: 650-342-8156. Web: www.sttims.us.
School—Tel: 650-342-6567; Fax: 650-342-5913. Web: www.sttimothyschool.org. Ms. Evelyn Rosa, Prin. Lay Teachers 9; Students 218.
Catechesis/Religious Program—Tel: 650-579-0901; Fax: 650-342-8156. Mr. Kohl Glau, C.R.E. Students 182.

SAN RAFAEL, MARIN CO.

1—BLESSED SACRAMENT (1951) Closed. For sacramental records please contact St. Isabella, San Rafael.

2—ST. ISABELLA (Terra Linda) (1961) [CEM] Revs. Kenneth M. Westray; Craig M. Forner; Alner Nambatac (Philippines); Deacons Jerry Friedman, (Retired); James Myers.
Mailing Address: P.O. Box 6166, 94903. In Res., Rev. Feliciano Mofan.
Res.: One Trinity Way, 94903. Tel: 415-479-1560; Fax: 415-479-8303. Email: office@stisabellasparish.org. Web: www.stisabellaparish.org.
School—P.O. Box 6188, 94903. Tel: 415-479-3727; Fax: 415-479-9961. Email: akalayjian@stisabellaschool.org. Web: www.stisabellaschool.org. Ann Kalayjian, Prin. Lay Teachers 23; Students 237.
Catechesis/Religious Program—Tel: 415-479-8303. Email: harpjoy@stisabellasparish.org. Web: www.stisabellasparish.org. Karen Morelli, D.R.E. Students 336.

3—ST. RAPHAEL (1817) Revs. Paul J. Rossi; Ngoan Phan; David S. Matz, C.P.P.S.; Deacon Eugene B. Smith. In Res., Rev. Denis McManus, C.S.Sp. (Retired).
Res.: 1104 Fifth Ave., 94901. Tel: 415-454-8141; Fax: 415-454-8193. Web: www.saintraphael.com.
School—1100 Fifth Ave., 94901. Tel: 415-454-4455; Fax: 415-454-5927. Mrs. Maureen Albritton, Prin. Lay Teachers 13; Students 161.
Catechesis/Religious Program—Tel: 415-459-7331; Fax: 415-454-8193. Students 378.
Mission—St. Sylvester 1115 Point San Pedro Rd., Marin Co. 94901.
Station—San Quentin State Prison San Quentin, NM. Tel: 415-456-8161.

4—ST. SYLVESTER (1961) Closed. For sacramental records please contact St. Raphael, San Rafael.

SAUSALITO, MARIN CO., ST. MARY STAR OF THE SEA (1881) Rev. Thomas M. Parenti. In Res., Rev. Eugene F. Duggan, Pastor Emeritus (Retired).
Res.: 180 Harrison Ave., 94965. Tel: 415-332-1765; Fax: 415-332-4962. Email: staroftheseа@starofthesea.us. Web: www.starofthesea.us.

SOUTH SAN FRANCISCO, SAN MATEO CO.

1—ALL SOULS (1913) Revs. Agnel De Heredia; Jose Eduardo Mendoza (Mexico).
Res.: 315 Walnut Ave., 94080. Tel: 650-871-8944; Fax: 650-871-5806. Email: info@allsoulschurchssf.org. Web: www.allsoulschurchssf.org.
School—479 Miller Ave., 94080. Tel: 650-583-3562; Fax: 650-952-1167. Rev. Vincent Riener, Prin. Lay Teachers 14; Students 252.
Catechesis/Religious Program—Tel: 650-873-5356. Benjamin Villa, D.R.E. Students 359.

2—ST. AUGUSTINE (1970) Revs. Rene R. Ramoso; Balaswamy Govindu (India); Deacons Frank Almeida; Robert Bertolani.
Res.: 3700 Callan Blvd., 94080. Tel: 650-873-2282; Fax: 650-873-1356. Email: staugustinessf@aol.com.
Catechesis/Religious Program—Tel: 650-873-2878. Email: staugustinessf@aol.com. Sr. Nona Barairo, S.F.C.C., D.R.E. Students 500.

3—MATER DOLOROSA (1961) Rev. Brian L. Costello; Deacon Alex Aragon. In Res., Very Rev. C. Michael Padazinski.
Res.: 307 Willow Ave., 94080. Tel: 650-583-4131; Fax: 650-616-9066. Email: fatherbrian@mdssf.org. Web: mdssf.org.
Catechesis/Religious Program—Tel: 650-588-0426. Email: rachael@mdssf.org. Rachael Smit, D.R.E. Students 84.

4—ST. VERONICA (1951) Revs. Charles Puthota; Linh Tien Nguyen; Deacons Roger Beaudry; Joseph LeBlanc.
Res.: 434 Alida Way, 94080. Tel: 650-588-1455; Fax: 650-588-1481. Email: churchoffice@stveronicassf.com. Web: www.stveronicassf.com.
School—Tel: 650-589-3909; Fax: 650-589-2826. Teresa Pallitto, Prin. Lay Teachers 19; Students 332.
Catechesis/Religious Program—Tel: 650-871-5607; Fax: 650-588-1481. Email: stveronicacatholicschool@yahoo.com. Students 270.

TIBURON, MARIN CO., ST. HILARY (1951) Revs. James T. Tarantino; Lawrence Vadakkan, S.D.B. (India).
Res.: 761 Hilary Dr., 94920-1498. Tel: 415-435-1122; Fax: 415-435-1862. Email: tibhilary@aol.com. Web: www.sthilary.org.
School—765 Hilary Dr., 94920. Tel: 415-435-2224; Fax: 415-435-5895. Web: www.sainthilaryschool.org. Mr. Bryan Clement, Prin. Lay Teachers 25; Students 268.
Catechesis/Religious Program—Tel: 415-435-1639; Fax: 415-435-1639. Diana Rittenhouse, D.R.E. Students 131.

TOMALES, MARIN CO., CHURCH OF THE ASSUMPTION (1860) [CEM] Rev. Robert Kevin White.
Res. & Mailing: 26825 Shoreline Hwy., P.O. Box 82, 94971-0082. Tel: 707-878-2208; Fax: 707-878-9422. Email: coatomales@yahoo.com.
Catechesis/Religious Program—Students 93.
Mission—St. Helen (1902) Marshall. P.O. Box 82, Marin Co. 94971-0082.

WOODSIDE, SAN MATEO CO., ST. MARCELLA MISSION, Closed. For sacramental records please contact St. Denis, Menlo Park.

Chaplains of Public Institutions

SAN FRANCISCO. *St. Anne's Home*. Rev. John T. Schwartz, Chap.
Catholic Healthcare West/Bay Area Region. Vacant.
St. Francis Hospital. Franciscans from St. Boniface Parish.
Kaiser Hospital San Francisco. Rev. Michael Greenwell, O.Carm.
Knights of Malta. The Sovereign Military Order of Malta (Western U.S.A. Association of the Sovereign Military Hospitaller Order of St. John of Jerusalem of Rhodes and of Malta--a Nonprofit Corporation). Rev. Msgr. Steven D. Otellini, Rev. John P. Kavanaugh (Retired).
Laguna Honda Home. Rev. Te Van Nguyen, Sr. Elizabeth Johnson, f.d.C.C.
St. Mary's Medical Center. Revs. Michael Greenwell, O.Carm., Edward K. Murray.
San Francisco Fire Department. Rev. John L. Greene.
San Francisco General Hospital. Rev. John Jimenez.
San Francisco Police Department. Rev. Michael J. Healy.
San Francisco State Univ., Newman Center. Rev. Msgr. Labib Kobti.
Serra Club of San Francisco (Downtown). Rev. Thomas A. Daly.
Serra Club of San Francisco (Golden Gate). Rev. Msgr. Edward P. McTaggart (Retired).
St. Thomas More Society. (Legal). Rev. Msgr. Labib Kobti.
Veterans' Hospital. Revs. John K. Coleman, Palo Alto, Lawrence Gould, S.A.C., San Francisco.
Young Ladies' Institute. Rev. Thomas M. Hamilton, Grand. Chap.

DALY CITY. *Seton Hospital*. Revs. Rory E. Murphy, Joseph Palathingal (India).

MARIN. *Serra Club of Marin*. Rev. Paul J. Rossi.

REDWOOD CITY. *Sequoia Hospital*. Rev. Kevin Kennedy, Chap.

SAN MATEO. *Serra Club of San Mateo*. Rev. James W. Livingstone.
Sheriff's Honor Camp and Medium Security Facility. Served by Archdiocese and St. Vincent de Paul volunteers, San Mateo District Council.

SAN QUENTIN. *California State Prison*, Tel: 415-454-1460. Rev. Stephen A. Barber, S.J., Chap.

On Special Assignment:
Rev. Msgrs.—
Arcamo, Floro B., Vicar for Filipinos
Rodriguez, Jose A., Vicar for Spanish Speaking
Schlitt, Harry G., Vicar for Admin.
Very Rev.—
Padazinski, C. Michael, J.C.D., Chancellor & Judicial Vicar
Revs.—
Daly, Thomas A., Dir. Vocations, President, Marin Catholic High School, Kentfield & St. Vincent School for Boys, San Rafael
Hoang, Thuan V., J.C.L., Tribunal
Johnson, Andrew R., Office, Devel.

On Duty Outside the Archdiocese:
Revs.—
Coleman, John, VA Hospital, Palo Alto, Diocese of San Jose
Ervin, Thomas, Ph.D., Oakland, California
Escalante, Augustin, Laredo, TX
Fredericks, James L., Faculty, Loyola-Marymount Univ., Los Angeles
Hagan, James, Mexico
Lopes, Steven J., S.T.L., Secretary to the Prefect of the Congregation for the Doctrine of Faith, Vatican
McElligott, Thomas J., St. Mary College, Moraga, Diocese of Oakland
Piechota, Lech, Particular Secretary to Cardinal Bertone, Vatican

---

Graduate Studies:
Rev.—
Previtali, Joseph F., North American College, Rome

Absent on Leave:
Rev. Msgr.—
O'Connor, John
Revs.—
Ingels, Gregory G.
Leach, Jerome
Walsh, Milton T.

Retired:
Most Rev.—
Quinn, John R., D.D.
Rev. Msgrs.—
Bitanga, Fred A.
Foudy, John T.
Holleran, J. Warren
Keane, James P.
Knapp, Richard L.
McCormick, Maurice M.
McKay, James P.
McTaggart, Edward P.
Pernia, John R.
Rodriguez, John F., Madrid, Spain.
Sullivan, Joseph P.
Very Rev.—
Wang, Ignatius C., J.C.D.
Revs.—
Aylward, James W.
Bain, Richard C.
Bitangjol, Albert P.
Bradley, Joseph A.
Bravo, Joseph
Brennan, Bernard F.
Burke, Ronald A.
Burns, Thomas J.
Calegari, Leonard J.
Caverte, Rolando A.
Chang, Benedict
Chung, Anthony
Cipriano, Robert P.
Cloherty, John J.
D'Angelo, Donald S.
Davenport, Clement A.
Decker, Raymond G.
Deitch, Richard S.
Duggan, Eugene F.
Filice, Francis P.
Gaffey, Kevin P.
Gordon, Joseph A.
Greenlaw, Martin F.
Hanson, Kirby C.
Horan, Terence J.
Jocson, Salvador
Kavanaugh, John P.
Kaylor, Lee
Knapp, William L.
Madden, J. Thomas
Marini, Joseph J.
McCormick, Kieran J.
McDonald, Peter
McDonnell, Donald C.
Moran, Thomas D.
Murray, Francis K.
Namocatcat, Felix S.
O'Connell, Joseph A.
O'Connell, William A.
O'Donnell, Hugh
O'Malley, James E.
O'Rourke, P. Gerard
Padilla, Aquino
Pettingill, David M.
Phelan, Edward
Piro, Frank R.
Quinn, William P.
Raimondi, Michele A.
Richard, Joseph E.
Riley, Miles O'Brien
Ring, Vincent D.
Rodriguez, Guillermo
Schipper, Carl A.

Shipp, Edmund N.
Shore, Zachary J.
Sigaran, Mamerto
Smith, Wilton S.
Thomas, George L.
Trainor, Henry J.
Ullery, Kirk J.
Ward, John J.
Worner, William H.
Young, William W.
Zohlen, Ray

Permanent Deacons:
Abu-Alshaer, Khaled, St. Thomas More, San Francisco
Aguilar, Angel, St. Timothy, San Mateo
Allen, Charles, St. Teresa, San Francisco
Almeida, Frank, St. Augustine, South San Francisco
Aragon, Alex, Mater Dolorosa, South San Francisco
Ayalin, Romeo P., Phoenix, AZ
Bacon, Nate, Guatemala
Beaudry, Roger, St. Veronica, South San Francisco
Bertolani, Bob, St. Augustine, San Francisco
Bettencourt, John, Palm Springs
Borg, Joe, (Retired), St. Anthony of Padua, Novato
Boulware, Peter I., St. Mary's Cathedral, San Francisco
Boyle, Tom, Our Lady of Mount Carmel, Redwood City
Bromberger, Brian, San Francisco
Brown, Rafeal, St. Matthew, San Mateo
Bruening, Bill, Our Lady of Perpetual Help, Daly City
Brumbaugh, Joe, St. Anthony of Padua, Novato
Buenavista, Tom, Pensicola
Cancilla, Charles, San Quentin Prison
Capetti, Virgil, Our Lady of the Pillar, Half Moon Bay
Carpenter, John W., New Orleans, LA
Cervantes, Vicente, Mission Dolores Basilica, San Francisco
Chatmon, Larry, St. Paul of the Shipwreck, San Francisco
Cunningham, Ed, St. Anselm, San Anselmo
Curran, Michael, St. Dominic, San Francisco
DeLaRosa, Ramon, St. Bruno, San Bruno
Dixon, Louis, St. Francis of Assisi, East Palo Alto
Doherty, Michael, Holy Name of Jesus, San Francisco
Duffey, Rusty, St. Robert, San Bruno
Dupre, John, St. Anne, San Francisco
Enos, Rick, Yreka
Foley, Richard, (On Leave)
Fox, Stephen, St. Gregory, San Mateo
Friedman, Jerome, Nazareth House, San Rafael
Gamarra, David, St. Peter, San Francisco
Garcia, Julio, Nicaragua
Ghiorso, Michael J., Our Lady of Mercy, Daly City
Grant, Richard, Tulsa, OK
Hackett, Steven, Immaculate Heart of Mary, Belmont
Hall, J. Bruce, Tiburon
Haug, James H., Church of the Good Shepherd, Pacifica
Ilao, Thomas J., St. Anne, San Francisco
Iskander, Fred, St. Gregory, San Mateo
Jacquemet, Hank, Immaculate Heart of Mary, Belmont
Kahn, Bob, Albany, OR
Kehrlein, Peter, St. Rita, Fairfax
Koloamatangi, Benjamin, St. Francis of Assisi Church, East Palo Alto
Kortenkamp, Leon, Diaconate Office
Lavulo, Joe, St. Bruno, San Bruno
LeBlanc, Joe, St. Veronica, South San Francisco
Lucia, Paul, St. Luke, Foster City
McGhee, John, Our Lady of Pillar, Half Moon Bay; Our Lady of Refuge, La Honda; St. Anthony Mission, Pescadero
McNeil, Chuck, St. Dominic, San Francisco
Meyer, John, St. Robert, San Bruno
Michaelson, Steven, Paso Robles, CA
Mitchell, William, (Retired), Our Lady of Loretto, Novato
Murphy, Michael, St. Charles, San Carlos
Myers, Jim, St. Isabella, San Rafael
O'Halloran, Bernard, St. Anselm, San Anselmo
Ocon, Manuel, Sacramento
Pagacz, Bruce, Our Lady of Fatima Byzantine Catholic Church, San Francisco
Paulino, Antonio, S. San Francisco
Pelimiano, Pete, Diaconate Office
Peloso, Dominick, Nativity, Menlo Park
Po'oi, Faiva, St. Timothy, San Mateo
Prudenciado, Lernito, Holy Angels, Colma
Reardon, Thomas, St. Gabriel, San Francisco
Rittenhouse, John H., (On Leave)
Rodriguez, Nicolas, St. Timothy, San Mateo
Rosen, Dan, St. Stephen, San Francisco
Ruiz, Juan, Holy Angels, Colma
Salinger, George A., St. Matthias, Redwood City
Salvan, Benjamin, Church of the Good Shepherd, Pacifica
Sandoval, R. Christoph, St. Mary's Cathedral, San Francisco
Santillan, Noel, Church of the Good Shepherd, Pacifica
Sequeira, John, St. Bartholomew, San Mateo
Sevilla, Wilfredo, Corpus Christi, San Francisco
Shea, James, St. Matthew, San Matteo
Simon, Tsui, Holy Family, San Francisco
Smith, Eugene B., St. Raphael, San Raphael
Solan, Peter, St. Peter, Pacifica
Solano, Jose, St. Paul, San Francisco
Sondergaard, Gerald, Albuquerque
Swanson, Fred, St. Dominic, San Francisco
Tano, Mar, St. Luke, Foster City
Turrentine, Bill, St. Rita, Fairfax
Twitty, Roy, St. Catherine of Sienna, Burlingame
Viray, Ding, Epiphany, San Francisco
West, Gary, St. Stephen, San Francisco
Young, Mike, Sacramento
Zamora, Ramon, Epiphany, San Francisco

INSTITUTIONS LOCATED IN THE ARCHDIOCESE

[A] SEMINARIES, ARCHDIOCESAN

MENLO PARK. *St. Patrick Seminary and University* (1898) Major Seminary of the Archdiocese of San Francisco, under the direction of the Society of St. Sulpice., 320 Middlefield Rd., 94025. Tel: 650-325-5621; 650-321-5655 (Library); Fax: 650-322-0997. Email: info@stpatricksseminary.org. Web: www.stpatricksseminary.org. Most Rev. George H. Niederauer, D.D., Ph.D., Chancellor.
(1891, 1944): The Roman Catholic Seminary of San Francisco Priests 15; Religious 3; Lay Teachers 4; Students 94.
Officers of the Administration: Revs. James L. McKearney, S.S., Vice Chancellor, Pres, & Rector; Gladstone H. Stevens, S.S., Vice Rector & Academic Dean; Gerald L. Brown, S.S., M.Div., Ph.D., (Sabbatical).
Resident Faculty: Rev. Msgr. J. Warren Holleran, Professor (Retired); Revs. Michael C. Barber, S.J., Dir. Spiritual Life Prog.; Frederick J. Cwiekowski, S.S., S.T.D., Prof. Emeritus; Jeffrey Hubbard, Instructor; Eugene J. Konkel, S.S., S.T.L.; Nam J. Kim, S.S., Asst. Prof./Dir. Pastoral Year; John S. Kselman, S.S., Assoc. Prof.; James L. McKearney, S.S., Pres., Rector & Vice Chancellor; Jose Antonio Rubio, Asst. Prof./Dir. Liturgy; George E. Schultze, S.J., Asst. Prof.; Gladstone H. Stevens, S.S., Vice Rector/Academic Dean; Noel de Lira, Instructor.
Non-Resident Faculty and Staff: Dr. Charles W. James, S.T.D., Assoc. Prof.; Revs. Andrews Amir, M.A., Ph.D., Assoc. Prof.; Howard P. Bleichner, Assoc. Prof.; Mrs. Nuria Ortiz, Registrar/Asst. to Academic Dean/Instructor; Sr. Mary Lange, S.H.F., M.A., Dir. Field Educ.; Ms. Jennifer Morris, Dir. Business Finance; Dr. Michael Neri, Ph.D., Prof. (On Sabbatical); Dr. Ruth Ohm, Asst.Prof. Sacred Scripture; Dr. Margaret M. Turek, S.T.D., Assoc. Prof.; Ms. Neva J. Turoff, Dir. Deaf Svcs.; Dr. Cecil White, Ph.D., Librarian; Mrs. Monica Haupt, Language Instructor; Rev. Msgr. Jeremiah J. McCarthy, Ph.D., Prof.
Vatican II Institute for Clergy Formation (1972) 320 Middlefield Rd., 94025. Tel: 650-325-9122; Fax: 650-325-6765. Web: www.stpatrickseminary.org. Rev. James E. Myers, S.S., M.Div., Dir.
St. Joseph's-St. Patrick's College Alumni Association, St. Patrick's Seminary, 320 Middlefield Rd., 94025. Tel: 650-591-3492; Fax: 650-654-3503. Email: murpur@aol.com. Web: www.saintjosephscollege.ws. Mr. James P. Murphy, Contact.

[B] SEMINARIES, RELIGIOUS OR SCHOLASTICATES

SAN FRANCISCO. *Capuchin Franciscan Order San Buenaventura Friary*, 750 Anza St., 94118. Tel: 415-387-7005; Fax: 415-831-5902. Revs. Martin Haggins, O.F.M.Cap, Hospital Chap.; Quoc Nguyen, O.F.M.Cap., Hospital Chap.; Alan Wilson, O.F.M.Cap, Hospital Chap. & Guardian; Gregory Coiro, O.F.M.Cap.; Bro. Mark Ortega, O.F.M.Cap., (Retired). Priests 4; Brothers 1.

[C] COLLEGES AND UNIVERSITIES

SAN FRANCISCO. **University of San Francisco* Established 1855; Chartered by State, 1859., 2130 Fulton St., 94117-1080. Tel: 415-422-5555; Fax: 415-422-2303. Web: www.usfca.edu. Rev. Stephen A. Privett, S.J., Pres.; Dr. James L. Wiser, Provost & Academic Vice Pres.; Rev. John Lo Schiavo, S.J., Chancellor; Mr. David F. Macmillan, Vice Pres., Univ. Advancement; Mr. Charles E. Cross, Vice Pres., Business & Finance; Dr. Margaret M. Higgins, Vice Pres., University Life; Mr. Jeffrey S. Brand, Dean, School of Law; Dr. Walter H. Gmelch, Dean, School of Educ.; Mr. Tyrone H. Cannon, Dean, University Library; Dr. Elizabeth J. Johnson, Dean, Academic Services; Dr. Judith F. Karshmer, Dean, School of Nursing; Dr. Jennifer E. Turpin, Dean, College of Arts & Sciences; Mr. Michael L. Duffy, Dean, School Business & Professional Studies. Jesuit Fathers. Priests 7; Sisters 2; Lay Faculty 371; Students 8,772.

BELMONT. *Notre Dame de Namur University* (1851) 1500 Ralston Ave., 94002. Tel: 650-508-3500; Fax: 650-508-3660. Email: cchu@ndnu.edu. Web: www.ndnu.edu. Dr. Judith Maxwell Greig, Pres.; Dr. Richard Giardina, Provost; Rev. Tom Splain, S.J.; Dr. Klaus Musmann, Librarian. Sisters of Notre Dame de Namur. Sisters 1; Lay Faculty 166; Students 1,613.

SAN RAFAEL. *Dominican University of California*, 50 Acacia Ave., 94901-2298. Tel: 415-457-4440; Fax: 415-485-3205. Email: enroll@dominican.edu. Web: www.dominican.edu. Dr. Joseph R. Fink, Pres.; Dr. Luis Calingo, Exec. Vice Pres./Chief Academic Officer; Rev. Robert Haberman, Campus Ministry; Alan Schut, Dir. Cataloging & Collections; Gary Gorka, Exec. Dir. Library. Resident and non-resident students. Priests 1; Sisters 4; Lay Teachers 337; Students 2,048.

[D] HIGH SCHOOLS, ARCHDIOCESAN

SAN FRANCISCO. *Archbishop Riordan High School (Boys)* (1949) 175 Phelan Ave., 94112. Tel: 415-586-8200, Ext. 216; Fax: 415-587-1310. Email: rkovacich@riordanhs.org. Web: www.riordanhs.org. Rev. Thomas French, S.M., M.Div., M.Ed., Pres.; Kevin Asbra, Prin.; Bro. Thomas M. Jalbert, S.M., Librarian. Priests 1; Sisters 1; Brothers 1; Lay Teachers 40; Students 571.
Sacred Heart Cathedral Preparatory (Coed) (1852) 1055 Ellis St., 94109. Tel: 415-775-6626; Fax: 415-931-6941. Email: margaret.baptista@shcp.edu. Web: shcp.edu. John Scudder, M.A., Pres.; Ken Hogarty, Ed.D., Prin.; Judy Scudder, Librarian. Sponsored by Daughters of Charity and Christian Brothers. Brothers 2; Sisters 3; Lay Teachers 89; Students 1,269.

KENTFIELD. *Marin Catholic College Preparatory (Coed)*, 675 Sir Francis Drake Blvd., 94904. Tel: 415-464-3800; Fax: 415-461-7161. Web: www.marincatholic.org. Email: tdaly@marincatholic.org. Rev. Thomas A. Daly, Pres.; Mr. Chris Valdez, Prin.; Mrs. Carol Teller, Librarian. Priests 1; Lay Teachers 63; Students 725.

SAN MATEO. *Junipero Serra High School (Boys)*, 451 W. 20th Ave., 94403-1385. Tel: 650-345-8207; Fax: 650-573-6638. Email: padres@serrahs.com. Web: www.serrahs.com. Mr. Lars Lund, Pres.; Mr. Barry Thornton, Prin.; Susan Cordes, Librarian. Lay Teachers 65; Students 1,000.

[E] HIGH SCHOOLS, PRIVATE

SAN FRANCISCO. *St. Ignatius College Preparatory (Coed)*, 2001 37th Ave., 94116-1165. Tel: 415-731-7500; Fax: 415-682-5003. Email: info@siprep.org. Web: www.siprep.org. Rev. Robert T. Walsh, S.J., Pres.; Mr. Patrick Ruff, Prin.; Revs. Anthony P. Sauer, S.J.; Thomas Allender, S.J.; Michael C. Barber, S.J.; Paul F. Capitolo, S.J.; Michael J. Kotlanger, S.J.; Andrew F. Maginnis, S.J.; Thomas H. O'Neill, S.J.; James V. Schaukowitch, S.J.; A. Francis Stiegeler, S.J.; Warren J. Wright, S.J.; Bros. Douglas E. Draper, S.J.; Arthur W. Lee, S.J.; John E. Maloney, S.J.; Mr. Jason W. Beyer, S.J.; Michelle Levine, Dean Students; William Gotch, Dean Students; Ms. Virtudes Gomez, Librarian. Priests 11; Seminarians 2; Brothers 3; Lay Teachers 110; Students 1,445.
Immaculate Conception Academy, (Girls) (1883) 3625 24th St., 94110. Tel: 415-824-2052; Fax: 415-821-4677. Email: ica@icacademy.org. Web: www.icacademy.org. Sr. Mary Virginia Leach, O.P., Pres.; Lisa Graham, Prin. Sisters 6; Lay Teachers 27; Students 248.
Mercy High School (Girls) (1952) 3250 19th Ave., 94132. Tel: 415-334-0525; Fax: 415-334-9726. Email: dmccrea@mercyhs.org. Web: www.mercyhs.org. Dorothy McCrea, Ed.D., Prin.; Rev. Gregory McGivern (Ireland), Chap.; Nancy Schaal, Librarian. Priests 1; Sisters 3; Lay Teachers 35; Students 503.
Schools of the Sacred Heart, Convent of the Sacred Heart High School (Girls) (1887) 2222 Broadway, 94115. Tel: 415-563-2900; Fax: 415-929-0553. Email: heart@sacredsf.org. Web:

www.sacredsf.org. Gordon Sharafinski, Dir.; Andrea Shurley, Head; Cynthia Velante, Librarian. Lay Teachers 25; Students 194.

Schools of the Sacred Heart, Stuart Hall High School (2000) (Boys), 1715 Octavia St., 94109. Tel: 415-345-5811; Fax: 415-931-9161. Email: heart@sacredsf.org. Web: www.sacredsf.org. Gordon Sharafinski, Dir.; Friar Anthony Farrell, Head; Sheila Chatterjee, Librarian. Lay Teachers 18; Students 153.

ATHERTON. *Sacred Heart Preparatory, Atherton (Co-Ed)* (1898) 150 Valparaiso, 94027. Tel: 650-322-1866; Fax: 650-327-7011. Web: www.shschools.org. Mr. Richard Dioli, Dir. Schools; Mr. James Everitt, Prin.; Bettie Bohler, Librarian. Religious of the Sacred Heart. Lay Teachers 76; Students 575.

BELMONT. *Notre Dame High School (Girls)*, 1540 Ralston Ave., 94002. Tel: 650-595-1913; Fax: 650-595-2116. Email: rgleason@ndhsb.org. Web: www.ndhsb.org. Ms. Rita Gleason, Prin.; Rev. Stephen H. Howell. Priests 1; Lay Teachers 45; Students 557.

BURLINGAME. *Mercy High School (Girls)*, 2750 Adeline Dr., 94010-5597. Tel: 650-343-3631; Fax: 650-343-2316. Web: www.mercyhsb.com. Laura M. Held, Prin. Lay Teachers 44; Students 495.

PORTOLA VALLEY. *Woodside Priory School* (Coed, Boarding)., 302 Portola Rd., 94028. Tel: 650-851-8221; Fax: 650-851-2839. Email: mmager@prioryca.org. Web: www.prioryca.org. Mr. Tim Molak, Headmaster; Peter Reinhardt, Librarian. *Benedictine Fathers of the Priory, Inc.* Priests 2; Brothers 1; Lay Teachers 53; Students 350.

SAN ANSELMO. *San Domenico School*, (Grades PreK-12) Mr. Dean Partlow, High School Div. Head; Mrs. Carol Chase, Primary School Div. Head; Mrs. Cecily Stock, Middle School Div. Head; Mr. Scott Fletcher, Librarian. (Grades PreK-8, Coed; Grades 9-12, Girls. Boarding and Day Students.); See separate listing under Elementary Schools, Private in the Institution section. Full-time 57.

[F] ELEMENTARY SCHOOLS, ARCHDIOCESAN

SAN FRANCISCO. *St. Brigid Elementary School* (1888) (Grades K-8), 2250 Franklin St., 94109. Tel: 415-673-4523; Fax: 415-674-4187. Email: office@saintbrigidsf.org. Web: www.saintbrigidsf.org. Sr. Carmen Santiuste, Prin. Sisters 4; Lay Teachers 14; Students 275.

St. Thomas More School (1954) (Grades PreSchool-8), 50 Thomas More Way, 94132. Tel: 415-337-0100; Fax: 415-333-2564. Email: office@stthomasmoreschool.org. Web: www.stthomasmoreschool.org. Marie Fitzpatrick, Asst. Prin.; Melody Oakley, Technology. Lay Teachers 11; Students 315.

[G] ELEMENTARY SCHOOLS, PRIVATE

SAN FRANCISCO. *DeMarillac Academy of San Francisco*, 175 Golden Gate Ave., 94102. Tel: 415-552-5220; Fax: 415-621-5632. Email: mike_daniels@demarillac.org. Web: www.demarillac.org. Michael Daniels, Pres. & CEO; Eileen Emerson, Prin. Lay Teachers 10; Students 115.

The Megan Furth Academy, 2445 Pine St., 94115. Tel: 415-346-9500; Fax: 415-346-8001. Email: nmcauliffe@meganfurthacademy.org. Robert LaLanne, Chair, Bd. Regents; Nicole McAuliffe, Prin. Sisters 2; Lay Teachers 8.

Schools of the Sacred Heart, Convent of the Sacred Heart Elementary School (1887) (Grades K-8), (Girls), 2222 Broadway St., 94115. Tel: 415-563-2900; Fax: 415-563-0438. Email: heart@sacred.sf.org. Web: www.sacredsf.org. Gordon Sharafinski, Dir.; Sr. Anne Wachter, R.S.C.J., Head; Tevis Jones, Librarian. Lay Teachers 42; Students 324.

Schools of the Sacred Heart, Stuart Hall For Boys, (Grades K-8), (Boys), 2222 Broadway St., 94115. Tel: 415-563-2900; Fax: 415-292-3165. Email: heart@sacredsf.org. Web: www.sacredsf.org. Gordon Sharafinski, Dir.; Jaime Dominguez, Headmaster; Tevis Jones, Librarian. Schools of the Sacred Heart. Lay Teachers 38; Students 324.

ATHERTON. *St. Joseph's School of the Sacred Heart* (1906) (Grades PreK-8), (St. Joseph's School), 50 Emilie Ave., 94027. Tel: 650-322-9931; Fax: 650-322-7656. Web: www.shschools.org. Mr. Richard Dioli, Dir. Schools; Mrs. Cee Salberg, Prin., (Grades PreK-K); Bridget Collins, Prin.; Joan Eagleson, Librarian. Sisters 1; Lay Teachers 53; Students 521.

BELMONT. *Notre Dame Elementary School*, 1200 Notre Dame Ave., 94002. Tel: 650-591-2209; Fax: 650-591-4798. Email: dgreggans@NDE.org. Web: NDE.org. Noreen Browning, Prin.; Sr. Catherine Davis, Librarian. Sisters 7; Lay Teachers 21; Students 228.

SAN ANSELMO. *San Domenico School*, (Grades PreK-12), (Grades PreK-8, Coed; Grades 9-12, Girls; Boarding & Day Students), 1500 Butterfield Rd., 94960-1099. Tel: 415-258-1900; Fax: 415-258-1901. Email: mheersche@sandomenico.org. Web: www.sandomenico.org. Matt Heersche, Ed.D., Head of School; Mrs. Cecily Stock, Middle School Div. Head (Grades 6-8); Carole Chase, Primary School Div. Head (Grades PreK-5). Lay Teachers 57; Students 527.

[H] ST. VINCENT DE PAUL SOCIETY

SAN MATEO. **The Society of St. Vincednt de Paul, Particular Council of San Mateo County, Inc.* (1931) Main Office, St. Vincent de Paul Society., 50 N. B St., 94401-3917. Tel: 650-373-0622; Fax: 650-343-9495. Email: svdplm@yahoo.com. Web: www.svdp-sanmateoco.org. Joseph Marchetti, Pres.; Lorraine Moriarty, Exec. Dir.; Margaret Jung, Dir. of Devel. & Pub. Rels.

Thrift Stores:

40 North B St., 94401. Tel: 650-347-5101; Fax: 650-244-0543.

344 Grand Ave., South San Francisco, 94080. Tel: 650-589-8445; Fax: 650-244-0543.

6256 Mision St., Daly City, 94014. Tel: 650-992-9271; Fax: 650-244-0543.

2406 El Camino Real, Redwood City, 94063. Tel: 650-366-6367; Fax: 650-244-0543.

Donation Pickups:

San Mateo County, San Francisco County, Santa Clara County Tel: 650-871-6844; Fax: 650-244-0543.

SVdP's Catherine's Center, 50 N. "B" St., 94401. Tel: 650-246-1520; Fax: 650-343-9495. Safe, supportive housing program for women previously incarcerated.

Vehicle Donation Program Tel: 800-937-7837; Fax: 415-977-1070. Web: www.yes-svdp.org.

St. Vincent de Paul Dining Room at St. Francis of Assisi Church, 1425 Bay Rd., East Palo Alto, 94303. Tel: 650-322-2152; Fax: 650-322-7319 Mon. evenings 4:30-6:00 pm.

Restorative Justice Ministry, 50 N. B St., 94401. Tel: 650-366-9847; Fax: 650-343-9495.

Peninsula Family Resource Center Tel: 650-343-4403; Fax: 650-343-9495.

San Mateo Homeless Help Center, 50 N. B St., 94401. Tel: 650-343-9251; Fax: 650-343-9495 Mon.-Fri. 10am-12noon.

North County Homeless Help Center, 344 Grand Ave., South San Francisco, 94080. Tel: 650-898-9039; Fax: 650-244-0543 Mon.-Sat.- 10am-12noon.

South County Homeless Help Center, 2600 Middlefield Rd., Redwood City, 94063. Tel: 650-343-4403 Mon.-Fri. 1pm-2pm.

Youth-Service Learning Opportunities Tel: 650-589-9039; Fax: 650-244-0543.

SAN RAFAEL. **St. Vincent de Paul Society Marin County District Council* (1946) 820 B St., P.O. Box 150527, 94915. Tel: 415-454-3303; Fax: 415-454-3406. Email: svdpmarin@vinnies.org. Web: vinnies.org. Michael Bromham, Pres.; Steven R. Boyer, Exec. Dir. Staff 15; Total Assisted 9,000; Meals Served 2,000,000.

Affordable Housing (1992) 822 B St., 94901. Tel: 415-454-3303; Fax: 415-454-3406.

Free Dining Room (1981) 820 B St., 94901. Tel: 415-454-0366; Fax: 415-454-3406.

Emergency Help Desk (1992) 822 B. St., 94915. Tel: 415-454-3303; Fax: 415-454-3406.

Thrift Store Pickups Tel: 800-584-1579.

Vehicle Donations Tel: 415-258-5226.

Vehicle Sales & Distribution Tel: 415-258-5226.

[I] DAY NURSERIES

SAN FRANCISCO. *Holy Family Day Home* (1900) 299 Dolores St., 94103. Tel: 415-861-5361; Fax: 415-703-0125. Email: admin@holyfamilydayhome.org. Web: www.holyfamilydayhome.org. Donna M. Cahill, Exec. Dir.

Holy Family Day Homes of San Francisco Religious 1; Lay Staff 50; Capacity 150.

[J] GENERAL HOSPITALS

SAN FRANCISCO. *Catholic Healthcare West* (1986) 185 Berry St., Ste. 300, 94107. Tel: 415-438-5500; Fax: 415-438-5726. Email: robert.sahagian@chw.edu. Web: www.chwHEALTH.org. Lloyd H. Dean, Pres. & CEO. A nonprofit public benefit corporation. CHW is a multi-congregational Health System co-sponsored by the Sisters of Mercy of the Americas West Midwest Community; the Sisters of St. Dominic of the Congregation of the Most Holy Rosary, Adrian, MI; the Sisters of the Third Order of St. Dominic, Congregation of the Most Holy Name, San Rafael, CA; the Congregation of the Sisters of St. Catherine of Siena of Kenosha, WI; the Sisters of St. Francis of Penance and Christian Charity, St. Francis Province; the Congregation of the Sisters of Charity of the Incarnate Word, Houston, Texas. CHW includes several affiliated hospitals, retirement homes, long-term care facilities, medical clinics and related corporations located in California, Arizona and Nevada. The System Office provides centralized management and support functions for the following affiliated nonprofit organizations in the Archdiocese of San Francisco (other affiliates are listed in their respective dioceses): St. Mary's Medical Center; St. Mary's Medical Center Foundation. Sisters 1.

St. Mary's Medical Center dba Catholic Healthcare West (1857) 450 Stanyan St., 94117. Tel: 415-668-1000; Fax: 415-750-4893. Web: www.stmarysmedicalcenter.org. Anna Cheung, Pres.; Revs. Edward K. Murray, Chap.; Michael Greenwell, O.Carm. Sponsored by Sisters of Mercy of the Americas West Midwest Community. Sisters 9; Bed Capacity 403; Total Staff 1,181; Patients Assisted Annually 137,566.

St. Mary's Medical Center Foundation, 450 Stanyan St., 94117-1079. Tel: 415-750-5790; Fax: 415-750-8132. Web: www.stmarysmedicalcenter.org. Margine Sako, Exec. Dir.

DALY CITY. *Seton Medical Center*, 1900 Sullivan Ave., 94015-2229. Tel: 650-992-4000; Fax: 650-991-6024. Email: srwilliameileendunne@dochs.org. Web: www.setonmedicalcenter.org. Lorraine P. Auerbach, Interim Pres. & CEO; Revs. Rory E. Murphy, Dir. Spiritual Care; Joseph Palathingal (India). Daughters of Charity of St. Vincent de Paul Province of the West., Member of Daughters of Charity Health System. Daughters of Charity 5; Bed Capacity 280; Total Staff 1,700; Patients Assisted Annually 511,000.

Seton Medical Center Foundation Tel: 650-991-6464; Fax: 650-991-6098. Web: www.setonfoundation-.org.

San Francisco Heart Institute Tel: 650-991-6712; Fax: 650-755-7315. Web: www.sfhi.com. Colman Ryan, M.D., Exec. Dir.

MOSS BEACH. *Seton Medical Center Coastside*, 600 Marine Blvd., 94038. Tel: 650-563-7100; Fax: 650-728-5314. Web: www.setonmedicalcenter.org. Lorraine P. Auerbach, Interim Pres. & CEO; Judy Cook, R.N., B.S.N., M.P.A., C.P.H.Q., Admin. Dir. Daughters of Charity of St. Vincent de Paul, Province of the West., Member of Daughters of Charity Health System. Religious 1; Patients Assisted Daily 116; Total Staff 160; Bed Capacity: Skilled Nursing 116.

[K] SENIOR CITIZEN RESIDENCES

SAN FRANCISCO. *Alexis Apartments of St. Patrick's Parish* (1973) 390 Clementina St., 94103-4138. Tel: 415-495-3690; Fax: 415-495-3629. Email: alexis@sco.net.

756 Mission St., 94103. Tel: 415-421-3730; Fax: 415-512-9730. Tessa Reed, Property Mgr. Residents 258.

Home for the Aged of the Little Sisters of the Poor, St. Anne's Home, 300 Lake St., 94118. Tel: 415-751-6510; Fax: 415-751-1423. Email: mslspsf@hotmail.com. Sr. Margaret Lennon, L.S.P., Supr. Religious 12; Residents 87. In Res. Revs. Heribert Duquet, M.E.P. (Retired); Thomas Hayes, O.P. (Retired); John T. Schwartz, Chap.; Mario Mich, S.D.B.; James Pratt, S.M. (Retired), (Marist).

Madonna Senior Center and Residence, 350 Golden Gate Ave., 94102. Tel: 415-592-2864; Fax: 415-928-5867. Email: ckoger@stanthonysf.org. Web: www.stanthonysf.org. Cathy Koger, Mgr. Nonprofit residence for women over 60 of low income. Total in Residence 51; Bed Capacity 51; Total Assisted Annually 56; Total Staff 13.

Mercy Housing California Holding Company (1982) 333 Baker St., 94117. Tel: 415-931-2325; Fax: 415-931-7206. Email: larmstrong@mercyhousing.org. Web: www.mercyhousing.org. The purpose of this corporation is to develop, construct, own, and operate housing for low and very low income seniors. Units 159; Bed Capacity 159; Total Assisted Annually 300; Staff 5.

SAN RAFAEL. *Nazareth House of San Rafael, Inc.*, 245 Nova Albion Way, 94903. Tel: 415-479-8282; Fax: 415-479-2217. Email: alice@nazarethhousesr.com. Web: www.sistersofnazareth.com. Sr. Catherine Rea, C.S.N., Supr.; Rev. Msgr. Joseph P. Sullivan, Chap. (Retired). Sisters of Nazareth 8; Bed Capacity 146; Residents 135; Total Staff 100. In Res. Rev. Msgr. Richard S. Knapp; Revs. Hugh O'Donnell (Retired); William L. Knapp (Retired); Wilton S. Smith (Retired); Jerald Thomas.

[L] RESIDENTIAL GROUP HOMES

SAN FRANCISCO. *The Good Shepherd Gracenter* (1986) 1310 Bacon St., 94134. Tel: 415-586-2845; Fax: 415-586-0355. Email: info@gsgracecenter.org. Web: www.gsgracecenter.org. Residential. Sisters 4; Lay Staff 12; Residence Capacity 13; Total Assisted 45.

Mount St. Joseph-St. Elizabeth (1976) 100 Masonic Ave., 94118. Tel: 415-567-8370; Fax: 415-351-5531. Email: slowery@msjse.org. Web: www.msjse.org. Sr. Eileen Kenny, D.C., Exec. Dir. Successor Corporation to Mount St. Joseph Home for Girls and St. Elizabeth Infant Hospital. Organization name: Epiphany Center for Families in (a program of Mt. St. Joseph-St. Elizabeth) Recovery. Sisters 3; Lay Staff 45; Total Assisted 171.

Epiphany Center for Families in Recovery Tel: 415-351-4052; Fax: 415-346-2356. 1. Comprehensive drug treatment with parenting, life skills, and health education groups.; 2. Epiphany In-Home Services for Families at Risk.; 3. Epiphany House -Transitional living for women and children. Families Served 60; Families Served by In-Home Services 85; Individuals Assisted 26.

[M] RETREAT HOUSES

BURLINGAME. *Sisters of Mercy of the Americas West Midwest Community, Inc. Mercy Retreat and Conference Center of Burlingame*, 2300 Adeline Dr., 94010. Tel: 650-340-7474; Fax: 650-340-1299. Web: mercy-center.org; mercywmw.org. Suzanne M. Buckley, Dir.; Constance Quirk, Reservations. Overnight Capacity 90; Daytime Capacity 300; Staff 14.

MENLO PARK. *Vallombrosa Center* (1946) 250 Oak Grove Ave., 94025. Tel: 650-325-5614; Fax: 650-325-0908. Web: www.vallombrosa.org. Rev. Patrick LaBelle, O.P., Dir.; Kathryn Gray, Dir. Mktg. & Opers.; Catherine Wolff, Prog. Dir.

Vallombrosa Center, Conference and Retreat Center of the Archdiocese of San Francisco Priests 1; Staff 11; Daytime Served 120; Overnight Served 100.

SAN RAFAEL. *Santa Sabina Center* (1939) 25 Magnolia, 94901. Tel: 415-457-7727; Fax: 415-457-2310. Email: info@santasabinacenter.org. Web: www.retreatsonline.net/santasabina. Sr. Margaret Diener, O.P., Dir. Dominican Sisters Retreat and Conference Center.

[N] MONASTERIES AND RESIDENCES OF PRIESTS AND BROTHERS

SAN FRANCISCO. *St. Dominic Priory* (1876) 2390 Bush St., 94115-3124. Tel: 415-567-7824; Fax: 415-931-3360; 415-567-1608 (Parish). Web: www.stdominics.org. Revs. Paul Scanlon, O.P., Prior; Xavier M. Lavagetto, O.P., Pastor & Sub-Prior; Anthony R. Rosevear, O.P., Novice Master & Vicar; Garry J. Cappleman, O.P.; Felix F. Cassidy, O.P.; Francis Goode, O.P.; Thomas Hayes, O.P. (Retired); Anselm Ramelow, O.P.; Paschal D. Salisbury, O.P.; Martin Walsh, O.P.; Bro. Gregory R. Lira, O.P. Priests 10; Brothers 1; Novices 3.

Jesuit Community at St. Ignatius College Preparatory, 2001 37th Ave., 94116-1165. Tel: 415-731-7500; Fax: 415-682-5003. Email: postmaster@siprep.org. Web: www.siprep.org. Rev. Robert T. Walsh, S.J., Pres.; Mr. Patrick Ruff, Prin.; Revs. Thomas Allender, S.J.; Paul F. Capitolo, S.J.; Michael C. Barber, S.J.; Michael J. Kotlanger, S.J.; Andrew F. Maginnis, S.J.; Thomas H. O'Neill, S.J., Supr.; Anthony P. Sauer, S.J.; James V. Schaukowitch, S.J.; A. Francis Stiegeler, S.J.; Warren J. Wright, S.J.; Bros. Douglas E. Draper, S.J.; Arthur W. Lee, S.J.; John E. Maloney, S.J.; Mr. Jason W. Beyer, S.J., Seminarian. Priests 11; Brothers 3; Seminarians 1.

Loyola House Jesuit Community (Corporate Title: Jesuit Community at University of San Francisco), 2600 Turk Blvd., 94118-4347. Tel: 415-422-4200; Fax: 415-422-5651. Web: www.usfca.edu/jesuit. Revs. Joseph T. Angilella, S.J., Prof. Emeritus Sociology; House Consultor; Ruben Arceo, S.J., Doctoral Student, School Educ.; Stephen A. Barber, S.J., Chap. San Quentin State Prison; James R. Blaettler, S.J., Assoc. Pastor, St. Ignatius Church; House Consultor; Mario J. Prietto, S.J., Rector, Univ. Leadership Team; Geoffrey R. Dillon, S.J., Asst. Prof., Educ./Dept.; Chair of Teacher Educ.; Project Dir. Learn Belize; Interim Dir., ICEL; Charles R. Gagan, S.J., Pastor, St. Ignatius Church; Albert A. Grosskopf, S.J., Assoc. Pastor, St. Ignatius Church; R. Daniel Kendall, S.J., Prof., Theology; John P. Koeplin, S.J., Assoc. Prof., SOBAM; House Consultor; John J. Lo Schiavo, S.J., Chancellor; Thomas M. Lucas, S.J., Assoc. Prof., Fine & Performing Arts; Sean D. Michaelson, S.J., Dir. St. Ignatius Institute; Chair, English Dept.; Stephen A. Privett, S.J., Pres., Univ. of San Francisco; Dennis C. Recio, S.J., Asst. Prof., English; Donal Godfrey, S.J., Exec. Dir. Univ. Ministry; Roger de la Rosa, S.J., Asst. Prof. Chemistry, Campus Ministry; House Minister; John A. Coleman, Assoc. Pastor St. Ignatius Church; James R. Stormes, S.J., Visiting Prof.; Bros. Jim Holub, S.J.; John Keck, S.J., House Sub-minister. Priests 19; Brothers 2.

Marianist Community (1949) 175 Phelan Ave., 94112. Tel: 415-586-8082; Fax: 415-586-9299. Revs. Thomas French, S.M., M.Div., M.Ed., Pres.; John F. Thompson, S.M., Supr.; Bros. Thomas Jalbert, S.M., B.A., M.A.L.S., M.A.; Richard Olsen, S.M., M.S. Priests 4; Brothers 2.

Marist Center of the West Atlanta Province of the Society of Mary (Marist), 625 Pine St., 94108-3210. Tel: 415-398-3543; Fax: 415-781-4937. Revs. Francis Springer, S.M. (Retired); Edward C. Blee, S.M. (Retired); Patrick J. Coyle, S.M. (Retired); Phillip d'Auby, S.M. (Retired); Robert E. Fahey, S.M. (Retired); Fortune C. Frenoy, S.M. (Retired); W. Thomas Jones, S.M. (Retired); Bros. John A. Hunt, S.M.; Patrick Souza, S.M., Admin.; Joseph Grima, S.M., (Retired). Priests 8; Brothers 2.

Paris Foreign Mission Society Residence (1948) 930 Ashbury St., 94117. Tel: 415-664-6747; Fax: 415-564-5335. Revs. Jacques R. Didier, M.E.P., Dir.; Heribert Duquet, M.E.P. (Retired). Priests 2.

Salesian Provincial Residence, 1100 Franklin St., 94109. Tel: 415-441-7144; Fax: 415-441-7155. Email: suosec@aol.com. Revs. Timothy Ploch, S.D.B., Prov.; Thomas Prendiville, S.D.B., Sec.; Ralph Murphy, S.D.B.; Bro. Michael Touchstone, S.D.B.; Rev. Jerry Wertz, S.D.B. Priests 11. In Res. Revs. Bernard Dabbene, S.D.B. (Retired); Larry Lorenzoni, S.D.B. (Retired); Laurence Byrne, S.D.B. (Retired); Richard Presenti, S.D.B. Military Chaplain: Rev. Robert Delis, S.D.B., Navy Chap., (MO).

San Buenaventura Friary, 750 Anza St., 94118. Tel: 415-387-7005; Fax: 415-831-5902. Residence of Capuchin Provincial House, Burlingame, CA.

Verbum Dei Missionary Fraternity (1969) 3373 19th St., 94110. Tel: 415-282-3005. Email: sfverbumdei@aol.com. Web: fmverbumdei.com/usa. Convent for missionary sisters. Sisters 14.

BURLINGAME. *Capuchin Provincial House* (1991) 1345 Cortez Ave., 94010. Tel: 650-342-1489; Fax: 650-342-5664. Email: ofmcap@aol.com. Web: www.olacapuchins.org. Revs. Matthew G. Elshoff, O.F.M.Cap., Prov.; James Stump, O.F.M.Cap., Hospital Chap.; Donal Burke, O.F.M.Cap., Devel. Dir.; Bro. Pius Higgins, O.F.M.Cap., Guardian; Revs. Richard Lopes, O.F.M.Cap., Hospital Chap.; Camillus MacRory, O.F.M.Cap. (Retired); Bertram Mulligan, O.F.M.Cap. (Retired); Miguel Angel Ortiz, O.F.M.Cap., Prov. Sec.; Fintan Whelan, O.F.M.Cap. *Capuchin Franciscan Seminarians Foundation*, 1345 Cortez Ave., 94010. Tel: 650-344-8321; Fax: 650-342-5664. Email: ofmcap@aol.com. Ms. Judy Steele, Contact Person. *Capuchin Franciscan Endowment Fund*, 1345 Cortez Ave., 94010. Tel: 650-344-8321; Fax: 650-342-5664. Ms. Judy Steele, Contact Person. *Capuchin Franciscan Mission Foundation*, 1345 Cortez Ave., 94010. Tel: 650-344-8321; Fax: 650-342-5664. Ms. Judy Steele, Contact Person. *Capuchin Franciscan Foundation for Retired Friars*, 1345 Cortez Ave., 94010. Tel: 650-344-8321; Fax: 650-342-5664. Ms. Judy Steele, Contact Person.

PORTOLA VALLEY. *Woodside Priory*, 302 Portola Rd., 94028. Tel: 650-851-8220; Fax: 650-851-2839. Email: mmager@prioryca.org. Web: www.prioryca.org. Very Rev. Martin J. Mager, O.S.B., Supr.; Revs. Pius L. Horvath, O.S.B.; Maurus B. Nemeth, O.S.B.; Bro. Edward Englund.

Benedictine Fathers of the Priory, Inc. Priests 3; Brothers 1.

[O] CONVENTS AND RESIDENCES FOR SISTERS

SAN FRANCISCO. *Carmelite Monastery of Cristo Rey, Discalced Carmelite Nuns* (1927) 721 Parker Ave., 94118-4227. Tel: 415-387-2640. Email: community@carmelitenunsusa.org. Professed Nuns 17; Novices 4.

Franciscan Missionaries of Our Lady of Peace (1941) *Our Lady of Guadalupe Convent* (1989) 46 Harrington St., 94112. Tel: 415-587-3729; Fax: 415-587-3729. Email: strhilda@gmail.com. Sr. Hilda Sandoval, M.F.P., Supr.

Mercy Place (Sisters of Mercy-Burlingame), 826 30th Ave., 94121-3522. Tel: 415-876-4303. Sisters 3; Candidates 1.

Monastery of Perpetual Adoration, Nuns of Perpetual Adoration, 771 Ashbury St., 94117. Tel: 415-566-2743; Fax: 415-564-4469. Email: mpador@aol.com. Sr. Rosalba Vargas, A.P., Supr. Cloistered Nuns 13.

Sisters of Social Service, 1850 Ulloa St., 94116. Tel: 415-681-9219. Web: www.socialservicesisters.org. Sisters 4.

Sisters of St. Francis - Mt. Alverno Marian Residence, 1330 Brewster Ave., Redwood City, 94062-1312. Tel: 650-369-1725; Fax: 650-369-0845. Email: blohm@sndden.org. Claire Blohm, Chief Fin. Officer.

Sisters of St. Joseph of Orange, 478 12th Ave., 94118-2904. Tel: 415-387-2493; Fax: 415-387-2493. Email: jmrmmcsj@sbcglobal.net. Sisters 2.

Sisters of St. Joseph of Orange (1912) 1737 Silliman St., 94134. Tel: 415-585-0159; Fax: 415-585-0159. Email: csjsf@comcast.net. Sisters 3.

Sisters of the Good Shepherd (1932) 1310 Bacon St., 94134. Tel: 415-586-2822; Fax: 415-586-0355. Email: lschillergs@aol.com. Sisters 7.

Sisters of the Holy Family, 331 Anza St., Apt. 307A, 94118. Tel: 415-221-6097. Sisters 2.

Sisters of the Presentation San Francisco (1854 - CA; 1775 - Ireland) 281 Masonic Ave., 94118-4416. Tel: 415-422-5001; Fax: 415-422-5026. Email: sstill@pbvmsf.org. Web: www.presentationsisterssf.org. Sr. Pamela Chiesa, P.B.V.M., M.A., M.B.A., Pres. Sisters in Archdiocese 60; Total in Congregation 98.

Verbum Dei Missionary Fraternity (1963) (Institute of Consecrated Life, Rome, Italy), 3373 19th St., 94110. Tel: 415-282-4979; Fax: 415-282-3005. Email: sfverbumdei@comcast.net. Web: www.fmverbumdei.com/usa. Sr. Julia D. E. Prinz, V.D.M.F., Supr. Prayer and ministry of the Word, working with youth, young adults & adults.

ATHERTON. *Religious of the Sacred Heart Oakwood*, 140 Valparaiso Ave., 94027. Tel: 650-323-8343; Fax: 650-326-2251. Sr. Marie Louise Flick, R.S.C.J., Dir. Infirmary for elderly Religious of the Sacred Heart. Sisters 50.

BURLINGAME. *Sisters of Mercy of the Americas West Midwest Community, Inc.* (As of July 1, 2008 the Sisters of Mercy of the Americas Regional Communities of Auburn, CA; Burlingame, CA; Cedar Rapids IA; Chicago, IL; Detroit, MI & Omaha, NE, merged to create Sisters of Mercy of the Americas West Midwest Community, Inc.), 2300 Adeline Dr., 94010-5599. Tel: 650-340-7410; Fax: 650-347-2550. Email: info@mercywmw.org. Web: www.mercywestmidwest.org. Sisters Norita Cooney, R.S.M., Pres.; Judith Frikker, R.S.M., Sub for Pres.; Sheila Megley, R.S.M., Treas.; Judith Cannon, R.S.M., Sec.; Kathy Thornton, R.S.M., Leadership Team; Michelle Gorman, R.S.M., Leadership Team; Kim Kinsel, Community Oper. Officer; Carol Kelley, Community Fin. Officer; Sandy Goetzinger-Comer, Dir. Communications. Sisters 810; Associates 565.

DALY CITY. *Daughters of Charity of St. Vincent de Paul* (1633) 2000 Sullivan Ave., 94015-2202. Tel: 650-991-6715. Email: docsmc@sbcglobal.net. Sr. William Eileen Dunn, Supr.

Quinhon Missionary Sisters of the Holy Cross (1988 - USA; 1926 - Vietnam) 298 Southgate Ave., 94015. Tel: 650-755-7231. Email: nhakhandaly@yahoo.com; josephinedao3@yahoo.com. Sisters Josephine Dao Vu, Nurse (Presentation Sisters); Maria Anh Nguyen, Student; Catherine Huong Nguyen, Student; Concepta Huong Thuy Nguyen, Student. Sisters 5.

Religious of the Virgin Mary, Our Lady of Mercy Convent, 15 Elmwood Dr., 94015. Tel: 650-992-5769; Fax: 650-755-3457. Email: bigwasfe@yahoo.com. Sisters Fe P. Bigwas, R.V.M.; Virginia Barcelona, R.V.M.; Ma. Auxencia Bitangjol, R.V.M.; Ma Nicolina Estevez, R.V.M.

MENLO PARK. *Corpus Christi Monastery* (1921) 215 Oak Grove Ave., 94025-3272. Tel: 650-322-1801; Fax: 650-322-6816. Email: nunsmenlo@comcast.net. Web: www.nunsmenlo.org. Sr. Mary Assumpta Rufo, O.P., Prioress. Nuns of the Order of Preachers. Cloistered Religious 15; Extern Sisters 1.

PACIFICA. *Missionaries of Charity* (1982) (India), 164 Milagra Dr., 94044. Tel: 650-355-3091. Sisters 8.

Noviciate (1982) 312 29th St., 94131. Tel: 415-647-1889. Sisters 4; Novices 31.

Queen of Peace (1984) 55 Sadowa St., 94112. Tel: 415-586-3449. Sisters 5.

REDWOOD CITY. *Daughters of St. Paul*, 3079 Oak Knoll Dr., 94062. Tel: 650-368-3184; Fax: 650-368-3189. Email: sanfrancisco@paulinemedia.com. Web: www.pauline.org. Sr. Armanda Santos, F.S.P., Supr. Sisters 5.

Santa Chiara Community, 5 Paddington Ct., Belmont, 94002. Tel: 650-593-3010; Fax: 650-593-3350. Email: norberta2@juno.com. Sr. Maureen Sinnott, Liaison. Sisters of St. Francis. Sisters 5.

SAN RAFAEL. *Carmelite Monastery of the Mother of God, Discalced Carmelite Nuns*, 530 Blackstone Dr., 94903. Tel: 415-479-6872; Fax: 415-491-4964. Email: sram@motherofgodcarmel.org. Sr. Anna Marie Vanni, O.C.D., Subprioress. Sisters 8.

Dominican Sisters of San Rafael Generalate & Convent (1850) 1520 Grand Ave., 94901-2236. Tel: 415-453-8303; Fax: 415-453-8367. Email: maureenmcinerney@sanrafaelop.org. Web: sanrafaelop.org. Sr. Maureen McInerney, O.P., Prioress Gen. Total in Community 121; Total in Archdiocese 83.

Dominican Convent, 1540 Grand Ave., 94901-2236. Tel: 415-454-9221. Sisters 20.

Jane d'Aza Convent, 60 Locust Ave., 94901-2237. Tel: 415-453-4784. Sisters 8.

Our Lady of Lourdes Convent, 77 Locust Ave., 94901-2237. Tel: 415-457-3171. Sisters 24.

Our Lady of Mt. Carmel Convent, 34 Buena Vista Ave., Mill Valley, 94941-1232. Tel: 415-389-0328. Sisters 5.

San Domenico Convent, 1500 Butterfield Rd., San Anselmo, 94960-1057. Tel: 415-453-9172. Sisters 7.

St. Margaret Convent, 40 Locust Ave., 94901-2237. Tel: 415-458-2952. Sisters 6.

St. Dominic Convent, 2517 Pine St., 94115-2609. Tel: 415-567-8282; Fax: 415-776-7384. Sisters 7.

St. Rose Convent, 2515 Pine St., 94115-2609. Tel: 415-441-2685. Sisters 6.

[P] CATHOLIC CHARITIES & THE CATHOLIC YOUTH ORGANIZATION

SAN FRANCISCO. *Catholic Charities CYO of the Archdiocese of San Francisco,* Dorothy Cartahena, Contact.

Administrative Office, 180 Howard St., Suite 100, 94105. Tel: 415-972-1200; Fax: 415-972-1201. Email: dcartahena@cccyo.org. Web: cccyo.org. Kimberly Watts, C.P.A., Dir. Finance; Martha Sullivan, C.F.R.E., Dir. Devel.; Tere Brown, Dir., Prog. & Svcs.; Mary Schembri, Dir. Parish & Community Response; Kent Eagleson, Dir. St. Vincent's Svcs. Board of Directors: Most Rev. George H. Niederauer, D.D., Ph.D., Chm.; Mrs. Cecilia Herbert, Pres.; Nanette Miller, Treas.; Carlos Alvarez; Nicholas Andrade; Steve Borden; Katie Cardinal; Gloria Carlos; Mark Cleary; Rev. Thomas A. Daly; Deborah Dasovich; Sr. M. Ellen Egan, R.S.M.; Jeffrey Fenton; Jack Fitzpatrick; Rev. Charles R. Gagan, S.J.; Bernard P. Hagan Sr.; Doug Hickey; John A. Knight; James McCabe; Sharon McCarthy-Allen; Robert P. McGrath; Ann Gray Miller; Steve Molinelli; Robert B. Morris III; Mark Okashima; Kathy Parish-Reese; Tim Rea; D. Paul Regan; William Ring; Rita Semel; Timothy Alan Simon; Maureen O'Brien Sullivan; Rev. Kenneth M. Weare; Jacqueline Woodford.

Behavioral Health Care and Senior Services:

Counseling Services:

SF Behavioral Healthcare Services, 2559 40th Ave., 94116. Tel: 415-564-7882; Fax: 415-731-1270. Email: dross@cccyo.org. Web: www.cccyo.org. Dave Ross, Ph.D., Admin.

Marin Counseling Services, St. Vincent's School for Boys, One St. Vincent Dr., San Rafael, 94903. Tel: 415-507-4244; Fax: 415-491-0532. Email: 1buntain@cccyo.org. Web: www.cccyo.org. Laurie Buntain, M.F.T., Prog. Dir.

San Mateo Behavioral Healthcare Services, 36 37th Ave., San Mateo, 94403. Tel: 650-295-2160; Fax: 650-286-1325. Email: dross@cccyo.org. Web: www.cccyo.org. Dave Ross, Ph.D., Dir.

Senior Services:

OMI Senior Center, 1948 Ocean Ave., 94127. Tel: 415-587-1443; Fax: 415-586-7960. Email: pclement@cccyo.org. Web: www.cccyo.org. Patty Clement, Prog. Dir.

San Carlos Adult Day Support, 787 Walnut St., San Carlos, 94070. Tel: 650-592-9325; Fax: 650-592-2316. Email: nkeegan@cccyo.org. Web: www.cccyo.org. Nancy Keegan, Prog. Dir.

San Francisco Adult Day Support, 50 Broad St., 94112. Tel: 415-452-3500; Fax: 415-452-3505. Email: pclement@cccyo.org. Web: www.cccyo.org. Patty Clement, Prog. Dir.

Children & Family Services:

Adoption Information & Referral

Canal Family Support Program, Pickelweed Community Center, 50 Canal St., San Rafael, 94901. Tel: 415-454-5896; Fax: 415-485-3185. Email: cgarcia@cccyo.org. Web: www.cccyo.org. Carlos Garcia, Prog. Dir.

Children's Village Child Development Center, 250 10th St., 94103. Tel: 415-865-2610; Fax: 415-503-0750. Email: mskuse@cccyo.org. Web: www.cccyo.org. Molly Skuse, Prog. Dir.

Mission Day Care, 180 Fair Oaks St., 94110. Tel: 415-826-6880; Fax: 415-920-2743. Email: lrossi@cccyo.org. Web: www.cccyo.org. Lilliana Rossi, Ph.D., Prog. Dir.

Family Services:

Refugee & Immigrant Services, 180 Howard St., Ste. 100, 94105. Tel: 415-972-1311; Fax: 415-972-1350. Email: cmartinez@cccyo.org. Web: www.cccyo.org. Christopher Martinez, Prog. Dir.

Information and Referral, 180 Howard St., Ste. 100, 94105. Tel: 415-972-1300; Fax: 415-972-1350. Email: aayala@cccyo.org. Web: www.cccyo.org. Ana Ayala, Admin.

Rita da Cascia, 1652 Eddy St., #8, 94115. Tel: 415-202-0941; Fax: 415-202-0937. Email: ehammerle@cccyo.org. Web: www.cccyo.org. Ellen Hammerle, Ph.D., Admin.

St. Joseph's Family Center, 899 Guerrero St., 94110. Tel: 415-550-4478; Fax: 415-550-4481. Email: ccallandrillo@cccyo.org. Web: www.cccyo.org. Chris Callandrillo, Prog. Dir.

Treasure Island Housing, P.O. Box 78037, 94107. Tel: 415-743-0017; Fax: 415-981-3039. Email: ngoncalves@cccyo.org. Web: www.cccyo.org. Nella Goncalves, Prog. Dir.

Youth Residential Services:

St. Vincent's School for Boys, One St. Vincent Dr., San Rafael, 94903. Tel: 415-507-4387; Fax: 415-491-0842. Email: dgallagher@cccyo.org. Web: www.cccyo.org. Dan Gallagher, Prog. Dir.

San Francisco Boys' and Girls' Home, 823 Euclid Ave., 94118. Tel: 415-221-3443; Fax: 415-387-1627. Email: dmayfield@cccyo.org. Web: www.cccyo.org. Denise Mayfield, Admin.

Assisted Housing and Health Services:

Derek Silva Community, 20 Franklin St., 94102. Tel: 415-553-8700; Fax: 415-575-3729. Email: kfauteux@cccyo.org. Web: www.cccyo.org. Kevin Fauteux, Ph.D., M.S.N., Acting Prog. Dir.

Assisted Housing & Health Programs, 180 Howard St., Suite 100, 94105. Tel: 415-972-1333; Fax: 415-972-1339. Email: gsimmons@cccyo.org. Web: www.cccyo.org. George Simmons, Prog. Dir.

Leland House, 141 Leland Ave., 94134. Tel: 415-405-2000; Fax: 415-337-1137. Email: kcunz@cccyo.org. Web: www.cccyo.org. Kevin Cruz, Prog. Dir.

Peter Claver Community, 1340 Golden Gate, 94115. Tel: 415-749-3800; Fax: 415-569-3153. Email: scerreta@cccyo.org. Web: www.cccyo.org/programs/hiv.php. Sally Cerreta, Admin.

Catholic Youth Organization Programs:

CYO Athletics:

CYO Athletics - San Francisco, 180 Howard St., Ste. 100, 94105. Tel: 415-972-1252; Fax: 415-972-1201. Email: cjohnson@cccyo.org. Web: www.cccyo.org. Courtney Johnson-Clendinen, Prog. Dir.

CYO Athletics - Marin, One St. Vincent Dr., San Rafael, 94903. Tel: 415-507-2000; Fax: 415-491-0842. Email: sfarbstein@cccyo.org. Web: www.cccyo.org. Steve Farbstein, Admin.

CYO Outdoor Programs:

CYO Camp/Outdoor Environmental Education, 2136 Bohemian Hwy., Occidental, 95465. Tel: 707-874-0200; Fax: 707-874-0230. Email: jwillford@cccyo.org. Web: www.cyocamp.org. Jim Willford, Exec. Dir.

CYO Transportation Services:

699 Serramonte Blvd., Ste. 210, Daly City, 94015. Tel: 650-757-2110; Fax: 650-758-1425. Email: mrea@cccyo.org. Web: www.cccyo.org. Marty Rea, Prog. Dir.

CYO Retreat Center:

Facility Manager, 2136 Bohemian Hwy., Occidental, 95465. Tel: 707-874-0210; Fax: 707-874-0230. Email: jwillford@cccyo.org. Web: www.cccyo.org. Jim Willford, Exec. Dir.

St. Vincent's Services:

St. Vincent's Foster Family, One St. Vincent Dr., San Rafael, 94903. Tel: 415-507-4387; Fax: 415-491-0842. Email: mchestnut@cccyo.org. Web: www.cccyo.org. Megan Chesnut, Prog. Dir.

Administration, 180 Howard St., 94105. Tel: 415-972-1230; Fax: 415-972-1201. Email: dcartahena@cccyo.org. Web: www.cccyo.org. Dorothy Carthahena, Exec. Asst.

[Q] NEWMAN CENTERS

SAN FRANCISCO. *Catholic Student Association of UCSF* (1967) 1290 Fifth Ave., 94122-2649. Tel: 415-566-5610; Fax: 415-566-5073. Email: stjohnofgod-sf@sbcglobal.net. Web: www.sjog.net.

Newman Center, San Francisco State University St. Thomas More Church, 1300 Junipero Serra Blvd., 94132-2913. Tel: 415-452-9634; Fax: 415-452-9653. Email: stmchurch2002@aol.com. Web: www.STMChurch.com. Rev. Msgr. Labib Kobti; Elvira Garcia, Admin. Office Mgr.

[R] PERSONAL PRELATURES

SAN FRANCISCO. *Prelature of the Holy Cross and Opus Dei* (1982) 765 14th Ave., 94118. Tel: 415-386-0431; Fax: 415-752-7177. Web: www.opusdei.org. Very Rev. John R. Meyer, D.D.S., S.T.D., Vicar for California; Rev. Msgr. James A. Kelly, Vicar Sec.; Revs. Matthew A. Bloomer, Spiritual Dir.; Torlach C. Delargy. Priests 4; Total Staff 45; Total Assisted 150.

Menlough Study Center, 1160 Santa Cruz Ave., Menlo Park, 94025. Tel: 650-327-1675.

[S] MISCELLANEOUS LISTINGS

SAN FRANCISCO. *Alliance of Mission District Catholic Schools (AMDCS)*, One Peter York Way, 94109. Tel: 415-614-5660; Fax: 415-614-5664. Email: dcs@sfarchdiocese.org. Ms. Maureen Huntington, Supt. Catholic Schools.

St. Anthony Foundation (1950) 150 Golden Gate Ave., 94102. Tel: 415-241-2600; Fax: 415-440-7770. Email: info@stanthonysf.org. Web: www.stanthonysf.org. Linda Pasquinucci, Interim Dir.; Sr. Andrea Tierbok, O.S.F., Chap.; Rev. Thomas B. West, O.F.M., Chap. A nonprofit, charitable corporation assisting the homeless and low-income. Priests 1; Staff 145.

Archdiocesan Council of Catholic Women, One Peter Yorke Way, 94109-6602. Tel: 415-614-5500; Fax: 415-353-5555. Mary Anne Bertken, Pres.; Rev. Msgr. Edward P. McTaggart, Moderator (Retired).

The Archdiocese of San Francisco Parish and School Juridic Persons Real Property Support Corporation, 1301 Post St., Ste. 102, 94109. Tel: 415-292-0800; Fax: 415-292-0805.

The Archdiocese of San Francisco Parish, School and Cemetery Juridic Persons Capital Assets Support Corporation, 1301 Post St., Ste. 103, 94109-6667. Tel: 415-292-3600; Fax: 415-292-3603.

St. Benedict Center for Deaf and Hearing Impaired at St. Francis Xavier Church, 1801 Octavia, 94109. Tel: 415-567-9855; 415-567-0438 (TDD); 866-896-0968 (Video Phone); Fax: 415-567-0916. Email: info@sfdeafcatholics.org. Web: www.sfdeafcatholics.org.

Masses for the Deaf & Hard of Hearing., Tel: 415-567-9855 (Video Phone); Fax: 415-567-0916. Email: info@sfdeafcatholics.org. Rev. Paul Zirimenya, Chap.

California Handicapables, Inc. (1965) 1274 30th Ave., 94122. Tel: 415-566-2331. Miss Nadine Calligiuri, Founder; Jack O'Keefe. To give shut-ins and handicapped people of all faiths an opportunity for monthly Mass, lunch and general fellowship. We generally meet the third Saturday of every month at St. Mary's Cathedral, San Francisco. Please call for more information.

Caritas Business Services, 203 Redwood Shores Pkwy., Redwood City, 94065. Tel: 650-551-6601; Fax: 650-551-6532. Email: wahidchoudhury@dochs.org. Web: www.dochs.org. Wahid Choudhury, Controller.

Catholic Kolping Society (1887) 440 Taraval St., 94116. Tel: 415-661-8305. Hubert Brinkmann, Pres.; Catherine Vennemeyer, Treas.

Catholic Scouting, Tel: 415-614-5652.

Catholics for Truth & Justice (1991) P.O. Box 26756, 94126-0756. Tel: 415-982-0920; Fax: 415-982-0921. Rev. Msgr. Harry G. Schlitt.

Congregation of the Holy Family of Blessed Mariam Thresia, India, 3112 Turk Blvd., 94118. Tel: 415-666-3237. Email: chfsfo@yahoo.com. Web: www.blessedmariamthresia.org.

Equestrian Order of the Holy Sepulchre of Jerusalem - Northwest Lieutenancy, 26 Lagoon Vista Rd., Tiburon, 94920. Tel: 415-789-1049; Fax: 415-789-1049. Mary Ellen Hoffman, Sec.

Father Raphael Piperni Charitable Trust, 1100 Franklin St., 94109. Tel: 415-441-7144; Fax: 415-441-7155. Email: suosec@aol.com. (The FRPC (R) Trust)

Italian Catholic Federation, St. Brendan Church, 29 Rockaway, 94127. Tel: 415-681-4225; Fax: 415-681-3976. Email: navigator@stbrendanparish.org. Revs. Michael F. Quinn, San Francisco District Chapter Chap.; Francis K. Murray, Chap. Archdiocese (Retired).

Legion of Mary (1921) 1425 Bay Rd., East Palo Alto, 94303. Tel: 650-322-2152; Fax: 650-322-7319. Email: sfofassisi@sbcglobal.net. Rev. Lawrence C. Goode, Spiritual Dir., San Francisco Senatus.

St. Mary's Medical Center Foundation, 450 Stanyan St., 94117-1079. Tel: 415-750-4828; Fax: 415-668-4531.

**Mercy Housing California*, 1360 Mission St., Suite 300, 94103. Tel: 415-355-7100; Fax: 415-355-7101. Email: VAgostino@mercyhousing.org. Web: www.mercyhousing.org. Housing development for low-income families, elderly, and singles.

Mercy Family Plaza, c/o Mercy Housing California, 1360 Mission St., Suite 300, 94103. Tel: 415-355-7100; Fax: 415-355-7101. Thirty-six affordable units for families.

M.H.R. AIDS Support Group, 100 Diamond St., 94114-2414. Tel: 415-863-1581; Fax: 415-552-8786. Email: mhr@mhr-asg.com. Web: www.mhr-asg.com.

**The Ordinary Mutual, RRG*, P.O. Box 191867, 94119-4002. Tel: 415-536-8440; Fax: 415-536-4002. Email: dennis_o'hara@ajg.com. Dennis O'Hara, Underwriting Mgr.; Randolph E. Steiner, Pres. A Risk Retention Group Corporation, incorporated in Vermont, serving the Dioceses of Tucson, Fresno, Monterey, Oakland, Orange, Sacramento, Santa Rosa, and Stockton, and the Archdioceses of Los Angeles and San Francisco.

St. Paul High School Alumnae Assoc., 221 Valley St., 94131. Tel: 415-648-7538. Email: sphsalumnae@yahoo.com. Sr. Maureen O'Brien, B.V.M., Mod. Not-for-profit charitable outreach.

Pauline Books & Media, 2640 Broadway, Redwood City, 94063. Tel: 650-369-4230; Fax: 650-369-4390. Email: sanfrancisco@paulinemedia.com. Web:

www.pauline.org. Sr. Armanda Santos, F.S.P., Supr. Daughters of St. Paul. Sisters 4.

Philip Rinaldi Charitable Trust, 1100 Franklin St., 94109. Tel: 415-441-7144; Fax: 415-441-7155. Email: suosec@aol.com. For the care of needy youth and for the formation needs of Salesians of St. John Bosco.

The Ricci Institute for Chinese-Western Cultural History at the Center for the Pacific Rim, University of San Francisco, 2130 Fulton St., 94117-1080. Tel: 415-422-6401; Fax: 415-422-2291. Email: ricci@usfca.edu. Web: www.usfca.edu/ricci. Xiaoxin Wu, Ed.D., Dir.; Mark Mir, Research Fellow & Chinese Library Cataloguer; May Lee, Prog. Asst.

St. Rose Corporation, 2501 Pine St., 94115. Tel: 415-440-9568; Fax: 415-440-9568. Email: lasop@sanrafaelop.org.

Officers of the Board: Sr. Lois Silva, O.P., Pres.; Thomas Bertelsen Jr., CFO & Sec.; Sr. Catherine Murray, O.P., Dir.; Jack R. Bertges, Dir.; Sr. Anne Bertain, O.P., Dir.; Rosario Bacon Billingsley, Dir.; Jeffrey K. Mori, Dir.; Cathy Murphy, Dir.; Sr. Lorna Walsh, S.H.J.M., Dir.

Shrine of St. Jude Thaddeus P.O. Box 15368, 94115-0368. Tel: 415-931-5919; Fax: 415-593-0350. Email: info@stjude-shrine.org. Web: www.stjude-shrine.org. Rev. Martin Walsh, O.P., Dir.; Stedman Matthew, Chief Admin. Officer.

Sisters of the Presentation Community Support Trust Fund, 2340 Turk Blvd., 94118. Tel: 415-422-5020. Email: sstill@pbvmsf.org. Mailing Address: 2340 Turk Blvd., 94118. Tel: 415-422-5020. Sisters Patricia Marie Mulpeters, P.B.V.M., Trustee; Patricia Boss, O.P., Trustee; Patricia Anne Cloherty, P.B.V.M., Trustee; Concepcion V. Del Rosario, Trustee; Sr. Giovanna Campanella, P.B.V.M., Trustee; Nanette Miller, Trustee; Sr. Stephanie Still, P.B.V.M., Chm. Trust used for the religious and charitable needs of the Sisters of the Presentation of the Blessed Virgin Mary.

BURLINGAME. *Music at Kohl Mansion, Inc.*, 2750 Adeline Dr., 94010. Tel: 650-762-1130; Fax: 650-343-8464. Email: director@musicatkohl.org. Web: www.musicatkohl.org. To develop and promote public knowledge and appreciation of musical arts by sponsoring chamber music concerts and other public performances of music, as well as music education activities.

DALY CITY. *Association of Catholic Student Councils*, 86 Cityview Dr., 94014-3400. Tel: 415-584-9877; Fax: 415-584-9877. Email: tacsc@tacsc.org. Web: www.tacsc.org. Marilyn Thickett, Exec. Dir.

Vincentian Service Corps West, 25 San Fernando Way, Suite B, 94015-2065. Tel: 650-991-6465; Fax: 650-991-3905. Email: vscwest@dochs.org. Web: www.vscorps.org. Sisters Camille Cuadra, D.C., Exec. Dir.; Eileen Kenny, D.C., Chairperson; James Comstock, M.A., Sec. & Treas.

REDWOOD CITY. *The Catholic Worker Community* (1975) 545 Cassia St., 94063. Tel: 650-366-4415. Lawrence P. Purcell, Dir. A foster home for teenagers.

**St. Francis Center of Redwood City*, 151 Buckingham Ave., 94063. Tel: 650-365-7829; Fax: 650-365-7829. Email: SChristina@aol.com. Web: www.stfrancisrwc.org. Sr. Christina Heltsley, O.P., Exec. Dir.

SAN RAFAEL. **Center Interfaith Housing*, 164 N. San Pedro Rd., 94903. Tel: 415-492-9340; Fax: 415-492-1340.

Mission Holding Corporation (1995) 1520 Grand Ave., 94901-2236. Tel: 415-453-8303; Fax: 415-453-8367. Email: maureenmcinerney@sanrafaelop.org. Web: sanrafaelop.org.

Governing Board: Sisters Maureen McInerney, O.P.; Margaret Diener, O.P.; Patricia Boss, O.P.; Susan Allbritton, O.P.; Patricia Farrell, O.P.

The Sisters of Nazareth of San Rafael Real Estate Holdings, Inc., 245 Nova Albion Way, 94903. Tel: 415-479-8282; Fax: 415-479-6413.

Sisters of the Third Order of St. Dominic Support Charitable Trust Fund, 1520 Grand Ave., 94901-2236. Tel: 415-453-8303; Fax: 415-453-8367. Email: maureenmcinerney@sanrafaelop.org. Web: sanrafaelop.org. Sisters Patricia Boss, O.P., Staff; Maureen McInerney, O.P., Trustee; Lois Silva, O.P., Trustee; Cathryn deBack, O.P.; Mr. Thomas Bertelsen, Staff; John R. Burgis, Trustee; Marcia A. Fitzgerald, Trustee; Eugene F. Lynch, Trustee; Sr. Imelda Maurer, C.D.P., Trustee; Patricia L. Weir, Trustee.

Sisters of the Third Order of St. Dominic, Congregation of the Most Holy Name, Support Charitable Trust Fund, Trust used for the religious and charitable needs of the Sisters of the Third Order of St. Dominic, Congregation of the Most Holy Name.

SOUTH SAN FRANCISCO. *The Contemplatives of Saint Joseph*, 377 Willow Ave., 94080-1446. Tel: 650-995-3660; Fax: 650-871-1685. A private preparatory religious association of the Archdiocese of San Francisco.

TIBURON. *Charismatic Movement* (1982) 761 Hilary Dr., 94920. Tel: 415-435-1122; Fax: 415-435-1862. Web: sfspirit.com. Revs. James T. Tarantino, Liason; Jose M. Corral, Liaison to Spanish Speaking; Ernie von Emster, Asst. Liaison, Anglo Charismatics.

[T] CLOSED INSTITUTIONS

SAN FRANCISCO. *All Hallows Church* For sacramental records please contact Our Lady of Lourdes, 1715 Oakdale Ave., San Francisco 94124, Tel: 415-285-3377; Fax: 415-285-2191.

St. Brigid Church For sacramental records please contact St. Vincent de Paul, 2320 Green St., San Francisco 94123, Tel: 415-992-1010; Fax: 415-922-7203.

St. Edward the Confessor Church For sacramental records please contact St. Dominic, 2390 Bush St., San Francisco, 94115, Tel: 415-567-7854; Fax: 415-567-1608.

St. Francis of Assisi Church For sacramental records please contact SS. Peter and Paul, 666 Filbert St., San Francisco, 94133, Tel: 415-421-0809; Fax: 415-421-0217.

Holy Cross Korean Church For sacramental records please contact Chancery Office, One Peter Yorke Way, San Francisco, 94109, Tel: 415-614-5500; Fax: 415-614-5555.

Immaculate Conception Church For sacramental records please contact St. Anthony of Padua, 3215 Cesar Chavez St., San Francisco, 94110, Tel: 415-647-2704; Fax: 415-647-7282.

St. Joseph Church For sacramental records please contact St. Patrick, 756 Mission St., San Francisco, 94103, Tel: 415-421-0547; 512-9730.

Our Lady of Guadalupe Church For sacramental records please contact SS. Peter and Paul, 666 Filbert St., San Francisco, 94133, Tel: 415-421-0809; Fax: 415-421-0217.

Sacred Heart Church For sacramental records please contact the Chancery Office, One Peter Yorke Way, San Francisco, 94109.

SAN RAFAEL. *Blessed Sacrament Church* For sacramental records please contact St. Isabella, One Trinity Way, San Rafael, 94901, Tel: 415-479-1560; Fax: 415-479-8303.

St. Sylvester Church For sacramental records please contact St. Raphael, 1104 Fifth Ave., San Rafael, 94901, Tel: 415-453-2314; Fax: 415-453-5402.

WOODSIDE. *St. Marcella Mission* , For sacramental records please contact St. Denis, 2250 Avy Ave., Menlo Park, 94025, Tel: 650-854-5976; Fax: 650-854-3754.

RELIGIOUS INSTITUTES OF MEN REPRESENTED IN THE ARCHDIOCESE

For further details refer to the corresponding bracketed number in the Religious Institutes of Men or Women section.

[]—*Apostolic Life Community of Priests* Moshe, Tanzania

[0200]—*Benedictine Monks* (Hungary)—O.S.B.

[0330]—*Brothers of the Christian Schools* (Prov. of San Francisco)—F.S.C.

[0470]—*The Capuchin Franciscans* (Irish Prov.)—O.F.M.Cap.

[0310]—*Congregation of Christian Brothers*—C.F.C.

[0480]—*Conventual Franciscans*—O.F.M.Conv

[0520]—*Franciscan Friars* (Santa Barbara Prov.)—O.F.M.

[0650]—*Holy Ghost Fathers*—C.S.Sp.

[0690]—*Jesuit Fathers and Brothers* (California Prov.)—S.J.

[0780]—*Marist Fathers* (American Prov.)—S.M.

[]—*Marist Fathers & Brothers* (Atlanta Prov.)—S.M.

[0800]—*Maryknoll*—M.M.

[]—*Order of Carmelites*—O.Carm.

[0430]—*Order of Preachers (Dominicans)* (Western Prov.)—O.P.

[0897]—*Paris Foreign Mission Society*—M.E.P.

[1030]—*Paulist Fathers*—C.S.P.

[1190]—*Salesian Don Bosco*—S.D.B.

[1260]—*Society of Christ* (Chicago Prov.)—S.Chr.

[0760]—*Society of Mary (Marianists)* (U.S. Prov.)—S.M.

[]—*Society of St. Paul* (Philippine-Macau Prov.)

[1290]—*Society of the Priests of Saint Sulpice* (American Prov.)—S.S.P.

[]—*Verbum Dei Missionary Fraternity*—V.D.M.F.

RELIGIOUS INSTITUTES OF WOMEN REPRESENTED IN THE ARCHDIOCESE

[]—*Apostolic Society, Society of the Divine Will*—D.D.W.

[]—*Congregation of Divine Providence*—C.D.P.

[1310]—*Congregation of the Franciscan Sisters of Little Falls, MN*

[]—*Congregation of the Holy Family of Blessed Mariam Thresia, India*

[3242]—*Congregation of the Sisters of Nazareth*—C.S.N.

[1920]—*Congregation of the Sisters of the Holy Cross* (Notre Dame, IN)—C.S.C.

[1940]—*Congregation of the Sisters of the Holy Faith*—C.H.F.

[1710]—*Congregation of the Third Order of St. Francis of Mary Immaculate, Joliet, IL*—O.S.F.

[0730]—*Daughters of Charity of Canossa*—F.D.C.C.

[0760]—*Daughters of Charity of St. Vincent de Paul* (Prov. of the West)—D.C.

[0880]—*Daughters of Mary and Joseph*—D.M.J

[0850]—*Daughters of Mary Help of Christians*—F.M.A.

[0420]—*Discalced Carmelite Nuns*—O.C.D.

[1050]—*Dominican Contemplative Nuns*—O.P.

[1070-03]—*Dominican Sisters*—O.P.

[1070-13]—*Dominican Sisters*—O.P.

[1070-19]—*Dominican Sisters of Houston*—O.S.F.

[1070-04]—*Dominican Sisters of San Rafael*—O.P.

[]—*Dominican Sisters of the Philippines*

[]—*Franciscan Missionaries of Mary*—F.M.M.

[]—*Franciscan Missionaries, Our Lady of Peace*—M.F.P.

[1310]—*Franciscan Sisters of Little Falls, Minnesota*—O.S.F.

[]—*Las Hermanas Misioneras*—M.S.C.Gpe.

[2340]—*Little Sisters of the Poor*—L.S.P.

[2390]—*Lovers of the Holy Cross Sisters*—L.H.C.

[2420]—*Marist Missionary Sisters, Society of Mary*—S.M.S.M.

[2470]—*Maryknoll Sisters of St. Dominic*—M.M.

[2720]—*Mission Helpers of the Sacred Heart*—M.H.S.H.

[2710]—*Missionary Sisters of Charity*—M.C.

[]—*Missionary Sisters of the Sacred Side*—M.C.S.

[3190]—*Nuns of the Perpetual Adoration of the Blessed Sacrament*—A.P.

[]—*Oblates Sisters of Jesus the Priest*—O.S.J.

[]—*Order of Preachers (Dominican Nuns)*—O.P.

[0950]—*Pious Society Daughters of St. Paul*—F.S.P.

[]—*Religious of the Sacred Heart of Jesus*—R.S.C.J.

[3465]—*Religious of the Sacred Heart of Mary*—R.S.H.M.

[]—*Religious of the Virgin Mary*—R.V.M.

[0440]—*Sisters of Charity of Cincinnati, Ohio*—S.C.

[0430]—*Sisters of Charity of the Blessed Virgin Mary*—B.V.M.

[2575]—*Sisters of Mercy of the Americas* West Midwest Community. (Omaha, NE)—R.S.M.

[2580]—*Sisters of Mercy of the United States of America*—R.S.M.

[3000]—*Sisters of Notre Dame de Namur* (Prov. of CA)—S.N.D.deN.

[3360]—*Sisters of Providence of Saint Mary-of-the-Woods, Indiana*—S.P.

[4080]—*Sisters of Social Service of Los Angeles, Inc.*—S.S.S.

[]—*Sisters of St. Dominic of Mission San Jose*—O.P.

[1570]—*Sisters of St. Francis of Holy Family*—O.S.F.

[1630]—*Sisters of St. Francis of Penance and Christian Charity*—O.S.F.

[]—*Sisters of St. Joseph* Nazareth, MI

[3840]—*Sisters of St. Joseph of Carondelet* (Los Angeles Prov.)—C.S.J.

[3930-03]—*Sisters of St. Joseph of Orange*—C.S.J.O.

[3890]—*Sisters of St. Joseph of Peace*—C.S.J.P.

[1830]—*The Sisters of the Good Shepherd*—R.G.S.

[1960]—*Sisters of the Holy Family* (San Francisco, CA)—S.H.F.

[1990]—*Sisters of the Holy Names of Jesus and Mary* (Provs. of CA; Oregon; Washington)—S.N.J.M.

[2130]—*Sisters of the Immaculate Conception* (Prov. of Madrid)—R.C.M.

[3260]—*Sisters of the Precious Blood (Dayton, Ohio)*—C.PP.S.

[3320]—*Sisters of the Presentation of the B.V.M.*—P.B.V.M.

[1720]—*Sisters of the Third Order Regular of St. Francis of the Congregation of Our Lady of Lourdes*—O.S.F.

[1890]—*Society of Helpers*—H.H.S.

[3330]—*Union Sisters of the Presentation of the Blessed Virgin Mary*—P.B.V.M.

[4110]—*Ursuline Nuns (Roman Union)*—O.S.U.

[]—*Ursuline Sisters of the Immaculate Conception* (Louisville, KY)—O.S.U.

[]—*Verbum Dei Missionary Fraternity*

ARCHDIOCESAN CEMETERIES AND MAUSOLEUMS

SAN FRANCISCO. *Holy Cross Cemetery and Mausoleum*, P.O. Box 1577, Colma, 94014. Tel: 650-756-2060; Fax: 650-757-0752. Email: keatkinson@holycrosscemeteries.com.

MENLO PARK. *Holy Cross*, P.O. Box 1577, Colma, 94014. Tel: 650-323-6375; Fax: 650-757-0752. Email: moreinfo@holycrosscemeteries.com.

SAN RAFAEL. *Mount Olivet*, P.O. Box 4368, 94903. Email: moreinfo@holycrosscemeteries.com.

NECROLOGY

† Armstrong, Rev. Msgr. Peter G., (Retired)—Died Nov. 17, 2009

† Dreier, Rev. Msgr. Bruce A., San Bruno, CA St. Robert—Died Aug. 10, 2009

† Heaney, Rev. Msgr. John P., (Retired)—Died Jan. 29, 2010

† Cleary, Edward M., (Retired)—Died July 7, 2009

† Duggan, William E., (Retired)—Died March 19, 2009

† Gomez, Rene J., (Retired)—Died June 7, 2009

† Healy, Joseph, San Francisco, CA Most Holy Redeemer—Died Dec. 4, 2009

† Keane, Patrick J., (Retired)—Died Jan. 20, 2009

† Robello, Louis J., (Retired)—Died Nov. 27, 2009

† Smith, Raymond K., (Retired)—Died March 30, 2009

† Wu, Stan, (Retired)—Died Nov. 5, 2009

An asterisk (*) denotes an organization that has established tax-exempt status directly with the IRS and is not covered by the USCCB Group Ruling.

Diocese of San Jose in California

(Dioecesis Sancti Josephi in California)

Most Reverend

PATRICK J. McGRATH, D.D., J.C.D.

Bishop of San Jose; ordained June 7, 1970; appointed Auxiliary Bishop of San Francisco and Titular Bishop of Allegheny December 6, 1988; Episcopal ordination January 25, 1989; appointed Coadjutor Bishop of San Jose June 29, 1998; succeeded to See November 27, 1999.

Most Reverend

PIERRE DuMAINE, D.D., Ph.D.

Bishop Emeritus of San Jose; ordained June 15, 1957; appointed Auxiliary Bishop of San Francisco and Titular Bishop of Sarda April 28, 1978; Episcopal ordination June 29, 1978; appointed Bishop of San Jose January 27, 1981; installed as Bishop of San Jose March 18, 1981; retired November 27, 1999. *Chancery Office: Diocese of San Jose, 1150 N. First St., Ste. 100, San Jose, CA 95112.*

Diocese of San Jose: 1150 N. First St., Ste. 100, San Jose, CA 95112. Tel: 408-983-0100; Fax: 408-983-0295.

Web: www.dsj.org

Email: chancellor@dsj.org

Established January 27, 1981.

Square Miles 1,300.

The Diocese of San Jose comprises the County of Santa Clara in the State of California.

Patrons of the Diocese of San Jose: St. Joseph, Husband of Mary, March 19; St. Clare of Assisi, August 11.

Legal Title: The Roman Catholic Bishop of San Jose, a Corporation Sole.
For legal titles of parishes and diocesan institutions, consult the Chancery Office.

STATISTICAL OVERVIEW

Personnel	
Bishop	1
Retired Bishops	1
Priests: Diocesan Active in Diocese	81
Priests: Diocesan Active Outside Diocese	7
Priests: Diocesan in Foreign Missions	1
Priests: Retired, Sick or Absent	50
Number of Diocesan Priests	139
Religious Priests in Diocese	208
Total Priests in Diocese	347
Extern Priests in Diocese	21
Ordinations:	
Diocesan Priests	7
Transitional Deacons	3
Permanent Deacons in Diocese	20
Total Brothers	64
Total Sisters	334
Parishes	
Parishes	49
With Resident Pastor:	
Resident Diocesan Priests	42
Resident Religious Priests	6
Without Resident Pastor:	
Administered by Priests	1
Missions	2
Pastoral Centers	4
Professional Ministry Personnel:	
Sisters	27
Lay Ministers	90
Welfare	
Catholic Hospitals	2
Total Assisted	220,000
Health Care Centers	1
Total Assisted	70
Homes for the Aged	1
Total Assisted	141
Day Care Centers	1
Total Assisted	100
Special Centers for Social Services	1
Total Assisted	50,000
Educational	
Diocesan Students in Other Seminaries	17
Total Seminarians	17
Colleges and Universities	1
Total Students	8,490
High Schools, Diocesan and Parish	2
Total Students	1,932
High Schools, Private	4
Total Students	4,712
Elementary Schools, Diocesan and Parish	28
Total Students	9,343
Elementary Schools, Private	2
Total Students	352
Catechesis/Religious Education:	
High School Students	5,500
Elementary Students	12,862
Total Students under Catholic Instruction	43,208
Teachers in the Diocese:	
Priests	6
Brothers	3
Sisters	22
Lay Teachers	1,056
Vital Statistics	
Receptions into the Church:	
Infant Baptism Totals	8,351
Minor Baptism Totals	333
Adult Baptism Totals	305
Received into Full Communion	499
First Communions	5,582
Confirmations	3,203
Marriages:	
Catholic	811
Interfaith	160
Total Marriages	971
Deaths	1,707
Total Catholic Population	575,000
Total Population	1,748,976

Former Bishop—Most Rev. Pierre DuMaine, D.D., Ph.D. (Retired), ord. June 15, 1957; appt. Auxiliary Bishop of San Francisco and Titular Bishop of Sarda, April 28, 1978; Episcopal ordination June 29, 1978; appt. Bishop of San Jose Jan. 27, 1981; installed as Bishop of San Jose March 18, 1981; retired Nov. 27, 1999.

Diocese of San Jose—1150 N. First St., Ste. 100, San Jose, 95112. Tel: 408-983-0100; Fax: 408-983-0295. Web: www.dsj.org.

Vicar General and Moderator of the Curia—Rev. Msgr. Francis V. Cilia, V.G. Tel: 408-983-0154; Fax: 408-983-0242.

Vicar General, Office for Special Projects—Very Rev. Brendan McGuire, V.G. Tel: 408-983-0198; Fax: 408-983-0121.

Lay Retirement Board—Rev. Msgr. Francis V. Cilia, V.G.; Joseph Bauer; Linda Bearie; Sarah Boskovich; Martin Chargin; Steve Duffy; Joe Guerra; Mary Lyons; Rosalie Marty; Robert Serventi; Charles Tully.

Chancellor—Linda Bearie. Tel: 408-983-0160; Fax: 408-983-0203.

Vicar for Clergy—Rev. Wilfredo S. Manrique, J.C.L. Tel: 408-983-0253; Fax: 408-983-0257.

Judicial Vicar—Rev. Andres C. Ligot, J.C.D.

Delegate to Religious—Sr. Marie Gertrude Roldan, C.S.J., J.C.L. Tel: 408-983-0216; Fax: 408-983-0181.

Director, Office of Stewardship & Development—Bill Matthews. Tel: 408-983-0245; Fax: 408-983-0290.

Diocesan Leadership Team—Most Rev. Patrick Joseph McGrath, D.D., J.C.D.; Rev. Msgr. Francis V. Cilia, V.G.; Very Rev. Brendan McGuire, V.G.; Linda Bearie; Robert Serventi.

College of Consultors—Rev. Msgrs. Francis V. Cilia, V.G.; J. Patrick Browne; Revs. Mark Arnzen; Thuc Si Ho; Very Rev. Brendan McGuire, V.G.; Revs. Wilfredo S. Manrique, J.C.L.; Rick Rodoni; Luis Vargas.

Council of Priests—Most Rev. Patrick Joseph McGrath, D.D., J.C.D.; Revs. Mark Arnzen, Chm.; Saju Joseph, Vice Chm. & Sec.; Rev. Msgr. Francis V. Cilia, V.G.; Revs. Ritche Bueza; Michael Carson; Wilfredo S. Manrique, J.C.L.; Very Rev. Brendan McGuire, V.G.; Revs. John Poncini; Roberto Adrian Rojas; Luis Vargas.

Council of Religious—Sisters Marie Gertrude Roldan, C.S.J., J.C.L., Chm.; Divina Caabay, A.R.; Ana Maria de Jesus Carrio, S.S.V.M.; Fran Ciluaga, D.C.; Rev. Kevin L. Dilworth, S.J.; Sr. Maria Griego, S.J.; Bro. James Siwicki, S.J.

Deans—Revs. Lawrence J. Percell, Deanery 2; Ritche Bueza, Deanery 3; Luis Vargas, Deanery 4; Hao Dinh, Deanery 5; Francisco Rios, Deanery 6; Christopher Bennett, Deanery 7.

Ecumenical and Interreligious Affairs—Rev. Jose Antonio Rubio, S.T.D., Dir. & Delegate to Eastern Rite Churches.

Chinese Catholic Community—Revs. Carlos Alberto Olivera, Chap.; Peter Kin Chung Sui, S.J., Part-time Chap.

Catholic Charities— Catholic Charities of Santa Clara County Gregory R. Kepferle, CEO.

Propagation of the Faith-Holy Childhood Association-Catholic Relief Service—Linda Batton, Dir. Tel: 408-983-0158.

Roman Catholic Welfare Corporation—Most Rev. Patrick Joseph McGrath, D.D., J.C.D., Pres.; Rev. Msgr. Francis V. Cilia, V.G., Vice Pres.;

LINDA BEARIE, Sec.; ROBERT SERVENTI, Treas.; KATHERINE ALMAZOL.

Roman Catholic Seminary Corporation—Most Rev. PATRICK JOSEPH MCGRATH, D.D., J.C.D., Pres.; Rev. Msgr. FRANCIS V. CILIA, V.G., Vice Pres.; LINDA BEARIE, Sec.; Rev. WILFREDO S. MANRIQUE, J.C.L.; ROBERT SERVENTI.

"The Valley Catholic" (Diocesan Newspaper)—ROBERTA WARD, Editor; MICHAEL HAWKINS, Business Mgr., Diocese of San Jose, 1150 N. First St., Ste. 100, San Jose, 95112. Tel: 408-983-0260.

Diocesan Tribunal—Diocese of San Jose, 1150 N. First St., Ste. 100, San Jose, 95112. Tel: 408-983-0219.

Judicial Vicar—Rev. ANDRES C. LIGOT, J.C.D.

Adjutant Judicial Vicar—Rev. ENGELBERTO GAMMAD, J.C.D.

Judges—Revs. ENGELBERTO GAMMAD, J.C.D.; WILFREDO S. MANRIQUE, J.C.L.; Sr. MARIE GERTRUDE ROLDAN, C.S.J., J.C.L.

Defender of the Bond—Rev. ROBERT E. HAYES, J.C.L.

Case Instructor—Sr. MICHELE MANGAN, O.S.F. Tel: 408-983-0224.

Administrative Assistant and Notary—Sr. SOFIA BERRONES, M.C.D.P. Tel: 408-983-0219.

Finance Office—ROBERT SERVENTI, CFO; JOHN HOFFMAN, Controller; IAN ABELL, Dir. Facilities; LUPE MONCIVAIS WARREN, Risk Mgr.; RON ROSS, Facilities Inspector & Coord.; TERESA CONVILLE, Compliance Officer.

Finance Council—MICHAEL HOPE, Chm.; MICHAEL BLACH; GEORGE DELUCCHI; STEVE DUFFY; DIANE S. GIANNINI; TROY JONES; VALERIE NICOLETTI; EUGENE TOOMEY; DONALD WAITE.

Building Committee—Rev. Msgr. FRANCIS V. CILIA, V.G.; Rev. CHRISTOPHER BRANSFIELD; IAN ABELL; PAMELA ANDERSON-BRULE; DAN BROWN; JAMES E. KOEPF; MARK LAUBACH; ROSANNA LERMA; PATRICK PFEIFFER; ROBERT SERVENTI; RICH SIMPSON.

Stewardship & Development Office—BILL MATTHEWS, Dir. Tel: 408-983-0244; Fax: 408-983-0290.

Department of Cemeteries—Mr. WILLIAM SOUSAE, Dir. Tel: 650-428-3730.

Office of the Vicar for Clergy—Rev. WILFREDO S. MANRIQUE, J.C.L., Episcopal Vicar for Clergy. Tel: 408-983-0253.

Associate for Deacon Life—Deacon DONALD SIFFERMAN.

Diocesan Clergy Personnel Board—Most Rev. PATRICK JOSEPH MCGRATH, D.D., J.C.D., Ex Officio; Revs. WILFREDO S. MANRIQUE, J.C.L., Ex Officio & Chm.; RITCHE BUEZA; ANDRES C. LIGOT, J.C.D.; Rev. Msgr. JOSEPH J. MILANI (Retired); Revs. ROBERT MORAN; JOHN PONCINI; LINDA BEARIE; DOROTHY CARLSON.

Ongoing Formation of Clergy—Revs. MARK ARNZEN; ROBERT E. HAYES, J.C.L.; RICHARD HILLIARD; PETER LOI HUYNH; G. ROBERT LEGER; WILFREDO S. MANRIQUE, J.C.L.; DAVID MERCER; JON PEDIGO; JOHN PONCINI; DANIEL C. URCIA, Ed.D.; Deacon RONALD HANSEN.

Priests' Retirement Board—Rev. Msgrs. J. PATRICK BROWNE, Chm.; FRANCIS V. CILIA, V.G., Ex Officio; ROBERT SERVENTI, Ex Officio; Revs. WILFREDO S. MANRIQUE, J.C.L., Ex Officio; MICHAEL CARSON; STEVEN P. BROWN; Rev. Msgr. JOSEPH J. MILANI (Retired); Rev. MATTHEW D. STANLEY; BRIAN BLACH; PHILIP CROY; RONALD PELZEL.

Vocation Office—Rev. JOHN PONCINI, Dir. Tel: 408-983-0255.

Deacon Formation—Rev. JOSEPH BENEDICT, S.T.D., Dir. Tel: 408-983-0256.

Department of the Chancellor—LINDA BEARIE, Chancellor. Tel: 408-983-0160.

Diocesan Archives and Records Management—BAYNE BENTLEY, 396 Martin Ave., Santa Clara, 95050. Tel: 408-970-9474.

Personnel Office—LINDA BEARIE, Dir.; PATRICIA WEIS, Assoc. for Personnel. Tel: 408-983-0149.

Education Department—KATHERINE ALMAZOL, Supt. of Schools; NANCY DOYLE, Asst. Supt. of Schools; CHARLENE LEMANN, Curriculum Consultant.

Office for Parish Services—Tel: 408-983-0125.

Director for Catechetics—WENDY SCHERBART. Tel: 408-983-0138.

Director for Hispanic Apostolate—LUPITA VITAL. Tel: 408-983-0133.

Director for Hispanic Youth and Young Adults—VACANT. Tel: 408-983-0134.

Director for Youth Ministry—JOHN RINALDO. Tel: 408-983-0135.

Director for Young Adult Ministry—ROBERT MALLON. Tel: 408-983-0123.

Missions Office—LINDA BATTON, Dir. Tel: 408-983-0158.

Director of Liturgy—DIANA MACALINTAL. Tel: 408-983-0136.

Director of Social Ministries—LINDA BATTON. Tel: 408-983-0158.

Detention Ministry—VACANT. Tel: 408-378-2464.

Human Concerns Commission—LINDA BATTON, Liaison. Tel: 408-983-0158.

Liturgical Commission—DIANA MACALINTAL, Liaison. Tel: 408-983-0136.

Pastoral Resource Committee for Ministry to Gay and Lesbian Catholics—Rev. G. ROBERT LEGER. Tel: 408-245-5554.

Respect Life Program—LINDA BATTON, Liaison. Tel: 408-983-0158.

Office for Evangelization—LINDA BATTON, Dir. Tel: 408-983-0158.

Institute for Leadership in Ministry—ANNE GRYCZ, Dir. Tel: 408-983-0111; VACANT, Asst. Dir. Tel: 408-983-0112.

Office for the Protection of Children and Vulnerable Adults—Deacon BERNARD V. NOJADERA, M.S.W., M.A. Tel: 408-983-0113; 408-983-0141 (Emergency Line); Fax: 408-983-0147.

Victim Assistance Coordinator—JOHN DUDLEY. Tel: 408-983-0141 (Emergency Line); Fax: 408-983-0147.

CLERGY, PARISHES, MISSIONS AND PAROCHIAL SCHOOLS

CITY OF SAN JOSE

1—CATHEDRAL BASILICA OF ST. JOSEPH (1849), (Hispanic—Latino), (Mexican National Church) Rev. Msgr. J. Patrick Browne; Rev. Francisco Miramontes. In Res., Rev. John Poncini.
Res. & Church: 80 S. Market St., 95113. Tel: 408-283-8100; Fax: 408-283-8110.
Catechesis/Religious Program—Susan Olsen, D.R.E. Students 269.

2—ST. ANTHONY (1982) Rev. Lawrence Hendel; Joann Maier, Pastoral Assoc.
Mailing Address: 20101 McKean Rd., 95120. Tel: 408-997-4800.
Old Church: 21800 Bertram Rd., 95120.
Catechesis/Religious Program—Tel: 408-997-4808; Fax: 408-997-4801. Students 145.

3—ST. BROTHER ALBERT CHMIELOWSKI POLISH CATHOLIC PASTORAL MISSION (1986), (Polish), Rev. Andrzej Salapata, S.Ch. (Poland); Deacon Andrzej Sobczyk. In Res., Rev. Edward Mroczynski, S.Ch.
Res.: 10250 Clayton Rd., 95127-4336. Tel: 408-251-8490; Fax: 408-251-8960.
Catechesis/Religious Program—Students 60.

4—CHRIST THE KING (1997) Revs. Jeronimo Gutierrez; Paul Duong.
Res.: 75 Cyclamen St., 95111.
Church: 5284 Monterey Rd., 95111. Tel: 408-362-9958; Fax: 408-362-9695.
Catechesis/Religious Program—Students 415.

5—ST. CHRISTOPHER (1951) Rev. Msgr. James Walsh; Revs. Mark Gazzingan; Saju Joseph.
Office: 2278 Booksin Ave., 95125. Tel: 408-269-2226; Fax: 408-269-2784.
School—(Grades K-8) Tel: 408-723-7223; Fax: 408-978-5458. Anne Ivie, Prin.; Dana Polini, Librarian. Sisters of the Presentation 2; Lay Teachers 36; Students 616.
Catechesis/Religious Program—Tel: 408-264-8764. Sr. Felicia Gross, O.S.F., D.R.E. Students 415.

6—CHURCH OF THE TRANSFIGURATION (1965) Rev. Walter M. McMahon; Deacon Steve Herrera.
Mailing Address: 4325 Jarvis Ave., 95118. Tel: 408-264-3600; Fax: 408-266-2745.
Catechesis/Religious Program—Tel: 408-264-3600, Ext. 5. Paula Ramos, Pastoral Assoc. Students 75.

7—FIVE WOUNDS PORTUGUESE NATIONAL CHURCH (1914), (Portuguese), Revs. W. Donald Morgan; Antonio Jose dos Reis (Brazil).
Res.: 1375 E. Santa Clara St., 95116. Tel: 408-292-2123; Fax: 408-292-0201.
Catechesis/Religious Program—Tel: 408-293-3938; Fax: 408-293-0431. Julie Meneses, D.R.E. Students 119.

8—ST. FRANCES CABRINI (1955) Revs. Lieu Vu; Robert Kiefer.
Res.: 15333 Woodard Rd., 95124. Tel: 408-879-1120; Fax: 408-377-3587.
School—(Grades PreSchool-8), 15325 Woodard Rd., 95124. Tel: 408-377-6545; Fax: 408-377-8491. Gail Cirone, Prin.; Connie Tomasello, Librarian. Sisters 1; Lay Teachers 29; Students 570.
Catechesis/Religious Program—Tel: 408-377-2111; Fax: 408-377-3587. Students 135.

9—ST. FRANCIS OF ASSISI (1997) Revs. Eugene P. O'Donnell; Peter Loi Huynh; Willy Agbayani, Pastoral Admin.; Deacons Andrzej Sobczyk; Sal Alvarez.
Res.: 5111 San Felipe Rd., 95135. Tel: 408-223-1562; Fax: 408-223-1759.
Catechesis/Religious Program—Students 445.

10—HOLY CROSS (1906), (Italian), Revs. Firmo Mantovani, C.S.; Humberto Chacon, C.S.
Res.: 580 E. Jackson St., 95112. Tel: 408-294-2440; Fax: 408-294-8609.
Catechesis/Religious Program—Tel: 408-294-1310; Fax: 408-294-8609. Bro. Charles Muscat, C.S., D.R.E. Students 400.

11—HOLY FAMILY (1905) Revs. Matthew D. Stanley; Peter Luc The Phan.
Office: 4848 Pearl Ave., 95136. Tel: 408-265-4040; Fax: 408-978-9979.
School—(Grades K-8), 4850 Pearl Ave., 95136. Tel: 408-978-0290; Fax: 408-978-0290. Gail Harrell, Prin.; Laurie Brant, Librarian. Lay Teachers 24; Students 446.
Catechesis/Religious Program—Tel: 408-265-6201. Katy Anderson, Dir. Faith Formation. Students 240.

12—HOLY SPIRIT (1963) Very Rev. Brendan McGuire; Rev. Andrew V. Nguyen; Penny Warne, Pastoral Assoc.
Church: 1200 Redmond Ave., 95120. Tel: 408-997-5101; Fax: 408-997-5102.
School—(Grades PreSchool-8), 1198 Redmond Ave., 95120. Tel: 408-268-0794; Fax: 408-268-5281. Mark Bistricky, Prin.; Anne-Marie Grusonik, Librarian. Lay Teachers 31; Students 588.
Catechesis/Religious Program—Tel: 408-997-5115. Linda Cunha-Ricchio, D.R.E. Students 300.

13—ST. JOHN VIANNEY (1952) Revs. Francisco Rios; Eduardo Obero. In Res., Rev. James K. Graham (NTN).
Rectory—4609 Alum Rock Ave., 95127.
Church: 4600 Hyland Ave., 95127. Tel: 408-258-7832 (Office); Fax: 408-258-6152 (Office).
School—(Grades K-8), 4601 Hyland Ave., 95127. Tel: 408-258-7677; Fax: 408-258-5997. Sr. Michele Anne Murphy, P.B.V.M., Prin.; Tudy Johnson, Librarian. Sisters of the Presentation of the B.V.M. 2; Lay Teachers 27; Students 573.
Catechesis/Religious Program—Tel: 408-258-7832, Ext. 24; Fax: 408-272-1045. Linda Rokita, D.R.E. Students 536.

14—ST. JULIE BILLIART (1974) Revs. Jon Pedigo; Allen Navarro; Deacon Bernard V. Nojadera.
Res.: 366 St. Julie Dr., 95119. Tel: 408-629-3030; Fax: 408-629-3343.
Catechesis/Religious Program—Tel: 408-226-3595. Yolanda Toulet, D.R.E. Students 530.

15—ST. LEO THE GREAT (1923) Revs. Marcelo Javier Navarro, I.V.E.; Jean-Marie Baudry, I.V.E. In Res., Rev. Matthew Koo (Retired).
Res.: 88 Race St., 95126. Tel: 408-293-3503; Fax: 408-293-3516.
School—(Grades K-8) Tel: 408-293-4846. Marie Bordeleau, Prin.; Mary Barber, Librarian. Lay Teachers 14; Students 275.
Catechesis/Religious Program—Sr. Mary of the Incarnation Creeden, S.S.V.M., D.R.E. Students 310.

16—ST. MARIA GORETTI (1961) Rev. Steven P. Brown; Rev. Msgr. Dominic Dinh Do; Revs. Roberto Gomez; Michael Gazzingan; Deacon Joseph Nhut Ho.
Res.: 2980 Senter Rd., 95111. Tel: 408-363-2300; Fax: 408-363-2305.
Catechesis/Religious Program—Tel: 408-363-2300, Ext. 23. Maureen Ickes, D.R.E. Students 820.
Mission—Santee Mission 1382 Tami Lee Dr. #4, Santa Clara Co. 95122. Tel: 408-292-7610.

17—ST. MARTIN OF TOURS (1914) Revs. Christopher Bransfield; Joselito Page.
Res.: 200 O'Connor Dr., 95128. Tel: 408-294-8953; Fax: 408-294-2624.
School—(Grades K-8), 300 O'Connor Dr., 95128. Tel: 408-287-3630; Fax: 408-287-4313. Karen DeMonner, Prin.; Trish Divis, Librarian. Lay Teachers 19; Students 320.
Catechesis/Religious Program—Tel: 408-289-9608. Liz Schoenwetter, D.R.E. Students 95.

18—ST. MARY OF THE ASSUMPTION (1975), (Croatian), (Croatian Mission) Rev. Ante Juric, O.F.M.
Res.: 901 Lincoln Ave., 95126. Tel: 408-279-0279; Fax: 408-292-5868.
Catechesis/Religious Program—Students 55.
Croatian Franciscan Fathers Corporation—Tel: 408-279-0279; Fax: 408-292-5868.
Franciscan Fathers—Tel: 408-276-0279; Fax: 408-292-5868.

19—MOST HOLY TRINITY (1961) Revs. Eduardo Samaniego, S.J.; Theodore Gabrielli, S.J.; Tien Nam, S.J.; Doanh "John" Nguyen, S.J. In Res., Revs. Chanh C. Nguyen, S.J.; Thomas Schwarz, S.J.
Res.: 2040 Nassau Dr., 95122. Tel: 408-729-0101; Fax: 408-258-4131.
School—(Grades K-8) Tel: 408-729-3431; Fax: 408-729-3432. Dorothy Suarez, Prin.; Mary Madamba, Librarian. Sisters 1; Lay Teachers 12; Students 261.

Catechesis/Religious Program—Sr. Patricia Galli, R.S.M., D.R.E. Students 600.

20—OUR LADY OF GUADALUPE (1962), (Hispanic), Revs. Javier Reyes, O.F.M.; Edgar Magana, O.F.M.; William Haney, O.F.M.; Alberto Villifan, O.F.M.; Deacon Eloy Chavez.
Office: 2020 E. San Antonio St., 95116. Tel: 408-926-9207; Fax: 408-258-8249.
Catechesis/Religious Program—Tel: 408-258-0544. Connie Torres, D.R.E. Students 684.

21—ST. PATRICK (1871), (Vietnamese), Revs. Hien Minh Nguyen; Anthony Tuong Nguyen; Truyen Nguyen; Martin Abrego; Deacons Dung Quoc Tran; Joseph Ngoc Huynh.
Res.: 389 E. Santa Clara St., 95113. Tel: 408-294-8120; Fax: 408-291-6277.
Vietnamese Ministry—Tel: 408-291-6280; Fax: 408-291-6289.
School—(Grades K-8), 51 N. 9th St., 95112. Tel: 408-283-5858; Fax: 408-283-5852. Sr. Rosemarie Carroll, C.S.J., Prin.; Ms. M. Delgado, Librarian. Sponsored by the Daughters of Charity. Sisters 1; Lay Teachers 11; Students 230.
Catechesis/Religious Program—Tel: 408-291-6270 (Vietnamese); Fax: 408-291-6289 (Vietnamese). Bro. Fortunat Tran Trong An Phong, F.S.C., D.R.E. (Vietnamese). Students 1,875.

22—QUEEN OF APOSTLES (1960) Revs. Michael Carson; Noel Sanvicente (Philippines); James J. Mifsud, S.M., Pastor Emeritus; Deacon Brian McKenna.
Res.: 4911 Moorpark Ave., 95129. Tel: 408-253-7560; Fax: 408-253-9530.
School—(Grades K-8), 4950 Mitty Way, 95129. Tel: 408-252-3659; Fax: 408-873-2645. Martin Chargin, Prin.; Joan Rehbock, Librarian. Lay Teachers 18; Students 299.
Catechesis/Religious Program—Tel: 408-255-9950; Fax: 408-253-9530. Patricia Sarria, D.R.E. Students 225.

23—SACRED HEART OF JESUS (1920), (Hispanic), Revs. Walter Suarez Lopez; Andres Parra.
Res.: 325 Willow St., 95110. Tel: 408-292-0146; Fax: 408-292-0172.
Catechesis/Religious Program—Tel: 408-292-0146, Ext. 202; Fax: 408-292-0172. Students 184.

24—SANTA TERESA (1967) Rev. Christopher Bennett. In Res., Rev. William Pegnam (Retired).
Res.: 794 Calero Ave., 95123. Tel: 408-629-7777; Fax: 408-629-5260.
Catechesis/Religious Program—Fax: 408-629-5260. Students 128.

25—ST. THOMAS OF CANTERBURY (1967) Rev. Hao Dinh.
Res.: 1522 McCoy Ave., 95130. Tel: 408-378-1595; Fax: 408-378-1215.
Catechesis/Religious Program—Tel: 408-364-8840. Sherry Scott, Catechetical Leader. Students 71.

26—ST. VICTOR (1961) Revs. Michael D. Hendrickson; Stephen F. Perata, Pastor Emeritus; Candido O. Lim, S.J.; Paul Cuong Phan.
Res.: 3108 Sierra Rd., 95132. Tel: 408-251-7055; Fax: 408-251-5528.
School—(Grades K-8), 3150 Sierra Rd., 95132. Tel: 408-251-1740; Fax: 408-251-1492. Patricia Wolf, Prin.; Joan Passalaqua, Librarian. Lay Teachers 17; Students 302.
Catechesis/Religious Program—Tel: 408-251-0154; Fax: 408-251-5528. Angela Giampaoli, D.R.E. Students 301.

OUTSIDE THE CITY OF SAN JOSE

ALVISO, SANTA CLARA CO., OUR LADY, STAR OF THE SEA (1984) Rev. Luis Vargas.
Mailing Address: P.O. Box 426, 95002-0426.
Res.: 1385 Michigan Ave., 95002-0426. Tel: 408-263-2121; Fax: 408-263-1182.
Catechesis/Religious Program—Students 60.

CAMPBELL, SANTA CLARA CO., ST. LUCY (1947) Revs. Kevin P. Joyce; Jonathan Cuarto; Tan Nguyen; Deacon Harry Collins.
Res.: 2350 Winchester Blvd., 95008. Tel: 408-378-2464; Fax: 408-378-5548.
School—(Grades K-8), 76 Kennedy Ave., 95008. Tel: 408-871-8023; Fax: 408-378-4945. Jennifer Martin, Prin.; Mary Casey, Librarian. Lay Teachers 17; Students 319.
Catechesis/Religious Program—Tel: 408-379-5900; Fax: 408-378-5548. Janet Ang, D.R.E. Students 452.

CUPERTINO, SANTA CLARA CO., ST. JOSEPH OF CUPERTINO (1913) Revs. Gregory C. Kimm; Normandy Segovia, Parochial Vicar; Peter Seimas, Parochial Vicar. In Res., Rev. Msgr. Joseph J. Milani, Pastor Emeritus (Retired).
Res.: 10110 N. De Anza Blvd., 95014. Tel: 408-252-7653; Fax: 408-252-5263.
School—(Grades K-8), 10120 N. DeAnza Blvd., 95014. Tel: 408-252-6441; Fax: 408-252-9771. Mary Lyons, Prin.; Barbara Hill, Librarian. Sisters 2; Lay Teachers 13; Students 259.
Catechesis/Religious Program—Tel: 408-252-7653, Ext. 60. Tam Tran, D.R.E. Students 204.

GILROY, SANTA CLARA CO., ST. MARY (1865) [CEM] Revs. Daniel Derry; Hugo Marcelo Rojas (Argentina); Tadeusz Terembula, S.V.D. (Poland); Deacon Pat Allen; Hilda Porcella, Pastoral Assoc.
Res.: 11 First St., 95020. Tel: 408-847-5151; Fax: 408-847-4851.
School—(Grades K-8), 7900 Church St., 95020-4499. Tel: 408-842-2827; Fax: 408-847-7679. Christa Hanson, Prin. Sisters 1; Lay Teachers 17; Students 279.
Catechesis/Religious Program—7950 Church St., 95020. Tel: 408-847-2652; Fax: 408-847-4851. Barbara Zarka, D.R.E. Students 1,561.

LOS ALTOS, SANTA CLARA CO.

1—ST. NICHOLAS (1947) Revs. Lawrence P. Percell; Vincent Tinh Dang.
Res.: 473 Lincoln Ave., 94022. Tel: 650-948-2158; Fax: 408-948-2056.
School—(Grades K-8), 12816 S. El Monte Ave., Los Altos Hills, 94022. Tel: 650-941-4056. Matt Komar, Prin.; Mary O'Shea, Librarian. Lay Teachers 15; Students 230.
Catechesis/Religious Program—Tel: 650-941-7672; Fax: 650-917-9872. Ginny Hinkle, D.R.E. Students 259.

2—ST. SIMON (1955) Revs. V. Warwick James; Randy Valenton; Abraham Antony (India). In Res., Rev. Michael J. Burns (Retired).
Res.: 1860 Grant Rd., 94024. Tel: 650-967-8311; Fax: 650-967-8876.
School—(Grades PreK-8), 1840 Grant Rd., 94024. Tel: 650-968-9952; Fax: 650-988-9308. Mr. Steve Clossick, Prin.; Patti Bo, Librarian. Lay Teachers 31; Students 552.
Catechesis/Religious Program—Tel: 650-967-8311, Ext. 32. Sr. Kathleen Hanley, R.S.M., D.R.E. Students 360.

3—ST. WILLIAM (1959) Rev. Joseph Benedict; Kathy Schlosser, Pastoral Assoc. In Res., Rev. Msgr. John Sandersfeld (Retired).
Res.: 611 S. El Monte Ave., 94022-4058. Tel: 650-559-2080; Fax: 650-968-8508.
Catechesis/Religious Program—Tel: 650-941-7672. Ginny Hinkle, D.R.E. Students 55.

LOS GATOS, SANTA CLARA CO., ST. MARY OF THE IMMACULATE CONCEPTION (1912) Revs. Rick Rodoni; Justin Le.
Res.: 219 Bean Ave., 95030. Tel: 408-354-3726; Fax: 408-354-9302.
School—(Grades K-8), 30 Lyndon Ave., 95030. Tel: 408-354-3944; Fax: 408-395-9151. Sr. Nicki Thomas, S.N.J.M., Prin.; Sheila Chavez, Librarian. Sisters of the Holy Names of Jesus and Mary 2; Lay Teachers 20; Students 287.
Catechesis/Religious Program—Tel: 408-354-4061; Fax: 408-354-9302. Terri Trotter, D.R.E. Students 465.

MILPITAS, SANTA CLARA CO.

1—ST. ELIZABETH (1968) Revs. Daniel C. Urcia; Victor Dinh Tran (Taiwan). In Res., Rev. Antonio Claudio (Philippines).
Res.: 750 Sequoia Dr., 95035. Tel: 408-262-8100; Fax: 408-946-8703.
Catechesis/Religious Program—Tel: 408-263-1995. Sr. Aqueda Poblete, C.H.S., D.R.E. Students 260.

2—ST. JOHN THE BAPTIST (1877) Rev. Norman Segovia.
Res.: 279 S. Main St., 95035. Tel: 408-262-2546; Fax: 408-263-2564.
School—(Grades PreSchool-8), 360 S. Abel St., 95035. Tel: 408-262-8110; Fax: 408-262-0814. Judy Perkowski, Prin.; Jaclyn George, Librarian. Augustinian Recollect Sisters 2; Lay Teachers 10; Students 241.
Catechesis/Religious Program—Tel: 408-262-3955; Fax: 408-262-7726. Sr. Susan Marie Alconcher, B.V.M., D.R.E. Students 274.

MORGAN HILL, SANTA CLARA CO., ST. CATHERINE OF ALEXANDRIA (1909) Revs. Mark Arnzen; Paul A. Mensah (Ghana); Roberto Rojas (Argentina); Deacon Erik Haeckel.
Res.: 17400 Peak Ave., 95037. Tel: 408-779-3959; Fax: 408-779-0289.
School—(Grades K-8), 17500 Peak Ave., 95037. Tel: 408-779-9950; Fax: 408-779-9928. Fabienne Esparza, Prin.; Catherine Graham, Vice Prin. Lay Teachers 13; Students 311.
Catechesis/Religious Program—Tel: 408-779-0542. Jeanne Gaffney, Pastoral Assoc./Youth Dir. Students 660.

MOUNTAIN VIEW, SANTA CLARA CO.

1—ST. ATHANASIUS (1959) Revs. Oscar Tabujara; Estanislao Mikalonis (Argentina); Deacon Leonel Mancilla.
Res.: 160 N. Rengstorff Ave., 94043. Tel: 650-961-8600; Fax: 650-968-5633.
Catechesis/Religious Program—Tel: 650-967-7900; Fax: 650-968-5633. Loretta Martinez Fennell, D.R.E. Students 245.

2—ST. JOSEPH (1901) Revs. Timothy Kidney, Admin.; Robert B. Moran.
Res.: 582 Hope St., 94041. Tel: 650-967-3831; Fax: 650-691-1522.
School—(Grades K-8), 1120 Miramonte Ave., 94040. Tel: 650-967-1839; Fax: 650-691-1530. Stephanie Mirenda-Knight, Prin.; Carmen Ayers, Librarian. Lay Teachers 17; Students 249.
Catechesis/Religious Program—Tel: 650-691-1525. Kevin Ross, D.R.E.; Amy Davis, D.R.E.; Erica Underwood, D.R.E. Students 119.

PALO ALTO, SANTA CLARA CO.

1—ST. ALBERT THE GREAT (1961) Merged with St. Thomas Aquinas Parish.

2—OUR LADY OF THE ROSARY (1959) Merged with St. Thomas Aquinas Parish.

3—ST. THOMAS AQUINAS (1901) Revs. George Aranha; Thierry Geris; Deacon Carl Bunje.
Office: 3290 Middlefield Rd., 94306. Tel: 650-494-2496; Fax: 650-494-3780.
School—St. Elizabeth Seton Catholic Community School, (Grades K-8), 1095 Channing Ave., 94301. Tel: 650-326-9004; Fax: 650-326-2949. Sr. Adella Armentrout, D.C., Prin.; Linda Brennan, Librarian. Sponsored by the Daughters of Charity. Sisters 4; Lay Teachers 13; Students 269.
Catechesis/Religious Program—Tel: 650-494-2496, Ext. 25; Fax: 650-494-3780. Susan Clingsmith, D.R.E. Students 484.

SANTA CLARA, SANTA CLARA CO.

1—CHINESE CATHOLIC COMMUNITY (1983), (Chinese), Revs. Carlos Alberto Olivera; Peter Kin Chung Siu, S.J.; Matthew Koo, Chap. (Retired).
900 Layfayette St., Ste. 301, 95050-4966. Tel: 408-983-0211; Fax: 408-983-0212.
Catechesis/Religious Program—Students 125.

2—ST. CLARE (1777) Revs. Paolo Gobbo (Italy); George Mancha. In Res., Rev. Carlos Alberto Olivera.
Church & Mailing Address: 725 Washington St., 95050. Tel: 408-248-7786; Fax: 408-248-8150.
School—(Grades K-8) Tel: 408-246-6797; Fax: 408-246-6726. Madeline Rader, Prin. Sisters 1; Lay Teachers 14; Students 299.
Catechesis/Religious Program—Tel: 408-248-7786; Fax: 408-248-8150. Sonia Delgado, D.R.E. Students 131.

3—ST. JUSTIN (1951) Revs. Ritche Bueza; Edsil Ortiz, O.F.M.; Joseph Bauer, Pastoral Assoc. In Res., Rev. Joseph Prendergast, C.S.Sp. (Retired).
Res.: 2655 Homestead Rd., 95051. Tel: 408-296-1193; Fax: 408-244-9437.
School—(Grades K-8) Tel: 408-248-1094; Fax: 408-248-0691. Kimberly Shields, Prin. Lay Teachers 15; Students 306.
Catechesis/Religious Program—Tel: 408-983-0361; Fax: 408-244-9437. Tracy Sevigny, D.R.E. Students 204.

4—ST. LAWRENCE, THE MARTYR (1959) Revs. Thuc Si Ho; Ernesto Orci. In Res., Rev. Wilfredo S. Manrique.
Res.: 1971 Saint Lawrence Dr., 95051. Tel: 408-296-3000; Fax: 408-296-3100.
School—(Grades PreSchool-5), 1977 St. Lawrence Dr., 95051. Tel: 408-296-2260; Fax: 408-296-1068. Priscilla Murphy, Prin.; Philip Dolan, Asst. Prin.; Suzanne Hunter, Librarian. Lay Teachers 9; Students 230.
School—(Grades 6-8) Tel: 408-296-2260. Priscilla Murphy, Prin.; Philip Dolan, Asst. Prin.; Suzanne Hunter, Librarian. Lay Teachers 7; Students 134.
School—2000 Lawrence Ct., 95051. Tel: 408-296-3013; Fax: 408-296-3794. Christie Filios, Prin. Sisters 1; Lay Teachers 21; Students 260.
Catechesis/Religious Program—Tel: 408-296-0208; Fax: 408-296-3100. Jennie de la Cerda, C.R.E. Students 124.

5—ORATORY OF OUR MOTHER OF PERPETUAL HELP (2004), (Forma Extraordinaria) Revs. Jean-Marie Moreau, Rector; Pedro Ottonello, O.A.D., Chaplain; Patrick L. Clark, Contact Person.
1298 Homestead Rd., 95050. Tel: 408-580-6548.

6—OUR LADY OF PEACE (1961) Revs. Walter Mallo, I.V.E. (Argentina); Jeffrey Obniski, I.V.E.; Joseph LoJacono, I.V.E.
Res.: 2800 Mission College Blvd., 95054. Tel: 408-988-4585; Fax: 408-988-0679.
Catechesis/Religious Program—Tel: 408-988-7543; Fax: 408-980-9436. Students 758.

SARATOGA, SANTA CLARA CO.

1—CHURCH OF THE ASCENSION (1964) Rev. Jose Galang. In Res., Rev. Andres Ligot.
Res.: 12033 Miller Ave., 95070. Tel: 408-725-3939.
Catechesis/Religious Program—Tel: 408-725-3930; Fax: 408-725-3932. Ann Liebmann, D.R.E. Students 147.

2—SACRED HEART (1951) Rev. Gary Thomas; Deacon Donald Sifferman.
Res.: 13716 Saratoga Ave., 95070. Tel: 408-867-3634; Fax: 408-867-5339.
Rectory—13724 Saratoga Ave., 95070.
School—(Grades PreSchool-8), 13718 Saratoga Ave., 95070. Tel: 408-867-9241; Fax: 408-867-9242. Tom Pulchny, Prin. Lay Teachers 18; Students 207.
Pre-School—Lay Teachers 2; Students 17.

Catechesis/Religious Program—Tel: 408-867-1530. Patrick DeLorenzo, Dir. Faith Formation. Students 155.

STANFORD, SANTA CLARA CO., CATHOLIC COMMUNITY AT STANFORD (1997) Revs. Nathan Castle, O.P.; Carl Schlichte, O.P.
Mailing Address: P.O. Box 20301, 94309. Tel: 650-725-0080; Fax: 650-723-6797.
Catechesis/Religious Program—

SUNNYVALE, SANTA CLARA CO.

1—CHURCH OF THE RESURRECTION (1963) Revs. G. Robert Leger; Vincent Pineda. In Res., Revs. Joseph N. Vanthu (Retired); Dennis Gilbert.
Res. & Church: 725 Cascade Dr., 94087. Tel: 408-245-5554; Fax: 408-245-5589.
School—(Grades PreSchool-8), 1395 Hollenbeck Ave., 94087. Tel: 408-245-4571; Fax: 408-733-7301. Sr. Georgianna Coonis, S.N.D., Prin. Sisters 3; Lay Teachers 14; Students 268.
Catechesis/Religious Program—Tel: 408-746-0172. Students 133.

2—ST. CYPRIAN (1961) Rev. Arturo Yabes.
Res.: 1133 W. Washington, 94086. Tel: 408-739-8506; Fax: 408-739-2815.
School—(Grades K-8), 195 Leota Ave., 94086. Tel: 408-738-3444; Fax: 408-733-3730. Paul Wilson, Prin. Lay Teachers 13; Students 174.
Catechesis/Religious Program—Tel: 408-739-1669. Porty Nevarez, D.R.E. Students 97.

3—HOLY KOREAN MARTYRS (2005), (Korean), Rev. Matthias Seon Ki Hwang.
Res.: 531 E. Weddell Dr., 94089-2162. Tel: 408-734-9721; Fax: 408-734-9723.
Catechesis/Religious Program—Tel: 408-225-9272. Richard Il-Young Hong, D.R.E. Students 390.

4—ST. MARTIN (1916) Revs. Jose Antonio Medina; David Mercer. In Res., Rev. Ed Samy (Retired).
Res.: 590 Central Ave., 94086. Tel: 408-736-3725; Fax: 408-736-4968.
School—(Grades PreSchool-8), 597 Central Ave., 94086. Tel: 408-736-5534. Eugenie Florczyk, Prin. Lay Teachers 11; Students 196.
Catechesis/Religious Program—593 Central Ave., 94086. Tel: 408-736-3725. Judy Kelch, D.R.E. Students 336.

Chaplains of Public Institutions

SAN JOSE. *Catholic Scouting*. Rev. Paul A. Soukup, S.J. Tel: 408-554-4124.
Detention Ministry for Juveniles. Rev. Antonio Claudio (Philippines). Tel: 408-739-8506.
Notre Dame Club of San Jose/Silicon Valley. Very Rev. Brendan McGuire, V.G.
Santa Clara County Jail. Rev. Antonio Claudio (Philippines).
Santa Clara County Sheriffs Dept. Rev. Paul Weisbeck.
Santa Clara County Women's Facility. Vacant.
Santa Clara Valley Medical Center. Rev. Eugene Corbett, S.J.

MILPITAS. *Stanford Medical Center*. Rev. John Hester. Tel: 650-723-4000.

Special Assignment:
Rev. Msgr.—
Cilia, Francis V., V.G., Vicar Gen.
Very Rev.—
McGuire, Brendan, V.G., Vicar General
Revs.—
Benedict, Joseph, S.T.D., Dir. Permanent Deacon Formation
Catalana, Mark, Sabbatical
Claudio, Antonio (Philippines), Detention Min.
Gammad, Engelberto, J.C.D., Tribunal - Adjutant Judicial Vicar
Hayes, Robert E., J.C.L., Tribunal Ministry, Defender of the Bond
Hilliard, Richard, Assoc.Continuing Education Clergy
Ligot, Andres C., J.C.D., Judicial Vicar, Vicar Filipino Min.
Mancuso, Anthony J., Ed.D., Sabbatical
Manrique, Wilfredo S., J.C.L., Vicar for Clergy
Nguyen, Hien Minh, J.C.D., Vicar Vietnamese Min.
Poncini, John, Dir. Vocations
Rios, Francisco, Vicar for Hispanic Min.
Rubio, Jose Antonio, S.T.D., Dir. Ecumenical & Interreligious Affairs & Delegate Eastern Rite Churches
Weisbeck, Paul, Sabbatical

On Duty Outside the Diocese:
Revs.—
Brocato, Robert S., Diocese of Montego Bay, Jamaica, WI
Menchaca, Luis Gerardo, Rome, Italy
Ovando, Sergio, Rome, Italy
Rich, Joseph, Newport Beach, CA
Saso, Michael, Macau

On Leave of Absence:
Revs.—
Arnone, Allan
Browne, Dennis
Day, Michael
Delgado, Joseph
Gray, Robert
Hernandez, Enrico
Keulman, Kenneth P.
Lagututta, Nunzio J.
Marx, Robert
Nabbefeld, Grant
Pereira, Anthony
Smith, Brian
Sullivan, Mervyn

Absent on Sick Leave:
Revs.—
Affonso, Alexander
Bonsor, Jack
Neary, Mark

Retired:
Most Rev.—
DuMaine, R. Pierre
Rev. Msgrs.—
Andre, Ludwig
Boyle, Eugene
Coleman, John
Larkin, Alexander C.
Lenane, William
Milani, Joseph J.
Mitchell, Michael J.
Sandersfeld, John
Sullivan, Terrence J.
Revs.—
Balthazar, Ayala
Burns, Michael J.
Davis, Terrence
Kilcoyne, Patrick
Koo, Matthew
Largente, Laurent
Leininger, William
Lopez, Abel, J.C.L.
Maher, Raymond
Manding, Benito O.
Passalacqua, Robert
Pegnam, William
Prendergast, Joseph, C.S.Sp.
Re, Angelo
Samy, Ed
Shea, Thomas
Tinh, Joseph Nguyen
Traverso, Leonard
Vanthu, Joseph N.
Zawadski, Justin

Permanent Deacons:
Allen, Pat, St. Mary, Gilroy
Alvarez, Salvador, St. Francis of Assisi
Bunje, Carl, St. Thomas Aquinas
Chavez, Eloy, Our Lady of Guadalupe
Collins, Harry, St. Lucy, Collins
Haeckel, Eric, St. Catherine
Hanson, Ron, St. Joseph of Cupertino
Herrera, Steven, Transfiguration
Ho, Joseph Nhut, St. Maria Goretti
Huynh, Joseph N., St. Patrick
Mancilla, Leonel, St. Athanasius
McKenna, Brian, Queen of Apostles
Nojadera, Bernard V., St. Julie Billiart
Perez, Vicente, Most Holy Trinity
Sifferman, Donald, Sacred Heart, Saratoga; Children's Hospital, Stanford
Sobezyk, Andrzej, St. Brother Albert Chmielowski Polish Mission & St. Francis of Assisi
Tran, Dung Quoc, St. Patrick

INSTITUTIONS LOCATED IN THE DIOCESE

[A] SHRINES

SANTA CLARA. *Shrine of Our Lady of Peace* 2800 Mission College Blvd., 95054. Tel: 408-988-4585; Fax: 408-988-0679. Rev. Walter Mallo, I.V.E. (Argentina), Dir.
Our Lady of Peace Gift Shop Tel: 408-980-9825; Fax: 408-988-2488.

[B] COLLEGES AND UNIVERSITIES

SANTA CLARA. *Santa Clara University*, 500 El Camino Real, 95053-0001. Tel: 408-554-4000; Fax: 408-554-2700. Email: username@scu.edu. Web: www.scu.edu. Elizabeth Salzer, Librarian. Society of Jesus., Mission Santa Clara. Founded in 1777. University established in 1851 and chartered by the State in 1855. Priest Teachers 47; Brothers 2; Scholastics 1; Sisters 3; Lay Teachers 400; Students 8,490.
Administrators: Revs. Michael E. Engh, S.J., Pres.; Kevin F. Burke, S.J., Dean Jesuit School Theology; Dr. Godfrey Mungal, Dean School of Engineering; Dr. Donald J. Polden, Dean School of Law; S. Andrew Starbird, Interim Dean Leavey School of Business Admin.; Mr. James M. Purcell, Vice Pres. Univ. Rels.; Mr. Robert Warren, Vice Pres. Finance Admin.; Dr. W. Atom Yee, Dean College of Arts & Sciences.
Jesuit Community, 500 El Camino Real, 95053-1600. Tel: 408-554-4124; Fax: 408-554-4795. Revs. Gardenio M. Manuel, S.J., Rector Jesuit Community; Jeffrey C. Baerwald, S.J.; Michael J. Buckley, S.J.; Luis F. Calero, S.J.; Christopher M. Cartwright, S.J.; Michael T. T. Castori, S.J.; Paul G. Crowley, S.J.; William F. Donnelly, S.J.; James W. Felt, S.J., Prof. Emeritus; Andrew J. Garavel, S.J.; Paul J. Goda, S.J.; Carl H. Hayn, S.J., Prof. Emeritus; Arthur F. Liebscher, S.J.; Paul L. Locatelli, S.J.; Paul P. Mariani, S.J.; Michael C. McCarthy, S.J.; Very Rev. John P. McGarry, S.J.; Revs. Gerald L. McKevitt, S.J.; John P. Mossi, S.J.; Alfred E. Naucke, S.J.; Chi V. Ngo, S.J.; Ugo Nweke, S.J.; Peter Pabst, S.J.; Dennis R. Parnell, S.J.; Charles T. Phipps, S.J., Min./Contact; Thomas J. Powers, S.J.; Kevin P. Quinn, S.J.; Mark A. Ravizza, S.J.; James W. Reites, S.J.; John Rose, S.J.; Theodore J. Rynes, S.J.; Nicky Santos, S.J.; Thomas Schwarz, S.J.; Peter Siu, S.J.; Francis R. Smith, S.J.; Dennis C. Smolarski, S.J.; Paul A. Soukup, S.J.; Robert L. St. Clair, S.J.; Salvatore A. Tassone, S.J.; Charles Tilly, S.J.; Frederick P. Tollini, S.J.; John P. Treacy, S.J.; Fidelis Udahemuka, S.J.; Tennant C. Wright, S.J.; Michael A. Zampelli, S.J.; Bros. Thomas C. Bracco, S.J., Asst. Min.; James Siwicki, S.J.; Mr. Matthew Farley, (Scholastic).
Jesuit Community at Santa Clara University, Inc. Priests 47; Brothers 2.

[C] HIGH SCHOOLS, DIOCESAN

SAN JOSE. *Archbishop Mitty High School* (Coed), 5000 Mitty Ave., 95129. Tel: 408-252-6610; Fax: 408-252-6967. Email: brosnan@mitty.com. Web: www.mitty.com. Mr. Timothy Brosnan, Prin.; Rev. John Russi, S.M., Campus Chap.; Billy King, Librarian. Lay Teachers 104; Students 1,672; Total Staff 163.

SANTA CLARA. *Saint Lawrence Academy*, 2000 Lawrence Ct., 95051. Tel: 408-296-3013; Fax: 408-296-3794. Email: cfilios@saintlawrence.org. Web: www.saintlawrence.org. Christie Filios, Prin.; Anne Eubanks, Asst. Prin. College Prep Coed. Sisters 1; Lay Teachers 25; Students 260; Total Staff 30.

[D] HIGH SCHOOLS, PRIVATE

SAN JOSE. *Bellarmine College Preparatory*, 960 W. Hedding St., 95126. Tel: 408-294-9224; Fax: 408-294-1894. Web: www.bcp.org. Chris Meyercord, Prin.; Ann Weber, Librarian; Revs. Kevin L. Dilworth, S.J., Supr. & Contact; Peter M.Q. Chu, S.J.; Ronald M. Clemo, S.J.; Richard E. Cobb, S.J.; Eugene J. Corbett, S.J.; Edwin B. Harris, S.J.; William Kelley, S.J.; Robert B. Mathewson, S.J.; Michael Moodie, S.J.; G. Max Oliva, S.J.; Paul G. Sheridan, S.J.; Robert J. Shinney, S.J.; Gerald T. Wade, S.J., Chancellor; Mr. Mark Doherty; Deacons Vincent Phuc Anh Duong; Quentin Dupont. Society of Jesus. Priests 10; Lay Teachers 111; Students 1,605.
Notre Dame High School, 596 S. Second St., 95112. Tel: 408-294-1113; Fax: 408-293-9779. Web: www.ndsj.org. Ann Gregg Skeet, Pres.; Mary Beth Riley, Prin.; Amy Huang, Librarian. Sisters of Notre Dame de Namur. Lay Teachers 53; Total Staff 78; Students 631.
Non-Resident Students: Ann Gregg Skeet, Pres.
Presentation High School, 2281 Plummer Ave., 95125. Tel: 408-264-1664; Fax: 408-266-7333. Web: www.Pres-Net.com. Mary Miller, Prin.; Rev. George Aranha, Chap.; Katy Lemon, Librarian. Sisters of the Presentation. Lay Teachers 66; Students 809; Total Staff 84.

MORGAN HILL. *South County Catholic High School*, 17190 Monterey Rd., Ste. 202, 95037. Tel: 408-778-0562. George Chiala, Pres.

MOUNTAIN VIEW. *St. Francis High School*, 1885 Miramonte Ave., 94040. Tel: 650-968-1213; Fax: 650-968-3241. Email: kemakley@sfhs.com. Web: www.sfhs.com. Mr. Kevin Makley, Pres.; Mr. Simon Raines, Dir. Activities; Mrs. Patricia Tennant, Prin.; Angelo Aguiar, Exec. Dir. Devel.; Ann Lane, Librarian. Brothers of Holy Cross. Brothers 1; Lay Teachers 107; Students 1,667; Total Staff 143.

[E] MIDDLE SCHOOLS, PRIVATE

SAN JOSE. *Sacred Heart Nativity School*, (Grades 6-8), 310 Edwards, 95110. Tel: 408-993-1293; Fax: 408-993-0675. Email: shnativity@shnativity.org. Web: www.shnativity.org. Rev. Peter Pabst, S.J., Pres.; Kevin Eagleson, Prin. Priests 1; Lay Teachers 23; Students 134; Total Staff 28.

CAMPBELL. *Canyon Heights Academy, Inc.*, (Grades PreSchool-8), 775 Waldo Rd., 95008. Tel: 408-370-6727; Fax: 408-370-7147. Email: wpparker@chamail.net. Web: www.canyonheightsacademy.com. W. Paul Parker, Prin. Lay Teachers 19; Students 224.

[F] THE CATHOLIC CHARITIES OF THE DIOCESE OF SAN JOSE

SAN JOSE. *Catholic Charities of Santa Clara County*, 2625 Zanker Rd., 95134. Tel: 408-468-0100; Fax: 408-944-0275. Web: www.ccsj.org. Gregory R. Kepferle, CEO; Margaret Williams, CAO & CFO; Deborah Baker, Human Resources; Ruben Solorio, Parish & Community Rels.; Marilou Cristina, Div. Dir. Older Adult Svcs.; Ellen Dumesnil, Div. Dir. Economic Dev. Svcs.; Jane Hills, Youth & Family Svcs.; Kitty Mason, Div. Dir., Behavioral Health Svcs.; Magi Young, Chief Devel. Officer; Cindy Zbin, Assoc. Devel. Dir.; Terrie Iacino, Dir. Community Devel. & Advocacy; Elizabeth Lilly, Div. Dir. Community & Parish Partnerships; Robin Reynolds, Dir. of Communications.

Service Divisions:
Community Dev. & Advocacy
Economic Development Svcs.
Older Adult Svcs.
Behavioral Health Svcs.
Children, Youth & Family Dev.
Community Development & Advocacy
Campaign to Cut Poverty Tel: 408-325-5130.
Handicapables Program Tel: 408-282-8606.
Partnership Tel: 408-325-5262.

Economic Development Services
Asylee Program Tel: 408-325-5170; 408-325-5227.
Citizenship Services - South County Tel: 408-914-8337.
Employment Services Tel: 408-325-5170; 408-325-5152.
Financial Education Services Tel: 408-325-5154.
Free Tax Preparation Tel: 408-325-5241.
Focus for Work Tel: 408-325-5285.
Housing Search and Stabilization Tel: 408-325-5277.
Immigration Legal Services Tel: 408-944-0691.
Refugee Foster Care Tel: 408-325-5159.
Refugee Resettlement Tel: 408-325-5170.
Training Tel: 408-325-5170; 408-325-5152.
Older Adult Services
Day Break Adult Day Care/Caregiver Support Tel: 408-270-4900.
Day Break Asian Model Tel: 408-282-1134.
Long Term Care Ombudsman Tel: 408-944-0567.
Senior Nutrition Program
Eastside Neighborhood Center Nutrition Tel: 408-937-3924.
John XXIII Multi-Service Center Nutrition Tel: 408-282-8607.
Gilroy Nutrition Tel: 408-846-0428.
Senior Programs at Neighborhood Centers
Eastside Neighborhood Center Tel: 408-251-0215.
John XXIII Multi-Service Center Tel: 408-282-8600.

Behavioural Health Services
Adult Mental Health Services Tel: 408-295-5288.
CalWORKs Tel: 408-325-5230.
Children and Family Services Tel: 408-325-5296.
Golden Gateway Tel: 408-295-5288.
OASIS (Older Adult Services) Tel: 408-955-9170; 408-295-5288.
Substance Abuse Recovery Services Tel: 408-325-5180.
Supportive Housing Tel: 408-920-0803.

Children, Youth & Family Development
CORAL (Communities Organizing Resources to Advance Learning) Tel: 408-283-6150.
El Toro Youth Center Tel: 408-779-6002.
FA'ATASI Tel: 408-938-6731.
First 5 Tel: 408-283-6150.
Intervention Services Tel: 408-938-6731.
Kinship Resource Center Tel: 408-200-0980.
LEAP Project (Leadership, Ethnic, & Academic Pride) Tel: 408-283-6150.
Peer Educators Tel: 408-823-6150.
Probation Suport Services Tel: 408-295-5288.
Raising A Reader Tel: 408-283-6150.
Successful Parents' Project Tel: 408-283-6150.
The Summit League Tech Lab Tel: 408-938-6731.
Washington United Youth Center Tel: 408-938-6731.
Young Women's Empowerment Tel: 408-938-6731.

[G] DAY CARE CENTERS

SAN JOSE. *St. Elizabeth's Day Home*, 950 St. Elizabeth Dr., 95126. Tel: 408-295-3456; Fax: 408-295-5917. Email: info@stelizabethdayhom.org. Web: www.stelizabethsdayhome.org. Diana Ballesteros, Exec. Dir. Lay Staff 25; Children 102.

[H] GENERAL HOSPITALS

SAN JOSE. *O'Connor Hospital*, 2105 Forest Ave., 95128. Tel: 408-947-2500; Fax: 408-995-0117. Web: www.oconnorhospital.org. James F. Dover, CEO; Rev. Robert McKay, Ph.D. (South Africa), Dir. Chap. Svcs.; Ms. Elsamma James, Staff Chap.; Mr. Raymond Dougherty, Staff Chap.

O'Connor Hospital, Sponsored by Daughters of Charity Health System. Total Staff 1,538; Bed Capacity 358; Patients Assisted Annually 150,000.

O'Connor Foundation, 2105 Forest Ave., 95128. Tel: 408-947-2717; Fax: 408-947-2649. Toni Harper, CEO Foundation.

GILROY. *Saint Louise Regional Hospital*, Admin. Office, 9400 No Name Uno, 95020. Tel: 408-848-2000; Fax: 408-842-2155. Email: joanneallen@dochs.org. Web: www.dochs.org. Sr. Paula Baker, P.B.V.M., Vice Pres. Mission Integration; Joanne Allen, Pres. & CEO. Sponsored by Daughters of Charity Health System. Sisters 3; Total Staff 470; Bed Capacity 93; Patients Assisted Annually 69,093.

[I] SPECIAL SANATORIUM AND HOSPITALS

SARATOGA. *Our Lady of Fatima Villa*, 20400 Saratoga-Los Gatos Rd., 95070. Tel: 408-741-2950; Fax: 408-741-4930. Web: www.fatimavilla.org. Bella Mahoney, Pres. & CEO; Sr. Susan Snyder, O.P., Prioress. Sponsored by Dominican Sisters of St. Catherine of Siena of Kenosha, Inc., Provides skilled nursing care and assisted living facility for aged women and men. Sisters 1; Residents 100; Total Staff 94.

[J] HOTEL, SENIOR CITIZENS RESIDENCE

SAN JOSE. *Giovanni Center, Inc.*, 85 S. Fifth St., 95112. Tel: 408-288-7436; Fax: 408-288-7264. Email: jeannedarc@jsco.net. Francisco Solis, Property Mgr. A California nonprofit charitable, public-benefit, housing project for low-income elderly. Sponsored by the Roman Catholic Bishop of San Jose, a corporation sole. Lay Staff 3; Residents 30.

Jeanne d'Arc Manor, 85 S. Fifth St., 95112. Tel: 408-288-7421; Fax: 408-288-7264. Email: jeannedarc@jsco.net. Francisco Solis, Property Mgr. Housing project for low-income elderly and disabled. Sponsored by the Roman Catholic Bishop of San Jose, A Corporation Sole. Lay Staff 10; Residents 110; Units 87.

[K] HOMES FOR THE AGED

MOUNTAIN VIEW. *Villa Siena*, 1855 Miramonte Ave., 94040. Tel: 650-961-6484; Fax: 650-961-6254. Email: vsiena@pacbell.net. Web: www.villa-siena.org. Mrs. Corine Bernard, Exec. Dir.; Sr. Judith Lynn Gardenhire, Pres. & Bd. Chm. Daughters of Charity of St. Vincent de Paul., Residential Care and Skilled Nursing Facility. Professed Sisters 3; Residents 66; In Nursing Care 20; Nursing Staff 27; Total Staff 60.

[L] RETREATS

LOS ALTOS. *Jesuit Retreat Center of Los Altos*, 300 Manresa Way, 94022. Tel: 650-948-4491; Fax: 650-948-0640. Email: retreat@jrclosaltos.org. Web: www.jrclosaltos.org. Revs. Thomas J. Carroll, S.J., Dir.; James Flynn, Supr.; Kevin Ballard, S.J., Retreat Dir.; Bernard J. Bush, S.J.; Robert J. Fabing, S.J.; Joseph J. Fice, S.J.; Gerald F. Hudson, S.J.; George E. Schultz, S.J.; Peter J. Togni, S.J.; Bro. Thomas J. Koller, S.J. Priests 9; Brothers 1.

LOS GATOS. *Presentation Center*, 19480 Bear Creek Rd., 95033-9519. Tel: 408-354-2346; Fax: 408-354-5226. Web: www.presentationcenter.org. Anna M. O'Connor, Exec. Dir. & Contact. Retreat and Conference Center. Religious 5; Lay People 3; Capacity 200; Staff 20.

Villa Holy Names, P.O. Box 907, 95031-0907. Tel: 408-354-2312; Fax: 408-354-8305. Email: jmvillalg@yahoo.com. Sr. Kathryn Ondreyco, S.N.J.M. Total Staff 1.

[M] MONASTERIES AND RESIDENCES OF PRIESTS AND BROTHERS

SAN JOSE. *Carmelite Monastery, Novitiate*, P.O. Box 3420, 95156-3420. Tel: 408-251-1361; Fax: 408-251-1854. Revs. James Geoghegan, O.C.D,; Donald Kinney, O.C.D., Novice Master; Ailbe Doolan, O.C.D.; John Colm Stone, O.C.D.; Patrick Sugrue, O.C.D.; Adam Gonzales, O.C.D., Vocation Dir.; Richard Mandoli, O.C.D.

CUPERTINO. *The Marianist Center*, 22683 Alcalde Rd., 95014. Tel: 408-207-4800; Fax: 408-253-3466. Revs. Joseph Stefanelli, S.M.; Robert Hertweck, S.M.; Thomas Hogan, S.M.; James Imhof, S.M.; Raymond Malley, S.M.; Lawrence Mann, S.M.; William O'Connell, S.M.; Daniel Triulzi, S.M.; Stephen Tutas, S.M.; Bros. Thomas Deasy, S.M.; Charles Ehrenfeld, S.M.; Paul Fennelly, S.M.; Eugene Frank, S.M.; Howard Hughes, S.M.; James Leahy, S.M.; Patrick McMahon, S.M.; Stanley Murakami, S.M., Sub-Dir.; Joseph Nu'uanu, S.M.; John Samaha, S.M.; Frank Spaeth, S.M.; Robert Wade, S.M. Marianist Center. Priests 9; Brothers 12; Total in Residence 21. *The Alcalde House*, 22683 Alcalde Rd., 95014-3903. Tel: 408-207-4808; Fax: 408-253-3466. Revs. David Schuyler, S.M., Community Dir.; Joseph Hartzler, S.M.; Bro. John Haster, S.M. Priests 2; Brothers 1; Total in Residence 3. *The Bordeaux House*, 22683 Alcalde Rd., 95014. P.O. Box 1775, 95015-1775. Tel: 408-207-4800; Fax: 408-253-3466. Revs. John McEnhill, S.M.; John Russi, S.M.; Bros. John Schlund, S.M.; Vincent Wayer, S.M. Priests 2; Brothers 4; Total in Residence 6. Living In Other Residences: Rev. Jorge da Silva, S.M., Los Gatos; Bros. Joseph Aspell, S.M., San Jose; Robert Juenemann, S.M., San Jose.

LOS ALTOS. *Maryknoll*, 23000 Cristo Rey Dr., 94024. Tel: 650-967-3822; Fax: 650-965-3473. Maryknoll Residence for Priests and Brothers. Priests 23; Brothers 8. In Res. Revs. Donald Allen, M.M.; William M. Boteler, M.M.; Bernard P. Byrne, M.M.; Robert J. Carleton, M.M.; Clyde F. Davis, M.M.; Marvin Deutsch, M.M.; Thomas F. Donnelly, M.M.; Arthur J. Dwyer, M.M.; John F. Felago, M.M.; Arthur J. Dwyer, M.M.; Joseph A. Klecha, M.M.; Joseph W. Kowalczyk, M.M.; Carmen G. LaMazza, M.M.; Richard G. Laszewski, M.M.; Donald P. McQuade, M.M.; Charles A. Murray, M.M.; Joseph C. Nerino, M.M.; Edward J. Quinn, M.M.; James Roth, M.M.; Alan J. Ryan, M.M.; Philip F. Sheerin, M.M.; James S. Stefaniak, M.M.; Cyril L. Vellicig, M.M.; John J. Vinsko, M.M.; Bros. Luke R. Baldwin, M.M.; Casimir Brezinski, M.M.; Duane S. Crockett, M.M.; Joseph Dowling, M.M.; Conrad Fleisch, M.M.; John H. Frangenberg, M.M.; Venard Ruane, M.M.; Leo Shedy, M.M.

LOS GATOS. *California Province of the Society of Jesus, Jesuit Provincial Office*, P.O. Box 519, 95031-0519. Tel: 408-884-1600; Fax: 408-884-1601. Email: calprovsj@calprov.org. Web: www.jesuitscalifornia.org. Very Rev. John P. McGarry, S.J., Regl. Prov.; Revs. Alfred E. Naucke, S.J., Exec. Asst. & Contact; Chi V. Ngo, S.J., Formation Dir.; Dennis R. Parnell, S.J., Treas.

Sacred Heart Jesuit Center, Provincial Office, P.O. Box 519, 95031. Tel: 408-884-1700; Fax: 408-884-1701. Revs. John Privett, S.J., Supr. & Contact; Thomas W. Foster, S.J., Asst. Supr.; Philip C. Blake, S.J.; Richard J. Blinn, S.J.; Francis J. Buckley, S.J.; Peter Burns, S.J.; William F. Cain, S.J.; J. Ripley Caldwell; Mario L. Capitolo, S.J.; William Carroll, S.J.; Bernard F. Cassidy, S.J.; John W. Clark, S.J.; Richard T. Coz, S.J.; George T. Dennis, S.J.; Raymond A. Devlin, S.J.; Ralph J. Drendel, S.J.; Donald J. Duggan, S.J.; Carlo A. Farina, S.J.; John G. Ferguson, S.J.; Thomas P. Finsterbach, S.J.; David T. Fisher, S.J.; John J. Flynn, S.J.; John L. Flynn, S.J.; Francis A. Frugoli, S.J.; Reynold J. Gatto, S.J.; John I. Geiszel, S.J.; Robert E. Griffin, S.J.; James R. Hanley, S.J.; Leo J. Hombach, S.J.; Carroll J. Keating, S.J.; George V. Kennard, S.J.; George J. Koch, S.J.; Gerald J. Lentz, S.J.; William F. Lester, S.J.; Jerold W. Lindner, S.J.; William J. Maring, S.J.; James P. McCauley, S.J.; Thomas F. McCormick, S.J.; Gerald P. McCourt, S.J.; Robert McDevitt, S.J.; Donald P. Merrifield, S.J.; Dare J. Morgan, S.J.; Stephen G. Olivo, S.J.; Lorenzo J. Palafax, S.J.; John J. Perlite, S.J.; Thomas J. Reilly, S.J.; Anton J. Renna, S.J.; F. Warren Schoeppe, S.J.; Robert R. Taheny, S.J.; Theodore T. Taheny, S.J.; Richard P. Vaughn, S.J.; Silvano P. Votto, S.J.; Duc Vu, S.J.; Francis X. Wang, S.J. (China); Carlton E. Whitten, S.J.; William J. Wood, S.J.; Michael J. Zimmers, S.J.; Bros. Charles L. Connor, S.J.; William C. Farrington, S.J.; Lawrence Thoo Fook, S.J.; Norbert J. Korte, S.J.; Thomas A. Marshall, S.J.; Charles J. Onorato, S.J.; Daniel J. Peterson, S.J.; Theodore C. Rohrer, S.J.; Edmund W. Ryan, S.J., (Retired); Leonard J. Sullivan, S.J.

California Province of the Society of Jesus dba Sacred Heart Jesuit Center Priests 60; Brothers 10.

Priests & Brothers of the Province residing elsewhere: Revs. Joseph D. Fessio, S.J.; Candido O. Lim, S.J.

SANTA CLARA. *Casa San Inigo, Jesuit Residence*, 1075 Benton St., 95050-4801. Tel: 408-200-1150; Fax: 408-200-1151. Rev. John P. Mossi, S.J.; Very Rev.

John P. McGarry, S.J.; Revs. Chi V. Ngo, S.J.; Peter Pabst, S.J.; Peter Kin Chung Siu, S.J.; Bro. James Siwicki, S.J.; Rev. Charles J. Tilley, S.J. Priests 6; Brothers 1.

Jesuit Community Please see listing under Santa Clara University, located under Colleges and Universities., 500 El Camino Real, 95053. Tel: 408-554-4124; Fax: 408-554-4795.

SARATOGA. *St. Patrick's Missionary Society* (St. Patrick Fathers), 19536 Eric Dr., 95070. Tel: 408-253-3135; Fax: 408-253-5433. Email: spsca@spms.org. Web: www.stpatrickfathers.org. Revs. Michael Moore, S.P.S., Dir. of Promotion; Steve Donohue, S.P.S. (Retired). Priests 2.

[N] CONVENTS AND RESIDENCES FOR SISTERS

SAN JOSE. *Community of the Holy Spirit*, 1275 Naglee Ave., 95126. Tel: 408-275-1710. Sr. Jolene M. Schmitz, C.H.S., Contact.

Daughters of Charity of St. Vincent de Paul, O'Connor Sisters Home, 350 O'Connor Dr., 95128. Tel: 408-289-9215. Email: dococon@sbcglobal.net. Sr. Michele Randall, D.C., Contact. Sisters 7.

Eucharistic Missionaries of the Most Holy Trinity, 815 S. Daniel Way, 95128. Tel: 408-243-3157; Fax: 408-243-3157. Sr. Gisela Enriquez, M.E.S.S.T., Supr. Sisters 5.

La Salle Sisters, 3867 Silver Creek Rd., 95121-1969. Tel: 408-238-9351; Fax: 408-258-4870. Email: nutulasan@yahoo.com. Web: saigon.com/-vietedu. Sr. Ann Olivia Thanh Vu, L.S.S., Contact Person. Sisters 12.

Pious Disciples of the Divine Master, 2076 Lincoln Ave., 95125. Tel: 408-265-8105; Fax: 408-265-8105. Email: sddmsjca@aol.com. Web: www.pddm.us. Sr. Fede Tanno, P.D.D.M., Supr. Sisters 2.

Quinhon Missionary Sisters of the Holy Cross, 368 Neilson Ct., 95111. Tel: 408-362-9719. Sr. Josefa Ngoc Nguyen, L.H.C., Regl. Supr. & Local Contact. Sisters 5.

Sinsinawa Dominican Congregation of the Most Holy Rosary, 2024 McDaniel Ave., #2, 95128. Tel: 408-298-4050. Sr. Virginia Pfluger, O.P., Local Contact. Sisters 2.

Sisters of the Holy Family, P.O. Box 3248, Fremont, 94539. Tel: 510-624-4500; Fax: 510-624-4550. *St. Elizabeth's Day Home Day Care Center* Children 102.

CONCORD. *Sisters of St. Joseph of Carondelet*, 2668 Concord Blvd., 94519. Tel: 925-691-9313. Web: www.csjla.org/membersonly. Sr. Diane Smith, Contact Person (Los Angeles Prov.). Sisters 5.

CUPERTINO. *Blessed Virgin Missionaries of Carmel (B.V.M.C.)*, 10130 N. De Anza Blvd., 95014. Tel: 408-257-1022; Fax: 408-257-3272. Sr. Gloria P. Solis, B.V.M.C., Supr. Sisters 3.

Intercommunity Convent, 10351 S. Blaney Ave., 95014-3122. Tel: 408-725-0898; 408-252-9696; Fax: 408-252-4848. Email: insyte@comcast.net.

LOS ALTOS HILLS. *Daughters of Charity of St. Vincent de Paul, Seton Provincialate*, 26000 Altamont Rd., 94022. Tel: 650-941-4490; Fax: 650-949-3874. Email: docpsec@aol.com. Web: www.daughtersofcharity.com. Rev. Andrew E. Bellisario, C.M., Dir. Sisters 55; Total in Province 126; Total in Diocese 55.

Immaculate Heart Monastery of the Poor Clares, 28210 Natoma Rd., 94022-3320. Tel: 650-948-2947. Sr. Maura Heinen, P.C.C., Abbess. Sisters 16.

LOS GATOS. *Sisters of the Holy Names of Jesus & Mary*, P.O. Box 907, 95031-0907. Tel: 408-395-2868; Fax: 408-354-8305. Email: snjmcadev@yahoo.com. Web: www.snjmusontario.org. Sisters Joan Saalfeld, S.N.J.M., Prov. Supr. & Contact; Emma Bezaire, S.N.J.M., Leadership Team; Jo'Ann De Quattro, S.N.J.M., Leadership Team; Mary Ellen Holohan, S.N.J.M., Treas. & Sec.; Judith Mayer, S.N.J.M., Leadership Team; Sr. Shirley Roberg, S.N.J.M., Vice Pres. Sisters of the Holy Names of Jesus and Mary US-Ontario Province., Other sisters reside in communities in Santa Clara, Los Gatos, San Jose, Cupertino, and Sunnyvale. *Convent of the Holy Names*, P.O. Box 1906, 95031. Tel: 408-354-1730; Fax: 408-395-6447. Ms. Dayna Hurst, Admin.; Sisters Molly Neville, S.N.J.M., Community Life Coord., Siena; Eleanore Maloney, S.N.J.M., Community Life Coord., Marian. Total in Convent 60.

MILPITAS. *Congregation of the Augustinian Recollect Sisters*, 307 Moretti Ln., 95035. Tel: 408-262-3536; Fax: 408-262-3536. Email: clairediane87@yahoo.com. Web: www.recoletas.org. Sr. Maria Divina N. Caabay, A.R., Contact Person.

Sisters of Mercy of Americas (Burlingame), 186 Beresford Ct. #F303, 95035. Tel: 408-946-5946. Email: mjvanbommel@att.net. Sr. Maria Juanita Van Bommel, R.S.M., Local Contact. Sisters 10.

REDWOOD CITY. *Sisters of St. Francis of Penance and of Christian Charity*, 1330 Brewster Ave., 94062. Tel: 650-369-1725; Fax: 650-369-0845. Web: www.stfrancisprovince.org. Sr. Patricia Rayburn, O.S.F., Prov. Min. Sisters 14.

SANTA CLARA. *Carmelite Monastery of the Infant Jesus, Discalced Carmelite Nuns*, 1000 Lincoln St., 95050. Tel: 408-296-8412; Fax: 408-248-4846. Email: santaclaracarmel@aol.com. Web: www.members.aol.com/santaclaracarmel. Sr. Irene Soos, O.C.D., Prioress. Sisters 13.

Dominican Sisters of San Rafael Congregation of the Most Holy Name, 1156 Santa Clara St., #11, 95050. Tel: 408-554-6431. Sr. Francine McCarthy, O.P., Contact Person.

Institute of the Servants of the Lord and the Virgin of Matara, 2800 Mission College Blvd., 95054. Tel: 408-988-4160. Email: c.ourladyofpeace@servidoras.org. Web: www.ssvmusa.org. Sisters 7.

Sisters of Charity of the Blessed Virgin Mary, 1220 Tasman Dr. #303, Sunnyvale, 94089. Tel: 408-744-9143; Fax: 408-734-9614. Web: www.bvmcong.org. Sr. Bette Gambonini, B.V.M., Contact. Sisters 5.

Society of the Sacred Heart, 1999 Lawrence Ct., 95051. Tel: 408-248-9058. Email: rstatt@rscj.org. Web: www.sofie.org/rscj/. Sr. Rosemary Statt, R.S.C.J., Contact. Sisters 3.

[O] MISCELLANEOUS LISTINGS

SAN JOSE. *Caritas Housing Corporation*, 1400 Parkmoor Ave., Ste. 190, 95126. Tel: 408-550-8300; Fax: 408-550-8339. Email: info@charitieshousing.org. Web: www.charitieshousing.org. Dan Wu, Exec. Dir.

The Catholic Foundation of Santa Clara County, 777 N. First St., Ste. 740, 95112. Tel: 408-995-5219; Fax: 408-995-5865. Email: info@cfoscc.org. Web: www.cfoscc.org. Carter Wells, Exec. Dir.

Charities Housing Development Corporation of Santa Clara County, 1400 Parkmoor Ave., Ste. 190, 95126. Tel: 408-550-8300; Fax: 408-550-8339. Email: info@charitieshousing.org. Web: www.charitieshousing.org. Dan Wu, Exec. Dir. Total Staff 52.

Christ Child Society of San Jose, 367 Santana Heights, #3107, 95128. Tel: 408-219-9884. Email: carriekrinock@yahoo.com. Carrie Krinock, Pres.

Hope Charities Housing Corporation, 1400 Parkmoor Ave., Ste. 190, 95126. Tel: 408-550-8300; Fax: 408-550-8339. Email: info@charitieshousing.org. Web: www.charitieshousing.org. Dan Wu, Exec. Dir.

San Antonio Charities, 1400 Parkmoor Ave., Ste. 190, 95126. Tel: 408-550-8300; Fax: 408-550-8339. Email: info@charitieshousing.org. Web: www.charitieshousing.org. Dan Wu, Exec. Dir.

San Jose Cathedral Foundation (A nonprofit, charitable, public-benefit California corporation.), 80 S. Market St., 95113. Tel: 408-283-8100, Ext. 2210; Fax: 408-283-8110. Email: atranchina@dsj.org. Web: www.stjosephcathedral.org. Rev. Msgr. J. Patrick Browne, Exec. Dir.; Sharon Miller, Assoc. Dir.

San Jose English Cursillo, P.O. Box 6648, 95150. Tel: 408-629-2928. Email: sanjosecursillo@yahoo.com. Web: www.sanjosecursillo.org. Mr. Kevin F. Eck, Lay Dir.

San Tomas/Charities Housing Corporation, 1400 Parkmoor Ave., Ste. 190, 95126. Tel: 408-550-8300; Fax: 408-550-8339. Email: info@charitieshousing.org. Web: www.charitieshousing.org. Dan Wu, Exec. Dir.

Serra International Region 11, District 31, 8690 Lomas Azules Pl., 95135. Tel: 650-520-3657. Roger Hagman, Dist. 31 Gov.

Sierra Vista I/Charities Housing Corporation, 1400 Parkmoor Ave., Ste. 190, 95126. Tel: 408-550-8300; Fax: 408-550-8339. Email: info@charitieshousing.org. Web: www.charitieshousing.org. Dan Wu, Exec. Dir.

Society of St. Vincent de Paul, District Council of Santa Clara County, P.O. Box 5579, 95150. Tel: 408-943-8292. Email: info@svdp.org. Web: www.svdp.org. Tammy Pottoroff, Pres. Total Assisted 70,000; Total Staff 1.

Stoney Pine Charities Housing Corporation, 1400 Parkmoor Ave., Ste. 190, 95126. Tel: 408-550-8300; Fax: 408-550-8339. Email: info@charitieshousing.org. Web: www.charitieshousing.org. Dan Wu, Exec. Dir.

Sunset Charities Housing Corporation, 1400 Parkmoor Ave., Ste. 190, 95126. Tel: 408-550-8300; Fax: 408-550-8339. Email: info@charitieshousing.org. Web: www.charitieshousing.org. Dan Wu, Exec. Dir.

Vietnamese Catholic Center, 2849 S. White Rd., 95148. Tel: 408-983-0215; Fax: 408-983-0181. Email: hnguyen@dsj.org. Web: www.dsj.org. Mailing Address: 389 E. Santa Clara St., 95113. Rev. Hien Minh Nguyen, J.C.D., Vicar for Vietnamese Ministry & Dir. Vietnamese Catholic Center.

Vietnamese Youth and Culture Association, La Salle Vietnam House, 1103 Maxey Ct., 95132. Tel: 408-926-4665; Fax: 408-926-4665. Email: valery@stmarys-ca.edu. Web: www.lasan.org. Bro. Valery Nguyen Van An, F.S.C., Dir. Brothers of the Christian Schools (San Francisco Prov.).

CUPERTINO. *St. Joseph Cupertino Retirement Residence*, 10130 N. DeAnza Blvd., 95014. Tel: 408-257-1022; Fax: 408-257-3272. Rev. Msgr. Joseph J. Milani, Dir. (Retired). Priests 4; Total Staff 3.

GILROY. *Saint Louise Regional Hospital Foundation*, 9400 No Name Uno, 95020. Tel: 408-779-4510; Fax: 408-782-0231. Email: micheleaverill@dochs.org. Web: www.saintlouisehospital.org.

LOS ALTOS. *Jesuit Institute for Family Life*, 300 Manresa Way, 94022. Tel: 650-948-4854; Fax: 650-948-0640. Web: www.elretiro.org. Rev. Robert J. Fabing, S.J., Dir.

Vincentian Marian Youth, 26000 Altamont Rd., 94022. Tel: 310-603-6007. Denise Collaro, Contact Person.

LOS ALTOS HILLS. *Daughters of Charity Health System*, 26000 Altamont Rd., 94022. Tel: 650-917-4500; Fax: 650-941-6309. Web: www.dochs.org. Mike Stuart, CFO; Robert Issai, Pres. & CEO.

LOS GATOS. *California Jesuit Missions*, P.O. Box 519, 95031-0068. Tel: 408-884-1645; Fax: 408-884-1601. Web: www.jesuits.org. Rev. Theodore Gabrielli, S.J., Dir.

Jesuit Seminary Association, P.O. Box 68, 95031-0068. Tel: 408-884-1647; Fax: 408-884-1631. Rev. John P. Mossi, S.J., Advancement Office Mgr.

LYNWOOD. *Daughters of Charity Ministry Services Corporation*, 3663 Martin Luther King Jr. Blvd., 90262.

MOUNTAIN VIEW. *Villa Siena Foundation*, 1855 Miramonte Ave., 94040. Tel: 650-961-6484; Fax: 650-961-6254. Email: vsiena@pacbell.net. Mrs. Corine Bernard, Exec. Dir.

SANTA CLARA. *Alexian Brothers of San Jose*, c/o 1150 N. First St., Ste. 100, 95112. Tel: 847-385-7147; Fax: 847-483-7036. Melissa Kulik, Contact Person.

Catholic Professionals, P.O. Box 6346, 95150. Tel: 408-491-9229. Email: info@sjcatholicprofessionals.com. Web: sjcatholicprofessionals.org. Rev. Justin Le, Chap.; James Parks, Pres.

Hand of Help Christian Service Program, 1150 N. First St., Ste. 100, 95112. Tel: 408-983-0158; Fax: 520-720-4004. Email: serve@theriver.com. Web: www.handofhelp.info. Bro. Fred Buerman, Exec. Dir.

Jesuit Volunteer Corps. Southwest, Braun, P.O. Box 459, 95050. Tel: 408-241-4200; Fax: 408-241-4201.

Roman Catholic Seminary Corporation of San Jose, 1150 N. First St., Ste. 100, 95112. Tel: 408-983-0154; Fax: 408-983-0242. Email: cilia@dsj.org. Rev. Msgr. Francis V. Cilia, V.G., Vice Pres. & Contact Person.

The Roman Catholic Welfare Corporation of San Jose, 1150 N. First St., Ste. 100, 95112. Tel: 408-983-0168; Fax: 408-983-0296. Email: serventi@dsj.org. Robert Serventi, Contact Person.

SARATOGA. *Our Lady of Fatima Villa Foundation*, 20400 Saratoga-Los Gatos Rd., 95070. Tel: 408-741-2950; Fax: 408-741-4930. Email: bmahoney@fatimavilla.org. Web: www.fatimavilla.org. Bella Mahoney, Pres., CEO & Admin.

RELIGIOUS INSTITUTES OF MEN REPRESENTED IN THE DIOCESE

For further details refer to the corresponding bracketed number in the Religious Institutes of Men or Women section.

[0330]—*Brothers of the Christian Schools*—F.S.C.

[0600]—*Brothers of the Congregation of the Holy Cross (Southwest Province)*—C.S.C.

[0260]—*Discalced Carmelite Friars*—O.C.D.

[]—*Franciscan Friars* (Croatia)—O.F.M.

[0650]—*Holy Ghost Fathers*—C.S.Sp.

[]—*Institute of Incarnate Word* (Argentina)—I.V.E.

[0690]—*Jesuit Fathers and Brothers (Society of Jesus)* (California Prov.)—S.J.

[0760]—*Marianists (Society of Mary)*—S.M.

[0800]—*Maryknoll (Catholic Foreign Mission Society of America, Inc.)*—M.M.

[1210]—*Missionaries of St. Charles - Scalabrinians (Province of St. John Baptist)*—C.S.

[1110]—*Missionaries of the Sacred Heart*—M.S.C.

[0520]—*Order of Friars Minor (Province of St. Barbara)*—O.F.M.

[0430]—*Order of Preachers (Province of the Most Holy Name of Jesus-Western Dominican Province)*—O.P.

[1260]—*Society of Christ (Society of Christ for Polonia)*—S.Ch.

[1170]—*St. Patrick's Missionary Society*—S.P.S.

RELIGIOUS INSTITUTES OF WOMEN REPRESENTED IN THE DIOCESE

[]—*Adrian Dominican Sisters*—O.P.

[]—*Blessed Virgin Missionaries of Carmel*—B.V.M.C.

[]—*Caritas Sisters of Miyazaki*—C.S.M.

[2020]—*Community of the Holy Spirit*—C.H.S.

[]—*Congregation of the Augustinian Recollects*—A.R.

[1070-12]—*Congregation of the Queen of the Holy Rosary (Dominican Sisters)*—O.P.

[0760]—*Daughters of Charity of St. Vincent De Paul*—D.C.

[0420]—*Discalced Carmelite Nuns*—O.C.D.

[1070-19]—*Dominican Sisters of Houston, Texas (Congregation of the Sacred Heart)*—O.P.

[1070-30]—*Dominican Sisters of Oakford*—O.P.

[]—*Dominican Sisters of San Rafael*—O.P.

[]—*Eucharistic Missionaries of the Most Holy Trinity* (Mexico)—M.E.S.S.T.

[]—*Franciscan Hospitalier Sisters of the Immaculate Conception*—F.H.IC.

[]—*Franciscans of Our Lady of the Poor*—F.L.P.

[]—*Institute of the Servants of the Lord and the Virgin of Matara*—S.S.V.M.

[]—*LaSalle Sisters* (Vietnam)—L.S.

[2470]—*Maryknoll Sisters of St. Dominic*—M.M.

[]—*Missionary Catechists of Divine Providence*—M.C.D.P.

[]—*Missionary Sisters Oblates of the Holy Family* (Taiwan)—O.H.F.

[3760]—*Order of St. Clare (Immaculate Heart Monastery of Poor Clares)*—P.C.C.

[0980]—*Pious Disciples of the Divine Master*—P.D.D.M.

[]—*Quinhon Missionary Sisters of the Holy Cross* (Vietnam)—L.H.C.

[1070-03]—*Sinsinawa Dominican Congregation of the Most Holy Rosary*—O.P.

[0430]—*Sisters of Charity of the Blessed Virgin Mary*—B.V.M.

[2516]—*Sisters of Mercy (Ireland)*—R.S.M.

[2570]—*Sisters of Mercy of the Americas (Regional Community of Burlingame)*—R.S.M.

[]—*Sisters of Notre Dame de Namur*—S.N.D.deN.

[3840]—*Sisters of St. Joseph of Carondelet (Province of Los Angeles)*—C.S.J.

[3840]—*Sisters of St. Joseph of Carondelet (Province of St. Louis)*—C.S.J.

[1960]—*Sisters of the Holy Family*—S.H.F.

[1990]—*Sisters of the Holy Names of Jesus and Mary (California Province)*—S.N.J.M.

[3320]—*Sisters of the Presentation of the Blessed Virgin Mary*—P.B.V.M.

[1630]—*Sisters of the Third Order of Saint Francis of Penance and Christian Charity*—O.S.F.

[]—*Society of Helpers*—H.H.S.

[4070]—*Society of the Sacred Heart*—R.S.C.J.

[]—*Ursuline Roman Union*—O.S.U.

DIOCESAN CEMETERIES AND MAUSOLEUMS

SAN JOSE. *Calvary Catholic Cemetery*, 2650 Madden Ave., 95116. Tel: 408-258-2940; Fax: 408-258-5614. Mr. William Sousae, Dir. (Santa Clara Co.)

LOS ALTOS. *Gate of Heaven*, 22555 Cristo Rey Dr., 94024. Tel: 650-428-3730; Fax: 650-428-3733. Mr. William Sousae, Dir.

NECROLOGY

† Dougherty, Charles, (Retired)—Died Jan. 27, 2009
† Freyne, Bernard, (Retired)—Died Feb. 2, 2009
† Fry, Richard C., (Retired)—Died Feb. 24, 2009
† Macedo, Charles, (Retired)—Died Oct. 1, 2009

An asterisk (*) denotes an organization that has established tax-exempt status directly with the IRS and is not covered by the USCCB Group Ruling.

Archdiocese of Santa Fe

(Archidioecesis Sanctae Fidei)

LOVE ONE ANOTHER CONSTANTLY

Most Reverend

MICHAEL J. SHEEHAN, S.T.L., J.C.D.

Archbishop of Santa Fe; ordained July 12, 1964; consecrated and installed as First Bishop of Lubbock June 17, 1983; appointed Apostolic Administrator of Santa Fe April 6, 1993; installed as Eleventh Archbishop of Santa Fe September 21, 1993. *Res.: Catholic Center, 4000 St. Joseph Pl., N.W., Albuquerque, NM 87120.*

Archdiocese of Santa Fe Catholic Center: 4000 St. Joseph Pl., N.W., Albuquerque, NM 87120. Tel: 505-831-8100.

ESTABLISHED IN 1850.

Square Miles 61,142.

Created an Archbishopric in 1875.

Solemnly consecrated to the Immaculate Heart of Mary on October 7, 1945.

Comprises the Counties of Colfax, Curry, DeBaca, Guadalupe, Harding, Los Alamos, Mora, Quay, Roosevelt, San Miguel, Santa Fe, Socorro, Taos, Torrance and Union with a part of Bernalillo, Sandoval, Rio Arriba and Valencia Counties.

Patron of the Archdiocese: St. Francis of Assisi.

For legal titles of parishes and archdiocesan institutions, consult the Chancery Office.

STATISTICAL OVERVIEW

Personnel	
Archbishops	1
Retired Archbishops	1
Abbots	1
Priests: Diocesan Active in Diocese	88
Priests: Retired, Sick or Absent	44
Number of Diocesan Priests	132
Religious Priests in Diocese	86
Total Priests in Diocese	218
Extern Priests in Diocese	16
Ordinations:	
Diocesan Priests	2
Transitional Deacons	2
Permanent Deacons	17
Permanent Deacons in Diocese	216
Total Brothers	70
Total Sisters	176
Parishes	
Parishes	92
With Resident Pastor:	
Resident Diocesan Priests	71
Resident Religious Priests	15
Without Resident Pastor:	
Administered by Deacons	1
Administered by Religious Women	4
Administered by Lay People	1
Missions	217
Pastoral Centers	4
Closed Parishes	1
Professional Ministry Personnel:	
Brothers	3
Sisters	31
Lay Ministers	72
Welfare	
Catholic Hospitals	1
Total Assisted	162,000
Health Care Centers	1
Total Assisted	1,500
Homes for the Aged	1
Total Assisted	25
Day Care Centers	1
Total Assisted	48
Specialized Homes	2
Total Assisted	2,100
Special Centers for Social Services	6
Total Assisted	367,809
Residential Care of Disabled	1
Total Assisted	16
Educational	
Diocesan Students in Other Seminaries	21
Total Seminarians	21
High Schools, Diocesan and Parish	1
Total Students	884
High Schools, Private	1
Total Students	768
Elementary Schools, Diocesan and Parish	15
Total Students	3,488
Catechesis/Religious Education:	
High School Students	4,651
Elementary Students	16,493
Total Students under Catholic Instruction	26,305
Teachers in the Diocese:	
Priests	3
Brothers	1
Sisters	12
Lay Teachers	380
Vital Statistics	
Receptions into the Church:	
Infant Baptism Totals	5,203
Minor Baptism Totals	928
Adult Baptism Totals	297
Received into Full Communion	465
First Communions	5,242
Confirmations	3,677
Marriages:	
Catholic	938
Interfaith	182
Total Marriages	1,120
Deaths	3,065
Total Catholic Population	314,183
Total Population	1,227,277

Former Archbishops—Most Revs. J. B. LAMY, cons. Nov. 24, 1850; created first Archbishop, 1875; resigned July 18, 1885; died Feb. 13, 1888; J. B. SALPOINTE, D.D., cons. Bishop of Doryla and Vicar Apostolic of Arizona, June 20, 1869; appt. Coadjutor of Santa Fe "cum jure successionis", April, 22, 1884; promoted to the Titular Archiepiscopal See of Anazarba, Oct. 11 of same year; succeeded to the See of Santa Fe, July 18, 1885; resigned Jan. 7, 1894 Titular Archbishop of Tomi; died July 15, 1898; P. L. CHAPELLE, cons. Nov. 1, 1891; Archbishop of Santa Fe, Jan. 7, 1894; transferred to New Orleans, Dec. 1, 1897; died Aug. 9, 1905; PETER BOURGADE, D.D., cons. May 1, 1885 Bishop of Thaumacum and Vic. Ap. of Arizona; Bishop of Tucson, May 8, 1897; transferred to Santa Fe, Jan. 7, 1899; died May 17, 1908; J. B. PITAVAL, D.D., cons. Titular Bishop of Sora and Auxiliary of Santa Fe, July 25, 1902; promoted to the See of Santa Fe, Jan. 3, 1909; resigned Feb., 1918; appt. Titular Archbishop of Amida, July 29, 1918; died May 23, 1928; ALBERT T. DAEGER, O.F.M., D.D., cons. May 7, 1919; died Dec. 2, 1932; RUDOLPH ALOYSIUS GERKEN, D.D., cons. Bishop of Amarillo, April 26, 1927; appt. Archbishop of Santa Fe, June 2, 1933; installed as Archbishop of Santa Fe, Aug. 23, 1933; died March 2, 1943; EDWIN V. BYRNE, D.D., cons. Bishop of Ponce, P.R.; transferred to Diocese of San Juan, P.R.; promoted to Archbishop of Santa Fe, June 15, 1943; died July 25, 1963; JAMES P. DAVIS, D.D., cons. Bishop of San Juan, P.R., Oct. 6, 1943; promoted to Archbishop, April 30, 1960; transferred to Archdiocese of Santa Fe, Jan. 3, 1964; retired Oct. 1974; died March 4, 1988; ROBERT F. SANCHEZ, cons. 10th Archbishop of Santa Fe, July 25, 1974; resigned April 6, 1993.

All offices are located at the Archdiocese of Santa Fe Catholic Center, 4000 St. Joseph Pl., N.W., Albuquerque, NM 87120. Tel: 505-831-8100, unless otherwise indicated.

Office of the Archbishop

Vicar-General—Rev. Msgr. LAMBERT J. LUNA, V.G., 5901 St. Joseph Dr., N.W., Albuquerque, 87120.

Secretary to the Archbishop—Ms. DOLORES CORDOVA. Tel: 505-831-8120.

Office of the Chancellor

Chancellor—Very Rev. TIMOTHY A. MARTINEZ. Tel: 505-831-8158.

Archivist and Artistic Patrimony—Mrs. MARINA OCHOA, 213 Cathedral Pl., Santa Fe, 87501. Tel: 505-983-3811.

Attorney for the Archdiocese—Mr. JUAN L. FLORES, 40 First Plaza, N.W., Ste. 740, Albuquerque, 87102. Tel: 505-247-0411; Fax: 505-842-8890. Mailing Address: P.O. Box 271, Albuquerque, 87103.

Communications-Media—Mrs. CELINE RADIGAN, Dir. Tel: 505-831-8180.

Ecumenical Commission and Interreligious Affairs—Rev. Msgr. RICHARD OLONA, Dir., 4000 St. Joseph Pl., N.W., Albuquerque, 87120. Tel: 505-831-8243; Fax: 505-831-8206.

Madonna Retreat and Conference Center—Ms. MARIE VILLANUEVA, Dir., 4040 St. Joseph Pl., N.W., Albuquerque, 87120. Tel: 505-831-8196.

Newspaper, Archdiocesan "People of God"—Most Rev. MICHAEL JARBOE SHEEHAN, S.T.L., J.C.D., Publisher; Mrs. CELINE RADIGAN, Editor, 4000 St. Joseph Pl., N.W., Albuquerque, 87120. Tel: 505-831-8180.

Parish Bulletin Service, "The Catholic Communicator"—JENNY CHILSON, Mailing Address: P.O. Box 93244, Albuquerque, 87199-3244. Tel: 505-856-0333; Fax: 505-822-5589.

Human Resources—Ms. CATHY SALCIDO, Dir. Tel: 505-831-8130.

Immaculate Heart of Mary Retreat and Conference Center—Mr. RANDOLPH DAUGHTERY, Dir. Tel: 505-988-1975.

Canonical Services Division

Judicial Vicar—Rev. JEROME PLOTKOWSKI, J.C.L. Tel: 505-831-8177.

College of Consultors—Most Rev. MICHAEL JARBOE SHEEHAN, S.T.L., J.C.D.; Rev. Msgr. LAMBERT J. LUNA, V.G.; Very Rev. JOHN CANNON; Rev. ADAM L. ORTEGA Y ORTIZ; Very Rev. TIMOTHY A. MARTINEZ; Rev. Msgr. FRANCIS EGGERT; Revs. WILLIAM YOUNG; JOHN C. DANIEL; MIKE SHEA; Rev. Msgr. RICHARD OLONA.

Council of Men and Women Religious—VACANT.

Holy Childhood Association— See Mission Office Svcs.

Mission Office—Rev. ARKAD BICZAK Dir. Propagation of the Faith; Holy Childhood; Catholic Relief Svcs. John XXIII Catholic Community, 4831 Tramway Ridge Dr., N.E., Albuquerque, 87111. Tel: 505-293-0088.

Office of Religious—VACANT.

Pastoral Planning—MICHELLE MONTEZ, Dir., 4000 St. Joseph Place, N.W., Albuquerque, 87120. Tel: 505-831-8221; Fax: 505-831-8206. Email: planning@archdiosf.org.

Permanent Diaconate Program—Deacon STEPHEN S. RANGEL, Dir., 4000 St. Joseph Pl., N.W., Albuquerque, 87120. Tel: 505-831-8229.

Pilgrimage for Vocations—Rev. EDMUND SAVILLA, Dir., Ascension Parish, 2150 Raymac Rd., S.W., Albuquerque, 87105. Tel: 505-877-8550.

Presbyteral Council of the Archdiocese of Santa Fe—Most Rev. MICHAEL JARBOE SHEEHAN, S.T.L., J.C.D., Pres. (Ex Officio); Rev. Msgr. LAMBERT J. LUNA, V.G., Vicar Gen. (Ex Officio Member); Very Revs. TIMOTHY A. MARTINEZ, Chancellor (Ex Officio Member); JOHN CANNON, Chm.; Revs. MICHAEL DEPALMA, Vice Chm.; CLARENCE MAES, Sec.; Very Rev. BENNETT J. VOORHIES, At Large Member; Revs. EDWARD DOMME, At Large Member; GERALD T. JOHNSON, Delegate At Large; NATHAN LIBAIRE, Delegate At Large; JUAN MENDEZ, Delegate At Large; Very Revs. FRANCIS MALLEY, Member; JAMES MCGOWAN, Member; DOUGLAS J. MITCHELL, Member; Rev. Msgrs. JEROME MARTINEZ Y ALIRE, J.C.L., Member; DOUGLAS A. RAUN, Member; Very Revs. BENNETT J. VOORHIES, Member; GABRIEL PAREDES, Member; Revs. MICHAEL DEPALMA; DENNIS M. GARCIA, J.C.L.; KEVIN W. NIEHOFF, O.P.; CLARENCE MAES; EDWARD DOMME; Rev. Msgr. FRANCIS EGGERT; Revs. THOMAS MAYEFSKE (Retired); RAFAEL GARCIA, S.J., Delegate for Relg.

Propagation of the Faith— See Mission Office.

Vicars Forane (Deans)—Rev. Msgrs. JEROME MARTINEZ Y ALIRE, J.C.L., Santa Fe Deanery; DOUGLAS A. RAUN, Albuquerque-Deanery A; Very Revs. BENNETT J. VOORHIES, Albuquerque-Deanery B; GABRIEL PAREDES, Albuquerque-Deanery C; DOUGLAS J. MITCHELL, Southwest Deanery; FRANCIS MALLEY, Northwest Deanery; JOHN CANNON, Northeast Deanery; JAMES MCGOWAN, Southeast Deanery.

Tribunal—Tel: 505-831-8177.

Judicial Vicar—Rev. JEROME PLOTKOWSKI, J.C.L.

Adjutant Judicial Vicar—Rev. KEVIN W. NIEHOFF, O.P.

Promoter of Justice—Rev. Msgr. JEROME MARTINEZ Y ALIRE, J.C.L.

Defenders of the Bond—Revs. DENNIS M. GARCIA, J.C.L.; STEPHEN SCHULTZ; ADAM LEE ORTEGA Y ORTIZ.

Associate Judges—Revs. JOHN R. CONWAY; RONALD J. BOWERS, J.C.D.; Deacons HARRY BEARE; GEORGE SANDOVAL; MARY ANN ECKLUND.

Notaries—Mr. JOSEPH SINICO; Ms. LOUELLEN N. MARTINEZ.

Delegate for Matrimonial Dispensations—Rev. JEROME PLOTKOWSKI, J.C.L.

Appeal Court—Tel: 505-831-8177.

Vocations—Rev. MICHAEL DEPALMA, Dir. Tel: 505-831-8143; Mr. ROBERT MARTINEZ, Asst. Dir.

Finance Division

Executive Director of Finance—Mr. TONY SALGADO, CPA. Tel: 505-831-8132.

Annual Catholic Appeal Foundation— Archdiocesan Annual Appeal Program, Dr. DOLORES SOKOL, Ph.D., Exec. Dir. Tel: 505-831-8155.

The Catholic Foundation of the Archdiocese of Santa Fe—MARY P. DUNN, Exec. Dir., 4333 Pan American Freeway, N.E., Ste. D, Albuquerque, 87107. Tel: 505-872-2901; Fax: 505-872-2905 Nonprofit corporation for financial support of Archdiocese of Santa Fe.

Finance Council—Most Rev. MICHAEL JARBOE SHEEHAN, S.T.L., J.C.D., Pres.; Mr. TIM SHEEHAN, Chm.; Very Rev. TIMOTHY A. MARTINEZ, Chancellor; Rev. Msgr. LAMBERT J. LUNA, V.G., Vicar Gen.; Rev. EDWARD C. DOMME; Mr. GIG BRUMMEL; Mrs. VIRGINIA SCHROEDER; Mr. TONY SALGADO, CPA, Exec. Dir. Finance; Ms. JENNIFER CANTRELL, CPA; Mr. WILLIAM F. RASKOB III.

Property Managers and Construction Contract Coord.—Mr. JOHN HUCHMALA. Tel: 505-831-8136.

Pastoral Ministries

Executive Director—FRANCES VOGEL-MONTANO, 4000 St. Joseph Pl., N.W., Albuquerque, 87120. Tel: 505-831-8151.

Catholic Campaign for Human Development—ANNE AVELLONE, Coord., 4000 St. Joseph Pl., N.W., Albuquerque, 87120. Tel: 505-831-8167.

Catholic Committee on Scouting— (Boy Scouts and Girl Scouts) Deacon DONALD BRUCKNER, Dir. Scouting.

Catholic Schools Office—SUSAN M. MURPHY, M.A., Supt. Tel: 505-831-8173.

Catholic Charities—JAMES GANNON, Dir., 6001 Marble, N.E., Albuquerque, 87110. Tel: 505-724-4670.

Cursillo Movement—Deacon MANUEL FACIO, Spiritual Dir.

Ministry to the Disabled—Deacon STEPHEN S. RANGEL, Dir. Tel: 505-831-8229.

Ministry to the Deaf—Mrs. ARDITH MONTANO, Coord. Tel: 505-831-8174.

Evangelization—MICHELLE MONTEZ, Dir. Tel: 505-831-8221.

Formation for Christian Service—DAN MCGILL, Dir. Tel: 505-831-8187.

Hospital Ministry—Deacon STEPHEN S. RANGEL, Coord. Tel: 505-831-8229.

Prison & Detention Ministry—Deacon STEPHEN S. RANGEL, Dir. Tel: 505-831-8229; Sr. JOSEFINA PERALTA, Fd.CC., Coord. Prison & Jail Ministry; Mr. CARL KOESTNER, Coord. Threshold Prog.

Archdiocesan Network for Catholic Legislative Advocacy—ANNE AVELLONE. Tel: 505-831-8167.

Liturgical Commission—Most Rev. MICHAEL JARBOE SHEEHAN, S.T.L., J.C.D., Pres.; Ms. BARBARA GUENTHER, Chm., 4000 St. Joseph Pl., N.W., Albuquerque, 87120. Tel: 505-831-8194.

Marriage and Family Life Office—Mrs. REMEDIOS (HEDDY) LONG, Dir. Tel: 505-831-8117.

Ministry to Spanish Speaking—Deacon JUAN BARAJAS, Dir. Tel: 505-831-8152.

African American Ministry—Ms. BRENDA DABNEY. Tel: 505-831-8167.

Native American Ministry—Mr. MIKE VALDO. Tel: 505-831-8100.

Newman Centers—

ALBQ: Aquinas Newman Center—Rev. THOMAS MARTIN JACKSON, O.P., Dir., Univ. of New Mexico, 1815 Lomas Rd., N.E., Albuquerque, 87106. Tel: 505-247-1095.

LAS VEGAS: Newman Center—Rev. GEORGE SALAZAR, Coord., Highlands University, 811 Sixth St., Las Vegas, 87701. Tel: 505-425-9295.

PORTALES: St. Thomas Moore Newman Center—Very Rev. JAMES MCGOWAN, Chap., Mailing Address: Eastern New Mexico University, P.O. Box 2253, Portales, 88130. Tel: 505-356-5615.

SANTE FE—

Santa Fe Community College—Bro. JAMES BROWN, Campus Min. Tel: 505-473-6587.

SOCORRO: St. Patrick Newman Center—Deacon NICHOLAS KELLER, 801 School of Mines Rd., Socorro, 87801. Tel: 575-838-2084.

Office of Worship—LINDA KREHMEIER, Dir. Tel: 505-831-8194.

RCIA—LINDA KREHMEIER. Tel: 505-831-8194.

Religious Education—Dr. CHELA GONZALEZ, Dir. Rel. Educ. Tel: 505-831-8127. 4000 St. Joseph Pl., N.W., Albuquerque, 87120. Tel: 505-831-8128.

Schools of Lay Ministry Formation—

Albuquerque Deanery A,B,C, "Emmaus Journey"—Deacon FRANK LUCERO, 4000 St. Joseph Pl., N.W., Albuquerque, 87120. Tel: 505-831-8151.

Northwest Deanery—JOANNE DUPONT-SANDOVAL, Coord., Mailing Address: P.O. Box 429, Truchas, 87578. Tel: 505-689-2404.

Santa Fe Deanery— (Jornada de Fe) JUANITA MONTOYA, Coord., 2727 Calle Cedro, Santa Fe, 87505. Tel: 505-471-6489.

Spanish School of Ministry—Deacon JUAN BARAJAS, Dir.; ROCIO GONZALEZ, Coord. Albuquerque Area; ANGIE KOLASH, Coord. Santa Fe Area. Tel: 505-831-8152.

St. Vincent de Paul Council—Deacon SANTOS ABEYTA, Spiritual Dir., Mailing Address: Holy Family Parish, P.O. Box 12127, Albuquerque, 87195. Tel: 505-842-5426.

Social Justice—ANNE AVELLONE. Tel: 505-831-8167.

Youth and Young Adult Ministry—BERNADETTE JARAMILLO, Dir. Tel: 505-831-8145.

Ministry Resource Center—DAN MCGILL, Dir. Tel: 505-831-8187.

Victim Assistance Coordinator—ANNETTE M. KLIMKA. Tel: 505-831-8159. Email: aklimka@archdiosf.org.

CLERGY, PARISHES, MISSIONS AND PAROCHIAL SCHOOLS

CITY OF SANTA FE

(SANTA FE COUNTY)

1—THE CATHEDRAL BASILICA OF ST. FRANCIS OF ASSISI (1610) [CEM] Rev. Msgr. Jerome Martinez y Alire, Rector; Rev. Oscar Coelho, Assoc. Rector; Deacons William Kollasch; Juan Martinez.
Res.: 131 Cathedral Pl., P.O. Box 2127, 87504. Tel: 505-982-5619; Fax: 505-989-1952. Email: santafecathedral@cbsfa.org. Web: www.cbsfa.org.
Catechesis/Religious Program—Tel: 505-982-3625; 505-820-3429; Fax: 505-989-3760. Sisters Josephine Macias, D.R.E.; Phyllis Stowell, D.R.E. Students 169.

2—ST. ANNE'S (1942) [JC] Rev. Leo W. Ortiz; Deacons Enrique M. Montoya; Andy Dimas.
Res.: 511 Alicia, 87501. Tel: 505-983-4430; Fax: 505-983-7483.
Catechesis/Religious Program—Students 191.

3—CRISTO REY (1940) [JC] Rev. Msgr. Jerome Martinez y Alire, Canonical Pastor; Deacon Thomas Van Valkenburgh, Parish Life Coord.
Office & Church: 1120 Canyon Rd., 87501. Tel: 505-983-8528; Fax: 505-992-6836. Email: cristorey@qwestoffice.net. Web: www.cristoreysantafe.parishesonline.com.
Mission—Our Lady of Guadalupe La Canada de los Alamos, Santa Fe Co. 87501.
Catechesis/Religious Program— Elementary Grades Twinned with Cathedral Basilica. Students 6.

4—ST. JOHN THE BAPTIST (1953) Rev. Nathan Libaire; Deacons Andres Carrillo; Joe Garcia, Coord. Faith Formation.
Res.: 1301 Osage Ave., 87505. Tel: 505-983-5034; Fax: 505-983-1861. Email: stjohns@qwestoffice.net. Web: stjohn-sf.org.
Catechesis/Religious Program—Students 169.

5—OUR LADY OF GUADALUPE (1882), (Hispanic), [CEM] [JC] Rev. Tien-Tri Nguyen; Deacons Carlos F. Pacheco, (Retired); Gilbert Valdez, Pastoral Assoc.; Jose Luis Burrola, Pastoral Assoc.; Thomas Stith, Pastoral Assoc.
Res.: 417 Agua Fria St., 87501. Tel: 505-983-8868; Fax: 505-983-4304.
Catechesis/Religious Program—Tel: 505-988-3336. Deacon Anthony Trujillo, D.R.E. Students 697.
Mission—San Ysidro P.O. Box 65, Tesuque, Santa Fe Co. 87574. Tel: 505-984-2930.
Mission—Our Lady of Sorrows Rio en Medio, Sante Fe Co. Tel: 505-982-5588.

6—SAN ISIDRO (1835), (Hispanic), [CEM 2] Rev. Franklin D. Pretto; Deacon Michael Siegel.
Res.: 3552 Agua Fria St., 87507. Tel: 505-471-0710; Fax: 505-471-9034. Email: sanisidro_1@juno.com.
Catechesis/Religious Program—Tel: 505-920-0569. Sr. Juanita Gonzalez, D.R.E. Tel: 505-471-6385 (Home). Students 344.
Mission—San Jose La Cienega, Santa Fe Co.

7—SANTA MARIA DE LA PAZ CATHOLIC COMMUNITY (1990) Revs. Adam Lee Ortega y Ortiz; Jim Wolff (Canada); Earl Rohleder (EVN) (Retired); Paul H. Lujan, Business Mgr.; Sisters Colleen Shanahan, O.S.F., Family Life Dir.; Felipa Lara, M.C.S.H., Dir. Spanish Speaking Ministry; Maria de Jesus Becerril, M.C.S.H.; Deacons Juan M. Rodriguez, (Retired); Manuel Montoya; Eloy Gallegos; John Cordova.
Res.: 11 College Ave., 87508. Tel: 505-438-9410; Fax: 505-473-1602. Email: smdlp@smdlp.org. Web: www.smdlp.org.
Catechesis/Religious Program—Mrs. Patricia Lopez, D.R.E. Students 416.

OUTSIDE THE CITY OF SANTA FE

ABIQUIU, RIO ARRIBA CO., ST. THOMAS APOSTLE (1745), (Hispanic), [CEM 5] Rev. James Marshall.
Res.: P.O. Box 117, 87510. Tel: 505-685-4462; Fax: 505-685-4209. Email: stthomas@valornet.com.
Catechesis/Religious Program—Tel: 505-685-4462 (All Missions). Isabel Trujillo, D.R.E.; Juan Chavez, D.R.E.; Pita Lopez, D.R.E.; Isabel Madrid, D.R.E. Students 96.
Mission— Canones, Rio Arriba Co.
Mission— Medanales, Rio Arriba Co.
Mission— Youngsville, Rio Arriba Co.
Mission— Coyote, Rio Arriba Co.
Mission— Mesa de Poleo, Rio Arriba Co.
Mission— Capulin, Rio Arriba Co.
Mission— Gallina, Rio Arriba Co.

ALBUQUERQUE, BERNALILLO CO.

1—ST. ANNE (1929) Rev. Irby C. Nichols; Deacons Tibo Chavez, Emeritus; Paul LeFebre; Juan Barajas; Benjamin Maes, Admin./ Dir. Music & Liturgy.
Res.: 1400 Arenal Rd., S.W., 87105. Tel: 505-877-3121; Fax: 505-877-0084. Email: stannes@lobo.net.
Catechesis/Religious Program—Tel: 505-877-0581. Jose Marcos Romero, D.R.E.; Brenda Romero, D.R.E. Students 235.
Mission—Morada de San Jose 2100 La Vega Rd., S.W., Bernalillo Co. 87105.

2—ANNUNCIATION (1959) Very Rev. Bennett J. Voorhies; Rev. Joel O. Bugas, Parochial Vicar; Deacons Harry Gogan; Victor J. Bachechi; Kevin Maloney; Robert Morrow. In Res., Rev. James Sampson, s.P.
Office & Res.: 2532 Vermont, N.E., 87110. Tel: 505-298-7553; 505-293-5462 (Res.); Fax: 505-294-7418. Email: contact@annunciationparishabq.org. Web: annunciationparishabq.org.
School—(Grades K-8), 2610 Utah N.E., 87110. Tel: 505-299-6783; Fax: 505-299-2182. Mrs. Cindy Shields, Prin. Sisters 1; Lay Teachers 30; Students 431.
Catechesis/Religious Program—Tel: 505-296-0411. Sr. Grace De Paoli, Fd.C.C., D.R.E. Students 185.

3—ASCENSION (1962) [CEM 2] Very Rev. Edmund Savilla; Deacons Bill Hoefler; Manuel Toquinto; Leon Jones.
Res.: 2150 Raymac Rd., S.W., 87105. Tel: 505-877-8550; Fax: 508-877-8508. Email:

ascension1@aol.com.
Catechesis/Religious Program—Tel: 505-877-8144. Anna Villegas, D.R.E.; Linda Sepulveda, D.R.E. Students 146.

4—ST. CHARLES BORROMEO (1934) [JC] Rev. Jerome D. Mueller, O.F.M.; Deacons William "Bill" Barry; Ron Schultz; Paul Dung Van Nguyen.
Res.: 1818 Coal Pl., S.E., 87106. Tel: 505-242-3462; Fax: 505-247-1292. Email: stcharlesborromeo@qwestoffice.net.
School—(Grades K-8) Tel: 505-243-5788; Fax: 505-764-8842. Ms. Barbara Rossow-Deming, Prin. Sisters 1; Lay Teachers 23; Students 274.
Catechesis/Religious Program—Tel: 505-247-1094, Ext. 15. Students 89.

5—ST. EDWIN (1965), (Hispanic), Rev. William E. Sanchez; Deacon Nestor Garcia, (Retired).
Res.: 2105 Barcelona Rd. S.W., 87105. Tel: 505-877-9118; Fax: 505-877-6810. Email: sechurch1@qwestoffice.net.
Catechesis/Religious Program—Tel: 505-877-2967. Students 49.

6—ST. FRANCIS XAVIER (1928), (Hispanic), [JC] Very Rev. Gabriel Paredes, Canonical Pastor; Sr. Bernice Garcia, Parish Life Coord. Tel: 505-268-0158.
Mailing Address: 820 Broadway, S.E., 87102.
Res.: 901 Adams, N.E., 87110.
Catechesis/Religious Program—Tel: 505-243-5201; Fax: 505-243-1179. Students 170.

7—HOLY FAMILY (1953), (Hispanic), Rev. Gerald Steinmetz, O.F.M.; Bro. Efren Quintero-Soto, Pastoral Assoc./C.R.E./Dir. Liturgy; Deacons Santos Abeyta; Eddie Blea. In Res., Revs. Richard Rohr, O.F.M.; Gonzalo Moreno, O.F.M.; Bro. Bart Wolff, O.F.M.
Res.: 562 Atrisco Dr., S.W., P.O. Box 12127, 87195. Tel: 505-842-5426; Fax: 505-842-9767. Email: holyfamilychurch@qwestoffice.net.
Catechesis/Religious Program—Tel: 505-842-5448; Fax: 505-842-5410. Email: religiousprogram@qwestoffice.net. Karen Mitchell, D.R.E. Students 229.

8—HOLY GHOST (1953) Rev. Mark A. Schultz; Deacons Ubaldo Chavez, (Retired); Ricardo Chavez; Faustin Archuleta.
Res.: 833 Arizona Ave., S.E., 87108. Tel: 505-265-5957; Fax: 505-265-5958. Email: hgparish2@aol.com.
School—(Grades K-8), (Elementary), 6201 Ross S.E., 87108. Tel: 505-256-1563; Fax: 505-262-9635. Email: hgschool964@aol.com. Web: www.holyghost-catholicschool.com. Dr. Noreen Copeland, Prin.; Christine Sedillo, Librarian. Sisters 1; Lay Teachers 18; Students 205.
Catechesis/Religious Program—Tel: 505-265-1975 (Spanish); 505-255-7798 (English). Email: hgengcat@aol.com (English); hghispanicmin@aol.com (Spanish). Marlene Torres, D.R.E. Spanish Program; Theresa Montoya, D.R.E. English Program. Students 96.

9—IMMACULATE CONCEPTION (1883), (Hispanic), Revs. Rafael Garcia, S.J.; Richard W. McGowan, S.J.; Leo V. Leise, S.J.; Deacons Gilbert Valverde, (Retired); George Sandoval. In Res., Revs. Thomas J. Steele, S.J.; Joseph Vanderholt, S.J.; Oren W. Key, S.J.; Arturo Araujo, S.J.
Res.: 619 Copper Ave., N.W., 87102. Tel: 505-247-4271; Fax: 505-243-0402.
School—St. Mary, (Grades K-8), 224 Seventh St., 87102. Tel: 505-242-6271; Fax: 505-242-4837. Sr. Marianella Domenici, S.C., Prin. Sisters 2; Lay Teachers 36; Students 561.
Catechesis/Religious Program—Tel: 505-247-2555; Fax: 505-247-2555. Students 160.

10—ST. JOHN THE APOSTLE (1984), (John XXIII Catholic Community) Rev. Arkad Biczak; Deacons John Russo; Alex Trujillo, (Retired); Earl Meyrick; Clara Maestas, Business Mgr.
4831 Tramway Ridge Dr., N.E., 87111. Tel: 505-293-0088; Fax: 505-293-7276. Web: www.johnxxiiic-c.org. In Res., Rev. Charles T. Doughterty, C.P.
Catechesis/Religious Program—Tel: 505-293-7756. Bernadette Downie, D.R.E. Students 202.

11—SAINT JOSEPH ON THE RIO GRANDE (1986) Rev. Msgr. Lambert J. Luna; Deacons Don Bruckner; Jerry Hietpas; Rene Greivel; Bert Dohle; Thomas Baca; George Miller; Sr. Kathleen Hurley, O.S.F., Pastoral Assoc.
Office: 5901 St. Joseph Dr., N.W., 87120. Tel: 505-839-7952; Fax: 505-839-7955. Email: sjrg@qwestoffice.net.
Catechesis/Religious Program—Tel: 505-244-2154; Fax: 505-833-1920. Students 481.

12—ST. JUDE THADDEUS (1968) Revs. John C. Daniel; Emmanuel Izuka (Nigeria), Parochial Vicar; Deacons Frank Lucero; Robert Aragon.
Mailing Address: P.O. Box 67710, 87193. Tel: 505-898-0826 (Church); 505-897-0391 (Res.); Fax: 505-792-9810. Email: stjude@stjudenm.org.
Catechesis/Religious Program—Students 685.

13—NATIVITY OF THE BLESSED VIRGIN MARY (1936) [CEM] [JC 2] Rev. Juan Mendez; Deacons Leonard Martinez; Juan Ortiz; Michael Illerbrun; Ralph Vigil.
Res.: 9502 Fourth St., N.W., 87114. Tel: 505-898-5253; Fax: 505-898-0496. Web: www.n-bvm.org.
School—(Grades PreK-K) Nancy A. Suedkamp, Prin. Religious Sisters 1; Lay Teachers 2; Students 20.
Catechesis/Religious Program—Tel: 505-898-1441. Michael Illebrun, D.R.E. Students 622.
Mission—Our Lady of Mount Carmel 7807 Edith, Bernalillo Co. 87114.

14—OUR LADY OF FATIMA (1949) [JC] Rev. Msgr. Francis X. Eggert; Deacons Thomas Jones; Steve Hall. In Res., Rev. Stephen A. Sanchez; Very Rev. Timothy A. Martinez, Chancellor.
Office: 4020 Lomas, N.E., 87110. Tel: 505-265-5868; Fax: 505-268-0680.
School—(Grades PreK-8) Tel: 505-255-6391; Fax: 505-268-3279. Tim Whalen, Prin. Lay Teachers 15; Students (K-5) 92; Students (6-8) 47.
Catechesis/Religious Program—Students 55.

15—OUR LADY OF GUADALUPE (1954), (Hispanic), Rev. Joe Vigil; Deacons Manuel Facio; George W. Valverde; Manuel Cabrera; Jim Garcia, Business Mgr.
Res.: 1860 Griegos, N.W., 87107. Tel: 505-345-4596; Fax: 505-342-2984.
Catechesis/Religious Program—Tel: 505-344-7153. Julia Martinez, D.R.E. (Children); Jacob Lucero, D.R.E. (Youth & Adult). Students 138.

16—OUR LADY OF LAVANG (1986), (Vietnamese), [JC] Rev. Tin Mahn Bui.
Church: 1015 Chelwood Park N.E., 87112. Tel: 505-275-3079.
Catechesis/Religious Program—Students 148.

17—OUR LADY OF MOST HOLY ROSARY (1950), (Hispanic), Revs. Joel P. Garner, O.Praem.; Eugene Gries, O.Praem., Parochial Vicar; Deacons Harry Beare; Frank Perez; Gene Tuma; James Beaudette; Joe Herrera Jr.; Joseph Silva; Dr. Christina Spahn, Pastoral Assoc.; Ms. Barbara Guenther, Pastoral Assoc.; Don Conklin, Pastoral Assoc.
Office:—5415 Fortuna Rd., N.W., 87105. Tel: 505-836-5011; Fax: 505-836-7562.
Santa Maria de la Vid Priory: 5825 Coors S.W., 87121. Tel: 505-873-4399; Fax: 505-873-4667.
Catechesis/Religious Program—Tel: 505-831-2525. Sr. Evangeline Salazar, O.S.B., D.R.E.; Michelle Montez, Youth Min. Students 528.

18—OUR LADY OF THE ASSUMPTION (1954) Revs. Edward C. Domme; Michael Cimino, Parochial Vicar; Deacons Jim Delgado; Jack Granato; Maurice Graff.
Office & Mailing Address: 811 Guaymas Pl., N.E., 87108-2398. Tel: 505-256-9818; 505-256-9877; Fax: 505-256-3131.
Res.: 8030 Fruit Ave., N.E., 87108. Tel: 505-255-5727.
School—(Grades K-8), 817 Guaymas Pl., N.E., 87108. Tel: 505-256-3167; Fax: 505-232-0282. Robert M. Kaiser, Prin.; Karen Gibbs, Librarian. Lay Teachers 17; Students 181.
Catechesis/Religious Program—Jason Rodarte, D.R.E. Students 175.

19—PRINCE OF PEACE CATHOLIC COMMUNITY (2000) Rev. Michael J. Shea; Deacon Steve Fraker, Pastoral Assoc.
Office:—12500 Carmel Ave., N.E., 87122. Tel: 505-856-7657; Fax: 505-856-2560. Email: mailpop@comcast.net. Web: www.popabq.org.
Catechesis/Religious Program—Tel: 505-797-9115. Robert Shields, Catechetical Leader. Students 363.

20—QUEEN OF ANGELS NATIVE AMERICAN CENTER AND ARCHDIOCESAN SHRINE TO KATERI TEKAKWITHA (1952), (Native American), Rev. Emeric Nordmeyer, O.F.M.
Office: 1100 Indian School Rd., N.W., P.O. Box 6881, 87197.
Catechesis/Religious Program—
Chapel—Queen of Angels Chapel 87197-6881.

21—QUEEN OF HEAVEN (1952) Revs. Johnny Lee Chavez; Vincent Dominguez, Parochial Vicar; Deacons Ruben Barela; Larry Cleveland; Pilar Garcia; Dan Lopez; Donna Duran, Admin. In Res., Rev. Fernando Rubio-Boitel (Retired).
Office: 5311 Phoenix, N.E., 87110. Tel: 505-881-1772; Fax: 505-883-5222.
School—(Grades PreK-8), 5303 Phoenix Ave., N.E., 87110. Tel: 505-881-2484; Fax: 505-837-1123. Dr. Richard Dodson, Prin. Lay Teachers 20; Students 203.
Catechesis/Religious Program— Donna Duran, D.R.E. Students 371.

22—RISEN SAVIOR CATHOLIC COMMUNITY (1979) Rev. Msgr. Richard Olona; Rev. Jerome Plotkowski; Deacons Mark Bussemeier, Pastoral Assoc.; Kenn Sinatra, Admin.; Merce Villareal; Manuel Garcia; Ken Trujillo; Dan Sheehan.
Church: 7701 Wyoming, N.E., 87109. Tel: 505-821-1571; Fax: 505-857-0065. Web: www.risensaviorcc.org.
Catechesis/Religious Program—Gerry Wood, D.R.E. (Adults); Jennifer Murphy-Dye, D.R.E. (Youth); Denise Sinatra, D.R.E. (Children). Students 759.

23—SACRED HEART (1903) [JC] Rev. Clarence Maes; Deacons Desiderio Luna; Robert Vigil; Edgar L. Torres, S.R. In Res., Rev. David Klein, C.S.B.
Res.: 412 Stover Ave., S.W., 87102. Tel: 505-242-0561; Fax: 505-243-7857. Email: sacredheartnm@comcast.net.
Catechesis/Religious Program—Students 80.

24—SAN FELIPE DE NERI (1706), (Hispanic), Rev. Dennis M. Garcia; Deacons Jose Lucero; James Robert (Bob) Lewis; Maurice Menke; Tom Perez; James Carbajal.
Mailing Address: P.O. Box 7007, 87194.
Res.: 2005 Plaza N.W. Old Town, 87104. Tel: 505-243-4628; Fax: 505-224-9495. Web: www.sanfelipedeneri.org.
School—(Grades PreK-8), 2000 Lomas Blvd., N.W., 87104. Tel: 505-242-2411; Fax: 505-242-7355. Nancy A. Suedkamp, Prin. Sisters 1; Lay Teachers 20; Students 250.
Catechesis/Religious Program—Maria E. Cruz-Cordoba, D.R.E. Students 225.
Mission—San Jose de los Duranes 2110 Los Luceros Rd., N.W., Bernalillo Co. 87104.

25—SAN IGNACIO (1916), (Hispanic), Rev. Dennis M. Garcia, Canonical Pastor; Sr. Annette Lucero, O.P., Parish Life Coord.
Res.: 1300 Walter, N.E., 87102. Tel: 505-243-4287; Fax: 505-243-7346.
Catechesis/Religious Program—Students 19.

26—SAN JOSE (1938) [CEM] Very Rev. Gabriel Paredes; Deacon Gregorio Henderson.
Res.: 2401 Broadway, S.E., 87102-5009. Tel: 505-242-3658; Fax: 505-248-0810. Email: sanjoseparish@msn.com.
Catechesis/Religious Program— Ivette Garcia, D.R.E.; Mirna Davila, D.R.E. Students 790.

27—SANGRE DE CRISTO (1972) Rev. Robert Lancaster; Deacons Lloyd Martinez; Paul Ortwerth.
Res.: 8901 Candelaria, N.E., 87112. Tel: 505-293-2327; Fax: 505-292-0590.
Catechesis/Religious Program—Tel: 505-293-2328. Students 137.

28—SANTUARIO SAN MARTIN DE PORRES (1979), (Hispanic), Rev. Leo L. Padget; Deacons Cresencio Salinas; Oscar Marquez.
Res.: 8321 Camino San Martin, S.W., 87121. Tel: 505-836-4676; Fax: 505-836-3253. Email: sanmartin31@aol.com.
Catechesis/Religious Program—Tel: 505-352-2571. Sr. Marcella Campos, D.R.E.; Deacon Constantino Avalos-Sanchez, D.R.E.; Lourdes Ceballos, Catechetical Leader (Spanish Program). Students 600.

29—SHRINE OF ST. BERNADETTE (1959) Rev. Thomas A. Zotter; Deacons Alfred McLane; Byron Wicker, Pastoral Assoc.; Joe Santana; Terry Palmer.
Res.: 1800 Martha, N.E., 87112. Tel: 505-298-7557; Fax: 505-271-8099. Email: stbernacc@aol.com. Web: www.shrineofstbernadette.com.
Catechesis/Religious Program—Tel: 505-293-7779; Fax: 505-298-2412. Students 469.

30—ST. THERESE OF THE INFANT JESUS OF THE LITTLE FLOWER (1947) Rev. Vincent P. Chavez; Deacons Manuel Montoya; Patrick Cooney, (Retired); Michael Wesley; Rudolph F. Baca.
Res.: 300 Mildred, N.W., 87107. Tel: 505-344-8050; 505-344-2884. Email: sttheresechurch@yahoo.com. Web: www.littleflower.uni.cc.
School—(Grades K-8), 311 Shropshire N.W., 87107. Tel: 505-344-4479; Fax: 505-345-6210. Donna Illerbrun, Prin. Lay Teachers 14; Students 129.
Catechesis/Religious Program—Tel: 505-344-7643; Fax: 505-345-3248. Students 202.

31—ST. THOMAS AQUINAS UNIVERSITY PARISH (1950), (Serving the University of New Mexico) Revs. Thomas Martin Jackson, O.P.; Joachim Culotta, O.P., Parochial Vicar; Rosie Chinea, Campus Min.; Steve Herrera, Liturgy Dir.; Deacons Bruce Eklund; Donald Contreras. In Res., Revs. George J.D. Reynolds., O.P.; Kevin W. Niehoff, O.P.; Matthew T.D. Strabala, O.P.
Res.: 1815 Las Lomas Rd., N.E., 87106-3803. Tel: 505-247-1094; Fax: 505-247-2933. Web: www.aquinasnm.org.
Catechesis/Religious Program—Tel: 505-247-1094, Ext. 226. Kyle Kemp, Dir. Faith Formation. Students 155.

ANTON CHICO, GUADALUPE CO., SAN JOSE (1857), (Hispanic), [CEM] [JC 5] Rev. Steven A. Sanchez, Canonical Pastor; Lugardita Romo, Pastoral Assoc.
Res.: 1081 Iglesia Rd., Box 99, 87711. Tel: 575-427-1164.
Catechesis/Religious Program—Tel: 505-427-4114. Students 27.
Mission— Dilia, Guadalupe Co.
Mission— Dahlia, Guadalupe Co.
Mission— Tecolotito, San Miguel Co.
Mission—Sangre de Cristo (1834)

ARROYO SECO, TAOS CO., LA SANTISIMA TRINIDAD (1834), (Spanish), [CEM] [JC 4] Rev. Titus Augustine Puravakkatt, C.M.I.; Deacon Romolo Arellano.

Res.: 498 Hwy. 150, Box 189, 87514. Tel: 575-776-2273; Fax: 575-776-1543. Email: trinityparish@taosnet.com.
Catechesis/Religious Program—Students 116.
Mission—Nuestra Senora de Dolores Upper Plaza, Arroyo Hondo, Taos Co. 87513.
Mission—San Antonio de Padua Valdez Plaza, Valdez, Taos Co. 87580.
Mission—Santo Nino de Atocha Santo Nino Rd., Las Colonias, Taos Co. 87529.
Mission—San Cristobal San Cristobal, Taos Co.

BELEN, VALENCIA CO., OUR LADY OF BELEN (1793) [CEM] [JC] Revs. Stephen Schultz; Bijoy Francis Valayil, O.Praem., Parochial Vicar; Deacons Felix Barela; Rudy Zamora; Robert Sanchez.
Res.: 101-A N. 10th St., 87002. Tel: 505-864-8043.
School—(Grades K-8) Tel: 505-864-0484; Fax: 505-864-2414. Dr. Gayle Fortna, Prin. Lay Teachers 12; Students 150.
Catechesis/Religious Program—Tel: 505-864-7869. Therese Salazar, D.R.E. Students 513.
Mission— Los Chavez, Valencia Co.
Mission— Jarales, Valencia Co.
Mission— Pueblitos, Valencia Co.
Mission— Bosque, Valencia Co.

BERNALILLO, SANDOVAL CO., OUR LADY OF SORROWS (1699), (Indian—Hispanic), [CEM 2] Rev. Stephen Imbarrato; Deacons Jose de Jesus Cervantes; Gonzalo Calderon.
Office & Res.: 301 Camino Del Pueblo, P.O. Box 607, 87004. Tel: 505-867-5252; 505-867-0585 (Res.); Fax: 505-867-0267.
Catechesis/Religious Program—Tel: 505-771-3568. Patsy Garcia, D.R.E. Students 393.
Mission— 43 San Antonio, Placitas, Sandoval Co. 87043.
Mission— 1416 Hwy. 313, Algodones, Sandoval Co. 87001.
Mission— 300 Parrot Blvd., Sandia Indian Pueblo, Sandoval Co. 87004.

CERRILLOS, SANTA FE CO., ST. JOSEPH (1850) [CEM 4] Rev. Msgr. Jerome Martinez y Alire, Canonical Pastor; Rev. Jonas Romea, Sacramental Min.
Res.: Box 98, 87010. Tel: 505-471-1562; Fax: 505-438-6584. Email: stjoseph@cnsp.com.
Catechesis/Religious Program—Students 42.
Mission— Golden, Santa Fe Co.
Mission— Galisteo, Santa Fe Co.

CHAMA, RIO ARRIBA CO., ST. PATRICK (1964), (Hispanic—Anglo), [JC] Rev. Clement Niggel.
Res.: 352 Pine Ave., Hwy. 29, P.O. Box 36, 87520-0036. Tel: 575-756-2926; Fax: 575-756-2926. Email: stpats@windstream.net.
Catechesis/Religious Program—Students 85.
Mission—Santo Nino Hwy. 84 & State Rd. 310, Cebolla, Rio Arriba Co. 87518.
Mission—San Juan Nepumoceno County Rd. 295, Canjilon, Rio Arriba Co. 87515.

CHIMAYO, RIO ARRIBA CO., HOLY FAMILY (1955), (Hispanic), [CEM] [JC 2] Revs. Julio Gonzalez, S.F.; Casimiro Roca, S.F.; James Suntum, S.F.; Ron Carrillo, S.F., Parochial Vicar.
Res.: P.O. Box 235, 87522. Tel: 505-351-4360; Fax: 505-351-4698. Email: holyfamily@cybermesa.com. Web: www.holychimayo.us.
Catechesis/Religious Program—Students 97.
Mission—Holy Rosary Truchas, Rio Arriba Co.
Mission—San Jose de Gracia Trampas, Taos Co.
Mission—Santo Domingo Cundiyo, Rio Arriba Co.
Mission—San Antonio Cordova, Rio Arriba Co.
Mission—Sagrado Corazon Rio Chiquito, Rio Arriba Co.
Mission—Santo Tomas Ojo Sarco, Rio Arriba Co.
Mission—San Miguel Archangel El Valle, Taos Co.
Shrine—El Santuario Shrine El Santuario, Santa Fe Co.

CIMARRON, COLFAX CO., IMMACULATE CONCEPTION CHURCH (1864), (Hispanic—Mexican), [JC] Very Rev. John Cannon.
Res.: 440 W. 18th St., 87714-9705. Tel: 575-376-2553; Fax: 575-376-2553.
Catechesis/Religious Program—Mrs. Marie Salas, D.R.E.; Maria Sedillo, D.R.E. Students 29.
Mission—St. Mel 200 Willow Creek, Eagle Nest, Colfax Co. 87718. Tel: 505-376-2553; 505-377-1937.
Mission—Holy Angels P.O. Box 73, Angel Fire, 87710.
Mission—St. Anthony Black Lake, Colfax Co.

CLAYTON, UNION CO., ST. FRANCIS XAVIER (1937) [JC] Rev. Glenn Jones; Deacon P. Louis Montoya.
Res.: 115 N. First St., 88415. Tel: 575-374-9500; Fax: 575-374-8897. Email: stfrancisxavier@plateautel.net.
Catechesis/Religious Program—Students 102.
Mission—Our Lady of Guadalupe Des Moines, Union Co.
Mission—St. Joseph Folsom, Union Co.
Mission—Sacred Heart Moses, Union Co.
Mission—Holy Trinity Hayden, Quay Co.

CLOVIS, CURRY CO.

1—OUR LADY OF GUADALUPE (1945) [CEM 2] [JC 2] Rev. Sotero A. Sena; Deacons Bob Pullings; Daniel Chavez.
Res.: 108 Davis St., 88101. Tel: 575-763-4445; Fax: 575-763-0261.
Catechesis/Religious Program—Tel: 575-762-7343. Sally Romero, D.R.E. (Grades K-6); David Briseno, D.R.E. (Grade 7-12); Margaret Briseno, D.R.E. (Grades 7-12). Students 200.
Mission— Box 122, Texico, Curry Co. 88135.

2—SACRED HEART (1908) Rev. Carlos Chavez; Deacons Juan A. Rodriguez; Michael A. Rowley.
Res.: 921 Merriwether St., 88101. Tel: 575-763-6947; Fax: 575-762-5557.
Catechesis/Religious Program—Students 187.
Mission— Melrose, Curry Co. 88124.

CORRALES, SANDOVAL CO., SAN YSIDRO (1966) [CEM] Rev. James L. Vance; Deacons Donald Roseborough; Steve Rangel.
Res.: 5015 Corrales Rd., Box 182, 87048. Tel: 505-898-1779; Fax: 505-897-6967.
Catechesis/Religious Program—Tel: 505-899-0276. Jennie Gonzales, D.R.E. Students 134.

DIXON, RIO ARRIBA CO., ST. ANTHONY (1929) [CEM 3] Rev. Vitus Ezeiruaku (Nigeria); Deacon Jerome Romero.
Res.: 1114 Private Dr. #5, P.O. Box 39, 87527-0039. Tel: 505-579-4389; Fax: 505-579-4389. Email: standixon@valornet.com. Web: www.stanthonydixon.parishesonline.com.
Catechesis/Religious Program—Students 60.
Mission—Nuestra Senora de Guadalupe Velarde, Rio Arriba Co.
Mission—Nuestra Senora de los Dolores Pilar, Taos Co.
Mission—San Jose Lyden, Rio Arriba Co.

EL RITO, RIO ARRIBA CO., SAN JUAN NEPOMUCENO (1832), (Spanish), [CEM] [JC 9] Rev. Patrick J. Chavez.
Res.: P.O. Box 7, 87530. Tel: 575-581-4714.
Catechesis/Religious Program—Students 47.
Mission— Gen. Del., La Madera, Rio Arriba Co. 87539.
Mission— Gen. Del., Las Tablas, Taos Co. 87539.
Mission— Gen. Del., Ojo Caliente, Rio Arriba Co. 87549.
Mission— Gen. Del., Petaca, Taos Co. 87539.
Mission— Gen. Del., Servilleta, Taos Co. 87539.
Mission— Gen. Del., Vallecitos, Rio Arriba Co. 87581.
Mission— Gen. Del., Canon de Vallecitos, Rio Arriba Co. 87581.
Mission— Gen. Del., Tres Piedras, Taos Co. 87579.
Mission— P.O. Box 7, Placitas, Rio Arriba Co. 87530.

ESPANOLA, RIO ARRIBA CO.

1—SACRED HEART (1950), (Hispanic), [CEM 2] Rev. Augustine J. Moore; Sr. Bernardita Abeyta, O.P.; Deacon Diego Herrera.
Res.: P.O. Box 69, 87532. Tel: 505-753-4225; Fax: 505-753-1282. Email: sacredheart@windstream.com.
Catechesis/Religious Program—Tel: 505-753-9413; 505-753-1695. Students 73.
Mission— Hernandez, Rio Arriba Co.
Mission— El Guache, Rio Arriba Co.
Mission— Guachupanque, Rio Arriba Co.
Mission— El Duende, Rio Arriba Co.

2—TEWA MISSIONS (2000) Rev. Terrence P. Brennan, Canonical Pastor.
Mailing Address: P.O. Box 1075, Ohkay Owingeh, 87566. Tel: 505-747-8220.
Catechesis/Religious Program—Sr. Patrick Marie Dempsey, S.B.S., D.R.E. Students 125.

FORT SUMNER, DE BACA CO., ST. ANTHONY OF PADUA formerly St. Anthony (1958), (Hispanic), [CEM] Rev. Steve Sanchez, Canonical Pastor; Sr. Phyllis Supancheck, O.P., Parish Life Coord.
Church & Mailing Address: 443 W. Richard Ave., P.O. Box 370, 88119. Tel: 575-355-2320; Fax: 575-355-2320.
Catechesis/Religious Program—Students 31.

ISLETA, PUEBLO BERNALILLO CO., ST. AUGUSTINE (1613), (Native American), [CEM] Rev. Hilaire Valiquette, O.F.M.
Res.: P.O. Box 849, 87022. Tel: 505-869-3398; Fax: 505-869-2447.
Catechesis/Religious Program—Students 140.

JEMEZ PUEBLO, SANDOVAL CO., SAN DIEGO INDIAN MISSIONS (1608), (Native American—Spanish), [CEM] [JC 4] Rev. Paul Juniet, O.F.M.; Bro. Ricardo Garcia, O.F.M.; Sr. Karen M Kuta, O.S.F.
Res.: 475 Mission Rd., P.O. Box 79, 87024. Tel: 575-834-7300; Fax: 575-834-7060.
Catechesis/Religious Program—Students 68.
Mission— Canon, Sandoval Co.
Mission— Ponderosa, Sandoval Co.
Mission— San Ysidro, Sandoval Co.
Mission— Santa Ana, Sandoval Co.
Mission— Zia, Sandoval Co.

JEMEZ SPRINGS, SANDOVAL CO., OUR LADY OF THE ASSUMPTION (1947) [CEM] Revs. Gregory McCormick, s.P.; Edward Rolph, s.P.
Res.: Tel: 575-829-3586; Fax: 575-829-3706. Email: servants@theservants.org.
Catechesis/Religious Program—Students 1.

LA JOYA, SOCORRO CO., OUR LADY OF SORROWS (1830), (Spanish), [CEM 6] Rev. Peter Hung Nguyen, S.O.L.T.; Deacon Alfred Edwin Esquibel.
Mailing Address: 19 Calle de la Iglesia, P.O. Box 32, 87028. Tel: 505-864-4461; 505-861-3522 (Rectory); Fax: 505-864-4461. Email: parishoffice@olslajoya.nm.org.
Catechesis/Religious Program—Students 124.
Mission—San Antonio Abeytas, Socorro Co.
Mission—San Jose Contreras, Socorro Co.
Mission—San Isidro Las Nutrias, Socorro Co.
Mission—San Juan Veguita, Socorro Co.
Mission—San Antonio Sabinal, Socorro Co.

LAS VEGAS, SAN MIGUEL CO.

1—IMMACULATE CONCEPTION (1885) [CEM] Rev. George Salazar.
Res.: 811 Sixth St., 87701. Tel: 505-425-7791; 505-425-6942; Fax: 505-425-6991. Email: icchurch2000@yahoo.com.
Catechesis/Religious Program—Tel: 505-454-0685. Velma Salazar, D.R.E. Students 234.
Mission—Los Vigiles (Our Lady of Refuge) 811 6th, San Antonio, San Miguel Co. 87701.

2—OUR LADY OF SORROWS CHURCH (1851), (Hispanic), [CEM 2] [JC 2] Rev. C. John Brasher; Deacons Jose Leroy Martinez; Reyes L. Sanchez.
Res.: 403 Valencia St., 87701. Tel: 505-454-1469; Fax: 505-425-0949.
Catechesis/Religious Program—Tel: 505-425-6823. Velma Salazar, D.R.E. Students 228.
Mission—Our Lady of Guadalupe HC 68, Box 11, Sapello, San Miguel Co. 87745. Tel: 505-425-8084.
Mission—San Isidro HC 32, Box 26, Trujillo, San Miguel Co. 87701. Tel: 505-641-5367.
Mission—Holy Family Garita. Box 1020, Variadero, San Miguel Co. 88421. Tel: 505-641-5339.
Mission—Santo Nino HC 69, Box 4, Rociada Abajo, San Miguel Co. 87742. Tel: 505-425-8251.
Mission—Santo Nino Montezuma. El Porvenir Rte., Box 63, Gallinas, San Miguel Co. 87731. Tel: 505-425-6015.
Chapel—Christ the King 2609 Encino St., 87701. Tel: 505-425-6894.
Chapel—San Jose Hot Springs.
Chapel—San Antonio Box 90, El Porvenir, 87731. Tel: 505-425-8010.
Chapel—San Ignacio HC 68, Box 15, Sapello, 87745. Tel: 505-425-3092; 505-454-1139.
Chapel—Our Lady of Sorrows Anton Chico Rte., Box 39, 87701. Tel: 505-421-5599.
Chapel—San Geronimo Mineral Hill Rte., Box 310, 87701. Tel: 505-425-3011.
Chapel—San Antonio P.O. Box 85, 87701. Tel: 505-425-3405.
Chapel—Lourdes
Chapel—San Jose HC 69, Box 12A, Rociada, 87742. Tel: 505-425-2809.
Chapel—San Rafael c/o Al Sanchez Jr., General Delivery, Trementina, 88439. Tel: 505-641-5384.
Chapel—Santo Nino de Atocha Anton Chico Rte., Box 20, 87701. Tel: 505-425-8014.
Chapel—Ojitos Frios
Chapel—Manuelitas
Chapel—Santo Nino, Tel: 505-454-0409.

LOS ALAMOS, LOS ALAMOS CO., IMMACULATE HEART OF MARY (1946) Rev. John F. Carney; Deacons Gerald Langner; Don Lucero; Ray Alcouffe; Roberto Villareal; Miracle Romero, Business Mgr.; Greg Smithhisler, Music Min. & Liturgy Dir.; Eric Horne, Youth Dir.
Mailing Address: 3700 Canyon Rd., 87544. Tel: 505-662-6193.
Res.: 3694 Canyon Rd., 87544. Tel: 505-662-6921; Fax: 505-662-5191. Web: www.ihmcc.org.
Catechesis/Religious Program—3580 Canyon Rd., 87544. Tel: 505-662-7773. Caren Stevens, D.R.E. Students 541.
Mission—St. Joseph 196 Meadow, White Rock, Los Alamos Co. 87544. Tel: 505-672-1270.

LOS LUNAS, VALENCIA CO., SAN CLEMENTE (1961) [CEM 2] [JC] Very Rev. Douglas J. Mitchell; Deacons Jim Snell, Business Mgr.; Robert Burkhard; Rudy Baca; Paul Baca; Brenda Sais, Family Life Coord.
Res.: 711 Canal Blvd., P.O. Box 147, 87031. Tel: 505-865-7385; Fax: 505-865-8323. Email: sanclemente@qwest.net. Web: www.sanclementeparish.org.
Catechesis/Religious Program—Tel: 505-865-9370. Students 487.
Mission—San Antonio Los Lentes, Valencia Co.
Mission—San Juan Diego P.O. Box 3320, 87031. Tel: 505-866-0443.

LOS OJOS, RIO ARRIBA CO., SAN JOSE (1883), (Hispanic), [CEM] [JC 2] Rev. Clement Niggel.
Res.: Box 6, 87551. Tel: 575-588-7473; Fax: 575-588-7239. Email: sjsncc@windstream.net.
Catechesis/Religious Program— Twinned with Santo Nino, Tierra Amarilla. Students 40.
Station— Ensenada.
Station— La Puente.
Station— Plaza Blanca.

MORA, MORA CO., ST. GERTRUDE (1851), (Hispanic), [CEM] [JC 9] Revs. John McHugh, S.O.L.T.; James Sanchez, S.O.L.T., Parochial Vicar; Deacons Reynaldo Cordova; Cristobal "Eloy" Roybal.
Res.: 1 Church Plaza, P.O. Box 599, 87732. Tel: 505-387-2336; Fax: 575-387-5786.
Catechesis/Religious Program—Deacon Eloy Roybal, D.R.E. Students 168.
Mission— Le Doux, Mora Co.
Mission— El Carmen, Mora Co.
Mission— Lucero, Mora Co.
Mission— Santiago-Talco, Mora Co.
Mission— Ojo Feliz, Mora Co.
Mission— Buenavista, Mora Co.
Mission— Golondrinas, Mora Co.
Mission— Rainsville, Mora Co.
Mission— Chacon, Mora Co.
Mission— Holman, Mora Co.
Mission— Cleveland, Mora Co.
Mission— Guadalupita, Mora Co.
Mission— Monte Aplanado, Mora Co.
Mission— Turquillo, Mora Co.
Mission— La Cueva, Mora Co.
Mission— Canoncito, Mora Co.

MORIARTY, TORRANCE CO., ESTANCIA VALLEY CATHOLIC PARISH (1972) [CEM 3] Revs. William Young; Kevin Iwuoha (Nigeria), Parochial Vicar; Deacons Juan S. Lucero; Don Cupps.
Res.: 1400 A 3rd St., S., P.O. Box 129, 87035. Tel: 505-832-6655; Fax: 505-832-6057. Email: parishoffice@estanciavalleycatholicch.org. Web: www.estanciavalleycatholicch.org.
Catechesis/Religious Program—Email: formation@estanciavalleycatholicch.org. Dorothy Ipiotis, D.R.E.; Jonathan Ipiotis, Dir. Youth Min. Students 267.
Mission—Sts. Peter & Paul 101 S. Ninth St., Estancia, Torrance Co. 87016.
Mission—San Antonio 8566 Hwy. 55 W., Tajique, 87016.
Mission—St. Elizabeth Ann Seton 85 Hwy. 344, Edgewood, 87015.

MOUNTAINAIR, TORRANCE CO., ST. ALICE (1946), (Hispanic), [CEM 5] [JC] Rev. Ronald G. Stone.
Res.: 206 Roosevelt St., P.O. Box 206, 87036. Tel: 505-847-2264; Fax: 505-847-0146. Email: stalicemtn@q.com.
Catechesis/Religious Program—Deacon Charles E. Schwenn, D.R.E. Students 96.
Mission— Abo, Torrance Co.
Mission— Punta de Agua, Torrance Co.
Mission— Manzano, Torrance Co.
Mission— Torreon, Torrance Co.
Mission— Willard, Torrance Co.

PECOS, SAN MIGUEL CO., ST. ANTHONY OF PADUA (1862) [CEM 5] Rev. Gerald Johnson.
Res.: HC 74 Box 23, 87552. Tel: 505-757-6345; Fax: 505-757-6377. Email: saintanthonys@wildblue.net.
Catechesis/Religious Program—Tel: 505-757-6305. Students 204.
Mission— Canoncito, Santa Fe Co.
Mission— Las Colonias, San Miguel Co.
Mission— Glorieta, Santa Fe Co.
Mission— Rowe, San Miguel Co.
Mission— El Macho, San Miguel Co.

PENA BLANCA, SANDOVAL CO., NUESTRA SENORA DE GUADALUPE (1877), (Hispanic—Native American), [CEM 3] Rev. Wayne Gibbeaut, O.F.M.; Deacons Albert Arquero; Joe Segura.
Res.: Hwy. 22, House #816, P.O. Box 1270, 87041. Tel: 505-465-2226; Fax: 505-465-1336.
Catechesis/Religious Program—Students 131.
Mission—St. Bonaventure, Indian Pueblo, Cochiti, Sandoval Co.
Mission—San Felipe, Indian Pueblo, San Felipe, Sandoval Co.
Mission—Santo Domingo, Indian Pueblo, Santo Domingo, Sandoval Co.
Mission—Santa Barbara Sile, Sandoval Co.
Mission—San Miguel La Bajada, Sandoval Co.

PENASCO, TAOS CO., SAN ANTONIO DE PADUA (1866) [CEM] Rev. Vitus Ezeiruaku (Nigeria); Deacon Jerome Romero.
Res.: 14079 N. Hwy. 75, P.O. Box 460, 87553-0460. Tel: 575-587-2111 (Office); 575-587-0399 (Res.); Fax: 575-587-2188.
Catechesis/Religious Program—Tel: 575-587-2216. Joyce Kilgore, D.R.E. Students 144.
Mission—Santa Cruz Mission Chamisal, Taos Co.
Mission—Sagrado Corazon Mission Rio Lucio, Taos Co.
Mission—Nuestra Senora de los Dolores Mission Vadito, Taos Co.
Mission—San Lorenzo Mission Picuris Indian Pueblo, Taos Co.
Mission—San Juan Nepomuceno Mission Llano San Juan, Taos Co.
Mission—Nuestra Senora de la Asuncion Mission Placita, Taos Co.
Mission—Santa Barbara Mission Rodarte, Taos Co.

PERALTA, VALENCIA CO., OUR LADY OF GUADALUPE (1970), (Hispanic), [CEM] Rev. Hoi Tran; Deacons Joe Trujillo, (Retired); Edward Espinosa.
Mailing Address: P.O. Box 10, 87042.
Res.: 3674 Hwy. 47, 87042. Tel: 505-869-2189; Fax: 505-869-5850. Email: ologper@aol.com. Web: home.flash.net/~gdc/olog/.
Catechesis/Religious Program—Tel: 505-869-6993; Fax: 505-869-6996. Karen Morgan, D.R.E. Students 389.
Mission—Sangre de Cristo Valencia, Valencia Co. Tel: 505-866-7254.
Station—Valencia

POJOAQUE, SANTA FE CO., N.S. DE GUADALUPE DEL VALLE DE POJOAQUE (1959), (Spanish—Native American), [CEM 2] Rev. Jose Flavio Santillanes; Deacons John Archuleta; Pedro Garcia; Daniel Valdez; Reuben Roybal.
Mailing Address: P.O. Box 3469, 87501.
Res.: 9 Grazing Elk, 87506-7140. Tel: 505-455-2472; Fax: 505-455-3849.
Catechesis/Religious Program—Tel: 505-455-2267. Donna Martinez, D.R.E. Students 200.
Mission— Nambe, Santa Fe Co.
Mission— El Rancho, Santa Fe Co.
Mission— Nambe Indian Pueblo, Santa Fe Co.

PORTALES, ROOSEVELT CO., ST. HELEN (1952) Very Rev. James McGowan; Deacon Roberto Herrera.
Res.: 1600 S. Avenue O, 88130. Tel: 575-356-4241; Fax: 575-359-1721. Email: sthelenofportales@yahoo.com.
Catechesis/Religious Program—Syliva Baca, D.R.E. Students 288.
Mission—Thomas More Center P.O. Box 2253, Roosevelt Co. 88130.

QUESTA, TAOS CO., ST. ANTHONY (1841) [CEM 6] Rev. Dino Candelaria; Deacons Marcus J. Rael; Jose Leroy Lucero.
Mailing Address: Box 200, 87556.
Res.: 10 Church Plaza, 87556. Tel: 575-586-0470; 575-586-0471; Fax: 575-586-1755. Email: sanantoniodelrio@qwestoffice.net.
Catechesis/Religious Program—Parish Center: 2453 St. Hwy 522, 87556. Tel: 575-586-2155. Students 75.
Mission— Cerro, Taos Co.
Mission— Red River, Taos Co.
Mission— Costilla, Taos Co.
Mission— Amalia, Taos Co.

RANCHOS DE TAOS, TAOS CO., SAN FRANCISCO DE ASIS (1936), (Hispanic), [CEM] Very Rev. Francis Malley; Deacon Pat Delozier.
Res.: P.O. Box 72, 87557-0072. Tel: 575-758-2754; Fax: 575-751-3923. Email: saintfrancis@kitcarson.net.
Catechesis/Religious Program—Students 200.
Mission—N.S. de San Juan de Los Lagos Talpa, Taos Co.
Mission—N.S. del Carmel Llano Quemado, Taos Co.
Mission—San Isidro Los Cordovas, Taos Co.

RATON, COLFAX CO., ST. PATRICK/ST. JOSEPH (1891) [CEM] [JC] Rev. Daniel M. Balizan; Deacon Thomas Alderette.
Res.: 105 Buena Vista St., Box 278, 87740. Tel: 575-445-9763; Fax: 575-445-7026. Email: stspatjoe@bacavalley.com.
Catechesis/Religious Program—104 Buena Vista St., 87740. Tel: 575-445-9563. Louise Ortiz, D.R.E. Students 194.

RIBERA, SAN MIGUEL CO., SAN MIGUEL DEL VADO (1804), (Hispanic—Native American), [CEM] [JC 7] Rev. Thomas Kayammakal.
Res.: P.O. Box 507, 87560. Tel: 575-421-2405; 575-421-2780 (Office); Fax: 575-421-2779. Email: sanmiguel@plateautel.net.
Catechesis/Religious Program—Students 73.
Mission— [CEM] [JC] San Isidro Norte, San Miguel Co.
Mission— [CEM] [JC] San Jose, San Miguel Co.
Mission— [CEM] [JC] San Juan, San Miguel Co.
Mission— [CEM] [JC] Santa Rita, San Miguel Co.
Mission—San Antonio de Padua [CEM] [JC] El Pueblo, San Miguel Co.
Mission— [CEM] [JC] La Lagunita, San Miguel Co.
Mission— [CEM] [JC] San Isidro Sur, San Miguel Co.

RIO RANCHO, SANDOVAL CO.

1—CHURCH OF THE INCARNATION (2003) Rev. Rick Zerwas; Deacons George Meyerson; Norbert Archibeque; Jerome Paszkiewicz.
Mailing Address: 2309 Monterey Rd., NE, 87144. Tel: 505-771-8331. Web: ccincarnation.org.
Catechesis/Religious Program—Mary Margaret Baca, D.R.E. Students 189.

2—ST. THOMAS AQUINAS (1974) Rev. Msgr. Douglas A. Raun; Rev. Scott Mansfield, Parochial Vicar; Deacons Rodger Ayers; James Baca; Thomas Burns; Kenneth Hill; David Little; Leroy Sanchez; Frank Smith. In Res., Rev. Michael DePalma.
Res.: 1502 Sara Rd., S.E., 87124. Tel: 505-892-1511; Fax: 505-891-3044.
School—(Grades K-8), 1100 Hood Rd., S.E., 87124. Tel: 505-892-3221; Fax: 505-892-3350. Sr. Anne Louise Abascal, M.P.F., Prin. Religious 3; Lay Teachers 23; Students 404.
Catechesis/Religious Program—Tel: 505-892-1497. Students 1,439.
Mission—St. John Vianney 1100 Hood Rd., S.E., Sandoval Co. 87124.

ROY, HARDING CO., HOLY FAMILY-ST. JOSEPH (1918), (Hispanic), [CEM 4] Rev. Paul Nkumbi (Uganda).
Res.: P.O. Box 37, 87743. Tel: 575-485-9633; Fax: 575-485-9633. Email: holyfamilyroy@yahoo.com.
Catechesis/Religious Program—Students 30.
Mission— Bueyeros, Harding Co.
Mission— Gallegos, Harding Co.
Mission— Sabinoso, San Miguel Co.

SAN JUAN PUEBLO, RIO ARRIBA CO. (INDIAN PUEBLO), ST. JOHN THE BAPTIST (1598) Revs. Terrence P. Brennan; Denis Kaggwa, Parochial Vicar; Deacons Eloy E. Martinez; Michael Salazar.
Res.: 1 Church Cir., P.O. Box 1075, Ohkay Owingeh Pueblo, 87566. Tel: 505-852-4179; Fax: 505-852-9719. Email: sjparish@cybermesa.com.
Catechesis/Religious Program—Tel: 505-852-2270; Fax: 505-852-9719. Frances Harney, D.R.E. Students 263.
Mission— Alcalde, Rio Arriba Co.
Mission— Chamita, Rio Arriba Co.
Mission— El Guique, Rio Arriba Co.
Mission— Ranchitos, Rio Arriba Co.
Mission— [CEM] Estaca, Rio Arriba Co.
Shrine—Our Lady of Lourdes, Pilgrimage shrine.

SANTA CRUZ, SANTA FE CO., HOLY CROSS (1695), (Hispanic), [CEM] Revs. Javier Gutierrez, S.F.; Jose Maria Blanch, S.F., Parochial Vicar; Sr. Dolores Abeyta, O.P., Dir. Homebound Min.
Res.: 124 S. McCurdy Rd., P.O. Box 1228, 87567-1228. Tel: 505-753-3345. Email: holycrosschurch@windstream.net.
School—(Grades K-6), P.O. Box 1260, 87567-1260. Tel: 505-753-4644; Fax: 505-753-7401. Mrs. Lorraine Sanchez, Prin.; Kathy Lujan, Librarian. Sisters 2; Lay Teachers 13; Students 149.
Catechesis/Religious Program—Tel: 505-753-4567; Fax: 505-753-7401. Sr. Angelina Gonzales, O.P., D.R.E. (Elementary); Janet Ortiz, D.R.E. (Junior & Senior High). Students 496.
Convent—P.O. Box 1137, 87567-1137. Tel: 505-753-3340.

SANTA ROSA, GUADALUPE CO., ST. ROSE OF LIMA (1907), (Hispanic), [CEM] Rev. Joseph Thomas Kanavalil, C.M.I.; Deacons Arsenio C. Sanchez; Marvin M. Marquez.
Res.: 439 Third St., 88435. Tel: 575-472-3724; Fax: 575-472-4724.
Catechesis/Religious Program—Tel: 505-472-3992. Sisters Helen Halligan, D.R.E.; Ann Kaufmann, D.R.E. Students 271.
Mission— Puerto de Luna, Guadalupe Co.
Mission— San Ignacio, Guadalupe Co.
Mission— Borica, Guadalupe Co.
Mission— Cuervo, Guadalupe Co.
Mission— Colonias, Guadalupe Co.
Mission— Pintada, Guadalupe Co.
Mission— Milagro, Guadalupe Co.

SOCORRO, SOCORRO CO., SAN MIGUEL (1615), (Native American—Hispanic), [CEM 8] [JC] Rev. Andrew J. Pavlak; Deacons Miguel Ybarra; Robert Jiron; Nicholas Keller; Raul Grajeda.
Res.: 403 El Camino Real, N.W., 87801. Tel: 575-835-2891; Fax: 575-835-1620.
Catechesis/Religious Program—Joyce Aguilar, D.R.E. Students 241.
Mission— Lemitar, Socorro Co.
Mission— Polvadera, Socorro Co.
Mission— Luis Lopez, Socorro Co.
Mission— San Antonio, Socorro Co.
Mission— Alamillo, Socorro Co.
Mission— Magdalena, Socorro Co.
Mission— Kelly, Socorro Co.
Mission— Riley, Socorro Co.

SPRINGER, COLFAX CO., ST. JOSEPH (1882), (Hispanic), [JC] Very Rev. John Cannon; Deacon Edward Olona.
Res.: 605 Fifth St., P.O. Box 516, 87747. Tel: 575-483-2775; Fax: 575-483-2518. Email: stjosephicc@aol.com.
Catechesis/Religious Program—Diane Alderette, D.R.E. Students 27.
Mission— Palo Blanco, Colfax Co.
Mission— Maxwell, Colfax Co.

Mission— Tinaja, Colfax Co.

TAOS, TAOS CO., NUESTRA SENORA DE GUADALUPE (1801), (Spanish), [CEM] Rev. Lawrence R. Brito; Deacons Donald Martinez; Jerry Quintana.
Res.: 205 Don Fernando St., 87571. Tel: 575-758-2095; Fax: 575-758-2745.
Catechesis/Religious Program—Tel: 575-758-9764. Students 148.
Mission—St. Jerome Taos Pueblo, Taos Co. 87571.
Chapel—El Prado, St. Theresa
Chapel—Canon, Our Lady of Sorrows
Chapel—Ranchitos, Immaculate Conception
Chapel—La Loma, San Antonio

TIERRA AMARILLA, RIO ARRIBA CO., SANTO NINO (1966), (Hispanic), [JC] Rev. Clement Niggel.
Mailing Address: Box 193, 87575. Tel: 575-588-7463.
Catechesis/Religious Program—Tel: 575-588-7473. Twinned with San Jose, Los Ojos. Students 45.

TIJERAS, BERNALILLO CO., HOLY CHILD (1962) [CEM 9] [JC 2] Rev. Mark E. Granito; Deacon Larry Carmony.
Res.: 19 Camino de Santo Nino, Box 130, 87059. Tel: 505-281-1502; 505-281-2297 (Office); Fax: 505-281-0355. Email: holychildparish@aol.com. Web: members.aol.com/holychildparish.
School—Holy Child Catholic School, Tel: 505-470-9011. Nancy Fitzpatrick, Prin. Lay Teachers 6; Students 41.
Catechesis/Religious Program—Students 336.
Mission—Holy Child Carnuel, Bernalillo Co.
Mission—San Juan de Nepumoceno Chilili, Bernalillo Co.
Mission—San Isidro Escobosa, Bernalillo Co.
Mission— San Antonio, Bernalillo Co.
Mission—San Isidro Sedillo, Bernalillo Co.
Mission— Canoncito, Bernalillo Co.
Mission—, Bernalillo Co.
Mission—Senor de Mapimi San Antonito.

TOME, VALENCIA CO., IMMACULATE CONCEPTION (1739), (Spanish), [CEM] Rev. Jose A. Hernandez.
Res.: 7 Church Loop, P.O. Box 100, 87060-0100. Tel: 505-866-9201; Fax: 505-865-7622. Web: icchurchtome.org.
Catechesis/Religious Program—7 Church Loop, Juan Diego Hall. Tel: 505-865-2958. Martha Sanchez, D.R.E. Students 170.
Mission— State Hwy. 304 S., Casa Colorada, Valencia Co. 87002.

TUCUMCARI, QUAY CO., ST. ANNE (1910) [JC] Rev. Hyginus Chucks Anuta (Nigeria); Deacons Robert Welch; Raphael (Ray) P. Aragon.
Res.: 306 W. High St., 88401. Tel: 575-461-2515; Fax: 575-461-3058.
Catechesis/Religious Program—Tel: 575-461-3568. Nancy Arias, D.R.E. Students 220.
Mission—San Antonio Logan, Quay Co.
Mission—Sacred Heart Nara Visa, Quay Co.
Mission—Our Lady of Guadalupe San Jon, Quay Co.

VAUGHN, GUADALUPE CO., ST. MARY (1936), (Hispanic), [JC] Rev. Steve Sanchez.
Res.: P.O. Box 276, 88353. Tel: 575-584-2954.
Catechesis/Religious Program—Students 33.
Mission— Encino, Torrance Co.
Mission— Duran, Torrance Co.
Mission— Pastura, Guadalupe Co.
Mission— Pinos Wells, Torrance Co.

VILLANUEVA, SAN MIGUEL, OUR LADY OF GUADALUPE (1830), (Hispanic), [CEM 6] Rev. Thomas Kayammakal, Canonical Pastor.
Mailing Address: P.O. Box 39, 87583. Tel: 575-421-2548; Fax: 575-421-2548. In Res., Sr. Elena L. Carney, O.L.V.M., Parish Life Coord.
Catechesis/Religious Program—Students 52.
Mission— Sena, San Miguel Co.
Mission— Cerrito, San Miguel Co.
Mission— Gonzales Ranch, San Miguel Co.
Mission— Leyba, San Miguel Co.
Mission— Aurora, San Miguel Co.

WAGON MOUND, MORA CO., SANTA CLARA (1882), (Hispanic), [CEM] Rev. Paul Nkumbi (Uganda); Deacon Charlie Duran.
Res.: P.O. Box 186, 87752. Tel: 575-666-2478; Fax: 575-666-2478.
Catechesis/Religious Program—Students 25.
Mission— Ocate, Mora Co.
Mission— Los Hueros, Mora Co.
Mission— Los Le Febres, Mora Co.
Mission— Watrous, Mora Co.

PILGRIMAGE SHRINES

ALBUQUERQUE
SHRINE—SHRINE OF ST. BERNADETTE 1800 Martha, N.E., 87112-3161.

CHIMAYO, SANTUARIO DE CHIMAYO, Attended by Holy Family, Chimayo. , 87522.

Priests Serving Private and Public Institutions

SANTA FE. *Hospital*. Deacon Steve Rangel, Dir. Outreach.
New Mexico State Penitentiary. Deacons Andy Carillo, Andy Dimas.
St. Vincent's Hospital. Rev. Pio O'Connor, O.F.M., Chap.

ALBUQUERQUE. *Lovelace Hospital*. Revs. Stephen A. Sanchez, Scott Mansfield, Binu Joseph Pazhayaveetil, O.Praem, Deacon Fabian Gagnon.
Presbyterian Hospital. Rev. Robert Campbell, O.Praem.
Prison Ministry. Deacon Steve Rangel, Dir. Outreach.
University Hospital. Rev. George Pavamkott, O.Praem.
Veterans Administration Medical Center. Rev. David Klein, C.S.B.

LAS VEGAS. *State Hospital*. Rev. George Salazar. Attended by Immaculate Conception Parish.

LOS LUNAS. *Correctional Facility (State)*. Deacon Lorenzo Castillo.

On Duty Outside the Archdiocese:
Revs.—
Phillipson, David
Steenson, Jeffery N., University of St. Thomas, Houston, TX.

Retired:
Rev. Msgrs.—
Gomez, Leo, (Gallup Diocese)
Lucero, Leo
Salas, Sipio
Revs.—
Amiro, Raymond M.
Aragon, Ramon
Auman, Robert
Bolman, Anthony P.
Bowers, Ronald J., (Archdiocese of St. Paul & Minneapolis)
Brand, Fred
Brown, Charles
Conway, John
Coughlan, Robert
DeFazio, Vincent G.
Duffy, Patrick
Falbo, Samuel
Furfaro, Virgil
Galli, Clarence F.
Garcia, Millan
Hendren, Lucian
Hickman, J. Stephen
Jakobiak, Arthur
Jaramillo, Luis
Kapitz, Donald
LaVoie, Joseph
Mayefske, Thomas
Mondragon, Antonio
Moore, James
Podvin, Albert J.
Prieto, Frank
Rivera, Guadalupe
Romero, Anthony E.
Rubio-Boitel, Fernando
Starkey, Donald

Permanent Deacons:
Abeyta, Santos, Holy Family, Albuquerque
Adams, Alton, St. Alice, Mountainair
Aguilar, Gregory, Santa Clara Pueblo, Tewa Missions
Alcouffe, Raymond, Immaculate Heart of Mary, Los Alamos
Alderette, Thomas, St. Joseph-St. Patrick, Raton
Allen, Charles, (Outside the Archdiocese)
Aragon, Raphael (Ray) P., St. Anne, Tucumcari
Aragon, Robert, St. Jude Thaddeus, Albuquerque
Archibeque, Norbert, Church of the Incarnation, Rio Rancho
Archuleta, Faustin, Holy Ghost, Albuquerque
Archuleta, John, Nuestra Senora de Guadalupe, Pojoaque
Archunde, Gregory, St. Bernadette Parish and Shrine, Albuquerque
Arellano, Romolo, La Santisima Trinidad, Arroyo Seco
Arquero, Albert, Our Lady of Guadalupe, Pena Blanca
Avalos-Sanchez, Constantino, Santuario de San Martin, Albuquerque
Avitia, Hector, San Clemente, Los Lunas
Ayala, Jose, St. Francis Xavier, Albuquerque
Ayers, Roger, St. Thomas, Rio Rancho
Baca, James, (Retired)
Baca, Paul, San Clemente, Los Lunas
Baca, Rudolph F., St. Therese, Albuquerque
Baca, Thomas, (Outside the Archdiocese)
Baca, Tomas, (Outside the Archdiocese)
Bachechi, Victor, Annunciation, Albuquerque
Bailey, Aston, (Retired)
Barajas, Juan, St. Anne, Albuquerque; Dir. of Hispanic Ministry; Assoc. Dir., Diaconate Program
Barela, Felix, Our Lady of Belen, Belen
Barela, Ruben, Queen of Heaven, Albuquerque
Barry, William, St. Charles, Albuquerque
Beare, Harry, Holy Rosary, Albuquerque
Beaudette, James, Holy Rosary, Albuquerque
Bird, John, St. John the Baptist, Ohkay Owingeh Pueblo
Blea, Edward, Holy Family, Albuquerque
Broussard, Peter, Our Lady of the Assumption, Albuquerque
Bruckner, Donald G., St. Joseph on the Rio Grande, Albuquerque
Burkhard, Robert, San Clemente, Los Lunas
Burns, Thomas, St. Thomas, Rio Rancho
Burrola, Jose Luis, Our Lady of Guadalupe, Santa Fe
Bussemeier, Mark, Risen Savior, Albuquerque, Director of Diaconate Formation
Cabrera, Juan, Our Lady of Guadalupe, Albuquerque
Calderon, Gonzalo, Our Lady of Sorrows, Bernalillo
Carbajal, James, San Felipe De Neri, Albuquerque
Carmony, Larry, Holy Child, Tijeras
Carrillo, Andres, St. John the Baptist, Santa Fe
Casaus, Luis, (Retired)
Castillo, Lorenzo, Immaculate Conception, Tome
Centenera, Leandro, Prince of Peace, Albuquerque
Cervantes, Jose de Jesus, Our Lady of Sorrows, Bernalillo
Chavez, Andrew, (Retired)
Chavez, Daniel, Our Lady of Guadalupe, Clovis
Chavez, Ernest, Immaculate Conception, Las Vegas
Chavez, Gerald, Our Lady of Guadalupe, Pena Blanca
Chavez, Ricardo, Holy Ghost, Albuquerque
Chavez, Tiburcio, (Retired)
Chavez, Ubaldo, Holy Ghost, Albuquerque
Cleveland, Larry, Queen of Heaven, Albuquerque
Contreras, Donald, Aquinas Newman Center, Albuquerque
Contreras, Robert, (Retired)
Cooney, Patrick, (Retired), St. Therese, Albuquerque
Cordova, John, Santa Maria De La Paz, Santa Fe
Cordova, Raynaldo A., (Retired), St. Gertrude the Great, Mora
Cullen, Charles, Prince of Peace, Albuquerque
Cupps, Donald, Estancia Valley Catholic Church, Moriarty
Delgado, James P., Our Lady of the Assumption, Albuquerque
DeLozier, Patrick, San Francisco de Asis, Ranchos De Taos
Dimas, Juan (Andy), St. Anne, Santa Fe
Dohle, Albert, St. Joseph, Albuquerque
Duran, Charles, Santa Clara, Wagon Mound
Eklund, Bruce, St. Thomas Aquinas Newman Center, Albuquerque
Elsberg, Alexander, San Miguel, Socorro
Escandon, Jose, (On Leave)
Espinosa, Edward, Our Lady of Guadalupe, Peralta
Esquibel, A. Edwin, Our Lady of Sorrows, La Joya
Facio, Manuel, Our Lady of Guadalupe, Albuquerque
Fraker, Steven, Prince of Peace, Albuquerque
Gagnon, Fabian, Pastoral Care, Sandia Health System, Albuquerque
Gallegos, Eloy, Santa Maria de la Paz, Santa Fe
Gallegos, Manuel A., (Retired)
Gallegos, Martin, Jr., San Isidro - San Jose, Santa Fe
Garcia, Joseph, St. John the Baptist, Santa Fe
Garcia, Manuel, Risen Savior, Albuquerque
Garcia, Nestor, (Retired), St. Edwin, Albuquerque
Garcia, Pedro, Nuestra Senora de Guadalupe, Pojoaque
Garcia, Pilar, Queen of Heaven, Albuquerque
Gogan, Harry L., Annunciation, Albuquerque
Gradeja, Raul, San Miguel, Socorro
Graff, Kenneth, Our Lady of Assumption, Albuquerque
Granato, John, Our Lady of the Assumption, Albuquerque
Greivel, Rene, St. Joseph on the Rio Grande, Albuquerque
Hackett, Hugh, (Retired), Our Lady of Fatima, Albuquerque
Hall, Sandy, Our Lady of Fatima, Albuquerque
Henderson, Gregorio, San Jose, Albuquerque
Herrera, Diego A., Sacred Heart, Espanola
Herrera, Joseph, Holy Rosary, Albuquerque
Herrera, Roberto, St. Helen, Portales
Hietpas, Gerald M., St. Joseph on the Rio Grande, Albuquerque
Hill, Kenneth, St. Thomas, Rio Rancho
Hoefler, William C., Ascension, Albuquerque
Illerbrun, Michael, Nativity of the Blessed Virgin Mary, Albuquerque
Jiron, Robert, San Miguel, Socorro
Johnson, Charles V., (Retired), P.L.C., San Ignacio, Albuquerque

Jones, Leon, Church of the Ascension, Albuquerque
Jones, Thomas E., Our Lady of Fatima, Albuquerque
Keller, Nicholas, San Miguel, Socorro
Kittredge, Michael, Holy Trinity, Arroyo Seco
Kollasch, William, St. Francis Cathedral Basilica, Santa Fe
Langner, Gerald, Immaculate Heart of Mary, Los Alamos
LeFebre, Paul, St. Anne, Albuquerque
Lente, Michael, Our Lady of Sorrows, Bernalillo
Lewis, James R. "Bob", San Felipe de Neri, Albuquerque
Little, David, St. Thomas, Rio Rancho
Lopez, Demetrio, Queen of Heaven, Albuquerque
Lopez, Jose O., Holy Family, Chimayo
Lucero, Charles, (Retired)
Lucero, Donato, Immaculate Heart of Mary, Los Alamos
Lucero, Frank, St. Jude Thaddeus, Albuquerque
Lucero, Jose E., San Felipe de Neri, Albuquerque
Lucero, Juan S., Estancia Valley Parish, Estancia
Lucero, Leroy, St. Anthony, Questa
Luna, Desiderio, Sacred Heart, Albuquerque
Maloney, Kevin, Annunciation, Albuquerque
Marquez, Mark Marvin, St. Rose of Lima, Santa Rosa
Marquez, Oscar, San Martin De Porres, Albuquerque
Martinez, Donald J., Our Lady of Guadalupe, Taos
Martinez, Eloy, St. John the Baptist, Ohkay Owingeh Pueblo
Martinez, Jose Leroy, Our Lady of Sorrows, Las Vegas
Martinez, Juan R., St. Francis Cathedral, Santa Fe
Martinez, Juan G., San Miguel, Ribera
Martinez, Leonard, Nativity, Albuquerque
Martinez, Lloyd, Sangre de Cristo, Albuquerque
McLane, Alfred, St. Bernadette, Albuquerque
Medina, Jesus, St. Francis Xavier, Albuquerque
Menke, Maurice, San Felipe, Albuquerque
Meyerson, George, Incarnation, Rio Rancho
Meyrick, Earl, (Retired)
Miller, George, St. Joseph on the Rio Grande, Albuquerque
Mishler, Richard, (Outside the Archdiocese)
Montoya, Enrique M., St. Anne, Santa Fe
Montoya, Filberto "Manny", Santa Maria, Santa Fe
Montoya, Manuel, St. Therese, Albuquerque
Montoya, P. Louis, St. Francis Xavier, Clayton
Morrow, Robert, Our Lady of the Annunciation, Albuquerque
Nguyen, Dung (Paul), St. Charles, Albuquerque
O'Hare, John J., (Outside the Archdiocese)
Olona, Edward, St. Joseph, Springer
Ortiz, Juan, Nativity of the Blessed Virgin Mary, Albuquerque
Ortwerth, Paul, Sangre de Cristo, Albuquerque
Pacheco, Carlos Felix, (Retired)
Pacheco, Charles, (Retired)
Padilla, Enrique, Prince of Peace, Albuquerque
Palmer, Terry, St. Bernadette, Albuquerque
Paszkiewicz, Jerome, Church of the Incarnation, Rio Rancho
Perez, Frank, Holy Rosary, Albuquerque
Perez, Tomas, Sacred Heart, Albuquerque
Porto, Tony, (Retired)
Pullings, Harold, Our Lady of Guadalupe, Clovis
Quintana, Jerry, Our Lady of Guadalupe, Taos
Rael, Felimon, St. Mel's Mission, Eagle Nest
Rael, Marcus, St. Anthony, Questa
Rangel, Stephen S., San Ysidro, Corrales; Dir. of Permanent Diaconate
Rasinski, John, Our Lady of the Sandias, Kirtland, AFB
Rodriguez, Juan, (Retired)
Rodriguez, Juan A., Sacred Heart, Clovis
Rodriguez, Randall, Holy Child, Tijeras
Romero, Jerome, San Antonio de Padua, Penasco
Roseborough, Donald, San Ysidro, Corrales
Rowley, Michael, Sacred Heart, Clovis
Roybal, Christobal, St. Gertrude, Mora
Roybal, Reuben, Nuestra Senora de Guadalupe, Pojoaque
Roybal, Richard, St. Anthony, Pecos
Russo, John L., John XXIII Catholic Community, Albuquerque
Salazar, Miguel, St. John the Baptist, Ohkay Owingeh Pueblo
Salazar, Phillip, (Outside the Archdiocese)
Salazar, Samuel, (On Leave)
Salinas, Cresencio, San Martin De Porres, Albuquerque
Sanchez, Arsenio, St. Rose of Lima, Santa Rosa
Sanchez, Leroy, St. Thomas, Rio Rancho
Sanchez, Norbert C., (Retired)
Sanchez, Reyes, Our Lady of Sorrows, Las Vegas
Sanchez, Robert, Our Lady of Belen, Belen
Sandoval, George, Immaculate Conception, Albuquerque
Santana, Joe, St. Bernadette, Albuquerque
Santistevan, Peter, (Retired)
Schultz, Ronald, St. Charles, Albuquerque
Schwenn, Charles E., St. Alice, Mountainair
Sedillo, Michael, Immaculate Conception, Cimarron
See, Frank C., Our Lady of Fatima, Albuquerque
Segura, Jose, Our Lady of Guadalupe, Pena Blanca
Sena, Edward, St. Anthony of Padua, Fort Sumner
Sheehan, Dan, Risen Savior, Albuquerque
Siegel, Michael, San Isidro/San Jose, Santa Fe
Silva, Joseph, Holy Rosary, Albuquerque
Sinatra, Kenneth, Risen Savior, Albuquerque
Smith, Frank, St. Thomas, Rio Rancho
Snell, Jimmie, San Clemente, Los Lunas
Stith, Thomas, Our Lady of Guadalupe, Santa Fe
Toliver, Jeffrey, (On Leave)
Toquinto, Jesus, Ascension, Albuquerque
Torres, Edgar L., S.R., Sacred Heart, Albuquerque
Trujillo, Alex, (Retired)
Trujillo, Anthony, Our Lady of Guadalupe, Santa Fe
Trujillo, Joseph, Our Lady of Guadalupe, Peralta
Trujillo, Kenneth, Risen Savior, Albuquerque
Tuma, Eugene, (Retired)
Valdez, Gilbert, Our Lady of Guadalupe, Santa Fe
Valdez, Jose, Nuestra Senora de Guadalupe, Pojoaque
Valkenburgh, Thomas Van, Cristo Rey, Santa Fe
Valverde, George W., Our Lady of Guadalupe, Albuquerque
Valverde, Gilbert, (Retired)
Vigil, Ralph, St. Anne, Santa Fe
Vigil, Robert, Sacred Heart, Albuquerque
Villareal, Merce A., Risen Savior, Albuquerque
Villarreal, Robert, Immaculate Heart of Mary, Los Alamos
Welch, Robert, St. Anne, Tucumcari
Wesley, Michael, St. Therese, Albuquerque
Wicker, Byron, St. Bernadette, Albuquerque
Ybarra, Miguel, San Miguel, Socorro
Zamora, Rudy R., Our Lady of Belen, Belen

INSTITUTIONS LOCATED IN THE ARCHDIOCESE

[A] SEMINARIES, RELIGIOUS OR SCHOLASTICATES

SANTA FE. *Sangre de Cristo Center* (1962) 410 State Rd. 592, 87506-0070. Tel: 505-983-7291; Fax: 505-983-6963. Email: SANGRE@newmexico.com. Web: www.sangredecristo.org. Bros. Vincent Pelletier, F.S.C., Dir.; Paul Kelly, C.S.C., Dir. Fin.; Dennis Galvin, FSC, Assoc. Dir.; Sisters Janet Franklin, C.S.J., Assoc. Dir.; Susan Kusz, S.N.D., Assoc. Dir. Program of refoundation for religious and priests, under the administration of the Christian Brothers. Participants 68 annually. Brothers 2; Sisters 2; Lay Persons 3; Total Staff 7.

[B] HIGH SCHOOLS, ARCHDIOCESAN AND PAROCHIAL

ALBUQUERQUE. *St. Pius X High School*, 5301 St. Joseph Dr., N.W., 87120. Tel: 505-831-8400; Fax: 505-831-8413. Web: www.saintpiusx.com. Barbara Rothweiler, Prin.; Rev. Anthony G. Maes, O.Praem. Priests 1; Sisters 2; Deacons 1; Lay Teachers 74; Students 884.

[C] HIGH SCHOOLS, PRIVATE

SANTA FE. *St. Michael's High School*, (Grades 7-12), (Coed Day School), 100 Siringo Rd., 87505. Tel: 505-983-7353; Fax: 505-982-8722. Email: mainoffice@stmikes.k12.nm.us. Web: www.stmichaelshs.org. Bill Armijo, Prin. Brothers of the Christian Schools 1; Lay Teachers 56; Students 769.

[D] ELEMENTARY REGIONAL SCHOOL

SANTA FE. *Santo Nino Regional Catholic School*, (Grades K-6), 23 College Ave., 87508. Tel: 505-424-1766; Fax: 505-473-1441. Email: snrcs@santonino.k12.nm.us. Web: www.santoninoregional.org. Theresa Vaisa, Prin. Lay Teachers 22; Students 351.

[E] SPECIAL HOSPITALS AND SANATORIA FOR INVALIDS

SANTA FE. *Villa Therese Catholic Clinic*, 219 Cathedral Pl., 87501. Tel: 505-983-8561; Fax: 505-982-7863. Email: vtcc@cnsp.com. Total Staff 3; Total Assisted Annually 1,500.

[F] SHELTER CARE HOMES

ALBUQUERQUE. *Good Shepherd Center, Inc.*, 218 Iron St., S.W., P.O. Box 749, 87103. Tel: 505-243-2527; Fax: 505-247-2207. Curits Marks, Pres. Direct Service Agency for the Homeless. Total Assisted 192,000; Total Staff 5.

Marie Amadea Shelter for Unwed Mothers (Alternative to Abortion), P.O. Box 708, 87103. Tel: 505-242-1516; Fax: 505-243-0402. Mrs. Dorothy Wickens, Dir. Home for unwed expectant women. Total Assisted 25; Total Staff 3.

[G] CARE HOMES FOR PHYSICALLY AND MENTALLY HANDICAPPED

ALBUQUERQUE. *Casa Angelica* (1967) 5629 Isleta Blvd., S.W., 87105. Tel: 505-877-5763; Fax: 505-873-2786. Email: lturner@casaangelica.org. Web: www.casaangelica.org. The Daughters of Charity of Canossa., Home for developmentally disabled children and young adults. Sisters 1; Residents 16; Lay Staff 54; Total Assisted 16; Total Staff 55.

[H] MONASTERIES AND RESIDENCES OF PRIESTS AND BROTHERS

ABIQUIU. *Monastery of Christ in the Desert* (1964) 87510. Tel: 801-545-8567; Fax: 419-831-9113. Email: cidguestmaster@christdesert.us. Web: www.christdesert.org. Rt. Rev. Philip Lawrence, O.S.B., Abbot; Revs. Christian Leisy, O.S.B., Subprior; Bernard Cranor, O.S.B.; Luis Regalado, O.S.B.; Dominic Nguyen, O.S.B.; Odon Nguyen, O.S.B.; Francisco Alanis Rios, Prior; Joseph Gabriel Cusimano, O.S.B.; Andrew Nguyen, O.S.B. Subiaco Congregation.

ALBUQUERQUE. *Little Brothers of the Good Shepherd, Villa Mathias-Foundation House*, 901 Bro. Mathias Pl., N.W., P.O. Box 389, 87103. Tel: 505-243-4238; Fax: 505-764-9721. Brothers 7; Total Staff 1.

Santa Maria de la Vid Priory, 5825 Coors Rd., S.W., 87121-6700. Tel: 505-873-4399; Fax: 505-873-4667. Email: norbertines@norbertinecommunity.org. Web: www.norbertine~community.org. Revs. Joel P. Garner, O.Praem., Prior & Vocation Dir.; Vincent J. DeLeers, O.Praem.; Eugene Gries, O.Praem.; Nicholas E. Nirschl, O.Praem.; Robert E. Campbell, O.Praem.; Francis W. Dorff, O.Praem.; Rod Fenzl, O.Praem.; Anthony G. Maes, O.Praem.; Bijoy Francis Valayil, O.Praem.; George Pavamkott, O.Praem.; Binu Joseph Pazhayaveetil, O.Praem; Bro. Dennis Butler. Canons Regular of Premontre (Norbertine Community)., Sponsor of the Hermitage Retreat and the Norbertine Library. Priests 11; Brothers 1.

The Province of Our Lady of Guadalupe formerly Curia Juan Diego (1985) 1204 Stinson, S.W., 87121-3440. Tel: 505-831-9199; Fax: 505-573-5584. Email: ofmprovsec@aol.com. Web: www.olgofm.org. Very Rev. Larry C. Dunham, O.F.M., (Sabbatical); Revs. Gino Correa, O.F.M., Provincial Min.; Don Billiard, O.F.M., Treas.; Bros. Duane Torisky, O.F.M., Sec./Notary Province; Bruce Michalek, O.F.M., Devel. Dir.; George Ward, O.F.M.; Revs. Crispin C. Butz, O.F.M.; Timon Cook, O.F.M. (Retired); Cecil Kleber, O.F.M.; Gonzalo Moreno, O.F.M., Province Vocation Dir.; Pio O'Connor, O.F.M.; Bros. Richardo Garcia, O.F.M.; Efren Quintero, O.F.M.; Jose Rodriguez, O.F.M.; Mark Schornack, O.F.M.; Bart Wolff, O.F.M.; Gordon Boykin, O.F.M.; Revs. Salvador Aragon, O.F.M.; Wayne Gibbeaut, O.F.M.; Emeric Nordmeyer, O.F.M.; Diego Mazon, O.F.M.; Ulric Pax, O.F.M.; Richard Rohr, O.F.M.; Chrysostom Partee, O.F.M.; Ramon Smith, O.F.M.; Gerald Steinmetz, O.F.M.; Hilaire Valiquette, O.F.M.
Franciscan Indian Missions
Franciscan Mission Center
The Province of Our Lady of Guadalupe of the Order of Friars Minor, Inc.
Southwest Franciscan Missions Priests 18; Brothers 9.

JEMEZ SPRINGS. *Our Lady of Lourdes*, P.O. Box 10, 87025-0010. Tel: 505-829-3004; Fax: 505-829-3706. Email: servants@theservants.org. Web: www.theservants.org. Revs. Gregory McCormick, s.P., Supr. & Father Servant; James Sampson, s.P.; Paul Valley, s.P.; Bros. John Paul Pelletier, s.P.; Conrad Rydelek, s.P.; Bernard Scollon, s.P. Priests 4; Brothers 3. In Res. Rev. Edward Rolph, s.P. *Formation House* Tel: 505-829-3720; Fax: 505-829-3706.

PECOS. *Our Lady of Guadalupe Abbey*, P.O. Box 1080, 87552-1080. Tel: 505-757-6415; Fax: 505-757-2285. Email: guestmaster@pecosmonastery.org. Web: www.pecosmonastery.org. Very Rev. Stephen M. Coffey, O.S.B., Prior; Revs. Paul Meaden, O.S.B.; Sam Dennis, O.S.B.; Colman Heffern, O.S.B.; Robert Lussier, O.S.B.; Bros. John M. Davies, O.S.B.; Joseph Janeczko, O.S.B.; Bernard M. Keele, O.S.B.; James M. Marrow, O.S.B.; William M. Woytavich, O.S.B. (Olivetan Benedictine Monks) Priests 5; Brothers 5.

[I] CONVENTS AND RESIDENCES FOR SISTERS

SANTA FE. *Discalced Carmelite Monastery* (1945) 49 Mount Carmel Rd., 87505-0352. Tel: 505-983-7232. Sr. Rose Teresa, O.C.D., Prioress; Revs. Crispin C. Butz, O.F.M., Chap.; Ricardo Russo, O.F.M., Chap.; Robert Lussier, O.S.B. Solemn Professed Nuns 6; Extern Sisters 2; Novices 1.

ABIQUIU. *Monastery of Our Lady of the Desert*, P.O. Box 1040, 87510. Tel: 801-545-8569. Email: benedcta@aol.com. Sisters Miriam Randall, O.S.B.; Helen Vasquez, O.S.B., Prioress. Benedictine Nuns Subiaco Congregation.

ALBUQUERQUE. *Cristo Rey Provincial House*, 5625 Isleta Blvd., S.W., 87105. Tel: 505-873-2854; Fax: 505-873-0678. Email: fdccalb@aol.com. Web: www.canossiansisters.org. Sr. Anne Bosio, Prov. Supr. Canossian Daughters of Charity. Sisters 13.

JEMEZ SPRINGS. *Cor Jesu Monastery* (1947) Motherhouse and Novitiate of the Handmaids of the Precious Blood., 87025. Tel: 575-829-3906; Fax: 575-829-3423. Sr. Marietta, H.P.B., Mother Prioress. Perpetually Professed Sisters 20.

RIO RANCHO. *Felician Sisters*, 4210 Meadowlark Ln., S.E., 87124-1021. Tel: 505-892-8862; Fax: 505-891-3893. Email: feliciansistersabvm@cableone.net. Web: southwestfeliciansisters.org. Sr. Danat Marie Brysch, C.S.S.F., Provincial Min. Assumption of the Blessed Virgin Mary. Residents 28; Professed Sisters of Province 50; Total Assisted Per Month 6,000; Total Staff 28. In Res. Revs. Ramon Smith, O.F.M., Chap.; Ron Walters, O.F.M.

[J] RETREAT HOUSES

SANTA FE. *Immaculate Heart of Mary Retreat and Conference Center*, 50 Mount Carmel Rd., 87505. Tel: 505-988-1975; Fax: 505-988-3963. Email: rdaughtery@archdiosf.org. Mr. Randolph Daughtery, Dir.

ALBUQUERQUE. *Madonna Retreat and Conference Center*, 4040 St. Joseph Pl., N.W., 87120. Tel: 505-831-8196; Fax: 505-831-8103. Email: madonnacenter@archdiosf.org. Web: www.archdiocesesantafe.org. Marie Villanueva, Dir. Total in Residence 2; Total Staff 3.

The Spiritual Renewal Center, Inc., 6400 Coors Blvd., N.W., 87120. Tel: 505-877-4211; Fax: 505-890-4110. Email: lynnbridgers@att.net. Web: www.spiritualrenewalretreats.com. P.O. Box 67860, 87193. Dominican Sisters (Elkins Park, PA)., Center for Retreats. Total Staff 3.

PECOS. *Our Lady of Guadalupe Olivetan Benedictine Abbey*, P.O. Box 1080, 87552. Tel: 505-757-6415; Fax: 505-757-2285. Email: guestmaster@pecosmonastery.org. Web: www.pecosmonastery.org.

[K] NEWMAN CENTERS

ALBUQUERQUE. *St. Thomas Aquinas (Newman Center) University Parish* (1950) 1815 Las Lomas Rd., N.E., 87106. Tel: 505-247-1094; Fax: 505-247-2933. Email: newmancenter@aquinasnm.org. Web: www.aquinasnm.org. Revs. Thomas Martin Jackson, O.P.; Joachim Culotta, O.P., M.A., J.C.D., Parochial Vicar; Deacons Donald Contreras; Bruce Eklund; Rosie Chinea, Campus Minister; Steve Herrera, Liturgy Dir.; Kyle Kemp, Rel. Formation Dir. Priests 2; Deacons 2; Total in Residence 5; Total Staff 13. In Res. Revs. Kevin W. Niehoff, O.P.; George J.D. Reynolds, O.P.; Matthew T.D. Strabala, O.P.

LAS VEGAS. *Highlands University Newman Center* Mailing Address: 811 - 6th St., 87701. Tel: 505-425-7791; Fax: 505-425-6991. Email: icchurch2000@yahoo.com. Attended by Immaculate Conception Parish, Las Vegas.

PORTALES. *University Catholic Center - St. Thomas More Chapel* E.N.M.U., P.O. Box 2253, 88130. Tel: 575-356-5615; Fax: 575-359-1721. Very Rev. James McGowan, Chap. Total Staff 1.

SOCORRO. *St. Patrick Newman Center* 801 School of Mines Rd., 87801. Tel: 575-835-8650. Deacon Nicholas Keller, Dir.

[L] MISCELLANEOUS LISTINGS

SANTA FE. *St. Michael's High School Foundation*, 100 Siringo Rd., P.O. Box 22563, 87505. Tel: 505-992-8000; Fax: 505-955-8921. Email: lmontoya@stmikessf.org. Dr. David Gonzales, M.D., Pres.

ALBUQUERQUE. *Annual Catholic Appeal Foundation of the Archdiocese of Santa Fe*, 4000 St. Joseph Pl., N.W., 87120. Tel: 505-831-8258; Fax: 505-831-8111. Email: aca@archdiosf.org. Web: www.archdiosf.org.

Anselm Weber Fund, P.O. Box 12315, 87195-0315. Tel: 505-877-6394. Rev. Don Billiard, O.F.M., Corp. Treas.

Archbishop's School Fund, 4000 St. Joseph Pl., N.W., 87120. Tel: 505-831-8120; Fax: 505-831-8101. Email: dc@archdiosf.org. Carol Zonski, Pres.

Archdiocesan Priests Retirement Fund, Inc., 5024 4th St., N.W., 87107.

**St. Bernadette Institute of Sacred Art* (1993) P.O. Box 8249, 87198. Tel: 505-265-9126; Fax: 505-266-4678. Email: sbi@nmia.com. Web: www.stbernadette.net. Dan Paulos, Dir. Sponsors and supports Catholic art and artists.

Brothers of the Good Shepherd Inc. of New Mexico, 901 Brother Mathias Pl., N.W., P.O. Box 389, 87102-7103. Tel: 505-243-4238; Fax: 505-764-9721. Web: www.lbgs.org. Brothers 7; Total Staff 1.

Caritas Deus Inc., P.O. Box 749, 87103. Tel: 505-243-2527; Fax: 505-247-2207. Property management nonprofit corporation.

Catholic Charismatic Center (1978) 1412 Fifth St., N.W., 87102. Tel: 505-247-0398; Fax: 505-843-9147. Email: mcgarrysmjccc@aol.com. Web: www.asfccc.web.com. Total in Residence 1; Total Staff 5.

The Catholic Foundation of the Archdiocese of Santa Fe (1991) 4333 Pan American Fwy., N.E., Suite D, 87107. Tel: 505-872-2901; Fax: 505-872-2905. Email: info@thecatholicfoundation.org. Web: www.thecatholicfoundation.org. Mary P. Dunn, Exec. Dir. Total Staff 5.

Center for Action and Contemplation, P.O. Box 12464, 87195. Tel: 505-242-9588; Fax: 505-242-9518. Email: info@cacradicalgrace.org. Web: cacradicalgrace.org. Rev. Richard Rohr, O.F.M., Founder & Animator; Stephen Picha, Exec. Dir. Total in Residence 1; Total Staff 18.

Charity Unlimited, Inc., P.O. Box 389, 87103. Tel: 505-243-4238; Fax: 505-764-9721. Property management nonprofit corporation.

Dominican Ecclesial Institute (D.E.I.) (1996) 1815 Las Lomas, N.E., 87106. Tel: 505-243-0525; Fax: 505-243-0005. Email: info@d-e-i.org. Web: www.d-e-i.org. Rev. Matthew T.D. Strabala, O.P., Exec. Dir. Total Staff 2.

Fraternidad Piadosa de Nuestro Padre Jesus Nazareno, 4000 St. Joseph Pl., N.W., 87120. Tel: 505-259-0254.

Good Shepherd Center, Inc. of New Mexico, 218 Iron St., S.W., P.O. Box 749, 87103. Tel: 505-243-2527; Fax: 505-247-2207. Total Staff 6; Total Assisted 190,000.

St. Joseph Community Health Foundation, P.O. Box 26926, 87125-6926. Tel: 505-924-8000; Fax: 505-924-8025. Email: sjch@catholichealth.net. Web: stjosephnm.org.

St. Joseph Fertility Care Center (1976) 4000 St. Joseph Pl., N.W., Lourdes Hall, #130, 87120. Tel: 505-831-8222; Fax: 505-831-8223. Email: angelgarcia@fertilitycare.net. Angelique N. Garcia, Pres. & Dir.

**The Marriage Enrichment Weekend Program, Inc.*, P.O. Box 94026, 87199-4026. Tel: 505-884-8250. Web: www.tmewpi.org. Ralph Johnson, Ph.D., Pres.

Norbertine Community of New Mexico, Inc., 5825 Coors Rd., N.W., 87121-6700. Tel: 505-873-4399; Fax: 505-873-4667. Email: santamariadelavid@hotmail.com; norbertines@norbertinecommunity.org. Web: www.norbertinecommunity.org. Rev. Joel P. Garner, O.Praem. Total in Residence 13; Total Staff 4.

St. Pius X High School Foundation, Inc., 5301 St. Joseph Dr., N.W., 87120. Tel: 505-831-8423; Fax: 505-831-8438. Email: lsanzero@spx.k12.nm.us. Web: www.saintpiusx.com. Barbara Rothweiler, Prin. Nonprofit corporation for the financial support of St. Pius X High School.

Roger Huser Fund, P.O. Box 12315, 87195-0315. Tel: 505-877-6394. Rev. Don Billiard, O.F.M., Corp. Treas.

Santo Nino Children's Foundation for Catholic Education, LLC, 4000 St. Joseph Pl., N.W., 87120. Tel: 505-831-8132; Fax: 505-831-8113.

SPX Towers, 5301 St. Joseph's Pl., N.W., 87120. Tel: 505-884-1309; Fax: 505-889-2720. Allen Jackson, Contact Person. To generate funds for use as financial aid for economically disadvantaged children to attend St. Pius X High School.

Villa Mathias Inc., P.O. Box 389, 87103. Tel: 505-243-4238; Fax: 505-764-9721.

JEMEZ SPRINGS. *EDSA Charitable Trust*, P.O. Box 10, 87025. Tel: 575-829-3586. Email: manilasp@aol.com. Rev. Gregory McCormick, s.P.

Fitzgerald Charitable Trust, P.O. Box 10, 87025. Tel: 575-829-3586; Fax: 575-829-3706. Web: www.theservants.org. Rev. Gregory McCormick, s.P.

RIO RANCHO. *St. Felix Pantry, Inc.*, 4020 Barbara Loop, 87124-1023. Tel: 505-891-8075. P.O. Box 44274, 87174. Sr. M. Edna Pearl Esquibel, C.S.S.F., Pres. Total Assisted Per Month 3,400; Total Staff 50.

RELIGIOUS INSTITUTES OF MEN REPRESENTED IN THE ARCHDIOCESE

For further details refer to the corresponding bracketed number in the Religious Institutes of Men or Women section.

[0170]—*Basilian Fathers* (Houston, TX)—C.S.B.

[0200]—*Benedictine Monks* (Our Lady of Guadalupe Abbey, Pecos; Abbey of Christ in the Desert, Abiquiu)—O.S.B.

[0330]—*Brothers of the Christian Schools* (Baltimore, Midwest & De La Salle Provinces)—F.S.C.

[0580]—*Brothers of the Good Shepherd* (Albuquerque, NM)—B.G.S.

[0900]—*Canons Regular of Premontre* (Norbertine Fathers and Brothers of De Pere, Wisconsin)—O.Praem.

[0520]—*Franciscan Friars* (Our Lady of Guadalupe, St. John the Baptist & St. Barbara Provinces)—O.F.M.

[0535]—*Franciscan Friars of the Renewal* (Bronx, NY)—C.F.R.

[0430]—*Order of Preachers-Dominicans* (St. Albert the Great Province)—O.P.

[1230]—*Servants of the Paraclete* (Jemez Springs, NM)—s.P.

[0690]—*Society of Jesus* (New Orleans Prov., Missouri Prov.)—S.J.

[0975]—*Society of Our Lady of the Most Holy Trinity* (Robstown, TX)—S.O.L.T.

[0640]—*Sons of the Holy Family* (Silver Spring, MD)—S.F.

RELIGIOUS INSTITUTES OF WOMEN REPRESENTED IN THE ARCHDIOCESE

[0200]—*Benedictine Sisters* (Pecos and Abiquiu, NM)—O.S.B.

[0230]—*Benedictine Sisters* (Colorado Springs, CO)—O.S.B.

[0730]—*Canossian Daughters of Charity* (Albuquerque, NM)—Fd.C.C.

[3832]—*Congregation of the Sisters of St. Joseph*—C.S.J.

[1780]—*Congregation of the Sisters of the Third Order of St. Francis of Perpetual Adoration* (La Crosse, WI)—F.S.P.A.

[0420]—*Discalced Carmelite Nuns* (Santa Fe, NM)—O.C.D.

[1070-03]—*Dominican Sisters* (Sinsinawa, WI)—O.P.

[1070-09]—*Dominican Sisters* (Racine, WI)—O.P.

[1070-14]—*Dominican Sisters* (Grand Rapids, MI)—O.P.

[1070-17]—*Dominican Sisters* (Elkins Park, PA)—O.P.

[1070-13]—*Dominican Sisters* (Adrian, MI)—O.P.

[1115]—*Dominican Sisters of Peace*—O.P.

[1170]—*Felician Sisters* (Congregation of Sisters of St. Felix of Cantalice)—C.S.S.F.

[1310]—*Franciscan Sisters* (Little Falls, MN)—O.S.F.

[1430]—*Franciscan Sisters of Our Lady of Perpetual Help* (St. Louis, MO)—O.S.F.

[1860]—*Handmaids of the Precious Blood* (Jemez Springs, NM)—H.P.B.

[2470]—*Maryknoll Sisters of St. Dominic* (Maryknoll, NY)—M.M.

[2760]—*Missionary Sisters of the Immaculate Conception of the Mother of God* (Paterson, NJ)—S.M.I.C.

[3130]—*Our Lady of Victory Missionary Sisters* (Huntington, IN)—O.L.V.M.

[3430]—*Religious Teachers Filippine* (St. Lucy Filippine Province, Morristown, NJ)—M.P.F.

[]—*Sisters for Christian Community*—S.F.C.C.

[0440]—*Sisters of Charity of Cincinnati, Ohio* (Mt. St. Joseph, OH)—S.C.

[0480]—*Sisters of Charity of Leavenworth, Kansas*—S.C.L.

[0990]—*Sisters of Divine Providence* (Allison Park, PA)—C.D.P.

[2360]—*Sisters of Loretto at the Foot of the Cross* (Denver, CO)—S.L.

[2575]—*Sisters of Mercy of the Americas* (Omaha, NE)—R.S.M.

[2990]—*Sisters of Notre Dame* (Toledo, OH)—S.N.D.

[0230]—*Sisters of Pontifical Jurisdiction* (Colorado Springs, CO)—O.S.B.

[1705]—*The Sisters of St. Francis of Assisi* (Milwaukee, WI)—O.S.F.

[1620]—*Sisters of St. Francis of Millvale, PA*—O.S.F.

[1630]—*Sisters of St. Francis of Penance and Christian Charity* (Sacred Heart & Holy Name Provinces, Stella Niagara, NY)—O.S.F.

[1640]—*Sisters of St. Francis of Perpetual Adoration* (St. Joseph Province, Colorado Springs, CO)—O.S.F.

[1530]—*Sisters of St. Francis of the Congregation of Our Lady of Lourdes, Sylvania, Ohio*—O.S.F.

[3830-01]—*Sisters of St. Joseph* (Boston, MA)—C.S.J.

[0260]—*Sisters of the Blessed Sacrament for Indians and Colored People* (Bensalem, PA)—S.B.S

[1760]—*Sisters of the Third Order of St. Francis of Penance and Charity* (Tiffin, OH)—O.S.F.

[1720]—*Sisters of the Third Order Regular of St. Francis of the Congregation of Our Lady of Lourdes* (Rochester, MN)—O.S.F.

[2150-60]—*Sisters, Servants of the Immaculate Heart of Mary* (Monroe, MI; Scranton, PA)—I.H.M.

[3105]—*Society of Our Lady of the Most Holy Trinity* (Skidmore, TX)—S.O.L.T.

[4120]—*Ursuline Nuns, of the Congregation of Paris* (Maple Mount, KY)—O.S.U.

ARCHDIOCESAN CEMETERIES

ALBUQUERQUE. *Catholic Cemetery Association,* 4000 St. Joseph Pl., N.W., 87120. Tel: 505-831-8100. Leah Detommaso, Exec. Dir. Tel: 505-248-1532. Diocesan Cemeteries, Rosario (Santa Fe), Mt. Calvary (Albuquerque) and Gate of Heaven (Albuquerque).

NECROLOGY

† Abeywickrema, Lionel Augustin—Died Nov. 12, 2008

† Bortolotti, Serafino, (Retired)—Died July 22, 2009

† Cushing, Alan, (Retired)—Died June 22, 2009

An asterisk (*) denotes an organization that has established tax-exempt status directly with the IRS and is not covered by the USCCB Group Ruling.

Diocese of Santa Rosa in California

(Dioecesis Sanctae Rosae in California)

Most Reverend

DANIEL F. WALSH, D.D.

Bishop of Santa Rosa in California; ordained March 30, 1963; appointed Titular Bishop of Tigia and Auxiliary of San Francisco September 24, 1981; appointed Bishop of Reno-Las Vegas June 9, 1987; installed August 6, 1987; appointed Bishop of Las Vegas March 21, 1995; installed June 28, 1995; appointed Bishop of Santa Rosa in California on April 4, 2000; installed May 22, 2000.

ESTABLISHED FEBRUARY 21, 1962.

Square Miles 11,711.

Comprises six Counties in the State of California-viz., Del Norte, Humboldt, Lake, Mendocino, Napa and Sonoma.

Legal Titles: "The Roman Catholic Bishop of Santa Rosa, a Corporation Sole" and "The Roman Catholic Welfare Corporation of Santa Rosa."
For legal titles of parishes and diocesan institutions, consult the Chancery Office.

Chancery Office: 985 Airway Ct., Santa Rosa, CA 95403. Tel: 707-545-7610; Fax: 707-542-9702. *Mailing Address: P.O. Box 1297, Santa Rosa, CA 95402-1297*

Web: www.srdiocese.org

STATISTICAL OVERVIEW

Personnel	
Bishop	1
Priests: Diocesan Active in Diocese	52
Priests: Diocesan Active Outside Diocese	2
Priests: Retired, Sick or Absent	18
Number of Diocesan Priests	72
Religious Priests in Diocese	10
Total Priests in Diocese	82
Extern Priests in Diocese	13
Ordinations:	
Transitional Deacons	3
Permanent Deacons in Diocese	32
Total Brothers	26
Total Sisters	42
Parishes	
Parishes	42
With Resident Pastor:	
Resident Diocesan Priests	39
Without Resident Pastor:	
Administered by Priests	2
Administered by Religious Women	1
Missions	18
Pastoral Centers	8
Professional Ministry Personnel:	
Sisters	4
Lay Ministers	26
Welfare	
Catholic Hospitals	5
Total Assisted	712,727
Homes for the Aged	1
Total Assisted	48
Residential Care of Children	1
Total Assisted	119
Special Centers for Social Services	9
Total Assisted	32,000
Educational	
Diocesan Students in Other Seminaries	7
Total Seminarians	7
High Schools, Diocesan and Parish	2
Total Students	802
High Schools, Private	3
Total Students	1,133
Elementary Schools, Diocesan and Parish	11
Total Students	2,385
Elementary Schools, Private	1
Total Students	80
Catechesis/Religious Education:	
High School Students	1,430
Elementary Students	4,895
Total Students under Catholic Instruction	10,732
Teachers in the Diocese:	
Priests	1
Brothers	1
Sisters	5
Lay Teachers	322
Vital Statistics	
Receptions into the Church:	
Infant Baptism Totals	3,265
Minor Baptism Totals	130
Adult Baptism Totals	104
Received into Full Communion	95
First Communions	2,495
Confirmations	1,068
Marriages:	
Catholic	406
Interfaith	132
Total Marriages	538
Deaths	873
Total Catholic Population	169,567
Total Population	909,361

Former Bishops—Most Revs. LEO T. MAHER, D.D., ord. Dec. 18, 1943; appt. First Bishop of Santa Rosa, Feb. 21, 1962; cons. April 5, 1962; translated San Diego, Aug. 27, 1969; died Feb. 23, 1991; MARK J. HURLEY, D.D., Ph.D., J.C.B., LL.D., ord. Sept. 23, 1944; appt. Titular Bishop of Thunusuda and Auxiliary of San Francisco, Oct. 12, 1967; cons. Jan. 4, 1968; translated Santa Rosa, Nov. 9, 1969; appt. member of the Vatican Secretariat for Non-Believers, consultor to the Congregation for Catholic Education; resigned as Bishop of Santa Rosa, April 15, 1986; died Feb. 5, 2001; JOHN T. STEINBOCK, D.D., ord. May 1, 1963; Titular Bishop of Midila and Auxiliary Bishop of Orange; appt. May 29, 1984; translated Santa Rosa, March 31, 1987; translated Fresno, Nov. 25, 1991; G. PATRICK ZIEMANN, D.D., ord. April 29, 1967; appt. Titular Bishop of Obba and Auxiliary Bishop of Los Angeles, Dec. 29, 1986; ord. Bishop, Feb. 23, 1987; appt. Bishop of Santa Rosa, July 14, 1992; resigned as Bishop of Santa Rosa, July 21, 1999; died Oct. 22, 2009.

Chancery Office—985 Airway Court, Santa Rosa, 95403. Tel: 707-545-7610; Fax: 707-542-9702. *Mailing Address: P.O. Box 1297, Santa Rosa, 95402-1297.* Office Hours: Mon.-Fri. 8:30-4:30; All applications for dispensations, faculties, etc., and all correspondence should be addressed to the Chancery Office.

Vicar General—Rev. Msgr. JAMES E. PULSKAMP, V.G.

Deans—Rev. Msgr. JOSEPH ALZUGARAY, Napa; Revs. ANGELITO PERIES, Sonoma-North; GARY LOMBARDI, Sonoma-South; RON SERBAN, Mendocino-Lake; FRANK EPPERSON, Humboldt-Del Norte.

Chancellor—Rev. Msgr. JAMES E. PULSKAMP, V.G.

Director of Clergy Personnel—Rev. Msgr. JAMES E. PULSKAMP, V.G.

Vicar for Priests—Rev. Msgr. DANIEL P. WHELTON, J.C.L.

Diocesan Finance Officer—Deacon MICHAEL URICK.

Secretary to the Bishop—PAM HAWKINS. Tel: 707-566-3325; Fax: 707-566-3310.

Diocesan Tribunal—Mailing Address: P.O. Box 1297, Santa Rosa, 95402-1297. Tel: 707-566-3370; Fax: 707-566-3385.

Judicial Vicar—Rev. Msgr. DANIEL P. WHELTON, J.C.L.

Adjutant Judicial Vicar—Rev. FERGAL MCGUINNESS, J.C.L.

Promoter of Justice—Rev. Msgr. JOHN J. BRENKLE, J.C.D.

Defender of the Bond—Rev. DAVID SHAW.

Diocesan Judges—Rev. Msgrs. JOHN J. BRENKLE, J.C.D.; JAMES P. GAFFEY (Retired); DANIEL P. WHELTON, J.C.L.; Revs. JOHN S. CREWS, Ed.D.; ABEL MENA, J.C.L.; FERGAL MCGUINNESS, J.C.L.

Advocates—Rev. WILLIAM P. DONAHUE; ANN LYNCH.

Auditor—Sr. ROSE MARY KUKLOK, O.S.B.

Notaries—Rev. Msgr. JAMES E. PULSKAMP, V.G.; PAM HAWKINS.

Board of Consultors—Rev. Msgrs. JAMES E. PULSKAMP, V.G.; DANIEL P. WHELTON, J.C.L.; JOSEPH ALZUGARAY; Revs. FRANK EPPERSON; GARY LOMBARDI; RON SERBAN; ANGELITO PERIES.

Priests' Council—Rev. Msgrs. JAMES E. PULSKAMP, V.G.; DANIEL P. WHELTON, J.C.L.; JOSEPH ALZUGARAY; Revs. GARY LOMBARDI; GORDON KALIL; ANGELITO PERIES; RON SERBAN; WILLIAM P. DONAHUE; RAUL LEMUS; MICHAEL W. CLONEY; FRANK EPPERSON; SEAN ROGERS; DAVID SHAW; OSCAR DIAZ.

Finance Committee—Rev. Msgr. JOHN J. BRENKLE, J.C.D.; Rev. DAVID SHAW; Rev. Msgr. JAMES E. PULSKAMP, V.G.; Rev. GARY LOMBARDI; Deacon FRANCIS DAHL; JUDY BARRETT; CLEM CARINALLI; WILLIAM CORNELISON; JANET HAGGEN; PEGGY FURTH; ROBERT FISH; PAUL LESAGE; MARY LEITTEM-THOMAS; HEDY MONTOYA; JOHN MOYNIER; GEORGE ORTIZ; RICK ROSA; JOHN SCHULTZ; GENE SENESTRARO.

Diocesan Building Committee—WILLIAM CORNELISON, Chm.; Rev. Msgr. JAMES E. PULSKAMP, V.G.; ANTHONY BATTAGLIA; LOWELL ALLEN; ED RONCHELLI; JOHN SCHULTZ.

Diocesan Communications Committee—DEIRDRE FRONTCZAK, Chm.; JUDY BARRETT; GEORGE ORTIZ; VALERIE PRESTON; KEVIN CONNOLLY.

Review Board—Rev. Msgrs. JAMES E. PULSKAMP, V.G.; JOHN J. BRENKLE, J.C.D.; ANTONIO MADRID, Ph.D.; FRANK SCALERCIO JR., Ph.D.; Hon. JOHN GALLAGHER; FRANK M. HEFFERNAN JR.; CATHY HUGHES, M.F.T.; BOB MCKEEVER; ELIZABETH MCKEE. Consultants: DAN GALVIN II, Esq.; JULIE SPARACIO, Dir. Office for the Protection of Children & Youth.

Diocesan Offices and Directors

Archivist—Rev. Msgr. JAMES E. PULSKAMP, V.G., 985 Airway Ct., Santa Rosa, 95403. Tel: 707-566-3312. Mailing Address: P.O. Box 1297, Santa Rosa, 95402-1297.

Director of the Office for the Protection of Children and Youth—JULIE SPARACIO, 985 Airway Ct., Santa Rosa, 95403. Tel: 707-566-3308. Mailing Address: P.O. Box 1297, Santa Rosa, 95402-1297.

Attorney for the Diocese—DANIEL J. GALVIN III, Shapiro, Galvin, Shapiro, Piasta & Moran, 640 Third St., Santa Rosa, 95401. Tel: 707-544-5858;

Fax: 707-544-6702.

Boy Scouts—STANLEY CORDERO, 985 Airway Court, Santa Rosa, 95403. Tel: 707-566-3343; Fax: 707-566-3320.

Catholic Charities, Central Administrative Office—LARRY R. LAKES, Exec. Dir., 987 Airway Ct., Santa Rosa, 95403. Tel: 707-528-8712; Fax: 707-575-4910. Mailing Address: P.O. Box 4900, Santa Rosa, 95402-4900.

Catholic Community Foundation—Rev. DAVID SHAW, Dir., 985 Airway Ct., Santa Rosa, 95403. Tel: 707-545-2311; 707-566-3357; Fax: 707-566-3310. Mailing Address: P.O. Box 1297, Santa Rosa, 95402-1297.

Catholic Youth Organization—KATHY DONLEY, Liaison, Office, 985 Airway Ct., Santa Rosa, 95403. Tel: 707-566-3349. Mailing Address: P.O. Box 1297, Santa Rosa, 95402-1297.

Cemeteries—Rev. Msgr. GERARD FAHEY, Dir., 2930 Bennett Valley Rd., P.O. Box 2098, Santa Rosa, 95404. Tel: 707-546-6290; Fax: 707-546-2773.

Clergy Formation—Rev. MICHAELRAJ PHILOMINSAMY, 985 Airway Ct., Santa Rosa, 95403. Tel: 707-545-7610; Fax: 707-542-9702.

Clergy Personnel Committee—Rev. Msgr. JAMES E. PULSKAMP, V.G.; Revs. LOREN ALLEN; MANUEL CHAVEZ; MICHAELRAJ PHILOMINSAMY; WILLIAM P. DONAHUE; DAVID SHAW; Deacon JAMES CARR.

Communications—DEIRDRE FRONTCZAK, Dir., 985 Airway Ct., Santa Rosa, 95403. Tel: 707-566-3302; Fax: 707-546-4239. Mailing Address: P.O. Box 1297, Santa Rosa, 95402-1297.

Custodian of Records—Rev. Msgr. JAMES E. PULSKAMP, V.G., 985 Airway Ct., Santa Rosa, 95403. Tel: 707-566-3312. Mailing Address: P.O. Box 1297, Santa Rosa, 95402-1297.

Restoration Justice & Detention Ministry—24A Ursuline Rd., Santa Rosa, 95403. Tel: 707-544-9080; Fax: 707-544-9081.

Development—DEBBIE DRAGO, Mailing Address: P.O. Box 1297, Santa Rosa, 95402. Tel: 707-566-3344.

Disabled—Chancery Office, 985 Airway Ct., Santa Rosa, 95403. Tel: 707-545-7610. *Mailing Address: P.O. Box 1297, Santa Rosa, 95402*.

Ecumenical and Interreligious Affairs—Rev. THOMAS W. DEVEREAUX, Mailing Address: P.O. Box 549, Cloverdale, 95425. Tel: 707-894-2535; Fax: 707-894-9603.

Hispanic Ministry—Rev. OSCAR DIAZ, Dir., Mailing Address: 150 St. Joseph Way, Cotati, 94931. Tel: 707-795-4807; Fax: 707-795-7851.

Cursillos De Cristiandad—Mailing Address: P.O. Box 1297, Santa Rosa, 95402. Tel: 707-545-7610.

Movimiento Familiar Cristiano—Mailing Address: P.O. Box 1297, Santa Rosa, 95402. Tel: 707-545-7610.

Renovacion Carismatica Catolica—Rev. CARLOS ORTEGA, Dir., Mailing Address: P.O. Box 666, Boyes Hot Springs, 95416. Tel: 707-996-8422; Fax: 707-996-3984.

National Council of Catholic Women—Rev. Msgr. THOMAS J. KEYS, Spiritual Dir., 495 White Oak Dr., Santa Rosa, 95409. Tel: 707-539-6262; Fax: 707-539-8620.

Newspaper—"North Coast Catholic" DEIRDRE FRONTCZAK, Editor, Mailing Address: P.O. Box 1297, Santa Rosa, 95402-1297. Tel: 707-566-3302; Fax: 707-546-4239.

Parish Priest Consultors—Rev. Msgr. GERARD J. BRADY; Revs. OSCAR DIAZ; MICHAELRAJ PHILOMINSAMY; MICHAEL M. KELLY.

Permanent Diaconate—Deacon JAMES CARR, Dir., Mailing Address: P.O. Box 1297, Santa Rosa, 95402-1297.

Pontifical Association of Holy Childhood—Deacon RAY NOLL, Ph.D., Mailing Address: P.O. Box 1297, Santa Rosa, 95402-1297. Tel: 707-762-2367.

Propagation of the Faith—Deacon RAY NOLL, Ph.D., Mailing Address: P.O. Box 1297, Santa Rosa, 95402-1297. Tel: 707-762-2367.

Religious Education—Sr. OLIVE MURPHY, R.S.M., Dir., 985 Airway Ct., Santa Rosa, 95403. Tel: 707-566-3366; Fax: 707-566-3320. Mailing Address: P.O. Box 11574, Santa Rosa, 95406.

Respect Life—Mailing Address: P.O. Box 1297, Santa Rosa, 95402. Tel: 707-545-7610; Fax: 707-542-9702.

Schools—Dr. JOHN COLLINS, Supt. of Schools, Office, 985 Airway Ct., Santa Rosa, 95403. Tel: 707-566-3311. Mailing Address: P.O. Box 6654, Santa Rosa, 95406.

Youth Ministry—STANLEY CORDERO, Dir., Mailing Address: P.O. Box 1297, Santa Rosa, 95402. Tel: 707-566-3343; Fax: 707-566-3320.

Vietnamese Martyrs Community—Rev. CHINH NGUYEN, Chap., 1798 E. Cotati Ave., Penngrove, 94951. Tel: 707-794-7957; Fax: 707-794-7957.

Vocations—Revs. THOMAS DIAZ, Dir., Mailing Address: P.O. Box 1297, Santa Rosa, 95402. Tel: 707-566-3395; Fax: 707-542-9702; MANUEL CHAVEZ, Mailing Address: 901 Washington St., Calistoga, 94515. Tel: 707-942-6894; Fax: 707-942-1091; Sr. OLIVE MURPHY, R.S.M., Rel. Life, 985 Airway Ct., Santa Rosa, 95403. Tel: 707-566-3366; Fax: 707-566-3320.

CLERGY, PARISHES, MISSIONS AND PAROCHIAL SCHOOLS

CITY OF SANTA ROSA

(SONOMA COUNTY)

1—CATHEDRAL OF ST. EUGENE (1950) [CEM] Rev. Msgr. James E. Pulskamp; Rev. Fergal McGuinness; Deacon Michael Heinzelman. In Res., Rev. Alvin M. Villaruel.
Res.: 2323 Montgomery Dr., 95405. Tel: 707-542-6984; Fax: 707-542-1621.
School—(Grades PreSchool-8), 300 Farmers Ln., 95405. Tel: 707-545-7252; Fax: 707-545-2594. Mrs. Barbara Gasparini, Prin.; Cindy Kirk, Librarian. Sisters 1; Lay Teachers 17; Students 352.
Catechesis/Religious Program—Tel: 707-542-1525. Diane Drew, D.R.E. Students 120.

2—HOLY SPIRIT (1964) Rev. Robert Blake; Deacon Jim Hercher.
Res.: 1244 St. Francis Rd., 95409. Tel: 707-539-4495; Fax: 707-539-3343.
Catechesis/Religious Program—Bernard Ciernick, D.R.E. Students 81.

3—RESURRECTION (1967) Revs. David Shaw; Jose Gonzalez; Deacon Stephen Ellis.
Res.: 303 Stony Point Rd., 95401. Tel: 707-544-7272; Fax: 707-544-2901.
Catechesis/Religious Program—Tel: 707-544-0708. Betty Kovanis, D.R.E. Students 500.

4—ST. ROSE OF LIMA (1877) Revs. Denis A. O'Sullivan; Andrew Metcalf; Ramon Pons.
Res.: 398 10th St., 95401. Tel: 707-542-6448; Fax: 707-542-3359.
School—(Grades PreSchool-8), 4300 Old Redwood Hwy., 95403. Tel: 707-545-0379; Fax: 707-545-7150. Kathy Ryan, Prin.; Louise Craighead, Librarian. Lay Teachers 15; Students 342.
Catechesis/Religious Program—Tel: 707-542-3080; Fax: 707-542-3359. Sr. Shelia Coffey, S.M., D.R.E. Students 365.

5—STAR OF THE VALLEY (1981) Rev. Msgrs. Thomas J. Keys; Gerard Fahey, Pastor Emeritus. In Res., Rev. Patrick J. Leslie (SAC).
Parish Center—495 White Oak Dr., 95409. Tel: 707-539-6262; Fax: 707-539-8620.

OUTSIDE CITY OF SANTA ROSA

AMERICAN CANYON, NAPA CO., HOLY FAMILY (1994) Rev. Patrick Stephenson; Deacons Michael Simmons; Charles Cancilla.
Res.: 402 Donaldson Way, 94503. Tel: 707-645-9331; Fax: 707-645-0424.
Catechesis/Religious Program—Tel: 707-554-1183. Lia Estupin, D.R.E. Students 110.

ARCATA, HUMBOLDT CO., ST. MARY'S (1883) [CEM] Rev. Gerard Gormley; Deacon John Gai.
Res.: 1690 Janes Rd., 95521. Tel: 707-822-7696; Fax: 707-822-6931.
School—(Grades PreSchool-8), 1730 Janes Rd., 95521. Tel: 707-822-3877; Fax: 707-822-8912. James Monge, Prin. Lay Teachers 7; Students 45.
Catechesis/Religious Program—Tel: 707-822-7696. Patricia Heavilin, D.R.E. Students 71.
Mission—St. Joseph Blue Lake.

BOYES HOT SPRINGS, SONOMA CO., ST. LEO (1966) Revs. William P. Donahue; Carlos Ortega.
Res.: 601 Agua Caliente Rd., Sonoma, 95476. Tel: 707-996-8422; Fax: 707-996-3984.
Church: P.O. Box 666, 95416.
Catechesis/Religious Program—Tel: 707-996-7503; Fax: 707-996-3984. Melissa Rodriguez, D.R.E. Students 200.

CALISTOGA, NAPA CO., OUR LADY OF PERPETUAL HELP (1915) Rev. Manual Chavez.
Res.: 901 Washington St., 94515. Tel: 707-942-6894; Fax: 707-942-1091.

CLEARLAKE, LAKE CO., OUR LADY, QUEEN OF PEACE (1967) Rev. Luis M. Penaloza; Deacon Ruben De Los Santos.
Res.: 14405 Uhl Ave., P.O. Box 6226, 95422. Tel: 707-994-6618; Fax: 707-994-2223.
Catechesis/Religious Program—Carol Combs, D.R.E. Students 143.
Mission—Queen of the Rosary Lucerne, 95458.

CLOVERDALE, SONOMA CO., ST. PETER'S (1917) Rev. Thomas W. Devereaux; Deacon Harry Martin.
Res.: 491 S. Franklin St., P.O. Box 549, 95425. Tel: 707-894-2535; Fax: 707-894-9603.
Catechesis/Religious Program—Fax: 707-894-9603. Students 74.
Mission—Our Lady of Mt. Carmel Asti.

COTATI, SONOMA CO., ST. JOSEPH (1913) Rev. Oscar Diaz; Deacons Jesus Fernandez; W. Everett Woodruff. In Res., Rev. Msgr. Daniel P. Whelton.
Res.: 150 St. Joseph Way, 94931-4117. Tel: 707-795-4807; Fax: 707-795-7851.
Catechesis/Religious Program—Tel: 707-795-7678; Fax: 707-795-7851. Students 280.

CRESCENT CITY, DEL NORTE CO., ST. JOSEPH (1869) [CEM] Rev. Frank Epperson.
Mailing Address: 440 Third St., 95531.
Res.: 319 E St., 95531. Tel: 707-465-1762; Fax: 707-465-1763.
School—(Grades PreSchool-8), 330 E St., 95531. Tel: 707-464-3477. Patricia Foht, School Admin. Lay Teachers 4; Students 40.
Catechesis/Religious Program—Students 110.
Mission—St. Robert and Ann Klamath.

EUREKA, HUMBOLDT CO.

1—ST. BERNARD (1864) [CEM] Revs. Loren Allen; Eric Freed; Deacons Frank Weber; Phillip Salazar.
Res.: 615 H St., P.O. Box 169, 95502. Tel: 707-442-6466; Fax: 707-443-0914.
Catechesis/Religious Program—115 Henderson St., 95501. Students 31.
Mission—St. Joseph 201 Henderson St., 95501.

2—SACRED HEART (1963) Rev. Ismael Mora; Deacons Anthony Viegas; Steven Justus.
Res.: 2085 Myrtle Ave., 95501. Tel: 707-443-8429; Fax: 707-443-8420.
Catechesis/Religious Program—Genoveva Gomez, C.R.E. Students 125.

FERNDALE, HUMBOLDT CO., CHURCH OF THE ASSUMPTION (1878) [CEM] Rev. Robert L. Benjamin.
Res.: 546 Berding St., P.O. Box 1097, 95536. Tel: 707-786-9551.
Catechesis/Religious Program—Sr. Marie Jeannette Ansberry, C.S.J., D.R.E. Students 25.
Mission—St. Patrick Petrolia.

FORT BRAGG, MENDOCINO CO., OUR LADY OF GOOD COUNSEL (1890) Rev. Michaelraj Philominsamy.
Res.: 255 S. Harold St., 95437. Tel: 707-964-0229; Fax: 707-222-4340.
Catechesis/Religious Program—Tel: 707-964-5727. Judy Williams, D.R.E. Students 68.

FORTUNA, HUMBOLDT CO., ST. JOSEPH (1909) [CEM] Revs. Louis Coddaire; Gary Sumpter; Deacons Thomas Silva; Francisco Nunez.
Res.: P.O. Box 430, 95540. Tel: 707-725-1148; Fax: 707-725-1149.
Catechesis/Religious Program—2292 Newburg Rd., 95540. Tel: 707-725-1216. Students 175.
Mission—St. Patrick Loleta.

GARBERVILLE, HUMBOLDT CO., OUR LADY OF THE REDWOODS (1950) Revs. Louis Coddaire; Gary Sumpter.
Mailing Address: P.O. Box 115, 95542.
Res.: 515 Maple Ln., 95542. Tel: 707-923-7864; Fax: 707-723-7864.
Catechesis/Religious Program—Students 4.

GUERNEVILLE, SONOMA CO., ST. ELIZABETH (1916) Rev. Ray Rioux.
Res.: 14095 Woodland Dr., 95446-9553. Tel: 707-869-2107; Fax: 707-869-2044.
Mission—St. Catherine Monte Rio.
Mission—St. Colman Cazadero.

HEALDSBURG, SONOMA CO., ST. JOHN THE BAPTIST (1884) Revs. Walter Rogina; Abel Mena.
Res.: 208 Matheson St., 95448. Tel: 707-433-5536; Fax: 707-433-1813.
School—(Grades PreSchool-8), 217 Fitch St., 95448. Tel: 707-433-2758; Fax: 707-433-0353. Donna Garcia, Prin. Lay Teachers 14; Students 265.
Catechesis/Religious Program—Students 289.

HOOPA, HUMBOLDT CO., BLESSED KATERI TEKAKWITHA MISSION (1955) Sr. Patricia Carson, R.S.M., Dir.; Deacon Ken Bond.
Res.: Pine Creek Rd. & Kateri Ln., P.O. Box 429, 95546. Tel: 530-625-4415; Fax: 530-625-4530.
Catechesis/Religious Program—Students 7.
Tekakwitha Center—P.O. Box 845, 95546. Tel: 530-625-4739. Sr. Patricia Carson, R.S.M., Dir.

LAKEPORT, LAKE CO., ST. MARY (1871) [CEM] Rev. Ron Serban.
Res.: 801 N. Main St., 95453. Tel: 707-263-4401; Fax: 707-263-6325.
Catechesis/Religious Program—Students 107.
Mission—St. Peter [CEM] Kelseyville.

MCKINLEYVILLE, HUMBOLDT COUNTY, CHRIST THE KING (1967) Rev. Michael W. Cloney; Deacon Robert Shell.
Res.: 1951 McKinleyville Ave., P.O. Box 2367, 95519. Tel: 707-839-2911; Fax: 707-839-9823.
Catechesis/Religious Program—Ann Friedman, D.R.E. Students 51.
Mission—Holy Trinity Trinidad.

MENDOCINO, MENDOCINO CO., ST. ANTHONY (1864) [CEM] Rev. Louis J. Nichols (SY).
Res.: 10700 Lansing St., P.O. Box 665, 95460. Tel: 707-937-5808; Fax: 707-937-2406.
Mission—Blessed Sacrament Elk.

MIDDLETOWN, LAKE CO., ST. JOSEPH (1894) Rev. James McSweeney.
Res.: P.O. Box 1350, 95461. Tel: 707-987-3676; Fax: 707-987-2792.
Catechesis/Religious Program—Students 40.
Mission—Our Lady of the Lake Loch Lomond.
Station—Our Lady of the Pines Forest Lake.

NAPA, NAPA CO.

1—ST. APOLLINARIS (1957) Rev. Msgr. Joseph Alzugaray; Rev. Dominic Malai (Kenya); Deacons Francis Dahl; Joel Momsen.
Res.: 3700 Lassen St., 94558. Tel: 707-257-2555; Fax: 707-224-5400.
School—(Grades K-8) Tel: 707-224-6525. Jack Kersting, Prin. Sisters 1; Lay Teachers 18; Students 276.
Catechesis/Religious Program—Tel: 707-255-7200; Fax: 707-255-0797. Sr. Peggy Cruise, S.M., D.R.E. Students 435.

2—ST. JOHN THE BAPTIST (1858) Revs. Gordon Kalil; Francisco Blandon (Nicaragua).
Res.: 960 Caymus St., 94559. Tel: 707-226-9379; Fax: 707-254-9262.
School—(Grades PreK-8), 983 Napa St., 94559. Tel: 707-224-8388; Fax: 707-224-0236. Nancy Jordan, Prin. Sisters 1; Lay Teachers 11; Students 200.
Catechesis/Religious Program—Tel: 707-255-3533. Celine Ford, C.R.E. (English); Eustolia Valasquez, C.R.E. (Spanish); Teresa Olguin, C.R.E. (Spanish); Luis Juarez, Youth Min. (Spanish); Michele DiMarco, Youth Min. (English); Milton Gallegos, Youth Min. (English). Students 499.
Station—State Hospital, St. Luke's Chapel Imola.

3—ST. THOMAS AQUINAS (1964) Rev. Msgr. Gerard J. Brady.
Res.: 2725 Elm St., 94558-6029. Tel: 707-255-2949; Fax: 707-255-2439.
Catechesis/Religious Program—Students 125.

OCCIDENTAL, SONOMA CO., ST. PHILIP (1903) Rev. Gary Logan, Admin.
Res.: 3730 Bohemian Hwy., P.O. Box 339, 95465. Tel: 707-874-3812; Fax: 707-874-9201.
Catechesis/Religious Program—Students 33.
Mission—St. Teresa [CEM] Bodega.

PETALUMA, SONOMA CO.

1—ST. JAMES (1964) Revs. Michael A. Culligan; Boniface Nzomo (Kenya); Deacon Ray Noll.
Res.: 125 Sonoma Mt. Pkwy., 94954. Tel: 707-762-4256; Fax: 707-762-4044.
Catechesis/Religious Program—Tel: 707-762-9063. Students 422.

2—ST. VINCENT DE PAUL (1857) Revs. Gary Lombardi; Sean Rogers; Deacons James Carr; John Norris.
Res.: 35 Liberty St., 94952. Tel: 707-762-4278; Fax: 707-763-8188.
School—(Grades K-8), Howard & Union Sts., 94952. Tel: 707-762-6426; Fax: 707-762-6791. Susan Roffmann, Prin. Lay Teachers 16; Students 289.
High School—849 Keokuk, P.O. Box 517, 94953. Tel: 707-763-1032; Fax: 707-763-9448. John Walker, Prin. Lay Teachers 32; Students 355.
Catechesis/Religious Program—Rose Marie Woodruff, D.R.E.; Abraham Solar, D.R.E.; Louise Martin, Coord. Youth Min. Students 528.

POINT ARENA, MENDOCINO CO., ST. ALOYSIUS (1889) [CEM] Rev. Thomas P. O'Sullivan (SAC), Admin.
Res.: P.O. Box 66, 95468. Tel: 707-884-4920.
Catechesis/Religious Program—Students 24.
Mission—Mary, Star of the Sea Gualala.

ROHNERT PARK, SONOMA CO., ST. ELIZABETH SETON (1981) Rev. John Griffin.
Res.: 4595 Snyder Ln., 94928. Tel: 707-585-3708; Fax: 707-585-1201.
Catechesis/Religious Program—Tel: 707-585-8821; Fax: 707-585-1202. Alicia Slaugh, D.R.E. Students 106.

SAINT HELENA, NAPA CO., ST. HELENA (1887) [CEM] Rev. Msgr. John J. Brenkle. In Res., Rev. Michael Angula (Nigeria).
Res.: 1340 Tainter St., St. Helena, 94574. Tel: 707-963-1228; Fax: 707-963-2894.
School—(Grades K-8), 1255 Oak Ave., St. Helena, 94574. Tel: 707-963-4677; Fax: 707-963-4659. Jim Ritchie, Prin. Lay Teachers 6; Students 90.
Catechesis/Religious Program—Lisa Hinz, D.R.E.; Ilona Falvy, Youth Min. Students 187.

SCOTIA, HUMBOLDT CO., ST. PATRICK (1905) Revs. Louis Coddaire, Admin.; Gary Sumpter.
Res.: 418 Church St., P.O. Box 98, 95565. Tel: 707-764-5446.

SEBASTOPOL, SONOMA CO., ST. SEBASTIAN (1898) Rev. Msgr. William Hynes.
Res.: 7983 Covert Ln., 95472. Tel: 707-823-2208; Fax: 707-823-1098.
Catechesis/Religious Program—Tel: 707-823-2208, Ext. 204. Mary McQuown, D.R.E. Students 94.

SONOMA, SONOMA CO., ST. FRANCIS SOLANO (1878) [CEM] Revs. Michael M. Kelly; Carlos Ortega.
Res.: 469 Third St., W., 95476. Tel: 707-996-6759; Fax: 707-996-2027.
School—(Grades K-8), 342 W. Napa St., 95476. Tel: 707-996-4994; Fax: 707-996-2662. Matt Vukicevich, Prin. Lay Teachers 25; Students 250.
Catechesis/Religious Program—Tel: 707-996-6994; Fax: 707-996-2662. Catherine Sawicki, D.R.E. Students 280.

UKIAH, MENDOCINO CO., ST. MARY OF THE ANGELS (1887) Rev. Raul Lemus.
Res.: 900 S. Oak St., 95482. Tel: 707-462-1431; Fax: 707-462-2879.
School—(Grades K-8), 991 S. Dora St., 95482. Tel: 707-462-3888; Fax: 707-462-6014. Mary Leittem-Thomas, Prin. Lay Teachers 16; Students 236.
Catechesis/Religious Program—Mary T. Koller, D.R.E. Students 329.
Mission—St. Francis Mission Hopland.
Mission—St. Elizabeth Seton Boonville, Mendocino Co. 95415.

WILLITS, MENDOCINO CO., ST. ANTHONY OF PADUA (1903) Rev. Tekle Dini (Ethiopia).
Res.: 61 W. San Francisco Ave., 95490. Tel: 707-459-2252; Fax: 707-459-0715.
Mission—Our Lady, Queen of Peace [CEM] Covelo, Mendocino Co.

WINDSOR, SONOMA CO., OUR LADY OF GUADALUPE (1969) Revs. Angelito Peries; Eric Arroyo (Mexico).
Mailing Address: 8400 Old Redwood Hwy., 95492. Tel: 707-837-8962; Fax: 707-837-9157.
Catechesis/Religious Program—Carole Pforsich, D.R.E. Students 384.

YOUNTVILLE, NAPA CO., ST. JOAN OF ARC (1920) Rev. Thomas Diaz, Admin.
Res.: 6404 Washington St., Box 2009, 94599. Tel: 707-944-2461; Fax: 707-944-2202.
Catechesis/Religious Program—Lilia Manzo, D.R.E. Students 55.
Mission—Holy Family Rutherford.

Chaplains Of Public Institutions

ELDRIDGE. *Sonoma Developmental Center.* Rev. Patrick J. Leslie (SAC), Chap.

IMOLA. *Napa State Hospital* 94558. Revs. James Lantsberger, O.M.I., Chap., Robert Castro, Chap.

PETALUMA. *U.S. Coast Guard Training Center.*

YOUNTVILLE. *Veterans Administration Home.* Rev. Paul F. Ledermann (OG), Chap.

Special Assignment:
Rev.—
Diaz De Leon, Juan Ramon

Unassigned:
Revs.—
McCormick, John
Talcott, Peter

On Duty Outside the Diocese:
Revs.—
Baptista, Diego
Boettcher, John

On Leave:
Revs.—
Hernandez, Apolinar
MacPherson, Stephen E.C.
Martinez, Luis
McAllister, Alex
Villalobos, David

Retired:
Rev. Msgr.—
Gaffey, James P.
Revs.—
Bernard, Andre
Bohner, Allan G.
Canny, Stephen
Healy, John
Ittiyappara, Mathew
Keogh, Thomas
Martin, John J.
McIntyre, Justin
Ryan, Philip
Sheehy, Wilfred
Thomas, Jerald

Permanent Deacons:
Begin, Kenneth, (Retired)
Bond, Ken, Arcata
Bromham, Paul, (Retired)
Cancilla, Charles, American Canyon
Carr, James, Petaluma
Dahl, Francis, Napa
De Los Santos, Ruben, Clearlake
Ellis, Stephen, Santa Rosa
Fernandez, Jesus, Cotati
Gai, John, Aracata
Heinzelman, Michael, Santa Rosa
Hercher, Jim, Santa Rosa
Jacobs, Jeff, (Ministry Outside the Diocese)
Justus, Steven, Eureka
Lemos, Armando, (Retired)
Martin, Harry, Cloverdale
Momsen, Joel, Napa
Moody, William, Palm Court, FL
Naumann, Richard, (Retired)
Noll, Ray, Ph.D., Petaluma
Norris, John, Petaluma
Nunez, Francisco, Fortuna
Olsen, Joseph, Rohnert Park
Ramirez, Arturo, Chehalis, WA
Robinson, David, Turlock
Salazar, Phillip, Eureka
Shell, Robert, McKinleyville
Silva, Thomas, Fortuna
Simmons, Michael, American Canyon
Vera, Juventino, Healdsburg
Viegas, Anthony, Eureka
Weber, Frank, Eureka
Woodruff, W. Everett, Cotati

INSTITUTIONS LOCATED IN THE DIOCESE

[A] SEMINARIES, RELIGIOUS, OR SCHOLASTICATES

NAPA. *Mont La Salle Novitiate*, 4405 Redwood Dr., 94558. Tel: 707-252-3821; Fax: 707-252-3731. Email: novitiate@dlsi.org. Web: www.delasalle.org. Brothers of the Christian Schools.

[B] HIGH SCHOOLS, DIOCESAN

SANTA ROSA. *Cardinal Newman High School*, 50 Ursuline Rd., 95403. Tel: 707-546-6470; Fax: 707-544-8502. Email: info@cardinalnewman.org. Web: cardinalnewman.org. Mike Truesdell, Pres. & CEO; Graham Rutherford, Prin.; Rev. Alvin M. Villaruel; Molly Bone, Librarian. Priests 1; Lay Teachers 33; Students 447.

[C] HIGH SCHOOLS, PRIVATE

SANTA ROSA. **Ursuline High School*, 90 Ursuline Rd., 95403. Tel: 707-524-1130; Fax: 707-542-0131. Email: jcarver@ursulinehs.org. Web: www.ursulinehs.org. Julie Carver, Pres. & Prin.; Mary Hart, Librarian.
Santa Rosa Ursuline Corporation Ursuline Sisters of the Roman Union. Sisters 1; Lay Teachers 29; Students 287.
**Ursuline Memorial Scholarship Fund* Fax: 707-542-0131.

NAPA. *Justin-Siena High School*, 4026 Maher St., 94558. Tel: 707-255-0950; Fax: 707-255-0334. Email: robertj@justin-siena.org. Web: justin-siena.org. Robert Jordan, Pres. & CEO; Noel Laird Hesser, Prin.; Robert Bailey, Vice Prin.; Alissa Kell, Librarian. Sisters 1; Brothers 1; Lay Teachers 51; Students 605.
**Justin-Siena High School Corporation, Inc.*
**Justin-Siena High School Foundation, Inc.*

[D] ELEMENTARY SCHOOLS, PRIVATE

EUREKA. **St. Bernard's Catholic School*, (Grades PreSchool-12), 222 Dollison St., 95501. Tel: 707-443-2735; Fax: 707-443-4723. Email: daly@saintbernards.us. Patrick W. Daly, Pres.; Michael O'Brien, Dean; Craig Brown, Dean; Nicole Matas, Librarian. Lay Teachers 25; Students 321.

[E] CATHOLIC CHARITIES

SANTA ROSA. *Catholic Charities of the Diocese of Santa Rosa*, P.O. Box 4900, 95402. Tel: 707-528-8712; Fax: 707-575-4910. Email: info@srcharities.org. Web: srcharities.org.
ADMINISTRATIVE SERVICES CENTER:, 987 Airway Ct., 95403. Tel: 707-528-8712; Fax: 707-575-4910. Larry R. Lakes, Exec. Dir.; Sharon K. McCarty, Dir. Human Resources & Admin. Svcs.; Albert Kovanis, Dir. Accounting & Finance; Betsy Timm, Com. Dir.; Angie Moeller, Dir. Development.
REGIONAL OFFICES:, c/o 1219 Jefferson St., Ste. 2, Napa, 94558. Tel: 707-224-4403; Fax: 707-224-2889. Mitchell Geis, Regl. Dir.
Lake County:
Rural Food Project Tel: 707-987-8139; Fax: 707-987-8139. Hedy Montoya, Regl. Dir.

Napa County:
HomeBase, 1219 Jefferson St., Ste. 2, Napa, 94558. Tel: 707-224-4403; Fax: 707-224-2889. Mitchell Geis, Regl. Dir.
Hale Nalu, c/o 1219 Jefferson St., Ste. 2, Napa, 94558. Tel: 707-224-4403; Fax: 707-224-2889. Mitchell Geis, Regl. Dir.
Rainbow House, c/o 1219 Jefferson St., Ste. 2, Napa, 94559. Tel: 707-224-4403; Fax: 707-224-2889. Mitchell Geis, Regl. Dir.
Sonoma County:
Alzheimer's Respite/Resource Center, 987 Airway Ct., 95403. Tel: 707-528-8712; Fax: 707-575-4910. P.O. Box 4900, 95402. Michele Osmon, Prog. Dir.
DeMeo House, P.O. Box 4900, 95402. Tel: 707-575-0215; Fax: 707-578-5210. Alison Mertz, Supportive Housing Coord.
Family Support Center, 465 A St., 95401. Tel: 707-542-5426; Fax: 707-542-3148. P.O. Box 4900, 95402. Nick Baker, Prog. Dir.
Homeless Services Center/Russell Avenue Shelter/Project Nightingale/Samuel L. Jones Hall, 600 Morgan St., 95401. Tel: 707-525-0226; Fax: 707-545-1920. P.O. Box 4900, 95402. Nick Baker, Prog. Dir.
Housing Counseling, 465 A St., 95401. Tel: 707-575-0215; Fax: 707-578-5210. P.O. Box 4900, 95402. Alison Mertz, Supportive Housing Coord.
Immigration and Resettlement Services, 987 Airway Ct., 95403. Tel: 707-578-6000; Fax: 707-575-4910. P.O. Box 4900, 95401. Brian O'Callaghan, Division Dir.
Parish/Community Services, 987 Airway Ct., 95403. Tel: 707-528-8712; Fax: 707-575-4910. P.O. Box 4900, 95402. Michele Osmon, Prog. Dir.
Coach 2 Career, 465 A St., 95401. Tel: 707-575-0215; Fax: 707-578-5210. P.O. Box 4900, 95402. Brian O'Callaghan, Division Dir.
Sonoma County, 465 A St., 95401. Tel: 707-542-5426; Fax: 707-542-3148. Brian O'Callaghan, Division Dir.
Transitional Housing, 465 A St., 95401. Tel: 707-575-0215; Fax: 707-578-5210. Alison Mertz, Supportive Housing Coord.
I'm Home Alone, 987 Airway Ct., 95403. Tel: 707-528-8712; Fax: 707-575-4910. Michele Osmon, Prog. Dir.

[F] GENERAL HOSPITALS

SANTA ROSA. *Santa Rosa Memorial Hospital*, 1165 Montgomery Dr., 95405. Tel: 707-546-3210; Fax: 707-547-4685. Email: katy.hillenmeyer@stjoe.org. Web: www.stjosephhealth.org. Kevin A. Klockenga, Pres. & CEO. Sisters of St. Joseph of Orange Corporation. Sisters 1; Employees 2,055; Bed Capacity 279; Patients Assisted Annually 200,269.

EUREKA. *St. Joseph Hospital of Eureka*, 2700 Dolbeer St., 95501. Tel: 707-445-8121; Fax: 707-269-3897. Web: www.stjosepheureka.org. Joseph Mark, Pres. & CEO; Ken Meece, Dir. of Spiritual Health. Sisters of St. Joseph of Orange. Bed Capacity 189; Sisters 6; Employees 1,038; Patients Assisted Annually 195,352.

FORTUNA. *Redwood Memorial Hospital*, 3300 Renner Dr., 95540. Tel: 707-725-3361; Fax: 707-725-7212. Web: www.redwoodmemorial.org. Joe Mark, Pres. & CEO. Sisters of St. Joseph of Orange. Sisters 1; Total Staff 219; Bed Capacity 25; Patients Assisted Annually 45,208.

NAPA. *Queen of the Valley Medical Center*, 1000 Trancas St., 94558. Tel: 707-252-4411; Fax: 707-257-4173. Web: www.thequeen.org. Dennis Sisto, Pres. & CEO; Kathleen Timm, Dir. of Mission Svcs. & Spiritual Care; Revs. Luis Antonio Lacson, Priest Chap.; Alan Wagner, S.D.S., Priest Chap.; Rev. Jim Warnock, Staff Chap. (Lutheran Min.). Sisters of St. Joseph of Orange, California. Priests 2; Sisters 3; Lay Staff 1,542; Bed Capacity 192; Patients Assisted Annually 234,598.

PETALUMA. *Petaluma Valley Hospital*, 400 N. McDowell Blvd., 94954. Tel: 707-778-1111; Fax: 707-778-9117. Web: www.stjosephhealth.org. Jane Read, R.N., Vice Pres. Opers. Sisters of St. Joseph of Orange. Lay Staff 500; Bed Capacity 80; Patients Assisted Annually 37,300.

[G] RESIDENTIAL TREATMENT CENTERS

SONOMA. *Hanna Boys Center*, P.O. Box 100, 95476. Tel: 707-996-6767; Fax: 707-996-4742. Web: www.hannacenter.org. Dennis Crandall, Prin.; Revs. John S. Crews, Ed.D., Exec. Dir.; Gregory Klaas.
Hanna Boys Center, For underprivileged and predelinquent boys, ages 12 to 18 years. Priests 2; Total Staff 110; Students 119.

[H] HOMES FOR SENIOR CITIZENS

SANTA ROSA. **Vigil Light Apartments (The Vigil Light, Inc.)*, 1945 Long Dr., 95405. Tel: 707-544-2810; Fax: 707-544-1219. Email: vigillightapts@sbcglobal.net. Sr. Sharon Fritsch, C.S.J., Mgr. Sisters 1; Residents 50.

[I] CAMPS AND COMMUNITY CENTERS

DUNCAN MILLS. *St. Joseph Camp*, 22776 Moscow Rd., P.O. Box 198, 95430-0198. Tel: 707-865-1942; Fax: 707-865-1025. Bro. Michael Saggau, F.S.C., Dir. Tel: 707-865-9304. Brothers of the Christian Schools.

LEGGETT. *Camp St. Michael* (Boys - Girls), P.O. Box 9447, 95405. Tel: 707-703-9171. Email: office@campstmichael.org. Web: www.campstmichael.org.

MIDDLETOWN. *Camp Salesian, Office, Salesian Provincial Office*, 1100 Franklin St., San Francisco, 94109. Tel: 415-441-7144; Fax: 415-441-7155. Conducted by the Salesians of St. John Bosco.

[J] NEWMAN CENTERS

ARCATA. *Newman Community, Humboldt State University* 700 Union St., 95521. Tel: 707-822-6057; Fax: 707-822-6057. Email: newmanct@humboldt1.com. Web: www.humboldT.edu/newman. Rev. Eric Freed; Deacon Kenneth M. Bond.

PENNGROVE. *Newman Hall, Sonoma State University, Intercollegiate Catholic Ministries* 1798 E. Cotati Ave., 94951. Tel: 707-794-7957; Fax: 707-794-7957. Rev. Chinh Nguyen.

[K] HOUSES OF PRAYER AND RETREAT HOUSES

SANTA ROSA. *Angela Center*, 535 Angela Dr., 95403. Tel: 707-528-8578; Fax: 707-528-0144. Email: angelacenter@juno.com. Web: www.angelacenter.com. Sisters Christine Van Swearingen, O.S.U., Dir.; Dianne Baumunk, O.S.U., Prog. Dir.
Cardinal Newman Retreat Center, 24 Ursuline Rd., 95403. Tel: 707-568-6822; Fax: 707-566-3360. Richard Boyer, Mgr.
The Santa Rosa Spiritual Enrichment Center, 360 Farmers Ln., 95405. Tel: 707-546-1781; Fax: 707-546-1781. Email: antoniaK@sonic.net. Mary Hart, Dir.

NAPA. *Christian Brothers Retreat and Conference Center*, 4401 Redwood Rd., P.O. Box 3720, 94558. Tel: 707-252-3810; 707-252-3811; 707-252-3897; Fax: 707-252-3818. Email: confctr@dlsi.org. Web: www.christianbrosretreat.com. Linda Bausch, CFO; Mary Jane Hagan, Conference Center Mgr.

OAKVILLE. *Carmelite House of Prayer*, P.O. Box 347, 94562. Tel: 707-944-2454; Fax: 707-944-8533. Email: ocdoakville@gmail.com. Rev. Gerald Werner, O.C.D., Dir.

[L] MONASTERIES AND RESIDENCES FOR PRIESTS AND BROTHERS

NAPA. *De La Salle Institute/Provincial Office*, 4401 Redwood Rd., 94558-9708. Tel: 707-252-0222; Fax: 707-252-0407. Email: bbrowne@dlsi.org. Web: www.delasalle.org. P.O. Box 3720, 94558-0372. Bro. Stanislaus Campbell, F.S.C., Provincial. Brothers of the Christian Schools. *Lasallian Education Corporation* Tel: 707-252-3870; Fax: 707-252-0407. *District of San Francisco Christian Brothers Charitable Trust* Tel: 707-252-0222; Fax: 707-252-7046. *Lasallian Education Fund*, 100 Shoreline Hwy., Ste. 386, Novato, 94945. Tel: 415-332-3471; Fax: 415-332-3962.
Holy Family Community, 4405 Redwood Rd., 94558-9708. Tel: 707-252-3887; 707-252-3857; Fax: 707-252-3842. Email: JRiordan@dlsi.org. Web: www.delasalle.org. Bro. James Riordan, F.S.C., Dir. Brothers of the Christian Schools. Brothers 17.
Provincialate Community, 4403 Redwood Rd., 94558. Tel: 707-252-0802; Fax: 707-252-7046. Email: twestberg@dlsi.org. Bros. Stanislaus Campbell, F.S.C., Prov.; Thomas Jones, F.S.C., Asst. Prov.; Thomas Westberg, F.S.C., Dir.; Arnold Stewart, F.S.C., Sub Dir.; Rev. David L. Deibel, Chap. Brothers of the Christian Schools. Priests 1; Brothers 8.

OAKVILLE. *Carmelite House of Prayer*, P.O. Box 347, 94562. Tel: 707-944-2454; 707-944-2460; Fax: 707-944-8533. Email: ocdoakville@gmail.com. Revs. Gerald Werner, O.C.D., Supr.; Michael Buckley, O.C.D.; David Costello, O.C.D.; Mark Kristy, O.C.D.; John R. McSweeney, O.C.D.; Xavier Pappalliyil, O.C.D.; Bros. Roger Larre, O.C.D.; Mark Moran, O.C.D. Discalced Carmelite Friars. Priests 6; Brothers 2.

SEBASTOPOL. *Franciscan Hermitage of St. Clare*, 6501 Orchard Station Rd., 95472. Tel: 707-792-5033. Brothers 1.

[M] CONVENTS AND RESIDENCES FOR SISTERS

SANTA ROSA. *Provincialate of Ursuline Nuns*, 639 Angela Dr., 95403. Tel: 707-545-6811; Fax: 707-579-8571. Email: stister2@aol.com. Web: www.ursulinewest.com. Sisters Margaret Johnson, O.S.U., Co-Prov. Tel: 208-301-0293; Shirley Ann Garibaldi, O.S.U., Co-Prov. Tel: 650-346-9897. Ursulines of the Roman Union - Western Province.

NAPA. *St. Apollinaris Convent*, 3700 Lassen St., P.O. Box 3012, 94558. Tel: 707-255-2185. Congregation of the Sisters of Mercy - The United States Province. Sisters 2.
Queen of the Valley Convent, 74 Catania Ln., 94558. Tel: 707-255-6169. Web: www.sistersofstjosephoforange.org. Sisters St. Joseph of Orange. Sisters 4.
Siena Convent, 4038 Maher St., 94558. Tel: 707-255-6110. Dominican Sisters of San Rafael. Sisters 4.

SEBASTOPOL. *Sisters of Christ the King*, 1520 Santa Maria Way, 95472. Sr. Mary Minette, S.C.K., Supr. Sisters of Christ the King. Assoc. Sisters 2.

WHITETHORN. *Our Lady of the Redwoods Abbey*, 18104 Briceland-Thorn Rd., 95589. Tel: 707-986-7419; Fax: 707-986-1176. Web: www.redwoodsabbey.org. Sr. Kathleen De Vico, O.C.S.O., Abbess; Rev. Maurice Flood, O.C.S.O., Chap. Cistercian Nuns of the Strict Observance. Priests 1; Sisters 11.

WINDSOR. *Ursuline Residence*, 9248 Lakewood Dr., 95492. Tel: 707-838-4232. Email: cvs535@aol.com. Web: www.ursulinewest.comFax: 707-528-0114. Ursuline Nuns. Sisters 1.

[N] MISCELLANEOUS

SANTA ROSA. **Angela Merici and John Henry Newman Foundation, Inc.*, 535 Angela Dr., 95403.
**Catholic Community Foundation*, P.O. Box 1297, 95402. Tel: 707-544-7272; Fax: 707-566-3310. Rev. David Shaw, Exec. Dir.

NAPA. **Life Legal Defense Foundation*, P.O. Box 2105, 94558. Tel: 707-224-6675; Fax: 707-224-6676. Email: info@lldf.org. Web: lldf.org. Mary Riley, Dir.

SAINT HELENA. **The Nurturing Network*, 1733 Fir Hill Dr., 94574. Tel: 707-963-3393 (Headquarters); 509-493-4026 (Administrative Office); Fax: 509-493-4027. Email: mary@nurturingnetwork.org. Web: www.nurturingnetwork.org. Mary Cunningham Agee, Pres.; Ann Granger, Dir. Communications.

RELIGIOUS INSTITUTES OF MEN REPRESENTED IN THE DIOCESE

For further details refer to the corresponding bracketed number in the Religious Institutes of Men or Women section.

[0330]—*Brothers of the Christian Schools* (San Francisco Prov.)—F.S.C.
[0350]—*Cistercian Order of the Strict Observance*—O.C.S.O.
[0260]—*Discalced Carmelite Friars* (Anglo-Irish Prov.)—O.C.D.
[0910]—*Oblates of Mary Immaculate*—O.M.I.
[1200]—*Society of the Divine Savior*—S.D.S.

RELIGIOUS INSTITUTES OF WOMEN REPRESENTED IN THE DIOCESE

[0670]—*Cistercian Nuns of the Strict Observance*—O.C.S.O.
[3110]—*Congregation of Our Lady of Retreat in the Cenacle*—R.C.
[1070-04]—*Dominican Sisters*—O.P.
[2575]—*Institute of the Sisters of Mercy of the Americas*—R.S.M.
[0440]—*Sisters of Charity of Cincinnati* (Cincinnati, Ohio)—S.C.
[0430]—*Sisters of Charity of the Blessed Virgin Mary* (Dubuque, IA)—B.V.M.
[]—*Sisters of Christ the King*—S.C.K.
[4090]—*Sisters of Social Service*—S.S.S.
[0230]—*Sisters of St. Benedict*—O.S.B.
[3740]—*Sisters of St. Casimir*—S.S.C.
[1570]—*Sisters of St. Francis* (Dubuque, IA)—O.S.F.
[3830-03]—*Sisters of St. Joseph*—C.S.J.
[3840]—*Sisters of St. Joseph of Carondelet*—C.S.J.
[3320]—*Sisters of the Presentation of the B.V.M.*—P.B.V.M.
[4110]—*Ursuline Nuns* (Western Prov.)—O.S.U.

DIOCESAN CEMETERIES

SANTA ROSA. *Calvary Catholic*
EUREKA. *St. Bernard*
PETALUMA. *Calvary Catholic*
ST. HELENA. *Holy Cross*
SONOMA. *St. Francis Solano*

NECROLOGY

✠ Ziemann, Most Rev. G. Patrick, Retired Bishop of Santa Rosa—Died Oct. 22, 2009

An asterisk (*) denotes an organization that has established tax-exempt status directly with the IRS and is not covered by the USCCB Group Ruling.

Diocese of Savannah

(Dioecesis Savannensis)

Most Reverend

J. KEVIN BOLAND, D.D.

Bishop of Savannah; ordained June 14, 1959; appointed Bishop of Savannah February 7, 1995; ordained and installed April 18, 1995.

Most Reverend

RAYMOND W. LESSARD, D.D.

Retired Bishop of Savannah; ordained December 16, 1956; appointed March 5, 1973; consecrated and installed April 27, 1973; retired February 7, 1995. *Catholic Pastoral Center, 601 E. Liberty St., Savannah, GA 31401-5196.* Tel: 912-201-4100.

Chancery: Catholic Pastoral Center, 601 E. Liberty St., Savannah, GA 31401-5196. Tel: 912-201-4100; Fax: 912-201-4101.

Web: www.dioceseofsavannah.org

Email: communications@diosav.org

Square Miles 37,038.

Established as Diocese of Savannah July 19, 1850. Name changed to Diocese of Savannah-Atlanta Jan. 5, 1937; Redesignated Nov. 8, 1956.

Comprises 90 Counties in the southern part of the State of Georgia.

Patrons of the Diocese: I. St. John the Baptist; II. Our Lady of Perpetual Help. This diocese was solemnly consecrated to the Sacred Heart of Jesus, May 7, 1872, and on Dec. 8, 1943, it was solemnly consecrated to the Immaculate Heart of Mary.

For legal titles of parishes and diocesan institutions, consult the Chancery.

STATISTICAL OVERVIEW

Personnel	
Bishop	1
Retired Bishops	1
Priests: Diocesan Active in Diocese	55
Priests: Diocesan Active Outside Diocese	7
Priests: Retired, Sick or Absent	19
Number of Diocesan Priests	81
Religious Priests in Diocese	24
Total Priests in Diocese	105
Extern Priests in Diocese	13
Ordinations:	
Diocesan Priests	4
Transitional Deacons	1
Permanent Deacons in Diocese	59
Total Brothers	3
Total Sisters	88
Parishes	
Parishes	55
With Resident Pastor:	
Resident Diocesan Priests	38
Resident Religious Priests	15
Without Resident Pastor:	
Administered by Priests	2
Missions	24
Pastoral Centers	11
Professional Ministry Personnel:	
Brothers	3
Lay Ministers	31
Welfare	
Catholic Hospitals	1
Total Assisted	200,000
Residential Care of Children	1
Total Assisted	13
Special Centers for Social Services	15
Total Assisted	27,000
Educational	
Diocesan Students in Other Seminaries	16
Total Seminarians	16
High Schools, Diocesan and Parish	2
Total Students	421
High Schools, Private	3
Total Students	1,092
Elementary Schools, Diocesan and Parish	16
Total Students	4,344
Catechesis/Religious Education:	
High School Students	695
Elementary Students	5,305
Total Students under Catholic Instruction	11,873
Teachers in the Diocese:	
Priests	2
Brothers	1
Sisters	15
Lay Teachers	450
Vital Statistics	
Receptions into the Church:	
Infant Baptism Totals	1,755
Minor Baptism Totals	155
Adult Baptism Totals	161
Received into Full Communion	349
First Communions	1,566
Confirmations	1,464
Marriages:	
Catholic	202
Interfaith	159
Total Marriages	361
Deaths	608
Total Catholic Population	77,473
Total Population	2,800,000

Former Bishops—Rt. Revs. FRANCIS X. GARTLAND, D.D., first bishop; cons. Nov. 10, 1850; died Sept. 20, 1854; JOHN BARRY, D.D., second bishop; cons. Aug. 2, 1857; died Nov. 21, 1859; AUGUSTIN VEROT, S.S., D.D., cons. April 25, 1858; Vic. Ap. of Florida; transferred to Savannah, July 14, 1861; returned to Florida as first Bishop of St. Augustine, 1870; died June 10, 1876; His Eminence IGNATIUS CARDINAL PERSICO, D.D., transferred to this See March 11, 1870; resigned 1872; created Cardinal Jan. 16, 1893; died Dec. 7, 1895; Rt. Revs. W. H. GROSS, C.Ss.R., D.D., cons. April 27, 1873; promoted to Oregon 1885; died Nov. 14, 1898; THOMAS A. BECKER, D.D., cons. Bishop of Wilmington, Aug. 16, 1868; transferred to Savannah, March 26, 1886; died July 29, 1899; BENJAMIN J. KEILEY, D.D., cons. June 3, 1900; resigned Feb. 13, 1922; appt. Titular Bishop of Scillium, March 24, 1922; died June 17, 1925; Most Revs. MICHAEL J. KEYES, S.M., D.D., appt. July 8, 1922; cons. Oct. 18, 1922; resigned Sept. 23, 1935; appt. Titular Bishop of Areopolis and Assistant at the Pontifical Throne; died July 31, 1959; GERALD P. O'HARA, D.D., J.U.D., appt. Titular Bishop of Heliopolis and Auxiliary Bishop of Philadelphia, April 26, 1929; cons. May 20, 1929; transferred to See of Savannah, Nov. 16, 1935; received personal title of Archbishop July 12, 1950; appt. Apostolic Nuncio to Ireland, 1951; appt. Apostolic Delegate to Great Britain, 1954; resigned Nov. 11, 1959; died July 16, 1963; THOMAS J. MCDONOUGH, D.D., J.C.D., appt. Titular Bishop of Thaenae and Auxiliary Bishop of St. Augustine, March 10, 1947; cons. April 30, 1947; transferred to Savannah, Jan. 2, 1957; succeeded to See, March 2, 1960; promoted to Archbishop of Louisville, March 1, 1967; resigned Sept. 29, 1981; died Aug. 4, 1998; GERARD L. FREY, D.D., appt. May 31, 1967; cons. Aug. 8, 1967; transferred to Bishop of Lafayette, Nov. 7, 1972; retired May 13, 1989; RAYMOND W. LESSARD, D.D., S.T.D., J.C.L. (Retired), appt. March 5, 1973; cons. April 27, 1973; resigned Feb. 7, 1995.

Chancellor—Rev. DANIEL F. FIRMIN, J.C.L. Tel: 912-201-4110.

Vicar General—Rev. Msgr. JOHN A. KENNEALLY, V.G., V.F., Catholic Pastoral Center, 601 E. Liberty St., Savannah, 31401-5196. Tel: 912-201-4126.

Chancery—Catholic Pastoral Center, 601 E. Liberty St., Savannah, 31401-5196. Tel: 912-201-4100; Fax: 912-201-4101. Rev. DANIEL F. FIRMIN, J.C.L., Chancellor. Tel: 912-201-4110; Fax: 912-201-4081.

Director Child and Youth Protection Services—Mr. STEPHEN B. WILLIAMS. Tel: 912-201-4073.

Director of Finance—Mr. LAWRENCE P. SAUNDERS, Catholic Pastoral Center, 601 E. Liberty St., Savannah, 31401-5196. Tel: 912-201-4123; Fax: 912-201-4101.

Diocesan Tribunal—Catholic Pastoral Center, 601 E. Liberty St., Savannah, 31401-5196. Tel: 912-201-4134; Fax: 912-201-4099.

Officialis—Rev. JEREMIAH J. MCCARTHY, J.C.L., J.V.

Director of the Tribunal—VACANT.

Tribunal Judges—Rev. JEREMIAH J. MCCARTHY, J.C.L., J.V.; Rev. Msgr. FRANCIS J. NELSON, J.C.L.; Rev. DANIEL F. FIRMIN, J.C.L.

Defender of the Bond—Rev. J. GERARD SCHRECK, J.C.D., V.F.

Case Assessors & Notaries—CAROLE BARRAS; EILEEN FLOYD; BERNADINE REGO; GILLIAN BROWN.

Promoter of Justice—Rev. Msgr. FRANCIS J. NELSON, J.C.L.

Censor Librorum—Rev. DOUGLAS K. CLARK, S.T.L.

Archivist—GILLIAN BROWN, Catholic Pastoral Center, 601 E. Liberty St., Savannah, 31401-5196. Tel: 912-201-4070.

Legal Counsel—Mr. JOSEPH P. BRENNAN, Catholic Pastoral Center, 601 E. Liberty St., Savannah, 31401-5196. Tel: 912-201-4100.

Finance Council—Mr. S. SCOTT VOYNICH, Chm.; Most Rev. JOHN KEVIN BOLAND, D.D.; Rev. Msgr. JOHN A. KENNEALLY, V.G., V.F.; Rev. MICHAEL J. KAVANAUGH; Mr. ROBERT W. O'DONNELL; Mr. ROBERT W. SCHIVERA; Mr. EUGENE MCMANUS; Ms. CELESTE SHEAROUSE; Mr. GARY MUSOLF; Dr. KENNETH L. STANLEY; Dr. FRANCIS P. ROSSITER; Mr. CHRISTOPHER S. EDWARDS. Staff: Mr. LAWRENCE P. SAUNDERS; Mr. JOSEPH P. BRENNAN;

Rev. DANIEL F. FIRMIN, J.C.L.

Investment Committee—Most Rev. JOHN KEVIN BOLAND, D.D.; Dr. KENNETH L. STANLEY, Chm.; Mr. EUGENE MCMANUS.

Audit—Mr. CHRISTOPHER S. EDWARDS, Chm.; Mr. ROBERT W. O'DONNELL; Mr. LAWRENCE P. SAUNDERS.

Clergy Personnel—Rev. Msgr. JOHN A. KENNEALLY, V.G., V.F.

Human Resources Director—Mrs. JO ANN GREEN.

Deans—

Savannah Deanery—Rev. Msgr. P. JAMES COSTIGAN, V.F., Mailing Address: P.O. Box 30859, Savannah, 31410-0859. Tel: 912-897-5156.

Augusta Deanery—Rev. GERALD RAGAN, V.F., 1420 Monte Sano Ave., Augusta, 30904-5394. Tel: 706-733-6627.

Albany Deanery—Rev. JACEK SZUSTER, V.F., 211 N. Pinetree Blvd., Thomasville, 31792-3973. Tel: 229-226-3624.

Columbus Deanery—Rev. J. GERARD SCHRECK, J.C.D., V.F., 2000 Kay Circle, Columbus, 31907-3229. Tel: 706-561-8678.

Macon Deanery—Rev. WALTER (MIKE) INGRAM, V.F., 4074 Chambers Rd., Macon, 31206-4702. Tel: 478-923-6386.

Statesboro Deanery—Rev. TIMOTHY P. MCKEOWN, V.F., 221 John Paul Ave., Statesboro, 30458-5076. Tel: 912-681-6726.

Valdosta-Brunswick Deanery—Rev. Msgr. JOHN A. KENNEALLY, V.G., V.F., 2300 Frederica Rd., Saint Simons Island, 31522-1965. Tel: 912-265-3249.

College of Consultors—Rev. ROBERT A. GIRARDEAU; Rev. Msgr. JOHN A. KENNEALLY, V.G., V.F.; Revs. DOUGLAS K. CLARK, S.T.L.; JEREMIAH J. MCCARTHY, J.C.L., J.V.; Rev. Msgr. FRANCIS J. NELSON, J.C.L.; Rev. GERALD RAGAN, V.F.

Presbyteral Council—Revs. JEREMIAH J. MCCARTHY, J.C.L., J.V.; ERIC R. FILMER; JUSTIN R. FERGUSON; DANIEL P. O'CONNELL; BRIAN LABURT; MARK N. VAN ALSTINE; DANIEL F. FIRMIN, J.C.L.; Rev. Msgr. FRED J. NIJEM, V.F.; Revs. MICHAEL J. KAVANAUGH; STEPHEN J. ANGELL; MARTINO BA THONG NGUYEN; THOMAS J. MURPHY.

Diocesan Offices and Directors

Office of Child and Youth Protection—Mr. STEPHEN B. WILLIAMS, Dir., 601 E. Liberty St., Savannah, 31401. Tel: 912-201-4073. Email: sbwilliams@diosav.org.

Newspaper— "The Southern Cross" Rev. DOUGLAS K. CLARK, S.T.L., Editor, Catholic Pastoral Center, 601 E. Liberty St., Savannah, 31401-5196. Tel: 912-201-4054; Fax: 912-201-4101. Email: editor@diosav.org; Printing Office, 601 E. 6th St., Waynesboro, 30830. Tel: 706-554-7888.

Director of Communications—Mrs. BARBARA KING, Catholic Pastoral Center, 601 E. Liberty St., Savannah, 31401-5196. Tel: 912-201-4052; Fax: 912-201-4101. Email: communications@diosav.org.

Superintendent of Schools—Sr. ROSE MARY COLLINS, S.S.J., Catholic Pastoral Center, 601 E. Liberty St., Savannah, 31401-5196. Tel: 912-201-4100; Fax: 912-201-4101. Email: rmcollins@diosav.org.

Director of African American Ministry—Rev. ROBERT E. CHANEY, Catholic Pastoral Center, 601 E. Liberty St., Savannah, 31401-5196. Tel: 912-201-4100; Fax: 912-201-4101. Email: af-am-ministry@diosav.org.

Director of Catholic Social Services—Sr. JACQUELINE GRIFFITH, S.S.J., 601 E. Liberty St., Savannah, 31401-5196. Tel: 912-201-4068; Fax: 912-201-4101. Email: jagriffith@diosav.org.

Director of Family Life—Sr. PATRICIA BROWN, S.S.M.N., Catholic Pastoral Center, 601 E. Liberty St., Savannah, 31401-5196. Tel: 912-201-4058. Email: familylife@diosav.org.

Director of Hispanic/Migrant Ministry—Mr. REY MORALES, 345 S. Fairview Dr., Harlem, 30814. Tel: 706-556-0334.

Director of Permanent Diaconate—Deacon GEORGE H. FOSTER, 4568 Betty's Branch Way, Evans, 30809. Tel: 706-651-8989; Fax: 706-651-0370.

Director of Faith Formation—Ms. ANN PINCKNEY, Catholic Pastoral Center, 601 E. Liberty St., Savannah, 31401-5196. Tel: 912-201-4041; Fax: 912-201-4101. Email: apinckney@diosav.org.

Director of Stewardship and Development—Ms. NANCY KOONS, Catholic Pastoral Center, 601 E. Liberty St., Savannah, 31401-5196. Tel: 912-201-4050.

Director of the Catholic Foundation of South Georgia—Mr. LIAM J. O'CONNOR, Catholic Pastoral Center, 601 E. Liberty St., Savannah, 31401-5196. Tel: 912-201-4061.

Vicar for Religious—Sr. CAMILLE COLLINI, C.S.J., Catholic Pastoral Center, 601 E. Liberty St., Savannah, 31401-5196. Tel: 912-201-4113.

Director of Vocations—Rev. TIMOTHY P. MCKEOWN, V.F., 221 John Paul Ave., Statesboro, 30458. Tel: 912-681-6726. Email: stmatthew101@yahoo.com.

Director of Youth Ministry—Mr. CHARLES R. FROST, Catholic Pastoral Center, 601 E. Liberty St., Savannah, 31401-5196. Tel: 912-201-4056; Fax: 912-201-4101. Email: youth&youngadultministry@diosav.org.

Apostleship of the Sea—Rev. RICHARD YOUNG, 912 E. 35th St., Savannah, 31401. Tel: 912-236-4547; Deacon MICHAEL WRIGHT, O.F.M.Conv., 729 Union St., Brunswick, 31520-8018. Tel: 912-265-3249.

Campaign for Human Development—Sr. JACQUELINE GRIFFITH, S.S.J., Catholic Pastoral Center, 601 E. Liberty St., Savannah, 31401-5196. Tel: 912-201-4067; Fax: 912-201-4101. Email: jagriffith@diosav.org.

Catholic Cemetery Advisory Board—Board Members: JOHN E. JAUGSTETTER, Ph.D.; Mr. JOE COUNIHAN, 601 E. Liberty St., Savannah, 31401-5196. Tel: 912-201-4100; Mr. THOMAS I. BRUNSON, 1030 Fisher St., Savannah, 31410. Tel: 912-897-3611; Mr. LAWRENCE P. SAUNDERS; Mr. ALEX HAGAN; Mr. WALTER E. PAIGE, Staff.

Catholic Relief Services—Rev. DANIEL F. FIRMIN, J.C.L., Dir., Catholic Pastoral Center, 601 E. Liberty St., Savannah, 31401-5196. Tel: 912-201-4110.

Council of Catholic Women—Ms. NEATRICE COLEY, Pres., 112 Kimmeridge Dr., Macon, 31220. Tel: 478-476-8382.

Diocesan Worship Commission—Rev. DOUGLAS K. CLARK, S.T.L., Chm., Catholic Pastoral Center, 601 E. Liberty St., Savannah, 31401-5196. Tel: 912-201-4054; Fax: 912-201-4101. Email: dkclark@diosav.org.

Diocesan Scout Chairman—Mr. CHARLES R. FROST; Ms. MEGHAN LOWE, Catholic Pastoral Center, 601 E. Liberty St., Savannah, 31401-5196. Tel: 912-201-4056.

Ecumenism and Interreligious Affairs—Rev. MICHAEL J. KAVANAUGH, Dir., Mailing Address: P.O. Box 4056, Port Wentworth, 31407-4056. Tel: 912-964-0219; Fax: 912-966-5468. Email: mjkavanaug@aol.com.

Georgia Catholic Conference—FRANCIS J. MULCAHY, Esq., Exec. Sec., Ste. 440, 100 N. Point Center E., Alpharetta, 30022-8261. Tel: 770-521-8799; Fax: 770-521-6337.

Mission Cooperative Appeal—Rev. DANIEL F. FIRMIN, J.C.L., Catholic Pastoral Center, 601 E. Liberty St., Savannah, 31401-5196. Tel: 912-201-4110; Fax: 912-201-4081.

Propagation of the Faith—Ms. ANN PINCKNEY, Catholic Pastoral Center, 601 E. Liberty St., Savannah, 31401-5196. Tel: 912-201-4041; Fax: 912-201-4101. Email: apinckney@diosav.org.

Victim Assistance Coordinator—ROSEMARY DOWNING. Pager: 912-495-3561.

CLERGY, PARISHES, MISSIONS AND PAROCHIAL SCHOOLS

CITY OF SAVANNAH

(CHATHAM COUNTY)

1—CATHEDRAL OF ST. JOHN THE BAPTIST (1873) Rev. Msgr. William O. O'Neill; Revs. Daniel F. Firmin; Douglas K. Clark; Bro. Robert Sokolowski, S.M., Pastoral Assoc.; Deacon Dewain Smith.
Res.: 222 E. Harris St., 31401-4699. Tel: 912-233-4709; Fax: 912-233-8229.

2—ST. BENEDICT THE MOOR (1874), (African American), Rev. Christian A. Alimaji, M.S.P.
Res.: 556 E. Gordon St., 31401. Tel: 912-232-7147; Fax: 912-238-0184.
School—Notre Dame Academy, (Grades 1-6) Tel: 912-232-5473; Fax: 912-232-3352. Mrs. Carole Foran, Prin. Lay Teachers 9; Sisters 1; Students 79.

3—ST. FRANCES XAVIER CABRINI (1968) Rev. Msgr. Francis J. Nelson; Rev. John C. Markham, Parochial Vicar.
Res.: 11500 Middleground Rd., 31419. Tel: 912-925-4725; Fax: 912-925-1379.
School—Tel: 912-925-6249; Fax: 912-925-5661. Web: www.cabrini-sav.org. Ms. Carrie Jane Williamson, Prin. Lay Teachers 8; Students 130.

4—ST. JAMES (1956) Revs. Mark J. Ross; David A. Koetter.
Res.: 8412 Whitfield Ave., 31406-6198. Tel: 912-355-1523; Fax: 912-353-7226. Email: general@stjamessav.com.
School—Tel: 912-355-3132; Fax: 912-355-1996. Web: www.sjcssavannahga.org. Sr. Lisa A. Golden, I.H.M., Prin. Sisters 4; Lay Teachers 24; Students 404.
Mission—Our Lady of Good Hope Isle of Hope, Chatham Co.

5—MOST BLESSED SACRAMENT (1920) Revs. Jeremiah J. McCarthy; Benjamin Dallas, Parochial Vicar; Deacon Michael F. Daly.
Res.: 909 E. Victory Dr., 31405-2499. Tel: 912-356-6980; Fax: 912-692-0010. Email: parish@mbschurch.org. Web: www.mbschurch.org.
School—Tel: 912-356-6987; Fax: 912-356-6988. Email: info@bss-savannah.org. Web: bss-savannah.org. Mrs. Lynn Brown, Prin. Lay Teachers 44; Students 434.

6—MOST PURE HEART OF MARY (1907) Closed. For inquiries for parish records contact the chancery.

7—STS. PETER AND PAUL (1980), (Vietnamese), Rev. Kim Son Nguyen.
Res.: 3115 Victory Dr., 31404-4598. Tel: 912-354-4014.

8—ST. PETER THE APOSTLE CHURCH (1993) Rev. Msgr. P. James Costigan; Rev. Mariusz K. Fuks, Parochial Vicar.
Mailing Address: 7020 Concord Rd., P.O. Box 30859, 31410.
Res.: 302 Bryson Dr., 31410. Tel: 912-897-5156; Fax: 912-897-7924.
School—Tel: 912-897-5224; Fax: 912-897-0801. Sr. Roberta Thoen, S.S.M.N., Prin. Lay Teachers 31; Sisters 3; Students 313.

9—RESURRECTION OF OUR LORD (2000) Rev. Robert E. Chaney.
112 Fell St., 31415-1828. Tel: 912-232-5258.

10—SACRED HEART OF JESUS (1880) Revs. John J. Lyons; Richard Young.
Res.: 1707 Bull St., 31401-7422. Tel: 912-232-0792; Fax: 912-236-0065. Email: sacredheartchurc@bellsouth.net. Web: www.sacredheartsavannah.org.

OUTSIDE THE CITY OF SAVANNAH

ALBANY, DOUGHERTY CO., ST. TERESA (1875) Revs. John Tran; Finbarr P. Stanton; Deacon John C. Dallas.
Res.: 421 Edgewood Ln., 31707. Tel: 229-432-0891; 229-439-2302 (Office); Fax: 229-439-0516. Email: stteresachurch@yahoo.com.
School—417 Edgewood Ln., 31707-3991. Tel: 229-436-0134; Fax: 229-436-0135. Mrs. Mary Lou Gamache, Prin. Lay Teachers 15; Students 181.

AMERICUS, SUMTER CO., ST. MARY (1891) Rev. Robert A. Girardeau. In Res., Rev. Msgr. Lawrence A. Lucree (Retired).
Res.: 332 S. Lee St., 31709-3916. Tel: 229-924-3495; Fax: 229-924-7124.

AUGUSTA, RICHMOND CO.

1—CHURCH OF THE MOST HOLY TRINITY (1810) Rev. Michael Lubinsky; Deacon Elmore J. Butler; Sr. Bernadette Quinlan, M.F.I.C., Pastoral Assoc.
Mailing Address: P.O. Box 2446, 30903-2446. Tel: 706-722-4944; Fax: 706-722-7774. Missionary Franciscan Sisters of the Immaculate Conception.
Res.: 303 Broad St., 30901. Tel: 706-724-4367.
School—Immaculate Conception School, Tel: 706-722-9964; Fax: 706-722-9994. Jonathan Pike, Prin. Lay Teachers 9; Students 100.

2—ST. JOSEPH (1954) Revs. Thomas Healy; Cheol Hyun Jung; Matthew Ericksen, Parochial Vicar; Deacons Gregory L. Bernard; Reinaldo Morales; James Lloyd.
Res.: 2607 Lumpkin Rd., 30906-3222. Tel: 706-798-1920; Fax: 706-798-8594.

3—ST. MARY ON THE HILL (1917) Revs. Gerald Ragan; Mark N. Van Alstine, Parochial Vicar; Deacons Don McArdle; Brian Goodman; Albert J. Sullivan Jr.; Kenneth R. Maleck. In Res., Revs. Charles Hughes, G.H.M. (Retired); Edward R. Frank (Retired).
Res.: 1420 Monte Sano Ave., 30904-5394. Tel: 706-733-6627; Fax: 706-733-4887. Email: smoth@knology.net. Web: www.stmaryonthehill.org.
School—1220 Monte Sano Ave., 30904-5394. Tel: 706-733-6193; Fax: 706-737-7985. Mr. Keith Darr, Prin. Lay Teachers 30; Students 490.
Chapel—Trinity Hospital, Tel: 706-481-7000; Fax: 706-481-7850.
Chapel—Aquinas Chapel, Tel: 706-736-5516; Fax: 706-736-2678.
Chapel—Adoration Chapel

BAINBRIDGE, DECATUR CO., ST. JOSEPH'S (1887) Revs. J. Roberto Mena, S.T.; Rudy V. Breunig, S.T.
Res.: 822 Ramsey St., P.O. Box 192, 39818-0192. Tel: 229-243-9146. Email: stjoebainbridge@hotmail.com.
Mission—Church of the Incarnation 5541 Hwy. 91, Donalsonville, Seminole Co. 31745.

BLAKELY, EARLY CO., HOLY FAMILY (1965) Rev. Joel S. Bladt, S.T.
Mailing Address: Box 425, 39823-0425. In Res., Rev. Victor Seidel, S.T. (Retired).
Res.: 533 Arlington Ave., P.O. Box 425, 39823. Tel: 229-723-3339.
Mission—St. Luke P.O. Box 491, Cuthbert, Randolph Co. 39840.

BRUNSWICK , GLYNN CO., ST. FRANCIS XAVIER (1884) Revs. Leo Kennedy, O.F.M.Conv.; Wilfrid Logsdon, O.F.M.Conv.; Cletus Pifher, O.F.M.Conv.; Bro.

Michael Wright, O.F.M.Conv.; Deacons Michael Murphy; Ntungwa Maasha.
Res. & Office: 405 Howe St., 31520-7526. Tel: 912-265-3249; Fax: 912-265-6797.
Friary: 729 Union St., 31520-8018. Tel: 912-554-8922.
School—1121 Union St., 31520. Tel: 912-265-9470; Fax: 912-265-9950. Ms. Erin Mary Finn, Prin. Lay Teachers 20; Students 252.
Catechesis/Religious Program—Christian Formation Center, 1116 Richmond St., 31520. Tel: 912-264-6805; Fax: 912-264-6885. Students 151.
Mission—Nativity of Our Lady 1000 N. Way St., Darien, McIntosh Co. 31305.

CLAXTON, EVANS CO., ST. CHRISTOPHER (1958) Rev. Robert Poandl; Sr. Janet Fischer, F.S.P.A., Pastoral Assoc.
Res.: 400 S. River St., 30417-2150. Tel: 912-739-3913.
Convent—Franciscan Sisters of Perpetual Adoration, 402 S. River St., 30417. Tel: 912-739-2275.
Mission—St. Jude Glennville, Tattnall Co. 30427-0772. Tel: 912-654-1908.
Mission—Holy Cross Pembroke, Bryan Co. 30417.
Mission—Our Lady of Guadalupe Sand Hill.

COLUMBUS, MUSCOGEE CO.

1—ST. ANNE (1961) Revs. J. Gerard Schreck; Scott Winchel, Parochial Vicar; Mrs. Margo Truett, Pastoral Assoc.
Mailing Address: 2000 Kay Cir., 31907-3229. Tel: 706-561-8678; Fax: 706-568-0179.
Res.: 3544 Trinity Dr., 31907-3229. Tel: 706-561-8678; Fax: 706-565-4845.
School—2020 Kay Cir., 31907. Tel: 706-561-8232. Email: stanne@aol.com. Web: www.stannecsg.com. Mrs. Danni Harris, Pres. Lay Teachers 44; Students 479.
High School—St. Anne Pacelli Catholic School formerly Pacelli High School Tel: 706-561-8243; Fax: 706-561-8232. Kristin Turner, Prin. (Grades 7-12); Jenn Ford, Prin. (Grades Pre-K - 6). Students 146.
Chapel—Mercy Chapel

2—ST. BENEDICT THE MOOR (1958), (African American), Rev. Donatus C. Mgbeajuo, M.S.P.
Church: 2935 Ninth St., 31906-0714. Tel: 706-323-1749; Fax: 706-324-2641. Email: stbenedict07@bellsouth.net.
Res.: 2939 Ninth St., 31906. Tel: 706-323-8300; Fax: 706-324-2641.

3—HOLY FAMILY (1835) [JC] Rev. Frank Patterson.
Res.: 320 12th St., 31901-2454. Tel: 706-323-6908; Fax: 706-323-2043. Email: holyfamily706@bellsouth.net. Web: holyfamilycolumbus.e-paluch.com.
Catechesis/Religious Program—Students 162.
St. Vincent de Paul—Mrs. Frances Cummings, Dir.

4—OUR LADY OF LOURDES (1958) Rev. Brian LaBurt. In Res., Rev. Robert T. Hand (Retired).
Res.: 1953 Torch Hill Rd., 31903-2745. Tel: 706-689-5720; Fax: 706-687-9579.
School—1973 Torch Hill Rd., 31903. Tel: 706-689-5644; Fax: 706-689-5644. Diana Hankins, Prin. Lay Teachers 10; Students 108.
Mission—St. Mary Magdalen S. Hwy. 41, Buena Vista, Marion Co. 31803-2745.

CORDELE, CRISP CO., ST. THERESA (1931) Rev. Robert A. Cushing.
Res.: 807 Third St. S., 31015-1705. Tel: 229-273-3446.
Mission—St. Michael 718 N. Dooly St., P.O. Box 685, Montezuma, Macon Co. 31063-1507. Tel: 478-472-5124; Fax: 478-924-7124.

DOUGLAS, COFFEE CO., ST. PAUL'S (1938) Rev. Raymond G. Levreault; Bertha Capetillo, Pastoral Assoc.
Mailing Address: 523 E. Ward St., 31533-3912.
Res.: 623 Briarwood Rd., 31533. Tel: 912-384-8212; Fax: 912-384-3560.
Mission—St. William 807 S. Merrimac, Fitzgerald, Ben Hill Co. 31750-0801.
Mission—Holy Family Willacoochee, Atkinson Co.

DUBLIN, LAURENS CO., IMMACULATE CONCEPTION (1911) Rev. Richard J. Hart.
Res.: 204 N. Church St., 31021-6152. Tel: 478-272-0266; Fax: 478-275-8806. Email: iccdublin@bellsouth.net. Web: immaculate-conception-church.net.
Mission—St. William 301 S. Smith St., Sandersville, Washington Co. 31082. Tel: 478-552-3352.

EASTMAN, DODGE CO., ST. MARK (1989) Rev. William Leahy; Domonica (Mecca) Gibbs, Pastoral Asst.
Mailing Address: P.O. Box 4304, 31023-4241. Tel: 478-374-0238; Fax: 478-374-4454.

GROVETOWN, COLUMBIA CO., ST. TERESA OF AVILA (1968) Revs. Michael E. Roverse; Martino Nguyen; Gaspar Hegedus, Parochial Vicar; Deacons William L. Johnson; Kerry C. Diver; Joseph S. Soparas.
Res.: 4921 Columbia Rd., 30813-5237. Tel: 706-854-7824; Fax: 706-863-5001.
Catechesis/Religious Program—Tel: 706-863-0252. Students 591.

HAZLEHURST, JEFF DAVIS CO., GOOD SHEPHERD (1967) Rev. Rafael A. Estrada.
Mailing Address: c/o P.O. Box 330, Baxley, 31515-0330. Tel: 912-366-0238. Email: elbuenpastor40@bellsouth.net.
Mission—St. Rose of Lima N. City Circle Rd., Baxley, Appling Co. 31513.
Mission—St. Raymond c/o P.O. Box 330, Baxley, Appling Co. 31515.

HINESVILLE, LIBERTY CO., ST. STEPHEN, FIRST MARTYR (1980) Rev. Thomas J. Murphy.
Res.: 399 Woodland Ave., 31313-2719. Tel: 912-876-4364; 912-876-4368 (Rectory); Fax: 912-876-3150. Email: sscc399@clds.net.

JESUP, WAYNE CO., ST. JOSEPH (1964) Rev. Keith O'Neill, O.F.M.Conv., Admin.
Res.: 1055 E. Plum St., 31546-4012. Tel: 912-427-8276.

KATHLEEN, HOUSTON CO., ST. PATRICK (1969) Rev. Kirk Mansell; Deacons Ralph H. McAtee; Ken Hutnick; James Roberge.
Res. & Church: 2410 GA Hwy. 127, 31047-2820. Tel: 478-987-4213; Fax: 478-988-3759. Email: saintpat@windstream.net. Web: stpatrickga.catholicweb.com.
Mission—St. Juliana 804 Martin Luther King Blvd. (US 341), P.O. Box 1022, Fort Valley, Peach Co. 31030.

LAKELAND, LANIER CO., QUEEN OF PEACE (1940) Rev. Fredy A. Angel; Ana D. Beltran, Sec.
Res.: 1706 S. Hutchinson Ave., P.O. Box 26, Adel, 31620. Tel: 229-896-7319. Email: sogamissions@windstream.net.
Mission—St. Mary Nashville, Berrien Co.
Mission—St. Margaret Mary Adel, Cook Co.
Mission—St. Jose Twin Lakes, Lowndes Co.

MACON, BIBB CO.

1—HOLY SPIRIT (1968) Rev. Walter (Mike) Ingram.
Res.: 4074 Chambers Rd., 31206-4702. Tel: 478-788-9820. Email: pastor@holyspiritmacon.org.
Parish Center—4074 Chambers Rd., 31206-4702. Tel: 478-788-2837.

2—ST. JOSEPH (1841) Revs. Allan J. McDonald; Justin R. Ferguson, Parochial Vicar; Deacons Donald R. Coates; Thomas J. Eden; Patrick F. Mongan.
Res.: 830 Poplar St., 31201-2093. Tel: 478-745-1631; Fax: 478-745-2254. Email: church@st-joseph.cc. Web: www.stjosephmacon.com.
School—Tel: 478-742-0636; Fax: 478-746-7685. Dr. Kaye Hlavaty, Prin. Lay Teachers 27; Students 315.

3—ST. PETER CLAVER (1915) Rev. Adam J. Kasela.
Res.: 131 Ward St., 31204-3193. Tel: 478-743-1454; Fax: 478-743-9868. Email: stpeterclaver@cbi.magcoxmail.com. Web: stpeterclaverchurch.org.
School—133 Ward St., 31204-3193. Tel: 478-743-3985; Fax: 478-743-0054. Email: info@spcschool.com. Sr. Margaret Mary Scally, Prin. Sisters 1; Lay Teachers 18; Students 229.

MCRAE, TELFAIR CO., HOLY REDEEMER (1968) Rev. William J. Leahy.
201 Telfair, 31055-1625. Tel: 478-868-2002; Fax: 478-868-2939. Email: holyredeemer@windstream.net.

MOULTRIE, COLQUITT CO., IMMACULATE CONCEPTION (1978) Rev. Eric R. Filmer; Deacons Philip J. Walsh; Richard F. Fetterman.
Res.: 1135 Second St., S.E., 31768. Tel: 229-985-6550; Fax: 229-217-4970. Email: icmoult@moultriega.net. Web: www.moultriegacatholic.org.
Mission—St. John Vianney P.O. Box 391, Camilla, Mitchell Co. 31730-0391. Tel: 229-336-8685.

PINE MOUNTAIN, HARRIS CO., CHRIST THE KING CHURCH (2006) Rev. John R. Madden.
Mailing Address: P.O. Box 899, 31822.
Res.: 6740 Hwy. 354, 31822. Tel: 706-663-0090; Fax: 706-663-0091. Email: christthekingpinemountain@att.net.

PORT WENTWORTH, CHATHAM CO., OUR LADY OF LOURDES (1940) Rev. Michael J. Kavanaugh; Sr. Georgette Cunniff, M.F.I.C., Pastoral Assoc.
Res.: 501 S. Coastal Hwy., (GA Hwy. 25), P.O. Box 4056, 31407-4056. Tel: 912-964-0219; Fax: 912-966-1476. Email: ololchurch@comcast.net.

RICHMOND HILL, BRYAN CO., ST. ANNE (1955) Rev. Joseph A. Smith; Deacon Paul Gutting.
Res.: P.O. Box 648, 31324-0601. Tel: 912-756-3338.

SPRINGFIELD, EFFINGHAM CO., ST. BONIFACE CHURCH (1987) Rev. Wes Lamb.
1952 GA Hwy. 21 S., 31329-5207. Email: pastor@sbcatholic.com.

ST. MARYS, CAMDEN CO., OUR LADY STAR OF THE SEA (1969) Rev. Gabriel Cummings; Deacon William H. Wilson.
Res.: P.O. Box 6900, 31558. Tel: 912-882-4718; Fax: 912-882-5845. Email: olssgc@tds.net. Web: www.stfrancisfolkston.com.
Mission—St. Francis of Assisi P.O. Box 487, Folkston, Charlton Co. 31537-0151. Tel: 912-496-3219. Email: carter47@windstream.net.

ST. SIMONS ISLAND, GLYNN CO., ST. WILLIAM (1968) Rev. Msgr. John A. Kenneally; Deacon George F. Ruehling III.
Res. & Mailing Address: 2300 Frederica Rd., 31522-1965. Tel: 912-638-2647; Fax: 912-638-7577. Email: stwilliamschurch@bellsouth.net.

STATESBORO, BULLOCH CO., ST. MATTHEW (1944) Rev. Timothy P. McKeown.
Res.: 221 John Paul Ave., 30458-5016. Tel: 912-681-6726; Fax: 912-681-6727.

SWAINSBORO, EMANUEL CO., HOLY TRINITY (1957) Rev. John T. Brown, G.H.M.; Sr. Mary Bordelon, C.D.P., Pastoral Coord.
Res.: 928 W. Main St., 30401-5502. Tel: 478-237-8722; Fax: 478-237-8722.
Mission—Holy Family P.O. Box 231, Metter, Candler Co. 30439-0231. Tel: 912-685-5811. Email: jbrown@glenmary.org.

SYLVANIA, SCREVEN CO., OUR LADY OF THE ASSUMPTION (1957) Rev. Louis Lussier, O.S.Cam.; Sr. Mary Ellen Barrette, G.H.M., Pastoral Assoc.
Res.: 121 Ridgecrest Dr., 30467-1840. Tel: 912-564-2312.
Mission—St. Bernadette P.O. Box 616, Millen, Jenkins Co. 30442-0501. Tel: 478-982-1445.
Chapel—Bay Branch, St. Joseph

THOMASVILLE, THOMAS CO., ST. AUGUSTINE (1936) Rev. Jacek Szuster; Deacons Howard G. Halladay; David Wendell; John Blaha.
Res.: 211 N. Pinetree Blvd., 31792-3973. Tel: 229-226-3624; Fax: 229-226-8808. Email: catholic@rose.net.
Mission—St. Elizabeth Ann Seton 11th Ave. N.W., Cairo, Grady Co. 31728-4007. Tel: 229-377-6996.

THUNDERBOLT, CHATHAM CO., NATIVITY OF OUR LORD, Closed. For inquiries for parish records contact the chancery.

TIFTON, TIFT CO., OUR DIVINE SAVIOUR (1953) Rev. Alfonso Gutierrez, Parochial Admin.; Deacon J. Brian Bergeron.
Res.: 2001 N. Central Ave., P.O. Box 212, 31793-0201. Tel: 229-382-3170; Fax: 229-382-7611. Email: ods@friendlycity.net.
Rectory—2001 N. Central Ave., 31794.
Mission—St. Ann 9007 U.S. Hwy. 82 E., Alapaha, Berrien Co. 31622. Tel: 229-382-4600. Email: ODS@friendlycity.net. ,

TYBEE ISLAND, CHATHAM CO., ST. MICHAEL (1892) Rev. Thomas J. Peyton; Deacons Fretwell G. Crider, (Retired); David V. Hayden; Sr. Terentia Hynes, Pastoral Assoc.
Res.: 802 Lovell Ave., 31328. Tel: 912-786-4505; Fax: 912-786-4661.
School—714 Lovell Ave., 31328. Tel: 912-786-4507; Fax: 912-786-4551. Ms. Holly Landford, Prin. Lay Teachers 12; Students 77.

VALDOSTA, LOWNDES CO., ST. JOHN THE EVANGELIST (1927) Revs. Daniel P. O'Connell; Luis Fonseca, Parochial Vicar; Deacons David Lasseter; Columbus Carter; Petra Faulkenhausen. In Res., Rev. Msgr. Marvin LeFrois (Retired).
Church Office: 800 Gornto Rd., 31602-1699. Tel: 229-244-2430; Fax: 229-244-5352.
Res.: 2402 Berkley Dr., 31602-1699. Tel: 229-244-9920. Email: stjohns@stjohnevang.org. Web: www.stjohnevang.org.
Newman Center— 412 Baytree Rd., 31602. Tel: 229-247-6707.
School—Sisters of St. Joseph, Tel: 229-244-2556; 229-244-0050 (Convent); Fax: 229-244-0865. Melanie Lasseter, Prin. Sisters 1; Lay Teachers 25; Students 232.

VIDALIA, TOOMBS CO., SACRED HEART (1967) Rev. Stephen J. Angell; Deacon Joseph P. Claroni.
Mailing Address: P.O. Box 1086, 30475.
Res.: 3119 E. North St., 30474. Tel: 912-538-7818.
Mission—St. Andrew the Apostle 138 Industrial Blvd., Reidsville, 30453. Tel: 912-537-7709. Email: shvidalia@bellsouth.net.

WARNER ROBINS, HOUSTON CO., SACRED HEART (1945) Rev. Msgr. Fred J. Nijem; Rev. Pablo Migone, Parochial Vicar; Deacon James A. Hunt.
Mailing Address: 251 S. Davis Dr., 31099-5052. Tel: 478-923-0124; Fax: 478-328-3078. Email: sacredheart@cbi.mgacoxmail.com.
School—Sacred Heart School formerly Sisters of Presentation , 1250 S. Davis Dr., 31088. Tel: 912-923-9668; Fax: 912-923-5822. Mrs. Staci Erwin, Prin. Students 200.

WAYCROSS, WARE CO., ST. JOSEPH'S (1960) Rev. Paul A. O'Connell.
Res.: 2011 Darling Ave., 31501-1846. Tel: 912-283-7700; Fax: 912-283-1944.

WAYNESBORO, BURKE CO., SACRED HEART (1961) Rev. Patrick A. Otor, Parochial Admin.
Res.: 115 S. Liberty St., P.O. Box 1100, 30830-4548. Tel: 706-554-2535.
Mission—St. Joan of Arc P.O. Box 175, Louisville, Jefferson Co. Tel: 478-625-3433.

Special Assignment:
Revs.—
Fisher, Albert, Chap., St. Joseph/Candler Hospital
Madden, John J., S.J., Chap., St. Joseph/Candler Hospital
Markham, John C., Memorial Medical Center & Candler General Hospital
Ryan, Timothy K., 1310 Primrose Dr., Roswell, 30076. Tel: 404-667-1313; Fax: 404-667-6305

On Duty Outside the Diocese:
Rev. Msgr.—
Schreck, Christopher J., S.T.B., S.S.L., Ph.D., S.T.D., Pontifical College Josephinum, 7625 N. High St., Columbus, OH 43235-1498. Tel: 614-885-5585
Revs.—
Brannen, Brett A. Tel: 301-447-5785 Mount St. Mary's Seminary, Emmitsburg, MD
Johnson, John R.
Osondu, Chidi E.
Pachence, Ronald A., University of San Diego, 5998 Alcala Park, San Diego, CA 92110. Tel: 619-260-4784
Pontzer, Stephen

Military Chaplains:
Rev.—
Quang, John, U.S.N.

Retired:
Most Rev.—
Lessard, Raymond W., D.D., S.T.D., J.C.L., St. Vincent DePaul Seminary, 10701 S. Military Tr., Boynton Beach, FL 33436-4899. Tel: 561-732-4424
Rev. Msgrs.—
Cuddy, John J., 830 Poplar St., Macon, 31201. Tel: 478-464-0731
LeFrois, Marvin, 800 Gornto Rd., Valdosta, 31602-1699. Tel: 912-253-0041
Lucree, Lawrence A., V.F., 332 S. Lee St., Americus, 31709. Tel: 229-924-3495
Revs.—
Brick, Paul T., S.D.S., 727 3rd Ave., Columbus, 31901.
Cerrone, Michael J., 6915 Chapelridge Dr., Dallas, TX 75249.
Drozd, Henry J. (LAR), P.O. Box 42063, 31409-1409. Tel: 912-353-8297
Frank, Edward R., 1420 Monte Sano Ave., Augusta, 30904. Tel: 706-738-5623
Gergel, Stephen J., 116 Lake Manor Dr., Kingsland, 31548-5639. Tel: 912-576-2716
Gorny, Edward V., G.H.M., P.O. Box 116, Claxton, 30417-0116. Tel: 912-739-7254
Greenway, George G., 220 Villager Dr., Saint Simons Island, 31522-5331. Tel: 912-634-6272
Hand, Robert T., Our Lady of Lourdes Church, 1953 Torch Hill Rd., Columbus, 31903. Tel: 706-689-5184
Higgins, Francis C., 2117 E. 41st St., 31404. Tel: 912-236-9267
Holloway, James, 500 Ocean Blvd., #7, Saint Simons Island, 31522. Tel: 912-634-2171
Hughes, Charles, G.H.M., 2504 McDowll St., Augusta, 30904. Tel: 706-667-6685
Keohane, Donal, St. Martin of Tours, 11967 Sunset Blvd., Los Angeles, CA 90049. Tel: 310-476-7403
Kumbalaprampil, Xavier, Ponel, P.O. Elamakkara, DT. Ernakulam 682026 India. Tel: 91-484-234-9268
Minch, Richard, 112 Katie Dr., Rincon, 31326. Tel: 912-826-0783
O'Brien, Patrick, 103 Winchester Dr., 31410. Tel: 912-898-7504
O'Keeffe, Michael, Blessed Trinity Church, 5 S.E. 17th St., Ocala, FL 34471.
Payne, Thomas H., P.O. Box 24683, St. Simons Island, 31522. Tel: 912-634-9189
Peterson, William, G.H.M., 147 Shadowwood Dr., Martinez, 30907-4509. Tel: 706-860-4738
Roxas, Rodolfo P., Chap., 11705 Mercy Blvd., 31419-1791. Tel: 912-819-3464
Searles, Thaddeus, P.O. Box 192, Bainbridge, 39818-9146. Tel: 229-243-9146
Seidel, Victor, S.T., P.O. Box 396, Cuthbert, 39840. Tel: 229-310-0094
Smith, Michael H., V.F., 222 John Paul Ave., Statesboro, 30458-5016. Tel: 229-891-6080
Szufel, Adam, 11 Atrium Dr., Warner Robins, 31088-5694. Tel: 478-328-6481; Fax: 478-328-3876. Email: ASzufel@aol.com

Permanent Deacons:
Andruzzi, Louis J., St. Jude, Glennville
Arcand, Dennis A., St. Juliana Church, Kathleen
Bergeron, J. Brian, Our Divine Saviour, Tifton
Bernard, Gregory L., St. Joseph's, Augusta
Blaha, John D., St. Augustine, Thomasville
Brown, Raymond E., Queen of Peace, Lakeland
Butler, Elmore J., Holy Trinity, Augusta
Carter, Columbus, Jr., St. John the Evangelist, Valdosta
Castillo, Tirso A., Immaculate Conception, Dublin
Clark, Gerald R., St. Frances Cabrini, Savannah
Claroni, Joseph B., Sacred Heart, Vidalia
Coates, Donald R., St. Joseph, Macon
Crider, Fretwell G., St. Michael's, Tybee Island
Dallas, John C., St. Teresa, Albany
Daly, Michael F., Blessed Sacrament, Savannah
Diver, Kerry C., St. Teresa of Avila, Grovetown
Eden, Thomas J., St. Joseph, Macon
Ensley, Edgar L., Jr., St. Anne, Columbus
Falkenhausen, Peter H., III, St. John the Evangelist, Valdosta
Fetterman, Richard F., Immaculate Conception, Moultrie
Foster, George H., St. Michael, Fort Gordon
Goodman, Brian, St. Mary on the Hill, Augusta
Gutting, Paul, St. Anne Church, Richmond Hill
Guyer, Lawrence A., St. William, St. Simons Island
Halbur, Richard A., St. Stephen, First Martyr, Hinesville
Halladay, Howard G., St. Augustine, Thomasville
Hayden, David V., St. Michael, Tybee Island
Herrmann, Robert, St. Anne, Columbus
Hubbard, James B., St. Peter Claver, Macon
Hunt, James A., Sacred Heart, Warner Robins
Hutnick, Kenneth P., St. Patrick Church, Perry
Johnson, William L., St. Teresa of Avila, Augusta
Kepshire, Robert J., St. Teresea of Avila, Grovetown
Kriegel, David L., St. Michael, Fort Gordon
Lasseter, R. David, St. John the Evangelist, Valdosta
Leslie, Cedric T., St. Peter Claver, Macon
Lloyd, James F., St. Joseph, Augusta
Maasha, Ntungwa, St. Francis Xavier, Brunswick
Maleck, Kenneth R., St. Mary on the Hill, Augusta
Marchek, Michael V., St. Michael's, Fort Gordon
McArdle, Donald R., St. Mary on the Hill, Augusta
McAtee, Ralph H., St. Patrick, Perry
McGrath, Michael J., St. Matthew, Statesboro
Mongan, Patrick F., St. Joseph, Macon
Morales-Morales, Reinaldo, St. Joseph, Augusta
Perez, Bienvenido, Jr., Hunter Army Air Field, Savannah
Plowman, Kenneth M., Most Holy Trinity, Augusta
Quillen, John R., Christ the King, Pine Mountain
Roberge, James D., Jr., St. Patrick, Kathleen
Ruehling, George F., III, 702 Cedar St., St. Simons Island, 31522-1259.
Smith, Dewain E., Cathedral of St. John the Baptist, Savannah
Soparas, Joseph S., St. Teresa of Avila, Grovetown
Sullivan, Albert J., Jr., St. Mary on the Hill, Augusta
Walsh, Philip J., Immaculate Conception, Moultrie
Wendell, David, St. Augustine, Thomasville
Wilson, William H., St. Francis of Assisi, Folkston
Wright, Michael, O.F.M.Conv., St. Francis Xavier, Brunswick

INSTITUTIONS LOCATED IN THE DIOCESE

[A] HIGH SCHOOLS, DIOCESAN

AUGUSTA. *Aquinas High School*, 1920 Highland Ave., 30904-5305. Tel: 706-736-5516; Fax: 706-736-2678. Email: cpaul@aquinashigh.org. Web: www.aquinashigh.org. Robert Larcher, Pres.; Mrs. Chris Paul, Prin.; Ms. Shannon Williams, Asst. Prin. Lay Teachers 28; Students 282.

COLUMBUS. *Pacelli Catholic High School*, 3556 Trinity Dr., 31907. Tel: 706-561-8243; Fax: 706-561-3243. Email: jford@sasphs.net; kturner@sasphs.net. Web: www.pacelli.net. Jenn Ford, Prin.; Kristin Turner, Prin.; Rev. J. Gerard Schreck, J.C.D., V.F., Diocesan Moderator. Lay Teachers 44; Students 468.

[B] HIGH SCHOOLS, PRIVATE

SAVANNAH. *Benedictine Military School*, 6502 Seawright Dr., 31406-2752. Tel: 912-644-7000; Fax: 912-356-3527. Email: deborah.antosca@bcsav.net. Web: bcsav.net. Rev. Frank Ziemkiewicz, Headmaster; Dr. Deborah Antosca, Prin.; Revs. Ronald P. Gatman, O.S.B.; Anthony P. Wesolowski, O.S.B.; Jeffrey S. Nyardy, O.S.B.; Bro. Timothy J. Brown, O.S.B. Secondary school conducted by the Dependent Priory of Benedictine Monks of St. Vincent Archabbey, Latrobe, PA. Brothers 1; Lay Teachers 28; Boys 314.

Convent and Academy of St. Vincent de Paul, 207 E. Liberty St., 31401-3577. Tel: 912-236-9541; Fax: 912-236-7877. Email: buttimer@svga.net. Web: www.stvincentsacademy.com. Sr. Helen Marie Buttimer, R.S.M., Prin. Sisters of Mercy of the Americas. Sisters 7; Lay Teachers 28; Girls 340.

MACON. *Mount de Sales Academy*, (Grades 6-12), 851 Orange St., 31201. Tel: 478-751-3240; Fax: 478-751-3241. Email: kprebble@mountdesales.net. Web: www.mountdesales.net. Ms. Katy Prebble, Pres.; Dr. Michael Franklin, Prin. (Upper); Dr. Bryn Gabriel, Prin. (Middle); Mr. Michael Vullo, Librarian. Sisters of Mercy of the Americas. Lay Teachers 76; Students 663.

[C] CHILD CARE HOMES

SAVANNAH. *St. Mary's Home*, 2170 E. Victory Dr., P.O. Box 3627-B, 31414. Tel: 912-236-7164; Fax: 912-236-9699. Email: STMARYHOME@aol.com. Sr. Mary Alvin Seubott, R.S.M., Admin. Sisters of Mercy of the Americas. Sisters 4; Lay Staff 16; Residents 8; Total Assisted 17.

Summer Program Total Assisted 30; Total Staff 23.

[D] SERVICES TO FAMILIES

MACON. *Nazareth Life Ministries*, 538 Orange St., 31201. Tel: 478-746-9803; Fax: 478-745-0847. Email: famsre@bellsouth.net. Sr. Elizabeth Greim, Exec. Dir. Pregnancy Services for birth parents/families/newborn, education & direct services.

[E] MONASTERIES AND RESIDENCES OF PRIESTS

SAVANNAH. *The Benedictine Priory*, 6502 Seawright Dr., 31406. Tel: 912-356-3520; Fax: 912-356-3527. Web: bccadets.org. Revs. Frank Ziemkiewicz, Prior; Anthony P. Wesolowski, O.S.B.; Ronald P. Gatman, O.S.B.; Jeffrey S. Nyardy, O.S.B.; Bro. Timothy Brown, O.S.B. Dependent Priory of St. Vincent Archabbey, Latrobe, PA.

[F] CONVENTS AND RESIDENCES FOR SISTERS

SAVANNAH. *Carmelite Monastery* (1958) 11 W. Back St., 31419-3219. Tel: 912-925-8505; Fax: 912-925-0797. Email: carmelite@savannahcarmel.org. Web: www.savannahcarmel.org. Sr. Mary Elizabeth Angaine, Contact Person. Professed Nuns 4.

Mercy Convent, 11801 McAuley Dr., 31419-1709. Tel: 912-925-3800; Fax: 912-925-3823. Email: mercy-convent@bellsouth.net. Ms. Maureen Shumard, Dir. Retired Sisters of Mercy. Sisters 8.

[G] NEWMAN CENTERS

MACON. *Mercer University, Wesleyan College Newman Center* c/o St. Joseph Church, 830 Poplar St., 31201-2093. Tel: 478-745-1631. Email: wilcox@st-joseph.cc. Web: www.sjcyouth.org. Tex Phelps, Campus Min.

STATESBORO. *St. Matthew Newman Center at Georgia Southern University* 221 John Paul Ave., 30458-5016. Tel: 912-681-6726; Fax: 912-681-6727.

VALDOSTA. *Valdosta State College Newman Center* 800 Gornto Rd., 31602. Bethany Brogdon, Campus Min.

[H] MISCELLANEOUS

SAVANNAH. *The Catholic Foundation of South Georgia*, 601 E. Liberty St., 31401-5196. Tel: 912-201-4100; Fax: 912-201-4101. Email: loconnor@diosav.org. Web: www.catholicfdn-southga.org. Paul Henchey, Chm., Bd. Trustees; Mr. Liam J. O'Connor, Exec. Dir.

Catholic Social Services, 601 E. Liberty St., 31401-5196. Tel: 912-201-4067; Fax: 912-201-4101. Email: catholicsocialservices@diosav.org. Web: www.diosav.org/socialservices. Sr. Jacqueline Griffith, S.S.J., Dir.

Mercy Properties Georgia, Inc. (1998) 1826 Florence St., 31415. Tel: 912-401-0008; Fax: 912-401-0012. Email: rhaddock@mercyhousing.org. Web: www.mercyhousing.org. Eugene P. Walker Jr., Pres.; John Corcoran, Vice Pres.

Social Apostolate of Savannah, 502 E. Liberty St., P.O. Box 8703, 31412. Tel: 912-233-1877; Fax: 912-651-3638. Email: socapsa@aol.com. Sr. Pauline O'Brien, M.F.I.C., Dir.

ALBANY. *St. Clare's Evangelization-Community Center*, 2005 Martin Luther King Dr., P.O. Box 4123, 31706-4123. Tel: 912-883-2566; Fax: 912-883-9116. Sr. Maura Molloy, M.F.I.C., Dir.

Neighbors in Need, 2005 Martin Luther King Dr., P.O. Box 3032, 31706-3001. Tel: 229-883-2872; Fax: 229-883-9116. Sr. Veronica Weygand, M.F.I.C., Dir.

AUGUSTA. *Alleluia Catholic Fellowship*, 2110 Richards St., P.O. Box 6805, 30916-6805. Tel: 706-798-1882; Fax: 706-560-2759. Mr. Dennis McBride, Moderator.

Catholic Social Services, 811 12th St., 30901-2749. Tel: 706-722-4390; Fax: 706-722-4758. Web: www.cssaugusta.com. Sr. Janet Roddy, M.F.I.C., Dir.

BRUNSWICK. *Society of St. Vincent de Paul (Glynn County)*, 1217 Newcastle St., 31520-7534. Tel: 912-262-6027; Fax: 912-265-6797. Marilee Williamson, Pres.

CLAXTON. *Clothesbasket*, 402 S. River St., 30417-2150. Tel: 912-739-2275. Email: jfischer0@bellsouth.net. Sr. Janet Fischer, F.S.P.A., Dir.

COLUMBUS. *St. Anne Community Outreach*, 3502 Kay Cir., 31907-3254. Tel: 706-568-1592. Mrs. Donna Bushaw, Dir.

St. Benedict Social Concerns, 2935 Ninth St., 31906-6354. Tel: 706-323-8300; Fax: 706-324-2641. Mrs. Helen Linton, Dir.

Holy Family Church-St. Vincent DePaul Society (Independent Conference), 320 12th St., 31901-2454. Tel: 706-322-0098; Fax: 706-327-8191. Email: holyfamily706@bellsouth.net. Web: holyfamilycolumbus.e-paluch.com. Mrs. Frances Cummings, Dir.

Holy Family Soup Kitchen-Lunch Program formerly Holy Family Soup Kitchen 320 12th St., 31901-2454. Tel: 706-322-0098; Fax: 706-327-8191. Email: holyfamily706@bellsouth.net. Web: holyfamilycolumbus.e-paluch.com. Mrs. Frances Cummings, Dir.

Our Lady of Lourdes, 1953 Torch Hill Rd., 31903-2754. Tel: 706-689-5720; Fax: 706-687-9579. Email: outreach@ololcol.org. Rev. Brian LaBurt.

HAMILTON. *(FOCUS)* (1984) Box 524, 31811. Tel: 706-628-9955; Fax: 706-628-9955. Web: www.focusfriends.org. Lynda Frerichs, Vice Pres./ Emergency Services.

MILLEN. *Catholic Thrift Shop*, 706 Bay St., 30442. Tel: 478-982-8361. Sr. Mary Ellen Barrette, G.H.M., Dir.

VALDOSTA. *St. Francis Center* (1975) P.O. Box 1331, 31601-1321. Tel: 229-242-8656; Fax: 229-244-2752. Email: jcarver@datasys.net. Mr. Dwight Carver, Dir.

WARNER ROBINS. *Sacred Heart Christian Service Center*, 251 S. Davis Dr., 31088. Tel: 478-929-3897; Fax: 478-328-3078. Email: sacredheart@cbi.magcoxmail.com. Web: www.sacredheartwr.com. Mr. Roberto Martinez-Perez, Dir.

RELIGIOUS INSTITUTES OF MEN REPRESENTED IN THE DIOCESE

For further details refer to the corresponding bracketed number in the Religious Institutes of Men or Women section.

[0200]—*Benedictine Monks* (St. Vincent Archabbey)—O.S.B.

[0240]—*Camillian Fathers & Brothers*—O.S.Cam.

[0480]—*Conventual Franciscans* (Provs. of Our Lady of Consolation & St. Anthony of Padua)—O.F.M.Conv

[0570]—*Glenmary Home Missioners* (Glendale, OH)—G.H.M

[0690]—*Jesuit Fathers & Brothers*—S.J.

[0854]—*Missionaries of St. Paul*—M.S.P.

[0840]—*Missionary Servants of Most Holy Trinity* (Dublin)—S.T.

[0780]—*Society of Mary*—S.M.

[1200]—*Society of the Divine Savior* (American Prov.)—S.D.S.

RELIGIOUS INSTITUTES OF WOMEN REPRESENTED IN THE DIOCESE

[1780]—*Congregation of the Sisters of the Third Order of St. Francis of Perpetual Adoration*—F.S.P.A.

[0760]—*Daughters of Charity of St. Vincent De Paul* (Emmitsburg, MD)—D.C.

[0420]—*Discalced Carmelite Nuns*—O.C.D.

[]—*Dominican Sisters*—O.P.

[1370]—*Franciscan Missionaries of Mary*—F.M.M.

[2080]—*Home Mission Sisters of America*—G.H.M.S.

[2690]—*Missionary Cathechists of Divine Providence*—M.C.D.P.

[1360]—*Missionary Franciscan Sisters of the Immaculate Conception*—M.F.I.C.

[3230]—*Poor Handmaids of Jesus Christ* (Indiana)—P.H.J.C.

[]—*Sisters for Christian Community*—S.F.C.C.

[]—*Sisters of Divine Providence* (San Antonio, TX)—C.D.P.

[2575]—*Sisters of Mercy of the Americas* (Baltimore, Burlingame, Erie)—R.S.M.

[3950]—*Sisters of Saint Mary of Namur*—S.S.M.N.

[3893]—*Sisters of St. Joseph* (Chestnut Hill, PA)—S.S.J.

[3840]—*Sisters of St. Joseph of Carondelet* (St. Louis, MO)—C.S.J.

[2170]—*Sisters, Servants of the Immaculate Heart of Mary*—I.H.M.

DIOCESAN CEMETERIES

SAVANNAH. *Catholic Cemetery and Properties, Catholic Pastoral Center*, 601 E. Liberty St., 31401-5196. Tel: 912-201-4100. Mr. Lawrence P. Saunders, Business Mgr.

AUGUSTA. *Catholic Cemetery*
Holy Trinity: 720 Telfair St., P.O. Box 2446, 30903. Tel: 706-722-4944.

DOUGLAS. *St. Paul's*, c/o 523 Ward St., 31533. Tel: 912-384-3560.

SYLVANIA. *Catholic Cemetery*
Our Lady of the Assumption: 121 Ridgecrest Dr., 30467. Tel: 912-564-2312.

WILLACOOCHEE. *Catholic Cemetery* Rev. Raymond G. Levreault.

NECROLOGY

(No Deaths)

An asterisk (*) denotes an organization that has established tax-exempt status directly with the IRS and is not covered by the USCCB Group Ruling.

Diocese of Scranton

(Dioecesis Scrantonensis)

Most Reverend

JOSEPH C. BAMBERA

Bishop of Scranton; ordained November 5, 1983; appointed Bishop of Scranton February 23, 2010; installed April 26, 2010.

Chancery Office: *300 Wyoming Ave., Scranton, PA 18503.* Tel: 570-207-2216; Fax: 570-207-2236.

Web: www.dioceseofscranton.org

Most Reverend

JOSEPH F. MARTINO, D.D., HIST. E.D.

Former Bishop of Scranton; ordained December 18, 1970; appointed Titular Bishop of Cellae in Mauretania and Auxiliary Bishop of Philadelphia January 24, 1996; consecrated March 11, 1996; appointed Bishop of Scranton July 25, 2003; resigned August 31, 2009. *Office: St. Charles Borromeo Seminary, 100 E. Wynnewood Rd., Wynnewood, PA 19096.*

Most Reverend

JAMES C. TIMLIN, D.D.

Bishop Emeritus of Scranton; ordained July 16, 1951; appointed Titular Bishop of Gunugo and Auxiliary Bishop of Scranton August 3, 1976; consecrated September 21, 1976; succeeded to See of Scranton April 24, 1984; installed June 7, 1984; resigned July 25, 2003. Tel: 570-343-6170.

Most Reverend

JOHN M. DOUGHERTY, D.D.

Former Auxiliary Bishop of Scranton; ordained June 15, 1957; appointed Titular Bishop of Sufetula and Auxiliary Bishop of Scranton February 7, 1995; Episcopal ordination received March 7, 1995; resigned August 31, 2009. *Office: 300 Wyoming Ave., Scranton, PA 18503.* Tel: 570-207-2216.

ESTABLISHED MARCH 3, 1868.

Square Miles 8,847.

Comprises the Counties of Luzerne, Lackawanna, Bradford, Susquehanna, Wayne, Tioga, Sullivan, Wyoming, Lycoming, Pike and Monroe in Pennsylvania.

For legal titles of parishes and diocesan institutions, consult the Chancery Office.

STATISTICAL OVERVIEW

Personnel	
Bishop	1
Retired Bishops	3
Priests: Diocesan Active in Diocese	162
Priests: Diocesan Active Outside Diocese	26
Priests: Retired, Sick or Absent	104
Number of Diocesan Priests	292
Religious Priests in Diocese	60
Total Priests in Diocese	352
Extern Priests in Diocese	16
Ordinations:	
Diocesan Priests	2
Religious Priests	1
Permanent Deacons in Diocese	65
Total Brothers	8
Total Sisters	523
Parishes	
Parishes	130
With Resident Pastor:	
Resident Diocesan Priests	125
Resident Religious Priests	5
Without Resident Pastor:	
Administered by Priests	13
Missions	54
Closed Parishes	40
Professional Ministry Personnel:	
Brothers	2
Sisters	10
Lay Ministers	35
Welfare	
Catholic Hospitals	5
Total Assisted	606,270
Health Care Centers	2
Total Assisted	118,714
Homes for the Aged	4
Total Assisted	526
Residential Care of Children	5
Total Assisted	682
Day Care Centers	9
Total Assisted	418
Specialized Homes	9
Total Assisted	1,638
Special Centers for Social Services	13
Total Assisted	211,798
Residential Care of Disabled	1
Total Assisted	155
Educational	
Diocesan Students in Other Seminaries	6
Seminaries, Religious	1
Students Religious	2
Total Seminarians	8
Colleges and Universities	4
Total Students	13,190
High Schools, Diocesan and Parish	4
Total Students	1,529
High Schools, Private	2
Total Students	924
Elementary Schools, Diocesan and Parish	21
Total Students	6,019
Non-residential Schools for the Disabled	1
Total Students	17
Catechesis/Religious Education:	
High School Students	4,885
Elementary Students	23,096
Total Students under Catholic Instruction	49,668
Teachers in the Diocese:	
Priests	4
Sisters	30
Lay Teachers	483
Vital Statistics	
Receptions into the Church:	
Infant Baptism Totals	3,484
Adult Baptism Totals	81
Received into Full Communion	111
First Communions	4,014
Confirmations	4,236
Marriages:	
Catholic	834
Interfaith	262
Total Marriages	1,096
Deaths	4,881
Total Catholic Population	323,047
Total Population	1,091,320

Former Bishops—Rt. Revs. WILLIAM O'HARA, D.D., ord. Dec. 21, 1842; First Bishop; cons. July 12, 1868; died Feb. 3, 1899; MICHAEL J. HOBAN, D.D., ord. May 22, 1880; Second Bishop; cons. Coadjutor, March 22, 1896; succeeded to See, Feb. 3, 1899; died Nov. 13, 1926; Most Revs. THOMAS C. O'REILLY, D.D., Third Bishop; ord. June 4, 1898; elected Dec. 19, 1927,; cons. Feb. 16, 1928; installed March 8, 1928; died March 25, 1938; WILLIAM J. HAFEY, D.D., Fourth Bishop; ord. June 16, 1914; appt. First Bishop of Raleigh, April 6, 1925; cons. June 24, 1925; transferred to Scranton as Coadjutor cum jure successionis and Apostolic Administrator, Oct. 2, 1937; succeeded to See, March 25, 1938; died May 12, 1954; JEROME D. HANNAN, D.D., Fifth Bishop; ord. May 22, 1921; appt. August 17, 1954; cons. Sept. 21, 1954; died Dec. 15, 1965; J. CARROLL MCCORMICK, D.D., Sixth Bishop; ord. July 10, 1932; appt. Titular Bishop of Ruspae and Auxiliary of Philadelphia, Jan. 11, 1947; cons. April 23, 1947; appt. Bishop of Altoona-Johnstown, June 25, 1960; transferred to the See of Scranton, March 4, 1966; installed May 25, 1966; retired Feb. 15, 1983; died Nov. 2, 1996; JOHN J. O'CONNOR, D.D., Seventh Bishop; ord. Dec. 15, 1945; appt. Titular Bishop of Cuzola and Auxiliary Bishop to the Military Vicar April 24, 1979; cons. May 27, 1979; appt. Bishop of Scranton, May 10, 1983; installed June 29, 1983; transferred to the See of New York, Jan. 31, 1984; died May 3, 2000; JAMES C. TIMLIN, D.D. (Retired), Eighth Bishop; ord. July 16, 1951; appt. Titular Bishop of Gunugo and Auxiliary Bishop of Scranton Aug. 3, 1976; cons. Sept. 21, 1976; succeeded to See of Scranton April 24, 1984; installed June 7, 1984; resigned July 25, 2003; JOSEPH F. MARTINO, D.D., Hist. E.D. (Retired), Ninth Bishop; ord. Dec. 18, 1970; appt. Titular Bishop of Cellae in Mauretania and Auxiliary Bishop of Philadelphia Jan. 24, 1996; cons. March 11, 1996; appt. Bishop of Scranton July 25, 2003; resigned Aug. 31, 2009.

Vicar General—VACANT.

Chancery Office—300 Wyoming Ave., Scranton, 18503-1279. Tel: 570-207-2216; Fax: 570-207-2236.

Moderator of the Curia—VACANT.

Episcopal Vicars—Rev. PHILIP A. ALTAVILLA, M.Th., V.E., Northern Pastoral Region. Tel: 570-587-5191; Rev. Msgr. NEIL J. VAN LOON, V.E., Western Pastoral Region. Tel: 570-326-4285; Revs. MARK G. BALCZENIUK, V.E., Eastern Pastoral Region. Tel: 570-243-4608; JOHN V. POLEDNAK, V.E., Southern Pastoral Region. Tel: 570-650-0954.

Chancellor—JAMES B. EARLEY. Tel: 570-207-2216; Fax: 570-207-2236.

Vice Chancellor—Rev. BRIAN J.W. CLARKE, J.C.L.

Diocesan Financial Office—ROBERT J. MILLER, Dir. Tel: 570-207-2237.

Diocesan Tribunal—300 Wyoming Ave., Scranton, 18503-1279. Tel: 570-207-2246; Fax: 570-207-2274. Direct all inquiries concerning marriage nullity, dispensations and permissions to this office.

Judicial Vicar—Rev. Msgr. ANTHONY J. GENEROSE, V.E., J.C.L.

Coordinator—JOSEPH V. FOX.

Judges—Most Rev. JOSEPH C. BAMBERA; Rev. BRIAN J.T. CLARKE, J.C.L.; CHARLES J. REID, J.D., J.C.L.; LINDA E. PRICE, J.C.L.

Defenders of the Bond—Rev. Msgrs. JOSEPH G. QUINN, J.D., J.C.L.; JOHN H. LOUIS, S.T.L., J.C.D.; Rev. JAMES J. WALSH, J.C.L.

Promoter of Justice—Rev. FRANCIS J. MARINI, J.D., J.C.O.D.

Auditors—JOSEPH A. BARRETT, Ph.D.; JOSEPH V. FOX.

Procurator/Advocates—JOSEPH V. FOX; Mr. TIMOTHY FERGUSON, J.C.L.; Rev. Msgr. PATRICK J. PRATICO, J.C.D.; Rev. PHILIP A. ALTAVILLA, M.Th., V.E.

Psychological Expert—JOSEPH A. BARRETT, Ph.D.

Notaries—ANN WALSH; JOSETTE JORDAN; PATRICIA VANCOSKY.

Diocesan Finance Council—Rev. Msgr. Vincent J. Grimalia; Revs. Thomas D. McLaughlin; Richard J. Polmounter; Joseph R. Kopacz; John H. Graham; James E. O'Brien Jr., Esq.; Mr. Frank Pellegrino; Carlon E. Preate; Josephine M. Rudick; Robert J. Miller; Frank Byrne; James B. Earley; Sr. Therese O'Rourke, I.H.M.

Diocesan Consultors—Most Rev. Joseph C. Bambera; Rev. Msgrs. Peter P. Madus; Vincent J. Grimalia; Neil J. Van Loon, V.E.; Revs. Charles J. Cummings (Retired); Joseph J. Manarchuck; Michael F. Quinnan; Philip A. Altavilla, M.Th., V.E.; Richard J. Loch, V.E.; Joseph R. Kopacz.

Ex Officio—Rev. Christopher T. Washington, S.T.L.

Diocesan Pastoral Council— Contact: Vacant, 300 Wyoming Ave., Scranton, 18503-1279. Tel: 570-207-2216.

Deans—Rev. Msgrs. John J. Bendik, Northern Luzerne; David L. Tressler, V.F., Mid-Valley/ Lackawanna; Revs. Richard J. Cirba, Southern Luzerne; Andrew S. Hvozdovic, Bradford/ Sullivan/Susquehanna; Charles J. Cummings, Lycoming/Tioga (Retired); John M. Lapera, Western Luzerne; Thomas D. McLaughlin, Monroe; Rev. Msgrs. William J. Feldcamp, V.E., Dunmore; Francis J. Callahan, Wilkes-Barre; Revs. August A. Ricciardi, Wayne/Pike; Samuel J. Ferretti, Scranton.

Presbyteral Council—Vacant.

Diocesan Building Commission— All plans for building should be sent to Chancery Office, *300 Wyoming Ave., Scranton, 18503-1279*. Rev. Msgr. Philip A. Gray (Retired); Revs. Joseph A. Greskiewicz; John M. Lapera; Al Brocavich; James Devers; John Pocius; Thomas Considine. Ex Officio: James B. Earley; Robert J. Miller; Frank M. Semanski.

Vicar for Administration—Vacant.

Episcopal Vicar for Priests—Rev. Richard J. Loch, V.E., 300 Wyoming Ave., Scranton, 18503-1279. Tel: 570-207-2269.

Vicar for Consecrated Life—Rev. Msgr. Anthony J. Generose, V.E., J.C.L. (pro tem) 300 Wyoming Ave., Scranton, 18503-1279. Tel: 570-207-2243.

Diocesan Offices and Directors

Blue Army of Our Lady of Fatima—Very Rev. Paul A. McDonnell, O.S.J., Spiritual Dir. Tel: 570-654-7542; Vacant, Chap.; Mr. John Witkosky.

Catholic Campaign for Human Development—David Clarke, Dir., Office of Parish Ministries, 400 Wyoming Ave., Scranton, 18503.

Campus Ministry—Sr. Catherine Ann Gilvary, I.H.M., Dir., Mailing Address: Lycoming College, 700 College Pl., Box 149, Williamsport, 17701. Tel: 570-321-4111; Fax: 570-321-4337.

Catholic Charismatic Renewal—Rev. Richard J. Loch, V.E., Spiritual Advisor; Robert Valiante, Coord., Mailing Address: P.O. Box 3306, Scranton, 18505. Tel: 570-344-2214.

Catholic Relief Services—James B. Earley, Chancellor, 300 Wyoming Ave., Scranton, 18503-1279. Tel: 570-207-2216.

Catholic Social Services—Rev. Msgr. Joseph P. Kelly, V.E., Sec. for Catholic Human Svcs. & Exec. Dir., 33 E. Northampton St., Wilkes-Barre, 18701. Tel: 570-822-7118; Fax: 570-829-7781.

Lackawanna County—

Scranton Office—Mr. Stephen R. Nocilla, M.A., Exec. Dir., 516 Fig St., Scranton, 18505-1753. Tel: 570-207-2283; Fax: 570-207-2206. Res.: 409-411 Olive St., Scranton, 18509. Tel: 570-342-1295; Fax: 570-341-6623.

Carbondale Office—*39 S. Main St., Carbondale, 18407*. Tel: 570-282-0460.

Luzerne County—

Wyoming Valley Office—Ronald G. Evans, Exec. Dir., 33 E. Northampton St., Wilkes-Barre, 18701. Tel: 570-822-7118; Fax: 570-829-7781.

Hazleton Office—Mr. Neil Oberto, M.A., Exec. Dir., 214 W. Walnut St., Hazleton, 18201. Tel: 570-455-1521; Fax: 570-455-2707.

Lycoming County—

Williamsport Office—Mr. Bernard Makos, L.S.W., Case Worker, 2110 Linn St., Williamsport, 17701. Tel: 570-322-4220.

Monroe County—

Stroudsburg Office—Sr. Vincentia Dorsey, I.H.M., Office Supvr., 411 Main St., Stroudsburg, 18360. Tel: 570-476-6460; Fax: 570-476-6466.

Pike County—

Milford Office—Erin Bustelos, Rte. 6, P.O. Box 1195, Milford, 18337. Tel: 570-296-1054; Fax: 570-296-9227.

Tioga County—

Wellsboro Office—Mr. Bernard Makos, L.S.W., 3892 Lambs Creek Rd., Mansfield, 16933. Tel: 570-662-7788; Fax: 570-662-7337.

Wayne County—

Honesdale Office—Joe Walsh, Case Worker, 414 Church St., Honesdale, 18431. Tel: 570-253-1777.

Natural Family Planning Coordinator—Brendan Murphy, Dir. Family Life, Marriage Prep. & Adult Formation, 400 Wyoming Ave., Scranton, 18503. Tel: 570-207-2213, Ext. 1133.

Cemeteries—Kevin Beck, Dir., 1708 Oram St., Scranton, 18504. Tel: 570-207-2209.

Censor Librorum—Rev. Charles P. Connor, c/o 300 Wyoming Ave., Scranton, 18503. Tel: 570-207-2216.

Cursillo Movement—Rev. Phillip J. Sladicka, Spiritual Moderator, St. Mary Rectory, 715 Hawthorne St., Avoca, 18641. Tel: 570-457-3412.

Diocesan Commission on Ethics for Catholic Health Care Facilities—Vacant.

Diocesan Commission on Ecumenism and Inter-Faith Matters—Rev. Philip A. Altavilla, M.Th., V.E., Diocesan Dir., Our Lady of the Snows Rectory, 301 S. State St., Clarks Summit, 18411. Tel: 570-587-5191.

Diocesan Facilities Manager—Frank M. Semanski, 300 Wyoming Ave., Scranton, 18503. Tel: 570-207-2232; Fax: 570-207-2273.

Diocesan Historian—Rev. Charles P. Connor, c/o Chancery Office, 300 Wyoming Ave., Scranton, 18503. Tel: 570-207-2216.

Diocesan Office for Communications—Mr. William R. Genello, Exec. Dir., 300 Wyoming Ave., Scranton, 18503-1272. Tel: 570-207-2219; 800-246-0288; Fax: 570-207-2281.

Diocesan Compliance Officer—Ms. Gail Fromm, 300 Wyoming Ave., Scranton, 18503. Tel: 570-207-2214; Fax: 570-207-2273.

Diocesan Office of Development—Frank Byrne, Dir., 300 Wyoming Ave., Scranton, 18503-1279. Tel: 570-207-2250; Fax: 570-207-1835.

Diocesan Appeal Office—Frank Byrne, Dir., 300 Wyoming Ave., Scranton, 18503-1279. Tel: 570-207-2250; Fax: 570-207-1835.

Diocese of Scranton Catholic Community Foundation—Frank Byrne, Dir., 300 Wyoming Ave., Scranton, 18503-1279. Tel: 570-207-2250; Fax: 570-207-1835.

Diocese of Scranton Scholarship Foundation—Frank Byrne, Dir., 300 Wyoming Ave., Scranton, 18503-1279. Tel: 570-207-2250; Fax: 570-207-1835.

Diocesan Office of Ecumenism—Rev. Philip A. Altavilla, M.Th., V.E., Dir., Our Lady of the Snows Rectory, 301 S. State St., Clarks Summit, 18411. Tel: 570-587-5191.

Diocesan Office for Parish Life and Evangelization—David Clarke, Acting Sec., Parish Life and Evangelization; Rev. Christopher T. Washington, S.T.L., Dir., Office for Worship; Sarah Mountain, Youth & Young Adult Ministry Dir.; Christopher Tigue, Dir, C.Y.O.; Brendan Murphy, Family Life Dir.; David Clarke, Social Concerns Dir., 400 Wyoming Ave., Scranton, 18503-1279. Tel: 570-207-2213.

Fatima Renewal Center—Sarah Mountain, Prog. Dir., 1000 Seminary Rd., Dalton, 18414. Tel: 570-563-8510.

Ministry for Persons with Disabilities—Sr. Mary Beth Makuch, SS.C.M., Dir., 400 Wyoming Ave., Scranton, 18503-1272. Tel: 570-207-2213.

Ministry with Deaf and Hard of Hearing—Sr. Mary Beth Makuch, SS.C.M., Dir.; Rev. Joseph G. Elston, Chap., 300 Wyoming Ave., Scranton, 18503-1272. Tel: 570-207-2213. Audiovisual Resource Center. Tel: 570-207-2284.

Diocesan Pro-Life Office—David Clarke, Diocesan Dir., 400 Wyoming Ave., Scranton, 18503-1279. Tel: 570-207-2213.

Pastoral Formation Institute—Mary Anne Malone, Dir., 400 Wyoming Ave., Scranton, 18503. Tel: 570-207-2213.

Religious Education—Mary Anne Malone, Dir., 400 Wyoming Ave., Scranton, 18503-1272. Tel: 570-207-2213.

Risk Management Office—*300 Wyoming Ave., Scranton, 18503*. Tel: 570-558-4310; Fax: 570-558-4311. Thomas Considine, Mgr. Tel: 570-558-4310, Ext. 1002; Sharon Porcello, Sec. Tel: 570-558-4310, Ext. 1015.

Consecrated Life Office—Rev. Msgr. Anthony J. Generose, V.E., J.C.L., Dir.

Hispanic Ministry Outreach—Rev. Msgr. Joseph P. Kelly, V.E., Episcopal Vicar, Catholic Social Services, 33 E. Northampton St., Wilkes Barre, 18701. Tel: 570-822-7118; Sr. Jacqueline Servick, I.H.M.; Alejandra Marroquin, c/o Nativity of Our Lord, 633 Orchard St., Scranton, 18505. Tel: 570-558-0848; Revs. John C. Ruth, Coord. Hispanic Min. Lackawanna County, 430 Pittston Ave., Scranton, 18505. Tel: 570-961-2297; Joseph R. Kopacz, Coord. Hispanic Min. Monroe County, c/o St. Mary of the Mount, 27 Fairview Ave., Mount Pocono, 18344. Tel: 570-839-7138; Albert Bellantonio, Mailing Address: c/o St. Ann, Main St., P.O. Box 188, Tobyhanna, 18466. Tel: 570-894-8018; Sr. Joel Marie Sheehe, I.H.M., Mailing Address: c/o St. Ann, Main St., P.O. Box 188, Tobyhanna, 18466. Tel: 570-894-8018; Rev. Victor Leon, O.S.J., c/o St. Gabriel, 122 S. Wyoming St., Hazleton, 18201. Tel: 570-454-0212.

Holy Childhood Association—Deacon Edward T. Kelly, Dir.; Miriam Heverline, Mission Educ. Coord., 300 Wyoming Ave., Scranton, 18503-1279. Tel: 570-207-2259; Fax: 570-207-2268.

Holy Name Society—Vacant, Spiritual Advisor.

Legion of Mary—Rev. David W. Cramer, Spiritual Dir., Mailing Address: St. Lawrence Rectory, 380 Franklin St., P.O. Box 592, Great Bend, 18821. Tel: 570-267-1366.

Liturgical Commission—Vacant.

Marriage Encounter—Vacant, Spiritual Advisor. Contact: Diane Zindell; Ed Zindell, 14 Evergreen Dr., Jermyn, 18433. Tel: 570-876-1610. Email: dz916@echoes.net.

D.C.C.M.—Vacant, Spiritual Moderator. Contact: David Clarke, Dir. Social Concerns. Tel: 570-207-2213, Ext. 1130.

D.C.C.W.—Vacant, Spiritual Moderator. Contact: David Clarke, Dir. Social Concerns. Tel: 570-207-2213, Ext. 1130.

Newspaper— "The Catholic Light" Mr. William R. Genello, Editor, 300 Wyoming Ave., Scranton, 18503-1279. Tel: 570-207-2229; 570-207-2272; Fax: 570-207-2271.

Office of Pastoral Planning—Rev. Msgr. Vincent J. Grimalia, Dir. Called to Holiness and Mission. Tel: 570-207-1452; Fax: 570-207-1833. Email: calledtoholinessandmission@dioceseofscranton.org.

Diocesan Television Station-CTV—Mr. William R. Genello, Exec. Dir.; James Brennan, Mgr., 400 Wyoming Ave., Scranton, 18503-1272. Tel: 570-207-2219; Fax: 570-207-2281.

Permanent Diaconate Office—Rev. Msgr. David A. Bohr, S.T.D., Dir., St. Peter's Cathedral, 315 Wyoming Ave., Scranton, 18503. Tel: 570-344-7231.

Pilgrimages—Vacant.

Priests' Purgatorial Society—Rev. Richard J. Loch, V.E., Sec., 300 Wyoming Ave., Scranton, 18503-1279. Tel: 570-207-2269.

Priests' Retirement Advisory Board—Revs. Richard J. Loch, V.E.; Walter F. Skiba (Retired); James R. Nash; Scott P. Sterowski; Andrew R. Sinnott; James B. Earley; Robert J. Miller.

Propagation of the Faith—Deacon Edward T. Kelly, Dir.; Miriam Heverline, Mission Educ. Coord., 300 Wyoming Ave., Scranton, 18503-1279. Tel: 570-207-2259; Fax: 570-207-2268. Email: miriam-heverline@dioceseofscranton.org.

Retirement Fund for Religious—Rev. Msgr. Anthony J. Generose, V.E., J.C.L., Dir. Tel: 570-207-1452; 570-207-2243.

Schools—Kathleen P. Hanlon, Acting Sec., Catholic Schools & Supt. of Schools. Tel: 570-207-2251; Mrs. Mary C. Tigue, Asst. Supt. Schools, 300 Wyoming Ave., Scranton, 18503. Tel: 570-207-2251; Patrick Cawley, Asst. Supt. Govt. Programs. Tel: 570-207-2235.

Regional School Systems—

Holy Cross Regional School System of the Diocese of Scranton, Inc.—Kathleen P. Hanlon, System Dir., 638 Hemlock St., Scranton, 18505. Tel: 570-342-1955. Mailing Address: c/o 300 Wyoming Ave., Scranton, 18503.

Holy Redeemer Regional School System of the Diocese of Scranton, Inc.—Kathleen P. Hanlon, System Dir., 316 N. Maple Ave., Kingston, 18704. Tel: 570-714-9611. Mailing Address: c/o 300 Wyoming Ave., Scranton, 18503.

Notre Dame Regional School System of the Diocese of Scranton, Inc.—Vacant, System Dir., 60 Spangenberg Ave., East Stroudsburg, 18301. Tel: 570-421-0466. Mailing Address: c/o 300 Wyoming Ave., Scranton, 18503.

Saint John Neumann Regional School System of the Diocese of Scranton, Inc.—Mrs. Susan Kaiser, System Dir., 901 Penn St., Williamsport, 17701. Tel: 570-323-9953. Mailing Address: c/o 300 Wyoming Ave., Scranton, 18503.

Scouts of America—Rev. Thomas M. Muldowney, Chap., St. Patrick Rectory, 200 Delaware Ave., Olyphant, 18447. Tel: 570-489-0752.

Victim Assistance Coordinator—Joan L. Holmes. Tel: 570-344-5216. Email: joan_holmes@verizon.net.

VIRTUS—Ms. Gail Fromm, Safe Environment Prog. Coord., 300 Wyoming Ave., Scranton, 18503. Tel: 570-207-2214; Fax: 570-207-2273.

Diocesan Office for Clergy Formation—Rev. Msgr. Vincent J. Grimalia, Dir., 300 Wyoming Ave., Scranton, 18503. Tel: 570-207-1452.

Vocations—Rev. Christopher T. Washington, S.T.L., Dir., 300 Wyoming Ave., Scranton, 18503. Tel: 570-207-2216.

CLERGY, PARISHES, MISSIONS AND PAROCHIAL SCHOOLS

CITY OF SCRANTON

(LACKAWANNA COUNTY)

1—ST. PETER'S CATHEDRAL (1853) Rev. Msgr. David A. Bohr; Deacon Edward R. Shoener. In Res., Most Rev. John M. Dougherty (Retired); Rev. Msgr. Vincent J. Grimalia; Revs. Christopher T. Washington; Brian J.W. Clarke.
Res.: 315 Wyoming Ave., 18503. Tel: 570-344-7231; Fax: 570-344-4749. Email: info@stpeterscathedral.org.
Convent—333 Wyoming, 18503. Tel: 570-344-9725.

2—ST. ANN'S BASILICA PARISH (1901) Revs. Francis Landry, C.P.; Michael Salvagna, C.P.
Res.: 1250 St. Ann St., 18504. Tel: 570-342-5166; Fax: 570-348-3750.
Catechesis/Religious Program—Tel: 570-344-8408. Katherine Stocki, D.R.E. Students 160.

3—ST. ANTHONY OF PADUA (1913), (Italian), Merged with St. Joseph, Scranton & Holy Rosary, Scranton. Rev. Cyril D. Edwards.
Mailing Address: *c/o Holy Rosary*, 316 William St., 18508. Tel: 570-342-4881; Fax: 570-342-4881.
Catechesis/Religious Program—Students 47.

4—ST. CLARE (1967), Restructured with St. Paul Scranton. Rev. Msgr. William J. Feldcamp.
c/o 1510 Penn Ave., 18509. Tel: 570-961-1549; Fax: 570-961-0335. In Res., Rev. Eric L. Bergman.

5—ST. DAVID'S (1946) Closed. For all inquiries see St. Patrick's, Scranton.

6—DIVINE MERCY (1875) [CEM], Restructured with Immaculate Conception, St. John the Baptist, Taylor & St. Mary Czestochowa, Moosic. Rev. Francis L. Pauselli.
Res.: 312 Davis St., 18505. Tel: 570-344-1724; Fax: 570-344-1787.
Catechesis/Religious Program—Nancy Mott, D.R.E. Students 265.

7—ST. FRANCIS (1920), (Italian), Consolidated - now part of St. Paul of the Cross Parish. Rev. Scott P. Sterowski.
c/o 1217 Prospect Ave., 18505. Tel: 570-343-6420; Fax: 570-343-3664.
Catechesis/Religious Program—Mary Ann Lucchi, D.R.E. Students 96.

8—HOLY FAMILY (1891) [CEM], Linked with St. Peter's Cathedral, Scranton Rev. Msgr. David A. Bohr.
Office: 510 E. Gibson St., 18509. Tel: 570-342-8548; Fax: 570-342-2581.
Catechesis/Religious Program—Mary Jule Kapacs, D.R.E. Students 21.

9—HOLY NAME OF JESUS (1938) Closed. Now part of St. John Neumann, Scranton.

10—HOLY ROSARY (1871), Restructured with St. Joseph, Scranton and St. Anthony of Padua, Scranton. Rev. Cyril D. Edwards.
Res.: 316 William St., 18508. Tel: 570-342-4881; Fax: 570-344-2130.

11—IMMACULATE CONCEPTION (1967), Restructured with Christ the King, Dunmore. Revs. Patrick J. McLaughlin; Joseph F. Sica. In Res., Rev. Edward F. Barrett.
Res.: 801 Taylor Ave., 18510. Tel: 570-961-5211; Fax: 570-961-0878.
Catechesis/Religious Program—Sandy Czyzyk, D.R.E. Students 271.

12—ST. JOHN THE EVANGELIST (1886) Closed. For inquiries for parish records please contact St. Paul of the Cross Parish, Scranton.

13—ST. JOSEPH'S (1894), (Lithuanian), [CEM], Merged with St. Anthony of Padua, Scranton and Holy Rosary, Scranton. Rev. Cyril D. Edwards.
Res.: c/o 316 William St., 18508. Tel: 570-342-4881; Fax: 570-342-4881.
Catechesis/Religious Program—Students 35.

14—ST. JOSEPH'S (1875) [CEM] Merged Restructured with Immaculate Conception & St. Mary of Czestochowa, Greenwood. For inquiries for parish records please contact Divine Mercy, Scranton.

15—ST. LUCY'S (1901), (Italian), Merged with SS. Peter & Paul, Scranton. Rev. Samuel J. Ferretti; Deacon Steven J. Napoli. In Res., Rev. Richard J. Loch.
Res.: 949 Scranton St., 18504. Tel: 570-347-9421; Fax: 570-341-8252. Web: stlucy-church.org.
Catechesis/Religious Program—Students 61.

16—ST. MARY CZESTOCHOWA (1904), (Polish), [CEM] Merged with churches in Taylor, PA. Now part of Divine Mercy Parish, Scranton.

17—ST. MARY OF THE ASSUMPTION (1854), (German), [CEM 2], Restructured with Holy Name of Jesus, Scranton. Consolidated, now known as St. John Neumann, Scranton. Rev. John C. Ruth.
Res.: 430 Pittston Ave., 18505. Tel: 570-961-2297; Fax: 570-961-1468.
Catechesis/Religious Program—Marie Merkel, D.R.E. Students 142.

18—ST. MICHAEL'S (1914), (Lithuanian), Revs. Michael O'Leary, F.S.S.P., Admin.; Dennis Gordon, F.S.S.P. In Res., Rev. Edmund A. Castronovo.
Res.: 1703 Jackson St., 18504. Tel: 570-961-1205; Fax: 570-961-2284. Email: stmichael@epix.net. Web: www.saintmichaelsrcc.org.

19—NATIVITY OF OUR LORD, Merged Restructured with Holy Name of Mary, Scranton & St. Mary of the Assumption, Scranton. For inquiries for parish records contact St. John Neumann, Scranton.

20—ST. PATRICK'S (1870) Rev. Peter J. O'Rourke. Restructured with St. David, Scranton. In Res., Rev. Msgr. Arthur J. Kaschenbach (Retired); Rev. James J. Walsh.
Res.: 1403 Jackson St., 18504. Tel: 570-344-2679; 570-343-4353; Fax: 570-343-2835. Email: stpatrick-scr@yahoo.com.
Catechesis/Religious Program—Linda Sepkowski, D.R.E. Students 450.
Chapel—Scranton, Immaculate Heart of Mary 1605 Oram St., 18504.

21—SAINT PAUL OF THE CROSS, SCRANTON (1885), (Polish), [CEM], Merged with St. John the Evangelist & St. Francis of Assisi, Scranton. Rev. Scott P. Sterowski.
1149 Providence Rd., 18505.
Res.: 1217 Prospect Ave., 18505. Tel: 570-343-6420; Fax: 570-343-3664.
Catechesis/Religious Program—Students 7.

22—ST. PAUL'S (1887), Restructured with St. Clare, Scranton. Rev. Msgr. William J. Feldcamp. In Res., Rev. Msgr. Michael J. Delaney; Rev. Jeffrey J. Walsh.
Res.: 1510 Penn Ave., 18509. Tel: 570-961-1549; Fax: 570-961-0335. Email: saintpaulsrectory@yahoo.com.
Catechesis/Religious Program—Jeanne Evans, D.R.E. Students 74.

23—SS. PETER AND PAUL (1910), (Polish), [CEM], Restructured with St. Lucy, Scranton. Rev. Samuel J. Ferretti.
Res.: 1309 W. Locust St., 18504. Tel: 570-343-7015; Fax: 570-343-7023. Email: ssppscr@verizon.net.
Catechesis/Religious Program—Christina Wasko, D.R.E. Students 23.

24—SACRED HEARTS OF JESUS AND MARY, Merged with St. John the Evangelist & St. Francis of Assisi, Scranton. See Saint Paul of the Cross, Scranton.

25—SAINT JOHN NEUMANN, SCRANTON (1903), Reconstructed with Holy Name of Mary, & St. Mary of the Assumption, Scranton. Rev. Michael Bryant; Deacon Joseph Donovan. In Res., Rev. William B. Pickard.
Res.: 633 Orchard St., 18505. Tel: 570-344-6159; Fax: 570-207-4932.
Catechesis/Religious Program—Maria Revesz, D.R.E. Students 165.

26—ST. VINCENT DE PAUL (1925) Closed. For inquiries for parish records contact the chancery. Merged with St. Joseph, Scranton & St. Anthony of Padua, Scranton.

OUTSIDE THE CITY OF SCRANTON

ARCHBALD, LACKAWANNA CO., ST. THOMAS AQUINAS (1858) [CEM], Restructured with St. Mary of Czestochowa, Eynon. Rev. Christopher S. Sahd, Admin.; Deacon Edward T. Kelly.
411 Church St., 18403.
Res.: 429 Church St., 18403. Tel: 570-876-1701; Fax: 570-876-3617. Email: st.tom@comcast.net.
Catechesis/Religious Program—Tel: 570-876-1411. Anne Walker, D.R.E. Students 338.

ASHLEY, LUZERNE CO.

1—HOLY ROSARY (1900), (Slovak), Closed. For inquiries for parish records please see St. Leo's, Ashley.

2—ST. LEO'S (1887) Rev. Thomas J. O'Malley.
Res.: 33 Manhattan St., 18706. Tel: 570-825-6669; Fax: 570-825-3055.
Catechesis/Religious Program—Michele Casey, D.R.E. Students 175.

ATHENS, BRADFORD CO., ST. JOSEPH (1852) Merged with St. John the Evangelist, South Waver. Linked with Epiphany. Sayre.

AVOCA, LUZERNE CO.

1—ST. MARY'S (1871) [CEM] Rev. Phillip J. Sladicka.
Res.: 715 Hawthorne St., 18641. Tel: 570-457-3412; Fax: 570-655-8218. Email: stmarysavoca@verizon.net.
Catechesis/Religious Program—Anthony Gueriglia, D.R.E. Students 77.

2—SS. PETER AND PAUL (1909), (Polish), [CEM] Rev. Phillip J. Sladicka.
Res.: 912 Vine St., 18641. Tel: 570-457-2483; 570-457-9806 (Auditorium); Fax: 570-451-2993. Email: ssppch@verizon.net.
Catechesis/Religious Program—Debby Yuschovitz, D.R.E. Students 60.

BASTRESS, LYCOMING CO., IMMACULATE CONCEPTION OF THE BLESSED VIRGIN MARY (1847), (German), [CEM] Rev. Msgr. Neil J. Van Loon, Admin.; Rev. Albert J. Leonard. Restructured with St. Luke, Jersey Shore.
Res.: 5973 Jacks Hollow Rd., Williamsport, 17702. Tel: 570-745-3301.
Catechesis/Religious Program—Students 125.

BEAR CREEK , LUZERNE CO.

1—ST. CHRISTOPHER (1962) Merged with Holy Saviour, Wilkes-Barre.

2—ST. ELIZABETH (1938) Rev. W. Jeffrey Paulish.
5700 Bear Creek Blvd., P.O. Box 25, 18602. Tel: 570-472-3061.
Catechesis/Religious Program—Theresa Kulakowski, D.R.E. Students 83.
Mission—St. Mark Thornhurst, Luzerne Co.

BENTLEY CREEK, BRADFORD CO., ST. ANN'S (1843) [CEM] Closed. Restructured with Epiphany, Sayre. For inquiries for parish records please see Epiphany, Sayre.

BLAKESLEE, MONROE CO., CHRIST THE KING (1976) Closed. For inquiries for parish records please see St. Maximilian Kolbe, Pocono Pines.

BLOSSBURG, TIOGA CO.

1—ST. JOHN NEUMANN, (Restructured with Holy Child, Mansfield) Rev. Jacek J. Bialkowski, Admin.
Office: c/o Holy Child Rectory, 237 S. Main St., Mansfield, 16933.

2—ST. MARY'S (1874), (Polish), [CEM 3] Closed. For inquiries for parish records contact Holy Child, Mansfield.

BRODHEADSVILLE, MONROE CO., OUR LADY QUEEN OF PEACE (1968) Revs. Michael F. Quinnan; Sean G. Carpenter; Deacon Robert A. O'Connor Jr.
Res.: Box 38, 18322. Tel: 610-681-6137; Fax: 610-681-6139.
Catechesis/Religious Program—Jacqueline Douglas, D.R.E. Students 889.

CANADENSIS, MONROE CO., ST. BERNADETTE (1967) Rev. Edward L. Michelini; Deacon Ronald P. Verkon.
Res.: Rte. 390, P.O. Box 14, 18325. Tel: 570-595-2139.
Catechesis/Religious Program—Dorothy Lewis, D.R.E. Students 121.
Mission—Our Lady of Fatima, Closed., State Park, Promised Land, Monroe Co.

CANTON, BRADFORD CO., ST. MICHAEL (1853) [CEM], Restructured with SS. Peter and Paul, Towanda. Revs. Martin M. Boylan; Gregory T. Villaescusa; Deacon William H. Graham.
Res.: 24 N. Washington St., 17724. Tel: 570-673-5253; Fax: 570-673-5630.
Catechesis/Religious Program—Deacon William H. Graham, D.R.E. Students 51.
Mission—St. John Nepomucene [CEM] Troy, Bradford Co. Tel: 570-297-4405.
Mission—St. Aloysius Ralston, Lycoming Co.

CARBONDALE, LACKAWANNA CO.

1—OUR LADY OF MT. CARMEL (1882), (Italian), [CEM] Rev. Russell E. Motsay.
Res.: 15 Fallbrook St., 18407. Tel: 570-282-5172.
Catechesis/Religious Program—Students 59.

2—ST. ROSE OF LIMA (1832) [CEM 2] Rev. Msgr. David L. Tressler; Rev. William D. Campbell; Deacon Edward Casey.
Res.: 6 N. Church St., 18407. Tel: 570-282-2991; Fax: 570-282-7580.
Catechesis/Religious Program—Patricia Dragwa, D.R.E. Students 241.

CARVERTON, LUZERNE CO., ST. FRANCES CABRINI (1947) Rev. Vincent H. Dang. In Res., Rev. Donald J. Williams.
Res.: 585 Mt. Olivet Rd., Kingston Twp., Wyoming, 18644-9333. Tel: 570-696-3737; Fax: 570-696-3737.
Catechesis/Religious Program—Students 50.
Mission—Blessed Sacrament, Closed., Centermoreland, Luzerne Co.

CLARKS GREEN, LACKAWANNA CO., ST. GREGORY (1974) Rev. Msgr. John H. Louis.
Res.: 330 N. Abington Rd., 18411. Tel: 570-587-4808; Fax: 570-586-4515. Email: churchofstgreg@yahoo.com.
Catechesis/Religious Program—Joanne Judge, D.R.E. Students 503.

CLARKS SUMMIT, LACKAWANNA CO., OUR LADY OF THE SNOWS (1911) Rev. Msgr. James J. McGarry; Rev. John C. O'Bell; Deacon Leo L. Lynn. In Res., Rev. Philip A. Altavilla.
Res.: 301 S. State St., 18411. Tel: 570-586-1741; Fax: 570-586-2504. Email: ols2@epix.net.
Catechesis/Religious Program—Nettie Goldate, D.R.E. Students 1,473.
Mission—St. Benedict Newton, Lackawanna Co.

CONYNGHAM, LUZERNE CO., ST. JOHN BOSCO (1964), Restructured with Good Shephard Drums. Revs. John C. Lambert; Connell A. McHugh.
Res.: 2 Charles Ave., P.O. Box 919, 18219. Tel: 570-788-1997; Fax: 570-788-6667.
Church: 573 State Rte. 93.
Catechesis/Religious Program—Robert Rock, D.R.E. Students 400.

DALLAS, LUZERNE CO., GATE OF HEAVEN (1951), Linked with Our Lady of Victory, Harveys Lake. Rev. Daniel A. Toomey; Deacon Thomas M. Cesarini.
Res.: 40 Machell Ave., 18612. Tel: 570-675-2121; Fax: 570-675-7143. Email: goh@epix.net.
Catechesis/Religious Program—Tel: 570-675-6488. Sonya Cesarini, D.R.E. Students 310.

DALTON, LACKAWANNA CO., OUR LADY OF THE ABINGTONS (1967) Rev. Kevin P. Mulhern.
Res.: 700 W. Main St., 18414. Tel: 570-563-1622; Fax: 570-563-0988.
Catechesis/Religious Program—Jacque Petherick, D.R.E. Students 235.

DICKSON CITY, LACKAWANNA CO.
1—ST. THOMAS THE APOSTLE, Closed. For inquiries for parish records please see Visitation of the Blessed Virgin Mary.
2—VISITATION OF THE BLESSED VIRGIN MARY (1890), (Polish), [CEM], Merged with St. Thomas the Apostle, Dickson City. Rev. Msgr. Patrick J. Pratico. In Res., Rev. Joseph C. Rusin (Retired).
Res.: 1090 Carmalt St., 18519. Tel: 570-489-2091; Fax: 570-489-0349.
Catechesis/Religious Program—Marie Piela, D.R.E. Students 145.

DORRANCE, LUZERNE CO., OUR LADY HELP OF CHRISTIANS (1948), (Polish), [CEM] Rev. Mark A. Honhart.
Res.: 3529 St. Mary's Rd. (Dorrance), Wapwallopen, 18660-1901. Tel: 570-868-5855; Fax: 570-868-5876.
Catechesis/Religious Program—Mrs. Patricia Heller, D.R.E. Students 104.

DRUMS, LUZERNE CO., CHURCH OF THE GOOD SHEPHERD (1940), Restructured with St. John Bosco, Conyngham. Revs. John C. Lambert; Connell A. McHugh.
Res.: 87 S. Hunter Hwy., 18222. Tel: 570-788-3141; Fax: 570-788-2916. Email: gsch@ptd.net.
Catechesis/Religious Program—Jean Klinger, D.R.E. Students 140.

DUNMORE, LACKAWANNA CO.
1—ALL SAINTS (1905), (Slovak), Closed. Merged with Our Lady of Mount Carmel, Dunmore.
2—ST. ANTHONY OF PADUA (1894), (Italian), Restructured with St. Rocco, Dunmore. Rev. David P. Cappelloni; Deacon Carmine Mendicino.
Res.: 303 Smith St., 18512. Tel: 570-344-1209; Fax: 570-344-1200.
Catechesis/Religious Program—Sr. Donna Cerminaro, M.P.F., D.R.E. Students 170.
Convent—Religious Teachers Filippini, 118 Kurtz St., 18512. Tel: 570-343-1422; Fax: 570-346-3099.
3—ST. CASIMIR, (Polish), Closed. Merged with Our Lady of Mount Carmel, Dunmore.
4—CHRIST THE KING (1949) Closed. For inquiries for parish records please see Immaculate Conception Parish, Scranton.
5—ST. MARY OF MOUNT CARMEL, Merged with All Saints and St. Casimir, Dunmore. See Our Lady of Mount Carmel Parish, Dunmore.
6—OUR LADY OF MOUNT CARMEL PARISH (1856) [CEM 2], (Merged with All Saints and St. Casimir, Dunmore.) Revs. John A. Doris; Rayanna Narisetti (India); Deacon David E. Marx; Roy E. Brehm, Pastoral Assoc. In Res., Rev. Brian F. Van Fossen.
Res.: 322 Chestnut St., 18512. Tel: 570-346-7429; Fax: 570-346-0523. Web: stmarysdunmore.com.
Catechesis/Religious Program—Lisa Murphy, D.R.E.; Ang Dempsey, D.R.E. Students 324.
7—ST. ROCCO'S (1905), (Italian), Restructured with St. Anthony of Padua, Dunmore. Rev. David P. Cappelloni.
Office: *St. Anthony of Padua*, 18510.
Res.: 303 Smith St., 18509-2919. Tel: 570-344-1209; Fax: 570-344-1200.
Catechesis/Religious Program—Students 39.

DUPONT, LUZERNE CO., SACRED HEART OF JESUS (1902), (Polish), [CEM] Rev. Joseph D. Verespy.
Res.: 215 Lackawanna Ave., 18641. Tel: 570-654-3713; Fax: 570-654-7952.
Catechesis/Religious Program—Elaine Starinski, D.R.E. Students 120.

DURYEA, LUZERNE CO.
1—HOLY ROSARY (1893), (Polish), [CEM] Rev. Charles W. Rokosz.
Res.: 127 Stephenson St., 18642. Tel: 570-457-3502; Fax: 570-457-3341. Email: holyrosaryrcc@aol.com.
Catechesis/Religious Program—Judy Lambert, D.R.E. Students 130.
2—ST. JOSEPH (1909), (Lithuanian), [CEM] Merged Sacred Heart of Jesus, Duryea.
3—SACRED HEART OF JESUS (1889), (German), Merged with Holy Rosary, Duryea in 2003. Rev. Charles W. Rokosz.
Res.: 529 Stephenson St., 18642. Tel: 570-457-2253; Fax: 570-451-2633.
Catechesis/Religious Program—Judy Lambert, D.R.E. Total Enrollment 87.

DUSHORE, SULLIVAN CO., ST. BASIL'S (1838) [CEM] Rev. Joseph R. Hornick; Deacon Joseph Roinick.
Res.: 101 Churchill St., P.O. Box 307, 18614-0307. Tel: 570-928-8865; Fax: 570-928-7972. Email: stbasilnfrancis@epix.net.
Catechesis/Religious Program—Carol Roinick, D.R.E. Students 148.
Mission—St. Francis Xavier, Closed. For inquiries for parish records please contact St. Basil the Great.
Mission—Sacred Heart, Closed. For inquiries for parish records please contact St. Basil the Great.
Mission—St. Francis of Assisi Eagles Mere, Sullivan Co.
Mission—St. Francis of Assisi Mildred, Sullivan Co.
Shrine—S. Philip and James Church-St. John Neumann Shrine Sugar Ridge.

EAST STROUDSBURG, MONROE CO.
1—ST. JOHN (1986) Rev. Alfred J. Vito; Deacon Thomas J. Dello Russo.
Mailing Address: 5171 Milford Rd., 18301. Tel: 570-223-9144; Fax: 570-223-9146. Email: stjohnch@ptd.net.
Catechesis/Religious Program—Tel: 570-223-0888. Mary Foglio, C.R.E. Students 389.
2—ST. MATTHEW'S (1902) Rev. Msgr. John A. Bergamo; Rev. L. Augustine (India); Deacons Svetko Jurjevic; Jose Oscar Langlois; Gerald M. Reynolds.
Res.: 200 Brodhead Ave., 18301. Tel: 570-421-2342; Fax: 570-421-8414.
Catechesis/Religious Program—Tel: 570-421-0113. Lisa Hoey, D.R.E. Students 520.

ELKLAND, TIOGA CO., ST. THOMAS THE APOSTLE (1907) Rev. John M. Kita.
Res.: 111 First St., 16920. Tel: 814-258-5121; Fax: 814-258-5122.
Catechesis/Religious Program—Michelle Whalen, D.R.E. Students 21.
Mission—St. Catherine Lincoln St., Westfield, Tioga Co. 16950.

ELMHURST, LACKAWANNA CO., ST. EULALIA (1950) Rev. Richard E. Fox. In Res., Rev. Peter D. Menghini.
Res.: P.O. Box 143, 18416. Tel: 570-842-7656; Fax: 570-842-7193. Email: steulaliachurch@aol.com.
Catechesis/Religious Program—Elizabeth Strasburger, D.R.E. Students 371.

EXETER, LUZERNE CO.
1—ST. ANTHONY OF PADUA (1928), (Italian), Revs. Joseph D. Sibilano, O.S.J.; Raymond Tabon, O.S.J.
Res.: 28 Memorial St., Pittston, 18643. Tel: 570-654-2103; Fax: 570-655-3313.
Catechesis/Religious Program—Denise Adams, D.R.E. Students 225.
2—ST. CECILIA (1900) [CEM], Merged with St. John the Baptist, Exeter. Rev. Daniel D. Hitchko; Deacon William A. Dervinis.
Res.: 1700 Wyoming Ave., 18643. Tel: 570-654-2133; Fax: 570-654-3449.
Catechesis/Religious Program—Students 178.
3—ST. JOHN THE BAPTIST (1898), (Polish), Merged with St. Cecilia, Exeter.

EYNON, LACKAWANNA CO.
1—ST. MARY OF CZESTOCHOWA (1915), (Polish), Merged with St. Mary of Vilna, Eynon; Restructured with St. Thomas Aquinas, Archbald. Rev. Christopher S. Sahd, Admin.; Deacon Edward T. Kelly.
Res.: 417 Main St., 18403. Tel: 570-876-2223; Fax: 570-876-3081.
Catechesis/Religious Program—Students 87.
2—ST. MARY OF VILNA, (Lithuanian), Merged with St. Mary's Czestochowa, Eynon.

FAIRMOUNT SPRINGS, LUZERNE CO., ST. MARTHA (1966), Restructured with St. Mary, Our Lady of Perpetual Help, Mocanaqua. (All records at Our Lady of Mt. Carmel, Lake Silkworth.) Rev. Stephen A. Krawontka.
Mailing Address: *St. Martha Church*, c/o 150 Main St., Mocanaqua, 18655. 260 Bonnieville Rd., Stillwater, 17878. Tel: 570-542-4157; Fax: 570-542-4158. Email: stmarychurch@frontier.net.
Catechesis/Religious Program—Kathleen Czeck, D.R.E. Students 29.

FOREST CITY, SUSQUEHANNA CO.
1—ST. JOSEPH'S (1904), (Slovenian), Merged with Sacred Heart of Jesus, Forest City.
2—SACRED HEART OF JESUS (1904), (Polish), Merged with St. Agnes, Forest City; Restructured with St. James, Pleasant Mount. Rev. Patrick L. Albert.
Res.: 612 Hudson St., 18421. Tel: 570-785-3838; Fax: 570-785-3713.

FREELAND, LUZERNE CO.
1—ST. ANTHONY, Closed. For inquiries for parish records please see Our Lady of the Immaculate Conception, Freeland.
2—ST. CASIMIR, Closed. For inquiries for parish records please see Our Lady of the Immaculate Conception, Freeland.
3—ST. JOHN NEPOMUCENE, Closed. For inquiries for parish records please see Our Lady of the Immaculate Conception, Freeland.
4—OUR LADY OF THE IMMACULATE CONCEPTION (1862) [CEM] Revs. J. Duane Gavitt; Joseph J. Mattey, Senior Priest; Deacon Cyril J. Kowalchick. In Res., Rev. Richard A. Zavacki (Retired).
Office: 898 Centre St., 18224. Tel: 570-636-3035; Fax: 570-636-1743.
Catechesis/Religious Program—Safko Centre, Chestnut St., 18224. Tel: 570-636-3698. Students 157.

FRIENDSVILLE, SUSQUEHANNA CO.
1—ST. FRANCIS XAVIER (1831) [CEM 3], Merged with St. Thomas the Apostle, Little Meadows and restructured with St. Joseph, St. Joseph. Rev. Casimir M. Stanis.
Res.: 17 Cottage St., P.O. Box 50, 18818. Tel: 570-553-2288; Fax: 570-553-2975. Email: stxc@epix.net.
Catechesis/Religious Program—Jane Conboy, D.R.E.; Liz Gleason, D.R.E. Students 48.
Mission—St. Patrick, Closed., Irish Hill, Rte. 3033, Middletown, Susquehanna Co.
2—ST. JOSEPH (1829) [CEM 2] [JC], Restructured with St. Francis Xavier, Friendsville. Rev. Casimir M. Stanis.
Mailing Address: Box 50, 18818.
Res.: Quinn Rd., R.R. 1, Box 1402, 18818. Tel: 570-553-2288; Fax: 570-553-2975.
Catechesis/Religious Program—Ann Reichlen, D.R.E. Students 50.
Mission—St. Augustine Silver Lake, Susquehanna Co.

GLEN LYON, LUZERNE CO.
1—ST. ADALBERT, Merged with Corpus Christi, Glen Lyon.
2—CORPUS CHRISTI (2001), (Merging of St. Adalbert, St. Denis & St. Michael's, Glen Lyon & St. Mary's, Wanamie. For inquiries for parish records, contact Corpus Christi.) Rev. Joseph P. Kutch.
Res.: 43 W. Main St., 18617. Tel: 570-736-6372; Fax: 570-736-6232.
Catechesis/Religious Program—Ann Marie O'Donnell, D.R.E. Students 90.
3—ST. DENIS, Merged with Corpus Christi, Glen Lyon.
4—ST. MARY (Wanamie) (1906), (Lithuanian), Merged with Corpus Christi, Glen Lyon.
5—ST. MICHAEL, Merged with Corpus Christi, Glen Lyon.

GOULDSBORO, WAYNE CO., ST. RITA (1975) Revs. Andrew Kurovsky; Deva Undralla (India).
Res.: P.O. Box 537, 18424. Tel: 570-842-4995; Fax: 570-842-5429.
Catechesis/Religious Program—Students 196.
Mission—St. Anthony of Padua Newfoundland, Wayne Co.

GREAT BEND, SUSQUEHANNA CO., ST. LAWRENCE (1872) [CEM], Linked with St. Martin of Tours, Jackson; St. John the Evangelist, Susquehanna. Revs. David W. Cramer; Alfhones Perikala (India).
Res.: 380 Franklin St., P.O. Box 592, 18821. Tel: 570-879-2392; Fax: 570-879-0126. Email: stlawrnc@epix.net.
Catechesis/Religious Program—Students 72.
Mission—St. John the Apostle [CEM], Closed., New Milford, Susquehanna Co.

HANOVER TOWNSHIP, WASHINGTON CO., EXALTATION OF THE HOLY CROSS (1917), (Polish), [CEM], Linked with St. Casimir, Hanover Twp. (Wilkes Barre); St. Aloysius, Wilkes Barre. Rev. Andrew R. Sinnott.
Res.: 420 Main Rd., 18706-6094. Tel: 570-823-6242; Fax: 570-829-4732. Email: exhc@aol.com.
Catechesis/Religious Program—Students 75.

HARDING-FALLS, LUZERNE CO., CHURCH OF THE HOLY REDEEMER (1952) Revs. Michael J. Piccola, Admin.; Arbogaste Satoun.
Res.: RR 1, Box 247-B, Pittston, 18643. Tel: 570-388-6300; Fax: 570-388-2034.
Catechesis/Religious Program—Kathy Justave, D.R.E. Students 102.

HARLEIGH, LUZERNE CO., SACRED HEART OF JESUS (1903) Consolidated Restructured with St. Nazarius, Pardeesvill; Our Lady of Grace, Hazleton & St. Mary, Lattimer. Consolidation - now known as Queen of Heaven, Hazleton. Rev. Thomas A. Cappelloni.
Res.: One Church Pl., 18225. Tel: 570-455-4402; Fax: 570-455-0306.
Catechesis/Religious Program—Students 7.
Shrine—National Shrine of the Sacred Heart (1975)
Shrine—Men of the Sacred Heart, National Office (1977)

HARVEYS LAKE, LUZERNE CO., OUR LADY OF VICTORY (1969), Linked with Gate of Heaven, Dallas. Rev. Daniel A. Toomey.
Res.: R.D. #1, Box 309, 18618. Tel: 570-639-1535; Fax: 570-639-1294. Email: olvhl309@aol.com.
Catechesis/Religious Program—Maureen Devine, D.R.E. Students 105.

HAWLEY, WAYNE CO., BLESSED VIRGIN MARY, QUEEN OF PEACE (1852) [CEM] Rev. Richard W. Beck.
Res.: 314 Chestnut Ave., 18428. Tel: 570-226-3183; Fax: 570-226-2126. Email: qofpeace1@verizon.net.
Catechesis/Religious Program—Tel: 570-226-2955. Marie Ribeiro, D.R.E. Students 245.

Mission—St. Veronica Lake Wallenpaupack, Pike Co.

HAZLETON, LUZERNE CO.

1—ANNUNCIATION, HAZELTON (1855) [CEM], Restructured with Sacred Heart of Jesus, Harleigh; St. Nazarius, Pardeesville & St. Mary, Lattimer. Revs. Gregory T. Finn, O.S.J.; Johnson Kochuparambil, O.S.J.; Victor Leon, O.S.J.; Deacon Bernardino Velez.
Res.: 122 S. Wyoming St., 18201. Tel: 570-454-0212; Fax: 570-459-5187.
Catechesis/Religious Program—Students 308.

2—CHURCH OF THE MOST PRECIOUS BLOOD (1885), (Italian), Rev. Louis A. Grippe.
Res.: 131 E. Fourth St., 18201. Tel: 570-454-8714; Fax: 570-454-8754.
Catechesis/Religious Program—Tel: 570-454-5916. Sr. Ursula Bower, D.R.E. Students 284.
Convent—221 E. Fourth St., 18201.

3—SS. CYRIL & METHODIUS, HAZLETON (1882), (Slovak), [CEM], Restructured with St. Stanislaus, Hazleton. Revs. Richard J. Cirba; Nalazala Irudayaraj; Deacon Leonard G. Kassick.
Res.: P.O. Box 2099, 18201. Tel: 570-454-0881; Fax: 570-454-1285.
Catechesis/Religious Program—Zelda Ondish, D.R.E. Students 73.
Mission—St. Ladislaus, Luzerne Co.

4—ST. GABRIEL'S, Merged Restructured with Our Lady of Mount Carmel, Hazelton. Now part of Annunciation, Hazelton.

5—HOLY ROSARY (1916), (Italian), Rev. Patrick J. Genello.
Res.: 240 S. Poplar St., 18201. Tel: 570-454-6693. Email: hrosaryhazleint@grafix.net.
Catechesis/Religious Program—Christine LaMonica, D.R.E. Students 350.

6—HOLY TRINITY (1887), (German), [CEM 2] Closed. For inquiries for parish records contact the chancery.

7—HOLY TRINITY (1907), (Slovak), [CEM] Closed. Restructured with Our Lady of Mt. Carmel (Tyrolese), Hazleton.

8—ST. JOSEPH (1882), (Slovak), [CEM] Consolidated Restructured with St. Stanislaus, Hazelton. For inquiries for parish record please contact SS. Cyril & Methodius, Hazleton.

9—OUR LADY OF GRACE (1910), (Italian), [CEM] Consolidated Restructured with Sacred Heart of Jesus, Harleigh; St. Mary, Lattimer & St. Nazarius, Pardeesville. For inquiries for parish records please contact Queen of Heaven, Hazelton.

10—OUR LADY OF MOUNT CARMEL (1905), (Tyrolese), Closed. Merged with Holy Trinity (Slovak), Hazleton. For inquiries for parish records please see SS. Cyril & Methodius Parish, Hazleton.

11—SS. PETER AND PAUL (1887), (Lithuanian), Closed. Merged with Transfiguration & St. Francis of Assisi, West Hazleton. For inquiries for parish records please see Transfiguration, West Hazleton.

12—QUEEN OF HEAVEN, HAZLETON (1910), (Italian), [CEM], Restructured with Sacred Heart of Jesus, Harleigh; St. Mary, Lattimer & St. Nazarius, Pardeesville. Rev. Thomas A. Cappelloni; Deacon Robert A. Roman.
Res.: 750 N. Vine St., 18201. Tel: 570-454-8797; Fax: 570-454-1922.
Catechesis/Religious Program—Students 94.

13—ST. STANISLAUS (1893), (Polish), [CEM], Restructured with St. Joseph (Slovak), Hazleton. Consolidation - now part of SS. Cyril & Methodius, Hazleton. Revs. Richard J. Cirba; Nalazala Irudayaraj.
Res.: 652 Carson St., 18201-4423. Tel: 570-454-0662; Fax: 570-454-0662.
Catechesis/Religious Program—Carol Baran, D.R.E. Students 31.

HONESDALE, WAYNE CO., ST. JOHN THE EVANGELIST (1842) [CEM 3], Restructured with St. Joseph, White Mills. Revs. William J.P. Langan; Balaraju Desam (India); Deacon Mark S. Jennings.
Office: 414 Church St., 18431. Tel: 570-253-4561; Fax: 570-253-1058.
Catechesis/Religious Program—Valeria Latona, D.R.E. Students 349.
Mission—St. Joseph Rileyville, Wayne Co.
Mission—St. Bernard, Beach Lake
Chapel—Honesdale, St. Mary Magdalene (1853)

HUDSON, LUZERNE CO., ST. JOSEPH'S (1889), (Polish), [CEM] Closed. Merged with Sacred Heart, Plains & Restructured with SS Peter and Paul, Plains.

HUGHESTOWN, LUZERNE CO., BLESSED SACRAMENT (1945), Restructured with St. Mary, Help of Christians, Pittston. Rev. Thomas J. Maloney.
Office: 535 N. Main St., Pittston, 18640.
Res.: 65 Rock St., 18640. Tel: 570-654-6553; Fax: 570-654-0466.
Catechesis/Religious Program—Sr. Mary Ann Cody, I.H.M., D.R.E. Students 66.

INKERMAN, LUZERNE CO., ST. MARK (1900) Closed. For inquiries for parish records please contact St. Maria Goretti, Laflin.

JACKSON, SUSQUEHANNA CO., ST. MARTIN OF TOURS (1940), Linked with St. Lawrence, Great Bend & St. John the Evangelist, Susquehanna. Revs. David W. Cramer; Alfhones Perikala (India).
Mailing Address: 8175 State Rte. 492, 18825. Tel: 570-853-4634. Email: parish@martinoftours.com.
Catechesis/Religious Program—Charlene Kempa, D.R.E. Students 40.
Convent—Capuchin Sisters of Nazareth
Mission—St. Paul Starrucca, Wayne Co.

JERMYN, LACKAWANNA CO.

1—SACRED HEART OF MARY (1889) [CEM] Consolidated Restructured with Sacred Heart of Jesus, Mayfield. For inquiries for parish records please contact Sacred Hearts of Jesus & Mary, Jermyn.

2—SACRED HEARTS OF JESUS & MARY, JERMYN (1889) [CEM], Restructured with Sacred Heart of Jesus, Mayfield. Rev. Thomas P. Shoback; Deacon Patrick J. Massino.
Res.: 624 Madison Ave., 18433-1697. Tel: 570-876-1061; Fax: 570-876-2493. Email: sachmary@verizon.net.
Catechesis/Religious Program—Students 117.

JERSEY SHORE, LYCOMING CO., ST. LUKE (1902), (Restructured with Immaculate Conception of the Blessed Virgin Mary, Bastress). Rev. Msgr. Neil J. Van Loon, Admin.; Rev. Albert J. Leonard.
Mailing Address: c/o Immaculate Conception, 5973 Jacks Hollow Rd., Williamsport, 17702.
Res.: 118 Kendall Ave., 17740. Tel: 570-398-2557; Fax: 570-398-0126.
Catechesis/Religious Program—Students 98.

JESSUP, LACKAWANNA CO.

1—ST. JAMES (1899) [CEM], Merged with St. Michael, Jessup and restructured with St. Mary's Assumption, Jessup. Revs. William B. Blake; Balaraju Eturi (India); Deacon Gerard L. Carpenter.
Res.: 605 Church St., 18434. Tel: 570-489-2252; Fax: 570-489-2527.
Catechesis/Religious Program—Mary Kay McHale, D.R.E. Students 268.

2—ST. MARY'S ASSUMPTION (1904), (Italian), [CEM], Restructured with St. James, Jessup. Revs. William B. Blake; Balaraju Eturi (India).
Mailing Address: c/o 605 Church St., 18434.
Res.: 516 Third Ave., 18434. Tel: 570-489-2252.
Catechesis/Religious Program—Angela Muchal, D.R.E. Students 174.

KINGSTON, LUZERNE CO.

1—ST. HEDWIG'S (1901), (Polish), [CEM] Closed. For inquiries for parish records please see St. Ignatius, Kingston.

2—ST. IGNATIUS LOYOLA, KINGSTON (1885) [CEM] Consolidated with St. Mary's Annunciation, Kingston. Rev. John M. Lapera; Deacon John E. O'Connor.
Res.: 339 N. Maple Ave., 18704. Tel: 570-288-6446; Fax: 570-288-0463.
Catechesis/Religious Program—Carmella Faust, D.R.E. Students 272.
Chapel—St. Ann's, Tel: 570-288-5919.

3—ST. MARY'S ANNUNCIATION (1902), (Lithuanian), Consolidated with St. Ignatius Loyola, Kingston. Rev. John M. Lapera.
Res.: 258 Zerbey Ave., 18704. Tel: 570-287-5096; Fax: 570-283-0162.
Catechesis/Religious Program—Students 55.

LAFLIN, LUZERNE CO., ST. MARIA GORETTI (1967) Rev. Michael J. Kirwin.
Res.: 42 Redwood Dr., 18702. Tel: 570-655-8956; Fax: 570-655-1746. Email: 42redwood@adelphia.net.
Catechesis/Religious Program—Mary Anne Susek, D.R.E. Students 235.

LAKE ARIEL, WAYNE CO., ST. THOMAS MORE (1941) [CEM] Rev. Michael E. Finn.
Mailing Address: Box 188, 18436. Tel: 570-698-5584; Fax: 570-698-8468. Email: stthomasstmary@echoes.net.
Catechesis/Religious Program—Tel: 570-698-7150. Marian Menapace, D.R.E. Students 195.
Mission—St. Mary Ledgedale, Wayne Co.

LAKE SILKWORTH, LUZERNE CO., OUR LADY OF MOUNT CARMEL (1923) [CEM] Rev. Joseph J. Pisaneschi.
Res.: 2011 State Rd. 29, Hunlock Creek, 18621. Tel: 570-477-5040; Fax: 570-477-3040. Email: olmcpastoralcent@aol.com.
Catechesis/Religious Program—Maggie Fishel, D.R.E. Students 137.

LAKE WINOLA, WYOMING CO., ST. MARY OF THE LAKE (1986), Restructured with Nativity B.V.M., Tunkhannock. Revs. Richard J. Polmounter; David R. Betts; Deacon Raymond A. Pieretti.
Mailing Address: *c/o Nativity of Blessed Virgin Mary*, P.O. Box 186, Tunkhannock, 18657.
Res.: 99 E. Tioga St., Tunkhannock, 18657. Tel: 570-836-3275; Fax: 570-836-4268.
Catechesis/Religious Program—Glenda Evans, D.R.E. Students 102.

LARKSVILLE, LUZERNE CO., ST. ANTHONY OF PADUA (1908) Closed. For inquiries for parish records please see St. John the Baptist, Plymouth.

LATTIMER, LUZERNE CO.

1—ST. MARY'S LATTIMER, (Italian), Merged with St. Nazarius, Pardeesville. Restructured with Our Lady of Grace, Hazleton & Sacred Heart of Jesus, Harleigh. For inquiries for parish records please contact Queen of Heaven (Hazelton).

2—QUEEN OF HEAVEN (HAZLETON) (1903), (Italian), Merged with St. Nazarius, Pardeesville; Restructured with Our Lady of Grace, Hazleton & Sacred Heart of Jesus, Harleigh., Mailing Address: 750 N. Vine St., Hazleton, 18201.
Res.: Main St., 18234.
Catechesis/Religious Program—Carol Matz, D.R.E. Students 10.

LITTLE MEADOWS, SUSQUEHANNA CO., ST. THOMAS THE APOSTLE (1887) Merged with St. Francis Xavier, Friendsville & restructured with St. Joseph, St. Joseph.

LORDS VALLEY, PIKE CO., ST. JOHN NEUMANN (1976), Linked with St. Ann, Shohola. Rev. Thomas J. Major; Deacons John Nash; Henry J. Ernst; Phil Bouwmann.
Res.: 705 Rte. 739, 18428. Tel: 570-775-6791; Fax: 570-775-1527.
Catechesis/Religious Program—Patricia Ohman, D.R.E. Students 94.
Mission—Good Shepherd Blooming Grove.

LUZERNE, LUZERNE CO.

1—ST. ANN'S (1924), (Lithuanian), Merged with Holy Family, Luzerne.

2—HOLY FAMILY (1999) Rev. Michael J. Zipay; Deacon John B. Ziegler.
Res.: 574 Bennett St., 18709. Tel: 570-287-6600; Fax: 570-283-0706.
Catechesis/Religious Program—Diane Janoski, D.R.E. Students 246.

3—ST. JOHN NEPOMUCENE (1907), (Slovak), Merged with Holy Family, Luzerne.

4—SACRED HEART CHURCH (1893), (German), Closed. For inquiries for parish records contact Holy Family, Luzerne.

MANSFIELD, TIOGA CO., HOLY CHILD (1953), (Restructured with St. John Neumann, Blossburg) Rev. Jacek J. Bialkowski. In Res., Rev. John M. Kita.
Res.: 237 S. Main St., 16933. Tel: 570-662-3568; Fax: 570-662-2113. Email: holychild@ptd.net.
Catechesis/Religious Program—Students 84.
Mission—St. Mary, Closed., Center St., Tioga, Tioga Co. 16946.

MATAMORAS, PIKE CO., ST. JOSEPH (1892) Rev. August A. Ricciardi.
Res.: 309 Ave. F, 18336. Tel: 570-491-2618; Fax: 570-491-4404.
Catechesis/Religious Program—Cristin Cavallaro, D.R.E. Students 161.
Mission—Holy Family Cemetery Rd., Mill Rift, Pike Co. 18340.

MAYFIELD, LACKAWANNA CO., SACRED HEART OF JESUS (1904), (Polish), [CEM] Consolidated with Sacred Heart of Mary, Jermyn. Now known as Sacred Hearts of Jesus & Mary, Jermyn.
Res.: 420 Hudson St., 18433. Tel: 570-876-1950; Fax: 570-876-1950.
Catechesis/Religious Program—Students 38.

MESHOPPEN, WYOMING CO., ST. JOACHIM (1873) [CEM], (Restructured with St. Mary's Assumption, Wyalusing) Rev. Joseph J. Manarchuck, Admin.
Mailing Address: *St. Mary's Assumption*, RR4, Box 4003, Wyalusing, 18853.
Res.: P.O. Box 67, 18630. Tel: 570-746-1006; Fax: 570-746-0389.
Catechesis/Religious Program—Valerie Trowbridge, D.R.E. Students 82.
Mission—St. Bonaventure [CEM], Closed.

MILDRED, SULLIVAN CO., ST. FRANCIS OF ASSISI (1894) Merged with St. Basil, Dushore.
Catechesis/Religious Program—Students 82.
Mission—St. Francis of Assisi Eagles Mere, Sullivan Co.
Mission—Sacred Heart, Closed.

MILFORD, PIKE CO.

1—ST. PATRICK (1946) Rev. Gerald F. Mullally; Deacon Clifford J. Jorgenson.
Res.: 111 E. High St., P.O. Box W, 18337. Tel: 570-296-7451; Fax: 570-409-1651.
Catechesis/Religious Program—Students 168.

2—ST. VINCENT DE PAUL (1976) Rev. Paul M. Mullen; Deacons Joseph A. LaCorte; Donald F. O'Brien; Joseph A. D'Aiello; Brian Drury.
Res.: 101 St. Vincent Dr., 18337-9672. Tel: 570-686-4545; Fax: 800-565-1762. Email: stvoff@ptd.net.
Catechesis/Religious Program—Tel: 570-686-3493. Students 465.

MOCANAQUA, LUZERNE CO.

1—ASCENSION OF THE LORD, (Slovak), For Parish records & information see St. Mary, Our Lady of Perpetual Help., Mailing Address: c/o 150 Main St., 18655.

2—ST. MARY, OUR LADY OF PERPETUAL HELP (1904), (Polish), [CEM], Restructured with St. Martha,

Fairmount Springs. Rev. Stephen A. Krawontka.
Res.: 150 Main St., 18655. Tel: 570-542-4157; Fax: 570-542-4158.
Catechesis/Religious Program—Tel: 570-542-4878. Students 24.

MONTDALE, LACKAWANNA CO.
1—CORPUS CHRISTI (1942) Consolidated Linked with St. Pius, Royal. For inquiries for parish records please contact St. John Vianney, Montdale.
2—ST. JOHN VIANNEY (1942), Linked with St. Pius, Royal - consolidated, now known as St. John Vianney Parish. Rev. James B. Shimsky; Deacon Edwin L. Salva Sr.
Res.: 704 Montdale Rd., Scott Twp., 18447. Tel: 570-254-9502; Fax: 570-254-6233.
Catechesis/Religious Program—Students 205.

MONTOURSVILLE, LYCOMING CO., OUR LADY OF LOURDES (1942) Rev. John K. Manno.
Res.: 800 Mulberry St., 17754. Tel: 570-368-8598; Fax: 570-368-2912.
Catechesis/Religious Program—Barbara Burchanowski, D.R.E. Students 156.

MONTROSE, SUSQUEHANNA CO., HOLY NAME OF MARY (1898) [CEM] Rev. Gerard F. Safko.
Res.: 60 S. Main St., 18801. Tel: 570-278-1504; Fax: 570-278-4751.
Catechesis/Religious Program—Francesca Calafut, D.R.E. Students 220.

MOSCOW, LACKAWANNA CO., ST. CATHERINE OF SIENA (1861) Rev. Robert J. Simon; Deacon John J. Franceschelli.
Res.: 220 Church St., P.O. Box 250, 18444. Tel: 570-842-4561; Fax: 570-842-6648.
Catechesis/Religious Program—Tel: 570-848-2158. Students 389.

MOUNT POCONO, MONROE CO., ST. MARY OF THE MOUNT (1909) Rev. Joseph R. Kopacz. In Res., Rev. Bryan B. Wright; Deacon Gregory F. Loushney.
Res.: 27 Fairview Ave., 18344. Tel: 570-839-7138; Fax: 570-839-7139.
Catechesis/Religious Program—Mary Lou Dumas, D.R.E. Students 173.

MOUNTAINTOP, LUZERNE CO., ST. JUDE (1953) Revs. Joseph J. Evanko; Anthony J. Gali (India); Deacon Eugene J. Kovatch.
Res.: 420 S. Mountain Blvd., 18707. Tel: 570-474-6315; Fax: 570-474-0775.
Catechesis/Religious Program—Pamela Urbanski, Youth Min. Students 550.

MUNCY, LYCOMING CO., RESURRECTION (1941) Rev. Glenn E. McCreary.
Res.: 75 Musser Ln., 17756. Tel: 570-546-3900; Fax: 570-546-0322.
Catechesis/Religious Program—Jennifer Frye, D.R.E. Students 168.

NANTICOKE, LUZERNE CO.
1—ST. FRANCIS OF ASSISI (1872) [CEM] Closed. For inquiries for parish records contact the chancery.
2—HOLY CHILD (1942), (Polish), Merged with Holy Trinity & St. Stanislaus, Nanticoke & Restructured with St. Mary of Czestochowa & St. Joseph, Nanticoke.
3—HOLY TRINITY (1894), (Polish), [CEM], Merged with St. Stanislaus & Holy Child, Nanticoke & Restructured with St. Mary of Czestochowa, Nanticoke. Rev. James R. Nash; Deacons Thaddeus Wadus; Florian G. Gyza.
Res.: 520 S. Hanover St., 18634-2799. Tel: 570-735-4833; Fax: 570-735-2281.
Catechesis/Religious Program—Students 159.
4—ST. JOSEPH'S (1888) [CEM], Merged with St. Stanislaus, St. Mary of Czestochowa, Holy Child, Holy Trinity, Nanticoke. Rev. James R. Nash.
Mailing Address: *c/o Holy Trinity*, 520 S. Hanover St., 18634.
Catechesis/Religious Program—Susan Saunders, D.R.E. Twinned with St. Francis of Assisi, Nanticoke. Students 17.
5—ST. MARY OF CZESTOCHOWA (1901), (Polish), [CEM], Restructured with Holy Trinity, Holy Child, St. Stanislaus, St. Joseph, St. Mary of Czestochowa, Nanticoke. Rev. James R. Nash.
Mailing Address: *c/o Holy Trinity*, 520 S. Hanover St., 18634. In Res., Rev. Raymond L. Deviney (Retired).
Res.: 1030 S. Hanover St., 18634. Tel: 570-735-6911; Fax: 570-735-6913.
Catechesis/Religious Program—Tel: 570-735-0313; Fax: 570-735-2123. Sr. Ursula Yerns, D.R.E. Students 17.
6—ST. STANISLAUS (1875), (Polish), [CEM], Merged with Holy Trinity, Holy Child, St. Joseph, Nanticoke & Restructured with St. Mary of Czestochowa, Nanticoke. Rev. James R. Nash; Deacons Florian J. Gyza; Thaddeus Wadus.
Mailing Address: 520 S. Main St., 18634.
Res.: 38 W. Church St., 18634. Tel: 570-735-0313; Fax: 570-735-2123.
Catechesis/Religious Program—Ann Morgas, D.R.E. Students 29.

NICHOLSON, WYOMING CO., ST. PATRICK (1888) [CEM] Rev. Gerard M. McGlone; Deacon Paul J. Brojack.
Res.: 100 Main St., P.O. Box 309, 18446. Tel: 570-942-6602; Fax: 570-942-5029.
Catechesis/Religious Program—Mary Smarkusky, D.R.E. Students 104.

OLD FORGE, LACKAWANNA CO.
1—ST. LAWRENCE O'TOOLE (1895) Consolidated Restructured with St. Mary, Old Forge. For inquiries for parish records please contact Prince of Peace, Old Forge.
2—ST. MARY (1897), (Italian), Restructured with St. Lawrence O'Toole, Old Forge. Consolidated, now known as Prince of Peace Parish. Revs. Louis T. Kaminski; Ronald J. Hughes.
Res.: 123 Grace St., 18518. Tel: 570-457-5900.
Catechesis/Religious Program—Sr. Geraldine, D.R.E. Students 198.
3—ST. MICHAEL (1905), (Polish), Closed. For inquiries for parish records contact the chancery.
4—PRINCE OF PEACE, OLD FORGE (1895), Restructured with St. Mary, Old Forge. Consolidated, now known as Prince of Peace Parish. Revs. Louis T. Kaminski; Ronald J. Hughes.
Res.: 123 Grace St., 18518. Tel: 570-457-5900.
Catechesis/Religious Program—JoAnn Wilbur, D.R.E. Students 74.
5—ST. STANISLAUS, Closed.

OLYPHANT, LACKAWANNA CO.
1—HOLY GHOST (1888), (Slovak), Merged with St. Patrick's Church, Olyphant.
Catechesis/Religious Program—Combined with St. Patrick & St. Michael the Archangel, Tel: 570-489-2023. Students 220.
Convent—Sisters of SS. Cyril and Methodius, 132 Lincoln Ave., 18447. Tel: 570-489-9551.
2—ST. MICHAEL THE ARCHANGEL (1909), (Polish), [CEM], Merged with St. Patrick and Holy Ghost, Olyphant. Rev. Thomas M. Muldowney.
Mailing Address: c/o 200 Delaware Ave., 18447.
Res.: 132 Lincoln St., 18447. Tel: 570-489-0752; Fax: 570-489-0225.
Catechesis/Religious Program—Michelle O'Brien, D.R.E. Total combined with St. Patrick & Holy Ghost 220.
3—ST. PATRICK'S (1875) [CEM], Merged with Holy Ghost (Slovak), Olyphant and St. Michael the Archangel, Olyphant. Rev. Thomas M. Muldowney.
Res.: 200 Delaware Ave., 18447. Tel: 570-489-0752; Fax: 570-489-0225.
Catechesis/Religious Program—Total combined with St. Michael the Archangel & Holy Ghost, Tel: 570-489-2023. Michelle O'Brien, D.R.E. Students 220.

PARDEESVILLE, LUZERNE CO., ST. NAZARIUS (1966), (Italian), Merged with St. Mary, Lattimer, Sacred Heart of Jesus, Harleigh. Consolidated wih Our Lady of Grace Parish, Hazleton (now known as Queen of Heaven Parish). Rev. Thomas A. Cappelloni; Deacon Robert A. Roman.
Mailing Address: 750 N. Vine St., Hazleton, 18201. Tel: 570-454-8797; Fax: 570-454-1922.
Catechesis/Religious Program—Jean Klinger, D.R.E. Students 7.

PECKVILLE, LACKAWANNA CO., SACRED HEART OF JESUS (1946) Rev. Msgr. Peter P. Madus.
Res.: 1101 Willow St., 18452. Tel: 570-383-3244; Fax: 570-383-8697.
Catechesis/Religious Program—Tel: 570-383-2777. Gayle Castellani, D.R.E. Students 221.

PITTSTON, LUZERNE CO.
1—ST. CASIMIR'S (1890), (Lithuanian), Closed. For inquiries for parish records please see St. John the Evangelist, Pittston.
2—ST. JOHN THE BAPTIST (1892), (Slovak), [CEM 2] Closed. For inquiries for parish records please see St. John the Evangelist, Pittston.
3—ST. JOHN THE EVANGELIST (1854) [CEM], Merged with St. Casimir and St. Joseph, Pittston. Restructured with St. John the Baptist, Pittston. Rev. Msgr. John J. Bendik; Rev. James P. Dougher; Deacons James G. Cortegerone; David E. Marx. In Res., Rev. Hugh H. McGroarty.
Res.: 35 William St., 18640. Tel: 570-654-0053; Fax: 570-654-3751. Email: angelsofsje@aol.com. Web: www.parishcommunity.com.
Catechesis/Religious Program—Patricia Marx, D.R.E. Students 196.
4—ST. JOSEPH (1909), (Polish), Closed. For inquiries for parish records please see St. John the Evangelist, Pittston.
5—ST. MARY'S ASSUMPTION (1863), (German), Merged with St. Mary, Help of Christians, Pittson and restructured with Blessed Sacrament, Hughestown.
Catechesis/Religious Program—Mary Pat Martarano, D.R.E. Students 71.
6—ST. MARY, HELP OF CHRISTIANS (1851) [CEM], Merged with St. Mary's Assumption, Pittston and restructured with Blessed Sacrament, Hughestown. Rev. Thomas J. Maloney.
Res.: 535 N. Main St., 18640. Tel: 570-654-0263; Fax: 570-654-0195.
Catechesis/Religious Program—Students 66.
7—OUR LADY OF MT. CARMEL (1904), (Italian), [CEM], Linked with St. Rocco, Pittston. Rev. Daniel L. Schwebs, O.S.J.
Res.: 237 William St., 18640. Tel: 570-654-6902; Fax: 570-655-5448.
Catechesis/Religious Program—Ann Hrobak, D.R.E. Students 181.
8—ST. ROCCO (1919), (Italian), [CEM], Linked with Our Lady of Mt. Carmel, Pittston. Rev. Daniel L. Schwebs, O.S.J.
Res.: 62 W. Oak St., 18640. Tel: 570-654-2914; Fax: 570-654-1614.
Catechesis/Religious Program—Students 140.

PLAINS, LUZERNE CO.
1—SS. PETER AND PAUL (1898), (Polish), [CEM] Consolidated Revs. Joseph A. Greskiewicz; Michael J. Kloton.
Res.: 13 Hudson Rd., 18705. Tel: 570-825-6663; Fax: 570-823-4556.
Catechesis/Religious Program—Sanrda Holena, D.R.E. Students 146.
2—SACRED HEART (1883) Closed. Merged with St. Joseph's, Hudson & Restructured with SS. Peter and Paul, Plains.

PLEASANT MOUNT, WAYNE CO., ST. JAMES (1887), Restructured with Sacred Heart of Jesus, St. Joseph, Forest City & St. Juliana, Rock Lake. Rev. Patrick L. Albert.
Res.: P.O. Box 53, 18453. Tel: 570-448-2211.
Office: *c/o St. Joseph Rectory*, 612 Hudson St., Forest City, 18421.
Catechesis/Religious Program—Students 4.
Mission—St. Cecilia, Closed.
Mission—Assumption of the B.V.M., Closed.

PLYMOUTH, LUZERNE CO.
1—ALL SAINTS (1885) [CEM 3], Merged with St Vincent de Paul, Plymouth. Rev. Robert J. Kelleher, Admin.; Deacon Joseph F. DeVizia.
Office: 66 Willow St., 18651. Tel: 570-779-5323; Fax: 570-779-4921.
Catechesis/Religious Program—Helen Cebula, D.R.E. Students 265.
2—ST. JOHN THE BAPTIST (1899), (Polish), Merged with St. Anthony of Padua, Larksville and SS. Cyril and Methodius, Edwardsville. Rev. Gerald J. Gurka.
3—ST. STEPHEN (1886), (Slovak), Closed. For Parish records see All Saints, Plymouth.
4—ST. VINCENT DE PAUL (1872) [CEM] Closed. For Parish records see All Saints, Plymouth.

POCONO PINES, MONROE CO.
1—OUR LADY OF THE LAKE (1985) Merged with Christ the King, Blakeslee. For inquiries for parish records please contact St. Maximilian Kolbe, Pocono Pines.
2—ST. MAXIMILIAN KOLBE, POCONO PINES (1985) Merged with Christ the King, Blakeslee and consolidated to become St. Maximilian Kolbe Parish. Rev. John B. Boyle; Deacon Frank Gisoldi.
Res.: Sullivan Rd., P.O. Box 0, 18350. Tel: 570-646-6424; Fax: 570-646-1047. Email: ourlady@ptd.net.
Catechesis/Religious Program—Lynnette Smith, D.R.E. Students 134.

ROCK LAKE, WAYNE CO., ST. JULIANA (1838) Merged with St. James, Pleasant Mount & restructured with Sacred Heart, & St. Joseph, Forest City.

ROYAL, SUSQUEHANNA CO., ST. PIUS X (1967), Linked with Corpus Christi, Montdale. Consolidated, now known as St. John Vianney Parish. Rev. James B. Shimsky.
Res.: Box 64, Clifford, 18413. Tel: 570-282-2991; Fax: 570-282-7580.
Office: *c/o St. John Vianney Parish*, 704 Montdale Rd., Scott Twp., 18447. Tel: 570-254-9502; Fax: 570-254-6233.
Catechesis/Religious Program—Students 64.

SAYRE, BRADFORD CO., CHURCH OF THE EPIPHANY (1888), Restructured with St. Ann, Bentley Creek (now closed), linked with St. John, South Waverly & St. Joseph, Athens. Revs. Andrew S. Hvozdovic; Wieslaw M. Ziebacz.
Res.: 304 S. Elmer Ave., 18840. Tel: 570-888-9641; Fax: 570-888-2608.
Catechesis/Religious Program—Students 70.

SHAVERTOWN, LUZERNE CO., ST. THERESE (1926) Rev. James J. Paisley.
Res.: 64 Davis St., 18708. Tel: 570-696-1144; Fax: 570-696-1210.
Catechesis/Religious Program—Denise Murphy, D.R.E. Students 542.

SHOHOLA, PIKE CO., ST. ANN'S (1928) [CEM], Linked with St. John Neumann, Lords Valley. Rev. Thomas J. Major; Deacon Glenn J. Biagi.
Mailing Address: 125 Richardson Ave., 18458.
Res.: 123 Richardson Ave., 18458. Tel: 570-832-4275.
Catechesis/Religious Program—Christine Barnansky, D.R.E. Students 144.
Mission—St. Mary of the Assumption Lackawaxen, Pike Co.

Mission—Sacred Heart of Jesus Greeley, Pike Co.

SIMPSON, LACKAWANNA CO., ST. MICHAEL (1903) [CEM] Rev. Joseph S. Sitko.
Res.: 46 Midland St., 18407. Tel: 570-282-2161; Fax: 570-282-4287.
Catechesis/Religious Program—Kathryn Yaklic, D.R.E. Students 103.

SOUTH WAVERLY, BRADFORD CO., ST. JOHN THE EVANGELIST (1902), Merged with St. Joseph, Athens, & Epiphany, Sayre. Rev. Andrew S. Hvozdovic. Mailing Address: c/o 304 S. Elmer Ave., Sayre, 18840. Tel: 570-888-9641.
Catechesis/Religious Program—Mary Costic, D.R.E.; LeAnn Steven, D.R.E. Students 98.

SOUTH WILLIAMSPORT, LYCOMING CO., ST. LAWRENCE (1931), linked with St. Boniface, Williamsport. Rev. Msgr. Stephen D. McGough.
Parish Office: 326 Washington Blvd., Williamsport, 17701. Tel: 570-326-1544; Fax: 570-326-6746.
Res.: 821 W. Central Ave., Williamsport, 17702.
Catechesis/Religious Program—Students 171.

STROUDSBURG, MONROE CO., ST. LUKE (1968) Revs. Thomas D. McLaughlin; Carmen J. Perry; Deacon Thomas W. Hogan Jr.
Office: 818 Main St., 18360. Tel: 570-421-9097; 570-421-9863; Fax: 570-421-6015.
Res.: 906 Main St., 18360. Tel: 570-421-8479; Fax: 570-421-6015.
Catechesis/Religious Program—Scott Fabian, D.R.E. Students 572.

SUGAR NOTCH, LUZERNE CO.

1—HOLY FAMILY PARISH (1901) [CEM], Consolidation. Rev. Joseph R. Kakareka.
Office: 828 Main St., 18706. Tel: 570-822-8983; Fax: 570-822-6016.
Catechesis/Religious Program—Mary Anne Malone, D.R.E. Students 75.

2—SS. PETER AND PAUL CHAPEL (1847), (Lithuanian), Merged with Holy Family, Sugar Notch.

SUSQUEHANNA, SUSQUEHANNA CO., ST. JOHN THE EVANGELIST (1847) [CEM], Linked with St. Lawrence, Great Bend & St. Martin of Tours, Jackson. Revs. David W. Cramer; Alfhones Perikala (India).
Res.: 101 Jackson Ave., 18847. Tel: 570-853-4634; Fax: 570-853-3356.
Catechesis/Religious Program—Victoria Mulligan, D.R.E. Students 100.

SWOYERSVILLE, LUZERNE CO.

1—HOLY NAME OF JESUS (1905) Merged with St. Mary of Czestochowa, Swoyersville.

2—HOLY NAME/ST. MARY'S, [CEM], Linked with Holy Trinity, Swoyersville. Revs. William J. Karle; Irudaya Raj Illuri (India); Deacon George Mochin Jr.
Office: 283 Shoemaker St., 18704. Tel: 570-287-2139; Fax: 570-287-6474.
Res.: *Holy Trinity*, 116 Hughes St., 18704.
Catechesis/Religious Program—Students 119.

3—HOLY TRINITY (1895), (Slovak), [CEM], Linked with Holy Name/St. Mary, Swoyersville. Rev. William J. Karle.
Res.: 116 Hughes St., 18704. Tel: 570-287-6624; Fax: 570-287-4704.
Catechesis/Religious Program—Margaret Semanek, D.R.E. Students 102.

4—ST. MARY OF CZESTOCHOWA (1909) Merged with Holy Name of Jesus, Swoyersville.

TANNERSVILLE, MONROE CO., OUR LADY OF VICTORY (1968) Rev. Richard E. Czachor; Deacon Ralph E. Weichand.
Res.: Cherry Lane Rd., P.O. Box 195, 18372. Tel: 570-629-4572; Fax: 570-629-5325.
Catechesis/Religious Program—Students 385.

TAYLOR, LACKAWANNA CO.

1—IMMACULATE CONCEPTION (1898), Closed. Merged with St. Joseph, Scranton; Restructured with St. John the Baptist, Taylor. Consolidated, now part of Divine Mercy Parish, Scranton. Rev. Francis L. Pauselli.
312 Davis St., 18505.
Catechesis/Religious Program—Nancy Mott, D.R.E. Students 37.

2—ST. JOHN THE BAPTIST (1904), (Slovak), Closed. Merged with Immaculate Conception, Taylor; Restructured with St. Joseph, Scranton. Consolidated, now part of Divine Mercy Parish, Scranton., 312 Davis St., 18505.

THROOP, LACKAWANNA CO.

1—ST. ANTHONY'S, Consolidated Now a part of Blessed Sacrament Parish, Throop.

2—BLESSED SACRAMENT, THROOP (1911), (Polish), [CEM], Merged with St. Bridget's and St. John the Baptist, Throop. Rev. Jeffrey J. Walsh, Admin.
Church & Office: 215 Rebecca St., 18519. Tel: 570-489-1963; Fax: 570-489-3291.
Catechesis/Religious Program—Students 103.

3—ST. BRIDGET'S (1916), Closed, see Blessed Sacrament Parish, Throop for records. Merged with St. John the Baptist & St. Anthony's, Throop. Rev. Jeffrey J. Walsh, Admin.
Office: 215 Rebecca St., 18519.

4—ST. JOHN THE BAPTIST (1905), (Slovak), [CEM] Closed. Merged with St. Bridget's and St. Anthony's, Throop. For inquiries for parish records please contact Blessed Sacrament Parish, Throop.

TOBYHANNA, MONROE CO., ST. ANN (1923) [CEM 2] Revs. Joseph R. Kopacz; Bryan B. Wright. In Res., Rev. Albert Bellantonio, Coord. Hispanic Ministry, Monroe Co.
Res.: Main St., P.O. Box 188, 18466-0188. Tel: 570-894-8018; Fax: 570-894-9619.
Catechesis/Religious Program—Students 674.

TOWANDA, BRADFORD CO., SS. PETER AND PAUL (1841) [CEM 3], Restructured with St. Michael, Canton. Revs. Martin M. Boylan; Gregory T. Villaescusa.
Res.: 106 Third St., 18848. Tel: 570-265-2113; Fax: 570-265-2114.
Catechesis/Religious Program—JeJe Barrett, D.R.E. Students 47.
Mission—Immaculate Conception, Closed.

TUNKHANNOCK, WYOMING CO., NATIVITY OF BLESSED VIRGIN MARY (1884) [CEM 2], Merged with St. Mary of the Lake, Lake Winola. Revs. Richard J. Polmounter; David R. Betts; Deacon Raymond A. Pieretti.
Res.: 99 E. Tioga St., 18657. Tel: 570-836-3275; Fax: 570-836-4268.
Catechesis/Religious Program—Tammy Nudo, D.R.E. Students 220.

WAYMART, WAYNE CO., ST. MARY (1915) [CEM] Rev. John T. Albosta.
Res.: 242 Carbondale Rd., P.O. Box 160, 18472. Tel: 570-488-6440; Fax: 570-488-7440.
Catechesis/Religious Program—Marion Menapace, D.R.E. Students 165.
Mission—St. Patrick, Closed.

WELLSBORO, TIOGA CO., ST. PETER'S (1879) [CEM 2] Rev. John J. Chmil.
Res.: 38 Central Ave., 16901. Tel: 570-724-3371; Fax: 570-724-6322.
Catechesis/Religious Program—Patti Mitchell, D.R.E. Students 175.
Mission—Sacred Heart, Closed.

WEST HAZLETON, LUZERNE CO.

1—ST. FRANCIS OF ASSISI (1940), Linked with SS. Peter & Paul, Hazleton & Transfiguration, West Hazleton. Rev. Philip S. Rayappan, Admin.
Res.: 544 N. Broad St., 18202. Tel: 570-454-3072; Fax: 570-454-2729.
Office: 213 W. Green St., 18202.
Catechesis/Religious Program—Joanne Karchner, D.R.E. Students 14.

2—TRANSFIGURATION (1907), (Polish), [CEM], Closed. Merged with SS. Peter & Paul, Hazleton, & St. Francis of Assisi, West Hazleton. Rev. Philip S. Rayappan.
Res.: 213 W. Green St., Hazleton, 18202. Tel: 570-454-3933; Fax: 570-454-8326.
Catechesis/Religious Program—Cheryl Krieger, D.R.E. Students 97.

WEST PITTSTON, LUZERNE CO., IMMACULATE CONCEPTION (1910), Linked with Holy Redeemer, Harding-Falls. Revs. Michael J. Piccola; Arbogaste Satoun.
Res.: 605 Luzerne Ave., 18643. Tel: 570-654-2753; Fax: 570-654-9244.
Catechesis/Religious Program—Juel Ann Klepadlo, D.R.E. Students 124.

WEST WYOMING, LUZERNE CO., OUR LADY OF SORROWS (1953), Restructured with St. Joseph, Wyoming. Revs. John V. Polednak, Admin.; Leonard M. Butcavage.
c/o St. Joseph Rectory, 97 E. 6th St., Wyoming, 18644.
Res.: 363 W. 8th St., 18644. Tel: 570-693-1991; Fax: 570-693-1399.
Catechesis/Religious Program—Students 132.

WESTON, LUZERNE CO., SACRED HEART (1888) [CEM] Rev. Patrick D. McDowell.
Res.: 554 Main St., P.O. Box A, 18256. Tel: 570-384-4121; Fax: 570-384-3976.
Catechesis/Religious Program—Students 5.
Mission—St. Joseph Nuremberg, Luzerne Co.

WHITE HAVEN, LUZERNE CO., ST. PATRICK'S (1874) [CEM] Rev. John F. McHale.
Office: 411 Allegheny St., 18661.
Res.: 521 Northumberland St., 18661. Tel: 570-443-9944; Fax: 570-443-9777.
Catechesis/Religious Program—Linda Kistler, D.R.E. Students 145.
Station—White Haven Center, Tel: 570-453-9564.

WHITE MILLS, WAYNE CO., ST. JOSEPH'S (1968) Closed. Restructured with St. John the Evangelist, Honesdale. For inquiries for parish records please contact St. John the Evangelist, Honesdale.

WILKES-BARRE, LUZERNE CO.

1—ST. ALOYSIUS (1899), Restructured with St. Casimir's, Wilkes-Barre & Exaltation of the Holy Cross, Hanover Twp. Revs. Andrew R. Sinnott; Thumma Savari. In Res., Rev. Msgr. Anthony J. Generose.
Res.: 143 W. Division St., 18706. Tel: 570-823-3791; Fax: 570-826-0233.
Catechesis/Religious Program—Lynn Sklanny, D.R.E. Students 193.

2—BLESSED SACRAMENT (1917) [CEM], Merged with St. Francis of Assisi and St. John the Baptist, Wilkes-Barre. Rev. Joseph A. Kearney.
Res.: 213 E. Main St., Miners Mills, 18705. Tel: 570-822-9561 (Rectory); Fax: 570-822-4347.
Catechesis/Religious Program—Cathy Riccetti, D.R.E. Students 163.
Station—Geisinger Wyoming Valley Hospital, Tel: 570-826-7300.

3—ST. BONIFACE (1896), (German), Linked with St. Patrick, Wilkes-Barre. Rev. James E. McGahagan; Deacon Francis J. Bradigan Jr.
Office: *c/o St. Patrick*, 316 Parish St., Wilkes Barre, 18702.
Res.: 225 Blackman St., 18702. Tel: 570-822-8330; Fax: 570-823-3177.
Catechesis/Religious Program—Marian Fadden, D.R.E. Students 28.

4—ST. CASIMIR'S (1889), (Lithuanian), [CEM], Restructured with St. Aloysius, Wilkes-Barre & Exaltation of the Holy Cross, Hanover Twp. Revs. Andrew R. Sinnott; Thumma Savari.
Res.: 301 Delaney St., 18706. Tel: 570-825-2598; Fax: 570-825-6525.
Catechesis/Religious Program—Ann Marie Piragus, D.R.E. Students 69.

5—ST. DOMINIC (1882), Linked with Blessed Sacrament, St. Francis of Assisi & St. John the Baptist, Wilkes-Barre. Rev. Joseph A. Kearney.
Res.: 155 Austin Ave., 18705. Tel: 570-822-8871.
Catechesis/Religious Program—Cathy Riccetti, D.R.E. Students 100.

6—ST. FRANCIS OF ASSISI (1913), (Lithuanian), Merged with St. John the Baptist, Blessed Sacrament, & St. Dominick, Wilkes-Barre.

7—HOLY ROSARY (1906), (Italian), Rev. Msgr. Joseph P. Kelly, Admin.
Res.: 363 Park Ave., 18702. Tel: 570-822-1183; Fax: 570-822-2755.
Catechesis/Religious Program—Mariam Rose Fadden, D.R.E. Students 12.

8—HOLY SAVIOUR (1895), Closed. Merged With St. Christopher, Bear Creek. Rev. Kenneth M. Seegar.
Res.: 54 Hillard St., 18702. Tel: 570-822-1186; Fax: 570-822-1074.
Catechesis/Religious Program—Students 4.

9—HOLY TRINITY (1893), (Lithuanian), [CEM 2], Closed. Restructured with St. Joseph, Wilkes-Barre Township. Rev. Paul L. Pudhota (India).
Res.: 416 E. South St., 18702. Tel: 570-823-1081.
Catechesis/Religious Program—Students 52.

10—ST. JOHN THE BAPTIST (1924), (Slovak), Merged with Blessed Sacrament, St. Francis of Assisi, & St. Dominick, Wilkes-Barre.

11—ST. JOHN THE EVANGELIST (1927) Merged with Sacred Heart of Jesus, Wilkes-Barre.

12—ST. JOSEPH (Georgetown) (1898) Rev. Theodore L. Obaza, Admin. (Retired).
Res.: 783 E. Northampton St., Wilkes Barre Township, 18702. Tel: 570-822-8023; Fax: 570-822-2891.
Catechesis/Religious Program—Students 72.

13—ST. JOSEPH (1927), (Slovak), Merged with St. Mary's Church of the Immaculate Conception, Wilkes-Barre.

14—ST. MARY OF THE IMMACULATE CONCEPTION (1845) [CEM] Rev. Msgr. Thomas V. Banick; Deacon Leo R. Thompson.
Res.: 134 S. Washington St., P.O. Box 348, 18703-0348. Tel: 570-823-4168; Fax: 570-822-3477.
Catechesis/Religious Program—Sr. Dolores M. Banick, I.H.M., D.R.E. Students 94.

15—MATERNITY OF THE BLESSED VIRGIN MARY (1885), (Polish), [CEM 2], Linked with St. Joseph, Wilkes-Barre Township, now closed. Rev. John S. Terry; Deacon Philip G. Harris Sr.
Res.: 40 Park Ave., 18702. Tel: 570-824-7832; Fax: 570-822-0765.
Catechesis/Religious Program—Frances Jacobs, D.R.E. Students 45.

16—ST. NICHOLAS (1856), (German), [CEM 2] Rev. Msgr. Joseph G. Rauscher; Rev. Stephen J. Stavoy; Deacon Peter G. Smith. In Res., Rev. John J. Victoria.
Res.: 226 S. Washington St., 18701-2897. Tel: 570-823-7736; 570-823-5842; Fax: 570-823-0256.
Catechesis/Religious Program—Mr. James McDermott, D.R.E. Students 562.

17—ST. PATRICK'S (1920), Linked with St. Boniface, Wilkes-Barre. Rev. James E. McGahagan; Deacon Francis J. Bradigan.
Res.: 316 Parrish St., 18702. Tel: 570-823-1948; Fax: 570-823-3177.
Catechesis/Religious Program—Marian Fadden, D.R.E. Students 32.

18—SACRED HEART-ST. JOHN (1896) [CEM], Merged with St. John the Evangelist, Wilkes-Barre and St. Stanislaus, Wilkes-Barre. Rev. Msgr. John J. Sempa;

Deacon Pete Hoegen.
Res.: 666 N. Main St., 18705-1794. Tel: 570-823-4988; Fax: 570-823-5932.
Catechesis/Religious Program—Joyce Cecconi, D.R.E. Students 41.

19—ST. STANISLAUS KOSTKA (1908), (Polish), [CEM], Restructured with Sacred Heart-St. John, Wilkes-Barre. Rev. Msgr. John J. Sempa.
Res.: 666 N. Main St., 18705. Tel: 570-823-4988.
Catechesis/Religious Program—Joyce Cecconi, D.R.E. Students 5.

20—ST. THERESE (1929) Rev. Msgr. Francis J. Callahan; Deacon James T. Atherton. In Res., Rev. James J. Alco (Retired).
Res.: 25 Old River Rd., 18702. Tel: 570-822-1075; Fax: 570-829-4147.
Catechesis/Religious Program—Mark Kalaus, D.R.E. Students 105.

WILLIAMSPORT, LYCOMING CO.

1—ST. ANN'S (1959) Rev. Paul C. Fontanella; Deacon Stephen Frye.
Res.: 1220 Northway Rd., 17701. Tel: 570-322-5935; Fax: 570-322-2451.
Catechesis/Religious Program—Marianne DePasqua, D.R.E. Students 150.
Mission—Assumption of the B.V.M. Cascade, Lycoming Co.

2—ANNUNCIATION, Consolidated with Holy Rosary, Williamsport. For inquiries for parish records please contact St. Joseph the Worker, Williamsport.

3—ASCENSION (1907), Merged with Holy Rosary & Mater Dolorosa, Williamsport. Now consolidated and known as St. Joseph the Worker, Williamsport., 2111 Linn St., 17701. Tel: 570-323-9456.

4—ST. BONIFACE (1853), (German), Linked with St. Lawrence, Williamsport. Rev. Msgr. Stephen D. McGough. In Res., Rev. Msgr. Neil J. Van Loon.
Res.: 326 Washington Blvd., 17701. Tel: 570-326-1544; Fax: 570-326-6746.

5—HOLY ROSARY (1915), (Polish), Closed. For inquiries for parish records please contact St. Joseph the Worker, Williamsport.

6—MATER DOLOROSA (1908), (Italian), Consolidated with Holy Rosary, Ascension & Assumption, Williamsport. For inquiries for parish records please contact St. Joseph the Worker, Williamsport.

7—ST. JOSEPH THE WORKER, WILLIAMSPORT (1865) [CEM], Consolidated with Holy Rosary (now closed), Ascension & Martin Dolorosa, Williamsport. Revs. Shane L. Kirby; David W. Bechtel; Deacon J. Morris Smith.
Office: 711 W. Edwin St., 17701. Tel: 570-323-9456; Fax: 570-323-3728.
Rectory—635 Hepburn St., 17701.
Catechesis/Religious Program—Tel: 570-323-3799. James Foran, D.R.E. Students 318.

WYALUSING, BRADFORD CO., ST. MARY'S ASSUMPTION (1950), (Restructured with St. Joachim, Meshoppen. Rev. Joseph J. Manarchuck, Admin.
Parish Office & Mailing Address—R.R. 4, Box 4003, 18853. Tel: 570-746-1006; Fax: 570-746-0389.
Res.: 200 Front St., 18853.
Catechesis/Religious Program—Cathy Hagadon, D.R.E. Students 46.
Mission—St. Anthony, Closed.

WYOMING, LUZERNE CO., ST. JOSEPH'S (1914), (Polish), [CEM], Restructured with Our Lady of Sorrows, West Wyoming. Revs. John V. Polednak, Admin.; Leonard M. Butcavage.
Res.: 97 E. Sixth St., 18644. Tel: 570-693-0510; Fax: 570-693-1652.
Catechesis/Religious Program—Frances Lisewski, D.R.E. Students 77.

Chaplains of Public Institutions

CLARKS SUMMIT. *Clarks Summit State Hospital* 18411. Rev. George A. Jeffrey (Retired). Tel: 570-822-1075.

DALLAS. *State Correctional Institution* 18612. Tel: 570-675-1101. Deacon Steve Napoli.

EAST STROUDSBURG. *East Stroudsburg State University*, 200 Prospect St., 18301. Tel: 570-422-3525; Fax: 570-422-3410. Vacant, Dir.

LA PLUME. *Keystone College*. Rev. Msgr. James J. McGarry.
Clarks Summit. Tel: 570-586-1741.

MUNCY. *Muncy Prison*, Tel: 570-546-3900. Rev. Glenn E. McCreary, Chap.
Rectory—Resurrection, 526 S. Main St., 17756.

WILKES-BARRE. *Geisinger Wyoming Valley Hospital*, Tel: 570-822-9561. Rev. Joseph A. Kearney.
Rectory—Blessed Sacrament, 213 E. Main St., 18705.
Veteran's Administration Hospital. Revs. David R. Betts, W. Jeffrey Paulish, Stephen J. Stavoy.

WILLIAMSPORT. *Lycoming College*, 700 College Pl., Box 149, 17701. Tel: 570-321-4111. Sr. Catherine Ann Gilvary, I.H.M., Campus Min.

On Special or Other Diocesan Assignment:
Revs.—
Bergman, Eric L., Chap., St. Thomas More Society of St. Clare Church, c/o 2301 N. Washington Ave., 18509. Tel: 570-343-0634
Elston, Joseph G., Chap. Ministry for the Deaf, 909 Grove St., Avoca, 18641.
Finn, Edward S. (Retired), 421 Layton Rd., Equinunk, 18417. Tel: 570-224-4380
Yaszcz, Thomas A., Chap., 52 W. Grove St., Nanticoke, 18634. Tel: 570-735-5447

On Duty Outside the Diocese:
Rev. Msgrs.—
Jordan, John J., Nativity Miguel Network of Schools, 729a Delaware Ave., S.W., Washington, DC 20024. Tel: 202-251-5274
Rossi, Walter R., Rector, Basilica of the National Shrine of the Immaculate Conception, 400 Michigan Ave., N.E., Washington, DC 20017. Tel: 202-526-8300
Rupert, Dalegord, The Liturgical Inst., St. Mary of the Lake Univ., 1000 E. Maple Ave., Mundelein, IL 60060. Tel: 847-970-4969
Revs.—
Clarke, Brian J.T., J.C.L., De Sales Hall, 721 Lawrence St., N.E., Washington, DC 20017. Tel: 202-269-9410, Ext. 52
Connor, Charles P., Jeanne Jugan Residence, 4200 Harewood Rd. N.E., Washington, DC 20017. Tel: 202-269-1831
Doherty, Daniel J., S.S., Society of St. Sulpice, St. Mary's Seminary & University, 5400 Roland Ave., Baltimore, MD 21210. Tel: 410-864-4005
Gabuzda, Richard J. (OM), Dir., Institute for Priestly Formation, 302 N. 22nd St., #802, Omaha, NE 68178. Tel: 402-546-6384
Gregoris, Nicholas L., 333 Pearl St., Apt. 15F, New York, NY 10038.
Melnick, John E., Society of St. Augustine, c/o St. Mary-St. Anthony Parish, 615 N. 7th St., Kansas City, KS 66101. Tel: 913-371-1408
Munkelt, Richard A., St. Anthony of Padua Church, 1360 Pleasant Valley Way, West Orange, NJ 07052. Tel: 201-319-1765
O'Connor, Dominic E., 27 Cavendish Rd. E. - The Park, Nottingham N67-1BB England.
Petro, Thomas J., Pontifical Gregorian Univ., Casa Santa Maria, Via dell Umilta 30, Rome 00187 Italy. 714 Tunkhannock Ave., Exeter, 18643.
Pilon, Jean-Pierre G., St. Patrick's Academy, Woodville House, Islandeady, Castlebar, Co. Mayo Ireland.
Rafferty, James A., S.T.L., PNAC, Casa Santa Maria, Via dell Umilta, 30, Rome 00187 Italy. Tel: 011 39 06 6900-1121. 301 Seymour Ave., 18505.
Reichlen, Gregory A., Casa Santa Maria, Via dell Umilta, 30, Rome 00187 Italy.
Sarnecki, Thomas G., Bay Pines Vet's Hospital, 10036 63rd Ave. N. Bldg. 5, Unit 18, Saint Petersburg, FL 33708. Tel: 727-946-0875
Shantillo, Gerald W., Pontifical North American College, Vatican City State, Rome 00120 Italy.
Terrera, C. Bernardo, Chapelle St. Augustin, Avenue de Bethusy 78, Lausanne 1012 Switzerland.
Walsh, John A., P.O. Box 1665, Minneola, FL 34755. Tel: 407-438-0990

Military Chaplains:
Revs.—
Dormer, David J., Chap. Major, U.S. Army, P.O. Box 4554, Fort Eustis, VA 23604. Tel: 570-441-7496
Fullerton, Daniel, Chap., USN, c/o 201 Woods Ln., Erin, NY 14838.
Hochreiter, Robert S., Chap., Col., U.S.A.F., 2270 White House Cove, Newport News, VA 23602. Tel: 757-874-8602
Kelly, Brian F., Chap., Cap., U.S.N., 7183 Willett Cir., Carlsbad, CA 92011. Tel: 858-577-1333
Kozen, Bert S., Chap., U.S. Army, c/o Chancery Office, Diocese of Scranton, 300 Wyoming Ave., 18503.
Petruska, William M., Cap., U.S.N., 4421 Collwood Ln., San Diego, CA 92115-2015. Tel: 619-795-8485
Stavoy, Stephen J., Chap., Commander, U.S.N.R., St. Nicholis Parish, 226 S. Washington St., Wilkes Barre, 18701.

Unassigned or Leave of Absence:
Rev. Msgrs.—
Crynes, J. Peter
O'Neill, Kevin P.
Revs.—
Alco, James J. (Retired)
Clay, Christopher R.
Ensey, Eric S.
Gibson, Robert J.
Harris, Michael B.
Hawley, Gerard L.
Hudak, Thomas R.
Kilpatrick, Andrew W.
Kringe, Charles J., Liberty Rehabilitation Home, 17th & Liberty Sts., Allentown, 18103. Tel: 610-782-7067
Kulik, Francis J.
Kurash, Stanley J.
Lyman, Edward P.
Marchetti, Michael H.
Roberts, Marshall M.
Sinnott, Thomas G.
Sokolowski, Thomas J.
Tetherow, Gabriel Francis
Timchak, Robert M.
Wysocki, Joseph A.
Young, Vincent J.

Retired:
Most Revs.—
Dougherty, John M., D.D., V.G., St. Peter's Cathedral Rectory, 315 Wyomins Ave., 18503. Tel: 570-344-7231 Former Auxiliary Bishop of Scranton
Martino, Joseph F., D.D., Hist. E.D., Former Bishop of Scranton
Timlin, James C., D.D., Villa St. Joseph, 1600 Green Ridge St., 18509. Tel: 570-343-6170 Bishop Emeritus of Scranton
Rev. Msgrs.—
Beeda, Francis J., Little Flower Manor, 200 S. Meade St., Rm. 204, Wilkes Barre, 18702. Tel: 570-822-3554
Castellano, Francis J., Rose View Court, 1251 Rural Ave., Ste. 328, 17701. Tel: 570-220-8702
Clarke, James T., Villa St. Joseph, Dunmore, 18509. Tel: 570-969-1235
Conlan, F. Allan, Ph.D., 1101 Tennyson Close, Moosic, 18507. Tel: 570-344-1396
Demuth, George R., Holy Family Pavilion, 2510 Adams Ave., Apt. 303, 18509-1597. Tel: 570-344-3719
Donovan, William L., Villa St. Joseph, Dunmore, 18509. Tel: 570-963-9383
Esseff, John A., Villa St. Joseph, 1600 Green Ridge St., Dunmore, 18509. Tel: 570-499-9044
Gajewski, Chester A., Villa St. Joseph, Dunmore, 18509. Tel: 570-347-1851
Gray, Philip A., Villa St. Joseph, 1600 Green Ridge St., Dunmore, 18509. Tel: 570-344-0897
Kulik, Alexander T., Villa St. Joseph, 1600 Green Ridge St., 18509. Tel: 570-341-8881
Lasky, Joseph J., St. Therese Residence, 260 S. Meade St., Wilkes-Barre, 18702. Tel: 570-823-6131
McAndrews, Donald A., Villa St. Joseph, 1600 Green Ridge St., 18509. Tel: 570-207-5586
Penkala, Edmund S., Villa St. Joseph, Dunmore, 18509. Tel: 570-344-6288
Piorkowski, Stanley W., Villa St. Joseph, Dunmore, 18509. Tel: 570-343-1184
Purcell, Paul J., Villa St. Joseph, 1600 Green Ridge St., Dunmore, 18509. Tel: 570-963-9453
Siconolfi, Constantine V., 207 Karen Dr., 18505. Tel: 570-343-1001
Ward, William P., Villa St. Joseph, 1600 Green Ridge St., Dunmore, 18509. Tel: 570-341-1558
Yarrish, Bernard E., S.T.L., St. Therese Residence, 260 S. Meade St., Wilkes-Barre, 18702. Tel: 570-208-5371
Revs.—
Adonizio, Joseph J., 154 Rock St., Pittston, 18640. Tel: 570-654-8032
Alisauskas, Peter J., Little Flower Manor, 200 S. Meade St., Wilkes-Barre, 18702. Tel: 570-823-6131
Bochinski, Mark J., Villa St. Joseph, 1600 Green Ridge St., Dunmore, 18509. Tel: 570-344-5001
Boles, Joseph M., Villa St. Joseph, Dunmore, 18509. Tel: 570-343-4791
Brogus, Albert G., 43 St. James St., Plains, 18705.
Brozena, Joseph M., 602 Sibley Ave., Old Forge, 18518.
Carr, Eugene R., P.O. Box 1063, Killington, VT 05751. Tel: 802-422-3589
Casey, John W., 1024 SE Fifth Ave., Apt. 404, Dania Beach, FL 33004. Tel: 954-920-0681
Cipriano, Joseph F., Villa St. Joseph, 1600 Green Ridge St., Dunmore, 18509. Tel: 570-961-0328
Cortese, Patrick S., 1007 Strawberry Ln., Hazle Township, 18202. Tel: 570-459-5929
Culnane, William R., Villa St. Joseph, 1600 Green Ridge St., 18509-2197. Tel: 570-343-4791
Cummings, Charles J., P.O. Box 3271, 17701. Tel: 570-220-2070
Deviney, Raymond L., 1030 S. Hanover St., Nanticoke, 18634. Tel: 570-735-4833
Fanucci, Santino J., Villa St. Joseph, 1600 Green Ridge St., Dunmore, 18509. Tel: 570-498-7091
Finn, Edward S., 421 Layton Rd., Equinunk, 18417. Tel: 570-224-4380
Flynn, Thomas A., St. Mary's Villa Nursing Home,

675 St. Mary's Villa Rd., Moscow, 18444. Tel: 570-348-0589
Flynn, William J., S.S., V.F., Villa St. Joseph, 1600 Green Ridge St., Dunmore, 18509. Tel: 570-344-4495
Gaiardo, Martin J., Mulberry Tower, 499 Mulberry St., Apt. 1216, 18503. Tel: 570-347-4826
Gallia, Andrew R., 620 Clark St., Rear, Old Forge, 18518. Tel: 570-457-3423
Gunning, Eugene L., May-Oct.: 35 Nevin Rd., P.O. Box J, Newfoundland, 18445. Nov.-April: 27595 Lime St., Bonita Springs, FL 34135. Tel: 270-881-2368
Hazzouri, Alex J., Villa St. Joseph, Dunmore, 18509. Tel: 570-343-2859
Healey, William B., Villa St. Joseph, 1600 Green Ridge St., Dunmore, 18509. Tel: 570-343-0239
Herhenrerder, Peter V., 54 Lincoln Ave., Carbondale, 18407. Tel: 570-282-0304
Horanzy, Joseph M., Villa St. Joseph, 1600 Green Ridge St., Dunmore, 18509. Tel: 570-479-0446
Kilpatrick, John J., The Meadows at Maria Joseph Manor, 19 Towerview Cir., Danville, 17821. Cell: 570-357-4158
Kizis, Kenneth G., Villa St. Joseph, 1600 Green Ridge St., Dunmore, 18509. Tel: 570-344-2142
Krafchak, John S., 134 Prichards Rd., Hunlock Creek, 18621. Tel: 570-256-3058
Langan, Vincent F., St. John the Evangelist Rectory (Res), 85 Division St., South Waverly, 18840-2847. Tel: 570-888-2123
Lewis, Harry J., St. Therese Residence, 260 S. Meade St., Wilkes-Barre, 18702. Tel: 570-823-6131
Litcheck, Michael P., Oblates of St. Joseph Seminry, 1880 Hwy. 315, Pittston, 18640.
Masakowski, Edward M., Cedar Village, 3 Bluebird Ct., Wilkes-Barre, 18706.
Matz, Joseph A., c/o Rev. William Blake, St. James Rectory, 605 Church St., Jessup, 18434.
McCawley, William J., P.O. Box 36, Brodheadsville, 18322. Tel: 610-681-6146
Motsay, Joseph R., 1930 Seeneytown Rd., Dover, DE 19904. Tel: 302-423-5383
Obaza, Theodore L., Two Joseph Ln., Wilkes Barre, 18702. Tel: 570-822-1473
Oldfield, Albert E., The Meadows at Maria Joseph Manor, 30 Mateo Dr., Danville, 17821.
Olszewski, Daniel D., 74 Pinewood Dr., Laflin, 18702. Tel: 570-655-2165
Ostrowski, Joseph C., Villa St. Joseph, Dunmore, 18509. Tel: 570-342-7220
Rable, Cyril J., Villa St. Joseph, 1600 Green Ridge St., Dunmore, 18509. Tel: 570-344-2113
Rafferty, Michael J., Villa St. Joseph, 1600 Green Ridge St., 18509. Tel: 570-961-3723
Rusin, Joseph C., Visitation of B.V.M., 1090 Carmalt St., Dickson City, 18519. Tel: 570-489-2091
Scott, Edward R., Villa St. Joseph, 1600 Green Ridge St., 18509. Tel: 570-941-0452
Skiba, Walter F., 1414 Schlager St., 18504. Tel: 570-963-7556
Skitzki, Francis P., St. Therese Residence, 260 S. Meade St., Wilkes-Barre, 18702.
Turi, John J., 3182 Hemlock Farms, Lords Valley, 18428. Tel: 570-775-8874
Urban, Anthony M., 635 Church St., Swoyersville, 18704. Tel: 570-283-1763
Weber, Joseph O., Holy Family Pavilion, Apt. 114, 2510 Adams Ave., 18509. Tel: 570-348-3535
Yenkevich, Daniel J., 846 Gibbons St., 18505. Tel: 570-961-0196
Zapotocki, Henry E., P.O. Box 847, Tannersville, 18372. Tel: 570-629-1235
Zavacki, Richard A., Our Lady of the Immaculate Conception, 898 Center St., Freeland, 18224. Tel: 570-823-3791
Zawadzki, Victor C., 5 O'Donnell St., Wilkes-Barre, 18702. Tel: 570-819-1629

INSTITUTIONS LOCATED IN THE DIOCESE

[A] SEMINARIES, DIOCESAN

DALTON. *Saint Pius X Seminary* (Collaborative College/Pre-Theology Seminary), 1000 Seminary Rd., 18414. Tel: 570-563-1131; Fax: 570-563-8520. Email: st-piusx-seminary@dioceseofscranton.org. Web: www.dioceseofscranton.org/stpius.

[B] SEMINARIES, RELIGIOUS

PITTSTON. *St. Joseph's Oblate Seminary*, 1880 Hwy. 315, 18640. Tel: 570-654-7542; Fax: 570-655-8652. Email: osjseminary@comcast.net. Very Rev. Paul A. McDonnell, O.S.J., Provincial Supr., Rector & Seminary Dir.; Revs. Gregory T. Finn, O.S.J., 1st Councilor; Joseph D. Sibilano, O.S.J., 2nd Councilor; Salvatore Bentivegna, O.S.J. In Res. Rev. Mario Buttini, O.S.J.

[C] COLLEGES AND UNIVERSITIES

SCRANTON. *Marywood University* 18509. Tel: 570-348-6211; Fax: 570-340-6014. Email: annemunley@marywood.edu. Web: www.marywood.edu. Sr. Anne Munley, I.H.M., Pres.; Dr. Peter Cimbolic, Provost & Vice Pres. Academic Affairs; Dr. Clayton N. Pheasant, Vice Pres. Univ. Advancement; Dr. Raymond P. Heath, Vice Pres. Student Life; Dr. Michael A. Foley, Dean, College of Liberal Arts & Sciences; Dr. Mary Anne Fedrick, Dean, College of Education & Human Devel.; Dr. Joyce Z. White, Dir., School of Social Work; Dr. Alan Levine, Dean, College of Health and Human Svcs.; Mr. Matthew R. Porse, Interim Dean, Insalaco College of Creative & Performing Arts; Rosemary Burger, Registrar; Ann Boland-Chase, M.A., Vice Pres. Enrollment Mgmt.; Dr. Ellen Boylan, Dir., Inst. Research & Assessment; Ms. Catherine Hanson Schappert, Dir., Library Svcs.; Mr. Gregory Keane Hunt, Dean, School Architecture. Sisters, Servants of the Immaculate Heart of Mary. Sisters 14; Lay Teachers 151; Students 3,480.

The University of Scranton (Society of Jesus), 18510. Tel: 570-941-7400; Fax: 570-941-4097. Email: info@scranton.edu. Web: www.scranton.edu. Rev. Scott R. Pilarz, S.J., Pres.; Dr. Harold W. Ballie, Provost & Vice Pres. for Academic Affairs; Dr. Joseph H. Dreisbach, Assoc. Provost, Academic Affairs; Dr. Steven Jones, Assoc. Provost, Community Engagement & Mission; Ms. Patricia Day, Vice Pres. Human Resources; Mr. Patrick F. Leahy, Vice Pres. Univ. Rels.; Mr. Edward J. Steinmetz, Vice Pres., Finance & Treas.; Mr. Gerald C. Zaboski, Vice Pres. Alumni & Public Rels.; Mr. Jerome P. DeSanto, Chief Information Officer & Vice Pres. for Planning; Dr. Paul F. Fahey, Acting Dean, College of Arts & Sciences; Dr. Michael Mensah, Dean, Kania School of Mgmt.; Dr. W. Jeffrey Welsh, Dean, College Graduate & Continuing Educ.; Ms. Helen Stager, Registrar; Dr. Debra A. Pellegrino, Dean, Panuska College of Professional Studies; Dr. Thomas Smith, Dir. Counseling Center; Dr. Vincent Carilli, Vice Pres., Student Affairs; Anitra Mcshea, Dean, Students; Mr. Charles E. Kratz, Dean, Library; Ms. Abigail Byman, Sec. of the Univ. & Gen. Counsel; Revs. John J. Begley, S.J., Prof., Theology; I. Michael Bellafiore, S.J., Prof. Theology; Louis A. Bonacci, S.J., Coord. Spiritual Direction; Timothy J. Cadigan, S.J., Prof., Biology; Terrence P. Devino, S.J., Vice Pres. Univ. Ministries; Peter Folan, S.J., Prof., Philosophy; Revs. Henry B. Haske, S.J., Pastoral Min.; Joseph Henry, S.J., Pastoral Min.; Herbert B. Keller, S.J., Pres., Scranton Prep; William Lamm, S.J., Pastoral Min.; John W. Lange, S.J., Pastoral Min.; John J. Levko, S.J., Prof., Mathematics; Francis J. MacEntee, S.J., Prof. Emeritus, Biology; William J. McGrath, S.J., Teacher Latin; Bernard R. McIlhenny, S.J., Min. Jesuit Community; Ronald H. McKinney, S.J., Prof., Philosophy; J. Patrick Mohr, S.J., Prof., Philosophy; G. Donald Pantle, S.J., Prof., German & Spanish; Thomas Roach, S.J., Rector; Thomas F. Sable, S.J., Prof., Theology; Daniel Sweeny, S.J., Prof. Political Science; Joseph N. Tylenda, S.J., Chap., Marian Convent; Bro. James C. Lemon, S.J., Admin. Asst., Scranton Prep; Sr. Carol Tropiano, R.S.M., Univ. Minister. Priests 23; Students 4,795.

DALLAS. *Misericordia University* 18612. Tel: 570-674-6400; Fax: 570-675-2441. Web: www.misericordia.edu. Conference for Mercy Higher Education Mid-Atlantic Region Division, Dallas, PA. Priests 1; Sisters Teaching 2; Students 2,358.
Administration: Michael A. MacDowell, Ed.D., Pres.; Mr. John Risboskin, Vice Pres. of Finance & Admin.; Rev. Donald J. Williams, Chap.; Dr. Mari King, Vice Pres. of Academic Affairs; Ms. Susan Helwig, Vice Pres. Institutional Advancement; Sr. Jean Messaros, R.S.M., Vice Pres. Student Affairs; Mrs. Jane Dessoye, M.S., Enrollment Mgr.; Mr. Edward Lahart, M.S., Registrar; Bernadette Rushmer, Dir., Career Svcs.; Ms. Jacqueline Ghormoz, M.S., Dir. Counseling Svcs.; Mr. Val Apanovich, Dir. Information Technology; Dr. John Sumansky, Chief Information & Planning Officer; Barbara Burd, Dir., Library Svcs.; Ms. Kathleen A. Foley, B.S., M.S., Asst. Vice Pres. Student Affairs; Mr. Ronald Hromisin, C.P.A., Controller; Mr. James Roberts, Dir. Mktg. & Public Rels.

WILKES-BARRE. **King's College* 18711. Tel: 570-208-5900; Fax: 570-208-9049. Web: www.kings.edu. Priests 8; Brothers 2; Lay Teachers 117; Students 2,557.
Officers of the College: Rev. Thomas J. O'Hara, C.S.C., Ph.D., Pres.; Dr. Nicholas A. Holodick, Vice Pres. Academic Affairs; Dr. Lisa Marie McCauley, Vice Pres. Business Affairs & Treas.; Ms. Janet Mercincavage, Vice Pres. Student Affairs; Dr. Frank H. Oliver, Vice Pres. Institutional Advancement; Revs. Richard C. Hockman, C.S.C., College Chap. & Dir. Campus Ministry; John J. Ryan, C.S.C., Dean, William J. McGowan School of Business; Mr. Paul J. Moran, Exec. Dir. Information and Instructional Technology Svcs.; Ms. Michelle Lawrence-Schmude, Dean Admissions & Interim Dir., College of Mktg. & Advertising; Mr. Daniel T. Cebrick, Registrar; Rev. Thomas C. Bertone, C.S.C., Rel. Supr. & Dir. Counseling Ctr. Holy Cross Community Revs. Genaro P. Aguilar, C.S.C., College Counselor; Thomas F. Carten, C.S.C., College Media; Anthony R. Grasso, C.S.C., Prof. English, Assoc. Vice Pres. Academic Affairs & Dean of Faculty; Richard C. Hockman, C.S.C., Dir. Campus Min.; Daniel J. Issing, C.S.C., Asst. Prof. Theology; Charles J. Kociolek, C.S.C., Dir. Academic Advisement; Thomas J. O'Hara, C.S.C., Ph.D., Pres.; John J. Ryan, C.S.C., Dean, McGowan School of Business; Bros. James H. Miller, C.S.C., Assoc. Prof. Theatre; George C. Schmitz, C.S.C., B.A., M.A., Dir. Community Outreach In Res. Revs. Joseph J. Long, C.S.C. (Retired); Fidel Ticona, C.S.C., Hispanic Min.; Bros. Jerome Matthews, C.S.C.; Harold J. Rogan, C.S.C.

[D] HIGH SCHOOLS, DIOCESAN

SCRANTON. *Holy Cross High School*, 501 E. Drinker St., Dunmore, 18512. Tel: 570-346-7541; 570-346-7542; Fax: 570-348-1070. Rev. Christopher T. Washington, S.T.L., Chap.; Mr. James P. Marcks, Prin. Priests 1; Sisters 4; Lay Teachers 40.

EAST STROUDSBURG. *Notre Dame High School* (member of the Notre Dame Regional School System of the Diocese of Scranton, Inc.), 60 Spangenburg Ave., 18301. Tel: 570-421-0466; Fax: 570-476-0629. Rev. Msgr. John A. Bergamo, J.C.L., Chap.; Mr. Jeffrey N. Lyons, Prin.; Mrs. Patricia Burke, Librarian.

WILKES-BARRE. *Holy Redeemer High School* (member of the Holy Redeemer Regional School System of the Diocese of Scranton, Inc.), 159 S. Pennsylvania Blvd., 18701. Tel: 570-829-2424; Fax: 570-829-4412. Rev. John J. Victoria, Chap.; Mr. James Redington, Prin.; Anita Sirak, Assoc. Prin.; Mary Francis Selecky, Librarian. Priests 1; Sisters 5; Deacons 1; Lay Teachers 40.

WILLIAMSPORT. *Saint John Neumann Regional Academy High School Campus*, (Grades 7-12), (member of the Saint John Neumann Regional School System of the Diocese of Scranton, Inc.), 901 Penn St., 17701. Tel: 570-323-9953; Fax: 570-321-7146. Ms. Denise Tobin, Prin.; Rev. David W. Bechtel, Chap.

[E] HIGH SCHOOLS, PRIVATE

SCRANTON. **Scranton Preparatory School*, 1000 Wyoming Ave., 18509. Tel: 570-941-7737; Fax: 570-941-6118. Email: pmarx@scrantonprep.com. Web: www.scrantonprep.com. Rev. Herbert B. Keller, S.J., Pres.; Patrick J. Marx, Prin.; Kathleen Dooley, Librarian. Society of Jesus. Priests 3; Brothers 1; Lay Teachers 63; Students 863.
Faculty: Revs. Henry B. Haske, S.J.; William J. McGrath, S.J.; Bro. James C. Lemon, S.J.

MOSCOW. *St. Gregory's Academy* (1993) R.R. 8, Box 8214, 18444. Tel: 570-842-8112; Fax: 570-842-4513. Email: sga@saintgregorysacademy.com. Rev. Justin Nolan, F.S.S.P., Chap.; Deacon John Rickert, Asst. Chap.; E. Howard Clark, Headmaster. Priestly Fraternity of St. Peter. Priests 1; Lay Teachers 12; Students 61.

[F] DIOCESAN ELEMENTARY SCHOOLS

SCRANTON. *All Saints Academy*, (Grades PreK-8), (member of the Holy Cross Regional School System of the Diocese of Scranton, Inc.), 1425 Jackson St., 18504. Tel: 570-343-8114; Fax: 570-343-0378. Mrs. Michele Long, Prin.; Sr. Jeanne McAuliffe, I.H.M., Librarian.

Saint Clare/Saint Paul Elementary School (Main Campus), (Grades 4-8), (member of the Holy Cross Regional School System of the Diocese of Scranton, Inc.), 1527 Penn Ave., 18509. Tel: 570-343-7880; 570-343-4485; Fax: 570-343-0069. Mrs. Elizabeth Murray, Prin.

Saint Clare/Saint Paul Elementary School (Primary Campus), (Grades PreK-3), (member of the Holy Cross Regional School System of the Diocese of Scranton, Inc.), 2215 N. Washington Ave., 18509. Tel: 570-343-2790; Fax: 570-343-4905. Mrs.

Elizabeth Murray, Prin.

Marian Catholic Elementary School, (Grades PreK-8), (member of the Holy Cross Regional School System of the Diocese of Scranton, Inc.), 638 Hemlock St., 18505. Tel: 570-346-9922; Fax: 570-207-2652. Mrs. Jeanne M. Rossi, Prin. Sisters 1; (Fulltime) 13.

CARBONDALE. *Sacred Heart Elementary School*, (Grades PreK-8), (member of the Holy Cross Regional School System of the Diocese of Scranton, Inc.), 27-33 Farview St., 18407. Tel: 570-282-0340; 570-282-5968; Fax: 570-281-3677. Mrs. Ellen M. Murphy, Prin.; Mrs. Barbara Carr, Librarian. Sisters 3; Lay Teachers 12.

CLARKS GREEN. *Our Lady of Peace Elementary School*, (Grades K-8), (member of the Holy Cross Regional School System of the Diocese of Scranton, Inc.), 410 N. Abington Rd., 18411. Tel: 570-587-4152; Fax: 570-586-5393. Mrs. Jane M. Quinn, Prin.; Mrs. Carol Harrison, Librarian.

CRESCO. *Monsignor McHugh Elementary School*, (Grades PreK-8), (member of the Notre Dame Regional School System of the Diocese of Scranton, Inc.), R.R. 1, Box 1780, 18326. Tel: 570-595-7463; Fax: 570-595-9639. Christopher Tigue, Prin.; Rev. Bryan B. Wright, Chap.

DALLAS. *Gate of Heaven Elementary School*, (Grades PreK-8), (member of the Holy Redeemer Regional School System of the Diocese of Scranton, Inc.), 40 Machell Ave., 18612. Tel: 570-675-6566; Fax: 570-674-0198. Abe Simon, Prin.

DUNMORE. *Saint Mary of Mount Carmel Elementary School*, (Grades PreK-8), (member of the Holy Cross Regional School System of the Diocese of Scranton, Inc.), 325 Chestnut St., 18512. Tel: 570-346-4429; 570-346-4560; Fax: 570-346-3016. Mr. Joseph Triano, Prin.

DURYEA. *Holy Rosary Elementary School*, (Grades PreK-8), (member of the Holy Redeemer Regional School System of the Diocese of Scranton, Inc.), 125 Stephenson St., 18642. Tel: 570-457-2553; Fax: 570-457-3537. Ms. Kathleen Gilmartin, Prin.

EAST STROUDSBURG. *Notre Dame Elementary School*, (Grades PreK-4), (member of the Notre Dame Regional School System of the Diocese of Scranton, Inc.), 78 Ridgeway St., 18301. Tel: 570-421-3651; Fax: 570-422-6935. Sr. Mary Alice Kane, I.H.M., Prin.; Mrs. Barbara Carr, Librarian.

Notre Dame Middle School, (Grades 5-8), (member of the Notre Dame Regional School System of the Diocese of Scranton, Inc.), 60 Spangenburg Ave., 18301. Tel: 570-421-7883; Fax: 570-421-2366. Mr. Thomas J. McCloskey, Prin.

EXETER. *Wyoming Area Catholic Elementary School*, (Grades PreK-8), (member of the Holy Redeemer Regional School System of the Diocese of Scranton, Inc.), 1690 Wyoming Ave., 18643. Tel: 570-654-7982; 570-655-8082; Fax: 570-654-0605. Mrs. Lucille Procopio, Prin.

HAZLETON. *Holy Family Academy*, (Grades PreK-8), (member of the Holy Redeemer Regional School System of the Diocese of Scranton, Inc.), 1700 W. Twenty-Second St., 18201. Tel: 570-455-9431; Fax: 570-455-2847. Mr. Stan Pavlick, Prin.

JESSUP. *La Salle Academy (Jessup Campus)*, (Grades 4-8), (member of the Holy Cross Regional School System of the Diocese of Scranton, Inc.), 309 First Ave., 18434. Tel: 570-489-2010; Fax: 570-489-3887. Sr. Donna Cerminaro, M.P.F., Prin.

LaSalle Academy (Dickson City Campus), (Grades PreK-3), (member of the Holy Cross Regional School System of the Diocese of Scranton, Inc.), 625 Dundaff St., Dickson City, 18519. Tel: 570-489-0061; Fax: 570-489-0157. Sr. Donna Cerminaro, M.P.F., Prin.

KINGSTON. *Good Shepherd Academy*, (Grades PreK-8), (member of the Holy Redeemer Regional School System of the Diocese of Scranton, Inc.), 316 N. Maple Ave., 18704. Tel: 570-718-4724; Fax: 570-718-4725. Mr. James A. Jones, Prin.

MOUNTAINTOP. *Saint Jude Elementary School*, (Grades PreK-8), (member of the Holy Redeemer Regional School System of the Diocese of Scranton, Inc.), 422 S. Mountain Blvd., Mountain Top, 18707. Tel: 570-474-5803; Fax: 570-403-6159. Mrs. Mary Ann Olszewski, Prin.; Linda Lawler, Librarian.

PITTSTON. *Saint Mary's Assumption Elementary School*, (Grades PreK-8), (member of the Holy Redeemer Regional School System of the Diocese of Scranton, Inc.), 41 Carroll St., 18640. Tel: 570-654-8313; Fax: 570-654-7052. Mrs. Mary Jane Kozick, Prin.

SAYRE. *Epiphany Elementary School*, (Grades PreK-8), (member of the Holy Cross Regional School System of the Diocese of Scranton, Inc.), 627 Stevenson St., 18840. Tel: 570-888-5802; Fax: 570-888-2362. Sr. Kathleen Kelly, I.H.M., Prin.

TOWANDA. *Saint Agnes Elementary School*, (Grades PreK-6), (member of the Holy Cross Regional School System of the Diocese of Scranton, Inc.), 102 Third St., 18848. Tel: 570-265-6803; Fax: 570-265-3065. Mrs. Kathleen DeWan, Prin.; Karen Troup, Librarian.

WILKES-BARRE. *Saint Nicholas/Saint Mary Elementary School*, (Grades K-8), (member of the Holy Redeemer Regional School System of the Diocese of Scranton, Inc.), 242 S. Washington St., 18701. Tel: 570-823-8089; Fax: 570-823-1402. Sr. Mary Catherine Slattery, S.C.C., Prin.

WILLIAMSPORT. *Saint John Neumann Regional Academy*, (Grades PreK-6), (member of the Saint John Newmann Regional School System of the Diocese of Scranton, Inc.), 710 Franklin St., 17701. Tel: 570-326-3738; 570-326-7385. Mrs. Susan Kaiser, Prin.

[G] PRESCHOOLS AND CHILD CARE CENTERS

SCRANTON. *Domiano Early Childhood Center* Marywood University, 2300 Adams Ave., 18509. Tel: 570-340-6085. Sr. Marilyn Muro, I.H.M., Dir.

Immaculate Care Preschool, 800 Taylor Ave., 18510. Tel: 570-344-4380. Ann Marie McDonald, Prin.

CLARKS GREEN. *St. Gregory Early Childhood Center*, 330 N. Abington Rd., Clarks Summit, 18411. Tel: 570-587-4808; Fax: 570-586-4515. Rev. Msgr. John H. Louis, S.T.L., J.C.D., Dir.

MILFORD. *St. Vincent de Paul Preschool*, 101 St. Vincent Dr., 18337-9672. Tel: 570-686-1867; 570-686-4545; Fax: 800-565-1762. Denise Spinetta, Dir.

MOSCOW. *St. Catherine Preschool* (1985) Church St., P.O. Box 250, 18444. Tel: 570-848-1258. Kathy Pierre, Dir.

MUNCY. *St. John Neumann Early Childhood Center*, 75 Musser Ln., 17756. Tel: 570-546-5272; Fax: 570-546-0322. Danielle Mc Fadden, Dir.

[H] RENEWAL CENTERS

CRESCO. *The Immaculate Heart of Mary Spiritual Renewal Center*, R.R. 1, Box 1781, 18326. Tel: 570-595-7548; 570-595-7549; Fax: 570-595-9698. Email: ihmcresco@yahoo.com. Web: ihm.marywood.edu. Sr. Anne Mary Boslett, I.H.M., Dir.

DALTON. *Fatima Renewal Center*, 1000 Seminary Rd., 18414. Tel: 570-563-8500; Fax: 570-563-1857. Email: fatima@dioceseofscranton.org. Web: www.dioceseofscranton.org/fatima. Mr. Robert Zigray, Facility Mgr.; Sarah Mountain, Prog. Coord. Total Staff 10.

NANTICOKE. *Holy Family Spiritual Renewal Center* (1996) 151 Old Newport St., 18634-1300. Tel: 570-735-2599; Fax: 570-735-2599. Email: mlhudak@verizon.net. Martin J. Hudak, Co-Dir.; Louise V. Hudak, Co-Dir. Total Staff 2; Total Assisted 4.

[I] GENERAL HOSPITALS

SCRANTON. *Mercy Community Care Corp*, 746 Jefferson Ave., 18510-1624. Tel: 570-348-7073; Fax: 570-348-7021. Email: tbisignani@health-partners.org. Web: mercyhealthpartners.com. Meg Hanson, Contact Person.

Mercy Health Partners Northeast Region, Inc., 746 Jefferson Ave., 18510-1624. Tel: 570-348-7100; Fax: 570-348-7639. Email: jstarcher@health-partners.org. Web: mercyhealthpartners.com. John Starcher, Pres. & CEO; Stephen Franko, CFO; Meg Hanson, Contact Person. Total Staff 93.

Mercy Hospital of Scranton, 746 Jefferson Ave., P.O. Box 994, 18510-1624. Tel: 570-348-7100; Fax: 570-348-7639. Email: jstarcher@health-partners.org. Web: mercyhealthpartners.com. John Starcher, Pres. & CEO, Mercy Health Partners; Rev. Eric L. Bersman, Chap.; Meg Hanson, Contact Person. Sisters of Mercy 7; Total Staff 1,105; Bed Capacity 320; Capacity 320; Patients Assisted Annually 186,458.

Mercy Healthcare Foundation, Inc., 746 Jefferson Ave., 18510-1624. Tel: 570-340-5902; Fax: 570-348-7208. Email: jhowells@health-partners.org. John Howells, Vice Pres. Total Assisted Annually 4,175.

Mercy Med-Care, Inc., 746 Jefferson Ave., 18510-1624. Tel: 570-348-7074; Fax: 570-348-7021. Email: sfranko@health-partners.org. Web: mercyhealthpartners.com. Total Staff 8; Patients Assisted Annually 16,677.

St. Stanislaus Medical Care Center dba Mercy Health Care Center 746 Jefferson Ave., 18510-1624. Tel: 570-348-7235; Fax: 570-348-7021. Meg Hanson, Contact Person.

CARBONDALE. *Marian Community Hospital*, 100 Lincoln Ave., 18407. Tel: 570-281-1000; Fax: 570-282-7177. Email: mariad@marianhospital.org. Web: www.mariancommunityhospital.org. Mary Theresa Vautrinot, Pres. & CEO. Sisters, Servants of the Immaculate Heart of Mary. Component of Maxis Health System, Member Catholic Health East. Sisters 4; Bed Capacity 70; Patients Assisted Annually 75,887.

Maxis Foundation, 100 Lincoln Ave., 18407. Tel: 570-281-1002; Fax: 570-281-7177. Web: www.mariancommunityhospital.org. Mary Theresa Vautrinot, Pres. & CEO.

Maxis Medical Services, 100 Lincoln Ave., 18407. Tel: 570-281-1315; Fax: 570-281-1256. Web: www.mariancommunityhospital.org. Mary Theresa Vautrinot, Pres. & CEO. Patients Assisted Annually 14,395.

MUNCY. *Muncy Valley Hospital*, 215 E. Water St., 17756. Tel: 570-546-8282; Fax: 570-546-4150. Email: jbednar@susquehannahealth.org. Web: www.susquehannahealth.org. Christine Ballard, Pres.; Sr. Sharon Hartman, S.C.C., Dir., Pastoral Care. Capacity 164; Patients Assisted Annually 111,285.

NANTICOKE. *Mercy Hospital of Nanticoke dba Mercy Special Care Hospital* 128 W. Washington St., 18634. Tel: 570-740-5204; 570-348-7235; Fax: 570-740-5220; 570-348-7021. Email: rwilliams@health-partners.org. Web: www.mercyhealthpartners.com. Robert D. Williams, Admin. Total Staff 166; Bed Capacity 67; Patients Assisted Annually 12,503.

WILLIAMSPORT. *Divine Providence Hospital of the Sisters of Christian Charity*, 1100 Grampian Blvd., 17701. Tel: 570-326-8181; Fax: 570-320-7979. Email: jbednar@susquehannahealth.org. Web: www.susquehannahealth.org. Ronald Reynolds, Pres.; Sr. Christina Marie Cables, S.C.C., Coord.; Rev. Fidelis Ekemgba, Chap. Bed Capacity 31; Patients Assisted Annually 201,142; Total Staff 464.

Sisters of Christian Charity Healthcare Corporation, 1100 Grampian Blvd., 17701. Tel: 570-320-7612; Fax: 570-320-7467. Email: jbednar@susquehannahealth.org. Web: www.susquehannahealth.org.

WILKES-BARRE. *Mercy Hospital of Wilkes-Barre*, c/o 746 Jefferson Ave., 18510-1624. Tel: 570-348-7073; Fax: 570-348-7021. Email: tbisignani@health-partners.org. Web: www.mercyhealthpartners.com.

[J] SPECIAL HOSPITALS

SCRANTON. *St. Joseph's Center* (1888) 2010 Adams Ave., 18509. Tel: 570-342-8379; Fax: 570-342-6080. Email: torourke@stjosephscenter.org. Web: www.stjosephscenter.org. Sr. Therese O'Rourke, I.H.M., Pres. & CEO; Rev. William B. Pickard, Chap. Priests 1; Bed Capacity 147; Patients Assisted Annually 155; Total Staff 535.

[K] SPECIAL EDUCATION SCHOOLS

CLARKS GREEN. *Lourdesmont* (1889) 537 Venard Rd., 18411. Tel: 570-587-4741; Fax: 570-586-0030. Email: msherman@lourdesmont.com. Web: www.lourdesmont.com. Sr. Mary Pauline Bilbrough, R.G.S., Coord.; Judy Neri, COO; John A. Antognoli, Ed.D., CEO.

Good Shepherd Corporation of Clarks Summit, PA Sisters of the Good Shepherd 6; Total Staff 70; Total Assisted 400.

PINE GROVE. *St. Michael's Group Home*, 25 Oak Grove Rd., 17963. Tel: 570-345-1160; Fax: 570-345-6307. Email: pggirls1995@yahoo.com. Web: www.dioceseofscranton.org. Total Assisted Annually 21; Total Staff 8; Bed Capacity 10.

TUNKHANNOCK. *St. Michael's Group Home-Tunkhannock*, 28 Putnam St., 18657. Tel: 570-836-6932; Fax: 570-836-6979. Email: stmikes@epix.net. Web: www.dioceseofscranton.org. Andrew Varzaly, Contact Person. Bed Capacity 6; Total Assisted Annually 9; Total Staff 5.

St. Michael's School, Box 370, 18657. Tel: 570-388-6155; Fax: 570-388-6979. Email: stmikes@epix.net. Web: www.dioceseofscranton.org. Mr. Andrew M. Varzaly, M.S.W., L.S.W., Exec. Dir.; Rev. John C. O'Bell, Chap. Bed Capacity 109; Total Staff 184; Students Assisted 338; Total Assisted Annually 232.

WEST PITTSTON. *St. Michael's Group Home-West Pittston*, 225-227 Damon St., 18643. Tel: 570-602-6579; Fax: 570-602-6979. Andrew Varzaly, Contact Person.

[L] HOMES FOR AGED

SCRANTON. *Home for Aged of the Little Sisters of the Poor, Holy Family Residence* (1907) 2500 Adams Ave., 18509. Tel: 570-343-4065; Fax: 570-346-1196. Sr. Charles Patricia Mary Mistretta, L.S.P., Supr. & Admin.; Rev. E. Francis Kelly, Chap. Little Sisters of the Poor 11; Aged Residents 52; Residents in Independent Living Apartments 23.

DALLAS. *Mercy Center Nursing Unit, Inc.*, Lake St., Box 370, 18612. Tel: 570-675-2131; Fax: 570-674-7606. Email: jwhite@mcnu.org. Web: www.mcnu.org. Sr. Sara Sweeney, R.S.M., Admin.; Sheila Heck, Dir. of Nursing; Rev. John J. Kulavich, Chap. Total Staff 155; Total Assisted 81;

Bed Capacity 140.

MOSCOW. *St. Mary's Villa Nursing Home* (1962) 675 St. Mary's Villa Rd., 18444. Tel: 570-842-7621; Fax: 570-842-2953. Email: lkanarr@stmarysvilla.com. Linda Kanarr, CEO/Admin.; Rev. Peter D. Menghini, Chap. A member of Covenant Health Systems, Lexington, MA Residents 112; Total Staff 200; Total Assisted 176; Bed Capacity 112.

St. Mary's Villa Residence (1999) One Pioneer Pl., 18444. Tel: 570-842-5274; Fax: 570-842-3472. Annette Chickey, Admin.; Rev. Peter D. Menghini, Chap. Residents 64; Total Staff 45.

WILKES-BARRE. *Little Flower Manor of the Diocese of Scranton*, 200 S. Meade St., 18702. Tel: 570-823-6131; Fax: 570-823-5171. Email: sjd@lfmstr.com. Andrew Durako, COO; Rev. Richard G. Ghezzi, Chap. Conducted by the Carmelite Sisters for the Aged and Infirm. Sisters 5; Aged Residents 133; Total Staff 230.

St. Therese Residence, 260 S. Meade St., 18702. Tel: 570-823-6131; Fax: 570-208-0143. Susan Kennan, Admin.; Rev. Richard G. Ghezzi, Chap. Conducted by the Carmelite Sisters for the Aged and Infirm. Residents 60; Total Staff 41.

[M] MONASTERIES AND RESIDENCES OF PRIESTS AND BROTHERS

SCRANTON. *Saint Ann's Passionist Monastery* (1909) 1233 St. Ann St., 18504. Tel: 570-347-5691; Fax: 570-347-9387. Email: rburke@cpprov.org. Very Rev. Richard Burke, C.P., Rector; Revs. Francis Landry, C.P., Asst. Rector; Brendan Breen, C.P.; Edward Deviny, C.P.; Brice Edwards, C.P.; Lee Havey, C.P.; John Connor, C.P. Sponsorship: Congregation of the Passion. In Res. Revs. Vincent Boney, C.P.; Edward Buchheit, C.P.; Malcolm Cornwell, C.P.; Roger Elliott, C.P.; Earl Keating, C.P.; Sebastian Kolinovsky, C.P.; Michael Salvagna, C.P.; Kenneth Walsh, C.P.; Cassian Yuhaus, C.P.; Bros. Joseph Rogers, C.P.; Daniel Turner, C.P.

ELMHURST. *Priestly Fraternity of St. Peter (F.S.S.P.), North American District Headquarters* (1991) *St. Peter's House*, Griffin Rd., P.O. Box 196, 18416. Tel: 570-842-4000; Fax: 570-842-4001. Email: info@fssp.com. Web: www.fssp.com. Revs. Edmund A. Castronovo, In Res., St. Michael's, Scranton; Michael O'Leary, F.S.S.P., Admin. St. Michael's, Scranton; Eric Flood, F.S.S.P., Dist. Supr.; Gregory Pendergraft, F.S.S.P., Exec. Dir. Devel.; Justin Nolan, F.S.S.P., Chap. St. Gregory's Academy, Elmhurst; Carl N. Gismondi, F.S.S.P., District Bursar; Deacon John Rickert, Chap., St. Gregory's Academy, Elmhurst. Priests 76; Seminarians 76.

LACEYVILLE. *Franciscan Missionary Hermits of St. Joseph* (1998) R.R. 1, Box 1590, 18623. Tel: 570-869-2918. Rev. Pio Mandato, F.M.H.J. In Res. Rev. Leo J. McKernan.

PITTSTON. *Our Lady of Sorrows Province of the Oblates of St. Joseph*, 1880 Hwy. 315, 18640. Tel: 570-654-7542; Fax: 570-654-8621. Very Rev. Paul A. McDonnell, O.S.J., Prov., Seminary Rector & Dir.; Revs. Gregory T. Finn, O.S.J., 1st Councilor; Joseph D. Sibilano, O.S.J., 2nd Councilor. Priests 10.

[N] DIOCESAN RESIDENCE FOR RETIRED PRIESTS

DUNMORE. *Villa St. Joseph*, 1600 Green Ridge St., 18509. Tel: 570-343-4791. Most Rev. James C. Timlin, D.D., Rector. Tel: 570-343-4791; Fax: 570-343-3040 In Res. Rev. Msgrs. James T. Clarke (Retired). Tel: 570-969-1235; J. Peter Crynes. Tel: 570-343-4791; William L. Donovan (Retired). Tel: 570-963-9383; John A. Esseff (Retired). Tel: 570-499-9044; Chester A. Gajewski (Retired). Tel: 570-347-1851; Philip A. Gray (Retired). Tel: 570-344-0897; Alexander T. Kulik (Retired). Tel: 570-341-8881; Donald A. McAndrews (Retired). Tel: 570-207-5586; Edmund S. Penkala (Retired). Tel: 570-344-6288; Stanley W. Piorkowski (Retired). Tel: 570-343-1184; Paul J. Purcell (Retired). Tel: 570-963-9453; William P. Ward (Retired). Tel: 570-341-1558; Revs. Mark J. Bochinski (Retired). Tel: 570-344-5001; Joseph M. Boles (Retired). Tel: 570-343-4791; Joseph F. Cipriano (Retired). Tel: 570-961-0328; William R. Culnane (Retired). Tel: 570-343-4791; Leo P. Cummings. Tel: 570-961-1815; Santino J. Fanucci (Retired). Tel: 570-498-7091; William J. Flynn, S.S., V.F. (Retired). Tel: 570-344-4495; Alex J. Hazzouri (Retired). Tel: 570-343-2859; William B. Healey (Retired). Tel: 570-343-0239; Joseph M. Horanzy (Retired). Tel: 570-479-0446; George A. Jeffrey (Retired). Tel: 570-814-2745; Kenneth G. Kizis (Retired). Tel: 570-344-2142; Joseph C. Ostrowski (Retired). Tel: 570-342-7220; Cyril J. Rable. Tel: 570-344-2113; Michael J. Rafferty (Retired). Tel: 570-961-3723; Edward R. Scott (Retired). Tel: 570-941-0452; Thomas J. Sokolowski. Tel: 570-343-4791.

[O] CONVENTS AND RESIDENCES FOR SISTERS

SCRANTON. *Immaculate Heart of Mary Center* (1971) 2300 Adams Ave., 18509. Tel: 570-342-6850; Fax: 570-346-5439. Email: communications@sistersofihm.org. Web: www.sistersofihm.org. Sisters Mary Persico, I.H.M., Pres. Tel: 570-346-5425; Mary Jo Gallagher, I.H.M., Vice Pres., Councilor Spiritual Devel. Tel: 570-346-5402; Barbara Jablonski, I.H.M., Councilor, Temporal Resources. Tel: 570-346-5405; Deborah Worlinsky, Business Mgr. Tel: 570-346-5406; Sisters Francine Fasolka, I.H.M., Dir. Communications. Tel: 570-346-5404; Ann Marie O'Brien, I.H.M., Dir. Coord. Missioning Resources. Tel: 570-346-5401; Kathryn Kurdziel, I.H.M., Dir. Candidates & Novices. Tel: 570-346-5414; Ruth Harkins, I.H.M., Dir. Vocations. Tel: 570-346-5413; Kathleen Mary Lunsmann, I.H.M., Dir. Devel. Tel: 570-346-5431. Sisters, Servants of the Immaculate Heart of Mary. Professed Sisters 457.

Councilors, Missioning & Community Life: Sisters Amy Zychal, I.H.M., Councilor, Missioning & Community Life. Tel: 570-346-5407; Kathryn Clauss, I.H.M., Councilor, Missioning & Community Life. Tel: 570-346-5409; Susan Hadzima, I.H.M., Councilor, Missioning & Community Life. Tel: 570-346-5410; Mary Mark Lowery, I.M.H., I.H.M. Center Admin. Tel: 570-346-5408; Jean Louise Bachetti, I.H.M., Dir. Associates. Tel: 570-963-2480.

Pascucci Family Our Lady of Peace Residence, 2300 Adams Ave., 18509. Tel: 570-346-5423; Fax: 570-346-5418. Sisters Mary Kathleen Faliskie, I.H.M., Asst. Admin. Tel: 570-346-5422; Jean Coughlin, I.H.M., Admin. Tel: 570-346-5421; Eleanor Mary Marconi, I.H.M., Asst. Admin. Tel: 570-346-5424; Rev. Joseph N. Tylenda, S.J., Chap. Sisters, Servants of the Immaculate Heart of Mary 99.

CLARKS SUMMIT. *St. Gabriel's Monastery*, 631 Griffin Pond Rd., South Abington Township, 18411. Tel: 570-586-2791; Fax: 570-586-8210. Email: cpnuns@intiques.com. Web: www.intiques.con/cpnuns/. Sr. Teresita Kho, Community Pres. Religious of the Passion of Jesus Christ; Passionist Nuns (Contemplative). Professed Sisters 8.

DALLAS. *Sisters of Mercy of the Americas, Mid-Atlantic Community*, 199 Lake St., 18612-0369. Tel: 570-675-2048; Fax: 570-675-9051. Email: cmcgroarty@mercymidatlantic.org. Web: www.mercymidatlantic.org. Sr. Christine McCann, R.S.M., Pres. Sisters 1,071.

TUNKHANNOCK. *Capuchin Sisters of Nazareth, Mother of God Convent*, 215 Wellwood Dr., 18657. Tel: 570-836-2737. Sr. Theresa May, Supr.

[P] RETREAT HOUSES

MOUNT POCONO. *Villa Our Lady Retreat House*, HCR 1, Box 41, Meadowside Rd., 18344-9714. Tel: 570-839-7217; Fax: 570-839-7553. Email: sbona@ptd.net. Web: www.villaourladyretreathouse.com. Sr. M. Bonaventa Radzai, O.S.F., Supr. & Admin. Bernardine Sisters 7.

SOUTH ABINGTON TOWNSHIP. *St. Gabriel's Retreat Center*, 631 Griffin Pond Rd., 18411. Tel: 570-586-4957; Fax: 570-587-3314. Email: kporter@epix.net. Religious of the Passion of Jesus Christ; Passionist Nuns (Contemplative).

[Q] CAMPS AND COMMUNITY CENTERS

TUNKHANNOCK. *Camp St. Andrew* (1940) 524 Stark Rd., P.O. Box 679, 18657. Tel: 570-836-2975. Off-Season Mailing Address: 33 E. Northampton St., Wilkes Barre, 18701. Tel: 570-226-4606; Fax: 570-829-7781. Rev. Msgr. Joseph P. Kelly, V.E., Exec. Dir. Regular Camp, Basketball Clinics 800.

WILKES-BARRE. *Catholic Youth Center*, 36 S. Washington St., 18701. Tel: 570-823-6121; Fax: 570-823-0175. Email: wvcyc@epix.net. Rev. John S. Terry, Dir.; Mr. Anthony D. English Jr., Exec. Dir.; Mr. Mark Soprano, Assoc. Dir.

[R] MISCELLANEOUS LISTINGS

SCRANTON. *African Sisters Education Collaborative(ASEC)* (2006) *Marywood University*, 2300 Adams Ave., 18509. Tel: 570-961-4700. Email: jernster@marywood.edu. Web: www.marywood.edu/asec/. Sr. Jacquelyn Ernster, O.S.B., Contact Person & Exec. Dir.

**Aid to the Church in Russia*, 300 Wyoming Ave., 18503-1279. Tel: 570-207-2216; Fax: 570-207-2236. James B. Earley, Dir., Scranton Office.

St. Ann's Foundation, 1239 St. Ann's St., 18504. Tel: 570-347-5691; Fax: 570-347-9387. Very Rev. Richard Burke, C.P., Exec. Dir.

Saint Ann's Media, Inc., 1230 St. Ann St., Box 111, 18504-0111. Tel: 570-941-2278; Fax: 570-941-0185. Email: webmaster@themass.com. Web: www.theMass.org; www.prayerline.org; www.theMass.com. Rev. Michael Salvagna, C.P., Dir.; Mr. Rich Shelp, Webmaster, Office Mgr. Sponsored by the Passionist Community.

St. Anthony's Haven, 409-411 Olive St., 18509. Tel: 570-342-1295, Ext. 204; Fax: 570-342-0985. Email: ghallinan@cssresidential.org. Men's & Women's Shelter.

St. James Manor, 600 Wyoming Ave., 18509. Tel: 570-342-1295, Ext. 202; Fax: 570-342-0985. Supportive Housing Program.

St. Francis of Assisi Kitchen, 500 Penn Ave., 18509. Tel: 570-342-5556; Fax: 570-963-8832. Web: www.stfranciskitchen.com. Rev. Msgr. Joseph P. Kelly, V.E., Dir.

Friends of the Poor (1984) *Jackson Terrace*, 148 Meridian St., 18503. Tel: 570-348-4428; Fax: 570-346-5412. Mailing Address: 2300 Adams Ave., 18509. Sr. Maryalice Jacquinot, I.H.M., CEO.

The Guild Studio, 400 Wyoming Ave., 18503. Tel: 800-367-6610; 570-342-8246; Fax: 570-342-5940. Email: guild01@aol.com. Trish Morrow, Gen. Mgr.

Religious Store, 400 Wyoming Ave., 18503. Tel: 800-367-6610; 570-342-8246; Fax: 570-342-5940. Email: guild01@aol.com.

I.H.M. Congregation Charitable Trust (1986) 2300 Adams Ave., 18509. Tel: 570-342-6850; Fax: 570-346-5439. Email: jablon@sistersofihm.org. Web: www.sistersofihm.org. Congregation of the Sisters, Servants of the Immaculate Heart of Mary.

Ministry for Religious Research and Consultancy (1984) 1233 St. Ann St., 18504. Tel: 570-586-9099; Fax: 570-586-9203. Email: cyuhaus@aol.com. Rev. Cassian J. Yuhaus, C.P., Exec. Dir.

VMR Charitable Trust (Vehicle Management for Religious) (1992) Tel: 570-586-9099; Fax: 570-586-9203.

DALLAS. *Mercy Consultation Center of Dallas*, S. Memorial Hwy., P.O. Box 370, 18612. Tel: 570-675-2284; Fax: 570-675-4390.

Studio I (1979) *Mercy Center*, Box 370, 18612. Tel: 570-675-1865; 570-674-3281; 570-675-2131; Fax: 570-674-5658. Email: srkiel@aol.com. Web: www.mercymall.com. Sr. Regina Kiel, R.S.M., Designer & Artist. Designing and handcrafting fine original custom jewelry and sculpture. Workshops in jewelry making using the lost wax casting technique: A. Couples - make their own wedding bands/engagement rings. B. All ages interested in learning the art of jewelry making.

HARLEIGH. *National Shrine of the Sacred Heart* 1 Church Pl., 18225. Tel: 570-455-4402. Rev. Thomas A. Cappelloni, Dir.

National Office: Men of the Sacred Heart, P.O. Box 500, 18225. Tel: 570-455-4402.

NANTICOKE. *People of God Community of Northeastern PA* (1984) 151 Old Newport St., 18634-1300. Tel: 570-735-2599; Fax: 570-735-2679. Email: jimmyg@epix.net. James Gialanella, Pres.

PITTSTON. *The Gabriel House*, 13 William St., 18640. Tel: 570-654-7157. Email: kitchenwb@aol.com. Anne Marie McCawley, Project Dir. Transitional housing facility for women and women with young children.

WILKES-BARRE. *Project REMAIN*, 215 High St., Apt. 100, 18701. Tel: 570-829-5373. Email: gkm@epix.net. Sr. Imelda Sherrett, R.S.M., Dir. Service for the elderly and the needy residents in the High Rises.

Project Remain Outreach to the Elderly dba John B. McGlynn Center Boulevard Townhomes, 72 Midland Ct., 18702. Tel: 570-824-8891; Fax: 570-970-1079. Sr. Miriam Francis Stadulis, R.S.M., Dir. Outreach to low income families in the housing projects.

St. Vincent De Paul Kitchen, 39 E. Jackson St., 18701. Tel: 570-829-7796; Fax: 570-208-9182. Email: amccawley@csswb.org. Thomas P. Cherry, Exec. Dir.; Anne Marie McCawley, Project Dir.

RELIGIOUS INSTITUTES OF MEN REPRESENTED IN THE DIOCESE

For further details refer to the corresponding bracketed number in the Religious Institutes of Men or Women section.

[1000]—*Congregation of the Passion* (Union City, NJ)—C.P.

[0690]—*Jesuit Fathers and Brothers* (Maryland Prov.)—S.J.

[0930]—*Oblates of St. Joseph* (Asti, Italy)—O.S.J.

[1065]—*Priestly Fraternity of St. Peter*—F.S.S.P.

[0610]—*Priests of the Congregation of Holy Cross* (Wilkes-Barre, PA)—C.S.C.

[1290]—*Society of the Priests of St. Sulpice*—S.S.

RELIGIOUS INSTITUTES OF WOMEN REPRESENTED IN THE DIOCESE

[1810]—*Bernardine Sisters of the Third Order of St. Francis*—O.S.F.

[0330]—*Carmelite Sisters of the Aged and Infirm*—O.Carm.

[2980]—*Congregation of Notre Dame*—C.N.D.

[0890]—*Daughters of Our Lady of Mercy*—D.M.

[]—*Dominican Sisters of Sparkhill*

[2575]—*Institute of the Sisters of Mercy of the Americas*—R.S.M.

[2340]—*Little Sisters of the Poor*—P.S.D.P.

[3240]—*Poor Sisters of Jesus Crucified and the Sorrowful Mother*—C.J.C.

[3170]—*Religious of the Passion of Jesus Christ*—C.P.

[3430]—*Religious Teachers Filippini*—M.P.F.

[0660]—*Sisters of Christian Charity*—S.C.C.

[3780]—*Sisters of Saints Cyril and Methodius*—SS.C.M.

[3840]—*Sisters of St. Joseph of Carondelet*—C.S.J.

[1830]—*Sisters of the Good Shepherd*—R.G.S.

[2160]—*Sisters, Servants of the Immaculate Heart of Mary*—I.H.M.

[]—*Society of the Sacred Heart of Jesus*—R.S.C.J.

[]—*Union Sisters of the Presentation of the Blessed Virgin Mary* (Ireland)—P.B.V.M.

DIOCESAN CEMETERIES

SCRANTON. *Cathedral*, 1708 Oram St., 18504. Tel: 570-347-9251; Fax: 570-347-4354.

Diocesan Cemeteries Office, 1708 Oram St., 18504. Tel: 570-207-2209; Fax: 570-347-4354. Kevin Beck, Dir.

CARVERTON. *Mount Olivet*, 612 Mt. Olivet Rd., 18644. Tel: 570-696-3636; Fax: 570-696-4705.

DRUMS. *Calvary*, Rte. 309, 49 S. Hunter Hwy., P.O. Box 485, 18222. Tel: 570-788-2150; Fax: 570-708-2938.

MOSCOW. *St. Catherine*, Main St., Rte. 435, P.O. Box 114, 18444. Tel: 570-842-8411; Fax: 570-842-8406.

OLD FORGE. *Holy Cross*, Oak & Keyser Ave., 18518. Tel: 570-347-9251; Fax: 570-347-4354. c/o 1708 Oram St., 18504.

WILLIAMSPORT. *Resurrection*, 4323 Lycoming Mall Dr., P.O. Box 12, Montoursville, 17754. Tel: 570-368-2727; Fax: 570-368-2727.

NECROLOGY

† Marra, Rev. Msgr. Anthony C., Dunmore, PA Saint Anthony of Padua Parish—Died May 12, 2009

† O'Brien, Rev. Msgr. John J., Scranton, PA Saint Paul Parish—Died Dec. 27, 2009

† Angelo, Girard F., Harleigh, PA Church of the Sacred Heart—Died June 20, 2009

† Everling, Robert M., Great Bend, PA Saint Lawrence Parish—Died April 1, 2009

† Fox, Joseph F., Bastress, PA Immaculate Conception Parish—Died July 26, 2009

† Malinowski, Hilary L., Simpson, PA Saint Micahel Parish—Died Oct. 1, 2009

† Plevyak, Valentine R., Sugar Notch, PA Holy Family Parish—Died May 30, 2009

† Prushinski, Carl T., (Retired)—Died Dec. 31, 2009

An asterisk (*) denotes an organization that has established tax-exempt status directly with the IRS and is not covered by the USCCB Group Ruling.

Archdiocese of Seattle

Archidioecesis Seattlensis

Most Reverend

ALEXANDER J. BRUNETT, Ph.D.

Archbishop of Seattle; ordained July 13, 1958; appointed Bishop of Helena April 19, 1994; consecrated and installed July 6, 1994; appointed Archbishop of Seattle October 28, 1997; installed December 18, 1997. *Office: 710 9th Ave., Seattle, WA 98104.* Tel: 206-382-4886; Fax: 206-382-3495.

Most Reverend

RAYMOND G. HUNTHAUSEN

Retired Archbishop of Seattle; ordained June 1, 1946; appointed Bishop of Helena, Montana July 8, 1962; consecrated August 30, 1962; appointed Archbishop of Seattle February 25, 1975; installed May 22, 1975; retired August 21, 1991. *Office: 710 9th Ave., Seattle, WA 98104.* Tel: 206-382-4886; Fax: 206-382-3495.

Most Reverend

EUSEBIO L. ELIZONDO

Auxiliary Bishop of Seattle; ordained August 18, 1984; appointed Auxiliary Bishop of Seattle and Titular Bishop of Acholla May 12, 2005; ordained June 6, 2005. *Office: 710 9th Ave., Seattle, WA 98104.* Tel: 206-274-3112.

Chancery Office: 710 9th Ave., Seattle, WA 98104. Tel: 206-382-4560; Fax: 206-382-4840.

Web: www.seattlearch.org

Email: info@seattlearch.org

Most Reverend

JOSEPH J. TYSON

Auxiliary Bishop of Seattle; ordained June 10, 1989; appointed Auxiliary Bishop of Seattle and Titular Bishop of Migirpa May 12, 2005; ordained June 6, 2005. *Office: 710 9th Ave., Seattle, WA 98104.* Tel: 206-382-4861.

Square Miles 28,731.

Established May 31, 1850. Name Changed to Seattle, September 11, 1907.

Created Archdiocese, June 23, 1951.

Comprises the Counties of Clallam, Clark, Cowlitz, Grays Harbor, Island, Jefferson, King, Kitsap, Lewis, Mason, Pacific, Pierce, San Juan, Skagit, Skamania, Snohomish, Thurston, Wahkiakum and Whatcom in the State of Washington.

Legal Title: "Corporation of the Catholic Archbishop of Seattle."
For legal titles of parishes and archdiocesan institutions, consult The Chancery.

STATISTICAL OVERVIEW

Personnel	
Archbishops	1
Retired Archbishops	1
Auxiliary Bishops	2
Abbots	1
Retired Abbots	1
Priests: Diocesan Active in Diocese	115
Priests: Diocesan Active Outside Diocese	4
Priests: Retired, Sick or Absent	77
Number of Diocesan Priests	196
Religious Priests in Diocese	92
Total Priests in Diocese	288
Extern Priests in Diocese	35
Ordinations:	
Diocesan Priests	6
Transitional Deacons	3
Permanent Deacons	5
Permanent Deacons in Diocese	118
Total Brothers	18
Total Sisters	420
Parishes	
Parishes	144
With Resident Pastor:	
Resident Diocesan Priests	97
Resident Religious Priests	9
Without Resident Pastor:	
Administered by Priests	30
Administered by Lay People	8
Missions	27
Pastoral Centers	9
New Parishes Created	1
Professional Ministry Personnel:	
Sisters	38
Lay Ministers	529
Welfare	
Catholic Hospitals	11
Total Assisted	1,192,915
Health Care Centers	2
Total Assisted	12,517
Homes for the Aged	19
Total Assisted	7,557
Residential Care of Children	227
Total Assisted	553
Day Care Centers	3
Total Assisted	276
Specialized Homes	10
Total Assisted	384
Special Centers for Social Services	111
Total Assisted	48,842
Educational	
Diocesan Students in Other Seminaries	27
Total Seminarians	27
Colleges and Universities	2
Total Students	9,438
High Schools, Diocesan and Parish	5
Total Students	2,459
High Schools, Private	6
Total Students	3,727
Elementary Schools, Diocesan and Parish	57
Total Students	15,772
Elementary Schools, Private	5
Total Students	1,059
Catechesis/Religious Education:	
High School Students	6,580
Elementary Students	29,850
Total Students under Catholic Instruction	68,912
Teachers in the Diocese:	
Priests	13
Brothers	3
Sisters	11
Lay Teachers	1,465
Vital Statistics	
Receptions into the Church:	
Infant Baptism Totals	6,822
Minor Baptism Totals	638
Adult Baptism Totals	482
Received into Full Communion	436
First Communions	6,015
Confirmations	4,300
Marriages:	
Catholic	825
Interfaith	540
Total Marriages	1,365
Deaths	2,685
Total Catholic Population	579,500
Total Population	5,202,500

Former Bishops—Rt. Revs. A. M. A. Blanchet, cons. Bishop of Walla Walla, Sept. 27, 1846; transferred to Nesqually, May 31, 1850; resigned 1879; made Bishop of Ibora; died Feb. 25, 1887; Aegidius Junger, D.D., cons. Oct. 28, 1879; died Dec. 26, 1895; Most Revs. Edward John O'Dea, D.D., cons. Bishop of Nesqually, Sept. 8, 1896; See transferred to Seattle, Sept. 11, 1907; died Dec. 25, 1932; Gerald Shaughnessy, S.M., S.T.D., appt. Bishop of Seattle July 1, 1933; cons. Sept. 19, 1933; died May 18, 1950; Thomas A. Connolly, D.D., cons. Aug. 24, 1939; succeeded, May 18, 1950; retired Feb. 25, 1975; died April 18, 1991; Raymond G. Hunthausen, D.D. (Retired), ord. June 1, 1946; appt. Bishop of Helena, Montana, July 8, 1962; cons. Aug. 30, 1962; appt. Archbishop of Seattle, Feb. 25, 1975; installed May 22, 1975; retired Aug. 21, 1991; Thomas J. Murphy, D.D., S.T.D., ord. April 12, 1958; appt. Bishop of Great Falls, July 5, 1978; appt. Coadjutor Archbishop of Seattle, May 26, 1987; succeeded to See Aug. 21, 1991; died June 26, 1997.

Chancery Office—Office of the Archbishop, 710 9th Ave., Seattle, 98104. Tel: 206-382-4886; Fax: 206-382-3495.

Vicar General—Most Revs. Joseph J. Tyson; Eusebio Elizondo, M.Sp.S., J.C.D., 710 9th Ave., Seattle, 98104. Tel: 206-274-3112.

Chancellor—Ms. Mary E. Santi, J.C.L., 710 9th Ave., Seattle, 98104. Tel: 206-264-2089; Fax: 206-274-3110.

Executive Assistant to the Archbishop—Ms. Angela Kison. Tel: 206-382-4525.

Presbyteral Council—Most Revs. Eusebio Elizondo, M.Sp.S., J.C.D.; Joseph J. Tyson; Rev. James D. Picton, J.D., J.C.L.; Very Revs. Paul A. Magnano, Ph.D.; Bryan L. Hersey; James P. Coyne; Anthony Bawyn, J.C.D.; Rev. Steven Sallis; Very Revs. K. Scott Connolly; Matthew L. O'Leary; Michael J. McDermott; David L. Mayovsky; David Mulholland; Rev. Tuan Nguyen; Very Rev. James Northrop; Rev. Hans M. Olson; Very Rev. James Johnson Jr.; Revs. Timothy Sauer; John C. Bentz, S.J.; Terrence J. Wager, O.S.B.

College of Consultors—Very Rev. Paul A. Magnano, Ph.D.; Rev. Tuan Nguyen; Very Rev. Michael J. McDermott; Revs. Hans M. Olson; Timothy Sauer; Steven Sallis; Kurt Nagel; Thomas L. Vandenberg (Retired).

Deans—Very Revs. K. Scott Connolly, Northern; Bryan L. Hersey, Snohomish; David L. Mayovsky, Olympic; James Johnson Jr., North Seattle; James Northrop, Eastside; John C. Madigan, South Seattle; James P. Coyne, South King; Michael J. McDermott, Pierce; David Mulholland, South Sound; Matthew L. O'Leary, Southern.

Metropolitan Tribunal

Judicial Vicar—Very Rev. Anthony Bawyn, J.C.D., 710 9th Ave., Seattle, 98104. Tel: 206-382-4830; Fax: 206-382-2071.

Adjunct Judicial Vicar—Rev. Paul R. Pluth, J.C.L.

Judges—Very Rev. Anthony Bawyn, J.C.D.; James L.

BROOKS, M.Ed.; Deacon JOHN LARUSSA; Ms. LYNDA ROBITAILLE, J.C.D.; Revs. PAUL R. PLUTH, J.C.L.; JAMES EBLEN, S.T.L., Ph.D. (Retired); ROBERT J.B. FLUMMERFELT, J.C.L.; Sr. CAROLYN ROEBER, O.P., J.C.L.

Defenders of the Bond—KAREN S. GIFFIN, M.Min.; Most Rev. EUSEBIO ELIZONDO, M.Sp.S., J.C.D.; Rev. ALAN DUSTON, O.P., J.C.D.

Notaries—VALERIE BLESENER; LIGIA MAHONEY; CHRISTINA MACHNIK.

Archdiocesan Offices and Directors

Accounting Services—NAN SEVERNS, Controller, 710 9th Ave., Seattle, 98104. Tel: 206-382-4377; Fax: 206-903-4624. Asst. Controllers: TOM GRECHIS. Tel: 206-382-4287; DOUG HITSMAN. Tel: 206-382-4849.

Administration and Finance, Office of—Mr. PATRICK J. SURSELY, Archbishop's Delegate, 710 9th Ave., Seattle, 98104. Tel: 206-382-4529; Fax: 206-274-3199.

African/African American/Black and Native American Ministry Services—Mr. PHILIP TRAN, Dir., 710 9th Ave., Seattle, 98104. Tel: 206-382-4828; 800-465-6862 (Toll Free); Fax: 206-382-2069.

Archdiocesan Building Commission—Mr. EDWARD FOSTER, Staff; Mr. BILL LEHTINEN, Chm., 710 9th Ave., Seattle, 98109. Tel: 206-382-4851; Fax: 206-382-4266.

Archdiocesan Finance Council—Mr. PATRICK J. SURSELY, Staff; Mr. LOU DELL'OSSO, Chm., 710 9th Ave., Seattle, 98104. Tel: 206-382-4529; Fax: 206-274-3199.

Archdiocesan Housing Authority—MICHAEL REICHERT, Pres., 100 23rd Ave. S., Seattle, 98144-2302. Tel: 206-328-5696; 800-499-5979 (Toll Free); Fax: 206-328-5699.

Archdiocesan Liturgical Commission—Ms. CAROLYN LASSEK, Chm., 710 9th Ave., Seattle, 98104. Tel: 206-382-4878; Fax: 206-903-4612.

Archdiocesan Women's Commission—LAURA TENISCI, Pres.; Ms. MARY CROSS, Liaison, 710 9th Ave., Seattle, 98104. Tel: 206-382-4268; Fax: 206-264-2084.

Archives and Information Services—Mr. SETH DALBY, 710 9th Ave., Seattle, 98104. Tel: 206-382-4352; Fax: 206-382-4840.

Asian Pacific American Ministry Services—Mr. PHILIP TRAN, Dir., 710 9th Ave., Seattle, 98104. Tel: 206-382-4509, Ext. 4828; 800-465-6862, Ext. 4828 (Toll Free); Fax: 206-382-2069.

Associated Catholic Cemeteries—Mr. RICHARD PETERSON, Dir., 710 9th Ave., Seattle, 98104. Tel: 206-522-0996; 253-838-2240; Fax: 206-525-9628.

Benefits Services—GERALYN MIRANTE-MARLEY, Dir., 710 9th Ave., Seattle, 98104. Tel: 206-382-4286; Fax: 206-382-3493.

Campaign for Human Development—Mr. J. L. DROUHARD, Dir., 710 9th Ave., Seattle, 98104. Tel: 206-382-4869; Fax: 206-382-3487.

Campus Ministry—Mr. STEPHEN J. HUEFFED, Dir., 710 9th Ave., Seattle, 98104. Tel: 206-382-4831; Fax: 206-903-4627.

Catholic Community Services of Western Washington—MICHAEL REICHERT, Pres., 100 23rd Ave. S., Seattle, 98144-2302. Tel: 206-328-5696; 800-499-5979 (Toll Free); 206-328-5646 (TTY); Fax: 206-328-5699.

Catholic Faith Formation, Office of—Dr. MARY CROSS, Archbishop's Delegate, 710 9th Ave., Seattle, 98104. Tel: 206-382-4835; Fax: 206-264-2084.

Catholic Relief Services—Mr. J.L. DROUHARD, Dir., 710 9th Ave., Seattle, 98104. Tel: 206-382-4580; 800-869-7028 (Toll Free); Fax: 206-382-3487.

Catholic Schools Department—Most Rev. JOSEPH J. TYSON, Supt. Catholic Schools, 710 9th Ave., Seattle, 98104. Tel: 206-382-4861; 800-473-5651 (Toll Free); Fax: 206-654-4651.

Catholic Youth Organization—Mr. TAUNO LATVALA, Exec. Dir., 710 9th Ave., Seattle, 98104. Tel: 206-382-2019; Fax: 206-903-4627.

Censor Librorum—Rev. MICHAEL RASCHKO, Ph.D.

Chancery Operations—Mr. DENNIS J. O'LEARY, Archbishop's Delegate, 710 9th Ave., Seattle, 98104. Tel: 206-382-4289; Fax: 206-382-4583.

Communications, Office of—Mr. GREG MAGNONI, Archbishop's Delegate, 710 9th Ave., Seattle, 98104. Tel: 206-382-4862; 800-473-5641 (Toll Free); Fax: 206-382-3487.

Newspaper "The Catholic Northwest Progress"—Mr. GREG MAGNONI, Delegate for Communications. Tel: 206-382-4850; 800-473-5641; Fax: 206-382-3487.

Criminal Justice Ministry Services—Mr. THOMAS WAGNER, Asst. Dir. Pastoral Care Svcs., 710 9th Ave., Seattle, 98104. Tel: 206-382-1477; 800-465-6862 (Toll Free); Fax: 206-382-2069.

Cultural and Ethnic Faith Formation—Mr. JOSE RAMIREZ-LOMELI, Dir., 710 9th Ave., Seattle, 98104. Tel: 206-654-4644; 800-950-4970 (Toll Free); Fax: 206-264-2084.

Deacon Services—Mr. PHILIP TRAN, 710 9th Ave., Seattle, 98104. Tel: 206-382-4828; Fax: 206-654-4654.

Disability Ministry Services—Mr. THOMAS WAGNER, Asst. Dir. Pastoral Care Svcs., 710 9th Ave., Seattle, 98104. Tel: 206-382-1477; 800-465-6862 (Toll Free); Fax: 206-382-2069.

Due Process—Very Rev. ANTHONY BAWYN, J.C.D., Contact, 710 9th Ave., Seattle, 98104. Tel: 800-950-4965 (Toll Free); 206-382-3484.

Ecumenical and Interfaith Commission—Sr. JOYCE M. COX, B.V.M., Archbishop's Delegate for Rel. Communities & Ecumenism, 710 9th Ave., Seattle, 98104. Tel: 206-382-4829; 800-406-6613 (Toll Free); Fax: 206-382-4840.

Hispanic/Latino Ministry Services—ISAAC GOVEA, Dir., 710 9th Ave., Seattle, 98104. Tel: 206-382-4825; 800-465-6862, Ext. 4825 (Toll Free); Fax: 206-382-2069.

Holy Childhood Association—Mr. J.L. DROUHARD, Dir., 710 9th Ave., Seattle, 98104. Tel: 206-382-4850; 800-869-7028 (Toll Free); Fax: 206-382-3487.

Human Resources—Ms. MARY E. SANTI, J.C.L., Archbishop's Delegate, 710 9th Ave., Seattle, 98104. Tel: 206-382-4570; 800-261-4749 (Toll Free); Fax: 206-382-4267.

Information Technology & Services—Mr. HOWARD CHANG, 710 9th Ave., Seattle, 98104. Tel: 206-382-4282; Fax: 206-382-4840.

Justice and Peace Ministry Resources—Dr. MARY CROSS, Archbishop's Delegate for Catholic Faith Formation, 710 9th Ave., Seattle, 98104. Tel: 206-382-4268; 800-950-4970 (Toll Free); Fax: 206-264-2084.

Koreans, Ministry to—Revs. JUNKOO YEO, Chap., St. Andrew Kim Korean Community, 11700 1st Ave., N.E., Seattle, 98125. Tel: 206-362-2278; 206-362-2492; THOMAS AQUINAS SEUNG-CHUL IM, St. Paul Chong Hasang Korean Community, 1316 62nd Ave. E., Fife, 98424. Tel: 253-896-4489.

Lay Ecclesial Ministry—Dr. MARY CROSS, Archbishop's Delegate for Catholic Faith Formation, 710 9th Ave., Seattle, 98104. Tel: 206-382-4268; 800-950-4970 (Toll Free); Fax: 206-264-2084.

Leadership Ministry Services—Ms. ERICA COHEN MOORE, Asst. Dir. Pastoral Svcs., 710 9th Ave., Seattle, 98104. Tel: 206-382-4852; 800-465-6862 (Toll Free); Fax: 206-382-2069.

Library Media Center—VACANT, 710 9th Ave., Seattle, 98104. Tel: 206-382-4883; 800-869-7027 (Toll Free); Fax: 206-382-3487.

Liturgy—Ms. CAROLYN LASSEK, 710 9th Ave., Seattle, 98104. Tel: 206-382-4878; 800-473-5657 (Toll Free); Fax: 206-903-4612.

Missions—Mr. J. L. DROUHARD, Dir., 710 9th Ave., Seattle, 98104. Tel: 206-382-4580; 800-869-7028 (Toll Free); Fax: 206-382-3487.

Native American Ministry Services—Mr. PHILIP TRAN, 710 9th Ave., Seattle, 98104. Tel: 206-382-4828; 800-465-6862 (Toll Free); Fax: 206-382-2069.

Parish and School Faith Formation—Ms. ANNE FREDERICK, Ed.D., Dir., 710 9th Ave., Seattle, 98104. Tel: 206-903-4614; 800-950-4970 (Toll Free); Fax: 206-264-2084.

Parish Financial Services—Mr. ED WILLIAMS, Dir., 710 9th Ave., Seattle, 98104. Tel: 206-382-7316; 800-768-7986 (Toll Free); Fax: 206-382-4279.

Parish Stewardship—Mr. SCOTT BADER, Dir., 710 9th Ave., Seattle, 98104. Tel: 206-903-4619; 866-381-2033 (Toll Free); Fax: 206-903-4610.

Pastoral Care of the Sick & Dying Ministry Services—Mr. THOMAS WAGNER, Asst. Dir. Pastoral Care Svcs., 710 9th Ave., Seattle, 98104. Tel: 206-382-1477; 800-465-6862 (Toll Free); Fax: 206-382-2069.

Pastoral Planning and Research—Mr. DENNIS J. O'LEARY, Dir. Tel: 206-382-4832; 800-327-5295 (Toll Free); Fax: 206-274-3161; MARY BETH CELIO, Dir. Research, 710 9th Ave., Seattle, 98104. Tel: 206-382-4272.

Planned Giving—Ms. JOANNE STROM, Dir., 710 9th Ave., Seattle, 98104. Tel: 206-903-4621; 800-752-5902 (Toll Free); Fax: 206-903-4610.

Polish Speaking, Ministry to—Revs. PIOTR DZIKOWSKI, S.Ch., 3422 Portland Ave., Tacoma, 98404. Tel: 206-272-5232; STANISLAW MICHALEK, S.Ch., 3221 14th Ave. W., Seattle, 98119. Tel: 206-282-1804.

Catholic Archdiocese of Seattle Clergy Medical Plan Veba Trust—Most Rev. ALEXANDER J. BRUNETT, D.D., Ph.D., Pres.; Rev. SEAN P. FOX, Chm. Trustees; GERALYN MIRANTE-MARLEY, Benefits Dir. Tel: 206-382-4286.

Priests' Pension Plan—Most Rev. ALEXANDER J. BRUNETT, D.D., Ph.D.; Rev. SEAN P. FOX, Chm. Trustees; GERALYN MIRANTE-MARLEY, Benefits Dir. Tel: 206-382-4286.

Propagation of the Faith, Society for the—Mr. J.L. DROUHARD, Dir., 710 9th Ave., Seattle, 98104. Tel: 206-382-4580; 800-869-7028 (Toll Free); Fax: 206-382-3487.

Property and Construction Services—Mr. EDWARD FOSTER, Dir., 710 9th Ave., Seattle, 98104. Tel: 206-382-4851; 800-809-4923 (Toll Free); Fax: 206-382-4266.

Religious Communities—Sr. JOYCE M. COX, B.V.M., Archbishop's Delegate, 710 9th Ave., Seattle, 98104. Tel: 206-382-4829; 800-406-6613 (Toll Free); Fax: 206-382-4840.

Samoan, Ministry to—Rev. POAO SAENA, Chap., 7025 S. Park Ave., Tacoma, 98408. Tel: 253-472-1360.

Seminarian Services—RICHARD SHIVELY, Assoc. Dir., 710 9th Ave., Seattle, 98104. Tel: 206-382-4595; 800-809-4919; Fax: 206-654-4654.

Sisters' Council—Sr. SHARON PARK, O.P., 508 2nd Ave. W., Seattle, 98119-3928. Tel: 206-301-0556; Fax: 206-301-0558.

Stewardship and Development Department—Mr. RICK FERSCH, Exec. Dir., 710 9th Ave., Seattle, 98104. Tel: 206-903-4620; Fax: 206-903-4610.

Theological Resources—Revs. JAMES EBLEN, S.T.L., Ph.D. (Retired), 131 Bellevue Ave. E., #203, Seattle, 98102-5566. Tel: 206-296-5339. Seattle University, 900 Broadway, Seattle, 98122; MICHAEL RASCHKO, Ph.D., 1614 Summit Ave., #502, Seattle, 98122. Tel: 206-296-5311. Seattle University, 900 Broadway, Seattle, 98122.

Vicar for Clergy, Office of—Very Rev. PAUL A. MAGNANO, Ph.D., 710 9th Ave., Seattle, 98104. Tel: 206-382-4839; 800-809-4919 (Toll Free); Fax: 206-654-4654.

Pastoral Outreach Coordinator—DENISE AUBUCHON. Tel: 206-382-4592; 800-446-7762 (Toll Free). Email: hotline@seattlearch.org.

Vietnamese, Ministry to—Very Rev. PHUONG HOANG, Vicar. Chaplains: Revs. FRANCIS MIEN; ANTHONY LAN TRAN, Church of the Vietnamese Martyrs, 1230 E. Fir St., Seattle, 98122. Tel: 206-325-5626; Fax: 206-324-5849.

Vocations—RICHARD SHIVELY, Assoc. Dir., 710 9th Ave., Seattle, 98104. Tel: 206-387-4595; Fax: 206-654-4654.

Youth and Young Adult Ministry, Office of—Mr. STEPHEN J. HUEFFED, Archbishop's Delegate, 710 9th Ave., Seattle, 98104. Tel: 206-382-4562; 800-950-4963; Fax: 206-903-4627.

CLERGY, PARISHES, MISSIONS AND PAROCHIAL SCHOOLS

CITY OF SEATTLE

(KING COUNTY)

1—ST. JAMES CATHEDRAL (1904) Very Rev. Michael G. Ryan. In Res., Rev. David A. Brant (Retired).
Res.: 804 Ninth Ave., 98104. Tel: 206-622-3559; Fax: 206-622-5303.
Station—Plymouth Congregational Church Chapel 1217 6th Ave., 98101.
Station—St. Ignatius Chapel Seattle University, 901 12th St., 98122.

2—ST. ALPHONSUS (1901) Rev. Danilo Abalon, S.O.L.T., Admin.
Res.: 5816 15th Ave., N.W., 98107. Tel: 206-784-6464; Fax: 206-789-5709.
School—(Grades PreSchool-8) Tel: 206-782-4363. Maureen Reid, Prin. Lay Teachers 16; Students 200.
Catechesis/Religious Program—Students 30.

3—ST. ANNE (1908) Revs. John Bowman, Parochial Vicar; Steven Sallis, Priest Moderator; Mr. Ron Ryan, Pastoral Coord.
Res.: 1411 1st Ave. W., 98119. Tel: 206-282-0223; Fax: 206-217-9541.
School—(Grades PreSchool-8), 101 W. Lee St., 98119. Tel: 206-282-3538; Fax: 206-284-4191. Mrs. Pat Durand, Prin. Lay Teachers 17; Students 260.

4—ASSUMPTION (1924) Rev. Oliver Duggan.
Office: 6201 33rd Ave. N.E., 98115. Tel: 206-522-7674; Fax: 206-522-6308.
School—(Grades K-8), 6220 32nd Ave., N.E., 98115-7233. Tel: 206-524-7452; Fax: 206-524-6757. Kathi Hand, Prin. Lay Teachers 28; Students 540.
Catechesis/Religious Program—Students 80.

5—ST. BENEDICT (1906) Rev. Steven Sallis.
Res.: 1805 N. 49th St., 98103. Tel: 206-632-0843; Fax: 206-632-2167. Web: www.stbens.net.
School—(Grades PreK-8), 4811 Wallingford Ave. N., 98103. Tel: 206-633-3375; Fax: 206-632-3236. Mrs. Maureen Blum, Prin.; Susan Lisi, Librarian. Lay Teachers 24; Students 225.
Catechesis/Religious Program—Students 60.

6—St. Bernadette (1958) Rev. Michael H. Wright. In Res., Rev. Donald Perea.
Res.: 861 S.W. 126th St., 98146. Tel: 206-242-7370; Fax: 206-242-7371. Web: www.saintbernadette.net.
School—(Grades PreK-8), 1028 S.W. 128th St., 98146. Tel: 206-244-4934; Fax: 206-244-4943. Robert Rutledge, Prin. Lay Teachers 16; Students 240.
Catechesis/Religious Program—Students 155.

7—Blessed Sacrament (1908) Revs. Daniel Syverstad, O.P.; Raphael Mary Salzillo, O.P.; Jordan Bradshaw, O.P. In Res., Rev. Augustine Hartman, O.P.
Res.: 5041 Ninth Ave., N.E., 98105. Tel: 206-547-3020; Fax: 206-547-6371.
Catechesis/Religious Program—Web: www.blessed-sacrament.org. Students 62.

8—St. Bridget (1968) [CEM] Rev. Timothy Sauer; Deacon Dennis T. Duffell.
Res.: 4900 N.E. 50th Ave., 98105. Tel: 206-523-8787; Fax: 206-528-7511. Web: www.stbridgetchurch.org.
Catechesis/Religious Program—Tel: 206-523-9760. Students 156.

9—St. Catherine of Siena (1929) Very Rev. Anthony Bawyn, Parochial Vicar; Rev. Oliver Duggan, Moderator; Victoria Ries, Pastoral Coord.
Res.: 814 N.E. 85th, 98115. Tel: 206-524-8800; Fax: 206-527-6339.
School—(Grades PreSchool-8), 8524 8th Ave., N.E., 98115. Tel: 206-525-0581; Fax: 206-985-0253. Steve Mezich, Prin.; Margaret Hartley, Librarian. Lay Teachers 14; Students 225.
Catechesis/Religious Program—Students 72.

10—Christ Our Hope Personal Parish Very Rev. Paul Magnano; Deacons Samuel Basta; Terrance Marcell; Lawrence McDonald.
710 9th Ave., 98104. 1902 2nd Ave., 98101.

11—Christ the King (1930) Rev. Raymond Cleaveland, Admin.
Res.: 405 N. 117th St., 98133. Tel: 206-362-1545; Fax: 206-364-8325.
School—(Grades PreSchool-8), 415 N. 117th St., 98133. Tel: 206-364-6890. Terence Maguire, Prin. Lay Teachers 16; Students 175.
Catechesis/Religious Program—Students 289.

12—St. Edward (1906) Revs. Felino Paulino; Robert J. Kenny, Parochial Vicar; Roy Baroma, Parochial Vicar.
Res.: 4212 S. Mead St., 98118. Tel: 206-722-7888; Fax: 206-722-7895. Web: www.stedwardparish.net.
School—(Grades PreK-8), 4200 S. Mead St., 98118. Tel: 206-725-1774; Fax: 206-725-4569. Mary Lundeen, Prin. Sisters 2; Lay Teachers 8; Students 160.
Catechesis/Religious Program—Students 32.

13—St. Francis of Assisi (1929) Rev. Richard K. Hayatsu; Deacon Lloyd Snider.
Mailing Address: P.O. Box 929, Seahurst, 98062. In Res., Rev. Michael Angelovic (Retired).
Res.: 15226 21st Ave., S.W., 98166. Tel: 206-242-4575; Fax: 206-242-1957.
School—(Grades K-8), P.O. Box 870, Seahurst, 98062. Tel: 206-243-5690; Fax: 206-433-8593. Sheila Keaton, Prin. Lay Teachers 30; Students 472.

14—St. George (1903) Revs. Felino Paulino; Roman Baroma, Parochial Vicar; Robert J. Kenny; Deacon Sagato Pele.
Catechesis/Religious Program—Students 130.
Res.: 5306 13th Ave. S., 98108. Tel: 206-762-7744; Fax: 206-762-4207.
School—(Grades PreSchool-8), 5117 13th Ave. S., 98108. Tel: 206-762-0656; Fax: 206-763-3220. Bernadette O'Leary, Prin. Lay Teachers 15; Students 205.
Catechesis/Religious Program—Students 181.

15—Holy Family (1921) Revs. Horacio Yanez; Armando Red, Parochial Vicar; Deacons Ted Wiese; Abel Magaña.
Res.: 9622 20th Ave., S.W., 98106. Tel: 206-767-6220; Fax: 206-767-0374. Web: www.hfseattle.org.
School—(Grades PreSchool-8), 9615 20th Ave. S.W., 98106. Tel: 206-767-6640; Fax: 206-767-9466. Francis Cantwell, Prin. Sisters 1; Lay Teachers 15; Students 137.
Catechesis/Religious Program—Students 240.

16—Holy Rosary (1907) Very Rev. John C. Madigan.
Res.: 4139 42nd Ave., S.W., 98116. Tel: 206-935-8353; Fax: 206-935-4303.
School—(Grades K-8), 4142 42nd Ave., S.W., 98116. Tel: 206-937-7255; Fax: 206-937-2610. Web: www.holyrosaryws.org. Kris Brown, Prin. Lay Teachers 30; Students 488.
Catechesis/Religious Program—Tel: 206-937-1488, Ext. 203. Students 60.

17—Immaculate Conception (1891) Very Rev. Phuong Hoang; Rev. Fabian MacDonald, Parochial Vicar; Deacons Joseph Connor; Frederic Cordova. In Res., Rev. Jaime Tolang (Retired).
Res.: 820 18th Ave., 98122. Tel: 206-322-5970; Fax: 206-322-9417.
Catechesis/Religious Program—Students 19.

18—St. John the Evangelist (1917) Rev. Crispin Okoth.
Office: 121 N. 80th St., 98103. Tel: 206-782-2810; Fax: 206-782-0242.
School—(Grades PreK-8), 120 N. 79th St., 98103. Tel: 206-783-0337; Fax: 206-706-2704. Web: www-.stjohnsea.org. Agnes Jacobson, Prin. Lay Teachers 30; Students 520.
Catechesis/Religious Program—Students 50.

19—St. Joseph (1907) Rev. John Whitney, S.J.; Deacon Stephen Wodzanowski, Pastoral Assoc.
Res.: 732 18th Ave. E., 98112. Tel: 206-324-2522; Fax: 206-329-5698. Web: www.stjosephparish.org.
School—(Grades K-8), 700 18th Ave. E., 98112. Tel: 206-329-3260; Fax: 206-324-7773. George Hofbauer, Prin. Sisters 1; Lay Teachers 42; Students 618.
Catechesis/Religious Program—Students 607.

20—St. Margaret of Scotland (1910) Rev. Stanislaw Michalek, S.Ch., Admin.
Res.: 3221 14th Ave. W., 98119. Tel: 206-282-1804; Fax: 206-282-6461.

21—St. Mary (1899) Revs. Anthony J. Haycock, Parochial Vicar; Felino Paulino, Moderator; Tricia Wittmann-Todd, Pastoral Coord.
Res.: 611 20th Ave. S., 98144. Tel: 206-324-7100; Fax: 206-329-4596. Web: www.stmarysseattle.org.
Catechesis/Religious Program—Students 137.

22—St. Matthew (1954) Rev. Rogelio Barcelona, S.O.L.T., Admin.
Res.: 1240 N.E. 127th St., 98125. Tel: 206-363-6767; Fax: 206-362-4863.
School—(Grades K-8), 1230 N.E. 127th St., 98125. Tel: 206-362-2785; Fax: 206-440-9476. Lillian Zadra, Prin. Lay Teachers 14; Students 215.
Catechesis/Religious Program—Students 27.

23—North American Martyrs Personal Quasi-Parish Rev. Gerard Saguto, F.S.S.P.
5901 8th Ave., N.W., 98107. Tel: 206-859-5161. Web: www.northamericanmartyrs.org.

24—Our Lady of Fatima (1952) Very Rev. James Johnson Jr.; Rev. Fidelis O. Umukoro, O.P.; Deacon Walter Shields. In Res., Rev. Robert Evenson.
Res.: 3218 W. Barrett, 98199. Tel: 206-283-1456; Fax: 206-283-5788. Web: www.olfatima.org.
School—(Grades K-8), 3301 W. Dravus St., 98199. Tel: 206-283-7031; Fax: 206-352-4588. Susan Burdett, Prin. Lay Teachers 20; Students 310.
Catechesis/Religious Program—Tel: 206-352-4571. Students 145.

25—Our Lady of Guadalupe (1960) Rev. John Walmesley.
Res.: 7000-35th Ave., S.W., 98126. Tel: 206-935-0358; Fax: 206-935-1230. Web: www.olgseattle.org.
School—(Grades PreK-8), 3401 S.W. Myrtle, 98126. Tel: 206-935-0651; Fax: 206-938-3695. Web: www.guadalupe-school.org. Kristin Dixon, Prin.; Loretta Kramer, Librarian. Lay Teachers 19; Students 253.
Catechesis/Religious Program—Students 50.

26—Our Lady of Lourdes (1892) Rev. Gerald L. Mayovsky.
Res.: 10243 12th Ave. S., 98168-1525. Tel: 206-762-3343; Fax: 206-762-3343.

27—Our Lady of Mount Virgin (1911) Very Rev. John C. Madigan; Revs. Clarence Edward Jones, C.O., Parochial Vicar; Patrick Twohy, S.J., Parochial Vicar (Native American Community); Deacons Joua Pao Yang, Pastoral Assoc. (Lao Community); Joseph Yuen, (Chinese Community); Charlene P. Collora, Pastoral Coord.
Res.: 1531 Bradner Pl. S., 98144. Tel: 206-324-8521; Fax: 206-322-6406.
Catechesis/Religious Program—Students 49.

28—Our Lady of the Lake (1929) Rev. Timothy Clark, Admin. In Res., Very Rev. Anthony Bawyn.
Res.: 8900 35th Ave., N.E., 98115. Tel: 206-523-6776; Fax: 206-524-0848. Web: www.ollseattle.org.
School—(Grades K-8), 3520 N.E. 89th St., 98115. Tel: 206-525-9980; Fax: 206-523-2858. Vince McGovern, Prin.; Carol Jez, Librarian. Lay Teachers 14; Students 147.
Catechesis/Religious Program—Tel: 206-522-2840. Students 25.

29—St. Patrick (1918) Rev. Patrick S. Clark.
Res.: 2702 Broadway E., 98102. Tel: 206-329-2960; Fax: 206-329-2961. Web: www.stpatsseattle.org.
Catechesis/Religious Program—Students 40.

30—St. Paul (1953) Revs. Felino Paulino; Roman Baroma, Parochial Vicar; Robert J. Kenny, Parochial Vicar.
Parish Office—5600 S. Ryan St., 98178. Tel: 206-725-2050; Fax: 206-725-7476.
School—(Grades PreSchool-8), 10001 57th Ave. S., 98178. Tel: 206-725-0780; Fax: 206-722-5732. Lay Teachers 15; Students 215.
Catechesis/Religious Program—Students 40.

31—St. Peter (1931) Very Rev. Michael G. Ryan, Priest Mod.; Rev. Peter Duggan, Senior Priest (Retired); Linda Lopez-Liang, Pastoral Coord.
Res.: 2807 15th Ave. S., 98144. Tel: 206-324-2290; Fax: 206-324-4020.
Catechesis/Religious Program—Students 29.

32—Sacred Heart of Jesus (1889) Revs. Harry Grile, C.Ss.R.; Joseph Thong Ngo, C.Ss.R., Parochial Vicar. In Res., Revs. Lyle Konen, C.Ss.R.; William Cleary, C.Ss.R.; Raymond Maiser, C.Ss.R.; Patrick O'Brien, C.Ss.R.; William Peterson, C.Ss.R.; Bro. Paul Jorns, C.Ss.R.
Res.: 205 2nd Ave. N., 98109. Tel: 206-284-4680; Fax: 206-284-3161. Web: www.sacredheartseattle.com.
Station—St. Joseph Chapel Josephinum, 1902 2nd Ave., 98101.

33—St. Therese (1926) Rev. Stephen Okumu, Admin.
Res.: 3416 E. Marion St., 98122. Tel: 206-325-2711; Fax: 206-329-8373. Web: www.sainttheresеparish.org.
School—(Grades K-8), 900-35th Ave., 98122. Tel: 206-324-0460; Fax: 206-324-8464. Mrs. Eileen Gray, Prin. Lay Teachers 12; Students 150.
Catechesis/Religious Program—Students 135.

OUTSIDE THE CITY OF SEATTLE

Aberdeen, Grays Harbor Co.

1—St. Mary (1885) Revs. Dennis E. Robb; Gerald Burns, Parochial Vicar.
Res.: 306 E. Third St., 98520. Tel: 360-532-8300; Fax: 360-538-9987.
School—(Grades PreSchool-8), 518 N. H St., 98520. Tel: 360-532-1230; Fax: 360-532-1209. Kathleen Beyer, Prin. Lay Teachers 15; Students 164.
Catechesis/Religious Program—Tel: 360-532-8300, Ext. 110. Students 35.
Mission—St. Paul P.O. Box 332, Westport, Grays Harbor Co. 98585.

2—SS. Peter and Paul (1907), (Polish), Revs. Dennis E. Robb; Gerald Burns, Parochial Vicar.
Res.: 306 E. Third St., 98520. Tel: 360-532-8300; Fax: 360-538-9987.

Anacortes, Skagit Co., St. Mary (1910) Rev. Vu Phong Tran.
Res.: 4001 St. Mary's Dr., 98221. Tel: 360-293-2101; Fax: 360-293-8556. Web: www.stmaryanacorteswa.org.
Catechesis/Religious Program—Tel: 360-293-6882. Students 85.

Arlington, Snohomish Co., Immaculate Conception (1890) Rev. James Dalton.
Res.: 1200 E. Fifth, P.O. Box 69, 98223. Tel: 360-435-8565; Fax: 360-435-9732. Web: www.immaculateconceptionarlington.net.
Catechesis/Religious Program—Tel: 360-435-8565, Ext. 13. Students 141.
Mission—St. John Mary Vianney 1150 Riddle St., Darrington, Snohomish Co. 98241.

Auburn, King Co., Holy Family (1904) Rev. Timothy McKenna.
Res.: 505 17th St., S.E., P.O. Box 290, 98071. Tel: 253-833-5130; Fax: 253-833-3421.
School—(Grades K-8), 505 17th St., S.E., 98002. Tel: 253-833-5130, Ext. 214; Fax: 253-833-9311. Daniel Hill, Prin. Lay Teachers 15; Students 196.
Catechesis/Religious Program—Tel: 253-833-5730; Fax: 253-833-5130. Students 382.

Bainbridge Island, Kitsap Co., St. Cecilia (1950) Rev. Emmett H. Carroll, S.J.
Church: 1310 Madison Ave. N., 98110. Tel: 206-842-3594; Fax: 206-842-6988. Web: www.saintcparish.org.
Catechesis/Religious Program—Tel: 206-842-3594, Ext. 102. Students 164.

Battle Ground, Clark Co., Sacred Heart (1877) [CEM] Very Rev. Matthew L. O'Leary; Deacons Jack Roscoe; Carl Anderson.
Mailing Address: 1603 N. Parkway Ave., P.O. Box 38, 98604. Tel: 360-687-4515; Fax: 360-687-3322. Web: www.sacredheartbg.org.
Catechesis/Religious Program—Tel: 360-687-4515; Fax: 360-687-3322. Students 123.
Mission—St. Joseph the Workman 200 W. Jones St., Yacolt, Clark Co. 98675. Tel: 360-686-8088.
Mission—St. Mary of Guadalupe (1888) 28309 N.W. 11th Ave., Ridgefield, Clark Co. 98642. Tel: 360-887-8194.

Bellevue, King Co.

1—St. Louise (1960) Rev. Thomas Belleque; Deacons William Haines Jr.; Samuel Basta.
Res.: 141 156th Ave., S.E., 98007. Tel: 425-747-4450; Fax: 425-644-3678.
School—(Grades K-8), 133 156th Ave., S.E., 98007. Tel: 425-746-4220; Fax: 425-644-3294. Web: www-.stlouiseschool.org. Dan Fitzpatrick, Prin.; Mary Carson, Librarian. Lay Teachers 31; Students 437.
Catechesis/Religious Program—Tel: 425-747-4450, Ext. 55. Students 433.

2—St. Madeleine Sophie (1968) Rev. James D. Picton; Deacon William Taube.
Res.: 4400 130th Pl., S.E., 98006-2014. Tel: 425-747-6770; Fax: 425-747-6349.
School—(Grades PreK-6) Tel: 425-747-6770, Ext. 202; Fax: 425-747-1825. Dan Sherman, Prin. Lay Teachers 6; Students 42.
Catechesis/Religious Program—Tel: 425-747-6770,

Ext. 124. Students 300.
3—SACRED HEART (1946) Rev. Patrick Ritter.
Res.: 9460 N.E. 14th St., 98004. Tel: 425-454-9536; Fax: 425-450-3909. Web: www.sacredheart.org.
School—(Grades K-8), 9450 N.E. 14th St., 98004. Tel: 425-451-1773; Fax: 425-450-3918. David Burroughs, Prin. Lay Teachers 29; Students 376.
Catechesis/Religious Program—Tel: 425-451-1775. Students 505.

BELLINGHAM, WHATCOM CO.
1—ASSUMPTION (1889) Very Rev. K. Scott Connolly; Deacon Lawrence Kheriaty.
Res.: 2116 Cornwall Ave., 98225. Tel: 360-733-1380; Fax: 360-733-5644. Web: www.assumption.org.
School—(Grades PreSchool-8) Tel: 360-733-6133; Fax: 360-647-4372. Web: www.school.assumption-.org. Ms. Rose Goeres, Prin. Lay Teachers 19; Students 326.
Catechesis/Religious Program—Students 227.
2—SACRED HEART (1905) [JC] Rev. Qui-Thac Nguyen, Admin.; Deacon Lawrence Gorman.
Res.: 1111 14th St., 98225. Tel: 360-734-2850; Fax: 360-734-0947.
Catechesis/Religious Program—Students 57.
Station—Newman Campus Ministry 714 N. Garden St., 98225. Tel: 360-410-0218.

BLACK DIAMOND, KING CO., ST. BARBARA (1912) Rev. David H. Young.
Res.: 32416 6th Ave., P.O. Box 189, 98010. Tel: 360-886-2229. Web: www.stbarbarachurch.org.
Catechesis/Religious Program—Students 261.

BOTHELL, KING CO., ST. BRENDAN (1949) Very Rev. James Northrop; Deacon Eamon Parsons.
Res.: 10051 N.E. 195th St., 98011-2931. Tel: 425-483-9400; Fax: 425-486-9735. Web: www.saintbrendan.org.
School—(Grades K-8) Tel: 425-483-8300; Fax: 425-483-2839. Chris Lunn, Prin. Lay Teachers 14; Students 264.
Catechesis/Religious Program—Students 453.

BOTHELL, SNOHOMISH CO., ST. ELIZABETH ANN SETON (1983) Revs. Edgar Sanchez, M.Sp.S., Admin.; Jorge Gomez del Valle, M.Sp.S., Parochial Vicar; Jose Ugalde, M.Sp.S., Parochial Vicar; Deacon Robert Dolan.
Res.: P.O. Box 12429, Mill Creek, 98082-0429. Tel: 425-481-0303; Fax: 425-485-8510.
Catechesis/Religious Program—Tel: 425-481-9358. Mavis Kalbrener, D.R.E. Students 815.

BREMERTON, KITSAP CO.
1—HOLY TRINITY (1964) Rev. Jack Buckalew.
Mailing Address: P.O. Box 910, Tracyton, 98393.
Res.: 4215 Pine Rd., 98310. Tel: 360-377-7674; Fax: 360-377-6181.
Catechesis/Religious Program—Tel: 360-479-9525. Students 290.
2—OUR LADY, STAR OF THE SEA (1902) Rev. Derek Lappe; Deacon William Hamlin.
Office: 1513-6th St., 98337. Tel: 360-479-3777; Fax: 360-479-1468. Web: www.starofthesea.net.
School—1516-5th St., 98337. Tel: 360-373-5162. Sally Merriwether, Prin. Lay Teachers 11; Students 200.
Catechesis/Religious Program—Students 194.

BUCKLEY, PIERCE CO., ST. ALOYSIUS (1892) Rev. Ambroise M. Ntumba, Admin.
Res.: 211 W. Mason St., 98321. Tel: 360-829-6515; Fax: 360-829-5190.
Catechesis/Religious Program—Tel: 360-829-9958. Students 53.
Mission—Our Lady of Lourdes (1894) [CEM] Wilkeson, Pierce Co.

BURLINGTON, SKAGIT CO., ST. CHARLES (1885) Revs. Martin Bourke; Milhton Scarpetta Molina; Emmanuel Azike, Parochial Vicar; Thomas McMichael, Parochial Vicar; Deacons Phil Meyer; Antonio Cavazos; George Peterson.
Res.: 935 Peterson Rd., 98233. Tel: 360-757-0128; Fax: 360-757-0418.

CAMAS, CLARK CO., ST. THOMAS AQUINAS (1870) [CEM] Rev. Peter Gillette, Admin.
Res.: 324 N.E. Oak, 98607. Tel: 360-834-2126; Fax: 360-834-5106. Web: www.st-thomascamas.org.
Catechesis/Religious Program—Tel: 360-834-2126, Ext. 2. Students 259.
Mission—Star of the Sea P.O. Box 901, Stevenson, Skamania Co. 98648. Tel: 509-427-8478; Fax: 509-427-8478. Deacon William Townsend.

CASTLE ROCK, COWLITZ CO., ST. MARY (1976) Rev. Mel Strazicich.
Mailing Address: P.O. Box 960, 98611-0960.
Church: 120 Powell Rd., 98611-0960. Tel: 360-274-7404; Fax: 360-274-7328.
Catechesis/Religious Program—Students 46.

CENTRALIA, LEWIS CO., ST. MARY (1910) Very Rev. David Mulholland, Admin.; Revs. Todd O. Strange, Parochial Vicar; Phuong D. Tran, Parochial Vicar.
Res.: 225 N. Washington Ave., 98531. Tel: 360-736-4356; Fax: 360-807-0758.
Catechesis/Religious Program—Tel: 360-736-3470. Students 175.

CHEHALIS, LEWIS CO., ST. JOSEPH (1888) Very Rev. David Mulholland; Revs. Todd O. Strange, Parochial Vicar; Phuong D. Tran, Parochial Vicar; Deacon Loren Lane.
Mailing Address: 157 S.W. 6th St., 98532.
Res.: 682 S.W. Cascade Ave., 98532. Tel: 360-748-4953; Fax: 360-748-3149. Web: www.wlpcatholic.org.
School—(Grades PreSchool-8), 123 S.W. 6th St., 98532. Tel: 360-748-0961; Fax: 360-748-8502. Lay Teachers 9; Students 127.
Catechesis/Religious Program—Students 50.

COVINGTON, KING CO., ST. JOHN THE BAPTIST (1990) Very Rev. James P. Coyne; Deacon Ted Childs.
Church: 25810 156th Ave., S.E., 98042. Tel: 253-630-0701; Fax: 253-630-3174. Web: www.sjtbcc.org.
Catechesis/Religious Program—Students 372.

DES MOINES, KING CO., ST. PHILOMENA (1927) Revs. Thanh X. Dao, Admin.; Simon Grillo, Parochial Vicar.
Res.: 1790 S. 222nd St., 98198. Tel: 206-878-8709; Fax: 206-824-3480.
School—(Grades K-8), 1815 S. 220th, 98198. Tel: 206-824-4051; Fax: 206-878-8646. Lay Teachers 17; Students 236.
Catechesis/Religious Program—Tel: 206-824-5582. Students 247.

DUVALL, KING CO., HOLY INNOCENTS Revs. David Rogerson; William Heric.
P.O. Box 850, 98019. Tel: 425-788-1400; Fax: 425-844-2384.

EDMONDS, SNOHOMISH CO., HOLY ROSARY (1940) Rev. Kenneth Haydock.
Res.: 760 Aloha St., P.O. Box 206, 98020. Tel: 425-778-3122; Fax: 425-672-4909. Web: www.holyrosaryedmonds.org.
School—(Grades PreSchool-8), 770 Aloha St., P.O. Box 206, 98020. Tel: 425-778-3197; Fax: 425-771-8144. Dr. Kathy Carr, Prin.; Carlotta Rojas, Librarian. Sisters 1; Lay Teachers 19; Students 260.
Catechesis/Religious Program—Tel: 425-778-3122. Students 247.

ELMA, GRAYS HARBOR CO., ST. JOSEPH (1890) [CEM] Rev. David Gese; Deacon Frank Hawkins.
Res.: 510 W. Waldrip St., P.O. Box 3027, 98541. Tel: 360-482-3190; Fax: 360-482-3107.
Catechesis/Religious Program—Tel: 360-495-3415. Students 45.
Mission—St. John Broadway and Church St., Montesano, Grays Harbor Co. 98563.

ENUMCLAW, KING CO., SACRED HEART OF JESUS (1888) [CEM] Rev. Jose C. Chcvenia Jr.
Res.: 1614 Farrelly St., 98022. Tel: 360-825-3759; Fax: 360-825-6832. Web: www.sacredheartenumclaw.com.
Catechesis/Religious Program—Tel: 360-825-2333. Students 212.
Station—Crystal Mountain, Crystal Mountain Chapel

EVERETT, SNOHOMISH CO.
1—IMMACULATE CONCEPTION (1904) Very Rev. Bryan L. Hersey; Rev. Sylvain Cibangu, Parochial Vicar; Deacon Matt Zuanich.
Mailing Address: 2619 Cedar St., 98201.
Res.: 2509 Hoyt Ave., 98201. Tel: 425-349-7014; Fax: 425-349-7015. Web: www.ic_olph.org.
Church: 2501 Hoyt Ave., 98201.
School—(Grades PreSchool-8), 2508 Hoyt Ave., 98201. Tel: 425-349-7777; Fax: 425-349-7048. Donna Ramos, Prin. Lay Teachers 28; Students 300.
Catechesis/Religious Program—Students 192.
2—ST. MARY MAGDALEN (1957) Revs. Hans M. Olson; Francis Thumbi; Deacon David P. Alcorta.
Res.: 8517 7th Ave., S.E., 98208. Tel: 425-353-1211; Fax: 425-348-0458. Web: www.smmparish.org.
School—(Grades PreSchool-8), 8615 7th Ave., S.E., 98208. Tel: 425-353-7559; Fax: 425-356-2687. Web: www.stmarym.org. Sr. Joanne McCauley, O.P., Prin. Sisters 1; Lay Teachers 26; Students 408.
Catechesis/Religious Program—Tel: 425-355-3133. Students 188.
Mission—St. John Mukilteo, Snohomish Co.
3—OUR LADY OF PERPETUAL HELP (1891) [CEM] Very Rev. Bryan L. Hersey; Rev. Sylvain Cibangu, Parochial Vicar; Deacon Matt Zuanich.
Res.: 2619 Cedar St., 98201. Tel: 425-349-7014; Fax: 425-349-7015.
Catechesis/Religious Program—Students 169.

FEDERAL WAY, KING & PIERCE COS., ST. THERESA (1924) Revs. Richard K. Hayatsu, Priest Moderator; Kevin Moran, Parochial Vicar; Linda M. DeMarce, Pastoral Coord.
Res.: 3939 S.W. 331st, 98023. Tel: 253-838-5924; Fax: 253-838-0300.
Catechesis/Religious Program—Students 280.

FEDERAL WAY, KING CO., ST. VINCENT DE PAUL (1961) Revs. William McKee; Leonardo Pestano, Parochial Vicar; Deacons Delbert Hoover; Juan Lezcano.
Res.: 30525 8th Ave. S., 98003. Tel: 253-839-2320; Fax: 253-839-1819.
School—(Grades K-8), 30527 8th Ave. S., 98003. Tel: 253-839-3532; Fax: 253-946-1247. Wanda Stewart, Prin. Lay Teachers 19; Students 315.
Catechesis/Religious Program—Students 414.

FERNDALE, WHATCOM CO., ST. JOSEPH (1893) Rev. Khanh Nguyen.
Res.: 5781 Hendrickson Ave., 98248. Tel: 360-384-3651; Fax: 360-384-1879.
Catechesis/Religious Program—Tel: 360-384-8818. Students 250.
Mission—St. Anne
Mission—St. Joachim (Indian Reservation) Bellingham. Kwina & Lummi Shore Rds., Lummi, Whatcom Co. 98226.

FIFE, PIERCE CO., ST. MARTIN OF TOURS (1947) Rev. Gary Weisenberger.
Res.: 2303-54th Ave. E., 98424. Tel: 253-922-7882; Fax: 253-922-2068.
School—All Saints at St. Martin of Tours, (Grades K-8), 2323 54th Ave. E., 98424. Tel: 253-922-5360; Fax: 253-922-6746. Web: www.allsaintspuyallup.org. Stephen Morissette, Prin.
Catechesis/Religious Program—Tel: 253-922-6858. Students 75.

FORKS, CLALLAM CO., ST. ANNE PARISH (1930) Revs. Thomas Nathe; Reynaldo Yu, Parochial Vicar.
Res.: 511-5th Ave., P.O. Box 2359, 98331. Tel: 360-374-9184.
Catechesis/Religious Program—Tel: 360-374-6405. Students 34.
Mission—St. Thomas the Apostle Clallam Bay, Clallam Co. Tel: 360-963-2556.

FRIDAY HARBOR, SAN JUAN CO., ST. FRANCIS (1860) [CEM] Rev. Raymond Heffernan, Admin.
Res.: 425 Price St., P.O. Box 1489, 98250. Tel: 360-378-6603 (Rectory); 360-378-2910 (Office); Fax: 360-378-1843.
Catechesis/Religious Program—Students 17.
Station—St. Francis-Eastsound 956 N. Beach Rd., Eastsound, 98245.
Station—St. Francis: Lopez Island Community, Center Church Davis Bay Rd., Lopez Island.
Station—Our Lady of Good Voyage Chapel Roche Harbor, WA. Lay Ministers 2.

GIG HARBOR, PIERCE CO., ST. NICHOLAS (1931) Rev. Hung Nguyen; Deacons John Ricciardi; Patrick Kelley.
Res.: 3510 Rosedale St., 98335. Tel: 253-851-8850; Fax: 253-851-8823.
School—(Grades K-8), 3555 Edwards St., 98335. Tel: 253-858-7632; Fax: 253-858-1597. Mike Sweeney, Prin. Lay Teachers 14; Students 149.
Catechesis/Religious Program—Tel: 253-851-9040. Students 235.

HOQUIAM, GRAYS HARBOR CO., OUR LADY OF GOOD HELP (1906) Revs. Dennis E. Robb; Fidelis O. Umukoro, O.P.; Gerald Burns, Parochial Vicar.
Mailing Address: 306 E. 3rd St., Aberdeen, 98520. 611 2nd St., 98550.
Res.: 208 L St., 98550. Tel: 360-532-6103; Fax: 360-538-9987.
Mission—Our Lady of the Olympics, Tel: 360-532-8300.

ISSAQUAH, KING CO., ST. JOSEPH (1962) Rev. Bryan Dolejsi, Admin.; Deacons Patrick Moynihan; Jack Bleile.
Res.: 220 Mt. Park Blvd., S.W., P.O. Box 200, 98027. Tel: 425-392-5516; Fax: 425-392-2722. Web: www.sjcissaquah.org.
School—Issaquah Campus, (Grades PreK-4) Tel: 425-313-9129; Fax: 425-313-7296. Peg Johnston, Prin. Lay Teachers 27; Students 355.
School—Snoqualmie Campus, (Grades PreSchool-3), 38645 S.E. Newton St., Snoqualmie, 98065. Tel: 425-888-9130. Peg Johnston, Prin.
Catechesis/Religious Program—Marge Barnette, D.R.E.; Tim Greer, D.R.E. Students 292.

KELSO, COWLITZ CO., IMMACULATE HEART OF MARY (1910) Rev. Mel Strazicich, Admin.
Res.: 2200 Allen St., 98626. Tel: 360-423-3650; Fax: 360-423-4165.
Catechesis/Religious Program—Tel: 360-423-3653; Fax: 360-423-4165. Students 118.

KENT, KING CO., HOLY SPIRIT PARISH (1890) [CEM] Rev. Vincent Pastro; Deacon Anselmo Pardo; Cathy Peters, Parish Admin.
Res.: 404 W. Titus, 98032. Tel: 253-859-0444; Fax: 253-859-5974. Web: www.holyspiritkent.org.
Catechesis/Religious Program—Students 247.

KIRKLAND, KING CO.
1—HOLY FAMILY (1915) Rev. Kurt Nagel.
Res.: 7355 120th Ave., N.E., 98033. Tel: 425-822-0295; Fax: 425-827-0648. Web: www.hfk2.org.
School—(Grades PreSchool-8), 7300 120th Ave. N.E., 98033. Tel: 425-827-0444; Fax: 425-827-0150. Web: www.hfkschool.org. Jacqueline Degel, Prin.; Anne Redman, Librarian. Lay Teachers 20; Students 265.
Catechesis/Religious Program—Students 345.
2—ST. JOHN MARY VIANNEY (1971) Rev. Ramon Santa Cruz, S.O.L.T.

Res.: 12600 84th Ave., N.E., 98034. Tel: 425-823-0787; Fax: 425-814-2115. Web: www.sjvkirkland.org.
Catechesis/Religious Program—Students 225.

LA CONNER, SKAGIT CO., SACRED HEART (1875) Revs. Martin Bourke; Milhton Scarpetta Molina, Parochial Vicar; Emmanuel Azike, Parochial Vicar; Thomas McMichael, Parochial Vicar; Deacons George Peterson; Philip Myer; Antonio Cavazos.
Res.: P.O. Box 757, 98257-0757. Tel: 360-466-3967; Fax: 360-466-3942.
Catechesis/Religious Program—Students 94.

LACEY, THURSTON CO., SACRED HEART OF JESUS (1923) Revs. Oliver Lee Hightower, Moderator; Magnus Attah, Parochial Vicar; Deacons Terry Barber; Ronald San Nicolas; Ms. Ferrell Gilson, Pastoral Coord.
Res.: P.O. Box 3805, 98509-3805. Tel: 360-491-0890; Fax: 360-456-1028. Web: www.sacredheartlacey.com.
Catechesis/Religious Program—Students 374.

LAKE STEVENS, SNOHOMISH CO., HOLY CROSS PARISH (2004) Rev. Joseph DeFolco.
P.O. Box 746, 98258. Tel: 360-691-2636. Email: administrator@holy-cross-parish.com. Web: www.holy-cross-parish.com.
Catechesis/Religious Program—Lee Ann Balbirona, D.R.E. Students 82.

LAKEWOOD, PIERCE CO.
1—ST. FRANCES CABRINI (1952) Rev. Peter Mactutis, Admin.; Deacon George Mounce III.
Res.: 5505 108th St., S.W., 98499. Tel: 253-588-2141; Fax: 253-582-5351. Web: www.cabrini.us.
School—(Grades PreSchool-8), 5621 108th St., S.W., 98499. Tel: 253-584-3850. Stephanie Van Leuven, Prin. Lay Teachers 15; Students 238.
Catechesis/Religious Program—Students 266.
2—ST. JOHN BOSCO (1968) Rev. Oliver Lee Hightower; Deacons Daniel Allen; Jeffrey Greer. In Res., Rev. Charles G. Crosse (Retired).
Res.: 10508 112 St., S.W., 98498. Tel: 253-582-1028; Fax: 253-584-0633. Web: www.stjbosco.org.
Catechesis/Religious Program—Students 175.
Mission—Immaculate Conception Nisqually & Main, Steilacoom, Pierce Co. 98388.

LANGLEY, ISLAND CO., ST. HUBERT (1938) Rev. Richard J. Spicer; Deacons Robert Huber; Lawrence Jesmer.
Mailing Address: P.O. Box 388, 98260-0388.
Res.: 815 Saratoga Ave., 98260. Tel: 360-221-5383; Fax: 360-221-2011. Web: www.sthubertchurch.org.
Catechesis/Religious Program—Students 54.

LONGVIEW, COWLITZ CO., ST. ROSE DE VITERBO (1928) Rev. Timothy W. Ilgen; Deacon Fred Johnson.
Res.: 701 26th Ave., 98632. Tel: 360-425-4660; Fax: 360-577-5820. Web: www.stroselongview.catholicweb.com.
School—(Grades PreSchool-8), 720 26th Ave., 98632. Tel: 360-577-6760; Fax: 360-577-3689. Web: www.strose-school.org. Rosemary Griggs, Prin. Lay Teachers 19; Students 208.
Catechesis/Religious Program—Tel: 360-577-7346. Students 178.
Mission—St. Catherine Cathlamet. 400 Columbia St., Cathlamet, Wahkiakum Co. 98612. Tel: 360-795-8725.

LYNDEN, WHATCOM CO., ST. JOSEPH (1897) Rev. Emilio Gonzalez.
Res.: 205 Twelfth St., 98264. Tel: 360-354-2334; Fax: 360-354-5889.
Catechesis/Religious Program—Students 150.
Mission—St. Peter [CEM 3] 6210 Mt. Baker Hwy., Deming, Whatcom Co. 98244.

LYNNWOOD, SNOHOMISH CO., ST. THOMAS MORE (1962) Rev. Maurice Mamba Ngalamulume, Admin. In Res., Rev. Ward B. Oakshott.
Res.: 6511-176th, S.W., 98037. Tel: 425-743-2929; Fax: 425-743-3652. Web: www.stmp.org.
School—(Grades PreSchool-8) Tel: 425-743-4242; Fax: 425-745-8367. Teresa Fewel, Prin. Sisters 1; Lay Teachers 15; Students 247.
Catechesis/Religious Program—Tel: 425-743-3652. Students 350.

MARYSVILLE, SNOHOMISH CO., ST. MARY (1888) [CEM] Rev. Mark A. Guzman; Deacon John Magnuson, (Retired).
Res.: 4200 88th St., N.E., 98270. Tel: 360-653-9400; Fax: 360-658-7439. Web: www.stmary-stanne.org.
Catechesis/Religious Program—Tel: 360-658-9400, Ext. 303 (Youth); 360-653-9400, Ext. 308 (Elementary). Students 263.
Mission—Tulalip Indian Reservation, St. Anne 7213 Totem Beach Rd., Tulalip, Snohomish Co. 98271. 4200 88th St. N.E., 98270.

MERCER ISLAND, KING CO., ST. MONICA (1958) Revs. Patrick Freitag; Negusse Fesseha Keleta (Eritrea); Anthony Davis, Parochial Vicar; Deacons Jack Warfield; Larry McDonald.
Res.: 4301 88th, S.E., 98040. Tel: 206-232-2900; Fax: 206-232-7875. Web: www.stmonica.cc.
School—(Grades K-8), 4320 87th, S.E., 98040. Tel: 206-232-5432; Fax: 206-275-2874. Mrs. Pamela Dellino, Prin. Lay Teachers 19; Students 245.
Catechesis/Religious Program—Tel: 206-232-9829; Fax: 206-232-3321. Students 503.

MONROE, SNOHOMISH CO., ST. MARY OF THE VALLEY (1902) Rev. Phillip A. Bloom.
Res.: 601 W. Columbia, P.O. Box 279, 98272-0279. Tel: 360-794-8945; Fax: 360-805-0201.
Catechesis/Religious Program—Students 119.

MORTON, LEWIS CO., SACRED HEART (1922) Rev. Roger J. Smith.
Res.: 277 7th St., P.O. Box 880, 98356. Tel: 360-496-5456; Fax: 360-496-5616.
Catechesis/Religious Program—Students 12.
Mission—St. Yves [CEM] Harmony, Lewis Co. Fax: 360-496-5658.
Station— Packwood.

MOUNT VERNON, SKAGIT CO., IMMACULATE CONCEPTION (1899) Revs. Martin Bourke; Milhton Scarpetta Molina, Parochial Vicar; Emmanuel Azike, Parochial Vicar; Thomas McMichael, Parochial Vicar.
Office: 215 N. 15th St., 98273. Tel: 360-336-6622; Fax: 360-336-5203. Web: www.svcc.us.
School—Immaculate Conception Regional School, (Grades PreSchool-8), 1321 E. Division St., 98273. Tel: 360-428-3912; Fax: 360-424-8838. Web: www.l-crsweb.org. Kathleen Cartee, Prin. Lay Teachers 19; Students 293.
Catechesis/Religious Program—Julie Wells, D.R.E.; Regla Wilson, D.R.E. (Hispanic). Students 191.
Skagit Valley Catholic Churches—215 N. 15th St., 98273. Tel: 360-336-6622; Fax: 360-336-5203. Email: admin@svcc.us. Web: www.svcc.us. Rev. Martin Bourke.

MOUNTLAKE TERRACE, SNOHOMISH CO., ST. PIUS X (1955) Revs. Sean P. Fox; Ronald Knudsen, Parochial Vicar.
Res.: 22301 58th Ave. W., 98043. Tel: 425-775-7545; Fax: 425-778-0413.
School—(Grades PreSchool-8), 22105 58th W., 98043. Tel: 425-778-9861; Fax: 425-776-2663. Web: www.stpx.org. Mrs. Ruth Foisy, Prin. Lay Teachers 8; Students 124.
Catechesis/Religious Program—Students 87.

OAK HARBOR, ISLAND CO., ST. AUGUSTINE (1939) Rev. Philip Raether, Admin.
Mailing Address: 185 N. Oak Harbor St., P.O. Box 1319, 98277.
Res.: 180 N.W. 1st Ave., 98277. Tel: 360-675-2303; Fax: 360-675-9490.
Catechesis/Religious Program—Tel: 360-675-2303, Ext. 25. Students 132.
Mission—St. Mary 207 N. Main, P.O. Box 1443, Coupeville, Island Co. 98239. Tel: 360-678-6536.

OCEAN SHORES, GRAYS HARBOR CO., ST. JEROME (1969) Revs. Dennis E. Robb; Gerald Burns, Parochial Vicar.
Mailing Address: 306 E. Third St., Aberdeen, 98520. In Res., Rev. Stephen Roman (Retired).
Res.: 15 Patrick Way, 98569. Tel: 360-289-2838; Fax: 360-538-9987.

OLYMPIA, THURSTON CO., ST. MICHAEL (1848) [CEM] Revs. James Lee; Patrick O'Hogan, Parochial Vicar; Deacons William Batstone; Robert Rensel.
Res.: 1208 11th Ave., S.E., P.O. Box 766, 98507. Tel: 360-754-4667; Fax: 360-754-0628. Web: www.saintmichaelparish.org.
School—(Grades K-8), 1204 11th Ave., S.E., 98501. Tel: 360-754-5131; Fax: 360-753-6090. Web: www-.stmikesolympia.org. Jack Nelson, Prin. Lay Teachers 16; Students 270.
Catechesis/Religious Program—P.O. Box 766, 98507. Students 614.

PE ELL, LEWIS CO., ST. JOSEPH (1894) [CEM 2] Very Rev. David Mulholland; Revs. Todd O. Strange, Parochial Vicar; Phuong D. Tran, Parochial Vicar.
Res.: 417 N. Main, P.O. Box 235, 98572. Tel: 360-291-3434; Fax: 360-291-3434.
Catechesis/Religious Program—Students 9.
Mission—Holy Family State Hwy. 6, Frances, Pacific Co. 98572.

PORT ANGELES, CLALLAM CO., QUEEN OF ANGELS (1891) Revs. Thomas Nathe, Admin.; Reynaldo Yu, Parochial Vicar; Deacons Peter Flatley; Richard Labrecque.
Res.: 209 W. 11th St., 98362. Tel: 360-452-2351; Fax: 360-452-1447. Web: www.olypen.com/qofa.
School—(Grades PreSchool-8), 1007 S. Oak, 98362. Tel: 360-457-6903; Fax: 360-457-6866. Web: www.olypen.com/qofaschool. Debra Brines, Prin. Lay Teachers 14; Students 135.
Catechesis/Religious Program—Tel: 360-457-4171. Students 155.

PORT ORCHARD, KITSAP CO., ST. GABRIEL (1942) Rev. Thomas R. Park.
Res.: 1150 Mitchell Ave., 98366-4416. Tel: 360-876-2762; Fax: 360-876-6085.
Catechesis/Religious Program—Tel: 360-876-2834. Students 284.
Mission—Prince of Peace (1970) N.E. 1171 Sand Hill Rd., P.O. Box 517, Belfair, Mason Co. 98528. Tel: 360-275-8760; Fax: 360-275-4418.
Catechesis/Religious Program—Students 44.

PORT TOWNSEND, JEFFERSON CO., ST. MARY STAR OF THE SEA (1859) [CEM] Rev. L. John Topel, S.J.
Res.: 1335 Blaine St., 98368. Tel: 360-385-3700; Fax: 360-379-1989. Web: www.sotsea.qwestoffice.net.
Catechesis/Religious Program—Tel: 360-385-1662. Students 50.

POULSBO, KITSAP CO., ST. OLAF (1968) Very Rev. David L. Mayovsky; Deacons Carlton Moyer; James Decker.
Res.: 18943 Caldart Ave., N.E., 98370. Tel: 360-779-4291.
Catechesis/Religious Program—Students 153.
Mission—St. Peter 910 South St., Suquamish, Kitsap Co. 98392.

PUYALLUP, PIERCE CO.
1—ALL SAINTS (1899) Revs. Richard McCallister; Justin D. McCreedy, O.S.B.; Deacons Michael McGillicuddy; Eric Paige.
Office: 204 6th Ave., S.W., 98371. Tel: 253-845-7521; Fax: 253-845-3105.
School—(Grades PreSchool-8), 504 2nd, S.W., 98371. Tel: 253-845-5025; Fax: 253-435-9841. Web: www.allsaintspuyallup.org. Stephen Morissette, Prin. Lay Teachers 23; Students 451.
Catechesis/Religious Program—Students 258.
2—HOLY DISCIPLES (1996) Most Rev. Joseph J. Tyson.
Res.: 10425 187th St. E., 98374. Tel: 253-875-6630; Fax: 253-846-9535.
Catechesis/Religious Program—Web: www.holydisciples.org. Students 395.
Mission—Our Lady of Good Counsel 229 Antonie Ave. N., Eatonville, Pierce Co. 98328. Tel: 360-832-6363. Web: www.ourladyofgoodcounseleatonville.org. Deacon Rodney McGuire.

RAYMOND, PACIFIC CO., ST. LAWRENCE (1904) Rev. Paul A. Kaech, Admin.
1112 Blake St., P.O. Box 31, 98577. Tel: 360-942-3000; Fax: 360-942-3000.
Catechesis/Religious Program—Students 25.

REDMOND, KING CO., ST. JUDE (1978) [CEM] Revs. David Rogerson; William Heric, Parochial Vicar; Deacon Carl Smith.
Res.: 10526 166th Ave., N.E., 98052. Tel: 425-883-7685; Fax: 425-881-2207.
Catechesis/Religious Program—Students 400.

RENTON, KING CO.
1—ST. ANTHONY (1901) Revs. Gary Zender; Duc Cong Nguyen, Parochial Vicar; Deacons Richard Combs; Teodoro Rodriguez.
Res.: 314 S. 4th St., 98057. Tel: 425-255-3132; Fax: 425-271-4729. Web: www.st-anthony.cc.
School—(Grades K-8), 336 Shattuck Ave. S., 98057. Tel: 425-255-0059; Fax: 425-235-6555. Web: www.sasr.org. Sr. Linda Riggers, S.N.J.M., Prin.; Trisha Swindal, Librarian. Sisters 2; Lay Teachers 29; Students 519.
Catechesis/Religious Program—Students 502.
2—ST. STEPHEN THE MARTYR (1966) Revs. Edward Goodwin White, Admin.; Brian Snyder, Parochial Vicar; Deacons Marshall Denby; William Eckert.
Res.: 13055 S.E. 192nd St., 98058. Tel: 253-631-1940.
Catechesis/Religious Program—Tel: 253-631-6175. Students 622.

SAMMAMISH, KING CO., MARY, QUEEN OF PEACE (1987) Rev. Kevin F.X. Duggan.
Res.: 1121 228th Ave., S.E., 98075. Tel: 425-391-1178; Fax: 425-391-3797. Web: www.mqp.org.
Catechesis/Religious Program—Students 664.

SEAVIEW, PACIFIC CO., ST. MARY (1965) Rev. Paul A. Kaech, Admin.; Deacon Glenn Cliffton.
Res.: P.O. Box 274, 98644. Tel: 360-642-2002; Fax: 360-642-7100.
Catechesis/Religious Program—Students 7.
Station— McGowan.

SEDRO-WOOLLEY, SKAGIT CO., IMMACULATE HEART OF MARY (1890) Revs. Martin Bourke; Emmanuel Azike, O.P., Parochial Vicar; Milhton Scarpetta Molina, Parochial Vicar; Thomas McMichael, Parochial Vicar; Deacon Phil Meyer.
Office:—719 Ferry St., Sedro Woolley, 98284. Tel: 360-855-0077; Fax: 360-855-2282.
Catechesis/Religious Program—Students 54.
Mission—St. Catherine 239 Limestone, Concrete, Skagit Co. 98237.

SEQUIM, CLALLAM CO., ST. JOSEPH (1916) Rev. Victor A. Olvida, Admin.
Res.: 121 E. Maple, P.O. Box 1209, 98382. Tel: 360-683-6076; Fax: 360-683-4674.
Catechesis/Religious Program—Students 100.

SHELTON, MASON CO., ST. EDWARD (1892) [JC] Rev. Ronald Belisle; Deacons Michael Samuel; William Batstone.
Res.: 601 W. C St., P.O. Box 758, 98584. Tel: 360-426-6134; Fax: 360-426-6231. Web: www.saintedwardshelton.org.
Catechesis/Religious Program—Students 188.

SHORELINE, KING CO.
1—ST. LUKE (1955) Rev. Robert Camuso.
Res.: 322 N. 175th St., 98133. Tel: 206-546-2451; Fax: 206-546-0328. Web: www.stlukecp.org.
School—(Grades K-8), 17533 St. Luke Pl. N.,

98133. Tel: 206-542-1133; Fax: 206-546-8693. Dr. Karen Matthews, Prin. Lay Teachers 20; Students 365.
Catechesis/Religious Program—Students 177.
2—ST. MARK (1954) Rev. William R. Harris.
Res.: 18033 15th Pl., N.E., 98155. Tel: 206-364-7900; Fax: 206-367-3919. Web: www.stmarkseattle.org.
School—(Grades K-8) Tel: 206-364-1633. Web: www.stmss.org. Kathryn Palmquist-Keck, Prin. Lay Teachers 16; Students 198.
Catechesis/Religious Program—Students 130.
SNOHOMISH, SNOHOMISH CO., ST. MICHAEL (1886) Revs. Joseph DeFolco; Armando Guzman, Parochial Vicar; Deacons Ed White; Gene Vanderzanden.
Res.: 1512 Pine Ave., 98290. Tel: 360-568-0821; Fax: 360-568-6426.
Catechesis/Religious Program—Students 159.
SNOQUALMIE, KING CO., OUR LADY OF SORROWS (1929) Rev. John J. Ludvik.
Mailing Address: P.O. Box 909, 98065.
Church: 39025 S.E. Alpha St., 98065.
Res.: 39025 S.E. Beta St., P.O Box 909, 98065. Tel: 425-888-2974; Fax: 425-888-7098. Web: www.olos.org.
Catechesis/Religious Program—Students 204.
Mission—St. Anthony P.O. Box 175, Carnation, King Co. 98014. Tel: 425-333-4930; Fax: 425-333-5001.
Station—St. Bernard's Chapel Snoqualmie Summit. Tel: 425-434-6287.
STANWOOD, SNOHOMISH CO., ST. CECILIA (1908) Rev. Laurence Poncini, O.C.D., Admin.
Res.: 26900 78th Ave., N.W., P.O. Box 1002, 98292. Tel: 360-629-3737; Fax: 360-629-6127. Web: www.home.catholicweb.com/saintcecelia.
Catechesis/Religious Program—Tel: 360-629-4425. Students 142.
SUMNER, PIERCE CO., ST. ANDREW (1921) Rev. Jack D. Shrum.
Office: 1401 Valley Ave. E., 98390. Tel: 253-863-2253; Fax: 253-863-3567.
Church: 1401 Valley Ave, 98390.
Catechesis/Religious Program—Students 500.
Mission—SS. Cosmas and Damian 213 W. Leber St., P.O. Box 215, Orting, Pierce Co. 98360. Tel: 360-893-3154. Deacon Gene Miller.
SWINOMISH, ST. PAUL (1867), (Native American), Revs. Martin Bourke; Jerry Graham, SJ; Thomas McMichael, Parochial Vicar.
17456 Pioneer Pkwy. Rd., 98257. Tel: 360-466-5737; Fax: 360-466-4039. Mailing Address: P.O. Box 2100, La Conner, 98257.
TACOMA, PIERCE CO.
1—ST. ANN (1924) Revs. Tuan Nguyen; Gilberto Mora Tapia, Parochial Vicar; Poao Saena, Parochial Vicar; Cal Christiansen, Parochial Vicar; Jacob M. Maurer, Parochial Vicar.
Res.: 7025 S. Park Ave., 98408. Tel: 253-472-1360; Fax: 253-475-6335. Web: www.catholic-tacoma.org.
Catechesis/Religious Program—Tel: 253-472-1360. Students 58.
2—ST. CHARLES BORROMEO (1956) Very Rev. Michael J. McDermott; Rev. Bryon A. Dickey, Parochial Vicar.
Res.: 7112 S. 12th St., 98465. Tel: 253-564-5185; Fax: 253-565-0936. Web: www.saintcharlesb.org.
School—(Grades PreK-8) Patrick Feist, Prin. Lay Teachers 29; Students 543.
Catechesis/Religious Program—Tel: 253-564-5185, Ext. 3036. Jodi Clark, D.R.E. Students 155.
3—HOLY CROSS (1915) Rev. John J. Renggli.
Res.: 5510 N. 44th St., 98407. Tel: 253-759-3368; Fax: 253-759-6126.
Catechesis/Religious Program—Tel: 253-759-3491. Students 27.
4—HOLY ROSARY (1891) Revs. Tuan Nguyen; Cal Christiansen, Parochial Vicar; Gilberto Mora Tapia, Parochial Vicar; Poao Saena, Parochial Vicar; Jacob M. Maurer, Parochial Vicar.
Res.: 424 S. 30th St., 98402. Tel: 253-383-4549; Fax: 253-779-0622.
School—(Grades K-8), 504 S. 30th, 98402. Tel: 253-272-7012; Fax: 253-404-1804. Rudy Navarro, Prin. Lay Teachers 16; Students 197.
5—ST. JOHN OF THE WOODS (1924) Revs. Tuan Nguyen; Gilberto Mora Tapia, Parochial Vicar; Poao Saena, Parochial Vicar; Cal Christiansen, Parochial Vicar; Jacob M. Maurer, Parochial Vicar.
7001 S. Park Ave., 98408.
Res.: 9903 24th Ave., E., 98445. Tel: 253-537-8551; Fax: 253-537-0459. Web: www.catholic-tacoma.org.
Catechesis/Religious Program—Tel: 253-531-7110. Students 90.
6—ST. JOSEPH (1911), (Slovak), Revs. Tuan Nguyen; Cal Christiansen, Parochial Vicar; Gilberto Mora Tapia, Parochial Vicar; Poao Saena, Parochial Vicar; Jacob M. Maurer, Parochial Vicar.
Res.: 608 S. 34th St., 98418. Tel: 253-472-2489; Fax: 253-473-1201.
7—ST. LEO THE GREAT (1879) Rev. Stephen C. Lantry, S.J.; Deacon Michael Riggio.
Res.: 710 S. 13th St., 98405. Tel: 253-272-5136; Fax: 253-272-6285.
Catechesis/Religious Program—Students 141.
8—OUR LADY, QUEEN OF HEAVEN (1893) Rev. John J. Wilkie.
Parish Office—14601 A St. S., 98444. Tel: 253-537-3252; Fax: 253-536-2662. Web: www.ourladyqueenofheaven.org.
Catechesis/Religious Program—Students 260.
9—ST. PATRICK (1891) Rev. Seamus Laverty.
Res.: 1001 N. J St., 98403. Tel: 253-383-2783; Fax: 253-627-5396. Web: www.stpats-tacoma.org.
School—(Grades PreSchool-8), 1112 N. G St., 98403. Tel: 253-272-2297; Fax: 253-383-2003. Mrs. Francie Jordan, Prin. Sisters 1; Lay Teachers 26; Students 440.
Catechesis/Religious Program—Students 175.
10—SS. PETER & PAUL (1892), (Polish), Rev. Piotr Dzikowski, S.Ch.
Res.: 3422 Portland Ave., 98404. Tel: 253-272-5232; Fax: 253-627-7848.
11—ST. RITA OF CASCIA (1922), (Italian), Rev. Carmine J. Sacco, S.J.
Res.: 1403 S. Ainsworth, 98405. Tel: 253-627-4851; Fax: 253-627-4851. Web: www.stritatacoma.org.
Catechesis/Religious Program—Students 40.
12—SACRED HEART (1912) Revs. Tuan Nguyen; Cal Christiansen, Parochial Vicar; Poao Saena, Parochial Vicar; Gilberto Mora Tapia, Parochial Vicar; Jacob M. Maurer, Parochial Vicar; Deacon Mauricio Anaya.
Res.: 4520 McKinley Ave., 98404. Tel: 253-472-7738; Fax: 253-475-0071.
Catechesis/Religious Program—Students 150.
13—VISITATION (1892) Revs. Tuan Nguyen; Cal Christiansen, Parochial Vicar; Poao Saena, Parochial Vicar; Gilberto Mora Tapia, Parochial Vicar; Jacob M. Maurer, Parochial Vicar.
Res.: 3314 S. 58th St., 98409. Tel: 253-473-4960; Fax: 253-474-8378.
School—(Grades PreSchool-8), 3306 S. 58th St., 98409. Tel: 253-474-6424; Fax: 253-474-6718. Web: www.visitationschool.net. Sheila Harrison, Prin. Lay Teachers 13; Students 134.
Catechesis/Religious Program—Students 89.
TOLEDO, LEWIS CO., ST. FRANCIS XAVIER (1838) [CEM] Very Rev. David Mulholland; Revs. Todd O. Strange, Parochial Vicar; Phuong D. Tran, Parochial Vicar; Deacon Clay Hartzell.
Res.: 139 Spencer Rd., 98591. Tel: 360-864-4126; Fax: 360-864-4130. Web: www.toledotel.com/~stfrancis.
Catechesis/Religious Program—Students 24.
TUKWILA, KING CO., ST. THOMAS (1912) Rev. Gerald L. Mayovsky.
Res.: 4415 S. 140th St., 98168. Tel: 206-242-5501; Fax: 206-244-9387.
Catechesis/Religious Program—Tel: 206-242-8189. Students 116.
VANCOUVER, CLARK CO.
1—HOLY REDEEMER (2000) Rev. Joseph P. Mitchell.
Mailing Address: P.O. Box 871417, 98687-1417. Tel: 360-885-7780; Fax: 360-944-7560.
Church: 17010 N.E. Ninth St., 98684. Tel: 360-885-7780, Ext. 11. Web: www.holyredeemervanc.org.
Catechesis/Religious Program—Students 252.
2—ST. JAMES (1836) [CEM] Rev. Dominic D. Hahn.
Res.: 218 W. 12th St., 98660. Tel: 360-693-3052; Fax: 360-693-3077. Web: www.saintjames-parish.com.
Catechesis/Religious Program—Students 98.
3—ST. JOHN THE EVANGELIST (1868) [CEM] Rev. Armando S. Perez. In Res., Rev. Joseph O'Shea (Retired).
Res.: 8701 N.E. 119 St., 98662. Tel: 360-573-3325; Fax: 360-573-3344.
Catechesis/Religious Program—Students 464.
4—ST. JOSEPH (1952) Revs. Gary Lazzeroni, Admin.; Emmanuel E. Iwen, Parochial Vicar.
Mailing Address: 6600 Highland Dr., 98661. Tel: 360-696-4407; Fax: 360-696-3959.
Church: 400 S. Andresen Rd., 98661. Web: www.stjoevan.org.
School—(Grades K-8), 6500 Highland Dr., 98661. Tel: 360-696-2586; Fax: 360-696-0977. Web: www.stjoevanschool.org. Lesley Harrison, Prin.; Stacie Hunt, Librarian. Lay Teachers 24; Students 403.
Catechesis/Religious Program—Students 329.
5—OUR LADY OF LOURDES (1958) Rev. Michael Radermacher, Admin.
Res.: 5007 N.W. Franklin St., 98663. Tel: 360-695-1366; Fax: 360-695-0610.
School—(Grades PreSchool-8), 4701 N.W. Franklin St., 98663. Tel: 360-696-2301; Fax: 360-696-6700. Mr. Anderson, Prin.; Beth Anderson, Librarian. Lay Teachers 37; Students 361.
Catechesis/Religious Program—Students 205.
VASHON, KING CO., ST. JOHN VIANNEY (1964) Rev. Marc L. Powell, Admin.
Mailing Address: P.O. Box 308, 98070. Tel: 206-567-4149; Fax: 206-567-4198.
Church: 16100 115th Ave. S.W., 98070.
Catechesis/Religious Program—Constance Walker, Asst. Faith Formation (Level 1). Students 94.
Chapel—St. Patrick 26100 99th Ave., S.W., Dockton, 98070.
WINLOCK, LEWIS CO., SACRED HEART (1909) [CEM] Very Rev. David Mulholland; Revs. Todd O. Strange, Parochial Vicar; Phuong D. Tran, Parochial Vicar; Deacon Clay Hartzell.
Res.: 216 N.W. Arden, P.O. Box 69, 98596. Tel: 360-864-4126; Fax: 360-864-4130.
WOODINVILLE, KING CO., BLESSED TERESA OF CALCUTTA (2004) Rev. Frank Schuster.
18712 N.E. 161st Pl., P.O. Box 705, 98072-6127. Tel: 425-806-8096. Web: www.blessedteresa.org.
WOODLAND, COWLITZ CO., ST. PHILIP (1950) [CEM] Rev. Gerald Woodman.
Res.: 430 Bozarth, Box 2169, 98674. Tel: 360-225-8308; Fax: 360-225-8866. Web: www.stphillip.org.
Catechesis/Religious Program—Students 80.
Mission—St. Joseph 136 S. 4th St., Kalama, Cowlitz Co. 98625.
YELM, THURSTON CO., ST. COLUMBAN (1960) Rev. Terrence J. Wager, O.S.B.
Res.: 506 1st St. S., 98597. Tel: 360-458-3031; Fax: 360-458-4094.
Mission—St. Peter Sussex & Keithan St., P.O. Box 744, Tenino, Thurston Co. 98589. Tel: 360-264-2124; Fax: 360-264-2666.
Catechesis/Religious Program—Tel: 360-458-2360. Students 132.

Chaplains of Public Institutions

SEATTLE. *Federal Detention Center*. Rev. Richard Gallagher, Catholic Chap. (Retired).
Immigration & Naturalization Services. Mara Eaton.
King County Jail. Ann Keller, Chap.
U.S. Public Health Hospital. Attended by St. Peter Church, Seattle.
Veterans Administration Medical Center. Rev. David Mani, Chap.
ABERDEEN. *Stafford Creek Correction Center*. Ray Moshofsky, Pastoral Care Min.
BUCKLEY. *Rainier School*. Vacant.
CLALLAM BAY. *Clallam Bay Correction Center*. Revs. Thomas Nathe, Reynaldo Yu.
EVERETT. *Snohomish County Jail*. Rev. Robert Evenson.
FORKS. *Clearwater / Olympic Correction Center*. Revs. Thomas Nathe, Reynaldo Yu.
GIG HARBOR. *Washington Corrections Center for Women*. Mary Rutter, Pastoral Care Min.
KENT. *Regional Justice Center*. Mary Rutter, Pastoral Care Min.
LAKEWOOD. *Western State Hospital*. Rev. Robert Tino.
LITTLE ROCK. *Cedar Creek Correction Center*. Mara Eaton, Pastoral Care Min.
MONROE. *Monroe Correctional Complex*. Bernadette Pauls, Pastoral Care Min.
Minimum Security Unit. Bernadette Pauls, Pastoral Min.
Special Offenders Center. Bernadette Pauls, Pastoral Min.
Twin Rivers Correction Center.
Washington State Reformatory. Bernadette Pauls, Pastoral Care Min. Part of Monroe Correctional Complex.
ORTING. *U.S. Soldiers' Home*. Attended by St. Andrew Church, Sumner.
PORT ORCHARD. *Washington Veterans Home Hospital*. Vacant. Attended by St. Gabriel Church, Port Orchard.
SHELTON. *Washington Corrections Center*, P.O. Box 900, 98584. Shannon O'Donnell, Pastoral Care Min.
SNOQUALMIE. *Echo Glen Children's Center*. Mr. Joseph Cotton, Pastoral Care Minister.
STEILACOOM. *McNeil Island Correction Center*. Vacant.
TACOMA. *Remann Hall*. Alice Jeffers, Pastoral Min.
Veterans Admin. Medical Center. Rev. Leo R. Rimmele, O.S.B.
VANCOUVER. *Veterans Administration Hospital*. Attended from Archdiocese of Portland in Oregon.
Washington State School for the Blind. Attended from St. James Church, Vancouver.
Washington State School for the Deaf. Attended from St. John Church, Vancouver.
YACOLT. *Larch Corrections Center*. Deacon Jack Roscoe, Pastoral Care Rep. Attended by Sacred Heart Church, Battle Ground.

Special Assignment:
Very Revs.—
Bawyn, Anthony, J.C.D., Judicial Vicar, 710 9th Ave., 98104.
Magnano, Paul A., Ph.D., Vicar for Clergy, 710 9th Ave., 98104.

Revs.—
Eblen, James, S.T.L., Ph.D. (Retired), Theologian, 710 9th Ave., 98104.
Evenson, Robert, c/o Office of Vicar for Clergy, 710 9th Ave., 98104.
Johnson, James
Perea, Donald, c/o Office of Vicar for Clergy, 710 9th Ave., 98104.
Peterson, C. Vincent (Retired), c/o Office of Vicar for Clergy, 710 9th Ave., 98104.
Raschko, Michael, Ph.D., Theologian, 1614 Summit, #602, 98122.
Sevilla, Dennis, Chap., c/o St. Joseph Medical Center, Tacoma, 710 9th Ave., 98104.
Silagan, Gorgonio, Jr., c/o Office of Vicar for Clergy, 710 9th Ave., 98104.
Stehly, Mark, Hospital Ministry, South Seattle, Deanery (Retired), 710 9th Ave., 98104. Tel: 201-382-3492

On Duty Outside the Archdiocese:
Rev.—
Larrivee, Leo J., S.S., c/o 710 9th Ave., 98104.

Military Chaplains:
Rev.—
Bailey, J. Lawrence, 746 Main St., McChord AFB, 98438.

Retired:
Revs.—
Angelovic, Michael, P.O. Box 929, Seahurst, 98062.
Basso, Richard, 6909 Weedin Pl., N.E. #B202, 98115.
Boyle, James, 2333 58th Ave. E., #6, Fife, 98424.
Brant, David A., 804 9th Ave., 98104.
Bulger, John, 54 Mitchell St., Pittson, PA 18640.
Chirico, Peter, S.S., 603 Maiden Choice Ln., Baltimore, MD 21228.
Cloquet, Victor, P.O. Box 1232, Allyn, 98524-1232.
Connole, Marlin J., P.O. Box 58, Salkum, 98582.
Crosse, Charles G., 10508 112th St., SW, Lakewood, 98498.
Domandich, Anthony, 4457 S.E. Oatfield Hill Rd. #1B, Milwaukie, OR 97267.
Douglas, Gordon W., 3212 40th Ave. W., 98199.
Duggan, Peter, 6704 S. 239th, #B102, Kent, 98032.
Eblen, James, S.T.L., Ph.D., 131 Bellevue Ave. E. #203, 98102.
Gallagher, Richard, 5809 S. 234th Pl., Kent, 98032.
Gallagher, William E., 6108 N. Park, Tacoma, 98407.
Godley, Patrick, 14950 W. Mountain View Blvd., Surprise, AZ 85374.
Hart, Brian
Heneghan, Jarlath, Knock, Claremorris, County Mayo, Ireland.
Horan, John, 4700 Dash Point Rd., #E4, Federal Way, 98023.
Jennings, John A., 4700 Dash Point Rd., #E2, Federal Way, 98023.
Jonientz, Bernard, 12028 71st Ave. S., #F-294, 98178.
Koehler, John, 2902 N. Carr St. #14, Tacoma, 98403.
Kramis, Joseph, 2009 Walker Park Rd., Shelton, 98584.
Lane, William, 4700 S.W. Dash Point Rd. #E1, Federal Way, 98023.
Lovett, Gerald F., 4700 S.W. Dash Point Rd. #G3, Federal Way, 98023.
Mallahan, James, 100 Crockett St., Rm. 415, 98109.
McCloskey, Lester, 502 43rd Ave. S.E. 14B, Puyallup, 98374.
McEnnis, Thomas, 9151 Greenway Rd., Peoria, AZ 85381.
McLaughlin, John, 1930 S.E. Oakview Dr., Chehalis, 98532.
McMullan, John, 6703 Pampus Dr., Orlando, FL 32819.
Meyer, Clayton, 13717 NN 2nd Ave. #U169, Vancouver, 98685.
Naumes, Matthew, 8818 East G St., Tacoma, 98445.
O'Brien, Patrick, Graigue, Cappagh, County Waterford, Ireland.
O'Brien, Roger, 7328 196th St., S.W., #203, Lynnwood, 98036.
O'Callaghan, Thomas, P.O. Box 346, Suquamish, 98392.
O'Neil, Michael, 8700 E. University Dr. #1712, Mesa, AZ 85207.
O'Neill, Patrick G., 16351 W. Labarynth Ln., Surprise, AZ 85374.
O'Shea, Joseph, c/o St. John Church, 8701 N.W. 119th St., Vancouver, 98662.
Palluck, M. Charles
Parle, Richard, 301 E. Wallace-Kneeland Blvd., Ste. 224-321, Shelton, 98584.
Peterson, C. Vincent
Petosa, Joseph, 17117 40th Ave. W., Lynnwood, 98037.
Phelan, Thomas, 512 S.E. 169th Ave., Vancouver, 98684-8413.
Quinn, Thomas, Aclare P.O., County Cligo, Ireland.
Rink, George, 1828 S.W. 318th Pl., Unit D, Federal Way, 98023.
Roman, Stephen, P.O. Box 190, Ocean Shores, 98569.
Ryan, Michael J., 40479 Bay Hill Way, Palm Desert, CA 92211.
Slate, William, P.O. Box 4258, Kent, 98032.
Stehly, Mark, 692 Panorama Blvd., Sequim, 98382.
Suss, Thomas J.
Szeman, Stephen J., 4814 N.E. 5th Ct., Renton, 98059.
Tolang, Jaime, 820 18th Ave., 98122.
Ton, Anthony, 3708 N.E. 40th Ave., Vancouver, 98661.
Treacy, William, 24880 Brotherhood Rd., Mount Vernon, 98274.
Vandenberg, Thomas L., 31080 9th Ave. S., Federal Way, 98003.
Wallace, Philip, 117 170th Ave., NE, #1504, Bellevue, 98004.
Ward, Richard J., 4700 S.W. Dash Pt. Rd., #64, Federal Way, 98023.
Williams, James, J.C.L., 14423 4th CRT St., 98168.

Permanent Deacons:
Anderson, David, S.J.
Aikin, Scott
Alcorta, David P.
Alexander, Richard
Allen, Daniel
Amlag, John
Anaya, Mauricio
Anderson, Carl
Barber, Terry
Basta, Samuel
Batstone, William
Bemis, James
Benedict, Nathan
Bleile, Jack
Carbajal, Adolfo
Cavazos, Antonio
Childs, Ted
Chin, Kwok
Combs, Richard
Connor, Joseph
Cordova, Frederick
Cummins, Donald
Dardis, Robert
Decker, James
Denby, Marshall
Dolan, Robert
Duffell, Dennis T.
Dunne, Joseph
Eckert, William
Edtl, Leland
Farrell, Daniel
Flatley, Peter
Fraczek, Henry
Gorman, Lawrence
Graddon, Gerald
Greer, Jeffrey
Haines, William, Jr.
Hamlin, William
Hanika, Donald
Harrington, Roy
Hartzell, Clay
Hawkins, F. Thomas
Henn, William
Hoover, Delbert
Huber, Robert
Huelett, William
Jesmer, Lawrence
Johnson, Frederick
Jones, David
Kelley, Patrick
Khieraty, Lawrence
Kim, Duk
Konold, Paul
Kreilkamp, Ben
La Russa, John
Labrecque, Richard
Lane, Loren
Lezcano, Juan
MacPherson, Bruce
Magaña, Abel
Magnuson, John
Maher, Dean
Marcell, Terrance
McDonald, Lawrence
McGillicuddy, Michael
McGlone, Stephen
McGuire, Rodney
McNabb, Joseph, III
Miller, Gene
Mounce, George, III
Moyer, Carlton
Moynihan, Patrick
Murdy, Don
Myer, Philip
Nguyen, Phillip
O'Loane, Philip
Olsen, David
Olsen, Richard
Paige, Eric
Pardo, Anselmo
Parsons, Eamon D.
Pele, Sagato
Pellegrino, Joseph
Pentony, Michael J.
Peterson, George
Ramirez, Artruro
Rapp, David
Rensel, Robert
Ricciardi, John
Riggio, Michael
Rodriguez, Teodoro
Roscoe, John
Rupno, Robert
Samuel, Michael
San Nicolas, Ronald
Sarver, Richard
Shields, Walter J.
Shriver, Joseph
Smith, Carl
Snider, Lloyd
Stenson, Mark
Stromberg, Alton
Swanson, Carl
Tanasse, William
Taube, William
Teskey, Michael
Townsend, William
Tulfua, Asipeli
Vanderzanden, Gene
Warfield, T. Jackson
White, Edward, Sr.
Wiese, Theodore
Wilson, Howard
Wodzanowski, Stephen
Yang, Joua Pao
Yuen, Joseph
Zellmer, Gary
Zuanich, Matthew

INSTITUTIONS LOCATED IN THE ARCHDIOCESE

[A] COLLEGES AND UNIVERSITIES

SEATTLE. *Seattle University*, 901 12th Ave., 98122-1090. Tel: 206-296-6000; Fax: 206-296-6200. Web: www.seattleu.edu. Revs. Stephen V. Sundborg, S.J., Pres.; David Anderson, S.J.; Michael S. Bayard, S.J., Dir. Campus Ministry; Frank Case, S.J.; Gerald T. Cobb, S.J.; Hugh P. Duffy, S.J.; Peter B. Ely, S.J., Vice Pres. Mission Ministry; John F. Foster, S.J.; Paul A. Janowiak, S.J.; Patrick Kelly, S.J.; David J. Leigh, S.J.; Roger S. Gillis, S.J.; Patrick J. Howell, S.J.; Michael M. Kelliher, S.J.; Fernando Alvarez Lara, S.J.; Thomas R.E. Murphy, S.J.; Patrick B. O'Leary, S.J.; Ignatius F. Ohno, S.J.; James B. Reichmann, S.J.; Josef V. Venker, S.J.; Eric J. Watson, S.J.; David Henry, S.J., Scholastic. Priests 21; Sisters 2; Lay Teachers 672; Students 7,560.

LACEY. *Saint Martin's University* (1895) 5300 Pacific Ave., S.E., 98503. Tel: 360-491-4700; Fax: 360-459-4124. Email: admissions@stmartin.edu. Web: www.stmartin.edu. Roy F. Haynderickx, Ph.D., Pres.; Barbara Gayle, Ph.D., Vice Pres. Academic Affairs; Revs. Benedict L. Auer, O.S.B., Campus Min.; Bede Classick, O.S.B., Treas.; Killian Malvey, O.S.B., Faculty, English & Religious Studies; Gerard D. Kirsch, O.S.B., Faculty, History; George J. Seidel, O.S.B., Faculty, Philosophy; Bros. Luke Devine, O.S.B., Assoc. Campus Min.; Boniface Lazzari, O.S.B., Faculty, Spanish; Aelred Woodard, O.S.B., Faculty, Religious Studies. Order of St. Benedict Master's Comprehensive University., Resident and non-resident students. Priests 5; Brothers 3; Lay Teachers 70; Students 1,700.

[B] HIGH SCHOOLS, ARCHDIOCESAN

SEATTLE. *Bishop Blanchet High School* (1954) (Coed), 8200 Wallingford Ave. N., 98103. Tel: 206-527-7711; Fax: 206-527-7712. Email: info@bishopblanchet.org. Web: www.bishopblanchet.org. Dr. Maureen O'Shaughnessy, Prin.; Rev. Gordon W. Douglas (Retired); Judy Baumgartner,

Librarian. Priests 1; Sisters 1; Lay Teachers 78; Students 1,000.

O'Dea High School (1923) (Boys), 802 Terry Ave., 98104-1238. Tel: 206-622-6596; Fax: 206-340-4110. Email: dmurray@odea.org. Web: www.odea.org. Bro. Dominic Murray, C.F.C., Prin.; Lawrence Kight, Librarian. Conducted by the Congregation of Christian Brothers. Brothers 5; Lay Teachers 36; Students 480.

Pope John Paul II High School, P.O. Box 3248, Lacey, 98509-3248. Tel: 360-438-7600; Fax: 360-438-7607.

BURIEN. *John F. Kennedy Catholic High School* (1966) (Coed), 140 S. 140th, 98168. Tel: 206-246-0500; Fax: 206-242-0831. Email: info@kennedyhs.org. Web: www.kennedyhs.org. Mr. Michael L. Prato, Prin.; Rev. Michael J. Batterberry. Priests 1; Lay Teachers 66; Students 964.

RIDGEFIELD. *St. Elizabeth Ann Seton High School*, 811 N.E. 112th Ave., Vancouver, 98684. Ed Little, Prin.

[C] HIGH SCHOOLS, PRIVATE

SEATTLE. *Holy Names Academy* (1880) (Girls), 728 21st Ave. E., 98112. Tel: 206-323-4272; Fax: 206-323-5254. Email: eswift@holynames-sea.org. Web: www.holynames-sea.org. Ms. Elizabeth Swift, Prin.; Sr. Ann Cornelia Sullivan, S.N.J.M., Librarian. Congregation of the Sisters of the Holy Names of Jesus and Mary. Sisters 5; Lay Teachers 42; Students 645.

Seattle Preparatory School (1891) (Coed), 2400-11th Ave. E., 98102. Tel: 206-324-0400; Fax: 206-323-6509. Email: tfields@seaprep.org. Web: www.seaprep.org. Mr. Kent Hickey, Pres.; Dr. Matt Barmone, Prin.; Janice Abe, Librarian. Priests 1; Lay Teachers 54; Students 680.

BELLEVUE. *Eastside Catholic School* (Coed), 232 228th Ave., S.E., Sammamish, 98074. Tel: 425-295-3000; Fax: 425-392-5160. Web: www.eastsidecatholic.org. Jim Kubacki, Pres.; Greg Marsh, High School Prin.; Karen O'Meara Pullen, Middle School Prin. Priests 1; Lay Teachers 67; Students 854.

Forest Ridge School of the Sacred Heart (1907) (Grades 5-12), (Girls), 4800 139th Ave., S.E., 98006. Tel: 425-641-0700; Fax: 425-643-3881. Email: marysm@forestridge.org. Web: www.forestridge.org. Mr. Mark Pienotti, Head of School; Carola Wittman, High School Dir.; Julie Grasseschi, Middle School Dir.; Joanne Boerth, Librarian. Religious of the Sacred Heart 3; Lay Teachers 56; Students 381.

EVERETT. *Archbishop Thomas J. Murphy High School* (Coed), 12911 39th Ave., S.E., 98208-6159. Tel: 425-379-6363; Fax: 425-385-2875. Web: www.archbishopmurphyhs.org. Dr. Robert Graby, Pres.; Dr. Kristine Brynildsen-Smith, Prin.; Nicolette Roberge, Librarian. Lay Teachers 44; Students 583.

TACOMA. *Bellarmine Preparatory School* (1928) (Coed), 2300 S. Washington, 98405. Tel: 253-752-7701; Fax: 253-761-3505. Web: www.bellarmineprep.org. Rev. John Fuchs, S.J., Rector; Mr. Jack Peterson, Pres.; Chris Gavin, Prin.; Revs. Gerard E. Chapdelaine, S.J., Teacher; Frederick P. Mayovsky, S.J., Teacher; Sr. Georgia Yianakulls, S.N.J.M., Librarian. Owned by the Jesuit Fathers. Board of Directors: 4 members of the Jesuit order and 16 others. Priests 9; Sisters 1; Lay Teachers 73; Students 1,002. In Res. Revs. William Bichsel, S.J.; Gerard E. Chapdelaine, S.J.; Thomas N. Gallagher, S.J.; Robert A. Goebel, S.J.; Craig Hightower, S.J.; Frederick P. Mayovsky, S.J.; Joseph O. McGowan, S.J.; Dominic Nguyen, S.J.; Thomas G. Williams, S.J.; Alan Yost, S.J.

[D] ELEMENTARY SCHOOLS, PRIVATE

SEATTLE. *Villa Academy*, (Grades PreK-8), (Coed), 5001 N.E. 50th St., 98105. Tel: 206-524-8885; Fax: 206-523-7131. Email: pskinner@thevilla.org. Web: www.thevilla.org. Pauline Skinner, Head of School; Karen Strand, Librarian. Lay Teachers 35; Students 343.

CAMAS. *Pacific Crest Academy*, (Grades PreK-8), 324 N.E. Oak St., P.O. Box 1031, 98607-1031. Tel: 360-834-9913; Fax: 360-834-9926. Web: www.pacificcrestacademy.org. Dr. Les White, Prin. Lay Teachers 13; Students 123.

LACEY. *Holy Family School*, (Grades PreK-8), 2606 Carpenter Rd., S.E., P.O. Box 3700, 98509. Tel: 360-491-7060; Fax: 360-456-3725. Web: holyfamilylacey.org. Linda Farrimond, Prin.; Debra Getty, Librarian. Lay Teachers 15; Students 102.

[E] CATHOLIC COMMUNITY SERVICES OF THE ARCHDIOCESE OF SEATTLE

SEATTLE. *Aloha Inn*, 1911 Aurora Ave. N., 98109. Tel: 206-283-6070; Fax: 206-283-7421.

Association for Catholic Childhood, 100 23rd Ave. S., 98144. Tel: 206-328-5973; Fax: 206-328-5699. Email: acc@ccsww.org. Web: www.forthechildrenww.org.

Catholic Charities Foundation, 100 23rd Ave., S., 98144-2302. Tel: 206-328-5696; Fax: 206-328-5699. Michael Reichert, Pres.

Catholic Community Services of Western Washington, 100 23rd Ave. S., 98144-2302. Tel: 206-328-5696; 206-328-5646 (TTY); Fax: 206-328-5699. Email: info@ccsww.org. Web: www.ccsww.org. Michael L. Reichert, Pres.

Catholic Community Services Northwest, 1918 Everett Ave., Everett, 98201. Tel: 425-257-2111; Fax: 425-257-2120.

Whatcom Family Center, 1133 Railroad Ave., Ste. 100, Bellingham, 98225-5054. Tel: 360-676-2164; Fax: 360-676-2144. Kathy McNaughton, Dir.

Skagit Family Center, 320 Pacific Pl., P.O. Box 2909, Mount Vernon, 98273-7909. Tel: 360-416-7546; Fax: 360-416-7541. Janet Simpson, Dir.

Snohomish Family Center, 1918 Everett Ave., Everett, 98201. Tel: 425-257-2111; Fax: 425-257-2120. Vicki Howell, Regional COO.

Skagit Community Mental Health Programs, 160 Cascade Pl., Ste. 201, Burlington, 98233-3126. Tel: 360-856-3054.

Catholic Community Services King County Family Centers, 100-23rd Ave. S., 98144-2302. Tel: 206-323-6336; 206-328-5646 (TDD); Fax: 206-324-4835. Bill Hallerman, Agency Dir. Tel: 206-328-5701.

Randolph Carter Family Learning Center, 100 23rd Ave. S., 98144-2302. Tel: 206-323-6336; Fax: 206-324-4835.

East King County Family Center, 875 140th Ave. N.E., Ste. 205, Bellevue, 98005. Tel: 425-213-1963; Fax: 425-213-1068.

South King County Family Center, 1229 W. Smith St., P.O. Box 398, Kent, 98035. Tel: 253-854-0077; Fax: 253-850-2503.

Catholic Community Services Southwest Family Centers, 1323 S. Yakima Ave., Tacoma, 98405. Tel: 253-383-3697; Fax: 253-572-3193. Denny Hunthausen, Agency Dir.

Grays Harbor Family Center, P.O. Box 1734, Aberdeen, 98520. Tel: 360-533-9470; Fax: 360-533-9473. Mike Curry, Dir.

Kitsap Family Center, 250 S. Cambrian Ave., Bremerton, 98312. Tel: 866-246-3642; Fax: 360-405-9487.

Benedict House, 250 S. Cambrian Ave., Bremerton, 98312. Tel: 360-405-9486; Fax: 360-405-9487.

Kitsap Family Center Counseling, Foster Grandparents and Volunteer Chore Services, 654 4th St., Ste. 202A, Bremerton, 98337. Tel: 866-246-3642; Fax: 360-377-5088.

Vancouver Family Center, 9300 N.E. Oakview Dr., Ste. A-1, Vancouver, 98662. Tel: 360-567-2211; Fax: 360-213-2402.

Longview Family Center, 676 26th Ave., Longview, 98632. Tel: 360-577-2200; Fax: 360-577-2205.

Tahoma Family Center, 1323 S. Yakima, Tacoma, 98405-4457. Tel: 253-383-3697; Fax: 253-572-3193. Susie Hofstedt, Dir.

Northend Family Preservation Center, 5410 N. 44th St., Tacoma, 98407. Tel: 253-759-9544; Fax: 253-759-9512. Mary Stone Smith, Dir.

Family Preservation Center, 285 Fifth St., Ste. 2, Bremerton, 98337. Tel: 360-792-2020; Fax: 360-478-6993.

Thurston County Family Center, 2940 Limited Ln., N.W., P.O. Box 11399, Olympia, 98508. Tel: 360-586-2960; Fax: 360-586-2930. Gary Sandwick, Dir.

Drexel House, 604 Devoe St., S.E., Olympia, 98501. Tel: 360-753-3340.

Community Kitchen, 505 E. 5th St. S.E., Olympia, 98501. Tel: 360-349-2808.

Archdiocesan Housing Authority dba Catholic Housing Services of Western Washington 100 23rd Ave. S., 98144. Tel: 206-328-5731; Fax: 206-328-5692. Michael L. Reichert, Pres.

Kincaid Housing/Kincaid Court Apartments, 6210 Parker Rd. E., Sumner, 98390. Tel: 253-863-8818; Fax: 253-826-1006. John Hickman, Dir. Finance & Opers.

Pioneer Court Housing/Pioneer Court Apartments, 507 W. Stewart Ave. #104, Puyallup, 98371. Tel: 253-863-8818; Fax: 253-826-1006.

Sunrise Court Housing/Sunrise Court Apartments, 110 140th St. S., Tacoma, 98444. Tel: 253-863-8818; Fax: 253-536-7148.

Redmond Elderly Housing Association/Emma McRedmond, 7960-169th Ave, N.E., Redmond, 98053. Tel: 425-869-2424. Michael L. Reichert, Pres.

AHA-Pierce County Association/Norm Fournier Court, 112 S. 127th, Tacoma, 98444. Tel: 253-845-3557. Michael L. Reichert, Pres.

Halcyon Foundation, 1200 134th Ave., N.E., Bellevue, 98005. Tel: 425-644-4344; Fax: 425-644-9867.

Catholic Community Services of Western Washington Long Term Care System Tel: 877-870-1582; Fax: 253-272-6356. Peter Nazzal, Dir. Email: petern@ccsww.org.

Seattle & North King Co. Office, 100 23rd Ave. S., 98144-2302. Tel: 800-310-5654.

Aberdeen Office, 3rd St. & H St., P.O. Box 1734, Aberdeen, 98520-4003. Tel: 877-870-1582.

Bellingham Office, 1133 Railroad Ave., Bellingham, 98225. Tel: 888-300-2493.

Bremerton Office, 285 5th St. Ste. 3, Bremerton, 98337. Tel: 800-642-8019.

Chehalis Office, P.O. Box 1152, Chehalis, 98532. Tel: 800-642-8021.

Everett Office, 2531 Wetmore, Everett, 98201. Tel: 800-562-4663.

Kelso Office

Kent Office, P.O. Box 398, Kent, 98035. Tel: 800-722-3479.

Port Angeles Office Tel: 800-642-1809. Carol Krula, Contact Person.

Shelton Office, P.O. Box 1228, Shelton, 98584-0947. Tel: 800-642-8026.

Tacoma Office, P.O. Box 1235, Tacoma, 98401. Tel: 253-502-2726; Fax: 253-272-6356.

Vancouver Office Tel: 800-733-8193; 877-870-1582.

St. Martin de Porres Shelter, 1561 Alaskan Way S., 98134. Tel: 206-323-6341; Fax: 206-328-5666.

St. Martin's Programs, 1561 Alaskan Way S., 98134. Tel: 206-323-6341; Fax: 206-328-5666.

Lazarus Day Center, 416 2nd Ave. Ext. S., 98104. Tel: 206-623-7219; Fax: 206-623-6191.

Sacred Heart Shelter, 232 Warren Ave. N., 98109. Tel: 206-285-7489; Fax: 206-285-9556.

Solanus Casey Center, 1008 James St., 98104. Tel: 206-223-0907.

Catholic Immigration Services, 4250 S. Mead St., 98118. Tel: 206-725-2090; Fax: 206-725-9046.

Matt Talbot Center, 2313 3rd Ave., 98121. Tel: 206-256-9865; Fax: 206-256-4065.

Noel House Programs, 2301 2nd Ave., 98121. Tel: 206-441-3210; Fax: 206-441-0350. Web: www.noel-house.org.

Rose of Lima, 120 Bell St., 98121. Tel: 206-441-1200; Fax: 206-770-9510. Web: www.rosehouse.org.

Women's Referral Center, 2030 3rd Ave., 98121. Tel: 206-441-3210; Fax: 206-441-0350.

Women's Wellness Center, 1900 2nd Ave., 98101. Tel: 206-256-0665; Fax: 206-448-8495.

First Nations Women's Housing and Recovery Program, 12794 78th Ave. S., 98178. Tel: 206-268-0880.

First Nations Men's Housing and Recovery Program, 610 Terry Ave., 98104. Tel: 206-268-0880.

Alder Crest Transitional Housing, 6520 35th Ave., S.W., 98126. Tel: 206-437-0341.

Hospitality Kitchen, 1323 S. Yakima Ave., Tacoma, 98405. Tel: 253-502-2696.

Tacoma Avenue Shelter, 1142 Ct. "E", Tacoma, 98405. Tel: 253-572-0131.

Phoenix Housing Network, 7050 S. "G" St., Tacoma, 98408. Tel: 253-471-5340.

Tacoma Indian Center, 1556 Market St., Tacoma, 98402. Tel: 253-593-2707.

Chemical Dependency Treatment System NW, 2806 Douglas Ave., Bellingham, 98225. Tel: 360-676-2184.

Frederic Ozanam House, 810 9th Ave., 98104. Tel: 206-441-4606.

Catholic Seamen's Club, 2330 1st Ave., 98121. Tel: 206-441-4773; Fax: 206-441-8059. Email: aosseattle@cablespeed.com. Rev. Anthony J. Haycock, Dir. & Chap. Total Assisted 18,000.

Sea-Tac Airport Tel: 206-324-7100, Ext. 14. Deacon Mark Stenson. Tel: 425-746-3547.

St. Mary Church: 611 20th Ave. S., 98144. Tel: 206-324-7100, Ext. 14.

[F] CHILD CARE SERVICES

SEATTLE. *Martin Luther King. Jr., Day Home Center*, 1855 S. Ln., 98144. Tel: 206-328-5670; Fax: 206-325-5922. Email: debb@ccsww.org. June Lombard-Allen, Dir. Total Staff 17; Total Assisted 75.

Providence Mt. St. Vincent Child Care, 4831 35th Ave., S.W., 98126-2799. Tel: 206-938-6784; Fax: 206-938-8999.

OLYMPIA. *St. Mike's Tikes*, 1010 Eastside St., S.E., 98501. Tel: 360-586-1585; Fax: 360-586-1584.

POULSBO. *St. Olaf's Daycare*, 18943 Caldart Ave., N.E., 98370. Tel: 360-779-5791; Fax: 360-598-5888.

[G] HOSPITALS AND HEALTH CARE SYSTEMS

SEATTLE. *Providence Health & Services*, 1801 Lind Ave. S.W., Renton, 98057-9016. Tel: 425-525-3355; Fax: 425-525-3984. Email: margaret.botch@providence.net. Sr. Margaret Botch, S.P., Prov. Supr.

Providence Health System-California Tel: 425-525-3355; Fax: 425-525-3984.

Providence Health System-Oregon Tel: 425-525-3355; Fax: 425-525-3984.

Providence Health & Services-Washington Tel: 425-525-3355; Fax: 425-525-3984.

BELLEVUE. *Sisters of St. Joseph of Peace, PeaceHealth, System Office*, 14432 S.E. Eastgate Way, Ste. 300, 98007-6412. Tel: 425-747-1711; Fax: 425-649-3825. Alan Yordy, Pres. & CEO.

BELLINGHAM. *St. Joseph Hospital*, 2901 Squalicum Pkwy., 98225. Tel: 360-734-5400; Fax: 360-738-6393. Web: www.peacehealth.org. Nancy Steiger, CEO; Chris Phillips, Dir. Mission and Community Outreach. Sisters of St. Joseph of Peace and PeaceHealth. Sisters 1; Bed Capacity 253; Patients Assisted Annually 25,426; Total Staff 2,020.

CENTRALIA. *Providence Centralia Hospital*, 914 S. Scheuber Rd., 98531. Tel: 360-736-2803; Fax: 360-330-8614. Web: www.providence.org.

Providence Health System dba Providence Centralia Hospital Bed Capacity 191; Patients Assisted Annually 140,000; Total Staff 690.

EVERETT. *Providence Everett Medical Center - Pacific Campus*, 916 Pacific Ave., P.O. Box 1067, 98206. Tel: 425-258-7992; Fax: 425-258-7307.

Providence General Foundation, 916 Pacific Ave., P.O. Box 1067, 98206. Tel: 425-258-7500; Fax: 425-258-7142. Sr. Anita Butler, S.P., Contact Person; Dottie Piasecki, Exec. Dir.

Providence Regional Medical Center Everett, 1321 Colby Ave., 98206. Tel: 425-261-2000; Fax: 425-261-4051. Web: www.providence.org/everett/. David Brooks, CEO; Tim Serban, Dir. Mission Integration & Spiritual Care; Sr. Dorothy Klingele, S.P., Sister Representative. Sisters 3; Bed Capacity 468; Patients Assisted Annually 268,023; Total Staff 2,669.

FEDERAL WAY. *St. Francis Hospital of Federal Way*, 34515 9th Ave. S., 98003-6761. Tel: 253-927-9700; 253-838-9700; Fax: 253-952-7988. Email: sydbersaute@chiwest.com. Web: www.fhshealth.org. Sisters of St. Francis of Philadelphia. Bed Capacity 110; Patients Assisted Annually 87,675; Total Staff 810.

GIG HARBOR. *St. Anthony Hospital*, 11567 Canterwood Blvd., N.W., 98332. Tel: 253-857-1431. Dianna Kielian, Vice Pres. Mission & Ministry.

LAKEWOOD. *St. Clare Hospital*, 11315 Bridgeport Way, S.W., 98499. Tel: 253-588-1711; Fax: 253-512-2833. Web: www.fhshealth.org. Kathy Bressler, COO; Dianna Kielian, Vice Pres., Mission & Ministry. Sisters of St. Francis of Philadelphia. Bed Capacity 106; Patients Assisted Annually 89,900; Total Staff 705.

Franciscan Health System, 11315 Bridgeport Way, S.W., 98499. Tel: 253-581-3111. Dianna Kielian, Contact Person.

LONGVIEW. *PeaceHealth, St. John Medical Center*, 1615 Delaware St., P.O. Box 3002, 98632. Tel: 360-414-2000; Fax: 360-414-7550. Web: www.peacehealth.org. Sisters of St. Joseph of Peace and PeaceHealth. Bed Capacity 346; Patients Assisted Annually 201,097; Total Staff 1,559.

OLYMPIA. *Providence St. Peter Hospital*, 413 Lilly Rd., N.E., 98506. Tel: 360-491-9480; Fax: 360-493-7268. Medrice Coluccio, Chief Exec.

Sisters of Providence - Mother Joseph Province Bed Capacity 390; Patients Assisted Annually 223,542; Total Staff 2,470.

Providence St. Peter Foundation, 413 Lilly Rd., N.E., 98506-5116. Tel: 360-493-7980; Fax: 360-493-4631. Sr. Anita Butler, S.P., Contact Person; Nancy Riordan, Exec. Dir., Foundation.

TACOMA. *Catholic Pastoral Care-Hospital Tacoma Ministry*, 1001 N. "J" St., 98403. Tel: 253-383-3496; Fax: 253-756-0290. Email: pcdeanery@juno.com. Rev. Justin D. McCreedy, O.S.B., Chap.

St. Joseph Medical Center, 1717 S. J St., P.O. Box 2197, 98405-2197. Tel: 253-426-4101; Fax: 253-426-6880. Web: www.fhshealth.org. Joseph Wilczek, CEO; Rev. Dennis Sevilla. Sisters of St. Francis of Philadelphia. Sisters 2; Bed Capacity 320; Patients Assisted Annually 469,776; Total Staff 2,520.

[H] NURSING HOMES

SEATTLE. *Providence Mount St. Vincent*, 4831 35th Ave., S.W., 98126. Tel: 206-937-3700; Fax: 206-938-8999. Email: charlene.boyd@providence.org. Web: www.providence.org/themount. Tom Mitchell, Admin.

Sisters of Providence - Mother Joseph Province Sisters 3; Bed Capacity 215; Apartments 109; Total Assisted Annually 750; Total Staff 500.

Providence Mt. St. Vincent Foundation, 4831 35th Ave., S.W., 98126. Tel: 206-938-8994; Fax: 206-938-8999. Email: cscollins@providence.org. Pat Welch, Bd.Pres.; Molly Swain, Exec. Dir.

ISSAQUAH. *Providence Marianwood*, 3725 Providence Point Dr., S.E., 98029. Tel: 425-391-2800; Fax: 425-391-5440. Web: www.providencemarianwood.org. Sisters of Providence Health System. Bed Capacity 120; Total Assisted Annually 450; Total Staff 175.

Providence Marianwood Foundation, 3725 Providence Point Dr., S.E., 98029. Tel: 425-391-2895. Sr. Anita Butler, S.P., Contact Person; Cindy Sharek, Foundation Dir.

OLYMPIA. *Providence Mother Joseph Care Center*, 3333 Ensign Rd., N.E., 98506. Tel: 360-493-4900; Fax: 360-493-4000. Rev. David Bates, M.Div., Chap.; Kate Gormally, Admin. Total Staff 210; Patients Assisted Annually 900.

[I] HOSPICES

EVERETT. *Providence Hospice and Home Care of Snohomish County*, 2731 Wetmore Ave., #500, 98201. Tel: 425-261-4800; Fax: 425-261-4850. Web: www.providence.org/phhc. Served 5,717; Total Staff 223.

Providence Hospice & Home Care of Snohomish Co. Foundation, 2731 Wetmore Ave., #500, 98201. Tel: 425-261-4805; Fax: 425-261-4850. Email: cwittren@providence.org. Connie Wittren, Devel. Dir.

OLYMPIA. *Providence Sound HomeCare and Hospice*, 3432 South Bay Rd., 98506. Tel: 800-869-7062; 360-459-8311; Fax: 360-493-4657. Web: www.providence.org. Lisa Rodriguez, COO Home Health. Total Staff 208; Patients Assisted Annually 6,800.

[J] RESIDENCES FOR ELDERLY, DISABLED, OR LOW INCOME

SEATTLE. *Chancery Place*, 910 Marion St., # 1307, 98104. Tel: 206-343-9415; Fax: 206-343-0680. Phoebe Klaer, Mgr. Total Apartments 84; Total Staff 5.

The Franciscan, 15237 21st Ave., S.W., 98166. Tel: 206-431-8001; Fax: 206-431-1254. Total Units 38; Total Staff 3.

Heritage House at The Market, 1533 Western Ave., 98101. Tel: 206-382-4119; Fax: 206-382-0201. Email: heritagehouse@providence.org. Total Assisted 75; Total Staff 40.

Providence ElderPlace, 4515 Martin Luther King Jr. Way S., 98118. Tel: 206-320-5325; Fax: 206-320-5326. Email: ellen.garcia@providence.org. Web: www.providence.org/long_term_care/elderplace. Ellen Garcia, Exec. Dir.

Providence Mount St. Vincent, 4831 35th Ave. S., 98126. Tel: 206-937-3700; Fax: 206-938-8999. Email: charlene.boyd@providence.org. Web: www.providence.org/themount. Jennifer Paquette, Dir. of Spiritual Care. Total Assisted 750; Residents 319; Bed Capacity 335; Total Staff 500.

Providence Peter Claver House, 7101 38th Ave. S., 98118. Tel: 206-721-6265; Fax: 206-721-1327. Email: duong.nguyen@providence.org. Duong Nguyen, Housing Dir. Units 79; Total Assisted Annually 79; Total Staff 5.

Providence Vincent House, 1423 First Ave., 98101. Tel: 206-682-9307; Fax: 206-682-0548. Sponsored by Providence Health and Services. Total Staff 4; Residents 61.

St. Martin's on Westlake, 2008 Westlake Ave., 98121. Tel: 206-340-0410; Fax: 206-682-8843. Email: marians@ccsww.org. Total Staff 10; Bed Capacity 53; Total Assisted Annually 63.

Spruce Park Apartments, 155 21st Ave., 98122. Tel: 206-322-0450; Fax: 206-328-6637. Staff 3; Assisted 125.

BELLEVUE. *Champion House*, 1800 145th Pl., S.E., 98007-6209. Tel: 425-644-4477; Fax: 425-746-0438. Total Staff 18; Total Assisted 8.

Elbert House, 16000 N.E. 8th St., 98008. Tel: 206-747-5111; Fax: 425-641-3141. Email: walterg@ccsww.org. Total Assisted Annually 49; Total Staff 4.

CENTRALIA. *Providence Blanchet House*, 1700 Providence Ln., 98531. Tel: 360-330-8748; Fax: 360-330-8795.

Providence Rossi House, 1700 Providence Ln., 98531. Tel: 360-330-8748; Fax: 360-330-8795.

CHEHALIS. *Providence Place*, 350 S.E. Washington Ave., 98532. Tel: 360-740-8389; Fax: 360-740-6504. Sponsored by The Sisters of Providence. Residents 60.

OLYMPIA. *Providence of St. Francis*, 3415 12th Ave., 98506. Tel: 360-493-5700; Fax: 360-493-5801.

Sunshine House, 413 N. Lilly Rd., 98506-5166. Tel: 360-493-7900; Fax: 360-493-5569. Email: ed.micas@providence.org. Web: www.providence.org/swsa/patient_resources/sunshine.htm.

Providence Health System, WA Total Staff 8; Total Assisted 95,000.

TUMWATER. *Tumwater Apartments*, 5701 6th Ave., S.W., 98501-8517. Tel: 360-352-4321; Fax: 360-352-3557. Units 50; Total Staff 3.

[K] SOCIAL SERVICES

SEATTLE. **L'Arche Noah Sealth of Seattle*, P.O. Box 22023, 98122-0023. Tel: 206-325-9434; Fax: 206-568-0367. Email: info@larcheseattle.org. Web: www.larcheseattle.org.

Providence Regina House, 8201 10th Ave. S. #6, 98108. Tel: 206-763-9204. Paige Collins, Mgr.

Sojourner Place, 5071 8th Ave., N.E., 98105. Tel: 206-545-4200; Fax: 206-633-3525. Sisters of Providence - Mother Joseph Province. Staff 4; Residents 11.

MONTESANO. *Archdiocesan Council of Catholic Women-Southern Deanery*, P.O. Box 535, Port Angeles, 98362. Tel: 360-249-2633. Email: eehig@lightstream.net. Edith Higginbothaan, Pres.

PORT ANGELES. *Archdiocesan Council for Catholic Women-Western Deanery*, P.O. Box 535, 98362. Tel: 360-461-0642. Patricia Pitsch, Pres.

Archdiocesan Council of Catholic Women, Northern Deanery, P.O. Box 535, 98362. Donna Rose, Pres.

RENTON. *Archdiocesan Council for Catholic Women-Central Deanery*, 17016 129th Ave., S.E., 98058. Tel: 425-226-6207.

[L] MONASTERIES AND RESIDENCES OF PRIESTS AND BROTHERS

SEATTLE. *Arrupe Jesuit Community at Seattle University*, 924 East Cherry St., 98122-4341. Tel: 206-296-6340; Fax: 206-296-6399. In Res. Revs. Patrick J. Howell, S.J., Seattle Univ. Rector; Stephen V. Sundborg, S.J., Seattle University Pres.; David Anderson, S.J.; Fernando Alvarez Lara, S.J.; Michael S. Bayard, S.J., Dir. Campus Ministry; Frank Case, S.J.; Gerald T. Cobb, S.J.; Emmett H. Carroll, S.J.; Denis Donaghue, S.J.; Hugh P. Duffy, S.J.; Robert J. Egan, S.J.; Peter B. Ely, S.J., Vice Pres. Mission & Ministry; John F. Foster, S.J.; Ronald R. Funke, S.J.; Jean Baptiste Ganza, S.J.; Roger S. Gillis, S.J.; David Henry, S.J.; Paul A. Janowiak, S.J.; Michael M. Kelliher, S.J.; Patrick Kelly, S.J.; David J. Leigh, S.J.; Thomas R.E. Murphy, S.J.; Ignatius F. Ohno, S.J.; Patrick B. O'Leary, S.J.; James B. Reichmann, S.J.; L. John Topel, S.J.; James Taiviet Tran, S.J.; Patrick Twohy, S.J.; Josef V. Venker, S.J.; Eric J. Watson, S.J.; William M. Watson, S.J.

Congregation of Christian Brothers (Irish Christian Brothers), 1021 Columbia St., 98104-2018. Tel: 206-622-2639; Fax: 206-340-4110. Bros. John Austin Pettit, C.F.C.; John Hugh Greenan, C.F.C., Community Leader; G. Greogry Lindeman, C.F.C.; D. Dominic Murray, C.F.C., Prin.; D. Thomas LeJeune, C.F.C. Brothers 5.

Jesuit House, Seattle, 621 17th Ave. E., 98112. Tel: 206-324-7496. Revs. John C. Bentz, S.J., Supr.; Richard P. Magner, S.J.; Joseph P. Carver, S.J.; Mr. Juan P. Manufo del Toro, S.J.; Mr. Edwin Martinez, S.J.; Revs. John Rashford, S.J.; Joseph Nguyen, S.J.; John O'Leary, S.J.; John Whitney, S.J.

Maryknoll Fathers & Brothers, 958-16th Ave. E., 98112. Tel: 206-322-8831; Fax: 206-324-6909. Email: mklseatl@maryknoll.org. Web: www.maryknoll.org. Bro. W. Timothy Raible, M.M., Regl. Dir.

The Redemptionist Society of Washington, 205 2nd Ave. N., 98109. Tel: 206-284-4680; Fax: 203-284-3161. Email: info@sacredheartseattle.com. Revs. William Cleary, C.Ss.R.; Harry Grile, C.Ss.R.; Lyle Konen, C.Ss.R.; Raymond Maiser, C.Ss.R.; Joseph Thong Ngo, C.Ss.R.; Patrick O'Brien, C.Ss.R.; William Peterson, C.Ss.R.; Bro. Paul Jorns, C.Ss.R.

Seattle Oratory 98144. Tel: 206-268-0043. Email: seattleoratory@aol.com. Revs. Robert Dell, C.O.; Clarence Edward Jones, C.O.

LACEY. *St. Martin's Abbey*, 5300 Pacific Ave, S.E., 98503-7500. Tel: 360-491-4700; 360-438-4440 (Abbot); Fax: 360-438-4441. Email: thabbot@stmartin.edu. Web: www.stmartin.edu. Rt. Revs. Neal G. Roth, O.S.B., Abbot; Conrad R. Rausch, O.S.B., Resigned Abbot; Very Rev. Alfred J. Hulscher, O.S.B., Prior, Treas. & Dir. Fiscal Affairs; Revs. Bede Classick, O.S.B., Vocation Team; Thaddaeus R. Arledge, O.S.B.; Benedict L. Auer, O.S.B., Postulant Dir.; Socius; Vocation Team; Edward R. Receconi, O.S.B., Novice Master, Junior Master; Urban C. Feucht; Gerard D. Kirsch, O.S.B.; Timothy J. Lamm, O.S.B.; Killian Malvey, O.S.B.; Justin D. McCreedy, O.S.B.; Very Rev. Clement Pangratz, O.S.B., Subprior; Revs. George J. Seidel, O.S.B.; John Scott, O.S.B.; Terrence J. Wager, O.S.B.; Paul M. Weckert, O.S.B., Guest Master, Vocation Dir.; Bros. Mark Bonneville, O.S.B.; Luke Devine, O.S.B.; Edmund Ebbers, O.S.B.; Vincent P. Francis, O.S.B.; Ignatius C. Kelly, O.S.B.; Boniface Lazzari, O.S.B.; Ramon Newell, O.S.B.; Bede Nicol, O.S.B.; Peter Tynan, O.S.B.; Theodore Vavrek, O.S.B.; Lawrence Vogel, O.S.B.; Nicolaus G. Wilson, O.S.B.; Aelred Woodard, O.S.B. Order of St.

Benedict, University, and Novitiate. Priests 19; Brothers 13.

[M] CONVENTS AND RESIDENCES FOR SISTERS

SEATTLE. *St. Joseph's Residence*, 4800 37th Ave., S.W., 98126. Tel: 206-937-4600; Fax: 206-923-4001 (8:30am-8:30pm). Email: jacqueline.fernandes@providence.org. Sr. Jacqueline Fernandes, S.P., Supr. & Admin. Sisters of Providence 37; Dominican Sisters of Tacoma 11; Sisters (Daughters of Mary) 2; Sisters (Carmelites) 1; Dominican Sisters of Adrian 5.

Lovers of the Holy Cross of Go Vap - St. Bernadette Convent, 1022 S.W. 128th St., 98146. Tel: 206-275-2283. Sr. Theresa Rose Tran, Supr.

Sisters of Providence, Mother Joseph Province, 1801 Lind Ave. S.W., #9016, Renton, 98057. Tel: 425-525-3355; Fax: 425-525-3984. Web: www.sistersofprovidence.net. Sr. Margaret Botch, S.P., Prov. Supr.

Providence Archives, 4800 37th Ave. S.W., 98126-2793. Tel: 206-937-4600; Fax: 206-923-4001. Email: archives@providence.org. Web: www.providence.org/phs/archives. Loretta Greene, Archivist; Peter Schmid, Visual Resources Archivist.

Providence Pariseau Corporation, 1801 Lind Ave. S.W., #9016, Renton, 98057-9016. Tel: 425-525-3360. Sisters Anita Butler, S.P., Treas.; Margaret Botch, S.P., Pres.

Sisters of Providence Retirement Trust Fund, 1801 Lind Ave. S.W., #9016, Renton, 98057. Tel: 425-525-3360. Email: lynn.chappell@providence.org. Sr. Anita Butler, S.P., Chair & Contact Person.

Sisters of St. Joseph of Peace, 1104 21st Ave. E., 98112. Tel: 206-324-1529. Web: csjp.org. Sisters 3.

Sisters of St. Joseph of Peace, Our Lady Province, Charitable Trust, 1663 Killarney Way, P.O. Box 248, Bellevue, 98009-0248. Tel: 425-451-1770; Fax: 425-462-9760. Web: www.csjp.org. Sr. Margaret Byrne, C.S.J.P., Congregation Leader.

BELLEVUE. *St. Mary's Residence and Novitiate*, P.O. Box 1763, 98009. 1663 Killarney Way, 98004. Tel: 425-451-1833; Fax: 425-462-9760. Web: www.csjp-olp.org. Sr. Judy Johnson, C.S.J.P., Admin. Sisters of St. Joseph of Peace 30.

St. Mary's Western U.S.Office for Sisters of St. Joseph of Peace, 1663 Killarney Way, Box 248, 98009-0248. Tel: 425-451-1770; Fax: 425-462-9760. Email: lhanson@csjp-olp.org. Web: www.csjp-olp.org. Sr. Margaret Byrne, C.S.J.P., Congregational Leader. Sisters of St. Joseph of Peace.

EDMONDS. *Rosary Heights*, 23120 Woodway Park Rd., P.O. Box 280, 98020-0280. Tel: 206-542-5450; Fax: 206-542-5450. Web: www.adriandominicans.org. (Dominican Sisters Congregation of the Most Holy Rosary, Adrian MI).

LACEY. *St. Placid Priory*, 500 College St., N.E., 98516. Tel: 360-438-1771; Fax: 360-438-9236. Email: stplacid@stplacid.org. Web: www.stplacid.org. Sr. Maureen O'Larey, O.S.B., Prioress. Includes The Priory Spirituality Center and The Priory Store. Sisters of St. Benedict 16.

SHAW ISLAND. *Our Lady of the Rock Priory* (Cloistered), P.O. Box 425, 98286. Tel: 360-468-2321; Fax: 360-468-2319. Web: www.rockisland.com/~mhildegard, Sr. Therese Critchley, O.S.B., Supr. Benedictine Nuns. Professed Nuns 8.

SHORELINE. *St. Joseph's Carmelite Monastery*, 2215 N.E. 147th, 98155. Tel: 206-363-7150; Fax: 206-365-7335. Email: seattlecarm@comcast.net. Sr. Sean Hennessy, O.C.D., Prioress. Discalced Carmelites 9; In Formation 3.

TACOMA. *III Order of St. Dominic*, Tacoma Dominican Center, 935 Fawcett Ave. S., 98402. Tel: 253-272-9688; Fax: 253-272-8790. Email: dominicans@tacoma-op.org. Web: www.tacomaop.org. Sr. Sharon Casey, O.P., Pres. (Congregation of St. Thomas Aquinas), Sisters of Saint Dominic of Tacoma Charitable Trust - Tacoma Dominican Center.

Sister of St. Francis of Philadelphia, St. Ann Retirement Convent, 6602 S. Alaska St., 98408. Tel: 253-474-8319; 253-475-0791; Fax: 253-474-0734. Email: saintann@worldnet.att.net. *Serra House*, 6602 S. Alaska St., 98408. Tel: 253-474-8026. *Evergreen House*, 6602 S. Alaska St., 98408. Tel: 253-474-9803. *Olympus House*, 6602 S. Alaska St., 98408. Tel: 253-474-8573. *Marian House*, 6802 47th St. W., 98466. Tel: 253-564-1816. *St. Marguerite Convent*, 4019 S. Thompson, 98408. Tel: 253-472-9702.

[N] RETREAT HOUSES, CONFERENCE CENTERS AND CAMPS

SEATTLE. *Camp Don Bosco*, 710 9th Ave., 98104. Tel: 206-382-4562 Contact CYO:. Email: cyo@seattlearch.org. Web: www.seattlearch.org/cyo.

Camp Gallagher, c/o 710 9th Ave., 98104.

Camp Hamilton, 710 9th Ave., 98104. Tel: 206-382-4562. Email: cyo@seattlearch.org. Web: www.seattlearch.org/cyo.

FEDERAL WAY. *The Palisades Archdiocesan Retreat & Faith Formation Center*, 4700 S.W. Dash Point Rd., #100, 98023. Tel: 253-927-9621 (Tacoma); 206-748-7991 (Seattle); Fax: 206-382-3482. Email: palisades@seattlearch.org. Web: www.seattlearch.org/palisades. David Jones, Dir.

[O] CAMPUS MINISTRY

SEATTLE. *Seattle University Campus Ministry* 901 12th Ave., P.O. Box 222000, 98122-1090. Tel: 206-296-6075; Fax: 206-296-6097. Email: campusministry@seattleu.edu. Web: www.seattleu.edu/campusministry/.

University of Washington, Catholic Newman Center 4502 20th Ave., N.E., 98105. Tel: 206-527-5072. Rev. Jordan Bradshaw, O.P., Chap.

Western Washington University (Bellingham) 102 Highland Dr., Bellingham, 98225. Tel: 206-733-3400. Rev. Qui-Thac Nguyen, Chap. Catholic Campus Ministry.

Saint Martin's College (Lacey) 5300 Pacific Ave., S.E., Lacey, 98503. Tel: 360-438-4381. Susan Leyster, Dir. Campus Ministry.

TACOMA. *Pacific Lutheran University Catholic Club* 121st St. & Park Ave. S., 98447. Email: catholic@plu.edu.

University of Puget Sound Catholic Campus Ministry 1500 N. Warner St., #1082, 98416. Tel: 253-879-3374.

[P] MISCELLANEOUS

SEATTLE. *Cursillo Movement*, P.O. Box 68803, 98168-0803. Tel: 206-537-4877. Jose Blakely, Dir.

The Food Bank at St. Mary's, 611 20th Ave. S., 98144. Tel: 206-324-7100, Ext. 21; Fax: 206-329-4596. Email: stmaryfb@yahoo.com.

St. Francis House, 169 12th Ave., 98122. Tel: 206-621-0945; Fax: 206-621-0945. Rose Flaherty, Dir.; Kathleen McKay, Dir. Third Order of St. Francis, Sponsor.

Fulcrum Foundation, 710 9th Ave., 98104. Tel: 206-748-7988; Fax: 206-219-5810. Email: joew@fulcrumfoundation.org. Web: www.fulcrumfoundation.org. Very Rev. Michael G. Ryan, Chm.

Intercommunity Housing Ferndale, 2505 3rd Ave., Ste. 204, 98121. Tel: 206-838-5700; Fax: 206-838-5705. Email: intercommunity@mercyhousing.org. Web: www.mercyhousing.org.

Intercommunity Mercy Housing, 2505 3rd Ave., Ste. 204, 98121. Tel: 206-838-5700; Fax: 206-838-5705. Email: intercommunity@mercyhousing.org. Web: www.mercyhousing.org. Cynthia Parker, Regl. Pres.

**Intercommunity Peace & Justice Center*, 1216 N.E. 65th St., 98115. Tel: 206-223-1138; Fax: 206-223-1139. Email: ipjc@ipjc.org. Web: www.ipjc.org. Sr. Linda Haydock, S.N.J.M., Exec. Dir.

South Seattle Catholic Schools, 4212 S. Mead, 98118. Tel: 206-722-7888; Fax: 206-722-7895.

Sterling Senior Housing, 2505 Third Ave., Ste. 204, 98121. Tel: 206-838-5700. Paul Chiocco, Contact Person.

Washington State Catholic Conference, 710 9th Ave., 98104. Tel: 206-301-0556; Fax: 206-301-0558. Email: wscc@thewscc.org. Sr. Sharon Park, O.P., Exec. Dir.

EDMONDS. *Edmonds Dominicans, Holy Angels Alumnae Assoc.*, 942 N.W. 60th, 98107. Tel: 206-782-1181; 206-546-6561; Fax: 206-789-2498.

TACOMA. *Pierce County Deanery*, 1001 N. J St., 98403. Tel: 253-383-3496; Fax: 253-756-0290. Email: pcdeanery@juno.com. Mary DeForrest, Admin.

RELIGIOUS INSTITUTES OF MEN REPRESENTED IN THE ARCHDIOCESE

For further details refer to the corresponding bracketed number in the Religious Institutes of Men or Women section.

[0200]—*Benedictine Monks* (Olympia, WA)—O.S.B.
[0310]—*Congregation of Christian Brothers* (Western U.S.)—C.F.C.
[0260]—*Discalced Carmelites Friars* (California Prov.)—O.C.D.
[0690]—*Jesuit Fathers and Brothers* (Oregon Province)—S.J.
[0800]—*Maryknoll*—M.M.
[]—*Oratorian Community*
[0430]—*Order of Preachers (Dominicans)* (San Francisco, CA)—O.P.
[1070]—*Redemptorist Fathers* (Denver Province)—C.SS.R.
[1250]—*Society of Christ* (American-Canadian Prov.)—S.Ch.
[1290]—*Society of the Priests of Saint Sulpice*—S.S.

RELIGIOUS INSTITUTES OF WOMEN REPRESENTED IN THE ARCHDIOCESE

[]—*Adrian Dominican Sisters*—O.P.
[0180]—*Benedictine Nuns of the Primitive Observance*—O.S.B.
[0230]—*Benedictine Sisters of Pontifical Jurisdiction* (Lacey, WA; Duluth, MN)—O.S.B.
[]—*Carmelite Sisters of Our Lady - Carm.*—O.L.
[2100]—*Congregation of the Humility of Mary*—C.H.M.
[1920]—*Congregation of the Sisters of the Holy Cross*—C.S.C.
[1780]—*Congregation of the Sisters of the Third Order of St. Francis*
[0420]—*Discalced Carmelite Nuns*—O.C.D.
[1070-04]—*Dominican Sisters* (Tacoma)—O.P.
[1070-19]—*Dominican Sisters* (Sinsinawa)—O.P.
[1115]—*Dominican Sisters of Peace*—O.P.
[]—*Franciscan Sisters of Perpetual Adoration*
[]—*Missionary Sisters of the Rosary of Fatima*—M.R.F.
[2860]—*Missionary Sisters of the Sacred Heart*—M.S.C.
[4070]—*Religious of the Sacred Heart*—R.S.C.J.
[]—*Religious Sisters of Mercy*—R.S.M.
[2970]—*School Sisters of Notre Dame*—S.S.N.D.
[]—*Sisters for Christian Community*—S.F.C.C.
[0430]—*Sisters of Charity of the Blessed Virgin Mary*—B.V.M.
[3000]—*Sisters of Notre Dame De Namur*—S.N.D.deN.
[]—*Sisters of Our Lady of Perpetual Help*—S.O.L.P.H.
[]—*Sisters of Our Lady of the Most Holy Trinity*—S.O.L.T.
[3350]—*Sisters of Providence*—S.P.
[]—*Sisters of St. Francis of Penance and Christian Charity*—O.S.F.
[1650]—*The Sisters of St. Francis of Philadelphia*—O.S.F.
[3840]—*Sisters of St. Joseph of Carondelet* (California Prov.)—C.S.J.
[3890]—*Sisters of St. Joseph of Peace*—C.S.J.P.
[1990]—*Sisters of the Holy Names of Jesus and Mary*—S.N.J.M.
[]—*Sisters of the Holy Names of Jesus and Mary* (Oregon Prov.)—S.N.J.M.
[]—*Sisters of the Holy Names of Jesus and Mary* (California Prov.)—S.N.J.M.
[]—*Sisters of the Lovers of the Holy Cross of Go Vap*—L.H.C.

ARCHDIOCESAN CEMETERIES

Associated Catholic Cemeteries: Central Office 910 Marion, 98104. Tel: 206-382-9281

SEATTLE

Calvary Cemetery, 5041 35th Ave., N.E., 98105. Tel: 206-522-0996; Fax: 206-525-9628.

FEDERAL WAY

Gethsemane Cemetery, 37600 Pacific Hwy. S., 98003. Tel: 206-838-2240.

KENT

St. Patrick Cemetery, 20400 Orillia Rd., 98032. Tel: 253-838-2240. c/o 37600 Pacific Hwy., S., Federal Way, 98003.

SHORELINE

Holyrood Cemetery, 205 N.E. 205th St., 98155. Tel: 206-363-8404.

NECROLOGY

† Beattie, Thomas W., (Retired)—Died June 23, 2009
† Doogan, Joseph H., Adjunct Judicial Vicar—Died May 12, 2009
† Rice, John A., (Retired)—Died Nov. 24, 2009

An asterisk (*) denotes an organization that has established tax-exempt status directly with the IRS and is not covered by the USCCB Group Ruling.

Diocese of Shreveport

(Dioecesis Sreveportuensis in Louisiana)

Most Reverend

MICHAEL G. DUCA, J.C.L.

Bishop of Shreveport; ordained April 29, 1978; appointed Bishop of Shreveport April 1, 2008; ordained May 19, 2008. *Chancery Office: 3500 Fairfield Ave., Shreveport, LA 71104.*

Most Reverend

WILLIAM B. FRIEND, D.D.

Retired Bishop of Shreveport; ordained May 7, 1959; appointed Titular Bishop of Pomaria and Auxiliary Bishop of Alexandria-Shreveport August 31, 1979; ordained Bishop October 30, 1979; appointed Bishop of Alexandria-Shreveport November 23, 1982; installed January 11, 1983; appointed Bishop of Shreveport June 16, 1986; retired December 20, 2006. *3575 Broken Woods Dr. #301, Coral Springs, FL 33065.* Tel: 954-344-6194.

Chancery Office: 3500 Fairfield Ave., Shreveport, LA 71104. Tel: 318-868-4441; Fax: 318-868-4469.

Web: www.dioshpt.org

ESTABLISHED AND CREATED A DIOCESE JUNE 16, 1986.

Comprises the Counties (parishes) of Bienville, Bossier, Caddo, Claiborne, DeSoto, East Carroll, Jackson, Lincoln, Morehouse, Ouachita, Red River, Richland, Sabine, Union, Webster and West Carroll.

For legal titles of parishes and diocesan institutions, consult the Chancery Office.

STATISTICAL OVERVIEW

Personnel	
Bishop	1
Retired Bishops	1
Priests: Diocesan Active in Diocese	25
Priests: Diocesan Active Outside Diocese	1
Priests: Retired, Sick or Absent	10
Number of Diocesan Priests	36
Religious Priests in Diocese	13
Total Priests in Diocese	49
Extern Priests in Diocese	2
Ordinations:	
Diocesan Priests	1
Permanent Deacons in Diocese	21
Total Brothers	5
Total Sisters	43
Parishes	
Parishes	27
With Resident Pastor:	
Resident Diocesan Priests	16
Resident Religious Priests	9
Without Resident Pastor:	
Administered by Priests	1
Administered by Deacons	1
Missions	14
Pastoral Centers	1
Professional Ministry Personnel:	
Sisters	4
Lay Ministers	23
Welfare	
Catholic Hospitals	2
Total Assisted	1,113
Health Care Centers	3
Total Assisted	429,108
Homes for the Aged	1
Total Assisted	190
Day Care Centers	3
Total Assisted	208
Special Centers for Social Services	23
Total Assisted	38,356
Other Institutions	2
Total Assisted	959
Educational	
Diocesan Students in Other Seminaries	4
Total Seminarians	4
High Schools, Diocesan and Parish	2
Total Students	656
Elementary Schools, Diocesan and Parish	5
Total Students	1,292
Catechesis/Religious Education:	
High School Students	466
Elementary Students	1,891
Total Students under Catholic Instruction	4,309
Teachers in the Diocese:	
Sisters	2
Lay Teachers	157
Vital Statistics	
Receptions into the Church:	
Infant Baptism Totals	410
Minor Baptism Totals	67
Adult Baptism Totals	60
Received into Full Communion	140
First Communions	534
Confirmations	472
Marriages:	
Catholic	71
Interfaith	56
Total Marriages	127
Deaths	329
Total Catholic Population	40,290
Total Population	793,222

Former Bishop—Most Rev. WILLIAM B. FRIEND, ord. May 7, 1959; appt. Titular Bishop of Pomaria and Auxiliary Bishop of Alexandria-Shreveport Aug. 31, 1979; ord. Bishop Oct. 30, 1979; appt. Bishop of Alexandria-Shreveport Nov. 23, 1982; installed Jan. 11, 1983; appt. Bishop of Shreveport June 16, 1986; retired Dec. 20, 2006.

Vicar General and Moderator of the Curia—Very Rev. DAVID T. RICHTER, J.C.L., V.G.

Vicars Forane—Very Rev. Msgr. EARL V. PROVENZA, V.F., Western Deanery; Very Revs. JOSEPH PUTHUPPALLY, V.F., Eastern Deanery; TIMOTHY C. HURD, V.F., Southern Deanery.

Chancery Office—Catholic Center, 3500 Fairfield Ave., Shreveport, 71104. Tel: 318-868-4441; Fax: 318-868-4469.

Chancellor—Mrs. CHRISTINE RIVERS.

Diocesan Tribunal—3500 Fairfield Ave., Shreveport, 71104. Tel: 318-868-4441; Fax: 318-219-7286.

Judicial Vicar—Very Rev. PETER B. MANGUM, J.C.L., J.V.

Adjutant Judicial Vicar—Rev. ROTHELL PRICE, J.C.L. Email: frprice@bellsouth.net.

Director of the Tribunal—Sr. MARILYN R. VASSALLO, C.S.J., J.C.L. Email: mvassallo@dioshpt.org.

Moderator of the Tribunal—RICOLE WILLIAMS. Email: rwilliam@dioshpt.org.

Secretary—ANN GOELDEN. Email: agoelden@dioshpt.org.

Judges—Very Rev. PETER B. MANGUM, J.C.L., J.V.; Rev. Msgr. FRANZ GRAEF, S.T.D. (Retired); Very Rev. DAVID T. RICHTER, J.C.L., V.G.; Rev. ROTHELL PRICE, J.C.L.; Sr. MARILYN R. VASSALLO, C.S.J., J.C.L.

Defenders of the Bond—Rev. PHILIP F. MICHIELS; Sr. MARY ANN HAYES, C.S.J., J.C.L., M.C.L.

Promoter of Justice—Sr. MARY ANN HAYES, C.S.J., J.C.L., M.C.L.

Advocates—Revs. KARL J. DAIGLE; RICHARD J. LOMBARD; Very Rev. TIMOTHY C. HURD, V.F.; Rev. MARK A. WATSON; Deacons TIMOTHY COTITA; CLARY NASH; WILLIAM ROCHE; MICHAEL STRAUB; MICHAEL SULLIVAN.

Notaries—RICOLE WILLIAMS. Email: rwilliam@dioshpt.org; ANN GOELDEN. Email: agoelden@dioshpt.org.

Corporate Council—Most Rev. MICHAEL GERARD DUCA, J.C.L., Bishop; Very Rev. DAVID T. RICHTER, J.C.L., V.G.; Mrs. CHRISTINE RIVERS.

College of Consultors—Very Rev. Msgr. EARL V. PROVENZA, V.F.; Very Revs. DAVID T. RICHTER, J.C.L., V.G.; TIMOTHY C. HURD, V.F.; PETER B. MANGUM, J.C.L., J.V.; JOSEPH PUTHUPPALLY, V.F.; Revs. PHILIP F. MICHIELS; LAVERNE (PIKE) THOMAS; MARK A. WATSON.

Presbyteral Council—Very Rev. PETER B. MANGUM, J.C.L., J.V.; Revs. PHILIP F. MICHIELS; LAVERNE (PIKE) THOMAS; MARK A. WATSON.

Ex Officio Members—Very Rev. TIMOTHY C. HURD, V.F.; Very Rev. Msgr. EARL V. PROVENZA, V.F.; Very Revs. JOSEPH PUTHUPPALLY, V.F.; DAVID T. RICHTER, J.C.L., V.G.

Deans—Very Rev. Msgr. EARL V. PROVENZA, V.F., Diocesan Admin.; Very Revs. JOSEPH PUTHUPPALLY, V.F., Ex Officio; TIMOTHY C. HURD, V.F.

Finance Council—Most Rev. MICHAEL GERARD DUCA, J.C.L., Bishop; Very Rev. DAVID T. RICHTER, J.C.L., V.G., Ex Officio; M. VAUGHN ANTLEY; Mrs. CHRISTINE RIVERS, Ex Officio; Rev. RICHARD J. LOMBARD; REGINALD W. ABRAMS; NONA DAILEY; LAWRENCE W. PETTIETTE JR.; MARGARET GREEN; GLENN KINSEY; Dr. JAMES ROBERT MICHAEL; PHYLLIS MURDOCK; Mr. NICHOLAS ROPPOLO.

Priests' Retirement Board—Revs. JOSEPH ROBERT INZINA (Retired); EDMUND A. (LARRY) NIEHOFF; Mr. NICHOLAS ROPPOLO; Mr. PAUL SKLAR; Very Rev. Msgr. EARL V. PROVENZA, V.F., Chm.; Revs. JAMES R. MCLELLAND; JOSEPH A. MARTINA JR.

The Catholic Foundation of North-Central Louisiana, Inc.— Contact the Catholic Center for information. Tel: 318-868-4441; Fax: 318-868-4469.

Diocesan Offices and Directors

Black Catholic Commission—Rev. ROTHELL PRICE, J.C.L., Chap., St. Mary of the Pines Church, 1050 Bert Kouns Industrial Loop, Shreveport, 71118. Tel: 318-687-5121.

Business Affairs—Mrs. JILL BRANIFF, CPA, Catholic Center, 3500 Fairfield Ave., Shreveport, 71104.

Tel: 318-868-4441; Fax: 318-868-4609.

Campaign for Human Development—Very Rev. DAVID T. RICHTER, J.C.L., V.G., Address Communications to: Catholic Center, 3500 Fairfield Ave., Shreveport, 71104. Tel: 318-868-4441; Fax: 318-868-4469.

Campus Ministry—VACANT, Dir., Catholic Center, 3500 Fairfield Ave., Shreveport, 71104. Tel: 318-868-4441; Fax: 318-868-4605.

Catechetics—VACANT, Catholic Center, 3500 Fairfield Ave., Shreveport, 71104. Tel: 318-868-4441; Fax: 318-868-4605.

Catholic Charities— Address Communications to the Chancery *Catholic Center, 3500 Fairfield Ave., Shreveport, 71104*. Tel: 318-868-4441; Fax: 318-868-4469.

Catholic Relief Services—Very Rev. DAVID T. RICHTER, J.C.L., V.G., Catholic Center, 3500 Fairfield Ave., Shreveport, 71104. Tel: 318-868-4441; Fax: 318-868-4469.

Cemeteries—Mrs. JILL BRANIFF, CPA, Catholic Center, 3500 Fairfield Ave., Shreveport, 71104. Tel: 318-868-4441; Fax: 318-868-4609.

Censor of Books—Rev. Msgr. FRANZ GRAEF, S.T.D. (Retired).

Church Vocations—Very Rev. DAVID T. RICHTER, J.C.L., V.G., Dir., 3500 Fairfield Ave., Shreveport, 71104. Tel: 318-868-4441; Fax: 318-868-4469.

Church Vocations Board & Vocations Office—Very Rev. DAVID T. RICHTER, J.C.L., V.G., Dir. Diocesan Vocations Office & Ex Officio; Revs. CHARLES GLORIOSO; KARL J. DAIGLE; Dr. J. MICHAEL COOK; Mr. E. B. POLSON; KAREN DILL, L.P.C.; Revs. ROTHELL PRICE, J.C.L.; MARK A. WATSON; Judge D. MILTON MOORE; Deacon CLARY NASH.

Clergy Continuing Formation Director—Rev. LAVERNE (PIKE) THOMAS.

Communications—Mr. JOHN MARK WILLCOX, Dir., 3500 Fairfield Ave., Shreveport, 71104. Tel: 318-868-4441; Fax: 318-868-4609.

Development Director—Mr. JOHN MARK WILLCOX, Catholic Center, 3500 Fairfield Ave., Shreveport, 71104. Tel: 318-868-4441; Fax: 318-868-4609.

Diocesan Publications—Mrs. JESSICA RINAUDO, Editor, Catholic Center, 3500 Fairfield Ave., Shreveport, 71104. Tel: 318-868-4441; Fax: 318-868-4609.

Ecumenism and Interreligious Affairs—Rev. Msgr. J. CARSON LACAZE, Cathedral of St. John Berchmans, 939 Jordan St., Shreveport, 71101. Tel: 318-221-5296.

Facility Manager, Catholic Center—Mr. JOHN TOWNLEY, Catholic Center, 3500 Fairfield Ave., Shreveport, 71104. Tel: 318-868-4441; Fax: 318-868-4605.

Fairview House (Residence for Clergy)—1000 Fairview, Shreveport, 71104. Tel: 318-868-4441; Fax: 318-868-4605.

Greco Institute—Rev. PATRICK J. MADDEN, Ph.D., Dir., Catholic Center, 3500 Fairfield Ave., Shreveport, 71104. Tel: 318-868-4441; Fax: 318-868-4456.

Hispanic Ministry and Immigration Services—Mrs. ROSALBA QUIROZ, Interim Dir., Catholic Center, 3500 Fairfield Ave., Shreveport, 71104. Tel: 318-868-4441; Fax: 318-868-4605; Rev. ALOYS JOST, O.F.M., Hispanic Ministry - Eastern Deanery, Res.: St. Thomas Aquinas Friary, 810 Carey Ave., Ruston, 71270.

Holy Childhood—Sr. CAROL SHIVELY, O.S.U., Contact Person, Catholic Center, 3500 Fairfield Ave., Shreveport, 71104. Tel: 318-868-4441; Fax: 318-868-4605.

Human Resources—Deacon MICHAEL STRAUB, Dir., Catholic Center, 3500 Fairfield Ave., Shreveport, 71104. Tel: 318-868-4441; Fax: 318-868-4609.

Information Systems Management—Ms. PATRICIA PILLORS, Dir., Catholic Center, 3500 Fairfield Ave., Shreveport, 71104. Tel: 318-868-4441; Fax: 318-868-4605.

Jail-Prison Ministry—Rev. RICHARD PUSCH, Chap., Forcht Wade Correctional Center, Mailing Address: P.O. Box 53043, Shreveport, 71135-3043.

Diocesan Liturgy Commission—MICHAEL KENNEY; JOHN GUERRIERO; CATHY COBB; Revs. PHILIP F. MICHIELS; LAVERNE (PIKE) THOMAS; CAROLE MOON; Very Revs. TIMOTHY C. HURD, V.F.; PETER B. MANGUM, J.C.L., J.V.; LARRY MEIER; Mrs. DIANNE RACHAL, Ex Officio.

Master of Ceremonies, Diocese of Shreveport—Rev. LAVERNE (PIKE) THOMAS.

Mission Director—Very Rev. DAVID T. RICHTER, J.C.L., V.G., Catholic Center, 3500 Fairfield Ave., Shreveport, 71104. Tel: 318-868-4441; Fax: 318-868-4469.

Mission Effectiveness—Mr. RANDY G. TILLER, Dir., Catholic Center, 3500 Fairfield Ave., Shreveport, 71104. Tel: 318-868-4441; Fax: 318-868-4469.

Permanent Deacon Formation Program—Deacon CLARY NASH, Dir., Catholic Center, 3500 Fairfield Ave., Shreveport, 71104. Tel: 318-868-4441; Fax: 318-868-4605.

Propagation of the Faith—Very Rev. DAVID T. RICHTER, J.C.L., V.G., Catholic Center, 3500 Fairfield Ave., Shreveport, 71104. Tel: 318-868-4441; Fax: 318-868-4469.

Religious Education—VACANT, Catholic Center, 3500 Fairfield Ave., Shreveport, 71104. Tel: 318-868-4441; Fax: 318-868-4605.

Resource Center (Library)—Mrs. DEBORAH SMITH, Library Technician, Catholic Center, 3500 Fairfield Ave., Shreveport, 71104. Tel: 318-868-4441; Fax: 318-868-4605.

Schools—Sisters CAROL SHIVELY, O.S.U., Supt.; ANN MIDDLEBROOKS, S.E.C., Assoc. Supt., Catholic Center, 3500 Fairfield Ave., Shreveport, 71104. Tel: 318-868-4441; Fax: 318-868-4605.

Child Nutrition Program—3500 Fairfield Ave., Shreveport, 71104. Tel: 318-868-4441; Fax: 318-868-5057.

Scouting—Rev. DARIUSZ PAWLOWSKI, Chap., Mailing Address: Chancery, 3500 Fairfield Ave., Shreveport, 71104.

St. Vincent de Paul Society—Ms. DOTYE STANFORD, Contact Person, Mailing Address: P.O. Box 3911, Shreveport, 71133-3911. Tel: 318-865-7807.

Victim Assistance Coordinator—Ms. GLENNDA LAWSON. Tel: 318-294-1031.

Worship—Mrs. DIANNE RACHAL, Dir., Catholic Center, 3500 Fairfield Ave., Shreveport, 71105. Tel: 318-868-4441; Fax: 318-868-4605.

Youth and Young Adult Ministry—VACANT, Dir., Catholic Center, 3500 Fairfield Ave., Shreveport, 71104. Tel: 318-868-4441; Fax: 318-868-4605.

CLERGY, PARISHES, MISSIONS AND PAROCHIAL SCHOOLS

CITY OF SHREVEPORT

(CADDO PARISH)

1—ST. JOHN BERCHMANS CATHEDRAL (1902) Very Rev. Peter B. Mangum, Rector; Rev. Msgr. J. Carson LaCaze, Parochial Vicar; Deacon John Basco.
Office: 939 Jordan St., 71101-4391. Tel: 318-221-5296; Fax: 318-221-8076.
School—(Grades PreK-8), 947 Jordan St., 71101. Tel: 318-221-6005; Fax: 318-425-0648. Mrs. Jo Cazes, Prin.; Judy Polhemus, Librarian. Lay Teachers 20; Students 235.
Catechesis/Religious Program—Students 115.
Mission—St. Catherine of Siena 331 E. 71st St., Caddo Parish 71106. Tel: 318-868-6506; Fax: 318-861-6177.

2—ST. ELIZABETH ANN SETON (1984) Rev. Philip F. Michiels; Deacon Homer Tucker.
Res.: 522 E. Flournoy-Lucas Rd., 71115-3802. Tel: 318-798-1887; Fax: 318-797-7302.
Catechesis/Religious Program—Students 205.

3—HOLY TRINITY (1856) Very Rev. Msgr. Earl V. Provenza; Deacons Jorge Martinez; Ronald Morris; Martha Martinez, Lay Ecclesial Min.
Res.: 315 Marshall St., P.O. Box 144, 71161-0144. Tel: 318-221-5990; Fax: 318-221-3545.
Catechesis/Religious Program—Students 10.

4—ST. JOSEPH (1949) Revs. Karl J. Daigle; Richard J. Lombard; Deacons Bruce Pistorius; William Roche.
Res.: 211 Atlantic Ave., 71105. Tel: 318-865-3581; Fax: 318-865-5125.
School—(Grades PreK-8), 1210 Anniston Ave., 71105. Tel: 318-865-3585; Fax: 318-868-1859. Mrs. Susan J. Belanger, Prin.; Ms. Nia Mitchell, Asst. Prin.; Joanne Creech, Librarian. Lay Teachers 28; Students 453.
Catechesis/Religious Program—Students 214.

5—ST. MARY OF THE PINES (1973) Revs. Rothell Price; Dariusz Pawlowski; Deacons Clary Nash, Community Coord., Sacred Heart; Thomas Latiolais.
Res.: 1050 Bert Kouns Industrial Loop, 71118-3499. Tel: 318-687-5121 Church Office; 318-687-1818 Rectory; Fax: 318-687-5124.
Catechesis/Religious Program—Students 196.
Mission—Sacred Heart of Jesus Mailing Address: P.O. Box 19467, 71149-0467.
Church: 4736 Lyba St., 71109. Tel: 318-635-2121; Fax: 318-635-5226.

6—OUR LADY OF THE BLESSED SACRAMENT (1923), (African American), Rev. Andre McGrath, O.F.M.; Deacon Harold Dean.
Res.: 1558 Buena Vista St., 71101-2448. Tel: 318-222-3790; Fax: 318-222-3793.
School—(Grades PreK-4), 2932 Murphy St., 71103-2241. Tel: 318-222-5051; Fax: 318-222-5840. Sr. John Mary Jackson, S.S.F., Prin. Sisters of the Holy Family 2; Lay Teachers 6; Students 121.
Catechesis/Religious Program—Students 5.

7—OUR LADY OF THE HOLY ROSARY (1952) Closed. For inquiries for parish records contact the chancery.

8—ST. PIUS X (1955) Rev. Joseph Kallookalam, C.M.I. (India); Deacons Mark Campbell; Jeff Chapman; Susan R. Lanier, Pastoral Assoc.
Res.: 4300 N. Market St., 71107-2953. Tel: 318-222-2165.
Child Development Center—Tel: 318-425-2192; Fax: 318-675-0132. Students 76.
Catechesis/Religious Program—Students 90.

9—ST. THERESA, Consolidated with St. John Berchmans Cathedral.

OUTSIDE THE CITY OF SHREVEPORT

BASTROP, MOREHOUSE PARISH

1—ST. JOSEPH (1943) [CEM] Rev. Richard Norsworthy.
Res.: 217 Harrington Ave., 71220. Tel: 318-281-4327; Fax: 866-473-1177. Email: stjoseph@sjccb.com.
Catechesis/Religious Program—Students 21.

2—OUR LADY HELP OF CHRISTIANS, Consolidated with St. Joseph, Bastrop.

BOSSIER CITY, BOSSIER PARISH

1—CHRIST THE KING (1939) Revs. Charles Glorioso; Rigoberto Betancurt; Deacon Burton Ainsworth.
Res.: 425 McCormick St., 71111-4692. Tel: 318-221-0238; Fax: 318-425-0011.
Catechesis/Religious Program—Students 70.

2—ST. JUDE (1964) Rev. LaVerne (Pike) Thomas; Deacons Larry Craig Mills; W. Freeman Ligon. In Res., Rev. Joseph Howard Jr.
Res. & Mailing Address: 3800 Viking Dr., 71111-7403. Tel: 318-746-2508; Fax: 318-742-4526.
Catechesis/Religious Program—Students 240.
Mission—Mary, Queen of Heaven 1659 Palmetto Rd., Benton, Bossier Parish 71006. Tel: 318-742-2508.

3—MARY, QUEEN OF PEACE (1999) Rev. Joseph Ampatt Chacko; Deacon Michael Straub.
Res.: 2101 Hope St, 71112. Tel: 318-752-5971; Fax: 318-752-5973.
Church & Mailing Address: 7738 Barksdale Blvd, 71112.
Catechesis/Religious Program—Students 103.
Mission—St. George 3076 Hwy. 155, Coushatta, Red River Parish 71019-0937. Tel: 318-752-5971; Fax: 318-752-5973.

GRAMBLING, LINCOLN PARISH, ST. BENEDICT THE BLACK (1966), (African American), Rev. Peter Pulivelil, C.M.I. (India).
Res.: 471 Main St., 71245-3088. Tel: 318-247-6734; Fax: 318-247-6288.
Catechesis/Religious Program—Students 6.

HODGE, JACKSON PARISH, ST. LUCY (1935) [CEM] Deacon Terry Walsworth, Pastoral Admin.; Rev. Msgr. Franz Graef (Retired); Alece Walsworth, Lay Ecclesial Min.
Res.: 1104 S. 2nd St., P.O. Box 100, 71247-0100. Tel: 318-259-2326; Fax: 318-259-2326 (Call first.).
Catechesis/Religious Program—(Grades PreK-2) Students 19.

LAKE PROVIDENCE, EAST CARROLL PARISH, ST. PATRICK (1870) [CEM] Rev. Zacharias Prakuzhy, C.M.I. (India).
Res.: 207 Scarborough St., P.O. Box 351, 71254-0351. Tel: 318-559-1276; Fax: 318-559-7733.
Catechesis/Religious Program—Students 13.

MANSFIELD, DESOTO PARISH, ST. JOSEPH (1907) [CEM 4] Rev. Edmund A. (Larry) Niehoff.
Res.: 305 Jefferson St., P.O. Box 760, 71052-0760. Tel: 318-872-1158.
Catechesis/Religious Program—Tel: 318-872-0905; Fax: 318-872-1161. Students 88.
Mission—St. Ann's Chapel 2260 Hwy. 171, Stonewall, DeSoto Parish 71078. Tel: 318-925-0591.

MANY, SABINE PARISH, ST. JOHN THE BAPTIST (1871) [CEM] Rev. Joseph A. Martina Jr.; Deacon Michael Sullivan.
Res.: 1130 E. San Antonio Ave., 71449-3226. Tel: 318-256-5680; 318-256-5689; Fax: 318-256-9177.
Catechesis/Religious Program—Students 68.
Mission—St. Terence 1130 E. San Antonio Ave., Hwys. 191 & 476, Sabine Parish 71449. Tel: 318-586-7444.

MINDEN, WEBSTER PARISH, ST. PAUL (1942) Rev. Mark Franklin.
Mailing Address: P.O. Box 799, 71058-0799. Tel: 318-377-5364; Fax: 318-377-5394.
Catechesis/Religious Program—Tel: 318-377-5364. Students 41.
Mission—Blessed Sacrament 2688 Military Rd., Ringgold, Bienville Parish 71068. Tel: 318-894-5785.
Mission—St. Margaret 600 E. 2nd St., Homer, Claiborne Parish 71040. Tel: 318-927-2865.
Mission—Sacred Heart 304 Gaisser St., Springhill, Webster Parish 71075. Tel: 318-539-4919.

MONROE, OUACHITA PARISH

1—JESUS THE GOOD SHEPHERD (1958) Revs. Mark A. Watson; Matthew Tyler Long; Deacon Timothy Cotita. In Res., Rev. Msgr. Edmund J. Moore (Retired).
Office: 2510 Emerson St., 71201-2699. Tel: 318-325-7549; Fax: 318-322-6969.

Priest's Residence—800 Marquette St., 71201. Tel: 318-325-6956.
School—(Grades PreK-6), 900 Good Shepherd Ln., 71201. Tel: 318-325-8569; Fax: 318-325-9730. Lisa Patrick, Prin.; Mary Jo Norris, Librarian. Lay Teachers 28; Students 305.
Catechesis/Religious Program—Students 64.

2—ST. JOSEPH (1956) Closed. For inquiries for parish records contact the chancery.

3—LITTLE FLOWER OF JESUS (1940), (African American), Rev. Adrian Fischer, O.F.M.; Bro. Roch Pfeifer, O.F.M.; Deacon Verdine Williams.
Res.: 616 S. 16th St., 71201. Tel: 318-324-9706.
Church Office: 600 S. 16th St., 71201. Tel: 318-322-1224; Fax: 318-322-1261.
School—(Grades PreSchool), 610 S. 16th St., 71201. Tel: 318-322-7379. Mrs. Emma Williams, Dir. Preschool. Lay Teachers 11; Students 76.
Catechesis/Religious Program—Students 28.

4—ST. MATTHEW (1851) [CEM] Very Rev. Joseph Puthuppally.
Res.: 121 Jackson St., 71201. Tel: 318-323-8878; 318-323-8879; Fax: 318-323-2537.
Catechesis/Religious Program—Students 63.

5—OUR LADY OF FATIMA (1952) [JC] Revs. Sebastian Kallarackal, C.M.I. (India); Job Edathinatt Scaria, C.M.I. (India).
Church: 3205 Concordia, P.O. Box 4136, 71201-4136. Tel: 318-325-7595; Fax: 318-325-8544.
Rectory—207 Sheridan, 71201.
School—(Grades PreK-3), 3202 Franklin St., 71201. Tel: 318-387-1851; Fax: 318-387-7593. Mrs. Donna Eichhorn, Prin. Lay Teachers 15; Students 178.
Catechesis/Religious Program—Tel: 318-325-7596. Students 36.
Mission—St. Lawrence 357 Swartz School Rd., Swartz, Ouachita Parish 71281. Tel: 318-343-1618.

OAK GROVE, WEST CARROLL PARISH, SACRED HEART (1947) Rev. Zacharias Prakuzhy, C.M.I. (India).
Church: 201 Purvis St., P.O. Box 419, 71263-0419. Tel: 318-428-2683.
Catechesis/Religious Program—Students 16.

RAMBIN, DESOTO PARISH, ST. MARY, Consolidated with St. Joseph, Mansfield.

RAYVILLE, RICHLAND PARISH, SACRED HEART (1920) Rev. Philip Pazhayakari, C.M.I.
Res. & Mailing Address: 716 Francis St., 71269. Tel: 318-728-2445; Fax: 318-728-2806.
Catechesis/Religious Program—Tel: 318-728-2445. Students 15.
Mission—St. Theresa 420 Main St., Delhi, Richland Parish 71232. Tel: 318-728-2445.

RUSTON, LINCOLN PARISH, ST. THOMAS AQUINAS (1941) Revs. Frank Folino, O.F.M.; Blane O'Neill, O.F.M.; Deacons John J. Serio; Oscar Hannibal.
Res.: 810 Carey Ave., 71270-4915. Tel: 318-255-2870; Fax: 318-254-8319.
Catechesis/Religious Program—Tel: 318-251-2142. Students 196.

VIVIAN, CADDO PARISH, ST. CLEMENT (1945) Rev. James R. McLelland.
Office: 819 N. Pine, 71082-3354. Tel: 318-375-2789; Fax: 318-375-3571.
Catechesis/Religious Program—Students 18.

WEST MONROE, OUACHITA PARISH, ST. PASCHAL (1940) [CEM] Rev. Frank Coens, O.F.M.
Res.: 711 N. Seventh St., 71291-4211. Tel: 318-323-1631; Fax: 318-361-0527.
Catechesis/Religious Program—Students 125.
Mission—Our Lady of Perpetual Help 600 Water St., Farmerville, Union Parish 71241. Tel: 318-368-9239.

ZWOLLE, SABINE PARISH, ST. JOSEPH (1881) [CEM 3] Very Rev. Timothy C. Hurd.
Res.: 307 Hammond St., P.O. Box 8, 71486-0008. Tel: 318-645-6155; 318-645-9198 (Rectory); Fax: 318-645-9852.
Catechesis/Religious Program—Students 354.
Mission—St. Ann [CEM] 5272 Hwy. 482, Noble, Sabine Parish 71462.

Chaplains of Public Institutions

SHREVEPORT. *Forcht Wade Correctional Center*. Rev. Richard Pusch, Chap.
Res.: P.O. Box 53043, 71135-3043.
Overton Brooks Veteran's Administration Medical Center, 510 E. Stoner Ave., 71101. Rev. Philip F. Michiels, Chap. Emergencies, St. Elizabeth Ann Seton Church, 522 E. Flournoy Lucas Rd., 71115. Tel: 318-798-1887.

Retired:
Rev. Msgrs.—
Clayton, Murray
Graef, Franz, S.T.D.
Moore, Edmund J.
Revs.—
Carey, William H., Ph.D.
Ebarb, Walter E.
Inzina, Joseph Robert
Kennedy, John D.
McMullen, Roger
Scully, Patrick A.
Williams, Kenneth

Permanent Deacons:
Ainsworth, Burton
Basco, John
Campbell, Mark
Chapman, Jeff
Cotita, Timothy
Dean, Harold
Hannibal, Oscar
Latiolais, Thomas
Ligon, Freeman
Martinez, Jorge
Mills, Larry Craig
Morris, Ronald J.
Nash, Clary
Pistorius, Bruce
Roche, William
Serio, John J.
Straub, Michael
Sullivan, Michael
Tucker, Homer
Walsworth, Terry
Williams, Verdine

INSTITUTIONS LOCATED IN THE DIOCESE

[A] HIGH SCHOOLS, DIOCESAN

SHREVEPORT. *Loyola College Prep*, 921 Jordan St., 71101-4390. Tel: 318-221-2675; Fax: 318-226-6334. Email: flyers@loyolaprep.org. Web: www.loyolaprep.org. Mr. Frank Israel, Prin.; Very Rev. Peter B. Mangum, J.C.L., J.V., Chap.; Mrs. Erin Berry, Librarian. Lay Teachers 36; Students 429.

MONROE. *St. Frederick High School*, (Grades 7-12), 3300 Westminster, 71201-3299. Tel: 318-323-9636; Fax: 318-323-7456. Email: warriors@stfrederickhigh.org. Web: www.stfrederickhigh.org. Jennifer Malone, Prin.; Elizabeth Craft, Librarian. Lay Teachers 24; Students 227.

[B] GENERAL HOSPITALS

SHREVEPORT. *Christus Health Northern Louisiana dba Christus Schumpert Health System* (1907) One St. Mary Pl., P.O. Box 21976, 71120-1976. Tel: 318-681-4500; Fax: 318-681-4177 (Admin.). Web: christusschumpert.org. Bonnie J. Burnett, M.Div., Vice Pres., Mission; Revs. Thomas John Vadakemuriyil, C.M.I. (India), Chap.; James R. McLelland, Chap.; Stephen F. Wright, Pres. & CEO; Sr. Jaya Xavier, S.D., Chap.; Mary Preziosi, Chap. Operated by Christus Health. Sisters 7; Bed Capacity 668; Patients Assisted Annually 220,309; Total Staff 1,763.
Christus Schumpert Bossier, 2105 Airline Dr., Bossier City, 71111. Tel: 318-848-8000; Fax: 318-848-8440. Stephen F. Wright, Pres. & CEO. (Sub. of Christus Schumpert Health System).
Christus Schumpert Highland, 1453 E. Bert Kouns Industrial Loop, 71105. Tel: 318-681-5000; Fax: 318-681-5475. Jason Rounds, Admin.; Rev. Thomas John Vadakemuriyil, C.M.I. (India), Chap.; Sr. Jaya Xavier, S.D., Chap. (Sub. of Christus Schumpert Health System).

COUSHATTA. *CHRISTUS Coushatta Health Care Center*, 1635 Marvel St., 71019. Tel: 318-932-2000; Fax: 318-932-2198. Karen Mixon, Admin. CHRISTUS Health Central Louisiana. Bed Capacity 25; Total Staff 157.

MONROE. *St. Francis Medical Center*, P.O. Box 1901, 71210-1901. Tel: 318-327-4000; Fax: 318-327-4142. Web: www.stfran.com. Louis H. Bremer Jr., FACHE, Pres. & CEO; Ronald E. Hogan, Senior Vice Pres. & CFO; Yvonne Boudreau, Vice Pres. Pastoral Care & Missions; Revs. Philip Chacko Theempalangattu (India), Chap.; James Dominic Thekkemury (India), Chap. Franciscan Missionaries of Our Lady 2; Bed Capacity 551; Patients Assisted Annually 208,774; Total Staff 2,148; Hospice & Ancillary Care 458,549.
Non-Catholic Chaplains: Rev. Everitt Slack; Rev. P.J. Wright; Rev. Fred Rushing.
**St. Francis Specialty Hospital* (1995) 309 Jackson St., P.O. Box 1532, 71210. Tel: 318-327-4600; Fax: 318-327-4082. Email: hightob@stfran.com. Web: www.specialtyhospital.com. Mr. Bill Hightower, Pres. & CEO. Licensed Beds 32; Physicians 195; Employees 140; Patient Admissions 368.
**St. Patrick Psychiatric Hospital, Inc.*, 3421 Medical Park Dr., 71203. Tel: 318-327-4686; Fax: 318-327-4951. Email: rogersc@stfran.com. Web: www.stpatrickshospital.net. Cindy J. Rogers, CEO, FACHE. Franciscan Missionaries of Our Lady Health System. Bed Capacity 24; Inpatients Assisted Annually 600; Outpatients 145; Total Staff 55.

[C] HOMES FOR AGED

MONROE. *CHRISTUS St. Joseph Home*, 2301 Sterlington Rd., P.O. Box 6057, 71211-6057. Tel: 318-323-3426; Fax: 318-387-7157. Larry N. Tucker, CEO. Operated by CHRISTUS Health Monroe. Licensed Capacity Nursing Care 130; Assisted Living Apartments 60; Sisters 2; Total Staff 150.

[D] SPECIAL CENTERS FOR SOCIAL SERVICES & ASSISTANCE

SHREVEPORT. *St. Catherine Community Center*, 331 E. 71st St., 71106-4305. Tel: 318-865-9817; Fax: 318-869-2549. Email: sccc@sport.rr.com. Web: www.rc.net/shreveport/stcatherine. Anthony Williams, Coord. Afterschool Enrichment, Summer Day Camp, Parenting, Arts, Anger Management, Computers, Health Services Program, Teen Mom Mentoring. Total Assisted 500; Total Staff 20.

LAKE PROVIDENCE. **LCWR Region V Lake Providence Collaborative Ministries*, 106 Ingram St., 71254. Tel: 318-559-3747. Learning programs for youth, employment skills development, adult literacy, and senior citizen programs. Staff 3.

[E] CONVENTS AND RESIDENCES FOR SISTERS

SHREVEPORT. *Motherhouse of the Daughters of the Cross in America*, 411 E. Flournoy-Lucas Rd., 71115-3901. Tel: 318-797-0887; Fax: 318-797-7102. Email: dcsrs@bayou.com. Sr. Maria Smith, Pres. Sisters 3.
Religious House of Formation and Retirement-Our Lady of Sorrows, 9894 Norris Ferry Rd., 71106-7724. Tel: 318-797-0213; Fax: 318-797-7003. Email: olsmotherhouse@aol.com. Web: www.ols.org. Sr. Seraphine Ricci, O.L.S., Supr. Sisters 10.

[F] NEWMAN CENTERS

GRAMBLING. *Student Center* 471 Main St., 71245-3088. Tel: 318-247-6734 (Office); Fax: 318-247-6288. Rev. Peter Pulivelil, C.M.I. (India); Deacon Oscar Hannibal, Assoc. Campus Min.

MONROE. *Catholic Campus Ministry at the University of Louisiana at Monroe*, (formerly Northeast Louisiana University), 911 University Ave., P.O. Box 7250, 71211-7250. Tel: 318-343-4897; Fax: 318-343-4812. Email: ccm1@bayou.com. Revs. Sebastian Kallarackal, C.M.I. (India); Job Edathinatt Scaria, C.M.I. (India), Campus Min.; Deacons Timothy Cotita, Assoc. Campus Min.; Verdine Williams, Assoc. Campus Min.; Margaret Horne, Business Admin.

RUSTON. *E. Donn Piatt Catholic Student Center at Louisiana Tech University* 600 S. Thornton St., 71270-4946. Tel: 318-251-0793; Fax: 318-254-8319. Email: acts@latech.edu. Web: www.stac-acts.com. Rev. Frank Folino, O.F.M.; Rose Serio, Campus Min.

[G] MISCELLANEOUS

SHREVEPORT. *Magnificat-Nowela Chapter*, 4686 Hwy. 71, 71107. Tel: 318-222-0007. Sandy Chapman, Coord.

RELIGIOUS INSTITUTES OF MEN REPRESENTED IN THE DIOCESE

For further details refer to the corresponding bracketed number in the Religious Institutes of Men or Women section.

[0275]—*Carmelites of Mary Immaculate (India)*—C.M.I.
[0520]—*Franciscan Friars* (Sacred Heart Prov.)—O.F.M.
[0520]—*Franciscan Friars* (Prov. of St. John the Baptist)—O.F.M.

RELIGIOUS INSTITUTES OF WOMEN REPRESENTED IN THE DIOCESE

[1070-14]—*Congregation of Our Lady of the Sacred Heart (Dominican)*—O.P.
[0470]—*Congregation of the Sisters of Charity of the Incarnate Word, Houston, Texas*—C.C.V.I.
[1950]—*Congregation of the Sisters of the Holy Family*—S.S.F.
[0760]—*Daughters of Charity of St. Vincent de Paul*—D.C.
[0895]—*Daughters of Our Lady of the Holy Rosary*—F.M.S.R.
[0770]—*Daughters of the Cross*—D.C.

[1380]—*Franciscan Missionaries of Our Lady*—O.S.F.

[1430]—*Franciscan Sisters of Our Lady of Perpetual Help*—O.S.F.

[]—*Marianites of the Holy Cross*—M.S.C.

[3120]—*Sisters of Our Lady of Sorrows*—O.L.S.

[3840]—*Sisters of St. Joseph of Carondelet*—C.S.J.

[]—*Sisters of the Destitute* India

[2050]—*Sisters of the Holy Spirit and Mary Immaculate*—S.H.Sp.

[4120-03]—*Ursuline Nuns of the Congregation of Paris*—O.S.U.

DIOCESAN CEMETERIES

SHREVEPORT. *St. Joseph, Catholic Center,* 3500 Fairfield Ave., 71104. Tel: 318-868-4441; Fax: 318-868-4609. Mrs. Jill Braniff, CPA, Contact Person.

NECROLOGY

(No Deaths)

An asterisk (*) denotes an organization that has established tax-exempt status directly with the IRS and is not covered by the USCCB Group Ruling.

Diocese of Sioux City

(Dioecesis Siopolitana)

Most Reverend

R. WALKER NICKLESS

Bishop of Sioux City; ordained August 4, 1973; appointed Bishop of Sioux City November 10, 2005; Episcopal ordination January 20, 2006. *Chancery: Administrative Offices, 1821 Jackson St., P.O. Box 3379, Sioux City, IA 51102-3379.* Tel: 712-255-7933; Fax: 712-233-7598.

Most Reverend

LAWRENCE D. SOENS, D.D.

Retired Bishop of Sioux City; ordained May 6, 1950; appointed Bishop of Sioux City June 15, 1983; consecrated and installed August 17, 1983; retired November 28, 1998. *Mailing Address: P.O. Box 3379, Sioux City, IA 51102-3379.* Fax: 712-233-7598.

ESTABLISHED JANUARY 15, 1902.

Square Miles 14,518.

Corporate Title: "The Diocese of Sioux City."

Comprises 24 Counties in the northwest part of Iowa, west of Winnebago, Hancock, Wright, Hamilton and Story Counties, and north of Harrison, Shelby, Audubon, Guthrie and Dallas Counties.

For legal titles of parishes and diocesan institutions, consult the Chancery.

Chancery: Administrative Offices, 1821 Jackson St., P.O. Box 3379, Sioux City, IA 51102-3379. Tel: 712-255-7933; Fax: 712-233-7598.

Web: www.scdiocese.org

Email: bishopnickless@scdiocese.org

STATISTICAL OVERVIEW

Personnel	
Bishop	1
Retired Bishops	1
Priests: Diocesan Active in Diocese	71
Priests: Diocesan Active Outside Diocese	3
Priests: Retired, Sick or Absent	69
Number of Diocesan Priests	143
Religious Priests in Diocese	1
Total Priests in Diocese	144
Permanent Deacons in Diocese	39
Total Sisters	69
Parishes	
Parishes	113
With Resident Pastor:	
Resident Diocesan Priests	62
Without Resident Pastor:	
Administered by Priests	51
Closed Parishes	2
Professional Ministry Personnel:	
Sisters	8
Lay Ministers	65
Welfare	

Catholic Hospitals	3
Total Assisted	213,160
Homes for the Aged	3
Total Assisted	316
Special Centers for Social Services	5
Total Assisted	3,457
Educational	
Diocesan Students in Other Seminaries	8
Total Seminarians	8
Colleges and Universities	1
Total Students	1,158
High Schools, Diocesan and Parish	8
Total Students	1,685
Elementary Schools, Diocesan and Parish	17
Total Students	4,575
Catechesis/Religious Education:	
High School Students	2,766
Elementary Students	6,442
Total Students under Catholic Instruction	16,634
Teachers in the Diocese:	

Priests	2
Sisters	4
Lay Teachers	546
Vital Statistics	
Receptions into the Church:	
Infant Baptism Totals	1,535
Minor Baptism Totals	108
Adult Baptism Totals	46
Received into Full Communion	166
First Communions	1,515
Confirmations	1,378
Marriages:	
Catholic	328
Interfaith	242
Total Marriages	570
Deaths	1,138
Total Catholic Population	94,821
Total Population	455,297

Former Bishops—Most Revs. PHILIP J. GARRIGAN, D.D., ord. June 11, 1870; appt. March 21, 1902; cons. May 25, 1902; died Oct. 14, 1919; EDMOND HEELAN, D.D., ord. June 24, 1890; cons. April 8, 1919; died Sept. 20, 1948; JOSEPH M. MUELLER, D.D., ord. June 14, 1919; cons. Oct. 16, 1947; died Aug. 9, 1981; FRANK H. GRETEMAN, D.D., ord. Dec. 8, 1932; appt. Titular Bishop of Vissalsa April 14, 1965; cons. May 26, 1965; appt. Bishop of Sioux City Oct. 20, 1970; installed Dec. 9, 1970; retired Aug. 17, 1983; died March 21, 1987; LAWRENCE D. SOENS, D.D. (Retired), ord. May 6, 1950; appt. Bishop of Sioux City June 15, 1983; installed Aug. 17, 1983; retired Nov. 28, 1998; DANIEL N. DINARDO, D.D., ord. July 16, 1977; appt. Coadjutor Bishop of Sioux City Aug. 19, 1997; Episcopal ord. Oct. 7, 1997; appt. Bishop of Sioux City Nov. 28, 1998; appt. Coadjutor Bishop of Galveston-Houston Jan. 16, 2004; installed March 26, 2004; appt. Coadjutor Archbishop Dec. 29, 2004; created Cardinal Priest Nov. 24, 2007.

Vicar General—Rev. Msgr. R. MARK DUCHAINE, V.G., J.C.L., Mailing Address: P.O. Box 3379, Sioux City, 51102-3379.

Episcopal Vicar for Canonical Affairs—Rev. Msgr. R. MARK DUCHAINE, V.G., J.C.L., Mailing Address: P.O. Box 3379, Sioux City, 51102. Tel: 712-255-7933.

Chancery—Administrative Offices, 1821 Jackson St., P.O. Box 3379, Sioux City, 51102-3379. Tel: 712-255-7933; Fax: 712-233-7598.

Chancellor—Dr. DAVID A. LOPEZ, Ph.D., Mailing Address: P.O. Box 3379, Sioux City, 51102. Tel: 712-233-7512.

Vice Chancellor—Rev. MARK J. STOLL, J.C.L., Immaculate Conception Church, 419 Jones St., P.O. Box 802, Moville, 51039. Tel: 712-233-7537.

Diocesan Tribunal— Address all marriage related materials to: *P.O. Box 3379, Sioux City, 51102-3379.* Tel: 712-233-7533; Fax: 712-233-7588.

Judicial Vicar—Rev. Msgr. R. MARK DUCHAINE, V.G., J.C.L., 1821 Jackson St., P.O. Box 3379, Sioux City, 51102-3379. Res.: St. Mary Church, 703 Heisler, Mapleton, 51034-1222. Tel: 712-882-1780.

Adjutant Judicial Vicar—Rev. MICHAEL J. ERPELDING, J.C.L.

Promoter of Justice—Rev. Msgr. RICHARD E. ZENK, J.C.D.

Defenders of the Bond—Rev. ROBERT P. BROWN, S.T.L.; Rev. Msgrs. RICHARD E. ZENK, J.C.D.; MICHAEL D. SERNETT, J.C.D., V.G.

Judges—Rev. Msgr. R. MARK DUCHAINE, V.G., J.C.L.; Rev. MICHAEL J. ERPELDING, J.C.L.; Mr. EUGENE J. ULSES, J.C.L.

Notary—TERRI NIEDERGESES.

Diocesan Finance Council—Most Rev. RALPH WALKER NICKLESS, Pres.; Rev. Msgr. R. MARK DUCHAINE, V.G., J.C.L. Directors: Rev. ROGER J. LINNAN; Mr. JEFFREY R. MOHRHAUSER; Mr. RICHARD MONTGOMERY; Mr. RANDY KRAMER; Dr. MICHAEL JUNG; Mr. JAMES COSGROVE; Ms. KAREN WALDSCHMITT; Ms. MARY SWANSON; Mr. MARK THOMPSON; Ms. DIANE DONNELLY; Mr. ROYCE RANNIGER.

Diocesan Legal Counsel—Mr. MAURICE NIELAND, (Rawlings, Nieland, Probasco, Killinger, Ellenwanger, Jacobs, Mohrhauser, Law Firm, Sioux City). Refer all legal matters to The Chancery.

Presbyteral Council—Most Rev. RALPH WALKER NICKLESS; Very Rev. RICHARD D. BALL, V.F.; Rev. Msgr. KEVIN C. MCCOY, S.T.D.; Very Revs. EDWARD M. GIRRES; ARMAND J. BERTRAND, V.F.; Revs. CRAIG A. COLLISON; STEVEN W. BRODERSEN; RANDY L. SCHON; TIMOTHY A. FRIEDRICHSEN; Rev. Msgrs. THOMAS DONAHOE (Retired); R. MARK DUCHAINE, V.G., J.C.L.; Revs. MICHAEL J. ERPELDING, J.C.L.; MATTHEW A. HEWITT; BRIAN C. HUGHES; ROGER J. LINNAN; Dr. DAVID A. LOPEZ,

Ph.D.; Revs. JOHN J. MCGUIRK; BRADLEY C. PELZEL; JEFFREY SCHLEISMAN; Very Revs. TIMOTHY SCHOTT, V.F.; MERLIN J. SCHRAD, V.F., Pres.; Rev. JOHN M. THOMAS.

Diocesan Consultors—Most Rev. RALPH WALKER NICKLESS; Rev. Msgr. R. MARK DUCHAINE, V.G., J.C.L.; Very Revs. MERLIN J. SCHRAD, V.F.; RICHARD D. BALL, V.F.; Revs. JOHN M. THOMAS; BRADLEY C. PELZEL; BRIAN HUGHES.

Deans—Very Rev. RICHARD D. BALL, V.F., Northwest Deanery; Rev. Msgr. KENNETH A. SEIFRIED, V.F., Northeast Deanery; Very Revs. MERLIN J. SCHRAD, V.F., Southwest Deanery; WILLIAM A. SCHREIBER, V.F., Southeast Deanery; TIMOTHY SCHOTT, V.F., South Central Deanery; ARMAND J. BERTRAND, V.F., Central Deanery.

Diocesan Offices and Directors

Board of Education—Most Rev. RALPH WALKER NICKLESS; Revs. PATRICK WALSH; TERRY A. RODER; GERALD F. FEIERFEIL; Sisters MARY LOUISE SCIESZINSKI; RUTH SCHOCK, O.S.F.; Mr. JAMES SCHALL; Mr. DAN RYAN; Mrs. KATHEE FROEHLICH; Mrs. LORI GOETZINGER; Mrs. LINDA EBEL.

Building Commission—Rev. BRIAN C. HUGHES; Very Rev. TIMOTHY SCHOTT, V.F.; Mr. BRAD MOLLET; Mr. THOMAS VOGT; Ms. GRETCHEN COONEY; Mr. CLETE WINDSCHITL.

Catholic School Foundation of the Diocese of Sioux City—Mr. ROYCE RANNIGER; Ms. DIANE DONNELLY; Mrs. KRISTIE ARLT; Most Rev. RALPH WALKER NICKLESS, Pres., 1821 Jackson St., Sioux City, 51105; ALLEN WILLETT; JAMES BRIDE; Rev. Msgr. R. MARK DUCHAINE, V.G., J.C.L.; MATT GRETEMAN; PAT HAGAN; MAUREEN HEFFERNAN; RICK KNEIP; Rev. BRUCE A. LAWLER; Mr. MIKE HURLBERT.

Archives—DANIEL P. BURNS, 1821 Jackson St., P.O. Box 3379, Sioux City, 51102-3379. Tel: 712-233-7525.

Catholic Youth Organization—Rev. RANDY L. SCHON, St. Joseph Church, 403 East St. S., P.O. Box 38, Wesley, 50483-0038.

Censor Librorum—VACANT.

Catholic Charities—Mr. JERRY EATON, Dir., 1601 Military Rd., Sioux City, 51103. Tel: 712-252-4547. Fort Dodge Office: 3 N. 16th, Fort Dodge, 50501. Tel: 515-576-4156. Carroll Office: 409 1/2 W. 7th St., P.O. Box 13, Carroll, 51401. Tel: 712-792-9597. Storm Lake Office: 1709 Richland St., Storm Lake, 50588.

Continuing Education for Priests—Rev. DANIEL C. GUENTHER, V.F., Dir., Mailing Address: Immaculate Conception Church, P.O. Box 2817, Sioux City, 51106-2817.

Council of Catholic Women—Rev. JAMES J. TIGGES, Moderator, St. James Church, 109 6th Ave., S.W., LeMars, 51031-3434. Tel: 712-546-5201.

Department of Formation and Ministry—Dr. DAVID A. LOPEZ, Ph.D., Exec. Dir. & Dir. Deacon Formation; Deacon TIMOTHY MURPHY, Dir., Deacon Personnel, 1607 N. West St., Carroll, 51401-1498. Tel: 712-792-0513; Mr. SEAN MARTIN, Rel. Educ. & Family Life; VACANT, Office of Worship; JESSICA LAFLEUR-MALM, Youth Ministry; Ms. GRACE ZAVALA, Diocesan Coord., Office of Hispanic Ministry.

Episcopal Representative for Religious—Sr. ROSALIE ERDMANN, S.L.W., 3636 Glen Oaks Blvd., Apt. 16, Sioux City, 51104-1564. Tel: 712-258-2579.

Episcopal Representative for Hospitals and Health Care—Rev. GERALD F. FEIERFEIL, Nativity Parish, 4242 Natalia Way, Sioux City, 51106-4099.

Holy Childhood Association—Rev. Msgr. RICHARD E. ZENK, J.C.D., Dir., Mailing Address: P.O. Box 3379, Sioux City, 51102-3379.

Liturgy Commission—Mrs. MARCY ANDERSON; Revs. BRUCE A. LAWLER; WILLIAM J. VIT JR.; Sisters JANICE HOFFMAN, O.S.F.; M. ARNOLD STAUDT, O.S.F.; Mrs. MARLENE FITZPATRICK; Mr. MATTHEW GEERLINGS; Mr. TIM PICK.

Office of "The Catholic Globe"—Ms. RENEE WEBB, Editor, 1825 Jackson St., P.O. Box 5079, Sioux City, 51102-5079. Tel: 712-255-2550 Editorial Office; Circulation.

Office of Catholic Education—Mr. DAN RYAN, Supt., 1821 Jackson, P.O. Box 3379, Sioux City, 51102-3379. Tel: 712-233-7589.

Priests' Personnel Board—Most Rev. RALPH WALKER NICKLESS, Chm.; Rev. Msgr. R. MARK DUCHAINE, V.G., J.C.L., Bishop's Liaison; Revs. DANIEL M. GREVING; TIMOTHY A. JOHNSON; BRUCE A. LAWLER; Rev. Msgr. KENNETH A. SEIFRIED, V.F.

Priests' Pension Plan - Board of Trustees—Most Rev. RALPH WALKER NICKLESS, Chm.; Rev. Msgrs. ROGER J. AUGUSTINE, V.G. (Retired); R. MARK DUCHAINE, V.G., J.C.L.; Revs. GARY B. SNYDER; ROGER J. LINNAN; HARRY D. MCALPINE (Retired); BRUCE A. LAWLER; Deacon RICHARD L. BILLINGS, Chm.; Mr. DAVID FLATTERY; Mr. THOMAS P. GRIMSLEY; Mr. PATRICK D. KUEHL; Ms. MARGARET FUENTES; Ms. DIANE DONNELLY; Mr. JEFFREY R. MOHRHAUSER; Mr. ROYCE RANNIGER; Ms. DEBRA M. PUHL.

Propagation of the Faith, Association of the Holy Childhood, Catholic Students' Mission Crusade—Rev. Msgr. RICHARD E. ZENK, J.C.D., Dir., 1821 Jackson St., P.O. Box 3379, Sioux City, 51102-3379.

Office of Communications—Mrs. KRISTIE ARLT, Dir., Mailing Address: P.O. Box 3379, Sioux City, 51102-3379.

Rural Life Conference—Mrs. MARILYN MURPHY, Dir., 1601 Military Rd., Sioux City, 51103. Tel: 712-252-4547.

St. Joseph Education Society— (Diocesan Seminarian Board). Rev. WILLIAM J. VIT JR., 1000 Douglas St., Sioux City, 51105-1399. Tel: 712-255-1637.

Victim Assistance Coordinator—ANGIE MACK, Mercy Child Advocacy Center. Tel: 712-279-5610; 866-435-4397 (Toll Free). Email: macka@mercyhealth.com.

Vocations—Rev. BRADLEY C. PELZEL, P.O. Box 3379, Sioux City, 51102. Tel: 712-233-7523; 712-255-3577.

CLERGY, PARISHES, MISSIONS AND PAROCHIAL SCHOOLS

CITY OF SIOUX CITY

(WOODBURY COUNTY)

1—CATHEDRAL OF THE EPIPHANY (1867) Revs. William J. Vit Jr., Admin.; Brent Lingle; Hieu Nguyen (Vietnam).
Res.: 1000 Douglas St., 51105-1399. Tel: 712-255-1637; Fax: 712-255-4194. Web: www.sccathedral.org.
See Bishop Heelan Catholic Schools under Inter-Parochial Schools located in the Institution section.
Catechesis/Religious Program—Tel: 712-258-4962; Fax: 712-258-4962. Students 279.

2—BLESSED SACRAMENT (1922) Very Rev. Merlin J. Schrad; Rev. Msgr. Roger J. Augustine, Senior Priest (Retired); Deacons John Heffernan; Fred Karpuk; Ronald C. Pietz, Dir. Opers.; Richard Billings.
Res.: 3012 Jackson St., 51104-2799. Tel: 712-277-2949; Fax: 712-277-2963. Email: tuckerd@bishopheelan.org. Web: www.blessedsac.com.
See Bishop Heelan Catholic Schools under Inter-Parochial Schools located in the Institution section.
Catechesis/Religious Program—Tel: 712-277-4739, Ext. 15; Fax: 712-258-3698. Email: drewalshp@bishopheelan.org. Patricia Walsh, D.R.E.; Ann Schultz, Liturgy Director. Students 164.

3—ST. BONIFACE (1887), (German), [JC] Rev. James A. Bruch; Deacon James Sands. In Res., Rev. Richard A. Sitzmann.
Res.: 703 W. Fifth St., 51103-3799. Tel: 712-255-3577; Fax: 712-279-0751.
See Bishop Heelan Catholic Schools under Inter-Parochial Schools located in the Institution section.
Catechesis/Religious Program—709 Iowa St., 51105. Tel: 712-258-4962; Fax: 712-258-7101. Students 64.

4—ST. CASIMIR (1915), (Lithuanian), Closed. For inquiries for parish records contact the chancery.

5—ST. FRANCIS OF ASSISI (1907), (Polish), Closed. For inquiries for parish records contact the chancery.

6—IMMACULATE CONCEPTION (1905) [JC] Rev. Daniel C. Guenther.
Res.: P.O. Box 2817, 51106-2817. Tel: 712-276-4821; Fax: 712-276-1321. Email: icchurch@cableone.net.
See Bishop Heelan Catholic Schools under Inter-Parochial Schools located in the Institution section.
Catechesis/Religious Program—Tel: 712-276-4571; Fax: 712-276-1321. Students 173.

7—ST. JOSEPH (1887) [JC] Rev. Michael J. Erpelding; Deacon Ronald Pietz. In Res., Rev. Bradley C. Pelzel.
Res.: 1112 Eighth St., 51105-1899. Tel: 712-258-3813; Fax: 712-255-4018.
Catechesis/Religious Program—Twinned with St. Boniface., Tel: 712-258-4962. Students 25.

8—ST. MICHAEL (1906) [JC] Rev. Gary B. Snyder; Sr. Jean Ann Rausch, F.S.P.A., Pastoral Min.; Deacons Larry Sitzman; William Berger, (Retired); Jerry Reicks, (Retired).
Office and Res.: 2223 Indian Hills Dr., 51104-1605. Tel: 712-239-2411; Fax: 712-239-4710.
See Bishop Heelan Catholic Schools under Inter-Parochial Schools located in the Institution section.
Catechesis/Religious Program—Tel: 712-239-2411. Students 142.

9—NATIVITY OF OUR LORD JESUS CHRIST (1966) Rev. Gerald F. Feierfeil; Deacon Michael J. Hand.
Res.: 4242 Natalia Way, 51106-4099. Tel: 712-276-3022; Fax: 712-274-2703.
See Bishop Heelan Catholic Schools under Inter-Parochial Schools located in the Institution section.
Catechesis/Religious Program—Tel: 712-274-0497. Students 386.

10—SACRED HEART (1907) [JC] Rev. Craig A. Collison; Deacon Mark Wyant.
Res.: 5000 Military Rd., 51103-1564. Tel: 712-233-1652; Fax: 712-255-3056. Email: collisonc@bishopheelan.org. Web: www.sacredheart-siouxcity.com.
See Bishop Heelan Catholic Schools under Inter-Parochial Schools located in the Institution section.
Catechesis/Religious Program—Students 126.

OUTSIDE SIOUX CITY

AKRON, PLYMOUTH CO., ST. PATRICK (1888) [CEM] Rev. Msgr. Richard E. Zenk.
Res.: 650 Dakota St., P.O. Box 317, 51001-0317. Tel: 712-568-3292.
Catechesis/Religious Program—Students 80.

ALGONA, KOSSUTH CO., ST. CECELIA (1880) [CEM] Very Rev. Edward M. Girres; Deacons Bob Larsen; Bill Black.
Res.: P.O. Box 633, 50511-0633. Tel: 515-295-3435; Fax: 515-295-9290. Email: scecelia@netamumail.com.
School—Seton Elementary, Tel: 515-295-3509; Fax: 515-295-7739. Email: seton@garrigan.put.k12.us. Web: www.garrigan.unlimitedweb.net. Consolidation of St. Cecelia, Algona, St. Benedict & St. Joseph, Wesley; St. Joseph, Bode. Presentation Sisters 1; Lay Teachers 25; Students 207.
Catechesis/Religious Program—Students 145.

ALTON, SIOUX CO., ST. MARY'S (1870), (German), [CEM] Rev. Paul F. Eisele.
Res.: 609 10th St., 51003. Tel: 712-756-4224; Fax: 712-756-4431.
School—Spalding Catholic, (Grades 3-4) Tel: 712-756-4532; Fax: 712-756-4532. Consolidation of Alton, Hospers and Granville. Lay Teachers 4; Students 67.
Catechesis/Religious Program— Cluster of St. Mary, St. Anthony's, and St. Joseph's. Students 61.

ANTHON, WOODBURY CO., ST. JOSEPH'S (1890) [CEM] Rev. Terry A. Roder.
Res.: 404 E. Randolph St., P.O. Box 285, 51004-0285. Tel: 712-373-5573; 712-883-2406; Fax: 712-883-2458.
Catechesis/Religious Program—Tel: 712-373-5573. Students 49.

ARCADIA, CARROLL CO., ST. JOHN THE BAPTIST (1875), (German), [CEM] Rev. Joseph A. Dillinger.
Res.: P.O. Box 23, 51430-0023. Tel: 712-689-2595.
Catechesis/Religious Program—Students 22.

ARMSTRONG, EMMET CO., ST. MARY'S (1892) [CEM] [JC] Rev. Brian Hughes.
Office: 404 Fifth Ave., P.O. Box 437, 50514-9301. Tel: 712-864-3160.
Catechesis/Religious Program—Tel: 712-362-4172. Students 30.

ASHTON, OSCEOLA CO., ST. MARY'S CATHOLIC CHURCH (1880) [CEM] Rev. John A. Vakulskas Jr.
Res.: P.O. Box 157, 51232-0157. Tel: 712-724-6411.
Catechesis/Religious Program—2191 Nettle Ave., 51232. Tel: 712-724-6297. Mrs. Nancy Marnach, D.R.E. Students 19.

AUBURN, SAC CO., ST. MARY'S (1893), (German), [JC] Rev. Lynn Bruch.
Res.: 301 E. 4th St., P.O. Box H, 51433. Tel: 712-688-2845.
Catechesis/Religious Program—Students 45.

BANCROFT, KOSSUTH CO., ST. JOHN THE BAPTIST'S (1891) [CEM] [JC] Rev. Paul D. Bormann; Deacon Philip Doocy.
Res.: 204 S. Summit Ave., P.O. Box 195, 50517-0195. Tel: 515-885-2462; Fax: 515-885-2424. Web: www.stjohnbancroft.com.
School—St. John's Elementary School, Tel: 515-885-2580; Fax: 515-885-2402. Lay Teachers 6; Students 34.
Catechesis/Religious Program— Lori Geitzenauer, D.R.E. Students 146.

BARNUM, WEBSTER CO., ST. JOSEPH'S (1891) [CEM] Closed. For inquiries for parish records contact Holy Trinity Parish of Webster County, Fort Dodge.

BODE, KOSSUTH CO., ST. JOSEPH'S (1876) [CEM] Rev. Victor Ramaeker.
Res.: 603 3rd St., Whittemore, 50598. Tel: 515-884-2614.
Catechesis/Religious Program—Tel: 515-295-3435. Students 7.

BOONE, BOONE CO., SACRED HEART (1868) [CEM] Rev. Steven W. Brodersen.
Res.: 915 12th St., 50036-2295. Tel: 515-432-1971. Email: shsecretary@mchsi.com. Web: www.sacredhrt.org.
Catechesis/Religious Program—Tel: 515-432-2884; Fax: 515-432-1975. Email: sh-youth@mchsi.com. Students 132.

BREDA, CARROLL CO., ST. BERNARD'S (1880) [CEM] Rev. Joseph A. Dillinger.
Res.: 206 N. 2nd St., P.O. Box 39, 51436-0031. Tel: 712-673-2351; Fax: 712-673-2351.
Parish is a member of the consolidated K-12 Kuemper Catholic School System, Carroll, IA. Please refer to Keumper Catholic School System under Inter-Parochial Schools in the Institution section.
Catechesis/Religious Program—Tel: 712-792-0513. Students 13.

CARROLL, CARROLL CO.

1—HOLY SPIRIT (1964) [JC], SS. Peter/Paul, and St. Joseph, Carroll merged to form Holy Spirit, Carroll. Revs. Timothy A. Johnson; John J. Gerald (India); Deacons Edward Miller; Greg Sampson.
Res.: 421 E. Bluff St., 51401-3099. Tel: 712-792-4386; Fax: 712-792-8038. Email: hsparish@mchsi.com. Web: www.holyspiritcarroll.org.
School—(Grades K-12) Tel: 712-792-3313; Fax: 712-792-8073. Parish is a member of the consolidated K-12 Kuemper Catholic School System, Carroll, IA. Please refer to Kuemper Catholic School System under Inter-Parochial Schools in the Institution section.
Catechesis/Religious Program—Tel: 712-792-0513; Fax: 712-792-9245. Deacon Timothy Murphy, D.R.E. Shared with St. Lawrence & surrounding parishes. Students 367.

2—ST. LAWRENCE (1914) [JC] Rev. Timothy R. Schott; Deacon Tim Murphy.
Res.: 1607 N. West St., 51401-1498. Tel: 712-792-9244; Fax: 712-792-9245.
Parish is a member of the consolidated K-12 Kuemper Catholic School System, Carroll, IA. Please refer to Keumper Catholic School System under Inter-Parochial Schools in the Institution section.
Catechesis/Religious Program—Tel: 712-792-0513. Shared with Holy Spirit and surrounding parishes. Students 114.

CHARTER OAK, CRAWFORD CO., ST. BONIFACE (1883), (German—Irish), [CEM] Rev. Andrew Bao Vo.
Res.: P.O. Box 317, Dow City, 51528. Tel: 712-678-3449.
Mission—St. Mary's [CEM] Box 317, Ute, Monona Co. 51528. Tel: 712-674-3329.
Catechesis/Religious Program—Tel: 712-678-3530. Students 38.

CHEROKEE, CHEROKEE CO., IMMACULATE CONCEPTION (1870) [CEM] Very Rev. Armand J. Bertrand; Deacon Leroy Rupp.
Res.: 709 W. Cedar St., P.O. Box 658, 51012-0658. Tel: 712-225-4606.
Catechesis/Religious Program—7th & Willow, 51012. Tel: 712-225-4466. Students 126.

CHURDAN, GREENE CO., ST. COLUMBKILLE (1886), (German—Irish), [CEM] Rev. Steven J. McLoud.
Res.: 807 Head St., P.O. Box 128, 50050-0128. Tel: 515-389-3625; Fax: 515-389-3797. Web: www.geocities.com/st_columbkilleparish.
Catechesis/Religious Program—Tel: 515-386-4010. Email: pastoralis@wccta.net. Students 40.

CLARE, WEBSTER CO., ST. MATTHEW'S (1886) [CEM] Closed. For inquiries for parish records contact Holy Trinity Parish of Webster County, Fort Dodge.

COON RAPIDS, CARROLL CO., ANNUNCIATION (1891) [CEM] Rev. Anthony Pick.
Res.: 724 Elm St., 50058-0076. Tel: 712-999-2823; Fax: 712-999-2823. Email: anchurch@longlines.com.
Catechesis/Religious Program—Tel: 712-999-5235. Students 80.

DANBURY, WOODBURY CO., ST. MARY'S (1897), (German), [CEM] Rev. Terry A. Roder.
Res.: 604 Peach St., 51019-5028. Tel: 712-883-2406; Fax: 712-883-2458.
School—Danbury Elementary, (Grades PreK-6) Tel: 712-883-2244; Fax: 712-883-2024. Kristi Liechti, Prin. Priests 1; Sisters 1; Lay Teachers 4; Students 39.
Catechesis/Religious Program—Students 36.

DAYTON, WEBSTER CO., CHRIST THE KING (1950) [CEM] Closed. For inquiries for parish records contact Holy Trinity Parish of Webster County, Fort Dodge.

DEDHAM, CARROLL CO., ST. JOSEPH'S (1892) [CEM] Rev. Anthony Pick.
Res.: P.O. Box 47, 51440-0047. Tel: 712-683-5744. Email: stjoes@iowatelecom.net.
School—Kuemper Catholic Grade Schools, Tel: 712-792-3596; Fax: 712-792-3365. Web: www.kuemper-.org. Consolidation of Dedham, Willey Elementary, Holy Spirit and St. Lawrence.
Catechesis/Religious Program—Students 30.

DENISON, CRAWFORD CO., ST. ROSE OF LIMA (1872) [CEM] Revs. Paul Kelly; Tim Friedrickson.
Res.: 916 2nd Ave. S., P.O. Box 280, 51442-0280. Tel: 712-263-2152; Fax: 712-263-2153.
School—Tel: 712-263-5408; Fax: 712-263-2153. Lay Teachers 9; Students 75.
Catechesis/Religious Program—Tel: 712-263-5408. Students 169.

DOW CITY, CRAWFORD CO., ST. MARYS (1947), (German—Irish), Rev. Andrew Bao Vo.
Res.: 215 Clark St., P.O. Box 317, 51528-0317. Tel: 712-674-3329.
Catechesis/Religious Program—Students 25.

DUNCOMBE, WEBSTER CO., ST. JOSEPH'S (1880) [CEM] Closed. For inquiries for parish records contact Holy Trinity Parish of Webster County, Fort Dodge.

EARLY, SAC CO., SACRED HEART (1882) [CEM] Rev. John J. McGuirk.
Res.: 501 Church St., 50535. Tel: 712-273-5482; Fax: 712-273-5798. Email: shchurch@frontiernet.net. Web: www.sacredheartearly.org.
Catechesis/Religious Program—Tel: 712-273-5577. Students 34.

EMMETSBURG, PALO ALTO CO.

1—HOLY FAMILY (1856), (Irish), [CEM] Rev. Clement W. Currans.
Res.: 2001 S. Broadway, P.O. Box 322, 50536-0322. Tel: 712-852-3187; Fax: 712-852-4406. Email: holyfamily@iowatelecom.net. Web: www.iowatelecom.net/~holyfamily.
School—Emmetsburg Catholic School, (Grades PreK-8) Tel: 712-852-3464; Fax: 712-852-3464. Email: jhyslop@emmetsburg-catholic.pvt.k12.ia.us. Mrs. Jean Hyslop, Prin. Lay Teachers 10; Students 83.
Catechesis/Religious Program—Tel: 712-852-3187. Students 129.

2—ST. THOMAS, Closed. For sacramental records contact Holy Family, Emmetsburg.

ESTHERVILLE, EMMET CO., ST. PATRICK'S (1891) [CEM] Rev. Brian C. Hughes.
Res.: 903 Central Ave., P.O. Box 383, 51334-0383. Tel: 712-362-5851; Fax: 712-362-5852. Email: dawnstpats@mchsi.com.
Catechesis/Religious Program—Duhigg Center, 902 Central Ave., P.O. Box 383, 51334. Tel: 712-362-4172. Students 162.

FONDA, POCAHONTAS CO., OUR LADY OF GOOD COUNSEL (1884) [CEM] Rev. Siby Punnoose (India), Admin.; Deacon Eldon Sullivan.
Res.: P.O. Box 339, 50540-0339. Tel: 712-288-6480; Fax: 712-288-6480. Email: olgc@ncn.net.
Catechesis/Religious Program—Students 64.

FORT DODGE, WEBSTER CO.

1—CORPUS CHRISTI (1856) [JC] Closed. For inquiries for parish records contact Holy Trinity Parish of Webster County, Fort Dodge.

2—HOLY ROSARY (1946) [JC] Closed. For inquiries for parish records contact Holy Trinity Parish of Webster County, Fort Dodge.

3—HOLY TRINITY PARISH OF WEBSTER COUNTY (2006) Rev. Msgr. Kevin C. McCoy.
Office: 2220 4th Ave. N., 50501. Tel: 515-573-3616; Fax: 515-955-8473.
See Fort Dodge Catholic Schools, Inc., Fort Dodge under Inter-Parochial Schools located in the Institution Section.
Catechesis/Religious Program—Students 137.

4—SACRED HEART (1897) [JC] Closed. For inquiries for parish records contact Holy Trinity Parish of Webster County, Fort Dodge.

GILMORE CITY, POCAHONTAS CO., ST. JOHN'S (1889) [CEM] Rev. James J. Tigges.
Res.: 311 4th St. N., Humboldt, 50548. Tel: 515-332-2856 (St. Mary's-Humboldt); Fax: 515-332-1487. Email: stmhbt@goldfieldaccess.net.
Catechesis/Religious Program—Tel: 515-332-2784. Students 5.

GRAETTINGER, PALO ALTO CO., IMMACULATE CONCEPTION (1891) [CEM] Rev. Msgr. Michael D. Sernett.
Res.: 305 N. Cameron Ave., P.O. Box 420, 51342. Tel: 712-859-3327; Fax: 712-859-3797. Email: icc@rvtc.net.
Catechesis/Religious Program—503 W. Olive St., 51342. Tel: 712-859-3482. Students 76.

GRAND JUNCTION, GREENE CO., ST. BRIGID'S (1873), (Irish), [CEM] Rev. Donald C. Ries.
Res.: 503 N. Chestnut, Jefferson, 50129. Tel: 515-738-2684; Fax: 515-386-3672.
Catechesis/Religious Program—St. Brigid Parish Center, 602 Hager St. E., 50107. Tel: 515-738-2254. Students 30.

GRANVILLE, SIOUX CO., ST. JOSEPH (1886) [CEM] Very Rev. Richard D. Ball.
Res.: 528 Elm St., P.O. Box 127, 51022-0127. Tel: 712-727-3551.
School—Spalding Catholic School, Tel: 712-727-3451; Fax: 712-727-3455. Mr. Gary Niichel, Prin. (Spalding Catholic High School); Judy Stokesberry, Librarian. Consolidation of Alton, Hospers and Granville. Lay Teachers 1; Students 39.
High School—Spalding Catholic High School, (Grades 7-8) Judy Stokesberry, Librarian. Lay Teachers 17; Students 61.
Catechesis/Religious Program—Tel: 712-752-8784. Pilgrim cluster held at St. Mary's, Alton. Students 15.

HALBUR, CARROLL CO., ST. AUGUSTINE'S (1904) [CEM] Rev. Dale E. Reiff.
Res.: P.O. Box 13, 51444-0013. Tel: 712-658-2464.
Parish is a member of the consolidated K-12 Kuemper Catholic School System, Carroll, IA. Please refer to Keumper Catholic School System under Inter-Parochial Schools in the Institution section.
Catechesis/Religious Program—Tel: 712-792-0513 (Carroll); 712-653-2131 (Manning). Students 17.

HAWARDEN, SIOUX CO., ST. MARY'S (1887) [JC] Rev. Roger J. Linnan.
Res.: 1125 Avenue L., P.O. Box 271, 51023-0271. Tel: 712-551-1501.
Catechesis/Religious Program—Tel: 712-551-2526. Students 168.

HOLSTEIN, IDA CO., OUR LADY OF GOOD COUNSEL (1884) [CEM] Rev. David Hemann; Deacon Mike Stover, Pastoral Min. In Res., Rev. Msgr. Kenneth A. Seifried.
Office: 513 Mueller St., 51025. Tel: 712-368-4755.
Catechesis/Religious Program—Tel: 712-368-2504. Students 72.

HORNICK, WOODBURY CO., ST. PHILIP'S (1900) Closed. For inquiries for parish records contact the chancery.

HOSPERS, SIOUX CO., ST. ANTHONY'S (1877) [CEM] Rev. Paul F. Eisele.
506 Elm, P.O. Box 86, 51238-0086. Tel: 712-752-8784. Email: stacc@nethtc.net.
Res.: *c/o St. Mary*, 609 10th St., Alton, 51003. Tel: 712-756-4224. Email: fatherpaul@midlands.net.
School—Spalding Elementary, (Grades K-3) Tel: 712-752-8286. Judy Stokesberry, Librarian. Consolidation of Alton, Hospers and Granville. Lay Teachers 4; Students 47.

HUMBOLDT, HUMBOLDT CO., ST. MARY'S (1878) [CEM] Rev. James J. Tigges.
Res.: 311 Fourth St. N., 50548-1647. Tel: 515-332-2856; Fax: 515-332-1487. Email: stmhbt@goldfieldaccess.net.
School—Tel: 515-332-2134. Sisters 1; Lay Teachers 14; Students 186.
Catechesis/Religious Program—Tel: 515-332-2784. Students 112.

IDA GROVE, IDA CO., SACRED HEART (1878) [CEM] Rev. David Hemann.
Res.: 800 N. Main, P.O. Box 244, 51445-1297. Tel: 712-364-2718. Email: igrectory@frontiernet.net. Web: fatherdavid.net.
Catechesis/Religious Program—Tel: 712-364-3628. Students 148.

JEFFERSON, GREENE CO., ST. JOSEPH'S (1875) Rev. Donald C. Ries.
Res.: 503 N. Chestnut St., 50129-1507. Tel: 515-386-2638; Fax: 515-386-3672. Email: joejeff@netins.net. Web: www.stjosephjefferson.com.
Catechesis/Religious Program—501 N. Locust, 50129. Tel: 515-386-4010. Students 115.
Mission—St. Brigid [CEM] 602 Hager, Grand Junction, Greene Co. 50107. Tel: 515-738-2254.

KINGSLEY, PLYMOUTH CO., ST. MICHAEL'S (1888) [CEM] Rev. Mark J. Stoll.
Res.: 403 Jones St., P.O. Box 802, Moville, 51039-0802. Tel: 712-378-2722; Fax: 712-873-3931. Email: icmoville@netins.net. Web: www.icmoville.catholicweb.com.
Catechesis/Religious Program—Tel: 712-378-2021. Students 122.

LAKE CITY, CALHOUN CO., ST. MARY'S (1894) [CEM] [JC] Rev. Lynn Bruch; Deacon Don Kunecke.
Res.: P.O. Box 131, 51449-0131. Tel: 712-464-3395; Fax: 712-464-7669.
Catechesis/Religious Program—Students 108.

LARCHWOOD, LYON CO., ST. MARY (1898), (German—Dutch), [JC] Rev. Jeffrey Schleisman; Deacon Jeff Gallagher.
Res.: 1413 Holder St., P.O. Box 37, 51241-0037. Tel: 712-477-2273; Fax: 712-477-2162. Email: amen1030@yahoo.com. Web: www.holymarycluster.wetpaint.com.
Catechesis/Religious Program—Students 115.

LAURENS, POCAHONTAS CO., SACRED HEART (1893) [CEM] Rev. Allan A. Reicks.
Res.: 708 Thomas St., P.O. Box 450, Sioux Rapids, 50585. Tel: 712-841-4596.
Catechesis/Religious Program—Tel: 712-289-6481. Students 46.

LE MARS, PLYMOUTH CO.

1—ST. JAMES (1883) [JC] Rev. Matthew A. Hewitt; Deacon Donald Kunkel, (Retired).
Res.: 109 Sixth Ave., S.W., 51031-3434. Tel: 712-546-5201; Fax: 712-546-8696. Email: saintjameslm@frontiernet.net.
School—Gehlen Catholic Elementary, (Grades PreK-6) Tel: 712-546-4181. Lay Teachers 21; Students 281.
High School—Gehlen Catholic High School, Tel: 712-546-4181. Lay Teachers 22; Students 145.

Catechesis/Religious Program—20 6th Ave. N.E., 51031. Tel: 712-546-5223. Students 234.

2—ST. JOSEPH'S (1875), (German), [CEM] [JC] Rev. Kevin M. Richter.
Res.: 35 6th Ave. N.E., 51031. Tel: 712-546-4813; Fax: 712-546-8346. Email: stjoelm@frontiernet.net.
School—Gehlen Catholic School, 709 Plymouth St., S.E., 51031. Tel: 712-546-4181; Fax: 712-546-8696. Email: 1.hatting@gehlencatholic.com. Jeff Alesch, Prin. Students 412.
Catechesis/Religious Program—Tel: 712-546-5223; Fax: 712-546-8346. Email: faithfor@frontier.net. Sr. Jeanette Homan, D.R.E. Students 184.

LEDYARD, KOSSUTH CO., SACRED HEART (1887) [CEM] [JC] Rev. Paul D. Bormann.
Mailing Address: P.O. Box 126, 50556-0067. Tel: 515-646-2525.
Res.: 204 S. Summit Ave., P.O. Box 195, Bancroft, 50517. Tel: 515-885-2462; Fax: 515-885-2424.
Catechesis/Religious Program— Twinned with St. John's, Bancroft. Students 16.

LIDDERDALE, CARROLL CO., HOLY FAMILY (1914), (German), [CEM] Rev. Timothy R. Schott.
Res.: P.O. Box 160, 51452-0160. Tel: 712-822-5522.
Parish is a member of newly consolidated K-12 Kuemper Catholic School System, Carroll, IA. Please refer to Keumper Catholic School System under Inter-Parochial Schools in the Institution section.
Catechesis/Religious Program—Tel: 712-792-0513. Students 9.
Mission—St. Elizabeth Seton Church Glidden, Carroll Co. Tel: 712-659-3051.

LIVERMORE, HUMBOLDT CO., SACRED HEART (1881) [CEM] Rev. Randy L. Schon.
Res.: 405 East St. S., P.O. Box 38, Wesley, 50483-0038. Tel: 515-679-4279.
Catechesis/Religious Program—Tel: 515-379-2508. Students 29.

LOHRVILLE, CALHOUN CO., ST. JOSEPH'S (1885), (Irish), [CEM] Rev. Lynn Bruch.
Res.: N. Lloyd St., P.O. Box 131, Lake City, 51449. Tel: 712-464-3395; Fax: 712-464-7669.
Catechesis/Religious Program—Students 14.

MADRID, BOONE CO., ST. MALACHY'S (1923) [JC] Rev. Timothy J. Boekelman.
Res.: 207 Gerald St., 50156-1464. Tel: 515-795-2731; Fax: 515-795-2731. Email: stmalachys@iowatelecom.net.
Church: 405 Gerald St., 50156. Tel: 515-795-2613.
Catechesis/Religious Program—Students 197.
Mission—St. John of God Woodward, 50276.

MALLARD, PALO ALTO CO., ST. MARY'S (1889) [CEM] Rev. Thomas J. Hart.
Mailing Address: P.O. Box 207, 50562-0236.
Res.: 206 1st Ave., N.W., West Bend, 50597. Fax: 515-887-3334.
Catechesis/Religious Program—Tel: 515-887-3333; Fax: 515-887-3334. Students 16.

MANILLA, CRAWFORD CO., SACRED HEART (1887) [CEM] Rev. Robert W. Gralapp.
Res.: 269 6th St., P.O. Box 339, 51454-0339. Tel: 712-654-9511.
Catechesis/Religious Program—Students 74.

MANNING, CARROLL CO., SACRED HEART (1916), (German), [CEM] Rev. Robert W. Gralapp.
Res.: 203 Sue St., 51455-1399. Tel: 712-655-3804; Fax: 712-655-9476.
Catechesis/Religious Program—Tel: 712-655-2933. Students 170.

MANSON, CALHOUN CO., ST. THOMAS (1885) [CEM 2] Rev. Richard S. Ries.
Res.: P.O. Box 99, 50563-0099. Tel: 712-469-3743; Fax: 712-469-3066.
Catechesis/Religious Program—Tel: 712-469-3334. Students 132.

MAPLE RIVER, CARROLL CO., ST. FRANCIS OF ASSISI (1904), (German), [CEM] Closed. For inquiries for parish records contact Our Lady of Mt. Carmel parish in Mt. Carmel, IA.

MAPLETON, MONONA CO., ST. MARY'S (1894) [CEM 2] Rev. Msgr. R. Mark Duchaine.
Mailing Address: 703 Heisler St., 51034. In Res., Rev. Gerald F. Zensen (Retired).
Res.: 620 State St., Oto, 51044. Tel: 712-827-4510. Email: stmarys@longlines.com.
Catechesis/Religious Program—Tel: 712-882-1780. Students 72.
Mission—St. Mary's Oto. 620 State St., Box 67, Oto, Woodbury Co. 51044-6007. Tel: 712-827-4467.

MARCUS, CHEROKEE CO., HOLY NAME (1877) [CEM] Very Rev. Armand J. Bertrand; Deacon Jerry Bertrand.
Res.: 102 N. Elm St., P.O. Box 366, 51035-0366. Tel: 712-376-2628.
Catechesis/Religious Program—Tel: 712-376-2625. Students 159.

MARYHILL, CHEROKEE CO., VISITATION OF THE B.V.M. (1895) [CEM] Closed. for inquiries for Parish records please contact Immaculate Conception, Cherokee.

MERRILL, PLYMOUTH CO., ASSUMPTION CHURCH (1890) [CEM 2] Rev. Daniel M. Greving.
Mailing Address: 527 Center St., P.O. Box 175, 51038.
Church: 527 Center St., 51038. Tel: 712-938-2236.
Catechesis/Religious Program—Students 31.
Mission—St. Joseph at Ellendale 23533 K22, Plymouth Co. 51038.
Catechesis/Religious Program—Students 41.

MILFORD, DICKINSON CO., ST. JOSEPH'S (1884) [CEM] Rev. Brian Danner.
1305 Okoboji Ave., 51351-1232.
Res.: 1413 Okoboji Ave., 51351. Tel: 712-338-2172; Fax: 712-338-2191.
Catechesis/Religious Program—Students 130.

MOORLAND, WEBSTER CO., OUR LADY OF GOOD COUNSEL (1902) [CEM] Closed. For inquiries for parish records contact Holy Trinity Parish of Webster County, Fort Dodge.

MOUNT CARMEL, CARROLL CO., OUR LADY OF MT. CARMEL (1869), (German), [CEM] Rev. Joseph A. Dillinger.
Res.: 206 2nd Ave., Breda, 51436. Tel: 712-673-2351.
Parish is a member of newly consolidated K-12 Kuemper Catholic School System, Carroll, IA. Please refer to Keumper Catholic School System under Inter-Parochial Schools in the Institution section.
Catechesis/Religious Program—Tel: 712-792-9244. Students 12.

MOVILLE, WOODBURY CO., IMMACULATE CONCEPTION (1892) Rev. Mark J. Stoll.
Office: 419 Jones St., P.O. Box 802, 51039-0802. Tel: 712-873-3644; Fax: 712-873-3931. Email: icmoville@netins.net. Web: www.icmoville.catholicweb.com.
Res.: 403 Jones St., P.O. Box 802, 51039-0802. Tel: 712-873-3745.
Catechesis/Religious Program—Tel: 712-873-3644. Students 137.

NEPTUNE, PLYMOUTH CO., ST. JOSEPH (Hinton) (1884), (German), [CEM] Rev. Daniel M. Greving.
Res.: 527 Center St., P.O. Box 175, Merrill, 51038. Tel: 712-938-2236.
Catechesis/Religious Program—LeMars Religious Education Program, 815 Plymouth St., N.E., P.O. Box 1103, LeMars, 51031. Tel: 712-546-5223. Students 27.

ODEBOLT, SAC CO., ST. MARTIN'S (1877) [CEM] Rev. David Hemann.
Res.: 400 Hansen Blvd., P.O. Box 500, 51458-0500. Tel: 712-668-2690.
Rectory—Sacred Heart, 200 N. Main, Ida Grove, 51445.
Catechesis/Religious Program—Students 95.

OGDEN, BOONE CO., ST. JOHN'S (1896) [CEM] Rev. Timothy J. Boekelman.
Res.: 801 W. Division St., 50212-0810. Tel: 515-275-2580; Fax: 515-275-2580. Email: stjohnogden@hotmail.com. Web: www.stjohncatholicchurch-ogden.org.
Catechesis/Religious Program—Tel: 515-275-4095. Students 77.

ONAWA, MONONA CO., ST. JOHN (1900) Rev. Patrick J. O'Kane; Deacons Thomas Morgan; Joseph Scurlock.
Res.: 1009 13th St., 51040-1508. Tel: 712-423-2656; Fax: 712-423-1040. Email: stjohnparishhall@msn.com.
Catechesis/Religious Program—Tel: 712-423-1004. Students 84.
Mission—St. Bernard Blencoe, Monona Co.

OYENS, PLYMOUTH CO., ST. CATHERINE'S (1900) [CEM] Rev. William A. McCarthy.
Res.: P.O. Box 366, Marcus, 51035. Tel: 712-376-2628.
School—St. Catherine-St. Mary's Elementary, Tel: 712-786-2764. Email: sacredhe@ionet.net. (Oyens-Remsen) Lay Teachers 11; Students 33.
Catechesis/Religious Program—321 Fulton St., Remsen, 51050. Tel: 712-786-1160. Students 18.

POCAHONTAS, POCAHONTAS CO., CHURCH OF THE RESURRECTION (1973) [CEM] Rev. Andrew W. Hoffman.
Res.: 21 S.W. 3rd St., 50574-0157. Tel: 712-335-3242; Fax: 712-335-3919.
School—Pocahontas Catholic Elementary, Tel: 712-335-3603; Fax: 712-335-3603. Email: pokycath@ncn.net. Ron Olberding, Prin. Lay Teachers 5; Students 71.
Catechesis/Religious Program—Students 101.

POMEROY, CALHOUN CO., ST. MARY'S (1881) [CEM] Rev. Richard S. Ries; Deacon Robert Lenz.
Mailing Address: P.O. Box 99, Manson, 50563-0099.
Res.: 1076 8th St., Manson, 50563. Tel: 712-469-3743; Fax: 712-469-3066.
Catechesis/Religious Program—Tel: 712-468-2248. Students 28.

REMSEN, PLYMOUTH CO., ST. MARY'S (1885) [CEM] Rev. William A. McCarthy.
Res.: 121 E. 4th St., Box #509, 51050. Tel: 712-786-1437; Fax: 712-786-1444. Email: smparish@midlands.net. Web: www.smparishinfo.org.
School—St. Catherine-St. Mary's Elementary, Tel: 712-786-1160; Fax: 712-786-1167. Ms. Elizabeth Gibney, Prin.; Ms. Mary Riedemann, Librarian. (Oyens-Remsen) Lay Teachers 11; Students 165. See St. Mary's High School, Remsen under Inter-Parochial Schools located in the Institution Section.
Catechesis/Religious Program—Tel: 712-786-2889; Fax: 712-786-1167. Students 249.

ROCK RAPIDS, LYON CO., HOLY NAME (1871), (Irish), [CEM] Rev. Jeffrey Schleisman.
Res.: 1108 S. Carroll St., 51246-9529. Tel: 712-472-3248; Fax: 712-472-3189. Email: holynamerr@yahoo.com. Web: www.alliancecom.net/campki.
Catechesis/Religious Program—Students 55.

ROCK VALLEY, SIOUX CO., ST. MARY'S (1895) [CEM] Rev. Douglas M. Klein.
Res.: 1821 14th St., 51247-0098. Tel: 712-476-2060; Fax: 712-476-9074. Email: smrv@hickorytech.net. Web: www.trinitycluster.org.
Catechesis/Religious Program— Totals include Sacred Heart and Christ the King, Sioux Center. Students 136.
Mission—Sacred Heart [CEM] 301 Seefield St., Alvord, Lyon Co. 51230. Tel: 712-473-2215.

ROCKWELL CITY, CALHOUN CO., ST. FRANCIS OF ASSISI (1899), (German), [CEM] Rev. Richard S. Ries.
Res.: 744 Main St., 50579-1399. Tel: 712-297-8263; Fax: 712-297-8330. Web: www.stfrancis-rc.org.
Catechesis/Religious Program—Tel: 712-297-5116. Students 67.

ROLFE, POCAHONTAS CO., ST. MARGARET'S (1895) [CEM] Rev. Andrew W. Hoffman.
Res.: 21 S.W. 3rd St., Pocahontas, 50574. Tel: 712-335-3242.
Catechesis/Religious Program—Tel: 712-848-3301. Janet Crowe, D.R.E. Students 30.

ROSELLE, CARROLL CO., HOLY ANGELS (1874) [CEM] Rev. Dale E. Reiff.
Res.: Box 13, Halbur, 51444-0013. Tel: 712-658-2464; Fax: 712-658-2464.
Parish is a member of the consolidated K-12 Kuemper Catholic School System, Carroll, IA. Please refer to Keumper Catholic School System under Inter-Parochial Schools in the Institution section.
Catechesis/Religious Program—Tel: 712-792-0513 (Carroll); 712-653-2131 (Manning). Students 8.

ROYAL, CLAY CO., ST. LOUIS (1923), (French—German), Rev. Robert P. Brown.
Res.: 300 1st Ave., P.O. Box 49, 51357. Tel: 712-933-2667. Email: stlouis@royaltelco.net.
Catechesis/Religious Program—Fax: 712-933-2356. Students 46.

RUTHVEN, PALO ALTO CO., SACRED HEART (1888), (German—Irish), [CEM] Rev. Peter Duc Hung Nguyen.
Church: P.O. Box 400, 51358-0400. Tel: 712-837-5240.
Catechesis/Religious Program—Students 25.
Mission—Sacred Heart P.O. Box 207, Ayrshire, Palo Alto Co. 50515. Tel: 515-426-3260.

ST. BENEDICT, KOSSUTH CO., ST. BENEDICT'S (1877) [CEM] Rev. Randy L. Schon.
Res.: P.O. Box 38, Wesley, 50483. Tel: 515-679-4279. Email: stjwesley@msn.com.
School—Seton Elementary, Tel: 515-295-3509; Fax: 515-295-7739. Consolidation of St. Cecelia, Algona, St. Benedict and St. Joseph, Wesley. Seton Students 17; Bishop Garrigan Students 4.
Catechesis/Religious Program—St. Patrick's Church, 139 3rd St., S.E., Britt, 50423. Tel: 641-843-3073. Students 10.

SAC CITY, SAC CO., ST. MARY'S (1892), (German—Irish), [CEM] Rev. John J. McGuirk.
Res.: P.O. Box 324, 50583-0324. Tel: 712-662-7240. Students 117.
Catechesis/Religious Program—Fax: 712-662-7240. Students 127.

SALIX, WOODBURY CO., ST. JOSEPH'S (1869) [CEM] [JC] Rev. Patrick J. O'Kane.
Res.: P.O. Box 270, 51052-0270. Tel: 712-946-5635.
Catechesis/Religious Program—Students 89.

SANBORN, O'BRIEN CO., ST. CECILIA'S (1882) [CEM] Rev. Timothy J. Hogan.
Res.: 310 E. 4th St., P.O. Box 555, 51248. Tel: 712-930-3423.
Catechesis/Religious Program—Tel: 712-928-2626. Nancy Williams, D.R.E. (Grades K-8). Students 90.
Mission—St. Joseph's, Tel: 712-728-2626.

SCHALLER, SAC CO., ST. JOSEPH'S (1891) [CEM] Rev. Bruce A. Lawler.
Res.: P.O. Box 457, 51053-0457. Tel: 712-275-4238. Email: stjoseph@evertek.net.
Catechesis/Religious Program—Students 35.

SCRANTON, GREENE CO., ST. PAUL'S (1926), (German—Irish), Rev. Steven J. McLoud.
403 State St., 51462-8419.
Res. & Mailing Address: 807 Head St., P.O. Box

128, Churdan, 50050. Tel: 515-389-3625 (Church); Fax: 515-389-3797. Email: timberhat@wccta.net. Web: www.st-paul-catholic-church.org.
Catechesis/Religious Program—Tel: 515-386-4010; Fax: 515-386-3672. Email: ssduffy@yahoo.com. Web: www.stjosephjefferson.net. Students 9.

SHELDON, O'BRIEN CO., ST. PATRICK'S (1873), (Irish), [CEM] Rev. Robert J. Schimmer.
Res.: 310 10th St., 51201-1530. Tel: 712-324-3220; Fax: 712-324-3559.
School—1020 4th Ave., 51201. Tel: 712-324-3181. Lay Teachers 11; Students 84.
Catechesis/Religious Program—Tel: 712-724-6513. Students 199.

SIBLEY, OSCEOLA CO., ST. ANDREW'S (1896) [CEM] Rev. John A. Vakulskas Jr.
Res.: 716 Eighth St., 51249-0130. Tel: 712-754-3311. Email: st.andrewsibley@yahoo.com.
Catechesis/Religious Program—Tel: 712-754-2739; Fax: 712-754-4042. Students 81.

SIOUX RAPIDS, BUENA VISTA CO., ST. JOSEPH (1886) [CEM] Rev. Allan A. Reicks.
Res.: 708 Thomas St., P.O. Box 450, 50585-0450. Tel: 712-283-2765.
Catechesis/Religious Program—Students 29.

SPENCER, CLAY CO., SACRED HEART (1883) Revs. William A. Schreiber; Thomas J. Flannagan; Deacon Jack Easter, (Retired).
Res.: 1111 4th Ave. W., P.O. Box 817, 51301-0817. Tel: 712-262-3047; Fax: 712-262-4067. Email: spncrsh@juno.com. Web: www.spencersacredheart.com.
School—Tel: 712-262-6428. Lay Teachers 13; Students 201.
Catechesis/Religious Program—Tel: 712-262-4486. Students 256.

SPIRIT LAKE, DICKINSON CO., ST. MARY'S (1914) [CEM] Rev. James R. Smith.
Res.: 1005 Hill Ave., P.O. Box 354, 51360-0354. Tel: 712-336-1742; Fax: 712-336-1013.
Catechesis/Religious Program—Tel: 712-336-1742. Students 212.

STORM LAKE, BUENA VISTA CO., ST. MARY'S (1872) [CEM] Rev. Bruce A. Lawler; Deacon Mark Prosser.
Res.: Third & Seneca Sts., P.O. Box 1106, 50588-1106. Tel: 712-732-3110; Fax: 712-732-8173. Email: parish@stormlakecatholic.com. Web: www.stormlakecatholic.com.
School—Elementary & High School, Tel: 712-732-1856 (Elementary); 712-732-4166 (High School); Fax: 712-732-4590. Email: bmach@stormlakecatholic.com. Web: www.stmarys-storm.pvt.k12.ia.us. Bev Mach, Prin. Lay Teachers 32; Students 389; Preschool 45.
Catechesis/Religious Program—Tel: 712-732-5160. Email: cary@iw.net. Web: www.stormlakecatholic.com. Students 474.

STRUBLE, PLYMOUTH CO., ST. JOSEPH'S (1903) [CEM 2] Rev. Daniel M. Greving.
Mailing Address: P.O. Box 175, Merrill, 51038. Tel: 712-938-2236.
Catechesis/Religious Program—Tel: 712-546-5223. Students 28.

SUTHERLAND, O'BRIEN CO., SACRED HEART (1883) [CEM] Rev. Timothy J. Hogan.
Res.: P.O. Box 555, Sanborn, 51248. Tel: 712-930-3423.
Catechesis/Religious Program—Tel: 712-928-2626. Students 64.
Mission—St. Anthony of Padua [CEM] Primghar.

TEMPLETON, CARROLL CO., SACRED HEART (1882) [CEM] Rev. Dale E. Reiff.
Res.: Box 13, Halbur, 51444. Tel: 712-658-2464; Fax: 712-658-2464.
Parish is a member of the consolidated K-12 Kuemper Catholic School System, Carroll, IA. Please refer to Kuemper Catholic School System under Inter-Parochial Schools in the Institution section.
Catechesis/Religious Program—Tel: 712-792-0513 (Carroll); 712-653-2131 (Manning). Students 13.

VAIL, CRAWFORD CO., ST. ANN'S (1878) [CEM] Rev. Paul Kelly.
Res.: P.O. Box 158, 51465-0158. Tel: 712-677-5556. See Kuemper Catholic School System, Carroll under Inter-Parochial Schools located in the Institution section.
Catechesis/Religious Program—Tel: 712-677-5556. Students 59.

VARINA, POCAHONTAS CO., ST. COLUMBKILLE'S (1882) [CEM] Rev. Siby Punnoose (India).
Res.: Box 339, Fonda, 50540-0339. Tel: 712-288-6480; Fax: 712-288-4465. Email: olgc@iowatelecom.net.
Catechesis/Religious Program—Students 12.

WALL LAKE, SAC CO., ST. JOSEPH'S (1878), (German), Rev. John J. McGuirk.
Res.: P.O. Box 130, 51466-0130. Tel: 712-664-2915.
Catechesis/Religious Program—Tel: 712-664-2910. Students 155.

WESLEY, KOSSUTH CO., ST. JOSEPH'S (1891) [CEM] Rev. Randy L. Schon.
Res.: 403 East St., S., P.O. Box 38, 50483-0038. Tel: 515-679-4279 (Residence); 515-679-4135 (Parish Hall). Email: stjwesley@msn.com.
School—Seton Elementary, Tel: 515-295-3509. Consolidation of St. Cecelia, Algona; St. Benedict & St. Joseph, Wesley; St. Michael's, Whittemore; St. Joseph, Bode. Students 18.
High School—Bishop Garrigan High School, Tel: 515-295-3521; Fax: 515-295-7739. Students 20.
Catechesis/Religious Program—Students 18.

WEST BEND, PALO ALTO CO., SS. PETER AND PAUL (1888) [CEM] Rev. Thomas J. Hart; Deacon Gerald Streit.
Res.: P.O. Box 16, 50597-0316. Tel: 515-887-3333; Fax: 515-887-3334.
Catechesis/Religious Program—Tel: 515-887-4586. Students 104.

WHITTEMORE, KOSSUTH CO., ST. MICHAEL'S (1889) [CEM] Rev. Victor Ramaeker; Deacon Joseph Straub.
Res.: P.O. Box 337, 50598-0337. Tel: 515-884-2669; Fax: 515-884-2618. Email: stmwhitt@ncn.net.
Catechesis/Religious Program— See separate listing at St. Cecelia, Algona. Students 21.

WILLEY, CARROLL CO., ST. MARY'S (1882) [CEM] Rev. Timothy A. Johnson.
Rectory—421 E. Bluff, Carroll, 51401.
Res.: 205 Olympic Ave., Carroll, 51401. Tel: 712-792-4386; Fax: 712-792-8038. Email: 1schreck@win-4-u.biz. Web: www.stmaryswilley.com.
Please see Kuemper Catholic School System under Inter-Parochial Schools located in the Institution Section
Catechesis/Religious Program—Tel: 712-792-4386. Students 11.

WOODWARD, BOONE CO., ST. JOHN OF GOD (1965), (State Hospital and School) Rev. Timothy J. Boekelman.
Res.: 207 Gerald St., Madrid, 50156-1464. Tel: 515-795-2731; Fax: 515-795-2731.

Chaplains of Public Institutions

SIOUX CITY. *Mercy Medical Center*. Rev. Richard A. Sitzmann.
CARROLL. *St. Anthony Regional Hospital*. Revs. John J. Gerald (India), Timothy A. Johnson.
CHEROKEE. *State Mental Health Institute*. Vacant.
FORT DODGE. *Marian Village*. Vacant.
Trinity Regional Hospital. Sr. M. Gertrude Keefe, R.S.M.
ROCKWELL CITY. *Calhoun County State Reformatory, Minimum Security for Men*. Rev. Richard S. Ries.
WOODWARD. *Woodward State Hospital and School*. Rev. Timothy J. Boekelman.

Special Assignment:
Revs.—
Larkin, Michael T., Sioux City Nursing Homes, 1122 Grandview Blvd., Apt. 7, 51103-4398. Tel: 712-258-5202
Meinen, Dennis W. (Retired), Ministry to People with Disabilities, 1701 W. 25th St., 51103-1799. Tel: 712-258-9120

On Duty Outside the Diocese:
Revs.—
Barrett, Miles J., 103 Shady Side Ln., New Bern, NC 28562.
Becker, Nickolas L.
Kurzak, John F., 9210 Jole Cove, San Antonio, TX 78239. Tel: 210-650-3238

Retired:
Rev. Msgrs.—
Augustine, Roger J., V.G., 3012 Jackson St., 51104.
Donahoe, Thomas, 916 3 Williams Dr., Fort Dodge, 50501. Tel: 515-573-8612
Hood, Mervin J., 629 Central Ave., #609, Fort Dodge. Tel: 515-576-3268
Lyon, Gerald F., Marian Hall, 1122 Grandview Blvd., 51105. Tel: 712-258-2033
Ruba, Nicholas J., 403 Cleveland Ct., Remsen, 51050. Tel: 712-786-2719
Ziegmann, Leonard M., P.O. Box 3379, 51102-3379.
Revs.—
Adams, Edmond F., 2661 3rd. Ave. N., Fort Dodge, 50501. Tel: 515-955-4859
Arts, Paul-Louis, 149 Stoney Point Drive, Storm Lake, 50588-7713.
Beacom, Vincent L., 1701 W. 25th St., 51103.
Boes, Clair L., 55 W. Clifton Ave., Apt. 303, 51104.
Boes, Marvin, 55 W. Clifton Ave., Apt. 303, 51104. Tel: 712-277-2046
Cain, John F., 1410 W. 4th St., Apt. B, Spencer, 51301.
Ceperley, Eugene F., Marian Village, 2320 6th Ave. N., Apt. 102, Fort Dodge, 50501.
Condon, Robert M., 900 N. 90th, Apt. 211, Omaha, NE 68114-2704.
Cosgrove, Jerome P., 1122 Grandview Blvd., Apt. 6, 51103.
Degen, Jerome A., Marian Village, 2320 6th Ave. N. Apt. 105, Fort Dodge, 50501. Tel: 515-295-3329
Devine, William B., 1703 W. 25th St., Apt. 212, 51103. Tel: 712-234-0857
Fangman, James E., 801 W. Division St., Ogden, 50212. Tel: 515-275-4799
Fangman, Robert M., 904 Amy Cir., Carroll, 51401.
Fisch, Gerald M., 122 Grandview Blvd., Apt. 6, 51103. Tel: 712-258-3892
Fransco, Peter J., 1803 Bruce St., Ruthven, 51358. Tel: 712-837-4323
Friedman, Cecil H., 1703 E. Lucas St., Algona, 50511. Tel: 515-295-5403
Geelan, Thomas E., 1806 Rolling St., Ruthven, 51358.
Grendler, Albert O., P.O. Box 34, Okoboji, 51355-0034.
Hartz, Gerald A., 3800 Littlefalls Ct., Bakersfield, CA 93312. Tel: 661-327-2744
Kielbasa, Richard, Marian Village, 2320 6th Ave., N., Apt. F3, Fort Dodge, 50501. Tel: 515-955-8990
Koster, Dale F., W. St., Apt. 8, P.O. Box 264, Auburn, 51433.
Leiting, Robert L., 240 S. Clark St., Carroll, 51401. Tel: 712-792-3122
Lynch, Daniel C., 407 S. 13th St., Sac City, 50583.
Macke, Richard J., 100 Circle Dr., Lake City, 51449.
McAlpin, James C.
McAlpine, Harry D., 1412 W. 4th St., Apt. C, Spencer, 51301. Tel: 712-580-4414
McCormick, James D., 301 E. 4th St., P.O. Box 187, Auburn, 51433-0187.
McCoy, Alfred E., P.O. Box 114, 51102. Tel: 712-279-5461
Meinen, Dennis W., 1701 W. 25th St., 51103-1705.
Nemmers, Francis J., P.O. Box 244, Bancroft, 50517-0244. Tel: 515-885-0212
Nooney, Patrick J., 2638 4th Ave. N., Apt. H, Fort Dodge, 50501-5795. Tel: 515-576-5567
Remmes, Richard R., P.O. Box 20, Arcadia, 51430. Tel: 712-689-2744
Riesberg, Leo L., Steffes Apts., 304 S. Clark St., Apt. 2, Carroll, 51401-3067. Tel: 712-792-8560
Sefcik, Dennis L., 53133 210 St., Pocahontas, 50574.
Seuntjens, LeRoy L., 112 Grandview Blvd., Apt. 1, 51103.
Sitzmann, Eugene E., 975 540th St., Cherokee, 51012-7151. Tel: 712-225-2131
Smith, Donald R., 2300 Indian Hills Dr., Apt. 1-114, 51104. Tel: 712-239-5865
Stapenhorst, Verne P., 106 N. Broadway St., West Bend, 50597.
Thiele, Robert A., 101 N. Earl, Lake City, 51449. Tel: 712-464-8024
Topf, Thomas J., 1122 Grandview Blvd., Apt. 8, 51103.
Waite, Patrick J., 5682 Tulane St., San Diego, CA 92122-3244.
Walding, Eugene F., 1707 W. 25th St., Apt. 409, 51103-1799.
Wieling, Raymond P., 3015 Chicago Ave., 51106-1259. Tel: 712-276-7065
Wingert, D. William, 110 W. Maple Dr., Hartley, 51346-7606. Tel: 712-728-9911
Wingert, Gerald R., 216 W. Nebraska, Algona, 50511-2608. Tel: 515-295-3123
Zensen, Gerald F., P.O. Box 65, Oto, 51044-0067.

Permanent Deacons:
Berger, William J., St. Michael's, Sioux City
Bertrand, Gerald L., Holy Name, Marcus
Billing, Richard, Blessed Sacrament, Sioux City
Black, William, St. Cecelia, Algona
Brown, David, Sacred Heart, Boone
Doocy, Philip F., St. John the Baptist, Bancroft
Easter, Jack L., (Unassigned)
Forrest, Ronald M., (Unassigned)
Gallagher, Jeffrey F., Holy Name, Rock Rapids
Hand, Michael J., Church of the Nativity, Sioux City
Hart, M. Peter, St. Joseph, Milford
Heffernan, John J., Blessed Sacrament Church, Sioux City
Karpuk, Fred P., Blessed Sacrament Church, Sioux City
Kunecke, Donald L., St. Columbkille, Churdan
Kunkel, Donald M., St. Joseph Church, LeMars
Larson, Robert, St. Cecelia, Algona
Lenz, Robert D., St. Mary's Church, Pomeroy
MacDonald, W. B., St. Cecelia Church, Algona
Meiners, Louis, St. Joseph, Dedham
Miller, Ed, Holy Spirit, Carroll
Morgan, Tom, St. John's, Onawa
Murphy, Tim, St. Lawrence, Carroll
Pietz, Ronald C., St. Joseph Church, Sioux City
Portz, Ray, St. Patrick, Sheldon
Prosser, Mark, St. Mary, Storm Lake

Reicks, Jerome A., St. Michael Church, Sioux City
Reuter, Anthony C., Bella Vista, AR 72715
Rosburg, Ray, St. Mary, Mapleton
Rupp, J. LeRoy, Immaculate Conception Church, Cherokee
Sampson, Gregory, Holy Spirit, Carroll
Sands, James H., St. Boniface, Sioux City
Schon, Gary, St. Elizabeth Seton, Glidden
Scurlock, Joseph, St. John, Onawa
Sitzman, Larry K., St. Michael's Church, Sioux City
Stone, Byron, St. Joseph, Wall Lake
Stover, Michael, Sacred Heart, Ida Grove
Straub, Joseph J., St. Michael's Church, Whittmore
Streit, Gerald B., Sts. Peter & Paul Church, West Bend
Sullivan, Eldon, Our Lady of Good Counsel, Fonda
Wyant, Mark, Sacred Heart Church, Sioux City

INSTITUTIONS LOCATED IN THE DIOCESE

[A] COLLEGES AND UNIVERSITIES

SIOUX CITY. *Briar Cliff University*, 3303 Rebecca St., P.O. Box 2100, 51104-2100. Tel: 712-279-5200; Fax: 712-279-5410. Web: www.briarcliff.edu. Bev Wharton, Pres.; Deidre Engel, Registrar; Sharisue Wilcoxon, Vice Pres. Enrollment Mgmt.; Rev. Bradley C. Pelzel; Debora Robertson, Librarian. Sisters of St. Francis of the Holy Family of Dubuque, Iowa., Liberal Arts University. Sisters 10; Lay Teachers 59; Lay Administrators & Staff 88; Students 1,158.

[B] INTER-PAROCHIAL SCHOOLS

SIOUX CITY. *Bishop Heelan Catholic Schools*, (Grades PreK-12), 1018 Grandview Blvd., 51103. Tel: 712-252-1350; Fax: 712-252-9086. Email: walsh@bishopheelan.org. Web: www.bishopheelan.org. Rev. Patrick Walsh, Pres. Serving the parishes of Nativity, Immaculate Conception, Cathedral, St. Boniface, St. Joseph, Blessed Sacrament, Sacred Heart, St. Michael. Priests 1; Sisters 2; Lay Teachers 125; Students 1,650; Total Staff 46.

Bishop Heelan High School, 1021 Douglas St., 51104. Tel: 712-252-0573; Fax: 712-252-4897. Web: www.bishopheelan.org. Mr. Chris Bork, Prin.; Sr. Colane Recker, Librarian. Priests 1; Lay Teachers 45; Students 525.

Holy Cross School-Blessed Sacrament Center, 3030 Jackson St., 51104. Tel: 712-277-4739; Fax: 712-258-3698. Michael Sweeney, Prin.; Pam Wilmes, Librarian. Consolidated with St. Michael. Lay Teachers 23; Students 318.

St. Michael (Grades K-2), 4105 Harrison, 51108. Tel: 712-239-1090; Fax: 712-239-8546. Web: www-.bishopheelan.org. Michael Sweeney, Prin.; Pam Wilmes, Librarian. Consolidated with Blessed Sacrament. Lay Teachers 11; Students 139.

Sacred Heart (Grades K-8), 5010 Military Rd., 51103. Tel: 712-233-1624; Fax: 712-233-1469. Email: ferrieb@bishopheelan.org. Web: www.bishopheelan-.org. Brenda Ferrie, Prin.; Sarah Case, Librarian. Lay Teachers 25; Students 334; Total Staff 52.

Mater Dei School Immaculate Conception Center (Grades K-5), 3719 Ridge Ave., 51106. Tel: 712-276-6216; Fax: 712-274-1221. Web: www.bishopheelan-.org. Ms. Mary Fischer, Prin.; Mrs. Vicky Samuelson, Librarian. Lay Teachers 22; Students 233.

Mater Dei School Nativity Center (Grades 6-8), 4242 Natalia Way, 51106-4099. Tel: 712-276-3022; Fax: 712-274-2703. Email: fischerm@bishopheelan.org. Web: www.bishopheel-an.org. Ms. Mary Fischer, Prin. Consolidated with Immaculate Conception Parish. Lay Teachers 12; Total Enrollment 104.

ALGONA. *Bishop Garrigan Catholic High School*, 1224 N. McCoy St., 50511. Tel: 515-295-3521; Fax: 515-295-7739. Email: stencem@garrigan.pvt.k12.ia.us. Web: www.garrigan.unlimitedweb.net. Mr. Eugene Meister, Pres.; Mr. Michael M. Stence, Prin. Serving the parishes at Algona, St. Benedict, Bode, Wesley, and Whittemore. Priests 1; Sisters 1; Deacons 1; Lay Teachers 18; Students 172.

CARROLL. *Kuemper Catholic School System*, 116 S. East St., 51401. Tel: 712-792-3313; Fax: 712-792-8073. Email: vrhenkenius@keumper.org. Web: www.kuemper.org. Mr. Vern Henkenius, Interim Pres. Grades K-12 Lay Teachers 93; Students 1,140.

Holy Spirit Center (Grades K-3), 201 S. Clark St., 51401. Tel: 712-792-3610. Mrs. Mary Dobson, Prin.

St. Angela Center (Grades 4-5), 116 N. East St., 51401. Tel: 710-792-8071. Mrs. Mary Dobson, Prin.

St. Lawrence Center (Grades 6-8), 1519 N. West St., 51401. Tel: 712-792-2123. Mr. Earl Schiltz, Prin.

Kuemper Catholic High School, 109 S. Clark St., 51401. Tel: 712-792-3596. Mrs. Penny Miller, Prin.

FORT DODGE. *Fort Dodge Catholic Schools, Inc.*, (Grades K-12), 2220 4th Ave. N., 50501. Tel: 515-955-6077; Fax: 515-955-8473. Web: www.st-edmund.pvt.k12.ia.us. Rev. Msgr. Kevin C. McCoy, S.T.D., Interim Pres.; Mr. Chuck Elbert, Prin.; Mr. Thomas Miklo, Dir. Devel.; Linda Mitchell, Prin. Sisters 1; Lay Teachers 62; Students 869.

GRANVILLE. *Spalding Catholic Schools, Inc.* 51022. Tel: 712-727-3451; Fax: 712-727-3455. Email: gniichel@spalding-catholic.pvt.k12.ia.us. Web: www.spalding-catholic.pvt.k12.ia.us. Very Rev. Richard D. Ball, V.F.; Mr. Gary Niichel, Prin.; Kathy Alons, Prin. Serving the parishes of Granville; Alton and Hospers. Priests 2; Lay Teachers 16; Students 189.

LE MARS. *Gehlen Catholic School* (1875) 709 Plymouth St. N.E., 51031. Tel: 712-546-4181; Fax: 712-546-9384. Email: l_niebuhr@gehlencatholic.com. Web: www.gehlencatholic.com. Rev. Kevin M. Richter, Pres.; Jeff Alesch, Prin. (7-12); Lorie A. Nussbaum, Prin. (K-6); Lisa Niebuhr, Devel. Dir.; Melinda Scheitler, Business Mgr.; Pat Beitelspacher, Librarian. Lay Teachers 36; Students 440.

REMSEN. *St. Mary's High School*, 523 Madison, 51050. Tel: 712-786-1433; Fax: 712-786-2499. Web: www.remsenstmarys.org. John Hughes, Prin. 9-12; Ms. Linda Loutsch, Librarian. Priests 1; Lay Teachers 12; Students 78.

STORM LAKE. *St. Mary's High School* 50588. Tel: 712-732-4166; Fax: 712-732-4590. Email: bmach@stmarys-storm.pvt-K12.ia.us. Ronald Olberding, Prin. (K-4); Bev Mach, Prin. (5-12). Serving St. Mary's. Sisters 1; Lay Teachers 11; Students 70.

[C] GENERAL HOSPITALS

SIOUX CITY. *Mercy Medical Center - Sioux City*, 801 Fifth St., 51101. Tel: 712-279-2010; Fax: 712-279-2494. Email: spencerj@mercyhealth.com. Web: www.mercy-siouxcity.com. Robert Peebles, Interim Pres. & CEO; Rev. Richard A. Sitzmann, Chap.; Sr. Marlys Becker, O.S.F., Chap.; Rev. Dennis Grohn, Lutheran Chap.; Rev. B. J. Van Kalsbeek, Reformed Presbyterian Chap.; Maria Baker, Chap.; Rev. Dennis W. Meinen, Chap. (Retired). Trinity Health, Catholic Health Ministries Sisters 1; Total Staff 1,296; Bed Capacity 484; Patients Assisted Annually 103,903.

CARROLL. *St. Anthony Regional Hospital*, 311 S. Clark St., P.O. Box 628, 51401. Tel: 712-792-3581; Fax: 712-792-2124. Email: garyr@stanthonyhospital.org. Web: www.StAnthonyHospital.org. Gary P. Riedmann, Pres.; Revs. Timothy A. Johnson; John J. Gerald (India). Bed Capacity 99; Patients Assisted Annually 73,976; Total Staff 650.

ESTHERVILLE. *Avera Holy Family Health*, 826 N. Eighth St., 51334. Tel: 712-362-2631; Fax: 712-362-2636. Email: info@avera-holyfamily.org. Web: www.avera-holyfamily.org. Sisters of the Presentation of the B.V.M. (Aberdeen, SD) & Benedictine Sisters of Sacred Heart Monastery, (Yanton, SD). Bed Capacity 25; Patients Assisted Annually 35,281; Total Staff 140.

Holy Family Hospital Foundation. Tel: 712-362-2631; Fax: 712-362-2636.

[D] HOMES FOR THE AGED

SIOUX CITY. *Holy Spirit Retirement Home*, 1701 W. 25th St., 51103. Tel: 712-252-2726. Patrick J. Tomscha, Admin.; Rev. Dennis W. Meinen (Retired). Total in Residence 100; Total Assisted 150; Total Staff 139.

CARROLL. *St. Anthony Nursing Home* (1963) 406 E. Anthony St., 51401. Tel: 712-792-3581; Fax: 712-792-8288. Email: stanthony@netins.net. Web: www.netins.net/showcase/sarh. Gary Riedmann, Admin.; Peg Scheidt, Dir. Pastoral Care. Residents 79; Total Staff 68.

FORT DODGE. *The Marian Home*, 2400 Sixth Ave. N., 50501. Tel: 515-576-1138; Fax: 515-576-5099. Email: marianhome1@dodgenet.com. Web: www.marianhome.com. Ms. Tracy Gailey, Admin. Guests 97; Total in Residence 115; Total Staff 125.

[E] CONVENTS AND RESIDENCES FOR SISTERS

SIOUX CITY. *Monastery of the Discalced Carmelite Nuns*, 2901 S. Cecelia St., 51106-3299. Tel: 712-276-1680; Fax: 712-276-5966. Email: carmelsc@msn.com. Web: www.carmelsc.org. Sr. Kateri Marie of the Eucharist, O.C.D., Prioress. Solemn Professed 10.

[F] SECULAR INSTITUTES

CARROLL. *Opus Spiritus Sancti* (1950) 301 E. 4th St., Auburn, 51433. Tel: 712-688-2253. Rev. James D. McCormick, Regl. Coord. Community Activities & Member Secular Institute of Priests (Retired).

[G] MISCELLANEOUS

SIOUX CITY. *The Catholic Schools Foundation of the Diocese of Sioux City* (1968) 1821 Jackson St., 51105. Tel: 712-255-7933; Fax: 712-233-7598. Email: danr@scdiocese.org. Web: www.scdiocese.org.

Holy Spirit Retirement Home Foundation, Inc., 1701 W. 25th St., 51103. Tel: 712-252-2726; Fax: 712-293-1953. Most Rev. Ralph Walker Nickless, Dir.; Patrick J. Tomscha, Dir.; Martha Burchard, Pres.

Monsignor Lafferty Tuition Foundation, 1821 Jackson St., 51105. Tel: 712-255-7933. Email: danr@scdiocese.org. Web: scdiocese.org. Mr. Dan Ryan, Contact Person & Supt. Schools.

ALGONA. *Friends of Garrigan High School, Inc.*, Garrigan High School, 1224 N. McCoy, 50511. Tel: 515-295-3521.

CARROLL. *St. Anthony Foundation*, 311 S. Clark St., 51401. Tel: 712-792-3581; Fax: 712-792-2124. Email: esmith@stanthonyhospital.org. Web: www.StAnthonyHospital.org. Mr. Gary P. Riedmann, CEO.

Kuemper Catholic Schools Foundation, Inc. (1985) 116 S. East St., 51401. Tel: 712-792-3313; Fax: 712-792-8073. Web: www.kuemper.org. Mr. Vern Henkenius, Pres.

Orchard View, Inc., 421 S. Clark St., 51401. Tel: 712-792-2042; Fax: 712-792-2124. Email: esmith@stanthonyhospital.org. Web: www.StAnthonyHospital.org. Gary P. Riedmann, Admin. Franciscan Sisters of Perpetual Adoration. Total in Residence 49.

FORT DODGE. *Saint Edmond Catholic Schools Foundation*, 2220 4th Ave. N., 50501. Tel: 515-955-6077; Fax: 515-955-8473. Email: frkevin@fdcatholic.com. Web: www.st-edmond.pvt.k12.ia.us. Rev. Msgr. Kevin C. McCoy, S.T.D., Interim Pres.; Linda Mitchell, Prin.; Tom Miklo, Devel. Dir.; Tim Hancock, Business Mgr.

Holy Trinity Parish Cemetery Improvement Society, 2220 4th Ave N., 50501. Tel: 515-573-3616. Rev. Msgr. Kevin C. McCoy, S.T.D., Contact Person.

Holy Trinity Parish Foundation of Webster County, 2220 4th Ave N., 50501. Tel: 515-573-3616; Fax: 515-955-8473. Email: fdcatholic@fdcatholic.com. Rev. Msgr. Kevin C. McCoy, S.T.D.

The Marian Home Foundation, 2400 6th Ave. N., 50501. Tel: 515-576-1138; Fax: 515-576-5099. Email: marianhome1@dodgenet.com.

STORM LAKE. *St. Mary's Foundation of Storm Lake, Iowa*, 320 Seneca St., P.O. Box 1106, 50588. Tel: 712-732-3110; Fax: 712-732-8173. Email: smalumni@iw.net. Web: www.stormlakecatholic.com. Rev. Bruce A. Lawler.

WEST BEND. *Grotto of the Redemption*, P.O. Box 376, 50597. Tel: 515-887-2371; Fax: 515-887-2372. Email: info@westbendgrotto.com. Web: www.westbendgrotto.com.

RELIGIOUS INSTITUTES OF WOMEN REPRESENTED IN THE DIOCESE

For further details refer to the corresponding bracketed number in the Religious Institutes of Men or Women section.

[0230]—*Benedictine Sisters of the Pontifical Jurisdiction*—O.S.B.
[1780]—*Congregation of the Sisters of the Third Order of St. Francis of Perpetual Adoration* (Central Prov.)—F.S.P.A.
[0420]—*Discalced Carmelite Nuns*—O.C.D.
[1070-20]—*Dominican Sisters Order of Preachers* (Tacoma, WA)—O.P.
[]—*Opus Spiritus Sancti*—O.S.S.
[1680]—*School Sisters of St. Francis*—S.S.S.F.
[]—*Sisters For Christian Community*—S.F.C.C.
[0430]—*Sisters of Charity of the Blessed Virgin Mary*—B.V.M.
[2575]—*Sisters of Mercy of the Americas* (Cedar Rapids Regional Community)—R.S.M.
[2575]—*Sisters of Mercy of the Union in USA Comm.* Cedar Rapids—O.S.F.
[1705]—*Sisters of St. Francis of Assisi*—O.S.F.
[1570]—*Sisters of St. Francis of the Holy Family*—O.S.F.
[1540]—*Sisters of St. Francis, Clinton, IA*—O.S.F.
[2350]—*Sisters of the Living Word*—S.L.W.
[3320]—*Sisters of the Presentation of the B.V.M.* Dubuque, IA & Aberdeen, SD—P.B.V.M.
[1720]—*Sisters of the Third Order Regular of St. Francis of the Congregation of Our Lady of Lourdes*—O.S.F.

DIOCESAN CEMETERIES

SIOUX CITY. *Calvary*, Office: 1821 Jackson St., P.O. Box 3379, 51102-3379. Tel: 712-233-7511; Fax: 712-233-7598.

LEMARS. *Calvary Cemetery*, 20 6th Ave. N.E., 51031. Tel: 712-546-5223; Fax: 712-546-8346. Janeen Reuter, Contact Person.

NECROLOGY

† Murray, Edward, Spencer, IA Sacred Heart—Died Oct. 6, 2009

† Schumacher, Eugene T., (Retired)—Died May 13, 2009

† White, Lloyd W., (Retired)—Died May 22, 2009

An asterisk (*) denotes an organization that has established tax-exempt status directly with the IRS and is not covered by the USCCB Group Ruling.

Diocese of Sioux Falls

(Dioecesis Siouxormensis)

Most Reverend

PAUL J. SWAIN

Bishop of Sioux Falls; ordained to priesthood May 27, 1988, Diocese of Madison; appointed Bishop of Sioux Falls August 31, 2006; Episcopal ordination October 26, 2006. *Chancery Office: 523 N. Duluth Ave., Sioux Falls, SD 57104.*

Chancery Office: 523 N. Duluth Ave., Sioux Falls, SD 57104. Tel: 605-334-9861; Fax: 605-334-2092.

Web: sfcatholic.org

Email: jklein@sfcatholic.org

ESTABLISHED NOVEMBER 12, 1889.

Square Miles 35,091.

Comprises that part of the State of South Dakota East of the Missouri River.

For legal titles of parishes and diocesan institutions, consult the Chancery Office.

STATISTICAL OVERVIEW

Personnel	
Bishop	1
Abbots	1
Retired Abbots	2
Priests: Diocesan Active in Diocese	75
Priests: Diocesan Active Outside Diocese	5
Priests: Retired, Sick or Absent	36
Number of Diocesan Priests	116
Religious Priests in Diocese	28
Total Priests in Diocese	144
Extern Priests in Diocese	10
Ordinations:	
Diocesan Priests	2
Permanent Deacons in Diocese	36
Total Brothers	8
Total Sisters	299
Parishes	
Parishes	150
With Resident Pastor:	
Resident Diocesan Priests	60
Resident Religious Priests	8
Without Resident Pastor:	
Administered by Priests	76
Administered by Professed Religious Men	1
Administered by Pastoral Teams, etc.	2
Completely Vacant	3
Professional Ministry Personnel:	
Brothers	1
Sisters	13
Lay Ministers	42
Welfare	
Catholic Hospitals	11
Total Assisted	720,000
Special Centers for Social Services	20
Total Assisted	50,400
Educational	
Diocesan Students in Other Seminaries	22
Total Seminarians	22
Colleges and Universities	2
Total Students	1,800
High Schools, Diocesan and Parish	3
Total Students	991
Elementary Schools, Diocesan and Parish	21
Total Students	4,157
Catechesis/Religious Education:	
High School Students	6,114
Elementary Students	7,188
Total Students under Catholic Instruction	20,272
Teachers in the Diocese:	
Priests	7
Sisters	2
Lay Teachers	332
Vital Statistics	
Receptions into the Church:	
Infant Baptism Totals	1,571
Minor Baptism Totals	70
Adult Baptism Totals	50
Received into Full Communion	242
First Communions	1,506
Confirmations	1,703
Marriages:	
Catholic	294
Interfaith	231
Total Marriages	525
Deaths	951
Total Catholic Population	124,972
Total Population	524,153

Former Bishops—Rt. Revs. MARTIN MARTY, O.S.B., D.D., ord. Sept. 14, 1856; appt. Bishop of Tiberias, Aug. 8, 1879; appt. Vicar Apostolic of Dakota, Aug. 12, 1879; consecrated Feb. 1, 1880; Bishop of Sioux Falls, 1889; transferred to St. Cloud, MN, 1894; died Sept. 19, 1896; THOMAS O'GORMAN, D.D., ord. Nov. 5, 1865; appt. Jan. 24, 1896; consecrated April 19, 1896; died Sept. 18, 1921; Most Revs. BERNARD J. MAHONEY, D.D., ord. Feb. 27, 1904; appt. May 22, 1922; consecrated June 29, 1922; died March 20, 1939; WILLIAM O. BRADY, S.T.D., D.D., appt. Bishop of Sioux Falls, June 10, 1939; consecrated Aug. 24, 1939; appt. Coadjutor of St. Paul, June 21, 1956; succeeded to the See, Oct. 11, 1956; died Oct. 1, 1961; LAMBERT A. HOCH, D.D., ord. May 30, 1928; Bishop of Bismarck; appt. Jan. 23, 1952; consecrated March 25, 1952; transferred to Sioux Falls, Nov. 27, 1956; retired June 13, 1978; died June 27, 1990; PAUL V. DUDLEY, D.D., ord. June 2, 1951; ord. Auxiliary Bishop of Archdiocese of St. Paul/Minneapolis, Jan. 25, 1977; appt. Bishop of Sioux Falls Sept. 26, 1978; installed Dec. 13, 1978; retired March 21, 1995; died Nov. 20, 2006; ROBERT J. CARLSON, ord. May 22, 1970; appt. Titular Bishop of Aviocala and Auxiliary Bishop of Saint Paul and Minneapolis Nov. 22, 1983; cons. Jan. 11, 1984; appt. Coadjutor Bishop of Sioux Falls Jan. 13, 1994; Succeeded to the See March 21, 1995; appt. Bishop of Saginaw Dec. 29, 2004; appt. Archbishop of St. Louis April 21, 2009.

Vicar General—Rev. CHARLES L. CIMPL, 523 N. Duluth Ave., Sioux Falls, 57104.

Episcopal Vicar for Clergy—VACANT.

Chancery Office—523 N. Duluth Ave., Sioux Falls, 57104. Tel: 605-334-9861; Fax: 605-334-2092. Refer all official business to this address.

Chancellor—Mr. JEROME KLEIN, 523 N. Duluth Ave., Sioux Falls, 57104. Tel: 605-988-3745.

Vice Chancellors—Mr. MATTHEW ALTHOFF. Tel: 605-988-3761; Rev. JAMES E. MASON. Tel: 605-988-3749. 523 N. Duluth Ave., Sioux Falls, 57104.

Diocesan Tribunal—523 N. Duluth Ave., Sioux Falls, 57104. Tel: 605-988-3757.

Judicial Vicar—Rev. GREGORY TSCHAKERT.

Promoter of Justice—VACANT.

Tribunal Judges—Revs. AL KRZYZOPOLSKI (Retired); RODNEY FARKE; KENNETH J. KOSTER; Miss THERESE IVERS, J.C.L.; Revs. JOHN LANTSBERGER; CHARLES L. CIMPL; GARY TERNES, J.C.L.; Deacon WILLIAM FRANKMAN; Rev. SCOTT TRAYNOR, J.C.L.

Defenders of the Matrimonial Bond—Rev. GREGORY TSCHAKERT; Sr. LYNN MARIE WELBIG, J.C.L., Ph.D.; Rev. JAMES FRIEDRICH.

Director of Matrimonial Tribunal—Sr. LYNN MARIE WELBIG, J.C.L., Ph.D.

Auditors—Deacon WILLIAM FRANKMAN; Sr. KATHLEEN BIERNE, P.B.V.M., J.C.L.; HEIDI EVERS.

Notary of Matrimonial Tribunal—Ms. VICKIE BEACH, Ecclesiastical Notary.

Diocesan Consultors—Revs. CHARLES L. CIMPL; DAVID A. DESMOND; DAVID KROGMAN; JAMES E. MASON; GREGORY TSCHAKERT; MICHAEL WENSING.

Consilium Administrationis— Most Rev. Bishop, Vicar General, Chancellor.

Presbyteral Council—Revs. CHARLES L. CIMPL; THOMAS CLEMENT; DAVID A. DESMOND; BRIAN SIMON; DAVID KROGMAN; JAMES E. MASON; SCOTT TRAYNOR; WILLIAM PITCAVAGE, S.C.J.; DEWAYNE KAYSER; SHANE STEVENS; GREGORY TSCHAKERT.

Diocesan Offices and Directors

Apostleship of Prayer—Mailing Address: 523 N. Duluth Ave., Sioux Falls, 57105.

Bishop's Bulletin—Rev. MICHAEL GRIFFIN, Exec. Editor; Mr. GENE YOUNG, Mgr. Editor, 523 N. Duluth Ave., Sioux Falls, 57104. Tel: 605-988-3789.

Building Commission—Mr. JEROME KLEIN, Chancellor; Mr. MICHAEL BANNWARTH, Finance Officer, Catholic Chancery Office, 523 N. Duluth Ave., Sioux Falls, 57104.

Catholic Charities—TRAVIS BENSON, J.D., Dir., 523 N. Duluth Ave., Sioux Falls, 57104. Tel: 605-988-3748.

Catholic Foundation for Eastern South Dakota—MARK CONZEMIUS, Pres.; ELIZABETH THEOBALD, Vice Pres. & Dir., Planned Giving, 523 N. Duluth Ave., Sioux Falls, 57104. Tel: 605-988-3788.

Catholic Relief Services—Mr. JEROME KLEIN, Chancellor, 523 N. Duluth Ave., Sioux Falls, 57104.

Catholic Family Services—Sr. MARTIN MERGEN, O.S.B., Interim Exec. Dir., 523 N. Duluth Ave., Sioux Falls, 57104. Tel: 605-988-3775.

Catholic Family Sharing Appeal and Stewardship—Mr. KEVIN MILES, Dir., 523 N. Duluth Ave., Sioux Falls, 57104. Tel: 605-988-3788.

Censor Librorum—Dr. CHRISTOPHER BURGWALD, S.T.L., 523 N. Duluth Ave., Sioux Falls, 57104.

Communications Office—Mr. JEROME KLEIN, Chancellor, 523 N. Duluth Ave., Sioux Falls, 57104. Tel: 605-988-3789.

Cursillo—Rev. RODNEY FARKE, 416 Walker St., Vermillion, 57069-3358. Tel: 605-624-4478.

Diocesan Archivist—Mr. JEROME KLEIN, Chancellor, 523 N. Duluth Ave., Sioux Falls, 57104. Tel: 605-334-9861.

Office of Catholic Schools—Mr. MATTHEW ALTOFF, Dir., 523 N. Duluth, Sioux Falls, 57104. Tel: 605-988-3761.

Office of Evangelization and Faith Formation—Dr. CHRISTOPHER BURGWALD, S.T.L., Dir., 523 N. Duluth Ave., Sioux Falls, 57104. Tel: 605-988-3766.

Ecumenical Commission—Rev. ANTHONY OPEM, 995 Sioux Point Rd., Dakota Dunes, 57049. Tel: 605-235-1942.

Family and Children Faith Formation—Ms. JEAN LORANG, 523 N. Duluth Ave., Sioux Falls, 57104. Tel: 605-988-3767.

Finance Officer—Mr. MICHAEL BANNWARTH, 523 N. Duluth Ave., Sioux Falls, 57104. Tel: 605-988-3759; Fax: 605-988-3746.

Worldwide Marriage Encounter—Rev. JAMES M. JOYCE, 900 E. 14th St., Apt. 112, Sioux Falls, 57104. Tel: 605-978-1592.

Newman Apostolate—VACANT.

Office of Planning and Office of Deacon Formation—Deacon ROGER R. HEIDT, 523 N. Duluth Ave., Sioux Falls, 57104. Tel: 605-988-3715.

Permanent Diaconate Council—Deacon JOSEPH GRAVES, 1008 Palmer Pl., Mitchell, 57301. Tel: 605-996-7997.

Personnel Board—Revs. CHARLES L. CIMPL, Vicar Gen.; MICHAEL GRIFFIN; ROBERT V. KRANTZ; JOHN LANTSBERGER; ANDREW SWIETOCHOWSKI; J. JOSEPH HOLZHAUSER; JOSEPH VOGEL; MARK LICHTER.

Propagation of the Faith—Rev. JEROME RANEK, Dir., Mailing Address: St. Margaret Church, P.O. Box 137, Kimball, 57355.

Respect Life Office—Directors: TRAVIS BENSON, J.D.; KELLY BENSON, J.D., 523 N. Duluth Ave., Sioux Falls, 57104. Tel: 605-988-3755.

Search—523 N. Duluth Ave., Sioux Falls, 57104. Tel: 605-334-9861.

Spanish-Speaking Apostolate—Rev. JOHN HELMUELLER, 105 S. Bates St., Flandreau, 57028-1809. Tel: 605-997-2610.

Teens Encounter Christ—523 N. Duluth Ave., Sioux Falls, 57104. Tel: 605-334-9861.

Victim Assistance Coordinator—Ms. JEAN LORANG. Tel: 605-334-9861. Email: jlorang@sfcatholic.org.

Vocations—Rev. PAUL A. RUTTEN, 523 N. Duluth Ave., Sioux Falls, 57104. Tel: 605-988-3772.

Adolescent Faith Formation—VACANT.

CLERGY, PARISHES, MISSIONS AND PAROCHIAL SCHOOLS

CITY OF SIOUX FALLS

(MINNEHAHA COUNTY)

1—ST. JOSEPH CATHEDRAL (1880) [JC] Revs. Thomas Fitzpatrick; Thomas Anderson.
Res.: 521 Duluth Ave., 57104. Tel: 605-336-7390; Fax: 605-330-0416. Email: cathedral@stcatholic.org. Web: www.cathedralofstjosephsiouxfalls.parishesonline.com.
See St. Joseph Cathedral Elementary, Sioux Falls under Inter-Parochial Schools located in the Institution section.
Catechesis / Religious Program—Students 158.

2—CHRIST THE KING (1949) Rev. Richard Fox; Deacon Leon Cantin. In Res., Rev. James Zimmer.
Res.: 1501 W. 26th St., 57105. Tel: 605-332-5477; Fax: 605-332-0552. Web: www.ctkparish-sf.org.
See Christ the King Elementary School, Sioux Falls under Inter-Parochial Schools located in the Institution section.
Catechesis / Religious Program—Students 161.

3—HOLY SPIRIT (1988) Revs. James P. Morgan; Shaun Thomas Haggerty; Deacon Thomas R. Bates.
Res.: 4008 Lisanne, 57103. Tel: 605-371-2320; Fax: 605-371-1957.
Church: 3601 E. Dudley Ln., 57103.
Catechesis / Religious Program—Students 579.

4—ST. JOSEPHINE BAKHITA CATHOLIC CHURCH (2004) Rev. Elias Rinaldo Gamboriko, A.J. (Sudan).
Mailing Address: 521 N. Duluth Ave., 57104. Tel: 605-336-7390.

5—ST. KATHARINE DREXEL CATHOLIC CHURCH (2004) Rev. Joseph Vogel.
Mailing Address: 1800 S. Katie Ste. 1, 57106.
Church: Email: stkatharinedrexel@midconetwork.com. Web: www.stkatharinedrexelsfsd.org.
Catechesis / Religious Program—Students 235.

6—ST. LAMBERT (1958) Revs. James E. Mason; Edward Anderson; Deacons Ralph C. Counter, (Retired); Roger R. Heidt; Jerome F. Wathen.
Res.: 3901 E. 16th St., 57103. Tel: 605-336-8808; Fax: 605-339-4389. Email: st.lambert.parish@sfcss.org. Web: www.stlambert-parish.org.
See St. Lambert Elementary, Sioux Falls under Inter-Parochial Schools located in the Institution section.
Catechesis / Religious Program—Tel: 605-338-4728. Students 213.

7—ST. MARY (1947) Rev. David Krogman; Deacon Henry Knapp. In Res., Rev. Greg Frankman.
Res.: 2109 S. Fifth Ave., 57105. Tel: 605-332-6391; Fax: 605-338-2953. Web: www.stmarysf.org.
See St. Mary, Sioux Falls under Inter-Parochial Schools located in the Institution section.
Catechesis / Religious Program—Tel: 605-334-1912. Students 152.

8—ST. MICHAEL (1979) [JC] Revs. Charles L. Cimpl; Kevin O'Dell; Deacon John P. Devlin.
Res.: 1600 S. Marion Rd., 57106. Tel: 605-361-1600; Fax: 605-361-4350.
See St. Michael Elementary School, Sioux Falls under Inter-Parochial Schools located in the Institution section.
Catechesis / Religious Program—Tel: 605-361-1317. Students 915.

9—OUR LADY OF GUADALUPE (1996) [JC] Revs. Thomas Fitzpatrick, Admin.; David Garza.
Res.: 1220 E. 8th St., 57103-1702. Tel: 605-338-8126; Fax: 605-338-0419.
Catechesis / Religious Program—Students 94.

10—ST. THERESE (1917) Rev. Hal Barber; Deacon Michael Conrads.
Res.: 1301 N. Dubuque Ave., 57110-6450. Tel: 605-338-2433; Fax: 605-339-2203.
Catechesis / Religious Program—Students 162.

OUTSIDE THE CITY OF SIOUX FALLS

ABERDEEN, BROWN CO.

1—ST. MARY, [CEM] Revs. J. Joseph Holzhauser; Jeffrey Thomas Norfolk; Deacon Peter Mehlaff.
Res.: 409 2nd Ave., N.E., 57401. Tel: 605-229-4422; Fax: 605-226-4908.
School— See separate listing under Inter-Parochial Schools in the Institution section.
Catechesis / Religious Program—Students 127.

2—SACRED HEART (1882) [CEM] Revs. Edward J. Pierce; Kevin Zilverberg.
Res.: 409 3rd. Ave., S.E., 57401. Tel: 605-225-7065; Fax: 605-226-5992. Email: jmecseji@parishmail.com. Web: parishesonline.com.
Church: 502 2nd Ave., S.E., 57401.
See Roncalli Schools, Aberdeen under Inter-Parochial Schools located in the Institution section.
Catechesis / Religious Program—Tel: 605-225-7065; Fax: 605-226-5992. Students 209.

ALEXANDRIA, HANSON CO., ST. MARY OF MERCY (1880) [CEM] Rev. Thomas Clement.
Res.: 220 W. 5th St., P.O. Box 158, 57311. Tel: 605-239-4833; Fax: 605-239-9833. Email: maryofmercy@triotel.net. Web: stamryofmercyalexandria.parishesonline.com.
Catechesis / Religious Program—Students 118.

ANDOVER, DAY CO., ALL SAINTS (1880) Closed. For inquiries for parish records contact the chancery.

ARLINGTON, KINGSBURY CO., ST. JOHN THE EVANGELIST (1907), Served from DeSmet., Mailing Address: Box 15, De Smet, 57231. Tel: 605-854-3564; Fax: 605-854-9961.
Catechesis / Religious Program—Students 49.

ARMOUR, DOUGLAS CO., ST. PAUL THE APOSTLE (1886) Rev. Cathal Gallagher, S.S.C.
Res.: Box 400, 57313. Tel: 605-724-2191; Fax: 605-724-2121.
Catechesis / Religious Program—Tel: 605-724-2121. Students 55.

ARTESIAN, SANBORN CO., ST. CHARLES (1908) [JC] Attended by St. Wilfrid, Woonsocket., Mailing Address: Box 266, Woonsocket, 57385. Tel: 605-796-4666; Fax: 605-796-4666.
Catechesis / Religious Program—Students 25.

ATHOL, SPINK CO., ST. MARY (1885) Closed. For inquiries for parish records contact All Saints, Mellette.

AURORA, BROOKINGS CO., ST. WILLIAM (1881) [CEM] Deacon Edwin Gruhot, Admin.
Mailing Address: 1647 Edgewater Dr., Lake Benton, MN 56149. Tel: 507-368-9406.
Catechesis / Religious Program—Students 12.

BERESFORD, UNION CO., ST. TERESA OF AVILA (1885) [CEM] Rev. Mark Axtmann.
Res.: 901 S. Third, P.O. Box 472, 57004. Tel: 605-763-2028 (Church); 605-763-5159 (Rectory). Email: markaxtmann@hotmail.com.
Catechesis / Religious Program—Students 101.

BIG BEND, HUGHES CO., ST. CATHERINE (1950) [CEM] Attended by Fort Thompson., Mailing Address: Box 47, Fort Thompson, 57339. Tel: 605-245-2350.
Catechesis / Religious Program—Students 45.

BIG STONE CITY, GRANT CO., ST. CHARLES (1882) [CEM] Rev. Daniel Wolfgram.
Res.: 106 3rd Ave., 57216. Tel: 605-862-8319; Fax: 605-862-8319.
Catechesis / Religious Program—Students 37.

BLUNT, HUGHES CO., HOLY SPIRIT, Closed. For inquiries for parish records contact the chancery.

BOWDLE, EDMUNDS CO., ST. AUGUSTINE (1894) [CEM] Rev. DeWayne Kayser.
Mailing Address: 3023 S. 3rd St., Box 310, 57428. Tel: 605-285-6466; Fax: 605-285-6160.
Catechesis / Religious Program—Students 26.

BRANDON, MINNEHAHA CO., RISEN SAVIOR (1979) [JC] Rev. Msgr. Joseph Wagner.
Res.: 312 9th Ave. N., 57005.
Church: 301 N. Splitrock Blvd., P.O. Box 80, 57005-0080. Tel: 605-582-8535 (Rectory); 605-582-6902 (Church); Fax: 605-582-3993.
Catechesis / Religious Program—Tel: 605-582-2292. Students 356.

BRIDGEWATER, MCCOOK CO., ST. STEPHEN (1883) [CEM] Rev. Paul Offerman.
Res.: Box 49, 57319. Tel: 605-729-2505. Email: stephen123@unitelsd.com.
Catechesis / Religious Program—Students 57.

BRISTOL, DAY CO., ST. ANTHONY (1885) [CEM], Attended from Groton.
Res.: Box 336, 57219. Tel: 605-492-3135.

BRITTON, MARSHALL CO., ST. JOHN DE BRITTO (1888) [JC] Rev. John L. Brophy (MIL).
Res.: 812 8th St., P.O. Box 108, 57430. Tel: 605-448-5379; Fax: 605-448-5388.
Catechesis / Religious Program—Students 46.

BROOKINGS, BROOKINGS CO., ST. THOMAS MORE (1904) [CEM] Rev. Rodney Farke.
Res.: 1700 8th St. S., 57006. Tel: 605-692-4361; Fax: 605-692-6176. Email: info@stmbrookings.org. Web: www.stthomasbrookings.parishesonline.com.
Catechesis / Religious Program—Tel: 605-692-6941. Students 539.

BRYANT, HAMLIN CO., ST. MARY (1881) [CEM] Attended by St. Michael, Clark., 110 N. Idaho St., Clark, 57225.
Catechesis / Religious Program—Students 7.

CANTON, LINCOLN CO., ST. DOMINIC Rev. Paul Pathiyamoola.
Res.: 800 E. Walnut, 57013. Tel: 605-764-5640; Fax: 605-764-3085.
Catechesis / Religious Program—Students 62.

CASTLEWOOD, HAMLIN CO., ST. JOHN (1885) [JC] Attended by Kranzburg., Mailing Address: Box 166, Kranzburg, 57245. Tel: 605-886-9166; Fax: 605-886-2715.
Catechesis / Religious Program—Students 55.

CAVOUR, BEADLE CO., ST. PATRICK (1883) Closed. For inquiries for parish records contact Holy Trinity, Huron.

CENTERVILLE, TURNER CO., GOOD SHEPHERD (1888) [JC] Attended by Beresford., Mailing Address: P.O. Box 98, 57014. Tel: 605-563-2220.
Catechesis / Religious Program—Students 61.

CHAMBERLAIN, BRULE CO., ST. JAMES (1891) [JC] Rev. William Pitcavage, S.C.J.; Deacon Alfred Bud Jetty.
Res.: 400 S. Main, 57325. Tel: 605-734-6122; Fax: 605-734-6729. Email: sjchamofc@parishmail.com. Web: www.stjameschamberlain.com.
Catechesis / Religious Program—Tel: 605-734-6122; Fax: 605-734-6729. Students 131.

CHELSEA, FAULK CO., SACRED HEART (1910) Closed. For records contact All Saints, Mellette.

CLARK, CLARK CO., ST. MICHAEL (1887) [CEM] Rev. William Hamak.
Res.: 110 N. Idaho St., 57225. Tel: 605-532-3855; Fax: 605-532-3855.
Catechesis / Religious Program—112 N. Idaho St., 57225. Tel: 605-532-3776. Students 54.

CLEAR LAKE, DEUEL CO., ST. MARY (1900) Rev. Brian Simon.
Res.: 408 Third St. W., Box 589, 57226. Tel: 605-874-2080; Fax: 605-874-1333.
Catechesis / Religious Program—Students 75.

COLMAN, MOODY CO., ST. PETER (1905) [CEM] Attended by SS. Simon & Jude, Flandreau., *c/o Ss. Simon & Jude*, 105 S. Bates St., Flandreau, 57028. Tel: 605-997-2610; Fax: 605-573-2080.
Catechesis / Religious Program—Students 77.

CONDE, SPINK CO., ST. JOHN THE BAPTIST (1906) [CEM]
Res.: 425 4th St., S. W., P.O. Box 129, 57434-0129. Tel: 605-382-5902; Fax: 605-382-5257.
Catechesis / Religious Program—Students 15.

DAKOTA DUNES, UNION CO., BLESSED TERESA OF CALCUTTA CATHOLIC CHURCH (1999) Rev. Anthony Opem; Deacon Joseph Twidwell.
Church: 995 Sioux Point Rd., 57049. Tel: 605-235-1942; Fax: 605-235-1492.
Catechesis / Religious Program—Students 97.

DANTE, CHARLES MIX CO., ASSUMPTION B.V.M. (1909) [CEM] Rev. Richard Baumberger.
Mailing Address: P.O. Box 36, 57329-0036. Tel: 605-384-5155.
Catechesis/Religious Program—Students 92.

DE SMET, KINGSBURY CO., ST. THOMAS AQUINAS (1901) [CEM] Rev. Shane Stevens.
Res.: 203 Harvey Dunn Ave., S.W., Box 15, 57231. Tel: 605-854-3564; Fax: 605-854-9961.
Catechesis/Religious Program—Students 87.

DELL RAPIDS, MINNEHAHA CO., ST. MARY'S (1898) [CEM] Rev. Gregory Tschakert.
Res.: 608 E. 8th St., 57022. Tel: 605-428-3390; Fax: 605-428-5304.
School—(Grades PreK-6) Tel: 605-428-3459. Lay Teachers 8; Students 118.
School—(Grades 7-12) Tel: 605-428-5591; Fax: 605-428-5377. Lay Teachers 7; Students 93.
Catechesis/Religious Program—Tel: 605-428-3597. Students 214.

DIMOCK, HUTCHINSON CO., SS. PETER AND PAUL (1885) [CEM] Rev. Joseph Thalanany, V.C. (India).
Res.: 146 W. 1st St., 57331. Tel: 605-928-3883. Email: sppaulpd@hotmail.com.
Catechesis/Religious Program—Students 58.

DOLAND, SPINK CO., ST. JOSEPH OF DOLAND (1909) Attended by Conde., Mailing Address: P.O. Box 393, 57436-0393. Tel: 605-635-6301.
Catechesis/Religious Program—Students 22.

DUNCAN, BUFFALO CO., ST. PLACIDUS (1887) [CEM] Attended by Woonsocket., P.O. Box 266, Woonsocket, 57385. Tel: 605-293-3484.
Church: HCR 3, Box 17, Gann Valley, 57341.
Catechesis/Religious Program—Students 13.

EDEN, MARSHALL CO., SACRED HEART (1917) [CEM]
Res.: Box 15, 57232. Tel: 605-486-4702; Fax: 605-486-4772. Email: sheden@venturecomm.net.
Catechesis/Religious Program—Students 35.

ELK POINT, UNION CO., ST. JOSEPH (1901) [CEM] Rev. David Roehrich.
605 E. Main St., Box 340, 57025. Tel: 605-356-2693; Fax: 605-356-3284. Email: stjoseph@iw.net. Web: www.parishesonline.com.
Catechesis/Religious Program—Students 200.

ELKTON, BROOKINGS CO., OUR LADY OF GOOD COUNSEL (1879) [CEM] Attended by Flandreau., Mailing Address: 105 S. Bates, Flandreau, 57028. Tel: 605-997-2610; Fax: 605-573-2080.
Res.: Box E, 57026. Tel: 605-542-8221; Fax: 605-542-8221.
Catechesis/Religious Program—Students 65.

EMERY, HANSON CO., ST. MARTIN (1884) [CEM] Rev. Thomas Clement.
Res.: Box 312, 57332. Tel: 605-449-4374. Web: www.stmartinemery.parishesonline.com.
Catechesis/Religious Program—Students 86.

EPIPHANY, HANSON CO., CHURCH OF THE EPIPHANY (1896) [CEM] Attended by Howard., Mailing Address: Box 100, Howard, 57349.
Catechesis/Religious Program—Students 41.

ESTELLINE, HAMLIN CO., ST. FRANCIS DE SALES (1884) [CEM] Attended by Clear Lake.
Res.: P.O. Box 589, Clear Lake, 57226. Tel: 605-873-2254; Fax: 605-874-1333.
Catechesis/Religious Program—Tel: 605-874-2080. Students 37.

ETHAN, DAVISON CO., HOLY TRINITY (1889) [CEM] Attended by Dimock., 146 W. 1st St., Dimock, 57331. Tel: 605-928-3883.
Catechesis/Religious Program—Tel: 605-227-4361. Nicole Nuegebauer, D.R.E. Students 57.

EUREKA, MCPHERSON CO., ST. JOSEPH (1896) Attended by Herreid., Mailing Address: P.O. Box 37, Herreid, 57632. Tel: 605-284-5190.
Church: 602 2nd St., 57437.
Catechesis/Religious Program—Students 29.

FARMER, HANSON CO., ST. PETER (1889) Closed. For inquiries for parish records contact the chancery.

FAULKTON, FAULK CO., ST. THOMAS THE APOSTLE (1903) [CEM] Rev. Joji Itukulapati (India); Deacon Arvid Holsing.
Res.: 206 10th Ave. S., P.O. Box 394, 57438. Tel: 605-598-6590; Fax: 605-598-6745. Email: stthomas@westtelco.com.
Church: 1013 Court St., 57438.
Catechesis/Religious Program—Kelly Bowar, D.R.E. Students 78.

FLANDREAU, MOODY CO., SS. SIMON AND JUDE (1882) [CEM] Rev. John Helmueller.
Res.: 105 S. Bates, 57028. Tel: 605-997-2610; Fax: 605-573-2080.
Catechesis/Religious Program—Students 129.

FLORENCE, CODINGTON CO., BLESSED SACRAMENT (1889) [CEM] Rev. Douglas Binsfeld.
Res.: Box 6, 57235. Tel: 605-758-2271; Fax: 605-758-2113.
Catechesis/Religious Program—Students 58.

FORT THOMPSON, BUFFALO CO., ST. JOSEPH (1889) [CEM] Revs. Joseph Dean, S.C.J.; Bernard Rosinski, S.C.J.; Deacon Steven A. McLaughlin.
Mailing Address: Box 47, 57339. Tel: 605-245-2350.
Catechesis/Religious Program—Students 100.

FRANKFORT, SPINK CO., ST. ANN (1884) Attended by Mellette., Mailing Address: Box 46, Mellette, 57461. Tel: 605-887-3414. Email: frhughes@nvc.net.

GARRETSON, MINNEHAHA CO., ST. ROSE OF LIMA (1898) [CEM] Rev. Kenneth Bain.
Res.: Drawer O, 57030. Tel: 605-594-3750; Fax: 605-594-2017.
Catechesis/Religious Program—Students 104.

GARRYOWEN, UNION CO., ST. MARY, Closed. For inquiries for parish records contact the chancery.

GARY, DEUEL CO., ST. PETER (1900) Attended by Clear Lake., 408 3rd St. W., Box 589, Clear Lake, 57226. Tel: 605-874-2080; Fax: 605-874-1333.
Catechesis/Religious Program—Students 16.

GEDDES, CHARLES MIX CO., ST. ANN (1902) [CEM] [JC] Attended by Platte., Mailing Address: P.O. Box 137, 57342. Tel: 605-337-3710; 605-337-9717; Fax: 605-337-9717. In Res., Rev. Roger Geditz (Retired).
Catechesis/Religious Program—Students 24.

GETTYSBURG, POTTER CO., SACRED HEART (1905) [CEM] Rev. Jerome Kopel.
Res.: 203 E. Garfield Ave., Box 285, 57442. Tel: 605-765-2161.
Catechesis/Religious Program—Tel: 605-765-2359. Students 73.

GRENVILLE, DAY CO., ST. JOSEPH (1885) [CEM] Attended by Eden.
Res.: Box 191, 57239. Tel: 605-486-4655; 605-486-4702 (Eden).
Catechesis/Religious Program—Students 25.

GROTON, BROWN CO., ST. ELIZABETH ANN SETON (1883), (formerly St. John the Baptist). Rev. Michael D. Kelly.
Res.: 803 1st St. N., P.O. Box 407, 57445. Tel: 605-397-8448; Fax: 605-397-8632.
Catechesis/Religious Program—Students 104.

GROVER, CODINGTON CO., ST. PETER (1901) Attended by Blessed Sacrament, Florence., Mailing Address: P.O. Box 6, Florence, 57235. Tel: 605-758-2271; Fax: 605-758-2113.
Catechesis/Religious Program—Students 17.

HARROLD, HUGHES CO., ST. JOHN THE EVANGELIST, [CEM] Attended by Highmore., Mailing Address: Box 457, Highmore, 57345. Tel: 605-852-2733; Fax: 605-852-2076.
Catechesis/Religious Program—Students 6.

HARTFORD, MINNEHAHA CO., ST. GEORGE (1882) [CEM] Rev. David A. Desmond; Sr. Muriel Spartz, O.S.B., Office Admin.
100 N. Mundt, Box 577, 57033. Tel: 605-528-3902; Fax: 605-528-3902. Email: stgeorgechurch@unitersd.com.
Res.: 300 W. Mickelson, 57033.
Catechesis/Religious Program—St. George Center, 408 S. Western Ave., 57033. Students 236.

HECLA, BROWN CO., ST. ANTHONY OF PADUA (1904) [JC] Attended by St. John, Britton., Mailing Address: Box 108, Britton, 57430. Tel: 605-448-5379; Fax: 605-528-3902.

HENRY, CODINGTON CO., ST. HENRY Rev. Douglas Binsfeld.
Mailing Address: 605 4th St., P.O. Box 73, 57243. Tel: 605-758-2271.
Catechesis/Religious Program—Students 29.

HERREID, CAMPBELL CO., ST. MICHAEL (1895) [CEM] Rev. Thomas Podimattam, C.M.I. (India).
Res.: 106 2nd Ave. W., Box 37, 57632. Tel: 605-437-2614; Fax: 605-437-2505. Email: stmichaels@valleytel.net.
Catechesis/Religious Program—Students 36.

HIGHMORE, HYDE CO., ST. MARY (1906) [CEM] Rev. Paul Nereparaampil, C.M.I. (India).
Res.: Box 457, 57345. Tel: 605-852-2733; Fax: 605-852-2076.
Catechesis/Religious Program—Students 59.

HOSMER, EDMUNDS CO., HOLY TRINITY (1912) [CEM] Attended by Bowdle.
Res.: P.O. Box 310, Bowdle, 57428. Tel: 605-285-6466.
Catechesis/Religious Program—Students 12.

HOVEN, POTTER CO., ST. ANTHONY OF PADUA (1887) [CEM] Rev. Lance Oser.
Res.: 546 Main St., Box 98, 57450. Tel: 605-948-2451; Fax: 605-948-2245. Web: www.stanthonys-hoven.com.
Catechesis/Religious Program—Students 72.

HOWARD, MINER CO., ST. AGATHA (1882) [CEM] Rev. Michael Schneider.
Res.: Box 100, 57349. Tel: 605-772-5564.
Catechesis/Religious Program—Students 91.

HUMBOLDT, MINNEHAHA CO., ST. ANN (1912) [CEM] Rev. Robert V. Krantz; Sr. Jane Schoenfelder, O.S.B.
Res.: 204 S. Jefferson, P.O. Box 195, 57035. Tel: 605-363-3330; Fax: 605-363-3856.
Catechesis/Religious Program—Students 82.

HUNTIMER, MINNEHAHA CO., ST. JOSEPH THE WORKMAN (1889) [CEM] Rev. Kenneth Bain.
Mailing Address: 520 Center Ave., P.O. Box O, Garretson, 57030. Tel: 605-594-3750.
Church: 46408 245th St., Colton, 57018.
Catechesis/Religious Program—Students 87.

HURON, BEADLE CO., HOLY TRINITY (1999) [CEM] Rev. Terence Anderson.
Mailing Address: 425 21st St. S.W., 57350.
Res.: 425 20th St., S.W., 57350. Tel: 605-352-2203; Fax: 605-353-0889. Email: hthuron@hur.midco.net. Web: www.holytrinityhuron.parishesonline.com.
School—Tel: 605-352-9344; Fax: 605-352-0889. Lay Teachers 8; Students 75.
Catechesis/Religious Program—Tel: 605-352-2237. Students 214.

IDYLWILDE, TURNER CO., ST. BONIFACE (1885) [CEM] Attended by St. George, Scotland., P.O. Box 449, Scotland, 57059.
Res.: Tel: 605-583-4318; Fax: 605-583-4457.
Catechesis/Religious Program—Students 48.

IPSWICH, EDMUNDS CO., HOLY CROSS (1886) [CEM] Rev. Randy Phillips.
Res.: Box 67, 57451. Tel: 605-426-6967; Fax: 605-426-6588.
School—13 6th St., P.O. Box 324, 57451. Tel: 605-426-6222. Lay Teachers 5; Students 29.
Catechesis/Religious Program—Students 68.

IROQUOIS, KINGSBURY CO., ST. PAUL (1914) [CEM] Attended by St. Thomas Aquinas, De Smet., Mailing Address: Box 15, De Smet, 57231. Tel: 605-854-3564; Fax: 605-854-9961.
Catechesis/Religious Program—Students 16.

JEFFERSON, UNION CO., ST. PETER (1867) [CEM] Rev. David Roehrich.
Res.: 400 Main St., P.O. Box 188, 57038-0188. Tel: 605-966-5716; Fax: 605-966-5492. Email: stpeter@longlines.com.
Preschool—P.O. Box 98, 57038-0098. Tel: 605-966-5746. Students 21.
Catechesis/Religious Program— (Combined with St. Joseph, Elk Point) Students 45.

KIMBALL, BRULE CO., ST. MARGARET (1884) [CEM] Rev. Jerome Ranek.
Res.: 417 S. Elm., Box 137, 57355. Tel: 605-778-6420. Web: www.stmargarets.midstatesd.net.
Preschool—Teachers 2; Students 27.
Catechesis/Religious Program—Tel: 605-778-6487. Students 119.

KRANZBURG, CODINGTON CO., HOLY ROSARY (1879) [CEM] Rev. Kenneth J. Koster.
Res.: 202 Minnesota Ave. N.E., Box 166, 57245. Tel: 605-886-3344; Fax: 605-886-2715.
School—(Grades K-6) Tel: 605-886-8114. Lay Teachers 4; Students 29.
Catechesis/Religious Program—Students 93.

LAKE ANDES, CHARLES MIX CO., ST. MARK (1904) [CEM] Bro. Martin Zatsick, T.O.R., Admin.
Res.: 251 3rd Ave., N., Box 250, 57356. Tel: 605-487-7300.
Catechesis/Religious Program—Tel: 605-487-7056. Students 29.

LAKE CITY, MARSHALL CO., ST. JOSEPH (1919) [CEM] Attended by Eden., Mailing Address: Box 15, Eden, 57232. Tel: 605-486-4702; Fax: 605-486-4772.

LENNOX, LINCOLN CO., ST. MAGDALEN, [CEM] Attended by St. Dominic, Canton., Mailing Address: Box 136, 57039. Tel: 605-647-2187. Email: stmagdalens@iw.net. Web: stmagdalenlennox.parishesonline.com.
Catechesis/Religious Program—Students 107.

LEOLA, MCPHERSON CO., OUR LADY OF PERPETUAL HELP (1891) [CEM] Rev. Randy Phillips.
Res.: P.O. Box 67, Ipswich, 57451. Tel: 605-426-6967; Fax: 605-426-6588.
Catechesis/Religious Program—Students 34.

LESTERVILLE, YANKTON CO., ST. JOHN THE BAPTIST (1904) [CEM] Attended by St. Wenceslaus, Tabor., Mailing Address: 205 N. Lidice, Tabor, 57063. Tel: 605-463-2336; Fax: 605-463-2518.
Catechesis/Religious Program—Students 36.

LETCHER, SANBORN CO., ST. SCHOLASTICA, Closed. For inquiries for parish records contact the chancery.

LILY, DAY CO., ST. JOSEPH, Closed. For sacramental records contact St. Anthony, Bristol.

MADISON, LAKE CO., ST. THOMAS AQUINAS (1881) [CEM] Rev. Robert B. Vinslauski.
Res.: 217 N.W. Fourth St., 57042. Tel: 605-256-2304; Fax: 605-256-9252.
School—Tel: 605-256-4419. Lay Teachers 11; Students 104.
Catechesis/Religious Program—Students 145.

MARION, TURNER CO., OUR LADY OF PERPETUAL HELP (1880) [CEM] Attended by St. Mary, P.O. Box 308, Salem, SD 57058.
Res.: 306 E. State St., Box 237, 57043. Tel: 605-648-3928.
Catechesis/Religious Program—Students 20.

MARTY, CHARLES MIX CO., ST. PAUL'S CHURCH (1913), (Native American), [CEM] Rev. David Tickerhoof, T.O.R.; Sr. Miriam Shindelar, O.S.B.S., Admin.
Res.: 102 Church Dr., P.O. Box 266, 57361. Tel: 605-384-3234; Fax: 605-384-3575. Email: stpaulsparish@hcinet.net.
Catechesis/Religious Program—Students 18.

Mayfield, Yankton Co., St. Columba (1902) [CEM] Unassigned. Attended by St. George, Scotland SD., P.O. Box 449, Scotland, 57059. Tel: 605-583-4318.
Catechesis/Religious Program—Students 19.

Mellette, Spink Co., All Saints (1944) [CEM] Rev. Christopher Hughes.
Mailing Address: Box 46, 57461. Tel: 605-887-3414.
Catechesis/Religious Program—Students 58.

Milbank, Grant Co., St. Lawrence (1882) [CEM] Rev. Ken Lulf.
Church/Office: 113 S. 6th St., 57252. Tel: 605-432-5353.
Res.: 101 S. 6th St., 57252.
School—Tel: 605-432-5673. Lay Teachers 9; Students 135.
Catechesis/Religious Program—Tel: 605-432-5353. Students 197.

Miller, Hand Co., St. Ann (1884) [CEM] Rev. Chester Murtha.
Res.: 709 E. 4th, P.O. Box 198, 57362. Tel: 605-853-2207; Fax: 605-853-3037. Email: stann1962@mncomm.com.
Catechesis/Religious Program—Tel: 605-853-2735. Students 101.

Mitchell, Davison Co.

1—Holy Family (1880) [JC] Rev. Larry Regynski; Deacon Joseph Graves.
Res.: 222 N. Kimball St., 57301. Tel: 605-996-3639; Fax: 605-996-3937. Email: holyfamily@mitchelltelecom.net.
Catechesis/Religious Program—1510 W. Elm, 57301. Tel: 605-996-3842. Students 341.

2—Holy Spirit (1962) Rev. Andrew Swietochowski; Deacon James M. Hayes.
Res.: 1401 W. Cedar Ave., 57301. Tel: 605-996-7424; Fax: 605-90-3401.
School—John Paul II Elementary, 1510 W. Elm Ave., 57301. Tel: 605-996-2365; Fax: 605-995-0378. Mrs. Michelle Ommen, Prin. Lay Teachers 14; Students 230.
Catechesis/Religious Program—See Holy Family for details., Tel: 605-996-3842.

Mobridge, Walworth Co., St. Joseph (1912) [JC] Rev. John Short.
Res.: 220 6th St., W., 57601. Tel: 605-845-2100. Email: stjoe@westriv.com.
Preschool—Lay Teachers 1; Students 30.
Catechesis/Religious Program—Students 120.

Montrose, McCook Co., St. Patrick (1904) [CEM] Rev. Robert V. Krantz.
211 S. Church, P.O. Box 158, 57048. Tel: 605-363-5068; Fax: 605-363-3856. Email: stpatmontrose@siouxvalley.net.
Catechesis/Religious Program—Students 123.

Mount Vernon, Davison Co., St. Michael (1900) Attended by Plankinton., Mailing Address: Box 430, Plankinton, 57368. Tel: 605-942-7125.
Catechesis/Religious Program—Students 45.

New Effington, Roberts Co., Sacred Heart (1913) Attended by Rosholt., Mailing Address: P.O. Box 45, Rosholt, 57260. Tel: 605-537-4583.
Catechesis/Religious Program—Students 10.

Oldham, Kingsbury Co., St. Catherine of Sienna (1899) Closed. For inquiries for parish records contact the chancery.

Onaka, Faulk Co., St. John the Baptist (1906) [CEM] Attended by St. Anthony of Padua, Hoven., Mailing Address: P.O. Box 98, Hoven, 57450. Tel: 605-948-2451; Fax: 605-948-2245.
Catechesis/Religious Program—Students 3.

Onida, Sully Co., St. Pius X (1959) [CEM] Attended by Sacred Heart, Gettysburg., Mailing Address: 102 6th St., P.O. Box 13, 57564. Tel: 605-258-2336. Email: stpiusx@venturecomm.net.
Catechesis/Religious Program—Students 44.

Orient, Faulk Co., St. Joseph (1884) Attended by Faulkton., 1985 354th Ave., 57467. Tel: 605-598-6590. P.O. Box 394, Faulkton, 57438.
Catechesis/Religious Program—Students 28.

Parker, Turner Co., St. Christina (1881) [CEM] Rev. David Stevens.
Mailing Address: P.O. Box 610, 57053. Email: stchristina@iw.net. Web: www.stchristinaparker.parishesonline.com.
Res.: Maple St., Box 116, Tea, 57064. Tel: 605-498-5449; Fax: 605-498-2110.
Catechesis/Religious Program—Students 72.

Parkston, Hutchinson Co., Sacred Heart (1887) [CEM 2] Rev. John Rader; Deacon Barry Wagner.
Res.: Box 460, 57366. Tel: 605-928-3676; Fax: 605-928-3862.
Catechesis/Religious Program—Students 211.

Pierre, Hughes Co.

1—Blessed Kateri Tekakwitha
Church & Office: 2815 E. Sully, 57501.

2—SS. Peter and Paul (1882) [CEM] Revs. Michael Griffin; Kevin Doyle.
Res.: 304 N. Euclid, 57501. Tel: 605-224-2483; Fax: 605-224-1483.
School—Tel: 605-224-7185; Fax: 605-224-1014. Benedictine Sisters 3; Lay Teachers 9; Students 164.
Catechesis/Religious Program—Students 360.

Plankinton, Aurora Co., St. John Rev. Msgr. Stephen Barnett.
Res.: Box 430, 57368. Tel: 605-942-7125. Email: sbarnett@siouxvalley.net. Web: www.stjohnplankinton.parishesonline.com.
Catechesis/Religious Program—Students 80.

Platte, Charles Mix Co., St. Peter the Apostle (1904) [CEM] Rev. Jesudas Thaliyan, C.M.I. (India).
Res.: 317 Ohio Ave., 57369. Tel: 605-337-3710; 605-337-2465; Fax: 605-337-9717.
Catechesis/Religious Program—Students 38.

Polo, Hand Co., St. Liborius (1904) [CEM] Attended by Miller., Mailing Address: 709 E. 4th, P.O. Box 198, Miller, 57362.
Catechesis/Religious Program—Students 12.

Pukwana, Brule Co., St. Anthony (1891) Attended by Chamberlain., 400 S. Main, Chamberlain, 57325. Tel: 605-734-6122; Fax: 605-734-6729.

Ramona, Lake Co., St. William of Vercelli (1899) Rev. Michael Schneider.
Mailing Address: Box 100, Howard, 57349. Tel: 605-482-8214; Fax: 605-482-8243.
Catechesis/Religious Program—Students 15.

Redfield, Spink Co., St. Bernard (1884) [CEM] Rev. William Osborn.
Res.: 213 E. 6th Ave., 57469-1249. Tel: 605-472-2500; Fax: 605-472-3397. Email: sbernard@abe.midco.net.
Catechesis/Religious Program—Tel: 605-472-1482. Students 159.

Revillo, Grant Co., Annunciation (1889) [CEM] Unassigned.
Res.: 301 W. 5th Ave., 57259.
Catechesis/Religious Program—Students 27.

Roscoe, Edmunds Co., St. Thomas Apostle (1906) [JC], Attended by Bowdle.
Res.: 605 N. Andrew St., 57471. Tel: 605-285-6466.
Catechesis/Religious Program—Students 42.

Rosholt, Roberts Co., St. John the Baptist (1911) [CEM] Rev. Dennis Deis, O.M.I.
Res.: 218 W. Dakota St., Box 45, 57260. Tel: 605-537-4583.
Catechesis/Religious Program—Students 70.

Salem, McCook Co., St. Mary (1885) [CEM] Rev. Martin E. Lawrence. In Res., Rev. Charles J. Duman (Retired).
Res. & Church: 340 N. Idaho, Box 308, 57058. Tel: 605-425-2600; Fax: 605-425-3310. Email: stmaryadm@triotel.net. Web: www.salemcatholic.org.
School—Tel: 605-425-2607. Lay Teachers 7; Students 68.
Catechesis/Religious Program—Students 70.

Scotland, Bon Homme Co., St. George (1906) [CEM] Rev. Mathew Vazhappilly, C.M.I. (India).
Res.: Box 449, 57059. Tel: 605-583-4318; Fax: 605-583-4457.
Catechesis/Religious Program—Tel: 605-583-4696. Students 41.

Selby, Walworth Co., St. Anthony (1900) Attended by Herreid., Mailing Address: 7209 5th Ave., P.O. ox 231, 57472. Tel: 605-649-6338; Fax: 605-437-2505.
Catechesis/Religious Program—Students 36.

Seneca, Faulk Co., St. Boniface (1903) Attended by St. Thomas the Apostle, Faulkton., Mailing Address: P.O. Box 394, Faulkton, 57438-0094. Tel: 605-598-6590.
Catechesis/Religious Program—Students 13.

Sigel, Yankton Co., St. Agnes (1885) [CEM], 29882 N. E. Jim River Rd., Mission Hill, 57046.
Catechesis/Religious Program—Students 18.

Sisseton, Roberts Co.

1—St. Catherine (1962) [CEM 2] Revs. Norman Volk, O.M.I.; Andrew Knop, O.M.I.
Office: 120 E. Chestnut, 57262. Tel: 605-698-7414; Fax: 605-698-7236.
Catechesis/Religious Program— (Combined with St. Peter, Sisseton). Students 19.

2—St. Peter (1899) [CEM] Revs. Norman Volk, O.M.I.; Andrew Knop, O.M.I.
Office: 120 E. Chestnut, 57262. Tel: 605-698-7414; Fax: 605-698-7236.
Catechesis/Religious Program—Students 90.

Spencer, McCook Co., St. Mary (1906) Merged with St. Peter, Farmer to form St. John Neumann, Spencer-Farmer.

Spencer-Farmer, McCook Co., St. John Neumann (1999) Attended by Bridgewater., Mailing Address: P.O. Box 49, Bridgewater, 57319. Tel: 615-729-2505.
Catechesis/Religious Program—Parish Center, 620 Cordo St., 57374. Tel: 605-246-2391. Students 16.

Springfield, Bon Homme Co., St. Vincent, Attended by Tyndall., Mailing Address: P.O. Box 130, 57062-0130. Tel: 605-589-3504.
Catechesis/Religious Program—Students 9.

Stephan, Hyde Co., Immaculate Conception (1886) [CEM] [JC] Attended by Ft. Thompson. Revs. Joseph Dean, S.C.J.; Bernard Rosinski, S.C.J.
Mailing Address: P.O. Box 185, Lower Brule, 57548. Tel: 605-852-2215.
Catechesis/Religious Program—Students 27.

Stickney, Aurora Co., St. Mary (1908) [CEM] Attended by Armour., Mailing Address: Box 400, Armour, 57313. Tel: 605-724-2191; Fax: 605-724-2121.
Catechesis/Religious Program—Students 21.

Tabor, Bon Homme Co., St. Wenceslaus (1872) [CEM] Rev. Joseph Puthenkulathil (India).
Res.: 205 N. Lidice St., 57063-2005. Tel: 605-463-2336; Fax: 605-463-2518.
Catechesis/Religious Program—Students 85.

Tea, Lincoln Co., St. Nicholas (1905) [JC] Rev. David Stevens.
Res.: 510 Maple St., P.O. Box 116, 57064. Tel: 605-498-2110. Email: stnick57064@yahoo.com. Web: www.stnicholas.parishesonline.com.
Church: 140 W. Brian St., P.O. Box 116, 57064. Tel: 605-498-5449.
Catechesis/Religious Program—Students 142.

Tripp, Hutchinson Co., Holy Rosary, Attended by Parkston., Mailing Address: P.O. Box 358, 57376-0358. Tel: 605-928-3676.
Catechesis/Religious Program—Students 14.

Turton, Spink Co., St. Joseph (1888) [CEM] [JC], Mailing Address: P.O. Box 127, 57477.
Catechesis/Religious Program—Students 3.

Tyndall, Bon Homme Co., St. Leo (1890) [CEM] Rev. Gerald Thury.
Res.: 100 E. 20th Ave., Box 47, 57066. Tel: 605-589-3504; Fax: 605-589-3392.
Catechesis/Religious Program—Students 118.
Station—Springfield Correctional Facility Springfield. Tel: 605-369-2201.

Veblen, Marshall Co., St. John Nepomucene (1907) [CEM] Attended by Catholic Community, Sisseton., 120 Chestnut St. E., Sisseton, 57262-1428. Tel: 605-698-7414; Fax: 605-698-7236.
Catechesis/Religious Program—Students 9.

Vermillion, Clay Co., St. Agnes (1860) [CEM 2] [JC] Rev. John Fischer.
Res.: 416 Walker St., 57069. Tel: 605-624-4478 (Church); 605-624-4479 (Rectory); Fax: 605-624-4479. Email: saintagneschurch@msn.com. Web: www.stagnesvermillian.parishesonline.com.
School—(Grades K-5), 909 E. Lewis St., 57069. Tel: 605-624-4144; Fax: 605-624-6239. Lay Teachers 7; Students 98.
Catechesis/Religious Program—Tel: 605-624-5161. Students 205.

Vodnany, Bon Homme Co., SS. Cyril and Methodius (1886) [CEM] Closed. For inquiries for parish records contact the chancery.

Wagner, Charles Mix Co., St. John the Baptist (1903) [CEM] Rev. Richard Baumberger; Deacon Albert J. Kocer.
Res.: Box 637, 57380. Tel: 605-384-5518; Fax: 605-384-5518.
Catechesis/Religious Program—Tel: 605-384-5157. Students 176.

Wakonda, Clay Co., St. Patrick (1904) [CEM 2] Attended by Newman Center, Vermillion. Deacon Thomas Vogel.
320 Cherry St., Vermillion, 57069. Tel: 605-624-2697.
Catechesis/Religious Program—Tel: 605-267-2676; Fax: 605-624-4145. Students 40.

Watertown, Codington Co.

1—Holy Name (1955) [JC] Rev. John Lantsberger.
Res.: 1009 Skyline Dr., 57201. Tel: 605-886-2628; Fax: 605-886-2142.
Catechesis/Religious Program—Tel: 605-886-3368; Fax: 605-886-2141. Students 357.

2—Immaculate Conception (1887) [CEM] Rev. Joseph Forcelle.
Res.: 309 Second Ave., S.E., 57201. Tel: 605-886-4049; Fax: 605-882-2911.
School—103 3rd St., S.E., 57201. Tel: 605-886-3883; Fax: 605-886-0199. Lay Teachers 16; Students 192.
Catechesis/Religious Program—103 Third St., S.E., 57201. Tel: 605-886-2772; Fax: 605-886-0199. Students 286.

Waubay, Day Co., Immaculate Conception (1894) [CEM] Attended by Webster., Mailing Address: 1101 E. 1st St., Webster, 57274. Tel: 605-345-3447; Fax: 605-345-4871.
Catechesis/Religious Program—Students 30.

Waverly, Codington Co., St. Joseph (1889) [CEM] Attended by Kranzburg., Mailing Address: 202 Minnesota Ave., Box 166, Kranzburg, 57245. Tel: 605-886-9166; Fax: 605-886-2715.
Catechesis/Religious Program—Students 37.

Webster, Day Co., Christ the King (1884) [CEM] Rev. David Axtmann.
Res.: 1101 E. 1st St., 57274. Tel: 605-345-3447; Fax: 605-345-4871. Email: ctkparish@abe.midco.net.
Catechesis/Religious Program—Students 131.

Wellington, Minnehaha Co., St. Joseph, Closed. For sacramental records contact St. Ann, Humboldt.

WESSINGTON SPRINGS, JERAULD CO., ST. JOSEPH (1906) [JC] Rev. James Friedrich.
Mailing Address: P.O. Box 266, Woonsocket, 57385. Tel: 605-539-9569; Fax: 605-539-9569. In Res., Rev. Msgr. Ed Burian (Retired).
Church: 510 N. Wallace St., 57382.
Catechesis/Religious Program—Students 46.

WESSINGTON, BEADLE CO., ST. JOSEPH, Attended by Miller., Mailing Address: P.O. Box 198, Miller, 57362-0198. Tel: 605-853-2207; Fax: 605-853-3037. Email: stann1962@mncomm.com.
Catechesis/Religious Program—Students 24.

WESTPORT, BROWN CO., SACRED HEART OF WESTPORT (1889) [CEM] Attended by Sacred Heart, Aberdeen., P.O. Box 87, 57481. Tel: 605-226-3713.
Catechesis/Religious Program—Students 55.

WHITE LAKE, AURORA CO., ST. PETER (1883) [CEM] Attended by Kimball
Res.: 101 S. Ellis, Box 277, 57383. Tel: 605-249-2700.
Catechesis/Religious Program—Students 80.

WHITE, BROOKINGS CO., ST. PAUL (1898) [JC] Rev. Andrew Dickinson.
Mailing Address: University Sta., Box 7019, Brookings, 57007. Tel: 605-692-9461.

WILLOW LAKE, CLARK CO., ST. JAMES (1895) Closed. For records, contact St. Michael, Clark.

WILMOT, ROBERTS CO., ST. MARY (1886) [CEM] Rev. John McMullen, O.S.B.
Res.: *Blue Cloud Abbey*, P.O. Box 98, Marvin, 57251.
Church: Box 204, 57279. Tel: 605-938-4289; Fax: 605-398-9201.
Catechesis/Religious Program—Students 62.

WOONSOCKET, SANBORN CO., ST. WILFRID (1884) [CEM] Rev. James Friedrich.
Res.: 203 N. 2nd Ave., Box 266, 57385. Tel: 605-796-4666; Fax: 605-796-4666.
Catechesis/Religious Program—Students 76.

WORTHING, LINCOLN CO., ST. EDWARD (1908) [CEM] Attended by St. Dominic, Canton., 800 E. Walnut, Canton, 57013. Tel: 605-764-5640; Fax: 605-764-3085.

YANKTON, YANKTON CO.
1—ST. BENEDICT (1993) [JC] Rev. Paul Josten; Deacon Ronald Kachena.
Res.: 1500 St. Benedict Dr., 57078. Tel: 605-664-6214; Fax: 605-664-2305.
Catechesis/Religious Program—1500 St. Benedict Dr., 57078. Tel: 605-665-6214. Students 214.
2—SACRED HEART (1871) [CEM] Revs. Mark Lichter; Robert Edward Lacey.
Res.: 509 Capitol St., 57078. Tel: 605-665-3655; Fax: 605-665-6768.
School—Tel: 605-665-5841; Fax: 605-668-9787. Sisters 1; Lay Teachers 15; Students 330.
Catechesis/Religious Program—Students 208.

ZELL, HAND CO., ST. MARY (1883) Attended by Mellette., Box 46, Mellette, 57461.

Chaplains of Public Institutions

SIOUX FALLS. *South Dakota State Penitentiary & Minnehaha County Correctional Centers*. Revs. Gary Ternes, J.C.L., A.W. Ramos.
Veteran's Hospital. Rev. Mark Axtmann.

FLANDREAU. *Government Indian School*. Attended by SS. Simon & Jude, Flandreau

SPRINGFIELD. *Mike Durfee Correctional Facility*. Attended by St. Leo, Tyndall

YANKTON. *Federal Prison Camp*. Rev. Lawrence J. Marbach (Retired).
Mickelson Center for the Neurosciences. Deacon Stillman Slassen.

On Duty Outside the Diocese:
Revs.—
Weber, Terry, St. Thomas Academy, 106 King St. W., Saint Paul, MN 55107.
Wensing, Michael, Institute for Continuing Education, Pontifical North American College 00120 Vatican City State.

Retired:
Rev. Msgrs.—
Andraschko, James, 3701 E. Peony Pl., 57103.
Burian, Ed, P.O. Box 267, Wessington Springs, 57382.
Doyle, James Michael, 2913 Ridgeview Way, 57105.
Hermann, Carlton P., 505 Burgess Rd., 57078-1819.
Mahowald, Richard J., P.A., Laurel Oaks #205, 4510 S. Prince of Peace Pl., 57103.
McPhee, Marvin (DEN), 1417 W. Ash Ave., Mitchell, 57301.
Revs.—
Brady, John, 509 Broadway, 57078.
Bream, James I., 4915 S. Glenview Rd., 57108.
Connolly, Thomas, Atria Baypoint Village #233, 7927 State Hwy. 52, Hudson, FL 34667.
Duman, Charles J., 330 N. Idaho, Salem, 57058.
Fox, Leonard, 600 E. Lincoln St., Elk Point, 57025.
Friedrich, Lawrence, 4500 S. Prince of Peace Pl., #A-8, 57103.
Geditz, Roger, P.O. Box 136, Geddes, 57342.
Holtzman, Jerome, 77 Paradise Dr., Watertown, 57201.
Imberi, Anthony, 25216 - 481st Ave., Garretson, 57030.
Imming, Donald, 30 Walker St., Vermillion, 57069.
Janes, David A., 1003 N. Dakota St., #8, Aberdeen, 57401.
Johnson, Doug, 930 W. 7th St., #7, 57104.
Joyce, James, 900 E. 14th St., #112, 57104.
Kayser, Leonard, 304 Greenview Dr., #11, 57078-1445.
Krzyzopolski, Al, 4700 S. Cliff Ave., #210, 57103.
Lantz, Gary, S.C.J., Rockford Apts. #3, 104 Cliffs Drive, P.O. Box 6, Chamberlain, 57325-0006.
Marbach, Lawrence J., 617 Maple St., 57078-3823.
Mardian, Pius, 4510 Prince of Peace Pl., #120, 57103.
Meier, Denis, 8728 Benet Place, 100 28th Ave, S.E. # 310, Watertown, 57201.
Molumby, Donald, Laurel Oaks, 4510 S. Prince of Peace Pl., #210, 57103.
Ortmeier, Richard J., Mother of God Monastery, Benet Place, 100 28th Ave., S.E., #311, Watertown, 57201.
Riedman, John, 501 North Buckboard Dr., Kerrville, TX 78028.

Permanent Deacons:
Barry, James T. "Tim", Ed.D., Mt. Marty College, Yankton
Bates, Thomas R., Holy Spirit, Sioux Falls
Boorman, James, (Out of diocese)
Cantin, Leon, Christ the King, Sioux Falls
Cheskie, Pete, (Out of Diocese)
Conrads, Michael, St. Therese, Sioux Falls
Counter, Ralph, (Retired), St. Lambert, Sioux Falls
Devlin, John P., St. Michael, Sioux Falls
Frankman, William, Marriage Tribunal
Graff, Francis, (Retired), Humboldt
Graves, Joseph, Holy Family, Mitchell
Gruhot, Edward, St. William, Aurora
Hayes, James M., Holy Spirit, Mitchell
Heidt, Roger, Chancery Office; St. Lambert, Sioux Falls
Holsing, Arvid, St. Thomas the Apostle, Faulkton
Huntington, Michael, Campus Minister, O'Gorman Junior High School
Jetty, Alfred "Bud", Native American Ministry, Chamberlain
Kachena, Ronald, St. Benedict, Yankton
Knapp, Henry J., St. Mary's, Sioux Falls
Kocer, Albert, St. John the Baptist, Wagner
McLaughlin, Steven A., Lower Brule Team Ministry, Fort Thompson
Mehlhaff, Peter, Sacred Heart, Aberdeen
Oliver, Edward B., (Retired), Canton
Pardew, Harold, Sioux Falls; St. Joseph Cathedral
Twidwell, Joseph, Blessed Teresa of Calcutta, Dakota Dunes
Vogel, Thomas, St. Patrick, Wakonda
Wagner, Barry, Sacred Heart, Parkston
Wagner, Donald, St. Rose of Lima, Garretson
Walden, James I., (Retired), Sioux Falls
Wambach, Micheal A., Holy Cross, Ipswich
Wathen, Jerome F., Hospital Chap., St. Lambert, Sioux Falls
Zephier, Edward P., (Retired), Marty

INSTITUTIONS LOCATED IN THE DIOCESE

[A] COLLEGES AND UNIVERSITIES

ABERDEEN. *Presentation College* (1951) 1500 N. Main St., 57401. Tel: 605-225-1634; Fax: 605-229-8330. Email: lorraine.hale@presentation.edu. Web: www.presentation.edu. Dr. Lorraine M. Hale, P.B.V.M., Pres.; Rev. Joseph Sheehan, O.Carm., Chap. Sisters of the Presentation of the B.V.M., Campuses also located at Eagle Butte, SD & Fairmont, MN Priests 1; Sisters 3; Lay Teachers 48; Students 700.

FAIRMONT. *Presentation College-Fairmont*, 115 S. Park St. Suite 210, MN 56031.

YANKTON. *Mount Marty College*, 1105 W. 8th St., 57078. Tel: 800-658-4552; Fax: 605-668-1357. Email: jbarry@mtmc.edu. Web: www.mtmc.edu. Deacon James T. "Tim" Barry, Ed.D.; Sandra Brown, Librarian. Benedictine Sisters. Sisters 7; Lay Teachers 45; Students 1,219.
Mount Marty College - Watertown Campus, 1225 Arrow Ave., P.O. Box 1385, Watertown, 57201. Tel: 605-886-6777; Fax: 605-882-6347. Email: mmcwatwn@dailypost.com. Linda Schurmann, Dir. Conducted by Benedictine Sisters.

[B] EDUCATION CENTERS, PRIVATE

CHAMBERLAIN. *St. Joseph Indian School*, P.O. Box 89, 57325. Tel: 605-234-3300; Fax: 605-234-3480. Web: www.stjo.org. Rev. Stephen Huffstetter, S.C.J.; Kathleen Donohue, Prin.; Judy Houska, Librarian. Priests 2; Lay Teachers 24; Students 210.

[C] INTER-PAROCHIAL SCHOOLS

SIOUX FALLS. *Sioux Falls Catholic School System*, 3100 W. 41st St., 57105. Tel: 605-336-6241; Fax: 605-373-1035. Email: tlorang@sfcss.org. Web: sfcss.org. Dr. Thomas Lorang, Supt.
O'Gorman High School, 3201 S. Kiwanis Ave., 57105. Tel: 605-336-3644; Fax: 605-336-9272. Kyle Groos, Prin.; Rev. David A. Desmond, Chap. Priests 1; Sisters 1; Lay Teachers 52; Students 761.
O'Gorman Catholic Junior High (Grades 7-8), 3100 W. 41st St., 57105. Tel: 605-988-0546; Fax: 605-336-9839. Colley Broveliet, Prin. Lay Teachers 24; Students 401.
St. Mary Elementary (Grades PreK-6), 2001 S. 5th Ave., 57105. Tel: 605-334-9881; Fax: 605-334-9224. Courtney Tielke, Prin. Lay Teachers 21; Students 373.
Holy Spirit Elementary (Grades PreK-6), 3601 E. Dudley Ln., 57103. Tel: 605-371-1481; Fax: 605-371-1483. Carol Loeffelholz, Prin. Lay Teachers 20; Students 397.
Christ the King Elementary School (Grades PreK-6), 1801 S. Lake Ave., 57105. Tel: 605-338-5103; Fax: 605-335-1231. Stephanie Wilson, Prin. Lay Teachers 7; Students 127.
St. Lambert Elementary School (Grades PreK-6), 1000 S. Bahnson Ave., 57103. Tel: 605-338-7042; Fax: 605-336-8727. Barbara Lockwood, Prin. Lay Teachers 20; Students 279.
St. Michael Elementary School (Grades PreK-6), 1600 S. Marion Rd., 57106. Tel: 605-361-0021; Fax: 605-361-0094. Lisa Huemoeller, Prin. Lay Teachers 20; Students 362.
St. Katherine Drexel Elementary, 1800 S. Katie Ave., Ste. 2, 57106. Tel: 605-275-6994. Katie Kerkuliet, Prin. Lay Teachers 3; Students 105.

ABERDEEN. *Aberdeen Catholic Schools Education Office*, 1400 N. Dakota St., S.E., 57401. Tel: 605-226-2100; Fax: 605-226-0616. Email: vickiehaiar@aberdeenroncalli.org. Web: www.aberdeenroncalli.org.
Roncalli Primary School (Grades PreK-2), 419 N.E. 1st. Ave., 57401. Tel: 605-225-3460. Email: mary.schwab@aberdeenroncalli.org. Mary Schwab, Prin. Lay Teachers 12; Students 193.
Roncalli Elementary School (Grades 3-6), 501 S.E. 3rd. Ave., 57401. Tel: 605-229-4100; Fax: 605-229-4101. Email: mary.schwab@aberdeenroncalli.org. Mary Schwab, Prin. (Elementary) Lay Teachers 11; Students 170.
Roncalli High School (Grades 7-12), 1400 N. Dakota St., 57401. Tel: 605-225-7440; Fax: 605-226-0616. Email: levens@midco.net. Web: www.aberdeenroncalli.org. Sandra Levsen, Dean; Peggy Cox, Prin.; Cathy McNeary, Librarian. Priests 3; Lay Teachers 26; Students 266.

YANKTON. *Sacred Heart School*, 1500 St. Benedict Dr., Ste. 200, 57078-6884. Tel: 605-665-5841; Fax: 605-260-3400. Email: regan.manning@k12.sd.us. Web: www.shs.k12.sd.us. Regan Manning, Prin.; Barb Rezac, Devel. Dir. Sisters 1; Lay Teachers 21; Total Enrollment 375.

[D] GENERAL HOSPITALS

SIOUX FALLS. *Avera McKennan* 57117-5045. Tel: 605-322-8000; Fax: 605-322-7822. Web: www.averamckennan.org. Mr. Fredrick W. Slunecka, Regl. Pres. & CEO; Rev. Greg Frankman, Chap. Sponsored by Sisters of the Presentation of the B.V.M. of Aberdeen, S.D., and Benedictine Sisters of Sacred Heart Monastery, Yankton, S.D. Sisters of the Presentation of the B.V.M. (Aberdeen, SD) 4; Bed Capacity 395; Total Staff 3,680; Patients Assisted Annually 200,200.
Avera McKennan aka Prince of Peace 4500 Prince of Peace, 57103. Tel: 605-322-5600; Fax: 605-322-5622. Justin Hinker, Admin. Skilled Nursing Care Units 90; Assisted Living 36; Total Staff 188.
Avera McKennan dba Avera Behavioral Health Center 57117. Tel: 605-322-8000; Fax: 605-322-4009. Sponsored by Sisters of the Presentation of the B.V.M. of Aberdeen, S.D. and Benedictine Sisters of Sacred Heart Monastery, Yankton, S.D. Staffed Beds 110; Total Staff 217.

ABERDEEN. *Avera St. Luke's*, 305 S. State St., 57401. Tel: 605-622-5000; Fax: 605-622-5127. Web: www.averastlukes.org. Ron Jacobson, Regl. Pres.; Rev. Charles Emezie (Nigeria), Chap.; Mike Sandsmark, Vice Pres. Mission. Sponsored by

Sisters of the Presentation of the B.V.M. of Aberdeen, SD, and Benedictine Sisters of Sacred Heart Monastery, Yankton, SD. Presentation Sisters of the B.V.M.(Aberdeen, SD) 2; Bed Capacity 139; Bassinets 20; Total Assisted Annually 232,656; Total Staff 1,463.

Avera St. Luke's dba Avera Mother Joseph Manor Retirement Community 1002 N. Jay St., 57401. Tel: 605-622-5850; Fax: 605-622-5851. Email: tom.snyder@averastlukes.org. Tom Snyder, Admin.; Rev. Charles Emezie (Nigeria). Adult Day Care, Community Outreach, Respite Care, Health Screening Clinics, and Family Support Council. Residents 81; Units for Apartment Living 58; Assisted Living Beds 34; Total Staff 130.

DELL RAPIDS. *Dells Area Health Center/Avera Health*, 909 N. Iowa St., 57022. Tel: 605-428-5431; Fax: 605-428-3906. Jim Faulwell, Admin. Acute Care Beds 23; Staff 55.

DE SMET. *Avera De Smet Memorial Hospital*, 306 Prairie Ave., S.W., P.O. Box 160, 57231. Tel: 605-854-3329; Fax: 605-854-3161. Janice Schardin, Admin. Bed Capacity 17; Staff 24.

EUREKA. *Avera St. Luke's dba Avera Eureka Health Care Center* 202 J Ave., P.O. Box 40, 57437. Tel: 605-284-2145; Fax: 605-284-2011. Web: www.averastlukes.org. Carmen Weber, Admin. Sponsored by Sisters of Presentation of the B.V.M of Abderdeen, SD & Benedictine Sisters of Sacred Heart Monastery, Yankton, SD. Nursing Home Beds 56; Total Staff 75.

GETTYSBURG. *Gettysburg Medical Center*, 606 E. Garfield, 57442. Tel: 605-765-2488; Fax: 605-765-2704. Mark C. Schmidt, Exec. Dir. Bed Capacity 50; Critical Access Hospital 10; Residential Living Units 12.

MILBANK. *Milbank Area Hospital/Avera*, 901 E. Virgil Ave., 57252. Tel: 605-432-4538; Fax: 605-432-5412. Marc Lemon, Admin. Bed Capacity 25; Staff 65.

MITCHELL. *Avera Queen of Peace*, 525 N. Foster, 57301. Tel: 605-995-2000; Fax: 605-995-2441. Email: tom.rasmusson@averaqueenofpeace.org. Web: www.averaqueenofpeace.org. Sponsored by Sisters of the Presentation of the B.V.M., Aberdeen, SD, and Benedictine Sisters of Sacred Heart Monastery, Yankton, SD. Sisters 3; Bed Capacity 120; Staff 586; Patients Assisted Annually 68,000.

Avera Queen of Peace dba Avera Brady Health & Rehabilitation, Avera Brady Assisted Living 500 S. Ohlman, 57301. Tel: 605-996-7701; Fax: 605-995-6134. Mrs. Veronica Smith, Admin. Sponsored by Sisters of the Presentation of the B.V.M., Aberdeen, SD, and Benedictine Sisters of Sacred Heart Monastery, Yankton, SD. Skilled Nursing Care Units 84; Assisted Living 30; Total Staff 128.

Bishop Hoch Villa, 500 S. Ohlman St., 57301. Tel: 605-996-7701; Fax: 605-995-6134. Units for Congregate Living 6; Additional Senior Units 2.

PARKSTON. *St. Benedict Health Center dba Avera St. Benedict Health Center* 401 W. Glynn Dr., 57366. Tel: 605-928-3311; Fax: 605-928-7368. Email: gale.walker@averastbenedict.org. Web: www.averastbenedict.org. Gale N. Walker, Pres. & CEO. Benedictine Sisters (Yankton, SD) 2; Bed Capacity 87; Total Assisted Annually 24,489; Total Staff 210.

PIERRE. *St. Mary's Foundation*, 800 E. Dakota, 57501. Tel: 605-224-3451; Fax: 605-224-3459. Email: ellenlee@catholichealth.net. Ellen J. Lee, Exec. Dir.

St. Mary's Healthcare Center of Pierre, South Dakota, 800 E. Sioux Ave., 57501. Tel: 605-224-3173; Fax: 605-224-3426. Email: chadcooper@catholichealth.net. Chad Cooper, CEO. Includes: Maryhouse Residential Nursing Facility and Parkwood Retirement Apartments. Sisters 1; Bed Capacity 60; Total Assisted Annually 27,758; Staff 435.

TYNDALL. *St. Michael's Hospital*, P.O. Box 27, 57066. Tel: 605-589-3341; Fax: 605-589-3288. Email: cdeurmier@smh-bhfp.org. Carol Deurmier, CEO. Bed Capacity 25; Total Assisted Annually 7,800; Total Staff 86.

WESSINGTON SPRINGS. *Avera Weskota Memorial Medical Center*, 604 First St., N.E., 57382. Tel: 605-539-1201; Fax: 605-539-4580. Gaea Blue, Admin. Bed Capacity 14; Staff 37.

YANKTON. *Sacred Heart Health Services dba Avera Sacred Heart Hospital* 501 Summit, 57078. Tel: 605-668-8000; Fax: 605-665-0170. Pamela Rezac, Pres. & CEO. Sponsored by Sisters of the Presentation of the B.V.M. of Aberdeen, S.D. and Benedictine Sisters of Sacred Heart Monastery, Yankton, S.D. Sisters 3; Bed Capacity 144; Total Staff 555.

Sacred Heart Health Services dba Avera Sister James Nursing Homes 2111 W. 11th, 57078. Tel: 605-668-8000; Fax: 605-665-0170. Total Bed Capacity for facilities at 501 Summit & 1212 W. Eighth St. 114; Total Staff 173.

Sacred Heart Health Services dba Avera Yankton Care Center 1212 W. Eighth St., 57078. Tel: 605-665-9429; Fax: 605-668-8966. Sponsored by Sisters of the Presentation of the B.V.M. of Aberdeen, S.D. and Benedictine Sisters of Sacred Heart Monastery, Yankton, S.D. Bed Capacity 73; Total Staff 82.

[E] HOMES FOR AGED

MILBANK. *St. William Care Center*, 100 S. 9th St., 57252. Tel: 605-432-5811; Fax: 605-432-3187. Conducted by Daughters of St. Mary of Providence, Milbank. Guests 60.

Angela Hall Tel: 605-432-3171; Fax: 605-432-3187. Assisted Living Center Sisters 4; Guests 6.

SISSETON. *Tekakwitha Nursing Center, Inc. dba Tekakwitha Living Center* (sub. of Benedictine Health System), 6 E. Chestnut, 57262. Tel: 605-698-7693; Fax: 605-698-3091. Email: jim.cornelius@bhshealth.org. James P. Cornelius, Admin.; Pearl Whelan, Dir. Pastoral Care. (Owned and operated by: Benedictine Health System) Bed Capacity 75; Total Assisted Annually 180; Total Staff 105.

Rainbow Daycare Center Tel: 605-698-3257; Fax: 605-698-3091.

[F] MONASTERIES AND RESIDENCES OF PRIESTS AND BROTHERS

MARVIN. *Blue Cloud Abbey*, 46561 147th St., P.O. Box 98, 57251-0098. Tel: 605-398-9200; Fax: 605-398-9201. Email: abbey@bluecloud.org. Web: www.bluecloud.org. Rt. Revs. Thomas Hillenbrand, Retired Abbot; Alan Berndt, O.S.B., Retired Abbot; Denis Quinkert, O.S.B., Abbot; Revs. John McMullen, O.S.B.; Basil Dilger, O.S.B.; Cletus Miller, O.S.B.; Odilo Burkhardt, O.S.B.; Bernardine Ness, O.S.B.; Christopher Uehlein, O.S.B.; Pedro Choc, O.S.B.; Francisco Arrivillaga Lemus, O.S.B.; Matthew Kowalski, O.S.B.; Carlos Antonio Pop, O.S.B.; Michael Peterson, O.S.B.; Elias Juan Tello Aburto, O.S.B.; Bro. Benet Tvedten, O.S.B., Prior. Priests 15; Brothers 19.

[G] CONVENTS AND RESIDENCES FOR SISTERS

SIOUX FALLS. *Adoration Sisters of the Blessed Sacrament*, 521 N. Duluth Ave., 57104. Tel: 605-336-2374; Fax: 605-357-7290. Email: adoratrices@msn.com. Sr. Angelica Morales Rendon, A.P., Supr. Sisters 8; Novices 3.

ABERDEEN. *Presentation Convent*, 1500 N. 2nd St., 57401. Tel: 605-229-8419; Fax: 605-229-8412. Email: pdonelan@presentationsisters.org. Web: www.presentationsisters.org. Sr. Pam Donelan, Pres. Motherhouse and Novitiate of the Sisters of the Presentation of the B.V.M. Final Professed Sisters 98.

ALEXANDRIA. *Monastery of Our Mother of Mercy and St. Joseph Discalced Carmelite Nuns*, 221 5th St. W., P.O. Box 67, 57311-0067. Tel: 605-239-4382; Fax: 605-239-4676. Sr. Marie Therese of the Child Jesus, O.C.D., Prioress.

Discalced Carmelite Nuns of Alexandria, South Dakota, Inc. Solemnly Professed Sisters 10; First Professed 2; Postulants 2.

MARTY. *Motherhouse Oblate Sisters of the Blessed Sacrament*Sr. Inez Jetty, O.S.B.S., Community Leader. *St. Sylvester's Convent*, 103 Church Dr., P.O. Box 217, 57361-0217. Tel: 605-384-3305; Fax: 605-384-3575. Email: osbs@cme.com. Professed Sisters 6.

MITCHELL. *Sisters of St. Francis of Our Lady of Guadulupe*, 1417 W. Ash, 57301. Tel: 605-996-1410. Email: sistersofstfrancis@mit.midco.net. Sr. M. Loretta Von Rueden, Sister Leader. Private Association of the Faithful. Professed Sisters 3.

WATERTOWN. *Mother of God Monastery*, 110 28th Ave., S.E., 57201-8419. Tel: 605-882-6600; Fax: 605-882-6658. Email: prioress@dailypost.com. Web: watertownbenedictines.org. Sr. Ramona Fallon, O.S.B., Prioress. Motherhouse and Novitiate of Benedictine Sisters. Sisters 56.

YANKTON. *Sacred Heart Monastery*, 1005 W. Eighth St., 57078-3389. Tel: 605-668-6000; Fax: 605-668-6153. Email: jkehrwald@mtmc.edu. Web: yanktonbenedictines.org. Sr. Jennifer Kehrwald, O.S.B., Prioress; Rev. Mel Patton, O.S.B., Chap. Motherhouse and Novitiate of the Benedictine Sisters. Sisters 119.

[H] NEWMAN CENTERS

ABERDEEN. *St. Thomas Aquinas Newman Center* Email: nsunewman@nvc.net.

Northern State University 310 15th Ave., S.E., 57401. Tel: 605-229-1011; Fax: 605-226-3274. Michala Heller, Campus Min. & Dir.

BROOKINGS. *Pius XII Student Center* Box 7019, University Station, 57007. Tel: 605-692-9461; Fax: 605-692-9461. Email: ccpoffice@brookings.net. Web: www.newmancenter.sdstate.org. Rev. Andrew Dickinson.

MADISON. *Dakota State University Newman Club Office* , Attended by St. Thomas Parish, Madison., 217 N.W. 4th St., 57042. Tel: 606-256-4135. Email: sistart@rapidnet.com.

VERMILLION. *St. Thomas More Catholic Newman Center* Email: newmanpc@usd.edu.

University of South Dakota 320 E. Cherry St., 57069. Tel: 605-624-2697; Fax: 605-624-4145. Rev. Scott Traynor.

[I] MISCELLANEOUS LISTINGS

SIOUX FALLS. *Avera Health*, 3900 W. Avera Dr., 57108-5721. Tel: 605-322-4700; Fax: 605-322-4799. Email: contactus@avera.org. Web: www.avera.org. Sponsored by the Sisters of the Presentation of the B.V.M., Aberdeen, SD, and the Benedictine Sisters of Sacred Heart Monastery, Yankton, SD.

Avera Health Foundation, 3900 W. Avera Dr., Ste. 100, 57108-5721. Tel: 605-322-4750; Fax: 605-322-4666. Email: jerry.soholt@avera.org. Web: www.avera.org.

The Berakhah House, 535 N. Duluth, 57104. Tel: 605-334-9861; Fax: 605-334-2092.

The Catholic Foundation for Eastern South Dakota, 523 N. Duluth Ave., 57104. Tel: 605-988-3788; Fax: 605-988-3746. Email: mconzemi@sfcatholic.org. Web: www.sfcatholic.org. Mark Conzemius, Pres.

City of Sioux Falls Catholic Schools Property Corporation, 523 N. Duluth Ave., 57104. Tel: 605-988-3759; Fax: 604-334-2092. Email: mbannwar@sfcatholic.org. Web: www.sfcatholic.org.

Community Outreach, 231 N. Weber Ave., 57103. Tel: 605-331-3935; Fax: 605-336-8924. Email: info@thecommunityoutreach.org. Angela Hyde, Dir. Total Staff 5; Total Families Assisted Annually 3,350.

St. Francis House, 1301 E. Austin St., 57103. Tel: 605-334-3879; Fax: 605-575-3999. Email: director@stfrancishouse.com. Julie Becker, Exec. Dir. Bed Capacity 39.

Good Shepherd Center, 300 N. Main Ave., 57104. Tel: 605-332-3176; Fax: 605-977-4807. Maria Krell, Dir. Total Staff 3; Total Assisted Annually 20,000.

Holy Spirit School Permanent Trust, 3601 E. Dudley Ln., 57103. Tel: 605-371-2320; Fax: 605-371-1957. Email: holyspiritsf@qwestoffice.net. Rev. James P. Morgan, Trustee.

St. Joseph Catholic Housing, Inc., Catholic Chancery Office, 523 N. Duluth Ave., 57104. Tel: 605-334-9861; Fax: 605-988-3746. Email: kbenson@SFCatholic.org.

Kateri Indian Center, 300 N. Main Ave., 57104. Tel: 605-335-3321; Fax: 605-977-4807. Total Staff 2; Total Assisted Annually 31,611.

Little Flower of Jesus School Foundation, Inc., 901 N. Tahoe Tr., 57110-5779. Tel: 605-338-2433; Fax: 605-339-2203.

St. Margaret's Fellowship, 1901 S. Grange Ave., 57105. Tel: 605-336-3151.

St. Matthew Stewardship, Inc., 523 N. Duluth Ave., 57104. Tel: 605-988-3759; Fax: 605-988-3746. Email: mbannwar@sfcatholic.org. Web: www.sfcatholic.org.

Pension Plan for Priests of the Diocese of Sioux Falls, 523 N. Duluth Ave., 57104. Tel: 605-334-9861; Fax: 605-334-2092. Web: www.sfcatholic.org.

Sioux Falls Catholic School Foundation, 3100 W. 41st St., 57105. Tel: 605-575-3364; Fax: 605-988-0581. Email: mflynn@stcss.org. Web: sfcss.org. Total Staff 2.

South Dakota Broadcasting Corporation, 523 N. Duluth Ave., 57104.

ABERDEEN. *The Presentation Sisters Heritage Trust*, 1500 North Second, 57401. Tel: 605-229-8419; Fax: 605-229-8412. Email: pdonelan@presentationsisters.org. Web: www.presentationsisters.org. Sr. Pam Donelan, P.B.V.M., Contact Person. Sponsored by: Sisters of the Presentation of the Blessed Virgin Mary of Aberdeen, South Dakota.

**Roncalli Foundation*, 1400 N. Dakota St., 57401.

IRENE. *Broom Tree Retreat and Conference Center*, Mailing Address: 523 N. Duluth, 57104. 29827 446th St., 57039. Tel: 605-263-1040; Fax: 605-263-1043.

MARVIN. *Blue Cloud Abbey Retirement Trust*, P.O. Box 98, 57251-0098. Tel: 605-398-9200; Fax: 605-398-9201. Email: mcmullen@tnics.com. Rev. John McMullen, O.S.B., Treas.

MITCHELL. *Foundation for Catholic Education*, 1510 W. Elm, 57301. Tel: 605-999-9127; Fax: 605-996-5738. Joan E. Roenfanz, Dir. Devel.

SISSETON. *Tekakwitha Housing Corp.*, Mailing Address: 711 Veteran's Ave., 57262. Tel: 605-698-7693; Fax: 605-698-3091.

Tekakwitha Indian Mission, Inc., 120 E. Chestnut, 57262. Tel: 605-698-7414; Fax: 605-698-7236.

WATERTOWN. *St. Ann's Corporation*, 100 28th Ave. S.E., 57201. Tel: 605-886-9177; Fax: 605-882-3193. Mary Beth Grape, Admin.

Benet Place (Independent Senior Apartments), 100 28th Ave., S.E., 57201. Tel: 605-886-9177; Fax: 605-882-3193. Units 36; Staff 13.

Evergreen Assisted Living, 90 28th Ave., S.E., 57201. Tel: 605-882-8555; Fax: 605-882-8556. Units 16; Staff 8.

The Benedictine Sisters Foundation of Watertown, 110 28th Ave., S.E., #55, 57201. Tel: 605-882-6633; Fax: 605-882-6658. Email: prioress@dailypost.com. Web: watertownbenedictines.org.

Holy Name Foundation, Inc., 1009 Skyline Dr., 57201. Tel: 605-886-2628; Fax: 605-886-2142.

Immaculate Conception School Foundation, Inc., 309 2nd Ave., S.E., 57201. Tel: 605-886-3883; Fax: 605-886-0199.

Retirement Trust, Mother of God Monastery, 110 28th Ave., S.E., 57201. Tel: 605-882-6654; Fax: 605-882-6658. Email: treasurer@dailypost.com. Web: watertownbenedictines.org.

YANKTON. *Benedictine Center, Inc.*, 1005 W. 8th, 57078. Tel: 605-668-6000; Fax: 605-668-6153.

Benedictine Health Foundation, Inc., 1000 W. 4th, Ste. 14, 57078. Tel: 605-668-8310; Fax: 605-665-0170. Email: BHF@SHHServices.com. Kelly Kathol, Exec. Dir.

The House of Mary Shrine, Inc., Lewis & Clark Lake, Box 455, 57078-0455. Tel: 605-668-0121. Jean Weller, Pres. Bd. of Directors; Rev. Kenneth Bain, Spiritual Dir.

Yankton Catholic Community Development Office, 509 Capital St., 57078. Tel: 605-665-4585; Fax: 605-665-4585. Email: yccdo@iw.net. Barb Rezac, Devel. Dir.

RELIGIOUS INSTITUTES OF MEN REPRESENTED IN THE DIOCESE

For further details refer to the corresponding bracketed number in the Religious Institutes of Men or Women section.

[]—*Apostles of Jesus* (Sudan)

[0200]—*Benedictine Monks* (Aurora, IL; Marvin, SD)—O.S.B.

[]—*Carmelite* (India)

[1130]—*Congregation of the Priests of the Sacred Heart* (Hales Corners, WI)—S.C.J.

[0910]—*Oblates of Mary Immaculate* (Central Prov.)—O.M.I.

[0560]—*Third Order Regular of Saint Francis* (Loretto, PA)—T.O.R.

[1335]—*Vincentian Congregation* (India)—V.C.

RELIGIOUS INSTITUTES OF WOMEN REPRESENTED IN THE DIOCESE

[0230]—*Benedictine Sisters of Pontifical Jurisdiction* (Yankton, Watertown, SD)—O.S.B.

[1310]—*Congregation of the Fransiscan Sisters of Little Falls, MN*

[0940]—*Daughters of St. Mary of Providence*—D.S.M.P.

[0420]—*Discalced Carmelite Nuns of the Monastery of Our Mother of Mercy* (Alexandria, SD)—O.C.D.

[3010]—*Oblate Sisters of the Blessed Sacrament*—O.S.B.S.

[3130]—*Our Lady of Victory Missionary Sisters*—O.L.V.M.

[]—*Perpetual Adoration Sisters of the Blessed Sacrament*—A.P.

[2970]—*School Sisters of Notre Dame* (Mankato Prov.)—S.S.N.D.

[2630]—*Sisters of Mercy of the Holy Cross*—S.C.S.C.

[3000]—*Sisters of Notre Dame de Namur*—S.N.D.deN.

[1030]—*Sisters of the Divine Savior*—S.D.S.

[3320]—*Sisters of the Presentation of the B.V.M.*—P.B.V.M.

[1720]—*Sisters of the Third Order Regular of St. Francis of the Congregation of Our Lady of Lourdes*—O.S.F.

INTER-PAROCHIAL CEMETERIES

SIOUX FALLS. *St. Michael*, 3001 N. Cliff, 57104. Tel: 605-338-3376; Fax: 605-338-4270.

NECROLOGY

† Fox, Robert J., (Retired)—Died Nov. 26, 2009
† Garvey, John M., (Retired)—Died Feb. 4, 2009

An asterisk (*) denotes an organization that has established tax-exempt status directly with the IRS and is not covered by the USCCB Group Ruling.

Diocese of Spokane

(Dioecesis Spokanensis)

Most Reverend

WILLIAM S. SKYLSTAD, D.D.

Bishop of Spokane; ordained May 21, 1960; appointed Bishop of Yakima February 22, 1977; consecrated and installed May 12, 1977; Transferred to Spokane April 17, 1990; succeeded to the See April 27, 1990. *Office: W. 1023 Riverside Ave., P.O. Box 1453, Spokane, WA 99210-1453. Res.: 1115 W. Riverside, Spokane, WA 99201-1195.*

Catholic Pastoral Center: W. 1023 Riverside Ave., P.O. Box 1453, Spokane, WA 99210-1453. Tel: 509-358-7300.

Web: www.dioceseofspokane.org

Email: chancellor@dioceseofspokane.org

ESTABLISHED DECEMBER 17, 1913.

Square Miles 24,356.

Solemnly consecrated to the Immaculate Heart of Mary on December 8, 1948.

Corporate Title: "The Catholic Bishop of Spokane, a Corporation Sole."

Comprises the following Counties in the State of Washington: Okanogan, Ferry, Stevens, Pend Oreille, Lincoln, Spokane, Adams, Whitman, Franklin, Walla Walla, Columbia, Garfield and Asotin.

For legal titles of parishes and diocesan institutions, consult the Catholic Pastoral Center.

STATISTICAL OVERVIEW

Personnel	
Bishop	1
Retired Abbots	1
Priests: Diocesan Active in Diocese	49
Priests: Diocesan Active Outside Diocese	4
Priests: Diocesan in Foreign Missions	1
Priests: Retired, Sick or Absent	29
Number of Diocesan Priests	83
Religious Priests in Diocese	79
Total Priests in Diocese	162
Extern Priests in Diocese	5
Permanent Deacons in Diocese	53
Total Brothers	7
Total Sisters	189
Parishes	
Parishes	82
With Resident Pastor:	
Resident Diocesan Priests	39
Resident Religious Priests	4
Without Resident Pastor:	
Administered by Priests	37
Administered by Religious Women	1
Administered by Lay People	1
Missions	2
Pastoral Centers	1
Professional Ministry Personnel:	
Brothers	5
Sisters	5
Lay Ministers	47
Welfare	
Catholic Hospitals	6
Total Assisted	562,984
Homes for the Aged	2
Total Assisted	205
Residential Care of Children	1
Total Assisted	31
Day Care Centers	1
Total Assisted	241
Specialized Homes	3
Total Assisted	2,544
Special Centers for Social Services	17
Total Assisted	194,049
Residential Care of Disabled	2
Total Assisted	12
Other Institutions	13
Total Assisted	693
Educational	
Seminaries, Diocesan	1
Students from This Diocese	10
Students from Other Diocese	10
Diocesan Students in Other Seminaries	7
Total Seminarians	17
Colleges and Universities	1
Total Students	7,701
High Schools, Diocesan and Parish	1
Total Students	113
High Schools, Private	2
Total Students	1,103
Elementary Schools, Diocesan and Parish	14
Total Students	3,305
Catechesis/Religious Education:	
High School Students	753
Elementary Students	2,140
Total Students under Catholic Instruction	15,132
Teachers in the Diocese:	
Lay Teachers	229
Vital Statistics	
Receptions into the Church:	
Infant Baptism Totals	1,259
Minor Baptism Totals	87
Adult Baptism Totals	127
Received into Full Communion	136
First Communions	1,321
Confirmations	1,620
Marriages:	
Catholic	231
Interfaith	82
Total Marriages	313
Deaths	592
Total Catholic Population	103,000
Total Population	792,306

Former Bishops—Most Revs. A. F. SCHINNER, D.D., cons. Bishop of Superior, July 25, 1905; resigned from that See, Jan. 15, 1913; appt. first Bishop of Spokane, March 18, 1914; resigned Dec. 17, 1925, and made Titular Bishop of Sala; died Feb. 7, 1937; CHARLES D. WHITE, D.D., ord. Sept. 24, 1910; appt. Dec. 20, 1926; cons. Feb. 24, 1927; died Sept. 25, 1955; BERNARD J. TOPEL, D.D., Ph.D., appt. Coadjutor Bishop Aug. 9, 1955; cons. Sept. 21, 1955; succeeded to the See Sept. 25, 1955; retired April 11, 1978; died Oct. 22, 1986; LAWRENCE H. WELSH, D.D., ord. May 26, 1962; appt. Bishop of Spokane Nov. 7, 1978; cons. and installed Dec. 14, 1978; resigned April 17, 1990; appt. Auxiliary of St. Paul-Minneapolis, Nov. 5, 1991; died Jan. 13, 1999.

Vicars General—Rev. STEVE DUBLINSKI, Mailing Address: P.O. Box 1453, Spokane, 99210-1453. Tel: 509-358-7303. Email: sdublinski@dioceseofspokane.org; Rev. Msgr. JOHN M. STEINER, St. Mary's Parish, 304 S. Adams Rd., Spokane Valley, 99216-2195. Tel: 509-928-3210. Email: jsteiner@dioceseofspokane.org.

Special Assistant to the Vicar General—ROBERTA SMITH, Asst. Coord., Mailing Address: P.O. Box 1453, Spokane, 99210-1453. Tel: 509-353-0442. Email: rsmith@dioceseofspokane.org.

Vicar for Priests—Rev. Msgr. ROBERT A. PEARSON (Retired), E. 429 Sharp, Spokane, 99202. Tel: 509-325-0681. Email: rpearson@dioceseofspokane.org.

Catholic Pastoral Center—W. 1023 Riverside Ave., P.O. Box 1453, Spokane, 99210-1453. Tel: 509-358-7300; Fax: 509-358-7302. Email: chancellor@dioceseofspokane.org. Office Hours: Mon.-Thurs. 8-5.

Moderator of the Curia—Rev. STEVE DUBLINSKI, Mailing Address: P.O. Box 1453, Spokane, 99210-1453. Tel: 509-358-7303. Email: sdublinski@dioceseofspokane.org.

Chancellor—Rev. MARK PAUTLER, J.C.L., Mailing Address: P.O. Box 1453, Spokane, 99210-1453. Tel: 509-358-7339. Email: mpautler@dioceseofspokane.org.

Archivist—Dr. ANTHONY CLARK, Ph.D.; Rev. THOMAS C. CASWELL (Retired), Mailing Address: P.O. Box 1453, Spokane, 99210-1453. Tel: 509-358-7349. Email: aclark@dioceseofspokane.org. Tues. & Thurs. 3-5pm.

Diocesan Tribunal—W. 1023 Riverside Ave., P.O. Box 1453, Spokane, 99210-1453. Tel: 509-358-7336; Fax: 509-693-3313. Email: tribunal@dioceseofspokane.org.

Judicial Vicar—Rev. MARK PAUTLER, J.C.L.

Defensor Vinculi—Rev. Msgr. JOHN M. STEINER; Rev. JOSE LUIS MILLAN.

Secretary—CHRISTY TONER.

Diocesan Consultors/Presbyteral Council—Members: Revs. MICHAEL L. ISHIDA; MICHAEL J. SAVELESKY, Chm.; PETER O. AMAH; DANIEL BARNETT; RICHARD CASE, S.J.; ROBERT J. MCNEESE; TYRONE J. SCHAFF; KEVIN CODD; JOSE LUIS MILLAN; ADRIAN PARCHER, O.S.B.; MICHAEL BLACKBURN, O.F.M.; STEVE DUBLINSKI; MARK PAUTLER, J.C.L.

Diocesan Pastoral Council—Most Rev. WILLIAM STEPHEN SKYLSTAD, D.D.; Rev. STEVE DUBLINSKI, Ex Officio; Mrs. MARY LOU BENTLEY (term expires 2009); Sr. JANYCE BOUTA, S.N.J.M. (term expires 2009); Mr. LEO LAPKE (term expires 2009); BETTY HEENEY; JACK HEENEY; Mr. DON KELLEY; Mr. JOE SCHNERT, (term expires 2009); DAVE OPBROEK; PAULA BACON; MARY DRUFFEL; DAVE KISHEL; DOREEN KISHEL; JOYCE MAYER; DENNY PENNA; LUCY STANZYK; JANICE STRIPES.

Diocesan Offices and Directors

Administrative Division: Diocesan Business Affairs—Deacon MICHAEL D. MILLER, Mailing Address: P.O. Box 1453, Spokane, 99210-1453. Email: mmiller@dioceseofspokane.org; 1023 W. Riverside Ave., Spokane, 99201. Tel: 509-358-7333; Fax: 509-358-7302.

Director of Fiscal Services—MERRILIN FULTON, Mailing Address: P.O. Box 1453, Spokane, 99210-1453. Tel: 509-358-7320. Email: mfulton@dioceseofspokane.org.

Catholic Foundation-Development Office—Mr. CHRIS SMITH, Mailing Address: P.O. Box 1453, Spokane, 99210-1453. Tel: 509-358-4280. Email: csmith@dioceseofspokane.org.

Computer Department—MARY GREEN, Mailing Address: P.O. Box 1453, Spokane, 99210-1453. Tel: 509-358-7346. Email: mgreen@dioceseofspokane.org.

Administrative Division: Catholic Schools—Dr. DUANE SCHAFER, Ph.D., Supt., Mailing Address: Office of Education, P.O. Box 1453, Spokane, 99210-1453.

Tel: 509-358-7330. Email: dschafer@dioceseofspokane.org.

Administrative Division: Evangelization and Ministries Formation—Sr. JUDITH NILLES, O.P., 1115 W. Riverside, Spokane, 99201. Tel: 509-358-4293. Email: jnilles@dioceseofspokane.org.

Communications Office—Deacon ERIC MEISFJORD, Dir. & Editor, Mailing Address: P.O. Box 1453, Spokane, 99210-1453. Tel: 509-358-7340. Email: emeisfjord@dioceseofspokane.org; NANCY LOBERG, Advertising Mgr. Tel: 509-358-7343. Email: nloberg@dioceseofspokane.org.

Charismatic Renewal—Rev. DANIEL WETZLER (Retired), 11517 Pebble Beach Dr., Harrison, ID 83833. Tel: 208-667-3232. Email: dwetzler@dioceseofspokane.org.

Ecumenical Relations—Rev. THOMAS C. CASWELL (Retired), 3534 W. Wellesley, Spokane, 99203. Tel: 509-624-1254. Email: tcaswell@dioceseofspokane.org.

Spanish Speaking Apostolates—VACANT.

Vietnamese Apostolate— Vietnamese Catholic Community of the Diocese of Spokane, Rev. JOACHIM L. HIEN, St. Anthony's Parish, 2320 N. Cedar, Spokane, 99205. Tel: 509-327-1162; Fax: 509-328-8728. Email: johien@dioceseofspokane.org.

Vocation Director—Rev. DARRIN CONNALL, 429 E. Sharp Ave., Spokane, 99202-1837. Tel: 509-326-3761. Email: bws@gonzaga.edu.

Diocesan Liturgical Commission—Rev. STEVE DUBLINSKI, Mailing Address: P.O. Box 1453, Spokane, 99210-1453. Tel: 509-358-7303. Email: sdublinski@dioceseofspokane.org.

Director of Deacon Formation—Rev. MICHAEL J. SAVELESKY, 3624 W. Indian Trail Rd., Spokane, 99208-4794. Tel: 509-326-0538. Email: abvm@icehouse.net.

Director of Deacons—Deacon JOHN SICILIA, St. Charles Parish, 4515 N. Alberta St., Spokane, 99205-1598. Tel: 509-327-9573.

Deacon Council—Deacon ERIC MEISFJORD, 1023 W. Riverside Ave., Spokane, 99201. Mailing Address: P.O. Box 1453, Spokane, 99210-1453. Tel: 509-358-7340.

Catholic Committee on Scouting—Deacon STEVE PRAWDZIK, Chap., 11828 S. Player Dr., Spokane, 99223-9524. Tel: 509-448-8934.

Bishop White Seminary—Rev. DARRIN CONNALL, Dir. Seminarians & Rector, 429 E. Sharp Ave., Spokane, 99202. Tel: 509-326-3255. Email: bws@gonzaga.edu. Web: bishopwhiteseminary.org.

Administrative Division: Social Ministries/Catholic Charities Diocesan Director—Dr. ROBERT J. MCCANN, Ph.D., W. 1023 Riverside, P.O. Box 1453, Spokane, 99210-1453. Tel: 509-358-4272. Email: rmcann@ccspokane.org.

Censor Liborum—Rev. MICHAEL J. SAVELESKY, Assumption of the Blessed Virgin Parish, 3624 W. Indian Trail Rd., Spokane, 99208-4794. Tel: 509-326-0144; Fax: 509-326-0538. Email: msavelesky@dioceseofspokane.org.

Continuing Education of Priests—Rev. Msgr. JOHN STEINER, St. Mary Parish, 304 S. Adams Rd., Spokane Valley, 99216. Email: jsteiner@dioceseofspokane.org.

Detention Ministry—Sr. MYRTA ITURRIAGA, S.P., Mailing Address: P.O. Box 1453, Spokane, 99210-1453. Tel: 509-358-7315. Email: miturriaga@dioceseofspokane.org.

Director of Cemeteries—JAMES G. FALKNER, Mailing Address: P.O. Box 18006, Spokane, 99228-0006. Tel: 509-467-5496. Email: info@cathcem.org. Web: www.cathcem.org.

Immaculate Heart Retreat Center—Deacon JOHN RUSCHEINSKY, Dir., 6910 S. Ben Burr Rd., Spokane, 99223. Tel: 509-448-1224. Web: www.ihrc.net. Email: ihrc@ihrc.net.

Priests' Personnel Board—Most Rev. WILLIAM S. SKYLSTAD, D.D.; Rev. Msgr. ROBERT A. PEARSON, Dir. (Retired), E. 429 E. Sharp, Spokane, 99202; Revs. JAMES KUHNS (Retired) (term expires May 2012) 304 S. Adams Rd., Spokane Valley, 99216; PATRICK KERST (term expires May 2010) 408 W. Poplar, Walla Walla, 99362; JOSE LUIS MILLAN (expires May 2010) 44 N.E. Ash St., Pullman, 99163; ROBERT J. MCNEESE; Rev. Msgr. PEDRO RAMIREZ (term expires May 2010).

Society for the Propagation of the Faith—Mr. CHRIS SMITH, W. 1023 Riverside Ave., P.O. Box 1453, Spokane, 99210. Tel: 509-358-4280. Email: csmith@dioceseofspokane.org.

Victim Assistance Coordinator—ROBERTA SMITH. Tel: 509-353-0442. Email: rsmith@dioceseofspokane.org.

CLERGY, PARISHES, MISSIONS AND PAROCHIAL SCHOOLS

CITY OF SPOKANE

(SPOKANE COUNTY)

1—CATHEDRAL OF OUR LADY OF LOURDES (1881) Revs. Steven L. Dublinski, Rector; Miguel Mejia; Deacon Gonzalo "Chalo" Martinez. In Res., Rev. Patrick Baraza.
Res.: 1115 W. Riverside Ave., 99201. Tel: 509-358-4290; Fax: 509-358-4277.
Catechesis/Religious Program—Tel: 509-358-4293. Sr. Judith Nilles, O.P., D.R.E. Students 10.

2—ST. ALOYSIUS (1890) Revs. Richard D. Case, S.J.; Charles Barnes, S.J., Parochial Vicar; Mr. Donald Weber, Parish Admin.
Res.: 330 E. Boone Ave., 99202. Tel: 509-313-5896; Fax: 509-313-5892. Email: stals@gonzaga.edu. Web: stalschurch.org.
School—(Grades PreK-8), 611 E. Mission Ave., 99202. Tel: 509-489-7825; Fax: 509-487-0975. Kerrie Rowland, Prin.
Montessori Education Center—Tel: 509-489-7825. Marta Schollenberger, Dir. Lay Teachers 18; Students 303.
Catechesis/Religious Program—Sr. Marianne Therese Wilkinson, S.N.J.M., D.R.E. Students 140.

3—ST. ANN (1902) Rev. Robert L. Fitts, S.J.; Craig Bartmess, Parish Admin.
Church: 2120 E. First Ave., 99202. Tel: 509-535-3031.

4—ST. ANTHONY (1909) Rev. Joachim L. Hien.
Res.: 2320 N. Cedar St., 99205. Tel: 509-327-1162; Fax: 509-328-8728.
See Trinity School, Spokane under Interparochial Grade Schools located in the Institution section.
Educare Center— Lay Teachers 4; Students 43.
Catechesis/Religious Program—Students 12.

5—ASSUMPTION OF THE BLESSED VIRGIN MARY (1958) Revs. Michael J. Savelesky; Lucas Ethan Tomson; Deacon Kelly Stewart.
Office: 3624 W. Indian Trail Rd., 99208. Tel: 509-326-0144; Fax: 509-326-0538.
School—(Grades PreK-8) Tel: 509-328-1115; Fax: 509-328-7872. Sonia Flores-Davis, Prin. Lay Teachers 14; Students 178.
Catechesis/Religious Program—Emily Klein, D.R.E. Students 66.

6—ST. AUGUSTINE (1914) Rev. Robert J. McNeese; Deacons Scott Brockway; Ken Dunlap.
Res.: 428 W. 19th Ave., 99203. Tel: 509-747-4421; Fax: 509-747-9086. Email: staugustine@dioceseofspokane.org.
School—Cataldo Catholic Interparochial, (Grades PreK-8), 455 W 18th Ave., 99203. Tel: 509-624-8759; Fax: 509-624-8763. Web: www.cataloo.org. Stephanie Johnson, Prin. Lay Teachers 23; Students 307.
Catechesis/Religious Program—Tel: 509-747-7972. Susan C. Harmon, D.R.E.; Christopher Ferrez, Youth Min. Students 93.

7—ST. CHARLES (1950) Rev. Eugene Tracy; Deacon John F. Sicilia.
Res.: 4515 N. Alberta St., 99205. Tel: 509-327-9573; Fax: 509-325-9353.
School—(Grades PreK-8) Tel: 509-327-9575; Fax: 509-325-9353. George Bonucelli, Prin. Religious 3; Lay Teachers 13; Students 261.
Catechesis/Religious Program—Students 40.

8—ST. FRANCIS OF ASSISI (1915) Revs. Michael Blackburn, O.F.M.; Alberic Smith, O.F.M.
Res.: 1104 W. Heroy Ave., 99205. Tel: 509-325-1321; Fax: 509-325-0927.
Catechesis/Religious Program—Geri Wasson, D.R.E. Students 10.

9—ST. FRANCIS XAVIER (1906) Revs. Victor M. Blazovich; Kenneth T. St. Hilare, Parochial Vicar; Deacon Gary Veale.
Mailing Address: 5021 N. Nelson St., 99217-6161.
Office:—545 E. Providence, 99207-1899. Tel: 509-487-1325.

10—ST. JOHN VIANNEY (1949) Revs. Joseph Bell; Charles Skok (Retired).
Mailing Address: P.O. Box 141125, Spokane Valley, 99214-1125.
Office: 503 N. Walnut Rd., 99206. Tel: 509-926-5428; Fax: 509-922-5282. Email: admin@sjvchurch.org. Web: www.sjvchurch.org.
School—(Grades PreK-8), 501 N. Walnut Rd., 99206. Tel: 509-926-7987; Fax: 509-891-9030. Web: st.johnvianney.com. Mr. Richard Pelkie Jr., Prin. Lay Teachers 11; Students 234.
Catechesis/Religious Program—Tel: 509-926-5553. Rita Crosby, D.R.E. Students 47.

11—ST. JOSEPH (1890) Rev. Joachim L. Hien; Deacon Gonzalo "Chalo" Martinez; Sr. Irene Knopes, S.N.J.M., Parish Admin.
Res.: 1503 W. Dean Ave., 99201. Tel: 509-328-4841; Fax: 509-328-4841.
See Trinity School, Spokane under Interparochial Grade Schools located in the Institution section.
Catechesis/Religious Program—Sr. Margarita Hernandez, S.P., Co-D.R.E.; Gail Wallace, Co-D.R.E. Students 30.

12—ST. MARY (1913) Rev. Msgr. John Steiner; Rev. Matthew Larsen; Deacons Cary Heth; Mike Miller.
Res.: 304 S. Adams Rd., Spokane Valley, 99216. Tel: 509-928-3210; Fax: 509-928-3215.
School—(Grades PreK-8), 14601 E. 4th Ave., 99216. Tel: 509-924-4300. Laurie Nauditt, Prin. Lay Teachers 14; Students 266.
Catechesis/Religious Program—Tel: 509-926-9559; Fax: 509-926-9550. Dona Mohr, D.R.E. Students 130.

13—MARY QUEEN (1957) Rev. Paul Vevik; Deacon Donald Whitney.
Res.: 3423 E. Carlisle Ave., 99217-7208. Tel: 509-483-4384; Fax: 509-483-0127.

14—OUR LADY OF FATIMA (1956) Rev. Tyrone J. Schaff; Deacon John Byrne.
Office:—1517 E. 33rd Ave., 99203. Tel: 509-747-7213; Fax: 509-747-7217.
School—All Saints Catholic School, (Grades 5-8) Tel: 509-624-5712; Fax: 509-624-7752. Ms. Kathy Hicks, Prin. Lay Teachers 12; Students 239.
Catechesis/Religious Program—Joan Leeds, D.R.E. Students 25.

15—OUR LADY OF THE LAKE (2002) Rev. Timothy R. Clancy, S.J.; Deacons George Lukach; Jack Crandell.
Mailing Address: P.O. Box 94, Nine Mile Falls, 99026. Tel: 509-276-7532.
Catechesis/Religious Program—Lucille Simmons, D.R.E. Students 5.

16—ST. PASCHAL (1916) Rev. W. Roy Floch.
Mailing Address: P.O. Box 11128, 99211-1128. Tel: 509-924-5090.
Educare Center—Tel: 509-922-7616. Ms. Mary Jo Paschall, Dir. Lay Teachers 2; Students 90.
Catechesis/Religious Program—Students 21.

17—ST. PATRICK (1893) Revs. Victor M. Blazovich; Kenneth T. St. Hilare.
Res.: 5021 N. Nelson St., 99217-6161. Tel: 509-487-1325; Fax: 509-484-3101.
School—(Grades PreK-8) Tel: 509-487-2830. Lay Teachers 9; Students 130.
Catechesis/Religious Program—Sandi Dotts, Children's Formation Dir. Students 36.
Convent—5008 N. Lacey St., 99207.

18—ST. PETER (1956) Revs. Michael (Brian) Mee, O.S.B.; George Haspedis (Retired).
Res. & Mailing Address: 3520 E. 18th Ave., 99223-3814. Tel: 509-534-2227; Fax: 509-534-5522. Email: stpeterspokane@yahoo.com.
School—All Saints Interparochial, (Grades PreK-4), 3510 E. 18th Ave., 99223. Tel: 509-534-1098; Fax: 509-534-1529. Web: allsaintsspokane.org. Ms. Kathy Hicks, Prin. Lay Teachers 22; Students 481.
Catechesis/Religious Program—Frank Ciccarello, D.R.E. Students 135.

19—SACRED HEART (1911) Rev. Mark Pautler; Ron Eberley, Pastoral Min.
Res.: 219 E. Rockwood Blvd., 99202. Tel: 509-747-5810; Fax: 509-747-5033. Email: shparish@qwestoffice.net.
Catechesis/Religious Program—Janet Maucione, D.R.E.; Christopher Ferrez, Youth Min. Students 65.

20—ST. THOMAS MORE (1957) Rev. Msgr. Pedro Ramirez-Alejos; Rev. David Kuttner.
Res.: 505 W. St. Thomas More Way, 99208. Tel: 509-466-0220; Fax: 509-466-0220.
School—(Grades PreSchool-8), 515 W. St. Thomas Way, 99208. Tel: 509-466-3811 (Option 2). Deacon Doug Banks, Prin.; Shelley Budig, Librarian. Lay Teachers 11; Students 258; Educare Enrollment 110.
Catechesis/Religious Program—Kate Bradley, D.R.E. Students 95.

OUTSIDE THE CITY OF SPOKANE

BREWSTER, OKANOGAN CO., SACRED HEART (1958) Rev. Miguel Angel Gusatvo Ruiz Juarez.
Res.: P.O. Box 548, 98812. Tel: 509-689-2931; Fax: 509-689-2931.

CHENEY, SPOKANE CO., ST. ROSE OF LIMA (1881) Rev. Jose Luis Hernandez; Deacon Eric Meisfjord.
Res.: 460 N. Fifth St., 99004. Tel: 509-235-6229.
Catechesis/Religious Program—Tel: 509-235-9330; Fax: 509-559-5188. Students 24.

CHEWELAH, STEVENS CO., ST. MARY OF THE ROSARY (1885) [CEM] Rev. Vincent Van Dao.
Res.: 3081 5th Ave., Valley, 99181. Tel: 509-937-2452.
Church: 502 E. Main St., P.O. Box 26, 99109. Tel: 509-935-8028.
Catechesis/Religious Program—Tel: 509-935-6367. Students 43.

CLARKSTON, ASOTIN CO., HOLY FAMILY (1914) [CEM] Rev. Thomas Connolly.
Res.: 917 Chestnut St., 99403. Tel: 509-758-6102. Email: holyfamily@cableone.net.

School—(Grades K-6) Tel: 509-758-6621; Fax: 509-758-7025. Email: hfschool@cableone.net. Mrs. Maribeth Richardson, Prin. Lay Teachers 7; Students 119.
Educare Preschool—Tel: 509-758-2737. Students 33.
Catechesis/Religious Program—Students 46.

CLAYTON, STEVENS CO., ST. JOSEPH, Closed. For inquiries for parish records contact the chancery.

COLBERT, SPOKANE CO., ST. JOSEPH (1910) Rev. Edgar Borchardt; Deacon Joe Schroeder.
Rectory—4305 E. Park Lane Rd., Mead, 99021.
Office: 3720 E. Colbert Rd., 99005. Tel: 509-466-4991; Fax: 509-466-4992. Email: stjoseph@cet.com.
Catechesis/Religious Program—Sr. Kathleen Reynolds, C.C.V.I., D.R.E. Students 229.

COLFAX, WHITMAN CO., ST. PATRICK (1878) Rt. Rev. Adrian Parcher, O.S.B.
Res.: 1018 S. Main St., 99111. Tel: 509-397-3921.
Catechesis/Religious Program—Linda Marler, D.R.E. Students 51.

COLTON, WHITMAN CO., ST. GALL (1893) [CEM] Rev. Edward Marier.
Res.: P.O. Box 108, 99113. Tel: 509-229-3548.
School—Guardian Angel-St. Boniface Interparochial, Tel: 509-299-3579. Lori Becker, Prin. Lay Teachers 4; Students 26.
See Guardian Angel-St. Boniface School, Colton under Interparochial Grade Schools located in the Institution section.

COLVILLE, STEVENS CO., IMMACULATE CONCEPTION (1861) Rev. Peter O. Amah.
Res.: 444 E. 4th St., 99114. Tel: 509-684-6223; Fax: 509-684-8084.
Catechesis/Religious Program—Dolores Cline, D.R.E. Students 70.

CONNELL, FRANKLIN CO., ST. VINCENT (1964) Rev. Pedro Bautista-Peráza.
Res.: P.O. Box 1030, 99326. Tel: 509-234-2262; Fax: 509-234-2262.
Catechesis/Religious Program—Maria Pena, D.R.E.; Marv Grassl, D.R.E. Students 95.

COULEE DAM, OKANOGAN CO., ST. BENEDICT, Closed. For sacramental records, contact St. Henry's, Grand Coulee (Diocese of Yakima).

CURLEW, FERRY CO., ST. PATRICK (1907) Rev. George H. Morbeck (Retired).
Res.: 756 S. Portland St., P.O. Box 333, Republic, 99166. Tel: 509-775-3935.

CUSICK, KALISPEL INDIAN RESERVATION, OUR LADY OF SORROWS Rev. Joseph Sullivan.
Res.: 612 W. First St., Box C, Newport, 99156. Tel: 509-447-4231.

DAVENPORT, LINCOLN CO., IMMACULATE CONCEPTION (1893) [CEM] Rev. Patrick MacMahon.
Res.: 1310 Adams, 99122. Tel: 509-725-1761.

DAYTON, COLUMBIA CO., ST. JOSEPH (1890) Rev. Robert D. Turner.
112 S. First St., 99328-1307.
Church: P.O. Box 3, 99328-1307. Tel: 509-382-2311.
Catechesis/Religious Program—Jeannie Lyonnais, D.R.E. Students 12.

DEER PARK, SPOKANE CO., ST. MARY PRESENTATION (1912) [CEM] Rev. Al Grasher; Deacon Richard Skok.
Res.: 316 N. Main St., P.O. Box 749, 99006. Tel: 509-276-2948.
Catechesis/Religious Program—Cathy Chase, D.R.E. Students 49.

ELTOPIA, FRANKLIN CO., ST. PAUL (1964) Rev. Pedro Bautista-Peráza.
Res.: 14181 Glade North Rd., 99330. Tel: 509-297-4371.
Catechesis/Religious Program—Jamie Gilmore, D.R.E.; Angie Manteroia, D.R.E. Students 74.

FORD, STEVENS CO., ST. PHILIP BENIZI (1912) Rev. Mark Hoelsken, S.J.
Indian-Spokane Reservation—P.O. Box 214, Wellpinit, 99040. Tel: 509-258-7233.

HARRINGTON, LINCOLN CO., ST. FRANCIS OF ASSISI (1906) Rev. Patrick MacMahon.
Res.: P.O. Box 166, 99134. Tel: 509-253-4310.

INCHELIUM, FERRY CO., ST. MICHAEL'S MISSION Revs. Jake Morton, S.J.; Robert J. Jones, S.J.; Joseph Schmert, Admin.; Deacon Alvin Toulou, (Retired).
Res.: P.O. Box 122, 99138. Tel: 509-722-4592.

IONE, PEND OREILLE CO., ST. BERNARD Rev. Joseph Sullivan.
Mailing Address: Box 731, 99139. Tel: 509-447-4231.
Res.: 612 W. First St., P.O. Box C, Newport, 99156. Tel: 509-447-4231.

KELLER, FERRY CO., ST. ROSE OF LIMA Revs. Robert J. Jones, S.J.; Jake Morton, S.J.
Res.: P.O. Box 70, Nespelem, 99155. 323 Edmonds, Omak, 98841-6401.

KETTLE FALLS, STEVENS CO., SACRED HEART OF JESUS (1906) Rev. Peter O. Amah.
Mailing Address: 320 N. Maple St., Colville, 99114. Tel: 509-684-6223; Fax: 509-684-8084.

LACROSSE, WHITMAN CO., ST. JOSEPH (1906) Rt. Rev. Adrian Parcher, O.S.B.
St. Patrick Parish: 1018 S. Main St., Colfax, 99111. Tel: 509-397-3921.
Catechesis/Religious Program—Students 26.

LIND, ADAMS CO., ST. AMBROSE (1920) Rev. Pedro Bautista-Peráza.
Mailing Address: 404 E. Fifth Ave., Ritzville, 99169. Tel: 509-659-0437.

MEDICAL LAKE, SPOKANE CO., ST. ANNE (1889) Rev. John P. Krier (GF).
Res.: 708 E. Lake St., P.O. Box 125, 99022. Tel: 509-252-0247; Fax: 509-351-3217. Email: stanne99022@hotmail.com.

METALINE FALLS, PEND OREILLE CO., ST. JOSEPH (1950) Rev. Joseph Sullivan.
Mailing Address: P.O. Box 417, 99153. Tel: 509-446-2651.
Res.: 612 W. First St., P.O. Box C, Newport, 99156. Tel: 509-447-4231; Fax: 509-299-9250.

NESPELEM, OKANOGAN CO., SACRED HEART MISSION (1915) [CEM] Revs. Jake Morton, S.J.; Robert J. Jones, S.J.
Res.: 209 9th St., P.O. Box 70, 99155. Tel: 509-634-4249; Fax: 509-634-4249.
Catechesis/Religious Program—Nancy Armstrong-Montes, D.R.E. Students 25.

NEWPORT, PEND OREILLE CO., ST. ANTHONY (1908) Rev. Joseph Sullivan.
Res.: 612 W. First St., P.O. Box C, 99156. Tel: 509-447-4231.

NORTHPORT, STEVENS CO., PURE HEART OF MARY (1898) Rev. Peter O. Amah.
Mailing Address: 320 N. Maple St., Colville, 99114. 720 South St., P.O. Box 29, 99157.

OAKESDALE, WHITMAN CO., ST. CATHERINE OF ALEXANDRIA Rev. Miguel Mejia.
Res.: P.O. Box 8, Rosalia, 99170. Tel: 509-523-3473.

ODESSA, LINCOLN CO., ST. JOSEPH (1905) Rev. Michael L. Ishida.
Res. & Mailing Address: P.O. Box 106, Wilbur, 99185. Tel: 509-647-2380.

OKANOGAN-OMAK, OKANOGAN CO., OUR LADY OF THE VALLEY (1976) Rev. Cyprien Niyitegeka.
Res.: 2511 N. Elmway, 98840. Tel: 509-422-5049.
Catechesis/Religious Program—Sheryl Potts, D.R.E. Students 40.

OMAK, OKANOGAN CO.
1—ST. JOSEPH (1945) Revs. Robert J. Jones, S.J.; Jake Morton, S.J.; Bro. Fred Mercy, S.J., Pastoral Assoc.
Res.: 323 Edmonds St., 98841-9661. Tel: 509-826-6401.
2—ST. MARY MISSION, [CEM] Bros. Fred Mercy, S.J., Asst. to Dir. of Rocky Mt. Missions; Fred Mercy, S.J.
Res.: 25 Mission Rd., 98841. Tel: 509-826-6401.

OROVILLE, OKANOGAN CO., IMMACULATE CONCEPTION (1898) Rev. Alejandro Zepeda.
Mailing Address: P.O. Box 308, 98844.
Res.: 1715 Main St., P.O. Box 2270, 98844. Tel: 509-476-2110; Fax: 509-476-2110.
Catechesis/Religious Program—Barbara Reed, D.R.E. Students 22.

OTHELLO, ADAMS CO., SACRED HEART (1956) Rev. Msgr. Kevin A. Codd; Deacons Antonio Beraza; Magdaleno Casillas; Joel Pruneda; Jesse Rodelo.
Res.: 616 E. Juniper St., 99344. Tel: 509-488-5653; Fax: 509-488-5654.
Catechesis/Religious Program—Anna Salmeron, D.R.E. Students 343.

OTIS ORCHARDS, SPOKANE CO., ST. JOSEPH (1892) Rev. Mike Kwiatkowski; Deacon Tom Heafey.
Res.: 4521 N. Arden Rd., 99027-9358. Tel: 509-926-7133; Fax: 509-926-9454.
Catechesis/Religious Program—Teresa McCann, D.R.E. Students 170.

PASCO, FRANKLIN CO., ST. PATRICK (1909), (Hispanic), Revs. Daniel Barnett; Fernando Maldonado; Matthew Nicks; Deacons Victor Ortega; Luis Ramos; Abraham Valdovinos; Antonio Rodriguez; James Ball; Gary Franz; Robert Kalinowski; Juanita Contreras, Pastoral Assoc. In Res., Rev. John G. Birk (Retired).
Res.: 1320 W. Henry, 99301. Tel: 509-547-8841; Fax: 509-547-3604.
School—(Grades PreK-8), 1016 N. 14th Ave., 99301. Tel: 509-547-7261; Fax: 509-547-2604. Antonio Vegas, Prin. Lay Teachers 33; Students 300; Educare Enrollment 63.
Catechesis/Religious Program—Peggy DeBord, D.R.E.; Maria Aguirre, D.R.E.; Maricela Rodriguez, D.R.E. (Grades 7-12). Students 1,100.

POMEROY, GARFIELD CO., HOLY ROSARY (1878) [CEM] Rev. Robert D. Turner.
Res.: 634 High St., 99347. Tel: 509-843-3801; 509-843-1110.
Catechesis/Religious Program—Mary Flerschinger, D.R.E. Students 23.

PULLMAN, WHITMAN CO., SACRED HEART (1913) Rev. Jose Luis Millan.
Office: 440 N.E. Ash St., 99163. Tel: 509-332-5312; Fax: 509-332-4402. Email: sacredheartpullman@verizon.net. Web: mysite.verizon.net/sacredheartpullman/.
Catechesis/Religious Program—Tel: 509-332-4402. Theresa Paul, D.R.E. Students 70.

REARDAN, LINCOLN CO., ST. MICHAEL (1907) Rev. Patrick MacMahon.
Mailing Address: 1310 Adams St., Davenport, 99122. Tel: 509-725-1761.

REPUBLIC, FERRY CO., IMMACULATE CONCEPTION (1898) Rev. George H. Morbeck (Retired).
Res.: 756 S. Portland, P.O. Box 333, 99166. Tel: 509-775-3935.

RITZVILLE, ADAMS CO., ST. AGNES (1915) Rev. Pedro Bautista-Peráza.
Res.: 404 E. Fifth Ave., 99169. Tel: 509-659-0437.

ROCKFORD, SPOKANE CO., ST. JOSEPH (1901) Rev. Msgr. William Van Ommeren (Retired).
c/o Immaculate Heart Retreat Center, 6910 Ben Burr Rd., 99223-1819.

ROSALIA, WHITMAN CO., HOLY ROSARY (1892) Rev. Miguel Mejia.
Res.: 601 N. Plaza Ave., P.O. Box 8, 99170. Tel: 509-523-4011.

ST. JOHN, WHITMAN CO., OUR LADY OF PERPETUAL HELP (1960) Rev. Miguel Mejia.
Mailing Address: 401 W. Liberty, 99171.
Res.: P.O. Box 8, Rosalia, 99170. Tel: 509-523-4011.

SPRAGUE, LINCOLN CO., MARY QUEEN OF HEAVEN (1885) [CEM] Rev. John Krier.
Mailing Address: P.O. Box 129, 99032. Tel: 509-263-5434.

SPRINGDALE, STEVENS CO., SACRED HEART (1911) Rev. Vincent Van Dao.
Res.: 3081 Fifth Ave., Valley, 99181. Tel: 509-937-2452.

TEKOA, WHITMAN CO., SACRED HEART (1893) [CEM] Rev. Miguel Mejia.
Res.: P.O. Box 8, Rosalia, 99170. Tel: 509-523-3473.

TONASKET, OKANOGAN CO., HOLY ROSARY Rev. Alejandro Zepeda.
Res. & Mailing Address: P.O. Box 308, Oroville, 98844. Tel: 509-476-2110; Fax: 509-476-2110.
Catechesis/Religious Program—Students 20.

TWISP, OKANOGAN CO., ST. GENEVIEVE (1907) Rev. Miguel Angel Gusatvo Ruiz Juarez.
Res.: P.O. Box 6, 98856. Tel: 509-997-4201.

UNIONTOWN, WHITMAN CO., ST. BONIFACE (1882) [CEM] Rev. Edward Marier.
Res.: P.O. Box 108, Colton, 99113. Tel: 509-229-3548.
See Guardian Angel-St. Boniface School, Colton under Interparochial Grade Schools located in the Institution section.

USK, PEND OREILLE CO., ST. JUDE (1941) Rev. Joseph Sullivan.
Res.: 612 W. First St., P.O. Box C, Newport, 99156. Tel: 509-447-4231.

VALLEY, STEVENS CO., HOLY GHOST (1914) Rev. Vincent Van Dao.
Res.: 3081 Fifth Ave., 99181. Tel: 509-937-2452.
Catechesis/Religious Program—Tel: 509-935-6367. Theresa Carr, D.R.E. Students 17.
Station—St. Joseph Jump-off Joe, Stevens Co., St. Joseph.

WAITSBURG, WALLA WALLA CO., ST. MARK (1888) Rev. Robert D. Turner.
Mailing Address: P.O. Box 0003, Dayton, 99328-0003. Office: 112 S. 1st St., Dayton, 99328-1307. Tel: 509-382-2311.
Catechesis/Religious Program—Mary Tompkins, D.R.E. Students 7.

WALLA WALLA, WALLA WALLA CO.
1—ASSUMPTION OF THE BLESSED VIRGIN MARY (1953) Revs. Timothy Hays; Kevin Oiland; Deacon Michael Breier.
Res.: 2098 E. Alder St., 99362. Tel: 509-525-8163; Fax: 509-525-5414.
School—Assumption Grade School, (Grades PreK-8) Tel: 509-525-9283. John Lesko, Prin. Lay Teachers 5; Priests 1; Sisters 2; Students 234.
2—ST. FRANCIS OF ASSISI (1915) Revs. Patrick Kerst; Jose Jaime Maldonado Reyna; Kevin Oiland; Deacon Jim Barrow.
Res.: 722 W. Alder St., 99362. Tel: 509-525-1663; Fax: 509-529-7849.
Catechesis/Religious Program—
3—ST. PATRICK (1859) Revs. Patrick Kerst; Jose Jaime Maldonado Reyna; Kevin Oiland; Deacons Olegario Reyes; James Barrow.
Office & Res.: 408 W. Poplar St., 99362. Tel: 509-525-1602; Fax: 509-529-7849.
Catechesis/Religious Program—Susan Logsdon, D.R.E. (Eng.). Tel: 509-529-5141; Carmen Garcia, D.R.E. (Hispanic). Students 130.

WASHTUNCA, ADAMS CO., HOLY TRINITY (1967) Rev. Pedro Bautista-Peráza.
Mailing Address: 404 E. 5th, Ritzville, 99169-1608.
Res.: 1418 Glade North Rd., Eltopia, 99330. Tel: 509-297-4371.

WELLPINIT, STEVENS CO., SACRED HEART (1943) [CEM] Rev. Mark Hoelsken, S.J.

Indian-Spokane Reservation—P.O. Box 214, 99040. Tel: 509-258-7233. Email: frjackoleary@aol.com.

WESTEND, STEVENS CO., OUR LADY OF LOURDES (1938) Rev. Mark Hoelsken, S.J.

Indian-Spokane Reservation—P.O. Box 214, Wellpinit, 99040. Tel: 509-258-7233.

WILBUR, LINCOLN CO., SACRED HEART (1900) Rev. Michael L. Ishida.

Res.: P.O. Box 106, 99185. Tel: 509-647-2380.

Catechesis/Religious Program—Students 13.

Chaplains of Public Institutions

WALLA WALLA. *Washington State Penitentiary.* Served by priests of Walla Walla.

Special Ministry:
Revs.—
Birk, John (Retired), Our Lady of Lourdes Health Center, Pasco
Obisike, Bonaventure, Holy Family Hospital, Spokane
Venneri, Michael D., Sacred Heart Medical Center, Spokane

On Duty Outside the Diocese:
Revs.—
Baronti, David, Diocese of Solola, Guatemala
Lucatero, Heliodoro

Absent on Leave:
Revs.—
Peak, James, US Army
Poole, Richard, US Air Force
Root, Richard, US Army

Retired:
Rev. Msgrs.—
Bach, Frank J., 1306 N. Blake Rd., Unit B, 99216-1149.
Pearson, Robert A., E. 429 Sharp, 99202.
Ribble, James M., Ph.D., 3204 W. Grandview Ave., 99204.
Van Ommeren, William, Immaculate Heart Retreat, 6910 S. Ben Burr Rd., 99203-1899.

Revs.—
Birk, John, 520 N. 4th St., Pasco, 99301.
Caffrey, Edward, 1105 S.W. Alver St., Pullman, 99163-2006.
Caswell, Thomas C., 117 E. 16th Ave., 99203.
Dugan, William M., 272 Kennedy St., No. 48, Chula Vista, CA 92011.
Eis, Charles R., 9202 Irvington Ave., San Diego, CA 92123-3129.
Haspedis, George, 3916 Salder Cir., 99228-7300.
Hullings, Clifford, 3110 E. Chattaroy Rd., No. 43, Chattaroy, 99003.
Kuhns, James, 304 S. Adams Rd., Spokane Valley, 99216.
Lorge, Felix P., 12011 S. Player Dr., 99223.
Morbeck, George H., P.O. Box 333, Republic, 99166-0333.
O'Brien, John P., P.O. Box 1808, Santa Rosa, CA 95402.
Sand, John, 1344 Mishaw Ave., Clarkston, 99403-2977.
Schoffelmeer, Arnold L., N. Findlay Rd., Box 36123, Deer Park, 99006.
Skok, Charles, 935 W. Glass #301, 99205.
Westbrook, J. Severyn, 221 E. Rockwood Blvd., No. 318, 99202.
Wetzler, Daniel, 11517 Pebble Beach Dr., Harrison, ID 83833.
Wietensteiner, Joseph M., P.O. Box 8087, 99203.

Permanent Deacons:
Back, Jack, St. Aloysius, Spokane; Prison Ministry
Ball, James, St. Patrick, Pasco
Banks, Douglas, St. Thomas More, Spokane
Barrow, Jim, St. Francis & St. Patrick, Walla Walla, WA
Bentley, Donald, St. Joseph, Rockfort
Beraza, Antonio, Sacred Heart, Othello
Blaine, Jim, (Retired)
Braungardt, Derwood "Brownie", (Retired), St. John Vianney, Spokane
Breier, Michael, Assumption, Walla Walla
Brockway, Scott, St. Augustine, Spokane
Byrne, John, Our Lady of Fatima, Spokane
Casillas, Magdaleno, Sacred Heart, Othello
Crandall, John
Crow, John, St. Joseph, Colbert
Dahl, Roy, St. Peter, Spokane
Dalecki, Robert, (On Duty Outside the Diocese)
Dudinsky, David, St. Francis of Assisi, Spokane
Dunlap, Kenneth, St. Augustine, Spokane
Fosmire, Charles, (On Leave)
Franz, Gary, St. Patrick, Pasco
Heafy, Thomas, St. Joseph, Ottis Orchards
Heth, Cary, St. Mary, Spokane
Kalinowski, Robert, St. Patrick, Pasco
King, Bob, St. Anne, Medical Lake
Lukach, George, Our Lady of the Lake, Tum Tum
Mackin, Francis, Sitka, AK
Malone, Richard, (Retired)
Martinez, Gonzalo "Chalo", Our Lady of Lourdes Cathedral & St. Joseph Cathedral, Spokane
Meisfjord, Eric, St. Rose of Lima, Cheney
Miller, Michael D., St. Mary, Spokane
Murphy, James E., Sacred Heart Medical Center, Spokane
Ortega, Victor, St. Patrick, Pasco
Phelps, Andrew
Polensky, Hugh, St. Francis Xavier & St. Patrick, Spokane
Prawdzik, Steve, Fairchild AFB; Holy Family, Clarkston
Pruneda, Joel, Sacred Heart, Othello
Ramos, Luis
Reyes, Olegario, St. Patrick, Walla Walla
Reyna, Romiro, St. Vincent, Connell
Riherd, John, (On Leave)
Ritchie, Dan, Sacred Heart Hospital, Spokane
Rodelo, Jesus, Sacred Heart, Othello
Rodriguez, Antonio, St. Patrick, Pasco
Ruscheinsky, John, St. Peter, Spokane
Sando, William, (Retired)
Schaefer, Edward, (On Leave)
Schroeder, Joe, St. Joseph, Colbert
Sicilia, John F., St. Charles, Spokane
Skok, Richard, St. Mary Presentation, Deer Park
Stewart, Kelly, Assumption, Spokane
Toulou, Alvin, (Retired)
Valdovines, Abraham, St. Patrick, Pasco
Veale, Gary, St. Francis Xavier, Spokane
Whitney, Donald, Mary Queen, Spokane
Wilson, Charles, (Retired)

INSTITUTIONS LOCATED IN THE DIOCESE

[A] SEMINARIES, DIOCESAN

SPOKANE. *Bishop White Seminary*, E. 429 Sharp Ave., 99202. Tel: 509-313-7100; Fax: 509-313-7101. Email: bws@gonzaga.edu. Web: www.bishopwhiteseminary.org. Revs. Darrin Connall, Rector; Kenneth T. St. Hilare, Spiritual Dir. Students 20.

[B] COLLEGES AND UNIVERSITIES

SPOKANE. *Gonzaga University* 99258. Tel: 509-323-6814; Fax: 509-323-6086. Email: cumlauder@gonzaga.edu. Revs. Joseph Conwell, S.J.; William C. Hausmann, S.J.; Stephen M. Hess, S.J.; Donald R. Cadden, S.J.; J. Alfred Carroll, S.J.; Richard Case, S.J.; Timothy R. Clancy, S.J.; Michael J. Connolly, S.J.; Michael L. Cook, S.J.; Frank B. Costello, S.J. (Retired); Bernard J. Coughlin, S.J.; Robert J. Egan, S.J.; Joe Fortier, S.J.; Tom Gallagher, S.J.; Richard H. Ganz, S.J.; Gerald R. Gordon, S.J. (Retired); Craig Hightower, S.J.; Kenneth R. Krall, S.J.; Stephen R. Kuder, S.J.; Michael W. Maher, S.J.; Mark McGregor, S.J.; James N. Meehan, S.J.; Alfred Morisette, S.J.; George O. Morris, S.J.; Louis Renner, S.J.; William F. Ryan, S.J.; Fredric Schlatter, S.J.; M. Delmar Skillingstad, S.J.; Robert J. Spitzer, S.J., Pres.; Bernard J. Tyrrell, S.J.; Gary D. Uhlenkott, S.J.; Anthony P. Via, S.J.; J. Kevin Waters, S.J.; Michael Woods, S.J.; Bro. Stephen J. Souza, S.J. College of Arts and Sciences, and Schools of Law, Engineering, Education, Business Administration, Graduate School. Professional Studies Education conducted by the Fathers of the Society of Jesus. Priests 13; Brothers 1; Sisters 2; Lay Teachers 324; Students 7,701.

The Ministry Institute (at Gonzaga University), E. 405 Sinto Ave., 99202-1849. Tel: 509-328-8332; Fax: 509-325-4011. Email: bartletts@gonzaga.edu. Web: gonzaga.edu/materdei. Shanna Bartlett, Prog. Dir.; Diane Imes, Business Mgr. Priests 5; Sisters 5; Lay Teachers 1; Full-Time Enrollment 12.

[C] HIGH SCHOOLS, INTERPAROCHIAL

WALLA WALLA. *Walla Walla Catholic School System*, (Grades PreK-12), E. 919 Sumach, 99362. Tel: 509-525-3030; Fax: 509-527-0361. Email: jlesko@wallawallacatholicschools.com. Web: wallawallacatholicschools.net. John Lesko, Prin.; Lynne Kuntz, Asst. Prin. Priests 1; Lay Teachers 14; Students: Elementary 234; High School 113.

[D] HIGH SCHOOLS, PRIVATE

SPOKANE. *Gonzaga Preparatory School*, E. 1224 Euclid Ave., 99207. Tel: 509-483-8511; Fax: 509-483-3124. Email: afalkner@gprep.com. Web: www.gprep.com. Mr. Al Falkner, Pres.; Revs. Kevin Connell, S.J., Prin.; Greg Vance, S.J.; Connie Robinson, Librarian. Priests 5; Lay Teachers 62; Students 967.

PASCO. *Tri Cities Prep, A Catholic High School*, 9612 St. Thomas Dr., 99301. Tel: 509-546-2465; Fax: 509-546-2490. Email: tcprep@tcprep.org. Arlene Jones, Prin.; Steve Potter, Pres. Sisters 1; Lay Teachers 15; Students 135.

[E] INTERPAROCHIAL GRADE SCHOOLS

SPOKANE. *All Saints Middle Bldg.*, (Grades 5-8), E. 1428 33rd Ave., 99203. Tel: 509-624-5712; Fax: 509-624-7752. Email: khicks@dioceseofspokane.org. Web: allstaintsspokane.org. Ms. Kathy Hicks, Prin.

All Saints Primary (Grades PreK-4), E. 3510 18th Ave., 99223. Tel: 509-534-1098, Ext. 215; Fax: 509-534-1529. Email: khicks@dioceaseofspokane.org. Ms. Kathy Hicks, Prin. Serving St. Peter, St. Ann, and Our Lady of Fatima Parishes. Lay Teachers 25; Students 473.

Cataldo Catholic School, (Grades PreK-8), 455 W. 18th Ave., 99203. Tel: 509-624-8759; Fax: 509-624-8763. Email: office@cataldo.org. Web: www.cataldo.org. Stephanie Johnson, Prin. Serving St. Augustine, Sacred Heart, and Our Lady of Lourdes Parishes. Lay Teachers 18; Students 310.

Trinity School, (Grades PreK-8), W. 1306 Montgomery Ave., 99205. Tel: 509-327-9369; Fax: 509-328-4128. Email: trinity@dioceseofspokane.org. Mrs. Sandra Nokes, Prin.; Ms. Nancy Likarish, Librarian. Serving St. Anthony and St. Joseph Parishes. Lay Teachers 8; Students 195.

COLTON. *Guardian Angel-St. Boniface School*, (Grades K-8), 306 Steptoe, P.O. Box 48, 99113. Tel: 509-229-3579. Email: gasbschool@colton-wa.com. Web: gasbschool.org. Lori Becker, Prin. Serving St. Gall and St. Boniface Parishes. Lay Teachers 5; Students 26.

WALLA WALLA. *Assumption Elementary School*, (Grades PreK-5), E. 2066 Alder St., 99362. Tel: 509-525-9283; Fax: 509-527-0848. Email: jlesko@wallawallacatholicschools.com. John Lesko, Prin.; Lynne Kuntz, Asst. Prin. Serving Assumption, St. Francis of Assisi, and St. Patrick Parishes. Lay Teachers 11; Students 234; High School 113.

Walla Walla Catholic School System, (Grades K-12), See listing under High Schools, Interparochial. John Lesko, Prin.; Agnes Lapke, Librarian.

[F] GENERAL HOSPITALS

SPOKANE. *Holy Family Hospital*, N. 5633 Lidgerwood St., 99208. Tel: 509-482-0111; Fax: 509-482-2456. Web: www.holy-family.org. P.O. Box 2555, 99220. Andrew Agwunobi, CEO; Ms. Joeine Enneking, Care Dir. Chaplains 1.

Sacred Heart Medical Center & Children's Hospital, W. 101 Eighth Ave., TAF-C9, 99220. Tel: 509-474-3131; Fax: 509-474-3153. P.O. Box 2555, 99220. Andrew Agwunobi, CEO; Mr. Michael D. Wilson, Pres.; Ms. Elaine Couture, COO; Rev. Michael D. Venneri, Chap. Chaplains 20; Total Staff 4,000; Bed Capacity 623; Patients Assisted Annually 195,000.

School of Radiology Tel: 509-624-5012; Fax: 509-624-3546. Students 41.

CHEWELAH. *St. Joseph's Hospital (of Chewelah)*, P.O. Box 197, 99109. Tel: 509-935-8211; Fax: 509-935-5257. Email: lori.johanson-fogle@providence.org. P.O. Box 2555, 99220. Gary V. Peck, CEO; Rev. Matt Kammer, Chap.; Sr. Margaret Retherfono, Chap.; Ed Grim, Chap. Bed Capacity 25; Patients Assisted Annually 21,318; Total Staff 200.

COLVILLE. *Mount Carmel Hospital*, 982 E. Columbia, 99114. Tel: 509-685-5100; Fax: 509-685-2492. Email: lori.johanson-fogle@providence.org. Web: www.mtcarmelhospital.org. P.O. Box 2555, 99220. Robert Campbell, CEO. Total Staff 270; Bed Capacity 25; Patients Assisted Annually 35,062.

PASCO. *Lourdes Medical Center*, 520 Fourth Ave., P.O. Box 2568, 99301-2568. Tel: 509-547-7704; 509-543-2483, Ext. 2483; Fax: 509-546-2291. John Serle, Pres. & CEO. Sisters of St. Joseph of Carondelet 4; Total Staff 700; Bed Capacity 127; Patients Assisted Annually 147,893. In Res. Rev. John Birk (Retired).

WALLA WALLA. *St. Mary Medical Center*, 401 W. Poplar St., 99362. Tel: 509-525-3320; Fax: 509-522-5509. Web: www.smmc.com. Steve Burdick, Pres. Sisters of Providence. Total Staff 1,005; Bed Capacity 141; Patients Assisted Annually 154,007.

[G] PROTECTIVE INSTITUTIONS

(Catholic Social Service)

SPOKANE

St. Anne's Children's Family Center, 25 W. 5th, 99204. Tel: 509-232-1111; Fax: 509-232-1118 (Childcare Center). Lee Williams, Dir. For children 1 month through 6 years of age. Staff 35.

Bernadette Place, Mailing Address: P.O. Box 2253, 99210-2253. Tel: 509-326-2023. 925 N. A St., #2, 99210-2253. This complex houses twelve developmentally delayed women; 6 units of affordable housing for persons with disabilities and special needs.

Office:, 12 E. Fifth Ave., P.O. Box 2253, 99210-2253. Tel: 509-358-4250.

Catholic Charities, Inc., 12 E. Fifth Ave., P.O. Box 2253, 99210-2253. Tel: 509-358-4250; Fax: 509-358-4259. Email: sgross@ccspokane.org. Web: www-.catholiccharitiesspokane.org. Dr. Robert J. McCann, Ph.D., Exec. Dir. Personnel 260.

Holy Family Adult Day Center, 6018 N. Astor, 99208. Tel: 509-482-2475; Fax: 509-482-2490. Web: www.hfadc.org. Mr. Jim Lippold, Exec. Dir. Purpose: to provide adult day health programs, including rehab & nursing, to the elderly and disabled.

House of Charity, 32 W. Pacific, P.O. Box 2253, 99210-2253. Tel: 509-624-7821; Fax: 509-742-3463. Email: emccarron@ccspokane.org. Web: catholiccharitiesspokane.org. Ed McCarron, Dir. Housing for homeless men. Total Assisted 75,902.

St. Joseph's Counseling Center dba St. Joseph Family Center N. 1016 Superior St., 99202-2059. Tel: 509-483-6495; Fax: 509-483-1541. Email: sjfc@stjosephfamilycenter.org. Web: www.stjosephfamilycenter.org. Sr. Elaine Thaden, O.S.F., M.A., Dir., St. Joseph Family Center. Bed Capacity 18; Total Assisted Annually 3,800; Total Staff 32.

St. Margaret's Shelter, P.O. Box 2253, 99210-2253. Tel: 509-624-9788; Fax: 509-624-1461. Nadine Van Stone, Dir. Emergency and transitional shelter for women & children. Total Staff 8; Total Assisted Annually 123.

Miryam's House, 1805 W. 9th St., 99204. Tel: 509-747-9222; Fax: 509-747-7261. Email: dcritchlow@help4women.com. Web: www.help4women.com. Transitional housing residential program and supportive services for women in transition. Total Staff 12; Total Assisted 70.

Morning Star Boys' Ranch, P.O. Box 8087, 99203. Tel: 509-448-1411; Fax: 509-448-1413. Email: msbr@msbranch.org. Web: morningstarboysranch.org. Joseph A. Pickert, Exec. Dir.; Mr. Daniel J. Kuhlmann, Finance Dir. Total Staff 36; Children in Residence 17; Total Assisted 31.

Spokane St. Vincent de Paul Social Services Center, P.O. Box 2906, 99220-2906. Tel: 509-323-9014 (Social Svc.); Fax: 509-535-2493. Mike Cain, Pres. *St. Vincent de Paul Social Service Office and Main Store St. Business Office* Total Assisted 74,101.

Summit View, P.O. Box 2253, 99201. 820 N. Summit Blvd., 99202. Tel: 509-327-9524. Email: claufer@ccspokane.org. Charlene Laufer, Property Mgr. 27 units of housing for families.

Transitional Living Center, 3128 N. Hemlock, 99205. Tel: 509-325-2959; 509-328-6702; Fax: 509-325-8319. Email: ktalbott@help4women.org. Web: www.help4women.org. Housing for homeless women & children.

Transitional Programs for Women, 1002 N. Superior St., 99202. Tel: 509-328-6702; Fax: 509-325-9877. Email: dmaurer@help4women.org. Web: www.help4women.org. Bed Capacity 35; Total Assisted Annually 1,500; Total Staff 38.

Women's Hearth, 920 W. Second Ave., 99201. Tel: 509-456-3531; Fax: 509-456-3531. Web: www.help4women.org. Sr. Mary Rathert, O.P., Prog. Dir. & Contact Person. A safe place for women at risk. Total Assisted Annually 1,500; Total Staff 15.

CHEWELAH

DominiCare, 110 S. Third St. E., P.O. Box 1070, 99109. Tel: 509-935-4925; Fax: 509-935-4082. Email: joan.sisco@providence.org. Web: www.providence-.org. Joan Sisco, Exec. Dir. A home care/chore service in Stevens & Spokane Counties. Total Assisted Annually 8,417; Total Staff 37; Hours of Home-Care Service 32,000.

CLARKSTON

Lewis and Clark District Council of St. Vincent de Paul, Office: 604 Second St., 99403. Tel: 509-758-7061; Fax: 509-758-9545. Email: shannonsvd@cableone.net.

Stores:

609 Third St., 99403. Tel: 509-758-7061; Fax: 509-758-9545.

3138 5th St., Lewiston, ID 83501. Tel: 208-746-7860.

COLVILLE

The Rhodena, 230 S. Wynne, 99114. Tel: 509-684-5671; Fax: 509-358-4259. Email: ghouston@ccspokane.org. A six unit affordable housing complex for families living in Colville, WA.

DAYTON

Project Timothy: Christian Service Center, 249 E. Main St., 99328. Tel: 509-382-2943. Sponsored by St. Joseph's & St. Mark's Churches. Total Assisted 4,550.

St. Vincent de Paul Store, 247 E. Main, 99328. Tel: 509-382-4146. Lydia C. Buettner, Treas.; Lynn Feeney, Mgr.

PASCO

St. Vincent de Paul Store, 1120 W. Sylvester, 99301. Tel: 509-547-2341; Fax: 509-547-7804. Cynthia Martinez, Mgr.

WALLA WALLA

Catholic Children and Family Service, 408 W. Poplar, Ste. 333, 99362. Tel: 509-525-0572; Fax: 509-525-0576. Email: wwcounseling@ccspokane.org. Richard A. Garcia, M.S.W., Dir.

St. Vincent de Paul Store, 308 W. Main St., 99362. Tel: 509-525-3903 (Store); 509-529-6778 (Office); Fax: 509-525-3903. Raymond Lane, Society Pres.; Julie Smith, Mgr.

[H] SENIOR CITIZEN HOUSING

SPOKANE. *Cathedral Plaza Apartments*, W. 1120 Sprague Ave., 99201. Tel: 509-747-6777. Email: rcoonse@ccspokane.org. Capacity 150.

The Delaney, W. 242 Riverside Ave., 99201. Tel: 509-747-5081. Email: delaney@ccspokane.org. Capacity 84.

Fahy Garden Apartments, W. 1411 Dean Ave., 99201. Tel: 509-326-6759; Fax: 509-323-5205. Email: fahys@ccspokane.org. Capacity 54.

Fahy West Apartments, W. 1523 Dean Ave., 99201. Tel: 509-326-6759; Fax: 509-323-5205. Email: fahys@ccspokane.org. Capacity 32.

The O'Malley, E. 707 Mission Ave., 99201. Tel: 509-487-1150. Email: omalley@ccspokane.org. Tandra Melville, Property Mgr. Capacity 99; Total Assisted Annually 101; Staff 5.

Rockwood Lane, E. 221 Rockwood Blvd., 99202. Tel: 509-838-3200; Fax: 509-838-1688. Email: jmcnally@ccspokane.org. Jeannette McNally, Property Mgr. Capacity 104.

Senior Service - Senior Nutrition, 12 E. Fifth Ave., P.O. Box 2253, 99210-2253. Tel: 509-495-6175.

CLARKSTON. *Austen Manor*, 1222 Chestnut St., 99403. Tel: 509-751-9640; Fax: 509-751-9610. Email: austenmanor@ccspokane.org. D.J. Joepino, Prop. Mgr. Capacity 29.

PULLMAN. *Pioneer Square*, 220 S. E. Kamiaken, 99163. Tel: 509-332-1106; Fax: 509-332-2516. Email: pioneersquare769@ccspokane.org. Capacity 45.

WALLA WALLA. *Garden Court / Mike Foye*, 420 W. Alder St., 99362. Tel: 509-529-4706. Email: sperez-garcia@ccspokane.org. Sara Perez-Garcia, Property Mgr. Capacity 25.

Mike Foye Apartments, 420 W. Alder St., #13, 99362. Tel: 509-529-4706. Email: ghouston@ccspokane.org. Web: www.catholiccharitiesspokane.org. Bed Capacity 53; Total Assisted Annually 25; Staff 3.

[I] HOMES FOR AGED

SPOKANE. *Emilie Court Assisted Living*, 34 E. 8th Ave., 99202-1202. Tel: 509-474-2550; Fax: 509-474-2618. Email: charlene.longworth@providence.org. Charlene Longworth, Dir. Bed Capacity 60; Total Staff 40; Total Assisted Annually 55.

St. Joseph Care Center (A Non-profit Corporation), E. 17 Eighth Ave., 99202. Tel: 509-474-5678; Fax: 509-455-4020. P.O. Box 2555, 99220. Andrew Agwunobi, CEO. Sisters of Providence-Mother Joseph Province. Bed Capacity 145.

[J] MONASTERIES AND RESIDENCES OF PRIESTS AND BROTHERS

SPOKANE. *Regis Community*, N. 1107 Astor St., 99202. Tel: 509-328-4220; Fax: 509-313-6086. Revs. Paul M. Cochran, S.J., Supr.; Charles Barnes, S.J., Asst. Supr.; Arnold R. Beezer, S.J. (Retired); Leo D. Davis; Joseph R. DeJardin, S. J.; Thomas R. Garvin, S.J. (Retired); Robert A. Goebel, S.J. (Retired); Laurence L. Gooley, S.J.; Henry G. Hargreaves, S.J.; Thomas F. Healy, S.J.; James Jacobson, S.J.; Robert J. Jones, S.J.; Leon Kapfer, S.J.; John J. Kindall, S.J.; Philip Lucid, S.J. (Retired); Paul P. Luger, S.J. (Retired); Alexander F. McDonald, S.J. (Retired); John J. Morse, S.J.; William M. O'Malley (Retired); Joseph L. Obersinner, S.J.; David S. Olivier (Retired); Robert F. Rekofke, S.J.; Joseph D. Ringwood, S.J. (Retired); Edmund J. Robinson, S.J. (Retired); Roberto B. Saenz, S.J. (Retired); Robert J. Schlim, S.J.; Charles Schmitz, S.J.; Joseph Shirey, S.J.; Joseph L. Showalter (Retired); Michael J. Taylor, S.J. (Retired); Thomas Williams, S.J.; Charles A. Wollesen, S.J.; Thomas E. Zeyen, S.J.; Bros. James J. Lee, S.J.; Frederick O. Mercy; Michael Richards.

[K] CONVENTS AND RESIDENCES FOR SISTERS

SPOKANE. *Convent of the Holy Names*, 2911 W. Fort George Wright Dr., 99224. Tel: 509-328-4310; Fax: 509-328-9824. Email: mafarley@snjmwa.org. Sr. Mary Ann Farley, S.N.J.M., Convent Community Dir. Sisters of the Holy Names of Jesus and Mary (U.S. Ontario Province). Professed Sisters 47.

Dominican Center, Sinsinawa Dominican Sisters, 3102 W. Fort George Wright Dr., 99224-5203. Tel: 509-328-8033; Fax: 509-328-8035. Email: dcentersp@comcast.net. Sisters 16.

Holy Names Foundation, 2911 W. Fort George Wright Dr., 99224. Tel: 509-328-7470; Fax: 509-328-9824. Support for educational activities of Sisters of the Holy Names of Jesus and Mary.

Holy Spirit Community, 2815 E. 63rd, 99223-6968. Tel: 509-448-6431. Email: Roy2815@msn.com. Margaret Breitenbach, Pres.

Monastery of St. Clare, 4419 N. Hawthorne St., 99205-1399. Tel: 509-327-4479; Fax: 509-327-5171. Sr. Rita Louise McLean, O.S.C., Abbess. Papal Enclosure Novitiate. Professed Cloistered Nuns 5; Poor Clare Nuns, Solemn Vows 5.

Mount St. Joseph Retirement residence and community., 12 W. Ninth Ave., 99204-2394. Tel: 509-474-2300; Fax: 509-474-2355. Laurie Crane, Gen. Mgr.; Sr. Sue Orlowski, Supr. Sisters of Providence, Mother Joseph, Province. Sisters 26.

Sisters of Providence Novitiate, 1016 N. Superior St., #4, 99202-2096. Tel: 509-487-7644; Fax: 509-489-0964. Sr. Marilyn Charette, S.P., Novitiate Dir.

NEWPORT. *Carmelite Sisters of Mary*, 2892 State Rte. 211, 99156. Tel: 509-292-0978. Sr. Leslie L. Lund, Prioress. Sisters 2; Hermitages 6; Postulants 1.

Renton

Sisters of Providence - Mother Joseph Province, 1801 Lind Ave. S.W., Renton, 98057-9016. Tel: 425-525-3355; Fax: 425-525-3984. Email: margaret.botch@providence.org. Web: www.sistersofprovidence.net. Sr. Margaret Botch, S.P., Leadership Team Coord. & Prov. Supr. Sisters of Providence, Mother Joseph Province (a Washington nonprofit corporation). Members of Providence Health and Services (a Washington nonprofit corporation). Sisters 46.

[L] ASSOCIATIONS OF THE FAITHFUL

SPOKANE. *Sisters of Mary, Mother of the Church*, 6910 S. Ben Burr Rd., 99223. Tel: 509-448-9890; Fax: 509-448-1623. Web: www.sistersofmarymotherofthechurch.org. Sisters Kathryn Joseph, S.M.M.C., Supr.; Marybeth, Business Mgr.

[M] RETREAT HOUSES

SPOKANE. *Clare Center, Franciscan Center*, P.O. Box 30250, 99223-3004. Tel: 509-448-0674; Fax: 509-448-1553. Sr. Rosile Pernsteiner, F.S.P.A., Admin. Sisters 2.

Immaculate Heart Retreat Center, 6910 S. Ben Burr Rd., 99223. Tel: 509-448-1224; Fax: 509-448-1623. Email: ihrc@ihrc.net. Web: www.ihrc.net. Deacon John Ruscheinsky, Exec. Dir.; Rev. Msgr. William Van Ommeren (Retired).

KAIROS House of Prayer, 1714 W. Stearns Rd., 99208. Tel: 509-466-2187. Sr. M. Florence Leone Poch, O.S.F., Coord.; Rita Beaulieu. Provides a place called to a prayerful, reflective environment for people of all faiths. Spiritual accompaniment is available.

Spiritual Exercise in Everyday Life (SEEL), 330 E. Boone, 99202. Tel: 509-323-5898; Fax: 509-323-5892. Email: seel-spokane@comcast.net. Diana Stoffregen, Dir.

TUM TUM. *House of the Lord Retreat Center, Inc.*, P.O. Box 1034, 99034. Tel: 509-276-2219. Web: www.houseofthelordministries.com. Ramona Salvatore, Dir.

[N] NEWMAN CENTERS

CHENEY. *Catholic Newman Center at Eastern Washington University* 837 Elm St., 99004. Tel: 509-235-8402. Mailing Address: 460 N. Fifth St., 99004.

PULLMAN. *"St. Thomas More Catholic Student Center" - Washington State University* 820 N.E. B St., 99163. Tel: 509-332-6311. Email: stthomasmorechapel@dioceseofspokane.org. Web: stmcatholicstudentcenter.catholicweb.com. Rev. Steven Werner, Pastor.

[O] MISCELLANEOUS

SPOKANE. *Catholic Charities Foundation*, P.O. Box 2253, 99210. Tel: 509-358-4255; Fax: 509-358-4259. Email: mheskett@ccspokane.org. Mary Ann Heskett, Contact Person & Planned Giving Coord.

The Catholic Foundation of the Spokane Diocese, W. 1023 Riverside Ave., P.O. Box 1453, 99210-1453.

Tel: 509-358-4280; Fax: 509-358-7302. Email: csmith@dioceseofspokane.org. Web: www.spokanecatholicfoundation.com. Mr. Chris Smith, Exec. Dir.

Dominican Outreach Foundation, c/o Dominican Center, W. 3102 Fort George Wright Dr., 99224. Tel: 509-328-8033; Fax: 509-328-0597. Email: lmcwilli@sinsinawa.org. Larry McWilliams, Treas. Supports the Sisters educational, religious, and charitable ministries.

Holy Names Music Center, 3910 W. Custer Dr., 99224. Tel: 509-326-9516; Fax: 509-326-7155. Email: music@hnmc.org. Web: www.hnmc.org. Craig Landron, Exec. Dir. Sponsored by Sisters of the Holy Names, Washington Province. Sisters 2; Lay Teachers 35; Students 700.

Immaculate Heart Retreat Center Foundation, S. 6910 Ben Burr Rd., 99223-1819. Tel: 509-448-1224; Fax: 509-448-1623.

Kateri Northwest Ministry Institute, 330 E. Boone, 99202-1710. Tel: 509-313-7024; Fax: 509-313-5892. Web: rockymtnmission.org. Rev. Michael Fitzpatrick, S.J., Co-Dir.; Cecelia Sheoships, Co-Dir.; Jen Edgren, Office Mgr. Kateri Northwest Ministry Institute is a Jesuit-sponsored formation program dedicated to the development of all ministries needed for reservation-and urban-based Indian Catholic church communities of the Northwest. Forming church communities to be fully Indian and fully Catholic, with indigenous leadership respectful of unique cultural expression, is the goal of the Institute. The Institute also develops active leadership for those who want to take on social justice issues in their church and local communities.

**L'Arche Spokane*, 703 E. Nora, 99207-2455. Tel: 509-483-0438; Fax: 509-483-0460. Email: info@larcheofspokane.org. Lura Southerland, Community Dir.

Providence Health & Services, 9 E. Ninth Ave., 99202-1295. Tel: 509-474-7337; Fax: 509-474-4882. Web: www.providence.org. John Koster, Pres. & CEO.

Providence Health Care, 101 W. 8th Ave., 99220. Tel: 509-474-3335; Fax: 509-474-4925. Andrew Agwunobi, CEO. Providence Health Care is an integrated healthcare delivery network made up of: Sacred Heart Medical Center & Children's Hospital, VNA Home Health Care Services, St. Joseph Care Center, Emilie Court, Pathology Associates Medical Laboratories, DominiCare, Holy Family Adult Day Centers, Deer Park Hospital and Holy Family Hospital, St. Joseph Hospital of Chewelah and Mount Carmel Hospital.

Providence Medical Research Center, 101 W. 8th Ave., 99204.

Serra Club of Spokane, P.O. Box 31536, 99223. Tel: 509-921-0141. Winnie Doohan.

Spokane Catholic Investment Trust, P.O. Box 30846, 99223-3014. Tel: 509-998-0654. Most Rev. William S. Skylstad, D.D., Pres.; Steven C. Kocharhook, Ph.D., Exec. Pres. A Washington Nonprofit Corporation established to invest funds on behalf of the charitable organizations organized within the Catholic Diocese of Spokane.

POMEROY. *Holy Rosary Catholic Church Foundation of Garfield County*, 634 High St., 99347.

WAITSBURG. *St. Mark Waitsburg and St. Joseph Dayton Catholic Parish Foundation*, 801 W. 7th St., 99361.

RELIGIOUS INSTITUTES OF MEN REPRESENTED IN THE DIOCESE

For further details refer to the corresponding bracketed number in the Religious Institutes of Men or Women section.

[0520]—*Franciscan Friars* (Santa Barbara Prov.)—O.F.M.

[0690]—*Jesuit Fathers and Brothers*—S.J.

RELIGIOUS INSTITUTES OF WOMEN REPRESENTED IN THE DIOCESE

[1780]—*Congregation of the Sisters of the Third Order of St. Francis of Perpetual Adoration*—F.S.P.A.

[1070-03]—*Dominican Sisters*—O.P.

[1180]—*Franciscan Sisters of Allegany, New York*—O.S.F.

[3760]—*Order of St. Clare*—O.S.C.

[]—*Sisters for Christian Community Eastern Washington Area Communication*

[3350]—*Sisters of Providence*—S.P.

[1650]—*The Sisters of St. Francis of Philadelphia*—O.S.F.

[3840]—*Sisters of St. Joseph of Carondelet*—C.S.J.

[1990]—*Sisters of the Holy Names of Jesus and Mary*—S.N.J.M.

[2110]—*Sisters of the Humility of Mary*—H.M.

DIOCESAN CEMETERIES

SPOKANE. *Catholic Cemeteries of Spokane*, P.O. Box 18006, 99228. 7200 N. Wall St., 99208. Tel: 509-467-5496; Fax: 509-467-6649. Jim Falkner, Exec. Dir.

Holy Cross, P.O. Box 18006, 99228. 7200 N. Wall St., 99208. Tel: 509-467-5496; Fax: 509-467-6649.

St. Joseph, P.O. Box 18006, 99228. 17825 E. Trent, 99216. Tel: 509-891-6420; Fax: 509-891-1912.

Mary Queen of Peace Cemetery, P.O. Box 18006, 99228. 6910 S. Ben Burr Rd., 99223. Tel: 509-467-5496.

NECROLOGY

† Rosage, Rev. Msgr. David E., (Retired)—Died Nov. 14, 2009

† Donnelly, Sean, (Retired)—Died Feb. 10, 2009

† Mangan, James—Died Jan. 11, 2009

† Mele, Thomas, (Absent on Leave)—Died April 19, 2009

† Rompa, John, Spokane, WA St. Ann—Died Nov. 13, 2008

† Schwemin, Ralph H., (Retired)—Died Oct. 31, 2009

An asterisk (*) denotes an organization that has established tax-exempt status directly with the IRS and is not covered by the USCCB Group Ruling.

Diocese of Springfield-Cape Girardeau

(Dioecesis Campifontis-Capitis Girardeauensis)

Most Reverend

JAMES V. JOHNSTON JR., D.D., J.C.L.

Bishop of Springfield-Cape Girardeau; ordained June 9, 1990; appointed Bishop of Springfield-Cape Girardeau January 24, 2008; ordained March 31, 2008. *Office: The Catholic Center, 601 S. Jefferson Ave., Springfield, MO 65806-3143.*

Most Reverend

JOHN J. LEIBRECHT, D.D., PH.D.

Bishop Emeritus of Springfield-Cape Girardeau; ordained March 17, 1956; appointed Bishop of Springfield-Cape Girardeau October 23, 1984; consecrated December 12, 1984; retired January 24, 2008. *Res.: 1152 W. Camino Alto St., Springfield, MO 65810.* Tel: 417-987-0884. Email: jleibrecht@mchsi.com.

Chancery Office: The Catholic Center, 601 S. Jefferson Ave., Springfield, MO 65806-3143. Tel: 417-866-0841; Fax: 417-866-1140.

Web: www.dioscg.org

Email: treidy@dioscg.org

ESTABLISHED AUGUST 24, 1956.

Square Miles 25,719.

Comprises the following Counties in the State of Missouri: Barry, Barton, Bollinger, Butler, Cape Girardeau, Carter, Cedar, Christian, Dade, Dallas, Dent, Douglas, Dunklin, Greene, Howell, Iron, Jasper, Laclede, Lawrence, McDonald, Madison, Mississippi, New Madrid, Newton, Oregon, Ozark, Pemiscot, Polk, Reynolds, Ripley, Scott, Shannon, Stoddard, Stone, Taney, Texas, Wayne, Webster and Wright.

For legal titles of parishes and diocesan institutions, consult The Catholic Center.

STATISTICAL OVERVIEW

Personnel	
Bishop	1
Retired Bishops	1
Retired Abbots	2
Priests: Diocesan Active in Diocese	45
Priests: Retired, Sick or Absent	20
Number of Diocesan Priests	65
Religious Priests in Diocese	53
Total Priests in Diocese	118
Extern Priests in Diocese	14
Ordinations:	
Religious Priests	6
Permanent Deacons in Diocese	16
Total Brothers	55
Total Sisters	82
Parishes	
Parishes	66
With Resident Pastor:	
Resident Diocesan Priests	41
Resident Religious Priests	6
Without Resident Pastor:	
Administered by Priests	16
Administered by Deacons	1
Administered by Religious Women	2
Missions	18
Pastoral Centers	4
Professional Ministry Personnel:	
Brothers	1
Sisters	19
Lay Ministers	34
Welfare	
Catholic Hospitals	7
Total Assisted	1,032,337
Homes for the Aged	1
Total Assisted	362
Day Care Centers	1
Total Assisted	39
Educational	
Diocesan Students in Other Seminaries	8
Seminaries, Religious	2
Students Religious	6
Total Seminarians	14
High Schools, Diocesan and Parish	3
Total Students	936
Elementary Schools, Diocesan and Parish	23
Total Students	3,580
Catechesis/Religious Education:	
High School Students	1,288
Elementary Students	3,408
Total Students under Catholic Instruction	9,226
Teachers in the Diocese:	
Brothers	1
Sisters	5
Lay Teachers	317
Vital Statistics	
Receptions into the Church:	
Infant Baptism Totals	878
Minor Baptism Totals	116
Adult Baptism Totals	122
Received into Full Communion	185
First Communions	1,182
Confirmations	817
Marriages:	
Catholic	173
Interfaith	152
Total Marriages	325
Deaths	532
Total Catholic Population	68,147
Total Population	1,226,079

Former Bishops—Most Revs. CHARLES H. HELMSING, D.D., cons. as Titular Bishop of Axomis and Auxiliary Bishop of Archdiocese of St. Louis, April 19, 1949; appt. Bishop of Springfield-Cape Girardeau, Aug. 24, 1956; transferred to Diocese of Kansas City-St. Joseph, Jan. 27, 1962; retired Aug. 17, 1977; died Dec. 20, 1993; IGNATIUS J. STRECKER, D.D., appt. April 7, 1962; cons. June 20, 1962; transferred to Archdiocese of Kansas City in Kansas, Sept. 10, 1969; retired Sept. 8, 1993; died Oct. 16, 2003; His Eminence WILLIAM CARDINAL BAUM, S.T.D. (Retired), appt. Feb. 18, 1970; cons. April 6, 1970; transferred to Archdiocese of Washington D.C., May 9, 1973; elevated to Cardinal, May 24, 1976; appt. Prefect, Congregation for Catholic Education in the Vatican, Jan. 15, 1980; Major Penitentiary, appt. April 6, 1990.; retired Nov. 22, 2001; BERNARD CARDINAL LAW, D.D., ord. May 21, 1961; appt. Bishop of Springfield-Cape Girardeau, Oct. 22, 1973; cons. Dec. 5, 1973; appt. Archbishop of Boston, Jan. 23, 1984; elevated to Cardinal, May 25, 1985; resigned Dec. 13, 2002; appt. Archpriest of St. Mary Major Basilica, Rome, Italy May 27, 2004; Most Rev. JOHN J. LEIBRECHT, D.D., Ph.D., ord. March 17, 1956; appt. Bishop of Springfield-Cape Girardeau Oct. 23, 1984; cons. Dec. 12, 1984; retired Jan. 24, 2008.

Vicar General—Rev. Msgr. THOMAS E. REIDY, V.G.

Chancery Office—The Catholic Center, 601 S. Jefferson Ave., Springfield, 65806-3143. Tel: 417-866-0841; Fax: 417-866-1140.

Chancellor—Rev. Msgr. THOMAS E. REIDY, V.G.

Vice Chancellor—Rev. THOMAS P. KIEFER, J.C.L.

Regional Priest Moderators—Region I: Rev. JUSTIN D. MONAGHAN. Region II: Rev. DAVID L. MILLER. Region III: Rev. Msgr. MICHAEL F. SWALINA, S.T.D. Region IV: Rev. J. FERGUS MONAGHAN. Region V: Rev. DANIEL J. HIRTZ. Region VI: Rev. JAMES J. UNTERREINER. Region VII: Rev. JOHN M. HARTH. Region VIII: Rev. ALLAN L. SAUNDERS. Region IX: Rev. DAVID J. DOHOGNE.

Office of Administration

Catholic Foundation Of The Diocese Of Springfield-Cape Girardeau—Most Rev. JAMES V. JOHNSTON JR., D.D., J.C.L., Pres.; Rev. Msgr. THOMAS E. REIDY, V.G., Vice Pres.; Ms. JANET L. SMITH, Sec. Treas.

Development and Properties—Dr. EUGENE AUG, Ph.D., Dir.

Diocesan Development Fund—Dr. EUGENE AUG, Ph.D., Dir. Devel. & Properties; Revs. RICK L. JONES; JOHN M. HARTH; Mrs. BARBARA GIBBS; Mr. MARK GRIESHABER; Mrs. KATHLEEN MITCHELL; Mrs. THERESA WITT.

Finance—Ms. JANET L. SMITH, Dir.

Financial Council—Ms. JANET L. SMITH, Dir. Finance; Dr. EUGENE AUG, Ph.D., Diocesan Dir., Devel. & Properties; Mrs. MAUREEN M. JERSAK, Diocesan Dir., Planned Giving; Mr. LARRY G. GRINSTEAD; Mrs. CATHY MEYER; Mr. TOM BARR; Mr. JAMES MOORE; Mr. KEVIN FITZGERALD; Mr. CHRIS CHURCHWELL; Mr. STAN IRWIN; Mrs. ANN SAUNDERS.

Planned Giving—Mrs. MAUREEN M. JERSAK, Dir.

Office of Education

Catholic Schools—Mr. LEON WITT, Supt. of Schools.

Communications (Public Relations)—Mrs. RECY MOORE, Dir.

Ecumenism—Rev. JOHN F. GAGNEPAIN, C.M.

Newspaper, Diocese of Springfield-Cape Girardeau—"The Mirror" Mrs. LESLIE A. EIDSON, Editor; Mrs. ANGIE TOBIN, Circulation & Administrative Asst. The Mirror Advisory Board: Mrs. LESLIE A. EIDSON, Editor; Mr. MICK T. GILLIAM; Rev. JOHN M. HARTH; Mrs. ANN K. HAYES; Mrs. EMELIE M. JOHNSON; Rev. J. FERGUS MONAGHAN; Mr. ANDY OSTMEYER; Sr. RITA MARIE SCHONHOFF.

Religious Education—Mrs. KAREN PESEK, Dir.

Office of Ministry

Campus Ministries—Revs. JOHN (J.) F. FRIEDEL, M.A., M.Div., Diocesan Dir. & Chap. Missouri Southern State Univ. Tel: 417-623-8643; THOMAS A. MCGANN, C.M.F., Missouri State Univ. Campus Min. Tel: 417-865-0802; PATRICK I. NWOKOYE, Ph.D., Southeast Missouri State Univ. Campus Min. Tel: 573-335-3899; THOMAS M. NGUYEN TUAN BINH, C.M.C., Part-Time Sacramental Asst. Missouri Southern State Univ. Tel: 417-358-7787; Mrs. LYNN MELENDEZ, Part-time Campus Minister, College of the Ozarks. Tel: 417-334-2928.

Diaconate (Permanent)—Deacon WILLIAM MCNAMEE. Tel: 417-887-0600, Ext. 106.

Diocesan Director of Continuing Formation of Clergy—Rev. JOHN F. GAGNEPAIN, C.M. Tel: 573-547-6533, Ext. 266.

Family Ministries—Mr. TROY S. CASTEEL, M.S., L.P.C., Dir.

Diocesan Council on Family Ministries—Mr. TROY S. CASTEEL, M.S., L.P.C., Dir. Family Ministries. Region I: DEANNA STREET, M.A., L.P.C.; ELIZABETH RUNKLE. Region II: VACANT. Region III: Rev. J. PATRICK WISSMAN. Region IV: Rev. MICHAEL V. MCDEVITT, M.A., M.Div.; SHARON WEIDELMAN; PATTI STRAUS; ERIC PICHLER; SHELLY PICHLER. Region V: Rev. ERNEST J. MARQUART. Region VI: Rev. JAMES J. UNTERREINER. Region VII: VACANT. Region VIII: JACK JACKOVIC; PAT JACKOVIC. Region IX: VACANT.

Natural Family Planning—Mr. TROY S. CASTEEL, M.S., L.P.C., Dir.

Rite of Christian Initiation of Adults—Co Directors: Rev. PAUL J. MCLOUGHLIN; Mrs. KAREN PESEK.

Hispanic Ministries—Mrs. MILAGROS CALVETTI, Dir.

Social Ministry—VACANT.

**Catholic Charities of Southern Missouri, Inc., 601 S. Jefferson Ave., Springfield, 65806.* Tel: 417-866-0841; Fax: 417-866-1140. Email: ccsomo@ccsomo.org. Dr. DONALD R. EMGE, Ph.D., Exec. Dir.

Safe Environment Coordinator—Mrs. KAREN PESEK.

Victim Assistance Coordinators—KATHLEEN P. GRIESEMER, Psy.D. Tel: 417-848-4601; JOHN K. KREYMER, Psy.D., DAPA.

Tribunal—

Judicial Vicar—Rev. Msgr. THOMAS E. REIDY, V.G.

Adjutant Judicial Vicars—Revs. VINCENT E. BERTRAND, J.C.L.; THOMAS P. KIEFER, J.C.L.

Coordinator & Auditor—Sr. ROBIN L. NORDYKE, C.D.P., J.C.L.

Judges—Revs. VINCENT E. BERTRAND, J.C.L.; THOMAS P. KIEFER, J.C.L.; Rev. Msgr. THOMAS E. REIDY, V.G.

Promoter of Justice—Sr. ROBIN L. NORDYKE, C.D.P., J.C.L.

Advocates for the Petitioners— Parish Priests, deacons, and pastoral ministers

Advocates for the Respondent—Revs. MICHAEL V. MCDEVITT, M.A., M.Div.; DAVID F. HULSHOF, M.A.

Defender of the Bond—Rev. Msgr. MICHAEL F. SWALINA, S.T.D.

Notary—Mrs. LINDA MURPHY.

Vicar For The Religious—Rev. Msgr. THOMAS E. REIDY, V.G.

Vocations-Seminarians—Revs. JOHN (J.) F. FRIEDEL, M.A., M.Div., Dir. Vocations/Seminarians; PATRICK I. NWOKOYE, Ph.D., Dir. of Vocation Promotion.

Youth Ministry—Ms. LEIGH STERTEN, Dir.

Catholic Scouting—Rev. PATRICK I. NWOKOYE, Ph.D., Diocesan Chap. Tel: 573-335-3899; Mr. BEN FRANCKA, Assoc. Diocesan Chap. Tel: 417-881-6518.

Camp Re-NEW-All—Ms. VIRGINIA SANDER, Camp Dir.; Mrs. MANDY WITT-AUBERT, Camp Dir.

Office of Worship

Office of Worship—Rev. PAUL J. MCLOUGHLIN, Dir.

Liturgical Commission—Rev. PAUL J. MCLOUGHLIN, Dir. Worship.

Priests' Eucharistic League Confraternity of The Most Blessed Sacrament—Rev. MICHAEL V. MCDEVITT, M.A., M.Div., Dir.

Officials And Committees

Catholic Relief Services—Rev. Msgr. THOMAS E. REIDY, V.G.

Cemeteries—Rev. Msgr. THOMAS E. REIDY, V.G.

Health Affairs—Mr. TROY S. CASTEEL, M.S., L.P.C., Dir.

Holy Childhood Association—Rev. Msgr. MICHAEL F. SWALINA, S.T.D. Tel: 417-532-4811.

Missionary Apostolate— Society for the Propagation of the Faith, Rev. Msgr. MICHAEL F. SWALINA, S.T.D. Tel: 417-532-4811.

Mission of the Laity— Apostleship of Prayer, Rev. Msgr. MICHAEL F. SWALINA, S.T.D. Tel: 417-532-4811.

National Shrine Of The Immaculate Conception—Rev. Msgr. THOMAS E. REIDY, V.G., Dir.

Priests' Mutual Benefit Society—Rev. Msgr. THOMAS E. REIDY, V.G., Exec. Sec.; Rev. THOMAS P. KIEFER, J.C.L., Vice Pres.; Rev. Msgrs. EDWARD M. EFTINK, Ph.D. (Retired); RAYMOND V. ORF (Retired); Revs. NORMAND G. VARONE (Retired); JOHN M. HARTH, Pres.; RALPH J. DUFFNER (Retired); PAUL J. MCLOUGHLIN.

Rural Life Movement—Rev. SYLVESTER W. BAUER (Retired). Tel: 573-744-5913.

Diocesan Consultative Groups

Diocesan Consultors—Rev. JOHN (J.) F. FRIEDEL, M.A., M.Div.; Rev. Msgr. MICHAEL F. SWALINA, S.T.D.; Rev. THOMAS P. KIEFER, J.C.L.; Rev. Msgr. THOMAS E. REIDY, V.G.; Revs. PAUL J. MCLOUGHLIN; JAMES J. UNTERREINER; DAVID F. HULSHOF, M.A.

Presbyteral Council—Revs. PAUL J. MCLOUGHLIN, Chm.; JAMES J. UNTERREINER; JOHN (J.) F. FRIEDEL, M.A., M.Div.; DAVID F. HULSHOF, M.A., Sec.; JOHN F. GAGNEPAIN, C.M.; RICK L. JONES, Vice Chm.; THOMAS A. MCGANN, C.M.F.; JAROSLAW Z. SKRZYPEK; Rev. Msgr. MICHAEL F. SWALINA, S.T.D.; Rev. JOSEPH WEIDENBENNER. Appointed Member: Rev. Msgr. THOMAS E. REIDY, V.G.

Diocesan Pastoral Council—Rev. DAVID J. DOHOGNE, Exec. Sec.

Diocesan School Board—Mr. LEON WITT, Supt.; Mrs. THERESA ADAMS; Mr. GREG BOONE; Mr. GENE KOESTER; Mrs. BECKI ESSNER; Mr. LOUIS GRIESEMER; Mr. DAVID KOCH; Bro. DAVID ANTHONY MIGLIORINO, O.S.F.; Mrs. JEANNE SKAHAM; Rev. Msgr. WILLIAM J. STANTON (Retired).

Diocesan Lay Endowment Board—Rev. DAVID F. HULSHOF, M.A., Chm.; Mrs. TONI GROJEAN; Mrs. TRACY DUMEY; Sr. MARY JANE JANSEN, S.S.N.D.; Mr. NORMAN LOOS; Deacon JAMES E. LONG JR.; Mrs. NORMA PARKER.

Catholic Organizations And Movements

Charismatic Prayer Groups—Mr. KLAUS TAMME; Rev. WILLIAM M. HODGSON.

Cursillo Movement—

Secretariat for Cursillo—Rev. WILLIAM M. HODGSON, Diocesan Chap.

St. Francis de Sales Association—Rev. FRANK C. PALERMO, Chap. (Retired); Rev. Msgr. WILLIAM J. STANTON, Chap. (Retired).

Diocesan Council of Catholic Women (DCCW)—Revs. JAMES J. UNTERREINER, Diocesan Spiritual Moderator; DAVID F. HULSHOF, M.A., Assoc. Spiritual Moderator; BEVERLY SWIHART, Pres. Tel: 417-326-7989.

Apostolates And Commissions

Apostolate to the Deaf—Rev. DAVID L. MILLER, Dir. Tel: 417-847-4948; 417-858-2518.

Diocesan Peace and Justice Commission—Dr. DONALD R. EMGE, Ph.D. Tel: 417-866-0841; Rev. SYLVESTER BAUER, Commissioner Emeritus (Retired). Tel: 573-744-5913.

State Office

Diocesan Delegates To The Missouri Catholic Conference—

Public Policy Committee—Mr. JAMES WIRTH.

CLERGY, PARISHES, MISSIONS AND PAROCHIAL SCHOOLS

CITY OF SPRINGFIELD

(GREENE COUNTY)

1—CATHEDRAL OF ST. AGNES (1908) [CEM] [JC] Revs. Michael V. McDevitt; Philip M. Lam Ba Trong, C.M.C.; Deacons William J. Keller; Mark A. Wand; Sr. Barbara Dingman, D.C., Min. of Care.

Res.: 533 S. Jefferson Ave., 65806. Tel: 417-831-3565; Fax: 417-865-0367.

School—(Grades PreSchool-8), 531 S. Jefferson Ave., 65806. Tel: 417-866-5038; Fax: 417-866-2906. Email: jskahan@scspk12.org. Web: www.scspk12.org. Mrs. Jeanne Skahan, Prin. Lay Teachers 14; Aides 2; Counselors 1; Students 233.

Catechesis/Religious Program—Ken Pesek, Liturgy & Music Dir.; Sabrina Schmidt, D.R.E. Students 118.

2—ST. ELIZABETH ANN SETON (1981) [CEM] Rev. Msgr. Thomas E. Reidy; Rev. Jeffery A. Fasching (WCH); Sr. Bernadette Goessling, S.S.N.D., Parish Min.; Deacon Thomas M. Brewer, Parish Min.

Church: 2200 W. Republic Rd., 65807. Tel: 417-887-6472; Fax: 417-887-7027.

School—(Grades PreSchool-4) Tel: 417-887-6056; Fax: 417-887-2189. Email: chall@scspk12.org. Web: www.scspk12.org. Mrs. Cheryl Hall, Prin. Lay Teachers 7; Aides 4; Students 158.

Catechesis/Religious Program—Melinda Lohkamp, Youth Min. Students 477.

3—HOLY TRINITY (1966) [JC] Rev. J. Fergus Monaghan. In Res., Rev. Frank C. Palermo (Retired).

Res.: 2818 E. Bennett, 65804. Tel: 417-883-3440; Fax: 417-883-0072.

Catechesis/Religious Program—Sr. Jeanne Goessling, S.S.N.D., D.R.E. Students 159.

4—IMMACULATE CONCEPTION (1868) [JC] Revs. Lewis E. Hejna; Simon Le Phuc Diem, C.M.C.; Deacon William McNamee. In Res., Rev. Msgr. Raymond V. Orf (Retired).

Res.: 3535 S. Fremont, 65804. Tel: 417-799-0062.

Church: 3555 S. Fremont, 65804. Tel: 417-887-0600; Fax: 417-887-0027.

School—(Grades PreSchool-8), 3555A S. Fremont, 65804. Tel: 417-881-7000; Fax: 417-881-7087. Mrs. Paula Baird, Prin. Lay Teachers 26; Aides 10; Students 504.

Catechesis/Religious Program—Mrs. Sharon Weidelman, D.R.E.; Dan Pfaff, Youth Min.; Mindy Pfaff, Youth Min.; Liz Kehl, Youth Min. Students 72.

5—ST. JOSEPH'S (1892) [JC] Rev. Denis Dougherty, O.S.B.; Deacons Mathey F. Fletcher; Norm Ridder. In Res., Rev. Eugene M. Klein (WIN).

Res.: 1115 N. Campbell Ave., 65802. Tel: 417-865-1112; Fax: 417-865-7488.

School—(Grades PreSchool-8), 515 W. Scott, 65802. Tel: 417-866-0667; Fax: 417-866-2862. Mrs. Marilyn Batson, Prin. Lay Teachers 11; Aides 3; Students 119.

Catechesis/Religious Program—Students 79.

6—SACRED HEART (1882) [JC] Rev. Daniel Robles; Deacon Edward Ellman.

Mailing Address: 1609 N. Summit, 65803. Tel: 417-869-3646; Fax: 417-869-2218.

Catechesis/Religious Program—Julia Valdes, C.R.E. Students 106.

CITY OF CAPE GIRARDEAU

(CAPE GIRARDEAU COUNTY)

1—CATHEDRAL OF ST. MARY OF THE ANNUNCIATION (1868) [CEM] [JC] Rev. Thomas P. Kiefer; Sr. Lucille Zerr, S.S.N.D., Pastoral Min.; Deacon James E. Long Jr.

Mailing Address: 615 William St., 63703.

Res.: 629 William St., 63703. Tel: 573-335-9347; Fax: 573-335-0649.

School—(Grades K-8), 210 S. Sprigg, 63703. Tel: 573-335-3840. Mrs. Carol Strattman, Prin. Lay Teachers 18; Aides 2; Students 255.

Catechesis/Religious Program—Brenda Kuhn, D.R.E.; Lisa Simmons, Youth Coord. Students 27.

Old St. Vincent's— (Chapel of Ease).

2—ST. VINCENT DE PAUL (1838) Revs. David F. Hulshof; Saviour Nundwe. In Res., Rev. Robert F. Manso.

Office: 1913 Ritter Dr., 63701.

Res.: 741 N. Forest, 63701. Tel: 573-335-7667; Fax: 573-335-0034.

School—(Grades K-8), 1919 Ritter Dr., 63701. Tel: 573-334-9594. Web: www.svscape.com. Mrs. Kay Glastetter, Prin. Lay Teachers 25; Aides 6; Students 422.

Catechesis/Religious Program—Kathy Hotop-Raines, D.R.E.; Sr. Theresa Davey, Christian Svc. Coord. Students 59.

OUTSIDE THE CITIES OF SPRINGFIELD AND CAPE GIRARDEAU

ADVANCE, STODDARD CO., ST. JOSEPH (1905) [CEM] Rev. Randolph G. Tochtrop.

Res.: P.O. Box 640, 63730. Tel: 573-722-3504.

Catechesis/Religious Program—Students 19.

AURORA, LAWRENCE CO., HOLY TRINITY (1906) [CEM] Revs. Michael V. McDevitt, Canonical Pastor; Milton Alvarez, C.M.F., Sacramental Priest; Sisters Francis Rose Rivers, S.S.N.D., Parish Min.; Mary Essner, S.S.N.D., Parish Life Coord.

Res.: Hwy. 60 & Carnation Rd., P.O. Box 533, 65605. Tel: 417-678-2403; Fax: 417-678-3714.

Catechesis/Religious Program—Mrs. Agnes Elsey, D.R.E. Students 52.

BENTON, SCOTT CO., ST. DENIS (1840) [CEM] Rev. Michael J. Casteel.

Res.: P.O. Box 127, 63736. Tel: 573-545-3864. Email: hukul23@aol.com.

School—(Grades K-8), P.O. Box 189, 63736. Tel: 573-545-3017; Fax: 573-545-9185. Email: kspowers1123@yahoo.com. Mrs. Karen Powers, Prin. Lay Teachers 8; Aides 1; Students 85.

Catechesis/Religious Program—Students 33.

BILLINGS, CHRISTIAN CO., ST. JOSEPH (1879) [CEM] Rev. Rahab Isidor, Parochial Admin.

Res.: P.O. Box 100, 65610. Tel: 417-744-2490; Fax: 417-744-2528.

Catechesis/Religious Program—Shelley Andrus, D.R.E.; Mrs. Margaret Baunach, Youth Min. Students 84.

BOLIVAR, POLK CO., SACRED HEART (1946) [CEM] Rev. J. Patrick Wissman.

Res.: 1405 W. Fair Play St., 65613. Tel: 417-326-5596; Fax: 417-326-5596.
Catechesis/Religious Program—Students 87.
Mission—St. Catherine P.O. Box 42, Humansville, Polk Co. 65674. Tel: 417-754-8825.

BRANSON, TANEY CO., OUR LADY OF THE LAKE (1951) Rev. Rick L. Jones.
Res.: 203 Vaughn Dr., 65616. Tel: 417-334-2928; Fax: 417-334-6883.
Catechesis/Religious Program—Mrs. Pat Hutcheson, D.R.E. & Youth Min. Students 206.

BUFFALO, DALLAS CO., ST. WILLIAM (1946) Rev. Gefford C. Lamprea.
Res.: P.O. Box 518, 65622. Tel: 417-345-2744.
Catechesis/Religious Program—Brenda Paul, D.R.E. Students 16.

CARTHAGE, JASPER CO., ST. ANN (1872) Rev. William M. Hodgson.
Res.: 908 S. Clinton St., P.O. Box 803, 64836. Tel: 417-358-1841; Fax: 417-358-1841.
School—(Grades PreSchool-6), 1156 Grand, 64836. Tel: 417-358-2674; Fax: 417-358-8976. Bonnie Schaefer, Prin. Lay Teachers 5; Students 82.
Catechesis/Religious Program—Ryan Kiniry, D.R.E. Students 112.

CARUTHERSVILLE, PEMISCOT CO., SACRED HEART (1900) Rev. Thomas Bartolomeo, Parochial Admin.
Res.: 605 Ward Ave., 63830. Tel: 573-333-4301.
Catechesis/Religious Program—Cynthia Hodge, C.R.E. Students 19.

CASSVILLE, BARRY CO., ST. EDWARD Rev. David L. Miller; Sr. Juilana Soto, M.C.M., Spanish Min.
Mailing Address: P.O. Box 492, 65625. Tel: 417-847-4948; Fax: 417-847-4947.
Office: 101 W. 17th St., 65625.
Res.: 1802 Y Hwy., P.O. Box 492, 65625. Tel: 417-847-8526.
Church: 107 W. 17th St., 65625.
Catechesis/Religious Program—Students 62.

CHAFFEE, SCOTT CO., ST. AMBROSE (1907) [CEM] Rev. Ralph J. Duffner, Admin. (Retired).
Office: 418 S. Third St., 63740. Tel: 573-887-3953.
Res.: 314 Elliott, 63740. Tel: 573-887-4283.
School—(Grades K-8), 419 S. Third St., 63740. Tel: 573-887-6711; Fax: 573-887-6711. Mrs. Jody Grim, Prin. Lay Teachers 9; Students 83.
Catechesis/Religious Program—Students 43.

CHARLESTON, MISSISSIPPI CO., ST. HENRY (1874) Rev. Glenn A. Eftink.
Res.: 304 Court St., 63834. Tel: 573-683-2114.
School—(Grades PreSchool-8), 306 Court St., 63834. Tel: 573-683-6218; Fax: 573-683-7800. Mrs. Alice Harvell, Prin. Lay Teachers 7; Aides 1; Students 123.
Catechesis/Religious Program—Students 6.

CONWAY, LACLEDE CO., SACRED HEART (1908) [CEM] Rev. Gefford C. Lamprea.
Res.: P.O. Box 8, 65632. Tel: 417-589-6782.
Church: 310 Spruce St., 65632.
Catechesis/Religious Program—Students 33.

DEXTER, STODDARD CO., SACRED HEART (1889) Rev. David J. Dohogne.
Office: 115 E. Market St., 63841.
Res.: 103 E. Market St., 63841. Tel: 573-624-8888.
Church: 102 E. Castor, 63841. Tel: 573-624-7333; Fax: 573-624-4076.
Catechesis/Religious Program—Shearon Harris, D.R.E. Students 72.

DONIPHAN, RIPLEY CO., ST. BENEDICT (1859) [CEM] Rev. David N. Coon.
Res.: 306 Kegler, 63935. Tel: 573-996-3301.
Catechesis/Religious Program—Terri Wright, C.R.E.; Sandra Kennon, C.R.E. Students 18.

EL DORADO SPRINGS, CEDAR CO., ST. ELIZABETH OF HUNGARY (1946) [CEM] Rev. Basil M. Doan Toan, C.M.C.
Res.: 609 S. Main, 64744. Tel: 417-876-3216; Fax: 417-876-6448.
Catechesis/Religious Program—Students 26.
Mission—St. Peter the Apostle 222 N. Hwy. J, P.O. Box 583, Stockton, Cedar Co. 65785. Tel: 417-276-5588.

FORSYTH, TANEY CO., OUR LADY OF THE OZARKS (1980) Revs. Rick L. Jones; Philip J. Conlon (MAD), Sacramental Min. (Retired); Dow Escalante, Pastoral Assoc.
Mailing Address: P.O. Box 639, 65653. Tel: 417-546-5208; Fax: 417-546-6615.
Church: 951 Swan Valley Dr., 65653.
Catechesis/Religious Program—Students 8.

FREDERICKTOWN, MADISON CO., ST. MICHAEL (1827) [CEM] Rev. Augustine Chibuzo Alilonu, Parochial Admin.
Res.: 304 W. Main St., 63645. Tel: 573-783-2182; Fax: 573-783-5230.
Catechesis/Religious Program—Mrs. Cynthia Belken, D.R.E. Students 76.

GLENNONVILLE, DUNKLIN CO., ST. TERESA (1905) [CEM] Rev. David J. Dohogne; Deacon Fred Hirtz.
Res.: 40694 State Hwy. JJ, Campbell, 63933-9148. Tel: 573-328-1226; 573-328-4544 (Office); Fax: 578-328-4544.
School—(Grades PreSchool-8) Mrs. Janet Kuper, Prin. Lay Teachers 7; Students 53; Aides 1.
Catechesis/Religious Program—Students 21.

HOUSTON, TEXAS CO., ST. MARK (1975) Rev. Matthew J. Rehrauer.
Res.: 117 E. South Oak Crest, 65483. Tel: 417-967-3589.
Catechesis/Religious Program—Students 33.
Mission—St. Vincent de Paul Roby, Texas Co.
Mission—St. John The Baptist Licking, Texas Co.

IRONTON, IRON CO., STE. MARIE DU LAC (1878) [CEM] Revs. James J. Unterreiner; Anthony M. Gaydos, O.S.M., Senior Priest.
Res.: 350 S. Main St., 63650. Tel: 573-546-2611; Fax: 573-546-3711.
Catechesis/Religious Program—Susan Wessel, C.R.E.; Dennis Trowbridge, Youth Min. Students 27.
Mission—Our Lady of Sorrows Lesterville, Reynolds Co.
Mission—St. Philip Benizi Viburnum, Iron Co.

JACKSON, CAPE GIRARDEAU CO., IMMACULATE CONCEPTION (1874) [CEM] Revs. John M. Harth; William Hennecke Jr.; Deacon Walter Biri.
Res.: 208 S. Hope St., Ste. 101, 63755. Tel: 573-243-3182; Fax: 573-243-6833.
School—(Grades PreSchool-8), 300 S. Hope St., 63755. Tel: 573-243-5013. Mrs. Tamara Nenninger, Prin. Lay Teachers 20; Students 239; Aides 2.
Catechesis/Religious Program—Alan Sellers, Youth Min.; Kim Sellers, Youth Min.; Eddie Laws, Educ. Min.; Misti Laws, Educ. Min.; Betty Starke, Educ. Min. Students 209.

JOPLIN, JASPER CO.
1—ST. MARY (1938) [JC] Rev. Justin D. Monaghan.
Res.: 2415 Moffet Ave., 64804. Tel: 417-623-3333; Fax: 417-623-4015.
School—(Grades PreSchool-5), 505 W. 25th St., 64804. Tel: 417-623-1465; Fax: 417-623-4749. Mr. Stephen Jones, Prin. Sisters 1; Lay Teachers 14; Students 222; Aides 5.
Catechesis/Religious Program—Patty Wheeler, C.R.E. Students 41.
2—ST. PETER THE APOSTLE (1877) [JC] Rev. John (J.) F. Friedel.
Res.: 812 S. Pearl Ave., 64801-4396. Tel: 417-623-8643; Fax: 417-623-0866.
School—(Grades 6-8), 802 Byers, 64801-4396. Tel: 417-624-5605; Fax: 417-624-6254. Mr. Greg Emory, Prin. Sisters 1; Lay Teachers 9; Students 78.
Catechesis/Religious Program—Elizabeth Runkle, C.R.E. Students 62.

KELSO, SCOTT CO., ST. AUGUSTINE (1878) Rev. M. Oliver Clavin.
Res.: 201 S. Messmer, Box 26, 63758. Tel: 573-264-4724; Fax: 573-264-4106.
School—(Grades K-8), 230 S. Hwy. 61, P.O. Box 97, 63758-0097. Tel: 573-264-4644; Fax: 573-264-1475. Mrs. Tracy Dumey, Prin. Lay Teachers 11; Students 111; Aides 1.
Catechesis/Religious Program—Students 1.

KENNETT, DUNKLIN CO., ST. CECILIA (1923) Rev. Allan L. Saunders; Sr. Carol Prenger, S.S.N.D., Pastoral Assoc. (Hispanic Ministry).
Res.: 1226 College St., P.O. Box 306, 63857. Tel: 573-888-2412; Fax: 573-888-0613.
Catechesis/Religious Program—Students 159.

KIMBERLING CITY, STONE CO., OUR LADY OF THE COVE (1979) Rev. Joseph Than Van Liem, C.M.C.
Res.: 20 Kimberling Blvd., P.O. Box 548, 65686. Tel: 417-739-4700; Fax: 417-739-5279.
Catechesis/Religious Program—Jim Dobbs, D.R.E. Students 93.

LAMAR, BARTON CO., ST. MARY (1904) [CEM] Rev. Frederick J. Lutz.
Res.: 200 E. 17th St., P.O. Box 89, 64759. Tel: 417-682-2492.
Catechesis/Religious Program—Students 32.

LEBANON, LACLEDE CO., ST. FRANCIS DE SALES (1870) [CEM] Rev. Msgr. Michael F. Swalina.
Res.: 345 Grand St., 65536. Tel: 417-532-4811; Fax: 417-532-8847.
Catechesis/Religious Program—Margaret Thessen, D.R.E.; Pat Hopkins, D.R.E. Students 106.
Chapel—Bennett Springs, Sportman's Chapel

LEOPOLD, BOLLINGER CO., ST. JOHN (1856) [CEM] Revs. John M. Harth; William Hennecke Jr.; Deacon Walter Biri.
Res.: 103 Main St., P.O. Box 83, 63760. Tel: 573-238-3300; Fax: 573-238-2450.
Catechesis/Religious Program—Cindy Jansen, Youth Dir. Students 196.
Mission—St. Anthony [CEM] Glennon, Bollinger Co.

MALDEN, DUNKLIN CO., ST. ANN (1890) Rev. David J. Dohogne; Deacon Fred Hirtz.
Mailing Address: *c/o St. Teresa Parish*, 40694 State Hwy. JJ, Campbell, 63933. Tel: 573-328-4544.
Church: 304 N. Douglas St., 63863.
Catechesis/Religious Program—Students 3.

MANSFIELD, WRIGHT CO., IMMACULATE HEART OF MARY (1943) Revs. Paul Wightman, O.M.I.; Jeffery A. Fasching (WCH), Sacramental Min.
Res.: Rte. 6, Box 6700, Ava, 65608. Tel: 417-683-5249; 417-924-3779 (Office).
Catechesis/Religious Program—Mrs. B. J. Sterling, C.R.E. (Ava); Nancy Stepro, C.R.E. (Mansfield); Sheri Richardson, C.R.E. (Gainesville). Students 42.
Mission—St. Leo the Great Rte. 6, Box 6700, Ava, Douglas Co. 65608. Tel: 417-683-5249.
Mission—St. William P.O. Box 367, Gainesville, Ozark Co. 65655. Tel: 417-679-4804.

MARSHFIELD, WEBSTER CO., HOLY TRINITY (1892) Rev. Scott M. Sunnenberg.
515 E. Washington, 65706-1865. Tel: 417-859-2228.
Res.: 125 N. Locust, 65706. Tel: 417-859-3489.
Catechesis/Religious Program—Students 118.

MONETT, BARRY CO., ST. LAWRENCE (1891) [CEM] Rev. Jaroslaw Z. Skrzypek; Sr. M. Socorro Lozoya, M.C.M., Hispanic Min.
Res.: 311 8th St., 65708. Tel: 417-236-9273; 417-235-3286 (Office); Fax: 417-235-3721.
Church: 405 Seventh St., 65708.
School—(Grades PreSchool-6), 407 Seventh St., 65708. Tel: 417-235-3721. Rita Donica, Prin.; Mrs. Teresa Verhoff, Asst. Prin. Sisters 1; Lay Teachers 8; Aides 2; Students 114.
Catechesis/Religious Program—Students 201.

MOUNT VERNON, LAWRENCE CO., ST. SUSANNE (1939) Rev. Patrick A. Teter.
Res.: P.O. Box 126, 65712. Tel: 417-466-4190; Fax: 417-466-2561.
Catechesis/Religious Program—Students 52.
Mission—St. Patrick Greenfield, Dade Co.

MOUNTAIN GROVE, WRIGHT CO., SACRED HEART (1893) Revs. Paul Wightman, O.M.I., Canonical Pastor; Jeffery A. Fasching (WCH), Sacramental Min.; Deacon Joseph Kurtenbach, Parish Life Coord.
Res.: 302 E. State St., 65711. Tel: 417-926-3803.
Catechesis/Religious Program—Students 20.
Mission—St. Michael Cabool, Texas Co.

MOUNTAIN VIEW, HOWELL CO., ST. JOHN VIANNEY (1951) Rev. Ernest J. Marquart.
Res.: 808 State Rd. Y, P.O. Box 38, 65548. Tel: 417-934-2649.
Catechesis/Religious Program—Patricia Einweck, C.R.E. Students 20.
Mission—St. Sylvester Eminence, Shannon Co.

NEOSHO, NEWTON CO., ST. CANERA (1871) [JC] Rev. Henry Grodecki, C.M.; Sr. Adelida Esquivel, M.C.M., Pastoral Assoc.
Res.: 504 S. Washington St., 64850. Tel: 417-451-3411; Fax: 417-451-3432.
Catechesis/Religious Program—Students 180.
Mission—Nativity of Our Lord P.O. Box 555, Noel, McDonald Co. 64854.

NEW HAMBURG, SCOTT CO., ST. LAWRENCE (1847) [CEM] Rev. Michael J. Casteel.
Mailing Address: P.O. Box 247, Benton, 63736-8159.
Church: 1001 State Hwy. A, Benton, 63736-0247. Tel: 573-545-3317; Fax: 573-545-3317.
Catechesis/Religious Program—Pat Moore, D.R.E. Students 91.

NEW MADRID, NEW MADRID CO., IMMACULATE CONCEPTION (1789) Rev. Thomas Bartolomeo (RCK), Parochial Admin.
Res.: 605 Davis St., 63869. Tel: 573-748-5183; Fax: 573-748-7718.
School—(Grades PreSchool-8), 560 Powell, 63869. Tel: 573-748-5123; Fax: 573-748-5123. Mrs. Mary Shy, Prin. Lay Teachers 4; Aides 1; Students 30.
Catechesis/Religious Program—Students 11.

NIXA, CHRISTIAN CO., ST. FRANCIS OF ASSISI (2004) Rev. Mark G. Boyer.
117 W. Sherman Way, P.O. Box 1920, 65714. Tel: 417-725-1975; Fax: 417-725-1975.
Catechesis/Religious Program—Leigh Sisk, C.R.E. Students 47.

ORAN, SCOTT CO., GUARDIAN ANGEL (1892) [CEM 2] Rev. Randolph G. Tochtrop; Sr. Mary Jane Jansen, S.S.N.D., Pastoral Assoc.
Res.: 604 Church St., P.O. Box 158, 63771. Tel: 573-262-3210; Fax: 573-262-3210.
School—(Grades K-8), 514 Church St., 63771. Tel: 573-262-3583. Ms. Michelle Huffman, Prin. Lay Teachers 8; Aides 1; Students 89.
Catechesis/Religious Program—Students 33.

OZARK, CHRISTIAN CO., ST. JOSEPH THE WORKER (1961) Rev. Paul J. McLoughlin.
Res.: 1796 N. State Hwy. NN, 65721. Tel: 417-581-6328; Fax: 417-581-4957.
Catechesis/Religious Program—Sr. Gale Bednarek, O.S.F., D.R.E. Students 159.

PIEDMONT, WAYNE CO., ST. CATHERINE OF SIENA (1873) Rev. Mark J. Binder; Sisters Mary Sheila Higdon, O.S.U., Pastoral Assoc.; Rita Schonhoff, Outreach Min.
Res.: 109 Piedmont Ave., 63957. Tel: 573-223-4924.
Catechesis/Religious Program—Students 48.
Mission—St. George Van Buren, Carter Co. Tel:

573-323-8576.
Mission—Our Lady of Sorrows Williamsville, Wayne Co.

PIERCE CITY, LAWRENCE CO., ST. MARY (1883) [CEM 2] Rev. Peter J. Morciniec.
Res.: 200 Front St., 65723. Tel: 417-476-2827.
School—(Grades PreSchool-8), 202 Front St., 65723. Tel: 417-476-2824; Fax: 417-476-2824. Mrs. Sally Heidlage, Prin. Lay Teachers 6; Aides 6; Students 81.
Catechesis/Religious Program—Mellanie Carder, D.R.E. Students 61.

POPLAR BLUFF, BUTLER CO., SACRED HEART (1891) [CEM] Revs. David N. Coon; Kizito Wenani.
Res.: 123 N. Eighth St., 63901. Tel: 573-785-9635; Fax: 573-785-2069.
School—(Grades PreSchool-8) Tel: 573-785-5836; Fax: 573-785-3908. Ms. Gloria Wilson, Prin. Sisters 3; Lay Teachers 13; Students 224; Aides 4.
Catechesis/Religious Program—Students 70.

PORTAGEVILLE, NEW MADRID CO., ST. EUSTACHIUS (1902) Rev. Allan L. Saunders.
Res.: 200 W. Fourth St., 63873. Tel: 573-379-3401.
School—(Grades PreSchool-8), 214 W. Fourth St., 63873. Tel: 573-379-3525; Fax: 573-379-3843. Mrs. Patricia Rone, Prin. Lay Teachers 6; Students 61.
Catechesis/Religious Program—Students 19.

PULASKIFIELD, BARRY CO., SS. PETER AND PAUL (1892) [CEM] Rev. Jaroslaw Z. Skrzypek.
Res. & Mailing Address: P.O. Box 396, Monett, 65708-0396. Tel: 417-476-2463.
Catechesis/Religious Program—Students 11.

SALEM, DENT CO., SACRED HEART (1880) Rev. Daniel J. Hirtz; Deacon Richard F. Cole.
Res.: 602 W. Butler, 65560. Tel: 573-729-4291; Fax: 573-729-3811.
Catechesis/Religious Program—June Cole, D.R.E. Students 67.
Mission—Christ the King P.O. Box 177, Bunker, Reynolds Co. 63629.
Chapel—Montauk, St. Jude

SARCOXIE, NEWTON CO., ST. AGNES (1870) [CEM] Rev. Peter J. Morciniec.
Res. & Mailing Address: P.O. Box 218, Pierce City, 65723-0218. Tel: 417-548-3540.
Catechesis/Religious Program—Jane Kutz, D.R.E. Students 12.

SCOTT CITY, SCOTT CO., ST. JOSEPH (1911) [CEM] Rev. M. Oliver Clavin.
Res.: 604 Sycamore, 63780. Tel: 573-264-4724; Fax: 573-264-1506.
School—(Grades K-8), 606 Sycamore, 63780. Tel: 573-264-2600; Fax: 573-264-1325. Clifford Lankheit, Prin. Lay Teachers 6; Students 38; Aides 1.
Catechesis/Religious Program—

SENECA, NEWTON CO., ST. MARY (1884) [CEM] Rev. Michael M. Do Van Quang, C.M.C., Admin. & Sacramental Priest.
Res.: P.O. Box 1169, 64865. Tel: 417-776-3786.
Church: 1209 Wyandotte, 64865.
Catechesis/Religious Program—Students 31.

SHELL KNOB, BARRY CO., HOLY FAMILY (1978) Rev. David L. Miller.
Res.: 24036 FR 1255, P.O. Box 229, 65747. Tel: 417-858-2518; 417-858-3678; Fax: 417-858-6029.
Catechesis/Religious Program—Penny Muckle, C.R.E.; Gretchen Brockman, Adult Educ. Coord. Students 2.

SIKESTON, SCOTT CO., ST. FRANCIS XAVIER'S (1893) Rev. Glenn A. Eftink.
Res.: 217 W. Center St., 63801. Tel: 573-471-5018; 573-471-2447 (Office); Fax: 573-471-9820.
School—(Grades PreSchool-8), 106 N. Stoddard, 63801. Tel: 573-471-0841. Mr. Pierre Antoine, Prin. Lay Teachers 10; Aides 3; Students 147.
Catechesis/Religious Program—Mrs. Toni Grojean, D.R.E. Students 43.

VERONA, LAWRENCE CO., SACRED HEART (1874) [CEM] Revs. Michael V. McDevitt, Canonical Pastor; Milton Alvarez, C.M.F., Sacramental Priest; Sr. Mary Essner, S.S.N.D., Parish Life Coord.
Mailing Address: P.O. Box 533, Aurora, 65605-0533.
Church: Adams & Second St., 65769. Tel: 417-678-2403; Fax: 417-678-3714.
Catechesis/Religious Program—Sr. Francis Rose Rivers, S.S.N.D., D.R.E. & Hispanic Min. Students 88.

WEBB CITY, JASPER CO., SACRED HEART (1908) Rev. John S. Braun.
Res.: 909 N. Madison, 64870. Tel: 417-673-2044.
Catechesis/Religious Program—Students 107.

WEST PLAINS, HOWELL CO., ST. MARY (1902) Rev. Joseph Weidenbenner; Deacon Patrick J. Keefe.
Mailing Address: P.O. Box 67, 65775.
Res.: 1551 Bill Virdon Blvd., 65775. Tel: 417-257-7912; 417-256-2556 (Office); Fax: 417-256-9251.
Catechesis/Religious Program—Students 81.
Mission—Sacred Heart Thayer, Oregon Co.

WILLOW SPRINGS, HOWELL CO., SACRED HEART (1897) [CEM] Rev. Sherman B. Wall, O.M.I.; Deacon G. Alan Bandy.
Church: 1050 W. Bus Hwy. 60-63, 65793. Tel: 417-469-2447.
Catechesis/Religious Program—Debbie Joerger, C.R.E. Students 48.
Mission—St. Joseph White Church, Howell Co. Robert Jones, C.R.E.

Chaplains of Public Institutions

SPRINGFIELD. *Diocesan Hospital Ministry*. Rev. Jeffrey A. Fasching. Tel: 417-887-6472.
St. John's Regional Health Center dba St. John's Hospital Tel: 417-820-2709. Rev. Augustine R. Njuu, A.J., Chap.
U.S. Medical Center, 1900 W. Sunshine, 65802. Tel: 417-862-7041, Ext. 1669. Rev. Eugene M. Klein, Chap.

CHARLESTON. *Southeast Correctional Center*, Tel: 573-748-5183. Rev. Randolph G. Tochtrop, Chap.

FORDLAND. *Ozark Correctional Center*, Tel: 417-887-6500. Rev. Eugene M. Klein, Chap. Tel: 417-865-1112.

JOPLIN. *Joplin Hospital Ministry*, Tel: 417-781-2727. Rev. Valery Burusu, (Diocese of Nyundo, Rwanda).

LICKING. *South Central Correctional Center*, Tel: 573-729-4291. Rev. Matthew J. Rehrauer, Chap. Tel: 417-967-3589.

POPLAR BLUFF. *Poplar Bluff Hospital Ministry*. Rev. David N. Coon. Tel: 573-785-9635.

Special Assignment:
Rev.—
Orthel, Joseph A., Chap., 2319 S. National Ave., 65804. Tel: 417-830-0496

Leave of Absence:
Revs.—
Carr, Gary M., 330 Emerson Rd. #200, High Ridge, 63049.
Hill, Kyle J.
Wilk, Mitchell S. (Retired), Temporary Address: The Catholic Center, 601 S. Jefferson Ave., 65806.

Retired:
Rev. Msgrs.—
Bucher, Philip A., V.G., 412 12th St. N.W., Albuquerque, NM 87102. Tel: 505-341-4514
Eftink, Edward M., Ph.D., 4009 N. Thistle Dr., Ozark, 65721. Tel: 417-551-4406
Ernstmann, Mark C., S.T.L., M.Ed., 3852 S. Jefferson Ave. Apt. D-6, 65807-5383. Tel: 417-889-8512
Orf, Raymond V., 3535 S. Fremont, 65804-4237. Tel: 417-887-0600; 417-799-0062
Rolwing, Richard C., 378 Etherton Dr., 63703. Tel: 573-335-3206
Stanton, William J., 358 Etherton Dr., 63703. Tel: 573-651-6465
Revs.—
Bauer, Sylvester W. (JC), 23 Bauer Ln., Freeburg, 65035. Tel: 573-744-5913
Biernacki, Jacob S., St. John's Mercy Villa, 1100 E. Montclair, 65807. Tel: 417-820-8303
Brath, John A., 3912 N. 15th St., Ozark, 65721. Tel: 417-581-1036
Duffner, Ralph J., 314 Elliott, Chaffee, 63740. Tel: 573-887-4283
Edwards, Byron H., P.O. Box 155, Morris Chapel, TN 38361. Tel: 731-632-9959
Huggins, William A., 203 Forrest Pkwy., Crestview, FL 32539.
Krudwig, William C., 25695 Mulberry Rd., Webb City, 64870. Tel: 417-642-5145
Landewe, Robert A., 645 Assisi Way, Republic, 65738. Tel: 417-350-3760
Palermo, Frank C., 2818 E. Bennett, 65804-1943. Tel: 417-883-3440
Seyer, James A., 150 S. Silver Springs Rd., #4, 63703-5076. Tel: 573-651-3939
Varone, Normand G., 383 Etherton Dr., 63703.

Permanent Deacons:
Bandy, G. Alan, Sacred Heart, Willow Springs
Biri, Walter, Immaculate Conception, Jackson; St. John, Leopold
Brewer, Thomas M., St. Elizabeth Ann Seton, Springfield
Cole, Richard F., Sacred Heart, Salem
Costello, Charles R.
Ellman, Edward V., Sacred Heart, Springfield
Fletcher, Mathey F., St. Joseph, Springfield
Hirtz, Fred, St. Teresa, Glennonville; St. Ann, Malden
Keefe, Patrick J., St. Mary, West Plains
Keller, William J., Cathedral of St. Agnes, Springfield
Kurtenbach, Joseph, Sacred Heart, Mountain Grove
Long, James E., Jr., Cathedral of St. Mary of the Annunciation, Cape Girardeau
McNamee, William, Immaculate Conception, Springfield
Ridder, Norm, Sacred Heart, Springfield
Vrooman, David
Wand, Mark A., Cathedral of St. Agnes, Springfield

INSTITUTIONS LOCATED IN THE DIOCESE

[A] SEMINARIES, RELIGIOUS, OR SCHOLASTICATES

AVA. *Assumption Novitiate (Trappists)*, Rte. 5, Box 1056, 65608-9142. Tel: 417-683-5110; Fax: 417-683-5658. Email: assumptionabbey@wildblue.net. Rt. Revs. Cyprian Harrison, O.C.S.O., Supr.; Robert Matter, O.C.S.O., Abbot Emeritus.

CARTHAGE. *Congregation of the Mother Co-Redemptrix*, 1900 Grand Ave., 64836. Tel: 417-358-7787; Fax: 417-358-9508. Email: cmc@dongcong.net. Web: www.dongcong.net. Very Rev. Michael M. Tran Mai, C.M.C., Prov.

[B] HIGH SCHOOLS, DIOCESAN

SPRINGFIELD. *Springfield Catholic High School* (Coed), 2340 S. Eastgate, 65809-2832. Tel: 417-887-8817; Fax: 417-885-1165. Email: tdilg@scspk12.org. Web: www.scspk12.org. Mr. Tim Dilg, Prin.; Revs. Philip M. Lam Ba Trong, C.M.C., Chap.; Scott M. Sunnenberg, Chap.; Mrs. Debbie Seitzer, Librarian. Lay Teachers 26; Students 326; Counselors 1.
Springfield Catholic School System, 3520 S. Culpepper Cir., Ste. C, 65804-4206. Tel: 417-865-5567; Fax: 417-865-5278. Email: ademleo@sscspk12.org. Web: www.scspk12.org. Mrs. Amy DeMelo, Dir.

CAPE GIRARDEAU. *Notre Dame Regional High School*, 265 Notre Dame Dr., 63701-8517. Tel: 573-335-6772; Fax: 573-335-3458. Email: principal@notredamehighschool.org. Web: www.notredamehighschool.org. Bro. David Anthony Migliorino, O.S.F., Prin.; Rev. Saviour Nundwe, Chap. Co-Instructional Regional High School Brothers 1; Lay Teachers 37; Counselors 2; Students 507.

JOPLIN. *St. Mary*, (Grades PreK-5), 505 W. 25th St., 64804. Tel: 417-623-1465; Fax: 417-623-4749. Email: sjones@jacss.org. Web: www.jacss.org. Mr. Stephen Jones, Prin. Sisters 1; Lay Teachers 14; Aides 5; Students 222.
McAuley Catholic High School, 930 Pearl Ave., 64801. Tel: 417-624-9320; Fax: 417-626-8334. Email: gkoester@jacss.org. Web: www.jacss.org. Mr. Gene Koester, Principal. Sisters 1; Lay Teachers 12; Counselors 2; Students 104.
St. Peter the Apostle Middle School, 802 Byers, 64801. Tel: 417-624-5605; Fax: 417-624-6254. Email: gemory@jacss.org. Web: www.jacss.org. Mr. Greg Emory, Prin. Sisters 1; Lay Teachers 9; Students 78.

[C] CATHOLIC CHARITIES

SPRINGFIELD. **Catholic Charities of Southern Missouri, Inc.*, 601 S. Jefferson Ave., 65806. Tel: 417-866-0841; Fax: 417-866-1140. Email: ccsomo@ccsomo.org. Dr. Donald R. Emge, Ph.D., Exec. Dir.

[D] GENERAL HOSPITALS

SPRINGFIELD. *St. John's Regional Health Center dba St. John's Hospital* 1235 E. Cherokee, 65804. Tel: 417-820-2710; Fax: 417-820-8730. Web: www.stjohns.com. Mr. Kim Day, Pres. & CEO, St. John's Health System; Jon Swope, Pres., St. John's Hospital; Rev. Augustine R. Njuu, A.J., Chap. Member of the Sisters of Mercy Health System, St. Louis. Sisters 4; Bed Capacity 866; Inpatients 32,319; Outpatients 567,708.

CAPE GIRARDEAU. **Saint Francis Medical Center*, 211 St. Francis Dr., 63703-8399. Tel: 573-331-3000; Fax: 573-331-5009. Email: sfmc@sfmc.net. Web: www.sfmc.net. Mr. Steven C. Bjelich, FACHE-D, Pres. & CEO; Rev. Augustine Chibuzo Alilonu, M.Div., Pastoral Care Mgr. & Chap. Owned and operated by a lay board with Diocesan sponsorship. Sisters 1; Bed Capacity 258; Inpatients 11,274; Outpatients 130,564.
**Saint Francis Foundation*, 211 St. Francis Dr., 63703. Tel: 573-331-5133; Fax: 573-331-5009.
**Saint Francis Healthcare System (formerly known as St. Francis Hospital of Franciscan Sisters)*, 211 St. Francis Dr., 63703.

AURORA. *St. John's Aurora, Inc. dba St. John's Hospital-Aurora* 500 Porter Ave., 65605. Tel: 417-678-2122; Fax: 417-678-7877. Web: www.stjohns.com. Gary W. Jordan, West Region Pres. Bed Capacity 25; Inpatients 1,088; Outpatients 27,604.

CASSVILLE. *St. John's Cassville, Inc. dba St. John's Hospital-Cassville* 94 S. Main St., 65625. Tel: 417-847-6000; Fax: 417-847-6083. Web: www.stjohnshospitalcassville.com. Gary W. Jordan, West Region Pres. Bed Capacity 18; Inpatients 352; Outpatients 21,120.

JOPLIN. *St. John's Regional Medical Center; Mercy Lifecare Systems* Affiliates of Sisters of Mercy Health System., 2727 McClelland Blvd., 64804-1694. Tel: 417-781-2727; Fax: 417-625-2910. Web: www.stj.com. George Caralis, Interim Pres. & CEO; Rev. Valery Burusu, Chap. Sisters of Mercy (St. Louis). Sisters 1; Bed Capacity 367; Inpatients 15,651; Outpatients 131,699.

St. John's Mercy Regional Foundation, 2727 McClelland Blvd., 64804.

LEBANON. **Breech Regional Medical Center, Inc. dba St. John's Hospital-Lebanon* 100 Hospital Dr., 65536. Tel: 417-533-6100; Fax: 417-533-6021. Email: Brenda.Parker@mercy.net. Web: stjohnslebanon.com. Mr. Mike Gillen, Pres. Sisters 1; Bed Capacity 62; Inpatients 2,933; Outpatients 67,382.

MOUNTAIN VIEW. *St. John's St. Francis Hospital*, P.O. Box 82, 65548. Tel: 417-934-7000; Fax: 417-934-7092. Jonathan Wade, Pres. Daughters of St. Francis of Assisi and Sisters of Mercy (Managed by St. John's Health System) Sisters 3; Bed Capacity 25; Total Assisted Annually 22,643.

The Sister Cornelia Blasko Foundation, Inc., 100 W. Hwy. 60, P.O. Box 82, 65548. Tel: 417-934-7090.

[E] SPECIAL HOSPITALS

SPRINGFIELD. *St. John's Mercy Villa*, 1100 E. Montclair, 65807. Tel: 417-820-8500; Fax: 417-820-8547. Donald Swafford, Admin., St. John's Mercy Villa, St. John's Health System. Skilled Care of Long Term Nursing Home, for the Aged and Chronically Ill. Bed Capacity 150.

[F] MONASTERIES AND RESIDENCES OF PRIESTS AND BROTHERS

SPRINGFIELD. *Claretians Missionaries' Residence-Villa Claret*, 1530 N. Summit, 65803. Tel: 417-869-0075. Revs. Milton Alvarez, C.M.F.; Thomas A. McGann, C.M.F.; Bro. Daniel Magner, C.M.F.

Congregation of Mother Coredemptrix, Our Lady of the Rosary House, 418 S. Kimbrough, 65806. Tel: 417-869-3822. Email: cmcspringfield@hotmail.com. Rev. Isidore M. Dinh Thanh Bac, C.M.C., Min. Priests 1.

AVA. *Assumption Abbey (Trappist)*, Rte. 5, Box 1056, 65608. Tel: 417-683-5110; Fax: 417-683-5658. Email: assumptionabbey@wildblue.net. Web: www.assumptionabbey.org. Rt. Revs. Robert Matter, O.C.S.O., Abbot Emeritus; Cyprian Harrison, O.C.S.O., Supr.; Revs. Leon Brockman, O.C.S.O.; Donald Joseph Hamilton, O.C.S.O.; Alberic Maisog, O.C.S.O.; Justin Trinidad, O.C.S.O., Oblate; Bros. Boniface Domas, O.C.S.O.; Francis Flaherty, O.C.S.O.; Gary Hunter, O.C.S.O., Oblate; Lazarus Mansi, Junior; Thomas Imhoff, O.C.S.O.; Dominic Pitagora, O.C.S.O. Priests 3; Brothers 5; Superior 1; Abbot Emeritus 2.

Our Lady of the Angels Friary, Rte. 5, Box 1042, 65608. Tel: 417-683-4303. Bros. Josef Anderlohr, O.F.M.; Joseph F. Manning, O.F.M.

CARTHAGE. *Congregation of the Mother Coredemptrix, United States Assumption Province*, 1900 Grand Ave., 64836. Tel: 417-358-7787; Fax: 417-358-9508. Email: cmc@dongcong.net. Web: www.dongcong.net. Very Rev. Michael M. Tran Mai, C.M.C., Prov.; Revs. Thomas M. Nguyen Tuan Binh, C.M.C., Asst. I; Raymond M. Nguyen Chau Dien, C.M.C., Asst. II; Louis M. Vu Minh Nhien, C.M.C., Asst. III; Lawrence M. Nguyen Chautly, C.M.C., Asst. IV; John M. Ngo Duc Vuong, C.M.C., Treas.; Philip M. Do Thanh Cao, C.M.C., Sec.; Felix M. Dinh Viet Luan, C.M.C.; Anselm M. Dinh Vuong Can, C.M.C.; Luke M. Do Minh Van, C.M.C.; Michael M. Do Quang Chinh, C.M.C.; Bartholomew M. Do Thai Iloa, C.M.C.; Mark M. Doan Quang Bau, C.M.C.; Francis Xavier M. Luong Minh Tuat, C.M.C.; Timothy M. Mai Vinh Loc, C.M.C.; John D.M. Ngo Duc Vuong, C.M.C., Treas.; Camillus M. Nguyen Duc Tuan, C.M.C.; Dominic M. Nguyen Hoan Luong, C.M.C.; Andrew M. Nguyen Hong An, C.M.C.; Tadeus M. Nguyen Ngoc Ban, C.M.C.; Dominic M. Nguyen Trung Chanh, C.M.C.; Albert M. Pham Kim Ban, C.M.C.; Bartholomew Pham Minh Van, C.M.C.; Matthias M. Tran Minh Man, C.M.C.; John M. Tran Quoc Toan, C.M.C.; Leo M. Vu Dinh Huyen, C.M.C.; John E. M. Vu Quang Huy, C.M.C.; Joseph M. Vu Toan Khoa, C.M.C.; Bros. John M. Bui Quang Trieu, C.M.C.; Michael M. Dao Trung Dan, C.M.C.; Giosaphat M. Do Cuong Phong, C.M.C.; Leo M. Do Quy Hien, C.M.C.; Alphonsus M. Do Van Kiet, C.M.C.; Maximilian Kolbe M. Do The Phat, C.M.C.; Martin M. Le Minh Lam, C.M.C.; Sylvester M. Lu Thuong Dien, C.M.C.; Stanis M. Nguyen An Phuc, C.M.C.; John B.M. Nguyen Duc Hien, C.M.C.; Thomas M. Nguyen Duc Hoc, C.M.C.; Anthony M. Nguyen Gia Huu, C.M.C.; Joachim M. Nguyen Khoa Cu, C.M.C.; Thomas More M. Nguyen Long Truong, C.M.C.; Henry M. Nguyen Minh Han, C.M.C.; Peter M. Nguyen Quang Thieu, C.M.C.; Bede M. Nguyen Quang Tuyen, C.M.C.; Thomas M. Nguyen Si Dien, C.M.C.; Titus M. Nguyen Si Hanh, C.M.C.; Ambrose M. Nguyen Tam Niem, C.M.C.; Justin M. Nguyen Tri Ky, C.M.C.; Pius V M. Nguyen Trung Thu, C.M.C.; Bonaventure M. Nguyen Tuan Bao, C.M.C.; Joseph C.M. Pham Cong Tho, C.M.C.; Mathew M. Pham Ngoc Thach, C.M.C.; Francis M. Pham Thuan Tu, C.M.C.; Justine M. Pham Xuan Binh, C.M.C.; Francis M. Ta Tan Van, C.M.C.; Paul M. Tran An Dinh, C.M.C.; Bernardine M. Tran Hien Si, C.M.C.; Stephen Tran Minh Giac, C.M.C.; Francis Tran Thanh Duy, C.M.C.; Norbert M. Truong Thinh Dat, C.M.C.; Cyril M. Vu Chuong Hao, C.M.C.; Anthony M. Vu Dinh Huan, C.M.C.; Matthew Vu Duc Kim, C.M.C.; Mr. Pius Nguyen Kim Duong, Collaborator. Priests 28; Brothers 34; Novices 3; Candidates 2. *Mater Dei Building*, 1900 Grand Ave., 64836. Tel: 417-358-7787; Fax: 417-358-9508. (Home for retired priests) In Res. Revs. Joseph Cao Phuong Ky, S.S.; Joseph Do Ba Ai; James Do Ba Cong; James Thuc Van Truong, O.S.B.; Joseph To Ngoc Lien.

MARIONVILLE. *The Society of Our Mother of Peace, Sons of Our Mother of Peace*, Queen of Heaven Solitude, 12494 Hwy. T, 65705. Tel: 417-744-2011. Revs. Placid Guste, S.M.P., Supr.; Augustine Ibok, S.M.P.; J. Peter Sirangelo, S.M.P.

The Society of Our Mother of Peace, Sons of Our Mother of Peace - Queen of Heaven Solitude

[G] CONVENTS AND RESIDENCES FOR SISTERS

SPRINGFIELD. *St. Anne Monastery*, 424 E. Monastery St., 65807-6099. Tel: 417-881-2115; Fax: 417-881-5570. Email: ozarkcarmel@juno.com. Sr. Marya Williams, O.C.D., Prioress. Discalced Carmelite Nuns 3.

Congregation of Mary Queen, 625 S. Jefferson Ave., 65806. Tel: 417-869-9842; Fax: 417-832-0852. Email: cmrusa@hotmail.com. Web: www.trinhvuong.org. Sr. Marguerite A. Tran, C.M.R., Regl. Supr. Sisters 6.

Sisters of Mercy of the Americas (St. Louis), 1330 E. Cherokee, 65804. Tel: 417-882-1297; Fax: 417-820-6960. Sisters 4.

AVA. *Nazareth Hermitage*, Rte. 5, Box 1122, 65608. Sisters 5.

MARIONVILLE. *The Society of Our Mother of Peace, Daughters of Our Mother of Peace*, 12494 Hwy. T, 65705-7121. Tel: 417-744-2011. Sr. Mary Fidelis Lane, S.M.P., Supr.

The Society of Our Mother of Peace, Daughters of Our Mother of Peace, Queen of Heaven Solitude Sisters 5.

PILOT KNOB. *Our Lady of the Valley Community*, 320 S. McCune St., Box 545, 63663-0545. Tel: 573-546-7229. Franciscan Sisters of Mary. Sisters 2.

REPUBLIC. *Little Portion Franciscans*, 645 Assisi Way, 65738. Tel: 417-732-6684. Email: lportion@juno.com. Sisters 3.

[H] RETREAT HOUSES

AVA. *Assumption Abbey* (Trappist), RR. 5, Box 1056, 65608. Tel: 417-683-5110; Fax: 417-683-5658. Email: avaguesthouse@hughes.net. Web: www.assumptionabbey.org. Rt. Rev. Cyprian Harrison, O.C.S.O.

MARIONVILLE. *The Society of Our Mother of Peace, Daughters of Our Mother of Peace*, 12494 Hwy. T, 65705. Tel: 417-744-2011. Sr. Mary Rachel Hain, S.M.P., Dir.

The Society of Our Mother of Peace, Daughters of Our Mother of Peace, Queen of Heaven Solitude

REPUBLIC. *Little Portion Retreat Center*, 645 S. Assisi Way, 65738-2190. Tel: 417-732-6684. Email: little.portion@att.net. Web: www.littleportionfranciscansisters.org. Sr. Lorraine Biebel, O.S.F., Coord.

[I] SHRINES

CARTHAGE. *Shrine of Immaculate Heart of Mary* 1900 Grand Ave., 64836. Tel: 417-358-8580; Fax: 417-358-3954. Email: heartofmaryshrine@yahoo.com. Web: www.dongcong.net/khiettam. Rev. Bartholomew M. Pham Minh Van, C.M.C., Dir.

[J] NEWMAN CENTERS

SPRINGFIELD. *Catholic Campus Ministry O'Reilly Catholic Student Center, Southwest MO State University, Drury College, Ozarks Technical Com* 847 S. Holland, 65806-3513. Tel: 417-865-0802; Fax: 417-865-0895. Web: www.ccm847.org. Rev. Thomas A. McGann, C.M.F., Dir.

CAPE GIRARDEAU. *Catholic Campus Ministry Southeast Missouri State University, Newman Center* 512 N. Pacific, 63701-4712. Tel: 573-335-3899; Fax: 573-334-0088. Email: catholic@ccmin.org. Web: www.ccmin.org. Rev. Patrick I. Nwokoye, Ph.D., Chap. & Dir.

BRANSON. *Catholic Christian Newman Association* , (College of the Ozarks), 203 Vaughn Dr., 65616. Tel: 417-334-2928; Fax: 417-334-6883. Email: lynnmelendez@aol.com. Web: www.ladyofthelakeparish.org. Mrs. Lynn Melendez, Campus Min.

JOPLIN. *Newman Club, Missouri Southern State University* 812 S. Pearl Ave., 64801-4336. Tel: 417-623-8643. Revs. John (J) F. Fricdel, M.A., M.Div., Dir. & Chap.; Thomas M. Nguyen Tuan Binh, C.M.C., Part-time Chap.

[K] MISCELLANEOUS

SPRINGFIELD. **St. John's Clinic*, 1965 S. Fremont St., Ste. 200, 65804. Tel: 417-820-2849; Fax: 417-820-7892. Web: www.stjohns.com.

St. John's Foundation for Community Health, Inc., 1235 E. Cherokee St., 65804. Tel: 417-820-3491; Fax: 417-820-3603. Email: michael.merrigan@mercy.net. Michael Merrigan, Gen. Counsel.

St. John's Health System, Inc., 1235 E. Cherokee, 65804. Tel: 417-820-2845; Fax: 417-820-8730. Web: www.stjohns.com.

St. John's Medical Research Institute, Inc., 1235 E. Cherokee St., 65804. Tel: 417-820-3491; Fax: 417-820-3603. Email: michael.merrigan@mercy.net. Michael Merrigan, Gen. Counsel.

**McAuley Counseling Services, Inc.*, 2200 E. Sunshine, Ste. 201, 65804. Tel: 417-823-0498. Sisters Ann Crouse, R.S.M., M.A., Exec. Dir.; Victoria Incrivaglia, R.S.M., L.S.C.W., Asst. Dir.

Queen of Angels Day Care Center, 625 S. Jefferson, 65806. Tel: 417-869-9842; Fax: 417-832-0852. Email: cmrusa@hotmail.com. Web: www.trinhvuong.org.

CARTHAGE. *Office of the Immaculate Heart of Mary Shrine*, 1749 Grand Ave., 64836. Tel: 417-358-8580; Fax: 417-358-3954. Web: www.dongcong.net/khiettam.

JOPLIN. *Mercy Village Joplin, Inc.*, 1148 W. 28th St., 64804. Tel: 417-623-7123.

RELIGIOUS INSTITUTES OF MEN REPRESENTED IN THE DIOCESE

For further details refer to the corresponding bracketed number in the Religious Institutes of Men or Women section.

[]—*Apostles of Jesus*—A.J.

[1330]—*Congregation of the Mission Western Province*—C.M.

[0865]—*Congregation of the Mother Coredemptrix*—C.M.C.

[0515]—*Franciscan Brothers of the Third Order Regular*—O.S.F.

[0520]—*Franciscan Friars*—O.F.M.

[0360]—*Missionary Sons of the Immaculate Heart of Mary (Claretians)*—C.M.F.

[0910]—*Oblates of Mary Immaculate (Oblates)* (United States Prov.)—O.M.I.

[0350]—*Order of Cistercians of the Strict Observance (Trappist)*—O.C.S.O.

[1240]—*Order of Friar Servants of Mary (Servites)* (United States Prov.)—O.S.M.

[0200]—*Order of St. Benedict (Benedictines)*—O.S.B.

[]—*The Society of Our Mother of Peace*—S.M.P.

[1290]—*Society of the Priests of Saint Sulpice*—S.S.

RELIGIOUS INSTITUTES OF WOMEN REPRESENTED IN THE DIOCESE

[0230]—*Benedictine Sisters of the Pontifical Jurisdiction* (Eau Claire, WI)—O.S.B.

[0397]—*Congregation of Mary, Queen*—C.M.R.

[0460]—*Congregation of the Sisters of Charity of the Incarnate Word* (San Antonio)—C.C.V.I.

[0725]—*Cordi-Marian Missionary Sisters Congregation*—M.C.M.

[0760]—*Daughters of Charity of St. Vincent de Paul* (St. Louis)—D.C.

[0920]—*Daughters of St. Francis of Assisi* (Lacon, Illinois)—D.S.F.

[0420]—*Discalced Carmelite Nuns*—O.C.D.

[1415]—*Franciscan Sisters of Mary* (St. Louis)—F.S.M.

[1430]—*Franciscan Sisters of Our Lady of Perpetual Help* (St. Louis, MO)—O.S.F.

[1240]—*Franciscan Sisters, Daughters of the Sacred Hearts of Jesus and Mary* (Wheaton)—O.S.F.

[2080]—*Home Mission Sisters of America (Glenmary)*—G.H.M.S.

[]—*Little Portion Franciscans*—O.S.F.

[]—*Nazareth Hermitage*

[]—*Poor Clare Missionaries*—M.C.

[2970]—*School Sisters of Notre Dame* (St. Louis)—S.S.N.D.

[0430]—*Sisters of Charity of the Blessed Virgin Mary* (Dubuque)—B.V.M.

[0990]—*Sisters of Divine Providence* (Marie de la Roche Prov.)—C.D.P.

[2360]—*Sisters of Loretto at the Foot of the Cross*—S.L.

[2575]—*Sisters of Mercy of the Americas* (West Midwest Community)—R.S.M.

[2575]—*Sisters of Mercy of the Americas* (Mid-Atlantic Community)—R.S.M.

[2575]—*Sisters of Mercy of the Americas* (South Central Community)—R.S.M.

[1720]—*Sisters of the Third Order Regular of St. Francis of Our Lady of Lourdes* (Rochester, MN)—O.S.F.

[]—*The Society of Our Mother of Peace*—S.M.P.

[4120]—*Ursuline Nuns of the Congregation of Paris* (Owensboro, KY)—O.S.U.

[4120]—*Ursuline Nuns of the Congregation of Paris* (Cleveland)

[4110]—*Ursuline Nuns (Roman Union)* (St. Louis, MO)—O.S.U.

NECROLOGY

† Nichols, Edward P. Jr., (Retired)—Died Aug. 5, 2009

An asterisk (*) denotes an organization that has established tax-exempt status directly with the IRS and is not covered by the USCCB Group Ruling.

Diocese of Springfield in Illinois

(Dioecesis Campifontis in Illinois)

Most Reverend

DANIEL L. RYAN

Retired Bishop of Springfield in Illinois; ordained May 3, 1956; ordained Titular Bishop of Surista in Mauritania and Auxiliary to the Bishop of Joliet in Illinois September 30, 1981; appointed Bishop of Springfield in Illinois November 22, 1983; installed January 18, 1984; retired October 19, 1999. *St. John Vianney Villa, 1464 Green Trail Dr., Naperville, IL 60540-8359.*

(VACANT SEE)

Catholic Pastoral Center: 1615 W. Washington St., P.O. Box 3187, Springfield, IL 62708-3187. Tel: 217-698-8500; Fax: 217-698-0802.

ERECTED JULY 29, 1853.

Square Miles 15,139.

Formerly Diocese of Quincy.

See Transferred to Alton, January 9, 1857. To Springfield, October 26, 1923.

Comprises the following Counties of Illinois: Adams, Bond, Brown, Calhoun, Cass, Christian, Clark, Coles, Crawford, Cumberland, Douglas, Edgar, Effingham, Fayette, Greene, Jasper, Jersey, Macon, Macoupin, Madison, Menard, Montgomery, Morgan, Moultrie, Pike, Sangamon, Scott and Shelby.

For legal titles of parishes and diocesan institutions, consult the Chancery Office.

STATISTICAL OVERVIEW

Personnel	
Retired Bishops	1
Priests: Diocesan Active in Diocese	73
Priests: Diocesan Active Outside Diocese	5
Priests: Retired, Sick or Absent	32
Number of Diocesan Priests	110
Religious Priests in Diocese	54
Total Priests in Diocese	164
Extern Priests in Diocese	4
Ordinations:	
Religious Priests	1
Transitional Deacons	2
Permanent Deacons	11
Permanent Deacons in Diocese	34
Total Brothers	28
Total Sisters	540
Parishes	
Parishes	131
With Resident Pastor:	
Resident Diocesan Priests	72
Resident Religious Priests	4
Without Resident Pastor:	
Administered by Priests	50
Administered by Deacons	2
Administered by Religious Women	3
Professional Ministry Personnel:	
Brothers	27
Sisters	525
Lay Ministers	45
Welfare	
Catholic Hospitals	6
Total Assisted	697,343
Homes for the Aged	1
Total Assisted	99
Residential Care of Children	1
Total Assisted	30
Day Care Centers	1
Total Assisted	142
Residential Care of Disabled	1
Total Assisted	128
Educational	
Diocesan Students in Other Seminaries	13
Total Seminarians	13
Colleges and Universities	2
Total Students	1,850
High Schools, Diocesan and Parish	5
Total Students	1,324
High Schools, Private	1
Total Students	793
Elementary Schools, Diocesan and Parish	42
Total Students	9,213
Catechesis/Religious Education:	
High School Students	1,915
Elementary Students	8,087
Total Students under Catholic Instruction	23,195
Teachers in the Diocese:	
Brothers	1
Sisters	29
Lay Teachers	648
Vital Statistics	
Receptions into the Church:	
Infant Baptism Totals	1,899
Minor Baptism Totals	106
Adult Baptism Totals	193
Received into Full Communion	310
First Communions	2,056
Confirmations	2,290
Marriages:	
Catholic	405
Interfaith	339
Total Marriages	744
Deaths	1,555
Total Catholic Population	146,692
Total Population	1,138,450

Former Bishops—Rt. Revs. HENRY DAMIAN JUNCKER, D.D., ord. 1834; cons. April 28, 1857; died Oct. 2, 1868; PETER JOSEPH BALTES, D.D., ord. 1853; cons. Jan. 23, 1870; died Feb. 15, 1886; JAMES RYAN, D.D., ord. 1871; cons. May 1, 1888; died July 2, 1923; Most Revs. JAMES A. GRIFFIN, D.D., ord. 1909; cons. Feb. 25, 1924; died Aug. 5, 1948; WILLIAM A. O'CONNOR, D.D., ord. 1927; cons. March 7, 1949; installed March 17, 1949; retired July 22, 1975; died Nov. 14, 1983; JOSEPH A. MCNICHOLAS, D.D., ord. 1949; cons. March 25, 1969; installed Sept. 3, 1975; died April 17, 1983; DANIEL L. RYAN, D.D., J.C.L. (Retired), ord. May 3, 1956; ord. Titular Bishop of Surista in Mauritania and Auxiliary to the Bishop of Joliet in Illinois, Sept. 30, 1981; appt. Bishop of Springfield in Illinois, Nov. 22, 1983; installed Jan. 18, 1984; retired Oct. 19, 1999; GEORGE J. LUCAS, ord. May 24, 1975; appt. Bishop of Springfield in Illinois Oct. 19, 1999; ord. and installed Dec. 14, 1999; appt. Archbishop of Omaha June 3, 2009.

Diocesan Administrator—Rev. Msgr. CARL A. KEMME.

Bishop's Cabinet—VACANT.

Chancellor—MARLENE MULFORD.

Vicars Forane—

Alton Deanery—VACANT.

Decatur Deanery—Very Rev. DAVID ZIMMERMAN, V.F.

Effingham Deanery—Rev. Msgr. LEO J. ENLOW, V.F., B.A. Theology.

Jacksonville Deanery—Very Rev. KENNETH J. VENVERTLOH, V.F.

Litchfield Deanery—Rev. Msgr. LAWRENCE AUDA, V.F.

Quincy Deanery—Rev. Msgr. MICHAEL KUSE, V.F.

Springfield Deanery—Rev. Msgr. THOMAS P. HOLINGA, V.F.

Diocesan Curia—

All diocesan agencies and councils are located at the Catholic Pastoral Center, unless otherwise indicated. *Catholic Pastoral Center, 1615 W. Washington St., P.O. Box 3187, Springfield, 62708-3187.* Tel: 217-698-8500; Fax: 217-698-0802.

Office of the Bishop—VACANT; CHERYL KANNALL, Exec. Asst.

Office for Campus Ministry—Mr. ROY LANHAM, M.A., Dir., 500 Roosevelt Ave., Charleston, 61920. Tel: 217-348-0188; Fax: 217-348-8964. Email: roylanham@eiunewman.org.

Office for Catholic Charities— (Central Administration) *1625 W. Washington, Springfield, 62702.* Tel: 217-523-9201; Fax: 217-523-5624. STEVEN E. ROACH, Exec. Dir. Associate Directors: ELAINE PERINE; MICHAEL SAKOLSKY.

Corporate Board Members—Rev. Msgr. CARL A. KEMME; Mr. JOHN J. MAXWELL, CPA; MARLENE MULFORD.

Corporate Board Directors—REGINALD COLEMAN; LARRY CLARK; THEODORE L. EILERMAN; JAMES M. GRAHAM; MICHAEL HOFFMANN, Chm.; BRIDGET HOGAN; Deacon WILLIAM KESSLER; AMY MAHER; Rev. JOSEPH G. RING; ROBERT SCHULTZ; EDWARD SHEEHAN; Sr. JOMARY TRSTENSKY, O.S.F., M.H.A., M.S.N.; JOHN C. WEBSTER; Senator DEANNA DEMUZIO; MICHAEL LUDVIGSEN; CLARE MCCULLA, Vice Chairperson.

Office for Catechesis—JONATHAN SULLIVAN, Dir.; CHRIS MALMEVIK, Assoc. Dir., Catechesis; BARB BURRIS, Assoc. Dir., School Planning; JEAN JOHNSON, Supt. Catholic Schools; MARILYN MISSEL, Assoc. Supt. Catholic Schools; CYNTHIA CLEMENS, Exec. Sec. Fax: 217-698-8620; KYLE HOLTGRAVE, Assoc. Dir., Youth & Young Adult Min.; ELIZABETH (BETH) SCHMIDT, Exec. Sec. School Personnel, Youth & Young Adult Min.

Board of Catholic Education—MARIAN ALTHOFF; Deacon DENNY BAKER; Sr. RUTH CHAUSSE, S.S.N.D.; JUDY CULP; KIM DIAZ, Pres.; REBECCA ESSELMAN; TOM HASSEN; TERRY KALLAL; Bro. ANTHONY JOSEPH MCCOY, F.F.S.C.; MARC MITALSKI, 1st Vice Pres.; KIM FERGUSON; Rev. Msgr. CARL A. KEMME, Ex-Officio; Sr. M. ELISE MIERENDORF, F.S.G.M., 2nd Vice Pres.; CAROLYN STEWART; Rev. JEFFERY A. GRANT; Sr. GERALDINE KEMPER, O.P.; Rev. DONALD L. WOLFORD; Sr. JOANN VOLK, S.S.N.D., 2nd Vice Pres.; Very Rev. DAVID ZIMMERMAN, V.F.

Office for Chancellor/Director of Pastoral Planning—MARLENE MULFORD.

Archives and Records Management—MICHELE MCVAY LEVANDOSKI, Dir.

Office for Communications—KATHIE SASS, Dir.; TAMMY WOLTERS, Sec. Tel: 217-698-8500; Fax: 217-698-0619.

"Catholic Times" Newspaper—KATHIE SASS, Editor; LAURIE WEAKLEY, Office Mgr.; WILLIAM CALLAN, Layout & Design Coord.; THERESA KELLY GEGEN, Projects Coord.; CATHY LOCHER, Reporter; PAULA RUOT, Advertising; DIANE SCHLINDWEIN, Reporter.

Office for the Diaconate—Rev. Msgr. DAVID S. LANTZ, Dir.; JOAN REED, Sec.

Office for Marriage and Family Life—PATRICK O'TOOLE, Dir.

Office for Finances—Mr. JOHN J. MAXWELL, CPA, Dir.; Mr. GREGORY FLECK, Assoc. Dir. Property, Bldgs. & Cemeteries; DAN JAMES, Assoc. Dir. Insurance, Fire, Extended Coverage, Vandalism, Multi-Peril Liability, Workers Compensation, Boiler, Unemployment, Lay Employee Pension Plan, Priests' Personal Property, Seminarians' Medical Care and Coordinator for Diocesan Health Insurance Program.; PATRICK KETCHUM, Insurance Assoc.; BERNADINE SMITH, Sec. Insurance; DAN GAUWITZ, Information Technology Assoc. Dir.; BOBBIE OZANIC, Asst. Information Technology Dept.; MICHAEL HOERNER, Web Master; JANET VESPA, Accounting Mgr.; AARON KUHN, Parish Financial Coord. Accountants: ROBYN DOOLEY; BARBARA SCOGGINS; HEATHER MCMILLEN, Coord., Annual Catholic Svcs. Appeal and Sec.; THOMAS REISER, Special Projects. Clerk, Annual Catholic Svcs. Appeal: KAREN REGAN.

Diocesan Health Insurance Program Committee—EDNA MAE BROWN; BARB BURRIS; DAN JAMES; Rev. Msgr. CARL A. KEMME; PATRICK KETCHUM; PATRICIA KORNFELD; LEO LENN; JOHN MAXWELL, Chairperson; THOMAS REISER; AUDRA SCHULTZ; KATHY WEAR; JULIE YOST.

Lay Employees' Pension Plan Administrative Committee—LEO LENN, Chm.; JOHN MAXWELL, Treas.; JERALD T. BARKMEIER, Consultant; EDNA MAE BROWN; BETH DALTON; THOMAS FRIER; DAN JAMES, Sec.; Rev. Msgr. CARL A. KEMME; PATRICK KETCHUM; PATRICIA KORNFELD; THOMAS REISER; Very Rev. KENNETH J. VENVERTLOH, V.F.; JANET VESPA, (Staff).

Commission for Buildings and Property—ANN CARR; GERALD L. GLAUS SR.; Rev. Msgr. CARL A. KEMME; JOHN MAXWELL; THOMAS C. PAVLIK JR., Chm. Consultants: GREGORY FLECK; THOMAS REISER.

Office for Human Resources—PATRICIA J. KORNFELD, Dir. & Victim Assistance Coord.; Mrs. SHERYL SPEARS, Administrative Asst.

Office for Ministry Formation—Rev. Msgr. DAVID S. LANTZ, Dir.; JOAN REED, Sec.

Advisory Board—Sr. JANE BOOS, S.S.N.D.; Rev. CHRISTOPHER A. HOUSE; ELIOT KAPITAN; CHRIS MALMEVIK.

Area Specialization Coordinators—Catechetical Leadership Ministry: CHRIS MALMEVIK. Catholic School Leadership Ministry: JEAN JOHNSON. Clinical Pastoral Care Ministry: MARY HANDLEY. Family Life Ministry: PATRICK O'TOOLE. Liturgical Ministry: Christian Initiation of Adult Leadership: ELIOT KAPITAN. Liturgical Ministry: Liturgical Leadership: Rev. CHRISTOPHER A. HOUSE. Parish Life Ministry: Rev. CHRISTOPHER A. HOUSE. Social Concerns Ministry: Sr. JANE BOOS, S.S.N.D. Tribunal Advocacy Ministry: VACANT. Youth Ministry: KYLE HOLTGRAVE.

Office for the Missions—VICKI COMPTON, Dir.; RUTH STAAB, Office Asst., Mailing Address: P.O. Box 7025, Springfield, 62791-7025.

Office for Social Concerns—Sr. JANE BOOS, S.S.N.D., Dir.; SHARON HAVEY, Sec.; ELAINE VONDERHEIDE, Assoc. Dir., Special Needs. Associate Directors for Rural Life: JAMES SCHUMACHER; KAREN SCHUMACHER; CHRISTINE LANSAW, Coord. Catholic Religious Education at Illinois School for the Deaf. Email: lansawfam@gmail.com; LEROY JORDAN, Coord., Black Catholic Ministry. Tel: 217-698-8500, Ext. 158 (TTY); Fax: 217-698-9581; Deacons DAVID G. SORRELL, Ministry of Charity and Justice; DAVID ERDMAN, Ministry of Charity and Justice.

Black Catholic Advisory Board—LEROY JORDAN, Chm.; Dr. LENORA BROWN, Alton Deanery; PAUL CONELL, Springfield Deanery; Rev. DELIX MICHEL, S.S.L., Litchfield Deanery; Mrs. FREDDIE MCEWEN-RANDLE, Decatur Deanery; RENEE SAUNCHES, Decatur Deanery; REGINALD COLEMAN, Quincy Deanery; HUGH HARRIS, Springfield Deanery; Mrs. DAPHINE SKRETVEDT, Alton Deanery; FRED ROBINSON, Springfield Deanery; SARAH GRIPPER, Springfield Deanery; Sr. JANE BOOS, S.S.N.D., Ex Officio; JIM FORSTALL, Ex Officio; JONATHAN SULLIVAN, Ex Officio.

Campaign for Human Development Advisory Board—Sr. JANE BOOS, S.S.N.D., Dir. Deanery Representatives: WALT UNGER, Alton Deanery; JUDY UNGER, Alton Deanery; GIL WEYHAUPT, Alton Deanery; KEN HANDLEY, Decatur Deanery; MARY MULCAHY, Decatur/Springfield Deaneries; MELISSA LYNCH, Decatur Deanery; KAREN MILLER, Effingham Deanery; JOSEPH KAUFMANN, Jacksonville Deanery; Deacon RAYMOND L. ROTH JR., Litchfield Deanery; THOMAS DETERS, Quincy Deanery; JANE DETERS, Quincy Deanery; HUGH HARRIS, Springfield Deanery; Sr. MAUREEN IRVIN, O.S.F., Springfield Deanery; Mr. KEN STEINER, Member At Large. Ex Officio: JONATHAN SULLIVAN, Ex Officio; MARTHA MAYFIELD, Coord.

Coordinator of Hispanic Ministry—Rev. CHRISTOPHER J. BREY.

Parish Hispanic Ministry—Sisters MARIA CHRISTINA MARTINEZ MESTIZO, M.A.G.; MARIA ANGELICA LOPEZ RODRIQUEZ, M.A.G.; MAGDALENA SERRANO-PAZ, M.A.G.

Comite Diocesano de Ministerio Hispano - Diocesan Committee for Hispanic Ministry—Sisters MARIA CHRISTINA MARTINEZ MESTIZO, M.A.G.; MARIA ANGELICA LOPEZ RODRIGUEZ, M.A.G.; MAGDALENA SERRANO-PAZ, M.A.G.; Revs. CARLOS M. BOHORQUEZ; CHRISTOPHER J. BREY; Mrs. JOHANNA GILLIAN DE OROZCO; Rev. BARRY J. HARMON; Rev. Msgr. CARL A. KEMME, Ex Officio; Rev. THOMAS C. MEYER; ANABELLA MELLADO; ARIEL MARTIN; CAROLINA MATA-WOODRUFF; CATHERINE BECKER; Revs. KENNETH ROSSWOG, O.F.M.; SYLVANO PERA, O.F.M.; GUILLERMO SOSA; Mrs. DORIS NORDIN; Sr. JANE BOOS, S.S.N.D., Ex Officio; Rev. ROBERT SPRIGGS; JONATHAN SULLIVAN, Ex Officio; Revs. THOMAS SHAUGHNESSY, O.F.M.; RICHARD W. WELTIN; Sr. MARY JEAN TRAEGER, O.P.; Rev. DANIEL L. WILLENBORG.

Task Force For Racial Justice—JAMES FORSTALL, Chm.; Rev. JOSEPH ZIMMERMAN, O.F.M., Vice Chm. (Retired); Deacon DAVID G. SORRELL, Office Liaison. Ex Officios: JONATHAN SULLIVAN; Sr. JANE BOOS, S.S.N.D.

Office for Stewardship and Development—Mr. SHAUN RIEDELL, Dir.; CATHY FURKIN, Sec.

Office for Tribunal Services—Revs. KEVIN LAUGHERY, J.C.L., Judicial Vicar; R. DEAN PROBST, J.C.L., Judge; Sr. M. MAXIMILIA UM, F.S.G.M., J.C.L., Defender of the Bond; BECKY DONALDSON, Office Mgr. & Notary; Bro. JOEL MARK ROUSSEAU, F.F.S.C., Sec. & Notary.

Office of the Vicar General—VACANT.

Moderator of the Curia—Rev. Msgr. CARL A. KEMME, Diocesan Admin.

Staff—JOAN REED, Exec. Sec.; CAROL MULLER, Records Mgmt.; Bro. ANTHONY JOSEPH MCCOY, F.F.S.C., Assoc. Exec. Sec.; PATRICIA POLONUS, Receptionist for Catholic Pastoral Center; RUTH STAAB, Special Projects.

Vicar for Clergy—Revs. JOSEPH G. RING, Dir.; DAVID L. PETERS, Assoc. Vicar for Retired Priests (Retired).

Ongoing Formation of Clergy—Rev. RICHARD L. CHIOLA, Dir.

Commission for the Care of Infirm and Retired Priests—Revs. MICHAEL B. HAAG; JOSEPH HAVRILKA; Rev. Msgr. THOMAS P. HOLINGA, V.F.; Revs. DONALD J. MEEHLING (Retired); ALOYSIUS OKEY NDEANAEFO; Rev. Msgr. JOHN R. OSSOLA; Revs. DAVID L. PETERS (Retired); JOSEPH G. RING. Consultant: Deacon WILLIAM E. KESSLER.

Priests' Personnel Board—Revs. PATRICK GIBBONS; JEFFREY GOECKNER; THOMAS HAGSTROM; DAVID J. HOEFLER; JOSEPH MOLLOY; JAMES NEUMAN; ROBERT SPRIGGS; Rev. Msgr. CARL A. KEMME, Consultant; MARLENE MULFORD, Chancellor, Dir. Pastoral Planning & Consultant; Rev. JOSEPH G. RING, Ex Officio.

Office for Vocations—Rev. CHRISTOPHER A. HOUSE, Dir.

Office for Worship and the Catechumenate—ELIOT KAPITAN, Dir.; VICKI WALKER, Sec.

Victim Assistance Coordinator—PATRICIA KORNFELD. Tel: 217-698-8500. Email: pkornfeld@dio.org.

Councils

Diocesan Finance Council—BARBARA BORDERS; JAMES DAVIS; Deacon WILLIAM KESSLER; LEO LENN, Chm.; LEE MARTEN; DAN MCGUIRE; Rev. JAMES L. NEUMAN; JOHN STAUDT. Consultants: Rev. Msgr. CARL A. KEMME; JOHN MAXWELL; MARLENE MULFORD; THOMAS REISER; JANET VESPA, Accounting Mgr.

Presbyteral Council— (suspended until the installation of a new bishop)

Catholic Charities Institutions

Administrative Office—

Springfield. Catholic Charities—STEVEN E. ROACH, Exec. Dir., 1625 W. Washington, Springfield, 62702. Tel: 217-523-9201; Fax: 217-523-5624.

Area Offices—

Alton. Madison County Catholic Charities—MAUREEN ROBINSON, Area Dir., 3512 McArthur Blvd., Alton, 62002. Tel: 618-462-0634; Fax: 618-462-3209.

Carlinville. Catholic Charities—PATRICIA A. POPE, Area Dir., 525 W. Second South St., P.O. Box 618, Carlinville, 62626-0618. Tel: 217-854-4511; Fax: 217-854-8049.

Decatur. Catholic Charities—MARIE RADEMACHER, Area Dir., 247 W. Prairie, Decatur, 62523. Tel: 217-428-3458; Fax: 217-428-4415.

Edwardsville, Madison County Catholic Charities—MAUREEN ROBINSON, Area Dir., 500 N. Main St., Edwardsville, 62025. Tel: 618-307-5420.

Effingham. Catholic Charities—Sr. CAROL BECKERMANN, O.S.F., Area Dir., Mailing Address: P.O. Box 1017, Effingham, 62401. Tel: 217-857-1458; Fax: 217-857-1481.

Granite City. Madison County Catholic Charities—MAUREEN ROBINSON, Area Dir., 2105 State St., Granite City, 62040. Tel: 618-877-1184; Fax: 618-798-4287.

Mattoon. Catholic Charities of Coles, Douglas and Edgar Counties—SANDY CLARK, Area Dir., 4217 DeWitt Ave., Mattoon, 61938. Tel: 217-235-0420; Fax: 217-235-0425.

Quincy. Catholic Charities—VACANT, 620 Maine St., Quincy, 62301. Tel: 217-222-0958; Fax: 217-222-8737.

Springfield. Catholic Charities—DANIELLE K. ZELLERS, Area Dir., 120 S. 11th St., Springfield, 62703. Tel: 217-525-0500; Fax: 217-525-0554.

Institutions—

Alton, Catholic Children's Home—STEVEN E. ROACH, Exec. Dir.; CANDACE HOVEY, Admin., 1400 State St., Alton, 62002. Tel: 618-465-3594; Fax: 618-465-4023. Email: info@catholicchildrenshome.com.

Springfield. St. John's Breadline—KEVIN KINDRED, Supvr., 430 N. Fifth St., Springfield, 62702. Tel: 217-528-6098; Fax: 217-528-3605.

Springfield. St. Clare's Health Clinic—CONNIE MARZINZIK, Clinic Supvr., 700 N. Seventh St., Ste. A, Springfield, 62702. Tel: 217-523-1474; Fax: 217-523-0194.

CLERGY, PARISHES, MISSIONS AND PAROCHIAL SCHOOLS

CITY OF SPRINGFIELD

(SANGAMON COUNTY)

1—CATHEDRAL OF THE IMMACULATE CONCEPTION (1928) [JC] Rev. Peter C. Harman; Deacon Irvin (Larry) Smith. In Res., Rev. Christopher A. House.
Res.: 524 E. Lawrence Ave., P.O. Box 1667, 62705. Tel: 217-522-3342; Fax: 217-522-1151.
School—Cathedral School, (Grades PreK-8), 815 S. Sixth St., 62703. Tel: 217-523-2652; Fax: 217-523-2750. Web: www.cathedralschoolil.org. Springfield Dominican Sisters 1; Lay Teachers 14; Students 158.
Catechesis/Religious Program—Students 69.

2—ST. AGNES (1889) Rev. Robert J. Jallas; Deacon Roy Harley.
Res.: 245 N. Amos Ave., 62702. Tel: 217-793-1330; Fax: 217-793-3212. Email: sac245@sbcglobal.net. Web: stagnes.dio.org.
School—(Grades PreSchool-8) Tel: 217-793-1370; Fax: 217-793-1238. Email: sjsorge@stagnes.dio.org. Lay Teachers 26; Students 443.
Catechesis/Religious Program—Students 177.

3—ST. ALOYSIUS (1928) [JC] Rev. Mark A. Schulte.
Res.: 2119 N. 20th St., 62702. Tel: 217-544-4554; Fax: 217-544-4963. Email: stals@saintaloysius.org. Web: www.saintaloysius.org.
School—(Grades PreSchool-8) Tel: 217-544-4553; Fax: 217-544-1680. Lay Teachers 14; Students 200.
Catechesis/Religious Program—Students 30.

4—BLESSED SACRAMENT (1924) Rev. David J. Hoefler; Deacons David R. Erdmann; Thomas G. Burns.
Res.: 1725 S. Walnut Ave., 62704. Tel: 217-528-7521; Fax: 217-528-3137. Email: bsacrament@dio.org. Web: www.bsps.org.
School—(Grades PreSchool-8), 748 West Laurel, 62704. Tel: 217-522-7534; Fax: 217-522-7542. Email: wear@bssbruins.org. Web: www.bssbruins.org. Leslie Shevlin, Librarian; Lori Criscione, Librarian. Lay Teachers 29; Students 448.
Catechesis/Religious Program—Students 58.

5—CHRIST THE KING (1963) Rev. Msgr. David S. Lantz; Deacon Allison (Al) Laabs.
Res.: 1930 Barberry Dr., 62704. Tel: 217-546-3527; Fax: 217-793-6393. Email: church@ctkparish.com.
School—1920 Barberry Dr., 62704. Tel: 217-546-2159; Fax: 217-546-0291. Web: www.ctkcougars.com. Lay Teachers 26; Students 465.
Catechesis/Religious Program—Elementary, 1920 Barberry Dr., 62704. Tel: 217-546-2159. Students 83.

6—ST. FRANCES CABRINI (1948) Rev. Richard L. Chiola.
Res.: 1020 N. Milton Ave., 62702. Tel: 217-522-8555; Fax: 217-523-1345.

7—ST. JOSEPH (1875) Rev. Msgr. Thomas P. Holinga; Deacon Larry Day.
Res.: 1300 N. 5th St., 62702.
Church & Office: 1345 N. Sixth St., 62702. Tel: 217-544-7426; Fax: 217-544-7467. Email: parish@stjoseph.dio.org. Web: http://stjoseph.dio.org.

School—(Grades K-8), 1345 N. 5th St., 62702. Tel: 217-523-6597; Fax: 217-523-6434. Lay Teachers 14; Students 129.
Catechesis/Religious Program—Students 68.

8—ST. KATHARINE DREXEL (2001) Revs. Peter C. Harman, Priest Moderator & Sacramental Priest; Christopher A. House, Sacramental Priest; Sr. Mary Jean Traeger, O.P., Parish Life Coord.
Mailing Address: 722 S. 12th St., 62703. Tel: 217-523-5963.
Sacred Heart Church: 730 S. 12th St., 62703. Tel: 217-523-5963; Fax: 217-523-5963.
St. Patrick Church: 1720 S. Grand Ave. East, 62703. Tel: 217-528-0453.
Catechesis/Religious Program—Tel: 217-744-0578; Fax: 217-753-3768. Students 25.

9—LITTLE FLOWER (1947) [JC] Rev. Msgr. John R. Ossola.
800 Stevenson Dr., 62703. Tel: 217-529-1606; Fax: 217-529-1649. Email: pax@littleflowerchurch.net. Web: littleflowerchurch.net.
School—(Grades PreK-8), 900 Stevenson Dr., 62703. Tel: 217-529-4511; Fax: 217-529-0405. Email: office@little-flower.org. Web: little-flower.org. Lay Teachers 24; Students 303.
Catechesis/Religious Program—Students 40.

10—ST. PATRICK, Merged with Sacred Heart of Jesus, Springfield to form St. Katharine Drexel, Springfield.

11—SS. PETER AND PAUL (1859), (German), Closed. For inquiries for parish records, contact the Cathedral of the Immaculate Conception, Springfield.

12—SACRED HEART OF JESUS (1884), (German), Merged with St. Patrick, Springfield to form St. Katharine Drexel.

OUTSIDE THE CITY OF SPRINGFIELD

ALEXANDER, MORGAN CO., VISITATION B.V.M. (1909) [CEM] Rev. Angel Sierra.
Mailing Address: P.O. Box 20, New Berlin, 62670. Tel: 217-488-3545; Fax: 217-488-3545. Email: visitation@quadpastoralunit.com.
Church: Old U.S. 36, 62601.
Catechesis/Religious Program—Students 4.

ALTAMONT, EFFINGHAM CO., ST. CLARE (1874), (German), [CEM] Rev. Joseph Simburger, Parochial Admin.
Res.: 216 N. Ninth St., 62411. Tel: 618-483-5346; Fax: 618-483-5345.
Catechesis/Religious Program—Students 64.
Mission—St. Mary St. Elmo, Fayette Co.

ALTON, MADISON CO.

1—ST. MARY'S (1858) [CEM] Revs. James Walther, O.M.V.; Shawn Monahan, O.M.V.; Nnamdi Moneme, O.M.V.; Bro. John Luong.
Mailing Address: 519 E. 4th St., 62002. Tel: 618-465-4284; Fax: 618-463-4637. Email: stmarylaurie@aol.com. Web: www.stmarysalton.com.
Res.: 525 E. Fourth St., 62002. Tel: 618-465-4284.
School—(Grades PreSchool-8), 536 E. 3rd St., 62002. Tel: 618-465-8523; Fax: 618-465-4725. Web: www.smsalton.com. Sisters of St. Francis of the Martyr St. George 6; Lay Teachers 16; Students 353; Preschool 33.
School—Middle School, 1015 Milton Rd., 62002. Tel: 618-465-9719.
Catechesis/Religious Program—Students 69.

2—ST. MATTHEW (1947) Closed. For inquiries for parish records please see St. Mary (Immaculate Conception), Alton.

3—ST. PATRICK (1883) Closed. For inquiries for parish records, contact St. Mary's, Alton.

4—SS. PETER AND PAUL (1855) [JC] Rev. Delix Michel, S.S.L., Parochial Admin.
Res.: 717 State St., 62002. Tel: 618-465-4221; Fax: 618-465-0346. Email: info@ssppalton.com. Web: www.ssppalton.com.
School—(Grades PreSchool-8), 801 State St., 62002. Tel: 618-465-8711; Fax: 618-465-6405. Lay Teachers 11; Students 135.
Catechesis/Religious Program—Students 140.

ARCOLA, DOUGLAS CO., ST. JOHN THE BAPTIST (1865) [JC] Rev. Barry J. Harmon, Parochial Admin.
Res.: 205 S. Locust St., Box 133, 61910. Tel: 217-268-3766; Fax: 217-268-3545. Email: johnbaptist@consolidated.net.
Catechesis/Religious Program—210 Pine St., 61910. Students 62.

ARENZVILLE, CASS CO., ST. FIDELIS (1853), (German—Irish), Rev. Christopher J. Brey.
Res.: *St. Augustine*, 320 N. Saratoga, Ashland, 62612. Tel: 217-323-4345.
Rectory—215 W. Fifth St., Beardstown, 62618.
Church: 601 W. North St., 62611.
Catechesis/Religious Program—Students 3.

ASHLAND, CASS CO., ST. AUGUSTINE (1875) [CEM] Rev. Christopher J. Brey.
Church & Res.: 320 N. Saratoga, P.O. Box 438, 62612. Tel: 217-476-8856.
Catechesis/Religious Program—Students 16.

ASSUMPTION, CHRISTIAN CO., ASSUMPTION B.V.M. (1870) [CEM] Rev. Donald L. Wolford; Deacon John O'Brien.
Res.: 301 St. Peter St., 62510. Tel: 217-226-3536; Fax: 217-226-3538.
Catechesis/Religious Program—Tel: 217-226-3205. Students 26.

ATHENS, MENARD CO., HOLY FAMILY (1903) [CEM] Rev. Anthony Pilli, Parochial Admin.
Mailing Address: 711 S. 6th St., Petersburg, 62675.
Res.: 212 Washington St., Petersburg, 62675. Tel: 217-632-2561; Fax: 217-632-7118. Email: stpeter234@sbcglobal.net.
Church: Springfield Rd., 62613. Tel: 217-632-7118. Web: hfa.dio.org.
Catechesis/Religious Program—Students 44.

AUBURN, SANGAMON CO.

1—ST. BENEDICT (1880) [JC] Merged with Sacred Heart, Divernon and St. Mary, Pawnee to form Holy Cross, Auburn.

2—HOLY CROSS (2006) Rev. Kevin Laughery.
Office & Res.: 125 E. Washington St., P.O. Box 168, 62615. Tel: 217-438-6222; Fax: 217-438-6732. Web: hcp.dio.org.
St. Benedict Church, 128 E. Washington St., 62615.
Sacred Heart Church: 224 S. Lincoln, Divernon, 62530.
Catechesis/Religious Program—Students 203.

BARRY, PIKE CO., HOLY REDEEMER (1954) [JC] Closed. For inquiries for parish records contact the chancery.

BATCHTOWN, CALHOUN CO., ST. BARBARA (1910) [CEM] Merged with St. Mary, Brussels and St. Joseph, Meppen to form Blessed Trinity, Brussels.

BEARDSTOWN, CASS CO., ST. ALEXIUS (1853) [CEM] Rev. Christopher J. Brey.
Res.: *St. Augustine*, 320 N. Saratoga, Ashland, 62612.
Church & Rectory: 215 W. 5th St., 62618. Tel: 217-323-4345 (Both tel. & fax).
Catechesis/Religious Program—Tel: 217-323-1888. Students 55.

BELLEVIEW, CALHOUN CO., ST. AGNES (1900) [CEM] Merged with St. Anselm, Kampsville, St. Norbert, Hardin and St. Michael, Michael to form St. Francis of Assisi, Hardin.

BELTREES, JERSEY CO., ST. MICHAEL (1877) [CEM] Rev. Stephen J. Pohlman, Admin.
Res.: 820 W. Homer Adams Pkwy., Godfrey, 62035. Tel: 618-466-2921; Fax: 618-466-2929. Email: stambrose820@yahoo.com.
Church: Beltrees Rd., 62022.
Catechesis/Religious Program—Students 10.

BENLD, MACOUPIN CO., ST. JOSEPH (1915) Rev. Msgr. Lawrence Auda, Parochial Admin.
Res.: 304 N. Macoupin, Gillespie, 62033. Tel: 217-839-3456.
Church: 310 W. Central Ave., 62009. Tel: 217-835-4701.
Catechesis/Religious Program—Students 22.

BETHALTO, MADISON CO., OUR LADY QUEEN OF PEACE (1945) Rev. Thomas R. Liebler.
Res.: 132 Butcher St., P.O. Box 100, 62010. Tel: 618-377-6519; Fax: 618-377-9550. Email: olqpchurch@ezl.com; frliebler@ezl.com.
School—(Grades K-8) Tel: 618-377-6401; Fax: 618-377-6146. Marian Connoyer, Librarian. Lay Teachers 13; Students 152.
Catechesis/Religious Program—Students 68.

BETHANY, MOULTRIE CO., ST. ISIDORE (1864) [CEM] Deacons James J. Ghiglione, Parish Life Coord.; Dennis W. Baker.
Res.: 400 Whitetail Cir., Mount Zion, 62549. Tel: 217-864-3467; Fax: 217-864-3091.
Catechesis/Religious Program—Tel: 217-873-8667. Students 16.

BISHOP CREEK, EFFINGHAM CO., ST. ALOYSIUS (1865) [CEM] Closed. For inquiries for parish records contact the chancery.

BLACK JACK, MADISON CO., ST. JOHN THE BAPTIST, Closed. For inquiries for parish records contact the chancery.

BLUFFS, SCOTT CO., ST. PATRICK (1871) Closed. For inquiries for parish records contact the chancery.

BRIGHTON, MACOUPIN CO., ST. ALPHONSUS (1868), (German), Rev. Raphael Paul.
Res.: 918 N. Main St., 62012. Tel: 618-372-3352; Fax: 618-372-8133. Email: stalchurch@sbcglobal.net.
Catechesis/Religious Program—Students 56.

BROCTON, EDGAR CO., ST. THOMAS AQUINAS (1899) Closed. For inquiries for parish records contact the chancery.

BRUSSELS, CALHOUN CO.

1—BLESSED TRINITY (2005) Rev. Don J. Roberts; Deacon Michael B. Hagen.
Office: 111 E. Main, P.O. Box 38, 62013-0038. Tel: 618-883-2400; Fax: 618-883-2511. Email: blessedtrinityom@gmail.com.
Res.: Meppen Ln., Meppen, 62013. Tel: 618-883-2309.
School—Tel: 618-883-2124. Mrs. Brenda Paynic, Prin. Lay Teachers 3; Students 42.
Catechesis/Religious Program—Students 23.

2—ST. MARY (1851) [CEM] Merged with St. Barbara, Batchtown and St. Joseph, Meppen to form Blessed Trinity, Brussels.

BUFFALO, SANGAMON CO., ST. JOSEPH (1882) Closed. For inquiries for parish records please see Resurrection Parish, Illiopolis.

BUNKER HILL, MACOUPIN CO., ST. MARY (1854) [CEM] Closed. For inquiries for parish records contact the chancery.

CAMP POINT, ADAMS CO., ST. THOMAS (1860) Rev. J. Thomas Henseler (PEO), Parochial Admin.; Deacon Michael P. Ellerman.
Mailing Address: P.O. Box 252, Mount Sterling, 62353.
Res.: 401 W. North St., Mount Sterling, 62353-0252. Tel: 217-773-3233; Fax: 217-773-3233. Email: holy.family@verizon.net.
Church: 109 E. Spring St., 62320.
Parish Hall:—103 E. Spring St., 62320. Tel: 217-593-6685.
Catechesis/Religious Program—Students 64.

CARLINVILLE, MACOUPIN CO.

1—SS. MARY & JOSEPH (1996) [JC], SS. Mary & Joseph was formed by the merger of St. Mary's of the Immaculate Conception & St. Joseph. Rev. Bernard Thomas Donovan; Deacon Thomas S. Lucia.
Office & Mailing Address: 2010 E. First S. St., P.O. Box 647, 62626-0647. Tel: 217-854-7151; Fax: 217-854-9228. Email: pastor@ssmjc.org. Web: ssmjc.org.
Catechesis/Religious Program—Email: dre@ssmjc.org. Students 172.

2—ST. MARY'S OF THE IMMACULATE CONCEPTION, Closed. For inquiries for parish records contact Ss. Mary and Joseph, Carlinville.

CARROLLTON, GREENE CO., ST. JOHN THE EVANGELIST (1858) [CEM] Rev. Henry Schmidt.
Res.: 414 Third St., 62016-1319. Tel: 217-942-3551; Fax: 217-942-6767.
School—(Grades PreK-8), 426 Third St., 62016-1319. Tel: 217-942-6814; Fax: 217-942-6767. Lori Loveless, Prin. Lay Teachers 8; Students 111.
Catechesis/Religious Program—426 Third St., 62016. Students 72.

CASEY, CLARK CO., ST. CHARLES BORROMEO (1878) Rev. Michael B. Haag.
Res.: 110 Lincoln Dr., P.O. Box 156, Greenup, 62428. Tel: 217-923-3523; Fax: 217-923-3523.
Church: 300 E. Jefferson, P.O. Box 72, 62420.
Catechesis/Religious Program—Students 17.

CHANDLERVILLE, CASS CO., ST. BASIL, Merged with St. Luke, Virginia.

CHARLESTON, COLES CO., ST. CHARLES BORROMEO (1873) Rev. John M. Titus; Deacon James Rupp.
Res.: 921 E. Madison St., 61920. Tel: 217-345-3332; Fax: 217-348-8449.
Catechesis/Religious Program—Students 191.

CHATHAM, SANGAMON CO., ST. JOSEPH THE WORKER (1920) Rev. John Nolan; Deacon Frank Maynerich Jr.; Sr. Judith Pfile, O.P., Pastoral Assoc.
Res.: 1505 Hoechester Rd., 62712. Tel: 217-529-8055.
Church: 700 E. Spruce St., 62629. Tel: 217-483-3772; Fax: 217-483-4581. Email: info@stjoschatham.org. Web: www.stjoschatham.org.
Catechesis/Religious Program— 62629. Tel: 217-483-4514. Email: lafolder@comcast.net. Web: www-.stjoschatham.org. Lee Ann Folder, Coord. Faith Formation (K-6) & Business Mgr.; Susan Carrigan, Coord. Faith Formation (7-11) & Youth Min.; John Kennedy, Dir. Music. Students 563.

COFFEEN, MONTGOMERY CO., ST. JOHN THE BAPTIST (1898) [CEM] [JC] Closed. For inquiries for parish records please see St. Agnes, Hillsboro.

COLLINSVILLE, MADISON CO., SS. PETER AND PAUL (1855), (Italian), [CEM] Rev. John P. Beveridge.
Res.: 200 Westview, 62234. Tel: 618-345-4343; Fax: 618-345-1145. Web: www.saintspeter-paul.org.
School—(Grades PreSchool-8) Tel: 618-344-5450; Fax: 618-344-5536. Web: www.sspeter-paulschool.org. Lay Teachers 22; Students 239.
Catechesis/Religious Program—Email: jeannet@saintspeter-paul.org. Students 68.

DALTON CITY, MOULTRIE CO., SACRED HEART (1891) Closed. For inquiries for parish records contact the chancery.

DECATUR, MACON CO.

1—HOLY FAMILY (1959) [JC] Rev. Joseph Molloy; Sisters Marianne Nolan, O.P., Pastoral Assoc.; Janet Pfile, O.P., Pastoral Assoc.
Convent—Holy Family Convent, 2450 S. Franklin St., 62521. Tel: 217-423-0240; Fax: 217-423-6237. Email: holyfamilychurch1@comcast.net. Sisters 4.
School—(Grades PreSchool-8), 2400 S. Franklin St., 62521. Tel: 217-423-7049; Fax: 217-423-0137. Web: www.hfschool.org. Sr. Geraldine Kemper, O.P., Prin. Springfield Dominican Sisters 2; Lay Teachers 18; Students 213; Preschool 22.
Catechesis/Religious Program—Students 43.

2—ST. JAMES (1877) [JC] Merged with St. Patrick, Decatur to form Saints James and Patrick Parish,

Decatur. For inquiries for parish records contact Saints James and Patrick Parish, Decatur.

3—SAINTS JAMES AND PATRICK PARISH (2007) Rev. Jeffery A. Grant; Deacon Gregory Sullivan; Sr. Chaminade Kelley, O.S.F., Parish Nurse; Anita Olson, Sec.; Therese Allen, Pastoral Assoc.; Thomas Cantwell, Business Mgr.; Karen Redden, Sec.; Molly Sykes, Sec. & Office Asst.
407 E. Eldorado St., 62523. Tel: 217-429-5363 (Office); 217-428-7733 (Office); Fax: 217-429-8206. Email: office@saintjamesandpatrick.org. Web: saintsjamesandpatrick.org.
School—St. Patrick School, (Grades K-12), 412 N. Jackson, 62523. Tel: 217-423-4351; Fax: 217-423-7288. Web: www.stpatricks.pvt.k12.il.us. Jan Sweet, Prin. Teachers 11; Students 143.
Catechesis/Religious Program—James Rossi, C.R.E. & Pastoral Assoc. Students 69.

4—OUR LADY OF LOURDES (1958) [JC] Revs. Richard W. Weltin; James Palakudy, S.A.C., Parochial Vicar.
Res.: 3850 Lourdes Dr., 62526. Tel: 217-877-4404; Fax: 217-877-5257.
School—(Grades PreSchool-8), 3950 Lourdes Dr., 62526-1799. Tel: 217-877-4408; Fax: 217-872-3655. Addie Heckman, Librarian. Lay Teachers 21; Students 292.
Catechesis/Religious Program—Email: ololpsr@yahoo.com. Students 153.

5—ST. PATRICK (1853) [JC] Merged with St. James, Decatur to form Saints James and Patrick Parish, Decatur. For inquiries for parish records contact Saints James and Patrick Parish, Decatur.

6—ST. THOMAS THE APOSTLE (1925) Revs. Richard W. Weltin; James Palakudy, S.A.C., Parochial Vicar; Deacon Kevin Richardson.
Res.: 2160 N. Edward St., 62526. Tel: 217-877-4146; Fax: 217-877-4147.
Catechesis/Religious Program—Students 73.

DIETERICH, EFFINGHAM CO.

1—IMMACULATE CONCEPTION (1905) [CEM] Closed. For inquiries for parish records contact the chancery.

2—ST. ISIDORE THE FARMER CHURCH (2004) [CEM] Rev. Joseph P. Carlos, O.F.M.
19812 E. 1000th Ave., 62424. Tel: 217-925-5579; Fax: 217-925-5879. Email: stalbc@mmtcnet.com.
Catechesis/Religious Program—Students 343.

DIVERNON, SANGAMON CO., SACRED HEART (1905) [CEM] Merged with St. Benedict, Auburn and St. Mary, Pawnee to form Holy Cross, Auburn.

EAST ALTON, MADISON CO., ST. KEVIN (1959) Merged with St. Bernard, Wood River to form Holy Angels, Wood River.

EDGEWOOD, EFFINGHAM CO., ST. ANNE (1865), (German), [CEM] Rev. Joseph Simburger, Parochial Admin.
Res.: 216 N. Ninth, Altamont, 62411. Tel: 618-483-5346; Fax: 618-483-5345.
Catechesis/Religious Program—Tel: 614-238-4513. Students 6.

EDWARDSVILLE, MADISON CO.

1—ST. BONIFACE (1869), (German), [CEM] Rev. Jeffrey Goeckner (India); Deacon Daniel L. Corbett.
Res.: 514 Chapman, 62025. Tel: 618-656-6450; Fax: 618-656-7669.
Church: 110 N. Buchanan St., P.O. Box 423, 62025. Email: stbchurch@st-boniface.com. Web: www.st-boniface.com.
Preschool—Tel: 618-692-9315. Students 72.
School—(Grades K-8) Tel: 618-656-6917. Email: stbschool@st-boniface.com. Lay Teachers 12; Students 199; Preschool 72.
Catechesis/Religious Program—Students 260.

2—ST. MARY (1842) [CEM] [JC] Rev. Thomas C. Meyer.
Res.: 1802 Madison Ave., 62025. Tel: 618-656-4857; Fax: 618-656-1715.
School—(Grades PreSchool-8) Tel: 618-656-1230. Sisters 1; Lay Teachers 15; Students 233.
Catechesis/Religious Program—Students 111.

EFFINGHAM, EFFINGHAM CO.

1—ST. ANTHONY OF PADUA (1858) [CEM] Rev. Msgr. Leo J. Enlow; Rev. Joseph Chandy Koyickal, S.A.C.; Deacon Joseph Emmerich.
Res.: 417 N. Third, P.O. Box 764, 62401. Tel: 217-347-7129; Fax: 217-342-6980. Web: www.stanthony.com.
School—St. Anthony Grade School, 405 N. Second St., 62401. Tel: 217-347-0419; Fax: 217-347-2749. Sisters 1; Lay Teachers 32; Students 327.
High School—St. Anthony High School, 304 E. Roadway Ave., 62401. Tel: 217-342-6969; Fax: 217-342-6997. Priests 2; Lay Teachers 22; Students 214.
Catechesis/Religious Program—Tel: 217-347-7129; Fax: 217-347-6980. Students 85.

2—SACRED HEART (1892) [JC] Rev. Robert Spriggs.
Res.: 405 S. Henrietta, P.O. Box 870, 62401. Tel: 217-347-7177; Fax: 217-347-0728. Email: shchurch@sheff.org. Web: www.sheff.org.
School—(Grades K-8) Tel: 217-342-4060; Fax: 217-342-9251. Email: shschool@sheff.org. Lay Teachers 14; Students 161.
Catechesis/Religious Program—Students 105.

FARMERSVILLE, MONTGOMERY CO., ST. MARY (1876) [CEM] [JC] Rev. Gerald L. Bunse, Parochial Admin.; Deacon Patrick J. O'Toole.
Res.: 310 Nobbie St., 62533. Tel: 217-227-3349; Fax: 217-227-3515.
Catechesis/Religious Program—Students 18.

FIELDON, JERSEY CO., ST. MARY, [CEM] Rev. William Hembrow, Parochial Admin.
Res.: 306 N. Washington, Jerseyville, 62052. Tel: 618-498-3416; Fax: 618-498-3414. Email: hgchurch@gtec.com.
Catechesis/Religious Program— Clustered with Holy Ghost, Jerseyville. Students 46.

FRANKLIN, MORGAN CO., SACRED HEART OF JESUS (1886) [CEM] Rev. Angel Sierra.
Mailing Address: P.O. Box 20, New Berlin, 62670. Tel: 217-488-3545; Fax: 217-488-3545. Email: sacredheart@quadpastoralunit.com.
Office & Res.: P.O. Box 20, New Berlin, 62670. Tel: 217-488-2410.
Church: Tel: 217-675-2631.
Parish Center—Tel: 217-675-2631.
Catechesis/Religious Program—Students 44.

GILLESPIE, MACOUPIN CO., SS. SIMON AND JUDE (1879) [CEM] Rev. Msgr. Lawrence Auda, Parochial Admin.
Res.: 304 N. Macoupin St., 62033. Tel: 217-839-3456. Email: simonjude@frontiernet.net.
Catechesis/Religious Program—Students 66.

GIRARD, MACOUPIN CO., ST. PATRICK (1887) Rev. Daren J. Zehnle.
Mailing Address: 721 N. Springfield St., Virden, 62690.
Church: 745 W. Center, 62640.
Catechesis/Religious Program—Students 59.

GLEN CARBON, MADISON CO., ST. CECILIA (1926) Rev. Joseph P. Kerber; Deacon Jerry L. Cato.
Res.: 155 N. Main St., 62034. Tel: 618-288-3200; Fax: 618-288-3292. Email: cecilia@stcparish.org. Web: www.stcparish.org.
Catechesis/Religious Program—St. Cecilia Family Life Center, Tel: 618-288-5523. Email: faithformation@stcparish.org. Web: www.stcparish.org. Students 194.

GODFREY, MADISON CO., ST. AMBROSE (1947) [JC] Rev. Stephen J. Pohlman; Deacon William E. Kessler.
Church: 820 W. Homer M. Adams Pkwy., 62035. Tel: 618-466-2921; Fax: 618-466-2959.
Res.: 3307 Morkel Dr., 62035. Tel: 618-466-6408.
School—(Grades PreSchool-8) Tel: 618-466-4216; Fax: 618-466-4575. Web: saintambrosegodfrey.org. Cathy McGarrahan, Prin. Lay Teachers 20; Students 257.
Catechesis/Religious Program—Students 88.

GRAFTON, JERSEY CO., ST. PATRICK (1871) Rev. Donald Patrick Gibbons, Admin.
11 N. Evans, P.O. Box 218, 62037. Tel: 618-786-3512; Fax: 618-786-2027. Email: stpatricks@gtec.com.
Res.: 506 S. State St., Jerseyville, 62052.
Catechesis/Religious Program—Students 21.

GRANITE CITY, MADISON CO.

1—ST. ELIZABETH (1871) [CEM] [JC] Rev. Christopher J. Comerford.
Office: 2300 Pontoon Rd., 62040. Tel: 618-877-3300; Fax: 618-877-9800. Email: secretary@stelizabethparish.net.
Res.: 3235 Edgewood, 62040. Tel: 618-877-0776.
School—(Grades PreK-8) Tel: 618-877-3300, Ext. 127; Fax: 618-877-3352. Email: steroyals@hotmail.com. Lay Teachers 12; Students 148.
St. Elizabeth Preschool—Tel: 618-877-3300, Ext. 124.
Catechesis/Religious Program—Students 96.

2—HOLY FAMILY (1988) [JC] Rev. Larry H. Brunette.
Res.: 2606 Washington Ave., 62040-4810. Tel: 618-877-7158; Fax: 618-877-7105.
School—(Grades K-8), 1900 St. Clair Ave., 62040. Tel: 618-877-5500; Fax: 618-877-5502. Lay Teachers 15; Students 210.
Catechesis/Religious Program—Tel: 618-452-8244. Students 25.

GRANTFORK, MADISON CO., ST. GERTRUDE (1872) [CEM] Rev. Carlos M. Bohorquez.
Mailing Address: P.O. Box 410, Pierron, 62273.
Church: 202 N. Locust St., 62249. Tel: 618-675-3383; Fax: 618-675-3388. Email: icsnsg@agtelco.com.
Catechesis/Religious Program—Tel: 618-675-3662. Maura Donnelly, C.R.E. Students 27.

GREEN CREEK, EFFINGHAM CO., ST. MARY HELP OF CHRISTIANS (1860), (German), [CEM] Rev. Robert L. DeGrand.
20057 N. 1525th St., Effingham, 62401. Tel: 217-844-2062; Fax: 217-844-2062. In Res., Rev. Sylvano Pera, O.F.M.
Res.: 200 N. Church St., P.O. Box 68, Sigel, 62462-0068. Tel: 217-844-3371; Fax: 217-844-2309.
Catechesis/Religious Program—Students 41.

GREENFIELD, GREENE CO., ST. MICHAEL (1880) [CEM] Rev. Henry Schmidt.
Res.: 411 Sheffield, 62044. Tel: 217-368-2176.
Catechesis/Religious Program—Students 28.

GREENUP, CUMBERLAND CO., CHRIST THE KING (1937) Rev. Michael B. Haag.
Res.: 110 Lincoln Dr., P.O. Box 156, 62428. Tel: 217-923-3523.
Catechesis/Religious Program—Students 30.

GREENVILLE, BOND CO., ST. LAWRENCE (1868) [CEM] Rev. Victor J. Kaltenbach, Parochial Admin.; Lisa Coleman, Contact Person.
Res.: 512 S. Prairie St., 62246. Tel: 618-664-9149; 618-664-9149. Email: stlawgrnvl@att.net.
Catechesis/Religious Program—Students 130.

GRIGGSVILLE, PIKE CO., HOLY FAMILY, Closed. For details for parish records see St. Mary, Pittsfield.

HAGAMAN, MACOUPIN CO., ST. CATHERINE (1905) Closed. For inquiries for parish records contact the chancery.

HARDIN, CALHOUN CO.

1—ST. FRANCIS OF ASSISI (2005) [CEM] Rev. Don J. Roberts.
Office:—304 French St, P.O. Box C, 62047. Tel: 618-576-2628; Fax: 618-576-9448. Email: stfrancisom@gmail.com. Web: www.stfrancisofassisiparish.com.
Res.: Meppen Ln., Meppen, 62013. Tel: 618-883-2309.
School—St. Norbert School, 401 Vineyard St., P.O. Box 525, 62047. Tel: 618-576-2514; Fax: 618-576-8074. Email: stnorbert@618connect.com. Lay Teachers 4; Aides 2; Students 57.
Catechesis/Religious Program—Tel: 618-576-2628; Fax: 618-576-9448. Email: sfaparishcre@gmail.com. Students 74.

2—ST. NORBERT (1872) [CEM] Merged with St. Agnes, Belleview, St. Anselm, Kampsville and St. Michael, Michael to form St. Francis of Assisi, Hardin.

HIGHLAND, MADISON CO., ST. PAUL (1844) [JC] Revs. Charles A. Edwards; Aloysius Okey Ndeanaefo, Parochial Vicar.
Res.: 1412 Ninth St., 62249. Tel: 618-654-2339; Fax: 618-654-9980. Web: stpaul-church.com.
School—(Grades PreK-8), 1416 Main St., 62249. Tel: 618-654-7525; Fax: 618-654-8795. Web: stpaul-highland.org. David Timmerman, Prin. Lay Teachers 29; Students 317.
Catechesis/Religious Program—1420 Ninth St., 62249. Tel: 618-654-2339, Ext. 216. Students 283.

HILLSBORO, MONTGOMERY CO., ST. AGNES (1840) [CEM] Rev. James L. Neuman.
Res.: 216 E. Tremont St., 62049. Tel: 217-532-5288; Fax: 217-532-2631. Email: fjnew@consolidated.net; agnesone_chris@consolidated.net. Web: www.stagneshillsboro.com.
Parish Office: 212 E. Tremont St., 62049.
Catechesis/Religious Program—Tel: 217-532-2631. Students 97.

HUME, EDGAR CO., ST. MICHAEL (1876) Rev. Paul H. Skelton.
Res.: 208 N. Pine, Box 17, Villa Grove, 61956. Tel: 217-832-8352; Fax: 217-832-8352.
Catechesis/Religious Program—Students 5.

ILLIOPOLIS, SANGAMON CO., RESURRECTION PARISH (1866) [CEM] [JC] Sr. Lois Kikkert, O.P., Parish Life Coord.; Rev. Joseph G. Ring, Priest Moderator.
Res.: 410 Anne St., P.O. Box 47, 62539-0047. Tel: 217-486-3851; Fax: 217-486-3851. Email: resurrectionparish@comcast.net.
Catechesis/Religious Program—Students 30.

ISLAND GROVE, JASPER CO., ST. JOSEPH (1874) [CEM] Closed. For inquiries for parish records contact the chancery.

JACKSONVILLE, MORGAN CO., OUR SAVIOUR (1851) [CEM 2] Very Rev. Kenneth J. Venvertloh; Rev. Jeffrey D. Long, Parochial Vicar.
Mailing Address: 453 E. State St., 62650. Tel: 217-245-6184; Fax: 217-245-6185. Email: osparish1@mchsi.com. Web: www.oursaviourparish.org.
School—(Grades K-8) Tel: 217-243-8621. Web: oss-shamrocks.com. Rita Carney, Prin. Lay Teachers 18; Students 217.
Catechesis/Religious Program—Tel: 217-245-7633. Students 93.

JERSEYVILLE, JERSEY CO.

1—ST. FRANCIS XAVIER (1857), (Irish—German), [CEM] [JC] Rev. Donald Patrick Gibbons.
Res.: 506 S. State St., P.O. Box 260, 62052-0260. Tel: 618-498-3518; Fax: 618-639-3519.
School—St. Francis/Holy Ghost School, (Grades K-8) Tel: 618-498-4823; Fax: 618-498-3827.
School—St. Francis, (Grades 5-8), 412 S. State St., 62052.
School—Holy Ghost, (Grades PreK-4), 309 N. Washington St., 62052. Tel: 618-498-4910; Fax: 618-498-2754. Mrs. Janet Goben, Prin. Lay Teachers 23; Students 418.
Catechesis/Religious Program—Twinned with Holy

Ghost, Jerseyville, IL., Tel: 618-498-5497. Students 97.

2—HOLY GHOST, (German), [JC] Rev. William Hembrow, Parochial Admin.
Res.: 306 N. Washington St., 62052. Tel: 618-498-3416; Fax: 618-498-3414. Email: hgchurch@gtec.com.
See St. Francis/Holy Ghost School, Jerseyville under St. Francis Xavier, Jerseyville for details.
Catechesis/Religious Program—Twinned with St. Francis, Jerseyville, IL.

KAMPSVILLE, CALHOUN CO., ST. ANSELM (1877) [CEM] Merged with St. Agnes, Belleview, St. Norbert, Hardin and St. Michael, Michael to form St. Francis of Assisi, Hardin.

KINCAID, CHRISTIAN CO., ST. RITA (1920) Rev. Alan M. Hunter; Deacon Raymond L. Roth Jr.
Res.: 30 St. Rita Ct., P.O. Box 439, 62540. Tel: 217-237-4339 (Rectory); 217-237-2333 (Office); Fax: 217-237-2477. Email: strita1@consolidated.net.
Catechesis/Religious Program—Students 30.

LIBERTY, ADAMS CO., ST. BRIGID (1860) [CEM] Rev. Jeffrey E. Stone; Deacon John M. Esselman.
Church: 706 N. Main St., P.O. Box 228, 62347. Tel: 217-645-3444; Fax: 217-645-3546. Email: sbtparishoffice@sbcglobal.net.
Rectory—806 N. Main St., 62347-0228.
Catechesis/Religious Program—Students 108.

LILLYVILLE, CUMBERLAND CO., SACRED HEART (1877), (German), [CEM] Rev. Robert L. DeGrand, Admin.
Res.: 200 N. Church St., P.O. Box 68, Sigel, 62462. Tel: 217-844-3371; Fax: 217-844-2309.
Church: 127 County Rd., 100 E., Sigel, 62462. Tel: 217-844-2062.
Catechesis/Religious Program—Tel: 217-844-2312. Students 26.

LITCHFIELD, MONTGOMERY CO., HOLY FAMILY (1988) [CEM], Formerly St. Mary, founded in 1857. Rev. James L. Neuman.
Res.: 216 E. Tremont St., P.O. Box 98, Hillsboro, 62049. Tel: 217-532-5288; Fax: 217-532-2631.
Church: 410 S. State St., P.O. Box 8, 62056. Tel: 217-324-2776; Fax: 217-324-2868.
Catechesis/Religious Program—411 S. Jackson St., 62056. Tel: 217-324-5834. Students 90.

LIVINGSTON, MADISON CO., SACRED HEART (1913) [CEM] Rev. George Radosevich. Tel: 618-635-8490.
Res.: 188 Livingston Ave., P.O. Box 458, 62058. Tel: 618-637-2211.
Catechesis/Religious Program— Combined with St. Michael Parish, Staunton.

LOVINGTON, MOULTRIE CO., ST. MARY, Closed. Sacramental records are located at Our Lady of the Holy Spirit, Mt. Zion.

MACON, MACON CO., ST. STANISLAUS (1866) Closed. For inquiries for parish records contact the chancery.

MADISON, MADISON CO., ST. MARY AND ST. MARK (2002) [JC] Rev. Eugene Prendiville, O.M.I., Sacramental Min.; Sisters Georgiana Stubner, O.P., Pastoral Assoc.; Mary Clare Fichtner, Parish Life Coord.
Res.: 1621 10th St., 62060. Tel: 618-452-5180; Fax: 618-877-4255. Email: clarefichtner@cbnstl.com.

MARINE, MADISON CO., ST. ELIZABETH (1856) [CEM] Rev. Msgr. Kenneth C. Steffen, Parochial Admin.
Res.: 120 N. Windmill St., P.O. Box 457, 62061. Tel: 618-887-4535.
Catechesis/Religious Program—1717 Parkview Dr., Highland, 62249. Tel: 618-654-3093. Kathy Ward, D.R.E. Students 21.

MARSHALL, CLARK CO., ST. MARY (1847) [CEM] Rev. Michael B. Haag.
Res.: 414 S. 6th St., 62441. Tel: 217-826-2845; Fax: 217-826-1137.
Catechesis/Religious Program—Students 76.

MARYVILLE, MADISON CO., MOTHER OF PERPETUAL HELP (1938) Rev. Stephen T. Sotiroff.
Church & Office: 200 N. Lange, 62062.
Res.: 7502 S. Ridge, 62062. Tel: 618-345-0331. Email: motherofperpetual@charterinternet.com.
School—St. John Neumann School, (Grades K-8) Tel: 618-345-7230; Fax: 618-345-4350. Lay Teachers 19; Students 343.
Catechesis/Religious Program—Students 55.

MATTOON, COLES CO., IMMACULATE CONCEPTION (1856) [CEM] Rev. Dennis D. Kollross.
Res.: 320 N. 21st St., P.O. Box 468, 61938-0468. Tel: 217-235-0539; Fax: 217-235-0593. Email: immaculate@mchsi.com.
School—(Grades K-5), 2000 Richmond Ave., 61938. Tel: 217-235-0431; Fax: 217-235-5447. Email: smschool1@consolidated.net. Web: www.stmary-schoolmattoon.org. Lay Teachers 8; Students 86.
Catechesis/Religious Program—Students 95.

MEDORA, MACOUPIN CO., ST. JOHN THE EVANGELIST (1914), (German), Rev. Raphael Paul, Admin.
Res.: *c/o St. Alphonsus Church*, 918 N. Main St., Brighton, 62012. Tel: 618-372-3352; Fax: 618-372-8133.
Catechesis/Religious Program— Clustered with St. Alphonsus, Brighton. Students 14.

MENDON, ADAMS CO., ST. EDWARD (1891) [CEM] Rev. Jeffrey E. Stone; Deacon John M. Esselman.
Mailing Address: P.O. Box 228, Liberty, 62347.
Res.: 806 N. Main St., Liberty, 62347. Tel: 217-645-3444; Fax: 217-645-3546. Email: sbtparishoffice@sbcglobal.net.
Church: 214 S. State Rd., 62351.
Catechesis/Religious Program—Students 52.

MEPPEN, CALHOUN CO., ST. JOSEPH (1864) [CEM] Merged with St. Barbara, Batchtown and St. Mary, Brussels to form Blessed Trinity, Brussels.

MICHAEL, CALHOUN CO., ST. MICHAEL (1864), (Irish), [CEM] Merged with St. Agnes, Belleview, St. Norbert, Hardin and St. Anselm, Kampsville to form St. Francis of Assisi, Hardin.

MONTROSE, EFFINGHAM CO., ST. ROSE OF LIMA (1879) [CEM] Revs. Austin Albers, O.F.M.; Ken Rosswog, O.F.M.; Vernon Olmer, O.F.M.
Mailing Address: 301 N. Springcreek Rd., P.O. Box 68, 62445. Tel: 217-924-4337; Fax: 217-924-4312.
Catechesis/Religious Program—Tel: 217-924-4465. Students 80.

MORRISONVILLE, CHRISTIAN CO., ST. MAURICE (1870) [CEM] Rev. Gerald L. Bunse, Parochial Admin.
Mailing Address: 706 E. 4th St., 62546.
Res.: 310 Nobbe St., Farmersville, 62533. Tel: 217-227-3349; Fax: 217-227-3515.
Catechesis/Religious Program—Students 17.

MOUNT OLIVE, MACOUPIN CO.

1—ASCENSION (1886), (Croatian), [CEM] Rev. Larry Anschutz, Admin.
Res.: 705 E. Main St., 62069. Tel: 217-999-4981; Fax: 217-999-4036.
Catechesis/Religious Program—Students 47.

2—HOLY TRINITY (1912), (Slovak), [CEM] Rev. Larry Anschutz, Admin.
Res.: 705 E. Main St., 62069. Tel: 217-999-4981; Fax: 217-999-4036.
Church: 410 E. Garfield, 62069.
Catechesis/Religious Program—Students 15.

MOUNT STERLING, BROWN CO., HOLY FAMILY (1864) [CEM] Rev. J. Thomas Henseler (PEO); Deacon Michael P. Ellerman.
Res.: 401 W. North St., 62353. Tel: 217-773-3233; Fax: 217-773-3233. Email: holy.family@verizon.net.
School—St. Mary, (Grades PreSchool-8), 408 W. Washington, 62353. Tel: 217-773-2825; Fax: 217-773-2399. Email: smseagle@adams.net. Charlotte J. Koch, Prin. Lay Teachers 7; Students 77.
Catechesis/Religious Program—Students 74.

MOWEAQUA, SHELBY CO., ST. FRANCES DE SALES (1895) [JC] Rev. Donald L. Wolford; Deacon John O'Brien.
Res.: 301 St. Peter St., Assumption, 62510. Tel: 217-226-3536; Fax: 217-226-3538.
Church: 231 E.Warren St., 62550.
Catechesis/Religious Program—Tel: 217-226-3205. Students 33.

MT. ZION, MACON CO., OUR LADY OF THE HOLY SPIRIT (1974) Deacons James J. Ghiglione, Parish Life Coord.; Dennis W. Baker.
Res.: 400 N. Whitetail Cir., 62549. Tel: 217-864-3467; Fax: 217-864-3091. Email: deaconjim@hotmail.com. Web: mtzolhs.org.
Catechesis/Religious Program—Tel: 217-864-4941. Students 86.

MURRAYVILLE, MORGAN CO., ST. BARTHOLOMEW (1884) [CEM] Closed. For inquiries for parish records contact the chancery.

NEOGA, CUMBERLAND CO., ST. MARY OF THE ASSUMPTION (1897), (German), [CEM] [JC] Rev. Robert L. DeGrand, Admin.
Res.: 200 N. Church St., P.O. Box 68, Sigel, 62462-0068. Tel: 217-844-3371; Fax: 217-844-2309.
Church: 670 Walnut Ave., 62447. Tel: 217-895-2166.
Catechesis/Religious Program—Students 80.

NEW BERLIN, SANGAMON CO., SACRED HEART OF MARY (1858) [CEM] Rev. Angel Sierra.
Res.: 404 E. Birch, P.O. Box 20, 62670. Tel: 217-488-2410 (Rectory); 217-488-3545 (Office). Email: stmarys@quadpastoralunit.com.
Catechesis/Religious Program—Tel: 217-488-3545; Fax: 217-488-3545. Students 39.

NEW DOUGLAS, MADISON CO., ST. UBALDUS (1872) [CEM] Closed. For inquiries for parish records contact the chancery.

NEWTON, JASPER CO., ST. THOMAS THE APOSTLE (1873) [CEM 3] Rev. Allen M. Kemme; Linda M. Hemrich, Contact Person.
Res.: 306 W. Jourdan St., P.O. Box 225, 62448. Tel: 618-783-8741; Fax: 618-783-8742. Email: stthomaschurch@psbnewton.com.
School—(Grades K-8), 306 W. Jourdan St., 62448. Tel: 618-783-3517; Fax: 618-783-2224. Web: www-.stthomassaints.com. Lay Teachers 9; Students 136.
Catechesis/Religious Program—Students 71.

NIANTIC, MACON CO., ST. ANN (1889) [JC] Closed. For inquiries for parish records please see Resurrection Parish, Illiopolis.

NOKOMIS, MONTGOMERY CO., ST. LOUIS (1870) [CEM] Rev. Daniel L. Willenborg.
Res.: 311 S. Elm St., 62075-1310. Tel: 217-563-7146; 217-563-7808 (Personal); Fax: 217-563-8671. Email: parish@stlouis-nokomis.k12.il.us. Web: www.stlouis-nokomis.k12.il.us.
School—(Grades PreK-8), 509 E. Union, 62075. Tel: 217-563-7445; Fax: 217-563-7450. Email: school@stlouis-nokomis.k12.il.us. Web: www.stlouis-nokomis.k12.il.us. Lay Teachers 6; Students 88.
Catechesis/Religious Program—Students 34.

NORTH ARM, EDGAR CO., ST. ALOYSIUS (1817) [CEM] Very Rev. David Zimmerman.
18925 E. 1350th Rd., P.O. Box 577, Paris, 61944.
Res.: 117 E. Edgar St., P.O. Box 577, Paris, 61944. Tel: 217-465-7667; Fax: 217-466-5215. Email: pj154@aol.com.
Catechesis/Religious Program— Combined with St. Mary's, Paris.

OBLONG, CRAWFORD CO., OUR LADY OF LOURDES (1954) Rev. William J. Overmann.
Res.: 207 E. Walnut St., Robinson, 62454. Tel: 618-544-7526; Fax: 618-544-9327. Web: www.crawfordcountycatholics.com.
Catechesis/Religious Program—Students 7.

OCONEE, SHELBY CO., SACRED HEART (1872) [CEM] Rev. William Kessler.
Res.: P.O. Box 45, 62553. Tel: 217-539-4325; Fax: 217-539-4569. Email: shparish@frontiernet.net.
Catechesis/Religious Program—Students 27.

PALMYRA, MACOUPIN CO., HOLY ROSARY (1954) Closed. For inquiries for parish records contact the chancery.

PANA, CHRISTIAN CO., ST. PATRICK (1858) [CEM] Rev. William Kessler.
Res.: 6 E. Fifth St., P.O. Box 440, 62557. Tel: 217-562-5396; Fax: 217-562-2308. Email: dhertz@stpatspana.org.
Church: 303 S. Locust St., 62557.
School—Sacred Heart, (Grades PreK-8) Tel: 217-562-2425. Mike Guidish, Prin. Lay Teachers 10; Students 141.
Catechesis/Religious Program—Tel: 217-562-2308. Students 78.

PANAMA, BOND CO., SACRED HEART (1916) [JC] Closed. For inquiries for parish records please see St. Agnes, Hillsboro.

PARIS, EDGAR CO., ST. MARY (1849) [CEM] Very Rev. David Zimmerman.
Church: 528 N. Main St., P.O. Box 577, 61944. Tel: 217-466-3355; Fax: 217-466-5215. Web: www.stmaryschurchparis.org.
School—(Grades PreSchool-8), 507 Connelly St., 61944. Tel: 217-463-3005; Fax: 217-465-4703. Email: barbara.moy@smsk8.com. Web: www.smsk8.com. Lay Teachers 7; Students 65.
Catechesis/Religious Program—Email: pat.catanzariti@stmaryschurchparis.org. Students 70.

PAWNEE, SANGAMON CO., ST. MARY (1899) [CEM] Merged with St. Benedict, Auburn and Sacred Heart, Divernon to form Holy Cross, Auburn.

PETERSBURG, MENARD CO., ST. PETER (1868) [CEM] Rev. Anthony Pilli, Parochial Admin.
Res.: 212 Washington, 62675. Tel: 217-632-7118; Fax: 217-632-7118. Email: stpeter234@sbcglobal.net. Web: www.spp.dio.org.
Catechesis/Religious Program—Tel: 217-632-7118. Students 78.

PIERRON, MADISON AND BOND COS., IMMACULATE CONCEPTION (1892) [CEM] Rev. Carlos M. Bohorquez.
Res.: 971 Main St., P.O. Box 410, 62273. Tel: 618-675-3383; Fax: 618-675-3388. Email: icsnsg@agtelco.com.
Catechesis/Religious Program—Students 55.

PITTSFIELD, PIKE CO., ST. MARY (1852) [CEM] [JC] Rev. Rodney A. Schwartz; Deacon Michael (Kim) Scott.
Mailing Address: 226 E. Adams, 62363. Tel: 217-285-4321; Fax: 217-285-9400.
Res.: 108 Pearl St., Winchester, 62694. Tel: 217-742-5224.
Catechesis/Religious Program—Students 40.

POCAHONTAS, BOND CO., ST. NICHOLAS (1871) [CEM] Rev. Carlos M. Bohorquez.
Res.: P.O. Box 410, Pierron, 62273. Tel: 618-675-3383; Fax: 618-675-3388. Email: icsnsg@agtelco.com.
Catechesis/Religious Program—Students 24.

QUINCY, ADAMS CO.

1—ALL SAINTS (1999) [JC] Merged with St. Boniface, Quincy and St. Mary (Immaculate Conception), Quincy to form Blessed Sacrament, Quincy.

2—ST. ANTHONY OF PADUA (1859) [CEM] Rev. Thomas Hagstrom; Deacons William K. Neuser; Harold Parn. In Res., Rev. John Carberry (Retired).
Res. & Church Address: 2223 St. Anthony Rd., 62305. Tel: 217-222-5996; Fax: 217-224-6477. Email: stanthonyparish@comcast.net.
School—St. Dominic, (Grades PreK-8) Tel: 217-224-0041; Fax: 217-224-0042. Email: stdominicschool@adams.net. Lay Teachers 14; Students 165.

Catechesis/Religious Program—Bonnie Nytes, D.R.E. Students 88.

3—BLESSED SACRAMENT (2006) Rev. Msgr. Michael Kuse; Deacons Terrence J. Ellerman; Leo Bistak; Phyllis Schulte, Business Mgr.; Steve Buckman, Music Min.; Carole Glosemeyer, Sec.
1119 S. Seventh St., 62301. Tel: 217-222-2759; Fax: 217-222-6463.
School—(Grades PreSchool-8), 1115 S. 7th, 62301. Tel: 217-228-1477. Email: info@blessedscs.org. Web: www.blessedsas.org. Lay Teachers 15; Students 122.
Catechesis/Religious Program—Tel: 217-222-2758. Web: quincycatholicyouth.org. Ann Gage, Pastoral Assoc.; Deacon Terrence J. Ellerman, Youth Min. Students 105.

4—ST. BONIFACE (1837) [JC] Merged with All Saints, Quincy and St. Mary (Immaculate Conception), Quincy to form Blessed Sacrament, Quincy.

5—ST. DOMINIC (1977) [JC] Merged with St. Anthony of Padua, Quincy.

6—ST. FRANCIS SOLANUS (1860) [JC] Revs. Donald Braeser, O.F.M., Parochial Admin.; James Wheeler, O.F.M.; Thomas Shaughnessy, O.F.M.; Deacon Wayne R. Zimmerman.
Res.: 1721 College Ave., 62301. Tel: 217-222-2898; Fax: 217-222-3020.
School—(Grades K-8) Tel: 217-222-4077; Fax: 217-222-5049. Lay Teachers 20; Students 252.
Catechesis/Religious Program—1721 College Ave., 62301. Students 152.

7—ST. JOHN THE BAPTIST (1880), (German), Merged with St. Rose of Lima, Quincy to form All Saints, Quincy. Records at Blessed Sacrament, Quincy.

8—ST. JOSEPH (1868) [CEM] Rev. Jeffrey E. Stone; Deacon John M. Esselman.
Mailing Address: P.O. Box 228, Liberty, 62347.
Church: 1435 E. 1500 St. Tel: 217-434-8442; Fax: 217-434-8058. Email: stjoe@adams.net.
Catechesis/Religious Program—Students 49.

9—ST. MARY (IMMACULATE CONCEPTION) (1867) [JC] Merged with All Saints, Quincy and St. Boniface, Quincy to form Blessed Sacrament, Quincy.

10—ST. PETER (1839) [JC] Rev. John Burnette.
Res.: 2600 Maine St., 62301. Tel: 217-222-3155; Fax: 217-222-3584. Email: church@cospq.org. Web: www.cospq.org.
School—(Grades PreK-8), 2500 Maine St., 62301. Tel: 217-223-1120; Fax: 217-223-1173. Web: www-.stpeterschool.com. Sisters 1; Lay Teachers 23; Students 409.
Catechesis/Religious Program—Students 113.

11—ST. ROSE OF LIMA (1892), (Irish), Merged with St. John the Baptist, Quincy to form All Saints, Quincy.

RAMSEY, FAYETTE CO., ST. JOSEPH (1870), (German—Irish), [CEM] Rev. Joseph Havrilka, Parochial Admin.
Res.: 118 E. Main, P.O. Box 455, 62080. Tel: 618-423-2424. Email: st.josephschurch_ramsey@yahoo.com.
Catechesis/Religious Program—Students 32.

RAYMOND, MONTGOMERY CO., ST. RAYMOND (1874) [CEM] Rev. Gerald L. Bunse, Admin.; Deacon Patrick J. O'Toole.
Office: P.O. Box 349, 62560.
Church: 306 S. McElroy, P.O. Box 349, 62560. Tel: 217-854-7151.
Catechesis/Religious Program—Students 33.

RIVERTON, SANGAMON CO., ST. JAMES (1871) Rev. Joseph G. Ring; Deacon Roch Magerl.
Res.: 112 N. Sixth St., P.O. Box 590, 62561-0590. Tel: 217-629-7717; Fax: 217-391-6590. Email: stjamesrctry@gcctv.com. Web: www.stjamesrivertonil.org.
Catechesis/Religious Program—Tel: 217-629-7717. Bro. Anthony Joseph McCoy, F.F.S.C., D.R.E. Lay Teachers 9; Students 79.

ROBINSON, CRAWFORD CO., ST. ELIZABETH (1907) Rev. William J. Overmann.
Res.: 207 E. Walnut St., 62454. Tel: 618-544-7526. Web: www.crawfordcountycatholics.com.
Catechesis/Religious Program—Fax: 618-544-9327. Students 105.

ROCHESTER, SANGAMON CO., ST. JUDE (1976) Rev. R. Dean Probst; Deacon Thomas A. Walker.
Res.: 633 S. Walnut St., 62563. Tel: 217-498-7133; Fax: 217-498-7180. Web: www.rochesterstjude.com.
Parish Center—635 S. Walnut St., 62563. Tel: 217-498-9524.
Catechesis/Religious Program—Tel: 217-498-9197. Students 306.

ST. ELMO, FAYETTE CO.

1—ST. BONAVENTURE (1843), (Irish—German), [CEM] Closed. For inquiries for parish records please see St. Mary, St. Elmo.

2—ST. MARY (1904), (German), Rev. Joseph Simburger, Admin.
Res.: 216 N. Ninth, Altamont, 62411. Tel: 618-483-5346; Fax: 618-483-5345.
Catechesis/Religious Program—Students 5.

ST. JACOB, MADISON CO., ST. JAMES (1894) Rev. Msgr. Kenneth C. Steffen, Parochial Admin.
Res.: 120 N. Windmill St., Box 457, Marine, 62061. Tel: 618-887-4535.
Catechesis/Religious Program—Students 22.

SHELBYVILLE, SHELBY CO., IMMACULATE CONCEPTION (1879) Rev. Donald L. Wolford; Deacon John M. O'Brien.
Res.: N. Rte. 128, P.O. Box 233, 62565. Tel: 217-774-3434; Fax: 217-774-3516. Email: icchurch@consolidated.net.
Catechesis/Religious Program—Students 35.

SHERMAN, SANGAMON CO., ST. JOHN VIANNEY (1931) [CEM] Rev. Msgr. Carl A. Kemme; Deacon David G. Sorrell.
Res.: 712 Lost Tree Dr., 62684. Tel: 217-523-3816; Fax: 217-523-3954. Email: parish@sjv.dio.org. Web: sjv.dio.org.
Catechesis/Religious Program—Students 150.

SHIPMAN, MACOUPIN CO., ST. DENIS (1876) [CEM] Closed. For inquiries for parish records contact the chancery.

SHUMWAY, EFFINGHAM CO., ANNUNCIATION (1879) [CEM] Rev. Msgr. Leo J. Enlow.
Res.: P.O. Box 96, 62461. Tel: 217-868-2752.
Catechesis/Religious Program—Tel: 618-487-5503. Students 51.

SIGEL, SHELBY CO., ST. MICHAEL THE ARCHANGEL (1867), (German), [CEM] Rev. Robert L. DeGrand, Admin.
Res.: 200 N. Church, Box 68, 62462-0068. Tel: 217-844-3371; Fax: 217-844-2309. Web: www.fourparishes.com.
School—Tel: 217-844-2231. Lay Teachers 10; Students 98.
Catechesis/Religious Program—Students 161.

STAUNTON, MACOUPIN CO., ST. MICHAEL THE ARCHANGEL (1875) [JC 2] Rev. George Radosevich.
Office: 428 E. North St., P.O. Box 240, 62088-0240. Tel: 618-635-3140; Fax: 618-635-2958. Email: stmikeof@madisontelco.com.
Res.: 322 E. Main, 62088-0240. Tel: 618-635-8490.
Church: 415 E. Main St., 62088-1451.
School—(Grades K-8), 419 E. Main, 62088. Tel: 618-635-3210; Fax: 618-635-3210. Lay Teachers 7; Students 78.
Catechesis/Religious Program—Students 108.

STE. MARIE, JASPER CO., ST. MARY (1837), (French—German), [CEM] [JC] Rev. Allen M. Kemme.
Res.: 112 W. Embarras St., P.O. Box 68, 62459. Tel: 618-455-3155; Fax: 618-455-3665.
Catechesis/Religious Program—112 W. Embarras St., P.O. Box 68, 62459. Students 38.

STONINGTON, CHRISTIAN CO., HOLY TRINITY (1879), (Irish—German), Rev. Alan M. Hunter; Deacon Raymond L. Roth Jr.
Res.: 108 N. Elm St., P.O. Box 257, 62567. Tel: 217-325-3697.
Church: 308 N. Pine, 62567. Tel: 217-824-8178.
Catechesis/Religious Program—Students 26.

SULLIVAN, MOULTRIE CO., ST. COLUMCILLE (1892) Rev. John E. Sohm, Parochial Admin.
Res.: 516 W. Jackson, P.O. Box 464, 61951. Tel: 217-728-4040.
Catechesis/Religious Program—Students 37.

TAYLORVILLE, CHRISTIAN CO., ST. MARY (1845) Rev. Alan M. Hunter; Deacon Raymond L. Roth Jr.
Res.: 116 W. Adams St., P.O. Box 470, 62568. Tel: 217-824-8178; Fax: 217-824-8225.
School—(Grades PreK-6), 422 S. Washington, 62568. Tel: 217-824-6501; Fax: 217-824-2803. Lay Teachers 13; Students 105.
Catechesis/Religious Program—Students 109.

TEUTOPOLIS, EFFINGHAM CO., ST. FRANCIS OF ASSISI (1839) [CEM] Revs. Austin Albers, O.F.M.; Kenneth Rosswog, O.F.M.; Jeffry Holtman, O.F.M.; Bro. Paulinus Johnson, O.F.M.; Revs. Vernon Olmer, O.F.M.; Sylvano Pera, O.F.M.; Theodore Bracco, O.F.M.; Maria Wargolet, Liturgy Director/Music Dir.
Res.: 203 E. Main St., 62467. Tel: 217-857-6404; Fax: 217-857-1031.
Catechesis/Religious Program—Tel: 217-857-6477. Sr. Ann Siemer, S.S.N.D., D.R.E.; Lisa Siemer, C.R.E.; Sr. Ann Pierre Wilken, O.S.F., D.R.E. Students 678.

TROY, MADISON CO., ST. JEROME (1870) [CEM 2] Rev. Pat G. Jakel.
511 S. Main St., 62294.
Res.: 64 Westbrooke, 62294. Tel: 618-667-6571; Fax: 618-667-2697. Web: www.stjeromeparish.org.
School—St. John Neumann, (Grades K-8), 142 Wilma Dr., Maryville, 62062. Tel: 618-345-7230; Fax: 618-345-4350. Email: jholmes@sjncrusaders.org. Web: www.sjncrusaders.org. Teachers 16; Students 257.
Catechesis/Religious Program—Fax: 618-667-2697. Email: mchomko@stjeromeparish.org. Students 156.

TUSCOLA, DOUGLAS CO., FORTY MARTYRS (1865) Rev. Barry J. Harmon, Parochial Admin.
Res.: 201 E. Van Allen St., P.O. Box 440, 61953. Tel: 217-253-9012; Fax: 217-253-5010.
Catechesis/Religious Program—Students 108.

VANDALIA, FAYETTE CO., MOTHER OF DOLORS (1850) [CEM] Rev. Joseph Havrilka.
Res.: 322 N. Seventh St., P.O. Box 377, 62471. Tel: 618-283-0214; Fax: 618-283-0278. Email: motherofdolors@att.net. Web: www.motherofdolors.com.
Catechesis/Religious Program—Students 68.

VENICE, MADISON CO., ST. MARK (1871) Closed. For inquiries for parish records contact the chancery.

VILLA GROVE, DOUGLAS CO., SACRED HEART (1906) Rev. Paul H. Skelton.
Res.: 208 N. Pine, Box 17, 61956. Tel: 217-832-8352; Fax: 217-832-8352. Email: sacht@royell.net; sacredheart@dio.org.
Catechesis/Religious Program—Students 39.
Mission—St. Michael's Center St., Hume, Edgar Co. 61932. Tel: 217-887-2482.

VIRDEN, MACOUPIN CO., SACRED HEART (1914), (Slovak), St. Catherine's (1866) Merged in 1978. Rev. Daren J. Zehnle.
Res.: 721 N. Springfield, 62690. Tel: 217-965-4545; Fax: 217-965-3889. Email: sacht@royell.net. Web: sacredheart.dio.org.
Catechesis/Religious Program—Tel: 217-965-5370. Students 61.

VIRGINIA, CASS CO., ST. LUKE (1840) Rev. Christopher J. Brey.
St. Augustine, 320 N. Saratoga, Ashland, 62612. Tel: 217-476-8856.
Church: 240 E. Myrtle St., 62691. Tel: 217-371-4713.
Catechesis/Religious Program—Students 11.

WAVERLY, MORGAN CO., ST. SEBASTIAN (1856) [CEM] Rev. Angel Sierra.
Office & Res.: 404 E. Birch St., P.O. Box 20, New Berlin, 62670. Tel: 217-488-2410 (Rectory); 217-488-3545 (Office); Fax: 217-488-3545. Email: stsebastian@quadpastoralunit.com.
Church: 265 E. Elm St., 62692.
Catechesis/Religious Program— Clustered with Sacred Heart, Franklin.

WHITE HALL, GREENE CO., ALL SAINTS (1883) Rev. Henry Schmidt, Parochial Admin.
Res.: 414 Third St., Carrollton, 62016. Tel: 217-942-3551; Fax: 217-942-6767.
Church: S. Main St., 62092.
Catechesis/Religious Program—Mary Beth Hawkins, D.R.E. Students 25.

WILSONVILLE, MACOUPIN CO., HOLY CROSS (1926) Closed. For inquiries for parish records contact the chancery.

WINCHESTER, SCOTT CO., ST. MARK (1860) [CEM] Rev. Rodney A. Schwartz; Deacon Michael (Kim) Scott.
Res.: 108 Pearl St., 62694. Tel: 217-742-5224; Fax: 217-742-5224.
Catechesis/Religious Program—Students 40.

WITT, MONTGOMERY CO., ST. BARBARA (1905) [CEM] Closed. For inquiries for parish records please see St. Louis, Nokomis.

WOOD RIVER, MADISON CO.

1—ST. BERNARD (1919) Merged with St. Kevin, Alton to form Holy Angels, Wood River.

2—HOLY ANGELS (2005) Rev. James A. Flach.
Church & Res.: 345 E. Acton Ave., 62095. Tel: 618-254-0679 (Office); Fax: 618-254-2690.
Catechesis/Religious Program—Students 40.

Chaplains of Public Institutions

ALTON. *Alton State Hospital*. Attended by the Catholic Churches in Alton. Vacant.

HILLSBORO. *Graham Correctional Center*. Rev. Gerald Bunse, Chap., St. Mary Church, 310 Nobbe St., Farmersville, 62533-7832. Tel: 217-227-3349.

JACKSONVILLE. *Illinois School for the Deaf*, 453 E. State St., 62650. Tel: 217-245-6184. Attended by Our Savior Parish.
Illinois School for the Visually Impaired, 453 E. State St., 62650. Tel: 217-245-6184. Attended by Our Savior Parish.
Jacksonville Correctional Center, 453 E. State St., 62650. Tel: 217-245-6184. Rev. Jeffrey D. Long, Chap.
Jacksonville Developmental Center, 453 E. State St., 62650. Tel: 217-245-6184. Attended by Our Savior Parish.

MOUNT STERLING. *Western Illinois Correctional Center*, 401 W. North St., 62353. Tel: 217-773-3233. Rev. J. Thomas Henseler (PEO), Chap. Attended by Holy Family Parish.

QUINCY. *Illinois Veterans' Home*, 1901 N. 18th, 62301. Tel: 217-224-0591. Rev. Donald Blickhan, Chap.

TAYLORVILLE. *Taylorville Correctional Center*, 116 W. Adams St., P.O. Box 248, 62658. Tel: 217-824-8178. Attended by St. Mary Parish.

VANDALIA. *Vandalia Correctional Center*, 322 N. Seventh, 62471. Tel: 618-283-0214. Rev. Delix

Michel, S.S.L., Chap. Attended by Mother of Dolors Parish.

Special or Other Diocesan Assignment:
Revs.—
Janoski, Steven A., 718 S. 7th St., Unit #803, 62703-2249. Tel: 217-753-3239
Trojcak, Ronald, 34 Gablewood Ct., London ON N6G 2Z9 Canada. Tel: 519-473-5007

On Duty Outside the Diocese:
Rev. Msgr.—
Renken, John, V.G., St. Paul University, Faculty of Canon Law, 223 Main St., Ottowa ON K1S 1C4 Canada.
Rev.—
Gallenbach, Thomas, 7075 Del Ray, Las Vegas, NV 89117. Tel: 702-254-5488 (Home); 702-363-1902 (Office)

Military Services:
Rev.—
Bergbower, Daniel J., Chap. Air National Guard

On Sabbatical:
Rev.—
Habing, Paul

Absent on Leave:
Revs.—
Dennis, Thomas J.
Jenkins, J. Michael
Miller, Tyler
Muniz, Kevin M.
Schmidt, David

Retired:
Rev. Msgrs.—
Mank, Virgil W., V.F., 169 Shadow Point Dr., Wentzville, MO 63385. Tel: 636-856-0524
Sheridan, Paul W., St. Clare's Villa, 915 E. 5th St., Rm. 218, P.O. Box 340, Alton, 62002-0340. Tel: 618-465-5880
Revs.—
Bauer, Roy R., 1329 Catherine Ct., Quincy, 62301. Tel: 217-641-0617
Becker, Robert T., St. Joseph Home, 3306 S. Sixth St. Rd., 62703. Tel: 217-789-1201
Carberry, John, P.O. Box 7, Quincy, 62306-0007. Cell: 217-430-3998
Dahlby, Charles, St. Joseph Home, 3306 S. 6th St. Rd., 62703. Tel: 217-679-2083
Donohoe, Peter, 714 Douglas Pl., Alton, 62002. Tel: 618-463-0521
Heintz, Robert L., Fountain Four, Rm. 209, 1000 Airport Rd., Godfrey, 62035. Tel: 618-466-3391
Kennedy, John, 411 Spring Lake Dr., Quincy, 62305-1051. Tel: 217-224-5288
Knuffman, Donald E., 1509 S. 15th St., Apt. 3, Quincy, 62301. Tel: 217-257-5717
Kraft, Philip G., P.O. Box 7492, 62791. Tel: 217-793-3218
Kromenaker, Joseph, Villa Health Care West, 100 Stardust Dr., Sherman, 62684. Tel: 217-525-8665
McCarthy, Joseph F., P.O. Box 638, Burlington, VT 05402. Tel: 802-862-3138
Meehling, Donald J., Cathedral of the Immaculate Conception, P.O. Box 1667, 62705-1667.
Meyer, Bernard A., 4725 W. Quincy Ave., #207, Denver, CO 80236. Tel: 303-738-9936
Morelock, George L., 816 Chestnut Ct., Chatham, 62629. Tel: 217-697-8377
Nelson, Charles T., 26 Pearl St., Winchester, 62694. Tel: 217-742-3689
O'Hara, Martin, 108 Pine St., Stonington, 62567. Tel: 217-325-3697
O'Reilly, Joseph, 1319 Tendick St., #3, Jacksonville, 62650-3120. Tel: 217-243-5483
O'Shea, James D., 1729 Dial Ct., 62704-3501. Tel: 217-679-0501
Peters, David L., 14 Kaeser Ct., Highland, 62249. Tel: 618-654-6801
Porter, Robert N., 203 Elizabeth Dr., Litchfield, 62056-1786. Tel: 217-324-2247
Savoree, John M., 15980 S. 1100th Rd., Paris, 61944.
Schlangen, Louis, 1905 N. 2800th Ave., Loraine, 62349. Tel: 217-938-4344
Schmidt, Anthony, 823 S. 36th St., Apt. 214, Quincy, 62301. Tel: 217-228-1097
Schmidt, Carl, 509 N. Main St., Effingham, 62401. Tel: 217-342-6487
Simpson, Roger, 271 E. Myrtle St., Virginia, 62691. Tel: 217-452-3168
Sperl, August J., St. Francis Convent, 4849 La-Verna Road, 62707. Tel: 217-522-3386
Sullivan, Kevin B., P.O. Box 44304, Phoenix, AZ 85064. Tel: 602-614-1207

Permanent Deacons:
Deacons—
Baker, Dennis W., Our Lady of the Holy Spirit, Mt. Zion; St. Isadore, Bethany
Burns, Thomas G., Blessed Sacrament, Springfield
Cato, Jerry L., St. Cecilia, Glen Carbon
Corbett, Daniel L., St. Boniface, Edwardsville
Day, Larry, St. Joseph, Springfield
Ellerman, Michael P., Holy Family, Mt. Sterling
Ellerman, Terrence J., Blessed Sacrament, Quincy
Emmerich, Joseph, St. Anthony of Padua, Effingham
Erdmann, David R., Blessed Sacrament, Springfield
Esselman, John M., St. Brigid, Liberty
Hagen, Michael B., Blessed Trinity, Brussels; St. Francis of Assisi, Hardin
Harley, Roy, St. Agnes, Springfield
Hoefler, Benedict P., St. Aloysius, Springfield
Kessler, William E., St. Ambrose, Godfrey
Laabs, Allison (Al), Christ the King, Springfield
Lucia, Thomas S., Ss. Mary and Joseph, Carlinville
Magerl, Roch, St. James, Riverton
Mauer, William J., St. Jerome, Troy
Maynerich, Frank, Jr., St. Joseph, Chatham
Neuser, William K., St. Anthony of Padua, Quincy
O'Brien, John, Immaculate Conception, Shelbyville; Assumption of the Blessed Virgin Mary, Assumption; St. Francis DeSales, Moweaqua
O'Toole, Patrick J., St. Mary, Farmersville; St. Maurice, Morrisonville, St. Raymond, Raymond
Richardson, Kevin, St. Thomas the Apostle, Decatur
Roth, Raymond L., Jr., St. Mary, Taylorville; St. Rita, Kincaid; Holy Trinity, Stonington
Rupp, James, St. Charles Borromeo, Charleston
Scott, Michael (Kim), St. Mark, Winchester; St. Mary, Pittsville
Smith, Irvin (Larry), Cathedral of the Immaculate Conception, Springfield
Sorrell, David G., St. John Vianney, Sherman
Sullivan, Gregory, Saints James & Patrick Parish, Decatur
Walker, Thomas A., St. Jude, Rochester
Zimmerman, Wayne R., St. Francis Solanus, Quincy

INSTITUTIONS LOCATED IN THE DIOCESE

[A] SEMINARIES, RELIGIOUS OR SCHOLASTICATES

GODFREY. *Immaculate Heart of Mary Novitiate*, 4300 Levis Ln., 62035. Tel: 618-466-2233; Fax: 618-466-2430. Email: ominov@aol.com. Web: www.ominov.itgo.com/ominov.htm. Revs. Thomas C. Horan, O.M.I.; Rudolph Nowakowski, O.M.I.; Mark Dean, O.M.I. Priests 3; Clerical Novices 7.

[B] COLLEGES AND UNIVERSITIES

QUINCY. *Quincy University* (1860) 1800 College Ave., 62301. Tel: 217-222-8020; 217-228-5489. Web: www.quincy.edu. Robert Gervasi, Ph.D., Pres.; Revs. John Doctor, O.F.M., Vice Pres. Mission & Ministry; Philibert Hoebing, O.F.M., Assoc. Prof. Emeritus (Retired); John J. Lakers, O.F.M., Assoc. Prof. Emeritus (Retired); Joseph Zimmerman, O.F.M. (Retired); Bros. Jack Hardesty, O.F.M., Systems Coord. & AV Supvr.; Edward Marc Arambasich, O.F.M., Dir. Campus Ministry & Chap.; Terrence Santiapillai, O.F.M., Reference & Archive Asst., Brenner Library. Franciscan Friars, Sacred Heart Province. Priests 4; Brothers 3; Lay Administrators 134; Lay Teachers 52; Students 1,323.

[C] JUNIOR COLLEGES

SPRINGFIELD. *Springfield College in Illinois* (1929) 1500 N. Fifth St., 62702. Tel: 217-525-1420; Fax: 217-789-1698. Email: mjrappe@sci.edu. Web: www.sci.edu. William J. Carroll, Pres.; Rev. Msgr. David S. Lantz, Dir.; Ms. Nancy Weichert, Librarian. Priests 1; Dominican Sisters 1; Lay Teachers 55; Students 527.

[D] HIGH SCHOOLS, PRIVATE

SPRINGFIELD. *Sacred Heart-Griffin* (1895) 1200 W. Washington St., 62702. Tel: 217-787-1595; Fax: 217-787-9856. Email: smjg@shg.org. Web: www.shg.org. Sisters Margaret Joanne Grueter, O.P., Prin.; Katherine O'Connor, O.P., Pres.; Mr. Robert Brenneisen, Asst. Prin.; Mrs. Beverly Neisler, Vice Pres. for Institutional Advancement; Mr. Thomas Fiaush, Business Mgr.; Dr. William Moredock, Dir. Student & Family Svcs. Springfield Dominican Sisters. Sisters 9; Lay Teachers 54; Additional Support Staff 29; Executive Team 4; Students 793.

DECATUR. *St. Teresa High School* (1930) 2710 N. Water St., 62526. Tel: 217-875-2431; Fax: 217-875-2436. Email: stadmin@st-teresahs.org. Web: www.st-teresahs.org. Dr. Kenneth C. Hendriksen, Prin. & CEO; Laura Brosamr Senger, B.S., M.S., Librarian. Ursuline Sisters 1; Lay Teachers 30; Students 304.

JACKSONVILLE. *Routt Catholic High School* (1902) 500 E. College, 62650. Tel: 217-243-8563; Fax: 217-243-3138. Email: gthoroman@routtcatholic.com. Web: www.routtcatholic.com. Gale Thoroman, Prin.; Dee Arendt, Librarian. Lay Teachers 8; Part Time 10; Students 131.

QUINCY. *Quincy Notre Dame High School*, 1400 S. 11th, 62301-7299. Tel: 217-223-2479; Fax: 217-223-0023. Email: rheilmann@quincynotredame.org. Web: www.quincynotredame.org. Ray E. Heilmann, Prin.; Lori Shepard, Vice Prin.; Barb Lieber, Librarian. Priests 1; School Sisters of Notre Dame 1; Lay Teachers 25; Students 411.

[E] HIGH SCHOOLS, DIOCESAN AND PAROCHIAL

ALTON. *Marquette Catholic High School* (1927) 219 E. Fourth St., 62002. Tel: 618-463-0580; Fax: 618-465-4029. Email: htomerlin@yahoo.com. Web: alton-marquette.com. Michael Slaughter, Prin. Sisters 1; Lay Teachers 29; Students 264.

EFFINGHAM. *St. Anthony High School*, 304 E. Roadway Ave., P.O. Box 545, 62401. Tel: 217-342-6969; Fax: 217-342-6997. Web: www.stanthony.com. Rev. Msgr. Leo J. Enlow, V.F., B.A. Theology, Supt.; Marianne Larimer, Prin.; Roberta Meyer, Librarian. Priests 2; Lay Teachers 22; Students 214.

[F] ELEMENTARY SCHOOLS, PRIVATE

SPRINGFIELD. *Saint Patrick Catholic Grade School* (1910) (Grades K-8), 1800 S. Grand Ave. E., 62703. Tel: 217-523-7670; Fax: 217-523-0760. Email: runkelmj@spdom.org. Sr. Marilyn Jean Runkel, O.P., Bd. Chairperson. Lay Teachers 7; Students 78.

[G] THE CATHOLIC CHARITIES OF THE DIOCESE OF SPRINGFIELD IN ILLINOIS

SPRINGFIELD. *Catholic Charities of Springfield*, 120 S. 11th St., 62703. Tel: 217-525-0500; Fax: 217-525-0554. Email: zellers_ccspfld@hansoninfosys.com. Web: www.cc.dio.org. 1625 W. Washington, 62702. Danielle K. Zellers, Area Dir. Total Families Assisted 490; Total Staff 28.

Catholic Charities Administrative Office, 1625 W. Washington, 62702. Tel: 217-523-9201; Fax: 217-523-5624. Email: roach@cc.dio.org. Web: www.cc.dio.org. Mr. Steven E. Roach, M.S., Exec. Dir. Total Staff 20.

Crisis Assistance & Advocacy and Holy Family Food Pantry, 1023 E. Washington, 62703. Tel: 217-523-4551; Fax: 217-523-8425. Web: www.cc.dio.org. Staff 4; Total Assisted 53,900.

St. Clare's Health Clinic, 700 N. 7th St., Ste. A, 62702. Tel: 217-523-1474; Fax: 217-523-0194. Web: www.cc.dio.org. Staff 7; Total Assisted 4,000.

St. John's Breadline, 430 N. Fifth St., 62702. Tel: 217-528-6098; Fax: 217-528-3605. Email: stjohnsbreadline@sbcglobal.net. Web: www.cc.dio.org. Meals Served Annually 208,000; Total Staff 8.

BEARDSTOWN. *St. Anne Residence*, 309 E. Ninth St., 62618. Tel: 800-745-5194; Fax: 217-523-5624. Web: www.cc.dio.org. Mailing Address: 1625 W. Washington, 62702. Mr. Steven E. Roach, M.S., Exec. Dir. Residents 23.

CARLINVILLE. *Carlinville Catholic Charities* (1990) 525 W. Second S., 62626. Tel: 217-854-4511; Fax: 217-854-8049. Email: pope_cccarl@frontiernet.net. Web: www.cc.dio.org. Mailing Address: 1625 W. Washington, 62702. Ms. Patricia Pope, Area Dir. Total Staff 8; Total Assisted 29,200.

DECATUR. *Catholic Charities of Decatur* (1944) 247 W. Prairie Ave., 62523. Tel: 217-428-3458; Fax: 217-428-4415. Web: www.cc.dio.org. Mailing Address: 1625 W. Washington, 62702. Marie Rademacher, Area Dir. Total Assisted Annually 96,400; Total Staff 24.

Catholic Charities Resale Store & Food Pantry, 239 W. Prairie Ave., 62523. Tel: 217-428-3458; Fax: 217-428-4415. 1625 W. Washington, 62702.

EDWARDSVILLE. *Madison County Catholic Charities*, 500 N. Main St., 62025. Tel: 618-307-5420. Web: www.cc.dio.org. Mailing Address: 1625 W. Washington, 62702. Total Assisted 23,122; Total Staff 2.

EFFINGHAM. *Effingham Catholic Charities*, 1502 E. Fayette, 62401. Tel: 217-857-1458; Fax: 217-857-1481. Web: www.cc.dio.org. Mailing Address: 1625

W. Washington, 62702. Sr. Carol Beckermann, O.S.F., Area Dir. Total Assisted Annually 59,000; Total Staff 23.

GRANITE CITY. *Madison County Catholic Charities* (1942) 2105 State St., 62040. Tel: 618-877-1184; Fax: 618-798-4287. Web: www.cc.dio.org. Mailing Address: 1625 W. Washington, 62702. Total Assisted 4,400; Total Staff 17.

MATTOON. *Mattoon Catholic Charities* (1996) 4217 Dewitt Ave., 61938. Tel: 217-235-0420; Fax: 217-235-0425. Email: clark_ccmatt@consolidated.net. Web: www.cc.dio.org. Mailing Address: 1625 W. Washington, 62702. Sandy Clark, Area Dir. Total Assisted 29,400; Total Staff 8.

QUINCY. *Quincy Catholic Charities*, 620 Maine St., 62301. Tel: 217-222-0958; Fax: 217-222-8737. Web: www.cc.dio.org. Mailing Address: 1625 W. Washington, 62702. Total Assisted 9,100; Total Staff 8.

WOOD RIVER. *Society of St. Vincent de Paul (Diocesan Central Council)*, 5 Eastmoor Ct., 62095. Tel: 618-254-9095. Email: cg9095@aol.com. Charles Goersch, Pres.

[H] CHILDREN'S HOMES

ALTON. *Catholic Children's Home*, 1400 State St., 62002. Tel: 618-465-3594; Fax: 618-465-4023. Email: info@catholicchildrenshome.com. Web: www.catholicchildrenshome.com. Mailing Address: 1625 W. Washington, 62702. Mr. Steven Roach, Exec. Dir.; Candace Hovey, Admin. Special Education 71; Lay Teachers 13; Residents 30; Total Staff 91.

[I] GENERAL HOSPITALS

SPRINGFIELD. *St. John's Hospital* (1875) 800 E. Carpenter St., 62769. Tel: 217-544-6464; Fax: 217-535-3989. Email: robert.ritz@st-johns.org. Web: www.st-johns.org. Robert P. Ritz, Pres. & CEO; Mary Jo Wasser, Dir. Pastoral Care. Patients Assisted Annually 270,132; Bed Capacity 457; Staff 3,224.

St. John's College, Department of Nursing Tel: 217-544-6464, Ext. 45165; Fax: 217-757-6870. Marjorie Beyers, Ph.D., M.S.N., B.S.N., Interim Chancellor. Students 71.

ALTON. *Saint Anthony's Health Center* (1925) 1 Saint Anthony's Way, 62002-0340. Tel: 618-465-2571; Fax: 618-465-4569. Web: www.sahc.org. E. J. Kuiper, Pres. & CEO. Three Campuses: Saint Anthony's Hospital, Saint Clare's Hospital and Saint Anthony's Medical Mall. Sisters of St. Francis of the Martyr St. George 8; Bed Capacity 220; Patients Assisted Annually 108,512; Staff 820.

DECATUR. *St. Mary's Hospital*, 1800 E. Lake Shore Dr., 62521. Tel: 217-464-2473; Fax: 217-464-1616. Web: www.stmarysdecatur.com. Hospital Sisters of the Third Order of St. Francis 5; Patients Assisted Annually 132,845; Bed Capacity 226; Staff 1,200.

EFFINGHAM. *St. Anthony's Memorial Hospital*, 503 N. Maple St., 62401. Tel: 217-342-2121; Fax: 217-347-1563. Email: hospital@effingham.net. Web: www.stanthonyshospital.org. Daniel J. Woods, Pres. & CEO; Rev. Ralph Zetzl, O.F.M., Chap. Bed Capacity 146; Patients Assisted Annually 95,157; Staff 708.

HIGHLAND. *St. Joseph's Hospital*, 1515 Main St., 62249. Tel: 618-651-2600; Fax: 618-651-2533. Email: jjohnson@sjh.hshs.org. Web: www.stjosephshighland.org. Peggy Sebastian, CEO. Hospital Sisters of the Third Order of St. Francis 2; Patients Assisted Annually 35,197; Bed Capacity 25; Staff 250.

LITCHFIELD. *St. Francis Hospital*, 1215 Franciscan Dr., P.O. Box 1215, 62056. Tel: 217-324-2191; Fax: 217-324-3081. Web: www.stfrancis-litchfield.org. Daniel Perryman, CEO; Rev. Theodosius A. Schelich, O.F.M., Chap.; Sr. Mary Flynn, O.S.F., Religious Coord. Hospital Sisters of the Third Order of St. Francis 1; Patients Assisted Annually 55,500; Bed Capacity 25; Staff 294.

[J] SPECIAL CARE INSTITUTIONS

SPRINGFIELD. *Brother James Court* (1975) 2508 St. James Rd., 62707. Tel: 217-544-4876; Fax: 217-747-5971. Email: administrator@brotherjamescourt.com. Web: www.brotherjamescourt.com. Mr. Ron Wampler, M.A., Exec. Admin. Franciscan Brothers of the Holy Cross., Residence for Mentally Retarded Male Adults. Franciscan Brothers of the Holy Cross 2; Bed Capacity 99; Residents 98; Total Staff 105.

[K] HOMES FOR AGED

SPRINGFIELD. *St. Joseph's Home* (1903) 3306 S. Sixth St. Rd., 62703. Tel: 217-529-5596; Fax: 217-529-8590. Sr. M. Lenore Highland, C.S.F.N., Admin. & Pres. of Board. Residence for the Elderly & Nursing Home. Sisters of St. Francis of the Immaculate Conception 6; Sisters of the Holy Family of Nazareth 1; Bed Capacity 113; Residents 90; Staff 129; Total Assisted Annually 128; Total Staff 129.

[L] MONASTERIES AND RESIDENCES OF PRIESTS AND BROTHERS

SPRINGFIELD. *Franciscan Brothers of the Holy Cross* (1862) (America 1928) *St. James Monastery*, 2500 Saint James Rd., 62707-9736. Tel: 217-528-4757; Fax: 217-528-4824. Email: stjamesmonastery@franciscanbrothers.net. Web: www.franciscanbrothers.net. Bros. John Francis Tyrrell, F.F.S.C., Supr.; Stephen Bissler, F.F.S.C., Treas.; Christian Guertin, F.F.S.C., Vicar. Represented in Arch/Diocese: Springfield, IL; St. Louis, MO; Madison, WI Total in Residence 7.

Our Lady of Angels Friary, P.O. Box 2153, 62705. Tel: 217-522-9822; Fax: 217-522-5004. Email: seniorfriars@aol.com; kleni70138@aol.com. Web: www.quincy.edu/shp-friar/senior-friars/. Bro. Kevin Lenihan; Revs. Louis Antl; Robert Behnen, O.F.M.; Bros. Earl Benz, O.F.M.; Greg Bumm, Vicar; John Bush; Revs. Vincent Callahan; Thomas Carolan; Peter Fritz, O.F.M.; Charles Hart, O.F.M.; Roger Niemeyer, O.F.M.; John Sullivan, O.F.M., Guardian; Victorian Haladus, O.F.M.; Sylvester Micek; Andre Schludecker, O.F.M.; Melchior Toczek, O.F.M.; Method Wilson, O.F.M.; Michael Ewert, O.F.M.; Fred Schneider, O.F.M.; Victor Kingery, O.F.M.; Zachary Hayes, O.F.M.; Nick Meyer; Bros. Theo Ballmann, O.F.M.; Kevin O'Connell, O.F.M.; Joseph Weithman, O.F.M.; Dan Piasecki, O.F.M.; James Finnegan, O.F.M.; Michel LeMier, O.F.M. Retirement Community of Our Lady of Friars Minor (Sacred Heart Province). Priests 21; Brothers 13.

QUINCY. *St. Francis Solanus Friary* (1860) 1721 College Ave., 62301. Tel: 217-222-2898; Fax: 217-222-3020. Email: church@stfrancissolanus.com. Web: www.stfrancissolanus.com. Revs. Donald Blaeser, O.F.M.; Thomas Shaughnessy, O.F.M., Senior Parochial Vicar; James Wheeler, O.F.M., Parochial Vicar. Priests 3.

Holy Cross Friary, 720 & 724 N. 20th St., 62301. Tel: 217-223-9920; Fax: 217-223-9992. Web: www.qufriary.org. Revs. John Doctor, O.F.M., Vice Pres. Mission, Quincy Univ.; Kenneth Capalbo, O.F.M.; Gary Bernhardt, O.F.M.; Irenaeus Kimminau, O.F.M. (Retired); John J. Lakers, O.F.M. (Retired); Joseph Zimmerman, O.F.M., Vicar (Retired); Philibert Hoebing, O.F.M. (Retired); John Leonard Ostdiek, O.F.M. (Retired); Bros. Edward Marc Arambasich, O.F.M., Guardian, Quincy Fire Chap., & Campus Min., Quincy Univ.; Terence Santiapillai, O.F.M., Asst. Librarian/Archives, Quincy Univ. Priests 8; Brothers 2.

TEUTOPOLIS. *St. Francis Assisi Friary* (1839) 203 E. Main St., P.O. Box 730, 62467-0730. Tel: 217-857-6404; Fax: 217-857-1031. Email: stfrancischurch@mchsi.com. Revs. Austin Albers, O.F.M.; Sylvano Pera, O.F.M.; Joseph P. Carlos, O.F.M.; Ralph Zetzl, O.F.M.; Theodore Bracco, O.F.M.; Jeffrey Holtman, O.F.M.; Kenneth Rosswog, O.F.M.; Vernon Olmer, O.F.M.; Bro. Paulinus Johnson, O.F.M. Priests 6; Brothers 1.

[M] CONVENTS AND RESIDENCES FOR SISTERS

SPRINGFIELD. *Congregation of Our Lady of Charity of the Good Shepherd*, 725 S. 12th St., 62703. Tel: 217-544-4613; Fax: 217-544-5356. Email: csgshepherd@aol.com. Web: www.goodshepherdsisters.org. Sr. Clare Szlachetka, C.G.S., Supr., Contact Person. Sisters 5.

Daughters of Divine Love Congregation (1969) 1713 S. Lincoln Ave., 62704. Tel: 217-787-8648. Email: fcokwara@yahoo.com. Sisters 4.

Dominican Sisters of Springfield, Il, 1237 W. Monroe St., 62704. Tel: 217-787-0481; Fax: 217-787-8169. Email: srriley@spdom.org. Web: www.springfieldop.org. Sisters Rose Marie Riley, O.P., Prioress Gen.; Bargara Blesse, O.P., Vicaress Gen.; Judith Anne Haase, O.P., Prioress; Rev. Peter Witchousky, O.P., Chap.

Dominican Sisters of Springfield, Illinois. Motherhouse of the Springfield Dominican Sisters. Motherhouse and Novitiate of the Dominican Sisters of Springfield, Illinois. Sisters in the Congregation 247; In Motherhouse 110.

St. Francis Convent (1844, Congregation); (1875, Province) 4849 LaVerna Rd., P.O. Box 19431, 62794-9431. Tel: 217-522-3386; Fax: 217-522-2483. Web: www.hospitalsisters.org. Sisters Jomary Trstensky, O.S.F., M.H.A., M.S.N., Prov. Supr.; Helen Marie Plummer, O.S.F., Community Life Leader; Revs. Vincent Callahan, Chap.; Andre Schludecker, O.F.M., Chap. The Motherhouse of the Hospital Sisters of St. Francis. Sisters 84.

Other Locations: *St. Francis Convent*, 2101 Shabbona, 62702. Tel: 217-789-4936. Sisters 3. *St. Francis Convent*, 4145 Sunderland Dr., Decatur, 62526. Tel: 217-877-2278. Sisters 3. *St. Francis Convent*, 52 Fairview, 62711. *St. Francis Convent*, 75 Sunflower Dr., Highland, 62249. Tel: 618-654-9759. Sisters 2. *St. Francis Convent*, 2717 Arrowhead, 62702. Tel: 217-528-6492. Sisters 2.

Hospital Sisters of St. Francis-USA, Inc., St. Francis Convent, La Verna Rd., P.O. Box 19431, 62794-9431. Tel: 217-522-3386; Fax: 217-522-2483. Web: www.hospitalsisters.org.

Missionary Sisters of the Sacred Heart of Jesus "Ad Gentes", 260 N. Amos Ave., 62702. Tel: 217-726-8159. Email: hnamagda@yahoo.com. Sr. Magdalena Serrano-Paz, M.A.G., Local Supr. Sisters 3.

Ursuline Convent (1857) 4849 LaVerna Rd., P.O. Box 670, 62705. Tel: 217-492-5940; Fax: 217-492-5945. Sr. Brendan Jacoby, O.S.U., Prioress. Ursuline Nuns of the Roman Union in Community 6.

ALTON. *St. Clare's Villa*, 915 E. 5th St., 62002. Tel: 618-604-5066. Web: www.divineprovidenceweb.org. Sr. Agnes Marie Geringer, C.D.P., Contact Person.

St. Francis Convent (1923) 1 Franciscan Way, P.O. Box 9020, 62002-9020. Tel: 618-463-2750; Fax: 618-465-5064. Email: vocations@altonfranciscans.org. Web: www.altonfranciscans.org. Sr. M. Regina Pacis Coury, F.S.G.M., Prov. Supr. Sisters 110; Final Professed 89; Junior Professed 21; Novices 6; Postulants 3.

Ursuline Convent of the Holy Family of the Ursuline Nuns of the Roman Union, 845 Danforth St., 62002. Tel: 618-465-9112; Fax: 618-465-0358. Sr. Chabanel Mathison, O.S.U., Prioress. Sisters 15.

Queen of Peace Health Care Center, 845 Danforth St., 62002. Tel: 618-465-0791; Fax: 618-465-0792. Sisters 28; Total Staff 63.

[N] NEWMAN CENTERS

CARLINVILLE. *Blackburn College Newman Club* 2010 E. 1st South St., P.O. Box 647, 62626. Tel: 217-854-7151; Fax: 217-854-9228. Web: ssmjc.org. Chaplains 1; Students 200.

CHARLESTON. *Eastern Illinois University Newman Catholic Center* 500 Roosevelt Ave., 61920. Tel: 217-348-0188; Fax: 217-348-8964. Email: newman@eiunewman.org. Web: www.eiunewman.org. Rev. John M. Titus, Chap.; Mrs. Doris Nordin, Campus Minister; Mr. Roy Lanham, M.A., Dir.; Ms. Edrianne Ezell, M.Div., Instructor; Mr. Louis Albarran, M.A., Instructor.

DECATUR. *Millikin University Newman Catholic Community* Campus: 1184 W. Main St., 62522. Tel: 217-348-0188; Fax: 217-348-8964. Email: rlanham@eiunewman.org. Mailing Address: 500 Roosevelt Ave., Charleston, 61920. Tel: 217-348-0188. Mr. Roy Lanham, M.A., Campus Min.

EDWARDSVILLE. *Southern Illinois University Catholic Campus Ministry The Center for Spirituality & Sustainability*, P.O. Box 1059, 62026. Tel: 618-650-3205; Fax: 618-650-3264. Email: ccalzet@siue.edu. Web: www.siue.edu/religion/catholic. Claudia Calzetta, S.L., Dir. Campus Min. Jesuit Priests 2; Diocesan Priests 1; Total Staff 4.

JACKSONVILLE. *Illinois College Newman Catholic Community* 453 E. State St., 62650. Tel: 217-245-6184; Fax: 217-245-6185. Email: frlong@mchsi.com. Rev. Jeffrey D. Long, Chap.

MacMurray College Newman Catholic Community c/o 453 E. State St., 62650. Tel: 217-245-6184; Fax: 217-245-6185. Rev. Jeffrey D. Long, Chap.

[O] MISCELLANEOUS LISTINGS

SPRINGFIELD. *Catholic Care Center, Inc., Catholic Pastoral Center*, P.O. Box 3187, 62708. Tel: 217-698-8500, Ext. 195; Fax: 217-698-0802. Email: gfleck@dio.org. Web: www.dio.org. Mr. Leo A. Lenn, Pres.; John Maxwell, Treas. & Dir.; Rev. Msgr. Carl A. Kemme, Diocesan Admin.; Gregory K.J. Fleck, Exec. Sec. & Dir.; Hugh Graham III, Dir.; Thomas Reiser, Dir.; Marlene Mulford, Dir.

Diocesan Care Management, Inc., Catholic Pastoral Center, P.O. Box 3187, 62708. Tel: 217-698-8500, Ext. 195; Fax: 217-698-0802. Email: gfleck@dio.org. Web: www.dio.org. Rev. Msgr. Carl A. Kemme, Diocesan Admin., Pres. & Dir.; Mr. John J. Maxwell, CPA, Treas. & Dir.; Gregory K.J. Fleck, Exec. Sec. & Dir.; Mr. Thomas E. Reiser, Dir.

Dominican Sisters of Springfield in Illinois Charitable Trust (1998) Sacred Heart Convent, 1237 W. Monroe, 62704-1680. Tel: 217-787-0481; Fax: 217-787-8169. Email: srriley@spdom.org. Web: www.springfieldop.org.

Foundation for the People of the Diocese of Springfield in Illinois, Catholic Pastoral Center, 1615 W. Washington, 62702. Tel: 217-698-8500, Ext. 114; Fax: 217-698-0802. Email: sriedell@dio.org. Web: dio.org.

The Foundation for the People of the Roman Catholic Diocese of Springfield in Illinois

Hospital Sisters Health System (1978) 4936 LaVerna Rd., P.O. Box 19456, 62794-9456. Tel: 217-523-4747. Mr. Leo A. Lenn, Sr. Vice Pres., Treas. & Legal Svcs.

Hospital Sisters Mission Outreach Corporation, P.O. Box 1665, 62705-1665. Tel: 217-522-3387, Ext. 648; Fax: 217-523-4742. Email: mission_outreach@hsosf-usa.org. Web: www.mission-outreach.org. Bruce Compton, Pres. & CEO.

Hospital Sisters of St. Francis Foundation, Inc. (1984) 4936 LaVerna Rd., P.O. Box 19456, 62794-9456. Tel: 217-523-4747. Julie Harmala, Contact Person.

Hospital Sisters Services, Inc. (1983) 4936 LaVerna Rd., P.O. Box 19456, 62794-9456. Tel: 217-523-4747; Fax: 217-523-0542. Mr. Leo A. Lenn, Sr. Vice Pres., Treas. & Legal Svcs.

Hospital Sisters Tanzania (2001) *Saint Francis Convent*, La Verna Rd., P.O. Box 19431, 62794-9431. Tel: 217-522-3386; Fax: 217-522-2483. Email: jschneider@hsosf-usa.org. Web: www.hospitalsisters.org. Sisters Jomary Trstensky, O.S.F., M.H.A., M.S.N., Pres.; Janice Schneider, O.S.F., Sec. & Treas.

Jubilee Farm, NFP, 6760 Old Jacksonville Rd., New Berlin, 62670-4767. Tel: 217-787-6927. Email: jubilee.farm@comcast.net. Web: www.jubileefarm.info. Sr. Sharon Zaynac, O.P., Exec. Dir.

Leadership Conference of Women Religious, 1237 W. Monroe, 62704. Tel: 217-787-0481; Fax: 217-787-8169. Sisters Patricia Crowley, O.S.B., Chm.; Carol Bredenkemp, S.C.C., Sec.; Geraldine Wodarczyk, C.S.F.N., Vice-Chair; Mary Ann Falbe, O.S.F., Treas.

Sponsored Activity: Project IRENE Sr. Rose Mary Meyer, B.V.M., Project Dir.

Legion of Mary, 30 Monica Ln., 62702-4346. Tel: 217-544-9022. Elsie P. Venvertloh, Comitium Pres.

Priests' Purgatorial Society Catholic Pastoral Center, 1615 W. Washington, P.O. Box 3187, 62708-3187. Tel: 217-698-8500; Fax: 217-698-0802. Email: ckemme@dio.org.

**Springfield Developmental Center Ltd.* (1976) 4595 LaVerna Rd., 62707. Tel: 217-525-8271; Fax: 217-525-5801. Email: sdcstjames@aol.com. Dawn Blisset, Dir. Franciscan Brothers of the Holy Cross., Developmental Training Program for Developmentally Disabled Adults. Lay Staff 26; Clients 110.

Theresian Foundation, Inc., 1237 W. Monroe St., 62704. Tel: 217-726-5484; Fax: 217-726-5631. Email: 5dimensions@att.net. Web: www.theresians.org. Victoria S. Schmidt, Exec. Dir.

Theresians International, Inc., 1237 W. Monroe St., 62704. Tel: 217-726-5484; Fax: 217-726-5631. Email: 5dimensions@att.net. Web: www.theresians.org. Victoria S. Schmidt, Exec. Dir. Sacred Heart Convent

Villa Maria - Catholic Life Center (Retreat and Conference Center), 1903 E. Lake Shore Dr., 62712-5514. Tel: 217-529-2213; Fax: 217-241-2485. Email: msmith@dio.org. Mary Ann Smith, Dir.

Weber House - Weber Care Corporation, 2520 St. James Rd., 62707. Tel: 217-522-8406. Email: webercare@sbcglobal.net. Bro. John Francis Tyrrell, F.F.S.C., Pres.; Laura Rape, Prog. Coord.; Bro. Gerald Voycheck, Business Mgr. Bed Capacity 8.

ALTON. *Saint Anthony's Foundation* (1993) 1 Saint Anthony's Way, 62002-0340. Tel: 618-465-2571; Fax: 618-465-4569. Email: foundation@sahc.org. Web: www.sahc.org.

Affiliates: Saint Anthony's Health System and Saint Anthony's Health Center. E. J. Kuiper, Pres. & CEO.

Saint Anthony's Health System, 1 Saint Anthony's Way, 62002-0340. Tel: 618-465-2571; Fax: 618-465-4569. Web: www.sahc.org. E. J. Kuiper, Pres. & CEO. Affiliates: Saint Anthony's Health Center and Saint Anthony's Foundation and Campus Network Sisters of St. Francis of the Martyr St. George 8.

Saint Clare's Hospital, 915 E. Fifth St., P.O. Box 340, 62002-0340. Tel: 618-463-5150; Fax: 618-463-5641. Web: www.sahc.org. E. J. Kuiper, Pres. & CEO. A Division of Saint Anthony's Health Center.

St. Francis Day Care Center, 710 College Ave., P.O. Box 9020, 62002-9020. Tel: 618-463-2766; Fax: 618-465-5064. Sr. M. Martha Weber, F.S.G.M., Dir. Day Care Center Sisters of St. Francis of the Martyr St. George 3; Assisted Daily 142; Total Staff 29.

QUINCY. *Latin Mass Society of Quincy*, P.O. Box 3006, 62305-3006.

Quincy Ladies of Charity, 510 S. 4th St., 62301. Tel: 217-222-6359. Jan Barnard, Pres.

RELIGIOUS INSTITUTES OF MEN REPRESENTED IN THE DIOCESE

For further details refer to the corresponding bracketed number in the Religious Institutes of Men or Women section.

[1320]—*Clerics of St. Viator* (Chicago Prov.)—C.S.V.

[0510]—*Franciscan Brothers of the Holy Cross*—F.F.S.C.

[0520]—*Franciscan Friars* (Sacred Heart Province)—O.F.M.

[0800]—*Maryknoll*—M.M.

[0910]—*Oblates of Mary Immaculate* (Central Province)—O.M.I.

[0940]—*Oblates of the Virgin Mary*—O.M.V.

[0430]—*Order of Preachers (Dominicans)*—O.P.

[]—*The Priestly Fraternity of St. Peter*—F.S.S.P.

[0990]—*Society of the Catholic Apostolate*—S.A.C.

RELIGIOUS INSTITUTES OF WOMEN REPRESENTED IN THE DIOCESE

[0100]—*Adorers of the Blood of Christ* (Ruma, IL; Wichita, KS)—A.S.C.

[]—*Congregation of Daughters of Divine Love*—D.D.L.

[1710]—*Congregation of the Third Order of St. Francis of Mary Immaculate, Joliet, IL*—O.S.F.

[1830]—*Contemplative Sisters of the Good Shepherd*—C.G.S.

[1070-10]—*Dominican Sisters*—O.P.

[1070-13]—*Dominican Sisters*—O.P.

[1770]—*Hospital Sisters of Third Order of St. Francis*—O.S.F.

[]—*Missionary Sisters of the Sacred Heart of Jesus "Ad Gentes"*—M.A.G.

[3230]—*Poor Handmaids of Jesus Christ*—P.H.J.C.

[2970]—*School Sisters of Notre Dame* (St. Louis, MO)—S.S.N.D.

[0990]—*Sisters of Divine Providence* (St. Louis Prov.)—C.D.P.

[1570]—*Sisters of St. Francis of the Holy Family*—O.S.F.

[1580]—*Sisters of St. Francis of the Immaculate Conception*—O.S.F.

[1600]—*Sisters of St. Francis of the Martyr St. George*—F.S.G.M.

[3270]—*Sisters of the Most Precious Blood (O'Fallon, MO)*—C.PP.S.

[4110]—*Ursuline Nuns (Roman Union)* (Central Prov.)—O.S.U.

[14120]—*Ursuline Sisters Mount Saint Joseph*—O.S.U.

DIOCESAN CEMETERIES

SPRINGFIELD. *Calvary Cemetery Association*

CARLINVILLE. *Calvary Cemetery Association*

DECATUR. *Calvary Cemetery Association*

EDWARDSVILLE. *Calvary Cemetery Association*

LITCHFIELD. *Holy Cross Cemetery Association*

MOUNT STERLING. *Catholic Cemetery Association*

QUINCY. *Catholic Cemetery Association*

NECROLOGY

† Kekeisen, William, (Retired)—Died Aug. 29, 2009

An asterisk (*) denotes an organization that has established tax-exempt status directly with the IRS and is not covered by the USCCB Group Ruling.

Diocese of Springfield in Massachusetts

(Dioecesis Campifontis)

Most Reverend

TIMOTHY A. McDONNELL

Bishop of Springfield in Massachusetts; ordained June 1, 1963; appointed Titular Bishop of Semina and Auxiliary Bishop of New York October 30, 2001; consecrated December 12, 2001; appointed Bishop of Springfield in Massachusetts March 9, 2004; installed April 1, 2004. *Mailing Address: P.O. Box 1730, Springfield, MA 01102-1730.*

Most Reverend

JOSEPH F. MAGUIRE, D.D.

Retired Bishop of Springfield; ordained June 29, 1945; appointed Auxiliary Bishop of Boston and Titular Bishop of Mactaris December 1, 1971; consecrated February 2, 1972; appointed Coadjutor Bishop of Springfield with right of succession April 3, 1976; officially installed as Bishop of Springfield on November 4, 1977; retired December 27, 1991. *Res.: 76 Elliot St., P.O. Box 1730, Springfield, MA 01102-1730.*

LOVE GOD AND LOVE NEIGHBOR

ESTABLISHED JUNE 14, 1870.

Square Miles 2,822.

Comprises the Counties of Berkshire, Franklin, Hampden and Hampshire in the State of Massachusetts.

For legal titles of parishes and diocesan institutions, consult the Chancery Office.

Chancery Office: P.O. Box 1730, Springfield, MA 01102-1730. Tel: 413-732-3175; Fax: 413-737-2337.

Web: www.diospringfield.org

Email: mail@diospringfield.org

STATISTICAL OVERVIEW

Personnel	
Bishop	1
Retired Bishops	2
Priests: Diocesan Active in Diocese	92
Priests: Diocesan Active Outside Diocese	6
Priests: Diocesan in Foreign Missions	2
Priests: Retired, Sick or Absent	45
Number of Diocesan Priests	145
Religious Priests in Diocese	37
Total Priests in Diocese	182
Extern Priests in Diocese	8
Ordinations:	
Permanent Deacons	14
Permanent Deacons in Diocese	78
Total Brothers	14
Total Sisters	427
Parishes	
Parishes	86
With Resident Pastor:	
Resident Diocesan Priests	67
Resident Religious Priests	6
Without Resident Pastor:	
Administered by Priests	13
Missions	9
Closed Parishes	15
Professional Ministry Personnel:	
Brothers	2
Sisters	12
Lay Ministers	10
Welfare	
Catholic Hospitals	1
Total Assisted	172,612
Health Care Centers	1
Total Assisted	7,000
Homes for the Aged	9
Total Assisted	454
Residential Care of Children	1
Total Assisted	36
Day Care Centers	1
Total Assisted	18
Special Centers for Social Services	8
Total Assisted	40,550
Other Institutions	2
Total Assisted	803
Educational	
Diocesan Students in Other Seminaries	27
Total Seminarians	27
Colleges and Universities	1
Total Students	1,323
High Schools, Diocesan and Parish	4
Total Students	1,170
Elementary Schools, Diocesan and Parish	16
Total Students	4,046
Catechesis/Religious Education:	
High School Students	6,398
Elementary Students	12,822
Total Students under Catholic Instruction	25,786
Teachers in the Diocese:	
Priests	1
Sisters	26
Lay Teachers	357
Vital Statistics	
Receptions into the Church:	
Infant Baptism Totals	2,466
Minor Baptism Totals	125
Adult Baptism Totals	96
Received into Full Communion	153
First Communions	2,506
Confirmations	2,246
Marriages:	
Catholic	511
Interfaith	121
Total Marriages	632
Deaths	3,546
Total Catholic Population	217,391
Total Population	816,953

Former Bishops—Most Revs. PATRICK THOMAS O'REILLY, D.D., cons. Sept. 25, 1870; died May 28, 1892; THOMAS DANIEL BEAVEN, D.D., cons. Oct. 18, 1892; died Oct. 5, 1920; THOMAS M. O'LEARY, D.D., cons. Sept. 8, 1921; died Oct. 10, 1949; CHRISTOPHER J. WELDON, D.D., cons. March 24, 1950; retired Oct. 15, 1977; died March 19, 1982; JOSEPH F. MAGUIRE, D.D. (Retired), cons. Auxiliary Bishop of Boston, Feb. 2, 1972; installed Bishop of Springfield, Nov. 4, 1977; retired Dec. 27, 1991; JOHN A. MARSHALL, D.D., cons. Bishop of Burlington, Jan. 25, 1972; installed Bishop of Springfield, Feb. 18, 1992; died July 3, 1994; THOMAS LUDGER DUPRE, D.D., J.C.D. (Retired), ord. May 23, 1959; appt. Auxiliary Bishop of Springfield and Titular Bishop of Hodelm April 19, 1990; cons. May 31, 1990; appt. Bishop of Springfield March 14, 1995; installed May 8, 1995; resigned Feb. 11, 2004.

Vicars General—Rev. Msgrs. CHRISTOPHER D. CONNELLY, J.C.L., Vicar General and Moderator of the Curia, 65 Elliot St., P.O. Box 1730, Springfield, 01102-1730; LEO A. LECLERC, V.G. (Retired), Assumption of the Blessed Virgin Mary Parish, 104 Springfield St., Chicopee, 01013-2695.

Chancery Office—76 Elliot St., P.O. Box 1730, Springfield, 01102. Tel: 413-732-3175; Fax: 413-737-2337.

Vicar for Canonical Affairs and Chancellor—Rev. Msgr. DANIEL P. LISTON, J.C.L.

Vice-Chancellor—Rev. ROBERT W. THRASHER, J.C.D. (Retired).

Judicial Vicar—Rev. Msgr. JOHN J. BONZAGNI, M.Ed., J.C.L., J.D.

Episcopal Vicars—Vicars for the Clergy: Rev. Msgrs. GEORGE A. FARLAND; MICHAEL SHERSHANOVICH, Berkshire Vicariate; RONALD G. YARGEAU, Franklin-Hampshire Vicariate; DAVID J. JOYCE, Hampden East Vicariate; HOMER P. GOSSELIN, Hampden Central and Hampden West Vicariate.

Vicar for Religious—Sr. JUDITH O'CONNELL, S.S.J., Vicar, 65 Elliot St., P.O. Box 1730, Springfield, 01102-1730. Tel: 413-452-0609.

Diocesan Tribunal—Sr. CLAIRE LAPOINTE, S.A.S.V., J.C.L., 65 Elliot St., P.O. Box 1730, Springfield, 01102. Tel: 413-452-0664; Fax: 413-747-8482.

Judges—Rev. Msgrs. DANIEL P. LISTON, J.C.L.; CHRISTOPHER D. CONNELLY, J.C.L.; Revs. DANIEL R. FOLEY, J.C.D. (Retired); JOHN L. SULLIVAN, J.C.L. (Retired).

Promoter of Justice—Rev. DANIEL R. FOLEY, J.C.D. (Retired).

Defenders of the Bond—Rev. Msgr. CHRISTOPHER D. CONNELLY, J.C.L.; Sr. CLAIRE LAPOINTE, S.A.S.V., J.C.L.; Rev. ROBERT W. THRASHER, J.C.D. (Retired).

Procurators-Advocate—Rev. Msgr. JUAN GARCIA, C.R.I.C.; Revs. JEDDIE P. BROOKS; DANIEL B. BRUNTON (Retired).

Psychotherapeutic Counselor—Rev. J. DONALD R. LAPOINTE, L.I.C.S.W.

Auditors—Rev. STEVEN F. MCGUIGAN; Deacons LEO COUGHLIN; JOHN ANTAYA; GEORGE KEATOR; FRANCIS RYAN; THEODORE T. TUDRYN.

Psychological Experts—MARTIN J. MARKEY, Ph.D.; ROBERT SAISI, Ph.D., Ed.D.; DAVID ARMSTRONG, L.I.C.S.W.

Notary—Ms. CYNTHIA CLARK.

Presbyteral Council—Most Rev. TIMOTHY A. MCDONNELL; Rev. Msgrs. CHRISTOPHER D.

CONNELLY, J.C.L., Vicar Gen.; DANIEL P. LISTON, J.C.L.; LEO A. LECLERC, V.G. (Retired); JUAN F. GARCIA; MICHAEL SHERSHANOVICH; JOHN J. BONZAGNI, M.Ed., J.C.L., J.D.; DAVID J. JOYCE; Revs. THOMAS M. SHEA; JEFFREY A. BALLOU; ROBERT A. GENTILE JR.; STANLEY J. AKSAMIT; MICHAEL ZIELKE, O.F.M.Conv.; DAVID M. DARCY; JOHN K. SHEAFFER; GARY M. DAILEY; HOWARD W. MCCORMICK (Retired); JOHN A. ROACH; CHRISTOPHER A. MALATESTA.

Deans—Revs. BRIAN F. MCGRATH, Hampden West Deanery; ROBERT J. COONAN, Hampshire Deanery; TIMOTHY J. CAMPOLI, Franklin Deanery; CHRISTOPHER A. MALATESTA, Berkshire Deanery; ROBERT A. GENTILE JR., Greater Holyoke Deanery; Rev. Msgr. GEORGE A. FARLAND, Springfield Deanery; Revs. DAVID M. DARCY, Hampden Central Deanery; STEFAN J. NIEMCZYK, Hampden East Deanery.

Diocesan Consultors—Rev. Msgrs. CHRISTOPHER D. CONNELLY, J.C.L.; JOHN J. BONZAGNI, M.Ed., J.C.L., J.D.; LEO A. LECLERC, V.G. (Retired); JUAN GARCIA, C.R.I.C.; DANIEL P. LISTON, J.C.L.; DAVID J. JOYCE; Revs. CHRISTOPHER A. MALATESTA; BRIAN F. MCGRATH; ROBERT A. GENTILE JR.; HOWARD W. MCCORMICK (Retired).

Bishop's Commission for Clergy—Rev. Msgrs. CHRISTOPHER D. CONNELLY, J.C.L.; LEO A. LECLERC, V.G. (Retired); GEORGE A. FARLAND; DAVID J. JOYCE; JOHN J. BONZAGNI, M.Ed., J.C.L., J.D.; DANIEL P. LISTON, J.C.L.; Revs. DAVID M. DARCY; CHRISTOPHER A. MALATESTA; BRIAN F. MCGRATH; FRANCIS J. MANNING (Retired); THOMAS M. SHEA; WILLIAM A. TOURIGNY.

Bishop's Cabinet—Rev. Msgrs. CHRISTOPHER D. CONNELLY, J.C.L.; DANIEL P. LISTON, J.C.L.; LEO A. LECLERC, V.G. (Retired); Sisters JUDITH O'CONNELL, S.S.J.; M. ANDREA CISZEWSKI, F.S.S.J.; WILLIAM F. LABROAD JR.; PATRICIA FINN MCMANAMY, L.I.C.S.W.; PETER SCHMIDT; VICKIE RIDDLE; JEAN RACZKOWSKI; MARK DUPONT; Sr. CATHERINE HOMROCK, S.S.J.

Diocesan Diaconate Council—Rev. Msgr. JOHN J. BONZAGNI, M.Ed., J.C.L., J.D., Advisor; Deacon LEO COUGHLIN, Dir.

Diocesan Diaconate Formation Board—Rev. TIMOTHY J. MURPHY, Dir.; Deacon LEO COUGHLIN, Asst. Dir.

Diocesan Commission for Ecumenism—Rev. WILLIAM A. POMERLEAU, 76 Elliot St., P.O. Box 1730, Springfield, 01101. Tel: 413-732-3175; MARTIN PION.

Diocesan Charismatic Renewal—Rev. GERALD BRADY, Dir. (Retired), Mailing Address: Office and Resource Center, P.O. Box 4668, Springfield, 01101.

Diocesan Commission for the Liturgy—Revs. VERNON P. DECOTEAU; GEOFFREY J. DEEKER, C.S.S., Chm., 65 Elliot St., P.O. Box 1730, Springfield, 01101-1730. Tel: 413-452-0839.

Co Vicars For Clergy—Rev. Msgrs. GEORGE A. FARLAND; DAVID J. JOYCE, 65 Elliot St., P.O. Box 1730, Springfield, 01102. Tel: 413-732-3175.

Diocesan Pastoral Council—RICHARD BUTLER; RICO CIRICOLA; ROBERT DIGAN; LYNN DUBREUIL; F. WILLIAM EULIANO JR.; LISA FUSINI; ROBERT GRENIER; Deacon DONALD HIGBY; EVERETT HUME; Rev. CHRISTOPHER A. MALATESTA; LUIS NEVAREZ; PAUL PAJAK; CAROL PIROG; Sr. MARY QUINN, S.S.J.; RITA STANISIEWSKI.

Finance Officer—WILLIAM F. LABROAD JR., 65 Elliot St., P.O. Box 1730, Springfield, 01102. Tel: 413-732-3175.

Diocesan Offices and Directors

Apostolate to the Handicapped—Sr. JOAN MAGNANI, S.S.J., Dir., Bureau for Exceptional Children and Adults, 537 Northampton St., P.O. Box 1039, Holyoke, 01041. Tel: 413-538-7450 (Voice and TTY); Fax: 413-536-5691.

Apostolate of the Suffering—Bro. ROBERT J. LETASZ, S.O.D.C., Pres.; JEANNINE GAGNON, Sec., P.O. Box 535, Chicopee, 01021.

Building Commission—Rev. J. DONALD R. LAPOINTE, L.I.C.S.W., Chm., 65 Elliot St., P.O. Box 1730, Springfield, 01102-1730.

Building Consultant—RICHARD WILK.

Campaign for Human Development—KATHRYN BUCKLEY-BRAWNER, Dir., 65 Elliot St., P.O. Box 1730, Springfield, 01102. Tel: 413-452-0697; Fax: 413-746-3421.

Counseling Office—PATRICIA FINN MCMANAMY, L.I.C.S.W., Dir. Tel: 413-452-0624; Dr. ALFRED A. D'AMATO, Ed.D., L.M.F.T.; Mrs. ROSEMARY CASTONGUAY, M.Ed., L.M.H.C., 65 Elliot St., P.O. Box 1730, Springfield, 01102-1730. Tel: 413-452-0273; Fax: 413-747-0273.

The Catholic Charismatic Renewal of Springfield, Inc.—Rev. GERALD BRADY (Retired), Mailing Address: Office and Resource Center, P.O. Box 4668, Springfield, 01101.

Catholic Charities Agency—VICKIE RIDDLE, Dir., 254 Bridge St., Springfield, 01103. Tel: 413-452-0605.

Annual Catholic Appeal—65 Elliot St., Springfield, 01101. Tel: 413-452-0629; Fax: 413-732-4297. *Mailing Address: P.O. Box 1730, Springfield, 01102.*

Catholic Relief Services—KATHRYN BUCKLEY-BRAWNER, 65 Elliot St., P.O. Box 1730, Springfield, 01102. Tel: 413-732-3175.

Cemeteries—JOSEPH KOSTEK, Pres. Cemeteries, 65 Elliot St., Springfield, 01101-1730. Tel: 413-782-0349; Fax: 413-785-5449. Saint Michael's Cemetery, 1601 State St., Springfield, 01109. Tel: 413-733-0659. Gate of Heaven Cemetery, 421 Tinkham Rd., Springfield, 01129. Tel: 413-782-4731. St. Aloysius Cemetery, 1601 State St., Springfield, 01109. Tel: 413-733-0695. St. Benedict Cemetery, Liberty St., Springfield, 01104. Tel: 413-782-4731. St. Matthew Cemetery, 366 Springfield St., Springfield, 01109. Tel: 413-733-0659. Calvary Cemetery, Northampton St., Springfield, 01040. Tel: 413-733-8140. St. Mary Cemetery, 203 Southampton Rd., Westfield, 01085. Tel: 413-568-7775. Notre Dame Cemetery, Lyman St., South Hadley, 01075. Tel: 413-782-4731. Calvary Cemetery, Northampton St., Holyoke, 01040. Tel: 413-782-4731. Precious Blood Cemetery, Willimansett St., South Hadley, 01075. Tel: 413-782-4731. St. Rose Cemetery, Lyman St., South Hadley, 01075. Tel: 413-420-0001.

Censor of Books—Rev. MARK S. STELZER, S.T.D.

Clergy Counseling Service—Rev. Msgr. GEORGE A. FARLAND, Sacred Heart Rectory, 395 Chestnut St., Springfield, 01104. Tel: 413-732-3721.

Communications and Public Relations—MARK DUPONT, Dir. Tel: 413-452-0648; Sr. CATHERINE HOMROCK, S.S.J., 65 Elliot St., P.O. Box 1730, Springfield, 01102-1730. Tel: 413-737-4744; Fax: 413-747-0273.

Catholic Communications Corporation—MARK DUPONT, Pres.; Sr. CATHERINE HOMROCK, S.S.J., COO, 65 Elliot St., P.O. Box 1730, Springfield, 01102-1730. Tel: 413-737-4744; Fax: 413-747-0273.

Services—

Chalice of Salvation (Televised Mass)—Bro. TERRENCE A. SCANLON, C.P., Exec. Dir., 65 Elliot St., P.O. Box 1730, Springfield, 01102-1730. Tel: 413-452-0642.

Real to Reel (Television News Magazine)—MARK DUPONT, Exec. Producer, 65 Elliot St., P.O. Box 1730, Springfield, 01102-1730. Tel: 413-452-0648.

The Catholic Observer (Newspaper)—REBECCA DRAKE, Editor, 65 Elliot St., P.O. Box 1730, Springfield, 01102-1730. Tel: 413-452-0636.

Continuing Education for Priests—Rev. JOHN T. SMEGAL, St. Brigid Rectory, 122 N. Pleasant St., Amherst, 01004. Tel: 413-256-6181.

Office of Religious Education-CCD—Sr. PAULA ROBILLARD, S.S.J., Dir.; CAROLYN GROVES, Consultant, Mailing Address: 65 Elliot St., P.O. Box 1730, Springfield, 01102-1730. Tel: 413-452-0807; Fax: 413-452-0817; CHARLES CONAGHAN, Berkshire Consultant, 191 Elm St., Pittsfield, 01201. Tel: 413-443-3187.

Cursillo Movement—Deacon JOHN BLEDSOE, V.F., Dir. English-Speaking Cursillo Movement, 84 Bardwell St., South Hadley, 01075. Tel: 413-532-6671; MARY VAZQUEZ, Spanish-Speaking Cursillo Movement. Tel: 413-535-0163.

Diocesan Office of Black Catholic Ministry—MARION M. JOHNSON, Administrative Dir., 235 Eastern Ave., Springfield, 01109. Tel: 413-788-9790. Email: marionmarie@rcn.com. Web: www.diospringfield.org/ministries/bc.html.

Diocesan Office for Communications—MARK DUPONT, 65 Elliot St., P.O. Box 1730, Springfield, 01102-1730. Tel: 413-737-4744; Fax: 413-747-0273.

Education—Sr. M. ANDREA CISZEWSKI, F.S.S.J., Supt. of Schools; Dr. GAIL FURMAN, Asst. Supt. Student Svcs., 65 Elliot St., P.O. Box 1730, Springfield, 01102-1730. Tel: 413-452-0830; Fax: 413-452-0817.

Family Life Bureau—Deacon JAMES CONROY; MARY CONROY, 65 Elliot St., P.O. Box 1730, Springfield, 01102-1730. Tel: 413-732-3175.

Fiscal Affairs—WILLIAM F. LABROAD JR., Finance Officer, 65 Elliot St., P.O. Box 1730, Springfield, 01102-1730. Tel: 413-452-0687; Fax: 413-785-5449.

Holy Childhood Association—Rev. DONALD LAPOINTE (Retired).

Holy Family League of Charity—c/o Office of Catholic Charities, P.O. Box 1730, Springfield, 01102-1730. Tel: 413-732-3175.

Human Resources—PETER SCHMIDT, Dir., Office: 65 Elliot St., P.O. Box 1730, Springfield, 01102-1730. Tel: 413-452-0691.

Counselors—Dr. ALFRED A. D'AMATO, Ed.D., L.M.F.T.; Mrs. ROSEMARY CASTONGUAY, M.Ed., L.M.H.C., 65 Elliot St., P.O. Box 1730, Springfield, 01101. Tel: 413-452-0621; Fax: 413-747-0273.

Office of Lay Ministry Formation—Revs. WILLIAM E. CYR, Dir.; THOMAS LISOWSKI, Coord.

Massachusetts Catholic Conference—Rev. Msgr. CHRISTOPHER D. CONNELLY, J.C.L.; Sr. ANNETTE MCDERMOTT, S.S.J.; JOHN EGAN ESQ., 65 Elliot St., P.O. Box 1730, Springfield, 01102-1730. Tel: 413-732-3175.

Ministry to the Deaf—Sr. CAROL LAREAU, S.S.J., 34 Nye St., Springfield, 01104. Tel: 413-736-0020.

Ministry to the Divorced and Separated—Pastoral Ministry Office, 65 Elliot St., P.O. Box 1730, Springfield, 01102-1730. Tel: 413-732-3175.

Newman Apostolate and Campus Ministry—Rev. DOUGLAS MCGONAGLE, Dir., Newman Center, 472 N. Pleasant St., Amherst, 01002. Tel: 413-549-0300.

Office for the Protection of Children and Youth—PATRICIA FINN MCMANAMY, L.I.C.S.W., Dir., 65 Elliot St., P.O. Box 1730, Springfield, 01102-1730. Tel: 413-452-0624.

Office of Social Concerns—PATRICIA FINN MCMANAMY, L.I.C.S.W., Dir., 65 Elliot St., P.O. Box 1730, Springfield, 01102-1730. Tel: 413-452-0615.

Pastoral Ministry—Mailing Address: 65 Elliot St., P.O. Box 1730, Springfield, 01102-1730. Tel: 413-732-3175.

Permanent Diaconate—Rev. TIMOTHY J. MURPHY, Dir.; Deacon LEO COUGHLIN, Asst. Dir., 65 Elliot St., P.O. Box 1730, Springfield, 01102-1730. Tel: 413-452-0674; Fax: 413-747-0273.

Priests' Retirement Program—Rev. FRANCIS MANNING, Liaison, 65 Elliot St., P.O. Box 1730, Springfield, 01102-1730.

Pro-Life Commission—TIMOTHY BIGGINS, Chm., 65 Elliot St., P.O. Box 1730, Springfield, 01102-1730. Tel: 413-732-3175.

Propagation of the Faith—Rev. J. DONALD R. LAPOINTE, L.I.C.S.W., Dir., 65 Elliot St., P.O. Box 1730, Springfield, 01102-1730. Tel: 413-452-0675.

Refugee Resettlement Program/Immigration Services—Catholic Charities Agencies, Inc., 254 Bridge St., Springfield, 01103. Tel: 413-452-0605.

Office of Social Concerns—65 Elliot St., P.O. Box 1730, Springfield, 01102-1730. Tel: 413-732-3175.

Representative of the Bishop at—Mercy Hospital, Springfield: Dr. KEVIN SCHMIDT. Mont Marie Health Care Center: Rev. Msgr. DANIEL P. LISTON, J.C.L. Sisters of Providence Care Centers, Inc.: Rev. JOHN L. SULLIVAN, J.C.L. (Retired). Our Lady of Providence Children's Center, West Springfield: Rev. J. DONALD R. LAPOINTE, L.I.C.S.W. Sisters of Providence Health System: WILLIAM COLLINS.

Retired Priests' Service—Rev. FRANCIS J. MANNING (Retired).

Southeast Asian Apostolate—Rev. QUYNH DINH TRAN, Dir., St. Paul the Apostle Church, 235 Dwight Rd., Springfield, 01108. Tel: 413-737-4422; Fax: 413-746-8378.

Catholic Latino Ministry—Mr. ANDRES LOPEZ, Dir.; LUCY RAMOS, Exec. Sec., Saint Francis of Assisi Center, 254 Bridge St., Springfield, 01103. Tel: 413-452-0631; Fax: 413-747-0273. Email: hispanicmin@diospringfield.org.

The Saint Thomas More Society—Mr. WILLIAM KERN, Esq., Pres.

Bishop Marshall Center—Ms. MARGO MORAN, Dir., St. Michael's Cathedral, 260 State St., Springfield, 01105. Tel: 413-732-2301.

Springfield Diocesan Council of Catholic Women—MARY BLAIS, Pres., Mailing Address: Diocese of Springfield, P.O. Box 1730, Springfield, 01102-1730.

Victim Assistance Coordinator—PATRICIA FINN MCMANAMY, L.I.C.S.W.

Vocations—Rev. GARY M. DAILEY, 65 Elliot St., P.O. Box 1730, Springfield, 01102-1730. Tel: 413-452-0816; Fax: 413-452-0817.

Office of Youth Ministry—ANGEL DELGADO, Youth Min., 65 Elliot St., P.O. Box 1730, Springfield, 01101-1730. Tel: 413-732-3175; Fax: 413-732-1944.

CLERGY, PARISHES, MISSIONS AND PAROCHIAL SCHOOLS

CITY OF SPRINGFIELD

(HAMPDEN COUNTY)

1—ST. MICHAEL'S CATHEDRAL (1847) Rev. Msgr. Christopher D. Connelly, Rector; Sisters Margaret McNaughton, S.S.J., Pastoral Min.; Eileen Sullivan, S.S.J., Outreach Min. In Res., Rev. Msgr. Daniel P. Liston; Revs. Gary M. Dailey; Steven F. McGuigan. Res.: 260 State St., 01103. Tel: 413-781-3656; Fax: 413-788-7752.

Catechesis/Religious Program—Students 35.
Mission—St. Francis Chapel 254 Bridge St., Hampden Co. 01102-1730. Tel: 413-452-0631.

2—ALL SOULS (1908), (Spanish), Rev. Msgr. Juan F. Garcia (Peru); Rev. Diomedes Calle (Peru). In Res., Deacon Jose Rivera.
Office & Res.: 445 Plainfield St., 01107. Tel: 413-736-8208; 413-736-2167; 413-736-0076 (Res.); Fax: 413-731-0962 (Res.).
Catechesis/Religious Program—Students 35.

3—ST. ALOYSIUS (1873), (French), Merged with St. Matthew, Springfield, to form St. Jude, Indian Orchard.

4—BLESSED SACRAMENT (1953), (Hispanic), Rev. Msgr. Juan F. Garcia (Peru); Rev. Diomedes Calle (Peru); Deacons Genaro Medina; Osvaldo Ramos.
Pastoral Center & Res.: 445 Plainfield St., 01107. Tel: 413-736-8208; 413-736-2167; 413-736-0076 (Res.); Fax: 413-731-0962.
Catechesis/Religious Program—Tel: 413-736-8208. Maria Ramos, D.R.E. Students 84.

5—ST. CATHERINE OF SIENA (1961) Rev. John K. Sheaffer; Deacons Joseph M. Garde; John Antaya.
Res.: 1023 Parker St., 01129. Tel: 413-783-8619; Fax: 413-783-2344. Email: stcatherine1023@comcast.net. Web: www.scsparish.4Lpi.com.
Catechesis/Religious Program—Students 240.

6—HOLY CROSS (1949) Rev. J. Victor Carrier; Deacon William Toller.
Res.: 221 Plumtree Rd., 01118. Tel: 413-783-4111; Fax: 413-783-4112. Email: hcparish@hcparish.org. Web: www.hcparish.org.
Catechesis/Religious Program—175 Eddywood St., 01118. Tel: 413-796-7675. Students 173.

7—HOLY FAMILY (1901), (African American—Hispanic), Merged into St. Michael's Cathedral with records being kept at St. Michael's Cathedral, Springfield. Rev. Msgr. Christopher D. Connelly.
Res.: 235 Eastern Ave., 01109. Tel: 413-732-1422. Email: holyfamilyrectory@verizon.net.
Catechesis/Religious Program—Cyndi Roberson, D.R.E. Students 40.

8—HOLY NAME (1909) Rev. Msgr. David J. Joyce, Parochial Vicar; Rev. Mark M. Mengel, S.S.C., Admin.; Sr. Catherine Leary, S.S.J., Pastoral Min.; Mary Reale, Finance Mgr.
Res.: 323 Dickinson St., 01108. Tel: 413-733-5823; Fax: 413-788-6481.
Center—57 Alderman St., 01108. Tel: 413-734-7113.
Catechesis/Religious Program—Tel: 413-736-4145. Claudine Bouchard Collins, C.R.E. Students 89.

9—IMMACULATE CONCEPTION (1905), (Polish), Rev. Dariusz P. Wudarski, Admin.
Res.: 25 Parker St. (Indian Orchard), 01151. Tel: 413-543-3627; Fax: 413-543-4301. Email: deaconrod@comcast.net.
Catechesis/Religious Program—Mrs. Mary Arabik, D.R.E. Students 80.

10—ST. JOSEPH'S (1873), (French), Closed. For inquiries for parish records please contact St. Michael's Cathedral, Springfield.

11—MARY MOTHER OF HOPE PARISH, 840 Page Blvd., 01104.

12—ST. MARY'S (1948), Merged with Our Lady of Hope, Springfield to form Mary Mother of Hope Parish, Springfield. All records located at Mary Mother of Hope Parish, Springfield. Rev. Michael F. Bernier, Admin.
Res.: 840 Page Blvd., 01104. Tel: 413-739-0456; Fax: 413-733-6155. Email: stmary@the-spa.com. Web: www.stmary-springfield.org.
Catechesis/Religious Program—Tel: 413-736-1622; Fax: 413-736-9299. Lee Lyon, D.R.E. Students 190.

13—OUR LADY OF HOPE (1906), Merged with St. Mary's, Springfield to form Mary Mother of Hope Parish, Springfield. All records located at Mary Mother of Hope Parish, Springfield. Rev. Msgr. David J. Joyce. In Res., Rev. Donatus Ironuma.
577 Carew St., 01104. Tel: 413-739-7369; Fax: 413-788-9313. Email: olohope@yahoo.com. Web: olohope.com.
Catechesis/Religious Program—Students 83.

14—OUR LADY OF MT. CARMEL (1907), (Italian), Revs. Robert S. White, C.S.S.; Paul D. Burns, C.S.S.; Sr. Elizabeth A. Matuszek, S.S.J., Pastoral Assoc. In Res., Rev. Anthony M. Corigliano, C.S.S.
Res.: 123 William St., 01105. Tel: 413-734-5433; Fax: 413-731-0680. Email: olmcspfld@aol.com. Web: www.olmcspfld.com.
Catechesis/Religious Program—Tel: 413-204-7789. Email: loisdegray@yahoo.com. Web: www.olmcspfld-.com. Students 125.

15—OUR LADY OF THE ROSARY (1917), (Polish), [JC] Rev. Stanislaw Sokol.
Res.: 28 Underwood St., 01104. Tel: 413-733-0508; Fax: 413-733-7512.
Catechesis/Religious Program—Tel: 413-739-2210. Students 70.

16—OUR LADY OF THE SACRED HEART (1929) Rev. William A. Pomerleau; Michael Maggipinto, Business Mgr.
Office: 51 Rosewell St., 01109. Tel: 413-782-8041; Fax: 413-783-9150. Email: churchinfo@olshaa.com.
Res.: 417 Boston Rd., 01109. Tel: 413-782-8041; Fax: 413-783-9150.
Catechesis/Religious Program—Kim Zeno, D.R.E. Students 150.
Mission—St. Jude Indian Orchard (1998)

17—ST. PATRICK'S (1961) Rev. Francis H. Crombie; Deacon George Kozach. Tel: 413-783-2458.
Res.: 1900 Allen St., 01118-1820. Tel: 413-783-6201; Fax: 413-783-7787. Email: stpatspringfield@aol.com.
Catechesis/Religious Program—Alan E. O'Dell, D.R.E. Students 99.

18—ST. PAUL THE APOSTLE (1960) Rev. Quynh Dinh Tran, Admin.; Deacons Francis D. Rogers; Ly X. Cao.
Res.: 235 Dwight Rd., 01108. Tel: 413-737-4422 (Parish Office); Fax: 413-746-8378. Email: stpaulsapostle@aol.com.
Catechesis/Religious Program—Students 87.

19—SACRED HEART (1872) Rev. Msgr. George A. Farland. In Res., Rev. Mark S. Stelzer.
Res.: 395 Chestnut St., 01104. Tel: 413-732-3721; Fax: 413-733-5731. Email: shc395@aol.com.
Catechesis/Religious Program—Students 150.

20—ST. THOMAS AQUINAS (1908), (French—Vietnamese), Closed. For inquiries for sacramental records contact Blessed Sacrament, Springfield.

OUTSIDE THE CITY OF SPRINGFIELD

ADAMS, BERKSHIRE CO.

1—NOTRE DAME DES SEPT DOULEURS (1882), (French), Merged with St. Thomas Aquinas, Adams, to form Notre Dame des Sept Douleurs and St. Thomas Aquinas, Adams.

2—NOTRE DAME DES SEPT DOULEURS AND ST. THOMAS AQUINAS (1998) Merged see Pope John Paul the Great, Adams.

3—POPE JOHN PAUL THE GREAT PARISH, (Merged parishes of Notre Dame/St. Thomas Aquinas & St. Stanislaus Kostka) Rev. Daniel J. Boyle; Deacons Robert R. Moulton; Gregory Lafreniere.
P.O. Box 231, 01220-0231.
Catechesis/Religious Program—Jill Staffin, D.R.E. (K-6); Sue LaFrance, D.R.E. (7-11). Students 250.

4—ST. STANISLAUS KOSTKA (1902), (Polish), [CEM] Merged with Notre Dame des Sept Douleurs and St. Thomas Aquinas, Adams, to form Pope John Paul the Great, Adams.

5—ST. THOMAS AQUINAS (1875) Merged with Notre Dame des Sept Douleurs, Adams, to form Notre Dame des Sept Douleurs and St. Thomas Aquinas, Adams.

AGAWAM, HAMPDEN CO.

1—ALL SAINTS (2001) Closed. For inquiries for parish records contact Sacred Heart, Feeding Hills.

2—ST. JOHN THE EVANGELIST (1946) Rev. John J. Brennan; Deacon Paul Briere; Mary Scannell, Pastoral Min. In Res., Rev. Warren J. Savage.
Res.: 833 Main St., 01001. Tel: 413-786-8105; Fax: 413-789-6266. Email: info@stjohnevangelistchurch.org. Web: www.stjohnevangelistchurch.org.
Catechesis/Religious Program—Tel: 413-789-2484. Students 550.

3—ST. THERESA OF THE CHILD JESUS (1883) Merged with Saint Anthony Mission to form All Saints, Agawam. For inquiries for parish records please see Sacred Heart, Feeding Hills.

AMHERST, HAMPSHIRE CO., ST. BRIGID'S (1872) [CEM] Rev. John T. Smegal.
Res.: 122 N. Pleasant St., P.O. Box 424, 01004-0424. Tel: 413-256-6181.
Catechesis/Religious Program—Students 120.

BELCHERTOWN, HAMPSHIRE CO., ST. FRANCIS OF ASSISI (1926) Rev. Vernon P. Decoteau.
Res.: 10 Park St., P.O. Box 612, 01007-0612. Tel: 413-323-6272; Fax: 413-323-6272. Web: stfrancisbtown.org.
Church: 24 Jabish St., P.O. Box 612, 01007.
Catechesis/Religious Program—Mrs. Judy Trickey, C.R.E.; Joan Murphy-Quinn, C.R.E. Students 524.

BONDSVILLE, HAMPDEN CO.

1—ST. ADALBERT'S (1910) Closed. Sacramental Records at Saint Thomas Parish, Palmer.

2—ST. BARTHOLOMEW'S (1878) [JC], Merged with St. Thomas the Apostle, Palmer. All records will be transferred to St. Thomas the Apostle, Palmer. Rev. Eugene J. Plasse.
1076 Thorndike St., Palmer, 01069. Tel: 413-283-5091; 413-283-8841 (Church).
Catechesis/Religious Program—Students 16.

BRIMFIELD, HAMPDEN CO., ST. CHRISTOPHER'S (1953) Rev. Jeddie P. Brooks.
Church: 20 Sturbridge Rd., Rte. 20, P.O. Box 387, 01010. Tel: 413-245-7274; Fax: 413-245-7372. Email: saintchris@verizon.net. Web: mysite.verizon.net/saintchris.
Rectory—16 Sturbridge Rd., Rte. 20, P.O. Box 387, 01010-0387.
Catechesis/Religious Program—Students 146.
Mission—St. Monica Wales, Hampden Co. (Closed)

CHESHIRE, BERKSHIRE CO., ST. MARY OF THE ASSUMPTION (1926) [JC] Rev. David R. Raymond; Deacon Robert Hitter.
Res.: 159 Church St., 01225. Tel: 413-743-2110. Email: stmarys159@verizon.net. Web: stmaryscheshire.com.
Catechesis/Religious Program—Tel: 413-743-5423; Fax: 413-743-5423. Email: mtamosfarm@roadrunner.com. Students 129.

CHICOPEE, HAMPDEN CO.

1—ST. ANNE'S (1912) Revs. William C. Rousseau; Richard M. Turner, Parochial Vicar.
Res.: 30 College St., 01020. Tel: 413-532-7503; Fax: 413-532-5970. Web: stanneparishchicopee.org.
Catechesis/Religious Program—Tel: 413-533-8038. Students 205.

2—ST. ANTHONY OF PADUA (1926), (Polish), St. Mary of the Assumption and Nativity of the B.V.M., Chicopee merged into St. Anthony. All records located at St. Anthony of Padua, Chicopee. Rev. Benedict Fagone, O.F.M.Conv. In Res., Bro. Frank Grimaldi, O.F.M.Conv.
Res.: 56 St. Anthony St., 01013. Tel: 413-538-9475; Fax: 413-538-9859.
Catechesis/Religious Program—Tel: 413-534-1493. Students 77.

3—ASSUMPTION (1885), (French), Merged with Holy Name of Jesus, Chicopee. All records kept at Holy Name of Jesus, Chicopee. Rev. David M. Darcy. In Res., Rev. Msgr. Leo A. Leclerc (Retired); Rev. Gerard A. LaFleur (Retired).
Res.: 104 Springfield St., 01013. Tel: 413-592-1597; Fax: 413-592-1597. Email: assumption.chicopee@charter.net.
Catechesis/Religious Program—Tel: 413-592-9344. Students 83.

4—ST. GEORGE'S (1893), (French), Merged into Holy Name of Jesus, Chicopee. All records kept at Holy Name of Jesus, Chicopee. Rev. Robert H. Riel; Deacon Leo Bergeron.
Res.: 202 E. Main St., 01020. Tel: 413-598-8622; Fax: 413-592-8353. Email: stgeorgeparish@charterinternet.net. Web: www.st-georgechicopee.org.
See St. Joan of Arc/St. George School, Chicopee under St. Rose de Lima, Chicopee for details.
Catechesis/Religious Program—Tel: 413-592-4456. Students 52.

5—HOLY NAME OF JESUS (1838) [CEM], Merged with Assumption, St. George's & St. Patrick's, Chicopee. All records for these parishes will be located at Holy Name of Jesus, Chicopee. Rev. David M. Darcy.
Office: 33 South St., 01013. Tel: 413-594-8700; Fax: 413-592-3871. Email: holynamechicopee@aol.com. Web: holynameassumption.org.
School—(Grades PreK-8), 63 South St., 01013. Tel: 413-592-6857; Fax: 413-598-0150. Email: hnprincipal@aol.com. Patricia Kern, Prin.; Ms. Carol Ann Robitaille, Librarian. Lay Teachers 11; Students 160.
Catechesis/Religious Program—Students 147.

6—ST. MARY'S (1939), Merged into St. Anthony of Padua, Chicopee. All records kept at St. Anthony of Padua, Chicopee. Rev. Norman B. Bolton, Admin. (pro-tem); Deacon Joseph A. Smith, (Retired).
Res.: 840 Chicopee St., 01013. Tel: 413-532-1854.
Catechesis/Religious Program—Students 84.

7—NATIVITY OF THE BLESSED VIRGIN MARY (1897), (French), [JC], Merged with St. Anthony of Padua, Chicopee. All records kept at St. Anthony, Chicopee. Rev. Norman B. Bolton, Admin. (pro-tem).
Res.: 840 Chicopee St., 01013-2747. Tel: 413-532-1854; Fax: 413-533-5121. Email: rnativity9421@charter.com.
Catechesis/Religious Program—Tel: 413-536-3310.

8—ST. PATRICK'S (1872), (Irish), [CEM], Merged into Holy Name of Jesus, Chicopee. All records kept at Holy Name of Jesus, Chicopee. Rev. Richard M. Turner.
Res.: 319 Broadway, 01020. Tel: 413-592-4178; Fax: 413-592-4170. Email: stpatrick5@verizon.net. Web: saint-patrickchurch.com.
Catechesis/Religious Program—Tel: 413-592-4344. Students 175.

9—ST. ROSE DE LIMA (1909), (French), [CEM] Rev. William A. Tourigny; Deacon Leon Mireault.
Res.: 600 Grattan St., 01020. Tel: 413-536-4558; Fax: 413-534-9130. Web: www.strosedelima.org.
School—St. Joan of Arc/St. George School, (Grades PreK-8), 587 Grattan St., 01020. Tel: 413-533-1475; Fax: 413-533-1418. Email: sjsg@stjoan-stgeorge.org. Web: www.stjoan-stgeorge.org. Paula Jenkins, Prin.; Rene Ruel, Librarian. Lay Teachers 20; Students 355.
Catechesis/Religious Program—Students 238.

10—ST. STANISLAUS BASILICA (1891), (Polish), [CEM] Revs. Michael Zielke, O.F.M.Conv.; Mieczyslaw Wit, O.F.M.Conv.; Marek Stybor, O.F.M.Conv.; Piotr

Tymko, O.F.M.Conv.; Deacons Charles Wainwright; Joseph Peters.
Res.: 566 Front St., 01013. Tel: 413-594-6669; Fax: 413-594-5259.
School—(Grades PreK-8), 534 Front St., 01013. Tel: 413-592-5135; Fax: 413-598-0187. Sr. Cecelia Haier, F.S.S.J., Prin. Franciscan Sisters of St. Joseph 2; Lay Teachers 28; Students 399.
Catechesis/Religious Program—Students 149.

DALTON, BERKSHIRE CO., ST. AGNES (1907) Rev. Christopher A. Malatesta; Deacons Pasqual Baldasaro; George Morrell.
Res.: 489 Main St., 01226. Tel: 413-684-0125; Fax: 413-684-0734. Email: stagnes@stagnes.cc.com. Web: www.stagnes.cc.com.
School—(Grades K-8), 30 Carson St., 01226. Tel: 413-684-3143; Fax: 413-684-3124. Theresa Dudziak, Prin. Sisters of St. Joseph 1; Lay Teachers 12; Students 125.
Catechesis/Religious Program—513 Main St., 01226. Tel: 413-684-1803. Students 500.
Chapel—St. Patrick Chapel 43 Church St., Hinsdale, 01235.

EAST LONGMEADOW, HAMPDEN CO., ST. MICHAEL'S (1894) Rev. James J. Scahill; Sisters Mary McGeer, S.S.J., Pastoral Assoc.; Betty Broughan, S.S.J., Pastoral Assoc.
Res. & Mailing Address: 128 Maple St., 01028. Tel: 413-525-4253; Fax: 413-525-2443. Email: stmichaelselong@aol.com.
Catechesis/Religious Program—Tel: 413-525-0371. Miss Rose Stella, D.R.E. Students 1,277.

EASTHAMPTON, HAMPSHIRE CO.
1—IMMACULATE CONCEPTION (1871) [CEM] Rev. Eugene D. Honan.
Res.: 33 Adams St., 01027. Tel: 413-527-9778; Fax: 413-527-9353. Email: icchurch@charter.net. Web: icparisheasthampton.org.
Catechesis/Religious Program—11 Clifford St., 01027. Tel: 413-527-7222. Students 284.
2—OUR LADY OF GOOD COUNSEL (1906), (French), Rev. Thomas R. Champigny.
Res.: 35 Pleasant St., 01027. Tel: 413-527-9588; Fax: 413-529-0517. Email: ndparish@charter.net. Web: www.notredameparish.us.
School—Our Lady's Child Care Center Perri Taylor, Dir. (Child Care). Lay Teachers 5; Students 23.
Catechesis/Religious Program—Email: ndparishgof@charter.net. Students 150.
3—SACRED HEART (1909), (Polish), [CEM] Rev. James A. Sipitkowski.
Res.: 33 Knipfer Ave., 01027. Tel: 413-527-9036; Fax: 413-529-0936.
Catechesis/Religious Program—Students 120.

FEEDING HILLS, HAMPDEN CO., SACRED HEART (1946) Rev. Steven Amo, Admin.
Res.: 1103 Springfield St., 01030. Tel: 413-786-8200; Fax: 413-786-7802. Email: office@sacredheartfeedinghills.org. Web: www.sacredheartfeedinghills.org.
Catechesis/Religious Program—Tel: 413-789-6705. Students 500.

FLORENCE, HAMPSHIRE CO., ANNUNCIATION (1878) Rev. John Gawienowski, Admin. Changed to a chapel under newly formed parish of Saint Elizabeth Ann Seton, Northampton. All records transferred to Saint Elizabeth All Seton, Northampton.
Res.: 87 Beacon St., P.O. Box 60055, 01062-0055. Tel: 413-584-1520; Fax: 413-586-7530. Email: annunciationchurch@verizon.net.
Catechesis/Religious Program—87 Beacon St., 01062-0055. Tel: 413-584-1520. Students 80.

GRANBY, HAMPSHIRE CO., IMMACULATE HEART OF MARY (1951) Rev. Charles H. Kuzmeski.
Res.: 256 State St., 01033. Tel: 413-467-9821; Fax: 413-467-2988. Email: parish@ihmgranby.org. Web: www.ihmgranby.org.
Catechesis/Religious Program—Tel: 413-467-3566. Email: faithformation@ihmgranby.org. Students 205.

GREAT BARRINGTON, BERKSHIRE CO., ST. PETER'S (1854) [CEM] Rev. William P. Murphy.
Res.: 16 Russell St., 01230. Tel: 413-528-1157; Fax: 413-644-8916. Email: stpeters@verizon.net.
Catechesis/Religious Program—Tel: 413-528-2037. Students 76.

GREENFIELD, FRANKLIN CO.
1—BLESSED SACRAMENT (1960) [CEM] Rev. Timothy J. Campoli.
Res.: 182 High St., 01301. Tel: 413-773-3311; Fax: 413-773-5785. Email: blessedsacrament@crocker.com. Web: blessedsacramentgreenfieldma.org.
Catechesis/Religious Program—Tel: 413-774-2918. Students 91.
2—HOLY TRINITY (1868) Rev. Msgr. Ronald G. Yargeau; Deacon Channing L. Bete Jr.
Res.: 133 Main St., 01301-3209. Tel: 413-774-2884; Fax: 413-774-3852. Email: churchlady@crocker.com. Web: www.holytrinitychurchgfld.org.
Catechesis/Religious Program—Students 175.
3—SACRED HEART (1912), (Polish), [CEM] Merged with St. Mary, Turner Falls & St. Ann, Turner Falls to form Our Lady of Peace, Turner Falls.

HADLEY, HAMPSHIRE CO.
1—HOLY ROSARY (1916), (Polish), Merged with St. John, Hadley, to form Most Holy Redeemer, Hadley.
2—ST. JOHN'S (1915) Merged with Holy Rosary, Hadley, to form Most Holy Redeemer, Hadley.
3—MOST HOLY REDEEMER (1998) [CEM] Rev. Shaun O'Connor.
Res.: 120 Russell St., P.O. Box 375, 01035-0375. Tel: 413-584-1326; Fax: 413-587-0224. Email: mhchurch@yahoo.com. Web: www.mhrparish.org.
Catechesis/Religious Program—Tel: 413-586-6209. Students 203.

HAMPDEN, HAMPDEN CO., ST. MARY'S (1951) [CEM] Rev. Timothy J. Murphy.
Res.: 27 Somers Rd., 01036. Tel: 413-566-8843; Fax: 413-566-5845.
Catechesis/Religious Program—Students 258.

HATFIELD, HAMPSHIRE CO.
1—HOLY TRINITY (1916), (Polish), [CEM] Rev. Robert J. Coonan.
73 Main St., P.O. Box 110, 01038. Tel: 413-247-3133; Fax: 413-247-5605. Email: holytrinityhatfield@yahoo.com.
Catechesis/Religious Program—Tel: 413-247-9079; Fax: 413-247-9080. Email: drehatfield@yahoo.com. Students 11.
2—ST. JOSEPH'S (1899) Rev. Robert J. Coonan.
Mailing Address: P.O. Box 34, 01038.
Res.: 11 School St., 01038. Tel: 413-247-9079; Fax: 413-247-9080. Email: stjosephhatfield@yahoo.com.
Catechesis/Religious Program—Students 102.

HAYDENVILLE, HAMPSHIRE CO.
1—ST. MARY'S (1889) [CEM] Merged with St. Catherine's, Leeds to form Our Lady of the Hills, Haydenville.
2—OUR LADY OF THE HILLS Rev. Galadima G. Goni, Admin. (pro-tem).
173 Main St., P.O. Box 277, 01039-0277. (Merged or yoked parishes St. Catherine of Alexandria Parish, Leeds & St. Mary of the Assumption, Haydenville.) In Res., Rev. Vincent M. O'Connor (Retired).
Catechesis/Religious Program—Students 101.

HINSDALE, BERKSHIRE CO., ST. PATRICK'S (1868) See separate listing. Now a chapel under St. Agnes, Dalton.

HOLYOKE, HAMPDEN CO.
1—BLESSED SACRAMENT (1913) Rev. Robert A. Gentile Jr. In Res., Rev. Richard A. Riendeau (Retired).
Res.: 1945 Northampton St., 01040. Tel: 413-532-0713.
School—(Grades K-8), 21 Westfield Rd., 01040. Tel: 413-536-2236; Fax: 413-534-0795. Anne Heston, Prin.; Kathleen Labon, Vice Prin. Sisters of St. Joseph 1; Lay Teachers 22; Students 303.
Catechesis/Religious Program—Fax: 413-322-7065. Roberta Cassidy, D.R.E. Students 122.
Mission—Holyoke Soldier's Home Chapel 110 Cherry St., Hampden Co. 01040. Tel: 413-532-9475.
2—HOLY CROSS (1905) Rev. Roland J. Galipeau; Deacon Thomas A. Callahan.
Church: 23 Sycamore St., 01040. Tel: 413-532-5661; Fax: 413-535-1759. Email: holycrholy@choiceonemail.com. Web: www.diospringfield.org/holycrossparish.
Catechesis/Religious Program—Tel: 413-536-8832. Dorothea MacNeil, C.R.E. Students 200.
3—HOLY FAMILY (1949) Closed. For inquiries for parish records please see Blessed Sacrament, Holyoke.
4—IMMACULATE CONCEPTION (1905) [JC] Rev. James Aherne, M.S.; Deacon Frederick Pelletier.
Res.: 54 N. Summer St., 01040-6279. Tel: 413-532-5784; Fax: 413-532-8852.
Catechesis/Religious Program—Students 47.
5—ST. JEROME (1854) [CEM] Rev. Anthony F. Cullen, Admin.
Res.: 169 Hampden St., 01040-4597. Tel: 413-532-6381; Fax: 413-540-9831. Email: st.jerome@comcast.net.
Catechesis/Religious Program—Students 44.
6—MATER DOLOROSA (1896), (Polish), [CEM] Revs. Alexander B. Cymerman, O.F.M.Conv.; Stanley Sobiech, O.F.M.Conv., Parochial Vicar; Bro. Stephen Murphy, O.F.M.Conv., Pastoral Assoc.
Offices—Tel: 413-532-7889; Fax: 413-538-6754.
Res.: 71 Maple St., 01041-4698. Tel: 413-532-8272.
School—(Grades K-8), 25 Maple St., 01040. Tel: 413-532-2831; Fax: 413-532-8588. Email: sunnyc515@aol.com. Web: www.mater-dolorosa.com. Sr. Corinne Gurka, F.S.S.J., Prin. Franciscan Sisters of St. Joseph 1; Lay Teachers 14; Students 273.
Catechesis/Religious Program—Tel: 413-532-8272. Students 115.
7—OUR LADY OF GUADALUPE (2001) [CEM 3] [JC] Revs. John G. Lessard-Thibodeau; Jose Bermudez.
Res.: 435 Maple St., 01040. Tel: 413-532-4282; Fax: 413-532-2182.
Catechesis/Religious Program—Students 154.
8—OUR LADY OF PERPETUAL HELP (1890), (French), Merged with Sacred Heart to form Our Lady of Guadalupe, Holyoke.
9—OUR LADY OF THE ROSARY (1886) Closed. For inquiries for parish records contact the chancery.
10—PRECIOUS BLOOD (1869) Closed. For inquiries for parish records contact Our Lady of Guadalupe, Holyoke.
11—SACRED HEART (1876) Merged with Our Lady of Perpetual Help to form Our Lady of Guadalupe, Holyoke.

HOUSATONIC, BERKSHIRE CO.
1—ALL SAINTS (1913), (Polish), Merged see Blessed Teresa of Calcutta.
2—BLESSED TERESA OF CALCUTTA PARISH, (Merged parishes of Corpus Christi & All Saints) Rev. William P. Murphy.
1085 Main St., P.O. Box 569, 01236. Tel: 413-274-3443.
Catechesis/Religious Program—Students 99.
3—CORPUS CHRISTI (1899) [CEM] Merged see Blessed Teresa of Calcutta.

HUNTINGTON, HAMPSHIRE CO., ST. THOMAS (1886) [CEM] Rev. Ronald F. Sadlowski; Deacon David Baillargeon.
Res.: 8 E. Main St., P.O. Box 547, 01050. Tel: 413-667-3350. Email: stthomashunt@aol.com.
Catechesis/Religious Program—Students 54.
Mission—St. John Middlefield St., Chester, Hampden Co. 01011.

LANESBORO, BERKSHIRE CO., NORTH AMERICAN MARTYRS (1969) Closed. For inquiries for parish records contact St. Mary, Cheshire.

LEE, BERKSHIRE CO., ST. MARY'S (1857) [CEM] Rev. Daniel R. Papineau.
Res.: 40 Academy St., 01238. Tel: 413-243-0275; Fax: 413-243-1926. Email: lcsmchurch@gmail.com.
School—(Grades PreK-8), 115 Orchard St., 01238. Tel: 413-243-1079; Fax: 413-243-1022. Email: jdavis@stmarysschoolonline.com. Web: stmarysschoolonline.com. Joan Davis, Prin. Lay Teachers 16; Students 155.
Catechesis/Religious Program—Tel: 413-243-1022. Students 135.
Mission—St. Mary of the Lakes Otis, Berkshire Co. Tel: 413-269-4200.
Mission—Saint Joseph Stockbridge, Berkshire Co. 01263. Tel: 413-298-3748.

LEEDS, HAMPSHIRE CO., ST. CATHERINE'S (1911) [JC] Closed. Yoked with St. Mary, Haydenville to form Our Lady of the Hills, Haydenville.

LENOX DALE, BERKSHIRE CO., ST. VINCENT DE PAUL'S (1904) Rev. Christopher J. Waitekus.
Mailing Address: P.O. Box 259, 01242-0259. In Res., Rev. Msgr. John J. Bonzagni. Tel: 413-637-1085.
Church & Res.: 29 Crystal St., 01242. Tel: 413-637-3525.
Catechesis/Religious Program—Tel: 413-637-0519. Students 26.

LENOX, BERKSHIRE CO., ST. ANN'S (1891) [CEM] Rev. Christopher J. Waitekus; Deacon George Keator.
Res.: 134 Main St., 01240. Tel: 413-637-0157; Fax: 413-637-2945. Email: stannlenox@verizon.net. Web: stannlenox.org.
Catechesis/Religious Program—Tel: 413-637-4027; Fax: 413-637-2945. Email: lindahermanski@yahoo.com. Students 329.

LONGMEADOW, HAMPDEN CO., ST. MARY'S (1936) Rev. Francis E. Reilly; Deacons Donald J. Higby; David Southworth.
Res.: 519 Longmeadow St., 01106. Tel: 413-567-3124; Fax: 413-567-4640. Email: parishoffice@stmarylong.org.
School—(Grades PreK-8), 56 Hopkins Pl., 01106. Tel: 413-567-0907; Fax: 413-567-7695. Email: stmarysacademy@comcast.net. Joan MacDonald, Prin. Lay Teachers 20; Students 242.
Catechesis/Religious Program—Tel: 413-567-3420; Fax: 413-567-0264. Students 1,070.

LUDLOW, HAMPDEN CO.
1—CHRIST THE KING (1948), (Polish), Rev. Raymond A. Soltys.
Res.: 41 Warsaw Ave., 01056. Tel: 413-583-2630; Fax: 413-583-2630.
Catechesis/Religious Program—Students 321.
2—SAINT ELIZABETH PARISH, 181 Hubbard St., 01056.
3—ST. JOHN THE BAPTIST (1904), (French), Merged with St. Mary, Ludlow to form Saint Elizabeth Parish. All records kept at Saint Elizabeth Parish, Ludlow. Rev. Msgr. Homer P. Gosselin; Deacons Edward Meyer; Norman Grodin. In Res., Rev. Norman B. Bolton.
Res.: 181 Hubbard St., 01056. Tel: 413-583-3467; Fax: 413-583-2036. Email: sjbrectory@yahoo.com.
School—(Grades PreK-8), 217 Hubbard St., 01056. Tel: 413-583-8550; Fax: 413-589-0544. Email: stjohnsprincipal@charterinternet.com. Web: diospringfield.org/sjbschool. Mrs. Shelly Rose, Prin. Lay Teachers 17; Students 274.
Catechesis/Religious Program—Tel: 413-529-9551.

Students 375.
4—ST. MARY (1968), Merged wtih St. John the Baptist, Ludlow to form Saint Elizabeth Parish, Ludlow. All records kept at Saint Elizabeth Parish, Ludlow. Rev. John E. Connors, Admin.; Deacon Robert L. Duval.
12 Cedar St., 01056. Tel: 413-583-2691; Fax: 413-589-1868. Email: diannestmarys@charter.net. Web: stmaryludlow.org.
Catechesis/Religious Program—Tel: 413-583-6710. Email: mbrownstmarys@charter.net. Maureen Brown, D.R.E. Students 348.
5—OUR LADY OF FATIMA (1948), (Portuguese), Rev. Vitor Oliveira.
Res.: 438 Winsor St., 01056. Tel: 413-583-2312; Fax: 413-547-0207.
Catechesis/Religious Program—Students 270.
MILLERS FALLS, FRANKLIN CO., ST. JOHN'S (1898) Closed. For inquiries for parish records contact Our Lady Peace, Turners Falls.
MONSON, HAMPDEN CO., ST. PATRICK'S (1878) [CEM] Rev. Jeddie P. Brooks; Deacon Bernard Pellissier; Wilfred Fredette, Pastoral Assoc.
Res.: 22 Green St., P.O. Box 473, 01057. Tel: 413-267-3622; Fax: 413-267-0272. Email: stpatmon@aol.com. Web: stpatrickmonson.org.
Catechesis/Religious Program—Students 251.
NORTH ADAMS, BERKSHIRE CO.
1—ST. ANTHONY OF PADUA (1903), (Italian), Merged see St. Elizabeth of Hungary, North Adams.
2—SAINT ELIZABETH OF HUNGARY PARISH Rev. William F. Cyr.
70 Marshall St., 01247.
3—ST. FRANCIS (1863) [CEM] Merged see St. Elizabeth of Hungary, North Adams.
4—HOLY FAMILY (1997) Merged with Our Lady of Incarnation, North Adams, to form Our Lady of Mercy, North Adams.
5—NOTRE DAME (1875) Closed. For inquiries for parish records contact the chancery.
6—OUR LADY OF MERCY (1997) Merged see St. Elizabeth of Hungary, North Adams.
7—OUR LADY OF MERCY SHRINE (1997), Consolidation of Holy Family, North Adams, and Our Lady of the Incarnation, North Adams. Rev. William F. Cyr.
1288 Massachusetts Ave., 01247. Tel: 413-663-7131; Fax: 413-664-4940.
8—OUR LADY OF THE INCARNATION (1955) Merged with Holy Family, North Adams, to form Our Lady of Mercy, North Adams.
NORTHAMPTON, HAMPSHIRE CO.
1—BLESSED SACRAMENT (1899), Merged with Saint Elizabeth Ann Seton Parish, Northampton. All records to Saint Elizabeth Ann Seton Parish, Northampton.
Res.: 336 Elm St., 01060. Tel: 413-584-1280. Email: blessedsacramentnorthampton@verizon.net.
Catechesis/Religious Program—Students 89.
2—SAINT ELIZABETH ANN SETON PARISH, Mailing Address: 3 Elm St., P.O. Box 180, 01061. Tel: 413-584-7310. 99 King St., 01060.
Chapel—Our Lady of the Annunciation, Changed to a chapel under newly formed parish of Saint Elizabeth Ann Seton, Northampton. All records transferred to Saint Elizabeth Ann Seton Parish, Northampton., 87 Beacon St., P.O. Box 60055, Florence, 01062-0055.
3—ST. JOHN CANTIUS (1904), (Polish), Merged with Saint Elizabeth Ann Seton Parish, Northampton. All records to Saint Elizabeth Ann Seton Parish, Northampton. Rev. Merle L. Lavoie (Retired).
Res.: 10 Hawley St., 01060. Tel: 413-584-1510; Fax: 413-586-5776.
Catechesis/Religious Program—101 King St., 01060. Tel: 413-584-7422. Students 25.
4—ST. MARY OF THE ASSUMPTION (1866), (Irish), [CEM], Merged with Saint Elizabeth Ann Seton Parish, Northampton. All records to Saint Elizabeth Ann Seton Parish, Northampton. Rev. William J. Hamilton; Mary McMahon, Pastoral Min.
Res.: 3 Elm St., P.O. Box 180, 01061. Tel: 413-584-7310; Fax: 413-584-4788.
Catechesis/Religious Program—Tel: 413-586-1111. Marie P. Noonan, D.R.E. Students 85.
5—SACRED HEART (1886), (French), Merged with St. Mary of the Assumption & St. John Cantius to form Saint Elizabeth Ann Seton Parish, Northampton. All records at Saint Elizabeth Ann Seton Parish, Northampton. Revs. John E. Connors; Sean O'Mannion, Parochial Vicar.
3 Elm St., P.O. Box 180, 01060. Tel: 413-584-7310. Church: 99 King St., 01060.
Catechesis/Religious Program—Students 35.
NORTHFIELD, FRANKLIN CO., ST. PATRICK (1973) [CEM] Deacon Arthur E. Ratte.
Res.: 80 Main St., 01360-1022. Tel: 413-498-2728; Fax: 413-498-2728. Email: stpats2@msn.com.
Catechesis/Religious Program—Students 17.
ORANGE, FRANKLIN CO., ST. MARY (1903) Rev. William H. Lunney; Deacon Joseph S. Bucci Jr.
Res.: 19 Congress St., 01364. Tel: 978-544-2900; Fax: 978-544-8105. Email: stmorang@earthlink.net.
Catechesis/Religious Program—Students 34.
PALMER, HAMPDEN CO., ST. THOMAS THE APOSTLE (1864) [CEM], Merged with St. Bartholomew's, Bondsville. Rev. Eugene J. Plasse.
Res.: 1076 Thorndike St., 01069. Tel: 413-283-5091; Fax: 413-289-1940.
Catechesis/Religious Program—Tel: 413-283-5651. Students 236.
PITTSFIELD, BERKSHIRE CO.
1—ST. CHARLES (1893) Rev. Peter A. Gregory; Sr. Barbara A. Faille, S.S.J., Pastoral Assoc.; Deacon William G. Moesley.
Res.: 89 Briggs Ave., 01201. Tel: 413-442-7470; Fax: 413-445-5267.
Catechesis/Religious Program—100 Briggs Ave., 01201. Tel: 413-442-0591. Students 276.
2—ST. FRANCIS (1960) Closed. For inquiries for parish records contact St. Joseph, Pittsfield.
3—HOLY FAMILY (1912), (Polish), Closed. For inquiries for parish records contact St. Joseph, Pittsfield.
4—ST. JOSEPH'S (1849) [CEM] Rev. Msgr. Michael Shershanovich; Deacon Pasqual Baldasaro. In Res., Rev. Geoffrey J. Deeker, C.S.S.
Res.: 414 North St., 01201. Tel: 413-445-5789; Fax: 413-443-5466. Email: msgrmike@berkshire.rr.com. Web: stjoemotherchurch.org.
Catechesis/Religious Program—Students 205.
5—ST. MARK'S (1913) Rev. John C. Salatino.
Office & Church: 400 West St., 01201. Tel: 413-447-7510; Fax: 413-448-2164.
Catechesis/Religious Program—400 Columbus Ave. Ext., 01201. Tel: 413-442-8444; Fax: 413-448-2164. Students 169.
6—ST. MARY THE MORNING STAR (1915) Closed. For inquiries for parish records contact St. Joseph, Pittsfield.
7—NOTRE DAME (1868) Closed. Sacramental Records at Saint Joseph, Pittsfield.
8—OUR LADY OF MT. CARMEL (1903), (Italian), Closed. For inquiries for parish records contact St. Joseph, Pittsfield.
9—SACRED HEART (1919) Rev. James K. Joyce; Deacon Robert Esposito; Sr. Kathryn Flanagan, Pastoral Min.; Deacon James A. Hager, Pastoral Min.; Kathleen Casella, Parish Nurse.
Res.: 191 Elm St., 01201. Tel: 413-443-6960; Fax: 413-442-9649. Email: pinkchurch@aol.com. Web: www.thepinkchurch.com.
Catechesis/Religious Program—Tel: 413-442-5564. Nicole Salvie, Admin. Asst.; Heather King, Admin. Asst. Students 410.
10—ST. TERESA (1926) Closed. For inquiries for parish records contact St. Joseph, Pittsfield.
RUSSELL, HAMPDEN CO.
1—HOLY FAMILY PARISH Rev. Ronald F. Sadlowski. P.O. Box 405, 01071-0405.
2—OUR LADY OF THE ROSARY (1969) [JC] Rev. Ronald F. Sadlowski; Deacon David Baillargeon.
Res.: 5 Main St., P.O. Box 16, 01071-0016. Tel: 413-862-4418. Email: ourladyofrosaryparish@juno.com.
Catechesis/Religious Program—Students 61.
SHEFFIELD, BERKSHIRE CO., OUR LADY OF THE VALLEY (1901) [CEM] Rev. Henry Kowalczyk (Poland); Deacons Herbert L. Cary; Richard Maginis.
Res. & Mailing Address: 99 Maple Ave., P.O. Box 515, 01257. Tel: 413-229-3028.
Catechesis/Religious Program—Students 98.
Mission—Immaculate Conception Main St., Mill River, Berkshire Co. 01244.
Mission—Our Lady of the Hills Beartown Rd., Monterey, Berkshire Co. 01245.
SHELBURNE FALLS, FRANKLIN CO., ST. JOSEPH'S (1883) Rev. Paul A. Bombardier; Deacon Thomas Rabbitt.
Res.: 34 Monroe Ave., 01370. Tel: 413-625-6405; Fax: 413-625-9951.
Catechesis/Religious Program—Students 55.
Mission—St. John the Baptist, (located in Colrain, MA), Colrain, Franklin Co. 01340.
Mission—St. Christopher Mailing Address: 01370. Charlemont, Franklin Co. 01339.
SOUTH DEERFIELD, FRANKLIN CO.
1—HOLY FAMILY PARISH, (Merged parishes of St. Stanislaus & St. James) Rev. Philippe D. Roux; Deacon Theodore J. Tudryn.
27 Sugarloaf St., 01373.
2—ST. JAMES (1895) Merged see Holy Family, South Deerfield.
3—ST. STANISLAUS B. AND M. (1908) [CEM] Merged see Holy Family, South Deerfield.
SOUTH HADLEY, HAMPSHIRE CO.
1—ST. PATRICK'S (1878) Rev. Thomas M. Shea; Deacon John Bledsoe.
Res.: 30 Main St., 01075. Tel: 413-532-2850; Fax: 413-552-0241.
Catechesis/Religious Program—Tel: 413-534-7080. Students 466.
2—ST. THERESA OF LISIEUX (1946) Rev. Richard A. Bondi.
Res.: 9 E. Parkview Dr., 01075-2103. Tel: 413-532-3228; Fax: 413-540-0964. Email: sainttheresachurch@comcast.net. Web: diospringfield.org/sttheresas.
Catechesis/Religious Program—Tel: 413-532-3228, Ext. 18; Fax: 413-540-0944. Anne Cormier, D.R.E. Students 95.
SOUTHWICK, HAMPDEN CO., OUR LADY OF THE LAKE (1951) Rev. Henry L. Dorsch; Deacon David Przybylowski.
Res.: 224 Sheep Pasture Rd., P.O. Box 1150, 01077. Tel: 413-569-0161. Web: ollsouthwick.org.
Catechesis/Religious Program—Lynda Daniele, D.R.E. Students 301.
STOCKBRIDGE, BERKSHIRE CO., ST. JOSEPH'S (1922) [CEM] Closed. Now a mission of St. Mary, Lee.
THORNDIKE, HAMPDEN CO., ST. MARY'S (1876) Closed. For inquiries for parish records contact the chancery.
THREE RIVERS, HAMPDEN CO.
1—ST. ANNE'S (1882), (French), [CEM], Merged with SS. Peter and Paul to form Divine Mercy Parish, Three Rivers. All records kept at Divine Mercy Parish, Three Rivers. Rev. Stefan J. Niemczyk.
Res.: 2230 Main St., 01080. Tel: 413-283-5041; Fax: 413-283-5041. Email: st.annes@samnet.net.
Catechesis/Religious Program—Tel: 413-283-7286. Students 90.
2—DIVINE MERCY PARISH, 2267 Main St., 01080.
3—SS. PETER AND PAUL (1903), (Polish), [CEM], Merged with St. Anne's to form Divine Mercy Parish, Three Rivers. All records kept at Divine Mercy Parish, Three Rivers. Rev. Stefan J. Niemczyk.
Mailing Address: P.O. Box 157, 01080.
Res.: 2267 Main St., 01080. Tel: 413-283-6030.
Catechesis/Religious Program—Tel: 413-283-4320. Students 195.
TURNERS FALLS, FRANKLIN CO.
1—ST. ANNE (1884), (French), [CEM] Merged with Sacred Heart, Greenfield & St. Mary, Turner Falls to form Our Lady of Peace, Turner Falls.
2—ST. MARY'S (1872) [CEM] Merged with Sacred Heart, Greenfield & St. Anne, Turner Falls to form Our Lady of Peace, Turner Falls.
3—OUR LADY OF CZESTOCHOWA (1909), (Polish), [CEM] Rev. Charles J. DiMascola.
Res.: 84 K St., 01376. Tel: 413-863-4748; Fax: 413-863-9263. Web: ourladyofczestochowa.org.
Catechesis/Religious Program—Students 129.
4—OUR LADY OF PEACE Rev. Stanley J. Aksamit.
Rectory—90 Seventh St., 01376. Tel: 413-863-2585; Fax: 413-863-8978. Email: frstan@ourladyofpeacetf.com. Web: ourladyofpeacetf.com.
Church: 80 Seventh St., 01376.
Catechesis/Religious Program—Carol Holubecki, D.R.E. Students 163.
WARE, HAMPSHIRE CO.
1—ALL SAINTS (1860) [CEM] [JC 2] Rev. Edward T. Fitzgerald.
Res.: 17 North St., 01082. Tel: 413-967-4963.
Catechesis/Religious Program—Students 145.
2—ST. MARY'S (1905), (Polish), [CEM] Rev. Jeffrey A. Ballou.
Res.: 60 South St., 01082. Email: smcrectory@comcast.net.
School—(Grades PreK-8), 59 South St., 01082. Web: www.stmarysware.org. Mrs. Paul Moran, Prin. Sisters of Immaculate Conception 4; Lay Teachers 13; Students 141.
Catechesis/Religious Program—Tel: 413-967-5913; Fax: 413-967-4679. Students 135.
3—OUR LADY OF MT. CARMEL (1871), (French), Closed. For inquiries for sacramental records contact All Saints, Ware.
WEST SPRINGFIELD, HAMPDEN CO.
1—ST. FRANCES XAVIER CABRINI PARISH, (Merged parishes of Immaculate Conception & St. Louis de France) Rev. Michael Lillpopp; Deacon Donald Philip.
495 Main St., 01089-3998.
Res. & Mailing Address: 475 Main St., 01089-3998. Tel: 413-736-4071; Fax: 413-734-5484.
Catechesis/Religious Program—Celeste Labbe, D.R.E. Students 36.
2—IMMACULATE CONCEPTION (1877) Merged see St. Frances Xavier Cabrini, West Springfield.
3—ST. LOUIS DE FRANCE (1895), (French), Merged see St. Frances Xavier Cabrini, West Springfield.
4—ST. THOMAS THE APOSTLE (1900) [CEM] Revs. Kenneth J. Tatro; Jonathan Reardon, Parochial Vicar; Deacon James Conroy.
Res.: 47 Pine St., 01089. Tel: 413-739-4779; Fax: 413-739-1608. Email: stthomassecretary@comcast.net.
School—(Grades PreK-8), 75 Pine St., 01089. Tel: 413-739-4131. Email: phottinssj@comcast.net. Sr. Patricia Hottin, S.S.J., Prin. Sisters of St. Joseph 5; Lay Teachers 23; Students 353.
Catechesis/Religious Program—89 Pine St., 01089.

Tel: 413-737-8267; Fax: 413-731-8768. Students 617.

WEST STOCKBRIDGE, BERKSHIRE CO., ST. PATRICK'S (1871) [CEM] Rev. Christopher J. Waitekus.
Res.: 30 Albany Rd., 01266. Tel: 413-232-4427; Fax: 413-232-4427. Email: stpatricksws@verizon.nt.
Catechesis/Religious Program—Students 17.

WESTFIELD, HAMPDEN CO.

1—ST. CASIMIR'S (1915) Merged with St. Peter's, Westfield to form St. Peter and St. Casimir, Westfield.

2—HOLY TRINITY (1903), (Polish), Revs. Rene L. Parent, M.S.; Lukasz Krzanowski, M.S., Parochial Vicar.
Res.: 335 Elm St., 01085. Tel: 413-568-1506; Fax: 413-572-2533. Email: htoffice@comcast.net.
Catechesis/Religious Program—Students 110.

3—ST. MARY'S (1862) Revs. Brian F. McGrath; James Longe, Parochial Vicar; Jose Alfredo Siesquen Flores (Peru); Deacon Pedro Rivera.
Res.: 30 Bartlett St., 01085. Tel: 413-562-5477; Fax: 413-562-5478.
School—St. Mary Elementary School, (Grades K-8), 35 Bartlett St., 01085. Tel: 413-568-2388; Fax: 413-568-7460. Sr. Christine Lavoie, S.S.J., Prin. Sisters 3; Lay Teachers 15; Students 185.
School—St. Mary Preschool, (Age 4 yrs.), 23 Bartlett St., 01085. Lay Teachers 2; Students 21.
High School—St. Mary High School, 27 Bartlett St., 01085. Tel: 413-568-5692; Fax: 413-562-3501. Mrs. Nichole Nietsche, Prin. Lay Teachers 17; Students 158.
Catechesis/Religious Program—Office of Rel. Educ., 86 Mechanic St., 01085. Tel: 413-568-1127; Fax: 413-562-5478. Mrs. Kay Mowatt, D.R.E. (Elementary); Mrs. Joanne Bagge, D.R.E. (High School). Students 684.
Convent—Sisters of St. Joseph 3.

4—OUR LADY OF THE BLESSED SACRAMENT (1910) Rev. Daniel S. Pacholec; Deacon Paul Federici.
Mailing Address: P.O. Box 489, 01086-0489.
Rectory—85 Ridgeview Terrace, 01085.
Church & Parish Center: 127 Holyoke Rd., P.O. Box 489, 01086-0489. Tel: 413-562-6978; Fax: 413-562-0399. Email: olbsoffice@aol.com. Web: diospringfield.org/olbs.
Catechesis/Religious Program—Tel: 413-562-3450. Email: olbsccd@verizon.net. Theresa Racine, D.R.E. Students 340.

5—ST. PETER AND ST. CASIMIR (2003) Rev. William H. Wallis.
Res.: 22 State St., 01085. Tel: 413-568-5421; Fax: 413-562-3879. Email: sspetetcas@comcast.net.
Catechesis/Religious Program—32 State St., 01085. Tel: 413-568-6261. Sr. Marcella Meluch, O.S.F., D.R.E. Students 182.

6—ST. PETER'S (1913) Merged with St. Casimir, Westfield to form St. Peter and St. Casimir, Westfield.

WILBRAHAM, HAMPDEN CO., ST. CECILIA'S (1951) Revs. Joseph M. Soranno; Mark Glover, Parochial Vicar; Sr. Mary McCue, S.N.D., Pastoral Min. Tel: 413-596-4232, Ext. 105.
Res.: 7 Maple St., 01095. Tel: 413-596-4232; Fax: 413-596-6272. Web: www.saintceciliawilbraham.org.
Catechesis/Religious Program—42 Main St., 01095. Tel: 413-596-4232, Ext. 104. Sr. Mary Patrice Mahoney, S.N.D., D.R.E. Students 1,260.

WILLIAMSTOWN, BERKSHIRE CO.

1—SS. PATRICK AND RAPHAEL (1997) Rev. Wayne C. Biernat; Deacon Francis Ryan.
Res. & Mailing Address: 54 Southworth St., 01267-2414. Tel: 413-458-4946; Fax: 413-458-4954. Email: saintpatrickandraphael@gmail.com. Web: www.williamstowncatholics.org.
Catechesis/Religious Program—53 Southworth St., 01267. Tel: 413-458-5443. Students 103.

2—ST. PATRICK'S (1887) Merged with St. Raphael, Williamstown, to form SS. Patrick and Raphael, Williamstown.

3—ST. RAPHAEL (1891) Merged with St. Patrick, Williamstown, to form SS. Patrick and Raphael, Williamstown.

Chaplains of Public Institutions

SPRINGFIELD. *Baystate Medical Center*, Office of Pastoral Ministry at Baystate, 01199.
Olympus Specialty Hospital, Sacred Heart Rectory, 395 Chestnut St., 01104. Tel: 413-732-3721.

HOLYOKE. *Soldiers' Home*, Tel: 413-532-0713. Served by Blessed Sacrament Parish.

MONSON. *State Hospital*. Bureau for Exceptional Children and Adults.
537 Northampton St., Box 1039, Holyoke, 01041. Tel: 413-538-7450. Deacon Gary Doane.

NORTHAMPTON. *Veterans Administration Hospital*, 421 N. Main St., 01060. Tel: 413-584-4040. Rev. Lionel E. Bonneville (Retired).

PITTSFIELD. *Berkshire Medical Center*, Tel: 413-447-2000. Rev. Leroy Smith.
One County Rte. 13, Chatham Center, NY 12184-9639. Tel: 413-392-4516.

WESTFIELD. *Western Massachusetts Hospital*, Tel: 413-562-3450. Served by Our Lady of the Blessed Sacrament Parish.

On Duty Outside the Diocese:
Revs.—
Cournoyer, Alfred C., A.P. 207, San Pedro Sula, Honduras.
Marchese, Joseph P., Boston College, Chestnut Hill, 02167. Chap.
McDonagh, John P., Catholic Student Ctr., Duke Univ., P.O. Box 90974, Durham, NC 27708.
Potvin, Raymond H., Ph.D., Prof. Emeritus (Retired), Catholic University, Box 1264, Washington, DC 20064.
Schmitt, Thomas F., Pope John XXII National Seminary, 558 South Ave., Weston, 02493.
Teague, Bruce N., Deaconess Medical Center, Dooley Chapel, 330 Brookline Ave., Boston, 02215-5400.
Tuohey, John F., Providence St. Vincent Medical Center, 9205 S.W. Barnes Rd., Portland, OR 97225.
Twardzik, Michael W.T., Holy Family Catholic Community, 40 Elizabeth St., Dansville, NY 14437.

On Sabbatical:
Rev.—
Noiseux, Donald A.

Absent on Leave:
Revs.—
Giroux, Regis J.
Minkler, Jeffrey R.
Twohig, Michael J.

Absent on Sick Leave:
Rev.—
Lis, John S.

Retired:
Rev. Msgrs.—
Leclerc, Leo A., V.G., Assumption of the Blessed Virgin Mary, 104 Springfield St., Chicopee, 01013.
Sniezyk, Richard S., 165 Sylvan Way, Wells, ME 04090.
Walsh, Francis E., Ripley Court Hotel, 37 Talbot St., Dublin, Ireland.
Revs.—
Begley, Thomas B., P.O. Box 517, Hinsdale, 01235.
Benoit, Adrian J., 281 Chauncey Walker St., #153, Belchertown, 01007.
Bombardier, Dennis P., 12 Myers Farm Ln., Greenfield, 01301.
Bonneville, Lionel E., P.O. Box 282, Wilbraham, 01095.
Brady, Gerald, P.O. Box 174, Northfield, 01360.
Breton, Albert, Mt. Marie, 34 Lower Westfield Rd., Ste. 1, Holyoke, 01040.
Brunton, Daniel B., 80 Brush Hill Ave., Unit 42, West Springfield, 01089.
Chwalek, John, 420 Old Cheshire Rd., P.O. Box 56, Windsor, 01270.
Crean, Hugh F., Providence Pl., 5 Gamelin St., Holyoke, 01040.
Creane, Anthony, Devonshire Place, 48 Holy Family Rd., Apt. W 315, Holyoke, 01040.
Darling, Franklin, 10 A Elm Ter., Greenfield, 01301. Tel: 413-772-6187
Dean, John T., 7 Corser St., Holyoke, 01040.
Diemand, James E., P.O. Box 141, Turners Falls, 01376.
Duquette, Roy H., 100 Wood Ave., East Longmeadow, 01028.
Foley, Daniel R., J.C.D., St. Michael's Residence, 86 Wendover Rd., 01118.
Gallerini, Philip G., 867 Knightbridge Cr., Davenport, FL 33896.
Gardner, Royal J., Sacred Heart Rectory, 191 Elm St., Pittsfield, 01201.
Gilbertson, Lee C., 29 Shoreline Dr., Belfast, ME 04915.
Gonet, Charles F., Saint Michael Residence, 86 Wendover Rd., 01118.
Greenway, George G., 220 Villager Dr., Saint Simons Island, GA 31522.
Hallahan, Timothy J., P.O. Box 150112, Cape Coral, FL 33915.
Hebert, Earl, 281 Chauncey Walker St., #350, Belchertown, 01007.
Jutt, Anthony J., 47 Bates Rd., 01085.
Kennedy, Francis M., P.O. Box 677, Southampton, 01073.
LaFleur, Gerard A., Assumption of the Blessed Virgin Mary Parish, 104 Springfield St., Chicopee, 01013-2695.
LaPointe, Donald, 6 Old Stagecoach Rd., Easthampton, 01027.
Lavoie, Merle L., 114 College Hwy., Southampton, 01073.
Manning, Francis J., 29 Oakhurst St., 01104.
McCormick, Howard W., Saint Michael Residence, 86 Wendover Rd., 01118.
Menge, James P., c/o 41c Nevada St., 01107.
O'Connor, Matthew J., 69 Beacon St., Holyoke, 01040.
O'Connor, Vincent M., P.O. Box 346, Leeds, 01053.
Pagano, Peter E., 1215 Massachusetts Ave., North Adams, 01247.
Perreault, Leonard J., Mt. Marie, 34 Lower Westfield Rd., Rm. 208, Holyoke, 01040.
Riendeau, Richard A., Blessed Sacrament Parish, 1945 Northampton St., Holyoke, 01040.
Sullivan, Francis X., 102 Allyn St., Holyoke, 01040.
Thrasher, Robert W., J.C.D., St. Michael's Residence, 86 Wendover Rd., 01118.

Permanent Deacons:
Antaya, John
Badame, Joseph, (Retired), 9541 W. Carol Ave., Peoria, AZ 85345.
Baillargeon, David, Our Lady of the Holy Rosary, Russell
Baldasaro, Pasqual, St. Joseph, Pittsfield
Bergeron, Leo, St. George, Chicopee
Bete, Joseph Channing, Holy Trinity, Greenfield
Bledsoe, John, V.F., St. Patrick, South Hadley
Brawner, William, St. Francis of Assisi, Belchertown
Briere, Paul, St. John the Evangelist, Agawam
Bucci, Joseph, St. Mary's, Orange
Callahan, Thomas A., Holy Cross, Holyoke
Carrier, Roger, St. Mary, Westfield
Cary, Herbert L., Our Lady of the Valley, Sheffield
Conroy, James, St. Thomas, West Springfield
Coughlin, Leo, St. Mary, Hampden
Cyr, Ralph R., Berkshire Medical Ctr. & Berkshire House of Correction
Diaz, Celso B., (On Duty Outside the Diocese)
Digiacomo, Enzo
Doane, Gary, St. Thomas, Palmer
Duval, Robert L., St. Mary of the Assumption, Ludlow
Esposito, Robert, Sacred Heart, Pittsfield
Faber, Edward H., (Retired), Hanward Hill E., East Longmeadow, 01028.
Federici, Paul, Our Lady of the Blessed Sacrament, Westfield
Fleury, Bernard J., 244 Main Rd., Westhampton, 01027.
Garde, Joseph, St. Catherine, Springfield
Gaudrault, Thomas, St. Theresa, South Hadley
Gois, Antonio, Our Lady of Fatima, Ludlow
Grodin, Norman, St. John, Ludlow
Hager, James A., Sacred Heart, Pittsfield
Herbert, Romeo, St. Anne, Chicopee
Higby, Donald, St. Mary, Longmeadow
Hitter, Robert, St. Mary, Cheshire
Hodges, Michael, Holy Name, Springfield
Kaiser, L. Joseph, (Retired)
Keator, George, St. Ann, Lenox
Kern, William, Sacred Heart, Springfield
Kolasinski, Mark, Most Holy Redeemer, Hadley
Kozach, George, St. Patrick Church, Springfield
Lafreniere, Gregory, Pope John Paul the Great, Adams
Leary, John, Blessed Sacrament, Greenfield
Magenis, Richard, Our Lady of the Valley, Sheffield
Mazzariello, Paul, Hampden Co. Correctional Facility
Medina, Genaro, Sr., All Souls, Latino Ministry, Springfield
Meyer, Edward, St. John the Baptist, Ludlow
Miller, Lucien M., Campus Ministry, University of Massachusetts, Amherst
Mireault, Leon, St. Rose de Lima, Chicopee
Moesley, William C., St. Charles, Pittsfield
Monat, Noe, 240 Skycrest Loop, Davenport, FL 33837.
Morrell, George, St. Agnes, Dalton
Moulton, Robert R., Pope John Paul the Great, Adams
Mulholland, Sean, St. Marks, Pittsfield
Mutti, Al, Our Lady of Hope, Springfield
O'Brien, John P., (On Duty Outside the Diocese)
O'Connell, Terrence, Providence Place and Providence Hospital, W. Springfield
Pelletier, Frederick J., Immaculate Conception, Holyoke
Pellissier, Bernard, St. Patrick, Monson
Pennell, Wendell, Blessed Sacrament, Holyoke
Perez, Angel, Holy Family, Springfield
Perkins, Michael, Our Lady of the Sacred Heart, Springfield
Peters, Joseph, St. Stanislaus, Chicopee
Phillip, Donald, St. Frances Xavier Cabrini, West Springfield
Przybylowski, David, Our Lady of the Lake, Southwick

Rabbitt, Thomas, St. Joseph, Shelburne Falls
Rael, Lincoln C., (Retired), 47 Nonotuck St., Holyoke, 01040.
Ramos, Oswaldo, Blessed Sacrament, Springfield
Ratte, Arthur E., St. Patrick, Northfield
Reagan, John, St. Mary, Haydenville
Rivera, Jose, All Souls, Springfield
Rivera-Burgos, Pedro, Our Lady of Guadalupe, Holyoke
Rivera-Moran, Pedro, St. Mary, Westfield
Rogers, Francis D., (Retired), St. Patrick, Chicopee
Ryan, Francis, Sts. Patrick & Raphael, Williamstown
Shaw, Edward, Sts. Patrick and Raphael, Williamstown
Smith, Joseph, St. Mary's, Chicopee
Southworth, David, St. Mary, Longmeadow
Talbot, Richard, Newman Center, Amherst
Toller, William, Holy Cross, Springfield
Tudryn, Theodore, St. Stanislaus, South Deerfield
Vernard, John, Holy Name, Springfield
Wainwright, Charles, St. Stanislaus, Chicopee
Wallen, Paul, (Retired), Springfield, MA
Ziemba, James, St. Cecilia, Wilbraham
Ziter, Bruce, Our Lady of Mercy & St. Francis, North Adams

INSTITUTIONS LOCATED IN THE DIOCESE

[A] COLLEGES AND UNIVERSITIES

CHICOPEE. *College of Our Lady of the Elms* 01013. Tel: 413-265-2293; Fax: 413-592-4871. Email: breauw@elms.edu. Web: www.elms.edu. Most Rev. Timothy A. McDonnell; Sr. Mary Reap, I.H.M., Ph.D., Pres.; Dr. Walter C. Breau, Vice Pres. Academic Affairs; Patricia Bombardier, Librarian. Sisters of St. Joseph. Sisters 3; Professors 63; Lay Teachers 63; Students 1,323; Total Staff 149.

[B] HIGH SCHOOLS, DIOCESAN

SPRINGFIELD. *Cathedral High School* (1883) 260 Surrey Rd., 01118. Tel: 413-782-5285; Fax: 413-782-5065. Email: info@cathedralhigh.org. Web: www.cathedralhigh.org. Mr. John Miller, Prin.; Ms. Susan French, Librarian. Sisters 3; Lay Teachers 40; Students 490.

CHICOPEE. *Holyoke Catholic High School*, 134 Springfield St., 01013. Tel: 413-331-2480; Fax: 413-331-2708. Email: gaels@holyokecatholichigh.org. Web: www.holyokecatholichigh.org. Mr. Michael S. Griffin, Ph.D., Prin.; Mrs. Jeanne O'Connell, Librarian. Sisters of St. Joseph. Sisters of St. Joseph 2; Lay Teachers 25; Students 302.

PITTSFIELD. *St. Joseph Central High School*, 22 Maplewood Ave., 01201. Tel: 413-447-9121; Fax: 413-443-7020. Web: www.stjoehigh.org. Donna Quallen, Prin.; Orion Hazard, Librarian. Sisters of St. Joseph. Lay Teachers 25; Students 220; Total Staff 35.

[C] ELEMENTARY SCHOOLS, DIOCESAN

SPRINGFIELD. *Saint Michael's Academy*, (Grades PreSchool-8), P.O. Box 1730, 01102-1730. Sisters 3; Lay Teachers 53; Students 821.

Preschool Campus, 90 Wendover Rd., 01118. Tel: 413-439-4310; Fax: 413-439-4396. Joanne Powers.

Elementary Campus, 153 Eddywood St., 01118. Tel: 413-782-5246; Fax: 413-782-8137. Claire Cote, Prin.; Ann Dougal, Asst. Prin.

Middle Campus, 99 Wendover Rd., 01118. Tel: 413-439-4300; Fax: 413-439-4399. Carol Raffaele, Prin.; David Nortz, Asst. Prin.; Maria-Manuels deCarvalho, Head of Academy.

ADAMS. *St. Stanislaus Kostka*, (Grades PreK-8), 108 Summer St., 01220. Tel: 413-734-1091. Sr. Jacqueline M. Kazanowski, C.S.S.F., Prin. Felician Sisters 1; Lay Teachers 11; Students 140.

PITTSFIELD. *Saint Mark School*, (Grades PreSchool-7), 400 Columbus Ave., Ste. 1, 01201. Tel: 413-442-6040; Fax: 413-448-5645. Email: stmark2@verizon.net. Web: www.stmarkpittsfield.com. Ms. Margaret (Meg) Skowron, Prin. Tel: 413-442-6040. Staff 22; Enrollment 132.

GREENFIELD. *Holy Trinity School*, (Grades PreK-8), 10 Beacon St., 01301. Tel: 413-773-3831; Fax: 413-774-7794. Email: holytrinityschool@comcast.net. Web: www.holytrinityschool-gfld.org. Arlene Ashby, Prin. Lay Teachers 10; Students 93.

[D] ORPHANAGES

WEST SPRINGFIELD. *Brightside, Inc.* Private, Nonprofit Agency., 2112 Riverdale St., P.O. Box 9012, 01089. Tel: 413-788-7366; Fax: 413-747-0182. Email: brightside.intake@sphs.com. Web: www.mercycares.com. *Sisters of Providence Health System*, P.O. Box 9012, 01102-9012. Tel: 413-827-4244; Fax: 413-827-4250. Mr. Vincent J. McCorkle, Pres.; Charles Ned Whitman, Vice Pres./Residential Svcs.; Vinnie Regan, Prin., Brightside Campus School; Barbara Gallagher Jarry, Chap. & Mgr. Spiritual Devel. Sisters of Providence. Children in Residence 36; Children in Day Treatment Program 18; Family Stabilization Team 250; Total Staff 180.

[E] GENERAL HOSPITALS

SPRINGFIELD. *CHE - The Mercy Hospital, Inc.*, 271 Carew St., Box 9012, 01102-9012. Tel: 413-748-9000; Fax: 413-781-7217. Web: www.mercycares.com. Mr. Vincent J. McCorkle, Pres.; Sr. Madeline Joy, S.P., Chap.; Rev. Donatus Ironuma, Chap.; David Teague, Chap.; Katherine Mastorakis, Chap.; Beverly Kiley Matakaetis, Chap.; Colleen O'Grady, Spiritual Care Coord. For both Mercy Campuses. Sisters of Providence 2; Bed Capacity 251; Patients Assisted Annually 172,612; Total Staff (Mercy Hospital) 1,443.

Providence Behavioral Health Hospital, 1233 Main St., Holyoke, 01040. Tel: 413-536-5111; Fax: 413-539-2992. Sr. Therese Dube, S.A.S.V. Spiritual Care Dept. 1; Bed Capacity 131; Total Staff 460.

TURNERS FALLS. *Farren Care Center, Inc.*, 340 Montague City Rd., 01376. Tel: 413-774-3111; Fax: 413-774-7049. Web: www.mercycares.com. Mailing Address: *Sisters of Providence Health Systems*, P.O. Box 9012, 01102. Email: jim.clifford@sphs.com. Sr. Madeline Joy, S.P., Chap.; James Clifford, Admin.; Christopher McLaughlin, COO Senior Care Network. Bed Capacity 122; Total Assisted Annually 121; Total Staff 175.

[F] FAMILY SERVICES

SPRINGFIELD. *Diocesan Office for Counseling, Prevention and Victim Services*, 65 Elliot St., P.O. Box 1730, 01102-1730. Tel: 413-732-3175; 413-452-0621; 413-452-0624; Fax: 413-452-0618. Web: www.diospringfield.org/MC.html. Dr. Alfred A. D'Amato, Ed.D., L.M.F.T., Counselor; Mrs. Rosemary Castonguay, M.Ed., L.M.H.C., Counselor; Barbara Conte, Admin. Asst. Total Assisted Annually 300; Total Staff 4.

HOLYOKE. *Mont Marie Child Care Center, Inc.* (1991) Mont Marie, 01040. Tel: 413-536-2964; Fax: 413-536-5557. Email: jfrappier@ssjspringfield.com. Sr. Eleanor T. Harrington, S.S.J., Dir. Sisters of St. Joseph 1; Total Staff 21; Children 107.

Providence Ministries for the Needy, Inc., 51 Hamilton St., P.O. Box 6269, 01041. Tel: 413-536-9109; Fax: 413-536-1137. Email: PMN3@hotmail.com. Web: www.providenceministries.freeservers.com. Karen M. Blanchard, Admin. Sponsored by the Sisters of Providence of Holyoke, MA. Total Assisted Annually 38,950; Total Staff 18.

Broderick House, 56 Cabot St., P.O. Box 6269, 01041. Tel: 413-534-7610; Fax: 413-536-8536. SRO (single room occupency), permanent housing for low income sober men/women. Capacity 20.

Margaret's Pantry Tel: 413-538-8026; Fax: 413-536-8536. Provides emergency food to families and individuals.

St. Jude's Center Tel: 413-534-7610; Fax: 413-536-8536. Distributes clothing and household items to the poor.

St. Jude's Furniture & Furnishing Store, 390 Main St., 01040. Tel: 413-536-9109; Fax: 413-536-1137. Provides new and pre-owned furniture and furnishings to the community.

Loreto House, 51 Hamilton St., 01041. Tel: 413-533-5909; Fax: 413-536-1137. An around-the-clock shelter for homeless men. Capacity 20.

Kate's Kitchen, 51 Hamilton St., 01040. Tel: 413-532-0233; Fax: 413-536-1137. A community kitchen which provides one meal daily to anyone in need - no questions asked. Capacity 99.

PITTSFIELD. *Catholic Charities Outreach Office*, 56 Newell St., 01202. Tel: 413-442-0103; Fax: 413-452-0605. 191 Elm St., 01202. Eryn Tobin, Social Worker BSW. Total Assisted 153.

TURNERS FALLS. *Montague Catholic Social Ministries, Inc.* (1994) 41 Third St., P.O. Box 792, 01376. Tel: 413-863-4804; Fax: 413-863-4844. Susan Mareneck, Exec. Dir. Purpose: To be a resource to children and families in the areas of parent education, family literacy, positive conflict resolution, communication skills, and community building; to assist in providing information and referral, the formation of community partnerships and neighborhood development and to facilitate parish concerns and social justice efforts. Total Assisted 1,600; Total Staff 8.

[G] HOMES FOR AGED

SPRINGFIELD. *St. Michael's Residence*, 86 Wendover Rd., 01118. Tel: 413-783-6773. Total Staff 2; Total in Residence 6. In Res. Revs. Daniel R. Foley, J.C.D. (Retired); Charles F. Gonet (Retired); Howard W. McCormick (Retired); John L. Sullivan, J.C.L. (Retired); Robert W. Thrasher, J.C.D. (Retired).

Sisters of Providence Care Centers, Inc., 271 Carew St., 01104. Tel: 413-748-9000; Fax: 413-781-7217. Web: www.mercycares.com. Total Assisted Annually 327; Total Staff 251.

Beaven Kelly Home (1909) 25 Brightside Dr., Holyoke, 01040. Tel: 413-532-4892; Fax: 413-535-2355. Sr. Sheila McGuirk, S.S.J., Chap.; Lori Naumowicz, Admin. Residents 55; Staff 22.

Mount St. Vincent Care Center (1972) 35 Holy Family Rd., Holyoke, 01040-2758. Tel: 413-532-3246; Fax: 413-532-0309. Persons Under Care 122; Total Staff 130. In Res. Sr. Ramona Williams, S.P., Chap.; Eriko Umana, Admin.

St. Luke's Home (1916) 85 Spring St., 01105. Tel: 413-736-5494; Fax: 413-746-5075. Albert Blanchard, Spiritual Care Coord.; Barbara Tadeo, Admin. Residents 84; Staff 30.

Providence Care Center of Lenox (1999) 320 Pittsfield Rd., Lenox, 01240. Tel: 413-627-2660; Fax: 413-637-3085. Email: colette.hanlon@sphs.com. Robert Post, Admin.; Sr. Colette Hanlon, S.S.J., Chap. Residents 67; Staff 69.

HOLYOKE. *Mont Marie Health Care Center, Inc.*, 36 Lower Westfield Rd., 01040-2739. Tel: 413-538-6050; Fax: 413-533-4505. Email: bsullivan@ssjspringfield.com. Sr. Elizabeth Sullivan, S.S.J., Admin. Priests 1; Total Resident Days 30,660; Total Census 84; Total Staff 132. In Res. Rev. Leonard J. Perreault (Retired).

Providence Place, Inc., 5 Gamelin St., 01040. Tel: 413-534-9700; Fax: 413-534-9782. Web: providenceplace.org. Richard Pelland, Exec. Dir.; Rev. Hugh F. Crean, Chap. (Retired). Sisters of Providence. Total in Residence 139; Total Staff 51.

St. Joseph Residence at Mont Marie, Inc., 38 Lower Westfield Rd., 01040. Tel: 413-536-0853, Ext. 280. Web: www.ssjspringfield.org. Email: jkeough@ssjspringfield.com. Jill Keough, Dir., Opers.

[H] MONASTERIES AND RESIDENCES OF PRIESTS AND BROTHERS

STOCKBRIDGE. *Congregation of Marian Fathers of The Immaculate Conception of the Most Blessed Virgin Mary*, Eden Hill, 2 Prospect Hill Rd., 01262. Tel: 413-298-1101; Fax: 413-298-0207. Email: provincial@marian.org. Web: www.marian.org; www.thedivinemercy.org. *Provincial Office* Tel: 413-298-1101; Fax: 413-298-0207. Very Revs. Daniel Cambra, M.I.C., Prov. Supr.; Kazimierz Chwalek, M.I.C., Vicar Prov.; Revs. Timothy Roth, M.I.C., 2nd Councilor & Prov. Sec.; Donald Callaway, M.I.C., 3rd Councilor; Bros. Brian Manian, M.I.C., 4th Councilor; Donald Schaefer, M.I.C., Prov. Treas. *The National Shrine of The Divine Mercy* Tel: 413-298-3931; Fax: 413-298-3910. Email: dmshrine@marian.org. Web: www.thedivinemercy.org/shrine. Rev. Anthony Gramlich, M.I.C., Rector; Bro. Kenneth Galisa, M.I.C., Sec. to Prov. *Association of Marian Helpers, Marian Helpers Center*, Eden Hill, 01263. Tel: 413-298-3691; Fax: 413-298-3583. Email: info@marian.org. Web: www.marian.org. Rev. Seraphim Michalenko, M.I.C., Dir.; Very Rev. Kazimierz Chwalek, M.I.C., Dir. Office of Evangelization & Devel.; Rev. Michael Callea, M.I.C., Coord. Divine Mercy Apostolates; Bros. Michael Opalacz, M.I.C., Grounds; Andrew Maczynski, M.I.C., Promoter of Marian Missions; Mr. Francis Bourdon, Exec. Dir. Marian Helpers Center. *John Paul II Institute of Divine Mercy* Tel: 413-298-1184; Fax: 413-298-4559. Email: jpii@marian.org. Web: www.thedivinemercy.org/jpii. Rev. Seraphim Michalenko, M.I.C., Dir. Emeritus; Dr. Robert Stackpole, S.T.D., Dir. Tel: 866-895-3236. Web: www.thedivinemercy.org/jpii.

Lay Outreach of the Province:

Eucharistic Apostles of the Divine Mercy (EADM) Tel: 877-380-0727. Email: eadm@marian.org. Web: www.thedivinemercy.org/eadm. Dr. Bryan Thatcher, M.D., Dir.

Mother of Mercy Messengers (MOMM) Tel: 830-634-0727. Email: momm@marian.org. Web: www.thedivinemercy.org/momm. Dave Maroney, Dir.; Joan Maroney, Dir. Tel: 877-380-0727. Web: www.thedivinemercy.org/momm.

Healthcare Professionals for Divine Mercy Tel: 877-380-0727. Email: marie@nursesfordivinemercy.org. Web: www.thedivinemercy.org/healthcare. Marie Romagnano, R.N., B.S.N., Dir. In Res. Very Rev. Kazimierz Chwalek, M.I.C.; Revs. Michael Callea, M.I.C.; Richard Drabik, M.I.C.; Andrzej Gorczyca, M.I.C.; Anthony Gramlich, M.I.C.; Walter Gurgul, M.I.C.; Victor Incardona, M.I.C.; Mariusz Jarzabek, M.I.C.; Seraphim Michalenko, M.I.C.; Anthony

Nockunas, M.I.C.; Martin Rzeszutek, M.I.C.; Bros. John Bryda, M.I.C.; Ken Galisa, M.I.C.; Leonard Kunda, M.I.C.; Andrew Maczynski, M.I.C.; Ronald McBride, M.I.C.; Albin Milewski, M.I.C.; Michael Opalacz, M.I.C.; Donald Schaefer, M.I.C.; Fred Wells, M.I.C.; Rev. Bernard Backiel, M.I.C. On Duty Outside of House: Revs. Ireneusz Chodakowski, M.I.C., Portland, ME; Donald Van Alstyne, M.I.C., Arch for the Military, MO On Duty Outside of the USA: Revs. Joseph Petraitis, M.I.C., Australia; Joseph Roesch, M.I.C., Generalate in Rome, Italy.

[I] CONVENTS AND RESIDENCES FOR SISTERS

HOLYOKE. *Daughters of the Heart of Mary Provincial Residence* (1791) 1339 Northampton St., 01040-1958. Tel: 413-533-6681; Fax: 413-533-4217. Email: clare1790@aol.com. Web: www.dhmna.org. Sr. Clare A. Thompson, D.H.M., Prov. Total in Residence 16; Total Staff 2.

Franciscan Missionary Sisters of Assisi Vice-Provincial House and Formation House, 1039 Northampton St., 01040-1320. Tel: 413-532-8156; Fax: 413-534-7741. Email: sistersofassisi@comcast.com. Web: www.sistersofassisi.org. Sr. Carol Woods, S.F.M.A., Vice Prov. Supr.

Franciscan Missionary Sisters of Assisi - Saint Francis Convent - Viceprovincial House and Formation House Sisters 7.

Marian Center, Inc., 1365 Northampton St., 01040. Tel: 413-534-4502; Fax: 413-534-7353. Sr. Marianna Mercurio, D.H.M., Supr. Daughters of the Heart of Mary 21; Total in Residence 16; Total Staff 50.

Mont Marie (1883) 34 Lower Westfield Rd., 01040. Tel: 413-536-0853; Fax: 413-533-3275. Email: mail@ssjspringfield.com. Sisters Mary Quinn, S.S.J., Pres.; Patricia Murphy, S.S.J., Vice Pres. The Congregation of the Sisters of St. Joseph of SpringfieldMotherhouse of the Sisters of St. Joseph of Springfield. Sisters 287; Total Staff 49.

Mont Marie Senior Residence, Inc., 32 Lower Westfield Rd., 01040. Tel: 413-532-9356; Fax: 413-532-9358. Sr. Denise Granger, S.S.J., Pres.

Sisters of Providence (1873) 5 Gamelin St., 01040. Tel: 413-536-7511; Fax: 413-536-7917. Email: sisters@sisofprov.org. Web: www.sisofprov.org. Motherhouse of the Sisters of Providence. Sisters 55.

Mary's Meadow, 12 Gamelin St., 01040. Tel: 413-420-2500; Fax: 413-322-7096.

Providence Ministries for the Needy, Inc., P.O. Box 6269, 01041-6269. Tel: 413-536-9109; Fax: 413-536-1137.

Genesis Spiritual Life Center, 53 Mill St., Westfield, 01085-4253. Tel: 413-562-3627; Fax: 413-572-1060.

TYRINGHAM. *Order of the Visitation of Holy Mary, Monastery of the Visitation*, P.O. Box 432, 01264. Tel: 413-243-3995; Fax: 413-243-3543. Email: vistyr@aol.com. Web: www.vistyr.org. Sr. Mary Ruth, V.H.M., Supr. Order of the Visitation of Holy Mary 19.

WEST SPRINGFIELD. *Monastery of the Mother of God, Dominican Nuns (Contemplative)*, 1430 Riverdale St., 01089-4698. Tel: 413-736-3639; Fax: 413-736-0850. Sr. Mary St. John, O.P., Prioress. Adoration to the Blessed Sacrament Chapel. Solemnly Professed Nuns 19.

[J] RETREAT HOUSES AND CHRISTIAN LIFE CENTERS

WESTFIELD. *Genesis Spiritual Life Center*, 53 Mill St., 01085. Tel: 413-562-3627; Fax: 413-572-1060. Email: genesis@genesiscenter.us. Web: www.genesiscenter.us. Sr. Ann Horgan, S.P., Admin.; Ms. Trisha Riga, Registrar; Mrs. Christine Morrissey, Asst. Prog. Coord. Retreats, workshops and spiritual guidance designed to promote health of body, mind and spirit. Also, host day and overnight conferences. Total Staff 15; Total in Residence 3.

[K] SPANISH APOSTOLATES

SPRINGFIELD. *Catholic Latino Ministry*, Saint Francis of Assisi Center, 254 Bridge St., 01103. Tel: 413-452-0631; Fax: 413-452-0647. Email: clm@diospringfield.org. Mr. Andres Lopez, Dir.; Lucy Ramos, Exec. Sec.

[L] BUREAU FOR EXCEPTIONAL CHILDREN AND ADULTS

HOLYOKE. *Bureau for Exceptional Children and Adults Inc.* (1972) 537 Northampton St., Box 1039, 01041. Tel: 413-538-7450; Fax: 413-536-5691. Email: jerichobeca@comcast.net. Sr. Joan Magnani, S.S.J., Dir.; Nicole Caron, Prog. Dir. Sisters 1; Lay Staff 5.

[M] YOUTH SERVICES

GOSHEN. *Holy Cross Camp Grounds*, 108 Cape St., 01032. Tel: 413-268-7819; Fax: 413-684-0125; Fax: 413-684-0734. Email: frcm@stagnes.cc.com. Web: www.campholycross.org. Mailing Address: 489 Main St., Dalton, 01226. Rev. Christopher A. Malatesta. Total Staff 2.

PITTSFIELD. *Catholic Youth Center*, 26 Melville St., 01201. Tel: 413-445-5496; Fax: 413-445-5248. Mr. Gary R. Collins, Interim Exec. Dir. Total Assisted 800; Total Staff 25.

[N] NEWMAN APOSTOLATES AND CAMPUS MINISTRIES

SPRINGFIELD. *Newman Apostolates and Campus Ministries* 65 Elliot St., P.O. Box 1730, 01102-1730. Tel: 413-452-0819; Fax: 413-452-0555. Email: n.bolton@diospringfield.org. Rev. Norman B. Bolton, Dir.

Campus Outreach in Higher Education 65 Elliot St., P.O. Box 1730, 01102-1730.

The Newman Catholic Center 472 N. Pleasant, Amherst, 01002-1739. Tel: 413-549-0300, Ext. 34; Fax: 413-548-9182. Email: fr.mcgonagle@gmail.com. Web: www.newmanumass.org. Rev. Douglas McGonagle, Dir. & Chap.

Amherst, MA:

Amherst College Cardigan Center for Religious Life, P.O. Box 5000, Amherst, 01002-5000. Tel: 413-542-8083. Email: ecarr@amherst.edu. Elizabeth E. Carr, Ph.D., Chap.

Center for Religious Life

University of Massachusetts Newman Center, 472 N. Pleasant St., Amherst, 01002-1739. Tel: 413-549-0300; Fax: 413-548-9182. Web: www.umass.edu/catholic. Rev. Douglas McGonagle, Dir. & Chap.; Mark Callahan, Campus Min.; Rev. John Gawienowski, Assoc. Dir.; Deacons Lucien Miller, Campus Min.; Richard Talbot, Campus Min.

Chicopee, MA:

College of Our Lady of the Elms College 291 Springfield St., Chicopee, 01013. Tel: 413-265-2289, Ext. 289; Fax: 413-594-6699. Web: www.elms.edu. Sr. Carol Allan, S.S.J., Dir. Campus Ministry.

American International College 202 E. Main St., Chicopee, 01020. Tel: 413-539-0835. Email: bolt1983@gmail.com. Rev. Norman B. Bolton, Chap.

Longmeadow, MA:

Bay Path College 202 E. Main St., Chicopee, 01020. Tel: 413-539-0835. Email: bolt1983@gmail.com. Rev. Norman B. Bolton. Diocese of Springfield, Campus Outreach

North Adams, MA:

Massachusetts College of Liberal Arts , Served by St. Anthony, North Adams, 375 Church St., North Adams, 01247. *St. Anthony Parish*, 70 Marshall St., North Adams, 01247. Tel: 413-663-3112. Rev. William F. Cyr; Deacon Bruce Ziter.

Northampton, MA:

Smith College Helen Hills, Hills Chapel, Northampton, 01063. Tel: 413-585-2752; Fax: 413-585-2794. Email: ecarr@email.smith.edu. Elizabeth E. Carr, Ph.D., Chap.

Pittsfield, MA:

Berkshire Community College 400 West St., Pittsfield, 01201-3194. Tel: 413-447-7510. Rev. John C. Salatino. Served by St. Mark's.

South Hadley, MA:

Mount Holyoke College Office of the Chaplain, Eliot House, South Hadley, 01075. Email: amagovern@mtholyoke.edu. Served by St. Theresa.

Res.: Office of the Chaplain, Eliot House, South Hadley, 01075. Tel: 413-538-2054; Fax: 413-538-2787. Anita Magovern, Rel. Advisor. Tel: 413-538-2787.

Springfield, MA:

Springfield College Campus Ministry Center Beveridge Center, 263 Alden St., 01109-3797. Tel: 413-748-3210; Fax: 413-748-3764.

Western New England College 1215 Wilbraham Rd., 01119-2684. Tel: 413-782-1221; Fax: 413-585-2752. Ms. Sheila Hanifan, Campus Min.

Westfield, MA:

Westfield State College Interfaith Center, Westfield, 01085. Tel: 413-572-5567; Fax: 413-562-3613. Rev. John T. Dean, Chap. (Retired).

Williamstown, MA:

Williams College , Served by St. Patrick's.

Res.: 39 Chapel Hill Dr., Williamstown, 01267-2569. Tel: 413-597-2483; Fax: 413-597-3955. Email: gary.c.caster@williams.edu. Rev. Gary C. Caster, Campus Min.

[O] MISCELLANEOUS

SPRINGFIELD. *The Foundation of the Roman Catholic Diocese of Springfield, Massachusetts, Inc.*, 65 Elliot St., P.O. Box 1730, 01102. Tel: 413-452-0630; Fax: 413-732-4297. Email: m.dupont@diospringfield.org. Web: www.diospringfield.org.

Sisters of Providence Health System, Inc., 271 Carew St., 01104. Tel: 413-748-9000; Fax: 413-781-7217. Web: www.mercycares.com. Mr. Vincent J. McCorkle, Pres. & CEO.

CHICOPEE. *The Friends of the Elms College, Inc.*, 291 Springfield St., 01013. Tel: 413-265-2372; Fax: 413-265-2346. Brian Doherty, Contact Person.

HOLYOKE. *Mary's Meadow at Providence Place, Inc.*, c/o Sisters of Providence, Inc., 12 Gamelin St., 01040. Tel: 413-536-7511, Ext. 2550. Sr. Kathleen Popko, S.P., Pres.

RELIGIOUS INSTITUTES OF MEN REPRESENTED IN THE DIOCESE

For further details refer to the corresponding bracketed number in the Religious Institutes of Men or Women section.

[]—*The Association of Marian Helpers of Stockbridge, MA*

[0470]—*The Capuchin Fathers* (St. Mary's Prov.)—O.F.M.Cap.

[0270]—*Carmelite Fathers and Brothers* (St. Elias Prov.)—O.Carm.

[0740]—*Congregation of Marians of the Immaculate Conception*—M.I.C.

[1000]—*Congregation of the Passion* (Union City, NJ)—C.P.

[0480]—*Conventual Franciscans*—O.F.M.Conv.

[0720]—*The Missionaries of Our Lady of La Salette*—M.S.

[1280]—*Stigmatine Fathers and Brothers*—C.S.S.

RELIGIOUS INSTITUTES OF WOMEN REPRESENTED IN THE DIOCESE

[0860]—*Daughters of Mary of the Immaculate Conception*—D.M.

[0810]—*Daughters of the Heart of Mary*—D.H.M.

[0820]—*Daughters of the Holy Spirit*—D.H.S.

[1050]—*Dominican Contemplative Nuns*—O.P.

[1170]—*Felician Sisters*—C.S.S.F.

[1330]—*Franciscan Missionary Sisters of Assisi*—S.F.M.A.

[1470]—*Franciscan Sisters of St. Joseph*—F.S.S.J.

[1180]—*Franciscan Sisters of the Allegany, New York*—O.S.F.

[]—*Little Sisters of St. Francis*—L.S.O.G.

[]—*Missionary Sisters of Our Lady of Africa*

[]—*Missionary Sisters of Our Lady of Perpetual Help*

[]—*Oblate Sisters of the Most Holy Eucharist*—O.S.S.E.

[]—*Schonestatt Sisters of Mary*

[1700]—*School Sisters of St. Francis*—O.S.F.

[]—*Sisters of Charity Seton Hill*—S.C.

[]—*Sisters of Mercy of the Americas*—R.S.M.

[3000]—*Sisters of Notre Dame de Namur*—S.N.D.deN.

[3340]—*Sisters of Providence*—S.P.

[3718]—*Sisters of St. Ann*—S.S.A.

[3830-16]—*Sisters of St. Joseph*—S.S.J.

[3850]—*Sisters of St. Joseph of Chambery*—C.S.J.

[0150]—*Sisters of the Assumption*—S.A.S.V.

[3310]—*Sisters of the Presentation of Mary*—P.M.

[4190]—*Visitation Nuns*—V.H.M.

DIOCESAN CEMETERIES

SPRINGFIELD. *St. Benedict Cemetery*, Mailing Address: *Springfield Diocesan Cemeteries, Inc.*, 421 Tinkham Rd., 01129. Liberty St., 01104. Tel: 413-782-0341; Fax: 413-782-5450. Web: www.diospringfield.org.

Gate of Heaven, 421 Tinkham Rd., 01129. Tel: 413-782-0341; Fax: 413-782-5450. Web: www.diospringfield.org. Joseph Kostek, Pres. Tel: 413-452-0692.

St. Matthew Cemetery, Mailing Address: *Springfield Diocesan Cemeteries, Inc.*, 421 Tinkham Rd., 01129. 366 Springfield St., 01109. Tel: 413-782-0341; Fax: 413-782-5450. Web: www.diospringfield.org.

St. Michael's Cemetery, 1601 State St., 01109. Tel: 413-782-0341; Fax: 413-782-5450. Web: www.diospringfield.org.

HOLYOKE. *Calvary Cemetery*, Mailing Address: *Springfield Diocesan Cemeteries, Inc.*, 1601 State St., 01109. Tel: 413-782-0341; Fax: 413-782-5450. Web: www.diospringfield.org. Office: Northampton St., 01040.

INDIAN ORCHARD. *St. Aloysius Cemetery*, Mailing Address: *Springfield Diocesan Cemetaries, Inc.*, 1601 State St., 01109. Tel: 413-782-0341; Fax: 413-782-5450. Web: www.diospringfield.org. Office: Berkshire Ave., 01151.

SOUTH HADLEY. *Notre Dame Cemetery*, *Springfield Diocesan Cemeteries, Inc.*, 63 Lyman St., 01075. Tel: 413-420-0001; Fax: 413-420-0004. Email: j.kostek@diospringfield.org. Web: www.diospringfield.org.

Precious Blood Cemetery, Springfield Diocesan Cemeteries, Inc., 63 Lyman St., 01075. Tel: 413-420-0001; Fax: 413-420-0004. Email: j.kostek@diospringfield.org. Web: www.diospringfield.org.

St. Rose Cemetery, Springfield Diocesan Cemeteries, Inc., 63 Lyman St., 01075. Tel: 413-420-0001; Fax: 413-420-0004. Email: jkostek@diospringfield.org. Web: www.diospringfield.org.

WESTFIELD. *Saint Mary Cemetery*, 203 Southampton Rd., 01085. Tel: 413-568-7775; Fax: 413-568-2727. Web: www.diospringfield.org. Joseph Kostek, Pres.

NECROLOGY

† Greene, Thomas S., (Retired)—Died Sept. 9, 2009
† Heberle, Frederick L., (Retired)—Died Nov. 10, 2009
† Remy, Adrien T., (Retired)—Died Feb. 28, 2009
† Varley, John J., (Retired)—Died March 31, 2009

An asterisk (*) denotes an organization that has established tax-exempt status directly with the IRS and is not covered by the USCCB Group Ruling.

Diocese of Steubenville

(Dioecesis Steubenvicensis)

Most Reverend

R. DANIEL CONLON, D.D., J.C.D., PH.D.

Bishop of Steubenville; ordained January 15, 1977; appointed Bishop of Steubenville May 22, 2002; consecrated and installed August 6, 2002. *Mailing Address: P.O. Box 969, Steubenville, OH 43952-5969.*

Most Reverend

ALBERT H. OTTENWELLER, D.D., S.T.L.

Retired Bishop of Steubenville; ordained June 19, 1943; appointed Titular Bishop of Perdices and Auxiliary of Toledo April 17, 1974; consecrated May 29, 1974; appointed to Steubenville October 11, 1977; installed November 22, 1977; retired April 2, 1992. *Res.: 2544 Parkwood Ave., Toledo, OH 43610-1317.*

Chancery Office: 422 Washington St., P.O. Box 969, Steubenville, OH 43952-5969. Tel: 740-282-3631; Fax: 740-282-3327.

Web: www.diosteub.org

Email: lnichols@diosteub.org

Most Reverend

GILBERT I. SHELDON, D.D., D.MIN.

Bishop Emeritus of Steubenville; ordained February 28, 1953; appointed Auxiliary and Titular Bishop of Taparura April 20, 1976; consecrated June 11, 1976; appointed to Steubenville January 28, 1992; installed April 2, 1992; retired August 6, 2002.

ESTABLISHED 1944.

Square Miles 5,913.

Comprises these thirteen Counties in the State of Ohio: Athens, Belmont, Carroll, Gallia, Guernsey, Harrison, Jefferson, Lawrence, Meigs, Morgan, Monroe, Noble and Washington.

For legal titles of parishes and diocesan institutions, consult the Chancery Office.

STATISTICAL OVERVIEW

Personnel	
Bishop	1
Retired Bishops	2
Priests: Diocesan Active in Diocese	49
Priests: Diocesan Active Outside Diocese	7
Priests: Retired, Sick or Absent	30
Number of Diocesan Priests	86
Religious Priests in Diocese	28
Total Priests in Diocese	114
Extern Priests in Diocese	6
Ordinations:	
Diocesan Priests	2
Permanent Deacons in Diocese	9
Total Brothers	7
Total Sisters	57
Parishes	
Parishes	58
With Resident Pastor:	
Resident Diocesan Priests	38
Without Resident Pastor:	
Administered by Priests	20
Missions	3
New Parishes Created	1
Closed Parishes	3
Professional Ministry Personnel:	
Brothers	1
Sisters	7
Lay Ministers	16
Welfare	
Catholic Hospitals	1
Total Assisted	243,845
Special Centers for Social Services	1
Total Assisted	23,743
Residential Care of Disabled	1
Total Assisted	185
Educational	
Seminaries, Diocesan	1
Students from This Diocese	2
Diocesan Students in Other Seminaries	5
Total Seminarians	7
Colleges and Universities	1
Total Students	2,449
High Schools, Diocesan and Parish	3
Total Students	494
Elementary Schools, Diocesan and Parish	13
Total Students	1,559
Catechesis/Religious Education:	
High School Students	362
Elementary Students	1,206
Total Students under Catholic Instruction	6,077
Teachers in the Diocese:	
Priests	1
Brothers	2
Sisters	6
Lay Teachers	178
Vital Statistics	
Receptions into the Church:	
Infant Baptism Totals	415
Minor Baptism Totals	77
Adult Baptism Totals	68
Received into Full Communion	80
First Communions	489
Confirmations	520
Marriages:	
Catholic	100
Interfaith	107
Total Marriages	207
Deaths	675
Total Catholic Population	38,693
Total Population	230,391

Former Bishops—Most Revs. JOHN KING MUSSIO, D.D., J.C.D., named First Bishop of Steubenville; ord. for Diocese of Cincinnati Aug. 15, 1935; appt. First Bishop of Steubenville March 16, 1945; cons. May 1, 1945; retired Oct. 11, 1977; died April 15, 1978; ALBERT H. OTTENWELLER, D.D., S.T.L. (Retired), named Second Bishop of Steubenville; ord. June 19, 1943; appt. Titular Bishop of Perdices and Auxiliary of Toledo April 17, 1974; cons. May 29, 1974; appt. Second Bishop of Steubenville Oct. 11, 1977; installed Nov. 22, 1977; retired April 2, 1992; GILBERT I. SHELDON, D.D., D.Min. (Retired), named Third Bishop of Steubenville.; ord. Feb. 28, 1953; appt. Auxiliary and Titular Bishop of Taparura April 20, 1976; cons. June 11, 1976; appt. Third Bishop of Steubenville Jan. 28, 1992; installed April 2, 1992; retired Aug. 6, 2002.

Vicar General—Rev. Msgr. KURT H. KEMO, J.C.L., V.G., 422 Washington St., P.O. Box 969, Steubenville, 43952-5969. Tel: 740-282-3631.

Moderator of the Curia—Rev. Msgr. KURT H. KEMO, J.C.L., V.G., 422 Washington St., P.O. Box 969, Steubenville, 43952-5969. Tel: 740-282-3631.

Episcopal Vicar for Pastoral Planning & Personnel—Rev. THOMAS A. CHILLOG, M.Div., 422 Washington St., P.O. Box 969, Steubenville, 43952-5969. Tel: 740-282-3631.

Chancellor—Mrs. LINDA A. NICHOLS.

Chancery Office—422 Washington St., P.O. Box 969, Steubenville, 43952-5969. Tel: 740-282-3631; Fax: 740-282-3327.

Diocesan Finance Office—Rev. Msgr. KURT H. KEMO, J.C.L., V.G., Finance Officer; Mr. DAVID FRANKLIN, Comptroller, Mailing Address: P.O. Box 969, Steubenville, 43952-5969. Tel: 740-282-3631.

Diocesan/Parish Share Campaign—Rev. Msgr. KURT H. KEMO, J.C.L., V.G., Dir.; Mr. MARTIN B. THOMPSON, Assoc. Dir. Tel: 740-282-3631.

Diocesan Tribunal—422 Washington St., P.O. Box 969, Steubenville, 43952-5969. Tel: 740-282-3631.

Judicial Vicar—Very Rev. WILLIAM D. CROSS, J.C.L.

Auditors—Revs. THOMAS A. CHILLOG, M.Div.; DANIEL HEUSEL, M.Div.

Notaries—Rev. DANIEL HEUSEL, M.Div.; Miss COLLEEN BAHEN.

Defenders of the Bond—Rev. Msgr. GERALD E. CALOVINI, V.F.; Revs. THOMAS A. CHILLOG, M.Div.; DANIEL HEUSEL, M.Div.

Director of the Tribunal & Notary—Miss COLLEEN BAHEN.

Judges—Most Rev. GILBERT I. SHELDON, D.D., D.Min. (Retired); Rev. Msgr. MARK J. FROEHLICH; Rev. JAMES M. DUNFEE, V.F.; Rev. Msgr. GENE W. MULLETT; Rev. VINCENT J. HUBER, M.Ed. (Retired).

Information & Technology—Mr. MARTIN B. THOMPSON, Dir.; Mr. ANTHONY TARGOSS, Mgr., 422 Washington St., P.O. Box 969, Steubenville, 43952-5969. Tel: 740-282-3631.

Diocesan Deaneries and Deans

Deans—Rev. JAMES M. DUNFEE, V.F., Mother of Hope Deanery; Rev. Msgr. PATRICK GAUGHAN, V.F., Nativity of Mary Deanery; Rev. DALE TORNES, Presentation Deanery; Rev. Msgr. ROBERT J. KAWA, Visitation Deanery.

Child Protection Review Board—Rev. Msgr. KURT H. KEMO, J.C.L., V.G., Contact Person, Mailing Address: P.O. Box 969, Steubenville, 43952-5969. Tel: 740-282-3631; Fax: 740-282-3327. Email: kkemo@diosteub.org. Members: MICHAEL DAVIS, M.A., B.A., Ph.D.; JANE ENGOTT; Judge FRANK A. FREGIATO; Dr. JOSEPH PALMA; Judge JULIE SELMON; DAN FRY, Esq.; Dr. FRANK JAMES, M.D., J.D., F.C.L.M.; Rev. DALE TORNES.

Pastoral Staff—Most Rev. ROBERT DANIEL CONLON, D.D., J.C.D., Ph.D.; Rev. Msgr. KURT H. KEMO, J.C.L., V.G.; Mrs. PAT DEFRANCIS; Mrs. LINDA A. NICHOLS; Rev. THOMAS A. CHILLOG, M.Div.; Mrs.

MARIANNE ENGELMANN; Mrs. MICHELE SANTIN; Revs. DAVID L. GAYDOSIK; TIMOTHY J. SHANNON; Mr. THOMAS S. WILSON; Mr. DAVID FRANKLIN; Very Rev. WILLIAM D. CROSS, J.C.L.; Mr. BRIAN HARVEY; Mr. MARTIN B. THOMPSON; Mr. PAUL WARD.

Presbyteral Council—Rev. Msgr. GERALD E. CALOVINI, V.F.; Revs. JOHN MUCHA; JOHN J. MCCOY JR.; CHARLES E. MASCOLINO (Retired); Rev. Msgr. J. MICHAEL CAMPBELL; Revs. DAVID CORNETT; TIMOTHY J. HUFFMAN; Rev. Msgr. KURT H. KEMO, J.C.L., V.G., Vice Chm.; Revs. THOMAS A. CHILLOG, M.Div., Chm.; JOSEPH YELENC, T.O.R.; PATTI PIASECKI, Recording Sec.

College of Consultors—Rev. Msgrs. GERALD E. CALOVINI, V.F.; KURT H. KEMO, J.C.L., V.G.; Revs. DAVID CORNETT; CHARLES E. MASCOLINO (Retired); Rev. Msgr. J. MICHAEL CAMPBELL; Revs. THOMAS A. CHILLOG, M.Div.; JOHN MCCOY JR.; TIMOTHY P. MCGUIRE; JASON PRATI; RICHARD J. TUTTLE.

Priests Personnel Board—Rev. Msgrs. GERALD E. CALOVINI, V.F., Northern Area; PATRICK GAUGHAN, V.F., Senior Clergy; Revs. THOMAS R. NAU, Middle Age Clergy; TIMOTHY J. HUFFMAN, Southern Area; WAYNE MORRIS, Younger Clergy; JOHN MUCHA, Central Area; Rev. Msgr. KURT H. KEMO, J.C.L., V.G.; Rev. THOMAS A. CHILLOG, M.Div., Ex Officio.

Diocesan Offices and Directors

Building Commission—Mr. BRIAN HARVEY, Chm., Mailing Address: P.O. Box 969, Steubenville, 43952-5969. Tel: 740-282-3631; Fax: 740-282-3327.

Building & Property Director—Mr. BRIAN HARVEY, Mailing Address: P.O. Box 969, Steubenville, 43952-5969. Tel: 740-282-3631; Fax: 740-282-3327.

Campus Ministry—Rev. MARTIN J. HOLLER, 75 Stewart St., Athens, 45701. Tel: 740-592-2711.

Censores Librorum—Rev. Msgr. KURT H. KEMO, J.C.L., V.G., Coord.; Rev. JAMES M. DUNFEE, V.F.; Dr. ALAN SCHRECK.

Office of Christian Formation and Schools—Mr. PAUL WARD, Mailing Address: P.O. Box 969, Steubenville, 43952-5969. Tel: 740-282-3631; Fax: 740-282-3327.

Diocesan Communications—Mrs. PATRICIA DEFRANCIS, Mailing Address: P.O. Box 160, Steubenville, 43952. Tel: 740-282-3631; Fax: 740-282-3238.

Office of Civil Law—Mr. THOMAS S. WILSON, Mailing Address: P.O. Box 969, Steubenville, 43952-5969. Tel: 740-282-3631; Fax: 740-282-3327.

Continuing Education of Priests—Rev. THOMAS A. CHILLOG, M.Div., Dir., Mailing Address: P.O. Box 969, Steubenville, 43952-5969. Tel: 740-282-3631; Fax: 740-282-3327.

Diocesan Finance Council—Mailing Address: 422 Washington St., P.O. Box 969, Steubenville, 43952-5969. Tel: 740-282-3631; Fax: 740-282-3327. Email: kkemo@diosteub.org. Most Rev. ROBERT DANIEL CONLON, D.D., J.C.D., Ph.D., Pres.; Rev. Msgr. KURT H. KEMO, J.C.L., V.G., Chm. Council Members: GREGORY J. AGRESTA; RICHARD DOLAN; COLLEEN OESS; MARK BRADLEY; DAVID A. FRANKLIN; THOMAS H. HISRICH; PETER STEIGERWALD; JAMES RILEY; Rev. Msgr. JOHN C. KOLESAR, V.F.

Diocesan Director of Cemeteries—Rev. Msgr. JOHN C. KOLESAR, V.F., 221 Hanna Ave., Adena, 43901. Tel: 740-546-3463.

Diocesan Director of Ecumenism—Rev. THOMAS F. HAMM JR., Mailing Address: St. Mary Church, 43700 Fulda Rd., Caldwell, 43724. Tel: 740-732-4576.

Diocesan Office of Worship—Mrs. MARIANNE ENGELMANN, Mailing Address: P.O. Box 969, Steubenville, 43952-5969. Tel: 740-282-3631; Fax: 740-282-3327.

Health Panel of the Clergy—Rev. THOMAS A. CHILLOG, M.Div., Contact Person, Mailing Address: P.O. Box 969, Steubenville, 43952-5969. Tel: 740-282-3631.

Hospitals— Trinity Health System: *Trinity Medical Center, West, 4000 Johnson Rd., Steubenville, 43952*. Tel: 740-264-8000; Fax: 740-283-7104. *Trinity Medical Center, East, 380 Summit Ave., Steubenville, 43952*. Tel: 740-283-7000; Fax: 740-283-7104. FRED B. BROWER, Pres. Tel: 740-283-7390; 740-264-8303; Rev. MARK J. MOORE, Chap. Tel: 740-264-4880.

Catholic Rural Life—Rev. DAVID L. GAYDOSIK, 334 S. Main St., Woodsfield, 43793. Tel: 740-472-0187; Fax: 740-472-0182.

Office of Family and Social Concerns— Services: Campaign for Human Devel.; Respect Life; Information & Referral; Marriage & Family Life. Mrs. MICHELE SANTIN, Dir., Mailing Address: P.O. Box 969, Steubenville, 43952-5969. Tel: 740-282-3631; 800-339-7890; Fax: 740-282-3327.

Priests' Retirement Board—Rev. VINCENT J. HUBER, M.Ed., Chm. (Retired).

Propagation of the Faith—Rev. TIMOTHY J. KOZAK, Asst. Dir.

Publication, "Steubenville Register"—Most Rev. ROBERT DANIEL CONLON, D.D., J.C.D., Ph.D., Pres. & Publisher; Mrs. PAT DEFRANCIS, Editor, 422 Washington St., P.O. Box 160, Steubenville, 43952-5969. Tel: 740-282-3631; Fax: 740-282-3238.

RCIA—Rev. THOMAS F. HAMM JR., Dir., 43700 Fulda Rd., Caldwell, 43724. Tel: 740-732-4576.

Schools—Mr. PAUL WARD, Supt., Mailing Address: P.O. Box 969, Steubenville, 43952-5969. Tel: 740-282-3631; Fax: 740-282-3327.

Stewardship and Development—Rev. Msgr. KURT H. KEMO, J.C.L., V.G., Dir., Mailing Address: P.O. Box 969, Steubenville, 43952-5969. Tel: 740-282-3631; Fax: 740-282-3327.

Vicar for Priests—Rev. THOMAS A. CHILLOG, M.Div., Mailing Address: P.O. Box 969, Steubenville, 43952-5969. Tel: 740-282-3631.

Vicar for Religious—Rev. Msgr. J. MICHAEL CAMPBELL, Mailing Address: St. Mary Church, 506 Fourth St., Marietta, 45750. Tel: 740-373-3643.

Vicar for Retired Priests—Rev. VINCENT J. HUBER, M.Ed. (Retired), 1225 N. River Ave., Toronto, 43964. Tel: 740-537-4433.

Victim Assistance Coordinator—Rev. Msgr. KURT H. KEMO, J.C.L., V.G., Contact, Mailing Address: P.O. Box 969, Steubenville, 43952. Tel: 740-282-3631; Fax: 740-282-3327. Email: kkemo@diosteub.org.

Vocations—Holy Name House of Formation, 411 S. 5th St., Steubenville, 43952. Tel: 740-282-0646. Email: tshannon@diosteub.org. Rev. TIMOTHY J. SHANNON, Dir. Assistant Directors: Revs. DANIEL HEUSEL, M.Div., Mailing Address: 411 S. 5th St., Steubenville, 43952. Tel: 740-282-3631; Fax: 740-282-3327. Email: dheusel@diosteub.org; MARK J. MOORE, Mailing Address: P.O. Box 908, Steubenville, 43952. Tel: 740-264-6177.

Woman's Club—Rev. TIMOTHY P. MCGUIRE; Mrs. DEDE KIDDER, Pres., Mailing Address: P.O. Box 31, Toronto, 43964. Tel: 740-544-5925.

CLERGY, PARISHES, MISSIONS AND PAROCHIAL SCHOOLS

CITY OF STEUBENVILLE

(JEFFERSON COUNTY)

1—HOLY NAME CATHEDRAL, [JC] Revs. Thomas R. Nau, Rector; Mark Moore; Deacons Lawrence Meagher; Gerald Hickey; Randall Redington.
Office: P.O. Box 908, 43952. Tel: 740-264-6177; Fax: 740-266-2844. Email: tnau@diosteub.org. Web: www.triumphofthecross.org.
Please see Catholic Central High School, Bishop John King Mussio Central Junior High School & Bishop John King Mussio Central Elementary Schools located in the Institution section

2—ST. ANTHONY OF PADUA, [JC] Closed. For inquiries for parish records contact Triumph of the Cross, Steubenville.

3—HOLY FAMILY, [JC] Rev. Msgr. Gerald E. Calovini.
Res.: 2608 Hollywood Blvd., 43952. Tel: 740-264-2825; Fax: 740-264-9348. Email: rectory@holyfamilyweb.org. Web: www.holyfamilyofsteubenville.4lpi.com.
Please see Catholic Central High School, Bishop John King Mussio Central Junior High School & Bishop John King Mussio Central Elementary Schools located in the Institution section

4—HOLY ROSARY, [JC] Closed. For inquiries for parish records contact Triumph of the Cross, Steubenville.

5—IMMACULATE HEART OF MARY CHAPEL, Closed. For inquiries for parish records contact the chancery.

6—OUR LADY OF NORTH AMERICA MARTYRS, Closed. For inquiries for parish records please see St. Peter's, Steubenville.

7—ST. PETER'S, [JC] Rev. Msgr. George W. Yontz; Bro. Patrick Geary, I.H.M., Pastoral Assoc.
Res.: 425 N. Fourth St., 43952. Tel: 740-282-7612; Fax: 740-282-9263. Email: jeanne@catholicweb.com. Web: www.stpeterschurch.catholicweb.com.
Please see Catholic Central High School, Bishop John King Mussio Central Junior High School & Bishop John King Mussio Central Elementary Schools located in the Institution section

8—ST. PIUS X, [JC] Closed. For inquiries for parish records contact Triumph of the Cross, Steubenville.

9—SERVANTS OF CHRIST THE KING, Closed. For inquiries for parish records contact Triumph of the Cross, Steubenville.

10—ST. STANISLAUS, [JC] Closed. For inquiries for parish records contact Triumph of the Cross, Steubenville.

11—TRIUMPH OF THE CROSS Revs. Thomas R. Nau; Mark J. Moore; Deacons Gerald Hickey; Randall Redington; Lawrence Meagher.
P.O. Box 908, 43952. Tel: 740-264-6177; Fax: 740-266-2844. Email: tofcmanager@comcast.net. Web: www.triumphofthecross.org.
Please see Catholic Central High School, Bishop John King Mussio Central Junior High School & Bishop John King Mussio Central Elementary Schools located in the Institution section

OUTSIDE THE CITY OF STEUBENVILLE

ADENA, JEFFERSON CO., ST. CASIMIR'S, [CEM] Rev. Msgr. John C. Kolesar.
Res.: 221 Hanna Ave., 43901. Tel: 740-546-3463; Fax: 740-546-3763. Email: stcadena@verizon.net.
Catechesis/Religious Program—Students 42.

AMSTERDAM, JEFFERSON CO., ST. JOSEPH, [CEM] Rev. John J. McCoy Jr.
Res.: 7457 State Hwy. 152, Richmond, 43944. Tel: 740-765-4142.
Church: 346 N. Main St., 43903.

ATHENS, ATHENS CO.

1—CHRIST THE KING UNIVERSITY PARISH Rev. Martin J. Holler.
Res.: 38 N. College St., 45701. Tel: 740-592-2711; Fax: 740-593-8908. Email: ctkinfo@ctkathens.org. Web: www.ctkathens.org.
Church: 75 Stewart St., 45701.
Catechesis/Religious Program—Email: ndenhart@ctkathens.org. Nancy Denhart, D.R.E. Students 139.

2—ST. PAUL'S, [CEM] Rev. Msgr. Patrick Gaughan.
Res.: 38 N. College St., 45701-2530. Tel: 740-593-7822.
Catechesis/Religious Program—Tel: 740-592-2711. Nancy Denhart, D.R.E. Students 71.
Chapel—Guysville, St. John

BARNESVILLE, BELMONT CO., ASSUMPTION, [CEM] Rev. Msgr. Mark J. Froehlich.
Res.: 306 W. Main St., P.O. Box 340, 43713. Tel: 740-425-2181; Fax: 740-425-3720. Email: mmjf6@comcast.net.
Catechesis/Religious Program—Students 56.

BARTON, BELMONT CO., OUR LADY OF ANGELS, Closed. For inquiries for parish records see St. Joseph, Bridgeport.

BELLAIRE, BELMONT CO.

1—ST. JOHN, [JC] Rev. Msgr. Gene W. Mullett.
Res.: 3745 Tallman Ave., 43906. Tel: 740-676-0051. Email: stjohns3745@comcast.net. Web: www.angelfire.com/falcon/stjohnstmichael.
School—Central Grade School, (Grades PreK-8) Tel: 740-676-2620; Fax: 740-676-8502. Email: bsje_jd@omeresa.net. Web: www.sjcgradeschool-.catholicweb.com. Joseph DeGenova, Prin. Lay Teachers 10; Students 120.

2—ST. MICHAEL'S, [CEM] [JC] Closed. For inquiries for parish records please see St. John, Bellaire.

BELLE VALLEY, NOBLE CO., CORPUS CHRISTI, [CEM] Rev. Wayne E. Morris.
Res.: P.O. Box 186, Caldwell, 43724. Tel: 740-732-4129; Fax: 740-732-1575. Email: ststephen@roadrunner.com.
Church: Main St., 43717. Tel: 614-732-7202.

BEVERLY, WASHINGTON CO., ST. BERNARD, [CEM] Rev. Msgr. Robert J. Kawa.
Res.: 309 Seventh St., P.O. Box 331, 45715. Tel: 740-984-2555; Fax: 740-984-2555. Email: stberbev@verizon.net.
Catechesis/Religious Program—Tel: 740-984-2387. Yvonne Huck, D.R.E. Tel: 740-984-4566. Students 112.

BLAINE, BELMONT CO., ALL SAINTS, Closed. For inquiries for parish records please see St. Joseph, Bridgeport.

BRIDGEPORT, BELMONT CO.

1—ST. ANTHONY OF PADUA, [JC] Rev. John Mucha.
Res.: 68210 Neola Ave., 43912. Tel: 740-635-0408.

2—ST. JOSEPH, [JC] Rev. John Mucha.
Res.: 68210 Neola Ave., 43912. Tel: 740-635-0408; Fax: 740-635-1166. Email: jmucha@diosteub.org. Web: www.stjoschurch.com.
School—(Grades PreK-8) Tel: 740-635-3313. Daniel Delande, Prin. Lay Teachers 12; Students 84.

BRILLIANT, JEFFERSON CO., OUR LADY OF FATIMA, Closed. Sacramental records are located at St. Agnes, Mingo Junction.

BUCHTEL, ATHENS CO., ST. PATRICK, Consolidated with St. Andrew to form St. Mary of the Hills, Nelsonville.

BURKHART, MONROE CO., ST. JOSEPH'S, [CEM 2] Closed. For inquiries for parish records please contact St. Sylvester, Woodsfield.

BYESVILLE, GUERNSEY CO., HOLY TRINITY, [CEM] Closed. For inquiries for parish records please contact Christ our Light, Cambridge.

CADIZ, HARRISON CO., ST. TERESA Rev. Timothy P. McGuire.
Res.: 143 E. South St., 43907. Tel: 740-942-2211. Email: harrcntcath@verizon.net.

CALDWELL, NOBLE CO., ST. STEPHEN, [CEM] Rev. Wayne E. Morris.
Res.: 1036 Belford St., Box 186, 43724. Tel: 740-732-4129; Fax: 740-732-1575. Email:

ststephencc@roadrunner.com.
CAMBRIDGE, GUERNSEY CO.
1—ST. BENEDICT, Closed. For inquiries for parish records see Christ Our Light, Cambridge.
2—CHRIST OUR LIGHT PARISH, [CEM 2] Revs. Robert D. Borer; Chester J. Pabin.
Office & Res.: 701 Gomber Ave., 43725. Tel: 740-432-7609; Fax: 740-439-0800. Email: stben_office@catholicweb.com.
School—St. Benedict, (Grades K-8), 220 N. 7th St., 43725. Tel: 740-432-6751; Fax: 740-432-4961. Sr. Theresa Feldcamp, O.S.F., Prin. Franciscan Sisters of Christian Charity 5; Lay Teachers 10; Students 102.
Catechesis/Religious Program—Patricia Farley, D.R.E. Students 83.
CARLISLE, NOBLE CO., ST. MICHAEL, [CEM] Rev. Thomas F. Hamm Jr.
Res.: 43700 Fulda Rd., Caldwell, 43724. Tel: 740-732-4576.
Church: 43925 County Rd. 43, Caldwell, 43724. Email: thamm@diosteub.org.
CARROLLTON, CARROLL CO., OUR LADY OF MERCY Rev. Thomas Marut.
Res.: 616 Roswell Rd., N.W., P.O. Box 155, 44615. Tel: 330-627-4664; Fax: 330-627-4664. Email: olm@voyager.net.
Catechesis/Religious Program—Sr. Rita Murphy, D.R.E. Students 56.
CHESAPEAKE, LAWRENCE CO., ST. ANN Rev. Charles Moran.
310 Third Ave., Box 428, 45619-0428. Tel: 740-867-4434; Fax: 740-867-5829. Email: stannchurch@verizon.net.
Catechesis/Religious Program—Tel: 740-867-4434, Ext. 10. Mrs. Marion Hutton, D.R.E. Students 56.
CHURCHTOWN, WASHINGTON CO., ST. JOHN THE BAPTIST, [CEM] Rev. Virgil Reischman.
Res.: 17784 State Rte. 676, Marietta, 45750. Tel: 740-896-2060; Fax: 740-896-3700.
School—Central Grade School, (Grades K-8) Tel: 740-896-2697; Fax: 740-896-2555. Jane Frances Hofbauer, Prin. Lay Teachers 10; Students 105.
COLERAIN, BELMONT CO., ST. FRANCES CABRINI Rev. Dale F. Tornes.
Res.: U.S. Rte. 250, P.O. Box 38, 43916. Tel: 740-635-9933; Fax: 740-738-0013. Email: dtornes@diosteub.org.
DILLONVALE, JEFFERSON CO., ST. ADALBERT, [CEM] Rev. Msgr. John C. Kolesar.
Res.: c/o 221 Hanna Ave., Adena, 43901. Tel: 740-546-3463; Fax: 740-546-3763. Email: stcadena@verizon.net.
Catechesis/Religious Program—Tel: 740-769-7858. Rosemary Zelek, D.R.E. Students 32.
FAIRPOINT, BELMONT CO., ST. JOSEPH Rev. Thomas J. Graven.
Mailing Address: 71793 Church St., P.O. Box 308, Maynard, 43937. Tel: 740-695-2618; Fax: 740-695-2618. Email: tgraven@diosteub.org.
Church: 46982 Columbia St., 8, 43927. Tel: 740-695-0840.
Catechesis/Religious Program—Students 55.
FLUSHING, BELMONT CO., ST. PAUL'S, [CEM] Rev. Frederick C. Kihm.
Res.: 115 Morristown Rd., Box 45, 43977. Tel: 740-968-4159.
Catechesis/Religious Program—Tel: 740-782-1223. Marianne Fraley, D.R.E. Students 14.
FULDA, NOBLE CO., IMMACULATE CONCEPTION, [CEM] Rev. Thomas F. Hamm Jr.
Res.: 43700 Fulda Rd., Caldwell, 43724. Tel: 740-732-4576.
GALLIPOLIS, GALLIA CO., ST. LOUIS, [CEM] Rev. Msgr. William R. Myers.
Res.: 85 State St., 45631. Tel: 740-446-0669; Fax: 740-446-9858.
GLOUSTER, ATHENS CO., HOLY CROSS, [CEM] Rev. David Cornett.
Mailing Address: 110 E. Washington St., Nelsonville, 45764. Tel: 740-753-1770; Fax: 740-753-4480.
Rectory—31 Republic Ave., 45732. Tel: 740-767-3068.
Church: Corner of Madison & Republic Avenues, 45732.
HARRIETTSVILLE, NOBLE CO., ST. HENRY, [CEM] Rev. Timothy J. Huffman.
Mailing Address: 5001 Lowell Hill Rd., Lowell, 45744. Tel: 740-896-2207; Fax: 740-896-2800.
Church: Rte. 1, 36575 Church St., CR 47, Lower Salem, 45745. Tel: 740-585-2383.
HOPEDALE, HARRISON CO., SACRED HEART, [JC] Rev. Timothy P. McGuire.
Res. & Mailing Address: 143 E. South St., Cadiz, 43907. Tel: 740-942-2211. Email: harrcntcath@verizon.net.
Church: 205 Cross St., 43976.
IRONTON, LAWRENCE CO.
1—ST. JOSEPH, [JC] Revs. David L. Huffman; Timothy J. Kozak, Parochial Vicar.
Res.: 905 S. Fifth St., P.O. Box 499, 45638. Tel: 740-532-0561; 740-532-0712; Fax: 740-534-0557. Email: stjoelaw@roadrunner.com. Web: www.irontoncatholicchurches.com.
Catechesis/Religious Program—Jane Rudmann, D.R.E. Students 49.
2—ST. LAWRENCE, [JC] Revs. David L. Huffman; Timothy J. Kozak, Parochial Vicar.
Res.: 905 S. Fifth St., P.O. Box 499, 45638-0499. Tel: 740-532-0561; Fax: 740-534-0557. Email: stjoelaw@roadrunner.com. Web: www.irontoncatholicchurches.com.
School—St. Lawrence Central Grade School, (Grades K-6) Tel: 740-532-5052; Fax: 740-532-5082. Web: irontoncatholicschools.com. James J. Mains III, Prin. Lay Teachers 9; Students 89.
High School—St. Joseph Central High School, (Grades 7-12), 912 S. 6th St., 45638. Tel: 740-532-0485; Fax: 740-532-3699. Web: irontoncatholicschools.com. James J. Mains III, Prin. Lay Teachers 10; Students 90.
Convent—615 Center St., 45638. Tel: 740-533-1206.
LAFFERTY, BELMONT CO., ST. MARY, [CEM] Rev. Frederick C. Kihm.
Res.: Box 45, Flushing, 43977. Tel: 740-968-4159.
Church: 70230 Church St., P.O. Box 188, 43951. Tel: 740-968-3200; Fax: 740-968-1881. Email: fkihm@diosteub.org.
Catechesis/Religious Program—Tel: 740-782-1487. Jill A. Clift, D.R.E. Students 19.
LITTLE HOCKING, WASHINGTON CO., ST. AMBROSE, [CEM] Rev. Robert A. Gallagher.
Res.: 5080 School House Rd., 45742. Tel: 740-423-7422.
Catechesis/Religious Program—Tel: 740-374-0848. Mrs. Joan Smith, D.R.E. Students 196.
LORE CITY, GUERNSEY CO., SS. PETER AND PAUL, [CEM] Closed. For inquiries for parish records please see Christ Our Light, Cambridge.
LOWELL, WASHINGTON CO., OUR LADY OF MERCY, [CEM] Rev. Timothy J. Huffman.
Res.: 5001 Lowell Hill Rd., 45744. Tel: 740-896-2207; Fax: 740-896-2800.
MALVERN, CARROLL CO., ST. FRANCIS XAVIER (1848) [CEM] Rev. Victor Cinson.
Res.: 125 Carrollton St., P.O. Box 275, Minerva, 44657. Tel: 330-863-0305; Fax: 330-863-0760.
Catechesis/Religious Program—Tel: 330-863-3050; Fax: 330-868-2188. Denise Laubacher, D.R.E. Students 42.
MARIETTA, WASHINGTON CO., ST. MARY'S, [CEM 2] Rev. Msgr. John Michael Campbell; Rev. Seth T. Wymer. In Res., Rev. Msgr. Edward Kakascik (Retired).
Res.: 506 Fourth St., 45750. Tel: 740-373-3643; Fax: 740-376-2956.
School—(Grades PreK-8), 320 Marion St., 45750. Tel: 740-374-8181; Fax: 740-374-8602. Rita Angel, Prin. Lay Teachers 22; Students 183.
Catechesis/Religious Program—Students 133.
MARTINS FERRY, BELMONT CO., ST. MARY, [CEM] Rev. Thomas A. Magary.
Res.: 20 N. Fourth St., 43935. Tel: 740-633-1416; Fax: 740-633-1490. Email: stmarymf@sbcglobal.net.
School—St. Mary Central, (Grades PreSchool-8), 24 N. Fourth St., 43935. Tel: 740-633-5424; Fax: 740-633-5462. Mary Carolyn Nichelson, Prin. Lay Teachers 9; Students 84; Aides 2.
Catechesis/Religious Program—Tel: 740-633-1416. Judy Kacsmar, D.R.E. Students 10.
MAYNARD, BELMONT CO., ST. STANISLAUS Rev. Thomas J. Graven.
Res.: 71793 Church St., P.O. Box 308, 43937. Tel: 740-695-2618; Fax: 740-695-2618. Email: tgraven@diosteub.org.
MCCONNELSVILLE, MORGAN CO., ST. JAMES Rev. Paul Walker.
Res.: 257 Bell Ave., 43756. Tel: 740-962-2856.
MILTONSBURG, MONROE CO., ST. JOHN THE BAPTIST, [CEM 2] Rev. David L. Gaydosik.
Res.: 334 S. Main St., Woodsfield, 43793.
Church: 35560 Miltonsburg-Calais Rd., Woodsfield, 43793. Tel: 740-472-0187; Fax: 740-472-0182. Email: dgaydosik@diosteub.org.
MINERVA, CARROLL CO., ST. GABRIEL THE ARCHANGEL Rev. Victor Cinson.
Res.: 400 West High, P.O. Box 275, 44657. Tel: 330-868-4498; Fax: 330-868-2188.
Catechesis/Religious Program—Students 162.
MINGO JUNCTION, JEFFERSON CO.
1—ST. AGNES, [JC] Rev. James M. Dunfee.
Mailing Address: 204 St. Clair Ave., 43938-1047. Tel: 740-535-1491.
Catechesis/Religious Program—Students 62.
2—ANNUNCIATION, Closed. Parish records can be found at St. Agnes Church, Mingo Junction.
3—ST. BERNADETTE, Closed. Sacramental records are located at St. Agnes, Mingo Junction.
MORGES, CARROLL CO., ST. MARY, [CEM] Rev. Thomas Marut.
Res.: P.O. Box 690, Waynesburg, 44688. Tel: 330-866-2023.
Catechesis/Religious Program—Suzanne Tozzi, D.R.E. Students 9.
NEFFS, BELMONT CO., SACRED HEART Rev. Msgr. Gene W. Mullett.
Res.: 54038 St. Mary Ave., P.O. Box 425, 43940-0425. Tel: 740-676-3277; Fax: 740-676-3400.
Catechesis/Religious Program—Students 7.
NELSONVILLE, ATHENS CO., ST. MARY OF THE HILLS, Consolidated with St. Andrew, Nelsonville and St. Patrick, Buchtel to form St. Mary of the Hills. Rev. David Cornett.
Res.: 110 E. Washington St., 45764. Tel: 740-753-1770; Fax: 740-753-4480.
PINE GROVE, LAWRENCE CO., ST. MARY, [CEM] Rev. David L. Huffman.
Res.: 905 S. Fifth St., Ironton, 45638. Tel: 740-532-0712; Fax: 740-534-0557.
PINEY FORK, JEFFERSON CO., ST. THERESE, Closed. For inquiries for Sacramental records please see St. Casimir, Adena.
POMEROY, MEIGS CO., SACRED HEART, [CEM] Rev. Walter E. Heinz.
Res.: 161 Mulberry Ave., 45769. Tel: 740-992-5898; Fax: 740-992-6771.
Catechesis/Religious Program—Cindy Nau, D.R.E. Students 67.
POWHATAN POINT, BELMONT CO., ST. JOHN VIANNEY Rev. Samuel Saprano.
Mailing Address: *St. Mary Church*, 350 E. 40th St., Shadyside, 43947. Tel: 740-676-3282.
Church: 295 Hwy. 7 N., 43942.
RICHMOND, JEFFERSON CO., ST. JOHN FISHER Rev. John J. McCoy Jr.
Res.: 7457 St. Hwy. 152, 43944. Tel: 740-765-4142.
ST. CLAIRSVILLE, BELMONT CO., ST. MARY'S Revs. Thomas A. Chillog; Anthony R. Batt; Bradley Greer, Parochial Vicar.
Office: 212 W. Main St., 43950. Email: stmarysc@comcast.net.
Res.: 230 W. Main St., 43950.
School—St. Mary Central Grade School, (Grades PreSchool-8), 226 W. Main St., 43950. Tel: 740-695-3189; Fax: 740-695-3851. Lay Teachers 10; Students 165.
Catechesis/Religious Program—Fax: 740-695-6503. Michael Zabrecky, D.R.E. Students 116.
SHADYSIDE, BELMONT CO., ST. MARY'S (1946) Rev. Samuel Saprano.
350 E. 40th St., 43947. Tel: 740-676-3282; Fax: 740-676-1424.
Catechesis/Religious Program—Lyn Velkovich, D.R.E. Students 23.
SMITHFIELD, JEFFERSON CO., OUR LADY, QUEEN OF PEACE, [JC] Closed. For inquiries for Sacramental records please see St. Casimir, Adena.
TEMPERANCEVILLE, BELMONT CO., ST. MARY'S, [CEM] Rev. Msgr. Mark J. Froehlich.
Res.: P.O. Box 340, Barnesville, 43713. Tel: 740-425-2181.
TILTONSVILLE, JEFFERSON CO., ST. JOSEPH (1917) Rev. Daniel Heusel.
Mailing Address: P.O. Box 8, 43963-0008.
Res.: 204 Mound St., 43963-1017. Tel: 740-859-4018; Fax: 740-859-6041. Email: dheusel@diosteub.org.
Catechesis/Religious Program—(Combined with St. Lucy, Yorkville) Students 16.
TORONTO, JEFFERSON CO.
1—ST. FRANCIS OF ASSISI, [JC] Rev. Thomas A. Vennitti; Bro. Anthony Motto, I.H.M., Pastoral Assoc.
Res.: 1225 N. River Ave., 43964. Tel: 740-537-4433; Fax: 740-537-9305. Web: home.catholicweb.com/sfsjtoronto.
School—(Grades PreK-6), 601 Loretta St., 43964. Tel: 740-537-2151; Fax: 740-537-9380. Mrs. Marian Barker, Prin. Lay Teachers 6; Students 63.
Catechesis/Religious Program—Judy Koehnlein, D.R.E. Students 19.
2—ST. JOSEPH'S, [JC] Rev. Thomas A. Vennitti; Bro. Anthony Motto, I.H.M., Pastoral Assoc.
Res.: 1225 N. River Ave., 43964. Tel: 740-537-4433; Fax: 740-537-9305. Web: home.catholicweb.com/sfsjtoronto.
Catechesis/Religious Program—Judy Koehnlein, D.R.E. Students 9.
VINCENT, WASHINGTON CO., ST. AMBROSE, Consolidated with St. Ambrose, Little Hocking.
WINTERSVILLE, JEFFERSON CO.
1—BLESSED SACRAMENT, [JC] Rev. Msgr. Kurt H. Kemo; Very Rev. William D. Cross; Revs. H. Christopher Foxhoven; Vincent J. Huber (Retired).
Res.: 852 Main St., 43953-3870. Tel: 740-264-0868; Fax: 740-264-5449. Email: mail@wintersvilleparishes.org. Web: www.wintersvilleparishes.org.
Please see Catholic Central High School, Bishop John King Mussio Central Junior High School & Bishop John King Mussio Central Elementary Schools located in the Institution section
Catechesis/Religious Program—Patty D'Anniballe, D.R.E. Students 22.

2—Our Lady of Lourdes, [JC] Rev. Msgr. Kurt H. Kemo; Very Rev. William D. Cross; Rev. H. Christopher Foxhoven.
Res.: 852 Main St., 43953-3870. Tel: 740-264-0868. Email: mail@wintersvilleparishes.org. Web: www.wintersvilleparishes.org.
Church: 1521 Bantam Ridge Rd., 43953-0612. Tel: 740-264-2798; Fax: 740-264-5449.
Please see Catholic Central High School, Bishop John King Mussio Central Junior High School & Bishop John King Mussio Central Elementary Schools located in the Institution section
Catechesis/Religious Program—Sam Rotella, D.R.E. Students 18.

Woodsfield, Monroe Co., St. Sylvester, [CEM] Rev. David L. Gaydosik.
Res.: 38867 Briar Ridge Rd., 43793. Tel: 740-472-0187; Fax: 740-472-0182. Email: dgaydosik@diosteub.org.
Rectory—334 S. Main St., 43793.
School—Central Grade School, (Grades PreSchool-8) Tel: 740-472-0321; Fax: 740-472-1994. Jill Schumacher, Prin. & D.R.E. Lay Teachers 8; Students 86.
Catechesis/Religious Program—Students 2.

Yorkville, Jefferson Co., St. Lucy's Rev. Daniel Heusel.
Mailing Address: P.O. Box 8, Tiltonsville, 43963-0008. Tel: 740-859-4018; Fax: 740-859-6041. Email: dheusel@diosteub.org.

DIOCESAN MISSIONS

Bloomingdale, Jefferson Co., St. Thomas More Mission, Closed. Sacramental records are located at St. John Fisher, Richmond.

Chauncey, Athens Co., St. Jude Mission, Closed. Sacramental records are located at St. Paul Church, Athens.

Crescent, Belmont Co., St. Elizabeth Mission, Closed. Sacramental records are located at St. Stanislaus Church, Maynard.

Freeport, Harrison Co., St. Matthias Mission Rev. Timothy P. McGuire.
Res.: 143 E. South St., Cadiz, 43907. Tel: 740-942-2211. Email: tmcguire@diosteub.org.
Church: Main St., Box 195, 43973. Tel: 740-658-3300.

Hammondsville, Jefferson Co., Nativity of Our Lord Mission, Closed. Sacramental records are located at St. Joseph Church, Toronto.

Jewett, Harrison Co., Our Lady of Perpetual Help Mission, Closed. Sacramental records located at 1435 E. South St., Cadiz, OH 43907.

Sardis, Monroe Co., St. John Bosco Mission, [CEM] Rev. David L. Gaydosik.
Res.: 334 S. Main St., Woodsfield, 43793. Tel: 740-472-0187; Fax: 740-472-1994.

Tappan Lake, Harrison Co., Christ the King Summer Mission, Closed. Sacramental records are located at: 143 E. South St., Cadiz 43907. Tel: 740-942-2211.

Tupper Plains, Meigs Co., Our Lady of Loretto Church, Closed. Sacramental records are located at Sacred Heart Church, Pomeroy.

On Duty Outside the Diocese:
Rev. Msgr.—
Wippel, John, Ph.D., 10105 Portland Pl., Silver Springs, MD 20901. Tel: 301-593-9345; 202-319-6648
Revs.—
Calabrese, Charles L., TCU, Box 297310, Fort Worth, TX 76129-0001. Tel: 817-923-2176; 817-921-7830
DiRenzo, Michael J. (LA), U.S.A.F. Chap. (Lt. Col.), 2731 Englewood Dr., Melbourne, FL 32940. Tel: 321-253-3303
Hrezo, Paul, Pontifical College Josephinum, 7625 N. High St., Columbus, 43235-1498. Tel: 614-885-5585
Massucci, Joseph D. (CIN), University of Dayton, 324 Chaminade Hall, Dayton, 45469-0534. Tel: 937-229-3737; 937-229-3730. Email: josephmassucci@notes.udayton.edu
Safraniec, Joseph N., Chap., St. Francis Way, Eagan, MN 55123-1167. Tel: 651-405-6705
Smith-Soucier, Martin D., 292 Durnan St., Rochester, NY 14621. Tel: 585-544-8778; 585-705-0188. Email: ms809oh@aol.com

---

On Leave:
Rev.—
Prati, Jason M.

Medical Leave:
Rev.—
Tuttle, Richard J., 436 Lauretta Dr., 43952. Tel: 740-264-5605

Administrative Leave:
Rev.—
Zaleski, Gary A.

Retired:
Most Revs.—
Ottenweller, Albert H., D.D., S.T.L.
Sheldon, Gilbert I., D.D., D.Min.
Rev. Msgrs.—
Adams, George J., 785 Broad St., Brockway, PA 15824. Tel: 814-265-8371
Boehm, James A., 501 W. Chestnut Dr., Hendersonville, NC 28739. Tel: 828-697-8269
Cornelius, William R., 4333 Steuben Woods Dr., 43953. Tel: 740-264-0741
Coyne, George R., 67330 Ebbert Rd., S. Unit 2, Saint Clairsville, 43950. Tel: 740-296-5038
Cymbor, John A., 54345 High Ridge Rd., Bridgeport, 43912. Tel: 740-676-5545
Giannamore, Anthony J., 709 Brockton Pl. E., Sun City Center, FL 33573. Tel: 813-633-3553
Horak, Donald E., 149 Otter Rd., Hilton Head Island, SC 29928. Tel: 843-363-2933
Kakascik, Edward, St. Mary Church, 506 4th St., Marietta, 45750. Tel: 740-373-3643
Metzger, Paul E., 428 Cambridge Dr., Middletown, 45042. Tel: 513-424-4576
Nealon, Joseph A., P.O. Box 158, Carrollton, 44615-0158. Tel: 330-627-7083
Nugent, James B., 25 Noe Bixby Rd., Unit 101, Columbus, 43213. Tel: 614-367-1924
Pasquinelli, Frederick A., 4337 Steuben Woods Dr., 43953. Tel: 740-264-0970
Petronek, Thomas C., 1810 National Rd., B3-109, Wheeling, WV 26003. Email: tpetronek@diosteub.org
Reasbeck, David E., Park Health, 100 Pine Ave., Rm. 217A, Saint Clairsville, 43950.
Uram, Kenneth J., 231 Woodridge Dr., Apt. A303, Wintersville, 43953. Tel: 740-264-9600
Revs.—
Belfield, John, P.O. Box 119, Avon Park, FL 33825. Tel: 941-386-0631
Cencula, Leonard T., 1127 Euclid Ave., Apt. 1405, Cleveland, 44115. Tel: 740-632-4624
Deasio, August J., M.A., 935 Yellow Mills Rd., Shortsville, NY 14548. Tel: 716-289-3074
Huber, Vincent J., M.Ed., 1688 Bantam Ridge Rd., Wintersville, 43953. Tel: 740-317-4939
Krajcovic, Bernard, 107 St. Lucy Ave., Yorkville, 43971. Tel: 740-859-0262
Lyden, Dennis P., St. Joseph Church, P.O. Box 98, Fairpoint, 43927. Tel: 740-695-0840
Martinosky, Joseph A., 603 Franklin Ave., Apt. #1, Columbus, 43215. Tel: 614-224-4498
Mascolino, Charles E., 4338 Steuben Woods Dr., Wintersville, 43953. Tel: 740-266-9032
Stabene, Edmondo, 2063 Bantam Ridge Rd., P.O. Box 2373, Wintersville, 43953. Tel: 740-264-9761
Stromski, Adam F.X., St. Joseph Care Center, 1882 Knob St., Louisville, KY 44541. Tel: 330-875-1491

Permanent Deacons:
Cerrato, Dominic, 162 Twp. Hwy. 202, Bloomingdale, 43910. Tel: 740-944-1846
Hickey, Gerald, 1803 Williams Pl., 43952. Tel: 740-283-1585
James, Joseph F., 1434 Magnolia Rd., S.W., Dellroy, 44620-9756. Tel: 330-340-4141
McKeating, Michael, 2012 Oregon Ave., 43952. Tel: 716-228-5129
Meagher, Lawrence, 4620 Lexington Dr., 43952. Tel: 740-264-3122
Miravalle, Mark, 315 High St., Hopedale, 43976. Tel: 740-283-6433; Fax: 740-937-2555; Tel: 740-444-4407
Pettie, Paul, (On Duty Outside the Diocese)
Piasecki, Stanley T., 67341 Ebbert South Rd., Saint Clairsville, 43950. Tel: 740-296-5123. Email: stpplpiasecki@aim.com
Poyo, Ralph, 1106 Jackson Pl., 43952. Tel: 740-314-5528
Redington, Randall, 401 Rosemont Ave., 43952. Tel: 740-266-7255; 740-765-5500

INSTITUTIONS LOCATED IN THE DIOCESE

[A] COLLEGES AND UNIVERSITIES

Steubenville. *Franciscan University of Steubenville*, 1235 University Blvd., 43952. Tel: 740-283-3771; Fax: 740-283-6472. Email: admissions@franciscan.edu. Web: www.franciscan.edu. Revs. Terence Henry, T.O.R., Pres.; Michael Scanlan, T.O.R., Chancellor; Mr. David M. Skiviat, Vice Pres. Finance & Admin.; Max Bonilla, Vice Pres., Academic Affairs; Mr. David Schmiesing, Vice Pres. Student Life; Dr. Robert Filby, Exec. Vice Pres.; Mr. Joel Recznik, Vice Pres., Enrollment Mgmt.; Mrs. Elizabeth Loizzo, Sec. to the Pres.; Revs. Bradley LePage, T.O.R., Chap., Austria Prog.; Brian Cavanaugh, T.O.R., Coord. Prog. Devel. & Tech. Initiatives; Richard Davis, T.O.R., Vice Pres. Community Rels. & Religious Admin.; Donald S. Frinsko, T.O.R., Theology Prog.; Dennis Gang, T.O.R., Chap., Student Life; Kenneth Cienik, S.A., Dir. Pre-Theology Prog.; Conrad Harkins, O.F.M., Assoc. Prof. Theology; Laurence Uhlman, T.O.R., Dir. Works of Mercy; Daniel Pattee, T.O.R, Asst. Prof. Theology; Dominic Scotto, T.O.R., Univ. Chap. & Lecturer in Theology; Joseph Yelenc, T.O.R., Biology Prof.; David Morrier, T.O.R., Coord. Household Life; Seraphim Beshoner, T.O.R., Asst. Prof. History; Dominic Foster, T.O.R., Dir. Evangelization; Bro. John Paul McMahon, T.O.R., Instr. Economy; Revs. Gregory Plow, T.O.R., Asst. Coord. Household Life; James Mormen, T.O.R, Counselor; Nicholas Polichnowski, T.O.R., Asst. Prof. Nursing; Richard Martignetti, O.F.M., Asst. Dir., Pre-Theology Prog.; Ronald J. Mohnickey, T.O.R., Dir. Austrian Prog.; Mr. Michael Hernon, Vice Pres. Advancement; Mr. Adam Scurti, Vice Pres. Human Resources & Legal Counsel; Mr. William Jakub, Librarian. Priests 21; Brothers 3; Sisters 1; Lay Teachers 105; Students 2,449.

[B] HIGH SCHOOLS, CENTRAL

Steubenville. *Catholic Central High School*, 320 West View, 43952. Tel: 740-264-5538; Fax: 740-264-5443. Email: r.wilinski@steubenvillecatholiccentral.org. Web: cchs.sbd.pvt.k12.oh.us. Mr. Richard Wilinski, Prin. Priests 1; Chaplain 1; Lay Teachers 20; Students 280.

Bellaire. *St. John Central High School*, (Grades 7-12), 3625 Guernsey St., 43906. Tel: 740-676-4932; Fax: 740-676-4934. Web: www.bellairestjohn.sbd.pvt.k12.oh.us. Mrs. Rhea Rosa, Interim Prin.; Edwin Jepson, Librarian. Sisters 1; Lay Teachers 15; Students 126.

[C] JUNIOR-SENIOR CENTRAL HIGH SCHOOLS

Ironton. *St. Joseph Central*, (Grades 7-12), 912 S. Sixth St., 45638. Tel: 740-532-0485; Fax: 740-532-3699. Email: jmains@Scoca-k12.org. James J. Mains III, Prin. Total Staff 13; Students 90.

[D] CENTRAL JUNIOR HIGH SCHOOLS

Steubenville. *Bishop John King Mussio Central Junior High School*, (Grades 7-8), 320 W. View, Ste. 2, 43952. Tel: 740-346-0028; Fax: 740-346-0070. Email: santinone@bishopmussiojh.org. Theresa Danaher, Prin. Lay Teachers 9; Students 146.

[E] ELEMENTARY SCHOOLS, CENTRAL

Steubenville. *Bishop John King Mussio Central Elementary School*, (Grades K-6), (Rosemont Campus): Etta Ave., 43952. Tel: 740-264-2550; Fax: 740-266-2843. Email: theresa.dipiero@omeresa.net. Theresa DiPiero, Prin. Lay Teachers 19; Students 285.
(Grades K-6), (Lovers Lane Campus): 625 Lovers Ln., 43953. Tel: 740-264-3651; Fax: 740-264-4277. Email: theresa.dipiero@omeresa.net. Theresa DiPiero, Prin. Lay Teachers 10; Students 157.

[F] GENERAL HOSPITALS

Steubenville. *Trinity Health System*, 380 Summit Ave., 43952. Tel: 740-283-7212; Fax: 740-283-7104. Web: www.trinityhealth.com. Sisters 4; Nurses 381; LPNs 29; Nurse Anesthetists 18; Admissions 12,349; Outpatients 185,559; Emergency Room 45,937; Births 627; Bed Capacity 500.
Trinity Medical Center, West, 4000 Johnson Rd., 43952. Tel: 740-264-8000; Fax: 740-283-7104. Web: www.trinityhealth.com. Rev. Mark J. Moore, Chap.
Trinity Medical Center, East, 380 Summit Ave., 43952. Tel: 740-283-7000; Fax: 740-283-7104. Sisters Magdala Davlin, O.S.F., Pastoral Care Coord.; Mary Patrick Gillen, O.S.F., Staff Chap.
Trinity Health System Foundation, 380 Summit Ave., 43952. Tel: 740-283-7212; Fax: 740-283-7104.

[G] RESIDENTIAL CARE FACILITY

Carrollton. *St. John Villa*, P.O. Box 457, 44615. Tel: 330-627-9789; Fax: 330-627-4826. Web: stjohnsvilla.net. Deacon Joseph F. James, Pres. Residential facility for persons with developmental disabilities. Faculty 100; Child

Care Services 120; Adult Day Care 10; Residents 55.

[H] MONASTERIES AND RESIDENCES OF PRIESTS AND BROTHERS

STEUBENVILLE. *Diocesan Brotherhood of Immaculate Heart of Mary*, Villa Maria Motherhouse, 609 N. Seventh St., 43952. Tel: 740-283-2462. Email: dcarroll@diosteub.org. Bro. Dominic Carroll, I.H.M., Supr. Gen. Professed Brothers 4.

Holy Spirit Friary, 1235 University Blvd., 43952. Tel: 740-283-6403; Fax: 740-283-6348. Web: www.franciscan.edu. Revs. Bradley LePage, T.O.R.; Seraphim Beshoner, T.O.R.; Brian Cavanaugh, T.O.R.; Richard Davis, T.O.R., Local Min.; Albert Driesch, T.O.R.; Dominic Foster, T.O.R.; Donald S. Frinsko, T.O.R.; Dennis Gang, T.O.R.; Terence Henry, T.O.R., Pres.; Ronald J. Mohnickey, T.O.R.; David Morrier, T.O.R.; James Morman, T.O.R.; Daniel Pattee, T.O.R; Gregory Plow, T.O.R.; Nicholas Polichnowski, T.O.R.; Michael Scanlan, T.O.R.; Dominic Scotto, T.O.R.; Joseph Yelenc, T.O.R.; Laurence Uhlman, T.O.R.; Bros. John Paul McMahon, T.O.R.; John Patrick Calvey, T.O.R.; Sean Mary Fitzwater, T.O.R. Priests 22; Brothers 3. In Res. Revs. Kenneth Cienik, S.A.; Conrad Harkins, O.F.M.; Richard Martignetti, O.F.M.

BLOOMINGDALE. *Holy Family Hermitage*, 1501 Fairplay Rd., 43910-7971. Tel: 740-765-4511; Fax: 740-765-4511. Web: www.camaldolese.org. Revs. Basil Corriere, E.C., Prior; Paul Vankeirsbilck, E.C.; Nicolas Luna, E.C.; Martin Flum, Postulant. Hermits 4.

[I] CONVENTS AND RESIDENCES FOR SISTERS

STEUBENVILLE. *Sacred Heart Villa*, 36 Villa Dr., 43953-7129. Tel: 740-282-3801; Fax: 740-282-3801. Sr. Ernestine Vitello, Supr. Handmaids of Reparation of the Sacred Heart of Jesus, Motherhouse of America Foundation. Engaged in Kindergarten, Pre-Kindergarten and Parish work.

CARROLLTON. *Union of Our Lady of Charity United States Province*, 620 Roswell Rd., N.W., P.O. Box 158, 44615-0158. Tel: 330-627-7647; Fax: 330-627-4415. Email: nauolc@eohio.net. Web: nauolc.org. Sr. Sheila Rooney, Local Supr. Professed Sisters 30.

[J] ASSOCIATIONS OF THE FAITHFUL

STEUBENVILLE. *Sisters of Reparation to the Most Sacred Heart of Jesus*, 354 Rinker Rd., P.O. Box 9, 43952. Tel: 740-282-2144; Fax: 740-282-7919. Email: srmwendy@sistersofreparation.org. Web: www.sistersofreparation.org. Sr. Wendy McMenamy, S.R., Local Supr. Sisters 6; Postulants 2.

BLOOMINGDALE. *Mount Carmel Hermitage of Ohio, Inc*, 1619 Township Rd. 204, 43910. Tel: 740-765-5409. Sisters Immaculata St. Anthony, O.C.D.; Barbara Wright, O.C.D. Sisters 2.

HOPEDALE. *The Order of the Sacred and Immaculate Hearts of Jesus and Mary*, 48765 Annapolis Rd., 43976. Tel: 740-946-9000. Email: twohearts1@mac.com. Revs. Benedict Suing, O.S.B.; Francis Dankoski; Sr. Teresa Condit, Vocations Dir. Priests 2; Brothers 2; Sisters 2.

TORONTO. *Franciscan Sisters Third Order Regular of Penance of the Sorrowful Mother*, 170 Little Church Rd., 43964. Tel: 740-544-5542; Fax: 740-544-5543. Email: franciscansisters@torsisters.org. Web: www.torsisters.org. Sr. Katherine Caldwell, T.O.R., Supr. Sisters 21; Novices 7; Postulants 3.

[K] SHRINES

FRANKLIN FURNACE. *Our Lady of Fatima Shrine* Old Rte. 52, 45629. P.O. Box 499, Ironton, 45638-0499. Rev. David L. Huffman. Tel: 740-532-0712; Fax: 740-534-0557.

[L] NEWMAN CENTERS

ATHENS. *Christ the King University Parish - Ohio University* 75 Stewart St., 45701. Tel: 740-592-2711; Fax: 740-593-8908. Email: mholler@ctkathens.org. Web: www.ctkathens.org. Rev. Martin J. Holler, Dir. Campus Ministry.

MARIETTA. *Marietta College* c/o St. Mary Church, 506 Fourth St., 45750. Tel: 740-373-3643; Fax: 740-376-2956. Email: info@stmarysmarietta.org. Web: www.stmarysmarietta.org. Rev. Msgr. John Michael Campbell, Dir.

NELSONVILLE. *Hocking Technical College* Rev. David Cornett, Dir.

Res.: 110 E. Washington St., 45764. Tel: 740-753-1770.

RIO GRANDE. *Rio Grande University* 91 State St., Gallipolis, 45631. Tel: 740-446-0669. Rev. Msgr. William R. Myers, Contact Person.

ST. CLAIRSVILLE. *Ohio University - Eastern* c/o St. Mary's Church, 212 W. Main St., 43950. Tel: 740-695-9993; Fax: 740-695-6503. Email: stmarysc@comcast.net. Rev. Thomas A. Chillog, M.Div., Contact Person.

[M] MISCELLANEOUS LISTINGS

STEUBENVILLE. *Boy Scouts*, P.O. Box 499, Ironton, 45638-0499. Tel: 740-532-0712. Email: smolloy@diosteub.org. Rev. David L. Huffman, Dir.

Campaign for Human Development, Office of Family & Social Concerns, P.O. Box 969, 43952. Tel: 740-282-3631; Fax: 740-282-3327. Email: msantin@diosteub.org. Web: www.diosteub.org. Mrs. Michele Santin, Diocesan Dir.

**Catholics United for the Faith, Inc.*, 827 N. Fourth St., 43952. Tel: 740-283-2484; Fax: 740-283-4011. Email: info@cuf.org. Web: www.cuf.org. Michael Sullivan, Pres.; Shannon Minch-Highes, Vice Pres. Opers.

**Dietrich Von Hildebrand Legacy Project*, 417 Belleview Blvd., 43952. Tel: 740-282-0883. Email: jimhostetler@sbcglobal.net. Web: www.hildebrandlegacy.org. James M. Hostetler, Trustee & Sec.

**Fraternity of Priests, Inc.*, 100 Belleview Blvd., 43952. Tel: 740-283-4400; Fax: 740-283-3622. Email: contact@fraternityofpriests.org. Web: www.fraternityofpriests.org.

Information & Referral, c/o Family & Social Concerns, P.O. Box 969, 43952. Tel: 740-282-6880; 800-339-7890; Fax: 740-282-3327. Email: msantin@diosteub.org. Web: www.diosteub.org.

Lay Employees Pension Plan, P.O. Box 969, 43952. Tel: 740-282-3631; Fax: 740-282-1409.

Mt. Calvary Cemetery Association, 94 Mt. Calvary Ln., 43952. Tel: 740-264-1331; Fax: 740-264-9203. Email: rap6477@hotmail.com.

**Pastoral Solutions Institute*, 234 St. Joseph Dr., 43952. Tel: 740-266-6461. Web: www.exceptionalmarriages.com. Gregory K. Popcak, Pres.

**St. Paul Center for Biblical Theology*, 2228 Sunset Blvd., Ste. 2A, 43952. Tel: 740-264-9535; Fax: 740-264-7908. Email: office@salvationhistory.com. Web: www.salvationhistory.com. Dr. Scott Hahn, Pres.

RCIA, 43700 Fulda Rd., Caldwell, 43724. Tel: 740-732-4576. Email: thamm@diosteub.org. Web: www.diosteub.org. Rev. Thomas F. Hamm Jr., Dir.

BEVERLY. *Marriage Encounter, c/o St. Bernard Church*, 307 Seventh St., P.O. Box 331, 45715. Tel: 740-984-2555; Fax: 740-984-2555. Email: stberbev@verizon.net. Rev. Msgr. Robert J. Kawa, Dir.

BLOOMINGDALE. *Apostolate for Family Consecration aka Catholic Familyland/John Paul II Holy Family Center* 3375 County Rd. 36, 43910-7903. Tel: 740-765-5500; Fax: 740-765-4941. Email: jconiker@familyland.org. Web: www.familycatechism.com. Mr. Jerome F. Coniker, Pres.

CARROLLTON. *Our Lady of Charity Center Caritas House, Inc.*, 620 Roswell Rd., N.W., P.O. Box 158, 44615. Tel: 330-627-5765; Fax: 304-627-4415. Sr. Mary Annunciata Mason, O.L.C., Prog. Dir.

RELIGIOUS INSTITUTES OF MEN REPRESENTED IN THE DIOCESE

For further details refer to the corresponding bracketed number in the Religious Institutes of Men or Women section.

[0680]—*Brothers of the Immaculate Heart of Mary*—I.H.M.

[0230]—*Camaldolese Hermits of the Congregation of Monte Corona*—ER. CAM.

[0740]—*Marians of the Immaculate Conception (St. Stanislaus Kostka Province)*—M.I.C.

[]—*The Order of the Sacred & Immaculate Hearts of Jesus & Mary*

[0560]—*Third Order of Saint Francis. (Sacred Heart Prov.)*—T.O.R.

RELIGIOUS INSTITUTES OF WOMEN REPRESENTED IN THE DIOCESE

[0370]—*Carmelite Sisters of the Most Sacred Heart of Los Angeles*—O.C.D.

[1230]—*Franciscan Sisters of Christian Charity, Manitowac, WI*—O.S.F.

[1880]—*Handmaids of the Sacred Heart of Jesus for Reparation*—A.R.

[]—*Institute of the Sisters of Mercy of the Americas*—R.S.M.

[3070]—*North American Union Sisters of Our Lady of Charity*—O.L.C.

[2970]—*School Sisters of Notre Dame*—S.S.N.D.

[0500]—*Sisters of Charity of Nazareth*—S.C.N.

[]—*Sisters of St. Francis of Perpetual Adoration*—O.S.F.

[1530]—*Sisters of St. Francis of the Congregation of Our Lady of Lourdes* (Sylvania, OH)—O.S.F.

[1600]—*Sisters of St. Francis of the Martyr St. George*—F.S.G.M.

NECROLOGY

† Manieri, Rev. Msgr. Frank P., (Retired)—Died June 28, 2009

† Battocletti, Richard L., (Retired)—Died March 23, 2009

† Cronin, Francis C., (Retired)—Died Aug. 2, 2009

An asterisk (*) denotes an organization that has established tax-exempt status directly with the IRS and is not covered by the USCCB Group Ruling.

Diocese of Stockton

(Dioecesis Stocktoniensis)

Most Reverend

STEPHEN E. BLAIRE, D.D.

Bishop of Stockton; ordained April 29, 1967; appointed Titular Bishop of Lamzella on March 20, 1990; ordained Auxiliary Bishop of Los Angeles May 31, 1990; appointed Bishop of Stockton January 18, 1999. *Office: 1105 N. Lincoln St., Stockton, CA 95203.* Tel: 209-466-0636.

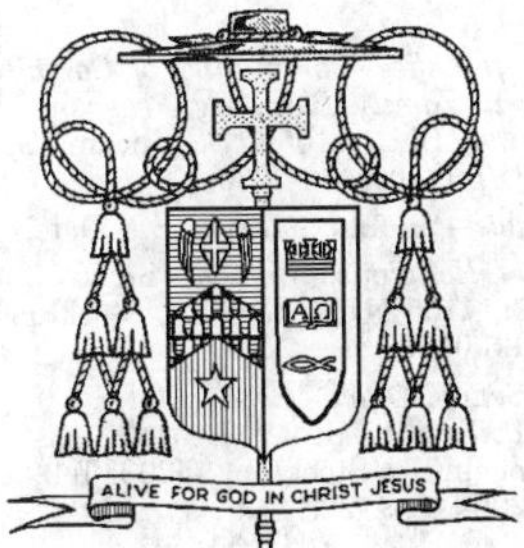

ESTABLISHED JANUARY 13, 1962

Square Miles 16,131.

Comprises six Counties in the State of California-viz., Alpine, Calaveras, Mono, San Joaquin, Stanislaus and Tuolumne.

Legal Title: The Roman Catholic Bishop of Stockton, a Corporation Sole.
For legal titles of parishes and diocesan institutions, consult the Chancery Office.

Chancery Office: 1105 N. Lincoln St., Stockton, CA 95203. Tel: 209-466-0636; Fax: 209-941-9722.

STATISTICAL OVERVIEW

Personnel	
Bishop	1
Priests: Diocesan Active in Diocese	48
Priests: Diocesan Active Outside Diocese	4
Priests: Retired, Sick or Absent	9
Number of Diocesan Priests	61
Religious Priests in Diocese	11
Total Priests in Diocese	72
Extern Priests in Diocese	22
Ordinations:	
Transitional Deacons	1
Permanent Deacons in Diocese	45
Total Brothers	4
Total Sisters	62
Parishes	
Parishes	34
With Resident Pastor:	
Resident Diocesan Priests	31
Resident Religious Priests	3
Missions	12
Professional Ministry Personnel:	
Brothers	4
Sisters	20
Lay Ministers	64
Welfare	
Catholic Hospitals	2
Total Assisted	560,832
Health Care Centers	1
Total Assisted	10,239
Homes for the Aged	2
Total Assisted	1,100
Special Centers for Social Services	1
Total Assisted	61,866
Educational	
Diocesan Students in Other Seminaries	10
Students Religious	10
High Schools, Diocesan and Parish	2
Total Students	1,503
Elementary Schools, Diocesan and Parish	11
Total Students	2,909
Catechesis/Religious Education:	
High School Students	790
Elementary Students	19,584
Total Students under Catholic Instruction	24,796
Teachers in the Diocese:	
Priests	3
Brothers	2
Sisters	2
Lay Teachers	279
Vital Statistics	
Receptions into the Church:	
Infant Baptism Totals	6,428
Minor Baptism Totals	233
Adult Baptism Totals	139
Received into Full Communion	158
First Communions	4,649
Confirmations	2,948
Marriages:	
Catholic	693
Interfaith	109
Total Marriages	802
Deaths	1,453
Total Catholic Population	218,605
Total Population	1,299,404

Former Bishops—Most Revs. HUGH A. DONOHOE, D.D., Ph.D., ord. June 14, 1930; appt. Titular Bishop of Taium and Auxiliary of San Francisco Aug. 2, 1947; cons. Oct. 7, 1947; appt. to Stockton Feb. 21, 1962; transferred to Fresno Aug. 27, 1969; died Oct. 26, 1987; MERLIN J. GUILFOYLE, D.D., J.C.D., ord. June 10, 1933; appt. Titular Bishop of Bulla and Auxiliary of San Francisco Aug. 15, 1950; cons. Sept. 21, 1950; translated to Bishop of Stockton Nov. 19, 1969; retired Feb. 26, 1980; died Nov. 20, 1981; ROGER M. MAHONY, D.D., ord. May 1, 1962; appt. Titular Bishop of Tamascani and Auxiliary of Fresno, Jan. 7, 1975; cons. March 19, 1975; translated Bishop of Stockton Feb. 26, 1980; elevated to Archbishop of Los Angeles July 16, 1985; elevated to Cardinal, June 28, 1991; DONALD W. MONTROSE, D.D. (Retired), ord. May 7, 1949; appt. Titular Bishop of Vescovio and Auxiliary of Los Angeles March 25, 1983; cons. May 12, 1983; translated Bishop of Stockton Dec. 19, 1985; installed Feb. 20, 1986; retired Jan. 18, 1999; died May 7, 2008.

Chancery Office—1105 N. Lincoln St., Stockton, 95203. Tel: 209-466-0636; Fax: 209-941-9722. Web: www.stocktondiocese.org.

Vicar General—Rev. Msgr. RICHARD J. RYAN, J.C.D., V.G.

Chancellor—Sr. BARBARA THIELLA, S.N.D.deN.

Vicar for Priests—Rev. Msgr. HARMON SKILLIN, J.C.D. (Retired).

Chief Financial Officer—Mr. DOUG ADEL.

Director of Human Resources—Mr. JOHN HALE.

Social Action Director—Mr. DAVE CORDER.

Diocesan Tribunal—1105 N. Lincoln St., Stockton, 95203. Tel: 209-466-0636; Fax: 209-941-9722. Web: stocktondiocese.org.

Judicial Vicar—Rev. JOVITO B. ROLDAN, J.C.L.

Vice-Officialis—Rev. Msgr. RICHARD J. RYAN, J.C.D., V.G.

Judges—Revs. KENNETH LAVERONE, O.F.M., J.C.L.; CHARLIE E. BLUM, J.C.L.; Rev. Msgr. HARMON SKILLIN, J.C.D. (Retired); Mrs. DEBORAH A. BARTON, J.C.L.

Tribunal Personnel—Notaries: MARY BARTON; DIANE LEWIS; JO ANNE GARCIA-JONES; DIANE TARICCO.

Defenders of the Bond—Revs. JOHN J.M. FOSTER, J.C.D.; JOVITO B. ROLDAN, J.C.L.

College of Consultors/Presbyteral Council—Rev. Msgrs. LAWRENCE MCGOVERN, S.T.L., Chm.; JOHN M. ARMISTEAD, Vice Chm.; Revs. JUAN SERNA, S.T.L., Sec. & Treas.; JORGE W. ARBOLEDA; LONACHAN W. AROUJE; MARK WAGNER; JOHN E. FITZGERALD; BERNARD J. QUINN, C.M.; ROLANDO C. PETRONIO; Rev. Msgrs. RICHARD J. RYAN, J.C.D., V.G.; HARMON SKILLIN, J.C.D., Consultant (Retired); Rev. RANDALL RAINWATER; Most Rev. STEPHEN E. BLAIRE, D.D.

Deans—Rev. Msgr. WILLIAM C. MOORE, Deanery 1; Revs. DEAN MCFALLS, Deanery 2; MICHAEL KELLY, V.F., Deanery 3; J. PATRICK WALKER, V.F., Deanery 4; Rev. Msgr. ALOYS CONRAD GRUBER, V.F., Deanery 5; Revs. BERNARD J. QUINN, C.M., Deanery 6; JOSEPH P. ILLO, Deanery 7; JOHN E. FITZGERALD, Deanery 8.

The Roman Catholic Welfare Corporation of Stockton—1105 N. Lincoln St., Stockton, 95203. Tel: 209-466-0636; Fax: 209-941-9722.

Diocesan Building Committee—Rev. Msgr. RICHARD J. RYAN, J.C.D., V.G., Chm.; Mr. DOUG ADEL; Rev. Msgr. WILLIAM MOORE; Deacons GREG YEAGER; ALAN MOZNETT; Mr. RAYMOND TUNKEL.

Diocesan Finance Council—Most Rev. STEPHEN E. BLAIRE, D.D.; Mr. PAUL SCHAEFER, Chm.; Mr. JOSEPH ARIAS; Mr. DOUG ADEL, Staff; Mr. KEVIN DOUGHERTY; Mr. TOM DRISCOLL; Mr. MICHAEL DUFFY; Revs. JOHN P. FALLON, O.S.F.S.; RANDALL RAINWATER; Mr. DAVID ROSE, CPA, C.F.E.; Mr. JOSE LOUIS SOLORIO; Mrs. MARIA STOKMAN; Rev. Msgr. RICHARD J. RYAN, J.C.D., V.G., Consultant.

Personnel Board—Rev. Msgr. HARMON SKILLIN, J.C.D. (Retired); Rev. ARMANDO VERGARA; Rev. Msgrs. LAWRENCE MCGOVERN, S.T.L.; RICHARD J. RYAN, J.C.D., V.G.; Revs. RAMON BEJARANO; JUAN SERNA, S.T.L.; MICHAEL KELLY, V.F.

Diocesan Offices and Directors

Apostleship of the Sea—Mr. MIKE DETORO. Tel: 209-466-0636.

Catholic Charities—ELVIRA RAMIREZ. Tel: 209-444-5900; Fax: 209-444-5933.

Catholic Youth Organization—Mr. DENNIS DEVINCENZI, Sports Dir., 1105 N. Lincoln St., Stockton, 95203. Tel: 209-466-0636.

Cemeteries—Mr. AL VIGIL, Supt. Cemeteries, Mailing Address: P.O. Box 1137, Stockton, 95201.

Censor Librorum—VACANT.

Apostolado Hispano—Mrs. DIGNA RAMIREZ-LOPEZ, Dir., 1105 N. Lincoln St., Stockton, 95203. Tel: 209-466-0636.

Development—Mrs. SHARON CAPORUSSO, Dir.

Continuing Education of Clergy—Rev. Msgr. ROBERT J. SILVA, 1105 N. Lincoln St., Stockton, 95203. Tel: 209-466-0636; Fax: 209-941-9722.

Communications Office—Sr. TERRY DAVIS, S.N.D.deN.

Cursillo Movement-English and Spanish—JESUS GONZALES, Dir.

Ecumenism—Deacon THOMAS CICCARELLI.

Office for Pastoral Leadership Development—Rev. Msgr. ROBERT J. SILVA.

Office of Religious Education—Sr. GLORIA DEJESUS SANCHEZ, E.F.M.S., Dir., 1105 N. Lincoln St., Stockton, 95203. Tel: 209-466-0636 Contact this office for various CCD Centers.

Office of Special Education—Ms. SANDRA NELSON, Consultant, 1105 N. Lincoln St., Stockton, 95203. Tel: 209-466-0636 Programs for physically & mentally impaired.

Ongoing Education for Clergy—Rev. Msgr. ROBERT J. SILVA.

Office for Deacon Formation—Rev. Msgr. ROBERT J. SILVA.

Engaged Encounter—PAT BIVENS; CONNIE BIVENS. Tel: 209-993-7198.

School of Ministry—Mrs. WANDA SCHEUERMANN, Dir., 1105 N. Lincoln St., Stockton, 95203. Tel: 209-466-0636; Rev. GILBERTO ARANGO, Assoc. Dir.

Episcopal Liaison of Catholic Charismatic Renewal—English: Deacon WILLIAM BRENNAN, Ph.D., 13 Pardee Ln., Stockton, 95207. Tel: 209-474-0571. Spanish: Rev. JOSE DOMINGO RUIZ. Tel: 209-465-0416.

Liturgical Commission—Mr. DAVID SPRINGER, Chm., 505 W. Granger Ave., Modesto, 95350. Tel: 209-524-7421.

Newman Apostolate— The Newman House at University of the Pacific Mr. GREG MCAVOY-JENSEN, Dir., Res.: 4101 N. Manchester, Stockton, 95207. Tel: 209-951-0881; Rev. SALVADOR LEDESMA, All Saints Newman Community at Stanislaus State University, 4040 McKenna Dr., Turlock, 95382. Tel: 209-669-0473.

Filipino Pastoral Ministry—Rev. JOSEPH MAGHINAY. Tel: 209-524-4381.

Office of Catechumenate—Mrs. LINDA HENKEL, Dir., 1105 North Lincoln St., Stockton, 95203. Tel: 209-466-0636.

Permanent Diaconate Program—Deacon DON BO, 215 W. Walnut St., Lodi, 95240. Tel: 209-369-1907.

Diaconate Formation—Rev. Msgr. ROBERT J. SILVA, Dir., 1105 N. Lincoln St., Stockton, 95203. Tel: 209-466-0636.

Pontifical Association of Holy Childhood—Mrs. MICHELLE ROMANO, 1105 N. Lincoln St., Stockton, 95203. Tel: 209-466-0636.

Propagation of the Faith—Mrs. MICHELLE ROMANO, 1105 N. Lincoln St., Stockton, 95203. Tel: 209-466-0636.

Respect Life Office--Community of Caring Program & Natural Family Planning Program—Mrs. NANCY BONNET, Dir., 1105 N. Lincoln St., Stockton, 95203. Tel: 209-466-0636.

Synod Office—Sr. TERRY DAVIS, S.N.D.deN.

Vicar for Religious Women—Sr. WANDA BILLION, M.S.C., 1105 N. Lincoln St., Stockton, 95203. Tel: 209-466-0636.

Catholic School Office—Sr. MARIAN CLARE VALENTEEN, R.S.M., Supt.; THOMAS BUTLER, Asst. Supt., 1105 N. Lincoln St., Stockton, 95203. Tel: 209-466-0636; Fax: 209-941-9722.

Vocations—Sr. WANDA BILLION, M.S.C., Dir., 1105 N. Lincoln St., Stockton, 95203. Tel: 209-466-0636; Rev. DAVID DUTRA, Assoc. Dir.

Office for Worship—Mrs. VIRGINIA MEAGHER, Coord., 1105 N. Lincoln St., Stockton, 95203. Tel: 209-466-0636.

Office of Youth Ministry—ANN MARIE AVANSINO, English Coord.; JOSE LOPEZ CEJA, Spanish Coord., 1105 N. Lincoln St., Stockton, 95203. Tel: 209-466-0636.

Catholic Committee on Scouting—LISA BALOGH. Tel: 209-815-8636.

Migrant Ministry Team—Mr. JOSE LOPEZ-CEJA, Leader; Sisters MARIA J. GARCIA, M.G.Sp.S.; LOURDES GONZALES, M.G.Sp.S.; TONI LOPEZ, M.G.Sp.S.

Victim Assistance Coordinator—Sr. BARBARA THIELLA, S.N.D.deN. Tel: 209-466-0636. Email: bthiella@stocktondiocese.org.

CLERGY, PARISHES, MISSIONS AND PAROCHIAL SCHOOLS

CITY OF STOCKTON

(SAN JOAQUIN COUNTY)

1—CATHEDRAL OF THE ANNUNCIATION (PASTOR OF) (1944) Rev. Msgr. John M. Armistead; Rev. Benjamin Puente (Mexico), Parochial Vicar; Deacons Michael Wofford; Matthew Joseph. In Res., Rev. Gilberto Arango.
Res.: 425 W. Magnolia St., 95203-2412. Tel: 209-463-1305; Fax: 209-463-0807.
School—1110 N. Lincoln St., 95203. Tel: 209-444-4000; Fax: 209-444-4013. Mrs. Carla Donaldson, Prin. Lay Teachers 20; Students 288.
Catechesis/Religious Program—Students 627.

2—ST. BERNADETTE CHURCH (PASTOR OF) (1955) Rev. Msgr. William C. Moore.
Res.: 2544 Plymouth Rd., 95204. Tel: 209-465-3081; Fax: 209-547-1327.
Catechesis/Religious Program—Students 145.

3—ST. EDWARD CHURCH (PASTOR OF) (1967), (Hispanic), Rev. Alvaro H. Delgado; Deacon Israel Lopez.
Res.: 731 S. Cardinal Ave., 95215. Tel: 209-466-3020; Fax: 209-466-0719. Email: stedwardsoffice@aol.com.
Catechesis/Religious Program—Students 379.

4—ST. GEORGE CHURCH (PASTOR OF) (1951) Revs. Javier Campechano; Edwin Musico (Philippines); Deacons Jim Janukites; Don Rodgers; Jesus Aguilar; Kevin Amen.
Res.: 120 W. Fifth St., 95206-2695. Tel: 209-463-3413; Fax: 209-463-0167. Email: st.george.church@comcast.net.
School—144 W. Fifth St., 95206. Tel: 209-463-1540; Fax: 209-463-2707. Mr. Frank Remkiewicz, Prin. Lay Teachers 4; Students 114.
St. George REALMS Foundation—
Catechesis/Religious Program—Tel: 209-463-3564. Students 640.
Mission—Good Shepherd P.O. Box 354, French Camp, San Joaquin Co. 95231. Tel: 209-982-0578; Fax: 209-858-4836.

5—ST. GERTRUDE CHURCH (PASTOR OF) (1913), (Mexican-American), [CEM] Revs. Alvaro U. Araque (Colombia); Jovito B. Roldan, Parochial Vicar; Deacons Louis Juarez; Dennis Monbureau.
Res.: 1663 E. Main St., 95205. Tel: 209-466-0278; Fax: 209-466-1927. Email: gertrudeschurch@sbcglobal.net.
Catechesis/Religious Program—Tel: 209-969-5345. Students 295.

6—ST. LINUS CHURCH (PASTOR OF) (1956), (Hispanic—Asian), Rev. Gustavo V. Quintero; Deacon Joe Orzal. In Res., Rev. Jose Domingo Ruiz.
Res.: 2620 S. B St., 95206. Tel: 209-465-1430; Fax: 209-465-0299.
Catechesis/Religious Program—Students 500.

7—ST. LUKE CHURCH OF STOCKTON (PASTOR OF) (1951), (Vietnamese), Revs. Matthew O'Donnell; Tuan Nguyen, S.D.B. (Vietnam); Joseph Maghinay; Deacons Haet Tansaeng; Glenn Sell; Ms. Victoria Kimball, Parish Admin.
Res.: 3847 N. Sutter St., 95204. Tel: 209-948-3450; Fax: 209-948-2841.
School—4005 N. Sutter St., 95204. Tel: 209-464-0801; Fax: 209-466-1150. Ms. Pat Simon, Prin. Lay Teachers 10; Students 210.
Catechesis/Religious Program—Tel: 209-462-0410. Paul C. DeValle, Dir. Youth Ministries; Sisters Odetta Bonini, Dir. Religious Ed.; Guia Jimenez, Dir. R.C.I.A. Students 555.
Convent—230 E. Atlee St., 95204. Tel: 209-463-6533.

8—ST. MARY OF THE ASSUMPTION CHURCH (PASTOR OF) (1851) Revs. Dean McFalls; David Dutra, Parochial Vicar; Deacons Jorge Torres; Mel R. Tahod. In Res., Revs. Christian Ezeh; Louis Garcia.
Res.: 203 E. Washington St., 95202. Tel: 209-948-0661; Fax: 209-948-0673.
Catechesis/Religious Program—Tel: 209-948-0665. Students 318.

9—ST. MICHAEL CHURCH OF STOCKTON (PASTOR OF) (1921), (Italian), Rev. Msgr. Agustin Gialogo; Deacon Allen Moznett.
Mailing Address: 5882 N. Ashley Ln., 95215-9307. In Res., Rev. Msgr. Richard J. Ryan.
Catechesis/Religious Program—Tel: 209-931-2696. Email: stmichaelcatmin@sbcglobal.net. Students 350.

10—PRESENTATION CHURCH (PASTOR OF) (1952) Rev. Msgr. Lawrence McGovern; Rev. Jose Luis Gutierrez, Parochial Vicar; Deacons William Brennan; Scott Johnson. In Res., Rev. George Okoro.
Res.: 6715 Leesburg Pl., 95207. Tel: 209-472-2150; Fax: 209-472-0541. Email: frontdesk@presentationchurch.net. Web: presentationchurch.net.
School—1635 W. Benjamin Holt Dr., 95207. Tel: 209-472-2140; Fax: 209-320-1515. Email: office@presentationschool.org. Web: presentationschool.org. Diane Rothschild, Prin. Lay Teachers 13; Students 284.
Catechesis/Religious Program—Tel: 209-320-5714. Email: religiousedpresentationchurch.net. Students 882.

OUTSIDE CITY OF STOCKTON

ANGELS CAMP, CALAVERAS CO., ST. PATRICK CHURCH OF ANGELS CAMP (PASTOR OF) (1856), (Italian), [CEM] [JC] Revs. Rolando C. Petronio (Philippines); Lonachan W. Arouje (India); Deacon Fred Ybarra.
Res.: 820 S. Main St., P.O. Box 576, 95222. Tel: 209-736-4575; Fax: 209-736-2217. Email: stpatricks_acamp@sbcglobal.net.
Catechesis/Religious Program—820 S. Main, 95222. Tel: 209-736-9180. Students 105.
Mission—St. Patrick 619 Sheep Ranch Rd., Murphys, Murphys Co. 95247. Tel: 209-728-2854.
Mission—Our Lady of the Sierra 1301 Linebaugh Rd., Arnold, Arnold Co. 95223. Tel: 209-795-7625.
Mission—St. Ignatius Mission

CERES, STANISLAUS CO., ST. JUDE CHURCH (PASTOR OF) (1962), (Hispanic), Revs. Jose Reyes-Cedillo, O.R.C. (Mexico); Ariel Munoz-Sanchez, O.R.C. (Mexico); Santos Licea-Anguiano, O.R.C. (Mexico).
Res.: 3824 Mitchell Rd., 95307-9422. Tel: 209-537-0516; Fax: 209-537-3412. Web: www.stjudesparish.org.
Catechesis/Religious Program—Tel: 209-537-7439. Students 1,546.
Mission—Ntra. Senora de Guadalupe 425 Broadway Ave., Modesto, Stanislaus Co. 95351. Tel: 209-537-0516.

HUGHSON, STANISLAUS CO., ST. ANTHONY CHURCH OF HUGHSON (PASTOR OF) (1921), (Hispanic), [CEM] Revs. Armando Vergara; Editho Mascardo; Deacon Raymond Flanders.
7820 Fox Rd., 95326-9309.
Res.: 2020 Euclid Rd., 95326. Tel: 209-883-4310; Fax: 209-883-2531.
Catechesis/Religious Program—Tel: 209-883-1632. Students 577.
Mission—St. Louis [CEM] Floto St., La Grange, Stanislaus Co. 95329. Tel: 209-852-0144; Fax: 209-852-0818. Doris Quinones, Contact Person.

LATHROP, SAN JOAQUIN CO., OUR LADY OF GUADALUPE CHURCH (PASTOR OF) (2002) Rev. Francisco Naranjo, Admin.; Deacon Jim Kottinger.
Church & Office: 16200 Cambridge Dr., 95330. Tel: 209-858-4466; Fax: 209-858-4978. Web: www.ourladyofguadalupelathrop.org.
Catechesis/Religious Program—Students 502.

LINDEN, SAN JOAQUIN CO., HOLY CROSS CHURCH (PASTOR OF) (1963), (Italian—Hispanic), Rev. Alexandre Pacheco (India).
Res.: 18633 E. Front St., P.O. Box 52, 95236. Tel: 209-887-3341; Fax: 209-887-2973.
Catechesis/Religious Program—Tel: 209-887-2263. Students 174.

LOCKEFORD, SAN JOAQUIN CO., ST. JOACHIM CHURCH OF LOCKEFORD (PASTOR OF) (1882), (Hispanic), [CEM] Rev. Michael Kelly; Deacon Bill Warren, Bible Study & Prayer Group Leader.
Mailing Address: P.O. Box 232, 95237. Tel: 209-727-3912; Fax: 209-727-0403. Email: joachim@sonnet.com.
Catechesis/Religious Program—Tel: 209-727-5192. Students 162.

LODI, SAN JOAQUIN CO., ST. ANNE CHURCH (PASTOR OF) (1904) [CEM] Revs. Brandon M. Ware, Admin.; Jairo H. Ramirez (Colombia); Hung Joseph Nguyen (Vietnam), Parochial Vicar; Deacons Juan Mendez; Porfirio Cisneros; Don Bo; Karl Welsbacher.
Mailing Address: P.O. Box 480, 95241. Tel: 209-369-1907; Fax: 209-369-1971.
Office: 215 W. Walnut St., 95240. Tel: 209-369-1907; Fax: 209-369-1971.
Res.: 150 S. Pleasant St., 95240.
School—200 S. Pleasant St., 95240. Tel: 209-333-7580. Mr. Dennis Taricco, Prin. Lay Teachers 15; Students 251.
Catechesis/Religious Program—Sisters Isabel de la Eucaristia Abril, E.F.M.S., D.R.E.; Rosalia Cano, E.F.M.S., D.R.E. Students 718.
Mission—Mater Ecclesiae 26500 Sacramento Blvd., Thornton, San Joaquin Co. 95686.

MAMMOTH LAKES, MONO CO., ST. JOSEPH CHURCH OF MAMMOTH LAKES (1939) Rev. Andrew C. Dachauer, S.J.; Bro. Daniel C. Corona, S.J., Pastoral Assoc.
Res.: 58 Ranch Rd., P.O. Box 372, 93546. Tel: 760-934-6276; Fax: 760-934-4047. Email: info@mammothcatholicchurch.org. Web: mammothcatholicchurch.org.
Mission—Infant of Prague Mission Church 74936 Hwy. 395, Bridgeport, Mono Co. 93517. Fax: 760-934-4047.
Mission—Our Savior of the Mountains 72 Mono Lake Ave., Lee Vining, Mono Co. 93541. Tel: 760-934-6276; Fax: 760-934-4047.
Catechesis/Religious Program—Students 246.

MANTECA, SAN JOAQUIN CO., ST. ANTHONY CHURCH OF MANTECA (PASTOR OF) (1917) Revs. J. Patrick Walker; Alvaro M. Lopez (Colombia); Dante U. Dammay (Philippines); Michael Brady; Deacons Harvey Parolari; Jeff Vierra.
505 E. North St., 95336.
Res.: 525 E. North St., 95336. Tel: 209-823-7197; Fax: 209-823-5238. Web: st-anthonys.org.
School—323 N. Fremont, 95336. Tel: 209-823-4513; Fax: 209-825-7447. Web: sasmanteca.org. Mary Lou Hoffman, Prin. Lay Teachers 10; Students 256.
Catechesis/Religious Program—Students 1,065.
St. Vincent de Paul Society—Tel: 209-823-8099.
St. Anthony School Educational Foundation—Tel: 209-239-4513.

MODESTO, STANISLAUS CO.

1—HOLY FAMILY CHURCH (PASTOR OF) (2006) Rev. Juan Serna; Deacon Philip Vallejo.
4220 Dale Rd., 95356. Tel: 209-545-3553; Fax: 209-545-3332.
Catechesis/Religious Program—Students 280.
Mission—Our Lady of San Juan de los Lagos 4643 Flint Ave., Salida, Stanislaus Co. 95368.

2—ST. JOSEPH CHURCH OF MODESTO (PASTOR OF) (1967) Revs. Joseph P. Illo; Camilo Garcia (Mexico); John Peter Pragasam (Italy); Benny Kottarathil (Italy); Deacon Kenneth Ochinero. In Res., Rev. Larry Guererro.

Res.: 1813 Oakdale Rd., 95355. Tel: 209-551-4973; Fax: 209-551-3213. Web: www.stjmod.com.
Catechesis/Religious Program—Students 1,162.

3—OUR LADY OF FATIMA CHURCH (PASTOR OF) (1951) Rev. Khoi Pham; Rev. Msgr. Bonifacio Baldonado, Parochial Vicar; Deacon James Johnson.
Res.: 505 W. Granger Ave., 95350. Tel: 209-524-7421; Fax: 209-524-7713.
School—501 W. Granger Ave., 95350. Tel: 209-524-4170; Fax: 209-524-3960. Linda Partlow, Prin. Lay Teachers 14; Students 255; Extended Day Care 125.
Catechesis/Religious Program—Tel: 209-491-3462; Fax: 209-524-7713. Students 915.
The Monsignor William P. Kennedy Education Foundation:—

4—ST. STANISLAUS CHURCH (PASTOR OF) (1881) Revs. Ramon Bejarano; John Lindsay, O.S.F.S.; Jorge W. Arboleda; David Dutra, Parochial Vicar; Deacons Jose Reyes; Jim Kottinger; Sam West.
Mailing Address: P.O. Box 292, 95353.
Res.: 709 J St., 95354. Tel: 209-524-4381; Fax: 209-524-1910. Email: ststancc@aol.com. Web: www.ststanscc.com.
School—1416 Maze Blvd., 95351. Tel: 209-524-9036; Fax: 209-524-4344. Web: www.ststansparish-school.com. Donna O'Connor, Prin. Lay Teachers 14; Students 224.
Catechesis/Religious Program—Tel: 209-522-6534; Fax: 209-523-9128. Students 1,184.

NEWMAN, STANISLAUS CO., ST. JOACHIM CHURCH OF NEWMAN (PASTOR OF) (1909), (Spanish—English), Rev. Hector Villegas; Deacon Lance Valez.
Res.: 1121 Main St., 95360. Tel: 209-862-3528; Fax: 209-862-3512. Email: hectovi@yahoo.com.
Catechesis/Religious Program—Tel: 209-862-2878. Students 230.

OAKDALE, STANISLAUS CO., ST. MARY OF THE ANNUNCIATION CHURCH (PASTOR OF) (1902) Rev. Msgr. Aloys Conrad Gruber; Rev. Misael Avila; Deacons Roberto Magdaleno, (Retired); Thomas Ciccarelli.
Res.: 1225 Olive St., 95361. Tel: 209-847-2715; Fax: 209-847-7348. Email: stmarysoakdale@aol.com.
Catechesis/Religious Program—Tel: 209-847-3498. Email: abcorissetto@gmail.com. Students 450.

PATTERSON, STANISLAUS CO., SACRED HEART CHURCH OF PATTERSON (PASTOR OF) (1925) Revs. Bernard J. Quinn, C.M.; Michael F. Walsh, C.M.
Res.: 529 I St., 95363. Tel: 209-892-9321; Fax: 209-892-2102. Email: sheartpatterson@juno.com. Web: www.sacredheartpatterson.org.
School—505 M St., 95363. Tel: 209-892-3544; Fax: 209-892-3214. Web: www.shcs-patterson.org. Jason Oliveira, Prin. Lay Teachers 13; Students 227.
Catechesis/Religious Program—503 M St., 95363. Tel: 209-892-6381; Fax: 209-892-6381. Students 417.
Mission—Immaculate Heart of Mary H St., Crows Landing, Stanislaus Co. 95313.

RIPON, SAN JOAQUIN CO., ST. PATRICK CHURCH OF RIPON (PASTOR OF) (1878) Rev. Peter Carota.
Res.: 19399 E St., Rte. 120 Hwy., 95366. Tel: 209-838-2133; Fax: 209-838-1077.
Catechesis/Religious Program—Tel: 209-838-3101. Students 641.

RIVERBANK, STANISLAUS CO., ST. FRANCES OF ROME CHURCH (PASTOR OF) (1953) Revs. Thomas M. Rajanayagam; Eduardo Perez, Parochial Vicar.
Res.: 2827 Topeka St., 95367. Tel: 209-869-2996; Fax: 209-863-1004. Email: francesofrome@aol.com.
Catechesis/Religious Program—Students 569.

SAN ANDREAS, CALAVERAS CO., ST. ANDREW CHURCH OF SAN ANDREAS (PASTOR OF) (1963) [CEM] Rev. Patrick Curran; Deacon Greg Yeager.
Res.: 162 Church Hill Rd., P.O. Box 550, 95249. Fax: 209-754-5116. Email: standrew@colisp.com.
Catechesis/Religious Program—Tel: 209-754-3815; Fax: 209-754-5116. Students 66.
Mission—St. Thomas Aquinas 8398 Lafayette St., Mokelumne Hill, Calaveras Co. 95245. Tel: 209-754-3815; Fax: 209-754-5116.
Mission—Our Lady of Fatima 22581 Hwy. 26, West Point, Calaveras Co. 95255. Tel: 209-754-3815; Fax: 209-754-5116.

SONORA, TUOLUMNE CO., ST. PATRICK CHURCH OF SONORA (PASTOR OF) (1851) [CEM 5] [JC] Rev. William Kraft; Deacon Michael Kubasek.
Res.: 116 Bradford St., 95370. Tel: 209-532-7139; Fax: 209-532-4389. Email: stpats@stpatssonora.org. Web: parishesonline.com.
Catechesis/Religious Program—Tel: 209-532-7139, Ext. 110; Fax: 209-532-4389. Students 120.
Mission—Our Lady of Mt. Carmel Cemetery Rd., Big Oak Flat, Tuolumne Co. 95305.
Mission—St. Anne 22518 Church Ln., Columbia, Tuolumne Co. 95310. Tel: 209-532-7139.

TRACY, SAN JOAQUIN CO., ST. BERNARD CHURCH (PASTOR OF) (1908) Rev. Msgr. Ivo D. Rocha (Portugal); Revs. Francis A. Joseph, O.C.D. (India), Parochial Vicar; Jorge A. Roman, Parochial Vicar; Deacons Ray Whitlock; Peter Ryza.
Res.: 163 W. Eaton Ave., 95376. Tel: 209-835-4560; Fax: 209-835-4588. Web: www.st-bernards.org.
School—165 W. Eaton Ave., 95376. Tel: 209-835-4560, Ext. 131; Fax: 209-835-2496. Web: www.st-bernardschool.org. Gary Abate, Prin. Lay Teachers 12; Students 261.
Catechesis/Religious Program—Tel: 209-835-4560, Ext. 128. Email: maryreardon@st-bernards.org. Mary Reardon, D.R.E. Students 1,545.
Convent—Daughters of the Cross, 165 W. Eaton Ave., 95376. Tel: 209-835-7391; Fax: 209-830-6137.

TURLOCK, STANISLAUS CO.

1—OUR LADY OF THE ASSUMPTION OF THE PORTUGUESE CHURCH (PASTOR OF) (1973), (Portuguese), Rev. Manuel F. Sousa; Deacon Edwin Santiago.
Mailing Address: P.O. Box 2030, 95381. Fax: 209-634-2366.
Res.: 1343 W. Greenway, 95380. Tel: 209-634-2222; 209-634-3140. Email: frmanuelsousa@att.net. Web: www.olassumption.net.
Catechesis/Religious Program—Connie Madruga, C.R.E. Students 403.

2—SACRED HEART CHURCH OF TURLOCK (PASTOR OF) (1910) Revs. Mark Wagner; Jesudasan Velichore, Parochial Vicar; Luis G. Navarro, Parochial Vicar.
Mailing Address: 1301 Cooper Ave., 95380.
Res.: 650 Rose St., 95380. Tel: 209-634-8578; 209-634-8579; Fax: 209-634-7124. Email: church@shparish.net.
School—1225 Cooper Ave., 95380. Tel: 209-634-7787; Fax: 209-634-0156. Mrs. Donna Noceti, Prin. Lay Teachers 13; Students 244.
Preschool—Tel: 209-667-5512; Fax: 209-669-9647. Debra Cannella, Prin. Lay Teachers 16; Students 122.
Catechesis/Religious Program—Sacred Heart Religious Education, 1250 Cooper #1, 95380. Tel: 209-634-5111. Students 1,048.

TWAIN HARTE, TUOLUMNE CO., ALL SAINTS CHURCH (PASTOR OF) (1962) [JC] Rev. John E. Fitzgerald; Deacon Edward Zoma.
Res.: 18674 Cherokee Dr., P.O. Box 642, 95383. Tel: 209-586-3161; Fax: 209-586-3161. Email: omnsanct@goldrush.com. Web: www.omnsanct.org.
Catechesis/Religious Program—Students 75.
Mission—St. Joseph Gardner St., Tuolumne, Tuolumne Co. 95379.
Station— Pinecrest. (Summer)

Chaplains of Public Institutions

STOCKTON. *DeWitt Nelson Training Center*, 7650 Newcastle Rd., P.O. Box 213003, 95213-9003. Tel: 209-944-6187. Rev. Randall Rainwater, Chap.
O.H. Close School, 7650 Newcastle Rd., P.O. Box 213002, 95213-9001. Tel: 209-944-6364. Deacon Louis Juarez.

FRENCH CAMP. *San Joaquin County Jail*, 999 W. Matthews Rd., 95231. Tel: 209-468-4562. Vacant.
San Joaquin General Hospital, 500 W. Hospital Rd., 95231. Tel: 209-468-6000. St. George Church.

JAMESTOWN. *Sierra Conservation Center*, P.O. Box 497, 95327-1213. Tel: 209-984-5291, Ext. 5281. Rev. Ray Abella, O.S.F.S., Chap.

TRACY. *Deuel Vocational Institution*, P.O. Box 400, 95376-3593. Tel: 209-835-4141, Ext. 5076. Deacon Edwin Santiago.

On Duty Outside the Diocese:
Revs.—
Bitterman, John L., S.S., S.T.B., M.A.
Foster, John J.M., J.C.D.
Myers, William
O'Neill, Robert
Pintacura, Michael

Absent on Leave:
Revs.—
Barrera, Fernando (Colombia)
McDonald, William
Pelaez, Oskar
Ryan, William
Suarez, Leo

Retired:
Rev. Msgrs.—
Cain, James E., Vicar Gen. Emeritus, 1105 N. Lincoln St., 95203.
Donohoe, Edward, 5835 Cherokee Rd., #69, 95215.
Skillin, Harmon, J.C.D.
Revs.—
Ford, William A., St. Mary Star of the Sea, 888 Blvd. of the Arts, #1508, Sarasota, FL 34236.
Johnson, Henry, P.O. Box 2147, Arnold, 95223.
Maguire, Enda J.
Miani, Titian A., Casa Manana, 3700 N. Sutter St., #207, 95204.
O'Dwyer, James, Pastor Emeritus, Casa Santa Fe, 24 Dillon St., Clonmel, Ireland.
Pereira, Robert J., P.O. Box 78072, 95267.
Wang, John, 3700 N. Sutter St. #352, 95204.
White, Nathan R., 6740 Deer Valley Rd., Ste. D107-#231.

Permanent Deacons:
Aguilar, Jesus, St. George, Stockton
Amen, Kevin, St. George, Stockton
Artesi, Joseph, (Retired), St. Luke's, Stockton
Bo, Donald, St. Anne, Lodi
Brennan, William, Ph.D., Church of the Presentation, Stockton
Broderick, Thomas, School of Ministry, Stockton
Ciccarelli, Thomas, St. Mary's of the Annunciation, Escalon
Cisneros, Porfirio, St. Anne, Lodi
Flanders, Raymond, St. Anthony, Hughson
Janukites, James, St. George, Stockton
Johnson, James, Our Lady of Fatima, Modesto
Johnson, Scott, Church of the Presentation
Joseph, Matthew, Annunciation, Stockton
Juarez, Louis, St. Gertrude's, Stockton
Kottinger, Jim, Our Lady of Guadalupe, Lathrop
Kubasek, Michael, St. Patricks, Twain Harte
Lopez, Isreal, St. Edward's, Stockton
Magdaleno, Roberto, St. Mary, Oakdale
Mendez, Juan, (Retired)
Monbureau, Denis, St. Gertrude, Stockton
Moznett, Al, St. Michael, Stockton
Ochinero, Kenneth, St. Jude's, Ceres
Orzal, Joe, St. George, Stockton
Parolari, Harvey, St. Anthony, Manteca
Pietras, Adam, St. Patrick, Angel's Camp
Reyes, Jose, St. Stanislaus, Modesto
Rodgers, Donald, Good Shepherd, French Camp
Ryza, Peter, St. Bernard's, Tracy
Santiago, Edwin, Our Lady of the Assumption, Turlock
Sell, William (Glenn), St. Luke's, Stockton
Tahod, Mel R., St. Mary's Assumption, Stockton
Tansaeng, Haet, St. Luke, Stockton
Torres, Jorge, St. Mary's, Stockton
Vallejo, Felipe, St. Frances of Rome, Riverbank
Velez, Lance, St. Joachim, Newman
Vierra, Jeffrey, Our Lady of Guadalupe, Lathrop
Warren, William E., St. Joachim, Lockeford
Welsbacher, Karl, St. Anne, Lodi
Whitlock, Ray, St. Bernard, Tracy
Wofford, Michael, Cathedral of Annunciation, Stockton
Ybarra, Fred, St. Patrick, Copperopolis
Yeager, Gregory, St. Andrews, San Andreas
Zoma, Edward T., All Saints, Twain Harte
Ryan, John G., St. Bernard, Tracy

INSTITUTIONS LOCATED IN THE DIOCESE

[A] HIGH SCHOOLS, DIOCESAN

STOCKTON. *St. Mary's High School* (1876) 5648 N. El Dorado St., P.O. Box 7247, 95267-0247. Tel: 209-957-3340; Fax: 209-957-0861. Email: jfallon@saintmaryshighshool.org. Web: www.saintmaryshighschool.org. Rev. John P. Fallon, O.S.F.S., Pres.; Mr. Peter Morelli, Prin.; Rev. Clark T. Kelley, O.S.F.S.; Bros. James Dorazio, O.S.F.S.; Neil McMenamin, O.S.F.S. Nonresident students. Priests 2; Brothers 2; Sisters 1; Lay Teachers 74; Students 1,075.
St. Mary's High School Foundation Tel: 209-957-3340; Fax: 209-957-0861.

MODESTO. *Central Catholic High School* (1966) 200 S. Carpenter Rd., 95351. Tel: 209-524-9611; Fax: 209-524-5646. Email: jehardee@cchsca.org. Web: www.cchsca.org. Mr. Jim Pecchenino, Pres.; Melissa Bengtson, Prin.; Wendy Habeeb, Asst. Prin.; Mrs. Theresa Hubert, Librarian. Nonresident students. Lay Teachers 30; Administrators 5; Students 425.
Central Catholic High School Foundation Tel: 209-524-6822; Fax: 209-524-5646.

[B] CATHOLIC CHARITIES

STOCKTON. *The Catholic Charities of the Diocese of Stockton* (1980) 1106 N. El Dorado St., 95202. Tel: 209-444-5900; Fax: 209-444-5933. Email: eramirez@ccstockton.org. Elvira Ramirez, Exec. Dir.; Jan Sturdivan, Chm. Corp. Bd.
Catholic Charities Services for Seniors & Caregivers, 1106 N. El Dorado St., 95202. Tel: 209-444-5923; Fax: 209-444-5929. Email: jhoman@ccstockton.org. Juliana Homan, Prog. Dir. Telephone Reassurance, Homemaker (Housekeeping), Personal Care, Respite Care Program, Caregiver Respite, Caregiver Chore & Home Improvement Modification. Clients 1,055.

Immigration Legal Services, 1106 N. El Dorado St., 95202. Tel: 209-444-5910; Fax: 209-460-1624. Email: rdarcy@ccstockton.org. Rosie D'Arcy, Prog. Coord. Naturalization/Citizenship, Green Card Renewal/ Replacement, Special Case Waivers, Adjustment of Status, Family Immigration, Affidavit of Support and Visa Application for Victims of Abuse and Crime. Clients 1,134.

Emergency Food Distribution, 1106 N. El Dorado, 95202. Tel: 209-444-5900; Fax: 209-444-5933. Allen Nesset, Coord. Clients 3,120.

ADVOCACY

Marriage Support, 1106 N. El Dorado St., 95202. Tel: 209-444-5937; Fax: 209-444-5933. Email: dcorder@ccstockton.org. Clients 3,000.

Golden Agers for Progress (GAP), 1106 N. El Dorado St., 95202. Tel: 209-444-5948; Fax: 209-460-1624. Email: srios@ccstockton.org. To support development of an active constituency of Senior Citizens that will advocate for the needs of the growing elderly, underserved population.

Environmental Justice Program (EJ), 1106 N. El Dorado St., 95202. Tel: 209-444-5925; Fax: 209-460-1624. Email: betsyr@accstockton.org. Serves to educate and motivate Catholics in the Stockton Diocese to a deeper reverence and respect for God's creation and to engage local parishes in activities to resolve environmental problems, particularly as they affect the poor.

Mission For Marriage For Life (MML), 1106 N. El Dorado St., 95202. Tel: 209-444-5937; Fax: 209-460-1624. Email: dcorder@ccstockton.org. MML program teaches couples how to be better communicators, gain knowledge and build relationship skills to transform their marriage. It is the goal of the program to train couples throughout the Diocese to become leaders of MML groups in their parishes.

Stanislaus County Senior Services, 400 12th St., Ste. 4, Modesto, 95354. Tel: 209-529-3784; Fax: 209-529-6083. Email: mramos@ccstockton.org. Monica Ramos, Prog. Dir. Homemaker Program, Respite Care, Ombudsman Program, Senior Transportation, Elder Abuse Program, Social Security Representative Payee Program, Stanislaus Elder Abuse Prevention Alliance. Clients 12,674.

Mother Lode Ombudsman Program Ombudsman Program, Legal Advocacy & Elder Abuse Prevention, Social Security Representative Payee Program., 14855 Mono Way, Ste. 105, Sonora, 95370. Tel: 209-532-7632; Fax: 209-532-8448. Email: ktoepel@ccstockton.org. Kathi Toepel, Prog. Dir. Clients 1,693.

Children's Health Initiative, 1106 N. El Dorado St., 95202. Tel: 209-444-5940; Fax: 209-444-5929. Email: jgalindo@ccstockton.org. Joanna Galindo, Prog. Dir. Services: Enroll Children to Medical Healthy Families or Healthy Kids Insurance Program & Parental Care Outreach Clients 1,375.

Nutritional Assistance Services Program (SNAP), 1106 N. El Dorado St., 95202. Tel: 209-444-5900; Fax: 209-444-5933. Email: eramirez@ccstockton.org. This program is an outreach and eligibility screening campaign designed to increase access by eligible individuals and families in San Joaquin county to the Supplemental Nutrition Assistance Program (SNAP). It is a new name for the federal food stamp program. The food stamp program is our nation's first line of defense against hunger and malnutrition and can be an effective way to increase a household's ability to purchase healthy food. Clients 37,815.

[C] GENERAL HOSPITALS

STOCKTON. *St. Joseph's Behavioral Health Center dba Catholic Healthcare West* (1993) 2510 N. California St., 95204. Tel: 209-948-2100; Fax: 209-464-2270. Web: www.stjosephscanhelp.org. Paul Rains, Pres. Sponsored by the Dominican Sisters of San Rafael, California. Bed Capacity 35; Total Assisted Annually 10,239; Total Staff 110.

St. Joseph's Medical Center of Stockton dba Catholic Healthcare West (1899) 1800 N. California St., 95204-9008. Tel: 209-943-2000; Fax: 209-461-3299. Web: www.stjosephscares.org. Donald J. Wiley, Pres. Sponsored by the Dominican Sisters of San Rafael, California. Sisters 5; Bed Capacity 294; Total Assisted Annually 560,832; Total Staff 2,420.

[D] HOMES FOR AGED

STOCKTON. *Casa Manana Inn*, 3700 N. Sutter St., 95204. Tel: 209-466-4046; Fax: 209-466-3450. Mary Berry, Admin. Total in Residence 162; Total Staff 4.

St. Joseph's Regional Housing Corp., 3400 Wagner Heights Rd., 95209. Tel: 209-956-3400; Fax: 209-952-6201. Email: info@oconnorwoods.org. Web: www.oconnorwoods.org. E. G. Schroeder, Pres.; R. Scot Sinclair, Exec. Dir. St. Joseph's Regional Housing Corp., sponsored by the Sisters of the Third Order of St. Dominic, Congregation of the Most Holy Name, provides a residential community for seniors offering a variety of living arrangements from active to assisted, skilled and rehabilitation services

O'Connor Woods Housing Corp., 3400 Wagner Heights Rd., 95209. Tel: 209-956-3400; Fax: 209-952-6201. E. G. Schroeder, Pres.; R. Scot Sinclair, Exec. Dir. O'Connor Woods Housing Corp., a nonprofit Corporation operates O'Connor Woods, Garden Oaks, Oak Creek and Meadowood Health and Rehabilitation Center. Bed Capacity 423; Total Assisted Annually 1,100; Total Staff 320.

O'Connor Woods, A Calif. Corp., 3400 Wagner Heights Rd., 95209. Tel: 209-956-3400; Fax: 209-952-6201. E. G. Schroeder, Pres. and CEO; R. Scot Sinclair, Exec. Dir. Bed Capacity 423; Total Assisted Annually 800; Total Staff 320.

[E] CONVENTS AND RESIDENCES FOR SISTERS

STOCKTON. *Eucharistic Franciscan Missionary Sisters*, 1205 N. San Joaquin St., 95202. Tel: 209-462-3906; Fax: 209-469-3759. Sisters 4.

Sacro Costato Missionary Sisters (1908) St. Luke's Convent, 230 E. Atlee St., 95204. Tel: 209-462-6533; Fax: 209-464-5342. Email: mscstockton@comcast.net. Sisters 4.

Sisters of Notre Dame de Namur (1804) 1105 N. Lincoln, 95203. Tel: 209-466-0636; Fax: 209-941-9722. Sisters Barbara Thiella, S.N.D.deN., Chancellor; Terry Davis, S.N.D.deN., Dir. Communication. Sisters 2.

MODESTO. *Sisters of the Cross of the Sacred Heart of Jesus* (1897) Cloistered Convent., 1320 Maze Blvd., 95351. Tel: 209-526-3525; Fax: 209-526-3525. Email: sistersofthecross@sbcglobal.net. Web: www.sistersofthecross.org. Sisters 12.

PATTERSON. *Daughters of the Holy Spirit* (1706) Sacred Heart Convent., *Daughters of the Holy Spirit*, 624 N. 64th St., 95363. Tel: 209-892-3410. Email: imeldadhs@gvni.com. Sisters Imelda Michaud, D.H.S., Dir.; Lucille Carreau, D.H.S., Chap. Sisters 2.

TRACY. *The Daughters of the Cross* (1833) St. Bernard Convent, 165 W. Eaton Ave., 95376. Tel: 209-835-7391; Fax: 209-830-6137. Email: fc1833@sbcglobal.net. Sisters 4.

TURLOCK. *Sisters of the Sacred Hearts of Jesus and Mary* Sacred Heart Convent, 1201 Lyons Ave., 95380-4120. Tel: 209-634-7708; Fax: 209-634-7124; 209-669-0173. Sr. Gillian Rosemary Chalk, S.H.J.M., Pastoral Min.

[F] RETREAT CENTERS

COPPEROPOLIS. *Madonna of Peace Renewal Center* (1982) (Youth Facility), 2010 Hunt Rd., P.O. Box 71, 95228. Tel: 209-785-2157 (Office); Fax: 209-785-2157. Total in Residence 2; Total Staff 2.

[G] MISCELLANEOUS

STOCKTON. *The Bishop's Educational Foundation, Diocese of Stockton*, 1105 N. Lincoln St., 95203. Tel: 209-466-0636; Fax: 209-941-9722.

Catholic Professional and Business Club, 1105 N. Lincoln St., 95203. Tel: 209-466-0636; Fax: 209-941-9722.

Church for Tomorrow Fund, 1105 N. Lincoln St., 95203.

Instituto Fe y Vida (1994) 1737 W. Benjamin Holt Dr., 95207. Tel: 209-951-3483; Fax: 209-478-5357. Email: info@feyvida.org. Web: www.feyvida.org. Total Staff 6.

St. John Vianney House of Formation, 4101 N. Manchester, 95207. Tel: 209-451-3220. Rev. David Dutra, Dir.

St. Joseph's Foundation of San Joaquin, 1800 N. California St., 95204. Tel: 209-467-6347; Fax: 209-461-6893. Email: linda.philipp@chw.edu. Web: www.stjosephscares.org.

St. Mary's High School Foundation (1982) Box 7247, 95267-0247. Tel: 209-957-3340; Fax: 209-957-0861. Email: jfallon@saintmaryshighschool.org. Web: www.saintmaryshighschool.org.

San Lorenzo Ruiz De Manila (1988) 2547 Dry Creek Way, 95206. Tel: 209-570-8222; Fax: 209-547-0248. Email: nbanasihan@yahoo.com. Natie R. Banasihan, Pres. & Founder.

SEEDS (Assistance for Catholic Education within the Roman Catholic Diocese of Stockton) (2004) 1105 N. Lincoln St., 95203. Tel: 209-466-0636; Fax: 209-941-9722.

LODI. *St. Anne's Endowment* (1986) 215 W. Walnut St., 95240. Tel: 209-369-1907; Fax: 209-369-1971.

MODESTO. *The Catholic Social Service Guild* (1975) 848 Ladd Rd., 95356. Tel: 209-545-3243. Ginger Ratto, Pres.

Central Catholic High School Foundation, 200 Carpenter Rd., 95351. Tel: 209-524-6822; Fax: 209-524-5646. Email: hart@cchsca.org. Web: www.cchsca.org. Volunteer Board Members 25.

Father John C. Silva Education Foundation, P.O. Box 4304, 95352. Tel: 209-524-4381; Fax: 209-524-1910.

**Mary Mother of God Mission Society*, 1813 Oakdale Rd., Ste. 11, 95355.

The Monsignor William P. Kennedy Education Foundation, 501 W. Granger Ave., 95350. Tel: 209-524-4170; Fax: 209-524-7713.

TURLOCK. *The Father McElligott Sacred Heart School Foundation*, 1225 Cooper St., 95380-4113. Tel: 209-634-7787; 209-669-5336; Fax: 209-634-0156. Email: shs.development@yahoo.com. Jackie Cotta, Exec. Dir. Students 245; Total Staff 28.

RELIGIOUS INSTITUTES OF MEN REPRESENTED IN THE DIOCESE

For further details refer to the corresponding bracketed number in the Religious Institutes of Men or Women section.

[0220]—*Congregation of the Blessed Sacrament*—S.S.S.

[]—*Congregation of the Mission* (Vincentians)—C.M.

[0260]—*Discalced Carmelite Friars*—O.C.D.

[0690]—*Jesuit Fathers and Brothers* (California, Columbia Prov.)—S.J.

[0920]—*Oblates of St. Francis De Sales* (Toledo-Detroit Prov.)—O.S.F.S.

[]—*Operarios del Reinode Christo*—O.R.C.

[1190]—*Salesians of St. John Bosco*—S.D.B.

[]—*Society of St. Sulpice (Sulpicians)*—S.S.

RELIGIOUS INSTITUTES OF WOMEN REPRESENTED IN THE DIOCESE

[1920]—*Congregation of the Sisters of the Holy Cross* (Notre Dame, IN)—C.S.C.

[]—*Daughters of Mary Immaculate Conception*

[0780]—*Daughters of the Cross of Liege*—F.C.

[0820]—*Daughters of the Holy Spirit* (Putnam, CT)—D.H.S.

[1070-04]—*Dominican Sisters* (San Rafael)—O.P.

[1150]—*Eucharistic Franciscan Missionary Sisters*—E.F.M.S.

[1310]—*Franciscan Sisters of Little Falls* (Minnesota)—O.S.F.

[1845]—*Guadalupan Missionaries of the Holy Spirit*—M.G.Sp.S.

[]—*Missionary Sisters of the Sacred Side of Jesus and the Sorrowful Mother* (Italy)—M.S.C.

[3465]—*Religious of the Sacred Heart of Mary*—R.S.H.M.

[]—*Sisters for Christian Community*—S.F.C.C.

[2575]—*Sisters of Mercy of the Americas*—R.S.M.

[3000]—*Sisters of Notre Dame de Namur*—S.N.D.deN.

[3340]—*Sisters of Providence*—S.P.

[1630]—*Sisters of St. Frances of Penance & Christian Charity*—O.S.F.

[1710]—*Sisters of St. Francis of Mary Immaculate*—O.S.F.

[3830-03]—*Sisters of St. Joseph of Orange*—C.S.J.O.

[]—*Sisters of the Cross of the Sacred Heart of Jesus* (Mexico City, Mexico)—R.C.S.C.J.

[1960]—*Sisters of the Holy Family* (San Francisco)—S.H.F.

[4070]—*Society of the Sacred Heart*—R.S.C.J.

DIOCESAN CEMETERIES AND MAUSOLEUMS

STOCKTON. *San Joaquin Cemetery and Mausoleum* Mr. Al Vigil, Supt.

ESCALON. *St. John Cemetery* Cynthia A. Rodriguez, Office Mgr.

MODESTO. *St. Stanislaus Cemetery and Chapel Crypts* Gretchen Storm, Office Mgr.

NECROLOGY

† Hayes, Rev. Msgr. Thomas P., Lodi, CA St. Anne (Pastor of)—Died April 13, 2009

† Coghlan, John A., (Retired)—Died Sept. 25, 2009

An asterisk (*) denotes an organization that has established tax-exempt status directly with the IRS and is not covered by the USCCB Group Ruling.

Diocese of Superior

(Dioecesis Superiorensis)

Most Reverend

PETER F. CHRISTENSEN

Bishop of Superior; ordained May 25, 1985; appointed Bishop of Superior June 29, 2007; consecrated September 14, 2007; installed September 23, 2007. *Office: 1201 Hughitt Ave., Superior, WI 54880.* Tel: 715-394-0205; Fax: 715-395-3149. *Res.: 1 Gitchinadji Dr., Superior, WI 54880. Mailing Address: Box 969, Superior, WI 54880.*

Most Reverend

RAPHAEL M. FLISS, D.D.

Retired Bishop of Superior; ordained May 26, 1956; appointed Coadjutor Bishop of Superior with right of succession November 6, 1979; ordained December 20, 1979; succeeded to See, June 27, 1985; retired June 28, 2007. *Res. & Mailing Address: 7218 Ogden Ave., P.O. Box 3067, Superior, WI 54880.* Tel: 715-392-2932; Fax: 715-392-0910.

Chancery Office: 1201 Hughitt Ave., Box 969, Superior, WI 54880. Tel: 715-392-2937; Fax: 715-392-2015.

ESTABLISHED MAY 3, 1905

Square Miles 15,715.

Comprises the Counties of Ashland, Barron, Bayfield, Burnett, Douglas, Iron, Lincoln, Oneida, Polk, Price, Rusk, Sawyer, St. Croix, Taylor, Vilas and Washburn in the State of Wisconsin.

Incorporated under the laws of the State of Wisconsin as the Diocese of Superior.

For legal titles of parishes and diocesan institutions, consult the Chancery.

STATISTICAL OVERVIEW

Personnel	
Bishop	1
Retired Bishops	1
Priests: Diocesan Active in Diocese	38
Priests: Retired, Sick or Absent	27
Number of Diocesan Priests	65
Religious Priests in Diocese	7
Total Priests in Diocese	72
Extern Priests in Diocese	2
Ordinations:	
Diocesan Priests	2
Transitional Deacons	2
Permanent Deacons	6
Permanent Deacons in Diocese	71
Total Sisters	77
Parishes	
Parishes	105
With Resident Pastor:	
Resident Diocesan Priests	33
Resident Religious Priests	3
Without Resident Pastor:	
Administered by Priests	49
Administered by Deacons	17
Administered by Religious Women	1
Administered by Lay People	2
Professional Ministry Personnel:	
Sisters	5
Lay Ministers	30
Welfare	
Catholic Hospitals	6
Total Assisted	328,992
Health Care Centers	2
Total Assisted	195
Homes for the Aged	12
Total Assisted	363
Day Care Centers	2
Total Assisted	256
Special Centers for Social Services	7
Total Assisted	2,985
Residential Care of Disabled	23
Total Assisted	248
Other Institutions	3
Total Assisted	1,305
Educational	
Diocesan Students in Other Seminaries	7
Total Seminarians	7
Elementary Schools, Diocesan and Parish	16
Total Students	2,482
Catechesis/Religious Education:	
High School Students	2,142
Elementary Students	4,996
Total Students under Catholic Instruction	9,627
Teachers in the Diocese:	
Sisters	5
Lay Teachers	244
Vital Statistics	
Receptions into the Church:	
Infant Baptism Totals	788
Minor Baptism Totals	25
Adult Baptism Totals	23
Received into Full Communion	79
First Communions	855
Confirmations	747
Marriages:	
Catholic	179
Interfaith	95
Total Marriages	274
Deaths	873
Total Catholic Population	78,826
Total Population	454,412

Former Bishops—Rt. Revs. AUGUSTIN FRANCIS SCHINNER, D.D., ord. March 7, 1886; cons. July 25, 1905; resigned Jan. 15, 1913; appt. Bishop of Spokane, WA, March 18, 1914; died Feb. 7, 1937; JOSEPH M. KOUDELKA, D.D., ord. Oct. 8, 1875; cons. Auxiliary Bishop of Cleveland and Titular Bishop of Germanicopolis, Feb. 25, 1908; transferred to Milwaukee as Auxiliary Bishop, Sept. 4, 1911; appt. to the See of Superior, Aug. 6, 1913; died June 24, 1921; JOSEPH G. PINTEN, D.D., ord. Nov. 1, 1890; elected Dec. 3, 1921; cons. May 3, 1922; transferred to the See of Grand Rapids, June 25, 1926; retired Nov. 1, 1940; died Nov. 6, 1945; Most Revs. THEODORE H. REVERMAN, D.D., ord. July 26, 1901; cons. Nov. 30, 1926; died July 18, 1941; WILLIAM PATRICK O'CONNOR, D.D., Ph.D., ord. March 10, 1912; cons. March 7, 1942; transferred to the See of Madison, Jan. 15, 1946; ALBERT GREGORY MEYER, S.S.L., D.D., ord. July 11, 1926; appt. Feb. 18, 1946; cons. April 11, 1946; promoted to Archbishop of Milwaukee, July 21, 1953; transferred to Archbishop of Chicago, Sept. 19, 1958; created Cardinal, Dec. 14, 1959; died April 9, 1965; JOSEPH JOHN ANNABRING, D.D., ord. May 3, 1927; appt. Jan. 27, 1954; cons. March 25, 1954; died Aug. 27, 1959; GEORGE A. HAMMES, D.D., Bishop Emeritus of Superior; appt. March 28, 1960; cons. May 24, 1960; retired June 27, 1985; died April 11, 1993; RAPHAEL M. FLISS, D.D., ord. May 26, 1956; appt. Coadjutor Bishop of Superior with right of succession Nov. 6, 1979; ord. Dec. 20, 1979; succeeded to See, June 27, 1985; retired June 28, 2007.

Chancery—1201 Hughitt Ave., Box 969, Superior, 54880. Tel: 715-392-2937; Fax: 715-392-2015.

Vicar General—Very Rev. DANIEL J. DAHLBERG, V.G., Office, 1500 Vine St., Hudson, 54016. Tel: 715-381-5120; Fax: 715-381-5125.

Moderator of the Curia—Very Rev. PHILIP J. HESLIN.

Chancellor—Mrs. DEBRA J. LIEBERG.

Secretary to Bishop—Mrs. PATRICIA WILDENBERG.

Diocesan Tribunal—

Judicial Vicar—Very Rev. JAMES F. TOBOLSKI, J.C.L.

Adjutant Judicial Vicar—Rev. JAMES P. POWERS, J.C.L.

Promoter of Justice— Appointed by case.

Defender of the Bond—Rev. WILLIAM G. HORATH.

Procurator and Advocate—Ms. PATTI J. HOLT.

Vicar for Canonical Affairs—Very Rev. JAMES F. TOBOLSKI, J.C.L.

Diocesan Pastoral Council—Most Rev. PETER F. CHRISTENSEN, M.A.S. South Central Deanery: CAROL EWAN; RODNEY MAHNER; ROGER RIVARD. Eastern Deanery: JANICE DONNER; JOHN MCGRAW; YVONNE GLONCHAK. Northwest Deanery: LOUISE POPE; ERNEST SWARTZ; CATE VAN LONE TAYLOR. North Central Deanery: JOHN GREK; SHIRLEY TRAUTT; MICHAEL PUTZER. Southwest Deanery: CATHERINE SMOLINSKE; RICHARD TRAYNOR; Deacon THOMAS J. WEISS, Bishop's Appointee. Ex Officio Members: Very Revs. DANIEL J. DAHLBERG, V.G.; PHILIP J. HESLIN; Sisters CELINE GOESSL, S.C.S.C.; THERESA SANDOK, O.S.M.

Deaneries and Deans—Northwest Deanery: Very Rev. JAMES F. TOBOLSKI, J.C.L. Southwest Deanery: Very Rev. JOHN A. DRUMMY. North Central Deanery: VACANT. South Central Deanery: Very Rev. PHILIP J. JUZA. East Deanery: Very Rev. JOHN C. ANDERSON.

Pastoral Consultors—Very Rev. PHILIP J. JUZA; Revs. JAMES J. KINNEY; RONALD OLSON, O.F.M.Conv.; MICHAEL J. TUPA.

Presbyteral Council & Diocesan Consultors—Most Rev. PETER F. CHRISTENSEN, M.A.S., Pres.; Rev. NORBERT D'MELLO, C.S.C.; Very Revs. JAMES F. TOBOLSKI, J.C.L., Sec.; DANIEL J. DAHLBERG, V.G.; Rev. JOHN R. GERRITTS, Treas.; Very Rev. KEVIN M. GORDON; Revs. GERALD A. HAGEN, Chm.; MICHAEL T. HAYDEN; EDWIN C. ANDERSON; ROBERT J. KOSZAREK; MICHAEL J. TUPA, Vice Chm.; THOMAS E. THOMPSON; GERARD I. WILLGER.

Personnel Placement Board—Very Revs. JOHN C. ANDERSON; KEVIN M. GORDON; Deacon TIMOTHY J. KUEHN; Rev. THOMAS E. THOMPSON; Very Revs. JOHN A. DRUMMY; PHILIP J. JUZA; JAMES F. TOBOLSKI, J.C.L.

Diocesan Offices and Directors

Bureau of Information—MEGAN MILLER, Dir., 1201 Hughitt Ave., P.O. Box 969, Superior, 54880. Tel: 715-394-0213.

Catholic Charities Bureau—Mr. BRIAN SOLAND, M.A., Exec. Dir., Office, 1416 Cumming Ave., Superior, 54880. Tel: 715-394-6617; Fax: 715-394-5951.

Catholic Boy and Girl Scout Chaplain—Rev. EDWIN C. ANDERSON, Mailing Address: St. Francis de Sales Church, 409 Summit St., Spooner, 54801. Tel: 715-635-3105; Fax: 715-635-7341.

Catholic Mutual Group—PAUL ALTMANN, Claims/Risk Mgr., 1201 Hughitt Ave., P.O. Box 969, Superior, 54880. Tel: 715-394-0222.

Catholic Women, Council of—PAT WILLIAMS, Pres., 701 N. State Rd. 46, Lot #40, Balsam Lake, 54810. Tel: 715-405-3727.

Moderator—Rev. GERARD I. WILLGER, Mailing Address: Our Lady of the Holy Rosary Church, P.O. Box 503, Medford, 54451.

Charismatic Renewal Liaison—Deacon MICHAEL D. CULLEN, St. Joseph Church, 827 E. LaSalle Ave., Barron, 54812. Tel: 715-637-3255; Fax: 715-637-3252.

Catholic Formation, Department of—VACANT.

Diocesan Coordinator of Health Affairs—Very Rev. KEVIN M. GORDON, 1201 Hughitt Ave., P.O. Box 969, Superior, 54880. Tel: 715-394-0229.

Diocesan Sisters Council—Sr. PHYLLIS WILHELM, O.S.F., Pres., 715 Third Ave. E., Ashland, 54806. Tel: 715-209-6825.

Ecumenical Commission—Very Rev. JAMES F. TOBOLSKI, J.C.L., Mailing Address: P.O. Box 969, Superior, 54880. Tel: 715-394-0207.

Evangelization, Office of—VACANT.

Finance, Department of—RONALD C. NELSON, Dir., 1201 Hughitt Ave., P.O. Box 969, Superior, 54880. Tel: 715-394-0221.

Holy Childhood Association—Rev. GREGORY J. HOPEFL, Dir., 13891 W. Mission Rd, Stone Lake, 54876. Tel: 715-865-3669.

Insurance/Employee Benefits and Payroll, Office of—CINDY GRONSKI, Dir., 1201 Hughitt Ave., P.O. Box 969, Superior, 54880. Tel: 715-394-0230; Fax: 715-395-3758.

Newman Apostolate— Superior: Newman and Young Adult Ministry Center, University of Wisconsin Directors: BRETT JONES; MEGHAN JONES, 823 N. 16th St., Superior, 54880. Tel: 715-394-7710. St. Thomas More Newman Center: Deacon THOMAS J. WEISS, Coord., Newman Ministry, 423 E. Cascade Ave., River Falls, 54022. Tel: 715-425-7234; Fax: 715-425-6959. Email: thomas.j.weiss@uwrf.edu.

Catholic Herald, Superior Edition—MEGAN MILLER, Editor, 1201 Hughitt Ave., P.O. Box 969, Superior, 54880. Tel: 715-394-0213.

Parish Accounting, Office of—CINDY GRONSKI, Contact, 1201 Hughitt Ave., P.O. Box 969, Superior, 54880. Tel: 715-394-0230.

Pastoral Services, Department of—VACANT.

Planning, Office of—VACANT.

Permanent Diaconate—Deacon TIMOTHY J. KUEHN, Dir., Mailing Address: 1201 Hughitt Ave., P.O. Box 969, Superior, 54880. Tel: 715-394-0217.

Respect Life Office—LLOYD CIZEK; JO CIZEK, 810 Wapogasset Lake Lane, Amery, 54001. Tel: 715-268-2496.

Propagation of the Faith—Rev. GREGORY J. HOPEFL, 13891 W. Mission Rd., Stone Lake, 54876. Tel: 715-865-3669.

Radio and Television—MEGAN MILLER, Dir., 1201 Hughitt Ave., P.O. Box 969, Superior, 54880. Tel: 715-394-0213.

The Bishop George A. Hammes Center—Deacon ROGER L. CADOTTE, Dir., 315 W. Fifth St., P.O. Box 280, Haugen, 54841. Tel: 715-234-5044; Fax: 715-234-5241.

St. Pius Priest Fund—Board of Directors: Most Rev. PETER F. CHRISTENSEN, M.A.S., Pres.; Revs. DENNIS M. MULLEN, Vice Pres.; JAMES P. POWERS, J.C.L., Sec.; Very Rev. JOHN C. ANDERSON; Revs. JAMES J. BRINKMAN; DENNIS T. MEULEMANS (Retired); DAVID P. OBERTS; DAVID R. LUSSON; WILLIAM J. MURPHY; THOMAS E. THOMPSON.

Stewardship and Development, Department of—Mr. STEVEN P. TARNOWSKI, Dir., 1201 Hughitt Ave., P.O. Box 969, Superior, 54880. Tel: 715-394-0223; Fax: 715-392-2015.

Superintendent of Schools—PEGGY SCHOENFUSS, Office: Bishop George A. Hammes Center, 315 W. Fifth St., P.O. Box 280, Haugen, 54841. Tel: 715-234-5044, Ext. 4405; Fax: 715-234-5241.

Diocesan Coordinators of Assistance—Mailing Address: P.O. Box 969, Superior, 54880. CATHY KOERPEL. Tel: 715-369-2676; GARY NELSON. Tel: 715-363-2623.

Vocations, Office of—Rev. THOMAS E. THOMPSON, Mailing Address: P.O. Box 399, Osceola, 54020.

Office of Worship—PAUL J. BIRCH, 1201 Hughitt Ave., P.O. Box 969, Superior, 54880. Tel: 715-394-0233.

CLERGY, PARISHES, MISSIONS AND PAROCHIAL SCHOOLS

CITY OF SUPERIOR

(DOUGLAS COUNTY)

1—CATHEDRAL OF CHRIST THE KING (1886) [CEM] Rev. Andrew P. Ricci, Rector; Deacon Arthur Gil de Lamadrid.
Mailing Address: 1410 Baxter Ave., 54880.
Church: Belknap Ave. & Grand, 54880. Tel: 715-392-8511; Fax: 715-392-3457.
School—Cathedral School, (Grades PreK-8), 1419 Baxter Ave., 54880. Tel: 715-392-2976; Fax: 715-392-2977. Timothy Johnson, Prin. Lay Teachers 22; Students 265.
Catechesis/Religious Program—Students 108.

2—ST. ANTHONY (1870), Also serves St. Anthony, Lake Nebagamon & St. William, Superior. Deacon Phillip J. Runser, Parish Life Coord.; Rev. Donald A. Kania, Parochial Vicar; Deacons Timothy J. Kuehn; Kevin Feind.
Church & Mailing Address: 4315 E. 3rd St., 54880. Tel: 715-398-3261; Fax: 715-398-3257.
Catechesis/Religious Program—Annette Minter, D.R.E. Students 48.

3—SS. CYRIL AND METHODIUS, (Slovak), Closed. For inquiries for sacramental records contact Cathedral of Christ the King.

4—ST. FRANCIS XAVIER (1854) [CEM] Very Rev. James F. Tobolski.
Church and Mailing Address: 2316 E. 4th St., 54880. Tel: 715-398-7174; Fax: 715-398-3074.
Catechesis/Religious Program—Ernest Swartz, D.R.E. Students 183.

5—HOLY ASSUMPTION OF THE B.V.M. (1891) Rev. Ronald Olson, O.F.M.Conv.; Deacon Robert J. Chammings.
Church & Mailing Address: 5601 Tower Ave., 54880. Tel: 715-394-7919; Fax: 715-394-4883.
Catechesis/Religious Program—Lucinda Wnuk, C.R.E. Students 74.

6—ST. LOUIS, Closed. For inquiries for sacramental records contact Cathedral of Christ the King.

7—ST. PATRICK, Closed. For inquiries for sacramental records contact Cathedral of Christ the King.

8—ST. STANISLAUS, (Polish), Closed. For inquiries for sacramental records contact Cathedral of Christ the King.

9—ST. WILLIAM (1908) [CEM] Deacon Phillip J. Runser, Parish Life Coord.; Rev. Donald A. Kania, Parochial Vicar.
Mailing Address: 4315 E. 3rd St., 54880.
Church: 3095 E. County Rd. B, 54880. Tel: 715-398-3261.
Catechesis/Religious Program—Students 32.

OUTSIDE THE CITY OF SUPERIOR

ALMENA, BARRON CO., SACRED HEART OF JESUS CHURCH (1890) [CEM] Rev. David R. Lusson.
Mailing Address: 900 St. Anthony St., Cumberland, 54829. Tel: 715-822-2948; Fax: 715-822-3588.
Church: 114 Soo Ave., 54805.
Catechesis/Religious Program—Steven Linton, D.R.E.

AMERY, POLK CO., ST. JOSEPH (1890) [CEM] Very Rev. John A. Drummy; Deacons Larry K. Bauer; Florian Heiser. Also serves Our Lady of the Lakes, Balsam Lake.
Church and Mailing Address: 1050 Keller Ave. N., 54001. Tel: 715-268-7717; Fax: 715-268-9986.
Catechesis/Religious Program—Mary Modjeski, D.R.E.; Joyce Holt, C.R.E. Students 147.

ASHLAND, ASHLAND CO.

1—HOLY FAMILY, (Polish), Closed. For inquiries for sacramental records contact Our Lady of the Lake Catholic Community, Ashland.

2—OUR LADY OF THE LAKE CATHOLIC COMMUNITY (1872) [CEM] Rev. Paul Pare, O.F.M.; Deacons William J. Holzhaeuser; Owen T. Gorman.
Mailing Address: 106 N. 2nd Ave. E., 54806. Also serves St. Mary, Odanah.
Church: 201 Lake Shore Dr. E., 54806. Tel: 715-682-7620; Fax: 715-682-7626.
School—(Grades PreK-8), 215 Lake Shore Dr. E., 54806. Tel: 715-682-7622. Mr. Dan Bell, Prin. Lay Teachers 20; Students 136.
Catechesis/Religious Program—Tim Mika, C.R.E. Students 120.

BALSAM LAKE, POLK CO., OUR LADY OF THE LAKES (1875) [CEM 2] Very Rev. John A. Drummy.
Mailing Address: P.O. Box 399, 54810.
Church: 507 W. Main, 58410. Tel: 715-405-2253; Fax: 715-405-2743.
Catechesis/Religious Program—Tel: 715-294-2243. Sally Christiansen, D.R.E. Tel: 715-405-2258. Students 76.

BARRON, BARRON CO., ST. JOSEPH (1907), Also serves St. Peter, Cameron and St. Boniface, Chetek. Deacon Michael D. Cullen, Parish Life Coord.; Rev. Norbert D'Mello, C.S.C.
Church and Mailing Address: 827 E. LaSalle Ave., 54812. Tel: 715-637-3255; Fax: 715-637-3252.
Catechesis/Religious Program—Anne Stephens, D.R.E. Students 89.

BAYFIELD, BAYFIELD CO., HOLY FAMILY (1878) [CEM] Revs. Michael Haney, O.F.M.; Lourdumar Reddy Mandapati; Deacon Roger L. Cadotte.
Mailing Address: P.O. Box 1290, 54814.
Church: 232 N. 1st. St., 54814. Tel: 715-779-3316; Fax: 715-779-9804.
Catechesis/Religious Program—Sr. Barbara Bogenschutz, O.P., D.R.E. Students 18.

BIRCHWOOD, WASHBURN CO., ST. JOHN EVANGELIST (1908) Deacon Dennis C. Geisler, Parish Life Coord.; Rev. David P. Oberts, Sacramental Min.
Mailing Address: 2411 23rd St., Rice Lake, 54868.
Church: 408 S. Main, 54817. Tel: 715-234-2917; Fax: 715-236-7865.
Catechesis/Religious Program—John Deering, D.R.E.; Kristine Deering, D.R.E. Students 36.

BLOOMVILLE, LINCOLN CO., ST. JOHN THE BAPTIST (1908) [CEM] Rev. Ronald Serrao, C.S.C.; Michele Rein, Parish Dir.
Mailing Address: N10090 County Rd. B., Tomahawk, 54487.
Church: Hwy. 17 & County Rd. J, Gleason, 54435. Tel: 715-453-2561; Fax: 715-453-4813.
Catechesis/Religious Program—Vincent Geisler, Youth Min. Students 44.

BOULDER JUNCTION, VILAS CO., ST. ANNE (1938) [CEM], Also serves St. Mary, Sayner, and St. Rita, Presque Isle. Rev. Bernard M. Byrne; Dorita Dolezal, C.R.E.
Mailing Address: P.O. Box 110, 54512.
Church: 10315 Main St., 54512. Tel: 715-385-2390; Fax: 715-385-2282.
Catechesis/Religious Program—Students 28.

BRUCE, RUSK CO., ST. MARY (1893) [CEM 2] Deacon Craig J. Voldberg, Parish Life Coord.
Mailing Address: P.O. Box 207, Weyerhaeuser, 54895. In Res., Rev. Ronald W. Levra, Parochial Vicar (Retired).
Church: 727 N. 2nd St., 54819. Tel: 715-353-2400; Fax: 715-353-4758.
Catechesis/Religious Program—Pat Stine, C.R.E. (K-6); Lenore Krajewski, C.R.E. Students 43.

BUTTERNUT, ASHLAND CO., IMMACULATE CONCEPTION (1880) [CEM] Rev. Daniel Gonzalez; Deacon Chester E. Ball Jr., Parish Life Coord.
Mailing Address: P.O. Box 6, 54514.
Church: 410 Michigan St., 54514. Tel: 715-769-3585; Fax: 715-769-3585.
Catechesis/Religious Program—Bette Hirtreiter, D.R.E. Students 32.

CABLE, BAYFIELD CO., ST. ANN (1902) Sr. Virginia Schwartz, O.S.M., Parish Dir.
Mailing Address: P.O. Box 37, 54821-0037.
Church: 13645 County Hwy. M, 54821. Tel: 715-798-3855; Fax: 715-798-3850.
Catechesis/Religious Program—Joyce Lenz, D.R.E. Students 18.

CAMERON, BARRON CO., ST. PETER (1908) Deacon Michael D. Cullen, Parish Life Coord.; Rev. Norbert D'Mello, C.S.C., Parochial Vicar; Deacon Russell E. Cabak.
Mailing Address: 827 E. LaSalle Ave., Barron, 54812.
Church: Creamery Rd. & Hwy. 8, 54822. Tel: 715-637-3255.
Catechesis/Religious Program—Patty Gerber, C.R.E. Students 102.

CATAWBA, PRICE CO., ST. PAUL THE APOSTLE (1907) [CEM] Rev. Gerald A. Hagen.
Mailing Address: 125 N. Argyle Ave., Phillips, 54555.
Church: W9485 Hwy. 8, 54515. Tel: 715-339-2222; Fax: 715-339-2216.
Catechesis/Religious Program—Andrea Bleck, D.R.E. Students 46.

CENTURIA, POLK CO., ST. PATRICK (1856) Closed. For inquiries for sacramental records, please contact Our Lady of the Lakes, Balsam Lake.

CHELSEA, TAYLOR CO., ASSUMPTION OF THE BLESSED VIRGIN MARY (1887) Closed. For Inquiries for sacramental records please contact Good Shepherd, Rib Lake., Mailing Address: 513 State Rd., Rib Lake, 54470.

CHETEK, BARRON CO., ST. BONIFACE (1880) [CEM] Deacon Michael D. Cullen, Parish Life Coord.; Rev. Norbert D'Mello, C.S.C., Parochial Vicar; Deacon James M. Dennis.
Mailing Address: 827 E. LaSalle Ave., Barron, 54812.
Church: 425 S. 3rd St., 54728. Tel: 715-924-3514; Fax: 715-924-3514.
Catechesis/Religious Program—Dawn Langman, C.R.E. Students 42.

CLAM LAKE, ASHLAND CO., ST. GEORGE (1890) Rev. Michael D. McLain.
Mailing Address: P.O. Box 17, Mellen, 54546.
Church: W. Hwy. 77, 54517. Tel: 715-264-3471.

CLEAR LAKE, POLK CO., ST. JOHN (1890) Very Rev. John A. Drummy.
Mailing Address: P.O. Box 337, 54005.
Church: 811 Fourth St., 54005. Tel: 715-263-2032; Fax: 715-263-2032.
Catechesis/Religious Program—Paul Mara, D.R.E. Students 45.

CORNUCOPIA, BAYFIELD CO., ST. ANN (1914) [CEM] Revs. Michael Haney, O.F.M.; Lourdumar Reddy Mandapati.
Mailing Address: P.O. Box 070, Washburn, 54891.
Church: Superior Ave. & Ash St., 54827. Tel: 715-373-2676; Fax: 715-373-0365.
Catechesis/Religious Program—

CRESCENT LAKE, BURNETT CO., SACRED HEARTS OF JESUS AND MARY (1857) [CEM] Rev. Michael J. Tupa.
Mailing Address: P.O. Box 7, Webster, 54893.
Church: County Rd. A & H, 54830. Tel: 715-866-7321; Fax: 715-866-7305.
Catechesis/Religious Program—Colleen Monfre, D.R.E. Students 4.

CUMBERLAND, BARRON CO., ST. ANTHONY ABBOT (1883) [CEM 2], Also serves Sacred Heart of Jesus, Almena and St. Ann, Turtle Lake. Rev. David R. Lusson.
Church and Mailing Address: 900 St. Anthony St., 54829. Tel: 715-822-2948; Fax: 715-822-3588.
Catechesis/Religious Program—Steven Linton, D.R.E. Students 155.

DANBURY, BURNETT CO., OUR LADY OF PERPETUAL HELP (1920) Rev. Michael J. Tupa.
Mailing Address: P.O. Box 7, Webster, 54893.
Church and Mailing: 7586 Main St., 54830. Tel: 715-866-7321; Fax: 715-866-7305.
Catechesis/Religious Program—Colleen Monfre, D.R.E. Students 7.

DAUBY, BAYFIELD CO., ST. PETER (1918) [CEM] Rev. Michael L. Crisp.
Mailing Address: P.O. Box 97, Iron River, 54847.
Church: Hwy. 2 & County Rd. F, 54847. Tel: 715-372-4756.
Catechesis/Religious Program—Betty Franzel, D.R.E. Students 5.

DOBIE, BARRON CO., OUR LADY OF LOURDES (1875) [CEM], (Also serves Holy Trinity, Haugen, and St. John the Evangelist, Birchwood.) Deacon Dennis C. Geisler, Parish Life Coord.; Rev. David P. Oberts, Sacramental Min.
Church and Mailing Address: 2411 23rd St., Rice Lake, 54868. Tel: 715-234-2917; Fax: 715-236-7865.
Catechesis/Religious Program—John Deering, C.R.E.; Kristine Deering, C.R.E. Students 114.

EAGLE RIVER, VILAS CO., ST. PETER THE FISHERMAN (1890) [CEM] Rev. Robert J. Koszarek; Sr. Jeanne Wiest, O.P., Pastoral Assoc.
Church and Mailing Address: 5001 County Rd. G, 54521. Tel: 715-479-8704; Fax: 715-477-2017.
Catechesis/Religious Program—Students 77.

ERIN, ST. CROIX CO., ST. PATRICK (1857) [CEM 2] Rev. James J. Brinkman.
Mailing Address: 151 S. Washington Ave., New Richmond, 54017.
Church: 1880 County Rd. G, 54017. Tel: 715-246-4652; Fax: 715-246-2526.
Catechesis/Religious Program—Jody Lenz, C.R.E. Students 17.

FARMINGTON, ST. CROIX CO., ASSUMPTION OF THE BLESSED VIRGIN MARY (1869) [CEM] Rev. Thomas E. Thompson.
Mailing Address: P.O. Box 399, Osceola, 54020-0399.
Church: 255 State Hwy. 35, 54025. Tel: 715-294-2243; Fax: 715-294-2495.
Catechesis/Religious Program—Barbara Ziegler, C.R.E. Students 15.

FIFIELD, PRICE CO., ST. FRANCIS OF ASSISI (1888) Rev. Daniel Gonzalez; Deacon Chester E. Ball Jr., Parish Life Coord.
Mailing Address: 276 S. 5th Ave., Park Falls, 54552.
Church: Balsam St., 54524. Tel: 715-762-4494.
Catechesis/Religious Program—Students 4.

FLAMBEAU, RUSK CO., ST. FRANCIS OF ASSISI (1866) [CEM] Deacon Craig J. Voldberg, Parish Life Coord.
Mailing Address: P.O. Box 207, Weyerhaeuser, 54895. In Res., Rev. Ronald W. Levra, Parochial Vicar (Retired).
Church: W10193 Lehman Rd., Holcombe, 54745. Tel: 715-353-2400; Fax: 715-353-4758.
Catechesis/Religious Program—Sally Meyer, D.R.E. Students 22.

FREDERIC, POLK CO., ST. DOMINIC (1904) [CEM], (Also serves Immaculate Conception, Grantsburg). Rev. Dennis M. Mullen; Deacon Stanley J. Marczak.
Mailing Address: P.O. Box 606, 54837.
Rectory & Parish Office: 107 W. Birch St., 54837.
Church: 103 W. Birch St., 54837. Tel: 715-327-8119; Fax: 715-327-8125.
Catechesis/Religious Program—Melody Dian, D.R.E. Students 55.

GEORGETOWN, POLK CO., OUR LADY OF THE HOLY ROSARY, Closed. For inquiries for sacramental records contact Our Lady of the Lakes Balsam Lake.

GILMAN, TAYLOR CO., SS. PETER AND PAUL (1910) [CEM], (Also serves St. Michael, Jump River; St. John the Apostle, Sheldon and St. Stanislaus, Lublin). Rev. John R. Long.
Church and Mailing: 315 E. Davlin St., 54433. Tel: 715-447-8510; Fax: 715-447-5742.
Catechesis/Religious Program—Sr. Marianna Ableidinger, F.S.P.A., D.R.E. Students 73.

GLENWOOD CITY, ST. CROIX CO., ST. JOHN THE BAPTIST (1886) [CEM] Rev. William J. Murphy.
Mailing Address: P.O. Box 18, Hammond, 54015.
Church: 757 1st St., 54013. Tel: 715-265-7133; Fax: 715-265-7339.
Catechesis/Religious Program—Deacon Wesley G. Tuttle, D.R.E. Students 180.

GLIDDEN, ASHLAND CO., MOST PRECIOUS BLOOD (1884) [CEM] Rev. Michael D. McLain, Admin.
Mailing Address: P.O. Box 17, Mellen, 54546. Tel: 715-264-3471.
Church: Grant St., 54527.
Catechesis/Religious Program—Larry Bay, C.R.E.; Kathy Witt, C.R.E. Students 45.

GORDON, DOUGLAS CO., ST. ANTHONY OF PADUA (1878) Rev. James J. Kinney.
Mailing Address: P.O. Box 303, Solon Springs, 54873.
Church: 9718 E. County Rd. Y, 54838. Tel: 715-378-4431.
Catechesis/Religious Program—Pat DenHartog, C.R.E.

GRANTSBURG, BURNETT CO., IMMACULATE CONCEPTION (1909) Rev. Dennis M. Mullen.
Mailing Address: P.O. Box 606, Frederic, 54837.
Church: 411 State Rd. 70, 54840. Tel: 715-327-8119.
Catechesis/Religious Program—Melody Dian, D.R.E.; Marie Ohnstad, C.R.E. Students 52.

HAMMOND, ST. CROIX CO., IMMACULATE CONCEPTION (1877) [CEM], Also serves St. John the Baptist, Glenwood City and St. Bridget, Wilson. Rev. William J. Murphy; Deacon Joseph F. Paron.
Mailing Address: P.O. Box 18, 54015-0018.
Church: 1265 Ridgeway, 54015. Tel: 715-796-2244; Fax: 715-796-2599.
Catechesis/Religious Program—Jackie Aune, C.R.E.; Diane Johnson, C.R.E. Students 238.

HARRISON, LINCOLN CO., ST. AUGUSTINE (1905) [CEM] Rev. Ronald Serrao, C.S.C.; Deacon Clarence D. Towle.
Mailing Address: Tomahawk N10090 Cty. B, Tomahawk, 54487. Tel: 715-453-2561; Fax: 715-453-4813.
Church: Highways B & D, Tomahawk, 54487.
Catechesis/Religious Program—Deacon Clarence D. Towle, D.R.E. Students 31.

HAUGEN, BARRON CO., HOLY TRINITY (1896) [CEM] Deacon Dennis C. Geisler, Parish Life Coord.; Rev. David P. Oberts, Sacramental Min.; Deacon Harvey G. Drost.
Mailing Address: 2411 23rd St., Rice Lake, 54868.
Church: 317 W. 5th St., 54841. Tel: 715-234-2917; Fax: 715-236-7865.
Catechesis/Religious Program—Kris Deering, Co-D.R.E.; John Deering, Co-D.R.E. Students 53.

HAWKINS, RUSK CO., ST. MARY OF CZESTOCHOWA (1913) [CEM] Rev. James P. Bartelme.
Mailing Address: 611 1st St. S., Ladysmith, 54848.
Church: N7386 Cty. Rd. M, 54530. Tel: 715-532-3051; Fax: 715-532-7368.
Catechesis/Religious Program—Gayle Spencer, D.R.E. Students 11.

HAYWARD, SAWYER CO., ST. JOSEPH (1882), Also serves St. Ann, Cable. Very Rev. Philip J. Juza.
Mailing Address: P.O. Box 877, 54843.
Church: 10586 N. Dakota Ave., 54843. Tel: 715-634-2867; Fax: 715-634-9037.
Catechesis/Religious Program—Teri Radcliffe, C.R.E. (Grades PreK-5). Students 174.

HIGHBRIDGE, ASHLAND CO., ST. ANTHONY (1880) Rev. Michael D. McLain, Admin.
Mailing Address: P.O. Box 17, Mellen, 54546.
Church: Hwy. 13, 54846. Tel: 715-274-3701; Fax: 715-274-3703.
Catechesis/Religious Program—Debbie Schutte, C.R.E. Students 7.

HUDSON, ST. CROIX CO., ST. PATRICK (1840) [CEM] Very Rev. Daniel J. Dahlberg; Rev. William D. Brenna; Deacons Peter R. Braum; Gregg Miller; Howard W. Cameron.
Church and Mailing Address: 1500 Vine St., 54016. Tel: 715-381-5120; Fax: 715-381-5125.
School—(Grades PreK-8), 403 St. Croix St., 54016. Tel: 715-386-3941. Mary Piasecki, Prin. Sisters 1; Lay Teachers 24; Students 360.
Catechesis/Religious Program—Tel: 715-386-9209. Larry Huiras, D.R.E.; Tim O'Brien, D.R.E. Students 565.

HURLEY, IRON CO., ST. MARY OF THE SEVEN DOLORS (1885) [CEM], Also serves St. Issac Jogues and Companions, Mercer. Rev. Michael T. Hayden.
Mailing Address: 404 Iron St., 54534.
Church: Iron St. & 5th Ave., 54534. Tel: 715-561-2606; Fax: 715-561-3739.
Catechesis/Religious Program—Ann Marie Batiste, C.R.E. Students 86.

INO, BAYFIELD CO., ST. FLORIAN (1913) [CEM] Rev. Michael L. Crisp.
Mailing Address: P.O. Box 97, Iron River, 54847.
Church: 19315 Keystone Rd., 54806. Tel: 715-372-4756.
Catechesis/Religious Program—Loretta Skaj, D.R.E. Students 4.

IRON RIVER, BAYFIELD CO., ST. MICHAEL (1892) [CEM], Also serves St. Peter, Dauby; St. Florian, Ino; SS. Peter & Paul, Moquah. Rev. Michael L. Crisp.
Mailing Address: P.O. Box 97, 54847.
Church: 68105 S. George St., 54847. Tel: 715-372-4756; Fax: 715-372-4753.
Catechesis/Religious Program—Cyndy Castro, C.R.E. Students 40.

JUMP RIVER, TAYLOR CO., ST. MICHAEL (1915) Rev. John R. Long.
Mailing Address: 315 E. Davlin St., Gilman, 54433. Tel: 715-447-8510; Fax: 715-447-5742.
Church: Hwy. 73, 54434.
Catechesis/Religious Program—Sr. Marianna Ableidinger, F.S.P.A., D.R.E.

LA POINTE, BAYFIELD CO., ST. JOSEPH (1669) [CEM] Revs. Michael Haney, O.F.M.; Lourdumar Reddy Mandapati.
Mailing Address: P.O. Box 1290, Bayfield, 54814.
Church: 266 Airport Rd., 54850. Tel: 715-779-3316; Fax: 715-779-9804.
Catechesis/Religious Program—Sr. Barbara Bogenschutz, O.P., D.R.E.

LAC DU FLAMBEAU, VILAS CO., ST. ANTHONY OF PADUA (1862), Also serves Our Lady Queen of Peace, Manitowish Waters. Rev. J. Patrick Hardy; Deacon John J. Bardos.
Mailing Address: P.O. Box 38, 54538.
Church: 650 Old Abe Rd., 54538. Tel: 715-588-3148; Fax: 715-588-3889.
Catechesis/Religious Program—Tel: 715-588-7439. Debra Ramsey, D.R.E. Students 10.

LADYSMITH, RUSK CO., OUR LADY OF SORROWS (1906), Also serves St. Mary, Hawkins, and St. Anthony de Padua, Tony. Rev. James P. Bartelme; Deacons Jerome J. Drahos; Richard D. Leonhard; Douglas L. Sorenson.
Church and Mailing Address: 611 1st St. S., 54848. Tel: 715-532-3051; Fax: 715-532-7368.
School—(Grades K-8), 105 E. Washington Ave., 54848. Tel: 715-532-3232. Tami Stewart, Prin. Lay Teachers 11; Students 103.
Catechesis/Religious Program—Tel: 715-532-3703. Gayle Spencer, C.R.E. Students 115.

LAKE NEBAGAMON, DOUGLAS CO., ST. ANTHONY (1899) [CEM] Deacon Phillip J. Runser, Parish Life Coord.; Rev. Donald A. Kania, Parochial Vicar.
Mailing Address: 4315 E. 3rd St., 54880.
Church: 11648 E. County Rd. B, 54849. Tel: 715-374-3570.
Catechesis/Religious Program—Tammy Brown, D.R.E. Students 47.

LAKE TOMAHAWK, ONEIDA CO., ST. JOHN VIANNEY (1859) Closed. For inquiries for sacramental records please contact Holy Family, Woodruff.

LAND-O'-LAKES, VILAS CO., ST. ALBERT (1894), Also serves St. Mary, Phelps. Michele Rein, Parish Dir.; Deacon Norman J. Mesun Jr.
Mailing Address: P.O. Box 237, Land O'Lakes, 54540.
Church: 4351 Hwy. B, Land O'Lakes, 54540. Tel: 715-547-3558; Fax: 715-547-3614.
Catechesis/Religious Program—Students 27.

LUBLIN, TAYLOR CO., ST. STANISLAUS (1907), (Polish), [CEM] Rev. John R. Long; Sr. Marianna Ableidinger, F.S.P.A., Pastoral Assoc.
Mailing Address: 315 E. Davlin St., Gilman, 54433.
Church: W13381 South St., 54447. Tel: 715-447-8510; Fax: 715-447-5742.
Catechesis/Religious Program—Sr. Marianna Ableidinger, F.S.P.A., D.R.E. Students 14.

MANITOWISH WATERS, VILAS CO., OUR LADY QUEEN OF PEACE (1958) Rev. J. Patrick Hardy.
Mailing Address: P.O. Box 325, 54545.
Church & Office: 193 S. Hwy. 51, 54545. Tel: 715-543-8428; Fax: 715-543-8428.
Catechesis/Religious Program—Veronica McGraw, D.R.E. Students 3.

MEDFORD, TAYLOR CO., OUR LADY OF THE HOLY ROSARY (1870) [CEM], Also serves Our Lady of Perpetual Help, Whittlesey. Rev. Gerard I. Willger; Deacon Joseph Stefancin, Pastoral Assoc.
Mailing Address: P.O. Box 503, 54451.
Church: 215 S. Washington Ave., 54451. Tel: 715-748-3336; Fax: 715-748-6643.

School—(Grades PreK-6) Fax: 715-748-5110. Daniel Minter, Prin. Sisters (Servants of Mary) 1; Lay Teachers 14; Students 168.
Catechesis/Religious Program—Julie Minter, C.R.E. (Grades K-6); Janine Rolfs, C.R.E. (Grades 7-12). Students 361.

MELLEN, ASHLAND CO., HOLY ROSARY (1886), Also serves St. Anthony, Highbridge; St. Anne, Sanborn; St. George, Clam Lake; Most Precious Blood, Glidden. Rev. Michael D. McLain, Parochial Admin.
Mailing Address: P.O. Box 17, 54546.
Church: 203 N. Main St., 54546. Tel: 715-274-3701; Fax: 715-274-3703.
Catechesis/Religious Program—Sara Schultz, C.R.E.; Shelia Dupee, C.R.E. Students 56.

MERCER, IRON CO., ST. ISAAC JOGUES AND COMPANIONS (1912) Rev. Michael T. Hayden; Deacon Norbert G. Brossmer.
Mailing Address: P.O. Box 575, 54547.
Church: 2611 W. Garnet St., 54547. Tel: 715-476-2697; Fax: 715-476-2704.
Catechesis/Religious Program—Laura Taylor, D.R.E. Students 20.

MERRILL, LINCOLN CO.
1—ST. FRANCIS XAVIER (1875) [CEM] Rev. James R. Horath; Deacon John E. Ramassini.
Church and Mailing Address: 1708 E. 10th St., 54452. Tel: 715-536-2803; Fax: 715-536-7536.
School—St. Francis, (Grades PreK-8) Tel: 715-536-6083. Jaclyn Behnke, Prin. Lay Teachers 15; Students 110.
Catechesis/Religious Program—Judy Warren, D.R.E. Students 262.
2—ST. ROBERT BELLARMINE (1886) Closed. For inquiries for sacramental records contact St. Francis Xavier, Merrill.

MINOCQUA, ONEIDA CO., ST. PATRICK (1894) [CEM] Closed. For inquiries for sacramental records, contact Holy Family, Woodruff.

MINONG, WASHBURN CO., ST. MARY (1904) Rev. James J. Kinney.
Mailing Address: P.O. Box 303, Solon Springs, 54873.
Office & Rectory: 11651 Business 53, Solon Springs, 54873.
Church: 506 Main St., 54859. Tel: 715-378-4431; Fax: 715-378-2480.
Catechesis/Religious Program—Pat DenHartog, C.R.E. Students 15.

MONTREAL, IRON CO., SACRED HEART OF JESUS (1904) Closed. For inquiries for parish records please see St. Mary of the Seven Dolors, Hurley

MOQUAH, BAYFIELD CO., SS. PETER AND PAUL (1912) [CEM 2] Rev. Michael L. Crisp; John Grek.
Mailing Address: P.O. Box 97, Iron River, 54847.
Church: 23505 County Rd. G, 54806. Tel: 715-372-4756.
Catechesis/Religious Program—Kathy Huybrecht, C.R.E. Students 22.

NEW POST, SAWYER CO., ST. IGNATIUS (1884) Rev. Gregory J. Hopefl.
Mailing Address: 13891 W. Mission Rd., Stone Lake, 54876. Tel: 715-865-3669; Fax: 715-865-3669.
Catechesis/Religious Program—Sr. Felissa Zander, S.S.S.F., D.R.E. Students 4.

NEW RICHMOND, ST. CROIX CO., IMMACULATE CONCEPTION (1883) [CEM], Also serves St. Patrick, Erin. Rev. James J. Brinkman; Deacon John P. Derrington.
Church and Office Address: 151 S. Washington Ave., 54017-1523. Tel: 715-246-4652; Fax: 715-246-2526.
School—(Grades K-8), 257 S. Washington Ave., 54017. Tel: 715-246-2469; Fax: 715-246-6195. Mari Zarcone-Patterson, Prin. Lay Teachers 17; Students 175.
Catechesis/Religious Program—Kim Palmer, D.R.E.; Patty Berger, C.R.E. Students 308.

ODANAH, ASHLAND CO., ST. MARY (1855) Rev. Paul Pare, O.F.M.; Sr. Phyllis Wilhelm, O.S.F., Pastoral Assoc.
Mailing Address: 106 N. Second Ave. E., Ashland, 54806. Tel: 715-682-7620; Fax: 715-682-7626.
Church: 300 Old Hwy. 2, 54861.

OSCEOLA, POLK CO., ST. JOSEPH (1915), Also serves Assumption of the Blessed Virgin Mary, Farmington. Rev. Thomas E. Thompson; Deacons Fred E. Johnson; Richard T. Peterson; Thomas P. Rausch.
Mailing Address: P.O. Box 399, 54020-0399.
Church: 255 10th Ave., 54020. Tel: 715-294-2243; Fax: 715-294-2495.
Catechesis/Religious Program—Tel: 715-294-4163. Gwen Nies, D.R.E. Students 131.

PARK FALLS, PRICE CO., ST. ANTHONY OF PADUA (1904), Also serves Immaculate Conception, Butternut; St. Francis of Assisi, Fifield. Rev. Daniel Gonzalez, Sacramental Min.; Deacon Chester E. Ball Jr., Parish Life Coord.
Church and Mailing Address: 276 S. 5th Ave., 54552. Tel: 715-762-4494; Fax: 715-762-0079.
School—(Grades PreK-8), 200 S. 5th Ave., 54552. Tel: 715-762-4476. Brent Balsavich, Prin. Lay Teachers 13; Students 123.
Catechesis/Religious Program— Deacon Chester E. Ball Jr., D.R.E. Students 149.

PELICAN LAKE, ONEIDA CO., ST. JOHN (1905) [CEM] Rev. John R. Gerritts.
Parish Office: 1350 N. Stevens St., Rhinelander, 54501.
Church: Appleton St. & Cty. Hwy. B, 54463. Tel: 715-362-3169.
Catechesis/Religious Program—Denise Jensen, C.R.E.; Madonna Jensen, C.R.E. Students 7.

PENCE, IRON CO., HOLY REDEEMER (1908) Closed. For inquiries for parish records please see St. Mary of the Seven Dolors, Hurley

PHELPS, VILAS CO., ST. MARY (1908) Michele Rein, Parish Dir.; Deacon Norman J. Mesun Jr.
Mailing Address: P.O. Box 237, Land O'Lakes, 54540.
Church: 4494 Town Hall Rd., 54554. Tel: 715-547-3558; Fax: 715-547-3614.
Catechesis/Religious Program—Students 20.

PHILLIPS, PRICE CO., ST. THERESE OF LISIEUX (1876) [CEM], Also serves St. Paul The Apostle, Catawba; St. John The Baptist, Prentice. Rev. Gerald A. Hagen; Deacons James J. Celba; Paul M. Ochodnicky.
125 N. Argyle Ave., 54555.
Church and Mailing Address: 655 S. Lake Ave., 54555. Tel: 715-339-2222; Fax: 715-339-2216.
Catechesis/Religious Program—Sherrie Kandutsch, C.R.E. Students 98.

PIER-WILLOW, ONEIDA CO., ST. FRANCIS OF ASSISI (1887) [CEM] Very Rev. John C. Anderson.
Mailing Address: 320 E. Washington Ave., Tomahawk, 54487.
Church: N. Willow Rd., Tripoli, 54564. Tel: 715-453-2878.

PRENTICE, PRICE CO., ST. JOHN THE BAPTIST (1886) Rev. Gerald A. Hagen.
Mailing Address: 125 N. Argyle Ave., Phillips, 54555.
Church: 935 Town St., 54556. Tel: 715-339-2222; Fax: 715-339-2216.
Catechesis/Religious Program—Andrea Bleck, D.R.E. Students 31.

PRESQUE ISLE, VILAS CO., ST. RITA (1950) Rev. Bernard M. Byrne.
Mailing Address: P.O. Box 110, Boulder Junction, 54512.
Church: Lake St., 54557. Tel: 715-385-2390.
Catechesis/Religious Program—Dorita Dolezal, C.R.E. Students 3.

RADISSON, SAWYER CO., SACRED HEART (1919) Rev. Shaji Joseph Pazhukkathara, Parochial Admin.; Deacon James E. Frederick.
Mailing Address: P.O. Box 216, Winter, 54896. In Res., Rev. Vincent M. Bromley (Retired).
Church: Hwy. 27, 54867. Tel: 715-266-3441; Fax: 715-266-3440.
Catechesis/Religious Program—Elna Korinke, C.R.E. (Elementary); Warren Wagner, C.R.E. (High School).

RED CLIFF, BAYFIELD CO., ST. FRANCIS (1861) [CEM] Revs. Michael Haney, O.F.M.; Lourdumar Reddy Mandapati.
Mailing Address: P.O. Box 1290, Bayfield, 54814.
Church: Church Rd., 54814. Tel: 715-779-3316; Fax: 715-779-9804.
Catechesis/Religious Program—Sr. Barbara Bogens, O.P., D.R.E.

RESERVE, SAWYER CO., ST. FRANCIS OF SOLANUS (1885), (Indian), [CEM], Also serves St. Ignatius, New Post; St. Philip, Stone Lake. Rev. Gregory J. Hopefl.
Church and Mailing Address: 13891 W. Mission Rd., Stone Lake, 54876. Tel: 715-865-3669; Fax: 715-865-3669.
School—St. Francis Solanus, (Grades PreK-8), 13885 W. Mission Rd., Stone Lake, 54876. Tel: 715-865-3662; Fax: 715-865-4055. Sr. Felissa Zander, S.S.S.F., Prin. Sisters of St. Francis 2; Lay Teachers 1; Students 30.
Catechesis/Religious Program—Sr. Felissa Zander, S.S.S.F., D.R.E. Students 7.

RHINELANDER, ONEIDA CO.
1—IMMACULATE CONCEPTION (1883) [CEM] Closed. For inquiries for sacramental records please contact Nativity of Our Lord, Rhinelander.
2—ST. JOSEPH'S (1909) [CEM] Closed. For inquiries for Sacramental Records contact Nativity of Our Lord, Rhinelander.
3—NATIVITY OF OUR LORD, Also serves St. John, Pelican Lake. Rev. John R. Gerritts; Deacons Ronald J. Bosi; Michael O. Harvey; Richard J. Meier; William D. Miller; Mathew C. Porten.
Mailing Address: 1350 N. Stevens St., 54501. Tel: 715-362-3169; Fax: 715-362-1811. Email: stjoe@frontiernet.net.
Worship Sites:—
St. Mary—125 E. King St., 54501.
St. Joseph—1360 N. Stevens St., 54501.
School—(Grades PreK-8), North Bldg.: 1360 N. Stevens St., 54501. Tel: 715-362-3366. South Bldg. (Main Office): 103 E. King St., 54501. Tel: 715-362-5588; Fax: 715-362-0952. Shirley Heise, Prin. Lay Teachers 24; Students 319.
Catechesis/Religious Program—Joyce Wagner, C.R.E. (Grades 9-12); Lori Novak, D.R.E. (Grades 6-7); Patti Shepard, D.R.E. (Grades K-5). Students 210.

RIB LAKE, TAYLOR CO.
1—GOOD SHEPHERD Rev. Otto N. Bucher, O.F.M.Cap.; Deacon Mark E. Priniski.
Mailing Address: P.O. Box 295, 54470. Tel: 715-427-5259; Fax: 715-427-0381. Email: goodshepherd@newnorth.net.
Church: 513 State Rd., 54470.
Catechesis/Religious Program—Mary Kauer, C.R.E. Students 90.
2—ST. JOHN THE BAPTIST (1896) Closed. For inquiries for sacramental records, contact Good Shepherd, Rib Lake.

RICE LAKE, BARRON CO., ST. JOSEPH (1878) [CEM] Rev. James P. Powers; Deacon Ronald J. Novotny.
Church and Mailing Address: 111 W. Marshall St., 54868. Tel: 715-234-2032; Fax: 715-234-7757.
School—St. Joseph School, (Grades PreK-8), 128 W. Humbird St., 54868. Tel: 715-234-7721; Fax: 715-234-5062. Sr. Claudine Balio, S.S.J.-T.O.S.F., Prin. Sisters 1; Lay Teachers 11; Students 166.
Catechesis/Religious Program—Rose Schullo, D.R.E. Students 155.

RIVER FALLS, ST. CROIX CO., ST. BRIDGET (1854) [CEM] Rev. Gerald P. Harris; Deacons Lawrence P. Hennemann; Thomas J. Weiss.
Mailing Address: P.O. Box 86, 54022. Tel: 715-425-1870; Fax: 715-425-1871.
Church: 211 E. Division St., 54022.
School—(Grades PreK-8), 135 E. Division St., 54022. Tel: 715-425-1872; Fax: 715-425-1873. Sue Steckbauer, Prin. Lay Teachers 16; Students 146.
Catechesis/Religious Program—Tel: 715-425-1874. Diane Wengelski, C.R.E.; Tessa Schuermann, D.R.E. Students 443.

SANBORN, ASHLAND CO., ST. ANNE (1895) Rev. Michael D. McLain, Parochial Admin.
Mailing Address: P.O. Box 17, Mellen, 54546.
Church: County Hwy. E, 54806. Tel: 715-274-3701; Fax: 715-274-3703.
Catechesis/Religious Program—Tom Henke, C.R.E. Students 12.

SARONA, WASHBURN CO., ST. CATHERINE (1917) Rev. Edwin C. Anderson, Parochial Admin.
Mailing Address: 409 Summit St., Spooner, 54801.
Church: W5262 County Hwy. D, 54870. Tel: 715-635-3105; Fax: 715-635-7341.
Catechesis/Religious Program—Susan Hughes, C.R.E.

SAXON, IRON CO., ST. ANN (1886) Very Rev. Kevin M. Gordon, Sacramental Min.
Mailing Address: P.O. Box 100, 54559.
Church: 14233 N. Church St., 54559. Tel: 715-893-2236.
Catechesis/Religious Program—Students 18.

SAYNER, VILAS CO., ST. MARY (1912) Rev. Bernard M. Byrne.
Mailing Address: P.O. Box 110, Boulder Junction, 54512.
Church: 2820 Hwy N, 54560. Tel: 715-542-3480.
Catechesis/Religious Program—Dorita Dolezal, C.R.E. Students 33.

SHELDON, RUSK CO., ST. JOHN THE APOSTLE (1955) Rev. John R. Long.
Mailing Address: 315 E. Davlin St., Gilman, 54433.
Church: N657 County Rd. VV, 54766. Tel: 715-447-8510; Fax: 715-447-5742.
Catechesis/Religious Program—Tel: 715-452-5374. Sr. Marianna Ableidinger, F.S.P.A., D.R.E. Students 40.

SHELL LAKE, WASHBURN CO., ST. JOSEPH (1880) [CEM] Rev. Edwin C. Anderson, Parochial Admin.
Mailing Address: 409 Summit St., Spooner, 54801.
Church: 502 N. 2nd St., 54871. Tel: 715-635-3105; Fax: 715-635-7341.
Catechesis/Religious Program—Susan Hughes, C.R.E. Students 32.

SOLON SPRINGS, DOUGLAS CO., ST. PIUS X (1878) [CEM], Also serves St. Anthony of Padua, Gordon; St. Mary, Minong. Rev. James J. Kinney.
Mailing Address: P.O. Box 303, 54873.
Church: 11651 Business 53, 54873. Tel: 715-378-4431; Fax: 715-378-2480.
Catechesis/Religious Program—Barbara Schuyler, C.R.E. Students 11.

SOMERSET, ST. CROIX CO., ST. ANNE (1851) [CEM] Deacon Richard T. Peterson, Parish Life Coord.; Rev. Barg G. Anderson, Parochial Vicar; Deacons A. Maurice Baillargeon; Lawrence E. Amell.
Mailing Address: P.O. Box 9, 54025.
Church: 141 Church Hill Rd., 54025. Tel: 715-247-3310; Fax: 715-247-3174.

School—(Grades PreK-8), 140 Church Hill Rd., 54025. Tel: 715-247-3762; Fax: 715-247-4335. Randall Stanke, Prin. Lay Teachers 10; Students 137.
Catechesis/Religious Program—Sara Measner, C.R.E. Students 163.

SPOONER, WASHBURN CO., ST. FRANCIS DE SALES (1886) [CEM 2], Also serves St. Joseph, Shell Lake; St. Catherine, Sarona. Rev. Edwin C. Anderson; Deacons Robert T. Jetto; Joseph J. Wesley; Gregory V. Ricci.
Church and Mailing Address: 409 Summit St., 54801. Tel: 715-635-3105; Fax: 715-635-7341.
School—(Grades PreK-8), 300 Oak St., 54801. Tel: 715-635-2774. Patricia Dougherty, Prin. Lay Teachers 8; Students 60.
Catechesis/Religious Program—Loree Nauertz, C.R.E.; Alan Nauertz, C.R.E.; Abbie Schmidt, C.R.E. Students 145.

STANTON, ST. CROIX CO., ST. BRIDGET (1875) Closed. For inquiries for parish records please see St. Joseph, Amery.

STETSONVILLE, TAYLOR CO., SACRED HEART OF JESUS (1884) [CEM] Rev. Frederick Brost; Deacon Joseph F. Roe.
Church and Mailing Address: 322 W. Cty. Hwy. A, 54480. Tel: 715-678-2395; Fax: 715-678-2395.
Catechesis/Religious Program—Karleen Sperl, D.R.E. Students 36.

STONE LAKE, SAWYER CO., ST. PHILIP (1905) Rev. Gregory J. Hopefl.
Mailing Address: 13891 W. Mission Rd., 54876.
Church: 5750 W. Frost Ave., 54876. Tel: 715-865-3669; Fax: 715-865-3669.

STRICKLAND, RUSK CO., ASSUMPTION OF THE BLESSED VIRGIN MARY (1897) [CEM] Deacons Craig J. Voldberg, Parish Life Coord.; James E. Roberge.
Mailing Address: P.O. Box 207, Weyerhaeuser, 54895. In Res., Rev. Ronald W. Levra (Retired).
Church: Old Hwy. 14, 54895. Tel: 715-353-2400; Fax: 715-353-4758.
Catechesis/Religious Program—Norbert Poch, C.R.E.; Barbra Poch, C.R.E.

SUGAR CAMP, ONEIDA CO., ST. KUNEGUNDA (1892) [CEM] Rev. William G. Horath; Deacon Albert A. Goodrich.
Mailing Address: P.O. Box 8, Three Lakes, 54562.
Church: 6895 Hwy. 17 N., 54501. Tel: 715-272-1191; Fax: 715-546-4046.
Catechesis/Religious Program—Patricia Sand, C.R.E. Students 58.

THREE LAKES, ONEIDA CO., ST. THERESA (1892), Also serves St. Kunegunda of Poland, Sugar Camp. Rev. William G. Horath; Deacon John McCaughn.
Church and Mailing Address: 6990 Forest St., 54562. Tel: 715-546-2159; Fax: 715-546-4046.
Catechesis/Religious Program—Deacon Al Goodrich, D.R.E. Students 91.

TOMAHAWK, LINCOLN CO., ST. MARY (1887) [CEM], Also serves St. Francis of Assisi, Pier-Willow. Very Rev. John C. Anderson; Deacons David C. Bablick; Bernard J. Lyngdal; Darrell P. Smerz; Clifford F. Eggett.
Church and Mailing Address: 320 E. Washington Ave., 54487. Tel: 715-453-2878; Fax: 715-453-6678.
School—(Grades PreK-5), 110 N. 7th St., 54487. Tel: 715-453-3542. Sonia Doughty, Prin. Lay Teachers 10; Students 129.
Catechesis/Religious Program—Kay Berg, C.R.E. Students 118.

TONY, RUSK CO., ST. ANTHONY DE PADUA (1901) [CEM] Rev. James P. Bartelme.
Mailing Address: 611 1st St. S., Ladysmith, 54848.
Church: N5323 Maple St., 54563. Tel: 715-532-3051; Fax: 715-532-7368.
Catechesis/Religious Program—Gayle Spencer, C.R.E. Students 36.

TURTLE LAKE, BARRON CO., ST. ANN (1882) [CEM 4] Rev. David R. Lusson.
Mailing Address: 900 St. Anthony St., Cumberland, 54829.
Church: 300 Pine St. S., 54889. Tel: 715-822-2948; Fax: 715-822-3588.
Catechesis/Religious Program—Steven Linton, D.R.E. Students 86.

WASHBURN, BAYFIELD CO., ST. LOUIS (1882) [CEM], Also serves Holy Family, Bayfield; St. Anne, Cornucopia; St. Joseph, La Pointe; St. Francis, Red Cliff. Revs. Michael Haney, O.F.M.; Lourdumar Reddy Mandapati; Deacon Kenneth D. Kasinski.
Mailing Address: Box 070, 54891. Tel: 715-373-2676; Fax: 715-373-0365.
Church: 217 W. 7th St., 54891.
School—(Grades PreK-6), 713 Washington Ave., P.O. Box 70, 54891. Tel: 715-373-5322. Karen Swanson, Prin. Lay Teachers 8; Students 55.
Catechesis/Religious Program—Wendie Libert, C.R.E. Students 42.

WEBSTER, BURNETT CO., ST. JOHN THE BAPTIST (1880) [CEM], Also serves Sacred Hearts of Jesus and Mary, Crescent Lake; Our Lady of Perpetual Help, Danbury. Rev. Michael J. Tupa.
Mailing Address: P.O. Box 7, 54893.
Church: 26455 S. Muskey Ave., 54893. Tel: 715-866-7321; Fax: 715-866-7305.
Catechesis/Religious Program—Colleen Monfre, D.R.E. Students 33.

WESTBORO, TAYLOR CO., ST. THERESA (1904) Closed. For Inquiries for sacramental records please contact Good Shepherd, Rib Lake.

WEYERHAEUSER, RUSK CO., SS. PETER AND PAUL (1897) [CEM], Also serves Assumption B.V.M., Strickland; St. Mary, Bruce and St. Francis of Assisi, Flambeau. Deacons Craig J. Voldberg, Parish Life Coord.; James E. Roberge; Thomas E. Fuhrmann.
Mailing Address: P.O. Box 207, 54895. In Res., Rev. Ronald W. Levra, Parochial Vicar (Retired).
Church: 251 First St., 54895. Tel: 715-353-2400; Fax: 715-353-4758.
Catechesis/Religious Program—Norbert Poch, Co-C.R.E.; Barbra Poch, Co-C.R.E. Students 42.

WHITTLESEY, TAYLOR CO., OUR LADY OF PERPETUAL HELP (1891) [CEM] Rev. Gerard I. Willger; Deacon Joseph Stefancin.
Mailing Address: P.O. Box 503, Medford, 54451.
Church: W5409 Whittlesey Ave., 54470. Tel: 715-748-3336; Fax: 715-748-6643.
Catechesis/Religious Program—Jayne Haenel, C.R.E. Students 45.

WILSON, ST. CROIX CO., ST. BRIDGET (1886) [CEM] Rev. William J. Murphy.
Mailing Address: P.O. Box 18, Hammond, 54015-0018.
Church: 120 Depot St., 54027. Tel: 715-796-2244; Fax: 715-796-2599.
Catechesis/Religious Program—Martha Erickson, D.R.E. Students 21.

WINTER, SAWYER CO., ST. PETER (1908) [CEM], Also serves Sacred Heart, Radisson. Rev. Shaji Joseph Pazhukkathara, Parochial Admin.
Mailing Address: P.O. Box 216, 54896.
Church: 5106 N. Main St., 54896. Tel: 715-266-3441; Fax: 715-266-3440. In Res., Rev. Vincent M. Bromley (Retired).
Catechesis/Religious Program—Elna Korinke, C.R.E.; Warren Wagner, C.R.E. Students 28.

WOODRUFF, ONEIDA CO.
1—HOLY FAMILY (2004) Very Rev. James A. Hoffman; Joan Laut, Pastoral Assoc.
Church & Office: 8950 County Rd. J., 54568. Tel: 715-356-6284; Fax: 715-356-2940.
Catechesis/Religious Program—Diana Maki, C.R.E.; Cheryl Vos, C.R.E. Students 253.
2—OUR LADY QUEEN OF THE UNIVERSE (1955) [CEM] Closed. For inquiries for sacramental records please contact Holy Family, Woodruff.

Chaplains of Public Institutions

On Special or Other Diocesan Assignment:
Very Revs.—
Gordon, Kevin M., Episcopal Vicar for Clergy, Chancery Box 969, 54880.
Heslin, Philip J., Moderator of the Curia, Chancery, Box 969, 54880.

Retired:
Revs.—
Briody, Hugh J., Woodmount, Ballinasloe, Co. Galway Ireland. Tel: 011-090-964-4439
Bromley, Vincent M., St. Peter Church, P.O. Box 216, Winter, 54896. Tel: 715-266-3441
Cary, William J., 1802 Dublin Tr., Apt. 36, Neenah, 54956. Tel: 920-486-7911
Dabruzzi, James S., WinterGreen, 1312 Wisconsin St., Apt. 119, Hudson, 54016. Tel: 715-381-2815
Fraher, Leonard W., 804 Woodland Ln., New Richmond, 54017. Tel: 715-246-7855
Green, William H., 1912 E. 2nd St., Apt. A, 54880. Tel: 715-392-2399
Heinen, Virgil O., 1336 A Carriage Dr., Hudson, 54016. Tel: 715-381-9778
Hornung, Eugene H., 10201 High Fishtrap Lake Rd., Apt. B, Boulder Junction, 54512. Tel: 715-671-8080
Kelchak, Joseph M., 4156 Oakmont Ct., Crown Point, IN 46307. Tel: 219-663-6726
Kleinheinz, Joseph L., 408 East St., Merrill, 54452.
Kowalski, Wladyslaw J., St. John the Baptist Parish (Peplin), 3308 Hwy. 153, Mosinee, 54455. Tel: 715-693-3604
Kraker, Lames J., P.O. Box 1247, 54568. Tel: 715-358-7785
Levra, Ronald W., Ss. Peter & Paul Church, P.O. Box 207, Strickland, 54895. Tel: 715-353-2400
Meulemans, Dennis T., 718 Holden Rd., Rib Lake, 54470. Tel: 715-728-3803; Fax: 715-427-0832
Meulemans, Edward G., Reflections, 2601 E. McKellips Rd., Apt. 2020, Mesa, AZ 85213. Tel: 480-969-3180
Pakosta, Francis J., 222 W. Hampton Ave., Apt. 309, Milwaukee, 53217. Tel: 414-967-9680
Powell, Edward F., W6771 Branch Rd., Tomahawk, 54487-9230. Tel: 715-453-1357
Spanjers, John J., P.O. Box 118, Turtle Lake, 54889.
Speerstra, William F., 9896 Morgan Oaks Dr., #4, Minocqua, 54548-8713. Tel: 715-358-3424
Trinka, Joseph C., 475 Golfview Ln., Apt. 101, Amery, 54001.
Urban, Robert M., 1715 Oakes Ave., #4, 54880. Tel: 715-394-3479
Verdegan, Albert L., 403 E. Corbett Ave., Apt. #3, Ladysmith, 54848-1954. Tel: 715-532-0861
Votruba, George L., 132 W. Marshall St., Rice Lake, 54868. Tel: 715-236-7091
Zepczyk, Gabriel C., 23515 County Rd. G, Ashland, 54806. Tel: 715-746-2549

Permanent Deacons:
Amell, Lawrence E., St. Anne, Somerset
Bablick, David C., St. Mary, Tomahawk
Baillargeon, Maurice A., St. Anne, Somerset
Ball, Chester E., Jr., St. Anthony, Park Falls
Bardos, John J., St. Anthony of Padua, Lac Du Flambeau
Bauer, Larry K., St. Joseph, Amery
Bosi, Ronald J., Nativity of Our Lord, Rhinelander
Braam, Peter R., (Retired), St. Patrick, Hudson
Brossmer, Norbert G., St. Isaac Joques and Companions, Mercer
Byrnes, Timothy J., Columbus, WI
Cabak, Russell E., St. Peter, Cameron
Cadotte, Roger L., Holy Family, Bayfield
Cameron, Howard W., St. Patrick, Hudson
Celba, James J., St. Therese of Lisieux, Phillips
Chammings, Robert J., Holy Assumption, Superior
Cullen, Michael D., St. Joseph, Barron
Dennis, James M., St. Boniface Parish, Chetek
Derrington, John P., St. Joseph, Amery
Drahos, Jerome J., Our Lady of Sorrows, Ladysmith
Drost, Harvey G., (Retired), Holy Trinity, Haugen
Eggett, Clifford, St. Mary, Tomahawk
Feind, Kevin L., St. Anthony, Superior
Frederick, James E., Sacred Heart, Radisson
Fuhrmann, Thomas E., Ss. Peter & Paul, Weyerhaeuser
Geisler, Dennis C., Our Lady of Lourdes, Dobie
Germain, Michael J., Immaculate Conception, New Richmond
Gil de Lamadrid, Arthur, Cathedral of Christ the King, Superior
Goodrich, Albert A., St. Kunegunda of Poland, Sugar Camp
Gorman, Owen T., Our Lady of the Lake, Ashland
Grek, John E., St. Peter & St. Paul, Moquah
Harvey, Michael O., Nativity of Our Lord, Rhinelander
Heiser, Florian H., St. Joseph, Amery
Hennemann, Lawrence P., St. Bridget, River Falls
Holzhaeuser, William J., Our Lady of the Lake, Ashland
Huntowski, Peter R., (Retired), Spooner
Jetto, Robert T., St. Francis de Sales Parish, Spooner
Johnson, Fred E., St. Joseph, Osceola
Kasinski, Kenneth D., St. Louis, Washburn
Kuehn, Timothy J., St. Anthony, Superior
Leonhard, Richard D., Our Lady of Sorrows, Ladysmith
Lundgren, Russell J., (Retired) Hurley
Lyngdal, Bernard J., St. Mary, Tomahawk
Marczak, Stanley J., St. Dominic, Frederic
Martineau, Philip L., (Retired)
McCaughn, John, St. Theresa, Three Lakes
McKenna, Jack, (Retired)
Meier, Richard J., Nativity of Our Lord, Rhinelander
Mercier, Stanley J., (Retired)
Mesun, Norman J., Jr., St. Albert, Land O'Lakes
Miller, Gregg St. Patrick, Hudson
Miller, William D. Nativity of Our Lord, Rhinelander
Novotny, Ronald J., St. Joseph, Rice Lake
Ochodnicky, Paul M., St. Therese of Lisieux, Phillips
Paron, Joseph F., Immaculate Conception, Hammond
Peterson, Richard T., St. Joseph, Osceola
Porten, Mathew C., Nativity of Our Lord, Rhinelander
Prinski, Mark, Good Shepherd, Rib Lake
Ramassini, John E., St. Francis Xavier, Merrill
Reuter, Joseph E., (Retired)
Ricci, Gregory J., St. Francis de Sales, Spooner
Roberge, James E., SS. Peter & Paul, Weyerhaeuser
Roe, Joseph F., Sacred Heart of Jesus, Stetsonville
Runser, Phillip J., St. Anthony, Superior
Smerz, Darrell P., St. Mary, Tomahawk

Sorenson, Douglas L., Our Lady of Sorrows, Ladysmith
Stefancin, Joseph, Our Lady of the Holy Rosary, Medford
Towle, C. Dan, St. Augustine, Harrison
Tuttle, Wesley G., St. John the Baptist, Glenwood City
Voldberg, Craig J., Ss. Peter & Paul, Weyerhaeuser
Weiss, Thomas J., St. Bridget Parish, River Falls
Wesley, Joseph J., St. Frances de Sales, Spooner

INSTITUTIONS LOCATED IN THE DIOCESE

[A] GENERAL HOSPITALS

SUPERIOR. *St. Mary's Hospital of Superior,* 3500 Tower Ave., 54880. Tel: 715-395-5403; Fax: 715-392-8395. Email: shawm@smdc.org. Web: www.smdc.org. Mary C. Shaw, Admin & COO; Ana Beier, Mgr. Spiritual Care Dept. Bed Capacity 25; Patients Assisted Annually 104,461; Total Staff 258.

EAGLE RIVER. **Eagle River Memorial Hospital, Inc.,* 201 Hospital Rd., 54521. Tel: 715-479-7411; Fax: 715-479-0395. Email: sheila.clough@ministryhealth.org. Web: www.ministryhealth.org. Sheila Clough, Pres. Corporate Sponsor: Ministry Health Care, Inc. (Milwaukee, WI). Sponsored by the Sisters of the Sorrowful Mother. Bed Capacity 25; Patients Assisted Annually 28,000; Total Staff 100.

MERRILL. *Good Samaritan Health Center of Merrill, Wisconsin, Inc.,* 601 S. Center Ave., 54452. Tel: 715-536-5511; Fax: 715-539-2170. Michael Hammer, Pres. Bed Capacity 25; Patients Assisted Annually 35,000; Total Staff 244.

RHINELANDER. *Sacred Heart-St. Mary's Hospital,* 2251 N. Shore Dr., 54501. Tel: 715-361-2000; Fax: 715-361-2011. Ms. Monica Hilt, Pres. Sisters of the Sorrowful Mother; Corporate Sponsor: Ministry Health Care., Inc. (Milwaukee, WI). Bed Capacity 73; Patients Assisted Annually 81,891; Shared Staff Rhinelander & Tomahawk Hospitals 700.

TOMAHAWK. *Sacred Heart-St. Mary's Hospitals, Inc.,* 401 W. Mohawk Dr., 54487. Tel: 715-453-7700; Fax: 715-453-7716. Ms. Monica Hilt, Pres. Corporate Sponsor: Ministry Health Care, Inc. (Milwaukee, WI). Bed Capacity 14; Patients Assisted Annually 13,164; Shared Staff Rhinelander & Tomahawk Hospitals 700.

WOODRUFF. **The Howard Young Medical Center, Inc.,* 240 Maple St., P.O. Box 470, 54568. Tel: 715-356-8000; Fax: 715-356-6097. Web: www.ministryhealth.org. Sheila Clough, Pres. Corporate Sponsor: Ministry Health Care, Inc. (Milwaukee, WI). Sponsored by the Sisters of the Sorrowful Mother. Bed Capacity 99; Patients Assisted Annually (Includes Inpatient Admissions) 66,476; Staff 561.

[B] HOMES FOR AGED

SUPERIOR. *St. Francis Home, Inc.,* 1416 Cumming Ave., 54880. Tel: 715-394-6617; Fax: 715-394-5951. Email: bosterlund@ccbsuperior.org. Mr. Brian Soland, M.A., Acting CEO.

MERRILL. *Bell Tower Residence, Inc.,* 1500 O'Day St., 54452. Tel: 715-536-5575; Fax: 715-536-1765. Email: dives@belltowerresidence.org. Web: www.belltowerresidence.org. Sr. Peggy Jackelen, S.C.S.C., Admin. Residence for the elderly. Bed Capacity 90; Total in Residence 87; Total Assisted Annually 79; Total Staff 103.

WOODRUFF. **Dr. Kate Newcomb Convalescent Center, Inc.,* P.O. Box 470, 54568-0470. Tel: 715-356-8560; Fax: 715-356-6097. Laurie Oungst, Vice Pres. Opers.; Sheila Clough, Pres. Sponsored by the Sisters of the Sorrowful Mother. Corporate Sponsor: Ministry Health Care, Inc. (Milwaukee, WI). Total Assisted 108; Total Staff 8.

[C] CONVENTS AND RESIDENCES FOR SISTERS

HUDSON. *Carmel of the Sacred Heart,* 430 Laurel Ave., 54016. Tel: 715-386-2156; Fax: 715-386-6946. Email: carmelit@pressenter.com. Web: www.pressenter.com/~carmelit/. Sr. Lucia LaMontagne, O.Carm., Prioress. Sisters 6.

LADYSMITH. *Servants of Mary,* 1000 College Ave. W., 54848-2199. Tel: 920-898-1142, Ext. 320; Fax: 920-898-4072. Email: info@servitesisters.org. Web: www.servitesisters.org. Sr. Theresa Sandok, O.S.M., Pres. Sisters 57.

MERRILL. *Sisters of Mercy of the Holy Cross,* 1400 O'Day St., 54452-3417. Tel: 715-539-1456; Fax: 715-539-1458. Email: provincialoffices@holycrosssisters.org. Web: www.holycrosssisters.org. Sr. Celine Goessl, S.C.S.C., Prov. Sisters 37.

[D] CATHOLIC CHARITIES BUREAU

SUPERIOR. *Catholic Charities Bureau, Inc.,* 1416 Cummings Ave., 54880. Tel: 715-394-6617; Fax: 715-394-5951. Web: www.ccbsuperior.org. Mr. Brian Soland, M.A., Exec. Dir.; William Anderson, CFO; Terry Hendrick, Dir. Devel. Svcs.; Marilyn Christopherson, Coord. Diocesan Rels.; Brenda Osterlund, Admin. Coord.; Gary Valley, Dir. Housing.

Catholic Community Services, Inc., 1416 Cumming Ave., 54880. Tel: 715-394-6617; Fax: 715-394-5951. Terry Hendrick, Dir.

Challenge Center, Inc., 39 N. 25th St. E., 54880. Tel: 715-394-2771; Fax: 715-394-2100. Eugene Chuzles, Dir.

Challenge Center A, Inc. dba Deer Haven Group Home 3105 Cumming Ave., 54880. Tel: 715-394-2771; Fax: 715-394-2100. Eugene Chuzles, Dir.

Cypress Group Home, 1415 Cypress, 54880. Tel: 715-394-2771; Fax: 715-394-2100. Eugene Chuzles, Dir.

The Dove, Inc., 1416 Cumming Ave., 54880. Tel: 715-392-3133; Fax: 715-392-3190. Web: thedovesuperior.com. Greg Leiviska, Admin.

The Dove Agency, Inc., 1416 Cumming Ave., 54880. Tel: 715-392-3133; Fax: 715-392-3190. Web: thedovesuperior.com. Greg Leiviska, Admin.

Foster Grandparent Program (NW WI, NE MN), 1416 Cumming Ave., 54880. Tel: 715-394-5384; Fax: 715-394-5951. Jennifer Jubenville, Dir.

Harborview Group Home, 910 E. 5th St., 54880. Tel: 715-394-2771; Fax: 715-394-2100. Eugene Chuzles, Dir.

Housing Counseling Program, 1416 Cumming Ave., 54880. Tel: 715-394-6617; Fax: 715-394-5951. Web: www.ccbsuperior.org. Sandy Alqudah, Dir.

McKenzie Manor, 3317 N. 21st St., 54880. Tel: 715-394-2771; Fax: 715-394-2100. Eugene Chuzles, Dir.

Missouri Gardens Adult Family Home, 2347 Missouri Ave., 54880. Tel: 715-394-2771; Fax: 715-394-2100. Eugene Chuzles, Dir.

Mountain View Group Home, 3319 N. 16th St., 54880. Tel: 715-394-2771; Fax: 715-394-2100. Eugene Chuzles, Dir.

Phoenix Villa, Inc., 1100 Weeks Ave., 54880. Tel: 715-394-6617; Fax: 715-394-5951. Gary Valley, Dir.

Phoenix Villa, Inc. dba Elmwood Apartments 1020 Weeks Ave., 54880. Tel: 715-394-6617; Fax: 715-394-5951. Gary Valley, Dir.

Phoenix Villa of Superior, Inc. dba Oakwood Apartments 1112 John Ave., 54880. Tel: 715-394-6617; Fax: 715-394-5951. Gary Valley, Dir.

Retired Senior Volunteer Program, 1416 Cumming Ave., 54880. Tel: 715-394-4425; Fax: 715-394-5951. Joan Nurminen, Dir.

Superior Housing Alliance, 1416 Cumming Ave., 54880. Tel: 715-394-6617; Fax: 715-394-5951. Terry Hendrick, Dir.

Westbay, Inc., 1104 John Ave., 54880. Tel: 715-394-6617; Fax: 715-394-5951. Gary Valley, Dir.

Woodview Adult Family Home, 6001 E. Third St., 54880. Tel: 715-394-2771; Fax: 715-394-2100. Eugene Chuzles, Dir.

AMERY. *Apple River, Inc.,* 401 Minneapolis Ave. S., 54001. Tel: 715-925-2015; Fax: 715-925-2014. Pam Kohnen, Mgr.

CHETEK. *Phoenix Villa, Inc. dba Evergreen Apartments* 707 Tainter St., 54728. Tel: 715-925-2015; Fax: 715-925-2014. Pam Kohnen, Mgr.

CRANDON. *Phoenix Villa, Inc. dba Acorn Apartments* 508 W. Washington, 54520. Tel: 715-369-2550; Fax: 715-369-5857. Paula Braun, Mgr.

CUMBERLAND. *Phoenix Villa, Inc. dba Phoenix Villa North* 1490 Arcade, 54829. Tel: 715-925-2015; Fax: 715-925-2014. Pam Kohnen, Mgr.

DULUTH. *Northfield Apartments, Inc.,* 2713 W. Superior St., MN 55806. Tel: 715-394-6617; Fax: 715-394-5951. Gary Valley, Dir.

HAYWARD. *Phoenix Villa, Inc. dba Phoenix Villa of Hayward* 15869 Muriel St., 54843. Tel: 715-236-2366; Fax: 715-236-3161. Cindy Lawrie, Mgr.

HUDSON. *United Day Care, Inc. dba Hudson Community Children's Center* 824 Fourth St., 54016. Tel: 715-386-5912; Fax: 715-386-1467. Linda Groom, Dir.

IRON RIVER. *Phoenix Villa, Inc. dba Phoenix Villa of Iron River* 62155 Cty Rd. H, 54847. Tel: 715-394-6617; Fax: 715-394-5951. Gary Valley, Dir.

LAKE NEBAGAMON. *Phoenix Villa, Inc. dba Phoenix Villa of Lake Nebagamon* 6250 S. Fitch Ave., 54849. Tel: 715-394-6617; Fax: 715-394-5951. Gary Valley, Dir.

MEDFORD. *Black River Industries, Inc.,* 650 Jensen Dr., 54451. Tel: 715-748-2950; Fax: 715-748-6363. Web: www.blackriverindustries.org. Paul Thornton, Dir.

Eastwood Apartments, Inc., 741-755 Del Rae Ct., 54451. Tel: 715-369-2550; Fax: 715-369-5857. Paula Braun, Mgr.

Phoenix Villa, Inc. dba Maywood Apartments 521 Lemke Ave., 54451. Tel: 715-369-2550; Fax: 715-369-5857. Paula Braun, Mgr.

MINONG. *Phoenix Villa, Inc. dba Acorn Apartments* 405 2nd St., 54859. Tel: 715-236-2366; Fax: 715-236-3161. Cindy Lawrie, Mgr.

PLOVER. *Phoenix Villa, Inc. dba Maywood Apartments* 2601 Madison Ave., 54467. Tel: 715-341-7616; Fax: 715-712-0387. Teri Obermeier, Mgr.

RHINELANDER. *Phoenix Villa, Inc. aka Evergreen Apartments/Timberlane* 880 E. Timber Dr., 54501. Tel: 715-369-2550; Fax: 715-369-5857. Paula Braun, Mgr.

Headwaters. Inc., 1441 E. Timber Dr., P.O. Box 618, 54501. Tel: 715-369-1337; Fax: 715-369-1793. Web: www.headwatersinc.org. Mary Hardtke, Dir.

Phoenix Villa, Inc. dba Phoenix Villa of Rhinelander 1011 Mason St., 54501. Tel: 715-369-2550; Fax: 715-369-5857. Paula Braun, Mgr.

Retired Senior Volunteer Program, 1835 N. Stevens St., Ste. 22, 54501. Tel: 715-362-1919. Lori Bushong, Dir.

Sumac Trail Apartments, Inc., 1313 Phillip St., 54501. Tel: 715-369-2550; Fax: 715-369-5857. Paula Braun, Mgr.

RICE LAKE. *Blue Valley, Inc.,* 1310 N. Wisconsin Ave., 54868. Tel: 715-236-2366; Fax: 715-236-3161. Cindy Lawrie, Mgr.

Phoenix Villa, Inc. dba Phoenix Villa North 1305 N. Wisconsin St., 54868. Tel: 715-236-2366; Fax: 715-236-3161. Cindy Lawrie, Mgr.

SHELL LAKE. *Phoenix Villa, Inc. dba Evergreen Apartments* 797 N. Lake Dr., 54871. Tel: 715-236-2366; Fax: 715-236-3161. Cindy Lawrie, Mgr.

SIREN. *Diversified Services Center, Inc.,* 7649 Tower Rd., P.O. Box 501, 54872. Tel: 715-349-5724; Fax: 715-349-5505. Web: www.sirentel.net/~dsi. Joe Wacek, Dir.

Lilac Grove Apartments, Inc., 24145 1st Ave., 54872. Tel: 715-925-2015; Fax: 715-925-2014. Email: pkohnen@ccbsuperior.org. Pam Kohnen, Mgr. Apartments (Low-Income) 14.

Phoenix Villa, Inc. dba Evergreen Apartments/Lakewood 24121 Fourth St., 54872. Tel: 715-925-2015; Fax: 715-925-2014. Pam Kohnen, Mgr.

WINTER. *Winterhaven Apartments, Inc.,* 5038 N. Ellen St., 54896. Tel: 715-236-2366; Fax: 715-236-3161. Cindy Lawrie, Mgr.

WISCONSIN RAPIDS. *Phoenix Villa, Inc. dba Acorn Apartments* 2721 Tenth St. S., 54494. Tel: 715-236-2366; Fax: 715-236-3161. Cindy Lawrie, Mgr.

[E] RETREAT HOUSES

AMERY. *Mount Carmel Hermitage,* 897 U.S. Hwy. 8, 54001-2541. Tel: 715-268-9313; Fax: 715-268-9313. Email: mtcarmel@amerytel.net. Sr. Kristine Haugen, O.C.D.H., Coord.

ARBOR VITAE. *Marywood Franciscan Spirituality Center (FSPA),* 3560 Hwy. 51 N., 54568-9538. Tel: 715-385-3750; Fax: 715-385-9118. Web: www.marywoodsc.org. Email: marywood.center@gmail.com. Sr. Elizabeth Amman, O.P., Dir.

[F] NEWMAN CENTERS

SUPERIOR. *Superior-UW* 823 N. 16th St., 54880. Tel: 715-394-7710. Newman Center Ministry to Young Adults.

RIVER FALLS. *St. Thomas More Newman Center* 423 E. Cascade, 54022. Tel: 715-425-7234; Fax: 715-425-6959. Email: thomas.j.weiss@uwrf.edu. Web: uwrfnewman.org. Deacon Thomas J. Weiss, Coord. for Newman Min.

[G] ASSOCIATION OF THE FAITHFUL

AMERY. *Hermits of Mt. Carmel,* 897 Hwy. 8, 54001-2541. Tel: 715-268-9313; Fax: 715-268-9313. Email: mtcarmel@amerytel.net. Sr. Kristine Haugen, O.C.D.H., Coord. Email: mtcarmel@amerytel.net.

[H] MISCELLANEOUS

SUPERIOR. *Society of St. Vincent de Paul Sacred Heart of Jesus Conference of Superior, WI,* 1416 Cumming Ave, 54880. Tel: 715-394-6617. Patricia Higgins, Pres.

LADYSMITH. *Mary Bradley Corporation,* 1000 College Ave. W., 54848-2199. Tel: 920-898-1142, Ext. 320; Fax: 920-898-4072. Sr. Theresa Sandok, O.S.M., Pres.

Servants of Mary Continuing Care Trust, 1000 College Ave. W., 54848. Tel: 920-898-1142, Ext. 320; Fax: 920-898-4072. Email: smueller@salvatoriancenter.com. Rev. Scott Wallenfelsz, S.D.S., OSM Fin. Dir.

MERRILL. *Good Samaritan Health Center Foundation of Merrill, Wisconsin, Inc.* A not for profit corporation for the purpose of soliciting and receiving contributions for the benefit of Good Samaritan Health Center of Merrill, WI, Inc., 601 S. Center Ave., 54452. Tel: 715-536-5511; Fax: 715-539-2170. Michael Hammer, Pres. Corporate Sponsor: Ministry Healthcare, Inc. Sponsored by Sisters of the Sorrowful Mother.

Sisters of Mercy of the Holy Cross Community Support Charitable Trust, 1400 O'Day St., 54452-3417. Tel: 715-539-1460; Fax: 715-539-1458. Email: gsbr@juno.com. Sisters Pat Cormack, S.C.S.C., Trustee; Rose Jochmann, O.S.F., Trustee; Grace Sbrissa, C.S.J., Trustee; John Tortolani, Trustee; Craig Nienow, Trustee.

RHINELANDER. **Ministry Medical Group, Inc.*, 2251 N. Shore Dr., 54501. Tel: 715-361-4700; 800-866-8673; Fax: 715-361-4877. Email: kathy.richards@ministryhealth.org. Web: www.ministryhealth.org. Stewart Watson, Pres. & CEO; Kathy Richards-Bess, Regl. Admin. Corporate Sponsor: Ministry Health Care, Inc., Milwaukee, WI.

Ministry Weight Mgmt., St. Mary's Hospital, 2251 N. Shore Dr., 54501. Tel: 715-361-2000; Fax: 715-361-2011. Duane Stefonek, Dir.

WEBSTER. *Thomas More Center for Preaching and Prayer, Inc.*, 27781 Leef Rd., 54893. Tel: 715-866-7436. Web: www.thomasmorecenter.org. Revs. Michael A. Champlin, O.P., Pres.; Nicholas W. Punch, O.P., Treas.; Sr. Joan Bukrey, O.S.F., Vice Pres.

WINTER. *Camp WeHaKee* (Girls), 8104 N. Barker Lake Rd., 54896. Tel: 715-266-3263; 800-582-2267; Fax: 608-787-8257. Email: camp@campwehakee.com. Web: www.campwehakee.com. Bob Braun, Co-Dir.; Maggie Braun, Co-Dir.

WOODRUFF. **Howard Young Health Care, Inc.*, 240 Maple St., P.O. Box 470, 54568. Tel: 715-356-8000; Fax: 715-356-6097. Email: sheila.clough@ministryhealth.org. Web: www.ministryhealth.org. Sheila Clough, Pres. Corporate Sponsor: Ministry Health Care, Inc. (Milwaukee, WI). Sponsored by the Sisters of the Sorrowful Mother. Total Staff 28.

RELIGIOUS INSTITUTES OF MEN REPRESENTED IN THE DIOCESE

For further details refer to the corresponding bracketed number in the Religious Institutes of Men or Women section.

[0470]—*Capuchin Franciscan Friars*—O.F.M.Cap.

[0480]—*Conventual Franciscans* (Arroyo Grande, CA)—O.F.M.Conv.

[0520]—*Franciscan Friars* (St. Louis, MO)—O.F.M.

[0430]—*Order of Preachers-Province of St. Albert the Great* Chicago—O.P.

[0610]—*Priests of the Congregation of the Holy Cross* (Indian Province, Inc.)—C.S.C.

RELIGIOUS INSTITUTES OF WOMEN REPRESENTED IN THE DIOCESE

[0320]—*Carmelite Nuns of the Ancient Observance*—O.Carm.

[1780]—*Congregation of the Sisters of the Third Order of St. Francis of Perpetual Adoration (Franciscan Sis*—F.S.P.A.

[1710]—*Congregation of the Third Order of St. Francis of Mary Immaculate* (Joilet, IL)—O.S.F.

[1070-13]—*Dominican Sisters of Adrian*—O.P.

[1070-40]—*Dominican Sisters of Grand Rapids*—O.P.

[1070-10]—*Dominican Sisters of Springfield*—O.P.

[2970]—*School Sisters of Notre Dame* (Mankato/Milwaukee)—S.S.N.D.

[1680]—*School Sisters of St. Francis*—S.S.S.F.

[3590]—*Servants of Mary (Servite Sisters)*—O.S.M.

[2630]—*Sisters of Mercy of the Holy Cross*—S.C.S.C.

[1705]—*Sisters of St. Francis of Assisi, Milwaukee*—O.S.F.

[1570]—*Sisters of St. Francis of the Holy Family*—O.S.F.

[3840]—*Sisters of St. Joseph of Carondelet* (Prov. of St. Paul)—C.S.J.

[3930]—*Sisters of St. Joseph of the Third Order of St. Francis* (Prov. of Immaculate Conception; St. Joseph Prov.)—S.S.J.-T.O.S.F.

[4100]—*Sisters of the Sorrowful Mother* (Third Order of St. Francis)—S.S.M.

[1720]—*Sisters of the Third Order Regular of St. Francis of the Congregation of Our Lady of Lourdes*—O.S.F.

NECROLOGY

† Kunda, Brendan J., (Retired)—Died May 14, 2009

An asterisk (*) denotes an organization that has established tax-exempt status directly with the IRS and is not covered by the USCCB Group Ruling.

Diocese of Syracuse

(Dioecesis Syracusensis)

Most Reverend

ROBERT JOSEPH CUNNINGHAM

Bishop of Syracuse; ordained May 24, 1969; appointed Bishop of Ogdensburg March 9, 2004; ordained and installed May 18, 2004; appointed Bishop of Syracuse April 21, 2009; installed as Tenth Bishop of Syracuse May 26, 2009. *Office: 240 E. Onondaga St., P.O. Box 511, Syracuse, NY 13201-0511.*

Most Reverend

JAMES M. MOYNIHAN, D.D.

Retired Bishop of Syracuse; ordained December 15, 1957; appointed Bishop of Syracuse April 4, 1995; consecrated and installed in See of Syracuse May 29, 1995; retired April 21, 2009. *Mailing Address: 240 E. Onondaga St., P.O. Box 511, Syracuse, NY 13201-0511. Res.: 420 Montgomery St., Syracuse, NY 13202.*

Chancery Office: P.O. Box 511, Syracuse, NY 13201. Tel: 315-422-7203; Fax: 315-478-4619.

Most Reverend

THOMAS J. COSTELLO, D.D., V.G.

Retired Auxiliary Bishop of Syracuse; ordained June 5 1954; appointed Auxiliary Bishop of Syracuse anc Titular Bishop of Perdices January 10, 1978; conse crated March 13, 1978; retired March 23, 2004. *Res. 1515 Midland Ave., Syracuse, NY 13205.*

ESTABLISHED NOVEMBER 26, 1886

Square Miles 5,749.

Corporate Title: The Roman Catholic Diocese of Syra cuse NY.

Comprises the Counties of Broome, Chenango, Cort land, Madison, Oneida, Onondaga and Oswego.

For legal titles of parishes and diocesan institutions, consult the Chancery Office.

STATISTICAL OVERVIEW

Personnel	
Bishop	1
Retired Bishops	2
Priests: Diocesan Active in Diocese	154
Priests: Diocesan Active Outside Diocese	11
Priests: Retired, Sick or Absent	77
Number of Diocesan Priests	242
Religious Priests in Diocese	36
Total Priests in Diocese	278
Extern Priests in Diocese	19
Ordinations:	
Diocesan Priests	1
Transitional Deacons	1
Permanent Deacons	8
Permanent Deacons in Diocese	85
Total Brothers	6
Total Sisters	317
Parishes	
Parishes	136
With Resident Pastor:	
Resident Diocesan Priests	131
Resident Religious Priests	5
Without Resident Pastor:	
Administered by Priests	14
Missions	11
Closed Parishes	6
Professional Ministry Personnel:	
Brothers	6
Sisters	317
Welfare	
Catholic Hospitals	3
Total Assisted	677,000
Health Care Centers	2
Total Assisted	500,000
Homes for the Aged	54
Total Assisted	2,500
Day Care Centers	1
Total Assisted	182
Specialized Homes	3
Total Assisted	125
Special Centers for Social Services	2
Total Assisted	1,500
Residential Care of Disabled	14
Total Assisted	212
Educational	
Diocesan Students in Other Seminaries	12
Seminaries, Religious	1
Students Religious	14
Total Seminarians	26
Colleges and Universities	1
Total Students	3,479
High Schools, Diocesan and Parish	5
Total Students	1,654
High Schools, Private	1
Total Students	750
Elementary Schools, Diocesan and Parish	22
Total Students	3,261
Catechesis/Religious Education:	
High School Students	6,939
Elementary Students	21,303
Total Students under Catholic Instruction	37,412
Teachers in the Diocese:	
Priests	4
Brothers	3
Sisters	21
Lay Teachers	461
Vital Statistics	
Receptions into the Church:	
Infant Baptism Totals	3,291
Minor Baptism Totals	106
Adult Baptism Totals	128
Received into Full Communion	385
First Communions	3,519
Confirmations	3,369
Marriages:	
Catholic	743
Interfaith	316
Total Marriages	1,059
Deaths	3,806
Total Catholic Population	284,000
Total Population	1,173,146

Former Bishops—Rt. Revs. PATRICK ANTHONY LUDDEN, D.D., ord. June 21, 1864; cons. May 1, 1887; died Aug. 6, 1912; JOHN GRIMES, D.D., ord. Feb. 19, 1882; cons. May 16, 1909; Coadjutor Bishop, 1909-1912; succeeded to the See, Aug. 6, 1912; died July 26, 1922; Most Revs. DANIEL JOSEPH CURLEY, D.D., ord. May 19, 1894; cons. May 1, 1923; died Aug. 3, 1932; JOHN ALOYSIUS DUFFY, D.D., ord. June 13, 1908; cons. June 29, 1933; installed July 11, 1933; appt. Bishop of Buffalo, Jan. 9, 1937; installed in See of Buffalo, April 14, 1937; died Sept. 27, 1944; WALTER A. FOERY, D.D., Ph.D., ord. June 10, 1916; appt. May 26, 1937; cons. Aug. 18, 1937; appt. assistant at the Pontifical Throne, Dec. 11, 1961; retired and named Titular Bishop of Miseno-Cape, Aug. 4, 1970; died May 10, 1978; DAVID F. CUNNINGHAM, D.D., ord. June 12, 1926; appt. Titular Bishop of Lampsacus and Auxiliary Bishop of Syracuse, April 5, 1950; cons. June 8, 1950; appt. Coadjutor Bishop "Cum jure successiones," June 19, 1967; succeeded to the See, Aug. 4, 1970; died Feb. 22, 1979; FRANK J. HARRISON, D.D., ord. June 4, 1937; appt. Titular Bishop of Aquae and Auxiliary Bishop of Syracuse, March 1, 1971; cons. April 22, 1971; appt. Bishop of Syracuse, Nov. 16, 1976; retired June 16, 1987; died May 1, 2004; JOSEPH T. O'KEEFE, D.D., ord. April 17, 1948; appt. Titular Bishop of Tre Taverne and Auxiliary Bishop of New York, July 3, 1982; cons. Sept. 8, 1982; appt. Bishop of Syracuse, June 16, 1987; installed in See of Syracuse, Aug. 3, 1987; retired April 4, 1995; died Sept. 2, 1997; JAMES M. MOYNIHAN, ord. Dec. 15, 1957; appt. Bishop of Syracuse April 4, 1995; cons. and installed in See of Syracuse May 29, 1995; retired April 21, 2009.

Vicar General—Rev. Msgr. J. ROBERT YEAZEL, V.G., Res.: Holy Cross, 4112 E. Genesee St., DeWitt, 13214.

Vicars Forane—Northern Area Vicar: Rev. GAETANO T. BACCARO, St. Paul, 50 E. Mohawk St., Oswego, 13126. Southern Area Vicar: Rev. JOHN P. PUTANO, 157 Clark St., Vestal, 13850. Eastern Area Vicars: Revs. PHILIP A. HEARN, 105 E. Liberty St., Rome, 13440; JOSEPH A. SALERNO, 2 Barton Ave., Utica, 13502. Western Area Vicars: Rev. Msgr. RICHARD M. KOPP; Rev. TIMOTHY S. ELMER, J.C.L., 240 E. Onondaga St., Syracuse, 13202.

Chancery Office—240 E. Onondaga St., Syracuse, 13202. Mailing Address: P.O. Box 511, Syracuse, 13201. Tel: 315-422-7203; Fax: 315-478-4619. Office Hours: Mon.-Fri. 8:30-4:30; Send official mail, including marriage dispensations, to Chancery.

Chancellor—Rev. CLIFFORD H. AUTH, J.C.L., 240 E. Onondaga St., Syracuse, 13202.

Assistant Chancellor—Mrs. DANIELLE CUMMINGS, 240 E. Onondaga St., Syracuse, 13202.

Board of Diocesan Consultors—Rev. PHILIP A. HEARN; Rev. Msgr. RICHARD M. KOPP; Revs. JAMES P. LANG; CLIFFORD H. AUTH, J.C.L.; STEPHEN P. WIRKES; Rev. Msgr. GEORGE F. SHEEHAN; Revs. JOSEPH A. SALERNO; JOHN P. PUTANO; Rev. Msgr. J. ROBERT YEAZEL, V.G.; Rev. TIMOTHY S. ELMER, J.C.L.

Management Team—Most Rev. ROBERT J. CUNNINGHAM, D.D.; Revs. JAMES P. LANG; TIMOTHY S. ELMER, J.C.L.; CLIFFORD H. AUTH, J.C.L.; JOSEPH H. PHILLIPS; JOSEPH E. SCARDELLA; Sr. KATIE EIFFE, C.S.J.; Rev. Msgr. GEORGE F. SHEEHAN; Mr. CHRISTOPHER PARKER; Mr. ROBERT WALTERS; Mr. JOSEPH G. SLAVIK; Sr. ELOISE EMM, O.S.F.; Mrs. DANIELLE CUMMINGS.

Pastoral Council—Most Rev. ROBERT J. CUNNINGHAM, D.D., Pres.; Ms. KATHLEEN M. DYER, Exec. Sec., Res.: 101 Ridge Rd., Fulton, 13069. Tel: 315-592-5566.

Pastoral Examiners—Revs. JOHN P. FENLON; MORITZ A. FUCHS (Retired); JAMES KENNEDY; RICHARD V. O'NEILL (Retired); DANIEL G. MURPHY (Retired); JOHN F. ROSE; JOSEPH A. SALERNO; JOSEPH S. ZARESKI.

Presbyteral Council—Most Rev. ROBERT J. CUNNINGHAM, D.D., Pres.; Revs. PAUL F. ANGELICCHIO; GAETANO T. BACCARO; JOHN CANARRO; PAUL V. CAREY; CHRISTOPHER CELENTANO; KEVIN CORCORAN; CLIFFORD H. AUTH, J.C.L.; ALFRED J. BEBEL (Retired); GERALD J. BUCKLEY (Retired); TIMOTHY S. ELMER, J.C.L.; PHILIP A. HEARN; Rev. Msgr. RICHARD M. KOPP; Revs. VALENTINE C. KRUL; JAMES P. LANG; GREGORY C. LESTRANGE; DANIEL J. MULHAUSER, S.J.; ROBERT L. KELLY; JOHN P. PUTANO; JOHN RUFFO, O.F.M.Conv.; JOSEPH A. SALERNO; Rev. Msgr. J. ROBERT YEAZEL, V.G.

Diocesan Tribunal—

Judicial Vicar—Rev. TIMOTHY S. ELMER, J.C.L. Tel: 315-470-1480; Fax: 315-474-6893.

Adjutant Judicial Vicar—Rev. JOHN P. DONOVAN, J.C.L.

Defender of the Bond—Rev. CLIFFORD H. AUTH, J.C.L.

Promoters of Justice—Rev. Msgr. JAMES A. MCCLOSKEY (Retired); Rev. ROBERT P. HYDE, J.C.L.

Notary of the Tribunal—BARBARA REITER.

Advocate—CLAIRE JOHNSON.

Case Coordinator/Staff—BARBARA REITER.

Vicar for Administration—Rev. CLIFFORD H. AUTH, J.C.L., 240 E. Onondaga St., P.O. Box 511, Syracuse, 13201. Tel: 315-470-1435.

Director for Community Services—Mr. JOSEPH G. SLAVIK, Dir., 240 E. Onondaga St., P.O. Box 511, Syracuse, 13201. Tel: 315-470-1415.

Vicar for Parishes—Rev. JAMES P. LANG, 240 E. Onondaga St., P.O. Box 511, Syracuse, 13201. Tel: 315-470-1437.

Vicar for Priests—Rev. Msgr. RICHARD M. KOPP, 240 E. Onondaga St., P.O. Box 511, Syracuse, 13201. Tel: 315-470-1460.

Vicar for Religious—VACANT.

Diocesan Offices

Accounting—VACANT, Mailing Address: P.O. Box 511, Syracuse, 13201. Tel: 315-422-9045; Fax: 315-422-9139.

Administration—Rev. CLIFFORD H. AUTH, J.C.L., Vicar, Mailing Address: P.O. Box 511, Syracuse, 13201. Tel: 315-422-7203.

Archives—Mr. EDWARD LONG, Archivist, Mailing Address: P.O. Box 511, Syracuse, 13201. Tel: 315-470-1493. Email: syrarchivesed@aol.com.

Asian Apostolate—Rev. THIENAN TRAN; Sr. JUDITH HOWLEY, C.S.J., 215 N. State St., Syracuse, 13203. Tel: 315-472-7043.

Benefits—Ms. CAROLYN CAIN, Admin., Mailing Address: P.O. Box 511, Syracuse, 13201. Tel: 315-422-9091.

Black Catholic Ministry—Mr. RALPH JONES, Mailing Address: P.O. Box 511, Syracuse, 13201. Tel: 315-470-1463.

Boy Scouts/Girl Scouts—Rev. JAMES P. LANG, Chap., 240 E. Onondaga St., P.O. Box 511, Syracuse, 13201-0511. Tel: 315-470-1437.

Building Commission—Most Rev. ROBERT J. CUNNINGHAM, D.D.; Revs. CLIFFORD H. AUTH, J.C.L.; JOSEPH E. SCARDELLA; Mr. EDWARD T. KING; Mr. JAMES W. MERRILL; Rev. Msgr. RICHARD M. KOPP; Rev. JAMES P. LANG.

Catholic Cemeteries—Mr. MARK LAZAROSKI, Dir., 2315 South Ave., Syracuse, 13207. Tel: 315-475-4639; Fax: 315-422-0363.

Catholic Charities—Mr. JOSEPH G. SLAVIK, Dir., Mailing Address: P.O. Box 511, Syracuse, 13201. Tel: 315-470-1416; Fax: 315-478-4619.

Onondaga County Director—Mr. MICHAEL F. MELARA, 1654 W. Onondaga St., Syracuse, 13204. Tel: 315-424-1800.

Broome County Director—LORI ACCARDI, Interim Dir., 232 Main St., Binghamton, 13905. Tel: 607-729-9166.

Chenango County Director—Dr. JANE CODDINGTON, Dir., 3 O'Hara Dr., Norwich, 13815. Tel: 607-334-8244.

Cortland County Director—MARIE WALSH, 33-35 Central Ave., Cortland, 13045. Tel: 607-756-5992.

Oneida and Madison Counties Director—KATHLEEN EICHENLAUB, 1404 Genesee St., Utica, 13502. Tel: 315-724-2158.

Oswego County Director—MARY MARGARET PEKOW, 365 First St., Fulton, 13069. Tel: 315-598-3980.

Catholic Deaf Community—MARY MARGARET VAN DAMME, Dir., P.O. Box 572, Rome, 13442. Tel: 315-404-5674 (TTY/Voice).

Catholic Relief Services—Mr. JOSEPH G. SLAVIK, Dir., Mailing Address: 240 E. Onondaga St., Syracuse, 13202. Tel: 315-470-1416.

Catholic Schools—Mailing Address: P.O. Box 511, Syracuse, 13201. Tel: 315-470-1450; Fax: 315-470-1470. Mr. CHRISTOPHER MOMINEY, Supt.; Rev. CHARLES S. VAVONESE, Asst. Supt.; Ms. CHERYL CANFIELD, Asst. Supt.; Mr. DOMINICK LISI, Dir. Technology.

Southern Region—Broome County Catholic School Office, 17 Adams St., P.O. Box 90, Binghamton, 13905. Tel: 607-723-1547; Fax: 607-723-5697.

Catholic School Endowment Fund of the Roman Catholic Diocese of Syracuse— (established to provide tuition assistance for students in diocesan Catholic schools) Most Rev. ROBERT J. CUNNINGHAM, D.D., Pres., 240 E. Onondaga St., P.O. Box 511, Syracuse, 13201-0511.

"The Catholic Sun"—CONNIE BERRY, Editor in Chief & Gen. Mgr.; Rev. DONALD E. BOURGEOIS, Episcopal Liaison, 420 Montgomery St., Syracuse, 13202. Tel: 315-422-8153; 800-333-0571; Fax: 315-422-7549. Email: catholicsun@yahoo.com. Web: www.sydio.org.

Catholic Television—Mr. ANDREW HAUFF, Production Coord., 1342 Lancaster Ave., Syracuse, 13210. Tel: 315-472-3584; Fax: 315-472-8409.

Christopher Community—Mr. DOUGLAS REICHER, Exec. Dir., 990 James St., Syracuse, 13203. Tel: 315-414-1821.

Clerical Fund Society of the Roman Catholic Diocese of Syracuse—Most Rev. ROBERT J. CUNNINGHAM, D.D., Pres.; Rev. Msgr. J. ROBERT YEAZEL, V.G., Vice Pres.; Rev. CLIFFORD H. AUTH, J.C.L., Sec. & Treas.

Office of Communications—Mrs. DANIELLE CUMMINGS, Dir., Mailing Address: P.O. Box 511, Syracuse, 13201. Tel: 315-470-1476; Fax: 315-478-4619. Email: dcummings@syracusediocese.org.

Stewardship & Development Office—Mr. CHRISTOPHER PARKER, 1342 Lancaster Ave., Syracuse, 13210. Tel: 315-472-0203; 315-472-7902; Fax: 315-472-8409.

Ecumenical Commission—Rev. Msgr. RONALD C. BILL, Dir. (Retired), 400 Salt Springs St., Fayetteville, 13066. Tel: 315-637-9846.

Family Life Education—Rev. JOSEPH H. PHILLIPS, Dir., 1342 Lancaster Ave., Syracuse, 13210. Tel: 315-472-6754; Fax: 315-472-8409.

Finance Committee—Most Rev. ROBERT J. CUNNINGHAM, D.D.; Rev. Msgrs. RICHARD M. KOPP; J. ROBERT YEAZEL, V.G., Chm.; Rev. CLIFFORD H. AUTH, J.C.L.; Mr. R. J. COLE; Ms. GRACE GHEZZI; Mr. WILLIAM MCAVOY; Mr. RICHARD DEGROOT; Ms. CAROL FLETCHER; Mr. JAMES MURPHY; Ms. CAROL PIEKLIK, Staff; Ms. DOREEN SIMMONS, Esq.; Mr. THOMAS PRINZING; Mr. J. DANIEL PLUFF, Consultant.

Formation for Ministry and Liturgy—Rev. JOSEPH E. SCARDELLA, Dir., Mailing Address: P.O. Box 511, Syracuse, 13202. Tel: 315-470-1420; Fax: 315-579-3564.

Health Care—Rev. JAMES H. CAREY, Dir., Mailing Address: P.O. Box 574, Tully, 13159. Tel: 315-696-5092.

Heritage Campaign—c/o Development Office, 1342 Lancaster Ave., Syracuse, 13210. Tel: 315-472-0203.

HOPE Appeal—Mr. CHRISTOPHER PARKER, 1342 Lancaster Ave., Syracuse, 13210. Tel: 315-472-0203; Fax: 315-472-8409.

Human Resources—PATRICIA MCMAHON, Dir., 240 E. Onondaga St., Syracuse, 13202. Tel: 315-422-7203.

Ruth Ministry— Syracuse Diocese Response to Domestic Violence LISA HALL, Dir., Mailing Address: P.O. Box 511, Syracuse, 13201. Tel: 315-470-1418; Fax: 315-478-4619.

Parish Services—Mr. NICK CROSBY, Mailing Address: P.O. Box 511, Syracuse, 13201. Tel: 315-422-9089.

Permanent Diaconate—Deacon LESLIE F. DISTIN, Dir., Mailing Address: P.O. Box 511, Syracuse, 13201. Tel: 315-470-1466.

Priest Personnel—Rev. Msgr. RICHARD M. KOPP, Mailing Address: P.O. Box 511, Syracuse, 13201. Tel: 315-470-1460; Fax: 315-478-4619.

Priests' Personnel Committee—Most Revs. JAMES M. MOYNIHAN, D.D. (Retired); THOMAS J. COSTELLO, D.D. (Retired); Revs. DARR F. SCHOENHOFEN; JOSEPH S. ZARESKI; THOMAS J. RYAN; JAMES P. SEROWIK; JOHN KURGAN; JOSEPH A. SALERNO; Rev. Msgrs. RICHARD M. KOPP; MICHAEL T. MEAGHER; Revs. CLIFFORD H. AUTH, J.C.L.; ANDREW E. BARANSKI, Ex Officio; JON K. WERNER; JAMES P. LANG, Ex Officio; JOHN P. DONOVAN, J.C.L.

Project Rachel— Post Abortion Healing LISA HALL, Dir., 240 E. Onondaga St., Syracuse, 13202. Tel: 315-424-3737.

Personal Resource Center—Rev. Msgr. NEAL QUARTIER, Ph.D., L.C.S.W., B.C.D., Dir., 215 N. State St., Syracuse, 13217-6482. Tel: 315-470-1462.

Propagation of the Faith—Rev. JOSEPH H. PHILLIPS, Dir.; Sr. JUDITH MARKERT, C.S.J., Coord., 1342 Lancaster Ave., Syracuse, 13210. Tel: 315-472-3442; Fax: 315-472-8409.

Public Policy—Rev. CHARLES S. VAVONESE, 240 E. Onondaga St., Syracuse, 13202.

Religious Education— (Office of Faith Formation) Sr. KATIE EIFFE, C.S.J., Dir., Mailing Address: P.O. Box 511, Syracuse, 13202. Tel: 315-470-1431; Fax: 315-478-4619.

Eastern Region—CATHERINE CORNUE, Dir., One Sherman St., New Hartford, 13413. Tel: 315-797-4030; Fax: 315-797-4031; CHERYL SMITH, Resource Center.

Northern Region—Sr. GERMANE HILSTON, Dir., 74 W. 6th St., Oswego, 13126. Tel: 315-596-4014; Fax: 315-343-5557; DEANNE HALL, Resource Center.

Southern Region—Sr. LOIS BARTON, C.S.J., Dir., 705 W. Main St., Endicott, 13760. Tel: 607-348-0746; Fax: 607-786-9650; ANDREA SCHAFFER, Resource Center. Tel: 607-786-9649.

Western Region—THERESA MAY, Dir., 1342 Lancaster Ave., Syracuse, 13210. Tel: 315-472-6753; Fax: 315-472-8409; MARGARET BABCOCK, Resource Center. Tel: 315-472-6752; BETH SCHAFER.

West (Cortland)—AMY WHITE, Resource Center, 44 N. Main St., Cortland, 13045. Tel: 607-753-3808; Fax: 607-753-1039.

Religious Retirement Fund— Retirement Plan for The Roman Catholic Diocese of Syracuse, NY. Est. January 1, 1988. Contact: VACANT, COO, Mailing Address: P.O. Box 511, Syracuse, 13201. Tel: 315-422-9045; Fax: 315-422-9139.

Respect for Life—LISA HALL, Dir., Mailing Address: P.O. Box 511, Syracuse, 13201. Tel: 315-470-1418.

Laymen & Laywomen Retreat Movements—Rev. MICHAEL J. CARMOLA, Dir., Christ the King Retreat House, 500 Brookford Rd., Syracuse, 13224. Tel: 315-446-2680.

Spanish Apostolate—Rev. ROBERT D. CHRYST, Dir., 170 Seymour St., Syracuse, 13204. Tel: 315-442-9390.

Syracuse Catholic Press Association, Inc.— "The Catholic Sun" CONNIE BERRY, Editor in Chief & Gen. Mgr.; Most Rev. ROBERT J. CUNNINGHAM, D.D., Pres., Mailing Address: P.O. Box 511, Syracuse, 13201. Tel: 315-422-8153; 800-333-0571; Fax: 315-422-7549.

Victim Assistance Coordinator—NUALA COLLINS, P.O. Box 511, Syracuse, 13201-0511. Tel: 315-470-1465; Fax: 315-478-4619.

Vocation Formation—Rev. THOMAS R. SERVATIUS, Dir., Mailing Address: P.O. Box 511, Syracuse, 13201. Tel: 315-470-1452; Fax: 315-478-4619.

Vocation Promotion—Rev. JOSEPH O'CONNOR, Dir., Mailing Address: P.O. Box 511, Syracuse, 13201. Tel: 315-470-1468; Fax: 315-478-4619.

Youth & Young Adult Ministry—Mr. ROBERT WALTERS, Dir., Mailing Address: P.O. Box 511, Syracuse, 13201. Tel: 315-470-1419; Fax: 315-478-4619.

CLERGY, PARISHES, MISSIONS AND PAROCHIAL SCHOOLS

CITY OF SYRACUSE

(ONONDAGA COUNTY)

SYRACUSE

1—THE CATHEDRAL OF THE IMMACULATE CONCEPTION (1841) Rev. Msgr. Neal Quartier, Rector; Most Rev. James M. Moynihan (Retired); Revs. John C. Schopfer; Mariusz Wirkowski (Poland), Parochial Vicar; Sr. Maureen D'Onofrio, C.S.J., Pastoral Assoc.; Deacon Fred Cholette.

Res.: 259 E. Onondaga St., 13202. Tel: 315-422-4177; Fax: 315-478-4619.

Consolidated with Our Lady of Pompei School, Syracuse

Catechesis/Religious Program—Students 66.

Station—Vivian Teal Howard, Tel: 315-478-1641.

Station—Clinton Plaza 13202. Tel: 315-475-2141.

Station—McCarthy Manor, Tel: 315-475-6390.

Station—Rosewood Heights, Tel: 315-474-4431.

2—ALL SAINTS Rev. Frederick D. Daley.

Res.: 112 Lancaster Pl., 13210. Tel: 315-472-9934; Fax: 315-472-9941.

Catechesis/Religious Program—Students 70.

3—ST. ANDREW THE APOSTLE (1953) Closed. For inquiries for parish records contact the chancery.

4—ST. ANN (1955) Rev. Brian G. Lang.

Res.: 4461 Onondaga Blvd., 13219. Tel: 315-468-1803; Fax: 315-487-6312. Email: stann4461@yahoo.com.

Catechesis/Religious Program—Tel: 315-487-6201. Students 171.

5—ST. ANTHONY OF PADUA (1901) Rev. Robert D. Chryst. In Res., Most Rev. Thomas J. Costello (Retired).

Res.: 1515 Midland Ave., 13205. Tel: 315-475-4114.

Catechesis/Religious Program—Students 12.

6—ASSUMPTION B.V.M. (1844), (German), [CEM] Revs. John Ruffo, O.F.M.Conv.; Jeffrey Keefe, O.F.M.Conv., Prov. Psychologist, Franciscan Counseling; Conrad Somerville, O.F.M.Conv.; Bro. Edward Falsey, O.F.M.Conv. In Res., Revs. Jim Stenberg, C.B.; Linus DeSantis, O.F.M.Conv.; Friar James Moore, O.F.M.Conv.; Bro. Joseph Freitag, O.F.M.Conv.; Rev. Adam Keltos, O.F.M.Conv.
St. Francis Friary: 812 N. Salina St., 13208. Tel: 315-422-4833; Fax: 315-422-4363.
Assumption Cemetery Corporation—2401 Court St., 13208. Tel: 315-454-3841; Fax: 315-454-4931. Email: assump812@aol.com.

7—BLESSED SACRAMENT (1921) Revs. E. Peter Reddick; Kevin Maloney. In Res., Rev. Joseph O'Conner.
Res.: 3127 James St., 13206. Tel: 315-437-3394; Fax: 315-432-9198.
School—(Grades PreK-6), 3129 James St., 13206. Tel: 315-437-1261; Fax: 315-463-1628. Mrs. Andrea Polcaro, Prin. Lay Teachers 18; Students 294.
Catechesis/Religious Program—Students 222.

8—ST. BRIGID AND ST. JOSEPH (1926 and 1869) Rev. Laurence W. Kennedy.
Res.: 318 Herkimer St., 13204. Tel: 315-488-7122; Fax: 315-484-9723. Email: lkennedy@syrdio.org.
Catechesis/Religious Program—Students 32.

9—ST. CHARLES BORROMEO (1929) Rev. Brian G. Lang; Sr. Jean A. Burns, C.S.J., Parish Min.; Deacons Peter P. Vanelli; Robert Connelly; Anthony J. Paratore. In Res., Rev. Philip S. Keane, S.S., (Weekend: In Res.).
Res.: 417 S. Orchard Rd., 13219. Tel: 315-468-4122; Fax: 315-468-4122.
School—200 W. High Ter., 13219. Tel: 315-488-7631; Fax: 315-488-0617. Sr. Donna Driscoll, Prin. Sisters 2; Lay Teachers 12; Students 212.
Catechesis/Religious Program—Tel: 315-488-7645. Students 260.
Convent—Missionary Franciscan Sisters of the Immaculate Conception, 401 E. Corey Rd., 13219. Tel: 315-468-6041.

10—ST. DANIEL (1932) Rev. Msgr. Eugene M. Yennock; Rev. Timothy S. Elmer.
Res.: 3004 Court St., 13208. Tel: 315-454-4946; Fax: 315-454-0978. Email: sdchurch@twcny.rr.com.
Catechesis/Religious Program—Students 200.

11—HOLY TRINITY (1891), (German), Rev. Jon K. Werner, Admin.
Res.: 501 Park St., 13203. Tel: 315-474-8681; Fax: 315-474-3154. Email: htrinity@twcny.rr.com.
Catechesis/Religious Program— Combined with St. John the Baptist, Syracuse & Our Lady of Pompei-St. Peter's, Syracuse

12—ST. JAMES (1925) Rev. John D. Manno, Admin. In Res., Rev. James P. Lang; Sr. Carolyn Chmielewski, C.S.J., Pastoral Assoc.
Res.: 4845 S. Salina St., 13205. Tel: 315-469-7789; Fax: 315-492-2707. Email: stjamessyrinfo@verizon.net.
Catechesis/Religious Program—Students 80.
Station—Onondaga Valley

13—ST. JOHN THE BAPTIST (1827) Rev. Jon K. Werner, Admin. In Res., Revs. Daniel C. Muscalino; Martin L. Dama (Africa).
Res.: 406 Court St., 13208. Tel: 315-478-0916; Fax: 315-423-8096. Email: johnthebaptist@twcny.rr.com.
Catechesis/Religious Program—Students 62.

14—ST. JOHN THE EVANGELIST (1851) Rev. Msgr. Neal E. Quartier, Admin.; Rev. Thienan Tran; Deacon John H. Collins.
Mailing Address: 215 N. State St., P.O. Box 6482, 13217-6482. Tel: 315-474-2363; 315-474-7322; Fax: 315-474-1045.
Catechesis/Religious Program—Tel: 315-474-7322. Students 130.

15—ST. LUCY (1872) Rev. James D. Mathews.
Res.: 432 Gifford St., 13204. Tel: 315-475-7273; Fax: 315-423-0128.
Catechesis/Religious Program—Tel: 315-478-6312. Students 86.

16—MOST HOLY ROSARY (1913) Rev. Frederick R. Mannara.
Res.: 111 Roberts Ave., 13207-1397. Tel: 315-478-5749; Fax: 315-478-8629.
School—(Grades PreK-6), 1031 Bellevue Ave., 13207. Tel: 315-476-6035; Fax: 315-476-0219. Web: www.mhrsyr.org. Sisters 2; Lay Teachers 15; Students 152.
Catechesis/Religious Program—Students 197.

17—OUR LADY OF LOURDES (1947) Rev. Thomas P. Fitzpatrick; Deacons Michael B. McGrath; Leo Needham.
Res.: 300 Valley Dr., 13207. Tel: 315-476-9576.
Catechesis/Religious Program—Tel: 315-478-6383. Students 72.

18—OUR LADY OF POMPEI (1924), (Italian), Merged with St. Peter, Syracuse to form Our Lady of Pompei-St. Peter, Syracuse.

19—OUR LADY OF POMPEI/ST. PETER (1924), (Italian), Rev. Paul F. Angelicchio. In Res., Revs. Frederick A. Pompei; Thienan Tran.
Res.: 301 Ash St., 13208. Tel: 315-422-7163; Fax: 315-422-7164.
School—915-917 N. McBride St., 13208. Tel: 315-422-8548; Fax: 315-472-0754. Charles La Barbera, Prin. Lay Teachers 12; Students 99.
Catechesis/Religious Program—Tel: 315-472-2260. Students 96.
Convent—Franciscan Missionary Sisters of the Immaculate Conception, 920 N. McBride St., 13208. Tel: 315-422-7922.

20—OUR LADY OF SOLACE (1926), with St. Therese the Little Flower of Jesus, Syracuse to form All Saints, Syracuse.

21—ST. PATRICK (1870) Rev. John P. Fenlon.
Res.: 216 N. Lowell Ave., 13204. Tel: 315-475-2185; Fax: 315-476-1565.
Catechesis/Religious Program—Students 85.

22—ST. PETER (1890), (Italian), Merged with Our Lady of Pompeii, Syracuse to form Our Lady of Pompeii-St. Peter, Syracuse.

23—SACRED HEART BASILICA (1892), (Polish), [CEM 2] Rev. Msgr. Peter W. Gleba; Revs. Stanley Dudkiewicz (Poland); Stanley Matula (Poland); Deacons James L. Morse; Joseph Daniszewski; Frank Timson.
Res.: 927 Park Ave., 13204. Tel: 315-422-2343; Fax: 315-422-2344.
Catechesis/Religious Program—Tel: 315-422-8883; Fax: 315-422-7372. Students 99.

24—ST. STEPHEN (1915), (Slovak), Closed. For inquiries for parish records please contact Sacred Heart, Syracuse.

25—ST. THERESE THE LITTLE FLOWER OF JESUS (1926) Merged with Our Lady of Solace, Syracuse to form All Saints, Syracuse.

26—TRANSFIGURATION (1911), (Polish), Rev. Thomas P. Kobuszewski. In Res., Rev. Tadeusz Rudnik (Poland).
Res.: 740 Teall Ave., 13206. Tel: 315-479-6129; Fax: 315-426-0684. Email: ctransfi@twcny.rr.com.

27—ST. VINCENT DE PAUL (1893) Rev. Wilbur J. Votraw, Admin. In Res., Revs. Wilbur J. Votraw; Theodore C. Sizing (Retired).
Res.: 342 Vine St., 13203. Tel: 315-479-6689; Fax: 315-479-6689.
Catechesis/Religious Program—Tel: 315-479-6301. Students 48.
Convent—Sisters of St. Joseph of Carondelet, 1101 Burnet Ave., 13203. Tel: 315-479-8012.

OUTSIDE THE CITY OF SYRACUSE

BAINBRIDGE, CHENANGO CO., ST. JOHN THE EVANGELIST (1914) Rev. Robert D. Dwyer.
Res.: 34 S. Main St., 13733. Tel: 607-967-4481.
Catechesis/Religious Program—Students 28.
Mission—St. Agnes Spring St., Afton, Chenango Co. 13730. Tel: 607-639-1200 (Hall).

BALDWINSVILLE, ONONDAGA CO.

1—ST. AUGUSTINE (1966) Rev. Abraham L. Esper. In Res., Rev. Clifford H. Auth.
Res.: 7333 O'Brien Rd., 13027. Tel: 315-638-0585; Fax: 315-635-0931. Email: staugustineparish@yahoo.com.
Catechesis/Religious Program—Tel: 315-638-0864. Students 323.

2—ST. ELIZABETH ANN SETON (1985) Rev. John S. Finnegan, Admin.; Deacon William A. Dotterer.
Res.: 3494 NY State Rte. 31, 13027. Tel: 315-652-4300; Fax: 315-622-1761. Email: mainoffice@stelizabethbville.org.
Catechesis/Religious Program—Tel: 315-652-3900. Students 910.

3—ST. MARY OF THE ASSUMPTION (1852) [CEM] Rev. Abraham L. Esper; Deacon Robert J. Talomie.
Res.: 47 Syracuse St., 13027. Tel: 315-635-5762; Fax: 315-635-8137. Email: stmarysbaldwinsville@gmail.com.
School—49 Syracuse St., 13027. Tel: 315-635-3977. Mrs. Debra Brillante, Prin. Sisters of the Third Franciscan Order M.C. 1; Lay Teachers 11; Students 153.
Catechesis/Religious Program—Tel: 315-635-5762, Ext. 110. Students 645.

BINGHAMTON, BROOME CO.

1—ST. ANDREW (1955) Merged with St. John the Evangelist, Binghamton to form Saints John & Andrew, Binghamton.

2—ST. ANN (1925), (Slovak), Merged with St. Joseph, Binghamton and St. Stanislaus Kostka, Binghamton to form Holy Trinity, Binghamton.

3—ST. CATHERINE OF SIENA (1929) Rev. Timothy J. Taugher; Sr. Karen Gaube, C.S.J., Pastoral Assoc.; Deacon Raymond Goskowski.
Res.: 1031 Chenango St., 13901. Tel: 607-722-4388; Fax: 607-722-1336.
Catechesis/Religious Program—1031 Chenango St., 13901. Tel: 607-722-4177. Students 530.

4—ST. CHRISTOPHER (1940) Revs. Timothy J. Taugher, Admin.; Robert A. Ours.
Res.: 103 Castle Creek Rd., 13901. Tel: 607-723-0677; Fax: 607-773-0268. Email: stchrisrectory@stny.rr.com.
Catechesis/Religious Program—Tel: 607-723-7010. Students 180.

5—SS. CYRIL AND METHOD (1904), (Slovak), Rev. George Sandor, O.F.M.Conv. In Res., Revs. Simeon Rukstalis, O.F.M.Conv.; Robert Amrhein, O.F.M.Conv.
Res.: 148 Clinton St., 13905. Tel: 607-724-1372; Fax: 607-724-1468.
Catechesis/Religious Program—Tel: 607-760-1372. Students 72.

6—HOLY TRINITY (2003) Revs. George Sandor, O.F.M-.Conv.; Robert Amrhein, O.F.M.Conv.; Simeon Rukstalis, O.F.M.Conv.
Res.: 346 Prospect St., 13905. Tel: 607-797-1856; Fax: 607-797-8452.
Catechesis/Religious Program—Students 66.

7—SAINTS JOHN & ANDREW Rev. Msgr. Michael T. Meagher; Rev. Christopher Celentano, Parochial Vicar. In Res., Revs. Krzysztof Boretto; Robert J. Sullivan (Retired).
Res.: 1263 Vestal Ave., 13903. Tel: 607-722-0493; Fax: 607-723-5171. Email: stjohn@stny.rr.com.
Res. & Parish Center: 356 Conklin Ave., 13903. Tel: 607-722-4049; Fax: 607-651-9140.
Catechesis/Religious Program—Students 385.

8—ST. JOHN THE EVANGELIST (1907) Merged with St. Andrew, Binghamton to form Saints John & Andrew, Binghamton.

9—ST. JOSEPH (1914), (Lithuanian), Merged with St. Ann, Binghamton and St. Stanislaus Kostka, Binghamton to form Holy Trinity, Binghamton.

10—ST. MARY OF THE ASSUMPTION (1887; 1913) Revs. Daniel Caruso; Joseph Mary Offeh (Africa). In Res., Rev. Francis W. Kocik (CAM).
Res.: 37 Fayette St., 13901. Tel: 607-723-5383. Email: stmaryrectory@aol.com.
Catechesis/Religious Program—Students 220.

11—ST. PATRICK (1838), (Irish), Rev. John A. Booth Jr.
Res.: 9 Leroy St., 13905. Tel: 607-722-1060.
Catechesis/Religious Program—Students 87.
Convent—Sisters of St. Joseph of Carondelet, 46 Oak St., 13905. Tel: 607-722-4745.

12—ST. PAUL (1896) Revs. Daniel M. Caruso; Joseph Mary Offeh (Africa), Parochial Vicar; Francis W. Kocik (CAM); Sr. Mary Rose De Donato, D.C., Pastoral Assoc.
Res.: 15 Doubleday St., 13901. Tel: 607-722-6492. Email: stpauls_binghamton@yahoo.com.
Catechesis/Religious Program—Tel: 607-724-5449; Fax: 607-724-3377. Students 170.

13—ST. STANISLAUS KOSTKA (1914), (Polish), Merged with St. Ann, Binghamton and St. Joseph, Binghamton to form Holy Trinity, Binghamton.

14—ST. THOMAS AQUINAS (1927) Rev. John J. Booth, Admin.
Res.: One Aquinas St., 13905. Tel: 607-797-4015; Fax: 607-729-9727.
Catechesis/Religious Program—4 Aquinas St., 13905. Tel: 607-797-3304. Students 98.

BOONVILLE, ONEIDA CO., ST. JOSEPH (1875) [CEM] Rev. Sean P. O'Brien.
Res.: 110 Charles St., 13309. Tel: 315-942-4618.
Catechesis/Religious Program—Tel: 315-942-5955; Fax: 315-942-4618. Students 104.

BREWERTON, ONONDAGA CO., ST. AGNES (1958) Rev. Frank Young.
Res.: 5472 Miller Rd., 13029. Tel: 315-676-7050; Fax: 315-668-8149. Email: ypf70@clearwire.net.
Catechesis/Religious Program—Tel: 315-676-5662. Twinned with St. Michael, Central Square. Students 12.

BRIDGEPORT, ONONDAGA CO., ST. FRANCIS OF ASSISI (1951) Rev. Raynald Yudin, O.F.M.Conv.; Deacon Guy W. Hart. In Res., Rev. Albert Scherer, O.F.M.Conv.
Friary—Res.: 7820 Rte. 298, P.O. Box 550, 13030-0550. Tel: 315-633-9682; Fax: 315-633-0672. Email: stfrancisofc@cnymail.com. Web: www.stfrancisbridgeport.org.
Parish Center— 13030-0550. Tel: 315-633-2561; Fax: 315-633-2743.
Catechesis/Religious Program—Tel: 315-633-5661. Students 186.

CAMDEN, ONEIDA CO., ST. JOHN THE EVANGELIST (1852) [CEM] Rev. Carlo C. Stirpe.
Res.: 22 Church St., 13316. Tel: 315-245-1603.
Catechesis/Religious Program—Students 148.

CAMILLUS, ONONDAGA CO., ST. JOSEPH (1852) Revs. Gregory C. LeStrange; Michael Galuppi.
Res.: 5600 W. Genesee St., 13031. Tel: 315-488-8490; Fax: 315-488-4214.
Catechesis/Religious Program—Students 1,084.

CANASTOTA, MADISON CO., ST. AGATHA (1883) [CEM] Rev. Kevin Corcoran; Deacon Adolph J. Uryniak.
Res.: 329 N. Peterboro St., 13032. Tel: 315-697-7104; Fax: 315-697-5821.
Catechesis/Religious Program—Tel: 315-697-7827. Students 239.

CAZENOVIA, MADISON CO., ST. JAMES (1847) [CEM] Rev. G. Peter Worn; Sr. Milice Bohrer, C.S.J.,

Pastoral Assoc.; Deacon Stephen Young.
Res.: 6 Green St., 13035. Tel: 315-655-3441; Fax: 315-655-3442. Email: stjpa@twcny.rr.com.
Catechesis/Religious Program—Tel: 315-655-4871. Students 530.

CENTRAL SQUARE, OSWEGO CO., ST. MICHAEL (1928) Rev. John J. Smegelsky.
Res.: 598 S. Main St., P.O. Box 514, 13036. Tel: 315-676-2898; Fax: 315-676-3103.
Catechesis/Religious Program—Tel: 315-676-4210. Students 210.

CHENANGO FORKS, BROOME CO., ST. RITA (1946) Closed. For inquiries for parish records contact the chancery.

CHITTENANGO, MADISON CO., ST. PATRICK (1853) [CEM] Rev. Edward J. Reimer.
Res.: 1341 Murray Dr., 13037. Tel: 315-687-6105; Fax: 315-687-0046.
Catechesis/Religious Program—Tel: 315-687-6561. Students 215.

CICERO, ONONDAGA CO., SACRED HEART (1888) Revs. James E. Gehl; James F. Quinn.
Res.: 8229 S. Main St., 13039. Tel: 315-699-2752; Fax: 315-699-3775. Email: sheart@twcny.rr.com.
Catechesis/Religious Program—Tel: 315-699-7678. Students 1,036.

CLARK MILLS, ONEIDA CO., CHURCH OF THE ANNUNCIATION (1908) Rev. Robert F. Bogan, Admin.
Mailing Address: 7616 E. South St., Clinton, 13323. Tel: 315-853-6138.
Catechesis/Religious Program—Tel: 315-853-6139. Students 200.

CLAYVILLE, ONEIDA CO.
1—ST. PATRICK (1864) [CEM] Closed. For inquiries for parish records contact St. Patrick-St. Anthony, Clayville.
2—ST. PATRICK-ST. ANTHONY (1907) Rev. Arthur Krawczenko, Admin.
Res.: 2398 Church St., P.O. Box 285, 13322. Tel: 315-839-5483; Fax: 315-839-5483.
Catechesis/Religious Program—Tel: 315-737-8692. Students 289.

CLEVELAND, OSWEGO CO., ST. MARY OF THE ASSUMPTION (1854) [CEM] Rev. R. Paul Mathis.
Res.: 148 State Rte. 49, 13042. Tel: 315-675-3542.
Catechesis/Religious Program—Tel: 315-675-3165. Students 153.
Mission—St. Bernadette State Rte. 49, Constantia, Oswego Co. 13044. Tel: 315-623-9803.

CLINTON, ONEIDA CO., ST. MARY (1850) [CEM] Rev. John P. Croghan.
Res.: 13 Marvin St., 13323. Tel: 315-853-2935; Fax: 315-859-1097. Email: stmarysc@borg.com.
Catechesis/Religious Program—Tel: 315-853-6196; Fax: 315-853-1440. Students 366.

CORTLAND, CORTLAND CO.
1—ST. ANTHONY OF PADUA (1917), (Italian), Rev. Mark P. Kaminski.
Res.: 45 Crandall St., 13045. Tel: 607-756-7533; Fax: 607-756-7697. Email: arectory@twcny.rr.com. Web: www.saintanthonyofcortland.com.
Catechesis/Religious Program—Diane Passalugo, D.R.E. Students 78.
2—ST. MARY (1855) Revs. Mark P. Kaminski, Admin.; Lukasz Kozlowski, Parochial Vicar; Deacons Joseph During; Steve Smith.
Res.: 44 N. Main St., 13045. Tel: 607-756-9967; Fax: 607-756-2494. Email: smc@odyssey.net.
School—61 N. Main St., 13045. Tel: 607-756-5614; Fax: 607-753-3444. Email: spmarycor@mail.odyssey.net. Mrs. Susan McInvale, Prin. Lay Teachers 17; Students 242.
Catechesis/Religious Program—59 N. Main St., 13045. Email: dreatsmc@odyssey.net. Mark T. Lickona, D.R.E. Students 172.

DEPOSIT, BROOME CO., ST. JOSEPH (1851) [CEM] Rev. John J. Booth.
Res.: 98 Second St., 13754. Tel: 607-467-2291; Fax: 607-467-2288.
Parish Center—74 Second St., 13754. Tel: 607-467-2226.
Catechesis/Religious Program—Students 69.

DEWITT, ONONDAGA CO., HOLY CROSS (1943) Rev. Msgr. J. Robert Yeazel; Rev. John V. Ahern, Parochial Vicar. In Res., Rev. Charles S. Vavonese.
Res.: 4112 E. Genesee St., 13214. Tel: 315-446-0473; Fax: 315-446-7608. Email: info@holycrossdewitt.org.
School—4200 E. Genesee St., 13214. Tel: 315-446-4890; Fax: 315-446-4799. David Wheeler, Prin. Lay Teachers 14; Students 213.
Catechesis/Religious Program—Students 960.

DURHAMVILLE, ONEIDA CO., ST. FRANCIS (1860), (German), [CEM] Rev. Joseph F. Kehoe.
Res.: 5334 Foster St., P.O. Box 189, 13054. Tel: 315-363-1572.
Chapel—St. Mary [CEM] Irish Ridge.
Catechesis/Religious Program—Students 28.

EAST SYRACUSE, ONONDAGA CO., ST. MATTHEW (1880) Revs. Joseph J. Clemente; Severine Yagaza.
Res.: 229 W. Yates St., 13057. Tel: 315-437-8318; Fax: 315-463-6399.
School—St. Daniel - St. Matthew Academy, 214 Kinne St., 13057. Tel: 315-437-1339; Fax: 315-463-1339. Deacon Joseph Celentano Sr., Prin. Lay Teachers 16; Students 196; Preschool 52.
Catechesis/Religious Program—Tel: 315-437-3685. Students 470.

ENDICOTT, BROOME CO.
1—ST. AMBROSE (1908) Revs. Charles A. Currie; Donald Bourgeois, Parochial Vicar. In Res., Rev. Benito Manding.
Res.: 203 Washington Ave., 13760. Tel: 607-754-2330; Fax: 607-785-6947.
Catechesis/Religious Program—Students 96.
2—ST. ANTHONY OF PADUA (1917), (Italian), Revs. James P. Serowik; Douglas D. Cunningham, Parochial Vicar; Deacon Frank Longo.
Res.: 306 Odell Ave., 13760. Tel: 607-754-4333; Fax: 607-786-3965. Email: stanthonys@stny.rr.com.
St. Anthony's Learning Center—906 Jenkins St., 13760. Tel: 607-748-5184; Fax: 607-786-3965. Email: stanthonytlc@stny.rr.com. (Pre-School)
Convent—Little Sisters of St. Francis, 304 Oak Hill Ave., 13760. Tel: 607-786-5006.
Catechesis/Religious Program—Email: stajannine@stny.rr.com. Students 279.
3—ST. CASIMIR (1928), (Polish), Rev. Matthew S. Wieczorek.
Res.: 212 N. McKinley Ave., 13760. Tel: 607-785-3262; Fax: 607-785-4772. Email: stcasimirs@verizon.net.
Catechesis/Religious Program— Twinned with St. Joseph, Endicott. Students 18.
4—ST. JOSEPH (1923), (Slovak), Rev. Charles Opondo-Owora (Africa); Deacon Dominick Rossi (Ghana). In Res., Rev. Robert A. Ours.
Res.: 207 Hayes Ave., 13760. Tel: 607-748-0442; Fax: 607-748-7725.
School—210 N. Jackson Ave., 13760. Tel: 607-748-8631; Fax: 607-748-7745. Angela Tierno, Prin. Lay Teachers 12; Students 120.
Catechesis/Religious Program—Students 179.
5—OUR LADY OF GOOD COUNSEL (1941) Rev. Edward J. Zandy; Deacon Thomas M. Harley.
Res.: 701 W. Main St., 13760. Tel: 607-748-7417; Fax: 607-785-6454.
Catechesis/Religious Program—Tel: 607-754-2213. Students 369.

ENDWELL, BROOME CO.
1—CHRIST THE KING (1949) Rev. Thomas F. Hobbes; Deacon Thomas N. Picciano.
Res.: 1501 Davis Ave., 13760. Tel: 607-785-3180; Fax: 607-785-3180 (call first); Tel: 607-754-1266 Linda Cargill-Questions.
Catechesis/Religious Program—Tel: 607-785-5016. Students 30.
2—CHURCH OF THE HOLY FAMILY (2008) Rev. Clarence F. Rumble.
Res.: 3011 Phyllis St., 13760. Tel: 607-754-1266; Fax: 607-754-7527. Email: churchoftheholyfamily@gmail.com.
Catechesis/Religious Program—Tel: 607-785-4581. Students 305.

FAIRMOUNT, ONONDAGA CO., HOLY FAMILY (1935) Revs. Richard Prior; Gregory J. Kreinheder; Deacon Nick Alvaro.
Parish Office—127 Chapel Dr., 13219. Tel: 315-488-3139; Fax: 315-487-1112.
Res.: 119 Chapel Dr., 13219. Tel: 315-488-5396.
School—130 Chapel Dr., 13219. Tel: 315-487-8515; Fax: 315-487-8515. Helen Chajka, Prin.
Catechesis/Religious Program—Tel: 315-488-5884. Students 1,000.

FAYETTEVILLE, ONONDAGA CO., IMMACULATE CONCEPTION (1869) [CEM] Rev. Thomas J. Ryan; Sr. Monica Zmolek, O.S.F., Pastoral Min. In Res., Rev. Msgrs. James A. McCloskey (Retired); Ronald C. Bill (Retired).
Res.: 400 Salt Springs St., 13066. Tel: 315-637-9846; Fax: 315-637-9846.
School—Tel: 315-637-3961; Fax: 315-637-2672. Mrs. Sally Lisi, Prin. Sisters of the Third Franciscan Order M.C. 1; Lay Teachers 28; Students 298.
Catechesis/Religious Program—Tel: 315-637-9840. Students 714.

FLORENCE, ONEIDA CO., ST. MARY (1845) [CEM] Rev. Joseph E. Moskal.
Res.: 22 Church St., Camden, 13316. Tel: 315-245-1603.

FORESTPORT, ONEIDA CO., ST. PATRICK (1848) [CEM] Revs. Sean P. O'Brien; Donald H. Karlen.
Mailing Address: P.O. Box 1, 13338. Tel: 315-392-2341; Fax: 315-392-5651.
Catechesis/Religious Program—Students 140.
Mission—St. Mary of the Snows Otter Lake, Oneida Co.

FULTON, OSWEGO CO.
1—HOLY FAMILY-ST. MICHAEL'S (1930) Rev. Robert B. Stephenson.
Office: 301 Buffalo St., 13069. Tel: 315-598-2118; Fax: 315-598-3355. Email: smarc@windstream.net.
Catechesis/Religious Program—Students 197.
2—IMMACULATE CONCEPTION (1854) [CEM] Rev. Stephen P. Wirkes.
Office: 309 Buffalo St., 13069. Tel: 315-598-2118.
Res.: Tel: 315-598-9094; Fax: 315-598-3355.
Rectory—57 S. 3rd St., 13069.
Catechesis/Religious Program—Students 107.
3—ST. MICHAEL (1924), (Polish), Merged with Holy Family, Fulton to form Holy Family-St. Michael's, Fulton.

GREENE, CHENANGO CO., IMMACULATE CONCEPTION (1889) Rev. Thomas I. Ward.
Res.: 1180 NY Hwy. 206, 13778. Tel: 607-656-9546; Fax: 607-656-7667. Email: officeiccgreene@frontiernet.net.
Catechesis/Religious Program—Students 55.

HAMILTON, MADISON CO., ST. MARY (1869) [CEM] Rev. Msgr. John R. Madden.
Res.: 16 Wylie St., 13346. Tel: 315-824-2164.
Catechesis/Religious Program—Tel: 315-824-5024. Twinned with St. Joan, Morrisville. Students 114.

HANNIBAL, OSWEGO CO., OUR LADY OF THE ROSARY (1954) Rev. Richard P. Morisette, Admin.
Office: 923 Cayuga St., P.O. Box 185, 13074-3138. Tel: 315-564-5201.
Catechesis/Religious Program—Students 107.
Mission—St. Joseph Southwest Oswego, Oswego Co. (Closed)

HINCKLEY, ONEIDA CO., ST. ANN (1895) [CEM] Rev. Vincent P. Long.
Res.: 7125 Main St., 13352. Tel: 315-896-2540.
Catechesis/Religious Program—Students 114.

HOLLAND PATENT, ONEIDA CO., ST. LEO (1882) Rev. Vincent P. Long; Constance Armstrong, Pastoral Assoc. In Res., Rev. Robert C. Weber.
Res.: 7937 Elm St., P.O. Box 185, 13354. Tel: 315-865-5371; Fax: 315-865-5868.
Catechesis/Religious Program—Students 410.

HOMER, CORTLAND CO., ST. MARGARET (1908) Rev. R. Daniel DeLorme. Pastoral Team, Lana Riley; Gary Smith; Donna Yacavone.
Res.: 14 Copeland Ave., P.O. Box 356, 13077. Tel: 607-749-2542; Fax: 607-749-4623.
Catechesis/Religious Program—

JOHNSON CITY, BROOME CO.
1—BLESSED SACRAMENT (1945) Rev. James D. Tormey.
Res.: 13 Cenacle Plaza, 13790. Tel: 607-797-5151; Fax: 607-797-8603. Email: info@bsacjc.org.
Catechesis/Religious Program—Tel: 607-797-8603. Students 95.
2—ST. JAMES (1900) Revs. John P. Donovan; Amedeo G. Guida, Parochial Vicar; Sr. Rose Margaret Noonan, C.S.J., Pastoral Assoc., Emerita; Deacon Edward Blaine; Mr. William P. Gallagher, Pastoral Assoc.
Office: 147 Main St., 13790. Tel: 607-729-6147; Fax: 607-797-5966.
Catechesis/Religious Program—Tel: 607-729-4083. Students 470.

JORDAN, ONONDAGA CO., ST. PATRICK (1858) [CEM] Rev. John R. DeLorenzo, Admin.
Res. & Office: 28 N. Main St., P.O. Box 567, 13080. Tel: 315-689-6240; Fax: 315-689-1695.
Catechesis/Religious Program—Students 125.

KIRKWOOD, BROOME CO., ST. MARY (1888) Rev. Thomas F. Catucci.
Res.: 975 NY Rte. 11, 13795. Tel: 607-775-0086. Email: stmaryskirkwood13795@verizon.net.
Catechesis/Religious Program—Tel: 607-775-2511. Students 174.

LACONA, OSWEGO CO., ST. FRANCES XAVIER CABRINI (1946) Closed. For inquiries for parish records contact the chancery.

LAFAYETTE, ONONDAGA CO., ST. JOSEPH (1866) Revs. James H. Carey, Admin.; John Kurgan.
Res.: 6104 Cherry Valley Rd., Box 169, 13084. Tel: 315-677-3439.
Catechesis/Religious Program—Tel: 315-677-7735; Fax: 315-677-3858. Students 175.

LAKELAND, ONONDAGA CO., OUR LADY OF PEACE (1935) Rev. John E. Fetcho.
Res.: 203 Halcomb St., 13209. Tel: 315-487-6832; Fax: 315-487-9722. Email: ourladyofpeace@centralny.twcbc.com.
Catechesis/Religious Program—Students 76.

LEE CENTER, ONEIDA CO., ST. JOSEPH (1923) Rev. Paul V. Carey.
Res.: 5748 Strokes Lee Center Rd., 13363. Tel: 315-336-2661; Fax: 315-336-8418.
Parish Center—Tel: 315-339-1890.
Catechesis/Religious Program—Tel: 315-339-3080. Students 257.

LIVERPOOL, ONONDAGA CO.
1—CHRIST THE KING (1964) Rev. James C. Fritzen; Deacon Thomas Hachey.
21 Cherry Tree Cir., 13090.
Res.: 26 Cherry Tree Cir., 13090. Tel: 315-652-3233; 315-652-9266 (Parish Office); Fax: 315-652-5680.
Catechesis/Religious Program—Tel: 315-652-5782. Students 299.

2—IMMACULATE HEART OF MARY (1950) Rev. Daniel J. O'Hara; Sr. Rose Marie Caravaglio, C.S.J., Pastoral Assoc.
Res.: 425 Beechwood Ave., 13088. Tel: 315-457-8060; Fax: 315-451-2110.
Catechesis/Religious Program—Tel: 315-457-5367. Students 225.

3—ST. JOHN (1971) Rev. James T. O'Brien.
Res.: 8290 Soule Rd., 13090. Tel: 315-652-6591; Fax: 315-652-6631. Email: saintjohnsliverpool@verizon.net.
Catechesis/Religious Program—Tel: 315-652-1094. Students 466.

4—ST. JOSEPH THE WORKER (1890) Rev. Charles M. Major.
Res.: 1001 Tulip St., 13088. Tel: 315-457-6060; Fax: 315-457-4119. Email: admin@sjwchurch.org. Web: www.sjwkrchurch.org.
Catechesis/Religious Program—Tel: 315-453-7970. Students 355.

MAINE, BROOME CO., MOST HOLY ROSARY (1944) Rev. Clarence Cerwonka, Admin.
Res.: 2596 Main St., Box 248, 13802. Tel: 607-862-3216; Fax: 607-862-0096.
Catechesis/Religious Program—Tel: 607-862-4758. Students 140.

MANLIUS, ONONDAGA CO., ST. ANN (1920) Rev. Kevin Hannon; Deacon Gerard T. Pittman.
Res.: 104 Academy St., 13104. Tel: 315-682-5181; Fax: 315-682-5248. Email: stannschurch@twcny.rr.com.
Catechesis/Religious Program—Tel: 315-682-9443. Students 673.

MARATHON, CORTLAND CO., ST. STEPHEN (1870) Rev. Jerome A. Katz; Deacon Joseph Caminiti.
Res.: 12 Academy St., P.O. Box 475, 13803-0475. Tel: 607-849-3480; Fax: 607-849-4078. Email: presbyter@odssey.net.
Catechesis/Religious Program—Students 96.
Mission—Our Lady of Perpetual Help Cincinnatus, Cortland Co.

MARCELLUS, ONONDAGA CO., ST. FRANCIS XAVIER (1873) [CEM] Rev. J. Michael Donovan.
Res.: 1 W. Main St., P.O. Box 177, 13108. Tel: 315-673-2531; Fax: 315-673-9305.
Catechesis/Religious Program—53 North St., 13108. Tel: 315-673-4107. Students 453.

MATTYDALE, ONONDAGA CO., ST. MARGARET (1926) Revs. Robert P. Hyde; Cleophas Oseso Tuka (Africa); Deacon Donald R. Whiting.
Res.: 203 Roxboro Rd., 13211. Tel: 315-455-5534; Fax: 315-454-4102.
School—Tel: 315-455-5791; Fax: 315-455-1250. Ms. Susanne Donze, Prin. Lay Teachers 19; Students 276.
Catechesis/Religious Program—200 Roxboro Rd., 13211. Tel: 315-455-2203. Students 404.

MEXICO, OSWEGO CO., ST. ANNE, MOTHER OF MARY (1914) Rev. John Canorro; Deacon Daniel Caughey.
Res.: 3352 Main St., P.O. Box 487, 13114. Tel: 315-963-7182; Fax: 315-963-4032. Email: sstarofs@twcny.rr.com.
Catechesis/Religious Program—Fax: 315-963-4032. Students 142.

MINETTO, OSWEGO CO., OUR LADY OF PERPETUAL HELP (1932) Rev. Joseph M. Larkin.
Res.: West River Rd., P.O. Box 236, 13115. Tel: 315-343-7922.

MINOA, ONONDAGA CO., ST. MARY (1834) [CEM] Rev. Raynald Yudin, O.F.M.Conv.; Deacon Guy W. Hart.
Mailing Address: P.O. Box 550, Bridgeport, 13030.
Res.: 7820 Rte. 298, Bridgeport, 13030. Tel: 315-633-0712; Fax: 315-633-0672.
Office: Tel: 315-656-3441.
Catechesis/Religious Program—Tel: 315-656-4220. Email: dresmary@twcn.rr.com. Students 292.

MORRISVILLE, MADISON CO., ST. JOAN OF ARC (1931) Rev. Msgr. John R. Madden.
Parish Office—6 Brookside Dr., P.O. Box 1087, 13408. Tel: 315-684-9551.
St. Mary: 16 Wylie St., Hamilton, 13346. Tel: 315-824-2164. Email: stjoan@dreamscape.com.
Catechesis/Religious Program—Tel: 315-684-9527. Students 99.

MUNNSVILLE, MADISON CO., ST. THERESE OF THE INFANT JESUS (1926) Rev. Joseph F. Kehoe.
Res.: Main St., P.O. Box 735, 13409.
Catechesis/Religious Program—Students 8.

NEW BERLIN, CHENANGO CO., ST. THERESA OF THE INFANT JESUS (1955) Rev. Lester E. Smith, Admin.
Res. & Mailing Address: P.O. Box 780, 13411-0780. Tel: 607-847-6851.
Catechesis/Religious Program—Tel: 607-847-8732. Students 30.

NEW HARTFORD, ONEIDA CO.

1—ST. JOHN THE EVANGELIST (1883) Rev. Joseph S. Zareski.
Res.: 66 Oxford Rd., 13413. Tel: 315-732-8521; Fax: 315-735-1569.
Catechesis/Religious Program—One Sherman St., 13413. Tel: 315-724-4347. Sr. Martha Vincent Larkin, C.S.J., D.R.E. Students 800.

2—OUR LADY OF THE ROSARY (1949) Rev. Felix R. Colosimo.
Res.: 1736 Burrstone Rd., 13413. Tel: 315-724-0402.
Catechesis/Religious Program—Students 360.

3—ST. THOMAS (1957) Rev. G. David Sears. In Res., Rev. John M. Quinn.
Res.: 150 Clinton Rd., 13413. Tel: 315-735-8381.
Catechesis/Religious Program—Students 65.

NEW LONDON, ONEIDA CO., HOLY CROSS (1968) Closed. For inquiries for parish records please see St. Francis, Durhamville.

NEW YORK MILLS, ONEIDA CO., CHURCH OF SACRED HEART AND ST. MARY (1909) [CEM] Rev. Valentine C. Krul.
Res.: 201 Main St., 13417. Tel: 315-736-4432; Fax: 315-736-8079.
School— Consolidated. See separate listing under Institutions located in the Diocese.
Catechesis/Religious Program—Tel: 315-736-9132. Students 165.

NORTH BAY, ONEIDA CO., ST. JOHN (1843) [CEM] Rev. Leo J. Wimett.
Res.: P.O. Box 289, 13123. Tel: 315-245-0853.
Catechesis/Religious Program—Students 200.
Mission—St. Mary Verona Beach, Oneida Co. 13162.

NORTH SYRACUSE, ONONDAGA CO., ST. ROSE OF LIMA (1926) Rev. Msgr. James M. Kennedy; Revs. Daniel Heintz (Retired); Jerome Amaechi; Corinne Mullen, Pastoral Min.
Parish Office—409 S. Main St., 13212. Tel: 315-458-0283; Fax: 315-458-1290.
Res.: 407 S. Main St., 13212. Tel: 315-458-0283.
Preschool—Tel: 315-458-6036. Students 103.
School—(Grades K-6), 411 S. Main St., 13212. Tel: 315-458-6036; Fax: 315-458-6038. Sisters Catherine Laboure, Prin.; Jogues, Librarian. Sisters of the Third Franciscan Order (Syracuse, NY) 2; Lay Teachers 22; Students 269; Preschool 101.
Catechesis/Religious Program—Tel: 315-458-6592; Fax: 315-458-1290. Patricia Decker, D.R.E.; Douglas Pyke, Music Dir. Students 988.

NORWICH, CHENANGO CO.

1—ST. BARTHOLOMEW THE APOSTLE (1919), (Italian), Merged with St. Paul, Norwich to form Church of the Holy Apostles, St. Paul Roman Catholic Community of Norwich, NY.

2—ST. PAUL (1851) Merged with St. Bartholomew the Apostle, Norwich to form Roman Catholic Community of Norwich, St. Paul & St. Bartholomew.

3—ROMAN CATHOLIC COMMUNITY OF NORWICH, ST. PAUL & ST. BARTHOLOMEW, [CEM] Rev. Ralph A. Bove; Deacons David Kirsch; Timothy McNerney; Sr. Soosai Raj Rose Mary, Pastoral Min.
Parish Office & Res.: 30 Pleasant St., 13815. Tel: 607-336-2222; Fax: 607-337-2218; 607-334-6521. Email: stpaulstbart@citlink.net. Web: www.stbartstpaul.com.
Catechesis/Religious Program—Tel: 607-337-2001. Sr. Sellapan Jacqueline Mary, D.R.E. Students 229.
Convent—79 E. Main St., 13815. Tel: 607-337-2219.

ONEIDA, MADISON CO.

1—ST. JOSEPH (1893) Rev. Richard J. Kapral; Rev. Msgr. Matthew C. Luczycki (Retired).
Res.: 121 St. Joseph Pl., 13421. Tel: 315-363-3280; Fax: 315-363-3280. Email: stjosephr@twcny.rr.com.
Parish Center—111 St. Joseph Pl., 13421. Tel: 315-363-5061.
Catechesis/Religious Program—Students 145.

2—ST. PATRICK (1843) [CEM] Rev. Richard J. Kapral.
Res.: 347 Main St., 13421. Tel: 315-363-7570. Email: stpatschurch@earthlink.net.
School—354 Elizabeth St., 13421. Tel: 315-363-3620; Fax: 315-363-5075. Peg Brown, Prin. Lay Teachers 8; Students 130.
Catechesis/Religious Program—Lisa Spooner, D.R.E. Students 124.

ONONDAGA HILL, ONONDAGA CO., ST. MICHAEL & ST. PETER (1874) Rev. Henry J. Pedzich; Deacon Gregory Cross, Pastoral Assoc.
Res.: 4782 W. Seneca Tpke., 13215. Tel: 315-469-6995; Fax: 315-469-4388.
Catechesis/Religious Program—Tel: 315-469-6600. Students 407.

ORISKANY FALLS, ONEIDA CO., ST. JOSEPH (1870) [CEM] Rev. Vincent J. Kelly.
Res.: 229 Main St., 13425. Tel: 315-821-6122. Email: stjoe@tds.net.
Catechesis/Religious Program—Students 56.

ORISKANY, ONEIDA CO., ST. STEPHEN, PROTOMARTYR (1929) Closed. For inquiries for Parish records contact St. Paul, Whitesboro.

OSWEGO, OSWEGO CO.

1—ST. JOHN THE EVANGELIST (1869) Closed. For inquiries for parish records please see St. Mary, Oswego.

2—ST. JOSEPH (1915), (Italian), Rev. Andrew E. Baranski; Deacon Joseph Chillemi.
Mailing Address: 178 W. Second St., 13126. Tel: 315-343-2160.
Catechesis/Religious Program—Tel: 315-342-3967. Students 100.

3—ST. LOUIS (1870), (French), Closed. For inquiries for parish records, please contact St. Peter, Oswego.

4—ST. MARY (1848) Rev. Richard P. Morisette.
Res.: 103 W. Seventh St., 13126. Tel: 315-343-3953; Fax: 315-342-5538. Email: srectory@twcny.rr.com.
For futher information please see Trinity Catholic School under Consolidated Schools located in the Institution section
School—76 W. 6th St., 13126. Tel: 315-342-5538.
Catechesis/Religious Program—Tel: 315-343-7210. Students 150.

5—ST. PAUL (1840), (Irish), Rev. Gaetano T. Baccaro; Deacon George E. Maynard.
Res.: 50 E. Mohawk St., 13126. Tel: 315-343-2333; Fax: 315-343-2334. Email: stpaulparish@cnymail.com.
Church: 134 E. Fifth St., 13126.
For further information see Trinity Catholic School under Consolidated Schools in the Institution section
Catechesis/Religious Program—Students 143.

6—ST. PETER (1862), (German), Rev. George E. Wurz, Admin.
Res.: 83 E. Albany St., 13126. Tel: 315-343-1352.
Catechesis/Religious Program—Students 64.
Mission—Sacred Heart Scriba, Oswego Co. Tel: 315-342-5705.

7—ST. STEPHEN THE KING (1908), (Polish), Rev. Andrew E. Baranski.
Res.: 138 Niagara St., 13126. Tel: 315-343-0350; Fax: 315-343-0736.
Catechesis/Religious Program—Students 40.

OXFORD, CHENANGO CO., ST. JOSEPH (1849) [CEM] Rev. Thomas I. Ward.
Res.: 3 Scott St., P.O. Box 352, 13830. Tel: 607-843-7021; Fax: 607-843-7021. Email: stjoseph04@frontiernet.net.
Church: 1180 NY Hwy. 206, Greene, 13778.
Catechesis/Religious Program—Students 41.
Station—New York State Veterans' Home 13830. Tel: 607-843-3100.

PARISH, OSWEGO CO., ST. ANNE (1950) [CEM] Closed. Merged with St. Mary, Star of the Sea, Mexico to form St. Anne, Mother of Mary, Mexico.

PHOENIX, OSWEGO CO., ST. STEPHEN (1880) Rev. Philip C. Brockmyre, Admin.; Deacon Frank Forish.
Res.: 469 Main St., 13135. Tel: 315-695-4531; Fax: 315-695-2176.
Catechesis/Religious Program—Tel: 315-695-4608. Students 147.

POMPEY, ONONDAGA CO., IMMACULATE CONCEPTION (1850) [CEM] Rev. James H. Carey, Admin.
Res.: 7386 Academy St., 13138. Tel: 315-677-3061; Fax: 315-677-2873.
Catechesis/Religious Program—Tel: 315-677-5126. Students 90.

PULASKI, OSWEGO CO., CHRIST OUR LIGHT (2003) Rev. Jozef Mucha (Poland).
23 Niagara St., 13142-4425. Tel: 315-298-5350; 315-298-3863 (Res.); Fax: 315-298-3749. Email: col23@gmail.com.
Catechesis/Religious Program—Students 105.

ROME, ONEIDA CO.

1—ST. JOHN THE BAPTIST (1909), (Italian), [CEM] Rev. John F. Hogan Jr.
Res.: 210 E. Dominick St., 13440. Tel: 315-337-0990; Fax: 315-336-3841. Email: rstjohn@twcny.rr.com.
Catechesis/Religious Program—Students 169.

2—ST. MARY OF THE ASSUMPTION (1848) [CEM] Rev. Philip A. Hearn. In Res., Rev. Msgr. Francis J. Culkin (Retired).
Res.: 210 W. Liberty St., 13440. Tel: 315-336-4832; Fax: 315-339-2744.
Catechesis/Religious Program—Students 48.
Station—Betsy Ross HRF

3—ST. PAUL (1954) Rev. Robert L. Kelly; Deacon Edgar Doyle Jr. In Res., Rev. Msgr. William M. Kelly, Pastor Emeritus (Retired).
Res.: 1807 Bedford St., 13440-2199. Tel: 315-336-3082; Fax: 315-336-3083. Email: stpaulsrome@twcny.rr.com.
Catechesis/Religious Program—Tel: 315-334-9570. Students 157.

4—ST. PETER (1837) [CEM] Revs. Philip A. Hearn; Bernard Osei Ampong (Ghana); Sisters Elizabeth Colby, C.S.J., Pastoral Assoc.; Phyllis Wulforst, C.S.J., Pastoral Assoc.; Rosaire Anne De Mare, C.S.J., Pastoral Assoc. & Admin. Asst. In Res., Rev. James A. Culver (Retired).
Res.: 105 E. Liberty St., P.O. Box 627, 13442. Tel: 315-336-5072; 315-337-8307. Email: rstpeter@twcny.rr.com.
Catechesis/Religious Program—Tel: 315-336-5066; Fax: 315-336-0855. Students 334.

5—TRANSFIGURATION (1909), (Polish), Rev. Lucian Urbaniak. In Res., Rev. William C. Cahill.
Res.: 111 Ridge St., 13440. Tel: 315-336-1152; Fax: 315-339-5931. Email: lucian1960@adelphia.net.
Catechesis/Religious Program—Students 33.

SANITARIA SPRINGS, BROOME CO., ST. JOSEPH (1914) Rev. Kevin J. Bunger, Admin.
Res.: 659 New York Rte. 7, P.O. Box 429, Port Crane, 13833. Tel: 607-648-5209; Fax: 607-648-3570.

SHERBURNE, CHENANGO CO., ST. MALACHY (1858) [CEM] Rev. Lester E. Smith, Admin.
Mailing Address: 29 E. State St., P.O. Box 722, 13460-0722. Tel: 607-674-9625; Fax: 607-674-2792. Email: st_malachy_sherburne@yahoo.com.
Catechesis/Religious Program—Tel: 315-674-4628. Students 80.

SHERRILL, ONEIDA CO., ST. HELENA (1917) Rev. William A. Mesmer.
Res.: 210 Primo Ave., 13461. Tel: 315-363-3882. Email: shelenarectory@twcny.rr.com.
Catechesis/Religious Program—Tel: 315-361-1566. Students 230.

SKANEATELES, ONONDAGA CO., ST. MARY OF THE LAKE (1855) [CEM] Rev. Thomas J. McGrath.
Mailing Address: 10 W. Austin St., 13152.
Res.: 81 Jordan St., 13152. Tel: 315-685-5083; Fax: 315-685-8327. Email: stmarys13152@yahoo.com.
Catechesis/Religious Program—Tel: 315-685-6377. Students 303.

SOLVAY, ONONDAGA CO., ST. CECILIA (1903), (Italian), Revs. George F. Hartnett; Paul Machira (Africa); Deacon Julius Kulak.
Res.: 1001 Woods Rd., 13209. Tel: 315-488-3221; Fax: 315-488-3222. Email: stcecilia@espeedusa.com.
Catechesis/Religious Program—Tel: 315-488-4648. Students 172.

SOUTH ONONDAGA, ONONDAGA CO., CORPUS CHRISTI (1938) Rev. Dennis J. Hayes.
Res.: P.O. Box 288, Marietta, 13110. Tel: 315-492-0814. Email: dennish@dreamscape.com.
Church: 3126 Cedarvale Rd., R.D. 1, Nedrow, 13120. Tel: 315-492-0814.
Catechesis/Religious Program—Students 152.
Mission—St. Patrick [CEM] P.O. Box 574, Marietta, Onondaga Co. 13110. Tel: 315-696-8601.

TABERG, ONEIDA CO., ST. PATRICK (1876) [CEM] Rev. Francis A. Wapen.
Res.: 9168 Main St., 13471. Tel: 315-336-4079.
Catechesis/Religious Program—Students 64.

TRUXTON, CORTLAND CO., ST. PATRICK (1854) [CEM] Revs. Daniel C. Muscalino, Admin.; James D. Tormey, Temporary Admin.; Deacon Laurence Brickner.
Res.: 3656 Rte. 13, Box 15, 13158. Tel: 607-842-6326.
Mission—St. Lawrence De Ruyter, Madison Co.

TULLY, ONONDAGA CO., ST. LEO (1891) Revs. James H. Carey; John Kurgan.
10 Onondaga St., P.O. Box 574, 13159. Tel: 315-696-5092.
Res.: 6104 US Rte. 20, P.O. Box 169, La Fayette, 13084. Tel: 315-677-3439; Fax: 315-696-8721.
Catechesis/Religious Program—Students 140.

UTICA, ONEIDA CO.

1—ST. AGNES (1887) Rev. Msgr. Francis J. Willenburg.
Res.: 700 Kossuth Ave., 13501. Tel: 315-735-5273; Fax: 315-735-2887. Email: agnes700@cs.com.
Catechesis/Religious Program—Program merged with St. Anthony of Padua, Utica. Students 150.
Convent—783 Blandina St., 13501. Tel: 315-732-1078.

2—ST. ANTHONY OF PADUA (1911), (Italian), Rev. Anthony LaFache; Deacon William Dischiavo, Sec.
Res.: 422 Tilden Ave., 13501. Tel: 315-732-1177.
Catechesis/Religious Program—Tel: 315-732-1177, Ext. 3151. Students 370.

3—BLESSED SACRAMENT (1924) Closed. Merged with St. Mary of Mt. Carmel, Utica to form St. Mary of Mt. Carmel/Blessed Sacrament.

4—ST. FRANCIS DE SALES (1876) Closed. Merged with St. John's, Utica. Parish records available at St. John's, Utica.

5—ST. GEORGE (1911), (Lithuanian), [CEM] Closed. For inquiries for parish records contact St. Joseph and St. Patrick, Utica.

6—HOLY TRINITY (1896), (Polish), [CEM] Rev. Arthur R. Hapanowicz.
Res.: 1206 Lincoln Ave., 13502. Tel: 315-724-7238.
Catechesis/Religious Program—Tel: 315-733-5492. Students 46.
Convent—1218 Lincoln Ave., 13502. Tel: 315-733-5492; Fax: 315-733-5492.

7—ST. JOHN (1819) Revs. John A. Buehler; Luis Olguin, Spanish Apostolate. Tel: 315-724-0389; Sisters Sharon Whellahan, C.S.J., Pastoral Assoc.; Joan Corcoran, D.C., Pastoral Assoc. & Outreach; Michelle Nguyen, D.C., Youth & Vietnamese Ministry; Deacon William R. Dischiavo, Pastoral Assoc. In Res., Rev. John P. Flanagan (Retired).
Res.: 240 Bleecker St., 13501. Tel: 315-724-6159. Email: historicstjohns@roadrunner.com.
Parish Center—520 John St., 13501. Tel: 315-732-2417. Nancy Manley.
Catechesis/Religious Program—Tel: 315-732-1334. Students 157.

8—ST. JOSEPH AND ST. PATRICK (1841 and 1849) [CEM] Rev. Richard E. Dellos; Deacon Gilbert Nadeau.
Res.: 702 Columbia St., 13502. Tel: 315-735-4429; Fax: 315-735-1691. Email: sjs@verizon.net.
Catechesis/Religious Program—Students 61.

9—ST. MARK (1963) Rev. Mark A. Pasik; Deacon Richard Prusko.
Res.: 440 Keyes Rd., 13502. Tel: 315-724-1645.
Catechesis/Religious Program—Students 200.

10—ST. MARY (1870), (German), Closed. For inquiries for parish records contact St. John, Utica.

11—ST. MARY OF MT. CARMEL/BLESSED SACRAMENT (1896) Rev. James M. Cesta; Anthony Elacqua, Dir. Maintenance; Mary Beth La Neve, Business Admin.; Peter Elacqua, Dir. In Res., Rev. Luis Olguin.
Res.: 648 Jay St., 13501. Tel: 315-735-1482; Fax: 315-735-9806. Email: mtcutica@aol.com.
Catechesis/Religious Program—Tel: 315-724-3950. Constance Armstrong, Dir. Faith Formation. Students 157.

12—OUR LADY OF LOURDES (1919) Revs. Joseph A. Salerno; Paul J. Alciati; Deacon William P. Hotaling; Sisters Julia Coyle, S.A.; Elizabeth Mary Paciello, C.S.J.; Lois Mary Paciello, C.S.J.
Res.: 2 Barton Ave., 13502. Tel: 315-724-3155; Fax: 315-732-3770.
See Our Lady of Lourdes, Utica under Consolidated Schools located in the Institution section.
Catechesis/Religious Program—Students 276.

13—ST. PETER (1872) [CEM] Rev. David J. Orzel.
Res.: 422 Coventry Ave., 13502. Tel: 315-724-6310; Fax: 315-724-4942.
Catechesis/Religious Program—Tel: 315-735-7077. Students 234.

14—SACRED HEART (1926) Closed. For inquiries for parish records contact St. Mary, New York Mills.

15—ST. STANISLAUS (1911), (Polish), [CEM] Rev. Msgr. Casimir J. Krzysiak.
Res.: P.O. Box 324, 13503. Tel: 315-732-5919.

VERNON, ONEIDA CO., HOLY FAMILY (1926; 1976) Rev. William A. Mesmer.
Res.: 4343 Peterboro St., P.O. Box 988, 13476. Tel: 315-829-3295.
Catechesis/Religious Program—Tel: 315-829-2820. Students 165.

VERONA, ONEIDA CO., OUR LADY OF GOOD COUNSEL (1913) Rev. Edmund J. Morelle.
Res.: 5259 Beacon Light Rd., P.O. Box 135, 13478. Tel: 315-363-7696. Email: ologcc@dreamscape.com.
Church: 5652 E. Main St., P.O. Box 135, 13478.
Catechesis/Religious Program—Students 100.

VESTAL, BROOME CO.

1—OUR LADY OF SORROWS (1941) Rev. John P. Putano; Deacon Dale Crotsley. In Res., Rev. Matthew F. Brown (Retired).
Res.: 157 Clark St., 13850-2494. Tel: 607-748-8287; Fax: 607-748-8016. Email: olsorrows@stny.rr.com.
Catechesis/Religious Program—Tel: 607-748-4766. Students 595.

2—ST. VINCENT DE PAUL (1965) Rev. James D. Tormey; Deacon James P. Crowley. In Res., Rev. Robert J. Sullivan (Retired).
Res.: 165 Clifton Blvd., 13850. Tel: 607-722-3988; Fax: 607-722-8787. Email: stvincentdepaul@stny.rr.com.
Catechesis/Religious Program—465 Clubhouse Rd., 13850. Tel: 607-722-8372. Students 169.

WARNERS, ONONDAGA CO., OUR LADY OF GOOD COUNSEL (1913) Merged with St. Joseph, Camillus.

WATERVILLE, ONEIDA CO., ST. BERNARD (1850) [CEM] Rev. Thomas R. Servatius.
Res.: 199 Stafford Ave., 13480. Tel: 315-841-4481. Email: sbwat1@yahoo.com.
Catechesis/Religious Program—Students 104.

WHITESBORO, ONEIDA CO.

1—ST. ANNE (1965), Merged with St. Paul's Whitesboro. Rev. Thomas M. Durant, Admin.
Res.: 16 Park Ave., 13492.
Church: 8539 Clark Mill Rd., 13492-2754. Tel: 315-736-7672.
Catechesis/Religious Program—Students 263.

2—ST. PAUL (1883) Rev. Thomas M. Durant.
Res.: 16 Park Ave., 13492. Tel: 315-736-1124; Fax: 315-768-7915.
Catechesis/Religious Program—Tel: 315-736-4807. Students 454.

WHITNEY POINT, BROOME CO., THE CATHOLIC COMMUNITY OF ST. STEPHEN-ST. PATRICK (1869) [CEM] Rev. Jerome A. Katz.
Res.: Box 711, 13862. Fax: 607-692-7171; Tel: 607-692-3911.
Catechesis/Religious Program—Students 65.
Mission—Our Lady of Perpetual Help Cincinnatus, Cortland Co. 13040.

WINDSOR, BROOME CO., OUR LADY OF LOURDES (1947) Rev. John J. Booth. In Res., Rev. Paul J. Keebler (Retired).
Res.: 594 Kent St., P.O. Box 361, 13865. Tel: 607-655-2116.
Catechesis/Religious Program—Tel: 607-655-8118. Students 89.

Chaplains of Public Institutions
Hospitals

SYRACUSE. *St. Camillus Health & Rehab Center*, 813 Fay Rd., 13219. Tel: 315-488-2951. Ms. Kathy Falso, Pastoral Care Coord.
Community General Hospital, 4900 Broad Rd., 13215. Tel: 315-492-5011. Sr. Winifred Guinan, O.S.F.
Crouse Irving Memorial Hospital, 736 Irving Ave., 13210. Tel: 315-470-7615. Rev. Robert P. Hyde, J.C.L., Sr. Mary Frances Cannon.
James Square Nursing Home. Attended from Blessed Sacrament Parish.
St. Joseph's Hospital Health Center, 301 Prospect Ave., 13203. Tel: 315-448-5116. Sisters Marie Therese Nicholson, O.S.F., Patrice Ward, O.S.F., Mary Louise Williams, O.S.F., Jacqueline Spiridlozzi, Dir., Frances Agnes Ryan, Mary Daniel Golmbieski, Patricia Scofield, Jane Patrick, Adelbert Durant, O.S.F.
Loretto Geriatric Center, 700 E. Brighton Ave., 13205. Tel: 315-469-5570.
Rosewood Heights Nursing Home, Tel: 315-474-4431. Sr. Frances Ann Thom, O.S.F.
University Hospital, 750 E. Adams St., 13210. Tel: 315-464-5540. Rev. Innocent Onyenagubo (Nigeria), Chap., Sr. Monica Czechowicz.
Van Duyn Home & Hospital, 5060 W. Seneca Tpke., 13215. Tel: 315-469-5511. Mrs. Janice Rosbrook.
Veterans Administration Hospital, Res: 800 Irving Ave., 13210. Tel: 315-476-7461. Revs. Wilfred F. Evans (Retired), David J. James, Chap.

BINGHAMTON. *Binghamton General Hospital*, Tel: 607-762-2200. Rev. John E. Mikalajunas, Sr. Annellen Kelly.
Binghamton Psychiatric Hospital. Revs. John J. Booth, Gerald J. Buckley (Retired).
Our Lady of Lourdes Memorial Hospital, 179 Riverside Dr., 13905. Tel: 607-798-5111. Sr. Ann Molesevick, D.C., Dir., Rev. Krzysztof Boretto, Bro. James Bagana, Sisters Kathleen Haley, Maureen Rainone, Laura Allen.

JOHNSON CITY. *Wilson Memorial Hospital*, 33 Harrison St., 13790. Tel: 607-763-6000.

LIVERPOOL. *Developmental Center*, 36 Grampian Rd., #5, 13090. Rev. Charles A. Aho.

UTICA. *St. Elizabeth Hospital*, 2209 Genesee St., 13501. Tel: 315-798-8100. Rev. John H. Comeskey (Retired), Sisters Irene Zegarelli, O.S.F., Anthony Marie Eddo.
Faxton Hospital, 1676 Sunset Ave., 13502. Tel: 315-738-6545. Sr. Maureen Denn, C.S.J.
St. Luke, 1656 Champlin Ave., 13503. Tel: 315-798-6000. Sr. Genevieve Ciscek, C.S.J.

VESTAL. *Binghamton Nursing Homes*, Our Lady of Sorrows, 157 Clark St., 13850. Tel: 607-748-8287. Rev. Matthew F. Brown, Pastoral Care Chap. (Retired).

Psychiatric Facilities

BINGHAMTON. *Binghamton Psychiatric Hospital*, Tel: 607-724-1391. Revs. John J. Booth, Gerald J. Buckley (Retired).

MARCY. *Central New York Psychiatric Center*, Old River Rd., Box 330, 13403. Tel: 315-736-8271. Rev. Richard V. O'Neill (Retired).

UTICA. *Mohawk Valley Psychiatric Center*, 1400 Noyes at York, 13502. Rev. Frederick D. Daley.

Jails

SYRACUSE. *Elmcrest Children's Center*, Salt Springs Rd., 13224. Vacant.
Hillbrook Detention Center, 4949 Velasko Rd., 13215. Tel: 315-492-1721. Sr. Judith Falk.
Jail Ministry Office, 208 Slocum Ave., 13204. Tel: 315-424-1877. Mary Czelusniak.
Public Safety Building, 259 E. Onondaga St., 13202. Rev. John C. Schopfer.

BINGHAMTON. *Broome County Jail*. Rev. Stanley J. Gerlock (Retired).

CORTLAND. *Cortland County Jail*. Vacant.

GEORGETOWN. *Camp Georgetown*, 31 E. State St., Sheburne, 13346. Tel: 315-837-4446. Rev. Edmund A. Castronovo.

JAMESVILLE. *Jamesville Penitentiary*, P.O. Box 143, 13078. Tel: 315-469-5581. Rev. Edward J. Reimer, Sr. Maura Rhode.

MARCY. *Mid-State Correctional Facility*, 210 W. Liberty St., 13403. Tel: 315-768-8581. Rev. Robert C. Weber.

MOHAWK. *Oneida Correctional Facility I.*, P.O. Box 8450, Rome, 13440. Tel: 315-339-6880. Rev. William C. Cahill.
Oneida Correctional Facility II, 578 Main St., P.O. Box 8450, Oneida, 13421. Deacon James Chappell.

NORWICH. *Norwich County Jail*. Vacant.

ORISKANY. *Oneida County Jail*, 120 Dexter Ave., 13424. Tel: 315-736-9033. Rev. Richard J. Stuczko (Retired).

OSWEGO. *Oswego County Jail*, 178 W. Second St., 13126. Tel: 315-343-2160. Rev. James M. Cesta.

ROME. *Walsh Facility*, Tel: 315-339-5232. Rev. Luis Olguin.

SOUTH PLYMOUTH. *Camp Pharsalia*. Rev. Edmund A. Castronovo.

UTICA. *Marcy Correctional Facility*, 15-8 Rox Pl., 13502. Tel: 315-768-1400. Deacon William Hotaling.

Special Assignment:
Most Revs.—
Costello, Thomas J., D.D. (Retired)
Cunningham, Robert J., D.D.
Moynihan, James M., D.D. (Retired)
Rev. Msgrs.—
Quartier, Neal E.
Sheehan, George F.
Revs.—
Aho, Charles A.
Auth, Clifford H., J.C.L.
Cahill, William C.
Carmola, Michael J.
Chryst, Robert D. Tel: 315-422-9390
Jones, Robert S.
Lang, James P.
Muscalino, Daniel C.
Olguin, Luis
Ours, Robert A.
Phillips, Joseph H.
Pompei, Frederick A.
Sambor, David R.
Schopfer, John C.
Sullivan, Robert J. (Retired)
Vavonese, Charles S.
Weber, Robert C.

On Duty Outside the Diocese:
Rev. Msgrs.—
Fahey, Charles J., Fordham University, New York.
Rossetti, Stephen
Revs.—
Bassano, Michael, M.M., Mary Knoll (Incardinated)
Cincotta, Anthony
Creed, Peter, St. Mary's Star of the Sea, Fort Monroe, VA 23651.
Gantley, Mark
Keane, Philip S., S.S.
Nichols, Louis J.
Wallace, Harry C.
Woolever, James

Military Chaplains:
Rev. Msgr.—
Elkin, Frederic F., 3942 Roebling Ln., Virginia Beach, VA 23452.
Revs.—
Dunn, Richard B., PSC 2 Box 953, APO, AP 96264.
Fukes, Gary M., 1st Lt. & Chap., 1420 Waterford Place #7, Manhattan, KS 66502.
Gryga, Theodore, U.S. Navy
Madej, Paul D., 3017 N. Institute St., Colorado Springs, CO 80907. U.S. Navy

On Sabbatical:
Rev.—
Jones, William R.

Absent on Leave:
Revs.—
Broderick, John W.
Carman, Paul
McNally, Edward F.
Wolak, Edmund

Retired:
Rev. Msgrs.—
Bill, Ronald C., Immaculate Conception Rectory, 400 Salt Springs St., Fayetteville, 13060.
Brigandi, Paul A.
Culkin, Francis J.
Davern, Robert
Donovan, William
Eckermann, Charles H.
Kane, James D.
Kantor, Adolph A.
Kelly, William M.
Luczycki, Matthew C.
Lutz, James M.
McCloskey, James A.
McGraw, John T.
Revs.—
Baehr, David, 1633 Leisure Dr., M-37, Bradenton, FL 34207.
Baker, William S., Clayville, NY
Bauer, Donald J., St. Joseph's Nursing Home.
Bebel, Alfred J., Binghamton, NY
Brown, Matthew F.
Buckley, Gerald J.
Comeskey, John H.
Culver, James A.
Durr, Edmund J., Bridgeport, NY
Esposito, William C., 104 David Dr., North Syracuse, 13212.
Evans, Wilfred F.
Flanagan, John P., St. John's Rectory, 240 Bleeker St., 13501-2216.
Florczyk, Walter
Fuchs, Moritz A.
Gerlock, Stanley J., Binghamton, NY
Gleba, William P.
Heagerty, John J.
Heintz, Daniel
Jutton, David J.
Kane, Joseph F.
Keebler, Paul J., Windsor, NY
Keeffe, Anthony J., 1124 Oak St., 13203.
Kiernan, Thomas
Lauducci, James V.
Libera, Angelo
Mattice, George F.
Morbito, Angelo L.
Murphy, Daniel G.
Nortz, Alfred E.
O'Neill, Richard V., St. George Rectory, 425 LaFayette St., 13502.
Pilat, Edmund S.
Pilla, P. Carl
Regan, William P.
Roark, John D.
Sizing, Theodore C.
Slater, Dennis
Stuczko, Richard J.
Thompson, Richard R., 1633 Leisure Dr., Apt. M37, Bradenton, FL 34207.
Tucker, Richard
Wagner, John P.
Wood, Raymond B.

Permanent Deacons:
Altmeter, Robert, Norwich
Alvaro, Nick A., Syracuse
Ashe, Wayne, (Retired), Kirkville
Ashley, John, (Retired), Binghamton
Blaine, Edward, Endicott
Bonocore, Steven J., Skaneateles
Borchert, Robert, (On Leave)
Brickner, Lawrence, Marathon
Brody, John P., (Retired)
Caminiti, Joseph, Cortland
Caughey, Daniel, Pulaski, NY
Celentano, Joseph, Sr., Syracuse
Chappell, James C., Oneida
Chillemi, Joseph, Oswego
Cholette, Frederick, Liverpool
Collins, John H., Pennellville
Connelly, Robert, Syracuse, NY
Crosby, James P., Syracuse (On Leave)
Cross, Gregory
Crossett, Thomas F., (Retired), Johnson City (On Leave)
Crotsley, Dale, Vestal
Crowley, James, (Retired), Vestal
Daniszewski, Joseph, Syracuse
Dischiavo, William R., Utica
Distin, Leslie, Johnson City
Dotterer, William A., Liverpool
Downes, Timothy, Tully
Doyle, Edgar A., Rome, NY
During, Joseph
Dwyer, Richard J., (Retired)
Engle, Christopher
Forish, Frank M., Baldwinsville
Goskowski, Raymond, Binghamton
Gudaitis, Michael, Rome
Hachey, Thomas, North Syracuse
Harley, Thomas, Endicott
Hart, Guy W., Bridgeport
Hazard, Wilbur, (Retired)
Heizman, Bernard, (Retired), La Fayette
Hotaling, William P., Utica
Joslin, Donald E., (On Leave)
Kearney, Garrett, Syracuse
Kehoe, Phillip, Fulton, NY
Kernan, Edward, New Hartford
Kirsch, David, Norwich
Kopec, John, NY Mills
Kotch, Myron, (Eastern Rite), Syracuse
Kulak, Jules F., Solvay
Lalande, John, Oswego
Longo, Frank, (On Leave)
Manzene, Stephen, Liverpool
Maynard, George E., Clay
McCabe, Donald, Syracuse
McGrath, Michael B., Syracuse
McNerney, Timothy, Norwich
Money, Kenneth, (On Leave)
Morse, James L., Syracuse
Mullin, Paul, (Retired)
Mulvey, John, (On Leave)
Murray, John, Manlius
Nadeau, Gilbert, Utica
Needham, Leo I., (Retired), Syracuse
Niles, Elbert, Oneida
Page, Warren C., Syracuse
Paparella, Anthony, Whitesboro
Paratore, Anthony J.
Phillips, George, Endwell
Picciano, Thomas N.
Pittman, Gerard, Fayetteville
Powers, Paul F., (Retired)
Prusko, Richard, Utica, NY
Riggalls, Robert, Sr., (Retired), Waterville
Rosher, Nicholas, Rome, NY
Rossi, Dominick (Ghana), (Retired)
Smith, Steve, Cortland
Stella, John, Binghamton
Sweenie, David, Oswego
Talomie, Robert J., Baldwinsville
Timson, Frank
Uryniak, Adolph J.
Vanelli, Peter P., Syracuse
Warren, Frank, (Retired), Oswego, NY
Whiting, Donald R., North Syracuse
Wilber, Richard, Chesire, CT, (On Leave)
Woloszyn, John, Liverpool
Young, Stephen, Cazenovia
Klockowski, Daniel A. (NTN), Utica; Eastern Rite

INSTITUTIONS LOCATED IN THE DIOCESE

[A] SEMINARIES, RELIGIOUS, OR SCHOLASTICATES

SYRACUSE. *Saint Andrew Hall*, 420 Demong Dr., 13214-1499. Tel: 315-445-3500; Fax: 315-446-9472. Revs. Joseph E. Lingan, S.J., Rector & Dir. Novices; Thomas G. Benz, S.J., Asst. Dir. Novices; Charles Healey, S.J., Asst. Dir. Novices. Novitiate for the Maryland, New England, and New York Provinces, Society of Jesus. Priests 3; Novices 14.

[B] COLLEGES AND UNIVERSITIES

SYRACUSE. *Le Moyne College*, 1419 Salt Springs Rd., 13214-1302. Tel: 315-445-4100; Fax: 315-445-4540. Web: www.lemoyne.edu. Dr. Fred P. Pestello, Ph.D., Pres.; Dr. Linda M. LeMura, Interim Provost & Vice Pres. for Academic Affairs; Dr. Shawn L. Ward, Vice Pres. Student Devel.; Mr. Roger W. Stackpoole, Vice Pres. Fin. & Admin.; Mrs. Barbara M. Karper, Asst. Vice Pres. Campus Programs & Multicultural Affairs; Mr. Mark G. Godelski, Dir. Residence Life & Coord. Judicial Affairs; Dr. Julie Grossman, Acting Dean, Arts & Sciences; Mrs. Mary M. Chandler, Registrar; Dr. Dennis DePerro, Vice Pres., Enrollment Mgmt.; Dr. Salwa Ammar, Dean Mgmt.; Mrs. Juliahn Galler Sims, Interim Vice Pres. for Inst. Advancement; Mr. Shawn Black, Acting Dir. for Information Technology. A private four-year comprehensive college founded in 1946 enrolling approximately 3,500 students in a program of liberal arts, sciences, business and pre-professional studies. Le Moyne offers 30 academic majors leading to BA and BS degrees and also offers graduate programs in business administration, education, nursing and physician assistant studies. Jesuits 5; Brothers 1; Sisters 1; Lay Teachers 151; Total Enrollment 3,479.

[C] HIGH SCHOOLS, DIOCESAN

SYRACUSE. *Bishop Ludden Junior/Senior High School*, (Grades 7-12), 815 Fay Rd., 13219. Tel: 315-468-2591; Fax: 315-468-0097. Email: blhs@syrdiocese.org. Mr. Curtis Czarniak, Prin.; John Bruzdzinski, Asst. Prin.; Parker O'Mara, Librarian. Priests 1; Sisters 1; Lay Teachers 41; Students 402.

BINGHAMTON. *Seton Catholic Central High School of Broome County*, 70 Seminary Ave., 13905. Tel: 607-723-5307; Fax: 607-723-4601. Email: secathb@syrdiocese.org. Ms. Kathleen M. Dwyer, Prin.; Dr. Anchen Schulz, Asst. Prin.; Rev. Robert A. Ours; Ms. Kathryn Frech, Librarian. Priests 1; Sisters 1; Deacons 1; Lay Teachers 28; Students 330.

EAST SYRACUSE. *Bishop Grimes Jr./Sr. High School*, (Grades 7-12), 6653 Kirkville Rd., 13057. Tel: 315-437-0356; Fax: 315-437-0358. Email: bghs@syrdiocese.org. Sr. James Therese Downey, Prin.; Mrs. Cathleen Hendrick, Librarian. Sisters 2; Brothers 2; Lay Teachers 41; Students 450.

UTICA. *Notre Dame Jr./Sr. High School*, 2 Notre Dame Ln., 13502. Tel: 315-724-5118; Fax: 315-724-9460. Email: amcollins@syrdiocese.org. Sr. Anna Mae Collins, C.S.J., Prin.; Mr. Roy Kane, Assoc. Prin.; Deborah Danquer, Librarian. Sisters 3; Lay Teachers 35; Students 385.

[D] HIGH SCHOOLS, PRIVATE

SYRACUSE. *Christian Brothers Academy*, (Grades 7-12), 6245 Randall Rd., 13214. Tel: 315-446-5960; Fax: 315-446-3393. Web: www.cbasyracuse.org. Bro. Joseph Jozwiak, F.S.C., Prin. Brothers of the Christian Schools 3; Lay Teachers 56; Students 750; Sisters of Third Order of St. Francis 2.

[E] CONSOLIDATED SCHOOLS

SYRACUSE. *Bishop's Academy at Most Holy Rosary*, (Grades PreK-6), 1031 Bellevue Ave., 13207-1399. Tel: 315-476-6035; Fax: 315-476-1029. Melanie Carroll, Prin. Consolidated Elementary Schools, Syracuse. Religious 2; Lay Teachers 16; Students 128.

Bishop's Academy at St. Charles, (Grades PreK-6), 200 W. High Terr., 13219-2497. Tel: 315-488-7631; Fax: 315-488-0617. Sr. Donna Driscoll, Prin. Consolidated Elementary Schools, Syracuse. Religious 2; Lay Teachers 14; Students 95.

Cathedral Academy at Pompei, (Grades PreK-6), 923 N. McBride St., 13208-2670. Tel: 315-422-8548; Fax: 315-472-0754. Charles LaBarbera, Prin.; Rose Ann Sunser, Librarian. Cathedral and Our Lady of Pompei. Religious 1; Lay Teachers 14; Students 100.

BINGHAMTON. *St. John the Evangelist*, (Grades PreK-8), 9 Livingston St., 13903. Tel: 607-723-0703; Fax: 607-772-6210. Email: mekelley@syrdiocese.org. Mary Ellen Kelley, Prin. Religious 2; Lay Teachers 17; Students 157.

St. Thomas Aquinas, (Grades PreK-3), 3 Aquinas St., 13905. Tel: 607-797-6528; Fax: 607-797-6541. Email: sthomasb@syracusediocese.org. Mrs. Suzanne Miller, Prin. Lay Teachers 15; Students 69.

ENDICOTT. *Seton Catholic Middle School*, (Grades 5-8), 1112 Broad St., 13760. Tel: 607-748-7423; Fax: 607-484-9576. Email: setonmid@syracusediocese.org. JoAnne Rowan, Prin. Lay Teachers 15; Students 129.

FAIRMOUNT. *Bishop's Academy at Holy Family*, (Grades PreK-6), 130 Chapel Dr., 13219-1920. Tel: 315-487-8515; Fax: 315-487-8515. Helen Chajka, Prin. Consolidated Elementary Schools, Syracuse. Lay Teachers 22; Students 203.

JOHNSON CITY. *St. James Middle School*, (Grades 4-8), 143 Main St., 13790. Tel: 607-797-5444; Fax: 607-797-6794. Email: ePrincipal@aol.com. George Clancy, Prin. Sisters 2; Lay Teachers 13; Students 122.

NORWICH. *Holy Family School*, (Grades PreK-8), 17 Prospect St., 13815. Tel: 607-337-2207; Fax: 607-337-2210. Email: hfamilyn@syrdiocese.org. Mr. Gene Chilion, Prin. Lay Teachers 15; Students 85.

OSWEGO. *Trinity Catholic School*, (Grades PreK-6), 115 E. 5th St., 13126. Tel: 315-343-6700; Fax: 315-342-9471. Mr. David Friedlander, Admin. Lay Teachers 7; Students 103.

ROME. *Rome Catholic School*, (Grades PreK-12), 800 Cypress St., 13440. Tel: 315-363-3620; Fax: 315-363-5075. Mrs. Barbara A. Jacques, Prin.; Mrs. Dyanna Gardinier, Librarian. Lay Teachers 20; Students 286.

UTICA. *Notre Dame Elementary School*, (Grades PreK-6), 11 Barton Ave., 13502. Tel: 315-732-4374; Fax: 315-738-9720. Email: lourdesu@syrdiocese.org. Web: www.lourdes-school.org. Ms. Judy Hauck, Prin.; Angeline Lubey, Librarian. Lay Teachers 25; Students 392.

VESTAL. *Our Lady of Sorrows - Seton Middle*, (Grades PreK-4), 1112 Broad St., Endicott, 13760. Tel: 607-748-7423. Email: setonmid@syrdiocese.org. Margaret Di Fulvio, Prin. Lay Teachers 15; Students 129.

[F] CATHOLIC CHARITIES OF SYRACUSE

SYRACUSE. *Bishop Joseph T. O'Keefe, Inc.*, c/o 240 E. Onondaga St., 13202. Tel: 315-424-1830; Fax: 315-478-4619. Most Rev. Robert J. Cunningham, D.D.; Rev. Clifford H. Auth, J.C.L., Chancellor; Most Rev. Thomas J. Costello, D.D., Vicar Gen. (Retired).

Catholic Charities of the Roman Catholic Diocese of Syracuse, 240 E. Onondaga St., 13202. Tel: 315-470-1415; Fax: 315-478-4619. Email: jslavik@syracusediocese.org. Web: www.syrdio.org. Mr. Joseph G. Slavik, Diocesan Dir.

Catholic Charities Onondaga County: Mr. Michael F. Melara, County Exec.

1654 W. Onondaga St., 13204. Tel: 315-424-1800; Fax: 315-424-6045. Email: mmelara@ccoc.us.

Jail Ministry, Slocum House, 208 Slocum Ave., 13204. Tel: 315-234-9262. Bill Cuddy, Coord.

Keener Seniors, 1654 W. Onondaga St., 13204. Tel: 315-424-1804; Fax: 315-424-6033. Nutrition Program for the Elderly.

BINGHAMTON. *Associated Catholic Charities*, 232 Main St., 13905. Tel: 607-729-9166; Fax: 607-729-2062. Web: www.catholiccharitiesbc.org. Lori Accardi, Exec. Admin.

Catholic Social Services of Broome County, 232 Main St., 13905. Tel: 607-729-9166; Fax: 607-729-2062. Email: dyeager@ccbc.net. Web: www.catholiccharitiesbc.org. Mr. Daniel L. Yeager, M.A., Exec. Dir.; Grazia Tonelli, L.C.S.W.-R., Supvr. of Clinical Svcs.; Shelly Kaminsky, L.C.S.W.-R., Supvr. Pregnancy, Parenting & Adopting Program.

CORTLAND. *Catholic Charities of Cortland County*, 33-35 Central Ave., 13045. Tel: 607-756-5992; Fax: 607-756-5999. Email: info@ccocc.org. Marie Walsh, Exec. Dir.

Case Management Services Tel: 607-756-5992; Fax: 607-756-5999. Email: info@ccocc.org. Ann Marie Phelps, Assoc. Dir.

Case Management Services for Psychiatrically Disabled Tel: 607-756-5992; Fax: 607-756-5999. Ann Marie Phelps, Assoc. Dir.

Residential Services Tel: 607-756-5992; Fax: 607-756-5999. Mike Pisa, Dir. Residential Svcs. Residential services for adult mental health and substance abuse recovery.

Residential Services Tel: 607-753-3550; 607-753-7780 (Lawrence House); Fax: 607-756-4697. Email: info@ccocc.org. Mike Pisa, Assoc. Dir. Lawrence House Community Residence: Supported Housing; Supportive Apartments; Alcohol Halfway House & Recovery Apartments, Independent Housing Option for Long-Term Mentally Ill Independent Housing Office.

Emergency Assistance Tel: 607-299-0029; Fax: 607-756-5999. Email: info@ccocc.org. Web: www.c-cocc.org. Ann Marie Phelps, Dir. of Community Svcs. Emergency & Basic Needs Assistance (Food Pantry, Clothing, Medication, Advocacy Referral & Support).; Summer Lunch Program for Children.

Catholic Charities-STEPS-TASA, 33-35 Central Ave., 13045. Tel: 607-756-5992; Fax: 607-756-5999. Email: info@ccocc.org. (Supportive Teen Education-Parents Services), TASA; Case Management; Adolescent Group Activities.

FULTON. *Catholic Charities of Oswego County*, 365 W. 1st St., 13069. Tel: 315-598-3980. Mary Margaret Pekow, Area Dir.

NORWICH. *Chenango County Catholic Charities*, 3 O'Hara Dr., 13815. Tel: 607-334-8244.

The Counseling Program See separate listing.

Chenango House, 49 Fair St., 13815. Tel: 607-336-8939. Supervised by Community Residence Program.

Intensive Supportive Apartment Program 49 Fair St., 13815. Tel: 607-336-4359.

Supported Housing Program 49 Fair St., 13815. Tel: 607-336-4492.

Community Residence Program Provides housing for mentally ill adults and adolescent boys.

Catholic Charities of Chenango County, 3 O'Hara Dr., 13815. Tel: 607-334-8244; Fax: 607-336-5779. Email: ccccharity@adelphia.net.

The Counseling Program Provides comprehensive counseling for children and adults, also specialized counseling for abused children.

Catholic Charities of Chenango County, 3 O'Hara Dr., 13815. Tel: 607-334-8244; Fax: 607-336-5779. Dr. Jane Coddington, Dir.

Crime Victims-Witness Assistance Program Tel: 607-334-3532; Fax: 607-336-5779. Provides 24-hour Hotline at 607-336-1101, Crisis Intervention, Safe Dwelling, Safe Housing; Court accompaniment; filing affidavits and claims with Crime Victims Board; advocacy with law enforcement agencies; information and referrals.

Catholic Charities of Chenango County, 3 O'Hara Dr., 13815. Tel: 607-336-1528; Fax: 607-336-5779.

ONEIDA. *Catholic Charities of Oneida - Madison Counties*, 258 Main St., 13421. Tel: 315-363-5274. Kathleen C. Eichenlaub, Area Dir.

Madison County Catholic Charities, 119 E. Walnut St., 13421. Tel: 315-363-5274; Fax: 315-363-4925. Kathleen C. Eichenlaub, Dir.

UTICA. *Catholic Charities of Oneida - Madison Counties*, 1408 Genesee St., 13502. Tel: 315-724-2158; Fax: 315-724-5318. Kathleen C. Eichenlaub, Area Dir.; Jan Stasaitis, Dir. Admin.; Anthony J. Conestabile, Dir. Finance; Jack Callaghan, Dir. Residential Support; Dianne DiMeo, Dir. Family & Community Support Svcs.

Catholic Social Services of Utica, 1408 Genesee St., 13502. Tel: 315-724-2158; Fax: 315-724-5318. Email: ddimeo@ccharityyom.org. Kathleen C. Eichenlaub, Area Dir.; Dianne DiMeo, Dir. Family & Community Support Svs. Div.

[G] OFFICES OF HUMAN DEVELOPMENT

SYRACUSE. *Bishop Foery Foundation*, 100 Edmond Ave., 13205. Tel: 315-475-8316.

BINGHAMTON. *Broome County Catholic Charities Office of Social Concerns*, 232 Main St., 13905. Tel: 607-729-9166; Fax: 607-729-2062. Web: www.catholiccharitiesbc.org. Lori Accardi, Contact Person.

[H] ST. VINCENT DE PAUL SOCIETY

FULTON. *Catholic Charities Thrift Shop*, 365 W. First St., 13069. Tel: 315-598-3980; Fax: 315-593-8440. Email: hhoefer@ccoswego.com.

[I] CATHOLIC YOUTH ORGANIZATIONS

SYRACUSE. *Catholic Charities of Onondaga County*, 1654 W. Onondaga St., 13204. Tel: 315-424-1800; Fax: 315-424-8262. Email: neron@ccoc.us. Mr. Michael F. Melara, Exec. Dir.

Children & Family Preservation Division, Catholic Charities of Onondaga County, 1654 W. Onondaga St., 13204. Tel: 315-424-1880; Fax: 315-424-6045. Email: mclary@ccoc.us. Mark Clary, Assoc. Dir.

Hawley Youth Organization, 716 Hawley Ave., 13203. Tel: 315-472-6343.

Northside CYO, 527 N. Salina St., 13208. Tel: 315-474-7428.

Salina Civic Center, 2826 Lemoyne Ave., Mattydale, 13211. Tel: 315-455-7096; Fax: 315-455-2352. Email: kcieplicki@ccoc.us.

Toomey Residential and Community Services Corp., 1654 W. Onondaga St., 13204. Tel: 315-424-1845; Fax: 315-424-7567. Email: jdamore@ccoc.us. Judith D'Amore, Exec. Dir.

Vincent House, 514 Seymour St., 13204. Tel: 315-475-9844; Fax: 315-474-3939.

BINGHAMTON. *Broome County CYO*, 86-88 Walnut St., 13905. Tel: 607-584-7800; Fax: 607-584-7801. Email: kmcgoff@stny.rr.com. Kevin McGoff, Exec. Dir.

FULTON. *Catholic Charities of Oswego Co.*, 365 W. First St., 13069. Tel: 315-598-3980. Mary Margaret Pekow, Exec. Dir.

UTICA. *Catholic Charities, Youth Services Division*, 1408 Genesee St., 13502. Tel: 315-724-6118; Fax: 315-724-5318. Dianne DiMeo, Dir. Family & Community Svcs.

[J] CHILDREN'S INSTITUTIONS AND DAY CARE CENTERS

SYRACUSE. *Catholic Charities of Onondaga County*, 1654 W. Onondaga St., 13204. Tel: 315-424-1847; Fax: 315-424-8262. Email: neron@ccoc.us. Web: www.ccoc.us. Mr. Michael F. Melara. Records only.

Gingerbread House Preschool & Childcare Center, 2500 Grant Blvd., 13208. Tel: 315-471-4198; Fax: 315-471-4198. Email: dcole-director@verizon.net. David Cole, Dir.

[K] DIOCESAN SUMMER CAMPS

SYRACUSE. *Lourdes Camp*, Office: 1654 W. Onondaga St., 13204. Tel: 315-424-1812; 315-673-2888 (Summer).

Camp Address:, 10 Mile Point, Skaneateles, 13152. Michael Preston, Dir.

UTICA. *Camp Nazareth*, Office: 1408 Genesee St., 13502. Tel: 315-724-2158.

112 Long Lake Rd., Woodgate, 13494. Tel: 315-392-3791; Fax: 315-392-6545. Dianne DiMeo, Dir. Family & Community Support Svcs.

[L] FAMILY LIFE BUREAUS

SYRACUSE. *Family Life Education*, 1342 Lancaster Ave., 13210. Tel: 315-472-6754; Fax: 315-472-8409. Email: familylifed@syracusediocese.org. Web: www.familylifeeducation.catholicweb.com. Rev. Joseph H. Phillips, Dir.; Jennifer Kerns, Coord., Family & Marriage Enrichment; Karen Bandoblu, Coord., Marriage Prep. & Speakers Bureau & Natural Family Planning; Cindy Fallon, Coord., Separated/Divorced, The Third Option, and Parenting; Sue & Ronald Kielar, Coordinators Eastern Region; Kathy Colligan, Coord. Southern Region.

Northern Region Office of Faith Formation & Special Education for Catechetics, 74 W. 6th St., Oswego, 13126. Tel: 315-596-4014; Fax: 315-596-4020. Email: germcsj@verizon.net. Sr. Germaine Hilston, C.S.J., Dir.; Deanne Hall, Resource Center Admin.

Western Region Office of Faith Formation, c/o 1342 Lancaster Ave., 13210. Tel: 315-472-6753; Fax: 315-472-8409. Email: tmay@syrdio.org. Theresa May, Dir.

Resource Center Bishop Harrison Diocesan Center, 1342 Lancaster Ave., 13210. Tel: 315-472-6752; Fax: 315-472-8409. Email: resctr@syrdio.org. Marge Babcock, Admin.

ENDWELL. *Southern Region Family Life Education*, 400 Corey Ave., 13760. Tel: 607-748-4743. Email: JColligan@stny.rr.com. John Colligan, Dir.; Kathleen Colligan, Dir.

Cortland Resource Center, 44 N. Main St., Cortland, 13045. Tel: 607-756-2532; Fax: 607-756-2532. Amy White.

[M] GENERAL HOSPITALS

SYRACUSE. *St. Joseph's Hospital Health Center*, 301 Prospect Ave., 13203. Tel: 315-448-5111; Fax: 315-448-6161. Email: teresa.lavalle@sjhsyr.org. Web: www.sjhsyr.org. Mr. Theodore M. Pasinski, Pres. & CEO. College for Nurses. Sisters of St. Francis of the Neumann Communities 20; Bed Capacity 431; Patients Assisted Annually 400,000; Total Staff 3,300; Students 279.

BINGHAMTON. *Our Lady of Lourdes Memorial Hospital*, 169 Riverside Dr., 13905. Tel: 607-798-5111; Fax: 607-798-7681. Web: lourdes.com. David Patak, Pres. Daughters of Charity of St. Vincent de Paul 9; Bed Capacity 267; Patients Assisted Annually 400,000; Total Staff 1,300.

UTICA. *St. Elizabeth Medical Center*, 2209 Genesee St., 13501. Tel: 315-798-8100; Fax: 315-734-3092. Email: sjohanna@STEMC.org. Web: www.stemc.org. Sr. M. Johanna Delelys, Pres. & CEO; Matthew Babock, Vice Pres. & COO; Rev. John H. Comeskey (Retired). College of Nursing. Sisters of the Third Franciscan Order 12; Bed Capacity 201; Patients Assisted Annually 434,277; Students 205; Total Staff 1,941.

[N] FACILITIES FOR THE AGED

SYRACUSE. *Bernardine Apartments, Inc.*, 417 Churchill Ave., 13205. Tel: 315-469-7786. Mr. Michael Sullivan, Pres.; Howard Jenkins, Admin.

St. Camillus Health & Rehabilitation Center, 813 Fay Rd., 13219. Tel: 315-488-2951; Fax: 315-488-3255. Email: aileen.balitz@st-camillus.org. Web: www.st-camillus.org. Mrs. Aileen M. Balitz, Pres.; Ms. Lisa Ferraro, Dir. Social Svcs. Bed Capacity 290; Total Assisted 2,700; Total Staff 670.

St. Camillus Foundation, 813 Fay Rd., 13219. Tel: 315-488-2951, Ext. 404. Mr. James Murphy, Foundation Chm.

Loretto, 700 E. Brighton Ave., 13205. Tel: 315-413-3733; Fax: 315-469-6558. Ms. Lisa Maxwell, Admin. Cunningham Bldg.; Sr. Cathleen Moore, S.S.V., Chap.

Loretto Health & Rehabilitation Center Bed Capacity 554; Total Assisted 2,000; Staff 800.

Loretto Geriatric Community Residences, Inc., 5018 S. Salina St., 13205. Tel: 315-492-0896.

700 E. Brighton Ave., 13205. Tel: 315-469-8562.

50 Syracuse St., Baldwinsville, 13027. Tel: 315-635-1647.

8659 Carpenter Rd., Baldwinsville, 13027. Tel: 315-635-1763.

Loretto Rest, Inc., 700 E. Brighton Ave., 13205. Tel: 315-469-5570; Fax: 315-469-6558. Mr. Michael Sullivan, Pres. & CEO; Sr. Cathleen Moore, S.S.V., Chap.; Mr. Mitchell Marsh, Admin. Adult Home.

Loretto and Loretto Apartments Housing Development Fund Co., Inc., c/o Loretto, 700 E. Brighton Ave., 13205.

OSWEGO. *Saint Luke's Health Care Services*, 299 E. River Rd., 13126. Tel: 315-342-3166; Fax: 315-343-6531. Email: tgorman@stlukehs.com. Web: www.stlukehs.com. Mr. Terrence Gorman, Admin. Bed Capacity 200; Total Assisted Annually 69,350; Total Staff 320.

UTICA. *St. Joseph Nursing Home*, 2535 Genesee St., 13501. Tel: 315-797-1230; Fax: 315-797-5171. Email: frank@stjosephnh.org. Web: www.stjosephnh.org. Mr. Frank Trimboli, Admin. Bed Capacity 120; Total Assisted Annually 182; Total Staff 180.

[O] SPECIALTY HOUSING

SYRACUSE. *Bartell Road Housing Development Co., Inc.* (Brewerton), 990 James St., 13203. Tel: 315-424-1821; Fax: 315-424-6048. Housing for well elderly.

Christopher Community, Inc. Professional management and consultants of housing programs for the elderly, families and special populations., 990 James St., 13203. Tel: 315-424-1821; Fax: 315-424-6048. Mr. Douglas Reicher, Exec. Dir.; Fred Zolna, Housing Devel. Specialist.

Churchill Manor, Inc., 750 E. Brighton Ave., 13205. Tel: 315-492-1329; Fax: 315-492-6076. Email: cahika@lorettosystem.org. A nonprofit corporation founded to provide housing for low and moderate income families and individuals.

Harbor View Housing Development Fund Co., Inc., c/o 1654 W. Onondaga St., 13204. Tel: 315-424-1821; Fax: 315-424-6048.

Hawley Winton Housing Development Fund, Inc., Walter Ludovico Apts., 340 Winton St., 13203. Tel: 315-422-0475; Fax: 315-471-1554. 32 one-bedroom units occupied. Christopher Community, (Managing Agent).

Ludden Housing Development Fund Company, Inc., 990 James St., 13203. Tel: 315-424-1821; Fax: 315-424-6048. Fifty one-bedroom apartments for the elderly and handicapped. Christopher Community Inc., (Managing Agent).

Marcellus Apartments Housing Development Fund Company, Inc., 990 James St., 13203. Tel: 315-424-1821; Fax: 315-424-6048. Christopher Community, Inc., (Managing Agent).

Mother Marianne Cope Housing Development Fund Co., Inc., 1047 E. Fayette St., 13210. Tel: 315-422-5611; Fax: 315-478-6972. 23 Units for HIV positive patients.

Mount St. James Corporation, 990 James St., 13203. Tel: 315-424-1821; Fax: 315-424-6048. Engaged in the operation of a nonprofit housing facility known as Mount St. James Apartments, at 338 Jamesville Ave., for persons of low to moderate income. Christopher Community, Inc., (Managing Agents).

St. Peter's Italian Church Housing Development Fund Co., Inc. Villa Scalabrini Apts., 301 Ash St., 13208. Operation of a nonprofit housing facility for aged, well persons of low income at the 800 block of E. Willow St. in Syracuse. 120 units, one-bedroom apartments. Christopher Community, Inc., (Managing Agent).

Pompei Housing Development Fund Company, Inc. 50 one-bedroom apartments for the elderly and handicapped. Christopher Community, Inc., (Managing Agent).

c/o Christopher Community, Inc., 990 James St., 13203. Tel: 315-424-1821; Fax: 315-424-6048.

Pond St. Housing Development Fund Co., Inc., Bishop Harrison Apartments, 300 Pond St., 13208. Tel: 315-476-8630; Fax: 315-474-0806. Email: kalibrandi@christopher-community.org. Operation of 47 units, one bedroom apartments for the elderly and handicapped. Christopher Community Inc., (Managing Agent).

Providence House Apartments, 1700 W. Onondaga St., 13204. Tel: 315-471-8427; Fax: 315-474-1224. Email: mquirk@christopher-community.org. Senior citizen housing, 100 units. Christopher Community, (Managing Agent).

Stoneleigh Housing Development Fund Co., Inc., Stoneleigh Apartments, 400 Lamb Ave., Canastota, 13032. Engaged in the construction and operation of a nonprofit housing facility for elderly and handicapped persons of low income. 100 units, one bedroom apartments. Christopher Community, Inc., (Managing Agent).

Tyson Place Housing Development Fund Company, Inc. (40 apartments for the elderly), *St. Joseph Manor*, 990 James St., 13203. Tel: 315-424-1821; Fax: 315-424-6048. Christopher Community, Inc., (Managing Agent).

AUBURN. *Mercy Housing Development Fund Co., Inc., Mercy Apartments*, 1 Thornton Ave., 13021. Tel: 315-424-1821; Fax: 315-424-6048. 990 James St., 13203. 40 one-bedroom units for the elderly and handicapped. Christopher Community, Inc., (Managing Agent).

BALDWINSVILLE. *Smokey Hollow Housing Development Fund Company, Inc., St. Mary's Apartments c/o Christopher Community*, 990 James St., 13203. Tel: 315-424-1821; Fax: 315-424-6048. Christopher Community, Inc., (Managing Agent).

BREWERTON. *Bartell Road Housing Development Fund Co., Inc. dba Long Manor Apts.* 5500 Miller Rd., 13029. Tel: 315-668-9871; Fax: 315-676-2544. Email: longmanor@christophercommunity.org. Justine Poplaski, Contact Person. 20 units, one bedroom apartments. Christopher Community, Inc., (Managing Agent).

CICERO. *Cicero Housing Development Fund Company Inc.*, 990 James St., 13203. Tel: 315-424-1821; Fax: 315-424-6048.

Sacred Heart Apartments, 990 James St., 13203. Christopher Community, Inc., (Managing Agent).

FAYETTEVILLE. *Redfield South Housing Development Fund Co., Inc.*, Redfield Village Apartments, 380 Salt Springs Rd., 13066. Tel: 315-637-8280; Fax: 315-637-2376. 50 one-bedroom units. Christopher Community, Inc., (Managing Agent). Total Assisted 50; Total Staff 2.

NORTH SYRACUSE. *Pitcher Hill-Christopher Housing Development Fund Co., Inc.*, 990 James St., 13203. Tel: 315-424-1821; Fax: 315-424-6048. Email: pitcherhill@christophercommunity.org. Engaged in the construction and operation of nonprofit housing facilities for elderly and handicapped persons of low income. 100 units, one bedroom apartments. Christopher Community, Inc., (Managing Agent). Total Assisted 98; Total Staff 4.

OSWEGO. *St. Luke's Housing Development Fund Co., Inc.*, St. Luke's Apartments, W. First St., 13126. Tel: 315-343-0821; Fax: 315-343-0619. Engaged in the construction and operation of a nonprofit housing facility for elderly and handicapped persons of low income. 100 units, one bedroom apartments. Christopher Community, Inc., (Managing Agent).

ROME. *C.N.C. Inc.*, 1003 W. Thomas St., 13440. Tel: 315-724-2185; Fax: 315-724-5318. *Catholic Charities of Oneida/Madison Counties*, 1408 Genese St., Utica, 13502. Facility for ten deinstitutionalized chronically mentally ill individuals living in a group home.

Rome Mall Housing Development Fund Company, Inc., 990 James St., 13203. Tel: 315-424-1821; Fax: 315-424-6048. 45 one-bedroom units for the elderly. Christopher Community, Inc., (Managing Agent).

Rome Mall Apts., 13440.

TOWN OF GATES. *Steger Housing Development Fund Co., Inc.*, 4100 Lyell Rd. 56 apartments for well elderly.

1654 W. Onondaga St., 13204. Tel: 315-424-1821; Fax: 315-424-6048.

UTICA. *Catherine St. Housing Development Fund Company, Inc., Mt. Carmel Apartments*, 990 James St., 13203. Tel: 315-424-1821; Fax: 315-424-6048. Christopher Community, Inc., (Managing Agent).

[P] PROGRAMS FOR THE HANDICAPPED

SYRACUSE. *L'Arche of Syracuse, Inc.*, 1232 Teall Ave., 13206. Tel: 315-479-8088; Fax: 315-479-8118. Email: larchesyracuse@cnymail.com. Web: www.larchesyracuse.com. Peggy Harper, Community Leader. A Christian Community concerned with life sharing between persons with a developmental disability and persons who assist them; Homes at 310 Galster Ave, 4550 Cleveland Rd., 211 Croyden Ln., 140 Highland Ave., Syracuse.

UTICA. *St. John and St. Joseph Home, Inc.*, 1408 Genesee St., 13502. Tel: 315-724-2158; Fax: 315-724-5318. Kathleen C. Eichenlaub, Contact Person.

[Q] MONASTERIES AND RESIDENCES OF PRIESTS AND BROTHERS

SYRACUSE. *Jesuits at LeMoyne, Inc.*, 1419 Salt Springs Rd., 13214. Tel: 315-445-4604; Fax: 315-445-4722. Email: jesuitres@lemoyne.edu. Web: www.lemoyne.edu/jesuitheritage/tabid/482/default.as Revs. William J. Bosch, S.J.; David J. Casey, S.J., Treas.; James H. Dahlinger, S.J.; William S. Dolan, S.J., Rector; Adelino P. Dunghe, S.J.; Vincent W. Hevern, S.J.; Donald J. Kirby, S.J.; Donald C. Maldari, S.J.; Carsten P. Martensen, S.J.; David C. McCallum, S.J.; Daniel J. Mulhauser, S.J.; Paul S. Naumann, S.J.; Joseph B. Neville, S.J.; Robert E. Scully, S.J.; James F. Smith, S.J.; Louis P. Sogliuzzo, S.J.; Andrew L. Szebenyi, S.J.; M. Donald Zewe, S.J. Priests 17; Scholastics 1.

Tommy Coyne Residence @ Dillon Hall, 714 E. Brighton Ave., 13205. Tel: 315-469-0078. Diocesan home for priests. In Res. Rev. Msgrs. Paul A. Brigandi (Retired); Robert B. Davern; Revs. Joseph F. Kane (Retired); Angelo L. Morbito (Retired); Alfred E. Nortz (Retired); P. Carl Pilla (Retired); William P. Regan (Retired); John D. Roock (Retired).

BINGHAMTON. *McDevitt Residence for Retired Priests*, 68 Seminary Ave., 13905. Tel: 607-771-6207. Rev. Msgr. James D. Kane (Retired); Revs. Gerald J. Buckley (Retired); Stanley J. Gerlock (Retired); Daniel G. Murphy (Retired).

EAST SYRACUSE. *Vianney House*, 6651 Kirkville Rd., 13057. Tel: 315-727-4631. Rev. Msgr. George F. Sheehan.

[R] CONVENTS AND RESIDENCES FOR SISTERS

SYRACUSE. *Dominican Monastery of the Perpetual Rosary*, 802 Court St., 13208-1766. Tel: 315-471-6762. Email: violetbop@juno.com. Sr. Bernadette Marie, O.P., Prioress. Cloistered Nuns 9; Extern Sisters 2.

Sisters of St. Francis of the Neumann Communities (1860) Congregational Offices: 2500 Grant Blvd., Ste. 3, 13208. Tel: 315-634-7000; Fax: 315-634-7023. Email: sisters@sosf.org. Web: www.sosf.org. Central New York Region: *St. Anthony and Jolenta Convents*, 1024 Court St., 13208. Tel: 315-422-8652; Fax: 315-422-9612. Sisters Patricia Burkard, O.S.F., Gen. Min.; Marian Rose Mansius, O.S.F., Gen. Councilor; Maria Salerno, O.S.F., Gen. Councilor; Barbara Woody, O.S.F., Gen Councilor; Frances Kowalski, O.S.F., Gen. Treas. & Regl. Councilor; Roberta Stark Smith,

O.S.F., Sec. Professed Sisters in the Region 165; Professed Sisters in the House 73; Associates in the Region 79; Total in Community 528.

ENDICOTT. *Little Sisters of Saint Francis of Assisi Mission*, 304 Oak Hill Ave., 13760. Tel: 607-786-5006; Fax: 607-786-5066. Email: lsosfabroad@yahoo.com. Sisters Anisia Muthoni, Dir.; Lilia Kagendo, Dir.

WINDSOR. *Transfiguration Monastery*, 701 NY Rte. 79, 13865-2700. Tel: 607-655-2366; Fax: 607-655-4024. Email: bendon@dep.tds.net. Sr. Donald Corcoran, O.S.B.Cam., Prioress. Camaldolese Benedictine Nuns. Sisters 4.

[S] RETREAT HOUSES

SYRACUSE. *Christ the King Retreat House*, 500 Brookford Rd., 13224. Tel: 315-446-2680; Fax: 315-446-2689. Email: retreats@christthekingretreat.com. Rev. Michael J. Carmola, Dir.; Charlene Oppedisano, Asst.; Marianne Carbone, Admin. Asst. General retreat house for priests, nuns, laity and youth of upstate New York. Priests 1.

SKANEATELES. *Stella Maris Retreat Center* 13152. Tel: 315-685-6836; Fax: 315-685-7008. Email: wwtkal@aol.com. Web: www.stellamarisretreat.org. Geraldine Kaluzny, Dir.; Sr. Stephanie Ward, Prog. Dir. Sisters of the Third Franciscan Order, M.C., Franciscan oriented center for renewal.

UTICA. *The Good News Foundation of Central New York*, 10475 Cosby Manor Rd., 13502. Tel: 315-735-6210; Fax: 315-735-7090. Email: goodnews@borg.com. Web: www.goodnewsfoundation.org. Michael Buckley, Exec. Dir. & CEC; Hilanne Meyers, Assoc. Dir.

[T] NEWMAN CENTERS

SYRACUSE. *LeMoyne College Campus Ministry* 1499 Salt Springs Rd., 13214. Tel: 315-445-4110; Fax: 315-445-4797. Revs. Louis P. Sogliuzzo, S.J., Dir.; William S. Dolan, S.J., Rector, Campus Min.

Syracuse University, St. Thomas More Foundation, Inc. Alibrandi Catholic Center, 110 Walnut Pl., 13210. Tel: 315-478-5959; Fax: 315-443-4465. Email: ldesanti@syr.edu. Rev. Linus DeSantis, O.F.M.Conv.

CAZENOVIA. *Cazenovia College Newman Center* 10 Seminary St., 13035. Tel: 315-655-7237; Fax: 315-655-7536. Email: jabaron@cazenovia.edu. Web: www.cazcollege.edu/zinterfaith.htm. Rev. G. Peter Worn, Chap.

CLINTON. *Hamilton College Newman Center* 198 College Hill Rd., 13323. Tel: 315-859-4129; Fax: 315-859-4041. Email: jcroghan@hamilton.edu. Web: www.hamilton.edu/college/newman. Rev. John P. Croghan, Chap.

CORTLAND. *Newman Foundation of Cortland, Inc. at the State University College of New York* 8 Calvert St., 13045. Tel: 607-753-6737. Email: marie.agen@cortland.edu. Web: www.cortland.edu/ministry/catholic.html. Marie C. Agen, Ph.D., Campus Min.

MORRISVILLE. *Newman Association at SUNY Morrisville* Mathasis Health Bldg., 13408. Tel: 315-684-6201. Email: YoungSR@morrisville.edu. Web: www.morrisville.edu/pages/newman. Deacon Steven R. Young, Chap.

St. Joan of Arc Newman Association at the State University of New York (SUNY) Morrisville Agricultural and Technical College

OSWEGO. *Newman Foundation, Inc., State University of New York Hall Newman Center*, 36 New St., P.O. Box 207, 13126. Tel: 315-312-7222; Fax: 315-312-7561. Email: newctr@oswego.edu.

UTICA. *Newman Center at SUNY Institute of Technology* P.O. Box 8087, 13505-8087. Tel: 315-792-3284; Fax: 315-792-4401. Rev. Paul J. Drobin, Chap.

State University of New York (SUNY) Institute of Technology Newman Center

Utica College Newman Center P.O. Box 8087, 13505-8087. Tel: 315-792-3284; Fax: 315-792-4401. Rev. Paul J. Drobin, Chap.

Res.: P.O. Box 8087, 13505-8087. Tel: 315-792-3284.

VESTAL. *Binghamton University Newman Center* 400 Murray Hill Rd., 13850. Tel: 607-798-7202. Email: frcorey@binghamton.edu. Rev. Corey S. Van Kuren, Chap.

[U] MISCELLANEOUS LISTINGS

SYRACUSE. **Brady Faith Center, Inc.*, 404 South Ave., P.O. Box 993, 13201. Tel: 315-472-9077; Fax: 315-472-9077. Web: www.bradyfaithcenter.org. Rev. John C. Schopfer, Pastoral Dir.

**David W. Barry Foundation*, 240 E. Onondaga St., P.O. Box 511, 13201-0511. Tel: 315-422-7203; Fax: 315-478-4619. Most Revs. Robert J. Cunningham, D.D., Pres.; Thomas J. Costello, D.D., Vice Pres. (Retired); Rev. Clifford H. Auth, J.C.L., Sec. & Treas.

St. Francis Social Adult Day Care, 1108 Court St., 13208. Tel: 315-424-1003; 315-424-1004; Fax: 315-472-9899. Email: info@stfrancisadc.com. Web: www.stfrancisadc.com. Sr. Barbara Jean Donovan, O.S.F., Admin. Sponsored by the Sisters of St. Francis of the Neumann Communities., A non-residential adult day-service providing holistic care for the frail elderly.

Grimes Foundation (Incorporated by special act of the New York State Legislature, May 1, 1916), 240 E. Onondaga St., 13202. Tel: 315-422-7203; Fax: 315-478-4619. Most Revs. Robert J. Cunningham, D.D., Pres. Ex-Officio; Thomas J. Costello, D.D., Vice Pres. (Retired); Rev. Clifford H. Auth, J.C.L., Treas. Corporation created to establish and maintain charitable, religious and educational facilities within the Roman Catholic Diocese of Syracuse, New York.

Guardian Angel Society, 259 E. Onondaga St., 13202. Tel: 315-422-7218; Fax: 315-422-2471. Email: angel003@twcny.rr.com. Kathy Fedrizzi, Devel. Dir.

Lasalle Syracuse, Inc., 6245 Randall Rd., 13214. Tel: 315-446-5960; Fax: 315-446-3393. Web: www.cbasyracuse.org.

Loretto Apartments Housing Development Fund Co., Inc., 700 E. Brighton Ave., 13205. Tel: 315-413-3277; Fax: 315-498-9073. Email: kcollins@lorettosystem.com.

Onondaga County Catholic School Foundation (Western Region Catholic School Foundation), 240 E. Onondaga St., P.O. Box 511, 13201-0511. Tel: 315-470-1450; Fax: 315-470-1470. (Vacant)

**Our Lady of Lourdes Hospitality - North American Volunteers, Ltd.*, P.O. Box 3820, 13220. Tel: 315-476-0026; Fax: 419-730-4540. A Public Association of the Christian Faithful founded in 2003 to share the Message of Lourdes, accompany the sick and handicapped on pilgrimage and serve the Sanctuaries at Lourdes, France.

**Sacred Heart Apostolate, Inc.*, 417 S. Orchard Rd., 13219-2407. Tel: 315-492-6308; Fax: 315-492-3407. Email: sacredhc@verizon.net. Web: www.sacredheartapostolate.com. Gloria Anson, Pres.; Thomas Mueller, Chm./Contact Person. Tel: 714-775-1246.

Spiritual Renewal Center, 1118 Court St., Ste. B., 13208. Tel: 315-472-6546. Email: mail@spiritualrenewalcenter.com. Web: www.spiritualrenewalcenter.com.

Saint Thomas Preparatory Seminary Fund, COO, P.O. Box 511, 13201. Incorporated under the Laws of the State of New York, 1963, as a Membership Corporation to solicit funds for the construction of a diocesan seminary.

BINGHAMTON. *Ladies of Charity*, 100 Main St., 13905. Tel: 607-723-0194.

Samaritan House, 11 Fayette St., 13901. Tel: 607-724-3969; Fax: 607-771-0356. Sr. Molly Smith, D.C., Co-Dir.; Brenda Kukwia, Co-Dir.

CANASTOTA. *Catholic Diocese of Nakuru Mission Office, Inc.*, 406 Spencer St., 13032. Tel: 315-697-8795; Fax: 315-697-8959. Email: cdnmission@yahoo.com. Rev. Cleophas Oseso Tuka (Africa), Dir.

DEWITT. *Joseph & Elaine Scuderi Foundation*, 5786 Widewaters Pkwy., P.O. Box 3, 13214.

ENDICOTT. *Little Sisters of St. Francis of Assisi Mission* 304 Oak Hill Rd., Broome Co. 13760. Tel: 607-273-4200. Elena Salerno Flash, Esq., Contact Person.

Roman Catholic Diocese - Bishop Harrison Education Trust (1994) P.O. Box 511, 13201-0511.

MAINE. *Mount St. Francis Hermitage, Inc.*, 120 Edison Rd., P.O. Box 236, 13802. Tel: 607-754-0001; Fax: 607-754-0001. Web: www.mtstfrancis.com. Revs. Johannes Michael Mary Smith, F.I.; John Joseph Mary Cook, F.I.; Friars Juniper Mary Gold, F.I.; Faustino Mary Fulnecky, F.I. Professed Friars 2; Postulants 5.

RICHLAND. *Rural & Migrant Ministry of Oswego Co. Inc.*, 15 Stewart St., P.O. Box 192, 13144-0192. Tel: 315-298-1154; Fax: 315-298-1154. Email: rmmoc@yahoo.com. Shawn Doyle, Exec. Dir.

UTICA. *Christ Child Society of Utica*, 140 Hawthorne Ave., 13502. Email: curling.kelly@verizon.net. Cindy Kelly, Treas.

RELIGIOUS INSTITUTES OF MEN REPRESENTED IN THE DIOCESE

For further details refer to the corresponding bracketed number in the Religious Institutes of Men or Women section.

[1350]—*Brothers of St. Francis Xavier* (St. Joseph Prov., Milton, MA)—C.F.X.

[0330]—*Brothers of the Christian Schools* (New York Prov.)—F.S.C.

[]—*Brothers of the Sacred Heart*

[0480]—*Conventual Franciscans*—O.F.M.Conv

[0690]—*Jesuit Fathers and Brothers* (New York Prov.)—S.J.

RELIGIOUS INSTITUTES OF WOMEN REPRESENTED IN THE DIOCESE

[0230]—*Benedictine Sisters of Pontifical Jurisdiction* (Erie, PA)—O.S.B.

[]—*Camaldolese Benedictine Sisters*—O.S.B.Cam.

[0330]—*Carmelite Sisters for the Aged and Infirm*—O.Carm.

[]—*Congregation of the Sisters of the Cross of Chavanod* (India)

[0760]—*Daughters of Charity of St. Vincent de Paul*—D.C.

[]—*Daughters of St. Mary of Providence*—D.S.M.P

[1050]—*Dominican Contemplative Nuns*—O.P.

[1070-01]—*Dominican Sisters*—O.P.

[1170]—*Felician Sisters*—C.S.S.F.

[1180]—*Franciscan Sisters of Allegany, New York*—O.S.F.

[1410]—*Franciscan Sisters of St. Joseph (Mill Hill)*—F.M.S.J.

[2575]—*Institute of the Sisters of Mercy of the Americas* (New York, NY; Omaha, NE)—R.S.M.

[]—*Little Sisters of St. Francis*—L.S.O.S.F.

[1360]—*Missionary Franciscan Sisters of the Immaculate Conception*—O.S.F.

[3160]—*Parish Visitors of Mary Immaculate*—P.V.M.I.

[0590]—*Sisters of Charity of Saint Elizabeth, Convent Station*—S.C.

[3340]—*Sisters of Providence (Holyoke)*—S.P.

[3950]—*Sisters of Saint Mary of Namur*—S.S.M.N.

[3780]—*Sisters of Saints Cyril and Methodius*—SS.C.M.

[1800]—*Sisters of St. Francis of the Neumann Communities*—O.S.F.

[3830-14]—*Sisters of St. Joseph* (Rochester, NY)—S.S.J.

[3840]—*Sisters of St. Joseph of Carondelet*—C.S.J.

[1970]—*Sisters of the Holy Family of Nazareth*—C.S.F.N.

[]—*Sisters of the Immaculate Heart of Mary, Mother of Christ* (Africa)—I.H.M.

[2160]—*Sisters, Servants of the Immaculate Heart of Mary*—I.H.M.

[4110]—*Ursuline Nuns (Roman Union)*—O.S.U.

DIOCESAN CEMETERIES

SYRACUSE. *St. Mary-St. Agnes*, 2315 South Ave., 13207. Tel: 315-475-4639. Mr. Mark Lazaroski, Dir.; Ralph D'Agostino, Supt.; Daniel Moorhead, Asst. Supt.

BALDWINSVILLE. *Our Lady of Peace Cemetery*, 8668 Oswego Rd., 13027. Tel: 315-303-4901. Christopher Nacey, Supt.

CORTLAND. *St. Mary*, 4101 West Road, 13045. Tel: 607-756-8838. Andrew Cook, Supt.

JOHNSON CITY. *Calvary-St. Patrick*, 501 Fairview St., 13790. Tel: 607-797-2906. Email: rramey@syracusecatholiccemeteries.org. Randy Ramey, Supt.; Ann Adams, Sec.

OSWEGO. *St. Peter & St. Paul*, 379 E. River Rd., R.R. 04, Box 4B, 13126. Tel: 315-343-5002. Christopher Nacey, Supt.

UTICA. *St. Agnes*, 601 Arthur St., 13501. Tel: 315-732-8588. John McCarthy, Supt.

Calvary Cemetery, 2407 Oneida St., 13501. Tel: 315-735-2727. David Pritchard, Supt.

Holy Trinity, Chaplain Ave., 13502. Tel: 315-724-0616. David Pritchard, Supt.

St. Mary Cemetery, Webster St., 13501. Tel: 315-735-2727. David Pritchard, Supt.

WHITESBORO. *Mount Olivet*, 70 Wood Rd., 13492. Tel: 315-736-4446. David Pritchard, Supt.

NECROLOGY

† Giblin, Rev. Msgr. Lawrence E., (Retired)—Died Sept. 26, 2009

† Drummond, Richard, (Retired)—Died May 1, 2009

† Guyder, Thomas F., (Retired)—Died April 25, 2009

† Zedar, Thomas, (Retired)—Died Feb. 8, 2009

An asterisk (*) denotes an organization that has established tax-exempt status directly with the IRS and is not covered by the USCCB Group Ruling.

Diocese of Toledo

(Dioecesis Toletana in America)

Most Reverend

LEONARD P. BLAIR

Bishop of Toledo; ordained June 26, 1976; appointed Titular Bishop of Voncariana and Auxiliary Bishop of Detroit July 9, 1999; consecrated August 24, 1999; appointed Bishop of Toledo October 7, 2003; installed December 4, 2003.

Most Reverend

ROBERT W. DONNELLY, D.D.

Retired Auxiliary Bishop of Toledo; ordained May 25, 1957; appointed Titular Bishop of Garba and Auxiliary Bishop of Toledo March 14, 1984; ordained Bishop May 3, 1984; retired May 30, 2006. *Res.: Blessed Sacrament Parish, 4227 Bellevue Rd., Toledo, OH 43613.*

Chancery: 1933 Spielbusch Ave., Toledo, OH 43604-5360. Tel: 419-244-6711; Fax: 419-244-4791.

Web: www.toledodiocese.org

Email: chancery@toledodiocese.org

ESTABLISHED APRIL 15, 1910.

Square Miles 8,222.

Comprises the following Counties of northwest Ohio: Williams, Fulton, Lucas, Ottawa, Defiance, Henry, Wood, Sandusky, Erie, Paulding, Putnam, Hancock, Seneca, Huron, Van Wert, Allen, Wyandot, Crawford and Richland.

For legal titles of parishes and diocesan institutions, consult the Chancery.

STATISTICAL OVERVIEW

Personnel	
Bishop	1
Retired Bishops	1
Priests: Diocesan Active in Diocese	121
Priests: Diocesan Active Outside Diocese	5
Priests: Diocesan in Foreign Missions	1
Priests: Retired, Sick or Absent	62
Number of Diocesan Priests	189
Religious Priests in Diocese	39
Total Priests in Diocese	228
Extern Priests in Diocese	8
Ordinations:	
Diocesan Priests	5
Religious Priests	3
Transitional Deacons	1
Permanent Deacons in Diocese	199
Total Brothers	8
Total Sisters	526
Parishes	
Parishes	128
With Resident Pastor:	
Resident Diocesan Priests	86
Resident Religious Priests	8
Without Resident Pastor:	
Administered by Priests	29
Administered by Religious Women	5
Closed Parishes	1
Professional Ministry Personnel:	
Brothers	5
Sisters	16
Lay Ministers	295
Welfare	
Catholic Hospitals	8
Total Assisted	1,266,598
Health Care Centers	4
Total Assisted	30,275
Homes for the Aged	7
Total Assisted	1,279
Specialized Homes	1
Total Assisted	87
Special Centers for Social Services	7
Total Assisted	11,806
Other Institutions	7
Total Assisted	1,407
Educational	
Diocesan Students in Other Seminaries	20
Total Seminarians	20
Colleges and Universities	2
Total Students	3,161
High Schools, Diocesan and Parish	10
Total Students	3,162
High Schools, Private	4
Total Students	2,553
Elementary Schools, Diocesan and Parish	66
Total Students	13,453
Elementary Schools, Private	2
Total Students	351
Non-residential Schools for the Disabled	1
Total Students	53
Catechesis/Religious Education:	
High School Students	4,973
Elementary Students	22,362
Total Students under Catholic Instruction	50,088
Teachers in the Diocese:	
Priests	16
Sisters	56
Lay Teachers	1,375
Vital Statistics	
Receptions into the Church:	
Infant Baptism Totals	2,784
Minor Baptism Totals	669
Adult Baptism Totals	359
Received into Full Communion	410
First Communions	3,717
Confirmations	3,521
Marriages:	
Catholic	686
Interfaith	538
Total Marriages	1,224
Deaths	2,840
Total Catholic Population	321,516
Total Population	1,461,436

Former Bishops—Most Rev. JOSEPH SCHREMBS, D.D., appt. Auxiliary Bishop of Grand Rapids, MI Jan. 8, 1911; cons. Feb. 22, 1911; transferred to Toledo, Aug. 11, 1911; transferred to Cleveland, OH, May 11, 1921; died Nov. 2, 1945; His Eminence SAMUEL CARDINAL STRITCH, D.D., cons. Bishop of Toledo, Nov. 30, 1921; appt. Archbishop of Milwaukee, Aug. 30, 1930; appt. Archbishop of Chicago, Dec. 27, 1939; created Cardinal, Feb. 18, 1946; named Pro-Prefect of the Sacred Congregation of the Propagation of the Faith, March 1, 1958; died in Rome, May 27, 1958; Most Revs. KARL J. ALTER, D.D., LL.D., appt. Bishop of Toledo, April 17, 1931; cons. June 17, 1931; appt. Archbishop of Cincinnati, June 21, 1950; retired July 23, 1969; died Aug. 23, 1977; GEORGE REHRING, D.D., cons. Oct. 7, 1937; appt. Auxiliary Bishop of Cincinnati, Oct. 7, 1937; appt. Bishop of Toledo, July 18, 1950; retired Feb. 25, 1967; died Feb. 29, 1976; JOHN A. DONOVAN, D.D., ord. Dec. 8, 1935; Titular Bishop of Rhasus and Auxiliary of Detroit, Michigan Sept. 6, 1954; ord. Bishop of Detroit, Michigan Oct. 26, 1954; appt. to Toledo, Feb. 25, 1967; retired July 29, 1980; died Sept. 18, 1991; JAMES R. HOFFMAN, D.D., J.C.L., ord. July 28, 1957; appt. Titular Bishop of Italica and Auxiliary Bishop of Toledo April 18, 1978; ord. June 23, 1978; appt. Bishop of Toledo Feb. 17, 1981; died Feb. 8, 2003.

Chancery

Episcopal Vicar, Moderator of the Curia and Chancellor—Very Rev. MICHAEL R. BILLIAN, V.E., Catholic Center, 1933 Spielbusch Ave., Toledo, 43604-5360. Tel: 419-244-6711; Fax: 419-244-4791. Email: mbillian@toledodiocese.org.

Archives—Catholic Center, 1933 Spielbusch Ave., Toledo, 43604-5360. Tel: 419-244-6711; Fax: 419-244-4791. Mr. PETER UEBERROTH, Archivist. Email: pueberroth@toledodiocese.org. Office House: Wed., Thurs., Fri. 8:30-2:30.

Canonical Services—Catholic Center, 1933 Spielbusch Ave., Toledo, 43604-5360. Tel: 419-244-6711; Fax: 419-244-4791.

Delegate of the Bishop—Very Rev. MICHAEL R. BILLIAN, V.E.

Promoter of Justice—Rev. DAVID M. ROSS, V.F., S.T.L., J.C.D.

Assessors—Rev. JOSEPH E. FOX, O.P., J.C.D.; Very Rev. CHRISTOPHER P. VASKO, V.J., J.C.D.

Advocate—Rev. JAMES E. AUTH, J.C.L.

Ecclesiastical Notary—Very Rev. MARVIN G. BORGER, V.G., J.C.L.

Catholic Center Services—Catholic Center, 1933 Spielbusch Ave., Toledo, 43604-5360. Tel: 419-244-6711; Fax: 419-244-4791. Ms. PATRICIA STEIN, Mgr. Email: pstein@toledodiocese.org. Provides building services and centralized purchasing for offices located in the Catholic Center.

Court of Equity— The Court of Equity has been granted jurisdiction and authority by the bishop to be a legally constituted body to consider complaints against administrative decisions and to resolve controversies by conciliation or arbitration. This court has jurisdiction over the parishes, departments and institutions that are under the authority of the bishop of Toledo. Ms. JUDITH GAJDOSTIK, Clerk, 3250 Hazelton Dr., Oregon, 43616. Tel: 419-691-7436; Mr. FRANK LINK, Presiding Judge.

Judges—Sr. JOANNE MARY FRANIA, S.N.D.; Mr. WAYNE GRAVES; Very Rev. GREGORY R. HITE, V.F.; Mr. FRANCIS LANDRY; Mr. COLIN MCQUADE; Rev.

DANIEL J. RING; Ms. LORI SMITH; Sr. DOROTHY THUM, R.S.M.; MARY GRACE TRIMBOLI; Mr. BRUCE WINTERS.

Conciliators—SHAWN T. BIESIADA; Deacon JAMES CARUSO; Mr. RICHARD HANUSZ; Sr. THERESE MILNE, I.H.M.; Ms. REGINA SCHIMMOELLER; Mr. JOHN F. WETLI.

Intake Officers— (pending)

Diocesan Case Manager—Catholic Center, 1933 Spielbusch Ave., Toledo, 43604-5360. Tel: 419-244-6711, Ext. 632; 800-926-8277, Ext. 632 (outside Toledo, within Ohio). Mr. FRANK DILALLO. Email: fdilallo@toledodiocese.org.

Review Board— The Review Board reviews cases involving allegations of sexual abuse of minors and makes recommendations to the bishop concerning those cases. The Review Board consists of a number of qualified lay volunteers with professional expertise as well as a canon lawyer and a priest who are appointed by the bishop. Mr. FRANK LINK, Chm. Members: Very Rev. CHRISTOPHER P. VASKO, V.J., J.C.D.; Mrs. MARY JO ANDERSON; Mr. FREDERICK FERRI; Ms. SHELLEY KILLEN; Dr. ROSALYN LISTON; Ms. SARAH MCHUGH; Dr. PAMELA OATIS; Ms. K. LAVERNE REDDEN.

Investigatory Team— The Investigatory Team is a designated group of individuals who are available to investigate allegations of sexual abuse. The Investigatory Team consists of a number of qualified lay volunteers with professional expertise and/or pastoral gifts to accomplish their task. They are appointed by the bishop. Members: Mr. LARRY ALBRIGHT; Mr. LAWRENCE KNANNLEIN; Mr. WILLIAM T. ROCCIA.

Pastoral Response Team— The Pastoral Response Team is a designated group of individuals who are available to respond to alleged victims of sexual abuse of minors and who are able to provide continuing pastoral care as needed. The Pastoral Response Team consists of a number of qualified lay volunteers with professional expertise. Members: Dr. TONY ALFANO; Ms. DIANE DERR; Miss SANDY HERMAN; Mr. JAMES HEYMAN; Ms. SHELLEY KILLEN; Mr. RICHARD KOHLER; Ms. ANDREA LOCH; Ms. ROSALIE STLUKA, L.I.S.W.; Mr. THOMAS WILLIAMS.

Human Resources—Catholic Center, 1933 Spielbusch Ave., Toledo, 43604-5360. Tel: 419-244-6711; Fax: 419-244-4791. Mr. GREGORY C. REED, Dir.; Mrs. RENE COUTTS, Generalist. Email: rcoutts@toledodiocese.org; Mrs. MEGHAN REED, Specialist. Email: mreed@toledodiocese.org; Mrs. JESSICA PARKER, HR Representative. Provides advice and counsel to diocesan offices, agencies and parishes in effective human resource practices; responsible for development, implementation and administration of personnel policies and programs in the areas of recruitment, employment, compensation/benefits and employee relations.

Retirement Plan for Lay Employees (RPLE)—Catholic Center, 1933 Spielbusch Ave., Toledo, 43604-5360. Tel: 419-244-6711; Fax: 419-244-4791. Mrs. LINDA MILLER, Admin. Email: lmiller@toledodiocese.org; Mrs. MARY P. BERNING, Asst. Email: mberning@toledodiocese.org. Maintains employees' contribution and benefit records and communicates with parishes, participants, trustees, investment and other professional counsel. Administers benefits including retirement, disability, death and survivor.

Employee Benefit Fund— Maintains employer's contribution records and administers certain employee benefits including life insurance, retiree health care stipend and the F. Edward Schaefer Scholarship.

Tax Deferred Savings Program for Employees— 403 (b). Savings plan to give lay employees' the opportunity to build savings for retirement through pre-tax paycheck.

Mareda, Inc.— MAREDA, Inc., is the Catholic diocesan low income housing corporation founded in 1978 by the late Bishop John A. Donovan. It is the successor corporation to the Catholic Better Community Development Corporation, which had been the diocesan housing corporation for the previous 11 years. This corporation extends the church's ministry of housing to the elderly and people with disabilities who are economically challenged. Very Rev. MICHAEL R. BILLIAN, V.E., Pres. Managed by Vistula Management Co. P.O. Box 4719, Toledo, 43620. Tel: 419-242-2300; Fax: 419-246-4703; Mr. JOHN KIELY, Dir. Email: jkiely@vmc.org.

Madonna Homes— (196 units) *722 Huron St., Toledo, 43604-5360.* Tel: 419-244-3758. Ms. TRACEY FRANKLIN, Mgr.

Regina Manor— (180 units) *3739 N. Erie St., #1B, Toledo, 43611.* Tel: 419-726-6186. Ms. KATRINA CONWAY, Mgr.

Delaware Acres— (68 units) *725 Buchanan St., Fremont, 43420.* Tel: 419-334-9558. Ms. MARCELLA WHITE, Mgr.

Moody Manor— (119 units) *2293 1/2 Kent St., Toledo, 43620.* Tel: 419-246-4737. Ms. ANNE FREEMAN, Mgr.

Hope Manor— (100 units) *4702 Violet Rd., Toledo, 43623.* Tel: 419-246-4733. Ms. CINDY KASPRZAK, Mgr.

Michaelmas Manor— (94 units) *3260 Schneider Rd., Toledo, 43614.* Tel: 419-389-4615. Ms. DIANE CLAUDA, Mgr.

Plaza Apartments— (160 units) *2520 Monroe St., Toledo, 43620.* Tel: 419-244-1881. Ms. ANGELA SHAW, Mgr.

Diocesan Outreach Centers—

Assumption Center—219 Page St., Toledo, 43620. Tel: 419-243-9213; Fax: 419-243-5405. Ms. SUZANNE STAPLETON, Facility Admin.; Ms. ELLEN MCCOMIS, Prog. Dir.

DeSales Center—501 Cherry St., Toledo, 43604. Tel: 419-243-4242; Fax: 419-243-4243. Deacon THOMAS CARONE, Dir.

Helping Hands of St. Louis—443 Sixth St., Toledo, 43605. Tel: 419-691-0613; Fax: 419-697-4223. Mr. PAUL COOK, Dir.

Office of Communications—Catholic Center, 1933 Spielbusch Ave., Toledo, 43604-5360. Tel: 419-244-6711; Fax: 419-244-0468. Ms. SALLY A. OBERSKI, Dir. Email: soberski@toledodiocese.org; VACANT, Pub. Rels. Asst. Represents the bishop and diocesan offices to the media; provides counsel for media and public relations and marketing efforts to the diocesan agencies, institutions and parishes; produces all news releases and places radio and television programming in the name of the diocese.

"Catholic Chronicle"—Catholic Center, 1933 Spielbusch Ave., Toledo, 43604-5360. Tel: 419-244-6711; Fax: 419-244-0468. Web: www.catholicchronicle.org. Email: ccnews@toledodiocese.org. Mrs. ANGELA KESSLER, Editor. Email: akessler@toledodiocese.org. The Catholic Chronicle is the official newspaper of the Diocese of Toledo. Its mission is to spread the good news of the Gospel by reporting information, providing education and including inspiring features about people and events in the diocese and the worldwide Catholic Church. It is published twice a month, except July.

Diocesan Directory—Catholic Center, 1933 Spielbusch Ave., Toledo, 43604-5360. Tel: 419-244-6711; Fax: 419-244-0468. ROSE ANNE CONRAD, Coordinating Sec. Email: rconrad@toledodiocese.org.

Information Technology—Catholic Center, 1933 Spielbusch Ave., Toledo, 43604-5360. Tel: 419-244-6711; Fax: 419-244-0468. Mr. JIM BRISTOW, Dir. Email: jbristow@toledodiocese.org; Ms. SHARON LANDIS, Assoc. Dir. Email: slandis@toledodiocese.org. Provides direct information technology services to organizations within the Catholic Center and its satellite locations. Consulting, technical guidelines, recommendations, procurement of hardware and software and other related system services are provided to parishes and schools.

Priests' Personnel Board—Tel: 419-644-6527 (Assumption Holy Trinity Rectory). Rev. RONALD A. SCHOCK, Chm., Assumption Holy Trinity, 2649 US Hwy. 20, Swanton, 43558. Email: father_@hotmail.com. Advises the diocesan bishop regarding the appointment of priests to the positions he identifies; serves as liaison between the bishop and the priests and the parishes in matters dealing with appointments. Members: Revs. KENT R. KAUFMAN; FRANKLIN P. KEHRES; Very Rev. DENNIS M. METZGER, V.F.; Revs. RONALD A. SCHOCK; JOSEPH R. STEINBAUER; DAVID A. REINHART.

Tribunal—Catholic Center, 1933 Spielbusch Ave., Toledo, 43604-5360. Tel: 419-244-6711; Fax: 419-244-4791. The mission of the Tribunal, under the guidance of our bishop, is to reflect and experience Christ in the ministry of justice through the compassionate and equitable application of church law, and to protect the rights and dignity of each person without discrimination, and to provide an opportunity for healing.

Judicial Vicar—Very Rev. CHRISTOPHER P. VASKO, V.J., J.C.D. Email: cvasko@toledodiocese.org.

Judges—Rev. JAMES E. AUTH, J.C.L.; Very Rev. MARVIN G. BORGER, V.G., J.C.L.; Rev. JOSEPH P. JAROS (Retired); Very Rev. GEORGE P. MILLER, J.C.L.; Revs. WILLIAM C. PARKER (Retired); DAVID M. ROSS, V.F., S.T.L., J.C.D.; Very Rev. DENNIS A. SCHROEDER, V.F.; Rev. RONALD R. WARNIMONT, J.C.L.

Defenders of the Bond—Revs. JOSEPH L. VAMOS (Retired); RONALD R. WARNIMONT, J.C.L.; Sr. MARCELLA HERMAN, O.S.F., J.C.L.; Rev. GARY D. YANUS, J.C.D.

Procurator-Advocate for Respondents—Mrs. PATRICIA A. EINGLE.

Ecclesiastical Notaries—Mrs. PAULA S. BUTLER; Mrs. ANGELA D. WALKER.

General Counsel— To support the Diocese of Toledo in its mission to serve the Body of Christ. This position serves as the principal legal advisor for the diocese, parishes, schools, cemeteries and other institutions that fall under the diocesan bishop's jurisdiction. Deacon JAMES CARUSO, Gen. Counsel.

Advisory Bodies

Priests' Council— Representing the presbyterate, the Priests' Council is to be like a senate of the bishop, assisting him in the governance of the diocese (canon 495). Rev. DAVID M. ROSS, V.F., S.T.L., J.C.D., Chm., 222 S. West St., Lima, 45801. Tel: 419-222-5521. Email: dmross@wcoil.com.

College of Consultors— The College of Consultors advises the bishop in the more important matters of diocesan administration (canon 502). Very Rev. MICHAEL O. BROWN, V.F.; Revs. GREGORY L. PEATEE, V.F.; DAVID M. ROSS, V.F., S.T.L., J.C.D.; Very Rev. GEORGE E. WENZINGER, V.F.; Revs. FREDERICK J. DUSCHL (Retired); EDWARD J. LITTELMANN; DENNIS G. WALSH; RONALD R. WARNIMONT, J.C.L.; HERBERT F. WEBER.

Deans— Also known as a vicar forane in the Code of Canon Law, each dean has the responsibility of promoting and coordinating the pastoral activity of his deanery according to the norm of law. Together, the deans serve as advisors to the bishop (canon 553-555). Blessed Junipero Serra Deanery: Very Rev. STEPHEN J. BLUM, V.F. Blessed Kateri Tekakwitha Deanery: Very Rev. MARK J. HERZOG, V.F. Blessed Teresa of Calcutta Deanery: Very Rev. DENNIS P. HARTIGAN, Ph.D., V.F. Our Lady of the Lake Deanery: Very Rev. JOHN C. MISSLER, V.F. Our Lady, Queen of Peace Deanery: Very Rev. DANIEL E. BORGELT, V.F. Precious Blood of Jesus Deanery: Very Rev. JOSEPH P. SZYBKA, V.F. St. Agnes Deanery: Very Rev. MICHAEL O. BROWN, V.F. St. Francis of Assisi Deanery: Very Rev. MICHAEL G. HOHENBRINK, V.F. St. George Deanery: Very Rev. GEORGE E. WENZINGER, V.F. St. John Neumann Deanery: Very Rev. FRANCIS J. SPEIER, V.F. St. Juan Diego Deanery: Very Rev. NELSON G. BEAVER, V.F. St. Katherine Drexel Deanery: Very Rev. GREGORY R. HITE, V.F. St. Luke Deanery: Very Rev. DENNIS M. METZGER, V.F. St. Maximilian Kolbe Deanery: Very Rev. G. ALLAN FILLMAN, V.F. St. Philomena Deanery: Very Rev. DENNIS A. SCHROEDER, V.F.

Diocesan Pastoral Advisory Council— The Diocesan Pastoral Advisory Council is a recommending body that will assist the bishop in setting the direction and vision for the diocese for pastoral ministry. The Diocesan Pastoral Advisory Council will engage in a planning process that includes assessment, development of strategies and evaluation. As it prays and works to carry out its mission, the council will promote and model collaboration, collegiality, cooperation and community. Members: Ms. SHARON BELISLE; Ms. IRMA CELESTINO; Ms. SHARON CHRISTY; Mr. BRAD COLON; Mrs. ALVINA COSTILLA; Deacon JAMES E. DUNN; Mrs. PATRICIA A. EINGLE; Mrs. PATRICIA ENGLEHART; Mr. ROBERT GEIGER; Mr. RICHARD HANUSZ; Ms. LIZ MILLER; Mr. JOSH MOCEK; Rev. JEFFREY J. NORDHAUS; Ms. CHERYL PRYOR; Ms. LINDA SALMONS; Mr. DAVID SANTO; Mr. BRUCE WINTERS.

Finance Council— The council reviews quarterly financial statements and advises the bishop on financial matters and investments. Ex Officio Members: Most Rev. LEONARD P. BLAIR, S.T.D.; Very Rev. MICHAEL R. BILLIAN, V.E.; Deacon RONALD D. HENDERSON. Members: Mr. RICHARD FAIST; Ms. BRENDA LEE, CPA; Ms. SUSAN MORGAN; Mr. HAL REED; Mr. SCOTT SAVAGE; Mr. SCOTT SCHOOK; Ms. SUE VERES.

Bishop's Education Council— The Council advises the bishop and the superintendent of schools on all matters concerning Catholic schools below the collegiate level in the diocese. Ex Officio Members: Most Rev. LEONARD P. BLAIR; Mr. JACK ALTENBURGER; Mrs. CAROLYN JAKSETIC; Mr. MICHAEL BEIER; Mrs. MARY CHALMERS. Members: Mr. WADE KAPSZUKIEWICZ; Mr. DAVID GERARDI; Dr. J.J. SREENAN; Mrs. JUDITH J. HALL; Rev. FRANK KEHRES; Mr. ROB LOEB; Dr. JANET ROBINSON; Mrs. TRESSA REITH; Very Rev. MARK J. HERZOG, V.F.; Mrs. MARY WERNER; Mr. WALTER KLIMASKI.

Project Review Board— The Project Review Board assists the bishop of Toledo by reviewing potential building, renovation and property expansion plans of the institutions of the diocese. Members: Most Rev. LEONARD P. BLAIR; Very Rev. MICHAEL R. BILLIAN, V.E.; Rev. KEITH A. STRIPE; Deacon

RONALD D. HENDERSON; Sisters JOYCE LEHMAN, C.PP.S.; KATHLEEN PADDEN, O.S.U.; Rev. HERBERT F. WEBER; Mr. JEFF MILLER.

Building Commission— The commission reviews all areas of architectural and structural design of plumbing, heating, air-conditioning and electrical systems involving the construction, repair or remodeling of church property. Dr. GEORGE MURNEN, Chm. Members: Rev. GERALD J. CHMIEL; Mr. JAMES CIHAK; Rev. FRANK K. ECKART; Dr. MARK A. PICKETT; Mr. FRANK RUGGIERO.

Liturgical Commission— At the invitation of the bishop, the Toledo Diocesan Liturgical Commission, in collaboration with the Office of Worship, assists the bishop in carrying out his function as promoter and guardian of the liturgical life of the diocese. Members: Sisters ANN CARMEN BARONE, O.S.F.; JOY BARKER, O.S.F.; Very Revs. MICHAEL R. BILLIAN, V.E.; MICHAEL O. BROWN, V.F.; Deacon JAMES CAVERA; Ms. RUTH FOSNAUGH; Mr. DANIEL J. DEMSKI; Mr. JACK GERDING; Ms. SANDRA HARDING; Dr. ROSALYN LISTON; Mr. CHARLES MCLAUGHLIN; Ms. KATHRYN L. MUMY; Mr. RONALD OSSOVICKI; Sr. CHRISTINE PRATT, O.S.U.; Rev. CHARLES E. SINGLER, D.Min.; Mr. JONATHON WALBERT; Mr. TONY ZSIGRAY.

Secretariat of Evangelization

Catechesis and Lifelong Formation Division—Sr. NANCY MATHIAS, O.S.U., Secretariat Leader, Catholic Center, 1933 Spielbusch Ave., Toledo, 43604-5360. Tel: 419-244-6711; Fax: 419-244-4791. Email: nmathias@toledodiocese.org.

Office of Evangelization and Catechesis—Catholic Center, 1933 Spielbusch Ave., Toledo, 43604-5360. Tel: 419-244-6711; Fax: 419-244-4791. Mr. DAVID MCCUTCHEN, Dir. Email: dmccutchen@toledodiocese.org. The Office of Evangelization and Catechesis oversees all religious education within the diocese. The work of the office can be divided into five primary areas: evangelization; adult faith formation; parish and school catechetical ministry; catechetical certification and lay ecclesial ministry and stewardship. Education and information in these areas is provided especially through the Mysterium Christi Diocesan Institute.

Media Resource Center—Web: www.toledocatholicmedia.org. The Media Resource Center, as part of the Catechetical Ministry Office, provides media resources to be used in the process of formation and spiritual development with parishes, schools and agencies of the diocese.

Office of Vocations: Priesthood and Consecrated Life—Catholic Center, 1933 Spielbusch Ave., Toledo, 43604-5360. Tel: 419-244-6711; Fax: 419-244-4791. Web: www.toledovocations.com. Rev. ADAM L. HERTZFELD, Dir. Email: ahertzfeld@toledodiocese.org; Mrs. YVONNE M. DUBIELAK, Assoc. Dir. Email: ydubielak@toledodiocese.org. The primary mission of the Office of Vocations is to assist those men who are called by God to the diocesan priesthood to recognize, discern and respond to their vocational call. In conjunction with seminary personnel, we assume responsibility for the formation of diocesan seminarians. We aim to empower all members of the local church to grow in awareness of their responsibility to foster and nourish vocations to the priesthood and consecrated life and seek to provide them with the necessary education and tools to do so.

Vicar for Deacons—Catholic Center, 1933 Spielbusch Ave., Toledo, 43604-5360. Tel: 419-244-6711; Fax: 419-244-4791. Deacon ALFREDO DIAZ. Email: adiaz@toledodiocese.org. The bishop's representative to permanent deacons of the diocese, providing pastoral care for deacons and their families and opportunities for spiritual and professional growth.

Deacon Formation—Catholic Center, 1933 Spielbusch Ave., Toledo, 43604-5360. Tel: 419-244-6711; Fax: 419-244-4791. Rev. WILLIAM J. KUBACKI, Dir. Email: wkubacki@toledodiocese.org. Coordinates the promotion, recruitment and discernment of a vocation to the diaconate. Provides a program in the areas of human, spiritual, and intellectual pastoral formation. Assists Vicar for Deacons in ministry to the diaconal community.

Vicar for Priests—Catholic Center, 1933 Spielbusch Ave., Toledo, 43604-5360. Tel: 419-244-6711; Fax: 419-244-4791. Rev. WILLIAM J. KUBACKI. Email: wkubacki@toledodiocese.org. Serves as a liaison for the bishop in providing pastoral care to the priests of the diocese.

Associate Vicar for Priests—Rev. THOMAS H. RADLOFF, S.J., 5901 Airport Hwy., Toledo, 43615. Tel: 419-865-5743, Ext. 242; Fax: 419-865-9675. Email: tradloff@gmail.com.

Continuing Formation for Priests— The provision for ongoing opportunities designed to enhance the human, spiritual, intellectual and pastoral growth for priests is mandated by the church. The office is at the service of the bishop and offers resources for the priests continuing formation and education. Rev. WILLIAM J. KUBACKI, Dir., Catholic Center, 1933 Spielbusch Ave., Toledo, 43604-5360. Tel: 419-244-6711; Fax: 419-244-4791. Email: wkubacki@toledodiocese.org.

Vicar For Religious—Catholic Center, 1933 Spielbusch Ave., Toledo, 43604-5360. Tel: 419-244-6711; Fax: 419-244-4791. Sr. NANCY MATHIAS, O.S.U. Email: nmathias@toledodiocese.org. Serves as the liaison for the diocesan bishop to religious women and men of the diocese, responds to the needs of the religious in the diocese and raises consciousness about the service that religious render in the diocese.

Women Blessing Women, Inc.—223 Page St., Toledo, 43620. Tel: 419-241-9789; Fax: 419-241-9791. Web: www.womenblessingwomen.org. VACANT, Dir. To serve, bless and empower women to achieve their potential, obtain living-wage jobs and break the cycle of poverty.

Youth, Young Adult and Campus Ministry—Catholic Center, 1933 Spielbusch Ave., Toledo, 43604-5360. Tel: 419-244-6711; Fax: 419-244-4791. Deacon JERRY ZIEMKIEWICZ, Coord. Youth Ministry. Email: jziemkiewicz@toledodiocese.org; Sr. RITA MARIE SCHROEDER, S.N.D., Coord. Young Adult & Campus Ministry. Email: rschroeder@toledodiocese.org; Revs. JEFFREY R. MCBETH, Chap. Catholic Youth Ministry. Email: jmcbeth@bex.net; MICHAEL G. DANDURAND, Chap. Young Adult & Campus Ministry. Email: frmichael@sttoms.com; CHRISTOPHER G. BAZAR, Chap. Catholic Scouting. Email: cbazar872@yahoo.com; VACANT, Chm. Toledo Diocese Catholic Committee on Scouting. Working with and supporting parishes and campuses to empower youth, young adults and college students to live as disciples of Jesus Christ by fostering a deeper understanding of and participation in the Catholic faith community.

Teens Encounter Christ (T E C)— A weekend experience for high school juniors, seniors and college freshmen to encounter Christ in a faith-filled community. Deacon JERRY ZIEMKIEWICZ, Contact. Email: jziemkiewicz@toledodiocese.org.

Mission of Accompaniment— The continued mission effort whereby the Diocese of Toledo supports financially the Diocese of Hwange in Zimbabwe in addressing the needs of the people of Binga and its outstations. Revs. BERNARD J. BOFF, Dir. (Retired). Email: bboff@toledodiocese.org; THOMAS J. MCQUILLEN, Seminary Professor. Email: frtombinga@yahoo.com.

Catholic Men's Fellowship— Catholic Men's Fellowship links men in supportive relationships, provides resources consistent with Catholic teaching and develops training and formation opportunities for men's ministry and evangelization. TADHG FARRELL, Coord.; Mr. DAVID MCCUTCHEN, Moderator.

Catholic Youth and School Services Division—Mr. JACK ALTENBURGER, Secretariat Leader & Supt. Catholic Schools, Catholic Center, 1933 Spielbusch Ave., Toledo, 43604-5360. Tel: 419-244-6711; Fax: 419-255-8269. Email: jaltenburger@toledodiocese.org.

Mission— To assist the bishop in his teaching mission by serving, challenging and supporting the leaders of youth formation and education who minister in parishes and the diocese.

Services— 1. To provide formation, direction and support for parish leaders responsible for catechesis and sacramental preparation of children and youth. 2. To provide leadership, support and services to the local Catholic school community and its leadership and staff. 3. To provide youth formation through CYO athletic programs.

Catholic Schools—Email: schools@toledodiocese.org. Web: www.cyss.org. Mrs. CAROLYN JAKSETIC, Asst. Supt. Email: cjaksetic@toledodiocese.org; MARTHA HASSELBUSCH, Curriculum Consultant. Email: mhasselbusch@toledodiocese.org; Mr. MICHAEL BEIER, Dir. Govt. Programs/High School. Email: mbeier@toledodiocese.org; Ms. KATHY TARASCHKE, Coord. Innovative Educators. Email: ktaraschke@toledodiocese.org; Mrs. SHARI BEIER, Technology Consultant. Email: sbeier@toledodiocese.org; Mr. FRANK DILALLO, Prevention Intervention. Email: fdilallo@toledodiocese.org; Mrs. VICKI FITTS, Teacher Certification. Email: vfitts@toledodiocese.org.

The Catholic Youth Organization (CYO)—Catholic Center, 1933 Spielbusch Ave., Toledo, 43604-5360. Tel: 419-244-6711; 419-243-4296 (Recorder); Fax: 419-244-3420. Web: www.cyss.org. Email: cyo@toledodiocese.org. Mr. JEFF MIELCAREK, Dir. Email: jmielcarek@toledodiocese.org; Ms. JULIE DUBIELAK, Asst. Dir. Email: jdubielak@toledodiocese.org.

Central City Ministry of Toledo Catholic School—Catholic Center, 1933 Spielbusch Ave., Toledo, 43604-5360. Tel: 419-244-6711; Fax: 419-255-8269. Mr. JACK ALTENBURGER, Interim Dir. Email: jaltenburger@toledodiocese.org. A consortium of two Catholic schools joined together to more effectively and efficiently minister to the central city community: Rosary Cathedral, Queen of Apostles.

Diocesan Schools— Tiffin, Calvert Catholic School; Defiance, Holy Cross Catholic School; Fremont St. Joseph Central Catholic School; Lima Central Catholic High School; Norwalk Catholic School; Oregon Cardinal Stritch High School; Sandusky Central Catholic School; Toledo Central Catholic High School; Central City Ministry of Toledo Catholic School; Toledo Kateri Catholic School.

Secretariat of Finance and Administration

Secretariat Leader and Canonical Finance Officer—Deacon RONALD D. HENDERSON, Catholic Center, 1933 Spielbusch Ave., Toledo, 43604-5360. Tel: 419-244-6711; Fax: 419-244-4791. Email: rhenderson@toledodiocese.org.

Financial Services— Provides centralized accounting and payroll services for diocesan offices (including CCMT school), responsible for investments, accountable for funds of the diocese. Provides auditing services to parishes of the diocese to ensure proper accounting of parish funds. Consulting and training is available for pastors, administrators, finance councils and parish staff. Mrs. RENE YUHAS SCHMIDBAUER, Finance & Database Mgr. Email: rschmidbauer@toledodiocese.org; Mr. STEVEN SICKMILLER, Diocesan Comptroller. Email: ssickmiller@toledodiocese.org; Ms. HONG XIAO, CPA/Inactive, Staff Accountant. Email: hxiao@toledodiocese.org; Ms. LISA ADAIR, Accounts Receivable. Email: ladair@toledodiocese.org; MICHELE POWERS, Accounts Payable; Ms. VICKI FINK, ParishSOFT Admin. Email: vfink@toledodiocese.org.

Development Office—Catholic Center, 1933 Spielbusch Ave., Toledo, 43604-5360. Tel: 419-244-6711; Fax: 419-720-0053. Ms. KAREN SZYMANSKI, Diocesan Fund Officer. Email: kszymanski@toledodiocese.org; Ms. JOELLEN CHOCHARD, Devel. Database Admin. Email: jchochard@toledodiocese.org. The Development Office is responsible for all fund development that includes the Annual Catholic Appeal, an annuity program and provides clearing house coordination for the sale of stocks and bonds for the diocese and affiliated parishes within the diocese. Provides support and direction to parishes, schools and departments within the diocese for major and planned gifts including but not limited to wills/bequests, life insurance and charitable gift annuities.

Central City Ministries of Toledo—Catholic Center, 1933 Spielbusch Ave., Toledo, 43604-5360. Tel: 419-244-6711; Fax: 419-270-0053. VACANT, Dir.; Ms. CLAIRE GUISFREDI, CCMT Fundraising Officer. Email: cguisfredi@toledodiocese.org. CCMT is a Catholic school with two campuses (Rosary Cathedral and Queen of Apostles) that offers educational opportunities to those families within the central city community. Underwriting opportunities include The Urban All-American Celebration, Celebrity Wait Night and Adopt-a-School.

Northwest Ohio Scholarship Fund—Catholic Center, 1933 Spielbusch Ave., Toledo, 43604-5360. Tel: 419-244-6711; Fax: 419-270-0053. Ms. ANN RIDDLE, Coord. Programs. Email: ariddle@toledodiocese.org. A program that supports parents' choice of a private education. Acceptance is based on family income and follows the federal standards for subsidized lunch program, as well as the number of members in a family. The family is expected to pay the first $500 of tuition and must live in Fulton, Wood or Lucas County. This program is affiliated with the National Children's Scholarship Fund.

Catholic Foundation, Inc.—Catholic Center, 1933 Spielbusch Ave., Toledo, 43604-5360. Tel: 419-244-6711; Fax: 419-270-0053. Ms. KAREN SZYMANSKI, Contact. Email: kszymanski@toledodiocese.org. Established in the fall of 1988 as an investment fund for Catholic parishes, schools, cemeteries and agencies of the diocese and the diocese itself.

Protected Self Insurance—Mailing Address: Protected Self Insurance Program (PSI), P.O. Box 30, Swanton, 43558. Tel: 419-826-5300; Fax: 419-826-5306. Mr. JOSEPH SPENTHOFF, Dir. Email: jspenthoff@toledodiocese.org; Mrs. VICKY SPENTHOFF, Administrative Asst. Email: vspenthoff@toledodiocese.org.

Catholic Cemeteries—5725 Hill Ave., (corner of Holland-Sylvania Rd.), Toledo, 43615-5852. Tel: 419-531-5747; Fax: 419-531-0946. Email: info@cathcemtoledo.org. Mr. DAVID CZECH, Diocesan Sexton. Assists parishes in bereavement ministry, provides appropriate products, services and burial sites, offers counsel to parish cemeteries in the diocese.

Cemeteries—Calvary Cemetery, 2224 Dorr St., Toledo, 43607. Tel: 419-536-3751. *Mount Carmel Cemetery, 15 E. Manhattan Blvd., Toledo, 43608.* Tel: 419-536-3751. *Resurrection Cemetery, 5725 Hill Ave., Toledo, 43615.* Tel: 419-531-5747.

Secretariat for Pastoral Leadership

Secretariat for Pastoral Leadership—Web: www.toledodiocese-spl.org. Email: pastoralleadership@toledodiocese.org.

Secretariat Leader—Sr. JOYCE LEHMAN, C.PP.S., Catholic Center, 1933 Spielbusch Ave., Toledo, 43624-1371. Tel: 419-244-6711; Fax: 419-244-4791. Email: jlehman@toledodiocese.org.

Mission Statement— The secretariat staff believes that baptism into Christ Jesus calls all to evangelize and to participate fully in the mission of the universal church. We serve the diverse peoples of the Diocese of Toledo by providing planning, resources, education and formation opportunities for the pastoral leadership of the Diocese of Toledo. Staff: Mrs. SUE FRENCH, Administrative Coord.; Mrs. FATIMA MARTINEZ, Administrative Staff; Mr. DANIEL J. DEMSKI, Exec. Admin.; Ms. JOETTE ROZANSKI, Technology Coord.; Mrs. TINA HORNYAK, Financial Coord.; Mr. MICHAEL L. WASSERMAN, Dir. Special Projects.

Office of Black Catholics—Catholic Center, 1933 Spielbusch Ave., Toledo, 43604-5360. Tel: 419-244-6711; Fax: 419-244-4791. Mr. MICHAEL YOUNGBLOOD, Dir. Email: myoungblood@toledodiocese.org. Assists parishes and deaneries in the area of African-American catechesis and Black Catholic celebrations and retreats; provides workshops on diversity and inclusion, racism and prejudice; facilitates diocesan Black Catholic events and promotes the National Black Catholic Congress.

Ecumenical and Interreligious Affairs Commission—709 W. Catawba Rd., Port Clinton, 43452. Tel: 419-797-4801. Rev. JAMES E. PEIFFER, Chm. (Retired). Supports local initiatives that express the Catholic commitment to the ecumenical movement and interreligious dialogue; develops suggestions for ways in which parishes can become ecumenically involved.

Office of Equal Access Ministries—Catholic Center, 1933 Spielbusch Ave., Toledo, 43604-5360. Tel: 419-244-6711; Fax: 419-244-4791; Teletype: 419-243-1475. Email: equalaccess@toledodiocese.org. Ms. MARSHA RIVAS, Dir. Email: mrivas@toledodiocese.org. Promotes ministry to people with disabilities ensuring inclusion in all aspects of the life of the church; assists parishes in assessing accessibility.

Office of Hispanic Ministries— (Oficina de Hispano Ministerio) *Catholic Center, 1933 Spielbusch Ave., Toledo, 43604-5360.* Tel: 419-244-6711; Fax: 419-244-4791. Rev. JUAN FRANCISCO MOLINA, Dir. Email: jmolina@toledodiocese.org; Mr. VIRGILIO GUERRA, Assoc. Dir. Email: vguerra@toledodiocese.org. Provides an active presence to, among and for the Hispanic population of northwest Ohio through support for Hispanic pastoral ministry; providing resources and collaborating with pastoral leadership in parishes and institutions to serve and advocate for the migrant and new immigrant populations at the local level.

Office of Global Concerns—Catholic Center, 1933 Spielbusch Ave., Toledo, 43604-5360. Tel: 419-244-6711; Fax: 419-244-4791. Deacon PAUL J. WHITE, Dir. Email: pwhite@toledodiocese.org. Provides resources for parishes and deaneries to deepen the mission consciousness and responsibility of the people of the diocese; informs them of needs; encourages prayer for the missions and missionaries; provides a conduit for material response to disasters within the country and around the world. Programs include the Society for the Propagation of the Faith, Catholic Relief Services, Holy Childhood Association and St. Peter the Apostle.

Office of Worship and Liturgical Music—Catholic Center, 1933 Spielbusch Ave., Toledo, 43604-5360. Tel: 419-244-6711; Fax: 419-244-4791. Rev. CHARLES E. SINGLER, D.Min., Dir. Email: csingler@toledodiocese.org; Mr. PAUL J. MONACHINO, Dir. Liturgical Music. Email: pmonachino@toledodiocese.org. Leads the continued development of the liturgical vision of the diocese guided by the documents and spirit of the Second Vatican Council and the directives of the USCCB; provides liturgical formation for pastoral leadership; provides liturgical resources to pastoral leadership and ministers. Promotes musical excellence in the liturgical life of the diocese; provides resources for ongoing evaluation and growth of music ministry for parishes.

Diocesan Council of Catholic Women (DCCW)—Catholic Center, 1933 Spielbusch Ave., Toledo, 43604-5360. Tel: 419-244-6711; Fax: 419-244-4791. Mrs. JAN HAZEN, Pres. Email: tdccw@toledodiocese.org; Very Rev. MARK J. HERZOG, V.F., Moderator. Affiliated with the National Council of Catholic Women, the Diocesan Council seeks to strengthen and broaden the network of affiliated parish women's organizations and individual Catholic women by providing programs, events and projects to respond to the spiritual and educational needs of diocesan women, their parishes, and communities.

Office of Pastoral Planning—Catholic Center, 1933 Spielbusch Ave., Toledo, 43604-5360. Tel: 419-244-6711; Fax: 419-244-4791. Sr. JOYCE LEHMAN, C.PP.S., Dir. Email: jlehman@toledodiocese.org. Provides resources and training for pastors/pastoral leaders, pastoral council members and pastoral staff in planning for a viable and sustainable parish; assists parishes in implementing the "Enhancing Parish Vitality" self-assessment process.

Secretariat of Catholic Charities

Catholic Charities—Web: www.catholiccharitiesnwo.org. Email: ccharities@toledodiocese.org. WILLIAM SANFORD, Secretariat Leader & Dir., Catholic Center, 1933 Spielbusch Ave., Toledo, 43604-5360. Tel: 419-244-6711; Fax: 419-244-5171.

Mission Statement— In the service ministry of the church Catholic Charities supports and enhances our parish communites' response to the social Gospel of Jesus Christ throughout the Diocese of Toledo.

History/Overview of Services— Catholic Charities began in 1914 to provide care and protection to orphans and single mothers. Since then the agency has grown to provide assistance to individuals, families and groups through direct social services, consultation, case management services, resources and in-service training for parish-based ministry programs, advocacy and justice education. While several programs are coordinated from a particular office, many services are available throughout the diocese.

Parish Community Services—Catholic Center, 1933 Spielbusch Ave., Toledo, 43604-5360. Tel: 419-244-6711; Fax: 419-244-4860. Ms. PATRICIA ULMER, Dir., 34 Woodlawn Ave., Norwalk, 44857. Tel: 419-668-3073; 800-668-3110. Email: pulmer@toledodiocese.org.

Family Connections/Healthy Beginnings—Catholic Center, 1933 Spielbusch Ave., Toledo, 43604-5360. Tel: 419-244-6711; Fax: 419-244-4860. Email: familyconnections@toledodiocese.org. Ms. ROBIN FOUSHEE, Coord. Email: rfoushee@toledodiocese.org. Provides diocesan-wide comprehensive support services for families and children including: Adoptions; Pregnancy Counseling; Domestic and International Home Studies; Post-Adoption Support; Infant Foster Care; Healthy Beginnings; Parenting Education.

Housing Services—Catholic Center, 1933 Spielbusch Ave., Toledo, 43604-5360. Tel: 419-244-6711; Fax: 419-244-4860. Provides qualified individuals and families with strategies to achieve future stability in their lives for home and financial management.

LaPosada (Family Emergency Shelter)—435 Eastern Ave., Toledo, 43609. Tel: 419-244-5931; Fax: 419-244-4993. Email: laposada@toledodiocese.org. Mr. MIKE KELLY, Coord. Email: mkelly@toledodiocese.org.

Miriam House (Huron County Transitional Housing)—249 W. Main St., Norwalk, 44857. Tel: 419-668-3073; 419-663-6341; 800-668-3110. Email: themiriamhouse@toledodiocese.org. Ms. LINDA RAPP, Coord. Email: lrapp@toledodiocese.org.

Permanent Supportive Housing Services Coordinator—VACANT.

Adult Advocacy Services— (Erie, Richland & Huron Counties) Guardianship services to adults 55 and older who are deemed incompetent by the court and who have no appropriate family support available. Payee services are focused on adults age 55 and older who voluntarily agree to assistance in maintaining their monthly budget.

Richland County - Mansfield—35 N. Park St., Mansfield, 44902. Tel: 419-524-0733. Ms. CAROL WHEELER, Contact. Email: cwheeler@toledodiocese.org.

Erie and Huron Counties - Norwalk—34 Woodlawn Ave., Norwalk, 44857. Tel: 419-668-3073; 800-668-3110. Ms. CAROL WHEELER, Coord. Email: cwheeler@toledodiocese.org.

Family Emergency Services—

Family Emergency Guidance—Catholic Center, 1933 Spielbusch Ave., Toledo, 43604-5360. Tel: 419-244-6711; Fax: 419-244-4860. Mr. BRIAN ROME, Coord. Email: brome@toledodiocese.org. Provides financial and lead paint education and limited financial assistance to people in need.

Community Emergency Assistance—35 N. Park St., Mansfield, 44902. Tel: 419-524-0733; Fax: 419-524-2055. Ms. REBECCA OWENS, Contact. Email: rowens@toledodiocese.org. Providing basic life sustaining services to people in need.

School Attendance Initiative Program—Catholic Center, 1933 Spielbusch Ave., Toledo, 43604-5360. Tel: 419-244-6711. Ms. THERESA ASHTON, Coord. Email: tashton@toledodiocese.org. This program focuses on Toledo parochial and public elementary students with beginning truancy problems by offering services that address the underlying family problems, enabling them to concentrate on their children's academic needs, school attendance and preventing future truancy issues.

Parish Ministries and Social Concerns—Catholic Center, 1933 Spielbusch Ave., Toledo, 43604-5360. Tel: 419-244-6711; Fax: 419-244-4860. VACANT, Dir., 537 Lime St., Fremont, 43420. Tel: 419-334-1331; Fax: 419-334-9837.

Social Ministry and Advocacy— Providing parish education promoting Catholic social teaching; parish social ministry formation; advocacy and legislative action; local, state and national networking for justice. VACANT.

Rural Life Ministry— Providing advocacy/education on rural and agricultural issues, annual Rural Life Day, Century Farm awards, Project Farm Hands, pastoral outreach, workshop and worship resources. VACANT, Contact.

Family Life Ministry—Catholic Center, 1933 Spielbusch Ave., Toledo, 43604-5360. Tel: 419-244-6711; Fax: 419-244-4860. Deacon TIMOTHY W. ETUE, Coord. Email: tetue@toledodiocese.org. Providing the following programs: Cana II, divorced/separated ministry, family spirituality, leadership in family ministry training, marriage enrichment/marriage preparation, natural family planning.

Respect Life Ministry—2200 W. Elm St., Lima, 45805. Tel: 419-796-8005. Ms. JAN KAHLE, Dir.

Respect Life/Pro-Life Issues—Email: familylife@toledodiocese.org.

Project Rachel— Confidential help for anyone suffering from the grief and guilt of abortion. *Information:* . Tel: 419-796-8005. *Project Rachel Help Line:* . Tel: 419-260-5811. Email: projectrachel@toledodiocese.org.

Diocesan Human Rights Commission— The Commission, through advocacy and prophetic voice, addresses human rights issues having an impact both within and outside the church. Ms. GERMAINE KIRK, Contact. Email: gkirk@toledodiocese.org.

Bereavement Action Committee— Providing support and training to parishes for bereavement ministry programs. Ms. GERMAINE KIRK, Contact. Email: gkirk@toledodiocese.org.

Jail and Prison Ministry— Coordinating ministry throughout the diocese; providing assistance, resources, retreats and workshops. Ms. GERMAINE KIRK, Contact. Email: gkirk@toledodiocese.org.

Catholic Campaign for Human Development— Anti-poverty, social justice program of the United States Catholic Conference of Bishops that funds self-help projects nationally and locally, assisting poor and low-income people help themselves. Ms. GERMAINE KIRK, Contact. Email: gkirk@toledodiocese.org.

Disaster Response— Coordinates response and collaborates with local response teams in providing services and resources to those affected by natural disasters. Ms. JAN KAHLE, Contact. Email: jkahle@toledodiocese.org.

Regional Offices—Fostoria: St. Wendelin Parish Center, 323 N. Wood St., Fostoria, 44830. Tel: 419-334-5061; Fax: 419-435-0733. *Fremont: 537 Lime St., Fremont, 43420.* Tel: 419-334-5061; 800-668-3110; Fax: 419-334-9737. *Mansfield: 35 N. Park St., Mansfield, 44902.* Tel: 419-524-0733; Fax: 419-524-2055. Email: rowens@toledodiocese.org. *Norwalk: 34 Woodlawn St., Norwalk, 44857.* Tel: 419-668-3073; 800-668-3110; Fax: 419-663-5070. Email: pulmer@toledodiocese.org. *Ottawa: SS. Peter and Paul Campus, 360 N. Locust St., Ottawa, 45875.* Tel: 419-796-8005. Email: jkahle@toledodiocese.org.

Affiliations and Licensures of Catholic Charities—

Ohio Catholic Conference—

Ohio Department of Human Services—

U.S. Catholic Conference of Bishops—

Catholic Club—1601 Jefferson Ave., Toledo, 43604. Tel: 419-243-7255; Fax: 419-243-6337. Email: info@catholicclub.org. Web: www.catholicclub.org. Mr. PAUL SZYMANSKI, Dir. Email: paul@catholicclub.org; Ms. BARB WITKOWSKI, Assoc. Dir. Email: barb@catholicclub.org.

Child Care— Mon.-Fri. 6:30 a.m. to 6:30 p.m. An educational child care and family center open to everyone, offering year-round state-licensed child care programs for infants through age 14. Infant care, toddler care, preschool care, before- and after-school care (transportation to and from school), calamity and snow day care, vacation day care and summer camp are available. Children participate in swimming, games, special events, field trips, crafts and more. Free of charge, all children receive breakfast, lunch and an afternoon snack. Children ages 3 and older receive free swim lessons as part of their child care enrollment.

Recreational Opportunities— Aquatic — Swim lessons for various levels of experience and age groups. School groups, scout troops and others may arrange group lessons. Transportation is available. Super Saturdays — 9 a.m.-1 p.m. (Oct.-May only) children in first through sixth grades enjoy a supervised day of activities including swimming, games and more.

Rentals— Facility — The pool and gym are available for parishes, class parties, birthday parties, team events, youth groups, etc. The facility is available for overnights and lock-ins. Vehicles — Two large school buses, one minibus and two 15-passenger vans are available for diocesan groups.

Licensed by: Ohio Department of Job and Family Services.

Accredited by: National Association for the Education of Young Children (NAEYC); National After School Association (NAA).

Other Organizations

Apostleship of the Sea— A ministry to the crews of ocean and lake ships that come to the Port of Toledo. Deacon EDWARD H. GRYCZEWSKI, Port Chap., 4448 289th St., Toledo, 43611. Email: ehgrycz@juno.com; Port of Toledo Ohio, 3332 St. Lawrence Dr., Toledo, 43605. Tel: 419-693-7678.

Christ Child Society of Toledo— A nonprofit, volunteer organization embracing members of all denominations. It is dedicated to the welfare of needy children in the Toledo area. The Toledo Chapter was founded in 1990 and has more than 60 members. *Mercy Professional Bldg., 2238 Jefferson Ave., Toledo, 43624.* Tel: 419-251-1218. Ms. LUCY ABU-ABSI, Pres.; Ms. KAREN SMITH, Vice Pres.; Ms. MARILYN ARBAUGH, Treas.; Ms. CAROL MORAVA, Sec.; Mrs. ANNE E. MALONE, Parliamentarian.

Cursillo Movement— Movement to form apostolic leaders and link them together for an effective, apostolic Christian life in the day-to-day environments where their lives take place. Spiritual Directors: Revs. EDWARD J. LITTELMANN, 4201 Heatherdowns Blvd., Toledo, 43614. Tel: 419-381-1540; JAMES E. BROWN, 6149 Hill Ave., Toledo, 43615. Tel: 419-865-2345; Deacon ALFREDO DIAZ, 1014 Garfield Rd., Fremont, 43420. Tel: 419-244-6711. Email: adiaz@toledodiocese.org; Sr. EDNA MICHEL, O.S.F., 200 St. Francis Ave., Tiffin, 44883. Tel: 419-447-0435. Email: emichel@tiffinfranciscans.org; Ms. MARGARET BOLTZ, Lay Dir., 322 Teal Dr., Toledo, 43615. Tel: 419-865-6959.

Fraternity of Communion and Liberation— Communion and Liberation is an ecclesial movement whose purpose is the education to Christian maturity of its adherents and collaboration in the mission of the church in all the spheres of contemporary life. *3454 Oak Alley Court, Toledo, 43606.* Tel: 419-578-0057. Dr. JEFFREY G. SCHMAKEL, Local Contact; Rev. STEPHEN R. MAJOROS, Priest Advisor (Retired).

Ministry To Catholic Charismatic Renewal (MCCR)— Provides pastoral guidance to parish charismatic prayer groups, promotes spiritual renewal through collaboration with prayer groups, parish staff and diocesan offices in integrating spirit baptism and spiritual gifts into the lives of Catholic people. *550 Clark St., Toledo, 43605-2273.* Tel: 419-691-6686; Fax: 419-691-1755. Web: www.mccrholyspirit.org. Email: mccr@toledolink.com. Mr. STEVEN TOTH, Dir.; Rev. JEROME F. NOWAKOWSKI, Spiritual Dir. (Retired).

Northwest Ohio Guild of the Catholic Medical Association—JEANNE WEISENBURGER, M.D., Contact, 1570 Elmore Rd., Pemberville, 43450. Tel: 419-287-4939. Email: rweisenb@verizon.net; Rev. ADAM L. HERTZFELD, Spiritual Advisor.

Philippine-American Catholic Council (PACC)— Provides opportunities for spiritual growth among members of the Filipino-American Catholic Community of greater Toledo and southeastern Michigan through Filipino liturgies, popular Marian devotions and other spiritual means. *3030 Tremainsville Rd., Toledo, 43613.* Tel: 419-471-1123. Rev. PETER V. ZAFE, Dir. Email: pvz64@aol.com.

Retrouvaille— An international program, offering help to couples who live in the disappointment and pain of a troubled marriage. It is a weekend experience with six follow-up sessions put on by couples who have rebuilt their own marriages. Rev. FREDERICK J. DUSCHL, Spiritual Dir. (Retired), 11312 County Rd. 6, Edon, 43518. Tel: 419-272-2475. Email: frfred@bright.net. Executive Team Couple: BONNIE LANGMEYER; SCOTT LANGMEYER, Mailing Address: 323 W. River St., P.O. Box 123, Deerfield, MI 49238. Tel: 517-447-3477. Email: bud@cass.net.

St. Vincent dePaul Society— A Catholic lay organization that leads women and men to grow spiritually and witness God's love by offering person-to-person service to those who are needy and suffering. *Diocesan Central Council, 1001 Washington St., Toledo, 43604-5360.* Tel: 419-243-6963. Mr. STEPHEN SANTO, Pres.; Ms. SANDRA BLOOMQUIST, Exec. Dir.; Rev. RONALD J. BRICKNER, Chap.

St. Vincent de Paul Thrift Store - Toledo—Tel: 419-243-2243.

Secular Franciscan Order—Tel: 800-372-6247. Web: www.nafra-sfo.org.

Divine Mercy Region, Lower Michigan and Toledo—Ms. MARY BITTNER, S.F.O., 1207 Collegewood St., Ypsilanti, MI 48197. Tel: 734-483-1956. Email: mbittner@umich.edu.

St. Paschal Fraternity (Toledo)—Mailing Address: P.O. Box 9118, Toledo, 43697. Tel: 419-868-8985; 800-372-6247. Ms. LISA CRAIG, S.F.O., Contact. Tel: 419-868-8985. Email: lisa5347@yahoo.com. Meetings: 3rd Sun. 2:30 pm at Mercy St. Vincent Medical Center Conference Room.

St. Maximilian Kolbe Fraternity (Toledo)—Mrs. MARIE CRISTE, S.F.O., Contact, 15275 S. Dixie Hwy. #419, Monroe, MI 48161. Tel: 734-240-2096. Email: mariecriste@comcast.net. Meetings: 2nd Tues. and 3rd Sun. 3 pm at St. Clement Church, 3030 Tremainsville Rd., Toledo.

St. Maximilian Kolbe Region, Northern Ohio—Mr. BERNARD F. WIRTZ, SFO, Regl. Min., 33049 Cobblestone Circle, North Ridgeville, 44039. Tel: 440-748-1580. Email: bfmaw@oh.rr.com.

St. Anthony of Padua Fraternity, Carey—Mr. KEITH COSSEY, SFO, 108 Rosewood Pl., Carey, 43316. Tel: 419-396-7373. Email: deadseascroller@aol.com.

St. Anthony of Padua Fraternity, Fostoria—Mrs. ANN MARIE JONES, SFO, 549 Maple St., Fostoria, 44830. Tel: 419-435-8707.

St. Maximilian Mary Kolbe Fraternity, Findlay—Ms. LORRAINE HENRY, 200 Shinkle St., Findlay, 45840. Tel: 419-422-5083.

St. Joseph Fraternity, Green Springs—Mr. DAVID LIPPOLD, SFO, Contact, 520 W. North St., McClure, 43534. Tel: 419-748-8173.

Queen of the Angels Fraternity, Lima—Ms. KATHY REEVES, SFO, Contact, 105 Chickadee Pl., Elida, 45807. Tel: 419-339-1507. Email: songbird482003@yahoo.com.

St. Michael Fraternity, Hicksville—Mr. ROBERT SILLIMAN, SFO, Contact, Mailing Address: P.O. Box 545, Antwerp, 45813. Tel: 419-258-3164. Email: msill@bright.net.

Secular Order of Discalced Carmelites—

Our Lady of the Holy Rosary Chapter (Toledo)—Ms. DONNA O'CONNELL, OCDS, Contact, 2155 Hawthorne Rd., Toledo, 43606. Tel: 419-531-3426.

Holy Family of the Infant Jesus' Flame of Love Chapter (Sandusky)—Ms. LOIS OPINCAR, OCDS, Contact, 30921 Walker Rd., Bay Village, 44140-1404. Tel: 440-871-3553. Email: lyo238@gmail.com. Meetings: 1st Tues. 6 pm at Sandusky St. Mary.

Serra International— Serra International is formally aggregated to the Pontifical Society for Priestly Vocations. Mr. GINO DIMATTIA, District Governor, 1824 University Blvd., Lima, 45805. Tel: 419-991-0289. Email: ginodimattia@juno.com; Mr. JOSEPH DIETRICH, Regl. Governor, 6958 Pennywhistle Cir., Painesville, 44077. Tel: 440-352-3846. Email: dietrich32@sbcglobal.net.

Defiance Serra Club—Mr. DAVID DIEHL, Pres., 2121 Baltimore St., Defiance, 43512. Tel: 419-782-2202. Email: diehltek@defnet.com. (1st Thurs. after 6:30 pm Mass Defiance St. John & 3rd Mon. 6 pm at Defiance K of C Hall).

Fremont Serra Club—Ms. CAROL WONDERLY, Pres., 5863 County Rd. 33, Helena, 43435. Tel: 419-638-4305 Meetings: 1st Wed. 7:30 pm at Pines Retreat Center; 2nd Wed. noon at Fremont Federation of Women's Home.

Lima Serra Club—Mr. RICHARD WOODFIELD, Pres., 1059 Westerly Dr., Lima, 45805. Tel: 419-991-5094; 419-995-8366 (work). Email: rwoodfield@woh.rr.com. Meetings: 2nd & 4th Thurs. 5:45 pm at Lima CCHS Library.

Mansfield Serra Club—Ms. ANN HARRAMAN, Pres., 588 Hawthorne Ln., Mansfield, 44907. Email: annha@earthlink.net. Meetings: 2nd & 4th Mon. 6 pm at Franciscan Activity Center.

St. John Neumann Serra Club—Mr. RICHARD ALGE, Pres., 144 Sycamore St., Norwalk, 44857. Tel: 419-668-7777. Email: ralge@ft.newyorklife.com. Meetings: 3rd Tues. of each month.

Tiffin Serra Club—Mrs. PATRICIA ENGLEHART, Pres., 54 Hancock St., Tiffin, 44883. Tel: 419-447-0347 Meetings: 1st & 3rd Tues. 6 pm upper room of St. Joseph Parish Activity Center.

Toledo Serra Club—RICHARD WEISENBURGER, Pres., 4282 Deepwood Ln., Toledo, 43614. Tel: 419-345-0371. Email: rfwsales@sbcglobal.net. Meetings: 1st & 3rd Fri. 11:45 a.m. at The Toledo Club.

Worldwide Marriage Encounter— Weekend experience, which provides tools for better communication and an atmosphere for husband and wife to evaluate and deepen their relationship with each other and God. Tel: 800-795-5683. Executive Team: JIM LEOPOLD; SUE LEOPOLD, 9452 Rd. 11, Ottawa, 45875. Tel: 419-539-6914. Liaison Team Priest: Rev. HAROLD C. BROWN, C.PP.S., Mailing Address: Bellevue Sorrowful Mother Shrine, P.O. Box 319, Bellevue, 44811-0319. Tel: 419-483-3435. Registration Couple: BRIAN SCHROEDER; CHRIS SCHROEDER, 13934 Rd. K, Ottawa, 45875. Tel: 419-538-7210. Email: bcschroeder@bright.net.

CLERGY, PARISHES, MISSIONS AND PAROCHIAL SCHOOLS

CITY OF TOLEDO

(LUCAS COUNTY)

1—QUEEN OF THE MOST HOLY ROSARY CATHEDRAL (1915) [JC] Rev. Charles E. Singler, Rector; Deacons Ronald D. Henderson; James D. Caruso. In Res., Most Rev. Albert H. Ottenweller; Very Rev. Michael R. Billian; Rev. William J. Kubacki.
Office: 2535 Collingwood Blvd., 43610. Tel: 419-244-9575; Fax: 419-242-1901. Email: roscath@totalink.net. Web: www.rosarycathedral.org.
Res.: 2544 Parkwood Ave., 43610-1317. Tel: 419-255-1890.
Church: 2561 Collingwood Blvd. and Islington St., 43610.
See Rosary Cathedral Campus under Consolidated Elementary Schools located in the Institution Section.
Catechesis/Religious Program—Students 15.

2—ST. ADALBERT (1907), (Polish), [JC] Revs. Richard Philiposki, S.Ch.; Leszek Wedziuk, S.Ch.; Deacon Gerald Ignatowski; Jackie Chmielewski, Business Mgr.
Office: 3233 Lagrange St., 43608-1898. Tel: 419-241-4179; Fax: 419-241-1136. Email: stadalbert2001@yahoo.com. Web: stadalbertsthedwig.org.
Catechesis/Religious Program—Cathy Rynski, D.R.E.

3—ST. AGNES (1910) Closed. For inquiries for parish records contact the chancery.

4—ST. ANN, Consolidated with St. Teresa to form St. Martin de Porres. See separate listing.

5—ST. ANTHONY (1882), (Polish), Closed. For inquiries for parish records contact the chancery.

6—BLESSED SACRAMENT (1924) [JC] Rev. P. Martin Donnelly; Deacons Patrick McCabe; Harold Welch; Richard D. Mishler; Dr. Bev Bingle, Pastoral Assoc.; Ms. Mary Janet L. Myers, Devel. Dir. In Res., Most Rev. Robert W. Donnelly.
Res.: 4227 Bellevue Rd., 43613-3999. Tel: 419-472-2288; Fax: 419-472-0493. Email: parishsecretary@bsctoledo.com. Web: www.bsctoledo.com.
School—(Grades PreK-8), 4255 Bellevue, 43613. Tel: 419-472-1121; Fax: 419-472-1679. Ms. Kathy C. White, Prin. Lay Teachers 20; Students 371.
Catechesis/Religious Program—Tel: 419-472-7526. Bev Bingle, D.R.E. Students 50.

7—ST. CATHERINE OF SIENA (1930) [JC] Rev. J. Douglas Garand; Deacons Curt R. Vogel; Michael R. Learned Sr.; Jim Riedy, Music Liturgy Dir.
Mailing Address: 4555 N. Haven Ave., 43612-2350. Tel: 419-478-9558. Email: stcatherine1@sbcglobal.net.

Res.: 4544 N. Haven Ave., 43612. Tel: 419-478-3281; Fax: 419-478-9434.
School—(Grades PreK-8), 1155 Corbin Rd., 43612-2366. Tel: 419-478-9900. Sandi Shinaberry, Prin. Students 255.
Catechesis/Religious Program—Vicki R. Mayfield, D.R.E.; Theresa Paredes, D.R.E. Students 45.

8—ST. CHARLES BORROMEO (1903) [JC] Rev. Gregory L. Peatee; Deacon Michael W. Pence; Mrs. Alison L. VanRynen, Admin.; Mrs. Lynn Van Doran, Finance Mgr.
Res. & Church: 1842 Airport Hwy., 43609-2069. Tel: 419-385-7431; Fax: 419-535-1813.
See St. Charles Borromeo Campus under Consolidated Elementary Schools located in the Institution section.
Catechesis/Religious Program—Mr. Jerry Mocek, D.R.E.; John VanRynen, Asst. Youth Min. Students 25.

9—CHRIST THE KING (1953) [JC 3] Revs. William J. Rose; Ronald W. E. Olszewski, O.S.F.S.; Dominic Savyo; Mrs. Suzanne Marciniak, Pastoral Assoc.; Deacons Jerome E. Sortman; Robert Beisser; Ms. Kathryn L. Mumy, Liturgy & Music Min.
Office: 4100 Harvest Ln., 43623-4399. Tel: 419-475-4348; Fax: 419-475-4050. Email: mail@cktoledo.org. Web: www.cktoledo.org.
School—(Grades PreK-8) Tel: 419-475-0909. Mrs. Karen Malcolm, Prin. Lay Teachers 23; Students 609.
Catechesis/Religious Program—Mrs. Sandra L. Trabbic, D.R.E. Students 204.

10—ST. CLEMENT (1947) [JC] Very Rev. Michael O. Brown; Rev. Alan D. Zobler, O.S.F.S.; Deacons Ronald J. Plenzler; LeRoy H. Houghton.
Res.: 3030 Tremainsville Rd., 43613-1901. Tel: 419-472-2111; Fax: 419-479-3215. Email: st.clement08@yahoo.com. Web: www.stclementparishtoledo.org.
School—(Grades K-8), 3020 Tremainsville Rd., 43613-1901. Tel: 419-474-9657; Fax: 419-474-3215. Patti Irons, Prin. Lay Teachers 22; Students 230.
Catechesis/Religious Program—Tel: 419-472-1259. Linda Gutierrez, D.R.E. Students 80.

11—COMMUNITY OF THE RISEN CHRIST (1972) Closed. For inquiries for parish records contact the chancery.

12—CORPUS CHRISTI (UNIVERSITY OF TOLEDO) (1970) [JC] Rev. James J. Bacik; Deacon James Moncher; Ms. Pamela A. Meseroll, Pastoral Admin.; Mary Lynn Delfino, Pastoral Assoc.
Res.: 2955 Dorr St., 43607-2023. Tel: 419-531-4992 (Office); Fax: 419-531-1775. Email: jbacik@ccup.org. Web: www.ccup.org.

13—ST. FRANCIS DE SALES (1841) Closed. For inquiries for parish records contact the chancery. Chapel remains open.

14—GESU (1920) [JC] Revs. James F. Cryan, O.S.F.S.; Shaun Lowery, O.S.F.S. In Res., Rev. Martin C. Lukas, O.S.F.S.; Very Rev. David Whalen, O.S.F.S.
Res.: 2049 Parkside Blvd., 43607-1597. Tel: 419-531-1421; Fax: 419-531-0270. Email: gesutoledo@buckeye-express.com. Web: www.gesutoledo.org.
School—(Grades PreK-8), 2045 Parkside Blvd., 43607-1555. Tel: 419-536-5634; Fax: 419-531-8932. Mrs. Beth Janke, Prin. Sisters of Notre Dame 2; Lay Teachers 25; Students 410.
Catechesis/Religious Program—Laurie Skowronski, D.R.E. Students 95.

15—GOOD SHEPHERD (1873) [JC] Rev. Jeffrey R. McBeth; Deacon Leon M. Holmer. In Res., Rev. Jerome F. Nowakowski (Retired).
Res.: 550 Clark St., 43605-2273. Tel: 419-691-5815; Fax: 419-693-6612.
Catechesis/Religious Program—Tel: 419-698-1519; Fax: 419-698-2050. Sr. Rita Rogier, C.P.P.S., Catechetical Leader. Students 15.

16—ST. HEDWIG (1875), (Polish), [JC] Revs. Richard Philiposki, S.Ch.; Leszek Wedziuk, S.Ch.; Jackie Chmielewski, Business Mgr. In Res., Rev. Francis Ejimofor, S.S.Sp. (Kenya).
Res. & Office: 3233 Lagrange St., 43608-1898. Tel: 419-241-4179; Fax: 419-241-1136. Email: stadalbert2001@yahoo.com. Web: www.stadalbertsthedwig.org.
Church: 2916 Lagrange St., 43608.
Catechesis/Religious Program—Cathy Rynski, D.R.E. Students 15.

17—HISTORIC CHURCH OF SAINT PATRICK (1863), (Irish), [JC] Very Rev. Dennis P. Hartigan; Deacons Thomas S. Carone; Trevor Fernandes. In Res., Very Rev. Christopher P. Vasko.
Res.: 130 Avondale Ave., 43604. Tel: 419-243-6452; Fax: 419-243-7032. Email: parish@stpatshistoric.org. Web: www.stpatshistoric.org.

18—HOLY ROSARY (1906), (Slovak), Closed. For inquiries for parish records contact the chancery.

19—ST. HYACINTH (1927), (Polish), [JC] Rev. Gregory L. Peatee; Deacon Michael W. Pence; Chris J. Jakutowicz, Business Admin.; Mrs. Lynn Van Doran, Finance Mgr.
Res.: 719 Evesham Ave., 43607-3806. Tel: 419-535-7077; Fax: 419-535-1813. Email: hyacinth.office@buckeye-express.com.
Church: Parkside Blvd. at Victory Ave., 43607.
Catechesis/Religious Program—Ms. Christine Kajfasz, D.R.E.

20—IMMACULATE CONCEPTION (1868) [JC] Revs. Juan Francisco Molina; James R. Sanford, O.S.F.S.
Res.: 434 Western Ave., 43609-2886. Tel: 419-243-1829; Fax: 419-243-0067. Email: toldarbyicc@sbcglobal.net.

21—ST. JAMES (1913) Closed. For inquiries for parish records contact the chancery.

22—ST. JOAN OF ARC (1978) [JC] Very Rev. Gregory R. Hite; Rev. Anthony L. Recker; Deacons Stanley F. Przybylek; Lawrence F. Lottier; Thomas M. Sheehan; Ms. Terri A. Pastura, Pastoral Assoc.
Res.: 5856 Heatherdowns Blvd., 43614-4570. Tel: 419-866-6181; Fax: 419-866-6142. Email: kaysja@yahoo.com. Web: www.joanofarc.org.
School—(Grades K-8), 5950 Heatherdowns Blvd., 43614-4500. Tel: 419-866-6177; Fax: 419-866-4107. Jayne Swemba, Prin. Lay Teachers 28; Students 403.
Catechesis/Religious Program—Tel: 419-866-6177. Sr. Elaine Marie Clement, S.N.D., D.R.E. Students 168.

23—ST. JOHN THE BAPTIST (1918) [JC] Rev. Gerald J. Chmiel; Deacons Edward Gryczewski; John Algee; Shirley Fischbach, Business Mgr.; Valerie Ademski, Music Min.
Res.: 5153 Summit St., 43611-2786. Tel: 419-726-2034; Fax: 419-726-1447. Email: stjohnptplace@buckeye-express.com. Web: www.stjohnthebaptisttoledo.parishesonline.com.
School—(Grades K-8), 2729 124th St., 43611-2240. Tel: 419-726-7761; Fax: 419-726-1031. Mary Jo Wilhelm, Prin. Sisters 1; Lay Teachers 21; Students 250.
Catechesis/Religious Program—Tel: 419-726-9141. Sr. Frances Herkender, S.N.D., D.R.E. Students 56.

24—ST. JOSEPH (1854) [JC] Rev. Joseph T. Poggemeyer.
Mailing Address: P.O. Box 790, 43697-0790. Tel: 419-255-5556. Email: stjodowntown@sbcglobal.net.
Res.: 626 Locust St., 43604.
Church: Erie & Locust Sts., 43604.

25—ST. JUDE (1955) [JC] Closed. For inquiries for parish records contact the chancery.

26—LITTLE FLOWER OF JESUS (1928) [JC] Rev. Joseph R. Steinbauer; Deacon Douglas Bullimore; Christine Lewinski, Business Mgr.; Daniel J. Meyer, Music Dir. & Liturgist.
Res.: 5522 Dorr St., 43615-3612. Tel: 419-537-6655; Fax: 419-537-1469. Email: littleflower@bex.net. Web: www.littleflowertoledo.org.
School—(Grades PreK-8), 1620 Olimphia Rd., 43615-3412. Tel: 419-536-1194; Fax: 419-531-5140. Carol Huss, Prin. Lay Teachers 13; Students 185.
Catechesis/Religious Program—Tel: 419-537-6655. Susan VanHersett, D.R.E.; Catherine A. Figliomeni, Dir., Youth Ministry. Students 132.

27—ST. LOUIS (1872), (French), Closed. For inquiries for parish records contact the chancery.

28—ST. MARTIN DE PORRES (1990) [JC] Sr. Virginia Welsh, O.S.F., Pastoral Leader; Very Rev. Christopher P. Vasko, Presbyteral Moderator & Chap.
Res.: 1119 W. Bancroft, 43606-4613. Tel: 419-241-4544; Fax: 419-241-6214. Email: stmartin@totalink.net. Web: www.saintmartindeporres.com.
Catechesis/Religious Program—Darla Depp, D.R.E.

29—ST. MARY OF THE ASSUMPTION (1854) Closed. For inquiries for parish records contact the chancery.

30—ST. MICHAEL THE ARCHANGEL (1900) [JC] Rev. Gerald J. Chmiel; Ms. Suzanne Stapleton, Parish Mgr.
Res.: 420 Sandusky St., 43611-3535. Tel: 419-726-1947; Fax: 419-726-3597. Email: stmichaels@sbcglobal.net.

31—OUR LADY OF LOURDES (1926) [JC] Rev. James E. Brown; Deacon Stephen J. Veselka.
Res.: 6149 Hill Ave., 43615-5699. Tel: 419-865-2345; Fax: 419-865-2545. Email: ollparishtoledo@sbcglobal.net. Web: www.olltoledo.com.
School—(Grades K-8), 6145 Hill Ave., 43615-5600. Tel: 419-866-0736; Fax: 419-866-1351. Carole Farnsworth, Prin. Lay Teachers 12; Students 106.
Catechesis/Religious Program—P.R.E.P., Tel: 419-754-9603. Ms. Sharon Christy, D.R.E.; Debbie E. Gray, Youth Min. Students 62.

32—OUR LADY OF PERPETUAL HELP (1918) [JC] Rev. Robert J. Reinhart; Deacons Robert J. Lesinski; Daniel R. Waters; Connie Skoski, Liturgy Dir.
Res.: 3464 Glynn Dr., 43614. Tel: 419-382-4992.
Church & Mailing Address: 2255 Central Grove, 43614-4321. Tel: 419-382-5511; Fax: 419-382-7360. Email: olph@bex.net. Web: www.olphtoledo.org.
School—(Grades PreK-8) Tel: 419-382-5696. Miss Lori Anderson, Prin. Lay Teachers 24; Students 300.
Catechesis/Religious Program—Mrs. Kathy Dusseau, D.R.E. Students 109.

33—ST. PATRICK OF HEATHERDOWNS (1956) [JC] Revs. Dennis G. Walsh; Edward J. Littelmann; Sr. Regina Marie Fisher, S.N.D., Pastoral Assoc.; Deacons Joel F. Junga; David J. Karpanty; Joseph H. Kest.
Mailing Address: 4201 Heatherdowns Blvd., 43614-3099. Tel: 419-381-1540; Fax: 419-381-2727. Email: dennis.walsh@toledostpats.org. Web: www.toledostpats.org.
Res.: 2424 Green Valley Dr., 43614-3936. Tel: 419-381-2533.
School—(Grades PreK-8) Tel: 419-381-1775; Fax: 419-389-1161. Mr. Eric Wagener, Prin. Lay Teachers 17; Students 149.
Catechesis/Religious Program—7743 Chestnut Ridge, Maumee, 43537-2727. Tel: 419-381-0240. Ms. Christine Kramer, D.R.E. Students 155.

34—SS. PETER AND PAUL (1866), (Hispanic), [JC] Revs. Juan Francisco Molina; James R. Sanford, O.S.F.S.; Deacons Salvador Sanchez; Jesus Villagomez; Ms. Linda Valadez, Sec.
Office: 728 S. St. Clair St., 43609-2432. Tel: 419-241-5822; Fax: 419-241-5822. Web: hosea.freewebpage.org/tolssp.
Catechesis/Religious Program—Tel: 419-283-0884. Ann Pasquinelly, D.R.E. Students 110.

35—ST. PIUS X (1953) [JC] Rev. Richard E. Morse, O.S.F.S.; Deacon Timothy Etue; Mrs. Patricia Urbaniak, Pastoral Assoc., Dir. Liturgy & Music; Thomas Gibney, Business Mgr.
Mailing Address: 3011 Carskaddon Ave., 43606-1662.
Res.: 2929 Ilger Ave., 43606. Tel: 419-535-7672; Fax: 419-535-7810. Email: stpius@bex.net. Web: www.saint-pius.org.
School—(Grades PreK-8), 2950 Ilger Ave., 43606-1661. Tel: 419-535-7688; Fax: 419-535-7829. Mrs. Debora E. O'Shea, Prin. Lay Teachers 16; Students 249.
Catechesis/Religious Program—3011 Carskaddon Ave., 43606. Ann Etue, D.R.E. Students 67.

36—REGINA COELI (1954) [JC] Rev. James E. Auth; Sr. Janice Ann Brown, O.S.U., Office Mgr.; Deacons James Dudley; George Mitchell; Jack Binder, Business Mgr.; Michael Soncrant, Music Min.
Mailing Address: 530 Regina Pkwy., 43612-3398. Tel: 419-476-0922; Fax: 419-478-5846. Email: auth1@juno.com. Web: www.regina-coeli.org.
Res.: 5505 Bennett, 43612. Tel: 419-476-2281 (Home); Fax: 419-478-5846 (7:30am-4pm).
School—(Grades PreK-8), 600 Regina Pkwy., 43612-3399. Tel: 419-476-0920; Fax: 419-476-6792. Barbara Lane, Prin. Lay Teachers 22; Students 390.
Catechesis/Religious Program—Sr. Janice Ann Brown, O.S.U., Catechetical Leader. Students 125.

37—SACRED HEART OF JESUS (1883), (German), [JC] Rev. Frank K. Eckart; Sr. Mary Madelena Pohlman, S.N.D., Pastoral Assoc.; Deacon Jose Garcia; Mr. Royce Wicks, Liturgy & Music Min.; Lynn K. Van Doren, Business Mgr.
Res.: 509 Oswald St., 43605-2131. Tel: 419-698-1664; Fax: 419-698-9708. Email: sacredheart@bex.net. Web: www.sacredhearttoledo.catholicweb.com.
See The Kateri Catholic School System, Oregon under Consolidated Elementary Schools located in the Institution Section.
Catechesis/Religious Program—Julie Marshall, D.R.E. Students 81.

38—ST. STANISLAUS (1908), (Polish), Closed. For inquiries for parish records contact the chancery.

39—ST. STEPHEN (1898), (Hungarian), [JC] Rev. Frank K. Eckart; Sr. Mary Madelena Pohlman, S.N.D., Pastoral Assoc.; Hank Rybaczewski, Music Dir. In Res., Revs. Juan Francisco Molina; Joseph L. Vamos (Retired).
Office: 1878 Genesee St., 43605-1440. Tel: 419-691-1673. Email: ststephen@bex.net. Web: ststephentoledo.catholicweb.com.
Res.: 1880 Genesee St., 43605-1440. Tel: 419-698-1031.
Catechesis/Religious Program—2565 York St., 43605. Tel: 419-693-2691. Julie Marshall, D.R.E.

40—ST. TERESA, Consolidated with St. Ann to form St. Martin de Porres. See separate listing.

41—ST. THOMAS AQUINAS (1915) [JC] Rev. Jeffrey R. McBeth; Deacon William Lochotzki; Mary VanderLinde, Pastoral Assoc.
Res.: 729 White St., 43605-2719. Tel: 419-698-1519; Fax: 419-698-2050. Email: stthomasaq@accesstoledo.com.
See The Kateri Catholic School System, Oregon under Consolidated Elementary Schools located in the Institution Section.
Catechesis/Religious Program—Sr. Rita Rogier, C.P.P.S., Catechetical Leader. Students 86.

42—ST. VINCENT DE PAUL (1928) Closed. For inquiries for parish records contact the chancery.

OUTSIDE THE CITY OF TOLEDO

ALVADA, SENECA CO., ST. PETER (1854) [CEM] Closed. For inquiries for parish records contact the chancery.

ANTWERP, PAULDING CO., ST. MARY (1868) [JC] Closed.

ARCHBOLD, FULTON CO., ST. PETER (1846) [CEM] Rev. Gary M. Ferguson.
Res.: 614 N. Defiance St., 43502-1105. Tel: 419-446-9288; Fax: 419-446-9288. Email: stpeter@rtecexpress.net.
Catechesis/Religious Program—Tel: 419-446-2150; Fax: 419-446-0282. Rita Kruse, D.R.E. Students 126.

ASSUMPTION, FULTON CO.

1—HOLY TRINITY (2003), (German—Irish), [CEM 4] Rev. Ronald A. Schock; Deacons Joseph Repka; Robert Gillen; Sr. Joy Barker, O.S.F., Pastoral Assoc. In Res., Rev. Frederick J. Snyder (Retired).
Res. & Mailing Address: 2649 U.S. Hwy. 20, Swanton, 43558-9558. Tel: 419-644-4014; Fax: 419-644-2159. Email: holytriparish@roadrunner.com. Web: www.holytrinityassumption.parishesonline.com.
Church: U.S. Hwy. 20 at State Rte. 64, Swanton, 43558.
School—(Grades PreK-8), 2639 U.S. Hwy. 20, Swanton, 43558-9558. Tel: 419-644-3971; Fax: 419-644-5018. Web: www.holytrinityschool-swanton.org. Linda R. Justen, Prin. Lay Teachers 16; Students 120.
Catechesis/Religious Program—Rosemary Ott, D.R.E. Students 160.

2—ST. MARY OF ASSUMPTION (1877), (German—Irish), Merged with Immaculate Conception, Marygrove and Saint Elizabeth of Hungary, Richfield Center to form Holy Trinity Catholic Parish, Assumption.

ATTICA, SENECA CO.

1—OUR LADY OF HOPE Rev. Paul A. Fahrbach.
Mailing Address: P.O. Box 461, 44807-0461. Tel: 419-426-3043; Fax: 419-426-1844. Email: oloh@sutton-ebank.com.
Res. & Church: 14204 E. County Rd. 56, 44807-0461.
Catechesis/Religious Program—Mrs. Linda Moylett, D.R.E. Students 195.

2—SS. PETER AND PAUL (1882) [CEM] Closed. For inquiries for parish records contact the chancery.

BASCOM, SENECA CO., ST. PATRICK (1864) [CEM] Rev. Arthur J. Niewiadomski; Deacon George Miller.
Res.: 6230 W. Tiffin, Box 226, 44809-0226. Tel: 419-937-2715; Fax: 419-937-2751. Email: patrick2@bright.net.
Catechesis/Religious Program—Cynthia L. Brickner, D.R.E. Students 130.

BELLEVUE, HURON CO., IMMACULATE CONCEPTION (1859) [CEM] Rev. Jonathan C. Wight; Deacon James J. Cavera; Ann Cavera, Pastoral Assoc.
Res.: 231 E. Center St., 44811-1404. Tel: 419-483-3417; 419-483-8254 (Res.); Fax: 419-483-2585. Email: parish@icbell.org. Web: www.icbell.org.
School—Immaculate Conception School, (Grades PreK-8), 304 E. Main St., 44811-1404. Tel: 419-483-6066; Fax: 419-483-2736. Mrs. Kathleen A. Bolen, Prin. Lay Teachers 16; Students 233.
Catechesis/Religious Program—Tel: 419-483-8374. Mrs. Jennifer Sanders, Youth Min. Students 148.

BETHLEHEM, RICHLAND CO., SACRED HEART OF JESUS (1833), (German), [CEM] Rev. Michael A. Geiger; Deacon Stephen Keller.
Office: 5742 State Rte. 61 S., Shelby, 44875-9080. Tel: 419-342-2256; Fax: 419-342-2256. Email: frgeiger@sacredheartbethlehem.org.
Church: State Rte. 61, Shelby, 44875.
School—(Grades PreK-8), 5754 State Rte. 61 S., Shelby, 44875-9802. Tel: 419-342-2797; Fax: 419-342-2797. Lisa Myers, Prin. Lay Teachers 6; Students 90.
Catechesis/Religious Program—Cheryl Rietsehlam, D.R.E. Students 25.

BISMARK, HURON CO., ST. SEBASTIAN (1846), (German), [CEM] Closed. For inquiries for parish records contact the chancery.

BLAKESLEE, WILLIAMS CO., ST. JOSEPH (1865), (German), [CEM] Closed. Church transferred to a chapel of Saint Mary, Edgerton

BLUFFTON, ALLEN CO., ST. MARY (1865) Sr. Carol Inkrott, O.S.F., Pastoral Leader; Rev. Timothy F. Ferris, Chap.
Mailing Address: 160 N. Spring, 45817. Tel: 419-358-8631; Fax: 419-358-0647. Email: cmschroede@embarqmail.com.
Res.: 144 N. Spring Rd., 45817. Tel: 419-358-1176.
Catechesis/Religious Program—Rebecca J. Meyer, D.R.E. Students 171.

BONO, LUCAS CO., OUR LADY OF MT. CARMEL (1917) Rev. David A. Reinhart.
Res.: 1105 Elliston Rd., Martin, 43445-9601. Tel: 419-836-7681; Fax: 419-836-7681. Email: olmc30@aol.com.
Catechesis/Religious Program—Julie Marshall, D.R.E. Students 58.

BOWLING GREEN, WOOD CO.

1—ST. ALOYSIUS (1862) Rev. Mark E. Davis; Deacons Ramon Llanas Jr.; Phillip Avina.
Mailing Address: P.O. Box 485, 43402-0485.
Church: S. Summit & Clough Sts., 43402-0485. Tel: 419-352-4195; Fax: 419-353-7865. Email: parishoffice@stalbg.org. Web: www.stalbg.org.
School—(Grades PreK-8), 148 S. Enterprise, 43402-4738. Tel: 419-352-8614; Fax: 419-352-4738. Andrea Puhl, Prin. Lay Teachers 15; Students 200.
Catechesis/Religious Program—Jean Bargiel, D.R.E. Students 236.

2—ST. THOMAS MORE UNIVERSITY PARISH (1967) Rev. Michael G. Dandurand; Deacon Gary M. Thrun; Kevin Schulze, Music Dir. In Res., Rev. Michael Ki-Sung Moon.
Res.: 425 Thurstin Ave., 43402-1901. Tel: 419-352-7555; Fax: 419-352-7557. Email: info@sttoms.com. Web: www.sttoms.com.
Catechesis/Religious Program—Julie Corrigan, D.R.E. Students 101.

BRYAN, WILLIAMS CO., ST. PATRICK (1857) Rev. James E. Halleron; Deacons Dennis F. Jackson; Thomas F. Dominique; Sr. Regina F. Smith, O.S.U., Pastoral Assoc.; Bill Beber, Music Dir.; Patricia Cox, Sec.
Church & Mailing Address: 610 S. Portland St., 43506-2059. Email: ritterc@cityofbryan.net. Web: www.stpatbryan.org.
Res.: 704 S. Portland, 43506.
School—(Grades PreK-8) Tel: 419-636-3592; Fax: 419-633-5054. Lisa Cinadr, Prin. Lay Teachers 11; Students 174.
Catechesis/Religious Program—Tel: 419-636-1044. Mrs. Judith F. Roy, D.R.E.; Ginny F. Coker, Dir., Youth Ministry. Students 166.

BUCYRUS, CRAWFORD CO., HOLY TRINITY (1865), (German), [CEM] Rev. Ronald J. LeJeune; Deacons Jerome A. Gubernath; Julius J. Fritz; Constance M. Widman, Liturgy Coord.
Res.: 760 Tiffin St., 44820-1551. Tel: 419-562-1346; Fax: 419-562-2784. Email: htc1@midohio.twcbc.com.
School—(Grades PreK-8), 740 Tiffin St., 44820-1551. Tel: 419-562-2741; Fax: 419-562-7659. Mary L. Radke, Prin. Lay Teachers 11; Students 59.
Catechesis/Religious Program—Tel: 419-562-2645. Danielle Skaggs, D.R.E. Students 98.

CAREY, WYANDOT CO., OUR LADY OF CONSOLATION, BASILICA-NATIONAL SHRINE (1867) [CEM] Revs. John R. Hadnagy, O.F.M.Conv.; Xavier Goulet, O.F.M.Conv.; Paul Faroh, O.F.M.Conv.; Florian Tiell, O.F.M.Conv.; Deacon James F. Kitzler. In Res., Revs. Kieran R. Kay, O.F.M.Conv.; Noel Drammer, O.F.M.Conv.; Bros. Bryan Hoban, O.F.M-.Conv.; Randy Kin, O.F.M.Conv.
Res.: 315 Clay St., 43316-1498. Tel: 419-396-1523; Fax: 419-396-3355. Email: olcparish@udata.com. Web: www.olcshrine.com.
School—401 Clay St., 43316-1496. Tel: 419-396-6166. Ms. Jean Schott, Prin. Lay Teachers 10; Students 164.
Catechesis/Religious Program—Tel: 419-396-1523. Sr. Dionne Sartor, O.S.F., D.R.E. Students 65.

CECIL, PAULDING CO., IMMACULATE CONCEPTION (1879) Closed. For inquiries for parish records contact the chancery.

CLOVERDALE, PUTNAM CO., ST. BARBARA (1898), (German), [CEM] Rev. John F. Stites. In Res., Rev. Roger D. Bonifas (Retired).
Res.: 160 Main St., P.O. Box 8, 45827. Tel: 419-488-2391; Fax: 419-488-2390. Email: kb8bia@nwbright.net.
Catechesis/Religious Program—Pamela Miller, C.R.E. Students 31.

CLYDE, SANDUSKY CO., ST. MARY (1890) [CEM] Very Rev. Dennis A. Schroeder; Judy Ann Hoffman, Business Mgr.
Res.: 609 Vine St., 43410-1537. Tel: 419-547-9610. Email: stmaryrec@winesburg.com. Web: www.clydestmary.org.
School—(Grades K-6), 615 Vine St., 43410-1537. Tel: 419-547-9687; Fax: 419-547-9687. Sharon Kinnear, Prin. Lay Teachers 6; Students 50.
Catechesis/Religious Program—Sr. Yvonne Fischer, D.R.E. Students 97.

COLUMBUS GROVE, PUTNAM CO., ST. ANTHONY OF PADUA (1912), (German), [CEM] Rev. Thomas E. Oedy; Deacon James E. Dunn; Jean A. Kohls, Music Dir.
Res.: 518 W. Sycamore St., 45830-1020. Tel: 419-659-2263; Fax: 419-659-5202. Email: mormanj@sa.noacsc.org.
School—(Grades K-8), 520 W. Sycamore, 45830-1020. Tel: 419-659-2103. Jan Schimmoeller, Prin. Lay Teachers 11; Students 209.
Catechesis/Religious Program—Judy Schroeder, C.R.E. Students 223.

CONTINENTAL, PUTNAM CO., ST. JOHN THE BAPTIST (1907) [JC] Rev. Matthew Jozefiak, C.PP.S.; Deacon Joseph Heeter.
Mailing Address: P.O. Box 8, Cloverdale, 45827-0008.
Church: 4893 St. Rte. 634, N, 45831. Tel: 419-488-2391; Fax: 419-488-2390. Email: kb8biq@nwbright.net. Web: www.stjohn-the-baptistchurch.org.
Catechesis/Religious Program—Denise J. Matthews, C.R.E.; Jean J. Tegenkamp, C.R.E. Students 97.

CRESTLINE, CRAWFORD CO., ST. JOSEPH (1861), (German), [JC] Rev. Michael A. Geiger; Deacons Joseph L. Burkhart; William E. Rall; Jodi Harsh, Business Mgr.
Res.: 331 N. Thoman St., 44827-1445. Tel: 419-683-2015; Fax: 419-683-3415. Email: parish@stjosephcrestline.org. Web: www.stjosephcrestline.org.
School—(Grades K-8), 333 N. Thoman St., 44827-1445. Tel: 419-683-1284. Carolyn Price, Prin. Lay Teachers 6; Students 95.
Catechesis/Religious Program—Sr. M. Samuel Lubeck, O.S.F., D.R.E.; Dustine E. May, Youth Min. Students 20.

CUBA, PUTNAM CO., ST. ISIDORE (1917) Closed. For inquiries for parish records contact the chancery. Shared with St. Michael, Kalida.

CUSTAR, WOOD CO., ST. LOUIS (1864) [CEM] [JC] Rev. Jeffrey J. Nordhaus.
Res.: 22792 Defiance Pike, 43511-9716. Tel: 419-669-1864; Fax: 419-669-3825. Email: stlouis@woh.rr.com. Web: www.stlouiscustar.parishesonline.com.
School—(Grades PreK-6), 22767 Defiance Pike, 43511-9716. Tel: 419-669-1875. Email: stlouis@wor.rr.com. Richelle L. Piercefield, Prin.; Ellen Boyer, Librarian. Lay Teachers 4; Students 43.
Catechesis/Religious Program—Janet L. Wilhelm, D.R.E.

CYGNET, WOOD CO., SACRED HEART (1890) Closed. For inquiries for parish records contact the chancery.

DEFIANCE, DEFIANCE CO.

1—ST. JOHN THE EVANGELIST (1850) [CEM] Rev. Todd M. Dominique; Deacons Donald Meyer; Domick J. Varano; Sr. M. Dean Pfahler, Generations of Faith Dir.; Mrs. Constance Moffitt, Pastoral Assoc.; Mr. David G. Moninger, Liturgy Dir.; Bonnie Nally, Office Mgr.
Office: 510 Jackson Ave., 43512-2189. Tel: 419-782-7121; Fax: 419-782-5813. Email: stjohncath@embarqmail.com. Web: www.stjohndefiance.org.
See Holy Cross Catholic School of Defiance under Consolidated Elementary Schools located in the Institution section.
Catechesis/Religious Program—Janice Elliott, Youth Min.

2—ST. MARY (1873) Rev. Timothy M. Kummerer; Deacons Jeff M. Mayer; George E. Newton; John M. Weber; Joanne Santo, Pastoral Admin.; Alyce Reinhart, Pastoral Assoc.; Rick Reed, Dir., Music & Worship.
Mailing Address: 715 Jefferson Ave., 43512. Tel: 419-782-2776; Fax: 419-782-1958. Email: stmarys@defnet.com. Web: www.stmarydefiance.org.
See Defiance Holy Cross Catholic School of Defiance under Consolidated Elementary Schools located in the Institution section.
Catechesis/Religious Program—Sr. M. Dean Pfahler, Generations of Faith Dir.

DELPHOS, ALLEN CO., ST. JOHN THE EVANGELIST (1844), (German), [CEM] Revs. Melvin T. Verhoff; Jacob A. Gordon; Deacons Frederick C. Lisk; David J. Ricker; Ms. Trina Schultz, Pastoral Assoc.; Mr. Ted I. Hanf, Business Mgr.; Mary Jo Duncan, Sec.
Mailing Address: 210 N. Pierce St., 45833. Email: bulletin@dsj.noacsc.org. In Res., Rev. Charles Obinwa (Nigeria).
Res.: 331 E. Second St., 45833-1788. Tel: 419-695-4050; Fax: 419-695-4060. Email: frmelverhoff@yahoo.com. Web: www.delphosstjohnparish.org.
School—(Grades PreK-8), 110 N. Pierce St., 45833-1799. Tel: 419-692-8561; Fax: 419-692-4501. Theresa Kemmann, Prin. Sisters of Notre Dame 1; Lay Teachers 23; Students 687.
High School—515 E Second St., 45833-1798. Tel: 419-692-5371; Fax: 419-879-6874. Nathan Stant, Prin. Lay Teachers 21; Students 339.
Catechesis/Religious Program—Mary Lou Pohlman, D.R.E.

DESHLER, HENRY CO., IMMACULATE CONCEPTION (1871) Rev. Jeffrey J. Nordhaus.
Mailing Address: 230 Allendale Ave., 43516-1103. Tel: 419-278-3686. Web: www.icdeshler.parishesonline.com.
Res.: 22767 Defiance Pike, Custar, 43511. Tel: 419-669-3920.
Catechesis/Religious Program—Janet L. Wilhelm, D.R.E. Students 32.

EDGERTON, WILLIAMS CO., ST. MARY (1865), (German), [CEM] Rev. Stephen L. Schroeder; Debra A. Schroeder, Business Mgr.

Mailing Address: P.O. Box 355, 43517. Tel: 419-298-2540; Fax: 419-298-3123. Email: stmarycatholic@verizon.net.
Office: 317 S. Locust St, 43517.
Res.: 133 W. Bement St., 43517. Tel: 419-298-2932.
Church: 300 S. Michigan Ave., 43517.
School—(Grades 1-6), 314 S. Locust St., P.O. Box 309, 43517. Tel: 419-298-2531. Mrs. Juliana M. Taylor, Prin. Lay Teachers 6; Students 105.
Catechesis/Religious Program—Mrs. Karrie Kimpel, C.R.E. Students 149.

FAYETTE, FULTON CO., OUR LADY OF MERCY (1943) Rev. Gary M. Ferguson.
Mailing Address: Box 429, 43521-0429.
Church: 409 E. Main St., 43521. Tel: 419-237-2441; Fax: 419-237-1042. Email: ourladyofmercy@verizon.net. Web: www.ourladyofmercyfayette.parishesonline.com.
Catechesis/Religious Program—P.O. Box 453, 43521. Tel: 419-237-3019. Anita VanZile, D.R.E. Students 77.

FINDLAY, HANCOCK CO., ST. MICHAEL THE ARCHANGEL (1834) [CEM] Very Rev. Michael G. Hohenbrink; Revs. Shaji R. Thomas; Christopher G. Bohnsak; Deacons Ray H. Parmelee; David Sadler; Mark Kern; Michael Eier.
Mailing Address: 750 Bright Rd., 45840-2448. Tel: 419-422-2646; Fax: 419-422-2602. Email: parish@findlaystmichael.org. Web: www.findlaystmichael.org.
Res.: 2008 Greendale Ave., 45840. Tel: 419-423-8776.
Church (Downtown): 617 W. Main Cross, 45840.
Church (East): 750 Bright Rd., 45840.
School—(Grades PreK-8), 723 Sutton Pl., 45840-6965. Tel: 419-423-2738; Fax: 419-423-2720. Anne Brehm, Prin.; Mr. Joseph Mihalik, Asst. Prin. Lay Teachers 34; Students 613.
Catechesis/Religious Program—Tel: 419-423-2123. Mrs. Geri Leibfarth, D.R.E. Students 324.

FORT JENNINGS, PUTNAM CO., ST. JOSEPH (1848), (German), [CEM] Rev. Joseph J. Przybysz.
Mailing Address: P.O. Box 68, 45844-0068. Tel: 419-286-2132; Fax: 419-286-3132. Email: stjoeparish@bright.net. Web: www.stjosephfortjennings.parishesonline.com.
Church: 135 N. Water St. at Second St., 45844.
Catechesis/Religious Program—Tel: 419-286-2019. Mrs. Margaret VonSossan, D.R.E. Students 330.

FOSTORIA, SENECA CO., ST. WENDELIN (1850) [CEM] Revs. Nicholas Weibl; Eric P. Schild; Deacon James E. Hammer; Jonathan B. Hay, Pastoral Assoc.; David Lang, Parish Mgr.
Mailing Address: P.O. Box 836, 44830-0836. Tel: 419-435-6692.
Res.: 222 N. Wood St., 44830. Tel: 419-435-1875; Fax: 419-435-7826. Email: parish@stwendelin.org. Web: www.stwendelin.org.
Church: 303 N. Wood St., 44830.
School—(Grades PreK-6), 300 N. Wood St., 44830-2246. Tel: 419-435-1809. Cathy Krupp, Prin. Sisters of Notre Dame 1; Lay Teachers 21; Students 320.
High School—(Grades 7-12), 533 N. Countyline St., 44830-1587. Tel: 419-435-8144; Fax: 419-436-4042. Angela Joseph, Prin. Lay Teachers 16; Students 153.
Catechesis/Religious Program—Tel: 419-435-6681. Mrs. Shellie Gabel, D.R.E.

FREMONT, SANDUSKY CO.

1—ST. ANN (1843) [JC] Rev. Thomas J. Extejt; Deacon James Heyman; Nancy Patterson, Business Mgr.
Res.: 1021 W. State St., 43420-2103. Tel: 419-332-7472; Fax: 419-332-3556. Email: stann_church@sbcglobal.net.
School—(Grades PreK-8), 1011 W. State St., 43420-2103. Tel: 419-332-2461. Mrs. Judith J. Hall, Prin. Lay Teachers 7; Students 106.
Catechesis/Religious Program—Sr. Janice M. Peer, O.S.F., D.R.E. Clustered with St. Joseph.

2—ST. CASIMIR (1915), (Polish), Closed. For inquiries for parish records contact the chancery.

3—ST. JOSEPH (1857), (German), [CEM] [JC] Rev. David R. Bruning; Deacons Norbert A. Wethington; William J. Snyder; Thomas Mosser, Business Mgr.; Fran R. Gonya, Music Dir.
Res.: 709 Croghan St., 43420-2482. Tel: 419-334-2638; Fax: 419-334-6929. Email: stjoefrem@sbcglobal.net.
School—(Grades PreK-8), 716 Croghan St., 43420-2477. Tel: 419-332-5161; Fax: 419-332-7299. Beverly Buckley, Prin. Sisters 1; Lay Teachers 17; Students (K-8) 232; Preschool 33.
Catechesis/Religious Program—Clustered with St. Ann, Fremont. Sr. Janice M. Peer, O.S.F., D.R.E.

4—SACRED HEART (1956) [JC] Rev. Kenneth J. Lill; Deacon Alfredo Diaz.
Res.: 550 Smith Rd., 43420-9567. Tel: 419-332-7339; Fax: 419-332-7511. Email: scrdhrt@sacredheart-fremont.org. Web: www.sacredheart-fremont.org.
School—(Grades PreK-8), 500 Smith Rd., 43420-9568. Tel: 419-332-7102; Fax: 419-332-1542. Cynthia Fought, Prin. Sisters 1; Lay Teachers 16; Students 327.
Catechesis/Religious Program—Rebecca Sorenson, D.R.E. Students 92.

FRENCHTOWN, SENECA CO., ST. NICHOLAS (1856), (German—French), [CEM] Closed. For inquiries for parish records contact the chancery.

GALION, CRAWFORD CO., ST. JOSEPH (1853) [CEM] Rev. John E. Brennen, Parochial Admin.; Deacons Alfred Sisson; Gregory Kirk.
Res.: 135 N. Liberty St., 44833-2017. Tel: 419-468-2884; Fax: 419-468-9464. Email: stjoegal@midohio.twcbc.com. Web: www.galionsaintjoseph.org.
School—(Grades PreK-8), 138 N. Liberty St., 44833-2016. Tel: 419-468-5436; Fax: 419-468-3611. Robert Lavengood, Prin. Sisters 1; Lay Teachers 8; Students 115.
Catechesis/Religious Program—141 N. Liberty St., 44833. Tel: 419-468-6330. Sr. M. Samuel Lubeck, O.S.F., D.R.E. Students 90.

GENOA, OTTAWA CO., OUR LADY OF LOURDES (1856) Rev. David L. Ritchie; Sr. Gemma M. Fenbert, O.S.F., Pastoral Assoc.
Church: 204 Main St., 43430-1609. Tel: 419-855-8501; Fax: 419-855-8159. Email: ollgenoa@verizon.net. Web: www.ollgenoa.parishesonline.com.
Catechesis/Religious Program—Tel: 419-855-7181. Sr. Alice Marie Schmersal, C.D.P., D.R.E. Students 170.

GIBSONBURG, SANDUSKY CO., ST. MICHAEL CHURCH (1892) [CEM], (Twinned with St. Mary, Millersville.) Rev. Theodore J. Miller; Sr. Mary Corese Floyd, S.N.D., Pastoral Assoc.; Deacon Rene S. Gonzalez.
Mailing: 317 E. Madison St., 43431-1498. Tel: 419-637-2255; Fax: 419-637-2255. Email: gburgstmichael@woh.rr.com.
Catechesis/Religious Program—Tel: 419-637-9929. Mrs. Patricia Hoffman, D.R.E. Students 214.

GLANDORF, PUTNAM CO., ST. JOHN THE BAPTIST (1834), (German), [CEM] [JC] Rev. Anthony Fortman, C.PP.S.; Sr. Carol Pothast, O.S.F., Pastoral Assoc.
Res.: 109 N. Main St., Box 48, 45848-0048. Tel: 419-538-6928; Fax: 419-538-6147. Email: stjohns@bright.net. Web: www.stjohnglandorf.parishesonline.com.
Catechesis/Religious Program—Tel: 419-538-6335. Students 680.

HAMLER, HENRY CO., ST. PAUL (1886) Closed. For inquiries for parish records contact the chancery. Chapel remains open.

HICKSVILLE, DEFIANCE CO., ST. MICHAEL (1878) Attended by Edgerton. Rev. Stephen L. Schroeder; Deacon Joseph Timbrook.
Mailing Address: 100 Antwerp Dr., 43526. Tel: 419-542-8202; Fax: 419-542-9513. Email: stmikehi@bright.net.
Res.: 133 W. Bement St., P.O. Box 355, Edgerton, 43517. Tel: 419-298-2932.
Church: W. High St. at Antwerp Dr., 43526.
Catechesis/Religious Program— Mrs. Suzanne M. Ankenbruck, D.R.E. Students 184.

HOLGATE, HENRY CO., ST. MARY (1886) [CEM], (Twinned with Sacred Heart of Jesus, New Bavaria.) Rev. Stephen L. Stanbery; Deacon James Schortgen; Mrs. Alain Miller, Music Dir.
Res.: 316 Chicago Ave., 43527-0487. Tel: 419-264-3321. Email: shchurch@metalink.net.
Catechesis/Religious Program—Tel: 419-264-6596. Sue Like, D.R.E.; Karen Schwiebert, D.R.E.; James Schortgen, D.R.E.; Anthony Klear, Youth Min. Students 82.

HURON, ERIE CO., ST. PETER (1888) [JC] Rev. Jeffery P. Sikorski; Deacon John Busam.
Res.: 430 Main St., 44839-1678. Tel: 419-433-5725; Fax: 419-433-2118. Email: opmgr@stpetershuron.com. Web: www.stpetershuron.com.
School—(Grades PreK-8), 429 Huron St., 44839-1753. Tel: 419-433-4640; Fax: 419-433-2118. Linda P. Smith, Prin. Lay Teachers 10; Students 172.
Catechesis/Religious Program—Sr. Patricia Ann Meyer, O.S.F., D.R.E.

JUNCTION, PAULDING CO., ST. MARY (1846) Closed. For inquiries for parish records contact the chancery.

KALIDA, PUTNAM CO., ST. MICHAEL (1878) [CEM] Rev. Mark Hoying, C.PP.S.; Deacon Robert Klausing; Miss Leslie A. Stechschulte, Sec.
Mailing Address: Box 387, 45853-0387.
Office: 312 N. Broad St., 45853-0387. Tel: 419-532-3474; Fax: 419-532-3470. Email: stmich@bright.net. Web: kalidastmichaels.org.
Res.: 206 N. Broad St., 45853. Tel: 419-532-3431.
Catechesis/Religious Program—Tel: 419-532-3494. Ms. Janice M. Kahle, Pastoral Council Facilitator; Mrs. Connie Cleemput, D.R.E.; Mrs. Mary Siefker, Youth Min. Students 547.

KANSAS, SENECA CO., ST. JAMES (1890) Closed. For inquiries for parish records contact the chancery.

KELLEY'S ISLAND, ERIE CO., ST. MICHAEL (1861) Sr. Lucille Kime, S.N.D., Pastoral Leader; Rev. Ronald J. Brickner, Presbyteral Moderator & Chap.
Mailing Address: P.O. Box 490, 43438-0490. Tel: 419-285-2741. Email: mos&sm@hmcltd.net.
Catechesis/Religious Program—Sr. Lucille Kime, S.N.D., D.R.E. Students 12.

KIRBY, WYANDOT CO., ST. MARY (1861) [CEM] Closed. For inquiries for parish records contact the chancery.

LANDECK, ALLEN CO., ST. JOHN THE BAPTIST (1866) [CEM] Rev. John W. Fleck; Rita Suever, Sec.
Res.: 14755 Landeck Rd., Delphos, 45833-9438. Tel: 419-692-0636; Fax: 419-692-0636. Email: schurch1@woh.rr.com.
Mission—St. Patrick 500 S. Canal, Spencerville, Allen Co. 45887. Tel: 419-695-4138.

LEIPSIC, PUTNAM CO., ST. MARY (1873) [CEM] Very Rev. George E. Wenzinger; Deacons Thomas B. Niese; Benjamin R. Valdez.
Res.: 318 State St., 45856-1332. Tel: 419-943-2952. Email: stmaryleipsic@fairpoint.net.
School—(Grades K-8), 129 St. Mary St., 45856-1328. Tel: 419-943-2801; Fax: 419-943-3555. Sr. Carol Ann Mary Smith, S.N.D., Prin. Sisters of Notre Dame 2; Lay Teachers 8; Students 143.
Catechesis/Religious Program—Sr. M. Francis Theresa Dorsey, S.N.D., D.R.E. Students 222.

LEXINGTON, RICHLAND CO., RESURRECTION (1969) Very Rev. Nelson G. Beaver; Deacons Thomas R. Dubois; Michael Yakir.
Res.: 2600 Lexington Ave., 44904-1426. Tel: 419-884-0060; Fax: 419-884-0261. Email: resparish@earthlink.net. Web: www.resurrectionlexington.org.
Catechesis/Religious Program—Barbara Ann Smith, D.R.E. Students 164.

LIBERTY, SENECA CO., ST. ANDREW (1834) [CEM] Rev. Arthur J. Niewiadomski; Leslie Brenamen, Sec.
Mailing Address: P.O. Box 226, Bascom, 44809-0266.
Res & Church: 3761 State Rte. 635 N., Bascom, 44809. Tel: 419-937-2715. Email: patrick2@bright.net.
Catechesis/Religious Program—Cynthia Brickner, D.R.E. Students 51.

LIMA, ALLEN CO.

1—ST. CHARLES BORROMEO (1953) [JC] Very Rev. Stephen J. Blum; Rev. Joseph Sekere; Deacon James S. Bronder.
Res.: 2200 W. Elm, 45805-2697. Tel: 419-228-7635; Fax: 419-229-2835. Email: office@st-charles.org. Web: www.st-charles.org.
School—(Grades PreK-8), 2175 W. Elm St., 45805-2673. Tel: 419-222-2536; Fax: 419-222-8720. Sarah Dee, Prin. Lay Teachers 29; Students 536.
Catechesis/Religious Program—Mrs. Mary S. Shak, D.R.E. Students 527.

2—ST. GERARD (1916) Very Rev. James McDonald, C.Ss.R.; Rev. Joy Poonoly, C.Ss.R.; Deacon Elias Pina. In Res., Rev. Thomas Lacey, C.Ss.R.
Res.: 240 W. Robb Ave., 45801-2899. Tel: 419-224-3080; Fax: 419-225-2231. Email: jimm@stgerardchurch.org. Web: www.stgerardchurch.org.
School—(Grades PreK-8), 1311 N. Main St., 45801-2818. Tel: 419-222-0431; Fax: 419-224-6580. Mary Camp, Prin. Lay Teachers 14; Students 189.
Catechesis/Religious Program—Amy Rohan, D.R.E. Students 140.

3—ST. JOHN THE EVANGELIST (1901) [JC] Rev. David M. Ross; Deacon Richard Gleason; David A. Dyer, Finance Mgr.; Mrs. Joyce M. Stombaugh, Admin. Asst.
Mailing Address: 222 S. West St., 45801-4842. Tel: 419-222-5521; Fax: 419-228-8439. Email: strchurch@wcoil.com. Web: limacatholic.org.
Church: 777 S. Main St., 45804.
Catechesis/Religious Program—Irene Alderman, C.R.E. Students 45.

4—ST. ROSE OF LIMA (1856) [JC] Rev. David M. Ross; Deacon Theodore J. Kaser Jr.; Mr. David A. Dyer, Business Mgr.; Mrs. Joyce M. Stombaugh, Admin. Asst.
Mailing Address: 222 S. West St., 45801-4842. Tel: 419-222-5521; Fax: 419-228-8439. Email: strchurch@wcoil.com. Web: www.stroselimaohio.org. In Res., Rev. Timothy F. Ferris.
Church: McKibben St. & N. West St., 45801-4294.
School—(Grades K-8), 523 N. West St., 45801-4237. Tel: 419-223-6361; Fax: 419-222-2032. Patricia Shanahan, Prin. Sisters 1; Lay Teachers 12; Students 116.
Catechesis/Religious Program—Tel: 419-222-2087. Mrs. Virginia J. Kiracofe, C.R.E. Students 76.

LYONS, FULTON CO., OUR LADY OF FATIMA (1946) Closed. For inquiries for parish records contact the chancery.

MANSFIELD, RICHLAND CO.

1—ST. MARY OF THE SNOWS (1949) [JC] Rev. Keith J. McCormack; Deacons Allan D. Kopp; Russell Shoemaker.
Res.: 1630 Ashland, 44905-1896. Tel: 419-589-5464; Fax: 419-589-7085. Email: pharoah@embarqmail.com. Web: www.mansfieldstmarys.org.
School—(Grades PreK-8) Tel: 419-589-2114; Fax: 419-589-7085. Roger Harraman, Prin. Lay Teachers 11; Students 148.
Catechesis/Religious Program—Judy Hess-Pompei, D.R.E.

2—ST. PETER (1844) [CEM] Revs. Anthony A. Borgia; Christopher G. Bazar; Deacon James Marshall; Sandy Lauer, Pastoral Assoc.; Bill Johnson, Dir. Liturgy & Music.
Mailing Address: 104 W. 1st St., 44902-2199. Tel: 419-524-2572; Fax: 419-522-2553. Email: vickie140@hotmail.com. Web: www.mansfieldstpeters.org.
Church: 54 S. Mulberry St., 44902.
School—(Grades PreK-6), 63 S. Mulberry St., 44902-1909. Tel: 419-524-3351; Fax: 419-524-3366. Mr. James Smith, Prin. Sisters of St. Francis of Mary Immaculate (Joliet, IL) 1; Lay Teachers 32; Students 468.
High School—(Grades 7-12), 104 W. First St., 44902-2199. Tel: 419-524-0979. Mrs. Tressa Reith, Prin. Sisters of St. Francis of Mary Immaculate (Joliet, IL) 1; Lay Teachers 24; Students 188.
Catechesis/Religious Program—Sheila Hershiser, Youth Min. Students 106.

MARBLEHEAD, OTTAWA CO., ST. JOSEPH (1867), (Slovak), [CEM] [JC] Rev. Daniel J. Ring; Carol Robertson, Business Mgr.; Mr. Ronald Ossovicki, Dir. Music & Liturgy.
Mailing Address: 113 James St., 43440-2118. Tel: 419-798-4177; Fax: 419-798-4260. Email: stjoseph@cros.net. Web: www.stjosephmarblehead.parishesonline.com.
Res.: 802 Barclay, 43440-2101.
Church: 822 Barclay St., 43440.
Catechesis/Religious Program—113 James St., 43440-2118. Tel: 419-798-5543. Carol Luebcke, Catechetical Leader. Students 74.

MARYGROVE, LUCAS CO., IMMACULATE CONCEPTION (1840) Merged with Saint Elizabeth of Hungary, Richfield Center, and St. Mary of Assumption, Assumption to form Holy Trinity Catholic Parish, Assumption.

MARYSDALE, DEFIANCE CO.

1—IMMACULATE CONCEPTION (1873) [CEM] Closed. For inquiries for parish records contact the chancery.

2—ST. ISIDORE (2005), (Twinned with St. Michael, St. Michael's Ridge.) Rev. Robert J. Kill.
Mailing Address: 05480 Moser Rd., Defiance, 43512-9150. Tel: 419-497-2161; Fax: 419-497-2058. Email: dtscherne@defnet.com. Web: www.saintisidoreparish.org.
Church: 06324 State Rte. 15 at Glenburg Rd., Defiance, 43512.
Catechesis/Religious Program—Tel: 419-658-2512. Mrs. Marie Nicely, D.R.E.; Mrs. Terry F. Guilford, C.R.E. Students 95.

MARYWOOD, SENECA CO.

1—ST. GASPAR DEL BUFALO (2005) Rev. Paul A. Fahrbach; Mrs. Leann Smith, Business Mgr.; Barb A. Miller, Sec.
Res.: 16209 E. County Rd. 46, Bellevue, 44811-4661. Tel: 419-483-3231; Fax: 419-483-4661. Email: stgaspar@hmcltd.net.
Catechesis/Religious Program—Mrs. Jane M. Miller, D.R.E. Students 136.

2—ST. MICHAEL'S (1839), (German), [CEM] Closed. For inquiries for parish records contact the chancery.

MAUMEE, LUCAS CO., ST. JOSEPH (1841) [CEM] Revs. Keith A. Stripe; Kishore Kottana; Deacons John E. Campbell; Edgar E. Irelan; E. Robert Pluciniak; Joseph Malenfant, Pastoral Assoc.
Res.: 104 W. Broadway, 43537-2137. Tel: 419-893-4848; Fax: 419-891-6968. Email: parish.office@stjosephmaumee.org. Web: www.stjosephfamily.org.
School—(Grades K-8), 112 W. Broadway St., 43537-2137. Tel: 419-893-3304. Gary Rettig, Prin. Lay Teachers 21; Students 303.
Catechesis/Religious Program—Tel: 419-893-7025; Fax: 419-891-6969. Mrs. Rilla Dunlevy, D.R.E. Students 420.

MILAN, ERIE CO., ST. ANTHONY (1862) [CEM] Very Rev. Francis J. Speier; Ms. Linda Salmons, Pastoral Assoc.
Mailing Address: P.O. Box 1200, 44846-9757.
Res.: 145 Center St., 44846-9757. Tel: 419-499-4274; Fax: 419-499-4584. Email: astanthonysc@neo.rr.com. Web: www.stanthonymilan.parishesonline.com.
Catechesis/Religious Program—130 S. Main St., 44846. Tel: 419-499-4300. Students 170.

MILLER CITY, PUTNAM CO., ST. NICHOLAS (1888) [CEM] Rev. A. Robert DeSloover.
Mailing Address: P.O. Box 40, 45864-0036. Tel: 419-876-3481; Fax: 501-665-8794. Email: snhf@fairpoint.net.
Church: 201 E. Main Cross, 45864-0036.
Catechesis/Religious Program—Combined with Holy Family, New Cleveland. Deborah Wehri, D.R.E.

MILLERSVILLE, SANDUSKY CO., ST. MARY (1859) [CEM], (Twinned with St. Michael, Gibsonburg.) Rev. Theodore J. Miller.
Res.: 875 State Rte. 635, Helena, 43435-9792. Tel: 419-638-3042; Fax: 419-638-3043. Email: msmparishoffice@cros.net.
Catechesis/Religious Program—Mrs. Rae L. Kistner, D.R.E. Students 59.

MONROEVILLE, HURON CO., ST. JOSEPH (1861) [CEM] Rev. William A. Pifher; Sr. Nancy Ferguson, O.S.F., Pastoral Assoc.
Res.: 66 Chapel St., 44847. Tel: 419-465-4142; Fax: 419-465-2170. Email: stjoseph@neo.rr.com. Web: stjosephmonroeville.org.
School—(Grades PreK-8), 79 Chapel St., 44847. Tel: 419-465-2625. James T. Francis, Prin. Lay Teachers 12; Students 152.
Catechesis/Religious Program—Students 50.

MONTPELIER, WILLIAMS CO., SACRED HEART (1911) Rev. James E. Halleron; Deacon Ralph J. Dominique.
Mailing Address: 220 S. East Ave., 43543-1504. Tel: 419-485-5914; Fax: 419-272-3400.
Res.: 610 S. Portland St., Bryan, 43506. Tel: 419-636-1044.
Catechesis/Religious Program—Christine Sheperd, D.R.E. Students 65.

NAPOLEON, HENRY CO., ST. AUGUSTINE (1856) [CEM] Very Rev. Daniel E. Borgelt; Deacon Robert Bost.
Office: 210 E. Clinton St., 43545-1602. Tel: 419-592-7656; Fax: 419-592-6316. Email: staugie@henry-net.com. Web: www.staugie.net.
School—(Grades PreK-8), 722 Monroe St., 43545-1631. Tel: 419-592-3641; Fax: 419-592-5156. Nancy Ann Schroeder, Prin. Lay Teachers 7; Students 110.

NEW BAVARIA, HENRY CO., SACRED HEART OF JESUS (1893), (German), [CEM] Rev. Stephen L. Stanbery; Deacon Kenneth Klear.
Res.: 13779 County Rd. Y, 43548-9738. Tel: 419-653-4157. Email: shchurch@metalink.net. Web: www.bright.net/~genos.
Catechesis/Religious Program—Tel: 419-635-4121. Raffaela Peck, D.R.E. Students 120.

NEW CLEVELAND, PUTNAM CO., HOLY FAMILY (1862) [CEM] Rev. A. Robert DeSloover; Deacon Doyle J. Erford; Jane Kuhlman, Pastoral Assoc.
Res. & Office: 7359 St. Rte. 109, c/o P. O. Box 40, Miller City, 45864-0036. Tel: 419-876-3481; Fax: 501-665-8794. Email: snhf@fairpoint.net.
Church: 7359 St. Rt. 109, 45864.
Catechesis/Religious Program—Tel: 419-876-3480. Deborah Wehri, D.R.E. Combined with St. Nicholas, Miller City. Students 259.

NEW LONDON, HURON CO., OUR LADY OF LOURDES (1853) [CEM] Rev. Douglas D. Taylor; Deacon John Busam; Lynn Detterman, Financial Admin.; Mary E. Harris, Sec.
Res.: 18 Park Ave., 44851-1163. Tel: 419-929-4401; Fax: 419-929-4430. Email: olonlondon@hmcltd.net.
Catechesis/Religious Program—43 S. Main St., 44851. Tel: 419-929-4402. Mary Lou Harris, Catechetical Leader; Melissa McIntosh, Catechetical Leader. Students 73.

NEW RIEGEL, SENECA CO.

1—ALL SAINTS (2005) Rev. Randy P. Giesige; Deacon Floyd J. Hohman; Ms. Lorrie J. Seiple, Business Mgr.; Mrs. Regina A. Wagner, Sec.
Mailing Address: P.O. Box 89, 44853-0089.
Church: 41 N. Perry St., 44853. Tel: 419-595-2567; Fax: 419-595-2303. Email: officeallsaintsparish@midohio.twcbc.com. Web: www.all-saints-parish.org.
Catechesis/Religious Program—Mrs. Kathy A. Reinhart, Catechetical Leader. Students 345.

2—ST. BONIFACE (1834) [CEM] Closed. For inquiries for parish records contact the chancery.

NEW WASHINGTON, CRAWFORD CO., ST. BERNARD (1844) [CEM] Rev. Tommy Rodrigues.
Mailing Address: P.O. Box 337, 44854-0337.
Church: 412 W. Mansfield, 44854-0337. Tel: 419-492-2295; Fax: 419-492-2135.
School—(Grades K-8), 320 Mansfield St., 44854-9704. Tel: 419-492-2693. Ben Lash, Prin. Lay Teachers 11; Students 108.
Catechesis/Religious Program—Carol Lassen, D.R.E. Students 52.

NORTH AUBURN, CRAWFORD CO., MOTHER OF SORROWS (1879) Closed. For inquiries for parish records contact the chancery. Chapel remains open.

NORTH BALTIMORE, WOOD CO.

1—HOLY FAMILY (2001) Rev. Stephen P. Cairns; Sr. Marguerite Lamberjack, O.S.F., Pastoral Assoc.
Mailing Address: 115 E. Cherry St., 45872-1134.
Res.: 410 Central Ave., 45872-1134. Tel: 419-257-2319; Fax: 419-257-2319. Email: mlamberjack@aol.com.
Catechesis/Religious Program—Margaret Bobb, C.R.E. Students 82.

2—OUR LADY OF THE MIRACULOUS MEDAL (1891) Consolidated with Sacred Heart, Cygnet to form Holy Family, North Baltimore.

NORTH CREEK, PUTNAM CO., ST. JOSEPH (1887), (German), Closed. For inquiries for parish records contact the chancery.

NORWALK, HURON CO.

1—ST. MARY, MOTHER OF THE REDEEMER (1860), (Irish), [CEM] Very Rev. Francis J. Speier; Ms. Linda Salmons, Pastoral Assoc.; Rita A. Bartholomew, Financial Admin.; Lynne E. Kleis, Admin. Asst.
Res.: 38 W. League St., 44857-1397. Tel: 419-668-2005; Fax: 419-663-6234. Email: lkleis@neo.rr.com. Web: www.stmarynorwalk.org.
School—*Norwalk Catholic Schools - Early Childhood Center*, 77 State St., 44857-1341. Tel: 419-668-8480; Fax: 419-668-3269. Cindy McLaughlin, Dir.
Norwalk Catholic School—93 E. Main St., 44857. Walt Klimaski, Supt.
Catechesis/Religious Program—P.O. Box 1200, Milan, 44846. Anne Daugherty, D.R.E. Combined with St. Anthony, Milan Students 38.

2—ST. PAUL (1876), (German), [CEM] Revs. Franklin P. Kehres; Eric Mueller; Deacon James A. Reichert; Marian Bermudez, Pastoral Assoc.; Pat Furlong, Business Mgr.
91 E. Main St., 44857-1798. Tel: 419-668-6044; Fax: 419-663-5770. Email: carolc@stpaulchurch.org. Web: stpaulnorwalk.parishesonline.com.
Res.: 47 Executive Dr., 44857. Tel: 419-668-0411.
School—*Norwalk Catholic Schools - St. Paul Campus*, (Grades 1-6), 31 Milan Ave., 44857-1341. Tel: 419-668-6091; Fax: 419-668-8276. Ms. Valerie French, Prin. Lay Teachers 26; Students 487.
High School—*Norwalk Catholic School*, (Grades 7-12), E. Main St., 44857-1797. Tel: 419-668-3005; Fax: 419-668-6417. Walt Klimaski, Supt.; James Tokarsky, Prin. Lay Teachers 26; Students 238.
Catechesis/Religious Program—Julie Wise, D.R.E. Students 137.

OAK HARBOR, OTTAWA CO., ST. BONIFACE (1866) Rev. David L. Ritchie; Sr. Gemma M. Fenbert, O.S.F., Pastoral Assoc.
Res.: 215 N. Church St., 43449-1216. Tel: 419-898-1389; Fax: 419-898-2212. Email: stboniface@verizon.net. Web: www.stbonifaceoakharbor.parishesonline.com.
School—(Grades K-5), 215 Oak St., 43449-1227. Tel: 419-898-1340; Fax: 419-898-4193. Millie Greggila, Prin. Lay Teachers 6; Students 50.
Catechesis/Religious Program—Tel: 419-855-7181; Fax: 419-855-8159. Sr. Alice Marie Schmersal, C.D.P., D.R.E. Students 76.

OREGON, LUCAS CO., ST. IGNATIUS (1883), (Territorial), [CEM] Very Rev. Mark J. Herzog; Anthony L. Romano, Business Mgr.
Res.: 212 N. Stadium Rd., 43616-1536. Tel: 419-693-1150; Fax: 419-693-0063. Email: church@stiggys.org. Web: www.stiggys.org.
Catechesis/Religious Program—Tel: 419-693-7662. Sr. Beth Hemminger, O.S.U., D.R.E. Students 330.

OTTAWA, PUTNAM CO., SS. PETER AND PAUL (1868) [CEM] Revs. Matthew Jozefiak, C.PP.S.; Alfons Minja, C.PP.S.; Deacon James A. Rump, Pastoral Assoc.; Mrs. Helen Schroeder, Music Min.; Mrs. Mary K. Durliat, Business Mgr.; Mrs. Julie Ellerbrock, Sec.
Res.: 307 N. Locust St., 45875-1495. Tel: 419-523-5216; Fax: 419-523-4048. Email: rectory1@spps.noacsc.org. Web: www.spppottawa.net.
School—320 N. Locust St., 45875-1496. Tel: 419-523-3697. William Kuhlman, Prin. Lay Teachers 17; Students 269.
Catechesis/Religious Program—Mrs. Teresa Lanwehr, D.R.E. Students 266.

OTTOVILLE, PUTNAM CO., IMMACULATE CONCEPTION (1848) [CEM] Rev. John F. Stites; Deacon Jose Flores.
Church & Mailing Address: 189 Church St., Box 296, 45876-0296. Email: immac@bright.net. Web: www.immaculateconceptionottoville.parishsonline.com.
Catechesis/Religious Program—Tel: 419-453-3702. Jean Byrne, D.R.E. Students 520.

PAULDING, PAULDING CO.

1—DIVINE MERCY PARISH Very Rev. G. Allan Fillman; Deacons David Jordan; Donald Coughlin; David

Laker; Rosalio M. Martinez; Robert Lee Nighswander; Leonard R. Roth; Heather Miller, Admin. Asst.
Mailing Address: 417 N. Main St., 45879-1291. Tel: 419-399-2576; Fax: 419-399-2581.
Church: 315 N. Main St., 45879.
School—(Grades PreK-6), 120 Arturus St., P.O. Box 98, Payne, 45880. Mrs. Cathy R. Schoenauer, Prin.
Catechesis/Religious Program—Combined with St. John the Baptist, Payne. Theresa R. Conley, D.R.E. Students 262.
2—St. Joseph (1894) Closed.
Payne, Paulding Co., St. John the Baptist (1892) [CEM] Closed. Church transferred to a chapel of Divine Mercy, Paulding
Perrysburg, Wood Co.
1—Blessed John XXIII (2005) Rev. Herbert F. Weber; Deacon Clifton Perryman.
Mailing Address: P.O. Box 48, 43552-0048. Web: www.blessedjohn.org.
Office: 24250 Dixie Hwy., 43551. Tel: 419-874-6502.
Catechesis/Religious Program—Marla Overholt, D.R.E.
2—St. Rose (1861) [CEM] Very Rev. Marvin G. Borger; Rev. John A. Miller; Deacons Lawrence Tiefenbach; Kenneth Cappelletty; Victor DeFilippis; Ms. Charlotte Mariasy, Dir. Liturgy & Music. In Res., Rev. Adam L. Hertzfeld.
Res.: 215 E. Front St., 43551-2193. Tel: 419-874-4559; Fax: 419-874-4375. Email: stroseoffice@stroseparish.com. Web: www.saintroseonline.org.
School—(Grades PreK-8), 217 E. Front St., 43551-2192. Tel: 419-874-5631; Fax: 419-874-1002. Barbara Jenks, Prin. Lay Teachers 26; Students 410.
Catechesis/Religious Program—Tel: 419-874-9474. Patricia Russo, D.R.E.; Craig Irwin, Youth Min. Students 388.
Peru, Huron Co., St. Alphonsus Liguori (1828), (German), [CEM] Rev. William A. Pifher; Deacon George C. Stepanic; Sr. Nancy Ferguson, Pastoral Assoc.
Res.: 66 Chapel St., Monroeville, 44847. Tel: 419-465-4142; Fax: 419-465-2170. Email: stalphonsus@neo.rr.com. Web: www.stalphonsusperu.org.
Church: 1360 Settlement Rd., Norwalk, 44857.
Catechesis/Religious Program—1360 Settlement Dr., Norwalk, 44857. Tel: 419-668-5030; Fax: 419-663-6234. Catherine Raftery, D.R.E. Students 61.
Plymouth, Huron Co., St. Joseph (1864) Rev. Stanley Szybka; Sr. Barbara Jean Miller, O.S.F., Pastoral Assoc.
Res.: 117 Sandusky St., 44865-1132. Tel: 419-687-4611; Fax: 419-687-4611. Email: stjoe@willard-oh.com.
Catechesis/Religious Program—Connie Donnersbash, D.R.E. Students 72.
Port Clinton, Ottawa Co., Immaculate Conception (1861) Very Rev. John C. Missler; Deacons Maury A. Hall; David A. Huffman.
Mailing Address: 414 Madison St., 43452-1922. Tel: 419-734-4004; Fax: 419-734-3477. Email: iccc@cros.net. Web: www.iccpc.org.
School—(Grades PreK-6), 109 W. Fourth St., 43452-1816. Tel: 419-734-3315; Fax: 419-734-6172. Sr. Rosemary Hug, S.N.D., Prin. Sisters of Notre Dame 1; Lay Teachers 9; Students 133.
Catechesis/Religious Program—Sr. Mary Jane Fisher, R.S.M., D.R.E.; Carol A. Fox, Youth Min. Students 147.
Providence, Lucas Co., St. Patrick (1842), (Irish), [CEM] Rev. David D. Tscherne.
Mailing Address: 14010 U.S. Rte. 24 W., Grand Rapids, 43522-9678. Tel: 419-832-5215; Fax: 419-832-4075. Email: spgr@verizon.net. Web: www.stpatrickgrandrapids.parishesonline.com.
Res.: 17680 Woodburn Ave., Grand Rapids, 43522-9745. Tel: 419-832-2414.
Catechesis/Religious Program—Students 140.
Put-In-Bay, Ottawa Co., Mother of Sorrows (1866) Sr. Lucille Kime, S.N.D., Pastoral Leader; Rev. Ronald J. Brickner, Presbyteral Moderator & Chap.
Mailing Address: 632 Catawba Ave., Box 179, 43456-0179. Tel: 419-285-2741; Fax: 419-285-2741 (call first). Email: mos&sm@hmcltd.net.
Reed, Seneca Co., Assumption (1867), (German), [CEM] Closed. For inquiries for parish records contact the chancery.
Republic, Seneca Co., St. Aloysius (1879) [CEM] Closed. For inquiries for parish records contact the chancery.
Richfield Center, Lucas Co., St. Elizabeth of Hungary (1914) Merged with Immaculate Conception, Marygrove and St. Mary of Assumption, Assumption to form Holy Trinity Catholic Parish, Assumption. Sacramental records at the Chancery.
Rossford, Wood Co., All Saints (1990) Rev. Kent R. Kaufman; Deacons Richard J. Vascik; Jerry Ziemkiewicz. Consolidated of SS. Cyril and Methodius and St. Mary Magdalene.
Church: 628 Lime City Rd., 43460. Tel: 419-666-1393; Fax: 419-666-5734. Email: allsaintsparish@juno.com. Web: www.allsaintsrossford.org.
School—(Grades PreK-8), 630 Lime City Rd., 43460. Tel: 419-661-2070; Fax: 419-661-2077. Teresa Richardson, Prin. Sisters 1; Lay Teachers 14; Total Staff 40; Students 260.
Catechesis/Religious Program—Cathleen Voyles-Baden, D.R.E. Students 138.
St. Michael's Ridge, Defiance Co., St. Michael (1861) [CEM] Rev. Robert J. Kill.
Res.: 05480 Moser Rd., Defiance, 43512-9150. Tel: 419-497-2161; Fax: 419-497-2058. Email: dtscherne@defnet.com.
Church: Moser Rd. at Behrens Rd., Defiance, 43512.
Catechesis/Religious Program—05537 Moser Rd., Defiance, 43512. Tel: 419-497-3122. Mary K. Imber, D.R.E. Students 132.
St. Stephen, Seneca Co., St. Stephen (1844) [CEM] Closed. For inquiries for parish records contact the chancery.
Salem Twp., Wyandot Co., St. Joseph (1849), (English), [CEM] Closed. For inquiries for parish records contact the chancery.
Sandusky, Erie Co.
1—Holy Angels (1839) [JC] Rev. Christopher Kardzis (Poland); Sr. Joyce Marie Bates, S.N.D., Pastoral Assoc.; Rose Hermes, Sec.
Res.: 428 Tiffin Ave., 44870. Tel: 419-625-3698; Fax: 419-625-5183. Email: rhermes@parishmail.com. Web: www.holyangelssandusky.parishesonline.com.
See Sandusky Central Catholic School, Sandusky under Consolidated Elementary Schools located in the Institution section.
2—St. Mary (1855), (German), [CEM] [JC 3] Revs. David W. Nuss; Jason J. Kahle; Deacons William G. Burch; Jeff Claar.
Res.: 429 Central Ave., 44870. Tel: 419-625-7465; Fax: 419-626-2834. Email: office@stmarysandusky.org. Web: www.stmary-sandusky.org.
See Sandusky Central Catholic School, Sandusky under Consolidated Elementary Schools located in the Institution section.
Catechesis/Religious Program—Tel: 419-621-7456. Debbie Geason, D.R.E. Students 155.
3—SS. Peter and Paul (1866) [CEM] [JC] Rev. Martin B. Nassr; Deacons Milton Opper; John F. Weeks; Linda A. Pedoli, Pastoral Assoc.
Res.: 510 Columbus Ave., 44870-2780. Tel: 419-625-6655; Fax: 419-625-6576. Email: office@stspeterpaul.com. Web: www.stspeterpaul-.com.
See Sandusky Central Catholic School, Sandusky under Consolidated Elementary Schools located in the Institution section.
Catechesis/Religious Program—Cheryl Pawlowski, D.R.E. Students 178.
Shelby, Richland Co., Most Pure Heart of Mary (1866), (German), [CEM] Rev. Nicholas J. Cunningham; Mrs. Barb Studer, Business Mgr.
Res.: 29 West St., 44875-1155. Tel: 419-347-2381; Fax: 419-347-3934. Email: toledomphm@impresso.com.
School—(Grades PreK-6), 26 West St., 44875-1148. Tel: 419-342-2626; Fax: 419-347-2763. Sally Dunbar, Prin. Lay Teachers 6; Students 105.
Catechesis/Religious Program—Lois Steele, D.R.E.; Mark Seitz, Youth Min. Students 220.
Spencerville, Allen Co., St. Patrick (1858) [JC] Rev. John W. Fleck; Theresa Jean Wolfe, Admin. Asst.
Office: 14755 Landeck Rd., Rte. 1, Delphos, 45833-9438.
Church & Res.: 500 S. Canal St., 45887. Tel: 419-692-0636; Fax: 419-692-0636. Email: schurch1@woh.rr.com.
Catechesis/Religious Program—Tel: 419-647-6202. Students 135.
Stryker, William Co., St. John the Evangelist (1861) [JC] Closed. For inquiries for parish records contact the chancery.
Swanton, Fulton Co., St. Richard (1893) [CEM] Rev. Daniel Zak; Deacons Timothy R. Worline; Michael J. Sarra; Joseph F. Panning, Business Mgr.; James A. Riedy, Dir. Liturgy & Music.
Res.: 333 Brookside Dr., 43558-1097. Tel: 419-826-2791; Fax: 419-826-7256. Email: pastor@saintrichard.org. Web: www.saintrichard.org.
School—(Grades PreK-8), 333 Brookside Dr., 43558-1062. Tel: 419-826-5041. Susan Richardson, Prin. Lay Teachers 11; Students 108.
Catechesis/Religious Program—Ann R. Geise, D.R.E. Students 156.
Sycamore, Wyandot Co., St. Pius X (1951) Revs. Gary R. Walters; Eric J. Culler; Deacon John Daniel.
Mailing Address: P.O. Box 282, 44882-0282. Tel: 419-447-2087; Fax: 419-927-6062.
Church: Saffel St., 44882.
Catechesis/Religious Program—Kelli Smith, D.R.E. Students 42.
Sylvania, Lucas Co., St. Joseph (1873) [CEM] Very Rev. Dennis M. Metzger; Revs. Vicente Antonio Vera (Philippines); Joseph P. Cardone; Sr. Patricia Gist, C.PP.S., Pastoral Assoc.; Deacons Robert Bodette; William A. Ulmer; Paul J. White; Gary L. Boudrie; Anthony J. Pistilli.
Res.: 5373 Main St., 43560-2177. Tel: 419-885-5791; Fax: 419-882-5235. Email: parish@stjoesylvania.org. Web: www.stjoesylvania.org.
School—(Grades PreK-8), 5411 Main St., 43560-2155. Tel: 419-882-6670. Sally Koppinger, Prin. Sisters 1; Lay Teachers 36; Students 784.
Catechesis/Religious Program—Tel: 419-885-2181; Fax: 419-885-8251. Jane Ross, D.R.E. Students 434.
The Bend, Defiance Co., St. Stephen (1855) [CEM] Closed. For inquiries for parish records contact the chancery.
Tiffin, Seneca Co.
1—St. Joseph (1845) [CEM] Very Rev. Joseph P. Szybka; Deacon Daniel Scherger.
Res.: 36 Melmore St., 44883-3098. Tel: 419-447-5848; Fax: 419-447-7580. Email: stjoetif@bright.net. Web: www.bright.net/stjoetif.
See Tiffin Calvert Schools under Consolidated Elementary Schools located in the Institution Section.
Catechesis/Religious Program—Jeannette Plisky, D.R.E. Students 136.
2—St. Mary (1831) [CEM] Revs. Gary R. Walters; Eric J. Culler; Thomas Fretz Jr., Liturgy & Music Dir.; William Booth, Opers. Dir.
Res.: 85 S. Sandusky St., 44883-2140. Tel: 419-447-2087; Fax: 419-447-9940. Email: tmfry@earthlink.net. Web: www.stmarychurch-.com.
See Tiffin Calvert Schools under Consolidated Elementary Schools located in the Institution Section.
Catechesis/Religious Program—Tel: 419-448-9341. Rose Ann Gaietto, D.R.E. Students 263.
Upper Sandusky, Wyandot Co.
1—St. Peter (1857) [CEM] [JC] Closed. For inquiries for parish records contact the chancery.
2—Transfiguration of the Lord (2005) Rev. Robert L. Dendinger; Deacon Kevin Wintersteller; Sr. Jeanette Zielinski, O.S.F., Pastoral Assoc.; Ilene M. Zender, Business Mgr.
Res.: 225 N. Eighth St., 43351-1299. Tel: 419-294-1268; Fax: 419-294-2030. Email: izender@parishmail.com. Web: www.totluppersandusky.parishesonline.com.
School—St. Peter Catholic School, (Grades K-6), 310 N. 8th St., 43351-1144. Tel: 419-294-1395; Fax: 419-209-0295. Mary Alice Harbour, Prin. Lay Teachers 8; Students 150.
Catechesis/Religious Program—Harriet Amendola, D.R.E. Students 80.
Van Wert, Van Wert Co., St. Mary of the Assumption (1876) Rev. Michael J. Zacharias; Deacon Andrew McMahon; Edward Fox, Business Mgr.
Res.: 601 Jennings Rd., 45891-9702. Tel: 419-238-3979; Fax: 419-238-3957. Email: info@stmarysvanwert.com. Web: www.stmarysvanwert.com.
School—(Grades K-6), 611 Jennings Rd., 45891-9701. Tel: 419-238-5186. David Mathew, Prin. Lay Teachers 7; Students 75.
Catechesis/Religious Program—Tel: 419-238-3079. Mrs. Cheryl Freewalt, D.R.E. Students 183.
Vermilion, Erie Co., St. Mary (1851) [JC] Rev. James J. Holmer; Sr. Claudia Bronsing, O.S.F.S., Pastoral Assoc.
Mailing Address: 731 Exchange St., 44089-1330. Tel: 440-967-8711; Fax: 440-967-8712. Email: parish@stmaryvermilion.org. Web: www.stmaryvermilion.org.
Res.: 5418 Ohio St., 44089. Tel: 440-967-8711; Fax: 440-967-8712.
School—(Grades PreK-6), 5450 E. Ohio St., 44089-1340. Tel: 440-967-7911; Fax: 440-967-8287. Barbara Bialko, Prin. Lay Teachers 8; Students 141.
Catechesis/Religious Program—Sandra J. Smith, D.R.E. Students 258.
Wakeman, Huron Co., St. Mary (1852) [CEM] Sr. Caroll Schemenauer, S.N.D., Pastoral Leader; Rev. Douglas D. Taylor, Chap.
Mailing Address: P.O. Box 576, 44889-0576.
Church: 46 E. Main St., 44889. Tel: 440-839-2023; Fax: 440-839-2881. Email: wakemanstmary@verizon.net. Web: www.stmarywakeman.parishesonline.com.
Catechesis/Religious Program—Mrs. Martha Tansey, D.R.E. Students 82.

WALBRIDGE, WOOD CO., ST. JEROME (1962) Rev. David J. Cirata.
Res.: 300 Warner St., 43465-1142. Tel: 419-666-2857; Fax: 419-661-2284. Email: stjeromeoffice@midohio.twcbc.com. Web: www.stjeromechurch.catholicweb.com.
See The Kateri Catholic School System, Oregon under Consolidated Elementary Schools located in the Institution Section.
Catechesis/Religious Program—Kathy Huffman, D.R.E. Students 85.

WAUSEON, FULTON CO., ST. CASPAR (1850) [CEM] [JC] Rev. Edward J. Schleter; Deacon Ivan James M. Dominique; Ms. Kathleen K. Sevenich, Admin.; Mrs. Vicki A. Smith, Sec.
Res.: 1205 N. Shoop Ave., 43567-1828. Tel: 419-337-2322; Fax: 419-337-2413. Email: stck@bright.net. Web: www.stcaspar.com.
School—
Catechesis/Religious Program—Ms. Barbara M. Bonfert, C.R.E.

WILLARD, HURON CO., ST. FRANCIS XAVIER (1875) [CEM] Rev. Stanley Szybka; Deacons Vincent Foos; Paul Jones.
Res.: 21 W. Perry St., 44890-1694. Tel: 419-935-1149; Fax: 419-933-6000. Email: parishangelj@willard-oh.com. Web: www.willardstfrancis.com.
School—(Grades K-6), 25 W. Perry St., 44890-1602. Tel: 419-935-4744. Donna McDowell, Prin. Lay Teachers 10; Students 146.
Catechesis/Religious Program—Mrs. Ruth Pifher, D.R.E. Students 151.

Chaplains of Public Institutions

TOLEDO. *St. Anne Mercy Hospital*, 3404 W. Sylvania Ave., 43623. Rev. Charles J. Denny, Deacon Michael W. Pence.
Sisters of Notre Dame, 3837 Secor Rd., 43623.
St. Vincent Mercy Medical Center, 2213 Cherry St., 43608-2691. Tel: 419-321-3232. Rev. Francis Ejimofor, S.S.Sp. (Kenya).

LIMA. *St. Rita Hospital and Medical Center*, 730 W. Market St., 45801. Rev. Charles Obinwa (Nigeria).

OREGON. *St. Charles Mercy Hospital*, 2600 Navarre, 43616. Rev. Charles J. Denny.

SANDUSKY. *Soldiers and Sailors Home*.

Special Assignment:
Rev.—
Cardone, Joseph P., Vice Pres. Mission & Values Integration, Mercy Medical Center.

On Duty Outside the Diocese:
Revs.—
McQuillen, Thomas J., St. Augustine's Seminary, P.O. Box 3800, Bulawayor, Zimbabwe, Africa.
Morman, Kenneth G., V.F., Mt. St. Mary Seminary, 6616 Beechmont Ave., Cincinnati, 45230-2006. Tel: 513-231-2223. Email: kmorman@athenaeum.edu

---

Graduate Studies:
Rev.—
Hoyles, Monte J., Catholic University of America

Military Chaplains:
Rev.—
Kirk, David R., Chap. U.S. Army

Health Leave:
Rev.—
Bowers, Mark R.

Retired:
Most Rev.—
Donnelly, Robert W., 4227 Bellevue Rd., 43613-3999.
Rev. Msgr.—
Dunn, Edward C., 157 Grover St., Mansfield, 44903.
Revs.—
Badger, Arthur A., 3607 Naples Dr., 43615-1155.
Beck, David J.
Blaser, John R., V.F.
Boff, Bernard J., 4035 Indian Rd., 43606.
Bonifas, Roger D., P.O. Box 8, Cloverdale, 45827-0008.
Caballero, Francisco, P.O. Box 985, 43697-0985.
Ceranowski, Albert B., 26324 Edgewater Dr, Perrysburg, 43551.
Ceranowski, Gerald L., V.F.
Dorley, Paul D., 4811 Estero Pl., 43623-3734.
Duschl, Frederick J., 11312 Cty Rd. 6, Edon, 43518. Tel: 419-272-2475 Mailing Address: P.O. Box 151 Blakeslee, OH 43505-0151
Ensman, Raymond E., 1800 Fulton St., Port Clinton, 43452.
Etzel, Raymond A., 4035 Indian Rd., 43606.
Feltman, Philip S., 2020 Sanford St., 44870.
Fraser, Daniel J., 1175 Raintree Blvd., Monroe, MI 48161.
Gallagher, Anthony, 6500 Carrietown Ln., 43615.
Gorman, Thomas J., 20420 W. River Rd., Grand Rapids, 43522.
Haas, Robert L., 135 N. Liberty St., Galion, 44833.
Holden, Robert A., 14900 County Rd. H., Unit 94, Wauseon, 43567.
Howe, J. Norbert, 165 N. Seriff Dr., Lima, 45807-2258.
Jaros, Joseph P., 29317 Bates Rd., Perrysburg, 43551.
Knueven, Gerald E., 29245 Hufford Rd., #8, Perrysburg, 43551.
Kwiatkowski, Paul M., 2200 Scottwood Ave., #303, 43620.
Laudick, John R., 2200 Scottwood, #107, 43620.
Lautermilch, David J., 318 Condley, 43608-1017.
Lester, John E., 4125 King Rd. #228, Sylvania, 43560.
Leyland, Thomas J., 213 West Indiana Ave., Perrysburg, 43551.
Loeffler, Earl A., 2967 Dorr St., 43607-2023.
Majoros, Stephen R., 3238 Seaman St., Oregon, 43616.
McClure, John A., J.C.L., Rosary Care Center, 6832 Convent Blvd., Sylvania, 43560.
Mueller, Donald R., 321 E. Madison St., Gibsonburg, 43431.
Niedermier, Jerome G., 5341 Glendale Dr., Harrison, MI 48625-9631.
Nieset, Frank E., 6832 Convent Blvd., Sylvania, 43560.
Nietfeld, Fred J., 3521 Environ Blvd. #301, Lauderhill, FL 33311.
Notter, Richard E., 5713 Bernath Ct., 43615.
Nowakowski, Jerome F., 550 Clark St., 43605-2273.
O'Brien, Joseph L., 930 S. Wynn #B213, Oregon, 43616.
Parker, William C., 3453 Woodley Rd., 43623.
Peiffer, James E., 709 N.W. Catawba Rd., Port Clinton, 43452.
Radvansky, Joseph R. (PRM), 350 N. Lighthouse Oval, Marblehead, 43440.
Reichert, Ralph J., 3230 Centennial Rd. #31, Sylvania, 43560-9744.
Rethinger, Omer, 1010 N. Brush, Apt. A, Fremont, 43420-1410.
Ricker, John Michael, 212 N. Stadium Rd., Oregon, 43616-1536.
Ringholz, Benedict E., 117 Leisure Ln., Norwalk, 44857-7032.
Risacher, James E., 8820 Walther Blvd. #4215, Baltimore, MD 21234.
Say, James K., 6584 N. California Dr., Long Beach, Oak Harbor, 43449.
Scherger, Herman F., Rte. 2, 21706 S.R. 114, Cloverdale, 45827-9632.
Schill, Frederick J., 586 Kaler, Bucyrus, 44820-2565.
Schmenk, Cleo S., 4337 Mt. Carmel Dr., Melbourne, FL 32901.
Shenk, Bertrand J., 59 Executive Dr., Norwalk, 44857-2471.
Sheperd, Raymond C., 11129 Dyke Rd., Curtice, 43412-9453.
Sherbno, John C., P.O. Box 26378, Fairview Park, 44126.
Snyder, Frederick J., 2645 U.S. Rte. 20, Swanton, 43558.
Steinle, James, 312 Greenfield St., Tiffin, 44883-2427.
Vamos, Joseph L., 1880 Genesee St., 43605.
Varney, Lawrence F., 27484 Oregon Rd. Lot 105, Perrysburg, 43551.
Wehinger, Thomas E., 2352 Cheyenne Blvd. #7, 43614.
Weithman, Robert J., 5055 Providence Dr., #112, 44870.
Wilhelm, Robert J., 4040 W. Bancroft, Apt. 3 E., 43606.
Wurzel, Richard T., S.T.D., 7445 Country Commons Ln., Sylvania, 43560.

Permanent Deacons:
Ackerman, Thomas
Algee III, John R., Historic St. Patrick, Toledo
Arbogast, Urban
Avina, Phillip, St. Aloysious, Bowling Green
Badenhop, Donald F.
Beat, Walter
Beisser, Robert A., Christ the King, Toledo
Betz, Eugene N.
Billmaier, Robert C.
Bistak, Leo T., Dir. Franciscan Center, Quincy University
Bleile, Jack, (Serving in Archdiocese of Seattle)
Bodette, Robert T., Sylvania St. Joseph
Bost, Robert, St. Augustine, Napoleon
Boudrie, Gary L., Sylvania St. Joseph
Bronder, James S., St. Charles Borromeo, Lima
Buckmaster, Bruce
Bullimore, Douglas, Little Flower of Jesus, Toledo
Burch, William G., St. Mary, Sandusky
Burkett, Dennis W., (Serving in Diocese of Charleston, SC)
Burkhart, Joseph L., St. Joseph, Crestline
Busam, John, St. Peter, Huron
Calvillo, Pedro
Campbell, John E., St. Joseph, Maumee
Cappelletty, Kenneth, St. Rose, Perrysburg
Carone, Thomas, Historic Church of St. Patrick, Toledo
Caruso, James D., Our Lady, Queen of the Most Holy Rosary, Toledo
Cavera, James J., Immaculate Conception, Bellevue
Claar, Jeff, St. Mary, Sandusky
Conkle, Walter H.
Coughlin, Donald J.
Daniel, John, St. Pius X, Sycamore
Dazley, Phillip
DeFilippis, Victor A., St. Rose, Perrysburg
Derr, Floyd
Diaz, Alfredo, St. Ann, Fremont
Dickey, Kenneth G.
Dominique, Ivan James M., St. Caspar, Wauseon
Dominique, Ralph J., Sacred Heart, Montpelier
Dominique, Thomas, St. Patrick, Bryan
Downey, John F., (Serving in Diocese of Cleveland)
Dubois, Thomas R., Resurrection, Lexington
Dudley, James M., Regina Coeli, Toledo
Dunn, James E., St. Anthony, Columbus Grove
Eier, Michael, St. Michael, Findlay
Erford, Doyle J., Holy Family, New Cleveland
Etue, Timothy W., Immaculate Conception, Toledo
Felter, Robert
Fernandez, Trevor, St. Patrick Historic, Toledo
Fisher, Clarence
Flores, Jose, Immaculate Conception, Ottoville
Foos, Vincent, St. Francis Xavier, Willard
Fox, Leonard
Fritz, Julius J., Holy Trinity, Bucyrus
Garcia, Jose, Sacred Heart of Jesus, Toledo
Garza, Ignacio
Gillen, Robert, Holy Trinity, Assumption
Gleason, Richard, St. John, Lima
Gonzalez, Rene S., St. Michael, Gibsonburg
Gryczewski, Edward, Chaplain, Port of Toledo
Gubernath, Jerome A., Holy Trinity, Bucyrus
Hall, Maury A., Immaculate Conception, Port Clinton
Hammer, James E., St. Wendelin, Fostoria
Hartings, Leo J., Sacred Heart of Jesus, Bethlehem
Hazelton, Dorsey A.
Heban, Richard D.
Heeter, Joseph M., St. John the Baptist, Continental
Henderson, Ronald D., Our Lady, Toledo; Queen of the Most Holy Rosary
Heyman, James, St. Mary, Clyde
Hohman, Floyd J., All Saints Parish, New Riegel
Holmer, Leon M., Good Sheperd, Toledo
Horning, William L.
Hostutler, James E., (Serving in Diocese of Phoenix)
Houghton, Leroy H.
Huffman, David A., Immaculate Conception, Port Clinton
Hulderman, Joseph
Ignatowski, Gerald, St. Helwig, Toledo
Irelan, Edgar E., St. Joseph, Maumee
Jackson, Dennis F., St. Patrick, Bryan
Jones, Paul R.
Jordan, David, Divine Mercy, Paulding
Junga, Joel F., St. Patrick of Heatherdowas, Toledo
Karpanty, David J., St. Patrick of Heatherdowas, Toledo
Kaser, Theodore J., Jr., St. Rose of Lima
Keller, Stephen, Sacred Heart of Jesus, Bethlehem
Kelley, Edward L.
Kern, Mark, St. Michael the Archangel, Findlay
Kest, Joseph, Jr., St. Patrick of Heatherdowas, Toledo
Kirk, Gregory, St. Joseph, Galion
Kitzler, James F., Our Lady of Consolation, Carey
Klausing, Robert R., St. Michael, Kalida
Klear, Kenneth, Sacred Heart of Jesus, New Bavaria
Koenn, Francis
Kopp, Allan D., St. Mary, Mansfield
Kozek, Richard
Kromer, John, St. Wendelin, Fostoria
Kujawa, Clifford
Lackney, Robert
Laker, David C., Divine Mercy, Paulding
Learned, Michael R., Sr., Our Lady of Perpetual Help, Toledo
Lesinski, Robert J., Our Lady of Perpetual Help, Toledo
Lisk, Frederick, St. John the Evangelist, Delphes
Llanas, Ramon, St. Aloysius, Bowling Green
Lochotzki, William, St. Thomas Aquinas, Toledo

Lopez, Valentin G., III
Lottier, Larry F., St. Joan of Arc, Toledo
Lyons, Raymond E., Jr., St. Joseph, Galion
Mack, La Von L.
Malenfant, Joseph, St. Joseph, Maumee
Marshall, James, St. Peter, Mansfield
Martinez, Rosalio M., Divine Mercy, Paulding
Mauer, Michael, (Serving in Diocese of Grand Rapids)
Mayer, Jeffrey L., St. Mary, Defiance
McCabe, Patrick, Blessed Sacrament, Toledo
McCauley, Terry L.
McMahon, Andrew P., St. Mary, Van Wert
Meyer, Donald, St. John, Defiance
Miller, George, St. Patrick; St. Andrew, Liberty
Mishler, Richard D.
Mitchell, George R., Regina Coeli, Toledo
Moncher, James, Corpus Christi, Toledo
Moore, Wilbur, St. Clement, Toledo
Morris, Paul J.
Newton, George E.
Niedermeier, Russell
Niese, Thomas B., St. Mary, Leipsic
Nighswander, Robert Lee, Divine Mercy, Paulding
Nissen, John
Nye, Harold
Opper, Milton C.
Ovalle, Eduardo
Pacholski, Robert
Parmelee, Ray H., St. Michael the Archangel, Findlay
Peeps, Ronald G.
Pence, Michael W., St. Charles and St. Hyacinth and St. Anne Mercy Medical Center, Toledo
Perez, Diego E.A.
Perez, William
Perryman, Clifton A., Blessed John XXIII, Perrysburg
Petersen, Laurence
Phillips, Eugene D., (Serving in Diocese of Phoenix)
Philpott, Terry B., St. Peter, Mansfield
Pina, Elias, St. Gerard, Lima
Pistilli, Anthony J., St. Joseph, Sylvania
Plenzler, Ronald J., St. Clement, Toledo
Pluciniak, Edward R.
Przybylek, Stanley, St. Joan of Arc, Toledo
Quinn, Daniel P.
Rall, William E., St. Joseph, Crestline
Reichert, James A., St. Paul, Norwalk
Reinhart, Lewis E.
Reinhart, Norbert
Repka, Joseph, Holy Trinity, Assumption
Ricker, David J., St. John, Delphias
Rodriguez, Guillermo
Rodriguez, Juan
Romo, Bernabe, (Serving in Archdiocese of Indianapolis)
Romo, Jose
Roth, Leonard R., St. Joseph, Paulding
Rump, James A., Saints Peter and Paul, Ottawa
Sadler, David L., St. Michael the Archangel, Findlay
Sanchez, Salvador, Saints Peter and Paul, Toledo
Sarra, Michael J., All Saints, Rossford
Saucedo, Juan
Schaupp, Lawrence
Scherger, Daniel, St. Joseph, Tiffin
Schimmoeller, Lawrence, St. Joseph, Fort Jennings
Schortgen, James, St. Mary, Holgate
Selmek, Zenon J.
Sheehan, Thomas K., St. Joan of Arc, Toledo
Shoemaker, Russell M., St. Mary, Mansfield
Sisson, Alfred N., St. Joseph, Galion
Snyder, William J.
Sortman, Jerome E., Christ the King, Toledo
Stepanic, George C., St. Alphonsus, Peru
Swartz, Robert L.
Thrun, Gary M., St. Thomas Moore University Parish, Bowling Green
Tiefenbach, Lawrence, St. Rose, Perrysburg
Timbrook, Joseph, St. Michael, Hicksville
Ulmer, William A., St. Joseph, Sylvania
Valdez, Benjamin R., St. Mary, Leipsic
Varano, Dominick J., St. John the Evangelist, Defiance
Vascik, Richard J., All Saints, Rossford
Veselka, Stephen J., Our Lady of Lourdes, Toledo
Villagomez, Jesus, Saints Peter and Paul, Toledo
Vogel, Curtis J.
Vrooman, David
Warren, Richard
Waters, Daniel R., Our Lady of Perpetual Help, Toledo
Weber, John C., St. Mary, Defiance
Weeks, John F., SS. Peter and Paul, Sandusky
Welch, Harold, Blessed Sacrament, Toledo
Westrick, Eugene
Wethington, Norbert A., St. Joseph, Freemont
White, Paul J., St. Joseph, Sylvania
Wiciak, John
Wilson, Larry J., (Serving in Diocese of Columbus)
Wintersteller, Kevin, Transfiguration of the Lord, Upper Sandusky
Worline, Timothy R., St. Richard, Swanton
Wurm, Eugene L.
Yakir, Michael, Resurrection, Lexington
Ziemkiewicz, Jerry, (Gesu)

INSTITUTIONS LOCATED IN THE DIOCESE

[A] COLLEGES AND UNIVERSITIES

TOLEDO. *Mercy College of Northwest Ohio* (1994) 2221 Madison Ave., 43604. Tel: 415-251-1313; Fax: 419-251-6711. Web: www.mercycollege.edu. John F. Hayward, Esq., Pres.; Janell Lang, Interim Vice Pres. Academic Affairs/Dean of Faculty; Mr. James Harter, Vice Pres. Admin. Svcs.; Ms. Joan Rutherford, Dir. College Finances & Resource Planning; Ms. Heather Hoppe, Registrar; Ms. Denise Hudgin, Dir. Communications; Kathryn Maluchnik, Librarian. Sisters of Mercy of the Americas, Mercy Sisters; Sister of Charity of Montreal, Grey Nuns. Sisters of Charity 1; Precious Blood Sisters 1; Sisters of Notre Dame 1; Students 803; Total Staff 97.

SYLVANIA. *Lourdes College*, 6832 Convent Blvd., 43560. Tel: 419-824-3969; Fax: 419-882-3987. Email: marquette@lourdes.edu. Web: www.lourdes.edu. Dr. Robert Helmer, Pres.; Dr. Janet Robinson, Vice Pres. Academic Affairs; Michael Killian, Vice Pres. Finance & Admin.; Kim Grieve, Interim Vice Pres. Student Svcs.; Sr. Ann Carmen Barone, O.S.F., Vice Pres. Mission & Ministry; Mary Arquette, Vice Pres. Institutional Advancement; Michelle Rable, Registrar. Sisters of St. Francis of the Congregation of Our Lady of Lourdes, (O.S.F.). Sisters 12; Faculty 71; Lay Instructors 59; Adjunct 140; Total Enrollment 2,200.

Franciscan Theatre and Conference Center of Lourdes College, 6832 Convent Blvd., 43560. Tel: 419-824-3969. Email: marquette@lourdes.edu. Web: www.franciscancenter.org. Penny Marks, Dir.; Sr. Sandra Rutkowski, Librarian. Total Staff 104.

[B] HIGH SCHOOLS, DIOCESAN

TOLEDO. *Central Catholic High School*, 2550 Cherry St., 43608-2394. Tel: 419-255-2280; Fax: 419-259-2848. Email: frdenny@centralcatholic.org. Web: www.centralcatholic.org. Very Rev. Dennis P. Hartigan, Ph.D., V.F., Pres.; Rev. Joseph T. Poggemeyer; Mr. Michael Kaucher, Prin.; Mr. William G. Axe, Asst. Prin.; Mr. Randal J. Euckert, Asst. Prin.; Kimberley Hoffman, Librarian. Conducted by Diocesan Priests, Sisters and Laity. Priests 2; Teaching Sisters 2; Lay Teachers 62; Students 1,098.

FREMONT. *St. Joseph Central Catholic High School* Consolidated from St. Joseph, Fremont, St. Ann, Fremont, Sacred Heart, Fremont, St. Mary, Clyde, St. Mary, Millersville, & Immaculate Conception, Bellevue., 702 Croghan St., 43420-2480. Tel: 419-332-9947; Fax: 419-332-4945. Web: www.fremontstjoe.org. Michael Gabel, Prin.; Rev. Ronald J. Brickner, Chap. Priests 1; Lay Teachers 24; Students 243.

LIMA. *Central Catholic High School* (1955) 720 S. Cable Rd., 45805. Tel: 419-222-4276; Fax: 419-222-6933. Email: rmitterholzer@lcchs.edu. Web: www.lcchs.edu. Richard Mitterholzer, Prin.; Rev. Timothy F. Ferris, Chap. Priests 1; Lay Teachers 28; Students 369.

TIFFIN. *Calvert High School*, 152 Madison St., 44883-0836. Tel: 419-447-3844; Fax: 419-447-2922. Email: amass@calverths.org. Web: www.calvertcatholicschools.org. Mr. Anthony J. Mass, Prin.; Rev. Eric J. Culler, Chap. Priests 1; Sisters 1; Lay Teachers 19; Students 207.

[C] HIGH SCHOOLS, PRIVATE

TOLEDO. *St. Francis de Sales High School*, 2323 W. Bancroft St., 43607-1399. Tel: 419-531-1618; Fax: 419-531-9740. Email: esmola@sfstoledo.org. Web: www.sfstoledo.org. Revs. Ronald W. E. Olszewski, O.S.F.S., Pres.; John I. Extejt, O.S.F.S., Vice Pres.; Very Revs. Michael O. Brown, V.F., Teacher; David Whalen, O.S.F.S., Teacher; Revs. Thomas A. Landgraff, O.S.F.S., Guidance; John Lehner, O.S.F.S., Chap. & Teacher; Alan D. Zobler, O.S.F.S., Teacher; Mr. Eric Smola, Prin.; Mrs. Christine Holliday, Librarian. Oblates of St. Francis de Sales., School for boys. Priests 7; Sisters 1; Lay Teachers 44; Students 620; Total Staff 79. In Res. Rev. Charles A. LaPenta, O.S.F.S. (Retired); Bros. Alfred D. Durant, O.S.F.S.; James Rago, O.S.F.S., (Retired).

St. John's Jesuit High School, (Grades 7-12), 5901 Airport Hwy., 43615-7344. Tel: 419-865-5743; Fax: 419-861-5002. Email: tmalone@sjjtitans.org. Web: www.sjjtitans.org. Brad Bonham, Prin.; Revs. Joaquin Martinez, S.J., Pres.; Thomas J. Pipp, S.J.; Thomas H. Radloff, S.J., Rector. Jesuits of the Detroit Province., School for boys. Priests 3; Lay Teachers 69; Students 940; Total Staff 121.

Notre Dame Academy, (Grades 7-12), 3535 Sylvania Ave., 43623-4479. Tel: 419-475-9359; Fax: 419-724-2640. Email: toledonda@nda.org. Web: www.nda.org. Sr. Mary Ann Culpert, S.N.D., Pres.; Kim Grilliot, Prin.; Ruthie Carnovale-Mitchell, Resource Ctr. Dir. Sisters of Notre Dame., School for girls. Sisters 4; Lay Teachers 53; Lay Staff 41; Students 654.

St. Ursula Academy (1854) 4025 Indian Rd., 43606-2291. Tel: 419-531-1693; Fax: 419-534-5777. Email: toledosua@toledosua.org. Web: www.toledosua.org. Mrs. Jane Charette, Pres. & Acting Prin.; Mrs. Sharon Meinerding, Librarian. Sponsored by Ursuline Sisters of the Sacred Heart. Sisters 1; Lay Teachers 61; Students 630; Total Staff 93.

[D] CONSOLIDATED ELEMENTARY SCHOOLS

TOLEDO. *Central City Ministry of Toledo Schools*, P.O. Box 985, 43697-0985. Tel: 419-244-6711; Fax: 419-255-8269. Sisters 5; Lay Teachers 43.

Central City Ministry of Toledo Schools (CCMT) (Grades PreK-8), 1933 Spielbusch Ave., P.O. Box 985, 43697-0985. Tel: 419-244-6711; Fax: 419-255-8269.

Queen of Apostles Campus, (Grades K-8), 235 Courtland Ave., 43609-2699. Tel: 419-241-7829; Fax: 419-241-4180. Email: smbrendah@yahoo.com. Sr. Mary Brenda Haynes, S.N.D., Prin.; Miss Virginia Hasselschwert, Librarian. Sisters 2; Lay Teachers 12; Students 165.

Rosary Cathedral Campus, (Grades PreK-8), 2535 Collingwood Blvd., 43610-1400. Tel: 419-243-4396; Fax: 419-242-1901. Web: rosarycathedralschool.org. Pamela Moors, Prin. Preschool 14; K-8 161.

DEFIANCE. *Holy Cross Catholic School of Defiance*, (Grades PreK-6), 1745 S. Clinton St., 43512. Tel: 419-784-2021; Fax: 419-784-2072. Web: www.defianceholycross.org. Rev. Todd M. Dominique, Supt.; Sr. Linda Snyder, S.N.D., Prin. St. John Campus (PreK-2), St. Mary Campus (Grades 3-6)

St. John Campus (Grades PreK-2), 800 Fifth St., 43512-2703. Tel: 419-782-2136; Fax: 419-784-5410. Preschool 22; Students (K-2) 76.

St. Mary Campus (Grades 3-6), 702 Washington St., 43512-2849. Tel: 419-782-2751; Fax: 419-782-8835. Students 90.

OREGON. *The Kateri Catholic School System*, (Grades PreSchool-12), 3225 Pickle Rd., 43616. Rev. David A. Reinhart, Pres.

SANDUSKY. *Sandusky Central Catholic School*, (Grades PreSchool-12), 410 W. Jefferson St., 44870-2427. Tel: 419-627-9718; Fax: 419-621-2252. Email: jmonaghan@sanduskycentralcatholic.org. Dr. Judy Monaghan, Supt.; Rev. Jason J. Kahle.

Sandusky Central Catholic Early Childhood Center (Grades PreSchool-K), 1603 W. Jefferson St., 44870-2124. Tel: 419-626-3075; Fax: 419-625-5183. Email: sdwight@sanduskycentralcatholic.org. Web: www.sanduskycentralcatholicschool.org. Sally Dwight, Dir. (Early Childhood Center) Students 108.

Sandusky Central Catholic School Elementary, 410 W. Jefferson St., 44870. Tel: 419-626-1892. Web: www.sanduskycentralcatholicschool.com. Ann Whitfield, Prin.

Sandusky Central Catholic School, St. Mary Central Catholic Jr. Hs/HS (Grades 7-12), SMCC Junior High-Grades 7-8., 410 W. Jefferson St., 44870-2427. Tel: 419-626-1892; Fax: 419-621-2252. Michael Savona, Prin. SMCC Junior High 104; SMCC High School 200.

TIFFIN. *Tiffin Calvert Schools*, (Grades K-12), 152 Madison St., 44883-2879. Tel: 419-443-0263. Mr. Anthony J. Mass, Prin.

[E] ELEMENTARY SCHOOLS, PRIVATE

SYLVANIA. *Sylvania Franciscan Academy*, (Grades PreSchool-8), 5335 Silica Dr., 43560. Tel: 419-885-3273; Fax: 419-882-5653. Email: sfa_sfa@nwoca.org. Web: www.s-f-a.org. Mr. Richard Kohler, Prin.; Roberta Handel, Librarian. Sisters 1; Lay Teachers 23; Students 260.

WHITEHOUSE. *Lial Elementary School* (1972) (Grades PreK-8), 5700 Davis Rd., 43571-9669. Tel: 419-877-5167; Fax: 419-877-9385. Email: lial_school@nwoca.org. Web: www.lialschool.org. Sr. Patricia M. McClain, S.N.D., Prin. Sisters of Notre Dame. Sisters 3; Lay Teachers 13; Students 197.

[F] ELEMENTARY SCHOOLS

TOLEDO. *Mary Immaculate School* (1960) 3835 Secor Rd., 43623-4402. Tel: 419-474-1688; Fax: 419-479-3062. Email: maryim_staudt@nwoca.org. Web: www.maryimmaculatetoledo.org. Ms. Shelli Staudt, Prin. Day School for Children with Learning Disabilities, Attention Deficit Disorder and Other Health Impairments. Sisters of Notre Dame 15; Lay Teachers 8; Total Staff 22; Students 68.

[G] GENERAL HOSPITALS

TOLEDO. *St. Anne Mercy Hospital* (2002) 3404 W. Sylvania Ave., 43623. Tel: 419-407-2663; Fax: 419-407-3888. Web: www.mercyweb.org. Rev. Charles J. Denny, Chap.; Deacon Michael W. Pence, Chap.; Richard E. Evens, Pres. & CEO. Patients Assisted Annually 181,157; Bed Capacity 128; Total Staff 768.

St. Vincent Mercy Medical Center, 2213 Cherry St., 43608-2691. Tel: 419-251-3232; Fax: 419-251-3810. Web: www.mercyweb.org. Elaine Ladd, Admin./Dir. Pastoral Care; Ms. Sharon Belisle, Chap.; Rev. Francis Ejimofor, S.S.Sp. (Kenya), Chap.; Sr. Maxine Young, N.D., Chap.; Mr. Ev Chavette, Chap. Grey Nuns., Affiliated with Mercy Health Partners. Sisters 1; Patients Assisted Annually 530,000; Bed Capacity 576; Total Staff 3,618.

Mercy Children's Hospital, 2222 Cherry St., 43608-2801. Tel: 419-251-3232; 800-860-6652; Fax: 419-251-3878. Web: www.mercyweb.org. Dr. John T. Schaeufele, M.D., Pres.

LIMA. *St. Rita's Medical Center* (1918) 730 W. Market St., 45801-4602. Tel: 419-227-3361; 800-467-0308; Fax: 419-226-9750. Web: www.stritas.org. Mr. James P. Reber, Pres.; William W. Roe, Vice Pres. Finance; Mr. Mark Skaja, Vice Pres. Mission Svcs.; Rev. Charles Obinwa (Nigeria), Chap.; Sr. Noel Frey, R.S.M., Chap. Sisters 1; Bed Capacity 437; Patients Assisted Annually 404,532; Total Staff 2,861.

OREGON. *St. Charles Mercy Hospital* (1953) 2600 Navarre Ave., 43616. Tel: 419-696-7200; Fax: 419-696-7328. Web: www.mercyweb.org. Carol A. Whittaker, Pres. & CEO; Revs. Charles J. Denny, Chap.; Don Corbin, Pastoral Care Dir. & Chap. Mercy Health Partners. Sisters 1; Bed Capacity 390; Patients Assisted Annually 164,559; Total Staff 1,427.

TIFFIN. *Mercy Hospital*, 45 St. Lawrence Dr., 44883. Tel: 419-455-7000; Fax: 419-455-7066. Email: john_halstead@mhsnr.org. Web: www.mercyweb.org. Mr. Dale E. Thornton, Pres. & CEO; Rev. John Halstead, Dir. of Mission & Values Integration. Sisters of Mercy of the Americas - Catholic Healthcare Partners. Sisters 2; Bed Capacity 62; Patients Assisted Annually 115,000; Total Staff 460.

WILLARD. *Mercy Hospital of Willard*, 110 E. Howard St., 44890. Tel: 419-964-5000; Fax: 419-964-5178 8. Email: paula_karr@mhsnr.org. Web: www.mercyweb.org. Paula Karr, R.N., Dir. Mission Integration; Sisters Diane Hay, O.S.F., Chap.; Rita Mary Wasserman, R.S.M., Chap. Sisters of Mercy of the Americas. Sisters 2; Bed Capacity 25; Total Staff 220; Patients Assisted Annually 56,917.

[H] HOMES FOR AGED

TOLEDO. *Oblate Residences* (1980) 1225 Flaire Dr., 43615. Tel: 419-536-3862; Fax: 419-536-6372. c/o 2043 Parkside Blvd., 43607-1597. Tel: 419-724-9851; Fax: 419-724-9853. Apartments 100.

OREGON. *Sacred Heart Home*, 930 S. Wynn Rd., 43616. Tel: 419-698-4331; Fax: 419-698-1109. Email: msoregon@littlesistersofthepoor.org. Sr. Anne Joseph Doyle, Supr./Pres.; Revs. Edward Donoher; Joseph L. O'Brien (Retired); Joseph A. Weigman, Chap. Little Sisters of the Poor. Sisters 10; Aged Residents 73; Independent Living Apartments 20; Total Assisted Annually 101; Total Staff 101.

SANDUSKY. **The Commons of Providence*, 5000 Providence Dr., 44870. Tel: 419-624-1171; Fax: 419-624-1175. Email: jwindisch@providencecenters.org. Web: www.providencecenters.org. Jane Windisch, Mktg. Dir. Apartment assisted living facility. Bed Capacity 56; Residents 62; Total Assisted Annually 147; Total Staff 75.

Providence Care Center, 2025 Hayes Ave., 44870. Tel: 419-627-2273; Fax: 419-627-5588. Email: dday@providencecenters.org. Web: www.providencecarecenters.org. Denice Day, Admin. Sisters 2; Bed Capacity 138; Patients Assisted Annually 236; Total Staff 160.

**Providence Residential Community Corp Apartment and Villa Home Independent Living*, 5000 Providence Dr., 44870. Tel: 419-624-1171; Fax: 419-624-1175. Email: jwindisch@providencecenters.org. Web: www.providencecenters.org. Jane Windisch, Mktg. Dir. Independent Apartments 62; Independent Villas 21; Residents 74.

[I] MONASTERIES AND RESIDENCES OF PRIESTS AND BROTHERS

TOLEDO. *Oblates of St. Francis de Sales* Tel: 419-724-9851; Fax: 419-724-9853. Web: www.oblates.us.

Provincial Residence, 2043 Parkside Blvd., 43607-1597. Tel: 419-724-9851; Fax: 419-724-9853. Very Rev. David Whalen, O.S.F.S., Prov.; Revs. Martin C. Lukas, O.S.F.S., Vocation Dir.; James F. Cryan, O.S.F.S., Pastor, Gesu Church.

Priests serving elsewhere: Revs. William G. Auth, O.S.F.S., Mexican Missions, 554 E. Second St., Salt Lake City, UT 84103. Tel: 801-359-8201; Kenneth N. McKenna, O.S.F.S., Novice Dir.; Thomas A. Ribits, O.S.F.S., Formation Council, 152 Plymouth Ave., Buffalo, NY 14201. Tel: 716-886-6597. *St. Francis de Sales High School Faculty House* 2323 W. Bancroft, 43607. Tel: 419-531-1619; Fax: 419-531-9740. Revs. Ronald W. E. Olszewski, O.S.F.S., Pres.; John I. Extejt, O.S.F.S., Vice Pres.; Thomas A. Landgraff, O.S.F.S., Guidance Office; John Lehner, O.S.F.S., Chap.; Alan D. Zobler, O.S.F.S., Instructor; Richard E. Morse, O.S.F.S., St. Pius X Church, Toledo; James F. Bradley, O.S.F.S. (Retired), Rosary Care Center, Sylvania, 43560; Bros. Alfred D. Durant, O.S.F.S.; James Rago, O.S.F.S., (Retired). *Annecy Hall*, P.O. Box 43, Childs, MD 21916-0043. Revs. Joseph Baraniewicz, O.S.F.S. (Retired); Edward P. Canavan, O.S.F.S. (Retired), Rosary Care Center, Sylvania, 43560. *St. Francis de Sale High School Endowment Fund, Inc.* Rev. Ronald W. E. Olszewski, O.S.F.S., Pres. Priests 13; Brothers 2.

BELLEVUE. **Mary Lay Center*, 4500 State Rte. 269, P.O. Box 319, 44811-0319. Tel: 419-483-0762; Fax: 419-483-6400. Total in Residence 4.

Residence for Staff of Sorrowful Mother Shrine. Revs. Robert Kunisch, C.PP.S.; George (Yuri) J. Kuzara, C.PP.S.; Bro. Charles McCafferty, C.PP.S.

[J] CONVENTS AND RESIDENCES FOR SISTERS

TOLEDO. *Monastery of the Visitation* (1915) (Contemplative), 1745 Parkside Blvd., 43607-1599. Tel: 419-536-1343; Fax: 419-536-0685. Email: vhm-toledo@toast.net. Web: www.toledovisitation.org. Sr. Mary Bernard Grote, V.H.M., Supr.

The Contemplative Order of the Visitation of Toledo, Ohio, Contemplative Order of the Sisters of the Visitation of Toledo, Ohio. Sisters 22; Perpetual Vows 17; Novices 2; Temporary Profession 3.

Notre Dame Academy Convent, 3535 Sylvania Ave., 43623. Tel: 419-475-4909; Fax: 419-724-2640. Email: chug@nda.org. Sr. Mary Charleen Hug, S.N.D. Sisters of Notre Dame. Sisters 27.

Notre Dame Provincial Center (1924) 3837 Secor Rd., 43623-4484. Tel: 419-474-5485; Fax: 419-474-1336. Email: awillman@sndtoledo.org. Web: www.sndtoledo.org. Sisters Mary Delores Gutliff, S.N.D., Prov. Supr.; Clarine Young, S.N.D., Local Supr. Sisters of Notre Dame. Sisters 232.

Ursuline Convent of the Sacred Heart (1854) *Congregational Offices*, 4045 Indian Rd., 43606. Tel: 419-536-9587; Fax: 419-536-0019. Email: ursulines@toledoursulines.org. Web: www.toledoursulines.org. Sr. Donna Frey, O.S.U., Pres.; Rev. Richard J. Saelzler, Chap. Professed Sisters 56; Health Care Assisted 23; Associates 150.

FREMONT. *St. Bernardine Home* (1970) 1220 Tiffin St., 43420. Tel: 419-332-8208; Fax: 419-332-4423. Email: mercyfre@ezworks.net. Sr. Kathleen Marie Noonan, R.S.M., Dir.; Arlene Fleming, Health Coord.; Rev. Raymond A. Fisher, Chap. Sisters of Mercy of the Americas, Cincinnati Regional Community. Sisters 35.

SYLVANIA. *Sisters of St. Francis of the Congregation of Our Lady of Lourdes*, 6832 Convent Blvd., 43560-2897. Tel: 419-882-2016; Fax: 419-885-8643. Email: cboratyn@sistersosf.org. Web: www.sistersosf.org. Sr. Diana Lynn Eckel, O.S.F., Congregational Min.

Sisters of St. Francis of the Congregation of Our Lady of Lourdes, Motherhouse and Novitiate Professed Sisters 204.

TIFFIN. *St. Francis Convent*, 200 St. Francis Ave., 44883-3458. Tel: 419-447-0435; Fax: 419-447-1612. Email: osftiffin@tiffinfranciscans.org. Web: www.tiffinfranciscans.org. Sr. Jacquelyn Doepker, O.S.F., Community Min.; Rev. Francis A. Murd, Chap. Motherhouse and Novitiate, Sisters of St. Francis of Tiffin. Sisters 110.

WHITEHOUSE. *Lial Residence, Sisters of Notre Dame*, 5908 Davis Rd., 43571. Tel: 419-877-0431. Email: jmfrania@toledosnd.org. Sr. Joanne Mary Frania, S.N.D., Community Coord. Sisters 4.

[K] RETREAT HOUSES AND CENTERS OF SPIRITUALITY

BELLEVUE. *Sorrowful Mother Shrine* (1850) 4106 State Rte. 269, P.O. Box 319, 44811-0319. Tel: 419-483-3435; Fax: 419-483-6400. Email: sorrowful@hughes.net. Web: www.sorrowfulmothershrine.com. Revs. Robert Kunisch, C.PP.S.; George (Yuri) J. Kuzara, C.PP.S., Shrine Dir.; Bro. Charles McCafferty, C.PP.S.

CAREY. *Our Lady of Consolation Retreat House*, 321 Clay St., 43316. Tel: 419-396-7970; Fax: 419-396-3355. Email: retreats@olcshrine.com. Web: www.olcshrine.com. Bro. Randy Kin, O.F.M.Conv., Retreat Dir. Diocese of Toledo, auspices of Shrine of Our Lady of Consolation, Carey, OH.

FREMONT. *Our Lady of the Pines Retreat Center* (1962) 1250 Tiffin St., 43420-3562. Tel: 419-332-6522; Fax: 419-333-0238. Email: olprc@ezworks.net. Web: www.pinesretreat.org. Sr. Christine Pratt, O.S.U., Dir. Sisters of Mercy. Total Staff 8.

SYLVANIA. *Sophia Center, Inc.*, 6832 Convent Blvd., 43560. Tel: 419-882-4529; Fax: 419-885-7612. Email: sophiacc@mindspring.com. 500 N. Main St., Findlay, 45840. Tel: 419-423-3292; Fax: 419-423-7662. Web: www.thesophiacenter.org. Sisters Rachel Marie Nijakowski, O.S.F.S., Psychologist (Ohio 4699); Sharon Pollnow, C.S.A., M.Ed., M.S.W., L.I.S.W., Counselor; Mary Ann Szydlowski, O.S.F.S., R.N., Massage & Polarity Therapy; Deborah Carney, C.F.O., Cert. Professional Organizer; Joan Dvorak, B.Ed., Learning Disability Specialist; Mary Goebel-Komala, Ph.D., Psychologist; Jeanne Holup, M.D., Psychiatrist; Bonnie Schrock, M.A., L.S.W., Counselor; Glennda Stelnicki, Psychologist; Norma Vorst, M.A., P.C.C., Licensed Professional Clinical Counselor; Craig Ward, L.I.S.W., Licensed Independent Social Worker & Counselor.

TIFFIN. *St. Francis Spirituality Center*, 200 St. Francis Ave., 44883-3491. Tel: 419-443-1485; Fax: 419-443-1612. Email: retreats@stfrancisspiritualitycenter.org. Web: www.stfrancisspiritualitycenter.org. Sr. Diane Mueller, O.S.F., Admin.; Martie J. Aiello, Prog. Dir. Sisters of St. Francis, Tiffin.

[L] CAMPUS MINISTRY

TOLEDO. *University of Toledo Campus Ministry* , Attended by Corpus Christi University Parish., 2955 Dorr St., 43607. Tel: 419-531-4992; Fax: 419-531-1775. Web: www.ccup.org. Rev. James J. Bacik; Pamela Meseroll, Pastoral Admin.

BLUFFTON. *Bluffton University Campus Ministry* 160 N. Spring St., 45817. Tel: 419-358-8631; Fax: 419-358-0647. Email: cinkrott@embarqmail.com. Sr. Carol Inkrott, O.S.F., Campus Min.

BOWLING GREEN. *Bowling Green State University Campus Ministry* , Attended by St. Thomas More University Parish., 425 Thurstin Ave., 43402. Tel: 419-352-7555; Fax: 419-352-7557. Email: info@sttoms.com. Web: www.sttoms.com. Rev. Michael G. Dandurand, Pastor. Total in Residence 27; Total Staff 15.

DEFIANCE. *Defiance College Newman Campus Ministry* 701 N. Clinton, 43512. Tel: 419-783-2563; Fax: 419-783-2597. Email: morzolek@defiance.edu. Mariah Orzolek, Advisor.

FINDLAY. *University of Findlay Campus Ministry* 750 Bright Rd., 45840. Tel: 419-422-2646; Fax: 419-422-2602. Email: dbrown@findlaystmichael.org. Donna Brown, Campus Min.

TIFFIN. *Heidelberg College Campus Ministry* 310 E. Market St., 44883. Email: bbishop@heidelberg.edu. Web: www.heidelberg.edu/offices/student/affairs/ religion.htmlTel: 419-448-2242; Fax: 419-448-2578. Bobbi Bishop, Campus Min.

[M] MISCELLANEOUS LISTINGS

TOLEDO. **Catholic Charities - Diocese of Toledo, Inc.*, 1933 Spielbusch Ave., P.O. Box 985, 43697-0985. Tel: 419-244-6711. Email: bsanford@toledodiocese.org. Web: www.catholiccharitiesnwo.org. William Sanford, Exec. Dir.

Catholic Club, The (1942) 1601 Jefferson Ave., 43604. Tel: 419-243-7255; Fax: 419-243-6337. Email: info@catholicclub.org. Web: www.catholicclub.org. Mr. Paul Szymanski, Dir.

Catholic Foundation of the Diocese of Toledo, P.O. Box 985, 43697-0985. Tel: 419-244-6711; Fax: 419-270-0053. Email: kszymanski@toledodiocese.org. Web: www.toledodiocese.org.

Christ Child Society of Toledo, 2238 Jefferson Ave., 43624. Tel: 419-251-1218; Fax: 419-824-8040. Web: www.ccsoftoledo.org. Ms. Lucy Abu-Absi, Pres.; Ms. Marilyn Arbaugh, Treas.; Ms. CeCe Rutherford, Sec.

Double ARC, 3837 Secor Rd., 43623-4484. Tel: 419-479-3060; Fax: 419-724-1372. Web: doublearc.org.

Sr. Linda Falquette, R.S.M., Exec. Dir.
Family Health Plan, 2200 Jefferson Ave., Sixth Fl., 43624. Tel: 419-241-6501; Fax: 419-241-1482. Web: www.familyhealthplan.org. Samatha Platzke, Dir. Affiliated with Mercy Health Partners.
Farley Health Care Corporation, 2200 Jefferson Ave., 43604. Tel: 419-251-2889. Email: barry_hudgin@mhsnr.org. Barry Hudgin, Legal Counsel.
St. Francis de Sales High School Endowment Fund, Inc., 2323 W. Bancroft St., 43607. Tel: 419-531-1618; Fax: 419-531-9740. Email: rolszewski@sfstoledo.org. Web: sfstoledo.org.
Franciscan Care Center, Sylvania, 4111 Holland Sylvania Rd., 43624. Tel: 419-882-6582; Fax: 419-885-1422. Web: www.fccsylvania.org.
Hope Manor, 4702 Violet Rd., 43623. Tel: 419-246-4733; Fax: 419-246-4734. Ms. Cindy Kasprzak, Mgr. Units 100.
Saint John's Jesuit High School Foundation, 5901 Airport Hwy., 43615. Tel: 419-865-5743; Fax: 419-861-5002. Email: tpipp@sjjtitnans.org. Web: sjjtitans.org. Rev. Thomas J. Pipp, S.J., Pres.
LifeStar Ambulance, Inc. Ambulance & medical transport company., 2200 Jefferson, 43604. Tel: 419-693-1611; Fax: 419-693-5931. Web: www.mercyweb.org. Cathy Nelson, Admin. Lifestar & Life Flight.
Madonna Homes, Inc., P.O. Box 4719, 43620. 722 N. Huron St., 43604. Tel: 419-244-3758; Fax: 419-246-4738. Email: tfranklin@vmc.org. Tracy Franklin, Mgr. Units 171.
Mareda, Inc., P.O. Box 4719, 43620. 1931 Scottwood Ave., Ste. 700, 43620. Tel: 419-242-2300; Fax: 419-246-4703. Email: jkiely@vmc.org. Mr. John Kiely, Exec. Dir. Housing Agency of the Diocese of Toledo.
St. Marguerite D'Youville Foundation II (1996) 2213 Cherry St., 43608.
Mercy College of Northwest Ohio Foundation, Inc., 2221 Madison Ave., 43604. Tel: 419-251-1314. Email: john.hayward@mercycollege.edu. Web: www.mercycollege.edu. John F. Hayward, Pres.
Mercy Health System-Northern Region dba Mercy Health Partners 2200 Jefferson Ave., 43604. Tel: 419-251-0700; Fax: 419-251-0733. Web: www.mercyweb.org. Mr. Steven L. Mickus, Pres. & CEO. Total Staff 625.
Michaelmas Manor, Inc., P.O. Box 4719, 43620. 3250-3260 Schneider Rd., 46314. Tel: 419-389-4615; Fax: 419-389-4620. Email: jkiely@vmc.org. Ms. Diane Clauda, Mgr. A corporation organized and operated for the purpose of providing housing facilities and services to elderly persons and handicapped persons. Units for the Elderly 70; Units for the Physically Handicapped 24.
Moody Manor, P.O. Box 4719, 43620. 2293 1/2 Kent St., 43620. Tel: 419-241-6985; Fax: 419-246-4737. Email: afreeman@vmc.org. Anglona Freeman, Mgr. Family & Elderly Units 119.
Office of Global Concerns, P.O. Box 985, 43697-0985. 1933 Spielbusch Ave., 43604-5360. Tel: 419-244-6711; Fax: 419-244-4791. Email: pwhite@toledodiocese.org. Web: www.toledodiocese.org/globalconcerns/index.html. Deacon Paul J. White, Dir. Society for the Propagation of the Faith; Holy Childhood Association; Catholic Relief Services.
Plaza Apartments, 2520 Monroe St., 43620. Tel: 419-244-1881; Fax: 419-246-4710. Email: ashaw@vmc.org. Mr. John Kiely, Vice Pres.; Ms. Angela Shaw, Project Mgr.
Regina Manor, Inc., 3731 N. Erie St., 43611. Tel: 419-726-6186; Fax: 419-726-6343. Email: jector@vmc.org. P.O. Box 4719, 43620. Patricia Hall, Mgr. Family & Elderly Units 180.
St. Vincent Mercy Medical Center Foundation, 2213 Cherry St., 43608. Tel: 419-251-2117. Tony Werner, Pres.
Toledo Catholic Charities Corporation, 1933 Spielbusch Ave., 43624. Tel: 419-244-6711; Fax: 419-720-0053. Email: rhenderson@toledodiocese.org. Deacon Ronald D. Henderson, Sec. Finance & Admin. The Catholic Charities Corporation is the Diocesan vehicle to collect and distribute endowment funds and bequests for charitable purposes.
U.T. Newman Foundation for Student Education and Development, 2955 Dorr St., 43607-3023. Tel: 419-531-4992; Fax: 419-531-1775. Rev. James J. Bacik.
Vision Time, Inc., 1618 W. Sylvania Ave., 43612. Tel: 419-476-0941; Fax: 419-476-8491. Email: nancy@servantleader.org. Sr. Nancy Westmeyer, O.S.F.
**Women Blessing Women* (1998) 223 Page St., 43620. Tel: 419-241-9789; Fax: 419-241-9791. Web: www.womenblessingwomen.org. Glenda Brown, Dir. Total Women Served 425.

CAREY. *Franciscan Mission Association*, 322 West St., 43316. Tel: 419-396-6455. Email: CarlosBH@aol.com. Bro. Bryan Hoban, O.F.M.Conv., Dir.

DELPHOS. *St. John Parish Foundation, Inc.*, Tel: 419-695-4050; Fax: 419-695-4060.
St. John the Evangelist Church: 331 E. Second St., 45833.

FINDLAY. *St. Michael Schools Educational Foundation*, 750 Bright Rd., 45840. Tel: 419-422-2646; Fax: 419-422-2602. Clifford Cook, Pres.

FREMONT. *Delaware Acres, Inc.* (1972) P.O. Box 4719, 43620. 725 S. Buchanan St., 43420. Tel: 419-334-9558; Fax: 419-334-9555. Email: jkiely@vmc.org. Ms. Marcella Miller, Mgr. Family Units 68.

GREEN SPRINGS. *St. Francis Hospital Foundation*, 401 N. Broadway, 44836. Tel: 419-639-2626; Fax: 419-639-6225. Email: jsmith@sfhcc.org. Web: www.sfhcc.org. Jean A. Smith, Exec. Dir.

LIMA. *Lima Central Catholic Educational Foundation* (1955) 720 S. Cable Rd., 45805. Tel: 419-222-4276; Fax: 419-222-6933. Email: lcary@lcchs.edu. Terrence J. Norton, Chm.
S.R.H.C. Foundation, 730 W. Market St., 45801-4667. Tel: 419-226-9775; Fax: 419-226-9750. Mr. James P. Reber, Pres.; William W. Roe, Sec. & Treas.

OREGON. *St. Charles Mercy Hospital Foundation*, 2600 Navarre Ave., 43616. Tel: 419-696-7245; Fax: 419-696-7644. Web: www.mercyweb.org/stcharlesfoundation. Holly Meyers, Foundation Chm.

SANDUSKY. *The Providence Fund* (1985) 2023 Hayes Ave., 44870. Tel: 419-627-8707; Fax: 419-627-9535. Email: ProvidenceFund@sbcglobal.net. Susan Daniel, Chm.; Nancy Beach, Exec. Dir. Eldercare Foundation.

SWANTON. *St. Richard's School Endowment Foundation* (1987) 333 Brookside Dr., 43558-1097. Tel: 419-826-2791; Fax: 419-826-7256. Email: busman@saintrichard.org. Web: saintrichard.org. Ed Snyder, Chmn.

SYLVANIA. **Franciscan Living Communities*, 6832 Convent Blvd., 43560. Tel: 419-882-8373; Fax: 419-882-7360. Email: rryan@fscsylvania.org. Rick Ryan, Pres.
Franciscan Properties, Inc. (1987) 6832 Convent Blvd., 43560. Tel: 419-824-3674; Fax: 419-824-3931. Email: dnolan@rosarycare.org. Sr. Jeanne Stack, O.S.F., Pres. Total in Residence 99; Total Staff 2; Apartments 98.
Franciscan Services Corporation (1984) 6832 Convent Blvd., 43560. Tel: 419-882-8373; Fax: 419-882-7360. Web: www.fscsylvania.org. Mr. John W. O'Connell, Pres.
Franciscan Shelters-Bethany House, P.O. Box 80596, 43608. Tel: 419-727-4948. Email: bethany_exdirector@yahoo.com. Kathleen Griffin, Exec. Dir.
Rosary Care Center (1975) 6832 Convent Blvd., 43560. Tel: 419-824-3600; Fax: 419-824-3931. Cheryl King, Admin.

TIFFIN. *St. Francis Home Inc.*, 182 St. Francis Ave., 44883. Tel: 419-447-2723; Fax: 419-448-1337. Email: ceo@stfrancishome.org. Web: www.stfrancishome.org. Robert G. Hauzie, Pres. & CEO; Ms. Anne Lange, Chairperson Bd. of Trustees. Residents 168; Total Assisted Annually 285; Total Staff 290.
St. Francis Senior Ministries Memorial Foundation, Inc., 182 St. Francis Ave., 44883. Tel: 419-447-2723; Fax: 419-448-1337. Email: ceo@stfrancishome.org. Web: www.stfrancishome.org. Cliff Farmer, Chm. Bd. of Trustees; Robert G. Hauzie, Pres. & CEO.
Saint Francis Senior Ministries, Inc., 182 Saint Francis Ave., 44883. Tel: 419-447-2723.
St. Francis Villas, Inc., 182 St. Francis Ave., 44883. Tel: 419-447-2723; Fax: 419-448-1337. Email: ceo@stfrancishome.inc. Web: www.stfrancishome.org. Robert G. Hauzie, Pres. & CEO; Ms. Anne Lange, Chairperson Bd. of Trustees.
Friedman Village at Saint Francis, LLC, 175 Saint Francis Ave., 44883. Tel: 419-447-2723.
Mercy Tiffin Health Foundation, 45 St. Lawrence Dr., 44883. Tel: 419-455-7049; Fax: 419-455-7066. Email: bernie_steinmetz@mhsnr.org. Web: www.mercyweb.org. Lee Martin, Chm.
St. Francis Senior Ministries Day Care, Inc., 182 St. Francis Ave., 44883. Tel: 419-447-2723; Fax: 419-448-1337. Email: ceo@stfrancishome.org. Web: stfrancishome.org. Robert G. Hauzie, Pres./CEO; Ms. Anne Lange, Chm. Bd. Trustees.
Tiffin Calvert Foundation (1974) 152 Madison St., 44883-0836. Tel: 419-447-3844. Michael Klepper, Pres.

VERMILION. *St. Mary's Church Education Endowment Foundation*, 731 Exchange St., 44089-1330. Tel: 440-967-8711; Fax: 440-967-8712. Email: parish@stmaryvermilion.org. Web: www.stmaryvermilion.org.

WILLARD. *Mercy Willard Hospital Foundation*, 110 E. Howard St., 44890. Tel: 419-964-5107; Fax: 419-964-5109. Email: marsha.danhoff@mhsnr.org. Web: mercyweb.org. Marsha Danhoff, Dir. Organizational Planning & Devel.

RELIGIOUS INSTITUTES OF MEN REPRESENTED IN THE DIOCESE

For further details refer to the corresponding bracketed number in the Religious Institutes of Men or Women section.

[]—*Congregation of the Holy Ghost of the Immaculate Heart of Mary (Holy Ghost Fathers)* (Nigeria)
[0480]—*Conventual Franciscans* (Our Lady of Consolation Prov.)—O.F.M.Conv.
[0690]—*Jesuit Fathers and Brothers*—S.J.
[0910]—*Oblates of St. Francis de Sales*—O.S.F.S.
[1070]—*Redemptorist Fathers* (Baltimore Prov.)—C.SS.R.
[1260]—*Society of Christ*—S.Ch.
[1060]—*Society of the Precious Blood* (Cincinnati Prov.)—C.PP.S.

RELIGIOUS INSTITUTES OF WOMEN REPRESENTED IN THE DIOCESE

[3710]—*Congregation of the Sisters of Saint Agnes*—C.S.A.
[1710]—*Congregation of the Third Order of St. Francis of Mary Immaculate, Joliet, IL*—O.S.F.
[4190]—*The Contemplative Order of the Sisters of the Visitation of Toledo, Ohio*—V.H.M.
[0793]—*Daughters of Divine Love*—D.D.L.
[1070-13]—*Dominican Sisters* (Adrian, MI)—O.P.
[1070-09]—*Dominican Sisters* (Racine, WI)—O.P.
[1430]—*Franciscan Sisters of Our Lady of Perpetual Help*—O.S.F.
[2575]—*Institute of the Sisters of Mercy of the Americas* (Cincinnati, OH)—R.S.M.
[2340]—*Little Sisters of the Poor* (Baltimore Prov.)—L.S.P.
[3130]—*Our Lady of Victory Missionary Sisters*—O.L.V.M.
[0440]—*Sisters of Charity of Cincinnati, Ohio*—S.C.
[0490]—*Sisters of Charity of Montreal (Grey Nuns)*—S.G.M.
[1000]—*Sisters of Divine Providence of Kentucky*—C.D.P.
[2990]—*Sisters of Notre Dame*—S.N.D.
[1530]—*Sisters of St. Francis of the Congregation of Our Lady of Lourdes, Sylvania, Ohio*—O.S.F.
[3930]—*Sisters of St. Joseph of the Third Order of St. Francis*—S.S.J.-T.O.S.F.
[]—*Sisters of the Imitation of Christ* (India)—S.I.C.
[2270]—*Sisters of the Little Company of Mary*—L.C.M.
[3260]—*Sisters of the Precious Blood* (Dayton, OH)—C.PP.S.
[1760]—*Sisters of the Third Order of St. Francis of Penance and Charity*—O.S.F.
[2150]—*Sisters, Servants of the Immaculate Heart of Mary*—I.H.M.
[4120-06]—*Ursuline Nuns of the Congregation of Paris*—O.S.U.
[4120]—*Ursuline Sisters of the Congregation of Paris*—O.S.U.-B.C.

DIOCESAN CEMETERIES

TOLEDO. *Calvary*, 2224 Dorr St., 43607. Tel: 419-536-3751. Web: www.cathcemtoledo.org. Deacon Ronald D. Henderson, Sec. Fin. & Admin.
Mount Carmel, 15 E. Manhattan Blvd., 43608. Mailing Address: 5725 Hill Ave., 43615. Tel: 419-531-5747; Fax: 419-531-0946.
Resurrection, 5725 Hill Ave., 43615. Tel: 419-531-5747; Fax: 419-531-0946. Web: www.cathcemtoledo.org. Deacon Ronald D. Henderson, Sec. Fin. & Admin.

FREMONT. *St. Joseph*, Tel: 419-332-8756.

LIMA. *Gethsemane*

SANDUSKY. *Calvary*, 2020 Sanford St., 44870. Tel: 419-625-2673; Fax: 419-502-3011.

NECROLOGY

† Dunn, Richard C., (Retired)—Died March 10, 2009
† Koerber, George M., (Retired)—Died 2009
† Kuhn, Thomas W., (Retired)—Died Dec. 3, 2009
† Miller, Richard G., (Retired)—Died March 30, 2009
† Walsh, James A., (Retired)—Died Feb. 8, 2009

An asterisk (*) denotes an organization that has established tax-exempt status directly with the IRS and is not covered by the USCCB Group Ruling.

Diocese of Trenton

(Dioecesis Trentonensis)

Most Reverend

JOHN M. SMITH, J.C.D., D.D.

Bishop of Trenton; ordained May 27, 1961; appointed Titular Bishop of Tre Taverne and Auxiliary Bishop of Newark December 1, 1987; consecrated January 25, 1988; appointed Bishop of Pensacola-Tallahassee June 25, 1991; installed July 31, 1991; appointed Coadjutor Bishop of Trenton November 21, 1995; appointed Bishop of Trenton July 1, 1997. *Res.: 901 W. State St., Trenton, NJ 08618.*

Most Reverend

JOHN C. REISS, D.D., J.C.D.

Retired Bishop of Trenton; ordained May 31, 1947; appointed Titular Bishop of Simidicca and Auxiliary of Trenton October 21, 1967; consecrated December 12, 1967; appointed Bishop of Trenton March 4, 1980; installed April 22, 1980; resigned July 1, 1997. *Res.: Villa Vianney, 2301 Lawrenceville Rd., Trenton, NJ 08648.*

SERVE THE LORD WITH GLADNESS

Pastoral Center: 701 Lawrenceville Rd., P.O. Box 5147, Trenton, NJ 08638. Tel: 609-406-7400; Fax: 609-406-7412.

ESTABLISHED AUGUST 11, 1881.

Square Miles 2,156.

Legal Corporate Title: "The Diocese of Trenton."

Comprises four Counties in the State of New Jersey: Burlington, Mercer, Monmouth and Ocean.

For legal titles of parishes and diocesan institutions, consult the Chancery Office.

STATISTICAL OVERVIEW

Personnel	
Bishop	1
Retired Bishops	1
Priests: Diocesan Active in Diocese	173
Priests: Diocesan Active Outside Diocese	10
Priests: Retired, Sick or Absent	58
Number of Diocesan Priests	241
Religious Priests in Diocese	58
Total Priests in Diocese	299
Extern Priests in Diocese	22
Ordinations:	
Diocesan Priests	3
Transitional Deacons	4
Permanent Deacons	13
Permanent Deacons in Diocese	357
Total Brothers	70
Total Sisters	366
Parishes	
Parishes	111
With Resident Pastor:	
Resident Diocesan Priests	98
Resident Religious Priests	9
Without Resident Pastor:	
Administered by Priests	4
Missions	6
New Parishes Created	1
Closed Parishes	3
Professional Ministry Personnel:	
Brothers	1
Sisters	32
Lay Ministers	96
Welfare	
Catholic Hospitals	2
Total Assisted	476,350
Health Care Centers	7
Total Assisted	4,500
Homes for the Aged	1
Total Assisted	430
Residential Care of Children	1
Total Assisted	24
Day Care Centers	6
Total Assisted	550
Specialized Homes	4
Total Assisted	200
Special Centers for Social Services	29
Total Assisted	27,750
Residential Care of Disabled	1
Total Assisted	180
Educational	
Diocesan Students in Other Seminaries	29
Students Religious	3
Total Seminarians	32
Colleges and Universities	1
Total Students	3,045
High Schools, Diocesan and Parish	8
Total Students	5,980
High Schools, Private	3
Total Students	1,181
Elementary Schools, Diocesan and Parish	36
Total Students	12,290
Elementary Schools, Private	3
Total Students	677
Non-residential Schools for the Disabled	1
Total Students	17
Catechesis/Religious Education:	
High School Students	1,077
Elementary Students	62,728
Total Students under Catholic Instruction	87,027
Teachers in the Diocese:	
Brothers	15
Sisters	68
Lay Teachers	952
Vital Statistics	
Receptions into the Church:	
Infant Baptism Totals	8,048
Minor Baptism Totals	101
Adult Baptism Totals	905
Received into Full Communion	295
First Communions	9,925
Confirmations	9,563
Marriages:	
Catholic	1,323
Interfaith	395
Total Marriages	1,718
Deaths	6,343
Total Catholic Population	831,707
Total Population	2,021,917

Former Bishops—Rt. Revs. MICHAEL J. O'FARRELL, D.D., cons. Nov. 1, 1881; died April 2, 1894; JAMES A. MCFAUL, D.D., LL.D., cons. Oct. 18, 1894; died June 16, 1917; Most Revs. THOMAS J. WALSH, S.T.D., J.C.D., cons. July 25, 1918; transferred to Newark, NJ, March 2, 1928; JOHN J. MCMAHON, D.D., cons. April 26, 1928; died Dec. 31, 1932; MOSES E. KILEY, S.T.D., cons. March 17, 1934; appt. Archbishop of Milwaukee, Jan. 1, 1940; WILLIAM A. GRIFFIN, D.D., appt. Bishop of Trenton, May 22, 1940; cons. May 1, 1938; died Jan. 1, 1950; GEORGE W. AHR, S.T.D., appt. Bishop of Trenton, Jan. 28, 1950; cons. March 20, 1950; retired June 23, 1979; died May 5, 1993; JOHN C. REISS, D.D., J.C.D. (Retired), appt. Bishop of Trenton, March 4, 1980; installed April 22, 1980; retired July 1, 1997.

Pastoral Center—701 Lawrenceville Rd., P.O. Box 5147, Trenton, 08638-0147. Tel: 609-406-7400; Fax: 609-406-7412.

Vicar General and Moderator of the Curia—Rev. Msgr. GREGORY D. VAUGHAN, V.G., 701 Lawrenceville Rd., Trenton, 08648.

Chancellor—Rev. Msgr. JOSEPH N. ROSIE, S.T.L., 701 Lawrenceville Rd., Trenton, 08648.

Episcopal Vicars—Ocean County: Rev. Msgr. CASIMIR H. LADZINSKI. Burlington County: Rev. Msgr. RICHARD L. TOFANI. Mercer County: Rev. Msgr. JOHN K. DERMOND, J.C.L. Monmouth County: Rev. Msgr. EUGENE M. REBECK.

Vice Chancellors—Rev. Msgr. EDWARD J. ARNISTER, J.C.L.; Rev. MICHAEL T. MCCLANE, J.C.L.

Assistant Chancellors—Rev. Msgrs. JOHN K. DERMOND, J.C.L.; JAMES G. INNOCENZI.

Secretary to the Bishop—Rev. CESAR A. RUBIANO.

Records Manager and Archivist—Sr. CATHERINE THIBAULT, S.S.J.

Diocesan Tribunal—701 Lawrenceville Rd., Trenton, 08648. Tel: 609-406-7411; Fax: 609-406-7424.

Judicial Vicar—Rev. Msgr. JOHN K. DERMOND, J.C.L.

Associate Judicial Vicars—Rev. Msgr. JAMES G. INNOCENZI; Rev. OSCAR B. SUMANGA, J.C.D.

Defenders of the Bond—Revs. PETER J. ALINDOGAN, J.C.L.; MICHAEL T. MCCLANE, J.C.L.; Deacon JOSEPH A. HANNAWACKER.

Promoter of Justice—Rev. PETER J. ALINDOGAN, J.C.L.

Tribunal Judges—Rev. Msgr. EDWARD J. ARNISTER, J.C.L.; Revs. AWTE WELDU, O.Cist.; EMMETT CARROLL, O.F.M.Conv.; LOUIS W. KRALOVICH (Retired); OSCAR B. SUMANGA, J.C.D.; Rev. Msgrs. WALTER E. NOLAN; EUGENE M. REBECK; Rev. JOHN J. SCULLY; Rev. Msgrs. JOSEPH C. SHENROCK, P.A. (Retired); RALPH W. STANSLEY.

Secretary of the Tribunal and Notary—Ms. EVELYN AGUIAR; Ms. JEANNETTE CAMERA.

Diocesan Consultors—Rev. Msgrs. GREGORY D. VAUGHAN, V.G.; WILLIAM F. FITZGERALD (Retired); Revs. JAMES J. MCCONNELL (Retired); THOMAS J. MULLELLY, J.D.; Rev. Msgrs. WALTER E. NOLAN; HUGH F. RONAN (Retired); KENARD J. TUZENEU; MICHAEL J. WALSH.

Diocesan Council of Priests—VACANT.

Council of Deacons and Vicariate Representatives—Deacon BARRY ZADWORNY, Pres. Burlington Co.: Deacons LEE ZITO; SALVATORE LANCIERI. Mercer Co.: Deacons BARRY ZADWORNY; ROBERT LAFOND. Monmouth Co.: Deacons VINCENT L. RINALDI; FERNANDO A. SORRENTINO. Ocean Co.:

Deacons ANTHONY MARTUCCI; JOHN R. PITT. At Large: Deacon JOSE RODRIQUEZ.

Diocesan Pastoral Council—Most Rev. JOHN MORTIMER SMITH, J.C.D., D.D., Chm.; Rev. Msgr. JOSEPH N. ROSIE, S.T.L., Liaison; Mr. JOSEPH MANZI, Pres.

Diocesan Finance Council—Most Rev. JOHN MORTIMER SMITH, J.C.D., D.D., Pres.; Mr. LAURENCE M. DOWNES, Chm.; Rev. Msgrs. GREGORY D. VAUGHAN, V.G.; JOSEPH N. ROSIE, S.T.L.; HARRY R. HILL, Esq.; Mr. BERNARD M. MCGLONE; Mr. ANTHONY J. MINGARINO; Ms. PATRICIA COSTANTE; Mr. ROBERT J. DUNNE III; Mr. EMIL A. SCHROTH JR.; Mr. RON NOWAK; Mr. MICHAEL CASTELLANO; Mr. WILLIAM N. DOOLEY.

Censores Librorum—Rev. Msgr. JOSEPH N. ROSIE, S.T.L.; Rev. PABLO T. GADENZ, S.T.D., S.S.L.

Secretariat for Temporal Administration

Secretary—Mr. ANTHONY J. MINGARINO, Pastoral Center, 701 Lawrenceville Rd., Trenton, 08648. Tel: 609-406-7400; Fax: 609-406-7414.

Office of Administrative Services—Mr. JOSEPH BIANCHI, S.P.H.R., Dir.; Mr. JOSEPH C. DAVIS, Assoc. Dir., Pastoral Center, 701 Lawrenceville Rd., Trenton, 08648. Tel: 609-406-7400; Fax: 609-406-7413.

Human Resources—Mr. JOSEPH BIANCHI, S.P.H.R., Dir.; ANGELA GITTO, HR Specialist.

Office of Computer Services—Ms. KATHLEEN MOORE, Dir., Pastoral Center, 701 Lawrenceville Rd., Trenton, 08648. Tel: 609-406-7400; Fax: 609-406-7414.

Office of Finance—Ms. DARYL ROWE, Dir., Pastoral Center, 701 Lawrenceville Rd., Trenton, 08648. Tel: 609-406-7400; Fax: 609-406-7414.

Office of Development—Mr. SHANNON JORDAN, Dir., Pastoral Center, 701 Lawrenceville Rd., Trenton, 08648. Tel: 609-406-7400; Fax: 609-406-7443.

Office of Major Gifts and Planned Giving—Mrs. BARBARA WARNER, Dir., Pastoral Center, 701 Lawrenceville Rd., Trenton, 08648. Tel: 609-406-7400; Fax: 609-406-7414.

Office of Pastoral Planning—Ms. TERRY GINTHER, Dir., Pastoral Center, 701 Lawrenceville Rd., Trenton, 08648. Tel: 609-406-7400; Fax: 609-406-7418.

Office of Property and Construction—Deacon WILLIAM A. WILSON, Dir. Associate Directors: Mr. KENNETH J. NOWAK; Deacon NEIL PIROZZI.

Expansion and Restructuring Commission—Rev. JEFFREY E. LEE, Chm., Pastoral Center, 701 Lawrenceville Rd., Trenton, 08648. Tel: 609-406-7400; Fax: 609-406-7444.

Building Commission—Rev. Msgr. RICHARD C. BRIETSKE, Chm. (Retired); Deacon WILLIAM A. WILSON, Asst., Pastoral Center, 701 Lawrenceville Rd., Trenton, 08648. Tel: 609-406-7400; Fax: 609-406-7412.

Cemeteries—Rev. Msgr. JAMES H. DUBELL, Dir., St. Mary of the Lakes, 40 Jackson Rd., Medford, 08055. Tel: 609-654-8208; Fax: 609-654-1734.

Secretariat for Catholic Education

Secretary—Mrs. JOANN TIER, Pastoral Center, 701 Lawrenceville Rd., Trenton, 08648. Tel: 609-406-7400; Fax: 609-406-7416.

Office of Catholic Schools

Office of Catholic Schools—Mrs. JOANN TIER, Supt.; Dr. MARGARET BOLAND, Assoc. Supt.; Ms. BETHANY DOROS-GREGG, Assoc. Dir. Educational Advancement; Ms. DONNA BACSIK, Assoc. Dir. Elementary Schools, Pastoral Center, 701 Lawrenceville Rd., Trenton, 08648. Tel: 609-406-7400; Fax: 609-406-7416.

Associate Director Athletics, School Boards, Marketing, and Government Programs—Ms. DONNA DAVIDSON, Pastoral Center, 701 Lawrenceville Rd., Trenton, 08648. Tel: 609-406-7400; Fax: 609-406-7416.

Office of Catechesis—Mr. MARTIN J. ARSENAULT, Dir. Associate Directors: Mr. MICHAEL FABIAN; Ms. JENNIFER HINTON.

Holy Innocents—Mr. ANGELO ROMANELLO, Pres., 5 Shelburne Dr., Trenton, 08638. Tel: 609-882-4567.

Office of Youth and Young Adult Ministries—Mr. MATTHEW GREELEY, Dir.

Scouting—Rev. MICHAEL A. SANTANGELO, Chap., St. Mary of the Lake Parish, 43 Madison Ave., Lakewood, 08701. Tel: 732-363-0139; Fax: 732-905-1410.

Campus Ministry—Mr. MATTHEW GREELEY, Coord., Pastoral Center, 701 Lawrenceville Rd., Trenton, 08648. Tel: 609-406-7400; Fax: 609-406-7416.

Secretariat for Community Relations

Secretary—Ms. RAYANNE BENNETT, Chief Communications Officer, Pastoral Center, 701 Lawrenceville Rd., Trenton, 08648. Tel: 609-406-7400; Fax: 609-409-7423.

Office of Communications and Public Relations—Ms. RAYANNE BENNETT, Dir. & Chief Communications Officer, Pastoral Center, 701 Lawrenceville Rd., Trenton, 08648. Tel: 609-406-7400; Fax: 609-406-7412.

The Monitor—Ms. RAYANNE BENNETT, Assoc. Publisher, Pastoral Center, 701 Lawrenceville Rd., Trenton, 08648. Tel: 609-406-7400; Fax: 609-406-7423; Mr. GEORGE W. STEVENSON, Business Dir.

Office of Radio and TV—Mrs. MARIANNE HARTMAN, Dir., Pastoral Center, 701 Lawrenceville Rd., Trenton, 08648. Tel: 609-406-7400; Fax: 609-406-7423.

Website Office—Mr. KENNETH PERRY, Dir., Pastoral Center, 701 Lawrenceville Rd., Trenton, 08648. Tel: 609-406-7400, Ext. 5602; Fax: 609-406-7423. Web: www.dioceseoftrenton.org.

Secretariat for Pastoral Life

Secretary—Very Rev. KEVIN J. KEELEN, V.F., St. Barnabas, 33 Woodland Rd., Box 1, Bayville, 08721. Tel: 732-269-2208; Fax: 732-269-2557.

Office of Pastoral Care of the Sick—Mrs. DEANNA V. SASS, M.A., Dir., 701 Lawrenceville Rd., Trenton, 08648. Tel: 609-406-7400; Fax: 609-406-7458.

Office of Family Life—Mrs. LINDA G. RICHARDSON, Dir.; Ms. MARILYN SCHIPP, Assoc. Dir., Pastoral Center, 701 Lawrenceville Rd., Trenton, 08648. Tel: 609-406-7400; Fax: 609-406-7403.

Office of Life and Justice Ministries—Rev. IAN W. TRAMMELL, Dir., Pastoral Center, 701 Lawrenceville Rd., Trenton, 08648. Tel: 609-406-7400; Fax: 609-406-7403.

Social Concerns—Rev. RONALD J. CIOFFI, Coord., St. Joseph, 376 Maple Pl., Keyport, 07735. Tel: 732-264-0322; Fax: 732-888-3280. Email: stjoeskeyport@aol.com.

Prison Ministry—Rev. ROBERT R. SCHULZE, Coord., Pastoral Center, 701 Lawrenceville Rd., Trenton, 08648. Tel: 609-406-7400; Fax: 609-406-7413.

The Hispanic and Portuguese Apostolate—Rev. JAVIER A. DIAZ-MUNOZ, Dir., St. Joseph Church, 540 N. Olden Ave., Trenton, 08638. Tel: 609-394-5757; Fax: 609-599-4402.

The Black Apostolate—Ms. ELLIEEN ANCRUM, Dir., Pastoral Center, 701 Lawrenceville Rd., Trenton, 08648. Tel: 609-406-7400; Fax: 609-406-7413.

The Haitian Apostolate—Mrs. MAGDA DORLEANS, Dir. (Trenton Area), The Haitian Community Center, 530 S. Olden Ave., Trenton, 08629. Tel: 609-588-8808; Fax: 609-588-8801; Rev. WILLIAM J. MCLAUGHLIN, Dir. (Asbury Park Area), Holy Spirit Church, 705 Second Ave., P.O. Box 617, Asbury Park, 07712. Tel: 732-775-0030; Fax: 732-775-7358.

The Korean Apostolate—Rev. CHA YONG LEE, Dir., Immaculate Conception, 64 Broad St., Eatontown, 07724. Tel: 732-542-0148; Fax: 732-389-2705.

Secretariat for Spiritual and Parish Life

Secretary—Rev. Msgr. RICHARD D. LAVERGHETTA, St. Gregory the Great Church, 4620 Nottingham Way, Trenton, 08690. Tel: 609-587-4877; Fax: 609-588-0192.

Office of Worship—Rev. SAM A. SIRIANNI, Dir.; Sr. ELEANOR MCCANN, Assoc. Dir., Pastoral Center, 701 Lawrenceville Rd., Trenton, 08648. Tel: 609-406-7400; Fax: 609-406-7403.

Office of Evangelization and Parish Development—Mr. JOHN BOUCHER, Dir.; Ms. JOLYNN KREMPECKI, Assoc. Dir., Pastoral Center, 701 Lawrenceville Rd., Trenton, 08648. Tel: 609-406-7400; Fax: 609-406-7415.

Charismatic Renewal—Rev. H. BRENDAN WILLIAMS, Liaison, St. Veronica Church, 4215 Hwy. 9 N., Howell, 08724. Tel: 732-363-4200; Fax: 732-370-3891. Email: willcron@world.net.att.net.

Cursillo—Rev. JOHN V. BOWDEN, Chap. (Retired), Villa Vianney, 2301 Lawrenceville Rd., Trenton, 08648.

Francis House of Prayer—Sr. MARCELLA SPRINGER, S.S.J., Dir., Mailing Address: P.O. Box 392, Rancocas, 08073. Tel: 609-877-0509; Fax: 609-877-5810. Web: www.francishouseofprayer.org. Email: fhop@pics.com.

Legion of Mary—Rev. MICHAEL J. BURNS, Chap., St. Mary Church, 45 Crosswicks St., Bordentown, 08505. Tel: 609-298-0261; Fax: 609-298-7178.

Upper Room—Co-Directors: Sisters MAUREEN CHRISTENSEN, R.S.M.; MAUREEN CONROY, R.S.M.; TRUDY AHERN, S.S.J., W. Bangs Ave. & Rte. 33, Neptune, 07754-1104. Tel: 732-922-0550; Fax: 732-922-3904. Web: www.theupper-room.org. Email: upperroom@bytheshore.com; Mailing Address: P.O. Box 1104, Neptune, 07754.

Secretariat for Personnel in Ministry

Secretary—Rev. Msgr. KENARD J. TUZENEU, St. Mary Church, 724 W. Bay Ave., P.O. Box 609, Barnegat, 08005. Tel: 609-698-5531; Fax: 609-698-6255.

Office of Continuing Education for Priests—Rev. THOMAS J. MULLELLY, J.D., Dir., Aquinas Institute, 65 Stockton St., Princeton, 08540. Tel: 609-924-1820; Fax: 609-924-8322.

Office of Permanent Deacons—Rev. Msgr. RALPH W. STANSLEY, Dir. Assistant Directors: Deacons LAWRENCE W. FINN SR.; JOSEPH M. DONADIEU, Pastoral Center, 701 Lawrenceville Rd., Trenton, 08648. Tel: 609-406-7400; Fax: 609-406-7417.

Office of Priest Personnel—Rev. Msgr. RONALD J. BACOVIN, Dir., Pastoral Center, 701 Lawrenceville Rd., Trenton, 08648. Tel: 609-406-7400; Fax: 609-406-7453.

Delegate for Consecrated Life—Sr. DONNA WATSON, I.H.M., Delegate, Pastoral Center, 701 Lawrenceville Rd., Trenton, 08648. Tel: 609-406-7409; Fax: 609-406-7413.

Office of Vocations—Rev. Msgr. GREGORY D. VAUGHAN, V.G., Dir. Seminarians, Pastoral Center, 701 Lawrenceville Rd., Trenton, 08648. Tel: 609-406-7400; Fax: 609-406-7412. Web: www.godiscallingyou.com.

Secretariat for Social Services

Secretary—Rev. THOMAS J. MULLELLY, J.D., Aquinas Institute, 65 Stockton St., Princeton, 08540. Tel: 609-924-1820; Fax: 609-219-9203.

Migration & Refugee Services—Sr. JANET YURKANIN, I.H.M., Dir., 149 N. Warren St., Trenton, 08608. Tel: 609-394-8299; Fax: 609-394-0240. Email: jyurkanin@aol.com.

Catholic Charities—Mr. FRANCIS E. DOLAN, Dir., 383 W. State St., P.O. Box 1423, Trenton, 08607-1423. Tel: 609-394-5181; Fax: 609-695-6978. Web: www.catholiccharitiestrenton.org.

Campaign for Human Development—Rev. JOSEPH A. JAKUB, Dir., Emmaus House, 2116 Lawrenceville Rd., Trenton, 08648. Tel: 609-896-0394.

Catholic Relief Services—Mrs. MARY GOSS, 10 Pumpshire Rd., Toms River, 08753. Tel: 732-929-9013.

Martin House—Rev. BRIAN MCCORMICK, Dir., 802 E. State St., P.O. Box 1025, Trenton, 08606. Tel: 609-989-8143; Fax: 609-989-0933. Email: mhlcmaster@aol.com.

Mount Carmel Guild—Ms. MARIE GLADNEY, Exec. Dir., 73 N. Clinton Ave., Trenton, 08609. Tel: 609-392-5159; Fax: 609-392-5903. Email: mtcarmelguild@aol.com.

St. Vincent DePaul Society—Ms. PATRICIA BROOKS, Diocesan Council Pres. Tel: 609-234-0628. Email: pbrooks@verizon.net.

CLERGY, PARISHES, MISSIONS AND PAROCHIAL SCHOOLS

CITY OF TRENTON

(MERCER COUNTY)

1—ST. MARY CATHEDRAL (1868) Rev. Msgr. John K. Dermond, Rector; Revs. Nilo Apura, Parochial Vicar; Alcides Castro Lopez; Deacons Emiliano Vazquez; Jose Beauchamps; Luis Ramos; Jose Rodriquez.
Res.: 151 N. Warren St., 08608. Tel: 609-396-8447; Fax: 609-396-5624. Email: stmaryscathedral@verizon.net.
Catechesis/Religious Program—Email: cathedralccd@aol.com. Sr. Luz Mery VeLez Quiroz, D.R.E.; Mrs. Marisol Rodriguez, C.R.E. Students 235.

2—ST. ANTHONY (1921) Closed. Sacramental records maintained at Our Lady of Sorrows-St. Anthony Parish, Hamilton.
High School—McCorristin High School, Closed. Records maintained at Trenton Catholic Academy, Hamilton.

3—BLESSED SACRAMENT (1912) Closed. Sacramental records maintained at Blessed Sacrament-Our Lady of the Divine Shepherd Parish, Trenton.

4—BLESSED SACRAMENT-OUR LADY OF THE DIVINE SHEPHERD PARISH (2005) Revs. Edward Tetteh, S.V.D.; Henry A. Militante; Guilherme A. Andrino, S.V.D.; Deacon Anthony D. Vogel.
Res.: 716 Bellevue Ave., 08618. Tel: 609-396-9231; Fax: 609-396-6432. Email: ols1948@juno.com. Web: www.cbs-olds.org.
Catechesis/Religious Program—Patricia Vincent, D.R.E. Students 40.
Station—Mercer Hospital 08618. Tel: 609-394-4000.

5—THE CHURCH OF THE INCARNATION-ST. JAMES (2006), (Merged July 1, 2006) Revs. Daniel Houde, O.SS.T.; Pradeep Puthenveettil, O.SS.T., Parochial Vicar; Deacons Thomas H. Rivella; Joseph A.

Hannawacker; Frances G. Golazeski. In Res., Rev. Kenneth G. Borgesen, O.SS.T.
Res.: 1545 Pennington Rd., 08618. Tel: 609-882-2860; Fax: 609-637-0460. Email: office@incarnationstjames.org. Web: www.incarnationstjames.org.
School—1555 Pennington Rd., 08618. Tel: 609-882-3228; Fax: 609-671-1629. Sr. Mary Patricia O'Donnell, I.H.M., Prin. Sisters, Servants of the Immaculate Heart of Mary (Immaculata, PA) 7; Lay Teachers 14; Students 207.
Catechesis/Religious Program—Tel: 609-882-8989. Sr. Mary Ellen Diehl, I.H.M., Dir. Faith Formation. Students 226.
Convent—45 Harrop Pl., 08618.

6—DIVINE MERCY PARISH (2005) Rev. Msgr. Edward J. Arnister; Revs. Leszek Tymoszuk; Armando Vazquez; Deacons John R. Grussler; Frank Sowa; Sisters Karen Crawford, F.S.S.J., Pastoral Assoc.; Loretta Janiszewski, F.S.S.J., Pastoral Assoc.; Carmen Bojorge, Pastoral Assoc.
Res.: 201 Adeline St., 08611. Tel: 609-393-4826; Fax: 609-278-1192.
Catechesis/Religious Program—233 Adeline St., 08611. Tel: 609-393-5233; Fax: 609-393-5233. Mrs. Rosemarie Micharski, D.R.E. Students 115.
Convent—333 Home Ave., 08611. Tel: 609-965-6424.

7—ST. FRANCIS OF ASSISIUM (1844) [CEM 2] Closed. Sacramental records maintained at Sacred Heart Church, Trenton.

8—ST. HEDWIG (1904), (Polish), [CEM 2] Rev. Jacek Labinski; Deacons Thomas H. Watkins Jr.; Barry Zadworny.
Res.: 872 Brunswick Ave., 08638. Tel: 609-396-9068; Fax: 609-396-3171.
Catechesis/Religious Program—Dorothy Zadworny, D.R.E. Students 240.

9—HOLY ANGELS (1921) Closed. Sacramental records maintained at St. Raphael-Holy Angels Parish, Hamilton.

10—HOLY CROSS (1891) [CEM] Closed. Sacramental records maintained at Divine Mercy Parish, Trenton.

11—IMMACULATE CONCEPTION (1874) Closed. Sacramental records maintained at Our Lady of the Angels Parish, Trenton.

12—INCARNATION (1947) Closed. For inquiries for parish records, see Incarnation-St. James Parish, Trenton.

13—ST. JAMES (1919) Closed. For inquiries for parish records, see Incarnation-St. James Parish, Trenton.

14—ST. JOACHIM (1901) Closed. Sacramental records maintained at Our Lady of Angels Parish, Trenton.

15—ST. JOSEPH (1891), (Spanish), Revs. Javier A. Diaz-Munoz; George A. Medina.
Res.: 540 N. Olden Ave., 08638. Tel: 609-394-5757; Fax: 609-218-6834.
Catechesis/Religious Program—Tel: 609-394-3580; Fax: 609-394-3418. Ms. Marlene Lao'-Collins, Dir. Students 80.
Station—Helene Fuld Hospital, Tel: 609-394-6000.

16—ST. MICHAEL (1921) Closed. Sacramental records maintained at Church of St. Ann, Lawrenceville.

17—OUR LADY OF GOOD COUNSEL (1942) Rev. Msgr. Ralph W. Stansley; Sr. Marie Therese Staiger, Pastoral Assoc.; Deacons Robert Brady; John Bonner.
Res.: 137 W. Upper Ferry Rd., West Trenton, 08628. Tel: 609-882-3277; Fax: 609-882-4375.
Catechesis/Religious Program—Tel: 609-883-9005. Brenda O'Callaghan, Dir. Students 150.

18—OUR LADY OF MOUNT CARMEL, Closed. For Sacramental records please contact St. Mary Cathedral, Trenton.

19—OUR LADY OF SORROWS (1939) Closed. Sacramental records maintained at Our Lady of Sorrows-St. Anthony Parish, Hamilton.

20—OUR LADY OF THE ANGELS PARISH (2005) Rev. Jeffrey E. Lee; Deacon Guido Mattozzi.
Res.: 19 Bayard St., 08611. Tel: 609-695-6089; Fax: 609-695-4375. Email: olatrenton05@aol.com.
Catechesis/Religious Program—Tel: 609-695-6089, Ext. 115. Mr. Edwin Sevilland, D.R.E. Students 53.

21—OUR LADY OF THE DIVINE SHEPHERD (1941) Closed. Sacramental records maintained at Blessed Sacrament-Our Lady of the Divine Shepherd Parish, Trenton.

22—SS. PETER AND PAUL (1899) [CEM] Closed. Sacramental records maintained at Divine Mercy Parish, Trenton.

23—ST. RAPHAEL (1943) Closed. Sacramental records maintained at St. Raphael-Holy Angels Parish, Hamilton.

24—SACRED HEART (1814) [CEM] Rev. Dennis A. Apoldite.
Res.: 343 S. Broad St., 08608. Tel: 609-393-2801; Fax: 609-989-8997. Web: www.trentonsacredheart.org.
Catechesis/Religious Program—Mrs. Linda Teresky, Dir. Students 135.

25—ST. STANISLAUS (1890) [CEM] Closed. Sacramental records maintained at Divine Mercy Parish, Trenton.

26—ST. STEPHEN (1903) [CEM] Closed. Sacramental records maintained at Our Lady of the Angels Parish, Trenton.

27—ST. VINCENT DE PAUL (1954) Revs. Stanley Krzyston; Rogatus Mpeka.
Res.: 555 Allentown Rd., Yardville, 08620. Tel: 609-585-6470; Fax: 609-585-0137.
Catechesis/Religious Program—Tel: 609-585-5484. Johanna Kraemer, D.R.E. Students 259.

OUTSIDE THE CITY OF TRENTON

ALLENTOWN, MONMOUTH CO., ST. JOHN (1878) [CEM] Rev. Patrick J. Castles; Deacon Joseph Hepp.
Res.: 1282 Yardville-Allentown Rd., 08501-1830. Tel: 609-259-3391; Fax: 609-259-0313. Email: stjohnallentown@optonline.net. Web: www.stjohnsallentownnj.org.
Catechesis/Religious Program—Tel: 609-259-3586; Fax: 609-259-0313. Mrs. Donna Millar, C.R.E. Students 526.

ASBURY PARK, MONMOUTH CO.

1—HOLY SPIRIT (1879) [CEM] Revs. William J. McLaughlin; Paul Janvier, Haitian Min.; Deacon Edner Andre.
Res.: 705 2nd Ave., P.O. Box 617, 07712. Tel: 732-775-0030; Fax: 732-775-7358.
Catechesis/Religious Program—Students 40.
Mt. Calvary Cemetery—Rte. 66 and Neptune Blvd., Box 2037, Ocean, 07712. Tel: 732-775-3320.

2—OUR LADY OF MT. CARMEL (1905), (Italian), Revs. Charles J. Flood, O.SS.T.; Boby Kurian Kumbakeel, O.SS.T., Parochial Vicar. In Res., Rev. Ireneusz Ekiert, O.SS.T.
Res.: 805 Pine St., 07712. Tel: 732-775-1056; Fax: 732-775-8767.
School—First Ave. & Pine St., 07712. Tel: 732-775-8989; Fax: 732-775-0108. Sr. Jude Catherine Boyce, S.S.J., Prin. Sisters 4; Lay Teachers 14; Students 152.
Catechesis/Religious Program—Tel: 732-988-5060. Sr. Christina Aldarelli, I.H.M., D.R.E. Students 216.

3—ST. PETER CLAVER (1943), (African American), Rev. William J. McLaughlin.
Res.: 705 2nd Ave., P.O. Box 617, 07712. Tel: 732-775-0030; Fax: 732-775-7358.
Catechesis/Religious Program—Mrs. Helen Jackson, D.R.E. Students 30.

ATLANTIC HIGHLANDS, MONMOUTH CO., ST. AGNES (1890) Rev. Michael B. Figler; Deacons Raymond Rainville; Robert J. Johnson.
Res.: 103 Center Ave., 07716. Tel: 732-291-0272; Fax: 732-291-4982. Email: sagneschur@aol.com.
Catechesis/Religious Program—Tel: 732-291-2035. Ms. Kerry Harvey, D.R.E. Students 552.
Convent—44 South Ave., 07716. Tel: 732-291-8246.

AVON, MONMOUTH CO., ST. ELIZABETH (1907) Rev. M. Joseph Mokrzycki.
Res.: 424 Lincoln Ave., Avon By The Sea, 07717. Tel: 732-774-4089; Fax: 732-774-5848. Email: stelizabeth@optonline.net.
Catechesis/Religious Program—Mrs. Beatrice Murday, C.R.E. Students 200.

BARNEGAT, OCEAN CO., ST. MARY (1942) [CEM] Rev. Msgr. Kenard J. Tuzeneu; Rev. Thomas Kunath; Deacons Patrick Martin; Joseph A. Fiorillo; Ronald Haunss; Joseph A. Vivona; Frank Campione; John R. Pitt; Daniel Miller; Robert Klein; Martin Hemberger.
Parish Center: 179 S. Main St., Manahawkin, 08050.
Res.: 747 W. Bay Ave., P.O. Box 609, 08005-0609. Tel: 609-698-5531; Fax: 609-698-6255. Web: stmary.shoresurfer.com.
Catechesis/Religious Program—Tel: 609-597-7600; Fax: 609-597-7178. Web: www.stmarysrep.com. Mrs. Joan Haldenwang, D.R.E. Students 1,800.
Mission—St. Mary of the Pines 100 Bishop Ln., Manahawkin, Ocean Co. 08050.

BAY HEAD, OCEAN CO., SACRED HEART (1913) Rev. Msgr. Casimir H. Ladzinski; Deacon James Lacey.
Res.: 751 Main Ave., 08742. Tel: 732-899-1398; Fax: 732-899-2233. Email: shrcbh@comcast.net. Web: sacredheartbayhead.com.
Catechesis/Religious Program—Students 96.

BAYVILLE, OCEAN CO., ST. BARNABAS (1966) Very Rev. Kevin J. Keelen; Rev. Alberto W. Tamayo; Deacons Guy C. Rasmussen; Michael A. Smigelski; George J. Swanson; Sr. Rosa Gamarra, Pastoral Assoc.
Res.: 33 Woodland Rd., P.O. Box I, 08721. Tel: 732-269-2208; Fax: 732-269-2557. Email: stbarnabas@sbrcc.com. Web: www.stbarnabasbayville.com.
Catechesis/Religious Program—Mary Britanak, C.R.E. Students 1,100.

BELMAR, MONMOUTH CO., ST. ROSE (1888) Revs. Douglas Freer; Joel R. Wilson; Deacons Normand C. Bailey; Eugene G. Malhame Jr.
Res.: 603 Seventh Ave., 07719. Tel: 732-681-0512; Fax: 732-280-3107. Email: parish@strose.k12.nj.us. Web: strosebelmar.org.
School—605 Sixth Ave., 07719. Tel: 732-681-5555; Fax: 732-681-5890. Williams Roberts, Prin. Sisters 1; Lay Teachers 18; Students 347.
High School—Tel: 732-681-2858; Fax: 732-280-2745. Sr. Kathleen Nace, S.S.J., Prin. Sisters 3; Lay Teachers 39; Students 555.
Catechesis/Religious Program—Tel: 732-681-6266. Sr. Cecilia Leipert, S.S.J., D.R.E. Students 360.
Convent—610 Eighth Ave., 07719. Tel: 732-681-1039.

BEVERLY, BURLINGTON CO., ST. JOSEPH (1864) Merged with St. Peter's, Riverside to form The Church of Jesus, the Good Shepherd, Riverside, N.J.

BORDENTOWN, BURLINGTON CO., ST. MARY (1837) [CEM] Rev. Michael J. Burns; Deacons David M. Harris Jr.; Harry A. Putnam, (Retired); Gary T. Richardson; Thomas F. Shea; Ronald F. Zalegowski; Lawrence W. Finn Sr. In Res., Rev. Felix F. Venza, Senior Priest.
Res.: 45 Crosswicks St., 08505. Tel: 609-298-0261; Fax: 609-298-7178. Email: office@stmarysbordentown.org. Web: www.stmarysbordentown.org.
School—30 Elizabeth St., 08505. Tel: 609-298-1448; Fax: 609-298-3803. Web: www.smsbordentown.org. Michael D. Rosenberg, Prin. Lay Teachers 14; Students 185.
Catechesis/Religious Program—Tel: 609-291-8281; Fax: 609-298-7178. Email: office@stmarysrc.org. Web: www.stmarysre.org. Mrs. Peg Corcoran, C.R.E. Students 443.

BRADLEY BEACH, MONMOUTH CO., ASCENSION (1907) Rev. Jerome M. Nolan; Deacon John Kopcak.
Res.: 501 Brinley Ave., 07720. Tel: 732-774-0456; Fax: 732-775-9335. Email: ascensionchurch@optonline.net.
Catechesis/Religious Program—Joan Rovere, Dir. Students 179.

BRANT BEACH, OCEAN CO., ST. FRANCIS OF ASSISI (1971) Revs. Stephen Kluge, O.F.M.; John R. Ullrich, O.F.M.; Thomas E. Conway, O.F.M., Parochial Vicar; James Scullion, O.F.M.; Deacons George Walker; Richard C. Titmas; Robert Cunningham.
Office: 4700 Long Beach Blvd., 08008-3926. Tel: 609-494-8813; Fax: 609-494-1466.
Catechesis/Religious Program—Ms. Sharon Desipio, D.R.E.
Mission—St. Thomas Aquinas 2nd & Atlantic, Beach Haven, Ocean Co. 08008. Tel: 609-492-2633.
Mission—St. Clare 56th & Long Beach Blvd., Loveladies, Ocean Co. 08008. Tel: 609-494-6662.
Mission—St. Thomas of Villanova 13th & Long Beach Blvd., Surf City, Ocean Co. 08008. Tel: 609-494-2371.

BRICK TOWN, OCEAN CO.

1—ST. DOMINIC (1962) Revs. James J. Brady; Joseph Gnarackatt; Dean A. Gaudio; Deacons Damian Ayers; Gerald Riedinger; Edward Buecker; Ms. Brigid Hughes, Pastoral Ministry.
Res.: 250 Old Squan Rd., 08724. Tel: 732-840-1410; Fax: 732-840-0522.
School—Tel: 732-840-1412; Fax: 732-840-6457. Carol Bathmann, Prin. Lay Teachers 30; Students 610.
Catechesis/Religious Program—Mrs. Ann M. Cramer, D.R.E. Students 850.

2—EPIPHANY (1973) Rev. Bernadino Esguerra; Deacons Ron Nowak; Michael Mullarkey; William Heard; Louis Commisso.
615 Thiele Rd., 08724.
Res.: 641 Thiele Rd., 08724. Tel: 732-458-0220; Fax: 732-458-0855. Web: www.churchofepiphany.org.
Epiphany Parish Hall—621 Herbertsville Rd., 08724. Tel: 732-840-8411.
Catechesis/Religious Program—Tel: 732-785-0576; 732-785-0872; Fax: 732-458-0855. Mrs. Sandra Mullarkey, C.R.E. Students 448.

3—VISITATION (1942) Revs. William M. Dunlap; Rodolfo Gonzalez-Ballesteros; Velanmarukudiyil Christudasl, O.S.B.; Deacons Edward Fischer III; Salvatore Vicari; Leonard Kruk; Bradford A. Krupa; David S. Kohut; Richard Johnston.
Res.: 730 Lynnwood Ave., 08723-5397. Tel: 732-477-0028; Fax: 732-477-1274.
Catechesis/Religious Program—Tel: 732-477-5217. Mrs. Nancy Grodberg, D.R.E. Students 1,310.

BROWNS MILLS, BURLINGTON CO., ST. ANN (1906) Rev. Edwin J. Mathias; Deacons Walter Price; Frank Sherpensky; Michael J. O'Brien.
Church & Res.: 22 Trenton Rd., 08015-3236. Tel: 609-893-3246; Fax: 609-893-8056. Web: stannschurch.org.
Catechesis/Religious Program—Students 195.
Station—Burlington Co. Minimum Security Jail Pemberton Township.
Station—Burlington Co. Juvenile Detention Center Pemberton.
Station—Deborah Heart & Lung Center, Tel: 609-893-6611.
Station—Evergreen Park, Buttonwood Hall, Tel:

609-726-7000.

BURLINGTON, BURLINGTON CO.

1—ALL SAINTS (1910), (Polish), Closed. For inquiries for parish records please see St. Katharine Drexel Parish, Burlington.

2—THE CHURCH OF ST. KATHARINE DREXEL, BURLINGTON, N.J. (1864) [CEM] Revs. Michael G. Dunn; Cesar R. Anson, Parochial Vicar; Deacons Francis A. Jones; Alfred Pennise; Alexander A. Punchello Sr.
Res.: 223 E Union St., 08016. Tel: 609-387-8191.
School—250 James St., 08016. Tel: 609-386-1645; Fax: 609-386-1345. Sr. Peter Damian, R.S.M., Prin. Sisters of Mercy 1; Lay Teachers 21; Students 415.
Catechesis/Religious Program—Miss Kathryn Besheer, D.R.E. Students 314.
Convent—122 James St., 08016-3319. Tel: 609-386-4083.

CINNAMINSON, BURLINGTON CO., ST. CHARLES BORROMEO (1961) Rev. Peter James Alindogan; Deacons William S. Sepich; William Gallagher; Carl Sondeen; Gerald Doughty; John Hvizdos.
Res.: 2226 Riverton Rd., P.O. Box 2220, 08077. Tel: 856-829-3322; Fax: 856-829-1852.
School—2500 Branch Pike, 08077. Tel: 856-829-2778; Fax: 856-829-3411. Mrs. Diane Kinnevy, Prin. Lay Teachers 19; Students 251.
Catechesis/Religious Program—Tel: 856-829-9119. Mrs. Patricia Hafner, C.R.E. Students 559.

COLTS NECK, MONMOUTH CO., ST. MARY'S (1887) Rev. Thomas J. Triggs; Deacons Paul Daniele; Caleb Weller; Fernando A. Sorrentino; Sr. Jeanne Belli, S.S.J., Pastoral Assoc.; Joe Noble, Business Mgr.; Tom Carter, Music Min.
Res.: 1 Phalanx Rd., 07722. Tel: 732-780-2666; Fax: 732-780-0394.
Catechesis/Religious Program—Tel: 732-294-8841. Mrs. Joan Celiano, D.R.E. Students 1,296.

DEAL, MONMOUTH CO., ST. MARY OF THE ASSUMPTION (1901) Revs. John G. DeSandre; Matthew Thelly; Deacon John McCabe.
Res.: 46 Richmond Ave., 07723. Tel: 732-531-1409; Fax: 732-531-3931.
Catechesis/Religious Program—Tel: 732-531-1889. Mrs. Maureen Melofchik, D.R.E. Students 250.

DELRAN, BURLINGTON CO.

1—CHURCH OF THE HOLY NAME (1972) Merged with St. Casimir, Riverside to form The Church of the Resurrection, Delran Township, N.J.

2—THE CHURCH OF THE RESURRECTION, DELRAN TOWNSHIP, N.J. (2008) Revs. David Stachurski, O.F.M.Conv.; Hilary Brzostowski, O.F.M.Conv.; Deacons Jim Manaloris; William E. Briggs; Daniel J. Meehan.
Office: 260 Conrow Rd., P.O. Box 1099, 08075. Tel: 856-461-6555; Fax: 856-461-1293. Email: resurrection2@comcast.net. Web: www.resurrection2.org.
Res.: 502 New Jersey Ave., Riverside, 08075. Tel: 856-461-0532; Fax: 856-461-5781.
Catechesis/Religious Program—Ms. Patricia Brooks, C.R.E. Students 320.

EATONTOWN, MONMOUTH CO.

1—ST. DOROTHEA (1905) Revs. G. William Evans; Vicente Magdaraog (Philippines); Deacons Stephen W. Andrews; John A. Notaro; Edward R. Herr; Nick Donofrio; Mary Escueta, Music Min.
Res.: 240 Broad St., 07724. Tel: 732-542-0148; Fax: 732-542-1531. Email: frbill@stdorothea.com. Web: www.stdorothea.com.
Catechesis/Religious Program—Tel: 732-542-0303. Email: john@stdorothea.com. Students 487.

2—IMMACULATE CONCEPTION (1984), (Korean), Rev. Rosario Kim, Admin.
Res.: 64 Broad St., 07724. Tel: 732-389-3830; Fax: 732-389-2705.
Catechesis/Religious Program—Mrs. Gratia Min, Dir. Students 59.

ENGLISHTOWN, MONMOUTH CO., OUR LADY OF MERCY (1948) [CEM] Merged with St. Thomas More, Manalapan.

EVESHAM TOWNSHIP, BURLINGTON CO., ST. ISAAC JOGUES (1996) Rev. Phillip C. Pfleger; Deacons Edward Gwiazda; Frank E. Giglio; George V. Lytle.
3 Lord Pl., Marlton, 08053. Tel: 856-797-0999; Fax: 856-797-0463. Email: saintisaacs@stisaacjogues.org.
Catechesis/Religious Program—Tel: 856-797-1811. Web: www.rc.net/trenton/st.isaac/. Sr. Clare Sabini, D.R.E. Students 808.

FAIR HAVEN, MONMOUTH CO., CHURCH OF THE NATIVITY (1954) Rev. Robert J.W. Schecker; Deacon James Kelly.
Res.: 180 Ridge Rd., 07704. Tel: 732-741-1714; Fax: 732-741-6837. Email: office@nativitychurchnj.org.
Catechesis/Religious Program—Email: dre@nativitychurchnj.org. Ms. Theresa Petrik, D.R.E. Students 800.

FARMINGDALE, MONMOUTH CO., ST. CATHERINE OF SIENA (1912) Rev. Michael S. Vona; Deacons Michael J. Principato; Joseph J. Prioli; Vincent L. Rinaldi.
Res.: 31 Asbury Rd., P.O. Box 667, 07727-0667. Tel: 732-938-5375; Fax: 732-938-3260. Email: frontoffice@sienachurch.org. Web: www.sienachurch.org.
Catechesis/Religious Program—Tel: 732-938-6229. Email: ccd@sienachurch.org. Dr. Anthony Novembre, C.R.E. Students 616.

FLORENCE, BURLINGTON CO., ST. CLARE (1874), (Irish—Italian), [CEM] Closed. For inquiries for parish records contact the chancery.

FORKED RIVER, OCEAN CO., ST. PIUS X (1961) Rev. Richard Basznianin; Cynthia Craft, Pastoral Assoc.; Deacons James Heller; Daniel Miller; Robert Klein; Anthony Martucci.
300 Lacey Rd., 08731-3598.
Res.: 203 W. Lacey Rd., 08731-3598. Tel: 609-693-5107; Fax: 609-693-6829.
Catechesis/Religious Program—Tel: 609-693-0368. Mrs. Patricia Colando, D.R.E. Students 1,120.

FREEHOLD, MONMOUTH CO.

1—ST. ROBERT BELLARMINE (1971) Rev. Edward M. Jawidzik; Deacons Francis J. Weber Jr.; Rolf B. Friedmann.
61 Georgia Rd., 07728. Tel: 732-462-7429; Fax: 732-409-3496. Web: www.strobert.com. In Res., Rev. Charles R. Valentine (Retired).
Catechesis/Religious Program—Tel: 732-431-3404. Deacon Rolf B. Friedmann, D.R.E. Students 1,480.

2—ST. ROSE OF LIMA (1871) [CEM] Revs. Richard R. Milewski; Roman Modino, Hispanic Ministry. Tel: 732-303-7800; Fax: 732-303-1228; Michael Brizio, I.M.C.; Stephen M. Piga; Deacons John Wanat; Andrew Luhman.
Res.: 16 McLean St., 07728. Tel: 732-462-0859; Fax: 732-462-8173. Email: stroseoflima@verizon.net. Web: www.stroseoflima.com.
School—51 Lincoln Pl., 07728. Tel: 732-462-2646; Fax: 732-462-0331. Email: stroseoflimaschool@comcast.net. Sr. Patricia Doyle, Prin. Sisters 2; Lay Teachers 28; Students 444.
Catechesis/Religious Program—Tel: 732-308-0215; Fax: 732-308-0257. Email: stroselimare@aol.com. Mr. Steven Olson, D.R.E. Students 1,183.
Convent—81 Randolph St., 07728. Tel: 732-462-0599.

HAINESPORT, BURLINGTON CO., OUR LADY QUEEN OF PEACE (1944) Rev. Msgr. Richard L. Tofani; Deacon John J. O'Donnell.
Res.: 1603 Marne Hwy., P.O. Box 188, 08036. Tel: 609-267-0230; Fax: 609-267-0372.
Catechesis/Religious Program—Tel: 609-267-3641. Mrs. Ginny Fama, D.R.E.

HAMILTON, MERCER CO.

1—ST. GREGORY THE GREAT (1953) Revs. Ian W. Trammell, Admin.; Thomas A. Fesen; Deacons Charles M. Moscarello; John Groffie, (Retired); Neil Pirozzi; William A. Wilson; Andrew A. Sabados Sr.; Joseph E. Latini.
Res.: 4620 Nottingham Way, Hamilton Square, 08690. Tel: 609-587-4877; Fax: 609-588-0192. Web: stgregorythegreat.org.
School—4680 Nottingham Way, Hamilton Square, 08690. Tel: 609-587-1131; Fax: 609-587-0322. Joan Pramberger, Prin.; Mr. Jason Briggs, Vice Prin. Sisters 1; Lay Teachers 51; Students 515.
Catechesis/Religious Program—Elizabeth Field, D.R.E. Students 1,632.
Convent—13 Stanley Dr., Robbinsville, 08691. Tel: 609-259-3384.

2—OUR LADY OF SORROWS-ST. ANTHONY PARISH (2005) Rev. Msgr. Thomas N. Gervasio; Revs. Oscar B. Sumanga (Philippines); Eugene K. Savarimuthu (India); Deacons James J. Challender; James Buchanan; Timothy Moore; Kevin J. O'Boyle; Dennis E. Slavin; Joseph Jaruszewski.
Res.: 3816 E. State St. Ext., 08619. Tel: 609-587-4372; Fax: 609-587-7998. Email: info@ols-sa.org. Web: ols-sa.org.
School—3800 E. State St. Ext., 08619. Tel: 609-587-4140; Fax: 609-584-8853. Web: olsschool.us. Teresa Carrick, Prin. Lay Teachers 22; Students 321.
Catechesis/Religious Program—Tel: 609-587-4140, Ext. 2; Fax: 609-587-4213. Email: mfrancis@ols-sa.org. Mariyan Iqbal Francis, D.R.E. Students 600.
Convent—626 S. Olden Ave., 08629. Tel: 609-586-4355.
Station—Mercer County Geriatric, Tel: 609-588-5859.

3—ST. RAPHAEL-HOLY ANGELS PARISH (2005) Revs. Jeffrey Kegley; Genaro Daguplo; Leandro Delacruz; Deacons Richard Arcari; Manuel Iglesias; Thomas Lavelle; Salvatore Marcello; Robert Tharp; John A. DiLissio.
Res.: 3500 S. Broad St., 08610. Tel: 609-585-7049; Fax: 609-585-5876. Web: www.straphael-holyangels.com.
School—151 Gropp Ave., 08610. Tel: 609-585-7733; Fax: 609-581-8436. Mr. Timothy M. Lynch, Prin.
Catechesis/Religious Program—Tel: 609-585-3848; Fax: 609-585-4925. Mr. John Margicin, D.R.E.; William Palmisano, D.R.E. Students 540.
Station—Robert Wood Johnson University Hospital at Hamilton, Tel: 609-585-7900.

HIGHLANDS, MONMOUTH CO., OUR LADY OF PERPETUAL HELP (1883) Rev. Daniel F. Gowen; Deacons James A. Kelly; Edward J. Moresco.
Res.: 141 Navesink Ave., 07732. Tel: 732-872-1290; Fax: 732-872-2796.
Catechesis/Religious Program—Mrs. Barbara Hardiman, D.R.E. Students 66.

HIGHTSTOWN, MERCER CO., ST. ANTHONY OF PADUA (1885) Revs. Patrick J. McDonnell; Miguel Valle; Deacons Thomas Garvey; Joseph Hepp; Patrick Kennedy.
Res.: 251 Franklin St., 08520-3223. Tel: 609-448-0141; Fax: 609-448-8878.
Catechesis/Religious Program—Tel: 609-443-3318; Fax: 609-443-3390. Mrs. Veronica Martella, D.R.E.; Mr. Michael Fabian, D.R.E. Students 1,095.

HOLMDEL, MONMOUTH CO.

1—ST. BENEDICT (1959) Revs. Daniel F. Swift; Richard C. Vila; Deacons Raymond R. Pelkowski; Stephen G. Scott; Catherine Warshaw, Parish Admin.; Tony Malone, Business & Finance Mgr.
Res.: 165 Bethany Rd., 07733-1699. Tel: 732-264-4712; Fax: 732-264-9080. Email: parish_office@stbenedictnj.org.
School—Tel: 732-264-5578; Fax: 732-264-8679. Mary Ellen Lilly, Prin. Lay Teachers 28; Students 516.
Catechesis/Religious Program—Tel: 732-264-4714; 732-264-4712, Ext. 24. Denise Contino, C.R.E.; Lori McCahill, Youth Min. Students 551.

2—ST. CATHARINE (1879) Rev. Msgr. Eugene M. Rebeck; Deacons John P. Flanagan; Christopher L. Hansen; Thomas J. DiCanio; Michael Lonie; Margaret Zavattieri, Pastoral Assoc.
Res.: P.O. Box 655, 07733. Tel: 732-842-3963; Fax: 732-842-9283. Email: parishoffice@stcatherine.net. Web: www.stcatherine.net.
Catechesis/Religious Program—Tel: 732-758-8568. Sr. Patricia Schladebeck, M.S.C., D.R.E.; Mrs. Dominica Vullo, C.R.E. Students 1,320.

HOPEWELL, MERCER CO., ST. ALPHONSUS (1877) [CEM] Rev. Mark Devlin; Deacons Robert Lafond; John Grant.
Res.: 54 E. Prospect St., 08525. Tel: 609-466-0332; Fax: 609-466-2023. Web: www.saintalphonsuschurch.org.
Catechesis/Religious Program—Tel: 609-466-2694. Sr. Rosemary Hendry, O.S.F., D.R.E. Students 225.

HOWELL TOWNSHIP, MONMOUTH CO.

1—ST. VERONICA (1962) Revs. H. Brendan Williams; Joy T. Chacko; Charles L. Griffiths; Deacons Gene F. Moir Sr.; Theodore V. Gularek; James Littlefield; Eugene Genovese; Tomasz Cechulski; Charles Daye Jr.
Res.: 4215 Hwy. 9 N., 07731. Tel: 732-363-4200; Fax: 732-370-3891.
School—4219 Hwy. 9 N., 07731. Tel: 732-364-4130; Fax: 732-363-4932. Sr. Cherree Ann Power, Prin. Sisters 5; Lay Teachers 30; Students 445.
Catechesis/Religious Program—Tel: 732-364-4137; Fax: 732-886-5064. Brenda Heffernan, D.R.E. Students 1,298.
Convent—4217 Hwy. 9 N., 07731. Tel: 732-364-2361.

2—ST. WILLIAM THE ABBOT (1985) Rev. Francis P. Tam.
Mailing Address & Church: 2740 Lakewood-Allenwood Rd., 07731. Tel: 732-840-3535; Fax: 732-840-3663. Email: stwilliam@optonline.net. Web: www.stwilliamtheabbot.com.
Res.: 2400 Allenwood-Lakewood Rd., P.O. Box 500, Allenwood, 08720. Tel: 732-840-3628.
Catechesis/Religious Program—Mrs. Mary Cleary, D.R.E. Students 645.
Station—Geraldine Thompson Nursing Home 2350 Hospital Rd., Allenwood, 08720. Tel: 732-938-5250.

JACKSON, OCEAN CO.

1—ST. ALOYSIUS (1964) Very Rev. G. Scott Shaffer; Rev. Brian P. Woodrow; Sr. Eileen Ivory, O.P., Pastoral Assoc.; Deacons Rene Perez; Frank Jackson; Uku Mannikus; Jennifer Schlameuss-Perry, Pastoral Assoc.
Res.: 935 Bennetts Mills Rd., P.O. Box 1285, 08527. Tel: 732-370-0500; Fax: 732-886-9336. Web: www.saintaloysiusonline.org.
School—Saint Aloysius Grammar School, Tel: 732-370-1515; Fax: 732-370-3555. Web: www.staloysiusschool.com. Ms. Elizabeth O'Connor, Prin. Lay Teachers 28; Students 400.
Catechesis/Religious Program—Tel: 732-370-1515. Ms. Rosemary V. Perry, D.R.E. Students 1,650.

2—CHURCH OF ST. MONICA (1953) Very Rev. G. Scott Shaffer; Rev. Thomas Petrillo.
679 W. Veteran's Hwy., 08527. Tel: 732-928-0279; Fax: 732-928-1853. Email: stmonica67@verizon.net. Web: www.saintmonica.com.
Catechesis/Religious Program—Tel: 732-928-4038. Email: stmonicaccd@verizon.net. Karen Badach, C.R.E. Students 415.

JOBSTOWN, BURLINGTON CO., ST. ANDREW'S CHURCH, JOBSTOWN (1880) Rev. Joseph G. Hlubik, Admin.; Deacons John F. Hoefling; Daniel Chase.
2489 Monmouth Rd., 08041. Tel: 609-723-4243.
Catechesis/Religious Program—Celeste Grant, D.R.E.

KEANSBURG, MONMOUTH CO., ST. ANN (1924) Revs. Daniel Cahill; Silvano B. Amora.
Res.: 311 Carr Ave., 07734. Tel: 732-787-0315; Fax: 732-787-5254. Email: stannkean@aol.com. Web: http://stannchurch.catholicworld.info/.
School—285 Carr Ave., 07734. Tel: 732-787-1027; Fax: 732-495-3338. Email: stannschool2003@yahoo.com. Web: stannsschool.org. Sr. Mary Dora McGrath, R.S.M., Prin. Sisters 2; Lay Teachers 12; Students 156.
Catechesis/Religious Program—Tel: 732-787-5744. John Clancy, D.R.E. Students 570.
St. Ann Child Care Center—121 Main St., 07734. Tel: 732-787-7220; Fax: 732-787-2136. Sisters 1; Students 65.
Bayshore Senior Health, Education & Recreation Center—100 Main St., 07734. Tel: 732-495-2454; Fax: 732-495-7897. Sisters 2; Seniors Served 1,350.
Hansel and Gretel Preschool—267 Carr Ave., 07734. Tel: 732-787-9237; Fax: 732-787-9237. Sisters 1; Children 60.
Project Paul—211 Carr Ave., 07734. Tel: 732-787-4887; Fax: 732-495-7072.

KEYPORT, MONMOUTH CO.

1—JESUS THE LORD (1978) Rev. Kenneth W. Ekdahl.
Res.: 123 Broad St., 07735-1203. Tel: 732-739-0323; Fax: 732-264-8276.
Church: 120 Broad St., 07735.
Catechesis/Religious Program—Ms. Anne Biagianti, C.R.E. Students 195.

2—ST. JOSEPH (1854) [CEM] Revs. James A. Conover; Francis P. Tam; Ronald J. Cioffi; Deacons Christopher O'Brien; Kenneth R. Sheehan.
Res.: 376 Maple Pl., 07735. Tel: 732-264-0322; Fax: 732-888-3280.
School—*St. Joseph School*, 376 Maple Pl., 07735. Tel: 732-264-2114; Fax: 732-264-8696. Ruth Mazzarela, Prin. Lay Teachers 28; Students 361.
Catechesis/Religious Program—Tel: 732-888-1274. Ms. Kay Hetherington, D.R.E. Students 400.

LAKEHURST, OCEAN CO., ST. JOHN (1969) Rev. Bernard Keigher; Deacons Edward Holowienka; Ronald Kerr; Robert Gooden; Michael Pirylis; Robert Diehl; Carol A. Kerr, Pastoral Assoc.
Res.: 619 Chestnut St., 08733. Tel: 732-657-6347; Fax: 732-657-8690.
Catechesis/Religious Program—Tel: 732-657-2348. Mrs. Mary Ann Dempkowski, D.R.E. Students 432.

LAKEWOOD, OCEAN CO.

1—ST. ANTHONY CLARET (1977), (Hispanic Parish for Ocean Co.) Revs. Jesus Briones, S.V.D.; Pelagio Calambia Pateno, S.V.D.
Res.: 780 Ocean Ave., 08701-3644. Tel: 732-367-8486; Fax: 732-367-0460. Email: svdclaret@aol.com.
Catechesis/Religious Program—Pilar Acosta, D.R.E. Students 320.

2—ST. MARY OF THE LAKE (1889) [CEM] Revs. Michael J. O'Connor; John O. Chang; Edward H. Blanchett; Bernadino Esguerra; Deacons Vincent Riccardi; Silverius Galvan; John Cullinane; Anthony Martucci, Pastoral Min.; Sr. Geraldine Contento, M.P.F., Pastoral Min.
Res.: 43 Madison Ave., 08701. Tel: 732-363-0139; Fax: 732-905-1410.
School—*Holy Family School*, 1141 E. County Line Rd., 08701. Tel: 732-363-4771; Fax: 732-363-3146. Elaine Bicher, Prin. Lay Teachers 26; Students 492.
Catechesis/Religious Program—Tel: 732-363-3043; Fax: 732-961-0382. Donna Marie Clancy, D.R.E. Students 550.
Mission—*Holy Family Church*, Ocean Co. Fax: 732-905-1410.

LAVALLETTE, OCEAN CO., THE CHURCH OF ST. PIO OF PIETRECLINA, LAVALLETTE, N.J. (1921) Rev. Msgr. Leonard F. Troiano.
Res.: 103 Washington Ave., 08735. Tel: 732-793-7291; Fax: 732-793-8204.
Catechesis/Religious Program—Tel: 732-793-3020. Sr. Patricia McClure, D.R.E. Students 79.

LAWRENCEVILLE, MERCER CO.

1—ST. ANN (1937) Rev. R. Vincent Gartland; Rev. Msgr. Joseph N. Rosie; Sr. Beth Dempsey, R.S.M., Pastoral Assoc.; Deacons Thomas J. Everist; Edward A. Hoag; James Scott; Mr. Gary Maccaroni, Pastoral Assoc.; Christine Barranco, Pastoral Assoc.
Res.: 1253 Lawrence Rd., 08648. Tel: 609-882-6491; Fax: 609-882-4366.
School—34 Rossa Ave., 08648. Tel: 609-882-8077; Fax: 609-882-0327. Mr. John McKenna, Prin. Lay Teachers 24; Students 283.
Catechesis/Religious Program—Tel: 609-882-1212. Students 550.

2—THE CHURCH OF THE KOREAN MARTYRS (1994), (Korean), Rev. Ki Ryong Shin, Admin.
Mailing Address: 1130 Brunswick Ave., 08638.
Catechesis/Religious Program—Students 56.

LINCROFT, MONMOUTH CO., ST. LEO THE GREAT (1958) Revs. John T. Folchetti, Dir. Min.; Selvam Gerald (India); Joseph M. Quinlan (Retired); Sr. Ann Barry, S.S.J., Pastoral Assoc.; Deacon Joseph DePaolis.
Res.: 50 Hurley's Ln., 07738. Tel: 732-747-5466; Fax: 732-219-5181. Email: stleoslincroft@comcast.net. Web: stleothegreat.com.
School—550 Newman-Springs Rd., 07738. Tel: 732-741-3133; Fax: 732-741-2241. Web: saintleothegreatschool.com. Joanne Kowit, Prin. Lay Teachers 33; Students 650.
Catechesis/Religious Program—Tel: 732-530-0717. Email: slreled@aol.com. Ms. Margaret Lang, D.R.E. Students 1,100.

LONG BRANCH, MONMOUTH CO.

1—THE CHURCH OF CHRIST THE KING, LONG BRANCH, N.J. (1878) [CEM] Revs. M. Joseph Mokrzycki; Thomas M. Vala; Deacon Donald A. Young; Sr. Diane Matera, R.S.M., Hospital Pastoral Min.
Res.: 380 Division St., 07740. Tel: 732-229-0526; Fax: 732-229-2886.
Catechesis/Religious Program—Tel: 732-229-0952. Mrs. Madeline Ottino, D.R.E. Students 111.

2—HOLY TRINITY (1906) Closed. For inquiries for parish records contact the chancery.

3—ST. JOHN THE BAPTIST (1984) Closed. For inquiries for parish records contact the chancery.

4—ST. MICHAEL (1885) Rev. Charles B. Weiser; Deacon Eugene A. Somma.
Res.: 800 Ocean Ave., West End, 07740. Tel: 732-222-8080; Fax: 732-870-1174. Email: stmichael@monmouth.com. Web: www.stmichaels-westend.com.
Catechesis/Religious Program—Tel: 732-483-0360; Fax: 732-483-0363. Email: outreachcenter@monmouth.com. Students 427.

MANALAPAN, MONMOUTH CO., ST. THOMAS MORE (1970) Revs. Mark W. Crane; Peter Kochery, Parochial Vicar; Deacons Keith J. Casey; James Davis; John J. Zebrowski; Mr. Steven Russell, Dir. Sacred Music; Mrs. Vincenza Magliano, Admin.
Res.: 186 Gordons Corner Rd., 07726. Tel: 732-446-6661; Fax: 732-446-6507.
Catechesis/Religious Program—Tel: 732-446-3232. Linda K. Andrew, D.R.E. Students 2,100.

MANASQUAN, MONMOUTH CO., ST. DENIS (1909) Very Rev. Stanley P. Lukaszewski; Rev. Msgr. Frederick A. Valentino (Retired); Rev. Joseph J. Miele (Retired); Sr. Josephine Wade, S.S.J., Pastoral Assoc.; Deacons George R. Kelder Jr.; Donald L. Perusi; Gary J. Pstrak.
Res.: 90 Union Ave., 08736. Tel: 732-223-0287; Fax: 732-528-1901. Email: stdenis@verizon.net. Web: www.churchofstdenis.org.
School—119 Virginia Ave., 08736. Tel: 732-223-4928; Fax: 732-223-1807. Web: stdenisonline.org. Trudy Bonavita, Prin. Lay Teachers 16; Students 187.
Catechesis/Religious Program—Tel: 732-223-1161. Sr. Maureen Christopher Loughlin, S.C., D.R.E. Students 945.
Chapel—*Our Lady Star of the Sea Chapel* 3rd Ave. and E. Main St., 08736.

MAPLE SHADE, BURLINGTON CO., OUR LADY OF PERPETUAL HELP (1920) Revs. John F. Wake; Robert Holtz; Deacons Joseph A. Card; Michael P. Boehm, Pastoral Assoc.; Ronald S. Meyers.
Res.: 236 E. Main St., 08052. Tel: 856-667-8850; 856-667-3772 (Pastoral Care Office); Fax: 856-667-1046. Email: parishsec@olphparish.com. Web: www.olphparish.com.
School—236 E. Main St., 08052. Tel: 856-779-7526, Ext. 225; Fax: 856-667-3083. Email: olphmsprn@yahoo.com. Donna Satkowski, Prin. Sisters 1; Lay Teachers 14; Students 241.
Catechesis/Religious Program—Tel: 856-779-7529. Email: religioused@olphparish.com. Mrs. Michelle Salvino, C.R.E. Students 372.

MARLBORO, MONMOUTH CO., ST. GABRIEL (1885) Revs. Eugene J. Roberts; Edward Kwoka, Parochial Vicar; Deacons James C. Russo; Lester Owens; Stephen Sansevere, Pastoral Admin.; Richard Scotti.
Res.: 100 N. Main St., 07746. Tel: 732-946-4487; Fax: 732-946-7276.
Catechesis/Religious Program—Fax: 732-946-2080. Dr. James J. Bridges, D.R.E. Students 1,640.

MARLTON, BURLINGTON CO., ST. JOAN OF ARC (1961) Rev. Msgr. Richard D. LaVerghetta; Rev. Michael Wallack; Sisters Eleanor O'Connell, S.S.J., Pastoral Assoc.; Peg Boyle, S.S.J., Pastoral Assoc.; Deacons Barry Tarzy; George Johnston; Jeffrey DeFrehn.
Church & Res.: 100 Willow Bend Rd., 08053. Tel: 856-983-0077; Fax: 856-983-7716. Web: stjoans.org.
School—101 Evans Rd., 08053. Tel: 856-983-0774; Fax: 856-983-3270. Web: stjoansk-8.org. Sr. Patricia Pycik, S.S.J., Prin. Sisters of St. Joseph 2; Lay Teachers 25; Students 418.
Catechesis/Religious Program—Tel: 856-983-7575; Fax: 856-983-3479. Email: linda.mueller@stjoans.org. Mrs. Linda Mueller, D.R.E. Students 1,175.
Convent—99 Evans Rd., 08053. Tel: 856-983-7575.

MATAWAN, MONMOUTH CO., ST. CLEMENT (1965) Revs. John J. Scully; Philip Ruggiero; Deacons Mark Micali; Tom Wadolowski.
Res.: 172 Freneau Ave., 07747. Tel: 732-566-3616; Fax: 732-566-9275.
Catechesis/Religious Program—Tel: 732-591-8090. Patricia Thein, C.R.E. Students 880.

MEDFORD, BURLINGTON CO., ST. MARY OF THE LAKES (1943) Rev. Msgr. James H. Dubell; Revs. Richard C. Vila; Charles Muorah; Deacons Joseph R. Patton; W. Norman Talbot; Joseph Tedeschi.
Res.: 40 Jackson Rd., 08055. Tel: 609-654-8208; Fax: 609-654-1734.
School—196 Rte. 70, 08055. Tel: 609-654-2546; Fax: 609-654-8125. Mrs. Paula P. Angilletta, Prin. Sisters of St. Francis of Philadelphia 2; Sisters of St. Joseph 4; Lay Teachers 23; Students 482.
Catechesis/Religious Program—196 Rte. 70, 08055. Tel: 609-654-8243; Fax: 609-953-8630. Mrs. Cathleen Sheridan, D.R.E. Students 1,388.
Convent—*Sisters of St. Francis*, 27 Schoolhouse Dr., 08055. Tel: 609-654-5896.
Convent—*Sisters of St. Joseph*, 24 Summerhill Lane, 08055. Tel: 609-654-1941.
St. Vincent DePaul Society-Medford—P.O. Box 1131, 08055. Tel: 609-953-0021; Fax: 609-953-2432. Mr. Paul V. Cannon, Treas.

MIDDLETOWN, MONMOUTH CO.

1—ST. CATHERINE (1948) Rev. Daniel C. Hesko; Deacons John C. Orlando; John G. McGrath; Martin K. McMahon; L. Jacqueline Callahan, Pastoral Ministry.
Res.: 5 Shore Acres Ave., 07748. Tel: 732-787-1318; Fax: 732-787-6139. Web: www.stcathek.org.
Catechesis/Religious Program—Tel: 732-495-7779; Fax: 732-495-7779. Mrs. L. Jackie Callahan, D.R.E. Students 610.

2—ST. MARY (1878) Rev. Msgr. Michael J. Walsh; Revs. Angelito Anarcon; David S. Swantek; Deacons Charles J. Smith; Robert F. Scharen.
Res.: 19 Cherry Tree Farm Rd., 07748. Tel: 732-671-0071; Fax: 732-671-6125. Email: stmarynm@aol.com. Web: www.stmarychurchnj.org.
School—538 Church St., New Monmouth, 07748. Tel: 732-671-0129; Fax: 732-671-2653. Web: stmaryes.org. Dr. William V. Smith, Prin.; Dennis Poracky, Asst. Prin. Lay Teachers 43; Students 717.
High School—*Mater Dei High School*, Tel: 732-671-9100; Fax: 732-671-9214. Web: www.materdeihs.org. Mr. Steven Sciarappa, Prin.; Charles Kroekel, Asst. Prin. Lay Teachers 41; Students 331.
Catechesis/Religious Program—Tel: 732-671-8550. Sr. Sharon Santos, F.C.L.G., D.R.E. Students 1,215.

MONMOUTH BEACH, MONMOUTH CO., CHURCH OF THE PRECIOUS BLOOD (1947) Rev. John T. Kielb.
Res.: 72 Riverdale Ave., 07750. Tel: 732-222-4756; Fax: 732-229-6448.
Catechesis/Religious Program—Tel: 732-870-1293. Mrs. Suzanne Goyette, D.R.E. Students 334.

MOORESTOWN, BURLINGTON CO., OUR LADY OF GOOD COUNSEL (1879) [CEM] Revs. Damian McElroy; James O'Neill, Parochial Vicar; Deacons James J. Grogan; Joseph A. Paul, (Retired); Stephen J. Lucasi, Dir. of Sacred Music; Deacons David F. Papuga, Business Mgr.; Edward A. Heffernan, Business Mgr.; Thomas D. Begley III.
Res.: 42 W. Main St., 08057. Tel: 856-235-0181; Fax: 856-235-4987. Web: www.olgcnj.org.
School—23 W. Prospect St., 08057. Tel: 856-235-7885; Fax: 856-235-2570. Jerome McGowan, Prin. Dominic Sisters of Hope 1; Lay Teachers 28; Students 515.
Catechesis/Religious Program—Tel: 856-235-2354. Dr. Linda M. Dix, D.R.E. Students 1,400.

MOUNT HOLLY, BURLINGTON CO.

1—CHRIST THE REDEEMER (1976), (Hispanic), Rev. Jamie Gonzalez, Temp. Admin.; Deacon Michael Adorno.
Res.: 35 South Ave., 08060. Tel: 609-261-0181; Fax: 609-702-0017.
Catechesis/Religious Program—426 Pine St., Mt. Holly, 08060. Students 59.

2—SACRED HEART (1848) [CEM] Rev. John P. Czahur; Deacons Louis C. Restivo; James Casa; Amado F. Acosta; William Rowley; Leo Zito; Stanley Orkis; Michael Auleta.
Res.: 260 High St., 08060-1404. Tel: 609-267-0209; Fax: 609-267-9293.
School—250 High St., 08060. Tel: 609-267-1728; Fax: 609-267-4476. Mrs. Priscilla Vimislik, Prin. Lay Teachers 27; Students 331.
Catechesis/Religious Program—Tel: 609-267-6319; Fax: 609-518-9010. Mrs. Deborah Clardy, D.R.E. Students 900.

Station—County Jail, Tel: 609-267-3300.
Station—Burlington County Hospital Extended Care Center, Tel: 609-367-0700.

MOUNT LAUREL, BURLINGTON CO., ST. JOHN NEUMANN (1978) Revs. Lino S. Parente, O.Cist. (Italy); Maurizio Nicoletti, O.Cist. (Italy); Deacons James Cattanea; Joseph Barbara.
Res.: 560 Walton Ave., 08054. Tel: 856-235-1330; Fax: 856-235-9632.
Catechesis/Religious Program—Tel: 856-235-6555; Fax: 856-235-6555. Email: stjohnneumannmtlre@comcast.net. Web: www.sjn-catholicchurch.org. Mrs. Helen Graziano, D.R.E. Students 735.

NEPTUNE, MONMOUTH CO.

1—HOLY INNOCENTS (1959) Revs. Brian T. Butch; Lawrence K. Kunnel (Retired); Deacons James Walsh; John Klincewicz.
Res.: 3455 W. Bangs Ave., P.O. Box 806, 07753. Tel: 732-922-4242; Fax: 732-922-2848.
School—3455 W. Bangs Ave., 07753. Tel: 732-922-3141; Fax: 732-922-6531. Elizabeth A. Barrella, Prin. Lay Teachers 14; Students 177.
Catechesis/Religious Program—Tel: 732-922-4242, Ext. 20; Fax: 732-922-3752. Sr. Bernadette Schuler, O.S.F., D.R.E. Students 502.
Station—Convacenter Nursing Home, Tel: 732-774-3500.
Station—Imperial Nursing Home, Tel: 732-922-3400.
Station—Heritage Hall Nursing Home 07754. Tel: 732-922-9330.
Station—Medicenter Nursing Home 07754. Tel: 732-774-8300.
Station—The Lodge, Kings Manor, Tel: 732-922-1900.

2—OUR LADY OF PROVIDENCE (1981), (Spanish), Rev. Miguel Virella, S.V.D.
Res.: 1228 Fifth Ave., 07753. Tel: 732-776-7164; Fax: 732-776-7825.
Catechesis/Religious Program—Vanessa Otero, D.R.E. Students 133.

NEW EGYPT, OCEAN CO., THE CHURCH OF THE ASSUMPTION (1853) [CEM] Revs. Joseph J. Farrell; Michael T. McClane, Parochial Vicar; Deacons Raymond W. Staub Jr.; Vincent P. Ricciardi Sr.; Mr. Mark Hoeler, Music Min.; Mary Steen, Business Mgr.
Res.: 76 Evergreen Rd., 08533. Tel: 609-758-2153; Fax: 609-758-6240. Email: assumptionoffice@aol.com. Web: www.churchoftheassumption.com.
Catechesis/Religious Program—Email: assumptionreled@aol.com. Mrs. Diane Gregorio, D.R.E. Students 630.

NORMANDY BEACH, OCEAN CO., OUR LADY OF PEACE (1979) Closed. For inquiries for parish records contact the chancery.

PENNINGTON, MERCER CO., ST. JAMES (1897) Rev. Msgr. Ronald J. Bacovin; Deacons James W. Palsir; Samuel Sciarrotta; Richard Currie; William Moore Hank.
Res.: 115 E. Delaware Ave., 08534. Tel: 609-737-0122; Fax: 609-737-6912. Email: stjames1@verizon.net. Web: www.stjames-nj.org.
Catechesis/Religious Program—Tel: 609-737-2717. Email: stjred@verizon.net. Nancy Lucash, D.R.E. Students 510.

PERRINEVILLE, MONMOUTH CO., ST. JOSEPH (1879) Rev. Michael P. Lang.
91 Stillhouse Rd., Millstone Township, 08510. Tel: 732-792-2270; Fax: 732-792-2271. Email: frmikestjoseph@optonline.net.
Catechesis/Religious Program—Jean Semanchick, C.R.E. Students 989.

POINT PLEASANT BEACH, OCEAN CO., ST. PETER'S (1882) Revs. Curt Kreml, O.F.M.Conv.; Crispin Fuino, O.F.M.Conv. (Retired); Paul Varga, O.F.M-.Conv.; Deacons George M. Korbelak; Thomas Loughran.
Res.: 406 Forman Ave., P.O. Box 1006, 08742. Tel: 732-892-0049; Fax: 732-295-9782. Web: www.saintpetersonline.org.
School—415 Atlantic Ave., 08742. Tel: 732-892-1260; Fax: 732-892-3488. Email: info@stpschool.org. Web: www.stpschool.org. Kathleen Berlino, Prin. Lay Teachers 13; Students 201.
Catechesis/Religious Program—Tel: 732-899-4839; Fax: 732-899-6841. Email: religiousèd@saintpetersonline.org. Mrs. Merrie Brambilla, D.R.E. Students 550.
Convent—401 Atlantic Ave., 08742. Tel: 732-899-2390.

POINT PLEASANT, OCEAN CO., ST. MARTHA (1972) Rev. Michael D. Sullivan; Deacons John Haney; John Gimblett; Francis Groff; Ted Kotz; John Fiorelli, Business Admin. & Lay Ecclesial Min.; Bridget L. Homes, Youth Min. & Pastoral Counselor; Maryann Collett, Pastoral Assoc. & Lay Ecclesial Min.; Richard Andrejack, Lay Ecclesial Min.; Anne Matthews, Lay Ecclesial Min.
Res. & Mailing Address: 3800 Herbertsville Rd., 08742. Tel: 732-295-3630; Fax: 732-295-9315. Web: www.saintmartha.net.
Catechesis/Religious Program—Tel: 732-295-3630, Ext. 48; Fax: 732-295-9325. Jane Shaheen, D.R.E.; Catherine Giza, C.R.E.; Florence Egan, Jr. High Youth Min. Students 1,030.

PRINCETON, MERCER CO., ST. PAUL (1864) [CEM] Rev. Msgr. Walter E. Nolan; Rev. Rene Mauricio Pulgarin; Deacons Paul LaChance; Joseph Kupin; Jim Knipper; Frank Crivello.
Res.: 214 Nassau St., 08542. Tel: 609-924-1743; Fax: 609-924-7510. Web: www.stpaulsprinceton.org.
School—218 Nassau St., 08542. Tel: 609-921-7587; Fax: 609-921-0264. Ryan Killeen, Prin. Sisters 3; Lay Teachers 28; Students 359.
Catechesis/Religious Program—Tel: 609-924-1743, Ext. 118. Mrs. Anne-Marie Calderone, D.R.E. Students 835.
Convent—216 Nassau St., 08540. Tel: 609-924-1743, Ext. 148.

RED BANK, MONMOUTH CO.

1—ST. ANTHONY (1920), (Italian), Revs. Anthony M. Carotenuto; Pedro L. Bou, S.V.D.; Deacon Arthur Fama.
Res.: 121 Bridge Ave., 07701. Tel: 732-747-0813; Fax: 732-224-0059. Email: st_anthonys@comcast.net.
Catechesis/Religious Program—Mrs. Michele McCue, D.R.E.; Roxane La Mont, Music Dir. Students 477.

2—ST. JAMES (1864) [CEM] Rev. Msgr. Philip A. Lowery; Revs. Alex Enriquez; Ariel Robles; Cesar Tolentino.
Res.: 94 Broad St., 07701. Tel: 732-741-0500; Fax: 732-741-1489.
School—St. James Grammar School, 30 Peters Pl., 07701. Tel: 732-741-3363; Fax: 732-933-4960. Janet Dolan, Prin. Lay Teachers 31; Students 528.
Preschool—Tel: 732-933-1041. Lay Teachers 3; Students 48.
High School—Red Bank Catholic High School, 112 Broad St., 07701. Tel: 732-747-1774; Fax: 732-747-1936. Robert Abatemarco, Prin. Sisters 5; Lay Teachers 106; Students 1,069.
Catechesis/Religious Program—Tel: 732-747-6006. Mrs. Mary Ellen Connolly, C.R.E. Students 650.
Convent—Sisters of Mercy, 25 Drummond Pl., 07701. Tel: 732-741-0724.
Station—Riverview Hospital, Tel: 732-530-2231; Fax: 732-530-2394.

RIVERSIDE, BURLINGTON CO.

1—ST. CASIMIR (1913), (Polish), Merged with Church of the Holy Name, Delran to form The Church of the Resurrection, Delran Township, N.J.

2—THE CHURCH OF JESUS, THE GOOD SHEPHERD, RIVERSIDE, N.J. (2008) Revs. Edward H. Blanchett; Angelo Amaral; Deacons Joseph Fuoco; Herman J. Mosteller; Matthew J. Stap, (Retired); Charles A. Perkins; Michael J. Hagan; Salvatore Lancieri; Debbie Cunningham, Music Min.
101 Middleton St., 08075. Tel: 856-461-0100; Fax: 856-764-6133.
Catechesis/Religious Program—Tel: 856-461-9343. Mrs. Maria B. Gimello, D.R.E. Students 368.

3—ST. PETER (1878) [CEM] Merged with St. Joseph, Beverly to form The Church of Jesus, the Good Shepherd, Riverside, N.J.

RIVERTON, BURLINGTON CO., SACRED HEART (1878) Revs. Michael J. Waites; Roberto Ignacio; Deacons Joseph M. Donadieu; Michael J. Stinsman; Kenneth W. Heilig; James E. Morton; Mark McKeever, Music Min. In Res., Rev. James T. Dever, O.S.F.S.
Res.: 103 Fourth St., 08077. Tel: 856-829-0090; Fax: 856-829-2087. Email: sacredheartriverton@comcast.net. Web: www.sacredheartriverton.org.
Catechesis/Religious Program—Tel: 856-829-1848; Fax: 856-829-7404. Mrs. Patricia Hutchinson, D.R.E. Students 779.

ROEBLING, BURLINGTON CO., THE CHURCH OF SAINTS FRANCIS AND CLARE, FLORENCE TOWNSHIP, N.J. (1913) Rev. Adam Midor; Deacons Robert D. Machion; Michael V. Scannella.
Res.: 1290 Hornberger Ave., 08554. Tel: 609-499-0161; Fax: 866-422-4690.
Catechesis/Religious Program—Mrs. Peggy Schwoebel, D.R.E. Students 150.

RUMSON, MONMOUTH CO., HOLY CROSS (1884) Rev. Michael Manning; Eugenia Kelly, Pastoral Assoc.; Jacqueline Mack, Business Admin.; Lori La Plante, Pastoral Assoc.
Res.: 30 Ward Ave., 07760. Tel: 732-842-0348; Fax: 732-842-3226. Email: webmaster@holycrossrumson.org. Web: www.holycrossrumson.org.
School—(Grades PreK-8), 40 Rumson Rd., 07760. Tel: 732-842-0348; Fax: 732-741-3134. Patricia Graham, Prin. Lay Teachers 30; Students 430.
Catechesis/Religious Program—Sally Kabash, C.R.E.; Michael Feerst, Youth Min. Students 621.

SEA GIRT, MONMOUTH CO., ST. MARK (1953) Rev. Msgr. Sean P. Flynn; Deacons Dennis Saake, Business Admin.; Michael P. Grogan.
Res.: 215 Crescent Pkwy., 08750. Tel: 732-449-6364; Fax: 732-449-1646. Email: st.markseagirt@verizon.net. Web: stmarkseagirt.com.
Catechesis/Religious Program—Tel: 732-449-6364, Ext. 105. Mrs. Mary Ann Hirsch, D.R.E. Students 505.

SEASIDE HEIGHTS, OCEAN CO., OUR LADY OF PERPETUAL HELP (1942) Rev. Richard Rossell, O.F.M.Conv. In Res., Bro. Nicholas Lorson.
Res.: 100 Grant Ave., 08751. Tel: 732-793-6881; Fax: 732-793-7632. Email: olph2@optonline.net. Web: ourladyph.com.
Catechesis/Religious Program—Tammy Garcia, C.R.E.

SEASIDE PARK, OCEAN CO., ST. CATHARINE OF SIENA (1906) Revs. Denis Hackett, O.F.M.Conv., Supr. & Pastor; Eric Fenner, O.F.M.Conv.; Emmett Carroll, O.F.M.Conv.; Otto Fouser, O.F.M.Conv.; Bro. Robert Lynch, O.F.M.Conv.
Res.: 50 E. St., Box A, 08752. Tel: 732-793-0041; Fax: 732-793-5483. Email: stcatharines@optonline.net. Web: www.stcatharinesiena.com.
Catechesis/Religious Program—Mary Britanak, D.R.E. Students 258.

SPRING LAKE, MONMOUTH CO., ST. CATHARINE (1901) [CEM 2] Rev. Msgr. Thomas A. Luebking; Rev. Joselito M. Noche; Deacons Edward Jennings; John L. Little.
Res.: 215 Essex Ave., 07762. Tel: 732-449-5765; Fax: 732-449-0916. Email: stcatharine@bytheshore.com. Web: www.stcatharine-stmargaret.com.
School—301 2nd Ave. Tel: 732-449-4424; Fax: 732-449-7876. Sr. Margo Kavanaugh, R.S.M., Prin. Sisters 2; Lay Teachers 24; Students 461.
Catechesis/Religious Program—Mrs. Diane Osieck, D.R.E. Students 660.
Convent—211 Essex Ave., 07762. Tel: 732-449-5765; Fax: 732-449-7876.
Mission—St. Margaret 300 Ludlow Ave., Monmouth Co. 07762.

TABERNACLE, BURLINGTON CO., HOLY EUCHARIST (1982) Rev. Andrew Jamieson; Deacons Joseph De Luca; Kenneth S. Domzalski; Anthony Repice; Sr. Geraldine Muller, S.S.J., Pastoral Assoc.; Lynette DeTata, Pastoral Assoc.; Linda Midura, Dir. of Music.
Office: 520 Medford Lakes Rd., 08088. Tel: 609-268-8383; Fax: 609-268-3294.
Catechesis/Religious Program—Tel: 609-268-7742. Dolores Wright, C.R.E. Students 750.
Station—New Lisbon Developmental Center New Lisbon. Tel: 609-726-1000.
Station—Leisuretown Senior Citizen Community Southampton.

TOMS RIVER, OCEAN CO.

1—ST. JOSEPH (Dover Township) (1883) [CEM] Revs. John P. Bambrick; Leon Salvador A. Buni; Patrick McPartland; Deacons Francis J. Babuschak; Edwin L. Voll Jr.; Frank J. McKenna; Romeo D. Aquino; Robert M. Barnes; Gerard Luongo; David L. Shapiro; Robert Degnon; Patrick J. Stesner Sr.; Michael A. Taylor; Thomas Genovese; Sr. Mary Anthony, Church Mgr.; Thomas Halpin, Music Min.; Jacqueline Mack, Business Admin.
Mailing Address: 685 Hooper Ave., 08753. Tel: 732-349-0018; Fax: 732-286-7064. Email: parish@stjosephtomsriver.org. Web: www.stjosephtomsriver.org.
School—711 Hooper Ave., 08753. Tel: 732-349-2355; Fax: 732-349-1064. Web: www.stjoesoftrk12njus.org. Mrs. Michele Williams, Prin. Lay Teachers 35; Students 718.
High School—Monsignor Donovan High School, Tel: 732-349-8801; Fax: 732-349-8956. Web: www-.mondonhs.com. Dr. Edward Gere, Prin. Lay Teachers 75; Students 896.
Catechesis/Religious Program—Tel: 732-349-0018, Ext. 2225. Email: sjcgodskids@yahoo.com. Celine Fowler, D.R.E.; Catherine Werner, Youth Min. Students 1,322.
Mission—St. Gertrude Ocean & Central Aves., Island Heights, Ocean Co. 08732. Tel: 732-288-0036.

2—ST. JUSTIN (Dover Township) (1972) Revs. Mark Kreder; John A. Bogacz; Deacons Richard Hauenstein; Richard J. Napolitano; Frederick C. Ebenau Sr.; James Gonzalez; James L. Campbell.
Res.: 975 Fischer Blvd., 08753. Tel: 732-270-3980; Fax: 732-929-9411. Web: www.stjustin.org.
Catechesis/Religious Program—Tel: 732-270-3797. Ellen Noble, D.R.E. Students 975.

3—ST. LUKE (Dover Township) (1982) Rev. Robert S. Grodnicki; Deacons Ronald R. Wicks; Stephen F. Delligatti; Joseph DeMaria; Louis Cartnick; Robert Puglisi. In Res., Rev. Louis W. Kralovich (Retired).
Res.: 1674 Old Freehold Rd., 08755. Tel: 732-286-2222; Fax: 732-914-1080.
Catechesis/Religious Program—Tel: 732-505-0108.

Students 950.

4—ST. MAXIMILIAN KOLBE (Berkeley Township) (1985) Revs. Francis E. Santitoro; Sheldon Amasa; Raymond E. Hughes. In Res., Deacons Raymond Shea; Albert M. Pacitti; Leo Montini.

Res. & Mailing Address: P.O. Box 4144, 08756. Tel: 732-914-0300; 732-914-8550 (Res.); Fax: 732-240-9517.

TUCKERTON, OCEAN CO., ST. THERESA (1944) Revs. K. Michael Lambeth; John C. Garrett; Deacons James Petrauskas; Charles Comito; Henry Palan; William Sulzmann; Robert Kratchman.

Parish Offices: 125 E. Main St., Ste. 3, 08087. Tel: 609-296-2504; Fax: 609-296-4530. Email: sttheresa450@verizon.net. Web: sttheresa-tuckerton.com.

Catechesis/Religious Program—Tel: 609-296-1940. Donnaann Powers, D.R.E. Students 615.

UNION BEACH, MONMOUTH CO., HOLY FAMILY (1942) Revs. Mark Devlin, Admin.; Francis Cheruparambil, V.C.; Sr. Gloria Jean Bateman, R.S.M., Pastoral Min.; Deacon John Clymore.

Res.: 727 Hwy. 36 W., P.O. Box 56, Keyport, 07735. Tel: 732-264-1484; Fax: 732-264-8369. Email: hfrccubnj@aol.com. Web: www.holyfamily.us.

Catechesis/Religious Program—Tel: 732-264-7043; Fax: 732-264-7043. Web: www.freewebs.com/hfreligiouseducation. Patricia McCarthy, C.R.E. Students 731.

Convent—Mercy Convent, 440 Sullivan Pl., 07735. Tel: 732-739-3065. Sisters 2.

WASHINGTON CROSSING, MERCER CO., ST. GEORGE (1924) Rev. Msgr. James G. Innocenzi; Sr. Dorothy Jancola, R.S.M., Pastoral Assoc.; Deacons Lawrence E. Gallagher; Michael Riley.

Res.: 1370 River Rd., P.O. Box 324, Titusville, 08560. Tel: 609-737-2015; Fax: 609-737-7863. Email: churchofstgeorge@aol.com. Web: www.thechurchofstgeorge.org.

Catechesis/Religious Program—Tel: 609-730-1703. Margaret Dziminski, C.R.E. Students 150.

Station—Mercer County Correction Center, Tel: 609-989-6901.

WAYSIDE, MONMOUTH CO., ST. ANSELM (1972) Rev. Eugene B. Vavrick.

Res.: 1028 Wayside Rd., 07712. Tel: 732-493-4411; Fax: 732-493-4272. Email: stanselm2@aol.com. Web: www.stanselm.com.

Catechesis/Religious Program—Students 580.

WEST LONG BRANCH, MONMOUTH CO., ST. JEROME (1956) Revs. Harold Cullen; Erin Brown, Parochial Vicar; Deacon Anthony N. DiCesare; James Palmer, Music Dir.

Res.: 254 Wall St., 07764. Tel: 732-222-1424; Fax: 732-222-2291. Email: stjeromec@aol.com. Web: saintjeromechurch.org.

School—250 Wall St., 07764. Tel: 732-222-8686; Fax: 732-263-0343. Sr. Angelina Pelliccia, Prin. Sisters 3; Lay Teachers 16; Students 267.

Catechesis/Religious Program—250 Wall St., 07764. Sr. Elizabeth Toft, D.R.E. Students 147.

Convent—250A Wall St., 07764. Tel: 732-222-2016.

WEST WINDSOR, MERCER CO., CHURCH OF ST. DAVID THE KING (1988) Rev. Timothy J. Capewell; Deacons Thomas Baker; Roger Dinella; Matthew V. Fung; Carol Sullivan, Dir. Music.

Res.: 517 Village Rd. W., Princeton Jct., 08550. Email: parishoffice@stdavidtheking.com. Web: www.stdavidtheking.com.

Church: One New Village Rd., Princeton Jct., 08550-2003. Tel: 609-275-7111; Fax: 609-799-1984.

Catechesis/Religious Program—Fax: 609-799-1964. Email: dre@stdavidtheking.com. Bro. Robert Ziobro, S.C., D.R.E.; Nancy Riddell, Youth Min.; Nancy Bachman, Adult Faith. Students 700.

WHITING, OCEAN CO., ST. ELIZABETH ANN SETON (1976) Rev. Pasquale A. Papalia; Rev. Msgr. Joseph C. Shenrock, Pastor Emeritus (Retired); Deacons Kyran J. Purcell; Joseph Rider; Ralph Cordasco; Donald W. Miller; Thomas Cater; Edward J. Hoefling; James Hendrix; Alvin Miester; Christopher O'Brien; Ms. Linda Quinn, Business Mgr.

Res.: 30 Schoolhouse Rd., 08759. Tel: 732-350-5001; Fax: 732-350-0912. Email: pastor@easeton.org. Web: www.seaswhiting.org.

Catechesis/Religious Program—Tel: 732-350-7391. Email: ccd@easeton.org. Deborah Milecki, D.R.E. Students 225.

WILLINGBORO, BURLINGTON CO., CORPUS CHRISTI (1959) Rev. Daniel J. Ryan; Deacons James E. Ayrer; John F. Vassallo Jr.; Jose J. Jimenez.

Res.: 63 Sylvan Ln., 08046. Tel: 609-877-5322; Fax: 609-877-1695. Email: corpuschristiparishnj@comcast.net. Web: www.mycorpuschristichurch.com.

Catechesis/Religious Program—Charleston & Sunset Rds., 08046. Tel: 609-871-4680; Fax: 609-871-5213. Sr. Rosemary Bucchi, O.S.F., D.R.E. Students 132.

Convent—150 Charleston Rd., 08046. Tel: 609-871-4226.

Chaplains of Public Institutions

TRENTON. *Capital Health System: Mercer Campus & Fluid Campus.* Attended from St. Michael Church, Tel: 609-393-4050 Rev. Henry A. Militante, Chap.

St. Francis Medical Center. Rev. Joel F. Szydlowski, O.F.M.

Katzenbach School for the Deaf. Vacant.

Mercer County Correction Center. Attended from St. George Church, Titusville, NJ 08560, Tel: 609-737-2015

New Jersey State Prison, CN 861, 08629. Sr. Elizabeth Gnaum.

Trenton Psychiatric Hospital. Rev. Joseph G. Hlubik, Chap.

BORDENTOWN. *Albert C. Wagner Youth Correction Facility.* Sr. Rose Huber, Chap.

Edward R. Johnstone Training and Research Center.

BURLINGTON. *Burlington County Hospital & Extended Care Center.* Attended from Sacred Heart Church.

260 High St., Mount Holly, 08060. Tel: 609-702-1848.

Burlington County Jail. Attended from Sacred Heart Church

260 High St., Mount Holly, 08060. Tel: 609-702-1848.

NEPTUNE. *Jersey Shore Medical Center.* Rev. Charles J. Flood, O.SS.T. Attended by St. Catherine Church, 215 Essex Ave. Spring Lake, NJ 07762, Tel: 732-449-5765

NEW LISBON. *New Jersey State Colony.* Attended from Holy Eucharist Church, Tabernacle, NJ 08088, Tel: 609-726-1000

Ocean County Jail. Attended by St. Joseph, Toms River, Tel: 732-349-0018

WAYSIDE. *Monmouth County Jail*, 1028 Wayside Rd., 07712. Tel: 732-493-4411. Attended from St. Rose Church, Freehold NJ, Tel: 732-462-7429

YARDVILLE. *Garden State Correctional Center*, P.O. Box 11401, 08620. Deacon James A. Manaloris. Tel: 609-298-6300, Ext. 2251.

Military Installations

COLTS NECK. *Naval Weapons Station Earle.* Served by chaplains. Assigned by the Archdiocese for the Military Service.

FORT DIX. *Fort Dix.* Served by chaplains. Assigned by the Archdiocese for the Military Service.

LAKEHURST. *U.S. Naval Air Warfare Center.* Served by chaplains. Assigned by the Archdiocese for the Military Service.

LITTLE SILVER. *Fort Monmouth.* Served by chaplains. Assigned by the Archdiocese for the Military Service.

MCGUIRE AIR FORCE BASE. *McGuire Air Force Base.* Served by chaplains. Assigned by the Archdiocese for the Military Service.

On Duty Outside the Diocese:

Rev. Msgr.—

Punderson, Joseph R., Villa Stritch, Via Della Nocetta 63, Rome 00164 Italy.

Revs.—

Bicomong, Sergio, Federal Correctional Institution, Fairton.

Gadenz, Pablo T., S.T.D., S.S.L., Seton Hall, South Orange, 07079.

Griswold, Edward J., St. Mary Seminary, Baltimore, MD 21210.

Hillier, David A., Our Lady of the Visitation, Shippensburg, PA 17257.

Kaeding, Robert F., The Center in Asbury Park, Asbury Park, 07712.

Krisak, Anthony F., S.S., 934 Kearny St., N.E., Washington, DC 20017-3516.

Kselman, John J., S.S., Weston School of Theology, Three Phillips Pl., Cambridge, MA 02138.

Lankford, Michael G., VAN-J Chaplain Service, East Orange, 07018.

Tedesco, Joseph A., Mepkin Abbey, Moncks Corner, SC 29461.

Military Chaplains:

Revs.—

Inghilterra, Vincent J., Honolulu, HI 96819.

Liguori, Henry A., 14 Rising Sun Ct., Las Vegas, NV 89014.

Leave of Absence:

Revs.—

Butch, Brian T.

Dobrosky, John M.

Donadio, Vincent J.

Gallagher, Richard

Hughes, Joseph W.

Inverso, Leon J.

Jackiewicz, Frederick W., 19 Pettit Ave., South River, 08882.

Lang, Leonard P.

Polczyk, Stanislaus

Tynski, Robert M.

Retired:

Most Rev.—

Reiss, John C., D.D., J.C.D., St. Lawrence Rehabilitation Center, 2381 Lawrenceville Rd., Lawrenceville, 08648.

Rev. Msgrs.—

Bogdan, Henry S., Villa Vianney, 2301 Lawrenceville Rd., West Trenton, 08628.

Brietske, Richard C.

Carton, William J.

Fitzgerald, William F., Villa Vianney, 2301 Lawrenceville Rd., Lawrenceville, 08648.

Flood, Peter J., Chap. Col., Headquarters AIA, 102 Halle Blvd., Suite 263, San Antonio, TX 78243.

Gibbons, John, 3300 N. Palm Aire Dr., Unit 703, Pompano Beach, FL 33069.

Kelty, Leo A., P.O. Box 281, Allenwood, 08720-0281.

McGovern, James J., 3225 Brunswick Ln., Sarasota, FL 34239.

Ronan, Hugh F., Villa Vianney, 2301 Lawrenceville Rd., Lawrenceville, 08648.

Shenrock, Joseph C., P.A.

Smith, Alfred D., 242 Peck Ave., West Haven, CT 06516.

Strano, Edward, 431 S.E. 3rd St, Apt. 403, Dania, FL 33004.

Valentino, Frederick A., 509 Woodland Ave., Brielle, 08730.

Revs.—

Adackapara, Matthew, c/o 5 Geraldine Dr., Monroe, 08831.

Albano, George M., Villa Vianney, 2301 Lawrenceville Rd., Lawrenceville, 08648.

Anderson, William C., 116 Crape Myrtle Dr., Holmdel, 07733.

Bausch, William J., Box 1068, Point Pleasant Beach, 08742.

Bianchi, Raymond S., Missionari Clarettiani, Via Del Banchi, Vecchi 12, Rome, Italy.

Bowden, John V.

Brennan, Thomas, 1122 Skiff Way, Forked River, 08731.

Byrnes, John P., 73 Connell St., Quincy, MA 02169.

Cammisa, James N., 15 Hastings Pl., Monmouth Beach, 07750.

Cenefeldt, Harry E., Villa Vianney, 2301 Lawrenceville Rd., Lawrenceville, 08648.

Cervenak, Andrew, Janosikova 21, Presov 08001 Slovakia.

Coley, James E., St. Lawrence Rehab, 2381 Lawrenceville Rd., Lawrenceville, 08648.

Conlon, Arthur F., 1015 Nottinghill Ln., 08619.

Cook, John B., 75 W. Shore Rd., House #25, Port Washington, NY 11050.

Cuomo, Rocco A.

Delzell, David G., Tower of David, P.O. Box 292, Uniondale, PA 18470.

Deutsch, George E., Pastor Emeritus, 1B Iowa Dr., Whiting, 08759. Tel: 609-242-9456

Dougherty, Edward J., Villa Vianney, 2301 Lawrenceville Rd., Lawrenceville, 08648.

Gardner, William P.

Halpin, Joseph A., 72A Belhaven Ct., Whiting, 08759.

Horvath, Stephen G., P.O. Box 78, Bushkill, PA 18324.

Kearns, Adam, Villa Vianney, 2301 Lawrenceville Rd., Lawrenceville, 08648.

Keenan, Eugene, 101-B Conestoga Dr., Manchester, 08759-1939.

Kralovich, Louis W.

Kunnel, Lawrence K.

Magee, Patrick F., 41 Osborne Ave., Bay Head, 08742.

Matera, Philip T., 1047 Lyndale Ave., 08629.

McCarron, Gerard J.

McConnell, James J., Villa Vianney, 2301 Lawrenceville Rd., Lawrenceville, 08648.

Miele, Joseph J., 388 Cherry Quay Rd., Brick, 08723-6308.

Milewski, Casimir, U1.M. Karlowicza 22 33-100, Tarnow, Poland.

Nolan, William J.

Pearson, Robert A., 16 Chestnut Pl., West Long Branch, 07764.

Petri, John C., 259 Squirrel Ridge Rd., Leasburg, NC 27291.

Poovakulam, Antony P., 9662 Hawaiian Summer St., Las Vegas, NV 89123.

Radomski, Joseph A., St. Lawrence Rehab, 2381 Lawrenceville Rd., 08648.

Rauch, Laszlo F., 1-D Yorktowne Pkwy., Whiting, 08759.

Sanchez, Castor G.

Sauchelli, James J.

Schabowski, Henry F., 240 Shepherd Ave., Middlesex, 08846.

Schneider, William T., The Manor at St. Mary's, 220 St. Mary's Dr., Cherry Hill, 08003.

Sloyan, Gerard S., 6216 41st Ave., Hyattsville, MD 27082.
Sweeney, Richard R., 633 Walden Cir., Robbinsville, 08691.
Thompson, James A., Emmaus House, 21 Main Ave., Ocean Grove, 07756.
Valentine, Charles R., 61 Woodstock Pl., Freehold, 07728-3143.
Zalewski, Francis, 66-15 Wetherole St., Apt. E17, Rego Park, NY 11374.

Permanent Deacons:
Acosta, Amado F., Sacred Heart-St. Andrew, Mt. Holly
Adorno, Miguel, Christ the Redeemer, Mt. Holly
Allen, John W., (Retired), St. George, Titusville
Andre, Edner, Holy Spirit, Asbury Park
Andrews, Stephen W., St. Dorothea, Eatontown
Aquino, Romeo D., St. Joseph's, Toms River
Arcari, Richard A., St. Raphael-Holy Angels, Hamilton
Armstrong, Robert B., St. Elizabeth, Avon-by-the-Sea
Auleta, Michael A., Sacred Heart, Mt. Holly
Ayers, Damian, St. Dominic, Brick
Ayrer, James E., (Retired), Corpus Christi, Willingboro
Babuschak, Francis J., St. Joseph, Toms River
Bailey, Normand C., (Retired), St. Rose, Belmar
Baker, Thomas, St. David the King, Princeton Junction
Barbara, Joseph F., St. John Newmann, Mt. Laurel
Barnes, Robert M., St. Joseph, Toms River
Beauchamps, Jose, St. Mary Cathedral, Trenton
Billbrough, Joseph C., (Retired), Corpus Christi, Willingboro
Bittner, Robert W., (Outside Diocese)
Blackwell, M. Darrell, On Duty Outside the Diocese (Maine)
Boehm, Michael P., Our Lady of Perpetual Help, Maple Shade
Bonner, John J., Our Lady Good Counsel, West Trenton
Bonocore, Steven J., On Duty Outisde the Diocese (Syracuse)
Briggs, William E., Church of the Resurrection, Delran
Buchanan, James, Our Lady of Sorrows-St. Anthony, Hamilton
Buecker, Edward J., St. Dominic, Brick
Byrne, Kevin M., On Duty Outside the Diocese (Washington, D.C.)
Campbell, James L., St. Justin, Toms River
Caponigro, Alfred E., On Duty Outside the Diocese (Arizona)
Card, Joseph A., (Retired), Our Lady of Perpetual Help, Maple Shade
Carlin, George M., (Retired), St. Paul, Burlington
Cartnick, Louis C., St. Luke, Toms River
Casa, James L., Sacred Heart, Mount Holly
Casey, Keith J., St. Thomas More, Manalapan
Cater, Thomas H., St. Elizabeth Ann Seton, Whiting
Cattanea, James F., St. John Neumann, Mt. Laurel
Cechulski, Thomas J., St. Veronica, Howell
Cerefice, Robert L., Holy Innocents, Neptune
Challender, James J., Our Lady of Sorrows-St. Anthony, Hamilton
Chase, Daniel A., (Retired), St. Andrew, Jobstown
Cheu, Richard A., On Duty Outside the Diocese (New York)
Clausen, Peter M., St. Barnabas, Bayville
Clymore, John L., Holy Family, Union Beach
Coccia, Brother Christopher A., On Duty Outside the Diocese (Florida)
Cole, John A., (Retired)
Comito, Charles, St. Theresa, Tuckerton
Commisso, Louis V., Epiphany, Brick
Cook, James P., On Duty Outside the Diocese (Florida)
Cordasco, Ralph, St. Elizabeth Ann Seton, Whiting
Cugini, Henry J., St. Robert Bellarmine, Freehold
Cullinane, John, On Duty Outside the Diocese (Cleveland)
Cummings, James H., St. Barnabas, Bayville
Cunningham, Robert, St. Francis of Assisi, Brant Beach
Currie, Richard J., St. James, Pennington
D'Angelo, V. Richard, On Duty Outside the Diocese (Charleston)
Davis, James R., (Retired), St. Thomas More, Manalapan
Daye, Charles, Jr., St. Veronica, Howell
DeFrehn, Jeffrey, St. Joan of Arc, Marlton
DelGuidice, John V., On Duty Outside the Diocese (Orlando)
Dello Russo, Thomas J., On Duty Outside the Diocese (Scranton)
DeLuca, Joseph W., Holy Eucharist, Tabernacle
DeLuca, Peter J., On Duty Outside the Diocese (Florida)
DeMauro, Gerald, On Duty Outside the Diocese (New York)
DePaolis, Joseph, (Retired), St. Leo the Great, Lincroft
DeValue, John M., Ascension, Bradley Beach
DiCanio, Thomas J., St. Catherine, Holmdel
DiCesare, Anthony N., St. Jerome, West Long Branch
DiLissio, John A., St. Raphael - Holy Angels, Hamilton
Dinella, Roger P., St. David the King, Princeton Junction
Domzalski, Kenneth S., Holy Eucharist, Tabernacle
Donadieu, Joseph M., Sacred Heart, Riverton
Donofeio, Nicholas, St. Dorothea, Eatontown
Doughty, Gerald A., St. Charles Borromeo, Cinnaminson
Ebenau, Frederick C., Sr., St. Justin, Toms River
Ernst, Henry J., On Duty Outside the Diocese (Scranton)
Ervin, Martin A., On Duty Outside the Diocese (Florida)
Evans, William G., (On Leave)
Everist, Thomas J., St. Ann, Lawrenceville
Fanelle, John D., On Duty Outside the Diocese (San Diego)
Fatovic, Andrew J., St. Vincent de Paul, Yardville
Finn, Lawrence W., Sr., St. Mary, Bordentown
Fiorillo, Joseph A., St. Mary, Barnegat
Fischer, Edward, III, Visitation, Brick
Flanagan, John P., (Retired), St. Catharine, Holmdel
Folinus, Robert, St. Joseph, Millstone Twp.
Friedmann, Rolf B., St. Robert Bellarmine, Freehold
Fullen, Michael P., Sr.
Fullen, Peter J., On Duty Outside the Diocese (Venice, FL)
Fung, Matthew V., St. David the King, Princeton Junction
Fuoco, Joseph R., (Retired), Jesus the Good Shepherd, Riverside
Gallagher, Lawrence E., St. George, Titusville
Gallagher, Paul A., San Alfonso Retreat House, Long Branch
Gallagher, William J., St. Charles Borromeo, Cinnaminson
Galvan, Silverius F., Epiphany, Brick
Garvey, Thomas J., St. Anthony of Padua, Hightstown
Genovese, Eugene, St. Veronica, Howell
Genovese, Thomas, St. Joseph, Toms River
Gettlefinger, Robert J., On Duty Outside the Diocese (North Carolina)
Giglio, Frank E., St. Isaac Jogues, Marlton
Glogoza, Richard T., St. John, Lakehurst
Golazeski, Frances G., Incarnation - St. James, Trenton
Gomez, Victor L., Jesus the Lord, Keyport
Gonzalez, James, St. Justin, Toms River
Gooden, Robert, (Retired), St. John, Lakehurst
Grant, John D., St. Alphonsus, Hopewell
Gray, William G., On Duty Outside the Diocese (Florida)
Gregory, Gabriel, On Duty Outside Diocese (Minnesota)
Gregory, Thomas J., (Retired) Arizona
Groff, Francis W., St. Martha, Point Pleasant
Groffie, John F., (Retired), St. Gregory the Great, Hamilton
Grogan, James J., Our Lady of Good Counsel, Moorestown
Grogan, Michael P., St. Mark, Sea Girt
Groh, Alfred, On Duty Outside the Diocese (Florida)
Grussler, John R., Divine Mercy, Trenton
Gularek, Theodore V., St. Veronica, Howell
Gwiazda, Edward J., St. Isaac Jogues, Marlton
Hagan, Michael J., Jesus, the Good Shepherd, Riverside
Hambleton, Richard N., On Duty Outside the Diocese (Charleston)
Haney, John J., St. Martha, Point Pleasant
Hank, William Moore, St. James, Pennington
Hanna, John H., St. Pio of Pietrelcina, Lavallette
Hannawacker, Joseph A., Incarnation-St. James, Trenton
Hansen, Christopher L., St. Catherine, Holmdel
Harbeck, Jay C., Holy Cross, Rumson
Harris, David M., (Retired), St. Mary, Bordentown
Hauenstein, Richard A., (Retired), St. Justin, Toms River
Haunss, Ronald J., St. Mary, Barnegat
Heard, William R., Epiphany, Brick Town
Heffernan, Edward A., Our Lady of Good Counsel, Moorestown
Heilig, Kenneth W., Sacred Heart, Riverton
Heller, James T., (Retired), St. Pius X, Forked River
Hemberger, Martin, (Retired), St. Mary, Bernegat
Hepp, Joseph L., St. John the Baptist, Allentown
Herr, Edward R., St. Dorothea, Eatontown
Hoag, Edward A., St. Ann, Lawrenceville
Hoch, Eugene, On Duty Outside the Diocese (Palm Beach, FL)
Hoefling, John F., St. Andrew, Jobstown
Hooker, George C., (Retired) South Carolina
Hughes, John P., (Retired), St. John Neumann, Mount Laurel
Hvizdos, John F., St. Charles Borromeo, Cinnaminson
Iadanza, John M., On Duty Outside the Diocese (Florida)
Iglesias, Manuel F., St. Raphael-Holy Angels, Hamilton
Imholte, Ralph, (Retired), St. Mary, Colts Neck
Jackson, Frank W., St. Aloysius, Jackson
Jaruszewski, Joseph, Our Lady of Sorrows-St. Anthony, Hamilton
Jennings, Edward F., St. Catharine, Spring Lake
Jimenez, Jose J., Corpus Christ, Willingboro
Johnson, James G., On Duty Outside Diocese (Washington, D.C.)
Johnson, Robert J., St. Agnes, Atlantic Highlands
Johnston, George A., St. Joan of Arc, Marlton
Johnston, Richard, Visitation, Brick
Jones, Francis A., (Retired), St. Paul, Burlington
Kelder, George R., Jr., St. Denis, Manasquan
Kelly, James A., Nativity, Fair Haven
Kennedy, Patrick W., (Retired)
Kerr, Ronald J., Sr., St. John, Lakehurst
Klein, Robert, St. Mary, Barnegat
Klimaszewski, Norbert J., On Duty Outside the Diocese (Florida)
Klincewicz, John G., Holy Innocents, Neptune
Knipper, James J., St. Paul, Princeton
Kohut, David S., Visitation, Brick
Kopcak, John, Ascension, Bradley Beach
Korbelak, George M., St. Peter's, Pt. Pleasant Beach
Krupa, Bradford A., On Duty Outside Diocese (Atlanta, GA)
Kupin, Joseph, St. Paul, Princeton
Lacey, James A., (Retired), Sacred Heart, Bay Head
Lachance, Paul A., (Retired), St. Paul, Princeton
Lafond, Robert H., St. Alphonsus, Hopewell
LaMachia, Ralph A., On Duty Outside the Diocese (Atlanta)
Lancieri, Salvatore, Office of Jail & Prison Ministry, Trenton
Latini, Joseph E., St. Gregory the Great, Hamilton
Laurita, Daniel J., On Duty Outside the Diocese (Alabama)
Lavalle, Thomas J., Jr., St. Raphael-Holy Angels, Hamilton
Little, John L., St. Catharine, Spring Lake
Little, Ronald J., On Duty Outside the Diocese (Phoenix)
Littlefield, James J., St. Veronica, Howell
Lombardo, Earl H., St. Pius X, Forked River
Lonie, Michael, St. Catherine, Holmdel
Lopez, Heriberto, On Duty Outside the Diocese (Florida)
Loughran, Thomas, St. Peter, Point Pleasant
Lovejoy, C. Doug, Jr., Aquinas Institute, Princeton
Luhman, Andrew G., Jr., St. Rose of Lima, Freehold
Luongo, Gerard, St. Joseph, Toms River
Lydick, Donald E., On Duty Outside the Diocese (Delaware)
Machion, Robert D., St. Francis & St. Clare, Florence Twp.
Malhame, Eugene G., Jr., St. Rose, Belmar
Manaloris, James A., Church of the Resurrection, Delran
Mannikus, Uku R., St. Aloysius, Jackson
Marcello, Salvatore, St. Raphael-Holy Angels, Hamilton
Martin, Patrick J., St. Mary, Barnegat
Martucci, Anthony R., St. Pius X, Forked River
Mattozzi, Guido J., Our Lady of the Angels, Trenton
McCabe, John, St. Mary, Deal
McGahran, Andrew R., On Duty Outside the Diocese (North Carolina)
McGrath, James G., St. Mary of The Lakes, Lakewood
McGrath, John G., St. Catherine, Middletown
McHugh, Joseph P., On Duty Outside the Diocese (Camden)
McKenna, Francis A., St. Joseph, Toms River
McKeon, James E., On Duty Outside Diocese (Richmond, VA)
McMahon, Martin K., St. Catherine, Middletown
McNally, Brent G., On Duty Outside Diocese (Venice, FL)
McNerny, Daniel J., On Duty Outside Diocese (Charleston, SC)
Meehan, Daniel J., Church of the Resurrection, Delran
Mendonca, Glen L., St. Joseph, Keyport

Meyer, Richard G., On Duty Outside the Diocese (Florida)
Meyers, Ronald S., Our Lady of Perpetual Help, Maple Shade
Micali, James Mark, St. Clement, Matawan
Miller, Daniel S., Sr., St. Mary, Barnegat
Miller, Donald C., (Retired), St. Elizabeth Ann Seton, Whiting
Mintz, Robert E., On Duty Outside the Diocese (St. Petersburg)
Moir, Gene F., Sr., St. Veronica, Howell
Moore, Timothy E., Our Lady of Sorrows-St. Anthony, Hamilton
Moresco, Edward J., Our Lady of Perpetual Help, Highlands
Morton, James E., Sacred Heart, Riverton
Moscarello, Charles M., St. Gregory The Great, Hamilton
Mosteller, Herman J., Jesus the Good Shepherd, Riverside
Motylinski, Kenneth E., Jr., St. Mary of The Lakes, Medford
Mroz, John J., St. Mary of The Lakes, Medford
Mullarkey, Michael F., Epiphany, Brick
Murray, William J., On Duty Outside Diocese (Palm Beach, FL)
Mylod, Philip J., (Retired)
Napolitano, Richard J., St. Justin, Toms River
Nimon, Robert R., On Duty Outside the Diocese (Florida)
Notaro, John A., St. Dorothea, Eatontown
Nowak, Ronald, Epiphany, Bricktown
O'Boyle, Kevin J., Our Lady of Sorrows-St. Anthony, Mercerville
O'Brien, Christopher D., St. Elizabeth Ann Seton, Whiting
O'Brien, Dennis R., St. Anthony of Padua, Hightstown
O'Brien, Michael J., St. Ann, Browns Mills
O'Connor, David W., St. Mary of The Lakes, Medford
O'Donnell, John J., Our Lady Queen of Peace, Hainesport
Olshevski, Stanley R., Sacred Heart, Mount Holly
Orkis, Stanley, Sacred Heart, Mt. Holly
Orlando, John C., St. Catherine, Middletown
Owens, Lester J., St. Gabriel's, Marlboro
Pacitti, Albert, (Retired), St. Maximilian Kolbe, Toms River
Palan, Henry N., St. Theresa, Tuckerton
Palsir, James W., St. James, Pennington
Papuga, David F., Our Lady of Good Counsel, Moorestown
Parr, Allan T., Sr., St. Gregory the Great, Hamilton
Patton, Joseph R., (Retired), St. Mary of the Lakes, Medford
Paul, Joseph A., Our Lady of Good Counsel, Moorestown
Peevost, George A., Jr., St. William the Abbot, Howell
Pelkowski, Raymond R., St. Benedict, Holmdel
Pennise, Alfred, St. Katherine Drexel, Burlington
Perez, Rene P., St. Aloysius, Jackson
Perkins, Charles A., Jesus the Good Shepherd, Riverside
Perusi, Donald L., St. Denis, Manasquan
Petrauskas, James J., St. Theresa's, Tuckerton
Pierfy, Jeffrey, On Duty Outside the Diocese (Charleston, SC)
Pirozzi, Neil, St. Gregory the Great, Hamilton
Pitt, John R., St. Mary, Barnegat
Policastro, Donald M., St. Joseph, Keyport
Porter, Thomas P., On Duty Outside the Diocese (Raleigh)
Price, Walter L., St. Ann, Browns Mills
Prihoda, Frank J., St. John, Allentown
Principato, Michael, St. Monica, Jackson
Prioli, Joseph J., St. Catherine, Farmingdale
Provencher, Conrad J., On Duty Outside the Diocese (Pennsylvania)
Pstrak, Gary J., St. Denis, Manasquan
Punchello, Alexander A., Sr., St. Katherine Drexel, Burlington
Purcell, Kyran J., St. Elizabeth Ann Seton, Whiting
Putnam, Harry A., (Retired), St. Mary, Bordentown
Rainville, Raymond R., St. Agnes, Atlantic Highlands
Ramos, Alfonso, St. Joseph, Trenton
Ramos, Luis A., St. Mary's Cathedral, Trenton
Rasmussen, Guy C., St. Barnabus, Bayville
Repice, Anthony, Holy Eucharist, Tabernacle
Ricciardi, Vincent P., Sr., Assumption, New Egypt
Richardson, Gary T., St. Mary, Bordentown
Richichi, Joseph, Diocesan Office of Worship
Rider, Joseph H., St. Elizabeth Ann Seton, Whiting
Riedinger, Gerald, St. Dominic, Brick
Riley, Michael, St. George, Titusville
Rinaldi, Vincent L., St. Catherine, Farmingdale
Rivella, Thomas H., Incarnation-St. James, Trenton
Rodriguez, Feliz, On Duty Outside the Diocese (Puerto Rico)
Rodriguez, Jose G., St. Mary Cathedral, Trenton
Ronning, Donald J., Jr., St. Agnes, Atlantic Highlands
Ross, Michael D., On Duty Outside Diocese (Columbus, OH)
Rowley, William R., Sacred Heart, Mt. Holly
Russo, James C., St. Gabriel, Marlboro
Saake, Dennis J., St. Mark, Sea Girt
Sabados, Andrew A., Sr., St. Gregory the Great, Hamilton
Sansevere, Stephen A., St. Gabriel, Marlboro
Scannella, Michael V., St. Francis & St. Clare, Florence Twp.
Scharen, Robert F., St. Mary, Middletown
Schwind, Albert, (Retired), St. Francis of Assisi, Brant Beach
Sciarrotta, Samuel P., St. James Church, Pennington
Scott, James M., III, St. Ann, Lawrenceville
Scott, Stephen G., St. Benedict, Holmdel
Scotti, Richard, St. Gabriel, Marlboro
Seaman, Joseph F., On Duty Outside Diocese (Camden)
Seaton, George L., On Duty Outside the Diocese (Florida)
Sepich, William S., (Retired), St. Charles Borromeo, Cinnaminson
Shapiro, David L., St. Justin, Toms River
Shea, Thomas F., St. Mary, Bordentown
Sheehan, Kenneth R., (Retired), St. Joseph, Keyport
Sherpensky, Frank, (Retired), St. Ann, Browns Mills
Slavin, Dennis E., Office of Family Life, Trenton
Slee, Louis F., (Retired)
Smigelski, Michael A., St. Barnabas, Bayville
Smith, Charles J., St. Mary, Middletown
Smith, Kevin M., St. William The Abbot, Howell
Somma, Eugene A., St. Michael, West End
Sondeen, Carl R., St. Charles Borromeo, Cinnaminson
Sorrentino, Fernando A., St. Mary, Colts Neck
Stap, Matthew J., (Retired), Jesus the Good Shepherd, Riverside
Staub, Raymond W., Jr., Assumption, New Egypt
Stesner, Patrick J., Sr., St. Joseph, Toms River
Stinsman, Michael J., Sacred Heart, Riverton
Sulzmann, William P., St. Theresa, Tuckerton
Swanson, George J., St. Barnabas, Bayville
Szmutko, Steven K., Our Lady of Good Counsel, W. Trenton
Tarzy, Barry R., St. Joan of Arc, Marlton
Taylor, Michael A., St. Joseph, Toms River
Tedeschi, Joseph R., (Retired), St. Mary of the Lakes, Medford
Tharp, Robert, St. Raphael-Holy Angels, Hamilton
Titmas, Richard C., St. Francis of Assisi, Brant Beach
Toca, Frederick M., On Duty Outside the Diocese (Atlanta)
Toolan, James W., On Duty Outside the Diocese (Allentown)
Torres, Benito, Our Lady of the Angels, Trenton
Trani, Eduardo, Christ the Redeemer, Mount Holly
Vagrin, Stephen R., St. Catherine, Seaside Park
Valentin, Juan E., On Duty Outside the Diocese (Florida)
Vassallo, John F., Jr., Corpus Christi, Willingboro
Vazquez, Emiliano, St. Mary Cathedral, Trenton
Vicari, Salvatore J., Jr., Visitation, Brick Town
Vignolini, Robert J., Christ the King, Long Branch
Vilches, Arnaldo, Christ the Redeemer, Mount Holly
Vivona, Joseph A., St. Mary, Barnegat
Vlcej, Robert J., On Duty Outside the Diocese (Baltimore)
Vogel, Anthony D.
Voll, Edwin L., Jr., (Retired), St. Joseph, Toms River
Wadolowski, Thomas P., St. Clement, Matawan
Walsh, James P., Holy Innocents, Neptune
Wanat, John A., St. Rose of Lima, Freehold
Watkins, Thomas H., Jr., St. Hedwig, Trenton
Weber, Francis J., Jr., St. Robert Bellarmine, Freehold
Weber, Richard J., St. Rose, Belmar
Weller, Caleb J., St. Mary, Colts Neck
White, Edward A., On Duty Outside the Diocese (Washington)
Wilson, William A., St. Gregory the Great, Hamilton Square
Young, Donald A., On Duty Outside the Diocese (Arlington, VA)
Zadworny, Barry J., St. Hedwig, Trenton
Zalegowski, Ronald F., St. Mary, Bordentown
Zebrowski, John J., St. Thomas More, Manalapan
Zito, Lee, Sacred Heard, Mount Holly

INSTITUTIONS LOCATED IN THE DIOCESE

[A] COLLEGES AND UNIVERSITIES

LAKEWOOD. *Georgian Court University*, 900 Lakewood Ave., 08701-2697. Tel: 732-987-2200; Fax: 732-987-2018. Email: bevacquak@georgian.edu. Web: www.georgian.edu. Sr. Rosemary E. Jeffries, R.S.M., Ph.D., Pres.; Dr. Joseph Gower, Provost; Rev. John Zec. Priests 3; Sisters 25; Lay Teachers 310; Students 3,579.

[B] HIGH SCHOOLS, DIOCESAN AND PARISH

TRENTON. *Notre Dame High School*, 601 Lawrence Rd., Lawrenceville, 08648. Tel: 609-882-7900; Fax: 609-882-5723. Email: ivins@ndnj.org. Web: www.ndnj.org. Ms. Mary E. Ivins, Prin.; Miss Joan Pilkington, Asst. Prin.; Salvatore Sciarrotta, Asst. Prin.; Rev. Joseph A. Jakub, Chap.; Mary Curtis, Librarian. Lay Teachers 92; Students 1,276.

BELMAR. *Saint Rose High School*, 607 Seventh Ave., 07719. Tel: 732-681-2858; Fax: 732-280-2745. Email: knace@strose.k12.nj.us. Web: www.strose.k12.nj.us. Sr. Kathleen Nace, S.S.J., Prin. Sisters 6; Lay Teachers 48; Students 580.

DELRAN. *Holy Cross High School*, 5035 Rte. 130 S., 08075. Tel: 856-461-5400; Fax: 856-764-0806. Email: dennis.guida@holycrosshighschool.org. Web: www.holycrosshighschool.org. Mr. Dennis M. Guida, Prin.; Sr. Bernadette Thomas, I.H.M., Librarian. Sisters of I.H.M., Scranton, PA. Priests 1; Sisters 4; Lay Teachers 43; Students 699.

HAMILTON. *Trenton Catholic Academy (Upper School)*, 175 Leonard Ave., 08610. Tel: 609-586-3705; Fax: 609-586-6584. Email: dpayne@trentoncatholic.org; jfoley@trentoncatholic.org. Sr. Dorothy Payne, S.S.J., Pres.; Ms. James Foley, Prin.; Miss Kathleen Faraglia, Librarian. Sisters 2; Lay Teachers 21.

HOLMDEL. *St. John Vianney High School*, 540 A Line Rd., 07733. Tel: 732-739-0800; Fax: 732-739-0824. Email: deroba@sjvhs.com. Web: www.sjvhs.com. Mr. Joseph F. Deroba, Prin. Sisters 2; Lay Teachers 63; Students 1,011.

NEW MONMOUTH. *Mater Dei High School*, 538 Church St., 07748. Tel: 732-671-9100; Fax: 732-671-9214. Email: materdeihighschool@nac.net. Web: www.materdeihs.org. Mr. Frank Poleski Jr., Prin. Students 380; Lay Teachers 28.

RED BANK. *Red Bank Catholic High School*, 112 Broad St., 07701. Tel: 732-747-1774; Fax: 732-747-1936. Web: www.redbankcatholic.org. Robert Abatemarco, Prin. Sisters 5; Lay Teachers 100; Students 1,039.

TOMS RIVER. *Monsignor Donovan High School*, 711 Hooper Ave., 08753. Tel: 732-349-8801; Fax: 732-349-8956. Email: egere@mondonhs.com. Web: www.mondonhs.com. Dr. Edward Gere, Prin. Priests 1; Lay Teachers 75; Students 896.

[C] HIGH SCHOOLS, PRIVATE

TRENTON. *Villa Victoria Academy*, 376 W. Upper Ferry Rd., 08628. Tel: 609-882-1700; Fax: 609-882-8421. Email: srlillian@villavictoria.org. Web: www.villavictoria.org. Sr. Mary Ann Gecina, M.P.F., Prin.; Jennifer Jacoppo, Librarian. Upper School, Grades 7-8 (Girls); Grades 9-12 (Girls). Sisters 3; Lay Teachers 13; Students 100.

LINCROFT. *Christian Brothers Academy*, 850 Newman Springs Rd., 07738. Tel: 732-747-1959; Fax: 732-747-1643. Email: adminoff@cbalincroftnj.org. Web: www.delasalle.org. Bros. Andrew O'Gara, F.S.C., Pres.; James Butler, F.S.C., Prin. Priests 1; Brothers 8; Lay Teachers 67; Students 958.

[D] REGIONAL SCHOOLS

WILLINGBORO. *Pope John Paul II Regional School*, 11 S. Sunset Rd., 08046.

[E] INTER-PARISH ELEMENTARY SCHOOLS

ATLANTIC HIGHLANDS. *Mother Teresa Regional School*, (Grades PreK-8), 55 South Ave., 07716. Tel: 732-291-1050; Fax: 732-872-2293. Mrs. Melissa Molloy, Prin.; Katey Patrizio, Librarian.

HAMILTON. *Trenton Catholic Academy (Lower School)*, 177 Leonard Ave., 08610. Tel: 609-586-5888; Fax: 609-631-9295. Email: dpayne@trentoncatholic.org. Anne Reap, Prin.; Candace Andrako, Librarian. Lay Teachers 21; Sisters 1.

MANAHAWKIN. *All Saints Regional Catholic School*, (Grades PreK-8), 400 Doc Cramer Blvd., 08050.

Tel: 609-597-3800; Fax: 609-597-2223. Email: asrc@asrcs.org. Web: asrcs.org. Sr. Jeannette Daily, Prin.; Pauline Barber, Librarian. Lay Teachers 22; Total Enrollment 400.

[F] ELEMENTARY SCHOOLS, PRIVATE

TRENTON. *Villa Victoria Academy*, (Grades PreK-6), (Girls), 376 W. Upper Ferry Rd., 08628. Tel: 609-883-5760; Fax: 609-882-8421. Email: sralice@villavictoria.org. Web: www.villavictoria.org. Sr. Alice Ivanyo, M.P.F., Prin.; Joanie Wentzel, Librarian. Lower School. Lay Teachers 8; Students 100.

PRINCETON. *Princeton Academy of the Sacred Heart*, 1128 Great Rd., 08540. Tel: 609-921-6499; Fax: 609-921-9198. Web: www.princetonacademy.org. Olen Kalkus, Headmaster; Ellen Dowling, Librarian. Private elementary school for boys.

Stuart Country Day School of the Sacred Heart, (Grades PreK-8), 1200 Stuart Rd., 08540. Tel: 609-921-2330; Fax: 609-497-0784. Email: stuart@school.org. Web: stuartschool.org. Sr. Frances de la Chapelle, Headmistress. Sisters 2; Lay Teachers 69; Students 520.

[G] CATHOLIC CHARITIES, DIOCESE OF TRENTON

TRENTON. *Catholic Charities*, 383 W. State St., P.O. Box 1423, 08607-1423. Tel: 609-394-5181; Fax: 609-695-6978. Email: fdolan@cctrenton.org. Web: catholiccharitiestrenton.org. Mr. Francis E. Dolan, Exec. Dir.; George Bontcue, Assoc. Exec. Dir., Fiscal Affairs; Kathryn Jean Turner, Assoc. Exec. Dir. Human Resources; Mary Anne Yeager, Development Officer; Joyce Campbell, M.S.W., Dir., Community & Government Rels.; Mary Ellen Blackwell, Dir., Parish Social Min.

Behavioral Health Services Burlington County, 25 Ikea Dr., Westampton, 08060. Tel: 609-267-9339; Fax: 609-267-6655. Email: hpostel@cctrenton.org. Harry Postel, Svc. Area Dir.

Behavioral Health Services Mercer County, 10 Southard St., 08609. Tel: 609-396-4557; Fax: 609-394-1412. Email: hpostel@cctrenton.org. Harry Postel, Svc. Area Dir.

Children & Family Services Monmouth/Ocean Counties, 145 Maple Ave., Red Bank, 07701. Tel: 732-747-9660; Fax: 732-747-7590. Email: rgering@cctrenton.org. Ronald C. Gering, Svc. Area Dir.

Emergency & Community Services, 801 Burlington Ave., Delanco, 08075. Tel: 856-764-6945; Fax: 856-764-6948.

Emergency and Community Services (Mercer), 132 N. Warren St., 08608. Tel: 609-394-8847; Fax: 609-599-9271.

Emergency and Community Services (Ocean), 200 Monmouth Ave., Lakewood, 08701. Tel: 732-363-5322; Fax: 732-363-3203.

Children & Family Services Mercer County, 55 N. Clinton Ave., 08609. Tel: 609-394-7680; Fax: 609-278-1836. Email: rgering@cctrenton.org. Ronald C. Gering, Svc. Area Dir. Services for victims and perpetuators of family violence.

Providence House Domestic Violence Services, 950A Chester Ave., Delran, 08075. Tel: 856-824-0599; Fax: 856-824-9340. Email: jmetz@cctrenton.org. Jean Metz, Svc. Area Dir. Services to women and children in danger of physical abuse.

Providence House Domestic Violence Services (Ocean), 88 Schoolhouse Rd., Whiting, 08759. Tel: 732-350-2120; Fax: 732-350-2725.

St. Michael Children's Home, c/o Diocese of Trenton, 701 Lawrenceville Rd., 08648.

[H] DAY CARE CENTERS

TRENTON. *Mount Carmel Guild Day Care Center*, 73 N. Clinton Ave., 08609. Tel: 609-392-5159. Email: mtcarmelguild@aol.com. Web: www.mcgtrenton.org. Mr. Russell J. Hansel, Exec. Dir.; Paula Maugans, Contact Person.

BRANT BEACH. *St. Francis of Assisi Day Care Center*, 4700 Long Beach Blvd., 08008. Tel: 609-494-8861; Fax: 609-494-0489. Joan Wickert, Contact Person.

HAMILTON. *Our Lady of Sorrows Preschool*, 3710 E. State St. Ext., 08619. Tel: 609-586-1422; Fax: 609-586-1214. Email: moboyle@ols-sa.org. Web: www.ols-sa.org. Mary O'Boyle, Dir. Preschool and Day Care Center. Lay Teachers 12.

KEANSBURG. *St. Ann Day Care*, 121 Main St., 07734. Tel: 732-787-7220; Fax: 732-787-2136. Sr. Mary Faith, Contact Person.

LONG BRANCH. *St. John the Baptist Family Center*, 272 Willow Ave., 07740. Tel: 732-229-8905; 732-229-8527; 732-571-1003; Fax: 732-571-0280. Email: roma1960@comcast.net. Day Care and Child Development Center. Children 154.

[I] CARE INSTITUTIONS FOR CHILDREN

EWING. *Sister Georgine School*, 180B Ewingville Rd., 08638. Tel: 609-771-4300; Fax: 609-771-8521. Email: sgs@srgeorgineschool.org. Web: www.srgeorgineschool.org. Sr. Barbara Furst, Prin. Sisters of St. Francis. Students 16; Staff 9.

HOPEWELL. *St. Michael's Orphanage and Industrial School, c/o the Diocese of Trenton*, 701 Lawrenceville Rd., 08648.

[J] GENERAL HOSPITALS

TRENTON. *St. Francis Medical Center*, 601 Hamilton Ave., 08629. Tel: 609-599-5000; Fax: 609-695-2744. Email: bdraper@che-east.org. Web: www.stfrancismedical.com. Affiliate of Catholic Health East. Sisters of St. Francis of Philadelphia 7; Bed Capacity 238; Patients Assisted Annually 128,953; Total Staff 1,049.

Schools for Nurses Tel: 609-599-5192; Fax: 609-599-5799. Bonny Ross, Dir. School of Nursing; Rev. Joel F. Szydlowski, O.F.M., Dir. Pastoral Care. Student Nurses 62.

WILLINGBORO. *The Combined Auxiliaries of Lourdes Medical Center of Burlington County*, 218A Sunset Rd., 08046. Tel: 609-835-2900; Fax: 609-835-3061.

Parent Organization: Our Lady of Lourdes Health Foundation, Inc.

Lourdes Medical Center of Burlington County, Inc. (Parent Corporation: Our Lady of Lourdes Health Care Services, Inc.), 218A Sunset Rd., 08046. Tel: 609-835-2900; Fax: 609-835-3061. Web: www.lourdesnet.org.

Lourdes Medical Center of Burlington County

[K] SPECIAL HOSPITALS AND SANATORIA FOR INVALIDS

LAWRENCEVILLE. *Morris Hall/Saint Lawrence, Inc.*, 2381 Lawrenceville Rd., 08648. Tel: 609-896-9500; Fax: 609-895-0242. Email: cbrennan@slrc.org. Web: www.slrc.org. Charles L. Brennan, CEO; Rev. Albert Ricciardelli, Chap. St. Lawrence Rehabilitation Center. Bed Capacity 166; Bed Licensure 139; Total Assisted Annually 2,558; Total Staff 409.

Morris Hall/Saint Lawrence, Inc. Morris Hall - St. Joseph's Nursing Center, 1 Bishops' Dr., 08648-2050. Tel: 609-896-0006; Fax: 609-896-8037; 609-895-0466. Email: epetroski@morrishall.org. Web: www.morrishall.org. Ellen Petroski, M.S.W., L.S.W., L.N.H.A., COO. Skilled Nursing Care Facility for the Chronically Ill. Bed Capacity 120; Total Assisted Annually 173; Staff 100.

Residences and Assisted Living for Senior Citizens Tel: 609-896-0006; Fax: 609-896-8037. Email: epetroski@morrishall.org. Web: www.morrishall.org.

Rosecliff Living-Inc., 2382 Lawrenceville Rd., 08648. Tel: 609-896-9500; Fax: 609-895-0242. Charles L. Brennan, CEO. Purpose is to provide housing, healthcare and social facilities and services to older adults.

[L] SPECIALIZED CHILD CARE AGENCIES

RED BANK. *Collier Group Home*, 180 Spring St., 07701. Tel: 732-842-8337; Fax: 732-530-7096. Email: pauldes21@comcast.net. Web: www.collieryouthservices.org. Mr. Paul DeSantis, Dir. Residential Programs. 24 Hour Program-Therapy and Educational Services. Provided Under the Supervision of the Sisters of the Good Shepherd. Capacity 10; Total Assisted Annually 19; Total Staff 8.

Collier House, 386 Maple Pl., Keyport, 07735. Tel: 732-264-3222; Fax: 732-264-3277. Email: pauldes21@comcast.net. Web: www.collieryouthservices.org. Mr. Paul DeSantis, Dir. Residential Prog. Transitional Aging-Out Program for Women 18-21 years old. Capacity 5; Total Staff 6.

WICKATUNK. *Collier Services, Collier High School*, 160 Conover Rd., 07765. Tel: 732-946-4771; Fax: 732-946-3519. Email: info@collieryouthservices.org. Web: www.collieryouthservices.org. Ms. Aideen Bugler, Prog. Dir.; Sr. Deborah Drago, Exec. Dir. Adolescent Boys and Girls. Capacity 150; Total Assisted Annually 230; Total Staff 120.

Kateri Environmental Education Center Tel: 732-946-9694; Fax: 732-946-9785. Web: www.collieryouthservices.org. Ms. Jeanne Navagh, Asst. Exec. Dir. Tel: 732-946-9694; Fax: 732-946-9785. Kateri Day Camp serves children 5-12 years old.; Project Eco- six week extended school year program.; JET-Summer Job Experience & Training program for teens. Capacity 75; Total Assisted Annually 4,471.

[M] HOMES FOR AGED

TRENTON. *Cathedral Square Housing, Inc.*, 26 W. Hanover Pl., 08608. Tel: 609-392-1111; Fax: 609-683-7227. Email: cs@gershengroup.com. Most Rev. John M. Smith, Dir. Senior Citizen Housing Project.

LAWRENCEVILLE. *Morris Hall-Saint Lawrence, Inc.*, 1 Bishops' Dr., 08648-2050. Tel: 609-896-0006; Fax: 609-896-8037; 609-895-0466. Email: epetroski@morrishall.org. Web: www.morrishall.org. Charles L. Brennan, CEO; Ellen Petroski, M.S.W., L.S.W., L.N.H.A., COO; Rev. Albert Ricciardelli. Morris Hall - St. Mary's Residence & Assisted Living. Guests 62; Bed Capacity 100; Total Assisted Annually 86; Total Staff 45.

YARDVILLE. *Villa Maria Sanitarium*, 109 Rte. 156, 08620. Tel: 609-585-4660; Fax: 609-585-2759. Rev. Severin Dietrich, O.F.M.Conv., Chap. Administration: Franciscan Sisters. Residents 7.

[N] MONASTERIES AND RESIDENCES FOR PRIESTS AND BROTHERS

TRENTON. *St. Lawrence Rehabilitation Center* (Lawrenceville), 2381 Lawrenceville Rd., 08648. Tel: 609-896-9500; Fax: 609-895-0242. Email: clb950@aol.com. Web: www.slrc.org. Charles Brennan, CEO. Nursing care for priests. In Res. Most Rev. John C. Reiss, D.D., J.C.D. (Retired); Rev. Msgr. Alfred D. Smith (Retired); Revs. George M. Albano (Retired); James N. Cammisa (Retired); James Coley (Retired); Stephen G. Horvath (Retired); John C. Petri (Retired); Stanislaus Polczyk; Laszlo F. Rauch (Retired).

Villa Vianney (Lawrenceville), 2301 Lawrenceville Rd., 08648. Tel: 609-219-0177; Fax: 609-896-8037. In Res. Rev. Msgrs. Henry S. Bogdan (Retired); William J. Carton (Retired); William F. Fitzgerald (Retired); Hugh F. Ronan (Retired); Edward Strano (Retired); Gregory D. Vaughan, V.G.; Revs. John V. Bowden (Retired); Harry E. Cenefeldt (Retired); Edward Dougherty (Retired); G. William Evans; Adam Kearns (Retired); Gerard J. McCarron (Retired); James J. McConnell (Retired); Richard R. Milewski; William J. Nolan (Retired); Joseph A. Radomski (Retired).

BORDENTOWN. *Society of the Divine Word*, 101 Park St., 08505. Tel: 609-298-0549; Fax: 609-298-6013. Revs. Victor Butler, S.V.D.; Patrick Connor, S.V.D.; Joseph Detig, S.V.D.; Leo Dusheck, S.V.D.; Raymond Hannah, S.V.D.; Raymond T. Lennon, S.V.D., Vice Rector; Martin Padovani, S.V.D., Admin.; Jefferson Pool, S.V.D.; Steven Schuler, S.V.D.; Gerhard Vogel, S.V.D.; Bros. Javier Eshman, S.V.D.; Louis Gagnon, S.V.D.; George Haegele, S.V.D.; Joseph Hornek, S.V.D.; Patrick Hogan, S.V.D., Rector; Henry Miller, S.V.D.; James Mullen, S.V.D.

LINCROFT. *Christian Brothers, St. La Salle Auxiliary*, 850 Newman Springs Rd., P.O. Box 238, 07738. Tel: 732-842-4359; Fax: 732-219-1619. Email: cards@dlsaux.org. Web: dlsaux.org. Bro. William Martin, F.S.C., Dir. *LaSalle Lincroft, Inc.*, 800 Newman Springs Rd., 07738. Tel: 732-842-7420; Fax: 732-530-3504. Bro. Frank Byrne, F.S.C., Contact Person. Brothers 3.

De La Salle Hall, 810 Newman Springs Rd., 07738. Tel: 732-530-9470; Fax: 732-530-3153. Bro. Michael Finnegan, F.S.C., Dir. Brothers Licensed Nursing Home. Brothers 3; Lay Staff 50; Patients 32.

La Salle Provincialate Inc., 800 Newman Springs Rd., 07738. Tel: 732-842-7420; Fax: 732-530-3504. Email: cbny@cbnewyork.org. Web: cbnewyork.org. Bro. Frank Byrne, F.S.C., Prov. Brothers of the Christian Schools.

The Vaugirard Religious & Charitable Trust, 800 Newman Springs Rd., 07738. Tel: 732-842-4359; Fax: 732-219-1619.

MOUNT LAUREL. *Cistercian Monastery of Our Lady of Fatima*, 564 Walton Ave., 08054-9582. Tel: 856-235-1330; Fax: 856-235-9632. Revs. Lino S. Parente, O.Cist. (Italy), Prior, (Italy); Maurizio Nicoletti, O.Cist. (Italy); Awte Weldu, O.Cist. Cistercian Fathers.

[O] CONVENTS AND RESIDENCES FOR SISTERS

TRENTON. *Morning Star House of Prayer*, 312 Upper Ferry Rd., 08628. Tel: 609-882-2766; Fax: 609-882-2766. Email: sisterjo@morningstarprayerhouse.org. Web: www.morningstarprayerhouse.org. Religious Sisters Filippini.

Notre Dame Diocesan Convent, 681 Lawrence Rd., 08648. Tel: 609-406-7437; Fax: 609-406-7412. Web: dioceseoftrenton.org. Lawrenceville; Intercongregational Living. Sisters 20.

Sisters of St. Francis of Philadelphia, St. Clare Convent, 917 Melrose Ave., 08629. Tel: 609-695-7805. Email: clareconl@verizon.net. Web: osfphila.org.

Villa Victoria Academy Convent, 376 W. Upper Ferry Rd., 08628. Tel: 609-883-0064; Fax: 609-882-8066. Web: www.villavictoria.org. Religious Sisters Filippini.

ASBURY PARK. *Missionaries of Charity*, 144 Ridge Ave., 07712. Tel: 732-775-1101.

CHESTERFIELD. *Monastery of Saint Clare*, 150 White Pine Rd., 08515. Tel: 609-324-2638; Fax: 609-324-2938. Email: mvarleyosc@verizon.net. Web: www.poorclaresnj.com. Sr. Miriam Varley, O.S.C., Abbess.

DELRAN. *Holy Cross High School Convent*, Sisters of the Immaculate Heart of Mary, 5035 Rte. 130 S., 08075. Tel: 856-461-1792.

HARVEY CEDARS. *Maris Stella Retreat and Conference Center*, 7201 Long Beach Blvd., 08008. Tel: 609-494-1182; Fax: 609-494-1182. Email: stmsalerno@comcast.net. Sr. Mary Morley, S.C., Admin. Sisters of Charity of St. Elizabeth, Convent Station.

LAKEWOOD. *Sisters of Mercy of the Americas, Mid-Atlantic Community, Georgian Court University Convent*, 900 Lakewood Ave., 08701. Tel: 732-987-2576; Fax: 732-987-2019.

LAWRENCEVILLE. *Religious of the Sacred Heart of Mary*, 43 Coral Ct., 08648. Tel: 609-896-2413.

NEW MONMOUTH. *Siena New Hope Home*, P.O. Box 518, 07748. Tel: 732-671-3622; Fax: 732-671-3691. Email: sienanewhopehome@comcast.net. Religious Teachers Filippini.

OCEAN GROVE. *Emmaus House*, 21 Main Ave., 07756. Tel: 732-776-5458; Fax: 732-776-7065. Email: dwiswll18@aol.com. Sr. Patricia Mary Walsh, O.P., Admin.

Memorare, 20 Pitman Ave., 07756. Tel: 732-774-3158; Fax: 732-776-7065. Sr. Patricia Mary Walsh, O.P., Admin.

WICKATUNK. *Convent of the Sisters of Good Shepherd*, 160 Conover Rd., 07765. Tel: 732-946-7877; 732-946-7886; Fax: 732-332-1240. Email: ddrago@collieryouthservices.org. Web: www.goodshepherdsisters.org. Sr. Deborah Drago, Coord. Sisters of Good Shepherd of New Jersey. Sisters 5.

YARDVILLE. *Congregation of the Servants of the Holy Child Jesus of the Third Order Regular of Sant Fra*, 109 Rte. 156, 08620. Tel: 609-585-4660; Fax: 609-585-2759. Sr. M. Antonia Cooper, Rel. Min. Properties owned and or sponsored: Villa Maria Sanitarium, Inc., Trenton, NJ. Ministry in Social Work; Health Care. Represented in the Dioceses of Trenton, Paterson, Metuchen. Total in American Region 19.

[P] CHAPELS

LAWRENCEVILLE. *Our Lady of the Rosary Chapel* 1 Bishops' Dr., 08648-2050. Tel: 609-896-0006; Fax: 609-895-0466. Email: info@morrishall.org. Web: www.morrishall.org. Located in Morris Hall.

[Q] HOUSES OF PRAYER

TRENTON. *Morning Star House of Prayer*, 312 W. Upper Ferry Rd., 08628. Tel: 609-882-2766; Fax: 609-882-2766. Email: sisterjo@morningstarprayerhouse.org. Web: morningstarprayerhouse.org. Sr. Josephine Aparo, M.P.F. Religious Teachers Filippini 2.

MOUNT HOLLY. *Francis House of Prayer*, P.O. Box 392, Rancocas, 08073. Tel: 609-877-0509. 39 Springside Rd., Westampton, 08060. Email: fhop@verizon.net. Web: www.fhop.org. Sr. Marcella Springer, S.S.J.

NEPTUNE. *The Upper Room Spiritual Center*, 3455 W. Bangs Ave. - Bldg. 2, 07753. Tel: 732-922-0550; Fax: 732-922-3904. Email: office@theupper-room.org. Web: www.theupper-room.org. Sisters Maureen Christensen, R.S.M., Co-Dir.; Maureen Conroy, R.S.M., Co-Dir.; Trudy Ahern, S.S.J., Co-Dir.

[R] RETREAT HOUSES

ELBERON. *Stella Maris Retreat Center*, 981 Ocean Ave., 07740. Tel: 732-229-0602; Fax: 732-229-8960. Email: smreservation@mycomcast.com. Web: www.stellamarisretreatcenter.com. Sr. Lois Jablonski, S.S.J., Admin.

LONG BRANCH. *San Alfonso Retreat House*, 755 Ocean Ave., P.O. Box 3098, 07740. Tel: 732-222-2731; Fax: 732-870-8892. Email: info@sanalfonsoretreats.org. Web: www.sanalfonsoretreats.org. Revs. Thomas J. Siconolfi, C.Ss.R., Rector/Dir.; Dennis Foley, C.Ss.R.; John M. Connor, C.Ss.R.; John McGowan, C.Ss.R.; Bro. Bernard Colleran, C.Ss.R.; Deacon Paul Gallagher. Priests 4; Brothers 1. In Res. Revs. John F. Murray, C.Ss.R.; John R. Cody, C.Ss.R.; William Gaffney, C.Ss.R.

SOUTH MANTOLOKING. *St. Joseph by the Sea Retreat House*, 400 Rte. 35 N., 08738. Tel: 732-892-8494; Fax: 732-892-9905. Email: sjbsea@comcast.net. Web: www.sjbsea.org. Sisters Frances Lauretti, M.P.F., Dir.; Barbara Ranere, M.P.F., Admin. Asst.; Brunilda Ramos, M.P.F., Admin. Asst. Sisters 3.

[S] PERSONAL PRELATURES

PRINCETON. *Opus Dei* Prelature of the Holy Cross and Opus Dei, 34 Mercer St., 08540. Tel: 609-497-9448; Fax: 609-497-0906. Email: mjm105@yahoo.com. Web: www.opusdei.org. Rev. Martin J. Miller.

[T] NEWMAN CENTERS

PRINCETON. *Campus Ministry for the Diocese of Trenton* Aquinas Institute, Princeton University, 65 Stockton St., 08540. Tel: 609-924-1820; Fax: 609-924-8322. Email: mullelly@princeton.edu. Rev. Thomas J. Mullelly, J.D., Dir. & Chap.

Emmaus House, Rider University 2116 Lawrenceville Rd., 08648. Tel: 609-896-0394; Fax: 609-219-9203. Email: bugliano@rider.edu. Rev. Bruno A. Ugliano, O.S.B., Chap.

Mercer County Community College 1200 Old Trenton Rd., Hamilton Township, 08690. Tel: 609-896-0394; Fax: 609-219-9203. Rev. Bruno A. Ugliano, O.S.B., Chap.

Bede House, College of New Jersey 492 Ewingville Rd., 08638. Tel: 609-771-9091. Rev. Joseph G. Hlubik, Chap.

Georgian Court College 900 Lakewood Ave., Lakewood, 08701. Tel: 732-364-2200, Ext. 600; Fax: 732-901-7151. Sr. Mariann Mahon, R.S.M., Dir. Campus Ministry.

Catholic Center at Monmouth University 16 Beechwood Ave., West Long Branch, 07764. Tel: 732-229-9300; Fax: 732-229-1050. Web: mvcatholic.com. Rev. Michael Lankford, Chap.; Mary Jakub, Assoc. Dir.

[U] MISCELLANEOUS LISTINGS

TRENTON. *Diocese of Trenton Charitable Trust for Aged, Infirm and Disabled Priests*, 701 Lawrenceville Rd., 08648. Mr. Anthony J. Mingarino, CAO & Contact Person.

**Foundation for Student Achievement, Inc.*, 701 Lawrenceville Rd., 08648.

The Haitian Community Center, 530 S. Olden Ave, 08629. Tel: 609-588-8808; Fax: 609-588-8801. Mrs. Magda Dorleans, Dir.

Martin House, 802 E. State St., P.O. Box 1025, 08606. Tel: 609-989-0961; Fax: 609-989-0933. Rev. Brian McCormick. Priests 1; Total Assisted 2,000; Total Staff 7.

Martin House Learning Center, 794 E. State St., P.O. Box 1025, 08606. Tel: 609-989-8143; Fax: 609-989-0933. Robert Donaldson, Min. Ministers 1; Total Assisted 700; Total Staff 25.

New Jersey Catholic Conference, 149 N. Warren St., 08608. Tel: 609-989-1120; Fax: 609-989-1152. Email: info@njcathconf.com. Web: www.njcathconf.com. Most Rev. John J. Myers, D.D., J.C.D., Pres.; Patrick R. Brannigan, Exec. Dir.

Trenton Diocesan Union of Holy Name Societies, 701 Lawrenceville Rd., P.O. Box 5147, 08638-0147. Tel: 732-295-2111; Fax: 732-295-2333. Email: hudsoncorp@comcast.net. Web: dioceseoftrenton.org.

Burlington County Federation of Holy Name Societies

Mercer County Federation of Holy Name Societies

Monmouth County Federation of Holy Name Societies

Ocean County Federation of Holy Name Societies

ASBURY PARK. *Mercy Center, Inc.*, 1106 Main St., 07712. Tel: 732-774-9397; Fax: 732-988-8709. Email: sistercarol@mercycenternj.org. Web: mercycenternj.org. Carol Ann Henry, R.S.M., Dir.

BRICK. *Mid-Life Directions*, 4 Palm Ave., 08723. Tel: 732-255-1239; Fax: 732-255-1239. Email: midlifedirections@comcast.net. Sr. Anne Brennan, C.S.J., Contact Person. Purpose: Ministry for personal and spiritual growth specifically for people in midlife and later years.

LAWRENCEVILLE. *The Foundation of Morris Hall/St. Lawrence, Inc.*, 2381 Lawrenceville Rd., 08648. Tel: 609-896-9500, Ext. 2215; Fax: 609-895-1602. Email: jmillner@slrc.org. Web: www.slrc.org. Mr. Thomas E. Boyle, CFO & Contact Person.

Morris Hall/St. Lawrence, Inc., 1 Bishops' Dr., 08648-2050. Tel: 609-896-0006; Fax: 609-896-8037. Email: epetroski@morrishall.org. Web: www.morrishall.org. Bed Capacity 220; Bed Licensure 220.

Morris Hall Tel: 609-896-0006; Fax: 609-896-8037. Email: epetroski@morrishall.org. Charles Brennan, CEO; Ellen Petroski, M.S.W., L.S.W., L.N.H.A., COO. Priests 1; Total Assisted 300; Total Staff 145.

LINCROFT. *The Bethlehem University Foundation, Inc.*, 800 Newman Springs Rd., 07738. Tel: 732-842-7420; Fax: 732-530-3504. Mr. Jack Steger, Bd. Chm.; Bros. Dominic Smith, F.S.C., Sec.; Benjamin Monastero, Treas.

Christian Brothers of Lincroft, NJ, Inc., 854 Newman Springs Rd., 07738. Tel: 732-842-6712; Fax: 732-758-8310. Bro. Michael Corry, F.S.C., Contact Person.

Christian Brothers Retirement and Continuing Care Trust, 800 Newman Springs Rd., 07738-1696.

District of Eastern North America Ministry Corporation, 800 Newman Springs Rd., 07738-1696.

FSC DENA Endowment Trust, 800 Newman Springs Rd., 07738-1696.

FSC DENA Real Estate Holding Corporation, 800 Newman Springs Rd., 07738-1696.

FSC DENA Real Estate Trust, 800 Newman Springs Rd., 07738-1696.

MIDDLETOWN. *The Gathering Place*, 130 Bray Ave., 07748. Tel: 732-495-7615; Fax: 732-495-6422. Email: pnoonel@comcast.net. Sr. Margaret Noone, R.S.M., Contact Person. Ministry which promotes systemic change through programs of human development and spiritual growth, with special emphasis on those who are poor.

TOMS RIVER. *Holy Redeemer Visiting Nurse Agency, Inc., (Ocean County Office)*, 1228 Rte. 37 W., 08755. Tel: 732-240-2449; Fax: 732-288-2669.

RELIGIOUS INSTITUTES OF MEN REPRESENTED IN THE DIOCESE

For further details refer to the corresponding bracketed number in the Religious Institutes of Men or Women section.

[0140]—*The Augustinians*—O.S.A.

[0200]—*Benedictine Monks* (St. Mary's Abbey, Morristown, NJ)—O.S.B.

[0330]—*Brothers of the Christian Schools*—F.S.C.

[1100]—*Brothers of the Sacred Heart*—S.C.

[0270]—*Carmelite Fathers and Brothers*—O.Carm.

[0340]—*Cistercian Fathers* (Cistercian Monastery of Our Lady of Fatima)—O.Cist.

[0390]—*Consolata Missionaries* (US Prov.)—I.M.C.

[0480]—*Conventual Franciscans* (Provs. of the Immaculate Conception & St. Anthony of Padua)—O.F.M.Conv.

[0520]—*Franciscan Friars* (Prov. of the Most Holy Name of Jesus)—O.F.M.

[1310]—*Order of the Holy Trinity*—O.SS.T.

[1070]—*Redemptorist Fathers & Brothers* (Baltimore & Denver Prov.)—C.SS.R.

[0420]—*Society of the Divine Word*—S.V.D.

[]—*Vincentian Congregation*—V.C.

RELIGIOUS INSTITUTES OF WOMEN REPRESENTED IN THE DIOCESE

[1810]—*Bernardine Sisters of Third Order of St. Francis*—O.S.F.

[1980]—*Congregation of the Servants of the Holy Child Jesus of the Third Order Regular of Sant Fra*—O.S.F.

[2980]—*Congregation of Notre Dame*—C.N.D.

[2410]—*Congregation of the Marianites of Holy Cross*—M.S.C.

[1170]—*Congregation of the Sisters of St. Felix (Felician Sisters)*—C.S.S.F.

[1830]—*Contemplative Sisters of the Good Shepherd*—R.G.S.

[0850]—*Daughters of Mary Help of Christians*—F.M.A.

[1070-05]—*Dominican Sisters* (Amityville, NY)—O.P.

[1070-11]—*Dominican Sisters* (Sparkhill, NY)—O.P.

[1070-15]—*Dominican Sisters* (Blauvelt, NY)—O.P.

[1070-18]—*Dominican Sisters* (Caldwell, NJ)—O.P.

[1105]—*Dominican Sisters of Hope* (Ossining, NY)—O.P.

[1115]—*Dominican Sisters of Peace*—O.P.

[1365]—*Franciscan Missionary Sisters of the Infant Jesus*—F.M.I.J.

[1180]—*Franciscan Sisters of Allegany, NY*—O.S.F.

[1470]—*Franciscan Sisters of St. Joseph* (Hamburg, NY)—F.S.S.J.

[1190]—*Franciscan Sisters of the Atonement (Graymoor)*—S.A.

[1840]—*Grey Nuns of the Sacred Heart*—G.N.S.H.

[]—*Hermanitas de la Anunciacion* (Columbia, South America)—H.A.

[2710]—*Missionaries of Charity*—M.C.

[2760]—*Missionary Sisters of the Immaculate Conception of the Mother of God*—S.M.I.C.

[3760]—*Order of St. Clare*—O.S.C.

[3465]—*Religious of the Sacred Heart of Mary*—R.S.H.M.

[3430]—*Religious Teachers Filippini*—M.P.F.

[2970]—*School Sisters of Notre Dame, Baltimore* (Province)—S.S.N.D.

[1700]—*School Sisters of the Third Order of St. Francis* (Bethlehem, PA)—O.S.F.

[1980]—*Servants of the Holy Infancy of Jesus*—O.S.F.

[]—*Sisters for Christian Community*—S.F.C.C.

[0590]—*Sisters of Charity of Saint Elizabeth, Convent Station*—S.C.

[2575]—*Sisters of Mercy of the Americas* (Mid-Atlantic Community)—R.S.M.

[3360]—*Sisters of Providence of Saint Mary of the Woods, IN*—S.P.

[3830]—*Sisters of Saint Joseph of Brentwood* (New York)—C.S.J.

[1630]—*Sisters of St. Francis of Penance and Christian Charity*—O.S.F.

[1650]—*The Sisters of St. Francis of Philadelphia*—O.S.F.

[]—*Sisters of St. Francis of the Neumann Communities*—O.S.F.

[3893]—*Sisters of St. Joseph of Chestnut Hill, Philadelphia*—S.S.J.

[3890]—*Sisters of St. Joseph of Peace*—C.S.J.P.

[1830]—*The Sisters of the Good Shepherd*—R.G.S.

[1970]—*Sisters of the Holy Family of Nazareth*—C.S.F.N.

[3480]—*Sisters of the Resurrection*—C.R.

[2170]—*Sisters, Servants of the Immaculate Heart of Mary* (Immaculata, PA)—I.H.M.

[2160]—*Sisters, Servants of the Immaculate Heart of Mary* (Scranton)—I.H.M.

[0810]—*Society of the Daughters of the Heart of Mary*—D.H.M.

[4060]—*Society of the Holy Child Jesus*—S.H.C.J.

[4070]—*Society of the Sacred Heart*—R.S.C.J.

NECROLOGY

† Wilus, Rev. Msgr. John M., (Retired)—Died 2007

† Becker, Ronald R.—Died Jan. 21, 2009

† Porazzo, Francis J. (Retired)—Died Oct. 10, 2009

An asterisk (*) denotes an organization that has established tax-exempt status directly with the IRS and is not covered by the USCCB Group Ruling.

Diocese of Tucson

(Dioecesis Tucsonensis)

Most Reverend

GERALD F. KICANAS, D.D.

Bishop of Tucson; ordained April 27, 1967; appointed Titular Bishop of Bela and Auxiliary Bishop of Chicago January 24, 1995; consecrated March 20, 1995; appointed Coadjutor Bishop of Tucson October 30, 2001; installed January 15, 2002; succeeded to See of Tucson March 7, 2003. *Mailing Address: P.O. Box 31, Tucson, AZ 85702.* Tel: 520-792-3410; Fax: 520-792-0291.

ESTABLISHED A VICARIATE-APOSTOLIC 1868.

Square Miles 42,707.

Erected by His Holiness Pope Leo XIII, May 8, 1897.

Comprises the Counties of Cochise, Gila, Greenlee, Graham, La Paz, Pima, Pinal, Santa Cruz and Yuma in the State of Arizona.

For legal titles of parishes and diocesan institutions, consult the Chancery Office.

Chancery Office: 111 S. Church Ave., P.O. Box 31, Tucson, AZ 85702. Tel: 520-792-3410.

Web: www.diocesetucson.org

Email: diocese@diocesetucson.org

STATISTICAL OVERVIEW

Personnel	
Bishop	1
Priests: Diocesan Active in Diocese	76
Priests: Diocesan Active Outside Diocese	1
Priests: Retired, Sick or Absent	16
Number of Diocesan Priests	93
Religious Priests in Diocese	81
Total Priests in Diocese	174
Extern Priests in Diocese	48
Ordinations:	
Religious Priests	1
Permanent Deacons in Diocese	113
Total Brothers	20
Total Sisters	200
Parishes	
Parishes	75
With Resident Pastor:	
Resident Diocesan Priests	52
Resident Religious Priests	15
Without Resident Pastor:	
Administered by Priests	6
Administered by Deacons	1
Administered by Religious Women	1

Missions	46
Professional Ministry Personnel:	
Brothers	2
Sisters	21
Lay Ministers	78
Welfare	
Catholic Hospitals	3
Total Assisted	470,500
Health Care Centers	1
Total Assisted	41,500
Special Centers for Social Services	2
Total Assisted	430,000
Educational	
Diocesan Students in Other Seminaries	17
Total Seminarians	17
High Schools, Private	6
Total Students	2,034
Elementary Schools, Diocesan and Parish	18
Total Students	4,519
Elementary Schools, Private	3
Total Students	627
Catechesis/Religious Education:	

High School Students	3,131
Elementary Students	12,746
Total Students under Catholic Instruction	23,074
Teachers in the Diocese:	
Priests	1
Brothers	6
Sisters	24
Lay Teachers	414
Vital Statistics	
Receptions into the Church:	
Infant Baptism Totals	5,748
Minor Baptism Totals	483
Adult Baptism Totals	234
Received into Full Communion	515
First Communions	5,511
Confirmations	3,250
Marriages:	
Catholic	660
Interfaith	153
Total Marriages	813
Deaths	2,118
Total Catholic Population	204,629
Total Population	1,822,276

Former Bishops—Most Revs. JOHN BAPTIST SALPOINTE, D.D., ord. Dec. 21, 1851; appt. Vicar Apostolic of Arizona and Titular Bishop of Doryla Sept. 25, 1868; ord. June 20, 1869; appt. Coadjutor Archbishop of Santa Fe with right of succession April 12, 1884 and Titular Archbishop of Anazarba Oct. 3, 1884; succeeded to the See of Santa Fe July 18, 1885; resigned; appt. Titular Archbishop of Tomi Jan. 27, 1894; died Tucson, July 15, 1898; PETER BOURGADE, D.D., ord. Nov. 30, 1869; appt. Vicar Apostolic of Arizona Jan. 23, 1885 and Titular Bishop of Thaumacum Feb. 7, 1885 and ord. May 1, 1885; appt. first Bishop of Tucson May 10, 1897; appt. fourth Archbishop of Santa Fe Jan. 7, 1899; died Chicago, May 17, 1908; HENRY REGIS GRANJON, D.D., ord. Dec. 17, 1887; appt. second Bishop of Tucson April 19, 1900; ord. June 17, 1900; died Brignais, France, Nov. 9, 1922; DANIEL JAMES GERCKE, D.D., ord. June 1, 1901; appt. third Bishop of Tucson June 21, 1923; ord. Nov. 6, 1923; resigned; appt. Titular Archbishop of Cotyaeum Oct. 26, 1960; died Tucson, March 19, 1964; FRANCIS JOSEPH GREEN, D.D., ord. May 15, 1932; appt. Titular Bishop of Serra in Proconsulari and Auxiliary Bishop of Tucson May 29, 1953; cons. Sept. 17, 1953; appt. Coadjutor "cum jure successionis" May 11, 1960; succeeded to See to become fourth Bishop of Tucson Oct. 26, 1960; retired July 28, 1981; died May 11, 1995; MANUEL D. MORENO, D.D. (Retired), ord. April 25, 1961; appt. Titular Bishop of Tanagra and Auxiliary of Los Angeles Dec. 20, 1976; cons. Feb. 19, 1977; appt. Bishop of Tucson Jan. 12, 1982; retired March 7, 2003; died Nov. 17, 2006.

Vicars General—Revs. RAUL P. TREVIZO, V.G.; ALBERT I. SCHIFANO, V.G., M.C.

Moderator of the Curia—Rev. ALBERT I. SCHIFANO, V.G., M.C.; Mrs. KATHY RHINEHART, Exec. Asst. Tel: 520-792-3410. Email: kathyr@diocesetucson.org.

Episcopal Vicar—Rev. Msgr. RICHARD W. O'KEEFFE, E.V., Yuma La Paz Vicariate.

Chancery Office—111 S. Church Ave., P.O. Box 31, Tucson, 85702. Tel: 520-792-3410; Fax: 520-792-0291.

Chancellor—Mr. ERNEST T. NEDDER, Office, 111 S. Church Ave., Tucson, 85701. Tel: 520-838-2500; Fax: 520-838-2581; Mrs. ANNA MARIA MAMMEN, Exec. Asst. Tel: 520-838-2511. Email: annamaria@diocesetucson.org.

Executive Assistants to the Bishop—Mrs. SONYA GUTIERREZ; Sr. CHARLOTTE ANNE SWIFT. Tel: 520-838-2500; Fax: 520-792-0291.

Fiscal Manager Office—THOMAS P. ARNOLD, CFO. Tel: 520-838-2500; DAVID KNIGHT, Senior Staff Acct., Mailing Address: P.O. Box 31, Tucson, 85702. Tel: 520-792-3410.

Matrimonial Tribunal—Office: 111 S. Church Ave., P.O. Box 31, Tucson, 85702. Tel: 520-792-3410.

Judicial Vicar—Rev. JOHN P. LYONS, J.C.L.

Adjutant Judicial Vicar—Rev. JOHN P. ARNOLD, J.C.L., V.F.

Promoter of Justice - Penal Cases—Rev. PATRICK R. LAGGES, J.C.D.

Judge—Rev. JOSEPH A. KRAUSE (Retired).

Defenders of the Bond—Revs. MICHAEL BUCCIARELLI; CHARLES KNAPP (Retired); JAMES M. HOBERT.

Advocates and Auditors—Mr. KEVIN ARNOLD; Mr. CHARLES ASHLEY; Mr. RICHARD COSGROVE; Mr. LUIS KAME; Mr. VINCENT LACSAMANA; Mr. PEDRO NAJERA; Mr. GERALD SWEENEY; Mr. MARK WILLIMANN.

Auditors, Notaries, Case Directors—MARTHA JORDAN; HELEN EVANS, Mailing Address: P.O. Box 31, Tucson, 85702. Tel: 520-838-2500.

Professional Consultant—STEPHEN J. SCHILTZ, M.S.W.; IRENE GRAM, Ph.D.

Finance Council—Ex Officio: Most Rev. GERALD FREDERICK KICANAS, D.D., Bishop of Tucson; Rev. ALBERT I. SCHIFANO, V.G., M.C., Moderator of the Curia; THOMAS P. ARNOLD, CFO. O.F.C. Members: NANCY STEPHEN; LUIS DABDOUB; HUMBERTO LOPEZ; LAWRENCE MCDONOUGH; Rev. MICHAEL SHAY, S.D.S.; RICHARD VAN EGEREN; LIRAIN URREIZTIETA; JOHN LAUER.

Diocesan Consultors—Revs. DALE A. BRANSON, V.F.; JOHN P. ARNOLD, J.C.L., V.F.; RAUL P. TREVIZO, V.G.; Rev. Msgr. THOMAS CAHALANE, V.F.; Revs. DOMENICO C. PINTI, V.F.; GONZALO J. VILLEGAS, V.F.; Most Rev. GERALD FREDERICK KICANAS, D.D.; Rev. ALBERT I. SCHIFANO, V.G., M.C.

Council of Priests—Most Rev. GERALD FREDERICK KICANAS, D.D.; Rev. Msgr. THOMAS CAHALANE, V.F.; Revs. JOHN P. LYONS, J.C.L.; JOHN P. ARNOLD, J.C.L., V.F.; Rev. Msgr. RICHARD W. O'KEEFFE, E.V.; Revs. JAVIER H. PEREZ, V.F.; ALBERT I. SCHIFANO, V.G., M.C.; ROBERT BRAZASKAS, V.F.; RICHARD E. TROUTMAN, V.F.; ARIEL G. LUSTAN, V.F.; RAUL P. TREVIZO, V.G., Vicar for Hispanic Affairs; DOMENICO C. PINTI, V.F.; ALEXANDER M. MILLS, V.F.; MICHAEL BUCCIARELLI, Co Dir. Vocations; VILIULFO VALDERRAMA; STEPHEN BARNUFSKY, O.F.M., V.F.; DALE A. BRANSON, V.F.; GONZALO J. VILLEGAS, V.F.

Vicar for Native Americans—Rev. STEPHEN BARNUFSKY, O.F.M., V.F.

Ministry to Priests Program—Rev. JAMES M. HOBERT.

Vicar for Priests—VACANT.

Vicar for Retired Priests—Rev. Msgr. THOMAS J. MILLANE (Retired), Mailing Address: P.O. Box 31, Tucson, 85702.

Vicar for Women Religious—Sr. RINA CAPPELLAZZO, O.P., Mailing Address: P.O. Box 31, Tucson, 85702. Tel: 520-792-3410. Email: srrc@diocesetucson.org.

Vicars Forane—Revs. ROBERT BRAZASKAS, V.F., Cochise Vicariate; DALE A. BRANSON, V.F., Gila-Pinal East Vicariate; ARIEL G. LUSTAN, V.F., Graham-Greenlee Vicariate; JOHN P. ARNOLD, J.C.L., V.F., Pima-Central Vicariate; Rev. Msgr. THOMAS CAHALANE, V.F., Pima-East Vicariate; Revs. GONZALO J. VILLEGAS, V.F., Pima-South Vicariate; RICHARD E. TROUTMAN, V.F., Pima-North Vicariate; STEPHEN BARNUFSKY, O.F.M., V.F., Pima West Vicariate; DOMENICO C. PINTI, V.F., Pinal-West Vicariate; ALEXANDER M. MILLS, V.F., Santa Cruz Vicariate; JAVIER H. PEREZ, V.F., Yuma-La Paz Vicariate.

Diocesan Offices and Directors

Archives—ELIZABETH WITTENBERG, Archivist, 300 S. Tucson Blvd., Tucson, 85716. Tel: 520-886-5201. Email: bettyw@diocesetucson.org.

Board of Education—Ex Officio Members: Most Rev. GERALD FREDERICK KICANAS, D.D.; Sisters ROSA MARIA RUIZ, C.F.M.M., Supt.; RUTHMARY POWERS, H.M., Ph.D., Asst. Supt. Members: PAT LOPEZ, Pres.; JAMES KLOSTER; Rev. KEVIN D. CLINCH; DANIELLE THU; SALLY DOYLE; Ms. JO ANN SAYRE; DENISE MCEVOY; JOHN FINA; THOMAS RANKIN.

Diocesan Building Committee—Most Rev. GERALD FREDERICK KICANAS, D.D., Honorary Chm.; Rev. ALBERT I. SCHIFANO, V.G., M.C., Moderator of the Curia; JAMES RONSTADT, Chm.; BRIAN MCCARTHY, Vice Chm.; LIZ AGUALLO, Sec.; JOHN C. SHAHEEN, A.I.A., Property & Insurance Mgr.; Rev. Msgr. TODD O'LEARY; HECTOR MARTINEZ; BOB SUAREZ; Mr. DAVID MILLER, Real Estate Specialist/Risk Mgmt.; CAROL E. SCHRADER; ERNIE DUARTE; DANIEL RORBACH; Sr. LOIS J. PAHA, O.P.

Cemeteries—Mr. JAMES DECASTRO, Dir., Mailing Address: Holy Hope Cemetery, 3555 N. Oracle Rd., P.O. Box 5158, Tucson, 85705. Tel: 520-888-0860; Fax: 520-888-7788.

Our Lady of the Desert Cemetery—2151 S. Avenida Los Reyes, Tucson, 85748. Tel: 520-885-9173.

Desert Vista Cemetery—2151 S. Avenida Los Reyes, Tucson, 85748. Tel: 520-885-9173.

Censor Librorum—VACANT.

Catholic Social Mission, Diocese of Tucson—JOANNE WELTER, Dir., P.O. Box 31, Tucson, 85702. Tel: 520-792-3410; Fax: 520-792-0291. Email: socialmission@diocesetucson.org. Includes following National Ministries: Catholic Campaign for Human Development; Catholic Relief Services

Catholic Schools—Sisters ROSA MARIA RUIZ, C.F.M.M., Supt.; RUTHMARY POWERS, H.M., Ph.D., Asst. Supt., Mailing Address: P.O. Box 31, Tucson, 85702. Tel: 520-838-2547; Fax: 520-838-2589.

Communications—FRED ALLISON, Dir., Mailing Address: P.O. Box 31, Tucson, 85702. Tel: 520-792-3410.

Human Resources—RICHARD M. SERRANO, Dir.; ALICIA CORTI, Employee Benefits Admin., 111 S. Church Ave., P.O. Box 31, Tucson, 85702. Tel: 520-792-3410; Fax: 520-838-2583.

Cursillo Movement—DICK GODDARD, Lay Dir., Mailing Address: P.O. Box 31, Tucson, 85702.

Detention Ministry—Ms. BARBARA MATTUS, M.A., Coord., 111 S. Church Ave., P.O. Box 31, Tucson, 85702. Tel: 520-298-0021.

Stewardship and Development—MARGIE PUERTA EDSON, Dir., 111 S. Church Ave., P.O. Box 31, Tucson, 85702. Tel: 520-838-2509.

Ecumenical Commission—Rev. Msgr. THOMAS CAHALANE, V.F., 1800 S. Kolb Rd., Tucson, 85710. Tel: 520-747-1321.

Chief Financial Officer—THOMAS P. ARNOLD, Mailing Address: P.O. Box 31, Tucson, 85702. Tel: 520-792-3410.

Holy Childhood Association—Rev. Msgr. VAN A. WAGNER, V.G., Dir. (Retired), Mailing Address: P.O. Box 31, Tucson, 85702. Tel: 520-792-3410.

Interfaith Council—LAUVER EDIE. Tel: 520-745-9443.

Legion of Decency—Chancery Office, 111 S. Church Ave., Tucson, 85701.

Diocesan Liturgical Coordinators—Rev. REMIGIO "MIGUEL" MARIANO; Sr. LOIS J. PAHA, O.P., 111 S. Church Ave., P.O. Box 31, Tucson, 85702. Tel: 520-838-2530.

Office of Catechesis for Children, Youth and Families—J. MICHAEL BERGER, Dir., 111 S. Church, P.O. Box 31, Tucson, 85702-0031. Tel: 520-792-3410; Fax: 520-838-2584. Email: mikeb@diocesetucson.org; JANET TOWNER, Admin. Support. Tel: 520-838-2544. Email: janett@diocesetucson.org.

Office of Evangelization and Hispanic Ministry—VACANT, Dir., Mailing Address: 111 S. Church Ave., P.O. Box 31, Tucson, 85702-0031. Tel: 520-792-3410; JANET TOWNER, Admin. Support.

Office of Formation—Sr. LOIS J. PAHA, O.P., Dir., 111 S. Church, P.O. Box 31, Tucson, 85702-0031. Tel: 520-792-3410; Fax: 520-838-2584. Email: srljp@diocesetucson.org; Mr. JOE PERDREAUVILLE, Asst. Dir. Email: joep@diocesetucson.org; Mrs. OFELIA JAMES, Administrative Support. Email: ofeliaj@diocesetucson.org; VACANT, Coord. Lay Ecclesial Ministry Formation.

Office of Worship—Rev. MIGUEL MARIANO, Dir., 111 S. Church, P.O. Box 31, Tucson, 85702-0031. Tel: 520-792-3410; Fax: 520-838-2584; Mrs. GRACE LOHR, Sec. Part-time. Email: gracel@diocesetucson.org.

Pastoral Diocesana De La Renovacion Carismatica Catolica—VIDAL HARO, Treas., Mailing Address: 4531 S. 11th Ave., Tucson, 85714. Tel: 520-889-0411.

Newspaper— "The New Vision/La Nueva Vision" BERNARD A. ZOVISTOSKI, Mng. Editor. Tel: 520-792-3410, Ext. 1062; Fax: 520-838-2599. Email: bernz@diocesetucson.org; OMAR RODRIGUEZ, Graphic Designer. Tel: 520-792-3410, Ext. 1063; Fax: 520-838-2599. Email: omarr@diocesetucson.org; CLAUDIA BORDERS, Advertising Rep., Mailing Address: P.O. Box 31, Tucson, 85702. Tel: 520-298-1265; Fax: 520-838-2599. Email: borders.c@worldnet.att.net. Web: www.newvisiononline.org.

Office of Child, Adolescent & Adult Protection—PAUL N. DUCKRO, Ph.D., P.O. Box 31, Tucson, 85702. Tel: 520-792-3410. Email: pauld@diocesetucson.org; Ms. JULIETA GONZALEZ, Exec. Asst. Tel: 520-838-2533. Email: julietag@diocesetucson.org.

Office of Due Process—Mailing Address: Chancery Office, P.O. Box 31, Tucson, 85702. Tel: 520-792-3410.

Office of Permanent Diaconate—Deacon KENNETH MORELAND, Dir., Mailing Address: P.O. Box 31, Tucson, 85702. Tel: 520-792-3410; Fax: 520-792-0291.

Associate Vicars—Deacons JOSEPH DELGADO; DAVID SAMPSON; ERNEST TRUJILLO.

Priests' Assurance Corporation—Most Rev. GERALD FREDERICK KICANAS, D.D., Pres. Ex Officio. Directors: Rev. Msgrs. ROBERT D. FULLER, M.R.E., D.Min.; THOMAS J. MILLANE (Retired); Revs. DOMENICO C. PINTI, V.F.; JOHN F. ALLT.

Priests' Placement Advisory Board—All Vicars Forane: Rev. Msgr. THOMAS CAHALANE, V.F.; Revs. JOHN P. ARNOLD, J.C.L., V.F.; JAVIER H. PEREZ, V.F.; DOMENICO C. PINTI, V.F.; DALE A. BRANSON, V.F.; GONZALO J. VILLEGAS, V.F.; ROBERT BRAZASKAS, V.F.; STEPHEN BARNUFSKY, O.F.M., V.F.; FRANCISCO MALDONADO, V.F.; ARIEL G. LUSTAN, V.F.; RICHARD E. TROUTMAN, V.F.

Chancellor—Mr. ERNEST T. NEDDER.

Episcopal Vicar—YUMA LAPAZ, Vicariate; Rev. Msgr. RICHARD W. O'KEEFFE, E.V.

Moderator of the Curia—Rev. ALBERT I. SCHIFANO, V.G., M.C.

Propagation of the Faith—Mr. ERNEST T. NEDDER, Dir. Pro Tem., P.O. Box 31, Tucson, 85702. Tel: 520-792-3410.

Property and Insurance Manager—JOHN C. SHAHEEN, A.I.A., Office, 111 S. Church Ave., Tucson, 85701. Tel: 520-792-3410; Fax: 520-792-0291.

Rural Life Bureau—Mailing Address: Box 31, Tucson, 85702. Tel: 520-792-3410.

Council of Women Religious, Leadership Team & Office for Religious—Sr. RINA CAPPELLAZZO, O.P., 111 S. Church Ave., P.O. Box 31, Tucson, 85702. Tel: 520-792-3410; Fax: 520-792-0291. Email: srrc@diocesetucson.org.

St. Gianna Oratory—Mailing Address: P.O. Box 87350, Tucson, 85754-7350. Rev. RICHARD VON MENSHENGEN. Tel: 520-883-4360.

Korean Catholic Community—3820 N. Sabino Canyon Rd., Tucson, 85750. Mailing Address: P.O. Box 14257, Tucson, 85732-4257. Rev. JINU ANDREW TAE. Tel: 520-885-0512.

Victim Assistance Coordinator—PAUL N. DUCKRO, Ph.D. Tel: 520-792-3410. Email: pauld@diocesetucson.org.

Vocations—Revs. MICHAEL BUCCIARELLI; VILIULFO VALDERRAMA; Mrs. MARTY HAMMOND, Exec. Asst., 111 S. Church Ave., P.O. Box 31, Tucson, 85702. Tel: 520-838-2531; Fax: 520-838-2593. Email: vocations@diocesetucson.org.

**Catholic Commission*JIM DOBRY, Pres., 231 W. Smoot Dr., Tucson, 85705.

CLERGY, PARISHES, MISSIONS AND PAROCHIAL SCHOOLS

CITY OF TUCSON

(PIMA COUNTY)

1—SAINT AMBROSE ROMAN CATHOLIC PARISH - TUCSON (1946) Rev. John P. Arnold.
Res.: 300 S. Tucson Blvd., 85716. Tel: 520-622-6749; Fax: 520-882-3057. Email: stambrose@sa.tuccoxmail.com.
School—(Grades PreK-8) Tel: 520-882-8678; Fax: 520-671-4860. Email: principal@stambroseschool.com. Martha G. Taylor, Prin. Lay Teachers 15; Students 265.
Catechesis/Religious Program—Tel: 520-623-2925. Students 76.

2—SAINT AUGUSTINE CATHEDRAL ROMAN CATHOLIC PARISH - TUCSON (1863) Revs. Patrick Crino, Rector; Jens-Peter (Jay) Jensen, Parochial Vicar.
Res.: 192 S. Stone Ave., 85701. Tel: 520-623-6351; Fax: 520-623-0088. Email: staugustinecathedral@staugustine.tuccoxmail.com. Web: www.staugustinecathedral.com.
Catechesis/Religious Program—Miss Barbara Valenzuela, D.R.E. Tel: 520-624-8627. Students 250.
Oratory—San Cosme 460 W. Simpson, 85701.

3—BLESSED KATERI TEKAKWITHA ROMAN CATHOLIC MISSIONS PARISH - TUCSON (1984), (Native American), Revs. Abram E. Dono, S.T.; Ermeregildo Saldana-Taneco, S.T.; Seraphim Molina, S.T.
Office: 507 W. 29th St., 85713. Tel: 520-622-5363; Fax: 520-792-0230. Email: bl_kateri_tekakwitha@yahoo.com.
Res. & Rectory: 101 W. 31st St., 85713-3336. Tel: 520-791-7774.
Catechesis/Religious Program—Tel: 520-622-5363. Students 425.
Parish Center—
Mission—Blessed Kateri Tekakwitha Parish Center 507 W. 29th St., South Tucson, Pima Co. 85713. Tel: 520-622-3681.
Mission—San Martin 418 W. 39th St., Pima Co. 85713.
Mission—Santa Rosa 2015 N. Calle Central, Pima Co. 85705. Tel: 520-622-3514.
Mission—Cristo Rey 7500 S. Camino Benem, Pima Co. 85747.
San Juan Diego Center—7465 S. Camino Benem, 85757. Tel: 520-578-0423.
Mission—El Senor de los Milagros 3410 S. 16th Ave., Pima Co. 85713.
Mission—San Ignacio de Loyola 785 W. Sahuaro, Pima Co. 85705.
Mission—San Juan Bautista Yoem Pueblo 1322 Sandario Rd., Marana, Pima Co. 85238.

4—CORPUS CHRISTI ROMAN CATHOLIC PARISH - TUCSON (1999) Rev. Richard M. Kingsley.
Res.: 300 N.Tanque Verde Loop, 85748. Tel: 520-751-4235; Fax: 520-751-1304. Email: adionne@cccctucson.org. Web: www.cccctucson.org.
Catechesis/Religious Program—Email: pwilliams@cccctucson.org. Peggy Williams, Dir. Children's Ministry; Danielle Kennedy, Dir. Youth Ministry. Students 197.

5—SAINT CYRIL OF ALEXANDRIA ROMAN CATHOLIC PARISH - TUCSON (1948) Revs. Ronald A. Oakham, O.Carm.; Glenn Snow, O.Carm.; Edward S. Pietrucha, C.S.P. (Retired).
Mailing Address: 4725 E. Pima St., 85712. Tel: 520-795-1633; Fax: 520-795-1639. In Res., Rev. Ivan Marsh, O.Carm.
Res.: 1722 N. Mountain View Ave., 85712. Tel: 520-795-7640. Web: www.stcyril.com.
School—(Grades K-8) Tel: 520-881-4240; Fax: 520-795-0325. Mrs. Ann Zeches, Prin.; Mary Botsford, Librarian; Jan Ladd, Librarian. Lay Teachers 26; Students 387.
Catechesis/Religious Program—Students 165.

6—SAINT FRANCES CABRINI ROMAN CATHOLIC PARISH - TUCSON (1961) Rev. Msgr. Robert D. Fuller.
Res.: 3201 E. Presidio Rd., 85716. Tel: 520-326-7670; Fax: 520-881-8480. Email: cabrini1962@aol.com. Web: www.cabrini.hagermans.com.
Catechesis/Religious Program—Tel: 520-795-1110. Students 104.

7—SAINT FRANCIS DE SALES ROMAN CATHOLIC PARISH - TUCSON (1971) Revs. Robert G. Tamminga; William T.J. Shuppert; Deacons Dennis Scalpone; William Vigil; Donald Ferris; Charles "Andy" Corder; John R. Martin; Russell Kingery; Shawn French. In Res., Rev. Robert E. Carney.
Res.: 1375 S. Camino Seco, 85710. Tel: 520-885-5908; Fax: 520-885-3109. Email: officemgr@saintfrancisdesalestucson.org. Web: www.saintfrancisdesalestucson.org.
Catechesis/Religious Program—Marian Gilbert, D.R.E.; Maureen Kingery, D.R.E. Students 448.

8—HOLY FAMILY ROMAN CATHOLIC PARISH - TUCSON (1915) Rev. Alonzo M. Garcia; Deacon David Nehmer.
Res.: 338 W. University Blvd., 85705. Tel: 520-623-6773; Fax: 520-623-3578. Email: jackie@hfc.phxcoxmail.com. Web: www.holyfamilychurchtucson.org.
Catechesis/Religious Program—Students 96.

9—SAINT JOHN THE EVANGELIST ROMAN CATHOLIC PARISH - TUCSON (1934) Revs. Raul P. Trevizo; Robert A. Gonzales, Parochial Vicar; Deacons Jose Ojeda; Don Baker; Jose Duarte.
Res.: 602 W. Ajo Way, 85713. Tel: 520-624-7409; Fax: 520-740-1145.
Casa San Juan Migrant Center—Tel: 520-798-0834; Fax: 520-740-1145. Beth Ann Johnson, Dir. Volunteer.
School—(Grades K-8) Tel: 520-901-1975. Roseanne Villanueva, Prin. Lay Teachers 7; Students 135.
Catechesis/Religious Program—Mrs. Lydia Lopez, D.R.E. Students 540.

10—SAINT JOSEPH ROMAN CATHOLIC PARISH - TUCSON (1953) Revs. Remigio "Miguel" Mariano; Frederic F. Curry, Pastor Emeritus (Retired); Lester Niez, A.M., Parochial Vicar; Robert A. Rodriguez, Parochial Vicar; Deacons George Herrick, (Retired); Leon Mazza; Philip Garcia; Richard Grijalva; Teodoro Perez. In Res., Revs. Isaac A. Fynn; William (Guillo) Kohler, C.Ss.R.
Res.: 215 S. Craycroft Rd., 85711. Tel: 520-747-3100; Fax: 520-745-4606.
School—(Grades K-8) Tel: 520-747-3060; Fax: 520-747-2024. Mrs. Ellen S. Kwader-Murphy, Prin.; Mrs. Donna Betterson, Vice Prin. Lay Teachers 23; Students 305.
Catechesis/Religious Program—Dee Dee Gradillas, D.R.E. Students 308.

11—SAINT MARGARET MARY ALACOQUE ROMAN CATHOLIC PARISH - TUCSON (1951) [CEM] Revs. Philip Sullivan, O.C.D.; Cyprian Killackey, O.C.D., Parochial Vicar; Albert Bunsic, O.C.D.; Deacons Miguel Lopez; Carlos Gelabert, Office Mgr.; Bro. Mark Silva, O.C.D., Pastoral Intern. In Res., Rev. Kevin McArdle, O.C.D.
Res.: 801 N. Grande Ave., 85745. Tel: 520-622-0168; Fax: 520-882-8022.
Catechesis/Religious Program—Tel: 520-622-5982. Students 542.

12—SAINT MARK ROMAN CATHOLIC PARISH - TUCSON (1999) Revs. Liam Leahy; Gregory Okafor; Deacons Timothy Krieski; John Scott Pickett; Charles Rasmussen.
Mailing Address: P.O. Box 68650, 85742. 2727 W. Tangerine Rd., 85742. Tel: 520-469-7835; Fax: 520-219-6003. Email: stmark0799@gmail.com. Web: www.stmarktucson.org.
Catechesis/Religious Program—Students 292.

13—SAINT MONICA ROMAN CATHOLIC PARISH - TUCSON (1964) Revs. James M. Hobert; Adolfo Martinez; Deacons Tomas Morales, (Retired); Eugene Fernandez; Nicolas De La Torre.
Res.: 212 W. Medina, 85756. Tel: 520-294-2694; Fax: 520-295-0339. Email: stmonica5@aol.com.
Catechesis/Religious Program—Tel: 520-889-1994. Students 1,116.

14—MOST HOLY TRINITY ROMAN CATHOLIC PARISH - TUCSON (1975) Rev. William Remmel, S.D.S.
Res.: 1300 N. Greasewood Rd., 85745. Fax: 520-620-0977. Email: office@mhtparish.org. Web: www.mhtparish.org.
Catechesis/Religious Program—Tel: 520-884-9021. Email: maredith@mhtparish.org. Students 335.

15—SAINT ODILIA ROMAN CATHOLIC COMMUNITY - TUCSON (1965) Revs. Richard E. Troutman; Frank G. Cady, Parochial Vicar; Deacon George Scherf.
Res. & Mailing Address: 7570 Paseo del Norte, 85704. Tel: 520-297-7271; 520-297-7272 (Office); Fax: 520-297-8247. Email: sodilias@comcast.net. Web: www.st-odilia.org.
Catechesis/Religious Program—Teresa Bier, D.R.E.; Susanna Chapman, Youth Min. Students 170.

16—OUR LADY OF FATIMA ROMAN CATHOLIC PARISH - TUCSON (1972) Revs. Raymond Ratzenberger; Jose Manuel Padilla, Parochial Vicar; Deacons Frank S. Lundgren Jr., (Retired); Robert Negrette.
Mailing Address: 1950 W. Irvington Pl., 85746. Tel: 520-883-1717.
Res.: 5576 S. Monroe St., 85746. Tel: 520-295-1211; Fax: 520-883-2450.
Catechesis/Religious Program—Tel: 520-883-1717. Students 216.
Mission—*St. Mary of the Desert* 1950 W. Irvington Pl., Pima Co. 85746.

17—OUR LADY OF LAVANG ROMAN CATHOLIC PARISH - TUCSON (1999), (Vietnamese), Revs. Dominic Trung Nguyen, C.Ss.R.; Peter Mau Nguyen, C.Ss.R.
Res.: 800 S. Tucson Blvd., 85716. Tel: 520-882-3891; Fax: 520-903-2895.
Catechesis/Religious Program—

18—OUR LADY QUEEN OF ALL SAINTS ROMAN CATHOLIC PARISH - TUCSON (1987), (Hispanic), Rev. Gonzalo J. Villegas; Deacon Armando L. Valenzuela.
Res.: 2915 E. 36th St., 85713-4041. Tel: 520-622-8602; Fax: 520-622-4581.
Catechesis/Religious Program—Ramora Borboa, D.R.E. (English). Students 322.

19—OUR MOTHER OF SORROWS ROMAN CATHOLIC PARISH - TUCSON (1958) Rev. Msgr. Thomas Cahalane; Revs. Madhu George; Virgilio "Jojo" Tabo Jr.; Deacons Paul J. Welsh; George Rodriguez; Scott Thrall; Chuck Chajewski; Charles Whalen.
Res.: 1800 S. Kolb Rd., 85710. Tel: 520-747-1321; Fax: 520-790-3308. Email: omosparish@omosparish.org. Web: www.omosparish.org.
School—(Grades PreK-8) Tel: 520-747-1027; Fax: 520-747-0797. David Keller, Prin. Lay Teachers 30; Students 408.
Catechesis/Religious Program—Email: lstehle@omosparish.org. Laura Stehle, D.R.E. Students 466.

20—SAINTS PETER AND PAUL ROMAN CATHOLIC PARISH - TUCSON (1930) Revs. John P. Lyons; Ricky V. Ordonez. In Res., Rev. Msgr. Van A. Wagner (Retired); Revs. Albert I. Schifano; Joseph Pottemmel, M.S.F.S.
Res.: 1946 E. Lee St., 85719-4337. Tel: 520-327-6015; Fax: 520-318-3918.
School—(Grades K-8), 1436 N. Campbell Ave., 85719. Tel: 520-325-2431; Fax: 520-881-4690. Web: sspp.k12.az.us. Mrs. Jean McKenzie, Prin.; Kellye Seeger, Librarian/Asst. Principal. Sisters of St. Francis 1; Lay Teachers 26; Students 432.
Catechesis/Religious Program—Tel: 520-321-1892. Students 140.
Convent—1947 E. Adams St., 85719. Tel: 520-325-2234.

21—SAINT PIUS X ROMAN CATHOLIC PARISH - TUCSON (1969) Revs. Harry Ledwith; Gerry Miriani (Retired); Bill Dougherty (Retired); Deacon Dennis Ranke.
Res.: 1800 N. Camino Pio Decimo, 85715. Tel: 520-885-3573; Fax: 520-885-0945.
Catechesis/Religious Program—Deanne Lialios, D.R.E. Students 474.

22—ROMAN CATHOLIC CHURCH OF SAINT ELIZABETH ANN SETON - TUCSON (1980) Revs. Joseph A. Lombardo; Clement Agamba, Parochial Vicar; Deacons James L. Burns; Leo Longoria; Alfred Caponigro; Jose Zapata; Robert P. Carlin; Francis C. Sherlock; Rodney J. Kulpa. In Res., Rev. Msgr. Thomas J. Millane, Pastor Emeritus (Retired).
Res.: 8650 N. Shannon Rd., 85742. Tel: 520-297-7357; Fax: 520-797-8886. Email: church@seastucson.org. Web: www.seastucson.org.
School—(Grades PreK-8) Tel: 520-219-7650; Fax: 520-297-1033. Email: school@seastucson.org. Web: www.school.seastucson.org. Suzanne Shadonix, Prin. Lay Teachers 41; Students 497.
Catechesis/Religious Program—Tel: 520-219-7626. Julie Espinoza, D.R.E. Tel: 520-219-7637; Sr. Gladys Echenique, O.P., Dir. Hispanic & Multicultural Ministry. Tel: 520-219-7628. Students 708.

23—SACRED HEART ROMAN CATHOLIC PARISH - TUCSON (1942) Revs. James Geaney, O.Carm.; Raymond Corkery, O.Carm., Parochial Vicar.
Res.: 601 E. Fort Lowell Rd., 85705. Tel: 520-888-1530; Fax: 520-888-1227.
Catechesis/Religious Program—Tel: 520-888-1530, Ext. 123. Students 230.

24—SAN XAVIER MISSION ROMAN CATHOLIC PARISH - TUCSON (1692), (Native American), Revs. Stephen Barnufsky, O.F.M.; Edward Sarrazin, O.F.M.
Res.: 1950 W. San Xavier Rd., 85746. Tel: 520-294-2624; Fax: 520-294-3438. Email: sfxsteve@hughes.net. Web: www.sanxaviermission.org.
School—(Grades K-8), 1980 W. San Xavier Rd., 85746. Tel: 520-294-0628; Fax: 520-294-3465. Shirley Kalinowski, Prin. Sisters 3; Students 158.
Catechesis/Religious Program—Tel: 520-294-4639. Email: scriach@yahoo.com. Students 136.
Convent—1996 W. San Xavier Rd., 85746. Tel: 520-746-4779.

25—SANTA CATALINA ROMAN CATHOLIC PARISH - TUCSON (1981) Rev. Peter Connolly, C.Ss.R.; Deacons William Krueger; Nick Santiago.
14380 N. Oracle Rd., 85739. Tel: 520-825-9611; Fax: 520-825-9866. Email: office@santacatalinaparish.org. Web: santacatalinaparish.org.
Catechesis/Religious Program—Students 116.

26—SANTA CRUZ ROMAN CATHOLIC PARISH - TUCSON (1919)
Res.: 1220 S. 6th Ave., 85713. Tel: 520-623-3833; Fax: 520-903-2742. Web: www.santacruzparish.org.
School—(Grades PreK-8) Tel: 520-624-2093; Fax: 520-624-2833. Sr. Leonette Kochan, O.S.F., Prin. Lay Teachers 12; Students 180.
Catechesis/Religious Program—Tel: 520-882-9687. Students 275.
Mission—*Our Lady of Guadalupe Capilla* 401 E. 31st St., Pima Co. 85713.
Mission—*St. Anthony's Catholic Instruction Center and Capilla* 225 W. 34th St., Pima Co. 85713.

27—SAINT THOMAS MORE ROMAN CATHOLIC NEWMAN PARISH - TUCSON (1926) Revs. Bartholomew J. Hutcherson, O.P.; James J. Moore, O.P.
1615 E. 2nd St., 85719. Tel: 520-327-4665; Fax: 520-327-6559. Email: newman@uacatholic.org. Web: www.uacatholic.org. In Res., Revs. Robert A. Burns, O.P.; Bede Wilks, O.P. (Retired); Michael S. Fones, O.P. (Retired).
Catechesis/Religious Program—Tel: 520-327-6663. Students 50.

28—SAINT THOMAS THE APOSTLE ROMAN CATHOLIC PARISH - TUCSON (1984) Rev. Msgr. Todd O'Leary; Deacon Edward P. Sheffer.
Office: 5150 N. Valley View Rd., 85718. Tel: 520-577-8780; Fax: 520-577-0441. Email: sttomapostle@yahoo.com.
Res.: 5010 N. Valley View Rd., 85718.
School—Tel: 520-577-0503. Email: sthomaspreschool@gmail.com. Lay Teachers 13; Students 76.
Catechesis/Religious Program—Tel: 520-577-8782; Fax: 520-577-0441. Students 314.

OUTSIDE THE CITY OF TUCSON

AJO, PIMA CO., IMMACULATE CONCEPTION ROMAN CATHOLIC CHURCH - AJO (1916) Rev. Peter C. Nwachukwu.
Office: 101 Rocalla, P.O. Box 550, 85321. Tel: 520-387-7049; Fax: 520-413-5567. Email: iccajo@tabletoptelephone.com. Web: www.iccajo.com.
Catechesis/Religious Program—Students 30.

APACHE JUNCTION, PINAL CO., SAINT GEORGE ROMAN CATHOLIC PARISH - APACHE JUNCTION (1968) Revs. Domenico C. Pinti; Stanley J. Nadolny; Deacons George Heise; Bill Jones.
Res.: 300 E. 16th Ave., 85119. Tel: 480-982-2929; Fax: 480-982-0036. Email: stgeorgeaz@mchsi.com. Web: stgeorge-apachejunction.e-paluch.com.
Catechesis/Religious Program—Students 350.

BENSON, COCHISE CO., THE ROMAN CATHOLIC PARISH OF OUR LADY OF LOURDES - BENSON (1895) Rev. Michael Bucciarelli; Deacons Thomas Adams; Ronald Desmarais.
Mailing Address: 244 S. Gila, P.O. Box 2198, 85602. Tel: 520-586-3394; Fax: 520-586-3919. Email: olol@theriver.com. Web: www.ololparish.org.
Res.: 210 Eighth St., 85602. Tel: 520-586-2447.
Catechesis/Religious Program—Students 87.

BISBEE, COCHISE CO., SAINT PATRICK ROMAN CATHOLIC PARISH - BISBEE (1902) Rev. Godfrey Oparaekwe; Deacons Tony Underwood, Pastoral Admin.; Guillermo Lugo; Joseph L. Delgado; Robert J. Gonzales.
Res.: P.O. Box 164, 85603. Tel: 520-432-5753. Email: stpatricks@cableone.net.
Catechesis/Religious Program—Students 161.
Mission—*St. Michael* 2090 W. Martinez, Naco, Cochise Co. 85620.

CASA GRANDE, PINAL CO., SAINT ANTHONY OF PADUA ROMAN CATHOLIC PARISH - CASA GRANDE (1932) Revs. Kevin D. Clinch; Felix Rodriquez, Parochial Vicar; Deacons Patrick L. Dugan; Francisco Solano; Florentino Tarango.
Office: P.O. Box 12335, 85130. Tel: 520-836-0601; Fax: 520-836-2985. Email: office@stanthonycg.org. Web: www.stanthonycg.org.
Res.: 309 Paseo de Paula, 85122. Tel: 520-836-0602.
School—(Grades PreK-8) Tel: 520-836-7247; Fax: 520-836-7289. Email: sas_secretary@qwest.net. Web: www.stanthonypaduaschool.org. Mr. Joe Parzych III, Prin. Lay Teachers 7; Students 252.
Catechesis/Religious Program—Students 612.
Mission—*St. Mary Mission* 89 N. Yaqui Way, Stanfield, Pinal Co. 85272.

CLIFTON, GREENLEE CO., SACRED HEART ROMAN CATHOLIC CHURCH AND ST. MARY'S MISSION - CLIFTON (1899) Rev. Bardo Fabian Antunez-Olea, Admin.; Deacon Samuel Fullen.
Mailing Address: P.O. Box 938, 85533. Tel: 928-865-2285; Fax: 928-865-1228.
Res.: 329 Chase Creek, 85533. Tel: 928-865-2285; Fax: 928-865-1228.
Catechesis/Religious Program—*North Cornado Boulevard Parish Center*, Tel: 928-865-3497. Students 60.
Mission—*St. Mary* Third St., P.O. Box 938, Greenlee Co. 85533. Tel: 928-359-2343.

COOLIDGE, PINAL CO., SAINT JAMES ROMAN CATHOLIC PARISH - COOLIDGE (1947), (Hispanic), Rev. Marco A. Basulto-Pitol; Deacon Viviano Leon.
Parish Center—437 W. Wilson Ave., 85228. Tel: 520-723-3063; Fax: 520-723-5137.
Res.: 809 W. Sunset Dr., 85228. Tel: 520-723-3063; Fax: 520-723-5137.
Catechesis/Religious Program—Tel: 520-723-3063. Students 157.

DOUGLAS, COCHISE CO.

1—IMMACULATE CONCEPTION ROMAN CATHOLIC PARISH - DOUGLAS (1905) Revs. Gilbert Malu Musumbu; Luis A. Espinoza (Argentina), Pastoral Assoc.; James Baka (Nigeria), Pastoral Assoc.; Deacons

Mario Castillo; Joaquin Carrasco.
Mailing Address: P.O. Box 1176, 85607. Tel: 520-364-8494; Fax: 520-364-8495.
Res.: 928 C Ave., 85607. Tel: 520-364-8494.
Lestonnac Kindergarten and Day Care Center—Tel: 520-364-3956; Fax: 520-364-3956. Rosa Delia Quintana, Dir. Sisters of the Company of Mary 4; Lay Teachers 3; Students 40.
Catechesis/Religious Program—Students 234.
Convent—Sisters of the Company of Mary, Tel: 520-364-7658; Fax: 520-364-3645.

2—SAINT LUKE ROMAN CATHOLIC CHURCH - DOUGLAS (1950) Revs. Gilbert Malu Musumbu; James Baka (Nigeria); Luis A. Espinoza (Argentina); Deacons Armando Moulinet; Gabe Saspe; Tom Willis; Guadalupe Yanez; Ed Gomez; Raul Cantua.
Res.: 1211 15th St., 85607. Tel: 520-364-4411; Fax: 520-364-2397.
School—Loretto Central Catholic, 1200 14th St., 85607. Tel: 520-364-5754; Fax: 520-364-7707. Sr. Mary Aloysius, O.C.D., Prin. Sisters 5; Lay Teachers 14; Students 264.
Catechesis/Religious Program—Tel: 520-364-4852; Fax: 520-364-2397. Students 230.
Convent—Carmelite Sisters of the Most Sacred Heart of Los Angeles, Loretto Convent, Tel: 520-364-7571; Fax: 520-364-7844.

ELOY, PINAL CO., SAINT HELEN OF THE CROSS ROMAN CATHOLIC CHURCH - ELOY (1952) Rev. Juan Carlos Aguirre; Deacon Leonard C. Dexter.
205 W. 8th St., 85231. Tel: 520-466-7258; 520-466-3313 (Rectory); Fax: 520-466-0486. Email: office@sthelenchurch.com. Web: www.sthelenchurch.com.
Catechesis/Religious Program—Tel: 520-466-9422. Students 168.

FLORENCE, PINAL CO., ASSUMPTION OF THE BLESSED VIRGIN MARY ROMAN CATHOLIC PARISH - FLORENCE (1870) Rev. Charles W. Cloud.
Res.: 177 E. 8th St., P.O. Box 2550, 85232. Tel: 520-868-5940; Fax: 520-868-0413. Web: www.assumptionbvm.onecause.com.
Catechesis/Religious Program—Tel: 520-868-3075. Students 162.
Convent—Chapel of the Gila, (Historical Site), 255 E. 8th St., P.O. Box 2550, 85232-0550.

GLOBE, GILA CO., HOLY ANGELS ROMAN CATHOLIC CHURCH - GLOBE (1905) Rev. Raul "Rudy" H. Rosales; Deacons Frank Castillo; Richard Le Mieux; Kennard G. Brusoe Jr.
Office: 201 S. Broad St., 85501. Tel: 928-425-3137; Fax: 928-425-3136. Email: ha-pastor@cableone.net. Web: www.holyangelscatholiccommunity.org.
Res.: 1312 Mesquite, 85501.
School—(Grades PreK-8), 1300 E. Cedar St., 85501. Tel: 928-425-5703; Fax: 928-425-5704. Rebecca Grant, Prin. & Admin. Presentation Sisters 3; Lay Teachers 8; Students 190.
Catechesis/Religious Program—Students 71.
Convent—Tel: 928-425-2034.

GREEN VALLEY, PIMA CO., OUR LADY OF THE VALLEY ROMAN CATHOLIC PARISH - GREEN VALLEY (1970) Rev. Francisco Maldonado; Deacons Rudy Noriega; Charles Pennington.
Res.: 505 N. La Canada Dr., 85614. Tel: 520-625-4536; Fax: 520-625-1084. Email: olvbusmgr@qwestoffice.net. Web: www.olvgvpima.org.
Catechesis/Religious Program— 85614. Tel: 520-625-4536. Students 200.

HAYDEN, GILA CO., SAINT JOSEPH ROMAN CATHOLIC PARISH - HAYDEN (1913) Rev. Dale A. Branson.
Res.: 300 Mountain View Dr., P.O. Box C, 85135-1007. Tel: 520-356-7223; Fax: 520-356-7376. Email: stjoeshayden@coppernet.net.
Catechesis/Religious Program—Tel: 520-356-7223. Students 18.

KEARNY, PINAL CO., INFANT JESUS OF PRAGUE ROMAN CATHOLIC PARISH - KEARNY (1961) Rev. James Aboyi, V.C. (Nigeria), Admin.
Res.: 501 Victoria Cir., P.O. Box 459, 85237. Tel: 520-363-7205; Fax: 520-363-7179. Email: ijpkearny@coppernet.net.
Catechesis/Religious Program—Tel: 520-363-7428. Students 75.

MAMMOTH, PINAL CO., BLESSED SACRAMENT ROMAN CATHOLIC PARISH - MAMMOTH (1970), (Hispanic), Rev. Walter Balduck, O.F.M.Cap., Admin.
Res.: 122 W. Church Dr., P.O. Box 220, 85618-0220. Tel: 520-487-2451; Fax: 520-487-0335.
Catechesis/Religious Program—Students 126.

MARANA, PIMA CO., SAINT CHRISTOPHER ROMAN CATHOLIC PARISH - MARANA (1954) Rev. Abran R. Tadeo.
Res.: 12101 W. Moore Rd., 85653. Tel: 520-682-3035; Fax: 520-682-4044. Email: stchristopher@comcast.net.
Catechesis/Religious Program—Students 65.

MARICOPA, PINAL CO., OUR LADY OF GRACE ROMAN CATHOLIC PARISH - MARICOPA (2007) Revs. Marcos Velasquez; Tersur Melchizedek Akpan, V.C.
P.O. Box 368, 85139-1801. Tel: 520-568-4605; Fax: 520-568-0861. Web: www.ourladygracechurch.org.
Catechesis/Religious Program—Priscilla Santi, D.R.E.

MIAMI, GILA CO., OUR LADY OF THE BLESSED SACRAMENT ROMAN CATHOLIC CHURCH - MIAMI (1915) Revs. Jay R. Luczak; Matthew Williams.
Res.: 844 W. Sullivan St., 85539. Tel: 928-473-3568.
Catechesis/Religious Program—Students 225.
Mission—St. Joseph 5678 Pineway St., Claypool, Gila Co. 85532.
Mission—St. Theresa Roosevelt Lake, Gila Co.

MORENCI, GREENLEE CO., HOLY CROSS ROMAN CATHOLIC CHURCH - MORENCI (1913) Rev. Bardo Fabian Antunez-Olea, Admin.
Res. & Mailing Address: 205 Fairbanks Rd., 85540. Tel: 928-865-3183; Fax: 928-865-1228. Email: hlycross@vtc.net.
Catechesis/Religious Program—Students 300.

NOGALES, SANTA CRUZ CO.

1—SACRED HEART OF JESUS ROMAN CATHOLIC PARISH - NOGALES (1897) Revs. Martin S. Martinez; Gustavo Benitez, Parochial Vicar.
Res.: P.O. Box 968, 85628. Tel: 520-287-9221; Fax: 520-287-9224.
School—(Grades K-8), 207 W. Oak St., 85621. Tel: 520-287-2223; Fax: 520-287-3373. Marlo Lopez, Librarian.
Catechesis/Religious Program—272 N. Rodriguez St., 85621. Tel: 520-397-0963; Fax: 520-397-0909. Students 324.

2—SAN FELIPE DE JESUS ROMAN CATHOLIC PARISH - NOGALES (1987) Revs. Viliulfo Valderrama; Abraham Guerrero, Parochial Vicar.
Mailing Address: P.O. Box 6600, 85628.
Res.: 444 Camino Dona Cydney, 85621. Tel: 520-281-1961.
Church: 1901 N. Jose Gallego Dr., #1, 85628. Tel: 520-761-3100; Fax: 520-281-4380. Email: sanfelipedejesusparish@hotmail.com. Web: www.sanfelipedejesusparish.org.
Catechesis/Religious Program—Students 690.

ORACLE, PINA CO., ST. HELEN (1927) Rev. Msgr. Ambrose O. Nwohu.
Mailing Address: HCR 01, Box 2000, 85623. Tel: 520-896-2708; Fax: 520-896-2631. Email: sthelensmissions@msn.com. Web: www.sthelensmission.com.
Catechesis/Religious Program—Students 51.

PARKER, LA PAZ CO., SACRED HEART ROMAN CATHOLIC PARISH - PARKER (1950) Rev. Manuel Fragoso Carranza; Deacon Leonel Bejarano; Ann Strawderman, Business Mgr.
Res.: 1101 Joshua Ave., 85344. Tel: 928-669-2502; Fax: 928-669-8196.
Catechesis/Religious Program—Students 98.
Mission—Kateri Tekakwitha Indian Mission Poston.
Mission—St. John the Baptist Wenden.
Mission—Queen of Peace Quartzsite.

PATAGONIA, SANTA CRUZ CO., SAINT THERESE OF LISIEUX ROMAN CATHOLIC PARISH - PATAGONIA (1955) Rev. Jose Maria A. Corvera (Philippines), Pastoral Admin.
Res.: Box 435, 85624. Tel: 520-394-2954; Fax: 520-394-2831. Email: sttheresa@dakotacom.net.
Catechesis/Religious Program—Tel: 520-394-0068. Students 15.
Mission—Our Lady of Angels Renzi Residence, Sonoita, Santa Cruz Co. 85637.

PAYSON, GILA CO., SAINT PHILIP THE APOSTLE ROMAN CATHOLIC CHURCH - PAYSON (1957) Rev. William Louis Gyure; Deacons Jesus Castillo; Ed Burgin; Tom Fox.
Res.: 511 S. St. Philip St., 85541-5144. Tel: 928-474-2392; Fax: 928-474-9661. Email: fatherbill@stphilippayson.org. Web: www.stphilippayson.org.
Catechesis/Religious Program—Tel: 928-474-1269. Judy Carroll, D.R.E. Students 100.
Mission—St. Benedict Mission 98 N. Winchester Dr., Young, Gila Co. 85554. Tel: 928-462-3871.
Mission—Tonto Basin/Punkin Center Rattlesnake Ln. & Hwy. 188, Tonto Basin, 85553.

PIRTLEVILLE, COCHISE CO., SAINT BERNARD ROMAN CATHOLIC CHURCH - PIRTLEVILLE (1914) Revs. Gilbert Malu Musumbu; Luis A. Espinoza (Argentina); James Baka (Nigeria).
Res.: 2308 N. McKinley, P.O. Box 3101, 85626. Tel: 520-364-2762; Fax: 520-364-2520.
Catechesis/Religious Program—340 Grace Ave., 85626. Tel: 520-364-5994. Students 102.
Chapel—Double Adobe, Our Lady of La Salette 3879 W. Mission Ln., Double Adobe, 85617.
Chapel—Douglas, Sacred Heart 300 17th St., Douglas, 85607.

RIO RICO, SANTA CRUZ CO., MOST HOLY NATIVITY OF OUR LORD JESUS CHRIST ROMAN CATHOLIC PARISH - RIO RICO (1987) Rev. Francisco Maldonado; Sr. Guadalupe Jurado, O.P., Pastoral Admin.
Mailing Address: P.O. Box 4024, 85648.
Res.: 395 Avenida Coatimundi, 85648. Tel: 520-281-7414; Fax: 520-281-1713. Email: mostholynativity@yahoo.com.
Catechesis/Religious Program—Javier Fierro, D.R.E. Students 107.

SAFFORD, GRAHAM CO., SAINT ROSE OF LIMA ROMAN CATHOLIC PARISH - SAFFORD (1937) Revs. Ariel G. Lustan; Thomas T. Dekaa, Parochial Vicar; Deacons Marcello Arbizo, (Retired); Carlos Vessels.
Res.: 311 Central Ave., 85546. Tel: 928-428-4920; Fax: 928-428-4922. Email: saintros@saintroselima-safford.com. Web: www.saintroselima-safford.com.
Catechesis/Religious Program—Tel: 928-348-4785. Students 455.
Mission—Pima Mission 28 S. Main, Pima, Graham Co. 85543.
Mission—Newman Center 528 4th St., Thatcher, Graham Co. 85552. Tel: 928-348-7539.

SAHUARITA, PIMA CO., ROMAN CATHOLIC PARISH OF SAN MARTIN DE PORRES - SAHUARITA (2002) Rev. Michael Shay, S.D.S.
Mailing Address: P.O. Box 65, 85629. Tel: 520-625-1154; Fax: 520-399-4480. Email: smdp@hughes.net.
Catechesis/Religious Program—Students 280.

SAN CARLOS, GILA CO., SAN CARLOS APACHE ROMAN CATHOLIC COMMUNITY - SAN CARLOS (1918), (Native American), Rev. Gino L. Piccoli, O.F.M.
Res.: 460 San Carlos Ave., P.O. Box 28, 85550. Tel: 928-475-2210. Email: fathergino@theriver.com.
School—(Grades K-6), P.O. Box 339, 85550. Tel: 928-475-2449; Fax: 928-475-2050. Email: stcharlessc@theriver.com. Web: www.stcharlesindianschool.com. Anna Dillon, Librarian. Sisters of Mercy 2; Students 123.
Catechesis/Religious Program—Students 15.
Convent—St. Charles, P.O. Box 338, 85550. Tel: 928-475-2460.
Mission—Blessed Kateri Tekakwitha Bylas, 85530.

SAN LUIS, YUMA CO., SAINT JUDE THADDEUS ROMAN CATHOLIC PARISH - SAN LUIS (1982) Revs. Raul Valencia Garcia; Jesus Alejandro Perez-Barrera; Deacon Jose Manuel Lopez.
984 N. Main St., P.O. Box 2888, 85349. Tel: 928-627-8011; Fax: 928-627-3916. Email: slaz_stjudastadeo_church@netzero.net.
Catechesis/Religious Program—Students 505.

SAN MANUEL, PINAL CO., SAINT BARTHOLOMEW ROMAN CATHOLIC PARISH - SAN MANUEL (1954) Rev. Msgr. Ambrose O. Nwohu; Rev. Sebastine Bula, V.C.
Res.: 609 Park Pl., Box 607, 85631. Tel: 520-385-4156; Fax: 520-385-4742. Email: stbarths@worldlinkisp.com. Web: www.stbartsparish.net.
Catechesis/Religious Program—Students 155.
Mission—St. Helen HCR 1, Box 2000, Oracle, Pinal Co. 85623. Tel: 520-896-2708; Fax: 520-896-2631. Email: sthelensmission@msn.com. Web: www.sthelensmission.com.

SIERRA VISTA, COCHISE CO.

1—SAINT ANDREW THE APOSTLE ROMAN CATHOLIC PARISH - SIERRA VISTA (1958) Revs. Gregory P. Adolf; German Bartolome Vasquez Johnston; Deacons George Gaun; Michael Milazzo; Joseph Kushner III.
Res.: 800 Taylor Dr., N.W., 85635. Tel: 520-458-2925; Fax: 520-452-0235. Email: office@standrewsv.org. Web: www.standrewsv.org.
Catechesis/Religious Program—Email: christine@standrewsv.org. Students 410.
Mission—Good Shepherd Whetstone, Cochise Co.

2—OUR LADY OF THE MOUNTAINS ROMAN CATHOLIC PARISH - SIERRA VISTA (1991) Rev. Robert Brazaskas; Deacons William Merritt; James Schaff; Gene Tackett; Jim Hill; Jim Burke; Reynaldo Romo.
1425 Yaqui St., 85650. Tel: 520-378-2720; Fax: 520-378-6825. Email: olmprincipal@ourladymtns.org. Web: www.olmaz.org.
School—
Catechesis/Religious Program—Tel: 520-378-2733. Students 69.

SOLOMON, GRAHAM CO., OUR LADY OF GUADALUPE ROMAN CATHOLIC PARISH - SOLOMON (1891) [CEM] Rev. John J. Ancharski.
Res.: P.O. Box 147, 85551. Tel: 928-428-0149.
Catechesis/Religious Program—Students 24.
Mission—San Jose San Jose, Graham Co.

SOMERTON, YUMA CO., IMMACULATE HEART OF MARY ROMAN CATHOLIC PARISH - SOMERTON (1954) Revs. Javier H. Perez; Jesus Acuna-Delgado.
310 W. Spring St., P.O. Box 597, 85350.
Res.: 324 W. Spring St., P.O. Box 597, 85350. Tel: 928-627-2918; Fax: 928-722-5962. Email: perezjavier@q.com.
Catechesis/Religious Program—Tel: 928-722-0004. Sr. Celia DeLeon, D.R.E. Students 489.

SUNSITES, COCHISE CO., SAINT JUDE THADDEUS ROMAN CATHOLIC PARISH - PEARCE SUNSITES (1983) Rev. Martin Atanga Baabuge.
Res.: P.O. Box 328, Pearce, 85625.
Church: 970 N. Hwy. 191, Mile Post 50, Cochise, 85606. Tel: 520-826-3869; Fax: 520-826-3869. Email: stjude@vtc.net.

Catechesis/Religious Program—Students 44.
Mission—St. Francis of Assisi Elfrida. *c/o St. Jude*, P.O. Box 328, Pearce, Cochise Co. 85625.

SUPERIOR, PINAL CO., SAINT FRANCIS OF ASSISI ROMAN CATHOLIC PARISH - SUPERIOR (1930) Rev. Mark J. Long, Admin.; Deacon Willard Kornovich.
Res.: 11 Church Ave., 85273. Tel: 520-689-2250; Fax: 520-689-5810.
Catechesis/Religious Program—St. Mary's Center, 100 Sunset Dr., 85273. Tel: 520-689-2116. Students 115.

TOMBSTONE, COCHISE CO., SACRED HEART OF JESUS ROMAN CATHOLIC PARISH - TOMBSTONE (1880) Rev. Sylvester N. Nwaogu, Admin.
Office: 592 E. Safford St., P.O. Box 547, 85638. Tel: 520-457-3364; Fax: 520-457-0017. Web: www.tombstone1880.com/sh.
Res.: 596 E. Safford St., P.O. Box 547, 85638. Tel: 520-457-3439.
Catechesis/Religious Program—Students 16.

TOPAWA, PIMA CO., SAN SOLANO MISSIONS ROMAN CATHOLIC PARISH - TOPAWA (1908), (Native American), (For office and sacramental records pertaining to Tohono O'odham Indians and mission churches on the reservation, please refer to San Solano Missions at the P.O. Box 210, Topawa, AZ, 85639 address). Friars Ponchie Vasquez, O.F.M.; David Paz, O.F.M., Guardian; Hajime Okuhara, O.F.M.; Chris Best, O.F.M.; Martin Sanabria, O.F.M.; Rev. Ignatius DeGroot, O.F.M.; Deacon Alfred M. Gonzales.
Mailing Address: P.O. Box 210, 85639. Tel: 520-383-2350; Fax: 520-383-3063. Email: ssmissions@toua.net.
Catechesis/Religious Program—San Solano Pastoral Center, P.O. Box 209, 85639. Tel: 520-383-2400.

TUBAC, SANTA CRUZ CO., SAINT ANN'S ROMAN CATHOLIC PARISH AND MISSIONS - TUBAC (1987) Rev. Alexander M. Mills.
Mailing Address: 2231 E. Frontage Rd., P.O. Box 2911, 85646-2911. Tel: 520-398-2646; Fax: 520-398-3036. Email: stannschurch@qwestoffice.net.
Catechesis/Religious Program—Students 22.
Mission—Assumption Chapel Amado, Santa Cruz Co.
Mission—St. Ferdinand Arivaca, Pima Co. 85646.

VAIL, PIMA CO., SAINT RITA IN THE DESERT ROMAN CATHOLIC PARISH - VAIL (1937) Rev. John F. Allt; Deacons Kenneth Hilliard; Efren Medrano.
Res.: 13260 E. Colossal Cave Rd., 85641. Fax: 520-762-5967. Email: strita400@aol.com. Web: www.stritainthedesert.org.
Catechesis/Religious Program—Tel: 520-762-9688. Students 218.

WELLTON, YUMA CO., SAINT JOSEPH THE WORKER ROMAN CATHOLIC PARISH - WELLTON Rev. Tomas G. Munoz, Admin.
Mailing Address: P.O. Box 157, 85356. Tel: 928-785-4275; Fax: 928-785-8706. Email: stjosephwellton@gmail.com.
Res.: 8674 S. Ave. 36 E., 85356.
Catechesis/Religious Program—Lisa Vouaux-Marlatt, D.R.E. Students 28.

WILLCOX, COCHISE CO., SACRED HEART OF JESUS ROMAN CATHOLIC CHURCH - WILLCOX (1936) Rev. Mark J. Stein.
Res.: 215 W. Maley St., 85643. Tel: 520-384-3432; Fax: 520-384-3573.
Catechesis/Religious Program—Students 99.
Mission—Our Lady of Perpetual Help San Simon, 85605.
Mission—Our Lady of Guadalupe Bowie, 85605.

YUMA, YUMA CO.

1—SAINT FRANCIS OF ASSISI ROMAN CATHOLIC PARISH - YUMA (1948) Revs. Christopher M. Orndorff II; Emilio Landeros Chapa; Deacons Paul Muthart; Gary Pasquinelli; Rick Hernandez; Rafael Vidal; Arnulfo Carbajal; Don Larson, (Retired); Jose Valadez; George Fischbach.
Res.: 1815 S. 8th Ave., 85364. Tel: 928-782-1875; Fax: 928-329-9479. Email: admin@stfrancisyuma.com. Web: www.stfrancisyuma.com.
School—(Grades K-8), 700 18th St., 85364. Tel: 928-782-1539; Fax: 928-782-0430. Susan Bostie, Prin.; Mary Slatcz, Librarian. Lay Teachers 13; Students 241.
Catechesis/Religious Program—Tel: 928-783-7461. Sr. Nancy Perez, D.R.E. Students 516.

2—IMMACULATE CONCEPTION ROMAN CATHOLIC PARISH & GUADALUPE MISSION - YUMA (1866) [JC] Rev. Msgr. Richard W. O'Keeffe; Revs. Eduardo Lopez; Richard Kusugh; Edward F. Lucero; Deacons Mark Nixen; David Sampson; Daniel L. Mulloy; Oscar F. Chavez; Antonio Gomez.
Res.: 509 S. Ave. B, 85364. Tel: 928-782-7516; Fax: 928-343-0172. Email: icchurchyumaaz@roadrunner.com.
School—(Grades K-8), 501 S. Ave. B, 85364. Tel: 928-783-5225. Email: icyuma@juno.com. Lydia A. Mendoza, Prin.; Denise Salgado, Librarian. Franciscan Sisters of Christian Charity 4; Lay Teachers 14; Students 240.
Catechesis/Religious Program—Tel: 928-783-1324. Deacon Mark Nixen, D.R.E.; Lourdes Cabrera, D.R.E. (Spanish Coord.). Students 822.
Mission—Our Lady of Guadalupe 417 15th Ave., Yuma Co. 85364. Tel: 928-376-6707.
Convent—500 24th Ave., 85364. Tel: 928-783-5224. Franciscan Sisters of Christian Charity 7.

3—SAINT JOHN NEUMANN ROMAN CATHOLIC CHURCH - YUMA (1986) Rev. John F. Friel; Deacon Rick Douglas.
Res.: 11545 E. 40th St., 85367. Tel: 928-342-3544; Fax: 928-342-7513. Email: admin@sjnyuma.com. Web: www.sjnyuma.com.
Catechesis/Religious Program—Students 134.

Chaplains of Public Institutions

TUCSON. *Arizona State Prison*, 10000 S. Wilmot Rd., 85777. Rev. Phong Bui.
Detention Ministry, P.O. Box 31, 85702. Tel: 520-792-3410, Ext. 131. Ms. Barbara Mattus, M.A., Dir.
Arizona Western College, 11750 S. Mesa Dr., 85365. Tel: 520-342-3544. Attended from St. John Neumann Parish, Yuma.
Christ the King Chapel, 355 WG/HC, Davis Monthan Air Force Base, 85707. Tel: 520-228-5411. Rev. Msgr. John J. Cusack, Revs. Timothy Butler, Michael Martinez, Chap.
St. Joseph's Hospital, 350 N. Wilmot Rd., 85732. Tel: 520-296-3211. Rev. Isaac A. Fynn.
Kino Community Hospital, 1220 S. Sixth, 85707. Tel: 520-623-3833.
2800 E. Ajo Way, 85713. Vacant.
St. Mary's Hospital, 1601 W. St. Mary's Rd., 85745. Tel: 520-622-5883. Rev. Joseph Saba.
Metropolitan Correctional Complex, 8901 S. Wilmot Rd., 85706. Tel: 520-741-3118.
Detention Ministry, P.O. Box 31, 85702. Tel: 520-792-3410, Ext. 131. Ms. Barbara Mattus, M.A., Dir.
Tucson Medical Center, 5301 E. Grant Rd., 85712. Rev. William (Guillo) Kohler, C.Ss.R., Chap. Tel: 520-324-1290; Fax: 520-324-1702.
U.S. Veterans Hospital, S. Sixth Ave., 85713. Tel: 520-792-1450. Rev. David H. Reinders.
Villa Maria Chapel, 4310 E. Grant Rd., 85712. Tel: 520-323-9351. Sr. Dorothy Ann Lesher, C.S.J., Dir. Pastoral Care.

CATALINA. *Catalina Juvenile Detention Center, Catalina Juvenile Detention Center*, 14500 N. Oracle Rd., 85713. Tel: 520-818-3484. Attended from Santa Catalina Mission.

FLORENCE. *Arizona State Prison, St. Dismas Chapel*, P.O. Box 550, 85232. Tel: 520-868-5940. Vacant.

FORT HUCHUCA. *Fort Huchuca Army Post* 85613. Rev. Krzysztof Kopec, Major.

SAFFORD. *Arizona State Prison* 85546. Tel: 928-428-4698.
Federal Correction Institute 85546. Tel: 928-428-6600. Vacant.

YUMA. *MCAS Chapel*, Marine Corps Air Station, 85369. Tel: 928-269-2371. Rev. James F. Finley, Chap.
Yuma Regional Medical Center, 1815 8th Ave., 85364. Tel: 928-782-1875. Attended from St. Francis of Assisi.

Special Assignment:
Rev. Msgr.—
O'Keeffe, Richard W., E.V., Episcopal Vicar
Revs.—
Lyons, John P., J.C.L., Adjutant Judicial Vicar
Schifano, Albert I., V.G., M.C., Moderator Curia & Vicar Gen.
Trevizo, Raul P., V.G., Vicar Gen. & Vicar Hispanic Affairs, P.O. Box 31, 85702. Tel: 520-792-3410

On Duty Outside the Diocese:
Rev.—
McCarthy, Jeremiah J., Rector, St. Patrick's Seminary, 320 Middlefield Rd., Menlo Park, CA 90524-3956.

Administrative Leave of Absence:
Revs.—
Cocio, Carlos
Guillen, Juan
Manzo, Fernando L.
Martinez, Felipe Antonio
Sanz, Julian
Stencil, Steven G.
Taylor, Daniel
Underwood, Gary E.

Leave of Absence:
Revs.—
Ancharski, John J.
Bradley, Michael
Cazares Haro, Salvador A.
Noriega, Arnoldo
Thuerauf, Jeffrey P.

Retired - Administrative Leave:
Rev. Msgrs.—
Coleman, James G. (HRT)
Oliver, John A.
Rosensweig, Walter F.
Rev.—
Hyman, Robert A.

Retired:
Rev. Msgrs.—
Brynda, Gerald J., 1724 Minnewawa, #53, Clovis, CA 93612.
Carrillo, Arsenio S., V.G., 9281 E. Summer Tr., 85749.
Carscallen, Edward C., 316 Via del Heroe, Green Valley, 85614.
Oliver, John A., 1020 W. 1st St., 85364.
Rosensweig, Walter F., 800 E. Baffert Dr., # 31, Nogales, 85621.
Wagner, Van A., V.G., 1946 E. Lee St., 85719.
Revs.—
Bryerton, Robert R., P.O. Box 1272, Hereford, 85615.
Chavez, Luis N., San Luis Potori, Mexico.
Cote, Gerald M., 5715 W. Box R St., 85713.
Curry, Frederic F., 870 Natachee, 85710.
Emanuel, John, 1230 Encintas Point, Colorado Springs, CO 80906.
Fahey, John M., 2701-3 Star Trails Dr., 85742.
Gagnon, Ronald P., 2727 W. Star Trails Dr., #1, 85742.
Gameros, Ignacio L., 20719 Flora View Ct., Spring, TX 77379.
Hyman, Robert A., 2240 E. Monte Vista Dr., 85719.
Knapp, Charles, 4675 S. Harrison #34, 85730.
Krause, Joseph A., 4800 S. Alma Schools Rd., #1026, Chandler, 85244.
Noriega, Arnoldo, 413 7th St., Douglas, 85607.
Padilla, Glibert, 1948 E. 5th St., 85716.
Pietrucha, Edward S., C.S.P., 6855 E. Dorado Blvd., 85715.
Ruiz, Antonio A., 7727 E. Black Crest Pl., 85750.
Sherry, Bryan W., J.C.L., 321 Washington Ave., Florence, 85232.

Permanent Deacons:
Ackerley, John K., St. Augustine Cathedral, Tucson
Adams, Thomas, Our Lady of Lourdes, Benson
Aguirre-Lopez, Felix Mario
Anderson, Elvon "Andy", St. George, Apache Junction
Arbizo, Marcello A., St. Rose of Lima, Safford
Baker, Don, St. John the Evangelist, Tucson
Bogushefsky, Joseph, St. Christopher Parish, Marana
Borquez, Henry S., (Retired)
Bracamonte, Gilbert, (Inactive)
Brusoe, Kennard G., Jr., Holy Angels Parish, Globe
Bueno, Oscar L., St. Augustine's, Tucson
Burgin, Edwin, St. Philip the Apostle, Payson
Burke, James, Our Lady of the Mountains, Sierra Vista
Burns, James, St. Elizabeth Ann Seton, Tucson
Callie, Albert, St. Joseph, Tucson
Campbell, Thomas, St. Peter & Paul Parish, Tucson
Cantua, Raul, St. Luke, Douglas
Caponigro, Alfred E., St. Elizabeth Ann Seton
Carbajal, Arnulfo, St. Francis of Assisi, Yuma
Carlin, Robert P., St. Elizabeth Ann Seton, Tucson
Carmona, Salvador, St. Augustine Cathedral, Tucson
Carrasco, Joaquin, Immaculate Conception, Douglas
Castillo, Frank R., Holy Angels, Globe
Castillo, Jesus, St. Philip the Apostle, Payson
Castillo, V. Mario, St. Luke, Douglas
Chajewski, Charles, Our Mother of Sorrows Parish, Tucson
Chavez, Oscar F., Immaculate Conception Parish, Yuma
Collura, Frank J., St. Francis de Sales, Tucson
Converse, Paul E., (Retired)
Corder, Charles "Andy", St. Francis de Sales Parish, Tucson
Crockette, Alvin, St. Francis de Sales, Tucson
De La Torre, Nicolas, St. Monica, Tucson
Delgado, Joseph, St. Patrick, Bisbee
Desmarais, Ronald, Our Lady of Lourdes, Benson
Dexter, Leonard C., St. Helen of the Cross, Eloy
Douglas, Rick, St. Francis of Assisi Parish, Yuma
Duarte, Carlos V., (Retired)
Duarte, Jose, St. John the Evangelist, Tucson
Dugan, Patrick, St. Anthony of Padua, Casa Grande
Fernandez, Eugene, St. Monica, Tucson
Ferris, Donald, St. Francis de Sales, Tucson
Fischbach, George, St. Francis of Assisi, Yuma
Fisher, Donald, St. Monica, Tucson

Flam, Richard, Corpus Christi, Tucson
Fox, Tom, St. Phillip the Apostle, Payson
French, Sean, St. Francis de Sales Parish, Tucson
Fugit, James, St. Thomas the Apostle Parish, Tucson
Fullen, Samuel, Holy Cross, Morenci
Gallegos, Charles A., St. Ann's Parish, Tubac
Gamboa, Henry W., San Xavier, Tucson
Garcia, John A., (Inactive)
Garcia, Marcario, Immaculate Heart of Mary, Somerton
Garcia, Philip, (Retired), St. Joseph, Tucson
Gaun, George, St. Andrew the Apostle, Sierra Vista
Gelabert, Carlos G., St. Margaret, Tucson
Geonnotti, Anthony, Jr., Our Lady of Fatima, Tucson
Gersitz, James M., Diocese of Phoenix
Glowdowski, Robert
Gomez, Antonio, Immaculate Conception, Yuma
Gomez, Edward, St. Luke Parish, Douglas
Gonzales, Alfred M., San Solano Missions, Sells
Gonzales, Jose U., (Out of Diocese)
Gonzales, Luciano, Jr., Immaculate Conception, Douglas
Gonzales, Robert J., St. Patrick, Bisbee & St. Michael Mission, Naco
Gonzalez, Richard A., (Inactive)
Grijalva, Richard, St. Joseph, Tucson
Grimaldo, Pedro, Our Lady of the Valley, Green Valley
Heise, George, St. George Parish, Apache Junction
Hernandez, Nieves J., Office of Catholic Chaplain, Yuma
Hernandez, Richard R., St. Francis of Assisi, Yuma
Herrick, George R., (Retired)
Hill, James, Our Lady of the Mountains, Sierra Vista
Hilliard, Kenneth, St. Rita in the Desert Parish, Vail
Hintze, Craig, (Inactive)
Hoerr, Michael "Danny", St. Joseph Parish, Hayden
Johnson, Ward, (Retired)
Kingery, Russell, St. Thomas the Apostle, Tucson
Kinnery, William J., (Retired)
Kornovich, William, St. Francis, Superior
Krieski, Timothy, St. Mark the Evangelist, Tucson
Krikawa, Joseph, Most Holy Trinity, Tucson
Krueger, William, Santa Catalina, Tucson
Kuebler, Myron, San Martin de Porres, Sahuarita
Kulpa, Rodney J., St. Elizabeth Ann Seton Parish, Tucson
Kushner, Joseph, III, St. Andrew the Apostle, Tucson
Lambert, Frank, (Retired)
Larson, Donald L., (Retired), St. Francis of Assisi Parish, Yuma
LaSalle, James F., (Retired), St. Thomas More Newman Center, Tucson
Leinfelder, Carl, Holy Family, Tucson
LeMieux, Richard, Holy Angels, Globe
Leon, Victor, (Out of Diocese)
Leon, Viviano, St. James, Coolidge
Long, James, Our Lady of Fatima, Tucson
Longoria, Leopoldo "Leo", St. Elizabeth Ann Seton, Tucson
Lopez, Jose, St. Jude Thaddeus Mission, San Luis
Lopez, Miguel, St. Margaret Mary, Tucson
Lugo, Guillermo A. (Bill), St. Patrick's, Bisbee
Lundgren, Frank S., Jr., Our Lady of Fatima, Tucson
Magallanes, Oscar, (Out of Diocese)
Martin, John R., St. Francis de Sales, Tucson
Martinez, Carlos C., St. Augustine Cathedral, Tucson
Mazza, Leon S., St. Joseph, Tucson
McNealy, Kenneth J., St. Thomas the Apostle, Tucson
Medrano, Efren, St. Joseph, Tucson
Merritt, William, Our Lady of the Mountains, Sierra Vista
Mezquita, Fernando, St. Andrew the Apostle, Sierra Vista
Milazzo, Mike, St. Andrew the Apostle, Sierra Vista
Miller, Anthony, St. Christopher, Marana
Miller, Rodger, Our Lady of the Mountains, Sierra Vista
Minetti, Bernard, (Inactive)
Morales, Tomas, (Retired), St. Monica, Tucson
Moreland, Kenneth, Vicar for Deacons, Most Holy Trinity, Tucson
Moreno, Florencio, Jr., (Retired)
Moulinet, Armando A., St. Luke's, Douglas
Mulloy, Daniel L., Immaculate Conception, Yuma
Munoz, Jorge, St. Christopher, Marana
Muthart, Paul, St. Francis of Assisi, Yuma
Negrette, Robert, Our Lady of Fatima, Tucson
Nehmer, David, Our Lady Queen of All Saints, Tucson
Nevins, Robert, St. Francis de Sales, Tucson
Nistler, Donald, St. John Neumann, Yuma
Nixen, Mark, Immaculate Conception, Yuma
Noriega, Rudy, Our Lady of the Valley, Green Valley
Ojeda, Jose, St. John the Evangelist, Tucson
Ornelas, Richard, Santa Cruz, Tucson
Ortega, Mario, St. Anthony of Padua, Casa Grande
Pasquinelli, Gary, St. Francis of Assisi, Yuma
Paulus, Raymond V., Sacred Heart, Tucson, (Inactive)
Pavlik, Keith F., (Out of the Diocese)
Pennington, Charles H., (Retired), St. Cyril of Alexandria, Tucson
Perez, Teodoro, St. Joseph Parish, Tucson
Pickett, John Scott, St. Mark Parish, Tucson
Prom, Mathas, Our Lady of the Valley, Green Valley
Radke, Robert, (Out of Diocese)
Ramirez, Frank, Santa Cruz, Tucson
Ranke, Dennis, St. Pius X, Tucson
Rasmussen, Charlie, St. Mark, Tucson
Rodriguez, George M., Our Mother of Sorrows, Tucson
Rombach, Lionel E., (Retired)
Romo, Reynaldo, Our Lady of the Mountains Parish, Sierra Vista
Roy, James, Our Lady of the Valley, Green Valley
Sadorf, Robert G., (Retired)
Saladin, Jerry, (Retired)
Sampson, David, Immaculate Conception, Yuma
Sanchez, Falvio, St. Bartholomew, San Manuel
Santiago, Nick, Santa Catalina, Tucson
Saspe, Gabriel, St. Luke, Douglas
Scalpone, Dennis R., St. Francis de Sales, Tucson
Schaff, James, Our Lady of the Mountains, Sierra Vista
Scherf, George, St. Odilia, Tucson
Sheffer, Edward P., St. Thomas the Apostle, Tucson
Sherlock, Francis C., St. Elizabeth Ann Seton, Tucson
Silva, Alfredo A., (Retired)
Solano, Francisco, St. Anthony of Padua, Casa Grande
Stotler, Jim, Our Lady of the Valley, Green Valley
Tackett, Gene, Our Lady of the Mountains, Sierra Vista
Tarango, Florentino, St. James, Coolidge
Terry, John, St. Rose of Lima, Safford
Thrall, Scott, Our Mother of Sorrows, Tucson
Trujillo, Ernest, Assumption of the Blessed Virgin Mary, Florence
Underwood, Anthony E., St. Patrick, Bisbee
Valadez, Jose, St. Francis of Assisi, Yuma
Valenzuela, Armando L., St. Monica, Tucson
Valenzuela, Carlos, St. Augustine Cathedral, Tucson
Vessels, Carlos, St. Rose of Lima, Safford
Vidal, Rafael, St. Francis of Assisi, Yuma
Vigil, William, St. Francis de Sales, Tucson
Welsh, Paul J., Our Mother of Sorrows, Tucson
Whalen, Charles, Our Mother of Sorrows, Tucson
Willis, Thomas, St. Luke Parish, Douglas
Yanez, Guadalupe, St. Elizabeth Ann Seton Parish, Tucson
Yanez, Jesus L. "Chuy", (Retired)
Zapata, Jose S., Immaculate Conception, Douglas

INSTITUTIONS LOCATED IN THE DIOCESE

[A] HIGH SCHOOLS, PRIVATE

TUCSON. *St. Augustine Catholic High School*, 8800 E. 22nd St., 85710. Tel: 520-751-8300; Fax: 520-751-8304. Email: sspaniol@staugustinehigh.com. Web: www.staugustinehigh.com. Kevin P. Kiefer, Prin. Lay Teachers 10; Students 130.

Salpointe Catholic High School (1950) 1545 E. Copper St., 85719. Tel: 520-327-6581; Fax: 520-327-8477. Email: president@salpointe.org. Web: www.salpointe.org. Mrs. Kay Sullivan, Interim Head of School & Pres. Carmelite Order. Priests 4; Sisters 3; Lay Teachers 80; Students 1,160.

Priory, 1540 E. Glenn St., 85719. Tel: 520-325-1537. In Res. Revs. Thomas Butler, O.Carm. (Retired); Roy Conry, O.Carm. (Retired); Foster Hanley, O.Carm.; Very Rev. William Harry, O.Carm.; Rev. Cyprian Hibner, O.Carm. (Retired); Very Rev. John Malley, O.Carm.; Revs. Vernon Malley, O.Carm. (Retired); Angelo Mastria, O.Carm.; Roy Ontiveros, O.Carm.; Jeffrey Smialek, O.Carm.; Bros. Daivd Balok, O.Carm.; Tom Conlon, O.Carm., (Retired); Matt Mateo, O.Carm.

San Miguel of Tucson Corporation - San Miguel Catholic High School, P.O. Box 22199, 85734. 6601 S. San Fernando Rd., 85756. Tel: 520-294-6403; Fax: 520-294-6417. Email: mirandac@sanmiguelhigh.com. Web: www.sanmiguelhigh.org. Leslie Schulz-Crist, Pres.; Bro. Nick Gonzalez, F.S.C., Prin.; Christine Miranda, Registrar & Asst. to Prin.; Sr. Judy Franz, S.B.S., Librarian. Brothers 4; Lay Teachers 15; Students 318.

ORO VALLEY. *Immaculate Heart School* (1930) (Grades PreK-12), 625 E. Magee Rd., 85704. Tel: 520-297-6672; Fax: 520-297-9152. Email: srevelyn@ihschool.org. Web: www.immaculateheartschool.com. Sisters Luisa Sanchez, I.H.M., Pres. (9-12); Mary Evelyn Soto, Pres. (PreK-8); Mrs. Lynn Cuffari, Prin. (PreK-8); Daniel Ethridge, Prin. (9-12); Sr. Miriam Claire, Librarian. Sisters of the Immaculate Heart of Mary 5; Lay Teachers 35; Students 452.

NOGALES. *Lourdes Catholic School*, (Grades PreK-12), (High School), 555 Patagonia Rd., P.O. Box 1865, 85628. Tel: 520-287-5659; Fax: 520-287-2910. Email: hsprincipal@lcsnogales.org. Web: www.lcsnogales.org. Sisters Barbara Monsegur, C.F.F.M., Prin. (High School); Esther Hugues, C.F.M.M., Prin. (Elementary). Minim Daughters of Mary Immaculate (C.F.M.M.) 4; Lay Teachers 20; Students 335.

YUMA. *Yuma Catholic High School* (2000) 2100 W. 28th St., 85364. Tel: 928-317-7900; Fax: 928-317-8558. Email: jbadgley@yumacatholic.org. Web: yumacatholic.org. Judeth Badgley, Prin.; Craig Koenigs, Media Specialist. Sisters 1; Lay Teachers 17; Students 278.

[B] CATHOLIC COMMUNITY SERVICES

TUCSON. *Catholic Community Service of Southern Arizona, Inc.* (1933) 140 W. Speedway, Ste. 230, 85705. Tel: 520-623-0344; Fax: 520-770-8514. Email: ccsinfo@ccs-soaz.org. Web: www.ccs-soaz.org. Deanna Lattari, Corp. Board Pres.; Marguerite Harmon, M.S., CEO.

Social Service Agencies: Pima County (Including City of Tucson), 140 W. Speedway, Ste. 230, 85705. Tel: 520-623-0344; Fax: 520-770-8514. Email: ccsinfo@ccs-soaz.org. Web: ccs-soaz.org.

Catholic Community Services of Southern Arizona, Inc. Marguerite Harmon, M.S., CEO of CCS; Ronald A. Dankowski, Ph.D., Exec. Dir., Catholic Social Svc.

Counseling Services, 140 W. Speedway, Ste. 130, 85705. Tel: 520-623-0344; Fax: 520-770-8578. Email: ccsinfo@ccs-soaz.org. Web: www.ccs-soaz.org. Michael Ponce, L.P.C., Clin. Dir.; Charles Fisher, M.Div., M.S.W., Exec. Dir.

Catholic Community Services in Southeastern Arizona, 155 Barton Ave., Sierra Vista, 85635. Tel: 520-458-4203; Fax: 520-432-2009. Chuck Fisher, Exec. Dir. of CCSSEAZ.

Sierra Vista Shelter, P.O. Box 1961, Sierra Vista, 85636. Tel: 520-459-0595. Chuck Fisher, Exec. Dir.

House of Hope, P.O. Box 121, Douglas, 85608. Tel: 520-364-2465. Chuck Fisher, Exec. Dir.

Migration and Refugee Services, 140 W. Speedway, Ste. 130, 85705. Tel: 520-623-0344; Fax: 520-770-8556. Ferdinand Lossou, Prog. Dir.

Santa Cruz Project, 848 S. 7th Ave., 85701. Tel: 520-770-8533; Fax: 520-770-8578. Sr. M. Teresa Apalategui, O.P., M.S.W., Assoc. Dir.

Senior Nutrition Services, 5009 E. 29th St., 85711. Tel: 520-624-1562; Fax: 520-519-1303. Ms. Linda Hutchings, M.S.R.D., Assoc. Dir.

Merilac Lodge and Casa de Crianza, 140 W. Speedway, Ste. 130, 85705. Tel: 520-623-0344; Fax: 520-770-8578. Sr. Mary Ann Bogosoff, C.S.A., Prog. Dir.

Immigration Counseling Service, 140 W. Speedway, Ste. 130, 85705. Tel: 520-623-0344; Fax: 520-770-8578. Rene Franco, Dir.

Field Offices:

Gila County Case Management, P.O. Box 1172, Globe, 85502. Tel: 520-425-5130; Fax: 520-425-2888. Sherlyn Harris-Ricketts, M.A., C.O.G., Program Dir.

Catholic Community Services in Western Arizona, 690 E. 32nd St., Yuma, 85365. Tel: 520-341-9400; Fax: 520-341-8428. Sarah Seneker, M.S.W., Exec. Dir.

Chaplaincy-Pastoral Ministry to Non-Denominational Nursing Homes, 140 W. Speedway, Ste. 230, 85705. Tel: 520-623-0344; Fax: 520-770-8514. Sr. Carolyn Nicolai, F.S.P., Prog. Coord.; Rev. Angelo Mastria, O.Carm., Chap.

Community Outreach Program for the Deaf, 268 W. Adams, 85705. Tel: 520-792-1906; Fax: 520-770-8544. Anne Levy, M.A., Exec. Dir.

Community Living Program, 268 W. Adams, 85705. Tel: 520-792-1906; Fax: 520-770-8544. Sue Henning-Mitchell, B.A., Deputy Dir.

Detention Ministry, 140 W. Speedway, Ste. 230, 85705. Tel: 520-623-0344; Fax: 520-770-8514. Ms. Barbara Mattus, M.A., Prog. Coord.

St. Elizabeth's Health Center, 140 W. Speedway, Ste. 100, 85705. Tel: 520-628-7871; Fax: 520-770-8528. Dana Pepper, Exec. Dir.

Pio Decimo Neighborhood Center, 848 S. 7th Ave., 85701. Tel: 520-622-2801; Fax: 520-622-4704. Joyce Walker, M.A., Exec. Dir.

Valley Center for the Deaf, 3130 E. Roosevelt, Phoenix, 85008. Tel: 602-267-1921; Fax: 602-273-1872. Anne Levy, M.A., Exec. Dir.

[C] GENERAL HOSPITALS

TUCSON. *Carondelet Health Network*, 2202 N. Forbes Blvd., Executive Ste., 85745-2682. Tel: 520-872-7790; Fax: 520-872-7838. Email: rbrinkley@carondelet.org. Web: www.carondelet.org. Ruth W. Brinkley, Pres. & CEO; Wes Colvin, COO.

Carondelet St. Joseph's Hospital, 350 N. Wilmot Rd., 85711. Tel: 520-873-3000; Fax: 520-872-3921. Email: gangle@carondelet.org. Greg Angle, CEO; Mrs. Cheryl Wilson-Weiss, Dir. Spiritual Care & Mission Integration; Revs. Charles Lehman; Ronald Yabut; Isaac A. Fynn; Rev. Wendy Hackler; Jude Magers, M.S., R.N., Chief Mission Integration Officer. Div. of Carondelet Health Network. Sisters of St. Joseph of Carondelet 5; Bed Capacity 478; Bassinets 30; Patients Assisted Annually 223,200.

Carondelet St. Mary's Hospital, 1601 W. St. Mary's Rd., 85745-2682. Tel: 520-872-3000; Fax: 520-872-6641. Email: obolano@carondelet.org. Odette Bolano, CEO; Revs. Edwin Emeli; Joseph Saba; Ukachukwu Oneyeabor. Div. of Carondelet Health Network. Sisters of St. Joseph 6; Bed Capacity 425; Patients Assisted Annually 197,800.

Carondelet Foundation, 120 N. Tucson Blvd., 85716. Tel: 520-873-5000; Fax: 520-873-5030. Web: www-.carondelet.org. Pamela Doherty, CEO.

St. Elizabeth of Hungary Clinic, 140 W. Speedway Blvd., Ste. 100, 85705. Tel: 520-628-7871; Fax: 520-205-8461. Email: njohnson@ccs-soaz.org. Web: www.ccs-soaz.org. Nancy Johnson, R.N., Ph.D., Exec. Dir., Admin. Patients Assisted Annually 42,000; Staff 75.

Tucson Heart Hospital - Carondelet, Inc., 4888 N. Stone Ave., 85704. Tel: 520-696-2328; Fax: 520-696-0449. Web: www.carondelet.org. Andrew R. Guarni, CFO.

NOGALES. *Holy Cross Hospital, Inc.* Div. of Carondelet Health Network, 1171 W. Target Range Rd., 85621. Tel: 520-285-3000; Fax: 520-285-8015. Email: winnie.fritz@carondelet.org. Web: carondelet.org. Sr. Isabelita Boquiren, Chap.; Ruth W. Brinkley, Pres. & CEO; Wanona Fritz, CEO, Holy Cross. Bed Capacity 25; Total Staff 252; Patients Assisted Annually 40,000.

Holy Cross Geriatric Center, 1171 W. Target Range, 85621. Tel: 520-285-8044; Fax: 520-397-5909. Patients Assisted Annually 125; Total Geriatric Patients Days 16,890; Admissions 1,935.

[D] MONASTERIES AND RESIDENCES OF PRIESTS AND BROTHERS

TUCSON. *Carmelite Priory* (1953) 1540 E. Glenn St., 85719. Tel: 520-325-1537; Fax: 520-318-4651. Very Rev. John Malley, O.Carm., Prior; Revs. Angelo Mastria, O.Carm.; Roy Conry, O.Carm. (Retired); Foster Hanley, O.Carm.; Very Rev. William Harry, O.Carm., Regl. Supr.; Revs. Vernon Malley, O.Carm. (Retired); Marlon Mateo, O.Carm.; Thomas Butler, O.Carm. (Retired); Cyprian Hibner, O.Carm. (Retired); Michael Higgins, O.Carm. (Retired); Jeffrey Smialek, O.Carm.; Bros. Daivd Balok, O.Carm.; Thomas Conlon, O.Carm., (Retired). Fathers and Brothers at Salpointe Catholic High School. Priests 11; Brothers 2.

Discalced Carmelite Friars of St. Margaret Mary's, 801 N. Grande Ave., 85745. Tel: 520-622-0168; Fax: 520-882-8022. Revs. Cyprian Killackey, O.C.D.; Kevin McArdle, O.C.D.; Philip Sullivan, O.C.D.; Albert Bunsic, O.C.D.

Jesuit Community of the Vatican Observatory, 2017 E. Lee St., 85719. Tel: 520-795-9866; Fax: 520-326-0756. Revs. Richard P. Boyle, S.J.; Christopher Corbally, S.J.; George V. Coyne, S.J.; William R. Stoeger, S.J., Acting Supr.; Andrew P. Whitman, S.J.; Bros. Guy Consolmagno, S.J.; John B. Hollywood, S.J.; Johnathan Stott, S.J. Jesuit Residence. **Vatican Observatory Foundation* Tel: 520-621-3225; Fax: 520-621-1532.

Offices of The Vatican Observatory, Steward Observatory, The University of Arizona, 85721. Tel: 520-621-3225; Fax: 520-621-1532.

CORTARO. *Redemptorist Society of Arizona Desert House of Prayer*, 7350 W. Picture Rocks Rd., P.O. Box 570, 85652. Tel: 520-744-3825; Fax: 520-744-0774. Web: deserthouseofprayer.org.

ST. DAVID. *Holy Trinity Monastery* (1974) P.O. Box 298, 85630. Tel: 520-720-4642; 520-720-4016; Fax: 520-720-4202. Email: frhenri@theriver.com. Web: www.holytrinitymonastery.org. Rev. Henri Capdeville, O.S.B., Prior. Benedictines. Professed 5; Novices 1; Perpetually Professed 5; Cloister Oblate 1.

SONOITA. *The Benedictine Monastery of Erlac in Sonoita*, Benedict's Ln., P.O. Box 534, 85637. Tel: 520-394-2961; Fax: 520-394-0163. Email: monksonoita@hughes.net. Web: benedictinemonastery.org.

[E] CONVENTS AND RESIDENCES FOR SISTERS

TUCSON. *St. Ann Convent*, 3820 Sabino Canyon Rd., 85750-6534. Tel: 520-298-0064; Fax: 520-885-8583. Email: stanns@q.com. Sr. Luisa Sanchez, I.H.M., Supr. Sisters of the Immaculate Heart of Mary 12.

Benedictine Monastery, 800 N. Country Club Rd., 85716-4583. Tel: 520-325-6401; Fax: 520-321-4358. Email: osbtucson@benedictinesisters.org. Web: www.benedictinesisters.org. Sr. Ramona Varela, O.S.B., Prioress & Contact. Sisters 23.

Carondelet Community, 6571 E. Carondelet Dr., 85710-2156. Tel: 520-873-3832. Email: mavonderahe@csjla.org. Sisters 4.

Convento Maria Nazareth - Minim Daughters of Mary (1986) 2821 W. Calle Gardenias, 85745. Tel: 520-743-0414. Email: rmrcfmm@yahoo.com. Sr. Rosa Maria Ruiz, C.F.M.M., Rgnl. Supr. Sisters 4.

Immaculate Heart Lodge Convent, 410 E. Magee Rd., 85704. Tel: 520-742-5896. Sr. Alice M. Martinez, Prov. Supr. Sisters of the Immaculate Heart of Mary 5.

Masmitja Community, 634 E. Magee Rd., 85704. Tel: 520-575-6002. Sr. Barbara Ann Gamboa, Supr. Sisters of the Immaculate Heart of Mary 3.

Immaculate Heart Novitiate, 3820 N. Sabino Canyon Rd., 85750-6534. Tel: 520-885-4981; Fax: 520-886-4273. Email: evelyn@theriver.com.

Immaculate Heart of Mary Provincial House Community, 3820 N. Sabino Canyon Rd., 85750-6534. Tel: 520-886-4273; Fax: 520-886-4273. Sr. Mary Evelyn Soto, Archivist. Sisters of the Immaculate Heart of Mary 3.

St. Joseph Community, 6569 E. Carondelet Dr., 85710-2156. Tel: 520-873-3816. Email: stjoetucson@aol.com. Sisters of the St. Joseph Community 3.

Maria Community, 1835 W. St. Mary's Rd., 85745-2653. Tel: 520-872-4940. Sisters 6.

Saints Peter and Paul Convent (1933) 1947 E. Adams St., 85719. Tel: 520-325-2234. Sisters of Charity of Seton Hill. Sisters of Charity of Seton Hill 5.

San Xavier Mission (1962) 1950 W. San Xavier Rd., 85746. Tel: 520-294-2624; Fax: 520-294-3438. Email: sfxsteve@hughes.net. Web: sanxaviermission.org.

DOUGLAS. *Loretto Convent*, 1200 - 14th St., 85607. Tel: 520-364-7571; Fax: 520-364-7844. Email: lorettodepazzi@hotmail.com. Web: carmelitegeneralate.homestead.com.

GLOBE. *Holy Angels Convent* (1956) 1300 E. Cedar, 85501. Tel: 928-425-2034; 928-425-5703 (School); Fax: 928-425-5704. Email: presglobe@yahoo.com. Web: www.pbvmunion.org. Convent Union of the Sisters of the P.B.V.M. 4.

NOGALES. *St. Joseph Convent*, 405 N. Carondelet Dr., 85621-2454. Tel: 520-287-7139; Fax: 520-287-2982. Email: clmrponce@yahoo.com. Sr. Celia Ma. Ponce, C.F.M.M., Supr. Minim Daughters of Mary Immaculate (C.F.M.M.) 7.

Our Lady of Lourdes Convent, P.O. Box 1865, 85628-1865. Tel: 520-287-3377; Fax: 520-287-2910. Minim Daughters of Mary Immaculate (C.F.M.M.) 7.

SAN CARLOS. *Saint Charles Convent*, 355 San Carlos Ave., 85550. Tel: 928-475-2460. Sisters of the Holy Cross.

SONOITA. *Santa Rita Abbey* (1972) HC 1, Box 929, 85637-9705. Tel: 520-455-5595; Fax: 520-455-5770. Email: sracommty@wildblue.net. Web: www.santaritabbey.org. Sr. Miriam Pollard, O.C.S.O., Prioress. Cistercian Nuns of the Strict Observance, O.C.S.O. Solemn Professed 8; Transfers 1; Postulants 1.

YUMA. *Immaculate Conception Convent*, 500 - 24th Ave., 85364. Tel: 928-783-5224; Fax: 928-343-0172. Email: acharleen@hotmail.com. Sisters 7.

[F] RETREAT HOUSES

TUCSON. *Redemptorist Society of Arizona Redemptorist Renewal Center*, 7101 W. Picture Rocks Rd., 85743. Tel: 520-744-3400; Fax: 520-744-8021. Email: office@desertrenewal.org. Web: www.desertrenewal.org. P.O. Box 569, Cortaro, 85652-0569. Revs. Thomas Santa, C.Ss.R., Dir.; Charles Wehrley, C.Ss.R.; Gregory Mayers, C.Ss.R.; Paul Coury, C.Ss.R., Supr.; Patrick Hawk, C.Ss.R.; Peter Connolly, C.Ss.R.; Bros. Michael Rhodes, C.Ss.R.; Steven Fruge, C.Ss.R. Priests 6; Brothers 2.

CORTARO. *Redemptorist Society of Arizona Desert House of Prayer*, P.O. Box 570, 85652. Tel: 520-744-3825; Fax: 520-744-0774. Web: deserthouseofprayer.org. In Res. Revs. William J. Parker, C.Ss.R.; Hugh Ricardo Elford, C.Ss.R.; Bro. William Cloughley, C.Ss.R.

ST. DAVID. *Holy Trinity Monastery* (1974) P.O. Box 298, 85630. Tel: 520-720-4642; Fax: 520-720-4202. Email: frhenri@theriver.com. Web: www.holytrinitymonastery.org.

SIERRA VISTA. *La Purisima Retreat Center, Inc.* (2001) Mailing Address: 800 Taylor Dr., N.W., 85635. Tel: 520-458-2925; Fax: 520-452-0235. Email: lapurisima@theriver.com. Web: lpretreat.org. 10301 E. Stone Ridge Rd., Hereford, 85615. Tel: 520-378-6783. Tom Felix, Facility Mgr.; Ann S. Dickson, Contact Person.

[G] NEWMAN CENTERS

TUCSON. *University of Arizona* , St. Thomas More Newman Center, 1615 E. 2nd St., 85719. Tel: 520-327-4665; Fax: 520-327-6559. Email: uacatholic@uacatholic.org. Web: www.uacatholic.org. Revs. Bartholomew J. Hutcherson, O.P.; James J. Moore, O.P.; Sr. Diane Bridenbecker, O.P. In Res. Revs. Robert A. Burns, O.P.; Michael S. Fones, O.P. (Retired); Bede Wilks, O.P. (Retired).

CASA GRANDE. *Central Arizona College, Holy Family Newman Center* P.O. Box 12335, 85230-2335. Tel: 520-836-0601; Fax: 520-836-2985. Email: stanthony@c2i2.com. Rev. Kevin D. Clinch.

DOUGLAS. *Cochise Community College* St. Luke, 1211 15th St., 85607. Tel: 520-364-4411; Fax: 520-364-2397. Rev. Gilbert Malu Musumbu; Marsha John, Office Mgr.

SAFFORD. *Eastern Arizona Junior College* 1705 8th Ave., 85546. Rev. Ariel G. Lustan, V.F.

St. Rose of Lima 311 Central Ave., 85546. Tel: 928-348-0232; Fax: 928-348-0232. Email: deacjbt@msn.com. Betty Terry, Campus Min.

[H] MISCELLANEOUS LISTINGS

TUCSON. *Carondelet Foundation*, 120 N. Tucson Blvd., 85716-4740. Tel: 520-873-5000; Fax: 520-873-5030. Email: pdoherty@carondelet.org. Web: www.carondelet.org. Mailing Address: 2202 N. Forbes, Executive Ste., 85745. Ms. Pamela Doherty, CEO.

Casa de los Ninos Crisis Center, 1101 N. 4th Ave., 85705. Tel: 520-624-5600; Fax: 520-623-2443. Email: info@casadelosninos.org. Web: www.casadelosninos.org. Susie Huhn, Exec. Dir.

Casa Maria (1981) 401 E. 26th St., 85713. Tel: 520-624-0312. Mr. Brian Flagg, Coord.

Catholic Community Services Foundation, 140 W. Speedway Blvd., Ste. 230, 85705. Tel: 520-670-0809; Fax: 520-770-8514. Email: lizm@ccs-soaz.org. Liz McMahon, Devel. Dir.

Catholic Foundation for the Diocese of Tucson 85702. Tel: 520-838-2507; Fax: 520-838-2585. Most Rev. Gerald Frederick Kicanas, D.D.; Martin Camacho, Exec. Dir.; John C. Woods, Past Pres.; Linda Tansik, Pres.; Mary Ann Hockstad, Treas.; Steven Thu, Vice Pres.; Clara I. Moreno, Exec. Asst.; Michele Antle, Fin. Specialist.

Ex Officio Members: Rev. Albert I. Schifano, V.G., M.C.; Tom Arnold, CFO.

Members: Rudy E. Ariate; Edith Auslander; William Bowen; Ann Charles; Annette Jones; Jane Kerr; Peter Likins; Richard Miranda; Mark Mistler; Jose Rincun; Dan Torrington.

Catholic Relief Services, 111 S. Church Ave., P.O. Box 31, 85702. Tel: 520-838-2534; Fax: 520-838-2588. Erica Dahl-Bredine, CRS Mexico Country Mgr.; Lourdes Aguilar, Office Coord., CRS/Mexico.

Catholic Tuition Support Organization (CTSO), P.O. Box 31, 85702. Tel: 520-838-2571; Fax: 520-838-2589. Email: gracieq@diocesetucson.org. Web: www.ctso-tucson.org. Gracie Quiroz, Dir. & Contact Person; Mr. Ernest T. Nedder, Pres.

Christ Child Society of Tucson, P.O. Box 36212, 85740-6212. Tel: 520-529-5858. Email: jan@msn.com. Donna Spackeen, Acting Pres.; Cheryl Rice, First Vice Pres.; Nancy Jones, Second Vice Pres.; Sylvia Blount, Treas.; Gail Toal, Sec.; Norma Greenbaum, Corresponding Sec.

Diocese of Tucson Catholic Cemeteries (Sole Corporation), 3555 N. Oracle Rd., 85705. Tel: 520-888-0860; Fax: 520-887-7360. Email: familyservice@dotcc.org. Web: www.dotcc.org.

Diocese of Tucson Catholic Committee on Scouting, P.O. Box 14256, 85732. Tel: 520-795-4210; Fax: 520-323-2026. Email: jhill548@aol.com. Web: www.diocesetucson.org/scoutindex.html.

The Diocese of Tucson Charity and Ministry Fund, Inc., P.O. Box 31, 85702-0031. Tel: 520-838-2509; Fax: 520-838-2598. Margie Puerta Edson, Exec. Dir.; Cheryl Ponzo, Pres.

St. Frances Cabrini Foundation, Inc., 3201 E. Presidio Rd., 85716. Tel: 520-326-7670; Fax: 520-881-8480. Rev. Msgr. Robert D. Fuller, M.R.E., D.Min., Contact Person.

Jordan Ministry Team, Inc., 48 N. Tucson Blvd., #101, 85716. Tel: 520-623-2563; Fax: 520-623-2585. Web: www.jordanministry.org. Rev. Joseph Rodrigues, S.D.S.; Sr. Jane Eschweiler, S.D.S., Dir.

Knights of Columbus, 14175 W. Indian School, Ste. B4-626, Goodyear, 85395. Tel: 602-369-4814; Fax: 623-691-8119. Web: www.kofc.org.

Magnificat - Tucson Chapter, 3560 N. Via San Juanito, 85749. Tel: 520-749-0633; Fax: 520-207-6211. Email: elizabeth962@juno.com. Mrs. L.J. Elizabeth Celenza, Pres. A ministry to Catholic women.

Parish Pooled Investment Trust, P.O. Box 31, 85702. Tel: 520-792-3410. Rev. Richard M. Kingsley, Chm.

**Reachout, Inc. dba Reachout Pregnancy Center* 2648 N. Campbell Ave., 85719. Tel: 520-321-4300; Fax: 520-391-4519. Email: reachout4life@q.com. Web: www.reachoutforlife.org. Angela Schneider, Exec. Dir.

Retorno (Marriage Retorno), 4321 N. Ventana Dr., 85750. Tel: 520-722-2931. Email: stogskk@mindspring.com. Web: www.marriageretorno.org. Kathie & Kevin Stogsdill, Contact Person. Tel: 520-722-2931. Prayer Retreat for Couples.

The Roman Catholic Diocese of Tucson Our Faith, Our Hope, Our Future, P.O. Box 31, 85702-0031. Tel: 520-838-2509; Fax: 520-838-2585. Email: margiee@diocesetucson.org. Web: www.diocesetucson.org. Margie Puerta Edson, Exec. Dir.; Thomas P. Arnold, Dir.

**Salpointe Catholic Education Foundation*, 1545 E. Copper St., 85719. Tel: 520-547-5878; Fax: 520-327-8477.

San Miguel Corporate Internship, 6601 S. San Fernando Rd., 85706. Tel: 520-294-6403; Fax: 520-294-6427. Leslie Schulz-Crist, Pres.

Society of St. Vincent de Paul Tucson Diocesan Council, 829 S. 6th Ave., 85701. Tel: 520-628-7837; Fax: 520-624-9102. Email: inbox@svdptucson.org. Web: www.svdptucson.org.

The St. Thomas More Society of Southern Arizona, 6818 N. Oracle Rd., Ste. 414, 85704. Tel: 520-838-2507. Ernest Skinner, Pres.; Mr. Mark T. Ralces, Treas.

HEREFORD. *Our Lady of the Sierras Foundation* (1993) 10310 S. Twin Oaks Rd., P.O. Box 269, 85615. Tel: 520-378-2950; Fax: 520-378-2950. Email: ourladysierrashrine@msn.com. Web: www.ourladyofthesierras.org. Mr. Gerald A. Chouinard, Pres.

NOGALES. *Kino Border Initiative* (2008) P.O. Box 259, 85628-0159. Tel: 520-287-2370; Fax: 520-287-2375. Web: www.kinoborderinitiative.org. Revs. Sean Carroll, S.J., Exec. Dir.; Donald Bahlinger, S.J., Chap.; Peter Neeley, S.J., Assoc. Educ. & Formation; Martin McIntosh, S.J., Assoc. Socio-Pastoral Outreach; Sisters Maria Engracia Robles, M.E., Migrant Aid Coord.; Imelda Ruiz, M.E., Asst. Migrant Aid Coord.; Lorena Leyva, M.E., Asst. Migrant Aid Coord.

MARANA. *Poverty 24/6 Trust*, 12101 W. Moore Rd., 85653. Tel: 520-682-3035. Email: poverty24-6@juno.com. Web: www.poverty24.6.org. Deacon Joseph Bogushefsky, Contact Person.

ST. DAVID. *San Pedro Valley Center for the Arts*, Box 298, 85630. Tel: 520-720-4642, Ext. 23. Patricia J. Don, Contact Person.

SOUTH TUCSON. *Blessed Kateri Tekakwitha Parish Center* (2003) 507 W. 29th St., 85713. Tel: 520-622-5363; Fax: 520-792-0230. Email: bl_kateri_tekakwitha@yahoo.com. Revs. Ermeregildo Saldana-Taneco, S.T.; Abram E. Dono, S.T.; Seraphim Molina, S.T.

[I] DIOCESAN CEMETERIES

TUCSON. *Holy Hope Cemetery and Mausoleum*, Office: 3555 N. Oracle Rd., 85705. Tel: 520-888-0860; Fax: 520-887-7360. Email: familyservice@dotcc.org.

Our Lady of the Desert Cemetery and Mausoleum, Office: 2151 S. Avenida Los Reyes, P.O. Box 5158, 85703. Tel: 520-885-9173.

[J] CLOSED INSTITUTIONS

TUCSON. *Diocese of Tucson Archives*, 300 S. Tucson Blvd., 85716. Tel: 520-886-5201; 520-792-3410. Email: bettyw@diocesetucson.org. The following parish, school or orphanage records may be found at the above address unless otherwise indicated. Notations to Sacramental Registers of closed parishes/missions on those listed below should be directed to the Archival Center and should specify the name of the parish. The location of records periodically changes. Inquiries for records of parishes, schools or institutions not on this list should be directed to the above address.

All Saints Parish (Tucson)
Blessed Martin de Porres (Tucson)
Sacred Heart Parish (Bisbee)
St. Anthony Parish (Tiger)
St. Bernard Mission Records located at: Our Lady, Queen of All Saints Parish, 2915 E. 36th St., Tucson, AZ 85713 Tel: 520-622-8602 Fax: 520-622-4581.
St. Helen Parish (Sonora)
All Saints Parochial School (Tucson)
Loretto Academy (Bisbee)
Regina Cleri Seminary (Tucson)
Sacred Heart Parochial School (Tucson)
St. Augustine Parochial School (Tucson)
St. Joseph Academy for Girls (Tucson)
St. Joseph Orphanage (Tucson)
St. Patrick Parochial School (Bisbee)

RELIGIOUS INSTITUTES OF MEN REPRESENTED IN THE DIOCESE

For further details refer to the corresponding bracketed number in the Religious Institutes of Men or Women section.

[0200]—*Benedictine Monks*—O.S.B.
[]—*Benedictine Monks of Erlac*—O.S.B.
[0330]—*Brothers of the Christian Schools*—F.S.C.
[0470]—*Capuchin Friars* (Prov. of St. Joseph)—O.F.M.Cap.
[0270]—*Carmelite Fathers and Brothers* (Prov. of Most Pure Heart of Mary)—O.Carm.
[1320]—*Clerics of St. Viator*—C.S.V.
[1330]—*Congregation of the Mission Western Province*—C.M.
[0260]—*Discalced Carmelites*—O.C.D.
[0520]—*Franciscan Friars*—O.F.M.
[]—*Friars of the Sick, Poor*—F.S.P.
[0300]—*Institute of Charity*—I.C.
[0690]—*Jesuit Fathers and Brothers*—S.J.
[0800]—*Maryknoll*—M.M.
[0720]—*Missionaries of Our Lady La Salette* (Immaculate Heart of Mary Prov.)—M.S.
[]—*Missionaries of St. Francis de Sales*
[0840]—*Missionary Servants of the Most Holy Trinity*—S.T.
[0430]—*Order of Preachers (Dominicans)*—O.P.
[1030]—*Paulist Fathers*—C.S.P.
[1070]—*Redemptorist Fathers* (Oakland Prov.)—C.SS.R.
[1200]—*Society of the Divine Savior*—S.D.S.
[]—*Via Christi Society*—V.C.

RELIGIOUS INSTITUTES OF WOMEN REPRESENTED IN THE DIOCESE

[0100]—*Adorers of the Blood of Christ*—A.S.C.
[1070-13]—*Adrian Dominican Sisters*—O.P.
[0233]—*Benedictine Nuns*—O.S.B.
[0220]—*Benedictine Sisters of Perpetual Adoration*—O.S.B.
[0370]—*Carmelite Sisters of the Most Sacred Heart of Los Angeles*—O.C.D.
[0670]—*Cistercian Nuns of the Strict Observance*—O.C.S.O.
[3710]—*Congregation of the Sisters of St. Agnes*—C.S.A.
[1920]—*Congregation of the Sisters of the Holy Cross*—C.S.C.
[1780]—*Congregation of the Sisters of the Third Order of St. Francis of Perpetual Adoration*—F.S.P.A.
[]—*Dominican Sisters of Mission San Jose*—O.P
[]—*Dominican Sisters of Oakford*—O.P.
[1115]—*Dominican Sisters of Peace*—O.P.
[1230]—*Franciscan Sisters of Christian Charity*—O.S.F.
[1310]—*Franciscan Sisters of Little Falls, Minnesota*—O.S.F.
[1415]—*Franciscan Sisters of Mary*—F.S.M.
[1425]—*Franciscan Sisters of Peace*—F.S.P.
[2575]—*Institute of the Sisters of Mercy of the Americas*—R.S.M.
[2490]—*Medical Mission Sisters*—M.M.S.
[2675]—*Minim Daughters of Mary Immaculate*—C.F.M.M.
[2720]—*Mission Helpers of the Sacred Heart*—M.H.S.H.
[]—*Oblates of St. Martha*—O.S.M.
[3130]—*Our Lady of Victory Missionary Sisters*—O.L.V.M.
[2970]—*School Sisters of Notre Dame*—S.S.N.D.
[1680]—*School Sisters of St. Francis*—S.S.S.F.
[3580]—*Servants of Mary*—O.S.M.
[3590]—*Servants of Mary (Servite Sisters)*—O.S.M.
[]—*Sisters for Christian Community*—S.F.C.C.
[0570]—*Sisters of Charity of Seton Hill, Greensburg, Pennsylvania*—S.C.
[2110]—*Sisters of Humility of Mary*—H.M.
[1705]—*The Sisters of St. Francis of Assisi*—O.S.F.
[1710]—*Sisters of St. Francis of Mary Immaculate*—O.S.F.
[1730]—*Sisters of St. Francis of Oldenberg*—O.S.F.
[1570]—*Sisters of St. Francis of the Holy Family*—O.S.F.
[3840]—*Sisters of St. Joseph of Carondelet*—C.S.J.
[0260]—*The Sisters of the Blessed Sacrament for Indians and Colored People*—S.B.S.
[1030]—*Sisters of the Divine Savior*—S.D.S.
[1990]—*Sisters of the Holy Names of Jesus and Mary*—S.N.J.M.
[2180]—*Sisters of the Immaculate Heart of Mary*—I.H.M.
[3320]—*Sisters of the Presentation of the Blessed Virgin Mary*—P.B.V.M.
[4070]—*Society of the Sacred Heart*—R.S.C.J.
[]—*Wheaton Franciscans*—O.S.F.

NECROLOGY

† Kattady, Augustine, Apache Junction, AZ St. George Parish—Died Jan. 24, 2009
† McGloin, Peter M.—Died June 15, 2009
† Moore, Tom, (Retired)—Died July 5, 2009
† Schlueter, Clemens M., (Retired)—Died Sept. 14, 2009
† Verbrugghe, Albert E., (Retired)—Died Aug. 20, 2009

An asterisk (*) denotes an organization that has established tax-exempt status directly with the IRS and is not covered by the USCCB Group Ruling.

Diocese of Tulsa

(Dioecesis Tulsensis)

Most Reverend

EDWARD J. SLATTERY

Bishop of Tulsa; ordained April 26, 1966; appointed Bishop of Tulsa November 11, 1993; ordained January 6, 1994 in Rome; installed January 12, 1994.

Chancery Office: 12300 E. 91st St. S., Broken Arrow, OK 74012. Mailing Address: P.O. Box 690240, Tulsa, OK 74169-0240. Tel: 918-294-1904; Fax: 918-294-0920.

Web: www.dioceseoftulsa.org

Email: bishop.office@dioceseoftulsa.org

ESTABLISHED FEBRUARY 7, 1973.

Square Miles 26,417.

The Diocese of Tulsa comprises the following 3 Counties: Adair, Atoka, Bryan, Cherokee, Choctaw, Coal, Craig, Creek, Delaware, Haskell, Hughes, Latimer, LeFlore, McCurtain, McIntosh, Mayes, Muskogee, Nowata, Okfuskee, Okmulgee, Osage, Ottawa, Pawnee, Payne, Pittsburg, Pushmataha, Rogers, Sequoyah, Tulsa, Wagoner and Washington.

For legal titles of parishes and institutions, consult the Chancery Office.

STATISTICAL OVERVIEW

Personnel	
Bishop	1
Priests: Diocesan Active in Diocese	50
Priests: Diocesan Active Outside Diocese	5
Priests: Retired, Sick or Absent	19
Number of Diocesan Priests	74
Religious Priests in Diocese	29
Total Priests in Diocese	103
Extern Priests in Diocese	11
Ordinations:	
Transitional Deacons	2
Permanent Deacons in Diocese	57
Total Brothers	18
Total Sisters	49
Parishes	
Parishes	76
With Resident Pastor:	
Resident Diocesan Priests	44
Resident Religious Priests	4
Without Resident Pastor:	
Administered by Priests	28
Missions	2
Closed Parishes	2
Welfare	
Catholic Hospitals	4
Total Assisted	1,200,000
Health Care Centers	1
Total Assisted	5,703
Homes for the Aged	4
Total Assisted	608
Specialized Homes	3
Total Assisted	270
Special Centers for Social Services	7
Total Assisted	45,756
Educational	
Diocesan Students in Other Seminaries	16
Total Seminarians	16
High Schools, Diocesan and Parish	1
Total Students	842
High Schools, Private	1
Total Students	556
Elementary Schools, Diocesan and Parish	9
Total Students	2,094
Elementary Schools, Private	2
Total Students	1,096
Catechesis/Religious Education:	
High School Students	1,340
Elementary Students	5,324
Total Students under Catholic Instruction	11,268
Teachers in the Diocese:	
Priests	4
Brothers	4
Sisters	5
Lay Teachers	346
Vital Statistics	
Receptions into the Church:	
Infant Baptism Totals	1,557
Minor Baptism Totals	132
Adult Baptism Totals	128
Received into Full Communion	342
First Communions	1,342
Confirmations	996
Marriages:	
Catholic	194
Interfaith	151
Total Marriages	345
Deaths	458
Total Catholic Population	57,938
Total Population	1,635,000

Former Bishops—Most Revs. BERNARD J. GANTER, D.D., ord. May 22, 1952; appt. Bishop of Tulsa, Dec. 19, 1972; ord. Feb. 7, 1973; transferred to Beaumont, Oct. 18, 1977; EUSEBIUS J. BELTRAN, ord. May 14, 1960; appt. Bishop of Tulsa, Feb. 28, 1978; ord. April 20, 1978; transferred to Archdiocese of Oklahoma City, Nov. 24, 1992.

Vicar General—Rev. Msgr. PATRICK J. GAALAAS, V.G.

Chancery Office—12300 E. 91st St. S., Broken Arrow, 74012. Mailing Address: P.O. Box 690240, Tulsa, 74169. Tel: 918-294-1904; Fax: 918-294-0920. Office Hours: Mon.-Fri. 9-5.

Chancellor—Deacon JOHN M. JOHNSON.

Finance Office—Mr. PHILIP J. CREIDER, Assets Mgr.; Mr. THOMAS SCHADLE, Finance Officer, Mailing Address: P.O. Box 690240, Tulsa, 74169-0240. Tel: 918-294-1904, Ext. 4926.

Diocesan Senators—Most Rev. EDWARD JAMES SLATTERY; Rev. Msgr. DENNIS C. DORNEY; Revs. MATTHEW J. GERLACH; SAMUEL PEREZ, J.C.L.; J. RICHARD BRADLEY; TIMOTHY L. DAVISON; JACK GLEASON; BRIAN O'BRIEN; LEONARD AHANOTU; PAUL EICHHOFF.

Ex Officio—Rev. Msgr. PATRICK J. GAALAAS, V.G.

Diocesan Consultors—Revs. JACK GLEASON; BERNARD C. SCIANNA, O.S.A.; Rev. Msgrs. PATRICK J. GAALAAS, V.G.; DENNIS C. DORNEY; DANIEL H. MUEGGENBORG; Revs. TAM N. NGUYEN; JOHN J. WADE (Retired); PAUL EICHHOFF; BRIAN O'BRIEN; SAMUEL PEREZ, J.C.L.

Diocesan Marriage Tribunal—

Judicial Vicar—Rev. MICHAEL J. KNIPE, J.C.L.

Adjutant Judicial Vicar—Rev. KENNETH J. HARDER, J.C.L.

Defender of the Bond—Rev. SAMUEL PEREZ, J.C.L.

Judges—Revs. MICHAEL J. KNIPE, J.C.L.; KENNETH J. HARDER, J.C.L.; KHIET NGUYEN, J.C.L.; Deacon KASPER E. WEIGANT.

Auditors—HENRY L. HARDER, Ph.D.; Deacon KENNETH LONGBRAKE.

Notary—Mrs. MARY JONES.

Promoter of Justice—Rev. SAMUEL PEREZ, J.C.L.

Priests' Personnel Committee—Rev. Msgr. PATRICK J. GAALAAS, V.G.; Revs. TAM N. NGUYEN; BRYAN V. BROOKS; Rev. Msgr. DENNIS C. DORNEY.

Seminary Board—Rev. Msgr. PATRICK J. GAALAAS, V.G.; Rev. DAVID MEDINA; Mr. ROBERT J. LAFORTUNE; Revs. MATTHEW J. GERLACH; JACK GLEASON; Rev. Msgr. DENNIS C. DORNEY; Ms. ANDREA HYATT.

Federation of Religious of the Diocese of Tulsa—Leadership Team: Sisters MARILYN NORWOOD, O.S.B.; EUGENIA BROWN, O.S.B., 2200 S. Lewis, Tulsa, 74114. Tel: 918-746-4211.

Diocesan Offices

Archivist—VACANT, Mailing Address: P.O. Box 690240, Tulsa, 74169-0240. Tel: 918-307-4956.

Campaign for Human Development—Deacon JOHN M. JOHNSON, Mailing Address: P.O. Box 690240, Tulsa, 74169. Tel: 918-307-4914.

Campus Ministry—Rev. MATTHEW J. GERLACH; LISA HOLDEN, Dir. Devel., St. Philip Neri Newman Center at The University of Tulsa, 440 S. Florence, Tulsa, 74104. Tel: 918-599-0204; Fax: 918-587-0115; Rev. STUART CREVCOURE, Chap., Oklahoma State University, 201 N. Knoblock St., Stillwater, 74075. Tel: 405-372-6408.

Catholic Charities of the Diocese of Tulsa—KEVIN SARTORIOUS, Exec. Dir., 2450 N. Harvard, Tulsa, 74115. Tel: 918-949-4673; Fax: 918-582-2123. Mailing Address: P.O. Box 580460, Tulsa, 74158.

Adoption Services—2450 N. Harvard, P.O. Box 580460, Tulsa, 74158. Tel: 918-949-4673.

Emergency Services—2450 N. Harvard, Tulsa, 74115. Mailing Address: P.O. Box 580460, Tulsa, 74158.

Madonna House—2450 N. Harvard, Tulsa, 74115. Mailing Address: P.O. Box 580460, Tulsa, 74158.

Immigration Office—2450 N. Harvard, Tulsa, 74115. Tel: 918-949-4673; Fax: 918-582-2123. *Mailing Address: P.O. Box 580460, Tulsa, 74158.*

Sallisaw Helping Center—Sallisaw. Tel: 918-775-6111.

St. Elizabeth Lodge—Tulsa. Tel: 918-949-4673.

St. Joseph Residence—Mailing Address: P.O. Box 580460, Tulsa, 74158. Tel: 918-587-6456.

Xavier Medical Center—2450 N. Harvard, Tulsa, 74115. Tel: 918-949-4673. *Mailing Address: P.O. Box 580460, Tulsa, 74158.*

Calvary Cemetery—9101 S. Harvard, Tulsa, 74137. Tel: 918-299-7348; Fax: 918-299-7558.

Clergy Education—Rev. Msgr. DENNIS C. DORNEY, Mailing Address: P.O. Box 690240, Tulsa, 74169. Tel: 918-294-1904, Ext. 4900.

Diocesan Catholic Committee on Scouting—Mr. DENNIS ZVACEK. Tel: 918-250-8787. Email: dzvacek@cox.net.

Diocesan Council of Catholic Women—MARIE BRASHER, 7798 E. Willow, Claremore, 74019. Tel: 918-266-3260.

Ecumenism—Rev. Msgr. PATRICK J. GAALAAS, V.G., Dir., 4001 E. 101st St., S., Tulsa, 74137.

Education—CAROL ROBINSON, Coord. Catechetical Svcs.; MARY MALCOM, Pastoral Studies Institute, Mailing Address: P.O. Box 690240, Tulsa, 74169. Tel: 918-294-1904, Ext. 4933.

Family Life Office—TRACY CALLICOAT, Mailing Address: P.O. Box 690240, Tulsa, 74169. Tel: 918-307-4940.

Parochial Schools—TODD GOLDSMITH, Supt. Catholic Schools, 820 S. Boulder, Tulsa, 74119. Tel: 918-582-9177; Fax: 918-582-1851.

Prison and Social Ministry—Deacon BILL DUNBAR, Mailing Address: P.O. Box 690240, Tulsa, 74169.

Hispanic Ministry—Mailing Address: P.O. Box 690240, Tulsa, 74169. Tel: 918-307-4950; Fax: 918-294-0920. Revs. DAVID MEDINA, Dir.; ROBERT M. DYE, Assoc. Dir., 1541 E. Newton Pl., Tulsa, 74106. Tel: 918-584-2424; LEONARDO MEDINA, Assoc. Dir.; DANIEL CAMPOS, Assoc. Dir.; SAMUEL PEREZ, J.C.L., Assoc. Dir.; ELKIN GONZALEZ, Assoc. Dir.; Deacon CARLOS MORENO.

Pastoral Studies Institute—MARY MALCOM, Mailing Address: P.O. Box 690240, Tulsa, 74169-0240. Tel: 918-307-4941.

Office of Divine Worship—Rev. Msgr. PATRICK M. BRANKIN, Dir., Mailing Address: P.O. Box 690240, Tulsa, 74169-0240. Tel: 918-307-4955.

Magazine "Eastern Oklahoma Catholic"—Ms. MARILYN DUCK, Editor, Mailing Address: P.O. Box 690240, Tulsa, 74169. Tel: 918-307-4946.

Office of Permanent Diaconate—Rev. Msgr. PATRICK M. BRANKIN, Vicar for Deacons, Mailing Address: P.O. Box 690240, Tulsa, 74169. Tel: 918-307-4955.

Diocesan Development Fund—Mr. JOE SOLENSKY, Mailing Address: P.O. Box 690240, Tulsa, 74169. Tel: 918-307-4929.

Propagation of the Faith—Rev. MATTHEW J. GERLACH, Coord., 440 S. Florence, Tulsa, 74104. Tel: 918-599-0204.

Victim Assistance Coordinator—Mr. QUENTIN HENLEY. Tel: 918-949-4673.

Te Deum Institute of Sacred Liturgy—Mailing Address: P.O. Box 690240, Tulsa, 74169. Rt. Rev. MARCEL ROONEY, O.S.B., Pres.

Vocations—Revs. MATTHEW J. GERLACH, Dir.; DAVID MEDINA, Assoc. Dir.; Mrs. THERESA WITCHER, Seminarians; Mr. WAYNE RZIHA, Promotion & Recruitment, 440 S. Florence, Tulsa, 74104. Tel: 918-599-0204; Fax: 918-587-0115.

Young Adult Ministry—VACANT, Mailing Address: P.O. Box 690240, Tulsa, 74169-0240. Tel: 918-307-4928.

Youth Ministry—VACANT, Mailing Address: P.O. Box 690240, Tulsa, 74169-0240. Tel: 918-307-4928.

CLERGY, PARISHES, MISSIONS AND PAROCHIAL SCHOOLS

CITY OF TULSA

(TULSA COUNTY)

1—HOLY FAMILY CATHEDRAL (1899) Rev. Msgrs. Gregory A. Gier, Rector; James F. Halpine, Rector Emeritus (Retired); Rev. James Van Nguyen; Deacons Millard Kizzia; Jerry Mattox; Thomas Gorman.
Res.: 122 W. 8th St., P.O. Box 3204, 74101. Tel: 918-582-6247; Fax: 918-599-8334. Email: tulsacathedral@gmail.com. Web: www.holyfamily-tulsa.org.
School—(Grades PreK-8), 820 S. Boulder St., 74119. Tel: 918-582-0422; Fax: 918-582-9705. Jay Luetkemeyer, Prin. Lay Teachers 10; Students 113.
Catechesis/Religious Program—Monica Skrzypczak, D.R.E.; Monika Davis, D.R.E. Students 85.

2—ST. AUGUSTINE'S (1955), (African American), Rev. Kenneth Iheanaho (Nigeria); Deacon Steve Litwack.
Church: 1728 E. Apache, 74110. Tel: 918-428-3280.
Catechesis/Religious Program—Students 22.

3—ST. BERNARD OF CLAIRVAUX (1978) [CEM] Rev. Msgr. Patrick J. Gaalaas; Deacons Richard Campbell; Alan Mikell; Robert Martin; David Johnson. In Res., Rev. James J. McGlinchey (Retired).
Res.: 4001 E. 101st St., 74137. Tel: 918-299-9406; Fax: 918-299-7796. Email: e-mailus@stbernardstulsa.org. Web: www.stbernardstulsa.org.
Preschool—Teachers 8; Students 42.
Catechesis/Religious Program—Sharon Lechtenberg, D.R.E. Students 530.

4—ST. CATHERINE (1925) Rev. Michael E. Cashen; Deacon Craig Victor.
Res.: 4532 S. 25th W. Ave., 74107. Tel: 918-446-8124; Fax: 918-446-4506.
School—(Grades PreSchool-8), 2515 W. 46th St., 74107. Tel: 918-446-9756. Vicky Adams, Prin. Sisters of St. Francis of the Martyr St. George 2; Lay Teachers 10; Students 130.
Catechesis/Religious Program—Students 19.
Mission—St. Joseph P.O. Box 603, Bristow, Creek Co. 74010. Deacon Tom Loney.

5—CHRIST THE KING (1917) Rev. Tam N. Nguyen; Sr. Connie Lennartz, O.P.; Deacons Loren F. Luschen; John M. Johnson.
Res. & Office: 1520 S. Rockford Ave., 74120. Tel: 918-584-4788; 918-584-4789; 918-584-6693 (Res.); Fax: 918-584-0055. Email: ctkparish@marquetteschool.org. Web: www.christthekingtulsa.org.
School—Marquette School, (Grades K-8), 1519 S. Quincy, 74120. Tel: 918-584-4631; Fax: 918-584-0055. Pete Theban, Prin. Lay Teachers 25; Students 403.
School—Marquette Early Childhood Development Center (ECDC), (6 mo. - 8th Grade), 1528 S. Quincy Ave., 74120. Tel: 918-583-3334. Web: www.marquetteschool.org. Lay Teachers 15; Students 80.
Catechesis/Religious Program—Students 150.

6—CHURCH OF ST. MARY (1954) Rev. Msgr. Dennis C. Dorney; Revs. Gary Kastl; William J. Swift; Deacon Richard Bender.
Office: 1347 E. 49th Pl., 74105. Tel: 918-749-1423; Fax: 918-747-9532. Email: church@churchofsaintmary.com. Web: www.churchofsaintmary.com.
School—(Grades PreSchool-8), 1365 E. 49th Pl., 74105. Tel: 918-749-9361; Fax: 918-712-9604. Maureen Clements, Prin. Lay Teachers 33; Students 340.
Catechesis/Religious Program—Linda Schoonover, D.R.E. Students 253.

7—CHURCH OF THE MADALENE (1946) Rev. Jack Gleason; Sr. Marie Pierre Fleming, O.S.B., Pastoral Assoc.; Deacon Robert DeWeese.
Res.: 3188 E. 22nd St., 74114. Tel: 918-744-0023; Fax: 918-744-0024. Web: www.madalenetulsa.org.
Catechesis/Religious Program—Tel: 918-744-0023, Ext. 15. Becky Holder, D.R.E. Students 150.

8—ST. FRANCIS XAVIER CHURCH AND DIOCESAN MARIAN SHRINE & EXPIATORY TEMPLE OF OUR LADY OF GUADALUPE (1926), (Hispanic), Revs. David Medina; Leonardo Medina; Robert M. Dye.
Church: 2434 E. Admiral Blvd., 74110. Tel: 918-592-6770; Fax: 918-592-2208.
Res.: 2510 E. 1st St., 74104. Tel: 918-592-6828.
Instituto Bilingue Guadalupano—(Grades PreSchool) Teachers 5; Students 38.
Catechesis/Religious Program—Gloria Gerardo, D.R.E. Students 504.

9—IMMACULATE CONCEPTION (1923) Closed. For inquiries for parish records contact the chancery.

10—ST. JOSEPH CHURCH (1977), (Vietnamese), Rev. Dovan Nguyen.
Res.: 14905 E. 21st St., 74134. Tel: 918-438-1380.
Catechesis/Religious Program—Tel: 918-438-6325. Students 175.

11—ST. MONICA'S (1926), (African American), Rev. Kenneth Iheanaho (Nigeria).
Church: 633 Marshall Pl., 74106. Tel: 918-587-2965 (Office); Fax: 918-582-0699.
Catechesis/Religious Program—Students 20.

12—OUR LADY OF GUADALUPE, Closed. For inquiries for sacramental records contact St. Francis Xavier, Tulsa.

13—PARISH OF SAINT PETER (1996) Revs. Peter Byrne, F.S.S.P.; Angelo Van der Putten, F.S.S.P.
Mailing Address: 1720 E. Apache, 74110. Tel: 918-425-0486; Fax: 918-425-2077.
Res.: 1728 E. Apache, 74110.
Catechesis/Religious Program—Students 51.

14—SS. PETER AND PAUL (1950) Revs. Timothy L. Davison; Elkin Gonzalez.
Res.: 1436 N. 67th E. Ave., 74115. Tel: 918-836-2596; Fax: 918-836-2597.
School—(Grades PreSchool-8), 1428 N. 67th E. Ave., 74115. Tel: 918-836-2165. Patrick Martin, Prin. Lay Teachers 18; Students 190.
Catechesis/Religious Program—Karen Campbell, D.R.E. Students 176.

15—ST. PIUS X (1955) Rev. Michael J. Knipe; Deacons Kasper Weigant; Anthony H. Tran.
Church: 1727 S. 75 E. Ave., 74112. Tel: 918-622-4488; Fax: 918-622-1239.
Res.: 7628 E. 17th St., 74112. Tel: 918-664-9723.
School—(Grades PreK-8), 1717 S. 75 E. Ave., 74112. Tel: 918-627-5367; Fax: 918-627-6179. Web: spxtulsa.org. Matthew Vereecke, Prin. Lay Teachers 26; Students 383.
Catechesis/Religious Program—Deborah Campbell, D.R.E. Students 120.

16—RESURRECTION (1968) Rev. Stephen E. Austin; Deacon James Scarpitti.
Mailing Address: P.O. Box 33169, 74153. Tel: 918-663-1907; Fax: 918-663-2533.
Res.: 4338 S. Braden Pl., 74135. Tel: 918-664-8319.
Church: 4804 S. Fulton, 74135. Tel: 918-663-1907.
Catechesis/Religious Program—Amy Synar, D.R.E. Students 110.

17—ST. THOMAS MORE (1972) Rev. Samuel Perez.
Church: 2720 S. 129 E. Ave., 74134-2411. Tel: 918-437-0168; 918-576-6446 (Hispanic); Fax: 918-437-0681; 918-576-6448 (Hispanic).
Catechesis/Religious Program—Sally Gonzalez, D.R.E. Students 817.

OUTSIDE CITY OF TULSA

ANTLERS, PUSHMATAHA CO., ST. AGNES (1897) Rev. Joseph Vadake Chirayath (India).
Church: 503 E. Main, 74523. Tel: 580-298-5204 (Parish Ctr.).
Res.: P.O. Box 99, Hugo, 74743. Tel: 580-326-7300.
Catechesis/Religious Program—Diann Baze, D.R.E. Students 10.
Station—McLeod Correctional Center Farris. Tel: 405-889-6651; Fax: 405-889-2264.

BARTLESVILLE, WASHINGTON CO.

1—ST. JAMES (1965) Rev. Archelito Fernandez (Philippines); Deacon Gerard Rutherford.
Church: 5500 Douglas Ln., 74006. Email: office_stjms@sbcglobal.net.
Catechesis/Religious Program—Tel: 918-335-0844; Fax: 918-333-0856. Students 90.

2—ST. JOHN'S (1906) [CEM] Rev. Festus Maliwa.
Res.: 715 S. Johnstone Ave., 74003. Tel: 918-336-4353; Fax: 918-336-4354.
School—(Grades PreK-8) Tel: 918-336-0624; Fax: 918-336-0603. Jane Sears, Prin. Lay Teachers 14; Students 108.
Catechesis/Religious Program—Dorlene Martin, D.R.E. Students 103.

BIXBY, TULSA CO., ST. CLEMENT OF ROME (1957) Rev. Leonard Ahanotu (Nigeria); Deacon Jose Guzman.
Church: 15501 S. Memorial Dr., 74008. Tel: 918-366-3166; Fax: 918-365-3164. Email: stclementchurch@tulsacoxmail.com. Web: www.stclement-bixby.org.
Catechesis/Religious Program—Students 101.

BROKEN ARROW, TULSA CO.

1—ST. ANNE (1937) [JC] Rev. Michael A. Dodd; Deacon Kenneth Schumacher.
Res.: 301 S. 9th St., 74012. Tel: 918-251-4000; Fax: 918-251-8719.
Catechesis/Religious Program—Tel: 918-251-5414. Becky Bryant, D.R.E. Students 141.

2—ST. BENEDICT (1980) Rev. Joe C. Townsend; Deacon John Donnelly.
Res.: 3105 S. Beech Ave., 74012. Tel: 918-455-4451.
Church: 2200 W. Ithica St., 74012. Fax: 918-451-2199.
Preschool—Teachers 16; Students 77.
Catechesis/Religious Program—Carol Bryan, C.R.E. Students 620.

CLAREMORE, ROGER CO., ST. CECILIA (1911) Rev. Paul Eichhoff.
Res.: 1304 N. Dorothy, 74017. Tel: 918-341-2343; Fax: 918-343-2893.
Catechesis/Religious Program—Tel: 918-341-4238. Students 274.

CLEVELAND, OSAGE, ST. JOSEPH (1905), (Native American), See separate listing. Now a mission of Sacred Heart, Fairfax.

COALGATE, COAL CO., BLESSED SACRAMENT ORATORY (1889) [CEM] Closed. For inquiries for parish records contact the chancery.

COLLINSVILLE, TULSA CO., ST. THERESE CHURCH AND DIOCESAN EUCHARISTIC SHRINE OF SAINT THERESE (1908) [CEM] Rev. Richard F. Cristler.
Church: 1007 N. 19th St., 74021. Tel: 918-371-2704; Fax: 918-371-3895.
Catechesis/Religious Program—Kelly Cassidy, D.R.E. Students 145.

COWETA, WAGONER CO., ST. VINCENT DE PAUL (1981) Rev. Joe C. Townsend; Deacon Lamar Yarbrough.
Mailing Address: P.O. Box 597, 74429-0597. Tel: 918-486-4757.
Catechesis/Religious Program—Students 41.

CUSHING, PAYNE CO., SS. PETER AND PAUL (1894) [CEM] Rev. Matthew G. LaChance; Deacons Kenneth Longbrake; Glenn Collum.
Mailing Address: P.O. Box 828, 74023.
Res.: 214 N. Steele Ave., 74023. Tel: 918-225-0644; Fax: 918-225-6569. Email: cushingcatholicchurch@yahoo.com.
Catechesis/Religious Program—Alice Patterson, C.R.E. Students 60.
Mission—St. Mary 321 S. Cimarron, Drumright, Creek Co. 74030. Tel: 918-352-9327 (Parish Hall).
Mission—St. John 333 S. 8th St., Pawnee, Pawnee Co. 74058.

DEWEY, WASHINGTON CO., OUR LADY OF GUADALUPE (1954) Rev. Orencio Mumar (Philippines); Deacon James Black.
400 W. Ninth St., 74029. Tel: 918-534-3420; Fax: 918-534-3013.
Catechesis/Religious Program—Susanna Mackie, C.R.E. Students 37.

Mission—St. Catherine 217 W. Modoc, Nowata, Nowata Co. 74048. Tel: 918-273-0737. P.O. Box 804, Nowata, 74048.

DURANT, BRYAN CO., ST. WILLIAM (1914) Rev. Valerian Gonsalves, O.S.B. (India).
802 University Blvd., 74701. Tel: 580-924-1989; Fax: 580-931-3044.
Catechesis/Religious Program—Students 38.
Mission—St. Patrick Church Hwy. 69 S., Atoka, Atoka Co. 74701. Tel: 580-931-3044.

FAIRFAX, OSAGE CO., SACRED HEART (1925), (Osage Indian), Rev. Bruce C. Brosnahan.
Mailing Address: 333 S. 8th St., 74637. Tel: 918-642-5053.
Catechesis/Religious Program—Students 15.
Mission—(1929) 421 S. Petit, Hominy, Osage Co. 74035.
Mission—St. Joseph Osage & C Ave., Cleveland, Pawnee Co. 74020.

GROVE, DELAWARE CO., ST. ELIZABETH (1949) Rev. Alex Kennedy.
Office: 1653 113th St., N.W., 74344. Tel: 918-256-2281.
Catechesis/Religious Program—Students 57.

HARTSHORNE, PITTSBURG CO., HOLY ROSARY (1895) [CEM] Rev. Hung Viet Le; Deacon Sid Starr.
Mailing Address: 912 Cherokee, P.O. Box 389, 74547. Tel: 918-297-2453.

HENRYETTA, OKMULGEE CO., ST. MICHAEL (1912) [JC] Rev. Chi Peter Phung.
1004 W. Gentry St., P.O. Box 148, 74437. Tel: 918-652-3445; Fax: 918-652-3445.
Catechesis/Religious Program—Students 9.

HOLDENVILLE, HUGHES CO., ST. STEPHEN'S (1905) Rev. Chi Peter Phung.
Mailing Address: P.O. Box 148, Henryetta, 74437.
Church: 515 E. Highway, 74848. Tel: 405-379-2512; Fax: 405-379-2512.
Mission—St. Teresa (1927) 8th and Broadway, Okemah, Okfuskee Co. 74859.

HOMINY, OSAGE CO., ST. JOSEPH (1929) See separate listing. Now a mission under Sacred Heart, Fairfax.

HUGO, CHOCTAW CO., IMMACULATE CONCEPTION (1903) Rev. Joseph Vadake Chirayath (India).
Res.: P.O. Box 99, 74743. Tel: 580-326-7300 (Rectory); 580-326-3602 (Church); Fax: 580-326-7300.
Mission—St. Jude 511 11th St., Boswell, Choctaw Co. 74727.
Catechesis/Religious Program—Students 21.

IDABEL, MCCURTAIN CO., ST. FRANCIS DE SALES (1945) Rev. Chet Artysiewicz, G.H.M.
Res.: 13 S.E. Jefferson, 74745. Tel: 580-286-3275.
Catechesis/Religious Program—Students 70.

KREBS, PITTSBURG CO., ST. JOSEPH'S (1886) [CEM] Rev. James A. Caldwell Jr.; Deacon Bill Anderson.
Res.: P.O. Box 621, 74554. Tel: 918-423-6695; Fax: 918-426-4255.
Catechesis/Religious Program—Tel: 918-423-7130. Bonnie DeGiacomo, D.R.E. Students 40.
Mission—St. Paul's [CEM] 6th & Forest, Eufaula, McIntosh Co. 74554.
Catechesis/Religious Program—Students 12.

LANGLEY, MAYES CO., ST. FRANCES OF ROME (1950) Rev. Celestine Obidiegwu.
Res.: Hwy. 28, P.O. Box 267, 74350-0267. Tel: 918-782-2248.
Catechesis/Religious Program—Students 12.

MCALESTER, PITTSBURG CO., ST. JOHN (1895) [CEM] Rev. Leonard H. Higgins.
Res.: 300 E. Washington Ave., P.O. Box 220, 74502. Tel: 918-423-0810; Fax: 918-423-0825. Email: stjohnmcalester@yahoo.com.
Catechesis/Religious Program—Students 106.
Station—Oklahoma State Penitentiary, Tel: 918-423-4700; Fax: 918-423-3862.

MIAMI, OTTAWA CO., SACRED HEART (1900) Rev. Carl Kerkemeyer.
Res.: 2515 N. Main, 74354. Tel: 918-542-5281; Fax: 918-542-7591.
Catechesis/Religious Program—Tel: 918-542-5898. Karen Painter, D.R.E. Students 75.
Mission—St. Ann P.O. Box 25, Welch, Craig Co. 74369. Tel: 918-788-3771.
Catechesis/Religious Program—Students 14.

MUSKOGEE, MUSKOGEE CO.

1—ASSUMPTION, Closed. For inquiries for sacramental records contact Saint Joseph Church, Muskogee.

2—SAINT JOSEPH CHURCH (1992) [CEM] Revs. Bryan V. Brooks; Daniel Campos; Deacon Edwin Falleur.
Mailing Address: P.O. Box 189, 74402.
Church: 321 N. Virginia, 74402.
Res. & Parish Office: 301 N. Virginia, 74403. Tel: 918-687-1351; Fax: 918-687-5541.
School—(Grades PreK-8), 323 N. Virginia, 74403. Tel: 918-683-1291; Fax: 918-682-5374. Sandra Brewer, Prin. Religious 1; Lay Teachers 16; Students 116.
Catechesis/Religious Program—Jimmy Perkins, D.R.E. Students 120.

3—SACRED HEART, Closed. For inquiries for sacramental records contact Saint Joseph Church, Muskogee.

OKMULGEE, OKMULGEE CO., ST. ANTHONY'S (1910) Rev. Benjamin A. Vima (India).
Res.: 515 S. Morton Ave., P.O. Box 698, 74447. Tel: 918-756-4385; Fax: 918-756-4385.
Catechesis/Religious Program—Freida Biddle, C.R.E. Students 40.
Mission—Uganda Martyrs 808 E. 3rd, Okmulgee Co. 74447. P.O. Box 698, 74447.

OWASSO, TULSA CO., ST. HENRY (1957) Revs. J. Richard Bradley; J. Paul Donovan, Pastor Emeritus (Retired); Deacons Vernon Foltz; Donald LeMieux; Edmundo Martinez.
Mailing Address: P.O. Box 181, 74055-0181. Tel: 918-272-3710; Fax: 918-272-1966.
Res.: 104 E. 16th St., 74055. Email: office@sthenryowasso.org. Web: www.sthenryowasso.org.
Church: 8500 Owasso Expy., 74055.
Catechesis/Religious Program—Tel: 918-272-3740. Elizabeth Gagner, D.R.E. Students 468.

PAWHUSKA, OSAGE CO., IMMACULATE CONCEPTION (1887), (Osage Indian), Rev. Christopher Daigle.
Res.: 1314 N. Lynn Ave., 74056. Tel: 918-287-1414.
Catechesis/Religious Program—Students 63.
Mission—St. Mary 3rd and Chestnut, Barnsdall, Osage Co. 74002.
Mission—St. Ann Gypsy St. & Taylor St., Shidler, Osage Co. 74652.

PAWNEE, PAWNEE CO., ST. JOHN (1907) Rev. Matthew G. LaChance; Deacon Glenn Collum.
Mailing Address: P.O. Box 828, Cushing, 74023.
Church: 8th St. & Oak, 74058.

PLUNKETVILLE, MCCURTAIN CO., ST. HENRY, Closed. For inquiries for parish records see St. Francis De Sales, Idabel.

POTEAU, LEFLORE CO., IMMACULATE CONCEPTION (1903) Rev. Valentine Ndebilie.
Church: 410 Bagwell St., P.O. Box 237, 74953. Tel: 918-647-3475.
Catechesis/Religious Program—Students 22.
Mission—St. Joseph 1204 N.W. 7th St., Stigler, Haskell Co. 74462.
Mission—St. Elizabeth Seton Hwy. 9, Spiro, Leflore Co. 74959.
Station—Ouachita Correctional Training Center Hodgens.

PRYOR, MAYES CO., ST. MARK'S (1942) Rev. Celestine Obidiegwu.
Res.: 1507 S. Vann, 74362. Tel: 918-824-4470; Fax: 918-825-2338. Email: stmarkspryor@sbcglobal.net.
Catechesis/Religious Program—Tel: 918-825-4186. Rose Craig, D.R.E.; Paula Kennedy, D.R.E. Students 96.

SALLISAW, SEQUOYAH CO., ST. FRANCIS XAVIER (1952) Rev. Desmond Okpogba; Deacon Robert Barnes, (Retired).
Church: 2110 N. Dogwood, 74955. Tel: 918-775-6217; Fax: 918-775-6217.
Catechesis/Religious Program—Students 32.
Mission—St. John the Evangelist P.O. Box 4, Cookson, Cherokee Co. 74427.
Mission—St. Joseph P.O. Box 53, Webbers Falls, Muskogee Co. 74470. Tel: 918-464-2422.
Mission—Blessed Kateri Tekakwitha P.O. Box 17, Roland, Sequoyah Co. 74954.

SAND SPRINGS, TULSA CO., ST. PATRICK'S (1919) Rev. Martin Morgan.
Res.: 204 E. Fourth, 74063. Tel: 918-245-5254; Fax: 918-241-3100. Email: stpartrickcathch@sbcglobal.net. Web: www.stpatrick-sandsprings.org.
Catechesis/Religious Program—Students 57.
Mission—Our Lady of the Lake 400 Cimarron Dr., Mannford, Creek Co. 74044.

SAPULPA, CREEK CO., SACRED HEART (1907) Rev. Jovita Okonkwo (Nigeria); Deacon Mark Pittman.
Church: 1777 E. Grayson Ave., 74066. Tel: 918-224-0944; Fax: 918-512-6830. Web: www.sacredheartsapulpa.org.
Catechesis/Religious Program—Students 60.

SKIATOOK, OSAGE CO., SACRED HEART (1921), (Formerly St. William). Rev. Khiet Nguyen.
Res.: 109 W. 5th St., 74070. Tel: 918-396-1179; Fax: 918-396-2112. Web: www.sacredheart-skiatook.org.
Catechesis/Religious Program—Students 65.

STILLWATER, PAYNE CO.

1—ST. FRANCIS XAVIER (1895) Rev. Kenneth J. Harder; Deacons Paul Govek; Roy Callison; Bill Moler, (Retired).
Church: 601 West St., 74074.
Res.: Box 909, 74076. Tel: 405-624-7243; Fax: 405-533-1728.
Catechesis/Religious Program—Students 125.

2—ST. JOHN THE EVANGELIST PARISH AND NEWMAN CENTER (1965) Revs. Stuart Crevcoure; Emmanuel Lugard Nduke; Deacons Bill Dunbar; Tom Haan; Richard Berberet; Thomas Doyle.
Res.: 201 N. Knoblock, 74075. Tel: 405-372-6408; Fax: 405-372-6409. Email: saintjohnparish@yahoo.com. Web: www.stjohn-stillwater.org.
Early Childhood Center—Lay Teachers 8; Students 72.
Catechesis/Religious Program—Tel: 405-372-7987. Students 108.

TAHLEQUAH, CHEROKEE CO., ST. BRIGID (1966) Rev. Jeffrey S. Polasek; Deacons Joseph Faulds; Mark Keeley.
Res.: 807 Crafton St., 74464. Tel: 918-456-8388; Fax: 918-456-8880. Email: stbrigid2@yahoo.com.
Catechesis/Religious Program—Tel: 918-207-1737. Patsy Clifford, D.R.E. Students 81.
Mission—San Juan Mission 23 W. Division St., Stilwell, Adair Co. 74960.

VINITA, CRAIG CO., HOLY GHOST (1892) Rev. Alex Kennedy.
Res.: 120 W. Sequoyah Ave., 74301. Tel: 918-256-2281.
Catechesis/Religious Program—Tel: 918-256-3118. Debbie Lauchner, C.R.E. Students 37.
Station—Northeastern Correctional Facility

VALIANT, MCCURTAIN CO., GOOD SHEPHERD, Closed. For inquiries for parish records see St. Francis De Sales, Idabel.

WAGONER, WAGONER CO., HOLY CROSS (1895) Rev. Edward Y. Yew; Deacon Jim Ruyle.
Mailing Address: P.O. Box 710, 74477. Tel: 918-485-5145; Fax: 918-485-0656. Email: hcrosswag@valornet.com.
Church: S.W. 15th & Pierce, 74477.
Catechesis/Religious Program—Students 21.

WILBURTON, LATIMER CO., SACRED HEART, [CEM] Rev. Joshua E. Litwack; Deacon Clement Bradley.
102 Center Point Rd., Latimer Co. 74578.
Catechesis/Religious Program—Students 15.
Mission—St. Catherine of Siena Second & Gann Sts., Talihina, Leflore Co. 74571. Tel: 918-567-2587.
Catechesis/Religious Program—Students 9.
Mission—Holy Trinity P.O. Box 747, Clayton, Pushmataha Co. 74523. Tel: 918-569-4767.

Chaplains of Public Institutions

Special Assignment:
Rt. Rev.—
Rooney, Marcel, O.S.B., Liturgical Institute of the Diocese of Tulsa
Rev. Msgr.—
Brankin, Patrick M., Office of the Diaconate, Chancery Office
Revs.—
Choorackunnel, John V., C.M.I., Chap., Saint Francis Hospital, Tulsa
Coleman, Gerald J., Chap., St. John Medical Center, Tulsa
Elliott, W. Gregg, Jane Phillips Medical Center, Bartlesville
Kirby, Mark, O.S.B., Spiritual Dir. Diocesan Priests & Deacons
Kodakarakaran, Paul, Chap., St. Francis Hospital, Tulsa
Sherman, Gary D., Chap., St. John Medical Center, Tulsa

On Duty Outside the Diocese:
Rev. Msgr.—
Mueggenborg, Daniel H., North American College, Rome
Revs.—
Amaliri, Paul Obi, Military Chap., U.S. Air Force
Cain, Robert K.C., Military Chap., U.S. Navy
Minh, Vu Duc, Holy Martyrs, Colorado Springs, CO
Wells, Peter B., Secretary of State Office, Section of General Affairs, Vatican

Retired:
Rev. Msgr.—
Halpine, James F., P.O. Box 3204, 74101.
Revs.—
Casey, Denis, 2121 S. Yorktown # 503, 74114.
Courtright, Lawrence P., 1921 S. Xanthus Ave., 74104.
Donovan, J. Paul, P.O. Box 181, Owasso, 74055.
Eastman, Patrick W., 30 N. Wall, Cricklade, Wiltshire SN66DE England.
Foken, Herman J., Franciscan Villa, 17110 E. 51st St., S., Broken Arrow, 74012.
Fulton, Kenneth S., 8437 E. 58th St., 74145.
Le, Hoang Viet, 2403 S. 141st East Ave., 74134.
Lundberg, John W., 43 California Ave., Middletown, NY 10940.
McGlinchey, James J., 4001 E. 101st St., 74137.
Melton, Thomas K., P.O. Box 151, 74578.
Perlinski, Daniel A., 17110 E. 51st St., Apt. 4, Broken Arrow, 74012.
Pickett, Robert T., 1414 E. 49th St., 74105-4798.
Richard, Edward, 1594 S. Chamberlain Blvd., North Port, FL 34286.

Skeehan, William K., 3008 E. 51st St., Apt. 27, 74105.
Swett, Charles J., 2009 Xanthus, 74104.
Swift, William V., 1779 S. Wheeling, 74104.
Wade, John J., 1171 S. Wheeling, 74104.
White, James D., 2800 E. Ramon Rd., Palm Springs, CA 92264.

Permanent Deacons:
Anderson, Bill, St. Joseph, Krebs
Barnes, Robert, (Retired)
Bender, Richard F., Church of St. Mary, Tulsa
Berberet, Richard, Stillwater Parishes
Black, James, Our Lady of Guadalupe, Dewey
Bradley, Clement W., Sacred Heart, Wilburton
Breazille, James E., Parishes of Stillwater
Callison, Roy, St. Francis Xavier, Stillwater
Campbell, Richard, St. Bernard, Tulsa
Campbell, Sam
Cardenas, Alfonso, (Retired)
Chamberlain, Richard, (Retired)
Collum, Glenn, St. John Parish, Pawnee
DeLeon, Felix, (Retired)
DeWeese, Robert, Church of the Madalene, Tulsa
Donnelly, John E., St. Benedict, Broken Arrow
Doty, Edward, (Retired)
Doyle, Thomas, Parishes of Stillwater
Dunbar, Bill, Stillwater Parishes
Falleur, Edwin E., St. Joseph, Muskogee
Faulds, Joseph M., St. Brigid, Tahlequah
Foltz, Vernon, St. Henry, Owasso
Garrett, James R., (Retired)
Gorman, Tom, Holy Family Cathedral, Tulsa
Govek, Paul, Stillwater Parishes
Guzman, Jose, St. Clement, Bixby
Haan, Tom, Stillwater Parishes
Hollingshead, Noel, (Retired)
Johnson, Dave, St. Bernard, Tulsa
Johnson, John M., Christ the King, Tulsa
Keeley, Mark, St. Brigid, Tahlequah
Kizzia, Millard H., Holy Family Cathedral, Tulsa
LeMieux, Donald J., St. Henry, Owasso
Litwack, Stephen J., St. Augustine, Tulsa & St. Monica, Tulsa
Loney, Tom, St. Joseph, Bristow
Longbrake, Kenneth, Sts. Peter and Paul, Cushing
Luschen, Loren F., Christ the King, Tulsa
Martin, Robert, St. Bernard of Clairvaux, Tulsa
Martinez, Edmundo S., St. Henry, Owasso
Mattox, Jerry, Holy Family Cathedral, Tulsa
Mikell, Alan G., St. Bernard, Tulsa
Moler, William J., (Retired)
Moreno, Carlos, Hispanic Apostolate
Morris, Marvin D., (Retired)
Mrasek, Vincent J., (Retired), St. Cecilia, Claremore
Perez, Jose, (Retired)
Pierret, James A., (Retired)
Pittman, Mark, Sacred Heart, Sapulpa
Richard, Joseph N., (Retired)
Rutherford, Gerard, St. James, Bartlesville
Ruyle, Jim, Holy Cross, Wagoner
Scarpitti, James, Church of the Resurrection, Tulsa
Schumacher, Kenneth, St. Anne, Broken Arrow
Starr, Sid, Holy Rosary, Hartshorne
Toppins, Charles A., (Retired)
Tran, Anthony, St. Pius X, Tulsa
Tucker, Donel, (Retired)
Victor, Craig, St. Catherine, Tulsa
Weigant, Kasper E., St. Pius X, Tulsa
Willis, Daniel H., (Retired)
Yarbrough, Lamar, St. Vincent de Paul, Coweta
Young, Thomas, (Retired)

INSTITUTIONS LOCATED IN THE DIOCESE

[A] HIGH SCHOOLS, DIOCESAN

TULSA. *Bishop Kelley High School* (1960) 3905 S. Hudson, 74135-5699. Tel: 918-627-3390; Fax: 918-664-2134. Email: frobrien@bkelleyhs.org. Web: www.bkelleyhs.org. Rev. Brian D. O'Brien, Pres.; Marianne Stich; Karen Govier, Librarian. Brothers 2; Lay Teachers 83; Students 845.

[B] HIGH SCHOOLS, PRIVATE

TULSA. *Cascia Hall Preparatory School*, (Grades 6-12), Box 52247, 74152. Tel: 918-746-2600; Fax: 918-746-2636. Email: info@casciahall.org. Web: www.casciahall.org. 2520 S. Yorktown Ave., 74114. Tel: 918-746-2600; Fax: 918-746-2636. Revs. Bernard C. Scianna, O.S.A., Headmaster; Donald Brennan, O.S.A.; Roland F. Follmann, O.S.A.; John H. Gaffney, O.S.A.; William A. Hamill, O.S.A.; William A. Perez, O.S.A.; Henry V. Spielmann, O.S.A.; Theodore E. Tack, O.S.A.; Bros. Jack H. Hibbard, O.S.A.; Paul L. Koscielniak, O.S.A.; Steve E. Mayfield, Prin.; Joan O'Brien Hubble, Librarian. Augustinians (Order of St. Augustine)., Coed College Preparatory School. Priests 8; Brothers 2; Sisters 1; Lay Teachers 55; Students 556.

[C] ELEMENTARY SCHOOLS, DIOCESAN

BROKEN ARROW. *All Saints School*, (Grades PreK-8), 299 S. 9th St., 74012. Tel: 918-251-3000; Fax: 918-258-9879. Anne Scalet, Prin.; LuAnn Cannon, Librarian. Lay Teachers 24; Students 289.

[D] ELEMENTARY SCHOOLS, PRIVATE

TULSA. *Monte Cassino School*, (Grades PreK-8), 2206 S. Lewis, 74114. Tel: 918-743-4471; Fax: 918-742-5206. Web: www.montecasino.org. Sr. Mary Clare Buthod, O.S.B., School Dir.; Nancy Henry, Librarian; Carmen Applegate, Librarian. Sisters 1; Lay Teachers 76; Students 933.

San Miguel School of Tulsa, Inc. (2004) (Grades 6-8), 2434 E. Admiral Blvd., 74110. Tel: 918-728-7337; Fax: 918-592-2208. Anne Edwards, Dir., Prin. & Contact Person. Lay Teachers 10; Students 64.

[E] GENERAL HOSPITALS

TULSA. *Saint Francis Hospital*, 6161 S. Yale Ave., 74136. Tel: 918-494-2200; Fax: 918-494-8435. Web: www.saintfrancis.com. Mr. Jake Henry Jr., Pres. & CEO; Lynn Sund, Sr. Vice Pres. & Admin.; Revs. Denis Casey, Chap. (Retired); John V. Choorackunnel, C.M.I., Chap.; Elias Abi-Sarkis, Chap. (Maronite); Paul Kodakarakaran. Bed Capacity 742; Bassinets 34; Patients Assisted Annually 706,546.

**Jane Phillips Health Corp.*, Mailing Address: 1923 S. Utica Ave., 74104. Tel: 918-331-1550. 3500 E. Frank Phillips Blvd., Bartlesville, 74006. Rev. Gregg Elliott, Pastoral Care. Bed Capacity 201; Total Assisted 146,000.

St. John Health System, Inc. (1982) 1923 S. Utica, 74104. Tel: 918-744-2180; Fax: 918-744-2716. Web: www.stjohnhealthsystem.com. Sr. M. Therese Gottschalk, Pres.

St. John Medical Center, Inc. (1926) 1923 S. Utica Ave., 74104. Tel: 918-744-2345; Fax: 918-744-2716. Web: www.sjmc.org. Charles Anderson, Pres.; Revs. Gary D. Sherman, Chap.; Gerald J. Coleman, Chap. Sisters of the Sorrowful Mother (Third Order of St. Francis). Sisters 17; Bed Capacity 567; Patients Assisted Annually 370,000.

Marian Health System, Inc. (1989) 1923 S. Utica Ave., 74104. Tel: 918-742-9988; Fax: 918-744-2716. Web: www.marianhealthsystem.com. Sr. M. Therese Gottschalk, Pres. & CEO.

OWASSO. *Owasso Medical Facility, Inc. dba St. John Owasso* 12451 E. 100th St. N., 74055.

[F] HOMES FOR THE AGED

TULSA. *Frances Streitel Senior Care Corporation*, 1923 S. Utica Ave., 74104. Tel: 918-355-1596.

St. John Villas, Inc. (1984) 1923 S. Utica, 74104. Tel: 918-355-1596. Web: www.stjohnhealthsystem.com/departments/seniorliving. Ron Hoffman, Pres.; Revs. Gary D. Sherman, Chap.; Jose K. Thottathil (SFE). Sisters of the Sorrowful Mother., Retirement Residence and Health Care Center for Intermediate Nursing Care. Bed Capacity 281; Apartments 67; Residents 242.

St. Teresa of Avila Villa, Inc., Mailing Address: 1923 S. Utica, 74104. Tel: 918-371-7771. 632 N. 19th St., Collinsville, 74021. Ron Hoffman, Pres. To assist in accommodating the elderly and disabled with housing facilities and services.

[G] MONASTERIES FOR MEN

HULBERT. *Our Lady of the Annunciation of Clear Creek Monastery* (1999) 5804 W. Monastery Rd., 74441-5698. Tel: 918-772-2454; Fax: 918-772-1044. Web: www.clearcreekmonks.org. Revs. Philip Anderson, O.S.B., Prior; Francois De Feydeau, O.S.B., Subprior; Christopher Andrews, O.S.B.; Mark Bachmann, O.S.B.; Francis Bales, O.S.B.; Francis Bethel, O.S.B.; Francis Xavier Brown, O.S.B.; Lawrence Brown, O.S.B.; Philippe Le Bouteiller des Haries, O.S.B.; Vincent Hulot, O.S.B.; Matthew Shapiro, O.S.B.; James Louis Ullmer. Priests 12; Brothers 20.

[H] CONVENTS AND RESIDENCES FOR SISTERS

TULSA. *St. Joseph Monastery* (1879) 2200 S. Lewis, 74114-3100. Tel: 918-742-4989; Fax: 918-744-1374. Email: sisters@stjosephmonastery.org. Web: www.stjosephmonastery.org. Sr. Christine Ereiser, O.S.B., Prioress. Motherhouse of Benedictine Sisters (Federation of St. Scholastica). Sisters in Community 22.

Sisters of Saint Joseph, 3942 S. Trenton, 74105. Tel: 918-749-8954. Sisters in Community 2.

BROKEN ARROW. *St. Clare Convent*, 700 E. Omaha, 74012. Tel: 918-355-0958; Fax: 918-355-3880. Sisters in Community 10.

[I] NEWMAN CENTERS

TULSA. *St. Philip Neri Newman Center at The University of Tulsa* 440 S. Florence, 74104. Tel: 918-599-0204; Fax: 918-587-0115. Email: tu-newman@utulsa.edu. Web: www.tu-newman.org. Rev. Matthew J. Gerlach, Chap.; Lisa Holden, Devel. Dir.; Daniel Bryan, Outreach Coord.

STILLWATER. *St. John's University Parish and Catholic Student Center* 201 N. Knoblock, 74075. Tel: 405-372-6408; Fax: 405-372-6409. Email: saintjohnparish@yahoo.com. Web: www.stjohn-stillwater.org. Rev. Stuart Crevcoure; Cathy Perry, Campus Min.

TAHLEQUAH. *Northeastern State University Catholic Student Organization* 807 Crafton St., 74464. Tel: 918-456-8388. Rev. Jeffrey S. Polasek.

[J] MISCELLANEOUS

TULSA. *Bishop Kelley High School Endowment Trust*, 3905 S. Hudson Ave., 74135. Tel: 918-627-3390; Fax: 918-664-2134. Email: frobrien@bkelleyhs.org. Web: bkelleyhs.org. Rev. Brian D. O'Brien, Pres.

Catholic Foundation of Eastern Oklahoma, Inc., P.O. Box 690240, 74169. Tel: 918-294-1904.

**Saint Francis Health System, Inc.*, 6161 S. Yale, 74136. Mr. Jake Henry Jr., Contact Person.

Saint Francis of Assisi Tuition Assistance Trust, Diocese of Tulsa, P.O. Box 690240, 74169-0240.

St. John Medical Center Foundation, Inc. (1981) 1923 S. Utica, 74104. Tel: 918-749-3553; Fax: 918-744-2716.

St. John Owasso, Inc., Mailing Address: 1923 S. Utica Ave., 74104. Tel: 918-744-2180. David Pynn, Pres.

Saint John Vianney Seminary Trust, Diocese of Tulsa, P.O. Box 690240, 74169-0240.

St. Joseph Residence, Inc., P.O. Box 580460, 74158. Tel: 918-587-6456; Fax: 918-587-3560. Total Assisted 21; Total Staff 6.

Priest Retirement Trust of the Roman Catholic Diocese of Tulsa, c/o Diocese of Tulsa, P.O. Box 690240, 74169-0240. Tel: 918-294-1904; Fax: 918-294-0920. Rev. Msgr. Patrick J. Gaalaas, V.G.

HASKELL. *Apostolate for the Most Holy Rosary and the Brown Scapular Association*, P.O. Box 1041, Coweta, 74429. Tel: 918-279-9158. Email: highlandhaven@windstream.net.

HULBERT. *Foundation for the Annunciation Monastery of Clear Creek* (1999) 5804 W. Monastery Rd., 74441-5698. Tel: 918-772-2454; Fax: 918-772-1044. Web: www.clearcreekmonks.org.

MUSKOGEE. *St. Joseph School Endowment Trust*, P.O. Box 189, 74402. Tel: 918-687-1351.

SAPULPA. *St. John Sapulpa Foundation, Inc.*, 1004 E. Bryan, 74066. Tel: 918-224-4280; Fax: 918-227-1093. Web: www.stjohnhealthsystem.com. Valerie Round, Exec. Dir.

RELIGIOUS INSTITUTES OF MEN REPRESENTED IN THE DIOCESE

For further details refer to the corresponding bracketed number in the Religious Institutes of Men or Women section.

[0140]—*The Augustinians (Province of Our Mother of Good Counsel)*—O.S.A.
[0200]—*Benedictine Monks (Solesmes Congregation)*—O.S.B.
[]—*Benedictine Monks (Conception Abbey)*
[]—*Benedictine Monks (Diocese of Tulsa)*
[0330]—*Brothers of the Christian Schools* (MIdwest Province, Burr Ridge, IL)—F.S.C.
[]—*Carmelites of Mary Immaculate*—C.M.I.
[0570]—*Glenmary Home Missioners*—G.H.M.
[0650]—*Holy Ghost Fathers*—C.S.Sp.
[1065]—*Priestly Order of St. Peter*—F.S.S.P.

RELIGIOUS INSTITUTES OF WOMEN REPRESENTED IN THE DIOCESE

[0220]—*Benedictine Sisters of Perpetual Adoration*—O.S.B.
[0230]—*Congregation of the Benedictine Sisters of the Sacred Hearts*—O.S.B.
[2330]—*Little Sisters of Jesus, Mexico*—L.S.J.
[]—*Medical Sisters of St. Joseph, India*
[2519]—*Religious Sisters of Mercy*—R.S.M.
[]—*Rose of Lima, Vietnam*—O.P.
[2970]—*School Sisters of Norte Dame*—S.S.N.D.
[1070-03]—*Sinsinawa Dominican Congregation*—O.P.
[1705]—*Sisters of St. Francis of Assisi*—O.S.F.

[1570]—*Sisters of St. Francis of the Holy Family*—O.S.F.

[1640]—*Sisters of St. Francis of the Martyr of St. George*

[3830]—*Sisters of St. Joseph*—S.S.J.

[4100]—*Sisters of the Sorrowful Mother (Third Order of St. Francis)*—S.S.M.

CEMETERIES

TULSA. *Calvary*, 9101 S. Harvard, 74136. Tel: 918-299-7348; Fax: 918-299-7558.

NECROLOGY

(No Deaths)

An asterisk (*) denotes an organization that has established tax-exempt status directly with the IRS and is not covered by the USCCB Group Ruling.

Diocese of Tyler

(Dioecesis Tylerensis)

Most Reverend

ALVARO CORRADA DEL RIO, S.J., D.D.

Bishop of Tyler; ordained July 6, 1974; appointed Auxiliary Bishop of Washington DC May 30, 1985; consecrated August 4, 1985; on assignment, as Apostolic Administrator, Diocese of Caguas; appointed Bishop of Tyler December 5, 2000; installed January 30, 2001. *Office: Diocese of Tyler, 1015 E.S.E. Loop 323, Tyler, TX 75701-9663.* Tel: 903-534-1077; Fax: 903-534-1370.

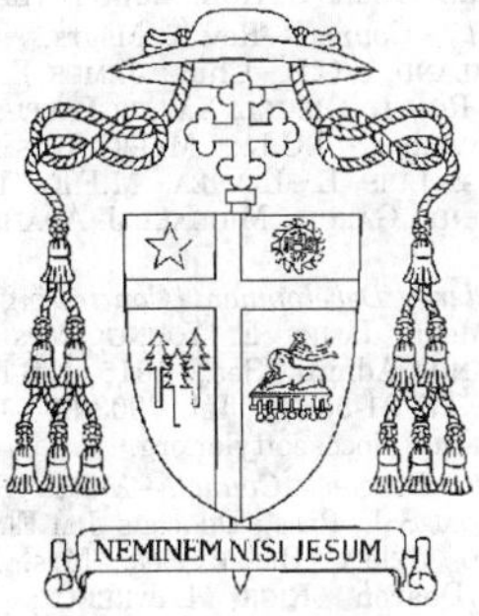

Chancery: 1015 E.S.E. Loop 323, Tyler, TX 75701-9663. Tel: 903-534-1077; Fax: 903-534-1370.

ESTABLISHED DECEMBER 12, 1986.

Square Miles 23,443.

Comprises the following Counties in the State of Texas: Anderson, Angelina, Bowie, Camp, Cass, Cherokee, Delta, Franklin, Freestone, Gregg, Harrison, Henderson, Hopkins, Houston, Lamar, Leon, Madison, Marion, Morris, Nacogdoches, Panola, Rains, Red River, Rusk, Sabine, San Augustine, Shelby, Smith, Titus, Trinity, Upshur, Van Zandt, and Wood.

For legal titles of parishes and diocesan institutions, consult the Chancery Office.

STATISTICAL OVERVIEW

Personnel	
Bishop	1
Priests: Diocesan Active in Diocese	54
Priests: Diocesan Active Outside Diocese	14
Priests: Retired, Sick or Absent	7
Number of Diocesan Priests	75
Religious Priests in Diocese	11
Total Priests in Diocese	86
Extern Priests in Diocese	16
Ordinations:	
Diocesan Priests	3
Transitional Deacons	2
Permanent Deacons in Diocese	93
Total Brothers	1
Total Sisters	54
Parishes	
Parishes	44
With Resident Pastor:	
Resident Diocesan Priests	36
Resident Religious Priests	4
Missions	28
Pastoral Centers	1
Professional Ministry Personnel:	
Brothers	1
Sisters	54
Lay Ministers	877
Welfare	
Catholic Hospitals	3
Total Assisted	1,167,073
Special Centers for Social Services	9
Total Assisted	25,000
Educational	
Diocesan Students in Other Seminaries	23
Total Seminarians	23
High Schools, Diocesan and Parish	1
Total Students	221
Elementary Schools, Diocesan and Parish	5
Total Students	814
Catechesis/Religious Education:	
High School Students	1,191
Elementary Students	5,703
Total Students under Catholic Instruction	7,952
Teachers in the Diocese:	
Priests	2
Lay Teachers	108
Vital Statistics	
Receptions into the Church:	
Infant Baptism Totals	2,492
Minor Baptism Totals	237
Adult Baptism Totals	102
Received into Full Communion	367
First Communions	2,056
Confirmations	2,948
Marriages:	
Catholic	278
Interfaith	77
Total Marriages	355
Deaths	338
Total Catholic Population	67,594
Total Population	1,359,507

Former Bishops—Most Revs. CHARLES E. HERZIG, D.D., First Bishop of Tyler; ord. May 31, 1955; appt. Bishop of Tyler Dec. 12, 1986; cons. Feb. 24, 1987; died Sept. 7, 1991; EDMOND CARMODY, D.D., Second Bishop of Tyler; ord. June 8, 1957; appt. Auxiliary Bishop of San Antonio, Nov. 8, 1988; cons. Dec. 15, 1988; appt. Bishop of Tyler, March 24, 1992; installed May 25, 1992; transferred to Diocese of Corpus Christi, March 17, 2000.

Office of Bishop—Most Rev. ALVARO CORRADA DEL RIO, S.J., 1015 ESE Loop 323, Tyler, 75701-9663. Tel: 903-534-1077; Fax: 903-534-1370. Email: bishopoffice@dioceseoftyler.org. Secretary to the Bishop: VACANT. Tel: 903-534-1077, Ext. 132. Email: bishopoffice@dioceseoftyler.org. Bishop Office Secretary: Ms. TERESA TISCARENO. Tel: 903-534-1077, Ext. 132. Email: mtiscareno@dioceseoftyler.org.

Vicar General—Rev. Msgr. XAVIER PAPPU, St. Matthew, 2800 Pine Tree Rd., Longview, 75604-1647. Tel: 903-295-3890. Email: vg@dioceseoftyler.org; Mrs. VIRGINIA S. MEDRANO, Admin. Sec. Tel: 903-534-1077, Ext. 160. Email: vmedrano@dioceseoftyler.org.

Chancery—1015 E.S.E. Loop 323, Tyler, 75701-9663. Tel: 903-534-1077; Fax: 903-534-1370. Office Hours: Mon.-Fri. 8:30-5.

Chancellor—Deacon RUBEN NATERA, 1015 ESE Loop 323, Tyler, 75701-9663. Tel: 903-266-2133. Email: chancellor@dioceseoftyler.org.

Administrative Assistant—Ms. ZAIRA AVILA. Email: zavila@dioceseoftyler.org.

Archivist—Deacon RUBEN NATERA, Chancellor. Tel: 903-534-1077, Ext. 133; 903-266-2133 (office). Email: chancellor@dioceseoftyler.org; Mrs. CINDY PLUMMER, Archivist Asst. Tel: 903-534-1077, Ext. 195.

College of Consultors—Rev. Msgrs. XAVIER PAPPU; JOSEPH E. STRICKLAND, J.C.L.; GERALD A. PRIEST; JAMES E. YOUNG; RONALD L. DIEGEL; ZACHARIAS S. KUNNAKKATTUTHARA; Revs. LUIS E. LARREA, M.F.E.; GAVIN N. VAVEREK, J.C.L.

Deans—Rev. Msgrs. RON L. DIEGEL, East Central Deanery; GERALD A. PRIEST, Northeast Deanery; JAMES E. YOUNG, Southeast Deanery; ZACHARIAS S. KUNNAKKATTUTHARA, Southwest Deanery; JOSEPH E. STRICKLAND, J.C.L., West Central Deanery; Rev. SUSAI AVULA, Northwest Deanery.

Tribunal Office—1015 E.S.E. Loop 323, Tyler, 75701-9663. Tel: 903-266-2140; Fax: 903-534-1370.

Judicial Vicar—Rev. Msgr. JOSEPH E. STRICKLAND, J.C.L. Tel: 903-534-1077, Ext. 139. Email: tribunal@dioceseoftyler.org; Mrs. TERRY BOLTON, Admin. Sec. Tel: 903-534-1077, Ext. 164. Email: tbolton@dioceseoftyler.org.

Judges—Rev. Msgr. JOSEPH E. STRICKLAND, J.C.L.; Revs. ANTHONY MCLAUGHLIN, J.C.L.; CHRISTOPHER V. RUGGLES, J.C.L.

Administrator—Mrs. MARGARET OPPENHEIMER. Tel: 903-266-2140. Email: tribunal@dioceseoftyler.org; moppenheimer@dioceseoftyler.org.

Defender of the Bond—Rev. GAVIN N. VAVEREK, J.C.L.

Advocates—Rev. STEPHEN J. DUYKA; Rev. Msgr. JOHN FLYNN (Retired). Tel: 903-534-1077, Ext. 172.

Candidates Approved as Canonical Advocates for Marriage Cases—

Southeast Deanery—Deacons RAY VANN, St. Patrick's, Lufkin; JOHN RAGLAND, Our Lady of Lourdes, Chireno.

Northeast Deanery—Mrs. OFELIA VALDEZ; Deacons CRAIG LASHFORD, Sacred Heart, Texarkana; TIMOTHY O'NEILL, St. Mary of the Cenacle, New Boston.

West Central Deanery—Rev. PAUL KEY, S.T.L.; Deacon JACK ROUNDS, Cathedral; VIRGINIA ROUNDS, Cathedral; Mrs. VIRGINIA S. MEDRANO, Cathedral; BEVERLY OHREN, Cathedral; BARBARA HAMPTON, St. Boniface, Chandler; Deacons DENNIS KING, Holy Family, Lindale; CLARENCE BLALOCK, St. Mary Magdalene's, Flint.

East Central Deanery—CAROL MOLINA, St. Mary's, Longview; BILL O'ROURKE, Christ the King, Kilgore; Deacon NELSON PETZOLD, St. Matthew's, Longview; CHARLOTTE SMITH, St. Joseph's Church, Marshall; LAURA BATE, St. William of Vercelli, Carthage; Deacon LARRY BATE, St. William of Vercelli, Carthage; DEBBIE SCHOLL, St. William of Vercelli, Carthage; Deacon LEN LUSCOMB, Our Lady Queen of Angels, Overton.

Northwest Deanery— (No candidates at the moment).

Southeast Deanery— (No candidates at the moment).

Auditor—Rev. JOSE CORTEZ.

Ecclesiastical Notaries—Mrs. MARGARET OPPENHEIMER; Mrs. CINDY PLUMMER; Deacon RUBEN NATERA, Chancellor.

DIOCESAN ADMINISTRATION

Finance Officer—Mr. JIM SMITH, 1015 E.S.E. Loop 323, Tyler, 75701-9663. Tel: 903-534-1077, Ext. 138. Email: jsmith@dioceseoftyler.org.

Diocesan Finance Council—Rev. Msgrs. JAMES E. YOUNG, Ex Officio; JOSEPH E. STRICKLAND, J.C.L.; Mrs. LAURA REDMAN; Mr. ROBERT BREEDLOVE; Mr. MICHAEL WEEKS; Mrs. FRED ARRAMBIDEZ; Mr. LOUIS OWEN; Rev. Msgr. XAVIER PAPPU, Ex Officio; Mr. JIM SMITH, Ex Officio; Deacon RUBEN NATERA, Chancellor; Mrs. YVETTE BRUNETTE.

Diocesan Building Board—Mr. BILLY CORDOVA, Chm.; Deacon RUBEN NATERA; Mr. TOM DEIBEL; Rev. GAVIN N. VAVEREK, J.C.L. Ex Officio: Rev. Msgr. XAVIER PAPPU; Mr. JIM SMITH.

East Texas Catholic Foundation—Mr. JIM SMITH, Dir., 1015 E.S.E. Loop 323, Tyler, 75701-9663. Email: jsmith@dioceseoftyler.org.

Priests' Pension Board—Rev. Msgrs. JAMES E. YOUNG; XAVIER PAPPU; Rev. BERNARD BOTEJU; Mr. JIM SMITH, Treas.; Rev. Msgrs. ZACHARIAS S. KUNNAKKATTUTHARA; RONALD L. DIEGEL; GERALD A. PRIEST; JOSEPH E. STRICKLAND, J.C.L.; Rev. GAVIN N. VAVEREK, J.C.L.

Catholic Campaign for Human Development—Mr. JIM SMITH. Tel: 903-534-1077, Ext. 138. Email: jsmith@dioceseoftyler.org.

Catholic Schools Office—Dr. C. CHARLES LEBLANC, Supt. Catholic Schools. Tel: 903-534-1077, Ext. 143. Email: cleblanc@dioceseoftyler.org; Mrs. MARY ELLIOTT, Sec., 1015 E.S.E. Loop 323, Tyler, 75701-9663. Tel: 903-534-1077, Ext. 142. Email: schooloffice@dioceseoftyler.org.

Diocesan Catholic School Advisory Council—Mrs. GRETCHEN COBB; Dr. JAMES KLASSEN; Mrs. KEISTAN MCBRIDE; Mrs. MARY LOU TYER; Dr. C. CHARLES LEBLANC, Exec. Officer; Most Rev. ALVARO CORRADA, S.J.; Mr. ALEX SUAREZ; Revs. THOMAS EDELEN, Chm.; DENZIL J. VITHANAGE; Ms. D. KIM SINE, Sec.; Mrs. DIANA HUMPHREYS, Chm.-Elect; Mrs. MARY ELLIOTT, Recording Sec.

Faith Formation Office—Mrs. LINDA PORTER, Dir. Email: lporter@dioceseoftyler.org; Ms. CECILIA ALLIGOOD, Sec. Email: calligood@dioceseoftyler.orgTel: 903-534-1077, Ext. 170.

Coordinator for Catechesis—Sr. ANGELICA OROZCO, E.F.M.S. Email: sistera@dioceseoftyler.org.

Diocesan Christian Initiation Team—Mrs. LINDA PORTER, Chm.; Rev. GAVIN N. VAVEREK, J.C.L., Consultant; Sr. SUSAN SEITZ, O.S.F., Tyler - Cathedral; Deacon DAVID DARBY, Nacog. - Sacred Heart; Mrs. TERESA DARBY, Nacog. - Sacred Heart; Deacon AUBREY FISK, Mineola - St. Peter the Apostle; Sr. GABRIELA DELGADO, Tyler - Cathedral; Rev. ARIEL CORTES, Pittsburgh - Holy Cross Parish; Sr. ANGELICA OROZCO, E.F.M.S., Diocese of Tyler; Ms. PEGGY HAMMETT, Tyler - Cathedral; Deacon TREVOR WELLS, Longview - St. Mary's; Mrs. MARY ANN CAVITT, Texarkana - Sacred Heart; Mrs. OFELIA VALDEZ, Tyler - Cathedral.

Pastoral Ministries—Deacon RUBEN NATERA, Coord. Email: rnatera@dioceseoftyler.org; Ms. ZAIRA AVILA, Administrative Asst.

Family Life Office—Co Directors: Deacon GERALD "JERRY" BESZE. Email: jbesze@dioceseoftyler.org; Mrs. MARY BESZE, 1015 E.S.E. Loop 323, Tyler, 75701-9663. Tel: 903-534-1077. Email: mbesze@dioceseoftyler.org.

Tyler Catholic Committee on Scouting—Mr. JOHN MCDOUGALD, Okee-Tukla District; Rev. FRANCIS O'DOWD, Chap., Mailing Address: P.O. Box 1071, Lindale, 75771-1078. Tel: 903-228-4079; Mr. BYRONE MEADS, Chm.; Mr. GARY L. HUBER, M.D.; Mr. TED KAMEL; Mr. CHARLES HEIMERDINGER; Mr. TIM RUSSELL; Mr. MIKE CONNOR, Professional Scouter, Mailing Address: 172 Luther Ln., Gun Barrel City, 75156. Tel: 903-757-7524.

Young Adult/Campus Ministries—Rev. JESUDOSS THOMAS, S.T.L., St. Mary Chapel, 211 E. College, Nacogdoches, 75965. Tel: 936-564-0661. Email: jesutomson@yahoo.com.

Hispanic Ministry Advisory Council—Revs. RUBEN C. FIGUEROA, O.F.M., Chm.; LUIS E. LARREA, M.F.E.; Deacon RUBEN NATERA, Chancellor.

Priests' Personnel Board—Rev. Msgrs. JAMES E. YOUNG, Chm.; XAVIER PAPPU; GERALD A. PRIEST; JOSEPH E. STRICKLAND, J.C.L., Sec.; Rev. SUSAI AVULA; Rev. Msgr. RONALD L. DIEGEL; Revs. RUBEN FIGUEROA; LUIS E. LARREA, M.F.E.; Rev. Msgr. ZACHARIAS S. KUNNAKKATTUTHARA.

Presbyteral Council—Rev. Msgrs. JOSEPH E. STRICKLAND, J.C.L., Chm.; JAMES E. YOUNG, Vice Chm.; RON L. DIEGEL; XAVIER PAPPU; Revs. GAVIN N. VAVEREK, J.C.L.; MARK KUSMIREK; ARIEL CORTES; LUIS E. LARREA, M.F.E.; EFREN NANO; RAYMUNDO GARCIA; MICHAEL J. ADAMS; TIMOTHY J. KELLY.

Office of Clergy Development/Continuing Education—Rev. Msgr. JAMES E. YOUNG; Mrs. VIRGINIA S. MEDRANO, Admin. Sec., 1015 E.S.E. Loop 323, Tyler, 75701-9663. Tel: 903-534-1077. Email: vmedrano@dioceseoftyler.org.

Permanent Deacon Council—Most Rev. ALVARO CORRADA, S.J., Pres.; Deacons JIM FINEGAN, Chm.; GERALD "JERRY" BESZE, Sec.; Mrs. MARY BESZE, Sec.; Deacon RICK LAWRENCE; Mrs. NELL LAWRENCE; Deacon NELSON PETZOLD; Mrs. REGINA PETZOLD; Deacon DAVID DARBY; Mrs. TERESA DARBY; Deacon BILLY MITCHELL; Mrs. DIANA MITCHELL; Deacon JOHN SARGENT; Mrs. KATHY SARGENT; Deacon REMIGIO ALFARO; Mrs. PATRICIA ALFARO; Deacon RUBEN NATERA; Mrs. MARIA GUADALUPE NATERA; Deacon LARRY BENZMILLER; Mrs. GLORIA BENZMILLER.

Vocations—Co Directors: Revs. JESUDOSS THOMAS, S.T.L. Tel: 903-534-1077, Ext. 184; JESUS RODRIGO ARROYAVE. Tel: 903-534-1077, Ext. 171. Email: vocations@dioceseoftyler.org.

Consecrated Life—Co Directors: Sisters CONCEPCION PONCE. Tel: 903-534-1077, Ext. 184. Email: sisterponce@dioceseoftyler.org; ANGELICA OROZCO, E.F.M.S., 1015 E.S.E. Loop 323, Tyler, 75701-9663. Tel: 903-534-1077, Ext. 145. Email: sistera@dioceseoftyler.org.

Communications Director—Mr. JIM H. D'AVIGNON, 1015 E.S.E. Loop 323, Tyler, 75701-9663. Tel: 903-534-1077, Ext. 144. Email: editorcet3@excite.com.

Discipleship and Stewardship—Deacon RICK LAWRENCE, Dir., 1015 ESE Loop 323, Tyler, 75701-9663. Tel: 903-534-1077, Ext. 161; Mrs. ADELA HERNANDEZ, Sec.

Bishop's Appeal—Deacon RICK LAWRENCE, Dir. Tel: 903-534-1077, Ext. 161. Email: rlawrence@dioceseoftyler.org; Mrs. ADELA HERNANDEZ, Sec., 1015 E.S.E. Loop 323, Tyler, 75701-9663. Tel: 903-534-1077, Ext. 162.

Catholic Charities—*J.J. Saleh Outreach Center, 202 W. Front St., P.O. Box 2016, Tyler, 75710.* Tel: 903-258-9492; Fax: 903-258-6012. Mrs. NELL LAWRENCE, Exec. Dir. Email: nlawrence@cctyler.com; Mrs. OFELIA VALDEZ, Administrative Sec. Email: ovaldez@cctyler.org.

Immigration Case Manager—Mrs. CLAUDIA MEAUX, VAWA (Violence Against Women Act). Email: cmeaux@cctyler.org; NYDIA MUNGIA, Asst. Email: nmungia@cctyler.org.

Society of St. Vincent de Paul—*Mailing Address: Immaculate Conception Conference, 410 S. College, Tyler, 75702.* Ms. SHAWN PICKETT, Dir. Tel: 903-592-0027; Cell: 903-363-5225; Fax: 903-593-7326. Email: cicsocialserv@suddenlinkmail.com; Mr. JOE MARTEL, Pres.; Mr. CHARLES CALSWELL, Vice Pres.; Mrs. TERRY BOLTON, Treas.; Mrs. CRISTINA RANDOLPH, Sec.

Newspaper "Catholic East Texas"—Mr. JIM H. D'AVIGNON, Editor. Reporters: Mrs. SUSAN DEMATTEO NECESSARY, Reporter; Mrs. JOANNE FLORES EMBLETON, Reporter, 1015 E.S.E. Loop 323, Tyler, 75701-9663. Tel: 903-534-1077; Fax: 903-534-1370.

DIOCESAN OFFICES

Diocesan Council of Catholic Women—CYNTHIA MCCOY, 3059 Smith Rd., Jefferson, 75657. Tel: 903-665-8909. Email: clmccoy63@yahoo.com; Rev. GAVIN N. VAVEREK, J.C.L., Moderator, 2108 Ridgewood, Longview, 75605-5199. Tel: 903-757-5855, Ext. 503. Email: frgavin@stmaryslgv.org.

Respect Life Program—Rev. GAVIN N. VAVEREK, J.C.L., Dir., 2108 Ridgewood, Longview, 75605-5199. Tel: 903-757-5855.

Victim Assistance Coordinator—Rev. GAVIN N. VAVEREK, J.C.L. Tel: 903-266-2159. Email: promoter@dioceseoftyler.org.

Diocesan Implementation Committee On Ethics and Integrity Policy for Church Personnel—Rev. GAVIN N. VAVEREK, J.C.L., Promoter of Justice; Rev. Msgr. JOSEPH E. STRICKLAND, J.C.L., Judicial Vicar; Deacon GERALD "JERRY" BESZE; Mrs. MARY BESZE; Deacon RUBEN NATERA; Mrs. LINDA PORTER.

Diocesan Liturgical Commission—Most Rev. ALVARO CORRADA DEL RIO, S.J.; Rev. MORGAN WHITE, Chm.; Deacon RUBEN NATERA; Rev. GAVIN N. VAVEREK, J.C.L.; Mr. BRIAN BRAQUET; Mrs. DIANNA BRAQUET; Ms. PEGGY HAMMETT; Mrs. LINDA PORTER; Ms. ZAIRA AVILA, Administrative Sec.; Deacon JOHN RAGLAND; MELBA RAGLAND; Sr. ANGELICA OROZCO, E.F.M.S.; Rev. JOSE LUIS VIDARTE; VINCENT MEINZER; Deacon SHAUN BLACK.

CLERGY, PARISHES, MISSIONS AND PAROCHIAL SCHOOLS

CITY OF TYLER

(SMITH COUNTY)

1—CATHEDRAL OF THE IMMACULATE CONCEPTION (1987) Rev. Msgr. Joseph E. Strickland, Rector; Revs. Jose Miguel Lopez (Puerto Rico); Augustine Tharappel, M.S.F.S. (India); Mike Snider, Parochial Vicar; Sisters Susan Seitz, O.S.F., Pastoral Assoc.; Sarah Kohles, O.S.F.; Deacons Ramiro Martinez; Ruben Natera; Bill Necessary; Jack Rounds Jr.; Steve Curry; Shaun Black; Rufino Cortez; Dwight (Sam) Hall; Mark D'Eramo.

Social Services:—Office, 423 S. Broadway, 75702. Tel: 903-592-0027; Fax: 903-593-7326.

Res.: 114 W. Front St., 75702. Tel: 903-592-5462.

School—*St. Gregory School*, (Grades PreK-5), 500 S. College St., 75702. Tel: 903-595-4109; Fax: 903-592-8626. Mrs. Kathy Shieldes Harry, Prin.; Diane Parker, Librarian. Lay Teachers 22; Students 333.

School—*Bishop T. K. Gorman Middle School*, (Grades 6-8), 1405 E.S.E. Loop 323, 75701. Tel: 903-561-2424; Fax: 903-561-2645. Mr. James P. Franz, Prin.; Chi-Shim Wellmon, Librarian. Lay Teachers 15; Students 181.

High School—*Bishop Gorman High School* Mr. James P. Franz, Prin. Lay Teachers 33; Students 282.

Catechesis/Religious Program—Tel: 903-592-1617. Lay Teachers 26; Students 150.

Society of St. Vincent de Paul—Tel: 903-592-0027; Fax: 903-592-0034.

Chapel—*St. Paul Chapel* 1015 E.S.E. Loop 323, 75701. Tel: 903-592-1617.

Mission—*St. Joseph the Worker Mission* 5075 FM 14, P.O. Box 4995, 75712. Tel: 903-593-5055. Rev. Scott W. Allen, F.S.S.P.

2—OUR LADY OF GUADALUPE (1999), (Hispanic), Rev. Ruben Figueroa.

Church & Mailing Address: 922 Old Omen Rd., 75701-3709. Tel: 903-593-2006; Fax: 903-593-6033. Email: rficar@att.net.

Catechesis/Religious Program—Students 350.

3—ST. PETER CLAVER (1936) [CEM] [JC] Revs. Luis Eduardo Larrea, M.F.E.; Paul Key; Bro. Simon L. Nila.

Res.: 615 W. Cochran St., 75702. Tel: 903-595-2612; Fax: 903-596-9659. Email: st.peterclaver@att.net. Web: stpeterclavertyler.com.

Catechesis/Religious Program—Fax: 903-596-9659. Students 470.

OUTSIDE THE CITY OF TYLER

ATHENS, HENDERSON CO., ST. EDWARD CHURCH (1947) [JC] Revs. Pancras Savarimuthu; Raymundo Garcia (Mexico), Pastoral Assoc.

Res.: 800 E. Tyler, 75751-2140. Tel: 903-675-2509; Fax: 903-675-8805. Email: pancrass@yahoo.com. Web: www.stedwards-athens.com.

Catechesis/Religious Program—Email: stedwardschurch12@suddenlink.net. Maria De Jesus Miranda, D.R.E. Tel: 903-203-1424. Students 218.

Mission—*St. Boniface* (1997) 318 S. Broad St., P.O. Box 762, Chandler, Van Sand Co. 75758-0762. Tel: 903-849-3234; Fax: 903-849-5634. Email: stboniface3234@earthlink.net. Web: www.home.earthlink.net. Deacon Steve Curry.

ATLANTA, CASS CO., ST. CATHERINE OF SIENA CHURCH (1965) [JC] Rev. Felix Chiraphurathel, O.Praem., Admin.

Res.: 309 N. Louise St., 75551. Tel: 903-796-4494; Fax: 903-796-9990. Email: stcathsienna@aol.com.

Catechesis/Religious Program—Tel: 903-756-5723. Irene Webster, D.R.E. Students 36.

BUFFALO, LEON CO., BLESSED KATERI TEKAKWITHA CHURCH (1979) Rev. Msgr. Theodore F. Rydelek.

Mailing Address: 208 N. Merrill, P.O. Box 878, 75831. Tel: 903-322-3705; Fax: 903-322-3155.

Catechesis/Religious Program—Email: bkateri@ezmailbox.net. Students 31.

CANTON, VAN ZANDT CO., ST. THERESE (1980) Rev. Selvaraj Sinnappan, Admin.; Deacons Richard Lawrence; Alan J. Stehsel; Jonathan Ben Fadely.

Mailing Address: 14786 FM 859, 75103-3676. Tel: 903-567-4286; Fax: 903-567-0586. Email: sttheresecanton@gmail.com.

Catechesis/Religious Program—Students 115.

Mission—*St. Luke* 312 W. O'Neal St., Wills Point, Van Zandt Co. 75169. Tel: 903-873-1238. Rev. Ouseph Thekumthala (India); Deacon Edilberto Reyes.

CARTHAGE, PANOLA CO., ST. WILLIAM OF VERCELLI (1948) Revs. Michael J. Adams; Carlos Rangel.

Res.: 4088 N.W. Loop, 75633-3346. Tel: 903-693-3766 (Office); Fax: 903-693-3759. Email: stwilliamofvercelli@hotmail.com. Web: www.angelfire.com/tx3stwilliam/index.html.

Catechesis/Religious Program—Students 89.

CENTER, SHELBY CO., ST. THERESE (1951) Rev. Jose Luis Vidarte, Admin.

Res.: 717 FM 2974, 75935-6006. Tel: 936-598-8458.

Catechesis/Religious Program—Students 120.

Mission—*Epiphany* 3072 U.S. Hwy. 59 S., Timpson, Shelby Co. 75975-9350. Tel: 936-254-9662.

CLARKSVILLE, RED RIVER CO., ST. JOSEPH (1870), (Hispanic), [CEM] Rev. Morgan White (Ireland), Admin.; Deacon Joe Ibarra Moreno.

Res.: 406 E. Broadway, 75426-3110. Tel: 903-427-5044.

Catechesis/Religious Program—Students 8.

CROCKETT, HOUSTON CO., ST. FRANCIS OF THE TEJAS (1931) Rev. Gary Rottman.

Res.: 609 N. 4th, 75835-4001. Tel: 936-544-5338; Fax: 866-591-9583.

Catechesis/Religious Program—Students 11.

Mission—*St. Leo the Great* P.O. Box 356, Centerville, Leon Co. 75833-0356. Tel: 903-536-5012; Fax: 903-536-1549. Rev. Luis Alphonse Roncancio (Colombia), Admin.; Deacon James Finegan.

Station—*St. Thomas More Hilltop Lake Chapel Fellowship Hall*, P.O. Box 1400, Hilltop Lakes. Tel: 936-855-2640; Fax: 936-855-2935. Rev. Luis Alphonse Roncancio (Colombia), Contact Person.

DAINGERFIELD, MORRIS CO., OUR LADY OF FATIMA (1951), (Hispanic), [CEM] Rev. Juan Carlos Sardinas.

Res.: 1305 Bert St., 75638. Tel: 903-645-5637.

Catechesis/Religious Program—Students 76.

DIBOLL, ANGELINA CO., OUR LADY OF GUADALUPE (1971), (Hispanic), [CEM] Rev. Victor Hamon (Colombia); Deacons Catarino Perez Jr.; Geraldo Trevino.
Mailing Address: P.O. Box 310, 75941-0310. Tel: 936-829-3659; Fax: 936-829-3659.
Res.: 100 Maynard St., 75941.
Catechesis/Religious Program—Students 175.

FAIRFIELD, FREESTONE CO., ST. BERNARD OF CLAIRVAUX (1986) Rev. Devaraj Arulappa (India).
Res.: 630 W. Main, 75840-1418. Tel: 903-389-4616; Fax: 903-389-3844.
Catechesis/Religious Program—Tel: 903-389-8221. Students 28.
Mission—St. Mary 609 Cedar, Teague, Freestone Co. 75840-1617. Tel: 254-739-3692. Rev. Jose Marin.

FLINT, SMITH CO., ST. MARY MAGDALENE CHURCH (1998) Rev. Timothy J. Kelly (Ireland); Deacon Clarence D. Blalock Jr.
Church: 18221 FM 2493, 75762. Tel: 903-894-7647; Fax: 903-894-7739.
Catechesis/Religious Program—Lisa Ellis, D.R.E. Students 139.

GILMER, UPSHUR CO., ST. FRANCIS OF ASSISI (1994) Rev. Hector Bruno de Jesus; Deacons Guylan Blasingame; Gonzalo Rojas.
Mailing Address: 2514 FM852, P.O. Box 704, 75644-0704. Tel: 903-797-3303.
Res.: 2514 FM 852, 75644. Tel: 903-797-3090; Fax: 903-797-3090. Email: stfrancisgilmer@gmail.com.
Catechesis/Religious Program—Tel: 903-797-3303. Students 64.
Mission—Holy Spirit Church 1612 S. FM 2869, Holly Lake Rach, Sulphur Co. 75755-9604. Tel: 903-769-3235; Fax: 903-769-1611. Rev. Msgr. Ronald L. Diegel; Deacon Sam Mullen.

GUN BARREL CITY, HENDERSON CO., ST. JUDE (1975) Rev. Francis O'Dowd; Rev. Msgr. John A. Brennan, Pastor Emeritus; Deacons Richard Sykora; Juan A. Cazares.
Res.: 172 Luther Ln., 75156. Tel: 903-887-1452 (Office); 903-887-5803 (Res.); Fax: 903-887-4906 (Office).
Catechesis/Religious Program—Tel: 903-887-9795 (Office). Mrs. Edna Beltz, D.R.E. Students 137.

HEMPHILL, SABINE CO., ST. PIUS I (1939) [CEM] Rev. Joseph M. Nasser, S.J.; Deacon Kenneth Horn.
309 Starr St., P.O. Box 1925, 75948-1925. Tel: 409-787-4189 (Res.).
Catechesis/Religious Program—Students 10.

HENDERSON, RUSK CO., ST. JUDE (1934) Revs. Jayaselanraj Lucas; Carlos Rangel.
200 Morningside, 75652.
Res.: 110 Millville Dr., 75652. Tel: 903-657-4398; 903-657-4080; Fax: 903-657-0078. Email: judes@eastex.net. Web: www.stjudehenderson.org.
Catechesis/Religious Program—Students 126.

JACKSONVILLE, CHEROKEE CO., OUR LADY OF SORROWS (1954) Revs. Mark Kusmirek; Freddy Celano, Vicar; Deacon Juventino Torres.
Res.: 1023 Corinth Rd., 75766-9801. Tel: 903-586-4538; Fax: 903-586-4996. Email: pastor@oloschurch.com. Web: www.oloschurch.com.
Catechesis/Religious Program—Email: ffl@oloschurch.com. Ana Maria Paredes, D.R.E. Students 377.
Mission—Sacred Heart P.O. Box 947, Rusk, Cherokee Co. 75785. Tel: 903-683-1862; Fax: 903-683-1853. Rev. Stephen Duyka; Deacon Ignacio Panuco.
Mission—Our Lady of Guadalupe Rt. 5, Box 357, Cherokee Co. 75766. Tel: 903-726-7272. Rev. Jose Cortez.
Mission—Venerable Antonio Margil 202 N. Marcus St., Alto, 75925. Tel: 903-683-1862.

JEFFERSON, MARION CO., IMMACULATE CONCEPTION (1867) [CEM] [JC] Rev. Mani Mathai (India), Admin.
Res.: 201 N. Vale St., 75657-2143. Tel: 903-665-2869; Fax: 903-665-8778.
Catechesis/Religious Program—Tel: 903-665-8909; Fax: 903-665-8778. Students 18.
Mission—St. Lawrence Brindisi P.O. Box 928, Waskom, Harrison Co. 75292-0928. Tel: 903-687-2385; Fax: 903-687-4503. Rev. Bernard Boteju, Admin.
Catechesis/Religious Program—Tel: 903-687-2951. Students 40.
Mission—St. Paul of Tarsus Mission 209 W. Lafaette, 75657.
Immaculate Conception Catholic Church, Jefferson, TX Foundation—209 W. Lafayette St., 75657-2143.

KILGORE, GREGG CO., CHRIST THE KING (1936) [JC] Revs. Matias Rodriguez (El Salvador); Patrick Fenton; Deacons Dennis Gilchrist; Alejandro Cisneros; Michael Heslin; Isidro Sanchez; Lino Huerta; William Holda; Len Luscomb.
Res.: 1407 Broadway, 75662-3209. Tel: 903-984-3716; Fax: 903-984-1426.
Catechesis/Religious Program—Tel: 903-986-3573; Fax: 903-984-1426. Sr. Luz del Carmen, E.F.M.S., D.R.E. Students 247.
Mission—Our Lady Queen of Angels 707 Bradford St., P.O. Box 322, Overton, Rusk Co. 75684. Tel: 903-834-6727; Fax: 903-834-6995. Email: ourladyqueenofangels@earthlink.net. Rev. Joby Cheradai Thomas, M.S.; Deacon Len Luscomb.

LINDALE, SMITH CO., HOLY FAMILY (1994) Rev. Mark Dunne, Admin.; Deacon Dennis King.
Mailing Address: P.O. Box 1071, 75771. Tel: 903-882-4079; Fax: 903-882-8382. Email: holy-family@sbcglobal.net.
Catechesis/Religious Program—Students 118.

LONGVIEW, GREGG CO.
1—ST. ANTHONY (1880), (Hispanic), Rev. Joseph B. Lincon; Deacons Joseph Pipak; Manuel Villalobos; Scott B. J. Daniel.
Res.: 908 E. Olive, 75601. Tel: 903-758-9550. Email: stanthonylgv@yahoo.comFax: 903-758-9066.
Church: 508 N. 6th St., 75601.
Catechesis/Religious Program—Shopka Center, 406 N. 6th St., 75601. Students 85.
2—ST. MARY (1982) Rev. Gavin N. Vaverek; Deacons John Borens; John Shaffer; Trevor Wells; Vincent James Wilson.
Res.: 2108 Ridgewood Dr., 75605-5199. Tel: 903-757-5855; Fax: 903-758-5074. Email: church@stmaryslgv.org. Web: www.stmaryslgv.org.
School—405 Hollybrook Dr., 75605-2464. Tel: 903-753-1657; Fax: 903-758-7347. Email: admin@stmaryslgv.org. Mrs. Amy Allen, Prin. Lay Teachers 20; Students 197.
Catechesis/Religious Program—Tel: 903-757-5891; Fax: 903-758-5074. Students 158.
Mission—Our Lady of Grace 415 Cypress St., Hallsville, Harrison Co. 75650. Tel: 903-668-5279; Fax: 903-668-5220. Rev. Peter McGrath, Parochial Vicar; Deacons Robert William Rhodes; Gregorio Sanchez.
3—ST. MATTHEW CATHOLIC CHURCH (1999) Rev. Msgr. Xavier Pappu; Deacon Nelson Petzold; Rev. Joel Gonzalez; Deacon Francisco Lopez.
Res.: 2900 Pinetree Road, 75604. Tel: 903-295-7558.
Church: 2800 Pine Tree Rd., 75604. Tel: 903-295-3890; Fax: 903-295-7559. Email: churchoffice@stmatthewlgv.org. Web: www.stmatthewlgv.org.
Catechesis/Religious Program—Email: dff@stmatthewlgv.org. Students 310.

LUFKIN, ANGELINA CO.
1—ST. ANDREW (1998) Rev. Jose J. Kannampuzha; Deacon Gary Trevino.
Office: 1611 Feagin Dr., 75904. Tel: 936-632-9100; Fax: 936-632-0627. Email: standrewlufkin@catholicweb.com.
Catechesis/Religious Program—Students 160.
2—ST. PATRICK (1928) Revs. William J. Slight, M.S.; Paul Rainville, M.S.; Deacons Martin Aguilar; Abelino Cordero; Juan Mijares; Manuel J. Ramos; Ray Vann.
Res.: 2118 Lowry St., 75901-1316. Tel: 409-634-6833; Fax: 409-634-6891.
School—St. Patrick School, (Grades PreK-8), 2116 Lowry St., 75901. Tel: 409-634-6719; Fax: 936-639-2776. Steve Coryell, Prin. Lay Teachers 13; Students 120.
Catechesis/Religious Program—Tel: 936-634-1090. Oralia Aguilar, D.R.E.; Brenda Dunn, C.R.E. Students 189.

MADISONVILLE, MADISON CO., ST. ELIZABETH ANN SETON (1978) [JC] Rev. Michael J. Barone; Deacon Burke J. Landry.
Mailing Address: 100 S. Tammye Ln., 77864. Tel: 936-348-6368; Fax: 936-348-5377. Email: pastor.stelizabeth@sbcglobal.net.
Catechesis/Religious Program—Students 90.

MALAKOFF, HENDERSON CO., MARY, QUEEN OF HEAVEN CHURCH Revs. William Palmer, Admin.; Raymundo Garcia (Mexico).
2269 CR 1730, P.O. Box 508, 75148-0508.
Catechesis/Religious Program—Neal Williams, D.R.E. Students 54.

MARSHALL, HARRISON CO., ST. JOSEPH (1874) [CEM] Revs. Denzil Vithanage, Admin.; Jesus Rodrigo Arroyave, Parochial Vicar; Deacons Santiago Suarez; Felipe Pena; Magdaleno Aguirre; John Sargent.
Res.: 410 N. Alamo Blvd., 75670-3450. Tel: 903-935-2536; Fax: 903-938-1591. Email: saintjosephmarshall@yahoo.com. Web: stjosephmarshall.com.
Catechesis/Religious Program—Tel: 903-935-5502. Students 175.
Convent—2305 S. Garrett, 75670. Tel: 903-938-3998.
Mission—San Pedro the Fisherman 1835 Chaparrall, Hwy. 43, P.O. Box 430, Tatum, Panola Co. 75691-0430. Tel: 903-947-2454. Deacon Jose Luis Mireles.

MINEOLA, WOOD CO., ST. PETER THE APOSTLE (1937) [JC] Rev. Efren Nano; Deacons Aubrey Fisk; William Faber.
203 Meadowbrook, P.O. Box 1022, 75773-7022. Email: stpeter75773@sbcglobal.net.
Rectory—
Catechesis/Religious Program—Students 102.
Mission—St. Celestine 116 W. Frank, Grand Saline, Van Zandt Co. 75140. Tel: 903-962-6350. Rev. Victor Hernandez (Colombia); Deacon William Flores.
Mission—St. John the Evangelist Church 551 E. FM 2795, Emory, Rains Co. 75140. Rev. Victor Hernandez (Colombia).

MOUNT PLEASANT, TITUS CO., ST. MICHAEL (1917) Revs. Octavio Suarez; Elpidio Lopez; Deacons Joe Ibarra Moreno; Lorenzo Martinez.
Mailing Address: 1403 E. 1st St., 75455-4715. Tel: 903-572-5227; Fax: 903-572-9659.
Res.: 310 Denman Dr., 75455-4157. Tel: 903-572-5611; Fax: 903-572-9659. Email: enfo@stmichaelmp.org. Web: www.stmichaelmp.org.
Catechesis/Religious Program—Ann Decious, Dir. Faith Formation. Students 510.

MOUNT VERNON, FRANKLIN CO., SACRED HEART (1986) Rev. Ambrose Chinnappa; Deacons Carl Miller; Donald R. Brown.
Mailing Address: P.O. Box 918, 75457. Tel: 903-537-2174; Fax: 903-537-2174.
Church: 406 S. SH-37, 75457. Tel: 903-537-2174; Fax: 903-537-2174.
Catechesis/Religious Program—Tel: 903-572-3390. Students 59.

NACOGDOCHES, NACOGDOCHES CO., SACRED HEART (1716) [CEM] [JC 2] Rev. Msgr. James E. Young; Rev. Luis F. Arroyave (Colombia); Deacons David Darby; Michael Doyle; Gary Giese; Ezequiel Tapia; Luis Alberto Hernandez; Rafael Landeros; Pedro Gonzalez; Librado Cruz Sosa.
Res.: 2508 Appleby Sand Rd., 75965-3632. Tel: 936-564-7134 (Rectory); 936-564-7807 (Office); Fax: 936-559-5442.
Catechesis/Religious Program—Tel: 936-564-5321. Deacon Gary Giese, D.R.E. Students 360.
Mission—Our Lady of Lourdes P.O. Box 241, Chireno, Nacogdoches Co. 75937. Tel: 936-598-8458. Rev. Joseph Lourdusamy.
Mission—Immaculate Conception - Moral [CEM] [JC 3] 1422 Co. Rd. 724, Nacogdoches Co. 75964. Tel: 936-560-3200; Fax: 936-462-8825. Rev. Joseph Lourdusamy.
Mission—Our Lady of Guadalupe 4401 Old Lufkin Rd., Nacogdoches Co. 75964. Tel: 936-560-5956. Rev. Luis F. Arroyave (Colombia), Contact Person.
Chapel—Nacogdoches, St. Mary's Chapel, Stephen F. Austin State University 211 E. College, 75961. Tel: 936-564-0661; Fax: 936-559-7377. Rev. Jesudoss Thomas.

NEW BOSTON, BOWIE CO., ST. MARY OF THE CENACLE (1918) Rev. Ronald G. Demski, Admin.; Deacon Timothy O'Neil.
Mailing Address: 216 W. Magnolia St., 75570-0914. Tel: 903-628-2323 Hall; Fax: 903-628-4161. Email: stmarycenacle@yahoo.com.
Res.: 216 Magnolia St., 75570. Tel: 903-628-6186.
Catechesis/Religious Program—Tel: 903-628-2323. Students 40.

PALESTINE, ANDERSON CO., SACRED HEART (1893) [CEM] Rev. Msgr. Zacharias S. Kunnakkattuthara (India); Rev. Renelmo Ramirez; Deacons Alex Kobar; Daniel Rose, Prison Chap.
Res.: 503 N. Queen St., 75801-2718. Tel: 903-729-2463; Fax: 903-723-9799. Email: shpalestine@earthlink.net.
Catechesis/Religious Program—Loiette Dixon, D.R.E.; Don Cumm, D.R.E.; Dr. Martin Flynn, Youth Min. Students 425.
Mission—St. Charles Borromeo 1101 Hwy. 155 N., Frankston, Anderson Co. 75763. Tel: 903-876-2089; Fax: 903-876-2089. Email: stch@gower.net. Rev. M. Jones Jayaraj.

PARIS, LAMAR CO., OUR LADY OF VICTORY (1880) [JC] Revs. Morgan White (Ireland); Jose Ruben Lobaton; James Rowland, Parochial Vicar.
Res.: 3300 Clarksville St., 75460. Tel: 903-784-1000; Fax: 903-784-3946. Email: ourladyofvictory@suddenlinkmail.com.
Catechesis/Religious Program—Nellie Denman, D.R.E. Students 235.

PITTSBURG, CAMP CO., HOLY CROSS (1987) [JC] Rev. Ariel Cortes Mojica.
501 Hill Ave., 75686-1810. Tel: 903-856-7609; 903-790-5252. Email: holycrosscc@hotmail.com.
Catechesis/Religious Program—Students 150.

SULPHUR SPRINGS, HOPKINS CO., ST. JAMES (1880) Revs. Maria Susai J. Avula; Jesus Eduardo Lazaro Angarita; Deacons Gerald "Jerry" Besze; Loren G. Seely.
297 Texas St., 75482. Tel: 903-885-1222; Fax: 903-885-5855.
Res.: 303 Texas St., 75482. Tel: 903-885-2873.
Catechesis/Religious Program— Cindy Lancaster, D.R.E. Students 188.
Mission—St. Clare Mission 10 E. Side Sq., Cooper, Delta Co. 75432.

TEXARKANA, BOWIE CO., SACRED HEART (1874) [CEM 2] Rev. Msgr. Gerald A. Priest; Rev. Christian

Zelaya; Deacons Keith A. Woods, (Retired); Larry Benzmiller; Craig Louis Lashford.
Res.: 4505 Elizabeth St., 75503-2998. Tel: 903-794-4444; Fax: 903-792-1529.
Catechesis/Religious Program—Tel: 903-792-6846. Students 200.

TRINITY, TRINITY CO., MOST HOLY TRINITY (1972) [JC] Rev. Thomas Edelen, Admin.; Deacon John Milton.
Res.: 401 Prospect Dr., 75862-9801. Tel: 936-594-6664; Fax: 936-594-5244. Email: mhtc@valornet.com.
Catechesis/Religious Program—Students 7.
Mission— Groveton, 75845.

UNION GROVE-GLADEWATER, UPSHUR CO., ST. THERESA OF THE INFANT JESUS (1945) [JC] Rev. Joseph Ezharath (India).
Mailing Address: 10138 Union Grove Rd., Gladewater, 75647-0967. Tel: 903-845-2306; Fax: 903-845-7126.
Catechesis/Religious Program—Students 26.

WHITEHOUSE, SMITH CO., PRINCE OF PEACE (1996) Rev. Daniel L. Daugherty.
Mailing Address: P.O. Box 456, 75791-0456. Tel: 903-581-9600; Fax: 903-561-4946. Web: officialprinceofpeacecatholicchurch.org.
Res.: 903 Langford Ln., 75791. Tel: 903-839-7599. Web: www.opopcc.org.
Catechesis/Religious Program—Email: srmmag@suddenlinkmail.com. Students 182.

Chaplains of Public Institutions

CROCKETT. *Crockett State School*, 1701 S.W. Loop 304, 75835. Tel: 936-852-5000; Fax: 936-544-2543. Email: crockett@tyc.state.tx.us. Rev. Jose George, Deacon Ramiro Romo. Attended by St. Francis of the Tejas Church, Crockett.

HENDERSON. *Bradshaw State Facility, Texas Department of Corrections*. Rev. Jayaselanraj Lucas. Attended by St. Jude Church, Henderson.
East Texas MTC (Management Training Corporation) Detention Center, 9000 Industrial Dr., 75652. Tel: 903-655-3300.

LOVELADY. *Eastham Unit, Texas Department of Corrections*. Attended by Most Holy Trinity Catholic Church 401 Prospect Dr., Trinity, TX 75862, P.O. Box 16, 75851-0016. Tel: 936-636-7321, Ext. 7204. P.O. Box 16, 75851-0016.

MIDWAY. *Ferguson Prison, Texas Department of Corrections*. Attended by Most Holy Trinity Catholic Parish, 401 Prospect Dr., Trinity, TX, 75862 (Tel: 936-594-6664), 12120 Savage Dr., 75852. Tel: 936-348-3751.

NEW BOSTON. *Telford Unit, Texas Department of Corrections*, P.O. Box 9200, 75570. Tel: 903-628-3171. Rev. Ronald G. Demski.

OVERTON. *Billy Max Moore Private Prison*, 8500 N. FM 3053, 75684-1000. Rev. Joby Cheradai Thomas, M.S., M.S., Chap.

PALESTINE. *Beto I Unit and Louie C. Powledge Unit, Texas Department of Corrections*, P.O. Box 2250, 75801. Rev. Msgr. Zacharias S. Kunnakkattuthara (India), Chap., Rev. Joseph Ezharath (India).

RUSK. *Jerry H. Hodge Unit and Sky View Unit, Texas Department of Corrections*, P.O. Box 999, 75785-0999. Tel: 903-683-5784. Revs. Mark Kusmirek, Chap., Jose Cortez, Chap., Stephen Duyka.

TEAGUE. *Boyd Unit, Texas Department of Correction*, Rte. 2, Box 500, 75860. Tel: 254-739-5555. Rev. Jose G. Marin, Chap.

TENNESSEE COLONY. *Coffield Unit, Texas Department of Corrections*, Rte. 1, Box 150, 75861-9710. Tel: 903-928-2211. Rev. Msgr. Zacharias S. Kunnakkattuthara (India), Chap., Rev. Harold P. Paulson (Retired).
Gurney Unit. Rev. Msgr. Zacharias S. Kunnakkattuthara (India), Chap., Rev. Harold P. Paulson (Retired). Attended by Sacred Heart, Palestine.
Michael Unit, P.O. Box 4500, 75886-4500. Tel: 903-928-2311. Rev. Msgr. Zacharias S. Kunnakkattuthara (India), Chap., Rev. Harold P. Paulson (Retired).

TEXARKANA. *Federal Corrections Institution*, P.O. Box 9500, 75505-9500. Tel: 903-838-4587. Rev. Msgr. Gerald A. Priest, Chap., Rev. Christian Zelaya, Deacon Joe Bruick. Attended by Sacred Heart, Texarkana.

WINNSBORO. *Clyde Johnston Unit, Texas Department of Corrections*, 703 Airport Rd., 75494-9999. Tel: 903-342-6166. Rev. Jose Kumblumkal, C.M.I.

On Duty Outside the Diocese:
Revs.—
Anthony, Alphonse
Bedoya, Dario
Dobosz, Jerzy George
Doyle, Michael A.
Duran, Said
Gonzalez, Daniel
Mathew, Thomas
Nevares, Eduardo
Ruggles, Christopher V., J.C.L.

Graduate Studies:
Rev.—
Gomez, Jhon Jairo, Continuing Education

Retired:
Rev. Msgrs.—
Flynn, John
Metzger, Sam S.
Revs.—
Hoan, Basil P., Lake House, Hemphill, 75948. Tel: 409-787-2310 (Residence)
Paulson, Harold P.
Walsh, Richard (Denis) L.
Zakshesky, Francis, 8409 CR 31, Sinton, 78387.

Absent on Sick Leave:
Rev.—
Zakshesky, Francis (Retired), 8409 CR 31, Sinton, 78387.

Permanent Deacons:
Aguilar, Martin, St. Patrick, Lufkin
Aguirre, Magdaleno, St. Joseph, Marshall
Alfaro, Remigio, Our Lady of Guadalupe, Tyler
Bate, Lawrence Foster, Jr., St. William of Vercelli, Carthage
Benzmiller, Lawrence, Sacred Heart Church, Texarkana
Besze, Gerald "Jerry", St. James the Apostle Church, Sulphur Springs
Black, Shaun, Cathedral of the Immaculate Conception, Tyler
Blalock, Clarence D., Jr., St. Mary Magdalene, Flint
Blas, Lorenzo Martinez, St. Michael, Mt. Pleasant
Blasingame, Guylan, St. Theresa, Union Grove
Borens, John, St. Mary, Longview
Brown, Donald R., Telford Unit, New Boston
Cazares, Juan A., St. Jude, Gun Barrel City
Cisneros, Alejandro, Christ the King, Kilgore
Cordero, Abelino, St. Patrick, Lufkin
Cortez, Rufino, Cathedral of the Immaculate Conception, Tyler
Curry, Steve, Cathedral of the Immaculate Conception, Tyler
D'Eramo, Mark, Cathedral of the Immaculate Conception, Tyler
Daniel, Scott B. J., St. Matthew, Longview
Darby, David, Sacred Heart Church, Nacogdoches
Doyle, Micheal, St. Augustine Church, San Augustine
Faber, William, St. Peter the Apostle Church, Mineola; St. Celestine Church, Grand Saline
Fadely, Jonathan Ben, St. Therese of Lisieux, Canton
Finegan, James, St. Thomas More Church, Hilltop Lakes; St. Leo the Great Church, Centerville; St. Elizabeth Ann Seton Church, Madisonville
Fisk, Aubrey, St. Peter the Apostle Church, Mineola
Flores, William, St. Celestine Church, Grand Saline
Giese, Gary, Sacred Heart Church, Nacogdoches
Gilchrist, Dennis S., Christ the King, Kilgore
Gonzales, Pedro, Sacred Heart, Nacogdoches
Gonzalez, Joel, St. Matthew, Longview
Hall, Dwight (Sam), Well Spring Spirituality Center
Hernandez, Jose, St. James, Sulphur Springs
Hernandez, Luis Alberto, Sacred Heart, Nacogdoches
Heslin, Mike, Christ the King Church, Kilgore; Bradshaw State Prison, Henderson; Bill Magmore Correctional Facility, Overton
Holda, William, Christ the King, Kilgore
Horn, Kenneth, St. Pius I, Hemphill
Huerta, Lino, Christ the King, Kilgore
King, Dennis G., Holy Family, Lindale
Kobar, Alex, Sacred Heart, Palestine
Landeros, Rafael, Our Lady of Guadalupe, Nacogdoches
Landry, Burke J., St. Elizabeth Ann Seton, Madisonville
Lashford, Craig Louis, Sacred Heart, Texarkana
Lawrence, Richard, St. Therese Church, Canton
Lopez, Francisco, St. Matthew, Longview
Luscomb, Len, St. Jude
Martinez, Lorenzo, St. Michael, Mount Pleasant
Martinez, Ramiro, Cathedral of the Immaculate Conception, Tyler
Mijares, Juan, St. Patrick, Lufkin
Miller, Carl, St. John the Evangelist, Emory
Milton, John, Assignment Outside Diocese
Mireles, Jose Luis, San Pedro the Fisherman, Tatum
Mitchell, Billy, St. Patrick Church, Lufkin
Moreno, Joe Ibarra, St. Michael, Mt. Pleasant
Mullen, Sam, Sacred Heart, Mt. Vernon
Natera, Ruben, Vice Chancellor, Cathedral of the Immaculate Conception, Tyler
Necessary, William, Tyler Cathedral, with additional ministry to St. Peter Claver Church, Tyler
O'Brien, William E., St. James, Sulphur Springs
O'Neill, Timothy Peter, St. Mary of the Cenacle, New Boston
Panuco, Ignacio, Sacred Heart, Rusk
Pena, Felipe, St. Joseph, Marshall
Perez, Catarino, Jr., Our Lady of Guadalupe, Diboll
Petzold, Nelson R., St. Matthew, Longview
Pipak, Joseph, St. Anthony, Longview
Ragland, John Allen, Our Lady of Lourdes, Chireno
Ramos, Manuel J., St. Patrick, Lufkin
Rhodes, Robert William, Our Lady of Grace, Hallsville
Rojas, Gonzalo, St. Anthony, Longview; St. Francis of Assisi, Gilmer
Romo, Ramiro, St. Francis of Tejas, Crockett
Rose, Daniel, Beto I & Powledge Unit, TDC, Palestine
Rounds, Jack, Jr., Cathedral of the Immaculate Conception, Tyler
Sanchez, Gregorio, Our Lady of Grace, Hallsville
Sanchez, Isidro, Christ the King, Kilgore
Sargent, John, St. Joseph, Marshall
Seely, Loren G., St. James, Sulphur Springs
Shaffer, John K., St. Mary, Longview
Sosa, Librado Cruz, Sacred Heart, Nacogdoches
Stehsel, Alan J., St. Therese of Lisieux, Canton
Suarez, Santiago, St. Joseph, Marshall
Sykora, Richard L., St. Jude, Gun Barrel City
Tapia, Ezequiel, Sacred Heart, Nacogdoches
Tiscareno, Jose Angel, Our Lady of Guadalupe, Tyler
Torres, Juventino, Our Lady of Sorrows, Jacksonville
Trevino, Gerardo, St. Patrick, Lufkin
Vann, Raymond Kiah, Jr., St. Patrick, Lufkin
Villalobos, Manuel, St. Anthony, Longview
Wells, Trevor, St. Mary Church, Longview
Wilson, Vincent James, St. Mary, Longview
Woods, Keith A., Sacred Heart, Texarkana
Yelverton, Ricky D., St. Francis of Assisi, Gilmer

INSTITUTIONS LOCATED IN THE DIOCESE

[A] GENERAL HOSPITALS

TYLER. *Trinity Mother Frances Health System* (1937) 800 E. Dawson St., 75701. Tel: 903-593-8441. Web: www.tmfhs.org. Mr. J. Lindsey Bradley Jr., Pres. & CAO; Rev. Paul Key, S.T.L., Chap. Sisters of the Holy Family of Nazareth 6; Bed Capacity 424; Staff 3,800; Total Assisted Annually 928,262.

MADISONVILLE. *Madison St. Joseph Health Center*, 100 W. Cross St., P.O. Box 698, 77864. Tel: 936-348-2631; Fax: 936-348-3404. Anthony D. Pfitzer, Trustee & Contact Person; Mr. Reed Edmundson, Admin. Bed Capacity 25; Total Assisted Annually 27,460; Total Staff 110.

TEXARKANA. *Christus Health Ark-La-Tex dba Christus St. Michael Health System* 2600 St. Michael Dr., 75503. Tel: 903-614-1000; Fax: 903-614-2030. Email: nancy.burleson@christushealth.org. Web: www.christusstmichael.org. Chris Karam, Pres & CEO. Rehabilitation Hospital., Operated by Christus Health Dallas, TX (Merged 2/1/1999). Bed Capacity 312; Total Staff 1,698; Total Assisted Annually 170,619.
Christus St. Michael Rehabilitation Hospital, 2400 St. Michael Dr., 75503. Tel: 903-614-4000; Fax: 903-614-4064. Rehabilitation Hospital., Operated by Christus Health. Bed Capacity 50; Total Staff 205; Total Assisted Annually 40,732.
St. Michael Rehabilitation Hospital, 2400 St. Michael Dr., 75503. Tel: 903-614-4000; Fax: 903-614-4064. Web: www.christusstmichael.org. Aloma R. Gender, R.N., M.S.W., Admin. Operated by Christus Health, Houston Texas. Bed Capacity 50; Total Assisted Annually 32,311; Total Staff 185.

[B] MONASTERIES AND RESIDENCES OF PRIESTS

PALESTINE. *Hermitage* (1968) 10020 An. Co. Rd. 404, 75803. Tel: 903-549-2950. Rev. Denis Walsh. Other Institutions: Houses of Religious Men 1; Total in Residence 1; Total Staff 1.
Prayer Mountain Hermitage (1985) 10089 An. Co. Rd. 404, 75803. Sr. Mary Vogel, H.S.S.R.

WHITEHOUSE. *The Missionaries of St. Francis de Sales* (1838) P.O. Box 440, 16828 FM 2964, 75791. Tel: 903-839-1280; Fax: 903-839-3486. Web:

www.wellsrpingcommunity.net. Rev. Augustine Tharappel, M.S.F.S. (India), Regl. Supr. MSFS USA Region Wellspring. *Fransalian Center for Spirituality*, P.O Box 440, 75791. Tel: 903-839-1280; Fax: 903-839-3486. Web: www.wellspringcommunity.net. Rev. Augustine Tharappel, M.S.F.S. (India), Dir. House of Prayer - Wellspring.

Priests of the Province Not Listed Elsewhere: Revs. Nithiyaselvam Arokiaselvam, M.S.F.S., East Lansing, MI; Sebastian Conrad, M.S.F.S., Deer Park, TX; Binu Edathumparambil, M.S.F.S., Elk Grove Village, IL; Mathew Elayidathamadam, M.S.F.S., Elk Grove Village, IL; Philip Thomas Kizhakumpurath, M.S.F.S. (India), Yonkers, NY; Jose Mudavankunnel, M.S.F.S., Mobile, AL; Tom Thomas, M.S.F.S., Elk Grove Village, IL.

Priests of the Region Serving Elsewhere: Revs. John Peter Arulanandam, M.S.F.S.; John Devore, M.S.F.S.; Martin Kopchik, M.S.F.S.; Paul Kunnumpuram, M.S.F.S.; Joseph Mullakkara, M.S.F.S.; George Puraidam, M.S.F.S.; John Peter Ambrose, M.S.F.S.; Dharmaraj Anthony, M.S.F.S.; Santhiyagu Arokiam, M.S.F.S.; Luckas Arulappa, M.S.F.S.; Anthony Bonela, M.S.F.S.; Davis Chackaleckel, M.S.F.S.; Johnbritto Chinnappa, M.S.F.S.; Benjamin Dande, M.S.F.S.; Luka U. Kalarickal, M.S.F.S.; Francis Kizhakkethazhe, M.S.F.S.; Santy Kochupurackal, M.S.F.S.; Kurian Kollapallil, M.S.F.S.; Joseph Kuzhupil, M.S.F.S.; Ananda Prasad, M.S.F.S.; Jojaiah Mandagiri, M.S.F.S.; Augustine Mannaparambil, M.S.F.S.; Joseph Mendes, M.S.F.S.; Joseph Charles Pednekar, M.S.F.S.; Joseph Pottemmel, M.S.F.S.; Tomy Puliynampattayil, M.S.F.S.; Johnny Puthiyaparampil, M.S.F.S.; Mathew Thayil, M.S.F.S.; George Thayilkuzhithottu, M.S.F.S.; Mathew Thottiyil, M.S.F.S.; George Vattappara, M.S.F.S.; Joseph Xavier, M.S.F.S.

[C] CONVENTS AND RESIDENCES FOR SISTERS

TYLER. *Instituto Santa Mariana de Jesus*, 2706 Shady Ln., 75702. Tel: 903-593-8933. Email: gadelmar85@aol.com.

LUFKIN. *Monastery of the Infant Jesus*, 1501 Lotus Ln., 75904-2699. Tel: 936-634-4233; Fax: 936-634-2156. Sr. Mary John, O.P., Prioress; Rev. J.D. Logan, O.P., Chap. Cloistered Dominican Nuns. Professed Sisters 26.

[D] CAMPUS MINISTRY

TYLER. *Tyler Junior College and The University of Texas at Tyler Newman Center* 423 S. Broadway, 75702. Tel: 903-592-1617. Attended from the Cathedral of the Immaculate Conception.

NACOGDOCHES. *Stephen F. Austin University Catholic Student Center* (1959) *SFA, Catholic Student Center*, P.O. Box 6125 SFA, 75962. Tel: 936-564-0661; Fax: 936-559-7377. Email: cscsfa@catholicweb.com. Web: www.sfacatholic.net. Rev. Jesudoss Thomas, S.T.L., Chap. Other Institutions: St. Mary's Chapel Total in Residence 1; Total Staff 1.

[E] MISCELLANEOUS

TYLER. *Catholic Charities East Texas - Diocese of Tyler, J.J. Saleh Outreach Ctr.*, 202 W. Front St., P.O. Box 2016, 75710. Tel: 903-258-9492; Fax: 903-258-6012. Mrs. Nell Lawrence, Exec. Dir.; Mrs. Claudia Meaux, BIA Immigration Case Worker; Mrs. Nydia Mungia, Immigration Case Worker; Mrs. Ofelia Valdez, Admin. Asst.

Society of St. Vincent de Paul, Immaculate Conception Conference, 410 S. College, 75702.

**Tyler Catholic School Foundation*, P.O. Box 131175, 75713. Tel: 903-526-5988; Fax: 903-526-0750. Email: tcsfnd@gmail.com. Web: www.tcsf.info. D. V. Emery, Exec. Dir.

LONGVIEW. **Longview Catholic School Endowment Fund*, 405 Hollybrook, 75605. Tel: 903-753-1657; Fax: 903-758-7347. Web: www.stmaryslgv.org.

LUFKIN. **St. Patrick School Foundation* (1983) 2116 Lowry, 75901. Tel: 936-634-6719; Fax: 936-639-2776. Email: webmaster@stpatricklufkin.com. Web: www.stpatricklufkin.com.

PARIS. *St. Joseph's Community Foundation* (2004) 2800 Lamar Ave., 75460. Tel: 903-784-5136; Fax: 903-784-5481. Web: www.sjparis.org. Mailing Address: P.O. Box 6427, 75460. Courtney Evdy, Pres. & Exec. Dir.

RELIGIOUS INSTITUTES OF MEN REPRESENTED IN THE DIOCESE

For further details refer to the corresponding bracketed number in the Religious Institutes of Men or Women section.

[]—*Carmelite of Mary Immaculate*—C.M.I.

[0220]—*Congregation of the Blessed Sacrament*—S.S.S.

[]—*Franciscan*—O.F.M.

[]—*Indian Missionary Society*—I.M.S.

[0720]—*The Missionaries of Our Lady of La Salette*—M.S.

[]—*Missionaries of St. Francis de Sales*—M.S.F.S.

[]—*Norbertine Fathers*—O.Praem.

[1065]—*Priestly Fraternity of St. Peter*—F.S.S.P.

RELIGIOUS INSTITUTES OF WOMEN REPRESENTED IN THE DIOCESE

[0230]—*Benedictine Sisters of Pontifical Jurisdiction*—O.S.B.

[]—*Congregation of the Mother of Carmel*—C.M.S.

[0470]—*Congregation of the Sisters of Charity of the Incarnate Word. Houston, Texas* (San Antonio, TX)—C.C.V.I.

[1070-19]—*Dominican Sisters of Houston, Texas (Congregation of the Sacred Heart)*—O.P.

[]—*Eucharistic Franciscan Sisters of Los Angeles*—E.F.M.S.

[]—*Franciscan Sisters of Dubuque*—O.S.F.

[]—*Hermit Sisters of St. Romuald*—H.S.S.R.

[]—*Instituto Santa Mariana de Jesus*—I.S.M.J.

[1570]—*Sisters of St. Francis of the Holy Family*—O.S.F.

[1970]—*Sisters of the Holy Family of Nazareth*—C.S.F.N.

NECROLOGY

† Whitsell, John L., (Retired)—Died July 28, 2009

An asterisk (*) denotes an organization that has established tax-exempt status directly with the IRS and is not covered by the USCCB Group Ruling.

Diocese of Venice

(Dioecesis Venetiae in Florida)

Most Reverend

FRANK J. DEWANE

Bishop of Venice; ordained July 16, 1988; appointed Coadjutor Bishop of Venice April 25, 2006; Episcopal ordination July 25, 2006; appointed Second Bishop of Venice January 19, 2007. *Res.: P.O. Box 2006, Venice, FL 34284-2006.*

Most Reverend

JOHN J. NEVINS, D.D.

Bishop Emeritus of Venice; ordained June 6, 1959; appointed Titular Bishop of Rusticiana and Auxiliary of Miami February 6, 1979; consecrated March 24, 1979; appointed First Bishop of Venice July 17, 1984; installed October 25, 1984; retired January 19, 2007. *Res.: P.O. Box 2006, Venice, FL 34284-2006.*

ESTABLISHED OCTOBER 25, 1984.

Square Miles 9,035.

Comprises the Counties of Charlotte, Collier, DeSoto, Glades, Hardee, Hendry, Highlands, Lee, Manatee and Sarasota in the State of Florida.

For legal titles of parishes and diocesan institutions, consult the Chancellor.

Catholic Center, 1000 Pinebrook Rd., Venice, FL 34285.
Mailing Address: P.O. Box 2006, Venice, FL 34284-2006.
Tel: 941-484-9543; Fax: 941-484-1121.

Web: dioceseofvenice.org

Email: info@dioceseofvenice.org

STATISTICAL OVERVIEW

Personnel	
Bishop	1
Retired Bishops	1
Priests: Diocesan Active in Diocese	81
Priests: Diocesan Active Outside Diocese	4
Priests: Retired, Sick or Absent	21
Number of Diocesan Priests	106
Religious Priests in Diocese	69
Total Priests in Diocese	175
Extern Priests in Diocese	94
Ordinations:	
Diocesan Priests	3
Transitional Deacons	2
Permanent Deacons	4
Permanent Deacons in Diocese	97
Total Brothers	19
Total Sisters	91
Parishes	
Parishes	57
With Resident Pastor:	
Resident Diocesan Priests	42
Resident Religious Priests	14
Without Resident Pastor:	
Administered by Priests	1
Missions	14
Pastoral Centers	1
Professional Ministry Personnel:	
Brothers	3
Sisters	39
Lay Ministers	106
Welfare	
Homes for the Aged	8
Total Assisted	594
Day Care Centers	1
Total Assisted	49
Specialized Homes	2
Total Assisted	57
Special Centers for Social Services	29
Total Assisted	39,966
Educational	
Diocesan Students in Other Seminaries	19
Seminaries, Religious	1
Students Religious	1
Total Seminarians	20
Colleges and Universities	1
Total Students	825
High Schools, Diocesan and Parish	3
Total Students	1,440
Elementary Schools, Diocesan and Parish	10
Total Students	2,863
Non-residential Schools for the Disabled	2
Total Students	110
Catechesis/Religious Education:	
High School Students	1,398
Elementary Students	11,631
Total Students under Catholic Instruction	18,287
Teachers in the Diocese:	
Priests	9
Brothers	3
Sisters	14
Lay Teachers	355
Vital Statistics	
Receptions into the Church:	
Infant Baptism Totals	4,185
Minor Baptism Totals	413
Adult Baptism Totals	425
Received into Full Communion	307
First Communions	3,710
Confirmations	3,060
Marriages:	
Catholic	439
Interfaith	133
Total Marriages	572
Deaths	2,237
Total Catholic Population	237,368
Total Population	1,959,795

Former Bishop—Most Rev. JOHN J. NEVINS, D.D., ord. June 6, 1959; appt. Titular Bishop of Rusticiana and Auxiliary of Miami Feb. 6, 1979; cons. March 24, 1979; appt. First Bishop of Venice July 17, 1984; installed Oct. 25, 1984; retired Jan. 19, 2007.

Catholic Center—1000 Pinebrook Rd., Venice, 34285. Tel: 941-484-9543; Fax: 941-484-1121. *Mailing Address: P.O. Box 2006, Venice, 34284.*

Office of the Bishop—Mrs. JOHANNA MARONE, Exec. Sec.; Mrs. CAROL COMPTON, Receptionist & Sec.

Vicar General—Very Rev. EDWARD D. MORETTI, V.G.

Chancellor—Dr. VOLODYMYR SMERYK, M.A., J.C.D., J.D.

Administrative Assistant to the Chancellor—Mrs. PHYLLIS M. CURLEY.

Treasurer—Very Rev. STEPHEN E. MCNAMARA, V.F.

College of Consultors—Very Revs. EDWARD D. MORETTI, V.G.; STEPHEN E. MCNAMARA, V.F.; FAUSTO STAMPIGLIA, S.A.C., V.F.; Revs. JOSEPH CONNOLLY, T.O.R.; MARCIAL I. GARCIA.

Deans—Very Revs. JOSE ANTONIO GONZALEZ, V.F., Eastern Deanery; STEPHEN E. MCNAMARA, V.F., Central Deanery; ROBERT KANTOR, V.F., Southern Deanery; FAUSTO STAMPIGLIA, S.A.C., V.F., Northern Deanery.

Presbyteral Council—Very Revs. EDWARD D. MORETTI, V.G.; STEPHEN E. MCNAMARA, V.F.; FAUSTO STAMPIGLIA, S.A.C., V.F.; JOSE ANTONIO GONZALEZ, V.F.; ROBERT KANTOR, V.F.; Revs. DONALD H. HENRY; LUIS PACHECO; JEAN-MARIE FRITZ LIGONDE; TEOFILO USECHE; TOMASZ ZALEWSKI; NICHOLAS MCLOUGHLIN; GEORGE RATZMANN; MARK L. HEUBERGER; HUGH MCGUIGAN, O.S.F.S.; ROBERT D. TABBERT, V.F.; Very Revs. JOHN J. LUDDEN; GERARD FINEGAN.

Theologian to the Bishop—Very Rev. FAUSTO STAMPIGLIA, S.A.C., V.F.

Vicar for Priests—Very Rev. JOHN J. LUDDEN.

Director for Deacons—Deacon FRANCIS J. CAMACHO.

Director for Religious—Sr. MONICA PAUL FRASER, O.P.

Priest Personnel Board—Very Rev. STEPHEN E. MCNAMARA, V.F., Chm.

Continuing Education of Clergy—VACANT.

Child Protection and Safe Environment Issues—Dr. VOLODYMYR SMERYK, M.A., J.C.D., J.D., Chancellor; Dr. KATHY KLEINLEIN, Dir. Awareness Training & Certification.

Victim Assistance Coordinator—Tel: 941-416-6114. Ms. BARBARA E. DICOCCO.

Official Archivist—Dr. VOLODYMYR SMERYK, M.A., J.C.D., J.D., Chancellor.

Historical Archivist—Ms. ROSEMARY GALLO.

Diocesan Tribunal— All Pastoral Center searches for information prior to October 25, 1984 should be directed to the Diocese of St. Petersburg for Manatee, Hardee, Sarasota, DeSoto, Glades, Charlotte and Lee Counties; to the Diocese of Orlando for Highlands Co. and to the Archdiocese of Miami for Hendry and Collier Counties

Judicial Vicar—Very Revs. ARTHUR J. ESPELAGE, O.F.M., J.C.D.; JOHN V. DOLCIAMORE, S.T.L., J.C.L., Judicial Vicar Emeritus.

Auditors—Revs. ANTHONY HEWITT, J.C.L.; JAROSLAW SNIOSEK, J.C.L.

Defenders of the Bond—Revs. ANTHONY HEWITT, J.C.L.; PATRICK DUBOIS, J.C.L.; JOEL SCHEVERS, O.Carm.

Promoter of Justice—Rev. RAFAEL PADILLA, J.C.L.

Judges—Very Rev. JOHN V. DOLCIAMORE, S.T.L., J.C.L.; Dr. VOLODYMYR SMERYK, M.A., J.C.D.,

J.D.; Revs. DENNIS C. KLEMME, S.T.L., J.C.D.; RAFAEL PADILLA, J.C.L.; JAROSLAW SNIOSEK, J.C.L.; SALVATOR STEFULA, T.O.R.

Ecclesiastical Notaries/Case Assessors—Mrs. ANN MANRODT; Mrs. MARIANA BARTOLILLO.

Diocesan Offices

Building Department—Mr. BOHDAN NEPIP, Assoc. Dir.; Mr. RICHARD VANNUCCI, Asst. Project Mgr.

Campaign for Human Development—VACANT.

**Catholic Charities of the Diocese of Venice, Inc.* Mr. PETER ROUTSIS-ARROYO, CEO.

Catholic Relief Services/Operation Rice Bowl—VACANT.

Communications Department—Mrs. ADELA GONZALEZ WHITE, Dir. Tel: 941-486-4702; Fax: 941-486-4761; Mrs. JUDY PIPER, Coord. Website.

The Florida Catholic, Venice Edition—Most Rev. FRANK J. DEWANE, Publisher; Mr. ROBERT REDDY, Editor, Venice Edition. Tel: 941-486-4701; Fax: 941-486-4763.

Stewardship and Development Office/Catholic Faith Appeal—Mrs. MARY CAMPO, Dir.

Diaconate—Very Rev. FAUSTO STAMPIGLIA, S.A.C., V.F.

Ecumenical and Interreligious Office—Deacon C. PATRICK MACAULAY, Dir.

Education—Dr. KATHLEEN SCHWARTZ, Dir. Educ.; Dr. KATHY KLEINLEIN, Dir., Catechetical Ministry; ANDREA LORENZO MOLINARI, Ph.D., M.A., Pres., Blessed Edmund Rice School for Pastoral Ministry; GEORGE L. SMITH, Dir. Youth Ministry.

Finance Department—Mr. BRAD WATSON, Dir.; Ms. DIONNE SPOO, Risk Mgmt. Coord.

Human Resources—Mr. ARTHUR FLEISCHER, Dir.

Information Technology—RICHARD HIBBARD, Dir.; Mr. DAVID DUDLEY, Technology Admin.

Internal Financial Services—Mrs. LORRAINE VANLEDE-BROWN, Dir.

Legal— DiVito and Higham, P.A., Gen. Counsel

Hispanic, Migrant and Spanish Speaking Apostolates—Revs. CELESTINO GUTIERREZ, Dir.; VICTOR CAVIEDES; JOSE DEL OLMO; Very Rev. JOSE GONZALEZ, V.F.; Rev. RAFAEL PADILLA, J.C.L.

Juventud Hispana (Hispanic Youth Ministry)—Very Rev. JOSE GONZALEZ, V.F., Dir.; Mrs. BLANCA ILDEFONSO, Coord.

Haitian Ministry—Rev. JEAN-MARIE FRITZ LIGONDE, Dir.

Lee County—Rev. JEAN-MARIE FRITZ LIGONDE.

West Collier County—Rev. TONY CHERMEIL.

Ministry to People with HIV/AIDS—Ms. CASANDRA GALLAGHER, Sarasota County; Sr. JUDY H. SIMONIS, C.S.J., Charlotte County.

Department of Worship and Ministries—Rev. JOHN MARK KLAUS, T.O.R., Dir. Liturgy; Deacon WILLIAM LADROGA, Dir. Ministries.

Charismatic Renewal—VACANT, Spiritual Dir.; Rev. JUAN LORENZO.

Prison Ministry—Sr. MARY HOPE RIEMENSCHNEIDER, C.E., Coord.; Mr. LOUIE FAUSTINO, Advisor.

Family Life Office— (includes Parenting and all Marriage Enrichment and Marriage Preparation programs) Deacon WILLIAM LADROGA; Mrs. BETTY KARSOKAS, Coord.

Divorced and Separated Ministry—Deacon WILLIAM LADROGA, Coord.

Scouting—Mr. JAMES FETTERMAN, Coord.

Peace and Social Justice Department—Mr. NEIL MICHAUD, M.S.W., Dir.

Respect Life Department—Rev. DENNIS J. COONEY, Moderator; Mrs. JEANNE BERDEAUX, Dir.; Ms. MARINA KOPKO, Asst. Dir.

Project Rachel—Tel: 877-908-1212 (Toll Free).

Real Estate Department—Dr. VOLODYMYR SMERYK, M.A., J.C.D., J.D., Dir.; Ms. BEVERLY KONDAS, Coord. Real Estate.

Vocations/Seminarian Formation—Rev. GREGG CAGGIANELLI, Dir.; Mrs. MARY MONTEDONICO.

Other Office

Propagation of the Faith/Mission Cooperative Program—Very Rev. JOHN J. LUDDEN, Dir.

Organizations

Catholic Volunteers in Florida—Mr. RICHARD GALENTINO, Exec. Dir., Mailing Address: P.O. Box 536476, Orlando, 32853. Tel: 407-382-7071. Email: volunteer@cvif.org.

Cursillo Movement—Rev. MICHAEL A. SCHEIP, Spiritual Advisor; Mr. GENE VENDITTO, Lay Dir.

Secretariado Hispano de Cursillos—Rev. SOFONIAS ORTEZ, Spiritual Dir.; JOSE GAUTIER, Lay Dir.

Equestrian Order of the Holy Sepulchre of Jerusalem—JOHN A. ROGGE, K.C.H.S., Diocesan Representative.

International Order of Alhambra, Diego Caravan 255—Mr. MARVIN A. PESCHEL, Supreme Dir.

Knights of Columbus—CHARLES KAHLER, Regl. Deputy; BRENT J. LABRECHE, Supreme Rep. Tel: 866-363-8022.

Legion of Mary—Rev. DAVID J. BAEHR, Manasota Curia.

St. Vincent DePaul Society—BARBARA REDMORE, Trustee.

Venice Diocesan Council of Catholic Women—Rev. JOSEPH CONNOLLY, T.O.R., Spiritual Dir.; Ms. MARILYNN BOGEN, Pres.

Advisory Groups to the Bishop

Audit Committee—Mr. ERNEST SKINNER, Chm.

Finance and Investment Committee—Mr. ERNEST SKINNER, Chm.

Pension Plan Board of Trustees (Archdiocese of Miami/Diocese of Venice)—Rev. JEROME A. CAROSELLA, Co Vice-Chm.

Liturgical Commission—Rev. JOHN MARK KLAUS, T.O.R., Chm.

Planning and Development Committee—Very Rev. EDWARD D. MORETTI, V.G., Chm.

Priest Personnel Board—Very Rev. STEPHEN E. MCNAMARA, V.F., Chm.

Real Estate Advisory Board—Dr. VOLODYMYR SMERYK, M.A., J.C.D., J.D., Chm.

Review Board—Mr. JACK DELLORTO, Chm.

CLERGY, PARISHES, MISSIONS AND PAROCHIAL SCHOOLS

CITY OF VENICE

(SARASOTA COUNTY)

1—EPIPHANY CATHEDRAL (1955) [CEM] Revs. John F. Costello, Rector; Richard York, Parochial Vicar; John Fitch, Parochial Vicar; Cory A. Mayer, Parochial Vicar; Joel Schevers, O.Carm.; James M. Shea (BUR) (Retired); Deacons Francis Cole; Brent McNally; Epimaco Roca Jr.; Robert Tomasso. In Res., Revs. Jaroslaw Sniosek; Jack Cosentino (FAR) (Retired).

Res.: 310 Sarasota St., 34285. Tel: 941-484-3505; Fax: 941-488-9333. Email: nault@epiphanycathedral.org. Web: www.epiphanycathedral.org.

School—(Grades PreK-8), 316 Sarasota St., 34285. Tel: 941-488-2215; Fax: 941-480-1565. Web: www.ecstigers.com. Irene Lynch, Prin. Lay Teachers 17; Students 240.

Catechesis/Religious Program—Sr. Frances Lalor, R.S.M., D.R.E. Students 240.

2—OUR LADY OF LOURDES (1986) Revs. Arnold Zebrowski, Admin.; Pawel Kawalec, Parochial Vicar; Deacon David Mulvaney. In Res., Very Rev. Arthur J. Espelage, O.F.M.; Revs. Patrick Dubois; Vincent J. Sheehy (Retired).

Res.: 1301 Center Rd., 34292. Tel: 941-497-2931; Fax: 941-497-5849.

Catechesis/Religious Program—Students 190.

OUTSIDE THE CITY OF VENICE

ARCADIA, DE SOTO CO., ST. PAUL (1885) Revs. Stanislaw Pierog, Admin.; Sofonias Ortez, Parochial Vicar.

Res.: 1208 E. Oak St., 34266. Tel: 863-494-2611; Fax: 863-494-6385.

Catechesis/Religious Program—Tel: 863-494-2835. Students 300.

Mission—Blessed Juan Diego 52417 S.W. Hwy. 17, Nocatee, De Soto Co. 34266. Tel: 863-993-4095.

AVE MARIA, COLLIER CO., QUASI-PARISH OF AVE MARIA ORATORY Rev. Robert Tatman Jr., Admin.

5068 Annunciation Cir., Ste. 101, 34142. Tel: 239-272-2077.

Catechesis/Religious Program—Students 106.

AVON PARK, HIGHLANDS CO., OUR LADY OF GRACE (1956) Rev. Nicholas McLoughlin.

Res.: 595 E. Main St., 33825. Tel: 863-453-4757; Fax: 863-453-2620. Web: ologap.org.

Catechesis/Religious Program—Tel: 863-453-7537. Students 207.

BOCA GRANDE, LEE CO., OUR LADY OF MERCY (1988) Rev. Jerome A. Carosella.

Res.: P.O. Box 181, 33921. Tel: 941-964-2254; Fax: 941-964-2173.

Catechesis/Religious Program—Students 12.

BOKEELIA, LEE CO., OUR LADY OF THE MIRACULOUS MEDAL (1965) Rev. Michael J. Hughes, O.S.A.

Church & Mailing Address: 12175 Stringfellow Rd., 33922. Tel: 239-283-0456; Fax: 239-283-1118. Email: olmmparish@embarqmail.com.

Catechesis/Religious Program—Students 44.

BONITA SPRINGS, LEE CO., ST. LEO (1962) Revs. Stanislaw Strycharz, Admin.; Luis Pacheco, Parochial Vicar.

Res.: 28290 Beaumont Rd., 34134. Tel: 239-992-0901; Fax: 239-992-5282. Web: stleocatholicchurch.org.

Catechesis/Religious Program—Tel: 239-267-8718. Mary Beth Geier, D.R.E. Students 345.

Mission—San Leo Hispanic Mission, Tel: 239-947-9098; Fax: 239-992-7700.

BRADENTON, MANATEE CO.

1—ST. JOSEPH (1927) Revs. Paul F. McLaughlin, Admin.; Piotr W. Zugaj, Parochial Vicar.

Res.: 2704 33rd Ave. W., 34205. Tel: 941-756-3732; Fax: 941-758-1244. Email: stjoechurch@aol.com. Web: saintjoechurch.com.

School—(Grades PreK-8), 2290 26th St. W., 34205. Tel: 941-755-2611; Fax: 941-753-6339. Robert Siccone, Prin.; Ms. Dory Stovall, Librarian. Lay Teachers 30; Students 300.

Catechesis/Religious Program—Tel: 941-755-4335; Fax: 941-753-5634. Michael John, D.R.E. Students 125.

2—SS. PETER AND PAUL THE APOSTLES (1987) Very Rev. Edward D. Moretti; Revs. Gordon Zanetti, Parochial Vicar; James J. Cogan, Parochial Vicar.

Office: 2850 75th St. W., 34209. Tel: 941-795-1228; Fax: 941-794-0127. Email: ss2850pp@hotmail.com. Web: www.sspeterandpaul.org. (Memorial Garden)

Catechesis/Religious Program—Tel: 941-798-9705; Fax: 941-794-3012. Michele Hogan, C.R.E. Students 372.

3—SACRED HEART (1969) Revs. Salvator Stefula, T.O.R.; David J. Baehr.

Mailing Address: 1220 15th St. W., 34205. Tel: 941-748-2221; Fax: 941-748-1744. Email: sacredheartchurch@tampabay.rr.com. Web: www.mysacredheart.com.

Catechesis/Religious Program—Tel: 941-748-2221, Ext. 118. Students 113.

CAPE CORAL, LEE CO.

1—ST. ANDREW (1964) Revs. Mark L. Heuberger; Philip Joly, Parochial Vicar; Remigious Ssekiranda, Parochial Vicar.

Res.: 2628 Del Prado Blvd., 33904. Tel: 239-574-4545; Fax: 239-574-2450. Email: sacc@standrewrcc.org. Web: www.standrewrcc.org.

School—(Grades PreK-8), 1509 S.E. 27th St., 33904. Tel: 239-772-3922; Fax: 239-772-7182. Sr. Elizabeth Meegan, Prin. Lay Teachers 15.

Catechesis/Religious Program—Tel: 239-574-2411. Mr. Carmine Macedonio, D.R.E. Students 500.

2—SAINT KATHARINE DREXEL (1990) Revs. John F. Deary, O.S.A.; John F. O'Rourke, O.S.A.; Deacon Richard Spiro.

Office: 1922 S.W. 20th Ave., 33991. Tel: 239-283-9501; Fax: 239-283-9502.

Catechesis/Religious Program—Theresa Idler, D.R.E. Students 631.

CLEWISTON, HENDRY CO., ST. MARGARET (1932), (Hispanic), Rev. Marcial I. Garcia, Admin.

208 N. Deane Duff Ave., 33440. In Res., Rev. Juan Lorenzo.

Res.: 312 N. Deane Duff Ave., 33440. Tel: 863-983-8585; Fax: 863-983-9673.

Catechesis/Religious Program—315 E. Pasadena Ave., 33440. Tel: 863-983-7589. Students 200.

Chapel—St. Margaret 208 N. Deane Duff Ave., 33440.

Mission—Santa Rosa de Lima 845 Mayoral St., Hendry Co. 33440. Tel: 863-983-8585; Fax: 863-983-9673.

ENGLEWOOD, SARASOTA CO., ST. RAPHAEL (1957) Revs. Mark Schaffner, O.Carm.; Niles Gillen, O.Carm.; Deacon Robert Godlewsky.

Res.: 770 Kilbourne Ave., 34223. Tel: 941-474-9595; Fax: 941-475-5697. Email: office@straphaelsonline.com. Web: www.straphaelsonline.org.

Catechesis/Religious Program—Tel: 941-473-2359. Jean M. Balmes, C.R.E. Students 45.

FORT MYERS BEACH, LEE CO., ASCENSION (1962) Rev. William Adams; Deacon Charles Kiesel.

Res.: 6025 Estero Blvd., 33931. Tel: 239-463-6754; Fax: 239-463-0690. Email: ascensionfmb@yahoo.com.

Catechesis/Religious Program—Students 13.

FORT MYERS, LEE CO.

1—BLESSED POPE JOHN XXIII (2002) Revs. Robert D. Tabbert; Ronnie Sison, Parochial Vicar; J. Patrick Boyhan, M.S.A., Parochial Vicar.

13060 Palomino Ln., 33912.

Catechesis/Religious Program—Tel: 239-561-7499; Fax: 239-561-3713. Students 366.

2—ST. CECILIA (1965) [CEM] Revs. Stanley J. Dombrowski, O.S.F.S.; Francis Hanlon, O.S.F.S., Parochial Vicar.

Res.: 5632 Sunrise Dr., 33919. Tel: 239-936-3635; Fax: 239-936-2108.

Catechesis/Religious Program—Kristine Neumayer Jenkins, D.R.E. Students 140.

3—CHURCH OF THE RESURRECTION OF OUR LORD (1974) Very Rev. Stephen E. McNamara; Rev. Oliver Toner, Parochial Vicar.

Parish Center & Mailing Address: 8121 Cypress Lake Dr., 33919. Tel: 239-481-7172; Fax: 239-481-8007. Email: parishoffice@resurrectionch.org. Web:

www.resurrectionch.org.
Church: 8051 Cypress Lake Dr., 33919. Tel: 239-481-7171.
Catechesis/Religious Program—Tel: 239-482-6883. Email: resurrectionoffice@yahoo.com. Lea Pascotto, D.R.E. Students 215.

4—ST. COLUMBKILLE (1993) [CEM] Rev. Joseph G. Clifford.
Church: 12171 Iona Rd., 33908. Tel: 239-489-3973; Fax: 239-432-0066. Email: office@stcolumbkille.com. Web: www.stcolumbkille.com.
Catechesis/Religious Program—Students 165.

5—ST. FRANCIS XAVIER (1910) Revs. Michael Mullen, Admin.; James G. Simko, Parochial Vicar.
Res.: 2133 Heitman St., P.O. Box 912, 33902. Tel: 239-334-2161; Fax: 239-332-4178. Web: stfrancisxavier-church.org.
School—(Grades PreK-8), 2055 Heitman St., 33901. Tel: 239-334-7707; Fax: 239-334-8605. Mrs. Janet Ortenzo, Prin. Franciscan Sisters of Allegany 3; Lay Teachers 30; Students 580.
Catechesis/Religious Program—2048 Heitman St., 33902. Tel: 239-246-2635. Students 50.
Mission—St. Therese (2003) 20115 N. Tamiami Tr., North Fort Myers, Lee Co. 33903. Tel: 239-567-2315; Fax: 239-567-2316. Email: sttheresech@aol.com. P.O. Box 3520, North Fort Myers, 33918. Rev. Mario Kono, Admin.

6—JESUS THE WORKER MISSION (JESUS OBRERO) (1973), (Hispanic), Revs. Patrick T. O'Connor, O.S.F.S., Admin.; Jaime Gonzalez, Parochial Vicar.
Office: P.O. Box 50909, 33994. Tel: 239-693-5333; Fax: 239-693-5626.

7—OUR LADY OF LIGHT (1990) [CEM] Revs. Hugh J. McGuigan, O.S.F.S.; Anthony Gilborges, O.S.F.S., Parochial Vicar; Deacon Francis J. Camacho.
Office: 19680 Cypress View Dr., 33967-6201. Tel: 239-267-7088; Fax: 239-267-5481. Email: info@ourladyoflight.com. Web: www.ourladyoflight.com.
Res.: 9404 Windlake Dr., 33967. Tel: 239-432-9095.
Catechesis/Religious Program—Students 210.

8—SAN JOSE MISSION (1968), (Hispanic), Revs. Patrick T. O'Connor, O.S.F.S., Admin.; Jaime Gonzalez, Parochial Vicar.
10750 Gladiolus Dr., 33908. Tel: 239-481-1143; Fax: 239-693-5626. Email: mmlcjo@earthlink.net.

9—ST. VINCENT DE PAUL (1986) Rev. David Arle.
Church & Mailing Address: 13031 Palm Beach Blvd., 33905. Tel: 239-693-0818; Fax: 239-693-8459. Email: thefamilyparish@embarqmail.com.
Catechesis/Religious Program—Students 55.

GROVE CITY, CHARLOTTE CO., ST. FRANCIS OF ASSISI (1978) Revs. Adrian Wilde, O.Carm.; Marcel Dube, O.Carm.
Res. & Church: 5265 Placida Rd., 34224. Tel: 941-697-4899; Fax: 941-697-0602.
Catechesis/Religious Program—Laurie Bryan, D.R.E. Students 125.

HOLMES BEACH, MANATEE CO., ST. BERNARD (1956) Revs. Robert Mongiello; Jean Woady Louis, Parochial Vicar.
Mailing Address: P.O. Box 1036, Bradenton Beach, 34217.
Res.: 246 S. Harbor Dr., Bradenton Beach, 34217. Tel: 941-778-4769; Fax: 941-778-4644. Email: stbernardcc@hotmail.com. Web: st-bernard-church.com.
Catechesis/Religious Program— Elizabeth Espinet, D.R.E. Students 47.

IMMOKALEE, COLLIER CO., OUR LADY OF GUADALUPE (1957) Revs. Pio Battaglia, C.S.; Onorio Benacchio, C.S., Parochial Vicar; Benjamin Casimir, C.S., Parochial Vicar.
Res.: 207 S. 9th St., 34142. Tel: 239-657-2666; Fax: 239-657-3431. Email: guadalupechurch@yahoo.com.
Catechesis/Religious Program—Mrs. Maria Marquez, D.R.E. Students 542.

LABELLE, HENDRY CO., OUR LADY QUEEN OF HEAVEN (1975) Revs. Chester Domaszewicz; Luis Albarracin, Parochial Vicar.
Res.: 355 S. Bridge St., P.O. Box 357, 33935. Tel: 863-675-0030; Fax: 863-675-0756.
Catechesis/Religious Program—Students 370.
Mission—Holy Martyrs Mission 4290 Crescent Ave., S.W., Hendry Co. 33935.

LAKE PLACID, HIGHLAND CO.

1—COMMUNIDAD CATOLICA HISPANA SANTIAGO APOSTOL (SANTIAGO MISSION) (1991), (Hispanic), [JC] Very Rev. Jose Gonzalez; Rev. Victor Caviedes.
685 CR 621 E, 33852. Tel: 863-699-1561. Mailing Address: 882 Bay St., Sebring, 33870. Tel: 863-385-6762; Fax: 863-358-5169. Email: frjose@stcathe.com.
Catechesis/Religious Program—Students 377.

2—ST. JAMES (1962) [JC] Rev. Michael J. Cannon, Admin.; Deacon Philip Coniglio.
Mailing Address: 3380 Placid View Dr., 33852. Tel: 863-465-3215; Fax: 863-465-0649. 779 Hawk Ave., 33852.
Catechesis/Religious Program—Students 33.

LAKEWOOD RANCH, MANATEE CO., OUR LADY OF THE ANGELS (1999) [CEM] Rev. Damian Vincent Amantia, T.O.R.; Deacons Ron Dains; Ronald Ochner.
12905 SR 70 E., 34202. Tel: 941-752-6770; Fax: 941-752-6821. Email: parishinfo@olangelscc.org. Web: www.olangelscc.org.
Catechesis/Religious Program—Ms. Chelle Maida, D.R.E. Students 202.

LEHIGH ACRES, LEE CO., ST. RAPHAEL (1962) Rev. Dennis J. Cooney; Deacon Joseph Allison.
Res.: 2514 Lee Blvd., 33971. Tel: 239-369-1831; Fax: 239-369-1039.
Catechesis/Religious Program—Tel: 239-369-6424. Students 335.

LONGBOAT KEY, MANATEE CO., ST. MARY STAR OF THE SEA (1973) Very Rev. Gerard Finegan.
Res. & Church: 4280 Gulf of Mexico Dr., 34228. Tel: 941-383-1255; Fax: 941-383-8758. Email: stmarylbk@comcast.net.
Catechesis/Religious Program—

MARCO ISLAND, COLLIER CO., SAN MARCO (1971) Revs. Timothy M. Navin; Andrew Malarz, Parochial Vicar; Deacons John Minicozzi; Michael Cristoforo; Norman F. McEnaney.
Res.: 851 San Marco Rd., 34145. Tel: 239-394-5181; Fax: 239-394-1385. Web: sanmarcochurch.com.
Catechesis/Religious Program—Tel: 239-394-4068. David Swierczek, D.R.E. Students 154.
Mission—St. Finbarr 13520 Tamiami Tr. E., Naples, Collier Co. 34114-8703. Tel: 239-417-2084. Rev. Jean-Marie Fritz Ligonde, Admin.
Mission—Holy Family Everglades City, Collier Co.

MOORE HAVEN, GLADES CO., ST. JOSEPH THE WORKER (1960), (Spanish), [JC] Rev. Lorenzo Gonzalez, Admin.
Res.: 25641 U.S. Hwy. 27, P.O. Box 1109, 33471. Tel: 863-946-0696; Fax: 863-946-3444.
Catechesis/Religious Program—Students 111.
Mission—St. Theresa of the Child Jesus 1027 Chobee Loop, Okeechobee, Okeechobee Co. 34974. Tel: 863-946-0696.

NAPLES, COLLIER CO.

1—ST. AGNES Very Rev. Robert Joseph Kantor, Admin.; Rev. Tomasz Zalewski, Parochial Vicar.
7775 Vanderbilt Beach Rd., 34120-1641. Tel: 239-592-1949.
Catechesis/Religious Program—Ivy O'Malley, D.R.E. Students 487.

2—ST. ANN (1955) Revs. Michael Vannicola, Admin.; Thomas J. Gillespie, O.S.F.S., Parochial Vicar; Stephen Shott, O.S.F.S., Parochial Vicar.
Res.: 475 Ninth Ave. S., 34102. Tel: 239-262-4256; Fax: 239-262-4296. Email: secretary@naplesstann.com. Web: www.naplesstann.com.
School—(Grades PreK-8), 542 Eighth Ave. S., 34102. Tel: 239-262-4110; Fax: 239-262-3991. Mr. Tommy Bridges, Prin. Sisters 3; Lay Teachers 35; Students 320.
Catechesis/Religious Program—Students 163.

3—ST. ELIZABETH SETON (1975) Revs. Dennis Harten, O.S.A.; Russel Ortega, O.S.A., Parochial Vicar.
Res.: 2760 52 Ter., S.W., 34116. Tel: 239-455-3900; Fax: 239-455-6895. Email: elizabethannseton@comcast.net.
School—(Grades PreK-8) Tel: 239-455-2262; Fax: 239-455-0549. Denny Denison, Prin. Lay Teachers 16; Students 226.
Catechesis/Religious Program— Ms. Christine Roberts, D.R.E. Students 299.

4—ST. JOHN THE EVANGELIST (1988) Very Rev. John J. Ludden; Revs. Marcin Koziola, Parochial Vicar; Daniel Smith, Parochial Vicar; Deacons Harold Brenner; Al Groh.
Res.: 625 111th Ave. N., 34108. Tel: 239-566-8740; Fax: 239-566-9117. Email: stjohnev1@aol.com.
Catechesis/Religious Program—Tel: 239-514-2927; Fax: 239-566-9117. Mrs. Margaret Lynch, D.R.E. Students 250.

5—ST. PETER THE APOSTLE (1974) Revs. Gerard F. Critch, Admin.; Tony Chermeil, Parochial Vicar; Russell Wright, S.T.L., Parochial Vicar; Pedro Roman, O.P., Parochial Vicar; Deacon David Nolan.
Res.: 5130 Rattlesnake Hammock Rd., 34113-7448. Tel: 239-774-3337; Fax: 239-774-3077. Email: stpeterschurch@embarqmail.com. Web: stpeternapels.org.
Catechesis/Religious Program—5025 Rattlesnake Hammock Rd., 34113. Tel: 239-775-9576; Fax: 239-775-6028. Liz McGuire, D.R.E. Students 407.

6—ST. WILLIAM (1973) Revs. George Ratzmann; Robert Murphy, Parochial Vicar; Raymond Hughes, C.R., Parochial Vicar; Paul R. D'Angelo, Parochial Vicar.
Res.: 750 Seagate Dr., 34103-2886. Tel: 239-261-4883; Fax: 239-261-8729. Email: cathy@saintwilliam.org. Web: www.saintwilliam.org.
Catechesis/Religious Program—Tel: 239-263-5429. Mary Jane Spirk, D.R.E. Students 366.

NORTH PORT, SARASOTA CO., SAN PEDRO (1964) Revs. Patrick C. Organ; Antonio Jean, Parochial Vicar; Deacons Eugene Willis; Thomas Caliguire.
Res.: 14380 Tamiami Tr., 34287. Tel: 941-426-2500; 941-426-6810; Fax: 941-423-8710. Email: sanpedroparish@hotmail.com. Web: www.sanpedrocc.org.
Catechesis/Religious Program—Tel: 941-426-2893; Fax: 941-429-8785. Email: spreligioused@hotmail.com. Students 348.

OSPREY, SARASOTA CO., OUR LADY OF MOUNT CARMEL (2000) Rev. Gregory L. Klein, O.Carm.; Deacon Thomas Grant.
Parish Center: 425 S. Tamiami Tr., P.O. Box 1097, 34229. Tel: 941-966-0807; Fax: 941-966-3909. Email: ol.mc@verizon.net. Web: www.olmc-osprey.org.
Res.: 554 Pine Ranch E. Rd., 34229. Tel: 941-918-2032.
Catechesis/Religious Program—Students 45.

PALMETTO, MANATEE CO., HOLY CROSS CHURCH (1956) Revs. Teofilo Useche; Vicente Moreno Martin, Parochial Vicar.
Church & Mailing Address: 505-26th St. W., 34221. Tel: 941-729-3891; Fax: 941-721-9402.
Catechesis/Religious Program—Tel: 941-729-4338. Students 105.

PARRISH, MANATEE CO., SAINT FRANCES XAVIER CABRINI (1992) Rev. Janusz Jay Jancarz.
Res.: 12001 69th St. E., 34219. Tel: 941-776-9097; Fax: 941-776-1307. Web: www.stfrancesxcabrini.org.
Catechesis/Religious Program—Tel: 941-776-8613. Students 233.

PORT CHARLOTTE, CHARLOTTE CO.

1—ST. CHARLES BORROMEO (1959) Revs. Thomas A. Heck, Admin.; Philip J. Scheff, Parochial Vicar; Leo Joseph Smith, Parochial Vicar; Bernard Chojnacki, Parochial Vicar; Deacon Michael DiMeglio.
Office & Church: 21505 Augusta Ave., 33952. Tel: 941-625-4754; Fax: 941-625-0256. Email: stcharlespcfl@hotmail.com.
School—(Grades PreK-8) Tel: 941-625-5533; Fax: 941-625-7359. Michael O'Loughlin, Prin.; Deborah Lambeth-Jones, Librarian. Lay Teachers 15; Students 190.
Catechesis/Religious Program—21505 Augusta Ave., 33952. Tel: 941-625-1292, Ext. 210. Nelson Perez, D.R.E. Students 138.

2—ST. MAXIMILIAN KOLBE (1988) Rev. Rafael Padilla, Admin.
Office: 1441 Spear St., 33948. Tel: 941-743-6877; Fax: 941-743-9176.
Res.: 1270 W. Corktree Cir., 33952.
Catechesis/Religious Program—Sr. Patricia Redmond, O.S.F., Dir. Faith Formation. Students 129.

3—SAN ANTONIO (1993) Revs. Jacek Mazur, Admin.; Leonard Gioeli, Parochial Vicar.
24445 Rampart Blvd., 33980. Tel: 941-624-3799; Fax: 941-624-6184. Web: sanantoniocatholicchurch.com.
Catechesis/Religious Program—Tel: 941-624-5156; Fax: 941-624-6631. Students 69.

PUNTA GORDA, CHARLOTTE CO., SACRED HEART (1954) Revs. Jerome P. Kaywell; Leo P. Riley, Parochial Vicar; Deacon Edward D. Lundy.
Res.: 211 W. Charlotte Ave., 33950-5546. Tel: 941-639-3957; Fax: 941-639-2061. Web: www.sacredheartfl.org.
Catechesis/Religious Program—Tel: 941-639-9545. Sr. Josine Perez, D.R.E. Students 129.

SANIBEL, LEE CO., ST. ISABEL (1973) Rev. Christopher Senk.
Res.: 3559 Sanibel Captiva Rd., 33957. Tel: 239-472-2763; Fax: 239-472-5351. Email: saintisabel@aol.com. Web: www.saintisabel.com.
Catechesis/Religious Program—Students 43.

SARASOTA, MANATEE CO., OUR LADY QUEEN OF MARTYRS (1959) Revs. Joseph F. Connolly, T.O.R.; John Mark Klaus, T.O.R., Parochial Vicar.
Res.: 833 Magellan Dr., 34243. Tel: 941-755-1826; Fax: 941-753-1654. Email: queenofmartyrs@olqm.net. Web: ourladyqueenofmartyrs.net.
Catechesis/Religious Program—Tel: 941-755-3497. Heather Felton, D.R.E. Students 156.

SARASOTA, SARASOTA CO.

1—INCARNATION (1958) Revs. Bernard P. Evanofski, Admin.; Edward Gibbons, Parochial Vicar; Michael Scheip, Parochial Vicar; Deacons Joseph Cirieco; John Crescitelli. In Res., Rev. Gregg Caggianelli.
Res.: 2929 Bee Ridge Rd., 34239. Tel: 941-921-6631; Fax: 941-927-2521. Web: www.incarnationchurch.org.
School—2911 Bee Ridge Rd., 34239. Tel: 941-924-8588; Fax: 941-925-1248. Ms. Regina Housel, Prin. Sisters 3; Lay Teachers 27; Students 206.
Catechesis/Religious Program—Tel: 941-924-9566. John Garisto, D.R.E. Students 272.

2—ST. JUDE (2006) Revs. Celestino Gutierrez; Jiobani Batista, Parochial Vicar; Anthony Hewitt, Parochial Vicar.

Mailing Address: 3930 17th St., 34235. Tel: 941-955-3934; Fax: 941-365-4760. Email: frcelestino@st-jude-parish.org. Web: www.stjudehispamerctr.com.
Catechesis / Religious Program—Students 240.

3—ST. MARTHA (1912) Very Rev. Fausto Stampiglia, S.A.C.; Revs. Andrew Kozminski, S.A.C., Parochial Vicar; Paul Van Nuyen, C.H.C., Parochial Vicar; C. Patrick Wilson, S.A.C., Parochial Vicar; Deacons C. Patrick Macaulay; William Ladroga; Kevin McKenney.
Mailing Address: 200 N. Orange Ave., 34236. Tel: 941-366-4210; Fax: 941-954-8434. Web: www.stmartha.org.
School—(Grades PreK-8), 4380 Fruitville Rd., 34232. Tel: 941-953-4181; Fax: 941-366-5580. Dr. Elizabeth Bowman, Prin.; Mrs. Siobhan Young, Dean. Religious 2; Lay Teachers 25; Students 465.
Catechesis / Religious Program—Email: sileo@mycomcast.com. Students 160.
Chapel—Christ the King (2009) 1900 Meadowood St., 34231-3949. Tel: 941-924-2777; Fax: 941-924-2797. Revs. James A. Fryar, F.S.S.P., Chap.; Brian Austin, F.S.S.P.
Mission—The Vietnam Catholic Community of Our Lady of Lavang Rev. Paul Van Nuyen, C.H.C., Contact Person.

4—ST. MICHAEL THE ARCHANGEL (1958) Rev. Joseph E. Stearns.
Mailing Address: 5394 Midnight Pass Rd., 34242. Tel: 941-349-4174; Fax: 941-349-6388.
Res.: 1014 Glebe Ln., 34242.
Catechesis / Religious Program—Tel: 941-349-4174, Ext. 14. Students 41.

5—ST. PATRICK (1988) Rev. Robert T. Dziedziak, Admin.
Res.: 7900 Bee Ridge Rd., 34241. Tel: 941-378-1703; Fax: 941-378-2153. Email: churchofstpatrick@churchofstpatrick.org.
Catechesis / Religious Program—Tel: 941-378-1521; Fax: 941-342-0543. Email: stpatff@churchofstpatrick.org. Students 266.

6—ST. THOMAS MORE (1979) Revs. Donald H. Henry; Jan Antonik, Parochial Vicar; Deacon Richard Zandy.
Mailing Address: 2506 Gulf Gate Dr., 34231. Tel: 941-923-1691; Fax: 941-923-1692. Email: stmsrq@aol.com. Web: sttmore.org.
Catechesis / Religious Program—Sr. Judy Baldino, S.S.J., D.R.E. Students 270.

SEBRING, HIGHLANDS CO., ST. CATHERINE (1929) [JC] Very Rev. Jose Gonzalez; Rev. Victor Caviedes, Parochial Vicar; Deacons James R. McGarry; Max Severe.
Mailing Address: 882 Bay St., 33870. Email: office@stcathe.com.
Res.: 862 Bay St., 33870.
Church: 820 Hickory St., 33870. Email: frjose@stcathe.com. Web: www.stcathe.com.
School—St. Catherine Catholic School (2008), (Grades PreK-2), 747 S. Franklin St., 33870. Tel: 863-385-7300. Email: school@stcathe.com. Arthur Balitz, Prin. Lay Teachers 5; Students 52.
Catechesis / Religious Program— Georgia Quick, D.R.E. Students 450.

WAUCHULA, HARDEE CO., ST. MICHAEL (1969), (Spanish—Creole), Revs. Vincent L. Clemente, Admin.; Teodoro Mata Taveras, Parochial Vicar.
Res.: 408 Heard Bridge Rd., 33873. Tel: 863-773-4089; Fax: 863-773-5641.
Catechesis / Religious Program—Tel: 863-773-4215. Students 525.
Convent—Sisters of Charity of Nazareth, 409 Alice St., 33873. Sisters 2.
Mission—Holy Child Chester Ave., Bowling Green, Hardee Co. 33834.
Mission—San Alfonso Catholic Center Schoolhouse Rd., Zolfo Springs, Hardee Co. 33890. Tel: 863-773-5889.

Military Chaplains:
Very Rev.—
Cannon, Col. Robert R., J.C.L., U.S. Air Force.
Revs.—
Kowalik, Jacek, U.S. Air Force, Germany.
Martin, Edward, U.S. Army
Sikorski, Leszek, U.S. Navy.

Absent on Leave:
Rev.—
Ochej, Tomasz

On Administrative Leave:
Rev.—
Joseph, Jean-Ronald

Retired:
Rev. Msgr.—
Mouch, Frank M.
Revs.—
Anglim, Thomas G.
Brennan, George
Brubaker, Claude
Duggan, Joseph P.
Ellis, John H.R.
Flemming, James K.
Glackin, Thomas J.
Gonzalez, Mario
Grogan, Gerald P.
Hickey, Michael
Lobato, Nicanor
Mattingly, Robert B.
McCarthy, Eugene
Murphy, Timothy
O'Connell, William
Pick, Edward, V.F.
Rourke, John
Ryan, Eugene
Sheehy, Vincent J.
Soy, Esteban
Sullivan, Charles K.
Walk, Donald J.

Permanent Deacons:
Allison, Joseph
Arnold, Maurice, (Retired)
Brenner, Harold
Caliguire, Thomas
Camacho, Francis, (Dir. Diaconate Personnel)
Cassidy, William
Cirieco, Joseph
Cole, Francis
DiMeglio, Michael
Fortier, W. Lorin, (Retired)
Grant, Thomas
Healy, M. Donald
Hedge, Dennis, (Leave of Absence)
Horan, Francis, (Retired)
Kiesel, Charles
Ladroga, William, (Dir. of Ministries; Dir. of Diaconate Formation)
Lundy, Edward
Macaulay, Patrick C.
McKenney, Kevin
Mueller, Martin, (Unassigned)
Mulvaney, David
Nolan, David W.
Roca, Epimaco, Jr.
Spiro, Richard
Willis, Eugene
Zandy, Richard

INSTITUTIONS LOCATED IN THE DIOCESE

[A] COLLEGES AND UNIVERSITIES

AVE MARIA. **Ave Maria Unversity*, 5050 Ave Maria Blvd., 34142-9505. Tel: 239-280-2500; 877-283-8648; Fax: 239-352-2392. Web: www.avemaria.edu. Nicholas J. Healy Jr., Pres.; Terence Gallagher, Librarian. Private Institution in the Catholic Tradition.

[B] HIGH SCHOOLS

FORT MYERS. *Bishop Verot High School* (1962) 5598 Sunrise Dr., 33919. Tel: 239-274-6700; Fax: 239-274-6798. Email: chris.beretta@bvhs.org. Web: www.bvhs.org. Rev. J. Christian Beretta, O.S.F.S, Prin.; Lillian Newman, Librarian. Oblates of St. Francis de Sales. Priests 3; Lay Teachers 48; Students 710; Total Staff 75.

NAPLES. **St. John Neumann High School* (1985) 3000 53rd St., S.W., 34116. Tel: 239-455-3044; Fax: 239-455-2966. Email: ddenison@sjnceltics.org. Web: www.sjnceltics.org. Dr. Denny Denison, Prin.; Mrs. Stephanie Sweeney, Librarian. Lay Teachers 22; Students 200; Total Staff 10.

SARASOTA. *Cardinal Mooney High School, Inc.*, 4171 Fruitville Rd., 34232. Tel: 941-371-4917; Fax: 941-371-6924. Email: schristie@cmhs-sarasota.org. Web: www.cmhs-sarasota.org. Sr. Mary Lucia Haas, S.N.D., Pres.; Mr. Stephen J. Christie, Prin.; Ms. Elaine Moore, Librarian. Sisters of Notre Dame of Chardon, OH. Sisters 1; Lay Teachers 45; Total Staff 60; Students 530.

[C] SCHOOLS FOR SPECIAL NEEDS

FORT MYERS. *Father Anglim Academy at Dreams are Free*, (Grades 1-12), *Fort Myers Campus*, 2045 Heitman St., 33901. Tel: 239-337-4010; Fax: 239-337-4044. Email: lmoreau@fatheranglimacademy.org. Web: www.fatheranglimacademy.org. Lori Moreau, Prin. Lay Teachers 8; Lay Speech Therapist 1; Lay Administrators 1; Students 70.

SARASOTA. *Dreams Are Free School at Bishop Nevins Academy, Sarasota Campus*, 4380 Fruitville Rd., 34232-1623. Tel: 941-366-4010; Fax: 941-366-3819. Email: jdickinson@dreamsarefree.org. Web: www.dreamsarefree.org. Judith Dickinson, Dir. Lay Teachers 8; Students 40.

[D] SCHOOLS FOR THEOLOGICAL, SPIRITUAL, PASTORAL AND PERSONAL FORMATION

ARCADIA. *Blessed Edmund Rice School for Pastoral Ministry* (1995) 10299 S.W. Peace River St., 34269-4068. Tel: 941-766-7334; Fax: 941-629-8555. Email: riceschool@daystar.net. Web: www.riceschool.org. Andrea Lorenzo Molinari, Ph.D., M.A., Pres.; Rev. C. Gerard Austin, O.P.; Clare Miller, Librarian. Priests 4; Sisters 1; Lay Teachers 2; Students 115; Total Staff 10.

[E] MIGRANT EDUCATION

BONITA SPRINGS. *Migrant Education Apostolate*, P.O. Box 716, 34133. Tel: 239-947-9098; Fax: 239-947-9098. Adult Education Outreach. Brothers 2.

[F] RESIDENCES FOR THE AGED

VENICE. *St. Mark's Housing of Venice, Inc. dba Villa San Marco* 1030 Albee Farm Rd., 34285. Tel: 941-483-1960; Fax: 941-483-3934. Email: manager@sanmarcos.affinitymembers.net; villasanmarcos@comcast.net. Total Staff 3; Total in Residence 80.
St. Vincent de Paul Housing, Inc., P.O. Box 2006, 34284-2006. Tel: 239-693-1333; Fax: 941-485-6344. Email: villa.vincente@earthlink.net. Most Rev. Frank J. Dewane. Total Staff 3; Total in Residence 63.

FORT MYERS. *Villa Francisco* (1984) 2140 Cottage St., 33901. Tel: 239-332-3229; Fax: 239-332-3229. Robert Little, Admin. Total in Residence 67; Total Staff 1.

PALMETTO. *Holy Cross Manor, Inc.*, 505 26th St. W., 34221. Tel: 941-729-2063. Total Staff 3; Total in Residence 68.

PORT CHARLOTTE. *St. Charles Housing I, Inc. aka Villa San Carlos* 2550 Easy St., 33952. Tel: 941-624-2266; Fax: 941-624-2283. Email: villasancarlos@comcast.net. Ms. Sheila Jones, Admin. Total in Residence 50; Total Staff 4.
St. Charles Housing II, Inc. dba Villa San Carlos II 22250 Vick St., 33980-2026. Tel: 941-624-4404; Fax: 941-624-5556. Email: villasancarlosii@comcast.net. Ms. Rebecca Murray, Admin. Residents 54; Total Staff 3.

SARASOTA. *St. Martha's Housing II, Inc.* (Casa Santa Marta II), 800 N. Lemon Ave., 34236. Tel: 941-365-7913; Fax: 941-365-8887. Email: casasantamarta.csm@verizon.net. Very Rev. Fausto Stampiglia, S.A.C., V.F., Pres.; Debra Greising, Site Mgr. Total in Residence 54; Total Staff 5.
St. Martha's Housing, Inc. (Casa Santa Marta), 1576 Eighth St., 34236. Tel: 941-366-4448; Fax: 941-366-2544. Email: casasantamarta.csm@verizon.net. Very Rev. Fausto Stampiglia, S.A.C., V.F., Pres.; Debra Greising, Site Mgr. Total in Residence 80; Total Staff 5.

[G] MONASTERIES AND RESIDENCES OF PRIESTS AND BROTHERS

VENICE. *Carmel in Venice*, 244 Harbor Dr. S., 34285. Tel: 941-485-0606. Rev. Bartholomew Larkin, O.Carm., Prior. Priests 2.
Xavieran Brothers, 609 Cornwell on the Gulf, 34285. Tel: 941-484-9641. Web: www.xaverianbrothers.org. Brothers of St. Francis Xavier Brothers 1.

ENGLEWOOD. *Society of Saint Edmund Residence*, 603 W. Harvard St., 34223. Tel: 941-474-7683.

FORT MYERS. *Oblates of St. Francis de Sales*, 5598 Sunrise Dr., 33919. Tel: 239-939-5334. Revs. Mark Wrightson, O.S.F.S.; Joseph A. Beattie, O.S.F.S.; J. Christian Beretta, O.S.F.S. Priests 4.

NOKOMIS. *Carmel at Mission Valley*, 955 Laurel Rd. E., 34275-4507. Tel: 941-412-0678; Fax: 941-485-5716. Email: ebell@carmelnet.org.

SARASOTA. *Congregation of the Holy Spirit*, 459 Beach Rd., 34242. Tel: 941-346-2083; Fax: 941-346-5512. Total in Residence 5.
Holy Cross Associates of Florida, Inc., 1635 4th St., 34236-5007. Tel: 941-365-0722. Bro. William Geenen, C.S.C., Contact Person.
Holy Cross Florida Regional Center (1973) 1635 4th St., 34236-5007. Tel: 941-365-0722. Email: sarasotacsc@verizon.net. Holy Cross Brothers Residence.

[H] CONVENTS AND RESIDENCES FOR SISTERS

FORT MYERS BEACH. *San Damiano Monastery of St. Clare.* (Solemn Vows, Papal Enclosure), 6029 Estero Blvd., 33931-4325. Tel: 239-463-5599; Fax: 239-463-4993. Email: saintclare@comcast.net.

Web: www.poorclare.com/fmb. Sr. Mary Frances Fortin, O.S.C., Abbess. Poor Clares. Cloistered Sisters 8.

[I] RETREAT CENTERS

VENICE. *Our Lady of Perpetual Help Retreat and Spirituality Center* (1996) 3989 S. Moon Dr., 34292. Tel: 941-486-0233; Fax: 941-486-1524. Email: olphsct@aol.com. Web: www.olph-retreat.org. Rev. Joseph McCarthy, C.Ss.R.; Sr. Carmella T. DeCosty, S.N.J.M., M.A., Admin.

LAKE PLACID. *Campo San Jose* (1996) 882 Bay St., Sebring, 33870. Tel: 863-385-6762; Fax: 863-385-5169. Email: frjose@camposanjose.com. Web: www.camposanjose.com. 170 S. Sun 'n' Lake Blvd., 33852. Very Rev. Jose Gonzalez, V.F., Dir.

[J] CATHOLIC CHARITIES

VENICE. *Catholic Charities, Diocese of Venice, Inc.*, 1000 Pinebrook Rd., 34285. Tel: 941-488-5581; Fax: 941-484-1121. Email: prarroyo@dioceseofvenice.org. Web: www.catholiccharitiesdov.org. Mr. Peter Routsis-Arroyo, CEO; Sharon Aragona, COO.

Catholic Charities, District I (Sarasota and Manatee Counties), 4930 Fruitville Rd., Sarasota, 34232. Tel: 941-379-5119; Fax: 941-379-3611. Email: dis1dir@comcast.net.

Catholic Charities, District II (Lee, Henry and Glades Counties), 4235 Michigan Ave. Link, Fort Myers, 33916. Tel: 239-337-4193; Fax: 239-332-2799. Email: cnolan@ccslee.org.

African Caribbean American Ministry (AFCAAM), 3861 Michigan Ave., Fort Myers, 33916. Tel: 239-461-0233; Fax: 239-461-0236. Email: aragona@dioceseofvenice.org.

Catholic Charities, District III (Collier County), 2210 Santa Barbara Blvd., Naples, 34116. Tel: 239-455-2655; Fax: 239-455-7235. Email: bob@catholiccharitiescc.org.

Catholic Charities, Rural Services (Charlotte, De Soto, Hardee and Highland Counties), 1210 E. Oak St., Arcadia, 34266. Tel: 863-494-1068; Fax: 863-494-1671. Email: charity2@embarqmail.com.

Casa San Jose, Inc., 3900 17th St., Sarasota, 34235. Tel: 941-952-1853; Fax: 941-952-1857. Email: prarroyo@dioceseofvenice.org.

Catholic Charities Housing, Diocese of Venice, Inc., 1000 Pinebrook Rd., 34285. Tel: 941-488-5581; Fax: 941-484-1121. Email: prarroyo@dioceseofvenice.org.

Casa San Juan Bosco, Inc., 1000 Pinebrook Rd., 34285. Tel: 941-488-5581; Fax: 941-484-1121. Email: arroyo@dioceseofvenice.org.

Marian Manor, Inc., 1000 Pinebrook Rd., 34285. Tel: 941-488-5581; Fax: 941-484-1121. Email: prarroyo@dioceseofvenice.org.

Catholic Charities Refugee Programs, 7810 S. Tamiami Tr., A-14, 34293. Tel: 941-493-8231; Fax: 941-493-8239.

Catholic Charities Immigration Programs, 1000 Pinebrook Rd., 34285.

SARASOTA. *Bethesda House - HIV/AIDS Ministries*, 1670 Fourth St., 34236. Tel: 941-366-1886; Fax: 941-362-9733. Email: hivaidsministriespd@verizon.net. Ms. Casandra Gallagher. (AIDS Ministry)

[K] FOUNDATIONS

VENICE. *Catholic Charities Foundation of the Diocese of Venice, Inc.*, 1000 Pinebrook Rd., 34285. Tel: 941-488-5581; Fax: 941-484-1121. Email: prarroyo@dioceseofvenice.org. Mr. Peter Routsis-Arroyo, Contact Person.

Catholic Community Foundation of Southwest Florida, Inc., 1000 Pinebrook Rd., P.O. Box 2006, 34284-2006. Tel: 941-484-9543; Fax: 941-486-4737. Email: flynn@ccfswf.org. Web: ccfswf.org. Joe Citro, Exec. Dir.; Dr. Volodymyr Smeryk, M.A., J.C.D., J.D., Contact Person.

FORT MYERS. *The Bishop Verot High School Foundation*, 5598 Sunrise Dr., 33919. Tel: 239-274-6700; Fax: 239-274-6797. Email: chris.beretta@bvhs.org. Web: www.bvhs.org. Rev. J. Christian Beretta, O.S.F.S.

St. Francis Xavier School Foundation, 2133 Heitman St., 33901. Tel: 239-334-2161; Fax: 239-332-4178. Email: mullenstfrancis@earthlink.net. Rev. Michael Mullen, Pres.; Dr. Michael Kyle, Chm.

NAPLES. *St. John Neumann High School Foundation*, 3000 53rd St., S.W., 34116. Tel: 239-455-3044; Fax: 239-455-2966. Email: ddenison@sjnceltics.org. Dr. Denny Denison, Prin.

PORT CHARLOTTE. *St. Charles Borromeo School Foundation*, 21505 Augusta Ave., 33952. Tel: 941-625-5533; Fax: 941-625-7359. Email: info@stcbs.org.

SARASOTA. *Cardinal Mooney High School Foundation*, c/o Cardinal Mooney High School, 4171 Fruitville Rd., 34232. Tel: 941-371-4917; Fax: 941-371-6924. Email: lhas@cmbs-sarasota.org. Web: www.cmhs-sarasota.org.

Incarnation School Foundation, 2911 Bee Ridge Rd., 34239. Tel: 941-924-8588; Fax: 941-925-1248. Email: monicafras@incarnationschool.edu. Web: www.incarnationschool.edu.

St. Martha School Foundation, 200 N. Orange Ave., 34236. Tel: 941-366-4210; Fax: 941-954-8434. Email: pastor@mycomcast.com. Web: www.stmarthaschool.net.

[L] MISCELLANEOUS LISTINGS

VENICE. *Catholic Charities Housing, Diocese of Venice, Inc.*, 1000 Pinebrook Rd., 34285. Tel: 941-488-5581; Fax: 941-484-1121. Email: prarroyo@dioceseofvenice.org. Mr. Peter Routsis-Arroyo, CEO.

Diocese of Venice in Florida, Inc., 1000 Pinebrook Rd., P.O. Box 2600, 34284-2600. Tel: 941-484-9543. Dr. Volodymyr Smeryk, M.A., J.C.D., J.D., Contact Person.

Trinity Enterprise Holdings, Inc., 1000 Pinebrook Rd., P.O. Box 2006, 34284-2006. Tel: 941-484-9543. Dr. Volodymyr Smeryk, M.A., J.C.D., J.D., Contact Person.

Trinity Trust, 1000 Pinebrook Rd., P.O. Box 2600, 34284-2006. Tel: 941-484-9543. Dr. Volodymyr Smeryk, M.A., J.C.D., J.D., Contact Person.

BONITA SPRINGS. *Iona House Corporation*, 26650 Noble Ln., 34135. Tel: 239-947-9098. Bro. Terence Connolly, C.F.C.

FORT MYERS. *Magnificat-Ft. Myers, FL-Mother of Mercy Chapter of the Diocese of Venice*, 1828 Pine Valley Dr., Apt. 206, 33907-4705. Tel: 239-267-2684; Fax: 239-267-2684. Email: loisamader@hotmail.com. Lois Mader, Contact Person & Coord.

Societies of St. Vincent de Paul, 3010 Cleveland Ave., 33901-7001. Tel: 239-274-0660; Fax: 239-274-0659. Barbara Redmore, Pres. District Council of Charlotte, District Council of Fort Myers, District Council of Manasota, District Council of Naples.

NAPLES. *Hope for Haiti, Inc.*, 1042 Sixth Ave., N., 34102. Tel: 239-434-7183. Email: hopeforhaiti@aol.com. Web: www.hopeforhaiti.com. JoAnne Kuehner, Pres. & Contact Person.

PALMETTO. *Holy Cross Manor II, Inc.*, 540 W. 26th St., 34221. 1000 Pinebrook Rd., 34286.

SARASOTA. *Christ Child Society of Sarasota, Inc.*, P.O. Box 52462, 34232-0320. Email: eb4runner@aol.com. Web: www.nationalchristchildsoc.org. Elaine Bokach, Pres. & Treas. Local affiliate of national non-profit organization whose member-volunteers serve needy children.

RELIGIOUS INSTITUTES OF MEN REPRESENTED IN THE DIOCESE

For further details refer to the corresponding bracketed number in the Religious Institutes of Men or Women section.

[0140]—*The Augustinians*—O.S.A.

[1350]—*Brothers of St. Francis Xavier*—C.F.X.

[]—*Brothers of the Catholic Apostolate*—S.A.C.

[0600]—*Brothers of the Congregation of Holy Cross*—C.S.C.

[0470]—*Capuchin Friars*—O.F.M.Cap.

[0270]—*Carmelite Fathers*—O.Carm.

[0310]—*Congregation of Christian Brothers*—C.F.C.

[0650]—*(Spiritans) Congregation of the Holy Spirit*—C.S.Sp.

[]—*Congregation of the Resurrection*—C.R.

[0430]—*Dominican Fathers*—O.P.

[0690]—*Jesuit Fathers*—S.J.

[0720]—*Missionaries of Our Lady of La Salette*—M.S.

[1210]—*Missionaries of St. Charles Scalabrians*—C.S.

[0590]—*Missionaries of the Holy Apostles*—M.Ss.A.

[0920]—*Oblates of St. Francis de Sales*—O.S.F.S.

[1065]—*Priestly Fraternity of St. Peter*—F.S.S.P.

[0110]—*Society of African Missions*—S.M.A.

[0440]—*Society of St. Edmund*—S.S.E.

[0990]—*Society of the Catholic Apostolate*—S.A.C.

[0560]—*Third Order Regular of St. Francis*—T.O.R.

RELIGIOUS INSTITUTES OF WOMEN REPRESENTED IN THE DIOCESE

[1070-15]—*Congregation of St. Dominic (Sisters of St. Dominic of Blauvelt, NY)*—O.P.

[]—*Congregation of the Sisters of St. Dominic of the Immaculate Heart of Mary*—O.P.

[3832]—*Congregation of the Sisters of St. Joseph*—C.S.J.

[1105]—*Dominican Sisters of Hope*—O.P.

[1070-13]—*Dominican Sisters/Congregation of the Most Holy Rosary (Adrian Dominicans)*—O.P.

[1070-03]—*Dominican Sisters/Sinsinawa Dominican Congregation of the Most Holy Rosary*—O.P.

[1180]—*Franciscan Sisters of Allegheny, NY*—O.S.F.

[]—*Missionaries Daughters of Our Blessed Lady of the Light, Yucatan, Mexico*—M.H.M.L.

[1360]—*Missionary Franciscan Sisters of the Immaculate Conception* (Newton, MA)—M.F.I.C.

[2800]—*Missionary Sisters of the Most Sacred Heart of Jesus of Hilltrup*—M.S.C.

[3070]—*North American Union of Sisters of Our Lady of Charity*—N.A.U.-O.L

[3760]—*Order of St. Clare*—O.S.C.

[3465]—*Religious of the Sacred Heart of Mary* (Eastern North American Province)—R.S.H.M.

[2970]—*School Sisters of Notre Dame* (St. Louis Prov. & Baltimore Prov.)—S.S.N.D.

[0590]—*Sisters of Charity of St. Elizabeth, Convent Station*—S.C.

[0430]—*Sisters of Charity of the Blessed Virgin Mary*—B.V.M.

[2575]—*Sisters of Mercy of the Americas* (New Jersey Prov.)—R.S.M.

[2549]—*Sisters of Mercy, Co. Sligo, Ireland*—R.S.M.

[2990]—*Sisters of Notre Dame* (Chardon, OH)—S.N.D.

[3360]—*Sisters of Providence of St. Mary-of-the-Woods, IN*—S.P.

[1650]—*Sisters of St. Francis of Philadelphia*—O.S.F.

[3830-01]—*Sisters of St. Joseph of Boston*—C.S.J.

[3840]—*Sisters of St. Joseph of Carondelet*—C.S.J.

[]—*Sisters of St. Joseph of Chestnut Hill, Philadelphia*—S.S.J.

[1990]—*Sisters of the Holy Name of Jesus and Mary*—S.N.J.M.

[1490]—*Sisters of the Third Franciscan Order* (Syracuse, NY)—O.S.F.

[1710]—*Sisters of the Third Order of St. Francis* (Newton, MA)—O.S.F.

[]—*Sisters of the Third Order of St. Francis* (Allegeny, NY)—O.S.F.

[4160]—*Vincentian Sisters of Charity*—V.S.C.

NECROLOGY

† Llaria, Vincente Ibanez, Lake Placid, FL St. James—Died Feb. 6, 2009

† Swiatecki, Emilian, (Retired)—Died Jan. 12, 2009

† Swietek, Walter, Lehigh Acres, FL St. Raphael—Died April 16, 2009

† Szabajkowicz, Dominik, Cape Coral, FL St. Andrew—Died Nov. 23, 2009

Diocese of Victoria in Texas

(Dioecesis Victoriensis in Texia)

Most Reverend

DAVID E. FELLHAUER, Ph.D., J.C.D.

Bishop of Victoria; ordained May 29, 1965; appointed Second Bishop of Victoria in Texas April 7, 1990; consecrated and installed May 28, 1990. *Mailing Address: P.O. Box 4070, Victoria, TX 77903.*

Chancery Office: P.O. Box 4070, Victoria, TX 77903. Tel: 361-573-0828; Fax: 361-573-5725.

Established and Created a Diocese, May 29, 1982.

Square Miles 9,609.

Comprises the Counties of Calhoun, DeWitt, Goliad, Jackson, Lavaca, Matagorda, Victoria, Wharton and Colorado; also Fayette County west of the Colorado River in the State of Texas.

Legal Title: Diocese of Victoria in Texas.
For legal titles of parishes and diocesan institutions, consult the Chancery Office.

STATISTICAL OVERVIEW

Personnel	
Bishop	1
Priests: Diocesan Active in Diocese	45
Priests: Diocesan Active Outside Diocese	4
Priests: Retired, Sick or Absent	6
Number of Diocesan Priests	55
Religious Priests in Diocese	6
Total Priests in Diocese	61
Extern Priests in Diocese	6
Ordinations:	
Religious Priests	1
Permanent Deacons in Diocese	29
Total Brothers	2
Total Sisters	85
Parishes	
Parishes	50
With Resident Pastor:	
Resident Diocesan Priests	39
Resident Religious Priests	2
Without Resident Pastor:	
Administered by Priests	9
Missions	17
Professional Ministry Personnel:	
Brothers	1
Sisters	19
Lay Ministers	8
Educational	
Diocesan Students in Other Seminaries	8
Total Seminarians	8
High Schools, Diocesan and Parish	2
Total Students	190
High Schools, Private	1
Total Students	407
Elementary Schools, Diocesan and Parish	11
Total Students	2,141
Elementary Schools, Private	1
Total Students	357
Catechesis/Religious Education:	
High School Students	2,478
Elementary Students	5,767
Total Students under Catholic Instruction	11,348
Teachers in the Diocese:	
Sisters	16
Lay Teachers	238
Vital Statistics	
Receptions into the Church:	
Infant Baptism Totals	1,547
Minor Baptism Totals	75
Adult Baptism Totals	57
Received into Full Communion	96
First Communions	1,349
Confirmations	1,019
Marriages:	
Catholic	331
Interfaith	98
Total Marriages	429
Deaths	894
Total Catholic Population	152,612
Total Population	276,846

Former Bishops—Most Rev. CHARLES V. GRAHMANN, D.D., ord. March 17, 1956; appt. Titular Bishop of Equilio and Auxiliary of San Antonio, June 30, 1981; cons. Aug. 29, 1981; appt. First Bishop of Victoria, April 14, 1982; installed May 29, 1982; appt. Coadjutor of Dallas, Dec. 18, 1989; succeeded to See, July 14, 1990; retired March 6, 2007.

Chancery Office—1505 E. Mesquite Ln., Victoria, 77901. Mailing Address: P.O. Box 4070, Victoria, 77903. Tel: 361-573-0828; Fax: 361-573-5725. Office Hours: Mon.-Fri. 8:30-4:30.

Vicars General—Rev. Msgrs. THOMAS C. MCLAUGHLIN, V.G., Mailing Address: P.O. Box 4070, Victoria, 77903. Fax: 361-572-8204; JAMES C. BRUNNER, V.G., Mailing Address: P.O. Box 2448, Victoria, 77902.

Chancellor—Rev. Msgr. THOMAS C. MCLAUGHLIN, V.G., Mailing Address: P.O. Box 4070, Victoria, 77903. Fax: 361-572-8204.

Vice-Chancellor—Rev. GARY W. JANAK, J.C.L., V.F., St. Philip the Apostle Church, 304 W. Church St., El Campo, 77437-3317. Tel: 979-543-3770.

Diocesan Consultors—Rev. Msgrs. THOMAS C. MCLAUGHLIN, V.G.; JAMES C. BRUNNER, V.G.; MICHAEL HARROLD, V.F.; Revs. GARY W. JANAK, J.C.L., V.F.; TIMOTHY KOSLER, V.F.; JOHN C. PETERS, V.F.; CHARLES DWOMOH, V.F.; KIRBY HLAVATY, V.F.

Vicars Forane—Victoria Deanery: Rev. Msgr. MICHAEL HARROLD, V.F., Our Lady of Victory Cathedral, 1309 E. Mesquite Ln., Victoria, 77901. Tel: 361-575-4741. Cuero Deanery: Rev. KIRBY HLAVATY, V.F., St. Michael Church, 302 E. Church St., Cuero, 77954-2906. Tel: 361-275-3554. Edna Deanery: Rev. CHARLES DWOMOH, V.F., Mailing Address: St. Anthony Church, P.O. Box 900, Palacios, 77465. Tel: 361-972-2446. El Campo Deanery: Rev. GARY W. JANAK, J.C.L., V.F., St. Philip the Apostle Church, 304 W. Church St., El Campo, 77437. Tel: 979-543-3770. Hallettsville Deanery: Rev. JOHN C. PETERS, V.F., Mailing Address: Sacred Heart Church, P.O. Box H, Hallettsville, 77964. Tel: 361-798-5888. Schulenburg Deanery: Rev. TIMOTHY KOSLER, V.F., St. Rose of Lima Church, 1010 Lyons Ave., Schulenburg, 78956. Tel: 979-743-3117.

Presbyteral Council—Rev. Msgrs. THOMAS C. MCLAUGHLIN, V.G.; JAMES C. BRUNNER, V.G.; Revs. JOHN C. PETERS, V.F.; CHARLES DWOMOH, V.F.; BRYAN O. HEYER; Rev. Msgr. MICHAEL HARROLD, V.F.; Revs. TIMOTHY KOSLER, V.F.; CHARLES SONNIER; MICHAEL PETERING; DOMINIC ANTWI-BOASIAKO, A.B.; KIRBY HLAVATY, V.F.; GARY W. JANAK, J.C.L., V.F.; ROBERT F. GUERRA; SAMUEL APPIASI; ROGER HAWES.

Diocesan Tribunal—1505 E. Mesquite Ln., Victoria, 77901. Tel: 361-573-0760; Fax: 361-572-8204.

Judicial Vicar—Rev. Msgr. THOMAS C. MCLAUGHLIN, V.G.

Judges—Rev. JOHN C. BILY; Rev. Msgr. MICHAEL HARROLD, V.F.; Revs. GARY W. JANAK, J.C.L., V.F.; GREGORY E. KORENEK; MATTHEW H. HUEHLEFELD, J.C.L.; CELESTINO SAY.

Promoter of Justice—Rev. GABRIEL MAISON, J.C.D.

Procurator Advocate—Revs. JOHNSON OWUSU-BOATENG; SAMUEL APPIASI; MICHAEL J. ROTHER.

Defenders of the Bond—Revs. DAN MORALES; TIMOTHY KOSLER, V.F.; DANIEL P. KAHLICH; FRANK B. LENZ; MICHAEL LYONS; CHARLES DWOMOH, V.F.

Notaries—Mrs. MINNIE BOCHAT; Mrs. MARY HAAS.

Priests' Personnel Board—Rev. Msgrs. THOMAS C. MCLAUGHLIN, V.G., Chancellor; JAMES C. BRUNNER, V.G.; Rev. JOHN C. PETERS, V.F.; Rev. Msgr. MICHAEL HARROLD, V.F.; Revs. GARY W. JANAK, J.C.L., V.F.; TIMOTHY KOSLER, V.F.; CHARLES DWOMOH, V.F.; KIRBY HLAVATY, V.F.

Building Board—Mr. MICHAEL J. BROWN; Mr. HENRY SCHROEDER; Mr. CHARLES BLUNTZER; Mr. JAMES MIORI; Mr. ED MARTINKA; Mr. DONALD NAISER; Mr. JOHN GEHRKE.

School Board—Most Rev. DAVID EUGENE FELLHAUER; Mr. JOHN QUARY; Mr. DARRELL COOPER; Mr. DAVID KAPAVIK; Mr. BOB LITTLE; Mrs. SHARON PARMA; Mrs. MARTHA SAWYERS; Mrs. YVONNE WAGNER; Sr. M. LEONITA BARRON, I.W.B.S.; Rev. GABRIEL BENTIL; Mr. ROBERT J. WHITWORTH JR.; Rev. ROBERT E. KNIPPENBERG.

Business Administration Office—Mr. MICHAEL J. BROWN, CFO; Mrs. SHARON JONES; Mrs. JERI JOSEPH, Mailing Address: P.O. Box 4070, Victoria, 77903. Tel: 361-573-0828.

Campaign For Human Development and Catholic Relief Services—Rev. DAN MORALES, Dir., Mailing Address: Our Lady of Gulf Church, P.O. Box 87, Port Lavaca, 77979. Tel: 361-552-6140.

Catholic Youth Ministry—Mrs. DEBBIE VANELLI, Dir.; Mr. JOSE ORTEGA III, Assoc. Youth Min., 1505 E. Mesquite Ln., P.O. Box 4070, Victoria, 77901. Tel: 361-573-0828.

Catholic Outreach Prison Ministry—P.O. Box 697, Cuero, 77954.

Council of Catholic Women (DCCW)—VACANT, Moderator; Mrs. JANICE OHRT, Chm., 2221 FM 237, Victoria, 77905. Tel: 361-575-2056.

Diocesan Cemeteries—GARY RANGNOW, Dir., P.O. Box 4070, Victoria, 77903. Tel: 361-573-0828.

Diocesan Finance Board—Mr. MICHAEL J. BROWN; Mrs. BEATRICE GONZALEZ; Mr. OTTO KALISCHKO; Mr. ROMAN SHIMEK; Mr. MARK WESTERMAN; Mr. HARDY MCCULLOUGH; Mr. JOHN ZACEK; Mr. JOHN HALL; Mr. GLEN VILLAFRANCA; Mr. JOHN STEVENSON; Rev. DONALD R. RUPPERT, V.F.; Rev. Msgrs. THOMAS C. MCLAUGHLIN, V.G.; JAMES C. BRUNNER, V.G.

Diocesan Services Appeal—Mrs. JERI JOSEPH, Dir., 1505 E. Mesquite Ln., P.O. Box 4070, Victoria, 77901. Tel: 361-573-0828.

Diocesan Office of Spiritual Renewal Center—RON FRIEDEL. Tel: 361-572-0836.

Ecumenical Commission—VACANT.

Presidio of La Bahia—Mr. NEWTON WARZECHA, Mailing Address: P.O. Box 57, Goliad, 77963. Tel: 361-645-3752.

Liturgical Commission—Mrs. CYNTHIA GOERIG, Mailing Address: Rte. 4, Box 26, El Campo, 77437. Tel: 979-543-5706.

Office of Catholic Schools—Mr. JOHN QUARY, Supt., Mailing Address: P.O. Box 4070, Victoria, 77903.

Permanent Diaconate Program—Rev. GABRIEL MAISON, J.C.D., Dir., 1505 E. Mesquite Ln., P.O. Box 4070, Victoria, 77903. P.O. Box 399, Moulton, 77975.

Propagation of the Faith, Holy Childhood Association—Rev. Msgr. THOMAS C. MCLAUGHLIN, V.G., Dir.

Mission Cooperative Plan—Rev. Msgr. THOMAS C. MCLAUGHLIN, V.G., Dir., Mailing Address: Chancery Office, P.O. Box 4070, Victoria, 77903.

Religious Education—Sr. DIGNA VELA, I.W.B.S., Dir., 1505 E. Mesquite Ln., P.O. Box 4070, Victoria, 77903. Tel: 361-573-0828.

Respect Life-Pro Life—Rev. Msgr. JAMES C. BRUNNER, V.G., Mailing Address: P.O. Box 2448, Victoria, 77902. Tel: 361-573-4328.

Rural Life Conference—VACANT.

Scouting—VACANT.

"The Catholic Lighthouse", Diocesan Newspaper—Mrs. CINDY BREWER, Mailing Address: P.O. Box 4070, Victoria, 77903. Tel: 361-573-0828.

Vietnamese American Apostolic Center—Rev. JOSEPH KHOA XUAN MAI, St. Anthony Church, P.O. Box 900, Palacios, 77465.

Vocations Director—Rev. DAN MORALES; Deacon CHARLES J. GLYNN, Assoc. Dir.

Director of Seminarians—Rev. DAN MORALES, Mailing Address: Our Lady of the Gulf Church, P.O. Box 87, Port Lavaca, 77979. Tel: 361-552-6140.

Victim Assistance Coordinator—Rev. GARY W. JANAK, J.C.L., V.F. Tel: 979-543-3770. Email: pastor@stphilipapostle.org.

CLERGY, PARISHES, MISSIONS AND PAROCHIAL SCHOOLS

CITY OF VICTORIA

(VICTORIA COUNTY)

1—OUR LADY OF VICTORY CATHEDRAL (1957) Rev. Msgr. Michael Harrold; Revs. David Berger; Charles E. Otsiwah.
Res.: 1309 E. Mesquite Ln., 77901. Tel: 361-575-4741; Fax: 361-573-5555. Web: www.olvcathedral.org.
School—(Grades PreK-8) Tel: 361-575-5391; 361-578-5454 (Convent); Fax: 361-575-3473. Web: ourladyvictory.org. Sr. M. Leonita Barron, I.W.B.S., Prin.; Norma Smolik, Librarian. Sisters 1; Lay Teachers 30; Students 501.
Catechesis/Religious Program—Tel: 361-575-8132. Betty Mitchell, D.R.E. Students 585.

2—HOLY FAMILY OF JOSEPH, MARY & JESUS (1981) [JC] Rev. Gregory E. Korenek; Rev. Msgr. Peter Agbenu; Deacon Steve Borowicz.
Office: 704 Mallette Dr., 77904. Tel: 361-573-5304; Fax: 361-573-6053. Web: www.hfccvic.org.
Catechesis/Religious Program—Tel: 361-573-5398; Fax: 361-573-6053. Students 435.

3—ST. MARY'S, [JC] Rev. Msgr. James C. Brunner; Rev. Anthony Boateng-Mensah; Deacons Richard Wearden; Jim Koenig.
Res.: 402 S. Main, P.O. Box 2448, 77902. Tel: 361-573-4328; Fax: 361-573-4308.
Catechesis/Religious Program—Diana Starnes, D.R.E. Students 44.

4—OUR LADY OF LOURDES (1875) Rev. Celestino Say, Admin.
Res.: 105 N. William, 77901. Tel: 361-575-3813.
Catechesis/Religious Program—Laurie Bautista, D.R.E. Students 69.

5—OUR LADY OF SORROWS (1913) [JC] Revs. Stanley De Boe, O.SS.T.; Adelson Silvestre Moreira, O.SS.T., Parochial Vicar; Deacons Edward Molina; Jesus Perez.
Res.: 208 W. River St., P.O. Box 2548, 77901. Tel: 361-575-2293; Fax: 361-582-0405.
Catechesis/Religious Program—Tel: 361-573-2681. Sr. Susana Islas, M.C., D.R.E. Students 1,028.
Convent—Missionary Catechists of the Sacred Hearts of Jesus and Mary (Violetas), 209 W. Murray St., 77901. Tel: 361-575-7654. Sisters 4.
Mission—Holy Trinity 2901 Pleasant Green Dr., Victoria Co. 77901.

OUTSIDE THE CITY OF VICTORIA

AMMANNSVILLE, FAYETTE CO., ST. JOHN THE BAPTIST, [CEM] Rev. Timothy Kosler, Admin.
Mailing Address: 7745 Mensik Rd., Schulenburg, 78956.
Mission—St. Wenceslaus [CEM] Holman, Fayette Co.

BAY CITY, MATAGORDA CO.

1—HOLY CROSS (1909) [CEM 2] [JC] Rev. Casimir Jarzombek; Deacon Guadalupe Rodriguez.
2001 Katy St., 77414.
Res.: 3813 Heather Glenn, 77414. Tel: 979-245-6379; Fax: 979-244-5481. Web: www.holycrossbaycity.org.
School—(Grades K-6) Tel: 979-245-5632; Fax: 979-245-6120. Stephanie Kucera, Prin.; Mita Bossley, Librarian. Lay Teachers 9; Students 129; Aides 2.
Catechesis/Religious Program—Terri Busha, D.R.E. Students 143.
Convent—Tel: 979-245-3173; Fax: 979-245-6120.
Mission—Sacred Heart Wadsworth, Matagorda Co.

2—OUR LADY OF GUADALUPE Rev. Gerard Cernoch.
Res.: 1412 12th St., 77414. Tel: 979-245-2010; 979-245-0774 (CCD Office); Fax: 979-245-1038. Email: olg2003@sbcglobal.net.
Catechesis/Religious Program—Esther Martinez, D.R.E. Students 515.

BLESSING, MATAGORDA CO., ST. PETER'S (1930) [CEM] [JC] Rev. Samuel Appiasi.
Res.: Box 395, 77419. Tel: 361-588-6241; Fax: 361-588-1421.
Catechesis/Religious Program—Scarlett Kacer, D.R.E.; Diana Gurecky, D.R.E. Students 154.
Mission—St. Robert Markham, Matagorda Co.

BLOOMINGTON, VICTORIA CO., ST. PATRICK'S (1959) Rev. Ty J. Bazar; Deacon Fred Soto.
Res. & Church: 13316 State Hwy. 185, P.O. Box 2122, 77951. Tel: 361-897-1155; Fax: 361-897-1064. Email: saintpatricks@tisd.net. Web: saintpatrickschurch.net.
Catechesis/Religious Program—Students 194.

CISTERN, FAYETTE CO., SS. CYRIL AND METHODIUS, [CEM 2] [JC 2] Rev. Joseph Hybner.
Mailing Address: P.O. Box 186, Flatonia, 78941. Tel: 361-865-3568.
Church: 113 Manchester St., Flatonia, 78941. Tel: 361-865-2222.

COLUMBUS, COLORADO CO., ST. ANTHONY'S (1930) [CEM] Rev. Daniel P. Kahlich; Deacons Bennie Holesovsky; Charlie Novosad.
Res.: P.O. Box 669, 78934. Tel: 979-732-2562; Fax: 979-732-8636.
School—(Grades PreK-8), 635 Bonham, 78934. Tel: 979-732-5505; Fax: 979-732-9758. Web: stanthony-school.homestead.com. John O'Leary, Prin.; Peggy Castillo, Librarian. Lay Teachers 13; Students 174.
Catechesis/Religious Program—Sr. Joyce Jilek, D.R.E. Students 86.

CUERO, DEWITT CO.

1—ST. MICHAEL (1875) Rev. Kirby Hlavaty; Deacons Anthony B. Warzecha; Leo Sharron.
309 E. Church St., 77954-2906.
Res.: 705 W. Broadway, 77954. Tel: 361-275-3554; Fax: 361-277-3924.
School—(Grades PreK-6), 208 N. McLeod, 77954. Tel: 361-277-3854; Fax: 361-275-3618. Web: www.stmichaels-cuero.org. Judy Roeder, Prin. Lay Teachers 7; Students 83.
Catechesis/Religious Program—Tel: 361-275-0955; Fax: 361-277-3924. Sr. Louise Miksch, D.R.E. Students 142.

2—OUR LADY OF GUADALUPE (1923) Rev. Kirby Hlavaty.
Res.: 705 W. Broadway, P.O. Box 547, 77954. Tel: 361-277-9062; Fax: 361-275-3135.
Catechesis/Religious Program—Tel: 361-275-0955; Fax: 361-277-3924. Students 142.

EAGLE LAKE, COLORADO CO., PARISH OF THE NATIVITY (1995) Rev. Robert F. Guerra.
Office: 545 S. Austin Rd., P.O. Box 307, 77434-0307. Tel: 979-234-2842; Fax: 979-234-5828.
Catechesis/Religious Program—Students 106.

EAST BERNARD, WHARTON CO., HOLY CROSS (1901) [CEM] Rev. Donald R. Ruppert.
Res.: 839 Church St., P.O. Box 1325, 77435-1325. Tel: 979-335-7551; Fax: 979-335-7038. Email: holycross@earth-comm.com. Web: www.eastbernardholycross.com.
Catechesis/Religious Program—Email: hcreled@elc.net. Students 246.
Religious Educ. & Cemetery Office: Tel: 979-335-4071. Email: hccemetery@elc.net.

EDNA, JACKSON CO., ST. AGNES (1880) Rev. Michael Petering.
Res.: 506 N. Allen, 77957. Tel: 361-782-3588; Fax: 361-782-8827. Email: stagnesedna@sbcglobal.net.
Catechesis/Religious Program—Doris Andel, D.R.E. (Elementary); Karen Morrow, D.R.E. (High School). Students 241.

EL CAMPO, WHARTON CO.

1—ST. PHILIP THE APOSTLE, [CEM] Revs. Gary W. Janak; Augustine Nsiah Asante, Parochial Vicar; Deacons Jarrel Nohavitza; Jerome Grahmann.
Res.: 304 W. Church St., 77437. Tel: 979-543-3770; Fax: 979-578-8831. Email: apostle@stphilipapostle.org.
School—(Grades PreK-8) Tel: 979-543-2901; Fax: 979-578-8835. Gwen Edwards, Prin. Lay Teachers 18; Students 262.
Catechesis/Religious Program—Students 229.

2—ST. ROBERT BELLARMINE (1928) Rev. Lawrence Matula; Deacon Margarito Cervantez Jr.
Res.: 512 Tegner St., 77437. Tel: 979-543-4298; Fax: 979-541-5399. Email: sanroberto@sbcglobal.net.
Catechesis/Religious Program—Janie Delgado, D.R.E. Students 439.

FLATONIA, FAYETTE CO., SACRED HEART (1912) [CEM] [JC] Rev. Joseph Hybner.
Res.: P.O. Box 186, 78941. Tel: 361-865-3568; Fax: 361-865-2518.
Catechesis/Religious Program—Students 65.

FRELSBURG, COLORADO CO., SS. PETER AND PAUL (1836) [CEM] Rev. Wayne N. Flagg.
Res.: 1031 Church Ln., New Ulm, 78950. Tel: 979-732-3430; Fax: 979-732-9204.
Catechesis/Religious Program—Lisa Janak, D.R.E.; Christine Feehery, D.R.E. Students 34.

GANADO, JACKSON CO., ASSUMPTION OF THE B.V.M. (1914) [CEM] Rev. Michael Lyons.
Mailing Address: P.O. Box 369, 77962. Tel: 361-771-3425; Fax: 361-771-3526.
Res.: 108 S. Sixth St., 77962. Tel: 361-771-3325.
Catechesis/Religious Program—Students 178.

GOLIAD, GOLIAD CO., IMMACULATE CONCEPTION, [CEM 2] Rev. Raphael Baidoo, O.SS.T.
P.O. Box 49, 77963. Tel: 361-645-3095.
Church: 238 N. Commercial St., 77963. Tel: 361-645-3095.
Shrine—Our Lady of Loreto (Old Franciscan Mission)

HALLETTSVILLE, LAVACA CO.

1—ST. MARY (1840) [CEM 4] Rev. John C. Peters.
Church: 1648 FM 340, P.O. Drawer H, 77964. Tel: 361-798-5888; Fax: 361-798-4970.
Catechesis/Religious Program—Cindy Svetlik, D.R.E. Students 70.

2—SACRED HEART (1882) [CEM] Revs. John C. Peters; Michael J. Rother; Deacons Joey Targac; W.S. (Sonny) Rogers.
Res. & Church: 400 E. Fifth St., P.O. Box H, 77964. Tel: 361-798-5888; Fax: 361-798-4970. Web: www.shcatholicchurch.org.
School—(Grades PreK-8) Tel: 361-798-4251; Fax: 361-798-4970. Mr. David Smolik, Prin. (Elementary & High School). Sisters 2; Lay Teachers 11; Students 212.
High School—313 S. Texana, 77964. Mr. David Smolik, Prin. Lay Teachers 18; Students 111.
Catechesis/Religious Program—Tel: 361-798-3124. Janice Busselman, D.R.E.; Angela McConnell, D.R.E. Students 204.

HIGH HILL, FAYETTE CO., NATIVITY OF THE BLESSED VIRGIN MARY, [CEM] Rev. Timothy Kosler, Admin.
Mailing Address: 2833 FM 2672, Schulenburg, 78956-5603. Tel: 979-561-8455.
Res.: 1010 Lyons Ave., Box 310, Schulenburg, 78956. Tel: 979-743-3117.

HILLJE, WHARTON CO., ST. ANDREW (1909) [CEM] Rev. Clement Quainoo; Deacon Edward Wendel.
Mailing Address: 270 St. Andrew St., El Campo, 77437. Tel: 979-648-2864; Fax: 979-648-2024. Email: standrew@ykc.com.
Catechesis/Religious Program—Ed Juroske, D.R.E. Students 101.
Mission—St. Procopius (1944) [CEM] Louise, Wharton Co.

HOSTYN, FAYETTE CO., HOLY ROSARY (1856) [CEM] Rev. Msgr. Stanley J. Petru; Deacon John McCourt.
Res.: 936 FM 2436, La Grange, 78945. Tel: 979-247-4441; Fax: 979-247-5008. Email: hostynch@cvctx.com.
Catechesis/Religious Program—Gina Kozelsky, D.R.E. Students 64.

HUNGERFORD, WHARTON CO., ST. JOHN THE BAPTIST (1917) [CEM] Rev. Henry C. Rachunek.
Res.: 101 Church St., P.O. Box 121, 77448. Tel: 979-532-4747; Fax: 979-532-8713.
Catechesis/Religious Program—Janet Bubela, D.R.E. Students 59.

INEZ, VICTORIA CO., ST. JOSEPH'S, [CEM] [JC 5] Rev. Gabriel Bentil, Parochial Admin.
Res. & Church: 403 Church St., P.O. Box 337, 77968. Tel: 361-782-3181; Fax: 361-781-0459. Email: stjosephchurch@tisd.net.
Catechesis/Religious Program—Ms. Kendall Pfuhl, D.R.E. Students 121.

KOERTH, LAVACA CO., ST. JOHN THE BAPTIST, [CEM] [JC] Rev. Charles Sonnier.
Res.: P.O. Box 201, Sweet Home, 77987. Tel: 361-741-3206; Fax: 361-741-3206.

MENTZ, COLORADO CO., ST. ROCH (1850) [CEM] Rev. Wayne N. Flagg; Deacons Douglas B. Tromblee; Chuck Glenn.
Mailing Address: 1600 Frelsburg Rd., Alleyton, 78935. Tel: 979-732-3460; Fax: 979-733-0908.
Catechesis/Religious Program—Students 34.

MEYERSVILLE, DEWITT CO., SS. PETER & PAUL (1858) [CEM] Rev. Frank B. Lenz.
Res.: 11220 FM 237, 77974. Tel: 361-275-3868; Fax: 361-277-8972. Email: stspp@gvec.net. Web: www.tisd.net/~stspp.
Catechesis/Religious Program—Mrs. Janice Ohrt, D.R.E. Students 50.
Mission—St. Aloysius Westhoff, DeWitt Co.

MOULTON, LAVACA CO., ST. JOSEPH'S (1888) [CEM] Rev. Gabriel Maison.
P.O. Box 399, 77975. Tel: 361-596-4674; Fax: 361-596-4826.
Res.: 601 N. Pecan St., 77975.
Catechesis/Religious Program—Tel: 361-596-7559. Students 95.

NADA, COLORADO CO., NATIVITY OF THE BLESSED VIRGIN MARY (1897) [CEM] Rev. Joseph L. Vrana.
Res. & Church: 1261 Old Nada Rd., P.O. Box 97, 77460. Tel: 979-758-3218; Fax: 979-758-3267.
Catechesis/Religious Program—Students 78.

NEW TAITON, WHARTON CO., ST. JOHN NEPOMUCENE (1912) [CEM] Rev. Gabriel Oduro Tawiah.
Res.: 1843 CR 469, El Campo, 77437. Tel: 979-543-6985; Fax: 979-543-3434. Email: stjohns@ykcwb.com.
Catechesis/Religious Program—Tel: 979-543-7397. Students 65.

PALACIOS, MATAGORDA CO., ST. ANTHONY'S (1912, Mission); (1954, Parish) Rev. Charles Dwomoh; Deacon Michael Vieira.
Res.: 1004 Magnusson, Box 900, 77465. Tel: 361-972-2446; Fax: 361-972-2606. Email: pasaop@wmconnect.com.
Catechesis/Religious Program—Mary Kay Beard, D.R.E. Students 334.
Vietnamese Apostolate—100 Vietnam, 77465. Tel: 361-972-2685.

PLUM, FAYETTE CO., SS. PETER AND PAUL (1897) [CEM 2] Rev. Msgr. Stanley J. Petru; Deacon John McCourt; Rev. Joseph Kariukikamau, Parochial Vicar.
Res.: 936 FM 2436, La Grange, 78945. Tel: 979-247-4441; Fax: 979-247-5008. Email: hostynch@cvtv.net.
Catechesis/Religious Program—Gina Kozelsky, D.R.E. Students 19.

PORT LAVACA, CALHOUN CO., OUR LADY OF THE GULF (1865) Revs. Dan Morales; Bryan O. Heyer; Deacons Kenneth Ryan; Alonzo Farias Calzada.
Res.: 303 S. Benavides St., P.O. Box 87, 77979. Tel: 361-552-6140; Fax: 361-552-4300. Email: olgulf@aol.com. Web: www.olgulf.org.
Preschool/Day Care—412 W. Austin St., P.O. Box 87, 77979. Tel: 361-552-6140, Ext. 503. Rosie Padron, Dir. Lay Teachers 10; Students 42.
School—(Grades PreK-8) Tel: 361-552-6140, Ext. 202; Fax: 361-552-7485. Theresa Dent, Prin. Sisters 2; Lay Teachers 15; Students 101.
Catechesis/Religious Program—Tel: 361-552-6140, Ext. 100. Linda Beard, D.R.E. Students 431.
Mission—St. Ann Point Comfort, Calhoun Co. Tel: 361-987-2855.
Mission—St. Joseph Port O'Connor, Calhoun Co. Tel: 361-983-4467.
Mission—St. Patrick Seadrift, Calhoun Co. Tel: 361-785-3405.

PRAHA, FAYETTE CO., ST. MARY'S (1855) [CEM] Rev. Edward C. Bartsch.
Res.: 821 FM 1295, Flatonia, 78941. Tel: 361-865-3560.
Catechesis/Religious Program—Students 11.

ST. JOHN, FAYETTE CO., ST. JOHN THE BAPTIST (1888) [CEM] Revs. John C. Peters; Michael J. Rother.
Res.: 400 E. Fifth St., P.O. Drawer H, Hallettsville, 77964. Tel: 361-798-5888; Fax: 361-798-4970. Email: rectory@shcatholicchurch.org.
Catechesis/Religious Program—Janis Hrncir, D.R.E. Students 34.
Mission—Ascension of Our Lord (1913) [CEM] 11134 FM 957 (Moravia), Hallettsville, Lavaca Co. 77964.

SCHULENBURG, FAYETTE CO., ST. ROSE OF LIMA (1889) [CEM] Revs. Timothy Kosler; Peter Yeboah-Amanfo.
Res.: 1010 Lyons Ave., Box 310, 78956. Tel: 979-743-3117; Fax: 979-743-4712.
School—(Grades PreK-8), 405 Black, 78956. Tel: 979-743-3080; Fax: 979-743-4228. Mrs. Rosanne Gallia, Prin. Lay Teachers 15; Students 160.
Catechesis/Religious Program—Nicole Michalke, (Grades 1-8); David Machac, (Grades 9-11). Tel: 979-743-4634. Students 230.

SHINER, LAVACA CO., SS. CYRIL AND METHODIUS, [CEM] Revs. Robert E. Knippenberg; Tommy Chen; Deacon Paul Patek.
Res.: 306 S. Ave. F, 77984. Tel: 361-594-3836; Fax: 361-594-2850. Email: rectory@sscmshiner.org. Web: www.sscmshiner.org.
School—St. Ludmila Elementary School, (Grades PreK-8) Tel: 361-594-3843; Fax: 361-594-8599. Email: principal@shinercatholicschool.org. Web: www.shinercatholicschool.org. Mr. Rob Whitworth, Prin. Sisters 2; Lay Teachers 14; Students 242.
High School—St. Paul High School, Tel: 361-594-2313; Fax: 361-594-8564. Mr. Rob Whitworth, Prin. Sisters 1; Lay Teachers 12; Students 79.
Catechesis/Religious Program—Tel: 361-594-3234. Email: spatek@sscmshiner.org. Web: www.sscmshiner.org. Sharon Patek, Youth Min. Students 204.

SWEET HOME, LAVACA CO., QUEEN OF PEACE, [CEM] [JC] Rev. Charles Sonnier.
Res.: 7372 FM 531, P.O. Box 201, 77987. Tel: 361-741-3206; Fax: 361-741-3206.
Catechesis/Religious Program—Students 113.

VANDERBILT, JACKSON CO., ST. JOHN BOSCO Rev. Johnson Owusu-Boateng.
Office: 232 Main St., P.O. Box 337, 77991-0337. Tel: 361-284-3361.
Res.: 121 Garcitas St., P.O. Box 337, 77991. Tel: 361-284-3361; Fax: 361-284-3391.
Catechesis/Religious Program—Debbie Kuchler, D.R.E. Students 100.
Mission—St. Theresa [CEM] 4612 CR 325, La Salle, Jackson Co. 77969.

WEIMAR, COLORADO CO., ST. MICHAEL (1883) [CEM] Rev. John C. Bily.
Res. & Church: 410 N. Center, Box 36, 78962. Tel: 979-725-6714; Fax: 979-725-8146.
School—(Grades PreK-8) Tel: 979-725-8461; Fax: 979-725-8344. Sr. Kathleen Goike, I.W.B.S., Prin. Sisters of the Incarnate Word and Blessed Sacrament 1; Lay Teachers 13; Students 140.
Catechesis/Religious Program—Students 61.
Mission—SS. Cyril and Methodius Dubina, Fayette Co.

WHARTON, WHARTON CO.
1—HOLY FAMILY, [JC] Revs. Dominic Antwi-Boasiako, A.B.; Gabriel D. Espinosa, Parochial Vicar; Varghese Kunnathu, M.C.B.S., Parochial Vicar; Deacon Alvin Matthys.
Res.: 2011 Briar Ln., 77488. Tel: 979-532-3593.
Catechesis/Religious Program—Tel: 979-532-3747. Students 265.
Mission—St. Joseph Boling, Wharton Co.
2—OUR LADY OF MT. CARMEL (1948) [JC] Revs. Dominic Antwi-Boasiako, A.B., Pastoral Admin.; Gabriel D. Espinosa, Parochial Vicar; Deacon David Valdez.
Res.: 506 S. East Ave., 77488. Tel: 979-532-3492; Fax: 979-532-2321. Email: olmc1948@sbcglobal.net.
Catechesis/Religious Program—Sr. Anna Lozano, M.C.S.H.J.M., D.R.E. Students 302.

YOAKUM, LAVACA CO., ST. JOSEPH (1869) [CEM] Rev. Matthew H. Huehlefeld; Deacons Linard Harper; Dennis Kutach.
Res.: 210 Schrimscher St., Box 734, 77995. Tel: 361-293-3518; 361-293-7572; Fax: 361-293-5355. Email: pastor@stjcatholicchurch.com. Web: www.stjcatholicchurch.com.
School—(Grades PreK-8) Tel: 361-741-5362; Fax: 361-293-3004. Web: www.stjcatholicschool.org. Susan Kelley, Prin.; Dorothy Harper, Librarian. Lay Teachers 19; Students 137.
Catechesis/Religious Program—Students 276.
Mission—St. Ann [CEM] Hochheim, DeWitt Co.

YORKTOWN, DEWITT CO., HOLY CROSS (1866) [CEM 2] Rev. Roger Hawes.
Res.: 1214 Zorn Rd., 78164-1907. Tel: 361-564-2893; Fax: 361-564-9315. Email: holycross1214@sbcglobal.net.
Catechesis/Religious Program—Students 84.
Mission—San Luis, DeWitt Co.
Mission—St. Ann's Nordheim, DeWitt Co.

On Special or Other Diocesan Assignment:
Rev. Msgr.—
McLaughlin, Thomas C., V.G., Vicar Gen. & Chancellor. Tel: 361-573-0828
Rev.—
Franks, Gabriel, Hospital Chap., 103 D Sherwood Dr., 77901. Tel: 361-579-6895

On Duty Outside the Diocese:
Rev. Msgr.—
Anders, Arnold
Revs.—
Henninger, George, Indianapolis, IN
Mensah, Gabriel, Military Chap., U.S. Navy
Nguyen, Thu Van, Diocese of Ft. Worth

Retired:
Rev. Msgrs.—
Hermes, Eustace
O'Shaughnessy, Michael A.
Rev.—
Higgins, Peter

Permanent Deacons:
Borowicz, Stephen James Michael
Calzada, Alonzo Farias
Cervantez, Margarito Candelario, Jr.
Glynn, Charles J.
Grahmann, Jerome J.
Harper, Linard
Holesovsky, Bennie
Koenig, James Nicholas
Kutach, Dennis
Matthys, Alvin
McCourt, John
Molina, Edwardo Pina
Nohavitza, Jarrel Joseph
Novosad, Charlie
Patek, Paul, Sr.
Perez, Jesus Castillo
Rodriguez, Guadalupe
Rogers, Walter Smith, Jr.
Ryan, Ken
Sharron, Leo
Soto, Fred
Targac, Joseph
Tran, Luan Van
Tromblee, Douglas B.
Valdez, David
Vieira, Michael
Warzecha, Anthony
Wearden, Arthur R.
Wendel, Edward

INSTITUTIONS LOCATED IN THE DIOCESE

[A] HIGH SCHOOLS, PRIVATE

VICTORIA. *St. Joseph High School*, 110 E. Red River, 77901. Tel: 361-573-2446; Fax: 361-573-4221. Email: bmcardle@stjvictoria.com. Web: www.stjvictoria.com. Mr. William H. McArdle Jr., Pres.; Debra Rigby Studer, Librarian; Anthony E. Winstead, Prin. Lay Teachers 30; Students 407.

[B] ELEMENTARY SCHOOLS, PRIVATE

VICTORIA. *Nazareth Academy* (1867) (Grades PreK-8), 206 W. Convent, 77901. Tel: 361-573-6651; Fax: 361-573-1829. Email: skloesel@nazarethacademy.org. Web: www.nazarethacademy.org. Scott Kloesel, Prin.; Sisters Liliane Janda, I.W.B.S., Librarian; M. Bernarda Bludau, Asst. Prin. Attended from St. Mary's, Our Lady of Lourdes, Our Lady of Victory, Holy Family and Our Lady of Sorrows' Churches. Sisters of the Incarnate Word and Blessed Sacrament 8; Lay Teachers 24; Students 357.

[C] PERSONAL PRELATURES

SCHULENBURG. *Opus Dei, Featherock Conference Center*, 934 Holub Rd., 78956-5324. Tel: 979-743-4642.

[D] CONVENTS AND RESIDENCES FOR SISTERS

VICTORIA. *Incarnate Word Convent*, 1101 N.E. Water St., 77901-9233. Tel: 361-575-2266; Fax: 361-575-2165. Web: www.iwbsvictoria.org. Sisters Evelyn Korenek, I.W.B.S., Gen. Supr.; Lois Marie Etzler, Local Supr. Sisters 49.
Missionary Catechists of the Sacred Hearts of Jesus and Mary, 209 W. Murray St., 77901. Tel: 361-575-7654. Sr. Susana Islas, M.C., Supr. Sisters 4.

PORT LAVACA. *Vietnamese Community, Our Lady of the Gulf Convent*, 415 W. Austin St., 77979. Tel: 361-552-3670. Sr. Francesca Bui, O.P., Supr.

[E] MONASTERIES & RESIDENCES OF PRIESTS & BROTHERS

VICTORIA. *Trinity House* Novitiate Holy Trinity Fathers., 1511 E. Commercial St., 77901. Tel: 361-573-7059.

[F] MISCELLANEOUS

VICTORIA. *Endowment Fund for the Catholic Diocese of Victoria in Texas*, P.O. Box 4070, 77903-4070. Tel: 361-573-0828; Fax: 361-573-5725. Email: mbrown@victoriadiocese.org. Web: www.victoriadiocese.org. Mr. Michael J. Brown, CFO.
Jeanne Chezard De Matel Fund, 1101 N.E. Water St., 77901-9233. Tel: 361-575-2266; Fax: 361-575-2165. Email: srevelynk@yahoo.com. Web: www.iwbsvictoria.org.
Sisters of the Incarnate Word and Blessed Sacrament of Victoria, Texas, Medical and Retirement Trust, 1101 N.E. Water St., 77901-9233. Tel: 361-572-9321; Fax: 361-575-2165. Email: iwbsbusofc@yahoo.com.
Sisters of the Incarnate Word and Blessed Sacrament, Victoria, Texas, Inc., 1101 N.E. Water St., 77901-9233. Tel: 361-575-2266; Fax: 361-575-2165. Email: srevelynk@yahoo.com. Web: www.iwbsvictoria.org. Sr. Evelyn Korenek, I.W.B.S., Gen Supr. & Mailing Contact. Perpetually Professed 83; Affiliate 3; Annually Professed 1.

RELIGIOUS INSTITUTES OF WOMEN REPRESENTED IN THE DIOCESE

For further details refer to the corresponding bracketed number in the Religious Institutes of Men or Women section.

[2200]—*Congregation of the Incarnate Word and Blessed Sacrament*—I.W.B.S.

[2700]—*Missionary Catechists of the Sacred Hearts of*

Jesus and Mary—M.C.SS.CC.

[0460]—*Sisters of Charity of Incarnate Word*—C.C.V.I.

[1010]—*Sisters of the Divine Providence of San Antonio, Texas*—C.D.P.

[]—*Vietnamese Dominican Sisters*—O.P.

NECROLOGY

† Thurmond, Rev. Msgr. Benton, (Retired)—Died Nov. 7, 2009

† Caponi, Jerome, (Retired)—Died Feb. 27, 2009

† Carolan, Charles B., (Retired)—Died Oct. 9, 2009

An asterisk (*) denotes an organization that has established tax-exempt status directly with the IRS and is not covered by the USCCB Group Ruling.

Archdiocese of Washington

(Archidioecesis Washingtonensis)

His Eminence

THEODORE CARDINAL MCCARRICK, PH.D., D.D.

Retired Archbishop of Washington; ordained May 31, 1958; appointed Auxiliary Bishop of New York and Titular Bishop of Rusibisir May 24, 1977; Episcopal ordination June 29, 1977; appointed First Bishop of Metuchen November 19, 1981; installed January 31, 1982; appointed Archbishop of Newark May 30, 1986; installed July 25, 1986; appointed Archbishop of Washington November 21, 2000; installed January 3, 2001; created Cardinal priest of Saints Nereus and Achilleus February 21, 2001; retired May 16, 2006. *Mailing Address: P.O. Box 29260, Washington, DC 20017-0260.*

Most Reverend

LEONARD J. OLIVIER, S.V.D., D.D.

Retired Auxiliary Bishop of Washington; ordained June 29, 1951; appointed Auxiliary Bishop of Washington and Titular Bishop of Legia November 10, 1988; Episcopal ordination December 20, 1988; retired May 18, 2004. *Res.: 619 Tenth St., N.W., Washington, DC 20001-4587.*

Most Reverend

FRANCISCO GONZALEZ, S.F., D.D., V.G.

Auxiliary Bishop of Washington; ordained May 1, 1964; appointed Auxiliary Bishop of Washington and Titular Bishop of Lamfua December 28, 2001; Episcopal ordination February 11, 2002. *Office: 5001 Eastern Ave., Hyattsville, MD 20782-3447. Mailing Address: P.O. Box 29260, Washington, DC 20017.*

Most Reverend

DONALD W. WUERL, S.T.D.

Archbishop of Washington; ordained December 17, 1966; appointed Titular Bishop of Rosemarkie and Auxiliary Bishop of Seattle December 3, 1985; consecrated January 6, 1986; appointed and canonically installed Bishop of Pittsburgh February 12, 1988; liturgically installed March 25, 1988; appointed Archbishop of Washington May 16, 2006; installed June 22, 2006. *Office: Archdiocesan Pastoral Center, 5001 Eastern Ave., Hyattsville, MD 20782-3447.* Tel: 301-853-4500; Fax: 301-853-5359. *Mailing Address: P.O. Box 29260, Washington, DC 20017-0260.*

Archdiocesan Pastoral Center: 5001 Eastern Ave., P.O. Box 29260, Washington, DC 20017. Tel: 301-853-4500; Fax: 301-853-5346.

Email: chancery@adw.org

Most Reverend

MARTIN D. HOLLEY, D.D., V.G.

Auxiliary Bishop of Washington; ordained priest May 8, 1987; appointed Auxiliary Bishop of Washington and Titular Bishop of Rusibisir May 18, 2004; Episcopal ordination July 2, 2004. *Office: 5001 Eastern Ave., Hyattsville, MD 20782-3447. Mailing Address: P.O. Box 29260, Washington, DC 20017.*

Most Reverend

BARRY C. KNESTOUT, D.D., V.G.

Auxiliary Bishop of Washington; ordained June 24, 1989; appointed Auxiliary Bishop of Washington and Titular Bishop of Leavenworth November 18, 2008; Episcopal ordination December 29, 2008. *Office: 5001 Eastern Ave., Hyattsville, MD 20782. Mailing Address: P.O. Box 29260, Washington, DC 20017.*

Square Miles 2,104.

Established Archdiocese July 22, 1939; Separated from Baltimore November 15, 1947; Became a Metropolitan See October 12, 1965.

Comprises the District of Columbia and Montgomery, Prince George's, St. Mary's, Calvert and Charles Counties in Maryland.

The Province of Washington has as a Suffragan, the Diocese of St. Thomas in the Virgin Islands.

For legal titles of parishes and archdiocesan institutions, consult the Chancery Office.

STATISTICAL OVERVIEW

Personnel	
Retired Cardinals	2
Archbishops	1
Auxiliary Bishops	3
Retired Bishops	1
Abbots	1
Retired Abbots	1
Priests: Diocesan Active in Diocese	203
Priests: Diocesan Active Outside Diocese	13
Priests: Diocesan in Foreign Missions	2
Priests: Retired, Sick or Absent	72
Number of Diocesan Priests	290
Religious Priests in Diocese	377
Total Priests in Diocese	667
Extern Priests in Diocese	146
Ordinations:	
Diocesan Priests	8
Transitional Deacons	8
Permanent Deacons in Diocese	199
Total Brothers	99
Total Sisters	562
Parishes	
Parishes	140
With Resident Pastor:	
Resident Diocesan Priests	117
Resident Religious Priests	17
Without Resident Pastor:	
Administered by Priests	3
Missions	9
Professional Ministry Personnel:	
Brothers	1
Sisters	26
Welfare	
Catholic Hospitals	3
Total Assisted	574,982
Health Care Centers	5
Total Assisted	89,176
Homes for the Aged	24
Total Assisted	2,010
Residential Care of Children	1
Total Assisted	280
Day Care Centers	6
Total Assisted	382
Specialized Homes	22
Total Assisted	14,909
Special Centers for Social Services	27
Total Assisted	181,000
Residential Care of Disabled	21
Total Assisted	360
Educational	
Seminaries, Diocesan	2
Students from This Diocese	41
Students from Other Diocese	63
Diocesan Students in Other Seminaries	26
Seminaries, Religious	11
Students Religious	152
Total Seminarians	219
Colleges and Universities	3
Total Students	12,250
High Schools, Diocesan and Parish	2
Total Students	786
High Schools, Private	16
Total Students	9,354
Elementary Schools, Diocesan and Parish	65
Total Students	16,687
Elementary Schools, Private	12
Total Students	1,741
Non-residential Schools for the Disabled	1
Total Students	61
Catechesis/Religious Education:	
High School Students	2,917
Elementary Students	30,680
Total Students under Catholic Instruction	74,695
Teachers in the Diocese:	
Priests	22
Brothers	12
Sisters	66
Lay Teachers	2,368
Vital Statistics	
Receptions into the Church:	
Infant Baptism Totals	4,300
Minor Baptism Totals	2,094
Adult Baptism Totals	774
Received into Full Communion	548
First Communions	5,470
Confirmations	4,602
Marriages:	
Catholic	997
Interfaith	548
Total Marriages	1,545
Deaths	2,680
Total Catholic Population	592,769
Total Population	2,694,405

Former Archbishops—Most Rev. MICHAEL J. CURLEY, cons. Bishop of St. Augustine, June 30, 1914; promoted to the See of Baltimore, Aug. 10, 1921; named Archbishop of Baltimore and Washington, July 22, 1939; died May 16, 1947; His Eminence PATRICK CARDINAL O'BOYLE, cons. Jan. 14, 1948; created Cardinal June 26, 1967; retired March 3, 1973; died Aug. 10, 1987; WILLIAM CARDINAL BAUM, S.T.D., installed May 8, 1973; appt. Prefect, Congregation for Catholic Education in the Vatican, Jan. 15, 1980; Major Penitentiary; appt. April 6, 1990; JAMES CARDINAL HICKEY, S.T.D., J.C.D., ord. Auxiliary Bishop of Saginaw April 14, 1967; appt. Bishop of Cleveland June 5, 1974; appt. Archbishop of Washington June 17, 1980; installed Aug. 5, 1980; created Cardinal June 28, 1988; retired Nov. 21, 2000; died Oct. 24, 2004; THEODORE CARDINAL MCCARRICK, Ph.D., D.D., ord. May 31, 1958; appt. Auxiliary Bishop of New York and Titular Bishop of Rusibisir May 24, 1977; Episcopal ord. June 29, 1977; appt. First Bishop of Metuchen Nov. 19, 1981; installed Jan. 31, 1982; appt. Archbishop of Newark May 30, 1986; installed July 25, 1986; appt. Archbishop of Washington Nov. 21, 2000; installed Jan. 3, 2001; created Cardinal priest of Saints Nereus and Achilleus Feb. 21, 2001; retired May 16, 2006.

Unless otherwise indicated, all Archdiocesan Offices, including the Chancery and the Tribunal, are located in the Archdiocesan Pastoral Center, 5001 Eastern Ave., Hyattsville, MD 20782. Mailing Address: P.O. Box 29260, Washington, 20017. Tel: 301-853-4500; Fax: 301-853-5346; Office Hours: Mon.-Fri. 8:30-5.

Vicars General—Most Revs. FRANCISCO GONZALEZ, S.F., D.D., V.G.; MARTIN D. HOLLEY, D.D., V.G.; BARRY C. KNESTOUT, D.D., V.G.

Moderator of the Curia—Most Rev. BARRY C. KNESTOUT, D.D., V.G.

Chancellor—JANE BELFORD, Esq. Tel: 301-853-4520; Fax: 301-853-7676.

Vice Chancellor—Rev. GEORGE E. STUART, J.C.D. Tel: 301-853-5327.

Office of Child Protection Services—Ms. MARCIA D. ZVARA, M.S.W., LCSW-C. Tel: 301-853-5328; Fax: 301-853-2787. Email: mzvara@adw.org.

Archivist—Rev. GEORGE E. STUART, J.C.D. Tel: 301-853-5327.

Secretary to the Archbishop—Rev. ADAM Y. PARK. Tel: 301-853-5350; Fax: 301-853-5359.

Secretariats—Mr. THOMAS W. BURNFORD, M.Div., Sec. Catholic Educ.; Rev. Msgr. MICHAEL W. FISHER, E.V., Vicar for Clergy & Sec. Ministerial Leadership; Mr. THOMAS P. DUFFY, CFO. Tel: 301-853-5312; Fax: 301-853-7693; Rev. WILLIAM D. BYRNE, Sec. Pastoral Ministry & Social Concerns, (See Separate sections for each Secretariat below).

Office of Canonical Services—

Episcopal Vicar for Canonical Services—Rev. Msgr. CHARLES V. ANTONICELLI, V.F. Tel: 301-853-5325; Fax: 301-853-7674.

Canonical Consultant—Sr. ELIZABETH MCDONOUGH, O.P.

The Tribunal

Tribunal—Tel: 301-853-4543; Fax: 301-853-7674.

Judicial Vicar—Rev. Msgr. JOSEPH F. SADUSKY, M.Div., M.Ch.A., J.C.D. Tel: 301-853-4544.

Adjutant Judicial Vicars—Rev. Msgr. GODFREY T. MOSLEY, J.C.D. Tel: 301-853-4543; Rev. BRIAN P. SANDERFOOT, J.C.L. Tel: 301-853-5324.

Judges—Rev. Msgrs. GEORGE E. DOBES, J.C.L. Tel: 301-853-4543, Ext. 253; CHARLES V. ANTONICELLI, V.F. Tel: 301-853-4543; Revs. G. PAUL HERBERT, J.C.L. Tel: 301-853-5326; VINCENT J. RIGDON, M.A., J.C.L., V.F. Tel: 301-853-4543; GEORGE E. STUART, J.C.D. Tel: 301-853-5327; MARK E. TUCKER, J.C.L. Tel: 301-853-5322.

Promoter of Justice—Rev. Msgr. KEVIN T. HART, J.C.D. Tel: 301-853-4543.

Defenders of the Bond—Revs. G. PAUL HERBERT, J.C.L. Tel: 301-853-5326; GEORGE E. STUART, J.C.D. Tel: 301-853-5327.

Advocates—Rev. Msgrs. PETER J. VAGHI, J.D., V.F. Tel: 301-853-4543; ROBERT G. AMEY. Tel: 301-853-4543; MARK E. BRENNAN. Tel: 301-853-4543; Revs. DONALD BRICE. Tel: 301-853-4536; JOHN T. DAKES, S.T.L. Tel: 301-853-4543; PAUL D. LEE, S.T.D. Tel: 301-853-4543; AGUSTIN MATEO AYALA. Tel: 301-853-4543; JEFFREY M. DEFAYETTE. Tel: 301-853-4543; WILLIAM H. GURNEE III. Tel: 301-853-4543.

Consultative Groups

Archdiocesan College of Consultors—Most Revs. FRANCISCO GONZALEZ, S.F., D.D., V.G.; MARTIN D. HOLLEY, D.D., V.G.; BARRY C. KNESTOUT, D.D., V.G.; Rev. Msgrs. JOHN J. ENZLER, E.V.; MICHAEL W. FISHER, E.V.; CHARLES E. POPE; PETER J. VAGHI, J.D., V.F.; EDDIE E. TOLENTINO, V.F.; Revs. MICHAEL A. SALAH, V.F.; JOHN J. DILLON, S.T.B., Ph.D.; JOHN T. DAKES, S.T.L.; FRANCISCO JAVIER SANTABALLA.

Archdiocesan Finance Council—Most Rev. DONALD W. WUERL; W. SHEPHERDSON ABELL, Esq.; THOMAS P. RODDY; GEORGE P. CLANCY JR.; CAROL G. BATES; Sr. CAROL KEEHAN, D.C.; J. PAUL MCNAMARA; LILA O'BRIEN SULLIVAN; WILLIAM J. SHAW. Staff: Most Rev. BARRY C. KNESTOUT, D.D., V.G., Vicar Gen. & Moderator of the Curia; Rev. Msgr. JOHN ENZLER, V.E., Vicar for Devel.; JANE G. BELFORD, Chancellor; Mr. THOMAS P. DUFFY, CFO; Mrs. KATHY MCKINLESS, CPA, Sr. Advisor.

Deans—Rev. Msgrs. MICHAEL WILSON, V.F., Northern Prince George's County; CHARLES J. PARRY, V.F., Middle Prince George's County; Rev. WILLIAM E. FOLEY, Southern Prince George's County; Rev. Msgrs. MICHAEL J. MELLONE, V.F., Upper Montgomery County; PETER J. VAGHI, J.D., V.F., Middle Montgomery County; EDDIE E. TOLENTINO, V.F., Lower Montgomery County; CHARLES V. ANTONICELLI, V.F., Northeast, D.C.; JAMES D. WATKINS, V.F., Northwest East, D.C.; W. RONALD JAMESON, Northwest West, D.C.; Revs. RAYMOND H. MOORE, V.F., Southeast, D.C.; MICHAEL J. KING, J.C.D., V.F., Calvert County; Rev. Msgrs. J. WILFRID PARENT, V.F., Charles County; KARL A. CHIMIAK, V.F., St. Mary's County.

Priest Council—Most Rev. DONALD W. WUERL, Pres.; Rev. Msgrs. JOHN ENZLER, V.E.; JAMES D. WATKINS, V.F.; CHARLES E. POPE; Revs. FREDERICK J. CLOSE JR., V.F.; RAYMOND J. WADAS; RONALD A. POTTS; Rev. Msgrs. PETER J. VAGHI, J.D., V.F.; EDDIE E. TOLENTINO, V.F.; Revs. RAYMOND H. MOORE, V.F.; LEVESTER JONES; RICHARD E. GARDINER; MICHAEL A. SALAH, V.F.; JOHN J. DILLON, S.T.B., Ph.D.; JOHN T. DAKES, S.T.L.; Rev. Msgrs. THOMAS M. DUFFY (Retired); JAMES T. BEATTIE; Rev. J. WILLIAM HINES; Rev. Msgr. MARK E. BRENNAN; Revs. JOHN P. CAULFIELD; STEVE SHAFRAN, S.D.B.; PATRICK A. SMITH; AN N. VU; FRANCISCO JAVIER SANTABALLA; MARIO E. DORSONVILLE; Most Revs. FRANCISCO GONZALEZ, S.F., D.D., V.G.; MARTIN D. HOLLEY, D.D., V.G.; BARRY C. KNESTOUT, D.D., V.G., Vicar Gen. & Moderator of the Curia; Rev. Msgr. MICHAEL W. FISHER, E.V.

Secretariat For Education

Secretary for Catholic Education—Mr. THOMAS W. BURNFORD, M.Div. Tel: 301-853-5331; Fax: 301-853-7691. Email: tburnford@adw.org.

Superintendent of Schools—PATRICIA A. WEITZEL-O'NEILL, Ph.D. Tel: 301-853-4518, Ext. 232; Fax: 301-853-7667. Email: weitzelp@adw.org.

Associate Superintendent of Catholic Schools—Ms. KELLY BRANAMAN. Tel: 301-853-4553; Fax: 301-853-7667. Email: branamank@adw.org.

Assistant Superintendent for Curriculum, Instruction, and Assessment—CATHY SPENCER. Tel: 301-853-4590; Fax: 301-853-7670. Email: spencerc@adw.org.

Director of Research and Planning—Mr. JEREMY MCDONALD. Tel: 301-853-4549; Fax: 301-853-7670. Email: mcdonaldj@adw.org.

Director of Special Education—Mrs. DOREEN ENGEL. Tel: 301-853-4569. Email: engeld@adw.org.

Director of Counseling—Mr. KENNETH GAUGHAN. Tel: 301-853-5353. Email: gaughank@adw.org.

Assistant Director for Funding and Educational Resources—Mr. THOMAS NAGLE. Tel: 301-853-5356. Email: naglet@adw.org.

Consortium of Catholic Academies of the Archdiocese of Washington, Inc.—MARGARET BOICE, Ed.D., Exec. Dir., 145 Taylor St., N.E., Washington, 20017. Tel: 202-234-4611; Fax: 202-234-4740. Email: margaret.boice@catholicacademies.org.

Board of Education—Ms. SUSAN DE PLATCHETT, Bd. Pres.

Office for Religious—Mr. HARRY DUDLEY, D.Min., D.R.E. Tel: 301-853-5368; Fax: 301-853-7387. Email: dudleyh@adw.org; JOSE AMAYA, Coord. Hispanic Catechesis & Catechist Formation. Tel: 301-853-5384; Fax: 301-853-7387. Email: amayaj@adw.org; ALICE NOE, Coord. Adult Faith Formation & Leadership Devel. Tel: 301-853-5385; Fax: 301-853-7387. Email: noea@adw.org.

Secretariat for Ministerial Leadership and Vicar for Clergy

Secretariat for Ministerial Leadership and Vicar for Clergy—Rev. Msgrs. MICHAEL WILLIAM FISHER, Secretariat for Ministerial Leadership & Vicar for Clergy. Tel: 301-835-4577; Fax: 301-853-7668; JOSEPH RANIERI, Coord. Pastoral Care of Priests. Tel: 301-853-5361; Fax: 301-853-7668; ROBERT J. PANKE, Dir. Priest Vocations & Formation. Tel: 301-853-4580; Fax: 301-853-7668; Revs. ROBERT WALSH, Asst. Dir. Priest Vocations & Formation. Tel: 301-853-5378; Fax: 301-853-7668; SCOTT HURD, Exec. Dir., Office of the Permanent Diaconate. Tel: 301-853-4582; Fax: 301-853-7668; Deacon KENNETH BARRETT, Dir. Formation for Permanent Diaconate. Tel: 301-853-4583; Fax: 301-853-7668; Sr. REBECCA BURKE, O.S.F., Delegate for Consecrated Life, Office for Consecrated Life. Tel: 301-853-4576; Fax: 301-853-7669.

Secretariat For Pastoral Ministry and Social Concerns

Secretary for Pastoral Ministry and Social Concerns—Rev. WILLIAM D. BYRNE, Sec. Email: byrnew@adw.org; Mr. STEPHEN DEMAURI, Administrative Asst. Tel: 301-853-4596; Fax: 301-853-7671. Email: spmsc@adw.org; demauris@adw.org.

Office for Ecumenical and Interreligious Affairs—Rev. PAUL D. LEE, S.T.D., Dir. Tel: 202-965-1610.

Charismatic Renewal Regional Service Committee—Rev. JOHN M. BARRY, St. Edward the Confessor, 16304 Pond Meadow Ln., Bowie, MD 20716. Tel: 301-249-9199.

Department of Special Needs Ministries—Ms. MARY O'MEARA, Exec. Dir., 7202 Buchanan St., Landover Hills, MD 20784. Tel: 301-459-7464 (V/TTY); Fax: 301-459-8186. Email: omearam@adw.org.

Ministry for the Deaf—Ms. LAUREEN LYNCH-RYAN, D.R.E. Tel: 301-459-7464 (V/TTY). Email: llynch-ryan@adw.org; Rev. GERARD A. TRANCONE, Gallaudet University, 800 Florida Ave., N.E., Washington, 20002. Tel: 301-577-3527 (Voice & TDD); Ms. MARGARET (PEG) KOLM, Coord. Special Needs Ministries. Tel: 301-853-4560. Email: mkolm@adw.org.

Holy Name Society—Mr. JOSEPH LATCHFORD, Vice Pres., Region IV, 141 Nottingham Ln., Berlin, MD 21811-1663. Tel: 410-641-7246. Email: joelatchford@verizon.net.

St. Ann's Infant & Maternity Home—Sr. MARY BADER, D.C., Dir., 4901 Eastern Ave., Hyattsville, MD 20782. Tel: 301-559-5500; Fax: 301-853-6985. Email: srmaryb@stanns.org; Mrs. PEGGY GATEWOOD, Dir., Faith House, 4903 Eastern Ave., Hyattsville, MD 20782. Tel: 301-559-5500; Fax: 301-853-6985. Email: peggy.gatewood@stanns.org.

St. Vincent de Paul Society—Ms. MARY LOUISE MAHONEY, Pres., Archdiocesan Council of Washington, 1438 Rhode Island Ave., N.E., Washington, 20018-3709. Tel: 202-281-2033. Email: svdpwashdc@aol.com.

Missionaries of Charity—

Gift of Peace House—Sr. M. LISSERIA, M.C., Supr., 2800 Otis St., N.E., Washington, 20018. Tel: 202-269-3313.

Casa Nuestra Senora de Guadalupe—Sr. CASIMIRA, M.C., Supr., Missionaries of Charity, 1646 Park Rd., N.W., Washington, 20010. Tel: 202-588-0091.

Community Center of the Missionaries of Charity—

Queen of Peace House—Sr. CLOVIS, M.C., Supr., 3310 Wheeler Rd., S.E., Washington, 20032. Tel: 202-562-6890.

Victory Housing, Inc.—Mr. JAMES A. BROWN JR., Pres., 5430 Grosvenor Ln., Ste. 210, Bethesda, MD 20814. Tel: 301-493-6000; Fax: 301-493-9788. Email: jbrown@victoryhousing.org; Ms. DEYSI FUENTES, Community Mgr., Andrew Kim House, Inc., 2100 Olney Sandy-Spring Rd., Olney, MD 20832. Tel: 301-260-2500; Fax: 301-260-2720. Email: andrewkimhouse@comcast.net; Ms. JONESY MAXSON, Dir., Raphael House, 1515 Dunster Rd., Rockville, MD 20854. Tel: 301-217-9116; Fax: 301-217-9119. Email: raphael@victoryhousing.org; Ms. KAREN KINNECOME, Dir., Byron House, 9210 Kentsdale Dr., Potomac, MD 20854. Tel: 301-469-9400; Fax: 301-765-8112. Email: byron@victoryhousing.org; Ms. MARGARET H. SMITH, Dir., Marian Assisted Living, 19109 Georgia Ave., Brookeville, MD 20833. Tel: 301-570-3190; Fax: 301-570-3638. Email: marian@victoryhousing.org; Sr. JEAN LOUISE FORKIN, C.S.C., FA.C.H.E., Dir., Malta House, 4916-18 LaSalle Rd., Hyattsville, MD 20782-3302. Tel: 301-699-8600; Fax: 301-699-1696. Email: malta@victoryhousing.org; Miss JEANNE BLUE, Dir., Bartholomew House, Inc., 6904 River Rd., Bethesda, MD 20817. Tel: 301-320-6151; Fax: 301-320-4420. Email: bartholomew@victoryhousing.org; Ms. BRIDGET DESNOES, Dir., Mary's House, 600-A Veirs Mill Rd., Rockville, MD 20852. Tel: 301-279-9520; Fax: 301-279-2080. Email: marys@victoryhousing.org; Ms. MEG DESCHRIVER, Dir., Grace House, 3214 Norbeck Rd., Silver Spring, MD 20906. Tel: 301-924-4424; Fax: 301-924-4427. Email: grace@victoryhousing.org.

Christ Child Society, Inc.—Ms. KATHLEEN CURTIN, Exec. Dir., 5101 Wisconsin Ave., N.W., Ste. 304, Washington, 20016. Tel: 202-966-9250; Fax: 202-966-2880. Email: kcurtin@christchilddc.org.

Cambridge Apartments, Inc.—Property Managers: Ms. KATHY CHAVIS, 676 Houston Ave., Ste. 104, Takoma Park, MD 20912. Tel: 301-585-3750; 301-585-4072. Email: cambridgeapts@verizon.net; Ms. BARBARA MILLER, Avondale Park Apartments, Inc., 4915 Eastern Ave., Hyattsville, MD 20782. Tel: 301-853-7787; Fax: 301-853-3988. Email: avondale1@verizon.net; Manor Apartments, Inc., 4907 Eastern Ave., Hyattsville, MD 20782. Tel: 301-853-2900; Fax: 301-853-3418. Email: manor417@verizon.net; Ms. BETTY SELLARS, Victory Forest, 10000 Brunswick Ave., Silver Spring, MD 20910. Tel: 301-589-4030; Fax: 301-589-7349. Email: manager106@habitatamerica.com; Ms. ARLITA MATTHEWS, Trinity Terrace, 6001 Fisher Rd., Temple Hills, MD 20748. Tel: 301-630-7717; Fax: 301-630-1798. Email: trinityterrace@verizon.net; Ms. DARCIA YOUNG, Victory Tower, 7051 Carroll Ave., Takoma Park, MD 20912. Tel: 301-270-1858; Fax: 301-270-4715. Email: manager412@habitatamerica.com; Ms. KATHY CHAVIS, Winslow House Apartments, 666 Houston Ave., Takoma Park, MD 20912. Tel: 301-585-3750. Email: cambridgeapts@verizon.net; Mr. INGRID GEISSLER, Victory Terrace Apartments, 9440 Newbridge Dr., Potomac, MD 20854. Tel: 301-983-9600; Fax: 301-983-9606. Email: victoryterrace@verizon.net; Ms. BRENDA WINES, Victory House of Palmer Park, 7801 Barlowe Rd., Palmer Park, MD 20785. Tel: 301-341-4995; Fax: 301-341-4997. Email: manager405@habitatamerica.com; Ms. SHAWN BARCUS, Cheval Court Apts., 2611 Luana Dr., Forestville, MD 20747. Tel: 301-736-0685; Fax: 301-736-0705. Email: chevalcourt@verizon.net; Ms. DELPHINE DUCKETT, Victory Heights, 1369 Irving St., N.W., Washington, 20010. Tel: 202-939-1431; Fax: 202-939-1433. Email: manager320@habitatamerica.com; Ms. MARCIA URQUIZA, Parkfair Apts., 1611 Park Rd., N.W., Washington, 20010. Tel: 202-986-1600; Fax: 202-986-4100. Email: 319manager@verizon.net.

Ladies of Charity—Ms. MARYANNE ROONEY, Pres., 5403 Linden Ct., Bethesda, MD 20814. Tel: 301-564-5793; Rev. CARL F. DIANDA, Spiritual Dir., St. Francis de Sales Parish, 2021 Rhode Island Ave.,

N.E., Washington, 20018. Tel: 202-529-7451.
Pastoral Care of Priests—Rev. Msgr. JOSEPH A. RANIERI, Coord. Tel: 301-853-5361.
Vocations for Men—Rev. Msgr. ROBERT J. PANKE, Dir. Tel: 301-853-4580; Rev. ROBERT E. WALSH, Asst. Dir. Tel: 301-853-5378.
Continuing Education for Clergy—Rev. Msgr. MICHAEL W. FISHER, E.V. Tel: 301-853-4577.
St. John Vianney House— Kensington, MD Tel: 301-942-1191.
Executive Director, Permanent Diaconate—Rev. SCOTT HURD. Tel: 301-853-4582.
Coordinator of Pastoral Care—Deacon JOSEPH F. CURTIS JR. Tel: 301-853-4586.
Director of Formation, Permanent Diaconate—Deacon KENNETH BARRETT. Tel: 301-853-4583.
Priests Retirement Board—Rev. Msgr. KEVIN T. HART, J.C.D., Chm. Tel: 301-292-0527.
Cardinal O'Boyle Residence for Priests—Rev. Msgr. LEONARD F. HURLEY, Mailing Address: P.O. Box 29206, Washington, 20017. Tel: 202-269-7818.
Serra Club of Washington, D.C.—Mr. JOSEPH F. SPANIOL JR., Pres., 5602 Ontario Cir., Bethesda, MD 20816. Tel: 301-229-2176.
Serra Club of Downtown Washington—Mr. GERRALD GIBLIN, Pres., 4409 Westover Pl., N.W., Washington, 20016. Tel: 202-362-2477.
Serra Club of Prince George's Co.—Miss JUDITH BARR, Pres., 4014 Nicholson St., Hyattsville, MD 20782. Tel: 301-779-3150.
Serra Club of Southern Maryland—Mrs. WALTER ROURKE, Pres. (Cathy) 10548 Wicomoco Ridge Rd., Charlotte Hall, MD 20622. Tel: 301-884-7464.
Delegate for Consecrated Life—VACANT.

Secretariat for Finance and Administration

Finance and Management—Mr. THOMAS P. DUFFY, CFO. Tel: 301-853-5365; Mr. SCOTT LANCASTER, Controller. Tel: 301-853-4504; Mrs. KATHY MCKINLESS, CPA, Senior Advisor. Tel: 301-853-5314.
Director of Parish and School Financial Operations—Mr. TERENCE FARRELL, CPA. Tel: 301-853-4511; Fax: 301-853-7664.
Property Risk & Liability Insurance—Mr. RICHARD B. GRAVES, Dir. Tel: 301-853-4522.
Facilities Management—Mr. RICHARD DE STWOLINSKI, Dir. Tel: 202-281-2491; Fax: 202-281-2498; Mr. SCOTT SULLIVAN, Asst. Dir. Tel: 202-281-2492; Ms. ALESSANDRA STYLES, Dir. Pastoral Center Mgmt. Tel: 301-853-4532; Fax: 301-853-7673.
Personnel and Benefits—Ms. DOROTHY MOORE, Dir. Human Resources. Tel: 301-853-4513; Fax: 301-853-7680.

Department for Evangelization and Family Life

Department for Evangelization and Family Life—Dr. SUSAN M. TIMONEY, S.T.D., Exec. Dir. Tel: 301-853-4558; Fax: 301-853-7660. Email: stimoney@adw.org.
Office of Family Life—Mr. PETER MURPHY, Dir. Tel: 301-853-4546; Fax: 301-853-7660. Email: murphyp@adw.org.
Coordinator for Hispanic Family Life—Mrs. ANA (PATTY) MAZARIEGOS. Tel: 301-853-4551; Fax: 301-853-7660. Email: mazariegosa@adw.org.
Coordinator of Ministry to Young Adults—Ms. LAURA FERSTL. Tel: 301-853-4559; Fax: 301-853-7660. Email: lferstl@adw.org.
Coordinator of Evangelization and Hispanic Christian Initiation—Ms. MAGDALENA GUTIERREZ. Tel: 301-853-5334; Fax: 301-853-7660. Email: mgutierrez@adw.org.
Coordinator of Christian Initiation—Mr. ALFRED D. TURNIPSEED JR. Tel: 301-853-5335; Fax: 301-853-7660. Email: turnipseeda@adw.org.

Office of Worship

Office of Worship—Rev. MARK D. KNESTOUT, Dir. Tel: 301-853-4595; Fax: 301-853-7684. Email: knestoutm@adw.org; Sr. CONSTANCE WARD, S.S.J., Administrative Asst. Tel: 301-853-4594. Email: cward@adw.org.
Commission on Sacred Art and Architecture—Rev. Msgr. W. RONALD JAMESON, Chm. Tel: 202-347-3215; Fax: 202-347-7184.

Office of the Missions

Office of the Missions—Sr. MARIE DE LA TRINITE SIOPONGCO, S.S.V.M., Dir. Tel: 301-853-4534; Fax: 301-853-7685. Email: siopongs@adw.org.
HCA Mission Education Coordinator—Sr. MARIA DE LA REVELACION CASTANEDA. Tel: 301-853-5388. Email: castanedar@adw.org.
Missionary Cooperative Plan Coordinator—Ms. CECILIA CORTES-PECK. Tel: 301-853-4528. Email: ccortes-peck@adw.org.

Department for Charity and Justice

Department for Charity and Justice—Ms. MARY C. MCGINNITY, Exec. Dir. Tel: 301-853-5339; Fax: 301-853-7671. Email: mmcginnity@adw.org.
Parish Social Ministry—Mr. ANTHONY BOSNICK, Coord. Tel: 301-853-5340; Fax: 301-853-7671. Email: bosnicka@adw.org.
Ministry to Persons with Disabilities— (see Margaret "Peg" Kolm under Dept. of Special Needs Ministries)
Catholic Relief Services/International Outreach and Global Solidarity—Ms. MARY C. MCGINNITY, CRS Diocesan Dir. Tel: 301-853-5339; Fax: 301-853-7671. Email: mmcginnity@adw.org.

Department for Life Issues

Department for Life Issues—Ms. CHRISTA LOPICCOLO, Exec. Dir. Tel: 301-853-5318; Fax: 301-853-7671. Email: clopiccolo@adw.org; Ms. MICHELLE CARPER, Prog. Coord. Tel: 301-853-4555; Fax: 301-853-7671. Email: mcarper@adw.org.
Birthing and Care Program—Ms. MICHELLE WILLIAMS, Dir. Tel: 301-853-5341; Fax: 301-853-7671. Email: mwilliams@adw.org.
Project Rachel—Ms. JULIA SHELAVA, Dir. Tel: 301-853-5386; Fax: 301-853-7671. Email: projectrachel@adw.org; Ms. LUZ MENJIVAR, Prog. Coord. Pastoral Care, Birthing and Care Prog. & Project Rachel. Tel: 301-853-4562; Fax: 301-853-7671.

Office of Black Catholics

Office of Black Catholics—Deacon AL TURNER, Dir. Tel: 301-853-5371; Fax: 301-853-7671. Email: obc@adw.org.

Office of Hispanic Pastoral Affairs

Office of Hispanic Pastoral Affairs—Mr. MANUEL ALIAGA, Dir. Tel: 301-853-4567; Fax: 301-853-7671. Email: maliaga@adw.org.

Office of Youth Ministry

Office of Youth Ministry—145 Taylor St., N.E., P.O. Box 29260, Washington, 20017. Tel: 202-281-2460; Fax: 202-281-2470. Ms. DEBORAH MCDONALD, Exec. Dir. Tel: 202-281-2466. Email: mcdonald@adw.org.
Associate Director, Coordinator of Athletic Ministry/CYO Sports—Mr. KEVIN DONOGHUE. Tel: 202-281-2463. Email: donoghuek@adw.org.
Associate Director, Coordinator of Youth Ministry Programs and Training—Mr. JOAQUIN TREJO. Tel: 202-281-2476. Email: jtrejo@adw.org.
African American Youth Ministry—Mr. DARREN FOSTER. Tel: 202-281-2469. Email: dfoster@adw.org.
OYM/CYO Programs Assistant—Deacon MICHAEL BOND. Tel: 202-281-2465. Email: mbond@adw.org.
Our Lady of Mattaponi Youth Retreat and Conference Center—Mrs. MARY DAWN WOODS, Dir. Tel: 301-952-9074; Fax: 301-952-0609. Email: dwoods2@adw.org.
Boy Scouts/Girl Scouts/Camp Fire Boys & Girls—Mr. FRANK ROSSOMONDO, Coord. Archdiocesan Catholic Committee on Scouting/Camp Fire. Tel: 301-770-7450. Email: fross2@juno.com.
Girl Scout Chair, Catholic Committee for Girl Scouts—Ms. BRENDA MURTHA. Tel: 301-349-4312. Email: breezegs@verizon.net.
Boy Scout Chair, Catholic Committee for Boy Scouts—Mr. RICHARD STEVICK. Tel: 301-490-7855. Email: dstevick@verizon.net.
Camp Fire Lay Coordinator—Ms. ROSEMARY PEZUTTO. Tel: 301-262-1631. Email: copier22@aol.com.
Archdiocesan Chaplain Coordinator/Catholic Committee on Boy Scouts, Girl Scouts & Camp fire—Rev. Msgr. JOHN B. BRADY (Retired). Tel: 301-769-3332.
Archdiocesan Chaplain - Catholic Committee on Boy Scouts—Rev. SCOTT WOODS. Tel: 301-862-4600.
Archdiocesan Chaplain - Catholic Committee on Girl Scouts—Rev. RONALD A. POTTS. Tel: 301-934-2261.

Lay Leadership Institute

Lay Leadership Institute—Cardinal McCarrick Center, 12247 Georgia Ave., Wheaton, MD 20902. Tel: 301-946-1621. Ms. CHRISTINA HIP-FLORES, M.P.P., Exec. Dir. Email: chip-flores@adw.org.

Secretariat for Development

Development Office— Coordinates all Archdiocesan development and fundraising efforts and oversees the Archbishop's Appeal, Parish Resource Development, planned giving, major donors, grant writing, Forward in Faith Campaign, and the Archdiocesan Tuition Assistance Fund. Tel: 301-853-4575; Fax: 301-853-7678; 301-853-7692. Email: development@adw.org.
Vicar of Development—Rev. Msgr. JOHN J. ENZLER, E.V. Tel: 301-853-5375; Fax: 301-853-7692. Email: jenzler@adw.org.
Executive Director of Development—Mr. KEVIN T. O'CONNOR. Tel: 301-853-4574; Fax: 301-853-7692. Email: oconnork@adw.org.
Archbishop's Appeal—Mr. KEVIN T. O'CONNOR, Dir. Tel: 301-853-4574; Fax: 301-853-7692. Email: oconnork@adw.org.
Planned Giving—Mr. EDWARD J. D'ANTONI, Dir. Tel: 301-853-4573; Fax: 301-853-7692. Email: dantonie@adw.org.
Forward in Faith—Mrs. WENDI M. WILLIAMS, Dir. Tel: 301-853-5376; Fax: 301-853-7692. Email: williamsw@adw.org.
Archdiocesan Tuition Assistance Fund—Mrs. WENDI M. WILLIAMS, Dir. Tel: 301-853-5376; Fax: 301-853-7692. Email: williamsw@adw.org.
Parish Resource Development—Mr. GEORGE REED, Dir. Tel: 301-853-5374; Fax: 301-853-7692. Email: reedg@adw.org.
Programs and Donor Relations—Ms. MARY MCNAMARA, Asst. Dir. Tel: 301-853-4572; Fax: 301-853-7692. Email: mmcnamara@adw.org; Mr. SEAN BROWN, Asst. Tel: 301-853-5344; Fax: 301-853-7692. Email: browns@adw.org.
Archdiocesan Building Commission—Rev. Msgr. JOSEPH A. RANIERI, Chm.
Archdiocesan Sacred Arts Committee—Rev. Msgr. W. RONALD JAMESON, 1725 Rhode Island Ave. N.W., Washington, 20036. Tel: 202-347-3215; Fax: 202-347-7184.
Cornerstone for Tomorrow, Inc.—Mr. THOMAS P. DUFFY, Mailing Address: P.O. Box 29260, Washington, 20017. Tel: 301-853-5375.
Priest Retirement Fund of the Archdiocese of Washington, Inc.—Mr. THOMAS P. DUFFY, Mailing Address: P.O. Box 29260, Washington, 20017. Tel: 301-853-5312.
Forward in Faith, Inc.—Mr. ROBERT F. COMSTOCK, Chm., Mailing Address: P.O. Box 29063, Washington, 20017-0063.

Office of Communications

Director—Ms. SUSAN GIBBS. Tel: 301-853-4516; Fax: 301-853-7672. Email: sgibbs@adw.org.
TV Mass Producer—Mr. JOHN CAPOBIANCO. Tel: 301-853-4517.
Carroll Publishing Company—Most Rev. DONALD W. WUERL, Publisher; Mr. THOMAS SCHMIDT, Pres. Tel: 202-281-2405; Fax: 202-281-2408.
Newspaper— "The Catholic Standard" Mr. MARK ZIMMERMANN, Editor. Tel: 202-281-2412; Fax: 202-281-2418. Email: mark@cathstan.org.
Newspaper "El Pregonero"—Mr. RAFAEL RONCAL, Editor. Tel: 202-281-2442; Fax: 202-281-2448. Email: rafael@elpreg.org.

CLERGY, PARISHES, MISSIONS AND PAROCHIAL SCHOOLS

DISTRICT OF COLUMBIA

1—ST. MATTHEW CATHEDRAL (1840) Rev. Msgr. W. Ronald Jameson; Rev. Kevin Regan; Deacons Ulysses Rice, (Retired); Bartholomew J. Merella; Boyd Work; Juan Cayrampoma; Pamela Erwin, Business Mgr. In Res., Revs. Mark D. Knestout; John Hurley (Retired); Evelis Menjiar.
Res.: 1725 Rhode Island Ave., N.W., 20036. Tel: 202-347-3215; Fax: 202-347-7184. Email: cathstmatt@stmatthewscathedral.org. Web: www.stmatthewscathedral.org.
Catechesis/Religious Program—Students 92.

2—ST. ALOYSIUS (1859) Revs. Thomas F. Clifford, S.J.; J-Glenn Murray, S.J., Parochial Vicar; Deacon Willis Daniels.
Res.: 19 Eye St., N.W., 20001. Tel: 202-336-7200; Fax: 202-842-3693. Email: stals@gonzaga.org. Web: www.stalschurchdc.org.
Father McKenna Center—Tel: 202-842-1112; Fax: 202-842-7401. Tom Howarth, Dir.
Catechesis/Religious Program—Students 45.

3—ST. ANN (1869) Rev. Msgr. Godfrey T. Mosley; Rev. William M. Brailsford; Deacon Robert W. Whitaker.
Res.: 4001 Yuma St., N.W., 20016. Tel: 202-966-6288; Fax: 202-966-7722. Email: stann@stanndc.org. Web: www.stanndc.org.
School—(Grades PreK-8), 4404 Wisconsin Ave., N.W., 20016. Tel: 202-363-4460, Ext. 1; Fax: 202-362-6560. Email: office@stannsacademy.org. Web: www.stannsacademy.org. Mr. Thomas Wharton, Prin.; Mr. Kevin Fosko, Librarian. Lay Teachers 18; Students 219.
Catechesis/Religious Program—Tel: 202-363-9524. Email: dre@stanndc.org. Students 87.
Mission— 4133 Yuma St., NW, 20016. Tel: 202-966-5676.

4—ANNUNCIATION (1948) Rev. Msgr. V. James Lockman; Rev. Donald Brice. In Res., Rev. Msgr. Barry C. Knestout.
Parish Office—Office: 3125 39th St., N.W., 20016-5409. Tel: 202-362-3323; Fax: 202-237-0652. Email: parish@annunciationdc.org. Web: www.annunciationdc.org.
Res.: 3915 Mass Ave., N.W., 20016.
School—3825 Klingle Pl., N.W., 20016-5434. Tel: 202-362-1408; Fax: 202-363-4057. Web: www.annunciationschool.net. Ms. K. Marguerite Conley, Prin. Lay Teachers 19; Students 123.
Catechesis/Religious Program—Ms. Patrice Morace, D.R.E. Students 98.
Convent—3200 39th St., N.W., 20016. Tel: 202-362-1464.

5—ST. ANTHONY (1892) Revs. Frederick J. Close Jr.; Berard L. Marthaler, O.F.M.Conv. (Retired). In Res., Revs. Tesfay Woldemarian Fesuh; John Milewski.
Res.: 1029 Monroe St., N.E., 20017. Tel: 202-250-8208; Fax: 202-250-6223. Email: stanthony.dc@adwparish.org.
School—Tel: 202-526-4657; Fax: 202-832-5567. Lay Teachers 19; Students 202.
Catechesis/Religious Program—Students 44.

6—ASSUMPTION (1916) Rev. Msgr. T. Ansgar Laczko (Retired).
Res.: 3401 Martin Luther King Jr. Ave., S.E., 20032-1597. Tel: 202-561-4178; Fax: 202-561-0336.

7—ST. AUGUSTINE (1858), (African American), Revs. Charles C. Green (Retired); Lowell D. Case, S.S.J., Admin.; Roy Edward Campbell.
Parish Office—1419 V St., N.W., 20009. Fax: 202-234-1787.
Res.: 1425 V St., N.W., 20009. Tel: 202-265-1470.
School—1421 V St., N.W., 20009. Tel: 202-667-2608. Donna Edwards, Prin. Lay Teachers 18; Students 173.
Catechesis/Religious Program—Students 155.

8—BASILICA OF THE NATIONAL SHRINE OF THE IMMACULATE CONCEPTION (1920) Mailing Address: 400 Michigan Ave., N.E., 20017-1566. Web: www.nationalshrine.com.

9—ST. BENEDICT THE MOOR (1946) Rev. Richard K. Gancayco.
Res.: 320 21st St., N.E., 20002. Tel: 202-397-3895; Fax: 202-398-3415. Email: rectory@stbenedictofdc.org. Web: www.stbenedictofdc.org.
Catechesis/Religious Program—Students 17.

10—ST. BLAISE (1984), (Croatian), (Croatian Pastoral Mission) Revs. Elvis Razov (Croatia); Damir Stojic, S.D.B. (Croatia).
Mailing Address: *Our Lady of Victory*, 4835 Macarthur Blvd., N.W., 20007. Tel: 202-492-9088; Fax: 202-338-4759.
Catechesis/Religious Program—Students 10.

11—BLESSED SACRAMENT, SHRINE OF THE MOST (1911) Rev. Msgrs. John J. Enzler; Maurice V. O'Connell, Senior Priest; Rev. James D. Boccabella; Deacon Daniel Thompson.
Mailing Address: 3630 Quesada St., N.W., 20015-2423. In Res., Rev. Tesfaye Fesuh (Ethiopia).
Res.: 6001 Western Ave., N.W., 20015. Tel: 202-966-6575; Fax: 202-966-9255. Web: www.blessedsacramentdc.org.
School—5841 Chevy Chase Pkwy., N.W., 20015. Tel: 202-966-6682; Fax: 202-966-4938. Web: www.b-sstoday.org. Mr. Christopher Kelly, Prin. Lay Teachers 41; Students 508.
Catechesis/Religious Program—Tel: 202-449-3989. Email: rmaro@blessedsacramentdc.org. Rob Maro, D.R.E. Students 521.

12—CHURCH OF ST. LOUIS (1972), (French), (Paroisse St. Louis de France-French-speaking Parish of Washington) Rev. Antoine De Romanet.
Res.: 4125 Garrison St., N.W., 20016. Tel: 202-537-0709; Fax: 202-244-9649. Email: stlouisdef@aol.com. Web: www.members.aol.com/stlouisdef.
Catechesis/Religious Program—Students 240.

13—ST. DOMINIC CHURCH & PRIORY (1852) Rev. Gregory R. Salomone, O.P.; Very Rev. George Muller, O.P., Prior; Revs. John A. McMahon, O.P.; Robert L. Walker, O.P.; Edmund J. Way, O.P.; V. F. McHenry, O.P.; Adrian L. Dionne, O.P.; J. Andrew Nicolicchia, O.P.; Eugene Cahouet, O.P.; David A. Butler, O.P.; Charles O'Brien, O.P.; Valerian LaFrance, O.P.; William Burke, O.P.; Peter J. Allen, O.P.; Bede Shipps, O.P.; Gerard Lessard, O.P.; Bro. Jude Locchetto, O.P. In Res., Rev. Robert Leo Pelkington.
Res.: 630 E St., S.W., 20024. Tel: 202-554-7863; Fax: 202-554-0231.

14—EPIPHANY (1923) Rev. Paul D. Lee.
Res.: 2712 Dumbarton St., N.W., 20007. Tel: 202-965-1610; Fax: 202-337-8377.
Catechesis/Religious Program—Jane Zilles-Soberano, D.R.E. Students 22.

15—ST. FRANCIS DE SALES (1722), (African American), Rev. Carl F. Dianda; Michael Howard, Pastoral Assoc. In Res., Rev. Henry Slevin.
Res.: 2021 Rhode Island Ave., N.E., 20018. Tel: 202-529-7451; Fax: 202-529-0050. Email: dcianda@adwparish.org. Web: www.stfrancisdesaleswdc.org.
Catechesis/Religious Program—Parish Family Center, 2017 St. Frances de Sales Pl., 20018. Tel: 202-529-2147; Fax: 202-529-1630. Email: etsm@prodigy.net. Students 6.

16—ST. FRANCIS XAVIER (1924) Rev. C. Gregory Butta.
Res.: 2800 Pennsylvania Ave., S.E., 20020. Tel: 202-582-5021; Fax: 202-581-7224.
School—Tel: 202-581-2010; 202-234-4611; Fax: 202-582-5244. Harold Thomas, Prin. Lay Teachers 12; Students 250.
Catechesis/Religious Program—Tel: 202-582-2607; Fax: 202-581-1142. Mr. Robert Fuller, D.R.E. Students 40.
Convent—Sisters of St. Joseph, 2812 Pennsylvania Ave., S.E., 20020. Tel: 202-584-5621. Sr. Marie Brigid Monahan, S.S.J., Pastoral Min.

17—ST. GABRIEL (1919) Rev. Agustin Mateo Ayala; Deacon Robert L. Berry. In Res., Rev. Tesfamariam Baraki.
Res.: 26 Grant Cir., N.W., 20011. Tel: 202-726-9092; Fax: 202-291-0334.
Catechesis/Religious Program—Tel: 202-726-9212; Fax: 202-291-0334. Students 160.

18—HOLY COMFORTER--ST. CYPRIAN (1893), (African American), Rev. Msgr. T. Ansgar Laczko (Retired); Rev. Mark D. White; Deacons Charles Edelin; Kevin Butler; Ralph Cyrus. In Res., Rev. F. Michael Bryant.
Res.: 1357 E. Capitol St., S.E., 20003. Tel: 202-546-1885; Fax: 202-544-1385.

19—HOLY NAME (1891), (African American—Hispanic), Revs. Everett Pearson; Robert Guillen; Deacon William Thomas. In Res., Rev. Francis M. Walsh.
Res.: 920 11th St., N.E., 20002. Tel: 202-397-2525; Fax: 202-397-6639.
Catechesis/Religious Program—Students 30.

20—HOLY REDEEMER (1919), (African American), Rev. David Bava.
Res.: 206 New York Ave., N.W., 20001. Tel: 202-347-7510; Fax: 202-638-4831. Email: holyredeemer.dc@adwparish.org.
School—Holy Redeemer School, (Grades PreK-8), 1135 New Jersey Ave., N.W., 20001. Tel: 202-638-5789; Fax: 301-628-0401. Ben Ketchum, Prin. Priests 1; Sisters 2; Deacons 1; Lay Teachers 15; Students 200.
Catechesis/Religious Program—Tel: 202-347-7510. Students 55.

21—HOLY ROSARY (1913), (Italian), Rev. Lydio F. Tomasi, C.S.
Res.: 595 Third St., N.W., 20001-2703. Tel: 202-638-0165; Fax: 202-638-0793. Email: casaitaldc@yahoo.com. Web: www.holyrosarychurchdc.org.
Catechesis/Religious Program—Students 12.

22—HOLY TRINITY (1787) Revs. Mark F. Horak, S.J.; Leo A. Murray, S.J.; Gregory A. Schenden, S.J.; Stephen F. Spahn, S.J.
Mailing Address: 36th St., N.W., between N and O Sts., 20007.
Parish Center Offices—3513 N St., N.W., 20007. Tel: 202-337-2840; Fax: 202-337-9048. Web: www.trinity.org.
Res.: 3514 O St., N.W., 20007.
School—1325 36th St. N.W., 20007-2604. Tel: 202-337-2339; Fax: 202-337-0368. Web: htsdc.org. Sisters of St. Joseph (Chestnut Hill, PA) 1; Lay Teachers 43; Students 333.
Catechesis/Religious Program—Students 680.

23—IMMACULATE CONCEPTION (1864), (African American), Rev. Msgr. James D. Watkins.
Res.: 1315 8th St., N.W., 20001. Tel: 202-332-8888; Fax: 202-332-0173. Web: www.immaculateconceptionchurchdc.org.
Catechesis/Religious Program—Students 10.

24—INCARNATION (1934), (African American), Rev. John A. Carroll, S.S.J.; Deacon Joseph E. Bell.
Res.: 880 Eastern Ave., N.E., 20019. Tel: 202-396-0942; Fax: 202-396-6064.
Catechesis/Religious Program—Students 123.

25—ST. JOSEPH ON CAPITOL HILL (1868) Rev. Msgr. Charles V. Antonicelli; Rev. Christopher T. Begg; Deacon Gary L. Bockweg. In Res., Rev. Eugene Hemrick (JOL).
Res.: 313 Second St., N.E., 20002. Tel: 202-547-1223; Fax: 202-547-4189. Web: www.st-josephs.org.
Catechesis/Religious Program—Email: ccd@st-josephs.org. Students 25.

26—KIDANE-MEHRET GE'EZ RITE CATHOLIC CHURCH (1984), (Ethiopian—Eritrean), Rev. Tesfamariam Baraki.
Mailing Address: 1001 Lawrence St., N.E., P.O. Box 29616, 20017. Tel: 202-529-8420.
Res.: 26 Grant Cir., N.W., 20011. Tel: 202-726-9092; Fax: 202-529-8523.
Catechesis/Religious Program—Students 127.

27—ST. LUKE (1957), (African American), Revs. Joseph F. Del Vecchio, S.S.J.; Joseph N. Begay, S.S.J.; Deacons Earle W. Coleman; Joseph M. Conrad.
Res.: 4925 E. Capitol St., S.E., 20019-5202. Tel: 202-584-8322; Fax: 202-584-3421.
Catechesis/Religious Program—Students 52.

28—ST. MARTIN OF TOURS (1901), (African American), Rev. Michael J. Kelley.
Res.: 1908 N. Capitol St., 20002. Tel: 202-232-1144; Fax: 202-832-6772. Web: www.stmartinsdc.org.
Catechesis/Religious Program—Students 58.

29—ST. MARY, MOTHER OF GOD (1845) [CEM] Rev. Alfred J. Harris. In Res., Revs. William Cleary; Daniel D'Alliessi (NY).
Res.: 727 Fifth St., N.W., 20001. Tel: 202-289-7771; Fax: 202-408-1989. Email: stmarys20001@gmail.com.
Catechesis/Religious Program—Tel: 202-289-7770.

30—NATIVITY (1901), (African American), Revs. George Hanna, S.D.B.; Dominic DeBlase, S.D.B.; John Serio, S.D.B.; Deacon Al Douglas Turner; Revs. Paul Grauls, S.D.B.; Steve Shafran, S.D.B.; Abraham Feliciano, S.D.B.; Bro. Thomas Sweeney, S.D.B.
Res.: 6000 Georgia Ave., N.W., 20011. Tel: 202-726-6262; Fax: 202-722-7170. Email: nativityccdc@aol.com. Web: www.nativitychurch.net.
Catechesis/Religious Program—Students 55.

31—NIGERIAN CATHOLIC COMMUNITY (1994), (Nigerian), Closed. For inquiries for parish records contact the chancery.

32—OUR LADY OF FATIMA PARISH (1999), (Portuguese-speaking Community) Revs. Sergio Dall Agnese, C.S.; Carlos Reyes Ramirez, C.S.
Mailing Address: 5700 St. Bernard's Dr., Riverdale, MD 20737. Tel: 301-277-1000; Fax: 301-277-3464.
Catechesis/Religious Program—10830 Eastwood Ave., Silver Spring, MD 20901. Tel: 301-949-2488. Students 75.

33—OUR LADY OF PERPETUAL HELP (1920), (African American), Revs. William L. Norvel, S.S.J.; Oswald Pierre Pierre-Jules Jr., S.S.J., Parochial Vicar; Bro. Marx Tyree, S.S.J., Pastoral Assoc.; Deacon Thomas Jones.
Res.: 1600 Morris Rd., S.E., 20020-6312. Tel: 202-678-4999; Fax: 202-610-3189. Web: www.olphchurchofdc.org.
Parish Life Center—1604 Morris Rd., S.E., 20020. Tel: 202-889-1662; 202-678-0211; Fax: 202-610-1519.
Catechesis/Religious Program—Students 72.

34—OUR LADY OF VICTORY (1909) Rev. David H. Werning; Rev. Msgr. Thomas M. Duffy, Co-Chap., Sibley Hospital (Retired); Deacon Leo Flynn. In Res., Rev. Leo D. Lefebure (CHI), Matteo Ricci Chair, Georgetown University; Prof. of Theology.
Res.: 4835 MacArthur Blvd., N.W., 20007. Tel: 202-337-4835; 202-337-4836; Fax: 202-338-4759.
School—4755 Whitehaven Pkwy., N.W., 20007. Tel: 202-337-1421; Fax: 202-337-2068. Email: info@olvschooldc.org. Web: olvschooldc.org. Mrs. Sheila Martinez, Prin. Lay Teachers 25; Students 187.
Catechesis/Religious Program—Students 38.

35—OUR LADY QUEEN OF PEACE (1948), (African American), Rev. Peter M. Giovanoni; Deacon Alfred Miller.
Res.: 3800 Ely Pl., S.E., 20019. Tel: 202-582-8600; Fax: 202-575-3317.
Catechesis/Religious Program—Tel: 202-581-4986. Students 64.
Convent—3740 Ely Pl., S.E., 20019. Tel: 202-581-4963; Fax: 202-584-1922.

36—OUR LADY QUEEN OF THE AMERICAS (1986), (Hispanic), Rev. Roberto J. Cortes-Campos; Deacon Jorge W. Vargas.
Mailing Address: 2200 California St., N.W., 20008.
Catechesis/Religious Program—Tel: 202-332-8838, Ext. 200; Fax: 202-332-2967. Steward Benalcazar, D.R.E. Students 260.

37—ST. PATRICK (1794) Rev. Msgr. Salvatore A. Criscuolo; Deacon John J. McGinness. In Res., Most Rev. Leonard J. Olivier, S.V.D.; Rev. Msgr. Robert J. Panke; Rev. Brian Sanderfoot.
Res.: 619 Tenth St., N.W., 20001-4587. Tel: 202-347-2713; Fax: 202-347-1401. Email: office@saintpatrickdc.org. Web: saintpatrickdc.org.
Catechesis/Religious Program—Robert Quinlan, D.R.E. (Adult); Ronald Stolk, Music Dir.

38—ST. PETER (1821) Revs. William D. Byrne; William Hegedusich, Parochial Vicar. In Res., Rev. Msgr. Joseph F. Sadusky.
Res.: 313 Second St., S.E., 20003. Tel: 202-547-1430; Fax: 202-547-5732. Email: stpetersdc@verizon.net. Web: www.saintpetersdc.org.
School—422 Third St., S.E., 20003. Tel: 202-544-1618; Fax: 202-547-5101. Email: admissions@stpetersinterparish.org. Web: stpetersinterparish.org. Jennifer Ketchum, Prin. Daughters of St. Anne 2; Lay Teachers 26; Students 235.

Catechesis/Religious Program—Fax: 202-547-5732. Students 76.

39—SHRINE OF THE SACRED HEART (1899) Revs. Stephen Carter, O.F.M.Cap.; Paul Zaborowski, O.F.M.Cap.; Kevin Thompson, O.F.M.Cap.; Andre Pierre, O.F.M.Cap. (Haiti), (Haitian Apostolate); Francis Hgi, (Vietnamese Apostolate); Deacon Sylvester Brown, (Retired). In Res., Bro. Thomas Wells, O.F.M.Cap.
Res.: 3211 Pine St., 20010. Tel: 202-234-8000 (Day); 202-234-8002 (Night); Fax: 202-234-9159.
School—1625 Park Rd., N.W., 20010. Tel: 202-265-4828; Fax: 202-265-0595. Juana Brown, Prin. Lay Teachers 16; Students 228.
Catechesis/Religious Program—Tel: 202-667-2446. Students 225.

40—ST. STEPHEN MARTYR (1867) Rev. Msgr. Robert J. Panke; Revs. Klaus J. Sirianni; Gregory W. Shaffer. In Res., Rev. Jamin S. David (BR).
Res.: 2436 Pennsylvania Ave., N.W., 20037. Tel: 202-785-0982; Fax: 202-785-1574. Email: st.stephenmartyrdc@verizon.net. Web: www.st-stephenmartyrdc.org.

41—ST. TERESA OF AVILA (1879), (African American), Rev. Msgr. Raymond G. East; Deacon William J. Hawkins.
1401 V St., S.E., 20020-5692.
Res.: 1430 Minnesota Ave., S.E., 20020-5692. Tel: 202-678-3037; Fax: 202-678-3325. Web: stachurch.org.
Church: 1244 V. St. S.E., 20020.
Catechesis/Religious Program—Students 70.
Parish Life Center: Tel: 202-678-3709; Fax: 202-678-3325.

42—ST. THOMAS APOSTLE (1913) Rev. Msgr. Michael J. Mellone; Deacon William C. Boesman.
Res.: 2665 Woodley Rd., N.W., 20008. Tel: 202-234-1488; Fax: 202-234-1480.
Catechesis/Religious Program—Students 36.

43—ST. THOMAS MORE (1952), (African American), Rev. Raymond H. Moore; Deacon Richard Walker. In Res., Rev. John P. Kinter.
Res.: 4275 4th St., S.E., 20032. Tel: 202-562-0431; Fax: 202-563-7347. Email: stmchurch@comcast.net.
School—Tel: 202-561-1189; Fax: 202-562-2336. Ms. Bridget Coates, Prin. Lay Teachers 15; Students 205.
Catechesis/Religious Program—Students 210.

44—ST. VINCENT DE PAUL (1903), (African American), Deacon Francis Kraemer. In Res., Bro. Marx Tyree, S.S.J.
Res.: 14 M St., S.E., 20003-3511. Tel: 202-488-1354; Fax: 202-488-7899.
Catechesis/Religious Program—Students 75.

CHURCHES IN MARYLAND

AVENUE, ST. MARY'S CO., HOLY ANGELS (1906) [JC] Rev. William H. Gurnee III; Deacon Joseph W. Lloyd Jr.
Res.: 21340 Colton Point Rd., MD 20609-2422. Tel: 301-769-3332; Fax: 301-769-2541. Email: angelsinavenue@gmail.com. Web: www.parishes.org/holyangels.html.
Catechesis/Religious Program—Students 38.

BADEN, PRINCE GEORGES CO., ST. MICHAEL (1957) Rev. Louis J. Faust; Deacon Tyrone Johnson.
Mailing Address: 17510 Horsehead Rd., Brandywine, MD 20613.
Catechesis/Religious Program—Tel: 301-579-6409; Fax: 301-579-0019. Students 90.
Mission—St. Dominic's [CEM] 22300 Aquasco Rd., Aquasco, Prince Georges Co., MD 20608. Tel: 301-888-1498; Fax: 301-579-0019.

BARNESVILLE, MONTGOMERY CO., ST. MARY CHURCH AND SHRINE OF OUR LADY OF FATIMA (1807) [CEM] Rev. Kevin P. O'Reilly; Deacon David Cahoon.
Res.: 18230 Barnesville Rd., P.O. Box 67, MD 20838. Tel: 301-972-8660; Fax: 301-349-0916. Email: stmarysb@yahoo.com. Web: www.stmaryonline.com.
Catechesis/Religious Program—Students 113.

BELTSVILLE, PRINCE GEORGES CO., ST. JOSEPH (1963) Rev. J. Michael Quill; Deacon Willis R. Wolfe. In Res., Rev. Joseph F. Wimmer, O.S.A.
Res.: 11007 Montgomery Rd., MD 20705. Tel: 301-937-7183; Fax: 301-937-7780. Email: stjoseph.beltsville.md@adwparish.org. Web: www.stjos.org.
School—11011 Montgomery Rd., MD 20705. Tel: 301-937-7154; Fax: 301-937-1467. Email: schooloffice@stjos.org. Lay Teachers 17; Students 195.
Catechesis/Religious Program—Email: dyoung@stjos.org. Students 94.

BENEDICT, CHARLES CO., ST. FRANCIS DE SALES (1903) Rev. Saverio T. Vitturino.
Res.: 7185 Benedict Ave., P.O. Box 306, MD 20612-0306. Tel: 301-274-3416; 301-870-4991; Fax: 301-274-0689. Email: francisben@comcast.net.
Catechesis/Religious Program—7209 Benedict Ave., P.O. Box 306, MD 20612. Tel: 301-274-0904. Email: religioused@stfrancisdesalescc.org. Students 42.

BETHESDA, MONTGOMERY CO.

1—ST. BARTHOLOMEW (1960) Rev. Msgr. James T. Beattie; Rev. Evelio Menjivar-Ayala.
Res.: 7212 Blacklock Rd., MD 20817. Tel: 301-229-7933; Fax: 301-229-7998.
School—6900 River Rd., MD 20817. Tel: 301-229-5586; Fax: 301-229-8654. Web: www.stbartholomew.org. Mrs. Kathleen Miller, Prin. Sisters 1; Lay Teachers 16; Students 224.
Catechesis/Religious Program—Tel: 301-229-3431; Fax: 301-229-7998. Students 201.

2—ST. JANE FRANCES DE CHANTAL (1950) Rev. Msgr. Donald S. Essex; Revs. Francis Alves; Paul Dean Nguyen; Deacons Kenneth Angell; Chester G. Chen. In Res., Rev. John F. McKay.
Res.: 9701 Old Georgetown Rd., MD 20814. Tel: 301-530-1550; Fax: 301-493-8953. Email: parish.office@stjanedechantal.org. Web: www.stjanedechantal.org.
School—9525 Old Georgetown Rd., MD 20814. Tel: 301-530-1221; Fax: 301-530-1688. Web: www-.dechantal.com. Mrs. Betsy Hamilton, Prin. Lay Teachers 26; Students 505.
Catechesis/Religious Program—Tel: 301-530-1640; Fax: 301-530-5881. Email: seton.center@stjanedechantal.org. Students 244.

3—LITTLE FLOWER (1948) Rev. Msgr. Peter J. Vaghi; Revs. Mark Ivany; George E. Stuart.
Res.: 5607 Massachusetts Ave., MD 20816. Tel: 301-320-4538; Fax: 301-320-4541. Email: paw@lfchurch.org. Web: lfparish.org.
School—5601 Massachusetts Ave., MD 20816. Tel: 301-320-3273; Fax: 301-320-2867. Email: rrynn@lfschool.org. Web: lfschool.org. Sisters of the Immaculate Heart of Mary 5; Lay Teachers 18; Students 269.
Catechesis/Religious Program—Tel: 301-320-5233. Students 325.

4—OUR LADY OF LOURDES (1926), (Spanish), Rev. Msgr. Edward J. Filardi; Revs. Javier Santaballa; Marco Federico Schad; Deacon John Shewmaker. In Res., Rev. Msgr. W. Louis Quinn (Retired); Rev. Robert Bozek.
Res.: 7500 Pearl St., MD 20814. Tel: 301-654-1287; Fax: 301-986-8716. Web: www.bethesdalourdes.org.
School—Tel: 301-654-5376; Fax: 301-654-2568. Web: www.bethesda-lourdes.org. Patricia K. McGann, Prin. Sisters 1; Lay Teachers 26; Students 220.
Catechesis/Religious Program—Tel: 301-654-5954. Students 312.

BOWIE, PRINCE GEORGES CO.

1—ASCENSION (1893) [CEM] Rev. Joseph A. Calis; Deacon Ted R. Pillman, (Retired).
Mailing Address: 12700 Lanham-Severn Rd., MD 20720. Tel: 301-262-2227; Fax: 301-805-5053. Email: ascensionbow@aol.com. In Res., Rev. William F. Goode (Retired).
Catechesis/Religious Program—Carolyn McCart, D.R.E. Students 110.

2—ST. EDWARD (1972) Rev. John M. Barry; Deacons David Barnes; Gary Perkins.
Res.: 16304 Pond Meadow Ln., MD 20716. Tel: 301-249-9199.
Catechesis/Religious Program—Tel: 301-249-9599; Fax: 301-249-1303. Students 300.

3—ST. PIUS X (1962) Revs. Michael T. Jones; Lawrence Swink; Deacon Andrew Nosacek, (Retired).
Res.: 3300 Moreland Pl., MD 20715. Tel: 301-262-2141; Fax: 301-262-2632.
Church: 14720 Annapolis Rd., MD 20715.
School—14710 Annapolis Rd., MD 20715. Tel: 301-262-0203; Fax: 301-805-8875. Lay Teachers 49; Students 786.
Catechesis/Religious Program—Tel: 301-262-3644. Debbie Langdon, D.R.E. Students 156.

4—SACRED HEART (1729) [CEM] Rev. Msgr. Charles J. Parry; Rev. Andrew Francis Royals, Parochial Vicar.
Res.: 16501 Annapolis Rd., MD 20715. Tel: 301-262-0704; Fax: 301-805-4686. Email: parishoffice@sacredheartbowie.org. Web: www.sacredheartbowie.org.
Catechesis/Religious Program—Tel: 301-262-1221. Email: schoolofreligion@sacredheartbowie.org. Mrs. Mimi Shea, C.R.E. Students 180.

BRYANTOWN, CHARLES CO., ST. MARY (1793) [CEM] Rev. Lawrence A. Young; Deacons Eugene Burroughs; Henry Middleton.
Res.: 13715 Notre Dame Pl., MD 20617-2224. Tel: 301-870-2220; 301-274-3187; Fax: 301-274-0253.
School—Tel: 301-932-6883; Fax: 301-274-0626. Lay Teachers 18; Students 258.
Catechesis/Religious Program—Tel: 301-274-3800. Students 206.

BURTONSVILLE, MONTGOMERY CO., RESURRECTION PARISH (1981) Revs. Robert F. Keffer; Charles E. Brown (Retired); Deacon Jon Thomas.
Res.: 3315 Greencastle Rd., MD 20866. Tel: 301-236-5200; Fax: 301-236-5204. Web: www.resurrectionadw.org.
Catechesis/Religious Program—Tel: 301-236-5200. Students 247.

BUSHWOOD, ST. MARY'S CO., SACRED HEART (1755) [JC] Rev. Francis J. Early.
Res.: 23080 Maddox Rd. (Rte. 238), P.O. Box 37, MD 20618. Tel: 301-769-3100; Fax: 301-769-2251.
Catechesis/Religious Program— See Holy Angels-Sacred Heart School, Avenue, MD, for details. Students 57.

CAMP SPRINGS, PRINCE GEORGES CO., ST. PHILIP THE APOSTLE (1957) Rev. Scott R. Hahn.
Res.: 5416 Henderson Way, MD 20746. Tel: 301-423-4244; Fax: 301-423-1226. Email: st.philipparish@comcast.net. Web: www.stphiliptheapostlechurch.org.
School—5414 Henderson Way, MD 20746. Tel: 301-423-4740; Fax: 301-423-4716. Lay Teachers 20; Students 283.
Catechesis/Religious Program—Students 48.

CHAPEL POINT, CHARLES CO., ST. IGNATIUS (1641) [CEM] Rev. Edward C. Dougherty, S.J.; Deacon Scott C. Stuart. In Res., Rev. Edward P. O'Connell, S.J.
St. Thomas Manor: 8855 Chapel Point Rd., Port Tobacco, MD 20677. Tel: 301-934-8245; Fax: 301-934-0944. Web: www.chapelpoint.org.
Catechesis/Religious Program—Tel: 301-392-0962. Angela Hume, D.R.E. Students 167.

CHAPTICO, ST. MARY'S CO., OUR LADY OF THE WAYSIDE (1938) Rev. Timothy K. Baer.
Tel: 301-884-3165; Fax: 301-884-3165.
Res. & Mailing Address: 37575 Chaptico Rd., P.O. Box 97, MD 20621. Tel: 301-884-2502; Fax: 301-884-0381.
School—Mother Catherine Spalding Tri Parish School, Tel: 301-884-3165. Lay Teachers 17; Students 172.
Catechesis/Religious Program—

CHEVERLY, PRINCE GEORGES CO., ST. AMBROSE (1886) Rev. Joseph B. Pierce. In Res., Rev. Alex Martinez.
Res.: 3107 63rd Ave., MD 20785. Tel: 301-773-9300; Fax: 301-773-2611. Email: stambrec@covad.net.
School—6310 Jason St., MD 20785. Tel: 301-773-0223; Fax: 301-773-9218. Mr. Carl Berger, Prin. Lay Teachers 24; Students 282.
Catechesis/Religious Program—Tel: 301-773-0627; Fax: 301-773-9647. Students 79.

CHILLUM, PRINCE GEORGES CO., ST. JOHN BAPTIST DE LA SALLE (1951) Rev. David Vidal, I.V.E.
Res.: 5706 Sargent Rd., MD 20782. Tel: 301-559-3636; Fax: 301-559-3062.
Catechesis/Religious Program—Tel: 301-559-3637. Students 90.

CLINTON, PRINCE GEORGES CO., CHURCH OF ST. JOHN THE EVANGELIST (1875) [CEM] Revs. Thomas W. Pollard; Charles McCann; Deacons Anthony Moll; Santiago T. Montalvo.
Res.: 8908 Old Branch Ave., MD 20735. Tel: 301-868-1070; Fax: 301-868-7915. Email: akarnezis@verizon.net. Web: www.sjreled.org.
Church: 8910 Old Branch Ave., MD 20735.
School—8912 Old Branch Ave., MD 20735. Tel: 301-868-2010; Fax: 301-856-8941. Email: scotts@adwschool.org. Web: saintjohnschool.org. Lay Teachers 21; Students 250.
Catechesis/Religious Program—Tel: 301-868-3026. Students 142.

COLLEGE PARK, PRINCE GEORGES CO.

1—ST. ANDREW KIM (1974), (Korean), Unassigned.17615 Old Baltimore Rd., Olney, MD 20832.
Res.: 3140 Saint Florence Ter., Olney, MD 20832. Tel: 301-924-8330; Fax: 301-924-8332.
Catechesis/Religious Program—Tel: 301-275-3734. Students 210.

2—HOLY REDEEMER (1912) Rev. George A. Wilkinson Jr.; Deacon Finis E. Thompson.
Res.: 4902 Berwyn Rd., MD 20740. Tel: 301-474-3920; Fax: 301-441-4954. Email: parish@holy-redeemer.org. Web: holy-redeemer.org.
School—Tel: 301-474-3993; Fax: 301-441-8137. Email: school@holy-redeemer.org. Maria Bovich, Prin. Lay Teachers 18; Students 243.
Catechesis/Religious Program—Tel: 301-474-4299. Email: mwinterson@holy-redeemer.org. Marie Winterson, D.R.E. & Youth Min. Students 62.

DAMASCUS, MONTGOMERY CO., ST. PAUL (1957) Rev. Peter T. Sweeney; Deacons John Finerty; David Terrar; Charles Weschler.
Res.: 9240 Damascus Rd., MD 20872. Tel: 301-253-2027; Fax: 301-391-6755.
Catechesis/Religious Program—Tel: 301-253-5941. Students 770.

DARNESTOWN, MONTGOMERY CO., OUR LADY OF THE VISITATION (1991) [CEM] Revs. Raymond L. Fecteau; Mathew Punchayil (India) (SYM); Deacon Robert Fischer.
Mailing Address: 14135 Seneca Rd., MD 20874-3337.
Res.: 14200 Darnestown Rd., MD 20874-3008. Tel: 301-948-5536; Fax: 301-948-7452.
Church: 14139 Seneca Rd., MD 20874. Tel: 301-948-5536. Email: parishoffice@olvp.org. Web: www.olvp.org.

Catechesis/Religious Program—Students 281.

DERWOOD, MONTGOMERY CO., ST. FRANCIS OF ASSISI (1972) Rev. David W. Beaubien; Deacons James J. Datovech; Pascal Hong. In Res., Rev. Msgr. Ralph J. Kuehner (Retired).
Res.: 6701 Muncaster Mill Rd., MD 20855. Tel: 301-840-1407; Fax: 301-258-5080. Email: sfaparishoffice@sfadw.org. Web: www.sfadw.org.
Catechesis/Religious Program—Tel: 301-258-9193. Email: sfareligiousedsfadw.org. Students 462.

FORESTVILLE, PRINCE GEORGE CO.
1—CHURCH OF THE HOLY SPIRIT (1966) Rev. Tam X. Tran. In Res., Rev. Jeffrey F. Samaha; Deacon Joseph Welch.
Res.: 1717 Ritchie Rd., MD 20747. Tel: 301-336-3707; Fax: 301-324-1649.
Catechesis/Religious Program— Combined with Mt. Calvary School, Forestville. Students 8.
2—MT. CALVARY (1942) [CEM] Rev. Michael A. Salah; Deacon Lawrence Miles. In Res., Rev. Msgr. Richard A. Hughes (Retired).
Res.: 6700 Marlboro Pike, MD 20747. Tel: 301-735-5532; Fax: 301-735-2005. Email: mtcalvary.md@adwparish.org. Web: www.mtccs.org.
School—6704 Marlboro Pike, MD 20747. Tel: 301-735-5262; Fax: 301-736-5044. Web: www.mtccs.org. Lay Teachers 19; Students 217.
Catechesis/Religious Program—6704 Marlboro Pike, MD 20747. Tel: 301-735-5262, Ext. 17. Students 26.

FORT WASHINGTON, PRINCE GEORGES CO., ST. IGNATIUS (1849) [CEM] Rev. Robert A. Finamore.
Res.: 2315 Brinkley Rd., MD 20744. Tel: 301-567-4740; Fax: 301-567-0046. Email: office@saint-ig.org.
School—2317 Brinkley Rd., MD 20744. Tel: 301-567-4090. Web: www.saintignatiusschool.org. Richard G. Gatto, Prin. Lay Teachers 14; Students 180.
Catechesis/Religious Program—Tel: 301-567-4740. Students 42.

GAITHERSBURG, MONTGOMERY CO.
1—ST. JOHN NEUMANN (1978) [CEM] Revs. Rory T. Conley; Gellert Jozsef Ailer; Deacons Robert Allen; Eugene Cummins; Carlo Caraballo; Michael W. Davy.
Mailing Address: 8900 Lochaven Dr., MD 20882-4460. Email: info@saintjohnneumann.org. Web: www.saintjohnneumann.org.
Church: 9000 Warfield Rd., MD 20882. Tel: 301-977-5492; Fax: 301-977-3559.
Catechesis/Religious Program—Tel: 301-977-7990; Fax: 301-330-3235. Students 407.
2—ST. MARTIN OF TOURS (1920) Rev. Msgr. Mark E. Brennan; Revs. Avelino Armando Gonzalez; Pawel Sass; Deacons Lawrence Bell; Ronald J. Meyer; William A. Vita Jr.
Res.: 201 S. Frederick Ave., MD 20877. Tel: 301-990-3203; Fax: 301-990-7538. Email: parish@stmartinsweb.com. Web: www.stmartinsweb.com.
School—115 S. Frederick Ave., MD 20877. Tel: 301-990-2441; Fax: 301-990-2688. Web: www.smsmd.org. Sr. Sharon Mihm, C.S.C., Prin. Lay Teachers 17; Students 234.
Catechesis/Religious Program—Tel: 301-990-2556; Fax: 301-990-2622. Email: religious-education@stmartinsweb.com. Ilsa Hernandez, D.R.E. Students 1,129.
3—ST. ROSE OF LIMA (1972) [CEM] Rev. Msgr. Paul M. Dudziak; Deacons John C. Liu; Mario F. Moreno; Patti Sullins, Dir Liturgy & Music.
Mailing Address: 11701 Clopper Rd., MD 20878-1024. Tel: 301-948-7545; Fax: 301-869-2170. Email: strose@strose.com. Web: www.strose.com.
Catechesis/Religious Program—Tel: 301-948-7545. Cheryl Shalgian, D.R.E. (Pre K-5, English). Tel: 301-948-7545, Ext. 245; Sr. Gisela Rodriguez, D.R.E. (K-12, Spanish); Meg Russell, D.R.E. (6-12, English); Kathryn Heetderks, Adult Faith Formation. Students 460.

GARRETT PARK, MONTGOMERY CO., HOLY CROSS (1960) Rev. Msgr. Robert Cary Hill; Rev. Joseph F. Perkins; Deacon Robert Hubbard.
Res.: 4900 Strathmore Ave., P.O. Box 249, MD 20896. Tel: 301-942-1020; Fax: 301-949-3543. Web: www.hcrosschurch.org.
School—Tel: 301-949-0053; Fax: 301-949-5074. Email: office@hcross.org. Web: www.hcross.org. Lisa Maio Kane, Prin. Lay Teachers 24; Students 227.
Catechesis/Religious Program—Tel: 301-942-8790. Email: keeney@hcrosschurch.org. Jeanmarie Keeney, D.R.E. Students 294.

GERMANTOWN, MONTGOMERY CO., MOTHER SETON PARISH (1974) [CEM] Revs. Mark W. Ervin; Louis J. Faust, Senior Priest; Emanuele DeNigris, Parochial Vicar; Deacons William Vita; Francis W. Bendel; Timothy Enright.
Res.: 19951 Father Hurley Blvd., MD 20874. Tel: 301-924-3838; Fax: 301-428-4951. Email: mspps@aol.com. Web: mothersetonparish.org.
Catechesis/Religious Program—Tel: 301-444-3496; 301-444-3495. Students 659.

GREAT MILLS, ST. MARY'S CO., HOLY FACE (1879) [CEM] Rev. Joseph Sileo.
Mailing Address: 20476 Point Lookout Rd., MD 20634. Tel: 301-994-0525; Fax: 301-994-1547. Email: holyface@md.metrocast.net.
School—Little Flower, 20410 Point Lookout Rd., MD 20634. Tel: 301-994-0404; Fax: 301-994-2055. Lay Teachers 15; Students 170.
Catechesis/Religious Program—Students 158.

GREENBELT, PRINCE GEORGES CO., SAINT HUGH OF GRENOBLE (1947) Rev. Walter J. Tappe.
Res.: 135 Crescent Rd., MD 20770. Tel: 301-474-4322; Fax: 301-474-9263. Web: www.sthughs.com.
School—145 Crescent Rd., MD 20770. Tel: 301-474-4071; Fax: 301-474-3950. Mrs. Tiffani James, Prin. Lay Teachers 14; Students 128.
Catechesis/Religious Program—Tel: 301-474-0239; Fax: 301-479-2950. Email: religioused@sthughs.com. Students 50.

HILLCREST HEIGHTS, PRINCE GEORGES CO., HOLY FAMILY (1952), (African American), Rev. Damian Shadwell.
Res.: 2210 Callaway St., MD 20748. Tel: 301-894-2222; Fax: 301-894-2938.
School—2200 Callaway St., MD 20748. Tel: 301-894-2323.
Catechesis/Religious Program—Students 191.

HILLTOP, CHARLES CO., ST. IGNATIUS LOYOLA (1851) [CEM] Rev. Robert J. Kosty; Deacon Frank L. Hopson, (Retired).
Mailing Address: P.O. Box 278, Port Tobacco, MD 20677. Tel: 301-934-9630; Fax: 301-934-8320. Email: pappybob46@aol.com.
Catechesis/Religious Program—Tel: 301-934-9080. Students 29.

HOLLYWOOD, ST. MARY'S CO., ST. JOHN FRANCIS REGIS (1690) [CEM] Rev. Raymond F. Schmidt; Rev. Msgr. Martin P. Harris, Pastor Emeritus (Retired). In Res., Rev. Eamon Dignan (Retired).
Res. & Mailing Address: 43950 St. John's Rd., MD 20636. Tel: 301-373-2281; Fax: 301-373-8984. Email: stjohnschurch1@verizon.net. Web: stjohnsparishhollywood.org.
School—Tel: 301-373-2142; Fax: 301-373-4500. Email: sjsoffice@adwschool.org. Web: www.stjohnsschoolhollywood.org. Patricia T. Suit, Prin. Students 190.
Catechesis/Religious Program—Email: sjcreled@verizon.net. Students 302.

HUNTINGTOWN, CALVERT CO., JESUS THE DIVINE WORD PARISH (1994) Rev. Daniel P. Leary.
Mailing Address: 885 Cox Rd., MD 20639. Tel: 410-414-8304; Fax: 410-535-9057. Email: office@jesusdivineword.org. Web: www.jesusdivineword.org.
Catechesis/Religious Program—Email: religioused@jesusdivineword.org. Students 336.

HYATTSVILLE, PRINCE GEORGES CO.
1—ST. JEROME (1886) Rev. James M. Stack; Deacon Neal T. Conway. In Res., Rev. Isadore Dixon.
Res.: 5205 43rd Ave., MD 20781. Tel: 301-927-6684; Fax: 301-927-9167. Email: ajstjerome@hotmail.com. Web: www.stjerome.org.
School—5207 42nd Pl., MD 20781. Tel: 301-277-4568; Fax: 301-779-2428. Mary Pat Donoghue, Prin. Sisters of Notre Dame de Namur 1; Lay Teachers 20; Students 300.
Convent—5300 43rd Ave., MD 20781. Tel: 301-864-2016.
Child Center—Tel: 301-699-1314.
Catechesis/Religious Program—Students 36.
2—ST. MARK (1958) Revs. John J. Dillon; Paul Sullins, Parochial Vicar; Jose Jesus Arriaga (Mexico); Deacons Jose Renato Molina; Curtis Turner. In Res., Rev. Msgr. Michael W. Fisher.
Res.: 7501 Adelphi Rd., MD 20783. Tel: 301-422-8300; Fax: 301-422-2313. Email: rectory@stmarkhyattsville.org. Web: www.stmarkhyattsville.4lpi.org.
School—Tel: 301-422-7440; Fax: 301-422-7710. Email: principal@stmarkhyattsville.org. Lay Teachers 18; Students 259.
Catechesis/Religious Program—Tel: 301-422-7822. Email: dmcnally@stmarkhyattsville.org. Deborah McNally, D.R.E. Students 374.

INDIAN HEAD, CHARLES CO., ST. MARY STAR OF THE SEA (1918) [CEM] Rev. William J. Thompson; Deacon Albert S. Tompa.
Res.: 30 Mattingly Ave., MD 20640. Tel: 301-753-9177; Fax: 301-743-6670. Email: sstarofthesea@aol.com.
School—6485 Indian Head Hwy., MD 20640. Tel: 301-283-6151; Fax: 301-283-4368. Email: office@stmarystar.net. Web: www.stmarystar.net. Lay Teachers 13; Students 111.
Catechesis/Religious Program—Students 38.

ISSUE, CHARLES CO., HOLY GHOST (1880) [CEM] Rev. Gregory S. Coan; Deacon Walter G. Rourke.
Res.: 15848 Rock Point Rd., Newburg, MD 20664. Tel: 301-259-2515; Fax: 301-259-2289. Email: holyghostchurch@verizon.net. Web: holyghostchurchissue.org.
Catechesis/Religious Program—Students 64.
Mission—St. Francis de Sales Newburg, MD. 13675 Furbush Rd., Rock Point, Charles Co., MD 20682. Tel: 301-259-0254.

KENSINGTON, MONTGOMERY CO., HOLY REDEEMER (1948) Revs. Mark Hughes; Mark Leo Smith.
Res.: 9705 Summit Ave., MD 20895. Tel: 301-942-2333; Fax: 301-942-1041.
School—9715 Summit Ave., MD 20895. Tel: 301-942-3701; Fax: 301-942-4981. Web: hrs-ken.org. Mrs. Harriann Walker, Prin. Lay Teachers 29; Students 440.
Catechesis/Religious Program—Tel: 301-942-2333, Ext. 105. John Buchanan, D.R.E. Students 167.

LA PLATA, CHARLES CO., SACRED HEART (1901) [CEM] Revs. Ronald A. Potts; Jaroslaw Gamrot; Deacons Anthony Barrasso; Albert E. Graham Jr.; Walter G. Rourke.
Res.: 201 St. Mary's Ave., P.O. Box 1390, MD 20646. Tel: 301-934-2261; Fax: 301-934-5435. Email: shclp@verizon.net. Web: www.shclp.org.
School—Archbishop Neale School, 104 Port Tobacco Rd., MD 20646. Tel: 301-934-9595; Fax: 301-753-1717. Anne Hedian, Prin. Lay Teachers 32; Students 430.
Catechesis/Religious Program—Tel: 301-934-3386. Deacon Anthony T. Barrasso, D.R.E. Students 245.

LANDOVER HILLS, PRINCE GEORGE'S CO.
1—ST. MARY'S CATHOLIC CHURCH (1948) Revs. Samuel C. Giese; Michael J. Blackwell (Retired); Deacons Stephen M. Robinson; Dennis J. Bingham. In Res., Rev. Jacob George Chirayath.
Res.: 7401 Buchanan St., MD 20784-2323. Tel: 301-577-8844; Fax: 301-306-5543. Email: secretary@saintmarylandoverhills.org. Web: www.saintmarylandoverhills.org.
School—7207 Annapolis Rd., MD 20784. Tel: 301-577-0031; Fax: 301-577-5485. Email: principal.stmarys@comcast.net. Web: stmarys-landoverhills.org. Susan Junge Varrone, Prin. Lay Teachers 20; Students 248.
Catechesis/Religious Program—Tel: 301-577-2478. Students 113.
2—SYRO-MALANKARA MISSION (1985), (Indian), Rev. Jacob C. George.
Res.: 7401 Buchanan St., MD 20784-9998. Tel: 301-577-8844; Fax: 301-306-5543. Email: frjacobchi02@yahoo.com.
Catechesis/Religious Program—Students 40.

LANHAM, PRINCE GEORGES CO., ST. MATTHIAS APOSTLE (1960) Rev. Jeffrey M. Defayette.
Res.: 9475 Annapolis Rd., MD 20706-3020. Tel: 301-459-4814; Fax: 301-306-4582.
School—9473 Annapolis Rd., MD 20706-3020. Tel: 301-577-9412; Fax: 301-577-2060. Web: www.stmatthias.org. Ms. Patricia F. Wilson, Prin. Lay Teachers 17; Students 200.
Catechesis/Religious Program—Tel: 301-459-4814, Ext. 205; Fax: 301-306-4582. Students 112.
Convent—9471 Annapolis Rd., MD 20706-3020. Tel: 301-459-8078.

LARGO, PRINCE GEORGES CO., ST. JOSEPH (1922), (African American), Rev. Levester Jones; Deacon Alton Davis.
Res.: 2020 St. Joseph Dr., MD 20774. Tel: 301-773-4838; Fax: 301-773-6832.
Catechesis/Religious Program—Tel: 301-773-2480. Students 14.

LAUREL, PRINCE GEORGES CO.
1—ST. MARY (1843) [CEM] Rev. Msgr. Michael Wilson; Revs. Grant Gaskin; Edward Anthony Hegnauer, Parochial Vicar; Deacons Donald Parker; Perfecto Santiago; Dan D. Abeyta; Robert L. Gigniliat.
Res.: 114 St. Mary's Pl., MD 20707. Tel: 301-725-3080; Fax: 301-725-2409. Web: www.stmarys.laurel.md.us.
School—106 St. Mary's Pl., MD 20707. Tel: 301-498-1433; Fax: 301-498-1170. Web: www.stmaryofthemill.org. James Pavlacka, Prin. Lay Teachers 28; Students 403.
Catechesis/Religious Program—Tel: 301-490-8770. Mrs. Carol Lee, Child Protection Coord.; Jennifer Juzwiak, D.R.E. (Adult). Students 431.
2—ST. NICHOLAS (1967) Rev. James S. Betz; Deacons Francis Hannagan; Perry Iannaconi. In Res., Rev. Samuel L. Craig (Retired).
Res.: 8603 Contee Rd., MD 20708. Tel: 301-490-5116; 301-490-5117; Fax: 301-490-1527.
Catechesis/Religious Program—Tel: 301-776-8303. Students 85.

LEONARDTOWN, ST. MARY'S CO., ST. ALOYSIUS (1710) [CEM] Rev. John T. Dakes.
Res.: 22800 Washington St., P.O. Box 310, MD 20650. Tel: 301-475-8064; Fax: 301-475-8762. Web: www.saintaloysiuschurch.org.
School—Father Andrew White, S.J., 22850 Washington St., P.O. Box 1756, MD 20650. Tel: 301-475-9795; Fax: 301-475-3537. Email:

fradwh@verizon.net. Web: www.fatherandrewwhite.org. Lay Teachers 18; Students 262.
Catechesis/Religious Program—Email: lwathen@saintaloysiuschurch.org. Students 209.

LEXINGTON PARK, ST. MARY'S CO., IMMACULATE HEART OF MARY (1947) [CEM] Revs. Roberto J. Cortes-Campos; Benton Lee Garrett, Parochial Vicar.
Mailing Address: 22375 Three Notch Rd., MD 20653-0166. Tel: 301-863-8144; Fax: 301-863-8180.
Catechesis/Religious Program—Tel: 301-863-8793. Janet Harmon, D.R.E. Students 244.

MCCONCHIE, CHARLES CO., ST. CATHERINE OF ALEXANDRIA (1911) [CEM] Rev. Robert J. Kosty; Deacon Frank L. Hopson, (Retired).
Mailing Address: P.O. Box 278, Port Tobacco, MD 20677. Tel: 301-934-9630; Fax: 301-934-8320. Email: pappybob46@aol.com.
Catechesis/Religious Program—Students 55.

MECHANICSVILLE, ST. MARY'S CO., IMMACULATE CONCEPTION (1876) Rev. Peter R. Alliata; Deacons James E. Conner, (Retired); William L. Kyte.
Mailing Address: 28297 Old Village Rd., P.O. Box 166, MD 20659. Tel: 301-884-3123; Fax: 301-884-7437. Email: immaculateconception.md@adwparish.org. Web: www.immaculateconceptionmechanicsville.com.
Catechesis/Religious Program—Tel: 301-884-3016. Email: icccddre@hotmail.com. Students 280.

MEDLEY'S NECK, ST. MARY'S CO., OUR LADY'S (1767) [CEM] Rev. Thomas G. LaHood; Deacon Thomas C. Spalding Sr.
Mailing Address: 41348 Medley's Neck Rd., Leonardtown, MD 20650. Tel: 301-475-8403; Fax: 301-475-6632.
Catechesis/Religious Program—Students 71.

MITCHELLVILLE, PRINCE GEORGES CO., HOLY FAMILY (1938) [CEM] Rev. Joseph A. Jenkins; Deacon Henry D. Dardy.
Mailing Address: 12010 Woodmore Rd., MD 20721. Tel: 301-249-2266; Fax: 301-249-2524. Web: holyfamilywoodmore.com.
Catechesis/Religious Program—Tel: 301-249-1167. Students 124.

MORGANZA, ST. MARY'S CO., ST. JOSEPH (1700) [CEM 2] [JC] Rev. Keith A. Woods; Deacon James A. Somerville, (Retired).
Res.: 29119 Point Lookout Rd., P.O. Box 175, MD 20660. Tel: 301-475-3293; Fax: 301-475-0491. Email: stjosephmorganza@yahoo.com.
Catechesis/Religious Program—Students 105.

MOUNT RAINIER, PRINCE GEORGES CO., ST. JAMES (1905) Rev. Pablo Daniel Munoz Iturreta, I.V.E.; Deacon John H. Turner. In Res., Rev. Pablo Bonello, I.V.E.
Res.: 3628 Rhode Island Ave., MD 20712. Tel: 301-927-0567; Fax: 301-927-5289. Email: st_james@verizon.net.
Catechesis/Religious Program—Tel: 301-927-0567. Students 545.

NEWPORT, CHARLES CO., ST. MARY (1674) [CEM] Rev. Msgr. Oliver McGready; Deacon Jerome Butkiewicz.
Res.: 11555 St. Mary's Church Rd., Charlotte Hall, MD 20622. Tel: 301-934-8825; Fax: 301-934-0245.
Catechesis/Religious Program—Students 115.

NEWTOWNE, ST. MARY'S CO., ST. FRANCIS XAVIER (1640) [CEM] Rev. John S. Mattingly; Deacon William J. Nickerson.
Res.: 21370 Newtowne Neck Rd., Leonardtown, MD 20650. Tel: 301-475-9885; Fax: 301-475-5662. Email: revmattingly@dishmail.net.
Catechesis/Religious Program—Students 58.

NORBECK, MONTGOMERY CO., ST. PATRICK (1966) Rev. Msgr. Kevin T. Hart; Rev. Joseph Everett Rogers; Deacon James T. Nalls.
Res.: 4101 Norbeck Rd., Rockville, MD 20853. Tel: 301-924-2284; 301-924-2285; Fax: 301-929-3017. Email: stpatrock@verizon.net. Web: www.stpatricksmd.org.
Catechesis/Religious Program—Tel: 301-929-9314. Students 351.

NORTH BEACH, CALVERT CO., ST. ANTHONY (1905) Rev. David P. Russell; Deacon John F. Lynch.
Res.: 8900 Bay Ave., P.O. Box 660, MD 20714. Tel: 410-257-2368; 301-855-7756 (Washington). Email: office@stanthonycal.us. Web: www.stanthonycal.com.
Catechesis/Religious Program—Tel: 202-855-0897. Deborah Wheeler, D.R.E. Students 213.

OLNEY, MONTGOMERY CO., ST. PETER (1953) Revs. Thomas M. Kalita; John Tung Nguyen; Patrick J. Riffle; Deacons James Cadigan; Thomas Cioffi; Rory P. Crawford; Mrs. Elizabeth Harper, Business Mgr.
Res.: 2900 Sandy Spring Rd., MD 20832. Tel: 301-924-3774; Fax: 301-774-5259. Email: info@stpetersolney.org. Web: www.stpetersolney.org.
School—Tel: 301-774-9112; Fax: 301-924-6698. Email: school@stpetersolney.org. Mrs. Mary Elizabeth Whelan, Prin. Lay Teachers 44; Students 414.
Catechesis/Religious Program—Tel: 301-570-4952. Angela Busby, D.R.E. (Grades K-4); Cindy Dixon, D.R.E. (Grades 5-8). Students 674.

OWINGS, CALVERT CO., JESUS THE GOOD SHEPHERD (1985) Rev. Michael J. King; Deacons Emmett (Chad) Martin; James G. Johnson; John Verdon.
Res.: 1555 W. Mt. Harmony Rd., MD 20736. Tel: 410-257-3810; Fax: 410-257-6334. Email: community@ccjgs.org. Web: www.ccjgs.org.
School—Cardinal Hickey Academy, 1601 W. Mt. Harmony Rd., MD 20736. Tel: 410-286-0404; Fax: 410-286-6334. Web: www.edline.net/pages/cardinal_hickey_academy. Sr. Mary Juliana Cox, O.P., Prin.
Catechesis/Religious Program—Tel: 410-257-3810, Ext. 18; Fax: 410-257-6334. Email: religioused@ccjgs.org. Students 650.

OXON HILL, PRINCE GEORGES CO., ST. COLUMBA (1960) Rev. Robert P. Buchmeier; Deacons Richard A. Fisher; Leandro Y. Espinosa.
Res.: 7804 Livingston Rd., MD 20745. Tel: 301-567-5506; Fax: 301-567-6546. Email: stcolumbachurch@comcast.net. Web: www.rc.net/washington/stcolumba.
School—7800 Livingston Rd., MD 20745. Tel: 301-567-6212; Fax: 301-567-6907. Email: schooloffice@stcolumbiafaculty.org. Lay Teachers 16; Students 268.
Catechesis/Religious Program—Tel: 301-567-6113; Fax: 301-567-3188. Students 85.

PISCATAWAY, PRINCE GEORGES CO., ST. MARY (1640) [CEM] Revs. Y. David Brault; Daniel T. Gallaugher; Deacons George Ames; Stephen McKimmie.
Res.: 13401 Piscataway Rd., Clinton, MD 20735-4564. Tel: 301-292-0527; Fax: 301-292-8786. Email: parish@stmaryspiscataway.org. Web: www.stmaryspiscataway.org.
School—13407 Piscataway Rd., Clinton, MD 20735. Tel: 301-292-2522; Fax: 301-292-2534. Email: school@stmaryspiscataway.org. Lay Teachers 14; Students 192.
Catechesis/Religious Program—Email: keimig@stmaryspiscataway.org. Students 98.

POMFRET, CHARLES CO., ST. JOSEPH (1763) [CEM] Rev. Mark Leo Smith; Deacon John R. Barnes.
Mailing Address: 4590 St. Joseph Way, MD 20675. Tel: 301-870-3041; 301-609-4670; Fax: 301-609-7564. Web: www.stjoepomfret.4lpi.com.
Catechesis/Religious Program—Students 160.

POOLESVILLE, MONTGOMERY CO., OUR LADY OF THE PRESENTATION (1992) Revs. Vincent J. Rigdon; G. Paul Herbert.
Mailing Address: P.O. Box 428, MD 20837. Tel: 301-349-2045; 301-349-2788; Fax: 301-349-5423. Email: ol-presentation.md@adwparish.org. Web: www.ol-presentation-md.org.
Catechesis/Religious Program—Students 129.

POTOMAC, MONTGOMERY CO.

1—NATIVITY OF THE BLESSED VIRGIN (GERMAN MISSION) (1992), (German), Rev. Michael Schapfel; Deacon Clayton A. Nickel.
Rectory—6330 Linway Ter., McLean, VA 22101-4150. Tel: 703-356-4473; Fax: 703-356-4558.

2—OUR LADY OF MERCY (1959), (Korean), [CEM] Rev. Msgr. William J. English; Revs. Stephen Bae (Korea, South); Donald P. Worch; Deacons F. Ian Ravenscroft; James Yun. In Res., Rev. Msgr. William J. Awalt (Retired).
Res.: 9200 Kentsdale Dr., MD 20854. Tel: 301-365-1415; Fax: 301-365-3104. Web: www.olom.org.
School—9222 Kentsdale Dr., MD 20854. Tel: 301-365-4477; Fax: 301-365-3423. Mrs. Joan C. Hosmer, Prin. Lay Teachers 30; Students 279.
Catechesis/Religious Program—Tel: 301-365-1318. Students 330.

PRINCE FREDERICK, CALVERT CO., ST. JOHN VIANNEY (1965) [CEM] Rev. Peter J. Daly.
Res.: 105 Vianney Ln., MD 20678-4123. Tel: 410-535-0223; Fax: 410-535-4422. Email: sjv@chesapeake.net. Web: www.sjvc.us.
Catechesis/Religious Program—Tel: 410-535-4395. Jeanette M. Pedone, D.R.E. Students 437.

RIDGE, ST. MARY'S CO., ST. MICHAEL (1824) [CEM] Rev. Msgr. Maurice V. O'Connell.
P.O. Box 429, MD 20680.
Res.: , MD 20680. Tel: 301-872-4321.
School—P.O. Box 429, MD 20680. Tel: 301-872-5454. Mrs. Regina Housel, Prin. Lay Teachers 14; Students 170.
Catechesis/Religious Program—Students 98.

RIVERDALE PARK, PRINCE GEORGES CO., ST. BERNARD (1950) Rev. John F. McKay; Deacon Alfredo Hidalgo. In Res., Rev. Pius T. Ajiki.
Res.: 5700 St. Bernard Dr., MD 20737-2185. Tel: 301-277-1000; Fax: 301-277-3464.
School—5811 Riverdale Rd., MD 20737. Tel: 301-864-3801; Fax: 301-864-2912. Philip Buckley, Prin. Lay Teachers 14; Students 242.
Catechesis/Religious Program—Tel: 301-277-4220; Fax: 301-277-3464. Mrs. Lucille Kolodrubetz, D.R.E. Students 349.

ROCKVILLE, MONTGOMERY CO.

1—ST. ELIZABETH (1964) Rev. Msgr. John F. Macfarlane; Rev. Brian Alick Coelho.
Res.: 917 Montrose Rd., MD 20852. Tel: 301-881-1380; Fax: 301-881-3068.
School—Tel: 301-881-1824; Fax: 301-881-6035. Lay Teachers 39; Students 508.
Catechesis/Religious Program—Students 320.

2—ST. MARY (1813) [CEM] Rev. Msgr. Robert G. Amey; Rev. Gary T. Villanueva; Deacon Daniel Kostka. In Res., Rev. M. Valentine Keveny.
Res.: 520 Veirs Mill Rd., MD 20852. Tel: 301-424-5550; Fax: 301-424-5579. Email: stmaryrockville@yahoo.com. Web: www.stmarysrockville.org.
School—600 Viers Mill Rd., MD 20852. Tel: 301-762-4179. Lay Teachers 21; Students 300.
Catechesis/Religious Program—Tel: 301-762-8750. Email: stmaryrockvilleym@yahoo.com. Students 288.

3—ST. RAPHAEL (1966) Revs. James P. Meyers; Carlos A. Benitez, Parochial Vicar; Deacons Richard Mattocks, (Retired); Frank Salatto, (Retired); Jorge Gatica. In Res., Rev. Msgr. Vincent S. Gatto (Retired).
Res. & Mailing Address: 1513 Dunster Rd., MD 20854. Tel: 301-762-2143; Fax: 301-762-0719. Web: www.straphaels.org.
Catechesis/Religious Program—Tel: 301-762-2143, Ext. 124. Students 754.

4—SHRINE OF ST. JUDE (1956) Revs. J. William Hines; G. Ralph Duffy (Retired); John R. Clark; Juan Esposito-Garcia; Deacons Nicholas E. Scholz; Donald Mays; Nathaniel Cordova.
Res.: 12701 Veirs Mill Rd., MD 20853. Tel: 301-946-8200; Fax: 301-946-4527. Web: www.shrinestjude.org.
School—4820 Walbridge St., MD 20853. Tel: 301-946-7888; Fax: 301-929-8927. Email: stjudemain@yahoo.com. Web: www.stjudesschool.org. Lay Teachers 21; Students 279.
Catechesis/Religious Program—Tel: 301-949-2336. Web: shrinestjude.org/organizations. Students 433.

ROSARYVILLE, PRINCE GEORGE'S CO., CHURCH OF THE MOST HOLY ROSARY (1966) [CEM] Rev. Roger A. Soley.
Res.: 11704 Duley Station Rd., Upper Marlboro, MD 20772. Tel: 301-856-3880; 301-856-3881; Fax: 301-856-3944. Email: holyrosary.md@adwparish.org. Web: www.mostholyrosarychurch.org.
Catechesis/Religious Program— Twinned with St. Mary of the Assumption, Upper Marlboro.

ST. INIGOES, ST. MARY'S CO., ST. PETER CLAVER (1903), (African American), [CEM] Rev. Scott Woods.
Res.: 16922 St. Peter Claver Church Rd., P.O. Box 240, MD 20684-0240. Tel: 301-872-5460; Fax: 301-872-5672.
Catechesis/Religious Program—Students 74.

ST. MARY'S CITY, ST. MARY'S CO., ST. CECILIA (1974) [JC] Rev. Damian Shadwell.
Res.: 47950 Mattapany Rd., P.O. Box 429, MD 20686. Tel: 301-862-4600.
Catechesis/Religious Program— Clustered with St. Michael's, Ridge. Students 8.

SEAT PLEASANT, PRINCE GEORGES CO., ST. MARGARET (1908), (African American), Revs. Columban Crotty, SS.CC.; Fintan Sheeran; Deacons Sam Minor; Valentine Oguledo.
Res.: 408 Addison Rd. S., MD 20743. Tel: 301-336-3345; Fax: 301-336-5501.
Catechesis/Religious Program—Tel: 301-336-5976. Students 108.

SILVER SPRING, MONTGOMERY CO.

1—ST. ANDREW APOSTLE (1959) Rev. Msgr. Michael J. Mellone; Rev. Andrew M. Morkunas, Parochial Vicar; Deacons Kevin M. Mukri; Michael Bond; Kenneth Barrett.
Res.: 11600 Kemp Mill Rd., MD 20902. Tel: 301-649-3700; Fax: 301-681-3527. Email: standrews11600@yahoo.com. Web: standrewapostle.org.
School—Tel: 301-649-3555; Fax: 301-649-2352. Email: standrew20902@yahoo.com. Kathleen Kilty, Prin. Lay Teachers 23; Students 294.
Catechesis/Religious Program—Tel: 301-649-4200. Students 116.

2—ST. BERNADETTE (Four Corners) (1948) Rev. Msgr. K. Bartholomew Smith; Rev. Vincent Derosa, Parochial Vicar; Deacon Thomas E. Roszkowski. In Res., Rev. Nicholas A. Zientarski (RVC).
Res.: 70 University Blvd., E., MD 20901. Tel: 301-593-0357; Fax: 301-593-3088. Email: parish@stbernadetteschurch.org.
School—80 University Blvd., E., MD 20901. Tel: 301-593-5611; Fax: 301-593-9042. Web: st_bernadetteelem.com. Lay Teachers 30; Students 430.
Catechesis/Religious Program—Tel: 301-593-5104. Email: baily@st-bernadetteelem.com. Mrs. Jane Baily, D.R.E. Students 150.

3—ST. CAMILLUS (1951) Revs. Lawrence J. Hayes, O.F.M.; Michael Johnson, O.F.M.; Jean-Marie Kabango, O.F.M.; Jacek Orzechowski, O.F.M.; Deacon Peter Barbernitz.
Res.: 1600 St. Camillus Dr., MD 20903. Tel:

301-434-8400; Fax: 301-434-8041. Web: stcamilluschurch.org.
School—1500 St. Camillus Dr., MD 20903. Tel: 301-434-2344; Fax: 301-434-7726. Email: drjblack@hotmail.com. Web: stcamillusschool.com. Lay Teachers 28; Students 320.
Catechesis/Religious Program—Tel: 301-434-2111. Email: re_office@yahoo.com. Mrs. Rosa Diaz, D.R.E. Students 754.
Mission—Catholic Community of Langley Park 1408 Merrimac Dr., Langley Park, Prince George's Co., MD 20787. Tel: 301-439-2045; Fax: 301-439-2355.

4—St. Catherine Laboure (Wheaton) (1951) Revs. Michael A. Salah; Thomas G. Morrow; Luis Marroquin; Bogumil Kosciesza; Deacon Raymond L. Chaput.
Res.: 11801 Claridge Rd., MD 20902. Tel: 301-946-3636; Fax: 301-946-5064.
School—11811 Claridge Rd., MD 20902. Tel: 301-946-1717; Fax: 301-946-9572. Lay Teachers 22; Students 322.
Catechesis/Religious Program—Tel: 301-946-3010 (English); 301-946-1020 (Hispanic Religious Education). Email: sclreligioused@aol.com. Students 692.

5—Christ the King (Wheaton) (1961) Rev. John F. Plans, S.F.; Deacon Stephen Mitchell.
Res.: 2300 East-West Hwy., 2301 Colston Dr., MD 20910. Tel: 301-589-8616; Fax: 301-587-1929.
Catechesis/Religious Program—Tel: 301-589-8620. Shawna Madison, D.R.E. Students 320.

6—St. John the Baptist (Spring Brook) (1960) Rev. Msgr. Francis G. Kazista; Rev. Michael Eugene Tietjen; Deacons John C. Cermak; James J. Gorman.
Res.: 12319 New Hampshire Ave., MD 20904. Tel: 301-622-1122; Fax: 301-625-9266. Email: stjohnbaptist.silverspring.md@adwparish.org. Web: www.sjbsilverspring.org.
School—Tel: 301-622-3076; Fax: 301-622-2453. Email: sjbsprincipal@yahoo.com. Marianne Moore, Prin. Lay Teachers 27; Students 259.
Catechesis/Religious Program—Email: dre@sjbsilverspring.org. Virginia Cohen, D.R.E. Students 238.

7—St. John the Evangelist (1774) [CEM] Rev. Msgr. John R. Pennington; Revs. Mark E. Tucker; Michael W. Briese; Sr. Theresa McElroy, I.H.M., Pastoral Min.; Mr. Michael White, Music Dir.
Res.: 10103 Georgia Ave., MD 20902. Tel: 301-681-7663; Fax: 301-681-8793. Web: sjcparish.org.
School—10201 Woodland Dr., MD 20902. Tel: 301-681-7656; Fax: 301-681-0754. Sr. Kathleen Lannak, I.H.M., Prin. Lay Teachers 14; (Part Time) 6; Students 227.
Catechesis/Religious Program—Tel: 301-681-7634. Sr. Roberta Harding, I.H.M., D.R.E. Students 170.

8—St. Michael (1930) Rev. Msgr. Eddie E. Tolentino; Rev. Daniel Malaver; Deacons Ronald Ealey, Life Dir.; Stephen B. Frye; Roberto Salgado.
Res.: 824 Pershing Dr., MD 20910. Tel: 301-589-1155; Fax: 301-589-3470. Web: www.stmichaelsilverspring.parishesonline.com.
School—824 Wayne Ave., MD 20910. Tel: 301-585-6873; Fax: 301-587-1142. Email: sms@adwschool.org. Web: st-michaelschool.org. Charles Eames, Prin. Lay Teachers 14; Students 191.
Catechesis/Religious Program—Tel: 301-587-2395; Fax: 301-589-3470. Email: stmichaelreled@yahoo.com. Students 376.

9—Our Lady of Grace (Leisure World) (1983) Rev. Peter T. Sweeney.
Mailing Address: 3134 Adderley Ct., MD 20906. Tel: 301-924-0067; Fax: 301-924-6809. In Res., Rev. Msgr. John J. Madigan (Retired).
Res.: 15665 Norbeck Blvd., MD 20906. Tel: 301-924-4927; Fax: 301-924-6809.

10—Our Lady of Vietnam (1990), (Vietnamese), Revs. Peter Nguyen-Thanh-Long; Hilary Tran-Khac Hy (Retired); Paul Tam X. Tran; Deacon John Huong Nguyen.
Res.: 11812 New Hampshire Ave., MD 20904. Tel: 301-622-4895; Fax: 301-625-9384.

11—Our Lady Queen of Poland and Saint Maximilian Kolbe (Leisure World) (1983), (Polish), Rev. Jan Fiedurek, S.Ch.
Res.: 9700 Rosensteel Ave., MD 20910. Tel: 301-589-1857; Fax: 301-589-4401.
Catechesis/Religious Program—Students 38.

Solomons, Calvert Co., Our Lady Star of the Sea (1888) [CEM] Rev. Richard E. Gardiner; Deacons Christopher Jensen; John G. Etzel, (Retired); Robert L. Connelly, (Retired).
Mailing Address: Box 560, MD 20688. Tel: 410-326-3535; Fax: 410-326-3679.
School—Tel: 410-326-3171; Fax: 410-326-9478. Email: olssschool@comcast.net. Sr. Rosella Summe, C.D.P., Prin. Sisters 2; Lay Teachers 15; Students 167.
Catechesis/Religious Program—Sr. Barbara Rohe, C.D.P., D.R.E. Students 242.

Suitland, Prince George's Co., St. Bernardine (1966) Rev. Kevin P. O'Reilly. In Res., Rev. Peter Ajibola.
Res.: 2400 Brooks Dr., MD 20746-1101. Tel: 301-736-0707; Fax: 301-736-2984. Email: st.bernardine@verizon.net. Web: www.saintbernardinechurch.org.
Catechesis/Religious Program—Students 56.

Takoma Park, Prince Georges Co., Our Lady of Sorrows (1932) Revs. Raymond J. Wadas; Jose Raul DeLeon; Deacon Trinidad Soc.
Res.: 1006 Larch Ave., MD 20912. Tel: 301-891-3500; Fax: 301-891-1523.
Catechesis/Religious Program—Tel: 301-891-2033. Students 345.

Upper Marlboro, Prince Georges Co., Saint Mary of the Assumption (1848) [CEM] Revs. William E. Foley; Kevin M. Cusick; Deacon Frank Klco.
Res.: 14908 Main St., MD 20772. Tel: 301-627-3255; Fax: 301-627-5533. Email: rectory@stmarysum.org. Web: www.stmarysum.org.
School—4610 Largo Rd., MD 20772. Tel: 301-627-4170; Fax: 301-627-6383. Email: tcampbell@stmarysum.org. Mr. Steven Showalter, Prin. Sisters, Servants of the Immaculate Heart of Mary 2; Students 240.
Catechesis/Religious Program—Tel: 301-627-3161; Fax: 301-627-5533. Mrs. Regina Piazza, D.R.E. Students 65.

Valley Lee, St. Mary's Co., St. George (1851) [CEM] Rev. Msgr. Karl A. Chimiak; Deacon George H. L'Heureux, (Retired).
Mailing Address: 19199 St. George Church Rd., P.O. Box 9, MD 20692. Tel: 301-994-0607; Fax: 301-994-1793. Email: stgeorge.md@adwparish.org. Web: stgeorgercc.org.
Catechesis/Religious Program—Tel: 301-994-0737. Students 70.
Chapel—St. George's Island, St. Francis Xavier

Waldorf, Charles Co.

1—Our Lady Help of Christians (1980) Rev. Thomas F. Crowley; Deacon Reginald A. Thomas.
Mailing Address: 100 Village St., MD 20602-2183. Tel: 301-645-7112; Fax: 301-645-3635. Email: olhc@verizon.net. Web: www.olhoc.org.
Res.: 930 Barrington Dr., MD 20602-2183. Tel: 301-843-8823; Fax: 301-645-3635.
Catechesis/Religious Program—Mrs. Kathleen White, D.R.E. Students 304.

2—St. Peter (1700) [CEM] Rev. Msgrs. J. Wilfrid Parent; Andrew J. Cassin, Pastor Emeritus (Retired); Rev. Alain M. Colliou.
Res.: 3320 St. Peter's Dr., MD 20601. Tel: 301-843-8916; Fax: 301-843-3163. Email: parishsecretary@stpeterswaldorf.org. Web: stpeterswaldorf.org.
School—3310 St. Peter's Dr., MD 20601. Tel: 301-843-1955; Fax: 301-843-6371. J.R. West, Prin. Lay Teachers 15; Students 262.
Catechesis/Religious Program—Alice Culbreth, Dir. Christian Formation. Students 245.

Chaplains of Public Institutions

Washington. *Children's Medical Center*, 111 Michigan Ave., N.W., 20010. Tel: 202-884-5050. Rev. Anthony Akinlolu, O.P., Chap.
St. Elizabeth's Hospital (Government Operated), 2700 Martin Luther King Jr. Ave., S.E., 20032. Tel: 202-671-1218. Rev. Maximo J. Ortiz, O.S.A., Chap.
National Rehabilitation Hospital, 102 Irving St., N.W., 20010. Tel: 202-877-1000. Rev. Anthony Akinlolu, O.P., Chap., Fredrick Allen.
Providence Hospital (1921) 1150 Varnum St., N.E., 20017-2180. Tel: 202-269-7000. Revs. Pratap Misal, C.M., Phelim Jordan, S.V.D. (Ireland), Chap.
Washington Hospital Center, 110 Irving St. N.W., 20010. Tel: 202-877-6691. Revs. Anthony Akinlolu, O.P., James Moran.

Bethesda, MD. *National Institutes of Health, Clinical Center*, MD. Tel: 301-496-3407. Vacant.

Lanham, MD. *Doctor's Hospital of Prince Georges County*, MD 20706. Served by the priests of St. Matthias Parish.

Special Ministries:
Rev. Msgrs.—
Criscuolo, Salvatore A., Chap., Police and Fire Dept.
Hurley, Leonard F., Rector, Cardinal Boyle Residence
Murray, Michael J., Priest Dir., Catholic Cemeteries
Revs.—
Adams, John E., Dir., S.O.M.E.
Begg, Christopher T., Ph.D., Ph.B., S.T.D., Catholic University of America
Bryant, F. Michael, Chap., District of Columbia Jail
Conley, Rory T., Archdiocesan Historian
Hurd, R. Scott, Permanent Diaconate
Ingels, Kyle Thomas, Chap., Newman Center, University of Maryland
Kemp, Raymond B., Fellow, Woodstock Theological Center, Georgetown University
Martin, Francis R., Chap., Mother of God Community; Instructor, John Paul II Institute (Retired)
Montgomery, William L., Teacher, Carroll High School
Mudd, John, Dir. Devel., Carroll High School
O'Brien, Raymond C., J.D., Asst. Dean, Catholic University
Shaffer, Gregory W., George Washington University Newman Medical Center
Trancone, Gerard A., Chap., Center for the Deaf & Gallaudet University

Pastoral Center Special Ministries:
Rev. Msgrs.—
Antonicelli, Charles V., V.F., V. Vicar Canonical Svcs.
Fisher, Michael W., E.V., Vicar for Clergy, Sec. Ministerial Leadership, Dir., Office of Continuing Educ.
Panke, Robert J., Dir. of Priestly Formation & Vocations
Ranieri, Joseph A., Coord. of Pastoral Care of Priests
Sadusky, Joseph F., M.Div., M.Ch.A., J.C.D., Judicial Vicar Tribunal
Revs.—
Byrne, William D., Sec. for Pastoral Ministry & Social Concerns
Herbert, G. Paul, J.C.L., Tribunal
Hurd, R. Scott, Office of Permanent Diaconate
Knestout, Mark D., Dir. Office of Worship
Park, Adam Y., Sec. to Archbishop Wuerl
Sanderfoot, Brian P., J.C.L., Tribunal
Stuart, George E., J.C.D., Tribunal, Vice Chancellor, Archivist
Walsh, Robert E., Assoc. Dir. Vocations, Sec. to Cardinal McCarrick

Hospital & Nursing Home Ministries:
Rev. Msgr.—
Hurley, Leonard F., Cardinal Boyle Residence, Carrol Manor
Revs.—
Baraki, Tesfamariam, Howard University Hospital
Brailsford, William M., Chap., Sibley Hospital
Kinter, John P., Greater S.E. Hospital
McKay, John F., Suburban Hosp.
Samaha, Jeffrey F., Southern Maryland Hospital
Valentine, Keveny M., Shady Grove Hospital

On Duty Outside the Archdiocese:
Rev. Msgrs.—
Albacete, Lorenzo, New York
Roensch, Roger, Vatican City State
Revs.—
Culkin, Michael, Lancaster, PA
DiNoia, Joseph Augustine, O.P., Ph.D., Sub-Secretary for the Congregation of the Doctrine of the Faith, Rome
Izac, Andre C. (R), North Carolina
Kuebler, A.M. Seamus, Maine
Oberle, James P., S.S., University of Dallas, Irving, TX
Sanz, Jose, D.L.P., California
Slevin, Henry, Vietnam
Ulshafer, Thomas, S.S., Baltimore, MD
Walsh, Francis M.

Graduate Studies:
Revs.—
Cortinovis, Charles
Griffin, Carter, Pontificia Universita della Santa Croce

Military Chaplains:
Revs.—
Fitz-Patrick, David M.
Garrett, Benton Lee
Holt, Paul-Stephen, Iowa
Mudd, David A.
Passamonti, Paul G.
Studniewski, Gary R.

Absent On Leave:
Revs.—
Bozek, Robert
Cocca, Stephen M.
Lee, John T. Matthew
Myslinski, John F.
Reeves, Harold Smith
Woods, Thomas Matthew

Retired:
Most Rev.—
Oliver, Leonard, S.V.D., 619 10th St., N.W., 20001.
Rev. Msgrs.—
Awalt, William J., Byron House, 9210 Kentsdale

Dr., Potomac, MD 20854.
Bazan, Joaquin, Jeanne Jugan Residence.
Brady, John B., 7201 Pyle Rd., Bethesda, MD 20817.
Burton, Richard W., O'Boyle Residence, P.O. Box 29206, 20017.
Cassin, Andrew J., St. Peter, Waldorf, MD.
Duffy, Thomas M., Our Lady of Victory, 20007.
Farina, Michael F., St. Patrick, 20001.
Gatto, Vincent S., St. Raphael, Rockville, MD 20854.
Gillen, James G., Rome, Italy.
Gozaloff, Paul J., P.O. Box 182, Compton, MD 20627.
Harris, Martin P., 44695 Whiteoak, #536, California, MD 20619.
Hughes, Richard A., Mt. Calvary, Forestville, MD 20747.
Kane, Thomas A., Severn House, 772A Fairview Ave., Annapolis, MD 21403-2957.
Kane, William J., Church of Little Flower, Bethesda, MD.
Kuehner, Ralph J., St. Francis of Assisi, Rockville, MD.
Laczko, T. Ansgar, 290 Devonshire Rd., Hedgesville, WV 25427.
Madigan, John J., Our Lady of Grace, 3134 Adderly Ct., Silver Spring, MD 20906.
Otero, Henry, 613 Old Stage Rd., S.W., Glen Burnie, MD 21061.
Quinn, W. Louis, Our Lady of Lourdes, Bethesda, MD.

Revs.—
Alvarez-Garcia, Julio, Carroll Manor, Miami, FL.
Barry, Paul, 5404 Bye St., Capitol Heights, MD 20743.
Berry, William F., Grace House, 3214 Norbeck Rd., Silver Spring, MD 20906.
Blackwell, Michael J., St. Mary, Landover Hills, MD 20784.
Brainerd, Winthrop J., O'Boyle Residence.
Brown, Charles E., Church of the Resurrection, Burtonsville, MD.
Caimi, Luke A., Charles Co. Nursing & Rehabilitation Center, 10200 LaPlata Rd., La Plata, MD 20646.
Conway, David, P.O. Box 173, Georgetown, DE 19947.
Craig, Samuel L., St. Nicholas, Laurel
De Porter, Arnold W., 15211 Elkridge Way, Apt. 94-24, Silver Spring, MD 20906.
DeRamos, Fidel, P.O. Box 60, Lucena City 4301 Philippines.
Dignan, Eamon, St. John, Hollywood, MD.
Dixon, J. Isidore, 6335 Bumpy Oak Rd., La Plata, MD 20646.
Dolan, Michael F., Our Lady of Grace, Silver Spring, MD 20906.
Duffy, G. Ralph, Shrine of St. Jude, Rockville, MD.
Evans, Edward, Sunapee, NH.
Gallagher, Roger P., Cardinal O'Boyle Residence, P.O. Box 29206, 20017.
Goode, William F., Ascension, Bowie, MD 20719.
Green, Charles C., Jeanne Jugan Residence.
Hill, W. Paul, 13901 Belle Chase Blvd., #313, Laurel, MD 20707.
Holloway, James P., 300 Ocean Blvd., #7, St. Simons Island, GA 31522.
Hurley, John, Cathedral of St. Matthew, Washington DC
Ihrie, Bernard R., Jr., 3736 Bay Dr., Edgewater, MD 21037.
Joyce, George V., Sisters of Providence Infirmary, 1233 Main St., 3rd Fl., Holyoke, MA 01040-5394.
Kennedy, Joseph P., 5 Brush Island Ct., Berlin, MD 21811.
Kleinstuber, Joseph J., 15345 Potomac River Dr., Cobb Island, MD 20625.
Liston, Paul F., O'Boyle Residence.
MacIntyre, Frederick H., Sacred Heart, La Plata, MD
Martin, Francis R., 20501 Goshen Rd., Gaithersburg, MD 20879.
McCaffrey, Patrick J., Malta House, 4918 LaSalle Rd., Hyattsville, MD 20782.
McManus, Eamon, Ave Maria University, 1025 Commons Cir., Naples, FL 34119.
Metzdorf, William C., St. Vincent de Paul Village, 3350 E. St., San Diego, CA 92102.
Muzzey, Charles H., Friendship Terrace, 4201 Butterworth Pl., N.W. #522, 20016-4562.
O'Sullivan, Michael J., Cardinal O'Boyle Residence, P.O. Box 29206, 20017.
Panares, Auxentius, 8787 Country Creek Blvd., Jacksonville, FL 32221.
Reid, George B., St. Catherine's Nursing Center, Emmitsburg, MD 21727.
Reynierse, Peter, 212 Creekside Dr., Locust Grove, VA 22508.
Richardson, Robert C., Hillcrest Bldg. 27, Unit 301, 3850 Washington St., Hollywood, FL 33021.
Salcedo, Luis G., 5G Castle Hills Rd., Agawam, MA 01001.
Stack, John P., 3501 Forest Edge Dr., 14-3F, Silver Spring, MD 20906.
Thompson, Matthew E., Marian Assisted Living, 19109 Georgia Ave., Brookeville, MD 20833.
Torsiello, Ralph C., 4 Winchester Dr., Ocean View, DE 19970.
Tou, Louis A., Cardinal O'Boyle Residence, P.O. Box 29206, 20017.
Tran-Khac-Hy, Hilarius, 14201 Schaeffer Rd., Boyds, MD 20841.
Ward, Neal A., St. Mary's Nursing Center, 21585 Peabody St., Rm. 431, Leonardtown, MD 20650.
Wintermyer, John S., 15316 Pine Orchard Dr., 2K, Silver Spring, MD 20906.

Permanent Deacons:
Abeyta, Dan D., St. Mary of the Mills, Laurel, MD
Allen, David A., (Retired)
Allen, Robert F., St. John Neumann, Gaithersburg, MD
Alvarez, Sergio, St. Ambrose, Cheverly, MD
Ames, George B., Jr., St. Mary, Piscataway, MD
Angell, Kenneth, St. Jane Frances de Chantal, Bethesda, MD
Barbernitz, Peter M., St. Camillus, Silver Spring, MD
Barnes, David, St. Edwards the Confessor, Bowie
Barnes, John R., St. Joseph, Pomfret, MD
Barrasso, Anthony T., (Retired)
Barrett, Kenneth, St. Andrew the Apostle, Silver Spring, MD
Barrett, Raymond J., Diocese of Venice, FL
Battaglia, Thomas D., Arlington
Bechet, Leon J., (Retired)
Bell, Joseph, Incarnation, Washington, DC
Bell, Lawrence G., St. Martin, Gaithersburg, MD
Beller, Edwin J., (Retired)
Bendel, Francis W., Mother Seton, Gaithersburg, MD
Berry, Robert L., St. Gabriel, Washington D.C.
Birkel, Richard, (On Leave of Absence)
Blanco-Eccleston, Julio, St. Bartholomew, Bethesda
Bobbitt, John W., (Retired)
Bockweg, Gary L., St. Joseph's on Capitol Hill, Washington, DC
Boesman, William C., St. Thomas the Apostle, Washington, DC
Bond, Stuart Michael, St. Andrew the Apostle, Silver Spring, MD
Brink, Edward J., Wilmington
Briscoe, John A., (Retired)
Brown, James E., (Retired), Holy Redeemer, Washington, DC
Brown, Sylvester, (Retired)
Burroughs, Eugene, St. Mary, Bryantown, MD
Butkiewicz, Jerome, St. Mary, Charlotte Hall
Butler, Kevin A., Sr., Holy Comforter-St. Cyprian, Washington, DC
Byrne, Kevin, St. Elizabeth, Rockville
Cadigan, James, St. Peter, Olney, MD
Cahoon, David L., Jr., St. Mary, Barnesville, MD
Cain, Leonard F., (Retired)
Caraballo, Carlo, St. John Neumann, Gaithersburg, MD
Carroll, Donald T., (Wilmington)
Cayrampoma, Juan, Cathedral of St. Matthew, Washington, DC
Cermak, John C., St. John the Baptist, Silver Spring
Chaput, Raymond L., St. Catherine Laboure, Wheaton, MD
Chase, Ira E., Basilica of the National Shrine of the Immaculate Conception, Washington, DC
Chavez, Antonio, (Retired)
Chen, Chester G., St. Jane de Chandal, Bethesda, MD
Choi, Chang Sup, St. Andrew Kim, Olney, MD
Chrzanowski, Edmund A., Jr., St. John Vianney, Prince Frederick, MD
Cioffi, Thomas, St. Peter, Olney, MD
Coates, Vincent J., Jr., (Retired), Fall River
Coleman, Earle W., (Retired)
Collins, Gerald A., Atlanta
Connelly, Robert L., (Retired)
Conner, James E., (Retired)
Connor, John E., (Retired)
Conrad, Joseph M., St. Luke, Washington, DC
Contreras, Carlos E., (Retired), VA
Conway, Neal T., St. Jerome, Hyattsville, MD
Cooper, Philip J., Charlotte
Cordova-Ferrer, Nathaniel, St. Jude, Rockville
Crawford, Rory P., St. Peter, Olney
Crowley, Ronald C., (Leave of Absence)
Cruz, George C., St. Bartholomew, Bethesda, MD
Cummins, Don E., Seattle
Cummins, Eugene, St. John Neumann, Gaithersburg, MD
Curtis, Joseph F., Jr., Basilica of the National Shrine of Immaculate Conception, Washington, DC
Cyrus, Ralph W., Holy Comforter-St. Cyprian, Washington, DC
Daniels, Willis, St. Aloysius, Washington, DC
Danko, Edward, Wilmington
Dardy, Henry, Holy Family, Mitchellville, MD
Datovech, James J., St. Francis of Assisi, Derwood
Davis, Alton, Jr., St. Joseph, Largo, MD
Davis, Harry, Holy Redeemer, Kensington
Davis, William E., Las Vegas
Davy, Michael W., St. John Newmann, Gaithersburg
DeRoze, Donald G., Resurrection, Burtonsville, MD
Ditewig, William, St. Petersburg
Dominic, James, St. Michael, Ridge
Draper, Harry R., (Retired)
Duggin, David, Harrisburg
Ealey, Ronald R., DC Correctional Treatment Center & DC Jail, Washington, DC; St. Michael the Archangel, Silver Springs, MD
Edelin, Charles E., Jr., (Retired)
Elliott, Thomas B., Richmond
Emley, William P., (Retired), VA
Enright, Timothy D., Mother Seton, Germantown, MD
Espinosa, Leandro Y., St. Columba, Oxon Hill, MD
Etzel, John G., (Retired)
Feeley, John, St. Anthony of Padua, Washington, DC
Feneis, Albert G., Raleigh
Fernandez, Elmer, Archdiocese of San Antonio
Finerty, John F., St. Paul, Damascus, MD
Fischer, Robert A., Our Lady of the Visitation, Darnestown
Fisher, Richard A., St. Columba, Oxon Hill, MD
Flores, Francisco, Diocese of Arlington
Flynn, Leo, Our Lady of Victory, Washington, DC
Frye, Stephen B., St. Michael the Archangel, Silver Spring, MD
Gallagher, Mark J., Camden; Blessed Sacrement, Washington, D.C.
Gallerizzo, William, Fall River
Garcia, David F., Santa Fe
Gatica-Delgado, Jorge, St. Raphael, Rockville
Genis, Thomas P., Immaculate Conception, Washington, DC
Gignilliat, Robert L., St. Mary of the Mills, Laurel
Glenn, Clark, (Retired), St. Ignatius, Oxon Hill, MD
Gorman, James J., St. John the Baptist, Silver Spring, MD
Gorospe, Santiago B., Honolulu
Graham, Albert E., Jr., (Retired), Sacred Heart, La Plata
Greenfield, William Mike, Incarnation, Washington, DC
Hannagan, Francis L., (Retired)
Hawkins, William J., St. Theresa of Avila, Washington DC
Haywood, Hiram H., Jr., (Retired)
Hidalgo, Alfredo, (Retired)
Hoen, David J., Fort Belvoir Army Base, VA
Hoffman, Michael R., Wilmington
Holson, Edward, Wilmington
Hong, Pascal, (Retired)
Hopson, Frank, (Retired)
Hubbard, Robert, Holy Cross, Garrett Park
Huber, Robert T., Seattle, WA
Huete, Stephen, The Netherlands
Huguley, Maury, Jr., St. Paul, Damascus, MD
Hume, W. Michael, Nashville
Iannaconi, Perry F., St. Nicholas, Laurel, MD
Interlandi, Joseph S., Orlando
Jackson, Harold I., Charleston
Jensen, Christopher, Our Lady Star of the Sea, Solomons, MD
Johnson, Alfred, St. Michael, Brandywine
Johnson, James G., Jesus the Good Shepherd, Owings, MD
Jones, Thomas R., Our Lady of Perpetual Help, Washington, DC
Keller, Grafton T., St. Augustine, FL
Keller, Norman B., (Retired)
Kelly, Richard F., St. Augustine, Washington, DC
Klco, Frank, St. Mary of the Assumption, Upper Marlboro, MD
Koeniger, Ludwig, St. John, Hollywood, MD
Kostka, Daniel S., St. Mary, Rockville, MD
Kraemer, Francis W., Sr., (Retired)
Kronschnabel, Michael C., Phoenix
Kyte, William L., Immaculate Conception, Mechanicsville, MD
L'Heureux, George G., (Retired)
L'Homme, Bertrand, St. Francis de Sales, Washington, D.C.
Lacovaro, James G., (Leave of Absence)
Lemon, John G., Wilmington
Leonard, John M., (Retired)
Levy, Richard A., Jr., (Leave of Absence)
Liu, John C., St. Rosa of Lima, Gaithersburg, MD

Lloyd, Joseph W., Jr., Holy Angels, Avenue, MD
Locke, John W., (Retired)
Luetjen, Palmer, (Retired)
Lynch, John F., St. Anthony, North Beach, MD
Lyons, Robert A., Arlington, VA
Lyons, Robert R., New York
Marinari, A. John, (On Leave of Absence)
Martin, E. Chad, Jesus the Good Shepherd, Dunkirk, MD
Mastrangelo, Eugene K., St. John Vianney, Prince Frederick, MD
Mattocks, Richard E., (Retired)
Mays, Donald, Shrine of St. Jude, Rockville, MD
McCann, James C., Archdiocese of Milwaukee
McCarthy, Michael, (Leave of Absence)
McGinness, John J., St. Patrick, Washington, DC
McGrath, Joseph B., LL.B., J.C.L., (Retired)
McKimmie, Stephen, St. Mary, Piscataway, MD
Merella, Bartholomew J., St. Matthew's Cathedral, Washington, DC
Meyer, Ronald J., St. Martin, Gaithersburg, MD
Middleton, Henry D., III, St. Mary, Bryantown, MD
Migliorini, Louis, Sr., (Retired)
Miles, Lawrence A., Mount Calvary, Forestville, MD
Miller, Alfred A., Jr., Our Lady Queen of Peace, Washington, DC
Miller, Lawrence L., Military Service
Minor, Samuel L., Jr., (Retired), St. Margaret, Seat Pleasant, MD
Mitchell, Stephen, Christ the King, Silver Spring, MD
Molina, Jose Renato, St. Mark the Evangelist, Hyattsville, MD
Molina, Nehemias J., Shrine of the Sacred Heart, Washington, DC
Moll, Anthony W., St. John the Evangelist, Clinton, MD
Montalvo, Santiago T., St. John the Evangelist, Clinton
Montgomery, John E., Jesus the Divine Word, Huntingtown, MD
Moreno, Mario F., St. Rose of Lima, Gaithersburg
Moskaitis, J. Vincent, (Leave of Absence)
Mukri, Kevin, St. Andrew the Apostle, Silver Spring, MD
Murati, George, St. Augustine
Nalls, James T., St. Patrick, Rockville, MD
Nguyen, John H., (Retired), Our Lady of Vietnam, Silver Spring, MD
Nickel, Clayton A., German Pastoral Mission, Washington, DC
Nickerson, William J., St. Francis Xavier, Newtowne, MD
Nosacek, Andrew J., (Retired), St. Pius X, Bowie, MD
Oettinger, Frank F., Las Vegas
Oguledo, Valentine, St. Margaret of Scotland, Seat Pleasant, MD
Om, Michael, Epiphany, Washington, DC
Parker, Donald A., St. Mary of the Mills, Laurel, MD
Perkins, Gary, St. Edward the Confessor, Bowie, MD
Picard, Adrien D., (Retired)
Pinder, Wilbur L., Jr., Wilmington
Pineda, Roberto L., Miami
Pitocco, Nickolas J., Ascension, Bowie, MD
Price, Robert, Raleigh
Ravenscroft, F. Ian, (Retired)
Reilly, Matthew B., Charlotte
Rice, Ulysses, (Retired)
Ricker, Philip W., Wilmington
Robinson, John E., Jr., Holy Redeemer, Washington, DC
Robinson, Stephen M., St. Mary, Landover Hills, MD
Roszkowski, Thomas E., St. Bernadette, Silver Spring, MD
Rourke, Walter G., Holy Ghost, Issue, MD
Ruffo, Paul, Arlington
Salatto, Frank J., Jr., (Retired)
Salgado, Roberto, St. Michael, Silver Spring, MD
Salinas, Rudolfo A., Seminarian of the Archdiocese of Washington
Santiago, Perfecto, St. Mary of the Mills, Laurel, MD
Schneider, Ronald W., Milwaukee
Scholz, Nicholas E., Shrine of St. Jude, Rockville, MD
Schopfer, Richard J., (Retired)
Serafini, Bartolo, St. Catherine Laboure, Wheaton
Sferrella, Joseph J., (Retired)
Shewmaker, John B., Our Lady of Lourdes, Bethesda, MD
Sinchak, J. Douglas, Archdiocese of Mobile
Smith, Anthony S., (Retired)
Smith, McBurnett J., Assumption, Washington, DC
Soc, Trinidad, Our Lady of Sorrows, Takoma Park, MD
Somerville, James, (Retired)
Somerville, John, (Retired)
Soto, Alfredo, Galveston-Houston
Spalding, Thomas C., Sr., (Retired)
Springer, James R., El Paso
Stackpole, Terrell U., (Retired)
Stuart, Scott C., St. Ignatius, Chapel Point, MD
Sweeney, Anthony J., III, St. Mary's County Detention Center; St. Cecilia & St. Mary City, MD
Tan, Domingo, (Retired)
Terrar, David B., St. Paul, Damascus, MD
Testudine, Joseph, (Retired)
Thomas, Reginald A., Our Lady Help of Christians, Waldorf, MD
Thomas, William, (Retired)
Thompson, Daniel R., (Retired)
Thompson, Finis E., Holy Redeemer, College Park, MD
Trichel, Allen J., (Leave of Absence)
Turner, Al Douglas, Nativity, Washington, DC
Turner, B. Curtis, St. Mark the Evangelist, Hyattsville, MD
Turner, John H., (Retired)
Vargas, Jorge W., Our Lady Queen of the Americas, Washington, DC
Verdon, John, Jesus the Good Shepherd, Dunkirk, MD
Vita, William A., Jr., St. Martin of Tours, Gaithersburg, MD
Wakefield, Walter W., III, Lexington
Walker, Richard, Jr., St. Thomas More, Washington, D.C.
Welch, Joseph, Holy Spirit, Forestville, MD
Weschler, Charles A., Wilmington
Whitaker, Robert W., St. Ann, Washington, DC
White, Robert C., Sr., St. Martin of Tours, Washington, DC
Wolfe, Willis R., St. Joseph, Beltsville
Work, Boyd, Jr., Cathedral of St. Matthew, Washington, DC
Yorke, Desmond, St. Bernard, Riverdale Park, MD
Yun, James, Our Lady of Mercy, Potomac, MD
Ziemianski, Lawrence L., (Retired)

INSTITUTIONS LOCATED IN THE ARCHDIOCESE

[A] SEMINARIES, ARCHDIOCESAN

WASHINGTON. *Theological College of the Catholic University of America*, 401 Michigan Ave., N.E., 20017. Tel: 202-756-4900; Fax: 202-756-4909. Email: decker@theologicalcollege.org. Web: www.theologicalcollege.org.

Theological College, Inc. Sulpician Fathers. Faculty: Priests 8; Students 84.

Faculty: Revs. David D. Thayer, S.S., S.T.L., Ph.D.; Melvin C. Blanchette, S.S., M.A., Ph.D., Rector; Daniel F. Moore, S.S., M.A., S.T.L., Vice Rector; Anthony J. Pogorelce, S.S., M.Div., M.S., Ph.D.; Gerald D. McBrearity, S.S., M.A., S.T.B., D.Min., Faculty Advisor; John Slovikovski, M.Div., M.A.; James P. Froehlich, O.F.M.Cap., M.A., M.S., Ph.D.; Daniel Greenleaf, S.T.B., S.T.L.

HYATTSVILLE, MD. *Redemptoris Mater Archdiocesan Missionary Seminary* (2002) 4900 Lasalle Rd., MD 20782. Tel: 301-277-4960; Fax: 301-277-5295. Email: seminary@rmwashington.org. Web: www.rmwashington.org. Revs. José Matías Díaz, Rector; Francisco Javier Santaballa, Vice Rector; Giovanni Buontempo, Spiritual Dir. Priests 3; Students 33.

[B] SEMINARIES, RELIGIOUS OR SCHOLASTICATES

WASHINGTON. *Atonement Seminary-Franciscan Friars of the Atonement*, 5207 Colorado Ave., N.W., 20011. Tel: 202-722-1893; Fax: 202-722-1716. Rev. John J. Keane, S.A., B.A., M.A., Admin. Priests 1.

St. Bonaventure Friary, 6706 Marlboro Pike, Forestville, MD 20747. Tel: 301-735-7979; Fax: 301-735-7955. Revs. Brad A. Milunski, O.F.M.Conv., M.Div., S.S.L., Guardian; Russell Governale, O.F.M.Conv., S.T.B., M.S.W., Vicar; Bro. Michael Austin, O.F.M.Conv., Treas.; Revs. Martin Day, O.F.M.Conv., M.A., L.C. Theol., Sec.; Berard L. Marthaler, O.F.M.Conv. (Retired). Priests 4; Brothers 1; Students 12.

Deshairs Community-Oblates of St. Francis de Sales Residence, 1621 Otis St., N.E., 20018-2321. Tel: 202-529-1926. Revs. Donald J. Heet, O.S.F.S.; John W. Crossin, O.S.F.S.

Diocesan Laborer Priests, House of Studies (1966) 3706 15th St., N.E., 20017. Tel: 202-832-4217; Fax: 202-526-5692. Email: info@solinstitutedc.com. Web: www.solinstitutedc.com. Revs. Juan A. Puigbo, US Delegate & Dir.; Gabriel Calvo; Victor Salomon; Ovidio Pecharroman. Priests 4; Total Enrollment 4.

Discalced Carmelite Friars (1918) 2131 Lincoln Rd., N.E., 20002-1199. Tel: 202-832-6622; Fax: 202-832-5711. Revs. Marc Foley, O.C.D., Prior; David Centner, O.C.D.; Regis Jordan, O.C.D.; Kieran Kavanaugh, O.C.D.; Francis Miller, O.C.D. (Retired); Thomas Ochieng Otanga, O.C.D.; Bros. Edward O'Donnell, O.C.D.; Bryan Paquette, O.C.D.; Michael Stoeghauer; Robert Sentman.

Discalced Carmelite Friars, Inc. Priests 7; Brothers 4.

Dominican House of Studies, 487 Michigan Ave., N.E., 20017. Tel: 202-495-3820; Fax: 202-495-3873. Web: www.dhs.edu. Very Rev. R. Giles Dimock, O.P., Prior; Rev. Basil Burr Cole, O.P.; Very Rev. Steven C. Boguslawski, O.P., M.A., M.Div., S.T.M., S.T.L., Ph.D., Pres. Pontifical Faculty; Revs. J. Raymond Vandegrift, O.P.; John A. Langlois, O.P., S.T.D., Student Master; William P. Garrott, O.P., M.A., Vocation Dir.; Kevin Anthony McGrath, O.P., S.T.L.; David John Paul Mott, O.P.; Gabriel O'Donnell, O.P., Vice Pres. & Academic Dean, Pontifical Faculty; Joseph Alobaidi, O.P.; Timothy Bellamah, O.P., S.T.L.; Brian Chrzastek, O.P., Subprior; John Dominic Corbett, O.P.; Henry Thomas Donoghue, O.P.; Bernard Dupont, O.P., M.A.; John Martin Egan, O.P.; Matthew Erickson, O.P., Procurator, Economic Admin.; Kenneth Harkins, O.P.; Elias Henritzy, O.P., S.T.D.; John Frederick Hinnebusch, O.P.; Theodore John Baptist Ku, O.P., S.T.L.; Michael J. McCormack, O.P., M.Div., M.A.; Matthew Bernard Mulcahy, O.P., Ph.D. (Cand.), Dir. Library; Jonah F. Pollock, O.P., B.A., S.T.B.; Kurt Pritzl, O.P., Ph.D.; Stephen Desmond Ryan, O.P.; Eugene M. Rzeczkowski, O.P., S.T.L.; John Gregory Schnakenberg, O.P., S.T.B.; Bruno M. Shah, O.P., M.A., S.T.B.; John Paul Walker, O.P., S.T.L.; Seth Thomas Joseph White, O.P., Ph.D.; Malcolm Sylvester Willoughby, O.P. Priests 33; Brothers 33; Clerical Brothers 2; Seminarians 34. In Res. Rev. John Thomas Mellein, O.P.

St. Francis Friary-Capuchin College, 4121 Harewood Rd., N.E., 20017-1593. Tel: 202-529-2188; Fax: 202-526-6664. Web: www.capcollege.net. Revs. James Menkhus, O.F.M.Cap., Guardian - Dir. Formation; William Graham, O.F.M.Cap.; Robert A. Barbato, O.F.M.Cap.; James P. Froehlich, O.F.M.Cap., M.A., M.S., Ph.D., Treas.; J. Daniel Mindling, O.F.M.Cap., Academic Dean, Mt. St. Mary, Emittsburgh, MD; Christopher Rengers, O.F.M.Cap., Pastoral Supply; Joseph Mindling, O.F.M.Cap., Prof., Washington Theological Union; Thaddeus Posey, O.F.M.Cap., Chap., Walter Reed Medical Center; Roberto Martinez, O.F.M.Cap. (Puerto Rico); Joseph Saviour, O.F.M.Cap. (India); Francis X. Russo, O.F.M.Cap., Hispanic Min.; Thomas Weinandy, O.F.M.Cap., Exec. Dir. of Sec. for Doctrine & Pastoral Practices USCCB; Charles Knoll, O.F.M.Cap; Bros. Michael Letosak, O.F.M.Cap.; Alfred Vincent, O.F.M.Cap.; Robert Toomey, O.F.M.Cap., Vicar & Coord Intl. Student Prog.; James Peterson, O.F.M.Cap.; Clifford Ledger, O.F.M.Cap., Cap Corps Lay Volunteer Dir. Priests 14; Scholastics 6; Brothers 5; Total Enrollment 6.

Franciscan Mission Service of North America, 1323 Quincy St., N.E., P.O. Box 29034, 20017. Tel: 202-832-1762; Fax: 202-832-1778. Email: info@franciscanmissionservice.org. Web: franciscanmissionservice.org. Ms. Kim Smolik, Exec. Dir. Lay Staff 2.

St. Joseph's Seminary (1888) 1200 Varnum St., N.E., 20017. Tel: 202-526-4231; 202-526-4229 (Student); Fax: 202-526-7811. Very Rev. John L.M. Filippelli, S.S.J., Spiritual Dir.; Rev. Albert Adeleke (Nigeria), Academic Dean; Very Rev. Brian Fox, S.S.J., Rector; Revs. Peter Weiss, S.S.J., Vocation Dir.; Robert DeGrandis, S.S.J.; Bros. Louis Tomasso, S.S.J., Assoc. Vocation Dir.; Thomas Vincent, S.S.J. St. Joseph's Society of the Sacred Heart-Josephite Fathers & Brothers. Priests 3; Brothers 1; Franciscan Sisters of St. Joseph 5; Seminarians 17. In Res. Revs. John Fritz (RCK); Howard Johnson (JKS) (Retired); William Lawrence, F.S.S.P.; John Nyoike (Kenya); Godwin Olugbami (Nigeria); Stephen Saawuan (Nigeria); Bro. David Andrews, C.S.C.

Josephite Pastoral Center, 1200 Varnum St., N.E., 20017. Tel: 202-526-9270; 202-526-9271; Fax: 202-526-7811. Email: ssjpastrcntr@aol.com. Rev. James E. McLinden, S.S.J., Dir.; Maria M. Lannon, Admin. Priests 1; Brothers 1; Deacons 1; Lay Women 3.

Marian Fathers Scholasticate (1673) 3885 Harewood Rd., N.E., 20017. Tel: 202-526-8884; Fax: 202-832-6551. Email: markbaron@hotmail.com. Web: www.marian.org. Revs. Mark Baron, M.I.C., Supr. & Novice Master; Lawrence Dunn, M.I.C.; Casimir Krzyzanowski, M.I.C.; Bro. Leonard Konopka, M.I.C., Treas. Priests 4; Brothers 1; Novices 3; Seminarians 7.

Marist College, The Scholasticate (1892) 815 Varnum St., N.E., 20017-2199. Tel: 202-529-2821; Fax: 202-635-4627. Rev. Timothy G. Keating, S.M., Rector. Priests 1; Scholastics 1.

Maryknoll Fathers and Brothers, 4834 16th St., N.W., 20011. Tel: 202-726-4252; Fax: 202-726-0466. Email: mkldc@aol.com. Web: www.maryknoll.org. Revs. William M. Boteler, M.M.; John Sullivan, M.M., Dir. Affiliates.

Office of Justice and Peace, P.O. Box 29132, 20017. Tel: 202-832-1780; Fax: 202-832-5159. Email: mknolldc@igc.org. Marie Dennis, Dir.; Rev. James W. Kofski, M.M.; Sisters Ann Braudis, M.M., Assoc.; Meg Gallagher, M.M., Assoc.; Judy Coode, Communications Dir.; David Kane, M.L.M., Assoc.; Susan Weissert, M.L.M.; Yamileth Coreas, Admin. Asst.

Oblates of St. Francis de Sales, 721 Lawrence St., N.E., 20017. Tel: 202-269-9410; Fax: 202-526-4323. Web: www.oblates.org. Priests 1; Brothers 1; Professed 2.

DeSales Hall Residence: Bro. Edward F. Ogden, O.S.F.S., Supr. & Dir. Formation; Rev. William F. Davis, O.S.F.S.

St. Paul's College, 3015 Fourth St., N.E., 20017-1199. Tel: 202-832-6262; Fax: 202-269-2507. Email: stpaulsdc@aol.com. Revs. John Behnke, C.S.P., Supr., Dir. Novices & Assoc. Dir. Formation; Stephen E. Bossi, C.S.P, Dir. Formation & Assoc. Dir. Novices; Kenneth G. Boyack, C.S.P., D.Min.; Francis P. DeSiano, C.S.P., D.Min.; John E. Lynch, C.S.P., Ph.D. (Retired); Ronald G. Roberson, C.S.P.; Paul G. Robichaud, C.S.P.; Thomas Ryan, C.S.P.; Ms. Denise Eggers, Librarian. Paulist Fathers. Priests 9; Novices 2; Students 6.

Queen of Pious Schools House of Studies-Piarist Fathers, 1339 Monroe St., N.E., 20017-2510. Tel: 202-529-7734; Fax: 202-529-7734 (Call first). Rev. Andrew C. Buechele, Sch.P., Ph.D., Rector, Librarian, Treas. & 1st Prov. Asst. Priests 1.

Washington Theological Union (1968) 6896 Laurel St., N.W., 20012-2016. Tel: 202-726-8800; Fax: 202-726-1716. Web: www.wtu.edu. Rev. Frederick J. Tillotson, O.Carm., Pres.; Dr. C. Colt Anderson, Ph.D., Vice Pres. for Academic Affairs & Academic Dean; Mr. Alexander Moyer, Librarian.

Washington Theological Union, Inc., Established in 1968 as the Coalition of Religious Seminaries. The Union is a school of theology and ministry. Among the numerous orders and societies that make up this institution are those whose Provincials or Superiors sit on the Provincials Council of the Board of Trustees including: the Order of Carmelites, Provinces of the Most Pure Heart of Mary and St. Elias; Order of Friars Minor, Province of the Most Holy Name of Jesus; Redemptorist Fathers and Brothers, Baltimore Province; Order of Friars Minor Conventual, Province of the Immaculate Conception. Priests 12; Sisters 4; Lay Teachers 8; Students 252.

Whitefriars Hall, 1600 Webster St., N.E., 20017. Tel: 202-526-1221; Fax: 202-526-9217. Email: qconners@carmelnet.org. Revs. Quinn Conners, O.Carm., Prior & Formation Dir.; Leopold Glueckert, O.Carm.; David Blanchard, O.Carm.; Donald W. Buggert, O.Carm.; Sam Citero, O.Carm.; John F. Horan, O.Carm.; Lijoy Jacob, O.Carm (India); Patrick McMahon, O.Carm., Ph.D.; Craig Morrison, O.Carm.; Elias O'Brien, O.Carm.; Joachim Smet, O.Carm.; Francis Sulistya, O.Carm (Indonesia); Frederick J. Tillotson, O.Carm. Priests 13; Brothers 8; Friars in Solemn Profession 13; Friars in First Profession 8.

The Carmelitana Library Tel: 202-526-1221, Ext. 121; Fax: 202-526-9217. Rev. Patrick McMahon, O.Carm., Ph.D.; Patricia O'Callagan, Librarian.

BELTSVILLE, MD. *The Saint LaSalle Auxiliary* (1918) P.O. Box 1710, MD 20704-1710. Tel: 301-210-7444; Fax: 301-210-0614. Email: Lasalleauxiliary@aol.com. Bro. John Patzwall, F.S.C., Dir. The Saint La Salle Auxiliary Inc. is the Development Office for the Christian Brothers of the Baltimore Province. Brothers 3; Lay Staff 1.

SILVER SPRING, MD. *Holy Family Seminary*, 401 Randolph Rd., P.O. Box 4138, MD 20914-4138. Tel: 301-622-1184; Fax: 301-622-2959. Email: holyfamilySeminary@gmail.com. Revs. Miguel Mateo, S.F., Vice Prov. Supr.; Hernando Cortes, S.F.; John A. Sierra, S.F.; Palmo Valente, S.F. Priests 4; Students 3.

Holy Name College (Residence), 1650 St. Camillus Dr., MD 20903. Tel: 301-434-3400; Fax: 301-434-4624. Rev. Francis J. Di Spigno, O.F.M., Supr. & Dir. Formation; Bro. David W. Schlatter, O.F.M., Vicar & Asst. Dir. Formation; Revs. Ronald Stark, O.F.M.; Agoston Bagyinski, O.F.M.; Hoan Dinh, O.F.M.; Lawrence Janiezic, O.F.M.; Lam Nguyen, O.F.M.; Bros. Juniper Capece, O.F.M.; Sebastian Tobin, O.F.M. House of Studies for Holy Name Province of the Order of Friars Minor. Solemnly Professed Friars 11; Simply Professed Friars 11.

Salvatorian Community (1888) 104 Bishop Dr., MD 20905. Tel: 301-933-3451; Fax: 301-384-5432. Email: flenwillis@verizon.net. Web: www.sds.org. Revs. Glen Willis, S.D.S., Area Coord.; Richard Maloney, S.D.S.; Eliot Nitz, S.D.S., First Consultor; Roman Stadtmueller, S.D.S. (Retired); Robert Nugent, S.D.S.; Julian Guzman, S.D.S.; Bogdan Palka, S.D.S.; Bros. Roger Nelson, S.D.S., M.A., Vicar Coord.; Marvin Kluesner, S.D.S.; James Rieden, S.D.S.; Sean McLaughlin, S.D.S. Society of the Divine Savior/Salvatorians. Priests 8; Brothers 5; Lay Members 20.

WEST HYATTSVILLE, MD. *Pallottine Seminary at Green Hill* (1961) 2009 Van Buren St., MD 20782-1761. Tel: 301-422-3777; Fax: 301-422-4070. Rev. Frank S. Donio, S.A.C., Rector, Formation Dir. Society of the Catholic Apostolate. Priests 1.

[C] COLLEGES AND UNIVERSITIES

WASHINGTON. *Catholic University of America, The* (1887) Nugent Hall/Executive Offices, 20064. Tel: 202-319-5000; Fax: 202-319-4441. Email: webmaster@cua.edu. Web: www.cua.edu. Most Rev. Donald W. Wuerl, Chancellor; Very Rev. David M. O'Connell, C.M., J.C.D., Pres.; James F. Brennan, Ph.D., Provost; Cathy Wood, M.F.A., Vice Pres. Finance & Treas.; Susan D. Pervi, M.A., Vice Pres. Student Life; Frank G. Persico, M.A., Vice Pres. for Univ. Rels. & Chief of Staff; Revs. Robert J. Kaslyn, S.J., Dean School of Canon Law; Kurt Pritzl, O.P., Ph.D., Dean School of Philosophy; Lawrence R. Poos, Ph.D., Dean School of Arts & Sciences; Charles C. Nguyen, Sc.D., Dean School of Engineering; Veryl V. Miles, J.D., Dean Columbus School of Law; Nalini Jairath, R.N., Ph.D., Dean School of Nursing; Murry Sidlin, M.M., Dean Benjamin T. Rome School of Music; James R. Zabora, S.C.D., Dean Natl. Catholic School of Social Svc.; Randall Ott, M.Arch., Dean School of Architecture & Planning; Sara M. Thompson, Ph.D., Dean Metropolitan College; Rev. Melvin Blanchette, S.S., Rector, Theological College; Shavaun M. Wall, Ph.D., Assoc. Vice Pres. Academic Planning; James J. Greene, Ph.D., Dean Graduate Studies; Ziaeddin Mafaher, M.A., M.S., CIO; Ralph Albano, M.B.A., Assoc. Provost for Sponsored Research; Rev. Robert Schlageter, O.F.M.Conv., S.T.L., Univ. Chap. & Dir. Campus Ministry; Kimberly Kelley, Ph.D., Assoc. Provost Libraries; Adriana Farella, B.A., Registrar; Victor Nakas, M.Phil., Assoc. Vice Pres. for Public Affairs; David J. McGonagle, Ph.D., Dir., CUA Press; W. Michael Hendricks, Ed.D., Vice Pres. Enrollment Mgmt.; Carl A. Petchik, M.Arch., M.C.R.P., Exec. Dir. Facility Opers.; Robert Sullivan, Ed.M., Vice Pres. Univ. Devel. Priests 27; Sisters 8; Lay Faculty 318; Students 6,768.

Priests Associated with the University Full-Time: Rev. Msgrs. Thomas J. Green, J.C.D. (BGP); Kevin W. Irwin (NY), Dean School of Theology & Rel. Studies; Paul McPartlan, D. Phil.; Robert S. Sokolowski (HRT); Robert F. Trisco, Hist.Eccl.D. (CHI), Prof. Emeritus, Church History (Retired); John Wippel, Ph.D. (STU); Revs. Regis Armstrong, O.F.M.Cap., M.Div., M.Theo., M.S.Ed., Ph.D.; John P. Beal, J.C.D.; Christopher T. Begg, Ph.D., Ph.B., S.T.D.; Alexander A. Di Lella, O.F.M., S.T.L., S.S.L., Ph.D., Prof. Emeritus (Retired); John T. Ford, C.S.C. T. Ford, M.A., S.T.D.; John P. Galvin, D.Th. (BO); Francis T. Gignac, S.J., S.T.L., D.Phil.; Patrick Granfield, O.S.B., Ph.D., S.T.D. (Retired); Jacques Gres-Gayer, D.Theo., S.T.D. (France); Sidney H. Griffith, S.T.D., Ph.D.; Donald J. Heet, O.S.F.S.; John P. Heil, S.S.D.; Joseph Jensen, O.S.B., S.S.L., S.T.D., Lecturer; Brian Johnstone, C.S.S.R., S.T.D.; Joseph A. Komonchak, S.T.L., Ph.D. (NY) (Retired); John E. Lynch, C.S.P., Ph.D. (Retired); Berard L. Marthaler, O.F.M.Conv., Prof. Emeritus (Retired); Frank J. Matera, M.A., Ph.D. (HRT); Mark Morozowich, S.E.O.D. (SJP); Raymond C. O'Brien, J.D.; Jon J. O'Brien, S.J. (Retired); Anthony J. Pogorelc, S.S., M.Div., Ph.D.; Kurt Pritzl, O.P., Ph.D., Dean, School of Philosophy; Dominic F. Serra, S.T.D.; Sean O. Sheridan, T.O.R.; Raymond Studzinski, O.S.B., Ph.D.; Paul Sullins; David D. Thayer, S.S., S.T.L., Ph.D.; James A. Wiseman, O.S.B., M.A., S.T.D.; Michael G. Witczak, M.Div., S.L.D. (MIL); Romuald Meogrossi, O.F.M.Conv.; John J. M. Foster; Melvin C. Blanchette, S.S., M.A., Ph.D.

Clerical Members, Board of Trustees: Most Rev. Michael J. Bransfield; His Eminence Francis Cardinal George, O.M.I., Ph.D., S.T.D.; Most Revs. Donald W. Wuerl, Chancellor; Frances B. Shulte, Trustee Emeritus; Philip M. Hannan, Trustee Emeritus; His Eminence Roger Cardinal Mahony; Justin Cardinal Rigali, J.C.D.; Sean Cardinal O'Malley, O.F.M.Cap., Ph.D.; Daniel N. DiNardo; Most Revs. Edward P. Cullen, D.D.; Timothy M. Dolan; Allen H. Vigneron, D.D., Bd. Chm.; Thomas G. Doran, D.D., J.C.D.; Jose H. Gomez, S.T.D.; Wilton D. Gregory, S.L.D.; John J. Myers, J.C.D., D.D.; Joseph A. Pepe, D.D., J.C.D.; Rev. Msgr. Walter R. Rossi; Most Revs. Michael F. Burbidge, D.D., Ed.D., V.G.; Paul S. Loverde, D.D., S.T.L., J.C.L. (ARL); Gregory J. Mansour; Robert J. McManus; Edwin F. O'Brien; Thomas G. Wenski.

**Georgetown University* (1789) 37th and O Sts., N.W., 20057. Tel: 202-687-0100. Web: www.georgetown.edu. John J. DeGioia, Ph.D., Pres.; James J. O'Donnell, Ph.D., Provost; Stuart Bondurant, Interim Exec. Vice Pres.; T. Alexander Aleinikoff, Vice Pres. & Dean of the Law Center; Spiros Dimolitsas, Ph.D., Senior Vice Pres.; Edward M. Quinn, Univ. Sec.; Christopher Joyce, M.B.A., Senior Vice Pres., CFO & Treas.; Todd A. Olson, Ph.D., Vice Pres. Student Affairs; Jo-Ann Henry, Vice Pres. & Chief Human Resources Officer; Daniel R. Porterfield, Ph.D., Vice Pres. Public Affairs & Strategic Devel.; H. David Lambert, Vice Pres. for Information Svcs. & CIO; Jane E. Genster, Vice Pres. & Gen. Counsel; Rev. Philip L. Boroughs, S.J., Vice Pres., Mission & Ministry; Michael D. McGuire, Exec. Dir. Planning & Institute Research; Revs. Charles G. Gonzalez, S.J.; William M. King, S.J.; Paul J. McCarren, S.J.; Patrick D. Rogers, S.J.; Mr. Jaroslow Chzanowski; Mr. Francois Kabore, S.J.; Mr. Richard Ross, S.J.; Mr. Rodrique Takoudjou. Jesuits 23; Sisters 5; Lay Teachers 1,067; Total Enrollment 12,688.

The following are the Schools and Colleges which compose the University: Undergraduate Admissions.

Georgetown College (1789) Jane Dammen McAuliffe, Ph.D., Dean.

Graduate School of Arts & Sciences (1820) David W. Lightfoot, Ph.D., Dean.

School of Medicine (1851) 3900 Reservoir Rd., N.W., 20007. Ray Mitchell, M.D., Senior Assoc. Dean Academic Affairs.

Law Center (1870) 600 New Jersey Ave., N.W., 20001. T. Alexander Aleinikoff, Exec. Vice Pres. & Dean of Law Center.

School of Nursing & Health Studies (1903) 3700 Reservoir Rd., N.W., 20007. Bette Keltner, R.N., F.A.A.N., Ph.D., Dean.

Edmund A. Walsh School of Foreign Service (1919) Hon. Robert L. Gallucci, Ph.D., Dean.

Robert Emmett McDonough School of Business (1957) George Daly, Dean Mibonough School of Business.

Georgetown Public Policy Institute (1990) 3600 N. St., N.W., Ste. 200, 20007. Judith Feder, Ph.D., Dean.

School of Summer and Continuing Education (1974) Robert J. Thomas, Ph.D., Dean.

Joseph Mark Lauinger Library Artemis G. Kirk, M.A., Univ. Librarian.

Office of the University Registrar John Q. Pierce IV, M.A., Univ. Registrar.

Office of Alumni & University Relations, Box 571253, 20057. Tel: 202-687-4111.

Affirmative Action Programs, G-10 Darnall Hall, 37th St. & O St., N.W., 20057. Tel: 202-687-4798; Fax: 202-687-7778. Rosemary Kilkenny, J.D., Special Asst. to Pres. for AAP.

Trinity College, 125 Michigan Ave., N.E., 20017. Tel: 202-884-9000; Fax: 202-884-9229. Email: pauleya@Trinitydc.edu. Web: www.trinitydc.edu. Patricia A. McGuire, Pres.; Sr. Mary Johnson, S.N.D., Community Representative; Dr. Robert Preston, Vice Pres. Academic Affairs. Sisters of Notre Dame de Namur. Priests 1; Sisters 5; Lay Professors 54; Students 1,600.

[D] HIGH SCHOOLS, ARCHDIOCESAN

WASHINGTON. *Archbishop Carroll High School*, 4300 Harewood Rd., N.E., 20017. Tel: 202-529-0900; Fax: 202-529-5989. Email: carroll@archbishopcarroll.org. Web: www.archbishopcarroll.org. Dr. David S. Stofa, Ph.D., Prin. & CEO; Ms. Mary Elizabeth Blaufuss, Vice Prin. Academic Affairs; Mr. Larry Savoy, Vice Prin. Student Affairs; Revs. William L. Montgomery; John Mudd; Ms. Nancy Berry, Librarian. (Coed) Priests 2; Sisters 1; 43 - full time; 1 - part time 44; Students 543; Staff 33.

Don Bosco Cristo Rey High School of the Archdiocese of Washington, Mailing Address: P.O. Box 56481, 20040-6481. Tel: 301-891-4750; Fax: 301-270-1459. Email: shafrans@dbcr.org. Web: www.donboscocristorey.org. Revs. Steve Shafran, S.D.B., Pres.; John Serio, S.D.B., Prin. Priests 3; Brothers 1; Lay Teachers 20; Students 241.

[E] HIGH SCHOOLS, PRIVATE

WASHINGTON. *St. Anselm's Abbey School, Inc*, (Grades 6-12), 4501 South Dakota Ave., N.E., 20017. Tel: 202-269-2350; Fax: 202-269-2373. Email: mainoffice@saintanselms.org. Web:

www.saintanselms.org. Rev. Dom Peter Weigand, O.S.B., Pres.; Louis Silvano, Headmaster; Bro. Marvin Kluesner, S.D.S., Librarian. Separate subsidiary corporation of The Benedictine Foundation at Washington, DC (St. Anselm's Abbey)., Seven-year college preparatory course. Priests 8; Brothers 2; Lay Faculty and Staff 45; Students 237.

Georgetown Visitation Preparatory School, 1524 35th St., N.W., 20007. Tel: 202-337-3350; Fax: 202-342-5733. Email: name@visi.org. Web: www.visi.org. Sr. Mary Berchmans Hannan, V.H.M., Pres. Emerita & Superior; Mr. Dan Kerns, Head of School; Elizabeth Burke, Librarian. Sisters 2; Lay Teachers 60; Students 480.

Gonzaga College High School, 19 Eye St., N.W., 20001. Tel: 202-336-7100; Fax: 202-336-7172. Email: anovotny@gonzaga.org. Web: www.gonzaga.org. Revs. Allen P. Novotny, S.J., Pres.; Vincent G. Conti, S.J., Headmaster; Robert J. Rokusek (DET), Chap.; Thomas F. Clifford, S.J., Rector; Patricia Tobin, Librarian. Society of Jesus, Jesuit Community. Priests 7; Sisters 2; Lay Teachers 76; Students 957; Scholastics 1. In Res. Revs. Kenneth E. Meehan, S.J.; Gerald V. O'Connor, S.J.; Bruce A. Steggert, S.J.; Timothy J. Stephens, S.J.; Mr. Stephen L. Surovick, S.J.

St. John's College High School (1851) (Coed Grades 9-12), 2607 Military Rd., N.W., 20015. Tel: 202-363-2316; Fax: 202-686-5162. Email: stjohnschs@stjohns-chs.org. Web: stjohns-chs.org. Bro. Thomas Gerrow, F.S.C., Pres.; Mr. Jeffrey Mancabelli, Prin.

St. John's College Brothers of the Christian Schools., College Preparatory, Elective Army Junior ROTC. Brothers 2; Sisters 1; Lay Teachers 78; Students 1,038.

**San Miguel School*, 7705 Georgia Ave., NW, 20012. Tel: 202-232-8345; Fax: 202-232-3987. Bro. Francis Eells, F.S.C., Prin.

BETHESDA, MD. *Mater Dei School, Inc.*, 9600 Seven Locks Rd., MD 20817. Tel: 301-365-2700; 301-365-2701; Fax: 301-365-2710. Mr. Edward N. Williams, Headmaster; Mr. Christopher S. Abell, Pres. Students 225.

Stone Ridge School of the Sacred Heart, 9101 Rockville Pike, MD 20814. Tel: 301-657-4322; Fax: 301-657-4393. Email: ckarrels@stoneridge.org. Web: www.stoneridge.org. Mrs. Catherine Ronan Karrels, Head of School. Religious of the Sacred Heart. Lay Teachers 82; Students 649.

BLADENSBURG, MD. *Elizabeth Seton High School* (1959) 5715 Emerson St., MD 20710-1844. Tel: 301-864-4532; Fax: 301-864-8946. Email: 269@setonhs.org. Web: www.setonhs.org. Sr. Ellen Marie Hagar, D.C., Pres.; Mrs. Sharon Pasterick, Prin.; Mrs. Kim Tremble, Librarian. Daughters of Charity of St. Vincent de Paul 7; Lay Teachers 48; Administration & Staff 33; Girls 650; Lay Staff 30.

FORESTVILLE, MD. *Bishop McNamara High School* (Coed), 6800 Marlboro Pike, MD 20747. Tel: 301-735-8401; Fax: 301-735-0934. Email: clarkm@bmhs.org. Web: www.bmhs.org. Ms. Heather Gossart, Pres.; Mr. Marco Clark, Prin. Holy Cross Brothers. Lay Teachers 75; Students 840.

HYATTSVILLE, MD. *De Matha Catholic High School*, 4313 Madison St., MD 20781. Tel: 240-764-2200; Fax: 240-764-2275. Email: dmmail@dematha.org. Web: www.dematha.org. Rev. Thomas J. Burke, O.SS.T., S.T.D., Rector & Vice Pres. Legal Affairs; Dr. Daniel J. McMahon, Ph.D., Prin.; Mrs. Zetha Ballinger, Librarian. Conducted by the Order of the Most Holy Trinity, Province of the Immaculate Heart of Mary., Boys, 9-12. Priests 2; Lay Teachers 79; Students 996.

KENSINGTON, MD. *The Academy of the Holy Cross, Inc.* (1868) 4920 Strathmore Ave., MD 20895. Tel: 301-942-2100; Fax: 301-929-6440. Email: schooloffice@academyoftheholycross.org. Web: academyoftheholycross.org. Claire M. Helm, Ph.D., Pres.; Mary Lynne Boss, Prin.; Mary Ann Grundborg, Librarian.

The Academy of the Holy Cross, Inc Sisters 2; Students 575; Lay Teachers 53.

LAUREL, MD. *St. Vincent Pallotti High School* (1921), MD 20707. Tel: 301-725-3228; Fax: 301-776-4343. Email: admissions@pallottihs.org. Web: www.pallottihs.org. Stephen J. Edmonds, Pres. & Prin.; Mrs. Amy Seigel, Librarian. Pallottine Missionary Sisters of the Catholic Apostolate. Priests 1; Sisters 1; Lay Teachers 36; Students 500.

LEONARDTOWN, MD. *St. Mary's Ryken High School* (1885) 22600 Camp Calvert Rd., MD 20650. Tel: 301-475-2814; 301-932-4422; Fax: 301-373-4195. Web: www.smrhs.org. Mrs. Mary Joy Hurlburt, Pres.; Rick Wood, Prin. Sponsored by the Xaverian Brothers. Lay Teachers 56; Students 668.

NORTH BETHESDA, MD. *Georgetown Preparatory School* , MD 20852. Tel: 301-493-5000; Fax: 301-530-9531. Web: www.gprep.org. Mr. Jeffrey Jones, Headmaster; Revs. Richard S. McCouch, S.J., Supr.; William L. George, Pres.; William J. Elliott, S.J.; Gerald P. Bell, S.J.; James P. Bradley, S.J.; George S. Williams, S.J.; Leonard A. Martin, S.J.; Philip J. Rosato, S.J. Jesuit Community; Society of Jesus. Priests 8; Lay Teachers 51; Students 476.

OLNEY, MD. *Our Lady of Good Counsel High School*, 17301 Old Vic Blvd., MD 20832. Tel: 240-283-3209; Fax: 240-283-3390. Email: raimo@olgchs.org. Web: olgchs.org. Mr. Arthur Raimo, Pres.; John Graham, Prin.; Rev. Barry R. Gross (LFT). Xaverian Brothers. Priests 1; Lay Teachers 89; Students 1,200.

POTOMAC, MD. *Connelly School of the Holy Child*, (Grades 6-12), 9029 Bradley Blvd., MD 20854. Tel: 301-365-0955; Fax: 301-365-0981. Web: www.holychild.org. Maureen K. Appel, Headmistress; Dr. Toni Bouillette, Head of Upper School; Ms. Martha Daly, Librarian. Sisters of the Holy Child Jesus., College Preparatory for Girls. Sisters 1; Lay Teachers 53; Students 382.

[F] ELEMENTARY SCHOOLS, ARCHDIOCESAN

DARNESTOWN, MD. *Mary of Nazareth Roman Catholic Elementary School* (1994) 14131 Seneca Rd., MD 20874. Tel: 301-869-0940; Fax: 301-869-0942. Email: marynaz@comcast.net. Web: www.maryofnazareth.org. Mr. Michael J. Friel, Prin.; Mrs. Denise Humphries, Librarian.

[G] ELEMENTARY SCHOOLS, PRIVATE

BETHESDA, MD. *The Woods Academy*, 6801 Greentree Rd., MD 20817. Tel: 301-365-3080; Fax: 301-469-6439. Email: mworch@woodsacademy.org. Web: www.woodsacademy.org. Mary Worch, Head of School; Judy Higgins, Librarian. Students 317; Lay Teachers 37.

GAITHERSBURG, MD. *Emmanuel, Inc.* (1987) 20501 Goshen Rd., MD 20879. Tel: 301-990-2088; Fax: 301-947-0574. Email: mog@mogschool.com. Web: www.mogschool.com. Ms. Mary Reinhard, Prin.; Sheila Martin, Librarian. Total Staff 22; Students 175.

POTOMAC, MD. *The Heights School*, 10400 Seven Locks Rd., MD 20854. Tel: 301-365-4300; Fax: 301-365-4303. Email: adevicente@heights.edu. Web: www.heights.edu. Mr. Alvaro de Vicente, Headmaster; Revs. Gerard Kolf, Chap.; John Debicki, Chap.; Mr. Michael Moynihan, Upper School Head; Mr. Andrew Reed, Middle School Head; Mr. Austin Hatch, Lower School Head; Mr. Joseph Cardenas, Dean Advisory; Mr. Thomas Royals, Asst. Headmaster; James Nelson, Librarian. Private, Independent, Spiritual Formation and Religious Education provided by the Prelature of Opus Dei. Priests 2; Lay Teachers 59.

[H] SPECIAL SCHOOLS

WASHINGTON. *Lt. Joseph P. Kennedy, Jr., Institute*, 801 Buchanan St., N.E., 20017. Tel: 202-529-7600; Fax: 202-529-2028. Email: gadair@kennedyinstitute.org. Web: www.kennedyinstitute.org. Deacon Richard C. Birkel, Ph.D., Pres. & CEO. The Lt. Joseph P. Kennedy, Jr., Institute of the Archdiocese of Washington is a private, nonprofit organization providing education, training and employment, therapeutic and residential services to children and adults with developmental disabilities.

Nonprofit Organizations Serving Children and Adults With Developmental Disabilities:

Adult Learning & Employment Services Tel: 202-529-0500; Fax: 202-529-8211. Participants 364.

Family & Personal Support Services Tel: 301-251-2860; Fax: 301-251-8559. Staff 25; Participants 102.

Early Intervention & Preventive Services Tel: 202-529-7600; Fax: 202-529-2028. Staff 45; Participants 82.

Kennedy Education Tel: 202-529-7600; Fax: 202-529-2028. (Includes Kennedy School, Outreach Program to Catholic Schools and Inclusion 2000) Staff 52; Students 140.

Residential Division Tel: 202-529-7600; Fax: 202-529-2028. Total Staff 81; Residents 61.

Administration Division Tel: 202-529-7600; Fax: 202-529-2028. Total Staff 25.

Community Living Partnership Total Staff 3; Families 50.

ROCKVILLE, MD. *The Frost Center, Society of the Divine Savior* (1976) 4915 Aspen Hill Rd., MD 20853. Tel: 301-933-3451; Fax: 301-933-0330. Email: seanmcl@frostcenter.com. Web: www.frostcenter.com. Bro. Sean McLaughlin, S.D.S., Center Dir.; Chris Eacho, Prin.; Rev. Glen Willis, S.D.S., Business Mgr.; Bros. Roger Nelson, S.D.S., M.A., Lead Teacher; Peter Farnesi, S.D.S., Plant Mgr. A School and Therapy Program for Emotionally Disturbed and Autistic Students. Grades 1-12. Priests 1; Brothers 3; Students 80; Total Staff 40.

[I] CATHOLIC CHARITIES OF THE ARCHDIOCESE

WASHINGTON. *Catholic Charities of the Archdiocese of Washington, Inc.*, 924 G St., N.W., 20001. Tel: 202-772-4300; Fax: 202-772-4308. Email: ed.orzechowski@catholiccharitiesdc.org. Web: catholiccharitiesdc.org. Mr. Edward Orzechowski, M.S.W., Pres.

Anchor Mental Health Association/Division of Adult and Family Services, 1001 Lawrence St., N.E., P.O. Box 29058, 20017. Tel: 202-635-5940; Fax: 202-481-1431. Email: denise.capaci@catholiccharitiesdc.org. Denise Capaci, Dir.

CCS Housing, Inc., 924 G St., N.W., 20001.

Calvert County Family Center, 855 Main St., Prince Frederick, MD 20678. Tel: 410-535-0309; Fax: 410-257-1002.

The Catholic Charities Foundation of the Archdiocese of Washington, 924 G St., N.W., 20001. Edward J. Orzechowski, M.S.W., Pres. Tel: 202-772-4373; Fax: 202-772-4411; Carol Shannon, Exec. Dir. Tel: 202-772-4395; Fax: 202-772-4411; Meha Desai, Dir. Div. of Children's Svcs. Tel: 202-526-4100; Fax: 202-526-1829.

Charles County Family Center, The Charles Bldg., 513 E. Charles St., La Plata, MD 20646. Tel: 301-934-2582; Fax: 301-934-3439.

St. Clement's Family Center, P.O. Box 113, Avenue, MD 20609. Tel: 301-769-2788; Fax: 301-769-2789.

Division of Catholic Charities Enterprises Tel: 202-635-5970; Fax: 202-481-1431. Email: scott.lewis@catholiccharitiesdc.org. Scott C. Lewis, Dir.

Division of Housing and Support Service Tel: 202-481-1435; Fax: 202-481-1430. Email: regine.clermont@catholiccharitiesdc.org. Regine Clermont, Dir.

Lt. Joseph P. Kennedy Institute/Division of Development Disabilities Services, 801 Buchanan St., N.E., 20017. Tel: 202-281-2759; Fax: 202-529-1673. Email: daphne.pallozzi@catholiccharitiesdc.org. Daphne Pallozzi, M.S., Dir.

Montgomery County Family Center, 12247 Georgia Ave., Silver Spring, MD 20902. Tel: 301-933-3164; Fax: 301-949-1371.

N.E. Family Center/Division of Children's Services, 1438 Rhode Island Ave., N.E., 20018. Tel: 202-526-4100; Fax: 202-526-1829. Email: meha.desai@catholiccharitiesdc.org.

Prince George's County Family Center, 6706 Marlboro Pike, Forestville, MD 20747. Tel: 301-568-9529; Fax: 301-568-9567.

Rollingcrest Commons, Inc., 924 G St., N.W., 20001-4532. Tel: 202-772-4308.

SHARE Food Network, 5170 Lawrence Pl., Hyattsville, MD 20781. Tel: 301-864-3115; Fax: 301-864-5370. P.O. Box 768, Bladensburg, MD 20710. Christopher Duke, Exec. Dir.

Southeast Family Center, 220 Highview Pl., S.E., 20032. Tel: 202-574-3442; Fax: 202-574-3474. Total Assisted 102,895; Total Staff 850.

Spanish Catholic Center, Inc./Division of Immigrant and Refuge Services, 1618 Monroe St., N.W., 20010. Tel: 202-939-2437; Fax: 202-234-7323. Email: mario.dorsonville@catholiccharitiesdc.org. Rev. Mario E. Dorsonville, Dir.

[J] ARCHDIOCESAN VOLUNTEER ORGANIZATIONS

WASHINGTON. *Archdiocesan Association of Ladies of Charity*, P.O. Box 10038, 20018. Vivian M. Chase, Pres. Purpose: Individual charity work, usually of emergency nature and supports various other agencies, foodbanks, child care centers and pregnancy aid centers.

Society of St. Vincent de Paul, Archdiocesan Council of Washington, 1438 Rhode Island Ave., N.E., 20018-3709. Tel: 202-281-2033.

Office of Archdiocesan Council

[K] ORPHANAGES AND INFANT HOMES

HYATTSVILLE, MD. *St. Ann's Infant and Maternity Home*, 4901 Eastern Ave., MD 20782. Tel: 301-559-5500; Fax: 301-853-6985. Email: donations@stanns.org. Web: www.stanns.org. Sisters Mary Bader, D.C., CEO; Virginia Ann Brooks, D.C., Local Supr. Daughters of Charity. Sisters 7; Residential Children 57; Day Care 75; Teen Mother-Baby Program: Mothers 20; Children 20; Faith House - 8 mothers & 8 children 16.

[L] GENERAL HOSPITALS

WASHINGTON. *Center for Life of Providence Hospital*, 1150 Varnum St., N.E., 20017. Tel: 202-269-7074;

Fax: 202-267-7470. Email: ghassin@provhosp.org. Nonprofit Corporation to Render Service, Support and Assistance in the Provision of Community Services which Foster Human Dignity, Family Unity and Respect for Life. Services Include: Reduced Fee Maternity Programs. Total Assisted 109,400; Total Staff 1,586.

De Paul Foundation, Inc., 1150 Varnum St., N.E., 20017. Tel: 202-269-7039; Fax: 202-269-7029. Email: jboland@provhosp.org. De Paul Foundation, Inc. was Organized to Provide Fund Development, Financial and Other Assistance to Provide Hospital and Other Subsidiaries of De Paul Foundation for the Health Care, Medical, Educational and Human Needs of the District of Columbia and Vicinity, by Functioning as a Charitable Nonprofit, Nonstock Corporation.

Providence Health Foundation, 1150 Varnum St., N.E., 20017. Tel: 202-269-7776; Fax: 202-269-7687. Providence Health Foundation, Inc. (PHF), a District of Columbia Charitable Nonprofit Corporation, was Organized to Support the Mission of Providence Hospital by Conducting Fundraising and Development Activities, by Receiving and Managing Donations, by Making Grants and by Promoting Educational Activities and Scientific Research.

Georgetown University Hospital, 3800 Reservoir Rd., N.W., 20007. Tel: 202-444-3000; Fax: 202-444-3095. Email: conleyb@gunet.georgetown.edu. Web: www.georgetownuniversityhospital.org. Richard Goldberg M.D., Interim Pres.; Revs. Brian J. Conley, S.J., Dir. Mission & Pastoral Care; Gustaaf M. Keppens, S.J., Chap.; Norman Schwartz, Chap.; Azuka Iwuchukwu, Chap. Priests 4; Bed Capacity 609; Total Assisted Annually 195,383; Total Staff 3,538.

Providence Health Services, Inc., 1150 Varnum St., N.E., 20017. Ambulatory-Outpatient Care, Promote Wellness and Carry Out Educational Activities and Scientific Research.

Providence Hospital, 1150 Varnum St., N.E., 20017. Tel: 202-269-7000; Fax: 202-269-7160. Email: srcarol@provhosp.org. Web: www.provhosp.org. Julius D. Spears Jr., Pres.; Revs. Phelim Jordan, S.V.D. (Ireland), Chap.; Carlo Napoli, T.O.R., Chap. Daughters of Charity of St. Vincent de Paul. Sisters 10; Bed Capacity 576; Patients Assisted Annually 182,000; Total Staff 2,325.

SILVER SPRING, MD. *Holy Cross Hospital of Silver Spring, Inc.*, 1500 Forest Glen Rd., MD 20910. Tel: 301-754-7000; Fax: 301-754-7012. Web: www.holycrosshealth.org. Mr. Kevin J. Sexton, CEO; Linda Arnold, Ph.D., Dir. Pastoral Care & Mission Opers.; Rev. George Markwell, M.Afr. A member of Trinity Health which is sponsored by Catholic Health Ministries. Sisters of the Holy Cross 9; Bed Capacity 450; Patients Assisted Annually 177,756; Total Staff 3,200.

[M] HOMES FOR AGED

WASHINGTON. *Cardinal O'Boyle Residence for Priests*, 1150 Varnum St., N.E., 20017. Tel: 202-269-7810 (Rector); Fax: 202-269-7820. P.O. Box 29206, 20017-0206. Suites 12; Residents 11; Total Staff 2. In Res. Rev. Msgrs. Leonard F. Hurley, Chap., Carroll Manor & Rector O'Boyle Residence for Retired Priests; Richard W. Burton (Retired); Michael D. Farina; Revs. Winthrop J. Brainerd (Retired); James Finan (Retired); Roger P. Gallagher (Retired); Paul F. Liston (Retired); Michael J. O'Sullivan (Retired); William J. Thompson; Louis A. Tou (Retired).

Little Sisters of the Poor of Washington, D.C., Inc. (1871) 4200 Harewood Rd., N.E., 20017-1554. Tel: 202-269-1831; Fax: 202-269-3910. Email: mswashington@littlesistersofthepoor.org. Web: www.littlesistersofthepoor.org. Sr. Benedict Armstrong, L.S.P., Supr.; Rev. Msgr. Joaquin Bazan (Retired). Little Sisters of the Poor. Sisters 13; Residents 75; Apartments 22; Total Staff 100.

BETHESDA, MD. *Palmer Park Seniors Housing, Inc.* (2001) c/o Victory Housing, Inc., 5430 Grosvenor Ln., Ste. 210, MD 20814-2142. Tel: 301-493-6000; Fax: 301-493-9788. Email: info@victoryhousing.org. Web: www.victoryhousing.org. John D. Spencer, Vice Pres. Apartment Units 69.

Takoma Tower, Inc. (2001) c/o Victory Housing, Inc., 5430 Grosvenor Ln., Ste. 210, MD 20814-2142. Tel: 301-493-6000; Fax: 301-493-9788. Email: info@victoryhousing.org. Web: www.victoryhousing.org. John D. Spencer, Vice Pres. Apartment Units 187.

Winslow House, Inc. (2002) c/o Victory Housing, Inc., 5430 Grosvenor Ln., Ste. 210, MD 20814-2142. Tel: 301-493-6000; Fax: 301-493-9788. Email: info@victoryhousing.org. Web: www.victoryhousing.org. John D. Spencer, Vice Pres. Apartment Units 46.

HYATTSVILLE, MD. *Sacred Heart Home Inc.*, 5805 Queens Chapel Rd., MD 20782. Tel: 301-277-6500; Fax: 301-277-3181. Email: sistervacha@sacredhearthome.org. Web: www.sacredhearthome.org. Sr. Waclawa Kludziak; Rev. Stan Ukwe. Sisters, Servants of Mary Immaculate. Sisters 6; Residents 102.

MITCHELLVILLE, MD. *Villa Rosa Nursing Home, Inc.*, 3800 Lottsford Vista Rd., MD 20721-4026. Tel: 301-459-4700; Fax: 301-429-0646. Rev. Dominic Rodighiero, C.S., Dir.; Mrs. Neva Babcock, R.N., B.S.N., L.N.H.A., Admin.; Sr. Teolide Cecagno, M.S.C.S., Supr. Comprehensive Care Nursing Facility. Sisters 4; Residents 100.

[N] MONASTERIES AND RESIDENCES OF PRIESTS AND BROTHERS

WASHINGTON. *St. Anselm's Abbey* (1923) 4501 S. Dakota Ave., N.E., 20017. Tel: 202-269-2300; Fax: 202-269-2312. Web: www.stanselms.org. Very Rev. Simon McGurk, S.T.L., Prior & Admin.; Rt. Rev. Aidan Shea, O.S.B.; Revs. James A. Wiseman, O.S.B., M.A., S.T.D.; John Farrelly, O.S.B., S.T.D.; David Granfield, O.S.B., L.L.B., S.T.D.; Patrick Granfield, O.S.B., Ph.D., S.T.D. (Retired); Michael Hall, O.S.B., M.A., Ph.D., Subprior; Hilary Hayden, O.S.B., S.T.L.; Edmund Henkels, O.S.B.; Joseph Jensen, O.S.B., S.S.L., S.T.D.; Gabriel Myers, O.S.B.; Mark Sheridan, O.S.B., S.S.L., Ph.D.; Philip Simo, O.S.B.; Boniface von Nell, O.S.B.; Peter Weigand, O.S.B.; Christopher Wyvill, O.S.B.; Bros. Dunstan Robidoux, O.S.B.; Matthew Nylund, O.S.B. Benedictine Foundation at Washington, DC, Order of St. Benedict. Priests 16; Brothers 2.

Brothers of Charity, 1359 Monroe St., N.E., 20017. Tel: 202-636-4306; Fax: 202-636-4307. Web: www.brothersofcharity.org. Email: donald.joyal.fc@fracarita.org. Bro. Donald Joyal, F.C., Dir. Formation.

Center for Assisted Living (1993) Dominican Fathers and Brothers., 630 E St., S.W., 20024. Tel: 202-488-4188; Fax: 202-554-5735. Email: jmcmahon@opfriars.org. Rev. John A. McMahon, O.P., S.T.B., M.A., Dir.

Commissariat of the Holy Land, Franciscan Monastery - Mount St. Sepulchre, 1400 Quincy St., N.E., 20017. Tel: 202-526-6800, Ext. 887; Fax: 202-529-9889. Email: commissarywdcusa@myfranciscan.com; secretariatusa@myfranciscan.com. Web: www.myfranciscan.com. Very Rev. Jeremy Harrington, O.F.M.; Rev. Garrett Edmunds, O.F.M., Vice Commissary; Friar John-Sebastian Laird-Hammond, O.F.M., Secretariat. Priests 9; Friars 18; Solemnly Professed 18. *Franciscan Monastery USA Inc.*, 1400 Quincy St. N.E., 20017. Tel: 202-526-6800; Fax: 202-529-9889. Email: secretariatusa@myfranciscan.com. Web: www.myfranciscan.com. Very Rev. Jeremy Harrington, O.F.M., Guardian; Friar Fadi Azar, O.F.M.; Rev. James Paul Brabandt, O.F.M., Mass Office; Friars Thomas Courtney, O.F.M.; John-Sebastian Laird-Hammond, O.F.M., Secretariat to Franciscan Monastery; Revs. Garrett Edmunds, O.F.M., Vice Commissary; Edward Flanagan, O.F.M.; Friar Alosius Florio, O.F.M., Vicar to Guardian; Rev. Romuald Green, O.F.M.; Friars Simon McKay, O.F.M.; Roger Petras, O.F.M.; Revs. Stephen F. Sabbagh, O.F.M. (Retired); Francis X. Sihuay, O.F.M. (Peru) (Retired); Jacob-Matthew Smith, O.F.M., Vocation Dir.; Friar Benedict Tade, O.F.M.; Revs. Kevin Treston, O.F.M.; David Wathen, O.F.M., Dir. Holy Land Tours; Friars Callistus Welch, O.F.M., Treas. Holy Land Foundation; Maximilian Wojciechowski, O.F.M., Gift Shop Mgr.; Rev. Manuel Ybarra, O.F.M., Finance Office. Priests 11; Deacons 1; Brothers 8; Solemnly Professed 20.

Divine Word House, 832 Varnum St., N.E., 20017. Tel: 202-635-7810; Fax: 202-635-7813. Email: phelimj@yahoo.com. Revs. Phelim Jordan, S.V.D. (Ireland), Rector; John Szukalski, S.V.D.; Michio Akao, S.V.D. (Japan); Phelim Jordan, S.V.D. (Ireland); John Rodney, S.V.D.; Rejimon Varghese, S.V.D. (India); Marianus Pale Hera, S.V.D. (Indonesia); Georges Kintiba, S.V.D.; Juan Antonio Romo-romo, S.V.D. Presently, 10 S.V.D. Priests. Residents 10.

Holy Redeemer College (1930) 3112 Seventh St., N.E., 20017. Tel: 202-529-4410; 202-529-4484; Fax: 202-832-1321. Very Rev. Gerard Chylko H., C.Ss.R., Rector/Superior; Revs. Kevin O'Neil, C.Ss.R.; James Wallace, C.Ss.R., Vicar; Thomas Forrest, C.Ss.R.; Matthew T. Allman, C.Ss.R.; Eric W. Fuchs (NEW); Brian Johnstone, C.Ss.R., Moral Theol. CUA; Tuan LeQuang, C.Ss.R.; James McEvoy; Paul Bao Vinh, C.Ss.R.; Bro. Thomas Rochacewicz, C.Ss.R.

Holy Redeemer College, Opened in 1930. Redemptorist House of Studies 2009. Priests 10; Religious Brother 1.

The Jesuit Community at Georgetown University, 37th and O Sts., N.W., 20057-1200. Tel: 202-687-4000; Fax: 202-687-7679. Email: langanj@georgetown.edu. Revs. John P. Langan, S.J., Rector; Pawel Adamczyk, S.J.; Edward W. Bodnar, S.J. (Retired); Philip L. Boroughs, S.J., Vice Pres. Mission & Ministry; Thomas J. Buckley, S.J.; Gerard J. Campbell, S.J. (Retired); Matthew E. Carnes, S.J.; Jaroslaw Chrzanowski, S.J.; David J. Collins, S.J.; Brian J. Conley, S.J., Treas.; Richard J. Curry, S.J.; James F. Duffy, S.J.; Stephen M. Fields, S.J.; Kevin T. FitzGerald, S.J.; Joseph A. Fitzmyer, S.J., S.T.L., S.S.L., Ph.D. (Retired); Gerald P. Fogarty, S.J.; Francis T. Gignac, S.J., S.T.L., D.Phil.; Timothy S. Godfrey, S.J.; Charles G. Gonzalez, S.J.; Howard J. Gray, S.J.; Patrick A. Heelan, S.J. (Ireland); Mark Henninger, S.J.; Otto H. Hentz, S.J.; Benedict Jung, S.J.; Mr. Francois Kabore, S.J.; Revs. Gustaaf M. Keppens, S.J.; John P. Langan, S.J.; Peter L'Estrange, S.J. (Australia); Lawrence J. Madden, S.J.; Daniel A. Madigan, S.J. (Australia); Ryan J. Maher, S.J.; John F. Martin, S.J.; Jean Baptiste Mazarati, S.J.; Paul J. McCarren, S.J.; William C. McFadden, S.J.; Dennis L. McNamara, S.J.; Ralph E. Metts, S.J.; G. Ronald Murphy, S.J.; Lan Ngo, S.J.; Eugene A. Nolan, S.J., Admin.; Jon J. O'Brien, S.J. (Retired); Kevin F. O'Brien, S.J., Exec. Dir. Campus Ministry; John W. O'Malley, S.J.; Ladislas Orsy, S.J.; Anatole France Pitroipa, S.J.; Alvaro Ribeiro, S.J.; Patrick D. Rogers, S.J.; Peter Rozic, S.J.; Andrew Rusatsi, S.J.; Solomon I. Sara, S.J.; James V. Schall, S.J.; Francis Schemel, S.J.; John R. Siberski, S.J.; Christopher W. Steck, S.J.; Rodrigue Takoudjou, S.J.; Anh Tran, S.J.; James P.M. Walsh, S.J.; John W. Witek, S.J.; Bro. Donald J. Dixon, S.J. Priests 55; Brothers 1.

The Jesuit Community of St. Aloysius Gonzaga, 19 Eye St., N.W., 20001. Tel: 202-336-7181; Fax: 202-336-7217. Email: rphillips@gonzaga.org. Revs. Thomas F. Clifford, S.J., Rector; Vincent G. Conti, S.J., Headmaster; George A. Aschenbrennen, S.J.; David R. Brooks, S.J.; Henry G. Heffernan, S.J.; Robert J. Kaslyn, S.J.; Raymond M. Lelii, S.J.; Joseph M. McCloskey, S.J.; Michael T. McNulty, S.J.; Kenneth E. Meehan, S.J.; J-Glenn Murray, S.J.; Allen P. Novotny, S.J.; Gerald V. O'Connor, S.J.; Bruce A. Steggert, S.J.; Timothy J. Stephens, S.J.

La Salette Formation Community (1968) 1243 Monroe St., N.E., 20017. Tel: 202-526-8070; Fax: 202-269-0775. Email: mlsadmin@aol.com. Web: www.lasalette.org. Revs. Clifford P. Hasler, Formation Dir., Post Novitiate; Peter D. Kohler, Dir., Pre-Novitiate; Romuald Rakotondraibe, In studies.; Bros. Joseph Lamartine Eliscar, M.S.; David Eubank, M.S.

Missionaries of La Salette Corporation

Leonard Neale House, 1726 New Hampshire Ave., N.W., 20009. Tel: 202-387-5375; 202-387-5376; Fax: 202-387-8220. Revs. Robert Ballecer, S.J., Dir. National Vocation Promotion of Jesuit Conference; Charles L. Currie, S.J., Pres., Assn. Jesuit Colleges & Univ.; Allan F. Deck, S.J., Exec. Dir. USCCB Secretariat Cultural Diversity in Church; Steven C. Dillard, S.J., Sec. for Formation, Jesuit Conference; Albert J. Diulio, S.J., Sec. for Finance & Higher Education, Jesuit Conference; Edward S. Fassett, S.J., Sec. Secondary & Pre-Secondary Educ. & Sec. Partnership Formation Jesuit Conference; Thomas P. Gaunt, S.J., Exec. Sec., Jesuit Conference; Kenneth J. Gavin, S.J., Supr. & Natl. Dir., Jesuit Refugee Svc. USA; James E. Hug, S.J., Pres., Center of Concern; Paul B. Macke, S.J., Sec. Pastoral Ministries, Jesuit Conference; James M. McCann, S.J., Dir., USCCB Office to Aid Church in Central & Eastern Europe; Very Rev. Thomas H. Smolich, S.J., Pres., Jesuit Conference; Revs. James A. Stoeger, S.J., Vice Pres. Jesuit Secondary Educ. Assoc.; Charles F. Kelley, S.J., Assistancy Planning Dir., Jesuit Conference. Priests 14; Total Staff 14.

St. Louis Friary, 831 Varnum St., N.E., 20017-2144. Tel: 202-529-0171; Fax: 202-832-8513. Revs. David Pivonka, T.O.R., Rel. Supr.; Alberto Bueno, T.O.R.; Ambrose Phillips, T.O.R.; John Shanahan, T.O.R.; Sean O. Sheridan, T.O.R.; Maurus Dolcic, T.O.R. House of Post-Novitiate Formation for Franciscan Friars, T.O.R., Province of the Most Sacred Heart of Jesus. Priests 6; Friars in Post-Novitiate Formation 9; Solemn Vows Relgious Brothers 1; First Vows (Students) 4; Total in Residence 15.

Marist Center (1900) 4408 8th St., N.E., 20017-2298. Tel: 202-529-4800; Fax: 202-526-2295. Revs. Thomas E. Dubay, S.M.; Joseph Fenton, S.M., Chap. Admin., The Claremont Colleges; James L. Hartnett, S.M. (Retired); Bruce Lery, S.M., Supr.; Thomas D. O'Donnell, S.M. (Retired); Joseph M. Pusateri, S.M. (Retired); Philip S. Gage, S.M.; Howard C. Smith, S.M.; Stanley W. Hosie, S.M. (Retired), 723 Palisades Beach Rd.,

Unit 211, Santa Monica, CA 90402-2479. Tel: 301-451-2479; Fax: 301-939-9562; Leonard P. Kellermann, S.M. (Retired), 4291 Richmond Rd., Warrensville, OH 44122-6199. Tel: 216-464-1222; Raymond J. Carr, S.M., Chap., Malta Court Apartments, 3500 Saint Claude Ave., New Orleans, LA 70117-6152. Tel: 504-943-6776; Fax: 504-948-9123; Richard K. Colbert, S.M. (Retired), Three Palms Pointe, Unit 801-W, 400 64th Ave., St. Petersburg Beach, FL 33706-2138. Tel: 727-367-8744; Joseph M. Fleury, S.M., Army Chap., CJTF 76 Chaplain, HSC, SETAF, Apo, AE 09354; H. Joseph Wilhelm, S.M. (Retired), Welty Apartments, 1276 National Rd., Apt. 409, Wheeling, WV 26003-5770. Tel: 304-242-5177. The Marist Finance Center of the Atlanta Province of the Society of Mary, Marist Fathers and Brothers.

Missionaries of Africa (1868) 1624 21st St., N.W., 20009-1003. Tel: 202-232-5154; Fax: 202-332-8640. Email: wcdyer@comcast.net. Revs. Sjef Donders, M.Afr. (Holland), Prof. Emeritus W.T.U.; John Lynch, M.Afr., Treas. & Dir of Devel. Office; George Markwell, M.Afr., Hospital Chap.; Jimmy McTiernan, M.Afr., Resident/Guestmaster; Jean-Claude Robitaille, M.Afr., Delegate Supr.; Richard Roy, M.Afr., Resident; Diego Ramon Sario Cucarella, M.Afr., Studies at Georgetown Univ.; Brian Denis Starkey, M.Afr., Treas.; Bro. James Heintz, M.Afr., Local Bursar Maintenance. Province of North America. Priests 8; Brothers 1; Total Staff 9.

Missionary Oblates of Mary Immaculate (1816) Tel: 202-529-4505; Fax: 202-529-4572. Email: province@omiusa.org. Web: www.omiusa.org.

Provincial Offices of the United States Province of the Missionary Oblates of Mary Immaculate (1999) 391 Michigan Ave., N.E., 20017-1516. Tel: 202-529-4505; Fax: 202-529-4572. Very Revs. Louis Lougen, O.M.I., Prov.; J. William Morell, O.M.I., Vicar Prov.; Revs. Seamus P. Finn, O.M.I., Dir. Justice & Peace; Bryan Silva, O.M.I., Dir. Special Svcs.; Thomas Ovalle, O.M.I., Councilor; Normand Bonneau, O.M.I., Prof.; Bro. William Johnson, O.M.I., Councilor-At-Large; Revs. Warren Brown, O.M.I., Councilor-At-Large; Joseph H. Hitpas, O.M.I., Treas.; Allen Maes, O.M.I., Councilor; William O'Donnell, O.M.I., Admin. Councilor & Personnel Dir.; Dale Schlitt, O.M.I., Prof.; Richard Sudlik, O.M.I., Councilor; William Antone, O.M.I., Councilor; Ronald Young, O.M.I., Prof.

Legal Titles and Holdings: *The United States Province of the Missionary Oblates of Mary Immaculate, Inc.* (1999) Tel: 202-529-4505; Fax: 202-529-4572. *Oblate Service Corporation* (1999) Tel: 202-529-4505; Fax: 202-529-4572. *Oblate Shrines and Renewal Centers, Inc.* (1999) Tel: 202-529-4505; Fax: 202-529-4572. *Oblate Title Holding Corporation* (1999) Tel: 202-529-4505; Fax: 202-529-4572. *Oblate Continuing Care Trust* (1999) Tel: 202-529-4505; Fax: 202-529-4572. *Oblate Education and Formation Trust* (1999) Tel: 202-529-4505; Fax: 202-529-4572. *Oblate Annuity Trust* (1999) Tel: 202-529-4505; Fax: 202-529-4572. *Oblate Endowment Trust* (1999) Tel: 202-529-4505; Fax: 202-529-4572. *Oblate Patrimony Trust* (1999) Tel: 202-529-4505; Fax: 202-529-4572. *Oblate Service Trust* (1999) Tel: 202-529-4505; Fax: 202-529-4572. *Oblate Real Estate Trust* (1999) Tel: 202-529-4505; Fax: 202-529-4572.

Oblate Community, 391 Michigan Ave., N.E., 20017-1516. Tel: 202-529-4505; Fax: 202-529-4572. Web: www.omiusa.org. Revs. William O'Donnell, O.M.I., Admin. Councilor & Personnel Dir.; Seamus P. Finn, O.M.I., Dir. of Justice & Peace; Charles Hurkes, O.M.I., Newsletter Editor; Very Rev. Louis Lougen, O.M.I., Prov.; Revs. Raymond A. Lebrun, O.M.I., Spiritual Dir. Natl. Shrine of the Immaculate Conception; George F. McLean, O.M.I., Dir. Center for Study of Culture & Values; Joseph H. Hitpas, O.M.I., Treas.; David N. Power, O.M.I., S.T.D., Prof.; Andrew Small, O.M.I., Policy Advisor, USCCB; Very Rev. J. William Morell, O.M.I., Vicar Prov.; Revs. Paul Waldie, O.M.I., Local Supr.; Bryan Silva, O.M.I., Dir. Special Svcs.; Daniel LeBlanc, O.M.I., Assoc. Justice & Peace Ministry; Bevil Bramwell, O.M.I., Prof. Priests 14.

Woodstock Jesuit Community, 1419 35 St., N.W., 20007. Tel: 202-337-7750; Fax: 202-687-5835. Email: woodstock@georgetown.edu. Revs. Gasper F. LoBiondo, S.J.; John C. Haughey, S.J.; J. Leon Hooper, S.J.; Thomas J. Reese, S.J.; George Karuvelil, S.J. (India); Daniel A. Madigan, S.J. (Australia). Priests 6.

ADELPHI, MD. *Father Judge Missionary Cenacle*, 1733 Metzerott Rd., MD 20783. Tel: 301-439-3171; Fax: 301-434-0848. Email: fjcenacle@aol.com. Bros. Richard McCann, S.T., Dir.; William Coombs, S.T., Asst. Dir.; Revs. Anselm Deehr, S.T.; Edwin Dill, S.T., M.A.; Stephen T. Ernst, S.T.; Bro. Boris Farrah, S.T.; Revs. Gabriel Hannan, S.T.; Maurice Haiss, S.T.; Daniel McLoughlan, S.J.; John McSpiritt, S.T.; Kevin Nugent, S.T.; Norbert Sharon, S.T.; Bros. Jordan Baxter, S.T.; Gregory Martin, S.T.; Hilary Mettes, S.T. Senior Ministry Residence.

Our Lady Missionary Cenacle (1992) 2717 Curry Dr., MD 20783-1725. Tel: 301-422-6100; Fax: 301-422-6199. Bro. Howard Piller, S.T., Supr.; Rev. Domingo Rodriguez, S.T.

BELTSVILLE, MD. *Ammendale Normal Institute of Prince George's County-La Salle Hall* (1880) 6001 Ammendale Rd., MD 20705. Tel: 301-210-7443; Fax: 301-210-7466. Email: ammendaleni@comcast.net. Bro. John P. McErlean, F.S.C., Dir. Brothers of the Christian Schools, Residence for Retired and Convalescent Brothers. Brothers 22.

BROOKEVILLE, MD. *Marian Monastery-Brookeville* Marian Residence & Marian Assisted Living, 19101 Georgia Ave., Box 220, MD 20833. Tel: 301-774-4478; 301-774-2242; Fax: 301-570-8645. Web: www.marian.org. Rev. Joseph Sielski, M.I.C. Priests 2.

HYATTSVILLE, MD. *Brothers of the Christian Schools*, 2301 Queens Chapel Rd., MD 20782-3673.

POTOMAC, MD. *Legionaries of Christ*, 10211 Norton Rd., MD 20854. Tel: 301-299-0806; Fax: 301-299-0809. Email: washington@legionaries.org. Revs. Anthony Sortino, L.C., Supr.; Ned Brown, L.C.; Steven Reilly, L.C.; John Hopkins; Michael Sliney, L.C.; Charles Sikorsky, L.C.; Daniel Wilson, L.C.; Bros. Andrew Gronotte, L.C.; Daniel Turski, L.C.

RIVERDALE, MD. *Holy Spirit Missionary Cenacle* (1996) 5809 Riverdale Rd., MD 20737. Tel: 301-277-7442; Fax: 301-209-0355. Rev. Louis Eugene Murphy, S.T., Local Supr. In Res. Revs. Sidney H. Griffith, S.T.D., Ph.D., Semantics & Early Christian Studies. Tel: 301-927-4919 Faculty, Catholic University of America; Edwin Dill, S.T., M.A., Dir., Office of Studies; John S. Edmunds, S.T., Supr. General; Bros. Stephen Vesely, S.T., Sec. General; Loughlan Sofield, S.T.

SILVER SPRING, MD. *Gemelli House* Franciscan Friars-Holy Name Province, 10400 Lorain Ave., MD 20901. Tel: 301-681-9478; Fax: 301-681-7170. Revs. Vincent de Paul Cushing, O.F.M., Guardian; Paul Lininger, O.F.M.Conv., Exec. Dir. Conference of Major Superiors of Men; John Burkhard, O.F.M.Conv., Pres., Washington Theological Union; Russel T. Murray, O.F.M., Washington Theological Union Faculty. Priests 5; Brothers 1. In Res. Bro. Hillary Hanrahan, O.S.B.

Missionary Servants of the Most Holy Trinity, Generalate, 9001 New Hampshire Ave., Ste. 300, MD 20903-3626. Tel: 301-434-0092; Fax: 301-434-0255. Email: generalate@trinitymissions.org. Web: www.mssst.org. Rev. John S. Edmunds, S.T., Gen. Custodian; Bro. Steven Vesely, S.T., Sec. Gen. & Gen. Councilor.

TAKOMA PARK, MD. *Society of African Missions (S.M.A.) House of Studies*, 209 Lincoln Ave., MD 20912-5738. Tel: 301-270-2008; Fax: 301-270-0132. Email: smausa-o@smafathers.org. Web: www.smafathers.org. Rev. Austin Charles Ochu, S.M.A., Local Supr. *Lay Missionary Program*, 256 N. Manor Cir., MD 20912-4551. Tel: 301-270-2009 (Home); 301-891-2037; Fax: 301-270-6370. Email: smausa-v@smafathers.org. Rev. Daniel Lynch, S.M.A.; Theresa Hicks, Dir.; Dr. Steve Price; Rev. Frank Wright, S.M.A.

[O] MINISTRY TO PRIESTS

KENSINGTON, MD. *St. John Vianney House*, 4214 Saul Rd., MD 20895. Tel: 301-942-1191; Fax: 301-942-1191.

[P] CONVENTS AND RESIDENCES FOR SISTERS

WASHINGTON. *Carmelite Sisters of Charity, U.S. Delegation Regional House*, 1222 Monroe St., N.E., 20017. Tel: 202-832-2114. Email: maureenfoltz@hotmail.com. Sisters Maureen Foltz, C.C.V., Regl. Supr.; Rosa M. Alvarez, C.C.V., First Councilor; Carmen Soto, C.C.V., Second Councilor; Francisca Mota, C.C.V., Sec.; Maria Pilar Chamorro, C.C.V., Treas.

Congregation of The Religious of Jesus and Mary, Provincialate (1818) 125 Michigan Ave. N.E., 4th Floor, 20017. Tel: 202-884-9795; Fax: 202-884-9794. Email: ereid@rjm-us.org. Sr. Eileen C. Reid, R.J.M., Prov. Administrative Team 4; Total Staff 1.

Other Residences: *Religious of Jesus and Mary* (1818) 6709 41st Ave., University Park, MD 20782. Tel: 301-779-0662; Fax: 301-779-3843. Sisters 4. *Religious of Jesus and Mary*, 4602 Clemson Rd., College Park, MD 20740. Tel: 301-699-3931; Fax: 301-927-4157. Sisters 3. *Religious of Jesus and Mary*, 3521 13th St., N.W., 20010. Tel: 202-265-8812; Fax: 202-265-1842. Sisters 4.

Franciscan Sisters of Atonement, 4000 Harewood Rd., N.E., 20017. Tel: 202-529-1111. Sr. Mary Harper, S.A., Dir. Sisters 7; Total Staff 9.

Georgetown Visitation Monastery (1799) 1500 35th St., N.W., 20007. Tel: 202-337-3350, Ext. 2283; Fax: 202-558-7976. Email: berchmans@visi.org. Web: www.georgetownvisitation.org. Sr. Mary Berchmans Hannan, Supr. Professed Sisters 16.

Institute of Our Lady of Mount Carmel (1854) *Scrilli Day Care Center*, 4415 8th St., N.E., 20017. Tel: 202-526-5106; Fax: 202-526-7101. Total Assisted 45; Total Staff 7.

Missionaries of Charity, 3310 Wheeler Rd., S.E., 20032. Tel: 202-562-6890. Sr. Mary Clovis, M.C., Supr. Sisters 7; Total Assisted 16,181.

Missionaries of Charity, Gift of Peace Convent (1986) 2800 Otis St., N.E., 20018. Tel: 202-269-3313. Sr. M. Lisseria, M.C., Supr. Total Assisted 75; Total in Residence 38.

Oblates Sisters of the Most Holy Eucharist, 2907 Ellicott Ter., N.W., 20008. Tel: 202-244-7714. Email: oblatesdc@hotmail.com. Sr. Margarita Jaime, O.S.S.E., Supr. Sisters 7.

Poor Clares of Perpetual Adoration (1954) 3900 13th St., N.E., 20017-2699. Tel: 202-526-6808; Fax: 202-526-0678. Email: ourprayer4u@poorclareswdc.org. Web: www.poorclareswdc.org. Cloistered Monastery of Perpetual Adoration. Cloistered Nuns 7.

Religious of the Sacred Heart Oakview Community., 1215 Perry St., N.E., 20017. Tel: 202-832-0071. Sr. Fleisa Garcia, Contact Person.

Rosary House of Studies-Dominican Sisters of The Presentation, 1201 Monroe St., N.E., 20017. Tel: 202-529-1768; Fax: 202-529-1768. Email: martesco@yahoo.fr. Sisters 4.

Sisters of Notre Dame de Namur, 145 Taylor St., N.E., 20017. Tel: 202-832-6240; Fax: 202-832-6270. Sr. Elizabeth Ann McFadden, S.N.D., Contact Person. Residence for Sisters. Sisters 4.

Sisters of the Holy Child Jesus, 1033 Newton St., N.E., 20017. Tel: 202-526-6832. Web: www.shcj.org. Novitiate Community. Sisters 3.

Other Convents:

St. Anthony's School Sisters 1.

Sisters of St. Francis of the Neumann Communities Emmaus Convent, 4309 19th St., N.E., 20018. Tel: 202-526-8017. Email: smcosf@aol.com. Web: www.sosf.org. Sisters Margaret Christi Karwowski, O.S.F., Contact Person & Treas.; Mary Farrell, O.S.F., Historian. Sisters 2.

Society of the Sacred Heart, 1235 Otis St., N.E., 20017. Tel: 202-832-1598; Fax: 202-526-3506. Email: kcollins@rscj.org. Web: www.rscj.org. Sr. Catherine Collins, R.S.C.J., Dir. Center for Educational Design & Communication. Tel: 202-635-7987. Sisters 3.

U.S. Delegation House of the Carmelites of Charity - Vedruna, 1222 Monroe St., N.E., 20017. Tel: 301-277-2963; 202-832-2114.

ANACOSTIA, WASHINGTON. *Missionaries of Charity (Contemplatives)*, 1244 V St., S.E., 20020-7016. Tel: 202-889-6100. Sr. M. Concepcion Membreno, M.C., Supr.

CLINTON, MD. *Religious Sisters of Mercy of Alma, MI* (1973) St. Andrew Home of Mercy, 6100 Wolverton Lane, MD 20735. Tel: 301-297-5617; Fax: 301-297-5618. Email: rsmofalma@comcast.com. Web: www.rsmofalma.com. Sr. Gabrielle Mary Braccio, R.S.M., Local Supr. & Contact Person. Sisters 10.

FORT WASHINGTON, MD. *The Missionary Catechists of St. Therese of the Infant Jesus, Inc.*, 2400 Brinkley Rd., MD 20744. Tel: 301-839-7751; Fax: 301-839-7751. Email: mcstusa@yahoo.com. Sr. Helen B. Sumander, M.C.S.T., Pres. Sisters 5.

KENSINGTON, MD. *Congregation of the Sisters of the Holy Cross*, St. Angela Hall, 4910 Strathmore Ave., MD 20895. Tel: 301-946-7750; Fax: 301-946-7751.

Sisters of the Holy Cross, Inc., Independent Living House for the Sisters of the Holy Cross. Sisters 29.

LA PLATA, MD. *Carmel of Port Tobacco* (1790) 5678 Mt. Carmel, MD 20646-3625. Tel: 301-934-1654; Fax: 301-934-0958. Web: www.carmelofporttobacco.com. Professed 11.

LAUREL, MD. *Pallotti Convent*, 404 Eighth St., MD 20707. Tel: 301-725-1717. Sr. M. Karen Lester, S.A.C., Sponsorship Dir. Professed Sisters 4; Total Staff 1.

NORTH BEACH, MD. *Sisters of St. Dominic of St. Cecilia of Nashville, TN, St. Anthony Convent*, 4104 First St., P.O. Box 600, MD 20714. Tel: 410-286-3393; Fax: 410-286-3275. Sr. Mary Juliana Cox, O.P., Convent Supr. Sisters 4.

RIVERDALE, MD. *Carmelite Sister of Christ - Vedruna*, 5410 56th Pl., #101, MD 20737. Tel: 301-277-2963.

SILVER SPRING, MD. *Sisters of Charity of St. Charles Borromeo, St. Elizabeth Convent*, 11320 Classical Ln., MD 20901. Tel: 301-681-9665; Fax: 301-681-0693.

Sisters of Mercy of the Americas - Institute Administrative Offices (1831) 8380 Colesville Rd., Ste. 300, MD 20910. Tel: 301-587-0423; Fax: 301-587-0533. Web: www.sistersofmercy.org. Legal Holdings: Mercy Action, Inc.; Mercy Volunteer Corps, Inc.; Sisters of Mercy of the Americas, Inc. Administrative Team 5; Total in Congregation 3,979.

Institute Leadership Team: Sisters Mary Waskowiak, R.S.M., Pres.; Patricia McDermott, R.S.M.; Eileen Campbell, R.S.M.; Anne Curtis, R.S.M.; Linda Werthman, R.S.M.

Sisters of the Good Shepherd, 504 Hexton Hill Rd., MD 20904-3300. Tel: 301-384-1169; Fax: 301-384-8889. Email: sg1504@aol.com. Web: www.goodshepherdsistersna.org. Sisters 4.

Sisters of the Holy Names (S.N.J.M.), 9603 Flower Ave., MD 20901. Tel: 301-587-1717. Email: kksnjml@gmail.com. Web: www.snjmusontario.org. Sisters 3.

Other Convents: *Sisters of the Holy Names (S.N.J.M.)*, 519 Varnum St., N.W., 20011. Tel: 202-829-8671. Sisters 3.

Sisters of the Holy Names (S.N.J.M.), 9212 Glenville Rd., MD 20901. Tel: 301-445-0309. Sisters 2.

Sisters of the Holy Names (S.N.J.M.), Church of the Annunciation, 3200 39th St. N.W., 20016. Sisters 2.

[Q] RETREAT HOUSES

WASHINGTON. *Washington Retreat House, Inc.* (1930) 4000 Harewood Rd., N.E., 20017. Tel: 202-529-1111; Fax: 202-259-2102. Email: washretreat@juno.com. Sr. Mary Harper, S.A., Dir. Franciscan Sisters of the Atonement. Sisters 7; Total in Residence 7; Total Staff 10.

FAULKNER, MD. *Loyola Retreat House*, P.O. Box 9, MD 20632. Tel: 301-392-0801; 301-870-3515; Fax: 301-392-0808. Email: director@loyolaretreat.org. Web: www.loyolaretreat.org. Rev. Frank T. Kaminski, S.J., Assoc. Dir. Total in Residence 4; Total Staff 5.

Staff: Revs. John Thomas Kelly, S.J.; Richard C. Schmidt, S.J.; Sr. Patricia McDermott, I.H.M., Dir.; Rev. Gerald J. Fitzpatrick, S.J.

UPPER MARLBORO, MD. *Our Lady of Mattaponi Youth Retreat and Conference Center* (1987) 11000 Mattaponi Rd., MD 20772. Tel: 301-952-9074; Fax: 301-952-0609. Email: mattaponi@adw.org. Total Staff 2.

[R] NATIONAL SHRINE

WASHINGTON. *Basilica of the National Shrine of the Immaculate Conception* 400 Michigan Ave., N.E., 20017-1566. Tel: 202-526-8300; Fax: 202-526-8313. Email: info@nationalshrine.com. Web: www.nationalshrine.com. Rev. Msgr. Walter R. Rossi (SCR), Rector; Revs. Raymond A. Lebrun, O.M.I., Spiritual Dir.; Michael D. Weston (ARL), Dir. Liturgy; Vito A. Buonanno (BRK), Dir. Pilgrimages.

[S] HOUSES OF PRAYER

WASHINGTON. *Catholic Information Center*, 1501 K St., N.W., Ste. 175, 20005-1401. Tel: 202-783-2062; Fax: 202-783-6667. Email: frarnep@cicdc.org. Web: www.cicdc.org. Rev. Arne A. Panula, S.T.D., Dir. Total Staff 7.

Madonna House, 220 C St., N.E., 20002. Tel: 202-547-0177; Fax: 202-547-8117. Web: www.madonnahouse.org. Cynthia Donnelly, Dir. Total in Residence 3; Total Staff 3.

[T] OFFICES OF CAMPUS MINISTRY

WASHINGTON. *Archdiocesan Campus Ministry*

American University Catholic Community Kay Spiritual Life Center, 4400 Massachusetts Ave., N.W., 20016-8010. Tel: 202-885-3327; Fax: 202-885-3317. Email: frwoods@stanndc.org. Rev. Keith A. Woods, Chap. Tel: 202-885-3327; Dr. Karin Thornton, Assoc. Chap. Tel: 202-885-3326.

Gallaudet University Catholic Community 800 Florida Ave., N.E., 20002. Tel: 202-651-5102. Rev. Gerard A. Trancone, Chap.

7202 Buchanan St., Landover Hills, MD 20784. Tel: 301-459-7467; 301-459-7464; Fax: 301-459-8186.

George Washington Univ. Newman Center 2210 F St., N.W., 20037. Tel: 202-676-6855; Fax: 202-676-6859. Very Rev. James J. Greenfield, O.S.F.S., Chap.

Howard Univ. Newman Center 818 Newman Center, 20059. Tel: 202-238-2687; Fax: 202-806-4641. Rev. John Raphael, S.S.J., Chap.

University of Maryland Catholic Student Center 4141 Guilford Dr., College Park, MD 20740. Tel: 301-864-6223; 301-864-6224; Fax: 301-864-8411. Rev. William D. Byrne, Chap.; Sr. Rita Ricker, R.J.M., Assoc.

St. Mary's College Campus Ministry P.O. Box 67, St. Mary's City, MD 20686. Tel: 301-862-4600. Rev. Francis W. Krastel.

[U] PERSONAL PRELATURES

WASHINGTON. *Prelature of the Holy Cross and Opus Dei*, 2301 Wyoming Ave., N.W., 20008. Tel: 202-234-1567; Fax: 202-238-0621. Web: www.opusdei.org. Revs. Arne A. Panula, S.T.D.; John Debicki; William G. Shaughnessy.

Other Centers:

Tenley Study Center, 4300 Garrison St., N.W., 20016. Tel: 202-362-2419; Fax: 202-362-0318. Revs. Gregory Coyne; Gerald S. Kolf.

[V] SECULAR INSTITUTES

WASHINGTON. *Community of Christ*, 1003 Kearney St., N.E., 20017. Tel: 202-832-9710; 202-797-8806; Fax: 202-265-3849. Email: frjohn@some.org. Rev. John E. Adams, Moderator. A Private Association Community of Archdiocesan Right for Priests, Lay Men and Lay Women. The Community of Christ Purpose is Simple Lifestyle, Poverty Ministry, Spiritual Growth and Prayer of Community Members.

HYATTSVILLE, MD. *Caritas Christi* (1937) 4619 LaSalle Rd., #15, MD 20782. Tel: 204-770-6450. Dr. Helen St. Denis, Former Pres. US-CSI (Retired). A Secular Institute of Pontifical Right.

WEST BETHESDA, MD. *Missionaries of the Kingship of Christ*, P.O. Box 34513, MD 20827-0513. Tel: 301-990-8630; Fax: 508-386-1417. Email: cdahlin@aol.com. Web: www.simkc.org. Rev. Gene Pistacchio, O.F.M. Tel: 617-542-6440.

A Franciscan Secular Institute of Pontifical Right., Tel: 301-990-8630; Fax: 508-386-1417. Rev. Gene Pistacchio, O.F.M., Ecclesiastical Asst. Tel: 617-542-6440.

[W] MISCELLANEOUS

WASHINGTON. **Africa Faith & Justice Network*, 125 Michigan Ave. N.E., 20017. Tel: 202-884-9780; Fax: 202-884-9774. Email: afjn@afjn.org. Web: www.afjn.org. Rev. Rocco Puopolo, S.X., Exec. Dir. Priests 1; Total Staff 3.

"The Americas" (1944) *Catholic University of America, Gibbons Hall*, Room B 17, 20064. Tel: 202-319-5890; Fax: 202-319-5569. Email: americas@cua.edu. Web: www.theamericasjournal.org.

Archbishop Carroll High School, 4300 Harewood Rd., N.E., 20017. Tel: 202-529-0900; Fax: 202-529-5989. Email: jbutler@archbishopcarroll.org. Web: www.archbishopcarroll.org. Records Center for the Archdiocese of Washington. Sisters 1; Lay Teachers 55; Students 654.

Alumni Office Tel: 202-529-0900, Ext. 160; Fax: 202-529-5989. Crystal Rucker, Dir. Devel. Tel: 202-529-0900, Ext. 160; Dr. David S. Stofa, Ph.D., Prin.; Ms. Nancy Berry, Librarian.

Archdiocese of Cotabato, 391 Michigan Ave., N.E., 20017. Tel: 202-529-4505; Fax: 202-529-4572. Most Rev. Orlando Quevedo, O.M.I., D.D.; Rev. Joseph H. Hitpas, O.M.I.

Association of Catholic Colleges & Universities (1899) One Dupont Cir., Ste. 650, 20036. Tel: 202-457-0650; Fax: 202-728-0977. Email: kladdbush@accunet.org. Web: www.accunet.org. Richard A. Yanikoski, Ph.D., Pres. & CEO. Total Staff 5.

Association of Jesuit Colleges and University, One Dupont Cir., N.W., Ste. 405, 20036. Tel: 202-862-9893; Fax: 202-862-8523. Email: office@ajcunet.edu. Web: www.ajcunet.edu. Rev. Charles L. Currie, S.J., Pres. Established in 1970, The Association of Jesuit Colleges and Universities (AJCU) is a national voluntary organization whose mission is to serve its member institutions, the 28 Jesuit colleges and universities in the United States, and its associate members. Though each institution is separately chartered and is legally autonomous under its own board of trustees, the institutions are bonded together by a common heritage, vision and purpose. They engage in a number of collaborative projects in the United States and around the world.

Black Leadership and Christ's Kingdom Society, P.O. Box 4579, 20017. Tel: 301-888-2566; Fax: 301-888-2566. Rev. Robert S. Pittman, S.S.S., Pres. Total Staff 2.

CARA, Center for Applied Research in the Apostolate (1964) 2300 Wisconsin Ave., N.W., Ste. 400, 20007. Tel: 202-687-8080; Fax: 202-687-8083. Email: cara@georgetown.edu. Web: cara.georgetown.edu. Sr. Mary E. Bendyna, R.S.M., Exec. Dir.

Carmelite Institute (1993) *Hecker Center*, 3025 4th St., N.E., Ste. 10, 20017-1102. Tel: 202-635-3534; Fax: 202-635-3538. Email: mail@carmeliteinstitute.org. Web: www.carmeliteinstitute.org. Dr. Keith Egan, T.O.Carm., Pres. Tel: 202-832-6622; Rev. John F. Horan, O.Carm., Exec. Dir.

Carroll Manor Nursing & Rehabilitation Center, 1150 Varnum St., N.E., 20017-2180. Tel: 202-269-7100; Fax: 202-269-7816. Rev. Msgr. Leonard F. Hurley, Chap.

Catholic Biblical Association (1936) *Catholic University of America*, 433 Caldwell Hall, 20064. Tel: 202-319-5519; Fax: 202-319-4799. Email: cua-cathbib@cua.edu. Web: cba.cua.edu. Rev. Joseph Jensen, O.S.B., S.S.L., S.T.D., Exec. Sec.

Catholic Daughters of the Americas Court #2344 - Our Lady of the Americas, 1510 Crittenden St., SW, 20011. Tel: 202-829-9034. Joan Tillery, Regent.

Catholic Historical Society of Washington, 619 10th St., N.W., 20001. Revs. William Richardson, S.F.O., Pres.; Paul F. Liston, Bd. Member (Retired).

Center of Concern (1971) 1225 Otis St., N.E., 20017-2516. Tel: 202-635-2757; Fax: 202-832-9494. Email: coc@coc.org. Web: www.coc.org. Rev. James E. Hug, S.J., Pres.

Centro Maria (1996) 650 Jackson St., N.E., 20017-1424. Tel: 202-635-1697; Fax: 202-526-1708. Email: centromaria@verizon.net. Web: www.religiosasdemariainmaculada.org. Sr. Clara Echeverria, R.M.I., Local Supr. Residence for young students and working women (18-30). Religious 6; Bed Capacity 40; Total Assisted Annually 160.

Christ Child Society of Washington, DC , Inc. (1887) 5101 Wisconsin Ave., N.W., #304, 20016. Tel: 202-966-9250; Fax: 202-966-2880. Email: info@christchilddc.org. Web: www.charityadvantage.com/christchilddc. Ms. Kathleen Curtin, Exec. Dir. A nonprofit, volunteer organization of approximately 600 persons serving children, regardless of race or creed, through layette distribution, school counseling, camp and uniform programs. Total Assisted 16,000; Total Staff 21.

Christ Our Hope Foundation, Inc., P.O. Box 29260, 20017.

Christian Brothers Conference, Hecker Center, 3025 Fourth St., N.E., #300, 20017-1102. Tel: 202-529-0047; Fax: 202-529-0775. Web: www.lasallian.info. Bros. Robert Schieler, F.S.C., Gen. Councilor; Gerard J. Frendreis, F.S.C., Dir. Finance & Admin.

Christian Brothers Major Superiors, Inc. Institutions owned and/or sponsored: Bethlehem University of the Holy Land; Sangre de Cristo Center, Santa Fe, NM; Christian Brothers Services, Romeoville, IL., Organizations and programs served by this office: Regional Conference of Christian Brothers; Lasallian Volunteers; Huether Lasallian Conference; Buttimer Institute of Lasallian Studies; Lasallian Leadership Institute; Lasallian Social Justice Institute.

Christian Life Communities, Washington Area Promoters: 5040 Nebraska Ave., N.W., 20008-2938. Tel: 202-363-4593. Ms. Margaret Fox. 201 E. Wayne Ave., Silver Spring, MD 20901-3808. Tel: 301-495-2969; Fax: 301-495-7318. Fred Leone; Betty Leone.

Communio: International Catholic Review, The Catholic University of America, McGivney Hall, 620 Michigan Ave., N.E., 20064. Tel: 202-526-0251; Fax: 202-526-1934. Email: communio@aol.com. Web: www.communio-icr.com. David L. Schindler, Contact Person.

Council for Research in Values and Philosophy (1983) The Catholic University of America, 20064. Tel: 202-319-6089; Fax: 202-319-6089. Email: mclean@cua.edu. Web: www.crvp.org. Rev. George F. McLean, O.M.I., Sec.

**Culture of Life Foundation*, 1413 K St., N.W., Ste. 1000, 20005. Tel: 202-289-2500; Fax: 202-289-2502. Email: info@culture-of-life.org. Web: www.culture-of-life.org.

Diocesan Laborer Priests, 3706 15th St., N.E., 20017.

District of Columbia Detention Facility, Office of Chaplain, 1357 E. Capitol St. S.E., 20003. Tel: 202-547-1715 (Office); Fax: 202-544-1385. Email: mbryantabc@msn.com. Rev. F. Michael Bryant, Chap. Total in Residence 2,500; Total Staff 15.

Don Bosco Cristo Rey Work-Study of the Archdiocese of Washington, Mailing Address: P.O. Box 56481, 20040-6481. Tel: 301-891-4750; Fax: 301-270-1459. Email: shafrans@dbcr.org. Web: www.donboscocristorey.org. 1010 Larch Ave., Takoma Park, MD 20912. Rev. Steve Shafran, S.D.B., Pres.; Ms. Alicia Bondanella, Exec. Dir.

**Education for Parish Service Program* (1978) 125 Michigan Ave., N.E., 20017-1094. Tel: 202-884-9020; Fax: 202-483-0253. Email: WaltzB@TrinityDC.edu. Web: eps.trinitydc.edu. Margaret McCarty, D.Min., Pres. Education for Parish Service Programs.

Engaged Encounter, 6514 7th Pl., N.W., 20012. Tel: 202-320-3254. Email: registration@dcengagedencounter.org. Adam Hughes, Registration Coord.; Mary Kate Hughes, Registration Coord.

Equestrian Order of the Holy Sepulchre of Jerusalem - Middle Atlantic Lieutenancy of the U.S., P.O. Box 29260, 20017-0260. Tel: 202-281-2480; Fax: 202-281-2488. Web: holysepulchre.net. His Eminence William Cardinal Keeler, D.D., J.C.D., Grand Prior; H.E. John C. Piunno, Lieutenant.

Ethiopian and Eritrean Catholic Mission, USA, 415 Michigan Ave., N.E., P.O. Box 29616, 20017. Tel: 202-529-8420; Fax: 202-529-8523. Web: www.catholic-forum.com/churches/kidanemehret. Rev. Tesfay Woldemarian Fesuh, Dir.

Fellowship of Catholic Scholars, John Paul II Institute, 415 Michigan Ave., N.E., 20017. Fax: 219-631-6371. Email: bdobranksi@avemarialaw.edu. Web: www.catholicscholars.org. Bernard Dobranski, Pres.

**Foundation for the Nativity & Miguel Schools*, 900 Varnum St., N.E., 20017. Tel: 202-832-3667; Fax: 202-832-8098. Email: jjordan@nativitymiguel.org. Web: www.nativitymiguelschools.org. Rev. Msgr. John W. Jordan, Exec. Dir.

The Franciscan Federation, Third Order Regular of the Sisters and Brothers of the United States, P.O. Box 29080, 20017. Tel: 202-529-2334; Fax: 202-529-7016. Email: franfed@aol.com. Web: www.franfed.org.

**Friends of the Pontifical Irish College, Rome, Inc.* (2000) 18 Beman Woods Ct., Potomac, MD 20854-5481. Tel: 301-983-3442; Fax: 301-649-1777. Email: frankcain@irishcollege.org. Web: www.irishcollege.org. Frank J. Cain, Pres.

**Imago Dei, Inc.*, 4393 Embassy Park Dr., NW, 20016. Tel: 202-962-0040.

Institute of Carmelite Studies and ICS Publications (1973) 2131 Lincoln Rd., N.E., 20002-1199. Tel: 800-832-8489; Fax: 202-832-8967. Email: brpaquette@aol.com. Web: www.icspublications.org. Rev. Kieran Kavanaugh, O.C.D., Publisher & Editorial Asst.; Bro. Bryan Paquette, O.C.D., Business Mgr. & Promotion Dir.

Jesuit Conference, Inc., 1016 16th St. N.W., Ste. 400, 20036. Tel: 202-462-0400; Fax: 202-328-9212. Email: usjc@jesuit.org. Web: www.jesuit.org. Very Rev. Thomas H. Smolich, S.J., Pres.; Rev. Thomas P. Gaunt, S.J., Exec. Sec.

Jesuit Missions, Inc., 1016 16th St., N.W., Ste. 400, 20036. Tel: 202-462-0400; Fax: 202-328-9212. Email: outreach@jesuit.org. Rev. Thomas P. Greene, S.J., Exec. Dir.

Jesuit Refugee Service (1984) 1016 16th St. N.W., Ste. 400, 20036. Tel: 202-462-0400; Fax: 202-328-9212. Email: kgavin@jesuit.org. Web: www.jrsusa.org. Rev. Kenneth J. Gavin, S.J., Natl. Dir.

Jesuit Secondary Education Association, 1016 16th St. N.W., 20036. Tel: 202-667-3888; Fax: 202-387-6305. Email: jsea@jsea.org. Web: www.jsea.org. Rev. Ralph E. Metts, S.J., Pres.; Bernard L. Bouillette, Ph.D., Vice Pres.; Rev. James A. Stoeger, S.J., Vice Pres.; Kathreja A. Mills, Communications Mgr. Total Staff 6.

Jesuit Social and International Ministries-National Office, 1016 16th St. N.W., Ste. 400, 20036. Tel: 202-462-0400; Fax: 202-328-9212. Email: outreach@jesuit.org. Web: www.jesuit.org. Rev. Thomas P. Greene, S.J., Sec.

Jesuit Volunteers International (1984) 1016 16th St. N.W., Ste. 400, 20036. Tel: 202-462-5200; Fax: 202-328-9212. Email: jvi@JesuitVolunteers.org. Web: www.JesuitVolunteers.org. Meghan Romey, Program Dir. Lay Volunteers 45; Foreign Missions 7; Total Staff 5.

Jesuit Volunteers, 1016 16th St., 20036.

The John Carroll Society, P.O. Box 454, Glen Echo, MD 20812. Tel: 202-537-6110. Email: jcs@johncarrollsociety.org. Web: www.johncarrollsociety.org. Gregory J. Granito, J.D., Pres.; Rev. Msgr. Peter J. Vaghi, J.D., V.F.

**John Paul II Fellowship*, P.O. Box 29482, 20017.

Knights of St. Jerome Bobby Gant, Pres.

McKenna House, 1501 Park Rd., N.W., 20010. Tel: 202-332-7333. Hagos Weldegiorgis, Prog. Mgr.

Morley Publishing Group, Inc., 2100 M St. N.W., #170-339, 20037. Tel: 202-861-7790; Fax: 202-403-3362. Email: mail@insidecatholic.com. Web: www.insidecatholic.com.

Mount Carmel House, 471 G Pl., N.W., 20001. Tel: 202-289-6315; Fax: 202-289-1710. Mary Bridget Klinkenbergh, Senior Program Mgr. Transitional Housing for Women with 20 beds.

National Black Sisters' Conference, 101 Q St., N.E., 20002-2166. Tel: 202-529-9250; Fax: 202-529-9370. Email: nbsc@igc.org. Web: www.nbsc68.tripod.com. Sr. Donna M. Banfield, S.B.S., Pres. Total Staff 3.

National Catholic Conference for Interracial Justice, 1200 Varnum St., N.E., 20017-2796. Tel: 202-529-6480; Fax: 202-526-1262. Deacon Joseph M. Conrad Jr., Exec. Dir.

National Institute for the Family (1979) 1200 Varnum St., N.E., 20017-2796. Tel: 202-302-1339; 202-557-4468 (alternate); Fax: 202-526-7811. Email: nationalinstituteforthefamily@gmail.com. Rev. Donald B. Conroy, S.T.L., Ph.D. (GBG), Pres.; Dr. Carolyn Gutowski, M.A.T., Ph.D., Assoc. Dir. Special Progs. Research Program: Parish Renewal, Intergenerational Ministry and Lay Leadership Formation in cooperation with the Christian Family Movement.

**Notre Dame Education Center* (1955) 330 21st St., N.E., 20002. Tel: 202-388-5029; 202-388-5027; Fax: 202-388-5028. Email: ndecdc@aol.com. Nonprofit, tax exempt adult education program for low income people. The center enables adults to earn a high school diploma and trains them in computers.

Oblate Missionary Society, Inc., 391 Michigan Ave., N.E., 20017.

Paulist National Catholic Evangelization Assoc. (1977) 3031 Fourth St., N.E., 20017-1102. Tel: 202-832-5022; Fax: 202-269-0209. Email: pncea@pncea.org. Web: www.pncea.org. Revs. Francis P. DeSiano, C.S.P., D.Min., Pres.; Kenneth G. Boyack, C.S.P., D.Min., Vice Pres.; Ms. Mary Weaver, Dir. Finance & Human Resources; Mr. Denny Marcotte, Dir. Production, Fulfillment & Facilities; Rev. Anthony F. Krisak, Dir. Training & Online Resources.

Pax Romana/Catholic Movement for Intellectual and Cultural Affairs-USA (1927) 1025 Connecticut Ave., NW, Ste. 1000, 20036. Tel: 202-269-6672; Fax: 202-269-6672. Email: pax.romana.cmica.usa@comcast.net. Web: www.paxromanausa.org. Edward "Joe" Holland, Ph.D., Pres.

RJM Endowment and Continuing Care Trust, 125 Michigan Ave., NE, 4th flr., 20017. Tel: 202-884-9795; Fax: 202-884-9794.

RJM Ministry Corporation, 125 Michigan Ave., NE, 4th Flr., 20017. Tel: 202-884-9795; Fax: 202-884-9794.

RJM Real Estate Trust, 125 Michigan Ave, NE, 4th Flr., 20017. Tel: 202-884-9795; Fax: 202-884-9794.

Rosary Shrine of St. Jude , Dominican Fathers and Brothers., St. Dominic's Church, 501 Sixth St., S.W., 20024. Tel: 202-554-7863; Fax: 202-554-3492. Rev. John A. Farren, O.P., M.A., S.T.L., S.T.D., Dir.

S.N.D.B.C. Charitable Trust, 1004 Newton St., N.E., 20017. Tel: 302-479-0077 (Day). Email: shsnd@comcast.net. Sisters Marie-Louise Rossi, S.N.D., Trustee; Theresa Kreibick, S.N.D., Trustee; Helen Bellew, S.N.D., Trustee.

Sisters of Notre Dame de Namur Base Communities, Inc. (1989) 125 Michigan Ave. N.E., 20017-1004. Tel: 202-884-9750. Email: sndbcunit@aol.com. Web: www.SNDdeN.org. Sisters 12.

Sovereign Military Order of Malta-Federal Association, 1730 M St., N.W., Ste. 403, 20036. Tel: 202-331-2494; Fax: 202-331-1149. Email: info@orderofmalta-federal.org. Web: www.orderofmalta-federal.org. Joseph J. Dempsey Jr., Exec. Dir.

Spanish Catholic Center, Administrative Office, P.O. Box 11450, 20008-0650. Tel: 202-939-2437; Fax: 202-234-7323. Email: infoscc@yahoo.com. Web: www.centrocatolicohispano.org. Rev. Donald F. Lippert, O.F.M.Cap.

Mt. Pleasant Branch, 1618 Monroe St., N.W., 20010. Tel: 202-939-2437; Fax: 202-234-7323.

Medical Clinic Tel: 202-939-2400; Fax: 202-232-1970.

Dental Clinic Tel: 202-939-2423; Fax: 202-234-7349.

Social Services Tel: 202-939-2414; Fax: 202-232-1970.

Immigration Services Tel: 202-939-2420; Fax: 202-234-7349.

Maryland Locations:

Langley Park Office, 1015 University Blvd. E., Silver Spring, MD 20903. Tel: 301-431-3773; Fax: 301-431-0886.

Adult Clinic Tel: 301-434-8381; Fax: 301-434-8067.

Pediatric Clinic Tel: 301-434-3999; Fax: 301-434-5160.

Piney Branch Office, 8545 Piney Branch Rd., Silver Spring, MD 20901.

Social, Employment & Immigration Services Tel: 301-587-0582; Fax: 301-587-8209.

Medical Clinic Tel: 301-929-0207; Fax: 301-929-0594.

Gaithersburg Branch, 117 N. Frederick Ave., Gaithersburg, MD 20877. Tel: 301-417-9113; Fax: 301-417-9895.

Social, Employment & Immigration Services Tel: 301-417-9113; Fax: 301-417-9895.

Spiritual Life (1954) 2131 Lincoln Rd., N.E., 20002-1199. Tel: 888-616-1713; Fax: 202-832-5711. Email: editor@spiritual-life.org. Web: www.spiritual-life.org. Rev. Regis Jordan, O.C.D., Notices Editor; Bros. Edward O'Donnell, O.C.D., Editor; Bryan Paquette, O.C.D., Business & Promotion Mgr.; Rev. David Centner, O.C.D., Book Review Editor. A Quarterly of Contemporary Spirituality. Priests 2; Total Staff 4.

**The Foundation for the Sacred Arts*, 1413 K St., N.W., Ste. 1000, 20005.

**The Paulus Institute*, 1201 Pennsylvania Ave., N.W., 5th Flr., 20004.

US Province of the Religious of Jesus and Mary, Inc., 125 Michigan Ave., NE, 4th Flr., 20017. Tel: 202-884-9795; Fax: 202-884-9794.

St. Vincent Pallotti Center for Apostolic Development, Inc. (1984) 415 Michigan Ave., N.E., 20017-1518. Tel: 202-529-3330; 877-865-5465 (Toll free); Fax: 202-529-0911. Email: pallotti@pallotticenter.org. Web: www.pallotticenter.org. Mr. Michael J. Goggin, M.A., Natl. Dir. Total Assisted 15,000; Total Staff 4.

**Washington Jesuit Academy*, 900 Varnum St., N.E., 20017. Tel: 202-832-7679; Fax: 202-832-8098. Email: wwhitaker@wjacademy.org. Web: www.wjacademy.org. William B. Whitaker, Pres.

**The Washington Middle School for Girls*, 1901 Mississippi Ave. SE, 20020. Tel: 202-678-1113; Fax: 202-678-1114. Email: smbourdon@washingtonmiddleschoolforgirls.org. Web: www.washingtonmiddleschoolforgirls.org. Sr. Mary Bourdon, Dir.

Womens Retreat League, 4000 Harewood Rd., N.E., 20017. Tel: 202-529-1111; Fax: 202-529-2102. Mrs. Leona Mahon, Pres.

Woodstock Theological Center, Box 571137, 20057-1137. Tel: 202-687-3532; Fax: 202-687-5837. Email: woodstock@georgetown.edu. Web: www.woodstock.georgetown.edu. Revs. J. Leon Hooper, S.J.; Raymond B. Kemp; Gasper F. LoBiondo, S.J., Dir.; John C. Haughey, S.J., Senior Research Fellow; Thomas J. Reese, S.J.; Daniel A. Madigan, S.J. (Australia), Senior Fellow.

ALEXANDRIA, VA. *Catholic War Veterans of the United States*, 411 N. Lee St., VA 22314. Tel: 703-549-3622; Fax: 703-684-5196. Fred Schwally, Natl. Commander; Lupita Martinez, Pres.

BETHESDA, MD. **Alliance for Communities in Action, Inc.*, 5403 Waneta Rd., MD 20816-2131. Tel: 301-229-0351. Email: allact@att.net. Deacon Richard Schopfer, Pres.; Juan Claudio Devincenti, Vice Pres.

Alpha Omega, Inc., Our Lady of Bethesda Retreat Center, 7007 Bradley Blvd., MD 20817. Tel: 301-365-0612; Fax: 301-469-7522. Email: manager@ourladyofbethesda.org. Web: www.ourladyofbethesda.org. Rev. John Hopkins, L.C., Pres.

Avondale Park Apartments, Inc. (1997) c/o Victory Housing, 5430 Grosvenor Ln., Ste. 210, MD 20814-2142. Tel: 301-493-6000; Fax: 301-493-9788. Email: info@victoryhousing.org. Web: www.victoryhousing.org.

Catholic Institute for the Psychological Science, Inc., 7007 Bradley Blvd., MD 20817. Tel: 203-281-4798. Bro. Juan Sabadell, L.C., Sec. & Treas.

Holy Family Hospital of Bethlehem Foundation, c/o James E. Murray Esq., 4706 Fort Sumner Dr., MD 20816. Tel: 301-320-1600; Fax: 301-320-0844. Email: info@hfhfoundation.org. Web: www.hfhfoundation.org.

Lay Women's Association, P.O. Box 34513, MD 20827. Tel: 301-990-8630; Fax: 508-386-1417. Email: cdahlin@aol.com. Web: www.simkc.org. National Headquarters of the LWA.

Mission Network Young Mens Program USA, Inc., 7007 Bradley Blvd., MD 20817. Tel: 301-365-7614; Fax: 301-299-0809. Email: msliney@legionaries.org. Rev. Jose Felix Ortega, L.C., Sec. & Treas.

National Christ Child Society, Inc. (1887) 4340 E. West Hwy., Ste. 202, MD 20814. Tel: 800-814-2149; Fax: 301-718-8822. Email: office@nationalchristchildsoc.org. Web: www.nationalchristchildsoc.org. Mrs. Margaret Saffell, Dir. Progs. & Chapter Rels. A national nonprofit organization with 40 affiliate chapters consisting of over 7,000 member volunteers serving needy children across the United States through educational and clothing programs.

Natural Family Planning Center of Washington, DC, Inc., 8514 Bradmoor Dr., MD 20817-3810. Tel: 301-897-9323; Fax: 301-571-5267. Email: hannaklaus@earthlink.net. Web: www.teenstarprogram.org. Sr. Hanna Klaus, M.D., M.D., Exec. Dir. Teen STAR & Holistic Sexuality Programs. Total in Residence 3; Total Staff 6.

Victory Crest, Inc., c/o Victory Housing, Inc., 5430 Grosvenor Ln., Ste. 210, MD 20814-2142. Tel: 301-493-6000; Fax: 301-493-9788. Email: info@victoryhousing.org. Web: www.victoryhousing.org. Mr. James A. Brown Jr., Pres. & CEO; John D. Spencer, Vice Pres. & COO.

Woodmont Educational Foundation, Inc., 7007 Bradley Blvd., MD 20817. Tel: 914-773-1368. Rev. Jose Felix Ortega, L.C., Contact Person.

BOWIE, MD. *Sodality Union*, 14720 Annapolis Rd., MD 20715. Tel: 301-262-2141; Fax: 301-262-2632. Rev. Lawrence Swink, Spiritual Dir. & Moderator; Elizabeth Coefield, Pres. Tel: 202-832-9226.

Washington Catholic Charismatic Service Committee, 16304 Pond Meadow Ln., MD 20716. Tel: 301-249-9199; Fax: 301-769-2541; 301-249-1303. Email: oremus2005@earthlink.net. Rev. John M. Barry, Dir.

COTTAGE CITY, MD. *Marriage Encounter-Worldwide*, 4011 Parkwood St., MD 20722. Tel: 301-395-5369. Email: dlf68@juno.com. Web: dc.wwme.org. Don Flanders, Contact Person; Wink Flanders, Contact Person.

FORT WASHINGTON, MD. *Birhen Ng Antipolo, USA, Inc.* (1997) 8504 Oxon Hill Road, MD 20744. Tel: 301-567-4914; Fax: 301-567-4914. Web: www.antipolo.us. Eddie D. Caparas, Pres. & Chm.

**Prison Outreach Ministry* (1982) P.O. Box 44325, MD 20749. Tel: 301-448-7026. Email: mbryantabc@msn.com. Rev. F. Michael Bryant, Chap.

GAITHERSBURG, MD. *Knights of Columbus*, 16584 Sioux Ln., MD 20878. Tel: 301-921-4035. Email: tryzub1@verizon.net. Lawrence Sosnowich, State Deputy.

GLEN ECHO, MD. *John Carroll Society*, P.O. Box 454, MD 20812. Tel: 202-537-6110. *Church of the Little Flower*, 5607 Massachusetts Ave., Bethesda, MD 20816. Rev. Msgr. Peter J. Vaghi, J.D., V.F., Chap.; Gregory Granitto, Pres.; Ms. Connie Mitchell, Exec. Dir. Tel: 202-537-6110.

HYATTSVILLE, MD. *Faith House, Inc.*, 4901 Eastern Ave., MD 20782. Tel: 301-559-5500; Fax: 301-853-6985. Email: maternity@stanns.org. Web: www.stanns.org. Sr. Mary Bader, D.C., CEO. Total Assisted Families 8.

KENSINGTON, MD. *Inter Mirifica*, 2812 Jutland Rd., MD 20895. Tel: 301-949-4840; Fax: 301-949-4840. Email: jdhoconnell@comcast.net. Rev. John Hardon, S.J., Founder; John O'Connell, Contact Person. Religious publications.

Victory Youth Centers, Inc., 10415 Armory Ave., MD 20895. Tel: 301-654-6200; Fax: 301-692-1990. Email: gdyer@dyercpa.com. Gregory B. Dyer, Pres.

LANDOVER HILLS, MD. *The Center for Deaf Ministries of the Archdiocese of Washington*, 7202 Buchanan, MD 20784. Tel: 301-459-7464 (TTY/Voice); Fax: 301-459-8186. Email: deafmindc@aol.com. Rev. Gerard A. Trancone, Dir. Total in Residence 1; Total Staff 3.

LAUREL, MD. *Pallotti Early Learning Center, Inc.*, 113 Saint Mary's Pl., MD 20707. Tel: 301-776-6471; 410-724-0097; Fax: 301-776-0019. Email: pelc.mia@verizon.net. Web: pallottiearlylearningcenter.com. Mia Laughlin, Dir.; Sr. Thomasine, S.A.C., Librarian. Sisters 2; Lay Teachers 11; Students 157; Day Care 76; After School 81.

MCLEAN, VA. *St. Francis de Sales Association*, 6671 McLean Dr., Mc Lean, VA 22101. Tel: 703-442-6615. Email: mitzijimison@cox.net. Mitzi Jimison, Directress of the Washington Group.

German Speaking Catholic Mission, Washington DC, 6330 Linway Ter., VA 22101-4150. Tel: 703-356-4473. Email: mschapfel@adwparish.org. Web: germancathwashington.com. Rev. Michael Schapfel.

MOUNT RAINIER, MD. *Dominican Fathers & Brothers Inc. Province of Nigeria, Development and Mission Office*, 4504 21st St., MD 20712. Tel: 301-927-0387; Fax: 301-927-0388. Email: nigopmissions@nig.op.org. Web: www.diafrica.org/nigeriaop. Rev. Anthony Akinlolu, O.P., Mission Dir. Priests 93; Total Assisted 153.

IVE Real Estate Trust, 3706 Rhode Island Ave., MD 20712.

MT. VICTORIA, MD. *Sacred Military Constantinian Order of St. George, American Delegation*, P.O. Box 7, Mount Victoria, MD 20661. Tel: 301-870-1033; Fax: 301-870-0993. Email: mountvictoria@aol.com. Web: www.realcasadiborbone.it. Michael J. Sullivan, Delegate & Contact Person.

POTOMAC, MD. *Potomac Pastoral Center Inc.*, 10211 Norton Rd., MD 20854. Tel: 301-299-0806; Fax: 301-299-0809.

ROCKVILLE, MD. *Archdiocesan Council of Catholic Women*, 520 Veirs Mill Rd., MD 20852. Tel: 301-424-5550; Fax: 301-424-5579. Rev. Msgr. Robert G. Amey, Moderator & Spiritual Dir.; Alice Wilson, Pres., 311 Wren Ct., Upper Marlboro, MD 20774. Tel: 301-249-1770.

SILVER SPRING, MD. *All Hallows Mission Fund, Inc.*, P.O. Box 3691, MD 20918. Tel: 301-593-4461; Fax: 301-593-4461.

Apostleship of Prayer, League of the Sacred Heart, 15107 Interlachen Dr., #722, MD 20906-5632. Tel: 301-438-3753; Fax: 301-441-4954. Web: www.apostleshipofprayer.org. Rev. Gerard P. Bell, S.J., Archdiocesan Dir.

Archdiocese of Washington Division, The Blue Army World Apostolate of Fatima, P.O. Box 4934, MD 20914. Tel: 301-589-7829. Mrs. Jane Baily, Pres.; Rev. Msgr. Charles E. Pope, Spiritual Dir.

Camp St. Charles, Inc. (1952) 104 Bishop Dr., MD 20905. Tel: 301-934-8799; 301-259-2645 (Summer); Fax: 240-523-9437. Email: glenwillis@verizon.net. Web: www.campstcharles.org. Rev. Glen Willis, S.D.S., Exec. Dir.; Ms. Laura Hall, Dir.; Bros. Roger Nelson, S.D.S., M.A., Asst. Dir.; Marvin Kluesner, S.D.S., Dir. Arts & Crafts. Priests 1; Brothers 2; Lay Staff 40; Children Served 600.

Catholics Committed to Support the Pope, 9402 Stateside Ct., MD 20903. Tel: 301-434-3245; 301-434-7763; Fax: 301-434-5486. Email: patmorse@comcast.net. George P. Morse, K.G.C.S.G., Pres. & Publisher; His Eminence Edward Cardinal Egan, Councilor; George Cardinal Pell, Councilor; Josef Cardinal Tomko, Councilor; Alfonso Cardinal Lopez Trujillo, Councilor; Most Revs. Timothy M. Dolan, Councilor; Donald W. Wuerl, Councilor; William E. Lori, Councilor; Peter J. Elliott, Councilor; Rev. Archimandrite Robert L. Stern, Councilor; Dr. William E. May, Councilor. Prepares, publishes and distributes world-wide thirteen-volume series of PRECIS OF OFFICIAL CATHOLIC TEACHING for use by rectors and faculty of seminaries, for seminarians, bishops, Catechetical Directors and DRE's, theologians and academics, for Catholic education courses and teaching, writers and teachers, Catholic Study Groups and laity. CCSP publishes and distributes "THE MASS: ITS MYSTERIES REVEALED."

Conference for Mercy Higher Education (2002) 8630 Fenton St., Ste. 934, MD 20910. Tel: 301-587-8988; Fax: 301-587-0077. Web: www.mercyhighered.org. Moya K. Dittmeier, Ed.D., Exec. Dir.; Paphasi Manickam, M.A., Exec. Asst. The Conference for Mercy Higher Education is separately incorporated for the preservation and development of the Catholic identity and mission of Mercy higher education in accord with the spirit, mission, and heritage of the Sisters of Mercy of the Americas. Each of the 16 active member institutions of the Conference is separately chartered and is legally incorporated with its own board of trustees.

Friends of John Paul II Foundation (1985) 9700 Rosensteel Ave., MD 20910. Tel: 703-790-1984. Email: virginiaegg@cox.net. Web: jp2friends.org. Rev. Klemens Dabrowski, S.Ch.; Raymond Glembocki, Pres. 2006-2007.

Holy Cross Health Corp., 1500 Forest Glen Rd., MD 20910-1484. Tel: 301-754-7000; Fax: 301-754-7413. Web: www.holycrosshealth.org. Mr. Kevin J. Sexton, Pres. & CEO. Includes Holy Cross Hospital, Home Health Agency, and other services.

Leadership Conference of Women Religious in the U.S.A., 8808 Cameron St., MD 20910. Tel: 301-588-4955; Fax: 301-587-4575. Email: director@lcwr.org. Web: www.lcwr.org. Sisters Marlene Weisenbeck, F.S.P.A., J.C.L., Ph.D., Pres.; Mary Hughes, O.P., Ed.D., Pres. Elect; J. Lora Dambroski, O.S.F., M.S., M.A., Past Pres.; Ellen Dauwer, S.C., Ph.D, Sec.; Elizabeth Ney, C.S.J., M.S.W., Treas.; Jane Burke, S.S.N.D., M.S.W., M.Ed, Exec. Dir.

Little Sisters of the Holy Family, 14000 New Hampshire Ave., MD 20904-6202. Tel: 301-236-4009; Fax: 301-236-4009. Sr. Domina Son, L.S.H.F., Supr.

Saint Luke Institute, Inc., 8901 New Hampshire Ave., MD 20903. Tel: 301-445-7970; Fax: 301-422-5400. Email: getinfo@sli.org. Web: www.sli.org. Rev. Edward J. Arsenault, S.T.L., Pres. & C.E.O. The Institute is a licensed and accredited treatment center for priests and religious, and a center for education and research. Total Assisted Annually 730; Total Staff 65.

Lumen Catechetical Consultants, Inc. (1982) P.O. Box 1761, MD 20915. Tel: 301-593-1066; 800-473-7980; Fax: 301-593-1689. Email: lumen@lifeaftersunday.com. Web: lifeaftersunday.com. Mr. John M. Capobianco, Pres. Provides Consulting & Production Services to Catholic Organizations; Assist in Development and Production of Catechetical Materials in Various Media. Publishes "Life After Sunday."

National Association for Treasurers of Religious Institutes (1981) 8824 Cameron St., MD 20910-4152. Tel: 301-587-7776; Fax: 301-589-2897. Email: trcri@trcri.org. Web: www.trcri.org. Sr. Hertha Longo, C.S.A., Pres.; Rev. Daniel Ward, O.S.B., Exec. Dir.

North American Conference of Provincials, Corporation National Advocacy Center of the Sisters of the Good Shepherd., 504 Hexton Hill Rd., MD 20904. Tel: 301-622-6838; Fax: 301-384-1025. Email: natlcor@gsadvocacy.org. Web: www.gsadvocacy.org. Sr. Gayle Lwanga Crumbley, R.G.S., Natl. Coord.

Sisters of Mercy of the Americas CCASA Community, Inc., 8380 Colesville Rd., Ste. 300, MD 20910.

Support Our Aging Religious, Inc. (SOAR!) (1986) (Support Our Aging Religious), 900 Varnum St., N.E., 20017. Tel: 202-529-7627; Fax: 202-529-7633. Email: info@soar-usa.org. Web: www.soar-usa.org. Sr. Patricia Sullivan, R.S.M., Pres.; Deborah H. Vornbrock, Dir. Grants Prog.

WHEATON, MD. *U.S. Foundation for the Congregation of the Holy Ghost and the Immaculate Heart of Mary, Inc.* (Sharelink - Spiritan Worldwide Aid Foundation), P.O. Box 2000, MD 20902. Tel: 877-443-1703; Fax: 301-942-5993. Email: spiritan@thespiritans.org. Web: www.thespiritans.org. Rev. George J. Spangenberg, C.S.Sp., Dir.

RELIGIOUS INSTITUTES OF MEN REPRESENTED IN THE ARCHDIOCESE

For further details refer to the corresponding bracketed number in the Religious Institutes of Men or Women section.

[0140]—*The Augustinians*—O.S.A.
[0200]—*Benedictine Monks*—O.S.B.
[]—*Brothers of Charity*—F.C.
[1350]—*Brothers of St. Francis Xavier*—C.F.X.
[0330]—*Brothers of the Christian Schools* (Baltimore Prov.)—F.S.C.
[0600]—*Brothers of the Congregation of Holy Cross*—C.S.C.
[0470]—*The Capuchin Friars* (Prov. of St. Augustine)—O.F.M.Cap.
[0270]—*Carmelite Fathers & Brothers*—O.Carm.
[]—*Congregation of the Sacred Hearts of Jesus and Mary*—SS.CC
[0480]—*Conventual Franciscans*—O.F.M.Conv.
[0260]—*Discalced Carmelite Fathers (Prov. of the Immaculate Heart of Mary)*—O.C.D.
[0520]—*Franciscan Friars (Commissariat of the Holy Land)*—O.F.M.
[0530]—*Franciscan Friars of the Atonement*—S.A.
[]—*Institute of the Incarnate Word*—IVE
[0690]—*Jesuit Fathers and Brothers (Prov. of Maryland)*—S.J.
[0730]—*Legionaries of Christ*—L.C.
[0740]—*Marian Fathers*—M.I.C.
[0780]—*Marist Fathers and Brothers*—S.M.
[0800]—*Maryknoll*—M.M.
[0850]—*Missionaries of Africa*—M.Afr.
[0720]—*The Missionaries of Our Lady of La Salette*—M.S.
[1210]—*Missionaries of St. Charles (Scalabrinians)*—C.S.
[0590]—*Missionaries of the Holy Apostle*—M.S.A.
[0840]—*Missionary Servants of the Most Holy Trinity*—S.T.
[0910]—*Oblates of Mary Immaculate (Eastern Prov.)*—O.M.I.
[0920]—*Oblates of St. Francis de Sales*—O.S.F.S.
[0430]—*Order of Preachers (Dominican) (Prov. of St. Joseph)*—O.P.
[1310]—*Order of the Holy Trinity (American Prov.)*—O.SS.T.
[1030]—*Paulist Fathers*—C.S.P.
[1040]—*Piarist Fathers*—Sch.P.
[0610]—*Priests of the Congregation of Holy Cross* (Indiana Prov.)—C.S.C.
[1070]—*Redemptorist Fathers* (Baltimore Prov.)—C.SS.R.
[]—*Salesians of Don Bosco*—S.D.B.
[0110]—*Society of African Missions*—S.M.A.
[1260]—*Society of Christ*—S.Ch.
[0990]—*Society of the Catholic Apostolate (Immaculate Conception Prov.)*—S.A.C.
[1200]—*Society of the Divine Savior* (Milwaukee, WI)—S.D.S.
[0420]—*Society of the Divine Word*—S.V.D.
[1290]—*Society of the Priests of Saint Sulpice*—S.S.
[0640]—*Sons of the Holy Family*—S.F.
[0700]—*St. Joseph Society of the Sacred Heart*—S.S.J.
[0560]—*Third Order Regular of Saint Francis (Prov. of the Immaculate Conception)*—T.O.R.

RELIGIOUS INSTITUTES OF WOMEN REPRESENTED IN THE ARCHDIOCESE

[0100]—*Adorers of the Blood of Christ*—A.S.C.
[1810]—*Bernardine Franciscan Sisters*—O.S.F.
[0340]—*Carmelite Sisters of Charity*—C.C.V.
[]—*Congregation of the Daughters of Mary Immaculate*—D.M.I.
[1170]—*Congregation of the Sisters of St. Felix Cantalice (Felician Sisters)*—C.S.S.F.
[3803-05]—*Congregation of the Sisters of St. Joseph* (Rockville Center, Brentwood, NY)—C.S.J.

[3832]—*Congregation of the Sisters of St. Joseph* (Baden, PA)—C.S.J.
[1920]—*Congregation of the Sisters of the Holy Cross*—C.S.C.
[0760]—*Daughters of Charity of St. Vincent de Paul*—D.C.
[]—*Daughters of Divine Love*—D.D.L.
[]—*Daughters of St. Anne*—F.S.A.
[0420]—*Discalced Carmelite Nuns*—O.C.D.
[1070-13]—*Dominican Congregation of the Most Holy Rosary* (Adrian, MI)—O.P.
[1070-03]—*Dominican Sisters* (Sinsinawa, WI)—O.P.
[1100]—*Dominican Sisters of Charity of the Presentation of the Blessed Virgin*—O.P.
[]—*Dominican Sisters of Our Lady of the Rosary of Fatima*—O.P.
[O.S.F.]—*Franciscan Sisters of Allegany, New York*—1180
[1470]—*Franciscan Sisters of St. Joseph*—H.F.S.J.
[1190]—*Franciscan Sisters of the Atonement*—S.A.
[0793]—*Handmaids of the Holy Child Jesus*—H.H.C.J.
[0410]—*Institute of the Sisters of Our Lady of Mt. Carmel*—O.Carm.
[]—*Institute Servants of the Lord and the Virgin of Matara*—S.S.V.M.
[2340]—*Little Sisters of the Poor*—L.S.P.
[2345]—*Little Workers of the Sacred Hearts of Jesus and Mary*—P.O.S.C.
[2490]—*Medical Mission Sisters*—M.M.S.
[2720]—*Mission Helpers of the Sacred Heart*—M.H.S.H.
[2710]—*Missionaries of Charity*—M.C.
[1475]—*Missionary Catechists of St. Therese*—M.C.S.T.
[2820]—*Missionary Sisters of Our Lady of Africa*—M.S.O.L.A.
[2900]—*Missionary Sisters of St. Charles Borromeo*—M.S.C.S.
[2865]—*Missionary Sisters of the Sacred Heart of Jesus and Our Lady of Guadalupe*—M.S.C.Gpe.
[]—*Oblate Sisters of the Most Holy Eucharist*—O.S.S.E.
[3210]—*Poor Clares of Perpetual Adoration*—P.C.P.A.
[3450]—*Religious of Jesus and Mary*—R.J.M.
[3460]—*Religious of Mary Immaculate*—R.M.I.
[2519]—*Religious Sisters of Mercy* (Alma, MI)—R.S.M.
[2970]—*School Sisters of Notre Dame*—S.S.N.D.
[3620]—*Sister Servants of Mary Immaculate*—S.S.M.I.
[0570]—*Sisters of Charity of Seton Hill, Greensburg, Pennsylvania*—S.C.
[]—*Sisters of Charity of St. Charles Borromeo*—S.C.B.
[]—*Sisters of Charity of the Blessed Virgin Mary*—B.V.M.
[0660]—*Sisters of Christian Charity*—S.C.C.
[1000]—*Sisters of Divine Providence* (Melbourne, KY)—C.D.P.
[2575]—*Sisters of Mercy of the Americas*—R.S.M.
[2630]—*Sisters of Mercy of the Holy Cross*—S.C.S.C.
[2990]—*Sisters of Notre Dame*—S.N.D.
[3000]—*Sisters of Notre Dame de Namur* (Maryland, Chesapeake & Base Communities Prov.)—S.N.D.deN.
[3360]—*Sisters of Providence of St. Mary-of-the-Woods, IN*—S.P.
[3893]—*Sisters of Saint Joseph of Chestnut Hill, Philadelphia*—S.S.J.
[1070-07]—*Sisters of St. Dominic of St. Cecilia* (Nashville, TN)—O.P.
[1650]—*Sisters of St. Francis of Philadelphia*—O.S.F.
[1600]—*Sisters of St. Francis of the Martyr St. George*—F.S.G.M.
[3830-13]—*Sisters of St. Joseph* (Brentwood, NY)—C.S.J.
[3890]—*Sisters of St. Joseph of Peace*—C.S.J.P.
[3850]—*Sisters of St. Joseph, Canondelet*—C.S.J.
[3980]—*Sisters of St. Paul de Chartres*—S.P.C.
[3150]—*Sisters of the Catholic Apostolate (Pallotine)*—S.A.C.
[1830]—*Sisters of the Good Shepherd*—R.G.S.
[1950]—*Sisters of the Holy Family*—S.S.F.
[1990]—*Sisters of the Holy Names of Jesus and Mary*—S.N.J.M.
[3270]—*Sisters of the Most Precious Blood*—C.P.P.S.
[3320]—*Sisters of the Presentation of the Blessed Virgin Mary*—P.B.V.M.
[4100]—*Sisters of the Sorrowful Mother*—S.S.M.
[1490]—*Sisters of the Third Franciscan Order* (Syracuse, NY)—O.S.F.
[1720]—*Sisters of the Third Order Regular of St. Francis of the Congregation of Our Lady of Lourdes*—O.S.F.
[2160]—*Sisters, Servants of the Immaculate Heart of Mary*—I.H.M.
[4060]—*Society of the Holy Child Jesus*—S.H.C.J.
[4070]—*Society of the Sacred Heart*—R.S.C.J.
[4120-06]—*Ursuline Nuns of the Congregation of Paris* (Toledo, OH)—O.S.U.
[]—*Vietnamese Dominican Sisters*—O.P.
[4190]—*Visitation Nuns*—V.H.M.

ARCHDIOCESAN CEMETERIES

WASHINGTON. *The Catholic Cemeteries of the Archdiocese of Washington, Inc.*, 13801 Georgia Ave., Silver Spring, MD 20906. Tel: 301-871-1300 (All offices 9-4:30 P.M.). Email: lkb@ccaw.org.
St. Mary's, 2121 Lincoln Rd., N.E., 20002. Tel: 202-399-3000. Anthony T. Covington, Mgr.
Mount Olivet Cemetery, 1300 Bladensburg Rd., N.E., 20002. Tel: 202-399-3000. Email: mto@ccaw.org. Anthony T. Covington, Mgr.

CLINTON, MD. *Resurrection Cemetery*, 8000 Woodyard Rd., P.O. Box 151, MD 20735. Tel: 301-868-5141. Email: res@ccaw.org. Christina S. Hammett, Mgr.

GERMANTOWN, MD. *All Souls Cemetery*, 11401 Brink Rd., MD 20876. Tel: 301-428-1995. Email: asc@ccaw.org. Michael R. Mazzuca, Mgr.

MECHANICSVILLE, MD. *St. Mary's Queen of Peace Cemetery*, 38888 Dr. Johnson Rd., P.O. Box 497, MD 20659. Tel: 301-932-1766. Email: qop@ccaw.org. John A. Spalding, Mgr.

SILVER SPRING, MD. *Gate of Heaven Cemetery*, 13801 Georgia Ave., MD 20906. Tel: 301-871-6500. Email: goh@ccaw.org. Samuel E. French Jr., Mgr.

NECROLOGY

† Jimenez, Rev. Msgr. Armando, (Retired)—Died Dec. 9, 2008
† O'Donnell, Rev. Msgr. William F., (Retired)—Died April 23, 2009
† Branch, Leslie, (Retired)—Died June 22, 2009
† Finch, G. William, Rockville, MD St. Raphael—Died April 9, 2009
† Higgins, John F., (Retired)—Died July 29, 2009
† Kemp, Patrick W., (Retired)—Died Nov. 18, 2008
† Murray, Paul Edward, (Retired)—Died Jan. 31, 2009
† Shaefer, Thomas S., (Retired)—Died July 22, 2009
† Sheehan, Thomas J., (Retired)—Died Aug. 24, 2009
† Twiddy, Paul, (Retired)—Died July 2, 2009

An asterisk (*) denotes an organization that has established tax-exempt status directly with the IRS and is not covered by the USCCB Group Ruling.

Diocese of Wheeling-Charleston

(Dioecesis Vhelingensis Carolopolitanus)

Most Reverend

MICHAEL J. BRANSFIELD

Bishop of Wheeling-Charleston; ordained May 15, 1971; appointed Bishop of Wheeling-Charleston December 9, 2004; ordained February 22, 2005.

Chancery Office: 1300 Byron St., P.O. Box 230, Wheeling, WV 26003. Tel: 304-233-0880; Fax: 304-233-4086.

Web: www.dwc.org

Email: acincinnati@dwc.org

Most Reverend

BERNARD W. SCHMITT, D.D.

Retired Bishop of Wheeling-Charleston; ordained May 28, 1955; appointed Titular Bishop of Walla Walla and Auxiliary Bishop of Wheeling-Charleston May 31, 1988; ordained to the Episcopacy August 1, 1988; appointed Seventh Bishop of Wheeling-Charleston March 30, 1989; installed May 17, 1989; retired December 9, 2004. *1300 Byron St., P.O. Box 230, Wheeling, WV 26003.*

Square Miles 24,282.

Established as Diocese of Wheeling July 19, 1850; Redesignated Diocese of Wheeling-Charleston October 4, 1974.

Comprises the entire State of West Virginia.

For legal titles of parishes and diocesan institutions, consult the Chancery Office.

STATISTICAL OVERVIEW

Personnel	
Bishop	1
Retired Bishops	1
Priests: Diocesan Active in Diocese	70
Priests: Diocesan Active Outside Diocese	1
Priests: Retired, Sick or Absent	41
Number of Diocesan Priests	112
Religious Priests in Diocese	52
Total Priests in Diocese	164
Extern Priests in Diocese	10
Ordinations:	
Diocesan Priests	3
Transitional Deacons	2
Permanent Deacons in Diocese	45
Total Brothers	12
Total Sisters	163
Parishes	
Parishes	111
With Resident Pastor:	
Resident Diocesan Priests	64
Resident Religious Priests	18
Without Resident Pastor:	
Administered by Priests	29
Missions	20
Pastoral Centers	4
Closed Parishes	1
Professional Ministry Personnel:	
Brothers	12
Sisters	163
Welfare	
Catholic Hospitals	3
Total Assisted	723,835
Residential Care of Children	1
Total Assisted	17
Day Care Centers	2
Total Assisted	200
Specialized Homes	1
Total Assisted	16
Special Centers for Social Services	11
Total Assisted	41,723
Educational	
Diocesan Students in Other Seminaries	10
Total Seminarians	10
Colleges and Universities	1
Total Students	1,288
High Schools, Diocesan and Parish	7
Total Students	1,649
Elementary Schools, Diocesan and Parish	25
Total Students	4,784
Catechesis/Religious Education:	
High School Students	861
Elementary Students	4,205
Total Students under Catholic Instruction	12,797
Teachers in the Diocese:	
Brothers	2
Sisters	4
Lay Teachers	469
Vital Statistics	
Receptions into the Church:	
Infant Baptism Totals	812
Minor Baptism Totals	140
Adult Baptism Totals	173
Received into Full Communion	185
First Communions	872
Confirmations	885
Marriages:	
Catholic	160
Interfaith	227
Total Marriages	387
Deaths	967
Total Catholic Population	82,996
Total Population	1,814,468

Former Bishops—Rt. Revs. RICHARD VINCENT WHELAN, D.D., cons. March 21, 1841; Bishop of Richmond; transferred to Wheeling in 1850; died July 7, 1874; JOHN JOSEPH KAIN, D.D., cons. May 23, 1875; transferred June 15, 1893, to the Titular Archiepiscopal See of Oxyrynchia; appt. July 6, 1893; Coadjutor "cum jure successionis" to the Most Rev. Archbishop of St. Louis, MO; created Archbishop of St. Louis, May 21, 1895; died Oct. 13, 1903; PATRICK JAMES DONAHUE, D.D., cons. April 8, 1894; died Oct. 4, 1922; Most Revs. JOHN J. SWINT, D.D., LL.D., appt. Auxiliary Bishop of Wheeling Feb. 22, 1922; cons. May 11, 1922; appt. Bishop of Wheeling Dec. 11, 1922; promoted to rank of Archbishop "ad personam," March 12, 1954; died Nov. 23, 1962; THOMAS J. MCDONNELL, D.D., LL.D., cons. Sept. 15, 1947; appt. Auxiliary Bishop of New York, June 21, 1947; appt. Coadjutor of Wheeling, "cum jure successionis," March 7, 1951; died Feb. 25, 1961; JOSEPH H. HODGES, D.D., ord. Dec. 8, 1935; appt. Titular Bishop of Rusadus and Auxiliary of Richmond Aug. 8, 1952; cons. Oct. 15, 1952; transferred to Wheeling See as Coadjutor, "cum jure successionis", May 24, 1961; succeeded to the See Nov. 23, 1962; died Jan. 27, 1985; FRANCIS B. SCHULTE, D.D., ord. May 10, 1952; appt. Titular Bishop of Afufenia and Auxiliary Bishop of Philadelphia June 27, 1981; cons. Bishop Aug. 12, 1981; transferred to Wheeling July 31, 1985; transferred to Archdiocese of New Orleans Feb. 14, 1989; retired Jan. 3, 2002.; BERNARD W. SCHMITT, D.D., ord. May 28, 1955; appt. Titular Bishop of Walla Walla and Auxiliary Bishop of Wheeling-Charleston May 31, 1988; ord. to the Episcopacy Aug. 1, 1988; app. Seventh Bishop of Wheeling-Charleston March 30, 1989; installed May 17, 1989; retired Dec. 9, 2004.

Vicar General and Moderator of the Curia—Rev. Msgr. FREDERICK P. ANNIE, V.G., Mailing Address: P.O. Box 230, Wheeling, 26003. Tel: 304-233-0880; Fax: 304-230-2231.

Chancery Office—Mailing Address: P.O. Box 230, Wheeling, 26003. Tel: 304-233-0880; Fax: 304-233-0890. Office Hours: Mon.-Fri. 8:30-4:30.

Chancellor—Mr. CHAD R. CARTER, M.B.A., B.A., Mailing Address: P.O. Box 230, Wheeling, 26003. Tel: 304-233-0880; Fax: 304-230-2029.

Assistant to the Bishop—Rev. Msgr. KEVIN M. QUIRK, J.C.D., J.V.

Priest-Secretary for Bishop—Rev. PAUL A. HUDOCK.

Diocesan Tribunal— All Rogatory Commissions should be addressed to the office of the Diocesan Tribunal, *Mailing Address: P.O. Box 230, Wheeling, 26003.* Tel: 304-233-0880.

Judicial Vicar—Rev. Msgr. KEVIN M. QUIRK, J.C.D., J.V.

Promotor Justitiae—Rt. Rev. JOHN M. LOGAN, O.Praem., J.C.L.

Defensor Vinculi—Deacon DENNIS W. NESSER, J.C.L.

Diocesan Consultors—Rev. Msgr. FREDERICK P. ANNIE, V.G.; Very Rev. ANTHONY CINCINNATI, S.T.D., V.E.; Rev. JOSEPH HAYDEN, S.J.; Very Rev. JOSEPH L. PETERSON, V.F.; Rev. Msgrs. SAMUEL S. SACUS, V.F.; P. EDWARD SADIE, S.T.L., V.F.

Delegate for Consecrated Life—Sr. ELLEN F. DUNN, O.P., Mailing Address: P.O. Box 230, Wheeling, 26003-0010. Tel: 304-233-0880; Fax: 304-233-4563.

Episcopal Vicar for Clergy—Very Rev. ANTHONY CINCINNATI, S.T.D., V.E., Mailing Address: P.O. Box 230, Wheeling, 26003-0010. Tel: 304-233-0880; Fax: 304-230-1583.

Vicars Forane—Very Rev. EUGENE S. OSTROWSKI, V.F., Wheeling Vicariate; Rev. Msgrs. SAMUEL S. SACUS, V.F., Beckley Vicariate; P. EDWARD SADIE, S.T.L., V.F., Charleston Vicariate; Very Revs. MARK WARD, C.P., V.F., Clarksburg Vicariate; WILLIAM P. LINHARES, T.O.R., Martinsburg Vicariate; JOSEPH L. PETERSON, V.F., Parkersburg Vicariate; DONALD X. HIGGS, V.F., Weston Vicariate.

Finance Council—Mailing Address: P.O. Box 230, Wheeling, 26003.

Finance Officer—Mr. WILLIAM G. FISHER, CPA, Mailing Address: P.O. Box 230, Wheeling, 26003. Tel: 304-233-0880.

Diocesan Offices and Directors

Apostleship of Prayer—Rev. Msgr. KEVIN M. QUIRK, J.C.D., J.V., Mailing Address: P.O. Box 230, Wheeling, 26003.

Archivists—Mr. RYAN RUTKOWSKI; Mr. CHAD R. CARTER, M.B.A., B.A., Chancellor, Mailing Address: West Virginia Catholic Heritage Center, 2000 Main St., Ste. 201, Wheeling, 26003. Tel: 304-230-2079; Fax: 304-230-2078. Email: rrutkowski@dwc.org.

Behavioral Counseling and Ministry—Rev. ROBERT G. PARK, Dir., Mailing Address: P.O. Box 230, Wheeling, 26003. Tel: 304-233-0880.

Diocesan School Board—Mr. BRANN ALTMEYER, Chm., Mailing Address: P.O. Box 230, Wheeling, 26003. Tel: 304-233-0880.

Buildings and Properties—Mr. DARRYL COSTANZO, Dir., Mailing Address: P.O. Box 230, Wheeling, 26003. Tel: 304-233-0880.

Catholic Charities West Virginia—Sr. MARY LOUISE LISOWSKI, S.C., Exec. Dir., Mailing Address: 1218 Eoff St., Wheeling, 26003. Tel: 304-233-0880; Fax: 304-233-9293. Email: mlisowski@dwc.org; Central Regional Office, 235 High St., Ste. 207, Morgantown, 26505. Tel: 304-292-6597. Eastern Regional Office, 521 W. Main St., #A, Romney, 26757. Tel: 304-822-5414. Northern Regional Office, 110 N. York St., Wheeling, 26003-0030. Tel: 304-230-1280. Parkersburg Regional Office, 521 Market St., #24, Parkersburg, 26101. Tel: 304-424-3457. Southern Regional Office, P.O. Box 386, Princeton, 24740-2909. Tel: 304-425-4306. Western Regional Office, 352 Mansion St., Hamlin, 25523. Tel: 304-824-5069. Weston Regional Office, 108 3rd St., Ste. #24, Elkins, 26241. Tel: 304-636-4875.

Child and Adult Care Food Program—Ms. ANNETTE "LYNN" WALLACE, CCWVa State Dir., 110 N. York St., Wheeling, 26003. Tel: 304-230-1280.

Child Care Resource Center—Mrs. TRACI KINNEY, Dir., Ste. #510, Mull Center, 1025 Main St., Wheeling, 26003. Tel: 304-232-1603.

Medicaid Program—Mrs. BARBARA HIGGINBOTHAM, CCWVa State Dir., 352 Mansion St., Hamlin, 25523. Tel: 304-824-5069.

WV Birth to Three - Region One—Ms. JUDITH BISCHOF, Dir., Ste. #502 Mull Center, 1025 Main St., Wheeling, 26003. Tel: 304-214-5775.

McDowell County Office—Ms. ANNETTE SHUMATE, Dir. (serving McDowell County) Mailing Address: P.O. Box 162, Eckman, 24829. Tel: 304-862-3320.

Catholic Community Homemaker Services, Inc.—Mrs. BARBARA HIGGINBOTHAM, CCWVa State Dir., Mailing Address: 352 Mansion St., Hamlin, 25523. Tel: 304-824-5069; Fax: 304-824-5070.

Diocesan Newspaper: "The Catholic Spirit"—Mrs. COLLEEN ROWAN, Editor, Mailing Address: P.O. Box 230, Wheeling, 26003-0030. Tel: 304-233-0880.

Diocesan Spokesperson—Mr. BRYAN MINOR, Mailing Address: P.O. Box 230, Wheeling, 26003-0030. Tel: 304-233-0880; Fax: 304-230-2029.

Catholic University, Friends of—Rev. Msgr. FREDERICK P. ANNIE, V.G., Mailing Address: P.O. Box 230, Wheeling, 26003. Tel: 304-233-0880.

Cemeteries—Mr. CHAD R. CARTER, M.B.A., B.A., Mailing Address: P.O. Box 230, Wheeling, 26003. Tel: 304-233-0880; Fax: 304-230-2029.

Censor Librorum—Rev. Msgr. KEVIN M. QUIRK, J.C.D., J.V.

Wheeling-Charleston Diocesan Council of Catholic Women—Sr. ELLEN F. DUNN, O.P., Diocesan Moderator, Mailing Address: P.O. Box 230, Wheeling, 26003. Tel: 304-233-0880; Very Rev. DONALD X. HIGGS, V.F., Diocesan Chap.; Mrs. BARBARA BELLDINA, Pres., PMB #102, 1111 Fledderjohn Rd., Charleston, 25314.

Computer Information Systems—Mr. RICHARD A. HARROLD, Dir. Technological Svcs.; Mrs. KAREN KOVACS, Coord. Technology Support Svcs.; Mr. ROBERT WICKHAM, Sr. Internet Technologies Engineer.

Stewardship and Development, Office of—Mr. BRYAN MINOR, Exec. Dir.; Mrs. KRISTEN BENSON, Dir.; Mrs. HEIDI SFORZA, Asst. Dir.; Ms. ANGELA ZAMBITO, Dir. Devel. Catholic Charities, Mailing Address: P.O. Box 230, Wheeling, 26003. Tel: 304-233-0880; Fax: 304-230-2029.

Diaconate Executive Committee—Deacon N. ROLLIN FAGERT, Chm., 202 E. Robinson St., Paden City, 26159. Email: rodgail2@verizon.net.

Finance Office—Mr. WILLIAM G. FISHER, CPA, CFO; Mr. ALEX J. NAGEM, CPA, Comptroller; Mr. FRANK BONACCI, Asst. Comptroller; Mr. JOHN L. HOFFMAN, Property Specialist; Mr. SCOTT M. MILLARD, Purchasing Agent, Mailing Address: P.O. Box 230, Wheeling, 26003-0010. Tel: 304-233-0880; Fax: 304-233-0890.

Office of Hispanic Ministry—

Martinsburg Vicariate—VACANT.

Holy Childhood Association—Rev. Msgr. FREDERICK P. ANNIE, V.G., Mailing Address: P.O. Box 230, Wheeling, 26003. Tel: 304-233-0880.

Diocesan and Foreign Missions, Office of—Rev. Msgr. FREDERICK P. ANNIE, V.G., Coord., Mailing Address: P.O. Box 230, Wheeling, 26003.

Diocesan (Home) Missions—Rev. Msgr. FREDERICK P. ANNIE, V.G., Dir., Mailing Address: P.O. Box 230, Wheeling, 26003.

Propagation of the Faith, Pontifical Society for—Rev. Msgr. FREDERICK P. ANNIE, V.G., Mailing Address: P.O. Box 230, Wheeling, 26003.

Human Resources, Office of—Mr. MICHAEL NAU, Dir., Mailing Address: P.O. Box 230, Wheeling, 26003. Tel: 304-233-0880.

Priests' Health and Retirement Association—Most Rev. MICHAEL J. BRANSFIELD, Pres.; Very Rev. ANTHONY CINCINNATI, S.T.D., V.E., Vice Pres. & Moderator; Mr. CHAD R. CARTER, M.B.A., B.A., Sec., Mailing Address: P.O. Box 230, Wheeling, 26003. Tel: 304-233-0880.

Justice and Life, Office of—Deacon TODD E. GARLAND, 1116 Kanawha Blvd. E., Charleston, 25301. Tel: 304-343-3360.

Migration and Refugee Services, Office of—Mrs. KIM KEENE, Dir., 1116 Kanawha Blvd. E., Charleston, 25301. Tel: 304-343-1036.

Health Ministry, Office of—VACANT, Dir., Mailing Address: P.O. Box 230, Wheeling, 26003. Tel: 304-233-0880.

Faith Formation, Office of—Ms. MICHELLE TOMSHACK, Dir., Mailing Address: 1322 Eoff St., P.O. Box 230, Wheeling, 26003. Tel: 304-233-0880.

Youth Ministry—Mr. JOSHUA WATTENBARGER, Coord., Mailing Address: 1322 Eoff St., P.O. Box 230, Wheeling, 26003. Tel: 304-233-0880.

Youth Adult and Campus Ministries—Ms. ANNA MARIE TROIANI, Coord., Mailing Address: 1322 Eoff St., P.O. Box 230, Wheeling, 26003. Tel: 304-233-0880.

Permanent Diaconate Formation—Very Rev. ANTHONY CINCINNATI, S.T.D., V.E., Dir.; Deacon LOUIS J. BELLDINA, M.S., Prog. Assoc., Mailing Address: P.O. Box 230, Wheeling, 26003. Tel: 304-233-0880.

Presbyteral Council—Very Rev. JOSEPH L. PETERSON, V.F., Chm., St. Margaret Mary, 2500 Dudley Ave., Parkersburg, 26101-2695.

Prison Ministry, Office of—

Federal Facilities—Deacon JOHN W. SARRAGA, Dir., Mailing Address: c/o St. Patrick, P.O. Box 99, Coalton, 26257-0099. Tel: 304-472-1216.

State Facilities—Deacon RUE C. THOMPSON JR., Dir., Mailing Address: c/o Holy Rosary, 35 Franklin St., Buckhannon, 26201. Tel: 304-472-1217.

Religious Unity, Diocesan Commission for—Rev. JOHN H. MCDONNELL, Chm. (Retired), 1116 Kanawha Blvd., E., Charleston, 25301. Tel: 304-925-2864.

Safe Environment, Office of—Deacon DOUGLAS W. BREIDING, Coord., 1310 Byron St., Wheeling, 26003. Tel: 304-233-0880.

Diocesan Committee on Scouting—Mr. DAVID TAMPLEN, Chm.; Rev. DENNIS R. SCHUELKENS JR., Diocesan Chap. to Boy Scouts of America.

Victim Assistance Coordinator—Dr. PATRICIA M. BAILEY, Ph.D., Professional Center III, Ste. 231, 30 Medical Park, Wheeling, 26003. Contacts to Report: Rev. Msgr. FREDERICK P. ANNIE, V.G. Email: fannie@dwc.org; Very Rev. ANTHONY CINCINNATI, S.T.D., V.E., Episcopal Vicar for Clergy. Email: acincinnati@dwc.org. Tel: 304-233-0880; Sr. ELLEN F. DUNN, O.P. Email: edunn@dwc.org; Mr. BRYAN MINOR. Email: bminor@dwc.org.

Vocations, Office of—Rev. PAUL A. HUDOCK, Dir., Mailing Address: P.O. Box 230, Wheeling, 26003-0010.

Vocations Promoters—Revs. CHRISTOPHER M. TURNER; DENNIS R. SCHUELKENS JR.

Catholic Conference of West Virginia—Rev. Msgr. P. EDWARD SADIE, S.T.L., V.F., Exec. Dir.; Rev. BRIAN P. O'DONNELL, S.J., Ph.D., Exec. Sec., Mailing Address: 1116 Kanawah Blvd. E., Charleston, 25301-2407.

Women, Office of—Sr. ELLEN F. DUNN, O.P., Dir., Mailing Address: P.O. Box 230, Wheeling, 26003-0010. Tel: 304-233-0880.

Catholic Charismatic Renewal—Deacon GARY W. LANE, Liaison, Mailing Address: Blessed John XXIII Pastoral Center, 100 Hodges Rd., Charleston, 25314. Tel: 304-342-0507; Fax: 304-342-4786.

Cursillo—Mr. EDWARD A. MARN, Lay Dir., 200 Church St., Paden City, 26159. Tel: 304-337-8005.

Pregnancy and Parenting Program—Mrs. ELLEN VANCE, Dir., 1116 Kanawha Blvd. E., Charleston, 25301. Tel: 304-380-0155; Fax: 304-380-0156.

Right from the Start Lead Agency—Mrs. SUELLEN FRIEND, Mull Center #500, 1025 Main St., Wheeling, 26003. Tel: 304-230-2229; Fax: 304-230-2228.

Office of Worship and Sacraments—Ms. BERNADETTE MCMASTERS, Dir., Mailing Address: P.O. Box 230, Wheeling, 26003-0030. Tel: 304-233-0880.

Diocesan Liturgical Commission—Ms. BERNADETTE MCMASTERS, Mailing Address: 1310 Byron St., P.O. Box 230, Wheeling, 26003. Tel: 304-233-0880.

Department of Catholic Schools—

Schools, Superintendent of—Sr. ELAINE POITRAS, C.S.C., Ph.D., Supt.

Associate Superintendent of Schools—Ms. ROBYN HAMMOND, Dir., Mailing Address: P.O. Box 230, Wheeling, 26003-0030. Tel: 304-233-0880.

Instructional Technology—Ms. JENNIFER L. HORNYAK, Dir., Mailing Address: P.O. Box 230, Wheeling, 26003. Tel: 304-233-0880.

CLERGY, PARISHES, MISSIONS AND PAROCHIAL SCHOOLS

CITY OF WHEELING

(OHIO COUNTY)

1—ST. JOSEPH'S CATHEDRAL (1828), Including former parishes: Blessed Trinity, St. Joan of Arc, and Sacred Heart. Rev. Msgr. Kevin M. Quirk, Rector; Mr. Chris Bayardi, Pastoral Assoc. In Res., Very Rev. Anthony Cincinnati; Rev. Robert G. Park.

Res.: 14 13th St., 26003-0051. Tel: 304-233-4121; Fax: 304-233-4129.

School—Wheeling Catholic Elementary School, 77 14th St., 26003. Tel: 304-233-1515. Mary Alice Florio, Prin.

2—ST. ALPHONSUS (1856), Including former parishes St. Mary and St. Ladislaus. Revs. Francis A. O'Kruta; Charles E. McGinnis Jr.; Deacon George Smoulder.

Church & Res. Address: 2111 Market St., 26003-3827. Tel: 304-232-4353; Fax: 304-232-1993.

School—Wheeling Catholic Elementary School 26003. Tel: 304-233-1515.

3—BLESSED TRINITY (1931) Closed. Merged with St. Joseph's Cathedral.

4—CORPUS CHRISTI (1916) Very Rev. Eugene S. Ostrowski; Deacon Douglas W. Breiding.

Mailing Address: 1518 Warwood Ave., 26003-7197.

Res.: 1516 Warwood Ave., 26003-7197. Tel: 304-277-2911; Fax: 304-277-1287.

School—Tel: 304-277-1220; Fax: 304-277-2823. Mr. Dick Taylor, Prin. Dominican Sisters 1; Lay Teachers 11; Students 188.

Catechesis/Religious Program—Students 71.

5—IMMACULATE CONCEPTION (ST. MARY) (1873) Closed. Merged with St. Alphonsus.

6—ST. JOAN OF ARC (1923) Closed. Merged with St. Joseph's Cathedral.

7—ST. LADISLAUS (1902) Closed. Merged with St. Alphonsus.

8—ST. MICHAEL (1897) [CEM] Revs. Jeremiah F. McSweeney; Joseph Daniel Pisano, Parochial Vicar.

Church & Res.: 1225 National Rd., 26003-5791. Tel: 304-242-1560; Fax: 304-243-5710. Email: stmikes@stmikesparish.org. Web: www.stmikesparish.org.

School—1221 National Rd., 26003. Tel: 304-242-3966; Fax: 304-214-6578. Email: school@stmikesparish.org. Mrs. Marilyn Richardson, Prin. Lay Teachers 25.

Catechesis/Religious Program—Students 90.

9—OUR LADY OF PEACE (Mt. Olivet) (1962) Rev. Dennis R. Schuelkens Jr., Admin.

Res.: 2 Allendale Rd., Mt. Olivet, 26003-4602. Tel: 304-242-6575.

School—Tel: 304-242-1383; Fax: 304-243-5410. Mrs. C'Ann Reilly, Prin. Lay Teachers 14; Students 192.

Catechesis/Religious Program—Students 22.

10—SACRED HEART (1903) Closed. Merged with St. Joseph's Cathedral.

11—ST. VINCENT DE PAUL (1895) [CEM] Revs. James F. McGoldrick, S.M; Edwin Keel, S.M.; Sr. Diane McCalley, C.S.J., Pastoral Assoc. In Res., Rev. William Seli, S.M.

Res.: 2244 Marshall Ave., 26003-7440. Tel: 304-242-0406; Fax: 304-243-0837. Email: stvincentdepaulparish@juno.com. Web: www.stratuswave.net/~vincent.

School—127 Key Ave., 26003. Tel: 304-242-5844; Fax: 304-243-1624. Mrs. Arica Holt, Prin. Lay Teachers 18; Students 196.

Catechesis/Religious Program—Students 81.

Mission—Our Lady of Seven Dolors [CEM] Chapel Hill Rd., Triadelphia, Ohio Co. 26059. Tel: 304-547-5342.

CITY OF CHARLESTON

(KANAWHA COUNTY)

1—ST. AGNES (1923) Rev. John McDonough.
Res.: 4807 Staunton Ave., S.E., 25304. Tel: 304-925-2836; Fax: 304-925-2854. Email: stagneschurch@suddenlink.net.
School—4801 Staunton Ave., S.E., 25304. Tel: 304-925-4341; Fax: 304-925-4423. Mrs. Theresa O'Leary, Prin. Lay Teachers 13; Students 130.
Catechesis/Religious Program—Students 44.

2—ST. ANTHONY (1905) Rev. Dennis J. Klemash, O.F.M.Cap.; Deacon David Wuletich. In Res., Rev. Kieran Quinn, O.F.M.Cap. (Retired); Bro. Thomas Wells, O.F.M.Cap.; Rev. Roy Schuster, O.F.M.Cap (Retired).
Res.: 1000 Sixth St., 25302. Tel: 304-342-2716; Fax: 304-342-2716.
School—1027 6th St., 25302. Tel: 304-346-8441. Mrs. Susan Maddox, Prin. Lay Teachers 11; Religious 1; Students 90.
Catechesis/Religious Program—Students 18.

3—BASILICA OF THE CO-CATHEDRAL OF THE SACRED HEART (1866) [CEM] Rev. Msgr. P. Edward Sadie, Rector; Rev. Carlos L. Melocoton Jr., Assoc. Rector; Mrs. Ann Weimar, Pastoral Assoc.
Rectory—1114 Virginia St. E., 25301-2879. Tel: 304-342-8175; Fax: 304-344-3907. Email: sacredheart@shccwv.us. Web: www.shccwv.us.
Church: 1032 Virginia St. E., 25301-2879. Tel: 304-414-4700.
School—1035 Quarrier St. E., 25301. Tel: 304-346-5491. Web: shgs.us. Mrs. Terri L. Maier, Prin. Lay Teachers 27; Students 390.
Catechesis/Religious Program—Students 115.

OUTSIDE THE CITIES OF WHEELING AND CHARLESTON

ALDERSON, GREENBRIER CO., ST. MARY (1978), See St. Patrick, Hinton

ANSTED, FAYETTE CO., MISSION OF JESUS OUR SAVIOR, Mission has been suppressed. Records are at Immaculate Conception, Montgomery.

BANCROFT, PUTNAM CO., ST. PATRICK Rev. Manuel T. Gelido, Admin.

BARRACKVILLE, MARION CO., ALL SAINTS, Merged with St. Joseph, Fairmont; St. Anthony, Grant Town, and Our Lady of the Assumption, Rivesville to form St. Peter the Fisherman, Fairmont.

BARTOW, POCAHONTAS CO., ST. MARK, See St. John Neumann, Marlinton

BECKLEY, RALEIGH CO., ST. FRANCIS DE SALES (1907) [CEM] Rev. Msgr. Samuel S. Sacus; Rev. Joshua R. Stevens; Deacons W. Donald Wise; John F. Ziolkowski.
Res.: 614 S. Oakwood Ave., 25801. Tel: 304-253-3695 (Parish Office); 304-256-3594 (Rectory); Fax: 304-253-3694. Email: church@stfrancis-wv.org. Web: www.stfrancis-wv.org.
School—622 S. Oakwood Ave., 25801. Tel: 304-252-4087; Fax: 304-252-4087. Email: sfschool@suddenlinkmail.com. Mrs. Karen Wynne, Prin. Lay Teachers 13; Students 158.
Montessori School—Lay Teachers 1; Students 10.
Catechesis/Religious Program—626 S. Oakwood Ave., 25801. Tel: 304-255-4694. Email: osfjanice@stfrancis-wv.org. Students 95.

BEECH BOTTOM, BROOKE CO., HOLY FAMILY, Closed. See St. John, Wellsburg.

BELLE, KANAWHA CO., ST. JOHN (1951) Rev. Albert Alexandrunas, O.F.M.Cap.
Res.: 321 E. Tenth St., 25015. Tel: 304-949-3063.
Catechesis/Religious Program—Students 12.
Mission—Good Shepherd 1013 First Ave., Box 16, Coalburg, Kanawha Co. 25067. Tel: 304-595-6002.

BENWOOD, MARSHALL CO., ST. JOHN'S (1875) Rev. Joseph Hayden, S.J.
Res.: 622 Main St., 26031. Tel: 304-232-6455; Fax: 304-232-6455.
School—Sts. James and John Consolidated School, Tel: 304-232-1587. Mrs. Jennifer Marsh, Prin. Lay Teachers 14; Students 103.

BERKELEY SPRINGS, MORGAN CO., ST. VINCENT DE PAUL (1931) [CEM] Rev. Leonard A. Smith; Deacons John W. Locke; Robert B. Lilly. In Res., Rev. Patrick J. Gillooly (Retired).
Res.: 38 S. Mercer St., 25411. Tel: 304-258-1311; Fax: 304-258-3936.
Catechesis/Religious Program—Students 50.
Mission—St. Charles

BLUEFIELD, MERCER CO., SACRED HEART (1895) Rev. Paul J. Wharton; Deacon Donald Hammond.
Res.: 1003 Wyoming St., P.O. Box 608, 24701-0608. Tel: 304-327-5623; Fax: 304-327-7769. Email: shcc@sacredheartblfd.org. Web: www.sacredheartblfd.org.
Catechesis/Religious Program—Students 72.

BOOMER, FAYETTE CO., ST. ANTHONY'S SHRINE (1954), See Immaculate Conception, Montgomery

BRIDGEPORT, HARRISON CO., ALL SAINTS (1946) Rev. Harry N. Cramer.
Res.: 317 E. Main St., 26330-1750. Tel: 304-842-2283; Fax: 304-842-2299. Email: ascwv1@verizon.net. Web: allsaintsbridgeport.com.
School—Harrison Co. Catholic School System, Tel: 304-624-5129.
Catechesis/Religious Program—Students 173.

BRUCETON MILLS, PRESTON CO., MARY HELP OF CHRISTIANS (1983), See St. Luke, Cheat Lake

BUCKHANNON, UPSHUR CO., HOLY ROSARY (1921) Rev. Ronald J. Nikodem, S.M.; Bro. Roy Madigan, S.M.; Deacon Rue Thompson Jr.
Church: 35 Franklin St., P.O. Box 848, 26201-0848. Tel: 304-472-3414; Fax: 304-472-6502.
Rectory—9 Lincoln Heights, 26021.
Catechesis/Religious Program—Students 56.
Mission—Sacred Heart (1902) [CEM] Pickens, Randolph Co. 26230.

BURNSVILLE, BRAXTON CO., ST. MICHAEL'S CENTER, See St. Thomas, Gassaway

CAIRO, RITCHIE CO., ST. WILLIAM CHURCH, Closed. See Christ Our Hope, Harrisville

CAMDEN, LEWIS CO., ST. BONIFACE (Leading Creek) (1875) [CEM] Rev. George Manjadi.
Res.: 9140 U.S. Hwy. 33 W., 26338-8256. Tel: 304-269-1767.
Chapel—St. Clare, St. Clare [CEM]
Catechesis/Religious Program—Students 3.

CAMERON, MARSHALL CO., ST. MARTIN (1871) [CEM] Unassigned.Mailing Address: RR 1, Box 203, Proctor, 26055.
Church: 5 Fitzgerald Ave., 26033. Tel: 304-455-4303.

CAROLINA, MARION CO., ST. MARY, See St. Peter, Farmington, 204 Furbee Ave., Mannington, 26582-1399.

CENTURY, UPSHUR CO., OUR LADY OF SORROWS, See Holy Rosary, Buckhannon

CHAPMANVILLE, LOGAN CO., ST. BARBARA, See St. Francis, Logan
Catechesis/Religious Program—Students 6.

CHARLES TOWN, JEFFERSON CO., ST. JAMES (1889) [CEM], Includes St. Peter, Harper's Ferry. Revs. S. Brian Owens; Carl E. Vacek, T.O.R., Dir. Hispanic Min.; Deacon David E. Galvin; Mrs. Jackie Moler, Pastoral Assoc.; Mr. Gary Penkala, Liturgy & Music.
49 Crosswinds Dr., 25414-0370.
Res.: 311 S. George St., 25414.
Catechesis/Religious Program—Students 450.

CHEAT LAKE, MONONGALIA CO., ST. LUKE THE EVANGELIST (1980) Rev. Ronald G. Prechtl.
Res.: 19 Jo Glen Dr., Morgantown, 26508-4434. Tel: 304-594-2353; Fax: 304-594-2359. Email: bulletin.stlukes1980@comcast.net.
School—St. Francis Central Catholic School, 41 Guthrie Ln., Morgantown, 26508. Tel: 304-291-5070; Fax: 304-291-5104. Mr. John Downey, Prin. Students 380.
Catechesis/Religious Program—Email: education.stlukes1980@comcast.net. Students 149.
Mission—Mary Help of Christians (1983) Bruceton Mills, Preston Co. 26525. Tel: 304-379-4220; Fax: 304-594-2359.

CHESTER, HANCOCK CO., SACRED HEART (1902) Rev. Eric B. Antwi.
Res.: 424 Fourth St., Box 313, 26034-0313. Tel: 304-387-0198.

CLARKSBURG, HARRISON CO.

1—HOLY ROSARY, See Immaculate Conception, Clarksburg

2—HOLY TRINITY, See Immaculate Conception, Clarksburg

3—IMMACULATE CONCEPTION (1864) [CEM] Rev. Casey B. Mahone. In Res., Rev. Christopher M. Turner.
Res.: 126 E. Pike St., 26301-2155. Email: immaculateconcep@ma.rr.com. Web: www.iolinc.net/icparish.
Parish Office—Tel: 304-622-8243.
Catechesis/Religious Program—Students 140.

4—ST. JAMES THE APOSTLE (1924) Rev. Benedict E. Kapa; Deacon Thomas Trunzo, Pastoral Assoc.
Res.: 2107 Pride Ave., 26301-1819. Tel: 304-622-1668; Fax: 304-622-4618. Email: stjameschurch@wvdsl.net.
School—Harrison County Catholic School System, Tel: 304-623-1026; 304-622-9831; Fax: 304-623-1026. See Immaculate Conception
Catechesis/Religious Program—Tel: 304-624-5811. Students 49.

5—ST. JOHN THE BAPTIST, See Immaculate Conception, Clarksburg

CLENDENIN, KANAWHA CO., ST. ANNE, See Our Lady of the Hills, Elkview

COALBURG, GOOD SHEPHERD, See St. John, Belle
Catechesis/Religious Program—Margaret Lucas, D.R.E. Students 9.

COALTON, RANDOLPH CO., ST. PATRICK CHURCH (1918) [CEM 4] Very Rev. Donald X. Higgs.
Res.: 200 Church St., P.O. Box 99, 26257-0099. Tel: 304-636-5754.
Catechesis/Religious Program—Students 15.

DAVIS, TUCKER CO., ST. VERONICA, See St. Thomas Aquinas, Thomas

DUNBAR, KANAWHA CO., CHRIST THE KING (1942) Rev. Manuel T. Gelido.
Mailing Address: P.O. Box 339, Nitro, 25143. Tel: 304-755-0791; Fax: 304-755-3473.
Church: 1504 Grosscup Ave., 25064-2925. Tel: 304-768-2527; Fax: 304-768-8547. Students 35.
Catechesis/Religious Program—Students 17.

ELIZABETH, WIRT CO., ST. ELIZABETH OF HUNGARY (1977), See Holy Redeemer, Spencer

ELKINS, RANDOLPH CO., ST. BRENDAN (1897) [CEM] Very Rev. Donald X. Higgs; Deacons John W. Sarraga; Raymond Godwin; Lou Belldina.
Res.: P.O. Box 2205, 26241-2205. Tel: 304-636-0467; 304-636-0546. Email: frdxh@aol.com. Web: www.stbrendanwv.org.
Catechesis/Religious Program—Students 105.
Chapel—St. John Bosco (1948) Rte. 1, Box 9D, Huttonsville, 26273-9737.
Station—Huttonsville Correctional Center Huttonsville. Tel: 304-338-6323.

ELKVIEW, KANAWHA CO., OUR LADY OF THE HILLS (1977) Rev. Dennis J. Klemash, O.F.M.Cap.
Res.: 100 Jackson Dr., 25071-9324. Tel: 304-965-7670.
Catechesis/Religious Program—Students 19.
Mission—St. Anne 63 Elk River Rd. S., Clendenin, Kanawha Co. 25045-9710. Tel: 304-548-7147. Sr. Kate Holohan, O.S.F., Pastoral Assoc.

FAIRMONT, MARION CO.

1—ST. ANTHONY (1964) Rev. John P. Mulcahy, Admin.
Res.: 1660 Mary Lou Retton Dr., 26554. Tel: 304-363-1328; Fax: 304-368-9191.
School—Fairmont Catholic Grade School, Tel: 304-363-5313.
Catechesis/Religious Program—Students 23.

2—IMMACULATE CONCEPTION (1960) Rev. Richard Ulam, O.S.B.; Sr. Stella Cronauer, C.S.J., Pastoral Assoc.
Mailing Address: 406 Alta Vista Ave., 26554. Tel: 304-363-5796; Fax: 304-366-4937.
School—Fairmont Catholic Grade School, Tel: 304-363-5313.
Catechesis/Religious Program—Students 120.

3—ST. JOSEPH'S (1909) Merged with St. Peter's, Fairmont to form The New St. Peter the Fisherman, Fairmont.

4—ST. PETER THE FISHERMAN CATHOLIC CHURCH (1873) [CEM 2], (Formerly St. Peter's, Fairmont.) Merged with St. Joseph, Fairmont; St. Anthony, Grant Town; Our Lady of the Assumption, Rivesville, and All Saints, Barrackville. Rev. Robert A. Perriello; Deacon David P. Lester.
Res.: 407 Jackson St., 26554-2941. Tel: 304-363-7434; Fax: 304-363-2660. Email: stpeterfisherman@verizon.net. Web: www.thefisherman.org.
School—Fairmont Catholic Grade School, Tel: 304-363-5313; Fax: 304-363-7701. Email: fcsschool@aol.com. Sr. Mary DiDomenico, S.S.J., Prin. Faculty 15; Students 182.
Catechesis/Religious Program—Students 135.

FARMINGTON, MARION CO., ST. PETER'S (1921) Rev. Douglas B. Sutton.
Mailing Address: 204 Furbee Ave., Mannington, 26582-1399. Tel: 304-986-2321; Fax: 304-986-1419.
Catechesis/Religious Program—Tel: 304-825-1397. Students 17.

FOLLANSBEE, BROOKE CO., ST. ANTHONY (1906) Revs. Gary P. Naegele; Pete A. Giannamore.
Res.: 1017 Jefferson St., 26037-1334. Tel: 304-527-2286; Fax: 304-527-2548.
Catechesis/Religious Program—Tel: 304-527-3966. Students 100.

FORT ASHBY, MINERAL CO., ANNUNCIATION OF OUR LORD (1981) Rev. William J. Kuchinsky.
Res.: 238 North Hwy. 28, P.O. Box 1560, 26719-1560. Tel: 304-298-3392; Fax: 304-298-3419. Email: annunciationchurch@atlanticbbn.net. Web: www.annunciationwv.org.
Catechesis/Religious Program—Students 52.

FRANKLIN, PENDLETON CO., ST. ELIZABETH ANN SETON (1975) Rev. Mario R. Claro; Deacons Robert W. Bittner; John E. Windett; Bro. William Lavigne, F.M.S., Pastoral Assoc.
Church & Res.: 141 Walnut St., P.O. Box 890, 26807. Tel: 304-358-7012.
Catechesis/Religious Program—Students 22.

GARY, MCDOWELL CO., OUR LADY OF VICTORY (1904) [CEM] Rev. That Son Ngoc Nguyen.
Church: 38 Church St., P.O. Box 130, 24836-0130. Tel: 304-448-2749.
Catechesis/Religious Program—Sr. Libby Delice, D.R.E. Students 3.

GASSAWAY, BRAXTON CO., ST. THOMAS (1973) Revs. Matheus B. Ro, S.V.D. (Indonesia); Dominikus Baok, S.V.D. In Res., Rev. Arnold Lang, S.V.D.
Res.: 624 Kanawha St., 26624-1208. Tel: 304-364-5895; Fax: 304-364-8099.
Catechesis/Religious Program—Students 37.

GLEN DALE, MARSHALL CO., ST. JUDE (1968) Rev. John R. Gallagher.
Res.: 710 Jefferson Ave., P.O. Box 147, 26038-0147. Tel: 304-845-8165 (Rectory); 304-845-2646 (Office); Fax: 304-845-3015.
Catechesis/Religious Program—Students 70.

GLENVILLE, GILMER CO., GOOD SHEPHERD (1958) Rev. J. Stephen Vallelonga, Temp. Admin.
Res.: 701 Mineral Rd., 26351-1310. Tel: 304-462-7130; Fax: 304-462-7130. Email: svdglenville@rtol.net.
Catechesis/Religious Program—Tel: 304-462-7130; Fax: 304-462-7130. Students 7.

GRAFTON, TAYLOR CO., ST. AUGUSTINE (1852), (Irish), [CEM 2] Rev. James E. O'Connor.
Res.: 17 W. Washington St., 26354-1398. Tel: 304-265-1848; 304-265-3861 (Office); Fax: 304-265-2810.
Catechesis/Religious Program—Students 65.

GRANT TOWN, MARION CO., ST. ANTHONY'S (1907) Merged with St. Joseph, Fairmont; Our Lady of the Assumption, Rivesville and All Saints, Barrackville to form St. Peter the Fisherman, Fairmont.

GRANTSVILLE, CALHOUN CO., JESUS CHRIST, PRINCE OF PEACE (1977), See Holy Redeemer, Spencer.

HAMLIN, LINCOLN CO., CHRIST IN THE HILLS, See St. Stephen, Ona or St. Mary, Madison

HARPERS FERRY, JEFFERSON CO., ST. PETER (1830) Closed. Merged with St. James, Charles Town.

HARRISVILLE, RITCHIE CO., CHRIST OUR HOPE (1980) [CEM] Rev. Paulous Manickathan; Sr. Linda Bates, O.S.F., Pastoral Assoc.
Res.: Rte. 1, Box 44A, 26362-9707. Tel: 304-643-4261. Email: slbatescoh@zoominternet.net.
Church: Pullman Rd. & E. Main, 26362-9707.
Catechesis/Religious Program—Students 20.
Chapel—Pennsboro, St. Joseph (1870) [CEM] Penn Ave., Pennsboro, 26415.

HEDGESVILLE, BERKELEY CO., ST. BERNADETTE (1982), See St. Joseph, Martinsburg

HINTON, SUMMERS CO., ST. PATRICK (1874), (Irish), [CEM 2] Rev. Arthur Bufogle Jr.
309 Second Ave., 25951-0008.
Mission—St. Mary of the Greenbrier 101 Davis St., State Rte. 12, P.O. Box 441, Alderson, Greenbrier Co. 24910.
Chapel—St. Colman (1882), (Irish Mountain, WV)
Catechesis/Religious Program—Students 12.

HOLDEN, LOGAN CO., ST. MARY'S (1961) Consolidated with Our Lady of Mount Carmel, Logan, to form St. Francis of Assisi, Logan.

HUNTINGTON, CABELL CO.
1—ST. JOSEPH'S (1872) [CEM] Rev. Msgr. Lawrence J. Luciana; Rev. Julian Marneni.
Res.: 1304 Sixth Ave., P.O. Box 369, 25708. Tel: 304-525-5202; Fax: 304-525-0951.
School—520 Thirteenth St., 25701. Tel: 304-522-2644; Fax: 304-522-2512. Karen Elk, Prin. Lay Teachers 10; Students 131.
2—OUR LADY OF FATIMA (1952) Rev. James M. Sobus.
Res.: 545 Norway Ave., 25705. Tel: 304-525-0866; Fax: 304-525-0390.
School—535 Norway Ave., 25705. Tel: 304-523-2861; 304-523-2863. Mr. Jeff Jackson, Interim Admin. Lay Teachers 18; Students 160.
Catechesis/Religious Program—Students 60.
3—ST. PETER CLAVER (1937), (African American), Rev. Livinus Uba.
Res.: 828 Fifteenth St., 25701. Tel: 304-523-7311.
Catechesis/Religious Program—Students 16.
4—SACRED HEART (1934) Rev. Livinus Uba; Deacon Michael R. Prestera Jr.; Sr. Mary Terence Wall, S.A.C., Pastoral Assoc.
Res.: 2015 Adams Ave., 25704-1419. Tel: 304-429-5088 (Rectory); 304-429-4318 (Office); Fax: 304-429-4319.
Catechesis/Religious Program—Students 33.

HURRICANE, PUTNAM CO., CATHOLIC CHURCH OF THE ASCENSION (1980) Rev. Neil R. Buchlein.
Res.: 905 Hickory Mill Rd., 25526. Tel: 304-562-5816; Fax: 304-562-3589. Email: ascensionwv@hotmail.com.
Catechesis/Religious Program—Students 202.

INWOOD, BERKELEY CO., ST. LEO (1982) Revs. D. Brian Shoda; Chapin Engler; Deacon Charles C. Quigley.
Res.: 2109 Sulphur Springs Rd., P.O. Box 93, 25428-0093. Tel: 304-229-8945; Fax: 304-229-9755.
Catechesis/Religious Program—Students 425.

KEYSER, MINERAL CO., ASSUMPTION (1874) [CEM] Rev. Ivan M. Lebar, T.O.R.; Bro. Luke D. Stone, T.O.R., Pastoral Assoc.
Res.: 34 James St., 26726-2721. Tel: 304-788-2488; Fax: 304-788-0647. Email: acckwv@verizon.net. Web: www.dwc.org.
Catechesis/Religious Program—Students 53.

KINGWOOD, PRESTON CO., ST. SEBASTIAN'S (1914) [CEM 3] Very Rev. Mark Ward, C.P.; Sisters Claude Vitale, C.S.J., Pastoral Assoc.; Mary Priscilla Weidenschlager, C.S.J., Pastoral Assoc.
Res.: P.O. Box 519, 26537. Tel: 304-329-1519; Fax: 304-329-2546. Email: ccpccath@verizon.net.
Church: 324 E. Main St., 26537.
Catechesis/Religious Program—Students 54.
Mission—St. Edward Rte. 17 E., Terra Alta, Preston Co.

LEWISBURG, GREENBRIER CO., ST. LOUIS, KING OF FRANCE, Closed. See St. Catherine, Ronceverte

LITTLETON, WETZEL CO., ASSUMPTION OF THE BLESSED VIRGIN MARY, See St. Patrick, Mannington

LOGAN, LOGAN CO., ST. FRANCIS OF ASSISI (1996) Rev. Thomas S. Charters, G.H.M.; Bros. Michael Springer, G.H.M., Pastoral Assoc.; Thomas Sheehy, Outreach Min.; Mrs. Connie Bazzilla, Pastoral Assoc.
Res.: 561 Main St., 25601-3899. Tel: 304-752-3017; Fax: 304-752-3017.
Church: Stratton St., 25601.
Catechesis/Religious Program—Students 15.

LOVEBERRY, ST. BERNARD, See St. Patrick, Weston

LUBECK, WOOD CO., ST. MONICA'S (1976) [CEM] Rev. Robert Eric Hall IV.
Res.: 532 Market St., Parkersburg, 26101. Tel: 304-422-6799; Fax: 304-422-6789.
Church: State Rte. 68, Lubeck Washington.
Catechesis/Religious Program—Students 20.

MADISON, BOONE CO., ST. MARY, QUEEN OF HEAVEN (1957) Rev. Soosai Arpudam Arokiadass, H.G.N. (India), Admin.
Res.: P.O. Box 467, 25130-0467. Tel: 304-369-4538; Fax: 304-369-6268. Email: stmaryofmadison@aol.com. Web: www.saintmaryofmadison.com.
Church: 51 Madison Ave., 25130.
Catechesis/Religious Program—Students 8.

MAN, LOGAN CO., ST. EDMUND (1961) Rev. Thomas S. Charters, G.H.M.; Bros. Michael Springer, G.H.M.; Thomas Sheehy, G.H.M.
Res.: 561 Main St., Logan, 25601-3899. Tel: 304-752-3017.
Church & Mailing Address: 110 S. Bridge St., 25635. Tel: 304-583-2476; Fax: 304-239-3131.

MANNINGTON, MARION CO., ST. PATRICK'S (1897), (Irish), Rev. Douglas B. Sutton.
Res.: 204 Furbee Ave., 26582-1399. Tel: 304-986-2321; Fax: 304-986-1419.
Catechesis/Religious Program—Tel: 304-986-1624. Students 23.
Mission—Assumption of the Blessed Virgin Mary (1859) [CEM 2] Long Drain Rd., Littleton, Wetzel Co. 26581. (Suppressed Sept. 1, 2001)

MARLINTON, POCAHONTAS CO., ST. JOHN NEUMANN (1977) [CEM] Rev. Mark T. Gallipeau, Admin.
Res.: 714 10th Ave., 24954-1314. Tel: 304-799-6778; Fax: 304-799-6778.
Mission—St. Mark the Evangelist (1977) Rt. 92-250, Bartow, Pocahontas Co. 24920.
Chapel—St. Bernard
Catechesis/Religious Program—Students 23.

MARTINSBURG, BERKELEY CO., ST. JOSEPH'S (1803) [CEM 2] Rev. Msgr. Patrick L. Fryer; Sisters Judith Rojas, D.C., Pastoral Assoc.; Patricia Endres, D.C., Pastoral Assoc.
Mailing Address: 336 S. Queen St., 25401-3213. In Res., Rev. Michael Cavanaugh, O.S.F.S.
Res.: 219 S. Queen St., 25401-3213. Tel: 304-264-8947; Fax: 304-263-7357. Email: stjoemart@verizon.net. Web: www.parishesonline.com/stjosephmartinsburg.
School—110 E. Stephen St., 25401. Tel: 304-267-6447; Fax: 304-267-6573. Email: info@stjosephparishschool.us. Web: www.stjosephparishschool.us. Daughters of Charity of St. Vincent de Paul 2; Lay Teachers 24; Students 355.
Catechesis/Religious Program—Students 74.
Mission—St. Bernadette 205 W. Main St., P.O. Box 11, Hedgesville, Berkeley Co. 25427. Tel: 304-754-7830; Fax: 304-754-7830. Email: stbernadette@verizon.net.

MASONTOWN, PRESTON CO., ST. ZITA'S (1962) Very Rev. Mark Ward, C.P.; Sisters Claude Vitale, C.S.J., Pastoral Assoc.; Mary Priscilla Weidenschlager, C.S.J., Pastoral Assoc.
Res.: P.O. Box 519, Kingwood, 26537-0519. Tel: 304-329-1519; Fax: 304-329-2546. Email: ccpccath@verizon.net.
Church: Tel: 304-864-5512.
Catechesis/Religious Program—Tel: 304-329-1063. Students 13.

MAYSEL, CLAY CO., RISEN LORD (1972) Rev. Matheus B. Ro, S.V.D. (Indonesia).
Mailing Address: 67 Wallback Rd., 25133. Tel: 304-587-4740; Fax: 304-587-4886.
Catechesis/Religious Program—Students 14.

MCMECHEN, MARSHALL CO., ST. JAMES (1900) Rev. Joseph Hayden, S.J.
Mailing Address: 328 Logan St., 26040. Tel: 304-232-1227.
School—Sts. James and John Consolidated Schools, Tel: 304-232-1587. Mrs. Jennifer Marsh, Prin. Lay Teachers 7; Students 98.
Catechesis/Religious Program—Students 254.

MIDDLEBOURNE, TYLER CO., ST. LAWRENCE, See Mater Dolorosa, Paden City
Catechesis/Religious Program—Darlene Koerber, D.R.E.

MONONGAH, MARION CO., HOLY SPIRIT (1975), (Polish—Italian), [CEM] Rev. John P. Mulcahy, Admin.
Res.: 687 Maple Ter., 26554-1116. Tel: 304-534-3020; Fax: 304-534-5910.
Catechesis/Religious Program—Students 38.

MONTGOMERY, FAYETTE CO., IMMACULATE CONCEPTION (1888) Rev. John Rice; Deacon John Divita.
Res.: P.O. Box 65, 25136. Tel: 304-442-2101; Fax: 304-442-2102. Email: ic_sa@verizon.net.
Shrine—St. Anthony Shrine (1928) P.O. Box 428, Boomer, Fayette Co. 25031. Tel: 304-779-2561.
Catechesis/Religious Program—Tel: 304-442-5224. Students 50.

MOOREFIELD, HARDY CO., EPIPHANY OF THE LORD (1980) [CEM] [JC] Rev. Giles LeVasseur; Bro. Philip Ouellette, F.M.S., Pastoral Assoc.
Church: 2029 State Rd. 55, 26836. Tel: 304-434-2547.
Catechesis/Religious Program—Tel: 304-257-1057; Fax: 304-257-9442. Students 12.

MORGANTOWN, MONONGALIA CO.
1—ST. FRANCIS DE SALES CATHOLIC CHURCH (2003), (Formerly St. Theresa's, Morgantown. Merged with St. Elizabeth Ann Seton, Westover to form The St. Theresa/St. Elizabeth Ann Seton, Morgantown.); (Formerly The New St. Theresa & St. Elizabeth Ann Seton) Rev. Leon Alexander; Sr. Nancy White, C.S.J., Pastoral Assoc.
Res.: One Guthrie Ln., 26508. Tel: 304-296-5353; Fax: 304-296-8200. Email: desaleswv01@comcast.net. Web: www.stfrancisdesalesparish.com.
School—St. Francis Central Catholic School, 41 Guthrie Ln., 26508. Tel: 304-291-5070. Mr. John Downey, Prin.
Catechesis/Religious Program—Students 85.
2—ST. JOHN UNIVERSITY PARISH, NEWMAN HALL (1966) Rev. William K. Matheny Jr.; Deacons Joseph Prentiss; Stephen A. Olenchock.
Res.: 1481 University Ave., 26505-5598. Tel: 304-296-8231; Fax: 304-296-4650. Email: stjohnmorgantown@comcast.net. Web: www.stjohnmorgantown.org.
School—St. Francis Central Catholic School, 41 Guthrie Ln., 26508. Tel: 304-291-5070; Fax: 304-291-5104. Sr. Patricia Ann Foley, C.S.J., Prin.
Catechesis/Religious Program—Students 160.

MOUNDSVILLE, MARSHALL CO., ST. FRANCIS XAVIER'S (1857) Revs. Edward G. Stafford, T.O.R.; Terrance Adams, T.O.R.
Church: 610 Jefferson Ave., 26041-2106.
Res.: 912 Seventh St., 26041-2106. Tel: 304-845-1593; Fax: 304-845-2006.
School—(Grades K-8), 600 Jefferson Ave., 26041. Tel: 304-845-2562; Fax: 304-845-0016. Mr. John Buffington, Prin. Lay Teachers 15; Students 123; Preschool 35.
Catechesis/Religious Program—Students 40.
Station—Northern Regional Jail and Correctional Facility, Tel: 304-843-4067.

MOUNT HOPE, FAYETTE CO.
MISSION—ST. ANTHONY, Suppressed as a mission June 21, 1994.

MULLENS, WYOMING CO., ST. JOHN THE EVANGELIST (1923) Rev. John C. Reich.
Res.: 13 Terry St., 25882-1624. Tel: 304-294-8128; Fax: 304-294-8128.
Catechesis/Religious Program—Students 9.
Mission—Holy Cross Rte. 10, P.O. Box 375, Pineville, Wyoming Co. 24874. Tel: 304-732-6199; 304-732-8128 (Rectory).

NEW CUMBERLAND, HANCOCK CO., IMMACULATE CONCEPTION (1904) Rev. Eric B. Antwi.
Res.: 1016 Ridge Ave., 26047-0666. Tel: 304-564-5068; Fax: 304-564-7063. Email: immaculateconceptionparish@comcast.net.
Catechesis/Religious Program—Students 28.

NEW MARTINSVILLE, WETZEL CO., ST. VINCENT DE PAUL (1901) Rev. Walter M. Jagela.
Res.: 21 Rosary Rd., 26155-1602. Tel: 304-455-4615; Fax: 304-455-4617. Email: office@svdpnm.org. Web: www.svdpnm.org.
Catechesis/Religious Program—Students 96.

NITRO, KANAWHA CO., HOLY TRINITY (1962) Revs. Manuel T. Gelido; Rey D. Landicho.
Mailing Address: P.O. Box 339, 25143-0339. Tel: 304-755-0791; Fax: 304-755-3473.
Res.: 2219-22nd St., P.O. Box 339, 25143-0339. Tel: 304-755-0791; Fax: 304-755-3473.
Catechesis/Religious Program—Students 61.
Mission—St. Patrick 207 Jefferson St., P.O. Box 238, Bancroft, Putnam Co. 25011. Tel: 304-586-3485; Fax: 304-586-3485.

OAK HILL, FAYETTE CO., SS. PETER AND PAUL (1906) [CEM] Rev. Paul D. Yuenger.
Res.: 122 Elmore St., 25901-2628. Tel: 304-465-5445. Email: pastor@ssppcatholic.org. Web:

www.ssppcatholic.org.
School—123 Elmore St., 25901-2628. Tel: 304-465-5045; Fax: 304-465-8726. Email: principal@ssppcatholic.org. Aaron Kemlock, Prin. Lay Teachers 8; Students 118.
Catechesis/Religious Program—Students 51.

ONA, CABELL CO., ST. STEPHEN (1980) Rev. James M. Sobus.
Res.: 2491 James River Tpke., 25545-9722. Tel: 304-743-3234. Email: ststephens@suddenlinkmail.com. Web: www.ststephens1.com.
Catechesis/Religious Program—Students 20.

PADEN CITY, TYLER AND WETZEL COS., MATER DOLOROSA (1921) Rev. James B. McCafferty, S.M.; Deacon N. Rollin Fagert.
Res.: 302 E. Main St., 26159-1736. Tel: 304-337-9837.
Catechesis/Religious Program—Students 8.
Mission—St. Lawrence P.O. Box 267, Middlebourne, Tyler Co. 26149. Tel: 304-758-4649.

PARKERSBURG, WOOD CO.

1—ST. FRANCIS XAVIER'S (1853) [CEM 3] Rev. R. Eric Hall IV; Deacons Douglas A. Deem; James R. Kelly.
Res.: 532 Market St., 26101-5144. Tel: 304-422-6799. Email: stxoffice@stx-pburg.org. Web: www.stx-pburg.org.
Catechesis/Religious Program—Tel: 304-422-6786; Fax: 304-422-6789. Students 93.

2—ST. MARGARET MARY (1923) Very Rev. Joseph L. Peterson; Rev. Douglas A. Ondeck; Deacons George B. Showalter; John Maher.
Res.: 2500 Dudley Ave., 26101-2695. Tel: 304-428-1262; Fax: 304-422-4905. Email: stmmpastor@suddenlinkmail.com. Web: stmmrcchurch.org.
Catechesis/Religious Program—Tel: 304-865-1470. Email: stmmdre@suddenlinkmail.com. Students 135.

PARSONS, TUCKER CO., OUR LADY OF MERCY, See St. Thomas, Thomas, P.O. Box 300, Thomas, 26292-0300.
Catechesis/Religious Program—Students 16.

PENNSBORO, RITCHIE CO., ST. JOSEPH CHAPEL, See Christ Our Hope, Harrisville

PETERSBURG, GRANT CO., ST. MARY'S (1971) [JC] Rev. Giles LeVasseur.
Rectory—5 Pierpont St., 26847-1633. Tel: 304-257-1057; Fax: 304-257-9442. Email: smcc@frontiernet.net.
Church: 4 Grant St., 26847-1633. Fax: 304-257-9442. Email: smcc2@frontiernet.net.
Catechesis/Religious Program—Students 4.

PHILIPPI, BARBOUR CO., ST. ELIZABETH PARISH (1953) Rev. James O'Connor; Deacon A. Ray Shaw III.
Res.: Rte. 3, Box 257, 26416-9581. Tel: 304-457-2641.
Catechesis/Religious Program— Patty Bowmar, D.R.E. Students 12.

PICKENS, RANDOLPH CO., SACRED HEART (1963), See Holy Rosary, Buckhannon, 35 Franklin St., P.O. Box 848, Buckhannon, 26201-0848.

PINEVILLE, WYOMING CO., HOLY CROSS (1963), See St. John the Evangelist, Mullens, 13 Terry St., Mullens, 25882-1624.
Catechesis/Religious Program—Students 1.

POINT PLEASANT, MASON CO., SACRED HEART (1948) Rev. David J. Schmitt.
Res.: 2222 Jackson Ave., 25550-2004. Tel: 304-675-4602.
Catechesis/Religious Program—Students 22.
Mission—St. Joseph (1856) [CEM] 3rd St. & Pomeroy St., Mason, Mason Co. 25260.
Catechesis/Religious Program—Students 6.

POWHATAN, MCDOWELL CO., SACRED HEART (1895) Rev. That Son Ngoc Nguyen.
Res.: HC 76, Box 402, 24877. Tel: 304-862-3494.
Catechesis/Religious Program—Students 3.

PRINCETON, MERCER CO., SACRED HEART (1915) Rev. Paul J. Wharton; Deacon Don M. Hammond, Campus Minister.
Res.: 507 Harrison St., 24740-3198. Tel: 304-425-3664; Fax: 304-425-3676. Email: sacheapar@citlink.net.
Catechesis/Religious Program—Students 96.
Campus Ministry, Concord College—Athens, 24712. Tel: 304-384-9502.

RAINELLE, GREENBRIER CO., SACRED HEART (1951) [CEM 2] Rev. Arthur Bufogle Jr.
401 13th St., 25962. Tel: 304-438-8687.
Res.: 309 2nd Ave., Hinton, 25951. Tel: 304-466-3966.
Chapel—SpringDale, Sacred Heart [CEM], (1876)
Catechesis/Religious Program—Students 6.

RAVENSWOOD, JACKSON CO., ST. MATTHEW (1957) Rev. Alfred Obiudu (Nigeria).
Res.: 600 Crooks Ave., 26164-1312. Tel: 304-273-2175. Email: stmatthewparish@msn.com.
Catechesis/Religious Program—Students 47.

RICHWOOD, NICHOLAS CO., HOLY FAMILY (1902) [CEM] Rev. Jerome D. Rawa, S.M.; Deacon John F. Ceslovnik; Bro. Richard McKenna, S.M., Pastoral Assoc.
Res.: 4 Maple St., 26261-1318. Tel: 304-846-2873; Fax: 304-846-2873. Email: hofam2@verizon.net.
Catechesis/Religious Program—Students 8.

RIDGELEY, MINERAL CO., ST. ANTHONY (1916) Rev. William J. Kuchinsky.
Res.: 121 Main St., P.O. Box 1350, 26753. Tel: 304-298-3392; Fax: 304-298-3419. Email: annunciationchurch@atlanticbbn.net. Web: www.stanthonywv.org.
Catechesis/Religious Program—Students 18.

RIVESVILLE, MARION CO., OUR LADY OF THE ASSUMPTION, Merged with St. Joseph, Fairmont; St. Anthony, Grant Town; Our Lady of the Assumption, Rivesville, and All Saints, Barrackville to form St. Peter the Fisherman, Fairmont.; See St. Anthony, Grant Town

ROANOKE, LEWIS CO., ST. BRIDGET, See St. Patrick, Weston

ROMNEY, HAMPSHIRE CO., OUR LADY OF GRACE (1951) Rev. William J. Kuchinsky; Deacon Lawrence Hammel.
Res.: 299 School St., 26757-0871. Tel: 304-822-5561.
Catechesis/Religious Program—Students 41.

RONCEVERTE, GREENBRIER CO., ST. CATHERINE OF SIENA (1892) Rev. Thomas W. Dagle; Deacon William B. Strange Jr.
Res.: 325 W. Main St., White Sulphur Springs, 24986-2413. Tel: 304-536-1813; Fax: 304-536-1813.
Catechesis/Religious Program—Tom Soper, D.R.E. Students 30.
Chapel—The Immaculate Conception of the Blessed Virgin Mary [CEM]
Chaplaincy—WV School of Osteopathic Medicine, Lewisburg, 24901.

ST. ALBANS, KANAWHA CO., ST. FRANCIS OF ASSISI (1947) [CEM] Rev. Patrick M. McDonough.
Res.: 1023 Sixth Ave., 25177. Tel: 304-727-3033; Fax: 304-727-6640.
School—(Grades PreK-5), 525 Holley St., Saint Albans, 25177. Tel: 304-727-5690; Fax: 304-727-5690. Priests 1; Lay Teachers 7; Students 140.
Catechesis/Religious Program—Students 40.

ST. CLARA, ST. CLARE, See St. Boniface, Camden

ST. JOSEPH SETTLEMENT, MARSHALL CO., ST. JOSEPH'S (1853), (German), [CEM] Unassigned.
Res.: R.D. 1, Box 203, Proctor, 26055. Tel: 304-455-4303; Fax: 304-455-4303.
Catechesis/Religious Program—Students 8.

ST. MARYS, PLEASANTS CO., ST. JOHN (1913) [JC] Rev. Paulose Manickathan.
Mailing Address: P.O. Box 338, 26170-0338.
Res.: 310 Washington St., 26170-1313. Tel: 304-684-7669. Email: stjohnsm@suddenlinkmail.com.
Catechesis/Religious Program—Students 30.

SALEM, HARRISON CO., SACRED HEART (1915) [CEM] Rev. Benedict E. Kapa.
Res.: Rte. 23 S. off Rte. 50, R.R. 5 Box 1424, 26426. Tel: 304-782-2277. Email: shp@verizon.net.
Catechesis/Religious Program—Students 16.

SHEPHERDSTOWN, JEFFERSON CO., ST. AGNES (1794) Rev. T. Matthew Rowgh; Deacon Anthony F. Maciorowski.
Mailing Address: P.O. Box 1603, 25443-1603.
Res.: 216 S. Duke St., 25443-1603. Tel: 304-876-6436; Fax: 304-876-6436. Email: stagnescenter@frontiernet.net. Web: www.lrwbf.com/st_agnes.
Catechesis/Religious Program—Students 87.

SHINNSTON, HARRISON CO., ST. ANN'S (1923) Rev. Karl R. Wohinc.
Res.: 610 Pike St., 26431-1451. Tel: 304-592-2733.
Mission—Holy Family (1925) Spelter, Harrison Co. 26438.

SISTERSVILLE, TYLER CO., HOLY ROSARY (1898) Rev. James B. McCafferty, S.M.; Deacon N. Rollin Fagert.
Church: 519 Main St., 26175-1405. Tel: 304-652-6381; 304-337-9837 (Rectory).
Catechesis/Religious Program—Students 6.

SOUTH CHARLESTON, KANAWHA CO., BLESSED SACRAMENT (1941) [CEM] Rev. John H. Finnell; Deacon John J. Hanna.
Res.: 305 E St., 25303-1597. Tel: 304-744-5523; Fax: 304-744-5669. Email: blessedsac@suddenlinkmail.com. Web: blessedsacramentwv.org.
Catechesis/Religious Program—Students 120.

SPELTER, HARRISON CO., HOLY FAMILY, See St. Ann's, Shinnston

SPENCER, ROANE CO., HOLY REDEEMER (1957) Rev. Tom Chacko.
Res.: 602 Parkersburg Rd., 25276-1024. Tel: 304-927-2013. Email: holy_redeemer@verizon.net. Web: mysite.verizon.net/holy_redeemer.
Catechesis/Religious Program—Students 21.
Mission—St. Elizabeth of Hungary (1977) Rt. 1, Box 118N3, Elizabeth, Wirt Co. 26143. Tel: 304-275-4226. Email: casamblanet@verizon.net. Web: mysite.verizon.net/stelizofhungary. Sr. Cheryl Samblanet, H.M., Pastoral Assoc.

STAR CITY, MONONGALIA CO., ST. MARY'S (1953) [CEM] Rev. John V. DiBacco Jr.
Res.: 3344 University Ave., 26505. Tel: 304-599-3747; Fax: 304-599-3769. Email: stmaryschurch@comcast.net. Web: www.stmarystarcity.com.
School—St. Francis Central Catholic School, 41 Guthrie Ln., Morgantown, 26508. Tel: 304-598-0133; Fax: 304-598-2690.
Catechesis/Religious Program—Tel: 304-225-1163. Email: kkerzak@comcast.net. Students 125.

STONEWOOD, HARRISON CO., OUR LADY OF PERPETUAL HELP (1955) Rev. John S. Ledford.
Res.: 707 3rd St., 26301-4854. Tel: 304-623-2334; Fax: 304-623-9988.
Catechesis/Religious Program—Tel: 304-623-2334, Ext. 19. Students 176.

SUMMERSVILLE, NICHOLAS CO., ST. JOHN THE EVANGELIST (1849) [CEM] Rev. Xavier Cooney, S.V.D.; Deacon John F. Ceslovnik.
Res.: 1704 Webster Rd., 26651-1096. Tel: 304-872-2554; Fax: 304-872-0580. Email: stjohnssummersville@verizon.net. Web: www.stjohnsummersville.com.
Catechesis/Religious Program—Students 52.

SWEET SPRINGS, MONROE CO., ST. JOHN, Closed. See St. Charles, White Sulphur Springs

TERRA ALTA, PRESTON CO., ST. EDWARD (1975) [CEM 2], See St. Sebastian, Kingwood
Catechesis/Religious Program—Sr. Priscilla Weidenschlager, D.R.E. Students 6.

THOMAS, TUCKER CO., ST. THOMAS AQUINAS (1897) [CEM] Rev. Timothy J. Grassi.
Res.: P.O. Box 300, 26292-0300. Tel: 304-463-4488.
Church: Brown St. & Third St., 26292.
Catechesis/Religious Program—Students 20.
Mission—Our Lady of Mercy (1960)

TRIADELPHIA, OHIO CO., OUR LADY OF SEVEN DOLORS (1869) [CEM], See St. Vincent de Paul, Wheeling

UNION, MONROE CO., ST. ANDREW, Closed. See St. Catherine of Siena, Ronceverte

VIENNA, WOOD CO., ST. MICHAEL'S (1956) [JC] Rev. Sajo Puthenpurackal Joseph, H.G.N.
Res.: 5501 Fourth Ave., 26105-2007. Tel: 304-295-6109; Fax: 304-295-2303. Email: stmoffice@verizon.net.
Catechesis/Religious Program—Students 99.

WAR, MCDOWELL CO., CHRIST THE KING (1942) Rev. That Son Ngoc Nguyen.
Church: Rt. 16 S., P.O. Box 728, 24892-0728. Tel: 304-875-3827.
Catechesis/Religious Program—Sr. Mary E. Deliee, R.S.M., D.R.E. Students 11.

WAYNE, WAYNE CO., NATIVITY OF OUR LORD (1980) Rev. Julian Marneni; Deacon Michael R. Prestera Jr.
Church: Rte. 4, Box 2502, 25570-9738. Tel: 304-272-5832; 304-525-5202; Fax: 304-272-6176.
Catechesis/Religious Program—Students 12.
Station—Genoa Christian Center P.O. Box 67, Genoa, 25517. Tel: 304-385-4583; Fax: 304-385-4583. Deacon Michael R. Prestera Jr.

WEBSTER SPRINGS, WEBSTER CO., ST. ANNE'S (1920) Rev. Matheus B. Ro, S.V.D. (Indonesia); Bro. James J. Zabransky, S.V.D., Pastoral Assoc.; Deacon Todd E. Garland.
Res.: 160 McGraw, 26288-1134. Tel: 304-847-5512; Fax: 304-847-5512.
Catechesis/Religious Program—Students 4.

WEIRTON, BROOKE CO., ST. PAUL'S (1910) [CEM] Rev. Larry W. Dorsch. In Res., Rev. Felix Owino, A.J.
Res.: 140 Walnut St., 26062-4521. Tel: 304-748-4118; Fax: 304-748-3749. Email: stpaulschurch@comcast.net.
School—Tel: 304-748-5225; Fax: 304-748-4163. Email: stpaulschool3@comcast.net. James S. Lesho, Prin. Lay Teachers 15; Students 267.
Catechesis/Religious Program—Debra Marino, D.R.E.; Michael Martocchio, D.R.E. Students 69.

WEIRTON, HANCOCK CO.

1—ST. JOSEPH THE WORKER (1957) Rev. Dean Borgmeyer.
Res.: 229 California Ave., 26062-3790. Tel: 304-723-2054; 304-723-2057; Fax: 304-723-3961.
School—St. Joseph the Worker Grade School, 151 Michael Ave., 26062. Tel: 304-723-1970; Fax: 304-723-5122. Mr. Alfred Boniti, Prin. Lay Teachers 13; Students 217.
Catechesis/Religious Program—Students 118.

2—SACRED HEART OF MARY (1911), (Polish), Rev. D. Kent Durig.
Office: 200 Preston Ave., 26062-3994. Tel: 304-723-7175; 304-723-0707 (Rectory); Fax: 304-723-7176. Email: shmparish@verizon.net.
Catechesis/Religious Program—Students 30.

WELCH, MCDOWELL CO., ST. PETER (1923) Rev. That Son Ngoc Nguyen.
Res.: 111 Virginia Ave., 24801-2424. Tel: 304-436-2014; Fax: 304-436-2332.
Chapel—Kimball, Our Lady Queen of the Apostles, (1959)
Catechesis/Religious Program—Students 8.

WELLSBURG, BROOKE CO., ST. JOHN THE EVANGELIST (1857) [CEM] Rev. Vincent Ezhanikatt Joseph (India).
Res.: 1300 Charles St., 26070-1408. Tel: 304-737-0429; Fax: 304-737-0429. Email: stjohn1300@comcast.net. Web: www.stjohnwellsburgwv.org.
School—Tel: 304-737-0511; Fax: 304-737-0988. Email: stjohns90ad@comcast.net. Lay Teachers 5; Students 57.
Catechesis/Religious Program—Students 40.
Mission—Holy Family (1980) Box 7, Beech Bottom, Brooke Co. 26030-0007. Tel: 304-394-5929; Fax: 304-394-1256.

WEST UNION, DODDRIDGE CO.
CHAPEL—ST. PATRICK CHAPEL (1856), See Sacred Heart, Salem

WESTON, LEWIS CO., ST. PATRICK'S (1845) Rev. J. Stephen Vallelonga.
Res.: 222 Center Ave., 26452-2029. Tel: 304-269-3048; Fax: 304-269-3048. Email: stpatrick4@verizon.net. Web: www.spchurchweston.net.
School—Tel: 304-269-5547. Email: st.pats@stpatswv.org. Paul Derico, Prin. Lay Teachers 8; Students 147.
Catechesis/Religious Program—Students 76.
Chapel—Loveberry, St. Bernard [CEM]
Chapel—Roanoke, St. Bridget [CEM]
Chaplaincy—Weston State Hospital. Tel: 304-269-3048.

WESTOVER, MONOGALIA CO., ST. ELIZABETH ANN SETON (1977) Merged with St. Theresa, Morgantown, to form The New St. Theresa & St. Elizabeth Ann Seton, Morgantown.

WHITE SULPHUR SPRINGS, GREENBRIER CO., ST. CHARLES BORROMEO (1903) [CEM] [JC] Rev. Thomas W. Dagle; Deacon William B. Strange Jr. Tel: 304-536-2333.
Res.: 325 W. Main St., 24986. Tel: 304-536-1813; Fax: 304-536-1813.
Catechesis/Religious Program—St. Louis Catholic Center, Lewisburg, 24901. Students 32.
Chapel—Sweet Springs, St. John The Evangelist [CEM 2] [JC 2]Tel: 304-536-1813. (1859)

WHITESVILLE, BOONE CO., ST. JOSEPH THE WORKER (1958) Closed. See St. Mary Queen of Heaven, Madison.

WILLIAMSON, MINGO CO., SACRED HEART (1911) Rev. Rey D. Landicho.
Res.: 110 W. Fourth Ave., 25661-3112. Tel: 304-235-2982; Fax: 304-235-3027.
School—126 W. Fourth Ave., 25661. Tel: 304-235-3027. Sisters 1; Lay Teachers 4; Students 35.
Catechesis/Religious Program—Students 45.

WINDSOR HEIGHTS, BROOKE CO., ST. THERESE, See St. John, Wellsburg

---

Graduate Studies:
Rev.—
DeViese, James R., Jr., Casa Santa Maria, Via dell'Umilta'30, Rome 00189 Italy.

Absent on Sick Leave:
Rev.—
Petro, William

Absent on Leave:
Revs.—
Kranyc, Andrew G.
Wash, Pat J.

Retired:
Very Rev.—
Anderson, William A., V.F., The Alphonsus House, P.O. Box 108, Salem, 26426.
Revs.—
Bandiera, Colombo F., 1117 University Ave., Apt. 103, Morgantown, 26505.
Bauer, Carl E., 106 Johnstone St., Hampton, SC 29924.
Bell, Edward M., V.F., 149 Otter Rd., Hilton Head Island, SC 29928.
Beyer, Leroy O., 889 Wess Rd., Mineral Point, PA 15942.
Campi, Vincent L., Welty Home, 21 Washington Ave., 26003.
Cann, Hilarion V., 174 Ridgeway Dr., Bridgeport, 26330.
Chalany, Robert, 17 Cedar Lake Rd., Chester, CT 06412.
Conlon, Anthony J., 8 Beech Park, Swinford Co., Mayo, Ireland.
Cullinane, Jeremiah J., Silver Lake College, 2406 S. Alverno Rd., Manitowoc, WI 54220-9319.
Cupp, Edwin F., Good Shepherd Nursing Home, 159 Edgington Ln., Room 209, 26003-1597.
Dene, Joseph, 6 Cool View Ln., Bridgeport, 26330.
Duhaime, John N., 327-13th Ave., P.O. Box 116, Rainelle, 25962.
Ebejer, Lino P., 1276 National Rd., #402, 26003.
Fahey, John H., P.O. Box 2226, Parkersburg, 26101.
Federico, Cesidio J., 112 Boley St., Weirton, 26062.
Getsinger, Ronald A., P.O. Box 2843, Weirton, 26062.
Gillooly, Patrick J., 517 S. Green St., Berkeley Springs, 25411.
Iaquinta, Patsy J., RR1 Box 605, Volga, 26238.
Lee, Michael G., Marcullen Nursing Home, Gollway, Ireland.
Lombard, Roy A., Welty Apartments, #405, 1276 National Rd., 26003-5743.
Lukas, Andrew F., P.O. Box 201, Fairmont, 26555-0201.
Lydon, Leo B., 236 Parkway Dr., Clarksburg, 26301.
Maguire, Seamus J., 1276 National Rd., #407, 26003.
Mascioli, Joseph M., P.O. Box 11, Morgantown, 26505.
McDonnell, John H., 4703 Kanawha Ave. S.E., 25304.
McGinnity, John C., P.O. Box B, Hot Springs, VA 24445.
Murphy, James J., 32 Elm Rd., Donnycarney, Dublin 9, Ireland.
Nash, Robert C., P.O. Box 1093, Deltaville, VA 23043.
O'Donovan, Donal, Westwood, Chapel St., Dunmanway, Co. Cork Ireland.
O'Reilly, Joseph F., P.O. Box 22303, Hilton Head Island, SC 29926.
Ralph, John, 1757 State St., Biloxi, MS 39531.
Stenger, William J., 3505 Kyle Ct., Wilmington, NC 28409.
Valdes, Bert W., 4306 Prices Creek Rd., Huntington, 25705.
Werner, Leo E., Good Shepherd Nursing Home, 159 Edgington Rd., Room 200, 26003.
Wrenn, Lawrence, Welty Apts., 1276 National Rd., #406, 26003.

Permanent Deacons:
Belldina, Louis J., M.S., Bishop Hodges Pastoral Center & St. John Bosco, Huttonsville
Bittner, Robert W. St. Elizabeth Ann Seton, Franklin
Breiding, Douglas W. Office of Safe Environment, Diocese of Wheeling-Charleston; Corpus Christi Parish, Wheeling
Ceslovnik, John F. St. John the Evangelist, Summersville & Holy Family, Richwood
Deem, Douglas A., St. Francis Xavier, Parkersburg
Divita, John, Immaculate Conception, Montgomery
Doerr, George J., (Absent on Leave)
Fagert, Rollin N., Mater Dolorosa, Paden City
Galvin, David E. St. James, Charles Town
Garland, Todd E. Executive Director Department of Social Ministries & St. Anne, Webster Springs
Godwin, Raymond G. St. Brendan, Elkins; St. Patrick, Coalton
Goetemann, Gerald B., (Retired)
Grant, Russell J., (On Leave Outside Diocese)
Hammel, Lawrence Our Lady of Grace, Romney
Hammond, Don M. Campus Ministry, Beckley Vicariate & Sacred Heart, Bluefield
Hanna, John J., Blessed Sacrament, South Charleston
Iafrate, Albert L., (Retired)
Kelly, James R. St. Francis Xavier, Parkersburg
Lane, Gary W. Director, Blessed John XXIII Pastoral Center, Charleston
Lester, David P., Pastoral Associate, St. Peter the Fisherman, Fairmont
Lilly, Robert B., St. Vincent De Paul, Berkeley Springs
Lipscomb, Truman A., Catholic Churches of Preston County
Locke, John W., St. Vincent de Paul, Berkeley Springs
Lynch, John J., (Retired)
Maciorowski, Anthony F. Priest Field Pastoral Center, Kearneysville & St. Agnes, Shepherdstown
Maher, John F., St. Margaret Mary Parish, Parkersburg
Mankowski, Richard W., (Retired)
Nedeff, George A., (Absent on Leave)
Nesser, Dennis W., J.C.L. Tribunal John XXIII Pastoral Center, Charleston
Olenchock, Stephen A. Engaged Encounter, Wheeling & Clarksburg Vicariates & St. John University, Morgantown
Prentiss, Joseph J., St. John University, Morgantown
Prestera, Michael R., Jr. Director, Genoa Christian Center; Pastoral Assoc., Sacred Heart, Huntington
Quigley, Charles C. Ecumenical Ministry, Martinsburg Vicariate & St. Leo, Inwood
Sarraga, John W. Office of Prison Ministry (Federal Prison) & St. Brendan, Elkins
Shaw, A. Ray, III, St. Elizabeth, Phillipi
Showalter, George B., St. Margaret Mary, Parkersburg
Shultz, John A., (Retired)
Smith, Paul J., (Retired)
Smoulder, George St. Alphonsus, Wheeling
Strange, William B., Jr., St. Charles Borromeo, White Sulphur Springs
Thompson, Rue C., Jr. Office of Prison Ministry (State Prisons and Regional Jails) & Holy Rosary, Buckhannon
Trunzo, Thomas Notre Dame High School, Clarksburg; St. James the Apostle, Clarksburg; Sacred Heart, Salem; St. Patrick, West Union
Windett, John E. Diocesan Planning and Pastoral Services (Home Health Care) & St. Elizabeth Ann Seton, Franklin
Wise, W. Donald, St. Francis De Sales, Beckley
Wojcicki, Ronald J., (Retired)
Wuletich, David E., St. Anthony, Charleston
Ziolkowski, John F., St. Francis De Sales, Beckley

INSTITUTIONS LOCATED IN THE DIOCESE

[A] COLLEGES AND UNIVERSITIES

WHEELING. *Wheeling Jesuit University*, 316 Washington Ave., 26003-6243. Tel: 304-243-2000; Fax: 304-243-2120. Web: www.wju.edu. Revs. Brian P. O'Donnell, S.J., Ph.D., Rector, Jesuit Community; Walter A. Buckius, S.J.; John J. Coll, S.J.; Harry F. Gieb; Joseph J. Hayden, S.J.; George R. Hohman, S.J.; Joseph E. Kolb, S.J.; James A. O'Brien, S.J.; Donald M. Serva, S.J.; Michael F. Steltenkamp, S.J. Jesuit Fathers. Priests 11; Lay Teachers 71; Students 1,304.

[B] HIGH SCHOOLS, CENTRAL

WHEELING. *Central Catholic High School*, 75-14th St., 26003. Tel: 304-233-1660; Fax: 304-233-3187. Web: www.cchsknights.org. Dr. Joseph F. Viglietta, Ph.D., Prin. Sisters of St. Joseph 1; Lay Teachers 33; Students 384.

CHARLESTON. *Charleston Catholic High School* (1923) (Grades 6-12), 1033 Virginia St. E., 25301. Tel: 304-342-8415; Fax: 304-342-1259. Email: debraksullivan@hotmail.com. Web: www.charlestoncatholic-crw.org. Mrs. Debra K. Sullivan, Prin.; Dara Krack, Librarian. Lay Teachers 33; Students 466.

CLARKSBURG. *Harrison Co. Catholic School System. Notre Dame High School* (1924) (Grades 7-12), 127 E. Pike St., 26301. Tel: 304-623-1026; Fax: 304-623-1026. Email: ndhs@iolinc.net. Dr. Carroll Kelly Morrison, Prin.; Shawn Williams, Librarian. Faculty 18; Lay Teachers 11; Students 162.

HUNTINGTON. *St. Joseph Catholic High School*, 600 13th St., 25701. Tel: 304-525-5096; Fax: 304-525-0781. Email: info@stjosephhs.org. Web: www.stjosephhs.org. Patrick Finneran, Prin.; Susan Popp, Librarian. Faculty 20; Students 196.

MCMECHEN. *Bishop Donahue Memorial High School* (1955) 325 Logan St., 26040. Tel: 304-233-3850; Fax: 304-233-8677. Email: dangalich@aol.com. Web: www.bishopdonahue.org. Daniel T. Angalich, Prin. (For Marshall Co.) Faculty 15; Students 144.

PARKERSBURG. *Parkersburg Catholic Junior-Senior High School*, (Grades 7-12), 3201 Fairview Ave., 26104. Tel: 304-485-6341; Fax: 304-485-4697. Email: pchs@pchs1.com. Web: pchs1.com. Mrs. Marie A. Held, Prin.; Mrs. Yvonne Powderly, Librarian. Faculty 22; Students 195.

WEIRTON. *Madonna High School*, 150 Michael Way, 26062. Tel: 304-723-0545; Fax: 304-723-0564. Email: jmihalyo@weirtonmadonna.org. Web: www.weirtonmadonna.org. John Mihalyo, Prin. Faculty 14; Students 160.

[C] ELEMENTARY SCHOOLS, CENTRAL

WHEELING. *Wheeling Catholic Elementary School*, (Grades PreK-8), Consolidation of the following parishes: St. Alphonsus; St. Ladislaus; St. Mary; St. Joseph; Sacred Heart; Blessed Trinity; St. Joan of Arc & Blessed Martin De Porres., 77-14th St., 26003. Tel: 304-233-1515; Fax: 304-233-1516.

Email: jstechly@access.k12.wv.us. Web: wheelingcatholicschool.com. Mary Alice Florio, Prin. Teachers 12; Students 114.

BENWOOD. *SS. James and John Elementary School*, (Grades PreK-8), 52 Seventh St., 26031. Tel: 304-232-1587; Fax: 304-232-4707. Email: saints527@yahoo.com. Mrs. Jennifer Marsh, Prin.; Mrs. Sandy Lantz, Librarian. Consolidation of the following parishes: St. John, Benwood; St. James, McMechen. Lay Teachers 12; Students 130.

CLARKSBURG. *Harrison County Catholic School System. St. Mary's Central Grade School* (1914) (Grades PreSchool-6), 107 E. Pike St., 26301. Tel: 304-622-9831; Fax: 304-622-9831. Email: smgs@iolinc.net. Nicole A. Folio, Prin. Consolidation of the following parishes: All Saints, Bridgeport; Immaculate Conception, Clarksburg; St. James, Clarksburg; Our Lady of Perpetual Help, Stonewood; St. Ann, Shinnston; Sacred Heart, Salem. Faculty 17; Students 151.

FAIRMONT. *Fairmont Catholic Grade School* (1928) (Grades K-8), Consolidation of the following parishes: St. Peter; Immaculate Conception; St. Anthony., 416-A Madison St., 26554. Tel: 304-363-5313; Fax: 304-363-7701. Email: FCSSSchool@aol.com. Sr. Mary DiDomenico, S.S.J., Prin. Sisters 1; Lay Teachers 13; Students 183.

MORGANTOWN. *St. Francis de Sales Central Catholic School*, (Grades PreK-8), 41 Guthrie La., 26508. Tel: 304-291-5070; Fax: 304-291-5104. Email: jdowney@stfrancismorgantown.com. Web: www.stfrancismorgantown.com. Mr. John M. Downey V., Prin.; Paige Buck, Librarian. Lay Teachers 26; Students 386.

PARKERSBURG. *Parkersburg Catholic Elementary School*, (Grades PreK-6), 810 Juliana St., 26101. Tel: 304-422-6694; Fax: 304-422-2469. Email: pces@pchs1.com. Web: pceswv.org. Mr. Kevin Simonton, Prin. Lay Teachers 9; Staff 22; Students 164.

[D] PASTORAL CENTERS

WHEELING. *Paul VI Pastoral Center*, 667 Stone & Shannon Rd., 26003. Tel: 304-277-3300; Fax: 304-277-4320. Email: info@paulvi.org. Web: www.paulvi.org. Revs. David Nestler, O.F.M.Cap., Dir.; Dismas Young, O.F.M.Cap.; Bro. Robert Herrick, O.F.M.Cap., Assoc. Dir. Capacity 72.

CHARLESTON. *Blessed John XXIII Pastoral Center* (1985) 100 Hodges Rd., 25314. Tel: 304-342-0507; Fax: 304-342-4786. Email: johnxxiii@charter.net. Deacon Gary W. Lane, Dir. Capacity 166.

HUTTONSVILLE. *Bishop Hodges Pastoral Center* (1977) Rte. 1, Box 9D, 26273. Tel: 304-335-2165; Fax: 304-335-2165. Email: groupservices@bhpc-dwc.org. Web: www.bhpc-dwc.org. Deacon Louis J. Belldina, M.S., Dir.; Barbara Bellding, Asst. Dir. Capacity 72.

KEARNEYSVILLE. *Priest Field Pastoral Center*, 4030 Middleway Pike, 25430. Tel: 304-725-1435; Fax: 304-725-1437. Email: priestfield@aol.org. Very Rev. William P. Linhares, T.O.R., Dir. Capacity 110.

[E] ASSOCIATED SPIRITUAL AND PASTORAL LIFE CENTERS

WHEELING. *St. Joseph Center*, 137 Mount St. Joseph Rd., 26003-1799. Tel: 304-232-8160; Fax: 304-232-0506. Email: mclark@dsjoseph.org. Web: www.csjoseph.org. Sr. Mary Clark, C.S.J., Dir. Congregation of St. Joseph Overnight Capacity 10; Daytime Capacity 25.

Maryhill Hermitage, 2264 Marshall Ave., 26003.

OLD FIELDS. *Holy Spirit Hermitage* (1979) Hickory Hill Rd., H.C. 66, Box 20, 26845-9201. Tel: 304-289-3997. In Res. Rev. Richard B. Hite, M.S.A.

[F] GENERAL HOSPITALS

WHEELING. *Bishop Joseph H. Hodges Continuous Care Center*, 600 Medical Park, P.O. Box 6316, 26003. Tel: 304-243-3800; Fax: 304-243-3398. Email: ctarr@wheelinghospital.com. Web: www.wheelinghospital.com. Christy Tarr, Admin. Skilled and Intermediate Care. Bed Capacity 120; Total Assisted Annually 310; Total Staff 170.

Wheeling Hospital (1850) One Medical Park, 26003. Tel: 304-243-3000; Fax: 304-243-3060. Web: www.wheelinghospital.com. Mr. Ronald L. Violi, CEO; Sr. Mary Ann Rosenbaum, S.S.J., Dir. of Pastoral Care Dept.; Rev. Michael McKay, O.S.B., Chap.; Bro. John McDonogh, F.M.S., Chap.; Sisters Mairead Scanlon, S.S.J., Chap.; Mona Farthing, S.S.J., Chap. Sisters of St. Joseph 3; Patients Assisted Annually 295,760; Total Staff 1,945; Bed Capacity 277.

BUCKHANNON. *St. Joseph's Hospital of Buckhannon, Inc.* (1921) 1 Amalia Dr., 26201. Tel: 304-473-2000; Fax: 304-472-6620. Web: www.stj.net. Sue Johnson-Phillippe, CEO. Attended by Marist Fathers. Sisters of the Pallottine Missionary Society 4; Bed Capacity 95; Patients Assisted Annually 69,994; Home Health Care & Hospice Patients 7,067; Total Staff 350.

St. Joseph's Foundation of Buckhannon, Inc. (1993) 1 Amalia Dr., 26201. Tel: 304-473-6819.

HUNTINGTON. *St. Mary's Medical Center*, 2900 First Ave., 25702. Tel: 304-526-1234; Fax: 304-526-1538. Web: www.st-marys.org. Michael G. Sellards, Pres. & CEO. Pallottine Missionary Sisters 6; Bed Capacity 393; Patients Assisted Annually 252,921.

School of Nursing Tel: 304-526-1270; Fax: 304-526-1538. Student Nurses 176; Total Staff 2,225.

[G] NURSING HOMES

WHEELING. *Good Shepherd Nursing Home*, 159 Edgington Ln., 26003. Tel: 304-242-1093; Fax: 304-242-1121. Mr. Donald R. Kirsch, Admin.; Revs. John Beckley, S.M., Chap.; Raymond Carr, S.M., Chap. Sisters 2; Bed Capacity 192; Total Assisted Annually 300; Total Staff 240.

[H] HOMES FOR AGED

WHEELING. *Welty Home for the Aged, Inc.*, 159 Edgington Ln., 26003-6261. Tel: 304-242-5233; Fax: 304-230-1132. Bed Capacity 52; Residents 52; Total Assisted Annually 66; Total Staff 46.

Welty Trust, Inc., 83 Edgington Ln., 26003. Tel: 304-242-2300; Fax: 304-243-0890.

Trustees: Most Rev. Michael J. Bransfield, Pres.; Very Rev. Anthony Cincinnati, S.T.D., V.E.; Mr. William Yaeger, Treas.

Welty Retirement Apartments, 1276 National Rd., 26003. Tel: 304-242-5820; Fax: 304-230-5600. 1315 National Rd., 26003. Tel: 304-230-5611.

[I] HEALTH SERVICES

HUNTINGTON. *Pallottine Health Services, Inc.* (1988) 2900 First Ave., 25702. Tel: 304-526-8915; Fax: 304-526-1538. Web: www.st-marys.org. Sr. M. Diane Bushee, S.A.C., Contact Person. Sponsored by the Pallottine Missionary Sisters.

Parent Corp. for:

St. Mary's Medical Center, Inc. (1924) 2900 First Ave., 25702. Tel: 304-526-1270; Fax: 304-526-1538. Web: www.st-marys.org.

St. Joseph's Hospital of Buckhannon, Inc. (1921) 1 Amalia Dr., Buckhannon, 26201. Tel: 304-473-2111; Fax: 304-472-6620. Web: www.stj.net. Bed Capacity 488; Total Assisted Annually 338,117; Total Staff 2,980.

PINEVILLE. *Children's Health Care, Inc.*, Box 430, 24874. Tel: 304-732-7069; Fax: 304-732-7098. Email: ecatters@marshall.edu. Sr. Eileen Catterson, D.W.M.D., Dir.; Donna Musgrave, Office Mgr. Total Assisted Annually 6,040; Total Staff 13.

RHODELL. *Rhodell Health Clinic* (1975) P.O. Box 158, 25915. Tel: 304-683-4318; Fax: 304-683-4791.

Appalachian Health Cooperative, Inc.

[J] SOCIAL SERVICE INSTITUTIONS

WHEELING. *Catholic Charities Neighborhood Center*, 125-18th St., P.O. Box 6176, 26003-0713. Tel: 304-232-7157; Fax: 304-238-7133. Email: wheelingccnc@comcast.net. Sr. Linda Sevcik, S.M., Dir.

HUTTONSVILLE. *Camp Tygart*, Rte. 1, Box 9D, 26273. Tel: 304-335-2130 (In Season); 304-233-0880 (Out of Season); Fax: 304-230-0508. Email: mhall@dwc.org. Mr. Joshua Wattenbarger, Admin. Diocesan Children's Camp.

KERMIT. *A.B.L.E. Families, Inc.* (1994) P.O. Box 1249, 25674. Tel: 304-393-4987; Fax: 304-393-4987. Web: www.ablefamilies.org. Barry M. Hudock, Exec. Dir.

SALEM. *Nazareth Farm, Inc.* (1979) Rte. 2, Box 194-3, 26426. Tel: 304-782-2742; Fax: 304-782-4358. Email: nazarethfarm@gmail.com. Web: www.nazarethfarm.org.

[K] HOMES FOR DEPENDENT CHILDREN

WHEELING. *St. John's Home for Children* (1856) 141 Key Ave., 26003-7412. Tel: 304-242-5633; Fax: 304-243-4911. Email: stjterry@stratuswave.net. Web: www.stjohnshomeforchildren.org. Terence A. McCormick, Exec. Dir. Children 8; Total Assisted 10.

[L] MONASTERIES AND RESIDENCES OF PRIESTS AND BROTHERS

WHEELING. *Capuchin Hermitage of St. Joseph, St. Joseph of Leonissa Capuchin Heritage*, 665 Stone & Shannon Rd., 26003. Tel: 304-277-2971; Fax: 304-277-2972. Email: caphermitage@att.net. Revs. Eric Gauchat, O.F.M.Cap.; David Nestler, O.F.M.Cap.; Bro. Robert Herrick, O.F.M.Cap.; Rev. Dismas Young, O.F.M.Cap.

CHARLESTON. *Capuchins-St. Anthony Friary*, 1000 Sixth St., 25302. Tel: 304-342-2716. Email: tonycap@city.net. Web: home.att.net/~stanthony/capuchinfranciscan.html. Revs. Dennis J. Klemash, O.F.M.Cap., Guardian; Regis Schlick, O.F.M.Cap., Vicar; Kieran Quinn, O.F.M.Cap. (Retired); Roy Schuster, O.F.M.Cap (Retired); Albert Alexandrunas, O.F.M.Cap.; Bro. Thomas Wells, O.F.M.Cap.

HINTON. *Monastery of Christ on the Mountain* (1968) P.O. Box 429, 25951-0429. Tel: 304-466-4782; Fax: 304-466-3716. Email: keving35@aol.com. Revs. Daniel Chowning; Anthony Haglof, Supr.; Bro. Gilbert Tovares, O.C.D. Discalced Carmelite Hermits.

[M] CONVENTS AND RESIDENCES FOR SISTERS

WHEELING. *Sisters of the Visitation*, Mount de Chantal, 410 Washington Ave., 26003. Tel: 304-232-1283; Fax: 304-233-8598. Email: sisters@mountdechantal.org. Web: www.mountdechantal.org; www.visitationsisters.org. Sr. Mary Alicia Sours, V.H.M., Mod.

Sisters of the Visitation of Holy Mary of Mount de Chantal, Inc., Attended by Jesuits from Wheeling Jesuit University. Professed Sisters 8.

Union of Our Lady of Charity United States Province (1900) 141 Edgington Ln., 26003. Tel: 304-242-7070; Fax: 304-242-0042. Web: nauolc.net. Sisters Deana Kohlman, Local Supr.; Deana Kohlman, Business Mgr.

North American Union Sisters of Our Lady of Charity, Inc.

Wheeling Center, Congregation of St. Joseph, 137 Mount St. Joseph Rd., 26003-1799. Tel: 304-232-8160; Fax: 304-232-0506. Email: ccrinkey@csjoseph.org. Web: www.csjoseph.org. Sr. Mary Alice Girrens, C.S.J., Admin. & Coord. Wheeling Center-Congregation of St. Joseph.

Attended by Wheeling Jesuit University.

[N] FOUNDATIONS

WHEELING. *Central Catholic High School Educational Foundation, Inc.*, 75-14th St., 26003. Tel: 304-233-1660; Fax: 304-233-3187.

**Clarence L. Christ Trust*, Office of the Chancellor: *Diocese of Wheeling-Charleston*, P.O. Box 230, 26003. Tel: 304-233-0880; Fax: 304-230-2029.

John S. Thoner Family Charitable Trust (1995) 1300 Byron St., P.O. Box 230, 26003. Tel: 304-233-0880; Fax: 304-233-4086.

Medical Park Foundation (1995) One Medical Park, 26003. Tel: 304-243-2969.

**Michael Christ Trust*, Office of the Chancellor: *Diocese of Wheeling-Charleston*, P.O. Box 230, 26003. Tel: 304-233-0880; Fax: 304-230-2029.

The Sisters of St. Joseph Health & Wellness Foundation, 137 Mount St. Joseph Rd., 26003-1799. Tel: 304-233-4500; Fax: 304-232-1404. Email: ssjhwf@aol.com; helenssj@aol.com. Web: www.ssjhealthandwellnessfoundation.org. Sisters Janice Landwehr, C.S.J., Co-Exec. Dir.; Helen Skormisley, C.S.J., Co-Exec. Dir.

Sisters of St. Joseph of Wheeling Foundation, Inc. (1974) 137 Mount St. Joseph Rd., 26003-1799. Tel: 304-232-8160; Fax: 304-232-0506. Email: ccrinkey@csjoseph.org. Web: www.csjoseph.org.

West Virginia Catholic Foundation, P.O. Box 230, 26003. Tel: 304-233-0880; Fax: 304-233-4086. Email: bminor@dwc.org. Web: wvcf.dwc.org. Mr. Bryan E. Minor, Exec. Dir.

CLARKSBURG. *Harrison County Catholic Education Foundation, Inc.*, 126 E. Pike St., 26301-2720.

PARKERSBURG. *Parkersburg Catholic Schools Foundation, Inc.*, 3201 Fairview Ave., 26104-2111. Tel: 304-428-7528; Fax: 304-428-8159. Email: pcsf@pchs1.com. Web: pchs1.com.

Sisters of St. Joseph Charitable Fund, Inc. (1997) 4420 Rosemar Rd., Ste. 204, P.O. Box 4440, 26104-4440. Tel: 304-424-6080; Fax: 304-424-6081. Email: info@ssjcharitablefund.org. Web: www.ssjcharitablefund.org. Sr. Jane Harrington, C.S.J., Exec. Dir.; Ms. Ann Y. Frost, Asst. Dir.; Sr. Molly Bauer, C.S.J., Prog. Dir.

[O] NEWMAN CENTERS

CHARLESTON. *John Paul II Campus Ministry Center* 310-26th St., 25304.

ATHENS. *Concord University Newman Center* , See Sacred Heart, Princeton, Hammond, P.O. Box 447, 24712. Tel: 304-384-9502. Email: sacheapar@citlink.net. Deacon Don M. Hammond.

BETHANY. *St. John Fisher Catholic Chapel* 201 Richardson St., Box W, 26032. Tel: 304-829-4622; Fax: 304-829-3417. Rev. Walter M. Jagela.

BUCKHANNON. *West Virginia Wesleyan College Newman Center* 35 Franklin St., Box 848, 26201-0848. Tel: 304-472-3414. Email: hrchurch@msys.net. Rev. Ronald J. Nikodem, S.M.; Bro. Ray Madigan, S.M.

FAIRMONT. *Fairmont State University Newman Center* 1200 College Park, 26554. Tel: 304-363-2300. Email: fatherj2@juno.com. Rev. Jude Molnar, T.O.R., Chap.

HUNTINGTON. *Marshall Newman Center* 1609 Fifth Ave., 25703. Tel: 304-525-4618; Fax: 304-522-4115. Email: mail@marshallcatholic.com. Web: www.marshallcatholic.com. Natalie Rohan, Dir. Campus Min.

PHILIPPI. *Alderson-Broaddus College Newman Center* Rte. 3, Box 257, 26416. Tel: 304-457-2641. Rev. Andrew G. Kranyc.

SHEPHERDSTOWN. *Good Shepherd Catholic Campus Ministry Center* P.O. Box 1163, 25443.

WEST LIBERTY. *West Liberty State College, St. Thomas Aquinas Campus Ministry* 134 Chatham St., 26074. Tel: 304-336-7751; 304-829-4622 (Bethany). Box W, Bethany, 26032. Rev. Walter M. Jagela.

[P] CHILD CARE CENTERS

WHEELING. *Holy Family Child Care & Development Center, Inc.*, 161 Edgington Ln., 26003. Tel: 304-242-5222; Fax: 304-242-5379. Email: hfcccoffice@wirefire.com. Michele Forsythe, Exec. Dir. Total Assisted 86; Total Staff 22.

CLARKSBURG. *Madonna Day Care Center*, 444 E. Pike St., 26031. Tel: 304-622-4453. Sandra Mitchell, Dir. Total Staff 6.

[Q] MISCELLANEOUS

WHEELING. *St. Joseph Health Initiative, Inc.*, 137 Mount St. Joseph Rd., 26003-1799. Tel: 304-232-8160; Fax: 304-232-0506. Email: ccrinkey@csjoseph.org. Sr. Marguerite O'Brien, C.S.J., Pres.

Retirement Trust Agreement of the Priests' Health and Retirement Association (1997) 1300 Bryon St., 26003. Tel: 304-233-0880; Fax: 304-233-4086.

Wheeling-Charleston Diocesan Council of Catholic Women, 1310 Byron St., P.O. Box 230, 26003. Tel: 304-233-0880, Ext. 264; Fax: 304-233-4563. Sr. Ellen F. Dunn, O.P., Diocesan Moderator; Barbara Belldina, Pres.; Toni DiStefano, Sec. & Treas.

PENCE SPRINGS. *Bethlehem Farm, Inc.*, P.O. Box 274, 24962.

RELIGIOUS INSTITUTES OF MEN REPRESENTED IN THE DIOCESE

For further details refer to the corresponding bracketed number in the Religious Institutes of Men or Women section.

[0470]—*The Capuchin Franciscan Friars*—O.F.M.Cap.
[1000]—*Congregation of the Passion*—C.P.
[0260]—*Discalced Carmelite Friars*—O.C.D.
[0520]—*Franciscan Friars*—O.F.M.
[0585]—*Heralds of Good News*—H.G.N.
[0690]—*Jesuit Fathers and Brothers*—S.J.
[0770]—*Marist Brothers*—F.M.S.
[0780]—*Marist Fathers*—S.M.
[0840]—*Missionary Servants of the Most Holy Trinity*—S.T.
[0920]—*Oblates of St. Francis de Sales*—O.S.F.S.
[0420]—*Society of the Divine Word*—S.V.D.
[0590]—*Society of the Missionaries of the Holy Apostles*—M.S.A.
[0570]—*The Glenmary Home Missioners*—G.H.M.
[0560]—*Third Order Regular of St. Francis*—T.O.R.

RELIGIOUS INSTITUTES OF WOMEN REPRESENTED IN THE DIOCESE

[0130]—*Apostles of the Sacred Heart of Jesus*—A.S.C.J.
[1000]—*Congregation of Divine Providence* (Melbourne, KY)—C.D.P.
[3110]—*Congregation of Our Lady of the Retreat in the Cenacle* (North American Prov.)—R.C.
[3832]—*Congregation of the Sisters of St. Joseph* (Wheeling Center)—C.S.J.
[1730]—*Congregation of the Sisters of the Third Order of St. Francis* (Oldenburg, IN)—O.S.F.
[0760]—*Daughters of Charity of St. Vincent De Paul* (Emmitsburg Prov.)—D.C.
[0960]—*Daughters of Wisdom*—D.W.
[1105]—*Dominican Sisters of Hope* (Ossining, NY)—O.P.
[1115]—*Dominican Sisters of Peace*—O.P.
[1070-02]—*Dominican Sisters of St. Mary of the Springs* (Columbus, OH)—O.P.
[2430]—*Marist Sisters*—S.M.
[3070]—*North American Union Sisters of Our Lady of Charity*—N.A.U.-O.L.C.
[3150]—*Pallottine Missionary Sisters*—S.A.C.
[2970]—*School Sisters of Notre Dame*—S.S.N.D.
[1680]—*School Sisters of St. Francis*—O.S.F.
[0570]—*Sisters of Charity of Seton Hill, Greensburg, PA*—S.C.
[0590]—*Sisters of Charity of St. Elizabeth Convent Station*—S.C.
[0990]—*Sisters of Divine Providence (Marie de la Roche Prov.)*—C.D.P.
[2575]—*Sisters of Mercy of the Americas*—R.S.M.
[3000]—*Sisters of Notre Dame de Namur* (Chesapeake Province)—S.N.D.DeN.
[1630]—*Sisters of St. Francis of Penance and Christian Charity*—O.S.F.
[1530]—*Sisters of St. Francis of the Congregation of Our Lady of Lourdes*—O.S.F.
[3893]—*Sisters of St. Joseph of Chestnut Hill* (Philadelphia)—S.S.J.
[3830-13]—*Sisters of St. Joseph of Pittsburgh* (Baden)—C.S.J.
[3830-05]—*Sisters of St. Joseph of Rockville Centre* (Brentwood)—C.S.J.
[]—*Sisters of the Holy Cross*—C.S.C.
[2110]—*Sisters of the Humility of Mary*—H.M.
[]—*Sisters of the Infant Jesus* Zimbabwe—S.J.I.
[3220]—*Sisters of the Poor Child Jesus*—P.C.J.
[1760]—*Sisters of the Third Order of St. Francis of Penance and Charity*—O.S.F.
[4120-03]—*Ursuline Nuns of the Congregation of Paris*—O.S.U.
[4190]—*Visitation Nuns* (Wheeling, WV)—V.H.M.

DIOCESAN CEMETERIES

WHEELING. *Mount Calvary* (1872) 1685 National Rd., 26003-5599. Tel: 304-242-0460; Fax: 304-242-9506.

NECROLOGY

† Neville, Franklin A., Proctor, WV St. Joseph's; Proctor, WV St. Martin—Died Nov. 16, 2009
† Schneider, Charles J., (Retired)—Died June 10, 2009

An asterisk (*) denotes an organization that has established tax-exempt status directly with the IRS and is not covered by the USCCB Group Ruling.

Diocese of Wichita

(Dioecesis Wichitensis)

Most Reverend

MICHAEL OWEN JACKELS

Bishop of Wichita; ordained May 30, 1981; appointed Bishop of Wichita January 28, 2005; ordained April 4, 2005. *The Chancery, 424 N. Broadway, Wichita, KS 67202.*

Most Reverend

EUGENE J. GERBER, D.D.

Bishop Emeritus of Wichita; ordained May 19, 1959; appointed Bishop of Dodge City October 16, 1976; ordained December 14, 1976; installed December 15, 1976; appointed Bishop of Wichita November 23, 1982; installed February 9, 1983; retired October 4, 2001. *Res.: 424 N. Broadway, Wichita, KS 67202.*

The Chancery: 424 N. Broadway, Wichita, KS 67202. Tel: 316-269-3900; Fax: 316-269-3902.

Web: www.cdowk.org

ESTABLISHED AUGUST 2, 1887.

Square Miles 20,021.

New boundaries established by Apostolic Letters dated May 19, 1951. Bounded on the west by the west lines of Rice, Reno, Kingman and Harper counties, south by Oklahoma, east by Missouri, and north by the north lines of Bourbon, Allen, Woodson, Greenwood, Morris, Marion, McPherson and Rice Counties in Kansas.

For legal titles of parishes and diocesan institutions, consult the Chancery Office.

STATISTICAL OVERVIEW

Personnel	
Bishop	1
Retired Bishops	1
Priests: Diocesan Active in Diocese	78
Priests: Diocesan Active Outside Diocese	6
Priests: Retired, Sick or Absent	34
Number of Diocesan Priests	118
Religious Priests in Diocese	1
Total Priests in Diocese	119
Extern Priests in Diocese	6
Ordinations:	
Diocesan Priests	1
Transitional Deacons	5
Permanent Deacons in Diocese	5
Total Sisters	278
Parishes	
Parishes	90
With Resident Pastor:	
Resident Diocesan Priests	66
Without Resident Pastor:	
Administered by Priests	24
Pastoral Centers	22
Closed Parishes	1
Professional Ministry Personnel:	
Brothers	1
Sisters	10
Lay Ministers	39
Welfare	
Catholic Hospitals	7
Total Assisted	493,471
Health Care Centers	2
Total Assisted	56,574
Homes for the Aged	7
Total Assisted	1,161
Specialized Homes	1
Total Assisted	42
Special Centers for Social Services	1
Total Assisted	22,734
Residential Care of Disabled	1
Total Assisted	210
Educational	
Diocesan Students in Other Seminaries	45
Total Seminarians	45
Colleges and Universities	1
Total Students	2,557
High Schools, Diocesan and Parish	4
Total Students	2,524
Elementary Schools, Diocesan and Parish	35
Total Students	8,283
Catechesis/Religious Education:	
High School Students	1,803
Elementary Students	5,068
Total Students under Catholic Instruction	20,280
Teachers in the Diocese:	
Priests	7
Sisters	11
Lay Teachers	668
Vital Statistics	
Receptions into the Church:	
Infant Baptism Totals	2,389
Minor Baptism Totals	183
Adult Baptism Totals	223
Received into Full Communion	379
First Communions	2,536
Confirmations	2,021
Marriages:	
Catholic	416
Interfaith	278
Total Marriages	694
Deaths	892
Total Catholic Population	115,023
Total Population	962,097

Former Bishops—Most Revs. JAMES O'REILLY, D.D., Bishop-Elect; died July 26, 1887; JOHN JOSEPH HENNESSY, D.D., cons. Nov. 30, 1888; died July 13, 1920; AUGUSTUS JOHN SCHWERTNER, D.D., ord. June 12, 1897; cons. June 8, 1921; installed June 22, 1921; died Oct. 2, 1939; CHRISTIAN HERMAN WINKELMANN, S.T.D., ord. June 11, 1907; cons. Auxiliary Bishop of St. Louis, Nov. 30, 1933; installed March 5, 1940; died Nov. 18, 1946; MARK K. CARROLL, S.T.D., ord. June 10, 1922; appt. Feb. 15, 1947; cons. April 23, 1947; installed May 6, 1947; resigned Sept. 27, 1967; died Jan. 12, 1985; LEO C. BYRNE, D.D., ord. June 10, 1933; appt. Titular Bishop of Sabidia and Auxiliary of St. Louis, May 21, 1954; cons. June 29, 1954; transferred to Wichita, "cum jure successionis" 1961; appt. Apostolic Administrator, Feb. 25, 1963; transferred to St. Paul and Minneapolis, Sept. 27, 1967; died Oct. 21, 1974; DAVID M. MALONEY, S.S., S.T.L., J.C.D., former Bishop of Wichita; ord. Dec. 8, 1936; appt. Titular Bishop of Ruspae Auxiliary of Denver, Nov. 9, 1960; cons. Jan. 4, 1961; transferred to Wichita, Dec. 6, 1967; resigned July 16, 1982; died Feb. 15, 1995; EUGENE J. GERBER, D.D., Bishop of Wichita; ord. May 19, 1959; appt. Bishop of Dodge City Oct. 16, 1976; ord. Dec. 14, 1976; installed Dec. 15, 1976; appt. Bishop of Wichita Nov. 23, 1982; installed Feb. 9, 1983; resigned Oct. 4, 2001; THOMAS J. OLMSTED, J.C.D., ord. July 2, 1973; appt. Coadjutor Bishop of Wichita Feb. 16, 1999; Episcopal ord. April 20, 1999; appt. Bishop of Wichita Oct. 4, 2001; appt. Bishop of Phoenix Dec. 20, 2003.

Chancery Office—424 N. Broadway, Wichita, 67202. Tel: 316-269-3900; Fax: 316-269-3902. Web: www.cdowk.org.

Vicar General—Rev. Msgr. ROBERT E. HEMBERGER, J.C.L.

Moderator of the Diocesan Curia—Rev. Msgr. ROBERT E. HEMBERGER, J.C.L., 424 N. Broadway, Wichita, 67202.

Vicar for Clergy—Rev. MATTHEW C. MCGINNESS.

Director of Diocesan Planning—Rev. Msgr. ROBERT E. HEMBERGER, J.C.L.

Chancellor—Rev. JOHN B. BRUNGARDT.

Administrative Assistant to the Bishop—Rev. THOMAS M. HOISINGTON, S.T.L.

Presbyteral Council/College of Consultors—Most Rev. MICHAEL O. JACKELS, S.T.D.; Revs. JEROME A. BEAT; JAMES J. BILLINGER; JOHN B. BRUNGARDT; Rev. Msgr. ROBERT E. HEMBERGER, J.C.L.; Revs. THOMAS M. HOISINGTON, S.T.L.; JOHN V. HOTZE, J.C.L.; JOHN P. LANZRATH, S.T.L.; Rev. Msgr. CHARLES W. REGAN (Retired); Revs. CHARLES F. SEIWERT, J.C.L.; JOHN P. SHERLOCK; MATTHEW C. MCGINNESS; JEROME J. SPEXARTH; KENNETH S. VAN HAVERBEKE.

Tribunal—424 N. Broadway, Wichita, 67202. Tel: 316-269-3960.

Judicial Vicar—Rev. JOHN V. HOTZE, J.C.L.

Adjutant Judicial Vicar—Rev. MICHAEL E. NOLAN, J.C.L.

Promoter of Justice—Rev. Msgr. JOHN P. GILSENAN, J.C.L.

Judges—Revs. STEPHEN R. BAXTER, J.C.L.; DOUGLAS CAMPBELL, J.C.L.; Rev. Msgr. ROBERT E. HEMBERGER, J.C.L.; Revs. JOHN V. HOTZE, J.C.L.; MICHAEL E. NOLAN, J.C.L.

Defenders of the Bond—Rev. Msgr. JOHN P. GILSENAN, J.C.L.; Revs. CHARLES F. SEIWERT, J.C.L.; STUART M. SMELTZER, J.C.L.

Notaries—Mrs. ROBERTA RAU; Mrs. CLAUDINE WALD; Mrs. JANET MILLER; Mrs. DENISE NORTHUP.

Ongoing Formation of the Clergy Committee—Revs. JOHN B. BRUNGARDT; JOSEPH M. GILE, S.T.D.; Rev. Msgr. ROBERT E. HEMBERGER, J.C.L.; Revs. JOHN P. LANZRATH, S.T.L., Prog. Dir.; MICHAEL E. NOLAN, J.C.L.; WAYNE L. SCHMID; JEROME J. SPEXARTH; KENNETH S. VAN HAVERBEKE; BENJAMIN N. NGUYEN; KENT A. HEMBERGER; MATTHEW D. MARNEY.

Diocesan Offices and Directors

Catholic Diocese of Wichita—Most Revs. MICHAEL O. JACKELS, S.T.D., Bishop of Wichita; EUGENE J. GERBER, D.D., Bishop Emeritus.

Apostleship of Prayer—Rev. MATTHEW C. MCGINNESS, 6900 E. 45th St., N., Wichita, 67226.

Catholic Charities—Ms. JANET PAPE, Dir., 532 N. Broadway, Wichita, 67214. Tel: 316-264-8344.

Catholic Care Center—Ms. WENDY MENDEZ, Admin., 6700 E. 45th St., N., Wichita, 67226. Tel: 316-744-2020; Fax: 316-744-2182.

Cemeteries—Mr. JIM SHELDON, 1640 N. Maize Rd., Wichita, 67212. Tel: 316-722-1971.

Communications Office—AMY PAVLACKA, Dir., 424 N. Broadway, Wichita, 67202. Tel: 316-269-3900; Fax: 316-269-3902.

Cursillo (Spanish language)—Rev. JEROME A. BEAT, Spiritual Dir., 3600 E. Harry, Wichita, 67218. Tel: 316-689-5242.

Cursillo (English language)—Rev. STEPHEN R. BAXTER, J.C.L., Spiritual Dir., P.O. Box 149, Halstead, 67056. Tel: 316-835-2173.

Building Commission—Rev. JAMES J. BILLINGER, Chm.; Mr. BRYAN R. COULTER, CPA; Rev. KENT A. HEMBERGER; Rev. Msgr. ROBERT E. HEMBERGER, J.C.L.; Mrs. LINDA SNOOK; Rev. MICHAEL E. NOLAN, J.C.L.; Mr. MICHAEL W. WESCOTT; Mrs. TERESA WHITE; Mr. WILLIAM WILHELM.

Stewardship Office—Rev. JOHN P. LANZRATH, S.T.L., Dir.; Mr. DANIEL L. LOUGHMAN, Coord.

Finance and Administrative Services Office—Mr. BRYAN R. COULTER, CPA, Dir. Finance, 424 N. Broadway, Wichita, 67202. Tel: 316-269-3900.

Finance Committee—Most Rev. MICHAEL O. JACKELS, S.T.D., Bishop of Wichita; Mr. MICHAEL AYLWARD; Rev. JOHN B. BRUNGARDT; Mr. BRYAN R. COULTER, CPA; Ms. JOYE HANEBERG; Rev. Msgr. ROBERT E. HEMBERGER, J.C.L.; Mr. RICHARD KERSCHEN; Mr. ALBERT LIEBERT; Mr. FRANK REMAR; Mr. DALE WIGGINS.

Health Affairs - Diocesan Liaison—Rev. Msgr. ROBERT E. HEMBERGER, J.C.L., 424 N. Broadway, Wichita, 67202. Tel: 316-269-3962.

Ministry with Persons with Disabilities Office—Mr. THOMAS K. RACUNAS, Dir., 424 N. Broadway, Wichita, 67202. Tel: 316-269-3900.

Catholic School Office—Mr. ROBERT VOBORIL, Supt., 424 N. Broadway, Wichita, 67202. Tel: 316-269-3950.

Religious Education Office—Ms. RHONDA LOHKAMP, Dir.; Ms. SHELLY BOLE, Prog. Coord. Catechist Formation & Special Projects, 424 N. Broadway, Wichita, 67202. Tel: 316-269-3940; Fax: 316-269-3967.

Mission Office—Sr. URSULA FOTOVICH, C.S.J., Dir., 424 N. Broadway, Wichita, 67202. Tel: 316-269-3946.

Legion of Mary—Rev. JAMES S. MAINZER, St. Mary Church, 106 E. Eighth, Newton, 67114. Tel: 316-282-0459.

Family Life and Natural Family Planning Office—Ms. JUDITH LEONARD, Dir.; Miss KRISTINA SAMPLE, Prog. Coord., 1515 S. Clifton, Ste. 400, Wichita, 67218. Tel: 316-685-6776.

Newspaper: "The Catholic Advance"—Mr. CHRISTOPHER M. RIGGS, Editor; Mr. BRYAN R. COULTER, CPA, Business Mgr., 424 N. Broadway, Wichita, 67202. Tel: 316-269-3965.

Development and Planned Giving Office—Mr. MICHAEL W. WESCOTT, Dir.; Mrs. SYNDI LAREZ, Coord., 424 N. Broadway, Wichita, 67202. Tel: 316-269-3917.

Worship Office—Rev. MICHAEL E. NOLAN, J.C.L., Dir.

Respect Life and Social Justice Office—VACANT, Dir.; Rev. THOMAS M. HOISINGTON, S.T.L., Spiritual Moderator, 424 N. Broadway, Wichita, 67202. Tel: 316-269-3935.

Retreats—Rev. KENT A. HEMBERGER, Dir., Spiritual Life Center, 7100 E. 45th St. N., Wichita, 67226. Tel: 316-744-0167.

Rural Life Ministry—VACANT, 424 N. Broadway, Wichita, 67202. Tel: 316-269-3900.

Social Service—Ms. JANET PAPE, Catholic Charities, 532 N. Broadway, Wichita, 67214. Tel: 316-264-8344.

Victim Assistance Coordinator—Ms. KATHERINE J. LAMBERTZ, L.M.S.W. Tel: 316-619-4804. Email: kit.lambertz@cdowk.org; Rev. Msgr. ROBERT E. HEMBERGER, J.C.L., Review Bd. Chm.

Vocations—Rev. MICHAEL M. SIMONE, S.T.L., Dir., 424 N. Broadway, Wichita, 67202. Tel: 316-269-3900.

Hispanic Ministry Office—Mrs. JOSEPHA FERNANDEZ, Dir., 437 N. Topeka, Wichita, 67202. Tel: 316-269-3919.

Youth and Young Adult Ministry—Ms. CHRISTINE EDMONDS, Dir.; Mr. DAVID WALKER, Prog. Coord., 424 N. Broadway, Wichita, 67202. Tel: 316-269-3930.

St. Dismas Ministry to the Incarcerated—Mrs. MARY RUBECK, 4826 S.W. Briarcliff Rd., Towanda, 67144. Tel: 316-778-1939. Email: mrubeck@aol.com.

Human Resource Office—Mrs. THERESE SEILER, Dir.; Mr. LARRY RANGE, Personnel/Benefits Dir., 424 N. Broadway, Wichita, 67202. Tel: 316-269-3900; Fax: 316-269-3902.

Harvest House—Sr. MARILYN STAHL, Dir.; Rev. PAUL J. OBORNY, Spiritual Moderator (Retired), 424 N. Broadway, Wichita, 67202. Tel: 316-269-3900.

Totus Tuus of Wichita—LISA SHARP, Dir., 424 N. Broadway, Wichita, 67202. Tel: 316-440-1732; Rev. JOHN F. JIRAK, Spiritual Moderator.

CLERGY, PARISHES, MISSIONS AND PAROCHIAL SCHOOLS

CITY OF WICHITA

(SEDGWICK COUNTY)

1—CATHEDRAL OF THE IMMACULATE CONCEPTION (1887) Revs. John P. Sherlock, Rector; Adam Keiter.
Res.: 307 E. Central Ave., 67202. Tel: 316-263-6574; Fax: 316-263-1316. Email: stmarys@cathedral.kscoxmail.com. Web: www.wichitacathedral.com.
Catechesis/Religious Program—Students 185.

2—ALL SAINTS (1946) [JC 3] Rev. H. Jay Setter.
Res.: 3205 E. Grand St., 67218. Tel: 316-682-1415; Fax: 316-682-1096.
School—(Grades K-8), 3313 E. Grand, 67218. Tel: 316-682-6021; Fax: 316-682-8734. Paul E. Spacil, Prin. Lay Teachers 16; Students 238.
Catechesis/Religious Program—Sandra Nettleton, D.R.E. Students 76.

3—ST. ANNE (1955) Rev. Thomas Leland; Tracy Winslow, Lay Pastoral Assoc.
Office: 2801 S. Seneca, 67217-2399. Tel: 316-522-2383; Fax: 316-524-2370. Email: church@stannewichita.org. Web: www.stannewichita.org.
School—(Grades PreK-8) Tel: 316-522-6131; Fax: 316-469-0096. Email: school@stannewichita.org. Mr. Winston Kenton, Prin. Lay Teachers 14; Students 215.
Catechesis/Religious Program—Students 149.

4—ST. ANTHONY (1887), (German), Rev. Hung Q. Pham.
Res. & Mailing Address: 325 Ohio, 67214. Tel: 316-269-4641; 316-264-9352.
Catechesis/Religious Program—Students 119.

5—BLESSED SACRAMENT (1927) [JC] Rev. W. Shawn McKnight. In Res., Rev. Joseph M. Gile.
Rectory—401 S. Roosevelt Ave., 67218. Tel: 316-681-2204.
Church Office: 124 N. Roosevelt, 67208. Tel: 316-682-4557; Fax: 316-682-4558. Web: www.blessedsacramentwichita.com.
School—(Grades PreK-8) Tel: 316-684-3752; Fax: 316-687-1082. Jim Grogan, Prin.; Pam Loyle, Librarian. Lay Teachers 27; Students 438.
Catechesis/Religious Program—Katie Lewis, D.R.E. Students 56.

6—ST. CATHERINE OF SIENA (2008) Rev. Daniel J. Spexarth.
7335 W. 33rd St. N., 67205. Tel: 316-425-0595; Fax: 316-425-0685. Email: nancy@saintcatherinewichita.com. Web: www.saintcatherinewichita.com.
Catechesis/Religious Program—Polly Blum, D.R.E. Students 134.

7—CHRIST THE KING (1950) [JC] Rev. John B. Brungardt; Deacon Len Fennewald. In Res., Revs. Michael M. Simone; Roger Lumbre.
Res.: 4411 Maple Ave., 67209. Tel: 316-943-4353; Fax: 316-943-8196. Email: maplestchurch@yahoo.com.
School—(Grades PreK-8), 4501 Maple Ave., 67209. Tel: 316-943-0111; Fax: 361-943-0147. Web: ctkwichita.org. Mrs. Cindy Chrisman, Prin. (ME Admin K-9). Sisters, Adorers of the Blood of Christ 1; Lay Teachers 10; Students 132.
Catechesis/Religious Program—Students 69.
Convent—4601 W. Maple Ave., 67209.

8—CHURCH OF THE MAGDALEN (1950) Revs. Patrick G. York; Aaron Spexarth; Sr. Connie Beiriger, C.S.J., Pastoral Assoc.
Res.: 12626 E. 21st St. N., 67206. Tel: 316-634-2315; Fax: 316-634-3948.
School—(Grades PreK-8), 2221 N. 127th St. E, 67226. Tel: 316-634-1572; Fax: 316-634-6957. Janice Palmer, Prin.; Margo Funk, Librarian. Lay Teachers 29; Students 542.
Catechesis/Religious Program—Students 170.

9—CHURCH OF THE RESURRECTION (1965) Rev. Sherman A. Orr.
Res.: 4910 N. Woodlawn, 67220. Tel: 316-744-2776; Fax: 316-744-3027. Email: church@resurrectionwichita.com. Web: www.resurrectionwichita.com.
School—(Grades PreK-8) Tel: 316-744-3576; Fax: 316-744-1582. James E. Finkeldei, Prin.; Lisa Hinson, Librarian. Lay Teachers 17; Students 239.
Catechesis/Religious Program—Dustin Gates, D.R.E. Students 74.

10—ST. ELIZABETH ANN SETON (1982) Revs. Kenneth S. Van Haverbeke; Matthew D. Marney.
Res.: 645 N. 119th St. W., 67235. Tel: 316-721-1686; Fax: 316-721-1723.
School—(Grades K-8) Tel: 316-721-5693. Mr. David Charles, Prin.; Mrs. Kitty Garcia, Asst. Vice Prin. Lay Teachers 38; Students 745.
Catechesis/Religious Program—Students 330.

11—ST. FRANCIS OF ASSISI (1959) Revs. Daryl Befort; Michael Linnebur. In Res., Rev. Thomas M. Hoisington.
Res.: 861 N. Socora, 67212. Tel: 316-722-4404; Fax: 316-722-4738.
School—(Grades PreSchool-8) Mary Carter, Prin.; Mary Bird, Vice Prin.; Barbara Fritz, Librarian; Margaret Raine, Librarian. Adorers of the Blood of Christ 1; Lay Teachers 39; Students 781.
Catechesis/Religious Program—Tel: 316-729-1350. Students 312.

12—HOLY SAVIOR (1948), (African American), Rev. James J. Billinger.
Res.: 1425 N. Chautauqua, 67214. Tel: 316-682-8712; Fax: 316-682-4797. Email: holysavior@holysavior.org.
School—(Grades PreK-8) Tel: 316-684-2141; Fax: 316-684-4318. Delia Barnett, Prin. Lay Teachers 15; Students 178.
Catechesis/Religious Program—Students 59.

13—ST. JOSEPH (1886) [JC] Rev. Stuart M. Smeltzer.
Res.: 132 S. Millwood Ave., 67213. Tel: 316-261-5800; Fax: 316-261-5806.
School—(Grades PreK-8), 139 S. Millwood Ave., 67213. Tel: 316-261-5801; Fax: 316-261-5804. Dan McAdam, Prin. Sisters 1; Lay Teachers 8; Students 124.
Catechesis/Religious Program—Mrs. Betty Ewing, D.R.E. Students 32.

14—ST. JUDE (1958) Rev. Thomas M. Hoisington, Admin.
Res.: 3130 Amidon Ave., 67204. Tel: 316-838-1963; Fax: 316-838-8513. Web: stjudewichita.net.
School—(Grades PreK-8) Tel: 316-838-0800; Fax: 316-838-0866. Mr. Dan Dester, Prin.; Carolyn Rooney, Librarian. Lay Teachers 15; Students 266.
Catechesis/Religious Program—Gayle Breth, D.R.E. Students 109.

15—ST. MARGARET MARY (1954) Rev. Richard Stuchlik.
Res.: 2701 Pattie St., 67216. Tel: 316-262-1821; Fax: 316-262-4057.
Church: 2635 Pattie St., 67216. Tel: 316-267-4911; Fax: 316-267-1707.
School—(Grades PreK-8), 2635 Pattie St., 67216. Tel: 316-267-4911; Fax: 316-267-1707. Mary Samms, Prin.; Lisa Hinson, Librarian. Lay Teachers 15; Students 215.
Catechesis/Religious Program—Tel: 316-522-4104. Esther Caire, C.R.E.; Sr. Rosa Cruz, C.R.E. Students 210.

16—OUR LADY OF GUADALUPE, Closed. For sacramental records contact St. Margaret Mary, Wichita.

17—OUR LADY OF PERPETUAL HELP (1927) [JC] Rev. Jose Machado.
Res.: 2351 N. Market St., 67219. Tel: 316-838-8373; Fax: 316-821-9250. Email: jmachado@cox.net.
Catechesis/Religious Program—Students 300.
Convent—2354 N. Market St., 67219. Tel: 316-838-3190.
Parish Center—2409 N. Market St., 67219. Tel: 316-838-5750.

18—ST. PATRICK (1910) [JC] Rev. Jerome J. Spexarth.
Church: 2007 Arkansas Ave., 67203. Tel: 316-262-4683; Fax: 316-262-0051. Email: stpatswichita@cox.net. Web: www.stpatswichita.org.
School—(Grades PreK-8), 2023 Arkansas Ave., 67203. Tel: 316-262-4071; Fax: 316-262-6217. Email: principal@stpatswichita.org. Mrs. Theresa Lam, Prin.; Joy Kirk, Librarian. Lay Teachers 16; Students 183.
Catechesis/Religious Program—Sr. Rosa Cruz, D.R.E., (English & Spanish). Students 304.
Convent—2045 Arkansas Ave., 67203. Tel: 316-267-0021.

19—ST. PAUL PARISH (1970) Rev. Eric M. Weldon.
Res.: 1810 N. Roosevelt, 67208. Tel: 316-684-6896; Fax: 316-684-2679.

20—ST. THOMAS AQUINAS (1957) Revs. Matthew C. McGinness; Benjamin S. Sawyer; Kim Scanlan, Parish Admin. In Res., Rev. Benjamin D. Shockey.
Res.: 1321 Stratford Ln., 67206. Tel: 316-683-6569; Fax: 316-683-6672. Email: church@stthomaswichita.com. Web: www.stthomaswichita.com.
School—(Grades PreK-8) Tel: 316-684-9201; Fax: 316-684-7421. Miss Mary Sweet, Prin.; Mr. Scott Landwehr, Asst. Prin.; Barbara Evans, Librarian. Lay Teachers 42; Students 734.

Catechesis/Religious Program—Students 153.
21—St. Vincent de Paul (1955) Rev. Michael E. Baldwin.
Res.: 123 N. Andover Rd., Andover, 67002. Tel: 316-733-1423; Fax: 316-733-1687. Email: office@svdpks.org. Web: www.svdpks.org.
Catechesis/Religious Program—Gayle Beuke, D.R.E.; Chris Porter, Youth Min. (MS/HS); Desirae Jensen, Youth Min. (HS). Students 340.

OUTSIDE THE CITY OF WICHITA

Aleppo, Sedgwick Co., Immaculate Conception (1890), (German), [CEM] Revs. Samuel J. Pinkerton; John C. Reinkemeyer.
Church: 25741 W. 13th St. N., Garden Plain, 67050. Tel: 316-531-2662.
Catechesis/Religious Program— With St. Anthony, Garden Plain. Students 8.

Andale, Sedgwick Co., St. Joseph (1890), (German), [CEM] Rev. Reinhard C. Eck.
Res.: 318 Rush Ave., Box 8, 67001. Tel: 316-444-2196.
Catechesis/Religious Program—Mary Jo Hieger, D.R.E. Students 327.

Anthony, Harper Co., Sacred Heart (1934) Closed. For inquiries for parish records contact St. Joan of Arc, 1023 W. Main St., Box 218, Harper, KS 67058. Merged with Immaculate Conception, Danville & St. Patrick, Harper to form Joan of Arc, Harper.

Arkansas City, Cowley Co., Sacred Heart (1886) Rev. Charles F. Seiwert.
Res.: 302 S. B St., 67005. Tel: 620-442-0566; Fax: 620-441-0935.
School—(Grades PreK-5), 312 S. B St., 67005. Tel: 620-442-6550; Fax: 620-441-0935. Richard Sleefe, Prin. Lay Teachers 5; Students 80.
Catechesis/Religious Program—Kyle Kisling, D.R.E. (Grades 1-12). Students 99.

Arma, Crawford Co., St. Joseph (1934) Rev. Lawrence D. Carney III.
Res.: 310 W. South St., P.O. Box 948, 66712. Tel: 620-347-4525. Email: stjoseph@ckt.net.

Augusta, Butler Co., St. James (1879) [CEM] Rev. Michael Schemm.
Res.: 1012 Belmont Ave., 67010. Tel: 316-775-2155; Fax: 316-775-2131.
School—(Grades K-6) Tel: 316-775-5721; Fax: 316-775-7160. Richard Guy, Prin.; Sharon Hoffman, Librarian. Lay Teachers 9; Students 88.
Catechesis/Religious Program—Bonnie Toombs, D.R.E. Students 140.

Baxter Springs, Cherokee Co., St. Joseph (1917) [JC] Rev. Chrysostom Ah Maung.
Res.: 115 W. Walnut, Columbus, 66725. Tel: 620-429-2639.
Catechesis/Religious Program—Students 12.

Burns, Marion Co., Immaculate Conception, Closed. For sacramental records contact Holy Family, Marion.

Bushton, Rice Co., Holy Name of Jesus (1878), (German), [CEM] Rev. Daniel S. Lorimer.
Res. & Office: 415 St. Francis St., Lyons, 67554. Tel: 620-257-3503.
Church: 296 3rd Rd., 67427. Tel: 316-562-3427.
Catechesis/Religious Program—Tel: 620-562-3662. Roxanna Habiger, D.R.E. Students 11.

Caldwell, Sumner Co., St. Martin of Tours (1888) [JC] Rev. Steven Scheier.
Res.: 428 N. Main, 67022. Tel: 620-845-6763; Fax: 620-845-6733.
Catechesis/Religious Program—Students 10.

Caney, Montgomery Co., Sacred Heart (1914) Rev. Sixtus Ye Myint (Burma).
Res.: 301 N. Hooker, 67333. Tel: 620-647-3577.
Catechesis/Religious Program—Tel: 620-879-2355. Students 29.

Capaldo, Crawford Co., St. Alice, Closed. For sacramental records contact Sacred Heart, Frontenac.

Castleton, Reno Co., St. Agnes (1872) Closed. For inquiries for sacramental records contact St. Teresa, Hutchinson.

Cedar Vale, Chautauqua Co., St. Joseph, Closed. For inquiries for parish records contact the chancery.

Chanute, Neosho Co., St. Patrick (1873) [CEM 2] Rev. Bernard X. Gorges.
Res.: 424 S. Central, 66720. Tel: 620-431-3165; Fax: 620-431-6587. Email: stpatschanute@cableone.net.
School—(Grades PreK-5) Tel: 620-431-4020. Jeff Brownfield, Prin. Sisters 1; Lay Teachers 7; Students 102.
Catechesis/Religious Program—Tel: 620-431-4287. Students 111.

Chase, Rice Co., St. Mary (1888), (German), Closed. For inquiries for sacramental records contact St. Paul, Lyons.

Cherokee, Crawford Co., St. Anastasia, Closed. For sacramental records contact Our Lady of Lourdes, Pittsburg.

Cherryvale, Montgomery Co., St. Francis Xavier's (1871), (German), [CEM] Rev. Daniel L. Vacca.
Res. & Office: 210 N. 4th, Independence, 67301. Tel: 620-331-1789; Fax: 620-331-6496.
Church: 202 S. Liberty St., 67335.
Catechesis/Religious Program—Tel: 620-336-2310. Students 39.

Chetopa, Labette Co., Sacred Heart (1873) [CEM] Closed. For sacramental records contact Mother of God Parish, Oswego.

Chicopee, Crawford Co., St. Barbara, Closed. For sacramental records contact Our Lady of Lourdes, Pittsburg.

Clonmel, Sedgwick Co., St. John (1878) [CEM] Rev. C. Jarrod Lies.
Church: 18630 W. 71st St., Viola, 67149. Tel: 316-545-7171; Fax: 620-545-7191.
Parish Center—Tel: 316-545-7211.
Catechesis/Religious Program—Deborah Tamburro, D.R.E.; Art Gentry, D.R.E. Students 63.

Coffeyville, Montgomery Co., Holy Name (1869), (Irish—German), [CEM 2] Rev. Benjamin N. Nguyen.
Res.: 408 Willow St., 67337. Tel: 620-251-0475; Fax: 620-251-0475. Email: holynamecoffeyville@gmail.com. Web: holynamecoffeyville.com.
School—(Grades PreK-6), 409 Willow St., 67337. Tel: 620-251-0480; Fax: 620-251-1651. Lisa Payne, Prin. Lay Teachers 10; Students 103.
Catechesis/Religious Program—Students 62.

Columbus, Cherokee Co., St. Rose (1887) [JC] Rev. Chrysostom Ah Maung.
Res.: 115 W. Walnut St., 66725. Tel: 620-429-2639; Fax: 620-429-2639.
Catechesis/Religious Program—Tel: 620-429-2938. Students 36.

Colwich, Sedgwick Co., Sacred Heart (1901) [CEM] Rev. Kenneth J. Schuckman.
Office: 311 S. Fifth St., P.O. Box 578, 67030. Tel: 316-796-1224; Fax: 316-796-0735.
Res.: 231 S. Fifth St., 67030. Tel: 316-796-0759.
Catechesis/Religious Program—Students 294.

Conway Springs, Sumner Co., St. Joseph (1886), (German), [CEM] Rev. Andrew J. Seiler.
Res.: 217 N. Sixth St., 67031. Tel: 316-456-2276; Fax: 316-456-3317.
School—(Grades K-6), 218 N. 5th St., 67031. Tel: 316-456-2270; Fax: 316-456-2272. Email: stjoeprinc@havilandtelco.com. Mr. Patrick Carl, Prin. Lay Teachers 7; Students 129.
Catechesis/Religious Program—Students 198.

Council Grove, Morris Co., St. Rose (1883) [CEM] [JC 2] Rev. Edmond G. Kline.
Res.: 300 Spencer St., 66846. Tel: 620-767-6412; Fax: 620-767-5370. Email: rosalima@tctelco.net.
Catechesis/Religious Program—Maureen Adams, C.R.E. Tel: 620-767-6607. Students 66.

Cunningham, Kingman Co., Sacred Heart (1908), (German), [CEM] Rev. John P. Miller.
Res.: P.O. Box 216, 67035. Tel: 316-298-2601; Fax: 316-298-2926.
Catechesis/Religious Program—Tel: 316-246-5241; 620-243-7666. Linda Kerschen, D.R.E.; Renee D. Adelhardt, D.R.E.

Danville, Harper Co., Immaculate Conception (1883) Closed. For inquiries for parish records contact St. Joan of Arc, 1023 W. Main St., Box 218, Harper, KS 67058. Merged with St. Patrick, Harper & Sacred Heart, Anthony to form Joan of Arc, Harper.

Derby, Sedgwick Co., St. Mary (1954) Rev. Wayne L. Schmid; Sr. Marie Zoglman, A.S.C., Pastoral Assoc., Liturgy Dir. & Music Min.
Parish Office: 2300 E. Meadowlark Rd., 67037. Tel: 316-788-5525; Fax: 316-788-1577. Web: www.stmarysderby.com.
School—(Grades K-8), 618 N. Derby Ave., 67037. Tel: 316-788-3151; Fax: 316-788-6895. Mr. Richard Montgomery, Prin. Lay Teachers 25; Students 300.
Catechesis/Religious Program—Tel: 316-788-1877. Janet Clark, Youth Dir.; Ms. Ann Hughes, D.R.E. Students 141.

El Dorado, Butler Co., St. John the Evangelist (1915) Rev. Brian D. Bebak.
Res.: 302 N. Denver Ave., 67042. Tel: 316-321-4796; Fax: 316-321-1831. Email: mail@stjohneldorado.com. Web: www.stjohneldorado.com.
Catechesis/Religious Program—Tel: 316-321-4933. Sedina Rardin, C.R.E. & Youth Min. Students 122.

Erie, Neosho Co., St. Ambrose (1915) Rev. Theodore Khin.
Res: P.O. Box 216, St. Paul, 66771. Tel: 620-449-2224; Fax: 620-449-8986.
Church: 519 N. Main, 66733.
Catechesis/Religious Program—

Eureka, Greenwood Co., Sacred Heart (1881), (German), [JC] Rev. Stephen F. Gronert.
Res.: 514 N. Elm St., 67045. Tel: 620-583-7100.
Catechesis/Religious Program—Students 27.
Mission—St. John Hamilton, Greenwood Co.
Mission—St. Teresa Of Avila Madison, Greenwood Co. Tel: 316-437-2504.

Florence, Marion Co., St. Patrick, Closed. Merged with St. Mark, Marion; St. John Nepomucene, Pilsen and Holy Redeemer, Tampa to form Holy Family, Marion.

Fort Scott, Bourbon Co., Mary Queen of Angels (1860) [CEM] Rev. Darrin M. May.
Res.: 705 S. Holbrook St., 66701-2506. Tel: 620-223-4340; Fax: 620-223-6060.
School—(Grades PreK-5) Tel: 620-223-6060; Fax: 620-223-6060. Krista Gorman, Prin.; Jill Gorman, Librarian. Lay Teachers 5; Students 68.
Catechesis/Religious Program—Peggy Niles, D.R.E. Students 60.

Fredonia, Wilson Co., Sacred Heart (1906) [CEM] Rev. Stephen M. Thapwa (Burma).
Res.: 428 N. 12th St., 66736. Tel: 620-378-2694. Email: sacredheart@twinmounds.com.
Catechesis/Religious Program—Tel: 316-204-6910. Jody Donahue, D.R.E. Students 38.

Frontenac, Crawford Co., Sacred Heart (1891), (Italian), [CEM] Rev. Robert K. Spencer.
Res.: 100 S. Cherokee St., 66763. Tel: 620-231-7747; Fax: 620-232-7006. Web: www.sacredheartsek.com.
Catechesis/Religious Program—Mona Wachter, D.R.E. Students 105.

Fulton, Bourbon Co., St. Patrick, Closed. For sacramental records contact Mary Queen of Angels, Fort Scott.

Galena, Cherokee Co., St. Patrick (1879) [JC] Rev. Chrysostom Ah Maung.
Res.: 115 W. Walnut, Columbus, 66725. Tel: 620-429-2639; Fax: 620-429-2639.
Church: 307 Galena, 66739.
Catechesis/Religious Program—Students 22.

Garden Plain, Sedgwick Co., St. Anthony (1901), (German), [CEM] Rev. Samuel J. Pinkerton.
Res.: 615 N. Main, 67050. Tel: 316-531-2252.
Catechesis/Religious Program—Tel: 316-535-2593. Students 353.
Mission—Immaculate Conception 25741 W. 13th St. N., 67050. Tel: 316-531-2662.

Girard, Crawford Co., St. Michael (1925), (Irish—German), Rev. Lawrence D. Carney III.
Res.: 106 N. Western St., 66743. Tel: 620-724-8717.
Catechesis/Religious Program—Joan Davied, D.R.E.; Nancy Bauer, D.R.E. Students 136.

Goddard, Sedgwick Co., Holy Spirit (1998) Rev. Michael E. Nolan.
Church: 18218 W. Hwy. 54, 67052. Tel: 316-794-3496; Fax: 316-794-3795. Web: www.holyspiritwichita.com.
Res.: 1206 Harvest Ln., 67052.
School—(Grades K-6) Tel: 316-794-8139; Fax: 316-794-2055. Kelly Bright, Prin. Teachers 6; Students 73.
Catechesis/Religious Program—Students 140.

Greenbush, Crawford Co., St. Aloysius, Closed. For sacramental records contact St. Michael, Girard.

Halstead, Harvey Co., Sacred Heart Parish (1874) [JC] Rev. Stephen R. Baxter.
Res.: 419 Poplar, P.O. Box 149, 67056. Tel: 316-835-2173; Fax: 316-830-2889.
Catechesis/Religious Program—Tel: 316-830-2764. Carolyn Armendariz, D.R.E. Students 110.

Hamilton, Greenwood Co., St. John (1888), (German), Rev. Stephen F. Gronert.
Res.: 514 N. Elm St., Eureka, 67045. Tel: 620-583-7100.
Catechesis/Religious Program—Students 8.

Harper, Harper Co.
1—St. Joan of Arc (1997), (Irish—German), Rev. Michael Peltzer. Consolidation of St. Patrick, Harper; Immaculate Conception, Danville & Sacred Heart, Anthony. Merged in 1997.
Rectory Office: 1023 W. Main, P.O. Box 218, 67058. Tel: 620-896-7886; Fax: 620-896-2249.
Catechesis/Religious Program—Cheryl Kernohan, D.R.E. Tel: 620-254-7792. Students 43.
2—St. Patrick (1882) Closed. For inquiries for parish records contact St. Joan of Arc, 1023 W. Main St., Box 218, Harper, KS 67058. Merged with Immaculate Conception, Danville & Sacred Heart, Anthony to form Joan of Arc, Harper.

Haysville, Sedgwick Co., St. Cecilia (1959) Rev. Thomas Than Wai (Burma).
Res.: 1900 W. Grand, 67060. Tel: 316-524-7801; Fax: 316-524-6183. Email: stcp.ftw@stceciliahaysville.com. Web: www.stceciliahaysville.com.
School—(Grades PreK-8), 1912 W. Grand, 67060. Tel: 316-522-0461. Email: cbuser@stceciliahaysville.com. Mr. Winston Kenton, Prin.; Jane Betzen, Librarian. Lay Teachers 10; Students 115.
Catechesis/Religious Program—Marcia Miller, D.R.E. Students 60.

Humboldt, Allen Co., St. Joseph (1867) [CEM] Rev. Bernard X. Gorges.
Church: 322 N. Sixth, 66748. Tel: 620-473-2636; Fax: 620-431-6587.
Res.: 424 S. Central Ave., Chanute, 66720. Tel:

620-431-3165.
Catechesis / Religious Program—Tel: 620-431-3165; Fax: 620-431-6587. Students 25.

HUTCHINSON, RENO CO.

1—CHURCH OF THE HOLY CROSS (1957) [CEM 3] [JC] Rev. Joseph A. Eckberg.
Res.: 2631 Independence Rd., 67502. Tel: 620-665-5163; Fax: 620-662-5085. Email: hcchurch@holycross.kscoxmail.com. Web: www.holycrosshutch.net.
School—(Grades K-6), 2633 Independence Rd., 67502. Tel: 620-665-6168; Fax: 620-665-6168. Mr. Kevin Hedrick, Prin. Lay Teachers 21; Students 223.
Catechesis / Religious Program—Students 134.

2—OUR LADY OF GUADALUPE (1927), (Hispanic), Rev. Brian D. Nelson.
Res.: 612 S. Maple, South Hutchinson, 67505-2099. Tel: 620-662-6443; Fax: 620-669-0215.
Catechesis / Religious Program—901 E. Ave. A, 67501. Tel: 620-474-3338. Deborah Castaneda, D.R.E. Students 147.

3—ST. TERESA (1897) [CEM] Rev. Nicholas A. Voelker.
Res.: 211 E. Fifth St., 67501. Tel: 620-662-7812; Fax: 620-662-7812.
School—(Grades PreSchool-6), 215 E. Fifth St., 67501. Tel: 620-662-5601; Fax: 620-662-5601. Ms. Ellen Albert, Prin. Lay Teachers 9; Students 139.
Catechesis / Religious Program—Students 40.

INDEPENDENCE, MONTGOMERY CO., ST. ANDREW (1869), (German—Mexican), [CEM 2] Rev. Daniel L. Vacca; Deacon Michael Steele.
Res.: 210 N. Fourth St., 67301. Tel: 620-331-1789; Fax: 620-331-6496. Email: standrewindp@sbcglobal.net.
School—(Grades PreK-8) Tel: 620-331-2870. Email: school@standrewindependence.com. Rebecca Brown, Prin. Lay Teachers 10; Students 169.
Catechesis / Religious Program—Tel: 620-331-8401. Students 38.

IOLA, ALLEN CO., ST. JOHN (1897) [CEM] [JC] Rev. Robert B. Wachter; Deacon Theodore Stahl.
Office: 310 S. Jefferson, 66749. Tel: 620-365-2277.
Res.: 314 S. Jefferson Ave., 66749. Tel: 316-365-3454.
Catechesis / Religious Program—Tel: 316-365-8488. Mrs. Annette Rexwinkle, D.R.E. Students 100.
Oratory—St. Martin 1368 Xylan Rd., Piqua, Woodson Co. 66761.

KINGMAN, KINGMAN CO., ST. PATRICK (1885), (Irish), [JC] Rev. James Weldon.
Res.: 638 Ave. D W., 67068. Tel: 316-532-5440; Fax: 316-532-5549. Web: stpatskingman.org.
School—(Grades PreK-8) Tel: 316-532-2791; Fax: 316-532-2966. Robert Lyall, Prin. Lay Teachers 12; Students 155.
Catechesis / Religious Program—Tel: 316-532-5440. Students 79.

LIBERTY, MONTGOMERY CO., ALL SAINTS, Closed. For inquiries for parish records contact the chancery.

LINDSBORG, MCPHERSON CO., ST. BRIDGET OF SWEDEN (1985) Rev. David J. Lies.
Church: 206 W. Swensson, P.O. Box 268, 67456. Tel: 785-227-3588; Fax: 620-245-9677. Email: stbridget@att.net.
Res.: 1524 Sonora Dr., McPherson, 67460. Tel: 620-241-0821; Fax: 620-241-8497.
Catechesis / Religious Program—Students 42.

LITTLE RIVER, RICE CO., HOLY TRINITY (1885) [JC] Rev. Nicholas A. Voelker.
Office: 415 St. Francis St., Lyons, 67554. Tel: 620-662-7812.
Res.: 211 E. Fifth Ave., Hutchinson, 67501.
Catechesis / Religious Program—Gary Grasser, D.R.E. Tel: 620-257-2969; Shayla Grasser, D.R.E. Students 42.

LYONS, RICE CO., ST. PAUL (1927) [JC] Rev. Daniel S. Lorimer.
Res.: 415 St. Francis St., 67554. Tel: 620-257-3503; Fax: 620-257-3021.
Catechesis / Religious Program—Tel: 620-257-3809. Donetta Birzer, D.R.E. Students 128.

MADISON, GREENWOOD CO., ST. TERESA OF AVILA (1954), (German), [JC] Rev. Stephen F. Gronert.
Res.: 514 N. Elm St., Eureka, 67045. Tel: 620-583-7100.
Catechesis / Religious Program—Students 2.

MARION, MARION CO., HOLY FAMILY (1992) [CEM 5] [JC 2], Parish formed from merger of St. Mark, Marion; St. John Nepomucene, Pilsen; St. Patrick, Florence; Holy Redeemer, Tampa and Immaculate Conception, Burns. Rev. Hien Paul Nguyen.
Res. & Mailing Address: 415 N. Cedar St., 66861. Tel: 620-382-3422; 620-382-3369 (Office). Email: hfpmarion@yahoo.com.
Catechesis / Religious Program— Jackie Palic, D.R.E., Marion; Sandra Oborny, D.R.E., Pilsen; Mary Jirak, D.R.E., Tampa; Jean Rziha, D.R.E., Tampa. Students 137.
Oratory—Holy Redemer Church Tampa, 67483.

MCPHERSON, MCPHERSON CO., ST. JOSEPH (1880) Rev. David J. Lies.
Church: 520 E. Northview, 67460. Tel: 620-241-0821; Fax: 620-245-9677. Web: www.stjosephmcpherson.com.
Res.: 1524 Sonora Dr., 67460. Tel: 620-504-6037.
School—(Grades PreK-6) Tel: 620-241-3913. Lay Teachers 10; Students 136.
Catechesis / Religious Program—Raschelle Jirak, D.R.E. Students 106.
Mission—St. Bridget of Sweden Box 268, Lindsborg, McPherson Co. 67456. Tel: 785-227-3588. Email: stbridget@att.net.

MOLINE, ELK CO., ST. MARY'S (1899) [CEM] Rev. Sixtus Ye Myint (Burma).
Res.: 320 N. Main, Box 276, 67353-0276. Tel: 620-647-3577.
Catechesis / Religious Program—Students 15.

MOUNT VERNON, KINGMAN CO., ST. ROSE (1911), (German—Irish), [CEM] Rev. Ivan C. Eck.
Res.: 13015 E. Maple Grove Rd., Mount Hope, 67108. Tel: 316-444-2210.
Catechesis / Religious Program—Tel: 316-542-3990. Students 141.

MULBERRY, CRAWFORD CO., ST. GABRIEL, Closed. For sacramental records contact Sacred Heart, Frontenac.

MULVANE, SUMNER CO., ST. MICHAEL THE ARCHANGEL (1948) Rev. Michael J. Maybrier.
Res.: 545 E. Main St., 67110. Tel: 316-777-4221; Fax: 316-777-9456. Email: stmichaelmulvane@sbcglobal.net. Web: www.mulvaneks.org/stmichaels/Home.html.
Catechesis / Religious Program— Karen Oblinger, D.R.E. Students 224.

NEODESHA, WILSON CO., ST. IGNATIUS (1876) [CEM] Rev. Stephen M. Thapwa (Burma).
P.O. Box 186, 66757. Tel: 620-325-5215.
Rectory—Res.: 428 N. 12th, Fredonia, 66736.
Catechesis / Religious Program—Tel: 620-325-8935. Jessica Busse, D.R.E. Students 31.

NEWTON, HARVEY CO.

1—ST. MARY (1872) [CEM] Rev. James S. Mainzer.
Res.: 106 E. Eighth St., 67114. Tel: 316-282-0459. Email: sschmidt@smcsnewton.org. Web: www.stmarynewton.org.
School—(Grades PreK-8) Tel: 316-282-1974; Fax: 316-283-3642. Email: mkellogg@smcsnewton.org. Philip Stutey, Prin. Lay Teachers 15; Students 164.
Catechesis / Religious Program—Mrs. Marie Morford, D.R.E. Students 81.

2—OUR LADY OF GUADALUPE (1919), (Hispanic), [JC] Rev. Juan G. Garza.
Res.: 415 S. Ash St., 67114.
Church: 421 S. Ash St., 67114. Tel: 316-283-3499; Fax: 316-283-6813.
Catechesis / Religious Program—Students 56.

OST, RENO CO., ST. JOSEPH (1880), (German), [CEM] Rev. Ivan C. Eck.
Res.: 13015 E. Maple Grove Rd., Mount Hope, 67108. Tel: 316-444-2210.
School—St. Joseph Catholic School - Ost, (Grades K-8), 12917 E. Maple Grove Rd., Mount Hope, 67108. Tel: 316-444-2548; Fax: 316-444-2448. Sisters 1; Lay Teachers 7; Students 90.
Catechesis / Religious Program—Tel: 316-444-2637. Students 25.

OSWEGO, LABETTE CO., MOTHER OF GOD (1878) [JC] Rev. Larry Parker.
Res.: 1105 4th St., 67356. Tel: 620-795-2262.
Catechesis / Religious Program—Students 54.

OXFORD, SUMNER CO., ST. MARY (1872) [JC] Rev. Michael A. Klag.
Res.: 412 E. Eighth St., Winfield, 67156. Tel: 620-221-3610; Fax: 620-221-3528.
Catechesis / Religious Program—Myra Jacobs, D.R.E. Students 25.

PARSONS, LABETTE CO.

1—MARY QUEEN OF PEACE (1909) Closed. For inquiries for parish records contact St. Patrick, Parsons.

2—ST. PATRICK (1872) [CEM 2] Rev. Jason W. Borkenhagen.
Res.: 1807 Stevens Ave., 67357. Tel: 620-421-6762; Fax: 620-421-1628.
School—(Grades PreK-8), 1831 Stevens Ave., 67357. Tel: 620-421-0710; Fax: 620-421-2429. Tim Born, Prin. Lay Teachers 13; Students 144.
Catechesis / Religious Program—Students 100.

PILSEN, MARION CO., ST. JOHN NEPOMUCENE, Closed. Merged with St. Mark, Marion; St. Patrick, Florence and Holy Redeemer, Tampa to form Holy Family, Marion.

PIQUA, WOODSON CO., ST. MARTIN (1884), (German), Closed. For inquiries for sacramental records contact St. John, Iola.

PITTSBURG, CRAWFORD CO., OUR LADY OF LOURDES (1881) [CEM] Revs. Thomas J. Stroot; John N. Hay; David Marstall.
Res.: 916 N. Locust St., P.O. Box 214, 66762. Tel: 620-231-2135; Fax: 620-231-4804. Email: kratz@ourladypittsburg.com. Web: www.ourladypittsburg.org.
School—St. Mary's Elementary School, (Grades PreK-6), (Elementary), 301 E. Ninth, 66762. Tel: 620-231-6941; Fax: 620-235-7442. Email: martinm@smcschools.org. Web: www.smcschools.com. Mr. John C. Kraus, Pres. Schools, Dir. Admin.; Mr. Mike Martin, Prin. (Pre-K-6); Janie Burrow, Librarian. Lay Teachers 21; Students 360.
School—St. Mary's Colgan Junior High, (Grades 7-8), 212 E. 9th, 66762. Tel: 620-231-4690. Email: gorman@smcschools.org. Web: www.smcschools.com. Mr. Tom Gorman, Prin., Jr. High & High Schools; Beverley Mitchelson, Librarian. Lay Teachers 5; Students 80.
High School—St. Mary's Colgan High School Lay Teachers 17; Students 149.
Catechesis / Religious Program—Jovanna Brackett-Oetinger, D.R.E. Students 66.

ST. LEO, KINGMAN CO., ST. LEO THE GREAT (1906), (German), [CEM] Rev. John P. Miller.
Res.: 8035 S.W. 160 Ave., Nashville, 67112. Tel: 316-246-5370.
Catechesis / Religious Program—P.O. Box 216, Cunningham, 67035. Tel: 316-298-2601. Students 15.

ST. MARK'S, SEDGWICK CO., ST. MARK (1876), (German), [CEM] Rev. Msgr. John P. Gilsenan.
Res.: 19230 W. 29th St. N., Colwich, 67030. Tel: 316-796-1604; Fax: 316-769-0511. Email: stmksec@pixius.net. Web: www.stmarkcolwich.org.
Catechesis / Religious Program—Tel: 316-640-8527. Vanessa Condreay, D.R.E. Students 200.

ST. PAUL, NEOSHO CO., ST. FRANCIS (1847) [CEM 2] Rev. Theodore Khin.
Res.: 208 Washington St., P.O. Box 216, 66771-0216. Tel: 620-449-2224; Fax: 620-449-8986.
Catechesis / Religious Program—Tel: 620-449-2672. Suzie Diskin, D.R.E. Students 160.

SCAMMON, CHEROKEE CO., ST. BRIDGET'S (1868) [CEM] Rev. Chrysostom Ah Maung.
Res.: 115 W. Walnut, Columbus, 66725. Tel: 620-429-2639; Fax: 620-429-2639.
Catechesis / Religious Program—Tel: 620-479-2236. Students 56.

SCHULTE, SEDGWICK CO., ST. PETER THE APOSTLE (1905) [CEM] Rev. Andrew Kuykendall.
Parish Offices—11000 S.W. Blvd., 67215. Tel: 316-524-4259; Fax: 316-524-0932. Email: psecretary@stpeterschulte.com. Web: www.stpeterschulte.com.
Res.: 10980 S.W. Blvd., 67215. Tel: 316-522-4728.
School—(Grades PreK-8), 11010 S.W. Blvd., 67215. Tel: 316-524-6585; Fax: 316-524-1656. Brenda Hickok, Prin.; Mattie McCuiston, Librarian. Sisters 2; Lay Teachers 21; Students 453.
Catechesis / Religious Program—Tel: 316-529-1681. Michelle Witthuhn, PSR Dir.; Mrs. Tama Dutton, D.R.E. & Dir. Formation. Students 143.

SEDAN, CHAUTAUQUA CO., ST. ROBERT BELLARMINE (1962) Rev. Sixtus Ye Myint (Burma).
Res.: 320 N. Main, P.O. Box 276, Moline, 67353-0276. Tel: 620-647-3577.
Catechesis / Religious Program—Tel: 620-725-3812. Students 8.

STRONG CITY, CHASE CO., ST. ANTHONY OF PADUA (1880) [CEM] [JC] Rev. Edmond G. Kline.
Res.: 300 Spencer, Council Grove, 66846. Tel: 620-767-6412; Fax: 620-767-5370.
Catechesis / Religious Program—Tel: 620-273-8617. Jeanette Black, C.R.E. Students 37.

TAMPA, MARION CO., HOLY REDEEMER, See separate listing. Now an oratory of Holy Family, Marion.

WALNUT, CRAWFORD CO., ST. PATRICK, Closed. For sacramental records contact St. Francis Church, St. Paul.

WATERLOO, KINGMAN CO., ST. LOUIS (1881), (German—Irish), [JC] Rev. Ivan C. Eck.
Res.: 13015 E. Maple Grove Rd., Mt. Hope, 67108. Tel: 316-444-2210.
Catechesis / Religious Program—Students 3.

WEIR, CHEROKEE CO., SACRED HEART, Closed. For sacramental records contact St. Rose of Lima, Columbus.

WELLINGTON, SUMNER CO.

1—ST. ANTHONY (1884) Merged with St. Rose of Lima, Wellington to form St. Anthony/St. Rose, Wellington. For inquiries for parish records contact St. Anthony/St. Rose.

2—ST. ANTHONY/ST. ROSE Rev. Andrew Heiman.
210 N. B St., 67152. Tel: 620-326-2522; Fax: 620-326-2527. Email: stanthony@sutv.com.
Catechesis / Religious Program—Tel: 620-326-3480. Carol Susong, D.R.E. Students 221.

3—ST. ROSE OF LIMA (1949), (Hispanic), Merged with St. Anthony, Wellington to form St. Anthony/St. Rose, Wellington. For inquiries for parish records, contact St. Anthony/St. Rose, Wellington.

WEST MINERAL, CHEROKEE CO., IMMACULATE CONCEPTION, Closed. For sacramental records contact St. Rose of Lima, Columbus.

WILLOWDALE, KINGMAN CO., ST. PETER'S (1884), (German), [CEM] Rev. John P. Miller.
Res.: P.O. Box 86, Zenda, 67159. Tel: 620-243-5451.

WINFIELD, COWLEY CO., HOLY NAME (1878) [JC] Rev. Michael A. Klag.
Res.: 412 E. Eighth St., 67156. Tel: 620-221-3610; Fax: 620-221-3528. Email: sec_holyname@yahoo.com. Web: www.holynamewinfield.org.
School—(Grades PreK-6) Tel: 620-221-0230; Fax: 620-221-4047. Email: holynamecatholicschool@yahoo.com. Kimberly Porter, Prin. Lay Teachers 4; Students 61.
Catechesis/Religious Program—Students 50.

YATES CENTER, WOODSON CO., ST. JOSEPH (1957) [JC] Rev. Robert B. Wachter.
Res.: 314 S. Jefferson, Iola, 66749.
Catechesis/Religious Program—Tel: 316-625-2672. Students 10.

ZENDA, KINGMAN CO., ST. JOHN (1908), (German), [CEM] Rev. John P. Miller.
Res.: P.O. Box 86, 67159. Tel: 620-243-5451.
Catechesis/Religious Program— Renee D. Adelhardt, D.R.E.

Chaplains of Public Institutions

WICHITA. *El Dorado Correctional Facility*. Rev. Brian D. Bebak.
Sedgwick County Adult Local Detention Facility. Rev. John P. Sherlock.
Veterans Administration Hospital. Rev. H. Patrick Malone (Retired).

HUTCHINSON. *Kansas State Industrial Reformatory*. Revs. Stephen R. Baxter, J.C.L., Juan G. Garza, Nicholas A. Voelker.

On Duty Outside the Diocese:
Revs.—
Birket, Dwight J.
Blick, Ned J.
Fasching, Jeffery A.
Jirak, John F.
McKinney, Floyd E.
Nguyen, Scott C.

Temporary Leave of Absence:
Revs.—
Campbell, Douglas, J.C.L.
McElwee, Robert W.

Retired:
Rev. Msgrs.—
Carr, William, 6900 E. 45th St., 67226.
Lampe, Irvin F., 13014 La Terraza Dr., Sun City West, AZ 85375.
McGread, Thomas, 6900 E. 45th St. N., 67226.
Regan, Charles W., 6900 E. 45th St. N., 67226.
Revs.—
Bieberle, Victor, 29 Tiburon Way, Hot Springs, AR 71909.
Boor, Colin J., 2823 River Park Dr., 67203.
Busch, Arthur, 6900 E. 45th St. N., 67226.
Cox, Francis, 6900 E. 45th St. N., 67226.
Dinan, John, 6900 E. 45th St. N., 67226.
Freed, Robert, P.O. Box 278, Bally, PA 19503.
Garrahy, Michael, 6900 E. 45th St. N., 67226.
Grabner, Eugene W., 82 Porterfield Ln., Noel, MO 64854.
Harvey, Charles K., 6900 E. 45th St. N., 67226.
Joyce, Raymond, 115 S. Rutan #4D, 67218.
Kerschen, Leon J., P.O. Box 432, Andale, 67001.
Larkin, Patrick, 6900 E. 45th St. N., 67226.
Linnebur, Leroy, 2101 W. MacArthur, Lot 902, 67217.
Malone, H. Patrick, 7077 E. Central, 67206.
Mannion, J. Patrick, 6900 E. 45th St., 67226.
Middleton, Charles, 723 First Capitol Dr., Saint Charles, MO 63301.
Nolan, Joseph T., 8 Wesley St., Newton, MA 02458.
O'Hare, Donal J., 6900 E. 45th St., 67226.
O'Shea, John J., 6900 E. 45th St., 67226.
Oborny, Paul J., 6900 E. 45th St. N., 67226.
Pepe, Robert F., 6900 E. 45th St. N., 67226.
Reinkemeyer, John, St. Mary, 25741 W. 13th St. N., Garden Plain, 67050.
Roth, James J., P.O. Box 515, Claflin, 67525.
Scaletty, Thomas F., 514 Central, Humboldt, 66748.
Slomski, Joseph P., 6900 E. 45th St. N., 67226.
Spexarth, James, R.R. 1, P.O. Box 30, Marion, 66861.
Thissen, Donald R., 6900 E. 45th St., 67226.

INSTITUTIONS LOCATED IN THE DIOCESE

[A] COLLEGES AND UNIVERSITIES

WICHITA. *Newman University*, 3100 McCormick Ave., 67213-2097. Tel: 316-942-4291; Fax: 316-942-4483. Web: www.newmanu.edu. Revs. Joseph C. Tatro, Chap.; Joseph M. Gile, S.T.D., Grad. Theology Dir. & Asst. Prof. Theology; Michael Austin, Ph.D., Provost & Vice Pres. Acad. Affairs; Mark Dresselhaus, Vice Pres. Finance & Admin.; Shirley Rueb, Registrar; Joseph Forte, Librarian; Noreen M. Carrocci, Ph.D., Pres.; Rhonda Cantrell, M.S., Vice Pres. Human Resources; John Clayton, M.Ed., Dean of Admissions; Tom Borrego, J.D., Vice Pres. Inst. Advancement; Victor Trilli, M.S.Ed., Dir. Athletics. Coeducational liberal arts college, founded in 1933 by the Sisters Adorers of the Blood of Christ. (Accredited by the Higher Learning Commission of the North Central Association of Colleges and Schools). Priests 2; Sisters 4; Lay Teachers 81; Total Staff 142; Total Faculty 83; Students 2,557.

[B] HIGH SCHOOLS, DIOCESAN

WICHITA. *Bishop Carroll Catholic High School* (1964) 8101 W. Central, 67212. Tel: 316-722-2390; Fax: 316-722-6670. Email: nielsenleticia@bcchs.org. Web: www.bcchs.org. Leticia C. Nielsen, Pres.; Mrs. Vanessa Harshberger, Prin.; Rev. C. Jarrod Lies, Chap. Tel: 316-682-1415; Peggy Ochs, Librarian. Sisters 2; Lay Teachers 69; Total Staff 71; Students 1,125.
Kapaun Mt. Carmel Catholic High School, 8506 E. Central, 67206. Tel: 316-634-0315; Fax: 316-636-2437. Email: mburrus@kapaun.org. Web: www.kapaun.org. Rev. Benjamin D. Shockey, Chap. & Instructor; David Kehres, Prin.; Mrs. Shirley Sharma, Librarian. Priests 1; Sisters 2; Lay Teachers 58; Total Staff 78; Students 918.

HUTCHINSON. *Trinity Catholic Endowment Fund*, (Grades 7-12), 1400 E. 17th, 67501. Tel: 620-662-5800; Fax: 316-662-1233. Email: suehall@trinity-hutch.com. Web: www.trinity-hutch.com. 424 N. Broadway, 67202. Tel: 316-269-3950. Joe Hammersmith, Prin. Priests 1; Sisters 3; Lay Teachers 15; Total Staff 22; Total Enrollment 250.
Trinity Catholic High School (1966) (Grades 7-12), 1400 E. 17th, 67501. Tel: 620-662-5800; Fax: 320-662-1233. Email: jhammersmith@trinity-hutch.com. Web: www.trinity-hutch.com. Joe Hammersmith, Prin.; Rev. Brian D. Nelson, Chap.; Bernadett Dillon, Librarian. Priests 1; Sisters 3; Lay Teachers 18; Total Staff 23; Students 250.

PITTSBURG. *St. Mary-Colgan High School*, (Grades 7-12), 212 E. 9th St., 66762. Tel: 620-231-4690; Fax: 620-231-0690. Email: smithd@smcschools.org. Web: www.smcschools.com. Rev. Thomas J. Stroot, Admin.; Mr. John C. Kraus, Pres. Schools; Mr. Tom Gorman, Prin.; Ms. Bev Mitchelson, Librarian. Priests 3; Lay Teachers 20; Total Staff 25; Students 231.

[C] GENERAL HOSPITALS

WICHITA. *Via Christi Regional Medical Center, Inc.*, 929 N. St. Francis, 67214. Tel: 316-268-5000; Fax: 316-291-7999. Web: www.Via-Christi.org. Ms. Michalene Maringer, Pres. & CEO; Sisters Sherri Marie Kuhn, S.S.M., Sr. Vice Pres. Mission Integration; Anne Dolores LaPlante, C.S.J., Vice Pres. Pastoral Care & Mission; Rev. Raymond Joyce (Retired). Bed Capacity 759; Licensed Beds 1,532; Inpatients 36,712; Outpatients 325,498; Total Assisted Annually 362,210; Total Staff 4,479.
St. Francis Campus, 929 N. St. Francis, 67214. Tel: 316-268-5000; Fax: 316-291-7999. Rev. Ruben Ortiz-Montelongo. Tel: 316-268-8522.
St. Joseph Campus, 3600 E. Harry, 67218. Tel: 316-685-1111; Fax: 316-689-4786. Rev. Jerry Beat.
Via Christi Rehabilitation Center, Inc. (1995) Our Lady of Lourdes Campus, 1151 N. Rock Rd., 67206. Tel: 316-634-3400; Fax: 316-634-1141. Email: cindy_lafleur@via-christi.org. Web: www.via-christi.org. Mr. Glen Baker, Bd. Chm.; Ms. Cindy LaFleur, Vice Pres. Rehabilitation Svcs. & Admin. Our Lady of Lourdes. Bed Capacity 60; Patients Assisted Annually 9,000; Staff 357.

COLUMBUS. *MNMCH, Inc. dba St. John's Maude Norton Memorial Hospital* 220 N. Pennsylvania Ave., 66725. Tel: 620-429-2545; Fax: 620-429-1984. Email: cneely@stj.com. Cynthia Neely, Vice Pres. Admin. Bed Capacity 25; Patients Assisted Annually 9,327; Total Staff 57.

FORT SCOTT. *Mercy Health Center*, 401 Woodland Hills Blvd., 66701. Tel: 620-223-7057; Fax: 620-223-5327. John Woodrich, Pres. & CEO. Sisters of Mercy 1; Pastoral Care Dir. 1; Lay Staff 425; Bed Capacity 69; Bassinets 6; Patients Assisted Annually 49,423; Home Health Visits 9,831.

INDEPENDENCE. *Mercy Health Systems of Kansas, Inc.-Independence*, 800 W. Myrtle St., P.O. Box 388, 67301. Tel: 620-331-2200; Fax: 620-332-3270. Email: john.woodrich@mercy.net. Web: www.mercykansas.com. John Woodrich, CEO. Sisters of Mercy 2; Total Staff 263; Bed Capacity 40; Patients Assisted Annually 41,468.

PITTSBURG. *Mount Carmel Regional Medical Center* (1903) 1102 E. Centennial, 66762. Tel: 620-231-6100; Fax: 620-232-0493. Web: www.mtcarmel.org. Jonathan Davis, Pres. & CEO. Sisters of St. Joseph 1; Total Staff 630; Bed Capacity 188; Patients Assisted Annually 22,043.
Mount Carmel Foundation (1983) Tel: 620-235-3512; Fax: 620-235-7862.

[D] HOMES FOR AGED

WICHITA. *Catholic Care Center, Inc.*, 6700 E. 45th St. N., 67226. Tel: 316-744-2020; Fax: 316-744-2182. Email: tom_church@via-christi.org. Web: www.catholiccarecenter.org. Thomas Church, CEO. Operated by Catholic Diocese of Wichita & the Via Christ Health System. Sisters 9; Total Staff 368; Bed Capacity 298; Total Assisted Annually 624.
Cornerstone Assisted Living, Inc. (2001) 1240 N. Broadmoor, 67206. Tel: 316-636-5101; Fax: 316-636-2576. Email: joanne_rogers@via-christi.org. Web: www.via-christi.org/cornerstonebroadmoor. Mr. Jerry Carley, CEO; Mr. Monty Warren, Admin. Total Assisted 37; Total Staff 23.
3636 N. Ridge Rd., Ste. 400, 67205. Tel: 316-462-3636; Fax: 316-462-3676. Mr. Jerry Carley, CEO; Ms. Joanne Rogers, Admin. Total Assisted 60; Total Staff 38.
Georgetown Village, Inc. (1985) 1655 Georgetown St., 67218. Tel: 316-685-0400; Fax: 316-685-0174. Web: www.via-christi.org. Erik Hatten, CEO. Staff 93; Total Assisted 68; Independent Living 130; Condominiums 17.
Riverside Village Inc., 777 N. McLean Blvd., 67203. Tel: 316-942-7000; Fax: 316-946-5727. Web: www.via-christi.org/riversidevillage. Mark Mains, CEO. Total Assisted 54; Total Staff 86; Total Nursing 36; Total Independent 42.
Sheridan Village, Inc., 1051 S. Bluffview, 67218. Tel: 316-681-1172; Fax: 316-681-0979. Mr. Jerry Carley, CEO. (HUD Low Income Senior Housing) Apartments 66; Total Staff 3.

MULVANE. *Villa Maria, Inc.* (1950) 116 S. Central, 67110. Tel: 316-777-1129; Fax: 316-777-4406. Email: rebecca@villamariainc.com. Rebecca Murray, Admin. & Pres. Home for Disabled Men and Women. Adorers of the Blood of Christ 2; Total Staff 140; Guests 98; Total Assisted 142.
Maria Court Assisted Living, 633 E. Main, 67110. Tel: 316-777-9917. Chad Bos, Dir. Bed Capacity 35; Total Assisted Annually 52; Total Staff 18.

PITTSBURG. *Cornerstone Village Inc.* (2003) 1502 E. Centennial, 66762. Tel: 620-235-0020; Fax: 620-235-0520. Email: cecil_nave@via-christi.org. Web: www.via-christi.org. Mr. Cecil Nave, CEO. Total Staff 150; Skilled Nursing Beds 96; Total Assisted 40.

[E] MONASTERIES AND RESIDENCES FOR PRIESTS AND BROTHERS

WICHITA. *Priests Retirement Center*, 6900 E. 45th St. N., 67226. Tel: 316-744-2020; Fax: 316-744-2182. Thomas M. Church, CEO. Residents 24.

[F] CONVENTS AND RESIDENCES FOR SISTERS

WICHITA. *Adorers of the Blood of Christ U.S. Region*, Wichita Center, 1165 Southwest Blvd., 67213. Tel: 316-942-2201; Fax: 877-942-0859. Web: www.adorers.org. Rev. Thomas Welk, C.PP.S., Chap. Professed Sisters 316.
Dominican House of Studies (1933) 201 S. Millwood, 67213. Tel: 316-267-4551. Residents 3.
Medical Sisters of St. Joseph-United States Foundation (1985) 3435 E. Funston, 67218. Tel: 316-686-4746. Email: msjchythania@cox.net. Sr. Rosamma C. Varkey, Supr. Professed Sisters 3.
Sisters of the Immaculate Heart of Mary of Wichita, Inc. (I.H.M.) (1979) 145 S. Millwood St., 67213. Tel: 316-722-9316; Fax: 316-722-4568. Email: mmb@sistersihmofwichita.org. Web: www.sistersihmofwichita.org. Sr. Marie Bernadette Mertens, I.H.M., Supr. Professed Sisters 17; Novices 1.
Wichita Center, Congregation of the Sisters of St. Joseph, 3700 E. Lincoln, 67218-2099. Tel: 316-686-7171; Fax: 316-689-4056. Email: pyoung@csjoseph.org. Web: www.csjoseph.org. Sr. Pam Young, C.S.J., Admin.; Rev. Msgr. Robert E. Hemberger, J.C.L., Chap. Professed Sisters 132.

VALLEY CENTER. *Discalced Carmelite Monastery of Divine Mercy and Our Lady of Guadalupe*, P.O. Box 278, 67147. Tel: 620-545-8386. Total Assisted 150.

[G] RETREAT HOUSES

WICHITA. *Spiritual Life Center,* 7100 E. 45th N., 67226. Tel: 316-744-0167; Fax: 314-744-8072. Email: slc@slcwichita.org. Web: www.slcwichita.org. Rev. Kent A. Hemberger, Dir. Residents 1; Staff 17; Total Assisted Annually 15,839.
Ministry Staff: Jim Rundell, Admin.; Chuck Weber, Prog. & Publicity Dir.; Kristine Ulhschmidt, Facility Coord.

[H] COMMUNITY CENTERS

WICHITA. **Center of Hope, Inc.,* 400 N. Emporia, 67202-2514. Tel: 316-267-3999; Fax: 316-267-7778. Email: george@centerofhopeinc.org. Web: www.centerofhopeinc.org. George Dinkel, Exec. Dir. Tel: 316-267-0222; Fax: 316-267-7778. Sponsored by Adorers of the Blood of Christ. Total Assisted Annually 7,065.

The Lord's Diner (2002) 520 N. Broadway, 67214. Tel: 316-266-4966; Fax: 316-265-6646. Email: wendyg@thelordsdiner.org. Web: www.thelordsdiner.org. Wendy Glick, Exec. Dir. Meals Served to Date 1,067,949.

Sisters of St. Joseph "Dear Neighbor" Ministries, Inc., 1329 S. Bluffview, 67218. Tel: 316-684-5120; Fax: 316-684-3983. Ms. Katherine J. Lambertz, L.M.S.W., Exec. Dir. Congregation of St. Joseph. Total Assisted 3,951; Total Staff 13.

[I] NEWMAN CENTERS

WICHITA. *St. Paul Newman Center (Wichita State University)* (1970) 1810 N. Roosevelt, 67208. Tel: 316-684-6896; Fax: 316-684-2679. Email: parish@wsunewmancenter.com. Web: www.wsunewmancenter.com. Rev. Eric M. Weldon, Chap.

PITTSBURG. *St. Pius X Newman Center (Pittsburg State University)* 301A E. Cleveland, 66762. Tel: 620-235-1138. Email: frdavid@catholicgorillas.org. Web: www.catholicgorillas.org. Rev. David Marstall, Chap.

[J] CATHOLIC CHARITIES

WICHITA. *Catholic Charities, Inc.* (1943) 532 N. Broadway, 67214. Tel: 316-264-8344; Fax: 316-264-4442. Email: info@catholiccharitieswichita.org. Web: www.catholiccharitieswichita.org. Ms. Janet Valente Pape, Exec. Dir. Total Agency Staff 133; Total Individuals Assisted 22,734.

Foster Grandparent Program (1981) 437 N. Topeka, 67202. Tel: 316-264-8344; Fax: 316-262-5356. Provides 119,114 hours of service. Hours of Service to Children 119,401; Total Foster Grandparents 145; Staff 2.

Help Center, 437 N. Topeka, 67202. Tel: 316-262-8898; Fax: 316-262-5356. Total Assisted 14,699; Total Staff 3; Total Assisted (Christmas Sharing Program) 1,491.

Immigration & Refugee Services, 437 N. Topeka, 67202. Tel: 316-264-0282; Fax: 316-262-5356. Total Assisted 1,364; Staff 3.

Pregnancy and Adoption Services, 425 N. Topeka, 67202. Tel: 316-263-0507; Fax: 316-263-5259. Total Assisted 315; Adoptions Completed 3; Total Staff 3.

Community Counseling Services, 425 N. Topeka, 67202. Tel: 316-263-6941; Fax: 316-263-5259. Individuals Served 1,267; Total Staff 11.

Adult Day Services (1975) 5920 W. Central, 67212. Tel: 316-942-2008; Fax: 316-942-2260. Total Assisted 98; Staff 19.

St. Anthony Family Shelter (1988) 256 N. Ohio, 67214. Tel: 316-264-7233; Fax: 316-267-3774. Individuals Assisted In Shelter 520; In Follow-Up 30; Staff 17.

Harbor House (1992) P.O. Box 3759, 67201. Tel: 316-263-6000; Fax: 316-263-8347. Women & Children Assisted and Victim's Advocate Program 1,522; Staff 35.

Interpreter Services (2001) 437 N. Topeka, 67202. Tel: 316-264-8344; Fax: 316-262-5356. Clients Served 144; Total Staff 1; Contracted Interpreters 4.

Catholic Charities Emergency Services - Pittsburg, 411 E. 12th St., Pittsburg, 66762. Tel: 620-235-0633; Fax: 620-235-0633. Clients Served 856; Staff 1.

Marriage For Keeps (A Project of Catholic Charities), 437 N. Topeka, 67202. Tel: 316-264-8344; Fax: 316-262-5356. Total Staff 19; Total Served 458.

[K] MISCELLANEOUS

WICHITA. *Engaged Encounter, St. Joseph Parish,* 520 E. Northview, Mc Pherson, 67460. Tel: 620-241-0821. Rev. David J. Lies, Contact Person.

Marriage Encounter, 6900 E. 45th St., N., 67226. Tel: 316-440-3087. Rev. Paul J. Oborny, Contact Person (Retired).

St. Dismas/Ministry to the Incarcerated (1991) 4826 S.W. Briarcliff Rd., Towanda, 67144. Tel: 316-778-1939; Fax: 316-744-8072. Email: mrubeck@aol.com. Web: www.cdowk.org. Total Staff 1; Inmates Served 6,100.

Father Kapaun Guild (Office for the Beatification and Canonization of Father Emil Kapaun), 424 N. Broadway, 67202. Tel: 316-269-3900. Email: hotzej@cdonk.org. Web: www.frkapaun.org. Revs. John V. Hotze, J.C.L., Episcopal Delegate; Thomas M. Hoisington, S.T.L., Promoter of Justice.

Gerard House, Inc. (1989) 3144 N. Hood, 67204. Tel: 316-832-0777; Fax: 316-832-1327. Deneen Dryden, Dir. Shelter for Needy Pregnant Women. Education Program 51; Total Assisted 42.

Guadalupe Clinic, Inc. (1985) 940 S. St. Francis, 67211. Tel: 316-264-8974; Fax: 316-262-4938. Email: guadalupe@guadalupeclinic.kscoxmail.com. Web: www.guadalupeclinic.com. Karl N. Hesse, Attorney; Marlene Dreiling, M.N., R.N., Exec. Dir. Total Assisted Annually 56,574; Total Staff 14.

Guadalupe Health Foundation, 940 S. St. Francis, 67202. Tel: 316-264-8974; Fax: 316-262-4938. Purpose: to support, assist and promote the interests and welfare of the programs and activities of the Diocese of Wichita which provide health care services and health education to poor, distressed and underprivileged individuals.

Harvest House (1989) 424 N. Broadway, 67202. Tel: 316-269-3900; Fax: 316-269-3902. Staff 1; Centers 32; Members Assisted 1,820.

Holy Family Special Needs Foundation, 424 N. Broadway, 67202. Tel: 316-269-3900; Fax: 316-269-3902. Web: cdowk.org/offices/disabilities/. Holly Goodwin, Member Bd. Directors.

Leaven International Corporation, 1165 Southwest Blvd., 67213. Tel: 316-943-1203; Fax: 316-943-1426. Email: biscang@adorers.org. Web: www.adorers.org. Sisters Jan E. Renz, A.S.C., Pres.; Vicki Bergkamp, A.S.C., Treas. A charitable organization of the Adorers of the Blood of Christ.

The Mary Magdalen Foundation, 12626 E. 21st St. N., 67206. Tel: 316-634-2315; Fax: 316-634-3948. Email: prange@magdalenwichita.com. Web: www.magdalenwichita.com. Priests 2.

Ministry with Persons with Disabilities Office, 424 N. Broadway, 67202. Tel: 316-269-3900; Fax: 316-269-3902. Web: cdowk.org/disabilities. Priests 10; Total Assisted 210; Volunteers 190; Total Staff 1.

Mother Mary Anne Clinic, Inc., 1152 S. Clifton Ave., 67218. Tel: 316-858-4907. Email: steve_clifton@via-christi.org.

Priests' Retirement and Education Fund of Wichita (2001) 424 N. Broadway, 67202. Tel: 316-269-3900; Fax: 316-269-3902. Rev. Matthew C. McGinness.

Serra Club of Reno County, 424 N. Broadway, 67202. Rev. Nicholas A. Voelker, Chap.

Serra Club of Wichita - Downtown, 424 N. Broadway, 67202. Tel: 316-269-3900. Rev. Kenneth J. Schuckman, Chap.

Serra Club of Wichita - Metro, 424 N. Broadway, 67202. Tel: 316-269-3900. Rev. Michael M. Simone, S.T.L., Chap.

Sisters of St. Joseph of Wichita, Kansas, 3700 E. Lincoln, 67218. Tel: 316-686-7171; Fax: 316-689-4056.

Via Christi Foundation, Inc. (1957) 723 N. McLean, Ste. 320, 67203. Tel: 316-946-5020; Fax: 316-946-5034. Email: james_barber@via-christi.org. Mr. James N. Barber, Pres. A subsidiary of Via Christi Regional Medical Center. Staff 12.

Via Christi Health Partners, Inc. (1982) 929 N. St. Francis, 67214. Tel: 316-268-5065; Fax: 316-291-7999. Web: www.Via-Christi.org. Total Staff 7.

Via Christi Health System, Inc. (1995) 3720 E. Bayley, 67218. Tel: 316-858-4900. Web: www.Via-Christi.org. Kevin P. Conlin, Pres. & CEO. Affiliated with the Marian Health System and Ascension Health and co-sponsored by the Sisters of the Sorrowful Mother and the sponsoring congregations of Ascension Health. Participating organizations include: three acute care facilities, fifteen senior care facilities and one 50% owned, managed acute care facility, located in two states.

Via Christi Healthcare Outreach Program for Elders, Inc. (HOPE) (2002) 2622 W. Central, Ste. 101, 67203. Tel: 316-858-1111; Fax: 316-858-1166. Email: justin_loewen@via-christi.org. Web: viachristihope.org. Justin Loewen, Prog. Dir. Long Term Care Bed Capacity 24; Total Assisted Annually 196; Total Staff 100.

Via Christi Home Health Inc. (1983) 555 S. Washington, 67211. Tel: 316-268-8588; Fax: 316-269-1556. Email: jscott@hmsvc.com. Web: www.via-christi.org. Registered Nurses 34; LPN's 3; Physical Therapists 7; CPTA's 5; Medical Social Workers 2; Speech Therapists 2; Occupational Therapists 4; COTA's 1; Total Staff 61.

Via Christi Property Services, Inc. (1998) 1100 N. St. Francis, Ste. 240, 67214. Tel: 316-268-5065; Fax: 316-291-7999 1. Web: www.Via-Christi.org. Total Staff 7.

Via Christi Senior Services, Inc. (1985) 2622 W. Central, Ste. 100, 67203. Tel: 316-946-5200; Fax: 316-946-5299. Email: jerry_carley@via-christi.org. Web: www.via-christi.org. Mr. Jerry Carley, CEO. Total Staff 70.

RELIGIOUS INSTITUTES OF MEN REPRESENTED IN THE DIOCESE

For further details refer to the corresponding bracketed number in the Religious Institutes of Men or Women section.

[1060]—*Society of the Precious Blood* (Kansas City Prov.)—C.PP.S.

RELIGIOUS INSTITUTES OF WOMEN REPRESENTED IN THE DIOCESE

[0100]—*Adorers of the Blood of Christ*—A.S.C.
[]—*Carmelite Sisters of St. Teresa*—C.S.S.T.
[3832]—*Congregation of the Sisters of St. Joseph*—C.S.J.
[]—*Discalced Carmelite Sisters of Divine Mercy and Our Lady of Guadalupe*—O.C.D.
[1115]—*Dominican Sisters of Peace*—O.P.
[]—*Guadalupan Missionaries of the Holy Spirit*—M.G.S.p.S.
[2500]—*Medical Sisters of St. Joseph*—M.S.J.
[]—*Missionaries of Little Flower*—M.L.F.
[]—*Missionary Catechists of the Poor*—M.C.P.
[]—*Sisters of Mercy South Central Regional Community*—R.S.M.
[]—*Sisters of St. Joseph of Concordia*—C.S.J.
[2185]—*Sisters of the Immaculate Heart of Mary of Wichita*—I.H.M.
[4100]—*Sisters of the Sorrowful Mother (Third Order of St. Francis)*—S.S.M.

NECROLOGY

† Hay, Francis J., (Retired)—Died Nov. 12, 2008
† O'Leary, David A., (Retired)—Died Aug. 24, 2009
† Wilkinson, James S., (Retired)—Died Jan. 1, 2009

An asterisk (*) denotes an organization that has established tax-exempt status directly with the IRS and is not covered by the USCCB Group Ruling.

Diocese of Wilmington

(Dioecesis Wilmingtoniensis)

Most Reverend

WILLIAM FRANCIS MALOOLY, D.D.

Bishop of Wilmington; ordained May 9, 1970; appointed Titular Bishop of Flumenzer and Auxiliary Bishop of Baltimore December 12, 2000; Episcopal ordination March 1, 2001; appointed Bishop of Wilmington July 7, 2008; installed September 8, 2008. *Chancery: 1925 Delaware Ave., P.O. Box 2030, Wilmington, DE 19899.* Tel: 302-573-3100; Fax: 302-573-6817.

Chancery Office: P.O. Box 2030, Wilmington, DE 19899-2030. Tel: 302-573-3100; Fax: 302-573-6836.

Web: www.cdow.org

Email: ccurtis@cdow.org

ESTABLISHED MARCH 3, 1868.

Square Miles Delaware 1,932; Maryland 3,375; Total 5,307.

Comprises the State of Delaware and the Counties of Caroline, Cecil, Dorchester, Kent, Queen Anne's, Somerset, Talbot, Wicomico and Worcester in Maryland.

For legal titles of parishes and diocesan institutions, consult the Chancery Office.

STATISTICAL OVERVIEW

Personnel	
Bishop	1
Priests: Diocesan Active in Diocese	87
Priests: Diocesan Active Outside Diocese	7
Priests: Retired, Sick or Absent	31
Number of Diocesan Priests	125
Religious Priests in Diocese	87
Total Priests in Diocese	212
Extern Priests in Diocese	14
Ordinations:	
Diocesan Priests	2
Permanent Deacons in Diocese	110
Total Brothers	34
Total Sisters	256
Parishes	
Parishes	57
With Resident Pastor:	
Resident Diocesan Priests	51
Resident Religious Priests	5
Without Resident Pastor:	
Administered by Priests	1
Missions	19
Closed Parishes	1
Professional Ministry Personnel:	
Brothers	1
Sisters	16
Lay Ministers	79
Welfare	
Catholic Hospitals	1
Total Assisted	174,158
Health Care Centers	1
Total Assisted	150
Homes for the Aged	6
Total Assisted	400
Residential Care of Children	1
Total Assisted	10
Day Care Centers	3
Total Assisted	170
Specialized Homes	3
Total Assisted	61
Special Centers for Social Services	15
Total Assisted	194,300
Residential Care of Disabled	1
Total Assisted	100
Other Institutions	6
Total Assisted	29,757
Educational	
Diocesan Students in Other Seminaries	9
Total Seminarians	9
High Schools, Diocesan and Parish	5
Total Students	2,784
High Schools, Private	3
Total Students	1,713
Elementary Schools, Diocesan and Parish	22
Total Students	7,530
Elementary Schools, Private	5
Total Students	1,007
Non-residential Schools for the Disabled	1
Total Students	80
Catechesis/Religious Education:	
High School Students	1,063
Elementary Students	10,012
Total Students under Catholic Instruction	24,198
Teachers in the Diocese:	
Priests	13
Brothers	8
Sisters	28
Lay Teachers	1,153
Vital Statistics	
Receptions into the Church:	
Infant Baptism Totals	2,673
Minor Baptism Totals	157
Adult Baptism Totals	143
Received into Full Communion	225
First Communions	2,502
Confirmations	2,241
Marriages:	
Catholic	426
Interfaith	217
Total Marriages	643
Deaths	1,689
Total Catholic Population	233,000
Total Population	1,314,050

Former Bishops—Rt. Revs. THOMAS A. BECKER, D.D., ord. June 18, 1859; cons. Aug. 16, 1868; transferred to Savannah, 1886; died July 29, 1899; ALFRED A. CURTIS, D.D., ord. Dec. 19, 1874; cons. Nov. 14, 1886; resigned 1896; named Titular Bishop of Echinus; died July 11, 1908; Most Revs. JOHN J. MONAGHAN, D.D., ord. Dec. 19, 1880; cons. May 9, 1897; resigned and named Titular Bishop of Lydda, July 10, 1925; died Jan. 7, 1935; EDMOND JOHN FITZMAURICE, D.D., ord. May 1904; cons. Nov. 30, 1925; resigned March 2, 1960 and named Titular Archbishop of Tomi; died July 25, 1962; HUBERT J. CARTWRIGHT, D.D., ord. June 11, 1927; cons. Coadjutor "with right of succession," Oct. 24, 1956; Titular Bishop of Neve; died March 6, 1958; MICHAEL W. HYLE, D.D., ord. March 12, 1927; cons. Sept. 24, 1958 as Titular Bishop of Christopolis and Coadjutor with right of succession; succeeded to See, March 2, 1960; died Dec. 26, 1967; THOMAS J. MARDAGA, D.D., ord. May 14, 1940; cons. Jan. 25, 1967; named Titular Bishop of Mutugenna; appt. Bishop of Wilmington, March 13, 1968; installed April 6, 1968; died May 28, 1984; JAMES C. BURKE, O.P., ord. June 18, 1956; cons. May 25, 1967; named Titular Bishop of Lamiggiga; Vicar Apostolic of Chimbote, Peru, 1962-1978; Served in Diocese of Wilmington, 1978-1994; died May 28, 1994; ROBERT E. MULVEE, D.D., J.C.D., ord. June 30, 1957; Auxiliary Bishop of Manchester and Titular Bishop of Summa, Feb. 15, 1977; cons. April 14, 1977; appt. Bishop of Wilmington, Feb. 19, 1985; installed April 11, 1985; appt. to Diocese of Providence as Coadjutor Bishop of Providence, Feb. 7, 1995; installed March 27, 1995; succeeded to See, June 11, 1997; MICHAEL A. SALTARELLI, D.D., ord. May 28, 1960; appt. Titular Bishop of Mesarfelta and Auxiliary Bishop of Newark, June 12, 1990; Episcopal ord. July 30, 1990; appt. Eighth Bishop of Wilmington Nov. 21, 1995; installed Jan. 23, 1996 retired July 7, 2008; died Oct. 8, 2009.

Office of the Bishop—Mailing Address: P.O. Box 2030, Wilmington, 19899. PATRICIA BOSSI, Sec. to Bishop & Notary for the Curia. Tel: 302-573-3100; Fax: 302-573-6817.

Chancellor—VACANT.

Vicar General for Administration and Moderator of the Curia—Rev. Msgr. J. THOMAS CINI, V.G., 1925 Delaware Ave., P.O. Box 2030, Wilmington, 19899. Tel: 302-573-3118; Fax: 302-573-6947.

Vicar General for Pastoral Services—Rev. Msgr. JOSEPH F. REBMAN, V.G., S.T.L., J.C.L., C.C.C.E., 1925 Delaware Ave., P.O. Box 2030, Wilmington, 19899. Tel: 302-573-3100; Fax: 302-573-6836.

Vicar for Priests—Rev. Msgr. CLEMENT P. LEMON, 1925 Delaware Ave., P.O. Box 2030, Wilmington, 19899. Tel: 302-573-3144; Fax: 302-573-6947.

Pastoral Services Department

Secretary, Pastoral Services Department—Rev. Msgr. JOSEPH F. REBMAN, V.G., S.T.L., J.C.L., C.C.C.E.

Chancery Office—VACANT, Mailing Address: P.O. Box 2030, Wilmington, 19899. Office, 1925 Delaware Ave., Wilmington, 19806. Tel: 302-573-3100; Fax: 302-573-6836. Email: ccurtis@cdow.org. Web: www.cdow.org. Office Hours: Mon.-Fri. 8:30-4:30; Send all marriage dispensation requests to Chancery Office.

Archives—Mr. DONN DEVINE, Archivist, 8 Old Church Rd., Greenville, 19807. Tel: 302-655-0597.

Censor of Books—Rev. LEONARD R. KLEIN, Immaculate Heart of Mary, 4701 Weldin Rd., Wilmington, 19803. Tel: 302-764-0357.

Diocesan Tribunal—Mailing Address: P.O. Box 2030, Wilmington, 19899. 1925 Delaware Ave., Wilmington, 19806. Tel: 302-573-3107; Fax: 302-573-6947.

Judicial Vicar—Very Rev. GEORGE J. BRUBAKER, J.C.L.

Office Supervisor—Mrs. JOANN KUBASKO.

Court of First Instance Judges—Rev. STANLEY R. DRUPIESKI, O.S.F.S.; Very Rev. GEORGE J. BRUBAKER, J.C.L.; Sr. JEANNE HAMILTON, O.S.U., J.C.L.; Ms. JACQUELINE E. HANNEM, J.C.L.

Auditor—Deacon FRANCIS STAAB.

Defenders of the Bond—Mr. JACK D. ANDERSON, J.C.D.; Rev. CYPRIAN ROSEN, O.F.M.Cap., S.T.L.; Sr. PATRICIA SMITH, O.S.F., J.C.D.

Secretaries/Notaries—Mrs. GAIL ESPOSITO; Mrs. PATRICIA KILLEN.

Catholic Cemeteries—Rev. Msgr. JOSEPH F. REBMAN, V.G., S.T.L., J.C.L., C.C.C.E., Dir.; Mr. MARK A. CHRISTIAN, C.C.C.E., Exec. Dir., Mailing Address: P.O. Box 2506, Wilmington, 19805. Tel: 302-656-3323; Fax: 302-656-1069.

Coordinator of Institutional Chaplains—Rev. JOHN J. MINK, Dir., 801 Dupont Blvd., New Castle, 19720. Tel: 302-328-1790.

Priest Personnel Committee—Rev. JOHN J. MINK, Dir., 801 Dupont Blvd., New Castle, 19720. Tel: 302-328-1790.

Office of Priestly and Religious Vocations and Seminarians and Newly Ordained—Rev. JOSEPH M.P.R. COCUCCI, Dir., 1626 N. Union St., P.O. Box 2030, Wilmington, 19899. Tel: 302-573-3113; Fax: 302-573-6944.

Office for Deacons—Deacon HAROLD D. JOPP JR., Dir., 1626 N. Union St., P.O. Box 2030, Wilmington, 19899. Tel: 302-573-2390; Fax: 302-573-6944.

Office of Worship—Rev. MICHAEL J. CARRIER, Dir., 1626 N. Union St., Wilmington, 19899. Tel: 302-573-3137; Fax: 302-573-6944.

Delegate for Religious—Sr. MARGARET CUNNIFFE, O.S.F., 1626 N. Union St., P.O. Box 2030, Wilmington, 19899. Tel: 302-573-3124; Fax: 302-573-6944.

Mission Office— Propagation of the Faith and Holy Childhood Association, Deacon JOSEPH C. ROMANS, Dir., 1626 N. Union St., P.O. Box 2030, Wilmington, 19899. Tel: 302-573-3104; Fax: 302-573-6944.

Apostolate for Ethnic Ministries—Mailing Address: P.O. Box 2030, Wilmington, 19899. Tel: 302-573-3100.

Ministry of Black Catholics—Mr. PRESTON TAYLOR, Dir., 2810 Monroe St., Wilmington, 19802. Tel: 302-762-6848; Fax: 302-764-8244.

Hispanic Ministry—

Wilmington Office—Rev. CHRISTOPHER J. POSCH, O.F.M., Dir., 1010 W. Fourth St., Wilmington, 19805. Tel: 302-655-0518; Fax: 302-655-7684; Sr. AGNES OMAN, C.S.B., Assoc. Dir., St. Francis de Sales Church, 417 Wicomico St., Salisbury, MD 21801. Tel: 443-235-7247; Fax: 410-742-9410; RONALDO TELLO, Coord. Hispanic Youth Ministry, 1010 W. Fourth St., Wilmington, 19805. Tel: 302-655-0518; Fax: 302-655-7684.

Korean Catholics—Rev. JOHN (B) LEE GYE-CHUN, Pastoral Min.; Mr. MATTHIAS MYUNG-GEUN LEE, Community Pres., 2710 Duncan Rd., Wilmington, 19808. Tel: 302-998-7609.

Native American Community—Contacts: SHERYL PERSINGER, 505 Rochelle Ave., Wilmington, 19804. Tel: 302-992-0708; DEBRA GOERGER, Mailing Address: P.O. Box 2030, Wilmington, 19899. Tel: 302-573-3100.

Catholic Education Department

Secretary—Mr. EDMUND F. GORDON.

Catholic Schools—Mrs. CATHERINE P. WEAVER, Supt. Assistant Superintendents: CAROL RIPKEN; LOUIS DEANGELO, 1626 N. Union St., Wilmington, 19806. Tel: 302-573-3133; Fax: 302-573-6945.

Catholic Education—Mr. EDMUND F. GORDON, Diocesan Dir.; Sr. SALLY RUSSELL, S.S.J., Assoc. Dir., 1626 N. Union St., Wilmington, 19806. Tel: 302-573-3130; Fax: 302-573-2393.

Education Ministry for Persons With Special Needs—Mrs. JO-ANN DORA, Coord. Spec. Rel. Educ. Tel: 302-573-3130; Mrs. MARGARET WYNN, Coord. Hearing Impaired, 1626 N. Union St., Wilmington, 19806. Tel: 302-573-3130.

Catholic Youth Ministry—Mr. PATRICK DONOVAN, Dir.; SUSAN MURRAY, Asst. Dir.; JOE MCNESBY, Dir. Athletics, 1626 N. Union St., Wilmington, 19806. Tel: 302-658-3800; Fax: 302-658-7617. Web: www.cdow.org.

Catholic Campus Ministry—Revs. AMBROSE ECKINGER, O.P.; STEPHEN ALCOTT, O.P.; MICHAEL DETEMPLE, O.P.; KIM ZITZNER, Campus Min., University of Delaware, 45 Lovett Ave., Newark, 19711. Tel: 302-368-4728; Fax: 302-368-2548.

Communications Department

Secretary—Mr. ROBERT KREBS.

Office of Public Relations, Radio and T.V.—Mr. ROBERT KREBS, Dir., 1626 N. Union St., Wilmington, 19899. Tel: 302-573-3116; Fax: 302-573-2393.

Finance Department

Chief Financial Officer and Secretary—Mr. JOSEPH P. CORSINI, Mailing Address: P.O. Box 2030, Wilmington, 19899. 1925 Delaware Ave., Wilmington, 19806. Tel: 302-573-3105; Fax: 302-573-6869.

Development Department

Secretary and Diocesan Development Director—Mrs. DEBORAH A. FOLS, Mailing Address: P.O. Box 2030, Wilmington, 19899. Tel: 302-573-3121; Fax: 302-573-6947.

Annual Catholic Appeal—Mrs. DEBORAH A. FOLS, Dir., Mailing Address: P.O. Box 2030, Wilmington, 19899. Tel: 302-573-3100; Fax: 302-573-6947.

Catholic Charities Department

Catholic Charities—Ms. RICHELLE A. VIBLE, M.B.A., Exec. Dir., Fourth St. & Greenhill Ave., P.O. Box 2610, Wilmington, 19805. Tel: 302-655-9624; Fax: 302-655-9753 (Refer to separate listings in the Institutions for detailed information on Catholic Charities and related organizations).

Parish Social Ministry—ANDREW A. ZAMPINI, S.F.O., Dir., Fourth St. & Greenhill Ave., P.O. Box 2610, Wilmington, 19805. Tel: 302-655-9624; Fax: 302-655-9753.

Family Life Bureau—Mr. THOMAS JEWETT, Dir., Mailing Address: P.O. Box 2610, Wilmington, 19805. Tel: 302-655-9624.

Offices Reporting to Vicar General for Administration/Moderator of the Curia

Catholic Press Inc., "The Dialog"—Most Rev. W. FRANCIS MALOOLY, D.D., Publisher; Mr. JIM GRANT, Editor & Gen. Mgr., Mailing Address: P.O. Box 2208, Wilmington, 19899. 1925 Delaware Ave., Wilmington, 19806. Tel: 302-573-3109 (Newsroom); 302-573-3112 (Advertising); Fax: 302-573-6948. Email: news@thedialog.org.

Human Resources Office—Sr. SUZANNE DONOVAN, S.C., Dir., Mailing Address: P.O. Box 2030, Wilmington, 19899. Tel: 302-573-3126; Fax: 302-573-6944.

Management Information System (MIS)—Mrs. NANCY MOORE, Dir., Mailing Address: P.O. Box 2030, Wilmington, 19899. 1925 Delaware Ave., Wilmington, 19806. Tel: 302-573-3122; Fax: 302-573-6947.

Diocesan Planning—Rev. Msgr. J. THOMAS CINI, V.G., Mailing Address: P.O. Box 2030, Wilmington, 19899. Tel: 302-573-3118; Fax: 302-573-6947.

Diocesan Real Estate Committee—Rev. Msgr. J. THOMAS CINI, V.G., Sec., Mailing Address: P.O. Box 2030, Wilmington, 19899. Tel: 302-573-3118; Fax: 302-573-6947.

Catholic Ministry to the Elderly—Rev. Msgr. J. THOMAS CINI, V.G., Sec., Mailing Address: P.O. Box 2030, Wilmington, 19806. Tel: 302-573-3118; Fax: 302-573-6947.

Other Ministries

Catholic Scouting Program—Revs. MICHAEL J. CARRIER, Chap. for Girl Scouts, 2500 Naamans Rd., Wilmington, 19810. Tel: 302-475-6486; MICHAEL P. DARCY, Chap. Boy Scouts, 691 Garfield Pkwy., Bethany Beach, 19930. Tel: 302-539-6449.

Liaison for Non-Christian Religions—Rev. LEONARD J. KEMPSKI, Liaison (Retired), Res.: St. Thomas the Apostle, 301 N. Bancroft Pkwy., Wilmington, 19805. Tel: 302-379-1261.

Liaison for Evangelization—Rev. WILLIAM J. LAWLER, Liaison, Mailing Address: P.O. Box 218, Cambridge, MD 21613. Tel: 410-228-4770.

Ecumenical Liaison—Rev. Msgr. JOSEPH F. REBMAN, V.G., S.T.L., J.C.L., C.C.C.E., Dir., Mailing Address: P.O. Box 2030, Wilmington, 19899. Tel: 302-573-3100.

Marian Devotions—Rev. Msgr. JOSEPH F. REBMAN, V.G., S.T.L., J.C.L., C.C.C.E., Dir. Associate Directors: Revs. TIMOTHY M. NOLAN; JOSEPH J. PIEKARSKI, Mailing Address: P.O. Box 2030, Wilmington, 19899. Tel: 302-573-3100.

Volunteer Liaison for the Physically Challenged—Mr. BOB CICHOCKI, M.H.S., 67 Lowry Dr., Wilmington, 19805. Fax: 302-995-1222.

Principal Advisory Groups to the Bishop

College of Consultors—Rev. Msgrs. JOSEPH F. REBMAN, V.G., S.T.L., J.C.L., C.C.C.E.; J. THOMAS CINI, V.G.; CLEMENT P. LEMON; Very Rev. GEORGE J. BRUBAKER, J.C.L.; Revs. JOHN P. HOPKINS; DAVID F. KELLEY; CLEMENS D. MANISTA.

Priests' Council—Rev. JOHN P. HOPKINS, Exec. Officer; Rev. Msgr. JOSEPH F. REBMAN, V.G., Sec., Mailing Address: P.O. Box 2030, Wilmington, 19899. Tel: 302-573-3100.

Deans—Very Revs. DANIEL W. GERRES, V.F.; PAUL F. JENNINGS JR., V.F.; Rev. CHARLES L. BROWN III, V.F.; Very Revs. RAYMOND L. FORESTER, V.F.; STEVEN B. GIULIANO, V.F.; JOHN MCKENNA, C.Ss.R., V.F.; STANLEY J. RUSSELL, V.F.

Finance Council—Mr. JOSEPH P. CORSINI, Sec., Mailing Address: P.O. Box 2030, Wilmington, 19899. Tel: 302-573-3105.

Priests' Personnel Committee—Rev. JOHN J. MINK, Dir., Mailing Address: P.O. Box 2030, Wilmington, 19899. Tel: 302-328-1790; Fax: 302-328-8364.

Women's Commission—Sr. MARGARET CUNNIFFE, O.S.F., Coord., Mailing Address: P.O. Box 2030, Wilmington, 19899. Tel: 302-573-3124; Fax: 302-573-6944. Co-Chairs: Ms. PAMELA NASH, Mailing Address: P.O. Box 2030, Wilmington, 19899; KIM ZITZNER, 45 Lovett Ave., Newark, 19711.

Other Advisory Groups

Priests' Continuing Formation Committee—Rev. JOHN P. HOPKINS, Chm., St. Margaret of Scotland, 2431 Frazer Rd., Newark, 19702. Tel: 302-834-0225; Fax: 302-834-0840.

Council of Religious—Sr. MARGARET CUNNIFFE, O.S.F., Contact, Mailing Address: P.O. Box 2030, Wilmington, 19899. Tel: 302-573-3124; Fax: 302-573-6944.

Diocesan School Board—Mrs. CATHERINE P. WEAVER, Sec., Mailing Address: P.O. Box 2030, Wilmington, 19899. Tel: 302-573-3133.

Diocesan Religious Education Board—Mr. EDMUND F. GORDON, Sec., Mailing Address: 1626 N. Union St., Wilmington, 19806. Tel: 302-573-3130; Fax: 302-573-6944.

Diocesan Building Committee—Mr. HENRY STEENHAMER, Chm.; Rev. Msgr. J. THOMAS CINI, V.G., Episcopal Liaison, Mailing Address: P.O. Box 2030, Wilmington, 19899. Tel: 302-573-3118; Fax: 302-573-6947.

Office for Pro-Life Activities—Mr. THOMAS JEWETT, Chm., Mailing Address: P.O. Box 2610, Wilmington, 19805. Tel: 302-655-9624; Fax: 302-655-9753.

Pastoral Council—Mr. MICHAEL RUSH, Exec. Officer, Mailing Address: P.O. Box 2030, Wilmington, 19899. Tel: 302-573-3100; Fax: 302-573-6836.

Public Affairs Advisory Committee—Rev. Msgr. J. THOMAS CINI, V.G., Chm., Mailing Address: P.O. Box 2030, Wilmington, 19899. Tel: 302-573-3118; Fax: 302-573-6947.

Respect Life Committee—Mr. THOMAS JEWETT, Chm., Fourth St. & Greenhill Ave., Wilmington, 19805. Tel: 302-655-9624; Fax: 302-655-9753.

Due Process Commission—Contact: Very Rev. GEORGE J. BRUBAKER, J.C.L., Clerk, Mailing Address: P.O. Box 2030, Wilmington, 19899. Tel: 302-573-3107; Fax: 302-573-6947.

Diocesan Corporations

Catholic Cemeteries, Inc.—Rev. Msgr. JOSEPH F. REBMAN, V.G., S.T.L., J.C.L., C.C.C.E., Vice Pres.; Mr. MARK A. CHRISTIAN, C.C.C.E., Sec., Mailing Address: P.O. Box 2506, Wilmington, 19805. Tel: 302-656-3323.

Catholic Diocese of Wilmington, Inc.— A corporation sole under the laws of the State of Delaware. Rev. Msgrs. JOSEPH F. REBMAN, V.G., S.T.L., J.C.L., C.C.C.E., Vice Pres.; J. THOMAS CINI, V.G., Sec., Mailing Address: P.O. Box 2030, Wilmington, 19899. Tel: 302-573-3118. Office, 1925 Delaware Ave., Wilmington, 19899.

Catholic Diocese Foundation—Mr. JOSEPH P. CORSINI, Exec. Dir., Mailing Address: P.O. Box 2030, Wilmington, 19899. Tel: 302-573-3105.

Catholic Ministry to the Elderly, Inc.—Rev. Msgr. J. THOMAS CINI, V.G., Vice Pres., Mailing Address: P.O. Box 2030, Wilmington, 19899. Tel: 302-573-3118.

Catholic Press of Wilmington, Inc.—Rev. Msgr. J. THOMAS CINI, V.G., Vice Pres., Mailing Address: P.O. Box 2208, Wilmington, 19899. Tel: 302-573-3118.

Catholic Charities, Inc.—Rev. Msgr. J. THOMAS CINI, V.G., Contact Person, Fourth St. & Greenhill Ave., P.O. Box 2610, Wilmington, 19806. Tel: 302-655-9624.

Catholic Youth Organization, Inc.—Rev. Msgr. J. THOMAS CINI, V.G., Vice Pres., Mailing Address: P.O. Box 2030, Wilmington, 19899. Tel: 302-573-3118.

Children's Home, Inc.—Rev. Msgr. J. THOMAS CINI, V.G., Contact Person, Fourth St. & Greenhill Ave., P.O. Box 2610, Wilmington, 19806. Tel: 302-655-9624.

Diocese of Wilmington Schools, Inc.—Mrs. CATHERINE P. WEAVER, Sec., 1626 N. Union St., Wilmington, 19806. Tel: 302-573-3133.

Seton Villa, Inc.—Rev. Msgr. J. THOMAS CINI, V.G., Contact Person, Fourth St. & Greenhill Ave., P.O. Box 2610, Wilmington, 19806. Tel: 302-655-9624.

Siena Hall, Inc.—Rev. Msgr. J. THOMAS CINI, V.G., Contact Person, Fourth St. & Greenhill Ave., P.O. Box 2610, Wilmington, 19806. Tel: 302-655-9624.

Activities

Apostleship of Prayer—Rev. JOSEPH R. MCMAHON, 7 Sharpley Rd., Wilmington, 19803. Tel: 302-652-6800.

Catholic Campaign for Human Development—ANDREW A. ZAMPINI, S.F.O., Diocesan Dir., Fourth St. & Greenhill Ave., P.O. Box 2610, Wilmington, 19806. Tel: 302-655-9624.

Catholic Charismatic Renewal—Rev. THOMAS A. FLOWERS, Chap., St. Polycarp, 135 Ransom Lane, Smyrna, 19977. Tel: 302-653-8279.

Catholic Relief Services, Inc.—Very Rev. GEORGE J. BRUBAKER, J.C.L., Diocesan Dir., 506 Seabury Ave., Milford, 19963. Tel: 302-422-5123.

Black & Native American Missions—Rev. Msgr. JOSEPH F. REBMAN, V.G., Diocesan Dir., Mailing Address: P.O. Box 2030, Wilmington, 19899. Tel: 302-573-3100; Fax: 302-573-6836.

Cursillo Movement—Ms. JUDITH A. LOVETT, Lay Dir., 2041 Dinah's Corner Rd., Dover, 19901. Tel: 302-741-2336.

Delmarva Catholic Network, Inc.—Mr. ROBERT KREBS, Contact Person, Mailing Address: P.O. Box 2030, Wilmington, 19899. Tel: 302-573-3116.

Diocesan Healing Ministry—JEANNE CASEY, Lay Dir., 533 Waterford Dr., Hockessin, 19707. Tel: 302-239-5982.

KAIROS Ministries, Inc.—Rev. GREGORY M. CORRIGAN, Contact Person, Corpus Christi, 905 New Rd., Wilmington, 19805. Tel: 302-994-2922.

Korean Catholic Community, Inc.—Rev. JOHN (B) LEE GYE-CHUN, Chap.; Mr. MATTHIAS MYUNG-GEUN LEE, Pres., Community Council, 2712 Duncan Rd., Wilmington, 19808. Tel: 302-998-7730.

St. Thomas More Society—Rev. LEONARD R. KLEIN, Chap., Immaculate Heart of Mary, 4701 Weldin Rd., Wilmington, 19803. Tel: 302-764-0357.

St. Vincent dePaul Society—Mr. PAUL COLLINS, 312 Hazlett Rd., New Castle, 19720. Tel: 302-328-5166.

Diocese of Wilmington - Serra Club In-formation—1626 N. Union St., Wilmington, 19806. Tel: 302-573-3116. Dr. HERBERT CASALENA, Pres.; Rev. JOSEPH M.P.R. COCUCCI, Chap.

Organizations With Which Diocese Has Liaison

**Birthright of Delaware, Inc.*Mrs. MARY JO FROHLICH, Dir., 1311 N. Scott St., Wilmington, 19806. Tel: 302-656-7080.

**Delaware Citizens for Life*Mr. THOMAS JEWETT, Chm., 4019 Greenmount Rd., Wilmington, 19810.

Delawareans United for Education—Rev. Msgr. J. THOMAS CINI, V.G., Mailing Address: P.O. Box 2030, Wilmington, 19899. Tel: 302-573-3118.

Maryland Catholic Conference— (An agency of the Archdiocese of Baltimore, Washington and the Diocese of Wilmington) MARY ELLEN RUSSELL, Exec. Dir., 10 Francis St., Annapolis, MD 21401. Tel: 410-269-1155; Fax: 410-269-1790. Mailing Address: P.O. Box 2030, Wilmington, 19899. Tel: 302-573-3118.

National Catholic Ministry to the Bereaved—Mr. THOMAS R. JEWETT, M.C., Contact, Mailing Address: P.O. Box 2610, Wilmington, 19805. Tel: 302-655-9624; Fax: 302-655-9753.

National Conference for Community and Justice—Rev. CLEMENS D. MANISTA, Vianney House, 905 Milltown Rd., Wilmington, 19808. Tel: 302-636-0200.

Regina Coeli Society—Rev. CORNELIUS J. BRESLIN, Chap., 1414 King St., Wilmington, 19801. Tel: 302-652-0743.

Victim Assistance Coordinator—PEGGY MCLAUGHLIN. Tel: 302-655-9624. Email: pmclaughlin@ccwilm.org.

World Wide Marriage Encounter—Contact Persons: ED THOMAS; BOBBIE THOMAS. Tel: 302-475-0925.

CLERGY, PARISHES, MISSIONS AND PAROCHIAL SCHOOLS

DELAWARE, CITY OF WILMINGTON

(NEW CASTLE COUNTY)

1—CATHEDRAL OF ST. PETER (1796) Rev. Joseph M.P.R. Cocucci, Rector.
Res.: 500 N. West St., 19801. Tel: 302-654-5920; Fax: 302-654-3197. Email: rector19801@comcast.net. Web: www.cathedralofstpeter.net.
School—310 W. 6th St., 19801. Tel: 302-656-5234; Fax: 302-658-6489. Sr. Barbara Ann Curran, D.C., Prin. Daughters of Charity of St. Vincent de Paul 2; Lay Teachers 13; Students 220.
Catechesis/Religious Program—Students 220.

2—ST. ANN (1887) Rev. Msgr. J. Thomas Cini; Rev. Steven P. Hurley; Sisters John Regina Lang, M.S.B.T., Pastoral Assoc.; Marie Bernadette Lang, M.S.B.T., Pastoral Assoc.
Res.: 2013 Gilpin Ave., 19806. Tel: 302-654-5519; 302-652-0152; Fax: 302-654-5527. Email: stannschurch1@verizon.net. Web: www.st-ann.net.
School—Tel: 302-652-6567; Fax: 302-652-4156. Sr. Virginia Pfau, I.H.M., Prin. Lay Teachers 22; Students 269.
Catechesis/Religious Program—Tel: 302-654-8504. Patricia Walker, D.R.E. Students 152.

3—ST. ANTHONY OF PADUA (1924), (Italian), Revs. John F. McGinley, O.S.F.S.; Francis Rinaldi, O.S.F.S.; Deacon Robert J. Leonzio. In Res., Revs. Roberto Balducelli, O.S.F.S.; Stanley R. Drupieski, O.S.F.S.; Bro. Michael J. Rosenello, O.S.F.S.
Res.: 901 N. DuPont St., 19805. Tel: 302-421-3700; Fax: 302-421-3709. Email: parish@stanthonynet.org. Web: www.stanthonynet.org.
School—9th & Scott Sts., 19805. Tel: 302-421-3743; Fax: 302-421-3796. Ms. Patricia O'Donnell, Prin. Sisters of St. Francis of Philadelphia 1; Lay Teachers 23; Students 272.
High School—Padua Academy, 905 N. Broom St., 19806. Tel: 302-421-3739; Fax: 302-421-3748. Web: www.paduaacademy.org. Cindy Hayes Mann, Prin. Lay Teachers 47; Students 580.
Catechesis/Religious Program—Fax: 302-421-3705. Students 65.
Convent—1710 W. 9th St., 19805. Tel: 302-421-3754. Sisters 2.
Convent—1401 W. 10th St., 19806. Tel: 302-421-3739. Sisters 3.
St. Anthony's Education Fund, Inc.—901 N. DuPont St., 19805. Tel: 302-421-3700; Fax: 302-421-3709.

4—CHRIST OUR KING (1926) Very Rev. John J. Kavanaugh, Temporary Admin. (Retired); Deacons William J. Johnston Jr.; William J. Maloney Jr., (Retired).
Res.: 2810 N. Monroe St., 19802. Tel: 302-762-4140; Fax: 302-762-8414. Web: www.christourkingcatholicchurch.org.
Catechesis/Religious Program—Students 3.

5—ST. ELIZABETH (1908) Revs. Norman P. Carroll; Anthony Giamello; Deacon Kenneth Pulliam Sr.
Res.: 809 S. Broom St., 19805-4296. Tel: 302-652-3626; Fax: 302-658-5957. Email: rectory809@aol.com.
School—1500 Cedar St., 19805-4249. Tel: 302-655-8208; Fax: 302-655-5457. Mr. William Beliveau, Prin. Lay Teachers 25; Aides 6; Students 384.
High School—Tel: 302-656-3369; Fax: 302-656-7513. Mrs. Shirley Bounds, Prin. Sisters 3; Lay Teachers 31; Students 441.
Catechesis/Religious Program—809 S. Broom St., 19805. Students 32.

6—ST. HEDWIG (1890), (Polish), Rev. Andrew Molewski; Deacon James Handlir.
Res.: 408 S. Harrison St., 19805. Tel: 302-594-1400; Fax: 302-594-1415.
Catechesis/Religious Program—Tel: 302-594-1400, Ext. 3. Students 21.

7—ST. JOSEPH'S R.C. CHURCH OF WILMINGTON, INC. (1889) Rev. John Frambes, O.F.M.; Deacons Robert J. Cousar Jr.; Robert J. Levesque.
Church: 1012 French St., 19801. Tel: 302-658-4535; Fax: 302-658-2006.
Res.: 1010 W. 4th St., 19805.

8—ST. MARY OF THE IMMACULATE CONCEPTION (1858) Rev. Cornelius J. Breslin, Admin.
Res.: 1414 King St., 19801. Tel: 302-652-0743; Fax: 302-652-7678.
Church: 6th & Pine Sts., 19801.

9—ST. PATRICK (1880) Rev. Cornelius J. Breslin, Admin.
Res.: 1414 King St., 19801. Tel: 302-652-0743; Fax: 302-652-7678.
Catechesis/Religious Program—Tel: 302-622-8581. Students 50.

10—ST. PAUL'S (1869) Revs. Todd Carpenter, O.F.M.; Michael Tyson, O.F.M., Parochial Vicar. In Res., Revs. John Frambes, O.F.M.; Christopher J. Posch, O.F.M.; Ronald J. Pecci, O.F.M.; Bro. William Herbst, O.F.M.
Res.: 1010 W. 4th St., 19805. Tel: 302-655-6596; Fax: 302-655-7684.
School—3rd & Van Buren Sts., 19805. Tel: 302-656-1372; Fax: 302-656-5238. Ms. Alexandria Cirko, Prin. Lay Teachers 20; Students 170.
Catechesis/Religious Program—Students 150.

11—SACRED HEART (1874), Reopened as Sacred Heart Oratory, Inc. (1998) A Center for Evangelization. Rev. Ronald Giannone, O.F.M.Cap.; Deacon Gianni Chicco; Sr. Mary Daniel Jackson, S.S.H.J., Assoc.; Joseph Graney, Pastoral Team.
Res.: 917 N. Madison St., 19801. Tel: 302-428-3658; Fax: 302-428-3655.

12—ST. STANISLAUS KOSTKA (1912), (Polish), Closed. For inquiries for parish records contact the chancery.

13—ST. THOMAS (1903) Very Rev. Daniel W. Gerres; Deacon Francis A. Quinlan. In Res., Rev. Leonard J. Kempski (Retired).

DELAWARE
OUTSIDE THE CITY OF WILMINGTON

BEAR, NEW CASTLE CO., ST. ELIZABETH ANN SETON (1978) Rev. Roger F. DiBuo; Deacon William Kibler.
Res.: 345 Bear-Christiana Rd., 19701-1048. Tel: 302-322-6430; Fax: 302-322-6297. Email: office@setonparish.net. Web: setonparish.net.
Catechesis/Religious Program—Tel: 302-322-6430, Ext. 102; Fax: 302-322-6297. Theresa Burke, C.R.E. Students 400.

BELLEFONTE, NEW CASTLE CO., ST. HELENA (Wilmington P.O.) (1936) Very Rev. Stanley J. Russell.
Res.: 602 Philadelphia Pike, 19809-2585. Tel: 302-764-0325; Fax: 302-764-1068.
Catechesis/Religious Program—Tel: 302-762-4280. Hummy Pennell, D.R.E. Students 98.
Convent—610 Philadelphia Pike, 19809. Tel: 302-764-3427.

BETHANY BEACH, SUSSEX CO., ST. ANN (1955) Revs. David F. Kelley; Michael P. Darcy; Deacons Edward Danko; Robert Tracy; Donald Lydick; Dennis Hayden; John Freebery.
Res.: 691 Garfield Ave., P.O. Box 149, 19930. Tel: 302-539-6449; Fax: 302-539-0657.
Catechesis/Religious Program—Tel: 302-539-5443; Fax: 302-539-5509. Students 165.
Mission—Our Lady of Guadalupe 35318 Church Rd., Frankford, Sussex Co. 19945.

BRANDYWOOD, NEW CASTLE CO., CHURCH OF THE HOLY CHILD (Wilmington P.O.) (1969) Revs. Michael J. Carrier; Michael A. Angeloni; Deacon Joseph Cilia Jr.; Sr. Ann Hughes, S.S.J., Pastoral Assoc.
Res.: 2500 Naamans Rd., 19810. Tel: 302-475-6486; Fax: 302-475-3458.
Catechesis/Religious Program—Students 285.

CLAYMONT, NEW CASTLE CO., HOLY ROSARY (1921) Rev. John J. Gayton; Deacons Richard J. Maichle; Allen Wolf. In Res., Rev. Edward J. Fahey.
Res.: 3200 Philadelphia Pike, 19703. Tel: 302-798-2904; 302-573-3113; Fax: 302-798-3609.
Catechesis/Religious Program—Tel: 302-798-0123. Students 130.

DELAWARE CITY, NEW CASTLE CO., ST. PAUL (1852) Rev. Roy F. Pollard.
Res.: 209 Washington St., P.O. Box 544, 19706. Tel: 302-834-4321; Fax: 302-834-7517.
Catechesis/Religious Program—Sr. Lawrence Therese Hudson, O.S.F.S., D.R.E. Students 24.

DOVER, KENT CO., HOLY CROSS (1870) [CEM] Revs. Daniel J. McGlynn; John B. Gabage; Carlos Ochoa Tello; Deacons Weston "Pete" Nellius; Robert McMullen; Philip Belt. In Res., Rev. James S. Lentini.
Res.: 631 S. State St., 19901. Tel: 302-674-5787; Fax: 302-674-5783.
School—Mrs. Denise Jacono, Prin. Lay Teachers 37; Students 635.
Catechesis/Religious Program—Carmella Jones, D.R.E. Students 500.

ELSMERE, NEW CASTLE CO., CORPUS CHRISTI (Wilmington P.O.) (1948) Rev. Gregory M. Corrigan; Deacon David M. DeGhetto.
Res.: 905 New Rd., Elsmere, 19805. Tel: 302-994-2922; Fax: 302-892-3315.
School—907 New Rd., Elsmere, 19805. Tel: 302-995-2231; Fax: 302-993-0767. Kathleen R. Connor, Prin. Sisters 2; Lay Teachers 22; Students 309.
Catechesis/Religious Program—Tel: 302-998-2864. Debbie Ciafre, C.R.E. Students 85.
Convent—912 New Rd., Elsmere, 19805. Tel: 302-998-2864.

FAIRFAX, NEW CASTLE CO., ST. MARY MAGDALEN (Wilmington P.O.) (1951) Revs. Joseph R. McMahon; James T. Kirk; Deacon Joseph C. Romans. In Res., Rev. Philip P. Sheekey.
Res.: 7 Sharpley Rd., 19803. Tel: 302-652-6800; Fax: 302-652-4771.
School—9 Sharpley Rd., 19803. Tel: 302-656-2745; Fax: 302-656-7889. Barbara Wanner, Prin. Lay Teachers 40; Students 540.
Catechesis/Religious Program—Tel: 302-652-7141. Karen Yasik, D.R.E. Students 235.

GARFIELD PARK, NEW CASTLE CO., HOLY SPIRIT (New Castle P.O.) (1954) Rev. Timothy M. Nolan; Deacon Patrick Johnston.
Res.: 12 Winder Rd., Garfield Park, New Castle, 19720. Tel: 302-658-1069; Fax: 302-658-6890. Email: hscathchurch@aol.com. Web: holyspiritcatholicchurchde.4lpi.com.
Catechesis/Religious Program—Students 30.

GEORGETOWN, SUSSEX CO., ST. MICHAEL THE ARCHANGEL (1956) Revs. Daniel J. McCloskey Jr.; Robert J. Burk, M.S.A.; Cesar Gomez (Honduras); Deacons Donald Carroll; David S. McDowell; Philip Ricker; Jose Rodriquez-Trejo; Martin J. Barrett.
Res.: 202 Edward St., 19947. Tel: 302-856-6451; Fax: 302-856-2353. Email: stmichre@comcast.net.
Catechesis/Religious Program—Students 261.
Mission—Mary Mother of Peace Rte. 24, Millsboro, Sussex Co. 19966. Tel: 302-856-6451; Fax: 302-856-2353.

GLASGOW, NEW CASTLE CO., ST. MARGARET OF SCOTLAND (1999) Rev. John P. Hopkins; Deacons Raymond R. Zolandz Jr.; Thomas E. Watts.
Res.: 2431 Frazer Rd., Newark, 19702. Tel: 302-834-0225; Fax: 302-834-0840.
Catechesis/Religious Program—Tel: 302-834-0225, Ext. 105. Students 590.

GREENVILLE, NEW CASTLE CO., ST. JOSEPH ON THE BRANDYWINE (1841) [CEM 2] Rev. Msgr. Joseph F. Rebman; Rev. David F. Murphy; Deacon F. Edmund Lynch.
Res.: 10 Old Church Rd., 19807. Tel: 302-658-7017; Fax: 302-428-0639. Web: www.stjosephonthebrandywine.org.

Catechesis/Religious Program—Tel: 302-656-7185; Fax: 302-658-8723. Ms. Maryanne Bemiller, D.R.E. Students 262.

HOCKESSIN, NEW CASTLE CO., ST. MARY OF THE ASSUMPTION (1882) [CEM] Revs. Charles C. Dillingham; James B. Smith; Deacons John Giacci; Joseph W. Jackson Sr.; Larry Morris. In Res., Rev. William T. Cocco.
Res.: 7200 Lancaster Pike, 19707. Tel: 302-239-7100; Fax: 302-239-8219. Web: www.stmaryoftheassumption.com.
Catechesis/Religious Program—Tel: 302-239-7100, Ext. 17. Sheila Meara, D.R.E. Students 747.

LEWES, SUSSEX CO., ST. JUDE THE APOSTLE (2002) Revs. James D. Hreha; Mark J. Connelly; Deacons R. Paul Woofter; Edward J. Brink, (Retired); William J. Pyrek; Kennet J. Hall; Robert J. Sprouse.
Office:—152 Tulip Dr., 19958. Tel: 302-644-7300; Fax: 302-644-7415.
Catechesis/Religious Program—Tel: 302-644-7413. Students 220.

LIFTWOOD, NEW CASTLE CO., IMMACULATE HEART OF MARY (Wilmington P.O.) (1955) Rev. Msgr. Clement P. Lemon; Revs. Robert A. Wozniak; Leonard R. Klein; Deacons Austin M. Snow Jr.; Francis C. Conway; Theresa H. Gerlach, Pastoral Assoc.
Res.: 4701 Weldin Rd., Liftwood, 19803. Tel: 302-764-0357; Fax: 302-764-4381.
School—(Grades PreK-8), 1000 Shipley Rd., Liftwood, 19803. Tel: 302-764-0977; Fax: 302-764-0375. Jan Chapdelaine, Prin.; Trish Melloy, Librarian. Lay Teachers 32; Students 503.
Catechesis/Religious Program—Tel: 302-762-5550. Claire D. Dasalla, C.R.E. Students 194.

MIDDLETOWN, NEW CASTLE CO., ST. JOSEPH (1883) [CEM 2] Very Rev. Steven B. Giuliano; Rev. John Grasing; Deacons Cruz Rodriguez; Fred Wendt.
Res.: 371 E. Main St., 19709. Tel: 302-378-5800; Fax: 302-378-5808. Email: office@stjosephmiddletown.com. Web: www.stjosephmiddletown.com.
Catechesis/Religious Program—Susan Pascoe, Co-ord.; Mark Winterbottom, Coord. Students 900.
Mission—St. Rose of Lima Lock St., Chesapeake City, Cecil Co., MD 21915.
Shrine—St. Francis Xavier-Old Bohemia Warwick, MD.

MILFORD, KENT AND SUSSEX COS., ST. JOHN THE APOSTLE (1910) Very Rev. George J. Brubaker; Revs. Michael J. McDermott; Salvador Magana; Deacons James D. Malloy; Anthony Bianco; John Yeager; J. Scott Landis.
Res.: 506 Seabury Ave., 19963-2217. Tel: 302-422-5123; Fax: 302-422-5720.
Catechesis/Religious Program—Tel: 302-422-5123, Ext. 12; Fax: 302-422-5720. Students 400.
Mission—St. Bernadette 109 Dixon, Harrington, Kent Co. 19952. Tel: 302-398-8269; Fax: 302-398-0253.

NEW CASTLE, NEW CASTLE CO., ST. PETER THE APOSTLE (1845) [CEM] Revs. John P. Klevence; John A. Lunness; Deacon Thomas G. Halko.
Church, Mailing & Res. Address: 521 Harmony St., 19720. Tel: 302-328-2335; Fax: 302-328-0519. Web: www.stpetertheapostlede.org. Email: parish@stpetertheapostlede.org.
School—515 Harmony Sts., 19720. Tel: 302-328-1191; Fax: 302-328-8049. Lay Teachers 14; Students 247.
Catechesis/Religious Program—Students 30.

NEWARK, NEW CASTLE CO.
1—ST. JOHN THE BAPTIST-HOLY ANGELS (1891) [CEM] Revs. Arthur B. Fiore; Michael J. Cook; Ralph T. Castelow; Deacons Angel L. Rivera; Charles Schauber Sr.; Heriberto Rodriguez.
Res.: 14 N. Chapel St., 19711. Tel: 302-731-2200; Fax: 302-731-2434. Email: aahar@holyangels.net. Web: www.holyangels.net.
School—Tel: 302-731-2210; Fax: 302-731-2211. Ms. Denise A. Winterberger, Prin. Lay Teachers 25; Students 379.
Catechesis/Religious Program—Tel: 302-731-2209. Students 392.
2—PARISH OF THE RESURRECTION (1969) Rev. William F. Graney; Deacons Joseph J. Conte, (Retired); Francis J. Huhn, (Retired); John J. Falkowski.
Office:—3000 Videre Dr., Skyline Ridge, 19808. Tel: 302-368-0146; Fax: 302-368-0146.
Catechesis/Religious Program—Tel: 302-368-0146, Ext. 104. Joanne Huhn, D.R.E. Students 140.
3—ST. THOMAS MORE ORATORY (1975), (Personal Parish for Students & Faculty of University of Delaware). Revs. Ambrose Eckinger, O.P.; Stephen Alcott, O.P.; Michael DeTemple, O.P.; Kim Zitzner, Pastoral Assoc. & Campus Min.
Church: 45 Lovett Ave., 19711. Tel: 302-368-4728.
Catechesis/Religious Program—Tel: 302-368-4728. Students 35.

OGLETOWN, NEW CASTLE CO., HOLY FAMILY (Newark P.O.) (1979) Revs. James Nash; Joseph F. Wisniewski; Deacon Joseph F. Certesio Sr. In Res., Rev. Antony William Rajayan.
Res.: 15 Gender Rd., Newark, 19713. Tel: 302-368-4665; Fax: 302-368-4667.
Catechesis/Religious Program—21 Gender Rd., Newark, 19713. Tel: 302-368-8976; Fax: 302-368-5184. Melody Duffy, D.R.E.; Mare Draper, Youth Min. Students 325.

PRICES CORNER, ST. CATHERINE OF SIENA (Wilmington P.O.) (1960) Rev. John M. Hynes; Deacons Francis J. Staab; Robert J. McNulty Jr. In Res., Rev. Alan Reyna.
Res.: 2503 Centerville Rd., 19808. Tel: 302-633-4900; Fax: 302-633-4960.
School—Tel: 302-633-4901; Fax: 302-633-4902. Deborah Ruff, Prin. Lay Teachers 20; Students 245.
Catechesis/Religious Program—Tel: 302-633-4903; Fax: 302-633-4960. Mrs. Eva Lyons, D.R.E. Students 202.

REHOBOTH BEACH, SUSSEX CO., ST. EDMOND (1952) Very Rev. Raymond L. Forester; Rev. James E. Downs; Deacons G. Jerry Shaw; John A. Smith; James M. Walls.
409 King Charles St., P.O. Box 646, 19971. Tel: 302-227-4550; Fax: 302-227-4557.
Res.: 402 King Charles St., P.O. Box 646, 19771.
Catechesis/Religious Program—Tel: 302-227-4553. James Walsh, C.R.E. Students 225.

SEAFORD, SUSSEX CO., OUR LADY OF LOURDES (1945) [CEM] Very Rev. John McKenna, C.Ss.R.; Deacon Arcy Passwaters.
Res.: 528 Stein Hwy., P.O. Box 719, 19973-0719. Tel: 302-629-3591; Fax: 302-629-6758.
Catechesis/Religious Program—Tel: 302-629-7999. Mrs. Debra Depta, D.R.E. Students 297.

SHERWOOD PARK, NEW CASTLE CO., ST. JOHN THE BELOVED (1955) Revs. Charles L. Brown III; Adrian F. Baranyuk; William D. Melnick; Deacons James Haley, (Retired); George Taylor; Dennis Wuebbels; Thomas A. Bailey.
Res.: 907 Milltown Rd., 19808. Tel: 302-999-0211; Fax: 302-999-9184. Email: sjbchurch907@yahoo.com. Web: www.sjbde.org.
School—905 Milltown Rd., 19808. Tel: 302-998-5525; Fax: 302-998-1923. Richard D. Hart, Prin. Sisters of St. Francis of Philadelphia 1; Lay Teachers 31; Students 594.
Catechesis/Religious Program—Tel: 302-994-7757; Fax: 302-996-9166. Pauline Berlingieri, D.R.E. Students 402.

SMYRNA, KENT CO., ST. POLYCARP (1883) Rev. Thomas A. Flowers; Deacons Charles Robinson; Michael Boyd.
Res.: 135 Ransom Ln., 19977. Tel: 302-653-8279; Fax: 302-653-3509.
Catechesis/Religious Program—Tel: 302-653-4101. Mrs. Carol Simpers, D.R.E. Students 286.

WILMINGTON MANOR, NEW CASTLE CO., OUR LADY OF FATIMA (New Castle P.O.) (1948) Revs. John J. Mink; Patrick Biegler, M.S.A.; Idongesit A. Etim; Deacon William Murrian.
Res.: 801 Dupont Blvd., New Castle, 19720. Tel: 302-328-3431; 302-328-5773; Fax: 302-328-6318.
School—Tel: 302-328-2803; Fax: 302-328-5427. Lay Teachers 20; Students 325.
Catechesis/Religious Program—Tel: 302-328-0307. Mrs. Madeline Romano, D.R.E. Teachers 20; Students 143.

WOODCREST, NEW CASTLE CO., ST. MATTHEW (1941) Revs. Joseph J. Drobinski; William J. Klapps (Retired); Deacons Harold Chalfant; Michael T. Wilber; William A. Kaper. In Res., Rev. William M. Hazzard (Retired).
Res.: 3 Curtis Ave., 19804. Tel: 302-633-5850; Fax: 302-633-5850.
School—One Fallon Ave., 19804. Tel: 302-633-5860. Mr. Bernard J. Fisher, Prin. Lay Teachers 23; Students 386.
Catechesis/Religious Program—Tel: 302-633-5860, Ext. 2. Students 158.

MARYLAND

BERLIN, WORCESTER CO., ST. JOHN NEUMANN ROMAN CATHOLIC CHURCH (2007) Revs. Thomas J. Protack, S.T.L.; Anthony M. Pileggi; Deacons John G. Lemon; Charles A. Weschler; Wilbur Pinder.
11211 Beauchamp Rd., MD 21811. Tel: 410-208-2956; Fax: 410-208-4584.
Catechesis/Religious Program—Nancy F. Groves, D.R.E. Students 214.

CAMBRIDGE, DORCHESTER CO., ST. MARY REFUGE OF SINNERS (1885) [CEM] Rev. William J. Lawler.
Res.: 1515 Glasgow St., Box 218, MD 21613. Tel: 410-228-4770; Fax: 410-228-0969.
Catechesis/Religious Program—Rosemary Robbins, D.R.E. Students 22.
Mission—St. Mary, Star of the Sea [CEM] Golden Hill, Dorchester Co., MD.

CENTREVILLE, QUEEN ANNE CO., OUR MOTHER OF SORROWS (1892) [CEM] Rev. Mark A. Kelleher.
Res.: 303 Chesterfield Ave., MD 21617. Fax: 410-758-5463. Web: www.sorrowsparish.org.
Catechesis/Religious Program—Tel: 410-758-0143. Mary Wood, D.R.E. Students 198.
Mission—St. Peter 5319 Ocean Gateway, Queenstown, Queen Anne Co., MD 21658. Tel: 410-827-8404.

CHESTER , KENT ISLAND QUEEN ANNE CO., ST. CHRISTOPHER (1954) Very Rev. Paul F. Jennings Jr.; Rev. Joseph V. Bozzelli; Deacon John E. Robinson Jr.
Res.: 1861 Harbor Dr., Box 660, MD 21619. Tel: 410-643-6220; Fax: 410-643-4055. Email: rectory@stchristopherki.org. Web: www.stchristopherki.org.
Catechesis/Religious Program—Tel: 410-643-8489. Students 450.

CHESTERTOWN, KENT CO., SACRED HEART (1876) [CEM] Rev. Paul J. Campbell; Deacon John Davis.
Res.: 508 High St., MD 21620. Tel: 410-778-3160; Fax: 410-810-0427.
Catechesis/Religious Program—Tel: 410-778-4650. Barbara Kelly, C.R.E. Students 94.
Mission—St. John W. Main St., Rock Hall, Kent Co., MD 21661. Tel: 410-778-3160.

EASTON, TALBOT CO., SS. PETER AND PAUL (1868) [CEM] Revs. Robert E. Coine; John E. Olson.
Res.: 7906 Ocean Gateway, MD 21601. Tel: 410-822-2344; Fax: 410-770-5080.
School—900 High St., MD 21601. Tel: 410-822-2251; Fax: 410-820-0136. Mrs. Connie Webster, Prin. Lay Teachers 30; Students 449.
High School—Tel: 410-822-2275; Fax: 410-822-1767. Mr. James Nemeth, Prin. Lay Teachers 25; Students 201.
Catechesis/Religious Program—Tel: 410-822-6581; Fax: 410-822-6581. Sr. Kathleen Boland, S.S.N.D., D.R.E. Students 242.
Mission—St. Joseph 13209 Church Ln., Cordova, Talbot Co., MD 21625.
Mission—St. Michael 109 Lincoln Ave., St. Michaels, Talbot Co., MD 21663.

ELKTON, CECIL CO., IMMACULATE CONCEPTION (1849) [CEM 2] Revs. Joseph J. Piekarski; Stanislao Esposito; Deacons Joseph J. Kosman; Michael Truman.
Office: 455 Bow St., P.O. Box 345, MD 21922. Tel: 410-398-1100; Fax: 410-398-1175. Email: icc@dol.net. Web: www.iccparish.org.
Res.: 300 Maryland Ave., MD 21922.
School—452 Bow St., MD 21921. Tel: 410-398-2636; Fax: 410-398-1190. Ms. Mary Kirkwood, Prin. Sisters of St. Francis of Philadelphia 1; Lay Teachers 22; Students 253.
Catechesis/Religious Program—Tel: 410-392-3551. Sr. Grace Andrew, D.R.E. Students 426.
Mission—St. Jude 928 Turkey Point, North East, Cecil Co., MD 21901.

GALENA, KENT CO., ST. DENNIS (1855) [CEM] Rev. Leonard J. Blakely.
Mailing Address: P.O. Box 249, MD 21635. Tel: 410-648-5145; Fax: 410-648-5767. Email: stdennischurch@aol.com. Web: stdennischurch.org.
Catechesis/Religious Program—Tel: 410-648-5287. Students 70.

MARYDEL, CAROLINE CO., IMMACULATE CONCEPTION (1916) Rev. Michael B. Roark; Deacons James M. Tormey; Sherman Mitchell III.
Res.: 522 Main St., MD 21649. Tel: 410-482-7687; Fax: 410-482-7253.
Catechesis/Religious Program—Tel: 410-482-8939. Students 140.

OCEAN CITY, WORCESTER CO.
1—ST. LUKE AND ST. ANDREW (1985) Revs. Richard Smith; Michael T. Casari; Deacons Edward Holson; Joseph Carraro.
Office: 14401 Sinepuxent Ave., MD 21842. Tel: 410-250-0300; Fax: 410-250-0417.
Catechesis/Religious Program—Students 40.
2—ST. MARY, STAR OF THE SEA (1877) Rev. Anthony F. Greco; Deacon Edward Gardner Sr.
Res.: 208 S. Baltimore Ave., MD 21842-4106.
Office: 1705 Philadelphia Ave., MD 21842. Tel: 410-289-0652; Fax: 410-289-1026.
Catechesis/Religious Program—Tel: 410-289-7038. Elizabeth A. Sacca-Kuczinski, D.R.E. Students 149.
Mission—Holy Savior 1705 Philadelphia Ave., Worcester Co., MD 21842.

PERRYVILLE, CECIL CO., CHURCH OF THE GOOD SHEPHERD (1949) Rev. Jay R. McKee; Deacon Luke Yackley.
810 Aiken Ave., MD 21903.
Res.: 828 Aiken Ave., MD 21903. Tel: 410-642-6534; Fax: 410-642-2234.
School—800 Aiken Ave., MD 21903. Tel: 410-642-6265; Fax: 410-642-6522. Scott Williams, Prin. Lay Teachers 15; Students 126.
Catechesis/Religious Program—Students 158.
Mission—St. Teresa 162 N. Main St., Port Deposit, Cecil Co., MD 21904.
Mission—St. Patrick, (Inactive), 287 Pleasant Grove Rd., Conowingo, Cecil Co., MD 21918.
Mission—St. Agnes 150 S. Queen St., Rising Sun,

Cecil Co., MD 21911.

POCOMOKE CITY, WORCESTER CO., HOLY NAME OF JESUS (1943) Rev. William J. Porter; Deacons Stephen J. Kuczma; Thomas S. Cimino, (Retired).

Res.: 1913 Old Virginia Rd., P.O. Box 179, MD 21851. Tel: 410-957-1215; Fax: 410-957-1214.

Catechesis/Religious Program—Jason Pfirman, C.R.E. Students 76.

Mission—St. Elizabeth 8734 Old Westover Rd., Westover, Somerset Co., MD 21871. Tel: 410-651-9117.

RIDGELY, CAROLINE CO., ST. BENEDICT (1896) [CEM 2] Rev. Hilary R. Rodgers; Deacons Harold D. Jopp Jr.; William G. Nickum.

Res.: 408 Central Ave., P.O. Box 459, MD 21660. Tel: 410-634-2253; Fax: 410-634-1997.

Catechesis/Religious Program—Students 153.

Mission—St. Elizabeth of Hungary [CEM] First St. & Franklin St., Denton, Caroline Co., MD 21629.

SALISBURY, WICOMICO CO., ST. FRANCIS DE SALES (1910) Revs. Edward M. Aigner Jr.; Raymond F. Weisman; Christopher W. LaBarge; Deacons James E. Dean; Bruce Abresch. In Res., Rev. Johnny Laura Lazo.

Res.: 514 Camden Ave., MD 21801. Tel: 410-742-6443; Fax: 410-742-9410.

School—500 Camden Ave., MD 21801. Tel: 410-749-9907; Fax: 410-749-9507. Mrs. Jude DeLucco, Prin. Lay Teachers 18; Students 246.

Catechesis/Religious Program—Tel: 410-546-2908. Pat Burbage, D.R.E.; Michele Harris, D.R.E.; Michele Ennis-Benn, Youth Min. Students 479.

Convent—413 Wicomico St., MD 21801.

Mission—Holy Redeemer Bi-State Blvd. & Chestnut St., Delmar, Wicomico Co., MD 21875.

SECRETARY, DORCHESTER CO., OUR LADY OF GOOD COUNSEL (1891) [CEM] Rev. Stephen C. Lonek, Admin.

Res.: 109 Willow St., P.O. Box 279, MD 21664. Tel: 410-943-4300; Fax: 410-943-1357.

Catechesis/Religious Program—Students 70.

Chaplains of Public Institutions

National Guard

WILMINGTON. *Delaware Air National Guard.* 801 DuPont Blvd., New Castle, 19720. Tel: 302-328-3431. Revs. John J. Mink, Chap., David F. Murphy, Chap.

Health Care

WILMINGTON. *St. Francis Hospital*, 7th St. & Clayton St., 19805. Tel: 302-421-4577. Revs. John A. Finn, O.S.F.S., Joseph J. McKenna, O.S.F.S.

DELAWARE CITY. *Governor Bacon Health Center.* Rev. Roy F. Pollard, Chap. Tel: 302-834-4321.

ELSMERE. *Veteran's Hospital*, 1601 Kirkwood Hwy., 19805. Tel: 302-994-2511. Revs. Sean P. Connery, O.S.F.S., Chap., William J. Dougherty, O.S.F.S., Chap.

NEW CASTLE. *Delaware Psychiatric Hospital.*

NEWARK. *Christiana Care Health Services, Inc.*, 4755 Ogletown-Stanton Rds., 19726. Tel: 302-733-1900; 302-733-1280.

Wilmington Hospital, 14th & Washington Sts., 19805. Tel: 302-733-1280. Revs. Cornelius J. Breslin, Leonard R. Klein, Antony William Rajayan.

PERRY POINT, MD. *Veterans Admin.* Rev. Mark E. Oguamana.

SMYRNA, MD. *Delaware Home & Hospital for the Chronically Ill.* Rev. Thomas A. Flowers, Chap. Tel: 302-653-8279.

Correctional Facilities

WILMINGTON. *Ferris School.* Vacant.

Howard R. Young Correctional Institution. Very Rev. Daniel W. Gerres, V.F., Chap. Tel: 302-764-0357.

NEW CASTLE. *Delores J. Baylor Women's Correctional Institution.* Vacant, Chap.

SMYRNA, MD. *Delaware State Correctional Center.* Rev. James M. Jackson, Chap. Tel: 302-653-9261, Ext. 487.

WESTOVER, MD. *Eastern Correctional Institution.* Rev. Edward M. Aigner Jr., Chap. Tel: 410-742-6443.

Campus Ministry

CHESTERTOWN, MD. *Washington College*, Sacred Heart, 508 High St., MD 21620. Tel: 410-778-3160. Rev. Paul J. Campbell, Chap.

DOVER. *Wesley College, Holy Cross Parish*, 631 S. State St., 19901. Tel: 302-674-5787; Fax: 302-674-5783. Vacant, Chap. Tel: 410-778-3160; Fax: 410-810-0427.

NEWARK. *University of Delaware*, St. Thomas More Oratory, 45 Lovett Ave., 19711. Tel: 302-368-4728. Revs. Ambrose Eckinger, O.P., Chap., Stephen Alcott, O.P., Chap., Michael DeTemple, O.P., Kim Zitzner, Pastoral Assoc./Campus Min.

SALISBURY, MD. *Salisbury State College*, 211 W. College Ave., MD 21801. Tel: 410-219-3376. Mrs. Regina Yankalunas, M.P.S., Campus Min.

University of Maryland, Eastern Shore, 211 W. College Ave., MD 21801. Tel: 410-219-3376. Mrs. Regina Yankalunas, M.P.S., Campus Min.

Nursing Homes:

Rev.—

Fahey, Edward J., NCC Health Care Facilities, 3200 Philadelphia Pike, Claymont, 19703. Tel: 302-798-2904

Special or Other Diocesan Assignment:

Rev.—

Grimm, John S., Immaculate Conception Seminary/School of Theology, Seton Hall University, South Orange, NJ 07079.

On Duty Outside the Diocese:

Rev. Msgrs.—

Koper, Francis B., SS. Cyril and Methodius Seminary, Orchard Lake, MI 48033.

McMahon, Kevin T., S.T.B., S.T.L., S.T.D., P.O. Box 2030, 19899.

Revs.—

Gallagher, Michael J., Trinity College, Theology Dept., 125 Michigan Ave., Washington, DC 20017.

Kauffman, William B., Chap., Mount St. Mary Seminary, 16300 Old Emmitsburg Rd., Emmitsburg, MD 21727. Tel: 302-994-2922

Mullen, Owen J., 9141 Ronda Ave., San Diego, CA 92123-3553.

Turley, Sean F., SS. Michael and James, Haunton near Tamworth, Staffordshire B799HL (1848) England.

Military Chaplains:

Rev.—

Kopec, Christopher A., c/o Archdiocese for the Military Service, P.O. Box 4469, Washington, DC 20017-0469.

Absent on Sick Leave:

Revs.—

Gomolski, Joseph T., 921 Begonia Rd., Apt. 201, Celebration, FL 34747.

Hanley, Thomas E., P.O. Box 2030, 19899.

Vazquez, Carlos R., P.O. Box 2030, 19899.

Retired:

Rev. Msgrs.—

Brady, Patrick A., Vianney House, 905 Milltown Rd., 19808.

Martin, Ralph L., 167 Cross Ave., New Castle, 19720.

Szupper, Michael F., Ph.D., 309 Apple Rd., Newark, 19711.

Very Rev.—

Kavanaugh, John J., P.O. Box 264, Charlestown, MD 21914.

Revs.—

Byrolly, Bruce, 2 Bay View Ave., P.O. Box 43, Cambridge, MD 21613.

Clark, Howard T., P.O. Box 147, Essington, PA 19029.

Connell, Stephen J., 71 Andersen Rd., Braintree, MA 02184.

Coppinger, Edmund, 225 28th St., Richmond, CA 94804.

Frundt, Oscar H., 417 Delaware Ave., 19803.

Gardocki, Thomas F., 4620 Sylvanus Dr., 19803.

Glapiak, Edward, ul. Krolowej Jadwig, #48, 63-400, Ostrow WLKP, Poland.

Hazzard, William M., 3 Curtis Ave., 19804.

Jennings, William E., Jeanne Jugan Residence, 185 Salem Church Rd., Newark, 19713-2997.

Kaczorowski, Edward J., 1012 Brandywine Dr., Bear, 19701.

Kandathiparampil, Joseph, India.

Kempski, Leonard J., 301 N. Bancroft Pkwy., 19805.

Klapps, William J., Caravel Farms, 260 Benjamin Blvd., Bear, 19701.

Kochan, Frederick A., 2201-A Baltimore Ave., Lavellette, NJ 08735.

Mathesius, William P., 103 Atlantic Ave., Washington Hgts., Rehoboth Beach, 19971.

McGann, L. Philip, 316 Cedar Ln., Mount Laurel, NJ 08054.

Peterman, Thomas J., #1 Photinia Dr., Newark, 19702.

Reissmann, Richard A., P.O. Box 2030, 19899.

Siry, Philip L., 417 Brandywine Dr., Bear, 19701.

Storck, Edward J., 1504-2 N. Broom St., #17, 19806.

Volmi, Dennis G., 10 E. Green Ln., Milford, 19963.

Permanent Deacons:

Abresch, Bruce, St. Francis de Sales, Salisbury, MD

Bailey, Thomas A., St. John the Beloved Parish, Wilington, DE

Baker, Joseph G., (Retired)

Barrett, Martin J., St. Michael the Archangel, Georgetown, DE

Belt, Philip, Holy Cross, Dover, DE

Bianco, Anthony A., (Retired)

Boyd, Michael, St. Polycarp, Smyrna, DE

Brink, Edward J., (Retired), St. Jude the Apostle, Lewes, DE

Campbell, Jack H., (Retired)

Carraro, Joseph, St. Luke & St. Andrew, Ocean City, MD

Carroll, Donald T., St. Michael the Archangel, Georgetown, DE

Certesio, Joseph F., Sr., Holy Family Parish, Newark, DE

Chalfant, Harold F., St. Matthew, Wilmington, DE

Chicco, Gianni, Sacred Heart Oratory and Howard Young Correctional Institution, Wilmington, DE

Cilia, Joseph A., Jr., Asst. Chap., Next Step Group, Church of the Holy Childhood, Wilmington, DE

Cimino, Thomas S., (Retired)

Conte, Joseph J., (Retired)

Conway, Francis C., Immaculate Heart of Mary, Wilmington, DE

Cousar, Robert J., Jr., St. Joseph Parish, Wilmington, DE

Danko, Edward, St. Ann, Bethany Beach, DE

Davis, John, Sacred Heart, Chestertown, MD

Dean, James E., St. Francis de Sales Parish, Salisbury, MD

DeGhetto, David M., Corpus Christi Parish, Wilmington, DE

Falkowski, John J., Resurrection Parish, Wilmington, DE

Freebery, John W., Jr., St. Ann, Bethany Beach, DE

Gardner, Edward, Sr., St. Mary Star of the Sea, Ocean City, MD

Giacci, John, St. Mary of the Assumption, Hockessin, DE

Haley, James J., (Retired)

Halko, Thomas G., St. Peter the Apostle Parish, New Castle, DE

Hall, Kenneth, St. Jude the Apostle, Lewes, DE

Handlir, James, St. Hedwig, Wilmington, DE

Hayden, Dennis L., St. Ann, Bethany Beach, DE

Holson, Edward G., St. Luke/St. Andrew, Ocean City, MD

Huhn, Francis J., (Retired)

Jackson, Joseph W., Sr., St. Mary of the Assumption Parish, Hockessin, DE; Jesus House, Wilmington, DE

Johnston, Patrick K., Holy Spirit Parish, New Castle, DE

Johnston, William J., Christ Our King Parish, Wilmington, DE

Jopp, Harold D., Jr., St. Benedict's, Ridgely, MD

Kaper, William A., St. Matthew Parish, Wilmington, DE

Kibler, William, III, St. Elizabeth Ann Seton, Bear, DE

Kosman, Joseph J., Immaculate Conception Parish, Elkton, MD

Kuczma, Stephen, Holy Name of Jesus, Pocomoke, MD

Lafferty, James J., Jr., (Retired)

Landis, Scott J., St. John the Apostle, Milford, PA

Lemon, John G., St. John Neumann, Berlin, MD

Leonzio, Robert J., St. Anthony of Padua Parish, Wilmington, DE

Levesque, Robert J., St. Joseph Parish, Wilmington, DE

Lydick, Donald E., St. Ann, Bethany Beach, DE

Lynch, Edmund F., St. Joseph on the Brandywine, Greenville, DE

Maichle, Richard J., Holy Rosary, Claymont, DE

Malloy, James D., St. John the Apostle, Milford, DE

Maloney, William, Jr., (Retired)

Masino, Thomas R., Our Lady of Perpetual Help, Dover AFB, DE

McDowell, David S., St. Michael the Archangel, Georgetown, DE

McMullen, Robert E., Holy Cross Parish, Dover, DE

McNulty, Robert J., St. Catherine of Siena, Wilmington, DE

Mitchell, Sherman, III, Immaculate Conception, Marydel, MD

Morris, Larry, St. Mary of the Assumption, Hockessin, DE

Murrian, William J., Our Lady of Fatima, New Castle, DE

Nellius, Weston E., Holy Cross Parish, Dover, DE

Nickum, William G., St. Benedict Parish, Ridgely, MD

O'Connor, Howard J., (Retired)

Ortiz, Hector, St. John the Apostle, Milford, DE

Paolucci, Robert, St. Mary Refuge of Sinners, Cambridge, MD

Parisi, John G., (Retired)

Passwaters, Arcy A., Our Lady of Lourdes, Seaford, DE

Perez, Jose, Holy Rosary, Claymont, DE

Pinder, Wilbur, St. John Neumann, Berlin, MD

Pisano, Vincent, Holy Cross, Dover, DE

Pulliam, Kenneth, Sr., St. Elizabeth, Wilmington, DE
Pyrek, William J., St. Jude the Apostle, Lewes, DE
Quinlan, Francis A., St. Thomas the Apostle, Wilmington, DE
Recce, Richard L., (Retired)
Ricker, Philip, St. Michael the Archangel; Mary, Mother of Peace
Rivera, Angel, St. Paul, Wilmington, DE
Robinson, Charles, St. Polycarp, Smyrna, DE
Robinson, John R., Jr., St. Christopher, Chester, MD
Rodriguez, Cruz, St. Paul, Wilmington, DE
Rodriguez, Heriberto, St. John, Holy Angels, Newark, DE
Rodriguez-Trejo, Jose N., St. Michael the Archangel, Georgetown, DE
Romans, Joseph C., Dir., Mission Office, Wilmington, DE; Mary Magdalen, Wilmington, DE
Schauber, Charles, Sr., St. John, Holy Angels, Newark, DE
Shaw, G. Jerry, St. Edmond, Rehoboth Beach, DE
Siers, Ronald, (Retired)
Smith, John A., St. Edmond, Rehoboth Beach, DE
Snow, Austin M., Jr., Immaculate Heart of Mary, Wilmington, DE
Soto, Eliezer, Our Lady of Fatima, New Castle, DE
Sprouse, Robert J., St. Jude the Apostle, Lewes, DE
Staab, Francis J., St. Catherine of Siena, Wilmington, DE
Taylor, Bradley D., SS. Peter & Paul, Easton, MD
Taylor, George M., Jr., St. John the Beloved & Ferris School, Wilmington, DE
Tormey, James M., Immaculate Conception, Marydel, MD
Tracy, Robert, St. Ann, Bethany Beach, DE
Truman, Michael, Immaculate Conception, Elkton, MD
VanBourgondien, Cornelius J., (Retired)
Walker, George W., Jr., St. John the Apostle, Milford, DE
Walls, James M., St. Edmond, Rehoboth, DE
Watts, Thomas, St. Margaret of Scotland, Newark, DE
Wendt, Fred, St. Joseph, Middletown, DE
Weschler, Charles A., St. John Neumann, Berlin, MD
Wilber, Michael T., St. Matthew Parish, Wilmington, DE
Wolf, Allen S., Claymont, DE, Holy Rosary; Christiana Div.
Woofter, R. Paul, St. Jude the Apostle, Lewes, DE
Wuebbels, Dennis, St. John the Beloved, Wilmington, DE
Yackley, Luke, Church of the Good Shepherd, Perryville, MD
Yeager, John A., St. John the Apostle, Milford, DE
Zolandz, Raymond R., Jr., St. Margaret of Scotland Parish, Glasgow, DE

INSTITUTIONS LOCATED IN THE DIOCESE

[A] HIGH SCHOOLS, DIOCESAN

WILMINGTON. *St. Mark's High School*, 2501 Pike Creek Rd., 19808. Tel: 302-738-3300; Fax: 302-738-5132. Email: principal@stmarkshs.net. Web: www.stmarkshs.net. Mr. Mark John Freund, Prin.; Rev. William T. Cocco, Chap.; Sr. Redempta Sweeney, I.H.M., Chap.; Voula Hadjipanayis, Librarian. Priests 1; Sisters 2; Lay Teachers 111; Students 1,357.

MAGNOLIA. *St. Thomas More Preparatory School* (1999) 133 Thomas More Dr., 19962. Tel: 302-697-8100; Fax: 302-697-8122. Email: dmckenzie@saintmore.org. Web: www.saintmore.org. David L. McKenzie, Prin.; Rev. James S. Lentini, Chap. Priests 1; Sisters 1; Lay Teachers 14; Students 230.

[B] HIGH SCHOOLS, PRIVATE

WILMINGTON. *Salesianum School*, 1801 N. Broom St., 19802. Tel: 302-654-2495; Fax: 302-654-7767. Email: principal@salesianum.org. Web: www.salesianum.org. Very Rev. James Dalton, O.S.F.S., Pres.; Revs. Dominic G. Ciriaco, O.S.F.S.; Michael C. Connolly, O.S.F.S.; Patrick J. Kifolo, O.S.F.S.; William T. McCandless, O.S.F.S., Prin.; John M. Mokluk, O.S.F.S.; Francis J. Pileggi, O.S.F.S.; Edward J. Roszko, O.S.F.S., B.A.; John P. Spellman, O.S.F.S.; Bros. Harry F. McGovern, O.S.F.S.; Harry G. Schneider, O.S.F.S.; Joseph G. Schodowski, O.S.F.S.; Elizabeth E. Diemer, Librarian; Mr. Michael A. Vogt, O.S.F.S., Seminarian. Priests 10; Brothers 3; Seminarians 1; Lay Teachers 68; Boys 1,035. In Res. Revs. Sean P. Connery, O.S.F.S.; Richard R. De Lillio, O.S.F.S., Supr.

Ursuline Academy of Wilmington, DE, Inc., 1106 Pennsylvania Ave., 19806. Tel: 302-658-7158; Fax: 302-658-4297. Web: www.ursuline.org. Susan L. Long, Prin. Middle & Upper School; Judy Teoli, Prin. Lower School; Cathie Field Lloyd, Pres. (Coed Grades Early Childhood-3, All Girls Grades 4-12) Lay Faculty 90; Ursuline Nuns 1; Students 600.

CLAYMONT. *Archmere Academy* (1932) 3600 Philadelphia Pike, 19703. Tel: 302-798-6632; Fax: 302-798-7290. Email: generale-mailbox@archmereacademy.com. Web: www.archmereacademy.com. Revs. Joseph P. McLaughlin, O.Praem., Headmaster; Michael T. Collins, O.Praem.; Blaise R. Krautsack, O. Praem; Dr. William J. Doyle, Prin.; Ms. Rosemary Conway-Bauer, Librarian. High School (Private Preparatory). Priests 3; Lay Teachers 58; Students 475.

[C] INTERPAROCHIAL SCHOOLS

WILMINGTON. *Pope John Paul II Elementary School*, (Grades PreSchool-8), 210 Bellefonte Ave., 19808. Tel: 302-762-5595; Fax: 302-762-6329. Monica Malseed, Prin.

BERLIN, MD. *Most Blessed Sacrament Catholic School*, 11242 Racetrack Rd., MD 21811. Tel: 410-208-1600; Fax: 410-208-4957. Mr. Mark J. Record, Prin.; Eileen Coyner, Librarian. Lay Teachers 18; Students 246; Total Staff 28.

NEWARK. *Christ the Teacher Catholic School*, (Grades PreK-8), 2451 Frazer Rd., 19702. Tel: 302-838-8850; Fax: 302-838-8854. Email: slking@christtheteacher.org. Web: ChristTheTeacher.org. Sr. La Verne King, R.S.M., Prin.; Mrs. Jane Keeper, Librarian. Sisters 1; Lay Teachers 28; Students 618; Total Staff 53.

[D] ELEMENTARY SCHOOLS, PRIVATE

WILMINGTON. *Saint Edmond's Academy*, (Grades PreK-8), 2120 Veale Rd., 19810. Tel: 302-475-5370; Fax: 302-475-2256. Web: stedmondsacademy.org. Michael A. Marinelli, Ed.D., Headmaster; Bros. Joseph Ash, C.S.C.; Thomas Meany, C.S.C.; Edward Quintal, C.S.C.; Tammy Hayes-Hartman, Librarian. Brothers of Holy Cross 3; Lay Teachers 30; Boys 285.

Nativity Preparatory School, 1515 Linden St., 19805. Tel: 302-777-1015; Fax: 302-777-1225. Email: dwoods@nativitywilmington.org. Web: nativitywilmington.org. Rev. Joseph A. Di Mauro, O.S.F.S., Prin.; David Kubacki, Librarian. Priests 1; Brothers 2; Lay Teachers 10.

CHILDS, MD. *Mount Aviat Academy*, (Grades PreK-8), 399 Childs Rd., MD 21916. Tel: 410-398-2206; Fax: 410-398-8063. Email: school@mountaviat.org. Web: www.mountaviat.org. Sr. John Elizabeth, O.S.F.S., Prin.; Gale Casini, Librarian. Oblate Sisters of St. Francis de Sales. Sisters 3; Lay Teachers 15; Students 260.

NEW CASTLE. *Serviam Girls Academy*, (Grades 5-8), 14 Halcyon Dr., 19720. Tel: 302-651-9700; Fax: 302-651-9703. Anne Weber, Pres.

RIDGELY, MD. *The Benedictine School*, 14299 Benedictine Ln., MD 21660. Tel: 410-634-2112; Fax: 410-634-2640. Email: nancy.mccloy@benschool.org. Web: www.benschool.org. Sr. Jeannette Murray, O.S.B., Dir. Sisters of St. Benedict. Sisters 3; Lay Teachers 17; Students 92.

Benedictine School for Exceptional Children Foundation, Inc., 14299 Benedictine Ln., MD 21660. Tel: 410-634-2292; Fax: 410-634-1855. Email: foundation@benschool.org. Web: benschool.org. Sr. Jeannette Murray, O.S.B., Dir. Sisters 1; Lay Staff 5.

[E] DIOCESAN CATHOLIC CHARITIES PROGRAM

WILMINGTON. *Catholic Charities, Inc.*, 2601 W. 4th St., P.O. Box 2610, 19805-0610. Tel: 302-655-9624; Fax: 302-655-9753. Web: www.cdow.org/charities.html. Ms. Richelle A. Vible, M.B.A., Exec. Dir; Ms. Katrina Eichler, B.A., Southern Regional Dir.; Mr. Frederick Jones, M.S., Northern Regional Dir. Total Staff 135; Individuals Served 80,000; Fuel Program 20,257.

Delaware Energy Assistance Program

New Castle County Office, 2601 W. 4th St., 19805. Tel: 302-655-9624; Fax: 302-654-9757. Evelyn Blackman, Prog. Mgr.

Sussex County Office, 406 S. Bedford St., Ste. 9, Georgetown, 19947. Tel: 302-856-6310; Fax: 302-856-6332.

Kent County Office, 1155 W. Walker Rd., Dover, 19904. Tel: 302-674-1782; Fax: 302-674-4018.

Counseling Services

Wilmington Office, 2601 W. 4th St., 19805. Tel: 302-655-9624; Fax: 302-654-6432. Mark Coffey, Prog. Mgr.

Dover Office, 1155 W. Walker Rd., Dover, 19904. Tel: 302-674-1600; Fax: 302-674-1005.

Georgetown Office, 406 S. Bedford St., Ste. 9, Georgetown, 19947. Tel: 302-856-9578; Fax: 302-856-6297.

Salisbury Office, 1201 Pemberton Dr., Ste. 1A, Salisbury, MD 21801. Tel: 410-749-1121; Fax: 410-543-0510.

Children's Services Pregnancy, Parenting and Adoption, 2601 W. 4th St., 19805-0610. Tel: 302-655-9624; Fax: 302-655-9753.

Wilmington Office, 2601 W. 4th St., 19805. Tel: 302-655-9624; Fax: 302-655-9753. Mr. Stephen LaPerle, Prog. Mgr.

Dover Office, 1155 W. Walker Rd., Dover, 19904. Tel: 302-674-1600; Fax: 302-674-1005.

Georgetown Office, 406 S. Bedford St., Ste. 9, Georgetown, 19947. Tel: 302-856-9578; Fax: 302-856-6297.

Salisbury Office, 1201 Pemberton Dr., Ste. 1A, Salisbury, MD 21801. Tel: 410-749-1121; Fax: 410-543-0510.

Family Life Bureau, 2601 W. 4th St., 19805. Tel: 302-655-9624; Fax: 302-654-9753. Mr. Thomas R. Jewett, M.C., Prog. Mgr.

Wilmington Office, 2601 W. 4th St., 19805. Tel: 302-655-9624; Fax: 302-654-9753.

HIV/AIDS Services, 2601 W. 4th St., 19805. Tel: 302-655-9624; Fax: 302-654-6432. Al Manganiello, Prog. Mgr.

Dover Office, 1155 W. Walker Rd., Dover, 19904. Tel: 302-674-1600; Fax: 302-674-4018.

Georgetown Office, 406 S. Bedford St., Ste. 9, Georgetown, 19947. Tel: 302-856-9578; Fax: 302-856-6297.

Community and Family Support Services

Crisis Alleviation

Wilmington Office, 2601 W. 4th St., 19805. Tel: 302-655-9624; Fax: 302-654-6432. Al Manganiello, Prog. Mgr.

Dover Office, 1155 W. Walker Rd., Dover, 19904. Tel: 302-674-4016; Fax: 302-674-4018.

Delaware Energy Assistance Program Evelyn Blackman, Prog. Mgr.

New Castle Co. Tel: 302-654-9295; Fax: 302-654-9759.

Kent Co. Tel: 302-674-1782; Fax: 302-674-4018.

Sussex Co. Tel: 302-856-6310; Fax: 302-856-6332.

Immigration & Refugee Services

4th St. and Greenhill Ave., P.O. Box 2610, 19805-0610. Tel: 302-654-6460; Fax: 302-654-9757. Maria Mesias, Supvr.

406 S. Bedford St., Ste. 9, Georgetown, 19947. Tel: 302-856-9578; Fax: 302-856-6297. Leila Krouse, Contact Person.

Catholic Charities Thrift Center, 1320 E. 23rd St., 19802. Tel: 302-764-2717; Fax: 302-764-2743. Diane Giovannozzi, Mgr.

CACFP (Child & Adult Care Food Program), 2604 W. 4th St., 19805. Tel: 302-655-9624; Fax: 302-654-9753.

Dover Office, 1155 W. Walker Rd., Dover, 19904. Tel: 302-674-1600; Fax: 302-674-4018. Ms. Katrina Eichler, B.A., Southern Region Dir.

Georgetown Office, 406 S. Bedford St., Ste. 9, Georgetown, 19947. Tel: 302-856-9578; Fax: 302-856-6332.

New Castle Co. Tel: 302-472-0639; Fax: 302-654-9757. Joanne Varnes, Contact Person.

Sussex Co. Tel: 302-856-3414; Fax: 302-856-6332. Karen Adams, Contact Person.

Counseling and Substance Abuse Services, 2601 W. 4th St., 19805. Tel: 302-655-9624; Fax: 302-654-6432. Mark Coffey, Prog. Mgr.

Dover Office, 1155 W. Walker Rd., Dover, 19904. Tel: 302-674-1600; Fax: 302-674-4018.

Georgetown Office, 406 S. Bedford St., Ste. 9, Georgetown, 19947. Tel: 302-856-9578; Fax: 302-856-6332.

Residential Services Marilyn Cockrell, Prog. Mgr.

Bayard House, 300 Bayard Ave., 19805. Tel: 302-654-1184; Fax: 302-654-8570. Shavonne Hines, Prog. Mgr.

Seton Villa Therapeutic Group Home For Children, 800 Bellevue Rd., 19809. Tel: 302-762-2982; Fax: 302-762-3187. Linda DiSabatino, Prog. Mgr.

Casa San Francisco, 127 Broad St., P.O. Box 38, Milton, 19968. Tel: 302-684-8694; Fax: 302-684-2808. William Post, Prog. Mgr.

Seton Center, 30632 Hampden Ave., P.O. Box 401, Princess Anne, MD 21853. Tel: 410-651-9608; Fax: 410-651-1437. Pippa McCullough.

Office for Parish Social Ministry, 2601 W. 4th St., 19805. Tel: 302-655-9624; Fax: 302-655-9753. Andrew A. Zampini, S.F.O., Prog. Mgr.

[F] CHILDREN'S SERVICES

WILMINGTON. *Seton Villa, Inc.*, 800 Bellevue Rd., 19809. Tel: 302-762-2982; Fax: 302-762-3187. Email: fjones@ccwilm.org. Web: www.cdow.org. Mr. Fritz Jones, Regl. Dir.; Marilyn Cockrell, Prog. Mgr. Capacity 10; Total Assisted 12; Total Staff 13.

[G] OTHER WELFARE AGENCIES (Not under jurisdiction of Department of Social Concerns)

WILMINGTON

Ministry of Caring, Inc. (1977) 506 N. Church St., 19801-4812. Tel: 302-652-5523; Fax: 302-652-1919. Email: mail@ministryofcaring.org. Barbara Krever, Pres., Bd. of Directors; Rev. Ronald Giannone, O.F.M.Cap., Exec. Dir.; Debbe Philips, Chief of Staff; Annie Halverson, Legal Asst. & Assoc. Devel. Dir.

Sacred Heart Administration, 903 N. Madison St., 19801. Tel: 302-888-1420; Fax: 302-594-9450. Anthea Piscarik, Grant Devel. Supr.

Nazareth Long Term Housing, 207 S. Van Buren St., 19805. Tel: 302-652-5523; Fax: 302-652-1919. Mark Poletunow, Prog. Dir. Transitional residence for families.

Nazareth Long Term Housing, 109-1/2 & 111 N. Jackson St., 19805. Tel: 302-652-5523; Fax: 302-652-1919. Mark Poletunow, Prog. Dir. Transitional residence for families.

Benedictine Park, 731 W. 9th St., 19801. Tel: 302-652-5523; Fax: 302-652-1919.

Andrisani Building (1996) 1801 W. 6th St., 19805. Tel: 302-428-3702; Fax: 302-428-3705. Mark Poletunow, Chief Fin. Officer & Deputy Dir. Programs; Ms. Louisa Teoli, Devel. Dir.

Sacred Heart House (1997) 917 N. Madison St., 19801. Tel: 302-428-3652; Fax: 302-428-3655. Marie Keefer, Deputy Dir. Human Resources.

Child Care Center (1992) 221 N. Jackson St., 19805-3649. Tel: 302-652-8992; Fax: 302-594-9442. Valerie Martin, Prog. Dir. Child care for homeless children, from infancy to 4 years old.

St. Clare Medical Outreach (1992) 7th & Clayton Sts., 19805-3156. Tel: 302-575-8218. Oswaldo Necastro, M.D., Medical Dir.; Maryann Merrylees, R.N. Mobile medical van which provides health services for the poor.

Mary Mother of Hope House Transitional Residence, 818-820 Jefferson St., 19801-1432. Tel: 302-594-9448; Fax: 302-594-9434. Email: mmatarese@ministryofcaring.org. Mary Anne Matarese, Prog. Dir. Transitional residence for single women. Capacity 12.

House of Joseph II, 9 W. 18th St., 19802-4833. Tel: 302-594-9473; Fax: 302-594-9494. Email: srjean@ministryofcaring.org. Sr. Jean Rupertus, O.S.F., Prog. Dir. Hospice for people with AIDS. Capacity 16.

Maria Lorenza Longo House (2003) 822 Jefferson St., 19801. Renee Mosley, Resident Mgr. Transitional Residence for Families. Capacity 5.

Pierre Toussaint Dental Office (1995) 830 Spruce St., 19801-4205. Tel: 302-652-8947; Fax: 302-652-8994. Gary Isaacs, D.M.D. Dental office for the homeless.

Angela Merici House (1993) 1105 W. 8th St., 19806-4605. Tel: 302-655-4817. Residence for Religious Sisters. Religious Sisters 3.

St. Francis Transitional Residence (1995) 103-107 & 111 N. Jackson St., 19805-3648. Renee Mosley, Prog. Dir. Transitional living for women and children.

House of Joseph Transitional Residence (1998) 704 West St., 19801-1523. Tel: 302-652-7968; Fax: 302-594-9472. Email: wnewson@ministryofcaring.org. Willie Newson, Prog. Dir. Transitional residence for employable, formerly homeless persons.

Samaritan Outreach (1995) 1410 N. Claymont St., 19802-5227. Tel: 302-594-9476; Fax: 303-594-9478. Sr. Pat Kerezsi, O.S.F., Prog. Dir. Social outreach for the homeless.

Mary Mother of Hope House I (1977) Temporary Address: 917 N. Madison St., 19801. Tel: 302-652-8532; Fax: 302-594-9434. Email: mmatarese@ministryofcaring.org. Mary Anne Matarese, Prog. Dir. Emergency shelter for homeless women. Capacity 20.

Mary Mother of Hope House II (1983) 121 N. Jackson St., 19805-3670. Tel: 302-652-1935; Fax: 302-594-9475. Renee Mosley, Prog. Dir. Emergency shelter for women with children. Capacity 23.

Mary Mother of Hope House III (1988) 515 N. Broom St., 19805-3114. Tel: 302-652-0970; Fax: 302-594-9496. Renee Mosley, Prog. Dir. Emergency shelter for women with children. Capacity 21.

Job Placement Center (1985) 1100 Lancaster Ave., 19805-4009. Tel: 302-652-5522; Fax: 302-652-0917. Email: mking@ministryofcaring.org. Ms. Marva King-Poynter, Prog. Dir. Employment agency to assist the poor.

House of Joseph I (1985) 1328 W. Third St., 19805-3662. Tel: 302-652-0904; Fax: 302-594-9472. Email: wnewson@ministryofcaring.org. Willie Newson, Prog. Dir. Shelter for homeless employable men who are seeking employment. Capacity 13.

Emmanuel Dining Room, West (1979) 121 N. Jackson St., 19805-3670. Tel: 302-652-3228; Fax: 302-652-2576. Bro. Rudolph Pieretti, O.F.M.Cap., Prog. Dir.

Emmanuel Dining Room, East, 226 N. Walnut St., 19801-3934. Tel: 302-652-2577; Fax: 302-652-2576. Mr. DeWitt Smith, Senior Mgr.

Emmanuel Dining Room, South, 500 Rogers Rd., New Castle, 19720. Tel: 302-577-2951; Fax: 302-652-2576. Sr. Bernadette McGoldrick, O.S.F., Senior Mgr.

Ministry of Caring Distribution Center, 1410 N. Claymont St., 19802-5227. Tel: 302-652-0969; Fax: 302-594-9478. Mr. Eugene McLaughlin, Dir. Maintenance & Safety.

Ministry of Caring Guild (1990) 506 N. Church St., 19801. Tel: 302-427-9447; Fax: 302-778-5286. Danielle Andrisani Nowaczyk, Pres.

Sacred Heart Housing, Inc. (1998) 506 N. Church St., 19801. Tel: 302-652-5523; Fax: 302-652-1919. Susan Canning, Pres., Board of Directors.

Guardian Angel Child Care (1998) 1000 Wilson St., 19801. Tel: 302-428-3620; Fax: 302-428-3622. Email: jchandler@ministryofcaring.org. Janet Chandler, Site Mgr.

Nazareth House I (1998) 106 N. Broom St., 19805. Tel: 302-652-0790; Fax: 302-594-9496. Renee Mosley, Prog. Dir. Capacity (Families) 3.

Bethany House (1999) 601 N. Jackson St., 19805-3241. Tel: 302-656-8391. Email: mmatarese@ministryofcaring.org. Mary Anne Matarese, Prog. Dir. Permanent housing for women with special needs. Capacity 8.

Nazareth House II (1998) 898 Linden St., 19805-4423. Tel: 302-428-3635; Fax: 302-428-3636. Renee Mosley, Prog. Dir. Transitional residence for families. Capacity 4.

Nazareth Long Term Housing (1998) 203 N. Jackson St., 19805-3649. Tel: 302-652-5523; Fax: 302-652-1919. Mark Poletunow, Deputy Dir. Programs. Long term housing

Nazareth Long Term Housing (1998) 807 W. 6th St., 19805. Tel: 302-652-5523; Fax: 302-652-1919. Mark Poletunow, Deputy Dir. Programs. Long term housing Capacity 1; Families 1.

Francis X. Norton Center (2002) 917 N. Madison St., 19801. Tel: 302-594-9455; Fax: 302-428-3655. Ms. Linda Richardson, Prog. Dir. Multigenerational community center.

Il Bambino (2002) 903 N. Madison St., 19801. Tel: 302-594-9449; Fax: 302-594-9450. Paulette Annane, Site Mgr. Infant day care program. Capacity 24.

Padre Pio House, 213 N. Jackson St., 19805. Email: wnewson@ministryofcaring.org. Willie Newson, Program Dir.; Gordon Corbitt, Resident Mgr. Permanent housing for men with special needs. Capacity 6.

Sacred Heart Convent, 700 W. 9th St., 19801. Tel: 302-692-8532. Capacity 3.

NEWARK

Our Lady of Grace Home for Children, Inc., 487 E. Chestnut Hill Rd., 19713-2682. Tel: 302-738-4658; 302-737-6650; Fax: 302-369-1395. Email: olghch@comcast.net. Felician Sisters 2.

RIDGELY, MD

St. Martin's Ministries, Inc. (1983) 14259 Benedictine Ln., MD 21660. Tel: 410-634-2497; Fax: 410-634-1410. Email: corta@juno.com. Web: www.stmartinsministries.org. Sr. Patricia Gamgort, O.S.B., Exec. Dir. Sisters of St. Benedict.

St. Martin's Barn, 14376 Benedictine Ln., MD 21660. Tel: 410-634-1140; Fax: 410-634-2684. Web: stmartinsministries.org. Odette Boyce-Galvez, Dir. Volunteers 40; Total Staff 5; Total Assisted 2,600.

St. Martin's House, 14374 Benedictine Ln., MD 21660. Tel: 410-634-2537. Denise Ransome, Dir. Volunteers 12; Staff 7; Total Assisted 41.

[H] HOMES FOR AGED

WILMINGTON. *The Antonian*, 1701 W. 10th St., 19805. Tel: 302-421-3758; Fax: 302-421-3759. Tori Daniello, Mgr. Congregate Housing for the Elderly Residents 143; Apartments 136; Total Staff 6.

St. Patrick's House, Inc., 115 E. 14th St., 19801. Tel: 302-654-6908. Affiliated with St. Patrick Parish. Congregate Independent Living Facility for the elderly Capacity 11; Total in Residence 7; Total Staff 2.

Vianney House (1997) 905 Milltown Rd., 19808. Tel: 302-636-0200. Lisa Winnington, Admin. Residents 3.

HOCKESSIN. *Franciscan Health System/Care at Brackenville* (1992) 100 St. Claire Dr., 19707. Tel: 302-234-5420; Fax: 302-234-5424. Email: jconnolly@che_east.org. Web: www.stfrancishealthcare.org. Jane Connolly, I.H.M., Chap. A 104-bed skilled nursing facility

NEWARK. *Jeanne Jugan Residence* (1978) 185 Salem Church Rd., 19713. Tel: 302-368-5886; Fax: 302-738-5610. Email: msnewark@littlesistersofthepoor.org. Sr. Chantal Peyton, L.S.P., Supr. Conducted by the Little Sisters of the Poor. Residents 80; Sisters 10.

Marydale Retirement Village, 135 Jeandell Dr., 19713. Tel: 302-368-2784; Fax: 302-731-0584. Michael Jester, Admin.; Sr. Mary Sheehan, I.H.M., Pastoral Care Coord. Apartments for Elderly. Apartments 108; Residents 112; Total Assisted 98.

[I] GENERAL HOSPITALS

WILMINGTON. *St. Francis Hospital, Inc.*, 7th and Clayton Sts., P.O. Box 2500, 19805-0500. Tel: 302-575-8301; Fax: 302-575-8320. Email: jmmonahan@che-east.org. Web: www.stfrancishealthcare.org. Julie A. Hester, Pres. & CEO; Revs. Joseph J. McKenna, O.S.F.S.; Joseph Monahan, T.O.R., Vice Pres. Mission & Min.; Linda Branco, Dir. Spiritual Care. Bed Capacity 395; Total Staff 900; Patients Assisted Annually 174,158.

[J] MONASTERIES AND RESIDENCES OF PRIESTS AND BROTHERS

WILMINGTON. *Brothers of Holy Cross, St. Edmond's Academy*, 2120 Veale Rd., 19810. Tel: 302-475-5321. Email: veal2120@aol.com. Bro. Joseph W. Ash, C.S.C., Dir. Religious. Brothers 3.

Capuchin Franciscan Friars, St. Francis Renewal Center, 1901 Prior Rd., 19809. Tel: 302-798-1454; Fax: 302-798-3360. Revs. Cyprian Rosen, O.F.M.Cap., S.T.L.; Francis Sariego, O.F.M.Cap., Vicar; William Arlia, O.F.M.

DeSales House, 1600 Brinckle Ave., 19806. Tel: 302-656-4342; Fax: 302-656-6108. Email: mmurray@osfs.org. Web: www.oblates.org. Very Rev. Michael S. Murray, O.S.F.S., Supr.; Revs. William J. Dougherty, O.S.F.S.; John A. Finn, O.S.F.S.; William R. Gore, O.S.F.S.; John J. Hurley, O.S.F.S.; William J. Keech, O.S.F.S.; Richard D. Leone, O.S.F.S.; Joseph J. McKenna, O.S.F.S. Priests 8.

St. Felix Friary, 119 N. Jackson St., 19805-3670. Tel: 302-652-7010; Fax: 302-652-8943. Email: mail@ministryofcaring.org. Rev. Ronald Giannone, O.F.M.Cap., Guardian; Bros. Roberto Perez, O.F.M.Cap.; Rudolph Pieretti, O.F.M.Cap. Priests 1; Brothers 2.

Wilmington-Philadelphia Province of the Oblates of St. Francis de Sales, 2200 Kentmere Pkwy., 19806. Tel: 302-656-8529; Fax: 302-658-8052. Email: bstrong@oblates.org. Web: www.oblates.org. Very Rev. James J. Greenfield, O.S.F.S.; Revs. Barry R. Strong, O.S.F.S., Dir. Prov. Admin.; Kevin M. Nadolski, O.S.F.S., Dir. Vocations & Communications; Georgiana Hoffmann, Controller; Bro. Daniel P. Wisniewski, O.S.F.S. Priests 5; Brothers 1.

Rev. Oblates Attached to the Provincial Residence: Revs. William J. Hultberg, O.S.F.S.; Mark A. Hushen, O.S.F.S.

OSFS Wilmington-Philadelphia Province, Inc.
Salesianum School Endowment Trust I
Salesianum School Endowment Trust II
Nativity Preparatory School of Wilmington Trust
OSFS Childs Real Estate Corporation
OSFS Real Estate Holding Corporation
OSFS Mission Corporation
OSFS Service Corporation
OSFS Real Estate Trust
OSFS Endowment Trust

CHILDS, MD. *Oblates of St. Francis De Sales* (1907) *Retirement and Assisted Care Facility*, 1120 Blue Ball Rd., MD 21916-0043. Tel: 410-398-3040; Fax: 410-620-6131. Email: wedavis52@yahoo.com. Web: www.oblates.org. Rev. William E. Davis, O.S.F.S., Supr. Priests 23; Brothers 8. In Res. Revs. Robert D. Ashenbrenner, O.S.F.S. (Retired); Joseph Baraniewicz, O.S.F.S. (Retired); Joseph D. Bowler, O.S.F.S. (Retired); John W. Brennan, O.S.F.S. (Retired); John J. Dennis, O.S.F.S. (Retired); John T. Doyle, O.S.F.S. (Retired); Hugh E. Duffy, O.S.F.S. (Retired); Joseph J. Griffin, O.S.F.S. (Retired); Peter J. Harvey, O.S.F.S. (Retired); Eugene L. Kelly, O.S.F.S. (Retired); John F. Kenny, O.S.F.S. (Retired); John A. Kowalewski, O.S.F.S.; Anthony J. Larry, O.S.F.S.; Eugene J. McBride, O.S.F.S. (Retired); A. Robert McGilvray, O.S.F.S. (Retired); John J. Muzdakis, O.S.F.S. (Retired); John M. O'Neill, O.S.F.S.; Edmund F. O'Rourke, O.S.F.S. (Retired); Thomas J. Tucker, O.S.F.S. (Retired); Bros. Thomas P. Brophy, O.S.F.S., (Retired); John M. Carroll, O.S.F.S.; Robert M. Carter, O.S.F.S.; John J. Dochkus, O.S.F.S.; Joseph H. Hayden, O.S.F.S.; Gerald M. Sweeney, O.S.F.S.

DOVER. *Oblate Apostles of the Two Hearts*, 749 Bison Rd., 19904. Tel: 302-697-6544. Revs. Edgardo M. Arellano, Supreme Moderator; Welthy Gorecho, Local Servant; John Richard F. Santos, National Servant; Robert Tiqual; Jose Viola, Foremater; Bros. Francis Platon, Foremater; Zidney Platon, Foremater.

MIDDLETOWN. *Immaculate Conception Priory of the Canons Regular of Premontre* (1997) 1269 Bayview Rd., 19709. Tel: 302-449-1840, Ext. 31; Fax: 302-449-1217. Very Rev. James D. Bagnato, O.Praem., Admin. Dir. Vocation & Novice Master; Revs. Francis J. Ciliberti, O.Praem.; Martin A. Frigo, O.Praem.; Brian Zielinski, O.Praem., Subprior. Priests 5.

Norbertine Fathers of Delaware, Inc. (1997) 1269 Bayview Rd., 19709. Tel: 302-449-1840; Fax: 302-449-1217. Very Rev. James D. Bagnato, O.Praem., Pres.; Rev. Brian Zielinski, O.Praem., Vice Pres.

[K] CONVENTS AND RESIDENCES FOR SISTERS

WILMINGTON. *St. Benedict*, 113 Canterbury Dr., 19803. Tel: 302-478-3754; Fax: 302-478-9305. Email: margosb@aol.com. Sisters of St. Benedict 3.

Monastery of St. Veronica Giuliani (Strict Enclosure), 816 Jefferson St., 19801. Tel: 302-654-8727; Fax: 302-652-3929. Email: stveronicagiuliani@MSN.com. Sr. Maria Magdalena Cacho, O.S.C.Cap., Abbess; Rev. Ronald Giannone, O.F.M.Cap., Chap. Capuchin Poor Clare Nuns of Delaware. Sisters 10.

Ursuline Academy Inc., The (1893) 1104 Pennsylvania Ave., 19806. Tel: 302-656-5890; Fax: 302-656-2315. Sr. Maureen Welch, O.S.U., Supr. Sisters 12.

CHILDS, MD. *Villa Aviat Convent*, 399 Childs Rd., MD 21916. Tel: 410-398-3699; Fax: 410-398-5801. Email: oblatesisters@mountaviat.org. Web: www.oblatesisters.org. Sr. Anne Elizabeth, O.S.F.S., Delegate. Oblate Sisters of St. Francis de Sales. Sisters 9.

DOVER. *Leaven of the Immaculate Heart of Mary (LIHM)*, 207 Northdown Dr., Village of Westover, 19904. Tel: 302-734-0847; Fax: 302-734-0847. Email: lihmdover@comcast.net. Sr. Maria Cecilia Garcia, Mother General; Rev. Edgardo M. Arellano, Spiritual Dir.; Sisters Gloria Tangan, L.I.H.M., Vocational Dir.; Eberlene Icalla, L.I.H.M., Legal Affairs & Local Servant.

NEW CASTLE. *Caterina Benincasa Dominican Monastery, Inc.*, 6 Church Dr., 19720. Tel: 302-654-1206. Sisters 3.

PRINCESS ANNE, MD. *St. Joseph Novitiate*, 10572 Anderson Rd., MD 21853. Tel: 410-651-5309; Fax: 410-742-3390. Email: lsjm@ezy.net. Web: thejosephhouse.org. Sr. Constance R. Ladd, L.S.J.M., Supr. Gen. Sisters 5; Novices 3.

Seton Center, Sisters of Charity (1983) (Convent Station), P.O. Box 401, MD 21853. Tel: 410-651-9608; Fax: 410-651-1437. Email: setoncenter@comcast.com. Sisters 4; Assisted 8,200.

RIDGELY, MD. *St. Gertrude's Monastery, Motherhouse and Novitiate of the Sisters of St. Benedict* (1857) 14259 Benedictine Ln., MD 21660-1434. Tel: 410-634-2497; Fax: 410-634-1410. Email: cashigley@aol.com. Web: www.ridgelybenedictines.org. Sr. Catherine Higley, O.S.B., Prioress. Sisters 26.

SALISBURY, MD. *Joseph House, Little Sisters of Jesus & Mary.*, P.O. Box 1755, MD 21802. Tel: 410-543-1645; Fax: 410-742-3390. Email: lsjm@comcast.net. Web: www.thejosephhouse.org. Sr. Constance R. Ladd, L.S.J.M., Supr. Gen. Sisters 7.

[L] SECULAR INSTITUTES

WILMINGTON. *De Sales Secular Institute*, 3127 Charing Cross, 19808. Tel: 302-234-8616. Web: www.secularinstitutes.org/sfs.htm. Mary Robinson, Dir.

Secular Franciscan Order (San Damiano Fraternity), 2508 Oakfield Ln., 19810. Tel: 610-388-6423. Email: carisio@yahoo.com. Bobbi O'Sullivan, Min.; Sr. Elise Betz, O.S.F., Spiritual Asst.

Secular Franciscan Order (St. Patrick's Fraternity), 1901 Prior Rd., 19809. Tel: 302-798-1454. John Oscar, S.F.O., Local Min.; Rev. William Arlia, O.F.M., Spiritual Asst.

BEAR, MD. *Secular Order of Discalced Carmelites*, 769 Fox Chase Cir., 19701. Tel: 302-836-3843. Email: malove@comcast.net. Mary An Love, Pres.; Bro. Bryan Paquette, O.C.D., Spiritual Asst. (Annunciation Community).

DOVER. *Secular Institute of the Two Hearts*, P.O. Box 1719, 19903. Tel: 302-678-1358; Fax: 302-678-3246. Email: ahfisecretariat@aol.com. Sisters Agnes Frias, S.I.T.H., Intl. Supr.; Deanna Crisologo, S.I.T.H., Intl. Vicar; Rev. Edgardo M. Arellano, Supr. Gen.

SALISBURY, MD. *Secular Order of Discalced Carmelites* (Mary, Mother of Life Community)., 631 Ridge Rd., MD 21811. Tel: 410-742-1777. Mrs. Marianne Chapin; Bro. Bryan Paquette, O.C.D., Spiritual Asst.

[M] RETREAT HOUSES, GENERAL

WILMINGTON. *De Sales Spirituality Center*, 2200 Kentmere Pkwy., 19806. Tel: 302-383-3585; Fax: 302-658-8052. Email: mmurray@osfs.org. Web: www.oblates.org/spirituality. Very Rev. Michael S. Murray, O.S.F.S., Dir.

St. Francis Renewal Center, 1901 Prior Rd., 19809. Tel: 302-798-1454; Fax: 302-798-3360. Revs. Cyprian Rosen, O.F.M.Cap., S.T.L.; Francis Sariego, O.F.M.Cap., Vicar; William Arlia, O.F.M. Priests 3.

**Jesus House*, 2501 Milltown Rd., 19808. Tel: 302-995-6859; Fax: 302-995-6833. Mr. Christian Malmgren, Dir.

[N] RETREAT HOUSES, WOMEN

CHILDS, MD. *Oblate Sisters of St. Francis de Sales*, Villa Aviat, 399 Childs Rd., MD 21916. Tel: 410-398-3699; Fax: 410-398-5801. Email: oblatesisters@mountaviat.org. Web: www.oblatesisters.org.

RIDGELY, MD. *Berg Retreat Center*, St. Gertrude's Monastery, 14259 Benedictine Ln., MD 21660. Tel: 410-634-2497; Fax: 410-634-1410. Email: cashigley@aol.com. Web: www.ridgelybenedictines.org. Benedictine Sisters.

[O] NEWMAN CENTERS

NEWARK. *Catholic Campus Ministry, Univ. of Delaware* St. Thomas More Oratory, 45 Lovett Ave., 19711. Tel: 302-368-4728; Fax: 302-368-2548. Web: www.udelcatholic.org. Revs. Stephen Alcott, O.P.; Ambrose Eckinger, O.P.

Delmar Organization of Catholic Students - DOCS Tel: 302-368-4728; Fax: 302-368-2548. Kimberly S. Zitzner, B.A., Dir.

Salisbury University 211 W. College Ave., Salisbury, MD 21801. Tel: 410-219-3376; Fax: 410-219-3376. Mrs. Regina Yankalunas, M.P.S., Campus Min.

University of Maryland Eastern Shore 211 W. College Ave., Salisbury, MD 21801. Tel: 410-219-3376; Fax: 410-219-3376. Email: campusministry@hotmail.com. Mrs. Regina Yankalunas, M.P.S., Campus Min.

Wesley College Newman Center Tel: 302-368-4728; Fax: 302-368-2548.

Washington College 45 Lovett Ave., 19711. Tel: 302-368-4728; Fax: 302-368-2548. Email: joe@delanet.com. Rev. Paul J. Campbell.

Wesley College Catholic Campus Ministry St. Thomas More Oratory, 45 Lovett Ave., 19711. Tel: 302-368-4728; Fax: 302-368-2548.

[P] MISCELLANEOUS

WILMINGTON. *Brisson Fund* (1989) 2200 Kentmere Pkwy., 19806. Tel: 302-656-8529. Very Rev. James J. Greenfield, O.S.F.S., Pres.

RELIGIOUS INSTITUTES OF MEN REPRESENTED IN THE DIOCESE

For further details refer to the corresponding bracketed number in the Religious Institutes of Men or Women section.

[1350]—*Brothers of St. Francis Xavier*
[0600]—*Brothers of the Congregation of Holy Cross* (Eastern Province)—C.S.C.
[0900]—*Canons Regular of Premontre*—O.Praem.
[0470]—*The Capuchin Friars* (Prov. of the Stigmata)—O.F.M.Cap.
[0520]—*Franciscan Friars* (Holy Name Province)—O.F.M.
[590]—*Missionaries of the Holy Apostles*—M.S.A.
[]—*Oblate Apostles of the Two Hearts*—O.A.T.H.
[0920]—*Oblates of St. Francis de Sales*—O.S.F.S.
[0430]—*Order of Preachers* (Prov. of St. Joseph)—O.P.
[1070]—*Redemptorist Fathers* (Baltimore, MD)—C.SS.R.
[1200]—*Society of the Divine Savior*—S.D.S.
[0560]—*Third Order Regular of Saint Francis*

RELIGIOUS INSTITUTES OF WOMEN REPRESENTED IN THE DIOCESE

[0100]—*Adorers of the Blood of Christ*—A.S.C.
[0230]—*Benedictine Sisters of Pontifical Jurisdiction*—O.S.B.
[3765]—*Capuchin Poor Clare Sisters*—O.S.C.Cap.
[]—*Carmelites of Charity of Verduna*—C.C.V.
[3735]—*Congregation of St. Brigid*—C.S.B.
[0760]—*Daughters of the Charity of St. Vincent de Paul*—D.C.
[1050]—*Dominican Contemplative Nuns*—O.P.
[1070-11]—*Dominican Sisters*—O.P.
[1170]—*Felician Sisters*—C.S.S.F.
[]—*Leaven of the Immaculate Heart of Mary Sisters*—L.I.H.M.
[2331]—*Little Sisters of Jesus and Mary*—L.S.J.M.
[2340]—*Little Sisters of the Poor*—L.S.P.
[2790]—*Missionary Servants of the Most Blessed Trinity*—M.S.B.T.
[3060]—*Oblates Sisters of St. Francis de Sales*—O.S.F.S.
[2575]—*Religious Sisters of Mercy Mid-Atlantic Community* (Baltimore, MD; Merion, PA)—R.S.M.
[2575]—*Religious Sisters of Mercy South Central Community*—R.S.M.
[2970]—*School Sisters of Notre Dame*—S.S.N.D.
[]—*Secular Institute of the Two Hearts*—S.I.T.H.
[3630]—*Servants of the Most Sacred Heart of Jesus*—S.S.C.J.
[]—*Sisters for Christian Community*—S.F.C.C.
[0440]—*Sisters of Charity of Cincinnati*—S.C.
[0590]—*Sisters of Charity of Saint Elizabeth, Convent Station* (Southern, Western Provs.)—S.C.
[3000]—*Sisters of Notre Dame* (Base Communities Prov.; Maryland Prov.)—S.N.D.deN.
[3770]—*Sisters of St. Clare*—O.S.C.
[1650]—*Sisters of St. Francis of Philadelphia*—O.S.F.
[3893]—*Sisters of St. Joseph of Chestnut Hill, Philadelphia*—S.S.J.
[]—*Sisters Servants of the Most Sacred Heart of Jesus*—S.S.C.J.
[2160]—*Sisters, Servants of Immaculate Heart of Mary* Scranton, PA—I.H.M.
[2150]—*Sisters, Servants of Immaculate Heart of Mary* Monroe, MI—I.H.M.
[4060]—*Society of the Holy Child Jesus*—S.H.C.J.
[4110]—*Ursuline Nuns (Roman Union)* (Eastern Prov.)—O.S.U.

DIOCESAN CEMETERIES

WILMINGTON. *All Saints Cemetery*, 6001 Kirkwood Hwy., 19805. Tel: 302-737-2524; Fax: 302-737-4091. Email: tkane@cathcemde.com. Web: www.cathcemde.com. Office: 6001 Kirkwood Hwy., 19808. Mr. Mark A. Christian, C.C.C.E., Exec. Dir.; Thomas J. Kane, Supt.

Cathedral Cemetery, P.O. Box 2506, 19805. Tel: 302-656-3323; Fax: 302-656-1069. Web: www.cathcemde.com. Office: 2400 Lancaster Ave., 19805. Mr. Mark A. Christian, C.C.C.E., Exec. Dir.; Larry Mann, Supt.

DAGSBORO. *Gate of Heaven Cemetery*, 32112 Vines Creek Rd., 19939. Tel: 302-732-3690; Fax: 302-732-3692. Mr. Mark A. Christian, C.C.C.E., Exec. Dir.; Nicholas Hoopes, Supt.

NECROLOGY

✠ Saltarelli, Most Rev. Michael A., Bishop Emeritus of Wilmington—Died Oct. 8, 2009
† Kenney, Francis P., (Absent on Sick Leave)—Died Feb. 14, 2009
† Plokhooy, Christopher H., (Retired)—Died March 2, 2009

An asterisk (*) denotes an organization that has established tax-exempt status directly with the IRS and is not covered by the USCCB Group Ruling.

Diocese of Winona

(Dioecesis Vinonaensis)

Most Reverend

JOHN M. QUINN, M.DIV.

Bishop of Winona; ordained March 17, 1972; appointed Auxiliary Bishop of the Archdiocese of Detroit and Titular See of Ressiana August 12, 2003; appointed Coadjutor Bishop of Winona October 15, 2008; Mass of Welcome December 11, 2008; Succeeded to See May 7, 2009. *Pastoral Center: 55 W. Sanborn St., P.O. Box 588, Winona, MN 55987.*

Most Reverend

BERNARD J. HARRINGTON, D.D.

Retired Bishop of Winona; ordained June 6, 1959; appointed Auxiliary Bishop of the Archdiocese of Detroit and Titular Bishop of Uzali November 23, 1993; ordained January 6, 1994; appointed Bishop of Winona November 5, 1998; installed January 6, 1999; retired May 7, 2009.

Pastoral Center: 55 W. Sanborn St., P.O. Box 588, Winona, MN 55987. Tel: 507-454-4643; Fax: 507-454-8106.

Web: www.dow.org

Email: dioceseofwinona@dow.org

ESTABLISHED NOVEMBER 26, 1889.

Square Miles 12,282.

Comprises the Counties of Winona, Wabasha, Olmsted, Dodge, Steele, Waseca, Blue Earth, Watonwan, Cottonwood, Murray, Pipestone, Rock, Nobles, Jackson, Faribault, Martin, Freeborn, Mower, Fillmore and Houston in the State of Minnesota.

For legal titles of parishes and diocesan institutions, consult the Pastoral Center.

STATISTICAL OVERVIEW

Personnel	
Bishop	1
Retired Bishops	1
Retired Abbots	1
Priests: Diocesan Active in Diocese	58
Priests: Diocesan Active Outside Diocese	4
Priests: Retired, Sick or Absent	53
Number of Diocesan Priests	115
Religious Priests in Diocese	8
Total Priests in Diocese	123
Extern Priests in Diocese	13
Ordinations:	
Diocesan Priests	1
Transitional Deacons	1
Permanent Deacons	12
Permanent Deacons in Diocese	28
Total Brothers	21
Total Sisters	387
Parishes	
Parishes	114
With Resident Pastor:	
Resident Diocesan Priests	47
Resident Religious Priests	1
Without Resident Pastor:	
Administered by Priests	54
Administered by Lay People	4
Pastoral Centers	2
Professional Ministry Personnel:	
Sisters	9
Lay Ministers	52
Welfare	
Catholic Hospitals	2
Total Assisted	86,550
Health Care Centers	1
Total Assisted	1,236
Homes for the Aged	10
Total Assisted	817
Day Care Centers	3
Total Assisted	17,935
Special Centers for Social Services	7
Total Assisted	4,563
Other Institutions	1
Total Assisted	100
Educational	
Seminaries, Diocesan	1
Students from This Diocese	6
Students from Other Diocese	51
Diocesan Students in Other Seminaries	3
Total Seminarians	9
Colleges and Universities	1
Total Students	1,404
High Schools, Diocesan and Parish	4
Total Students	996
Elementary Schools, Diocesan and Parish	21
Total Students	4,097
Catechesis/Religious Education:	
High School Students	3,375
Elementary Students	7,874
Total Students under Catholic Instruction	17,755
Teachers in the Diocese:	
Priests	1
Sisters	2
Lay Teachers	325
Vital Statistics	
Receptions into the Church:	
Infant Baptism Totals	1,807
Adult Baptism Totals	27
Received into Full Communion	125
First Communions	1,572
Confirmations	1,621
Marriages:	
Catholic	296
Interfaith	249
Total Marriages	545
Deaths	1,048
Total Catholic Population	131,280
Total Population	573,635

Former Bishops—Rt. Revs. JOSEPH B. COTTER, D.D., ord. May 3, 1871; cons. Dec. 27, 1889; died June 28, 1909; PATRICK R. HEFFRON, D.D., ord. Dec. 22, 1884; cons. May 19, 1910; died Nov. 23, 1927; Most Revs. FRANCIS M. KELLY, D.D., ord. Nov. 1, 1912; cons. June 9, 1926; transferred to Diocese of Winona, Feb. 10, 1928; transferred to Titular See of Nasal, Oct. 17, 1949; died June 24, 1950; EDWARD A. FITZGERALD, D.D., ord. July 25, 1916; cons. Sept. 12, 1946; appt. Titular Bishop of Cantanus and Auxiliary Bishop of Dubuque; transferred to Winona, Oct. 20, 1949; retired and transferred to the Titular See of Zerta, Jan. 8, 1969; died March 30, 1972; LORAS J. WATTERS, D.D. (Retired), ord. June 7, 1941; appt. Titular Bishop of Fidoloma and Auxiliary Bishop of Dubuque, June 23, 1965; cons. Aug. 26, 1965; transferred to Winona, Jan. 8, 1969; retired Oct. 14, 1986; appt. Apostolic Administrator, Oct. 14, 1986; died March 30, 2009; JOHN G. VLAZNY, D.D., ord. Dec. 20, 1961; appt. Auxiliary Bishop of Chicago and Titular Bishop of Stagno, Oct. 31, 1983; cons. Dec. 13, 1983; appt. Bishop of Winona, May 19, 1987; installed July 29, 1987; appt. Archbishop of Portland, Oct. 28, 1997; BERNARD J. HARRINGTON, D.D., ord. June 6, 1959; appt. Auxiliary Bishop of Archdiocese of Detroit and Titular Bishop of Uzali Nov. 23, 1993; ord. Jan. 6, 1994; appt. Bishop of Winona Nov. 5, 1998; installed Jan. 6, 1999; retired May 7, 2009.

Vicar General—Very Rev. JAMES P. STEFFES, Mailing Address: 55 W. Sanborn St., P.O. Box 588, Winona, 55987. Tel: 507-454-4643; Fax: 507-454-8106.

Moderator of the Curia—Very Rev. JAMES P. STEFFES.

Chancellor—Mrs. P. J. THOMPSON, Mailing Address: 55 W. Sanborn St., P.O. Box 588, Winona, 55987. Tel: 507-454-4643; Fax: 507-454-8106.

Vice Chancellor—Mr. WILLIAM L. DANIEL, J.C.L., Mailing Address: 55 W. Sanborn St., P.O. Box 588, Winona, 55987. Tel: 507-454-4643; Fax: 507-454-8106.

Deans—Very Revs. THOMAS J. HARGESHEIMER, Winona; TIMOTHY T. REKER, S.T.L., Rochester; DALE E. TUPPER, Austin-Albert Lea; JOHN M. KUNZ, Mankato; GERALD C. KOSSE, Worthington.

Diocesan Consultors—Very Rev. JAMES P. STEFFES; Rev. Msgr. DONALD P. SCHMITZ, M.Ch.A.; Revs. GLENN K. FRERICHS; ROBERT G. MEYER (Retired); Very Revs. RICHARD M. COLLETTI; THOMAS J. HARGESHEIMER.

Finance Council—Most Rev. JOHN M. QUINN, M.Div.; Very Rev. JAMES P. STEFFES; Rev. THOMAS A. LOOMIS; Mr. LAWRENCE J. DOSE, Dir. & Exec. Sec.; Sr. JEAN KENIRY, O.S.F.; Mr. JAMES ANDERSON, CPA; Mr. JAMES WIEKAMP; Ms. MARGARET V. MICHALETZ; Mr. ROBERT WOODEN.

Diocesan Board of Administration— (Civil Corporation): Most Rev. JOHN M. QUINN, M.Div., Pres.; Very Rev. JAMES P. STEFFES, Vicar Gen.; Mrs. P. J. THOMPSON, Chancellor & Sec.; Mr. JAMES ANDERSON, CPA; Ms. MARGARET V. MICHALETZ.

Deposit and Loan Board—Most Rev. JOHN M. QUINN, M.Div.; Very Rev. JAMES P. STEFFES; Mr. LAWRENCE DOSE, Treas.; Rev. JOSEPH P. PETE; Ms. CAROL ORLOWSKE, Sec.; Mr. MICHAEL KIEFFER; Mr. MICHAEL SPELTZ.

Tribunal— (First and Second Instance); Please direct all inquiries concerning marriage nullity, dispensations and permissions, and pre-marriage documentation to this office: *Tribunal: 55 W.*

Sanborn St., P.O. Box 588, Winona, 55987-0588. Tel: 507-454-4643; Fax: 507-454-8106.

Judicial Officers—Very Rev. R. PAUL HEITING, J.C.L., Judicial Vicar; Mr. WILLIAM L. DANIEL, J.C.L., Dir.

Censors of Books and Periodicals—Revs. WILLIAM M. BECKER, S.T.D.; JOHN M. SAUER, S.T.L.; Very Revs. TIMOTHY T. REKER, S.T.L.; ANDREW J. BEERMAN, S.T.L.; Rev. ROBERT S. HORIHAN, S.T.D. (Cand.).

Associate Judges—Revs. WILLIAM J. KULAS, J.C.L.; DAVID WECHTER, O.C.S.O., J.C.L.; Mr. LAWRENCE G. PRICE, J.D., J.C.L.; Mr. WILLIAM L. DANIEL, J.C.L.

Defenders of the Bond—Sr. VICTORIA VONDENBERGER, R.S.M., J.C.L.; Mr. TIMOTHY FERGUSON, J.C.L.; Rev. JOHN GRIFFITHS, J.C.D. Experts: Dr. JOHN JOHNSON; Deacon DAVID PLEVAK.

Advocates—Very Rev. GERALD C. KOSSE; Rev. MARTIN T. SCHAEFFER; Mr. THOMAS HEALY, J.D.; Mr. TIMOTHY FERGUSON, J.C.L.; Sr. RITA MARIE SCHNEIDER, S.S.N.D.

Second Instance Court— Archdiocesan Tribunal of St. Paul/Minneapolis

Promoter of Justice—Mr. TIMOTHY FERGUSON, J.C.L.

Ecclesiastical Notaries—Ms. PAULA WATEMBACH; Mrs. JULIE WRIGHT.

Diocesan Offices and Directors

All Diocesan Offices and Directors are located at the Pastoral Center (unless otherwise indicated), 55 W. Sanborn St., P.O. Box 588, Winona, 55987. Tel: 507-454-4643; Fax: 507-454-8106. Web: www.dow.org.

Curia—

Vicar General—Very Rev. JAMES P. STEFFES. Email: jsteffes@dow.org.

Chancellor—Mrs. P. J. THOMPSON, P.O. Box 588, Winona, 55987. Email: pjthompson@dow.org.

Vice Chancellor—Mr. WILLIAM L. DANIEL, J.C.L. Email: wldaniel@dow.org.

Finances—Mr. LAWRENCE J. DOSE, Dir. Email: ldose@dow.org.

Catholic Charities—Mr. ROBERT TEREBA, Exec. Dir., 111 Market St., P.O. Box 379, Winona, 55987. Tel: 507-454-2270; Fax: 507-457-3027. Email: rtereba@ccwinona.org.

Communications - "The Courier"—Miss ROSE HAMMES. Email: rhammes@dow.org.

Office of RCIA, Liturgy and Evangelization—Ms. PEGGY LOVRIEN. Email: plovrien@dow.org.

Education, Human Resources and Schools—Mrs. P. J. THOMPSON. Email: pjthompson@dow.org.

Lifelong Faith Formation—Mr. MARK NUEHRING. Email: mnuehring@dow.org.

Diaconate Formation—Deacon JUSTIN GREEN. Email: jgreen@dow.org.

Vocations—Rev. THOMAS P. MELVIN, Dir., Immaculate Heart of Mary Seminary #43, 700 Terrace Heights, Winona, 55987-1399. Tel: 507-457-7373. Email: tmelvin@dow.org.

Lay Ministry Formation—Mr. TODD GRAFF. Email: tgraff@dow.org.

Stewardship and Development—Deacon LEONARD L. FULLER. Email: lfuller@dow.org.

Hispanic Ministry—Deacon EDUARDO FORTINI, Dir. Email: efortini@dow.org.

Additional Ministries—

Annual Diocesan Appeal—Deacon JUSTIN GREEN, Dir. Email: jgreen@dow.org.

Continuing Formation and Education for Clergy—Very Rev. JAMES P. STEFFES, Dir., IHM Seminary, 700 Terrace Hts., #43, Winona, 55987. Tel: 507-457-7371; Fax: 507-457-8601. Email: jsteffes@dow.org.

Continuing Education for Deacons—Deacon JUSTIN GREEN, Dir. Email: jgreen@dow.org.

Vicar for Senior Priests—Rev. Msgr. DONALD P. SCHMITZ, M.Ch.A., Church of Nativity of the Blessed Virgin Mary, 640 First Ave., S.W., Harmony, 55939. Tel: 507-886-2393; Fax: 507-886-2394. Email: fdpsch@harmonytel.net.

Ecumenism—Mr. TODD GRAFF. Email: tgraff@dow.org.

Emmaus House of Formation—Rev. TIMOTHY E. BIREN, Dir., 1502 Warren St., Mankato, 56001. Tel: 507-385-0647; Fax: 507-385-0679. Email: timothy.biren@mnsu.edu.

Propagation of the Faith—Rev. CHARLIE I. COLLINS, 55 W. Sanborn St., P.O. Box 588, Winona, 55987. Tel: 507-454-4643; Fax: 507-454-8106. Email: jherdina@dow.org.

Coordinator of Diocesan Health Ministry—Rev. JAMES F. BURYSKA, Diocesan Dir. of Hospitals, Rochester Methodist Hospital Chaplain Services, 201 W. Center St., Rochester, 55902. Tel: 507-255-5551; Fax: 507-255-3125. Email: buryska.james@mayo.edu.

Advisory Bodies—

Presbyteral Council—

Ex Officio—Very Rev. JAMES P. STEFFES.

Elected Senior Member—Rev. CHARLES J. QUINN (Retired).

Appointed Members—Revs. JAMES J. SEITZ; PATRICK O. ARENS; MATTHEW J. FASNACHT; GLENN K. FRERICHS; MARREDDY POTHIREDDY; MARTIN T. SCHAEFER.

Elected At-Large Representatives—Revs. HILARY R. BRIXIUS; KEVIN CONNOLLY.

Elected Deanery Representatives—Revs. THOMAS J. JENNINGS; THOMAS P. MELVIN; JOHN M. SAUER, S.T.L.; DONALD J. SCHMITZ; MARK C. MCNEA.

Priest Assignments Committee—Very Rev. JAMES P. STEFFES; Revs. JOSEPH B. FOGAL; PAUL W. SURPRENANT; THOMAS A. LOOMIS; KEVIN CONNOLLY; THOMAS P. MELVIN; PETER J. KLEIN.

Priests' Pension Board—Most Rev. JOHN M. QUINN, M.Div.; Very Rev. JAMES P. STEFFES; Mr. LAWRENCE J. DOSE, Treas.; Revs. WILLIAM J. KULAS, J.C.L.; STEVEN J. PETERSON; PAUL E. NELSON; Mr THOMAS CROWLEY; Mr. DANIEL KUTZKE; Mr. ROBERT HOODECHECK.

Commission on Sacred Liturgy—Ms. PEGGY LOVRIEN, Dir.; Very Rev. TIMOTHY T. REKER, S.T.L.; Sr. LORRAINE LOECHER, O.S.F.; Ms. SUE VIEHAUSER; Ms. MARY BASSETT; Ms. JACI JAMES; Ms. BOBBIE SNOW; Ms. JOANN FAGAN; Mr. DAVID U'REN; Deacons EDUARDO FORTINI; MICHAEL ELLIS.

Diocese of Winona Incardination Board—Very Rev. JAMES P. STEFFES; Rev. THOMAS P. MELVIN, Chm.; Rev. Msgr. DONALD W. GRUBISCH (Retired); Rev. JOHN M. SAUER, S.T.L.; Deacon LEONARD L. FULLER.

Winona Diocesan Organizations-Agencies-Programs

Archives—Mrs. P. J. THOMPSON, Pastoral Center, 55 W. Sanborn St., P.O. Box 588, Winona, 55987. Tel: 507-454-4643; Fax: 507-454-8106.

Boy Scouts—Mr. MARK NUEHRING, Coord., Pastoral Center, 55 W. Sanborn St., P.O. Box 588, Winona, 55987. Tel: 507-454-4643; Fax: 507-454-8106.

Chaplain—Rev. THOMAS P. MELVIN, Immaculate Heart of Mary Seminary #43, 700 Terrace Heights, Winona, 55987-1399. Tel: 507-457-7373.

Catholic Charities—Mr. ROBERT TEREBA, Exec. Dir., Administrative and Winona Regional Office, 111 Market St., P.O. Box 379, Winona, 55987. Tel: 507-454-2270; Fax: 507-457-3027. Email: rtereba@ccwinona.org. Web: www.ccwinona.org.

Catholic Charities Board—Mr. PETE CONNOR, Chm. Email: cepha6@msn.com. Web: www.ccwinona.org.

Regional Offices—Mankato: 816 Hubbell Ave., Mankato, 56001. Tel: 507-387-5586; Fax: 507-387-5587. *Rochester: 903 W. Center St., Ste. 220, Rochester, 55902.* Tel: 507-287-2047; Fax: 507-287-2050. *Worthington: 1234 Oxford St., Worthington, 56187.* Tel: 507-376-9757; Fax: 507-376-9758.

Field Offices—Albert Lea: 308 E. Fountain, Albert Lea, 56007. Tel: 507-377-3664. *Austin: 405 4th St., N.W., Austin, 55912.* Tel: 507-433-3062. *Owatonna: 577 State Ave., Owatonna, 55060.* Tel: 507-455-2008.

Parish and Community Social Action Office—Ms. SUZANNE BELONGIA, Dir., 111 Market St., P.O. Box 379, Winona, 55987. Tel: 507-454-2270; Fax: 507-457-3027. Email: sbelongia@ccwinona.org. Coordination of: Parish Social Ministry, Rural Life Ministry, Catholic Campaign for Human Development, Catholic Relief Services, HIV-AIDS Ministry, Disaster Relief Services.

Refugee Resettlement—Ms. MARY ALESSIO, Dir., 903 W. Center St., Ste. 220, Rochester, 55902. Tel: 507-287-2047; Fax: 507-287-2050. Email: malessio@ccwinona.org.

Clinical Counseling and Pregnancy, Parenting and Adoption—Mrs. VALERIE CUNNINGHAM, Dir., 903 W. Center St., Ste. 220, Rochester, 55902. Tel: 507-287-2047; Fax: 570-287-2050. Email: valerie@ccwinona.org.

Senior Services—Mrs. JENNIFER HALBERG, Dir., 111 Market St., P.O. Box 379, Winona, 55987. Tel: 507-454-2270; Fax: 507-457-3027. Email: jhalberg@ccwinona.org.

Court Appointed Services—Mrs. MARY BORGEN, Dir., 111 Market St., P.O. Box 379, Winona, 55987. Tel: 507-454-2270; Fax: 507-457-3027. Email: mborgen@ccwinona.org.

Cemeteries—Mrs. P. J. THOMPSON, Pastoral Center, 55 W. Sanborn St., P.O. Box 588, Winona, 55987. Tel: 507-454-4643; Fax: 507-454-8106.

Council of Catholic Women—Ms. BEV MCCARVEL, Pres., 39574 160th St., Brewster, 56119. Tel: 507-842-5460. Email: bmccarvel@roundlk.net; Very Rev. THOMAS J. HARGESHEIMER, Diocesan Moderator, St. Stanislaus Kostka Church, 625 E. 4th St., Winona, 55987. Tel: 507-452-5430.

Diocesan Self-Insurance Plan—Mr. RYAN CHRISTIANSON, Catholic Mutual Group, 111 Riverfront, Ste. 209, Winona, 55987. Tel: 507-454-6452; 800-494-6452; Fax: 800-335-8141; 507-454-8141.

Diocese of Winona Foundation—Deacon LEONARD L. FULLER, Exec. Dir., 55 W. Sanborn St., P.O. Box 588, Winona, 55987. Tel: 507-454-4643; Fax: 507-454-8106. Email: lfuller@dow.org. Web: www.dow.org.

Hospitals—Rev. JAMES F. BURYSKA, Rochester Methodist Hospital, 201 W. Center St., Rochester, 55902. Tel: 507-255-5551; Fax: 507-255-3125.

Catholic Medical Association—Dr. JOHN I. LANE, M.D., 200 First St., S.W., Rochester, 55905. Tel: 507-266-3412; Fax: 507-266-1657. Email: lane.john@mayo.edu.

Girl Scouts—Mr. MARK NUEHRING, Coord.; Rev. THOMAS P. MELVIN, Chap., Immaculate Heart of Mary Seminary #43, 700 Terrace Heights, Winona, 55987-1399. Tel: 507-457-7373.

Marriage Preparation/Enrichment—Mr. MARK NUEHRING, 55 W. Sanborn St., P.O. Box 588, Winona, 55987. Tel: 507-454-4643; Fax: 507-454-8106.

Pathways TEC (Teens Encounter Christ)—Mr. MARK NUEHRING, Diocesan Liaison, 55 W. Sanborn St., P.O. Box 588, Winona, 55987. Tel: 507-454-4643; Fax: 507-454-8106; Rev. MARTIN T. SCHAEFER, Spiritual Dir., Sacred Heart Church, 111 4th St., N.W., Waseca, 56093. Tel: 507-835-1222; Fax: 507-833-1498. Email: sheart@hickorytech.net.

Respect Life—Mr. MARK NUEHRING, 55 W. Sanborn St., P.O. Box 588, Winona, 55987. Tel: 507-454-4643; Fax: 507-454-8106.

Misconduct Issues—Very Revs. R. PAUL HEITING, J.C.L., Mailing Address: 55 W. Sanborn St., P.O. Box 588, Winona, 55987. Tel: 507-454-4643; Fax: 507-454-8106. Email: pheiting@dow.org; JAMES P. STEFFES, Mailing Address: 55 W. Sanborn St., P.O. Box 588, Winona, 55987. Tel: 507-454-4643; Fax: 507-454-8106. Email: jsteffes@dow.org; Mrs. P. J. THOMPSON, 55 W. Sanborn St., P.O. Box 588, Winona, 55987. Tel: 507-454-4643; Fax: 507-454-8106. Email: pjthompson@dow.org; Mr. ROBERT TEREBA, Catholic Charities, 111 Market St., P.O. Box 379, Winona, 55987. Tel: 507-454-2270; Fax: 507-457-3027. Email: rtereba@ccwinona.org.

Retrouvaille—Rev. THEODORE J. HOTTINGER, S.J., 423 W. 7th St., Mankato, 56001. Tel: 507-317-8194.

Victim Assistance Coordinator—Mrs. P. J. THOMPSON, Mailing Address: 55 W. Sanborn St., P.O. Box 588, Winona, 55987. Tel: 507-454-4643, Ext. 223. Email: pjthompson@dow.org.

CLERGY, PARISHES, MISSIONS AND PAROCHIAL SCHOOLS

CITY OF WINONA

(WINONA COUNTY)

1—CATHEDRAL OF THE SACRED HEART (1950) [JC] Very Revs. Richard M. Colletti, Rector; James P. Steffes; Revs. Ubaldo Huerta Roque; Thomas M. Niehaus; Deacons James Welch; Eduardo Fortini.
Res.: 360 Main St., 55987-3299. Tel: 507-452-4770; Fax: 507-454-1974. Email: info@cathedralwinona.org. Web: www.cathedralwinona.org.
School— See listings under Centralized Catholic Schools.
Catechesis/Religious Program—Students 88.

2—ST. CASIMIR'S (1906) [JC] Attended by Cathedral of the Sacred Heart, 360 Main St., Winona. Very Rev. Richard M. Colletti; Rev. Roque Huerta; Deacons James Welch; Eduardo Fortini.
Church: 624 W. Broadway, 55987-2721. Tel: 507-452-4770; Fax: 507-454-1974. Email: info@cathedralwinona.org.
Catechesis/Religious Program—Students 52.

3—ST. JOHN NEPOMUCENE (1888) Attended by St. Stanislaus, Winona. Very Rev. Thomas J. Hargesheimer; Deacon Justin Green.
625 E. Fourth St., 55987-4297. Tel: 507-452-5430; Fax: 507-452-3355. Email: ststans@hbci.com. Web: ststans-stjohn-winonamn.4lpi.com.
Catechesis/Religious Program—626 E. Fifth St., 55987. Students 19.

4—ST. MARY'S (1911) [JC] Rev. William M. Becker.
Res.: 1303 W. Broadway, 55987-2395. Tel: 507-452-5656; Fax: 507-452-5477. Email: stmarys@wacsl.org. Web: www.stmaryswinona.org.
See St. Mary's Primary School, Winona under Centralized Catholic Schools located in the Institution section.

Catechesis/Religious Program—Tel: 507-452-5656; Fax: 507-452-5477. Students 145.

5—St. Stanislaus (1871) Very Rev. Thomas J. Hargesheimer; Deacon Justin Green.
Res.: 625 E. Fourth St., 55987-4297. Tel: 507-452-5430; Fax: 507-452-3355. Email: ststans@hbci.com. Web: ststans-stjohn-winonamn.4lpi.com.
See St. Stanislaus Middle School, Winona under Centralized Catholic Schools located in the Institution section.
Catechesis/Religious Program—626 E. Fifth St., 55987. Students 113.

OUTSIDE THE CITY OF WINONA

Adams, Mower Co., Sacred Heart (1886) [CEM] Rev. James J. Seitz.
Res.: 412 Main St., P.O. Box 352, 55909-9998. Tel: 507-582-3321; Fax: 507-582-1033. Email: fatherjseitz@smig.net.
School—Tel: 507-582-3120. Mr. Shawn Kennedy, Prin. Lay Teachers 8; Students 92.
Catechesis/Religious Program—Tel: 507-582-3321. Students 66.

Adrian, Nobles Co., St. Adrian (1877) [CEM] Rev. Timothy J. Hall.
Res.: 512 Maine Ave., P.O. Box 475, 56110-0475. Tel: 507-483-2317; Fax: 507-483-2460. Email: stadrian@frontiernet.net. Web: www.frontiernet.net/~stadrian.
Catechesis/Religious Program—108 E. Sixth St., 56110. Tel: 507-483-2480; Fax: 507-483-2480. Email: stafaith@frontiernet.net. Students 118.

Albert Lea, Freeborn Co., St. Theodore (1882) [CEM] Rev. James C. Berning; Deacon Michael Ellis.
Mailing Address: 308 E. Fountain St., 56007-2456. Tel: 507-373-0603; Fax: 507-373-0604. Web: www.sttheo.org.
Res.: 311 E. Clark St., 56007-2456. Tel: 507-373-9661.
Parish Center & School—323 E. Clark St., 56007. Tel: 507-373-9657; Fax: 507-373-9657. See listings under Centralized Catholic Schools.
Catechesis/Religious Program—Tel: 507-373-2987; Fax: 507-373-9657. Students 463.

Altura, Winona Co., St. Anthony's (1919) [JC] Attended by St. Rose of Lima. Rev. Marreddy Pothireddy.
180 S. Fremont, Lewiston, 55952-0727. Tel: 507-796-6271; 507-523-2428 (Rectory). Email: dowstrose@embarqmail.com. Web: www.st-rose.org.
Catechesis/Religious Program—Included with St. Rose of Lima, Lewiston, MN. Students 189.

Austin, Mower Co.

1—St. Augustine's (1857) [JC] Attended by St. Edward, Austin. Rev. Joseph B. Fogal; Deacons John Kluczny; Richard Aho.
Mailing Address: 2000 Oakland Ave. W., 55912-1599. Tel: 507-433-1841; Fax: 507-433-9680.
Church: 405 Fourth St. N.W., 55912-3091. Tel: 507-437-4537; Fax: 507-437-4537.
See Austin Catholic Elementary School, under Centralized Catholic Schools located in the Institution section.
Catechesis/Religious Program—Tel: 507-437-3250. Austin Tri-Parish Students 300.

2—St. Edward's (1960) [JC] Rev. Joseph B. Fogal; Deacons John Kluczny; Richard Aho; Sr. Lorraine Loecher, Pastoral Assoc. In Res., Rev. Richard P. Loomis (Retired).
Res.: 2000 Oakland Ave. W., 55912-1599. Tel: 507-433-1841; Fax: 507-433-9680.
See Austin Catholic Elementary School, under Centralized Catholic Schools located in the Institution section.
Catechesis/Religious Program—Tel: 507-437-3250. Austin Tri-Parish Students 330.

3—Queen of Angels (1936) [JC] Very Rev. Dale E. Tupper; Deacon David Blake.
Res.: 1001 Oakland Ave. E., 55912-3896. Tel: 507-433-1888; Fax: 507-433-1889. Email: qofaparish@chartermi.net. Web: www.austincatholic.org.
See Austin Catholic Elementary School, under Centralized Catholic Schools located in the Institution section.
Catechesis/Religious Program—311 4th St., N.W., 55912. Tel: 507-437-3250. Austin Tri-Parish Students 71.
Catechesis/Religious Program—Spanish Catechesis, Tel: 507-433-8474. Total Enrollment 80.
Queens of Angels Hermitage—1009 E. Oakland Ave., 55912. Tel: 507-437-4015. Rev. Jon H. Moore.

Blooming Prairie, Steele Co., St. Columbanus (1878) [CEM] Rev. William J. Kulas.
Res.: 114 E. Main St., 55917-1427. Tel: 507-583-2529; 507-583-2784; Fax: 507-583-7738.
Catechesis/Religious Program—Tel: 507-583-2784; Fax: 507-583-7738. Students 70.

Blue Earth, Faribault Co., SS. Peter and Paul's (1866) [CEM] Rev. Leo Charles Koppala, Parochial Admin.
Res.: 214 S. Holland, 56013-1331. Tel: 507-526-5626.
Catechesis/Religious Program—Tel: 507-526-2816. Students 137.

Brewster, Nobles Co., Sacred Heart (1901) [CEM] Attended by St. Francis Xaiver, Windom. Rev. James Von Tobel, S.J.
548 17th St., P.O. Box 39, Windom, 56101-1217. Tel: 507-831-3300; Fax: 507-831-3300. Email: sacreds@centurytel.net.
Catechesis/Religious Program—P.O. Box 187, 56119. Tel: 507-842-5584; Fax: 507-842-5523. Loretta Smith, Dir. Faith Formation. Students 44.

Brownsdale, Mower Co., Our Lady of Loretto (1946) Attended by Queen of Angels, Austin. Very Rev. Dale E. Tupper; Deacon David Blake.
1001 Oakland Ave. E., Austin, 55912-1599. Tel: 507-433-1888; Fax: 507-433-1889. Email: qofaparish@chartermi.net.
Catechesis/Religious Program—Tel: 507-567-2456. Students 11.

Brownsville, Houston Co., St. Patrick's (1871) [CEM] [JC 2] Attended by St. Mary, Caledonia. Rev. Gregory P. Leif.
Mailing Address: P.O. Box 406, Caledonia, 55921-0406. Tel: 507-725-3804. Email: stpatricks@acegroup.cc.
Church: 604 Adams, 55919. Tel: 507-482-6818; Fax: 507-482-6818.
Catechesis/Religious Program—P.O. Box 155, 55919. Students 40.

Byron, Olmsted Co., Christ the King (1965) Rev. Paul W. Surprenant.
Res.: 202 Fourth St., N.W., P.O. Box 1000, 55920-1000. Tel: 507-775-6455; Fax: 507-775-6473. Email: ckhf@charterinternet.com.
Catechesis/Religious Program—Tel: 507-775-0501. Students 164.

Caledonia, Houston Co., St. Mary (1975) [CEM] Rev. Gregory P. Leif.
Mailing Address: P.O. Box 406, 55921-0406. Email: stmary1@acegroup.cc. Web: www.churchofstmary.net.
Office: 453 S. Pine St., 55921.
Res.: 513 S. Pine St., 55921-0406. Tel: 507-725-4408.
School—(Grades PreK-8) Tel: 507-725-3355. Mr. Thomas Reichenbacher, Prin. Priests 1; Lay Teachers 14; Students 161.

Canton, Fillmore Co., The Assumption (1891) [CEM] [JC] Attended by Nativity of B.V.M. Rev. Msgr. Donald P. Schmitz.
640 First Ave., S.W., Harmony, 55939-0596. Tel: 507-886-2393; Fax: 507-886-2394.
Catechesis/Religious Program—(Students attend Rel. Educ. programs at Nativity, Harmony or St. Olaf, Mabel.) Email: fdpsch@harmony.net. Total Enrollment 32.

Chatfield, Fillmore Co., St. Mary's (1866) [CEM 2] Rev. Russell G. Scepaniak.
405 Bench St., S.W., 55923. Tel: 507-867-3148; Fax: 507-867-0073.
Catechesis/Religious Program—Tel: 507-867-3922. Students 136.

Claremont, Dodge Co., St. Francis de Sales (1869) [CEM] [JC] Attended by St. John Baptist de La Salle, Dodge Center. Rev. Kurt Farrell.
20 Second St., N.E., P.O. Box 310, Dodge Center, 55927-0310. Tel: 507-374-6830; Fax: 612-605-4315. Email: tritonparishes@frontiernet.net.
Catechesis/Religious Program—P.O. Box 117, West Concord, 55985. Tel: 507-527-2384. Students 35.

Currie, Murray Co., Immaculate Heart of Mary (1883) Attended by St. Gabriel, Fulda. Rev. Jeffrey L. Dobbs, Parochial Admin.
Mailing Address: 307 W. Lake Ave., Fulda, 56131. Tel: 507-763-3145; Fax: 507-763-3545.
Church: 510 Mill St., 56123.
Catechesis/Religious Program—Students 50.

Dakota, Winona Co., Holy Cross (1890) Attended by Crucifixion Church, LaCrescent. Rev. Gregory G. Havel; Deacons Gerald Trocinski; Robert Yerhot.
Res. & Mailing Address: 423 S. 2nd St., La Crescent, 55947-1326. Tel: 507-895-4720; Fax: 507-895-6880. Email: cruxch@acegroup.cc.
Church: 820 River St., 55925.
Catechesis/Religious Program—Tel: 507-895-4120. Students 6.

Deerfield, Steele Co., Corpus Christi (1869) Attended by Christ the King, Medford. Ms. Amy Hellevik, Parish Dir.
205 N.W. Second Ave., P.O. Box 120, Medford, 55049-0120. Tel: 507-451-6353; Fax: 507-451-6353. Email: christtheking@myclearwave.net.
Catechesis/Religious Program—Tel: 507-451-8898. Students 38.

Delavan, Faribault Co., Mater Dolorosa (1889) Closed. For inquiries for parish records contact the chancery.

Dodge Center, Dodge Co., St. John Baptist de La Salle (1945) Rev. Kurt Farrell.
Res.: 20 Second St., N.E., P.O. Box 310, 55927-0310. Tel: 507-374-6830; Fax: 612-605-4315. Email: stjohnscatholic@kmtel.com.
Catechesis/Religious Program—Tel: 507-374-6765; 507-527-2384; Fax: 612-605-4315. Students 63.

Dundee, Nobles Co., St. Mary, Closed. For inquiries for parish records contact the chancery.

East Chain, Martin Co., Holy Family (1897) [CEM] [JC] Attended by St. John Vianney, Fairmont. Rev. Kevin Connolly; Deacon Edwin C. Bonnarens.
Res.: 901 S. Prairie Ave., Fairmont, 56031-3098. Tel: 507-235-5535; Fax: 507-235-5536. Email: sjv-church@midconetwork.com.
Catechesis/Religious Program—Tel: 507-773-4491. Students 40.

Easton, Faribault Co., Our Lady of Mount Carmel (1866) [CEM] Attended by S. Casimir, Wells. Rev. Mark C. McNea; Deacon Eugene Paul.
Res.: 320 2nd Ave., S.W., Wells, 56097-1399. Tel: 507-553-5391. Email: olmc@bevcomm.net.
Church: 27 Main St., 56025. Tel: 507-787-2303; Fax: 507-787-2221.
Catechesis/Religious Program—Students 80.

Elba, Winona Co., St. Aloysius (1877) [CEM] Attended by St. Charles Borromeo, St. Charles. Rev. James F. Callahan; Deacon Placido Zavala.
1900 E. 6th St., St. Charles, 55972-1426. Tel: 507-932-3294; Fax: 507-932-3393. Email: borromeo@hbcsc.net.
Catechesis/Religious Program— Attending St. Charles Borromeo program, Tel: 507-932-3303. Students 30.

Ellendale, Freeborn Co., St. Aidan (1857) [CEM] Attended by All Saints, New Richland. Rev. Swaminatha R. Pothireddy.
Mailing Address: 307 SW First St., P.O. Box 185, New Richland, 56072-0185. Tel: 507-465-8217. Email: asbulletin@earthlink.net.
Catechesis/Religious Program—Tel: 507-684-2245. Students 30.

Ellsworth, Nobles Co., St. Mary's (1885) [CEM] Attended by St. Catherine, Luverne. Rev. Thomas J. Jennings.
203 E. Brown St., Luverne, 56156-1599. Tel: 507-283-8502. Email: stcatherine@iw.net. Web: www.stmaryellsworth.org.
Catechesis/Religious Program—Tel: 507-283-8071; Fax: 507-449-3638. Email: kbaustian@iw.net. Students 20.

Eyota, Olmsted Co., Holy Redeemer (1891) Attended by St. Charles Borromeo, St. Charles. Rev. James F. Callahan; Deacon Placido Zavala.
Mailing Address: 1900 E. 6th St., St. Charles, 55972-1426. Tel: 507-932-3294; Fax: 507-932-3393.
Catechesis/Religious Program—Tel: 507-545-2161; Fax: 507-545-2161. Students 167.

Fairmont, Martin Co., St. John Vianney (1952) [CEM] Rev. Kevin Connolly; Deacon Edwin C. Bonnarens.
Parish Office—901 S. Prairie Ave., 56031-3023. Tel: 507-235-5535; Fax: 507-235-5536. Email: sjv-church@midconetwork.com.
School—(Grades PreK-6), 911 S. Prairie Ave., 56031. Tel: 507-235-5304; Fax: 507-235-9099. Email: jschaffer@sjvschool.net. Joan Schaffer, Prin. Priests 1; Lay Teachers 10; Students 130.
Catechesis/Religious Program—Tel: 507-235-5639; Fax: 507-235-5536. Email: joni@midconetwork.com. Students 234.

Fountain, Fillmore Co., St. Lawrence O'Toole (1872) Closed. For inquiries for parish records contact the chancery.

Fulda, Murray Co., St. Gabriel's (1882) [CEM] Rev. Jeffrey L. Dobbs, Parochial Admin.
307 W. Lake Ave., 56131-9402.
Church: 309 W. Lake Ave., 56131-9402. Tel: 507-425-2595; 507-425-2369 (Office). Email: stgab2369@centurytel.net (Office).
Catechesis/Religious Program—Tel: 507-425-2369. Students 100.

Geneva, Freeborn Co., St. Mary (1867) [CEM] Attended by All Saints, New Richland. Rev. Swaminatha R. Pothireddy.
307 1st St., S.W., P.O. Box 185, New Richland, 56072-0185. Tel: 507-465-8217; Fax: 507-465-8381.
Catechesis/Religious Program—Tel: 507-583-7530. Students 30.

Good Thunder, Blue Earth Co., St. Joseph (1879) [CEM] Attended by St. Teresa, Mapleton. Rev. Brian F. Sutton, Parochial Admin.
Mailing Address: 104 Silver St., W., Mapleton, 56065. Tel: 507-524-3127; Fax: 507-524-4423.
Catechesis/Religious Program—Tel: 507-278-3444. Students 37.

Grand Meadow, Mower Co., St. Finbarr's (1878) [CEM] Attended by St. Ignatius, Spring Valley. Rev. Steven J. Peterson.
Mailing Address: 213 W. Franklin St., Spring Valley, 55975-1312. Tel: 507-346-7565.
Church: 504 1st St., S.W., P.O. Box 326, 55936. Tel: 507-754-5190.
Catechesis/Religious Program—Students 71.

GUCKEEN, FARIBAULT CO., OUR LADY OF MERCY (1902) Closed. For inquiries for parish records contact the chancery.

HAMMOND, WABASHA CO., ST. CLEMENT'S, Closed. For inquiries for parish records contact SS. Peter and Paul, Mazeppa.

HARMONY, FILLMORE CO., THE NATIVITY OF THE BLESSED VIRGIN (1906) Rev. Msgr. Donald P. Schmitz.
Res.: 640 First Ave., S.W., 55939-0596. Tel: 507-886-2393; Fax: 507-886-2394.
Catechesis/Religious Program—Students 36.

HAYFIELD, DODGE CO., SACRED HEART (1935) Attended by St. Columbanus, Blooming Prairie. Rev. William J. Kulas.
114 E. Main St., Blooming Prairie, 55917-1427. Tel: 507-583-2529; Fax: 507-583-7738. Email: stcolumbanus@frontiernet.net.
Church: 150 2nd St., N.E., 55940. Tel: 507-477-2256; Fax: 507-477-2938.
Catechesis/Religious Program—Students 91.

HERON LAKE, JACKSON CO., SACRED HEART (1884) [CEM] Attended by St. Francis Xavier, Windom. Rev. James Von Tobel, S.J.
548 17th St., P.O. Box 39, Windom, 56101-1217. Tel: 507-831-3300; Fax: 507-831-3300. Email: ssacred@centurytel.net.
Catechesis/Religious Program—Tel: 507-793-2773. Students 89.

HOKAH, HOUSTON CO., ST. PETER'S (1876) [CEM] [JC 2] Attended by St. Joseph, Rushford. Rev. Joseph P. Pete.
101 Rushford Ave. W., P.O. Box 577, Rushford, 55971-0577. Tel: 507-864-2257; Fax: 507-864-3716. Email: paradm@acegroup.cc.
Church: 34 Main St., P.O. Box 355, 55941-0355. Tel: 507-894-4242; Fax: 507-894-4375.
School—(Grades PreK-8) Tel: 507-894-4375; 507-894-4944. Email: stpeter@acegroup.ccc. Mrs. Rachel Fishel, Prin. Students 60.
Catechesis/Religious Program—Students 23.

HOUSTON, HOUSTON CO., ST. MARY'S (1873) [CEM] Attended by St. Joseph, Rushford. Rev. Joseph P. Pete.
101 Rushford Ave. W., P.O. Box 577, Rushford, 55971-0557. Tel: 507-864-2257. Email: paradm@acegroup.cc. Web: www.sjsmsp.org.
Catechesis/Religious Program—Students 65.

IONA, MURRAY CO., ST. COLUMBA'S (1891) [CEM] Attended by St. Ann, Slayton. Rev. Patrick O. Arens.
2747 29th St., Slayton, 56172-1485. Tel: 507-836-8030; Fax: 507-836-6261.
Catechesis/Religious Program—Email: triparish@frontiernet.net. Students 18.

JACKSON, JACKSON CO., GOOD SHEPHERD (1891) [CEM] Rev. Peter L. Schuster.
Res.: 311 N. Sverdrup Ave., P.O. Box 65, 56143-1329. Tel: 507-847-2504; Fax: 507-847-3734. Email: goodshep@msn.com.
Catechesis/Religious Program—Tel: 507-847-2719. Susanne Foster, D.R.E. Students 111.

JANESVILLE, WASECA CO., ST. ANN'S (1876) [CEM] Rev. Peter J. Klein.
307 W. Second St., P.O. Box 218, 56048-0218. Tel: 507-234-6244; Fax: 507-234-6237. Email: stannjan@hickorytech.net.
Catechesis/Religious Program—Tel: 507-234-5753. Students 142.

JASPER, PIPESTONE CO., ST. JOSEPH'S (1890) [CEM] Attended by St. Leo's, Pipestone. Very Rev. Gerald C. Kosse.
415 Hiawatha Ave. S., P.O. Box 36, Pipestone, 56164. Tel: 507-825-3152; Fax: 507-825-4492. Email: om@triparishmn.org.
Rectory—121 Smith St., N., Woodstock, 56186. Tel: 507-777-4160; Fax: 507-825-4492.
Church: 415 2nd St. E., 56144.
Catechesis/Religious Program—Students 23.

JEFFERS, COTTONWOOD CO., ST. AUGUSTINE'S (1912) Closed. For inquiries for parish records contact the chancery.

JOHNSBURG, MOWER CO., ST. JOHN'S (1859) [CEM] Attended by Sacred Heart, Adams. Rev. James J. Seitz.
412 Main St., P.O. Box 352, Adams, 55909. Tel: 507-582-3321; Fax: 507-582-1033.
Catechesis/Religious Program—Students 29.

KASSON, DODGE CO., HOLY FAMILY (1976) [CEM] Attended by Christ the King, Byron. Rev. Paul W. Surprenant.
202 Fourth St., N.W., P.O. Box 1000, Byron, 55920-1000. Fax: 507-634-7200. Email: ckhf@charterinternet.com; holyfamilyjen@kmtel.com.
Church: 1904 N. Mantorville Ave., P.O. Box 171, 55944. Tel: 507-634-7520.
Catechesis/Religious Program—Tel: 507-634-7599. Students 238.

KELLOGG, WABASHA CO.

1—ST. AGNES (1900) Attended by St. Felix, Wabasha. Rev. Glenn K. Frerichs; Deacon John Hust.
117 3rd St. W., Wabasha, 55981-1201. Tel: 651-565-3931; Fax: 651-565-4363. Email: stfelix@hbci.com.
Catechesis/Religious Program—Tel: 651-565-3718; Fax: 651-565-0244. Email: stfelixgrowthinfaith@yahoo.com. Students 27.

2—IMMACULATE CONCEPTION (1881) Attended by St. Joachim, Plainview. Rev. Thien Van Nguyen.
900 W. Broadway, Plainview, 55964-1039. Tel: 507-534-3321; Fax: 507-534-3687. Email: stjoachimchurch@hotmail.com. Web: immconception-church.org.
Catechesis/Religious Program—Tel: 507-534-3588. Students 95.

LA CRESCENT, HOUSTON CO., THE CHURCH OF THE CRUCIFIXION (1856) [CEM 2] Rev. Gregory G. Havel; Deacons Gerald Trocinski; Robert Yerhot.
407 S. Second St., 55947-1326.
Res.: 423 S. Second St., 55947-1326. Tel: 507-895-4720; Fax: 507-895-6880. Email: cruxch@acegroup.cc.
School—(Grades PreK-6), 420 S. Second St., 55947. Tel: 507-895-4402; Fax: 507-895-4403. Robert Formanek, Prin. Lay Teachers 10; Students 108.
Catechesis/Religious Program—1380 Lancer Blvd., 55947. Tel: 507-895-2700. Students 165.
Parish Office: 423 S. Second St., 55947. Tel: 507-895-6867.

LAKE CITY, WABASHA CO., ST. MARY'S OF THE LAKE (1877) Rev. Richard J. Dernek; Deacon David Dose.
Res.: 419 Lyon Ave., 55041-1649. Tel: 651-345-4134; Fax: 651-345-6134.
Catechesis/Religious Program—Email: stmarysff@embarqmail.com. Students 250.

LAKE CRYSTAL, BLUE EARTH CO., HOLY FAMILY (1900) [CEM] Attended by St. Joseph the Worker, Mankato. Rev. John P. Wilmot; Deacon Preston Doyle.
Church: 201 N. Hunt St., 56055. Tel: 507-726-2070. Email: sjwhf@hickorytech.net.
Res.: 423 W. 7th St., Mankato, 56001-2197. Tel: 507-388-3766; Fax: 507-388-2101.
Catechesis/Religious Program—Tel: 507-726-2725. Students 108.

LAKE WILSON, MURRAY CO., ST. MARY (1916) [JC] Attended by St. Ann, Slayton. Rev. Patrick O. Arens.
2747 29th St., Slayton, 56172-1485. Tel: 507-836-8030; Fax: 507-836-6261.
Catechesis/Religious Program—Students 26.

LAKEFIELD, JACKSON CO., ST. JOSEPH (1897) [CEM] Attended by Good Shepherd, Jackson. Rev. Peter L. Schuster.
311 N. Sverdrup Ave., P.O. Box 65, Jackson, 56143-1329. Tel: 507-847-2504; Fax: 507-847-3734. Email: sjcc@frontiernet.net; goodshep@msn.com.
Catechesis/Religious Program—410 Broadway Ave., Box 517, 56150. Tel: 507-662-5819; Fax: 507-662-5924. Students 83.

LAMOILLE, WINONA CO., PRECIOUS BLOOD (1900) Closed. For inquiries for parish records contact the chancery.

LANESBORO, FILLMORE CO., ST. PATRICK (1871) [JC] Attended by St. Mary's, Chatfield. Rev. Russell G. Scepaniak.
Mailing Address: 405 Twiford St., S.W., Chatfield, 55923. Tel: 507-867-3922; Fax: 507-867-0073. Email: tostmarys@gamil.com.
Church: 200 Ridgeway Ln., P.O. Box 307, 55949. Tel: 507-467-2480.
Catechesis/Religious Program—Students 15.

LE ROY, MOWER CO., ST. PATRICK'S (1878) [CEM] Attended by St. Ignatius, Spring Valley. Rev. Steven J. Peterson.
213 W. Franklin St., Spring Valley, 55975-1312. Tel: 507-346-7565; Fax: 507-324-5203.
Catechesis/Religious Program—Students 76.

LEWISTON, WINONA CO., ST. ROSE OF LIMA (1876) [CEM] Rev. Marreddy Pothireddy.
Res.: 180 S. Fremont, 55952-0727. Tel: 507-523-2428; Fax: 507-523-2645. Email: dowrose@embarqmail.com. Web: www.st-rose.org.
Catechesis/Religious Program—Included with St. Anthony, Altura, MN., Tel: 507-523-3548. Email: dowstrose@embarqmail.com. Students 237.

LISMORE, NOBLES CO., ST. ANTHONY'S (1887) [CEM] Rev. Timothy J. Hall, Priest Moderator; Roxanne Kemper, Parish Dir.
Mailing Address: 310 Third Ave. S., P.O. Box 158, 56155-0158. Tel: 507-472-8262; Fax: 507-472-8454. Email: santhony@myclearwave.net. Web: www.frontiernet.net/~stadrian.
Catechesis/Religious Program—Tel: 507-472-8262; Fax: 507-472-8454. Students 55.

LITOMYSL, STEELE CO., HOLY TRINITY (1877) Attended by Sacred Heart, Owatonna. Rev. John M. Sauer; Deacon Adam McMillan.
810 S. Ceder Ave., Owatonna, 55060. Tel: 507-451-1588; Fax: 507-446-9979.
Church: 9946 S.E. 24th Ave., Owatonna, 55060.
School—St. Isidore, (Grades PreK-5) Tel: 507-451-5876; Fax: 507-433-9680. Jenny Deml, Prin. Lay Teachers 3; Students 23.
Catechesis/Religious Program—Tel: 507-583-7591. Students 36.

LUVERNE, ROCK CO., ST. CATHERINE'S (1881) [CEM] Rev. Thomas J. Jennings.
203 E. Brown, 56156-1599. Tel: 507-283-8502. Email: stcatherine@iw.net. Web: www.stcatherineluverne.org.
Catechesis/Religious Program—Tel: 507-283-8071; Fax: 507-449-3638. Email: kbaustian@iw.net. Students 230.

LYLE, MOWER CO., QUEEN OF PEACE (1946), (German), Attended by Sacred Heart, Adams. Rev. James J. Seitz.
Mailing Address: 412 Main St., P.O. Box 352, Adams, 55909-0352. Tel: 507-582-3321; Fax: 507-582-1033.
Catechesis/Religious Program—Tel: 507-325-4677. Students 40.

MABEL, FILLMORE CO., ST. OLAF (1954) [JC] Attended by Nativity of B.V.M., Harmony. Rev. Msgr. Donald P. Schmitz.
640 First Ave., S.W., Harmony, 55939-0596. Tel: 507-886-2393; Fax: 507-886-2394.
Catechesis/Religious Program—Students 41.

MADELIA, WATONWAN CO., ST. MARY (1872) Revs. Thomas E. Cook; Luis Vargas, (Hispanic Ministry).
Res.: 212 First St., N.E., 56062-1702. Tel: 507-642-8305; Fax: 507-642-8310.
School—(Grades PreK-6) Tel: 507-642-3324; Fax: 507-642-3899. John DeZeeuw, Prin. Priests 1; Lay Teachers 4; Students 46.
Catechesis/Religious Program—Students 124.

MADISON LAKE, BLUE EARTH CO., ALL SAINTS (1894) [CEM] Rev. Robert J. Schneider.
Parish Endowment Fund, Inc. of All Saints Church—601 4th St., P.O. Box 217, 56063-0217. Tel: 507-243-3319; Fax: 507-243-4308. Email: asoffice@hickorytech.net. Web: as-ic.org.
School—(Grades PreK-4), P.O. Box 158, 56063-0158. Tel: 507-243-3819. Email: ascs@hickorytech.net. Priests 1; Lay Teachers 4; Students (K-4) 22; Preschool 30.
Catechesis/Religious Program—Tel: 507-327-2976. Email: colleenterrell@hotmail.com. Students 141.

MANKATO, BLUE EARTH CO.

1—ST. JOHN THE BAPTIST (1884) [JC] Very Rev. John M. Kunz.
Church: 632 S. Broad St., 56001-3890. Tel: 507-625-3131; Fax: 507-625-3270. Email: stjohnch@hickorytech.net. Web: www.stjohnscatholicchurch.com.
Rectory—321 E. Liberty St., 56001-3890.
School—Tel: 507-388-2997; Fax: 507-388-3081. Web: www.mankatoareacatholicschools.org. See listings under Centralized Catholic Schools.
Catechesis/Religious Program—Tel: 507-387-6928. Email: mbn@hickorytech.net. Students 368.

2—ST. JOSEPH THE WORKER (1957) [JC] Rev. John P. Wilmot; Deacon Preston Doyle.
Res.: 423 W. 7th St., 56001-2197. Tel: 507-388-3766; Fax: 507-388-2101. Email: sjwhf@hickorytech.net.
School— See listings under Centralized Catholic Schools.
Catechesis/Religious Program—423 W. 7th St., 56001. Tel: 507-625-3450. Students 172.
Convent—Tel: 507-388-2515.

3—SS. PETER AND PAUL'S (1854) Revs. Mariano O. Varela; Samuel H. Leonard, I.V.E.; Deacon Christopher Walchuk.
Res.: 105 N. Fifth St., 56001-4442. Tel: 507-388-2995; Fax: 507-388-7661. Email: sspp@hickorytech.net.
School—Tel: 507-388-2997. See listings under Centralized Catholic Schools.
Catechesis/Religious Program—Students 98.

MAPLETON, BLUE EARTH CO., ST. TERESA'S (1876) [CEM] Rev. Brian F. Sutton, Parochial Admin.
104 Silver St., W., P.O. Box 305, 56065-0305.
Catechesis/Religious Program—Tel: 507-524-4606. Students 83.

MAZEPPA, WABASHA CO., SS. PETER AND PAUL (1860) Attended by Pax Christi, Rochester. Rev. Joseph L. Keefe; Deacon Christopher Orlowski.
4135 18th Ave., NW, Rochester, 55901-0460. Tel: 507-282-8542; Fax: 507-289-8741.
Church: 280 First St., P.O. Box 224, 55956-0224. Tel: 507-843-3885; Fax: 507-843-3900. Email: office@sspnp.com.
Catechesis/Religious Program—Tel: 507-843-4600. Students 73.

MEDFORD, STEELE CO., CHRIST THE KING (1943) Ms. Amy Hellevik, Parish Dir.; Rev. Robert D. Herman, Priest Moderator (Retired).
Res.: 205 N.W. Second Ave., P.O. Box 120, 55049-0120. Tel: 507-451-6353; Fax: 507-451-6353. Email: christtheking@myclearwave.net.
Catechesis/Religious Program—Tel: 507-451-8898. Students 135.

MINNEISKA, WABASHA CO., ST. MARY'S (1867) Attended by Holy Trinity, Rollingstone. Rev. Donald J. Lovas.
83 Main St., Rollingstone, 55969-9759. Tel: 507-689-2351; Fax: 507-689-2251. Email: holymary@charter.net.
Catechesis/Religious Program—Total Enrollment 3.

MINNESOTA CITY, WINONA CO., ST. PAUL'S (1924) [CEM] Attended by Holy Trinity, Rollingstone Rev. Donald J. Lovas.
Res.: 83 Main St., Rollingstone, 55969-9759. Tel: 507-689-2351; Fax: 507-689-2251. Email: holymary@charter.net.
Catechesis/Religious Program—Students 3.

MINNESOTA LAKE, FARIBAULT CO., ST. JOHN THE BAPTIST (1865) [CEM] Attended by St. Casimir, Wells. Rev. Mark C. McNea; Deacon Eugene Paul.
Mailing Address: 320 2nd Ave. S.W., Wells, 56097-1399. Tel: 507-553-5391. Email: scasimir@bevcomm.net.
Church: 100 Park St., P.O. Box 158, 56068. Tel: 507-462-3636; Fax: 507-462-3212. Email: stjb@bevcomm.net.
Catechesis/Religious Program—25 Higbie Ave., P.O. Box 158, 56068. Email: stjbff@bevcomm.net. Students 46.

NEW RICHLAND, WASECA CO., ALL SAINTS (1879) [CEM] Rev. Swaminatha R. Pothireddy.
Res.: 307 1st St., S.W., P.O. Box 185, 56072-0185. Tel: 507-465-8217; Fax: 507-465-8381. Email: asbulletin@earthlink.net.
Catechesis/Religious Program—Students 39.

OAK RIDGE, WINONA CO., IMMACULATE CONCEPTION (1875) Closed. For inquiries about sacramental records contact Holy Trinity, Rollingstone.

OWATONNA, STEELE CO.

1—ST. JOSEPH'S (1891) Rev. Edward F. McGrath, Parochial Admin.; Deacon Patrick Fagan.
Res.: 512 S. Elm St., 55060-3399. Tel: 507-451-4845; Fax: 507-451-4651. Email: stjosephparishowatonna@charter.net.
School— See listings under Centralized Catholic Schools.
Catechesis/Religious Program—Students 411.

2—SACRED HEART (1866) [JC] Revs. John M. Sauer; Gregory Parrott, Parochial Vicar.
Res.: 810 S. Cedar Ave., 55060-3297. Tel: 507-451-1588; Fax: 507-446-9979. Web: www.sacredheartowatonna.org.
School—Tel: 507-446-2300; Fax: 507-446-2304. See listings under Centralized Catholic Schools.
Catechesis/Religious Program—730 S. Cedar Ave., 55060. Tel: 507-446-2302. Students 350.

PIPESTONE, PIPESTONE CO., ST. LEO'S (1887) [CEM] Very Rev. Gerald C. Kosse.
Mailing Address: 415 Hiawatha Ave. S., P.O. Box 36, 56164-0036. Tel: 507-825-3152. Email: om@triparishmn.org.
Res.: 121 Smith St., N., Woodstock, 56186. Tel: 507-777-4160; Fax: 507-825-4492.
Catechesis/Religious Program—Students 188.

PLAINVIEW, WABASHA CO., ST. JOACHIM'S (1858) [CEM] Rev. Thien Van Nguyen.
Res.: 900 W. Broadway, 55964-1039. Tel: 507-534-3321; Fax: 507-534-3687. Email: stjoachimchurch@hotmail.com.
Catechesis/Religious Program—Tel: 507-534-2887. Students 350.

PRESTON, FILLMORE CO., ST. COLUMBAN (1869) [CEM 2] [JC] Attended by St. Mary's, Chatfield. Rev. Russell G. Scepaniak.
Mailing Address: *Tri-Parish*, 405 Bench St. N.W., Chatfield, 55923.
Church: 408 N.W. Preston St., 55965. Tel: 507-765-3886; Fax: 507-765-9886. Email: singwjoy@acegroup.com.
Catechesis/Religious Program—Students 47.

ROCHESTER, OLMSTED CO.

1—ST. BRIDGET'S (1857) [CEM] Attended by St. Bernard, Stewartville. Rev. Matthew J. Fasnacht, Parochial Admin.
116 4th Ave., S.E., Stewartville, 55976. Tel: 507-533-8257; Fax: 507-533-1053. Email: stbernard116@aol.com. Web: www.stbernardsparish.org.
Catechesis/Religious Program—Students 49.

2—ST. FRANCIS OF ASSISI (1937) [JC] Very Rev. Timothy T. Reker; Rev. William Thompson, Parochial Vicar; Deacons Richard Mangen; David Plevak.
Res.: 1114 3rd St., S.E., 55904-7293. Tel: 507-288-7313; Fax: 507-281-5997. Email: francis@stfrancis-church.org. Web: www.stfrancis-church.org.
See St. Francis of Assisi School, Rochester under Centralized Catholic Schools located in the Institution section.
Catechesis/Religious Program—Tel: 507-289-2427. Students 147.

3—HOLY SPIRIT (1990) [JC] Rev. Donald J. Schmitz; Deacons Richard Quinn; Joseph Weigel; Mary Margaret Yaeger, Pastoral Assoc.
Office: 5455 50th Ave., N.W., 55901. Tel: 507-280-0638; 507-281-8323 (Res.); Fax: 507-292-9547. Email: hspirit@holyspiritrochester.org.
See Holy Spirit School, Rochester under Centralized Catholic Schools located in the Institution section.
Catechesis/Religious Program—Students 123.

4—ST. JOHN THE EVANGELIST (1863) [JC] Rev. Msgr. Gerald A. Mahon; Deacons Gerald Freetly; John DeStazio. In Res., Rev. John Lugala Lasuba.
Res.: 11 4th Ave., S.W., 55902-3098. Tel: 507-288-7372; Fax: 507-288-7373. Email: stjohn@sj.org. Web: www.sj.org.
See St. John School, Rochester under Centralized Catholic Schools located in the Institution section.
Catechesis/Religious Program—Students 256.

5—PAX CHRISTI (1973) [JC] Revs. Joseph L. Keefe; Caesar Dralega; Deacon Christopher Orlowski.
Res.: 4135 18th Ave., N.W., 55901-0460. Tel: 507-282-8542; Fax: 507-289-8741. Email: paxchristichurch@charter.net. Web: www.paxchristichurch.org.
School—Tel: 507-280-0349; Fax: 507-289-4008. See listings under Centralized Catholic Schools.
Catechesis/Religious Program—Students 262.

6—ST. PIUS X (1954) [JC] Revs. Charlie I. Collins; Paul E. Nelson.
Res.: 4833 Salley Ln., NW, 55901.
Church: 1315 12th Ave., N.W., 55901-1744. Tel: 507-288-8238; Fax: 507-286-8769. Email: church@piusx.org. Web: www.piusx.org.
See St. Pius X School, Rochester under Centralized Catholic Schools located in the Institution section.
Catechesis/Religious Program—Tel: 507-289-6317; Fax: 507-286-8769. Students 113.

7—RESURRECTION (1967) [JC] Revs. Thomas A. Loomis; Matthew J. Fasnacht, Parochial Vicar; Deacon Thomas DeRienzo.
Res.: 1600-11th Ave., S.E., 55904-5499. Tel: 507-288-5528; Fax: 507-252-0763. Email: office@resurrection-catholic.org. Web: www.resurrection-catholic.org.
School— See listings under Centralized Catholic Schools.
Catechesis/Religious Program—Students 210.

ROLLINGSTONE, WINONA CO., HOLY TRINITY (1862) [CEM] Rev. Donald J. Lovas.
Res.: 83 Main St., 55969-9759. Tel: 507-689-2351; Fax: 507-689-2251. Email: holymary@charter.net.
Catechesis/Religious Program—Students 60.

ROSE CREEK, MOWER CO., ST. PETER'S (1885) [CEM] Attended by Sacred Heart, Adams. Rev. James J. Seitz.
Mailing Address: 412 Main St., P.O. Box 352, Adams, 55909. Tel: 507-582-3321.
Church: 302 Maple St., S.W., 55970-9701. Tel: 507-433-1532.
Catechesis/Religious Program—Tel: 507-433-6472. Students 67.

RUSHFORD, FILLMORE CO., ST. JOSEPH'S (1868) [CEM] Rev. Joseph P. Pete.
Res.: 101 Rushford Ave. W., P.O. Box 577, 55971-0577. Tel: 507-864-2257. Email: jpete@acegroup.cc. Web: home.catholicweb.com/stspetermaryjoseph/index.cfm.
Catechesis/Religious Program—Students 70.

ST. CHARLES, WINONA CO., ST. CHARLES BORROMEO (1867) [CEM] Rev. James F. Callahan; Deacon Placido Zavala.
Church: 1900 E. 6th St., 55972-1426.
Catechesis/Religious Program—Students 275.

ST. CLAIR, BLUE EARTH CO., IMMACULATE CONCEPTION (1874) [CEM] Attended by All Saints Church, 600 3rd St., P.O. Box 217, Madison Lake 56063-0217. Rev. Robert J. Schneider.
Tel: 507-243-3319. Email: icoffice@hickorytech.net. Web: www.as-ic.org.
Catechesis/Religious Program—Students 141.

ST. JAMES, WATONWAN CO., ST. JAMES (1876) [CEM] Attended by St. Mary Church, 212 First St., N.E., Madelia, MN, 56062. Revs. Thomas E. Cook; Luis Vargas, (Hispanic Ministry).
Church: 707 4th St. S., 56081-1808. Tel: 507-375-3542; Fax: 507-375-4170.
Catechesis/Religious Program—Nonnie Hanson, D.R.E. Students 181.

ST. KILIAN, NOBLES CO., ST. KILIAN (1903) [CEM] Attended by St. Anthony, Lismore. Roxanne Kemper, Parish Dir.; Rev. Timothy J. Hall, Priest Moderator.
Mailing Address: 310 Third Ave. S., P.O. Box 158, Lismore, 56155-0158. Tel: 507-472-8262; Fax: 507-472-8454. Email: santhony@myclearwave.net. Web: frontiernet.net/~stadrian.
Catechesis/Religious Program—Students 23.

SHERBURN, MARTIN CO., ST. LUKE'S (1888) [CEM] Attended by Good Shepherd, Jackson. Rev. Peter L. Schuster.
Res.: 311 N. Sverdrup Ave., P.O. Box 65, Jackson, 56143-1329. Tel: 507-764-7831; Fax: 507-847-3734. Email: goodshep@msn.com.
Catechesis/Religious Program—Tel: 507-764-7831; Fax: 507-764-7831. Students 60.

SLAYTON, MURRAY CO., ST. ANN'S (1897) [CEM] Rev. Patrick O. Arens.
Res.: 2747 29th St., 56172-1485. Tel: 507-836-8030; Fax: 507-836-6261.
Catechesis/Religious Program—Email: triparish@frontiernet.net. Students 123.

SPRING VALLEY, FILLMORE CO., ST. IGNATIUS (1878) [CEM] Rev. Steven J. Peterson.
Res.: 213 W. Franklin St., 55975-1312. Tel: 507-346-7565; Fax: 507-346-7725.
Catechesis/Religious Program—Tel: 507-346-7194. Students 103.

STEWARTVILLE, OLMSTED CO., ST. BERNARD'S (1894) [CEM] Rev. Matthew J. Fasnacht, Parochial Admin.
Res.: 116 Fourth Ave., S.E., 55976. Tel: 507-533-8257; Fax: 507-533-1053. Email: stbernard116@aol.com. Web: www.stbernardsparish.org.
Catechesis/Religious Program—Tel: 507-533-8192. Students 208.

THEILMAN, WABASHA CO., ST. JOSEPH'S (1903) [CEM] Closed. For inquiries for sacramental records, contact St. Mary of the Lake, Lake City.

TRIMONT, MARTIN CO., ST. JOSEPH, Closed. For inquiries for parish records contact the chancery.

TRUMAN, MARTIN CO., ST. KATHERINE (1954) Attended by St. Mary, Madelia. Rev. Thomas E. Cook.
212 First St., N.E., Madelia, 56062-1702. Tel: 507-642-8305; Fax: 507-642-8310.
Church: 518 E. 2nd St. S., 56088.
Catechesis/Religious Program—

TWIN LAKES, FREEBORN CO., ST. JAMES (1876) Attended by St. Theodore, Albert Lea. Rev. James C. Berning; Deacon Michael Ellis.
Mailing Address: 308 E. Fountain St., Albert Lea, 56007. Tel: 507-373-0603; Fax: 507-373-0604.
Church: 106 W. Main St., 56089.
Catechesis/Religious Program—Email: dlm@sttheo.org. Students 13.

VERNON CENTER, BLUE EARTH CO., ST. MATTHEW (1911) [CEM] Attended by St. Teresa, Mapleton. Rev. Brian F. Sutton, Parochial Admin.
104 Silver St., W., P.O. Box 305, Mapleton, 56065-0305. Tel: 507-524-3127; Fax: 507-524-4423.
Catechesis/Religious Program—Students 34.

WABASHA, WABASHA CO., ST. FELIX (1858) [CEM] Rev. Glenn K. Frerichs; Deacon John Hust.
Res.: 117 W. Third St., 55981-1201. Tel: 651-565-3931; Fax: 651-565-4363. Email: stfelix@hbci.com. Web: www.stfelixschool.org/st_felix_parish.htm.
School—(Grades PreK-6), 130 Third St. E., 55981. Tel: 651-565-4446; Fax: 651-565-0244. Email: mainoffice@stfelixschool.org. Web: stfelixschool.org. Marsha Stenzel, Prin. Lay Teachers 10; Students 62.
Catechesis/Religious Program—Tel: 651-565-3718. Email: stfelixgrowthinfaith@yahoo.com. Students 105.
Convent—36 Bailey Ave., 55981. Tel: 651-565-4578.

WALDORF, WASECA CO., ST. JOSEPH'S (1878) [CEM] Attended by St. Ann, Janesville, 307 W. 2nd St., P.O. Box 218, Janesville, MN 56048-0218. Rev. Peter J. Klein.
Catechesis/Religious Program—Students 34.

WASECA, WASECA CO., SACRED HEART (1869) [JC 2] Revs. Martin T. Schaefer; James Von Tobel, S.J.
Res.: 111 Fourth St., N.W., 56093-2413. Tel: 507-835-1222; Fax: 507-833-1498. Email: sheart@hickorytech.net. Web: www.sacredheartwaseca.org.
School—(Grades PreK-4), 308 W. Elm Ave., 56093. Tel: 507-835-2780. Email: shschool@hickorytech.net. LeAnn Dahle, Prin. Priests 1; Lay Teachers 9; Students 155.
Sacred Heart Children's House—(Grades PreSchool), 400 Second Ave., N.W., 56093. Tel: 507-835-1044. Pauline Holman, Dir. Students 84.
Catechesis/Religious Program—Tel: 507-835-1500. Students 475.

WELLS, FARIBAULT CO., ST. CASIMIR'S (1880) [CEM] Rev. Mark C. McNea; Deacon Eugene Paul.
Res.: 320 Second Ave., S.W., 56097-1399. Tel: 507-553-5391; Fax: 507-553-5391. Email: scasimir@bevcomm.net.
School—(Grades K-8), 330 Second Ave., S.W., 56097. Tel: 507-553-5822. Email: casimir@bevcomm.net. Joanne Tibodeau, Prin. Lay Teachers 8; Students 87.
Catechesis/Religious Program—Students 114.

WEST ALBANY, WABASHA CO., ST. PATRICK OF WEST ALBANY (1865) [CEM] Attended by St. Mary of the Lake, Lake City. Rev. Richard J. Dernek.
419 W. Lyon Ave., P.O. Box 224, Lake City, 55041. Tel: 651-345-4134. Email: fatherdernek@embarqmail.com.
Catechesis/Religious Program—Tel: 507-753-2424; Fax: 507-843-3900. Students 51.

WEST CONCORD, DODGE CO., ST. VINCENT DE PAUL (1945) [CEM] Attended by St. John Baptist de La Salle, Dodge Center. Rev. Kurt Farrell.
20 Second St., N.E., P.O. Box 310, Dodge Center, 55927-0310. Tel: 507-374-6830. Email: tritonparishes@frontiernet.net.
Church: 310 Clyde St., 55985.
Catechesis/Religious Program—P.O. Box 117, 55985. Tel: 507-527-2384; Fax: 612-605-4315. Students 56.

WESTBROOK, COTTONWOOD CO.
1—ST. ANTHONY'S (1909) [CEM], Attended by St. Gabriel, Fulda. Rev. Jeffrey L. Dobbs, Parochial Admin.
307 Lake Ave., Fulda, 56131. Tel: 507-274-5946. Email: anthonys@centurytel.net.
Church: 1153 1st Ave., P.O. Box 278, 56183.
Catechesis/Religious Program—Students 38.

WILMONT, NOBLES CO., OUR LADY OF GOOD COUNSEL (1903) [CEM] Attended by St. Adrian, Adrian. Rev. Timothy J. Hall.
512 Main Ave., P.O. Box 475, Adrian, 56110-0475. Tel: 507-483-2317; Fax: 507-483-2460. Email: stadrian@frontiernet.net. Web: www.frontiernet.net/~stadrian.
Catechesis/Religious Program—Tel: 507-926-5305. Email: faithform4@frontiernet.net. Students 69.

WILSON, WINONA CO., IMMACULATE CONCEPTION (1874) Attended by St. Rose of Lima, Lewiston. Rev. Marreddy Pothireddy.
180 S. Fremont St., Lewiston, 55952-0727. Tel: 507-523-2428; Fax: 507-523-2645. Email: dowstrose@embarqmail.com.
Catechesis/Religious Program—Students 41.

WINDOM, COTTONWOOD CO., ST. FRANCIS XAVIER'S (1898) Rev. James Von Tobel, S.J.
Res.: 548 17th St., P.O. Box 39, 56101-1217. Tel: 507-831-3300; Fax: 507-831-3300.
Catechesis/Religious Program—532 17th St., 56101. Tel: 507-831-1985. Email: stfxavier@msn.com. Students 140.

WINNEBAGO, FARIBAULT CO., ST. MARY'S (1893) [CEM] Attended by Ss. Peter and Paul, Blue Earth. Rev. Leo Charles Koppala, Parochial Admin.
Mailing Address: 214 S. Holland, Blue Earth, 56013.
Church: 32 1st St., N.E., 56098-0308. Tel: 507-526-5626; Fax: 507-526-2456. Email: markmcnea@juno.com.
Catechesis/Religious Program—Students 25.

WOODSTOCK, PIPESTONE CO., ST. MARTIN'S (1882) [CEM] Attended by St. Leo, Pipestone. Very Rev. Gerald C. Kosse.
Mailing Address: 415 Hiawatha Ave. S., P.O. Box 36, Pipestone, 56164. Tel: 507-825-3152; Fax: 507-825-4492. Email: om@triparishmn.org.
Rectory—121 Smith St. N., 56186.
Church: 101 Smith St. N., 56186. Tel: 507-777-4160.
Catechesis/Religious Program—Students 26.

WORTHINGTON, NOBLES CO., ST. MARY'S (1886) [CEM] Rev. Hilary R. Brixius; Deacon Vernon Behrends.
Res.: 1215 Seventh Ave., 56187-2297. Tel: 507-376-6005; Fax: 507-376-9167. Email: hbrixius@yahoo.com.
School—(Grades K-6), Twelfth St. & Eighth Ave., 56187. Tel: 507-376-5236; Fax: 507-376-6159. Barbara Daly, Prin. Lay Teachers 11; Students 106.
Catechesis/Religious Program—Tel: 507-372-2090. Students 289.
Convent—1221 Seventh Ave., 56187. Tel: 507-376-4035.

WYKOFF, FILLMORE CO., ST. KILIAN'S (1887) Closed. For inquiries for parish records contact the chancery.

Chaplains of Public Institutions

WINONA. *Winona County Law Enforcement Center*, 466 Chestnut St., 55987. Tel: 507-452-4723. Deacon Justin Green, Chap.

ROCHESTER. *Federal Medical Center, Bureau of Prisons*, 2110 Center St. E., 55904. Sr. Emile Bormann, P.B.V.M., Chap.

WASECA. *Federal Correctional Institution*. Vacant.

On Special or Other Diocesan Assignment:
Revs.—
Buryska, James F., Chap., Rochester Methodist Hospital, 201 W. Center St., Rochester, 55902. Tel: 507-255-5551
Byrne, David, Chap., Church of the Resurrection, 1600 S.E. 11th Ave., Rochester, 55904. Tel: 507-255-4074 Mayo Clinic Hospitals
Chacko, Joseph P., Chap., Saint Mary's Hospital, 1216 2nd St., S.W., Rochester, 55902. Tel: 507-255-9025
Kunz, James H., Chap., Mayo Medical Center, 1216 2nd St., S.W., Rochester, 55902. Tel: 507-255-5780
Marek, Dean V., Chap., Mayo Medical Center, 1216 2nd St., S.W., Rochester, 55902. Tel: 507-266-7283

On Duty Outside the Diocese:
Revs.—
Brandenhoff, Peter B., 8859 Spring Ln., Woodbury, 55125. Tel: 651-578-0957
Klein, Eugene M., U.S. Medical Center for Federal Prisoners, 1900 W. Sunshine St., Springfield, MO 65807. Tel: 417-227-0264

Absent on Leave:
Revs.—
Cashman, Joseph C.
Cronin, Michael J., J.C.L., Diocese of Winona, 55 W. Sanborn St., P.O. Box 588, 55987.
Hodapp, Timothy L., 224 Lexington Pkwy. S., St. Paul, 55105. Tel: 651-848-0805
Murray, Daniel L.
Taylor, Robert H., Diocese of Winona, P.O. Box 588, 55987.

Additional Diocesan Assignments:
Very Rev.—
Beerman, Andrew J., S.T.L., Immaculate Heart of Mary Seminary, 700 Terrace Heights, #43., 55987. Tel: 507-457-7371
Revs.—
Dittmer, Antonio, Immaculate Heart of Mary Seminary, 700 Terrace Heights, #43, 55987. Tel: 507-457-7373
Dralega, Caesar, Pax Christi, 4135 18th Ave., N.W., Rochester, 55901. Tel: 507-282-8542
Fabian, Andrew C., O.P., Saint Mary's University of Minnesota, 700 Terrace Hts., 55987. Tel: 507-457-1539
Nienaber, Paul J., S.J., St. Mary's University of Minnesota, 700 Terrace Hts., #32, 55987. Tel: 507-457-1532

Retired:
Rev. Msgrs.—
Egan, Eugene E., 401 N. Maple St., Ellsworth, 56129.
Evers, Paul C., 12106 Grant Blvd. W., Wabasha, 55981.
Galles, Francis A., 500 Preston St., N.W., Preston, 55965. Tel: 507-765-2756
Grubisch, Donald W., 14035 658th St., Wabasha, 55981. Tel: 651-565-4625
Habiger, James D., Univ. of St. Thomas, 2115 Summit Ave., Box 4174, St. Paul, 55105. Tel: 651-962-8065 (Res); 651-227-8777
Literski, Roy E., 1328 D. McNally Dr., 55987. Tel: 507-452-7685
Mountain, Joseph W., 4001 N.W. 19th Ave., Apt. 804, Rochester, 55901.
Revs.—
Arnoldt, David L., 118 Central Park Ln., Evans, GA 30809. Tel: 706-650-9222
Breza, Paul J., 102 Liberty St., 55987. Tel: 507-643-0441
Brown, Sylvester F., 302 N.W. 4th St., P.O. Box 232, Elysian, 56028. Tel: 507-267-4876
Connelly, Donald F., 1200 W. Grant Blvd., Apt. 105, Wabasha, 55981-1098. Tel: 651-565-4531
Conway, Gerald W., 14208 N. Newcastle Dr., Sun City, AZ 85351. Tel: 623-505-7106
Dandelet, James D., P.O. Box 46, Easton, 56025-0046. Tel: 507-787-2520
Eikens, Leroy F., 1200 5th Grant Blvd. W., Apt. 103, Wabasha, 55981. Tel: 651-560-4313
Engels, Richard J., 205 Dugan St., Wabasha, 55981. Tel: 651-565-3432
Ernster, Milo L., 64540 140th Ave., Wabasha, 55981. Tel: 651-565-2191
Ginther, Lawrence P., 5125 W. Seventh St., Apt. 8, 55987-5616. Tel: 507-454-4789
Gits, Douglas J., 1420 4th St. S.E., Rochester, 55904-4716. Tel: 507-286-7874
Haberman, Clayton J., 5371 Elkton Tr., Faribault, 55021-8453. Tel: 507-334-0610
Halloran, Paul F., 7646 Sixth Lake Rd., N.W., Akeley, 56433-9507.
Hennessy, James W., S1629 Lisowski Rd., Alma, WI 54610. Tel: 608-685-4095
Herman, Robert D., 205 N.W. 2nd Ave., P.O. Box 120, Medford, 55049. Tel: 507-451-6353
Jewison, Harry P., 1024 Ninth St., N.E., Rochester, 55906. Tel: 507-285-5515
Kellen, Elmer W., 12104 W. Grant Blvd., Wabasha, 55981. Tel: 651-565-5513
Kerrigan, Bernard A., St. Elizabeth Health Care Center, 626 Shields Ave., Wabasha, 55981.
Kulas, Robert A., 7510 Cahill Rd., #201B, Edina, 55439. Tel: 952-946-8972
Kunz, Francis P., 240 Hudson Ave. E., Mankato, 56001. Tel: 507-625-6217
LaPlante, Joseph A., 67643 154th Ave, Wabasha, 55981. Tel: 651-565-2441
Leary, Donald G., 220 S. Broadway, #1504, Rochester, 55902. Tel: 507-288-5813
Loomis, Richard P., St. Edward Church, 2000 Oakland Ave. W., Austin, 55912. Tel: 507-433-1841
Maher, Robert G., 9505 Salem Hills Court, Las Vegas, NV 89134-4600. Tel: 702-804-2718
McCauley, James A., P.O. Box 203, Brownsville, 55919. Tel: 507-482-6631
Meyer, Robert G., 1312 N. 7th St., Apt. 134, Lake City, 55041. Tel: 651-345-4022
Mountain, Edward C., 420 11th St., S.E., Owatonna, 55060-4008. Tel: 507-451-6752
Olsem, Andrew D., 610 Reed St., Mankato, 56001.
Ozbun, John W., Diocese of Winona, 55 W. Sanborn St., P.O. Box 588, 55987.
Quinn, Charles J., 405 S. Lake St., Sherburn, 56171. Tel: 507-764-4069
Russell, James D., 202 B Alpine Ridge, Wabasha, 55981. Tel: 651-565-3632
Schaefer, Edgar J., 9659 111th Ave. N, Sun City, AZ 85351. Tel: 623-875-9749
Schiltz, Roger J., 1532 Glenrosa Dr., North Las Vegas, NV 89031-5548.
Smith, Leland J., 468 Center St., 55987. Tel: 507-454-8464
Speck, James A., 528 Maceman St., Apt. 108, 55987-2479. Tel: 507-454-2129
Spinler, Ruben C., 302 Maple St. S.W., Rose Creek, 55970. Tel: 507-433-1532
Stamschror, Robert P., 2480 Goodview Rd., 55987. Tel: 507-452-4202
Stenzel, Eugene F.
Traufler, John F., 200 18th St. N.W., Austin, 55912. Tel: 507-434-7702
Trocinski, LaVern F., 4513 Ruby Ln., N.W., Rochester, 55901. Tel: 507-536-0747
Verdick, Jerome F., 210 E. Paddock, P.O. Box 87, Alpha, 56111-0087. Tel: 507-847-2939
Zenk, Donald W., 602 31st St., N.W., Austin, 55912. Tel: 507-437-3579

Permanent Deacons:
Aho, Richard, St. Edward, Austin; St. Augustine Austin
Behrends, Vernon, St. Mary, Worthington
Blake, David, Queen of Angels, Austin; Our Lady of Loretto, Brownsdale
Bonnarens, Edwin C., St. John Vianney, Fairmont; Holy Family, East Chain
DeRienzo, Thomas, Resurrection, Rochester
DeStazio, John, St. John the Evangelist, Rochester
Dose, David, St. Mary, Lake City; St. Patrick, West Albany
Doyle, Preston, St. Joseph, Mankato; Holy Family, Lake Crystal
Ellis, Michael, St. Theodore, Albert Lea; St. James, Twin Lakes
Fagan, Patrick, St. Joseph, Owatonna
Fortini, Eduardo, Cathedral of the Sacred Heart, Winona; St. Casimir, Winona
Freetly, Gerald, St. John the Evangelist, Rochester
Fuller, Leonard L., Diocese of Winona
Green, Justin, St. Stanislaus, Winona; St. John Nepomucene, Winona
Hust, John, St. Felix, Wabasha; St. Agnes, Kellogg
Kluczny, John, St. Edward, Austin; St. Augustine, Austin
Kunkel, Jerrold, St. Thomas More Newman Center, Mankato
Mangen, Richard, St. Francis of Assisi, Rochester.
McMillan, Adam, St. Philip, Litchfield, MN
Orlowski, Christopher, Pax Christi, Rochester; Ss. Peter & Paul, Mazeppa
Paul, Eugene, St. Casimir, Wells; Our Lady of Mt. Carmel, Easton; St. John the Baptist, Minnesota Lake
Plevak, David, St. Francis of Assisi, Rochester
Quinn, Richard, Holy Spirit, Rochester
Trocinski, Gerald, Crucifixion, LaCrescent; Holy Cross, Dakota
Vogel, Andrew, Sacred Heart Major Seminary, Detroit, MI
Walchuk, Christopher, Ss. Peter & Paul, Mankato
Weigel, Joseph, Holy Spirit, Rochester
Welch, James, Cathedral of the Sacred Heart, Winona; St. Casimir, Winona
Yerhot, Robert, Crucifixion, LaCrescent; Holy Crescent, Holy Cross, Dakota
Zavala, Placido, St. Charles Borromeo, St. Charles; St. Aloysius, Elba; Holy Redemer, Eyota

INSTITUTIONS LOCATED IN THE DIOCESE

[A] SEMINARIES, DIOCESAN

WINONA. *Immaculate Heart of Mary Seminary*, 700 Terrace Hts. #43, 55987-1399. Tel: 507-457-7373; Fax: 507-457-8601. Email: ihms@smumn.edu. Web: www.ihmseminary.org. Very Revs. Andrew J. Beerman, S.T.L., Rector; R. Paul Heiting, J.C.L., Dean of Formation; Revs. Jon H. Moore, Spiritual Dir.; Antonio Dittmer, Spiritual Life Dir.; Thomas P. Melvin, Extern Spiritual Dir.; Rev. Msgr. Donald P. Schmitz, M.Ch.A., Extern Spiritual Dir.; Revs. Martin T. Schaefer, Extern Spiritual Dir.; Glenn K. Frerichs, Extern Spiritual Dir.; David Wechter, O.C.S.O., J.C.L., Extern Spiritual Dir.; Ellen Speltz, Dir. Devel. Affiliated with Saint Mary's University of MN. Priests 4; Lay Staff 6; Students 59.

[B] COLLEGES AND UNIVERSITIES

WINONA. *Saint Mary's University of Minnesota* (Coed), 700 Terrace Hts., 55987-1399. Tel: 507-457-1600; Fax: 507-457-1722. Email: admissions@smumn.edu. Web: www.smumn.edu. Bros. William Mann, F.S.C., D.Min., Pres.; Louis De Thomasis, F.S.C., Chancellor; Sr. Judith Schaefer, O.P., Ph.D., University Dean for Univ. Affairs; Mr. Anthony Piscitiello, Vice Pres. Admissions & Financial Aid; Cynthia Marek, Vice Pres. Fin. Affairs; Ann Merchlewitz, Exec, Vice Pres. & Gen. Counsel; James Bedtke, Vice Pres. Schools of Graduate & Professional Programs & the College; Dr. Thomas Mans, Vice Pres. Academic Affairs; Robert Conover, Vice Pres. Communications & Mktg.; Linka Holey, Assoc. Vice Pres. Graduate & Professional Programs, Academic Dean; Chris Kendall, Vice Pres. Student Devel.; Rachel Thomas, Librarian. DeLaSalle Christian Brothers. Priests 5; Brothers 7; Sisters 4; Lay Faculty 96; Students 1,404.

[C] CENTRALIZED CATHOLIC SCHOOLS

WINONA. *Cotter High School & Junior High School*, (Grades 7-12), 1115 W. Broadway, 55987. Tel: 507-453-5002; Fax: 507-453-5006. Email: sblank@cotterschools.org; dforney@cotterschools.org. Web: www.cotterschools.org. Sandra Blank, Prin.; Dave Forney, Dir. Cotter Junior High School; Marisa Corcoran, Campus Min.; Patrick Bowlin, Activities Dir.; John Broadwater, CFO; Will Gibson, Admissions Dir.; Megan Sadowski, Devel. Dir. Tel: 507-453-5102; David Williams, Librarian. Lay Teachers 36; Students 399.

Winona Area Catholic Schools, 602 E. 5th St., 55987. Tel: 507-452-3766; Fax: 507-452-5497. Email: dlueck@wacsl.org. Web: www.wacsl.org. Dawn Waller Lueck, Prin. Lay Teachers 31.

St. Mary's Primary School (Grades PreK-K), 1315 W. Broadway, 55987. Tel: 507-452-2890; Fax: 507-452-2898. Email: dlueck@wacsl.org. Dawn Waller Lueck, Prin.; Christine Nichols, Prog. Dir. Students 175.

St. Stanislaus Elementary School (Grades 1-6), 602 E. Fifth St., 55987. Tel: 507-452-3766; Fax: 507-452-5497. Email: dlueck@wacsl.org. Dawn Waller Lueck, Prin. Students 285.

Winona Area Catholic Schools Foundation (Grades PreK-12), 1115 W. Broadway, 55987. Tel: 507-453-5102; Fax: 507-453-5013. Sara Brandon, Pres.

ALBERT LEA. *St. Theodore School*, (Grades K-6), 323 E. Clark St., 56007. Tel: 507-373-9657; Fax: 507-373-9657. Email: jfc@sttheo.org. Web: www.sttheo.org. Rev. James C. Berning, Admin.; Deacon Michael Ellis, Admin.; Jean Calderon, Admin. Lay Teachers 6; Students 100.

AUSTIN. *Austin Catholic Elementary School*, (Grades PreK-6), 511 N.W. Fourth Ave., 55912. Tel: 507-433-8859; Fax: 507-433-6630. Web: www.austincatholic.org. Lay Teachers 15; Students 218.

Pacelli High School (Grades 7-12), 311 Fourth St., N.W., 55912. Tel: 507-437-3278; Fax: 507-433-5693. Web: www.austincatholic.org. Alice Duffy-Meyer, Campus Min.; Mary P. Holtorf, Dir. Schools. Lay Teachers 9; Students 124.

United Catholic Schools Foundation of Austin, MN, Inc., 511 N.W. Fourth Ave., 55912. Tel: 507-433-6630; Fax: 507-433-6630.

MANKATO. *Loyola Catholic Schools*, (Grades PreK-12), 145 Good Counsel Dr., 56001-3146. Tel: 507-388-2997; Fax: 507-388-3081. Email: bblaisdell@macsmn.com. Web: loyolacatholicschool.org. Bette Blaisdell, Pres.; Sr. Mary Beth Schraml, S.S.N.D., Prin.; William Schumacher, Prin.; Ruth Corcoran, Librarian; Diane Jewison, Librarian. Priests 1; Sisters 1; Lay Teachers 60; Total Enrollment 650.

OWATONNA. *St. Mary's School*, (Grades PreK-8), 730 South Cedar Ave., 55060. Tel: 507-446-2300; Fax: 507-446-2304. Web: www.stmarys-owatonna.org. Mrs. Mary Hawkins, Prin.; Sharleen Berg, Media Specialist. Lay Teachers 24; Students 385.

ROCHESTER. *Rochester Catholic Schools*, (Grades N-12), 1710 Industrial Dr., 55902. Tel: 507-280-0349; Fax: 507-292-9682. Web: rochestercatholic.K12.mn.us. Mr. Dennis L. Nigon, Pres.

St. Francis of Assisi School (Grades PreK-8), 318 11th Ave., S.E., 55904. Tel: 507-288-4816; Fax: 507-288-4815. Email: bplenge@rochestercatholic.k12.mn.us. Mrs. Barb Plenge, Prin. Priests 2; Lay Teachers 30; Students 520.

St. John School (Grades 5-8), 424 W. Center St., 55902. Tel: 507-282-5248; Fax: 507-282-1343. Email: dvalentine@rochestercatholic.k12.mn.us. Mr. Don Valentine, Prin. Priests 2; Lay Teachers 16; Students 202.

St. Pius X School (Grades PreK-4), 1205 12th Ave., 55901. Tel: 507-282-5161; Fax: 507-282-5107. Email: dvalentine@rochestercatholic.k12.mn.us. Mr. Don Valentine, Prin. Priests 2; Lay Teachers 19; Students 266.

Lourdes High School of Rochester, Inc., 621 W. Center St., 55902. Tel: 507-289-3991; Fax: 507-289-4008. Email: tdonlon@rochestercatholic.k12.mn.us. Mr. Thomas Donlon, Prin.; Rita Hendrickson, Campus Min.; Rev. William Thompson, Instructor. Priests 1; Lay Teachers 37; Students 442.

Holy Spirit School (Grades PreK-8), 5455 50th Ave., N.W., 55901. Tel: 507-288-8818; Fax: 507-288-5155. Email: mklebe@rochestercatholic.k12.mn.us. Mr. Matthew Klebe, Prin. Priests 1; Lay Teachers 27; Students 348.

[D] GENERAL HOSPITALS

ROCHESTER. *Catholic Medical Association*, 200 First St., S.W., 55905. Tel: 507-266-3412; Fax: 507-266-1657. Email: lane.john@mayo.edu. Dr. John I. Lane, M.D.

**Saint Mary Hospital* 55902-1970. Tel: 507-255-5123; Fax: 507-255-3125. B. Lynn Frederick, Admin.; Revs. James H. Kunz. Tel: 507-255-4743; James F. Buryska. Tel: 507-255-5551; Dean V. Marek. Tel: 507-266-7283; William D. Byrne. Tel: 507-255-5123; Joseph P. Chacko. Tel: 507-255-9025; John Evans. Tel: 507-255-5780. Sisters of the Third Order Regular of St. Francis of the Congregation of Our Lady of Lourdes 21; Bed Capacity 1,157; Patients Assisted Annually 60,700.

WABASHA. *Saint Elizabeth's Medical Center*, 1200 Grant Blvd., W., 55981. Tel: 651-565-4531; Fax: 651-565-2482. Email: carmen.tiffany@ministryhealth.org. Web: www.StElizabethsWabasha.org. Mr Thomas Crowley, Pres.; Rev. Elmer W. Kellen (Retired). Corporate Sponsor: Ministry Health Care, Inc. (Milwaukee, WI); Sponsored by Sisters of the Sorrowful Mother. Sisters of the Third Order of St. Francis of the Sorrowful Mother 2; Bed Capacity 25; Patients Assisted Annually 25,850; Total Staff 170.

[E] SPECIAL HOSPITALS AND REHABILITATION FACILITIES

ROCHESTER. *Guest House*, 4800 48th St., N.E., P.O. Box 954, 55903. Tel: 800-634-4155; Fax: 507-288-1240. William C. Morgan, Dir. Residential treatment center for priests, brothers, deacons and seminarians. Bed Capacity 37; Total Assisted 100.

[F] HOMES FOR AGED

WINONA. *Saint Anne of Winona*, 1347 W. Broadway, 55987. Tel: 507-454-3621; Fax: 507-452-2556. Rand Gettler, CEO & Admin. Subsidiary of Benedictine Health Systems, sponsored by the Sisters of St. Scholastica Monastery.

St. Anne of Winona Callista Court, 1455 W. Broadway, 55987. Tel: 507-457-0280; Fax: 507-494-5117. Subsidiary of Benedictine Health Systems, sponsored by the Sisters of St. Scholastica Monastery., Assisted living for seniors. Units 75; Residents 80; Total Staff 45; Resident Days 29,000.

St. Anne of Winona Benedictine Adult Day Center, 1455 W. Broadway, 55987. Email: tammy.ross@bhshealth.org. Tammy Ross, Dir. Guest Days 11,600.

St. Anne of Winona Extended Health Care, 1347 W. Broadway, 55987. Tel: 507-454-3621; Fax: 507-452-2556. Email: rand.gettler@bhshealth.org. Rand Gettler, CEO & Admin.; Jo Hassinger, Dir. of Nursing Svcs. Nursing care for the aged, chronically ill or rehab. Bed Capacity 109; Residents 107; Resident Days 39,055; Total Staff 210.

St. Anne of Winona Training Center, 1455 W. Broadway, 55987. Tel: 507-457-3811; Fax: 507-494-5117. Email: rand.gettler@bhshealth.org. Joyce Nelson, Contact Person.

AUSTIN. *Sacred Heart Care Center, Inc.*, 1200 Twelfth St., S.W., 55912. Tel: 507-433-1808; Fax: 507-433-8012. Rebecca Mathews Halverson, Admin.; Rev. Donald W. Zenk, Chap. (Retired). Bed Capacity 59; Residents 59; Assisted Living Apartments (filled) 26; Adult Day Care (Client Days) 3,392; Alzheimer's Day Program (Client Days) 2,943; Home Health Care (Clients) 120; Total Staff 157.

PLAINVIEW. *Benedictine Care Centers, St. Isidore Health Center of Greenwood Prairie*, 800 2nd Ave., N.W., 55964. Tel: 507-534-3191; Fax: 507-534-2778. Email: paula.lewis@bhshealth.org. Paula Lewis, Admin. Benedictine Health System, sponsored by Srs. of St. Scholastica Monastery Total Staff 116; Long Term Care Bed Capacity 63.

Benedictine Care Centers, Green Prairie Place, 810 2nd Ave., N.W., 55964. Tel: 507-534-4204; Fax: 507-534-0139. Email: joann.klavetter@bhshealth.org. Joann Klavetter, Resident Services Mgr.; Paula Lewis, Admin. Benedictine Health System, sponsored by Srs. of St. Scholastica Monastery Total Assisted 10; Total Staff 15; Independent Apts. 26.

ROCHESTER. *Madonna Meadows of Rochester*, 3035 Salem Meadows Dr., S.W., 55902. Tel: 507-252-5400. Email: mark.cairns@bhshealth.org. Mark Cairns, Admin. & Corp. Exec. Officer. Benedictine Health System and Sisters of St. Scholastica Monastery., Assisted living facility. Bed Capacity 78; Guests 70; Total Staff 72.

Madonna Towers of Rochester, Inc., 4001 19th Ave., N.W., 55901. Tel: 507-288-3911; Fax: 507-288-0393. Email: mark.cairns@bhshealth.org. Mark Cairns, Admin. & Corp. Exec. Officer. Independent, assisted and nursing care facility; T. Emil Gauthier Memory Care. Subsidiary of Benedictine Health System. Bed Capacity 62; Total Staff 210; Apartments 107.

Chapel of St. Benedict and Chapel of St. Scholastica Tel: 507-288-3911; Fax: 507-288-0393.

Madonna Living Community Foundation of Rochester, 4001 19th Ave., N.W., 55901. Tel: 507-288-3911; Fax: 507-288-0393.

WABASHA. *St. Elizabeth's Health Care Center*, 626 Shields Ave., 55981. Tel: 651-565-4581; Fax: 651-565-3414. Web: www.ministryhealth.org. Mr Thomas Crowley, Admin.; Rev. Bernard A. Kerrigan (Retired). (Conducted in connection with St. Elizabeth's Medical Center.) Skilled Beds 100; Admissions 86; Total Staff 130; Total Assisted Annually 265.

[G] CONVENTS AND RESIDENCES FOR SISTERS

HOUSTON. *Hermits of St. Mary of Carmel, (H.S.M.C.)* Carmelite Eremitical Community of Diocesan Right, 33005 Stinson Ridge Rd., 55943-4033. Tel: 507-896-2125; Fax: 507-896-4349. Sr. Rosemary Therese Quinn, H.S.M.C., Prioress; Rev. David Wechter, O.C.S.O., J.C.L. Tel: 507-896-2125. Sisters 5.

JACKSON. *Convent of Religious Sisters of Mercy*, 51437 800th St., 56143. Tel: 507-847-5498; Fax: 507-847-5689. Web: www.rsmofalma.org. Sr. Mary Charles Mayer, R.S.M., Local Supr. Sisters 3.

MANKATO. *Provincial House of the School Sisters of Notre Dame*, Convent of Our Lady of Good Counsel, 170 Good Counsel Dr., 56001-3138. Tel: 507-389-4200; Fax: 507-389-4125. Email: mklein@ssndmankato.org. Web: www.ssndmankato.org. Sisters Marjorie Klein, S.S.N.D., Prov. Leader; Julie Brandt, S.S.N.D., Vocation Dir. Religious in Province 319; Sisters in Motherhouse 129; Lay Staff 120.

School Sisters of Notre Dame at Mankato, MN, Inc. Tel: 507-389-4200; Fax: 507-389-4125.

School Sisters of Notre Dame at Mankato, MN, Inc. Charitable Trust Tel: 507-389-4200; Fax: 507-389-4125.

School Sisters of Notre Dame Cooperative Investment Fund Tel: 507-389-4200; Fax: 507-389-4125.

ROCHESTER. *Sisters of St. Francis of the Third Order Regular of the Congregation of Our Lady of Lourdes*, Assisi Heights Admin. Ctr., 1001 14th St., N.W., Ste. 100, 55901-2511. Tel: 507-282-7441; Fax: 507-282-7762. Web: www.rochesterfranciscan.org. Sr. Tierney Trueman, O.S.F., Pres. & Community Min.

Academy of Our Lady of Lourdes Religious in Province 265; Sisters in Motherhouse 120; Lay Staff 98.

[H] RETREAT HOUSES AND CENTERS OF SPIRITUALITY

AUSTIN. *Annunciation Hermitage, Carmelites of St. Joseph*, 1009 Oakland Ave. E., 55912. Tel: 507-437-4015. Rev. Jon H. Moore, Prior. Brothers 3.

JANESVILLE. *Holy Spirit Retreat Center*, 3864 420th Ave., 56048. Tel: 507-234-5712; Fax: 507-234-6188.

Email: retreat@frontiernet.net. Web: www.RochesterFranciscan.org. Sisters Monique Schwirtz, O.S.F., Dir.; JoAnn Haney, O.S.F.; Marita Johnson, O.S.F.; Charlotte Hesby, O.S.F.

[I] NEWMAN CENTERS

WINONA. *St. Thomas Aquinas Newman Center* 475 Huff St., 55987. Tel: 507-452-2781. Email: newman@hbci.com. Web: studentsclubs.winona.edu/cnc. Mr. Thomas Parlin, Dir.; Rev. Thomas P. Melvin, Chap.

MANKATO. *St. Thomas More Newman Center, Minnesota State University* 1331 Warren St., 56001. Tel: 507-387-4154. Email: mccabes@mnsu.edu. Ms. Sydelle McCabe, Dir.; Rev. Timothy E. Biren, Chap.

[J] MISCELLANEOUS LISTINGS

WINONA. *Diocese of Winona Deposit & Loan*, 55 W. Sanborn St., P.O. Box 588, 55987. Tel: 507-454-4643; Fax: 507-454-8106. Email: ldose@dow.org. Web: www.dow.org.

Diocese of Winona Foundation, 55 W. Sanborn St., P.O. Box 588, 55987. Tel: 507-454-4643; Fax: 507-454-8106. Email: lfuller@dow.org. Web: www.dowgift.org. Deacon Leonard L. Fuller, Exec. Dir.

Saint Mary's Press, Christian Brothers Publications, 702 Terrace Hts., 55987. Tel: 800-533-8095; Fax: 800-344-9225. Email: smpress@smp.org. Web: www.smp.org. Bro. Damian Steger, F.S.C., Chm. Corp.; John M. Vitek, Pres. & CEO.

ALBERT LEA. *St. Theodore Catholic School Endowment*, 308 E. Fountain St., 56007-2456. Tel: 507-373-0603; Fax: 507-373-0603. Email: jcb@sttheo.org. Web: www.sttheo.org. Rev. James C. Berning, Contact.

JACKSON. *Sacred Heart Mercy Health Care Center* (Pro Life Clinic, N.F.P. Family Practice), 803 Fourth St., 56143. Tel: 507-847-3571; Fax: 507-847-5664. Email: sacredheartmercl@qwest.net. Sr. Mary Charles Meyer, R.S.M., Admin. Patients Assisted Annually 1,236; Total Staff 6.

MANKATO. *IVE Formation Program*, 512 E. Mulberry St., 56001. Tel: 507-388-2995; Fax: 507-388-7661. Email: mvarela@hickorytech.net. Rev. Mariano O. Varela, Dir.

ROCHESTER. *Poverello Foundation*, St. Mary's Hospital, 1216 S.W. Second St., 55902. Tel: 507-255-5158; Fax: 507-255-3125. Email: hanson.sandra@mayo.edu. Sr. Generose Gervais, O.S.F., Pres.

The Roman Catholic Pontifical Lay Association Memores Domini, 6006 Woodridge Ct., N.E., 55906. Tel: 507-292-0551. Email: smodarelli@sj.org. Web: www.comunioneliberazione.org.

RELIGIOUS INSTITUTES OF MEN REPRESENTED IN THE DIOCESE

For further details refer to the corresponding bracketed number in the Religious Institutes of Men or Women section.

[0330]—*Brothers of the Christian Schools*—F.S.C.

[0340]—*Cistercian Fathers* (Abbey of Our Lady of New Malleray)—O.S.C.O.

[]—*Institute of the Incarnate Word*—I.V.E.

[0690]—*Jesuit Fathers and Brothers* (Wisconsin Province)—S.J.

[0430]—*Order of Preachers (Dominicans)* (Chicago Province)—O.P.

RELIGIOUS INSTITUTES OF WOMEN REPRESENTED IN THE DIOCESE

[1780]—*Congregation of the Sisters of the Third Order of St. Francis of Perpetual Adoration* (Eastern, Central Regions)—F.S.P.A.

[1310]—*Franciscan Sisters of Little Falls*—O.S.F.

[]—*Hermits of St. Mary of Carmel (Contemplative Community)*—H.S.M.C.

[2519]—*Religious Sisters of Mercy of Alma, Michigan*—R.S.M.

[2970]—*School Sisters of Notre Dame*—S.S.N.D.

[1680]—*School Sisters of St. Francis*—O.S.F.

[]—*Sinsinawa Dominican Sisters*—O.P.

[0430]—*Sisters of Charity of the Blessed Virgin Mary*—B.V.M.

[1705]—*The Sisters of St. Francis of Assisi*—O.S.F.

[1570]—*Sisters of St. Francis of the Holy Family*—O.S.F.

[3320]—*Sisters of the Presentation of the B.V.M.*—P.B.V.M.

[4100]—*Sisters of the Sorrowful Mother (Third Order of St. Francis)*—S.S.M.

[1720]—*Sisters of the Third Order Regular of St. Francis of the Congregation of Our Lady of Lourdes*—O.S.F.

DIOCESAN CEMETERIES

WINONA. *Catholic Cemeteries of Winona*, 55 W. Sanborn St., P.O. Box 588, 55987. Tel: 507-454-4643; Fax: 507-454-8106. Mrs. P.J. Thompson.

NECROLOGY

(No Deaths)

Diocese of Worcester

(Dioecesis Wigorniensis)

Most Reverend

ROBERT J. McMANUS

Bishop of Worcester; ordained May 27, 1978; appointed Auxiliary Bishop of Providence and Titular Bishop of Allegheny December 1, 1998; consecrated February 22, 1999; appointed Bishop of Worcester March 9, 2004; installed May 14, 2004. *Chancery Office: 49 Elm St., Worcester, MA 01609.*

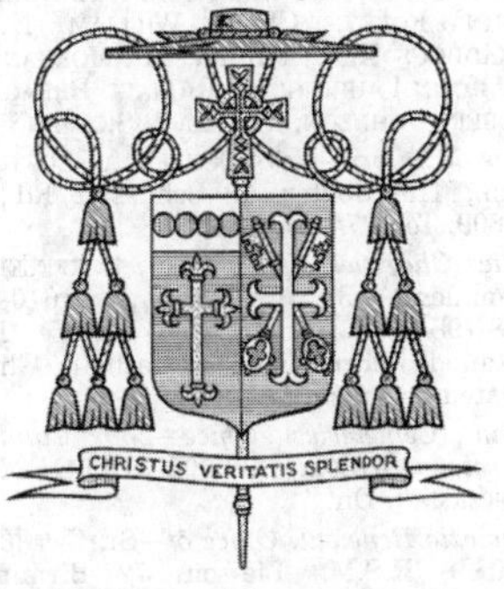

Chancery Office: 49 Elm St., Worcester, MA 01609. Tel: 508-791-7171; Fax: 508-754-2768.

Web: www.worcesterdiocese.org

Most Reverend

DANIEL P. REILLY, D.D.

Retired Bishop of Worcester; ordained May 30, 1953; appointed Bishop of Norwich June 17, 1975; consecrated August 6, 1975; appointed Bishop of Worcester October 27, 1994; installed December 8, 1994; retired March 9, 2004. *Res.: St. Paul Cathedral, 38 High St., Worcester, MA 01609.*

Most Reverend

GEORGE E. RUEGER, D.D., V.G.

Retired Auxiliary Bishop of Worcester; ordained January 6, 1958; appointed Auxiliary Bishop of Worcester and Titular Bishop of Maronana January 19, 1987; consecrated February 25, 1987; retired January 25, 2005. *Res.: St. Stephen's Rectory, 16 Hamilton St., Worcester, MA 01604.*

ESTABLISHED JANUARY 14, 1950.

Square Miles 1,532.

Comprises the County of Worcester in the State of Massachusetts.

For legal titles of parishes and diocesan institutions, consult the Chancery Office.

STATISTICAL OVERVIEW

Personnel	
Bishop	1
Retired Bishops	2
Abbots	3
Priests: Diocesan Active in Diocese	132
Priests: Diocesan Active Outside Diocese	11
Priests: Diocesan in Foreign Missions	1
Priests: Retired, Sick or Absent	45
Number of Diocesan Priests	189
Religious Priests in Diocese	106
Total Priests in Diocese	295
Extern Priests in Diocese	5
Ordinations:	
Diocesan Priests	1
Religious Priests	1
Transitional Deacons	2
Permanent Deacons	7
Permanent Deacons in Diocese	106
Total Brothers	74
Total Sisters	427
Parishes	
Parishes	116
With Resident Pastor:	
Resident Diocesan Priests	103
Resident Religious Priests	2
Without Resident Pastor:	
Administered by Priests	11
Missions	4
New Parishes Created	2
Closed Parishes	2
Professional Ministry Personnel:	
Brothers	1
Sisters	9
Lay Ministers	70
Welfare	
Catholic Hospitals	1
Total Assisted	228,139
Health Care Centers	5
Homes for the Aged	3
Residential Care of Children	1
Total Assisted	24
Day Care Centers	14
Total Assisted	1,500
Specialized Homes	3
Total Assisted	300
Special Centers for Social Services	7
Total Assisted	65,000
Educational	
Diocesan Students in Other Seminaries	25
Total Seminarians	25
Colleges and Universities	3
Total Students	8,917
High Schools, Diocesan and Parish	4
Total Students	1,879
High Schools, Private	5
Total Students	1,524
Elementary Schools, Diocesan and Parish	19
Total Students	4,601
Elementary Schools, Private	3
Total Students	450
Non-residential Schools for the Disabled	1
Total Students	30
Catechesis/Religious Education:	
High School Students	5,647
Elementary Students	17,942
Total Students under Catholic Instruction	41,015
Teachers in the Diocese:	
Priests	15
Brothers	1
Sisters	31
Lay Teachers	1,127
Vital Statistics	
Receptions into the Church:	
Infant Baptism Totals	2,634
Minor Baptism Totals	153
Adult Baptism Totals	75
Received into Full Communion	150
First Communions	3,290
Confirmations	2,757
Marriages:	
Catholic	436
Interfaith	100
Total Marriages	536
Deaths	3,167
Total Catholic Population	305,000
Total Population	784,992

Former Bishops—His Eminence JOHN CARDINAL WRIGHT, D.D., S.T.D., ord. Dec. 8, 1935; appt. Titular Bishop of Aegea and Auxiliary Bishop of Boston, May 10, 1947; cons. June 30, 1947; transferred to new See of Worcester, Jan. 14, 1950; enthroned March 7, 1950; appt. Bishop of Pittsburgh, Jan. 28, 1959; created Cardinal, April 28, 1969; transferred to the Roman Curia Prefect, Sacred Congregation for the Clergy; died Aug. 10, 1979; Most Revs. BERNARD J. FLANAGAN, D.D., J.C.D., retired March 31, 1983; died Jan. 28, 1998; TIMOTHY J. HARRINGTON, D.D., retired Oct. 27, 1994; died March 23, 1997; DANIEL P. REILLY, D.D., ord. May 30, 1953; appt. Bishop of Norwich June 17, 1975; cons. Aug. 6, 1975; appt. Bishop of Worcester Oct. 27, 1994; installed Dec. 8, 1994; retired March 9, 2004.

Vicar General—Most Rev. GEORGE E. RUEGER, D.D., V.G. (Retired), St. Stephen's Rectory, 16 Hamilton St., Worcester, 01604. Tel: 508-755-3165.

Chancery Office—Rev. Msgr. THOMAS J. SULLIVAN, Chancellor. Tel: 508-929-4346; Fax: 508-754-2768; Mr. RAYMOND L. DELISLE, Vice Chancellor, 49 Elm St., Worcester, 01609. Tel: 508-929-4313.

Diocesan Director of Fiscal Affairs—Rev. Msgr. THOMAS J. SULLIVAN, 49 Elm St., Worcester, 01609. Tel: 508-929-4346.

Director of Catholic Relief Services—Rev. Msgr. THOMAS J. SULLIVAN, Res.: 49 Elm St., Worcester, 01609. Tel: 508-929-4346.

Diocesan Expansion Fund—Rev. Msgr. THOMAS J. SULLIVAN; Mr. PETER J. DAWSON, 49 Elm St., Worcester, 01609.

Diocesan Finance Committee—JOSEPH GIOVINO, Chm., 49 Elm St., Worcester, 01609.

Diocesan Tribunal—Address all communications to, 49 Elm St., Worcester, 01609. Tel: 508-791-7171.

Judicial Vicar and Vicar for Canonical Affairs—Rev. Msgr. F. STEPHEN PEDONE, J.C.L., 49 Elm St., Worcester, 01609.

Associate Judicial Vicar—Rev. PAUL T. O'CONNELL, J.C.D.

Judges—Rev. PAUL T. O'CONNELL, J.C.D.; Rev. Msgr. F. STEPHEN PEDONE, J.C.L.; Rev. BRICE A. LEAVINS, O.F.M.

Promoter of Justice—Sr. MARY L. WALSH, S.N.D., J.C.L.

Psychologist—Sr. MARY DANIEL MALLOY, R.S.M.

Auditor—Rev. BRICE A. LEAVINS, O.F.M.

Secretary to the Tribunal—EILEEN CHARBONNEAU.

Defender of the Bond—Rev. Msgr. ANTHONY S. CZARNECKI, J.C.L.

Advocates—Revs. THOMAS E. MAHONEY; JAMES P. KERRIGAN; GEORGE J. RIDICK; MICHAEL A. DIGERONIMO; WILLIAM F. SANDERS; TERENCE T. KILCOYNE, D.Min.

Notary—EILEEN CHARBONNEAU Address all requests for dispensations to: Diocesan Tribunal, 49 Elm St., Worcester, 01609.

Diocesan College of Consultors—Most Rev. GEORGE E. RUEGER, D.D., V.G. (Retired); Rev. Msgr. THOMAS J. SULLIVAN; Revs. H. EDWARD CHALMERS; JOSEPH M. NALLY; Rev. Msgr. FRANCIS T. GOGUEN; Revs. GEORGE L. O'BRIEN (Retired); BRIAN P. O'TOOLE; Rev. Msgrs. THOMAS J. SULLIVAN; F. STEPHEN PEDONE, J.C.L.; ROCCO M. PICCOLOMINI; FRANCIS J. SCOLLEN; Rev. JOSEPH F. SZWACH; Rev. Msgr. EDMOND T. TINSLEY, P.A. (Retired).

Deans—Rev. WILLIAM E. CHAMPLIN, Area I; Rev. Msgr. JAMES P. MORONEY, Area II; Revs. JAMES B. O'SHEA, Area III; WILLIAM F. SANDERS, Area IV; PAUL M. LAPALME, Area V; MICHAEL F. ROSE,

Area VI; Rev. Msgr. ANTHONY S. CZARNECKI, J.C.L., Area VII; Revs. PAUL M. BOMBA, Area VIII; RICHARD T. CAREY, Area IX; Rev. Msgr. FRANCIS T. GOGUEN, Area X; Revs. ROBERT D. BRUSO, Area XI; TERENCE T. KILCOYNE, D.Min., Area XII; MARTIN P. DONAHUE, Area XIII (Retired).

Director of Priest Personnel—Rev. JOSE A. RODRIGUEZ.

Vicar for Religious—Sr. PAULA KELLEHER, S.S.J., 49 Elm St., Worcester, 01609. Tel: 508-791-7171.

Diocesan Offices and Directors

The Adopt-A-Student Endowment Trust—ROBERT PAPE, 49 Elm St., Worcester, 01609. Tel: 508-791-7171.

African Ministry—Rev. ANTHONY MPAGI, Chap., St. Peter, 929 Main St., Worcester, 01610. Tel: 508-752-4674.

Haitian Apostolate—Sr. JUDITH DUPUY, S.S.A., Dir. Tel: 508-929-4328.

Hmong Ministry—St. Anthony, Fitchburg, 01420. Tel: 978-342-4706. Rev. ROBERT D. BRUSO, Contact Person.

Vietnamese Ministry—Our Lady of Vilna, Worcester, 01610. Tel: 508-752-1825. Rev. TAM M. BUI.

Brazilian Ministry—Revs. ROBERTO APARACIDO DE LIMA, C.Ss.R.; HERIVELTO JEDER PEREIRA, C.Ss.R.; RONIVAL REIS, Office: 4 Caroline St., Worcester, 01604. Tel: 508-752-6364.

European Ministries—

Lithuanian Churches— St. John, Worcester. VACANT.

Polish Ministry—St. Joseph, Webster, 01570. Tel: 508-943-0467. Rev. Msgr. ANTHONY S. CZARNECKI, J.C.L., Natl. Delegate, Our Lady Czestochowa, Worcester; Jasna Gora, Clinton; St. Andrew Bobola, Dudley; St. Joseph, Gardner; St. Hedwig, Southbridge; St. Stanislaus, West Warren.

Portuguese Ministry—St. Mary, Milford, 01757. Tel: 508-473-2000. Rev. DANIEL R. MULCAHY JR.

Hispanic Ministry—

St. Paul—19 Chatham St., Worcester, 01609. Tel: 508-754-3195. Rev. ANGEL R. MATOS; Sr. MARIA DALLARI, X.M.M.; Deacon FRANCISCO ESCOBAR.

St. Peter—929 Main St., Worcester, 01610. Tel: 508-752-4674. Rev. EDWIN A. GOMEZ; Sr. ANN MARSHALL, R.S.M.

St. Joan of Arc—570 Lincoln St., Worcester, 01605. Tel: 508-852-3232. Rev. JOSE A. RODRIGUEZ; Sr. YENNY RAMIREZ, R.O.D.A.

Our Lady of Providence—7 Auburn St., Worcester, 01605. Tel: 508-755-3820. Rev. WILLIAM E. REISER, S.J.; Sr. REBECCA SANCHEZ, X.M.M.

St. John—149 Chestnut St., Clinton, 01510. Tel: 978-368-0366. Rev. MIGUEL PAGAN; Sr. PATRICIA VENEGAS, S.S.A.

St. Francis—63 Sheridan St., Fitchburg, 01420. Tel: 978-342-9651. Rev. EMERITO ORTIZ; Deacon WILLIAM COLON.

Holy Spirit—45 Metcalf St., Gardner, 01440. Tel: 978-632-3333. Rev. JESUS E. MARTINEZ; Deacon STANLEY H. BACZEWSKI.

Holy Trinity—69 Lincoln Terr., Box 667, Leominster, 01453. Tel: 978-534-5258. Chaplains: Revs. MIGUEL PAGAN; KEVIN F. HARTFORD.

St. Mary—27 Pearl St., Milford, 01757. Tel: 508-473-2000. Rev. MANUEL A. CLAVIJO.

St. Mary—263 Hamilton St., Southbridge, 01550. Tel: 978-764-3226. Rev. PETER JOYCE; Sr. XINIA RODRIGUEZ, R.O.D.A.; Deacon TEODORO CAMACHO.

St. Louis—15 Lake St., Webster, 01570. Tel: 508-943-0240. Rev. EDWIN A. GOMEZ; Ms. NOELIA RIVERA.

St. Luke—70 W. Main St., Westborough, 01581. Tel: 508-366-5502. Sr. SOLEDAD CHACON, R.O.D.A.; ELENA TELLO.

Black Catholics: African American—St. Peter, 929 Main St., Worcester, 01610. Tel: 508-752-4674. Rev. Msgr. FRANCIS J. SCOLLEN, Contact Person.

Catholic Charities—10 Hammond St., Worcester, 01609. Tel: 508-798-0191.

Refugee Apostolate—Little Store, 27 Chandler St., Worcester, 01609. Tel: 508-831-7455.

Apostleship of Prayer and Eucharistic Crusade—Rev. THADDEUS X. STACHURA, Our Lady of Czestochowa, 34 Ward St., Worcester, 01610. Tel: 508-755-5959.

Apostolate of Divine Mercy—Rev. RALPH A. DIORIO, Dir., Mailing Address: P.O. Box 668, Worcester, 01613-0668. Tel: 508-791-0427.

Archivist—Rev. Msgr. THOMAS J. SULLIVAN, Chancellor, 49 Elm St., Worcester, 01609. Tel: 508-929-4346.

The Annual Partners in Charity Appeal—Rev. Msgr. THOMAS J. SULLIVAN, Dir., 49 Elm St., Worcester, 01609. Tel: 508-929-4346.

Diocesan Building Commission Members—Rev. Msgrs. THOMAS J. SULLIVAN; ROBERT K. JOHNSON; Revs. JOHN FOLEY, Chm.; WILLIAM N. CORMIER; THADDEUS X. STACHURA; Mr. JORDAN O'CONNOR; Mr JOHN LAURING; Mr RICHARD BREAGY, Staff; Mr. ROBERT JOHNSON; Mr. KEVIN SEAMAN.

Campus Ministry—Rev. ROBERT A. LOFTUS, Campus Min., The Center, 19 Schussler Rd., Worcester, 01609. Tel: 774-262-6562.

Catholic Charities—CATHERINE LOEFFLER, Dir., 10 Hammond St., Worcester, 01610-1513. Tel: 508-798-0191 (Refer to separate listings for detailed information on Catholic Charities and related organizations).

Diocesan Cemeteries Office—260 Cambridge St., Worcester, 01603. Tel: 508-757-7415. Mr. ROBERT ACKERMAN, Dir.

Charismatic Renewal, Office of—Sr. CATHERINE MARIE WALSH, R.S.M., Liaison, 72 Birmingham Ct., Milford, 01757. Tel: 508-381-0987.

Clergy Benefit Plan—Rev. EDWARD D. NICCOLLS, Treas., Mailing Address: P.O. Box 498, North Uxbridge, 01538; Ms. MARY LOU VERLA, Admin. Tel: 508-887-8623.

Communication Office—Mr. RAYMOND L. DELISLE, Dir., 49 Elm St., Worcester, 01609. Tel: 508-929-4313; Mr. STEPHEN KAUFMAN, TV Ministry Production Mgr. Tel: 508-791-2039.

Office of Ongoing Priestly Formation—Rev. RONALD G. FALCO, Dir., 40 Brattle St., Worcester, 01606. Tel: 508-853-0183.

Cursillo—Rev. ROBERT A. GRATTAROTI, Dir., Mailing Address: P.O. Box 338, Charlton City, 01508. Tel: 508-248-7862.

Stewardship and Development Office— The Annual Partners in Charity Appeal, Annual Catholic School Appeal. Rev. Msgr. THOMAS J. SULLIVAN, Dir., 49 Elm St., Worcester, 01609. Tel: 508-929-4346; Fax: 508-929-4387; Mr. MICHAEL GILLESPIE, Dir. Stewardship. Tel: 508-929-4368.

Diocesan Expansion Fund—49 Elm St., Worcester, 01609. Members: Rev. Msgr. JOHN E. DORAN; Rev. RICHARD A. JAKUBAUSKAS; Mr. TERRENCE SULLIVAN; JANET CHAMBERS; Mr. JEROME JUSSAUME, Staff; MARTIN CONNORS JR.; JOHN GRAHAM; Mr. PETER J. DAWSON, Chm.; WILLIAM JONES.

Diocesan Scouts—Boy Scout Office/Girl Scout Office, 120 Hill St., Whitinsville, 01588. Tel: 508-234-0346. Rev. JAMES S. MAZZONE, Chap.

Ecumenical and Interreligious Affairs, Diocesan Office for—VACANT.

Evangelization, Office of—VACANT.

Office of Marriage and Family—ALLISON LEDOUX, Dir., 49 Elm St., Worcester, 01609. Tel: 508-929-4311.

Finance Office—Rev. Msgr. THOMAS J. SULLIVAN, Fiscal Affairs; Mr. JEROME D. JUSSAUME, Mgr. Finance; Mrs. CAROL ADAMS, Mgr. Accounting, 49 Elm St., Worcester, 01609. Tel: 508-791-7171.

Haitian Apostolate of the Diocese of Worcester—Sr. JUDITH DUPUY, S.S.A., Dir., 49 Elm St., Worcester, 01609. Tel: 508-929-4328; Fax: 508-753-7180. Email: sjudith41@yahoo.com.

Holy Childhood Association—Most Rev. GEORGE E. RUEGER, D.D., V.G., Dir. (Retired), 16 Hamilton St., Worcester, 01604. Tel: 508-755-3165.

Meet-the-Father Ministry, Inc.—Mrs. EILEEN GEORGE, Contact Person, 363 Greenwood St., Millbury, 01527.

Newspaper— "The Catholic Free Press" Mrs. MARGARET M. RUSSELL, Exec. Editor, 51 Elm St., Worcester, 01609. Tel: 508-757-6387.

Office for Divine Worship—Rev. Msgr. ROBERT K. JOHNSON, Dir.; ELIZABETH MARCIL, 19 Chatham St., Worcester, 01609. Tel: 508-798-0417.

Permanent Diaconate—Deacon ANTHONY R. SUROZENSKI, Dir., 49 Elm St., Worcester, 01609. Tel: 508-929-4332.

Presbyteral Council—Most Rev. ROBERT JOSEPH MCMANUS, Pres.; Rev. Msgrs. F. STEPHEN PEDONE, J.C.L., Ex Officio; THOMAS J. SULLIVAN, Ex Officio; JAMES P. MORONEY; Revs. WILLIAM E. CHAMPLIN, Chm.; RICHARD T. CAREY; Rev. Msgr. ANTHONY S. CZARNECKI, J.C.L.; Revs. WILLIAM F. SANDERS; TERENCE T. KILCOYNE, D.Min.; PAUL M. BOMBA; Rev. Msgr. FRANCIS T. GOGUEN; Revs. JAMES B. O'SHEA; PAUL M. LAPALME, Vice Chm.; MARTIN P. DONAHUE (Retired); MICHAEL F. ROSE; ROBERT D. BRUSO, Sec. & Treas., Chancery Bldg.: 49 Elm St., Worcester, 01609. Tel: 508-791-7171.

Priests' Personnel Board—Rev. JOSE A. RODRIGUEZ, Dir., 570 Lincoln St., Worcester, 01605. Tel: 508-852-3232.

Ministry to Retired Priests—Sr. MARY ANN BARTELL, C.S.E., 188 Old Worcester Rd., Charlton, 01507. Tel: 508-868-9239.

Respect Life—ALLISON LEDOUX, 49 Elm St., Worcester, 01609. Tel: 508-791-7171.

Propagation of the Faith—Most Rev. GEORGE E. RUEGER, D.D., V.G., Dir. (Retired), 16 Hamilton St., Worcester, 01604. Tel: 508-755-3165.

Religious Education Office—ELIZABETH MARCIL, Dir., 49 Elm St., Worcester, 01609. Tel: 508-929-4303.

St. Paul Catholic Schools Consortium—MARCUS MORAN, Chm., 49 Elm St., Worcester, 01609. Tel: 508-929-4317; Fax: 508-929-4386.

School Department—Dr. DELMA JOSEPHSON, Supt.; Mr. WILLIAM J. MULFORD, Assoc. Supt.; Ms. BERNA MANN, Assoc. Supt.

Office of Justice & Peace—49 Elm St., Worcester, 01609. Tel: 508-791-7171.

Diocesan Hispanic Apostolate—Rev. ANGEL R. MATOS, Dir., 49 Elm St., Worcester, 01609. Tel: 508-791-7171.

St. Vincent dePaul Society--— Central and Greater Worcester District Council Mrs. FRANCES PIKE, Pres.; Rev. WILLIAM E. CHAMPLIN, Spiritual Dir.

Northern Worcester County District Council—JOHN YOVINO, Pres.

Central Worcester County District Council—ROBERT K. SMITH.

Tri-Conference Retirement Fund for Religious—Sr. PAULA KELLEHER, S.S.J., Diocesan Coord., 49 Elm St., Worcester, 01609. Tel: 508-791-7171.

Director of Priest Personnel—Rev. JOSE A. RODRIGUEZ, 570 Lincoln St., Worcester, 01605.

Vicar for Religious—Sr. PAULA KELLEHER, S.S.J., 49 Elm St., Worcester, 01609. Tel: 508-791-7171.

Vietnamese Apostolate—Rev. TAM M. BUI, 153 Sterling St., Worcester, 01610. Tel: 508-752-1825.

Victim Assistance Coordinator—FRANCES J. NUGENT. Tel: 508-929-4363. Email: fnugent@worcesterdiocese.org.

Vocation Office—Rev. JAMES S. MAZZONE, Dir., 51 Illinois St., Worcester, 01610. Tel: 508-799-2792.

Minister to Priests—Rev. RICHARD F. TRAINOR, Mailing Address: P.O. Box 488, North Oxford, 01537.

Worcester Diocesan Commission for Women—ANNE ARCONA, Chm., 21 Searhill Rd., Boylston, 01505. Tel: 508-869-6748.

Youth Ministry—Deacon EDUARDUS MEILUS, Dir. Youth Ministry, Office, 120 Hill St., Whitinsville, 01588. Tel: 508-234-0346.

CLERGY, PARISHES, MISSIONS AND PAROCHIAL SCHOOLS

CITY OF WORCESTER

(WORCESTER COUNTY)

1—ST. PAUL CATHEDRAL (1866) Rev. Msgr. James P. Moroney (BO), Rector; Rev. Angel R. Matos; Deacon Francisco Escobar. In Res., Most Rev. Daniel P. Reilly; Rev. Msgrs. Thomas J. Sullivan; Robert K. Johnson.

Res.: 38 High St., 01609. Tel: 508-799-4193; Fax: 508-752-6308. Email: rectorsaintpauls@aol.com. Web: www.cathedralofstpaul.com.

Catechesis/Religious Program—Tel: 508-755-1414; Fax: 508-755-1414. Students 276.

2—ST. ANDREW THE APOSTLE (1954), Now a mission of St. Peter, Worcester.

3—ASCENSION (1911) Closed. For inquiries for parish records, please see St. John's, Worcester.

4—ST. BERNARD (1916) Closed. Merged with Our Lady of Fatima, Worcester to form Our Lady of Providence, Worcester.

5—BLESSED SACRAMENT (1912) Rev. Msgr. F. Stephen Pedone; Rev. Henry A. Donoghue, Senior Priest.

Res.: 551 Pleasant St., 01602. Tel: 508-755-5291; Fax: 508-755-6891. Email: blessedsacrament@charter.net. Web: www.blessedsacrament.us.

Catechesis/Religious Program—Epiphany House, Tel: 508-752-4368. Students 335.

6—ST. CASIMIR (1894), (Lithuanian), Closed. For inquiries for parish records contact St. John, Worcester.

7—ST. CATHERINE OF SWEDEN (1952) Merged with Sacred Heart of Jesus, Worcester to form Sacred Heart of Jesus-St. Catherine of Sweden, Worcester.

8—ST. CHARLES BORROMEO (1954) Rev. Chester J. Misiewicz.

Res.: 341 June St., 01602. Tel: 508-799-4031; Fax: 508-792-6675.

Catechesis/Religious Program—Mrs. Jean Urbanowski, C.R.E. Students 78.

9—CHRIST THE KING (1936) Revs. Thirburse F. Millott; Walter J. Riley; Deacon Joseph M. Baniukiewicz.

Res.: 1052 Pleasant St., 01602. Tel: 508-754-5361; Fax: 508-753-0448.

Catechesis/Religious Program—Tel: 508-752-5514.

Kathleen Cushing, D.R.E. Students 216.
10—ST. CHRISTOPHER (1956) Rev. Edward D. Niccolls; Deacon Christopher C. Meyers.
Res.: 950 W. Boylston St., 01606. Tel: 508-853-1492; Fax: 508-853-4338.
Catechesis/Religious Program—Tel: 508-853-3302; Fax: 508-854-4338. Students 77.
11—ST. GEORGE (1951) Rev. Ronald G. Falco.
Res.: 40 Brattle St., 01606. Tel: 508-853-0183; Fax: 508-854-0864. Email: office@saintgeo.com. Web: www.saintgeo.com.
Catechesis/Religious Program—Tel: 508-852-1784. Peggy Moynahan, D.R.E. Students 415.
12—HOLY FAMILY PARISH Rev. Richard G. Roger.
St. Joseph Church, 35 Hamilton St., 01604. In Res., Rev. Robert A. Loftus.
Rectory—5 Whitman Rd., 01609. Tel: 508-754-6722; Fax: 508-438-0368.
Catechesis/Religious Program—Michaelle Zellmer, C.R.E. Students 37.
13—HOLY NAME OF JESUS (1893), (French), Closed. For inquiries for parish records, please see Holy Family, Worcester.
14—IMMACULATE CONCEPTION (1873) Rev. William E. Champlin.
Res.: 353 Grove St., 01605. Tel: 508-754-8419; Fax: 508-754-8508. Web: www.icworc.com.
Catechesis/Religious Program—Father Connors Center, Tel: 508-791-5887; Fax: 508-754-8508. Web: www.icworc.com. Students 82.
15—ST. JOAN OF ARC (1950) Revs. Jose A. Rodriguez; Anthony Mpagi; Patrick Ssekyole; Sisters Yenny Ramirez, R.O.D.A., Pastoral Assoc.; Frances Barry, S.S.J., Pastoral Assoc.
Res.: 570 Lincoln St., 01605. Tel: 508-852-3232; Fax: 508-852-3223. Email: stjoan570@hotmail.com. Web: www.stjoanofarcworcester.com.
Catechesis/Religious Program—Luz Diaz, C.R.E. Students 216.
16—ST. JOHN'S (1834) Rev. John F. Madden, Admin.; Rev. Msgr. Edmond T. Tinsley (Retired).
Res.: 44 Temple St., 01604. Tel: 508-756-7165; Fax: 508-754-5153. Web: stjohnsworcester.org.
Catechesis/Religious Program—Mrs. Donna Mastrovito, D.R.E. Students 118.
17—ST. MARGARET MARY (1922) Closed. For inquiries for parish records, please see St. Anne, Shrewsbury.
18—NOTRE DAME DES CANADIENS - ST. JOSEPH (1869), (French), [CEM] Closed. For inquiries for parish records please see Holy Family, Worcester.
19—OUR LADY OF CZESTOCHOWA (1903), (Polish), Revs. Thaddeus X. Stachura; Ryszard Polek.
Res.: 34 Ward St., 01610. Tel: 508-755-5959; Fax: 508-767-1644.
School—St. Mary's Elementary, (Grades PreK-6), 50 Richland St., 01610. Tel: 508-753-0484; Fax: 508-767-1384. Corey E. Maloney, Prin. Lay Teachers 8; Students 125.
High School—St. Mary's Jr. & Sr. High School, (Grades 7-12) Tel: 508-753-1170; Fax: 508-795-0560. Michael E. Dudek, Prin. Lay Teachers 16; Students 144.
Catechesis/Religious Program—Students 138.
20—OUR LADY OF FATIMA (1952), (Spanish), Closed. Merged with St. Bernard, Worcester to form Our Lady of Providence, Worcester.
21—OUR LADY OF LORETO (1966), (Italian), Rev. Charles R. Armey; Deacon Paul T. Audette, Pastoral Assoc.
Res.: 33 Massasoit Rd., 01604. Tel: 508-753-5001; Fax: 508-754-1537. Email: aloreto@aol.com.
Catechesis/Religious Program—37 Massasoit Rd., 01604. Tel: 508-799-2445. JoAnn Bafaro, D.R.E. Students 42.
22—OUR LADY OF LOURDES (1949) Rev. James B. O'Shea. In Res., Rev. Francis J. Roach.
Res.: 1290 Grafton St., 01604. Tel: 508-757-0789; Fax: 508-757-0048.
Catechesis/Religious Program—Tel: 508-753-5773. Jo-Ann Bafaro, D.R.E. Students 176.
23—OUR LADY OF MT. CARMEL AND ST. ANN (1872), (Italian—Irish), Rev. Msgr. Rocco M. Piccolomini; Rev. Michael P. Bafaro, Senior Priest.
Res.: 53 E. Central St., 01605. Tel: 508-797-4546; Fax: 508-755-3506. Web: www.mtcarmel.ws.
Catechesis/Religious Program—Tel: 508-791-6139. Joan D'Argenis, D.R.E. Students 158.
24—OUR LADY OF PROVIDENCE PARISH Rev. Edward M. Ryan.
Rectory—7 Auburn St., 01605. Tel: 508-755-3820; Fax: 508-755-7196.
St. Bernard Church: 228 Lincoln St., 01605.
Catechesis/Religious Program—Students 36.
25—OUR LADY OF THE ANGELS (1916) Rev. Charles F. Monroe; Deacon Alphonse Desautels, Pastoral Assoc.; Karen Barrows, Pastoral Asst. In Res., Rev. Terrence Dougherty, O.C.D.
Res.: 1222 Main St., 01603. Tel: 508-791-0951; Fax: 508-753-9531. Web: www.ourladyoftheangels.org.
School—(Grades PreK-8), 1220 Main St., Rear, 01603. Tel: 508-752-5609; Fax: 508-798-9634. Doreen J. Albert, Prin.; Jodi L. Zaparakas, Asst. Prin. Lay Teachers 17; Students 291.
Catechesis/Religious Program—Students 230.
26—OUR LADY OF THE ROSARY (1911) Rev. William F. Sanders.
Res.: 23 Fales St., 01606. Tel: 508-853-1640; Fax: 508-853-2426.
Catechesis/Religious Program—Father Riley Center, 9 Emerson Rd., 01606. Tel: 508-852-5474. Sr. Irene Moran, M.P.V., D.R.E. Students 209.
27—OUR LADY OF VILNA (1925), (Lithuanian—Vietnamese), Rev. Peter Tam Bui. In Res., Rev. Son Anh Nguyen.
Res.: 153 Sterling St., St. 2, 01610. Tel: 508-752-1825; Fax: 508-752-9245.
Catechesis/Religious Program—Students 119.
28—ST. PETER (1884) Rev. Msgr. Francis J. Scollen; Revs. Edwin A. Gomez; Anthony Mpagi; John-Rita Adegboyega, Chap. African Community; Deacons Robert Devine; Scott R. Reisinger; Sr. Ann Marshall, R.S.M., Pastoral Assoc.
Res.: 929 Main St., 01610. Tel: 508-752-4674; Fax: 508-767-1511. Email: stpeters_standrewsparish@verizon.net.
Catechesis/Religious Program—Tel: 508-752-0797. Students 210.
Mission—St. Andrew the Apostle Mission Spaulding St., 01603. Tel: 508-752-4674; Fax: 508-767-1511.
29—SACRED HEART OF JESUS-ST. CATHERINE OF SWEDEN (1880) Rev. George J. Ridick.
Res.: 596 Cambridge St., 01610. Tel: 508-752-1608; 508-753-2555; Fax: 508-757-2462. Web: www.home.catholicweb.com/sacredheartworcester.
Catechesis/Religious Program—Students 46.
30—ST. STEPHEN'S (1887) Rev. Joseph M. Nally; Deacon David F. Vaillancourt. In Res., Most Rev. George E. Rueger (Retired); Rev. Joseph P. Mahoney.
Res.: 16 Hamilton St., 01604. Tel: 508-755-3165; Fax: 508-755-0937.
School—(Grades PreK-8), 355 Grafton St., 01604. Tel: 508-755-3209; Fax: 508-770-1052. Ms. Elizabeth Drake, Prin. Sisters 1; Lay Teachers 16; Students 218.
Catechesis/Religious Program—Ramona Kneeland, D.R.E. Students 99.

OUTSIDE THE CITY OF WORCESTER

(In the County of Worcester)

ASHBURNHAM, ST. DENIS (1951) [CEM] Rev. John E. Horgan; Deacon Richard DesJardins.
Res.: 85 Main St., P.O. Box 418, 01430. Tel: 978-827-5806; Fax: 978-827-1191. Email: stdenis@comcast.net.
Catechesis/Religious Program—Tel: 978-827-4892. Students 285.
ATHOL
1—ST. FRANCIS (1912), (Lithuanian), Revs. Richard A. Jakubauskas; Frederick D. Fraini III; Deacon Scott Colley.
Res.: 105 Main St., 01331. Tel: 978-249-3361.
Catechesis/Religious Program—Included in Our Lady Immaculate. Students 2.
2—OUR LADY IMMACULATE (1882) Revs. Richard A. Jakubauskas; Frederick D. Fraini III; Deacon James L. Linderman.
Res.: 192 School St., 01331-2399. Tel: 978-249-2738; Fax: 978-249-0447. Email: ourladyrectory@hotmail.com. Web: www.nqcatholic.org.
Catechesis/Religious Program—Tel: 978-249-7690; Fax: 978-249-7639. Donna Findlay, D.R.E. Students 150.
Mission—Our Lady Queen of Heaven Rte. 68, South Royalston, Worcester Co. 01368. Tel: 978-249-4103.
AUBURN
1—ST. JOSEPH'S (1907) Revs. Patrick J. Hawthorne; Paul W. Lemire; Deacons Peter Ryan; Bruce R. Vidito.
Res.: 194 Oxford St. N., 01501. Tel: 508-832-2074; Fax: 508-832-8894. Email: stjoesbulletin@charter.net. Web: www.stjosephauburn.org.
Catechesis/Religious Program—Tel: 508-832-0492; Fax: 508-832-6629. Lisa Wass, D.R.E. Students 678.
2—NORTH AMERICAN MARTYRS (1952) Rev. John F. Gee.
Res.: 8 Wyoma Dr., 01501. Tel: 508-798-8779; Fax: 508-791-6614. Email: namoffice@verizon.net. Web: www.auburncatholiccommunity.org.
Catechesis/Religious Program—Tel: 508-798-0612; Fax: 508-798-0612. Email: namparish@aol.com. Joan Sundstrom, C.R.E. Students 245.
BALDWINVILLE, ST. VINCENT DE PAUL (1955) Rev. Francis A. Roberge; Deacon James A. Connor.
Res.: 18 Pleasant St., 01436. Tel: 978-939-8851; Fax: 978-939-2120. Email: stvindepaul05@aol.com. Web: svdponline.com.
Catechesis/Religious Program—Tel: 978-939-8290. Students 121.
BARRE, ST. JOSEPH'S (1896) [CEM] Rev. Thomas H. Hultquist.
Res.: 90 Common St., P.O. Box 598, 01005. Tel: 978-355-4463; Fax: 978-355-0136.
Catechesis/Religious Program—Tel: 978-355-6402. Students 88.
BERLIN, ST. JOSEPH THE GOOD PROVIDER (1973) Rev. Robert M. Spellman.
Res.: 52 West St., Box 284, 01503-0284. Tel: 978-838-9922; Fax: 978-838-9933.
Catechesis/Religious Program—Students 180.
BLACKSTONE
1—ST. PAUL'S (1850) [CEM] Rev. Conrad S. Pecevich.
Res.: 48 St. Paul St., 01504. Tel: 508-883-6726; Fax: 508-883-2079. Email: stpaulblackstone@comcast.net. Web: www.stpaulblackstone.org.
Catechesis/Religious Program—Tel: 508-883-2590. Email: religioused@stpaulblackstone.org. Students 243.
2—ST. THERESA (1929), (French), Rev. Paul M. Bomba.
Res.: 630 Rathbun St., 01504. Tel: 508-883-7206; Fax: 508-883-5250.
Catechesis/Religious Program—Tel: 508-883-7527. Students 228.
BOLTON, ST. FRANCIS XAVIER (1954) Merged with St. Theresa's, Harvard to form Holy Trinity, Harvard.
BOYLSTON, ST. MARY OF THE HILLS (1952) Rev. Paul J. Tougas; Marcella Wilson, Pastoral Assoc.
Res.: 620 Cross St., 01505. Tel: 508-869-6771.
Catechesis/Religious Program—Tel: 508-869-6771; Fax: 508-869-0418. Anne Dowen, D.R.E. (Asst. grades 3-10). Students 285.
BROOKFIELD, ST. MARY'S (1885) Rev. David B. Galonek.
Res.: 10 Milk St., West Brookfield, 01585. Tel: 508-867-6469; Fax: 508-867-3670.
Catechesis/Religious Program—Students 50.
CHARLTON CITY, ST. JOSEPH'S (1900) Revs. Robert A. Grattaroti; J. Normand Tremblay, Senior Priest; Deacons Lawrence F. Miskell; Robert F. Dio.
Res.: 10 H. Putnam Ext., Box 338, 01508. Tel: 508-248-7862; Fax: 508-248-5832. Email: stjoecharlton@aol.com. Web: stjosephcharlton.com.
Catechesis/Religious Program—Tel: 508-248-7986. Elizabeth Cotrupi, D.R.E. (High School); Cheryl Kingston, D.R.E. (Junior High); Sr. Agnes Patricia, D.R.E. (Grades 1-5). Students 525.
CLINTON
1—ST. JOHN THE EVANGELIST (1849) [CEM] Revs. Thomas V. Walsh; Miguel Pagan; Deacon Dennis J. Cormier; Sisters Patricia Venegas, S.S.A., Pastoral Assoc. & Hispanic Min.; Sheila Finnigan, S.N.D., Pastoral Assoc.
Res.: 149 Chestnut St., 01510. Tel: 978-368-0366; Fax: 978-368-4359. Web: www.stjohnsclinton.org.
Catechesis/Religious Program—Tel: 508-368-0052; Fax: 978-368-4360. Students 470.
2—OUR LADY OF JASNA GORA (1913), (Polish), Rev. Tomasz J. Borkowski.
1 Cross St., 01510.
Res.: 128 Franklin St., 01510. Tel: 978-365-3621. Email: frtomasz@msn.com. Web: www.jasna-gora.org.
Catechesis/Religious Program—Tel: 508-393-2724. Students 55.
3—OUR LADY OF THE ROSARY (1909) Rev. Tomasz J. Borkowski.
Res.: One Cross St., 01510. Tel: 978-365-2724; Fax: 978-365-5705.
Catechesis/Religious Program—Students 32.
DOUGLAS, ST. DENIS (1870) [CEM] Rev. William N. Cormier.
Res.: 23 Manchaug St., 01516. Tel: 508-476-2002; Fax: 508-476-2022. Email: wcormier@saintdenischurch.com.
Catechesis/Religious Program—Students 531.
DUDLEY
1—ST. ANDREW BOBOLA (1963), (Polish), [JC] Rev. Joseph F. Szwach.
Res.: 54 W. Main St., P.O. Box 98, 01571. Tel: 508-943-5633; Fax: 508-949-6701.
Catechesis/Religious Program—Students 59.
2—ST. ANTHONY (1905) [CEM] Rev. Paul F. Campbell.
Res.: 22 Dudley Hill Rd., Box 277, 01571-0277. Tel: 508-943-0470; Fax: 508-943-5663.
Catechesis/Religious Program—Tel: 508-949-0335. Email: stanthonyreled@charter.net. Linda Brink, D.R.E. Students 267.
EAST BROOKFIELD, ST. JOHN THE BAPTIST (1952) Rev. George A. Charland.
Res.: 121 Blaine Ave., 01515. Tel: 508-867-3738; Fax: 508-867-3301.
Catechesis/Religious Program—Tel: 508-885-4506. Students 81.
EAST TEMPLETON, HOLY CROSS (1952) Rev. Joseph J. Jurgelonis; Deacon Richard J. Tatro.
Res.: 25 Lake Ave., P.O. Box 418, 01438. Tel: 978-632-2121; Fax: 978-630-3890. Email: hcchurchet@comcast.net.

Catechesis/Religious Program—Tel: 978-632-2194. Students 198.
Mission—St. Martin 247 State Rd., Otter River, 01438. Tel: 978-939-5588; Fax: 978-939-2305.
Catechesis/Religious Program—Students 31.

FISKDALE, ST. ANNE'S AND ST. PATRICK'S (1883) [CEM] Revs. Peter Precourt, A.A., Shrine Dir. & Pastor; Philip Bonvouloir; Deacon Richard Olson.
Res.: 16 Church St., 01518. Tel: 508-347-7338; Fax: 508-347-2982. Web: stannestpat.org.
Catechesis/Religious Program—Tel: 508-347-9353; Fax: 508-347-9353. Students 275.

FITCHBURG

1—ST. ANTHONY OF PADUA (1908), (Italian), Rev. Robert D. Bruso; Deacon Salvatore Tantillo.
Res.: 2 Beekman St., 01420. Tel: 978-342-4706; Fax: 978-342-8160. Email: saintanthony@net1plus.com. Web: stanthonyfitchburg.net.
School—(Grades PreK-8), 123 Salem St., 01420. Tel: 978-345-7785; Fax: 978-342-5110. Email: principal@stanthony.net. Web: stanthony.net. John Ginnity, Prin. Sisters 2; Lay Teachers 18; Students 252.
Catechesis/Religious Program— Ellen DePatie, D.R.E. Students 89.

2—ST. BERNARD (1847) [CEM] Rev. H. Edward Chalmers. In Res., Rev. Theodore R. Laperle (Retired).
Res.: 240 Water St., 01420. Tel: 978-343-7459; Fax: 978-343-0193.
School—(Grades PreK-8), 254 Summer St., 01420. Tel: 978-342-1948; Fax: 978-342-1153. Mr. David Farnsworth, Prin. Sisters of the Presentation of the Blessed Virgin Mary 2; Lay Teachers 10; Students 240.
Catechesis/Religious Program—Students 86.

3—ST. CAMILLUS DE LELLIS (1953) Rev. Joseph M. Dolan; Deacon Benjamin A. Nogueira.
Res.: 333 Mechanic St., 01420. Tel: 978-342-7921; Fax: 978-345-2688. Email: st.camillus@verizon.net. Web: www.saintcamillusparish.org.
Catechesis/Religious Program—Students 59.

4—ST. FRANCIS OF ASSISI (1903), (French), Rev. Emerito Ortiz.
Res.: 63 Sheridan, 01420. Tel: 978-342-9651; Fax: 978-342-7936. Web: www.stfrancisfitchburg.org.
Catechesis/Religious Program—Tel: 978-342-3521. Robert Jones, D.R.E. Students 105.

5—IMMACULATE CONCEPTION (1886), (French), Rev. Thien Nguyen.
Res.: 59 Walnut St., 01420. Tel: 978-342-5851; Fax: 978-345-2491.
Catechesis/Religious Program—Students 30.

6—ST. JOSEPH'S (1890) [CEM] Rev. Robert D. Bruso, Admin.; Deacon James Couture. In Res., Revs. Laurie L. Leger, M.S.; John Hughes, M.S.
Res.: 49 Woodland St., 01420. Tel: 978-345-7997; Fax: 978-345-7678.
Catechesis/Religious Program—Tel: 978-345-7997. Bette Brunell, D.R.E. Students 67.

7—MADONNA OF THE HOLY ROSARY (1955) Rev. Frank J. Liistro.
Res.: 118 Theresa St., 01420. Tel: 978-342-1290; Fax: 978-345-3032.
Catechesis/Religious Program—Tel: 978-345-4906. Maureen Beauvais, C.R.E. Students 46.

8—SACRED HEART OF JESUS (1878), (Irish), Rev. Frank J. Liistro, Admin.
Res.: 118 Theresa St., 01420. Tel: 978-342-1290; Fax: 978-345-3032.
Catechesis/Religious Program—Students 16.

GARDNER

1—HOLY SPIRIT (1955) Rev. Thomas M. Tokarz; Deacon Stanley H. Baczewski.
Res.: 45 Metcalf St., 01440. Tel: 978-632-3333; Fax: 978-632-3630.
Catechesis/Religious Program—Holy Spirit & St. Joseph Combined Rel. Educ. Prog. Students 83.

2—ST. JOSEPH'S (1908), (Polish), [CEM] Rev. Thomas M. Tokarz.
Res.: 358 Pleasant St., 01440. Tel: 978-632-0375; Fax: 978-632-1282.
Catechesis/Religious Program—Combined with Holy Spirit, Gardner. Students 9.

3—OUR LADY OF THE HOLY ROSARY (1884) [CEM] Rev. Andre E. Dargis.
Res.: 135 Nichols St., 01440. Tel: 978-632-0253; Fax: 978-630-1773. Web: holyrosarynet.com.
School—(Grades PreK-8), 99 Nichols St., 01440. Tel: 508-632-8656; Fax: 508-630-1433. Email: holyrosary@holyrosarynet.com. Web: holyrosarynet.com/school.htm. Lay Teachers 26; Students 283.
Catechesis/Religious Program—Students 145.

4—SACRED HEART OF JESUS (1874) [CEM] Revs. Brian P. O'Toole; Gerald A. Dorais, Senior Priest; Jesus E. Martinez; Deacon Paul J. Carrier.
Res. & Parish Hall: 166 Cross St., 01440. Tel: 978-632-0237; Fax: 978-630-2459. Email: shrectory@hotmail.com. Web: www.sacredheartgardner.org.
Parish Center—100 Central St., 01440. Tel: 978-632-0217 (Deacon's Office).
School—Sacred Heart of Jesus School, (Grades PreK-8), 53 Lynde St., 01440. Tel: 978-632-0950; Fax: 978-630-2448. Maureen Lapan, Prin. Lay Teachers 13; Students 284.
Catechesis/Religious Program—Tel: 978-632-0218. Students 231.
Day Care—Tel: 978-632-5745. Mrs. Jane Pineo, Dir.

GILBERTVILLE, ST. ALOYSIUS (1872) [CEM] Rev. Richard Lembo (PRT).
Res.: 58 Church St., P.O. Box 542, 01031-0542. Tel: 413-477-6493; Fax: 413-477-0140.
Catechesis/Religious Program—Students 53.
Mission—St. Augustine 98 Church Ln., Wheelwright, Hardwick Co. 01094.

GRAFTON, ST. PHILIP'S (1869) [CEM] Rev. Raymond M. Goodwin.
12 West St., 01519. Tel: 508-839-3325; Fax: 508-839-1310.
Catechesis/Religious Program—Tel: 508-839-9130. Students 129.

HARVARD

1—HOLY TRINITY (2009) Rev. Dennis J. O'Brien.
15 Still River Rd., P.O. Box 746, 01451. Tel: 978-456-3563; Fax: 978-456-8352. Email: sttheresaparish@aol.com. Web: www.st-theresas.org.
Catechesis/Religious Program—Tel: 978-456-8807.

2—ST. THERESA'S (1950) Merged with St. Francis Xavier, Bolton to form Holy Trinity, Harvard.

HOPEDALE, SACRED HEART OF JESUS (1935) Rev. William C. Konicki; Deacon Joseph Manella; Pam Chaplin, Ministry Coord.
Res.: 187 Hopedale St., 01747. Tel: 508-473-1900; Fax: 508-473-1745. Email: parishoffice@shchopedale.org. Web: www.shchopedale.org.
Catechesis/Religious Program—Tel: 508-473-1701. Students 622.

JEFFERSON, ST. MARY (1884) [CEM] Rev. Andre N. Remillard; Grace Riley, Pastoral Staff.
Res.: 114 Princeton St., P.O. Box 2200, 01522. Tel: 508-829-4508; Fax: 508-829-0429. Email: stmaryjeff@charterinternet.com. Web: www.stmarysjeff.com.
Catechesis/Religious Program—Tel: 508-829-6758. Email: stmaryreled@charterinternet.com. Students 587.

LANCASTER, IMMACULATE CONCEPTION (1915) Rev. Edward P. Lettic.
Res.: 28 Packard St., P.O. Box 95, 01523. Tel: 978-365-6582; Fax: 978-365-3097.
Catechesis/Religious Program—Students 138.

LEICESTER

1—ST. ALOYSIUS-ST. JUDE (1904) Rev. Peter H. White.
Res.: 491 Pleasant St., 01524. Tel: 508-892-8296; Fax: 508-892-9054.
Catechesis/Religious Program—Mrs. Cynthia Garabedian, C.R.E. Students 85.

2—ST. JOSEPH (1851) [CEM] Rev. Stephen D. Johnson; Carol Cornacchioli, Pastoral Assoc.
Res.: 759 Main St., 01524. Tel: 508-892-7407; Fax: 508-892-4753. Email: stpiusx@aol.com. Web: www.stjoseph-stpiusx.com.
Catechesis/Religious Program—Tel: 508-892-0660. Combined with St. Pius X. Students 140.

3—ST. PIUS X (1956) Rev. Stephen D. Johnson; Carol A. Cornacchioli, Pastoral Assoc.
Mailing Address: 759 Main St., 01524. Tel: 508-892-7407; Fax: 508-892-4753.
Church: 1161 Main St., 01524.
Catechesis/Religious Program— Combined with St. Joseph's, Leicester.

LEOMINSTER

1—ST. ANNA (1937), (Italian), Rev. James B. Callahan.
Res.: 199 Lancaster St., 01453. Tel: 978-537-5293; Fax: 978-537-2950.
School—(Grades PreK-8) Tel: 978-534-4770; Fax: 978-466-1167. Web: www.stannaschool.org. Danielle Colvert, Prin. Priests 1; Lay Teachers 16; Students 147.
Catechesis/Religious Program—Tel: 978-537-2945. Students 106.

2—ST. CECILIA (1900), (French), [CEM] Rev. Msgr. Francis T. Goguen; Rev. Edward Michalski; Deacon Ronald J. Aubuchon.
Res.: 170 Mechanic St., 01453. Tel: 978-537-6541; Fax: 978-840-1965.
Catechesis/Religious Program—Tel: 978-537-4673. Patricia Secino, D.R.E. Students 255.

3—HOLY FAMILY OF NAZARETH (1963) Rev. Thomas F. Egan.
Res.: One S. Flagg St., 01602.
Church: 750 Union St., 01453. Tel: 978-537-3016; Fax: 978-534-1119. Email: churchonhill@aol.com.
Catechesis/Religious Program—Tel: 978-537-5660. Email: churchonhill@aol.com. Anne Booth, D.R.E. Students 185.

4—ST. LEO (1872) [CEM] Rev. Msgr. John E. Doran; Rev. Kevin F. Hartford.
Res.: 108 Main St., 01453. Tel: 978-537-7257; Fax: 978-840-6182. Email: stleoparish@verizon.net. Web: stleosparish.org.
School—(Grades PreK-8), 120 Main St., 01453. Tel: 978-537-1007; Fax: 978-537-2828. Web: www-.stleoschool.org. Mrs. Carolyn Polselli, Prin.; Sr. Mary Anne Seliga, P.B.V.M., Librarian. Sisters of the Presentation of the Blessed Virgin Mary 2; Lay Teachers 32; Students 292.
Catechesis/Religious Program—Tel: 978-537-1194; Fax: 978-840-6182. Web: www.stleosparish.org. Students 295.

5—OUR LADY OF THE LAKE (1952) Rev. Timothy M. Brewer; Deacon Fred A. Harkins.
Res.: 1400 Main St., 01453. Tel: 978-342-2978; Fax: 978-342-8738. Email: ourladylake@comcast.net. Web: www.ourladylake.org.
Catechesis/Religious Program—Tel: 978-345-7469. Lisa Sciacca, D.R.E. Students 646.

LINWOOD, GOOD SHEPHERD (1904) Rev. Lawrence J. Esposito; Deacon Marc E. Gervais.
Res.: 121 Linwood St., P.O. Box 517, 01525. Tel: 508-234-7726; Fax: 508-234-0964. Email: gshepherd7726@charter.net. Web: www.gdshphrd.com.
Catechesis/Religious Program—Tel: 508-234-5340. Carol A. Zabinski, Music Min. Students 188.

LUNENBURG, ST. BONIFACE (1950) Rev. John A. Dwyer.
Res.: 817 Massachusetts Ave., 01462. Tel: 978-582-4008; Fax: 978-582-9355. Email: stbonifaceparish@verizon.net.
Catechesis/Religious Program—Tel: 978-582-6650; Fax: 978-582-9355. Maura L. Sweeney, D.R.E. Students 220.

MANCHAUG, ST. ANNE (1900) Rev. Stanley F. Krutcik.
Res.: 31 Main St., P.O. Box 311, 01526. Tel: 508-476-2405; Fax: 508-476-4443.
Catechesis/Religious Program—Students 56.

MENDON, ST. MICHAEL (1952) Rev. Thomas E. Mahoney.
Res.: 29 North Ave., P.O. Box 33, 01756. Tel: 508-478-4456; Fax: 508-634-2664. Email: stmichaels@comcast.net. Web: www.stgabrielma.org.
Catechesis/Religious Program—Students 260.

MILFORD

1—ST. MARY OF THE ASSUMPTION (1848), (Portuguese—Spanish), [CEM] Revs. Daniel R. Mulcahy Jr.; Manuel A. Clavijo; Sr. Theresa Lucier, S.P., Pastoral Assoc.
Res.: 27 Pearl St., 01757. Tel: 508-473-2000; Fax: 508-473-6907. Email: administrator@stmarymilford.org. Web: www.stmarymilford.org.
Catechesis/Religious Program—St. Mary's Parish Center, 17 Winter St., 01757. Tel: 508-478-7440. Sandra Piwko, C.R.E. (Children & Teens); Robert Daly, D.R.E. (Adult). Tel: 508-478-7441. Students 717.

2—SACRED HEART OF JESUS (1905) [CEM] Rev. Richard A. Scioli, C.S.S.; Deacon Pasquale G. Mussulli.
Res.: 5 E. Main St., 01757. Tel: 508-634-5435; Fax: 508-478-4993. Email: shbulletineditor@comcast.net (For Bulletin News); office@sacredheartmilford.org. Web: sacredheartmilford.org.
Catechesis/Religious Program—Tel: 508-473-1036. Amy Donahue, C.R.E.; Donna Niro, C.R.E. Students 426.

MILLBURY

1—ASSUMPTION (1884), (French), Rev. Richard A. Fortin.
Res.: 12 Waters St., 01527. Tel: 508-865-2657; Fax: 508-865-4866. Email: apsecretary@charter.net.
School—(Grades PreK-8), 17 Grove St., 01527. Tel: 508-865-5404; Fax: 508-581-8974. Dr. Rita Bernard, Prin. Lay Teachers 11; Students 213.
Catechesis/Religious Program—Students 41.

2—ST. BRIGID (1849) Rev. Paul M. LaPalme; Deacon Ronald B. Buron.
Res.: 59 Main St., 01527. Tel: 508-865-6624; Fax: 508-865-3101. Email: stbrigidchurch@charter.net.
Catechesis/Religious Program—Tel: 508-865-2752. Students 271.

MILLVILLE, ST. AUGUSTINE (1884) Rev. Maurice L. Gilbert; Deacon William Lucier.
Res.: 17 Lincoln St., P.O. Box 710, 01529. Tel: 508-883-6678; Fax: 508-883-5878. Email: st.augustinemillville@charter.net.
Catechesis/Religious Program—15 Lincoln St., 01529. Tel: 508-883-8794. Students 78.

NORTH BROOKFIELD, ST. JOSEPH (1867) [CEM] Rev. Richard T. Carey.
Res.: 28 Mt. Pleasant St., 01535. Tel: 508-867-6811; Fax: 508-867-7756. Email: stjosephsrectory@verizon.net. Web: www.nbstjosephs.org.
Church: 296 N. Main St., 01535.
Catechesis/Religious Program—27 Mt. Pleasant St., 01535. Tel: 508-867-9302; Fax: 508-867-7756. Students 130.

NORTH GRAFTON, ST. MARY (1952) Rev. Raymond M. Goodwin; Lisa Stewart, Business Mgr.

Res.: 17 Waterville St., 01536. Tel: 508-839-3993; Fax: 508-839-1330. Web: stmarysgrafton.org.
Catechesis/Religious Program—Tel: 508-839-3993, Ext. 12. Sr. Yvonne Millman, S.S.A, D.R.E. Students 278.

NORTH OXFORD, ST. ANN (1906) Rev. Richard F. Trainor; Sr. Jeanne Rouillard, S.A.S.V., Pastoral Assoc.
Res.: 652 Main St., P.O. Box 488, 01537. Tel: 508-987-8892; Fax: 508-987-1598. Email: stannsrectory@charterinternet.com.
Catechesis/Religious Program—P.O. Box 488, 01537. Tel: 508-987-1869. Students 177.

NORTHBORO

1—ST. BERNADETTE (1959) Rev. Stephen M. Gemme; Deacon George O'Connor.
Res.: 266 Main St., 01532. Tel: 508-393-2223; Fax: 508-393-2718. Email: stbernadetteparish@charter.net. Web: www.stb-parish.org.
School—(Grades PreK-8), 266 Main St., 01532. Tel: 508-351-9905; Fax: 508-351-2941. Email: principal@stb-school.org. Deborah O'Neil, Prin.; Nancy Berry, Librarian; Suzana Bardellini, Librarian. Sisters 1; Lay Teachers 53; Students 542.
Catechesis/Religious Program—Tel: 508-393-7445. Students 407.

2—ST. ROSE OF LIMA (1883) Rev. James A. Houston.
Res.: 244 W. Main St., P.O. Box 685, 01532. Tel: 508-393-2413; Fax: 508-393-4922. Email: strose@charterinternet.com. Web: www.saintroseoflima.com.
Catechesis/Religious Program—P.O. Box 387. Tel: 508-393-6444. Mrs. Susan McGoldrick, D.R.E. Students 649.

NORTHBRIDGE, ST. PETER (1904) Rev. James F. Carmody; Deacon Lee Packard.
Res.: 39 Church Ave., P.O. Box 446, 01534. Tel: 508-234-2156; Fax: 508-234-5123.
Catechesis/Religious Program—Tel: 508-234-6355. Students 128.

OTTER RIVER, ST. MARTIN MISSION (1864) Rev. Joseph J. Jurgelonis.
Res.: 248 State Rd., 01438. Tel: 978-632-2121; Fax: 978-939-5588. Email: info@saintmartinchurch.org. Web: saintmartinchurch.org.
Church: 18 Pleasant St., P.O. Box 14, Baldwinville, 01436.
Catechesis/Religious Program—Students 29.

OXFORD, ST. ROCH (1886) [CEM] Rev. Msgr. Louis R. Piermarini; Deacon Wesley Stevens. In Res., Rev. Robert E. Kelley.
Res.: 334 Main St., 01540. Tel: 508-987-8987; Fax: 508-987-8938. Web: www.strochoxford.parishesonline.com.
Catechesis/Religious Program—Tel: 508-987-2382. Students 192.

PAXTON, ST. COLUMBA (1951) Rev. David E. Doiron.
Res.: 10 Richards Ave., 01612. Tel: 508-755-0408; Fax: 508-767-0759. Email: stcolumba@charter.net. Web: www.rc.net/worcester/stcolumba.
Catechesis/Religious Program—Tel: 508-755-0601. Students 254.

PETERSHAM, ST. PETER (1968) Revs. Richard A. Jakubauskas; Frederick D. Fraini III; Deacon Paul Mello.
Mailing Address: 18 North St., 01366. Tel: 978-249-3361.
Res.: 192 School St., Athol, 01331. Tel: 978-249-2738.
Catechesis/Religious Program—Tel: 978-249-7690. High School is done with Our Lady Immaculate. Students 23.

PRINCETON, PRINCE OF PEACE (1967) Rev. James J. Caldarella; Sr. Teresa Rose Carchidi, M.P.V., Pastoral Assoc.
Res.: 5 Worcester Rd., P.O. Box 305, 01541. Tel: 508-464-2871; Fax: 508-464-0449. Email: princeofpeace@verizon.net. Web: www.princeofpeace.41pi.com.
Catechesis/Religious Program—Students 173.

RUTLAND, ST. PATRICK (1938) Rev. James P. Kerrigan; Deacon Pierre G.L. Gemme.
Res.: 290 Main St., Box 939, 01543. Tel: 508-886-4309; Fax: 508-886-2897. Email: stpatsrutland@aol.com. Web: stpatrickrutland.org.
Church: 258 Main St., 01543. Tel: 508-886-6131.
Catechesis/Religious Program—Tel: 508-886-4984; Fax: 508-886-7414. Michele Curtis, D.R.E. Students 423.

SHREWSBURY

1—ST. ANNE (1950) [CEM] Revs. John J. Foley; Paul T. O'Connell, Senior Priest; Deacon Dennis J. Klug. In Res., Rev. Bernard E. Gilgun (Retired).
Res.: 130 Boston Tpke., 01545. Tel: 508-757-5154; Fax: 508-797-9520. Email: starec@aol.com. Web: www.stannesparish.org.
Catechesis/Religious Program—Tel: 508-752-5040. Karen Etre, D.R.E. Students 488.

2—ST. MARY'S (1922) Revs. Michael F. Rose; Leo Lancaster; Adam R. Reid.
Res.: 18 Summer St., 01545. Tel: 508-845-0161; Fax: 508-842-9132.
School—(Grades PreK-8) Tel: 508-842-1601; Fax: 508-845-1535. Joan Barry, Prin. Sisters 1; Lay Teachers 26; Students 295.
Catechesis/Religious Program—Tel: 508-845-1154. Students 948.

SOUTH ASHBURNHAM, ST. ANNE (1895) Rev. John E. Horgan; Deacon Richard DesJardins.
Pastoral Office—85 Main St., P.O. Box 418, Ashburnham, 01430-0418. Tel: 978-827-5806; Fax: 978-827-1191. Email: stdenis@comcast.net.
Catechesis/Religious Program—Tel: 978-827-4892. Combined with St. Denis.

SOUTH BARRE, ST. THOMAS-A-BECKET (1918) Rev. Ernest Allega.
Res.: 398 Vernon Ave., P.O. Box 186, 01074. Tel: 978-355-2228; Fax: 978-355-0042. Email: e.allegra@yahoo.com.
Catechesis/Religious Program—Tel: 508-882-3353; Fax: 508-882-9517. Students 80.

SOUTH GRAFTON, ST. JAMES (1887) Rev. Edward J. Hanlon; Deacon Edward Richards.
Res.: 89 Main St., 01560. Tel: 508-839-5354; Fax: 508-839-5430.
Catechesis/Religious Program—Tel: 508-839-6800. Students 358.

SOUTHBOROUGH

1—ST. ANNE (1886) Revs. Thomas B. Garlick; Krzysztof Korcz.
Res.: 20 Boston Rd., 01772. Tel: 508-485-0141; Fax: 508-481-9374. Email: stanne403@charter.net. Web: stanne-southboro.org.
Catechesis/Religious Program—Tel: 508-481-3159. Cynthia dela Pena, D.R.E. Students 485.

2—ST. MATTHEW (1956) [JC] Rev. James B. Flynn.
Res.: 105 Southville Rd., 01772. Tel: 508-485-2285; Fax: 508-485-4437. Email: office@stmatthewsb.org. Web: stmatthewcatholic-southboro.org.
Catechesis/Religious Program—Tel: 508-229-2429; Fax: 508-229-0837. Email: reled@stmatthewsb.org. Students 700.

SOUTHBRIDGE

1—ST. HEDWIG (1916), (Polish), [CEM] Rev. Charles E.J. Borowski.
Res.: 29 Summer St., 01550. Tel: 508-764-6947; Fax: 508-764-7707.
Catechesis/Religious Program—Students 39.

2—ST. MARY (1861) [CEM] Rev. Peter Joyce; Deacons W. Steve Miller; Teodoro Camacho.
Res.: 263 Hamilton St., 01550. Tel: 508-764-3226; Fax: 508-764-3209. Web: www.stmarysbge.com.
See Trinity Catholic Academy, Southbridge in the Institution Section (G) under Elementary School, Parochial.
Catechesis/Religious Program—Tel: 508-765-0394 (Spanish). Sr. Xinia Rodriguez, R.O.D.A., D.R.E.; Antonia Correa, C.R.E. (K-12); Brandon Vennink, Music Dir. Students 348.

3—NOTRE DAME (1869), (French-Canadian), Rev. Leo-Paul J. LeBlanc; Deacons Michael J. Corby; Thomas A. Skonieczny.
Res.: 61 Marcy St., 01550. Tel: 508-765-0601; Fax: 508-764-4148.
Catechesis/Religious Program—Religious Education Center, 20 Marcy St., 01550. Tel: 508-764-8018. Students 123.

4—SACRED HEART OF JESUS (1908), (French), Rev. Leo-Paul J. LeBlanc, Admin.; Deacons Michael J. Corby; Thomas A. Skonieczny.
Res.: 61 Marcy St., 01550. Tel: 508-765-0601; Fax: 508-764-4148. Email: sacredheartofjesus@charterinternet.com.
Catechesis/Religious Program—Students 22.

SPENCER

1—MARY, QUEEN OF THE ROSARY (1994) [CEM], Merger of St. Mary, Spencer and Our Lady of the Rosary, Spencer. Rev. James F. Hoey; Deacon Harry M. Sweet.
Office: 60 Maple St., 01562. Tel: 508-885-3111; Fax: 508-885-4905. Email: office@maryqueenoftherosary.org. Web: www.maryqueenoftherosary.org.
Res.: 46 Maple St., 01562. Tel: 508-885-3806.
Catechesis/Religious Program—Tel: 508-885-0211. Mrs. Judith Brennan, D.R.E. Students 340.

2—OUR LADY OF THE ROSARY (1854) Merged with St. Mary's, Spencer to form Mary, Queen of the Rosary, Spencer.

STERLING, ST. RICHARD OF CHICHESTER (1953) Rev. James M. Steuterman; Sr. Anne Marie Wildenhain, S.S.J., Pastoral Assoc.; Kathleen Majikas, Admin. Asst.
Res.: 4 Bridge St., P.O. Box 657, 01564. Tel: 978-422-8881; Fax: 978-422-0291. Email: strichardsterling@comcast.net. Web: www.strichardsterling.org.
Catechesis/Religious Program—Tel: 508-422-8921. Karen Casey, D.R.E. Students 442.

SUTTON, ST. MARK (1964) [CEM] Rev. Michael A. DiGeronimo; Deacon John Dugan.
Res.: 356 Boston Rd., 01590. Tel: 508-865-3860; Fax: 508-865-5095. Email: st.mark-office@verizon.net. Web: www.stmarksparish.org.
Catechesis/Religious Program—Tel: 508-845-3860, Ext. 16. Elizabeth Gorman, D.R.E. Students 140.

UPTON, HOLY ANGELS (1900) Rev. Laurence V. Brault.
Res.: 2 Nelson St., 01568. Tel: 508-529-6981; Fax: 508-529-6317. Email: holyangels1@charter.net. Web: www.stgabrielma.org.
Catechesis/Religious Program—Tel: 508-529-3109. Simone Caron, D.R.E. Students 636.

UXBRIDGE, ST. MARY'S (1853) [CEM] Rev. Steven M. LaBaire; Deacon Paul Brown.
Res.: 77 Mendon St., 01569. Tel: 508-278-2226; Fax: 508-278-7949.
Catechesis/Religious Program—Tel: 508-278-3777. Students 184.

WARREN, ST. PAUL (1872) [CEM] Rev. Daniel J. Becker.
Res.: 1082 Main St., P.O. Box 1027, 01083-1027. Tel: 413-436-7327.
Catechesis/Religious Program—Tel: 413-436-7492. Clustered with St. Thomas Aquinas, West Warren. Students 50.

WEBSTER

1—ST. JOSEPH BASILICA (1887), (Polish), [CEM] Rev. Msgr. Anthony S. Czarnecki.
Res.: 53 Whitcomb St., 01570. Tel: 508-943-0467; Fax: 508-943-0808. Email: rectory@stjosephwebster.com. Web: www.saintjosephbasilica.com.
School—(Grades PreK-8) Tel: 508-943-0378; Fax: 508-949-0581. Email: principal@saintjosephwebster.com. Web: www.saintjosephschool.net. Donald Cushing, Prin. Felician Sisters 2; Lay Teachers 16; Students 108.
Catechesis/Religious Program—Students 75.

2—ST. LOUIS (1853) Rev. Joseph A. Marcotte. In Res., Rev. Edwin A. Gomez.
Res.: 15 Lake St., 01570. Tel: 508-943-0240; Fax: 508-943-0801. Email: saintlouischurch@verizon.net. Web: www.stlouischurchwebster.org.
School—(Grades K-8) Tel: 508-943-0257; Fax: 508-943-0257. Mrs. Katherine Kelly, Prin. Lay Teachers 12; Students 209.
Catechesis/Religious Program—Tel: 508-943-0817; Fax: 508-943-0817. Email: stlouisreled@stlouisschool.org. Students 329.

3—SACRED HEART OF JESUS (1870) [CEM] [JC] Rev. Michael J. Roy; Deacons Anthony R. Surozenski; Laurent Mongeau, (Retired).
Res.: 18 E. Main St., 01570. Tel: 508-943-3140; Fax: 508-943-2213. Email: shp1870@verizon.net.
School—St. Anne, (Grades PreK-8), Day St., 01570. Tel: 508-943-2735; Fax: 508-943-6215. Sr. Constance Bayeur, S.S.A., Prin. Sisters of St. Anne 2; Lay Teachers 12; Students 209.
Catechesis/Religious Program—Tel: 508-943-0113. Students 57.

WEST BOYLSTON, OUR LADY OF GOOD COUNSEL (1869) [CEM] Rev. Kenneth R. Cardinale. In Res., Rev. John M. Lizewski.
Res.: 111 Worcester St., 01583. Tel: 508-835-3606; Fax: 508-835-5456. Email: goodcounsel@charter.net.
Catechesis/Religious Program—Tel: 508-835-6336. Sr. Elaine Potvin, S.S.A., D.R.E. Students 236.

WEST BROOKFIELD, SACRED HEART OF JESUS (1950) Rev. David B. Galonek.
Res.: 10 Milk St., 01585-0563. Tel: 508-867-6469; Fax: 508-867-3670.
Parish Center—Tel: 508-867-4460.
Catechesis/Religious Program—Tel: 508-867-4460. Students 123.

WEST WARREN

1—ST. STANISLAUS (1913), (Polish), Rev. Daniel J. Becker.
Res.: 2270 Main St., P.O. Box 723, 01092-0723. Tel: 413-436-5110.
Catechesis/Religious Program—Students 10.

2—ST. THOMAS AQUINAS (1893) Closed. For inquiries for parish records contact St. Paul, Warren.

WESTBOROUGH, ST. LUKE THE EVANGELIST (1870) [CEM] Rev. Msgr. Michael G. Foley; Rev. Dennis O'Mara.
Res.: 70 W. Main St., 01581. Tel: 508-366-5502; Fax: 508-366-6049. Email: office@stlukes-parish.org. Web: www.stlukes-parish.org.
Catechesis/Religious Program—One Ruggles St., 01581. Tel: 508-366-8509. Email: religiouseducation@stlukes-parish.org. Diane Patrick, D.R.E.; Gloria Josephs, Youth Dir. Students 770.

WESTMINSTER, ST. EDWARD THE CONFESSOR (1951) Rev. Terence T. Kilcoyne; Deacon Roderick F. Cashes.
Res.: 10 Church St., 01473. Tel: 978-874-2362; Fax: 978-874-1024.
Catechesis/Religious Program—Tel: 978-874-1559. Students 269.

WHITINSVILLE, ST. PATRICK (1889) [CEM] Rev. C. Michael Broderick; Deacon Patrick W. Stewart.

Res.: 7 East St., P.O. Box 60, 01588. Tel: 508-234-5656; Fax: 508-234-6845. Web: www.mystpatricks.com.
Catechesis/Religious Program—Tel: 508-234-3511. Mary Lou Petty, D.R.E. Students 489.

WINCHENDON, IMMACULATE HEART OF MARY (1870) [CEM] Rev. Francis A. Roberge; Deacon Mark J. Carrier.
Res.: 52 Spruce St., 01475. Tel: 508-297-0280; Fax: 508-297-3577. Email: ihmwinchendon@aol.com.
Catechesis/Religious Program—Tel: 508-297-2699. Sr. Pauline Grenier, P.M., D.R.E. Students 127.
Convent—110 Summer St., 01475. Tel: 508-297-0275. Sisters of the Presentation of Mary 3.

Chaplains of Public Institutions

WORCESTER. *Memorial Hospital*.
University of Mass Medical Center. Rev. Francis J. Roach.
Worcester Belmont House. Serviced by St. Anne Church, Shrewsbury.
Worcester State Hospital. Rev. Msgr. Rocco M. Piccolomini.

BOYLSTON. *Worcester County Jail and House of Correction*. Deacon Gary Miller.

GARDNER. *Massachusetts Correctional Institution*.

LEOMINSTER. *Leominster Hospital*. Sr. Cathleen Pimley, Catholic Pastoral Min.

OTTER RIVER. *Templeton Developmental Center*. Rev. Joseph J. Jurgelonis.

On Administrative Leave of Absence:
Revs.—
Doherty, Paul J.
Martinez, Jesus E.

On Special or Other Diocesan Assignment:
Rev. Msgr.—
Banach, Michael, Vatican Diplomatic Corp.
Rev.—
Diorio, Ralph A., Apostolate of Healing

On Duty Outside the Diocese:
Rev. Msgrs.—
Banach, Michael, Dir., Theresianumgasse 33/4, Vienna A-1040 Austria.
Kelly, Francis D., Rector, Superior, Casa Santa Maria, Via dell'Umitta, 30, Rome 00187 Italy.
Mongelluzzo, James A., 158 Berrington Rd., Leominster, 01453.
Roy, F. Gilles, Apartado 46, Sicuani (Via Cuzco), Peru.
Revs.—
Boucher, Roger R., C.D.R., C.H.C., U.S.N., P.O. Box 148, Gilmanton Iron Works, NH 03837.
Damian, Ronald, Chap., V.A. Medical Center, Miami, FL
Dunkley, George, St. Mark, San Marcos, CA 92069.
Gelineau, Raymond H., Diocese of Knoxville
Hill, George H., 1759 Castle Hill Ave., Bronx, NY 10462.

Graduate Studies:
Rev.—
Reidy, Richard F. Canonical Law The Catholic University of America, Washington, DC 20064.

Military Chaplains:
Rev.—
Kazarnowicz, Anthony S., Chap., U.S. Army, 1319-A Mississippi Ave., P.O. Box 1134, Fort Campbell, KY 42223.

On Medical Leave of Absence:
Rev.—
Landry, Thomas

Retired:
Rev. Msgrs.—
Collette, Richard, Southgate, 30 Julio Dr., Shrewsbury, 01545.
Sirois, Joseph V. House of Formation for Pre-Seminary Studies
Tinsley, Edmond T., P.A.
Revs.—
Banach, Henry S., 64 Oakwood Ln., 01604.
Burke, John F., 30 Julio Dr., Shrewsbury, 01545.
Connell, John F., P.O. Box 43, Northbridge, 01534.
Debitetto, Ronald E., 66 Stetson St., Hyannis, 02601.
Donahue, Martin P., 101 Wilson Ave., Spencer, 01562.
Dutram, Charles J., 12 Elizabeth St., Dudley, 01571.
Falvey, Edmund F., St. Patrick Manor, Framingham, 01701.
Gallagher, William J., 38 High St., 01609.
Gariepy, Andre M., 855 John Fitch Hwy., Unit 27, Fitchburg, 01420.
Gariepy, Robert E., Southgate, 35 Julio Drive, Apt. 311, Shrewsbury, 01545.
Gionet, Urbain J., Southgate of Shrewsbury, 30 Julio Dr., Apt. 112, Shrewsbury, 01545.
Gould, Louis J., 875 John Fitch Hwy., #15, Fitchburg, 01420.
Grochowski, Bernard J., Box 9839, Las Vegas, NV 89191.
Hamernik, Peter P., Immaculate Conception Rectory, 25 Parker St., Indian Orchard, 01151.
Hebert, Roland G., Southgate of Shrewsbury, 30 Julio Dr., Apt. 109, Shrewsbury, 01545.
Labonte, Richard H., 41 Providence St., 01604.
Lamothe, C. Romero, Southgate of Shewsbury, 30 Julio Dr., Shrewsbury, 01545.
Lange, George O., Southgate, 30 Julio Dr., Apt 236, Shrewsbury, 01545.
Laperle, Theodore R., St. Bernard Rectory, 240 Water St., Fitchburg, 01420.
Lewandowski, Richard P., M.A., 49 Elm St., 01609.
McGovern, William W., 34 Mild Bay Cir., Dennis Port, 02639-1003.
McNamara, Philip D., 30 Julio Dr., Shrewsbury, 01545.
O'Brien, George L., 143 Breezy Point Rd., South Yarmouth, 02664.
O'Brien, Thomas F., 662 Windsurf Ln., Naples, FL 34108.
O'Brien, William G., P.O. Box 362, West Brookfield, 01585.
O'Donoghue, Brendan W., 30 Julio Dr., Apt. 246, Shrewsbury, 01545.
O'Leary, Cornelius F., Notre Dame Assisted Living.
Ouillette, Arthur A., 30 Julio Dr., Shrewsbury, 01545.
Thomas, John D., Christ the King, 1052 Pleasant St., 01602.

Permanent Deacons:
Aliskevicz, John J., Immaculate Conception, Fitchburg; D'Youville Senior Care Center, Lowell
Archibald, Norbert H., St. George, Worcester, MA
Arsenault, Roger D., (Retired), Holy Rosary, Gardner
Aubuchon, Ronald J., St. Cecilia, Leominster
Audette, Paul T., Our Lady of Loreto, Worcester, MA
Baczewski, Stanley H., Holy Spirit, Gardner
Baniukiewicz, Joseph M., Christ the King, Worcester
Benvenuti, Clement E., (Retired)
Blackwelder, Edgar B., (Retired)
Bosse, Raymond J., (Retired)
Briggs, Roy F., Blessed Sacrament, Worchester
Brown, Paul E., Deaf Ministry; St. Mary, Uxbridge
Buron, Ronald B., St. Brigid, Millbury
Camacho, Teodoro, St. Mary, Southbridge
CaraDonna, Nicholas M., Jr., St. Mary's, North Grafton
Carrier, Mark, Immaculate Heart of Mary, Winchendon
Carrier, Paul J., Sacred Heart of Jesus, Gardner
Cashes, Roderick F., St. Edward the Confessor, Westminster
Clonan, Joseph V., St. Joseph the Good Provider, Berlin
Colley, Scott, St. Francis of Assisi, Athol
Colon, William B., Hispanic Community, St. Francis, Fitchburg
Connor, James A., St. Vincent de Paul, Baldwinville
Connor, Michael P., N. Charleston, NC
Corby, Michael P., Notre Dame, Southbridge
Cormier, Dennis J., St. John the Evangelist, Clinton
Couture, James, St. Joseph, Fitchburg
Croteau, Andre W., (Retired)
Daluga, Richard B., Henderson, NV
Denning, James, St. Catherine of Sweden, Worcester
Desautels, Alphonse T., Our Lady of the Angels, Worcester
Desjardin, Richard C., St. Dennis/St. Ann, Ashburnham
Desmarais, Ernest E., (Retired)
Devine, Philip E., Chaplain, N. Central Correctional Institute, Gardner
Devine, Robert, St. Peter, Worcester
DeVito, Frederick A., (Retired)
Dio, Robert F., St. Joseph, Charlton City
DiPadua, James F., Jr., 49 Elm St., Worcester
Doyle, Walter F., Refugee Apostolate, Worcester
Driscoll, Patrick M., Refugee Apostolate, Our Lady of the Rosary, Worcester
Dugan, John, St. Mark, Sutton
Dunphy, Melvin A., New Port Richey, FL
DuVarney, Joseph T., (Retired)
Escobar, Francisco, St. Paul Cathedral, Worcester
Faford, Peter R., Les Calles, Haiti
Fiore, Anthony, St. Boniface, Lunenburg
Franchi, John A., St. Brigid, Millbury
Gemme, Pierre G.L., St. Patrick, Rutland
Gendron, Steven P., St. Bernard, Fitchburg
Gervais, Mark E., Good Shepherd, Linwood
Giard, Arthur J., Jr., (Retired)
Graves, James E., St. Anna, Leominster
Green, Amos H., Sr., (Retired)
Harkins, Frederick A., Our Lady of the Lake, Leominster
Hayes, Myles, Our Lady of Fatima, St. Bernard, Worcester
Isabel, David R., Souza-Baranowski Correction Center, Lancaster
King, Loren M., (Retired)
Klug, Dennis J., St. Anne, Shrewsbury
Ladroga, William J., (On Duty Outside the Diocese)
Leger, Robert, (Retired)
Linderman, James L., Our Lady Immaculate, Athol
Lucier, William J., St. Augustine, Millville
Manella, Joseph R., Sacred Heart, Hopedale
Martino, Richard C., St. Rose of Lima, Northboro
McCaffrey, Joseph A., (Retired)
Meilus, Eduardas, Youth Ministry & St. Mark, Sutton
Mello, Paul, St. Peter, Petersham
Meyers, Christopher C., St. Christopher, Worcester
Michaud, Roland R., (Leave of Absence)
Miller, Gary, (Worcester County Jail and House of Correction)
Miller, William S., St. Mary, Southbridge
Miskell, Lawrence F., St. Joseph, Charlton
Mongeau, Laurent M., (Retired)
Montiverdi, Gerald M., University of Massachusetts Medical Center, Worcester
Motyka, Peter J., St. Louis, Webster
Mussulli, Pasquale, Sacred Heart, Milford
Myska, Frank B., Jr., St. Mary, Shrewsbury
Nogueira, Benjamin A., Campus Ministry, Fitchburg State College, Fitchburg
O'Connor, George, St. Bernadette, Northborough
Olson, Richard V., St. Anne, St. Patrick, Sturbridge
Packard, Lee, St. Peter, Northbridge
Prince, Norman A., (Retired)
Reisinger, Scott R., St. Peter, Worcester
Richards, Edward J., St. James, South Grafton
Ryan, Peter, St. Joseph, Auburn
Skonieczny, Thomas A., Sacred Heart, Notre Dame, Southbridge
Stevens, Wesley, St. Roch, Oxford
Stewart, Patrick W., St. Patrick, Whitinsville
Surozenski, Anthony R., Office of the Diaconate; Sacred Heart, Webster
Sweet, Harry M., Mary Queen of the Rosary, Spencer
Tantillo, Salvatore, St. Anthony di Padua, Fitchburg
Tatro, Richard J., Holy Cross, East Templeton
Vaillancourt, David F., St. Stephen, Worcester
Vidito, Bruce R., St. Joseph, Auburn
Wagner, Thomas A., (On Duty Outside the Diocese)
Weiss, Stephen J., El Mirage, AZ

INSTITUTIONS LOCATED IN THE DIOCESE

[A] COLLEGES AND UNIVERSITIES

WORCESTER. *Assumption College* (1904) 500 Salisbury St., 01609. Tel: 508-767-7000; Fax: 508-756-1780. Email: info@assumption.edu. Web: www.assumption.edu. Dr. Francesco C. Cesareo, Pres.; Christian McCarthy, Exec. Vice Pres.; Frederick F. Travis, Interim Provost; Rev. Dennis Gallagher, A.A., Vice Pres. Mission; Thomas E. Ryan, Vice Pres. Inst. Advancement; Catherine M. Woodbrooks, Vice Pres. Student Life; Doris Ann Sweet, Dir. Library Svcs. A Catholic Liberal Arts College under the auspices of the Augustinians of the Assumption (Assumptionists). Priests 2; Sisters 1; Lay Teachers 155; Students 2,776; Total Enrollment 4,422.

College of the Holy Cross, Inc. (1843) 01610. Tel: 508-793-2011; Fax: 508-793-3030. Email: relias@holycross.edu. Web: www.holycross.edu. Rev. Michael C. McFarland, S.J., Pres.; Dr. James Hogan, Librarian. A College for Boarders and Day Scholars. Sisters 1; Lay Teachers 321; Students 2,901; Jesuit Teachers 13.

PAXTON. *Anna Maria College*, 50 Sunset Ln., 01612. Tel: 508-849-3300; Fax: 508-849-3334. Email: pgreen@annamaria.edu. Web: www.annamaria.edu. Jack P. Calareso, Ph.D., Pres.; Barbara Zawalich, Registrar; Paula Green,

Dir. Mktg.; Ms. Ruth Pyne, Librarian. Sisters of St. Anne., A Coeducational Catholic College. Priests 1; Sisters 1; Lay Teachers 172; Students 1,594.

[B] HIGH SCHOOLS, CENTRAL

WORCESTER. *Holy Name Central Catholic Junior/Senior High School* (1942) (Grades 7-12), 144 Granite St., 01604. Tel: 508-753-6371; Fax: 508-831-1287. Email: ereynolds@holyname.net. Web: www.holyname.net. Mrs. Mary E. Riordan, B.A., M.Ed., M.A., Dir. Inst. Advancement; Mr. Edward M. Reynolds, B.A., M.Ed., Headmaster; Mr. Ray Greenwood, B.A., Prin., Upper School; Mrs. Arlene Maurello, M.Ed., Prin., Lower School; Rev. James B. Flynn, B.A., L.S.T., Ph.D., Senior Counselor; Susan Hughes, Librarian. Priests 1; Lay Teachers 38; Students 655.

St. Peter-Marian Central Catholic Junior/Senior High School (1976) (Grades 7-12), 781 Grove St., 01605-3196. Tel: 508-852-5555; Fax: 508-852-7238. Email: spmsroffice@spmguardians.org. Mr. Matthew R. Sturgis, B.A., M.A., M.Ed., Headmaster; Mrs. Joanne Ethier, Prin. Jr. High; Mrs. Denise Allain, B.A., M.A., Prin., High School; Mary Andrysick, Librarian. Sisters 1; Lay Teachers 43; Students 710.

FITCHBURG. *St. Bernard's Central Catholic High School* (1926) 45 Harvard St., 01420. Tel: 978-342-3212; Fax: 978-345-8067. Web: stb.echalk.com. James Conry, Headmaster; Robert Blanchard, M.A., Prin. Priests 1; Lay Teachers 21; Students 370; Total Staff 12.

[C] HIGH SCHOOLS, PAROCHIAL

WORCESTER. *St. Mary's Junior/Senior High School*, (Grades 7-12), 50 Richland St., 01610. Tel: 508-753-1170; Fax: 508-795-0560. Email: mdudekstmaryshigh@gmail.com. Michael E. Dudek, Prin. Congregation of the Sisters of the Holy Family of Nazareth. Lay Teachers 15; Students 145.

[D] HIGH SCHOOLS, PRIVATE

WORCESTER. *Notre Dame Academy*, 425 Salisbury St., 01609. Tel: 508-757-6200; Fax: 508-757-7200. Email: amorrison@nda-worc.org. Web: www.nda-worc.org. Sr. Ann Morrison, S.N.D., Prin. A Private Day School for Girls. Sisters of Notre Dame de Namur 2; Other Religious Orders 1; Lay Teachers 31; Girls 270.

FITCHBURG. *Notre Dame Preparatory School*, 171 South St., 01420. Tel: 978-343-7635; Fax: 978-343-4379. Email: jheffh@hotmail.com. Web: www.notredameprepfitchburg.citymax.com. Mr. Jeff Hammond, Headmaster. Lay Teachers 7; Students 43.

LANCASTER. *Trivium School* (1979) (Grades 7-12), 471 Langen Rd., 01523. Tel: 978-365-4795; Fax: 978-365-4795. Email: triviumschool@aol.com. Web: triviumschool.com. Dr. William M. Schmitt, Headmaster. Lay Teachers 15; Students 76.

SHREWSBURY. *St. John's High School* (1898) 378 Main St., 01545. Tel: 508-842-8934; Fax: 508-842-3670. Email: jconca@stjohnshigh.org. Web: www.stjohnshigh.org. Mr. Michael W. Welch, Headmaster; Dr. Jacob A. Conca, Prin.; Elizabeth Kavanagh, Librarian. Xaverian Brothers. Lay Teachers 63; Boys 1,000.

STILL RIVER. *Immaculate Heart of Mary School* (1976) 282 Still River Rd., Box 1000, 01467. Tel: 978-456-8877; Fax: 978-456-9052. Email: smt@saintbenedict.com. Web: www.saintbenedict.com. Sr. Miriam Teresa, Prin.; Ann Cutress, R.N., Librarian. Sisters 11; Students 135; Total Staff 20.

[E] MIDDLE SCHOOLS, PRIVATE

WORCESTER. *The Nativity School of Worcester*, (Grades 7-9), 10 Irving St., 01606. Tel: 508-799-0100; Fax: 508-799-3951. Email: info@nativityworcester.org. Web: www.nativityworcester.org. Matthew Brunell, Exec. Dir. Tel: 508-799-0100; David Roach, Prin.; Charles Weiss, Chm. Bd. Teachers 13; Boys 55.

[F] ELEMENTARY SCHOOLS, CENTRAL

WORCESTER. *St. Peter's Central Catholic Elementary School* (1921) 865 Main St., 01610. Tel: 508-791-6496; Fax: 508-770-0818. Web: www.stpetercc.com. Mrs. Meg Kursonis, Head of School. Lay Teachers 21; Students 324; Preschool 60; Total Enrollment 384.

MILFORD. *Milford Catholic Elementary School* (1975) (Grades PreK-6), 11 E. Main St., 01757. Tel: 508-473-7303; Fax: 508-478-4902. Email: info@milfordcatholic.org. Web: milfordcatholic.org. Mrs. Andrea Tavaska, Prin. Lay Teachers 14; Aides 3; Students 175.

UXBRIDGE. *Our Lady of Valley Regional Elementary School* (1964) 75 Mendon St., 01569. Tel: 508-278-5851; Fax: 508-278-0391. Pauline Hayward, Librarian. Lay Teachers 9; Part-Time Teachers 4; Students 186.

[G] ELEMENTARY SCHOOLS, PAROCHIAL

SOUTHBRIDGE. *Trinity Catholic Academy*, 11 Pine St., 01550. Tel: 508-765-5991; Fax: 508-765-0017. Email: mbrouillard@worcesterdiocesek12.org. Web: www.trinitycatholicacademy.net. Mrs. Madeleine Brouillard, Prin.; Gale Splaine-Belanger, Librarian. Lay Teachers 14; Students 200; Total Staff 24.

[H] ELEMENTARY SCHOOLS, PRIVATE

WORCESTER. *Venerini Academy*, (Grades PreK-8), 27 Edward St., 01605. Tel: 508-753-3210; Fax: 508-754-6050. Email: snap@veneriniacademy.com. Web: www.veneriniacademy.com. Sr. Sandra Napier, S.N.D.deN., B.A., M.Ed., Prin.; Patricia Avis, Librarian. Sisters 3; Lay Teachers 19; Students 329.

NEW BRAINTREE. *Magnificat Academy & Choir School*, 1115 Worcester Rd, 01531. Tel: 508-755-6096; Fax: 508-867-2205. Email: magnificatacademy@verizon.net. Web: magnificatacademy.org. Paul Jernberg, Headmaster. Lay Teachers 2; Students 21.

[I] CATHOLIC CHARITIES

WORCESTER. *Catholic Charities* (1950) 10 Hammond St., 01610-1513. Tel: 508-798-0191; Fax: 508-797-5659. Web: www.ccworc.org. Catherine Loeffler, Diocesan Dir.; Cynthia Ross, Dir. Financial Mgmt.; Judith Zeh, Manager, Personnel & Training.

Northern Worcester Co. Offices, 196 Mechanic St., Leominster, 01453. Tel: 978-840-0696; Fax: 978-345-4161.

12 Riverbend St., Athol, 01331-2520. Tel: 978-249-4563; Fax: 978-249-2545. Jacqueline Hager, Area Admin.

Southern Worcester Co. Offices

Southbridge Office, 79 Elm St., Southbridge, 01550-2601. Tel: 508-765-5936; Fax: 508-764-4153. Lisa Genest, Area Admin.

Blackstone Valley/Greater Milford Area Office, 9 Spring St., Whitinsville, 01588-1409. Tel: 508-234-3800; Fax: 508-234-2321.

126 Main St., Rm. 6, Milford, 01757. Tel: 508-478-9632; Fax: 508-478-9632. Noreen Landry, Area Admin.

Senior Employment Service, 10 Hammond St., 01610-1513. Tel: 508-798-0191; Fax: 508-797-5659. Susan Maedler, Prog. Admin. Senior Aid Employment.

Refugee Resettlement, 10 Hammond St., 01610-1513. Tel: 508-798-0191; Fax: 508-797-5659. Debra Spangler, Prog. Admin. Homeless Prevention Refugee Resettlement & Community Educ.

Family & Community Services, 10 Hammond St., 01610-1513. Tel: 508-798-0191; Fax: 508-797-5659. Diane Lambert, Admin. Family Community Svcs.

Literacy Volunteers, 10 Hammond St., 01610-1513. Tel: 508-798-0191; Fax: 508-797-5659. Madelyn Hennessy, Prog. Admin. Literacy.

Crozier House, 10 Hammond St., 01610-1513. Tel: 508-798-0191; Fax: 508-797-5659. J. David Mulrooney, Prog. Admin. A Half-Way House for Substance Abusing Men.

Mercy Centre (Developmental Disabilities), 25 W. Chester St., 01605-1136. Tel: 508-852-7165; Fax: 508-856-9755. Heather MacDonald, Admin. Special Education Day Program and Sheltered Workshop for Developmentally Disabled Youngsters and Adults.

Youville House Shelter for Homeless Families, 133 Granite St., 01604-4500. Tel: 508-753-3084; Fax: 508-754-0139. Kenneth Michaud, Prog. Admin. Family Shelter. Total Assisted 30,000; Total Staff 250.

[J] CHILD CARE AGENCIES

WORCESTER. *Guild of St. Agnes*, 133 Granite St., 01604. Tel: 508-755-2238; Fax: 508-754-2026. Email: swoodbury@guildofstagnes.org. Web: www.guildofstagnes.org. Mr. Edward Madaus, Dir. Day Care Centers for Infants, Toddlers, Preschoolers & School-age Children. Children aged 4 weeks-12 years.; Family Day Care Program ages 6 weeks-5 years. Children 1,327; Total Staff 225.

FITCHBURG. *Guild of St. Agnes*, 62 Dover St., 01420. Tel: 978-343-3042; Fax: 978-343-2610. Total Assisted 110; Total Staff 7.

LEICESTER. *McAuley Nazareth Home for Boys* (1901) 01524. Tel: 508-892-4886; Fax: 508-892-9736. Email: naz1901@verizon.net. Web: www.nazareth-home.org. Sr. Janet Ballentine, R.S.M., Exec. Dir.; Rev. Msgr. Edmond T. Tinsley, P.A., Chap. (Retired). Diocese of Worcester. Sisters 3; Lay Teachers 5; Boys 20; Special Education School: Boys 24.

[K] GENERAL HOSPITALS

WORCESTER. *Saint Vincent Hospital, Inc.* (1893) 123 Summer St., 01608. Tel: 508-363-5000; Fax: 508-363-5387. Email: teri.hegarty@stvincenthospital.com. Web: www.stvincenthospital.com. Mr. John E. Smithhisler, Pres. & CEO; Rev. Peggy Kieras, Supvr., Clinical Pastoral Educ.; Revs. Terrence M. Curry, S.J., Chap.; Son Anh Nguyen, Chap.; Peter R. Beaulieu, Dir., Mission Integration & Pastoral Care; Sisters Mary O'Leary, S.P., Chap.; Ann Marie Boudreau, S.S.A., Chap.; Adrienne Lamoureux, P.F.M., Chap. Sisters 3; Bed Capacity 321; Patients Assisted Annually 228,139; Total Staff 1,824.

[L] SPECIAL HOSPITALS AND SANATORIA

WORCESTER. *Saint Francis Home* (1898) 101 Plantation St., 01604. Tel: 508-755-8605; Fax: 508-791-6954. Email: ceo@saintfrancishome.org. Lisa Piekarczkyk, Admin. Bed Capacity 137; Employees 210.

Notre Dame Health Care Center, Inc., 559 Plantation St., 01605. Tel: 508-852-3011; Fax: 508-852-0397. Email: klemay@notredameltcc.org. Web: www.notredameltcc.org. Katherine Lemay, Admin. Bed Capacity 123; Total Staff 170.

WHITINSVILLE. *St. Camillus Hospice, Inc.*, 447 Hill St., 01588. Tel: 508-234-7306; Fax: 508-234-7597. Rev. John J. Gallagher, O.S.Cam.

St. Camillus Nursing Home Inc., 447 Hill St., 01588. Tel: 508-234-7306. William Graves, Admin.; Bro. Thomas Farrell, O.S.Cam., Dir. Pastoral Care. Priests 1; Brothers 2; Bed Capacity 123.

St. Camillus Institute, 497 Hill St., 01588.

St. Camillus, 495 Hill St., 01588. Rev. Jack Gallagher, O.S.Cam.

[M] HEALTH SERVICES

WORCESTER. *Pernet Family Health Service*, 237 Millbury St., 01610. Tel: 508-755-1228; Fax: 508-797-3477. Email: sdooley@pernetfamilyhealth.org. Web: pernetfamilyhealth.org. Sheilah Dooley, Exec. Dir. Mission of the Little Sisters of the Assumption.; Certified Home Health and Social Service Agency. Focus of services toward the parent and young child. Parenting groups, family activities available, Early Childhood Development services also available. Total Staff 28; Little Sisters of the Assumption 2; Total Volunteers 50.

[N] HOMES FOR AGED

WORCESTER. *Notre Dame du Lac*, 555 Plantation St., 01605. Tel: 508-852-5800; Fax: 508-852-1700. Email: csessions@charter.net. Web: www.notredamedulac.org. Margaret Coffin, Exec. Dir. Apartments 108; Total Staff 97.

LEOMINSTER. *Presentation Health Care Center* (1993) 99 Church St., 01453-3147. Tel: 978-537-7856; Fax: 978-840-1564. Email: admjuliec@juno.com. Sr. Patricia Anastasio, P.B.V.M., Pres. Purpose: To operate and maintain a rest home for aged and/or infirmed sisters at Presentation Convent. Total in Residence (Closed Skilled Unit) 10; Total Staff 25.

SPENCER. *St. Joseph's Abbey Resident Care Facility, Inc.* (2003) 167 N. Spencer Rd., 01562-1233. Tel: 508-885-8702; Fax: 508-885-8701. Web: www.spencerabbey.org. Bro. Amadeus Hamilton, O.C.S.O., M.S.N., N.P., Admin. Bed Capacity 12; Total Staff 7; Total Assisted 14.

[O] MONASTERIES AND RESIDENCES OF PRIESTS AND BROTHERS

WORCESTER. *Assumptionists (Augustinians of the Assumption)* (1845) 50 Old English Rd., 01609. Tel: 508-754-6276; Fax: 508-797-1789. Web: www.assumptio.org. Revs. Alexis A. Babineau, A.A.; Eugene LaPlante, A.A., College Chap. (Retired); Paul Vaudreuil, A.A., A.A., Supr.; Robert Fortin, A.A.; Aidan M. Furlong, A.A.; Oliver (Robert) Blanchette, A.A.; Theodore L. Fortier, A.A.; Norman Meiklejohn, A.A.; Bros. Armand Lemaire, A.A.; John-Thomas McHugh, A.A.; Richard Gagnon, A.A., Treas. & College Admissions Officer. Priests 8; Brothers 3; Total Staff 2.

Assumptionists of Assumption College, Emmanuel House, 512 Salisbury St., 01609-1326. Tel: 508-767-7523; Fax: 508-793-9701. Email: dgallagh@assumption.edu. Web: www.assumptionists.com. Revs. Donat R. Lamothe, A.A., Treas.; Barry Bercier, A.A.; Dennis Gallagher, A.A., Regional Supr.; Roger R. Corriveau, A.A.; John Franck, A.A., Local Supr.; Salvatore Musuande, A.A.; Bro. Vo Tran Gia Dinh, A.A. Total in Residence 8; Total Staff 1.

Jesuits of the Holy Cross, Inc. (1843) 1 College St., 01610. Tel: 508-793-2427; Fax: 508-793-2624.

Web: www.holycross.edu/index.html. Revs. John E. Brooks, S.J.; William A. Clark, S.J.; Terrence M. Curry, S.J.; Charles J. Dunn, S.J.; John E. Fagan, S.J.; J. Thomas Hamel, S.J.; Paul F. Harman, S.J.; James M. Hayes, S.J., Rector; Eduardo T. Henriques, S.J.; Anthony J. Kuzniewski, S.J.; Vincent A. Lapomarda, S.J.; Gregory A. Lynch, S.J.; Michael C. McFarland, S.J.; Earle L. Markey, S.J.; James J. Miracky, S.J.; John P. Reboli, S.J.; William E. Reiser, S.J.; Philip C. Rule, S.J.; John D. Savard, S.J.; Thomas J. Sheehan, S.J.; Simon E. Smith, S.J.; William E. Stempsey, S.J.; Edward J. Vodoklys, S.J.; Thomas W. Worcester, S.J.; Christopher Ryan, S.J., (Scholastic). Priests 24; Scholastics 1.

FITCHBURG. *Missionaries of La Salette (MA), Inc.*, St. Joseph, 46 Woodland St., 01420. Tel: 978-342-7907; Fax: 978-345-7678. Total in Residence 2.

PETERSHAM. *St. Mary's Monastery*, N. Main St., P.O. Box 345, 01366. Tel: 978-724-3350; Fax: 978-724-3549. Email: smm1petersham@juno.com. Web: www.stmarysmonastery.org. Revs. Anselm Atkinson, O.S.B., Supr.; Bede Kierney, O.S.B.; Gregory Phillips, O.S.B. Priest-Monks 3; Monks 4.

SHREWSBURY. *Xaverian Brothers*, 378 Main St., 01545. Tel: 508-845-1878; Fax: 508-842-3670. Email: pfeeney@stjohnshigh.org. Bros. Paul Feeney, C.F.X., Dir.; James Mahoney, C.F.X.; Plunket Doherty, C.F.X.; Regis Moynihan, C.F.X.; J. Conal Owens, C.F.X. Brothers 5.

SPENCER. *St. Joseph's Abbey* 01562-1233. Tel: 508-885-8700; Fax: 508-885-8701. Email: monks@spencerabbey.org. Web: www.spencerabbey.org. Rt. Rev. Damian Carr, O.C.S.O.; Revs. Dominic Whedbee, O.C.S.O., Prior; Laurence Bourget, O.C.S.O.; Adrian Proback, O.C.S.O.; Basil Byrne, O.C.S.O.; Eugene Lacasse, O.C.S.O.; Robert Kevin Anderson, O.C.S.O., (In Service Outside the Community); Edward Steriti, O.C.S.O.; Matthew Flynn, O.C.S.O.; Gabriel Bertoniere, O.C.S.O.; Patrick Brown, O.C.S.O.; Kevin Hunt, O.C.S.O.; Robert Morhous, O.C.S.O.; Henry Scarborough, O.C.S.O.; Peter Schmidt, O.C.S.O.; Gerald Sears, O.C.S.O.; Kizito Thompson, O.C.S.O.; Aquinas Keane, O.C.S.O.; Luke Truhan, O.C.S.O.; Aidan (Arthur H.) Logan, O.C.S.O., (On Leave to Military Ordinariate); Francis Rodriguez, O.C.S.O.; Andrew Johnson, O.C.S.O., (In Service Outside Community); David Lavich, O.C.S.O., (In Service Outside the Community); James Palmigiano; Isaac Keeley, O.C.S.O.; Timothy Scott, O.C.S.O., Novice Dir.

Cistercian Abbey of Spencer, Inc. Cistercian Order of the Strict Observance (Trappists). Solemnly Professed 68; Simply Professed 1; Novices 2; Total Priests in Community 27; Total in Community 71.

STILL RIVER. *Benedictine Monks, St. Benedict Abbey* (Harvard), 252 Still River Rd., P.O. Box 67, 01467. Tel: 978-456-3221; Fax: 978-456-8181. Email: saintbenedict@abbey.org. Web: www.abbey.org. Rt. Rev. Gabriel Gibbs, O.S.B., Abbot; Very Rev. Xavier Connelly, O.S.B., Prior; Revs. Basil Rechenburg, O.S.B.; Peter Connelly, O.S.B.; Anthony Kloss, O.S.B.; Marc Crilly, O.S.B.; James Doran, O.S.B.; Augustine Senz, O.S.B. Priests 8; Brothers 6; Oblates 1.

WHITINSVILLE. *St. Camillus Community*, 447 Hill St., 01588. Tel: 508-234-7306; Fax: 508-234-7597. Email: bgraves@stcamillus.com. Web: www.stcamillus.com. Rev. John Gallagher, M.I., Chap. Priests 1.

[P] CONVENTS AND RESIDENCES FOR SISTERS

WORCESTER. *Harper Residence*, 11 Beechmont St., 01609. Tel: 508-792-1619; Fax: 508-792-2067. Email: lcsasv@yahoo.com. Sr. Lucille Cermier, S.A.S.V., Supr. & Contact. Sisters 5.

Little Franciscans of Mary (1889) 55 Moore Ave., 01602-1819. Tel: 508-755-0878; Fax: 508-755-6822. Email: sjalix@yahoo.com. Sr. Jacquelyn Alix, P.F.M., Regl. Supr. Tel: 508-755-0878. Sisters 5.

Little Sisters of the Assumption, Pernet Family Health Service, Inc., 237 Millbury St., 01610. Tel: 508-755-1228; Fax: 508-797-3477. Email: sdooley@pernetfamilyhealth.org. Web: www.pernetfamilyhealth.org. Family Health Agency. Nursing and Family Development Services-Home Based.

Religious Venerini Sisters Provincial Office, 23 Edward St., 01605. Tel: 508-745-1020; Fax: 508-745-6715. Email: himpv4@veneriniacademy.com. Web: www.venerinisisters.org. Sr. Hilda Ponte, M.P.V., Prov. Sisters 23.

Sisters of St. Anne, Esther House (1973) 1015 Pleasant St., 01602. Tel: 508-757-6053. Email: smdugas@hotmail.com. Web: www.sistersofsaintanne.org. Sisters 4; Total in Residence 4; Total Staff 4.

Sisters of St. Joseph, S.S.J., 783 Grove St., 01605. Tel: 508-852-1659. Sisters 3.

Sisters of the Assumption of the Blessed Virgin, 316 Lincoln St., 01605. Tel: 508-856-9383; Fax: 508-853-0881. Email: lono9595@aol.com. Sisters Lorraine Normand, S.A.S.V., Treas. Tel: 508-856-9450; Muriel Lemoine, S.A.S.V., Gen. Asst.

Xaverian Missionary Society of Mary, Inc., Headquarters: 242 Salisbury St., 01609-1639. Tel: 508-757-0514; Fax: 508-757-0514. Email: xavsistersusa@msn.com. Sr. Rosa Maria G. Serra, X.M.M., Supr. Sisters 5.

CHARLTON. *Carmelite Sisters of the Eucharist of Worcester, MA*, 188 Old Worcester Rd., 01507. Tel: 508-248-2936; Fax: 508-248-3814. Sisters 4.

LEOMINSTER. *The Sisters of the Presentation of the Blessed Virgin Mary, New Windsor, NY*, 99 Church St., 01453. Tel: 978-537-7108; Fax: 978-537-3789. Email: campjoynh@hotmail.com. Web: www.sistersofthepresentation.org. Ministries are in the areas of education in parochial elementary schools; pastoral services; health care; social services. Professed Sisters 133.

Mt. St. Joseph, 880 Jackson Ave., New Windsor, NY 12553. Tel: 914-564-0513 (Admin. Office); Fax: 845-567-0219 (Admin. Office). Sisters Patricia Anastasio, P.B.V.M., Pres.; Mary Anne Seliga, P.B.V.M., House Coord.

PETERSHAM. *Assumption Residence of the Sisters of the Assumption of the Blessed Virgin*, 211 N. Main St., 01366. Tel: 978-724-3468; Fax: 978-724-0200. Email: gloriatet@verizon.net. Web: www.sasv.ca. Sisters Estelle Dube, S.A.S.V., Co-Admin.; Lucille Tetreault, Co-Admin.; Sandra Dupre, S.A.S.V., Co-Admin. Professed Sisters 41.

St. Scholastica Priory (1980) 271 N. Main St., Box 606, 01366-0606. Tel: 978-724-3213; Fax: 978-724-3216. Email: sspriory@aol.com. Web: www.stscholasticapriory.org. Very Sr. Mary Elizabeth Kloss, O.S.B., Prioress; Sr. Mary Angela Kloss, O.S.B., Subprioress. Benedictine Nuns (Cloistered). Nuns in Solemn Vows 12.

STILL RIVER. *Sisters of Saint Benedict Center, Slaves of the Immaculate Heart of Mary Inc.* (1949) *St. Ann House*, 254 Still River Rd., P.O. Box 22, 01467. Tel: 978-456-8017; Fax: 978-456-8508. Email: micm@verizon.net. Sr. Maria Cordata Baravella, M.I.C.M. Professed Sisters 12.

WEBSTER. *St. Joseph Convent*, 5 Maynard St., 01570-2433. Tel: 508-943-2228. Email: cssfwebster@yahoo.com. Sr. Jeanne Marie Akalski, C.S.S.F., Supr. Felician Sisters 2.

[Q] RETREAT HOUSES AND HOUSE OF PRAYER

SPENCER. *St. Joseph Abbey*, 167 N. Spencer Rd., 01562-1233. Tel: 508-885-8710; Fax: 508-885-8701. Web: www.spencerabbey.org. Rev. Aquinas Keane, O.C.S.O., Abbot. Guest house and Retreat house.

Mary House, Inc. (1969) 186 N. Spencer Rd. (Rte. 31), P.O. Box 20, 01562. Tel: 508-885-5450. Email: maryhousespencer@netzero.com. Web: maryhousespencer.com. Ms. Joyce Thomasmeyer, Pres. House of Prayer and Contemplation.

STILL RIVER. *Benedictine Monks, St. Benedict Abbey* (Harvard); (See separate listing under Monasteries and Residences for Men.), 252 Still River Rd., P.O. Box 67, 01467. Tel: 978-456-3221; Fax: 978-456-8181. Email: saintbenedict@abbey.org. Web: www.abbey.org. Rt. Rev. Gabriel Gibbs, O.S.B., Abbot.

[R] NEWMAN CHAPLAINS AND CENTERS

WORCESTER. *Campus Ministry* P.O. Box 903, 01613. Tel: 508-925-5004. Email: priest@WPI.edu. Web: www.wpi.edu/~newman. Rev. Peter J. Scanlon, S.T.L., Vicar.

Assumption College 500 Salisbury St., 01609. Tel: 508-767-7419. Email: godonline@assumption.edu. Rev. Dennis Gallagher, A.A.; Mr. Peter Hart; Mr. John Fleming; Sr. Cecilia Hervas, R.A.; Frank Corbin, Ph.D.

Becker College 19 Schussler Rd., 01609. Tel: 774-262-6562. Email: priest@wpi.edu. Rev. Robert A. Loftus, Chap., Religious Center at W.P.I.

Clark University 930 Main St., 01610. Tel: 508-793-7737. Rev. Msgr. Francis J. Scollen, Chap.

Holy Cross College The Office of the College Chaplain. Tel: 508-793-2448. Email: kbarrowsola@aol.com. Ms. Katherine McElaney, Dir.; Rev. James M. Hayes, S.J., Chap. Sisters 1.

Becker College at Leicester Tel: 508-757-6097. Email: priest@wpi.edu. Refer to Diocesan Office.

Worcester State College Campus Ministry Center, 486 Chandler St., 01602. Tel: 508-793-8017. Email: rmcginn@juno.com. Ruth O. McGinn, Chap.

Worcester Polytechnic Institute Religious Center at WPI, 19 Schussler Rd., 01609. Tel: 774-262-6562. Email: lrob@wpi.edu. Rev. Robert A. Loftus.

Fitchburg State College (Fitchburg) Newman Center, 333 Mechanic St., Fitchburg, 01420. Tel: 978-342-7921. Rev. Joseph M. Dolan, Chap.; Deacon Benjamin A. Nogueira; Lois I. Nogueira, Chap.

Anna Maria College Box 35, Paxton, 01612. Tel: 508-849-3399. Rev. John M. Lizewski, Chap.

PAXTON. *Anna Maria College* Office of Campus Ministry, 01612-1198. Tel: 508-849-3399; Fax: 508-849-3319. Web: www.annamaria.edu. Total Staff 1.

[S] MISCELLANEOUS

WORCESTER. *The Charlton Charitable Corporation, Inc.* Diocese of Worcester., 49 Elm St., 01609. Tel: 508-791-7171; Fax: 508-754-2768.

Dismas House of Massachusetts, P.O. Box 30125, 01603. Tel: 508-799-9389; Fax: 508-767-9930. Email: cmdismashouse@aol.com. Web: www.dismashouse.org. David McMahon, Co-Dir.; Colleen Hilferty, Co-Dir. To provide transition for those who are leaving prison.

The Guild of Our Lady of Providence, Chancery Office of the Diocese of Worcester, 49 Elm St., 01609. Tel: 508-791-7171; Fax: 508-753-7180.

Mendon Charitable Corporation, Inc., 49 Elm St., 01609. Tel: 508-791-7171; Fax: 508-754-2768. Mr. Jerome D. Jussaume, Mgr. Finance.

Monsignor Thomas Griffin Foundation, 49 Elm St., 01609. Tel: 508-929-4339; Fax: 508-929-4380. Email: mtinsley@worcesterdiocese.org. Rev. Msgr. Edmond T. Tinsley, P.A., Contact Person (Retired).

Notre Dame Development Fund, Inc., 340 Plantation St., 01604-1637. Tel: 508-770-1744; Fax: 508-770-1745. Email: SNDNEdev@aol.com. Web: www.SNDDEN.org/dev/ne. Sr. Anne-Louise Nadeau, S.N.D., Pres.

St. Peter-Marian Endowment Trust (1998) c/o St. Peter-Marian Central Catholic Junior/Senior High School, 781 Grove St., 01605. Tel: 508-852-5555; Fax: 508-852-7238. Email: alumni@spmguardians.org; spmsroffice@spmguardians.org. Mr. Matthew R. Sturgis, B.A., M.A., M.Ed., Headmaster; Mrs. Joanne Ethier, Jr. High Prin.; Mrs. Denise Allain, B.A., M.A., Prin. Staff 63; Total Assisted 850.

Visitation House, P.O. Box 60115, 01606. 119 Endicott St., 01610. Tel: 508-798-0762; Fax: 508-798-8902. Email: evelindquist@visitationhouse.org. Eve Lindquist, Exec. Dir.; Susan Arraje, House Mgr. A home of hospitality and life for pregnant women in need.

AUBURN. *Kateri Tekakwitha Development, Inc.*, 8 Wyoma Dr., 01501. Tel: 508-798-8779; Fax: 508-791-6614. Email: namoffice@verizon.net. Rev. John F. Gee, Contact Person.

Kateri Tekakwitha Housing Corp., 8 Wyoma Dr., 01501.

CHARLTON. *Ministry to Retired Priests*, 188 Old Worcester Rd., 01507. Tel: 508-868-9239; Fax: 508-248-3814. Sr. Mary Ann Bartell, C.S.E., Dir.

LANCASTER. *Community of St. John*, 471 Langen Rd., 01523. Tel: 978-365-4795; Fax: 978-365-4795. Email: wmschmitt@triviumschool.com. Dr. William M. Schmitt, Contact Person. Total in Residence 1.

PETERSHAM. *St. Bede's Publications* (1977) 271 N. Main St., P.O. Box 545, 01366-0545. Tel: 978-724-3217; Fax: 978-724-3216. Web: www.fordhampress.com. Sr. Mary Clare Vincent, O.S.B.

St. Mary and St. Scholastica Church, Inc. (1996) P.O. Box 606, 01366-0606.

SHREWSBURY. *New England Intercommunity Support Services (NEISS)* (1991) 89 Hill St., 01545-1930. Tel: 508-842-3555. Email: marna.rogers@sndden.org. Sr. Marna Rogers, S.N.D., Contact Person.

SOUTHBRIDGE. *The Worcester Guild of the Catholic Medical Association*, 141 Main St., 01550. Tel: 508-764-9800; Fax: 508-764-0333. Web: www.worcestercma.org. Dr. John Howland, Contact Person, Sec. & Treas.

WHITINSVILLE. *St. Camillus Institute, Inc.*, 447 Hill St., 01588. Tel: 617-234-7306. Very Rev. William F. Cronin, O.S.Cam., Pres. Order of the Servants of the Sick (St. Camillus).

RELIGIOUS INSTITUTES OF MEN REPRESENTED IN THE DIOCESE

For further details refer to the corresponding bracketed number in the Religious Institutes of Men or Women section.

[]—*Augustinians of the Assumption*

[1350]—*Congregation of St. Francis Xavier*—C.F.X.

[]—*Congregation of the Most Holy Redeemer*

[1000]—*Congregation of the Passion*—C.P.

[]—*Congregation of the Sacred Stigmata*

[0790]—*Maronite Monks of Adoration*—M.M.A.

[0720]—*Missionaries of Our Lady of LaSalette* (Seven Dolors Prov.)—M.S.

[0200]—*Order of St. Benedict* (Petersham; Still River)—O.S.B.

[0240]—*Order of St. Camilus*—O.S.Cam.

[]—*Society of Jesus*—S.J.

[0370]—*Society of St. Columban*—S.S.C.
[0350]—*The Cistercians Order of the Strict Observance (Trappists)*—O.C.S.O.

RELIGIOUS INSTITUTES OF WOMEN REPRESENTED IN THE DIOCESE

[0192]—*Carmelite Sisters of the Eucharist, Inc.*—C.S.E.
[2980]—*Congregation of Notre Dame*—C.N.D.
[]—*Congregation of Sisters of St. Felix of Cantauce*
[3830-01]—*Congregation of St. Joseph* (Boston, Brighton)—C.S.J.
[0820]—*Daughters of the Holy Spirit*—D.H.S.
[1070-06]—*Dominican Sisters* (Newburgh, NY)—O.P.
[1115]—*Dominican Sisters of Peace*—O.P.
[]—*Franciscan Sisters of the Immaculate Heart of Mary* (India)—F.I.H.M.
[]—*Fransciscan Sisters Minor*—F.S.M.
[2575]—*Institute of the Sisters of Mercy of the Americas* (New York, NY)—R.S.M.
[2280]—*Little Franciscans of Mary*—P.F.M.
[2310]—*Little Sisters of the Assumption*—L.S.A.
[]—*Order of St. Benedict* Petersham—O.S.B.
[3390]—*Religious of the Assumption*—R.A.
[4180]—*Religious Venerini Sisters*—M.P.V.
[]—*Servants of the 11th Hour of St. John Evdas*—E.S.E.H.
[]—*Sisters Oblates of Divine Love*—R.O.D.A.
[2540]—*Sisters of Mercy*—R.S.M.
[3000]—*Sisters of Notre Dame de Namur* (Boston, Ipswich, Japan and Connecticut Provs.)—S.N.D.deN.
[3340]—*Sisters of Providence* (Holyoke)—S.P.
[3720]—*Sisters of Saint Anne*—S.S.A.
[3830-16]—*Sisters of St. Joseph* (Springfield)—S.S.J.
[0150]—*Sisters of the Assumption*—S.A.S.V.
[1830]—*The Sisters of the Good Shepherd*—R.G.S.
[3310]—*Sisters of the Presentation of Mary*—P.M.
[3320]—*Sisters of the Presentation of the B.V.M.*—P.B.V.M.
[]—*Slaves of the Immaculate Heart of Mary*—M.I.C.M.
[4230]—*Xaverian Missionary Society of Mary, Inc.*—X.M.M.

DIOCESAN CEMETERIES

WORCESTER. *St. John's*

NECROLOGY

† Adamo, Joseph A., (Retired)—Died April 20, 2009
† Anger, Raymond G., (Retired)—Died Oct. 8, 2009
† Baker, Donald H., Gardner, MA Sacred Heart of Jesus—Died April 9, 2009
† Barry, Thomas M., (Retired)—Died Dec. 14, 2009
† Cahill, John, (Retired)—Died Sept. 24, 2009
† Gothing, Donald B., (Retired)—Died Oct. 19, 2009
† Lange, Raymond L., (Retired)—Died July 10, 2009
† Nally, J. Brendan, (Retired)—Died Nov. 3, 2009
† Rocheford, Dennis J, North Oxford, MA St. Ann—Died Sept. 10, 2009

An asterisk (*) denotes an organization that has established tax-exempt status directly with the IRS and is not covered by the USCCB Group Ruling.

Diocese of Yakima

(Dioecesis Yakimensis)

Most Reverend

CARLOS A. SEVILLA, S.J., D.D.

Bishop of Yakima; ordained June 3, 1966; appointed Auxiliary Bishop of San Francisco December 6, 1988; Episcopal ordination January 25, 1989; appointed Bishop of Yakima December 31, 1996; installed February 17, 1997. *Address all correspondence to: 5301-A Tieton Dr., Yakima, WA 98908.*

ESTABLISHED JUNE 23, 1951.

Square Miles 17,787.

Comprises the following Counties in the State of Washington: Benton, Chelan, Douglas, Grant, Kittitas, Klickitat and Yakima.

Legal Title: Corporation of the Catholic Bishop of Yakima.
For legal titles of parishes and diocesan institutions, consult the Pastoral Office.

Pastoral Office (Chancery): 5301-A Tieton Dr., Yakima, WA 98908. Tel: 509-965-7117; Fax: 509-966-8334.

Email: info@yakimadiocese.org

STATISTICAL OVERVIEW

Personnel	
Bishop	1
Priests: Diocesan Active in Diocese	42
Priests: Diocesan Active Outside Diocese	1
Priests: Retired, Sick or Absent	32
Number of Diocesan Priests	75
Religious Priests in Diocese	7
Total Priests in Diocese	82
Extern Priests in Diocese	1
Ordinations:	
Diocesan Priests	4
Permanent Deacons in Diocese	26
Total Brothers	3
Total Sisters	33
Parishes	
Parishes	41
With Resident Pastor:	
Resident Diocesan Priests	39
Resident Religious Priests	2
Without Resident Pastor:	
Administered by Priests	8
Missions	3
Pastoral Centers	1
Professional Ministry Personnel:	
Brothers	3
Sisters	33
Lay Ministers	17
Welfare	
Health Care Centers	1
Total Assisted	73,658
Day Care Centers	1
Total Assisted	174
Special Centers for Social Services	5
Total Assisted	49,389
Educational	
Diocesan Students in Other Seminaries	10
Total Seminarians	10
High Schools, Private	1
Total Students	190
Elementary Schools, Diocesan and Parish	6
Total Students	1,572
Catechesis/Religious Education:	
High School Students	1,862
Elementary Students	5,709
Total Students under Catholic Instruction	9,343
Teachers in the Diocese:	
Brothers	3
Sisters	6
Lay Teachers	112
Vital Statistics	
Receptions into the Church:	
Infant Baptism Totals	3,315
Minor Baptism Totals	175
Adult Baptism Totals	109
Received into Full Communion	205
First Communions	2,501
Confirmations	1,164
Marriages:	
Catholic	342
Interfaith	100
Total Marriages	442
Deaths	521
Total Catholic Population	78,317
Total Population	649,846

Former Bishops—Most Revs. JOSEPH P. DOUGHERTY, D.D., First Bishop of Yakima; ord. June 14, 1930; appt. July 9, 1951; cons. Sept. 26, 1951; resigned Feb. 5, 1969; died July 10, 1970; CORNELIUS M. POWER, D.D., Second Bishop of Yakima; ord. June 3, 1939; appt. Feb. 5, 1969; cons. May 1, 1969; elevated to Metropolitan See of Portland in Oregon, Jan. 24, 1974; died May 22, 1997; NICOLAS E. WALSH, D.D., Third Bishop of Yakima; ord. June 6, 1942; appt. Sept. 5, 1974; cons. Oct. 28, 1974; installed Oct. 30, 1974; transferred to Archdiocese of Seattle as Auxiliary Bishop, Aug. 10, 1976; resigned Sept. 6, 1983; died April 22, 1997; WILLIAM S. SKYLSTAD, D.D., Fourth Bishop of Yakima; ord. May 21, 1960; appt. Feb. 22, 1977; cons. May 12, 1977; transferred to Spokane as Bishop of Spokane, April 17, 1990; FRANCIS E. GEORGE, O.M.I., Ph.D., S.T.D., Fifth Bishop of Yakima; ord. Dec. 21, 1963; appt. July 10, 1990; cons. Sept. 21, 1990; appt. Metropolitan See of Portland in Oregon, April 30, 1996; appt. Metropolitan See of Chicago, April 8, 1997; created Cardinal Priest, Feb. 21, 1998.

Pastoral Office (Chancery)—5301-A Tieton Dr., Yakima, 98908. Tel: 509-965-7117; Fax: 509-966-8334.

Vicar General—Rev. Msgr. JOHN A. ECKER, 5301-A Tieton Dr., Yakima, 98908-3493.

Vicar for Priests—Revs. MARIO A. SALAZAR; LAWRENCE T. REILLY.

Moderator of the Curia—Rev. ROBERT M. SILER.

Chancellor—Rev. ROBERT M. SILER.

Vice Chancellor—Mrs. ELVIA GONZALEZ.

Office of Canonical Concerns—5301-D Tieton Dr., Yakima, 98908. Tel: 509-965-7123.

Judicial Vicar—Very Rev. MICHAEL J. IBACH, J.C.L.

Adjutant Judicial Vicar—Rev. DAVID J. JIMENEZ.

Judges—Very Rev. MICHAEL J. IBACH, J.C.L.; Revs. JOHN F. HENEGHAN (Retired); DAVID J. JIMENEZ.

Defenders of the Bond—Revs. THOMAS C. CHAMPOUX; SALOMON COVARRUBIAS-PINA; Ms. KAY SHEPARD.

Advocates— Clergy and pastoral ministers by appointment.

Notaries—Mrs MARIA G. FLORES; Mrs. EILEEN M. WALKER; Rev. ROBERT M. SILER.

Diocesan Consultors—Revs. OSMAR R. AGUIRRE; JAIME H. CHACON, M.Div.; Very Rev. MICHAEL J. IBACH, J.C.L.; Rev. NEILL R. MEANY, S.J.; Rev. Msgr. JOHN A. ECKER; Revs. ARGEMIRO OROZCO; FELIPE PULIDO; LAWRENCE T. REILLY; ROBERT M. SILER.

Diocesan Offices, Commissions, Committees

Adults with Developmental Disabilities—MICHELE WALL, 12203 Klendon Dr., Yakima, 98908. Tel: 509-965-4642.

Calvary Cemetery—KATHY DEAN, Dir., 1405 S. 24th Ave., Yakima, 98902. Tel: 509-457-8462; Fax: 509-457-6267.

CYO—DON ERICKSON, 410 S. 47th Ave., Yakima, 98908. Tel: 509-965-3382.

Campaign for Human Development—Rev. ROBERT M. SILER, 5301-A Tieton Dr., Yakima, 98908.

Catholic Charities—Mr. JOHN L. YOUNG, Exec. Dir., Office, 5301-C Tieton Dr., Yakima, 98908. Tel: 509-965-7100.

Charismatic Renewal, English—5301-A Tieton Dr., Yakima, 98908. Tel: 509-965-7117.

Charismatic Renewal, Spanish—Rev. GUSTAVO GOMEZ, Mailing Address: Our Lady of the Desert, P.O. Box 2268, Mattawa, 99349. Tel: 509-932-5424.

Cursillo, English—Rev. JOHN M. SHAW, Spiritual Dir. (English) (Retired), 213 N. Beech, Toppenish, 98948. Tel: 509-865-4725; JUDY KITCHEN, Lay Dir., 118 Fairwood Ct., Richland, 99352. Tel: 509-628-3428.

Spanish—Deacon FRANK MARTINEZ, Spiritual Dir., 3790 Rd. 10.2 S.W., Royal City, 99357. Tel: 509-346-9536; JOSE GONZALEZ, Coord., 2467 N. Ashland Ave., East Wenatchee, 98802. Tel: 509-884-6009.

Native American—Rev. JOHN M. SHAW, Spiritual Dir. (Retired), 213 N. Beech St., Toppenish, 98948. Tel: 509-865-2400; JIM ARNOUX, Liaison, P.O. Box 421, White Swan, 98952; MARY GARCIA, Mailing Address: P.O. Box 191, White Swan, 98952.

Director of Planned Giving—Rev. BROOKS F. BEAULAURIER, 5301-A Tieton Dr., Yakima, 98908. Tel: 509-965-7117.

Development Office/Stewardship—Rev. BROOKS F. BEAULAURIER, Dir., 5301-A Tieton Dr., Yakima, 98908. Tel: 509-965-7117.

Diocesan Coordinator for Health Affairs—Rev. THOMAS C. CHAMPOUX, 5301-C Tieton Dr., Yakima, 98908. Tel: 509-965-7100.

Diocesan Commission for the Catechumenate—Most Rev. CARLOS ARTHUR SEVILLA, S.J., D.D.; Rev. JUAN M. FLORES ALFEREZ; Ms. KAY SHEPARD, Chm.; Mrs DANETTE HESTER; Mr. RICK PINNELL; Deacon ROBERT J. SCHROM; Sr. MARIA ELENA CASILLAS, M.D.P.V.M.; Deacon KERRY TURLEY.

Diocesan Commission on Public Worship—Revs. JUAN MANUEL FLORES; THOMAS S. KUYKENDALL, Chm.; Mrs. PAT MANDELAS; Deacon RAY MILLER.

Diocesan Pastoral Council—Most Rev. CARLOS ARTHUR SEVILLA, S.J., D.D.; Deacon BERNEY ALVARADO; Sr. MARIA ELENA CASILLAS, M.D.P.V.M.; RITA KEENE; Ms. KITTY T. RYAN; RONNI ROYLANCE; KEN GOEDDE; DON HALEY; JOE GALLEGOS; VICTORIA PERKIS; STEVE SANCHEZ.

Ecumenical Liaison—Rev. Msgr. JOHN A. ECKER, 15 S. 12th Ave., Yakima, 98902. Tel: 509-575-3713.

Engaged Encounter—FRANK BECKER; TRACY BECKER, 2080 New Haven Loop, Richland, 99352.

Diocesan Finance Council—Most Rev. CARLOS ARTHUR SEVILLA, S.J., D.D., Pastoral Center, 5301-A Tieton Dr., Yakima, 98908; Rev. Msgr. JOHN A. ECKER; Mrs. COLLEEN KELLEHER; Mrs. PAT MYERS; Rev. DANIEL G. DUFNER; JEFF PETERSON, Consultant; JAMES PERKO, CFO; Mr. PETER SPADONI; Rev. ROBERT M. SILER, Ex Officio.

Gang Outreach Ministry—VACANT.

Home Schooling—Deacon DUANE BERGER, Chap., 1706 Lower Ahtanum, Yakima, 98903. Tel: 509-457-1926; JONELLA LEADON.

Lay Advisory Board—Mr. RUSSELL MAZZOLA, Chm. Tel: 888-276-4490; Mr. THOMAS DITTMAR; Rev. Msgr. JOHN A. ECKER; Dr. MARK MAIOCCO; Dr. JORGE TORRES-SAENZ, PsyD.; Mrs. YVONNE SMITH.

Marriage Encounter, English—VACANT.

Spanish—Rev. JOSE DE JESUS RAMIREZ, Mailing Address: P.O. Box 340, Royal City, 99357-0340. Tel: 509-346-2730.

Natural Family Planning Advisory Committee—Rev. JUAN MANUEL GODINA, Dir. Tel: 509-965-7117; SHIRA WISE; ANNE NEALEN, M.D.; THEODORE F. O'DONNELL, M.D.; Dr. JAN HEMSTAD; Mrs. JAN R. HEMSTAD, M.D.

Ministry & Education Center—Rev. THOMAS S. KUYKENDALL, Dir. Catholic Schools, 5301-B Tieton Dr., Yakima, 98908. Tel: 509-965-7117.

Hispanic Ministries/Hispanic Ministry Formation—Rev. JAIME H. CHACON, M.Div., Dir. Hispanic Ministry, 5301-B Tieton Dr., Yakima, 98908. Tel: 509-965-7117.

Evangelization, Deacon Formation, Pastoral Council, Small Church Communities—VACANT, Dir.

Family Ministries—VACANT.

Religious Education and Hispanic Catechesis—Rev. TOMAS VASQUEZ TELLEZ, 5301-B Tieton Dr., Yakima, 98908. Tel: 509-965-7117.

Youth/Young Adult Director—Rev. WILMAR ZABALA, 5301-B Tieton Dr., Yakima, 98908. Tel: 509-965-7117.

Youth/Young Adult Hispanic Ministry—Rev. MIGUEL GONZALEZ CASTILLO, 5301-B Tieton Dr., Yakima, 98908. Tel: 509-965-7117.

Deacon Council—Deacon INDALECIO "ANDY" GONZALEZ; Mrs. ELVIA GONZALEZ; Deacon BILL MICH; MARGO MICH; Deacon ROBERT J. SCHROM; TERESA SCHROM.

Permanent Diaconate Liaison—Deacon ROBERT J. SCHROM, 7240 Rd. 17 S.W., Royal City, 99357. Tel: 509-346-9464.

Clergy Personnel Board—Most Rev. CARLOS ARTHUR SEVILLA, S.J., D.D.; Rev. Msgr. JOHN A. ECKER; Revs. DANIEL G. DUFNER; WILLIAM E. SHAW; MARIO A. SALAZAR; THOMAS C. CHAMPOUX; ROBERT M. SILER; LAWRENCE T. REILLY, Ex Officio; RICARDO A. VILLARREAL.

Press (Central Washington Catholic)—Rev. ROBERT M. SILER.

Presbyteral Council Executive Committee—Most Rev. CARLOS ARTHUR SEVILLA, S.J., D.D.; Rev. Msgr. JOHN A. ECKER; Revs. L. MICHAEL POPE, S.J.; RICARDO A. VILLARREAL; FELIPE PULIDO; THOMAS S. KUYKENDALL; SALOMON COVARRUBIAS-PINA; ARGEMIRO OROZCO; ROBERT M. SILER; RICHARD D. SEDLACEK; JOHN M. SHAW (Retired).

Native American Ministries—Rev. JOHN M. SHAW (Retired), 213 N. Beech, Toppenish, 98948. Tel: 509-865-4725.

Natural Family Planning—Rev. JUAN MANUEL GODINA, 5301-B Tieton Dr., Yakima, 98908. Tel: 509-965-7117.

Jail Ministry—Deacon NESTOR CHAVEZ, 710 E. Race St., Yakima, 98901; Rev. SALOMON COVARRUBIAS-PINA; Mrs. GAYLE A. MILLER; Mr. RAY MILLER.

Respect Life Committee—Mr. GEORGE BRIGGS; Mr NORM HILBERT; Mrs CATHY HILBERT; VICKIE MONTGOMERY; Rev. JUAN MANUEL GODINA, 5301-B Tieton Dr., Yakima, 98908. Tel: 509-965-7117.

Diocesan Catholic Committee on Scouting—Deacon WILLIAM A. DRONEN, Chap., 306 Railroad Ave., Cashmere, 98815. Tel: 509-782-3976; Mr PHIL PIEPEL, Chm., 2897 Riviera Blvd., Malaga, 98828. Tel: 509-665-0892; Mr. MARC DESGROSEILLIER; Mr RICHARD MANKA; Mr SCOTT MELTON; Rev. NEILL R. MEANY, S.J.; Mr CURT NEALEN; Mr RICK URLACHER; Ms DONNA VAN DOREN; Rev. SAMUEL P. BELLINO, S.J.

Social Justice and Human Life Commission—Rev. JUAN MANUEL GODINA; Mr. JOHN L. YOUNG; Rev. WILLIAM VOGEL, S.J.

St. Joseph Mission at the Ahtanum—Directors: ED CAMPBELL; CARY CAMPBELL, 17740 Ahtanum Rd., Yakima, 98903. Tel: 509-966-0865; Fax: 509-966-5649. Email: casprus2@prodigy.net.

St. Vincent de Paul Society—Rev. THOMAS C. CHAMPOUX, Spiritual Dir., 1126 Long Ave., Richland, 99352. Tel: 509-946-1675.

Serra Club—BILL HAYES, 800 S. 46th St., Yakima, 98908. Tel: 509-966-7056; JOAN TOTH, 504 N. Rd. 40, Pasco, 99301.

Victim Assistance Coordinators—Mrs. JANET ERICKSON. Email: jerickson@cfcsyakima.org; BLANCA VARGAS. Email: bvargas@cfcsyakima.org.

Vocations—Revs. FELIPE PULIDO; WILMAR ZABALA.

CLERGY, PARISHES, MISSIONS AND PAROCHIAL SCHOOLS

CITY OF YAKIMA

(YAKIMA COUNTY)

1—ST. PAUL CATHEDRAL (1914) [CEM] Rev. Msgr. John A. Ecker; Rev. Rafael Hinojosa; Deacon Ray Miller; Alma Jauregui, Pastoral Care for Senior Citizens.
Res.: 15 S. 12th Ave., 98902. Tel: 509-575-3713; Fax: 509-453-7497. Email: parish@stpaulyakima.org. Web: www.stpaulyakima.org.
School—(Grades PreK-8), 1214 W. Chestnut Ave., 98902. Tel: 509-575-5604; Fax: 509-577-8817. Email: ebalch@stpaulsch.org. Web: www.stpaulcathedralschool.org. Lay Teachers 17; Students 220.
Catholic Student Center—810 S. 16th Ave., 98902. Tel: 509-249-6238.
Catechesis/Religious Program—Students 308.

2—HOLY FAMILY (1959) Revs. Cesar M. Vega; Gary L. Desharnais, Parochial Vicar; Deacons John Cornell; James Kramper. In Res., Rev. Thomas V. Lane (Retired).
Res.: 5315 Tieton Dr., 98908. Tel: 509-966-0830; Fax: 509-965-1742. Email: office@holyfamilyyakima.org. Web: www.holyfamilyyakima.org.
Catechesis/Religious Program—Tel: 509-966-0788; Fax: 509-965-0288. Students 265.
Mission—St. Joseph Mission at the Ahtanum 17740 Ahtanum Rd., Yakima Co. 98908. Tel: 509-966-5649; Fax: 509-966-5649.

3—HOLY REDEEMER (1962), (Hispanic), [JC] Rev. Francisco Gutierrez; Deacon Duane Berger.
Res.: 1607 Landon Ave., 98902. Tel: 509-248-2241; Fax: 509-457-3312. Email: holyredeemer_o@questoffice.net. Web: www.holyredeemeryakima.org.
Church: 1707 S. Third Ave., 98902.
Catechesis/Religious Program—Students 72.

4—ST. JOSEPH PARISH (1847) Revs. L. Michael Pope, S.J.; Eugene Delmore, S.J.; Alan Yost, S.J.; Deacon Nestor Chavez.
212 N. 4th St., 98901-2426. Tel: 509-248-1911; Fax: 509-248-2604. In Res., Rev. Neill R. Meany, S.J.
School—St. Joseph/Marquette, 202 N. 4th St., 98901. Tel: 509-575-5557; Fax: 509-457-5621. Lay Teachers 29; Students 318.
Catechesis/Religious Program—Students 428.

OUTSIDE THE CITY OF YAKIMA

BENTON CITY, BENTON CO., ST. FRANCES XAVIER CABRINI (1963) Revs. Richard D. Sedlacek; Juan Manuel Godina; Jaime H. Chacon.
Mailing Address: P.O. Box 179, 99320-0179. Fax: 509-588-3636.
Church: 1000 Horn Rd., 99320. Tel: 509-588-3636; Fax: 509-588-3636. Email: sfxc-secretary@verizon.net. Web: www.benton-cabrini.org.
Catechesis/Religious Program—Students 70.

BRIDGEPORT, DOUGLAS CO., ST. ANNE'S (1964) Revs. Ricardo Villarreal; Juan Carlos Chiarinoti.
Mailing Address: P.O. Box 1089, Chelan, 98816-1089. Tel: 509-682-2433; Fax: 509-682-9147. Email: stfrancischurch@nwi.net.
Catechesis/Religious Program—Students 52.
Mission—St. Mary (1909) Mansfield Blvd. & 2nd, Mansfield, Douglas Co. 98830. Tel: 509-682-2433; Fax: 509-682-9147. Email: stfrancischurch@nwi.net.

CASHMERE, CHELAN CO., ST. FRANCIS XAVIER (1915) Rev. Daniel G. Dufner; Deacon Bill Dronen.
Res.: 307 Angier, 98815. Tel: 509-782-2643; Fax: 509-782-2686.
Catechesis/Religious Program—Students 76.

CHELAN, CHELAN CO., ST. FRANCIS DE SALES (1904) [CEM] Revs. Ricardo Villarreal; Juan Carlos Chiarinoti.
215 W. Allen Ave., P.O. Box 1089, 98816-1089. Tel: 509-682-2433; Fax: 509-682-9147. Email: stfrancischurch@nwi.net.
Catechesis/Religious Program—Students 65.

CLE ELUM, UPPER KITTITAS CO., ST. JOHN THE BAPTIST (1913) Rev. Lawrence T. Reilly.
Office: 303 W. 2nd St., 98922. Tel: 509-674-2531; Fax: 509-674-1894.
Catechesis/Religious Program—Students 30.

COWICHE, YAKIMA CO., ST. JUAN DIEGO (1959), (Spanish), (Formerly known as St. Peter the Apostle). Rev. Jorge A. Granados Lopez.
Res.: 15800 Summitview Rd., 98923. Tel: 509-678-4164; Fax: 509-678-4165. Email: stjuandiego@centurytel.net.
Catechesis/Religious Program—Students 105.

EAST WENATCHEE, DOUGLAS CO., HOLY APOSTLES (1962) Rev. Argemiro Orozco; Deacon Thomas Richtsmeier.
Res.: 1315 NE Eight St., 98802. Tel: 509-884-5444; Fax: 509-886-3424. Email: holyapostles@nwi.net. Web: www.holyapostlesparish.org.
Catechesis/Religious Program—1315 8th St. N.E., 98802. Tel: 509-884-5444. Students 85.

ELLENSBURG, KITTITAS CO., ST. ANDREW'S (1884) [CEM] Rev. Tomas Vazquez.
Mailing Address: 401 S. Willow St., 98926.
Res.: 403 S. Willow St., 98926. Tel: 509-962-9821. Email: standrewparish@yahoo.com.
Catechesis/Religious Program—Students 230.

EPHRATA, GRANT CO., ST. ROSE OF LIMA (1915) [CEM] Rev. Gary Norman.
Mailing Address: 323 D St., S.W., 98823. Email: strose@nwi.net.
Parish Office—560 Nat Washington Way, 98823. Tel: 509-754-3640; Fax: 509-754-4064. Email: strose@nwi.net.
School—(Grades PreK-6), 520 Nat Washington Way, 98823. Tel: 509-754-4901; Fax: 509-754-9274. Lay Teachers 7; Students 97.
Catechesis/Religious Program—Students 127.

GOLDENDALE, KLICKITAT CO., HOLY TRINITY (1884) [CEM] Rev. William Byron.
Res.: 210 S. Schuster St., 98620. Tel: 509-773-4516; Fax: 509-773-6983. Email: holytrinity@gorge.net.
Catechesis/Religious Program—Jackie Bugler, D.R.E. Students 33.

GRAND COULEE, GRANT CO., ST. HENRY'S (1955) [JC] Rev. Robert P. Himes.
Res.: 590 Grand Coulee Ave. W., P.O. Box P, 99133. Tel: 509-633-1180; Fax: 509-633-6859.
Catechesis/Religious Program—Students 9.

GRANDVIEW, YAKIMA CO., BLESSED SACRAMENT (1954) Revs. Jaime H. Chacon; Jose M. Herrera.
Res.: 1201 Missouri, 98930. Tel: 509-882-1657; Fax: 509-882-1107. Email: blessedsacramentchurch@embarqmail.com.
Catechesis/Religious Program—Students 380.

GRANGER, YAKIMA CO., OUR LADY OF GUADALUPE (1966), (Hispanic), [JC] Rev. Mario P. Salazar.
Res.: 608 Granger Ave., P.O. Box 308, 98932. Tel: 509-854-1558; Fax: 509-854-7326.
Catechesis/Religious Program—Tel: 509-854-2164. Students 97.

HARTLINE, GRANT CO., ST. PATRICK'S (1955) [CEM], Served from St. Henry's, P.O. Box P, Grand Coulee 99133. Rev. Robert P. Himes.
Mailing Address: P.O. Box 925, Coulee City, 99115. Tel: 509-633-1180; Fax: 509-633-6859.
Catechesis/Religious Program—
Mission—Holy Angels P.O. Box 925, Coulee City, Grant Co. 99115.

KENNEWICK, BENTON CO.

1—HOLY SPIRIT (1980) Rev. Perron J. Auve; Deacon John E. Powers. In Res., Rev. John G. O'Shea.
Office: 7409 W. Clearwater, 99336. Tel: 509-735-8558; Fax: 509-735-8559. Email: pohs@amerion.com. Web: www.holyspiritkennewick.org.
Catechesis/Religious Program—Jennifer Moore, D.R.E.; Pat Moore, D.R.E. & Youth Min. Students 184.

2—ST. JOSEPH'S (1911) Revs. Richard D. Sedlacek; Juan Manuel Godina; Sr. Robert Joseph Doucette, C.S.J., Pastoral Assoc.; Deacon William Mich. In Res., Rev. Msgr. Desmond P. Dillon (Retired).
Res.: 520 S. Garfield, 99336. Tel: 509-586-3820; Fax: 509-586-3558. Email: parish.office@stjoseph-kennewick.org.
School—(Grades PreSchool-8), 901 W. 4th Ave., 99336. Tel: 509-586-0481; Fax: 509-585-9781. Sisters of St. Joseph of Carondelet 1; Lay Teachers 22; Students 378.
Catechesis/Religious Program—Tel: 509-582-8460. Students 488.

LEAVENWORTH, CHELAN CO., OUR LADY OF THE SNOWS (1912) Rev. Daniel G. Dufner.
Res.: 145 Wheeler St., 98826. Tel: 509-548-5119; Fax: 509-548-5051.
Catechesis/Religious Program—Students 73.

MABTON, YAKIMA CO., IMMACULATE CONCEPTION (1910) Revs. Jaime H. Chacon; Jose M. Herrera.
Mailing Address: P.O. Box 275, 98935. Tel: 509-882-1657; Fax: 509-882-1107.
Res.: 1201 Missouri, Grandview, 98930. Tel: 509-882-1657; Fax: 509-882-1107.
Catechesis/Religious Program—Students 52.

MATTAWA, GRANT CO., OUR LADY OF THE DESERT (1987) [JC] Rev. Gustavo Gomez.
Mailing Address: 301 8th St., P.O. Box 2268, 99349. Tel: 509-932-5424; Fax: 509-932-4055.
Catechesis/Religious Program—Students 215.

MOSES LAKE, GRANT CO., OUR LADY OF FATIMA (1955), (Spanish), [CEM] Revs. Felipe Pulido; Tomas Vidal; Deacons Robert J. Schrom; Agapito Gonzales Jr. In Res., Rev. Msgr. Martin O. Skehan (Retired).
Res.: 200 N. Dale Rd., 98837. Tel: 509-765-6729; Fax: 509-765-0114. Email: ldy_fatima@yahoo.com.
Parish Center—210 N. Dale Rd., 98837. Tel: 509-765-6729.
Catechesis/Religious Program—Students 530.

MOXEE CITY, YAKIMA CO., HOLY ROSARY (1900) [CEM] Rev. John J. Murtagh.
Res.: 201 N. Iler., P.O. Box 279, 98936. Tel: 509-453-4061; Fax: 509-576-6290.
Catechesis/Religious Program—Tel: 509-453-6754. Students 235.

NACHES, YAKIMA CO., ST. JOHN (1959) Rev. Msgr. John A. Ecker, Admin.; Rev. Neill R. Meany, S.J.; Deacon Don Griek.
Res.: 204 Moxee Ave., P.O. Box 128, 98937-0128. Tel: 509-653-2534; Fax: 509-653-2534.
Catechesis/Religious Program—Tel: 509-653-2534. Students 12.

PROSSER, BENTON CO., SACRED HEART (1899) Rev. Osmar R. Aguirre.
Res.: 1905 Highland Dr., 99350. Tel: 509-786-1783; Fax: 509-786-1747. Email: shcc@embarqmail.com.
Catechesis/Religious Program—Cynthia O'Brien, D.R.E., (English Prog.). Tel: 509-786-1783; Cathy Moore, D.R.E. (English Prog.); Maria Zepeda, D.R.E., (Spanish Program). Tel: 509-786-1783. Students 405.

QUINCY, GRANT CO., ST. PIUS X (1955), (Hispanic), Rev. Mario A. Salazar.
Res.: 805 N. Central Ave., P.O. Box 308, 98848. Tel: 509-787-2622; Fax: 509-787-6068. Email: st.piusx@verizon.net.
Catechesis/Religious Program—Rita Keene, D.R.E.; Ana Argueta, D.R.E., (Spanish). Students 267.

RICHLAND, BENTON CO., CHRIST THE KING (1946) Revs. Thomas C. Champoux; Teodulo G. Taneo, S.V.D. (Philippines); Vandennis Nguyen; Deacons Robert DaValle; LeRoi Rice; Alfred Rizzo.
Office: 1111 Stevens Dr., 99354. Tel: 509-946-1675; Fax: 509-946-9940. Web: www.ckparish.org.
School—1122 Long Ave., 99354. Tel: 509-946-6158; Fax: 509-943-8402. Web: www.CKschoolRichland.org. Lay Teachers 27; Students 416.
Catechesis/Religious Program—Tel: 509-946-1154; Fax: 509-946-9940. Email: erin@ckparish.org. Lori Wasner, D.R.E. Students 262.

ROSLYN, UPPER KITTITAS CO., IMMACULATE CONCEPTION (1887) Rev. Lawrence T. Reilly.
Mailing Address: 303 W. 2nd St., Cle Elum, 98922. Tel: 509-674-2531; Fax: 509-674-1894.
Res.: 211 N. B St., 98941.
Catechesis/Religious Program— Twinned with St. John the Baptist, Cle Elum.

ROYAL CITY, GRANT CO., ST. MICHAEL THE ARCHANGEL (1966), (Hispanic), Rev. J. Jesus Ramirez; Deacon Francisco Martinez.
Res.: 145 Daisy St., N.W., P.O. Box 340, 99357. Tel: 509-346-2730; Fax: 509-346-2901. Email: fr.jesusramirez@centurytel.net.
Catechesis/Religious Program—Tel: 509-346-2236. Students 76.

SELAH, YAKIMA CO., OUR LADY OF LOURDES (1975) Rev. David J. Jimenez.
Res.: 1112 W. Fremont, 98942. Tel: 509-697-4633; Fax: 831-664-4633. Email: ollselah@hotmail.com.
Catechesis/Religious Program—1111 W. Fremont, 98942. Students 179.

SUNNYSIDE, YAKIMA CO., ST. JOSEPH'S (1936) Revs. Thomas J. Bunnell, S.J.; Miguel Gonzalez Castillo; Deacon Kerry Turley.
Res.: 920 S. 6th St., 98944. Tel: 509-837-2243; Fax: 509-837-7063.
Catechesis/Religious Program—Tel: 509-839-4758. Students 650.
Convent—Tel: 509-837-2242. Missionary Daughters of the Most Pure Virgin Mary 4.

TOPPENISH, YAKIMA CO., ST. ALOYSIUS (1908) Rev. Juan M. Flores; Deacon Berny Alvarado.
Mailing Address: 213 N. Beech St., 98948. Tel: 508-865-4725; Fax: 508-865-7882. Email: st.aloysius@charter.net. In Res., Rev. John M. Shaw (Retired).
Religious Education Center—214 N. Beech St., 98948. Tel: 509-865-2565.
Catechesis/Religious Program—Fax: 509-865-3077. Ms. Elizabeth Torres, D.R.E. Students 577.

WAPATO, YAKIMA CO., ST. PETER CLAVER (1906) Rev. Salomon Covarrubias-Pina; Deacon John Kassinger.
509 S. Satus Ave., 98951. Tel: 509-877-2813.
Catechesis/Religious Program—Tel: 509-877-2081. Students 162.

WARDEN, GRANT CO., QUEEN OF ALL SAINTS (1966), (Spanish), Revs. Felipe Pulido; Tomas Vidal; Deacon Andres Escamilla.
c/o 200 N. Dale Rd., Moses Lake, 98837. Tel: 509-765-6729; Fax: 509-765-0114.
Catechesis/Religious Program—Ronni Roylance, D.R.E. (K-12). Students 200.

WATERVILLE, DOUGLAS CO., ST. JOSEPH'S (1892) [CEM] [JC] Rev. Juan Manuel Godina.
Res.: 103 Poplar St., P.O. Box 519, 98858. Tel: 509-745-8205.
Catechesis/Religious Program—Tel: 509-745-8787. Noreen Daling, D.R.E. Students 32.

WENATCHEE, CHELAN CO., ST. JOSEPH'S (1903) Revs. Thomas S. Kuykendall; Rogelio Gutierrez; Deacon Bill Osborn.
Res.: 625 Elliott, 98801. Tel: 509-662-4569; Fax: 509-663-8437. Email: stjoewen@stjoewen.org.
School—(Grades PreK-5), 600 St. Joseph Pl., 98801. Tel: 509-663-2644; Fax: 509-663-8474. Religious 3; Lay Teachers 10; Students 143.
Catechesis/Religious Program—600 St. Joseph Pl., 98801. Students 341.

WHITE SALMON, KLICKITAT CO., ST. JOSEPH (1912), (Spanish), Rev. Alejandro E. Trejo.
Res.: 240 N.W. Washington, P.O. Box 2049, 98672. Tel: 509-493-2828; Fax: 509-493-2175. Web: church.gorge.net/stjoes-ws/. Email: stjosephs@embarqmail.com.
Catechesis/Religious Program—Tel: 509-493-2386. Email: hshultzy5@yahoo.com. Students 61.

WHITE SWAN, YAKIMA CO., ST. MARY'S (1889), (Native American), Rev. William E. Shaw; Deacon Andy Gonzalez.
Res.: 360 Signal Peak Rd. (UPS), P.O. Box 417, 98952-0417. Tel: 509-874-2436; Fax: 509-874-1197.
Catechesis/Religious Program—Students 50.

ZILLAH, YAKIMA CO., RESURRECTION (1963) Rev. Juan M. Flores.
Mailing Address: P.O. Box 567, 98953-0567. Tel: 509-829-5433; 509-829-5312 (Spanish Ministries); Fax: 509-829-5312. Email: zresurrection@aol.com.
Catechesis/Religious Program—Tel: 509-829-5433; 509-829-6139 Jane Schneider. Students 65.

Special Assignment:
Revs.—
Magaña, Alberto O., 5301-A Tieton Dr., 98908.
Minder, Kevin, 5301-A Tieton Dr., 98908.
Mitchell, Darell J., 5301-A Tieton Dr., 98908.
Vogl, John C., 5301-A Tieton Dr., 98908.

On Duty Outside the Diocese:
Revs.—
DeLoza, Jose, Mexico
Hernandez, Francisco J. (Retired), 214 San Bernardo Ave., Laredo, TX 78040.
Higuera, Francisco, 521 Fair St., Lodi, WI 53555.
Inman, Robert D.
Kenna, Joseph J. (Retired), 9103 Wellington Pl., Lanham, MD 20706.
Keolker, Richard F., Mount Angel Seminary, 119 Anselm, St. Benedict, OR 97373.
Milich, Nicohlas, 1335 Byron Dr., Salinas, CA 93901.
Rodriguez, Felix M., P.O. Box 12335, Casa Grande, AZ 85230.

Military Chaplains:
Rev.—
House, Richard M., U.S.S. Ronald Reagan CVN 76, 3311 West Ave., #608, Newport News, VA 23607.

Retired:
Rev. Msgrs.—
Dillon, Desmond P., St. Joseph Parish, 520 S. Garfield, Kennewick, 99336.
Skehan, Martin O., 200 N. Dale Rd., Moses Lake, 98837.
Revs.—
Cerezo, Alberto F., 11637 100th Ave., N.E., #C2, Kirkland, 98034-6518.
Greene, Daniel (ORL), 7851 54th Ave. N., St. Petersburg, FL 33709-2338.
Hannick, Anthony S., 1600 Roosmoor Pkwy., Walnut Creek, CA 94553.
Heneghan, John F., Waverly Collacoon, Mayo, Ireland.
Hernandez, Francisco J., 214 San Bernardo Ave., Laredo, TX 78040.
Kenna, Joseph J.
Kerr, Seamus
Lane, Thomas V., 304 S. 50th, 98908.
Patnode, Ronald J.
Peterson, Maurice F., 5301-A Tieton Dr., 98908.
Sarsfield, Emmett
Senvello, Robert, P.O. Box 6, Plentywood, MT 59254.
Shaw, John M.
Shields, Robert J., 4602 Tieton Dr., Apt. D 24, 98908.
Surman, Darrell, P.O. Box 12523, Thorndon Wellington, New Zealand.
Tholen, John, 5301-A Tieton Dr., 98908.

Permanent Deacons:
Alvarado, Berney, 15 S. Date St., Toppenish, 98948.
Berger, Duane, 1706 Lower Ahtanum, 98903.
Chavez, Nestor, 710 E. Race St., 98901.
Cornell, John, 2504 W. Chestnut, 98902.
DaValle, Robert, 1837 Marshall Ave., Richland, 99352.
Dronen, Bill, 306 Railroad Ave., Cashmere, 98815.
Escamilla, Andres, 4765 Rd. V., S.E., Warden, 98857.
Farrell, Daniel J., 923 Straitview Dr., Port Angeles, 98362.
Garcia, Gilberto, 2702 W. 6th. Ave., Kennewick, 99336.
Gonzales, Agapito, Jr., P.O. Box 551, Warden, 98857.
Gonzalez, Indalecio, 2760 Brownstown Rd., Harrah, 98933.
Griek, Don, P.O. Box 1023, Leavenworth, 98826.
Hudson, William D., 8819 S.E. 213th St., Renton, 98058.
Kassinger, John, 1314 N. Ave., #4, Sunnyside, 98944.
Kramper, James, 7304 Tieton Dr., 98908.
Martinez, Frank, 3790 Rd. 104, S.W., Royal City, 99357.
Mich, William, 601 N. Reed, Kennewick, 99336.
Miller, Ray, 2412 W. Chestnut, 98902.
Osborn, Bill, 1613 Fairview Ave., Wenatchee, 98801.
Osorio, Antonio, 14 S. I St., Toppenish, 98948.
Powers, John, 3614 S. Green St., Kennewick, 99337.
Reyna, Lupe, 1130 S. Grand, Moses Lake, 98837.
Rice, LeRoi, 1845 Mahan Ave., Richland, 99352.
Richtsmeier, Thomas, 2901 8th St., S.E., East Wenatchee, 98802.
Rizzo, Al, 135 MacArthur St., Richland, 99352.
Schrom, Robert J., 7240 Rd. 17, S.W., Royal City, 99357.
Turley, Kerry, 304 E. Woodin Rd., Sunnyside, 98944.

INSTITUTIONS LOCATED IN THE DIOCESE

[A] COLLEGES AND UNIVERSITIES

TOPPENISH. **Heritage University* (1982) (Interdenominational University with an Independent Board), 3240 Fort Rd., 98948. Tel: 509-865-8600; Fax: 509-865-7976. Email: ross_k@heritage.edu. Web: www.heritage.edu. Bill McCay, Librarian. Sisters 5; Lay Teachers 48; Students 1,500; Lay Staff 83.

[B] HIGH SCHOOLS

UNION GAP. *La Salle High School*, 3000 Lightning Way, 98903. Tel: 509-225-2900; Fax: 509-225-2950. Email: office@lasalleyakima.org. Web: www.lasalleyakima.org. Timothy McGree, Pres.; Bro. James Joost, F.S.C., Prin. Brothers 3; Sisters 1; Lay Teachers 12; Staff 8; Students 190.

[C] HOSPITALS

RICHLAND. *Lourdes Counseling Center*, 1175 Carondelet Dr., 99354. Tel: 509-943-9104; Fax: 509-943-7206. Email: bmead@lourdesonline.org. Web: www.lourdeshealth.net. Barbara Mead, Exec. Dir. Bed Capacity 32; Total Assisted Annually 73,658; Total Staff 165.

[D] CATHOLIC SOCIAL SERVICE CATHOLIC CHARITIES

YAKIMA. *Carroll Children's Center*, 5301 Tieton Dr., Ste. C, 98908. Tel: 509-965-7104; Fax: 509-966-9750. Email: khelseth@cfcsyakima.org. Kathy Helseth, Prog. Mgr. Capacity 121; Total Assisted Annually 174; Total Staff 25.

Catholic Charities of the Diocese of Yakima, 5301-C Tieton Dr., 98908. Tel: 509-965-7100; Fax: 509-972-0167. Email: jyoung@ccyakima.org. Web: www.ccyakima.org. Mr. John L. Young, Exec. Dir.

Catholic Family and Child Service, 5301 Tieton Dr., Ste. C, 98908. Tel: 509-965-7100; Fax: 509-966-9750. Email: info@cfcsyakima.org. Web: www.cfcsyakima.org. Mrs. Darlene Darnell, M.S.W., Agency Dir. Total Assisted Annually 37,489; Total Staff 125.

Child Care Nutrition, 4704 Tieton Dr., Ste. A, 98908. Tel: 509-965-7107; 800-449-9005; Fax: 509-965-8337. Email: coliphant@cfcsyakima.org.

St. Vincent Center, 2629 Main St., Union Gap, 98903. Tel: 509-457-5111; Fax: 509-457-3526. Email: stores@stvincentyakima.org. Web: www.ccyakima.org. Mr. John L. Young, Pres. Total Staff 14.

ELLENSBURG. *St. Vincent Center*, 1200 S. Canyon Rd., 98926. Tel: 509-925-2167; Fax: 509-925-9547. Email: stores@stvincentyakima.org. Web: www.ccyakima.org. Total Staff 8.

KENNEWICK. *St. Vincent Center*, 120 N. Morain, 99336. Tel: 509-783-7020; Fax: 509-783-7039. Email: ksvc@verizon.net. Web: www.ccyakima.org.

MOSES LAKE. *Catholic Family and Child Service of Moses Lake-Ephrata*, 1017 W. Broadway, 98837. Tel: 509-765-1875; Fax: 509-766-1836. Email: jyoung@cfcsyakima.org. Web: www.ccyakima.org. Total Assisted 1,500; Total Staff 4.

RICHLAND. *Catholic Family and Child Service*, 2139 Van Giesen, 99354. Tel: 509-946-4645; Fax: 509-943-2068. Email: jyoung@ccyakima.org. Maureen C. McGrath, M.A., Agency Dir. Total Assisted 6,700; Total Staff 57.

SUNNYSIDE. *Catholic Family and Child Service of Yakima*, 320 N. 16th St., 98944. Tel: 800-793-4453. Email: jyoung@cfcsyakima.org. Web: www.ccyakima.org. Total Assisted 1,200; Total Staff 6.

WENATCHEE. *Catholic Family and Child Service*, 640 S. Mission St, 98907. Tel: 509-662-6761; Fax: 509-663-3182. Email: jyoung@cfcsyakima.org. Web: www.ccyakima.org. Total Assisted 2,500; Total Staff 35.

[E] RETIREMENT HOMES

YAKIMA. **The Gamelin Association-Providence House*, 312 N. 4th St., 98901. Tel: 509-452-5017; Fax: 509-452-1947. Email: Dawn.Rodrigues@providence.org. Web: www.providence.org/Long_Term_Care/Housing/e20ProvHouse.htm. Dawn Rodrigues, Dir. Low income housing for elderly.

[F] VOLUNTEER SERVICES

YAKIMA. *Holy Family Parish Conference*, 5315 Tieton Dr., 98908. Tel: 509-966-0830; Fax: 509-965-1742. Email: office@holyfamilyyakima.org. Web: www.holyfamilyparish.org.

St. Joseph's Parish Conference, 212 N. 4th St., 98901. Tel: 509-248-1911; Fax: 509-248-2604. Omer G. Gress, Pres.

St. Paul's Parish Conference, 15 S. 12th Ave., 98902. Tel: 509-575-3713; Fax: 509-453-7497. Email: stpaul@wolfenet.com. Bob Rogers, Pres.; Fred Baur, Treas.; Mrs. Patty Schuanms, Sec.

Society of St. Vincent de Paul, Particular Council of Yakima, 269 D St., S.E., #209, Ephrata, 98823. Tel: 509-754-4246.

EAST WENATCHEE. *Holy Apostles Parish*, 1315 8th St., N.E., 98801. Tel: 509-884-5444; Fax: 509-886-3424. Email: holyapostles@nwi.net. Web: www.holyapostlesparish.org. Lee Gale, Pastoral Council Pres.; Rev. Argemiro Orozco.

KENNEWICK. *St. Joseph Parish Conference*, 520 S. Garfield, 99336. Tel: 509-586-3820; Fax: 509-586-3558. Email: parish.office@stjoseph-kennewick.org.

RICHLAND. *Christ the King Parish Conference* (1955) 1111 Stevens Dr., 99354. Tel: 509-946-1675; Fax: 509-946-9940. Email: bulletin@ckparish.org. Web: www.ckparish.org. Bob Morford, Pres.

WENATCHEE. *St. Joseph Parish Conference, St Vincent de Paul*, 625 S. Elliott, 98801. Tel: 509-662-4569; Fax: 509-663-8437. Pat Lynam, Pres.

[G] CAMPUS MINISTRY

ELLENSBURG. *Catholic Campus Ministry at Central Washington University* 706 N. Sprague, 98926. Tel: 509-925-3043. Email: ccmcwu@fairpoint.netFax: 509-925-3043. Rev. Wilmar Zabala, Dir. & Campus Min. Total in Residence 4; Total Staff 1.

[H] MISCELLANEOUS LISTINGS

YAKIMA. **Catholic Charities Housing Services, Diocese of Yakima*, 5301 Tieton Dr., Ste. C, 98908-3478. Tel: 509-853-2794; Fax: 509-853-2805. Mr. John L. Young, Pres.

**Central Washington Catholic Foundation* (2002) 5301 Tieton Dr., Ste. F, 98908-3479. Tel: 509-972-3732; Fax: 509-972-2417. Email: info@cwcatholicfoundation.org. Web: www.cwcatholicfoundation.org. Rev. Samuel P. Bellino, S.J., Exec. Dir.

St. Vincent Centers of the Diocese of Yakima, 5301-C Tieton Dr., 98908. Tel: 509-853-2796; Fax: 509-972-0167. Email: stores@stvincentyakima.org. Web: www.ccyakima.org. Mr. John Young, Pres.

COWICHE. *Catholics In Action* (200) P.O. Box 130, 98923. Tel: 509-678-8754; Fax: 888-457-9498. Email: mail@reachym.com. Mr Richard Sevigny, Pres.

TOPPENISH. *Association of Catholic Sisters for Educational Opportunities for the Poor*, 3240 Fort Rd., 98948. Tel: 509-865-3836. Sr. Kathleen Ross, S.N.J.M., Pres.

UNION GAP. *La Salle Foundation of Yakima*, 3000 Lightning Way, 98903. Tel: 509-225-2991; Fax: 509-225-2994. Email: foundation@lasalleyakima.org. Web: www.lasalleyakima.com. Timothy McGree, Pres.

RELIGIOUS INSTITUTES OF MEN REPRESENTED IN THE DIOCESE

For further details refer to the corresponding bracketed number in the Religious Institutes of Men or Women section.

[0200]—*Benedictine Monks (American Cassinese Congregation)*—O.S.B.

[0330]—*Brothers of the Christian Schools* (Prov. of San Francisco)—F.S.C.

[0690]—*Jesuit Fathers and Brothers (Oregon Province)*—S.J.

RELIGIOUS INSTITUTES OF WOMEN REPRESENTED IN THE DIOCESE

[1070-20]—*Dominican Sisters*—O.P.

[1115]—*Dominican Sisters of Peace*—O.P.

[]—*Misioneras Trabajadoras Sociales de la Inglesia*—M.T.S.I.

[]—*Missionary Daughters of the Most Pure Virgin Mary*—M.D.P.V.M.

[3350]—*Sisters of Providence* (Mother Joseph Prov.)—S.P.

[]—*Sisters of St. Francis*—O.S.F.

[3840]—*Sisters of St. Joseph of Carondelet*—C.S.J.

[1990]—*Sisters of the Holy Names of Jesus and Mary*—S.N.J.M.

[2160]—*Sisters, Servants of the Immaculate Heart of Mary*—I.H.M.

NECROLOGY

(No Deaths)

An asterisk (*) denotes an organization that has established tax-exempt status directly with the IRS and is not covered by the USCCB Group Ruling.

Diocese of Youngstown

(Dioecesis Youngstoniensis)

Most Reverend

GEORGE V. MURRY, S.J.

Bishop of Youngstown; ordained June 9, 1979; appointed Auxiliary Bishop of Chicago and Titular Bishop of Fuerteventura January 24, 1995; appointed Coadjutor Bishop of Saint Thomas in the Virgin Islands May 5, 1998; succeeded June 29, 1999; appointed Bishop of Youngstown January 30, 2007; installed March 28, 2007. *Chancery Office: 144 W. Wood St., Youngstown, OH 44503*. Tel: 330-744-8451; Fax: 330-742-6448.

Chancery Office: 144 W. Wood St., Youngstown, OH 44503. Tel: 330-744-8451; Fax: 330-742-6448; 330-744-2848.

Web: www.doy.org

Email: chancery@doy.org

ESTABLISHED MAY 15, 1943.

Square Miles 3,404.

Canonically Erected July 22, 1943.

Comprises six Counties in the northeastern part of the State of Ohio, namely, Ashtabula, Columbiana, Mahoning, Portage, Stark and Trumbull Counties.

For legal titles of parishes and diocesan institutions, consult the Chancery Office.

STATISTICAL OVERVIEW

Personnel	
Bishop	1
Priests: Diocesan Active in Diocese	98
Priests: Diocesan Active Outside Diocese	4
Priests: Retired, Sick or Absent	51
Number of Diocesan Priests	153
Religious Priests in Diocese	17
Total Priests in Diocese	170
Extern Priests in Diocese	6
Ordinations:	
Transitional Deacons	4
Permanent Deacons in Diocese	80
Total Brothers	13
Total Sisters	198
Parishes	
Parishes	113
With Resident Pastor:	
Resident Diocesan Priests	91
Resident Religious Priests	2
Without Resident Pastor:	
Administered by Priests	20
Missions	2
Professional Ministry Personnel:	
Sisters	29
Lay Ministers	106
Welfare	
Catholic Hospitals	4
Total Assisted	53,269
Health Care Centers	29
Total Assisted	1,307,395
Homes for the Aged	10
Total Assisted	2,010
Day Care Centers	1
Total Assisted	120
Specialized Homes	5
Total Assisted	577
Special Centers for Social Services	14
Total Assisted	44,244
Educational	
Diocesan Students in Other Seminaries	14
Total Seminarians	14
Colleges and Universities	1
Total Students	2,936
High Schools, Diocesan and Parish	6
Total Students	2,321
Elementary Schools, Diocesan and Parish	32
Total Students	6,155
Elementary Schools, Private	2
Total Students	345
Catechesis/Religious Education:	
High School Students	2,920
Elementary Students	12,032
Total Students under Catholic Instruction	26,723
Teachers in the Diocese:	
Priests	4
Sisters	9
Lay Teachers	561
Vital Statistics	
Receptions into the Church:	
Infant Baptism Totals	1,877
Minor Baptism Totals	170
Adult Baptism Totals	191
Received into Full Communion	301
First Communions	2,238
Confirmations	2,258
Marriages:	
Catholic	460
Interfaith	305
Total Marriages	765
Deaths	2,766
Total Catholic Population	201,857
Total Population	1,193,021

Former Bishops—Most Revs. JAMES A. MCFADDEN, S.T.D., LL.D., appt. Titular Bishop of Bida and Auxiliary of Cleveland, May 13, 1932; cons. Sept. 8, 1932; appt. Bishop of Youngstown, June 2, 1943; died Nov. 16, 1952; EMMET M. WALSH, D.D., ord. Jan. 15, 1916; appt. Bishop of Charleston, June 20, 1927; appt. Titular Bishop of Rhaedestus and Coadjutor, Sept. 8, 1949; succeeded to See, Nov. 16, 1952; died March 16, 1968; JAMES W. MALONE, D.D., ord. May 26, 1945; appt. Titular Bishop of Alabanda and Auxiliary, Jan. 2, 1960; appt. Apostolic Administrator, Jan. 22, 1966; succeeded to See, May 2, 1968; retired Dec. 4, 1995; died April 9, 2000; THOMAS J. TOBIN, D.D., ord. July 21, 1973; appt. Titular Bishop of Novica and Auxiliary Bishop of Pittsburgh, Nov. 3, 1992; appt. Fourth Bishop of Youngstown installed Feb. 2, 1996; appt. Bishop of Providence March 31, 2005.

All Diocesan offices and personnel can be reached at 144 W. Wood St., Youngstown, OH, 44503. Tel: 330-744-8451, Fax: 330-742-6448; 744-2848 unless otherwise indicated.

Chancery Office

Vicar General & Moderator of the Curia—Rev. Msgr. ROBERT J. SIFFRIN.

Vicar for Administration—Rev. Msgr. JOHN A. ZURAW, J.C.L.

Chancellor—Mrs. NANCY YUHASZ.

"The Catholic Exponent", Diocesan Newspaper—Most Rev. GEORGE VANCE MURRY, S.J., Publisher; Mr. LOUIS JACQUET, Editor & Gen. Mgr. Tel: 330-744-5251.

College of Consultors—Rev. Msgrs. MICHAEL J. CARIGLIO, J.C.L.; JOHN P. ASHTON, Ph.D. (Retired); DAVID W. RHODES; ROBERT J. SIFFRIN; Revs. BERNARD R. BONNOT; GREGORY F. FEDOR; JOSEPH W. WITMER; JOHN JEREK.

Priests Council—Rev. Msgrs. MICHAEL J. CARIGLIO, J.C.L.; JOHN P. ASHTON, Ph.D. (Retired); DAVID W. RHODES; ROBERT SIFFRIN; LEWIS F. GAETANO, Ph.D.; Revs. BERNARD R. BONNOT; GREGORY F. FEDOR; DONALD E. KING; JAMES E. MCKARNS (Retired); EDWARD P. NOGA; JOSEPH W. WITMER; THOMAS G. BISHOP; BERNARD N. GAETA; JOHN KEEHNER, J.C.L.; WILLIAM J. LOVELESS; JOHN JEREK.

Finance Council—Rev. Msgrs. ROBERT J. SIFFRIN, Chm.; FRANK A. CARFAGNA; JOHN H. DEMARINIS; PETER M. POLANDO, J.C.L.; THERESA DELLICK; MARY BETH HOUSER; Sr. ANDRIENE IHNOT, H.M.; ROBERT MARKS; PARKER MCHENRY; EUGENE ROSSI; Mr. PAT KELLY; Mr. ROBERT A. HOFFMAN.

Diocesan Pastoral Council— To be reestablished.

Communications—

Catholic Television Network of Youngstown (CTNY)—Rev. JOHN-MICHAEL LAVELLE, D.Min., Pastoral Dir.; BOB GAVALIER, Gen. Mgr., Mailing Address: P.O. Box 430, Canfield, 44406-0430. Tel: 330-533-2243.

Public-Media Relations—Mrs. NANCY YUHASZ.

Development/Stewardship—Mr. PAT PALOMBO, Dir.

Ecumenism—Rev. JOSEPH W. WITMER, Dir., Ecumenical Commission, 342 S. Chillicothe, Aurora, 44202. Tel: 330-562-8519.

Office of Missions/Evangelization—Bro. THOMAS AQUINAS DOLAN, O.P., Dir.

Scouting, Diocesan Office—Rev. TERRENCE HAZEL.

Department of Canonical Services

Department of Canonical Services—Rev. Msgr. MICHAEL J. CARIGLIO, J.C.L., Exec. Dir., 141 W. Rayen Ave., Youngstown, 44503. Tel: 330-744-8451; Fax: 330-742-6450.

Office of Conciliation—

Matrimonial Dispensations—

Tribunal—

Judicial Vicar—Rev. Msgr. MICHAEL J. CARIGLIO, J.C.L.

Adjutant Judicial Vicar—Rev. Msgr. PETER M. POLANDO, J.C.L.

Judges—Rev. Msgrs. FRANK A. CARFAGNA; WILLIAM J. CONNELL, J.C.L.; DAVID W. RHODES; MARTIN S. SUSKO (Retired); Revs. BERNARD N. GAETA; ROBERT G. GIBAS (Retired); JOHN E. KEEHNER, J.C.L.; DANIEL J. KULESA (Retired); THOMAS J. MCCARTHY; JOHN R. OLSAVSKY, J.C.L.; ROBERT F. PFEIFFER, J.C.L.; GARY D. YANUS, J.C.D.

Defenders of the Bond—Rev. Msgr. JOHN A. ZURAW, J.C.L.; Revs. TERRENCE J. HAZEL; RAYMOND L. PAUL; JOHN F. WARNER.

Advocates—Revs. MARTIN CELUCH; BERNARD N. GAETA; PHYLLIS KULICS; Mrs. BARBARA ROGICH; VICKI KIDD.

Promoter of Justice—Rev. Msgr. JOHN A. ZURAW, J.C.L.

Notary—LINDA TEDDE.

Department of Catholic Charities Services

Department of Catholic Charities Services—Mr. BRIAN CORBIN, Exec. Dir., Health & Human Svcs. Commission; Liaison to St. Vincent DePaul Society.

Office of Social Action—Mr. BRIAN CORBIN, Dir.; Mr. GEORGE GARCHAR, Assoc. Dir. Rural Life; Catholic Relief Services; Criminal Justice Ministry; Migration and Refugee Services; Catholic Campaign for Human Development; Parish Social Ministry.

Office of Social Services—Mrs. MARY ELLEN ANDERSEN, Pres., Diocese of Youngstown Catholic Charities Corp.; Dir., Social Svcs. Dept.

Hispanic Ministry—Sr. PATRICIA FLORES, H.M., Coord., 394 Tenney Ave., Campbell, 44405. Tel: 330-755-3633.

Immigrant Services—EFRAIN RUANO, Coord., Pastoral Care for Migrants and Refugees, 144 W. Wood St., Youngstown, 44503. Tel: 330-744-8451; 330-755-3633.

Diocese of Youngstown Legal Immigration Services—(an affiliate of CLINIC) NAOMI HOKKY, J.D., Senior Attorney; JOSEPH MILES, Interpreter & Asst. Tel: 866-901-3700. Offices: 206 W. Main St., Ravenna, OH 44266; 3112 Cleveland Ave., N.W., Canton, OH 44709; 4200 Park Ave., Ashtabula, OH 44004.

Department of Clergy and Religious Services

Department of Clergy and Religious Services—Rev. JOHN JEREK, Vicar Clergy & Rel. Svcs.

Office of Vocations—Revs. JOHN JEREK; CHRISTOPHER LUONI.

Serra Club of Trumbull County—Rev. FREDERICK LUKEHART, Chap. (Retired), 127 Royal Troon, S.E., Warren, 44484.

Serra Club of Mahoning County—VACANT.

Serra Club of Stark County—VACANT.

Office of Clergy Services—Rev. JOHN JEREK.

Office of Continuing Education and Formation of Priests—Rev. STEPHEN POPOVICH, Dir., 4490 Norquest Blvd., Youngstown, 44515. Tel: 330-793-9988.

Office of Priests' Personnel Advisor—Rev. THOMAS MCCARTHY, 935 E. State St., Salem, 44460. Tel: 330-332-0336.

Office of Permanent Diaconate—Rev. Msgr. JOHN A. ZURAW, J.C.L., Dir.

Office of Religious—Sr. JOYCE CANDIDI, O.S.H.J., Dir.

Diocesan Conference of Religious—Sr. JOYCE CANDIDI, O.S.H.J., Dir.

Department of Financial Services

Department of Financial Services—Mr. PATRICK A. KELLY, CFO.

Office of Finance—Mrs. MARGARET FISHER, Dir. Finance; Mrs. CHRISTINE JICKESS, Assoc. Dir. Finance; Mrs. LINDA DIGAETANO, Benefits Coord.

Office of Information Systems Services—Mr. LOUIS ORBIN, Dir.; Ms. MARIJO ORBIN, Assoc. Dir.

Department of Pastoral and Educational Services

Pastoral and Educational Services—

Office of Catholic Schools—Dr. MICHAEL SKUBE, Supt.; Dr. ALAN DIGIANANTONIO, Dir. Curriculum Instruction & Technology; Dr. LOIS CAVUCCI, Dir. Certificated Personnel; Mr. WALLACE DUNNE, Dir., Govt. Programs & Resource Devel.

The Catholic Diocese of Youngstown Educational Fund, Inc.—

Office of Religious Education—BARBARA WALKO, Diocesan Dir., 225 Elm St., Youngstown, 44503. Tel: 330-744-8451; THOMAS SAULINE, Consultant; CARLA HLAVAC, Consultant.

Council for Catechesis—Mrs. KATHLEEN SWEET, Chm.; Rev. JOHN-MICHAEL LAVELLE, D.Min., Vice Chm.

Office of Youth and Young Adult Ministry—CINDEE CASE, Dir.; FAYE ABBONDANZA, Assoc. Dir.

Office of Campus Ministry—Ms. CARMEN ROEBKE, Diocesan Dir., 1424 Horning Rd., Kent, 44240. Tel: 330-678-0240.

Hiram College—Rev. LEO J. WEHRLIN, St. Ambrose Parish, 10692 Freedom St., Garrettsville, 44231. Tel: 330-527-4105.

University Parish Newman Center (Kent State)—Rev. CHRISTOPHER LUONI, Pastor.

Walsh University—Rev. CHRISTOPHER M. SALIGA, O.P., Chap.; MIGUEL CHAVEZ, Dir., 2020 Easton St., N.W., North Canton, 44720. Tel: 330-490-7344; 330-490-7341; 330-490-7182.

Youngstown State University—Mr. THOMAS BAGOLA, Dir., 254 Madison Ave., Youngstown, 44504. Tel: 330-747-9202.

Office of Worship—FRAN AMER, Dir.

Office of Lay Ministry Formation—Mr. JOHN DAMICO, Dir.

Office of Pro-Life, Marriage & Family Ministry—MELINDA KNIGHT, Dir.; Mr. DANIEL THIMONS, Assoc. Dir.

Other Ministries

Bishop's Delegate for Retired Priests—Rev. THOMAS MCCARTHY.

Catholic Women, Diocesan Council of—Rev. FREDERICK LUKEHART, Moderator (Retired), 127 Royal Troon, S.E., Warren, 44484.

Charismatic Prayer Group—Rev. ROBERT EDWARDS, Dir., 271 Chestnut St., Lisbon, 44432. Tel: 330-424-7648.

Disabled Services—

Physically and Developmentally—Rev. TERRENCE J. HAZEL, Chap., 281 Glenview Dr., Canfield, 44406. Tel: 330-533-6839.

Deaf and Hearing Impaired—Rev. TERRENCE J. HAZEL, Chap., 281 Glenview Dr., Canfield, 44406. Tel: 330-533-6839.

Victim Assistance Coordinator—Mrs. NANCY YUHASZ. Tel: 330-744-8451. Email: nyuhasz@youngstowndiocese.org.

CLERGY, PARISHES, MISSIONS AND PAROCHIAL SCHOOLS

CITY OF YOUNGSTOWN

(MAHONING COUNTY)

1—CATHEDRAL OF ST. COLUMBA (1847) [JC] Rev. John Keehner, Rector; Sr. Isabel Rudge, Pastoral Min.; Deacon Roy West III; Dr. Daniel Laginya, Music Min. In Res., Rev. Edward R. Brienz.
Res.: 159 W. Rayen Ave., 44503. Tel: 330-744-5233; Fax: 330-744-2282.
Catechesis/Religious Program—Tel: 330-744-4233. Students 78.

2—ST. ANTHONY (1898), (Italian), Rev. Msgr. John H. DeMarinis; Deacon Nicholas Boccieri.
Res.: 1125 Turin Ave., 44510. Tel: 330-744-5091; Fax: 330-744-1407.
Catechesis/Religious Program—Students 11.

3—ST. BRENDAN (1923) Rev. James M. Daprile.
Res.: 2800 Oakwood Ave., 44509. Tel: 330-792-3875; Fax: 330-792-9080. Email: pastor@stbrendanyo.org. Web: www.stbrendanyo.org.
Catechesis/Religious Program—Tel: 330-792-3875, Ext. 12. Email: dff@stbrendanyo.org. Students 47.

4—ST. CASIMIR (1906) Rev. John Keehner.
Church: 145 Jefferson St., P.O. Box 2209, 44510-1325. Tel: 330-743-3951; 330-744-5233 (Pastor).
Catechesis/Religious Program—Students 2.

5—ST. CHRISTINE (1953) Rev. Msgr. David W. Rhodes; Rev. Kevin Peters; Deacons Robert Cuttica, Pastoral Min.; David Beil; Ronald Layko; Jim Brown.
Res.: 3165 S. Schenley Ave., 44511. Tel: 330-792-3829; Fax: 330-792-6587. Email: parishoffice@stchristine.org. Web: www.stchristine.org.
School—(Grades PreK-8), 3125 S. Schenley Ave., 44511. Tel: 330-792-4544; Fax: 330-792-6888. Marge Gatto, Librarian. Lay Teachers 19; Students 407.
Catechesis/Religious Program—Tel: 330-793-0544. Email: stchcb@aol.com. Colleen Boyle, Dir. Faith Formation. Students 441.

6—SS. CYRIL AND METHODIUS (1896), (Slovak), Rev. Nicholas J. Mancini.
Res.: 252 E. Wood St., 44503. Tel: 330-743-5291; Fax: 330-746-1207.
Catechesis/Religious Program— Twinned with St. Stephen of Hungary & Our Lady of Mt. Carmel. Students 5.

7—ST. DOMINIC (1923) Very Rev. Gregory Maturi, O.P., Prior; Revs. Christopher M. Saliga, O.P.; Peter Fegan, O.P.; Regis Heuschkel, O.P.; Paul J. Keller, O.P.; William J. Rock, O.P.; Deacon Thomas Aquinas Dolan, O.P.
Res.: 77 E. Lucius Ave., 44507. Tel: 330-783-1900; Fax: 330-783-2396. Email: stdomsytn@yahoo.com. Web: www.saintdominic.org.
Parish Center—3403 Southern Blvd., 44507. Tel: 330-782-1123.
Catechesis/Religious Program—Students 85.

8—ST. EDWARD (1917) Rev. Msgr. Robert J. Siffrin, Admin.; Deacon James Smith.
Res.: 240 Tod Ln., 44504. Tel: 330-743-2308; Fax: 330-743-8321.
Catechesis/Religious Program—Email: treerichosu@yahoo.com. Web: www.saintedwardparish.org. Students 36.

9—ST. ELIZABETH (1922), (Slovak), Rev. Michael Swierz, Admin.; Deacon Anthony Falasca Jr.
Res.: 633 Porter Ave., Campbell, 44405. Tel: 330-747-4085 (Office); 330-755-0266 (Rectory, St. Joseph the Provider); Fax: 330-747-8647.
Church: 124 Keystone, Campbell, 44405. Tel: 330-750-6085; Fax: 330-755-1988.
Catechesis/Religious Program—Tel: 330-726-7775. Students 18.

10—HOLY NAME OF JESUS (1916), (Slovak), Rev. Msgr. Peter M. Polando, Admin.
Res.: 613 N. Lakeview Ave., 44509. Tel: 330-799-8873; Fax: 330-799-1721.
Catechesis/Religious Program—Students 16.

11—IMMACULATE CONCEPTION (1882) Rev. Msgr. John A. Zuraw, Admin.; Sr. Mary Lee Nalley, O.S.U., Pastoral Min.
Res.: 811 Oak St., 44506. Tel: 330-747-3533; Fax: 330-747-0219.
Catechesis/Religious Program—Email: skmccarragher@yahoo.com. Sr. Kathleen McCarragher, O.S.U., D.R.E. Students 33.

12—IMMACULATE HEART OF MARY (1954) Rev. Stephen Popovich; Deacon Nicholas G. Moliterno.
Res.: 4490 Norquest Blvd., 44515. Tel: 330-793-9988; Fax: 330-799-9288.
School—St. Joseph and Immaculate Heart of Mary School, (Grades K-8), 4470 Norquest Blvd., 44515. Tel: 330-799-1944; Fax: 330-799-0151. Sisters 1; Lay Teachers 21; Students 254.
Catechesis/Religious Program—Tel: 330-799-4202. Students 267.

13—ST. JOSEPH (1966) Rev. Gregory F. Fedor; Deacons Michael Roberts, Pastoral Assoc.; Gerald L. Savo.
Res.: 4545 New Rd., Austintown, 44515. Tel: 330-792-1919; Fax: 330-792-5233. Email: austjoseph@zoominternet.net. Web: saintjosephaustintown.org.
Catechesis/Religious Program—Mrs. Sheila Palombo, C.R.E. Students 282.

14—ST. MATTHIAS (1914), (Slovak), Rev. Msgr. Peter M. Polando; Deacon Salvatore DiFrancesco.
Mailing Address: 915 Cornell St., 44502-2765.
Catechesis/Religious Program—Tel: 330-788-5082. Students 23.

15—OUR LADY OF HUNGARY (1929), (Hungarian), Rev. Joseph Rudjak.
Office: 545 N. Belle Vista Ave., 44509. Tel: 330-799-6829; Fax: 330-799-6829. Email: olh545@yahoo.com. Web: www.ourladyhungary.catholicweb.com.
Catechesis/Religious Program—Students 40.

16—OUR LADY OF MT. CARMEL (1908), (Italian), Rev. Msgr. Michael J. Cariglio; Deacon Joseph Nohra.
Res.: 343 Via Mt. Carmel, 44505. Tel: 330-743-4144; Fax: 330-743-1035.
Catechesis/Religious Program—Tel: 330-743-3508. Sr. Karen Marie Barile, O.S.H.J., C.R.E.; Mark Izzo, Music Min. Students 242.

17—ST. PATRICK (1911) Rev. Edward P. Noga.
Res.: 1420 Oak Hill Ave., 44507. Tel: 330-743-1109; Fax: 330-743-8810. Email: stpatricks@neo.rr.com. Web: www.stpatsyoungstown.com.
Catechesis/Religious Program—Students 108.

18—SS. PETER AND PAUL (1911), (Croatian), Rev. Joseph Rudjak.
Res.: 421 Covington St., 44510. Tel: 330-747-6762; Fax: 330-747-6763. Email: jrudjakdoy@yahoo.com. Web: www.sspeterpaulcroatian.catholicweb.com.
Catechesis/Religious Program—Students 19.

19—SACRED HEART OF JESUS (1888) Rev. Msgr. Kenneth E. Miller, Admin.
Res.: 5235 South Ave., 44512.
Rectory—400 Lincoln Park Dr., 44506. Tel: 330-747-6080; Fax: 330-747-7003. Email: churchofsacredheart@yahoo.com.
Catechesis/Religious Program—Tel: 330-747-3533. Sr. Kathleen McCarragher, O.S.U., D.R.E. Students 32.

20—ST. STANISLAUS KOSTKA (1902), (Polish), Rev. Edward J. Neroda; Deacon Michael Schlais.
Res.: 430 Williamson Ave., 44507. Tel: 330-747-8503; Fax: 330-747-6334. Email: stans430@yahoo.com. Web: www.ststansyoungstown.org.
Catechesis/Religious Program—Tel: 330-747-3015. Students 21.

21—ST. STEPHEN OF HUNGARY (1905), (Hungarian), Rev. Nicholas J. Mancini.
Church: 854 Wilson Ave., 44506. Tel: 330-743-1905; Fax: 330-743-1905.
Catechesis/Religious Program— Twinned with SS. Cyril and Methodius, 252 E. Wood St., Youngstown Tel: 330-743-5291. Students 5.

OUTSIDE THE CITY OF YOUNGSTOWN

ALLIANCE, STARK CO.

1—ST. JOSEPH (1854) [CEM] Rev. Donald L. Feicht. In Res., Rev. Msgr. James Kolp (Retired).
Res.: 427 E. Broadway, 44601. Tel: 330-821-5760; Fax: 330-821-5783. Web: www.stjoseph-alliance.org.
Catechesis/Religious Program—Students 56.

2—REGINA COELI (1958) [JC] Rev. Michael D. Seifert.
Res.: 663 Fernwood Blvd., 44601-2796. Tel: 330-821-5880; Fax: 330-821-8837. Email: rcchurch@rcyd.net.
School—(Grades PreK-8), 733 Fernwood Blvd., 44601-2796. Tel: 330-829-9239; Fax: 330-823-1877. Lay Teachers 14; Students 153.

Catechesis/Religious Program—Amy Benedetti, D.R.E. Students 119.

ANDOVER, ASHTABULA CO., OUR LADY OF VICTORY (1949) [CEM] Rev. Kevin McCaffrey.
Res.: 481 S. Main St., P.O. Box 669, 44003-0669. Tel: 440-293-6218; Fax: 440-293-7778.
Catechesis/Religious Program—Students 26.

ASHTABULA, ASHTABULA CO.

1—ST. JOSEPH (1862) [CEM] Rev. Philip Miller; Deacons Richard Johnson; Alan Prasek; Donald Johnson; Peter Olsen, Business Mgr.
Res.: 3312 Lake Ave., 44004. Tel: 440-992-0330; Fax: 440-993-3579. Email: stjoeparish@hotmail.com. Web: www.stjcc.com.
Mission—Our Lady of Miracles (St. Joseph Mission) 4313 West Ave., Ashtabula Co. 44004.
Catechesis/Religious Program—Students 157.

2—MOTHER OF SORROWS (1890), (Irish—Finnish), [JC] Rev. Joseph Ruggieri.
1464 W. 6th St., 44004-3310. Tel: 440-964-3277; Fax: 440-964-6780. Email: mosorrows@windstream.net.
1200 E. 21st St., 44004.
Catechesis/Religious Program—Students 99.

3—OUR LADY OF MT. CARMEL (1897), (Italian), [CEM] Rev. Joseph Ruggieri.
Res.: 1200 E. 21st St., 44004. Tel: 440-998-4111; Fax: 440-998-7829. Email: mtcarmel@mtcarmel-ash.org. Web: www.mtcarmel-ash.org.
Catechesis/Religious Program—Students 125.

AURORA, PORTAGE CO., OUR LADY OF PERPETUAL HELP (1955) Rev. Joseph W. Witmer; Sr. Lu Haidnick, C.D.P., Pastoral Assoc.; Deacon Joseph Pepoy.
Res.: 342 S. Chillicothe Rd., 44202-7814. Tel: 330-562-8519; Fax: 330-562-2529. Web: www.olphaurora.org.
Catechesis/Religious Program—Margaret A. Clapp, D.R.E. Students 457.

BOARDMAN, MAHONING CO.

1—ST. CHARLES BORROMEO (1926) Revs. Philip E. Rogers; Shawn Conoboy, Parochial Vicar; Deacons Paul Lisko, Pastoral Assoc.; Michael A. Kocjancic, Pastoral Assoc.; Mark Heagerty, Dir. Finance; Janette Koewacicn, Pastoral Assoc.; Linda O'Brien, Pastoral Assoc.; Natalie Wardle, Coord. Youth Min.; Jacek Sobieski, Dir. Music.
Res.: 7345 Westview Dr., 44512. Tel: 330-758-2325; Fax: 330-758-2004.
School—(Grades K-8), 7325 Westview Dr., 44512. Tel: 330-758-6689; Fax: 330-758-7404. Mary Welsh, Prin. Lay Teachers 25; Students 470.
Catechesis/Religious Program—Tel: 330-758-8063. Mrs. Geraldine M. Jacquet, D.R.E. Students 528.
Convent—7515 Oregon Tr., 44512. Tel: 330-758-2396.

2—ST. LUKE (1962) Rev. Joseph A. Fata; Deacons Richard Milanek; Robert T. Redig. In Res., Rev. Msgr. Kenneth E. Miller; Rev. James E. O'Brien (Retired).
Res.: 5235 South Ave., 44512. Tel: 330-782-9783; Fax: 330-782-1574. Email: saintlukes@zoominternet.net.
School—(Grades PreK-8), 5225 South Ave., 44512. Tel: 330-782-4060; Fax: 330-782-4842. Email: ygnluk@doy.org. Lay Teachers 10; Students 152.
Catechesis/Religious Program—Students 198.

BREWSTER, STARK CO., ST. THERESE (1928) [JC] Rev. Robert W. Kaylor.
Res.: 456 Wabash Ave. S., 44613. Tel: 330-767-3622; Fax: 330-478-6086. Email: rkaylor@cchsweb.com.
Catechesis/Religious Program—Students 71.

CAMPBELL, MAHONING CO.

1—ST. JOHN THE BAPTIST (1919), (Slovak), [CEM] Rev. John M. Jerek, Admin.; Deacon Ronald J. Bunofsky.
Res.: 159 Reed Ave., 44405. Tel: 330-755-4141 (Office); Fax: 330-755-1022.
Catechesis/Religious Program—Marge O'Malley, D.R.E. Students 20.

2—ST. JOSEPH THE PROVIDER (1919), (Polish), Rev. Michael Swierz; Deacon Anthony Falasca Jr. In Res., Rev. Paul R. Tobin (Retired).
Res.: 633 Porter Ave., 44405. Tel: 330-755-0266; Fax: 330-755-1988.
School—(Grades K-8) Tel: 330-755-4747; Fax: 330-755-4749. Pat Tirpack, Librarian. Lay Teachers 9; Students 132.
Catechesis/Religious Program—Tel: 330-747-4085; Fax: 330-747-8647. Students 31.

3—ST. LUCY (1937), (Italian), Rev. Gerald M. DeLucia, Admin.
Res.: 394 Tenney Ave., 44405-1695. Tel: 330-755-4132; Fax: 330-755-1367.
Catechesis/Religious Program—Tel: 330-755-1367. Marge O'Malley, D.R.E. Students 40.

4—ST. ROSE OF LIMA (1961), (Hispanic), Rev. Gerald M. DeLucia, Admin.; Deacons John Rentas; Enrique Santiago.
394 Tenney Ave., 44405. Tel: 330-755-3633; Fax: 330-755-3683.
Catechesis/Religious Program—Students 70.

CANAL FULTON, STARK CO., SS. PHILIP AND JAMES (1845) [CEM] Rev. John F. Warner.
Res.: 412 High St., 44614. Tel: 330-854-2332; Fax: 330-854-2599. Email: sspj@sssnet.com.
School—(Grades PreSchool-8) Tel: 330-854-2823; Fax: 330-854-1109. Email: spjoffice@yahoo.com. Web: www.saintsphilipandjames.org. Patricia Yacucci, Prin. Lay Teachers 11; Students 148.
Catechesis/Religious Program—Tel: 330-854-3988. Jackie Prosise, D.R.E. Students 157.

CANFIELD, MAHONING CO., ST. MICHAEL (1962) Rev. Terrence J. Hazel; Sr. Brendan Sherlock, O.S.U., Pastoral Min.; Deacon Tom Soich; Mrs. Barbara Spencer, Pastoral Min.
300 N. Broad St., 44406.
Res.: 281 Glenview Dr., 44406. Tel: 330-533-6839; Fax: 330-702-0432. Email: info@stmichaelcanfield.org. Web: www.stmichaelcanfield.org.
Catechesis/Religious Program—Tel: 330-533-5275. Vicki Vicars, Pastoral Min. Catechesis; Maureen Hall, Pastoral Min., Youth. Students 448.

CANTON, STARK CO.

1—ALL SAINTS (1920), (Polish), Rev. Thomas G. Bishop.
Res.: 1386 Henry Ave., S.W., 44706. Tel: 330-453-6429; 330-456-0266 (Hall); Fax: 330-453-2071. Email: allsaints@allsaintscanton.org. Web: www.allsaintscanton.org.
Catechesis/Religious Program—Tel: 330-452-9539; Fax: 330-452-4870. Mary Lou Vega, D.R.E. Students 7.

2—ST. ANTHONY (1908), (Italian), Rev. Thomas G. Bishop.
Res.: 1530 11th St., S.E., 44707. Tel: 330-452-9539; 330-453-9722 (Hispanic); Fax: 330-452-4870. Email: office@stanthonycanton.org. Web: www.stanthonycanton.org.
Catechesis/Religious Program—Mary Lou Vega, D.R.E.; Sr. Karen Lindenberger, Coord. Hispanic Ministry; Roger Herstine, Dir. Youth Min. (English & Hispanic) 204.

3—ST. BENEDICT (1923) Rev. Benson Claret Okpara (Nigeria), Admin.
Res.: 2207 Third St., S.E., 44707. Tel: 330-452-0751; Fax: 330-452-7299.
Benedict Center—Tel: 330-453-3642.
Church: E. Tuscarawas St. & Girard Ave., S.E., 44707.
Catechesis/Religious Program—Students 67.

4—ST. JOAN OF ARC (1944) Rev. William B. Kraynak; Deacon David Conversino.
Res.: 4940 Tuscarawas St. W., 44708-5012. Tel: 330-477-6796; 330-477-6797; Fax: 330-477-0594. Email: rstjoanofar@neo.rr.com. Web: www.sjacanton.com.
School—(Grades PreK-8), 120 Bordner Ave., S.W., 44710. Tel: 330-477-2972; Fax: 330-478-2606. Lay Teachers 23; Students 322.
Catechesis/Religious Program—166 Bordner Ave., S.W., 44710. Students 229.

5—ST. JOHN THE BAPTIST (1823) [CEM] Rev. Ronald M. Klingler; Deacon Carl Burkhardt.
Res.: 627 McKinley Ave., N.W., 44703. Tel: 330-454-8044; Fax: 330-454-1397. Email: canton-stjohn@ameritech.net. Web: www.stjohncanton.com.
Catechesis/Religious Program—Students 94.

6—ST. JOSEPH (1902) Rev. Msgr. Frank A. Carfagna; Deacon Wilbur J. Bagley.
Res.: 2427 W. Tuscarawas St., 44708. Tel: 330-453-2526. Email: stjosephcanton@catholicweb.com. Web: stjosephcanton.catholicweb.com.
School—(Grades K-8), 126 Columbus Ave., N.W., 44708. Tel: 330-454-9787; Fax: 330-454-9866. Lay Teachers 10; Students 126.
Catechesis/Religious Program—Tel: 330-454-2144. Students 88.

7—ST. MARY OF THE IMMACULATE CONCEPTION (1899) Rev. Benson Claret Okpara (Nigeria), Admin.
Res.: 1602 Market Ave. S., 44707. Tel: 330-453-2110; Fax: 330-453-4008. Email: stmaryschrh@neo.rr.com.
Catechesis/Religious Program—Students 72.

8—ST. MICHAEL THE ARCHANGEL (1952) Revs. Bradford N. Helman; Matthew Albright, Parochial Vicar; Sisters Carol McHenry, S.N.D., Pastoral Assoc.; Dorothy Fuchs, S.N.D., Pastoral Assoc.; Deacons Mark J. Fuller; Peter P. Pohl; Mrs. Faith Wackerly, Pastoral Assoc.; Mrs. Mary Germann, Parish Admin.; Mr. Jeff Fricker, Youth Min.; Mr. Kevin Kutz, Music Dir.
Res.: 3430 St. Michael Blvd., N.W., 44718. Tel: 330-492-3119; Fax: 330-492-0339. Web: www.stmichaelcanton.org.
School—(Grades PreK-8), 3431 St. Michael's Blvd., N.W., 44718. Tel: 330-492-2657; Fax: 330-492-9618. Mrs. Sally Roden, Prin.; Mrs. Connie Benner, Librarian. Lay Teachers 25; Students 439.
Catechesis/Religious Program—Email: mike@stmichaelcanton.org. Mr. Michael Ress, D.R.E. Students 515.

9—OUR LADY OF PEACE (1952) Rev. Msgr. Lewis F. Gaetano, Admin.
Res.: 833 39th St., N.W., 44709. Tel: 330-492-0757; Fax: 330-492-1214. Web: www.ourladyofpeace.org.
School—(Grades K-8), 1001 39th St., N.W., 44709. Tel: 330-492-0622; Fax: 330-492-0959. Lay Teachers 15; Students 237.
Catechesis/Religious Program—Tel: 330-492-0929. Students 75.

10—ST. PAUL (1907) [JC] Rev. Msgr. Lewis F. Gaetano.
Res.: 1459 Superior Ave., N.E., 44705. Tel: 330-456-7555; Fax: 330-452-7716. Email: stpaulscanton44705@yahoo.com. Res.: 423 Pebblebrook Dr., SW, North Canton, 44709. Tel: 330-685-2867.
Catechesis/Religious Program—Email: a4jtm@yahoo.com. Students 16.

11—ST. PETER (1845) [CEM] Rev. Msgr. John C. Finnigan.
Res.: 726 Cleveland Ave., N.W., 44702. Tel: 330-453-8493; Fax: 330-453-8083. Web: www.stpeter.org.
School—(Grades PreK-8), 702 Cleveland Ave., N.W., 44702. Tel: 330-452-0125. Email: office@stpetercanton.org. Lay Teachers 12; Students 162.
Catechesis/Religious Program—Students 112.

CHAMPION, TRUMBULL CO., ST. WILLIAM (1963) Rev. Michael D. Balash.
Res.: 5411 Mahoning Ave., N.W., Warren, 44483. Tel: 330-847-8677; Fax: 330-847-6275. Web: www.stwilliamchampion.org.
Catechesis/Religious Program—Tel: 330-847-8627. Carol Timko, C.R.E. Students 145.

COLUMBIANA, COLUMBIANA CO., ST. JUDE (1966) Rev. Thomas G. Ziegler; Deacons Louis Cosentino; Terry L. Coulter.
Res.: 180 Seventh St., 44408. Email: stjude@comcast.net.
Catechesis/Religious Program—Tel: 330-482-2888. Dr. Thomas Brozich, D.R.E. Students 119.

CONNEAUT, ASHTABULA CO.

1—ST. FRANCES CABRINI (1955) [JC] Merged with St. Mary of the Immaculate Conception, Conneaut to form Saint Mary/Saint Frances Cabrini, Conneaut.

2—ST. MARY OF THE IMMACULATE CONCEPTION (1888) [CEM] [JC] Merged with St. Frances Cabrini, Conneaut to form Saint Mary/Saint Frances Cabrini, Conneaut.

3—SAINT MARY/SAINT FRANCES CABRINI Rev. Raymond J. Thomas.
Office: 744 Mill St., P.O. Box 619, 44030. Tel: 440-599-8570; Fax: 440-593-6772. Email: stmsfc@hotmail.com. Web: www.stmsfc.org.
Church: 744 Mill St., 44030.
Church: 480 State St., P.O. Box 619, 44030. Tel: 440-599-8570.
School—(Preschool), Tel: 440-593-1677.
Catechesis/Religious Program—Students 80.

CORTLAND, TRUMBULL CO., ST. ROBERT BELLARMINE PARISH (1952) Rev. Carl Kish.
Res.: 4659 Niles-Cortland Rd., N.E., 44410. Tel: 330-637-4886; Fax: 330-637-0608.
Catechesis/Religious Program—Students 475.

DUNGANNON, COLUMBIANA CO., ST. PHILIP NERI (1817) [CEM] Rev. John P. Tully.
Mailing Address: P.O. Box 309, Hanoverton, 44423-0309.
Office & Res.: 16017 Smith Rd., Summitville, 43962. Tel: 330-223-1871.
Church: 11328 Gavers Rd., 44423. Tel: 330-223-1973.
Catechesis/Religious Program—Students (At St. John) 3.

EAST LIVERPOOL, COLUMBIANA CO.

1—ST. ALOYSIUS (1838), (Irish), [CEM] Rev. Peter Haladej, Admin.
Office & Mailing Address: 512 Monroe St., 43920. Tel: 330-385-7131; Fax: 330-385-3025. Email: st_aloysius@sbcglobal.net.
Res.: 235 W. 5th St., 43920.
School—(Grades PreK-8), 335 W. 5th St., 43920. Tel: 330-385-5963; Fax: 330-385-6455. Email: ygnaloysius@doy.org. Web: www.staloysius.k12.oh.us. Donna Hall, Librarian. Lay Teachers 10; Students 100.
Catechesis/Religious Program— (H.S. refer to Immaculate Conception Church, Wellsville). Elementary 36.

2—ST. ANN (1915) Rev. George J. Balasko.
Res.: 1506 Pennsylvania Ave., 43920. Tel: 330-385-5582. Email: frgeo@stannchurch.comcastbiz.net.
Catechesis/Religious Program— Twinned with St. Aloysius, East Liverpool.

EAST PALESTINE, COLUMBIANA CO., OUR LADY OF LOURDES (1880) [CEM] Rev. Daniel Cipar, Admin. (Retired); Rev. Msgr. Dezso Torok, Pastor Emeritus (Retired).
Res.: 200 E. Main St., 44413. Tel: 330-426-9346; Fax: 330-426-9846.
Catechesis/Religious Program—20 N. James St., 44413. Tel: 330-426-2254. Students 80.

GARRETTSVILLE, PORTAGE CO., ST. AMBROSE (1944) Rev. Leo J. Wehrlin; Deacons Robert Rapp; Gerolome P. Scopilliti.
Res.: 10692 Freedom St., 44231. Tel: 330-527-4105; Fax: 330-527-2500. Email: st_ambrose44231@yahoo.com. Web: www.stambroseonline.com.
Catechesis/Religious Program—Students 140.

GENEVA, ASHTABULA CO., ASSUMPTION B.V.M. (1915) [JC] Rev. Melvin E. Rusnak.
Res.: 594 W. Main St., 44041. Tel: 440-466-3427; Fax: 440-466-4670. Web: assumptiongeneva.org.
School—(Grades PreK-6), 30 Lockwood St., 44041. Tel: 440-466-2104; Fax: 440-466-7769. Web: www-.genevaassumption.com. Mrs. Cheryl Woodward, Prin. Lay Teachers 6; Students 130.
Catechesis/Religious Program—Students 85.

GIRARD, TRUMBULL CO., ST. ROSE (1892) Revs. J. James Korda; Steven J. Agostino, S.J., Parochial Vicar; Deacon Paul Milligan.
Res.: 48 E. Main St., 44420. Tel: 330-545-4351; Fax: 330-545-0119.
School—(Grades K-8), 61 E. Main St., 44420. Tel: 330-545-1163. Web: www.stroseschool.info. Mrs. Linda Borton, Prin. Sisters 1; Lay Teachers 16; Students 267.
Sunny Days Day Care Center—Tel: 330-545-1490; Fax: 330-545-1584. Email: sunnydaysccc@att.net. Michelle Frease, Dir. (Preschool)
Catechesis/Religious Program—Tel: 330-545-1216. Susan Lipkovich, Christian Formation Dir. Students 247.

HUBBARD, TRUMBULL CO., ST. PATRICK (1869) [CEM] Rev. Timothy H. O'Neill; Deacon Robert Friedman, Pastoral Assoc.
Mailing Address & Res.: 225 N. Main St., 44425. Tel: 330-534-1928; Fax: 330-534-0820.
School—(Grades K-8), 38 E. Water St., 44425. Tel: 330-534-2509; Fax: 330-534-0305. Lay Teachers 14; Students 132.
Catechesis/Religious Program—225 N. Main St., 44425. Tel: 330-534-8304. Email: spreled@aol.com. Web: www.stpatshub.org. Karen Bartos, C.R.E.; Roger Leckfor, Coord. Youth Min. Students 567.

JEFFERSON, ASHTABULA CO., ST. JOSEPH CALASANCTIUS (1858) Rev. Stephen M. Wassie.
Res.: 32 E. Jefferson St., 44047. Tel: 440-576-3651; Fax: 440-576-3651.
Catechesis/Religious Program—Tel: 440-576-3339. Students 87.

KENT, PORTAGE CO.
1—ST. PATRICK'S (1864) [JC] Rev. Richard J. Pentello; Deacons Timothy DeFrange; Michael W. Stabilla.
Res.: 313 N. Depeyster St., 44240. Tel: 330-673-5849; Fax: 330-673-5849.
School—(Grades K-8), 127 Portage St., 44240. Tel: 330-673-7232; Fax: 330-678-6612. Lay Teachers 21; Students 305.
Catechesis/Religious Program—Tel: 330-677-4453. Students 210.
2—UNIVERSITY PARISH NEWMAN CENTER (1953) Rev. Christopher Luoni.
Res.: 1424 Horning Rd., 44240. Tel: 330-678-0240; Fax: 330-678-7780. Web: www.kentnewmancenterparish.org.
Catechesis/Religious Program—Students 80.

KINGSVILLE, ASHTABULA CO., ST. ANDREW (1936) Rev. Stephen M. Wassie.
Res.: 3700 Rte. 193, 44048. Tel: 440-224-0987 (Church).
Catechesis/Religious Program—Students 28.

KINSMAN, TRUMBULL CO., ST. PATRICK (1957) Attended by Our Lady of Victory, Andover. Rev. Kevin McCaffrey.
Res.: 481 S. Main St., P.O. Box 669, Andover, 44003-0669. Tel: 440-293-6218; Fax: 410-293-7778.
Catechesis/Religious Program—Students 28.

LAKE MILTON, MAHONING CO., ST. CATHERINE (1956) Rev. David W. Merzweiler.
50 Rosemont Rd., North Jackson, 44451. Tel: 330-538-2602; Fax: 330-538-9580.
Res.: 1254 Grandview Rd., 44429-9542. Tel: 330-654-4001.
Catechesis/Religious Program—Carol Muldowney, D.R.E. Students 38.

LEETONIA, COLUMBIANA CO., ST. PATRICK (1861) [CEM] Revs. Thomas Eisweirth, Canonical Admin.; Thomas McCarthy; Deacon Lawrence Parks.
Res.: 167 W. Main St., 44431. Tel: 330-427-6577; Fax: 330-332-7982.
Catechesis/Religious Program—Students 30.

LISBON, COLUMBIANA CO., ST. GEORGE (1820) Rev. Robert Edwards.
Res.: 271 W. Chestnut St., 44432. Tel: 330-424-7648.
Catechesis/Religious Program—Tel: 330-424-0109. Students 75.
Mission—St. Agatha, Tel: 330-424-0155 (Sunday only).

LOUISVILLE, STARK CO.
1—ST. LOUIS (1838), (French—German), [CEM] Rev. David C. Menegay (PIT).
Res.: 300 N. Chapel St., 44641. Tel: 330-875-1658; Fax: 330-875-1657. Web: stlouiscatholicchurchlouisvilleoh.4lpi.com.
School—(Grades PreSchool-8) Tel: 330-875-1467; Fax: 330-875-2511. Email: ygnlouis@doy.com. Web: stlouiscatholicschool.com. Carole von Buelow, O.S.F., Prin.; Samor Salvino, Librarian. Lay Teachers 12; Students 108.
Catechesis/Religious Program—Stephanie Bole, C.R.E.; Michelle May, Youth Min.; Daniel Kelly, Music Min.; Marsha Dalsky, Ministry Coord. Students 180.
2—SACRED HEART OF MARY (1833) [CEM] Rev. Howard Ziemba, Admin.
Res.: 8277 Nickelplate Ave., N.E., 44641. Tel: 330-875-2827; Fax: 330-875-5511. Email: rsacred@neo.rr.com.
Catechesis/Religious Program—Students 77.

LOWELLVILLE, MAHONING CO., OUR LADY OF THE HOLY ROSARY (1867) [CEM] Rev. Charles Poore, Admin.
Res.: 131 E. Wood St., 44436. Tel: 330-536-6436; Fax: 330-536-9188.
Catechesis/Religious Program—Students 205.

MANTUA, PORTAGE CO., ST. JOSEPH (1923) Rev. Michael Garvey; Deacon Gary Keefer.
Res.: 4534 Pioneer Tr., 44255. Tel: 330-274-2114.
Parish Office Center—Tel: 330-274-2253; Fax: 330-274-2254. Email: parishoffice@stjosephmantua.com. Web: www.stjosephmantua.com.
School—(Grades K-8) Tel: 330-274-2268; Fax: 330-274-2269. Lay Teachers 7; Students 89.
Catechesis/Religious Program—Tel: 330-274-2253; Fax: 330-274-2254. Students 177.

MASSILLON, STARK CO.
1—ST. BARBARA (1867), (German), [CEM] Rev. Thomas W. Cebula; Deacon Peter P. Pohl, Pastoral Assoc.
Res.: 2813 Lincoln Way, N.W., 44647. Tel: 330-833-6898; Fax: 330-833-5164. Email: stbarbmassillon@aol.com. Web: www.stbarbmassillon.com.
School—(Grades PreK-8), 2809 Lincoln Way, N.W., 44647. Tel: 330-833-9510; Fax: 330-833-3297. Email: ygnbarbara@doy.org. Sisters (Humility of Mary) 1; Lay Teachers 9; Students 122.
Catechesis/Religious Program—Henry Kappel, D.R.E. Students 117.
2—ST. JOSEPH (1863) [CEM] Rev. Raymond L. Paul; Deacons Steven A. Wyles; Donald F. Molinari.
Res., Parish Center & Office: 322 Third St., S.E., 44646. Tel: 330-833-2607; 330-833-4907; 330-833-6088; Fax: 330-833-3907. Web: www.stjoemassillon.catholicweb.com.
Catechesis/Religious Program—Students 110.
3—SAINT MARY (1839) [CEM] Revs. A. Edward Gretchko; Robert M. Miller; Deacon Joseph Fries.
Parish Office—726 1st St., N.E., 44646. Tel: 330-833-8501; Fax: 330-833-3359. Email: stmarysmassilon@yahoo.com. Web: www.stmarysonline.org.
Res.: 206 Cherry Rd., N.E., 44646. Tel: 330-832-1270.
School—(Grades PreK-8), 640 First St., N.E., 44646. Tel: 330-832-9355; Fax: 330-832-9030. Lisa Channel, Librarian. Sisters 1; Lay Teachers 16; Students 229.
Catechesis/Religious Program—Tel: 330-832-5719; Fax: 330-832-9020. Students 97.

MASURY, TRUMBULL CO., ST. BERNADETTE (1940) Rev. Frank L. Zanni; Deacon Frank Marino.
Res.: 7800 Locust St., 44438. Tel: 330-448-8015; Fax: 330-448-6653. Email: st_bernadette@hotmail.com.
Catechesis/Religious Program—*Brookfield Junior High*, Twinned with St. Vincent de Paul Parish, Vienna., Brookfield. Tel: 330-394-2361.

MAXIMO, STARK CO., ST. JOSEPH (1850) [CEM] Rev. Thomas Ungashick.
Res.: P.O. Box 219, 44650. Tel: 330-823-7809.
Catechesis/Religious Program—Tel: 330-823-5233. Students 59.

MCDONALD, TRUMBULL CO., OUR LADY OF PERPETUAL HELP (1943) Rev. John P. Madden.
Res.: 618 Ohio Ave., 44437. Tel: 330-530-6929; Fax: 330-530-2488. Email: olphmcdonald@aol.com. Web: ourladymcdonald.com.
Catechesis/Religious Program—601 Indiana Ave., 44437. Tel: 330-530-1111. Email: olphmcdonaldccd@aol.com. Students 179.

MIDDLEBRANCH, STARK CO., ST. THERESE LITTLE FLOWER (1929) Revs. John E. Zuzik; Robert J. Hannon, Admin. (Retired).
Res.: 2040 Diamond St., N.E., Canton, 44721. Tel: 330-494-2759; Fax: 330-494-2536.
Catechesis/Religious Program—Email: bbuzenski@littleflowerparish.com. Web: www.littleflowerparish.com. Students 313.

MINERAL RIDGE, TRUMBULL CO., ST. MARY (1870) Rev. Richard Murphy.
Res.: 3504 Main St., 44440. Tel: 330-652-7761; Fax: 330-652-7765. Email: saintmary@zoominternet.net.
Catechesis/Religious Program—Students 83.

NAVARRE, STARK CO., ST. CLEMENT (1832) [CEM] Rev. Edward L. Beneleit.
Res.: 216 Wooster St. E., 44662. Tel: 330-879-5900; Fax: 330-879-5138.
Catechesis/Religious Program—Students 33.

NEW MIDDLETOWN, MAHONING CO., ST. PAUL THE APOSTLE (1952) [JC] Rev. Nicholas R. Shori.
Res.: 10143 Main St., P.O. Box 515, 44442. Tel: 330-542-3466; Fax: 330-542-2448.
Catechesis/Religious Program—Tel: 330-542-3824. Students 450.

NEWTON FALLS, TRUMBULL CO.
1—ST. JOSEPH (1923), (Slovak), [CEM] Merged with St. Mary, Newton Falls to form Saint Mary and Saint Joseph, Newton Falls.
2—ST. MARY (1928), (Polish), [JC] Merged with St. Joseph, Newton Falls to form Saint Mary and Saint Joseph, Newton Falls.
3—ST. MARY AND ST. JOSEPH PARISH (1923) [CEM] Rev. Maciej Mankowski.
Res.: 131 W. Quarry St., 44444-1560. Tel: 330-872-5742; Fax: 330-872-5744. Email: parishssmaryjoseph@yahoo.com. Web: www.stmaryandstjosephparish.com.
School—(Grades PreK-8) Tel: 330-872-7676; Fax: 330-872-1013. Web: www.ssmj.org. Sr. Carol Suhar, O.S.U., Prin.; Mrs. Brasko, Librarian. Students 91.
Catechesis/Religious Program—Students 70.

NILES, TRUMBULL CO.
1—OUR LADY OF MT. CARMEL (1906), (Italian), [CEM] Rev. Lawrence Frient.
Res.: 381 Robbins Ave., 44446. Tel: 330-652-5825; Fax: 330-544-1872. Email: mountcarmelniles@yahoo.com. Web: www.mountcarmelniles.org.
Catechesis/Religious Program—Students 125.
2—ST. STEPHEN (1853) [CEM] Rev. Thomas P. Kraszewski.
Res.: 129 W. Park Ave., 44446. Tel: 330-652-4396; Fax: 330-652-9317. Email: churchofsaintstephen@yahoo.com.
School—(Grades PreK-8), 45 S. Chestnut, 44446. Tel: 330-652-5511; Fax: 330-652-4264. Religious 1; Lay Teachers 14; Students 136; Preschool 39.
Catechesis/Religious Program—Students 196.

NORTH CANTON, STARK CO., ST. PAUL (1845) Rev. Msgr. James A. Clarke; Revs. James E. McKarns (Retired); Donald J. Oser (Retired); Christopher Henyk; Judy Piero, Pastoral Min.; Deacons William Lambert; Ron Reolfi, Business Admin.; Edward Loubacher; Peter D. Watry; Carl Jerzyk.
Res.: 241 S. Main St., 44720. Tel: 330-499-2201; Fax: 330-499-8106. Web: stpaulncanton.org.
School—(Grades K-8), 303 S. Main St., 44720. Tel: 330-494-0223; Fax: 330-494-3226. Jackie Zufall, Prin.; Kathy Yackshaw, Librarian. Lay Teachers 21; Students 377.
Catechesis/Religious Program—Marcy Fessler, D.R.E. Students 716.

NORTH JACKSON, MAHONING CO., ST. JAMES PARISH (1943) Rev. David W. Merzweiler.
Mailing & Office Address: 50 Rosemont Rd., 44451. Tel: 330-538-2602.
Res.: 1254 Grandview Rd., Lake Milton, 44429. Tel: 330-654-4001.
Catechesis/Religious Program—Carol Muldowney, D.R.E. Students 73.

ORWELL, ASHTABULA CO., ST. MARY (1922) [CEM] Rev. G. David Weikart, Admin.
Res.: 103 N. Maple, Box 217, 44076-0217. Tel: 440-437-6262; Fax: 440-437-8216. Email: stmaryofc@fairpoint.net.
Catechesis/Religious Program—Tel: 440-437-8216. Students 112.

POLAND, MAHONING CO., HOLY FAMILY (1956) Rev. Msgr. William J. Connell; Rev. Richard Whetstone (PBR); Deacons Ray Hatala; Ernest Formichelli.
Res.: 2729 Center Rd., 44514. Tel: 330-757-1545; Fax: 330-757-4443. Email: holy_family@sbcglobal.net. Web: www.massintransit.com/oh/hlyfam-poland.
School—(Grades K-8) Tel: 330-757-3713; Fax: 330-757-7648. Email: ygnholyfamily@doy.org. Web: holyfamilypoland.org. Lay Teachers 20; Students 299.
Catechesis/Religious Program—Students 464.

RANDOLPH TOWNSHIP, PORTAGE CO., ST. JOSEPH (1831) [CEM] Rev. Edward R. Wieczorek; Deacons James White; Steven Gies, Parish Life & Family Life Chairperson.
Res.: 2643 Waterloo Rd., Mogadore, 44260. Tel: 330-628-9941; Fax: 330-628-9942. Email: stjoerandolph@yahoo.com. Web: www.stjosephrandolph.org.
School—(Grades K-8), 2617 Waterloo Rd., Mogadore, 44260. Tel: 330-628-9555; Fax: 330-628-9942. Email: ygnjosephran@day.org. Web: www.stjoerandolph.org. Lay Teachers 10; Students 111.
Catechesis/Religious Program—Tel: 330-628-4844; Fax: 330-628-9942. Email: msgrlin@aol.com. Linda Shaw, D.R.E. Students 225.

RAVENNA, PORTAGE CO., IMMACULATE CONCEPTION (1854) [CEM] Rev. John-Michael Lavelle; Deacon Russell J. Brode.
Res.: 409 W. Main St., 44266. Tel: 330-296-6434; Fax: 330-296-9193.
Catechesis/Religious Program—Tel: 330-296-4549. Students 150.

ROCK CREEK, ASHTABULA CO., SACRED HEART (1956) [JC] Rev. G. David Weikart, Admin.
Office: 3049 SR 45, P.O. Box 310, 44084. Tel: 440-563-3010. Email: shc305@windstream.net.
Catechesis/Religious Program—Tel: 440-563-5253. Students 40.

ROOTSTOWN, PORTAGE CO., ST. PETER OF THE FIELDS (1868), (German), [CEM] Rev. David M. Misbrener; Deacons Thomas Shay; James Louis Massacci.
Mailing Address: 3487 Old Forge Rd., 44272. Tel: 330-325-7543.
Catechesis/Religious Program—Students 220.

SALEM, COLUMBIANA CO., ST. PAUL (1881) Rev. Thomas Eisweirth; Donna Lynn, Pastoral Min.; David Markovich, Pastoral Min. In Res., Rev. Thomas McCarthy.
Res.: 157 Ohio Ave., 44460. Tel: 330-332-0336; Fax: 330-332-7982.
Parish Administration Center—935 E. State St., 44460.
School—925 E. State St., 44460. Tel: 330-337-3451; Fax: 330-337-3452. Lay Teachers 12; Students 105.
Catechesis/Religious Program—Sr. Mary McFadden, S.N.D., Pastoral Assoc.; Donna Dermotta, D.R.E. Students 285.

SALINEVILLE, COLUMBIANA CO., ST. PATRICK (1873) [CEM] Rev. John P. Tully.
Office, Res. & Mailing Address: P.O. Box 309, Hanoverton, 44423-0309. Tel: 330-223-1871.
Church: 611 Jefferson St., 43945.
Catechesis/Religious Program—Twinned with St. John, Summitville. Students 4.

SEBRING, MAHONING CO., ST. ANN (1908) Rev. Thomas P. Dyer, Admin.; Deacon Ralph Chase.
Res.: 323 S. 15th St., 44672. Tel: 330-938-2033; Fax: 330-938-6544. Email: stannsebring@sbcglobal.net.
Catechesis/Religious Program—Students 60.

STREETSBORO, PORTAGE CO., ST. JOAN OF ARC (1965) Rev. Pat Ferraro; Deacon John F. Carney.
Res.: 8894 State Rte. 14, 44241. Tel: 330-626-3424; Fax: 330-626-3422.
Catechesis/Religious Program—Students 187.

STRUTHERS, MAHONING CO.

1—HOLY TRINITY (1907), (Slovak), Rev. William Petrunak.
Res.: 250 N. Bridge St., 44471. Tel: 330-755-2115; Fax: 330-750-9431.
Catechesis/Religious Program—Tel: 330-755-4133. Students 28.

2—ST. NICHOLAS (1865) Rev. Bernard R. Bonnot; Deacon John Terranova.
Res.: 764 5th St., 44471-1795. Tel: 330-755-9819.
Parish Office—764 5th St., 44471-1704. Tel: 330-755-9819; Fax: 330-755-9949.
School—(Grades K-8), 762 5th St., 44471-1704. Tel: 330-755-2128. Lay Teachers 16; Students 177.
Catechesis/Religious Program—Tel: 330-755-6245. Miss Stephanie Tarajcak, D.R.E. Students 259.

SUMMITVILLE, COLUMBIANA CO., ST. JOHN (1839) [CEM] Rev. John P. Tully.
Mailing Address: P.O. Box 309, Hanoverton, 44423-0309.
Office & Res.: 16017 Smith Rd., 43962. Tel: 330-223-1871.
Catechesis/Religious Program—Students 54.

UNIONTOWN, STARK CO., HOLY SPIRIT (1979) Rev. John Zapp.
Res.: 2952 Edison St., N.W., 44685. Tel: 330-699-4500. Email: holyspiritunoh@sbcglobal.net. Web: www.holyspiritunoh.org.
Catechesis/Religious Program—Students 204.

VIENNA, TRUMBULL CO.

1—QUEEN OF THE HOLY ROSARY (1997) Revs. Denis Bouchard, F.S.S.P.; Joseph Orlowski, F.S.S.P.
Res.: 291 Scoville Dr., 44473. Tel: 330-856-4204; Fax: 330-856-9587.
Catechesis/Religious Program—Students 53.

2—ST. VINCENT DE PAUL (1879) Rev. Frank L. Zanni.
Res.: 4453 Warren-Sharon Rd., 44473. Tel: 330-394-2461; Fax: 330-609-0320.
Catechesis/Religious Program—Twinned with St. Bernadette, Masury., Tel: 330-394-2361. Students 179.

WARREN, TRUMBULL CO.

1—BLESSED SACRAMENT (1959) Rev. Donald E. King.
Res.: 3020 Reeves Rd., N.E., 44483. Tel: 330-372-2215; Fax: 330-372-6380. Email: bsp3722215@aol.com. Web: e-blessedsacramentparish.org.
See Notre Dame School, Inc., Blessed Sacrament Campus in the Institution Section under Diocesan Schools.
Catechesis/Religious Program—Fax: 330-372-6380. Students 386.

2—CHRIST OUR KING (1951) Rev. James P. Walker.
Res.: 1000 Tod Ave., S.W., 44485. Tel: 330-395-3747; Fax: 330-395-1631.

3—SS. CYRIL AND METHODIUS (1928), (Slovak), Rev. James P. Walker; Deacon Joseph P. Toth.
Res.: 185 Laird Ave., N.E., 44483. Tel: 330-393-9766; Fax: 330-393-0555. Email: warrenstcyril@aol.com. Web: www.sscmwarren.org.
Catechesis/Religious Program—Tel: 330-393-0781. Students 34.

4—ST. JAMES (1947) Rev. Charles W. Crumbley.
Res.: 2532 Burton St., S.E., 44484. Tel: 330-369-3518; Fax: 330-369-2761.
Catechesis/Religious Program—2106 Arbor St., S.E., 44484. Tel: 330-369-3518. Sr. Yvonne Horning, O.P., D.R.E. Students 50.

5—ST. JOSEPH (1928) [CEM] Rev. Fred E. Trucksis.
Res.: 1346 Vernon St., N.W., 44483. Tel: 330-393-0226; Fax: 330-393-4764.

6—ST. MARY (1835) [CEM] Rev. Bernard R. Schmalzried.
Res.: 232 Seneca St., N.E., 44481. Tel: 330-393-8721; 330-394-3426.
Catechesis/Religious Program—Students 85.

7—ST. PIUS X (1959) Rev. William J. Loveless.
Res.: 1401 Moncrest Ave., N.W., 44485. Tel: 330-399-8881; 330-399-8882; Fax: 330-399-1361.
See Notre Dame School, Inc., St. Pius X Campus in the Institution Section under Diocesan Schools.
Catechesis/Religious Program—Tel: 330-394-4343. Students 37.

WAYNESBURG, STARK CO., ST. JAMES (1928) Rev. Joseph Zamary.
Res.: 400 W. Lisbon St., 44688. Tel: 330-866-9449; Fax: 330-866-1750. Email: jjzamary@aol.com.
School—(Grades PreK-6) Tel: 330-866-9556; Fax: 330-866-1750. Sharon Brown, Librarian. Lay Teachers 8.
Catechesis/Religious Program—Tel: 330-866-9449. Students 75.

WELLSVILLE, COLUMBIANA CO., IMMACULATE CONCEPTION (1842) [CEM] Rev. Peter Haladej, Admin.; Mary E. Frost, Business Mgr.
1021 Riverside Ave., 43968. Tel: 330-385-7131; Fax: 330-385-3025.
Office: 512 Monroe St., East Liverpool, 43920.
Res. & Rectory: 235 W. 5th St., East Liverpool, 43920.
Catechesis/Religious Program—Tel: 330-385-5963. Mr. Robert Barto, D.R.E. Students 38.

WINDHAM, PORTAGE CO., ST. MICHAEL'S (1943) Rev. James Paul Lang.
Res.: 9736 E. Center St., 44288. Tel: 330-326-3531.
Catechesis/Religious Program—Students 25.

On Duty Outside the Diocese:
Revs.—
Deffenbaugh, Joseph T., Pensacola, FL
Nuzzi, Ronald, Notre Dame, IN

Graduate Studies:
Rev.—
Celuch, Martin, Canon Law Studies, Catholic University of America, Washington, DC.

Military Chaplains:
Rev.—
Mikstay, Michael, U.S. Navy

Retired:
Rev. Msgrs.—
Adamko, Cyril A.
Ashton, John P., Ph.D.
Kelly, Thomas F.
Kolp, James
Reidy, Robert
Ronik, Michael
Sabatino, Robert
Slaven, Frederick
Susko, Martin S.
Torok, Dezso
Revs.—
Bantz, William
Brobst, Richard A.
Cavanaugh, James K.
Cipar, Daniel
Czaja, Joseph S.
Dobosiewcz, Leon W.
Esposito, Anthony
Fasline, Anthony
Forgach, Carl J.
Franko, George M.
Friedrich, Ralph
Gibas, Robert G.
Grabowski, Dennis
Hannon, Robert J.
Horvath, Stephen
Johnson, James
Karas, Stephen
Kulesa, Daniel J.
Lehnerd, Frank M.
Lody, John
Loperfido, Ernest
Lukehart, Frederick
Lyons, John F.
McKarns, James E.
Mintjal, Frank
Mulqueen, John D.
Murray, John A.
Nentwick, John
O'Brien, James E.
O'Leary, Patrick D.
Oser, Donald J.
Platt, Stewart
Pleban, Leo
Reiss, John E.
Santucci, Louis
Smar, Michael J.
Summers, John
Tamburrini, Joseph
Tobin, Paul R.
Witt, William
Yablonsky, Gabriel

Permanent Deacons:
Arend, David H., (On Duty Outside Diocese)
Bagley, Wilbur J., St. Joseph, Canton
Beil, David C., St. Christine, Youngstown
Boccieri, Nicholas J., St. Anthony, Youngstown
Brode, Russell J., Immaculate Conception, Ravenna
Brown, James, St. Christine, Youngstown
Bunofsky, Ronald J., St. John, Campbell
Burkhardt, Carl R., St. John the Baptist, Canton
Carney, John F., St. Joan of Arc, Streetsboro
Chase, Ralph, St. Ann, Sebring
Conversino, David, St. Joan of Arc, Canton
Cosentino, Louis A., St. Jude, Columbia
Coulter, Terry L., D.C., St. Jude, Columbiana
Cuttica, Robert J., St. Christine, Youngstown
Davies, Martin H., (On Duty Outside Diocese)
DeFrange, Tim, St. Patrick, Kent
DiFrancesco, Salvatore, St. Matthias, Youngstown
Falasca, Anthony, Jr., St. Joseph, Campbell
Formichelli, Ernest, Holy Family, Poland
Friedman, Robert J., St. Patrick, Hubbard
Fries, Joseph K., St. Mary, Massillon
Fuller, Mark J., St. Michael, Canton
Gies, Steven R., Immaculate Conception, Ravenna
Harvey, James G., St. William, Warren
Hatala, Ray H., (Office of Permanent Diaconate)
Hawkins, Edward, St. Patrick, Youngstown
Heinz, Edward, Sts. Peter and Paul, Youngstown
Ivan, Ellis C., Holy Spirit, Uniontown
Jerzyk, Carl, St. Paul, North Canton
Johnson, Don, St. Joseph, Ashtabula
Johnson, Richard M., St. Joseph, Ashtabula
Keefer, Gary, St. Joseph, Mantua
Klein, Robert E., St. Peter, Canton
Kocjancic, Michael A., St. Charles, Boardman
Krause, Harold R., (On Duty Outside the Diocese)
Lamar, Kevin T., St. Vincent dePaul, Vienna
Lambert, William H., St. Paul, North Canton
Laubacher, Edward, St. Paul, North Canton
Layko, Ronald J., St. Christine, Youngstown
Lisko, Paul, St. Nicholas, Struthers
Marino, Frank, St. Bernadette, Masury
Massacci, James Louis, St. Peter, Rootstown
Milanek, Richard, St. Luke, Boardman
Milligan, Paul, St. Rose, Girard
Mintus, Robert, St. Pius X, Warren
Molinari, Donald F., St. Joseph, Massillon
Moliterno, Nicholas G., Immaculate Heart of Mary, Youngstown
Nohra, Joseph S., St. Maron & Mt. Carmel, Youngstown
O'Neill, Russell, Holy Spirit, Uniontown
Pallo, John D., Sacred Heart, Rock Creek
Pasko, Lawrence, St. Patrick, Leetonia
Pepoy, Joseph E., Our Lady of Perpetual Help, Aurora
Pfleger, James W., (On Duty Outside the Diocese)
Pohl, Peter P., SS. Philip & James, Canal Fulton
Prasek, Alan, St. Joseph, Ashtabula
Rapp, Robert, St. Ambrose, Garrettsville
Redig, Robert T., St. Luke, Boardman
Rentas, John, St. Rose of Lima, Youngstown
Reolfi, Ron, St. Paul, North Canton
Roberts, Michael R., Jr., St. Joseph, Austintown
Rohr, Thomas J., SS. Philip & James, Canal Fulton
Santiago, Enrique, St. Rose of Lima, Youngstown
Savo, Gerald L., St. Joseph, Austintown
Schlais, Michael, St. Stanislaus, Youngstown
Scopilliti, Gerolome P., St. Ambrose, Garrettsville
Seaman, Michael T., St. Peter, Canton
Shay, Thomas R., Sr., St. Peter of the Fields, Rootstown
Sherwood, Ronald D., (Serving Outside the Diocese)
Simmerly, Robert, St. James, Warren

Smith, James, St. Edward, Youngstown
Soich, Thomas G., St. Michael, Canfield
Stabilla, Michael W., St. Patrick, Kent
Terranova, John, St. Nicholas, Struthers
Toth, Joseph P., Blessed Sacrament, Warren
Waldron, Michael K., Sts. Philip & James, Canal Fulton
Watry, Peter D., St. Paul, North Canton
West, Raymond F., III, St. Columba, Youngstown
White, James A., (On Duty Outside Diocese)
Wood, Gregory J., St. Peter, Canton
Wyles, Steve, St. Joseph, Massillon

INSTITUTIONS LOCATED IN THE DIOCESE

[A] SEMINARIES, RELIGIOUS, OR SCHOLASTICATES

CANFIELD. *Society of St. Paul*, 9531 Akron-Canfield Rd., P.O. Box 595, 44406. Tel: 330-533-5503; 330-533-1076; Fax: 330-533-1076. Email: paultheapostle@msn.com. Web: www.albahouse.org. Revs. Ignatius Staniszewski, S.S.P., Local Supr.; Anthony Chenevy, S.S.P.; Thomas Fogarty, S.S.P.; Jeffrey Mickler, S.S.P.; Anthony Warren, S.S.P.; Bros. Dismas Beique, S.S.P.; Dominic Calabro, S.S.P.; Augustine Condon, S.S.P.; Paschal Duesman, S.S.P.; James Mann, S.S.P.; John Naranjo, S.S.P.; Gerard Roche, S.S.P.; Peter Scalise, S.S.P. Priests 5; Brothers 8; Total Staff 13.

[B] COLLEGES AND UNIVERSITIES

NORTH CANTON. *Walsh University* (Coed), 2020 E. Maple St., 44720-3396. Tel: 330-490-7090; Fax: 330-490-7165. Email: admissions@walsh.edu. Web: www.walsh.edu. Rev. Christopher M. Saliga, O.P., Univ. Chap.; Richard Jusseaume, Pres.; Mr. Dale Howard, Vice Pres. Student Affairs; Brett Freshour, Vice Pres. Enrollment Mgmt.; Philip Daniels, Vice Pres. Business & Finance; Bridgette Neisel, Vice Pres. Devel. & Univ. Rels.; Rev. J. Patrick Manning, Chair, Theology Dept.; Daniel Suvak, Librarian. Brothers of Christian Instruction. Priests 5; Sisters 1; Lay Teachers 109; Total Staff 174; Students 2,936.

[C] HIGH SCHOOLS, DIOCESAN

YOUNGSTOWN. *Cardinal Mooney High School* (1956) 2545 Erie St., 44507. Tel: 330-788-5007; Fax: 330-788-4511. Email: jmkudlacz@aol.com. Web: www.cardinalmooney.com. Sr. Jane Marie Kudlacz, H.M., Prin.; Debra Scarnechia, Librarian. Sisters 1; Lay Teachers 54; Students 635.

Ursuline High School (1905) 750 Wick Ave., 44505. Tel: 330-744-4563; Fax: 330-744-3358. Email: ygnursuline@doy.org. Web: www.ursuline.com. Patricia Fleming, Prin.; Kristina Martinez, Librarian. Priests 1; Sisters 3; Lay Teachers 30; Students 447.

ASHTABULA. *SS. John & Paul School* (1953) (Grades 7-12), St. John High School Building, 541 W. 34th St., 44004. Tel: 440-997-5531; Fax: 440-998-1661. Web: www.ssjp.org. Miss Albina Larson, Prin.; Janis Brown, Librarian. Lay Teachers 10; Students 111.

CANTON. *Central Catholic High School* (1905) 4824 Tuscarawas St. W., 44708-5198. Tel: 330-478-2131; Fax: 330-478-6086. Email: rkaylor@cchsweb.com. Web: www.cchsweb.com. Rev. Robert W. Kaylor, Prin.; Mr. John Korecki, Asst. Prin.; Mr. Leo DeMatteis, Dean of Students; Mr. James Naegeli, Campus Ministry Dir.; Lue Schwing, Librarian. Priests 1; Lay Teachers 39; Total Staff 43; Students 460.

LOUISVILLE. *St. Thomas Aquinas High School* (1964) 2121 Reno Dr., N.E., 44641. Tel: 330-875-1631; Fax: 330-875-8469. Web: www.stahs.org. Rev. Thomas P. Dyer, Pres. & CEO; Mr. Joseph Vagedes, Prin.; Mrs. Sally Deckard, Campus Min. Lay Teachers 27; Religious 1; Total Staff 49; Students 346.

[D] ELEMETARY SCHOOLS, DIOCESAN

ASHTABULA. *SS. John & Paul School* (1996) (Grades K-6), Our Lady of Mt. Carmel Building, 2150 Columbus Ave., 44004. Tel: 440-997-5821; Fax: 440-998-0514. Email: thomas.thornton@neomin.org. Web: www.ssjp.org. Lay Teachers 7; Students 146.

Consolidated school for Mother of Sorrows, St. Joseph & Our Lady of Mt. Carmel. Mr. Thomas Thornton, Prin.; Michelle Martino, Librarian.

[E] PRIVATE SCHOOLS

CANFIELD. *Ursuline Preschool/Kindergarten*, 4300 Shields Rd., 44406. Tel: 330-792-4150; Fax: 330-792-8177. Email: upsk@sbcglobal.net. Sr. Charlotte Italiano, O.S.U., Dir. & Prin. Ursuline Sisters 1; Lay Teachers 10; Assistants 8; Students 255.

HUBBARD. *Villa Maria Teresa Daycare and Kindergarten*, 50 Warner Rd., 44425. Tel: 330-759-7383; Fax: 330-759-7290. Sr. Vittoria Nisi, O.S.H.J., Prin. & Dir. Sisters 5; Lay Teachers 4; Students 90.

[F] DIOCESAN SCHOOLS

WARREN. *Notre Dame School, Inc.*, 2550 Central Pkwy, S.E., 44484.

Notre Dame School, Inc., Blessed Sacrament Campus (Grades PreK-6), 3000 Reeves Rd., N.E., 44483. Tel: 330-372-2375; Fax: 330-372-2465. Email: ygnb/sacrament@doy.org. Mrs. Theresa A. Dolan-Dixon, Prin.; Mrs. Donna Zahler, Librarian. Lay Teachers 21; Students 271.

Notre Dame School, Inc., John F. Kennedy Jr. and Sr. High School (1964) (Grades 7-12), 2550 Central Pkwy., S.E., 44484. Tel: 330-369-1804; Fax: 330-369-1125. Web: www.warrenjfk.com. Rev. William Petrunak, Chap.; Mr. Brian Sinchak, Prin.; Staci Raab, Dean of Students. Priests 2; Lay Teachers 30; Students 336.

Notre Dame School, Inc., St. Pius X Campus (Grades PreK-6), 1461 Moncrest Ave., N.W., 44485. Tel: 330-399-5411; Fax: 330-399-7364. Email: ygnapostles@doy.org. Web: www.ndsdoy.com. Mary Jo Dugan, Prin.; Christina Thompson, Librarian. Lay Teachers 10; Students 91.

[G] GENERAL HOSPITALS

YOUNGSTOWN. *Humility of Mary Health Partners, St. Elizabeth Health Center* (1911) 1044 Belmont Ave., Box 1790, 44501. Tel: 330-746-7211; Fax: 330-480-7974. Web: www.hmpartners.org. Mr. Robert W. Shroder, Pres. & CEO; Donald Koenig, Exec. Vice Pres., HMHP. Bed Capacity 580; Bassinets 60; Patients Assisted Annually (Includes Boardman Facility) 348,358; Total Staff 2,455.

BOARDMAN. *Humility of Mary Health Partners St. Elizabeth Boardman Health Center*, 8401 Market St., 44512. Tel: 330-729-2929. Mr. Robert W. Shroder, Pres. & CEO; Eugenia L. Aubel, Pres. St. Elizabeth Boardman Health Center. Bed Capacity 108; Total Assisted 71,966; Total Staff 411.

CANTON. **CSAHS/UHHS - Canton, Inc. dba Mercy Medical Center* (1908) 1320 Mercy Dr., N.W., 44708. Tel: 330-489-1000; Fax: 330-489-1312. Email: mail@cantonmercy.com. Web: www.cantonmercy.com. Thomas Cecconi, Pres. & CEO. Bed Capacity 523; Bassinets 47; Total Staff 2,534; Total Assisted Annually 575,372.

WARREN. *St. Joseph Health Center* (1924) 667 Eastland Ave., S.E., 44484. Tel: 330-841-4000; Fax: 330-841-4019. Web: www.hmpartners.org. Mr. Robert W. Shroder, Pres. & CEO; John Finizio, Pres. Sisters of the Humility of Mary 3; Bed Capacity 219; Bassinets 17; Total Assisted Annually 177,039; Total Staff 795.

[H] SPECIAL CARE FACILITIES

GIRARD. *Humility of Mary Health Partners, Home Health Services*, 979 Tibbetts-Wick Rd., Ste. A, 44420. Tel: 330-480-3776; Fax: 330-480-4584. Robert Shroder, Pres. & CEO; Rodney Carnifax, Dir. Home Health Svcs. Patients Assisted Annually 11,250; Total Staff 106.

NORTH LIMA. *The Assumption Village, Marian Living Center (Assisted Living Facility)*, 9800 Market St., 44452. Tel: 330-549-0740; Fax: 330-549-0701. Mary Lou Clatterbuck, L.N.H.A., Exec. Dir. LTC; Kristine Mariotti, Dir. Assisted Living Svcs.; Loretta Morell, RN Wellness Mgr. Sponsorship: Sisters of the Humility of Mary., Member: Catholic Healthcare Partners and Humility of Mary Health Partners.; Special Care Unit for residents with Alzheimer's or Dementia; Skilled Nursing Unit with Subacute Care Program; Intermediate Care. Assisted Living Rooms 48; Assisted Living Total Staff 29; Total Assisted Annually 65.

POLAND. *Hospice of the Valley, Hospice House*, 9803 Sharrott Rd, 44514. Tel: 330-549-5850; Fax: 330-549-5859. Richard T. Bell, Dir. Bed Capacity 16; Staff 40; Total Assisted Annually 1,400.

[I] HOMES FOR AGED

AUSTINTOWN. *Humility House*, 755 Ohltown Rd., 44515. Tel: 330-505-0144; Fax: 330-544-5694. Mary Lou Clatterbuck, L.N.H.A., Exec. Dir. LTC. Nursing Home Beds 70; Assisted Living Beds 32; Total Assisted 134; Total Staff 120.

CANTON. *House of Loreto*, 2812 Harvard Ave., N.W., 44709. Tel: 330-453-8137; Fax: 330-453-8140. Sisters Marilee Heuer, C.D.S., Admin.; Janet Harold, C.D.S., Admin.; Michele Beauseigneur, Sec. Administered by the Congregation of the Divine Spirit. Sisters of the Congregation of the Divine Spirit 18; Bed Capacity 50; Residents 50; Total Assisted Annually 65; Total Staff 50. In Res. Rev. Msgr. Homer C. DeWalt (E) (Retired); Rev. Gerald J. Sommer, M.S.C. (Retired).

HUBBARD. *Villa Maria Teresa* (1894) 50 Warner Rd., 44425. Tel: 330-759-9329 (Villa); 330-875-4635 (Emmaus House); Fax: 330-759-7290. Email: jcoblate@aol.com. Web: www.oblatesistersofshj.com. Retired Priests' Residence. Villa Residents 6; Emmaus House Residents 1; Bed Capacity 15; Total Assisted Annually 10; Total Staff 4.

LOUISVILLE. *Emmaus House* (1977) 1515 California Ave., 44641. Tel: 330-875-4635. Rev. Howard Ziemba, Admin. Retired Priests' Residence. Bed Capacity 10; Residents 1; Total Assisted Annually 5; Total Staff 4.

St. Joseph Care Center, 2308 Reno Dr., 44641. Tel: 330-875-5562; Fax: 330-875-8947. Email: sjcc@neo.rr.com. Web: www.thealsatian.com. John T. Banks, Admin.; Sr. Andriene Ihnot, H.M., Assoc. Admin. Sisters of St. Joseph of St. Mark 8; Sisters of the Humility of Mary 1; Notre Dame Sisters 1; Sisters of Our Lady of Kilimanjaro 1; Nursing Home 100; Assisted Living 67; Independent Living 66; Adult Day Care 25; Bed Capacity 273; Total Assisted Annually 340; Total Staff 235.

NORTH LIMA. *The Assumption Village, Humility Health Center (Nursing Care)*, 9800 Market St., 44452. Tel: 330-549-0740; Fax: 330-549-0701. Mary Lou Clatterbuck, L.N.H.A., Exec. Dir. Long Term Care; Lisa Peretti, R.N., Dir. Nursing. Sponsorship: Sisters of the Humility of Mary., Member: Catholic Healthcare Partners and Humility of Mary Health Partners; Skilled Nursing Unit with Subacute Care Program; Special Care Unit for residents with Alzheimer's or cognitive impairment. Nursing Home Beds 150; Total Assisted 325; Total Staff 164.

[J] MONASTERIES AND RESIDENCES OF PRIESTS AND BROTHERS

YOUNGSTOWN. *Mt. Alverna Friary*, 517 S. Belle Vista Ave., 44509. Tel: 330-799-1888; Fax: 330-799-0723. Revs. Jules Wong, O.F.M.; Vit Fiala, O.F.M., Guardian. Franciscan Friars. Total in Residence 2; Total Staff 2.

[K] CONVENTS AND RESIDENCES FOR SISTERS

CANFIELD. *Motherhouse and Educational Center of the Ursuline Sisters* (1874) 4250 Shields Rd., 44406. Tel: 330-792-7636; Fax: 330-792-9553. Email: admainosuyo@yahoo.com. Web: www.theursulines.org. Sr. Nancy Dawson, O.S.U., Gen. Supr. Total in Community 54; Total in Residence 32; Total Staff 5.

Ursuline Center, 4280 Shields Rd., 44406. Tel: 330-799-4941; Fax: 330-799-4988.

CANTON. *Sancta Clara Monastery* (1946) 4200 N. Market Ave., 44714. Tel: 330-492-1171; Fax: 330-492-8657. Email: srmagdalenpcpa@hotmail.com. Web: www.poorclares.org. Rev. Process Milton Kiocha, A.J., Chap.; Sr. Marion Zeltmann, P.C.P.A., Abbess. Poor Clares of Perpetual Adoration. Cloistered Professed Nuns 9.

HUBBARD. *Oblate Sisters of the Sacred Heart of Jesus Institute, Villa Maria Teresa* (1984) 50 Warner Rd., 44425. Tel: 330-759-9329; Fax: 330-759-7290. Email: jcoblate@aol.com. Web: www.oblatesistersofshj.com. Sr. Vittoria Nisi, O.S.H.J., Regl. Supr. & Convent Supr. Novitiate and American Headquarters of Oblate Sisters of the Sacred Heart of Jesus. Sisters 17; Total Staff 8.

[L] CATHOLIC CHARITIES SOCIAL SERVICE AGENCIES

YOUNGSTOWN. *Catholic Charities Housing Opportunities Corporation*, 225 Elm St., 44503. Tel: 330-744-8451; Fax: 330-742-6447. Email: ggarchar@youngstowndiocese.org. Web: www.catholiccharitiesyoungstown.org. Richard P. Clautti, Pres.; Mr. George Garchar, Exec. Dir. Purpose: Provides coordination, integration and leadership in the provision of housing services which promote affordable housing in the community. Total Families Assisted 50; Total Staff 1.

Catholic Charities Regional Agency (1946) 2401 Belmont Ave., 44505. Tel: 330-744-3320; Fax: 330-744-3677. Email: nvoitus@ccregional.org. Nancy Voitus, Exec. Dir. Family and child welfare work in various social services and counseling in Mahoning, Trumbull and Columbiana Counties. Total Staff 52.

Diocese of Youngstown Catholic Charities Corporation (1999) 144 W. Wood. St., 44503. Tel: 330-744-8451; Fax: 330-742-6447. Email: ccdoy@att.net. Web: www.catholiccharitiesyoungstown.org.

ASHTABULA. *Catholic Charities of Ashtabula County* (1944) 4200 Park Ave., 3rd Fl., 44004. Tel: 440-992-2121; Fax: 440-992-5974. Email: lynnz@doyccac.org. Web: www.doyccac.org. Lynn M. Zalewski, Exec. Dir. Total Assisted 10,800; Total Staff 15.

CANTON. *Catholic Charities of Stark County* (1999) 3112 Cleveland Ave., N.W., 44709. Tel: 330-491-0896; Fax: 330-491-1298. Email: ccstark@sbcglobal.net. Diana Gray Stromsky, Exec. Dir. Total Assisted (Estimated) 6,000; Total Staff 22.

Catholic Charities Adult Day Services - West, 59 Lincoln Way, E., Massillon, 44646. Tel: 330-832-9758; Fax: 330-832-9849.

Catholic Charities Adult Day Services - East, 2308 Reno Dr., Louisville, 44641. Tel: 330-875-7979; Fax: 330-875-3006.

RAVENNA. *Catholic Charities of Portage County*, 206 W. Main St., 44266. Tel: 330-297-7745; Fax: 330-297-7763. Email: dmorrow@ccpcdoy.org. Deborah Morrow, Exec. Dir.

[M] HOMES FOR WOMEN

YOUNGSTOWN. *Beatitude House* (1991) 238 Tod Ln., 44504. Tel: 330-744-3147; Fax: 330-744-3991. Email: info@beatitudehouse.com. Web: www.beatitudehouse.com. Sr. Patricia McNicholas, O.S.U., Exec. Dir. Permanent supportive housing, transitional housing, job preparation, job training, counseling, education and case management for economically disadvantaged women and children. Bed Capacity 115; Total Assisted 530; Total Staff 25.

[N] RETREAT HOUSES

YOUNGSTOWN. *Our Lady of the Woods Pastoral Center* (1994) 144 W. Wood St., 44503. Tel: 330-744-8451; Fax: 330-744-1702.

[O] NEWMAN CENTERS

YOUNGSTOWN. *Newman Center at Youngstown State University* 254 Madison Ave., 44504-1627. Tel: 330-747-9202; Fax: 330-747-1667. Email: ysunewmancenter@sbcglobal.net. Web: www.ysunewmancenter.org. Total Staff 1.

KENT. *Kent State University Newman Center* 1424 Horning Rd., 44240. Tel: 330-678-0240; Fax: 330-678-7780. Web: www.kentnewmancenterparish.org. Rev. Christopher Luoni; Ms. Carmen Roebke, Pastoral Assoc. Total in Residence 1; Total Staff 4.

[P] MISCELLANEOUS LISTINGS

YOUNGSTOWN. *Caritas Communities*, 225 Elm St., 44503. Tel: 330-744-8451; 330-384-1555; Fax: 330-742-6447. Email: ggarchar@youngstowndiocese.org. Web: www.catholiccharitiesyoungstown.org. Mr. George Garchar, Pres. & CEO; Ken Radigan, Chm. As a member Corporation of Catholic Charities Housing Opportunities and the Humility of Mary Housing Program, Caritas Communities will serve as Property Management Corporation for low income and special needs housing. Families Assisted 200; Total Staff 1.

"The Catholic Exponent", P.O. Box 6787, 44501-6787. Tel: 330-744-5251; Fax: 330-744-5252. Email: exponent@doyweb.org. Web: www.cathexpo.org.

Declaration of Trust of Trumbull, Department of Education, 144 W. Wood St., 44503. Tel: 330-744-8451; Fax: 330-744-8451; 330-744-5099. Email: mskube@doy.org. County Catholic School Endowment Fund.

First Friday Club of Greater Youngstown, P.O. Box 11146, 44511. Tel: 330-533-1023; Fax: 330-533-1023.

Humility of Mary Health Partners Development Foundation (1966) 250 DeBartolo Pl., Ste. 2560, 44512. Tel: 330-729-1182; Fax: 330-729-1180. Email: james_schultis@hmis.org. Web: www.hmpartners.org. James Schultis, Pres. & CEO. Total Staff 8.

Humility of Mary Information Systems, Inc., 250 Federal Plaza E., 2nd Fl., 44503. Tel: 330-884-6641; Fax: 330-746-6824. Email: mike_seiser@hmis.org. Web: www.hmpartners.org. Mike Seiser, Vice Pres. Information Systems.

Lake to River Telecommunications Corporation, 144 W. Wood St., 44503.

Roman Catholic Diocese of Youngstown "Today's Sacrifice...Tomorrow's Church" Capital Campaign, 144 W. Wood St., 44503. Tel: 330-744-8451; Fax: 330-742-6447. Web: www.doy.org. Mr. Pat Palombo, Dir. Devel. & Stewardship, 144 W. Wood St., 44503. Tel: 330-744-8451; Mr. Patrick A. Kelly, CFO.

Roman Catholic Diocese of Youngstown Foundation, 144 W. Wood St., 44503. Tel: 330-744-8451; Fax: 330-744-2848. Mr. Patrick A. Kelly, CFO.

Roman Catholic Diocese of Youngstown Property Corporation, 144 W. Wood St., 44503. Tel: 330-744-8451; Fax: 330-744-2848. Mr. Patrick A. Kelly, CFO.

CANFIELD. *The Ursuline Center* (1993) 4280 Shields Rd., 44406. Tel: 330-799-4941; Fax: 330-799-4988. Email: ndawsonosu@aol.com. Web: www.theursulines.org. Resource and outreach services for the poor, including prison ministry, AIDS ministry, retreats, water therapy, adult formation, speech and hearing services, school of music, massage therapy, college courses, Walsh University Masters Programs, undergrad degree programs, preschool, and kindergarten. Total Assisted Annually 40,000; Sisters 11; Total Staff 28.

CANTON. *CSA Mercy Ministries*, 3114 Cleveland Ave., N.W., 44709. Tel: 216-696-5560. Web: www.sistersofcharityhealth.org. Sr. Judith Ann Karam, C.S.A., Pres. & CEO.

Sisters of Charity Foundation of Canton (1996) 400 Market Ave. N., Ste. 300, 44702-1556. Tel: 330-454-5800; Fax: 330-454-5909. Email: jclose@scfcanton.org. Web: www.scfcanton.org. Joni T. Close, Pres.

LOUISVILLE. *St. Thomas Aquinas High School Endowment Fund* (1964) 2121 Reno Drive, N.E., 44641. Tel: 330-875-1631; Fax: 330-875-8469. Web: www.stahs.org. Rev. Thomas P. Dyer, Pres. & CEO; Victoria Frustaci, Business Mgr.

MASSILLON. *National Shrine of St. Dymphna* (1938) 3000 Erie St. S., P.O. Box 4, 44648-0004. Tel: 330-833-8478; Fax: 330-833-5193. Rev. A. Edward Gretchko, Chap. Located on the grounds of Heartland Behavioral Healthcare.

[Q] DIOCESAN CEMETERIES

YOUNGSTOWN. *Calvary*, 248 S. Belle Vista Ave., 44509. Tel: 330-792-4721; Fax: 330-792-1885.

Catholic Cemeteries of the Diocese of Youngstown, Inc., 144 W. Wood St., 44503. Tel: 330-744-8451; Fax: 330-742-6448. Rev. Msgr. Frank A. Carfagna, Dir.; Mr. Joseph Kun, Asst. Dir.

Resurrection, 300 N. Raccoon Rd., 44515. Tel: 330-799-1900; Fax: 330-799-5241.

CORTLAND. *All Souls*, 3823 Hoagland Blackstub Rd., 44410. Tel: 330-637-2761; Fax: 330-637-9522.

MASSILLON. *Calvary*, 3469 Lincoln Way E., 44646. Tel: 330-832-1866; Fax: 330-832-0059. Becky Tully, Supt.

RELIGIOUS INSTITUTES OF MEN REPRESENTED IN THE DIOCESE

For further details refer to the corresponding bracketed number in the Religious Institutes of Men or Women section.

[]—*Apostles of Jesus*—AJ

[0320]—*Brothers of Christian Instruction*—F.I.C.

[0520]—*Franciscan Friars* (Immaculate Conception Prov. of New York)—O.F.M.

[]—*Missionaries of the Sacred Heart*—M.S.C.

[0430]—*Order of Preachers (Dominicans)* (Prov. of St. Joseph)—O.P.

[1065]—*Priestly Fraternity of St. Peter*—F.S.S.P.

[]—*Society of Jesus*—SJ

[1020]—*Society of St. Paul*—S.S.P.

RELIGIOUS INSTITUTES OF WOMEN REPRESENTED IN THE DIOCESE

[0100]—*Adorers of the Blood of Christ*—A.S.C.

[]—*Antonine Sisters*—A.S.

[]—*Benediction Sisters (Byzantine Sisters)*—O.S.B.

[1040]—*Congregation of the Divine Spirit*—C.D.S.

[1115]—*Dominican Sisters of Peace*

[]—*Little Sisters of Mary Immaculate*—L.S.M.I.G.

[3050]—*Oblate Sisters of the Sacred Heart of Jesus*—O.S.H.J.

[3210]—*Poor Clares of Perpetual Adoration*—P.C.P.A.

[]—*Sisters of Charity of Seton Hill* (Greensburg, PA)—S.C.

[0580]—*Sisters of Charity of St. Augustine*—C.S.A.

[0990]—*Sisters of Divine Providence*—C.D.P.

[2990]—*Sisters of Notre Dame*—S.N.D.

[]—*Sisters of Our Lady of Kilimanjaro*—C.D.N.K.

[1710]—*Sisters of St. Francis of Mary Immaculate, Joliet, IL*—O.S.F.

[]—*Sisters of St. Francis of Tiffin, OH*—OSF/T

[3910]—*Sisters of St. Joseph of St. Mark*—S.J.S.M.

[]—*Sisters of St. Joseph of the Third Order of St. Francis*—SSJ-TOSF

[2110]—*Sisters of the Humility of Mary*—H.M.

[3730]—*Sisters of the Order of St. Basil the Great*—O.S.B.M.

[]—*Ursuline Sisters of Cleveland*—O.S.U.

[4120-07]—*Ursuline Sisters of Youngstown*—O.S.U.

NECROLOGY

† Fye, Rev. Msgr. Lawrence C., (Retired)—Died July 25, 2009

† Chonko, Michael J., (Retired)—Died April 18, 2009

† Duritsa, George M., (Retired)—Died June 4, 2009

† Lettau, David, (Retired)—Died May 21, 2009

† Nist, Arthur, (Retired)—Died Sept. 10, 2009

† Popovich, George, (Retired)—Died June 18, 2009

† Shelton, Matthew, (Absent on Sick Leave)—Died June 11, 2009

† Slipski, William P., (Retired)—Died March 7, 2009

Apostolate to Hungarians

Most Reverend

FERENC CSERHATI, S.T.D.

Titular Bishop of Centuria, Auxiliary to Esztergom-Budapest, especially entrusted with the coordination of the pastoral service of Hungarians abroad; ordained April 18, 1971 in Alba Julia; appointed June 15, 2007; consecrated in Esztergom August 15, 2007. *Res.: Ung.Kath.Delegatur, Landwehrstr.66, Munchen D-80336 Germany*. Tel: 49-89-532-8288; Fax: 49-89-532-8245.

ESTABLISHED MAY 20, 1983.

The Apostolate of the Bishop of Hungarians living outside of Hungary extends territorially to all the Hungarian communities existing outside of Hungary. The main purpose of the Apostolate is to give spiritual assistance to them through and in cooperation with the local ordinary and pastors.

Former Bishop—Most Revs. LADISLAUS A. IRANYI, Sch.P., ord. March 13, 1938; appt. May 20, 1983; cons. July 27, 1983; died March 6, 1987; ATTILA MIKLOSHAZY, S.J., S.T.D., Titular Bishop of Castel Minore and Bishop for the Spiritual Assistance to the Hungarian Emigrant People; ord. June 18, 1961; appt. Aug. 12, 1989; cons. Nov. 4, 1989; resigned April 5, 2006.

Delegate in North America—Rev. BARNABAS G. KISS, O.F.M., Holy Cross Hungarian R.CX. Church, 8423 South St., Detroit, 48209-2709. Tel: 313-842-1133; Fax: 313-842-2773. Email: szthereszt@comcast.net.

Hungarian Priests' Association in Canada—Rev. SZABOLCS SAJGO, S.J., St. Elizabeth of Hungary, 432 Sheppard Ave. E., Toronto ON M2N 3B7 Canada. Tel: 416-225-3300; Fax: 416-225-3814.

American Hungarian Catholic Priests' Association (USA)—Rev. BARNABAS G. KISS, O.F.M., Holy Cross Hungarian R.CX. Church, 8324 South St., Detroit, 48209-2709. Tel: 313-842-1133; Fax: 313-842-2773. Email: sztkereszt@comcast.net.

Hungarian Catholic League of America, Inc.—Rev. Msgr. WILLIAM I. VARSANYI, P.A., J.C.D., Chm., One Cathedral Sq., Providence, RI 02903. Tel: 401-278-4520; Fax: 401-278-4548.

Newspapers & Magazines—

"Eletunk" (Our Life)—Rev. Msgr. FERENC CSERHATI, Editor, Landwehrstrasse 66, D-80336, Munchen 2, Germany. Tel: 49-89-532-8288; Fax: 49-89-532-8245.

"Tavlatok"— (Perspectives), Quarterly on Worldview, Spirituality and Culture, ed. by the Unio Cleri Hungarici. Rev. FERENC SZABO, S.J.

"A Sziv"— (Sacred Heart Messenger), monthly, published by the Hungarian Jesuit Fathers. Rev. ARPAD HORVATH, S.J., Editor, H-1085, Horanslky U.20, Hungary. Tel: 30-820-3775. Email: asziv@jezsuita.hu; Address in Canada, 432 Sheppard Ave. E., Toronto ON M2N 3B7 Canada.

STATISTICS

Most personnel and institutions are under the jurisdiction of their local ordinaries.

NECROLOGY

Incorporated in diocesan and archdiocesan listings.

An asterisk (*) denotes an organization that has established tax-exempt status directly with the IRS and is not covered by the USCCB Group Ruling.

Apostolate For Lithuanian Catholics

Living Outside Lithuania

Very Reverend Monsignor

EDMOND PUTRIMAS, J.C.L.

Delegate of the Lithuanian Bishops Conference appointed August 19, 2003 to coordinate the pastoral care of Lithuanian Catholics living outside of Lithuania. *Office: 1 Resurrection Rd., Toronto ON M9A 5G1 Canada*. Tel: 416-233-7819; Fax: 416-233-5765. Email: putrimas@sielovada.org.

Most Reverend

PAUL A. BALTAKIS, O.F.M.

Former Bishop For Lithuanian Catholics; ordained August 24, 1952; appointed Titular Bishop of Egara and Bishop for Spiritual Assistance of Lithuanian Catholics June 1, 1984; cons. Sept. 14, 1984; retired July 12, 2003. *Res.: St. Anthony's Friary, 28 Beach Ave., P.O. Box 980, Kennebunkport, ME 04046*. Tel: 207-967-2011, Ext. 30.

ESTABLISHED JUNE 1, 1984.

The Apostolate for Lithuanian Catholics, extends worldwide to all Lithuanian communities existing outside Lithuania. Seventy-five percent of them in the U.S.A. The purpose of the apostolate is to give spiritual assistance to them in cooperation with the local ordinaries and pastors.

(VACANT SEE)

Email: putrimas@sielovada.org

Former Lithuanian Bishops—Most Revs. VINCENTAS BRIZGYS, Ph.D., J.C.D., cons. May 19, 1940; Titular Bishop of Bosana; Auxiliary Bishop of Kaunas, Lithuania (Impeditus); died April 23, 1992; ANTANAS DEKSNYS, Ph.D., cons. Jan. 15, 1969; Titular Bishop of Lavello; died May 5, 1999; PAUL A. BALTAKIS, O.F.M. ord. Aug. 24, 1952; appt. Titular Bishop of Egara and Bishop of Spiritual Assistance of Lithuanian Catholics in diaspora June 1, 1984; cons. Sept. 14, 1984; retired July 12, 2003.

Office of General Counsel—SAULIUS V. KUPRYS, 150 S. Wacker Dr., Ste. 1050, Chicago, IL 60606. Tel: 312-346-5275; Fax: 312-346-5640. Email: viskas@aol.com.

Lithuanian R. Catholic Priests' League of Canada—Rev. VYTAUTAS STASKEVICIUS, Pres., Lithuanian Martyr's Parish, 494 Isabella Ave., Mississauga, Ontario L5B 2G2 Canada. Tel: 905-277-4320.

Lithuanian R. Catholic Priests' League of America—Rev. Msgr. ALBERT CONTONS, Pres., P.O. Box 1025, Humarock, MA 02047. Tel: 781-834-4079.

Lithuanian Franciscan Province of St. Casimir—Very Rev. PLACIDAS BARIUS, O.F.M., Delegate, Kennebunkport, ME 04046. Tel: 207-967-2031; Fax: 207-967-5721.

Lithuanian Jesuit Province—Very Rev. ANTANAS GRAZULIS, S.J., Delegate, 2345 W. 56th St., Chicago, IL 60636. Tel: 773-737-8400.

Marian Province of Mary Mother of Mercy—Very Rev. DANIEL CAMBRA, Prov., Stockbridge, MA 01262.

Pontifical Lithuanian College of St. Casimir—Rev. PETRAJ SIURYS, L.I.C., Rector, via Casalmonferrato 20, Rome 00182 Italy. Tel: 06-70-24-908; Fax: 06-70-11-659.

Sisters of the Immaculate Conception of the Blessed Virgin Mary—Sr. IGNE MARIJOSIUTE, Prov., Rte. 21, R.D. 2, Putnam, CT 06260. Tel: 860-928-7955; Fax: 860-928-1930.

Poor Sisters of Jesus Crucified and the Sorrowful Mother—Sr. MARY J. VALLERE, Supr. Gen., 261 Thatcher St., Brockton, MA 02402. Tel: 617-588-5070.

Sisters of St. Casimir—Sr. IMMACULATA WENDT, Gen. Supr., 2601 W. Marquette Rd., Chicago, IL 60609. Tel: 773-776-1324.

Sisters of St. Francis—Sr. JANET GARDNER, O.S.F., Supr. Gen., 3603 McRoberts Rd., Pittsburgh, PA 15234. Tel: 412-882-9911.

**Lithuanian R. Catholic Religious Aid, Inc.*Rev. Msgr. ALGIMANTAS BARTKUS, J.C.L., Pres.; Mrs. VIDA JANKAUSKAS, Mgr., 64-25 Perry Ave., Maspeth, 11378. Tel: 718-326-5202; Fax: 718-326-5206. Email: lcra@earthlink.net.

Lithuanian American R. Catholic Federation—Youth Camp, 15100 Austin Rd., Manchester, MI 48158.

Lithuanian Roman Catholic Charities, Inc.—4545 W. 63rd St., Chicago, IL 60629.

Publications— Draugas (Chicago, IL); The Observer (Chicago, IL); Teviskes Ziburiai (Toronto, Ontario, Canada); Teviskes Aidai (Adelaide, Australia)

INSTITUTIONS LOCATED IN THE DIOCESE

[A] SCHOOLS

CHICAGO. *Maria High School*

THOMPSON. *Marionapolis Prep School*

[B] HOSPITALS

CHICAGO. *Holy Cross Hospital*

[C] NURSING HOMES AND HOMES FOR THE AGED

BROCKTON. *St. Joseph Manor Nursing Home*

ELMHURST. *St. Mary's Villa*

HOLLAND. *St. Joseph Nursing Home*

LEMONT. *Holy Family Villa*

PUTNAM. *Matulaitis Nursing Home*

[D] MISCELLANEOUS

CHICAGO. *Catholic Action Fund*

Jesuit Lithuanian Center

**Lithuanian Catholic Press Society*, 4545 W. 63rd St., IL 60629.

Lithuanian Roman Catholic Charities, 4545 W. 63rd St., IL 60629.

Matulaitis Institute

MANCHESTER. *Lithuanian American R. Catholic Federation Youth Camp*, 15100 Austin Rd., MI 48158.

PUTNAM. *American Lithuanian Catholic Archives*

WEST BRATTLEBORO. *Camp Neringa*

[E] CEMETERIES

CHICAGO. *St. Casimir Lithuanian*

RELIGIOUS INSTITUTES OF MEN REPRESENTED IN THE DIOCESE

For further details refer to the corresponding bracketed number in the Religious Institutes of Men or Women section.

[]—*Congregation of the Marians Province of Mary Mother of Mercy* (Stockbridge, MA)

[]—*Franciscan Fathers of the Lithuanian Province of St. Casimir* (Kennebunkport, ME)

[]—*Jesuit Fathers of Della Strada* (Chicago, IL)

RELIGIOUS INSTITUTES OF WOMEN REPRESENTED IN THE DIOCESE

[3240]—*Poor Sisters of Jesus Crucified and the Sorrowful Mother* (Brockton, MA)—C.J.C.

[2140]—*Sisters of Immaculate Conception of the Blessed Virgin Mary* (Putnam, CT)

[3740]—*Sisters of St. Casimir* (Chicago, IL)—S.S.C.

[1690]—*Sisters of St. Francis* (Pittsburgh, PA)—O.S.F.

STATISTICS

Most personnel and institutions are under the jurisdiction of their local ordinaries.

NECROLOGY

(No Deaths)

An asterisk (*) denotes an organization that has established tax-exempt status directly with the IRS and is not covered by the USCCB Group Ruling.

Prelature of the Holy Cross and Opus Dei

(Praelatura Sanctae Crucis et Operis Dei)

Most Reverend

JAVIER ECHEVARRIA, J.D., J.C.D.

Prelate of the Prelature of the Holy Cross and Opus Dei ordained August 7, 1955; appointed April 20, 1994; episcopal ordination January 6, 1995. *Curia of the Prelature, Viale Bruno Buozzi 73, Rome 00197 Italy.* Tel: 011-39-06-808-961.

PRELATURE OF OPUS DEI

Erected by the Apostolic Constitution, "Ut sit," on November 28, 1982 by Pope John Paul II.

Opus Dei was founded on October 2, 1928 by Saint Josemaria Escriva, to spread in all sectors of society a profound awareness of the universal call to sanctity in ordinary life and, more specifically, in the exercise of one's work.

Curia of the Prelature—Viale Bruno Buozzi 73, Rome 00197 Italy. Tel: 011-39-06-808-961.

Vicar General—Rev. Msgr. FERNANDO OCARIZ, Ph.D., S.T.D., Viale Bruno Buozzi 73, Rome 00197 Italy.

Regional Vicar for the United States—Rev. Msgr. THOMAS G. BOHLIN, Ph.D., S.T.D., 139 E. 34th St., New York, NY 10016. Tel: 646-742-2700.

Vicar for the Midwest—Very Rev. PETER V. ARMENIO, B.S., Ph.D., 5800 N. Keating Ave., Chicago, IL 60646. Tel: 312-283-5800. Embracing the states of Illinois, Indiana, Missouri and Wisconsin.

Vicar for California—Very Rev. JOHN R. MEYERS, D.D.S., S.T.D., 765 14th Ave., San Francisco, CA 94118. Tel: 415-386-0431.

Vicar for Texas—Very Rev. PAUL D. KAIS, B.A., M.A., Ph.D., 5505 Chaucer Dr., Houston, TX 77005. Tel: 715-523-4351.

Represented in the Archdioceses of Boston, Chicago, Galveston-Houston, Los Angeles, Milwaukee, Newark, New York, St. Louis, San Antonio, San Francisco, Washington and in the Dioceses of Burlington, Dallas, Fort Wayne-South Bend, Gary, Oakland, Palm Beach, Peoria, Pittsburgh, Providence, Trenton and Victoria.

Regional Vicar for Puerto Rico—Rev. Msgr. VICENTE ARIZA, Ph.D., J.C.D., Villa Caparra, 35 A St., Guaynabo, PR 00966. Tel: 787-781-9123.

Represented in the Archdiocese of San Juan and the Dioceses of Mayaguez and Ponce.

CHAPLAINS FOR THE UNITED STATES

State of New York

New Rochelle. Revs. Bradley K. Arturi, J.C.D. (NY), John R. Waiss (NY), Orestes Gonzalez (NY), 99 Overlook Cir., New Rochelle, NY 10804.

New York. Rev. Msgrs. Thomas G. Bohlin, Ph.D., S.T.D. (NY), Reg. Vicar, Javier Garcia de Cardenas (NY), Revs. James W. Albrecht (NY), John C. Agnew (NY), Robert A. Brisson (NY), Deo G. Rosales (NY), 139 E. 34th St., New York, NY 10016. Tel: 646-742-2700, Malcolm M. Kennedy (NY), 330 Riverside Dr., New York, NY 10025. Tel: 212-222-3285.

District of Columbia

Washington. Revs. Arne A. Panula, Ph.D., S.T.D. (NY), William G. Shaughnessy, John P. Debicki (CHI), 2301 Wyoming Ave., N.W., Washington, DC 20008. Tel: 202-234-1567, Gregory Coyne (WDC), Very Rev. Gerald S. Kolf, B.S., M.B.A., S.T.D. (GAL), 4300 Garrison St., N.W., Washington, DC20016. Tel: 202-362-2419.

State of Massachusetts

Cambridge. Revs. Thomas J. Lamb (BO), David J. Cavanagh (BO), 25 Follen St., Cambridge, MA 02138. Tel: 617-354-3204.

Chestnut Hill. Revs. Richard W. Rieman (BO), Jose P. Ruisanchez (BO), Salvador S. Vahi (PMB), Alvaro Silva (BO), 481 Hammond St., Chestnut Hill, MA 02467. Tel: 617-738-7348.

State of New Jersey

Princeton. Rev. Martin J. Miller (TR), 34 Mercer St., Princeton, NJ 08540. Tel: 609-497-9448.

South Orange. Rev. Robert A. Connor, 170 Montrose Ave., South Orange, NJ 07079. Tel: 201-763-8397.

State of Pennsylvania

Pittsburgh. Revs. Rene J. Schatteman (PIT), Charles Trullols (PIT), 5090 Warwick Ter., Pittsburgh, PA 15213. Tel: 412-683-8448.

State of Florida

Delray Beach. Rev. Francis Vera, 4409 Frances Dr., Delray Beach, FL 33445. Tel: 305-498-1249.

Miami. Revs. Victor Cortes (DAL), Christopher Schmitt (PMB), 4415 S.W. 88th Ave., Miami, FL 33165. Tel: 305-551-7965.

State of Rhode Island

Providence. Rev. George A. Crafts, 224 Bowen St., Providence, RI 02906. Tel: 401-272-7834.

State of Illinois

Chicago. Very Rev. Peter V. Armenio, B.S., Ph.D. (CHI), Vicar for the Midwest, Revs. Javier del Castillo (WDC), Edward G. Maristany (CHI), Frank J. Hoffman (CHI), 5800 N. Keating Ave., Chicago, IL 60646. Tel: 312-283-5800, Joseph P. Landauer (PIT), Hilary F. Mahaney (CHI), Charles M. Ferrer (CHI), C. John McCloskey (CHI), 1825 N. Wood St., Chicago, IL 60622. Tel: 312-278-2644, Paul Grant (CHI), 7225 N. Greenview Ave., Chicago, IL 60646. Tel: 312-465-3486.

Oak Park. Revs. Richard L. Schendt (CHI), James Socias (CHI), Martin J. Miller (PIT), 829 S. Euclid, Oak Park, IL 60304. Tel: 708-383-0928.

Urbana. Rev. G. Barry Cole, 715 W. Michigan, Urbana, IL 61801. Tel: 217-367-6650.

State of Indiana

South Bend. Rev. Mark S. Mannion (FTW), 1121 N. Notre Dame Ave., South Bend, IN 46617. Tel: 219-232-0550.

State of Missouri

Kirkwood. Revs. Michael E. Giesler (STL), John J. Alvarez (STL), 100 E. Essex Ave., Kirkwood, MO 63122. Tel: 314-821-1608.

State of Wisconsin

Brookfield. Revs. Timothy J. Uhen (MIL), John C. Kubeck (MIL), 12900 W. North Ave., Brookfield, WI 53005. Tel: 414-784-1523.

State of California

San Francisco. Very Rev. John R. Meyer, D.D.S., S.T.D. (SFR), Vicar for California, Rev. Matthew A. Bloomer (SFR), 765 14th Ave., San Francisco, CA 94118. Tel: 415-386-0431.

Menlo Park. Rev. Torlach C. Delargy (SFR), 1160 Santa Cruz Ave., Menlo Park, CA 94025. Tel: 415-327-1675.

Los Angeles. Revs. Paul A. Donlan, Luke J. Mata, Juan R. Velez (LA), Rev. Msgr. James A. Kelly (SFR), 655 Levering Ave., Los Angeles, CA 90024. Tel: 213-208-0941.

Berkeley. Rev. Jerome L. Jung (SFR), 2710 College Ave., Berkeley, CA 94705. Tel: 510-548-2819.

State of Texas

Houston. Very Rev. Paul D. Kais, B.A., M.A., Ph.D. (GAL), Vicar for Texas, Rev. Msgr. William H. Stetson (WDC), Revs. Michael J. Barrett, S.T.D., Michael J. Manz (GAL), 5505 Chaucer Dr., Houston, TX 77005. Tel: 713-523-4351.

Irving. Revs. John E. Solarski, Derrick Esclanda (DAL), 3610 Wingren, Irving, TX 75062. Tel: 214-650-0064.

San Antonio. Rev. Eduardo Castillo, 1979 Summit Ave., San Antonio, TX 78212. Tel: 210-732-3065.

State of Virginia

Reston. Revs. Ronald S. Gillis, Lawrence A. Kutz, 1810 Old Reston Ave., Reston, VA 20190. Tel: 703-689-3433.

Puerto Rico

Guaynabo. Rev. Msgr. Vicente Ariza, Ph.D., J.C.D. (SJN), Reg. Vicar, Revs. Justiniano Garcia (SJN), Juan Aramendi (SJN), Javier Bernaola (SJN), Villa Caparra, A35 A St., Guaynabo, PR 00966-2211. Tel: 787-781-9123, Gonzalo Diaz (SJN), Alfredo Gastalver (SJN), Villa Caparra, 48 A St., Guaynabo, PR 00966. Tel: 787-783-1987.

San Juan. Revs. Pablo J. Concepcion (SJN), Martin Llambias (SJN), 51 Margarita St., San Juan, PR 00925. Tel: 787-759-6193.

Ponce. Revs. Ramon Alvarez (PCE), Jaime E. Bermudez (PCE), 8 Alcazar St., La Alhambra, Ponce, PR 00731. Tel: 787-844-2661.

Mayaguez. Rev. Andres Eiroa (MGZ), 69 Orquideas St., Ensanche Martinez, Mayaguez, PR 00680. Tel: 787-833-6461.

Eparchy of Newton (Melkite-Greek Catholic)

Most Reverend

CYRIL SALIM BUSTROS, S.M.S.P.

Eparch of Newton; ordained June 29, 1962; appointed Archbishop of Baalbek (Melkite) Lebanon October 25, 1988; ordained November 27, 1988; appointed Eparch of Newton June 22, 2004; enthroned August 18, 2004.

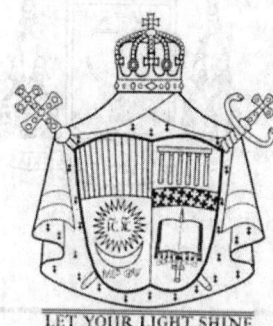

Most Reverend

JOHN A. ELYA, B.S.O., D.D.

Retired Eparch of Newton; ordained February 17, 1952; appointed Auxiliary Bishop of Newton April 2, 1986; appointed Eparch of Newton November 25, 1993; installed January 25, 1994; retired August 18, 2004. *Res.: 30 East St., Methuen, MA 01844.* Tel: 978-683-2471. Email: bpjohn3@aol.com.

Most Reverend

NICHOLAS J. SAMRA, D.D.

Retired Auxiliary Bishop of Newton; ordained May 10, 1970; appointed Auxiliary Bishop of Newton June 29, 1989; retired January 11, 2005. *Mailing Address: 3 Veterans of Foreign Wars Pkwy., West Roxbury, MA 02132.*

ESTABLISHED AS AN APOSTOLIC EXARCHATE JANUARY 10, 1966.

Elevated to Eparchy, June 28, 1976; Embraces all members of the Melkite Greek Catholic Church in the United States.

For legal titles of parishes and institutions, consult the Chancery Office.

The Chancery: 3 Veterans of Foreign Wars Pkwy., West Roxbury, MA 02132. Tel: 617-323-9922; Fax: 617-323-0944.

Web: melkite.org

STATISTICAL OVERVIEW

Personnel	
Archbishops	1
Retired Bishops	2
Priests: Diocesan Active in Diocese	37
Priests: Diocesan Active Outside Diocese	3
Priests: Retired, Sick or Absent	6
Number of Diocesan Priests	46
Religious Priests in Diocese	14
Total Priests in Diocese	60
Ordinations:	
Permanent Deacons	5
Permanent Deacons in Diocese	51
Parishes	
Parishes	40
With Resident Pastor:	
Resident Diocesan Priests	36
Resident Religious Priests	4
Missions	4
Educational	
Diocesan Students in Other Seminaries	1
Seminaries, Religious	1
Students Religious	2
Total Seminarians	3
Catechesis/Religious Education:	
High School Students	200
Elementary Students	1,199
Total Students under Catholic Instruction	1,402
Vital Statistics	
Receptions into the Church:	
Infant Baptism Totals	210
Adult Baptism Totals	10
Received into Full Communion	12
First Communions	219
Confirmations	230
Marriages:	
Catholic	53
Interfaith	16
Total Marriages	69
Total Catholic Population	24,791

Former Eparchs—Most Revs. JUSTIN A. NAJMY, B.A.O., D.D., born April 23, 1898; ord. Dec. 25, 1926; cons. May 29, 1966; installed June 4, 1966; died June 11, 1968; JOSEPH E. TAWIL, D.D., LL.D., ord. July 20, 1936; cons. Jan. 1, 1960; appt. Apostolic Exarch, Oct. 30, 1969; appt. Eparch, June 28, 1976; became emeritus Dec. 2, 1989; died Feb. 17, 1999; IGNATIUS GHATTAS, B.S.O., D.D., born Dec. 25, 1920; ord. July 7, 1946; appt. Dec. 2, 1989; cons. Feb. 23, 1990; died Oct. 11, 1992; JOHN A. ELYA, B.S.O., D.D., ord. Feb. 17, 1952; appt. Auxiliary Bishop of Newton April 2, 1986; appt. Eparch of Newton Nov. 25, 1993; installed Jan. 25, 1994; retired Eparch of Newton Aug. 18, 2004.

Diocesan Administration

Chancery Office—3 VFW Pkwy., West Roxbury, 02132. Tel: 617-323-9922; Fax: 617-323-0944. Office Hours: Mon.-Fri. 9-5.

Protosyncellus—Rt. Rev. Exarch JOSEPH HAGGAR.

Chancellor—Rev. Deacon PAUL J. LEONARCZYK.

Eparchial Tribunal—6458 Tapestry Circle, Spring Hill, FL 34606. Tel: 352-683-7637.

Judicial Vicar—Rt. Rev. Archimandrite GERASIMOS MURPHY, J.C.D., 6458 Tapestry Cir., Spring Hill, FL 34606.

Judges—Revs. MICHAEL K. SKROCKI, J.C.L.; JOSEPH KOURY, J.C.D.; HERBERT MAY, J.C.L.; Rev. Msgr. MICHAEL SOUCKAR, J.C.D.

Defender of the Bond and Promoter of Justice—Rt. Rev. Exarch JOSEPH S. HAGGAR, J.C.L.

Notaries—Rev. Archdeacon GEORGE YANY; Rev. Deacon PAUL J. LEONARCZYK; LUCILLE LAROCHE; JANICE M. TERRIS.

Chief Finance Officer—Rev. Deacon ROBERT SHALHOUB. Tel: 973-785-4144; Fax: 973-890-9599.

Protopresbyters—Rt. Rev. JOSEPH FRANCAVILLA, Mid-Atlantic; Rt. Rev. Exarch JOSEPH S. HAGGAR, J.C.L., New England; Rt. Revs. FRANK J. MILIENEWICZ, Southeast; PHILIP RACZKA, Great Lakes; ALEXEI SMITH, West.

Consultative Bodies

College of Eparchial Consultors—Rt. Rev. JOSEPH FRANCAVILLA; Rt. Rev. Exarch GABRIEL GHANOUM, B.S.O.; Very Rev. PHILARET LITTLEFIELD; Rt. Rev. Exarch JOSEPH S. HAGGAR, J.C.L.; Rt. Revs. FRANK J. MILIENEWICZ; ALEXEI SMITH; Rt. Rev. Archimandrite ROBERT RABBAT.

Presbyteral Council—Rt. Revs. CHARLES ABOODY (Retired); JOSEPH F. FRANCAVILLA; LAWRENCE GOSSELIN; Rt. Rev. Exarch JOSEPH S. HAGGAR, J.C.L.; Rt. Revs. FRANK J. MILIENEWICZ; PHILIP RACZKA; KENNETH SHERMAN; ALEXEI SMITH; Very Rev. PHILARET LITTLEFIELD; Rev. PETER BOUTROS; Rt. Rev. Archimandrite ROBERT RABBAT; Rt. Rev. JOHN AZAR; Revs. MICHAEL K. SKROCKI, J.C.L.; NAIM KHALIL, B.S.O.; CHRISTOPHER MANUELE; SAMIR ABU-LAIL; ANTOINE RIZK, B.S.O.

Diocese of Newton for the Melkites in the USA, Inc., a Massachusetts Corporation—Most Rev. CYRIL SALIM BUSTROS, S.M.S.P.; Rt. Rev. Economos SAMI W. BAROODY; Rt. Rev. Exarch JOSEPH S. HAGGAR, J.C.L.; Rt. Rev. Archimandrite ROBERT RABBAT; Rev. Deacon PAUL J. LEONARCZYK.

Finance Council—Rt. Rev. Exarch JOSEPH S. HAGGAR, J.C.L.; Dr. JOHN NAZARIAN; CHARLES JOSEPH; Rev. Deacon ROBERT SHALHOUB; CAMILLE F. SARROUF JR.; BASIL ZALOOM.

Legal Consultants—CAMILLE F. SARROUF; CAMILLE F. SARROUF JR., 95 Commercial Wharf, Boston, 02110. Tel: 617-227-5800.

Pastoral Offices and Commissions

Continuing Education of Clergy Office—Rt. Rev. PAUL G. FRECHETTE; Rt. Rev. Exarch GABRIEL GHANOUM, B.S.O.; Rt. Rev. ALEXEI SMITH; Rev. IGNATIUS HARRINGTON.

National Association of Melkite Youth—Rev. THOMAS P. STEINMETZ, 140 Mitchell St., Manchester, NH 03102.

MAYA (Melkite Assoc. of Young Adults)—Rev. JUSTIN ROSE, 923 W. Congress St., San Bernardino, CA 92410. Tel: 909-889-3579.

Ambassadors—Rev. PETER BOUTROS, 3718 E. Greenway Rd., Phoenix, AZ 85032. Tel: 602-787-4787.

National Association of Melkite Women—Rt. Rev. EDWARD KAKATY, 41 Cross Rd., Waterford, CT 06385. Tel: 860-442-2211.

Liturgical Commission—Rev. DAMON GEIGER, O.SS.T.

Office of Communications—Rev. Deacon PAUL LEONARCZYK, Dir., 3 VFW Pkwy., West Roxbury, 02132.

Educational Services—FRANCES COLIE, Ph.D., Dir., 1710 Surf Ave., Belmar, NJ 07719. Tel: 732-280-1774.

Vocations Office—Rt. Rev. PHILIP RACZKA, Coord., 8525 Cole Ave., Warren, MI 48093. Tel: 586-751-6017; Fax: 586-751-1877; Rt. Rev. Archimandrite ROBERT RABBAT; Rev. SABA SHOFANY.

"Sophia" (A Journal)—Rt. Rev. Archimandrite ROBERT RABBAT, Editor-in-Chief; Rev. Deacon PAUL LEONARCZYK, Production.

Order of St. Nicholas—Mailing Address: 3 VFW Pkwy., West Roxbury, 02132. Tel: 617-323-9922; Fax: 617-323-0692. GREGORY OUSSANY, Natl. Chm.; Rt. Rev. Exarch GABRIEL GHANOUM, B.S.O., Chap.

Associated Melkite Charities—Very Rev. PHILARET LITTLEFIELD, 1617 W. State St., Milwaukee, WI 53233. Tel: 414-342-1543.

Sophia Press—Rev. Deacon PAUL J. LEONARCZYK; Rev. MICHAEL K. SKROCKI, J.C.L., Office: 3 VFW Pkwy., West Roxbury, 02132. Tel: 617-323-9922, Ext. 206; Fax: 617-323-0692.

Victim Assistance Coordinator—Rt. Rev. Exarch GABRIEL GHANOUM, B.S.O., Mailing Address: 126 S.E. 15 Rd., Miami, FL 33129. Tel: 305-856-8666; Fax: 305-859-7982.

CLERGY, PARISHES, MISSIONS AND PAROCHIAL SCHOOLS

STATE OF MASSACHUSETTS

BOSTON, SUFFOLK CO., ANNUNCIATION CATHEDRAL Rt. Rev. Archimandrite Robert Rabbat, Rector; Rev. Charles Kattan; Rev. Deacons John Moses; Ibrahim Zeinieh; Thomas Burke.
Res.: 7 V.F.W. Pkwy., 02132. Tel: 617-323-5242; Fax: 617-325-2662. Email: ourlady3@verizon.net.

LAWRENCE, ESSEX CO., ST. JOSEPH Rev. Imad Barakeh, B.S.O.; Protodeacon Bryan McNeil; Rev. Deacon John MacMillan.
Res.: 241 Hampshire St., 01841. Tel: 978-682-8152; Fax: 978-682-6114.

WORCESTER, WORCESTER CO., OUR LADY OF PERPETUAL HELP Rt. Rev. Paul G. Frechette; Rev. Deacons Dennis J. McCarthy; Elias (Richard) Bailey.
Res.: 256 Hamilton St., 01604. Tel: 508-752-4174; Fax: 508-752-8351.

STATE OF ALABAMA

BIRMINGHAM, JEFFERSON CO., ST. GEORGE Rt. Rev. Frank J. Milienewicz; Rev. Deacon Seraphim Ritchey.
Res.: 425 Sixteenth Ave. S., AL 35205. Tel: 205-252-5788; Fax: 205-252-0063.

STATE OF ARIZONA

PHOENIX, MARICOPA CO., ST. JOHN OF THE DESERT Rev. Peter Boutros; Rev. Deacon Marion Rimmer.
Res.: 3718 E. Greenway Rd., AZ 85032. Tel: 602-787-4787; Fax: 602-795-4752. Email: frpeter@stjohnofthedesert.com.

STATE OF CALIFORNIA

EL SEGUNDO, LOS ANGELES CO., ST. PAUL Rt. Rev. Alexei Smith, Admin.; Rev. Deacon Irenaeus Dionne.
Res.: 538 Concord St., CA 90245. Tel: 310-322-1892; Fax: 310-322-1919.

NORTH HOLLYWOOD, LOS ANGELES CO., ST. ANNE Rev. Albert Wehby, B.A.O.; Rt. Rev. George Said Bisharat; Protodeacon George Sayegh; Rev. Deacons George Karout; Tareq Nasrallah; Thom O'Malley; Estephanos Helo.
Res.: 11245 Rye St., CA 91602. Tel: 818-761-2034; Fax: 818-761-2922.
Mission—Annunciation Mission 381 Center St., Covina, CA 91723. Tel: 626-359-3976.

PLACENTIA, ORANGE CO., HOLY CROSS Rt. Rev. James K. Babcock.
Church & Res.: 451 W. Madison Ave., CA 92870. Tel: 714-985-1710; Fax: 714-985-1765. Email: hcmelkite@earthlink.net.

SACRAMENTO, SACRAMENTO CO., ST. GEORGE Rt. Rev. Mark E. Melone.
Church: 1620 Bell St., CA 95825. Tel: 916-920-2900; Fax: 916-920-2900. Email: stgeorge@cwnet.com.

SAN BERNARDINO, SAN BERNARDINO CO., ST. PHILIP Rev. Justin Rose; Protodeacon Stephen Ghandour; Rev. Deacons Jacob Pesta; Joseph Kaiser.
Mailing Address: 923 W. Congress St., CA 92410. Tel: 909-889-3579. Email: comeandsee@earthlink.net.

SAN DIEGO, SAN DIEGO CO., ST. JACOB MISSION, Services at Holy Angels Church, San Diego. Rev. Saba Shofany; Protodeacon Edward Bagdasar; Rev. Deacon Antoine Kabane.
Mailing Address: 6281 Cowles Mountain Blvd., CA 92119. Tel: 619-825-9344; Fax: 619-825-9344.

SAN JOSE, SANTA CLARA CO., ST. ELIAS Rev. James K. Graham.
Church: 4411 Hyland Ave., CA 95127. Tel: 408-259-0259. Email: frjamie@earthlink.net.

WILDOMAR, RIVERSIDE CO., VIRGIN MARY MISSION, Services at St. Mark Church, San Marcos. Rt. Rev. Nassir Matta, Admin.; Rev. Deacon Habib Khasho.
Mailing Address: 33881 Orange St., CA 92595. Tel: 909-674-3162.

STATE OF CONNECTICUT

DANBURY, FAIRFIELD CO., ST. ANN Rev. Michael K. Skrocki; Rev. Deacons Nicholas Bourjaili; Thomas Davis.
Mailing Address: 181 Clapboard Ridge Rd., CT 06811. Tel: 203-743-5119.

WATERFORD, NEW LONDON CO., ST. ANN Rt. Rev. Edward G. Kakaty.
Res.: 41 Cross Rd., CT 06385. Tel: 860-442-2211; Fax: 860-442-2211. Email: edkakaty@gmail.com.

STATE OF FLORIDA

DELRAY BEACH, PALM BEACH CO., ST. NICHOLAS, Served by Miami. Rt. Rev. Exarch Gabriel Ghanoum, B.S.O.; Protodeacon Magdi Negm.
Res.: 5715 Lake Ida Rd., FL 33484. Tel: 305-856-8666.

MIAMI, DADE CO., ST. JUDE Rev. Eugene Mitchell, B.S.O.; Protodeacon Magdi Negm.
Res.: 126 S.E. 15 Rd., FL 33129. Tel: 305-856-8666; Fax: 305-859-7982.

STATE OF GEORGIA

ATLANTA, DEKALB CO., ST. JOHN CHRYSOSTOM Rt. Rev. John Azar.
Res.: 1428 Ponce de Leon Ave., N.E., GA 30307. Tel: 404-373-9522; Fax: 404-373-9755. Email: stjchrys@bellsouth.net.

AUGUSTA, RICHMOND CO., ST. IGNATIOS OF ANTIOCH Rev. Miguel Grave de Peralta; Rev. Deacons Kent Plowman; Robert Pride; Michael Willoughby.
Mailing Address: P.O. Box 3351, GA 30914-3351.
Res.: 4220 Wood Creek Ct., Martinez, GA 30907. Tel: 706-228-4938.
Church: 1003 Merry St., GA 30904. Tel: 706-738-9388; Fax: 706-738-6559. Email: stignatios@aol.com.

STATE OF ILLINOIS

NORTHLAKE, COOK CO., ST. JOHN THE BAPTIST Rt. Rev. Fouad Sayegh; Rev. Archdeacon Elias Sahyouni; Protodeacon Antoine Shehata; Rev. Deacon Fadi Rafidi.
Res.: 318 E. Hirsch Ave., IL 60164. Tel: 708-938-5804; Fax: 708-492-0391. Email: stjohnthebaptistchicago@hotmail.com.

STATE OF INDIANA

HAMMOND, LAKE CO., ST. MICHAEL THE ARCHANGEL (1978) Rt. Rev. Philip Raczka.
Res.: 606 141st St., IN 46327. Tel: 219-933-1457; Fax: 219-852-0727. Email: michaelarchangel@comcast.net.

SOUTH BEND, ST. JOSEPH CO., ST. JOHN OF DAMASCUS Rt. Rev. Philip Raczka.
Church: 839 Woodcliff Dr., IN 46615. Tel: 574-282-2140.

STATE OF MICHIGAN

LANSING, INGHAM CO., ST. JOSEPH Rt. Rev. Lawrence Gosselin.
Res.: 921 Westover Circle, MI 48917. Tel: 517-327-6394; Fax: 517-327-6965. Email: lansingmelkite@aol.com.

PLYMOUTH, WAYNE CO., ST. MICHAEL Rev. Elie Eid, Admin.; Protodeacon Joseph Daratony.
Church: 585 N. Mill St., MI 48170. Tel: 734-414-6110.

WARREN, MACOMB CO., OUR LADY OF REDEMPTION Rev. Michel Cheble; Protodeacon James Soloman; Rev. Deacon David Herr.
Res.: 29293 Lorraine, MI 48093. Tel: 586-574-0140; Fax: 586-751-1877.

STATE OF NEW HAMPSHIRE

MANCHESTER, HILLSBOROUGH CO., OUR LADY OF THE CEDARS Rev. Thomas P. Steinmetz; Rt. Rev. Andre St. Germain (Retired); Rev. Deacons Robert Spencer; Paul J. Leonarczyk.
Res.: 140 Mitchell St., NH 03103. Tel: 603-623-8944; Fax: 603-645-6017. Email: oloc.church@comcast.net.

STATE OF NEW JERSEY

CLIFFSIDE PARK, BERGEN CO., ST. DEMETRIUS Rev. Jean Ghaby.
Church: 184 Cliff St., NJ 07010. Tel: 201-840-8554.

WEST PATERSON, PASSAIC CO., ST. ANN Revs. George Batikha; Jean Ghaby; Rev. Archdeacon Edward Bsarany; Rev. Deacons Roland Basinski; Robert Shalhoub; Choukri Sabbagh.
Res.: 802 Rifle Camp Rd., NJ 07424. Tel: 973-785-4144; Fax: 973-890-9599.

STATE OF NEW YORK

BROOKLYN, KINGS CO., CHURCH OF THE VIRGIN MARY Rev. Antoine Rizk, B.S.O.; Rev. Deacon Nagi Youssef.
Res.: 216 Eighth Ave., NY 11215. Tel: 718-788-5454; Fax: 718-499-7702.

ROCHESTER, MONROE CO., ST. NICHOLAS Rt. Rev. Kenneth Sherman; Rev. Deacons Edmond Elhilow; Elias Sarkis.
Res.: 1492 Spencerport Rd., NY 14606. Tel: 585-426-4218.

UTICA, ONEIDA CO., ST. BASIL Rt. Rev. Julien A. Eliane; Rev. Deacon Daniel A. Klockowski.
Res.: 901 Sherman Dr., NY 13501. Tel: 315-732-4662.

YONKERS, WESTCHESTER CO., CHRIST THE SAVIOR CHURCH Rev. Patrick W. Moloney; Protodeacon Saleem Naber.
Church: 491 Palisade Ave., NY 10703. Tel: 914-963-6680.

STATE OF OHIO

AKRON, SUMMIT CO., ST. JOSEPH Rev. Basil Samra; Rev. Deacon Dennis Jebber.
Church & Res.: 600 W. Exchange St., OH 44302. Tel: 330-535-7364; Fax: 330-535-8037. Email: stjomelk@sbcglobal.net.

BROOKLYN, CUYAHOGA CO., ST. ELIAS Rev. Naim Khalil, B.S.O.
Res.: 8023 Memphis Ave., OH 44144. Tel: 216-661-1155; Fax: 216-661-3838.

COLUMBUS, FRANKLIN CO., HOLY RESURRECTION Rev. Ignatius Harrington.
Res.: 8148 Wildflower Ln., Westerville, OH 43081. Tel: 614-987-7239; Fax: 614-987-7239.
Church: 4611 Glen Mawr Ave., OH 43224.

ZANESVILLE, MUSKINGUM CO., HOLY TRINITY Rev. Ignatius Harrington.
Res.: 8148 Wildflower Ln., Westerville, OH 43081. Tel: 614-987-7239; Fax: 614-987-7239.
Church: 3745 W. Pike, OH 43701.

STATE OF PENNSYLVANIA

SCRANTON, LACKAWANNA CO., ST. JOSEPH Rev. Christopher Manuele; Protodeacon Michael Jolly.
130 St. Francis Cabrini Ave., PA 18504. Tel: 570-343-6092. Email: scrantonmelkite@comcast.net.

STATE OF RHODE ISLAND

LINCOLN, PROVIDENCE CO., ST. BASIL THE GREAT Rt. Rev. Exarch Joseph S. Haggar; Rev. Archdeacon George M. Yany; Rev. Deacon Edmond Raheb.
Church: 15 Skyview Dr., RI 02865.
Res.: 111 Cross St., Central Falls, RI 02863. Tel: 401-722-1345; Fax: 401-722-2436.

WOONSOCKET, PROVIDENCE CO., ST. ELIAS Rt. Rev. Exarch Joseph S. Haggar.
Church: 80 Hamilton St., RI 02895.
Res.: 111 Cross St., Central Falls, RI 02863. Tel: 401-722-1345.

STATE OF SOUTH CAROLINA

HANAHAN, CHARLESTON CO., OUR LADY PROTECTRESS OF ALL CHRISTIANS Rev. Titus Fulcher; Rev. Deacon David W. Richardson.
Res.: 9 Otranto Blvd., SC 29406. Tel: 843-824-5831.
Our Lady of Mercy: 77 America St., Charleston, SC 29403.

STATE OF VIRGINIA

MCLEAN, FAIRFAX CO., HOLY TRANSFIGURATION Rt. Rev. Joseph F. Francavilla; Rev. Ephrem Handal; Protodeacon David Baroody; Rev. Deacons David Black; Joseph Olt; John Fleshman.
Res.: 8501 Lewinsville Rd., VA 22102. Tel: 703-734-9198; Fax: 703-734-5148. Email: office@holytransfiguration.org.

STATE OF WASHINGTON

SEATTLE, KING CO., ST. JOSEPH MISSION Rev. Samir Abu-Lail.
Res.: 12038 31st Ave. N.E. #306, WA 98125. Tel: 206-362-2519; Fax: 206-888-6355. Email: samirabulail@gmail.com.

STATE OF WISCONSIN

MILWAUKEE, MILWAUKEE CO., ST. GEORGE Very Rev. Philaret Littlefield.
Res.: 1617 W. State St., WI 53233. Tel: 414-342-1543.

Military Chaplain:
Rev.—
Brown, Shaun S.

Leave of Absence:
Revs.—
Golini, Ronald
Koury, James
Saato, Fred

Retired:
Rt. Revs.—
Aboody, Charles
Dagher, George, B.S.O.
Samaha, Victor, B.C.O.
St. Germain, Andre
Revs.—
Alam, Alam
Azoon, Philip

Kerby, Robert
King, James E.
Leonard, John

Deacons:
Rev. Archdeacons—
Bsarany, Edward
Sahyouni, Elias
Yany, George M.
Protodeacons—
Bagdasar, Edward, El Cajon, CA
Baroody, David, McLean, VA
Daratony, Joseph, Plymouth, MI
Ghandour, Stephen, San Bernardino, CA
Jolly, Michael, Scranton, PA
McNeil, Bryan, Lawrence, MA
Naber, Saleem, (Yonkers, NY)
Negm, Magdi, Miami, FL
Negm, Magdi
Sayegh, George, North Hollywood, CA
Shehata, Antoine, Northlake, IL
Soloman, James, Warren, MI
Rev. Deacons—
Bailey, Elias (Richard), Worcester, MA
Basinski, Roland, West Paterson, NJ
Black, David, McLean, VA
Burke, Thomas, Boston, MA
Dionne, Irenaeus, El Segundo, CA
Elhilow, Edmond, Rochester, NY
Fleshman, John, McLean, VA
Herr, David, Warren, MI
Jebber, Dennis, Akron, OH
Kaiser, Joseph, San Bernardino, CA
Karout, George, North Hollywood, CA
Khasho, Habib, Northlake, IL
Klockowski, Daniel A., Utica, NY
Leonarczyk, Paul J., Manchester, NH
MacMillan, John, Lawrence, MA
Moses, John, Boston, MA
Nasrallah, Tareq, North Hollywood, CA
O'Malley, Thom, N. Hollywood, CA
Olt, Joseph, McLean, VA
Pesta, Jacob, San Bernardino, CA
Plowman, Kent, Augusta, GA
Pride, Robert, Augusta, GA
Rafidi, Fadi, Northlake, IL
Raheb, Edmond, Lincoln, RI
Richardson, David W., Charleston, SC
Rimmer, Marion, Phoenix, AZ
Ritchey, Seraphim, Birmingham, AL
Sabbagh, Choukri
Sarkis, Elias, Rochester, NY
Shalhoub, Robert, West Paterson, NJ
Spencer, Robert, Manchester, NH
Trabulsy, Rick, Warren, MI
Willoughby, Michael, Augusta, GA
Youssef, Nagi, Brooklyn, NY
Zeinieh, Ibrahim, Boston, MA
Deacons—
Bourjaili, Danbury, CT
Davis, Thomas J., Jr., Danbury, CT
McCarthy, Dennis, (Worcester, MA)

Priests Serving Outside the Eparchy:
Rt. Rev.—
Russo, Romanos V.
Revs.—
Gallaro, George D., J.C.O.D.
McCarthy, Emmanuel Charles
Parent, Basil R.

Deacons Serving Outside the Eparchy:
Rev. Deacons—
Haddad, Gregory (HT)
Hill, James A.
Nasser, Andre P. (FR)
Versage, Joseph V.

INSTITUTIONS LOCATED IN THE DIOCESE

[A] SEMINARIES

STATE OF MASSACHUSETTS

METHUEN. *Seminary of St. Basil the Great*, 30 East St., 01844. Tel: 978-683-2471. Rev. Joseph Thomas, B.S.O., Dean. Priests 4.

WEST ROXBURY. *Seminary of St. Gregory the Theologian*, 3 VFW Pkwy., 02132. Rt. Rev. Philip Raczka, Rector. Priests 1.

[B] MONASTERIES AND RESIDENCES FOR PRIESTS AND BROTHERS

STATE OF MASSACHUSETTS

METHUEN. *Basilian Salvatorian Order*, 30 East St., 01844. Tel: 978-683-2471; Fax: 978-794-3452. Rt. Rev. George Dagher, B.S.O. (Retired); Revs. Youssef Clement, B.S.O.; Martin A. Hyatt, B.S.O., Local Supr.; Eugene Mitchell, B.S.O., Gen. Economos; Joseph Thomas, B.S.O.; Lawrence Tumminelli, B.S.O.

[C] CONVENTS AND RESIDENCES FOR SISTERS

STATE OF CONNECTICUT

DANBURY. *Community of The Mother of God of Tenderness*, 79 Golden Hill Rd., CT 06811-4631. Tel: 203-794-1486. Email: sophiamic711@sbcglobal.net. Sr. Mary Ann Socha, C.M.G.T., Pres. Sisters 3.

[D] MISCELLANEOUS

STATE OF MASSACHUSETTS

METHUEN. *St. Basil's Salvatorian Center*, 30 East St., 01844. Tel: 978-683-2959; Fax: 978-794-3379. Patricia Paduano, Dir.

STATE OF PENNSYLVANIA

WARREN CENTER. *Our Lady of Solitude Cloister & Retreat*, Mailing Address: P.O. Box 111, PA 18851. Tel: 570-395-0234. Physical Address: 550 Lake of Meadows Rd., Little Meadows, PA 18830. Fax: 570-395-0235. Rev. Angelus Ferrara, Supr.

RELIGIOUS INSTITUTES OF MEN REPRESENTED IN THE EPARCHY

For further details refer to the corresponding bracketed number in the Religious Institutes of Men or Women section.

[]—*Basilian Chouerite Order* (St. John Monastery, Khonchara, Lebanon)—B.C.O.

[0190]—*Basilian Salvatorian Order* (Holy Saviour Monastery, Sidon, Lebanon)—B.S.O.

NECROLOGY

(No Deaths)

An asterisk (*) denotes an organization that has established tax-exempt status directly with the IRS and is not covered by the USCCB Group Ruling.

Diocese of Our Lady of Deliverance

For Syriac Catholics in the United States and Canada

(Editor's Note: 2010 information was not received)

Most Reverend

YOUSIF HABASH

Bishop of Our Lady of Deliverance; ordained August 31, 1975; appointed Bishop of Our Lady of Deliverance April 12, 2010. *Chancery Office: 317 Ave. E., Bayonne, NJ 07002-4678.*

DIOCESE ESTABLISHED NOVEMBER 18, 1995.

Comprises the United States and Canada.

Chancery Office: 317 Ave. E, Bayonne, NJ 07002-4678. Tel: 201-455-8151; Fax: 201-455-8152.

Web: www.syriac-catholic.org

Email: FRSYRIAC@aol.com

STATISTICAL OVERVIEW

Personnel	
Bishop	1
Priests: Diocesan Active in Diocese	9
Priests: Diocesan Active Outside Diocese	2
Number of Diocesan Priests	11
Total Priests in Diocese	11
Permanent Deacons in Diocese	3
Parishes	
Parishes	9
With Resident Pastor:	
Resident Religious Priests	8
Without Resident Pastor:	
Administered by Priests	1
Missions	4
Educational	
Diocesan Students in Other Seminaries	2
Total Seminarians	2
Catechesis/Religious Education:	
High School Students	54
Elementary Students	324
Total Students under Catholic Instruction	380
Vital Statistics	
Receptions into the Church:	
Infant Baptism Totals	54
Adult Baptism Totals	6
Received into Full Communion	6
First Communions	60
Confirmations	60
Marriages:	
Catholic	32
Interfaith	6
Total Marriages	38
Deaths	22
Total Catholic Population	18,200

Former Bishop—Most Rev. JOSEPH YOUNAN, ord. Sept. 12, 1971; ord. Bishop of Our Lady of Deliverance Jan. 7, 1996; installed Feb. 10, 1996; appt. Patriarch of Antiochia, Lebanon; confirmed Jan. 22, 2009; installed Feb. 15, 2009.

Chancery—317 Ave. E., Bayonne, 07002-4678. Tel: 201-455-8151; Fax: 201-455-8152.

Chancellor—Very Rev. ST SUTTON, J.C.L. Tel: 201-455-8151; Fax: 201-455-8152.

Officialis—Very Rev. ST SUTTON, J.C.L. Tel: 201-583-1067.

CLERGY, PARISHES, MISSIONS AND PAROCHIAL SCHOOLS

STATE OF NEW JERSEY

UNION CITY, HUDSON CO., OUR LADY OF DELIVERANCE (1986) Mr. Nabil Cherbaka, Parish Council Chair.
Res.: 502 Palisade Ave., 07087-5213. Tel: 201-583-9590; Fax: 201-583-9639.
Catechesis/Religious Program—Mrs. Nahla Mensi, D.R.E. Students 49.

STATE OF CALIFORNIA

LOS ANGELES, LOS ANGELES CO., SACRED HEART PARISH Rev. Yousif A. Habash; Deacon George Qatto.
Res.: 10837 Collins St., North Hollywood, CA 91601-2009. Tel: 818-766-7001; Fax: 818-766-7254.
Catechesis/Religious Program—Mrs. Layla Touma, D.R.E. Students 52.

OCEANSIDE, SAN DIEGO CO., SAINT JOSEPH'S MISSION Rev. Emad Hanna Al-Shaikh, Admin.

SAN DIEGO, SAN DIEGO CO., OUR MOTHER OF PERPETUAL HELP PARISH Rev. Emad Hanna Al-Shaikh, Admin.
Mailing Address: 9911 Bonnie Vista Dr., La Mesa, CA 91941. Fax: 619-660-1492.
Res.: 9800 San Juan St., Spring Valley, CA 91977.
Catechesis/Religious Program—Mrs. Khouloud Habbosh, D.R.E. Students 42.

STATE OF FLORIDA

JACKSONVILLE, DUVAL CO., SAINT EPHREM Rev. Selwan A. Sulaiman; Mr. Jack Albanna, Parish Council Chair.
Res.: 14608 Stacey Rd., FL 32250. Tel: 904-992-0025.
Catechesis/Religious Program—Mrs. Emtethal Yazji, D.R.E. Students 64.

STATE OF ILLINOIS

TECHNY, COOK CO., SAINT MARY VIRGIN IMMACULATE MISSION, Served by Chancery personnel.
Res.: 2001 Waukegan Rd., IL 60082. Tel: 847-272-2700; Fax: 847-272-1233.

STATE OF MICHIGAN

FARMINGTON HILLS, OAKLAND CO., SAINT TOMA'S Rt. Rev. Chorbishop Toma B. Azizo; Mr. Charles Halabo, Parish Council Chair.
Mailing Address: 18290 W. 12 Mile Rd., Southfield, MI 48076. Tel: 248-569-3107; Fax: 248-478-0814.
Res.: 29000 W. 11 Mile Rd., MI 48336.
Catechesis/Religious Program—Mrs. Dhamia Albert Mansour, D.R.E. Students 68.

STATE OF PENNSYLVANIA

ALLENTOWN, LEHIGH CO., OUR MOTHER OF MERCY MISSION, Unassigned.

STATE OF RHODE ISLAND

PROVIDENCE, PROVIDENCE CO., SAINT JAMES SYRIAC MISSION Mr. Samir Mansourati, Admin.
Mailing Address: *Saint Francis Chapel*, 58 Weybosset St., RI 02903.

CANADA

HAMILTON, SYRIAC MISSION Rev. Yousif Mansour Abba, Admin.

LAVAL, PAROISSE SAINT EPHREM Rev. Paskal Kassis.
Mailing Address: 3000 Edouard Monpetit QC H7T 2T5 Canada. Tel: 450-682-7546; Fax: 450-682-7603.
Res.: 7055 Jean Bourdon, Montreal QC Canada.
Catechesis/Religious Program—Michel Jiji, D.R.E. Students 160.

MONTREAL, NOTRE DAME DE L'ASSOMPTION Rev. Richard Daher.
Mailing Address: 1625 Montee Massom, Laval QC H7E 2P2 Canada.

TORONTO, SAINT JOSEPH'S Rev. Yousif Mansour Abba.
Res.: 222 Ridley Blvd. ON M5M 3M6 Canada. Tel: 416-487-0960; Fax: 416-489-4183.
Catechesis/Religious Program—Mrs. Samira Raffi, D.R.E. Students 78.

Special Assignment:

Very Rev.—

Sutton, ST, J.C.L., Chancellor & Sec. to the Bishop

NECROLOGY

(No Deaths)

An asterisk (*) denotes an organization that has established tax-exempt status directly with the IRS and is not covered by the USCCB Group Ruling.

Eparchy of Our Lady of Lebanon of Los Angeles

Most Reverend

ROBERT J. SHAHEEN

Bishop of the Eparchy of Our Lady of Lebanon of Los Angeles; ordained May 2, 1964; appointed December 5, 2000; consecrated February 15, 2001.

Comprises the States of Ohio, West Virginia, Illinois, Alabama, Michigan, Minnesota, Missouri, Texas, Utah, Arizona, Nevada, Oregon, California, Alaska, Hawaii, Indiana, Kentucky, Tennessee, Mississippi, Wisconsin, Iowa, Arkansas, Louisiana, North Dakota, South Dakota, Kansas, Oklahoma, Nebraska, Montana, Wyoming, Colorado, New Mexico, Idaho and Washington.

Pastoral Center: 1021 S. 10th St., St. Louis, MO 63104. Tel: 314-231-1021; Fax: 314-231-1418.

Web: www.usamaronite.org

Email: mdenny@usamaronite.org

STATISTICAL OVERVIEW

Personnel	
Bishop	1
Retired Bishops	1
Priests: Diocesan Active in Diocese	28
Priests: Diocesan Active Outside Diocese	3
Priests: Retired, Sick or Absent	3
Number of Diocesan Priests	34
Religious Priests in Diocese	15
Total Priests in Diocese	49
Ordinations:	
Transitional Deacons	1
Permanent Deacons in Diocese	17
Total Sisters	5
Parishes	
Parishes	28
With Resident Pastor:	
Resident Diocesan Priests	20
Resident Religious Priests	7
Missions	10
Professional Ministry Personnel:	
Sisters	5
Welfare	
Residential Care of Children	1
Total Assisted	25
Day Care Centers	1
Total Assisted	150
Other Institutions	1
Total Assisted	70
Educational	
Diocesan Students in Other Seminaries	4
Total Seminarians	4
Elementary Schools, Private	1
Total Students	39
Catechesis/Religious Education:	
High School Students	555
Elementary Students	1,456
Total Students under Catholic Instruction	2,054
Teachers in the Diocese:	
Lay Teachers	1
Vital Statistics	
Receptions into the Church:	
Infant Baptism Totals	406
Adult Baptism Totals	32
Received into Full Communion	16
First Communions	348
Confirmations	411
Marriages:	
Catholic	104
Interfaith	30
Total Marriages	134
Deaths	192
Total Catholic Population	45,232

Former Bishop—Most Rev. JOHN GEORGE CHEDID, D.D. (Retired), ord. Dec. 21, 1951; appt. Titular Bishop of Callinicum and Auxiliary Bishop of St. Maron of Brooklyn, Oct. 28, 1980; cons. Jan. 25, 1981; appt. Bishop of Our Lady of Lebanon of Los Angeles, Feb. 19, 1994; retired Dec. 5, 2000.

Pastoral Center—Chorbishop FAOUZI ELIA, Vicar Gen. & Chancellor; Mrs. MARY DENNY, Vice Chancellor & Chief Fiscal Officer; Deacon WISSAM G. AKIKI, Pastoral Assoc., 1021 S. 10th St., St. Louis, 63104. Tel: 314-231-1021; Fax: 314-231-1418.

College of Consultors—Chorbishops FAOUZI ELIA; RICHARD D. SAAD; MICHAEL J. KAIL; Rev. ABDALLAH E. ZAIDAN, M.L.M.; Rev. Msgr. SHARBEL MAROUN; Rev. GARY GEORGE, C.Ss.R.

Commission for Lebanon—Rev. ABDALLAH E. ZAIDAN, M.L.M.

Tribunal—

Defender of the Bond—Rev. ROBERT BISHOP, S.T.L., C.F.M.

Judicial Vicar—Chorbishop WILLIAM LESER, S.T.B.

Moderator of the Tribunal—Most Rev. ROBERT JOSEPH SHAHEEN.

Procurator/Advocate—Revs. ABDALLAH E. ZAIDAN, M.L.M.; ELIAS SLEIMAN, M.L.M.

Promoter of Justice—Rev. ROBERT BISHOP, S.T.L., C.F.M.

Notary—Ms. KATARINA LEIGH.

Eparchial Newsletter— "The Maronite Voice" Rev. Msgr. GEORGE SEBAALI, St. Anthony, 4611 Sadler Rd., Glen Allen, VA 23060. Tel: 804-762-4301; Fax: 804-273-9914. Email: gmsebaali@aol.com.

Office for Immigration—Chorbishop FAOUZI ELIA.

Office for Missions—Rev. Msgrs. DONALD J. SAWYER, D.Mim.; ANTHONY SPINOSA.

Office of Communications—Chorbishop RICHARD D. SAAD.

Office of Inter-faith/Ecumenical Affairs—Rev. Msgr. ANTHONY SPINOSA.

Office of Liturgy—Chorbishop MICHAEL J. KAIL.

Office of Ministries—Deacon LOUIS PETERS.

Office of Priestly Vocations—Rev. Msgr. SHARBEL MAROUN; Rev. ARMANDO EL KHOURY.

Office of Religious Education—Deacon LOUIS PETERS.

Office of Youth Ministries—Rev. GARY GEORGE, C.Ss.R.

Master of Ceremonies—VACANT.

Office of Young Adult Ministry—Rev. ELIAS SLEIMAN, M.L.M.

Presbyteral Council—Chorbishops FAOUZI ELIA, Ex Officio; RICHARD D. SAAD; Rev. ABDALLAH E. ZAIDAN, M.L.M.; Rev. Msgr. ALFRED BADAWI; Chorbishop MICHAEL J. KAIL; Rev. Msgr. SHARBEL MAROUN; Revs. GARY GEORGE, C.Ss.R.; NABIL MOUANNES; ARMANDO EL KHOURY; PETER KARAM.

Pro-Life & Family Life Office—VACANT.

Eparchial Webmaster—Rev. ARMANDO EL KHOURY.

Properties Owned—

Los Angeles Chancery Office— Los Angeles, CA

Father Tobia Retirement Home— North Jackson, OH

Maronite Catholic Pastoral Center— St. Louis, MO

Protopresbyters—Rev. Msgr. SHARBEL MAROUN, Mid-America Region; Chorbishop MICHAEL J. KAIL, Midwest Region; Rev. ABDALLAH E. ZAIDAN, M.L.M., Southwest Region; Chorbishop RICHARD D. SAAD, Southern Region.

Spiritual Director for the National Apostolate of Maronites—Chorbishop RICHARD D. SAAD.

Order of St. Sharbel—Chorbishop JOSEPH KADDO, Spiritual Dir.; Ms. BEVERLY NARD-MIKE, Natl. Pres.; Mrs. WANDA ELKHOURIE, Vice Pres., Eparchy of Our Lady of Lebanon of Los Angeles, 1021 S. 10th St., St. Louis, 63104.

Victim Assistance Coordinator—Rev. PETER KARAM Cleveland, OH.

Office of Protection of Minors—Rev. PETER KARAM, Dir., 1245 Carnegie Ave., Cleveland, OH 44115. Tel: 216-781-6161; Fax: 216-781-6162. Web: www.usamaronite.org.

Personnel Board—Rev. ABDALLAH E. ZAIDAN, M.L.M.; Chorbishop RICHARD D. SAAD; Rev. Msgr. SHARBEL MAROUN.

Board of Pastors—Chorbishop RICHARD D. SAAD; Rev. ABDALLAH E. ZAIDAN, M.L.M.; Chorbishop WILLIAM LESER, S.T.B.

Advisor for Priests—Chorbishop RICHARD D. SAAD.

CLERGY, PARISHES, MISSIONS AND PAROCHIAL SCHOOLS

STATE OF CALIFORNIA

LOS ANGELES, LOS ANGELES CO.

1—OUR LADY OF MT. LEBANON-ST. PETER MARONITE CATHOLIC CATHEDRAL (1923) Revs. Abdallah E. Zaidan, M.L.M., Rector; Elias Sleiman, M.L.M.; Deacon Edward Corey.

Res.: 333 S. San Vicente Blvd., CA 90048. Tel: 310-275-6634; Fax: 310-858-0856.

Catechesis/Religious Program—Students 100.

2—ST. JUDE MARONITE CATHOLIC CHURCH (1999) Rev. Samuel Madel; Subdeacon Pierre El-Khoury.

1437 W. Badillo St., West Covina, CA 91790.

Res.: Tel: 909-592-9090; Fax: 909-592-9494. Email: maronitechurch@yahoo.com. Web: saintjudemaronitemission.com.

Catechesis/Religious Program—P.O. Box 885, San Dimas, CA 91773. Tel: 626-840-4134.

ANAHEIM, ORANGE CO., ST. JOHN MARON MARONITE CATHOLIC CHURCH (1988) Rev. Antoine Bakh; Deacon Alfred Harb; Subdeacons John Younes; Sharbel Abi-Saber.

Mailing Address: c/o 601 N. Woods, Fullerton, CA 92832-1027. Tel: 714-520-5303; Fax: 714-784-7503. Email: email@johnmaron.org. Web:

www.johnmaron.org.
Catechesis/Religious Program—Students 70.
Mission—St. Joseph Maronite Catholic Mission
MILLBRAE, SAN MATEO CO., OUR LADY OF LEBANON MARONITE CATHOLIC CHURCH (1979) [JC] Rev. John Nahal.
Mailing Address: 600 El Camino Real, CA 94030. Email: ollsf@aol.com. Web: www.maronite-sf.org.
Res.: 19 Hermosa Ave., CA 94030. Tel: 650-652-6445; Fax: 650-652-6445.
Catechesis/Religious Program—Minaise Minaise, D.R.E. Students 65.
Mission—St. Sharbel Maronite Catholic Mission Stockton, San Joaquin Co., CA. Tel: 209-954-0200.
SAN DIEGO, SAN DIEGO CO., ST. EPHREM MARONITE CATHOLIC CHURCH (1989) [CEM] Rev. Nabil Mouannes; Deacon Georges Ghosn.
Mailing Address: 750 Medford St., El Cajon, CA 92020. Tel: 619-337-1350.
Res.: 766 Medford St., El Cajon, CA 92020. Tel: 619-697-3040; Fax: 619-697-3042. Email: stephrem@sbcglobal.net. Web: www.stephrem.org. Students 39.
School—Saint Ephrem Maronite Catholic Academy, Tel: 619-337-1350. Rachael Farich, Prin. Students 39.
Catechesis/Religious Program—Students 100.
Mission—Maronite Catholic Community of Sacramento
THOUSAND OAKS, VENTURA CO., SAINTS PETER AND PAUL MARONITE CATHOLIC MISSION (2002) Rev. Jean Yammine, M.L.M., Admin.
P.O. Box 4455, CA 91359-1455. Tel: 818-620-0100; Fax: 818-889-5963.
Catechesis/Religious Program—Elie ElHage, D.R.E. Students 43.

STATE OF ALABAMA

BIRMINGHAM, JEFFERSON CO.
1—ST. ELIAS MARONITE CATHOLIC CHURCH (1910) Chorbishop Richard D. Saad; Deacons Joseph Stephens; Samuel J. Wehby.
Res.: 836 Eighth St. S., AL 35205-4567. Tel: 205-251-5057; 205-252-3867; Fax: 205-251-5028. Email: eliasbham@aol.com. Web: stelias.org.
Catechesis/Religious Program—Beverly Kimes, D.R.E.; Dora Bolus, D.R.E. Students 105.
2—MARONITE CATHOLIC COMMUNITY OF LOUISIANA (1910) Chorbishop Richard D. Saad, Parochial Admin.
Mailing Address: St. Elias Church, 836 8th St. S., AL 35205. Tel: 205-251-5057; Fax: 205-251-5028.
Catechesis/Religious Program—Students 42.

STATE OF ARIZONA

PHOENIX, MARICOPA CO., ST. JOSEPH MARONITE CATHOLIC CHURCH (1992) Rev. Ghattas Khoury.
Res.: 5406 E. Virginia Ave., AZ 85008. Tel: 602-667-3280; Fax: 602-468-0174. Email: ghattaskhoury@cox.net. Web: www.stjosephmaronitechurch.org.
Catechesis/Religious Program—Danielle Gorayeb, D.R.E. Students 70.
Mission—Maronite Catholic Mission of Tuscan

STATE OF COLORADO

LAKEWOOD, JEFFERSON CO, ST. RAFKA MARONITE CATHOLIC CHURCH Rev. Armando Elkhoury.
Res.: 2301 Wadsworth Blvd., CO 80214. Tel: 720-833-0354; Fax: 720-833-0390. Email: father@saintrafka.org. Web: www.saintrafka.org.
Catechesis/Religious Program—Students 15.

STATE OF ILLINOIS

LOMBARD, DUPAGE CO., OUR LADY OF LEBANON MARONITE CATHOLIC CHURCH (1952) Rev. Msgr. Alfred Badawi; Deacon John Sfire.
Res.: 950 N. Grace St., IL 60148. Tel: 630-932-9640; Fax: 630-932-9463. Email: abouna65!@sbcglobal.net.
Catechesis/Religious Program—Students 117.
Mission—Maronite Catholic Community Sacred Heart Church, Eighth St., Michigan City, La Porte Co., IN 46360.
PEORIA, PEORIA CO., ST. SHARBEL MARONITE CATHOLIC CHURCH (1973) Chorbishop Faouzi Elia; Rev. Bechara Awada; Deacons James Siedlecki; George Gaegea.
Res.: 2914 W. Scenic Dr., IL 61615. Tel: 309-688-5555; Fax: 309-688-0431. Email: stsharbel@sbcglobal.net.
Catechesis/Religious Program—Students 37.

STATE OF KENTUCKY

LOUISVILLE, JEFFERSON CO., MARONITE CATHOLIC COMMUNITY OF LOUISVILLE (1910) Closed.

STATE OF LOUISIANA

Maronite Community of Louisiana, Closed. For inquiries for parish records contact the chancery.
BATON ROUGE, EAST BATON ROUGE PARISH, ST. SHARBEL MARONITE CATHOLIC MISSION Chorbishop Richard D. Saad, Admin.
c/o 1021 S. 10th St., 63104.
LAFAYETTE, CONTRA COSTA PARISH, MARONITE CATHOLIC COMMUNITY, Closed. For inquiries for parish records contact the chancery.
LAKE CHARLES, CALCASIEU PARISH, MARONITE CATHOLIC COMMUNITY, Closed. For inquiries for parish records contact the chancery.
NEW ORLEANS, ORLEANS PARISH, MARONITE CATHOLIC COMMUNITY, 1021 S. 10th St., 63104. Tel: 314-231-1021; Fax: 314-231-1418.

STATE OF MICHIGAN

DETROIT, WAYNE CO., ST. MARON MARONITE CATHOLIC CHURCH (1910) [CEM] Rev. Msgr. Louis Baz.
Res.: 11466 Kercheval/St. Jean, MI 48214. Tel: 313-824-0196; Fax: 313-824-6418.
Catechesis/Religious Program—
FLINT, GENESEE CO., OUR LADY OF LEBANON MARONITE CATHOLIC CHURCH (1973) Rev. Hanna Tayar, O.M.M.; Deacons Martin J. Rachid; Earl Matte.
Res.: 4133 Calkins Rd., MI 48532. Tel: 810-733-1259; Fax: 810-732-2760.
Catechesis/Religious Program—
WARREN, MACOMB CO.
1—ST. RAFKA MARONITE CATHOLIC MISSION (2003) Chorbishop Michael J. Kail, Admin.; Deacon Al Morad, (Retired).
Mailing Address: 32801 Lydon Ave., Livonia, MI 48154. Tel: 734-634-9225.
Catechesis/Religious Program—
2—ST. SHARBEL MARONITE CATHOLIC CHURCH (1987) Chorbishop Michael J. Kail; Subdeacons Michael Magyar; Anthony Brown; Elias Aouad; Michael Coakley; Paul Makhoul; Melissa Hamama, Youth Min.
Res.: 31601 Schoenherr Rd., MI 48088-1977. Tel: 586-826-9688; Fax: 586-826-3521. Email: stsharbelwarren@aol.com. Web: stsharbelwarren.com.
Catechesis/Religious Program—

STATE OF MINNESOTA

MINNEAPOLIS, HENNEPIN CO., ST. MARON MARONITE CATHOLIC CHURCH (1903) [CEM] [JC] Rev. Msgr. Sharbel Maroun.
Res.: 600 University Ave., N.E., MN 55413. Tel: 612-379-2758; Fax: 612-379-7647. Email: abouna@stmaron.com. Web: www.stmaron.com.
Catechesis/Religious Program—Tel: 651-714-4740. Carla Bedros, D.R.E.
ST. PAUL, RAMSEY CO., HOLY FAMILY MARONITE CATHOLIC CHURCH (1918) [CEM] Rev. Rodrigue Constantin.
Res.: Tel: 651-291-1116; Fax: 651-222-3033. Email: holyfamilychurch@comcast.net; rodriguec@hotmail.com. Web: www.holyfamilymaronite.org.
Catechesis/Religious Program—

STATE OF MISSOURI

ST. LOUIS, ST. LOUIS CITY CO., ST. RAYMOND MARONITE CATHOLIC CATHEDRAL (1913) Rev. Jibran BouMerhi, Rector; Deacons Louis Peters; Wissam G. Akiki; Subdeacons George Simon; Fadi MouHanna.
Res.: 931 Lebanon Dr., 63104. Tel: 314-621-0056; Fax: 314-231-9057. Web: www.straymonds.net. Email: straymondscathedral@hotmail.com.
Catechesis/Religious Program—

STATE OF NEVADA

LAS VEGAS, CLARK CO., ST. SHARBEL MARONITE CATHOLIC MISSION (1991) Rev. Nadim Abou Zeid, M.L.M., Admin.
10325 Rancho Distino Rd., NV 89183. Tel: 702-824-1444; Fax: 702-616-4032. Email: abnadim@hotmail.com; stsharbel.lv@gmail.com. Web: www.stsharbellasvegas.org.
Catechesis/Religious Program—Danelle Marek, D.R.E. Students 30.

STATE OF OKLAHOMA

TULSA, TULSA CO.
1—ST. THERESE OF THE CHILD JESUS MARONITE CATHOLIC CHURCH (1998) Rev. Elias Abi-Sarkis.
Rectory—8311 S. 107th Ave., E., OK 74133. Tel: 918-872-7400; Fax: 918-286-6619. Email: padre@saintherese.org. Web: www.sainttherese.org.
Church & Office: 8315 S. 107th Ave., E., OK 74133.
Catechesis/Religious Program—

STATE OF OHIO

CINCINNATI, HAMILTON CO., ST. ANTHONY OF PADUA MARONITE CATHOLIC CHURCH (1910) [CEM] [JC] Rev. David Fisher; Subdeacons Joseph Mousie; Tom Simon.
Res.: 2530 Victory Pkwy., OH 45206. Tel: 513-961-0120; Fax: 513-861-5075. Email: david_andrew1@mal.com.
Catechesis/Religious Program—Kim Simon, D.R.E. Students 10.
CLEVELAND, CUYAHOGA CO., ST. MARON MARONITE CATHOLIC CHURCH (1915) [JC] Rev. Peter Karam; Deacon George M. Khoury; Subdeacons James Peters; Lattouf Lattouf; Ghazi Faddoul; Georges Faddoul; Bechara Daher.
Res.: 1245 Carnegie Ave., OH 44115. Tel: 216-781-6161; Fax: 216-781-6162.
Catechesis/Religious Program—
DAYTON, MONTGOMERY CO.
1—SAINT IGNATIUS OF ANTIOCH MARONITE CATHOLIC CHURCH (1993) [JC] Rev. Pierre Bassil.
Mailing Address: 5915 Springboro Pike, OH 45449. Tel: 937-428-0372; Fax: 937-428-0371.
Catechesis/Religious Program—William Thomas, D.R.E.; Laura Thomas, D.R.E.
2—OUR LADY OF LEBANON MARONITE CATHOLIC MISSION (2003) Rev. Pierre Bassil, Admin.
5915 Springboro Pike, OH 45449. Tel: 937-428-0372; Fax: 937-428-0371. Web: www.ourladyoflebanon.info.
FAIRLAWN, SUMMIT CO., OUR LADY OF THE CEDARS OF MT. LEBANON MARONITE CATHOLIC CHURCH (1937) Rev. Toufic M. Nasr; Deacon Robert Foster; Subdeacon Tom Maroon.
Res.: 507 S. Cleveland-Massillon Rd., OH 44333-3019. Tel: 330-666-3598; Fax: 330-666-3897.
Catechesis/Religious Program—
TOLEDO, LUCAS CO., MARONITE CATHOLIC COMMUNITY (1999) Closed.
YOUNGSTOWN, MAHONING CO., ST. MARON MARONITE CATHOLIC CHURCH (1902) Rev. Gary George, C.Ss.R.; Deacons Joseph Nohra; William George; Subdeacons Michel Bassil; James Essad.
Res.: 1555 S. Meridian Rd., OH 44511-1199. Tel: 330-792-2371; 330-792-7671 (Center); Fax: 330-792-3026. Email: parishoffice@stmaronyoungstown.org. Web: stmaronyoungstown.org.
Catechesis/Religious Program—Tel: 330-538-2567; Fax: 330-538-9820.

STATE OF OREGON

PORTLAND, MULTNOMAH CO., SAINT SHARBEL MARONITE CATHOLIC CHURCH (1970) [CEM 2] Rev. Jonathan Decker, S.J.M.J.; Deacon Antoine Karam.
Res.: 1804 S.E. 16th Ave., OR 97214. Tel: 503-231-3853; Fax: 503-533-8524. Web: www.saintsharbel.com.
Catechesis/Religious Program—Email: n.redmond@comcast.net. Nadia Redmond, D.R.E.

STATE OF TEXAS

AUSTIN, TRAVIS CO., OUR LADY'S MARONITE PARISH (1982) Rev. Msgr. Donald J. Sawyer; Deacons Joseph Crowley; Ron Lastovica.
Mailing Address: 1320 E. 51st St., TX 78723. Tel: 512-458-3693; Fax: 512-451-9554. Email: email@ourladysmaronite.org. Web: www.ourladysmaronite.org.
Catechesis/Religious Program—
EL PASO, EL PASO CO., ST. ANTHONY OF THE DESERT MARONITE CATHOLIC MISSION/HOLY FAMILY CHURCH (1997) Rev. Msgr. Victor Kayrouz; Subdeacon George Karam.
Res. & Church: 104 Fewel St., TX 79902. Tel: 915-532-8462; Fax: 915-577-0236.
Catechesis/Religious Program—Email: victor_kayrouz_msgr.@yahoo.com. Students 5.
HOUSTON, HARRIS CO., OUR LADY OF THE CEDARS MARONITE CATHOLIC CHURCH (1990) [JC] Revs. Milad T. Yaghi, M.L.M.; Andre S. Estephan, M.L.M.; Pierre El Khoury.
Res.: 11935 Belfort Village Dr., TX 77031. Tel: 281-568-6800; Fax: 281-564-6961. Web: www.ourladyofthecedars.net.
Catechesis/Religious Program—
LEWISVILLE, DENTON CO., OUR LADY OF LEBANON MARONITE CATHOLIC CHURCH (1990) Rev. Assaad El Basha, M.L.M.
Res.: 719 University Pl., TX 75067. Tel: 972-436-7617; Fax: 972-221-3430. Web: ourladylebanon.com.
Catechesis/Religious Program—
SAN ANTONIO, BEXAR CO., ST. GEORGE MARONITE CATHOLIC CHURCH (1925), (Maronite), [JC] Revs. Ghassan Mattar, M.L.M.; Charles H. Khachan, M.L.M.; Subdeacon Raymond E. Casillas.
Church: 6070 Babcock Rd., TX 78240. Tel: 210-690-9569; Fax: 210-690-5093.
Catechesis/Religious Program—

STATE OF UTAH

MURRAY, SALT LAKE CO., SAINT JUDE MARONITE CATHOLIC CHURCH (1975) Rev. Msgr. William D. Bonczewski.
Res.: 4893 Wasatch St., UT 84107. Tel: 801-268-2820; Fax: 801-268-4404. Email: frtom48@gmail.com. Church: 4900 Wasatch St., UT 84107. Email: stjudechurch@stinger.net.
Catechesis/Religious Program—

STATE OF WEST VIRGINIA

WHEELING, OHIO CO., OUR LADY OF LEBANON MARONITE CATHOLIC CHURCH (1906) [JC] Rev. Bakhos Chidiac.
Res.: 2216 Eoff St., WV 26003. Tel: 304-233-1688; Fax: 304-233-4714.
Catechesis/Religious Program—

STATE OF WASHINGTON

SEATTLE, KING CO., ST. JOSEPH MARONITE CATHOLIC MISSION (2001) Unassigned.
Catechesis/Religious Program—

Special Assignment:
Revs.—
Kimes, John Paul, Congregation for the Doctrine of the Faith, Vatican City, Rome.
Mhanna, Andre, Studying in Rome/Ph.D. in Liturgy.
Salim, Anthony, St. Theresa Church, P.O. Box 2567, Brockton, MA 02305-2567. Tel: 508-586-1428; Fax: 508-587-8139

Retired:
Rev. Msgr.—
Michael, Kenneth
Rev.—
Grunewald, Bernard, Er.O.L.S, M.A., S.T.B.
Chorbishop—
Khachan, Bernard C.

INSTITUTIONS LOCATED IN THE DIOCESE

[A] MONASTERIES AND RESIDENCES OF PRIESTS AND BROTHERS

LOS ANGELES. *The Congregation of Maronite Lebanese Missionaries,* 333 San Vicente Blvd., CA 91016. Tel: 310-275-6634; Fax: 310-858-0856. Rev. Abdallah Zaidan, M.L.M.

ANN ARBOR. *Maronite Order of the Blessed Virgin Mary,* 4405 Earhart Rd., MI 48105. Tel: 734-662-4822; Fax: 734-662-4822. Email: josephkhalil@sbcglobal.net. Revs. Ziad Antoun, O.M.M.; Hanna Tayar, O.M.M.; Joseph Khalil, O.M.M., Supr.; Paul Tarabay, O.M.M.; Nabil Habchi, O.M.M. Total in Residence 4.

HOUSTON. *The Congregation of Maronite Lebanese Missionaries* (1865) Our Lady of the Cedars, 11935 Bellfort Village, TX 77031. Tel: 281-568-6800; Fax: 281-564-6961. Email: azaidan@earthlink.net. Revs. Abdallah E. Zaidan, M.L.M., Supr.; Pierre El Khoury; Milad T. Yaghi, M.L.M.; Andre S. Estephan, M.L.M.; Assaad El Basha, M.L.M.; Ghassan Mattar, M.L.M.; Samuel Tanios Madel, M.L.M.; Elias Sleiman, M.L.M.; Charles H. Khachan, M.L.M., Asst.; Jean Yammine, M.L.M.; Nadim Abou Zeid, M.L.M.

[B] CONVENTS AND RESIDENCES FOR SISTERS

NORTH JACKSON. *Antonine Maronite Sisters of Youngstown, Inc.,* 2691 N. Lipkey Rd., OH 44451. Tel: 330-538-2567; 330-538-9822; Fax: 330-538-9820. Email: anto9srs@aol.com. Web: www.antoninesisters.com. Sr. Marie M. Iskandar, A.S., Dir. Sisters 5. *Antonine Sisters Adult Day Care, Inc.,* 2675 N. Lipkey Rd., OH 44451. Tel: 330-538-9822; Fax: 330-538-9820. Email: anto9sis@aol.com. Web: www.antoninesistersadultdaycare.com. Total Staff 12; Total Assisted 65.

[C] NATIONAL SHRINES

NORTH JACKSON. *National Shrine of Our Lady of Lebanon* 2759 N. Lipkey Rd., OH 44451. Tel: 330-538-3351; Fax: 330-538-0455. Email: ololshrine@aol.com. Web: www.ourladyoflebanonshrine.com. Rev. Msgr. Anthony Spinosa, Rector.

[D] RELIGIOUS COMMUNITIES OF MEN

PHILIPPI. *Our Lady of Solitude Maronite Hermitage, Inc.* (1966) 334 S. Main St., WV 26416-1252. Tel: 304-457-3330; Fax: 304-457-3330. Email: monkbg7@aol.com. Revs. Bernard Grunewald, Er.O.L.S, M.A., S.T.B., Supr. (Retired); W. Johnathan Decker, S.J.M.J., Canonical Hermit, 1804 S. E. 16th Ave., Portland, OR 97214. Tel: 503-231-3853; Fax: 503-533-8524. Total in Residence 1.

[E] RESIDENCES FOR CLERGY

NORTH JACKSON. *Father Tobia Retirement Home,* 2759 N. Lipkey Rd., OH 44451. Tel: 330-538-3351; Fax: 330-538-0455. Email: ololshrine@aol.com. Web: www.ourladyoflebanonshrine.com. Rev. Msgr. Anthony Spinosa, Rector & Contact Person.

[F] MISCELLANEOUS

ST. LOUIS. *Bishop's Charities,* 1021 S. 10th St., 63104. Tel: 314-231-1021; Fax: 314-231-1418. Email: mdenny@usamaronite.org. Most Rev. Robert J. Shaheen, Chm.

Caritas Lebanon, 1021 S. 10th St., 63104. Tel: 314-231-1021; Fax: 314-231-1418. Email: mdenny@usamaronite.org.

Catholic School Assistance Fund, 1021 S. 10th St., 63104. Tel: 314-231-1021; Fax: 314-231-1418. Email: mdenny@usamaronite.org. Web: www.usamaronite.org. Most Rev. Robert Joseph Shaheen.

Eparchial Endowments, 1021 S. 10th St., 63104. Tel: 314-231-1021; Fax: 314-231-1418. Chorbishop Faouzi Elia.

LEAF USA, Inc., 1021 S. 10th St., Saint Louis, 63104. Tel: 314-231-1021; Fax: 314-231-1418.

Maronite Heritage Institute, 1021 S. 10th St., 63104. Tel: 314-231-1021; Fax: 314-231-1418. Most Rev. Robert J. Shaheen, Contact Person.

Maronite Outreach, 1021 S. 10th St., 63104. Tel: 314-231-1021; Fax: 314-231-1418. Email: info@maroniteoutreach.org. Web: www.maroniteoutreach.org. Most Rev. Robert Joseph Shaheen, Chm.

Our Lady of Smiles Orphanage, 1021 S. 10th St., 63104. Tel: 314-231-1021; Fax: 314-231-1418. Email: mdenny@usamaronite.org. Rev. Mansour Labaky, Pres.

Priest's Retirement Fund, 1021 S. 10th St., 63104. Tel: 314-231-1021; Fax: 314-231-1418. Email: mdenny@usamaronite.org. Web: www.usamaronite.org.

RELIGIOUS INSTITUTES OF MEN REPRESENTED IN THE DIOCESE

For further details refer to the corresponding bracketed number in the Religious Institutes of Men or Women section.

[0785]—*The Congregation of Maronite Lebanese Missionaries* (Houston, TX)—M.L.M.

[0782]—*Maronite Order of Blessed Virgin Mary* (Ann Arbor, MI)—O.M.M.

[]—*The Congregation of Maronite Lebanese Missionaries* (Los Angeles, CA)—M.L.M.

NECROLOGY

(No Deaths)

Armenian Catholic Eparchy of Our Lady of Nareg in the United States of America and Canada

Most Reverend

MANUEL BATAKIAN

Armenian Catholic Eparch of Our Lady of Nareg; born November 5, 1929; ordained December 8, 1954; appointed Titular Bishop of Caesarea of Cappadocia January 8, 1995; ordained March 12, 1995; appointed third Apostolic Exarch for Armenian Catholics in United States and Canada November 30, 2000; installed January 20, 2001; nominated as the first Eparch of Our Lady of Nareg September 12, 2005. *Office: 167 N. 6th St., Brooklyn, NY 11211.*

Chancery & Vicar General Office: 167 N. 6th St., Brooklyn, NY 11211. Tel: 718-388-4218; Fax: 718-486-0615.

Legal Title: Armenian Catholic Eparchy of Our Lady of Nareg in the United States and Canada.

STATISTICAL OVERVIEW

Personnel	
Bishop	1
Priests: Diocesan Active in Diocese	3
Number of Diocesan Priests	3
Religious Priests in Diocese	8
Total Priests in Diocese	11
Permanent Deacons in Diocese	1
Total Sisters	7
Parishes	
Parishes	7
With Resident Pastor:	
Resident Diocesan Priests	3
Resident Religious Priests	4
Professional Ministry Personnel:	
Sisters	7
Educational	
Diocesan Students in Other Seminaries	1
Total Seminarians	1
High Schools, Private	1
Total Students	76
Elementary Schools, Diocesan and Parish	3
Total Students	1,048
Total Students under Catholic Instruction	1,125
Vital Statistics	
Receptions into the Church:	
Infant Baptism Totals	81
Minor Baptism Totals	2
Adult Baptism Totals	4
First Communions	39
Confirmations	87
Marriages:	
Catholic	32
Interfaith	29
Total Marriages	61
Total Catholic Population	25,000

Former Bishops—Most Revs. NERSES MIKAEL SETIAN, ord. April 13, 1941; appt. Titular Bishop of Ancera and Apostolic Exarch for the Armenian Catholics in the U.S.A. and Canada July 3, 1981; ord. Dec. 5, 1981; installed Dec. 27, 1981; retired Sept. 18, 1993; died Sept. 9, 2002; HOVHANNES TERTZAKIAN, O.M.Ven., ord. Sept. 8, 1948; appt. Titular Bishop of Trebisonda and Apostolic Exarch for Armenian Catholics in the United States and Canada Jan. 6, 1995; ord. April 29, 1995; installed May 7, 1995; retired Nov. 30, 2000; died Jan. 28, 2002.

Chancery & Vicar General Office—167 N. 6th St., Brooklyn, 11211. Tel: 718-388-4218; Fax: 718-486-0615.

Vicar General—Rev. GEORGES ZABARIAN. Tel: 718-388-4218.

Business Chancellor—Rev. RAPHAEL ANDONIAN, O.Mech. Tel: 718-388-4218; 617-489-2280.

Newspaper Diocesan Bulletin— "The Eternal Flame" *167 N. 6th St., Brooklyn, 11211.* Tel: 718-388-4218.

Newspaper Diocesan Bulletin "VERELK"—Office: 1327 Pleasant Ave., Los Angeles, CA 90033-2328. Tel: 323-267-1740.

CLERGY, PARISHES, MISSIONS AND PAROCHIAL SCHOOLS

STATE OF NEW YORK

NEW YORK, NEW YORK CO., ST. ANN'S ARMENIAN CATHOLIC CATHEDRAL (1983) Rev. Antoine Noradounghian.
Res.: 167 N. 6th St., 11211. Tel: 718-388-4218; Fax: 718-486-0615.

STATE OF CALIFORNIA

GLENDALE, LOS ANGELES CO., ST. GREGORY ARMENIAN CATHOLIC CHURCH (1998) Rev. Antoine Saroyan.
Res.: 1510 E. Mountain St., CA 91207-1226. Tel: 818-243-8400; Fax: 818-243-0095.

LOS ANGELES, LOS ANGELES CO., OUR LADY QUEEN OF MARTYRS (1951) Rev. Antoine Panossian.
Res.: 1327 Pleasant Ave., CA 90033-2328. Tel: 323-261-9898; Fax: 323-261-0522.

STATE OF MASSACHUSETTS

BOSTON, MIDDLESEX CO., HOLY CROSS (1940) Rev. Raphael Andonian, O.Mech.; Deacon M.J. Connolly.
Res.: 200 Lexington St., Belmont, MA 02478-1241. Tel: 617-489-2280; Fax: 617-484-0218.

STATE OF MICHIGAN

DETROIT, WAYNE CO., ST. VARTAN'S (1948) Rev. Antoine Adamian.
Res.: 34080 Edmonton St., Farmington, MI 48335. Tel: 248-877-3718 (Cell); 248-991-3766 (Church).

STATE OF NEW JERSEY

PATERSON, PASSAIC CO., SACRED HEART (1927) Rev. George Kalousieh.
Res.: 155 Long Hill Rd., Little Falls, NJ 07424-2374. Tel: 973-890-0447; Fax: 973-890-0292.

STATE OF PENNSYLVANIA

PHILADELPHIA, PHILADELPHIA CO., ST. MARK'S ARMENIAN CATHOLIC (1924) Rev. Armenag Bedrossian.
Res.: 400 Haverford Rd., Wynnewood, PA 19096-2699. Tel: 610-896-7789; Fax: 610-896-0915.

INSTITUTIONS LOCATED IN THE DIOCESE

[A] SCHOOLS

STATE OF CALIFORNIA

MONTROSE. *Armenian Sisters of the Immaculate Conception,* 2361 Florencita Dr., CA 91020-1817. Tel: 818-249-8783; Fax: 818-249-7288. Sr. Lucia Al-Haik, Prin.

TUJUNGA. *Mekhitarist School,* 6470 Foothill Blvd., CA 91042-2729. Tel: 818-353-3003; Fax: 818-353-0815. Rev. Augustin Szekula, O.Mech., Prin.
6507 Alta Gracia Dr., CA 91042-3403. Tel: 818-352-3048; Fax: 818-352-2647.

STATE OF MASSACHUSETTS

LEXINGTON. *Armenian Sisters Academy,* 20 Pelham Rd., MA 02421-5702. Tel: 781-861-8303; Fax: 781-862-8479. Sr. Cecile Keheyan, Prin.

STATE OF PENNSYLVANIA

RADNOR. *Armenian Sisters Academy,* 440 Upper Gulph Rd., PA 19087-4699. Tel: 610-687-4100; Fax: 610-687-2430. Web: ameniansrsacademy.org. Sr. Louisa Kassarjian, Supr. & Prin.

[B] RELIGIOUS INSTITUTES AND CONVENTS FOR WOMEN

STATE OF CALIFORNIA

MONTROSE. *Armenian Sisters of the Immaculate Conception,* 2361 Florencita Dr., CA 91020-1817. Tel: 818-249-7493 (convent). Sr. Lucia Al-Haik, Prin.

STATE OF MASSACHUSETTS

LEXINGTON. *Armenian Sisters of the Immaculate Conception,* 6 Eliot Rd., MA 02173. Tel: 781-863-5962; Fax: 781-674-0410. Sr. Cecile Keheyan, Prin.

STATE OF PENNSYLVANIA

RADNOR. *Armenian Sisters of the Immaculate Conception,* 440 Upper Gulph Rd., PA 19087-4699. Tel: 610-687-4100; 610-688-9360 (convent); Fax: 610-687-2430. Sr. Louisa Kassarjian, Supr. & Prin.

NECROLOGY

(No Deaths)

An asterisk (*) denotes an organization that has established tax-exempt status directly with the IRS and is not covered by the USCCB Group Ruling.

Byzantine Eparchy of Parma

Most Reverend

JOHN M. KUDRICK

Bishop of Parma; ordained May 3, 1975; consecrated and installed July 10, 2002.

Chancery Office: 1900 Carlton Rd., Parma, OH 44134. Tel: 216-741-8773; Fax: 216-741-9356.

Web: www.parma.org

ESTABLISHED FEBRUARY 21, 1969.

Embraces all Byzantine Ruthenian Rite Catholics in the States of Illinois, Indiana, Iowa, Kansas, Michigan, Minnesota, Missouri, Nebraska, North Dakota, South Dakota and Wisconsin. Also the entire State of Ohio excluding the Counties of Ashtabula, Trumbull, Mahoning, Columbiana, Carroll, Harrison, Guernsey, Noble, Morgan, Athens, Meigs, Gallia and Lawrence.

For legal titles of parishes and diocesan institutions, consult the Chancery Office.

STATISTICAL OVERVIEW

Personnel	
Bishop	1
Priests: Diocesan Active in Diocese	27
Priests: Diocesan Active Outside Diocese	3
Priests: Retired, Sick or Absent	12
Number of Diocesan Priests	42
Religious Priests in Diocese	1
Total Priests in Diocese	43
Extern Priests in Diocese	6
Ordinations:	
Transitional Deacons	1
Permanent Deacons	1
Permanent Deacons in Diocese	13
Total Sisters	8
Parishes	
Parishes	30
With Resident Pastor:	
Resident Diocesan Priests	28
Without Resident Pastor:	
Administered by Priests	2
Missions	5
Pastoral Centers	1
Closed Parishes	1
Professional Ministry Personnel:	
Sisters	6
Welfare	
Day Care Centers	1
Total Assisted	57
Special Centers for Social Services	5
Total Assisted	16,500
Educational	
Diocesan Students in Other Seminaries	2
Total Seminarians	2
Elementary Schools, Diocesan and Parish	1
Total Students	170
Catechesis/Religious Education:	
High School Students	118
Elementary Students	375
Total Students under Catholic Instruction	665
Teachers in the Diocese:	
Sisters	3
Lay Teachers	9
Vital Statistics	
Receptions into the Church:	
Infant Baptism Totals	73
Minor Baptism Totals	1
Adult Baptism Totals	6
Received into Full Communion	19
First Communions	50
Confirmations	69
Marriages:	
Catholic	19
Interfaith	3
Total Marriages	22
Deaths	138
Total Catholic Population	8,752

Former Bishops—Most Revs. EMIL J. MIHALIK, D.D., ord. Sept. 21, 1945; appt. first Bishop of the Ruthenian Eparchy of Parma, March 22, 1969; installed June 12, 1969; died Jan. 27, 1984; ANDREW PATAKI, D.D., appt. Titular Bishop of Tellmisus and Auxiliary of Passaic, NJ, May 30, 1983; installed Aug. 23, 1983; succeeded to See, June 19, 1984; transferred to Parma See, Aug. 16, 1984; transferred to Byzantine Eparchy of Passaic, Nov. 21, 1995; BASIL MYRON SCHOTT, O.F.M., ord. Aug. 29, 1965; cons. and installed as Bishop of Parma July 11, 1996; transferred to Archeparchy of Pittsburgh July 9, 2002.

Chancery Office—1900 Carlton Rd., Parma, 44134. Tel: 216-741-8773; Fax: 216-741-9356.

Protosyncellus—Rt. Rev. Mitred Archpriest JOHN S. KACHUBA, M.A.

Syncellus for Clergy and Religious—Very Rev. STEVEN KOPLINKA, M.Div.

Syncellus for Parishes and Laity—Very Rev. THOMAS LOYA, S.T.B., M.A.

Syncellus for Doctrine and Worship—Very Rev. Archpriest MICHAEL HAYDUK.

Chancellor—Very Rev. Archpriest DENNIS M. HRUBIAK.

Presbyteral Council—Rt. Rev. Mitred Archpriest JOHN S. KACHUBA, M.A.; Very Rev. NICHOLAS RACHFORD, J.C.L.; Very Rev. Archpriest MICHAEL HAYDUK; Very Revs. DAVID A. HANNES, J.C.L.; STEVEN KOPLINKA, M.Div.; JAMES KUBAJAK, M.Div.; THOMAS LOYA, S.T.B., M.A.; Revs. BASIL HUTSKO; BRUCE RIEBE; TERRENCE FARMER; Rev. Msgr. FRANK KORBA, V.F.; Rev. JAMES J. BATCHA.

Eparchial Pastoral Council—Rt. Rev. Mitred Archpriest JOHN S. KACHUBA, M.A.; Very Rev. Archpriest MICHAEL HAYDUK; Very Revs. STEVEN KOPLINKA, M.Div.; THOMAS LOYA, S.T.B., M.A.; Rev. JOSEPH REPKO, M.Div.; Deacon JOHN PETRUS, M.D.; CATHERINE BARANKO; VIRGILDEE DANIEL; NICHOLAS J. NAGRANT; LORETTA NEMETH; MICHAEL ROBUSTO; ANN SEABRIGHT; KATHRYN SZILAGYE.

Eparchial Finance Council—Rev. JAMES J. BATCHA, Finance Officer.

Eparchial Finance Officer—Rt. Rev. Mitred Archpriest JOHN S. KACHUBA, M.A.; JENNIFER L. CLAIR, Sec.; JEROME J. LUCAS; EDWARD MAHER; THOMAS PERCIAK.

Eparchial Consultors—Rt. Rev. Mitred Archpriest JOHN S. KACHUBA, M.A.; Very Rev. Archpriest DENNIS M. HRUBIAK; Very Rev. NICHOLAS RACHFORD, J.C.L.; Rev. Msgr. FRANK KORBA, V.F.; Very Rev. Archpriests DAVID PETRAS, S.E.O.D.; MICHAEL HAYDUK.

Protopresbyters—Ohio: Very Rev. BRYAN R. EYMAN, D.Min. Midwest: Rev. Msgr. FRANK KORBA, V.F. Great Lakes: Very Rev. JAMES KUBAJAK, M.Div.

Vicar Judicialis—Very Rev. NICHOLAS RACHFORD, J.C.L.

Vicar Adjutant—Rev. MICHAEL J. HUSZTI.

Judge—Very Rev. DAVID A. HANNES, J.C.L.

Secretary of the Tribunal—VACANT.

Defender of the Bond—Very Rev. JAMES KUBAJAK, M.Div.

Promoter of Justice—Very Rev. JAMES KUBAJAK, M.Div.

Notaries—MARILYN MUCHA; Rev. RICHARD PLISHKA.

Eparchial Censor—Very Rev. Archpriest DAVID PETRAS, S.E.O.D.

Priest Secretary to the Bishop—Rev. RICHARD PLISHKA.

Eparchial Commissions

Sacred Liturgy—Very Rev. Archpriest DAVID PETRAS, S.E.O.D., Chm.; Rev. ROBERT BARTER (Retired); Very Rev. Archpriest MICHAEL HAYDUK; Very Rev. STEVEN KOPLINKA, M.Div.

Building Commission—Very Rev. Archpriest DAVID PETRAS, S.E.O.D.; Very Rev. BRYAN R. EYMAN, D.Min., Chm.; Deacon WILLIAM FREDRICK; FRANK TOMBAZZI.

Cantors' Institute—NICOLETTE BOROS, Dir. Cantors' Institute Faculty: Very Rev. Archpriests DAVID PETRAS, S.E.O.D.; DENNIS M. HRUBIAK; MICHAEL HAYDUK; Revs. MICHAEL J. HUSZTI; JAMES J. BATCHA; Very Rev. NICHOLAS RACHFORD, J.C.L.

Office of Religious Education—Rt. Rev. Mitred Archpriest JOHN S. KACHUBA, M.A., Dir. Tel: 216-741-4102. Associates: Rev. Msgr. FRANK KORBA, V.F., Midwest; Deacon WILLIAM FREDRICK, Safe Environment Coord.

Catechetical Board—Rev. Msgr. FRANK KORBA, V.F.; LISA STANICH.

Office of Youth Ministry—Rev. BRUCE RIEBE, Dir.; Very Rev. THOMAS LOYA, S.T.B., M.A., Midwest.

Young Adults—Revs. TERRENCE FARMER; RICHARD PLISHKA; JULIE HRITZ.

Office of Family Life—VIRGILDEE DANIEL, Dir.

Office of Evangelization and Missionary Activity—Revs. JAMES J. BATCHA, Dir.; STEPHEN TITKO; LORETTA NEMETH.

Office of Vocations—Very Rev. Archpriest DENNIS M. HRUBIAK, Dir.

Seminary Education Formation Board—Very Rev. Archpriests DAVID PETRAS, S.E.O.D., Chm.; MICHAEL HAYDUK; DENNIS M. HRUBIAK; Rt. Rev. Mitred Archpriest JOHN S. KACHUBA, M.A.; Very Rev. STEVEN KOPLINKA, M.Div.

Priest's Pension Board—Rt. Rev. Mitred Archpriest JOHN S. KACHUBA, M.A.; Revs. BASIL HUTSKO; JOSEPH MARQUIS; Very Rev. Archpriest DENNIS M. HRUBIAK; Revs. SIDNEY SIDOR; JAMES J. BATCHA, Chm.

Office of Ecumenical Activity—Very Rev. Archpriest DAVID PETRAS, S.E.O.D., Dir.

Stewardship Office—Rev. JAMES J. BATCHA.

Eparchial Shrine of the Weeping Madonna of Mariapoch— (Burton, OH): President, The Most Rev. Ordinary of the Parma Eparchy. Tel: 440-834-0700. Revs. JAMES J. BATCHA, Admin.; GARY FRANCISKO, Pastoral Ministry. Tel: 440-834-4078.

Respect Life Office—Very Rev. THOMAS LOYA, S.T.B., M.A.

Pre-Cana Office—VIRGILDEE DANIEL; LOUISE DANIEL.

Victim Assistance Coordinator—SHARON DILAURO PETRUS, M.D. Tel: 216-741-8773, Ext. 246. Email: jpetrus@adelphia.net.

Office of Communications—LORETTA NEMETH, Dir. Tel: 216-741-3312. Email: viscom@parma.org.

Boy Scout Chaplain—Very Rev. NICHOLAS RACHFORD, J.C.L.

Sexual Allegation Review Board—MADELINE ZAWORSKI, Chm.; MICHAEL ROBUSTO, Sec.; Rev. JAMES J. BATCHA; RITA BASALLA; WILLIAM BOCKANIC; ROBERT KINKELA; JEAN MCNOSKY; LISA NEWBURGER; JODI STARRE. Ex Officio: Rt. Rev. Mitred Archpriest JOHN S. KACHUBA, M.A.; Very Rev. JAMES KUBAJAK, M.Div.

CLERGY, PARISHES, MISSIONS AND PAROCHIAL SCHOOLS

STATE OF OHIO

PARMA, CUYAHOGA CO.

1—SAINT JOHN THE BAPTIST, CATHEDRAL (1898), (Ruthenian), Very Rev. Archpriest Michael Hayduk; Deacon John Petrus.
Church: 1900 Carlton Rd., 44134-3129. Tel: 216-661-8658; Fax: 216-661-8221.
Res.: 1703 Carlton Rd., 44134.
Catechesis/Religious Program—Students 30.

2—HOLY SPIRIT (1969) [CEM 2] Rev. James J. Batcha.
Res.: 5500 W. 54th St., 44129-2274. Tel: 440-884-8452; Fax: 440-884-8453. Email: church@holyspiritchurch.ohiocoxmail.com. Web: holyspiritbyzantine.org.
Catechesis/Religious Program—

AKRON, SUMMIT CO., ST. MICHAEL THE ARCHANGEL (1916) [CEM] Rev. Robert Stash.
Res.: 847 Crouse St., 44306-1125. Tel: 330-376-6633; Fax: 330-376-7007.
Catechesis/Religious Program—Students 11.

BARBERTON, SUMMIT CO., ST. NICHOLAS (1918) [CEM] Rev. Miron Kerul'-Kmec, Admin.
Church: 1051 E. Robinson St., 44203-3852. Tel: 330-753-2031; Fax: 330-745-5500. Email: stnickbyz@gmail.com. Web: www.stnickbyz.com.
Catechesis/Religious Program—Students 18.

BEDFORD, CUYAHOGA CO., ST. EUGENE (1963) Rev. Joseph Repko.
Res.: 264 Warrensville-Center Rd., 44146-2741. Tel: 440-232-7302; Fax: 440-439-9537. Email: frrepko@ameritech.net.
Catechesis/Religious Program—Students 7.

BRECKSVILLE, CUYAHOGA CO., ST. JOSEPH (1913) Rev. Bruce Riebe; Deacon William Fredrick.
Res.: 8111 Brecksville, 44141-1204. Tel: 440-526-1818; Fax: 440-526-6464. Email: stjoebyz@sbcglobal.net. Web: www.stjoebyz.com.
Catechesis/Religious Program—Students 64.

BRUNSWICK, MEDINA CO., ST. EMILIAN (1975) Rev. Marek Visnovsky.
Res.: 4705 Hickory Ridge Rd., 44212.
Church: 1231 Substation Rd., 44212-0843. Tel: 330-225-9857; Fax: 330-220-5963.
Catechesis/Religious Program—Students 7.

BURTON, GEAUGA CO., CHURCH OF MARIAPOCH (1956) Revs. James J. Batcha, Admin.; Gary Francisko.
Church: 17486 Mumford Rd., P.O. Box 388, 44021-9640. Tel: 440-834-8807.
Shrine—Shrine of Mariapoch, Tel: 440-834-0700.

CLEVELAND, CUYAHOGA CO.

1—HOLY GHOST (1909) Closed. For inquiries for parish records contact the chancery.

2—ST. MARY (1938) Very Rev. Steven Koplinka; Deacon Joseph Hnat.
Res.: 4600 State Rd., 44109-5243. Tel: 216-741-7979; Fax: 216-741-6622.
School—(Grades K-8) Tel: 216-749-7980; Fax: 216-749-7775. Rita Basalla, Prin.; Mary Somrak, Librarian. Sisters of St. Basil the Great 3; Lay Teachers 9; Students 170.
Catechesis/Religious Program—Students 4.
Convent—Sisters of St. Basil the Great., 3518 Stickney Ave., 44109. Tel: 216-398-5939.

3—ST. NICHOLAS (1902), (Croatian), Rev. Robert D. Kelly.
Res.: 2035 Quail Ave., Lakewood, 44107. Tel: 216-521-1081; Fax: 216-521-1020.
Church: 3431 Superior Ave., 44114-4160. Tel: 216-361-5069; Fax: 216-361-2455.
Catechesis/Religious Program—

COLUMBUS, FRANKLIN CO., ST. JOHN CHRYSOSTOM (1961) Rev. Terrence Farmer; Deacon Jeffrey Martin.
Res.: 5858 Cleveland Ave., 43231-2862. Tel: 614-882-7578; Fax: 614-890-6048.
Catechesis/Religious Program—Students 25.

DAYTON, MONTGOMERY CO., ST. BARBARA, Closed. For inquiries for parish records contact the chancery.

EUCLID, CUYAHOGA CO., ST. STEPHEN (1955) Rt. Rev. Mitred Archpriest John S. Kachuba.
Res.: 532 Lloyd Rd., 44132-1721. Tel: 216-732-7292; Fax: 216-732-9434.
Catechesis/Religious Program—Students 45.

FAIRPORT HARBOR, LAKE CO., ST. MICHAEL (1926) Very Rev. Bryan R. Eyman.
Mailing Address: *St. Andrew*, c/o 5768 Andrews Rd., Mentor-on-the-Lake, 44060-2608.
Res.: 630 Plum St., 44077-5660. Tel: 440-257-3620; Fax: 440-257-6524.
Catechesis/Religious Program—Students 3.

FAIRVIEW PARK, CUYAHOGA CO., ST. MARY MAGDALENE (1966) Very Rev. Archpriest Dennis M. Hrubiak; Deacon Daniel Surniak.
Res.: 5390 W. 220th St., 44126-2968. Tel: 440-734-4644; Fax: 440-734-4645. Email: fdhrubiak@yahoo.com. Web: ebni.com/stmarymagdalene.
Catechesis/Religious Program—Students 20.

LAKEWOOD, CUYAHOGA CO., ST. GREGORY THE THEOLOGIAN (1905) Rev. Robert D. Kelly.
Res.: 2035 Quail Ave., 44107-5217. Tel: 216-521-1081; Fax: 216-521-1020.
Catechesis/Religious Program—

LORAIN, LORAIN CO.

1—ST. MICHAEL, Closed. For inquiries for parish records contact the chancery.

2—ST. NICHOLAS (1914) Very Rev. Nicholas Rachford.
Res.: 2711 W. 40th St., 44053-2252. Tel: 440-282-7525; Fax: 440-282-9185. Email: info@stnicks.org. Web: www.stnicks.org.
Catechesis/Religious Program—Students 27.

MARBLEHEAD, OTTAWA CO., ST. MARY (1897) [CEM] Rev. Basil Hutsko.
Res.: 506 E. Main St., 43440-2232. Tel: 419-798-4283; Fax: 419-798-4095.
Catechesis/Religious Program—Students 5.

MENTOR-ON-THE-LAKE, LAKE CO., ST. ANDREW THE APOSTLE (1974) Very Rev. Bryan R. Eyman.
Res.: 630 Plum St., Fairport Harbor, 44077.
Church: 5768 Andrews Rd., 44060-2608. Tel: 440-257-3620; Fax: 440-257-6524.
Catechesis/Religious Program—Students 18.

NORTHWOOD, LUCAS CO., ST. MICHAEL THE ARCHANGEL (1915) Very Rev. James Kubajak; Deacon James Sofalvi.
Res.: 2526 Skagway Dr., 43619. Tel: 419-691-5656; Fax: 419-691-7669.
Church: 4001 Navarre Ave., Oregon, 43616.
Catechesis/Religious Program—Students 1.

SOLON, CUYAHOGA CO., ST. JOHN THE BAPTIST (1892) Rev. Joseph Repko.
Res.: 264 Warrensville Center Rd., Bedford, 44146. Tel: 440-232-7302.
Church: 36125 Aurora Rd., 44139-3841. Tel: 440-248-0417; Fax: 440-248-8044.
Catechesis/Religious Program—Students 2.

STATE OF ILLINOIS

CHICAGO, COOK CO., ST. MARY, Closed. For inquiries for parish records contact the chancery.

HOMER GLEN, WILL CO., ANNUNCIATION BYZANTINE CATHOLIC CHURCH (1999) [CEM] Very Rev. Thomas Loya; Deacons Michael Kenes; J. Timothy Tkach; John Evancho.
Res.: 14610 S. Will-Cook Rd., IL 60491-9212. Tel: 708-645-0241; Fax: 708-645-0243. Email: annuncbyzchurch@aol.com. Web: www.byzantinecatholic.com.
Catechesis/Religious Program—Students 50.

JOLIET, WILL CO., ST. MARY ASSUMPTION, Closed. For inquiries for parish records contact the chancery.

STATE OF INDIANA

EAST CHICAGO, LAKE CO., ST. BASIL'S, Closed. For inquiries for parish records contact the chancery.

INDIANA, HARBOR CO., HOLY GHOST, Closed. For inquiries for parish records contact the chancery.

INDIANAPOLIS, MARION CO., ST. ATHANASIUS CHURCH (1980) Rev. Sidney Sidor.
Res.: 1117 S. Blaine Ave., IN 46221-1110. Tel: 317-632-4157; Fax: 317-632-2988. Email: stathanasius@pngusa.net. Web: http://r-fol.com./st.athanasius.
Catechesis/Religious Program—Students 6.

MERRILLVILLE, LAKE CO., ST. MICHAEL (1911) Very Rev. Michael Evanick.
Res.: 557 W. 57th Ave., IN 46410-2540. Tel: 219-980-0600; Fax: 219-980-0127.
Catechesis/Religious Program—Students 19.

MUNSTER, LAKE CO., SAINT NICHOLAS (1922) [CEM] Rev. Msgr. Frank Korba.
Res.: 8103 Columbia Ave., IN 46321-1802. Tel: 219-838-9380; Fax: 219-838-1265.
Catechesis/Religious Program—Students 10.

WHITING, LAKE CO., ASSUMPTION OF THE BLESSED VIRGIN (1899) [CEM] Rev. John Kovach; Deacons Richard Guiden, (Retired); J. Timothy Tkach.
Res.: 2011 Clark St., IN 46394-2023. Tel: 219-659-0277; Fax: 219-659-1687.
Catechesis/Religious Program—Students 12.

STATE OF MICHIGAN

ALLEN PARK, WAYNE CO., ST. STEPHEN (1941) Rev. Cyril Attak.
Res.: 4141 Laurence Ave., MI 48101-3049. Tel: 313-382-5901; Fax: 313-382-5902.
Catechesis/Religious Program—Students 14.

BAY CITY, BAY CO., SAINT GEORGE (1967) Rev. Innokentij Stikhin, Admin.
Res.: 204 N. Van Buren St., MI 48706-6519. Tel: 616-322-6462; Fax: 989-892-0763.
Catechesis/Religious Program—Students 6.

DETROIT, WAYNE CO.

1—ST. JOHN THE BAPTIST, Closed. For inquiries for parish records contact the chancery.

2—ST. NICHOLAS (1921) Rev. Robert Barter (Retired).
Res.: 34475 Jefferson, Harrison Township, MI 48045. Tel: 586-792-1677.
Church: 23300 King Dr., Clinton Township, MI 48035. Tel: 586-791-1052; Fax: 586-791-1059.
Catechesis/Religious Program—Students 5.

FLUSHING, GENESEE CO., ST. MICHAEL (1917) Very Rev. David A. Hannes.
Res.: 2333 N. Elms Rd., MI 48433-9426. Tel: 810-659-4887; Fax: 810-659-8363. Email: stmichaelbyz@aol.com. Web: www.stmichaelbyz.com.
Catechesis/Religious Program—Students 45.

LIVONIA, WAYNE CO., SACRED HEART (1957) Rev. Joseph Marquis; Deacon Lawrence Hendricks.
Res.: 16881 Savoie St., MI 48154.
Church: 29125 W. Six-Mile Rd., MI 48152-3661. Tel: 734-522-3166; Fax: 734-261-8562. Email: shbyzantine@sbcglobal.net.
Catechesis/Religious Program—Students 10.

OMER, ARENAC CO., ST. JOHN (1981) Rev. Innokentij Stikhin.
Res.: 204 N. Van Buren St., Bay City, MI 48706-6519. Tel: 616-322-6462; Fax: 989-892-0763.
Church: 125 High St., P.O. Box 236, MI 48749-0236.

STERLING HEIGHTS, MACOMB CO., ST. BASIL (1962) Rev. Mychail Rozmarynowycz, Admin.; Deacon Paul Latcha.
Res.: 4700 Metropolitan Pkwy., MI 48310-3905. Tel: 586-268-1082; Fax: 586-268-2548.
Catechesis/Religious Program—Students 9.

TAYLOR, WAYNE CO., CHRIST THE KING, Closed. For inquiries for parish records contact the chancery.

STATE OF MINNESOTA

MINNEAPOLIS, HENNEPIN CO., ST. JOHN THE BAPTIST (1907) Rev. Ihar Labacevich.
Res.: 2215 Third St., N.E., MN 55418-3422. Tel: 612-789-6252; Fax: 612-789-2607. Email: stjohnminneapolis@comcast.net.
Catechesis/Religious Program—Students 10.

STATE OF MISSOURI

ST. LOUIS, ST. LOUIS CO., ST. LOUIS MISSION (1981) Revs. Eugene P. Selzer; Paul Niemann; Joseph A. Weber.
Mailing Address: 796 Buckley Rd., MO 63125. Tel: 314-892-5109; Fax: 314-892-0629.
Blessed John XXIII Center: 8300 Morganford Rd., MO 62123.

SUGAR CREEK, JACKSON CO., ST. LUKE, BYZANTINE CATHOLIC PARISH (1980) Revs. Stephen Muth; John Mack, Parochial Vicar; Deacon Nicholas Szilagye.
Mailing Address: P.O. Box 8673, MO 64054.
Church: 11411 Chicago, MO 64054. Tel: 816-231-7100.

STATE OF WISCONSIN

BRISTOL, KENOSHA CO., ST. IRENE, Closed. For information regarding the Byzantine Catholic Community contact the Chancery.

On Duty Outside the Diocese:
Revs.—
Atkins, James, Archeparchy of Pittsburgh
Huszti, Michael J., Sisters of St. Basil the Great, 500 W. Main St., Uniontown, PA 15401. Tel: 724-439-4475
Very Rev. Archpriest—
Petras, David M., Byzantine Catholic Seminary, 3605 Perrysville Ave., Pittsburgh, PA 05214. Tel: 412-321-5133; Fax: 412-321-9936

Absent on Leave:
Revs.—
Chelena, Thomas
Rebovich, John
St. Germain, Brian

Retired:
Rev. Msgr.—
Smochko, Basil, 66399 Estrella Ave., Desert Hot Springs, CA 82240-4525. Tel: 760-251-0802
Very Rev.—
Zavell, Edward, 11644 Katherine, Taylor, MI 48180. Tel: 734-250-8594

Revs.—

Barter, Robert, 34475 Jefferson, Harrison Township, MI 48045.

Ivan, Nicholas, Mt. Macrina Manor, 520 W. Main St., Uniontown, PA 15401.

Jadwisiak, Edmund, 5000 Providence Dr. #321, Sandusky, 44870-1414. Tel: 419-625-1354

Linowski, Eugene R., 2221 Glenmere Rd., Columbus, 43220. Tel: 614-488-0427

Pohorlak, Joseph, 1511 Warwick Ave., Apt 1S, Whiting, IN 46394. Tel: 219-473-0197

Radvansky, Joseph R. Tel: 419-503-0507

Wojciechowski, Edward C., Albertine Home, 1501 Hoffman St., Hammond, IN 46327. Tel: 219-937-0575

Permanent Deacons:

Evancho, John

Fredrick, William, St. Joseph, Brecksville, OH

Guiden, Richard, (Retired)

Hendricks, Lawrence, Sacred Heart, Livonia, MI

Hnat, Joseph, St. Mary, Cleveland, OH

Kenes, Michael, Annunciation Byzantine Church, Homer Glen, IL

Kirschner, Robert

Latcha, Paul, St. Basil, Sterling Heights, MI

Martin, Jeffrey, St. John Chrysostom, Columbus, OH

Petrus, John, M.D., St. John Cathedral, Parma, OH

Sofalvi, James, St. Michael, Northwood, OH

Surniak, Daniel, St. Mary Magdalene, Fairview Park, OH

Szilagye, Nicholas, M.D., St. Luke, Sugar Creek, MO

Tkach, J. Timothy, Annunciation Byzantine Church, Homer Glen, IL; St. Mary, Whiting, IN

INSTITUTIONS LOCATED IN THE DIOCESE

[A] CONVENTS AND RESIDENCES FOR SISTERS

NORTH ROYALTON. *Motherhouse and Novitiate*, 6688 Cady Rd., 44133. Tel: 440-237-6800. Sr. Mary Lucille Tepper, B.P.C.N., Supr.

[B] RELIGIOUS SHRINES

BURTON. *Shrine of Mariapoch* 17486 Mumford Rd., 44021. Tel: 440-834-0700.

[C] MISCELLANEOUS

CLEVELAND. *St. Mary Hospitality House*, 5500 W. 54th St., 44129. Tel: 440-884-8452; Fax: 440-884-8453. Dorothy Papke, Dir.

DAYTON. *St. Barbara Prayer Community* Prayer Center., 5915 Springboro Pike, 45449. Tel: 513-434-9205. Rev. John Kapitan Jr., O.F.M.

RELIGIOUS INSTITUTES OF WOMEN REPRESENTED IN THE DIOCESE

For further details refer to the corresponding bracketed number in the Religious Institutes of Men or Women section.

[]—*Byzantine Nuns of St. Clare* (Parma Eparchy)—B.P.C.N.

[3730]—*Sisters of the Order of St. Basil the Great*—O.S.B.M.

[]—*Social Mission Sisters of Mariapoch*—S.M.S.

NECROLOGY

(No Deaths)

An asterisk (*) denotes an organization that has established tax-exempt status directly with the IRS and is not covered by the USCCB Group Ruling.

Byzantine Catholic Eparchy of Passaic

MAY THE LORD GIVE YOU PEACE

Most Reverend

WILLIAM C. SKURLA

Bishop of Passaic; ordained May 23, 1987; appointed Bishop of the Eparchy of Van Nuys February 19, 2002; consecrated and enthroned April 23, 2002; transferred to the Eparchy of Passaic December 6, 2007; enthroned January 29, 2008.

Chancery Office: 445 Lackawanna Ave., Woodland Park, NJ 07424. Tel: 973-890-7777; Fax: 973-890-7175.

Web: www.eparchyofpassaic.com

Email: bishop@dioceseofpassaic.org

ESTABLISHED JULY 31, 1963.

Embraces all Catholics of the Byzantine-Ruthenian Rite in the States of New Jersey, Connecticut, Delaware, District of Columbia, Florida, Georgia, Maine, Maryland, Massachusetts, New Hampshire, New York, North Carolina, Rhode Island, South Carolina, Vermont, Virginia and all Eastern Pennsylvania within the western boundaries of the Counties of Franklin, Juniata, Lycoming, Mifflin, Union and Tioga.

For legal titles of parishes and diocesan institutions, consult the Chancery Office.

STATISTICAL OVERVIEW

Personnel	
Bishop	1
Retired Bishops	1
Priests: Diocesan Active in Diocese	52
Priests: Diocesan Active Outside Diocese	4
Priests: Retired, Sick or Absent	14
Number of Diocesan Priests	70
Religious Priests in Diocese	13
Total Priests in Diocese	83
Extern Priests in Diocese	3
Permanent Deacons in Diocese	27
Total Brothers	1
Total Sisters	17
Parishes	
Parishes	84
With Resident Pastor:	
Resident Diocesan Priests	50
Resident Religious Priests	5
Without Resident Pastor:	
Administered by Priests	28
Administered by Deacons	1
Missions	4
Educational	
Catechesis/Religious Education:	
High School Students	184
Elementary Students	752
Total Students under Catholic Instruction	936
Vital Statistics	
Receptions into the Church:	
Infant Baptism Totals	124
Minor Baptism Totals	2
Adult Baptism Totals	5
Received into Full Communion	6
First Communions	131
Confirmations	126
Marriages:	
Catholic	37
Interfaith	11
Total Marriages	48
Deaths	478
Total Catholic Population	17,360

Former Bishops—Most Revs. STEPHEN J. KOCISKO, D.D., ord. March 30, 1941; appt. Titular Bishop of Theveste and Auxiliary of Exarchate of Pittsburgh, July 20, 1956; appt. First Eparch of Passaic, July 31, 1963; appt. Eparch of Pittsburgh, Dec. 21, 1967; installed March 5, 1968; elevated to Metropolitan Archbishop of Pittsburgh, Feb. 21, 1969; retired June 12, 1991; died March 7, 1995; MICHAEL J. DUDICK, D.D. (Retired), ord. Nov. 13, 1945; appt. Bishop of Passaic, Aug. 21, 1968; installed Oct. 24, 1968; retired Nov. 21, 1995; died May 30, 2007.; ANDREW PATAKI, J.C.L., D.D., ord. Feb. 24, 1952; appt. Titular Bishop of Tellmisus and Auxiliary Bishop of Passaic, May 30, 1983; cons. Aug. 23, 1983; appt. Bishop of Parma June 19, 1984; enthroned Aug. 16, 1984; transferred to Passaic Nov. 6, 1995; enthroned Feb. 8, 1996; retired & appt. Apostolic Administrator Dec. 6, 2007.

Protosyncellus-Vicar General and Moderator of the Curia—Most Rev. ANDREW PATAKI, J.C.L., D.D.

Syncellates and Protopresbyterates—

Susquehanna Valley Syncellate—

Syncellus—Very Rev. FRANCIS M. TWARDZIK, S.D.B., St. Mary's Church, 310 Mifflin Ave., Scranton, PA 18503. Tel: 570-342-8429.

Northern Pennsylvania/Northern New York Protopresbyterate—Rev. Msgr. JOHN T. SEKELLICK, J.C.L., Protopresbyter, Holy Ghost Church, 313 First St., Jessup, PA 18434. Tel: 570-489-2353.

Wyoming Valley Protopresbyterate—Very Rev. JAMES HAYER, Protopresbyter, St. Mary's Church, 695 N. Main St., Wilkes-Barre, PA 18705. Tel: 570-822-6028.

Central Pennsylvania Syncellate—

Syncellus—Very Rev. RONALD BARUSEFSKI, SS. Peter & Paul Church, 107 S. Fourth St., Minersville, PA 17954. Tel: 570-544-2074.

Mid-Pennsylvania Protopresbyterate—VACANT.

South Pennsylvania Protopresbyterate—Very Rev. PETER J. HOSAK, M.S., Protopresbyter, SS. Peter & Paul Church, 1140 Johnston Dr., Bethlehem, PA 18017-1934. Tel: 610-867-2322.

New Jersey Syncellate—

Syncellus—Very Rev. MICHAEL MONDIK, St. Thomas the Apostle Church, 1410 Church St., Rahway, 07065. Tel: 732-382-5300.

Northern New Jersey Protopresbyterate—Very Rev. MARCEL SZABO, Protopresbyter, St. Michael Cathedral, 96 First St., Passaic, 07055. Tel: 973-777-2553.

Central New Jersey Protopresbyterate—Very Rev. GREGORY J. NOGA, M.A., Protopresbyter, St. Mary Church, 411 Adeline St., Trenton, 08611. Tel: 609-394-5004.

New York-New England Syncellate—

Syncellus—Very Rev. ROBERT J. HOSPODAR, J.C.L., St. Mary Church, 246 E. 15th St., New York, NY 10003. Tel: 212-677-0516.

New York/New England Protopresbyterate—VACANT.

Middle States Syncellate—

Syncellus—Very Revs. JOHN G. BASARAB, M.A., Epiphany of Our Lord Church, 3410 Woodburn Rd., Annandale, VA 22003. Tel: 703-573-3986; CONAN H. TIMONEY, Ph.D., Protopresbyter, Patronage of Mother of God Church, 1260 Stevens Ave., Baltimore, MD 21227. Tel: 410-247-4936.

Southern States Syncellate—

Syncellus—Very Revs. PETER LICKMAN, St. Basil Church, 1475 N.E. 199th St., Miami, FL 33179. Tel: 305-651-0991; ROBERT EVANCHO, Protopresbyter, St. Therese Church, 4265 13th Ave. N., St. Petersburg, FL 33713. Tel: 727-323-4022.

Chancery Office—Eparchial Center, 445 Lackawanna Ave., Woodland Park, 07424. Tel: 973-890-7777; Fax: 973-890-7175. Office Hours: Mon.-Fri. 9-12 & 1-4.

Chancellor—Very Rev. ROBERT J. HOSPODAR, J.C.L.

Eparchial Finance Officer—Mr. MARK KOSCINSKI.

Eparchial Financial Controller—Mr. GEORGE ESCHENBACH.

Eparchial Finance Council—Mr. MARK KOSCINSKI; Mr. THOMAS P. DEVITA, Attorney at Law; Mr. BERT REIMAN; Mr. JERRY LUCAS, CPA; Mr. GEORGE ESCHENBACH.

Eparchial College of Consultors—Very Revs. FRANCIS M. TWARDZIK, S.D.B.; MICHAEL MONDIK; JOHN G. BASARAB, M.A.; PETER LICKMAN; RONALD BARUSEFSKI; ROBERT J. HOSPODAR, J.C.L., Sec.

Presbyteral Council—Most Rev. ANDREW PATAKI, J.C.L., D.D.; Very Revs. RONALD BARUSEFSKI; JOHN G. BASARAB, M.A.; ROBERT J. HOSPODAR, J.C.L.; PETER LICKMAN; MICHAEL MONDIK; CONAN H. TIMONEY, Ph.D.; FRANCIS M. TWARDZIK, S.D.B.; Rev. Msgr. JOHN T. SEKELLICK, J.C.L.; Revs. JOHN J. CIGAN, J.C.B.; PETER M. DONISH; EDWARD J. HIGGINS; GARY J. MENSINGER; SALVATORE A. PIGNATO; MICHAEL G. POPSON; CARMEN SCUDERI, O.F.M.; CHARLES YASTISHOCK; MICHAEL J. YURISTA.

Eparchial Tribunal—445 Lackawanna Ave., Woodland Park, 07424. Tel: 973-890-7777.

Judicial Vicar—Rev. Msgr. JOHN T. SEKELLICK, J.C.L.

Defender of the Bond—Very Rev. MICHAEL M. WALTERS, J.C.L.

Advocate—VACANT.

Promoter of Justice—Very Rev. ROBERT J. HOSPODAR, J.C.L.

Notary—Rev. GARY J. MENSINGER.

Commissions, Departments and Institutions

Building and Properties Commission—Very Rev. MICHAEL MONDIK, Chm.

Cemeteries Commission—VACANT.

Clergy Continued Education—VACANT.

Commission for Ecumenism—Rev. EDWARD J. HIGGINS, Chm.

Communications and Telecommunications—Very Rev. JAMES HAYER.

Evangelization—Rev. JOSEPH BERTHA, Ph.D., Chm.

Respect Life—Very Rev. ROBERT J. HOSPODAR, J.C.L., Dir.

Family Life—Rev. Msgr. JOHN T. SEKELLICK, J.C.L., Dir.

Eparchial Historian—Very Rev. ROBERT J. HOSPODAR, J.C.L.

Eparchial Liturgy and Art Commission—Very Rev. MICHAEL MONDIK, Chm.

Eparchial Music Commission—Mr. ELIAS ZAREVA, Member & Representative.

Eparchial Newspaper— "The Eastern Catholic Life" Very Rev. JAMES HAYER, Editor; Rev. G. SCOTT BOGHOSSIAN. Tel: 973-890-7794.

Office for Eastern Christian Formation (formerly: Office of Religious Education)—Very Rev. GREGORY J. NOGA, M.A., Dir.

Secretariat for Youth—Mrs. ANDREA BABILYA, Moderator.

Retirement Plan Board—Most Rev. ANDREW PATAKI, J.C.L., D.D.; Very Rev. ROBERT J. HOSPODAR, J.C.L., Chm.; Mr. MARK KOSCINSKI, Treas.; Revs. MICHAEL J. YURISTA; HARRY P. UNTEREINER, Sec.; JOSEPH BERTHA, Ph.D.; GARY J. MENSINGER; PETER M. DONISH; STEVEN SAFKO; MICHAEL KERESTES, Vice Chm.; SALVATORE A. PIGNATO; JOHN J. CIGAN, J.C.B.

Saint Nicholas Shrine - Carpathian Village—Rev. MICHAEL SALNICKY, Dir., Mailing Address: P.O. Box 616, Canadensis, PA 18325. Tel: 570-595-3265; Fax: 570-595-6177.

Vocations—Rev. SALVATORE A. PIGNATO.

Priesthood & Diaconate Formation Programs—Rev. EDWARD G. CIMBALA, D.Min., Dir.

Eastern Catholic Associates— Publication: "God With Us" *445 Lackawanna Ave., Woodland Park, 07424.*

CLERGY, PARISHES, MISSIONS AND PAROCHIAL SCHOOLS

STATE OF NEW JERSEY

PASSAIC, PASSAIC CO., ST. MICHAEL CATHEDRAL, [CEM] Very Rev. Marcel Szabo; Rev. Jody Baran.
Res.: 96 First St., 07055. Tel: 973-777-2553; Fax: 973-777-9474.
Chapel— 415 Lackawanna Ave., 07424. Tel: 973-256-0134; Fax: 973-777-9474.

BAYONNE, HUDSON CO., ST. JOHN THE BAPTIST Rev. Michael J. Yurista.
Res.: 15 E. 26th St., 07002. Tel: 201-339-1840; Fax: 201-339-6255.

CARTERET, MIDDLESEX CO., ST. ELIAS Rev. Edward Semko.
Res.: 42 Cooke Ave., 07008. Tel: 732-541-5213; Fax: 732-541-9637.

DUNELLEN, MIDDLESEX CO., ST. NICHOLAS, Administered from Nativity, East Brunswick, NJ.
Res.: 121 Madison Ave., 08812. Tel: 732-968-3337.

EAST BRUNSWICK, MIDDLESEX CO., NATIVITY OF OUR LORD Rev. Gregory Hosler, Admin.
Res.: 700 Old Bridge Tpke., 08816. Tel: 732-238-0865; Fax: 732-238-2950.

EDISON, MIDDLESEX CO., ST. NICHOLAS, Closed. For inquiries for parish records, please contact St. Nicholas, Perth Amboy, NJ.

ELIZABETH, UNION CO., SS. PETER AND PAUL, Administered from St. George's, Linden, NJ.
Res.: 316 First Ave., 07206. Tel: 908-353-7246; Fax: 908-353-7791.

FLANDERS, MORRIS CO., HOLY WISDOM, Administered from St. Michael Cathedral, Passaic, NJ.
Res.: 197 Emmans Rd., 07836. Tel: 973-584-0414.

HILLSBOROUGH TOWNSHIP, SOMERSET CO., ST. MARY'S Rev. Edward G. Cimbala.
Res.: 1900 Brooks Blvd., 08844. Tel: 908-725-0615; Fax: 908-725-9615.

JERSEY CITY, HUDSON CO., ST. MARY'S, Administered from St. John the Baptist, Bayonne, NJ.
Res.: 231 Pacific Ave., 07304. Tel: 201-333-2975.

LINDEN, UNION CO., ST. GEORGE'S Rev. G. Scott Boghossian.
Res.: 417 McCandless St., 07036. Tel: 908-486-6500; Fax: 908-486-6523.

MAHWAH, BERGEN CO., HOLY SPIRIT, Administered from St. Michael Cathedral, Passaic, NJ. , Mailing Address: c/o 96 First St., Passaic, 07055.
Church: Island Rd. at Church St., 07430.

NEW BRUNSWICK, MIDDLESEX CO., ST. JOSEPH Rev. Harry P. Untereiner.
Res.: 30 High St., 08901. Tel: 732-545-1686.

NEWARK, ESSEX CO., ST. GEORGE, Administered from St. John the Baptist, Bayonne, NJ.
Res.: 214 Warwick St., 07105. Tel: 973-589-7202; Fax: 973-589-7202.

PERTH AMBOY, MIDDLESEX CO.
1—ST. MICHAEL, [CEM] Deacon Mark Koscinski.
Res.: 401 Hall Ave., 08861. Tel: 732-826-0792; Fax: 732-826-7993.
2—ST. NICHOLAS, [CEM] Most Rev. Andrew Pataki, Admin.
Church: 320 Washington St., 08861. Tel: 732-442-0418.

PHILLIPSBURG, WARREN CO., SS. PETER AND PAUL Rev. Steven Safko.
Res.: 723 S. Main St., 08865. Tel: 908-454-5482; Fax: 908-859-6174.

RAHWAY, UNION CO., ST. THOMAS THE APOSTLE Very Rev. Michael Mondik.
Res.: 1410 Church St., 07065. Tel: 732-382-5300; Fax: 732-382-3265.

ROEBLING, BURLINGTON CO., ST. NICHOLAS, [CEM], Administered from St. Mary's, Trenton, NJ.
Res.: 191 Norman Ave., 08554. Tel: 609-499-0058; Fax: 609-499-9539.

SOMERSET, SOMERSET CO., SS. PETER AND PAUL Rev. Robert Kemeter.
Res.: 285 Hamilton St., 08873. Tel: 732-545-5500; Fax: 732-545-2525.

TOMS RIVER, OCEAN CO., OUR LADY OF PERPETUAL HELP Rev. Charles Yastishock.
Res.: 1937 Church Rd., 08753. Tel: 732-255-6272; Fax: 732-255-6272.

TRENTON, MERCER CO.
1—ST. MARY, [CEM] Very Rev. Gregory J. Noga.
Res.: 411 Adeline St., 08611. Tel: 609-394-5004; Fax: 609-394-5045.
2—ST. NICHOLAS, Closed. For parish records contact St. Mary of the Assumption, Trenton, NJ.

STATE OF CONNECTICUT

BRIDGEPORT, FAIRFIELD CO., HOLY TRINITY, Closed. For inquiries for parish records contact the chancery.

DANBURY, FAIRFIELD CO., ST. NICHOLAS Rev. Michael G. Popson.
Res.: 13 Pembroke Rd., CT 06811. Tel: 203-743-1106; Fax: 203-743-5326.

MERIDEN, NEW HAVEN CO., ST. NICHOLAS OF MYRA, Administered from St. Nicholas, Danbury, CT., Mailing Address: c/o 13 Pembroke Rd., Danbury, CT 06810.
Church: 89 Summer St., CT 06450. Tel: 203-743-1106.

NEW BRITAIN, HARTFORD CO., HOLY TRINITY, [CEM] Rev. Frank A. Hanincik, Admin.
Res.: 121 Beaver St., CT 06051. Tel: 860-229-2531; Fax: 860-827-0564.

TRUMBULL, FAIRFIELD CO., ST. JOHN THE BAPTIST Rev. Frank A. Hanincik.
Res.: 100 St. John's Dr., CT 06611. Tel: 203-377-5967; Fax: 203-377-5968.

STATE OF FLORIDA

COCONUT CREEK, BROWARD CO., OUR LADY OF THE SIGN Rev. Michael Kane.
Res.: 7311 Lyons Rd., FL 33073. Tel: 954-429-0056.

FORT PIERCE, PORT ST. LUCIE CO., SS. CYRIL AND METHODIUS Rev. Michael Sopoliga, Admin.
Res.: Tel: 772-595-8862.
Church: 1002 Bahama Ave., FL 34982. Tel: 772-595-1021.

JACKSONVILLE, DUVAL CO., PROTECTION OF THE MOTHER OF GOD, Closed. For parish records, contact Holy Dormition, Ormond Beach, FL.

LAKE WORTH, DUVAL CO., HOLY APOSTLES, Closed. For parish records contact St. Basil, Miami, FL.

MIAMI, DADE CO., ST. BASIL (1966) Very Rev. Peter Lickman.
Res.: 1475 N.E. 199 St., FL 33179-5162. Tel: 305-651-0991; Fax: 305-651-4902.

NEW PORT RICHEY, PASCO CO., ST. ANNE'S Rev. Michael Krulak.
Church: 7120 Massachusetts Ave., FL 34653. Tel: 727-849-1190.

NORTH FORT MYERS, LEE CO., ALL SAINTS BYZANTINE CATHOLIC, Administered from St. Basil's, Miami, FL., Mailing Address: c/o 1475 N.E. 199 St., Miami, FL 33179. Tel: 305-651-0991.
Res.: 10291 Bayshore Rd., FL 33917. Tel: 239-543-6363; Fax: 239-543-6363.

ORLANDO, ORANGE CO., ST. NICHOLAS OF MYRA Rev. Salvatore A. Pignato.
Res.: 5135 Sand Lake Rd., FL 32819. Tel: 407-351-0133; Fax: 407-351-0133.

ORMOND BEACH, VOLUSIA CO., HOLY DORMITION, Administered from St. Nicholas of Myra, Orlando, FL. Rev. Vincent M. Brady.
Mailing Address: 5135 Sand Lake Rd., Orlando, FL 32819.
Church: 17 Buckskin Ln., FL 32174. Tel: 407-351-0133; Fax: 407-351-0133.

ST. PETERSBURG, PINELLAS CO., ST. THERESE Very Rev. Robert Evancho.
Res.: 4236 13th Ave. N., Saint Petersburg, FL 33713. Tel: 727-323-4022; Fax: 727-323-8351.
Convent—Sisters of Saint Basil the Great, 1200 37th St. N., FL 33713. Tel: 727-322-0003.

STATE OF GEORGIA

ROSWELL, FULTON CO., EPIPHANY BYZANTINE CHURCH Rev. Philip P. Scott.
Res.: 2030 Old Alabama Rd., GA 30076. Tel: 770-993-0973; Fax: 770-993-2419.

STATE OF MARYLAND

BALTIMORE, BALTIMORE CO., PATRONAGE OF THE MOTHER OF GOD Very Rev. Conan H. Timoney.
Church: 1260 Stevens Ave., MD 21227. Tel: 410-247-4936; Fax: 410-247-1542.
Mission—St. Francis Abingdon, Harford Co., MD.
Mission—St. Ann's Hagerstown, Washington Co., MD.

BELTSVILLE, PRINCE GEORGE'S CO., ST. GREGORY OF NYSSA Rev. Michael Kerestes.
Res.: 12420 Old Gunpowder Rd. Spur, MD 20705. Tel: 301-953-9323; Fax: 301-953-1529.

STATE OF MASSACHUSETTS

SOUTH HADLEY, HAMPSHIRE CO., ST. MICHAEL'S, Closed. For parish records contact Holy Trinity, New Britain, CT.

STATE OF NEW YORK

AMHERST, ERIE CO., ST. STEPHEN'S, Closed. For inquiries for parish records contact the chancery.

BINGHAMTON, BROOME CO., HOLY SPIRIT, [CEM] Rev. John J. Cigan, J.C.B.
Res.: 360 Clinton St., NY 13905. Tel: 607-797-2122; Fax: 607-797-2167.

BROOKLYN, KINGS CO., ST. ELIAS, Closed. For inquiries for parish records please contact St. Mary's, New York., Mailing Address: c/o 246 E. 15th St., New York, NY 10003.

ENDICOTT, BROOME CO., SS. PETER AND PAUL'S, [CEM], Administered from Holy Spirit, Binghamton, NY., Mailing Address: c/o 360 Clinton St., Binghamton, NY 13905.
Church: 106 N. Rogers Ave., NY 13763. Tel: 607-797-2122.

GRANVILLE, WASHINGTON CO., SS. PETER AND PAUL, [CEM], Administered from St. Mary's, New York, NY., Mailing Address: c/o 246 E. 15th St., New York, NY 10003. Tel: 212-677-0516. In Res., Rev. Harold R. Stockert.
Church: 2 Park Ave., NY 12832.

NEW YORK, NEW YORK CO.
1—EXALTATION OF HOLY CROSS, Administered from St. Mary's, New York, NY., Mailing Address: 246 E. 15th St., NY 10003.
Church: 323 E. 82nd St., NY 10028. Tel: 914-681-0659.
2—ST. MARY'S Very Rev. Robert J. Hospodar.
Res.: 246 E. 15th St., NY 10003. Tel: 212-677-0516; Fax: 212-260-6071.

OLEAN, CATTARAGUS CO., ST. MARY'S Very Rev. Francis M. Twardzik, S.D.B., Admin.
Church: 718 Fountain St., NY 14760. Tel: 716-688-9290.

PEEKSKILL, WESTCHESTER CO., SS. PETER AND PAUL Rev. Msgr. Robert Senetsky.
Res.: 705 Shenandoah Ave., NY 10566. Tel: 914-737-8249; Fax: 914-737-8438.

SMITHTOWN, SUFFOLK CO., RESURRECTION, [CEM] Rev. John S. Custer.
Res.: 225 Ellison Ave., Westbury, NY 11590. Tel: 631-759-6083.

WESTBURY, NASSAU CO., ST. ANDREW THE APOSTLE Rev. John S. Custer, Admin.
Church: 275 Ellison Ave., NY 11590. Tel: 631-759-6083.

WHITE PLAINS, WESTCHESTER CO., ST. NICHOLAS OF MYRA Very Rev. Robert J. Hospodar, Admin.
Res. & Church: 768 North St., NY 10605. Tel: 914-681-0659; Fax: 914-681-0238.

YONKERS, WESTCHESTER CO., ST. NICHOLAS OF MYRA, Administered from St. Nicholas of Myra, White Plains, NY., Mailing Address: 768 North St., White Plains, NY 10605.
Church: 75 Ash St., NY 10701. Tel: 914-681-0659.

STATE OF NORTH CAROLINA

CARY, WAKE CO., SS. CYRIL & METHODIUS BYZANTINE CATHOLIC Rev. Richard Rohrer.
Res.: 2510 Piney Plains Rd., NC 27518. Tel: 919-851-9266; Fax: 919-233-3997.

STATE OF PENNSYLVANIA

ALLENTOWN, LEHIGH CO.
1—ST. ANDREW THE APOSTLE, Closed. For parish records, contact St. Michael, Allentown.
2—ST. MICHAEL Rev. J. Michael Venditti.
Res.: 156 Green St., PA 18102. Tel: 610-432-6773; Fax: 610-432-6773.

BEAVER MEADOWS, CARBON CO., SS. PETER AND PAUL, [CEM] Rev. James J. Demko.
Res.: P.O. Box 206, PA 18216. Tel: 570-455-1442; Fax: 570-455-7144.

BETHLEHEM, NORTHAMPTON CO., SS. PETER AND PAUL Very Rev. Peter J. Hosak.
Res.: 1140 Johnston Dr., PA 18017. Tel: 610-867-2322; Fax: 610-867-7274.

BROCKTON, SCHUYLKILL CO., ST. MARY'S, [CEM], Administered from St. Mary's, Mahanoy City, PA., Mailing Address: c/o 621 Mahanoy Ave., Mahanoy City, PA 17948.
Church: Green St., PA 17925.

CLARKS SUMMIT, LACKAWANNA CO., TRANSFIGURATION, Closed. For parish records contact St. Mary, Scranton, PA.

COATESVILLE, CHESTER CO., ST. MARY'S, Administered from St. Michael, Mont Clare, PA.
Church: 88 Gap Rd., PA 19320.

DUNMORE, LACKAWANNA CO., ST. MICHAEL, [CEM] Rev. Robert W. Lozinski, C.S.C.
Res.: 511 E. Drinker St., PA 18512. Tel: 570-344-2521; Fax: 570-344-4535.

FOREST CITY, SUSQUEHANNA CO., ST. JOHN THE BAPTIST, [CEM], Administered from Holy Ghost, Jessup, PA., Mailing Address: c/o 313 First Ave., Jessup, PA 18434.
Church: 306 Susquehanna St., PA 18421.

FREELAND, LUZERNE CO., ST. MARY'S, [CEM] Rev. Msgr. Nicholas I. Puhak.
Res.: 643 Fern St., PA 18224. Tel: 570-636-0700; Fax: 570-636-1955.

GLEN LYON, LUZERNE CO., ST. MICHAEL, Closed. For parish records contact St. Mary's, Kingston, PA.
Church: 47 Spring St., PA 18617.

HARRISBURG, DAUPHIN CO., ST. ANN Rev. Leonard Martin, S.J.
Res.: 5408 Locust Ln., PA 17109. Tel: 717-652-1415; Fax: 717-652-5471.

HAZLETON, LUZERNE CO.
1—ST. JOHN THE BAPTIST CHURCH, [CEM] Rev. Carmen Scuderi, O.F.M.
Res.: 5 E. 20th St., PA 18201. Tel: 570-454-1142; Fax: 570-454-6120.
2—ST. MARY'S Rev. Peter M. Donish.
Res. & Church: 227 E. Beech St., PA 18201. Tel: 570-455-3232; Fax: 570-455-5654.

HILLTOWN, BUCKS CO., BYZANTINE CATHOLIC MISSION OF BUCKS COUNTY, PA, Closed. For mission records contact Holy Ghost, Philadelphia, PA.

JESSUP, LACKAWANNA CO., HOLY GHOST, [CEM] Rev. Msgr. John T. Sekellick.
Res.: 313 First Ave., PA 18434. Tel: 570-489-2353; Fax: 570-489-7049.

KINGSTON, LUZERNE CO., ST. MARY'S, [CEM] Rev. Mykhaylo Prodanets.
Res.: 321 Chestnut Ave., PA 18704. Tel: 570-287-0282; Fax: 570-283-0464.

LANSFORD, CARBON CO., ST. JOHN THE BAPTIST, [CEM] Rev. Ronald Hatton.
Church: 116 E. Bertsch St., PA 18232. Tel: 570-645-2640; Fax: 570-645-8718.

LEVITTOWN, BUCKS CO., OUR LADY OF PERPETUAL HELP Rev. Myron M. Badnerosky.
Res.: 1787 Woodburne Rd., PA 19056. Tel: 215-945-5122.

LOPEZ, SULLIVAN CO., SS. PETER AND PAUL, [CEM] Closed. For inquiries for parish records please contact St. Mary's, Scranton, PA.

MAHANOY CITY, SCHUYLKILL CO., ST. MARY'S, [CEM] Rev. James Carroll, O.F.M., Admin.
Res.: 621 W. Mahanoy Ave., PA 17948. Tel: 570-773-2631.

MCADOO, SCHUYLKILL CO., ST. MICHAEL, [CEM] Rev. George A. Bujnak.
Res.: 17 E. Blaine St., PA 18237. Tel: 570-929-1062; Fax: 570-929-3239.

MINERSVILLE, SCHUYLKILL CO., SS. PETER AND PAUL, [CEM] Very Rev. Ronald Barusefski.
Res.: 107 S. Fourth St., PA 17954. Tel: 570-544-2074; Fax: 570-544-2074.

MONT CLARE, MONTGOMERY CO., ST. MICHAEL, [CEM] Rev. James Badeaux.
Church: 203 Jacob St., PA 19453. Tel: 610-933-2819; Fax: 610-935-9460.

NANTICOKE, LUZERNE CO., ST. MARY'S, Closed. (Hanover) For inquiries for parish records contact St. John's, Wilkes-Barre, PA.

NESQUEHONING, CARBON CO., ST. MARY'S, [CEM], Administered from St. John the Baptist, Lansford, PA.
Church: 141 W. High St., PA 18240.

OLD FORGE, LACKAWANNA CO., ST. NICHOLAS, [CEM] Rev. Gary J. Mensinger.
Res.: 140 Church St., PA 18518. Tel: 570-457-3042; Fax: 570-457-1906.

PALMERTON, CARBON CO., SS. PETER AND PAUL, Administered from St. Michael's, Allentown, PA., Mailing Address: c/o 156 Green St., Allentown, PA 18102.
Church: 142 Lafayette Ave., PA 18071.

PHILADELPHIA, PHILADELPHIA CO.
1—HOLY GHOST Rev. Edward J. Higgins.
Res.: 2310 S. 24th St., PA 19145. Tel: 215-334-5129; Fax: 215-334-1797.
2—HOLY TRINITY, Administered from Holy Ghost, Philadelphia, PA., Mailing Address: c/o 2310 S. 24th St., PA 19145.
Church: 6801 N. 10th St., PA 19126. Tel: 215-548-2837.

PITTSTON, LUZERNE CO., ST. MICHAEL, [CEM] Rev. Joseph Bertha.
Res.: 205 N. Main St., PA 18640. Tel: 570-654-4564; Fax: 570-654-5349.

POCONO SUMMIT, MONROE CO., ST. NICHOLAS Rev. Michael Salnicky, Admin.
Rte. 940 & Commerce St., P.O. Box 515, PA 18346. Tel: 570-839-8090; Fax: 570-595-6177.

POTTSTOWN, MONTGOMERY CO., ST. JOHN THE BAPTIST, [CEM] Rev. Nicholas DeProspero.
Res.: 301 Cherry St., PA 19464. Tel: 610-326-1877; Fax: 610-326-1890.

ST. CLAIR, SCHUYLKILL CO., ST. MARY'S, [CEM], Administered from SS. Peter and Paul, Minersville, PA., Mailing Address: c/o 107 S. 4th St., Minersville, PA 17954.
Church: 131 S. Morris St., PA 17970.

SCRANTON, LACKAWANNA CO.
1—ST. JOHN THE BAPTIST, [CEM], Administered from St. Mary's, Scranton, PA., Mailing Address: c/o 310 Mifflin Ave., PA 18503.
Church: 310 Broadway, PA 18505.
2—ST. MARY'S, [CEM] Very Rev. Francis M. Twardzik, S.D.B.
Res.: 310 Mifflin Ave., PA 18503. Tel: 570-342-8429; Fax: 570-342-6773.

SHEPPTON, SCHUYLKILL CO., ST. MARY'S, [CEM], Administered from SS. Peter and Paul, Beaver Meadows., Mailing Address: c/o P.O. Box 206, Beaver Meadows, PA 18216.

SWOYERSVILLE, LUZERNE CO., ST. NICHOLAS, [CEM], Administered from St. Michael, Pittston, PA., Mailing Address: c/o 205 N. Main St., Pittston, PA 18640.
Church: 271 Tripp St., PA 18704.

TAYLOR, LACKAWANNA CO., ST. MARY'S, [CEM], Administered from St. Nicholas, Old Forge., Mailing Address: c/o 140 Church St., Old Forge, PA 18518.
Church: 700 Oak St., PA 18517.

WILKES-BARRE, LUZERNE CO.
1—ST. JOHN'S, Administered from St. Mary's, Kingston, PA.
Res.: 526 Church St., PA 18702. Tel: 570-825-4338; Fax: 570-825-0786.
2—ST. MARY'S, [CEM] Very Rev. James Hayer.
Res.: 695 N. Main St., PA 18705. Tel: 570-822-6028; Fax: 570-822-5423.

WILLIAMSTOWN, DAUPHIN CO., HOLY SPIRIT, [CEM] Closed. For inquiries for parish records contact SS. Peter and Paul, Minersville, PA.

STATE OF VIRGINIA

ANNANDALE, FAIRFAX CO., EPIPHANY OF OUR LORD Very Rev. John G. Basarab.
3410 Woodburn Rd., VA 22003. Tel: 703-573-3986; Fax: 703-573-0344.
Mission—Mother of God Community School 20501 Goshen Rd., Gaithersburg, MD 20879.

WILLIAMSBURG, YORK CO., ASCENSION OF OUR LORD Rev. Alex Shuter.
Mailing Address: P.O. Box 5096, VA 23188. Tel: 757-253-5641; Fax: 757-253-9423.
Church: 114 Palace Ln., VA 23185. Tel: 757-220-8098.
Mission—Our Lady of Perpetual Help 216 S. Parliament Dr., Virginia Beach, Virginia Beach Co., VA 23462. Tel: 757-456-0809.

Special or Other Diocesan Assignment:
Rev.—
DeFronzo, Anthony P.

On Duty Outside Diocese:
Revs.—
Fulton, Eugene, Larchmont Trinity Retreat, One Pryer Manor Rd., Larchmont, NY 10538. Tel: 914-632-3743
Hamperzonian, Jerry, Chap., VA Medical Center, 3350 Lajolla Village Dr., San Diego, CA 92161. Tel: 619-582-5722
Siroki, David

Leave of Absence:
Revs.—
Kapron, Alan
Malitz, George M.
Mitchko, James
Woytek, Robert

Retired:
Revs.—
Bitsko, Daniel J.
Brown, Charles, M.D., Santa Teresita del Nino Jesus, 2 Poniente #2714, Puebla CP 72140 Mexico. Tel: 011-22-48-38-78
Drucker, James N.
Eles, Joseph, 150 Horizons E., Apt. 305, Boynton Beach, FL 33435. Tel: 407-731-2682
Gera, Francis
Kraynak, Nicholas, 328 S. Belle Vista Ave., Youngstown, OH 44509.
Mohrbacher, Austin
Petruska, Christopher, 15544 Bellflower Blvd., Apt. C, Bellflower, CA 90706.
Skurla, Robert J., c/o Little Sisters of the Poor, 110-30 221 St., Queen of Peace Rm. 215, Queens Village, NY 11429.
Tigyer, Paul, P.O. Box 658, Hamlin, PA 18427. Tel: 717-689-2153
Zeyack, John, S.T.L., 53 Blue Ridge Dr., Brick, 08724.

Permanent Deacons:
Behrens, Robert
Daddona, Nicholas
Dunlop, Richard
Erdek, Michael A.
Foran, Lawrence
Frey, Edward
Guze, John G.
Hook, Thomas
Kolesar, Verlan
Koscinski, Mark
Kotlar, Anthony, (Leave of Absence)
Kubik, Alexander
Laskowski, Charles J.
McDonnell, Gerald E.
Opalka, Michael
Pataki, Michael
Pekarik, Elmer
Russo, Stephen
Senoyuit, Michael, III
Soroka, Basil
Sotack, Nicholas
Szewczyk, William
Thomas, David
Tizio, William, (Retired)
Vanisko, Thomas L.
Wolf, Daniel
Worlinsky, Lawrence

INSTITUTIONS LOCATED IN THE DIOCESE

[A] MONASTERIES

MATAWAN. *Basilian Fathers of Mariapoch*, 360 Monastery Ln., 07747-9703. Tel: 732-566-8445; Fax: 732-566-8762. Very Rev. Joseph J. Erdei, O.S.B.M., Supr.; Rev. Lawrence Robert Wolf, O.S.B.M.

SYBERTSVILLE, PA. *Holy Dormition Friary*, P.O. Box 270, PA 18251. Tel: 570-788-1212; Fax: 570-788-2431. Revs. Carmen Scuderi, O.F.M.; Anthony Skurla, O.F.M.; James Carroll, O.F.M.; Paul Guthrie, O.F.M.; Laurian Janicki, O.F.M., Guardian; Jerome Wolbert, O.F.M.; Bro. Augustine Paulik, O.F.M.

[B] CONVENTS AND RESIDENCES FOR SISTERS

SUGARLOAF, PA. *Holy Annunciation Monastery*, 403 W. County Rd., PA 18249. Tel: 570-788-1205; Fax: 570-788-3329. Discalced Carmelite Nuns of the Byzantine Rite Nuns with Solemn Vows 13.

WILKES-BARRE, PA. *Sisters of Saint Basil The Great Saint Mary of the Assumption Convent*, 522 Madison St., Wilkes Barre, PA 18705. Tel: 570-824-3973.

[C] SHRINES AND SPIRITUAL RENEWAL CENTERS

CANADENSIS, PA. *Carpathian Village* RR3, Box 3180, Snow Hill Rd., Cresco, PA 18326. Tel: 570-595-3265; Fax: 570-595-6177. Rev. Michael Salnicky, Dir.

[D] MISCELLANEOUS

WEST PATERSON. *Eastern Catholic Associates*, 445 Lackawanna Ave., 07424. Tel: 973-890-7777; Fax: 973-890-7175.

God with Us Publications Most Revs. Basil Schott, Pres.; John M. Kudrick, Vice Pres.; Richard S. Seminack, Sec.; William Charles Skurla, Registered Agent.

RELIGIOUS INSTITUTES OF MEN REPRESENTED IN THE DIOCESE

For further details refer to the corresponding bracketed number in the Religious Institutes of Men or Women section.

[0520]—*Franciscan Friars*—O.F.M.

[0180]—*Order of St. Basil the Great*—O.S.B.M.

RELIGIOUS INSTITUTES OF WOMEN REPRESENTED IN THE DIOCESE

[0420]—*Discalced Carmelite Nuns (Byzantine Rite)*—O.C.D.

[3730]—*Sisters of the Order of St. Basil the Great*—O.S.B.M.

NECROLOGY

(No Deaths)

An asterisk (*) denotes an organization that has established tax-exempt status directly with the IRS and is not covered by the USCCB Group Ruling.

Metropolitan Archeparchy of Philadelphia Ukrainian

Most Reverend

STEFAN SOROKA

Archbishop of Philadelphia Ukrainian; ordained June 13, 1982; appointed Auxiliary Bishop of Winnipeg (Ukrainian) March 29, 1996; ordained Auxiliary Bishop of Winnipeg (Ukrainian) June 13, 1996; appointed Archbishop of Philadelphia Ukrainian November 29, 2000; installed Archbishop of Philadelphia Ukrainian February 27, 2001.

Most Reverend

JOHN BURA

Auxiliary Bishop of Philadelphia Ukrainian; ordained February 14, 1971; appointed Auxiliary Bishop of Philadelphia Ukrainian and Titular Bishop of Limisa January 3, 2006; ordained February 21, 2006.

Most Reverend

STEPHEN SULYK

Archbishop Emeritus of Philadelphia Ukrainian; ordained June 14, 1952; appointed Archbishop of Philadelphia Ukrainian December 29, 1980; ordained March 1, 1981; retired November 29, 2000.

ESTABLISHED MAY 28, 1913.

The jurisdiction of the Metropolitan Archdiocese of Philadelphia includes the District of Columbia, the States of Virginia, Maryland, Delaware, New Jersey and eastern Pennsylvania to the eastern boundaries of the following Counties: Potter, Clinton, Center, Mifflin, Huntington and Fulton. With regard to persons, his subjects are all Catholics of the Byzantine Rite: 1. Who immigrated to this country from Galicia, Bucovina and other Ukrainian provinces; 2. Who descend from such persons (can. 755); 3. Women married to men referable to 1. and 2. if they comply with can. 98, n. 4; 4. Who in accordance with can. 98, n. 3 changed their Rite; 5. Converts to the Catholic Church of the Byzantine Rite; 6. And in fact all other Catholics of the Byzantine Rite who are attached to parishes subject to the jurisdiction of the Archbishop.

For legal titles of parishes and archdiocesan institutions, consult the Chancery Office.

Chancery Office: 827 N. Franklin St., Philadelphia, PA 19123-2097. Tel: 215-627-0143; Fax: 215-627-0377.

Email: ukmet@catholic.org

STATISTICAL OVERVIEW

Personnel	
Archbishops	1
Retired Archbishops	1
Auxiliary Bishops	1
Priests: Diocesan Active in Diocese	39
Priests: Retired, Sick or Absent	8
Number of Diocesan Priests	47
Religious Priests in Diocese	5
Total Priests in Diocese	52
Extern Priests in Diocese	8
Ordinations:	
Diocesan Priests	1
Transitional Deacons	1
Permanent Deacons	2
Permanent Deacons in Diocese	7
Total Sisters	55
Parishes	
Parishes	66
With Resident Pastor:	
Resident Diocesan Priests	42
Resident Religious Priests	2
Without Resident Pastor:	
Administered by Priests	22
Professional Ministry Personnel:	
Sisters	33
Lay Ministers	2
Welfare	
Homes for the Aged	2
Total Assisted	280
Educational	
Seminaries, Diocesan	1
Students from This Diocese	2
Students from Other Diocese	12
Diocesan Students in Other Seminaries	1
Total Seminarians	3
Colleges and Universities	1
Total Students	969
High Schools, Private	1
Total Students	380
Elementary Schools, Diocesan and Parish	4
Total Students	674
Catechesis/Religious Education:	
High School Students	120
Elementary Students	509
Total Students under Catholic Instruction	2,655
Teachers in the Diocese:	
Priests	1
Sisters	6
Lay Teachers	64
Vital Statistics	
Receptions into the Church:	
Infant Baptism Totals	222
Minor Baptism Totals	5
Adult Baptism Totals	7
Received into Full Communion	52
First Communions	217
Confirmations	250
Marriages:	
Catholic	55
Interfaith	14
Total Marriages	69
Deaths	417
Total Catholic Population	14,980

Former Bishops—Most Revs. STEPHEN SOTER ORTYNSKY, O.S.B.M., D.D., First Ukrainian Catholic Bishop of the United States; ord. July 18, 1891; cons. May 12, 1907; died March 24, 1916; CONSTANTINE BOHACHEVSKY, D.D., S.T.D., appt. Bishop in the United States, May 20, 1924; appt. Metropolitan Archbishop of the Philadelphia Archeparchy, Byzantine Rite, Aug. 6, 1958; cons. June 15, 1924; died Jan. 6, 1961; AMBROSE SENYSHYN, O.S.B.M., D.D., appt. Auxiliary Bishop to the Philadelphia Bishop, July 6, 1942; appt. Exarch of Stamford, July 20, 1956; appt. Eparch of Stamford, Nov. 1, 1958; appt. Metropolitan Archbishop of Philadelphia, Aug. 14, 1961; died Sept. 11, 1976; JOSEPH M. SCHMONDIUK, D.D., appt. Titular Bishop of Zeugma and Auxiliary of the Archeparchy of Philadelphia, July 20, 1956; cons. Nov. 8, 1956; transferred to the Diocese of Stamford See, Nov. 9, 1961; appt. Metropolitan Archbishop of Philadelphia, Oct. 1, 1977; died Dec. 25, 1978; His Eminence MYROSLAV CARDINAL LUBACHIVSKY, D.D., appt. Metropolitan Archbishop of Philadelphia, Sept. 21, 1979; appt. Apostolic Administrator of Philadelphia, Oct. 3, 1979; cons. in Rome, Nov. 12, 1979; named Coadjutor Major Archbishop of Lviw, March 24, 1980; transferred to Rome; Assumed position of Major Archbishop of Lviw, Sept. 7, 1984. Created Cardinal, May 25, 1985; died Dec. 14, 2000; Most Rev. STEPHEN SULYK, D.D. (Retired), appt. Archbishop of Philadelphia for Ukrainians and Metropolitan of the Ukrainian Catholic Church in the USA, Dec. 29, 1980; ord. March 1, 1981; retired Nov. 29, 2000.

Protosyncellus—Rev. Msgr. PETER D. WASLO, J.C.L.

Chancellor—Rev. Msgr. PETER D. WASLO, J.C.L. Tel: 215-627-0143. Email: chancellor@catholic.org.

Vice Chancellor—Very Rev. ANDRIY RABIY, J.C.L.

Secretary to the Archbishop—Sr. LYDIA SAWKA, O.S.B.M.

Chancery Office—827 N. Franklin St., Philadelphia, 19123-2097. Tel: 215-627-0143; Fax: 215-627-0377.

College of Archeparchial Consultors—Rev. Msgr. PETER D. WASLO, J.C.L.; Very Rev. ANDRIY RABIY, J.C.L.; Rev. Archpriest JOHN M. FIELDS; Very Revs. IVAN DEMKIV; ROBERT HITCHENS; JOSEPH SZUPA.

Presbyteral Council—Rev. Msgr. PETER D. WASLO, J.C.L.; Very Revs. ANDRIY RABIY, J.C.L.; IVAN DEMKIV; ROBERT HITCHENS; Very Rev. Archpriest DANIEL TROYAN; Very Rev. VOLODYMYR POPYK; Very Rev. Archpriest DANIEL GUROVICH; Very Revs. NESTOR IWASIW; ROMAN PITULA; MARK FESNIAK; WASYL KHARUK; JOHN CIURPITA; JOSEPH SZUPA; Rev. Archpriest JOHN M. FIELDS.

Archeparchial Corporation—Most Rev. STEFAN SOROKA, D.D., Ph.D., Pres.; JOHN DROZD, Treas.; Rev. Msgr. PETER D. WASLO, J.C.L., Sec.

Archdiocesan Tribunal—827 N. Franklin St., Philadelphia, 19123. Tel: 215-627-0143. Email: metropolitantribunal@catholic.org.

Judicial Vicar—Rev. Msgr. PETER D. WASLO, J.C.L.

Adjunct Judicial Vicars—Very Rev. Archpriest DANIEL GUROVICH; Revs. PAUL LUNIW, Eparchy of Stamford; RICHARD WHETSTONE, Archeparchy of Pittsburgh.

Procurator/Advocate—Very Revs. JOSEPH SZUPA; NESTOR IWASIW.

Auditor—Very Rev. ANDRIY RABIY, J.C.L.

Defender of the Bond—Rev. MYKOLA IVANOV, Ukraine.

Notary—GLORIA LEINART.

Director of Evangelization—Very Rev. Archpriest DANIEL TROYAN.

Archeparchial Council for Economic Affairs—Most Rev. STEFAN SOROKA, D.D., Ph.D.; Rev. Msgr. PETER D. WASLO, J.C.L.; JOHN DROZD; HELEN CHELOC; LEONARD MAZUR; ANDREW FYLYPOWYCH; KEN HUTCHINS; ALBERT SCHULZE; Sr. LYDIA SAWKA, O.S.B.M., Sec.

Financial Officer—JOHN DROZD.

Protopresbyters (Deans)—Rev. Msgr. RONALD P. POPIVCHAK, Ph.D., Lehigh-Schuylkill Valley; Very Revs. IVAN DEMKIV, Philadelphia; JOHN SENIW, North Anthracite; JOSEPH SZUPA, New Jersey; Rev. Archpriest JOHN M. FIELDS, South Anthracite; Very Rev. TARAS LONCHYNA, Washington.

Diocesan Offices and Directors

Youth Ministry—VACANT, Dir.

Pro-Life and Family Ministry—Very Rev. TARAS LONCHYNA.

Apostolate—Most Rev. STEFAN SOROKA, D.D., Ph.D.; JOHN DROZD.

Cemeteries—TARAS HANKEWYCH.

Censor—Rev. Msgr. RONALD P. POPIVCHAK, Ph.D.

Ecumenical Relations—Rev. Msgr. PETER D. WASLO, J.C.L.

Insurance Commission—JOHN DROZD.

Director of Communication—Rev. Msgr. PETER D. WASLO, J.C.L. Email: comm@ukrarcheparchy.us.

The Way - Online Newspaper—Web: www.ukrarcheparchy.us. Email: theway@ukrarcheparchy.us. TERESA SIWAK, Editor; Rev. IHOR ROYIK, Asst. Editor; Rev. Msgr. PETER D. WASLO, J.C.L.

Archdiocesan Bulletin—Office: 827 N. Franklin St., Philaldephia, 19123. Rev. Msgr. PETER D. WASLO, J.C.L.; Very Rev. ANDRIY RABIY, J.C.L.

Priests Beneficial Fund—Most Rev. STEFAN SOROKA, D.D., Ph.D., Pres.; Very Rev. Archpriest DANIEL GUROVICH, Sec. & Treas. Board Members: Rev. Archpriests MICHAEL HUTSKO; JOHN M. FIELDS; Very Rev. JOHN SENIW; Rev. Msgr. JAMES T. MELNIC; Very Rev. WASYL KHARUK, Alternate Member.

Office of Vocations—Rev. Msgr. PETER D. WASLO, J.C.L., Dir. Tel: 202-529-1177, Ext. 115. Email: ukrvocations@catholic.org.

Archeparchial Seminary Advisory and Admissions Board—Most Rev. STEFAN SOROKA, D.D., Ph.D.; Very Revs. ROBERT HITCHENS; NESTOR IWASIW; ANDRIY RABIY, J.C.L.

Sheptytsky Educational Center—Most Rev. STEFAN SOROKA, D.D., Ph.D.

Evangelization Center—Very Rev. Archpriest DANIEL TROYAN.

Department of Religious Education—Very Rev. VOLODYMYR POPYK, Dir. Email: ukrcatecheticaloffice@catholic.org.

Byzantine Church Supplies—Mrs. MYROSLAVA DEMKIV. Tel: 215-627-0660. Email: supplies@ukrarcheparchy.us.

Archeparchial Museum— Treasury of Faith. Tel: 215-627-3389. Email: tofmuseum@catholic.org. Sisters NADIA BARANICK, M.S.M.G.; EVHENIA PRUSNAY, M.S.M.G.; TIMOTHEA KONYU, M.S.M.G.; Very Rev. Archpriest DANIEL TROYAN.

Victim Assistance Coordinator—Very Rev. ANDRIY RABIY, J.C.L. Tel: 215-873-6162. Email: ukrchildprotection@catholic.org.

Deacon Formation—Deacon PAUL MAKAR.

CLERGY, PARISHES, MISSIONS AND PAROCHIAL SCHOOLS

CITY OF PHILADELPHIA

(PHILADELPHIA COUNTY)

1—IMMACULATE CONCEPTION OF BLESSED VIRGIN MARY, CATHEDRAL, [CEM] Very Rev. Ivan Demkiv; Rev. Myron Myronyuk (Ukraine).
Res.: 833 N. Franklin St., 19123. Tel: 215-922-2845; Fax: 215-922-4635. Email: cathedralonfranklin@comcast.net. Web: www.ukrcathedral.com.
Mission—St. Nicholas 871 N. 24th St., Philadelphia Co. 19130. Tel: 215-769-3863; Fax: 215-769-2018.
Chapel—Missionary Sisters of Mother God Convent Chapel—Chapel of St. Joseph of Arimathea and the Holy Myrrh-Bearing Women

2—ST. ANDREW, Closed. For inquiries for parish records contact the Cathedral of the Immaculate Conception, Philadelphia.

3—ANNUNCIATION OF THE B.V.M. Rev. Ihor Royik.
Res.: 1206 Valley Rd., Melrose Park, 19027-3035. Tel: 215-635-1627; Fax: 215-635-9203. Email: a.b.v.m@comcast.net.
Church: 1204 Valley Rd., Melrose Park, 19027-3035.

4—CHRIST THE KING (1949) Rev. Yaroslav Kurpel.
Res.: 1629 W. Cayuga St., 19140. Tel: 215-455-2416; Fax: 215-455-6614. Email: ctkucc@aol.com.

5—ST. JOSAPHAT'S Rev. Ihor Bloshchynskyy (Ukraine), Admin.
Res.: 6932 Ditman St., 19135. Tel: 215-332-8488; Fax: 215-332-0315.
School—(Grades K-8), 4521 Longshore Ave., 19135. Tel: 215-332-8008; Fax: 215-332-1876. Christine McIntyre, Prin. Sisters 1; Lay Teachers 14; Students 235.

6—ST. NICHOLAS (1943) Attended by the Cathedral of the Immaculate Conception, Philadelphia.
Res.: 871 North 24th St., 19130. Tel: 215-769-3863; Fax: 215-769-2018.
Church: 24th & Poplar Sts., 19130-1988.

7—PROTECTION OF BLESSED VIRGIN MARY, Closed. For inquiries for parish records please see SS. Peter and Paul, Clifton Heights.

8—SACRED HEART, Closed. For inquiries for parish records contact the chancery.

STATE OF DELAWARE

WILMINGTON, NEW CASTLE CO., ST. NICHOLAS Rev. Volodymyr Klanichka.
Res.: 801 Lea Blvd., DE 19802. Tel: 302-762-5511; Fax: 302-762-5849. Email: stnicholas2@verizon.net. Web: st-nicholas-church.org.

STATE OF MARYLAND

BALTIMORE, BALTIMORE CO., ST. MICHAEL'S, [CEM] Rev. Vasyl Sivinskyi, Admin.
Res.: 2401 Eastern Ave., MD 21224. Tel: 410-675-7557; Fax: 410-732-0839. Email: tserkva@yahoo.com.

CHESAPEAKE CITY, CECIL CO., ST. BASIL THE GREAT, Attended by St. Nicholas, Wilmington., Mailing Address: 801 Lea Blvd., Wilmington, DE 19802.

CURTIS BAY, BALTIMORE CO., SS. PETER AND PAUL, Attended by St. Michael's, Baltimore., Mailing Address: 2401 Eastern Ave., Baltimore, MD 21224. Church: 1506 Church St., MD 21226-1440.

SILVER SPRING, MONTGOMERY CO., HOLY TRINITY (1980) Very Rev. Taras Lonchyna.
Res.: 16631 New Hampshire Ave., MD 20905-3919. Tel: 301-421-1739; Fax: 301-421-1869.

STATE OF NEW JERSEY

BAYONNE, HUDSON CO., ASSUMPTION B.V.M. (1916) Attended by SS. Peter and Paul, Jersey City., Mailing Address: *c/o SS. Peter and Paul*, 30 Bentley Ave., Jersey City, NJ 07304. Tel: 201-432-3122; Fax: 201-432-0111.
Church: 30 E. 25th St., Box 260, NJ 07002.

CARTERET, MIDDLESEX CO., ST. MARY'S (1949) Rev. Vasyl Vladyka.
719 Roosevelt Ave., NJ 07008. Tel: 732-366-2156.

CHERRY HILL, CAMDEN CO., ST. MICHAEL'S Rev. Ruslan Romanyuk.
Res.: 675 Cooper Landing Rd., NJ 08002. Tel: 856-482-0938; Fax: 609-482-9092. Email: stmichaelucc@comcast.net.

ELIZABETH, UNION CO., ST. VLADIMIR'S (1903) Very Rev. Joseph Szupa.
Res.: 312 Grier Ave., NJ 07202-3310. Tel: 908-352-8823; Fax: 908-352-7648.
Catechesis / Religious Program—Students 8.

GREAT MEADOWS, WARREN CO., ST. NICHOLAS (1923) Attended by Holy Ghost, West Easton, PA. Rev. Petro Zvarych, Admin.
Mailing Address: c/o 315 Fourth St., West Easton, 18042. Tel: 610-252-4266; Fax: 610-252-8533.
Church: Rte. 46, P.O. Box 162, NJ 07838.

HILLSIDE, UNION CO., IMMACULATE CONCEPTION (1957) Attended by St. Vladimir, Elizabeth.
Church: Bloy St. and Liberty Ave., NJ 07205.

JERSEY CITY, HUDSON CO., SS. PETER AND PAUL (1886) Rev. Vasyl Putera.
Res.: 30 Bentley Ave., NJ 07304. Tel: 201-432-3122; Fax: 201-432-0111.

HILLSBOROUGH, SOMERSET CO., ST. MICHAEL'S Very Rev. Roman Pitula.
Res.: 63 N. 18th Ave., Manville, NJ 08835. Tel: 908-725-5089; Fax: 908-725-2370.
Church: 1700 Brooks Blvd., NJ 08844.

MARLBORO, MONMOUTH CO., ST. VOLODYMYR'S, Closed. For inquiries for parish records contact the chancery.

MILLVILLE, CUMBERLAND CO., ST. NICHOLAS, [CEM], Attended from St. Stephen, Toms River, NJ. Rev. Ivan Turyk.
Church: 801 Carmel Rd., NJ 08332. Tel: 856-825-4826; Fax: 856-825-4826.

NEW BRUNSWICK, MIDDLESEX CO., NATIVITY OF B.V.M., Attended by St. Michael, Hillsborough, NJ. Very Rev. Roman Pitula.
Mailing Address: 80 Livingston Ave., NJ 08901.

NEWARK, ESSEX CO., ST. JOHN THE BAPTIST Revs. Leonid Malkov, C.Ss.R.; Andriy Manko, C.Ss.R.; Taras Svirchuk, C.Ss.R.
Res.: 719 Sandford Ave., NJ 07106. Tel: 973-371-1356; Fax: 973-416-0085.
Catechesis / Religious Program—Students 20.

PASSAIC, PASSAIC CO., ST. NICHOLAS Rev. Andriy Dudkevych (Ukraine).
Res.: 60 Holdsworth Ct., NJ 07055. Tel: 973-471-9727; Fax: 973-471-4714.
School—(Grades K-8) Tel: 973-779-0249; Fax: 973-779-6309. Sisters 2; Lay Teachers 10; Students 98.

PERTH AMBOY, MIDDLESEX CO., ASSUMPTION OF B.V.M. (1908) Rev. Roman Dubitsky; Deacon Paul Makar.
Res.: 684 Alta Vista Pl., NJ 08861. Tel: 732-826-0767; Fax: 732-826-6744. Email: assumptionchurch@verizon.net. Web: www.assumptioncatholicchurch.net.
School—(Grades PreK-8) Tel: 732-826-8721; Fax: 732-826-5013. Michael Szpyhulsky, Prin. Missionary Sisters of Mother of God 2; Lay Teachers 11; Students 170.

RAMSEY, BERGEN CO., ST. PAUL, Attended by St. John the Baptist, Whippany. Rev. Archpriest Mitrat Roman Mirchuk.
Mailing Address: 60 N. Jefferson Rd., Whippany, NJ 07981. Tel: 973-887-3616; 845-356-1634.
Church: 79 Cherry Ln., NJ 07446.

RUTHERFORD, BERGEN CO., ANNUNCIATION B.V.M., Closed. For inquiries for parish records please see St. Vladimir, Elizabeth.

TOMS RIVER, OCEAN CO., ST. STEPHEN'S Rev. Ivan Turyk.
1344 White Oak Bottom Rd., NJ 08755. Tel: 732-505-6053. Web: www.ststephenchurch.us.

TRENTON, MERCER CO., ST. JOSAPHAT'S (1949) Very Rev. Volodymyr Popyk.
Res.: 1195 Deutz Ave., NJ 08611. Tel: 609-695-3771; Fax: 609-815-0232.

WHIPPANY, MORRIS CO., ST. JOHN THE BAPTIST Rev. Archpriest Mitrat Roman Mirchuk.
Res.: 60 N. Jefferson Rd., NJ 07981. Tel: 973-887-3616; Fax: 973-585-7188.

WILLIAMSTOWN, GLOUCESTER CO., SS. PETER AND PAUL (1920) [CEM] Rev. Paul Labinsky.
Mailing Address: 1101 Heartwood Dr., Cherry Hill, NJ 08003. Tel: 856-616-0677.
Church: Black Horse Pike & Cecil Rd., NJ 08094.

WOODBINE, CAPE MAY CO., ST. NICHOLAS, Closed. For inquiries for parish records contact St. Nicholas, Millville, NJ

STATE OF PENNSYLVANIA

ALDEN STATION, LUZERNE CO., ST. VLADIMIR, Closed. For inquiries for parish records contact St. Nicholas, Glen Lyon, PA.

ALLENTOWN, LEHIGH CO., IMMACULATE CONCEPTION OF B.V.M., Closed. For inquiries for parish records contact St. Josaphat, Bethlehem, PA.

BERWICK, COLUMBIA CO., SS. CYRIL AND METHODIUS (1909) [CEM] Very Rev. John Seniw.
Res.: 706 Warren St., 18603. Tel: 717-752-3172; Fax: 570-752-0378. Email: sscm1@verizon.net.
Catechesis / Religious Program—Students 2.

BETHLEHEM, LEHIGH CO., ST. JOSAPHAT'S (1918) [CEM] Very Rev. Archpriest Daniel Gurovich.
Res.: 1826 Kenmore Ave., 18018-3305. Tel: 610-865-2521; Fax: 610-865-4490. Email: yaroway@aol.com.
Catechesis / Religious Program—Students 42.

BRIDGEPORT, MONTGOMERY CO., SS. PETER AND PAUL (1924) [CEM] Rev. Msgr. Ronald P. Popivchak.
Res.: 519 Union Ave., P.O. Box 126, 19405. Tel: 610-272-7035; Fax: 610-272-5620.
Catechesis / Religious Program—George Maxim, D.R.E. Students 100.

BRISTOL, BUCKS CO., ST. MARY'S (1954) Rev. Gregory Maslak.
Res.: 2026 Bath Rd., 19007. Tel: 215-788-7117; Fax: 215-788-7175.
Catechesis / Religious Program—Students 10.

CENTRALIA, COLUMBIA CO., ASSUMPTION OF B.V.M., [CEM] Attended by Shamokin. Rev. Stepan Bilyk. Tel: 570-648-5932; Fax: 570-648-3871.
Mailing Address: 303 N. Shamokin St., Shamokin, 17872-5460.
Church: N. Paxton St., 17927.

CHESTER, DELAWARE CO., HOLY GHOST Very Rev. John Ciurpita.
Res.: 3015 W. Third St., 19013. Tel: 610-494-7899; Fax: 610-494-2350.
Catechesis / Religious Program—Students 13.

CLIFTON HEIGHTS, DELAWARE CO., SS. PETER AND PAUL Very Rev. John Ciurpita, Admin.
Res.: 104 S. Penn St., 19108.
Church: 100 S. Penn St., 19018. Tel: 610-626-9495; Fax: 610-626-0346. Email: revjnc@aol.com.

EDWARDSVILLE, LUZERNE CO., ST. VLADIMIR'S (1910) [CEM] Rev. Orest Kunderevych.
Mailing Address: 70 Zerby Ave., 18704. Tel: 570-287-9718.
Catechesis / Religious Program—Tel: 717-822-1589. Christine Mash, D.R.E. Students 3.

FRACKVILLE, SCHUYLKILL CO., ST. MICHAEL'S (1921) [CEM] Rev. Archpriest John M. Fields.
Res.: 45 S. Second St., 17931. Tel: 570-874-1101; Fax: 570-874-0448. Email: IBAH@aol.com.
Catechesis / Religious Program—Tel: 717-874-1101. Students 27.

GLEN LYON, LUZERNE CO., ST. NICHOLAS, Attended by Ss Cyril and Methodius, Berwick., Mailing Address: 706 Warren St., Berwick, 18603. Tel: 570-752-3172.
Church: 153 Main St., 18617.
Catechesis / Religious Program—Students 2.

HAZLETON, LUZERNE CO., ST. MICHAEL'S (1910) [CEM] Attended by St. Mary's, McAdoo. Rev. Msgr. James T. Melnic.
Mailing Address: 210 W. Blaine St., McAdoo, 18237. Tel: 570-455-0643. Email: stmarysmcadoo@aol.com.
Church: 74 N. Laurel St., 18201.
Catechesis/Religious Program—Students 3.

JENKINTOWN, MONTGOMERY CO., ST. MICHAEL THE ARCHANGEL Rev. Volodymyr Kostyuk (Ukraine), Admin.
Res.: 1013 Fox Chase Rd., 19046. Tel: 215-576-5827; Fax: 215-576-8500.

LANSDALE, MONTGOMERY CO., PRESENTATION OF OUR LORD (1969) Attended by St. Anne's, Warrington. Rev. Wasyl Bunik, Admin.
Mailing Address: 1545 Easton Rd., Warrington, 18976.
Church: 1564 Allentown Rd., 19446. Tel: 215-368-3993; Fax: 215-343-8060. Web: www.presentationukrainiancc.com.
Catechesis/Religious Program—Students 9.

MAHANOY CITY, SCHUYLKILL CO., ST. NICHOLAS, [CEM] Closed. For inquiries for parish records contact the chancery.

MAIZEVILLE, SCHUYLKILL CO., ST. JOHN THE BAPTIST (1908) [CEM] Attended by St. Michael, Frackville. Rev. Archpriest John M. Fields.
Mailing Address: 45 S. Second St., Frackville, 17931. Tel: 570-874-1101.
Church: Main St., 17934. Tel: 570-874-1101; Fax: 570-874-0448.

MARION HEIGHTS, NORTHUMBERLAND CO., PATRONAGE OF THE MOTHER OF GOD (1911) Attended by SS. Peter & Paul, Mount Carmel., Mailing Address: 131 N. Beech St., Mount Carmel, 17851.

MCADOO, SCHUYLKILL CO., ST. MARY'S (1891) [CEM] Rev. Msgr. James T. Melnic.
Church: 210 W. Blaine St., 18237. Tel: 570-929-2804.

MIDDLEPORT, SCHUYLKILL CO., NATIVITY OF B.V.M. (1910) [CEM] Rev. Mark Fesniak, Admin.
Mailing Address: 415 N. Front St., Minersville, 17954. Tel: 570-544-4581; Fax: 570-544-9653.
Church: Kaska St., 17953.

MINERSVILLE, SCHUYLKILL CO., ST. NICHOLAS (1896) [CEM] Rev. Mark Fesniak.
Res.: 415 Front St., 17954. Tel: 570-544-4581; Fax: 570-544-9653.
School—(Grades K-8) Tel: 570-544-2800; Fax: 570-544-6471. Email: altssn@ptd.net. Karen Rogers, Prin.; Sofie Smith-Frantz, Librarian. Sisters 2; Lay Teachers 13; Students 161.
Catechesis/Religious Program—Students 12.

MOSCOW, LACKAWANNA CO., HOLY GHOST, Closed. For inquiries for parish records contact St. Vladimir, Scranton, PA.

MOUNT CARMEL, NORTHUMBERLAND CO., SS. PETER AND PAUL (1891) [CEM] Rev. Thaddeus Krawchuk, C.Ss.R., Admin.
Res.: 131 N. Beech St., 17851. Tel: 570-339-0650; Fax: 570-339-2715.

NANTICOKE, LUZERNE CO.
1—ST. NICHOLAS, Closed. For inquiries for parish records contact Transfiguration of Our Lord, 240 Center St., Nanticoke.
2—TRANSFIGURATION OF OUR LORD (1912) [CEM] Rev. Roman Petryshak (Ukraine), Admin.
Res.: 240 Center St., 18634. Tel: 570-735-2262; Fax: 570-735-6020. Email: holytransfiguration@verizon.net. Web: transfigurationofourlord.org.

NORTHAMPTON, NORTHAMPTON CO., ST. JOHN THE BAPTIST, [CEM] Rev. Archpriest David Clooney.
Res.: 1343 Newport Ave., 18067. Tel: 610-262-4104; Fax: 610-262-7393. Email: stjohn1900@verizon.net.

OLYPHANT, LACKAWANNA CO., SS. CYRIL AND METHODIUS (1888) [CEM] Very Rev. Nestor Iwasiw.
Res.: 135 River St., 18447. Tel: 570-489-2271; Fax: 570-489-6918. Email: sscyrilmethodius@verizon.net.

PALMERTON, CARBON CO., ST. VLADIMIR'S Rev. Evhan Moniuk.
Res.: 101 Lehigh Ave., 18071. Tel: 610-826-2359.

PHOENIXVILLE, CHESTER CO., SS. PETER AND PAUL, [CEM] Attended by St. Michael, Pottstown. Rev. Mykola Ivanov, Admin.
Mailing Address: 425 W. Walnut St., Pottstown, 19464-6654. Tel: 610-933-5453; Fax: 610-933-9826.
Church: 472 Emmett St., 19460.

PLYMOUTH, LUZERNE CO., SS. PETER AND PAUL Rev. Roman Petryshak (Ukraine), Admin.
Res.: 20 Turner St., 18651. Tel: 570-779-9728; Fax: 570-735-6020.

POTTSTOWN, MONTGOMERY CO., ST. MICHAEL'S (1936) [CEM] Rev. Mykola Ivanov, Admin.
Res.: 425 W. Walnut St., 19464. Tel: 610-326-2150; Fax: 610-326-2150. Email: mykolaivan1977@yahoo.com.

READING, BERKS CO., NATIVITY OF BLESSED VIRGIN MARY, [CEM] Very Rev. Andriy Rabiy, Admin.
Res.: 1814 Philadelphia Ave., 19607. Tel: 610-376-0586; Fax: 610-376-0586. Email: nativitybvmucc@catholic.org.

ST. CLAIR, SCHUYLKILL CO.
1—HOLY TRINITY, [CEM] Closed. For inquiries for parish records contact the chancery.
2—ST. NICHOLAS, [CEM] Attended by Holy Trinity, St. Clair. Rev. Oleksandr Dumenko (Ukraine), Admin.
Mailing Address: *Holy Trinity*, 254 N. Mill St., 17970. Tel: 570-462-0809; Fax: 570-462-0517.
Church: N. Morris St., 17970.

SAYRE, BRADFORD CO., ASCENSION OF OUR LORD, [CEM] Attended by St. Nicholas, Elmiria, NY. Rev. Vasile Godenciuc (STF). Tel: 607-734-1221.
Church: 110 N. Higgins Ave., 18840. Tel: 570-888-2207.

SCRANTON, LACKAWANNA CO., ST. VLADIMIR'S, [CEM] Rev. Paul Wolensky, Admin.
Res.: 430 N. Seventh Ave., 18503. Tel: 570-342-7023; Fax: 570-342-7130. Email: stvladimirscr430@verizon.net.

SHAMOKIN, NORTHUMBERLAND CO., TRANSFIGURATION OF OUR LORD, [CEM] Rev. Stepan Bilyk; Deacon Theodore Spotts.
Res.: 303 N. Shamokin St., 17872-5460. Tel: 570-648-5932; Fax: 570-648-3871.
Catechesis/Religious Program—Students 8.

SHENANDOAH, SCHUYLKILL CO., ST. MICHAEL'S (1884) [CEM] Rev. Oleksandr Dumenko (Ukraine), Admin.
Res.: 114 S. Chestnut St., 17976. Tel: 570-462-0809; Fax: 570-462-0517. Web: www.firstukrainian.com.

SIMPSON, LACKAWANNA CO., SS. PETER AND PAUL (1905) [CEM] Very Rev. Nestor Iwasiw, Admin. In Res., Rev. Edward Levandusky.
Res.: 43 Rittenhouse St., 18407. Tel: 570-282-0331.

WARRINGTON, BUCKS CO., ST. ANNE'S (1963) Rev. Wasyl Bunik, Admin.
Res.: 1545 Easton Rd., 18976. Tel: 215-343-0779; Fax: 215-343-8060. Web: www.stanneukrainiancc.com.
Catechesis/Religious Program—Students 20.

WEST EASTON, NORTHAMPTON CO., HOLY GHOST (1921) [CEM] Rev. Petro Zvarych, Admin.
Res.: 315 Fourth St., 18042. Tel: 610-252-4266; Fax: 610-252-8533.
Catechesis/Religious Program—Christine Mattes, D.R.E. Students 6.

WILKES-BARRE, LUZERNE CO., SS. PETER AND PAUL, [CEM] Rev. Orest Kunderevych.
Church: 635 N. River St., 18701. Tel: 570-823-1821; Fax: 570-822-7391. Email: sspeterandpaulwb@gmail.com.
Catechesis/Religious Program—Christine Mash, D.R.E. Students 21.

STATE OF VIRGINIA

MANASSAS, PRINCE WILLIAM CO., ANNUNCIATION OF THE BLESSED VIRGIN MARY (1925) [CEM] Attended by Holy Trinity, Silver Spring, MD. Very Rev. Taras Lonchyna.
Mailing Address: 16631 New Hampshire Ave., Silver Spring, MD 20905-3919.
Church: 6719 Token Valley Rd., VA 20108-0878. Tel: 703-791-6635.
Catechesis/Religious Program—Helen Troy, D.R.E. Students 16.

RICHMOND, HENRICO CO., ST. JOHN THE BAPTIST (1966) Attended by Holy Trinity, Silver Spring, MD. Very Rev. Taras Lonchyna.
Mailing Address: 16631 New Hampshire Ave., Silver Spring, MD 20905-3919. Tel: 301-421-1739.
Chapel—Comboni Sisters Chapel 1307 Lakeside Ave., VA 23228. Tel: 804-272-3844.

DISTRICT OF COLUMBIA

WASHINGTON, DISTRICT OF COLUMBIA, UKRAINIAN CATHOLIC NATIONAL SHRINE OF THE HOLY FAMILY Very Revs. Robert Hitchens; Wasyl Kharuk, Parochial Vicar; Deacon Theophil Staruch.
Res.: 4250 Harewood Rd., N.E., DC 20017. Tel: 202-526-3737. Web: www.ucns-holyfamily.org.
Catechesis/Religious Program—Pamela White, D.R.E.

Absent on Leave:
Rev. Archpriest—
Hutsko, Michael

Special Assignment:
Rev. Msgr.—
Grabowsky, Myron
Very Rev. Archpriest—
Troyan, Daniel, Dir., Evangelization

Retired:
Most Rev.—
Sulyk, Stephen, D.D., 1113 Cobble Creek Cir., Cherry Hill, NJ 08003.
Very Rev. Msgr.—
Hrynuck, Stephen
Rev. Msgr.—
Fedorowich, Michael, 415 N. Front St., Minersville, 17954.
Very Rev. Archpriest—
Markewych, Uriy, 990 Summerhill Rd., Auburn, 17922.
Revs.—
Molodowitz, Augustine, Ascension Manor, 911 N. Franklin St. Apt. #708, 19123-2077.
Patrylak, Frank, St. Mary's Catholic Home, 210 St. Mary's Dr., Cherry Hill, NJ 08003.
Sinatra, Leonard, 1114 Chestnut St. Alden, Nanticoke, 18634.
Wysochansky, John, 118 Second St., Blakely, 18447.

Permanent Deacons:
Latrick, Donald, (On Leave)
Makar, Paul, Assumption B.V.M., Perth Amboy
Schultz, Charles, III, Cathedral of I.C., Philadelphia
Spotts, Paul, St. Michael, Frackville, PA
Spotts, Theodore, Transfiguration, Shamokin, PA; Assumption B.V.M., Centralia, PA
Staruch, Theophil, Holy Family Ukrainian Catholic National Shrine, Washington, DC
Waak, Michael P., Cathedral of the Immaculate Conception, Philadelphia

INSTITUTIONS LOCATED IN THE ARCHDIOCESE

[A] SEMINARIES, ARCHEPARCHY

WASHINGTON. *St. Josaphat Seminary*, 201 Taylor St., N.E., DC 20017. Tel: 202-529-1177; Fax: 202-529-9366. Email: stjosaphatseminary@catholic.org. Web: www.sjucs.org. Very Revs. Robert Hitchens, Rector; Wasyl Kharuk, Spiritual Dir.

[B] COLLEGES AND UNIVERSITIES

JENKINTOWN. *Manor College*, 700 Fox Chase Rd., 19046. Tel: 215-885-2360; Fax: 215-576-6564. Email: scecilia@manor.edu. Web: www.manor.edu. Sr. M. Cecilia Jurasinski, O.S.B.M., Pres.; Sally Mydlowec, Exec. Vice Pres. & Dean Academic Affairs; Barbara Ozer, Contact Person; Beth Lauder, Librarian. Sisters of St. Basil the Great., Approved by the Commonwealth of Pennsylvania and accredited by the Middle States Association of Colleges and Secondary Schools. Sisters 3; Professors 23; Students 969.

[C] HIGH SCHOOLS, PRIVATE

JENKINTOWN. *St. Basil Academy*, 711 Fox Chase Rd., 19046. Tel: 215-885-3771; Fax: 215-885-4025. Email: admissions@stbasilacademy.org. Web: www.stbasilacademy.org. Sr. Carla Hernandez, O.S.B.M., Prin. High School Sisters 5; Lay Teachers 50; Students 380.

[D] HOMES FOR SENIOR CITIZENS

PHILADELPHIA. *Ascension Manor, Inc.*, 911 N. Franklin St., 19123. Tel: 215-922-1116. Most Revs. Stefan Soroka, D.D., Ph.D.; John Bura; Rev. Msgrs. James T. Melnic; Peter D. Waslo, J.C.L., Sec. Treas.; Rev. Archpriest John M. Fields, Exec. Vice Pres.; Andrew Fylypowych, Dir.; Jeanne Karbiwnyk, Dir.; Ihor Shust, Dir.; John Siwak, Gen. Mgr.

Ascension Manor I, 911 N. Franklin St., 19123. Tel: 215-922-1116; Fax: 215-922-3735. Bill Malinowski, Asst. Mgr.

Ascension Manor II, 970 N. Seventh St., 19123. Tel: 215-923-3907; Fax: 215-922-3735. Tonja Starkey, Asst. Mgr.

[E] MONASTERIES AND RESIDENCES OF PRIESTS AND BROTHERS

WASHINGTON. *Monastery of the Holy Cross*, 1302 Quincy St., N.E., DC 20017-2614. Tel: 202-832-8519; Fax: 202-526-3316. Email: holycrossdc@aol.com. Rev. Archimandrite Joseph (Richard) Lee.

[F] CONVENTS AND RESIDENCES FOR SISTERS

PHILADELPHIA. *Motherhouse of the Missionary Sisters of Mother of God*, 711 N. Franklin St., 19123. Tel: 215-627-7808; Fax: 215-627-4225. Sr. Nadia Baranick, M.S.M.G., Supr. Gen.

Sacred Heart Convent, 160 W. Carpenter Ln., 19119. Tel: 215-843-2266. Sr. Daniella, P.O.S.C., Supr.

FOX CHASE MANOR. *Provincial Motherhouse of the Sisters of St. Basil the Great*, 710 Fox Chase Rd., 19046. Tel: 215-379-3998; Fax: 215-728-6129.

Email: Basilians@aol.com. Web: www.basiliansfoxchase.org. Sisters Laura Palka, O.S.B.M., Prov. Supr.; Dolores Ozel, O.S.B.M., Asst. Prov.; Maria Rozmarynowycz, Councilor; Monica Lesnick, O.S.B.M., Councilor; Joan Sosler, O.S.B.M., Councilor; Rev. D. George Worschak, Chap. Professed Sisters 44.

[G] MISCELLANEOUS

PHILADELPHIA. *Archieparchial Museum and Educational Center*, 814 N. Franklin St., 19123. Tel: 215-627-3389; Fax: 215-627-0377. Sr. Nadia Baranik, M.S.M.G., Admin.

FOX CHASE MANOR. *Basilian Spirituality Center*, 710 Fox Chase Rd., 19046. Tel: 215-780-1227; Fax: 215-780-1743. Email: basilcenter@stbasils.com. Sr. Marina Bochnewich, O.S.B.M., Dir.

JENKINTOWN. *The Basileiad Library*, 700 Fox Chase Rd., 19046. Tel: 215-885-2360, Ext. 238; Fax: 215-576-6564. Email: basileiad@manor.edu. Web: library.manor.edu. Beth Lauder, Library Dir. Sisters of St. Basil the Great.

RELIGIOUS INSTITUTES OF MEN REPRESENTED IN THE ARCHEPARCHY

For further details refer to the corresponding bracketed number in the Religious Institutes of Men or Women section.

[1070]—*Redemptorist Fathers*—C.SS.R.

RELIGIOUS INSTITUTES OF WOMEN REPRESENTED IN THE ARCHEPARCHY

[2345]—*Little Workers of the Sacred Heart of Jesus and Mary*—P.O.S.C.

[2810]—*Missionary Sisters of Mother of God*—M.S.M.G.

[3730]—*Sisters of the Order of St. Basil the Great*—O.S.B.M.

[3610]—*Sisters Servants of Mary Immaculate*—S.S.M.I.

ARCHDIOCESAN CEMETERIES

LANGHORNE. *Mother of Sorrows*, Langhorne & Yardley Rd., 19047. Tel: 215-627-0143; Fax: 215-627-0377. 827 N. Franklin St., 19123.

NECROLOGY

(No Deaths)

An asterisk (*) denotes an organization that has established tax-exempt status directly with the IRS and is not covered by the USCCB Group Ruling.

Metropolitan Archeparchy of Pittsburgh, Byzantine

Most Reverend

BASIL M. SCHOTT, O.F.M.

Metropolitan Archbishop for Pittsburgh, Byzantine; ordained August 29, 1965; appointed Eparch of Parma May 3, 1996; enthroned July 11, 1996; appointed Metropolitan Archbishop of Pittsburgh May 3, 2002; enthroned July 9, 2002. *Chancery: 66 Riverview Ave., Pittsburgh, PA 15214.*

Chancery: 66 Riverview Ave., Pittsburgh, PA 15214. Tel: 412-231-4000; Fax: 412-231-1697.

ESTABLISHED FEBRUARY 25, 1924.

Raised to Archeparchy February 21, 1969.

Embraces all Byzantine Ruthenian Rite Catholics in that part of the State of Pennsylvania west of the western boundaries of the Counties of Tioga, Lycoming Union, Mifflin, Juniata and Franklin. In the State of Ohio, the Counties of Ashtabula, Athens, Belmont, Carroll, Columbiana, Gallia, Guernsey, Harrison, Jefferson, Lawrence, Mahoning, Meigs, Morrow, Morgan, Noble, Trumbull and Washington and also the States of Alabama, Arkansas, Kentucky, Louisiana, Mississippi, Oklahoma, Tennessee, Texas and West Virginia.

For legal titles of parishes and diocesan institutions, consult the Chancery.

STATISTICAL OVERVIEW

Personnel	
Archbishops	1
Abbots	1
Priests: Diocesan Active in Diocese	41
Priests: Diocesan Active Outside Diocese	1
Priests: Retired, Sick or Absent	13
Number of Diocesan Priests	55
Religious Priests in Diocese	7
Total Priests in Diocese	62
Extern Priests in Diocese	9
Ordinations:	
Diocesan Priests	1
Transitional Deacons	1
Permanent Deacons in Diocese	16
Total Brothers	3
Total Sisters	80
Parishes	
Parishes	79
With Resident Pastor:	
Resident Diocesan Priests	40
Resident Religious Priests	3
Without Resident Pastor:	
Administered by Priests	36
Missions	2
Pastoral Centers	3
Professional Ministry Personnel:	
Sisters	10
Welfare	
Homes for the Aged	2
Total Assisted	553
Educational	
Seminaries, Diocesan	1
Students from This Diocese	1
Students from Other Diocese	7
Total Seminarians	1
Catechesis/Religious Education:	
High School Students	311
Elementary Students	933
Total Students under Catholic Instruction	1,245
Vital Statistics	
Receptions into the Church:	
Infant Baptism Totals	159
Minor Baptism Totals	5
Adult Baptism Totals	16
Received into Full Communion	44
First Communions	189
Confirmations	193
Marriages:	
Catholic	47
Interfaith	21
Total Marriages	68
Deaths	458
Total Catholic Population	58,763

Former Bishops—Most Revs. BASIL TAKACH, ord. Dec. 12, 1902; appt. May 20, 1924; cons. June 15, 1924; died May 13, 1948; DANIEL IVANCHO, D.D., Titular Bishop of Europus; ord. Sept. 30, 1934; appt. Coadjutor Bishop, Aug. 29, 1946; cons. Nov. 5, 1946; succeeded to May 13, 1948; retired Dec. 2, 1954; died Aug. 2, 1972; NICHOLAS T. ELKO, D.D., ord. Sept. 30, 1934; cons. March 6, 1955; transferred to Rome, Dec. 22, 1967; died May 18, 1991; STEPHEN J. KOCISCKO, D.D., ord. March 30, 1941; appt. Titular Bishop of Theveste and Auxiliary Bishop of Pittsburgh July 20, 1956; cons. Oct. 23, 1956; appt. First Eparch of Passaic July 31, 1963; appt. Eparch of Pittsburgh Dec. 21, 1967; enthroned March 5, 1968; elevated to Metropolitan Archbishop of Pittsburgh Feb. 21, 1969; retired June 12, 1991; died March 7, 1995; THOMAS V. DOLINAY, ord. May 16, 1948; appt. Titular Bishop of Thyatira and Auxiliary of Passaic, Sept. 23, 1976; cons. Nov. 23, 1976; appt. First Ordinary of the Byzantine Catholic Eparchy of Van Nuys; installed March 1982; appt. Coadjutor Archbishop of Pittsburgh, March 13, 1990; installed May 29, 1990; succeeded to June 12, 1991; died April 13, 1993; JOHN M. BILOCK, ord. Feb. 3, 1946; appt. Titular Bishop of Pergamo and Auxiliary Bishop to the Metropolitan Archbishop of Pittsburgh; installed March 1, 1973; cons. May 15, 1973; appt. Archieparchial Administrator, April 20, 1993; died Sept. 8, 1994; JUDSON M. PROCYK, ord. May 19, 1957; appt. Metropolitan Archbishop of Pittsburgh Nov. 15, 1994; installed Feb. 7, 1995; died April 24, 2001.

Chancery—66 Riverview Ave., Pittsburgh, 15214. Tel: 412-231-4000; Fax: 412-231-1697. Email: archpitt@aol.com. Office Hours: Mon.-Fri. 9:30-12 and 12:30-4.

Protosyncellus—Rev. Msgr. RUSSELL A. DUKER, S.E.O.D.

Vicar for Canonical Services—Rev. GEORGE D. GALLARO, J.C.O.L., J.C.O.D., S.T.L.

Finance Officer—GREGORY S. POPIVCHAK.

Consultors—Very Rev. Archpriest DENNIS M. BOGDA; Rev. Msgr. RUSSELL A. DUKER, S.E.O.D.; Very Rev. RICHARD I. LAMBERT; Revs. SIMEON B. SIBENIK; JAMES A. SPONTAK; Very Rev. EUGENE P. YACKANICH.

Protopresbyters—Very Rev. JOSEPH BORODACH, Clairton; Rev. Msgr. RAYMOND A. BALTA, Johnstown; Very Revs. JOHN H. SALKO, Mon-Valley; JOHN J. MIHALCO, S.E.O.L., North-Central; EUGENE P. YACKANICH, Pittsburgh; ELIAS L. RAFAJ, Southwest; JOSEPH J. JUGAN, Tri-State; RICHARD I. LAMBERT, Youngstown.

Finance Council—Most Rev. BASIL SCHOTT, O.F.M.; GREGORY S. POPIVCHAK; Very Rev. EUGENE P. YACKANICH; MICHAEL I. ROMAN; BERNARD J. KOSAR SR.; CATHY A. CHROMULAK, Attorney.

Tribunal—

Judicial Vicar—Rev. GEORGE D. GALLARO, J.C.O.L., J.C.O.D., S.T.L.

Pro-Synodal Judges—Revs. MICHAEL HUSZTI, J.C.O.L.; MICHAEL K. SKROCKI, J.C.O.L.; Rev. Msgr. PETER WASLO, J.C.L.

Defender of the Bond—Very Rev. JOHN J. MIHALCO, S.E.O.L.

Promoter of Justice—Rev. RICHARD J. WHETSTONE, J.C.O.L.

Secretary—Sr. ELAINE KISINKO, O.S.B.M.

Notaries—Rev. GREGORY J. MICHALISIN; Sr. VALERIA EVANYO, O.S.B.M.; DONNA OBSINCS.

Archieparchial Choir—DARLENE FEJKA, Dir.

Archives—Revs. JOHN L. MINA, Ph.D., Archivist; ROBERT F. ORAVETZ, Asst.; Sr. ELAINE KISINKO, O.S.B.M., Asst.

Clergy Continuing Formation—

Presbyteral Council—Very Rev. Archpriest JOHN G. PETRO; Revs. GEORGE D. GALLARO, J.C.O.L., J.C.O.D., S.T.L.; FRANK A. FIRKO, S.T.L., Sec.; Very Rev. Archpriest DENNIS M. BOGDA; Rev. ANDREW J. DESKEVICH; Rev. Msgr. RUSSELL A. DUKER, S.E.O.D.; Revs. ROBERT J. KARL; RONALD P. LARKO; KEVIN E. MARKS; Rt. Rev. LEO R. SCHLOSSER; Rev. JAMES A. SPONTAK; Very Rev. EUGENE P. YACKANICH.

Communications—DARLENE FEJKA; TIMOTHY P. WEBER, Asst.; Rev. ANDREW J. DESKEVICH, Asst. Dir. Media.

Diaconate Program—Very Rev. Archpriest JOHN G. PETRO, Dir.

Evangelization, Mission Activity and Ecumenism—Rev. ROBERT F. ORAVETZ, Dir.

Vocations—Very Rev. Archpriest DENNIS M. BOGDA, Dir.; Rev. KEVIN E. MARKS, Assoc. Dir.; DARLENE FEJKA, Admin. Coord.

Priests' Pension Board— Ex Officio Members: Most Rev. BASIL SCHOTT; GREGORY S. POPIVCHAK, Finance Officer; Rev. Msgr. RUSSELL A. DUKER, S.E.O.D., Protosyncellus & Chancellor.

Elected Deanery Representatives—Revs. JOSEPH R. RAPTOSH, Sec., Clairton; DAVID A. BOSNICH, Greater Pittsburgh; GREGORY J. MICHALISIN, Johnstown; JEROME G. BOTSKO, Mon Valley; Very Rev. JOHN J. MIHALCO, S.E.O.L., North Central; Revs. DANIEL J. LOYA, Tri State; FRANK A. FIRKO, S.T.L., Youngstown.

Office of Religious Education—Sr. MARION DOBOS, O.S.B., Dir.; Very Rev. ELIAS L. RAFAJ, Asst. Dir., Archeparchial Catechetical Center, 3605 Perrysville Ave., Pittsburgh, 15214. Tel: 412-322-8773; Fax: 412-322-8737.

Revitalization and Renewal Commission—Very Rev. Archpriest DENNIS M. BOGDA; Revs. JOSEPH KAPUSNAK; ROBERT J. KARL; ANDREW J. DESKEVICH; HELEN KENNEDY; Deacon DENNIS M. PRESTASH; SANDRA SIMKO; Deacon RAYMOND J. ZADZILKO.

Archieparchial Newspaper— "Byzantine Catholic World" DARLENE FEJKA, Layout & Graphics; STEVEN HORGER, Business Mgr.; DONNA OBSINCS, Circulation Mgr.; Sr. ELAINE KISINKO, O.S.B.M., Copy Editor, 66 Riverview Ave., Pittsburgh, 15214. Tel: 412-231-4000; Fax: 412-231-1697.

Byzantine Catholic Seminary Press—Sr. JOSETTA KRISS, O.S.B.M., Dir., 3643 Perrysville Ave., Pittsburgh, 15214. Tel: 412-322-8307; Fax: 412-322-9530.

Victim Assistance Coordinator—Sr. BARBARA JEAN MIHALCHICK, O.S.B.M., 500 W. Main St., P.O. Box 878, Uniontown, 15401-0878. Tel: 724-438-7149.

Safe Environment Coordinator—Sr. AGNES KNAPIK, O.S.B., Queen of Heaven Monastery, 8640 Squires Lane, N.E., Warren, OH 44484. Tel: 330-856-1813.

CLERGY, PARISHES, MISSIONS AND PAROCHIAL SCHOOLS

STATE OF PENNSYLVANIA

ALIQUIPPA, BEAVER CO., ST. GEORGE THE GREAT MARTYR (1915) Rev. Kevin E. Marks.
Res.: 1001 Clinton St., 15001-3903. Tel: 724-375-2742; Fax: 724-375-8776.

AMBRIDGE, BEAVER CO., ST. MARY'S (1940) Rev. Kevin E. Marks.
Res.: 624 Park Rd., 15003. Tel: 724-266-2030; Fax: 724-266-1834.

ARCADIA, INDIANA CO., ASCENSION, [CEM] Closed. For inquiries for parish records contact the chancery.

AVELLA, WASHINGTON CO., ST. JOHN THE BAPTIST (1916) [CEM] Attended by St. Mary's, Weirton, WV.
Res.: 176 Cross Creek Rd., P.O. Box 565, 15312. Tel: 304-748-2087; Fax: 304-748-7550.

BEAVER, BEAVER CO., SAINT NICHOLAS CHAPEL (1995) Very Rev. Archpriest John G. Petro, Admin.
5400 Tuscarawas Rd., 15009-9513. Tel: 412-321-7550. Web: www.gcuusa.com. Mailing Address: 3605 Perrysville Ave., 15214.

BEAVERDALE, CAMBRIA CO., ST. MARY'S (1906) [CEM] Attended by Sts. Peter and Paul, Portage.
Church: 513 Cameron Ave., P.O. Box 610, 15921. Tel: 814-736-9780.

BRADDOCK, ALLEGHENY CO., SS. PETER AND PAUL (1896) Attended by Sts. Peter and Paul, Duquesne.
Church: 431 George St., P.O. Box 441, 15104. Tel: 412-466-3578.

BRADENVILLE, WESTMORELAND CO., ST. MARY'S (1902) [CEM] Very Rev. Joseph Borodach.
Res.: 112 St. Mary's Way, 15620-1017. Tel: 724-537-5839; Fax: 724-532-1499.

BROWNSVILLE, FAYETTE CO., ST. NICHOLAS (1911) [CEM] Rev. Jerome G. Botsko.
Res.: 302 Third Ave., 15417. Tel: 724-785-7573; Fax: 724-785-4649.

CANONSBURG, WASHINGTON CO., ST. MICHAEL (1912) [CEM] Very Rev. Joseph J. Jugan; Deacon Lance D. Weakland.
Res.: 166 E. College St., 15317. Tel: 724-745-7117; Fax: 724-745-3097.

CHARLEROI, WASHINGTON CO., HOLY GHOST (1899) Rev. James A. Ragan.
Res.: 828 Meadow Ave., 15022. Tel: 724-483-8622; Fax: 724-483-0696. Email: hgbyz.midmon@lcsys.net.

CLAIRTON, ALLEGHENY CO., ASCENSION OF OUR LORD (1907) [CEM] Rev. John L. Mina.
Res.: 318 Park Ave., 15025. Tel: 412-233-7422. Email: ascension1@ypgs.net.

CLARENCE, CENTRE CO., DORMITION OF THE MOTHER OF GOD (1906) [CEM] Attended by St. John the Baptist Church, Hawk Run., Mailing Address: *c/o St. John the Baptist Church*, P.O. Box 2, Hawk Run, 16840. Tel: 814-342-4315. Web: www.byzcath.org/centralpa.

CLYMER, INDIANA CO., ST. ANNE (1907) Attended by St. Mary, Homer City., Mailing Address: 279 Yellow Creek St., Homer City, 15748. Tel: 724-479-2206; Fax: 724-479-9506.

COAL RUN, INDIANA CO., HOLY CROSS, Closed. For inquiries for parish records contact the chancery.

CONEMAUGH, CAMBRIA CO., HOLY TRINITY (1908) [CEM] Attended by St. Mary, Johnstown.
Church: 217 Fourth St., 15909. Tel: 814-535-4132.

DONORA, WASHINGTON CO., ST. MICHAEL (1904) [CEM] Rev. Stephen J. Wahal.
Church: 511 Murray Ave., 15033. Tel: 724-379-9751; Fax: 724-379-9752.

DU BOIS, CLEARFIELD CO., NATIVITY OF THE MOTHER OF GOD (1910) Attended by Holy Trinity, Sykesville. Very Rev. John J. Mihalco; Deacons Paul M. Boboige; George M. Fatula.
Res.: 200 McCullough St., 15801. Tel: 814-894-5440; Fax: 814-894-2412.

DUNLO, CAMBRIA CO., SS. PETER AND PAUL (1909) [CEM] Attended by Sts. Peter and Paul, Portage., Mailing Address: 143 Church Rd., Portage, 15946. Tel: 814-736-9780.

DUQUESNE, ALLEGHENY CO.
1—ST. MARY'S (1915) Closed. For inquiries for parish records contact the chancery.
2—SS. PETER AND PAUL (1904) [CEM] Rev. David A. Bosnich.
Res.: 701 Foster Ave., 15110. Tel: 412-466-3578; Fax: 412-466-3578.

EAST PITTSBURGH, ALLEGHENY CO., ST. MARY'S (1930) Attended by Resurrection, Monroeville.
Res.: 317 Howard St., 15112. Tel: 412-372-8650.

ERIE, ERIE CO., SS. PETER AND PAUL (1912) Rev. Andrew J. Deskevich.
Res.: 3415 Wallace St., 16504. Tel: 814-825-8140; Fax: 814-825-7582. Email: eriecountybyzantines@verizon.net.

ERNEST, INDIANA CO., ST. JUDE THADDEUS (1949) Attended by Sts. Peter and Paul, Punxsutawney. Rev. Simeon B. Sibenik.
Res.: 320 Main St., Box 130, 15739. Tel: 814-938-6564.

GIBSONIA, ALLEGHENY CO., ST. ANDREW THE APOSTLE (1975) Rev. George D. Gallaro.
Res.: 235 Logan Rd., 15044-6093. Tel: 724-625-1160; Fax: 724-625-1160.

GIRARD, ERIE CO., SS. CYRIL AND METHODIUS (1952) Attended by Sts. Peter and Paul, Erie
Res.: 1022 Tilden Ave., 16417. Tel: 814-774-3281; Fax: 814-774-5405. Email: eriecountybyzantines@verizon.net.

GREENSBURG, WESTMORELAND CO., ST. NICHOLAS OF MYRA (1955) Rev. Regis J. Dusecina.
Res.: 624 E. Pittsburgh St., 15601. Tel: 724-837-0295; Fax: 724-837-9042.

HANNASTOWN, WESTMORELAND CO., ST. MARY'S (1906) Attended by St. Nicholas of Myra, Greensburg., 624 E. Pittsburgh St., Greensburg, 15601. Tel: 724-837-0295.

HAWK RUN, CLEARFIELD CO.
1—ST. JOHN THE BAPTIST (1904) [CEM] Rev. Robert F. Oravetz; Deacons John A. Custaney; Dennis M. Prestash.
Mailing Address: 24 Fulton St., P.O. Box 2, 16840. Tel: 814-342-4315; Fax: 814-342-3254. Web: www.byzcath.org/centralpa.
2—STATE COLLEGE PA BYZANTINE CATHOLIC COMMUNITY (2005) Rev. Robert F. Oravetz, Admin.
P.O. Box 431, State College, 16804-0431. Tel: 814-861-2005; Fax: 814-342-3254. Email: byzbob@aol.com. Web: www.byzcath.org/centralpa.

HERMINIE, WESTMORELAND CO., ST. MARY'S (1923) Attended by St. Stephen's, North Huntington., 5 Second St., 15637. Tel: 724-446-5570.

HERMITAGE, MERCER CO., ST. MICHAEL (1905) [CEM] Rev. Frank A. Firko.
Res.: 2230 Highland Rd., 16148. Tel: 724-981-6680; Fax: 724-981-7422.

HOMER CITY, INDIANA CO., ST. MARY'S HOLY PROTECTION formerly Holy Protection of Mary, The Mother of God (1919) Rev. Cuthbert A. Jack, O.S.B.; Deacon Richard A. Ciganko.
Res.: 279 Yellow Creek St., 15748. Tel: 724-479-2206; Fax: 724-479-9506.

JEROME, SOMERSET CO., SS. PETER AND PAUL (1913) [CEM] Attended by St. Mary, Windber. Rev. Gregory J. Michalisin; Deacon Paul J. Pipta.
803 Somerset Ave., Windber, 15963. Tel: 814-467-8044; Fax: 814-467-8044.

JOHNSTOWN, CAMBRIA CO., ST. MARY'S (1895) [CEM] Rev. Msgr. Raymond A. Balta.
Res.: 411 Power St., 15906. Tel: 814-535-4132; Fax: 814-536-9017.

LATROBE, WESTMORELAND CO., ST. MARY'S (1894) [CEM] Rev. Julian Anthony.
Res.: 4480 Rte. #981, 15650. Tel: 724-423-3673; Fax: 724-423-1808.

LEISENRING, FAYETTE CO., ST. STEPHEN (1892) [CEM] Rev. Joseph Kapusnak.
Res.: P.O. Box 128, 15455. Tel: 724-628-6611; Fax: 724-628-5009.

LYNDORA, BUTLER CO., ST. JOHN THE BAPTIST (1910) [CEM] Rt. Rev. Leo R. Schlosser, Abbot; Deacon Paul Simko.
Res.: 105 Kohler Ave., 16045. Tel: 724-287-5000; Fax: 724-287-6769.

MCKEES ROCKS, ALLEGHENY CO., HOLY GHOST (1907) Rev. Ronald P. Larko.
Res.: 225 Olivia St., 15136. Tel: 412-771-3324; Fax: 412-331-1870.

MCKEESPORT, ALLEGHENY CO.
1—ST. NICHOLAS (1901) [CEM] Rev. Donald J. Voss.
Res.: 410 Sixth Ave., 15132. Tel: 412-664-9131; Fax: 412-664-0854.
2—TRANSFIGURATION OF OUR LORD (1913) Attended by St. Nicholas, McKeesport.
Res.: 121 Sixth Ave., 15132. Tel: 412-672-0728.

MONESSEN, WESTMORELAND CO., ASSUMPTION OF THE BLESSED VIRGIN (1902) [CEM] Rev. Stephen J. Wahal; Deacon John M. Hanchin.
Res.: 125 McKee Ave., 15062. Tel: 724-684-5662; Fax: 724-684-3301.

MONONGAHELA, WASHINGTON CO., ST. MACRINA, Closed. For inquiries for parish records contact the chancery.

MONROEVILLE, ALLEGHENY CO., CHURCH OF THE RESURRECTION (1969) Rev. Richard Joseph Raptosh, Admin.
Res.: 455 Center Rd., 15146. Tel: 412-372-8650; Fax: 412-372-1442.

MUNHALL, ALLEGHENY CO.
1—ST. JOHN THE BAPTIST CATHEDRAL (1897) [CEM] Very Rev. Archpriest Dennis M. Bogda, Rector; Deacon Timothy J. Corbett.
Res.: 210 Greentree Rd., 15120. Tel: 412-461-0944; Fax: 412-462-3495.
2—ST. ELIAS (1907) [CEM] Very Rev. Eugene P. Yackanich; Rev. Daniel A. Forsythe, Parochial Vicar.
Res.: 4200 Homestead-Duquesne Rd., 15120. Tel: 412-461-1712; Fax: 412-461-1712.

NANTY-GLO, CAMBRIA CO., ST. NICHOLAS (1919) Attended by St. Mary, Johnstown.
Church: 1191 Second St., 15943. Tel: 814-535-4132.

NEW SALEM, FAYETTE CO., ST. MARY'S (1903) [CEM] Attended by St. Nicholas, Brownsville., Mailing Address: P.O. Box 487, 15468. Tel: 724-245-7188.

NORTH HUNTINGDON, WESTMORELAND CO., ST. STEPHEN'S (1972) Rev. James D. Hess, O.Carm.
Res.: 90 Bethel Rd., 15642. Tel: 724-863-6776; Fax: 724-864-9685. Email: jimocarm@mac.com.

NORTHERN CAMBRIA, CAMBRIA CO., ST. JOHN THE BAPTIST (1897) [CEM] Rev. Oliver J. Hebert, T.O.R.
Res.: 719 Chestnut Ave., 15714-1459. Tel: 814-948-8242; Fax: 814-948-8252. Email: stjohn@pennswoods.net. Web: ssppandjbyzcatholic.com.

PATTON, CAMBRIA CO., SS. PETER AND PAUL (1900) [CEM] Attended by St. John, Northern Cambria. Rev. Oliver J. Hebert, T.O.R.; Deacon Raymond J. Zadzilko.
Church: 516 Palmer Ave., 16668. Tel: 814-674-5552; Fax: 814-948-8252. Email: stjohn@pennswoods.net. Web: ssppandjbyzcatholic.com.

PERRYOPOLIS, FAYETTE CO., ST. NICHOLAS (1911) [CEM] Rev. Robert E. Halus.
Res.: 102 Railroad St., 15473. Tel: 724-736-4344; Fax: 724-736-4642.

PITTSBURGH, ALLEGHENY CO.
1—HOLY GHOST (1902) Attended by Holy Ghost, McKees Rocks.
Church: 1437 Superior Ave., 15212. Tel: 412-321-5072; Fax: 412-321-0260.
2—HOLY SPIRIT (1907) Rev. Msgr. Russell A. Duker, S.E.O.D.
Res.: 4815 Fifth Ave., 15213. Tel: 412-687-1220; Fax: 412-687-1520.
3—ST. JOHN CHRYSOSTOM (1910) Rev. John J. Cuccaro.
Res.: 506 Saline St., 15207. Tel: 412-421-0243; Fax: 412-422-3624.
4—ST. JOHN THE BAPTIST (1900) [CEM] Rev. Thomas Schaefer.
Res.: 1720 Jane St., 15203. Tel: 412-431-1090; Fax: 412-431-2059.
5—NATIVITY OF B.V.M. (1932) Attended by St. John Chrysostom, Pittsburgh
Res.: 4027 Beechwood Blvd., 15217. Tel: 412-421-5231.
6—ST. PIUS X (1954) Rev. Msgr. Russell A. Duker, S.E.O.D.
Res.: 2336 Brownsville Rd., 15210. Tel: 412-881-8344.

PORTAGE, CAMBRIA CO., SS. PETER AND PAUL (1917) [CEM] Rev. James A. Spontak.
Res.: 143 Church Rd., 15946. Tel: 814-736-9780; Fax: 814-736-8701.

PUNXSUTAWNEY, JEFFERSON CO., SS. PETER AND PAUL (1893) [CEM 2] Rev. Simeon B. Sibenik.
Res.: 714 Sutton St., 15767. Tel: 814-938-6564; Fax: 814-938-6551.

RANKIN, ALLEGHENY CO., ST. JOHN'S, Closed. For inquiries for parish records contact the chancery.

SAGAMORE, ARMSTRONG CO., ST. MARY'S, [CEM] Closed. For inquiries for parish records contact the chancery.

SCOTTDALE, WESTMORELAND CO., ST. JOHN THE BAPTIST (1912) [CEM] Very Rev. John H. Salko.
Res.: 525 Porter Ave., 15683. Tel: 724-887-5072; Fax: 724-887-3365.

SHEFFIELD, WARREN CO., ST. MICHAEL (1905) [CEM] Rev. Roy R. Schubert.
Res.: 407 School St., P.O. Box 801, 16347. Tel: 814-968-5478; Fax: 814-968-4445.

SOUTH FORK, CAMBRIA CO., ST. MICHAEL'S, [CEM] Attended by SS. Peter and Paul Church, Portage., 143 Church Rd., Portage, 15946. Tel: 814-736-9780; Fax: 814-736-8701.

SYKESVILLE, JEFFERSON CO., HOLY TRINITY (1907) [CEM] Very Rev. John J. Mihalco; Deacon Lucas M. Crawford.
Res.: 104 Shaffer St., 15865. Tel: 814-894-5440; Fax: 814-894-2412.

TARENTUM, ALLEGHENY CO., STS. PETER AND PAUL (1918) Rev. Wesley M. Mash.
Res.: 339 E. 10th Ave., 15084-1003. Tel: 724-224-3026; Fax: 724-224-5242. Web: www.stspeterpaul-byz.org.

UNIONTOWN, FAYETTE CO., ST. JOHN THE BAPTIST (1911) [CEM] Rev. Thomas J. Wesdock.
Res.: 185 E. Main St., 15401. Tel: 724-438-6027; Fax: 724-438-1382.

UPPER ST. CLAIR, ALLEGHENY CO., ST. GREGORY NAZIANZUS (1971) Rev. Jerome J. Wolbert, O.F.M.
Res.: 2005 Mohawk Rd., 15241. Tel: 412-835-7800; Fax: 412-835-7898.

WALL, ALLEGHENY CO., HOLY TRINITY (1928) Rev. Anselm Orlosky.
Res.: 470 Wall Ave., 15148. Tel: 412-824-9803.

WINDBER, SOMERSET CO., ST. MARY (DORMITION) CHURCH (1900) [CEM] Rev. Gregory J. Michalisin.
Res.: 803 Somerset St., 15963. Tel: 814-467-8044; Fax: 814-467-8044.

STATE OF LOUISIANA

NEW ORLEANS, ST. NICHOLAS OF MYRA MISSION (1976) Rev. James M. Deshotels, S.J.; Deacon Gregory A. Haddad, Admin.
2435 S. Carrollton Ave., LA 70118. Tel: 504-861-0806; Fax: 985-872-9123. Email: stnicholasnola@yahoo.com. Mailing Address: P.O. Box 1359, Gray, LA 70359-1359.

STATE OF OHIO

ASHTABULA, ASHTABULA CO., ST. NICHOLAS (1906) Rev. A. Edward Gretchko.
Res.: 206 Cherry Rd., N.E., Massillon, OH 44646.
Church: 1104 E. Fifteenth St., OH 44004. Tel: 330-833-8501; Fax: 330-833-3359.

BOARDMAN, MAHONING CO., INFANT JESUS OF PRAGUE (1907) Rev. Christopher R. Burke.
Res.: 7754 S. Ave., OH 44512. Tel: 330-758-6019; Fax: 330-758-0768.

CAMPBELL, MAHONING CO., ST. MICHAEL (1922) [CEM] Rev. Msgr. Victor G. Romza.
Res.: 463 Robinson Rd., Box 426, OH 44405. Tel: 330-755-4831; Fax: 330-755-1818.

MINGO JUNCTION, JEFFERSON CO., ST. JOHN THE BAPTIST (1923) Attended by St. Joseph, Toronto.
Church: 207 Standard St., OH 43938. Tel: 740-535-0271; Fax: 740-537-9802.

NEWTON FALLS, TRUMBULL CO., ST. MICHAEL (1924) Attended by Assumption of the Blessed Virgin, Youngstown.
Church: 737 Ridge Rd., P.O. Box 485, OH 44444. Tel: 330-872-5216.

PLEASANT CITY, GUERNSEY CO., ST. MICHAEL (1898) [CEM] Rev. Daniel J. Loya.
Res.: 408 Walnut St., OH 43772. Tel: 740-685-3292; Fax: 740-685-3292.

TORONTO, JEFFERSON CO., ST. JOSEPH (1901) Rev. James Atkins.
Res.: 814 N. Fifth St., OH 43964. Tel: 740-537-1026; Fax: 740-537-9802. Email: fr.james@sbcglobal.net.

WARREN, TRUMBULL CO., SS. PETER AND PAUL'S (1925) [CEM] Rev. Robert J. Karl.
Res.: 180 Belvedere Ave., N.E., OH 44483. Tel: 330-372-1875; Fax: 330-372-1896.

YOUNGSTOWN, MAHONING CO.

1—ASSUMPTION OF THE BLESSED VIRGIN (1899) [CEM] Very Rev. Richard I. Lambert.
Res.: 356 S. Belle Vista, OH 44509. Tel: 330-799-8163; Fax: 330-793-5360.

2—ST. GEORGE (1914) Attended by St. Nicholas, Youngstown., 1726 Canfield Rd., OH 44511. Tel: 330-782-2865.

3—ST. JOHN THE BAPTIST, Closed. For inquiries for parish records contact St. Nicholas, 1898 Wilson Ave., Youngstown, OH 44506. Tel: 330-743-0419.

4—ST. NICHOLAS (1912) [CEM] Rev. David J. Shortt.
Res.: 1898 Wilson Ave., OH 44506. Tel: 330-743-0419; Fax: 330-743-6888. Email: stnick9000@aol.com.

STATE OF TEXAS

HOUSTON, HARRIS CO., ST. JOHN CHRYSOSTOM (1982) Very Rev. Elias L. Rafaj; Deacon Andrew F. Veres.
Res.: 5402 Acorn St., TX 77092-4255. Tel: 713-681-3580; Fax: 713-681-3466. Email: houstonelias@gmail.com. Web: www.st-john-chrysostom-houston.org.

IRVING, DALLAS CO., ST. BASIL THE GREAT (1988) Very Rev. Elias L. Rafaj.
Res.: 1118 E. Union Bower Rd., TX 75061. Tel: 972-438-5644; Fax: 972-721-0696. Web: stbasilsinirving.org.

STATE OF TENNESSEE

KNOXVILLE, KNOX CO., HOLY RESURRECTION MISSION (1999) Rev. Thomas P. O'Connell, Admin.
1041 N. Central St., TN 37917.
Res.: 806 Villa View Way, TN 37920. Tel: 865-256-4880.

STATE OF WEST VIRGINIA

MORGANTOWN, MONONGALIA CO., ST. MARY HOLY PROTECTION (1918) Attended by Chaplain, Mt. St. Macrina, Uniontown, PA, Mailing Address: 2115 Listravia Ave., WV 26505.
Church: Tel: 304-296-2455; 724-439-4475 (Res.). Web: www.saintmarybyz.org.

WEIRTON, HANCOCK CO., ST. MARY'S (1924) Rev. Edward M. Lucas.
Res.: 3116 Elm St., WV 26062. Tel: 304-748-2087; Fax: 304-748-7550.

On Duty Outside the Diocese:
Rev.—
Wolbert, Jerome J., O.F.M.

Retired:
Rev. Msgrs.—
Mihalik, Alexis E., 4300 Westford Pl., #6-C, Canfield, OH 44406-7010.
Rosack, Edward V., P.O. Box 603, Perryopolis, 15473-0603.
Tay, Peter P., 1200 San Pedro St., 15212.
Revs.—
Borsuk, Ronald W., 180 Van Buren St., Johnstown, 15909.
Chewning, Seraphim John, 821 Clark St., Cambridge, OH 43725.
Chornyak, Joseph I., 660 Cherry Tree Lane #129, Uniontown, 15401.
Evancho, George, P.O. Box 568, Avella, 15312-0568.
Kolcun, Stephen J., 4469 Country Club Dr., 15236.
Petruska, Gregory, 15544 Bellflower Blvd., #C, Bellflower, CA 90706.

INSTITUTIONS LOCATED IN THE ARCHDIOCESE

[A] SEMINARIES, ARCHDIOCESAN

PITTSBURGH. *Byzantine Catholic Seminary of SS. Cyril and Methodius*, 3605 Perrysville Ave., 15214-2297. Tel: 412-321-8383; Fax: 412-321-9936. Email: byzcathsem@verizon.net. Web: www.byzcathsem.org. Very Rev. Archpriest John G. Petro, Rector. Tel: 412-321-7550; Rev. David M. Petras, Spiritual Dir. Tel: 412-321-8383, Ext. 12; Sandra A. Collins, Ph.D., Academic Dean & Librarian. Tel: 412-321-8383, Ext. 23; Rev. George D. Gallaro, J.C.O.L., J.C.O.D., S.T.L., Coord. Student Life. Tel: 412-321-8383, Ext. 15. Students for Priesthood 7.

[B] HOMES FOR AGED

UNIONTOWN. *Mt. Macrina Manor*, 520 W. Main St., 15401-2602. Tel: 724-437-1400; Fax: 724-430-1095. Email: pbenford@mtmacrinamanor.com. Web: www.mtmacrinamanor.com. Patricia A. Benford, Admin. Sisters of St. Basil the Great 1; Bed Capacity 139.

WARREN. *Infant of Prague Manor*, 169 Kenmore, N.E., OH 44483. Tel: 330-372-4700. Rev. Robert J. Karl. Housing for the elderly. Apartments 46; Total Staff 3; Total in Residence 31.

[C] MONASTERIES AND RESIDENCES OF PRIESTS AND BROTHERS

BUTLER. *Holy Trinity Monastery*, 134 Trinity Ln., P.O. Box 990, 16003. Tel: 724-287-4461; Fax: 724-287-6160. Rt. Rev. Leo R. Schlosser, Abbot/Hegumen; Rev. Anselm Orlosky, Prior; Bros. Michael Zetzer, Procurator; James Merva. Priests 2; Brothers 2.

[D] CONVENTS AND RESIDENCES FOR SISTERS

ALIQUIPPA. *St. George Convent*, 1000 Clinton St., 15001. Tel: 724-378-0238.

UNIONTOWN. *Monastery and Novitiate of the Sisters of St. Basil the Great*, 500 W. Main St., P.O. Box 878, 15401. Tel: 724-438-8644; Fax: 724-438-8660. Email: osbmolph@verizon.net. Web: www.sistersofstbasil.org. Sr. Seraphim Olsafsky, O.S.B.M., Prov. Supr.; Rev. Michael Huszti, J.C.O.L. Professed Sisters 72.

WARREN. *Queen of Heaven Monastery*, 8640 Squires Ln., N.E., OH 44484. Tel: 330-856-1813; Fax: 330-856-9528. Email: qohm@netdotcom.com. Web: www.benedictinebyzantine.org. Sr. Margaret Mary Schima, O.S.B., Prioress. Benedictine Sisters of the Byzantine Rite 7.

YOUNGSTOWN. *Byzantine Convent*, 5512 Youngstown-Poland Rd., OH 44514. Tel: 330-757-9186; Fax: 330-757-1950. Sisters of St. Basil the Great 2.

[E] MISCELLANEOUS

UNIONTOWN. *Mt. St. Macrina House of Prayer*, 510 W. Main St., P.O. Box 878, 15401-0878. Tel: 724-438-7149; Fax: 724-438-3048. Email: hpmsm@verizon.net. Web: www.sistersofstbasil.org. Sr. Carol Petrasovich, O.S.B.M., Dir.

RELIGIOUS INSTITUTES OF WOMEN REPRESENTED IN THE ARCHDIOCESE

For further details refer to the corresponding bracketed number in the Religious Institutes of Women section.

[0230]—*Benedictine Sisters of the Byzantine Church*—O.S.B.

[3730]—*Sisters of the Order of St. Basil the Great*—O.S.B.M.

NECROLOGY

† Asturi, Bruno, Upper St. Clair, PA St. Gregory Nazianzus—Died Jan. 26, 2009
† Kasarda, John, (Retired)—Died Dec. 8, 2008
† Mokris, Michael, (Retired)—Died April 22, 2009

An asterisk (*) denotes an organization that has established tax-exempt status directly with the IRS and is not covered by the USCCB Group Ruling.

Romanian Catholic Diocese of Saint George in Canton

Most Reverend

JOHN MICHAEL BOTEAN, D.D.

Bishop for the Romanian Catholic Diocese of Canton; ordained May 18, 1986; appointed Bishop for the Romanian Catholic Diocese of Canton July 15, 1996; Episcopal Ordination August 24, 1996. *Res.: 1325 Skyway St., N.E., Canton, OH 44721.* Tel: 330-493-9355; Fax: 330-493-9963.

Chancery: P.O. Box 7189, Canton, OH 44705-0189. Tel: 330-493-9355; Fax: 330-493-9963.

Web: www.romaniancatholic.org

Email: chancery@romaniancatholic.org

Elevated from Apostolic Exarchate for Romanian Byzantine to the Rank of an Eparchy (Diocese) March 26, 1987

The Jurisdiction of the Romanian Catholic Diocese of Canton extends territorially to all of the United States

Legal Title: The Romanian Catholic Diocese of Canton.

STATISTICAL OVERVIEW

Personnel	
Bishop	1
Abbots	1
Priests: Diocesan Active in Diocese	14
Priests: Retired, Sick or Absent	6
Number of Diocesan Priests	20
Religious Priests in Diocese	3
Total Priests in Diocese	23
Extern Priests in Diocese	2
Ordinations:	
Diocesan Priests	1
Permanent Deacons in Diocese	3
Total Brothers	5
Total Sisters	4
Parishes	
Parishes	13
With Resident Pastor:	
Resident Diocesan Priests	10
Resident Religious Priests	1
Without Resident Pastor:	
Administered by Priests	3
Administered by Lay People	1
Missions	5
Closed Parishes	1
Professional Ministry Personnel:	
Lay Ministers	6
Educational	
Diocesan Students in Other Seminaries	2
Total Seminarians	2
Catechesis/Religious Education:	
High School Students	47
Elementary Students	68
Total Students under Catholic Instruction	117
Vital Statistics	
Receptions into the Church:	
Infant Baptism Totals	39
Minor Baptism Totals	2
Adult Baptism Totals	2
Received into Full Communion	8
First Communions	39
Confirmations	38
Marriages:	
Catholic	10
Interfaith	5
Total Marriages	15
Deaths	23
Total Catholic Population	5,869

Former Bishop—Most Rev. LOUIS PUSCAS, D.D., ord. May 14, 1942; appt. Exarch, Dec. 4, 1982; Episcopal ordination, June 26, 1983; installed Aug. 28, 1983; promoted to first Eparch, April 16, 1987; retired July 15, 1993; died Oct. 3, 2009.

Protosyncellus—Very Rev. GEORGE DAVID, V.G.

Chancery—Mailing Address: P.O. Box 7189, Canton, 44705-0189.

Chancellor—Rev. OVIDIU IOAN MARGINEAN.

Economos—JAMES P. DERSHAW, CPA, Reader.

College of Consultors—Very Revs. GEORGE DAVID, V.G.; AUREL PATER; ANDRE MATTHEWS, Vicar for Clergy; Rev. MICHAEL MOISIN; Rt. Rev. Msgr. GREGORY DUMA; Rev. GEORGE GAGE.

Protopresbyters: Deans—

Canton Deanery—Rt. Rev. Msgr. GREGORY DUMA.

Aurora Deanery—Very Rev. AUREL PATER.

Trenton Deanery—Very Rev. GEORGE DAVID, V.G.

Vicar for Theological Affairs—Sr. THERESA KOERNKE, I.H.M., Ph.D.

Vicar for Clergy—Very Rev. ANDRE MATTHEWS.

Director of Religious Education—Rev. ANDREW KOLITSOS.

Pro-Life Commission—Dr. DAN FARCASIU.

Director of Scouting Svcs.—Deacon GARY A. BOYCE, Dir.

Formation Council—Rev. RICHARD J. MUCOWSKI, O.F.M., Ph.D.; Sr. THERESA KOERNKE, I.H.M., Ph.D.; Revs. AUGUST J. DEASIO, M.A. (Retired); EMMANUEL G. SAMAYOA.

Director of Vocations—Very Rev. GEORGE DAVID, V.G.

Office to Aid the Church in Romania—Rev. MICHAEL MOISIN, Coord.

Diocesan Collections Coordinator—Rev. GEORGE GAGE.

Evangelization—Rev. PAUL VOIDA.

Finance Council—Most Rev. JOHN MICHAEL BOTEAN, D.D.; Very Revs. GEORGE DAVID, V.G.; AUREL PATER, Protopresbyter; Revs. MICHAEL MOISIN; OVIDIU IOAN MARGINEAN.

Victim Assistance Coordinator—CAROL ANN GALL, Mailing Address: 335 Southampton Dr., Aurora, 44202. Tel: 216-444-4095. Email: gallc@ccf.org.

Communications Director—Rev. ALIN NADIR DOGARU.

Tribunal of the Eparchy— The Romanian Catholic Eparchy of St. George in Canton has as its Tribunal the Tribunal of the Eparchy of St. Maron of Brooklyn.

Judicial Vicar—Very Rev. FRANCIS J. MARINI, J.D., J.C.D.

CLERGY, PARISHES, MISSIONS AND PAROCHIAL SCHOOLS

STATE OF OHIO

ALLIANCE, STARK CO., ST. THEODORE, Attended by St. George Cathedral. Rev. Ovidiu Ioan Marginean, Admin.
Mailing Address: 1121 44th St. N.E., 44714-1297. Tel: 330-492-8413; Fax: 330-493-9963.
Church: 820 S. Linden St., 44601.

CANTON, STARK CO., ST. GEORGE CATHEDRAL Rt. Rev. Msgr. Gregory Duma, Rector; Rev. Ovidiu Ioan Marginean.
Church & Res.: 1121 44th St., N.E., 44714-1297. Tel: 330-492-8413; Fax: 330-493-9963.
Bishop's Residence:—1325 Skyway St., N.E., 44721. Tel: 330-493-9355; Fax: 330-493-9963.
Catechesis/Religious Program—Michael Polnik, D.R.E. Students 9.

CHESTERLAND, GEAUGA CO., MOST HOLY TRINITY
Church: 8549 Mayfield Rd., 44026-2625. Tel: 216-729-7636; Fax: 216-729-7636.

CLEVELAND, CUYAHOGA CO., ST. HELENA (1904) Very Rev. Andre Matthews; Adrian V Rosca, Lector; Florentin O. Popa, Cantor.
Church & Res.: 1367 W. 65th St., 44102-2109. Tel: 216-651-0965; Fax: 216-631-3853.
Catechesis/Religious Program—Students 5.

YOUNGSTOWN, MAHONING CO., ST. MARY Rev. George Gage.
Church & Res.: 7782 Glenwood Ave., Boardman, 44512-5823. Tel: 330-726-8573; Fax: 330-726-8573.

STATE OF CALIFORNIA

LOS ANGELES, LOS ANGELES CO., ST. MARY ROMANIAN CATHOLIC MISSION, See separate listing. Rev. Calin Tamiian.
5329 Sepulveda Blvd., Sherman Oaks, CA 91411.
Res. & Mailing Address: 1447 Iguana Cir., Ventura, CA 93003-6337. Tel: 805-671-9936. Email: ctamiian@hotmail.com.

STATE OF ILLINOIS

AURORA, DU PAGE CO., ST. MICHAEL (1906) Very Rev. Aurel Pater.
Res. & Church: 609 N. Lincoln Ave., IL 60505-2112. Tel: 630-897-8115; Fax: 630-897-5923.

AURORA, KANE CO., ST. GEORGE (1935) Rev. Frederick Peterson, O.S.B.
Res.: 850 Butterfield Rd., IL 60502-8609. Tel: 630-897-7215, Ext. 326; Fax: 630-897-0393.
Church: 720 Rural St., IL 60505-2551. Tel: 630-851-4002.
Catechesis/Religious Program—Carol Glover, D.R.E. Students 22.

CHICAGO, COOK CO., SS. PETER AND PAUL CHURCH (1994) Rev. Sergiu Cornea.
Res.: 1472 Burr Oak Cir., Aurora, IL 60506-1396. Tel: 630-205-4806; Fax: 630-896-4807. Email: slcornea@aol.com.
Church: 3107 Fullerton Ave., IL 60647-2809. Tel: 773-342-7373; Fax: 773-342-7373.

STATE OF INDIANA

EAST CHICAGO, LAKE CO., ST. NICHOLAS (1913) Rev. Alin Nadir Dogaru, Admin.

Church & Res.: 4309 Olcott Ave., IN 46312-2649. Tel: 219-398-3760; Fax: 219-398-3760. Email: adogaru@romaniancatholic.org.

STATE OF MASSACHUSETTS

BOSTON, MIDDLESEX CO., ROMANIAN CATHOLIC MISSION OF BOSTON (2000) Rev. Michael Moisin, Admin. Res. & Mailing Address: 8 Druce St., Brookline, MA 02445-4213. Tel: 617-216-4980; Fax: 617-566-3073.

STATE OF MICHIGAN

DEARBORN, WAYNE CO., ST. MARY Rev. Gheorghe Opris, Admin.
Church & Res.: 823 S. Military, MI 48124-2109. Tel: 313-274-2347.

DETROIT, WAYNE CO., ST. JOHN THE BAPTIST Rev. Emmanuel G. Samayoa.
Res.: 2371 Woodstock Dr., MI 48203-1060. Tel: 313-386-1046; Fax: 313-368-5358.

STATE OF NEW JERSEY

ROEBLING, BURLINGTON CO., ST. MARY, Attended by St. Basil, Trenton. Very Rev. George David.
Church: 180 Alden Ave., NJ 08554-1125. Tel: 609-695-6093.

TRENTON, MERCER CO., ST. BASIL (1909) Very Rev. George David.
Church & Res.: 238 Adeline St., NJ 08611-2420. Tel: 609-695-6093; Fax: 609-695-6093.

STATE OF NEW YORK

ASTORIA, QUEENS CO., ST. MARY ROMANIAN CATHOLIC MISSION
Holy Cross Church: 31-12 30th St., Long Island City, NY 11106-2802. Tel: 718-845-5366. Rev. Radu N. Titonea; Radu Costiu, Contact Person. Tel: 201-693-8986.

STATE OF PENNSYLVANIA

MCKEESPORT, ALLEGHENY CO., ST. MARY Rev. Paul Voida.
Church & Res.: 318 26th St., PA 15132-7014. Tel: 412-673-5552.

SHARON, MERCER CO., ST. JOHN THE BAPTIST, Closed.

Unassigned:
Revs.—
Brown, Konstantin K.
Kolitsos, Andrew
Yossa, Kenneth F.

Retired:
Revs.—
Buga, John
Kirila, Michael
Streza, Charles V.

INSTITUTIONS LOCATED IN THE DIOCESE

[A] MONASTERIES

NEWBERRY SPRINGS, CA. *Holy Resurrection Monastery*, Mailing Address: P.O. Box 826, Pearblossom, CA 93553. 31001 N. Valyermo Rd., Valyermo, CA 93563. Tel: 661-944-2178; Fax: 661-944-1076. Web: www.hrmonline.org. Rt. Rev. Archimandrite Nicholas Zachariadis, Abbot; Revs. Maximos Davies, Hieromonk; Moses Wright, Hierodeacon.

OLYMPIA, WA. *Holy Theophany Monastery*, 10220 66th Ave., S.E., WA 98513-9207. Tel: 360-491-8233. Email: htheophany@earthlink.net. Sr. Anastasia, Abbess.

NECROLOGY

✠ Puscas, Most Rev. Louis, Bishop Emeritus for the Romanian Catholic Diocese of Canton—Died Oct. 3, 2009

An asterisk (*) denotes an organization that has established tax-exempt status directly with the IRS and is not covered by the USCCB Group Ruling.

Ukrainian Catholic Diocese of St. Josaphat in Parma

Most Reverend

JOHN BURA

Auxiliary Bishop of Philadelphia Ukrainian and Apostolic Administrator of St. Josaphat in Parma; ordained February 14, 1971; appointed Auxiliary Bishop of Philadelphia Ukrainian and Titular Bishop of Limisa January 3, 2006; ordained February 21, 2006; appointed Apostolic Administrator of St. Josaphat in Parma July 29, 2009.

(VACANT SEE)

Chancery: 5720 State Rd., P.O. Box 347180, Parma, OH 44134-7180. Tel: 440-888-1522; Fax: 440-888-3477.

Email: josaphateparchy@cs.com

Most Reverend

ROBERT M. MOSKAL, D.D.

Retired Bishop of St. Josaphat in Parma; ordained March 25, 1963; appointed Titular Bishop of Agathopolis and Auxiliary Bishop of the Archeparchy of Philadelphia August 3, 1981; consecrated October 13, 1981; appointed First Bishop of St. Josaphat in Parma December 5, 1983; retired July 29, 2009. *Res.: 5720 State Rd., P.O. Box 347180, Cleveland, OH 44134.*

ESTABLISHED DECEMBER 3, 1983.

The jurisdiction of the Bishop of St. Josaphat in Parma extends territorially through all the States of Ohio, Mississippi, West Virginia, Kentucky, Tennessee, Alabama, Georgia, North Carolina, South Carolina, Florida and western Pennsylvania. With regards to persons, his subjects are Catholics of the Byzantine Ukrainian Rite: 1. Who immigrated to this country from Galicia, Bucovina and other Ukrainian provinces; 2. Who descend from such persons (Can. 755); 3. Women married to men referable to 1 and 2, if they comply with (Can. 98, n.4); 4. Who in accordance with (Can. 98, n.3) changed their Rite; 5. Converts to the Catholic Church of the Byzantine Ukrainian Rite; 6. And in fact, all other Catholics of the Byzantine Ukrainian Rite who are attached to parishes subject to the jurisdiction of the Bishop of St. Josaphat in Parma.

For legal titles of parishes and diocesan institutions, consult the Chancery.

STATISTICAL OVERVIEW

(Editor's Note: 2010 information was not received)

Personnel	
Retired Bishops	1
Priests: Diocesan Active in Diocese	29
Priests: Diocesan Active Outside Diocese	6
Priests: Retired, Sick or Absent	12
Number of Diocesan Priests	47
Religious Priests in Diocese	1
Total Priests in Diocese	48
Extern Priests in Diocese	9
Ordinations:	
Diocesan Priests	4
Transitional Deacons	2
Permanent Deacons	1
Permanent Deacons in Diocese	8
Total Brothers	3
Total Sisters	3
Parishes	
Parishes	38
With Resident Pastor:	
Resident Diocesan Priests	31
Without Resident Pastor:	
Administered by Priests	7
Missions	4
Professional Ministry Personnel:	
Sisters	2
Welfare	
Homes for the Aged	3
Total Assisted	173
Educational	
Diocesan Students in Other Seminaries	8
Total Seminarians	8
Catechesis/Religious Education:	
High School Students	43
Elementary Students	120
Total Students under Catholic Instruction	171
Vital Statistics	
Receptions into the Church:	
Infant Baptism Totals	89
Adult Baptism Totals	5
First Communions	32
Confirmations	94
Marriages:	
Catholic	29
Interfaith	8
Total Marriages	37
Deaths	189
Total Catholic Population	10,685

Former Bishop—Most Rev. ROBERT M. MOSKAL, ord. March 25, 1963; appt. Titular Bishop of Agathopolis and Auxiliary Bishop of the Archeparchy of Philadelphia Aug. 3, 1981; cons. Oct. 13, 1981; appt. First Bishop of St. Josaphat in Parma Dec. 5, 1983; retired July 29, 2009.

Chancery—*5720 State Rd., P.O. Box 347180, Parma, 44134-7180.* Tel: 440-888-1522; Fax: 440-888-3477. Web: stjosaphateparchy.org. Office Hours: Mon.-Thurs. 10-12 & 2-4, Fri. 10-12

Chancellor—Very Rev. Canon STEVEN PALIWODA.

Vice Chancellor—Rev. VALERIAN MICHLIK.

Vicar General—Rev. Msgr. GEORGE APPLEYARD.

Judicial Vicar—VACANT.

Consultors—Rev. Msgr. GEORGE APPLEYARD; Very Rev. Canon STEVEN PALIWODA; Very Rev. MICHAEL POLOSKY; Very Rev. Canon ANDREW HANOWSKY; Rev. MICHAEL KRUPKA; Very Rev. IGNATIUS KURY.

Eparchial Corporation—Most Rev. JOHN BURA, Pres.; Rev. Msgr. GEORGE APPLEYARD, Vice Pres.; Very Rev. Canon STEVEN PALIWODA, Sec. & Treas.

Administrative Council—Most Rev. JOHN BURA; Very Rev. Canon ANDREW HANOWSKY; Revs. MARK MOROZOWICH, S.E.O.D.; IHOR KASIYAN; Deacons DONALD BILLY; MARK PROKOPOWICH.

Vicar for Clergy—Very Rev. ANTHONY BALISTRERI.

Vicar for Religious—Rev. Msgr. GEORGE APPLEYARD.

Tribunal—

Judicial Vicar—VACANT.

Judge—VACANT.

Defender of the Bond—VACANT.

Notary—VACANT.

Liturgical Commission—Most Rev. JOHN BURA; Revs. VALERIAN MICHLIK; IVAN CHIROVSKY; Rev. Msgr. GEORGE APPLEYARD; Rev. MARK MOROZOWICH, S.E.O.D.

Examiners of Clergy—Rev. Msgr. GEORGE APPLEYARD; Rev. JOSEPH TAMBURRO.

Personnel Board—Very Rev. ANTHONY BALISTRERI, Chm.; Very Rev. Canon STEVEN PALIWODA, Sec.; Very Rev. MICHAEL POLOSKY; Revs. VALERIAN MICHLIK; MICHAEL KRUPKA.

St. Josaphat Sacerdotal Society— (next election in May 2011) Most Rev. JOHN BURA, Ex Officio; Very Rev. Canons STEVEN PALIWODA, Ex Officio; ANDREW HANOWSKY, Sec.; Rev. IVAN CHIROVSKY; Very Rev. IGNATIUS KURY; Rev. PETER TOMAS. Alternates: Revs. VALERIAN MICHLIK; IHOR KASIYAN; GREGORY MAYDYA; IHOR HOHOSHA.

Religious Education—Sr. ANN LASZOK, O.S.B.M., Dir.

League of Ukrainian Catholics—Rev. VALERIAN MICHLIK, Western PA Spiritual Dir.

Obnova Societies—Rev. Mitred Archpriest WOLODYMYR WOLOSZCZUK (Retired).

Vocations—Rev. MARK MOROZOWICH, S.E.O.D.

Acolyte Confraternity—Deacon DONALD BILLY; Mr. JOSEPH LEVY.

Permanent Deacon Program—Rev. Msgr. GEORGE APPLEYARD.

Priests' Continuing Education—Rev. JOSEPH TAMBURRO.

Eparchial Convention—Rev. Msgr. GEORGE APPLEYARD.

Youth Ministries—Very Rev. MICHAEL POLOSKY.

Lay Ministries—Sisters ANN LASZOK, O.S.B.M.; OLGA MARIE FARYNA, O.S.B.M.

Presbyteral Council—Most Rev. JOHN BURA; Rev. Msgr. GEORGE APPLEYARD; Rev. Msgr. Mitred JOHN STEVENSKY; Rev. IHOR HOHOSHO; Very Rev. ANTHONY BALISTRERI; Very Rev. Canon STEVEN PALIWODA; Very Rev. MICHAEL POLOSKY; Revs. JOSEPH TAMBURRO; VALERIAN MICHLIK.

Arbitration Board—Rev. Msgr. GEORGE APPLEYARD; Rev. Archpriest PHILIP BUMBAR; Rev. IVAN CHIROVSKY; Rev. Msgr. Mitred JOHN STEVENSKY; Rev. XAVIER ELAMBASSERY.

Protopresbyteries—

Western Protopresbytery—Very Rev. Canon STEVEN PALIWODA, 3038 Charleston Ave., Lorain, 44055-2464. Tel: 440-277-7114 Akron, OH; Austintown, OH; Brunswick, OH; Canton, OH; Cleveland, OH; Lorain, OH; Parma, OH (Cathedral); Parma, OH (St. Andrew); Parma, OH (Pokrova); Rossford, OH; Solon, OH; Youngstown, OH.

Central Protopresbytery—Rev. Msgr. GEORGE APPLEYARD, 726 Washington Ave., Carnegie, PA 15106. Tel: 412-279-4652 Aliquippa, PA; Ambridge, PA; Arnold, PA (New Kensington); Carnegie, PA; Jeannette, PA; Lyndora, PA; McKees Rocks, PA; McKeesport, PA; Pittsburgh, PA (St. George); Pittsburgh, PA (St. John); Wheeling, WV; Wilmerding, PA.

Eastern Protopresbytery—Very Rev. ANTHONY BALISTRERI, 22 Bentz St., Ramey, PA 16671. Tel: 814-378-7688 Altoona, PA; Ford City, PA; Johnstown, PA; Latrobe, PA; New Alexandria, PA; Northern Cambria, PA (Barnesboro); Ramey, PA; Revloc, PA; West Leechburg, PA.

Southern Protopresbytery—Rev. Msgr. Mitred JOHN STEVENSKY, 434 90th Ave., N., St. Petersburg, FL 33702. Tel: 727-576-1001 Apopka, FL; Conyers, GA; Spring Hill (Brooksville), FL; Miami, FL; North Port, FL; St. Petersburg, FL.

Mid-Atlantic Protopresbytery—Very Rev. MARK SHUEY, 4801 Topstone Rd., Raleigh, NC 27603. Tel: 919-779-7246 Garner, NC (Ss. Volodymyr and Olha); Raleigh, NC (St. Nicholas); Charlotte,

NC (St. Basil); Knoxville, TN (St. Thomas the Apostle).

Presbyters—Rev. Msgr. Mitred LEO ADAMIAK, V.G. (Retired), 1216 Fifth Ave., Youngstown, 44502. Tel: 330-743-6606; Rev. Msgr. GEORGE APPLEYARD, Holy Trinity, 726 Washington Ave., Carnegie, PA 15106-4109. Tel: 412-279-4652; Fax: 412-279-5109; Cell: 724-290-6561; Tel: 814-385-6775 (Cabin). Email: apple@cboss.com; Revs. RICHARD ARMSTRONG, St. Thomas the Apostle, 2044 Farmstead Ln., Powell, TN 37849; ORYST BALABAN (Retired), 1532 Fourth Ave., Arnold, PA 15068-4402. Tel: 724-335-2238; Very Rev. ANTHONY BALISTRERI, Annunciation BVM, 22 Bentz St., Ramey, PA 16671. Tel: 814-378-7688; Rev. MICHAEL BLISZCZ (on loan to St. Nicholas Eparchy) St. Michael, 4390 Woodside Oaks Dr., S.E., Grand Rapids, MI 49546-6216. Tel: 616-949-1151; Rev. Archpriest PHILIP BUMBAR, 726 Washington Ave., Carnegie, PA 15106-4109. Tel: 412-279-4652; Fax: 412-279-5109; Rev. Msgr. Mitred MARTIN A. CANAVAN, 2850 N. Palm Aire Dr. #604, Pompano Beach, FL 33069. Tel: 305-450-8003. Email: pmsgr@en.com; Revs. JASON CHARRON, Ss. Volodymyr and Olha, 8312 White Oak Rd., Garner, NC 27529. Tel: 919-376-8099; IVAN CHIROVSKY, St. John the Baptist, 109 S. 7th St., Pittsburgh, PA 15203-1028. Tel: 412-431-2531; Fax: 412-431-0727; Cell: 786-251-9522. Email: ugveg@aol.com; CRAIG DE PAULO (on leave); MICHAEL DERBISH, O.F.M. (Retired), 2001 Main St., Aliquippa, PA 15001-2724. Tel: 724-375-7016; IHOR HOHOSHO, St. John the Baptist, 204 Olivia St., Mc Kees Rocks, PA 15136. Tel: 412-331-5605; MICHAEL DROZDOVSKY, Pokrova, 6790 Broadview Rd., Parma, 44134. Tel: 216-524-0918 (Residence & Office); Fax: 216-524-0919; Tel: 216-524-6872 (Hall Office); 216-524-6871 (Hall); BORIS DUKELEY (Retired), 415 Montpellier Court, Spring Hill, FL 34608. Tel: 352-684-4876; XAVIER ELAMBASSERY, Assumption BVM/Nativity BVM, 4827 Rte. 982, Latrobe, PA 15650. Tel: 724-537-6450; JOHN GRIBIK, St. Demetrius/Ss. Peter and Paul, 1013 Gaskill Ave., Jeannette, PA 15644. Tel: 724-523-9389; VOLODYMYR GRYTSYUK, Protection BVM, 27275 Aurora Rd., Solon, 44139-1804. Tel: 440-248-4549; Cell: 440-539-2621; Very Rev. Canons ANDREW HANOWSKY, Ss. Peter & Paul, 2280 W. 7th St., Cleveland, 44113. Tel: 216-861-2176; Cell: 216-401-0004; ROBERT HNATYSHYN (Retired), 452 E. McMurray Rd., Mc Murray, PA 15317. Tel: 724-969-5003; Revs. JERRY IKALOWYCH, Mother of God, 2880 Hwy. 138, N.E., Conyers, GA 30013. Tel: 770-760-1111; Fax: 770-922-2992. 143 McBride, Canonsburg, PA 15317; JOHN IZRAL, St. Vladimir, 1601 Kenneth Ave., Arnold, PA 15068-4219. Tel: 724-339-9622; OLEH KACHUR (on loan to Toronto Eparchy) 251 Bolton St., Apt. 20, Ottawa, Canada ON K1N 5B5; IHOR KASIYAN, St. Andrew, 7700 Hoertz Rd., Parma, 44134-6404. Tel: 440-843-9149; 440-845-2270 (Residence); Cell: 440-391-8500. Email: pastor@standrewucc.org. Web: www.standrewucc.org; MICHAEL KOUTS, St. Andrew, 8064 Weeping Willow St., Brooksville, FL 34613. Tel: 352-596-2433; SEVERYN KOVALYSHIN (Entrance BVM into Temple) 1078 N. Biscayne Dr., North Port, FL 34291. Tel: 941-426-7931. Email: severinokov@yahoo.it. Web: www.ukrainiancatholicflorida.com; ANDREW KRASULSKI, St. John/Protection BVM, 606 Maple Ave., Johnstown, PA 15901. Tel: 814-535-2634. Email: stjohnbaptist@yahoo.com; MICHAEL KRUPKA, Our Lady of Perpetual Help, 4136 Jacob St., Wheeling, WV 26003. Tel: 304-232-2168; 304-232-1774 (Hall). Email: krupka@juno.com; IVAN KUBISHYN, St. Mary's Protection, 305 Lake McCoy Dr., Apopka, FL 32712. Tel: 407-880-1640; MICHAEL KULICK, 8455 Sunnydale Dr., Brecksville, 44141. Tel: 440-526-4517; 440-888-8811 (Office); Fax: 440-888-5818; Cell: 440-537-0175; Pager: 440-948-2976. Email: dddfriend@sbcglobal.net; Very Rev. IGNATIUS KURY, Holy Ghost/St. Nicholas, 1859 Carter Ave., Akron, 44301-3198. Tel: 330-724-8277; Cell: 202-270-6153; Revs. SEAN J. LABAT, St. Basil Mission, Charlotte, NC. 1315 Pickens St., Apt. 1, Columbia, SC 29201. Tel: 803-381-7073. Email: sjlabat@yahoo.com; DOUGLAS LORANCE, 610 Hansen Ave., Lyndora, PA 16045-1325. Tel: 724-283-6230; Fax: 724-283-0363; GREGORY MADEYA, B.H.S., St. John the Baptist, 1907 Eden Park Blvd., Mc Keesport, PA 15132. Tel: 412-672-0923. 111 Third St., Dravosburg, PA 15034. Tel: 412-896-1668; Cell: 412-805-3451. Email: greggorio2@aol.com; ANDREW MARKO (Retired), 33225 Electric Blvd., Avon Lake, 44012. Tel: 440-933-6954; VALERIAN MICHLIK, St. George, 3455 California Ave., Pittsburgh, PA 15212-2180. Tel: 412-766-8801; Fax: 412-766-3379; Tel: 412-766-8800 (Hall); 412-766-8802 (Sheptytsky Hall). Email: frvalmichlik@yahoo.com; saintgeorgepghs@aol.com. Web: saintgeorgepittsburgh.org; MARK MOROZOWICH, S.E.O.D., 3900 B Watson Pl., N.W., Apt. G3A, Washington, DC 20016. Tel: 202-965-1572 (House); Cell: 202-468-5166; Tel: 202-319-6515 (Voice Mail); Fax: 202-319-4967. Email: morozowich@cua.edu; GEORGE MULLONKAL, St. Michael, 133 Walnut St., Rossford, 43460-1248. Tel: 419-666-5627; Rev. Msgr. MICHAEL NESTOR (Retired), 867 N. Concord St., Gilbert, AZ 85234. Tel: 480-507-5015. Email: imike@worldnet.att.net; Very Rev. Canon STEVEN PALIWODA, Protopresbyter, Western, St. John the Baptist, 3038 Charleston Ave., Lorain, 44055-2464. Tel: 440-277-7114. Email: steve@eriennet.net; Rev. VASYL PETRIV, St. Josaphat Cathedral, 5720 State Rd., Parma, 44134. Tel: 440-886-2108; Very Rev. MICHAEL POLOSKY, Ss. Peter & Paul, 404 Sixth St., Ambridge, PA 15003. Tel: 724-266-2262 (Office); Fax: 724-266-2262. Email: sspandp@aol.com; Rev. Msgrs. Mitred MICHAEL POLOWAY (Retired), Shevchenko Manor, 5620 W. 24th St., #211, Parma, 44134. Tel: 216-741-8106; Cell: 216-235-7001; MICHAEL REWTIUK (Retired) (on leave) 3112 Marioncliff Dr., Parma, 44134. Email: 2stm@buckeye-express.com; markmorozowich@comcast.net; THOMAS A. SAYUK (on leave); Revs. MATTHEW SCHROEDER, Assumption BVM, 11000 S.W. 128th St., Miami, FL 33176. 39 N.W. 57th Court, Miami, FL 33126. Tel: 305-262-4192; Fax: 305-261-9759; Tel: 786-242-8146 (Home). Email: father@uccm.us. Web: www.uccm.us; JAROSLAV SHUDRAK; Very Rev. MARK SHUEY, St. Nicholas Mission; St. Basil the Great, Charlotte. Email: george.gulyas@lpl.com. Web: www.saintbasilcharlotte.org; 4801 Topstone Rd., Raleigh, NC 27603. Tel: 919-779-7246. Email: rfmark@nc.rr.com; Revs. JOHN SMEREKA (visiting priest) 410 7th Ave., Carnegie, PA 15106; MICHAEL SOPP (on leave of absence) P.O. Box 49, Kittanning, PA 16201; ANIBAL SOUTIS, 2941 Lookout, Atlanta, GA 30035. Tel: 404-723-7396; Rev. Msgr. Mitred JOHN STEVENSKY, Protopresbyter, Southern, Epiphany of Our Lord, 434 90th Ave., N., St. Petersburg, FL 33702-3022. Tel: 727-576-1001. Email: msgrjps@mindspring.com; Revs. JOSEPH TAMBURRO, Immaculate Conception/Imm. Con., 3711 Campbell Ave., P.O. Box 1335, Northern Cambria, PA 15714-1335. Tel: 814-948-9193 (Res.). Email: rublievht@sbcglobal.net; PETER TOMAS, St. Anne, Holy Trinity, 3055 S. Raccoon Rd., Austintown, 44515-5351. Tel: 330-793-5436 (Res.); Fax: 330-793-5436. Office: 4310 Kirk Rd., Austintown, 44511-1899. Tel: 330-792-8555. Email: stannechurch@yahoo.com; frpetertomas@yahoo.com; Rev. Mitred Archpriest WOLODYMYR WOLOSZCZUK (Retired), 4240 Timberline Blvd., Venice, FL 34293. Tel: 941-493-7299; Rev. Canon WALTER WYSOCHANSKY (Retired), 404 Sixth St., Ambridge, PA 15003. Tel: 724-266-2262; Rev. STEVEN ZARICHNY, Holy Trinity, 526 W. Rayen Ave., Youngstown, 44502-1124. Tel: 330-744-5820.

CLERGY, PARISHES, MISSIONS AND PAROCHIAL SCHOOLS

STATE OF OHIO

PARMA

1—ST. ANDREW Rev. Ihor Kasiyan; Deacon Roman Turchyn.
Res.: 7700 Hoertz Rd., 44134-6404. Tel: 440-843-9149; Fax: 440-845-2986.
Catechesis/Religious Program—Mary Sulhan, D.R.E. Students 17.

2—ST. JOSAPHAT CATHEDRAL (1959) Revs. Michael Kulick; Vasyl Petriv; Archdeacon Jeffrey Smolilo.
Res.: 5720 State Rd., 44134-2536. Tel: 440-886-2108.

3—POKROVA UKRAINIAN CATHOLIC PARISH, [CEM] Rev. Michael Drozdovsky.
Res.: 6790 Broadview Rd., 44134-4804. Tel: 216-524-0918; Fax: 216-524-0919.

AKRON, SUMMIT CO., HOLY GHOST Very Rev. Ignatius Kury.
Res.: 1859 Carter Ave., 44301. Tel: 330-724-8277.

AUSTINTOWN, MAHONING CO., ST. ANNE (1967) [JC] Rev. Peter Tomas.
Res.: 3055 S. Raccoon Rd., 44515-5351. Tel: 330-792-8555; Fax: 330-793-5436.
Catechesis/Religious Program—Mrs. Michelle Tomas, D.R.E. Students 5.

CANTON, STARK CO., ST. NICHOLAS, Attended by Akron. Very Rev. Ignatius Kury.
Res.: 1859 Carter Ave., Akron, 44301. Tel: 330-724-8277.

CLEVELAND, CUYAHOGA CO., SS. PETER AND PAUL, [CEM] Very Rev. Canon Andrew Hanowsky.
Res.: 2280 W. 7th St., 44113. Tel: 216-861-2176.

LORAIN, LORAIN CO., ST. JOHN THE BAPTIST (1913) Very Rev. Canon Steven Paliwoda.
Res.: 3038 Charleston Ave., 44055-2164. Tel: 440-277-7114.
Church: 2445 E. 31st St., 44055.

ROSSFORD, WOOD CO., ST. MICHAEL Rev. George Mullonkal.
Res.: 133 Walnut St., 43460-1248. Tel: 419-666-5627; Fax: 419-666-3077.

SOLON, CUYAHOGA CO., PROTECTION B.V.M. Rev. Volodymyr Grytsyuk.
Res.: 27275 Aurora Rd., 44139-1804. Tel: 440-248-4549.
Catechesis/Religious Program—Students 7.

YOUNGSTOWN, MAHONING CO., HOLY TRINITY Rev. Steven Zarichny.
Res.: 526 W. Rayen Ave., 44502-1124. Tel: 330-744-5820.

STATE OF FLORIDA

APOPKA, ORANGE CO., ST. MARY'S Rev. Ivan Kubishyn; Deacon Richard Wilhelm.
Res.: 305 Lake McCoy Dr., FL 32712. Tel: 407-880-1640.
Catechesis/Religious Program—

BROOKSVILLE, HERNANDO CO., ST. ANDREW Rev. Michael Kouts.
Mailing Address: 8064 Weeping Willow St., FL 34613. Tel: 352-597-4366.

MIAMI, DADE CO., ASSUMPTION OF B.V.M. Rev. Matthew Schroeder.
Res.: 11000 S.W. 128th St., FL 33126. Tel: 305-262-4192; Fax: 305-261-9759.
Church: 39 N.W. 57th Ct., FL 33126.
Catechesis/Religious Program—Students 10.
Mission— Lantana, Palm Beach Co., FL.

NORTH PORT, SARASOTA CO., ENTRANCE OF B.V.M. INTO THE TEMPLE (ST. MARY'S) Rev. Severyn Kovalyshin.
Res.: 1078 N. Biscayne Dr., FL 34286. Tel: 941-426-7931; Fax: 941-426-7931.

ST. PETERSBURG, PINELLAS CO., EPIPHANY OF OUR LORD Rev. Msgr. Mitred John Stevensky.
Res.: 434 90th Ave. N., FL 33702. Tel: 727-576-1001 (Res.); Fax: 727-576-6821.

STATE OF GEORGIA

CONYERS, ROCKDALE CO., MOTHER OF GOD Rev. Jerry Ikalowych.
Res.: 2880 Hwy. 138, N.E., GA 30013. Tel: 770-760-1111.

STATE OF NORTH CAROLINA

CHARLOTTE, MECKLENBURG CO., ST. BASIL THE GREAT MISSION Very Rev. Mark Shuey; Rev. Sean J. LaBat.
c/o Rev. Mark Shuey, 4801 Topstone Rd., Raleigh, NC 27603. Tel: 919-779-7246.
Res.: 729 Aiken St., Columbia, SC 29201. Tel: 803-381-7073.

GARNER, WAKE CO., SS. VOLODYMYR AND OLHA MISSION (2006) Rev. Jason Charron.
8312 White Oak Rd., NC 27529. Tel: 919-376-8099.
Catechesis/Religious Program—Students 17.

RALEIGH, WAKE CO., ST. NICHOLAS MISSION Very Rev. Mark Shuey.
4801 Topstone Rd., NC 27603. Tel: 919-779-7246.

STATE OF PENNSYLVANIA

ALIQUIPPA, BEAVER CO., SS. PETER AND PAUL (1916) Rev. Ihor Hohosha. Served from St. John the Baptist, McKees Rocks.
Res.: 2001 Main St., PA 15001. Tel: 412-375-7016.

ALTOONA, BLAIR CO., IMMACULATE CONCEPTION, [CEM], Served by Northern Cambria , Mailing Address: 2024 20th St., PA 16601.

AMBRIDGE, BEAVER CO., SS. PETER AND PAUL (1907) [CEM] Very Rev. Michael Polosky.
Res.: 404 6th St., PA 15003. Tel: 412-266-2262; Fax: 412-266-2262. In Res., Rev. Canon Walter Wysochansky (Retired).
Catechesis/Religious Program—Michael Cross, D.R.E. Students 70.
Convent—542 Melrose Ave., PA 15003. Tel: 724-266-5578. Sisters of St. Basil the Great.

CARNEGIE, ALLEGHENY CO., HOLY TRINITY (1951) [CEM] Rev. Msgr. George Appleyard; Rev. John Smereka; Rev. Canon Philip Bumbar.
Res.: 730 Washington Ave., PA 15106. Tel: 412-279-4652; Fax: 412-279-5109.
Catechesis/Religious Program—Donna Sradomski, D.R.E. (Elementary); Mark Medwig, D.R.E. (High School). Students 29.

FORD CITY, ARMSTRONG CO., ST. MARY, [CEM] Rev. John Izral.
Res.: 514 Ninth St., PA 16226. Tel: 724-763-1203.

JEANNETTE, WESTMORELAND CO., ST. DEMETRIUS Rev. John Gribik.
Res.: 1013 Gaskill Ave., PA 15644-3307. Tel: 724-523-9389.

JOHNSTOWN, CAMBRIA CO., ST. JOHN THE BAPTIST, [CEM] Rev. Andrew Krasulski.
Res.: 606 Maple Ave., PA 15901. Tel: 814-535-2634; Fax: 814-535-2634.
Catechesis/Religious Program—Miss Mary Anne Varholak, D.R.E. Students 4.

LATROBE, WESTMORELAND CO., ASSUMPTION OF B.V.M. Rev. Xavier Elambassery.
Res.: 4827 Rt. 982, PA 15650. Tel: 412-537-6450.

LYNDORA, BUTLER CO., ST. MICHAEL Rev. Douglas Lorance.
Res.: 610 Hansen Ave., PA 16045-1325. Tel: 724-283-6230; Fax: 724-283-0363. Email: stmikeschurch@zoominternet.net.
Catechesis/Religious Program—Students 10.

MCKEES ROCKS, ALLEGHENY CO., ST. JOHN THE BAPTIST (1941) Rev. Ihor Hohosha.
Res.: 204 Olivia St., PA 15136. Tel: 412-331-5605; Fax: 412-331-8809.

MCKEESPORT, ALLEGHENY CO., ST. JOHN THE BAPTIST Rev. Gregory Madeya, B.H.S.
Res.: 1907 Eden Park Blvd., PA 15132. Tel: 412-672-0923.

NEW ALEXANDRIA, WESTMORELAND CO., NATIVITY B.V.M., [CEM] Attended by Assumption of B.V.M., Latrobe., Mailing Address: 4827 Rte. 982, Latrobe, PA 15650. Tel: 412-537-6450.
Church: Shersburg Rd., PA 15670.

NEW KENSINGTON (ARNOLD), WESTMORELAND CO., ST. VLADIMIR (1912) Rev. John Izral; Deacon Stephen Aftanas.
Res.: 1601 Kenneth Ave., Arnold, PA 15068. Tel: 724-339-9622.

NORTHERN CAMBRIA, CAMBRIA CO., IMMACULATE CONCEPTION Rev. Joseph Tamburro.
Res.: 300 Campbell Ave., P.O. Box 1335, PA 15714. Tel: 814-948-9193.

PITTSBURGH, ALLEGHENY CO.

1—ST. GEORGE Rev. Valerian Michlik.
Res.: 3455 California Ave., PA 15212. Tel: 412-766-8801; Fax: 412-766-3379.

2—ST. JOHN THE BAPTIST, [CEM] Rev. Ivan Chirovsky.
Res.: 109 S. Seventh St., PA 15203. Tel: 412-431-2531; Fax: 412-431-6404.

RAMEY, CLEARFIELD CO., ANNUNCIATION B.V.M., [CEM] Unassigned.Mailing Address: P.O. Box 205, PA 16671.
Res.: 22 Bentz St., PA 16671-0205. Tel: 814-378-7688.

REVLOC, CAMBRIA CO., PROTECTION BLESSED VIRGIN MARY (1926) Attended by Johnstown., 606 Maple Ave., Johnstown, PA 15901. Tel: 814-535-2634.
Church: 560 Cambria Ave., P.O. Box 194, PA 15948-0914.
Catechesis/Religious Program—Mrs. Robin Wagner, D.R.E. Students 6.

WEST LEECHBURG, ARMSTRONG CO., ST. MICHAEL, Attended by Ford City, PA., Mailing Address: 514 Ninth St., Ford City, PA 16226. Tel: 724-763-1203.
Church: Main St., PA 15656.

WILMERDING, ALLEGHENY CO., SS. PETER AND PAUL, Attended by Jeannette, PA., Mailing Address: 1013 Gaskill Ave., Jeannette, PA 15644-3307. Tel: 724-523-9389.
Church: 163 State St., PA 15148-1323. Tel: 724-829-1833.

STATE OF WEST VIRGINIA

WHEELING, OHIO CO., OUR LADY OF PERPETUAL HELP Rev. Canon Michael Krupka.
Res.: 4136 Jacob St., WV 26003. Tel: 304-232-2168; Fax: 304-232-8719.

On Assignment Outside the Diocese:
Revs.—
Bliszcz, Michael, St. Michael, 4390 Woodside Oaks Dr., S.E., Grand Rapids, MI 49506.
Kachur, Oleh, 251 Bolton St., Apt. 20, Ottawa ON K1N5B5 Canada.
Morozowich, Mark, S.E.O.D., 3900 B Watson Pl., N.W., Apt. G3A, Washington, DC 20016.
Shudrak, Jaroslav, 1555 Bloor St. W., Toronto ON M6P 1A4 Canada.
Soutos, Hannibal, On Loan to Diocese of Kiev, Ukraine

On Leave:
Rev. Msgrs. Mitred—
Rewtiuk, Michael (Retired), 3112 Marioncliff Dr., 44134.
Sayuk, Thomas A.
Revs.—
de Paulo, Craig
Sopp, Michael, P.O. Box 49, Kittanning, PA 16201.

Retired:
Rev. Msgr.—
Nestor, Michael, 867 N. Concord St., Gilbert, AZ 85234. Tel: 602-507-5015
Revs.—
Balaban, Oryst, 1532 Fourth Ave., Arnold, PA 15068-4402.
Derbish, Michael, O.F.M., 2001 Main St., Aliquippa, PA 15001.
Dukeley, Boris, 415 Montpellier Ct., Spring Hill, FL 34608.
Marko, Andrew, 33225 Electric Blvd., Avon Lake, 44012.
Very Rev. Canon—
Hnatyshyn, Robert, 452 E. McMurray Rd., Mcmurray, PA 15317.
Rev. Msgrs. Mitred—
Adamiak, Leo, V.G., 526 W. Rayen Ave., Youngstown, 44502-1124.
Poloway, Michael, 5620 W. 24th St., #211, 44134.
Rev. Mitred Archpriest—
Woloszczuk, Wolodymyr, 4240 Timberline Blvd., Venice, FL 34293.
Rev. Canon—
Wysochansky, Walter, 404 6th St., Ambridge, PA 15003.

Permanent Deacons:
Aftanas, Stephen, 3009 Wachter Ave., Lower Burrell, PA 15068.
Billy, Donald, 2515 McCollum Rd., Youngstown, 44509. Tel: 330-792-3166
Dozier, Daniel, P.O. Box 2264, Southern Pines, NC 28388. Tel: 860-938-2582
Dozier, Gordon, 15 Village By the Lake, Southern Pines, NC 28387.
Gregory, John, 7629 Normandy Blvd., Apt. B28, Middleburg Heights, 44130-6560.
Prokopovich, Mark, 38 Anthony Wayne Ter., Baden, PA 15005.
Smolilo, Jeffery, 4546 Shelly Dr., Seven Hills, 44131. Tel: 216-328-0743 (Home); 216-344-8315 (Office)
Suchan, Stephen, 133 Willow Village Dr., Pittsburgh, PA 15239.
Wirag, Joseph, 807 Pine St., Ambridge, PA 15003-1734. Cell: 724-709-9640
Wroblicky, Alexander, 818 Hershire Dr., Bethel Park, PA 15102. Tel: 412-527-8456

INSTITUTIONS LOCATED IN THE DIOCESE

[A] MONASTERIES AND RESIDENCES FOR PRIESTS AND BROTHERS

BROOKLYN. *Holy Spirit Monastery*, 4150 Rabbit Run, 44144. Tel: 216-741-3653. Email: brotherdale@catholicweb.com. Bros. Dale Sefcik, B.H.S.; David Robert, B.H.S.

[B] CONVENTS

PARMA. *St. Josaphat Cathedral Convent*, 5710 State Rd., 44134-2536. Tel: 440-885-1245. Email: janinajp3@yahoo.com. Sisters of St. Basil the Great.

AMBRIDGE. *Ss. Peter & Paul Convent*, 542 Melrose Ave., PA 15003. Tel: 724-266-5578. Sisters of St. Basil the Great

[C] HOMES FOR THE AGED

PARMA. *Shevchenko Manor*, 5620 W. 24th St., 44134-2751. Tel: 216-459-1440; Fax: 216-459-1442. Jean Waschtschenko, Mgr.

PITTSBURGH. *St. George's Close*, 3505 Mexico St. at Chidel St., PA 15212. Jennifer Verdi, Mgr.
Sheptytsky Arms, 3503 Mexico St., PA 15212. Tel: 412-766-8802. Jennifer Verdi, Mgr.

[D] MISCELLANEOUS

PITTSBURGH. *Pastoral Ministry Office*, 727 E. Carson St., PA 15203. Tel: 412-481-9778; Fax: 412-481-4914.

NECROLOGY

† Ropke, John, (On Leave)—Died June 7, 2009
† Poorman, James E., Ramey, PA Annunciation B.V.M.—Died May 26, 2009

An asterisk (*) denotes an organization that has established tax-exempt status directly with the IRS and is not covered by the USCCB Group Ruling.

Eparchy of St. Maron of Brooklyn

Most Reverend
GREGORY J. MANSOUR

Bishop of Saint Maron of Brooklyn; ordained September 18, 1982; appointed Bishop of Saint Maron of Brooklyn January 10, 2004; consecrated March 2, 2004; installed April 27, 2004. *109 Remsen St., Brooklyn, NY 11201.*

Most Reverend
STEPHEN HECTOR DOUEIHI, S.T.D.

Retired Bishop of Saint Maron of Brooklyn; born June 25, 1927; ordained August 14, 1955; appointed Second Eparchial Bishop of the Eparchy of Saint Maron of Brooklyn November 23, 1996; consecrated January 11, 1997; enthroned February 5, 1997; retired January 10, 2004. *Res.: 113 Remsen St., Brooklyn, NY 11201.*

Most Reverend
FRANCIS M. ZAYEK, D.D., S.T.D., J.C.D.

Retired Archbishop of St. Maron of Brooklyn; born October 18, 1920; ordained March 17, 1946; appointed Titular Bishop of Callinicum May 30, 1962; consecrated August 5, 1962; appointed Bishop of the Diocese of Saint Maron November 11, 1971; installed June 4 1972; elevated to Archbishop December 22, 1982, retired November 11, 1996. *Res.: 4010 Galt Ocean Dr., Apt. 1203, Fort Lauderdale, FL 33308.* Established as an Apostolic Exarchate January 10, 1966; Elevated to a Diocese November 11, 1971.

The jurisdiction of the Diocese extends to all the Maronite Catholics in New York, New Jersey, Pennsylvania, Florida, Georgia, North Carolina, South Carolina, Delaware, Virginia, District of Columbia, Maine, New Hampshire, Vermont, Massachusetts, Rhode Island, Connecticut and Maryland.

For legal titles of parishes and diocesan institutions, consult the Chancery Office.

Chancery Office, 109 Remsen St., Brooklyn, NY 11201. Tel: 718-237-9913; Fax: 718-243-0444.

Email: chancerystmaron@verizon.net

Web: www.stmaron.org

STATISTICAL OVERVIEW

Personnel	
Retired Archbishops	1
Bishop	1
Retired Bishops	1
Abbots	1
Priests: Diocesan Active in Diocese	35
Priests: Diocesan Active Outside Diocese	3
Priests: Diocesan in Foreign Missions	1
Priests: Retired, Sick or Absent	12
Number of Diocesan Priests	51
Religious Priests in Diocese	12
Total Priests in Diocese	63
Extern Priests in Diocese	7
Ordinations:	
Transitional Deacons	2
Permanent Deacons	2
Permanent Deacons in Diocese	17
Total Brothers	7
Total Sisters	1
Parishes	
Parishes	34
With Resident Pastor:	
Resident Diocesan Priests	33
Resident Religious Priests	1
Missions	5
Pastoral Centers	1
Welfare	
Other Institutions	1
Total Assisted	75
Educational	
Seminaries, Diocesan	1
Students from This Diocese	4
Students from Other Diocese	4
Total Seminarians	4
Catechesis/Religious Education:	
High School Students	315
Elementary Students	1,597
Total Students under Catholic Instruction	1,916
Vital Statistics	
Receptions into the Church:	
Infant Baptism Totals	391
Minor Baptism Totals	8
Adult Baptism Totals	17
Received into Full Communion	18
First Communions	320
Confirmations	461
Marriages:	
Catholic	87
Interfaith	21
Total Marriages	108
Deaths	264
Total Catholic Population	30,200

Former Bishops—Most Revs. FRANCIS M. ZAYEK, D.D., S.T.D., J.C.D., born Oct. 18, 1920; ord. March 17, 1946; appt. Titular Bishop of Callinicum May 30, 1962; cons. Aug. 5, 1962; appt. Bishop of the Diocese of Saint Maron Nov. 11, 1971; installed June 4, 1972; elevated to Archbishop Dec. 22, 1982; retired Nov. 11, 1996.; STEPHEN HECTOR DOUEIHI, S.T.D., born June 25, 1927; ord. Aug. 14, 1955; appt. Second Eparchial Bishop of the Eparchy of Saint Maron of Brooklyn Nov. 23, 1996; cons. Jan. 11, 1997; enthroned Feb. 5, 1997; retired Jan. 10, 2004.

Protosyncellus (Vicar General)—Chorbishop MICHAEL G. THOMAS, J.C.D.

Chancellor—Chorbishop MICHAEL G. THOMAS, J.C.D.

The Chancery—109 Remsen St., Brooklyn, 11201. Tel: 718-237-9913; Fax: 718-243-0444. Email: chancerystmaron@verizon.net. Office Hours: Mon.-Fri. 9-4. Closed on holy days of obligation and national holidays.

Tribunal of the Eparchy of Saint Maron of Brooklyn—300 Wyoming Ave., Scranton, PA 18503-1279. Tel: 570-207-2246; Fax: 570-207-2274. Email: maronitetribunal@aol.com.

Tribunal—

Judicial Vicar—Very Rev. FRANCIS J. MARINI, J.D., J.C.D.

Judges—Chorbishop MICHAEL G. THOMAS, J.C.D.; Rev. Msgr. ANDREW L. ANDERSON, J.C.D.; Rev. JOHN PAUL KIMES, J.C.D.; Rev. Msgr. PATRICK J. PRATICO, J.C.D.

Promoter of Justice—Very Rev. WILLIAM J. KING, J.C.D.

Defender of the Bond—Rev. Msgr. JOSEPH G. QUINN, J.D., J.C.L.

Advocates—Rev. TANIOS KOZHAYA AKOURY, J.C.L.; Rev. Msgr. NEVIN J. KLINGER, J.C.L.

Notaries—Mrs. JOAN MATELIS; Ms. CAMILLE P. MANNING; Ms. PAT VANCOSKY; Ms. CARYN BUTLER.

Presbyteral Council—Rev. Msgr. PETER F. AZAR, Ex Officio; Chorbishop SEELY BEGGIANI, S.T.D., Ex Officio; Revs. PETER BOULOS, Ex Officio; GEORGES Y. EL-KHALLI, Ph.D., Ex Officio; Chorbishop JOSEPH F. KADDO; Very Rev. FRANCIS J. MARINI, J.D., J.C.D.; Rev. SAMUEL A. NAJJAR, Ex Officio; Very Rev. JAMES A. ROOT, Ex Officio; Rev. BASSAM SAADE; Rev. Msgr. GEORGE M. SEBAALI; Chorbishop MICHAEL G. THOMAS, J.C.D., Ex Officio; Rev. JEAN YOUNES.

Protopresbyters (Deans)—Rev. Msgr. PETER F. AZAR, New England Region; Revs. PETER BOULOS, Far South Region; GEORGES Y. EL-KHALLI, Ph.D., Mid-Atlantic West Region; Very Rev. JAMES A. ROOT, Mid-Atlantic East Region; Rev. SAMUEL A. NAJJAR, South Region.

Lebanon Commission—Chorbishop SEELY BEGGIANI, S.T.D., Chm., 7164 Alaska Ave., N.W., Washington, DC 20012. Tel: 202-723-8831. Email: ololsem@maroniteseminary.org.

National Apostolate of Maronites National Office—MIKE J. NABOR, Exec. Dir., Mailing Address: P.O. Box 717, Yonkers, 10702. Tel: 914-964-3070; Fax: 914-964-3071. Email: nam@namnews.org.

Diocesan Offices and Directors

Communications—Rev. Msgr. GEORGE M. SEBAALI, 4611 Sadler Rd., Glen Allen, VA 23060. Tel: 804-270-7234; Fax: 804-273-9914. Email: gmsebaali@aol.com.

(Diocesan Newspaper) "The Maronite Voice"—Rev. Msgr. GEORGE M. SEBAALI, Editor, 4611 Sadler Rd., Glen Allen, VA 23060. Tel: 804-762-4301; Fax: 804-273-9914. Email: gmsebaali@aol.com.

Finance Council—Chorbishops MICHAEL G. THOMAS, J.C.D., Finance Officer; SEELY BEGGIANI, S.T.D.; Mr. ANTHONY BUDWAY; Ms. CLAIRE HABIB; Mr. RODNEY THOMAS; Mr. ALBERT ASHKOUTI; Dr. PETER GABRIEL.

Ministries (Permanent Deacons and Subdeacons)—Rev. JACK MORRISON, 11 Franklin St., New Bedford, MA 02740. Tel: 508-996-8934; Fax: 508-996-2744. Email: aboonajack@aol.com.

Order of Saint Sharbel—Mrs. BEVERLY MIKE-NARD, Pres., 3330 Partridge Park Dr., Poland, OH 44514; BERNADETTE SHALHOUB, Vice Pres., 8429 W. Lake Dr., Lake Clarke Shores, FL 33406.

Office of Outreach—Rev. Msgr. RONALD BESHARA, Dir., 5200 N. Flaglar 1404, West Palm Beach, FL 33407. Tel: 561-596-8176; Fax: 561-841-1153. Email: rbeshara@hanleycenter.org.

Office of Ecumenism and Interreligious Dialogue—Rev. SAMUEL A. NAJJAR, St. Michael the Archangel Church, 806 Arsenal Ave., Fayetteville, NC 28305. Tel: 910-484-1531; Fax: 910-484-5387. Email: stmikemcc@embarqmail.com.

Pro-Life Director—Rev. Kevin Beaton, 2 W. Reynolds St., New Castle, PA 16101. Tel: 724-658-0787; Fax: 724-658-2711. Email: stjohnbaptist@netzero.com.

Religious Education—Rev. Georges Y. El-Khalli, Ph.D., 2040 Wehrle Dr., Williamsville, 14221. Tel: 716-634-0669; Fax: 716-634-0674. Email: stjmaron@buffnet.net.

Victim Assistance Coordinator—Rosanne Solomon, 15 Raven Rd., Canton, MA 02021. Tel: 781-828-5183. Email: rosannesolomon@hotmail.com.

Vocations—Very Rev. James A. Root, Our Lady of Lebanon Cathedral, 113 Remsen St., Brooklyn, 11201. Tel: 718-624-7228; Fax: 718-624-8034. Email: cathrectory@verizon.net.

Youth Ministry Office—Rev. Gary George, Saint Maron Church, 1555 S. Meridian Rd., Youngstown, OH 44511. Tel: 330-792-2371; Fax: 330-792-3026. Email: abounag1@hotmail.com.

Young Adult Ministry—Rev. Elie Hares Mikhael, Our Lady of Lebanon, 2055 Coral Way, Miami, FL 33145. Tel: 305-856-7449; Fax: 305-856-5740. Email: ololmiami@bellsouth.net.

Board of Pastors—Rev. Msgr. Peter F. Azar; Very Rev. Francis J. Marini, J.D., J.C.D.; Rev. Msgr. George M. Sebaali.

College of Consultors—Rev. Msgr. Peter F. Azar; Revs. Peter Boulos; Georges Y. El-Khalli, Ph.D.; Very Rev. Francis J. Marini, J.D., J.C.D.; Rev. Msgr. George M. Sebaali.

Immigration Office—Michael J. Koury Jr., Attorney. Tel: 610-905-3781; Fax: 610-253-0673. Email: kourylaw@msn.com.

CLERGY, PARISHES, MISSIONS AND PAROCHIAL SCHOOLS

STATE OF NEW YORK

Brooklyn, Kings Co., Cathedral of Our Lady of Lebanon (1902) [JC] Very Rev. James A. Root, Rector. In Res., Rev. Geoffrey Abdallah.
Res.: 113 Remsen St., 11201. Tel: 718-624-7228; Fax: 718-624-8034.
Catechesis / Religious Program—Students 94.
Mission—

Olean, Cattaraugus Co., St. Joseph (1919) [JC] Rev. Joseph G. Akiki.
Res.: 225 N. 4th St., 14760. Tel: 716-372-4311. Email: stjosepholean@roadrunner.com.
Catechesis / Religious Program—Students 11.

Troy, Rensselaer Co., St. Ann (1905) Rev. Elie G. Kairouz.
Church: 184 Fourth St., 12180. Tel: 518-272-6073; Fax: 518-272-6073. Email: st.ann_mc_church@yahoo.com. Web: www.sainteann.com.
Catechesis / Religious Program—Email: stann_reled@yahoo.com. Students 16.

Utica, Oneida Co., St. Louis Gonzaga (1910) Chorbishop John D. Faris; Deacon Paul A. Salamy.
Res.: 520 Rutger St., 13501. Tel: 315-732-6019; Fax: 315-732-6018. Email: stlouisgonzaga@gmail.com.
Catechesis / Religious Program—Students 84.

Williamsville, Erie Co., St. John Maron (1903), (Lebanese), Rev. Georges Y. El-Khalli.
Res.: 2040 Wehrle Dr., 14221-7041. Tel: 716-634-0669; Fax: 716-634-0674. Email: stjmaron@gmail.com. Web: www.stjohnmaron.org.
Catechesis / Religious Program—Students 111.

STATE OF CONNECTICUT

Danbury, Fairfield Co., St. Anthony (1932) Rev. Jean Younes.
Res.: 17 Granville Ave., CT 06810. Tel: 203-744-3372; Fax: 203-794-0949. Email: stanthonyoffice@yahoo.com.
Catechesis / Religious Program—Students 51.

Torrington, Litchfield Co., St. Maron (1909) Rev. Lawrence P. Michael; Subdeacon Paul Comeau; Deacon Steve Marcus.
Mailing Address: 605 Main St., CT 06790.
Res.: 613 Main St., CT 06790. Tel: 860-489-9015; Fax: 860-482-1614. Email: stmaronchurch@aol.com.
Catechesis / Religious Program—Students 140.

Waterbury, New Haven Co., Our Lady of Lebanon (1975) Rev. Naji Kiwan.
Mailing Address: 8 E. Mountain Rd., CT 06706. Email: our_lady_lebanon@sbcglobal.net.
Res.: 1544 Hamilton Ave., CT 06706. Tel: 203-753-9428; Fax: 203-573-8384.
Catechesis / Religious Program—Students 20.

STATE OF FLORIDA

Jacksonville, Duval Co., St. Maron Maronite (1995) [JC] Rev. Elie Abi-chedid; Deacon Elias Shami.
Res.: 7032 Bowden Rd., FL 32216. Tel: 904-448-0203; Fax: 904-448-8277. Email: frchedid@hotmail.com. Web: stmaronjax.com.
Catechesis / Religious Program—Students 40.

Miami, Dade Co., Our Lady of Lebanon (1973) Rev. Elie Hares Mikhael.
Mailing Address: 2055 Coral Way, FL 33145. Tel: 305-856-7449; Fax: 305-856-5740. Email: ololmiami@bellsouth.net. Web: www.ololmiami.org.
Res.: 420 Como Ave., Coral Gables, FL 33146.
Catechesis / Religious Program—Students 55.

Orlando, Orange Co., St. Jude (2003) Rev. Bassam Saade.
Res.: 5555 Dr. phillips Blvd., FL 32819. Tel: 407-363-7405; Fax: 407-363-7793. Email: saintjudechurch@saintjudechurch.org. Web: www.saintjudechurch.org.
Catechesis / Religious Program—Students 45.

Tampa, Pasco Co., Mission of Sts. Peter & Paul (2000) Rev. Peter Boulos.
6201 Sheldon Rd., FL 33615. Tel: 813-886-7413 (church & Rectory); Fax: 813-885-6346. Email: peterandpaulmcc@gmail.com. Web: www.maronitetampa.com.
Catechesis / Religious Program—Students 8.

West Palm Beach, Palm Beach Co., Mary Mother of Light Maronite Mission Rev. Msgr. Ronald Beshara; Subdeacon Dennis Somerville.
Mailing Address & Church: 4891 Lake Worth Rd., Greenacres, FL 33463. Tel: 561-433-8831; Fax: 561-841-1153. Email: rbfish1404@gmail.com.
Catechesis / Religious Program—Students 25.

STATE OF GEORGIA

Atlanta, Fulton Co., St. Joseph's Maronite Church (1911) [JC] Rev. Dominique Hanna, Admin.; Deacon Robert Calabrese.
Res.: 502 Seminole Ave., N.E., GA 30307. Tel: 404-525-2504; Fax: 404-524-8572. Email: sjmcc@sjmcc.org. Web: www.sjmcc.org.
Catechesis / Religious Program—Students 70.

STATE OF MAINE

Waterville, Kennebec Co., St. Joseph (1927) Rev. Larry Jensen; Deacon Peter P. Joseph.
Res.: 3 Appleton St., ME 04901. Tel: 207-872-8515; Fax: 207-872-8089. Email: stjoesinmaine@yahoo.com.
Catechesis / Religious Program—Students 20.

STATE OF MASSACHUSETTS

Brockton, Plymouth Co., St. Theresa (1932) Rev. Anthony J. Salim.
Mailing Address: P.O. Box 2567, MA 02305-2567. Fax: 508-587-8139.
Res.: 343 N. Main St., MA 02301. Tel: 508-586-1428; Fax: 508-587-8139. Email: sainttheresa@comcast.net.
Catechesis / Religious Program—Students 19.

Fall River, Bristol Co., St. Anthony of the Desert (1911) Chorbishop Joseph F. Kaddo; Rev. Nadim Helou, M.L.M., Parochial Vicar; Deacons Donald P. Massoud; Andre Nasser.
Res.: 300 N. Eastern Ave., MA 02723. Tel: 508-672-7653; Fax: 508-678-1474. Email: saotd@saotd.com. Web: www.saotd.com.
Catechesis / Religious Program—Students 66.

Jamaica Plain, Suffolk Co., Our Lady of the Cedars of Lebanon (1893) Rev. Msgr. Joseph F. Lahoud.
Res.: 61 Rockwood St., MA 02130. Tel: 617-522-0225; Fax: 617-522-0194. Email: rockcedars@yahoo.com. Web: www.ourladyofthecedars.org.
Catechesis / Religious Program—Students 35.

Lawrence, Essex Co., St. Anthony (1903) [CEM] Rev. Msgr. Peter F. Azar; Rev. Milad Zein, Parochial Vicar; Deacons Allan Ramey; Simon Abi Nader; Subdeacon Abraham Abdulla.
Res.: 145 Amesbury St., MA 01841. Tel: 978-685-7233; Fax: 978-688-4475. Email: rectory@stanthonylawrence.org. Web: stanthonylawrence.org.
Catechesis / Religious Program—Students 147.

New Bedford, Bristol Co., Our Lady of Purgatory (1917) Rev. John A. Morrison; Deacon Jean E. Mattar; Subdeacon Joseph Abraham.
Res.: 11 Franklin St., MA 02740. Tel: 508-996-8934; Fax: 508-996-2744.
Catechesis / Religious Program—Students 10.

Springfield, Hampden Co., St. Anthony (1905) Unassigned. Deacon Enzo DiGiacomo.
Mailing Address: 375 Island Pond Rd., MA 01118-1002.
Res.: 419 Island Pond Rd., MA 01118-1002. Tel: 413-732-0589; Fax: 413-732-6320. Email: stanthony419@comcast.net.
Catechesis / Religious Program—Students 25.

Worcester, Worcester Co., Our Lady of Mercy (1923) Rev. Paul Mooradd.
Res.: 74 Mulberry St., MA 01605. Tel: 508-752-4287; Fax: 508-798-4189. Web: www.ourladyofmercy.parishesonline.com.
Catechesis / Religious Program—Students 21.

STATE OF NEW HAMPSHIRE

Dover, Strafford Co., St. George (1949) Rev. Joseph Khoueiry.
Mailing Address: 15 Chapel St., P.O. Box 2210, NH 03821-2210.
Res.: 46 Hough St., NH 03820. Tel: 603-742-1149; Fax: 603-740-9624. Email: stgeorgemaronite@myfairpoint.net.
Church: 15 Chapel St., NH 03821. Tel: 603-740-4287 (Church).

STATE OF NEW JERSEY

Somerset, Somerset Co., St. Sharbel Rev. Msgr. Maroun Asmar; Subdeacon Joseph Chebli.
Res.: 7 Reeve St., NJ 08873. Tel: 732-828-2055; Fax: 732-828-5488.
Catechesis / Religious Program—Email: secretary@saintsharbelnj.us. Students 150.
Mission—Our Lady Star of the East 220 N. Main St., Pleasantville, Atlantic Co., NJ 08232. Tel: 609-484-8817 (Res.); Fax: 609-383-8644 (Bus.).

STATE OF NORTH CAROLINA

Cary, Wake Co., Saint Sharbel Mission (2000) Rev. Kamil Alchouefati.
Mailing Address: P.O. Box 4093, NC 27513. Tel: 610-905-2859; 919-931-5781; 866-748-8522. Email: stsharbelnc@yahoo.com. Web: www.marsharbel.org.
Rectory—c/o 806 Arsenal Ave., Fayetteville, NC 28305-5363. Tel: 910-484-1531.
Catechesis / Religious Program—Students 22.

Fayetteville, Cumberland Co., St. Michael the Archangel (1973) Rev. Samuel A. Najjar.
Res.: 212 Bradford Ave., NC 28301. Tel: 910-484-1531; Fax: 910-484-5387. Email: stmikemcc@embarqmail.com. Web: www.stmichaelsmaronite.org.
Catechesis / Religious Program—Students 20.

STATE OF PENNSYLVANIA

Carnegie, Allegheny Co., Our Lady of Victory Rev. Rodolph Wakim.
Res.: 1000 Lindsay Rd., PA 15106. Tel: 412-278-0841; Fax: 412-278-0846. Email: abounarodolph@gmail.com. Web: www.olov.info.
Catechesis / Religious Program—Students 30.
Mission—Maronite Mission of Aliquippa 2001 Main St., Aliquippa, Beaver Co., PA 15001.

Easton, Northampton Co., Our Lady of Lebanon (1931) Rev. Paul Damien; Deacon Anthony P. Koury.
Res.: 54 S. Fourth St., PA 18042. Tel: 610-252-5275; Fax: 610-252-1737. Email: oLoLchurch@yahoo.com. Web: www.mountlebanon.org.
Catechesis / Religious Program—Students 45.

New Castle, Lawrence Co., St. John the Baptist (1926) Rev. Kevin J. Beaton, S.F.O.; Deacon Richard E. Stone.
Res.: 2 W. Reynolds St., PA 16101. Tel: 724-658-0787; Fax: 724-658-2711. Email: stjohnthebaptist@netzero.com.
Catechesis / Religious Program—Students 42.

Newtown Square, Delaware Co., St. Sharbel (1983) Deacon Martin LoMonaco.
Res.: 3679 Providence Rd., PA 19073. Tel: 610-353-5952; Fax: 610-353-0343.
Catechesis / Religious Program—Students 23.

Philadelphia, Philadelphia Co., St. Maron (1862) Rev. Msgr. Sharbel Lischaa; Deacon Joseph Regan.
Res.: 1010 Ellsworth St., PA 19147-4622. Tel: 215-389-2000.
Catechesis / Religious Program—Students 35.

Scranton, Lackawanna Co., St. Ann (1903) [JC] Very Rev. Francis J. Marini; Subdeacon Robert Rade.
Res.: 1320 Price St., PA 18504-3336. Tel: 570-344-2129; Fax: 570-344-3920. Email: stannscranton@aol.com.
Catechesis / Religious Program—Students 18.

Uniontown, Fayette Co., St. George (1927) Rev. Tony Akoury; Subdeacon Thomas George.
Res.: 6 Lebanon Ter., PA 15401-3011. Tel: 724-437-5589; Fax: 724-437-3819. Email: sixleb@atlanticbb.net. Web: www.stgeorgemaronite.com.
Catechesis / Religious Program—Students 36.

Wilkes-Barre, Luzerne Co., St. Anthony + St. George (1911) Rev. Hanna Karam; Subdeacon Oliver Crosby Sparks.
Res.: 79 Loomis St., PA 18702-4610. Tel: 570-824-3599; Fax: 570-824-1747.
Catechesis / Religious Program—Students 38.

STATE OF RHODE ISLAND

LINCOLN, PROVIDENCE CO., ST. GEORGE (1911) Rev. Edward T. Nedder.
Church & Res.: 171 Twin Rivers Rd., RI 02865. Tel: 401-723-8444 (Rectory); Fax: 401-728-2032. Email: maronitechurch@earthlink.net.
Catechesis/Religious Program—Students 34.

STATE OF SOUTH CAROLINA

GREENVILLE, GREENVILLE CO., ST. RAFKA MARONITE MISSION (2002) Rev. Bartholomew Leon, O.S.B., Admin.
Res.: *St. Mary's Church*, 111 Hampton Ave., SC 29601. Tel: 864-271-8422; Fax: 864-370-9880. Email: saintrafkasc@aol.com. Web: www.saintrafka.net.
Catechesis/Religious Program—Mr. Elie Alam, D.R.E. Students 4.

STATE OF VIRGINIA

GLEN ALLEN, HENRICO CO., ST. ANTHONY (1913) [JC] Rev. Msgr. George M. Sebaali; Rev. Georges Bouchaaya, M.L.M., Parochial Vicar.
Res.: 4611 Sadler Rd., VA 23060. Tel: 804-270-7234; Fax: 804-273-9914. Email: stanthonymaronitechurch@verizon.net. Web: www.stanthonymaronitechurch.org.
Catechesis/Religious Program—Students 200.

ROANOKE, ROANOKE CITY CO., ST. ELIAS (1917) Rev. Claude W. Franklin Jr.
Res.: 4730 Cove Rd., N.W., VA 24017. Tel: 540-562-2525; Fax: 540-562-1300. Email: fr@steliaschurch.org. Web: www.steliaschurch.org.
Catechesis/Religious Program—Students 52.

DISTRICT OF COLUMBIA

WASHINGTON, DISTRICT OF COLUMBIA, OUR LADY OF LEBANON CHURCH (1967) Chorbishop Dominic F. Ashkar; Deacon John Jarvis.
Res.: 7237 15th Pl. N.W., DC 20012. Tel: 202-291-5153; Fax: 202-291-5153. Web: ourladyoflebanon-dc.org.
Church: 7142 Alaska Ave., N.W., DC 20012. Tel: 202-829-5154.
Catechesis/Religious Program—Students 84.

On Duty Outside the Diocese:
Chorbishop—
Faris, John D.
Revs.—
Amar, Joseph P.
Bartoul, William
Michael, David C. (BO)
Mouannes, Tanios

On Leave:
Rev.—
Zina, George

On Sabbatical:
Rev. Msgr.—
George, David M.

Retired:
Most Revs.—
Doueihi, Stephen Hector, S.T.D.
Zayek, Francis M.
Rev. Msgrs.—
Hayek, Sami
Khoury, James T.
Sadek, Ignace
Revs.—
Andary, John S.
Basinow, Leonard
Boackle, Paul H.
El-Hayek, Nehmatallah
Henderson, Christopher
Shaheen, Joseph

Permanent Deacons:
Abi Nader, Simon, Bow, NH
Calabrese, Robert, Cummings, GA
DiGiacomo, Enzo, Springfield, MA
Gebron, Charles, Springfield, MA
Joseph, Peter P., Waterville, ME
Koury, Anthony P., Easton, PA
Massoud, Donald P., Fall River, MA
Mattar, Jean E., New Bedford, MA
Nasser, Andre, Fall River, MA
Ramey, Allan, Lawrence, MA
Regan, Joseph W., Sewell, NJ
Salamy, Paul A., Utica, NY
Shami, Elias, Jacksonville, FL
Stone, Richard E., New Castle, PA

INSTITUTIONS LOCATED IN THE DIOCESE

[A] SEMINARIES, DIOCESAN

WASHINGTON. *Our Lady of Lebanon Maronite Seminary*, 7164 Alaska Ave., N.W., DC 20012. Tel: 202-723-8831; Fax: 202-829-6053. Email: ololsem@maroniteseminary.org. Web: www.maroniteseminary.org. Chorbishop Seely Beggiani, S.T.D., Rector. Priests 1. In Res. Rev. Msgr. Ignace Sadek (Retired).

[B] RELIGIOUS COMMUNITIES OF MEN

PETERSHAM. *Maronite Monks of Adoration Most Holy Trinity Monastery*, 67 Dugway Rd., MA 01366-9725. Tel: 978-724-3347. Rt. Rev. William J. Driscoll, O.Mar., Abbot; Very Rev. Louis Marie Dauphinais, M.M.A., Prior; Revs. Michael Gilmary Cermak, O.Mar.; John Marie Choiniere, O.Mar.; Ignatius (Allen) Dec, O.Mar.; Martin Ferland, O.Mar.; Giles R. Goyette, O.Mar.; Elias Havel, O.Mar.; Robert Nortz; Bros. Joseph Brady; Benedict Henricks; Patrick Kokorian; John Baptist Livingston; Augustine Martin; Ephrem Martin; Jerome Sander; Simon Peter Williams. Priests 9; Brothers 8; Novices 1.

[C] RELIGIOUS COMMUNITIES OF WOMEN

BROOKLYN. *Servants of Christ the Light, c/o Eparchy of Saint Maron of Brooklyn*, 109 Remsen St., 11201. Tel: 202-213-7700. Email: sister@maroniteservants.org. Web: www.maroniteservants.org.

[D] RESIDENCES FOR CLERGY

BROOKLYN. *Bishop's Residence*, 8070 Harbor View Ter., 11209.

[E] ASSISTED LIVING

NEW BEDFORD. *Cedar Holdings, Inc.*, c/o 11 Franklin St., MA 02740. Tel: 508-996-8934; Fax: 508-996-2744. Web: www.thecedarsassistedliving.com. Rev. Jack Morrison.

[F] MISCELLANEOUS

BROOKLYN. *Bishops Retirement Trust Fund*, 109 Remsen St., 11201.
Order of St. Sharbel Trust Fund, 109 Remsen St., 11201.
Priest Retirement Trust Fund, 109 Remsen St., 11201.
Tele Lumiere / Noursat, 109 Remsen St., 11201.

SHELBURNE. *Saint Rafka Retreat Center*, 6420 Rte. 116, VT 05482-7191. Tel: 802-660-2528; Fax: 802-660-2528. Rev. Kurt Apfelbeck.

NECROLOGY

† Abi-Nader, Chorbishop Joseph, (Retired)—Died June 6, 2009

An asterisk (*) denotes an organization that has established tax-exempt status directly with the IRS and is not covered by the USCCB Group Ruling.

Diocese of St. Nicholas in Chicago for Ukrainians

Most Reverend

RICHARD S. SEMINACK

Bishop of St. Nicholas in Chicago; ordained May 25, 1967; appointed Bishop of St. Nicholas in Chicago March 25, 2003; ordained June 4, 2003. *Office: 2245 W. Rice St., Chicago, IL 60622.* Tel: 773-276-5080.

Most Reverend

INNOCENT LOTOCKY, O.S.B.M.

Retired Bishop of St. Nicholas in Chicago; ordained November 24, 1940; appointed Second Bishop of Chicago January 29, 1981; consecrated March 1, 1981; installed April 2, 1981; retired September 28, 1993. *Mailing Address: 2245 W. Rice St., Chicago, IL 60622.* Tel: 773-276-8981.

Chancery Office: 2245 W. Rice St., Chicago, IL 60622. Tel: 773-276-5080; Fax: 773-276-6799; 773-276-0314.

Email: sneparchy@iols.com

Comprises all of the United States west of the western borders of Ohio, Kentucky, Tennessee and Mississippi.

For legal titles of parishes and diocesan institutions, consult the Chancery Office.

STATISTICAL OVERVIEW

Personnel	
Bishop	1
Retired Bishops	1
Abbots	1
Priests: Diocesan Active in Diocese	29
Priests: Retired, Sick or Absent	5
Number of Diocesan Priests	34
Religious Priests in Diocese	8
Total Priests in Diocese	42
Extern Priests in Diocese	7
Ordinations:	
Diocesan Priests	2
Transitional Deacons	2
Permanent Deacons in Diocese	8
Total Sisters	4
Parishes	
Parishes	40
With Resident Pastor:	
Resident Diocesan Priests	32
Resident Religious Priests	3
Without Resident Pastor:	
Administered by Priests	5
Missions	6
Closed Parishes	1
Educational	
Elementary Schools, Diocesan and Parish	2
Total Students	245
Catechesis/Religious Education:	
High School Students	40
Elementary Students	105
Total Students under Catholic Instruction	390
Teachers in the Diocese:	
Priests	1
Sisters	2
Lay Teachers	20
Vital Statistics	
Receptions into the Church:	
Infant Baptism Totals	150
Adult Baptism Totals	4
Received into Full Communion	7
First Communions	132
Confirmations	161
Marriages:	
Catholic	45
Interfaith	3
Total Marriages	48
Deaths	183
Total Catholic Population	13,915

Former Bishops—Most Revs. JAROSLAV GABRO, D.D., appt. First Bishop of Chicago, July 12, 1961; cons. Oct. 26, 1961; died March 28, 1980; INNOCENT LOTOCKY, O.S.B.M., D.D., Ph.D., ord. Nov. 24, 1940; appt. Second Bishop of Chicago, Jan. 29, 1981; cons. March 1, 1981; installed April 2, 1981; retired Sept. 28, 1993; MICHAEL WIWCHAR, C.Ss.R., D.D., ord. June 28, 1959; appt. Third Bishop of St. Nicholas July 2, 1993; ord. Sept. 28, 1993; appt. Bishop of Saskatoon (Ukrainian), Nov. 29, 2000; secondary appt. Apostolic Administrator of St. Nicholas in Chicago, Dec. 9, 2000.

Protosyncellus—Very Rev. Canon WAYNE RUCHGY.

Chancellor—Very Rev. JAMES M. KAREPIN, O.P.

Vice Chancellor—VACANT.

Chief Financial Officer and Eparchial Finance Director—JAROSLAW HANKEWYCH. Tel: 773-772-6131. Email: hankewych@msn.com.

Chancery Office—2245 W. Rice St., Chicago, 60622. Tel: 773-276-5080; Fax: 773-276-6799; 773-276-0314. Email: sneparchy@iols.com. Office Hours: Mon.-Fri. 9-4. Closed all major holy days and legal holidays.

Diocesan Consultors—Very Rev. Canon WAYNE RUCHGY; Very Revs. JAMES M. KAREPIN, O.P.; VARCILIO BASIL SALKOVSKI, O.S.B.M.; Rev. RICHARD JANOWICZ; Very Rev. Canon MICHAEL STELMACH; Very Rev. Archpriest MYKHAILO KUZMA.

Presbyteral Council—Most Rev. RICHARD S. SEMINACK, D.D., Ex Officio; Very Rev. Canon WAYNE RUCHGY; Very Rev. JAMES M. KAREPIN, O.P.; Very Rev. Archpriest MYKHAILO KUZMA; Revs. HUGO SOUTUS, Chm.; YAROSLAV MENDYUK, Sec.; MYRON MYKYTA; RICHARD JANOWICZ; BASIL SALKOVSKI, O.S.B.M.; Very Rev. VOLODYMYR PETRIV.

Personnel Board—Most Rev. RICHARD S. SEMINACK, D.D.; Very Rev. Canon WAYNE RUCHGY, Chm.; Very Rev. Archpriest MYKHAILO KUZMA; Very Rev. JAMES M. KAREPIN, O.P.; Rev. RICHARD JANOWICZ.

Tribunal— Through Special Permission of the Holy See, Local Latin Rite Tribunals Handle the Cases Within the Diocese.

Protopresbyteries (Deans)—Detroit: Very Rev. VOLODYMYR PETRIV, Protopresbyter. Chicago: Very Rev. VARCILIO BASIL SALKOVSKI, O.S.B.M., Protopresbyter; Very Rev. Archpriest MYKHAILO KUZMA, Vice Protopresbyter. Minneapolis: Very Rev. Canon MICHAEL STELMACH, Protopresbyter. South-West: Rev. RICHARD JANOWICZ, Protopresbyter.

Eparchial Censor—Rev. DEMETRIUS WYSOCHANSKY, O.S.B.M.

Eparchial Office of Religious Education & Catechesis—Rev. OLEH KRYVOKULSKY, Dir.; NAZAR SLOBODA, Assoc. Dir.

Eparchial Ecumenical Officer—Very Rev. JAMES M. KAREPIN, O.P.

Stewardship and Development Office—Mr. SERGE MICHALUK, Dir., 2245 W. Rice St., Chicago, 60622. Tel: 773-276-9500; Fax: 773-276-9502.

Office for Protection of Children and Youth—Mr. SERGE MICHALUK, Dir.

Task Force for a Safe Environment—Dr. LINDA HRYHORCZUK, Chm.

"New Star" - Eparchial Newspaper—Rev. JOHN P. LUCAS, English Editor. Tel: 773-291-0168; Subdeacon PETRO RUDKA, Ukrainian Editor.

CLERGY, PARISHES, MISSIONS AND PAROCHIAL SCHOOLS

STATE OF ILLINOIS

CHICAGO, COOK CO.

1—ST. NICHOLAS UKRAINIAN CATHOLIC CATHEDRAL (1906), (Ukrainian), [CEM] Revs. Bohdan Nalysnyk, Rector; Volodymyr Hudzan, Vice Rector; Pavlo Popov; Deacons Mychajlo Horodysky; Michael Huskey.

Res.: 2238 W. Rice St., 60622. Tel: 773-276-4537 (parish phone); Fax: 773-276-5558. Email: office@stnicholaschicago.org. Web: www.stnicholaschicago.org.

School—(Grades PreK-8), 2200 W. Rice St., 60622-4811. Tel: 773-384-7243; Fax: 773-384-7283. Sr. Irenea Hankewych, O.S.B.M., Supr.; Maria Klysh-Finiak, Prin. Sisters 2; Lay Teachers 12; Students 100.

Convent—Sisters of St. Basil the Great, 2230 W. Rice St., 60622-4811. Tel: 773-486-6820.

2—ST. JOSEPH (N.W. Chicago) (1956), (Ukrainian), Rev. Mykola Buryadnyk. Tel: 312-421-5230; Very Rev. Canon Thomas Glynn; Rev. Volodymyr Kushnir. Tel: 773-979-4737.

Res.: 5000 N. Cumberland Ave., 60656. Tel: 773-625-4833; 773-625-4805 (Office); Fax: 773-625-4148.

Catechesis/Religious Program—Students 35.

3—ST. MICHAEL'S (1917), (Ukrainian), [JC] In Res., Rev. John Lucas.

Church & Mailing Address: 12211 S. Parnell, 60628. Tel: 773-291-0168; 773-291-0168.

4—SS. VOLODYMYR AND OLHA (1968), (Ukrainian), [JC] Rev. Oleh Kryvokulsky, Admin. Tel: 312-829-6805; Rt. Rev. Mitred Archpriest Ivan Krotec, Pastor Emeritus. Tel: 312-455-0178; Revs. Ihor Koshyk. Tel: 773-276-1493; Stepan Kostiuk.
Parish Office—2245 W. Superior St., 60612. Tel: 312-829-5209; Fax: 312-829-4113.

MADISON, MADISON CO., ST. MARY'S, [JC] Rev. Robert Piorkowski, Admin.
Res.: 1312 Iowa St., 62060. Tel: 616-452-9118.

PALATINE, COOK CO., IMMACULATE CONCEPTION (1963), (Ukrainian), Very Rev. Archpriest Mykhailo Kuzma.
Res.: 745 S. Benton, 60067. Tel: 847-991-0820; Fax: 847-991-7873. Email: mykhailo-marian@sbcglobal.net.
Catechesis / Religious Program—Tel: 847-639-9188. Students 31.

PALOS PARK, COOK CO., NATIVITY OF B.V.M. (1911), (Ukrainian), Very Rev. Varcilio Basil Salkovski, O.S.B.M.; Rev. Demetrius Wysochansky, O.S.B.M.; Deacon Michael Cook.
Res.: 8530 W. 131 St., 60464. Tel: 708-361-8876; Fax: 708-361-8820. Email: nativityukrainian@sbcglobal.net.
Catechesis / Religious Program—Patricia Kuzmak, D.R.E. Students 7.

STATE OF ARIZONA

PHOENIX, MARICOPA CO., ASSUMPTION OF B.V.M. (1959) Rev. Hugo Soutus.
Res.: 3730 W. Maryland Ave., AZ 85019. Tel: 602-973-3667; Fax: 602-973-3667.
Church: 3720 W. Maryland Ave., AZ 85019.
Mission—Flagstaff Mission 16 W. Cherry Ave., Flagstaff, AZ 86001. Served by Phoenix.

TUCSON, PIMA CO., ST. MICHAEL (1978), (Ukrainian), [JC] Rt. Rev. Andriy Chirovsky, Temporary Admin. Mailing Address: 715 W. Vanover Rd., AZ 85705-4137.
Res.: 1557 N. Brown Way, AZ 85715-5578. Tel: 520-298-4967.
Res.: 1135 E. Balboa Dr., Tempe, AZ 85282-3906. Tel: 480-217-8505.
Catechesis / Religious Program—Mrs. Halyna Chirovsky, D.R.E. Students 4.

STATE OF CALIFORNIA

LOS ANGELES, LOS ANGELES CO., NATIVITY OF B.V.M. (1947), (Ukrainian), Rev. Myron Mykyta.
Res.: 5154 De Longpre Ave., Hollywood, CA 90027. Tel: 323-663-6307; Fax: 323-663-0369.

CITRUS HEIGHTS, SACRAMENTO CO., HOLY WISDOM (2001) Rev. Theodore P. Wroblicky.
Mailing Address: 1324 La Serra Dr., Sacramento, CA 95864.
Chapel— Christ the King Retreat Center, 6520 Van Maren Ln., CA 95621. Tel: 916-486-0632.

DESERT HOT SPRINGS, RIVERSIDE CO., ST. SOPHIA, Closed. For inquiries for parish records contact the chancery.

LA MESA, SAN DIEGO CO., OUR LADY OF PERPETUAL HELP (1960), (Ukrainian), Rev. James Bankston.
Church: 4400 Palm Ave., CA 91941. Tel: 619-697-5085; Fax: 619-697-7374.
Catechesis / Religious Program—Students 8.

SACRAMENTO, SACRAMENTO CO., ST. ANDREW THE APOSTLE Rev. Petro Kozar.
Res.: 7001 Florin Rd., CA 95828. Tel: 916-383-8614; 916-381-1179.
Catechesis / Religious Program—Tel: 916-381-2529; Fax: 916-381-2529.

SAN FRANCISCO, SAN FRANCISCO CO., IMMACULATE CONCEPTION CATHOLIC CHURCH (1957), (Ukrainian), Rev. Petro Dyachok, Admin.
Res.: 215 Silliman, CA 94134. Tel: 415-468-2601; Fax: 415-468-2601.
Catechesis / Religious Program—Tel: 415-468-2601.

SANTA CLARA, SANTA CLARA CO., ST. VOLODYMYR (1963) Attended by San Francisco. Rev. Petro Dyachok, Admin.
445 Washington St., CA 95050. Email: yhryciw@gmail.com. Web: www.homestead.com/calukes.
Catechesis / Religious Program—Yarema Hryciw, D.R.E. Students 20.

UKIAH, UKIAH CO., ST. PETER EASTERN CATHOLIC MISSION (1999), (Ukrainian), Rev. David Anderson, Admin.
Res.: 190 Orr St., CA 95482. Tel: 707-468-4348; Fax: 707-467-0505.

STATE OF COLORADO

DENVER, DENVER CO., TRANSFIGURATION OF OUR LORD (1954), (Ukrainian), [JC] Rev. Vasyl Hnatkivskyy, Admin.; Deacon Michael Bozio.
Res.: 4118 Shoshone St., CO 80211. Tel: 303-433-2347. Email: denverukrainian@comcast.net.

STATE OF HAWAII

HONOLULU, ST. SOPHIA BYZANTINE MISSIONS Revs. George Busto, C.O., Admin.; Michael Owens.
Res.: 5919 Kalanianaole Hwy., HI 96821. Tel: 808-396-0551.

STATE OF INDIANA

MISHAWAKA, ST. JOSEPH CO., ST. MICHAEL (1962) Very Rev. James Karepin, O.P.
Res.: 712 E. Lawrence St., IN 46544. Tel: 574-259-7173. Email: archangelmishawaka@comcast.net.

MUNSTER, LAKE CO., ST. JOSAPHAT (1958), (Ukrainian), Rev. Yaroslav Mendyuk.
Res.: 8624 White Oak Ave., IN 46321. Tel: 219-923-0984; Fax: 219-923-0984.
Catechesis / Religious Program—Students 11.

STATE OF KANSAS

WICHITA, SEDGWICK
MISSION—HOLY APOSTLES 7100 E. 45th St. N., KS 67226. Tel: 316-734-1295; 316-744-0167, Ext. 118. Deacon Randall Brown, Temporary Admin.

STATE OF MICHIGAN

DEARBORN, WAYNE CO., ST. MICHAEL'S (1962) Very Rev. Canon Wayne J. Ruchgy.
Res.: 6340 Chase Rd., MI 48126. Tel: 313-582-1424; Fax: 313-582-8157.
Mission—Holy Ascension Salem, MI 48175.

DEARBORN HEIGHTS, WAYNE CO., OUR LADY OF PERPETUAL HELP (1963), (Ukrainian), Very Rev. Volodymyr Petriv; Rev. Andriy Burda.
Res.: 26606 Ann Arbor Trail, MI 48127. Tel: 313-278-0470. Email: olphukr@gmail.com.
Catechesis / Religious Program—Students 7.

DETROIT, WAYNE CO., ST. JOHN THE BAPTIST (1918), (Ukrainian), Rev. Valeriy Kandyuk, Admin.
Res.: 3877 Clippert Ave., MI 48210. Tel: 313-897-7300; Fax: 313-897-7304.

FLINT, GENESEE CO., ST. VLADIMIR'S (1950) Rev. Bogdan Rybchuk.
Res.: c/o 24932 Marigold Ave., Warren, MI 48089. Tel: 586-757-3834.

GRAND RAPIDS, KENT CO., ST. MICHAEL'S (1949), (Ukrainian), [JC] Rev. Michael Bliszcz (SJP), Admin.
Mailing Address: 154 Gold Ave., N.E., MI 49504. Tel: 616-742-0874.

HAMTRAMCK, WAYNE CO., IMMACULATE CONCEPTION OF B.V.M. (1914), (Ukrainian), Revs. Daniel Schaicoski, O.S.B.M., Supr. & Pastor; Roman Hykavy, O.S.B.M.
Res.: 11700 McDougall St., MI 48212. Tel: 313-893-1710; Fax: 313-893-0770.
School—(Grades K-8), 29500 Westbrook, Warren, MI 48093. Tel: 586-574-2480; Fax: 586-574-2723. Christine Juzych, Librarian. Priests 1; Lay Teachers 17; Students 145.
Catechesis / Religious Program—Students 145.

WARREN, MACOMB CO., ST. JOSAPHAT (1961), (Ukrainian), [CEM] Revs. Mario Dacechen, O.S.B.M.; Walter Rybicky, O.S.B.M.
Res.: 26401 St. Josaphat Dr., MI 48091. Tel: 586-755-1740; Fax: 586-755-1399.
Catechesis / Religious Program—Marie Heshchuk, D.R.E. Students 16.

STATE OF MINNESOTA

MINNEAPOLIS, HENNEPIN CO., ST. CONSTANTINE (1913), (Ukrainian), [CEM] Very Rev. Canon Michael Stelmach.
Res.: 515 University Ave., N.E., MN 55413-1944. Tel: 612-379-2394; Fax: 612-379-2470.
Catechesis / Religious Program—Students 17.

STATE OF MISSOURI

ST. JOSEPH, BUCHANAN CO., ST. JOSEPH'S (1918), (Ukrainian), Attended by Omaha, NE. Rev. Bohdan Kudleychuk.
Church: 526 Virginia, MO 64504. Tel: 816-238-1187; Fax: 402-345-1552.

ST. LOUIS, ST. LOUIS CO., ASSUMPTION B.V.M. (1894), (Ukrainian), Rev. Andrew Plishka, Admin. Served by Chicago.
Church: 11363 Oak Branch Dr., MO 63129. Tel: 314-487-1786.

STATE OF NEBRASKA

LINCOLN, LANCASTER CO., ST. GEORGE'S (1950), (Ukrainian), Rev. Bohdan Kudleychuk.
Res.: 1513 Martha St., Omaha, NE 68108.
Church: 3330 N. 13th St., NE 68521. Tel: 402-435-5882; 402-345-1552.

OMAHA, DOUGLAS CO., ASSUMPTION OF B.V.M. (1950), (Ukrainian), Rev. Bohdan Kudleychuk.
Res.: 1513 Martha St., NE 68108. Tel: 402-345-1552.

STATE OF NORTH DAKOTA

BELFIELD, STARK CO.

1—ST. DEMETRIUS (1905), (Ukrainian), [CEM 2] Rev. Michael Taras Miles; Deacon Leonand Kordonowy.
Res.: P.O. Box 428, ND 58622-0428. Tel: 701-575-4281.
Catechesis / Religious Program—Students 15.

2—ST. JOHN THE BAPTIST (1946), (Ukrainian), [CEM 2] Rev. Michael Taras Miles; Deacon Leonard Kordonowy.
Mailing Address: P.O. Box 428, ND 58622-0428.
Res.: 307 6th St., N.E., P.O. Box 428, ND 58622-0428. Tel: 701-575-4281; Fax: 701-575-4281.
Catechesis / Religious Program—Tel: 701-575-8645. Students 3.

WILTON, MCLEAN CO., SS. PETER AND PAUL (1906), (Ukrainian), [CEM] Rev. George L. Pruys, Admin.
Res.: 106 N. 7th St., P.O. Box 275, ND 58579. Tel: 701-734-6464.
Catechesis / Religious Program—Students 38.
Mission—St. Michael 812 N. Main St., Minot, Ward Co., ND 58703. Tel: 701-839-4756.

STATE OF OREGON

SPRINGFIELD, LANE CO., NATIVITY OF THE MOTHER OF GOD (1981), (Ukrainian), Rev. Richard Janowicz.
Res.: 704 Aspen St., OR 97477. Tel: 541-726-7309; Fax: 541-726-7309.
Catechesis / Religious Program—Students 18.

STATE OF TEXAS

HOUSTON, HARRIS CO., PROTECTION OF THE MOTHER OF GOD (1957), (Ukrainian), [JC] Rev. Mykola Dovzhuk, Admin.
Res.: 9102 Meadowshire St., TX 77037. Tel: 713-447-2749; Fax: 713-447-2749.
Catechesis / Religious Program—Students 27.

THE COLONY, ST. SOPHIA UKRAINIAN CATHOLIC CHURCH (1999), (Ukrainian), Rev. Vasyl Savchyn.
Church & Res.: 5600 N. Colony Blvd., TX 75056-1927. Tel: 972-379-4700; Fax: 972-379-4700. Email: info@stsophiaukrainian.cc. Web: www.st-sophiaukrainian.cc.

STATE OF WASHINGTON

SEATTLE, KING CO., OUR LADY OF ZAVARNYTSYA (1959) Rev. Abraham Miller.
5321 17th Ave., S., WA 98108. Tel: 206-762-1055.
Catechesis / Religious Program—Ulana Petersen, D.R.E. Students 3.

STATE OF WISCONSIN

MILWAUKEE, MILWAUKEE CO., ST. MICHAELS (1950), (Ukrainian), [JC] Rev. Volodymyr Zaiats; Deacon Michael Chabin.
Res.: 1025 S. 11th St., P.O. Box 64012, WI 53204. Tel: 414-672-5616; Fax: 414-672-5616.

Chaplains of Public Institutions
Hospitals

Rev. Mykola Buryadnyk, Resurrection Health Care Center, Very Rev. Archpriest Mykhailo Kuzma, Resurrection Health Care Center, Alexian Brothers, Rev. Jaroslav Mendyuk, Illinois Masonic Hospital.

Retired:
Revs.—
Bucsek, Basil, 17648 W. Voltaire St., Surprise, AZ 85388-5057. Tel: 623-243-5207
Marick, Thomas D., 1801 Dallas Ave., Royal Oak, MI 48067. Tel: 248-398-9196
Very Rev. Archpriests—
Dobrowolski, Thomas. Tel: 313-768-5474
Lazar, John, 26606 Ann Arbor Trail, Dearborn Heights, MI 48127.
Rev. Msgr. Canon—
Bilinsky, William M., 84031 Pine Dr., Folsom, LA 70437.

Permanent Deacons:
Bozio, Michael, Transfiguration of Our Lord, Denver, CO
Brown, Randall, Holy Apostles Mission, Wichita, KS
Chabin, Nicholas, St. Michael, Milwaukee, WI
Cook, Michael, Nativity of the Blessed Virgin Mary
Horodysky, Mychajlo, St. Nicholas Cathedral, Chicago, IL
Huskey, Michael, St. Nicholas Cathedral, Chicago, IL
Kordonowy, Leonard, St. John the Baptist, Belfield, ND; St. Demetrius, Belfield, ND
Logusch, Eugene, St Mary's Assumption, St. Louis, MO

INSTITUTIONS LOCATED IN THE DIOCESE

[A] MONASTERIES

EAGLE HARBOR. *Holy Transfiguration Skete* (1983) Society of St. John, 6559 State Hwy. M26, MI 49950. Tel: 906-289-4484; Fax: 906-289-4388. Email: skete@societystjohn.com. Web: societystjohn.com. Very Rev. Nicholas Glenn, Hegumen; Deacon Ambrose Nemeth; Rev. Basil Paris. Priests 2; Deacons 1; Professed Monks 5.

REDWOOD VALLEY. *Holy Transfiguration Monastery*, 17001 Tomki Rd., CA 95470. Tel: 707-485-8959; Fax: 707-485-1122. Email: mttabor@pacific.net. Web: www.byzantines.net/monastery. P.O. Box 217, CA 95470. Very Rt. Rev. Joseph Homick, Abbot; Rev. Theodore Zientek. Monks of Mount Tabor. Priests 2; Deacons 1; Professed Monks 6.

[B] MISCELLANEOUS

CHICAGO. **Ukrainian Catholic Education Foundation*, 2247 W. Chicago Ave., 60622. Tel: 773-235-8462; Fax: 773-235-8464. Email: ucef@ucef.org. Web: www.ucef.org. Daniel R. Szymanski Jr., Exec. Dir.

TEMPE. *Metropolitan Andrey Sheptytsky Institute of Eastern Christian Studies*, 1135 E. Balboa Dr., AZ 85282-3906. Tel: 480-736-0202. Web: www.ustpaul.ca/sheptytsky.

RELIGIOUS INSTITUTES OF MEN REPRESENTED IN THE DIOCESE

For further details refer to the corresponding bracketed number in the Religious Institutes of Men or Women section.

[]—*Dominicans, Province of St. Albert the Great*

[]—*Monks of Mt. Tabor*

[]—*Oratorians of Honolulu*

[0180]—*Order of St. Basil the Great*—O.S.B.M.

[]—*Skete of Mt. Tabor*

RELIGIOUS INSTITUTES OF WOMEN REPRESENTED IN THE DIOCESE

[3730]—*Sisters of the Order of St. Basil the Great*—O.S.B.M.

NECROLOGY

(No Deaths)

An asterisk (*) denotes an organization that has established tax-exempt status directly with the IRS and is not covered by the USCCB Group Ruling.

Eparchy of St. Peter the Apostle (Chaldean)

Most Reverend

SARHAD Y. JAMMO

First Bishop-Eparch of the Eparchy of Saint Peter the Apostle-Chaldean; ordained December 19, 1964; appointed Chaldean Bishop May 4, 2002; consecrated Bishop July 18, 2002 in Detroit, Michigan; installed July 25, 2002 in San Diego, California; appointed First Bishop Eparch to the Eparchy of Saint Peter the Apostle-Chaldean Catholic Diocese of America July 25, 2002. *Res.: St. Peter Chaldean Diocese, 1627 Jamacha Way, El Cajon, CA 92019.*

Chancery Office: 1627 Jamacha Way, El Cajon, CA 92019. Tel: 619-579-7913; 619-579-7997; Fax: 619-588-8281.

Email: sjammo@gmail.com

ESTABLISHED JULY 25, 2002.

The Jurisdiction of the Eparchy extends territorially to all Western States in the United States of America inclusive. With regards to persons, its subjects are all Catholics of the Chaldean or Assyrian Ancestry: (1) Who immigrated to this country from the Middle East, especially from Iraq and Iran; (2) Who descends from such persons (can. 755); (3) Women married to men referable to (1) & (2) if they comply with can. 98, n.4; (4) Who in accordance with can. 98, n. 3, changed their Rite; (5) converts to the Catholic Church of the Chaldean Rite; (6) And in fact, all other Catholics of the Chaldean Rite who are attached to the parishes subject to the jurisdiction of the Eparch. For legal titles of parishes and diocesan institutions, consult the Chancery Office.

Legal Title: The Chaldean Catholic Diocese of St. Peter the Apostle.

STATISTICAL OVERVIEW

Personnel	
Bishop	1
Priests: Diocesan Active in Diocese	12
Priests: Diocesan Active Outside Diocese	1
Number of Diocesan Priests	13
Religious Priests in Diocese	5
Total Priests in Diocese	18
Ordinations:	
Permanent Deacons	3
Permanent Deacons in Diocese	9
Total Sisters	12
Parishes	
Parishes	9
With Resident Pastor:	
Resident Diocesan Priests	5
Resident Religious Priests	4
Welfare	
Homes for the Aged	2
Total Assisted	96
Vital Statistics	
Receptions into the Church:	
Infant Baptism Totals	401
Adult Baptism Totals	2
First Communions	333
Confirmations	405
Marriages:	
Catholic	123
Total Marriages	123
Deaths	111
Total Catholic Population	49,563

Chancery Office—1627 Jamacha Way, El Cajon, 92019. Tel: 619-579-7913; 619-579-7997; Fax: 619-588-8281.

Vicar General—Rev. Msgr. Archdeacon SABRI A. KEJBO, 799 E. Washington Ave., El Cajon, 92020. Tel: 619-444-9911; Fax: 619-444-7989.

Chancellor—Rev. Msgr. Chorbishop SAEED D. SAEED (Felix Shabi).

Judicial Officer—Rev. Msgr. Chorbishop SAEED D. SAEED (Felix Shabi).

Director of Finance—Rev. Msgr. Chorbishop SAEED D. SAEED (Felix Shabi).

Diocesan Advisory Council—Mr. AZIZ RAZOKY.

Director of Religious Education—Ms. KHELOUD ALLOS.

Media Center—WASAN JARBO, Mgr. Tel: 619-590-9028; Fax: 619-590-8273.

Child Protection Review Board—NADIA NAJOR; KUSAY ARABO.

Victim Assistance Coordinator—Rev. Msgr. Archdeacon SABRI A. KEJBO. Tel: 619-444-9911; Fax: 619-444-7989. Email: st.michaels@cox.net.

CLERGY, PARISHES, MISSIONS AND PAROCHIAL SCHOOLS

STATE OF CALIFORNIA

CERES, STANISLAUS CO., ST. MATTHEW'S ASSYRIAN-CHALDEAN CATHOLIC CHURCH Rev. Michael Barota. 3005 6th St., 95307. Tel: 209-541-1660; Fax: 209-541-3952.

EL CAJON, SAN DIEGO CO.

1—**ST. PETER CHALDEAN CATHEDRAL* (1973), (Chaldean), Rev. Michael J. Bazzi; Rev. Msgr. Polis Karkees; Rev. Andrew Younan.
Res.: 1627 Jamacha Way, 92019. Tel: 619-579-7913; 619-588-9921; Fax: 619-588-8281.
Catechesis/Religious Program—Tel: 619-447-8876; Fax: 615-588-8281. Ms. Kheloud Allos, D.R.E. Students 720.
Convent—Chaldean Sisters, 1591 Jamacha Way, 92019. Tel: 619-447-4842; Fax: 619-590-0052.
Convent—Worker of the Vineyard, 552 E. Camden Ave., 92020. Tel: 619-440-4078.

2—ST. MICHAEL CHALDEAN CATHOLIC CHURCH (1999), (Chaldean), Rev. Msgr. Archdeacon Sabri A. Kejbo; Rev. Peter Lawrence.
Church: 799 E. Washington Ave., 92020. Tel: 619-444-9911; Fax: 619-444-7989.
Catechesis/Religious Program—Sr. Miskenta Mariam (Reem) Salman, D.R.E. Students 170.

EL DORADO HILLS, EL DORADO CO., OUR LADY OF PERPETUAL HELP CHALDEAN/ASSYRIAN CATHOLIC CHURCH, (Sacramento, CA) Rev. Kamal Warda Bidawid, Admin.; Tom Simon, Parochial Board Pres.
P.O. Box 4154, 95762. Tel: 916-709-3784.

NORTH HOLLYWOOD, LOS ANGELES CO., ST. PAUL ASSYRIAN-CHALDEAN CATHOLIC PARISH (1980), (Chaldean—Assyrian), [JC] Revs. Noel Gorgis, Admin.; Tomy Tomikeh.
Res.: 13050 Vanowen St., 91605. Tel: 818-765-3665; Fax: 818-765-0493.
Catechesis/Religious Program—Students 20.

PERRIS, RIVERSIDE CO., ST. HORMIZDAH MISSION Revs. Awraha Mansoor, Admin.; Pieter Georgis.
13985 Descanso Dr., 92570. Tel: 951-780-1593.

POWAY, SAN DIEGO CO., MAR ADDAI MISSION Rev. Peter Lawrence.
17252 Bernardo Center Dr., San Diego, 92128.

SAN JOSE, SANTA CLARA CO., ST. MARY ASSYRIAN-CHALDEAN PARISH (1987) Revs. Yoshia Sana; Samuel Dinkha.
Assyrian Chaldean Catholic Church California Corporation—
Church & Rectory: 109 N. First St., Campbell, 95008. Tel: 408-378-6212; Fax: 408-379-0496.
Catechesis/Religious Program—Students 70.

SANTA ANA, ORANGE CO., ST. GEORGE CHALDEAN CATHOLIC CHURCH (2001), (Chaldean), [JC] Rev. Awraha Mansoor, Admin.
Church: 4807 W. McFadden, 92704. Tel: 714-531-7760; Fax: 714-531-3409.
Catechesis/Religious Program—Students 25.

TURLOCK, STANISLAUS CO., ST. THOMAS ASSYRIAN-CHALDEAN PARISH (1964), (Chaldean), [CEM] [JC] Rev. Kamal Warda Bidawid.
Res.: 2901 N. Berkeley Ave., 95380. Tel: 209-668-4500; Fax: 209-668-2762.
Catechesis/Religious Program—Students 30.
Convent—Chaldean Sisters, 2937 N. Berkeley Ave., 95380. Tel: 209-634-2043; Fax: 209-668-2762.
St. Thomas Retirement Center—Tel: 209-634-7252.

STATE OF ARIZONA

GLENDALE, MARICOPA CO., HOLY FAMILY MISSION Rev. Msgr. Chorbishop Saeed D. Saeed, (Felix Shabi).
3847 W. Bluefield Ave., AZ 85305.

SCOTTSDALE, MARICOPA CO., MAR AURAHA CHALDEAN CATHOLIC PARISH (1992), (Chaldean), [JC] Rev. Poulos Ghozairan, Admin.
The Chaldean Catholic Church of Arizona Corporation—
Res.: 6816 E. Cactus Rd., AZ 85254. Tel: 480-596-6798; Fax: 480-596-9067.
Catechesis/Religious Program—Students 75.
Convent—Chaldean Sisters, 6308 E. Shea Blvd., AZ 85254. Tel: 480-596-1012. Sisters 2.

STATE OF NEVADA

LAS VEGAS, CLARK CO., ST. BARBARA ASSYRIAN-CHALDEAN CATHOLIC CHURCH Rev. Zuhair G. Toma.
4514 Meadows Ln., NV 89107. Tel: 702-870-0045; Fax: 702-430-8566.

INSTITUTIONS LOCATED IN THE DIOCESE

[A] SEMINARIES

EL CAJON. *Seminary of Mar Abba the Great*, 1245 Jamacha Rd., 92019. Tel: 619-334-8427. Rev. Andrew Younan, Rector.

[B] RETIREMENT CENTERS

EL CAJON. *Good Samaritan Retirement Center*, 1515 Jamacha Way, 92019. Tel: 619-590-1515; Fax: 619-590-0052. Web: www.goodsamretirement.org. Sr. Alexandra Matti, Exec. Dir.

[C] MONASTERIES AND RESIDENCES FOR PRIESTS AND BROTHERS

PERRIS. *St. George Monastery/Retreat Center*, 13985

Descanso Dr., 92570. Rev. Awraha Mansoor, Admin.

[D] MISCELLANEOUS

EL CAJON. *Chaldean Media Center*, 1627 Jamacha Way, 92019. Tel: 619-590-9028; Fax: 619-590-8273. Email: infokaldu@yahoo.com. Web: www.kaldu.org. Wasan Jarbo, Dir.

NECROLOGY

(No Deaths)

An asterisk (*) denotes an organization that has established tax-exempt status directly with the IRS and is not covered by the USCCB Group Ruling.

Eparchy of Saint Thomas the Apostle (Chaldean)

(Editor's Note: 2010 information was not received)

Most Reverend

IBRAHIM N. IBRAHIM, D.D.

First Bishop-Eparch of the Eparchy of Saint Thomas the Apostle-Chaldean Catholic Diocese of America; ordained December 30, 1962; appointed Chaldean Apostolic Exarch and Titular Bishop of Anbar January 26, 1982; consecrated Bishop March 7, 1982 in Baghdad, Iraq; installed April 18, 1982 in Detroit; appointed First Bishop Eparch to the Eparchy of Saint Thomas the Apostle-Chaldean Catholic Diocese of America September 14, 1985. *Res.: St. Thomas the Apostle, Chaldean Catholic Diocese of U.S.A., 25603 Berg Rd., Southfield, MI 48033.*

Exarchate Erected January 26, 1982. Elevated to the Rank of Eparchy September 14, 1985.

The Jurisdiction of the Eparchy extends territorially to all Eastern States in the United States of America inclusive. With regard to persons, its subjects are all Catholics of the Chaldean or Assyrian Ancestry: (1) Who immigrated to this country from the Middle East, especially from Iraq and Iran; (2) Who descends from such persons (can. 755); (3) Women married to men referable to (1) & (2) if they comply with can. 98, n. 4; (4) Who in accordance with can. 98, n. 3., changed their Rite; (5) Converts to the Catholic Church of the Chaldean Rite; (6) And in fact, all other Catholics of the Chaldean Rite who are attached to the parishes subject to the jurisdiction of the Eparch.

For legal titles of parishes and diocesan institutions, consult the Chancery Office.

STATISTICAL OVERVIEW

Personnel	
Bishop	1
Priests: Diocesan Active in Diocese	14
Priests: Retired, Sick or Absent	1
Number of Diocesan Priests	15
Total Priests in Diocese	15
Permanent Deacons in Diocese	120
Total Sisters	11
Parishes	
Parishes	8
With Resident Pastor:	
Resident Diocesan Priests	8
Welfare	
Homes for the Aged	1
Total Assisted	60
Special Centers for Social Services	1
Total Assisted	130
Educational	
Diocesan Students in Other Seminaries	6
Total Seminarians	6
Total Students under Catholic Instruction	6
Vital Statistics	
Receptions into the Church:	
Infant Baptism Totals	901
Adult Baptism Totals	14
First Communions	609
Marriages:	
Catholic	336
Interfaith	6
Total Marriages	342
Deaths	194
Total Catholic Population	120,000

Chancery Office—25603 Berg Rd., Southfield, 48033. Tel: 248-351-0440; Fax: 248-351-0443. Email: chaldeandiocese-detroit@comcast.net. Web: www.chaldeandiocese.org.

Vicar General—Rev. MANUEL Y. BOJI, 25585 Berg Rd., Southfield, 48033. Tel: 248-356-0565; Fax: 248-356-5235.

Eparchial College of Consultors—Revs. MANUEL Y. BOJI; STEPHEN H. KALLABAT; JACOB O. YASSO; SULEIMAN DENHA; JIRJIS ABRAHIM; WISAM MATTI; EMANUEL ISHO SHALETA; FRANK KALABAT.

Diocesan Corporation-The Chaldean Catholic Church of U.S.A.—Most Rev. IBRAHIM N. IBRAHIM, D.D., S.T.D., Pres.; Revs. MANUEL Y. BOJI, Treas.; FRANK KALABAT, Sec.

Eparchial Tribunal—Rev. STEPHEN H. KALLABAT, Court of the First Instance, Chancery Office, 25603 Berg Rd., Southfield, 48033. Tel: 248-351-0440.

CLERGY, PARISHES, MISSIONS AND PAROCHIAL SCHOOLS

STATE OF MICHIGAN

DETROIT, WAYNE CO., SACRED HEART CHALDEAN PARISH (1973), (Chaldean), Rev. Jacob O. Yasso.
Res.: 310 W. Seven Mile Rd., 48203. Tel: 313-368-6214 (Church); Fax: 313-891-0132. Email: fryasso@hotmail.com.
Catechesis/Religious Program—Tel: 248-548-0066. Students 50.

OAK PARK, OAKLAND CO., MAR ADDAI CHALDEAN PARISH (1979), (Chaldean), Revs. Stephen H. Kallabat; Suleiman Denha; Fadi Habib.
Res.: 24010 Coolidge Hwy., 48237. Tel: 248-547-4648; Fax: 248-399-9089.
Catechesis/Religious Program—Students 220.

SHELBY TWP., OAKLAND CO., ST. GEORGE CALDEAN CATHOLIC CHURCH (2005) Revs. Emanuel Isho Shaleta; Basel Yaldo.
Mailing Address: 45700 Dequinder Rd., 48317. Tel: 586-254-7221; Fax: 586-254-2874.
Catechesis/Religious Program—Students 140.

SOUTHFIELD, OAKLAND CO., OUR LADY OF CHALDEANS CATHEDRAL, MOTHER OF GOD CHALDEAN PARISH (1948), (Chaldean), Most Rev. Ibrahim N. Ibrahim; Revs. Manuel Y. Boji, Rector; Wisam Matti.
Res.: 25585 Berg Rd., 48033. Tel: 248-356-0565; 248-356-0569; 248-356-9809 (Hall); Fax: 248-356-5235.
Catechesis/Religious Program—Tel: 248-356-2448. Students 180.
Convent—Chaldean Sisters, Daughters of Mary Immaculate Conception, 24900 Middlebelt Rd., Farmington, 48336. Tel: 248-615-2951; Fax: 248-615-3482.
Chaldean Manor Housing for Elders—25775 Berg Rd., 48033. Tel: 248-355-9491. (Middle age & up).

TROY, OAKLAND CO., ST. JOSEPH CHALDEAN PARISH (1981), (Chaldean), Rev. Msgr. Zouhair Toma; Rev. Ayad Hanna.
Res.: 2442 E. Big Beaver Rd., 48083. Tel: 248-528-3676; 248-524-1144 (Church); Fax: 248-524-1957.

WEST BLOOMFIELD, OAKLAND CO., ST. THOMAS CHALDEAN CATHOLIC PARISH (1992), (Chaldean), Revs. Frank Kalabat; Jirjis Abrahim.
Res. & Mailing Address: 6900 Maple Rd., 48322. Tel: 248-788-2460; Fax: 248-788-2153.
St. Ephrem Re-Evangelization Center—4875 Maple Rd., Bloomfield Township, 48301. Tel: 248-538-9903; Fax: 248-538-0969.
Catechesis/Religious Program—Tel: 248-306-6004. Students 370.

STATE OF ILLINOIS

CHICAGO, COOK CO.

1—ST. EPHREM'S CHURCH (1904), (Chaldean-Assyrian), [JC] Rev. Msgr. Edward J. Bikoma.
Res.: 2537 W. Bryn Mawr Ave., IL 60659-4996. Tel: 773-271-8899; Fax: 773-271-8866.
Catechesis/Religious Program—Tel: 773-506-9957. Students 50.
Convent—Chaldean Sisters, Daughters of Mary Immaculate Conception, 2908 Morse, IL 60645. Tel: 773-338-8832.

2—MART MARIAM PARISH (1986), (Chaldean-Assyrian), [JC] Rev. Sanharib Youkhanna.
Church: 2849 W. Chase Ave., IL 60645. Tel: 773-761-9401; Fax: 773-761-9045. Web: www.martmariamchurch.org.

Retired:

Rev.—

Rayes, Emanuel, 6900 Maple Rd., West Bloomfield, 48322. Tel: 248-788-2460

INSTITUTIONS LOCATED IN THE DIOCESE

RELIGIOUS INSTITUTES OF WOMEN IN THE EPARCHY

For further details refer to the corresponding bracketed number in the Religious Institutes of Men or Women section.

[]—*Daughters of Mary Immaculate* (Baghdad, Iraq); (Farmington Hills, MI; Chicago, IL)—D.M.I.

NECROLOGY

(No Deaths)

An asterisk (*) denotes an organization that has established tax-exempt status directly with the IRS and is not covered by the USCCB Group Ruling.

St. Thomas Syro-Malabar Catholic Diocese of Chicago

Most Reverend

JACOB ANGADIATH

Bishop of St. Thomas Syro-Malabar; ordained January 5, 1972; appointed Bishop of St. Thomas Syro-Malabar Catholic Diocese of Chicago March 13, 2001; Episcopal Ordination July 1, 2001. *Office: 372 S. Prairie Ave., Elmhurst, IL 60126-4020.* Tel: 630-279-1386; 630-279-1383; Fax: 630-279-1479.

ESTABLISHED MARCH 13, 2001.

Comprises all of the United States and Canada.

Diocesan Office: 372 S. Prairie Ave., Elmhurst, IL 60126-4020. Tel: 630-279-1386; 630-279-1383; Fax: 630-279-1479.

STATISTICAL OVERVIEW

Personnel	
Bishop	1
Priests: Diocesan Active in Diocese	35
Number of Diocesan Priests	35
Religious Priests in Diocese	9
Total Priests in Diocese	44
Total Sisters	15
Parishes	
Parishes	18
With Resident Pastor:	
Resident Diocesan Priests	14
Resident Religious Priests	2
Without Resident Pastor:	
Administered by Priests	2
Missions	38
New Parishes Created	4
Educational	
Catechesis/Religious Education:	
High School Students	1,492
Elementary Students	3,139
Total Students under Catholic Instruction	4,631
Vital Statistics	
Receptions into the Church:	
Infant Baptism Totals	259
Minor Baptism Totals	32
Adult Baptism Totals	38
Received into Full Communion	57
First Communions	617
Confirmations	633
Marriages:	
Catholic	67
Interfaith	10
Total Marriages	77
Deaths	42
Total Catholic Population	85,000

Diocesan Office—372 S. Prairie Ave., Elmhurst, 60126-4020. Tel: 630-279-1386; 630-279-1383; Fax: 630-279-1479.

Administration

Vicar General (Protosyncellus)—Rev. GEORGE MADATHIPARAMPIL, V.G., 372 S. Prairie Ave., Elmhurst, 60126-4020. Tel: 630-279-1386; 630-279-1453; Fax: 630-279-1479.

Vicar General (Syncellus)—Rev. ABRAHAM MUTHOLATH JACOB, Our Lady of Victory Church, 5212 W. Agatite Ave., Chicago, 60630. Tel: 773-286-2950; Cell: 773-412-6254.

Chancellor & Secretary to Bishop—Rev. ROY JOSEPH KADUPPIL, 372 S. Prairie Ave., Elmhurst, 60126-4020. Tel: 630-279-1386; 630-279-1383; Fax: 630-279-1479.

Procurator—Rev. VINOD MADATHIPARAMBIL, 372 S. Prairie Ave., Elmhurst, 60126-4020. Tel: 630-279-1386; 630-279-1383; Fax: 630-279-1479.

Eparchial Consultors—Revs. GEORGE MADATHIPARAMPIL, V.G.; ABRAHAM MUTHOLATH, V.G.; ROY JOSEPH KADUPPIL, Chancellor; VINOD MADATHIPARAMBIL, Procurator; ANTONY C. THUNDATHIL; JOS KANDATHIKUDY; JOHN MELEPURAM.

Cathedral—Mar Thoma Sleeha Cathedral, 5000 St. Charles Rd., Bellwood, 60104. Tel: 708-544-7250; Fax: 708-544-5890.

Victim Assistance Coordinator—Dr. O. JOSEPH. Tel: 630-964-2151 (USA). Email: ojoseph27@yahoo.com.

CLERGY, PARISHES, MISSIONS AND PAROCHIAL SCHOOLS

STATE OF ILLINOIS

BELLWOOD, COOK CO.

1—MAR THOMA SLEEHA CATHEDRAL (1985), (Indian), [JC 2] Rev. Antony C. Thundathil.
5000 St. Charles Rd., 60104. Tel: 708-544-7250; Fax: 708-544-5890.
Catechesis/Religious Program—Mr. Thomas Moolayil, D.R.E. Students 725.

2—SYRO-MALABAR CATHOLIC MISSION OF THE DIOCESE OF CHICAGO (1985), (Indian), Closed. For inquiries for parish records contact the chancery.

MAYWOOD, COOK CO., SACRED HEART KNANAYA CATHOLIC PARISH (2006), (Indian), [JC] Rev. Abraham Mutholathu, Dir.
611 Maple St., 60153. Tel: 773-412-6254; Fax: 773-286-8579. Email: mutholath2000@yahoo.com. Web: www.knanayaregion.us/chicago.
Catechesis/Religious Program—John Mathew, D.R.E. Students 394.
St. Mary's Parish Unit— (2007) Mailing Address: 5212 W. Agatite Ave., Chicago, 60630. 7800 W. Lyons St., Morton Grove, 60053. Tel: 773-412-6254. Email: mutholath2000@yahoo.com. Web: www.knanayaregion.us/chicago.
Our Lady of Victory—5212 W. Agatite Ave., Chicago, 60630. Tel: 773-412-6254.
Catechesis/Religious Program—Saji Poothrukayil, D.R.E. Students 132.

STATE OF ARIZONA

PHOENIX, MARICOPA CO., HOLY FAMILY SYRO-MALABAR CATHOLIC CHURCH (2007) Rev. Mathews Kurian Munjanath.
Mailing Address: 2936 N. 81st Ave., AZ 85033. Cell: 602-410-8843; Tel: 623-328-5784; Fax: 623-328-5784. Email: info@holyfamilychurchphx.org. Web: www.syromalabaraz.org.
Catechesis/Religious Program—Tom Joe, D.R.E. Students 89.

STATE OF CALIFORNIA

LOS ANGELES, LOS ANGELES CO.

1—ST. ALPHONSA SYRO-MALABAR CATHOLIC CHURCH OF LOS ANGELES (2001), (Asian—Indian), Rev. Paul Kottackal, Dir.
Mailing Address: 11320 Laurel Cyn., San Fernando, CA 91340.
Church: 607 Fourth St., San Fernando, CA 91340. Tel: 818-365-5522; 818-361-1706; Fax: 818-365-5522. Email: frpaulkottackal@gmail.com. Web: www.syromalabar.org.
Catechesis/Religious Program—Students 70.

2—ST. PIUS X KNANAYA CATHOLIC MISSION OF LOS ANGELES (2001), (Indian), Rev. Thomas Mulavanal, Dir.
Mailing Address: 8912 S. Gate Ave., South Gate, CA 90280. Tel: 310-709-5111; Fax: 323-563-0161. Email: tmulavan@gmail.com. Web: www.knanyaregion.us/losangeles.
Church: 20124 Saticoy, Winnetka, CA 91306.
Catechesis/Religious Program—Students 23.

SAN FRANCISCO, SAN FRANCISCO CO., ST. THOMAS SYRO-MALABAR CATHOLIC CHURCH OF SAN FRANCISCO (2001), (Indian), Rev. Kurian Neduvelichalumkal, Dir.
Mailing Address: 4861 Central Ave., #207, Fremont, CA 94536. Tel: 510-688-7805; 510-648-2539; Fax: 510-648-2539. Email: frneduveli@gmail.com. Web: www.syromalabarsf.org.
Church: 200 N. Abbott Ave., Milpitas, CA 95035.
Catechesis/Religious Program—Students 92.

SAN JOSE, SANTA CLARA CO., ST. MARY KNANAYA CATHOLIC MISSION OF SAN JOSE (1997), (Indian), Rev. Msgr. Jacob Vellian, Dir.
Mailing Address: 6983 Rockton Pl., CA 95119. Tel: 408-281-9458; Cell: 408-284-9753.
St. Mary's Knanaya Catholic Mission—
Catechesis/Religious Program—Tel: 510-745-9244. Binoya Chennathy, D.R.E. Students 95.

SANTA ANA, ORANGE CO., ST. THOMAS APOSTLE SYRO-MALABAR CATHOLIC CHURCH (2001), (Indian), Rev. Jacob Kattackal.
Mailing Address: 5021 W. 16th St., CA 92703. Tel: 714-530-2900; Cell: 714-200-7796; Fax: 714-784-7699. Web: www.stthomassyromalabar.com.
Catechesis/Religious Program—Shary Joseph, D.R.E. Students 105.

STATE OF CONNECTICUT

HARTFORD, HARTFORD CO., ST. THOMAS SYRO-MALABAR MISSION OF HARTFORD (1998), (Indian), Rev. Thomas Puthiyadom, Dir.
133 Woodland St., Apt. 10, CT 06105. Tel: 860-247-4549; Cell: 860-748-1986; Fax: 860-714-8030. Email: puthiya@stfranciscare.org.

STATE OF FLORIDA

CORAL SPRINGS, BROWARD CO., OUR LADY OF HEALTH CATHOLIC CHURCH, FLORIDA (2003), (Indian), Rev. Zacharias Thottuvelil.
Mailing Address: 159 N.W. 95th Ln., FL 33071. Tel: 754-366-6765. Email: fr_zacharias@yahoo.com. Web: syromalabarflorida.org.
Church: 201 N. University Dr., FL 33071.
Catechesis/Religious Program—Tel: 954-296-7527.

Email: sabsangeltz@yahoo.com. Students 200.
Mission—St. Joseph Syro-Malabar Catholic Mission West Palm Beach, FL.
Mission—St. George Syro-Malabar Catholic Mission Miami, FL.

MIAMI BEACH, MIAMI-DADE CO., SYRO-MALABAR KNANAYA CATHOLIC MISSION OF SOUTH FLORIDA (2007) Rev. Stephen J. Vettuvelil, Dir.
Mailing Address: 7193 Pembroke Rd. #A, Pembroke Pines, FL 33023. Tel: 786-370-8649. Email: vettuvelilstephen@gmail.com.

TAMPA, HILLSBOROUGH CO., ST. JOSEPH SYRO-MALABAR CATHOLIC CHURCH (2008) Rev. George Maliekal Paulos.
3001 W. Dr. Martin Luther King Jr. Blvd., FL 33607-6387. Cell: 813-420-3436. Email: vamaliva@yahoo.com. Web: www.stjosephsmcc.org.
St. Lawrence Catholic Church, 5225 N. Himes Ave., FL 33614.
Mary Help of Christians Church—6400 E. Chelsea St., FL 33610. (Mass & religious education classes held here.)
Catechesis/Religious Program—Sr. Christy Kanjirakkattu, D.R.E. Students 70.

VALRICO, HILLSBOROUGH CO., SACRED HEART KNANAYA CATHOLIC MISSION (2009) Rev. Abey Vadakkekara.
2620 Washington Rd., FL 33594. Tel: 813-446-9868. Email: gampaknanayamission@gmail.com.
St. Stephen Catholic Church, 5049 Bell Shoals Rd., FL 33596.
Catechesis/Religious Program—Kunjumol Puthusseril, D.R.E. Students 115.

STATE OF GEORGIA

ATLANTA, HOLY FAMILY KNANAYA CATHOLIC CHURCH (2008) Rev. Thomas Adathiparampil, Dir.
Mailing Address: 2140 Beaver Run Rd., Norcross, GA 30071. 3885 Rosebud Rd., Loganville, GA 30052. Tel: 770-310-4291; Fax: 770-448-7046. Email: aptom@rediffmail.com.
Catechesis/Religious Program—Students 65.

LOGANVILLE, GWINNETT CO., ST. ALPHONSA SYRO-MALABAR CATHOLIC CHURCH, ATLANTA (2001), (Indian), Rev. Abraham P. Schariah.
Mailing Address: 4561 Rosebud Rd., GA 30052. Tel: 404-935-8658; 404-921-1267; Fax: 678-512-0295. Email: frjohnyp@gmail.com. Web: www.stalphonsacatholicchurch.org.
Catechesis/Religious Program—John C. Koikara, D.R.E. Students 161.

STATE OF KENTUCKY

LOUISVILLE, JEFFERSON CO., SYRO-MALABAR CATHOLIC MISSION LOUISVILLE, KENTUCKY (2006) Rev. George Madathiparampil.
Assumption Cathedral, 433 S. Fifth St., KY 40202. Tel: 630-279-1453; Fax: 630-279-1479. Email: georgempqrampil@yahoo.com.

STATE OF MARYLAND

BALTIMORE, BALTIMORE CO., SYRO-MALABAR CATHOLIC MISSION OF BALTIMORE (2003), (Asian—Indian), Rev. James Nirappel, Dir.
St. Mary Catholic Church—224 W. Washington St., Hagerstown, MD 21740. Tel: 301-739-0390; Cell: 443-414-2250; Fax: 301-739-7082. Email: nirappeljames@yahoo.com. Web: www.syromalabarbaltimore.com.
Catechesis/Religious Program—Students 61.

STATE OF MASSACHUSETTS

BOSTON, SUFFOLK CO., ST. THOMAS SYRO-MALABAR CATHOLIC CHURCH (2006) Rev. Kuriakose Vadana.
41 Brook St., Framingham, MA 01701. Tel: 508-877-6574; Cell: 617-717-4018; Fax: 508-877-6574. Email: syromalabarchurchboston@gmail.com. Web: www.malayamchurchboston.com.
Catechesis/Religious Program—Students 56.

STATE OF MICHIGAN

FARMINGTON HILLS, OAKLAND CO., KNANAYA CATHOLIC MISSION OF DETROIT (2009) Rev. Mathew Meladath.
30689 Grand River Ave., MI 48336. Mailing Address: 1040 Birchway Ct., South Lyon, MI 48178. Tel: 248-820-2086; Fax: 248-423-4570.

SOUTHFIELD, OAKLAND CO., ST. THOMAS SYRO-MALABAR CATHOLIC CHURCH, DETROIT (1995), (Indian), [JC] Rev. Varghese Naickamparambil, Vicar.
Mailing Address: 17235 Mt. Vernon St., MI 48075. Tel: 248-552-6620; Fax: 248-552-6620. Email: vicar@syromalabardetroit.org. Web: www.syromalabardetroit.com.
Catechesis/Religious Program—James Varghese, D.R.E. Students 125.

STATE OF MINNESOTA

ST. PAUL, RAMSEY CO., ST. ALPHONSA SYRO-MALABAR CATHOLIC CHURCH MINNESOTA (1999), (Indian), Rev. Joseph J. Arackal, V.C., Dir.
Mailing Address: *Syro-Malabar Catholics of MN*, 210 5th Ave., S.E., St. Cloud, MN 56304. Tel: 651-230-7662; 320-229-7759; Fax: 320-217-8237.
Catechesis/Religious Program—Sr. Tresa Margret, D.R.E. Students 10.

STATE OF NEVADA

LAS VEGAS, CLARK CO., BL. MOTHER THERESA SYRO-MALABAR CATHOLIC CHURCH (2006) Rev. Paul Kottackal.
St. Thomas More, 130 N. Pecos Rd., Henderson, NV 89074. Tel: 818-361-1706; 818-297-9696; Fax: 818-360-5964. Email: frpaulkottackal@gmail.com. Web: www.syromalabar.org. Mailing Address: 11320 Laurel Canyon, San Fernando, CA 91340.

STATE OF NEW JERSEY

EAST MILLSTONE, SOMERSET CO., ST. THOMAS SYRO-MALABAR CATHOLIC CHURCH (2001), (Indian), Rev. Thomas Kadukappillil.
Mailing Address: 44 Livingston Ave., Somerset, NJ 08873. Tel: 908-837-9484; Fax: 732-957-8222. Email: kadukappilly@yahoo.com. Web: www.stthomassyronj.org.
Catechesis/Religious Program—46 Livingston Ave., NJ 08875. Students 160.

GARFIELD, BERGEN CO., SYRO-MALABAR CATHOLIC MISSION OF NEW JERSEY (2004), (Indian), Rev. Joy Alappat (NEW), Dir. Tel: 973-772-7889; Fax: 973-772-7806.
Mailing Address: 69 Market St., NJ 07026. Email: joyalappat@gmail.com. Web: www.syromalabarmissiongarfield.com.
Catechesis/Religious Program—Students 145.

NEWARK, ESSEX CO., KNANAYA CATHOLIC MISSION OF NEWARK NEW JERSEY (1996), (Indian), [JC] Rev. Joseph Tharackal, Dir.
Res.: 1969 Crompond Rd., Cortlandt Manor, NY 10567. Tel: 847-322-9503; Fax: 914-737-6882. Email: josetharackal@yahoo.com.

STATE OF NEW YORK

BRONX, WESTCHESTER CO., ST. THOMAS SYRO-MALABAR CATHOLIC CHURCH (2002), (Asian—Indian), [CEM] [JC] Rev. Jos Kandathikudy.
Mailing Address: 810 E. 221 St., NY 10467. Tel: 718-944-4747; Cell: 201-681-6021; Fax: 347-920-4296. Email: stsmcc@optonline.net. Web: www.stsmcc.org.
Catechesis/Religious Program—Tel: 718-944-4747. Sabu Ooluthua, D.R.E. Students 124.

FLORAL PARK, NASSAU CO.

1—KNANAYA CATHOLIC MISSION OF BROOKLYN, NY (1993), (Asian—Indian), [JC] Rev. Joseph Tharackal, Dir.
Res.: 1969 Crompond Rd., Cortlandt Manor, NY 10567. Tel: 847-322-9503; Fax: 914-737-6882. Email: josetharackal@yahoo.com.
Catechesis/Religious Program—Rena Joseph Thadathil, D.R.E. Students 60.

HAVERSTRAW, ROCKLAND CO., KNANAYA CATHOLIC MISSION OF ROCKLAND, NY (1994), (Indian), [JC] Rev. James Mathew (India), Dir.
Res.: 1969 Compond Rd., Cortlandt Manor, NY 10567. Tel: 914-309-5822; Fax: 914-737-6882. Email: jponganayil@yahoo.com.
Catechesis/Religious Program—Students 55.

ROCKLAND, SULLIVAN CO., SYRO-MALABAR CATHOLIC MISSION, ROCKLAND (2001), (Indian), Rev. Anthony K. Joseph Kudukkamthadam, Dir.
St. Mary Church—71 Grand St., P.O. Box 730, Marlboro, NY 12542. Tel: 845-236-4340; Cell: 845-271-8846; Fax: 845-236-4050. Email: antokudukka@gmail.com.
Catechesis/Religious Program—James Kanachery, D.R.E. Students 80.

STATEN ISLAND, RICHMOND CO., BLESSED KUNJACHAN SYRO-MALABAR CATHOLIC MISSION, STATEN ISLAND, NY (2002), (Indian), Rev. Joy Alappat, Dir.
Mailing Address: 69 Market St., Rosebank, Garfield, NJ 07026.
Catechesis/Religious Program—Students 21.

WEST HEMPSTEAD, NASSAU CO., ST. MARY SYRO-MALABAR CATHOLIC CHURCH (1994) Rev. Ligory Johnson Philips.
Mailing Address: 24 Westminster Rd., NY 11552. Tel: 516-505-7940; Cell: 281-491-5805; Fax: 516-292-2651. Email: kattiakaran@yahoo.com. Web: www.stmaryssyromalabar.org.
Catechesis/Religious Program—James Cherian, D.R.E. Students 190.

WESTCHESTER, WESTCHESTER CO., KNANAYA CATHOLIC MISSION OF WESTCHESTER AND BRONX, NY (1994), (Indian), [JC] Rev. James Mathew (India), Dir.
Mailing Address: 1969 Crompond Rd., Cortlandt Manor, NY 10567. Tel: 845-309-5822; Fax: 914-737-6882. Email: jponganayil@yahoo.com.
Catechesis/Religious Program—

STATE OF NORTH CAROLINA

RALEIGH-DURHAM, WAKE CO., LOURDES MATHA SYRO-MALABAR CATHOLIC CHURCH (2006) Rev. Augustine Kizhakkedam.
Mailing Address: 1412 Park Ave., Morrisville, NC 27560. Tel: 919-439-0305; 919-749-4455. Email: akizhakkedam@yahoo.com.
Catechesis/Religious Program—Biju Parayil, D.R.E. Students 62.

STATE OF OHIO

CINCINNATI, CLERMONT CO., BLESSED CHAVARA SYRO-MALABAR CATHOLIC CHURCH CINCINNATI, OH (2005) Rev. Baby Shepherd, C.M.I.
St. Francis Xavier—Mailing Address: 202 Second St., Falmouth, KY 41040. Tel: 615-400-4725.

CLEVELAND, CUYAHOGA CO., ST. RAPHEL SYRO-MALABAR MISSION CLEVELAND, OH (2005) Rev. John Thomas.
Mailing Address: 893 Hamlet St., Columbus, OH 43201.
Our Lady of Peace Catholic Church—12503 Buckingham Ave. & Shaker Blvd., OH 44120.

COLUMBUS, DELAWARE CO., ST. MARY SYRO-MALABAR CATHOLIC MISSION COLUMBUS, OH (2004) Rev. John Thomas.
c/o Sacred Heart Church, 893 Hamlet St., OH 43201. Tel: 614-372-5249. Email: jthachara@gmail.com. Web: www.columbusnazrani.googlepages.com.
Catechesis/Religious Program—Medona Jose, D.R.E. Students 25.

STATE OF OKLAHOMA

OKLAHOMA CITY, OKLAHOMA CO., HOLY FAMILY SYRO-MALABAR CATHOLIC CHURCH OKLAHOMA (2005) Rev. Davis Cherayath, Dir.
Mailing Address: P.O. Box 267, OK 73101. Cell: 405-677-7976.
Church: 3916 S. Highland Park Dr., OK 73129.
Catechesis/Religious Program—Tel: 972-303-5404; Cell: 630-901-6416. Email: frdavis@gmail.com. Students 49.

STATE OF PENNSYLVANIA

AMBLER, MONTGOMERY CO., ST. ANTONY KNANAYA CATHOLIC MISSION OF GREATER PHILADELPHIA (1999), (Indian), Rev. Joseph Tharackal, Dir.
St. Anthony Rectory—259 Forest Ave., PA 19002. Tel: 847-322-9503; Fax: 914-737-6882.
Catechesis/Religious Program—Students 16.

PHILADELPHIA, PHILADELPHIA CO., ST. THOMAS SYRO-MALABAR CATHOLIC CHURCH (2005), (Asian—Indian), Rev. John Melepuram.
Church: 608 Welsh Rd., PA 19115. Tel: 215-808-4052; Fax: 215-464-4055. Email: johnmelepuram@gmail.com. Web: www.syromalabarphila.org.
Catechesis/Religious Program—Dr. James Kurichy, D.R.E. Students 272.

PITTSBURGH, ALLEGHENY CO., SYRO-MALABAR CATHOLIC MISSION PITTSBURGH, PA (2006) Rev. Vinod Madathiparambil.
Mailing Address: 372 S. Prairie Ave., 60126. Tel: 630-279-1383; 630-901-5724; Fax: 630-279-1479. Email: frvinod@gmail.com.
St. Simon & Jude Church—Church: 1607 Green Tree Rd., PA 15220.

STATE OF TENNESSEE

NASHVILLE, DAVIDSON CO., BLESSED MOTHER THERESA SYRO-MALABAR MISSION NASHVILLE, TN (2008) Rev. Tomy Joseph Puiyanampattayil, M.S.F.S.
Mailing Address: *Sacred Heart Church*, 305 Church St., Loretto, TN 38469. Tel: 931-853-4370 (office); 931-853-4371 (Res.); Cell: 615-943-8706. Email: tomypjosephmsfs@gmail.com.
Assumption Church—Church: 1227 Seventh Ave., N., TN 37208.

STATE OF TEXAS

AUSTIN, HAYS CO., ST. ALPHONSA SYRO-MALABAR CATHOLIC CHURCH AUSTIN, TX (2008) Rev. Prince Kuruvilla.
Mailing Address: *St. John of the Corss Church*, 200 S. Metz St., P.O. Box 329, Orange Grove, TX 78372. Tel: 361-756-9028; Fax: 361-384-0056. Email: princekuruvila@gmail.com.
Dolores Catholic Church—1111 Montopolis Dr., TX 78741.

COPPELL, DALLAS CO., ST. ALPHONS SYRO MALABAR CATHOLIC CHURCH (2008) Rev. Sajy Chakkittamuriyil.
Mailing Address: 2225 E. Peters Colony Rd., Carrollton, TX 75007. Tel: 630-709-5077; Cell: 214-914-4670; Fax: 972-240-1489. Email: frsajy@gmail.com.
200 S. Heartz Rd., TX 75019.
Catechesis/Religious Program—Students 200.

GARLAND, DALLAS CO., ST. THOMAS THE APOSTLE CATHOLIC CHURCH (SYRO-MALABAR) (1984), (Indian), Rev. Sebastian Kaniampadickal.

4922 Rosehill Rd., TX 75043. Tel: 972-240-1100; Fax: 972-240-1489. Email: jojiachan@gmail.com. Web: www.syromalabarchurchdallas.org.
1210 Columbine Dr., TX 75043. Tel: 972-303-7063.
Catechesis/Religious Program—Josey Angiliuelil, D.R.E. Students 278.

HOUSTON, HARRIS CO., ST. MARY'S KNANAYA CATHOLIC MISSION OF HOUSTON (1996), (Indian), [JC] Rev. James Chandy, Dir.
Mailing Address: 10415 Huntington Wood Dr., TX 77099-3721. Tel: 281-568-3281. Email: jamescheruvil@yahoo.com. Web: www.houstonknanayacatholics.com.
Church: 2210 Staffordshire, Missouri City, TX 77489.
Catechesis/Religious Program—Students 301.

MCALLEN, HIDALGO CO., DIVINE MERCY MALABAR CATHOLIC CHURCH (2007) Rev. Cyriac John Valachanath.
102 W. Nolane Loop #B, P.O. Box 123, Pharr, TX 78577. Tel: 361-520-4680; Cell: 361-389-8205; Fax: 361-664-1688. Email: divinemercymalabar@gmail.com.

MESQUITE, DALLAS CO., KNANAYA CATHOLIC MISSION DALLAS/FORTWORTH (1996) Rev. Joseph Sauriamakkel, Mission Dir.
1900 Pinehurst Ln., TX 75150. Tel: 469-248-3045; Fax: 469-248-3045. Email: jsauriamakel@gmail.com.

SAN ANTONIO, BEXAR CO., ST. THOMAS SYRO-MALABAR CATHOLIC MISSION OF SAN ANTONIO (2006) Rev. Prince Kuruvilla, Dir.
4603 Manitou Dr., TX 78228. Tel: 210-647-2947.
Mailing Address: 8735 Sarasota Woods, TX 78250. Email: princekuruvila@gmail.com.

SUGAR LAND, FORT BEND CO., ST. JOSEPH SYRO-MALABAR CATHOLIC CHURCH (2001), (Indian), Rev. Jacob Christy Parampakattil.
Mailing Address: 211 Present St., P.O. Box 2247, Missouri City, TX 77489. Tel: 281-261-7700; 281-904-6622; Fax: 281-969-7088.
231 Boardwalk Pkwy., Stafford, TX 77477. Tel: 281-904-6622. Email: jacobchristy@gmail.com.
Catechesis/Religious Program—Students 419.

DISTRICT OF COLUMBIA

DISTRICT OF COLUMBIA, SYRO-MALABAR CATHOLIC MISSION OF GREATER WASHINGTON (1980) Rev. Mathew Punchayil (India), Dir.
Mailing Address: 14135 Seneca Rd., Darnestown, MD 20874. Tel: 301-948-5536, Ext. 101; Cell: 301-873-7006; Fax: 301-948-7452. Email: matpunchayil@yahoo.com. Web: syromalabargw.org.
St. Rose of Lima—11701 Clopper Rd., Gaithersburg, MD 20878.
Catechesis/Religious Program—Roy Mathew, D.R.E. Students 50.

INSTITUTIONS LOCATED IN THE DIOCESE

[A] CONVENTS AND RESIDENCES FOR SISTERS

CHICAGO. *Congregation of Mother of Carmel*, 8120 S. California Ave., 60652. Tel: 773-737-9440. Sr. Gina, C.M.C., Mother Supr.

MARGATE. *Sisters of Adoration of Blessed Sacrament, St. Thomas Adoration Convent*, 6981 N.W. 18th Ct., FL 33063. Tel: 954-978-9639. Sr. Mercitta, S.A.B.S., Mother Supr.

SAN ANTONIO. *Missionary Sisters of Mary Immaculate*, 19 Kenrock Ridge, TX 78254. Tel: 210-647-2947. Sr. Licy George, M.S.M.I., Mother Supr.

STAFFORD. *Missionary Sisters of Mary Immaculate*, 630 Easy Jet Dr., TX 77477. Tel: 281-499-0030. Sr. Agnes, M.S.M.I., Mother Supr.

RELIGIOUS INSTITUTES OF MEN REPRESENTED IN THE ARCHDIOCESE

For further details refer to the corresponding bracketed number in the Religious Institutes of Women section.

[]—*Missionary Society of St. Thomas the Apostle*—M.S.T.

[]—*Vincentian Congregation - Marymatha Province*

RELIGIOUS INSTITUTES OF WOMEN REPRESENTED IN THE ARCHDIOCESE

[]—*Congregation of Mother of Carmel* (Chicago, IL)

[]—*Missionary Sisters of Mary Immaculate* (Stafford, TX)

[]—*Missionary Sisters of Mary Immaculate* (San Antonio, TX)

[]—*Sisters of Adoration of Blessed Sacrament* (Margate, FL)

NECROLOGY

(No Deaths)

An asterisk (*) denotes an organization that has established tax-exempt status directly with the IRS and is not covered by the USCCB Group Ruling.

Ukrainian Catholic Diocese of Stamford

Most Reverend

PAUL PATRICK CHOMNYCKY, O.S.B.M.

Bishop of Stamford; ordained October 1, 1988; appointed Apostolic Exarch of Great Britain, Faithful of Eastern Rite & Titular Bishop of Buffada April 5, 2002; ordained June 11, 2002; appointed Bishop of Stamford for Ukrainians January 3, 2006; installed February 20, 2006. *Office: 14 Peveril Rd., Stamford, CT 06902-3019.*

Most Reverend

BASIL H. LOSTEN, D.D., S.T.L., LL.D. (HON.)

Retired Bishop of Stamford; ordained June 10, 1957; appointed Titular Bishop of Arcadiopolis and Auxiliary of Ukrainian Catholic Archeparchy of Philadelphia March 15, 1971; consecrated May 25, 1971; appointed Apostolic Administrator of Archeparchy of Philadelphia June 8, 1976; Transferred to the Stamford See September 20, 1977; retired January 3, 2006. *Res.: 122 Clovelly Rd., Stamford, CT 06902.*

ESTABLISHED AUGUST 8, 1956.

The jurisdiction of the Bishop of Stamford extends territorially throughout all of New York State and the New England States. With regard to persons, his subjects are all members of the Ukrainian Catholic Church (Byzantine Rite), irrespective of where they received Baptism.

For legal titles of parishes and diocesan institutions, consult the Chancery Office.

Chancery Office: 14 Peveril Rd., Stamford, CT 06902-3019. Tel: 203-324-7698; Fax: 203-967-9948.

Email: stamfordeparchy@optonline.net

STATISTICAL OVERVIEW

Personnel	
Bishop	1
Retired Bishops	1
Priests: Diocesan Active in Diocese	30
Priests: Retired, Sick or Absent	6
Number of Diocesan Priests	36
Religious Priests in Diocese	17
Total Priests in Diocese	53
Extern Priests in Diocese	25
Ordinations:	
Transitional Deacons	1
Permanent Deacons in Diocese	10
Total Brothers	1
Total Sisters	33
Parishes	
Parishes	51
With Resident Pastor:	
Resident Diocesan Priests	46
Resident Religious Priests	5
Without Resident Pastor:	
Administered by Priests	4
Missions	3
Welfare	
Homes for the Aged	1
Total Assisted	21
Day Care Centers	1
Total Assisted	44
Educational	
Seminaries, Diocesan	1
Students from This Diocese	3
Diocesan Students in Other Seminaries	8
Total Seminarians	11
High Schools, Diocesan and Parish	1
Total Students	200
Elementary Schools, Diocesan and Parish	2
Total Students	200
Catechesis/Religious Education:	
High School Students	330
Elementary Students	919
Total Students under Catholic Instruction	1,660
Teachers in the Diocese:	
Sisters	5
Lay Teachers	20
Vital Statistics	
Receptions into the Church:	
Infant Baptism Totals	183
Adult Baptism Totals	4
Received into Full Communion	2
First Communions	137
Confirmations	186
Marriages:	
Catholic	62
Interfaith	16
Total Marriages	78
Deaths	347
Total Catholic Population	16,000

Former Bishops—Most Revs. AMBROSE SENYSHYN, O.S.B.M., D.D., installed as first Bishop of Stamford, Dec. 15, 1956; transferred to the Archeparchy of Philadelphia, Oct. 26, 1961; died Sept. 11, 1976; JOSEPH M. SCHMONDIUK, D.D., Bishop of Stamford, Nov. 9, 1961; transferred to the Archeparchy of Philadelphia, Sept. 20, 1977; died Dec. 25, 1978; BASIL H. LOSTEN, D.D., S.T.L., LL.D. (Hon.), ord. June 10, 1957; appt. Titular Bishop of Arcadiopolis and Auxiliary of Ukrainian Catholic Archeparchy of Philadelphia March 15, 1971; cons. May 25, 1971; appt. Apostolic Administrator of Archeparchy of Philadelphia June 8, 1976; transferred to the Stamford See Sept. 20, 1977; retired Jan. 3, 2006.

Chancery Office—14 Peveril Rd., Stamford, 06902-3019. Tel: 203-324-7698; Fax: 203-967-9948. Email: chancellor@optonline.net. Web: www.stamforddio.org. Office Hours: Mon.-Fri. 9-12 & 1-5.

Vicar General—Rt. Rev. Mitred Archpriest IHOR MIDZAK.

Econome—Rt. Rev. Mitred Msgr. JOHN TERLECKY, B.A., M.A., M.L.S.

Vice Econome—Very Rev. Archpriest MIHAI DUBOVICI, B.A., S.T.B.

Chancellor & Archivist—Very Rev. Archpriest PHILIP CANON WEINER.

Chancery Secretary—OKSANA DRAGAN.

Notary Publics—Very Rev. Archpriest MIHAI DUBOVICI, B.A., S.T.B.; OKSANA DRAGAN.

Diocesan Consultors—Rt. Rev. Mitred Archpriest IHOR MIDZAK; Very Rev. Archpriest PHILIP CANON WEINER; Rt. Rev. Mitred Msgr. JOHN TERLECKY, B.A., M.A., M.L.S.; Rev. PAUL LUNIW; Very Revs. EDWARD P. YOUNG; KIRIL ANGELOV; Rev. MAXIM KOBASIUK, O.S.B.M.

Diocesan Tribunal—14 Peveril Rd., Stamford, 06902-3019. Tel: 203-324-7698.

Judicial Vicar—Rev. PAUL LUNIW.

Judge—Rev. THEODOSIUS ILNICKI, O.S.B.M., J.C.L.

Defender of the Bond— "Ad Hoc" Appointment

Notary—Rev. MARK HIRNIAK.

Diocesan Protopresbyters (Deans)—Albany: Rev. VLADIMIR MARUSCEAC. Boston: Rev. JAROSLAW NALYSNYK. Brooklyn: Very Rev. VASILE TIVADAR. Buffalo: Very Rev. MARIJAN PROCYK. Hartford: Rev. PAUL LUNIW. New York: Very Rev. Archpriest PHILIP CANON WEINER. Syracuse: Very Rev. KIRIL ANGELOV.

Presbyteral Council—Most Rev. PAUL P. CHOMNYCKY, O.S.B.M.; Rt. Rev. Mitred Archpriest IHOR MIDZAK; Very Rev. Archpriest PHILIP CANON WEINER; Very Rev. MARIJAN PROCYK; Very Rev. Archpriests MIHAI DUBOVICI, B.A., S.T.B.; IVAN KASZCZAK, Ph.D., M.A., B.A.; Revs. IVAN MAZURYK; BERNARD J. PANCZUK, O.S.B.M.; Rev. Msgr. ROMAN GOLEMBA; Rt. Rev. Mitred Msgr. JOHN TERLECKY, B.A., M.A., M.L.S.; Revs. PAUL LUNIW; BOHDAN DANYLO, B.A., S.T.B.

Diocesan Offices and Directors

All offices are located at the following address unless otherwise noted *14 Peveril Rd., Stamford, 06902-3019.* Tel: 203-325-2116; Fax: 203-967-9948. Email: chancellor@optonline.net.

Administrative Council—Most Rev. PAUL P. CHOMNYCKY, O.S.B.M.; Very Rev. Archpriest PHILIP CANON WEINER; Rt. Rev. Mitred Msgr. JOHN TERLECKY, B.A., M.A., M.L.S.; Rev. YAROSLAW KOSTYK; Very Rev. KIRIL ANGELOV; Very Rev. Archpriest MIHAI DUBOVICI, B.A., S.T.B.; Rt. Rev. Mitred Archpriest IHOR MIDZAK.

Priest Personnel Board—Rt. Rev. Mitred Archpriest IHOR MIDZAK; Very Revs. VASILE TIVADAR; PAWLO MARTYNIUK; Very Rev. Archpriest PHILIP CANON WEINER.

Apostleship of Prayer—Very Rev. MARIJAN PROCYK.

Catechetics (Heritage Schools)—Revs. ALBERT FORLANO; VASILE COLOPELNIC.

Cemeteries—Holy Spirit Ukrainian Catholic Cemetery, 141 Sarah Wells Trail, Campbell Hall, NY 10916. Tel: 845-496-5506. Directors: Most Rev. PAUL P. CHOMNYCKY, O.S.B.M., Pres. & Chm.; Rev. JAROSLAW KOSTYK, Exec. Dir.; Very Rev. Archpriest PHILIP CANON WEINER, Sec.; Rt. Rev. Mitred Archpriest IHOR MIDZAK; Rt. Rev. Mitred Msgr. JOHN TERLECKY, B.A., M.A., M.L.S.; Mr. LOUIS NIGRO; Mr. JOHN SENKO.

Censor—Very Rev. EDWARD P. YOUNG.

Communications—Rev. MARK HIRNIAK.

Development Office—Very Rev. Archpriest MIHAI DUBOVICI, B.A., S.T.B.

Diaconate, Permanent—Very Rev. Archpriest PHILIP CANON WEINER.

Diocesan Charities and Missions—Most Rev. PAUL P. CHOMNYCKY, O.S.B.M.

Ecumenical Commission—Most Rev. PAUL P. CHOMNYCKY, O.S.B.M.; Very Rev. Archpriest MIHAI DUBOVICI, B.A., S.T.B.; Rev. THEODOSIUS ILNICKI, O.S.B.M., J.C.L.; Very Rev. EDWARD P. YOUNG.

Educational Institutions—Most Rev. PAUL P. CHOMNYCKY, O.S.B.M.; Rev. JAMES MORRIS; Sr. JONATHAN DUCHENSKY, S.S.M.I.; Mr. PETER SHYSHKA, Supt. Schools.

Family Life—Rev. ALBERT FORLANO.

Holy Name Societies—Rev. ROBERT BATCHO.

League of Ukrainian Catholics—Very Revs. PAWLO MARTYNIUK, Spiritual Dir. (New England); MARIJAN PROCYK, Spiritual Dir. (New York).

Liturgical Commission—Very Rev. Archpriest PHILIP CANON WEINER; Revs. BOHDAN DANYLO, B.A., S.T.B.; VOLODYMYR SYBIRNYY.

Missionaries, Diocesan—Rev. BERNARD J. PANCZUK, O.S.B.M.

Ukrainian Museum and Library of Stamford, Inc.—161 Glenbrook Rd., Stamford, 06902. Museum Library Research Center, 39 Clovelly Rd., Stamford, 06902. Tel: 203-327-7899. Ms. LUBOW WOLYNETZ, B.A., M.L.S., Curator, Librarian & Archivist; Rt. Rev. Mitred Msgr. JOHN TERLECKY, B.A., M.A., M.L.S., Librarian.

Press, Diocesan: "The Sower"—Ms. MYROSLAVA ROZDOLSKA, Ukrainian Editor; Sr. NATALYA STOCZANYN, S.S.M.I., Editor-in-Chief. Email: thesower@optonline.net.

Priests' Benevolent Association—Rev. MIKHAIL MYSHCHUK, Sec. & Treas.

Religious Communities, Vicar—Very Rev. PHILIP SANDRICK, O.S.B.M.

Religious Education—Rev. ALBERT FORLANO, Dir.

Sodalities, B.V.M.—Rev. STEPHEN YANOWSKI.

Vocations—Rev. BOHDAN DANYLO, B.A., S.T.B.

Youth Apostolate—Rev. IVAN MAZURYK.

Youth-For-Christ Association—Rev. IVAN MAZURYK.

Office of Safe Environment—Sr. NATALYA STOCZANYN, S.S.M.I.

CLERGY, PARISHES, MISSIONS AND PAROCHIAL SCHOOLS

STATE OF CONNECTICUT

ANSONIA, NEW HAVEN CO., SS. PETER AND PAUL (1897), (Ukrainian), [CEM] Rt. Rev. Mitred Msgr. John Terlecky; Rev. Stepan Yanovsky, Parochial Vicar.
Res.: 105 Clifton Ave., 06401. Tel: 203-734-3895; Fax: 203-732-3191. Email: st_peter_st_paul@sbcglobal.net. Web: st-peter-st-paul.com.

BRIDGEPORT, FAIRFIELD CO., PROTECTION OF B.V.M. (1950), (Ukrainian), Very Rev. Archpriest Mihai Dubovici.
Holy Protection of B.V.M. Ukrainian Catholic Church: 457 Noble Ave., 06608. Tel: 203-367-5054; Fax: 203-367-5054.
Res.: 255 Barnum Ave., 06608. Tel: 203-367-5054.

COLCHESTER, NEW LONDON CO., ST. MARY DORMITION (1948), (Ukrainian), [CEM] Rev. Kiril Manolev.
Res.: 178 Linwood Ave., 06415. Tel: 860-537-2069; Fax: 860-537-2069. Email: frcyril@sbcglobal.net.

GLASTONBURY, HARTFORD CO., ST. JOHN THE BAPTIST (1925), (Ukrainian), Attended by St. Mary Dormition, Colchester. Rev. Kiril Manolev.
Church: 26 New London Tpke., 06033.
Res.: 178 Linwood Ave., Colchester, 06415. Tel: 860-537-2069.

HARTFORD, HARTFORD CO., ST. MICHAEL (1910), (Ukrainian), [CEM] Very Rev. Pawlo Martyniuk.
Church: 125 Wethersfield Ave., 06114.
Res.: 135 Wethersfield Ave., 06114. Tel: 860-525-7823; Fax: 860-548-1049.
School—Saturday Ukrainian School, (Grades K-8) Tel: 860-728-8792. Lesia Paslavsky, Prin. Priests 1; Lay Teachers 6; Students 64.

NEW BRITAIN, HARTFORD CO., ST. JOSAPHAT (1951), (Ukrainian), Rev. Stepan Bereza.
Res.: 303 Eddy Glover Blvd., 06053. Tel: 860-225-7340; Fax: 860-229-5490.
Catechesis/Religious Program—Priests 1; Lay Teachers 2; Students 18.

NEW HAVEN, NEW HAVEN CO., ST. MICHAEL (1909), (Ukrainian), Rev. Iura Godenciuc.
Res.: 569 George St., 06511. Tel: 203-865-0388; Fax: 203-752-0327.
School—St. Michaels Ukrainian Heritage School Myron Melnyk, Prin. (Saturdays) Priests 1; Lay Teachers 5; Students 37.

STAMFORD, FAIRFIELD CO., ST. VLADIMIR CATHEDRAL (1916), (Ukrainian), Rt. Rev. Mitred Archpriest Ihor Midzak.
Res.: 24 Wenzel Ter., 06902. Tel: 203-324-0242; Fax: 203-316-8284.
Catechesis/Religious Program—Priests 1; Sisters 1; Lay Teachers 3; Students 39.

TERRYVILLE, LITCHFIELD CO., ST. MICHAEL (1910), (Ukrainian), [CEM] Rev. Paul Luniw.
Res.: 35 Allen St., 06786. Tel: 860-583-7588; Fax: 860-582-8064. Email: stmichael@adelphia.net. Web: www.stmichaelterryville.org.
Catechesis/Religious Program—Tel: 860-582-1850. Kristine Meinert, D.R.E.; Ann Kerry, D.R.E.; Dan Czuchta, D.R.E.; John Stefanczyk, D.R.E. Priests 1; Students 11; Lay Teachers 4.

WILLIMANTIC, WINDHAM CO., PROTECTION OF B.V.M. (1950), (Ukrainian), Rev. Ivan Bilyk.
Res.: 69 Oak St., 06226. Tel: 860-423-5031; Fax: 860-423-5031.

STATE OF MASSACHUSETTS

BOSTON, SUFFOLK CO., CHRIST THE KING (1968) [CEM] Rev. Jaroslaw Nalysnyk, Admin.
Res.: 146 Forest Hills St., Jamaica Plain, MA 02130. Tel: 617-522-9720; Fax: 617-983-0309. Email: yaroslavnalysnyk@aol.com.
School—Saturday Ukrainian School Priests 1; Lay Teachers 2; Students 40.
Catechesis/Religious Program—Priests 1; Lay Teachers 2; Students 12.

FALL RIVER, BRISTOL CO., ST. JOHN-THE-BAPTIST (1914) [JC] Attended by Woonsocket, RI. Rev. Msgr. Roman Golemba.
Church: 339 Center St., MA 02724. Tel: 508-673-2353.

LUDLOW, HAMPDEN CO., SS. PETER AND PAUL (1912)(1924), (Ukrainian), Very Rev. Archpriest Edward P. Young.
Res.: 45 Newbury St., MA 01056. Tel: 413-583-2140; Fax: 413-583-2140. Email: eyoung8073@aol.com.
Catechesis/Religious Program—Priests 1; Students 1.

PITTSFIELD, BERKSHIRE CO., ST. JOHN THE BAPTIST (1921), (Ukrainian), Attended by Hudson, New York Rev. Janusz Jedrychowski.
Res.: Tel: 518-828-5226; Fax: 518-828-6749.

SALEM, ESSEX CO., ST. JOHN THE BAPTIST (1918), (Ukrainian), Rev. James Morris, Admin.
Mailing Address: P.O. Box 206, MA 01970-0206. Tel: 978-745-3151.
Church: 124 Bridge St., MA 01970. Email: saintjohnsukr@comcast.net.
Catechesis/Religious Program—Tel: 617-599-8138. Students 3.

SOUTH DEERFIELD, FRANKLIN CO., HOLY GHOST (1920), (Ukrainian), Very Rev. Archpriest Edward P. Young.
Res.: 44 Sugarloaf St., MA 01373. Tel: 413-665-3880.
Catechesis/Religious Program—Priests 1; Students 6.

STATE OF NEW HAMPSHIRE

MANCHESTER, HILLSBORO CO., PROTECTION OF B.V.M. (1908), (Ukrainian), Rev. Robert Smolley.
Church: 54 Walnut St., NH 03104. Tel: 603-622-0034; Fax: 603-642-8961.
Catechesis/Religious Program—Priests 1; Lay Teachers 2; Students 14.

STATE OF NEW YORK

AMSTERDAM, MONTGOMERY CO., ST. NICHOLAS (1909), (Ukrainian), [CEM] Rev. Marian Kostyk.
Res.: 24 Pulaski St., NY 12010. Tel: 518-842-8731; Fax: 518-842-1384.

AUBURN, CAYUGA CO., SS. PETER AND PAUL (1901), (Ukrainian), Rev. Ivan Mazuryk.
Res.: 136 Washington St., NY 13021. Tel: 315-252-5573; Fax: 315-252-7469.
School—(Grades K-8) Tel: 315-252-5567. Sr. Kathleen Hutsko, S.S.M.I., Prin. Lay Teachers 8; Students 102.
Catechesis/Religious Program—Lay Teachers 3; Students 15.

BATH, STEUBEN CO., CHRIST THE KING, Closed. For inquiries for parish records contact the chancery.

BEDFORD HILLS, WESTCHESTER CO., HOLY PROTECTION OF THE MOTHER OF GOD (2000) Very Rev. Archpriest Ivan Kaszczak.
Res.: 195 Glenbrrok Rd., 06902. Tel: 203-324-4578.

BRONX, BRONX CO., ST. MARY PROTECTRESS (1943), (Ukrainian), [JC] Rev. Lawrence Lawryniuk, O.S.B.M.
Church: 1745 Washington Ave., NY 10457. Tel: 718-731-9392.
Res.: E. Beach Dr., Glen Cove, NY 11542. Tel: 516-671-0545; Fax: 516-676-7465.

BROOKLYN, KINGS CO.

1—HOLY GHOST (1913), (Ukrainian), Rev. Ivan Tykhovytch.
Mailing Address: 161 N. Fifth St., NY 11211.
Church: 160 N. 5th St., NY 11211. Tel: 718-782-9592; Fax: 718-599-2905.

2—ST. NICHOLAS (1916), (Ukrainian), Rev. Robert Markowitch.
256 19th St., NY 11215. Tel: 718-389-8744.
Mission—Blessed Nicholas Chernetsky, Manhattan Beach, NY

BUFFALO, ERIE CO., ST. NICHOLAS (1894), (Ukrainian), Very Rev. Marijan Procyk; Rev. Raymond Palko.
Res.: 308 Fillmore Ave., NY 14206. Tel: 716-852-7566; Fax: 716-855-1319.
Catechesis/Religious Program—Elaine P. Nowadly, D.R.E. Priests 2; Students 26.

COHOES, ALBANY CO., SS. PETER AND PAUL (1907), (Ukrainian), Rev. Vladimir Marusceac.
Res.: 198 Ontario St., NY 12047. Tel: 518-237-0535; Fax: 518-237-2397.
Catechesis/Religious Program—Priests 1; Lay Teachers 1; Students 7.

ELMIRA HEIGHTS, CHEMUNG CO., ST. NICHOLAS (1895), (Ukrainian), Rev. Vasile Godenciuc.
Res.: 410 E. McCanns Blvd., NY 14903. Tel: 607-734-1221; Fax: 607-737-7569.
Catechesis/Religious Program—Irene Moffe, D.R.E. Priests 1; Lay Teachers 4; Students 12.

FRESH MEADOWS, QUEENS CO., ANNUNCIATION OF THE B.V.M. (1957), (Ukrainian), Very Rev. Zbigniew Canon Brzezicki.
Res.: 48-26 171st St., NY 11365. Tel: 718-939-4116; Fax: 718-939-3696.

GLEN SPEY, SULLIVAN CO., ST. VOLODYMYR (1961), (Ukrainian), [JC] Attended by Campbell Hall, New York Rev. Yaroslaw Kostyk.
Res.: 141 Sarah Wells Tr., Campbell Hall, NY 10916. Tel: 845-496-5506.

HAMPTONBURGH, ORANGE CO., ST. ANDREW'S (1983), (Ukrainian), Rev. Yaroslaw Kostyk.
Res.: 141 Sarah Wells Tr., Campbell Hall, NY 10916. Tel: 845-496-5506; Fax: 845-496-5564.
Catechesis/Religious Program—Priests 1; Lay Teachers 1; Students 4.

HEMPSTEAD , NASSAU CO., ST. VLADIMIR (1944), (Ukrainian), Rev. Wasyl Hrynkiw.
Res.: 709 Front St., NY 11550. Tel: 516-481-7717; Fax: 516-481-3435.
Parish Center—226 Uniondale Ave., Uniondale, NY 11553. Tel: 516-485-0775.
School—Saturday Ukrainian School, (Grades 1-12) Priests 1; Lay Teachers 8; Students 60.
Catechesis/Religious Program—Priests 1; Lay Teachers 9; Students 38.

HUDSON, COLUMBIA CO., ST. NICHOLAS (1923), (Ukrainian), Rev. Janusz Jedrychowski.
Res.: 206 Union St., NY 12534. Tel: 518-828-5226; Fax: 518-828-6749.

HUNTER, GREENE CO., ST. JOHN THE BAPTIST (1962), (Ukrainian),Rte. 23A, P.O. Box 284, NY 12442. Tel: 518-263-3862.

JOHNSON CITY, BROOME CO., SACRED HEART UKRAINIAN CATHOLIC CHURCH (1944), (Ukrainian), [CEM] Rev. Teodor Czabala.
Res.: 230 Ukrainian Hill Rd., NY 13790. Tel: 607-797-6293; Fax: 607-797-6295. Email: shucc@stny.rr.com. Web: www.sacredheartucc.org.
School—Saturday Ukrainian School, Tel: 607-797-6294. Lay Teachers 3; Students 11.
Catechesis/Religious Program—Tel: 607-797-6294. Luba Woytew, D.R.E. Lay Teachers 3; Students 20.

KENMORE, ERIE CO., ST. JOHN THE BAPTIST (1902), (Ukrainian), Rev. Stepan Kuklich.
Res.: 3275 Elmwood Ave., NY 14217. Tel: 716-873-5011; Fax: 718-462-5243.

KERHONKSON , ULSTER CO., HOLY TRINITY (1965), (Ukrainian), Rev. Volodymyr Pyso.
Mailing Address: 211 Foordmore Rd., NY 12446.
Church: 211 Foordmore Rd., NY 12446. Tel: 845-626-2864; Fax: 845-626-3548.
School—Saturday Ukrainian School Olha Rawluk, Prin. Priests 1; Lay Teachers 6; Students 17.

LACKAWANNA, ERIE CO., OUR LADY OF PERPETUAL HELP (1925), (Ukrainian), Rev. Andriv Kasiyan.
Res.: 1182 Ridge Rd., NY 14218. Tel: 716-823-6182; Fax: 716-823-6550.
Catechesis/Religious Program—Maria Slabyk, D.R.E.; Oksana Kasiyan, D.R.E. Priests 1; Lay Teachers 2.

LANCASTER, ERIE CO., ST. BASIL (1921), (Ukrainian), Rev. Robert Moreno.
Res.: 12 Embry Pl., NY 14086. Tel: 716-683-0313; Fax: 716-651-9873.
Church: 3657 Walden Ave., NY 14086.
Catechesis/Religious Program—Michele Forkl, D.R.E. Students 20.

LINDENHURST, SUFFOLK CO., HOLY FAMILY (1924), (Ukrainian), Rev. Olvian Popovici.
Res.: 225 N. 4th St., NY 11757. Tel: 631-225-1168; Fax: 631-225-1177.
Catechesis/Religious Program—Priests 1; Lay Teachers 2; Students 39.

LITTLE FALLS, HERKIMER CO., ST. NICHOLAS (1912) Attended by Amsterdam. Rev. Marian Kostyk.
Res.: 24 Pulaski St., Amsterdam, NY 12010. Tel: 518-842-8731; Fax: 518-842-1384.

LONG ISLAND CITY, QUEENS CO., HOLY CROSS (1944), (Ukrainian), Revs. Christopher Woytyna, O.S.B.M.; Januario Lucavei, O.S.B.M.; Melecio Kraizyi.
Res.: 31-12 30th St., NY 11106. Tel: 718-932-4060; Fax: 718-932-6370. Web: www.geosites.com/church11106.
Catechesis/Religious Program—Priests 1; Lay Teachers 1; Students 4.

NEW YORK, NEW YORK CO., ST. GEORGE (1905), (Ukrainian), Rev. Bernard J. Panczuk, O.S.B.M.; Very Rev. Cyril Izczuk, O.S.B.M.
Res.: 30 E. Seventh St., NY 10003. Tel: 212-674-1615; Fax: 212-475-7017.
School—215 E. Sixth St., NY 10003. Tel: 212-473-3130; Fax: 917-534-0819. Sr. Theodosia, O.S.B.M., Prin. Sisters of St. Basil the Great 2; Lay Teachers 8; Students 100.
High School—Tel: 212-473-3323; Fax: 917-534-0819. Mr. Peter Shyshka, Prin. Lay Teachers 13; Students 100.

NIAGARA FALLS, NIAGARA CO., PROTECTION OF B.V.M. (1920), (Ukrainian), Rev. Raymond Palko.
Res.: 2713 Ferry Ave., NY 14301. Tel: 716-284-7066; Fax: 716-282-6902.

OZONE PARK , QUEENS CO., ST. MARY PROTECTRESS (1954), (Ukrainian), Very Rev. Vasile Tivadar.
Res.: 97-06 87th St., NY 11416. Tel: 718-845-5366; Fax: 718-529-1477.

RIVERHEAD, SUFFOLK CO., ST. JOHN THE BAPTIST (1924), (Ukrainian), [CEM] Rev. Vasyl Kornitsky.
Res.: 820 Pond View Rd., NY 11901. Tel: 631-727-2766; Fax: 631-727-4141.
Church: Franklin St., NY 11901.

ROCHESTER, MONROE CO.
1—EPIPHANY OF OUR LORD (1958), (Ukrainian), [JC] Rev. Roman Sydorovych.
Res.: 202 Carter St., NY 14621. Tel: 585-266-4036; Fax: 585-323-9691. Email: vasylcolopelnic@yahoo.com.
Catechesis/Religious Program—Teachers 8; Students 41.
2—ST. JOSAPHAT (1909), (Ukrainian), Very Rev. Kiril Angelov; Rev. Roman Malyarchuk.
Res.: 940 Ridge Rd. E., NY 14621. Tel: 585-467-6457; Fax: 585-467-7296.
Catechesis/Religious Program—Lay Teachers 9; Students 43.

ROME, ONEIDA CO., ST. MICHAEL (1914), (Ukrainian), [CEM] Attended by St. Vladimir, Utica. Rev. Michael Bundz.
Res.: 296 Genessee St., Utica, NY 13502. Tel: 315-735-5138; Fax: 315-735-0443.
Church: 133 River St., NY 13440.

SPRING VALLEY , ROCKLAND CO., SS. PETER AND PAUL (1913), (Ukrainian), Rev. Vasile Colopelnic.
Res.: 41 Collins Ave., NY 10977. Tel: 845-356-1634; Fax: 845-425-2749.
Catechesis/Religious Program—Tel: 201-529-4208. Maria-Liusea Colopelnic, D.R.E. Lay Teachers 2; Students 14.

STATEN ISLAND, RICHMOND CO., HOLY TRINITY (1949), (Ukrainian), Rev. Mykhaylo Dosyak.
Res.: 288 Vanderbilt Ave., NY 10304. Tel: 718-442-2555.

SYRACUSE, ONONDAGA CO., ST. JOHN THE BAPTIST (1900) Rev. Robert Batcho.
Res.: 207 Tompkins St., NY 13204. Tel: 315-478-5109; Fax: 315-471-9867.
Catechesis/Religious Program—Priests 1; Lay Teachers 8; Students 60.

TROY, RENSSELAER CO., PROTECTION OF B.V.M. (1952), (Ukrainian), [JC] Attended by St. Nicholas Watervilet. Revs. Mikhail Myshchuk; Volodymyr Sibirnij.
Church: 459 Second St., NY 12180. Tel: 518-274-5318.

UTICA, ONEIDA CO., ST. VOLODYMYR THE GREAT (1950), (Ukrainian), [CEM] Rev. Michael Bundz, Admin.
Res.: 296 Genessee St., NY 13502. Tel: 315-735-5138; Fax: 315-735-0443.

WATERVLIET, ALBANY CO., ST. NICHOLAS (1905), (Ukrainian), [CEM] [JC] Revs. Mikhail Myshchuk; Volodymyr Sibirnij.
Res.: 2410-4th Ave., NY 12189. Tel: 518-273-6752; Fax: 866-751-4103. Email: office@cerkva.com. Web: www.cerkva.com.
School—Saturday Ukrainian School Lay Teachers 8; Students 34.
Catechesis/Religious Program—Students 28.

YONKERS, WESTCHESTER CO., ST. MICHAEL (1899), (Ukrainian), Very Rev. Archpriest Philip Canon Weiner; Revs. Mykola Drofych; Mark Hirniak.
Res.: 21 Shonnard Pl., NY 10703. Tel: 914-963-0209; Fax: 914-969-6269. Email: stmich@optonline.net.
Catechesis/Religious Program—School of Ukrainian Studies Priests 2; Lay Teachers 8; Students 140.

STATE OF RHODE ISLAND

WOONSOCKET, PROVIDENCE CO., ST. MICHAEL (1908) [CEM] [JC] Rev. Msgr. Roman Golemba.
Res.: 394 Blackstone St., RI 02895. Tel: 401-762-2733; Fax: 401-762-2733.
Church: 396 Blackstone St., RI 02895.

Retired:
Rev. Msgr.—
Skrincosky, Peter, 222 Broad St., Arnot, St. Clair, PA 17970.
Rev.—
Mudry, Lubomyr, St. Joseph's, P.O. Box 8, Sloatsburg, NY 10974.
Rt. Rev. Mitred Msgrs.—
Mosko, Leon, 195 Glenbrook Rd., 06902.
Squiller, John, B.A., S.T.L.

Permanent Deacons:
Behay, Vasyl, St. Vladimir Cathedral, Stamford, CT
Coleman, Paul, SS. Peter & Paul, Auburn, NY
Evans, Michael, SS. Peter & Paul, Auburn, NY
Galvin, Edward, St. John the Baptist, Syracuse, NY
Gutch, Thomas, St. Nicholas, Waterlivet, NY
Hedz, Bodhan, St. John the Baptist, Syracuse, NY
Hobczuk, John, St. Nicholas, Elmira Heights, NY
Homick, Willis, SS. Peter & Paul, Auburn, NY
Kotch, Myron, St. John the Baptist, Syracuse, NY
Malachowsky, Yourij, Holy Cross, Long Island City, NY
Stadnick, Thomas, Holy Ghost, Brooklyn, NY
Wanat, John, Protection of the BVM, Bridgeport, CT

INSTITUTIONS LOCATED IN THE DIOCESE

[A] SEMINARIES, DIOCESAN

STAMFORD. *Ukrainian Catholic Seminary Inc. St. Basil College*, 195 Glenbrook Rd., 06902-3099. Tel: 203-324-4578; Fax: 203-357-7681. Most Rev. Paul P. Chomnycky, O.S.B.M., Chm., Bd. Trustees; Revs. Bohdan Danylo, B.A., S.T.B., Pres. & Rector; Maxim Kobasiuk, O.S.B.M.; Very Rev. Archpriests Ivan Kaszczak, Ph.D., M.A., B.A., Acting Academic Dean; Mihai Dubovici, B.A., S.T.B., Bursar; Ms. Lubow Wolynetz, B.A., M.L.S., Librarian; Mr. Vasile Popovici, Procurator.

[B] SEMINARIES, RELIGIOUS

GLEN COVE. *Basilian Fathers Novitiate of the Order of St. Basil the Great*, E. Beach Dr., NY 11542. Tel: 516-671-0545; Fax: 516-676-7465. Revs. Roberto (Tarcisio) Lucavei, O.S.B.M., Vicar, Provincial Treas.; Athanasius B. Pekar, O.S.B.M.; Taras Prokopiw, O.S.B.M.; Theodosius Ilnicki, O.S.B.M., J.C.L., Provincial Sec. Priests 3; Brothers 1.

[C] NURSERY SCHOOLS

STAMFORD. *St. Ann's Nursery School*, 111 W. North St., 06902. Tel: 203-323-1237; 203-348-5675; Fax: 203-323-0262. Missionary Sisters of Mother of God 6; Nursery 44; Staff 3.

[D] ADULT FACILITIES

SLOATSBURG. *St. Joseph's Adult Care Home, Inc.*, 125 Sisters Servants Ln., NY 10974-0008. Tel: 845-753-2555; Fax: 845-753-6910. Sisters Bernardine Symionow, S.S.M.I., Admin.; Barbara Stefaniak, S.S.M.I., Asst. Admin. Sisters Servants of Mary Immaculate 6; Residents 28; Total Staff 12.

[E] MONASTERIES AND RESIDENCES OF PRIESTS AND BROTHERS

NEW YORK. *Provincialate of Basilian Fathers*, Res.: 29 Peacock Ln., Locust Valley, NY 11560. Tel: 516-609-3262; Fax: 516-609-3264. Email: USAOSBM@aol.com. Very Rev. Philip Sandrick, O.S.B.M., Protohegumen. Priests 24; Brothers 3.

[F] MONASTERIES OF NUNS

STAMFORD. *Missionary Sisters of Mother of God*, 111 W. North St., 06902. Tel: 203-323-1237; Fax: 203-323-0262. Sr. Nadia Baranik, M.S.M.G., Supr.; Rev. Peter Gronski, Chap.

MIDDLETOWN. *Nuns of St. Basil the Great*, Sacred Heart Monastery, 209 Keasel Rd., NY 10940-6287. Tel: 845-343-1308; Fax: 845-343-1308. Sr. Georgianna Snihur, O.S.B.M., Supr. Sisters 4; Novices 1.

SLOATSBURG. *Sister Servants of Mary Immaculate, Inc.*, 150 Sisters Servants Ln., 9 Emmanuel Dr., P.O. Box 9, NY 10974-0009. Tel: 845-753-2840; Fax: 845-753-1956. Email: ssminy@aol.com. Sr. Michele Yakymovitch, S.S.M.I., Prov. Supr. Sisters Servants of Mary Immaculate Conception Province. Sisters 33.

[G] MISCELLANEOUS

STAMFORD. *Institute of Catechists of the Heart of Jesus*, 161 Glenbrook Rd., 06902. Tel: 203-327-6374.

SLOATSBURG. *St. Mary's Villa Spiritual, Cultural & Educational Center*, 150 Sisters Servants Ln., P.O. Box 9, NY 10974-0009. Tel: 845-753-5100; Fax: 845-753-1956. Sr. Albina Gregory, S.S.M.I., Coord.

RELIGIOUS INSTITUTES OF MEN REPRESENTED IN THE DIOCESE

For further details refer to the corresponding bracketed number in the Religious Institutes of Men or Women section.

[0180]—*Order of St. Basil the Great*—O.S.B.M.
[1070]—*Redemptorists*—C.Ss.R.

RELIGIOUS INSTITUTES OF WOMEN REPRESENTED IN THE DIOCESE

[]—*Institute of Catechists of the Heart of Jesus*
[2810]—*Missionary Sisters of Mother of God*—M.S.M.G.
[3730]—*Sisters of the Order of St. Basil the Great*—O.S.B.M.
[3610]—*Sisters Servants of Mary Immaculate*—S.S.M.I.

NECROLOGY

† Lazor, Joseph—Died Sept. 23, 2009
† Sharanevych, Emile, (Retired)—Died Dec. 12, 2008

Byzantine Eparchy of Van Nuys

Most Reverend

GERALD N. DINO

Bishop of Van Nuys; ordained March 21, 1965; appointed Bishop of Van Nuys December 6, 2007; ordained March 27, 2008. *Office: 8105 N. 16th St., Phoenix, AZ 85020.*

ESTABLISHED DECEMBER 3, 1981.

Embraces all Catholics of the Byzantine-Ruthenian Church in the States of California, Oregon, Washington, Idaho, Nevada, Arizona, Utah, Wyoming, Montana, Colorado, New Mexico, Alaska and Hawaii.

Principal Patron-Patronage of the Mother of God (Pokrov).

For legal titles of parishes and diocesan institutions, consult the Chancery Office.

Chancery Office: 8105 N. 16th St., Phoenix, AZ 85020. Tel: 602-861-9778; Fax: 602-861-9796.

Web: eparchy-of-van-nuys.org

Email: evnbishop@qwestoffice.net

STATISTICAL OVERVIEW

Personnel	
Bishop	1
Priests: Diocesan Active in Diocese	19
Priests: Diocesan Active Outside Diocese	2
Priests: Retired, Sick or Absent	4
Number of Diocesan Priests	25
Religious Priests in Diocese	1
Total Priests in Diocese	26
Permanent Deacons in Diocese	11
Total Brothers	2
Total Sisters	3
Parishes	
Parishes	19
With Resident Pastor:	
Resident Diocesan Priests	18
Resident Religious Priests	1
Missions	1
Professional Ministry Personnel:	
Brothers	2
Sisters	3
Welfare	
Other Institutions	1
Total Assisted	28
Educational	
Diocesan Students in Other Seminaries	3
Total Seminarians	3
Catechesis/Religious Education:	
High School Students	82
Elementary Students	328
Total Students under Catholic Instruction	413
Vital Statistics	
Receptions into the Church:	
Infant Baptism Totals	73
Adult Baptism Totals	12
First Communions	95
Confirmations	96
Marriages:	
Catholic	18
Interfaith	6
Total Marriages	24
Deaths	27
Total Catholic Population	2,561

Former Bishops—Most Revs. THOMAS V. DOLINAY, D.D., ord. May 16, 1948; cons. Nov. 23, 1976; appt. Tutular Bishop of Thyatira and Auxiliary of Passiac, Sept. 23, 1976; appt. First Ordinary of the Byzantine Catholic Diocese of Van Nuys, CA; installed March 9, 1982; appt. Coadjutor Archbishop of Pittsburgh Byzantine Rite, March 13, 1990; succeeded to June 12, 1991; died April 13, 1993; GEORGE M. KUZMA, D.D. (Retired), ord. May 29, 1955; appt. Auxiliary Bishop of the Byzantine Eparchy of Passaic, Nov. 11, 1986; cons. Feb. 4, 1987; appt. Bishop of Eparchy of Van Nuys Oct. 23, 1990; installed as Second Bishop of Van Nuys, Jan. 15, 1991; retired Dec. 5, 2000; died Dec. 7, 2008.; WILLIAM C. SKURLA, ord. May 23, 1987; appt. Bishop of Eparchy of Van Nuys Feb. 19, 2002; ord. April 23, 2002; appt. Bishop of Passaic Dec. 6, 2007; enthroned Jan. 29, 2008.

Chancery Office—Byzantine Catholic Eparchy of Van Nuys, Pastoral Center, 8105 N. 16th St., Phoenix, 85020. Tel: 602-861-9778; Fax: 602-861-9796. Email: evnsecretary@qwestoffice.net. Web: www.eparchy-of-van-nuys.org. Office Hours: Mon.-Fri. 10-3.

Chancellor—Rt. Rev. WESLEY W. IZER.

Protosyncellus—Rt. Rev. STEPHEN G. WASHKO. Email: sstparish@qwestoffice.net.

College of Consultors—Very Revs. KURT BURNETTE, J.C.L.; JOSEPH HUTSKO; Rt. Rev. WESLEY W. IZER; Very Rev. ROBERT M. PIPTA; Rt. Revs. FRANCIS VIVONA, J.C.L.; STEPHEN G. WASHKO.

Finance Officer—Rt. Rev. WESLEY W. IZER. Email: evntreasurer@qwestoffice.net.

Finance Assistant—Sr. ALPHONSA DANOVICH, O.S.B.M.

Presbyteral Council— All priests having a Pastoral Assignment within the Eparchy.

Secretary for the Presbyteral Council & The College of Consultors—Rev. JAMES M. LANE.

Eparchial Tribunal—Office of the Tribunal Eparchy of Van Nuys, 2120 Lindell Rd., Las Vegas, NV 89146. Tel: 702-873-5102; Fax: 702-873-5104.

Judicial Vicar—Rt. Rev. FRANCIS M. VIVONA, S.T.M., J.C.L.

Adjutant Judicial Vicar—Very Rev. KURT BURNETTE, J.C.L.

Promoter of Justice—Rev. PETER ROMEO, J.C.L.

Secretary—Mr. PAUL KILROY.

Defender of the Bond—Rev. KEVIN MCAULIFFE.

Judge—Rev. KEVIN MCAULIFFE.

Auditors—Rev. MARCUS GOMORI; Deacon STEPHEN CASMUS, M.A.

Notaries—Rev. KEVIN MCAULIFFE; Deacon STEPHEN CASMUS, M.A.; Mr. PAUL KILROY.

Bishop's Appeal—Sr. CHRISTOPHER MALCOVSKY, O.S.B.M.

Building and Sacred Arts—Rt. Revs. STEPHEN WASHKO; WESLEY W. IZER; Rev. Msgr. GEORGE N. VIDA; Deacon JOHN MONTALVO III; Mr. KEVIN KOWALCHUK.

Building Commission—Rt. Revs. STEPHEN G. WASHKO; WESLEY W. IZER; Deacon JOHN MONTALVO III; Mr. JOEL WEISHEIT.

Director of Religious Education—Rev. ANTHONY HERNANDEZ; Sr. JEAN MARIE CIHOTA, O.S.B.M., Asst. Dir.

Director of Evangelization—Rt. Rev. JOSEPH STANICHAR.

Ecumenism—Rt. Rev. STEPHEN WASHKO.

Eparchial Finance Commission—Rt. Revs. STEPHEN G. WASHKO, Chm.; WESLEY W. IZER; Sr. ALPHONSA DANOVICH, O.S.B.M.; Deacon JAMES DANOVICH.

Finance Officer—Rt. Rev. WESLEY W. IZER.

Finance Council—Rt. Revs. WESLEY W. IZER; STEPHEN G. WASHKO; Sr. ALPHONSA DANOVICH, O.S.B.M.; Deacon JAMES DANOVICH.

Safe Environment Coordinator—Sr. JEAN MARIE CIHOTA, O.S.B.M. Email: evnoffice@qwestoffice.net.

Victim Assistance Coordinators—ROSEMARIE LUDWIG, Ph.D. Tel: 602-997-1550. Email: rstussy@cox.net.

Victim Rights Advocates—ROSEMARIE LUDWIG, Ph.D. Email: rstussy@cox.net.

Vocations Office—Very Rev. ROBERT M. PIPTA, Dir.; Rev. MICHAEL O'LOUGHLIN, Asst. Dir.; Deacon JAMES DANOVICH; Sr. JEAN MARIE CIHOTA, O.S.B.M.

Ecclesiatical Notaries—Mrs. DIANE RABIEJ; Rt. Rev. STEPHEN WASHKO.

Liturgy & Music Commission—Rt. Rev. STEPHEN WASHKO, Chm.; Very Rev. ROBERT M. PIPTA; Sr. CHRISTOPHER MALCOVSKY, O.S.B.M.; Mr. BASIL RABAYDA JR.

Newsletter— "Eparchial Newsletter" Mrs. DIANE RABIEJ. Email: evnsecretary@qwestoffice.net.

Director of Development & Stewardship—Sr. CHRISTOPHER MALCOVSKY, O.S.B.M.

Director of Ecumenical Affairs—Rt. Rev. STEPHEN WASHKO.

Censor—Rt. Rev. FRANCIS M. VIVONA, S.T.M., J.C.L.

Administrative Secretary—Mrs. DIANE RABIEJ. Email: evnsecretary@qwestoffice.net.

Commission for the Implementation of the Particular Law—Very Rev. KURT BURNETTE, J.C.L.; Rt. Revs. FRANCIS M. VIVONA, S.T.M., J.C.L.; STEPHEN G. WASHKO.

Pro-Life Coordinator—Rev. LEE PERRY.

Communication and Eparchial Web Site—Mrs. DIANE RABIEJ.

Pension Committee—Rt. Revs. STEPHEN WASHKO; WESLEY W. IZER; Rev. Msgr. GEORGE N. VIDA; Very Rev. KURT BURNETTE, J.C.L.; Rev. MARCUS GOMORI.

Personnel Board—Rt. Revs. STEPHEN WASHKO; WESLEY IZER; Very Rev. ROBERT M. PIPTA.

Youth—Very Rev. JOSEPH HUTSKO; Rev. ROBERT RANKIN.

CLERGY, PARISHES, MISSIONS AND PAROCHIAL SCHOOLS

STATE OF ARIZONA

GILBERT, MARICOPA CO., ST. THOMAS THE APOSTLE (1982) Rt. Rev. Wesley W. Izer; Deacon Michael Sullivan.
Mailing Address: P.O. Box 667, 85299-0667. Tel: 480-497-6726; Fax: 480-497-6726. Web: www.stthomasbcc.org.
Church: 19 W. Bruce Ave., 85233.
Catechesis/Religious Program—Students 11.

PHOENIX, MARICOPA CO., ST. STEPHEN (1968), (Byzantine Catholic Pro-Cathedral) Rt. Rev. Stephen G. Washko, Rector; Sr. Christopher Malcovsky, O.S.B.M., Pastoral Assoc.; Deacons John Montalvo III; James Danovich; Michael Hanafin.
Res.: 8141 N. 16th St. Frnt., 85020-3999. Tel: 602-943-5379; Fax: 602-997-4093. Email: sstparish@qwestoffice.net. Web: www.ststephenbyzantine.org. Sisters 2.
Catechesis/Religious Program—Sr. Jean Marie Cihota, O.S.B.M., D.R.E. Students 72.
Convent—St. Stephen Convent, 8141 N. 16th St. #27, 85020. Tel: 602-944-5121; Fax: 602-997-4093. Sisters 3.

TUCSON, PIMA CO., ST. MELANY (1974) Rev. Robert Rankin.
Church: 1212 N. Sahuara, 85712-5018. Tel: 520-886-4225; Fax: 520-751-4574. Web: byzantinetucson.com.
Catechesis/Religious Program—Students 23.

STATE OF ALASKA

ANCHORAGE, ANCHORAGE CO., SAINT NICHOLAS OF MYRA (1958) Rev. James Barrand.
Res.: 2200 Arctic Blvd., AK 99503-1909. Tel: 907-277-6731; Fax: 907-222-6891.
Catechesis/Religious Program—Students 9.
Mission—Blessed Theodore Romzha Mission Old Sacred Heart Church, 1201 Bogard Rd., Wasilla, AK 99654.

STATE OF CALIFORNIA

SHERMAN OAKS, LOS ANGELES CO., CATHEDRAL OF ST. MARY (1956) Very Rev. Melvin Rybarczyk, C.R., Rector.
Res.: 5329 Sepulveda Blvd., CA 91411-3441. Tel: 818-907-5511; Fax: 818-981-7107.
Catechesis/Religious Program—5335 Sepulveda Blvd., CA 91411. Cynthia Bosak, D.R.E. Students 9.

ANAHEIM, ORANGE CO., ANNUNCIATION (1969) Rev. Msgr. George N. Vida.
Res.: 995 N. West St., CA 92801-4305. Tel: 714-533-6292; Fax: 714-991-9738.
Rectory—999 N. West St., CA 92801-4305.
Catechesis/Religious Program—Students 31.

FONTANA, SAN BERNARDINO CO., ST. NICHOLAS (1958) Very Rev. Joseph Hutsko; Mrs. Georgie Block, Fin. Admin.
Res.: 9112 Oleander Ave., CA 92335-5599. Tel: 909-822-9917; Fax: 909-822-7663. Email: huts1009@roadrunner.com.
Catechesis/Religious Program—Pager: 909-822-7663. Students 3.

FRESNO, FRESNO CO., BYZANTINE CATHOLIC COMMUNITY OF FRESNO, CA, Closed. For inquiries for parish records contact the chancery.

LOS GATOS, SANTA CLARA CO., ST. BASIL THE GREAT (1986) Rev. Anthony Hernandez.
Res.: 14263 Mulberry Dr., CA 95032-1208. Tel: 408-871-0919; Fax: 408-871-0911. Email: pastor@stbasil.org. Web: www.stbasil.org.
Catechesis/Religious Program—Students 6.
Salinas Monterey Byzantine Catholic Outreach—, Location: Blessed Edmund Rice Chapel at Palma High School, 919 Iverson St., Salinas, CA. (Div. Liturgy 2nd & 4th Sat. of month at 4:30 PM), 14263 Mulberry Dr., CA 95032. Email: pastor@stbasil.org. Web: www.bcmonterey.org.

PALM SPRINGS, RIVERSIDE CO., BYZANTINE CATHOLIC COMMUNITY OF PALM SPRINGS, CA, Closed. For inquiries for parish records contact the chancery.

SACRAMENTO, SACRAMENTO CO., ST. PHILIP THE APOSTLE (1971) Rev. Frantisek Murin; Margaret Dean, Fin. Admin.
Mailing Address: P.O. Box 245098, CA 95824.
Church: 3866 65th St., CA 95824. Tel: 916-452-1888 (Office); Fax: 916-452-6333. Email: stphilpastor @juno.com.

SAN DIEGO, SAN DIEGO CO., HOLY ANGELS (1958) Very Rev. Robert M. Pipta.
Mailing Address: 2235 Galahad Rd., CA 92123-3931. Tel: 858-277-2511; Fax: 858-277-5792. Web: www.holyangelssandiego.com.
Catechesis/Religious Program—Students 40.

SAN LUIS OBISPO, SAN LUIS OBISPO CO., SAINT ANNE (1986) Revs. James Lane; Edmund M. Idranyi, Pastor Emeritus (Retired); Deacon John Bradley; Mr. Paul Sawko, Fin. Admin.
Mailing Address: 222 E. Foothill Blvd., CA 93405-1540. Tel: 805-543-8883; Fax: 805-543-8832.
Catechesis/Religious Program—Students 38.

SAN MATEO, SAN MATEO CO., ST. MACRINA, Closed. All records at the Chancery Office.

STOCKTON, SAN JOAQUIN CO., BYZANTINE CATHOLIC COMMUNITY OF STOCKTON, Closed. For inquiries for parish records contact the chancery.

STATE OF COLORADO

COLORADO SPRINGS, EL PASO CO., BYZANTINE CATHOLIC MISSION, Closed. For inquiries for parish records contact the chancery.

DENVER, DENVER CO., HOLY PROTECTION OF THE MOTHER OF GOD (1974) Rev. Michael O'Loughlin; Deacon Andrew Bodnar.
Mailing Address: 1074 S. Cook St., CO 80209-4923. Tel: 303-778-8283; Fax: 303-778-8283. Email: pastor@holyprotection.org. Web: www.holyprotection.org.
Church: 1201 S. Elizabeth St., CO 80210.
Catechesis/Religious Program—Students 17.

STATE OF NEVADA

LAS VEGAS, CLARK CO.
1—ST. GABRIEL THE ARCHANGEL (1977) Rev. Mark A. Gomori.
Church: 2250 E. Maule Ave., NV 89119-4607. Tel: 702-361-2431 (Office); 702-433-1935 (Rectory); Fax: 702-361-3772.
Catechesis/Religious Program—Students 27.
2—OUR LADY OF WISDOM ITALO-GREEK (1993) Rt. Rev. Francis Vivona; Deacon Stephen Casmus.
Church: 2120 Lindell Rd., NV 89146. Tel: 702-873-5101; Fax: 702-873-5104. Web: www.ourladyofwisdom.net.
Catechesis/Religious Program—Students 35.
Outreach: 8530 Robertson Rd., NV 89146.

STATE OF NEW MEXICO

ALBUQUERQUE, BERNALILLO CO., OUR LADY OF PERPETUAL HELP (1974) Very Rev. Kurt Burnette; Deacon Brian Escobedo. In Res., Rev. Christopher L. Zugger (Retired).
Church: 1837 Alvarado Dr., N.E., NM 87110. Tel: 505-256-1539; 505-268-2877 (Rectory); Fax: 505-256-1278. Web: www.olphnm.org.
Catechesis/Religious Program—Students 14.

LAS CRUCES, DONA ANA CO., BYZANTINE CATHOLIC MISSION, Closed. Records are located at Albuquerque Parish.

STATE OF OREGON

PORTLAND, MULTNOMAH CO., ST. IRENE BYZANTINE CATHOLIC CHURCH Rev. Frank Knusel.
Mailing Address: 34799 N. Honeyman Rd., Scappoose, OR 97056. Tel: 503-543-2188. Email: fknusel@gmail.com.
Church: 4630 N. Maryland Ave., OR 97217.

STATE OF UTAH

SALT LAKE CITY, SALT LAKE CO., BYZANTINE CATHOLIC MISSION, Closed. For inquiries for parish records contact the chancery.

STATE OF WASHINGTON

OLYMPIA, THURSTON CO., ST. GEORGE BYZANTINE CATHOLIC CHURCH (1989) Rev. Lee Perry; Deacon Joseph Wargacki.
Res.: 9730 Yelm Hwy., WA 98513. Tel: 360-413-5651; Fax: 360-413-5651.
Catechesis/Religious Program—Students 26.

SEATTLE, KING CO., ST. JOHN CHRYSOSTOM (1981) Rt. Rev. Joseph Stanichar, Pastor; Deacon Michael J. Mandelas.
Res.: 1305 S. Lander St., WA 98144-5038. Tel: 206-329-9219; Fax: 206-322-6930. Web: www.stjohnchrysostom.org.
Catechesis/Religious Program—Students 72.
Whatcom, Skagit & Island Outreach—, Location: Immaculate Conception Church, Mt. Vernon, WA. (Div. Liturgy Sunday at 5:30 PM)

SPOKANE, SPOKANE CO., SS. CYRIL & METHODIUS (1979) Rev. William O'Brien.
Mailing Address: P.O. Box 15314, Spokane Valley, WA 99216-5314.
Res.: 4317 N. Evergreen Rd., WA 99216-1298. Tel: 509-922-4527.
Boise Outreach—, Location: St. Mary Church, 2612 W. State St., Boise, ID. (Sun. Liturgy at 7:30 PM).

WALLA WALLA, WALLA WALLA CO., BYZANTINE CATHOLIC MISSION, Closed. For inquiries for parish records contact the Spokane parish.

On Special Assignment:
Revs.—
Daigle, Robert E., 6505 O'Bannon Dr., Las Vegas, NV 89146.
Gnall, Julian, 11986 Tivoli Park Row #3, San Diego, CA 92128. Tel: 619-532-6043
Michalenko, Alexei, Chap., Georgetown Law Center, 600 New Jersey Ave., N.W., Washington, DC 20001.

On Leave:
Rev.—
Greskowiak, Stephen
Deacon—
Martonick, Gregory, Spokane, WA

Retired:
Revs.—
Idranyi, Edmund M., Rancho Del Bordo, 10025 El Camino Real, Space 25, Atascadero, CA 93422.
Ridella, Joseph, 66295 Hacienda Ave., Desert Hot Springs, CA 92240.
Zugger, Christopher L., 1838 Palomas Dr. N.E., Albuquerque, NM 87110.
Very Rev. Archpriest—
Moran, Michael, J.C.D., 6745 E. Superstition Springs, Blvd. #1020, Mesa, 85206.

Permanent Deacons:
Bodnar, Andrew, Denver, CO
Bradley, John, San Luis Obispo, CA
Casmus, Stephen, M.A., Las Vegas, NV
Danovich, James, Phoenix, AZ
Escobedo, Brian, Albuquerque, NM
Hanafin, Michael, Phoenix, AZ
Hess, David, P.O. Box 139, Granville, OH 43023. San Diego, CA
Mandelas, Michael, Seattle, WA
Montalvo, John, III, Phoenix, AZ
Sullivan, Michael, Gilbert, AZ
Wargacki, Joseph, Olympia, WA

INSTITUTIONS LOCATED IN THE DIOCESE

[A] RELIGIOUS COMMUNITIES

PHOENIX. *St. Stephen Convent*, 8141 N. 16th St., #27, 85020. Tel: 602-944-5121; Fax: 602-861-9796. Sisters Jean Marie Cihota, O.S.B.M.; Christopher Malcovsky, O.S.B.M.; Alphonsa Danovich, O.S.B.M.

[B] RETIREMENT HOMES

PHOENIX. *St. Stephen Senior Citizen Apartments*, 8141 N. 16th St., 85020. Tel: 602-943-5379; Fax: 602-997-4093. Web: www.ststephenbyzantine.org. Rt. Rev. Stephen G. Washko, Contact Person. Senior Citizens Apartments 26; Residents 28.

[C] MONASTERIES AND RESIDENCES OF PRIESTS AND BROTHERS

CALIMESA. *Byzantine Brothers of St. Francis, St. Francis Monastery*, 9443 Sharondale Rd., CA 92320. Tel: 909-795-0848. Bros. Michael Sullivan, B.B.S.F., Supr.; John Gray, B.B.S.F., Treas.

RELIGIOUS INSTITUTES OF MEN REPRESENTED IN THE DIOCESE

For further details refer to the corresponding bracketed number in the Religious Institutes of Men or Women section.

[]—*Byzantine Brothers of St. Francis*—B.B.S.F.

[1080]—*Congregation of the Resurrection*—C.R.

RELIGIOUS INSTITUTES OF WOMEN REPRESENTED IN THE DIOCESE

[3730]—*Sisters of the Order of St. Basil the Great*—O.S.B.M.

NECROLOGY

(No Deaths)

An asterisk (*) denotes an organization that has established tax-exempt status directly with the IRS and is not covered by the USCCB Group Ruling.

Archdiocese of Agana

Most Reverend

ANTHONY SABLAN APURON, O.F.M.Cap., D.D.

Archbishop of Agana; ordained August 26, 1972; appointed Auxiliary Bishop December 8, 1983; ordained Titular Bishop of Muzuca February 19, 1984; appointed Apostolic Administrator to the Archdiocese October 27, 1985; succeeded to Metropolitan See May 11, 1986. *Res.: Archbishop's Residence, 196-B Cuesta San Ramon, Agana, GU 96910.* Tel: 671-472-6116; Fax: 671-477-3519.

Erected by Pope Pius X, March 1, 1911 and Committed to the Order of Friars Minor Capuchin. Extended to all the Marianas Islands, July 4, 1946, Wake Island, June 14, 1948. Elevated to a Diocese, October 14, 1965, as a Suffragan of San Francisco. Elevated to Metropolitan Archdiocese, May 20, 1984 with a Suffragan See, Diocese of Caroline-Marshalls and Diocese of Chalan Kanoa (subsequently added January 13, 1985). Member of CEPAC Conference. Member of Federation of Catholic Bishops Conference of Oceania. Observer to NCCB-USCC Conference.

Guam is a Territory of the U.S.A. by Act of the U.S. Congress July 21, 1949.

Legal Title: Archbishop of Agana, a Corporation Sole.

STATISTICAL OVERVIEW

Personnel	
Archbishops	1
Priests: Diocesan Active in Diocese	42
Priests: Diocesan Active Outside Diocese	3
Priests: Retired, Sick or Absent	1
Number of Diocesan Priests	46
Religious Priests in Diocese	11
Total Priests in Diocese	57
Ordinations:	
Diocesan Priests	4
Permanent Deacons in Diocese	19
Total Brothers	2
Total Sisters	90
Parishes	
Parishes	24
With Resident Pastor:	
Resident Diocesan Priests	19
Resident Religious Priests	5
Welfare	
Homes for the Aged	1
Total Assisted	60
Day Care Centers	4
Total Assisted	592
Special Centers for Social Services	2
Total Assisted	8,109
Educational	
Seminaries, Diocesan	1
Students from This Diocese	36
Diocesan Students in Other Seminaries	1
Total Seminarians	37
High Schools, Diocesan and Parish	4
Total Students	927
High Schools, Private	1
Total Students	353
Elementary Schools, Diocesan and Parish	7
Total Students	3,158
Catechesis/Religious Education:	
High School Students	1,837
Elementary Students	2,370
Total Students under Catholic Instruction	8,682
Teachers in the Diocese:	
Priests	5
Brothers	2
Sisters	35
Lay Teachers	349
Vital Statistics	
Receptions into the Church:	
Infant Baptism Totals	1,838
Minor Baptism Totals	74
Adult Baptism Totals	64
Received into Full Communion	476
First Communions	1,246
Confirmations	1,122
Marriages:	
Catholic	217
Interfaith	10
Total Marriages	227
Deaths	585
Total Catholic Population	142,000
Total Population	166,000

Former Vicars-Apostolic—Most Revs. FRANCIS X. VILLA Y MATEU, O.F.M.Cap., D.D., cons. Titular Bishop of Adraha, Oct. 1, 1911; died at Agana, Jan. 1, 1913; AUGUSTIN BERNAUS Y SERRA, O.F.M.Cap., D.D., cons. Titular Bishop of Milopotamo, May 9, 1913; transferred to Vicariate-Apostolic of Bluefields, Nicaragua, 1914; JOAQUIN FELIPE OLAIZ Y ZABALZA, O.F.M.Cap., D.D., cons. Titular Bishop of Docimeo, Nov. 30, 1914; died at Pamplona, Spain, Dec. 8, 1945; MIGUEL ANGEL OLANO Y URTEAGA, O.F.M.Cap., D.D., cons. Titular Bishop of Lagina, May 5, 1935; resigned and made Asst. at Pontifical Throne Aug. 20, 1945; died at Agana, Guam May 21, 1970; APOLLINARIS W. BAUMGARTNER, O.F.M.Cap., D.D., cons. Sept. 18, 1945; appt. First Bishop of Agana, Oct. 14, 1965; died at Agana, Guam Dec. 18, 1970; FELIXBERTO CAMACHO FLORES, ord. April 30, 1949; appt. Apostolic Admin., Diocese of Agana, May 2, 1969; appt. Titular Bishop of Stonj, March 19, 1970; cons. May 17, 1970; succeeded to See, May 15, 1971; died Oct. 25, 1985.

Chancery Office—196 B Cuesta San Ramon, Hagatna, 96910. Tel: 671-472-6116; 671-472-6573; Fax: 671-477-3519. Office Hours: Mon.-Fri. 8-12 & 1-4.

Moderator of the Curia and Vicar General—Rev. Msgr. DAVID C. QUITUGUA, J.C.D.

Chancellor—Sr. ANA LEE, O.P., J.C.L.

Finance Officer and Business Mgr.—Deacon STEPHEN W.M. MARTINEZ.

Archdiocesan College of Consultors—Rev. Msgr. DAVID C. QUITUGUA, J.C.D.; Very Rev. ERIC FORBES, O.F.M.Cap.; Revs. KENNETH HEZEL, S.J.; JOSE ALBERTO RODRIGUEZ; Rev. Msgr. JAMES L.G. BENAVENTE.

Archdiocesan Finance Council—Rev. Msgr. JAMES L.G. BENAVENTE; RICHARD UNTALAN, Pres.; Mr. JOSEPH RIVERA; Sr. MARY STEPHEN TORRES, R.S.M.

Archdiocesan Presbyteral Council—Rev. Msgr. DAVID C. QUITUGUA, J.C.D.; Very Rev. ERIC FORBES, O.F.M.Cap.; Rev. KENNETH HEZEL, S.J.; Rev. Msgr. JAMES L.G. BENAVENTE; Very Rev. Msgr. DAVID I.A. QUITUGUA; Revs. JOSEPH ENGLISH, O.F.M.Cap.; AGUSTIN GUMATAOTAO, O.F.M.Cap.; JOSE ALBERTO RODRIGUEZ; JOSE ANTONIO P. ABAD; JEFFREY SAN NICOLAS; MICHAEL CRISOSTOMO; PATRICK CASTRO, O.F.M.Cap.; Rev. Msgr. BRIGIDO ARROYO.

Metropolitan Tribunal—

Judicial Vicar—Rev. Msgr. DAVID C. QUITUGUA, J.C.D.

Promoter of Justice—Rev. JOSE VILLAGOMEZ, O.F.M.Cap.

Defender of the Bond—Rev. JONATHAN ALVAREZ.

Associate Judges—Rev. CARLOS S. VILA, J.C.L.; Sr. ANA LEE, O.P., J.C.L.

Notary—Rev. FELIX LEON GUERRERO, O.F.M.Cap.

Chancery Records Department—Mrs. JUNE UNGACTA.

Catholic Schools Office—Mrs. CYNTHIA AGBULOS, Supt.

Division of Pastoral Ministries—Sr. MARIAN ARROYO, R.S.M., Exec. Dir. Tel: 671-472-6116; Fax: 671-472-4406; Ms. CATHERINE LEON GUERRERO, Exec. Asst.

Office of Faith Formation—Deacon LARRY CLAROS, Dir.

Office of Family Ministry—Deacon LARRY CLAROS, Dir.

Office of Pastoral Planning—Sr. MARIAN ARROYO, R.S.M., Dir.

Office of Worship—Sr. MARIAN ARROYO, R.S.M., Dir.

Office of Communications—Mr. TONY DIAZ, Dir., 196 B Cuesta San Ramon, Hagatna, 96910. Tel: 671-472-6427; Fax: 671-477-5656.

Catholic Educational Radio, KOLG—196 B Cuesta San Ramon, Hagatna, 96910. Tel: 671-477-5654; Fax: 671-477-5656.

Pacific Voice—Mr. TONY DIAZ, Editor, 193 B Cuesta San Ramon, Hagatna, 96910. Tel: 671-472-6427; Fax: 671-477-5224. Email: pacvoice@ite.net; Ms. MARIQUITA CRUZ, Production Supvr.; Ms. LUZ OBERIANO, Office Asst.

Procurement Clerk—Ms. ANN GOGUE.

Information Resource Officer—HELEN FLORES.

Family Ministry Coordinator—CARMELITA MONDIA.

Other Archdiocesan Pastoral Offices and Directors

Catholic Campus Ministry, Newman Center, University of Guam—Rev. MICHAEL CRISOSTOMO, Dir., 196 B Cuesta San Ramon, Hagatna, 96910. Tel: 671-734-3507; Fax: 671-734-2943.

Catholic Cemetery Office—FRANK SANTOS, Exec. Dir.; Rev. Msgr. JAMES L.G. BENAVENTE, Dir., 196 B Cuesta San Ramon, Hagatna, 96910. Tel: 671-472-6201; Fax: 671-472-1729.

Office of Vocations—

Formation Program for the Permanent Diaconate—Rev. JEFFREY C. SAN NICOLAS, Dir.

Associations and Charitable Organizations in the Archdiocese

Alee Shelter Program for Spousal Abuse—Sr. BRIGID PEREZ, R.S.M., Dir., c/o Catholic Social Service, 234-A US Army Juan C. Fejeran St., Barrigada, 96913. Tel: 671-635-1409; Fax: 671-635-1444.

Catholic Charities Appeal—Deacon LARRY CLAROS, 196 B Cuesta San Ramon, Hagatna, 96910. Tel: 671-472-6116; Fax: 671-477-3519.

Catholic Pro-Life Committee—

Gentle Refuge Crisis Pregnancy Center—

Project Rachel (Abortion Aftermath Counseling)—Deacon FRANCISCO TENORIO, Exec. Dir., Mailing Address: P.O. Box 23006, GMF, 96921. Tel: 671-477-1724.

Catholic Social Service—Mrs. CERILA MATIAS RAPADAS, Exec. Dir., 234-A US Army Juan C. Fejeran St., Barrigada, 96913. Tel: 671-635-1410; Fax: 671-635-1444. Email: css@guam.net. Web: www.catholicsocialservice.net.

Pontifical Holy Childhood Association & Pontifical Society for the Propagation of the Faith—Rev. Msgr. DAVID C. QUITUGUA, J.C.D., Contact Person, 196 B Cuesta San Ramon, Hagatna, 96910. Tel: 671-472-6116; 671-472-6573; Fax: 671-477-3519.

Groups, Ecclesial Movements and other Organizations in the Archdiocese

Catholic Daughters of the Americas—Rev. Msgr. BRIGIDO ARROYO, Chap., P.O. Box 7707, Tamuning, 96931. Tel: 671-646-7181.

Court 2047, Our Lady of Camarin—ELIZABETH UNTALAN, Regent.

Court 2450, Maria Rainan Y Familia—Mrs. DORA SALAZAR, Regent.

Confraternity of Christian Mothers—Rev. FELIX LEON GUERRERO, O.F.M.Cap., Spiritual Dir.

United Catholic Charismatic Community—

Catholic Covenant Community—CARLOS SAN AGUSTIN. Tel: 671-477-9118.

Cell Prayer Community—ROQUE MENDIOLA.

El Shaddai (PPFI), Prayer Partner International, Guam Chapter—ALBINA SANTOS, Coord.; Rev. PAUL M. GOFIGAN, Spiritual Dir.

Our Lady of Lourdes Catholic Charismatic Group—LINDA ESTRELLA. Tel: 671-653-2584.

Worship and Praise—FLO SANCHEZ. Tel: 671-646-8044.

Cursillo in Christianity—Rev. JOEL DE LOS REYES, Spiritual Dir., Santa Barbara Church, Dededo, 96929. Tel: 671-632-5659; Fax: 671-632-1713; Mr. SIMON PEREZ, Pres.

Evenings for the Engaged—229 San Roke St., Barrigada, 96913. Tel: 671-734-4573; Fax: 671-734-5858.

Knights of Columbus—JOE YATAR, State Deputy; Rev. JOSE VILLAGOMEZ, O.F.M.Cap., State Chap.

Knights of St. Gregory the Great—Sir Knight CRISTOBAL DUENAS.

Knights of St. Sylvester—FRANK CRUZ; PEDRO M. CAMACHO; RICHARD UNTALAN; FRANK SANTOS; THOMAS J. CALVO; EDWARD S. TERLAJE; GONZALO REYES.

Legion of Mary—Rev. Msgr. DAVID C. QUITUGUA, J.C.D., Spiritual Dir.; Mrs. REMEDIOS SILVERIO, Pres., Mailing Address: P.O. Box 2890, Hagatna, 96932. Tel: 671-632-2281; 671-734-2829; Fax: 671-477-3519.

Marriage Encounter—Coordinators: CHARLES KEONE; ESTHER KEONE, 196 B Cuesta San Ramon, Hagatna, 96910. Tel: 671-632-7654; Fax: 671-477-3519.

Neo Catechumenal Way— Dulce Nombre de Maria Cathedral-Basilica Most Rev. ANTHONY SABLAN APURON, O.F.M.Cap., D.D., 207 Archbishop Flores St., Agana, 96910. Tel: 671-472-6201; Fax: 671-472-1729. San Vicente Ferrer Parish: Rev. JOSE ALBERTO RODRIGUEZ, Presbyter, 229 San Roke St., Barrigada, 96913. Tel: 671-734-4573; Fax: 671-734-5858. Saint Anthony Parish: Rev. Msgr. BRIGIDO ARROYO, Presbyter, P.O. Box 7707, Tamuning, 96931. Tel: 671-646-8044; Fax: 671-649-1039. Our Lady of Lourdes Parish: Rev. JEFFREY C. SAN NICOLAS, Presbyter, P.O. Box 11001, Yigo, 96929. Tel: 671-653-2584; Fax: 671-653-4746. Nino Perdido Parish (Asan): Rev. ANTONINO CAMINITI, Presbyter, P.O. Box 45, Agana, 96910. Tel: 671-477-2211.

Secular Franciscans (Third Order)—Rev. DANIEL CRISTOBAL, O.F.M.Cap., Spiritual Dir.; Mrs. CARMEN MANIBUSAN, Pres., 135 Chalan Kapuchino, Agana Heights, 96910.

Sponsor Couple Program—Deacon LARRY CLAROS.

Natural Family Planning Program—Deacon LARRY CLAROS, 196 B Cuesta San Ramon, Hagatna, 96910. Tel: 671-472-6116; 671-472-6573; Fax: 671-477-3519.

Youth and Young Adults Ministry—Rev. MICHAEL CRISOSTOMO.

CLERGY, PARISHES, MISSIONS AND PAROCHIAL SCHOOLS

CITY OF AGANA

ISLAND OF GUAM

1—DULCE NOMBRE DE MARIA CATHEDRAL - BASILICA (1669) Most Rev. Anthony Sablan Apuron, O.F.M.Cap., Pastor; Rev. Msgrs. James L.G. Benavente, Rector; David C. Quitugua; Rev. Thomas B. McGrath, S.J.; Deacons John Dierking; Augusto F. Cepeda.
Res.: 207 Archbishop Felixberto C. Flores St., 96910. Tel: 671-472-6201; 671-477-1842; Fax: 671-472-1729. Email: info@aganacathedral.org. Web: www.aganacathedral.org.
Catechesis/Religious Program—Students 200.

2—ST. ANDREW KIM (1998), (Korean), Under the Jurisdiction of Santa Barbara Parish, Dededo., Mailing Address: P.O. Box 1555, 96910. Tel: 671-637-4148; 671-637-1116; Fax: 671-637-4149. Email: sungjoox@hanmail.net. Web: www.guam.cath.kr.
Catechesis/Religious Program—Email: bin200p@hanmail.net. Students 60.

OUTSIDE THE CITY OF AGANA

AGANA HEIGHTS, OUR LADY OF THE BLESSED SACRAMENT (1948) Rev. Patrick Castro, O.F.M.Cap.
Res.: 135 Chalan Kapuchino, 96919. Tel: 671-472-6246.
Catechesis/Religious Program—Cynthia Agbulos, D.R.E. Students 211.

AGAT, OUR LADY OF MOUNT CARMEL (1957) [CEM] Rev. Jason Granado.
Mailing Address: P.O. Box 8353, 96928.
Res.: 157S Eugenio St., 96928. Tel: 671-565-2136; Fax: 671-565-9678.
Catechesis/Religious Program—Students 178.
Chapel—Santa Ana Chapel Lot No. 306-4-2, 96928.

ASAN, NINO PERDIDO Y SAGRADA FAMILIA (1947) Rev. Antonino Caminiti; Deacon R. Larry Claros.
Res.: Nino Perdido St., 96910. Tel: 671-477-2211; Fax: 671-477-2211.
Catechesis/Religious Program—Students 70.

BARRIGADA, SAN VICENTE FERRER (1947) Revs. Jose Alberto Rodriguez, Admin.; Edward M. Gallagher, Parochial Vicar; Edivaldo daSilva Oliveira.
Res.: 229 San Roke St., 96913. Tel: 671-734-4573; Fax: 671-734-5858.
Catechesis/Religious Program—Geraldine Dela Rosa, D.R.E. Students 308.

CHALAN PAGO, NUESTRA SENORA DE LA PAZ Y BUEN VIAJE (1959) Revs. Santiago Flor Caravia; Aurelio Stoia.
Res.: 520 S. Chalan Kanton Tasi, 96910. Tel: 671-734-3723; Fax: 671-734-3722. Email: olopsj@gmail.com. Web: www.olopsj.org.
Catechesis/Religious Program—Tel: 671-734-4223. Students 189.

DEDEDO, SANTA BARBARA (1947) Revs. Paul M. Gofigan; Vito San Andres, Parochial Vicar; Joel de los Reyes (Philippines), Parochial Vicar; Dan Bien, Parochial Vicar; Deacons Herbert Cruz; Peter L. Kaai.
Office: 330 Iglesias Cir., 96929. Tel: 671-632-5659; 671-632-9534; Fax: 671-632-1713. Email: welcome@sbparish.org.
Res.: 372 Gloria Cir., 96929. Tel: 671-633-7253.
Catechesis/Religious Program—Virginia Avaricio, C.R.E.; Cristeta Deliquina, C.R.E. Students 611.

INARAJAN, ST. JOSEPH (1680), (Chamorro), [CEM] Rev. Lonilo R. Torres, Admin.
Res.: P.O. Box 170022, 96917. Tel: 671-828-8102; Fax: 671-828-7062.
Catechesis/Religious Program—Students 132.

MAINA, OUR LADY OF THE PURIFICATION (1949) Rev. Simeon Balmeo.
Res.: P.O. Box 4477, 96910. Tel: 671-477-7256; Fax: 671-635-1444.
Catechesis/Religious Program—Students 31.

MALOJLO, SAN ISIDRO (1950) [JC] Rev. Hector U. Canon.
Res.: 131 San Isidro St., HC 1 Box 17083, 96915. Tel: 671-828-8454; Fax: 671-828-8454.
Catechesis/Religious Program—Students 169.

MANGILAO, SANTA TERESITA (1951) Rev. Felixberto C. Leon Guerrero, O.F.M.Cap.; Deacon Itoy Ruda.
Res.: 192 Vietnam Veterans Hwy., 96913. Tel: 671-734-2100; 671-734-2171; Fax: 671-734-2172. Email: santateresitaguam@gmail.com.
Catechesis/Religious Program—Email: youthandfaith@mail2kevin.com. Students 320.

MERIZO, SAN DIMAS AND OUR LADY OF THE ROSARY (1680), (Chamorro), [CEM] Rev. Wojciech B. Jaskowiak; Deacon Jeff Barcinas.
Res.: P.O. Box 6099, 96916. Tel: 671-828-8056; Fax: 671-828-3100.
Catechesis/Religious Program—Students 206.

MONGMONG, NUESTRA SENORA DE LAS AGUAS (1969) Rev. Manuel Trenchera Jr.; Deacons Stephen W.M. Martinez; Louis J. Rama.
139-A Roy T. Damian St., 96927.
Res.: P.O. Box 163, 96932. Tel: 671-477-6754; Fax: 671-472-6569. Email: nuestra@guam.net.
Catechesis/Religious Program— Rosa C. Santos, D.R.E. Students 59.

ORDOT, SAN JUAN BAUTISTA (1947), (Chamorro), Very Rev. Msgr. David I.A. Quitugua; Rev. Manny Ombao.
Res.: P.O. Box 49, 96910. Tel: 671-472-8341; Fax: 671-472-2324.
Catechesis/Religious Program—Students 139.

PITI, ASSUMPTION OF OUR LADY (1930), (Chamorro), Rev. Willy O. Lorilla.
Res. & Mailing Address: 314 Assumption Dr., 96915. Tel: 671-472-2272; Fax: 671-477-1955. Email: pitichurch@guam.net.
Catechesis/Religious Program—Students 93.

SANTA RITA, OUR LADY OF GUADALUPE (1944) Rev. Fabio Faiola.
Res.: P.O. Box 4632, 96932. Tel: 671-565-2160; Fax: 671-565-7078.
Catechesis/Religious Program—Mrs. Cecilia Cruz, D.R.E. Students 206.

SINAJANA, SAINT JUDE THADDEUS (1962) Rev. Agustin Gumataotao, O.F.M.Cap.; Deacons Joseph Barcinas; Anthony Leon Guerrero.
Church: 122 Bien Avenida Ct., 96910. Tel: 671-475-6530; Fax: 671-477-5353.
Catechesis/Religious Program—Cindy Eclavea, D.R.E. Students 321.

TALOFOFO, SAN MIGUEL (1945), (Chamorro), Rev. Daniel Cristobal, O.F.M.Cap.
Res.: 138 San Miguel St., 96915-3606. Tel: 671-789-1069; Fax: 671-789-7665.
Catechesis/Religious Program—Tel: 671-789-0130. Marie E. Meno, D.R.E.; Goring Duenas, D.R.E. Students 195.

TAMUNING, ST. ANTHONY AND ST. VICTOR (1946) Rev. Msgr. Brigido Arroyo; Revs. James Ch'e; Carlos S. Vila (Philippines); Mario S. Palanca; Rodolfo G. Arejola; Miguel Angel Cervantes Pardo.
Res.: P.O. Box 7707, 96931. Tel: 671-646-7181; 671-646-8044; Fax: 671-646-1039.
Catechesis/Religious Program—Students 244.

TOTO, IMMACULATE HEART OF MARY (1948) Rev. Michael Crisostomo; Deacon Jose E. Santos.
Res.: P.O. Box 2552, Hagatna, 96932. Tel: 671-477-9118; Fax: 671-472-2514.
Catechesis/Religious Program—Tel: 671-472-6754. Students 94.

TUMON BAY, BLESSED DIEGO LUIS DE SAN VITORES CHURCH (1970) Rev. Jose Antonio P. Abad, Pastor; Deacon William Hagen.
Res.: 884 Pale' San Vitores Rd., 96913-4013. Tel: 671-646-5649; Fax: 671-648-6887.
Catechesis/Religious Program—Students 81.

UMATAC, SAN DIONISIO (1680), (Chamorro), [CEM] Revs. Wojciech B. Jaskowiak; Julio Cesar Sanchez Malangon; Deacon Jeff Barcinas.
Res.: P.O. Box 6099, Merizo, 96915. Tel: 671-828-8056; Fax: 671-828-3100.
Catechesis/Religious Program—Students 60.

YIGO, OUR LADY OF LOURDES (1947) Revs. Jeffrey C. San Nicolas; Patrick Kenny Q. Garcia, Parochial Vicar; Jonathan Alvarez, Parochial Vicar; Deacons Fred Otte; Len Stohr; David Richards.
Res.: 153 Chalan Pale Ramon Lagu, 96929. Tel: 671-653-2584; Fax: 671-653-4746. Email: ourlady@ite.net. Web: www.lourdesguam.com.
Catechesis/Religious Program—Tel: 671-653-1102. Femelyne Wesolowski, D.R.E.; Veronica Lizama, Coord. (Children's Div.); Glenda Luke, Registrar. Students 572.
Mission—Santa Bernadita Mission Chapel
Catechesis/Religious Program—Students 34.

YONA, SAN FRANCISCO D'ASSISI (1954) [CEM] Rev. Jose Villagomez, O.F.M.Cap.
San Fidelis Friary: 135 Chalan Kapuchino, Agana Heights, 96910. Tel: 671-789-1491; 671-789-1492; Fax: 671-789-1400. Email: stfrancis@teleguam.net.
Catechesis/Religious Program— Sharon O'Mallan, D.R.E. Students 344.

On Duty Outside the Archdiocese:
Rev.—
Adversario, Efren, Military Chap., U.S. AF

Retired:
Rev.—
Brouillard, Louis A., 525 9th St., Pine City, MN 55063.

Permanent Deacons:
Agbulos, Louis T., Jr.
Barcinas, Jeff
Barcinas, Joseph
Cepeda, Augusto F.
Claros, Larry
Cruz, Herbert
Diaz, Ramon
Dierking, John
Hagen, William
Kaai, Peter L.
Leon Guerrero, Anthony
Martinez, Steve
Otte, Fred
Rama, Louis J.
Richards, David
Ruda, Itoi
Santos, Jose E.
Stohr, Leonard
Tenorio, Francisco

INSTITUTIONS LOCATED IN THE ARCHDIOCESE

[A] SEMINARIES

YONA. *Redemptoris Mater Archdiocesan Missionary Seminary* (1999) 130 Chalan Seminariu, 96915. Tel: 671-789-2400; Fax: 671-789-2800. Email: rmsguam@ite.net. Web: www.seminaryguam.com. Revs. Pablo Ponce Rodriguez (Italy), Rector;

Wojciech B. Jaskowiak, Prefect of Studies; Giovanni Rizzo, M.Div. (NEW), Vice-Rector. Seminarians 36.

[B] HIGH SCHOOLS

AGANA. *Academy of Our Lady of Guam*, 233 W. Archbishop Felixberto C. Flores St., 96910. Tel: 671-477-8203; Fax: 671-477-8555. Email: acad@aolg.edu.gu. Web: www.aolg.edu.gu. Sr. Francis Jerome Cruz, R.S.M., Pres.; Ms. Lourdes Babauta, Dean Student Affairs; Mrs. Mary Meeks, Prin.; Mrs. Daphne Castillo, Vice Prin.; Mrs. Margaret Mesa, Admission Dir.; Sr. Orlean Pereda, R.S.M., Librarian. Sisters of Mercy. Sisters 4; Lay Teachers 29; Staff 15; Students 419.

HAGATNA. *The Father Duenas Memorial School* (1949) P.O. Box FD, 96932. Tel: 671-734-2261; 671-734-2263; Fax: 671-734-5738. Email: fdms@guam.net. Web: www.fatherduenas.com. Rev. Vitaliano Dimaranan, S.D.B., Prin.; Dante Perez, Librarian. Priests 4; Lay Teachers 28; Students 428.

ORDOT. *St. Aquinas High School, Ordot*, P.O. Box AC, 96932. Dr. Hauhoriat Diambra-Odi, Ph.D., Prin. Students 40.

TALOFOFO. *Notre Dame High School*, 480 S. San Miguel St., 96915-3540. Tel: 671-789-1676; 671-789-1745; Fax: 671-789-4847. Email: info@ndroyals.net. Web: ndroyals.net. Sr. Jean Ann Crisostomo, S.S.N.D., Pres.; Mariesha Cruz-San Nicolas, Prin. Sisters 3; Lay Teachers 25; Students 353.

[C] ELEMENTARY AND JUNIOR HIGH SCHOOLS

AGAT. *Our Lady of Mt. Carmel School* (1957) P.O. Box 7830, 96928. Tel: 671-565-3822; 671-565-5128; Fax: 671-565-3539. Email: mcsourlady@gmail.com. H. delos Santos, Prin.; Ms. Maria Florig, Librarian. Sisters 2; Lay Teachers 26; Students 515.

BARRIGADA. *San Vicente Catholic School*, 196 Bejong St., 96913. Tel: 671-735-4240; Fax: 671-734-8718; 671-735-4243. Email: braves@ite.net. Web: www.geocities.com/sanvicentebraves2000/index.htm. Sr. Joseph Ann Quinene, S.S.N.D., Prin.; Maria Camacho, Library Tech; Sr. Lydia Marie Borja, S.S.N.D., Librarian. Brothers 1; Sisters 3; Lay Teachers 19; Students 280.

DEDEDO. *Santa Barbara Catholic School* (1950) 274-A W. Santa Barbara Ave., 96929-5308. Tel: 671-632-5578; Fax: 671-632-1414. Email: info@santabarbaraschool.org. Web: www.santabarbaraschool.org. Sr. Jeanette Marie Pangelinan, R.S.M., Prin.; Margaret Catabay, Librarian. Sisters 2; Lay Teachers 39; Students 491.

GMF. *St. Francis School*, P.O. Box 22199, 96921. Tel: 671-789-1270; 671-789-1350; Fax: 671-789-3900. Email: sfcsyona@ite.net. Web: www.sfguam.com. Sr. Marsha Nededog, S.S.N.D., Prin.; Mr. Francisco Pangelinan, Librarian. Sisters 2; Lay Teachers 20; Students 301.

SINAJANA. *Bishop Baumgartner Memorial Catholic School*, 281 Calle Angel Flores St., 96910. Tel: 671-472-6670; 671-477-2677; 671-477-4010; 671-477-4003; Fax: 671-477-4028. Email: jmartero1938@hotmail.com. Web: www.bbmcs.org. Sr. Mary Emiline Artero, R.S.M., Pres.; Mrs. Rita D. Duenas, Prin.; Merly Lacaden, Librarian. Cathedral Grade School merged with Bishop Baumgartner Middle School to form Bishop Baumgartner Memorial Catholic School. Brothers 1; Sisters 3; Lay Teachers 43; Students 710.

TAMUNING. *Saint Anthony School*, 529 Chalan San Antonio, 96913. Tel: 671-647-1140; Fax: 671-649-7130. Email: sasadm@ite.net. Web: www.stanthonyschoolguam.org. Sr. Doris San Agustin, R.S.M., Prin.; Mrs. Arlene Rodriguez, Librarian. Sisters 3; Lay Teachers 48; Students 716.

YIGO. *Dominican Catholic School* (1995) 114 Chalan Pale Ramon-Lagu Rte. 1, 96929. Tel: 671-653-3021; Fax: 671-653-3090. Email: cormosd@ite.net. Web: dominicancatholicschool.com. Sr. Zenaida T. Ancheta, O.P., Prin.; Ms. Bernadette Alicante, Librarian. Sisters 6; Lay Teachers 18; Students 223.

[D] KINDERGARTEN AND NURSERY SCHOOLS

AGANA HEIGHTS. *Maria Artero Catholic Preschool & Kindergarten*, 161 A Sunset Dr., 96910-6451. Tel: 671-472-8777; Fax: 671-472-2326. Email: macpk@teleguam.net. Web: www.macpk.brinkster.net. Sr. Katherine E. Bromwell, M.M.B., Prin. Sisters 5; Lay Teachers 2; Students 64.

ORDOT. *Dominican Child Development Center*, P.O. Box 5668, 96932. Tel: 671-477-7228; 671-472-1524; Fax: 671-472-4282. Email: dcdcj1980@yahoo.com. Sisters Ma. Ana Lee, O.P., Local Prioress & Contact Person; Jessica Quipit, O.P., Prin. Sisters 3; Lay Teachers 9; Aides 4; Students 151.

PEREZVILLE-TAMUNING. *Mercy Heights Nursery and Kindergarten, Inc.*, 211 Fr. San Vitores St., Tamuning, 96913. Tel: 671-646-1185; Fax: 671-649-1822. Ms. Cecilia Crisostomo, Admin. Lay Teachers 16; Students 197.

TAI. *Infant of Prague Nursery and Kindergarten, Inc.*, 164 Sabanan Magas Rd., Mangilao, 96913. Tel: 671-734-2785; Fax: 671-734-1055. Email: sbu@ite.net. Sr. Barbara Ungacta, R.S.M., Admin. Institute of the Sisters of the Mercy of the Americas, South Central Community on Guam. Sisters 4; Lay Teachers 19; Students 180.

[E] CATHOLIC CHARITIES

BARRIGADA. *Catholic Social Services of Guam*, 234A U.S. Army Juan C. Fejeran St., 96913. Tel: 671-635-1409; 671-635-1406; Fax: 671-635-1444. Email: css@guam.net. Web: www.catholicsocialservices.net. Mrs. Cerila Matias Rapadas, Exec. Dir.; Leo G. Casil, Deputy Dir. Total Elderly Assisted 1,349; Total Adults Assisted 846; Total Children Assisted 557; Total Families Assisted 874; Total Staff 230.
Elderly Programs:
Case Management Lisa Kenworthy, Prog. Mgr.
Adult Day Care Lia Ponce, Prog. Mgr.
Dementia Care Julie Perez, Prog. Mgr.
Emergency Receiving Home Juliet Baroga, Acting Prog. Mgr.
Shelter Programs:
Alee I Shelter for Abused Spouses & Children Sr. Brigid Perez, R.S.M., Project Dir.
Alee II Shelter for Abused Children Sr. Brigid Perez, R.S.M., Project Dir.
Caridad I Shelter for Children with Disabilities R. Arlene Santos, Project Dir.
Caridad II Shelter for Adults R. Arlene Santos, Project Dir.
Guma San Jose Josephine Rosario, Project Dir.
Transitional Homeless (Liheng) Jesse Catahay, Project Dir.
Programs for Persons with Disabilities:
Respite Care Norbert Ungacta, Project Dir.
Community Habilitation Program Lourdes Bitanga, Project Dir.
Guma Hinemlo Ray Aromin, Prog. Mgr.
Literacy Programs:
Literacy Program Jesse Catahay, Project Dir.
GED Prep Program Jesse Catahay, Project Dir.
Support Services Division:
Support Services Juan C. Chargualaf, Support Svc. Dir. & Facilities Maintenance Coord.
Federal Grant
FEMA (Food & Shelter Grant)
Emergency Food Bank
Msgr. David I.A. Quitugua Foundation
Finger Printing
Food Catering
Monthly Rummage Sale
Hidden Treasure

[F] MONASTERIES AND RESIDENCES OF PRIESTS

AGANA HEIGHTS. *St. Fidelis Friary*, 135 Chalan Kapuchino, 96910. Tel: 671-472-6339; Fax: 671-472-3335. Web: www.thepacificaps.org. Revs. Joseph English, O.F.M.Cap., Vice Prov., Guardian; Felix Leon Guerrero, O.F.M.Cap., Councilor; George Maddock, O.F.M.Cap.; Jose Villagomez, O.F.M.Cap., Councilor; Agustin Gumataotao, O.F.M.Cap.; Randolph Nowak, O.F.M.Cap.; Daniel Cristobal, O.F.M.Cap.; Patrick Castro, O.F.M.Cap.; Very Rev. Eric Forbes, O.F.M.Cap.; Revs. Michael Tenorio, O.F.M.Cap.; Andre Eduvala, O.F.M.Cap.; Bros. Brian Champoux, O.F.M.Cap.; Joseph R. Meno Jr., O.F.M.Cap.; Brian Champoux, O.F.M.Cap. Headquarters of Capuchin Friars (Vice Province, Star of the Sea).

BARRIGADA. *Society of Jesus Micronesia*, P.O. Box 315244, Tamuning, 96931. Tel: 671-649-0073; Fax: 671-649-0074. Email: khezel@ite.net. Revs. Kenneth J. Hezel, S.J., Supr.; Thomas B. McGrath, S.J., Chap.

[G] CONVENTS AND RESIDENCES FOR SISTERS

AGANA HEIGHTS. *Mercedarian Missionaries of Berriz*, 161 A Sunset Dr., 96910-6451. Tel: 671-477-8303; Fax: 671-472-2326. Email: mmbmicro@teleguam.net. Web: www.mmberriz.com. Sisters Isabel T. Seman, M.M.B., Regl. Coord.; Anotia Addy, M.M.B., Regl. Vicar; Fudalina Umwech, M.M.B., Admin.; Katherine E. Bromwell, M.M.B., Prin.; Marlihsa Suzumu, M.M.B., Teacher Aide MACPK & Student UOG; Ancherin Koto, M.M.B., Teacher Aide MACPK & Student UOG; Brenda Mwarike, M.M.B., Teacher Aide MACPK; Rosemary Laigeluw, M.M.B., Teacher Aide MACPK. Sisters 8.

BARRIGADA. *San Vicente Community*, 201 Bejong St., 96913. Tel: 671-734-3010; Fax: 671-734-8718. Email: ssndbarr@ite.net. Sr. Joseph Ann Quinene, S.S.N.D., Prin. Sisters teach at San Vicente Elementary, St. Francis School. Sisters 4.

DEDEDO. *Santa Barbara Convent*, 274 B. W. Santa Barbara St., 96929. Tel: 671-632-2384; Fax: 671-632-1414. Institute of the Sisters of Mercy of the Americas, South Central Community on Guam. Sisters 4.

HAGATNA. *Cathedral Mercy Convent*, 221 Archbishop F. C. Flores St., 96910-5102. Tel: 671-477-9291; Fax: 671-477-9293. Email: mercy@aolg.edu.gu. Sisters 5.

ORDOT. *Religious Missionaries of St. Dominic*, P.O. Box 5668, 96932. Tel: 671-472-1524. Email: tribunal@ite.net. Religious 3; Total in Residence 4.

PEREZVILLE-TAMUNING. *MERCY ACTION MARIANAS, Ltd. (MAML)*, 211 Fr. San Vitores St., Tamuning, 96913. Tel: 671-649-7561; Fax: 671-649-1822. Email: guamrsm@ite.net. Sr. Trinie Pangelinan, R.S.M., Pres. Institute of the Sisters of Mercy of the Americas, South Central Community on Guam.

Mercy Heights Convent, 211 Fr. San Vitores St., Tamuning, 96913. Tel: 671-646-7246; Fax: 671-649-1822. Email: guamrsm@ite.net. Sr. Mary Cecilia Camacho, R.S.M., Local Admin. Sisters in residence teaching and working in Tamuning, Agana, Sinajana and infirmed; Residence, retirement residence & administrative offices of the Institute of the Sisters of Mercy of the Americas, South Central Community on Guam. Sisters 20.

SINAJANA. *St. Jude Thaddeus Convent*, P.O. Box 394, Hagatna, 96932. Tel: 671-477-7852. Email: sgamakaka@teleguam.net. Franciscan Sisters of Perpetual Adoration.

TAI. *Tai Mercy Convent and Formation House*, P.O. Box 22865 GMF, Barrigada, 96921-2865. Tel: 671-734-3312; Fax: 671-734-2260. Institute of the Sisters of Mercy of the Americas, South Central Community on Guam.; Professed Sisters in various Apostolates and Sisters in basic formation as well as retired sisters. Sisters 14.

TALOFOFO. *S.S.N.D. Notre Dame Center*, 480 San Miguel St., 96915-3540. Tel: 671-789-7763; 671-789-0501; Fax: 671-789-3810. Email: maryjuancamacho@yahoo.com. Sr. Mary Juan Camacho, S.S.N.D., Coord. Sisters 22.

Mother Theresa Tel: 671-789-0501; Fax: 671-789-3810.

Notre Dame Community Tel: 671-789-1629; Fax: 671-789-3810.

TAMUNING. *Discalced Order Of Carmelites Monastery*, P.O. Box 315225, 96931. Tel: 671-646-8972; 671-727-7737 (Work); Fax: 671-922-7737. Email: guam@carmelite-nuns.org. Web: www.carmelite-nuns.info. Sr. Dawn Marie, O.C.D., Prioress. Order of Discalced Carmelites. Sisters 9.

[H] MISCELLANEOUS LISTINGS

AGANA. *Our Lady of the Waters House of Prayer* (Retreat Center), P.O. Box 163, 96932. Tel: 671-472-6201; 671-472-1842; Fax: 671-477-3766; 671-472-1729.

Secular Franciscans, 135 Chalan Kapuchino, 96910. Tel: 671-472-6023; 671-472-6339; Fax: 671-789-7665. Rev. Daniel Cristobal, O.F.M.Cap., Spiritual Dir.; Mrs. Carmen Manibusan, Pres.

BARRIGADA. *Saint Dominic's Senior Care Home*, 350 N. Sabana Dr., Barrigada Heights, 96913-1262. Tel: 671-632-9370; 671-632-9378; Fax: 671-637-1679. Email: stdom@ite.net. Sr. Emelita Cinco, O.P., Admin. Bed Capacity 60; Total Assisted Annually 60; Total Staff 75.

MANGILAO. *Office of Youth, Young Adult & Campus Ministry* 196-B Cuesta San Ramon, Hagatna, 96910. Tel: 671-734-3507; Fax: 671-734-2943. Email: palemike@yahoo.com. Rev. Michael Crisostomo, Dir. Total Assisted Annually 15; Total Staff 2.

RELIGIOUS INSTITUTES OF MEN REPRESENTED IN THE ARCHDIOCESE

For further details refer to the corresponding bracketed number in the Religious Institutes of Men or Women section.

[0470]—*The Capuchin Friars* (Vice Prov. of Mary, Star of the Sea)—O.F.M.Cap.

[0690]—*The Society of Jesus- Jesuit Fathers and Brothers* (N.Y. Prov.)—S.J.

RELIGIOUS INSTITUTES OF WOMEN REPRESENTED IN THE ARCHDIOCESE

[1780]—*Congregation of the Sisters of the Third Order of St. Francis of Perpetual Adoration* (La Crosse, WI)—F.S.P.A.

[0420]—*Discalced Carmelite Nuns*—O.C.D.

[2510]—*Mercedarian Missionaries of Berriz*—M.M.B.

[]—*Religious Missionaries of St. Dominic*—O.P.

[2970]—*School Sisters of Notre Dame* (Mequon, WI)—S.S.N.D.

[2575]—*Sisters of Mercy of the Americas* (Belmont, NC)—R.S.M.

NECROLOGY

† Perez, Antonio, (On Duty Outside the Archdiocese)—Died Sept. 12, 2009

An asterisk (*) denotes an organization that has established tax-exempt status directly with the IRS and is not covered by the USCCB Group Ruling.

Diocese of Arecibo, Puerto Rico

(Dioecesis Arecibensis)

Most Reverend

INAKI MALLONA TXERTUDI, C.P.

Bishop of Arecibo; ordained March 17, 1956; appointed December 14, 1991; consecrated January 6, 1992; installed January 25, 1992. *Res.: 206 Dr. Salas St., P.O. Box 616, Arecibo, PR 00613.*

The Chancery: 206 Dr. Salas St., P.O. Box 616, Arecibo, PR 00613. Tel: 787-878-3180; 787-878-3110; Fax: 787-880-2661.

Email: obispado@xsn.net

ESTABLISHED APRIL 30, 1960.

Square Miles 833.

Comprises the mid-northern part of the Island.

STATISTICAL OVERVIEW

Personnel	
Bishop	1
Priests: Diocesan Active in Diocese	39
Priests: Diocesan Active Outside Diocese	11
Priests: Retired, Sick or Absent	11
Number of Diocesan Priests	61
Religious Priests in Diocese	45
Total Priests in Diocese	106
Extern Priests in Diocese	9
Ordinations:	
Religious Priests	1
Transitional Deacons	1
Permanent Deacons in Diocese	3
Total Brothers	6
Total Sisters	170
Parishes	
Parishes	59
With Resident Pastor:	
Resident Diocesan Priests	42
Resident Religious Priests	17
Without Resident Pastor:	
Administered by Priests	1
Completely Vacant	1
Missions	241
Welfare	
Homes for the Aged	4
Total Assisted	255
Residential Care of Children	3
Total Assisted	45
Specialized Homes	1
Total Assisted	9
Special Centers for Social Services	1
Total Assisted	858
Educational	
Seminaries, Diocesan	1
Students from This Diocese	14
Diocesan Students in Other Seminaries	11
Total Seminarians	25
Colleges and Universities	1
Total Students	685
High Schools, Diocesan and Parish	9
Total Students	4,926
High Schools, Private	5
Total Students	7,068
Elementary Schools, Diocesan and Parish	5
Total Students	4,926
Elementary Schools, Private	5
Total Students	2,142
Catechesis/Religious Education:	
High School Students	1,372
Elementary Students	19,740
Total Students under Catholic Instruction	40,884
Teachers in the Diocese:	
Priests	10
Brothers	3
Sisters	25
Lay Teachers	445
Vital Statistics	
Receptions into the Church:	
Infant Baptism Totals	3,150
Minor Baptism Totals	600
Adult Baptism Totals	363
First Communions	3,489
Confirmations	3,500
Marriages:	
Catholic	530
Interfaith	27
Total Marriages	557
Deaths	2,000
Total Catholic Population	370,000
Total Population	603,469

Former Bishops—Most Revs. ALFRED F. MENDEZ, C.S.C., ord. 1935; cons. Oct. 28, 1960; retired Jan., 1974; died Jan. 28, 1995; MIGUEL RODRIQUEZ, C.S.S.R., D.D., ord. June 22, 1958; appt. Jan. 21, 1974; cons. March 23, 1974; retired March, 1990; died Aug. 13, 2001.

Secretary to the Bishop—Miss SYLVIA HERNANDEZ.

Chancery Office—206 Dr. Salas St., P.O. Box 616, Arecibo, 00613-0616. Tel: 787-878-3180; 787-878-3110; Fax: 787-880-2661.

Vicar General—Rev. JOSE D. SOBERAL, V.G., Mailing Address: P.O. Box 616, Arecibo, 00613. Tel: 787-878-3180; 787-878-3110.

Secretary and Receptionist—Mrs. WALESKA CORDERO.

Administrator—Mr. MIGUEL GONZALEZ.

Accountant—VACANT.

Chancellor—Rev. JORGE L. VIRELLA VAZQUEZ, Mailing Address: P.O. Box 616, Arecibo, 00613. Tel: 787-878-3180.

Vice Chancellor & Secretary—Miss SYLVIA VARGAS.

Diocesan Tribunal of Arecibo—Rev. EDWIN MERCADO VIERA, J.C.L., Judicial Vicar & Presiding Judge.

Adjutant Judges—Revs. JUAN R. MORA DELGADO, J.C.L., Mailing Address: P.O. Box 775, Vega Alta, 00692; JORGE L. VIRELLA VAZQUEZ, Official, Mailing Address: P.O. Box 9018, Sabana Branch, Vega Baja, 00694.

Promoter of Justice—Rev. GABRIEL MADURO LOPEZ.

Defenders of the Bond—Revs. ALBERTO DIAZ COLON; GABRIEL MADURO.

Advocate—Rev. JOSE COLON OTERO, J.C.L., Mailing Address: P.O. Box 142142, Arecibo, 00614. Fax: 787-815-0022.

Notary—Miss DIANA GONZALEZ.

Secretary—Mrs. LIVIA E. SERRANO.

Vicar of Diocesan Pastoral Affairs—Rev. ADRIAN N. JIMENEZ ORTIZ; Mrs. MIRIAM NEGRON, Sec.

Diocesan Consultors—Revs. P. JESUS MONREAL PUJANTE, O.Carm.; JOSE D. SOBERAL, V.G.; VICTOR ROJAS; EDWIN A. MERCADO; JORGE L. VIRELLA VAZQUEZ; FERNANDO MORELL DOMINGUEZ; CARMELO URARTE.

Priest's Senate (Consejo Presbiteral)—Revs. VICTOR SANCHEZ VELEZ; JOSE D. SOBERAL, V.G.; EDWIN A. MERCADO; TOMAS SANTOS RODRIGUEZ; MIGUEL MERCADO RIVERA; VICTOR ROJAS; ELVIN A. IRIZARRY ROMAN; CARMELO URARTE; ROBERTO ATZENI MARINI, C.M.V.; WILFREDO CALDERON CALDERON, S.D.B.; JOSE B. ZAPIEN GOMEZ, M.N.M.; ADRIAN N. JIMENEZ ORTIZ; ROBERTO VEGA; ALBERTO DIAZ COLON; JORGE L. VIRELLA VAZQUEZ.

Diocesan Offices and Directors

Ayuda Social Movimiento Juan XXIII—BRENDA RIVERA, Coord., Mailing Address: P.O. Box 241, Sabana Hoyos, 00688-0241. Tel: 787-881-7141; 787-881-2342; Fax: 787-881-7141. Email: ayudasoc@coqui.net.

Confraternity of Christian Doctrine—Sr. MARIA ELISA GONZALEZ, H.C., Mailing Address: 5 Calle Mariano Abril, Box 1151, Arecibo, 00613. Tel: 787-878-8401. Email: catequesis_arecibo@hotmail.com.

Cursillos de Cristiandad—Rev. OMAR A. BEDOYA, P.O. Box 1826, Arecibo, 00613. Tel: 787-872-2563.

Diocesan Council of Catholic Women—Mrs. BLANCA RUIZ.

Propagation of Faith—Rev. ORLANDO CAMACHO, C.S.Sp.

Holy Childhood—Rev. ORLANDO CAMACHO, C.S.Sp.

Director of Youth—Revs. OVIDIO PEREZ; JOSE A. ACABA.

Legion of Mary—VACANT.

Movimiento Familiar Cristiano (CFM)—Rev. JORGE L. VIRELLA VAZQUEZ.

Prison Services—Rev. ELVIN A. IRIZARRY ROMAN, Mailing Address: P.O. Box 2525 CMB - 75, Utuado, 00641-2525. Tel: 787-894-7144; Fax: 787-894-7144.

Seminario Jesus Maestro College Seminary—Rev. OVIDIO PEREZ, Mailing Address: Box 2164, Arecibo, 00613. Tel: 787-878-1528.

Seminary Board and Vocation Program—Rev. OVIDIO PEREZ.

Pastoral Vocational Program—Revs. OVIDIO PEREZ; JORGE L. VIRELLA VAZQUEZ; FERNANDO MORELL DOMINGUEZ; JOSE D. SOBERAL, V.G.; TOMAS SANTOS RODRIGUEZ; VICTOR ROJAS; ROBERTO VEGA.

Superintendent of Schools—JUAN A. VALDES; Mrs. TRINIDAD GONZALEZ, Sec., Mailing Address: P.O. Box 1683, Arecibo, 00613. Tel: 787-878-1095; Fax: 787-878-1095.

Oficina para la Promocion y el Desarrollo Humano, Inc.—

Catholic Charities—EURELIA PEREZ OLIVO, Dir.; VACANT, In Charge of the Mission; Sr. VERONICA ORAVEC, C.D.P., Admin.; Dr. ZULMA CUEVAS, Psychology Asst., Mailing Address: P.O. Box 353, Arecibo, 00613. Tel: 787-817-6951; Fax: 787-817-7597.

Programs—

Women Head of Household—VIVIAN TORRES.

Domestic Violence Unit—VIVIAN TORRES.

Parenting with Love—MARIA GONZALEZ.

Community Development—CARMEN NORIS ARBELO.

Improving Your Self Esteem—LUZ I. SOTO.

Retreat House, Centro Diocesano Mons. Mendez—Rev. OVIDIO PEREZ, Apdo. 2164, Arecibo, 00613. Tel: 787-878-4796.

Boy Scouts—VACANT.

Hospital Chaplains—

Arecibo Hospital—Dr. COLL Y TOSTE; Miss ESTHER COSTA; Rev. P. GABRIEL MADURO. Cathedral of San Felipe Apostol: Rev. ROBERTO VEGA.

Susoni Hospital—Rev. P. GABRIEL MADURO.

Vocations—Rev. OVIDIO PEREZ, Apdo. 2164, Arecibo, 00613. Tel: 787-878-1528.

Police Chaplain—Rev. LUIS A. VAZQUEZ.

Sociedad San Vincente de Paul (Vincentinos)—Mr. ANGEL GINES, Pres. Consejo Diocesano. Tel: 787-884-5087; 787-854-2562.

CLERGY, PARISHES, MISSIONS AND PAROCHIAL SCHOOLS

CITY OF ARECIBO

1—CATHEDRAL OF SAN FELIPE APOSTOL (1616) [JC] Revs. Roberto Vega, Rector; Gabriel Maduro.
De Diego St.—Box 577, 00613. Tel: 809-878-1149; Fax: 787-816-5719. Email: catedralarecibo@hotmail.com.
Catechesis/Religious Program—Students 259.
Chapel—Islote II, Sagrada Familia
Chapel—Islote III (Sector Vibora), San Juan Evangelista
Chapel—Sector Boam, Maria Reina
Chapel—Islote I (Vigia), N.S. del Carmen

2—CHURCH OF CHRIST THE KING (1967) Rev. Eugenio Gayarre.
Res.: Box 1932, 00613. Tel: 809-878-9214.
Catechesis/Religious Program—Students 174.
Chapel—Bo. Hato Arriba, Maria Auxiliadora

3—CHURCH OF SAGRADO CORAZON DE JESUS (1961) [JC] Rev. Melquiades Rojas.
Res.: Box 140637, 00614. Tel: 787-878-4910; Fax: 787-879-2124.
School—Colegio San Felipe, (Grades PreK-12), Box 673, 00613. Tel: 809-878-3532; Fax: 787-879-2124. Email: colegio-san-felipe@yahoo.com. Judith Colon, Prin. Lay Teachers 38; Students 500.
Catechesis/Religious Program—Students 130.
Chapel—Bo. Obrero, Inmaculada Concepcion

4—CHURCH OF SAN MARTIN DE PORRES (1973) Revs. Francisco R. Tejada, Admin.; Miguel A. Blanco; Hipolito Crespo.
Res.: Calle 6 F-12, Box 14-2142, Urb. Univ. Gardens, 00613. Tel: 787-878-1822.
Catechesis/Religious Program—Students 288.
Chapel—Victor Rojas II, San Jose Obrero

5—CHURCH OF SANTA CECILIA (1981) [JC] Unassigned. Rev. Roberto Vega, Admin.
Res.: HC-02, Box 13674, 00612. Tel: 787-879-3364. Email: peregrino59@aol.com.
Catechesis/Religious Program—Students 176.
Chapel—Calichosa, San Jose
Chapel—Los Canos, San Martin de Porres
Chapel—La Guinea, La Milagrosa

6—CHURCH OF SANTA TERESITA (1980) [JC] Rev. Jose D. Soberal, Admin.
Res.: Road 492, KM 1.9, P.O. Box 9242, Cotto Station, 00613. Tel: 787-878-7015.
Catechesis/Religious Program—Students 143.
Chapel—Hato Arriba, N.S. La Providencia
Chapel—Barranca La Milagrosa

7—INMACULADO CORAZON DE MARIA (1987) [JC] Rev. Lisimaco Hincapie, Admin.
Res.: Box 1282, Sabana Hoyos, 00688.
Catechesis/Religious Program—Students 111.
Chapel—Bo. Asomante, San Isidro
Chapel—Bo. Carolina, Sagrado Corazon de Jesus
Chapel—Bo. Arrozal, San Jose
Chapel—Los Muertos, San Francisco

8—LA MILAGROSA (1973) [JC] Rev. Omar A. Bedoya, Admin.
Res.: Box 204, Bajadero, 00616. Tel: 787-878-3899. Email: lamilagrosaare@hotmail.com.
Catechesis/Religious Program—Students 258.
Chapel—Bajadero, Immaculada Concepcion
Chapel—Domingo Ruiz, N.S. La Providencia
Chapel—Carreras, San Judas
Chapel—Biafara, N.S. La Virgen del Carmen

9—NUESTRA SENORA DE FATIMA (1967) [JC] Revs. Roberto Atzeni; Raul Mamani; Johnny C. Iturrizaga, C.M.V.; Michele Querin, C.M.V.
Res.: Box 667, Sabana Hoyos, 00688. Tel: 787-881-8274.
Catechesis/Religious Program—Students 227.
Chapel—Garrochales, S. Fco. de Asis
Chapel—Ballaja, N.S. del Carmen
Chapel—Garrochales, La Milagrosa, San Luis
Chapel—Espino, Immaculada Concepcion

10—NUESTRA SENORA DEL CARMEN (1961) [JC] Rev. Miguel Mercado.
Res.: Bo. Cotto No. 985, P.O. Box 9949, Cotto Sta., 00613. Tel: 787-878-1268; Fax: 787-817-5062.
School—Hogar-Colegio La Milagrosa, (Grades K-12), Ave. Francisco Jimenez Gonzalez, 00612-4912. Tel: 787-878-0341; 787-879-4912; Fax: 787-817-7822. Email: hogarcolegiolamilagrosa@yahoo.com. Sr. Maria D. Vicens, Prin. Sisters of Charity 2; Lay Teachers 33; Students 411.
Catechesis/Religious Program—Students 181.
Chapel—Abra S. Francisco, San Antonio
Chapel—Rodriguez Olmo, San Francisco

11—OUR LADY OF HOPE (1986) [JC] Rev. Ivan Martinez Adorno.
Res.: Box 489, 00613. Tel: 787-880-1943.
Catechesis/Religious Program—Students 214.
Chapel—Cantagallo, Sgdo. Corazon de Jesus
Chapel—Plan Bonito, San Rafael

12—SAN JUAN BOSCO (1971) Rev. Efraín Montesino, Dir.
Res.: Urb. Jardines de Arecibo, Calle R-Y-26, 00612. Tel: 787-879-1070; Fax: 787-817-4107. Email: col.sanjuanboscoare@yahoo.com.
School—(Grades PreK-9) Tel: 787-879-2069. Nilda Gonzalez, Prin. Lay Teachers 34; Students 472.
Catechesis/Religious Program—Students 233.
Chapel—Las Canelas, N.S. La Dolorosa, San Daniel Sisters of Nazaret 3.

13—SANTA ANA (1961) [JC] Rev. Edwin A. Mercado.
Res.: Bo. Santana, Box 318, 00613. Tel: 787-881-6005.
Catechesis/Religious Program—Tel: 787-881-6882. Students 193.
Chapel—Factor II, N.S. del Carmen
Chapel—Santuario Cristo de los Milagros

14—SANTISIMO SACRAMENTO (1990) [JC] Rev. Jorge L. Virella.
Res.: Ste. 109, P.O. Box 4015, 00613. Tel: 787-880-6513.
Catechesis/Religious Program—Students 105.
Chapel—Del Valle, La Milagrosa
Chapel—Jobos, San Pascual

OUTSIDE OF ARECIBO

BARCELONETA

1—CHURCH OF OUR LADY OF MT. CARMEL (1882) [JC] Rev. Victor Rojas.
Res.: P.O. Box 2062, 00617. Tel: 809-846-5625; Fax: 787-846-5690. Email: senoradelcarmen@coqui.net.
Catechesis/Religious Program—Tel: 787-846-7343. Students 282.
Chapel—Garrochales I, N.S. de Fatima
Chapel—Palmas Altas, San Antonio
Chapel—Punta Palma, N.S. del Mar

2—OUR LADY OF VICTORY (1963) [JC] Rev. Antonio Ramos, Admin.
Res.: Ste. 125, Call Box 2020, 00617. Tel: 809-846-6120.
Catechesis/Religious Program—Students 154.
Chapel—Parcelas Imberry, San Jose Obrero
Chapel—Quebrada, Immaculate Heart of Mary
Chapel—Tiburones, N.S. de Fatima
Chapel—Palenque, San Juan Bautista

CAMUY

1—ST. JOSEPH (1827) [JC] Revs. Pedro N. Montoya; Rodolfo R. Cabrera.
Res.: P.O. Box 414, 00627. Tel: 787-898-3620; Fax: 787-898-3620.
Catechesis/Religious Program—Students 542.
Convent—San Jose Hermanas Terciarias Capuchinas 4.
Chapel—Membrillo, N.S. La Monserrate
Chapel—Puente (Zarzas), Sagrado Corazon
Chapel—Puente (Zarza Parcelas), N.S. La Milagrosa
Chapel—Puente (Sector Pica), N.S. del Rosario
Chapel—Abra Honda, Espiritu Santo
Chapel—Zanjas, Immaculada Concepcion

2—OUR LADY OF ASUMPTION (1984) [JC] Rev. Marcos A. Cepeda Contreras, M.N.M.
Res.: HC-02, Box 8047, 00627. Tel: 787-898-8038.
Catechesis/Religious Program—Students 247.
Chapel—Cibao Ocasio, N.S. del Perpetuo Socorro
Chapel—Callejones, Sagrado Corazon
Chapel—Callejones II, San Pablo de la Cruz
Chapel—Cibao Lugo, Maria Auxiliadora

3—OUR LADY OF MONSERRATE (1961) [JC] Revs. Joaquín J. Rojas, M.N.M.; Salvador Diaz Llamas, M.N.M.
Res.: HC-03, Box 16512, Quebradillas, 00678-9820. Tel: 787-898-6784.
Catechesis/Religious Program—Students 341.
Convent—Tel: 787-896-6176. Hermanas Angeles Custodios 2.
Chapel—Piletas (Lares), N.S. del Carmen
Chapel—Guajataca (Queb.), N.S. de Fatima
Chapel—Aibonito Beltran, San Antonio
Chapel—Cibao (S. Sebastian), Santa Ana
Chapel—Planas I (Isabela), Santa Cruz
Chapel—Planas II, N.S. del Rosario

4—OUR LADY OF THE MIRACULOUS MEDAL (1962) [JC], (El Calvario) Rev. Jose B. Zapien, M.N.M.
Res.: HC-01 Buzon 5240, 00627. Tel: 787-898-5825.
Catechesis/Religious Program—Tel: 787-898-4841. Students 586.
Chapel—Planas II, Santiago Apostol
Chapel—Puertos, Sagrado Corazon
Chapel—Cienaga, Cristo Rey
Chapel—Camuy Arriba, N.S. del Carmen
Chapel—Sector Riego, Santa Clara
Chapel—Sector Mani, Sagrado Corazon

CIALES

1—HOLY ROSARY (1820) [JC] Revs. Jorge R. Betancourt, O.Carm.; Antonio Soto, O.Carm.; Tomas Ciscar Nadal, O.Carm.
Res.: P.O. Box 26, 00638. Tel: 787-871-2205; 787-871-3485.
School—P.O. Box 1334, 00638. Tel: 787-871-2222; Fax: 787-871-5797. Email: cnsrciales@hotmail.com. Blanca Marrero, Prin. Sisters 3; Lay Teachers 23; Students 293.
Catechesis/Religious Program—Tel: 787-871-1492. Students 754.
Chapel—Pozas, San Elias
Chapel—Cialitos, Buen Pastor
Chapel—Hato Viejo, Corazon de Jesus
Chapel—Hato Viejo, San Antonio
Chapel—Jaguas, Santa Clara
Chapel—Pesa, San Ignacio
Chapel—Cialitos-Cruces, Corazon de Maria
Chapel—Toro Negro, N.S.
Chapel—Bo. Marias, Maternidad de la Virgen

2—N.S. MADRE DEL REDENTOR (1988) [JC] Rev. Wiktor Tarnawski.
Res.: P.O. Box 1181, 00638. Tel: 787-871-2404.
Catechesis/Religious Program—Students 125.
Chapel—Yunes, San Jose
Chapel—Fronton (Sabana), Perpetuo Socorro
Chapel—Cordillera 5, N.S. La Providencia
Chapel—Limon, Smo. Rosario
Chapel—Cordillera 7, Sagrada Familia

COROZAL, HOLY FAMILY (1804) [JC] Revs. Alberto Diaz; Delfin Rodriguez; Jorge Y. Morales.
Res.: P.O. Box 474, 00783. Tel: 787-859-2595; Fax: 787-859-5018.
School—(Grades PreK-12) Tel: 787-859-2420; Fax: 787-859-4115. Email: csfcorbiblio@yahoo.com. Sr. Maria Salvador, Prin. Sisters of St. Joseph 9; Lay Teachers 53; Students 1,187.
Catechesis/Religious Program—Students 816.
Chapel—Guarico Palmarejo I, San Judas Tadeo
Chapel—Palmarejo II, San Vicente
Chapel—Palmarejo II, San Francisco de Asis
Chapel—Dos Bocas II, Santa Teresita
Chapel—Cibuco, N.S. del Carmen
Chapel—Abras, San Jose
Chapel—Urb. Sylvia, Perpetuo Socorro

COROZAL-PADILLA, OUR LADY OF THE SEVEN SORROWS (1984) Rev. Miguel Rivera, Admin.
Res.: P.O. Box 740, 00783-0740. Tel: 787-859-1900. Email: 7dolores@catholicnet.zzn.co.
Catechesis/Religious Program—Students 564.
Chapel—Padilla Hermita, San Rafael
Chapel—Padilla Hormiga, San Martin
Chapel—Cieneguita (V.A.), N.S. del Perpetuo Socorro

COROZAL-PALMARITO, LA MILAGROSA Revs. Rafael J. Gonzalez, C.R.L.; Nicolas De la Cruz, C.R.L., Vicar.
Res.: HC-03, Box 13976, 00783-9803. Tel: 787-859-5306. Email: crl-milagrosa@hotmail.com.
Catechesis/Religious Program—Students 484.
Convent—P.O. Box 80267, Bo. Palmarito, Corozal, 00783-8267. Tel: 787-859-5181. Hermanas de San Francisco (Secular Institute) 1.
Chapel—Maguelles, Cristo Rey
Chapel—Mana, N.S. de Fatima
Chapel—Radio Oro, Nuestra Senora del Carmen

COROZAL-PALOS BLANCOS, CHRIST THE KING (1968) [JC] Rev. Edison Navarro, C.R.L.
Res.: P.O. Box 1091, 00783-1091. Tel: 787-859-7313.
Catechesis/Religious Program—Students 401.
Chapel—Cuchillas, N.S. del Perpetuo Socorro
Chapel—Negros, N.S. del Rosario
Chapel—Palos Blancos, Santa Teresita
Chapel—Palos Blancos, San Antonio

FLORIDA, OUR LADY OF MERCY (1887) [JC] Rev. Cesar E. Santos.
Res.: P.O. Box 437, 00650. Tel: 787-822-2670; Fax: 787-822-2670.
Catechesis/Religious Program—Tel: 787-822-2045. Students 196.
Chapel—Monte Bello, N.S. del Carmen
Chapel—Pajornal (Bta.), Santa Rosa de Lima

HATILLO

1—OUR LADY OF GUADALUPE (1961) [JC] Revs. Rene A. Colon, Admin.; Kenneth D. Moore Irizarry, S.E.M.V., Vicar; Marcos A. Conelly, Vicar; Luis R. Banchs, S.E.M.V., Vicar; Victor R. Borrero, S.E.M.V., Vicar; Sr. Teresa Maria V. de la Eucaristia.
Res.: Carr. Ins. 129, Arecibo to Lares, P.O. Box 1131, 00613. Tel: 787-898-8035. Email: laguadalupe@prtc.net.
Catechesis/Religious Program—Students 264.
Chapel—Pajuil, Santa Rosa de Lima

Chapel—Buena Vista, Inmaculada Concepcion
Chapel—Bda Colon, N.S. La Providencia
Chapel—Sector Naranjito, San Jose

2—OUR LADY OF MT. CARMEL (1830) [JC] Revs. Fernando Morell, Pastor; Luis J. Rivera.
Res.: P.O. Box 2, 00659. Tel: 809-898-5300.
School—(Grades PreK-12) Tel: 787-898-2800; 787-898-5235; Fax: 787-820-5258. Email: mmielescnsc@yahoo.com. Rev. Fernando Morell, Dir.; Carmen Diaz, Prin. (Elementary); Mr. Frederico Lopez, Prin. (High School). Sisters 3; Lay Teachers 54; Students 743.
Catechesis/Religious Program—Tel: 787-898-3302. Students 352.
Chapel—Carrizales, Sagrado Corazon
Chapel—Corcovados, Immaculada Concepcion
Chapel—Capaez, N.S. Perpetuo Socorro
Chapel—Carrizales, San Jose
Chapel—Santa Rosa, Santa Rosa de Lima
Chapel—Lechuga: San Pio X
Chapel—Palma Gordo: Sagrada Familia

3—PERPETUAL HELP (1961) [JC] Rev. Antonio Portalatin.
Res.: Ste. 393, P.O. Box 69001, 00659. Tel: 787-898-7771.
Catechesis/Religious Program—Tel: 787-820-2819. Students 258.
Chapel—Aibonito, Cristo Rey
Chapel—Berrocal, Sagrado Corazon de Jesus
Chapel—Sonadora, La Milagrosa
Chapel—Mariposa, N.S. del Carmen
Chapel—Cantera, Ntra. Sra. de la Providencia

ISABELA

1—ST. ANTHONY (1835) [JC] Revs. Elias Fernandez, O.SS.T.; Manuel E. Salgado, O.SS.T., Vicar.
Res.: Box 525, 00662. Tel: 787-872-2563; Fax: 787-872-4393.
School—(Grades K-12)Email: csaisabela@yahoo.com. Sr. Ida Negrón, O.P., Prin. Sisters of St. Dominic 3; Lay Teachers 36; Students 526.
Catechesis/Religious Program—Students 726.
Chapel—Medina, Sma. Trinidad
Chapel—Curva, Santa Rosa de Lima
Chapel—Cotto, San Martin de Porres
Chapel—Arenales Bajo, N.S. La Monserrate
Chapel—Vendrel, N.S. La Providencia
Chapel—Jobos, Buen Pastor
Chapel—Guayabos, Espiritu Santo
Chapel—Arenales A., El Salvador
Chapel—Arenales Alto, Sagrado Corazon, Tel: 787-872-0015. Sisters of Trinity (Valencia) 4.
Chapel—Hogar Infantil/Jesus Nazareno, Isabella Sisters of Trinity (Valencia) 2.

2—OUR LADY OF MOUNT CARMEL (1983) [JC] Rev. German LLona, O.SS.T.
Res.: Box 1555, 00662. Tel: 787-872-5550.
Catechesis/Religious Program—Students 217.
Chapel—Poncito, Santos Inocentes
Chapel—Planas, San Juan Bautista
Chapel—La Tuna, San Juan de Mata
Chapel—Galateo Bajo, La Milagrosa

LARES

1—ST. JOSEPH (1827) [JC] Revs. Carlos L. Rodriguez, C.P.; Juan B. Bengurria, C.P.; Dennys W. Cruz, C.P.
Res.: P.O. Box 103, 00669-0103. Tel: 787-897-2067.
School—(Grades PreK-9) Tel: 787-897-2640; Fax: 787-897-2640. Maritza Lopez Pol, Prin. Hermanas Pasionistas 3; Lay Teachers 17; Students 136.
Catechesis/Religious Program—Tel: 787-897-2717. Students 545.
Chapel—Piletas II, San Carlos
Chapel—Sebruguillo, La Resurreccion
Chapel—Piletas Arece, La Milagrosa
Chapel—Piletas, Saint Maria Goretti
Chapel—Tabonuco, La Providencia Hermanas Josefinas de Mexico 4.

2—ST. JUDAS TADEOS (1986) [JC] Rev. David Rivas, Admin.
Res.: P.O. Box 1109, 00669. Tel: 809-897-3540.
Catechesis/Religious Program—Students 219.
Chapel—Palmar Llano, Perpetuo Socorro
Chapel—Vega de los Acevedo, La Dolorosa
Chapel—Buenos Aires, Sgda. Familia de Nazaret
Chapel—Matilde, San Antonio

MANATI

1—LA CANDELARIA (1738) [JC] Revs. Emilio Tovar, C.M.; Ignacio Alonso.
Res.: Calle Padial #2, 00674. Tel: 787-854-2013. Email: manaticm@atenas.com.
School—(Grades PreK-12) Tel: 787-854-2079; Fax: 787-854-2202. Email: cinmacul@yahoo.com. Sr. Rosalina Santiago, Prin. Sisters of Charity 3; Lay Teachers 50; Students 945.
Catechesis/Religious Program—Tel: 787-854-4021. Students 241.
Chapel—Pugnado, N.S. del Perpetuo Socorro
Chapel—Villa Amalia, La Milagrosa
Chapel—Cortes, Sagrado Corazon
Chapel—Polvorin, La Monserrate
Chapel—Ceiba, Espiritu Santo

2—NUESTRA SENORA DEL MAR (1978) [JC] Rev. Alvaro Silva.
Res.: Apdo. 1183, 00674. Tel: 787-854-5388.
Catechesis/Religious Program—Tel: 787-854-9252. Students 399.
Chapel—Tierras Nuevas, Santa Rosa de Lima
Chapel—Sector Cantito, La Milagrosa
Chapel—Boquillas, Nuestra Senora de Lourdes

3—OUR SAVIOR Rev. Victor Sanchez.
Res.: P.O. Box 465, 00674. Tel: 787-884-3664. Email: parrelsalv@ad.com.
School—Colegio Marista, (Grades K-12), P.O. Box 462, 00764. Tel: 787-854-1075; 787-854-2485; Fax: 787-854-6733. Email: maristamanote@yahoo.com. Bro. Carlos Velez, Dir.; Margarita Santiago, Prin. Marist Brothers 3; Lay Teachers 35; Students 520.
Catechesis/Religious Program—Students 316.
Chapel—San Jose, San Jose
Chapel—Lagunas Tierra Nueva, N.S. de Lourdes
Chapel—Guayaney, San Martin de Porres

4—SAGRADA FAMILIA (1972) [JC] Revs. Francisco J. Marrodan, C.M.; Bernardo Hernandez, C.M.
Res.: P.O. Box 704, 00674. Tel: 787-854-2858.
Catechesis/Religious Program—Students 423.
Chapel—Parcelas Marquez, San Judas Tadeo
Chapel—Palo Alto, N.S. La Monserrate
Chapel—Polvorin, La Milagrosa

MOROVIS

1—NUESTRA SENORA DEL CARMEN (1820) [JC] Revs. Jesus Monreal, O.Carm.; Enrique Oria, O.Carm.; Jose Oliveras.
Res.: Box 428, 00687. Tel: 787-862-2620.
Catechesis/Religious Program—Students 1,701.
Chapel—San Lorenzo, N.S. del Rosario
Chapel—Perchas, N.S. del Carmen
Chapel—Pastos, N.S. del Carmen
Chapel—Rio Grande, La Milagrosa
Chapel—Morovis Sur, San Jose
Chapel—Unibon, San Miguel
Chapel—Vaga III, La Milagrosa
Chapel—MPatron I, Sagrada Familia
Chapel—Cuchillas, Segrado Corazon
Chapel—Morovis Sur, Inmaculada Concepcion

2—ST. PAUL APOSTLE (1985) [JC] Rev. Tomas Santos, Admin.
Res.: P.O. Box 537, 00687. Tel: 787-862-3445.
Catechesis/Religious Program—Students 731.
Chapel—Franquez, Nino de Praga
Chapel—Franquez Carretera, La Providencia
Chapel—Torrecillas, Senor de los Milagros

OROCOVIS

1—OUR LADY OF FATIMA (1975) [JC] Revs. Jose Alamo, C.S.Sp.; Tosello Giangiacomo, C.S.Sp.; Bro. Irving Oquendo Romero.
Res.: Box 2118, 00720. Tel: 787-867-3277. Email: fatimaorocovis@hotmail.com.
Catechesis/Religious Program—Students 394.
Chapel—Bermejales, Cristo de la Salud
Chapel—Bauta, N.S. La Dolorosa
Chapel—Damian Arriba, N.S. del Perpetuo Socorro
Chapel—Pellejas I, Espiritu Santo
Chapel—Miraflores, San Martin

2—SAN JUAN BAUTISTA (1838) [JC] Revs. Demetrio Coello, S.D.B.; Wilfredo Calderon, S.D.B.; Antonio Robles, S.D.B.; Jose R. Patino, S.D.B., Vicar; Francisco Juan.
Res.: P.O. Box 2114, 00720. Tel: 787-867-2210; Fax: 787-867-5675. Email: sdboro@coqui.net.
School—(Grades PreK-6) Tel: 787-867-2295; Fax: 787-867-6269. Email: smmmfma@yahoo.com. Sr. Magna M. Martinez, Prin. Salesian Sisters 3; Lay Teachers 19; Students 317.
Catechesis/Religious Program—Students 1,108.
Chapel—Sabana, Angeles Custodios
Chapel—Botijas I, Cristo Resucitado
Chapel—Botijas II, Santa Clara
Chapel—El Puente, San Pablo
Chapel—Mata de Cana, Sagrado Corazon
Chapel—Damian Arriba, Espiritu Santo
Chapel—Montebello, N.S. del Carmen
Chapel—Guadalupe, N.S. La Guadalupe
Chapel—Gato Bajura, N.S. La Providencia
Chapel—Gato, San Judas Tadeo

QUEBRADILLAS

1—SACRED HEART (1977) [JC] Rev. Carmelo Urarte.
Res.: Box 1569, 00678. Tel: 787-895-3033; Fax: 787-895-3033.
Catechesis/Religious Program—Students 631.
Chapel—San Antonio, San Miguel
Chapel—Yeguada, N.S. del Perpetuo Socorro
Chapel—El Verde, Madre Dolorosa

2—SAN RAPHAEL (1828) [JC] Revs. Jose A. Acaba; Miguel S. Bido, Vicar.
Res.: Box 57, 00678. Tel: 787-895-3463.
School—(Grades K-9) Tel: 809-895-2280; Fax: 787-895-2280. Email: csrque@q.mail.com. Wilfredo Lopez, Prin. Lay Teachers 22; Students 282.
Catechesis/Religious Program—Students 722.
Chapel—San Jose, San Jose
Chapel—Quebrada, N.S. del Carmen
Chapel—Chivos, Santa Cruz

Chapel—Cacao, La Milagrosa
Chapel—Parcelas San Antonio, N.S. La Monserrate
Chapel—San Antonio, San Antonio
Chapel—Charcas, N.S. del Perpetuo Socorro
Chapel—Las Talas, La Guadalupe

UTUADO

1—NUESTRA SENORA DEL MONTE CARMELO (1981) [JC] Rev. Angel R. Díaz.
Res.: P.O. Box 299, Caonillas-Utuado, 00641. Tel: 787-894-7340. Email: parrmontecarmelo@yahoo.com.
Catechesis/Religious Program—Students 134.
Chapel—Mameyes, San Antonio
Chapel—Tetuan III, Sagrado Corazon
Chapel—Tetuan I, Cristo Salvador
Chapel—Don Alonso, La Milagrosa

2—OUR LADY OF ANGELS (1967) [JC] Rev. Salomon J. Morales.
Res.: Box 98, Angeles, 00611. Tel: 809-894-3964.
Catechesis/Religious Program—Students 97.
Chapel—Corcho, San Jose
Chapel—Santa Isabela, N.S. La Monserrate
Chapel—Las Vegas, Sagrada Familia

3—OUR LADY OF SORROWS (1983) [JC] Rev. Elvin A. Irizarry.
Res.: CMB-73, P.O. Box 2525, 00641-2525. Tel: 787-894-7144.
Catechesis/Religious Program—Students 238.
Chapel—Roncador, San Martin de Porres
Chapel—Cayuco, Cristo Rey
Chapel—Jacanas, N.S. la Monserrate

4—SAN MIQUEL (1746) [JC] Revs. Edward Maldonado, O.F.M.Cap.; Jose A. Villaran, O.F.M.Cap. In Res., Bros. Jose E. Sanchez, O.F.M.Cap.; Reynaldo Saliva, O.F.M.Cap.
Res.: 8 Barcelo St., P.O. Box 10, 00641-0010. Tel: 787-894-2696; 787-894-3108; Fax: 787-894-3812. Email: parroquiasanmiguel@utuadoweb.com.
School—Elementary School, (Grades K-12), Progreso St., Box 10, 00641. Bro. Jorge Macias, O.F.M.Cap., Prin. Lay Teachers 22; Students 184.
School—Intermediate and High School, San Miguel Ave., Box 10, 00641. Tel: 809-894-9386; Fax: 787-894-3994. Lydia M. Giusti, Prin.
Catechesis/Religious Program—Students 375.
Chapel—Puente Blanco, San Fidel
Chapel—Arenas, San Martin
Chapel—Sabana Grande, N.S. del Perpetuo Socorro

5—SAN PEDRO Y SAN PABLO (1988) [JC] Rev. Rafael Nuno.
Res.: Box 679, 00641. Tel: 787-894-0696.
Catechesis/Religious Program—Students 133.
Chapel—Las Palmas, San Francisco
Chapel—Vivi Arriba, Inmaculada Concepcion
Chapel—La Pica, La Milagrosa
Chapel—Consejo, San Jose
Chapel—Vivi Abajo, Nuestra Senora de la Divina Providencia Sisters (Monastery Mother of God Cloistered) 38.

VEGA-ALTA

1—IMMACULATE CONCEPTION OF BLESSED VIRGIN MARY (1805) Revs. Adrian N. Jimenez; Carlos S. Henriquez.
Res.: P.O. Box 775, 00692. Tel: 787-883-4875.
Catechetical Center—Calle Colon 17, 00692. Students 445.
Chapel—Maricao IV, Sagrado Corazon
Chapel—Bajura II, San Vicente
Chapel—Bajura I, Santa Ana
Chapel—Candelaria, Inmaculado Corazon de Maria
Chapel—Maricao II, N.S. La Guadalupe

2—PERPETUO SOCORRO (1975) [JC] Rev. Luis A. Vazquez.
Res.: Sabana Branch, Box 9018, Vega-Baja, 00694-9018. Tel: 787-883-5776; Fax: 787-270-3103.
Catechesis/Religious Program—Students 173.
Chapel—Sabana (V.B.), San Vicente
Chapel—Cerro Gordo, N.S. del Carmen

3—SANTA ANA (1967) Rev. Angel Diaz Caceres.
Res.: Urb. Santa Ana, Apartado 2105, Calle 3H9, 00692. Tel: 787-883-2502.
Catechesis/Religious Program—Students 238.
Chapel—Espinosa, N.S. del Carmen

VEGA-BAJA

1—THE BLESSED TRINITY (1971) Rev. Angel M. Santos, Admin.
Res.: P.O. Box 58, Almirante Sur Station, 00694-0058. Tel: 809-858-8743.
Catechesis/Religious Program—Students 220.
Chapel—Almirante Norte, Sagrada Familia
Chapel—Patron II, N.S. La Providencia

2—HOLY ROSARY (1794) [JC] Revs. Jorge Paredes; Marc A. Santiago.
Res.: P.O. Box 1388, 00694. Tel: 787-858-2969.
School—(Grades K-12) Tel: 787-858-2538; 787-858-4111; Fax: 787-858-6648. Email: melendez@colros.org. Lay Teachers 39; Students 542. Principals:, Nilda Fontan, Elementary; Miguelina Melendez, High School.
Catechesis/Religious Program—Students 244.
Chapel—Arenales, San Jose

Chapel—Almirante, N.S. de Fatima

3—N.S. DE LA PROVIDENCIA (1970) [JC] Rev. Carlos E. Granados, Admin.
Res.: Box 4056, Vega Baja, 00694-4056. Tel: 809-858-2171; Fax: 809-858-2171.
Catechesis/Religious Program—Students 422.
Chapel—Brisas de Tortuguero, San Jose
Chapel—Vega Baja Lakes, San Pedro

4—OUR LADY OF CARMEN-PLAYA (1976) [JC] Rev. Jesus A. Rodriguez, Admin.
Res.: Apdo. 4095, 00694-4095. Tel: 787-855-5226; Fax: 787-855-5115.
Catechesis/Religious Program—Students 224.
Chapel—Naranjos, San Judas Tadeo
Chapel—San Demetrio, Divino Nino Jesus

5—OUR LADY OF LOURDES (1984) [JC] Rev. Ramon Olivencia.
Res.: P.O. Box 4414, 00694-4414. Tel: 787-855-4942; Fax: 787-807-9249.
Catechesis/Religious Program—Students 368.
Convent—Tel: 787-855-0341. Hermanas Terciarias Capuchinas 3.
Chapel—Rio Abajo, Santa Rosa de Lima
Chapel—Quebrada Arenas, San Juan Bautista
Chapel—Las Granjas, S. Francisco de Asis

6—OUR LADY OF MT. CARMEL (1968) [JC] Rev. Pedro Hernandez, Admin.
Camelia St. #48-A, Bo. Carmelita, Vega Alta, 00692.
Res.: P.O. Box 1417, 00694-1417. Tel: 787-855-0159; Fax: 787-855-0159.
Catechesis/Religious Program—Students 167.
Chapel—Pueblo Nuevo, La Milagrosa
Chapel—Sabana Hoyos, San Judas
Chapel—Santa Rosa, La Guadalupe

7—PARROQUIA DE SAN MARTIN DE PORRES (1967) [JC] Rev. Jose Colon.
Res.: P.O. Box 254, Vega Baja, 00694. Tel: 787-858-1485; Fax: 787-858-1485.
Catechesis/Religious Program—Tel: 787-858-8651. Students 233.
Chapel—Panaini, Del Carmen
Chapel—Pugnado Adentro, San Jose
Chapel—Villa Colombo, St. Anthony

On Duty Outside the Diocese:
Revs.—
Davila, Andres, Mexico
Guerrero, Jose Ma., Espana
Irizarry, Alan M., Favetteville, NC
Lopez, Carlos A., Boston, MA
Lopez, Jose M., Tyler, TX
Lopez, Juan J., Sunrise, FL
Munoz, Jesus M., Military Service
Nunez, Philip, III, Archdiocese of San Juan
Pagan, Angel M., Archdiocese of San Juan
Rodriguez, Jose A., Archdiocese of San Juan
Santana, Edward, J.C.L., Homestead, FL
Velazquez, Luis A. Archdiocese of San Juan

Retired:
Revs.—
Acevedo, Bertulfo, Colombia
Caraballo, Antonio, Spain
Estensoro, Jose, Hogar Sta. Teresa Jornet, San Juan, PR
Fernandez Minguez, Serapio
Garcia, Jose L., Sevilla, Espana
Hernandez, Jimmy, Quebradillas, Puerto Rico
Jimenez, Francisco, Hogar Sta. Teresade Jesus Jornet, San Juan
Jimenez, Victorino, Spain
Perez, Leon, Zaragoza, Espana
Zayas, Hector, Utando, Puerto Rico

INSTITUTIONS LOCATED IN THE DIOCESE

[A] EDUCATIONAL

ARECIBO. *Pontificia Universidad Catholica de Puerto Rico, Recinto de Arecibo*, P.O. Box 144045, 00614-4045. Tel: 787-881-1212; Fax: 787-881-0777. Web: www.pucpr.edu. Rev. Omar Bedoya Gaviria (PCE), Chap.; Mrs. Nora Garcia de Lopez, Dir. Priests 3; Lay Teachers 71; Students 685.

Seminario de Jesus Maestro, P.O. Box 2164, 00613. Tel: 787-878-1528; Fax: 787-880-2661. Email: jesusmaestro1@gmail.com. Rev. Ovidio Perez, Dir. Total Enrollment 23.

[B] HOMES FOR AGED AND ORPHANS

ARECIBO. *Hogar de Ancianos San Vicente de Paul*, P.O. Box 4196, Vega Baja, 00694. Bo. Almirante Sur-Carr 645 Km. 6.6, Vega Baja, 00693. Tel: 787-855-0487; Fax: 787-858-3103. Email: svpaulpr@aol.com. Nelson De Leon, Dir. Tel: 787-862-5257; Cell: 787-318-6695. Sisters of Charity 1; Guests 50.

Hogar Sta. Maria Eufrasia, P.O. Box 1909, 00613. Fax: 787-880-2632. Carr. Est. 651-10, Sector Junco, 00612. Tel: 787-878-5166. Email: eufrasia86@gmail.com. Web: www.hogareufrasia.org. House for pregnant teens. Good Shepherd Sisters 4; Unwed Mothers 9; Babies 5.

La Milagrosa Home for Orphan Girls, Ave. Francisco Jimenez Gonzalez #987, 00612. Tel: 787-878-6231; 787-878-0341; Fax: 787-817-7822. Email: hogarcolegiolamilagrosa@yahoo.com. Sisters of Charity 5; Girls 15.

San Rafael Home for Aged, Calle Cervantes, 00612. Tel: 787-878-3813; Fax: 787-879-4592. Sisters of Charity 5; Guests 25.

Centro Geriatrico San Rafael, Calle Cervantes #49, 00612. Tel: 787-878-3813; Fax: 787-879-4592. Email: asilosanrafael@gmail.com. Mrs. Sylvia M. Mestres Torres, Admin.

ISABELA. *Hogar Infantil Jesus Nazareno, Inc.*, P.O. Box 1671, 00662. Tel: 787-872-0015; Fax: 787-872-0015. Email: hijn@coqui.net. Sisters 3; Residential Care of Children 14.

LARES. *Hogar Envejecientes Irma Fe Pol Mendez, Inc.*, P.O. Box 1185, 00669. Tel: 787-897-6090; Fax: 787-897-0612. Charity Sisters of St. Joseph (Mexico) 4; Guests 25.

VEGA-ALTA. *Centro Actividades Multiples/Conferencia San Vicente de Paul*, P.O. Box 1613, 00692. Tel: 787-270-4517; Fax: 787-883-2370. Email: centrojan@coqui.net. Orlando Garcia, Dir. Tel: 787-270-4517. Guests 155.

Centro Geriatrico Juan de los Olivos, P.O. Box 1613, 00692. Tel: 787-883-2370; Fax: 787-883-2370.

[C] MISCELLANEOUS

ARECIBO. *Hogar Infantil Santa Teresita del Nino Jesus, Inc.*, P.O. Box 140057, 00614-0057. Tel: 787-817-6651; 787-650-7731; Fax: 787-817-6651. Email: hogarsantateresita@hotmail.com. Mrs. Melva Arbelo Mangual, Dir.; Mrs. Maria del Carmen Alonso, Admin. Hermanas Dominicas de la Presentacion 3; Children 15.

Oficina para la Promocion y el Desarrollo Humano, Inc., P.O. Box 353, 00613. Tel: 787-817-6951; 787-817-6954; 787-817-6955; Fax: 787-817-7597. Email: opdhinc@gmail.com.

UTUADO. *Fondita Santa Marta*, #1 Calle Betances, P.O. Box 10, 00641. Tel: 787-814-0735; Fax: 787-814-0735. Bro. Jose Enrique Sanchez, O.F.M.Cap., Pres.

RELIGIOUS INSTITUTES OF MEN REPRESENTED IN THE DIOCESE

For further details refer to the corresponding bracketed number in the Religious Institutes of Men or Women section.

[]—*Canonigos Regulares Lateranenses de San Agustin* (Bronx, NY)—C.R.L.
[0470]—*Capuchin Friars* (Province of Pittsburgh)—O.F.M.Cap.
[0270]—*Carmelite Fathers and Brothers* (Province de Aragon, Valencia, Espana)—O.Carm.
[]—*Comunidad Misionera de Villaregia*—C.M.V.
[1330]—*Congregation of the Mission* (Vice-Province of Puerto Rico)—C.M.
[1000]—*Congregation of the Passion* (Bilbao, Spain)—C.P.
[]—*Esclavos de la Eucaristia y Maria Virgen*—E.E.M.V.
[0650]—*Holy Ghost Fathers* (Eastern Province)—C.S.Sp.
[0770]—*Marist Brothers*—F.M.S.
[]—*Misioneros Natividad de Maria* (Mexico)—M.N.M.
[1310]—*Order of the Holy Trinity* (Viscaya, Spain Province)—O.SS.T.
[1190]—*Salesians of Don Bosco* (Province of Madrid)—S.D.B.

RELIGIOUS INSTITUTES OF WOMEN REPRESENTED IN THE DIOCESE

[]—*Comunidad Misionera de Villaregia*—C.M.V.
[]—*Congregation of Sisters of Passion* (Mexico)
[]—*Convento Madre de Dios, Inc.*
[0760]—*Daughters of Charity of St. Vincent de Paul*—H.C.
[]—*Dominican Sisters of Amityville, N.Y.*
[1100]—*Dominican Sisters of Charity of the Presentation of the Blessed Virgin*—O.P.
[]—*Dominican Sisters of Fatima* (Yauco PR)
[]—*Dominicas Divina Misericordia* (Lares, Puerto Rico)
[]—*Hermanas de San Jose de Corozal* (Corozal)
[]—*Hermanas del Buen Pastor*
[]—*Hermanas Esclaves del Santisimo y la Inmaculada*
[]—*Hermanas Josefinas* (Mexico)
[]—*Hermanas San Francisco* (Instituto Secular)
[]—*Hnas. Apostolado Corzon de Jesus* (Madrid)—R.A.
[]—*Hnas. de Nazaret* (El Salvador)
[]—*Hnas. Misioneras de Jesus* (Colombia)
[]—*Hnas. Religiosas Angeles Custodios* (Madrid, Spain)
[]—*Instituto Sma. Trinidad* (Valencia, Spain)
[]—*Misioneras de la Sagrada Familia* (Instituto Secular)
[]—*Salesian Sisters* (Roma)
[]—*Siervas de Maria* (Roma)
[0990]—*Sisters of Divine Providence* (Pittsburgh)—C.D.P.
[]—*Terciarias Capuchina Sgda. Familia* (Roma)

NECROLOGY

† Concepcion, Rev. Msgr. Francisco, Vega-Alta, PR Immaculate Conception of Blessed Virgin Mary—Died Oct. 22, 2009
† Burgos, Jose Casco, (Retired)—Died June 16, 2009
† Irizarry, Rafael, (Retired)—Died March 27, 2009

Diocese of Caguas, Puerto Rico

(Dioecesis Caguana)

Most Reverend

RUBEN ANTONIO GONZALEZ MEDINA, C.M.F.

Bishop of Caguas; ordained February 9, 1975; appointed Bishop of Caguas December 12, 2000; consecrated February 4, 2001.

Most Reverend

ENRIQUE HERNANDEZ RIVERA, D.D.

Bishop Emeritus of Caguas; ordained June 8, 1968; appointed Titular Bishop of Vanalla, North Africa and Auxiliary Bishop of San Juan June 11, 1979; consecrated August 17, 1979; appointed Bishop of Caguas February 13, 1981; officially installed March 8, 1981; retired July 28, 1998. *Res.: Bishop's House, Box 8698, Caguas, PR 00726.* Tel: 787-747-5885; 787-747-5787; Fax: 787-747-5616; 787-747-5767.

Web: www.home.coqui.net/obicag

Email: obicag@coqui.net

ESTABLISHED NOVEMBER 1964.

Square Miles 737.

Comprises east and southeast portion of Puerto Rico.

Patroness of the Diocese: Maria, Madre de la Iglesia - November 12, 1988.

STATISTICAL OVERVIEW

Personnel	
Bishop	1
Retired Bishops	2
Priests: Diocesan Active in Diocese	44
Priests: Diocesan Active Outside Diocese	3
Priests: Diocesan in Foreign Missions	1
Number of Diocesan Priests	48
Religious Priests in Diocese	36
Total Priests in Diocese	84
Ordinations:	
Transitional Deacons	2
Permanent Deacons in Diocese	102
Total Sisters	96
Parishes	
Parishes	34
With Resident Pastor:	
Resident Diocesan Priests	27
Resident Religious Priests	7
Welfare	
Specialized Homes	2
Total Assisted	186
Educational	
Seminaries, Diocesan	2
Students from This Diocese	10
Students from Other Diocese	1
Diocesan Students in Other Seminaries	3
Total Seminarians	13
High Schools, Diocesan and Parish	2
High Schools, Private	7
Elementary Schools, Diocesan and Parish	2
Elementary Schools, Private	7
Total Students under Catholic Instruction	13
Vital Statistics	
Receptions into the Church:	
Infant Baptism Totals	3,421
Minor Baptism Totals	81
Adult Baptism Totals	275
First Communions	3,645
Confirmations	2,757
Marriages:	
Catholic	490
Interfaith	21
Total Marriages	511
Deaths	1,942
Total Catholic Population	350,000
Total Population	503,000

Former Bishops—Most Revs. RAFAEL GROVAS, D.D., S.T.D., Ph.D., J.C.L., ord. April 7, 1928; appt. Jan. 19, 1965; cons. March 28, 1965; retired Feb. 13, 1981; died Sept. 9, 1991; ENRIQUE HERNANDEZ RIVERA, D.D. (Retired), ord. June 8, 1968; cons. Aug. 17, 1979; appt. Feb. 13, 1981; retired July 28, 1998.

Vicar General—Rev. ANTONIO CARTAGENA.

Sec. Chancellor—Rev. ANGEL MOLINA.

Sec. Vice Chancellor—VACANT.

Diocesan Consultors—Revs. HIPÓLITO TORRES; AURELIO ADAN; ANTONIO CARTAGENA; OSCAR RIVERA; CAMPO E. ARIZA; ISRAEL BERRIOS.

Diocesan Tribunal of Caguas—Rev. FELIX NUNEZ, Judicial Vicar; Sr. CARMEN GONZALEZ, C.D.P., J.C.L., Dir.; Revs. MIGUEL A. MERCED; ORLANDO DE JESUS, Mailing Address: P.O. Box 9779, Caguas, 00726. Tel: 787-286-8595; Fax: 787-286-8620.

Board of Diocesan Government—Rev. FELIX OLIVERAS VILLANUEVA.

Priests Senate—Revs. HIPÓLITO TORRES; ANTONIO CARTAGENA; AURELIO ADAN; FELICIANO RODRIGUEZ; ANGEL MOLINA; OSCAR RIVERA; CAMPO E. ARIZA; FELIX NUNEZ; ISRAEL BERRIOS; ROBERTO SOLIVAN; JORGE D. CARDONA; YAMIL A. VELAZQUEZ; JHON J. FLOREZ; BORIS ESPINOZA; Revs. MIGUEL A. DE ANGEL; JOSE VICENTE MARTINEZ, C.M.F.

Diocesan Offices and Directors

Economic Administrator—Rev. FELIX OLIVERAS VILLANUEVA; Mr. ABDEL ALVAREZ GONZALEZ; Deacon JOSE RODRIGUEZ, Mailing Address: P.O. Box 8698, Caguas, 00726. Tel: 787-747-5885; 787-747-5787, Ext. 227.

Planning Vicar—VACANT, Mailing Address: P.O. Box 8698, Caguas, 00726. Tel: 787-747-5885; 787-747-5787.

Movimientos y Organizaciones Diocesanas—

Cursillos de Cristiandad—FELIPE SANCHEZ RAMOS. Tel: 787-734-7068.

Legion de Maria—ANTONIO RODRIGUEZ.

Renovacion Carismatica—ADELAIDA CRUZ.

Juan XXIII—FLORENCIO MARTINEZ. Tel: 787-747-3748.

Apostolado de la Cruz—ELVIN PENA. Tel: 787-715-1768.

Caballeros de Colon—JOSE SOTO CARMONA. Tel: 787-746-4747.

Equipos Ntra. Sra.—GUILLERMO TORRES; MILAGROS ORTIZ.

Equipo Ntra. Sra.—LUIS Y AMPARO URBINA. Tel: 787-739-8581.

Hijas Catolicas—IRMA RUIZ DE MERCED.

Hnos. Cheos—ESTEBAN RIVERA. Tel: 787-850-5224.

Misioneros Padre Ntro.—RAMON L. RAMOS.

Schoenstatt—JOSE N. BRACERO. Tel: 787-722-3941.

Vicentinos—CARMENCITA COLON. Tel: 787-747-6546.

Talleres de Oracion y Vida—PETRONILA RUIZ. Tel: 787-745-4123.

Sociedad del Santo Nombre—VICTOR COTTO.

La Piedra que Cristo edifico en mi—JAVIER LEBRON.

Camino Neo Catecumenal—DOMINGO VEGA.

CASSE—Sr. CARMEN D. ROSADO. Tel: 787-286-3333.

Comisiones Diocesanas—

Pastoral de Multitudes—MARINY VAZQUEZ. Tel: 787-738-1941.

Pastoral Familiar—Deacon VICTOR M. CRUZ. Tel: 787-733-3592.

Pastoral Preadolescentes—*Hnas. Salesianas.* Tel: 787-744-0858.

Pastoral Social—Rev. FELICIANO RODRIQUEZ. Tel: 787-745-8183.

Espiritualidad Comunitaria—HERMINIA FONSECA. Tel: 787-746-2669.

Misiones—Deacon JOSE BERRIOS. Tel: 787-869-3042.

Pastoral Penitenciaria—D. ANIBAL GONZALEZ. Tel: 787-263-0976.

Pastoral Nec. Especiales—VACANT.

Formacion Diac. Permanentes—Rev. FRANCISCO HERNANDEZ.

Catholic Youth—Rev. MIGUEL CLAUDIO, Mailing Address: P.O. Box 8698, Caguas, 00726. Tel: 787-744-6738, Ext. 229.

Catholic Social Action—VACANT, Mailing Address: P.O. Box 8698, Caguas, 00726. Tel: 787-747-5885; 787-747-5787.

Catholic School Consultors—MARIA MERCEDES AGOSTO, Mailing Address: P.O. Box 8699, Caguas, 00726. Tel: 787-743-1171.

Catechetical Vicar—Sr. CLETA M. LOPEZ.

Building Commission—VACANT, Mailing Address: P.O. Box 8698, Caguas, 00726. Tel: 787-747-5885; 787-747-5787.

Liturgical Consultor—Rev. MELVIN MONTANEZ, Mailing Address: P.O. Box 8698, Caguas, 00626. Tel: 787-747-5885, Ext. 222.

Communication Office—MARINY VAZQUEZ, Mailing Address: P.O. Box 8698, Caguas, 00726. Tel: 809-746-3783.

Red de Esperanzay Solidaridad (REDES)—MAGALY MILLAN; Sr. MARIA JESUS MOMPO, Mailing Address: P.O. Box 8698, Caguas, 00726. Tel: 787-747-5767.

Vincentian Society—CARMENCITA COLON, Mailing Address: P.O. Box 8698, Caguas, 00726.

Hospitals—VACANT, Mailing Address: P.O. Box 8698, Caguas, 00726.

Legion of Mary—Mr. ISABELO HUERTAS, Mailing Address: P.O. Box 8698, Caguas, 00726.

Master of Ceremonies—Rev. MELVIN MONTANEZ, Mailing Address: P.O. Box 8698, Caguas, 00726. Tel: 809-747-5885.

Pastoral Vicar—Rev. FELICIANO RODRIGUEZ, Mailing Address: P.O. Box 8698, Caguas, 00726. Tel: 787-286-0475, Ext. 245.

Schools—Mailing Address: P.O. Box 8699, Caguas, 00726. Tel: 787-743-1171.

School Superintendent—MARIA MERCEDES AGOSTO.

Vocations—Revs. JOSE A. DE LEON, Rector; ISRAEL BERRIOS, Mailing Address: P.O. Box 8698, Caguas, 00726. Tel: 787-747-5885, Ext. 243; Fax: 787-857-3585.

Catholic Charities—VACANT, Mailing Address: P.O. Box 8698, Caguas, 00726. Tel: 787-703-0775; Fax: 787-747-5616.

Commission of Permanent Deacons—Deacon CARLOS LUGO.

CLERGY, PARISHES, MISSIONS AND PAROCHIAL SCHOOLS

CITY OF CAGUAS

1—CATHEDRAL DULCE NOMBRE DE JESUS (1771) Revs. Campo E. Ariza, Rector; Melvin Montanez (FAJ).
Res.: 44 Betances St., Box 665, 00726-0665. Tel: 787-743-4311; 787-743-2927; Fax: 787-746-5399.
Chapel—Nuestra S. Perpetuo Socorro (1929) 24 Aguayo St., 00726.
Chapel—San Gerardo (1940) 221 B St., B-14, Jardines de Caguas, 00726.
Chapel—San Vicente de Paul 221 B St., Brooklyn, NY 11209.
Chapel—La Sagrada Familia (1978) 1004 P St., Bda. Morales.

2—DIVINO NINO (1995) Rev. Hermenegildo Alayón; Deacons Moise's Vargas; Rolando Rocafort.
Mailing Address: P.O. Box 9416, 00726. Tel: 787-746-1450; Fax: 787-744-3497.
Catechesis/Religious Program—Fax: 787-744-3497. Students 120.
Chapel—San Francisco Javier, Tel: 787-286-0440.

3—EL SALVADOR (1970) Rev. Victor G. Ortiz; Deacon Pablo Gonzalez.
Parcelas Bo. Boringuen—HC 08, Buzon 38888, 00725-9723. Tel: 787-747-0091; Fax: 787-747-0091 (call first). Email: elsalvador@caribe.net.
Catechesis/Religious Program—Students 300.
Chapel—Bo. San Salvador, Cristo Rey (1922)
Chapel—Sector Anon, San Alfonso (1929)
Chapel—Sector Hato, Nuestra S. del Carmen (1911)

4—INMACULADO CORAZON DE MARIA (1971) [JC] Revs. Jose Vicente Martinez, C.M.F. (Spain); Vincent Penalba; Tomas Cabello, C.M.F.; Deacon Jose A. Velez Velazquez.
Mailing Address: HC 05, P.O. Box 57564, 00725-9233. Tel: 787-747-6336; Fax: 787-258-4910.
Catechesis/Religious Program—Students 435.
Chapel—Bo. La Barra, Cristo Rey (1971)
Chapel—San Antonio (1950)
Chapel—Bo. La Mesa, N.S. Providencia (1982)
Chapel—Bo. La Mesa, Nuestra S. del Carmen
Chapel—Bo. Quebrada Arenas, San Felipe
Chapel—Guasabara, Sta. Teresa del Nino Jesus (1995)

5—MARIA MADRE DE LA IGLESIA (1972) Rev. Miguel Claudio; Deacons Genaro Estrella Martinez; Francisco Gonzalez; Hipolito Montanez; Felix Cotto Velez.
Calle Juan M. Morales D-23 Urb Valle Tolima, 00725. Tel: 787-258-4481; Fax: 787-747-5616.
Chapel—Bo. Canabon, Maria Reina
Chapel—Las Carolinas, Ntra. Sra. del Carmen

6—NUESTRA SENORA DE LA PROVIDENCIA (1966) Rev. Pedro Ortiz; Deacon Ruben Villodas.
Res.: Urb. Villa del Carmen, Box 6318, 00726. Tel: 787-743-8200; Fax: 787-743-8200.
Station—Urb. Mariolga
Station—Caserio Publico
Station—Los Flamboyanes
Station—Rio Verde
Station—Villa Carmen
Station—Villa del Rey I
Station—Residencial San Carlos 00726.
Station—Residencial San Alfonso

7—NUESTRA SENORA DEL PERPETUO SOCORRO (1966) Revs. Angel Molina; Francisco Hernandez; Deacons Francisco Santiago; Miguel Laguerre; Mario Cardona; Domingo Bousono; Jose M. Garcia.
Res.: Calle 2, A-13, Villa Nueva, 00725. Tel: 787-744-1420; Fax: 787-258-4341. Email: vpsocorro@hotmail.com.
Station—San Patricio (1926) Bo. Canaboncito.
Station—San Judas Tadeo (1960) Villa Esperanza.
Station—Sagrado Corazon Bo. Canaboncito (Las Parcelas).
Station—Nuestra S. del Carmen (1988) Urb. Turabo Gardens.

8—SAGRADO CORAZON DE JESUS (1963) Rev. Hipólito Torres.
Res.: HC 04, Box 45078, Bo. Beatriz, 00726. Tel: 787-747-5170.
Chapel—Bo. Beatriz, Cristo Rey (1960)
Chapel—San Martin (1994)

9—SAN JOSE (1960), (Discalced Carmelites from Spain) Revs. Miguel Arroyo, O.C.D.; Alejandro Moral, O.C.D.; Samuel Fernandez, O.C.D.; Deacons Rafael Torres; Kenny Figueroa; Bruno Dueno.
Res.: Coral St., Villa Blanca, P.O. Box 1749, 00726. Tel: 787-743-5889; Fax: 787-258-0683. Email: sanjose_caguas@yahoo.com. Web: www.parroquiasanjose.net.
School—P.O. Box 1101, 00726. Tel: 787-743-2032; Fax: 787-258-0683. Email: csje-sec@csje-sec.org. Web: www.csje-sec.org. Sr. Nelly O. Rodriguez, C.M., Prin. (Spanish Carmelite Missionaries Sisters) Priests 2; Sisters 5; Lay Teachers 29; Students 596.
High School—Tel: 787-744-8993; Fax: 787-744-4111. Email: webmaster_csjs@yahoo.com. Mrs. Brenda Figueroa de Soler, Prin. Priests 1; Lay Teachers 21; Students 450.
Chapel—Nuestra Senora del Rosario (1981) Boi Bairoa La 25, Puerto Rico. Tel: 787-743-5889.
Catechesis/Religious Program—Norma Otie, D.R.E.; Helen Nolasco, D.R.E. Students 120.

10—SAN JUAN APOSTOL Y EVANGELISTA (1982) Rev. Antonio Cartagena; Deacons Francisco Gonzalez; Jose Rodriquez; Ruben Huertas.
Res.: Apartado 459, Avenida Bairoa, 00726. Tel: 787-744-6359; Fax: 787-743-8266.
Catechesis/Religious Program—Tel: 787-743-8266. Students 200.

11—SAN PABLO APOSTOL (1980), (Hispanic), Rev. Jhon Jaime Florez Gallo.
Res.: Kennedy U-32-B Urb. Jose Mercado, 00725. Tel: 787-743-3546; Fax: 787-743-3546.
Chapel—Bo. Tomas de Castro I, Nuestra S. de Guadalupe (1928)
Chapel—Bo. Tomas de Castro II, Santa Rose de Lima
Chapel—Sector Ramal, San Martin de Porres (1969)
Chapel—Sector Buenos Aires, San Juan Bautista y Santa Ines
Chapel—Sector RM5, Ntra. Sra. de la Monserrate
Catechesis/Religious Program—Students 134.

12—SAN PEDRO APOSTOL (1982) Rev. Antonio Munoz Alcarria.
Res.: Urb. Bonneville, P.O. Box 8878, 00726. Tel: 787-744-2036; Fax: 787-743-4695.

13—SANTISIMA TRINIDAD (1986) Rev. Efrain Zabala; Deacon Esteban Dominguez.
Res.: P.O. Box 9630, 00726-9630. Tel: 787-747-6967; Fax: 787-747-6967. Email: pstcaguaspr@yahoo.com.

14—SANTISIMO SACRAMENTO (1967), Blessed Sacrament Fathers. Revs. Jose Martin Eguiguren; Jesus Maria Maiza, S.S.S.
Res.: Calle Caney A-11, Caguax, 00725. Tel: 787-743-8444; Fax: 787-745-5165.
Chapel—Urb. Caguas Norte, San Antonio de Padua
Chapel—Nuestra S. de Guadalupe 5th St., 00725.

OUTSIDE THE CITY OF CAGUAS FROM LAS AMERICAS EXPRESSWAY TOWARD THE WEST

AGUAS BUENAS, AGUAS BUENAS CO.

1—CHURCH OF TRES SANTOS REYES (1838), Redemptorist Fathers. Revs. Miguel A. Torres, C.Ss.R.; Antonio Hernandez, C.Ss.R.; Clemente Cahill, C.Ss.R.; Jose Checchia, C.Ss.R.; Hector Colon, C.Ss.R.
Res.: 4 Munoz Rivera St., P.O. Box 1, 00703. Tel: 787-732-2741; Fax: 787-732-2185.
School—Academia San Alfonso, Tel: 787-732-8288; Fax: 787-732-4115. Email: sanalfonso@prtc.net. Mrs. Luz Rodriguez, Prin. Religious 1; Lay Teachers 16; Students 172.
Chapel—Bo. Sumidero, Nuestra S. del Perpetuo Socorro (1933)
Chapel—Sector Las Corujas del Barrio Sumidero, Buen Pastor (1984)
Chapel—Bo. Sonadora, Sagrado Corazon (1937)
Chapel—Bo. Jagueyes Abajo, San Jose (1939)
Chapel—Bo. Jagueyes Quintas, Santisimo Redentor (1947)
Chapel—Bo. Caguitas, Madre del Perpetuo Socorro (1941)
Chapel—Bo. Caguitas, Sector La Brusca, Ntra. del Rosario (1996)
Chapel—Parcelas Santa Clara, Santa Clara (1974)

2—ESPIRITU SANTO (1991) Rev. Felix Nunez; Deacons Juan Lopez; Jose Rivera; Domingo Falcon; Nelson Garcia.
Res.: P.O. Box 1250, 00703. Tel: 787-732-1270.
Chapel—Carr. 156, Santa Teresita (1929)
Chapel—Bo. Mulitas Alvelo, De Todos los Santos (1974)
Chapel—Bo. Mulitas Tiza, San Gerardo Mayela (1974)
Chapel—Bo. Juan Ascencio, San Alfonso

AIBONITO, AIBONITO CO., CHURCH OF ST. JOSEPH (1897) Revs. Israel Berrios; Israel Ramos Cintron; Deacons Modesto Reyes; Ezequiel Collazo; Cristobal Rolon; Carlos Lugo; Humberto Martinez.
Res.: P.O. Box 2038, 00705. Tel: 787-735-3741; 787-735-7235; Fax: 787-735-4436.
Catechesis/Religious Program—Tel: 787-735-4856. Students 1,900.
Mission—Barrio Algarrobo Barrio La Plata, Amoldadero. Tel: 787-735-5032.
Chapel—Bo. Asomante (Cuadritos), Nuestra S. del Carmen (1959)Tel: 787-735-1811.
Chapel—Bo. Asomante (Abejas), Inmaculada Concepcion (1965), Tel: 787-735-6455.
Chapel—Bo. Pasto, Nuestra S. de Guadalupe (1970)Tel: 787-735-6977.
Chapel—Nuestra S. de la Providencia (1982) Palestina St. Tel: 787-735-3072.
Chapel—Bo. Rabanal (Parcelas), Nuestra S. de Fatima (1972)Tel: 787-735-0395.
Chapel—Ext. San Luis, Nuestra S. del Carmen (1986)Tel: 787-735-7189.
Chapel—La Plata, La Milagrosa (1986)Tel: 787-735-4038.
Chapel—Llanos, Sector El Juicio, Tel: 787-735-1973.
Chapel—La Sierra, San Judas Tadeo, Tel: 787-735-2835.

BARRANQUITAS, BARRANQUITAS CO.

1—CHURCH OF ST. ANTHONY OF PADUA (1808; 1988) Revs. Juan Colon Pineiro; Edwin R. Hernández; Deacon Carlos Colon Bernardi.
Res.: P.O. Box 1099, 00794. Tel: 787-857-3585; Fax: 787-857-3585.
Catechesis/Religious Program—Students 1,800.
Chapel—San Francisco de Asis (1960)
Chapel—Bo. Mana, Virgen del Carmen (1963)
Chapel—Bo. Canabon, Virgen de la Providencia (1968)
Chapel—Bo. Helechal, San Jose Obrero (1968)
Chapel—Bo. Quebrada Grande, Nuestra Sra. de la Monserrate (1968)
Chapel—Bo. Palo Hincado, Virgen del Perpetuo Socorro (1975)
Chapel—Bo. Lajitas, Nuestra S. del Pilar (1970)
Chapel—Sector La Torre, Santa Cruz (1975)
Chapel—Bo. Helechal, San Martin de Porres (1950)

2—SAN ANDRES APOSTOL (1986) Rev. Jose A. de Leon; Deacons Optaciano Rivera Ortiz; Angel Mercado. In Res., Rev. Raúl Santos.
Res.: Bo. Quebradillas, Box 490, 00794. Tel: 787-875-5424; Fax: 787-875-5424.
Catechesis/Religious Program—Students 241.
Chapel—Bo. Palomas, Comerio, San Jose (1925)
Chapel—Bo. Quebradillas, Barranquitas, Corazon de Jesus (1940; 1987)
Chapel—Bo. Cedro Arriba, Naranjito, San Antonio de Padua (1864)
Chapel—Bo. Quebradillas, Barranquitas, Inmaculada Concepcion y Santa Cruz (1957)
Chapel—Bo. Cedro Arriba, Naranjito, Santuario Maria Auxiliadora (1992)

CAYEY, CAYEY CO.

1—NUESTRA SENORA DE LA ASUNCION (1787), Mercedarian Fathers. Revs. Jose Munoz, O.M.; Antonio Garcia, O.M.
Casa Parroquial: P.O. Box 372887, 00737-2887. Tel: 787-738-2763; Fax: 787-738-2763. Email: asuncion.cayey@hotmail.com.
Catechesis/Religious Program—Students 1,069.
Chapel—Bo. Jajome, Sagrado Corazon de Jesus (1935)
Chapel—Bo. Pasto Viejo, Nuestra S. del Carmen (1937; 1988)
Chapel—Bo. Toita, Nuestra S. de la Merced (1946)
Chapel—Res. Brisas de Cayey, San Ramon Nonato (1978)
Chapel—Bo. Maton Arriba, Santa Teresita del Nino Jesus (1987)

2—NUESTRA SENORA DE LA MERCED (1968) Revs. Elias Lorenzana; Wilfredo Riveros; Gregorio Dafonte Vaz.
Reparto Montellano—P.O. Box 372798, 00737. Tel: 787-738-3872; Fax: 787-263-1810.
Chapel—Bo. Vegas, San Ramon Nonato (1961)
Chapel—Bo. Culebras, Nuestra S. del Carmen (1973)
Chapel—Bo. Farallon, San Pedro Nolasco (1980)
Chapel—San Pedro Armengol (La Plata) (1994)

3—SAN ESTEBAN PROTOMARTIR (1985) Rev. Oscar Rivera; Deacons Anibal Gonzalez Vazquez; Felix Montanez Perez; Silvestre Rodriguez Flores.
Res.: Bo. Guavate, 22601 Sector Nieves, 00736-9522. Tel: 787-747-4555.
Chapel—Bo. Borinquen Pradera, Nuestr Senora del Carmen (1910)
Chapel—Bo. Guavate, San Jose de la Montana (1951; 1990)

CIDRA, CIDRA CO.

1—NUESTRA SENORA DE FATIMA (1963) Rev. Roberto Soliván; Deacons Reyes Santos; Israel Santiago.
Bo. Rabanal—Box 214, 00739. Tel: 787-739-0633.

Catechesis/Religious Program—Students 596.
Chapel—Bo. Toita, Sagrado Corazon de Jesus (1960)
Chapel—Bo. Salto, San Vicente (1965)
Chapel—Bo. Honduras, Perpetuo Socorro (1970)
Chapel—Bo. Rabanal, Jesus Salvador (1970)
Chapel—Bo. Parcelas, La Milagrosa (1978)
Chapel—Bo. Salto, Nuestra Senora de la Providencia
Chapel—Bo. Salto, Santa Teresita (1982)
Chapel—Santo Cristo de Los Milagros (1987)

2—NUESTRA SENORA DEL CARMEN (1818) Revs. Orlando de Jesus Gomez; David Díaz; Deacons Diego Reyes Vasquez; Hector Orlando Santos Reyes; Jose Antonio Flores Colon; Ramon Hernandez Zayas; Angel Alberto Perez Arroyo; Rafael Santos Cruz.
Centro Plaza Municipal—P.O. Box 359, 00739. Tel: 787-739-2406; Fax: 787-739-4991.
Chapel—Bo. Rio Abajo, Madre del Salvador
Chapel—Urb. Treasure Valley, La Milagrosa
Chapel—Bo. Bayamon-Centenejas I, La Inmaculada
Chapel—Bo. Montellano, Santa Teresa del Nino Jesus
Chapel—Bo. Bayamon-Certenejas II, Perpetuo Socorro
Chapel—Bo. Bayamon-Juan del Valle, Nuestra Senora del Rosario
Chapel—Bo. Arena-Santa Clara, San Joaquin
Chapel—Bo. Ceiba-Hevia, Nuestra Senora del Rosario
Chapel—Bo. Arenas, Nuestra Senora de la Providencia
Chapel—Bo. Ceiba, Cristo Rey
Chapel—Bo. Bayamon-San Jose, San Jose
Chapel—Bo. Rincon, San Francisco de Asis
Chapel—Bo. Sud, La Milagrosa
Chapel—Bo. Sud, San Pablo

COMERIO, COMERIO CO., SANTO CRISTO DE LA SALUD (1832) Rev. Encarnación Nieves; Deacon Manuel Rivera Gonzalez.
Mailing Address: P.O. Box 1139, 00782. Tel: 787-875-4525; Fax: 787-875-3481.
Res.: Calle Santiago R Palmer #12, 00782.
Chapel—Bo. Sabana, Nuestra Senora del Santisimo Rosario (1966)
Chapel—Bo. Rio Hondo, Nuestra Senora de Fatima (1953)
Chapel—Bo. Palomas, Santa Ceceilia (1954)
Chapel—Bo. Cedrito, Virgen de la Providencia (1958)
Chapel—Bo. Rio Hondo-Sector Las Parcelas, San Pablo (1965)
Chapel—Bo. Pinas Arriba, Nuestra Senora del Carmen (1973)
Chapel—Bo. Naranjo-Sector Las Parcelas, San Antonio de Padua (1977)
Chapel—Bo. Vega Redonda, San Francisco de Asis (1977)
Chapel—Bo. Cejas, Santa Rose de Lima (1980)
Chapel—Bo. Dona Elena, San Martin de Porres (1950)
Chapel—Rio Hondo II, Maria Madre de la Iglesia

NARANJITO, NARANJITO CO., SAN MIGUEL ARCANGEL (1831) Revs. Felix Oliveras Villanueva; Yamil A. Velazquez; Deacons Abigail Matos; Jose Berrios.
Res.: Centro Parroquial, P.O. Box 68, 00719. Tel: 787-869-2840; 787-869-4080; 787-869-4690; Fax: 787-869-3050.
Chapel—Bo. Nuevo, Santa Rosa de Lima (1953)
Chapel—Bo. Lomas Centro, Virgen del Carmen (1954)
Chapel—Bo. Anones, La Milagrosa (1962)
Chapel—Bo. Lomas Valles, San Judas Tadeo (1963)
Chapel—Bo. Guadiana, La Monserrate (1967)
Chapel—Bo. Achiote, Sagrado Corazon (1978)
Chapel—Bo. Nuevo Parcelas, San Vicente de Paul (1981)
Chapel—Bo. Cedro Abajo, San Jose (1981)

OUTSIDE THE CITY OF CAGUAS FROM LAS AMERICAS EXPRESSWAY TOWARD THE EAST COAST

GURABO, GURABO CO., SAN JOSE (1822) Rev. Angel Colon.
Res.: 7 Santiago Iglesias St., P.O. Box 733, 00778. Tel: 787-737-2656; Fax: 787-737-2656.
Catechesis/Religious Program—Students 240.
Chapel—Bo. Jagual, Sagrado Corazon de Jesus (1951)
Chapel—Bo. Jaguas Llano, Virgen del Carmen (1967)
Chapel—Bo. Santa Rita, Santa Rita (1968)
Chapel—La Milagrosa (1973) Bo. Hato Nuevo, 00778.
Chapel—Bo. Celada, Santa Francisca Javier Cabrini (1967)
Chapel—Bo. Hato Nuevo, La Milagrosa (1982)
Chapel—Bo. Jaguas Loma, San Miguel (1989)
Chapel—Bo. Mamey II, Ntra. Sra. del Carmen

JUNCOS, JUNCOS CO., INMACULADA CONCEPCION (1797) Rev. Feliciano Rodriquez; Deacons Luis Almodovar; Avelino Perez; Carlos Sola.
Res.: Munoz Rivera St. #25 B, 00777.
Office: Algarin St., #6, P.O. Box 1728, 00777. Tel: 787-734-2431; Fax: 787-734-0350. Email: immaculada_juncos@hotmail.com.
Catechesis/Religious Program—Students 200.
Chapel—Bo. Canta Gallo, Cristo Redentor (1975)
Chapel—Bo. Ceiba Sur, Sagrado Corazon (1976)
Chapel—Bo. Valenciano Sector Amigo, Espiritu Santo (1976)
Chapel—Bo. Ceiba Norte, Cristo Rey (1978)
Chapel—Bo. Valenciano Arriba, San Juan Bautista (1979)
Chapel—Bo. Ceiba Norte Sector Chinos, Buen Pastor (1979)
Chapel—Bo. Pinas, Santa Cruz (1981)
Chapel—Bo. Lirios, San Jose (1978)
Chapel—Bo. Canta Gallo Secto Reparto Valenciano, Maria Madre de la Iglesia (1993)
Chapel—Santisima Trinidad Bo. Placita.

LAS PIEDRAS, LAS PIEDRAS CO.

1—INMACULADA CONCEPCION (1801) Revs. Boris Espinoza Perez; Enrique Gómez.
Res.: Box 324, 00771. Tel: 787-733-2381; Fax: 787-733-1180.
Catechesis/Religious Program—Tel: 787-733-8325. Hnas Fatima, D.R.E.; Sr. M. Ines Zayas, O.P., C.R.E. Students 450.
Chapel—Bo. Montones I, Perpetuo Socorro (1935)
Chapel—Bo. Tejas Asomante, Nuestra Senora de la Providencia (1955)
Chapel—Bo. La Fermina, Jesus de Nazaret (1979)
Chapel—Bo. Montones IV, Santa Teresa del Nino Jesus (1980)
Chapel—Bo. Montones II, San Juan Bautista (1982)
Mission— Salon Usos Multiples-Urb. April Gardens, Las Piedras.

2—SAN JUAN BAUTISTA (Bo. Pueblito del Rio) (1971) Rev. Pastor A. Arroyave; Deacons Angel Luis Santiago; Efrain Gomez.
Bo. Pueblito del Rio—HC 02, Buzon 4467, 00771. Tel: 787-733-6444; Fax: 787-733-1479. Email: psjb@prtc.net.
Chapel—Finca Roig, San Juan Bautista (1911; 1940)
Chapel—Bo. Boqueron, La Sagrada Familia (1957)
Chapel—Bo. Pena Pobre, Sagrado Corazon (1964)
Chapel—Bo. Rio Blanco, La Milagrosa (1972)
Chapel—Bo. Mango, San Francisco Javier
Chapel—Bo. Pasto Seco, El Buen Pastor 00771.

MAUNABO, MAUNABO CO., SAN ISIDRO LABRADOR (1799) Rev. Jorge D. Cardona.
Res.: P.O. Box 248, 00707. Tel: 787-861-2595; Fax: 787-861-2595.
Chapel—Nuestra Senora del Carmen (1962)
Chapel—Bo. Calzada, Nuestra Senora de la Providencia (1971)
Chapel—Bo. Matuyas, Nuestra Senora de la Candelaria (1974)
Chapel—Bo. Palo Seco, San Judas Tadeo (1975)
Chapel—Bo. Emajaguas, San Antonio de Padua (1977)
Mission— Bo. Quebrada Arenas.
Mission— Bo. Lizas.
Chapel—N.S. del Rosario de Fatima Bo. Talante.
Mission— Bo. Paloseco.
Mission— Bo. Talante (La Pica).
Mission— Bo. Calzada.

SAN LORENZO, SAN LORENZO CO.

1—NUESTRA SENORA DE LA MERCEDES (1810), (Hispanic), Revs. Angel Lopez, C.Ss.R.; Juan Ramon Hernandez, C.Ss.R.; Andres Spacht, C.Ss.R.; Santiago Mallen, C.Ss.R.; Rafael Torres, C.SS.R.
Res.: Munoz Rivera 55, Apartado 1280, 00754-1280. Tel: 787-736-2571; Fax: 787-736-1213.
Chapel—Bo. Jagual, Nuestra Senora del Carmen (1952)
Chapel—Bo. Quemados, Nuestra Senora del Perpetuo Socorro (1957)
Chapel—Bo. Cerro Gordo Abajo, Cristo Redentor (1965)
Chapel—Bo. Quebrada, Jesus Maestro
Chapel—Bo. Florida, Santa Monica
Chapel—Bda. Roosevelt, Nuestra Senora del Carmen (1968)
Chapel—Bo. Hato Km. 6, Nuestra Senora del Perpetuo Socorro (1968)
Chapel—Bo. Cerro Gordo Arriba, Nuestra Senora del Perpetuo Socorro (1977)
Chapel—Bo. Lorenzo del Valle, Inmaculado Corazon de Maria (1978)
Chapel—Bo. Santa Clara, San Gerardo (1986)
Chapel—Urb. Los Flamboyanes, Bo. Florida, Nuestra Senora de Lourdes (1988)
Catechesis/Religious Program—Students 1,115.

2—SAGRADO CORAZON DE JESUS Y 12 APOSTOLES (Bo. Espino) (1986) Revs. Luis Antonio Rivera Cruz; Franklin Rodriguez; Giovanni Ruiz.
Bo. Espino—HC 30, Box 32716, 00754-9726. Tel: 787-715-6947; Fax: 787-715-6947.
Chapel—San Francisco de Asis (1988) Carr. 181, 00754.
Chapel—Santa Rosa de Lima (1989) Carr. 181, 00754.
Chapel—San Jose (1959) Carr. 181, 00754.
Chapel—Nstra. Sra. del Rosario (1994) Carr. 181, Ramal 745, 00754.
Chapel—Maria Madre de la Iglesia (1990) Carr. 181, 00754.
Chapel—San Pedro (1998) 00754.
Chapel—Santa Teresita del Nino Jesus (1950) 00754.

YABUCOA, YABUCOA CO., SANTOS ANGELES CUTODIOS (1793) Revs. Jose A. Flores; Miguel A. de Angel; Deacon Carlos M. Ramos.
Res.: Degetau St. #2, P.O. Box 7, 00767. Tel: 787-893-2250 (Res.); 787-893-3347 (Office); Fax: 787-266-0841.
Catechesis/Religious Program—Students 930.
Chapel—Bo. Rosa Sanchez, Santa Rosa de Lima
Chapel—Bo. Jacanas Granjas, San Juan Evangelista
Chapel—Bo. Jac. Piedra Blanca, Sagrado Corazon (1976)
Chapel—Bo. Tejas Piedra Azul, Sta. Maria Reina Paz
Chapel—Bo. Martorell, Santa Teresita del Nino Jesus
Chapel—Bo. Tejas, Ntra. Sra. de la Divina Providencia
Chapel—Bo. Playita Cuesta, San Bernardo
Chapel—Bo. Playita Arriba, S. Antonio de Padua (1947)
Chapel—Bo. Playita Parcelas, Virgen Milagrosa
Chapel—Bo. Quebradillas, Ntra. Sra. del Carmen
Chapel—Bo. Guayabota, La Sagrada Familia (1948)
Chapel—Bo. Calabazas Arriba, San Jose (1942)
Chapel—Bo. Quebrada Grande, San Benito
Chapel—Bo. Playa Guayanes, Ntra. Sra. del Carmen
Chapel—Bo. Aguacate, Ntra. Sra. del Perpetuo Socorro (1937)
Chapel—Bo. Jagueyes, Inmaculada Concepcion (1910)
Chapel—Bo. Ingenio, Santisima Trinidad
Chapel—Bo. Camino Nuevo, San Jeronimo
Chapel—Bo. Jacanas Sur, Divino de Jesus y Beato Diego (1999)
Chapel—Bo Tejas Valerio, Corpus Christi.
Chapel—Camino Nuevo, El Guano, San Esteban
Chapel—Jacanas, Piedra Blanca, Sagrado Corazon de Jesus
Chapel—Limones, Campo Alegre, San Francisco de Asis

Chaplains of Public Institutions

CAGUAS. *Hospital Interamericano de Medicina Avanzada (HIMA)*Vacant.
San Juan Bautista Hospital

Retired:
Revs.—
Chocarro, Antonio
Martinez, Alfredo

INSTITUTIONS LOCATED IN THE DIOCESE

[A] PAROCHIAL SCHOOLS

CAGUAS. *Academia Cristo de los Milagros* (1982) Box 7618, 00726-7618. Tel: 787-743-3131; 787-743-4242; 787-743-4855; Fax: 787-746-1428. Email: acdlm@caribe.net. Mrs. Leonides Parrilla de Carrión, Prin.; Mrs. Nilda Aponte, Librarian. Priests 1; Deacons 1; Lay Teachers 63; Students 1,304.

Colegio Catolico Notre Dame Elemental (1916) P.O. Box 967, 00726. Tel: 787-743-2385; 787-743-2524; Fax: 787-743-7567; 787-744-6464. Email: prsbm@yahoo.com.du. Web: www.ccnde.org. Sr. Bernardine Fontanez, S.S.N.D., Prin. Priests 1; Sisters 3; Lay Teachers 65; Aides 16; Students 1,021.

Colegio Catolico Notre Dame Superior, Box 937, 00726. Tel: 787-743-3693; 787-743-5501; Fax: 787-258-9648. Web: www.ccnd.org. Mr. Jose G. Grillo, Prin.; Aurora Vazquez, Librarian. Priests 2; Lay Teachers 86; Students 1,174.

Colegio San Jose Elemental (1963) P.O. Box 1749, 00726. Tel: 787-743-2032; 787-743-3205; Fax: 787-258-0683. Email: csje-sec@csje-sec.org. Web: www.csje-sec.org. Sr. Soledad Diaz, C.M., Prin.; Rev. P. Samuel Fernandez Paulino, O.C.D., Dir.; Mrs. Judith Perez, Librarian. Priests 1; Sisters 4; Lay Teachers 26; Students 409.

Colegio San Jose Superior (1977) Y/O 1749, P.O. Box 1101, 00726. Tel: 787-744-8993; Fax: 787-744-4111. Email: colegiosanjosesuperior@hotmail.com.

Rev. Alejandro Moral, O.C.D., Dir.; Mrs. Brenda Figueroa de Soler, Prin.; Mrs. Sonia Fernandez, Librarian. Priests 1; Lay Teachers 21; Students 294.

Colegio San Juan Apostol y Evangelista (1992) P.O. Box 459, 00726-0459. Tel: 787-743-8266; 787-747-4302; 787-744-6359; Fax: 787-747-4301. Zaida Flores, Prin.; Wilma Roman, Admin.; Carmen Martinez, Librarian. Lay Teachers 43; Students 790.

AGUAS BUENAS. *Academia San Alfonso*, (Grades PreK-7), Pio Rechani St., P.O. Box 97, 00703. Tel: 787-732-8288; Fax: 787-732-4115. Luz E. Rodriguez-Marrero, Prin. Lay Teachers 16; Students 172.

BARRANQUITAS. *Colegio San Francisco de Asis Elemental y Superior*, P.O. Box 789, 00794. Tel: 787-857-2123; Fax: 787-857-2123. Email: matriculateya@csfa-sec.org. Mr. Celestino Mercado Cartagena, Dir. Students 137.

CAYEY. *Colegio Nuestra Senora de la Merced*, P.O. Box 372678, 00736. Tel: 787-738-3438; Fax: 787-263-5837. Email: www.lamercedcayey@yahoo.com. Mrs. Nancy Diaz Morales, Prin.; Maricarmen Lopez, Librarian. (Nuestra Senora de la Asuncion Parish) Priests 1; Lay Teachers 47; Students 826.

GURABO. *Colegio Ntra. Sra. De Pilar*, P.O. Box 1332, 00778. Tel: 787-737-1400; 787-737-1401; Fax: 787-737-1400. Mrs. Adelaida Cruz Zayas. Priests 1; Lay Teachers 11; Total Staff 24; Students 146.

NARANJITO. *Academia Santa Teresita*, P.O. Box 244, 00719. Tel: 787-869-7968; 787-869-6731; 787-869-8357; Fax: 787-869-8357. Email: astnar@prtc.net. Mrs. Josefina Lopez Caldero, Prin. Lay Teachers 21; Students 360.

[B] RETREAT HOUSES

AGUAS BUENAS. *Casa Cristo Redentor* (1967) P.O. Box 8, 00703-0008. Tel: 787-732-5161; Fax: 787-732-1115. Email: pdamian@coqui.net. Revs. Terence Damian Wall, C.Ss.R., S.T.D., Supr.; Hipolito Vicens, C.Ss.R., Dir.; Hector Garcia, C.Ss.R. In Res. Rev. Harold Spacht, C.Ss.R.

AIBONITO. *Casa Manresa*, P.O. Box 1319, 00705. Tel: 787-735-8016; 787-735-8017; Fax: 787-735-2421. Email: manresa@caribe.net. Web: www.casamanresaaibonito.org. Rev. Aurelio Adan, Dir.

JUNCOS. *Casa Cursillos de Cristiandad of Caguas* (Lay Corp. of Cursillistas), Salida de Juncos Carretera 919, P.O. Box 1762, 00777. Tel: 787-734-7068; Fax: 787-713-9725.

SAN LORENZO. *Casa Charlie Rodriguez*, P.O. Box 1190, 00754. Tel: 787-736-5750; Fax: 787-715-8946. Email: santuariopr@gmail.com. Web: www.santuario pr.org. Rev. Giovanni Ruiz Esquivel.

[C] MONASTERIES AND RESIDENCES OF PRIESTS

CAGUAS. *Misioneros Hijos del Inmaculado Corazon de Maria (Claretianos)*, Bo. Rio Canas HC-05, Box 57564, 00725-9233. Tel: 787-747-6336; Fax: 787-258-4910. Email: jvicente@coqui.net; jvmsg@hotmail.com.

AIBONITO. *Casa Salesiana de Retiros*, P.O. Box 2019, 00705. Tel: 787-735-2486; Fax: 787-735-5501. Email: sdbaibon@coqui.net. Revs. Luis Dalbon; Jorge Santiago, S.D.B.; Johnny R. Guzman, S.D.B.; Julian San Nicasio, S.D.B.

[D] CLOISTER SISTERS

CAGUAS. *Hnas. Hijas de Santa Maria de la Ternura*, Calle Naranjito 220 - Barrio Boringuen Parcelas Viejas, P.O. Box 5097, 00726. Tel: 787-653-5813; Fax: 787-653-5813. Sr. Sonia Maria La Luz, H.S.M.I, Prior.

AGUAS BUENAS. *Santa Clara Monastery* Hermanas Clarisas, P.O. Box 884, 00703. Tel: 787-732-5339.

[E] SHRINES

SAN LORENZO. *Diocesan Shrine Our Lady of Mount Carmel* P.O. Box 1190, 00754. Tel: 787-736-5750; Fax: 787-715-8946. Email: santuariopr@gmail.com. Web: www.santuariopr.org. Rev. Giovanni Ruiz Esquivel, Rector.

[F] MISCELLANEOUS

CAGUAS. *Centro de Acompanamiento Sico Social Espiritual (CASSE)*, P.O. Box 656, 00726. Tel: 747-286-3333; Fax: 787-286-3612.

Diocesan Tribunal of Caguas, P.O. Box 9779, 00726. Tel: 787-286-8595; Fax: 787-286-8620. Rev. Felix Nunez, Judicial Vicar.

Instituto Secular de Ntra. Sra. de la Altagracia, Calle 13, L23. Urb. Delgado, 00725. Tel: 787-744-3628; Fax: 787-744-3628. Isabel Vazquez Rivera; Maria Melendez Sanchez; Ramonita Lopez Diaz; Zoraida Santos Santos; Judith Colon Cruz; Olga Rodriguez Berrios; Maria Isabel Colon; Prixda Santos Agosto; Doris Roque Julia; Natividad Ramos Ramos; Evelyn Rosado Rivera; Brenda Y. Abreu Garcia.

Movimiento Juan XXIII, P.O. Box 7229, 00726. Tel: 787-747-3748. Rev. Hipólito Torres.

NARANJITO. *Seminario Pablo VI - Theological*, P.O. Box 302, 00719. Tel: 787-869-0861; Fax: 787-869-0861. Email: jcardona@prtc.net.

Casa del Apostol San Andres Revs. Israel Berrios; Baltazar Nunez.

RELIGIOUS INSTITUTES OF MEN REPRESENTED IN THE DIOCESE

For further details refer to the corresponding bracketed number in the Religious Institutes of Men or Women section.

[]—*Claretian Fathers*—C.M.F.

[0220]—*Congregation of the Blessed Sacrament* (N. Spain Prov.)—S.S.S.

[]—*Mercedarian Fathers* (Spain)

[]—*Order of Carmelites*—O.Carm.

[1070]—*Redemptorist Fathers* (San Juan Prov.)—C.SS.R.

[1190]—*Salesians of Don Bosco* (Antillas)—S.D.B.

RELIGIOUS INSTITUTES OF WOMEN REPRESENTED IN THE DIOCESE

[0420]—*Discalced Carmelite Nuns* (Spain)—O.C.C.

[]—*Doninicas de la Santisima Virgen*

[]—*Dominicas del Rosario de Fatima*

[]—*Hermanas Carmelitas Misioneras*

[]—*Hermanas Clarisas*

[]—*Hermanas de Notre Dame*

[]—*Hermanas Dominicas del Rosario de Fatima*

[]—*Hermanas Hijas de Santa Maria de la Ternura*

[]—*Hermanas Mercedarias*

[]—*Hermanas Misioneras de los Sagrados Corazones*

[]—*Hermanas Misioneras del Buen Pastor*

[]—*Hermanas Misioneras Dominicas del Santo Rosario*

[]—*Hijas de Maria Auxiliadora*

[]—*Misioneras de Maria Corredentora*

[]—*Misioneras del Sagrado Corazon*

[2790]—*Missionary Servants of the Most Holy Trinity* (Spain)—M.S.B.T.

[3760]—*Order of St. Clare*—P.C.C.

[]—*Religiosas del Sagrado Corazon*

[]—*Sacred Heart Sisters*

[]—*Salesian Sisters*

[2970]—*School Sisters of Notre Dame* (Wilton, CT)—S.S.N.D.

[]—*Siervas de Maria* (Spain)

[]—*Siervas de Maria*

[0640]—*Sisters of Charity of St. Vincent de Paul* (Puerto Rico Prov.)—S.C.

[]—*Sisters of Fatima* (P.R.)

[2150]—*Sisters Servants of the Immaculate Heart of Mary*—I.H.M.

NECROLOGY

(No Deaths)

An asterisk (*) denotes an organization that has established tax-exempt status directly with the IRS and is not covered by the USCCB Group Ruling.

Diocese of the Caroline Islands

Editor's Note: 2010 information was not received)

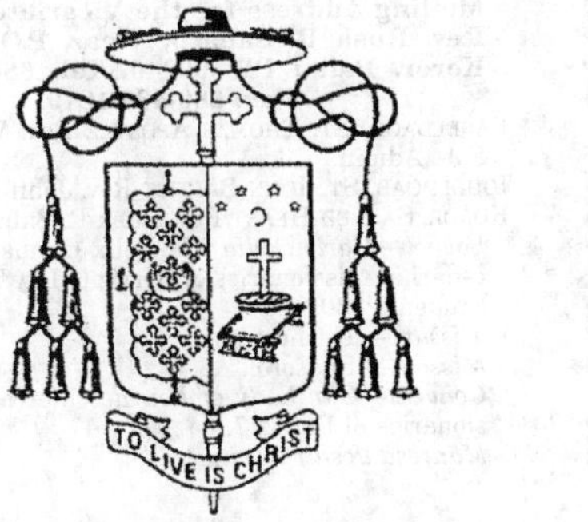

Most Reverend

AMANDO SAMO, D.D.

Bishop of the Caroline Islands; ordained Priest December 10, 1977; appointed Titular Bishop of Libertina and Auxiliary Bishop of the Caroline and Marshalls May 10, 1987; ordained Bishop August 15, 1987; named Coadjutor February 3, 1994; named Bishop of the Diocese March 25, 1995; installed June 6, 1995. *Res.: P.O. Box 939, Chuuk, FM 96942.* Tel: 691-330-2399; Fax: 691-330-4585.

Chancery Office: P.O. Box 939, Chuuk, FM 96942. Tel: 691-330-2399; Fax: 691-330-4585.

Web: www.diocesecarolines.org

Email: diocese@mail.fm

Square Miles Ocean 1,725,000.

Total Population of 135,831.

Vicariate of the Caroline Islands erected December 10, 1905 and committed to the Order of Friars Minor Capuchin, extended to the Mariana Islands March 1, 1911.

Vicariate of the Marianas and Caroline and Marshall Islands erected May 4, 1923 and committed to the Society of Jesus. Marianas Islands separated July 4, 1946. Diocese of the Caroline-Marshalls created February 3, 1980. The Marshalls made a separate Prefecture Apostolic August 15, 1993, and the Diocese renamed "Diocese of the Caroline Islands."

Civilly it includes the four Federated States of Micronesia (Chuuk, Kosrae, Pohnpei and Yap) and the Republic of Palau.

STATISTICAL OVERVIEW

Personnel	
Bishop	1
Priests: Diocesan Active in Diocese	10
Priests: Diocesan Active Outside Diocese	2
Priests: Retired, Sick or Absent	1
Number of Diocesan Priests	13
Religious Priests in Diocese	15
Total Priests in Diocese	28
Ordinations:	
Diocesan Priests	1
Transitional Deacons	3
Permanent Deacons	23
Permanent Deacons in Diocese	65
Total Brothers	2
Total Sisters	34
Parishes	
Parishes	29
With Resident Pastor:	
Resident Diocesan Priests	10
Resident Religious Priests	7
Without Resident Pastor:	
Administered by Priests	2
Administered by Deacons	12
Missions	2
Professional Ministry Personnel:	
Brothers	2
Sisters	34
Educational	
Diocesan Students in Other Seminaries	12
Total Seminarians	12
High Schools, Diocesan and Parish	3
Total Students	620
High Schools, Private	1
Total Students	175
Elementary Schools, Diocesan and Parish	4
Total Students	1,221
Catechesis/Religious Education:	
High School Students	798
Elementary Students	1,309
Total Students under Catholic Instruction	4,135
Teachers in the Diocese:	
Scholastics	2
Brothers	2
Sisters	24
Lay Teachers	134
Vital Statistics	
Receptions into the Church:	
Infant Baptism Totals	1,424
Minor Baptism Totals	345
Adult Baptism Totals	113
First Communions	1,171
Confirmations	886
Marriages:	
Catholic	245
Interfaith	31
Total Marriages	276
Total Catholic Population	77,733
Total Population	140,368

Former Bishops—Most Revs. SALVADOR WALLAESER, O.F.M.Cap., cons. Vicar Apostolic and Titular Bishop of Tanagra, Aug. 21, 1912; resigned June 23, 1919; died Jan. 1, 1946; SANTIAGO LOPEZ DE REGO, S.J., cons. Vicar Apostolic and Titular Bishop of Dionisiopolis, Aug. 26, 1923; resigned June 2, 1939; died Aug. 5, 1940; THOMAS J. FEENEY, S.J., cons. Vicar Apostolic and Titular Bishop of Agno, Sept. 8, 1951; died Sept. 9, 1955; VINCENT I. KENNALLY, S.J., cons. Vicar Apostolic and Titular Bishop of Sassura, March 25, 1957; resigned Sept. 20, 1971; died April 12, 1977; MARTIN J. NEYLON, S.J., D.D., ord. Bishop, Feb. 2, 1970; succeeded to as Vicar Apostolic, Sept. 20, 1970; named to be Bishop of the new diocese, May 3, 1979; installed as first Bishop of the Diocese of the Carolines-Marshalls, Feb. 3, 1980; retired June 6, 1995; died April 13, 2004.

Chancery Office—Mailing Address: P.O. Box 939, Chuuk, 96942. Tel: 691-330-2399; Fax: 691-330-4585.

Vicar General—Rev. JOHN F. CURRAN, S.J., J.C.L.

Chancellor—Rev. ROSENDO RUDOLF.

Diocesan Consultors—Revs. DAVID ANDRUS, S.J.; RUSK SABURO; JOHN S. HAGILEIRAM, S.J.; NICHOLAS P. RAHOY.

Finance Committee—Rev. JOHN F. CURRAN, S.J., J.C.L.; Mr. SANTI ASANUMA; Mr. IGNACIO STEPHEN; Mr. TONY GANNGIYAN; Mr. ALBINO KERMAN; Rev. ROSENDO RUDOLF.

Episcopal Vicars—

Chuuk—Rev. NICHOLAS P. RAHOY, Mailing Address: P.O. Box 337, Chuuk, 96942. Tel: 691-330-2672; Fax: 691-330-4394.

Palau—Rev. RUSK SABURO, Mailing Address: P.O. Box 128, Palau, PW 96940. Tel: 680-488-6539; 680-488-2226; Fax: 680-488-1819.

Pohnpei-Kosrae—Rev. DAVID ANDRUS, S.J., Mailing Address: P.O. Box 160, Pohnpei, 96941. Tel: 691-320-4661; Fax: 691-320-5876.

Yap—Rev. JOHN S. HAGILEIRAM, S.J., Mailing Address: P.O. Box "A", Yap, 96943. Tel: 691-350-2265; Fax: 691-350-2784.

Diocesan Tribunal—

Judical Vicar—Rev. WILLIAM J. RAKOWICZ, S.J., Mailing Address: P.O. Box 128, Palau, PW 96940. Tel: 680-488-2226; Fax: 680-488-1819.

Defenders of the Bond—Revs. NICHOLAS P. RAHOY; RUSK SABURO.

Notaries—Rev. JOHN F. CURRAN, S.J., J.C.L.; Mrs. MIRIAM CHIN; Ms. FILIPANA PHILLIP.

Vocations—Rev. JULIO ANGKEL.

CLERGY, PARISHES, MISSIONS AND PAROCHIAL SCHOOLS

CHUUK (TRUK) STATE, CAROLINE ISLANDS

Mailing Address for the Vicariate of Chuuk: Rev. Nicholas Rahoy, P.O. Box 250, Chuuk, Caroline Islands, FM 96942. Tel: 691-330-2672; Fax: 691-330-4394 (unless otherwise noted).

FEFAN, SACRED HEART Deacon Iowanes Reim, Admin.
Mission— Parem.

MORTLOCK ISLANDS, MORTLOCK Revs. John Ikataere, M.S.C.; Tatieru Eweneteang, M.S.C.; Deacons Soichy Buliche; Petrus Soumwei.
Mission— Satowan.
Mission— Kuttu.
Mission— Moch.
Mission— Ettal.
Mission— Namoluk.
Mission— Lukunor.
Mission— Oneop.
Mission— Ta.
Mission— Nama.
Mission— Piis.
Mission— Losap.

NEEPWUKOS, HOLY FAMILY CHURCH Rev. Basilio Dilipy; Deacons Eliot Cholymay; Bername Itiraw; Rikarto Fabian; Julio Akapito.

TOL, ASSUMPTION OF THE BLESSED VIRGIN MARY Rev. Fernando Titus; Deacons Angken Rapun; Roke Rokop; Kintin Rawit; Itoi Ruta; Oiken Victus; Missa Sewell; Francisco Ykuta; Lukas Paulus; Gabriel Ykuda; Krispino Raphael; Siano Pius; Enato Rapun.

TOLOWAS, ST. ANTHONY'S Rev. Julio Angken; Deacons Tobias Soram; Rinder Fidel.

TUNNUK, IMMACULATE HEART OF MARY CATHEDRAL Rev. Nicholas P. Rahoy; Deacons Chitaro William; Yostaro Noporu; Edwin Shuru, (Retired); Angken Xymoon.
School—St. Cecilia's, Tel: 691-330-4525; Fax: 691-330-4394. Mr. Kaspar Berry, Prin. Mercedarian Missionaries of Berriz 4; Peace Corps Volunteer 1; Lay Teachers 25; Students 634.

UDOT, ST. FRANCIS ASSISI Rev. Fernando Titus; Deacons John Fritz; Eichy Karsom; Julian Ranu; Kerno Sam.
Mission—St. Joseph Romanum.

UMAN, HOLY CROSS Revs. Edmond Ludwick; Lomano Kauvaetupu, M.S.C.; Deacons Audreas Nimas; Carlos Sam; Salvador Mailos; Akiuo Meisa; Joseph Albert; Nori Oneitam; Atitor Edmond; Istor Aien.

POHNPEI STATE, CAROLINE ISLANDS

Mailing Address for the Vicariate of Pohnpei: Rev. Dave Andrus, S.J., P.O. Box 160, Pohnpei, Caroline Islands, FM 96941. Tel: 691-320-4661; Fax: 691-320-5876 (unless otherwise noted).

AWAK, ST. JOSEPH Deacons Adelino Lorens, Admin.; Manuel Amor, (Retired).
Tel: 691-320-6025.

IPWUTEK, ST. AUGUSTINE Deacon Tarsisio Amon, Admin.
Tel: 691-320-8930.

KOLONIA, OUR LADY OF MERCY Revs. Cuthbert Yiftheg; Kasiano Paul (Special Studies Philippines).; Deacons Edgar Martin; Martiniano Rodriguez.
Tel: 691-320-2557; Fax: 691-320-5876.
School—Pohnpei Catholic School, Tel: 691-320-2556. Sisters 3; Lay Teachers 11; Students 213.

PALIKIR, STS. PAUL AND BARNABAS Deacon Thomas Santos, Admin.
Tel: 691-320-5822.

PORRASSAPW, CHRIST THE KING Deacons Saulus Olbet, Admin.; Koropin Kermen.
Tel: 691-320-3744.

SEINWAR, MOST PURE HEART OF MARY Deacon Luciano Iowanis.
Tel: 691-320-3573.

SOKEHS, ST. PETER'S Deacon Albert Linny, Admin.
Tel: 691-320-4667; 691-320-6923.

TAMOROI, SACRED HEART Rev. Gregory F. Muckenhaupt, S.J.
Mission— Pohnpei, 96941.

YAP STATE, CAROLINE ISLANDS

Mailing Address for the Vicariate of Yap: Rev. Paul L. Horgan, S.J., Vicar, P.O. Box A, Yap, FM 96943. Tel: 691-350-2265; Fax: 350-2784.

GAGIL-TOMIL, ST. JOSEPH Rev. Eddy Anthony, S.J.
Tel: 691-350-2598.

NEMAR, ST. MARY
School—St. Mary's Sr. Vincent Marie Balajadia, S.S.N.D., Prin. Priests 1; Sisters 1; Lay Teachers 13; Students 310.

ULITHI AND NEIGHBORING ISLANDS, QUEEN OF HEAVEN Deacon John Rulmal.
Mission— Ngulu.

WOLEAI AND NEIGHBORING ISLANDS, ST. IGNATIUS Rev. John S. Hagileiram, S.J.

REPUBLIC OF PALAU, CAROLINE ISLANDS

Mailing Address for the Vicariate of Palau: Rev. Rusk R. Sabaro, Vicar, P.O. Box 128, Koror, Palau PW 96940. Tel: 680-488-1758; Fax: 680-488-1819.

BABELDAOB, ST. THOMAS APOSTLE Rev. Wayne Tkel, S.J., Admin.

IOUELDOAB, ST. JOHN BAPTIST Rev. John Paul Ililau.

KOROR, SACRED HEART Rev. Rusk R. Saburo.
School—Maris Stella Mr. Felix Okabe, Prin. Mercedarian Missionaries of Berriz 6; Lay Teachers 23; Students 330.
Mission— Ngcheangl.
Mission— Sonsorol.
Convent—Our Lady of Lourdes Mercedarian Missionaries of Berriz 7.
Manresa Jesuit Novitiate—

Permanent Deacons:
Afeiluk, Christino, Weno, Chunk
Aien, Istor, Uman, Chuuk
Akapito, Camirino, Fefan, Chuuk
Akapito, Julio, Fefan, Chuuk
Albert, Joseph, Uman, Chuuk
Amor, Manuel, Awak, Pohnpei
Amor, Tarsisio, Ipwutek, Pohnpei
Buliche, Soichy, Satawan, Chuuk
Cholymay, Eliot, Neepwokos, Moen, Chuuk
Easu, Mariano, Polowot, Chuuk
Edgar, Martin, Kolonia, Pohnpei
Edmond, Atitor, Uman, Chuuk
Else, Pelsiano, Sapwuahfik, Pohnpei
Elukan, Augustine, (Retired), Maap, Yap
Fabian, Rikarto, Weno, Chuuk
Felichoo, Francisco, Gagil-Tomil, Yap
Fichiman, Donald, Gagil-Tomil, Yap
Fidel, Rinder, Tolas, Chuuk
Fritz, John, Udot, Chuuk
Iowanis, Tuciano, Seinwar, Pohnpei
Itiraw, Bername, Neepwukos, Chuuk
James, Kawaichy, Murilo, Chuuk
Kanas, Patrick, Fefan, Chuuk
Karsom, Eichy, Udot, Chuuk
Kermen, Koropin, Kiti, Pohnpei
Kerno, Sam, Udot, Chuuk
Linny, Albert, Sokehs, Pohnpei
Lorens, Adelino, Uh, Pohnpei
Mailos, Salvador, Uman, Chuuk
Meisa, Akiuo, Uman, Chuuk
Naich, Julio, Pollap, Chuuk
Nimas, Andreas, Uman, Chuuk
Noporu, Yostaro, Fono, Chuuk
Olbet, Saulus, Porrassapw, Pohnpei
Oneitam, Nory, Uman, Chuuk
Paulus, Lucas, Fanapanges, Chuuk
Pius, Siano, Wonei, Chuuk
Rano, Julian, Romanum, Chuuk
Raphael, Krispino, Polle, Chuuk
Rapun, Angken, Tol, Chuuk
Rapun, Enato, Tol, Chuuk
Rawit, Kintin, Wonei, Chuuk
Reim, Iowanes, Fefan, Chuuk
Robert, Pisek, Mekur (Weito), Chuuk
Rodriguez, Martiniano, Kolonia, Pohupei
Rokop, Roke, Tol, Chuuk
Rulmal, John B., Ulithi, Yap
Ruta, Itoi, Tol, Chuuk
Sadlin, Anasio, Fefan, Chuuk
Sam, Karlos, Uman, Chuuk
Santos, Thomas, Palikir, Pohnpei
Sewell, Meisa, Tol, Chuuk
Shuru, Edwin, (Retired), Moen, Chuuk
Silbanuz, Peter, Tamworoi, Pohnpei
Soram, Tobias, Tolowas, Chuuk
Sos, Iakim, Uman, Chuuk
Soumwei, Petrus, Kuttu, Chuuk
Victus, Oiken, Pwene, Chuuk
William, Chitaro, Tunnuk, Moen, Chuuk
Xymon, Angken, Fefan, Chuuk
Ykuda, Gabriel, Polle, Chuuk
Ykuta, Francisco, Pwene, Chuuk

INSTITUTIONS LOCATED IN THE DIOCESE

[A] PASTORAL RESEARCH INSTITUTE

POHNPEI. *Micronesian Seminar*, P.O. Box 160, 96941. Tel: 691-320-4067; Fax: 691-320-5876. Rev. Francis X. Hezel, S.J., Dir. Lay Assistants 2.

[B] HIGH SCHOOLS

CHUUK. *Saramen Chuuk Academy*, P.O. Box 662, 96942. Tel: 691-330-4442; Fax: 691-330-4452. Mr. Wayne Olap, Prin. Sisters 4; Lay Teachers 18; Students 249.
Xavier High School, P.O. Box 220, 96942. Tel: 691-330-4266; Fax: 691-330-4753. Rev. Richard McAuliff, S.J., Dir.; Ms. Anne Traynor, Prin. Lay Teachers 13; Scholastics 2; Students 153.

PALAU. *Mindszenty High School*, P.O. Box 69. Tel: 680-488-2437. Ms. Justa Polloi, Prin. Priests 1; Mercedarian Sisters 1; Lay Teachers 17; Students 197.

POHNPEI. *Our Lady of Mercy Vocational Training School*, P.O. Box 73, 96941. Tel: 691-320-3168. Sr. Maria Perez-Caballero, M.M.B., Prin. Mercedarian Sisters 3; Lay Teachers 6; Students 61.

[C] RESIDENCES OF PRIESTS AND BROTHERS

KOLONIA, POHNPEI. *Jesuit House*, P.O. Box 160, 96941. Tel: 691-320-2317; Fax: 691-320-5876. In Res. Revs. Joseph A. Cavanagh, S.J.; John F. Curran, S.J., J.C.L., Vicar Gen. & E. Vicar; Francis X. Hezel, S.J., Supr.; Dave Andrews, S.J.; Gregory F. Muckenhaupt, S.J.

KOROR, PALAU. *Manresa Jesuit House*, P.O. Box 128. Tel: 680-488-2226; Fax: 680-488-1819; 680-488-1725. Revs. Kenneth J. Hezel, S.J., Regl. Supr.; Rusk R. Saburo; John Paul Ililau; Wayne Tkel, S.J.

TUNNUK, CHUUK. *Vicariate Residence*, P.O. Box 250, 96942. Tel: 691-330-2313; Fax: 691-330-4394. In Res. Revs. Julio Angkel; Basilio Dilipy, Admin.; David Lewis; Edmond Ludwick; Nicholas P. Rahoy; Rosendo Rudolf; Fernando Titus.

[D] RESIDENCES OF SISTERS

AWAK, POHNPEI. *Sisters of Marie Auxiliatrice*, P.O. Box 1375, 96942. Tel: 691-320-2626. Sisters 6.

COLONIA, YAP. *Maryknoll Sisters*, P.O. Box 26, 96943. Tel: 691-350-2148 (Colonia). Sr. Joanne McMahon, M.M., Contact Person. Sisters 3.
School Sisters of Notre Dame, P.O. Box 111, 96943. Tel: 691-350-2345. Sr. Vincent Marie Balajadia, S.S.N.D., Contact Person. Sisters 2.

KOLONIA, POHNPEI. *Mercedarian Missionaries of Berriz*, P.O. Box 73, 96941. Tel: 691-320-2558. Sr. Gloria Billimont, M.M.B., Coord. Sisters 4.

KOROR, PALAU. *Mercedarian Missionaries of Berriz*, P.O. Box 56. Tel: 680-488-2272. Sr. Micaela Udui, M.M.B., Coord. Sisters 7.

NEEPWUKOS, CHUUK. *Religious Sisters of Mercy* 96942. Tel: 691-330-3363. Sr. Grace Joseph, R.S.M., Coord. Sisters 1.

WENO, CHUUK. *Mercedarian Missionaries of Berriz*, P.O. Box 67, 96942. Tel: 691-330-4587. Sr. Faustina Nedelec, M.M.B., Coord. Sisters 5.

RELIGIOUS INSTITUTES OF MEN REPRESENTED IN THE DIOCESE

For further details refer to the corresponding bracketed number in the Religious Institutes of Men or Women section.

[0690]—*Jesuit Fathers and Brothers* (New York Prov.)—S.J.

[1110]—*Missionaries of the Sacred Heart*—M.S.C.

RELIGIOUS INSTITUTES OF WOMEN REPRESENTED IN THE DIOCESE

[2470]—*Maryknoll Sisters of St. Dominic*—M.M.

[2510]—*Mercedarian Missionaries of Berriz*—M.M.B.

[2970]—*School Sisters of Notre Dame*—S.S.N.D.

[]—*Sisters of Marie Auxiliatrice*—M.A.

[2575]—*Sisters of Mercy of the Americas*—R.S.M.

[]—*Sisters of the Immaculate Heart of Mary*—S.I.H.M.

NECROLOGY

(No Deaths)

An asterisk (*) denotes an organization that has established tax-exempt status directly with the IRS and is not covered by the USCCB Group Ruling.

Diocese of Chalan Kanoa

(Dioecesis Vialenbensis)

Most Reverend

TOMAS A. CAMACHO, D.D.

Bishop Emeritus of Chalan Kanoa; ordained June 14, 1961; appointed Prelate of Honor by Pope Paul VI in 1974; appointed Bishop of Chalan Kanoa November 8, 1984; consecrated and installed January 13, 1985; retired April 6, 2010. *Res.: Bishop's Residence, P.O. Box 500745 CK, Saipan, MP 96950.* Tel: 670-235-1114.

ESTABLISHED NOVEMBER 8, 1984.

Square Miles 184.

Corporate Title: "Bishop of Chalan Kanoa, a Corporation Sole."

Comprises the Mariana Island chain except for Guam, known legally as the Commonwealth of the Northern Mariana Islands.

For legal titles of parishes and diocesan institutions, consult the Diocesan Curia.

(VACANT SEE)

Web: www.cnmicatholic.org

Email: diocese@pticom.com

STATISTICAL OVERVIEW

Personnel	
Retired Bishops	1
Priests: Diocesan Active in Diocese	16
Number of Diocesan Priests	16
Religious Priests in Diocese	1
Total Priests in Diocese	17
Parishes	
Parishes	12
With Resident Pastor:	
Resident Diocesan Priests	11
Resident Religious Priests	1
Missions	1
Pastoral Centers	1
Professional Ministry Personnel:	
Lay Ministers	36
Welfare	
Specialized Homes	1
Total Assisted	262
Special Centers for Social Services	2
Total Assisted	2,232
Educational	
Diocesan Students in Other Seminaries	1
Total Seminarians	1
Elementary Schools, Diocesan and Parish	3
Total Students	462
Catechesis/Religious Education:	
High School Students	618
Elementary Students	528
Total Students under Catholic Instruction	1,609
Teachers in the Diocese:	
Priests	1
Sisters	4
Lay Teachers	36
Vital Statistics	
Receptions into the Church:	
Infant Baptism Totals	606
Minor Baptism Totals	15
Adult Baptism Totals	18
First Communions	597
Confirmations	618
Marriages:	
Catholic	55
Interfaith	3
Total Marriages	58
Deaths	169
Total Catholic Population	43,000
Total Population	71,850

Former Bishop—Most Rev. TOMAS A. CAMACHO, ord. June 14, 1961; appt. Prelate of Honor by Pope Paul VI in 1974; appt. Bishop of Chalan Kanoa Nov. 8, 1984; cons. and installed Jan. 13, 1985; retired April 6, 2010.

Diocesan Curia—Mailing Address: P.O. Box 500745, Saipan, 96950. Tel: 670-234-3000; Fax: 670-235-3002.

Vicar General—Rev. MANUEL R. CORCUERA.

Chancellor—Rev. RYAN JIMENEZ.

Finance Officer—Rev. PRIMITIVO T. LOPEZ.

Personnel Officer—VACANT.

Director of Vocations—Rev. JESSE T. REYES, Dir.

Director of Religious Education—Sr. ESTELA V. ALTEA, S.G.B.P., Dir.

Superintendent of Catholic Schools—Rev. RYAN JIMENEZ.

Director of Worship—Rev. ISAAC M. AYUYU.

Director of Youth Ministry—Rev. FLORENTINO E. RECAIDO JR.

Diocesan Curia Staff—Mrs. LOLITA M. BABAUTA, Office Mgr.; Rev. RYAN JIMENEZ, Bishop's Sec.; Mrs. MARITES L. VILLANUEVA, Accountant.

Consultative Bodies

Presbyteral Council—Rev. RYAN JIMENEZ; Rev. Msgr. LOUIS ANTONELLI; Revs. MANUEL R. CORCUERA; ISAAC M. AYUYU; EMMANUEL ALPARCE; CHARLITO A. BORJA; PRIMITIVO T. LOPEZ; KYE MANSOO ANTONY; REY ROSAL; ISIDRO T. OGUMORO; JESSE T. REYES; ALBERTO DELA CRUZ; FLORENTINO E. RECAIDO JR.; FRANCISCO M. SANTOS; CELSO MAGBANUA.

College of Consultors—Rev. MANUEL R. CORCUERA.

Diocesan Finance Council—Mr. MICHAEL JOHNSON; Mr. KARL REYES; JOAQUIN Q. DELA CRUZ.

Diocesan Pastoral Council— Representatives from every Parish, Clergy and Religious. Rev. MANUEL R. CORCUERA; Sr. MARYANN HARTMAN, M.M.B.; CHRISTOPHER TENORIO; VIRGINIA C. VILLAGOMEZ; HERBERT S. DELROSARIO; JAMES LG. SABLAN; ROSIKY F. CAMACHO; JOSEFA C. TAITANO; MARIE T. MUNA; Sr. VERONICA A. BENAVENTE; FRANCES T. JOHNSON; TRICIA T. TENORIO; FRANCISCO LG. CAMACHO; NIEVES L. BABAUTA; NOMINANDA L. KOSAKA; PRESCILLA SN. MUNA; MARGARET C. DELACRUZ; MARCELINA P. CEPEDA; MARIA MALUA T. PETER; FRANCISCO M. DIAZ; BAE IN HWA; HAN GI YANG; RITA A. MANGLONA; ROSA P. ACQUININGOC; ANICETO MUNDO; FRANCISCO S. CALVO; VINCENT M. CALVO.

Diocesan Tribunal

Judicial Vicar—Rev. Msgr. DAVID C. QUITUGUA, J.C.D.

Marriage Tribunal Judge—VACANT.

Defender of the Bond—VACANT.

Tribunal Auditor—VACANT.

Diocesan Commissions

Commission on Worship—VACANT.

Commission on Justice and Development—VACANT.

Commission on Evangelization—VACANT.

Commission on Family Life—Rev. MANUEL R. CORCUERA, Chm.

Commission on Ministerial Development—VACANT.

Commission on Heritage Cultural of the Church—Rev. RYAN JIMENEZ, Chm.

Apostolic Works of the Diocese

Diocesan Publications Office—Revs. RYAN JIMENEZ, Dir.; EMMANUEL ALPARCE, Editor of "North Star" (Diocesan Newspaper); Ms. JOCELYN GUERRERO, Advertising Mgr.

Electronic Media—Rev. RYAN JIMENEZ.

Hospital Chaplaincy (Saipan)—Rev. ISAAC M. AYUYU.

Mt. Carmel Catholic Cemetery—Mr. MARLON CARLOS, Consultant.

Prison Chaplaincy—Rev. JESSE T. REYES.

Police and Fire Departments Chaplaincy—Rev. JESSE T. REYES.

St. Joseph Catholic School (Tinian)—Sr. LUCIA ANIBAN, S.I.H.M.

Civilly Incorporated Activities of the Diocese

Mount Carmel School, Inc. (Saipan)—Mrs. LYNETTE L. VILLAGOMEZ, Chm.; Mrs. MARGARET C. DELA CRUZ, Pres.; Mrs. LOURDES T. MENDIOLA; VACANT, Chap. Mt. Carmel School.

Eskuelan San Francisco de Borja School, Inc. (Rota)—Mr. FRANK CALVO, Chm.; Sr. ZOSIMA CAPUA, R.V.M., Admin.

Karidat, Inc.—Mr. NED ARRIOLA, Pres. Bd. Directors; Ms. ANGIE V. GUERRERO, Exec. Dir.

Associations of the Faithful

A.G.A.P.E. (Almighty God and People Encounter)—Adult Leaders: CRIS SABLAN; LUCINDA SABLAN; Rev. FLORENTINO E. RECAIDO JR., Spiritual Dir.

Catholic Daughters of America—Mrs. FELICIDAD OGUMORO, Regent.

Children of God the Father, Inc.—Ms. ROXANN D. ARANDA, Pres.; Rev. FLORENTINO E. RECAIDO JR., Spiritual Dir.

Confraternity of Christian Mothers—Mrs. ESTHER S. FLEMING, Diocesan Bd. Pres.; Rev. JESSE T. REYES, Spiritual Dir.

Couples for Christ—Household Leaders: Mrs. CECILIA PAGAPULAR; Rev. FRANCISCO M. SANTOS.

Cursillo Movement—Mr. JESUS ELAMETO, Acting Pres.; Rev. RYAN JIMENEZ, Spiritual Dir.

El Shaddai Movement—VACANT, Leader; Rev. PRIMITIVO T. LOPEZ, Spiritual Dir.

Eucharistic Adoration Society—Most Rev. TOMAS AGUON CAMACHO; ELIZABETH CHO; FRANCISCO PALACIOS.

Knights of Columbus—Sir Knight VINCENT MARFALEN, District Deputy; Rev. FRANCISCO M. SANTOS, Spiritual Dir. for Rev. Msgr. Vicente T. Martinez Council & Pale Luis Medina Council.

Legion of Mary—Rev. MANUEL R. CORCUERA, Diocesan Spiritual Dir.

San Roque Parish - Mother of Divine Love Praesidium—Mrs. RIZALINA CANO, Pres.; Rev. PRIMITIVO T. LOPEZ, Spiritual Dir.

Legion of Mary at San Antonio Parish/Mother of Perpetual Help Praesidium—Mrs. MARIA N. ALDAN, Pres.; Rev. FRANCISCO M. SANTOS, Spiritual Dir.

Legion of Mary at Kristo Rai Parish/Mother Refuge of Sinners, Praesidium—VACANT, Spiritual Dir.

Legion of Mary at San Jose Parish/Rainan i Gef Santos Na Lisayo—Rev. JESSE T. REYES, Spiritual Dir.

Light & Salt Catholic Charismatic Community—CELY ZAMORA, Head Servant; VACANT, Spiritual Dir.

Marriage Encounter—Main Contact: Mr. CHARLES V. CEPEDA, Ecclesial Team; Mrs. CATHY S. CEPEDA; Rev. ISAAC M. AYUYU, Spiritual Dir.

CLERGY, PARISHES, MISSIONS AND PAROCHIAL SCHOOLS

ISLAND OF SAIPAN

CHALAN KANOA VILLAGE, CATHEDRAL OF OUR LADY OF MT. CARMEL Most Rev. Tomas Aguon Camacho; Revs. Ryan Jimenez; Isaac M. Ayuyu; Florentino E. Recaido.

Rectory—Mt. Carmel, P.O. Box 500745, 96950. Tel: 670-234-3000.

Mission—Korean Catholic Community P.O. Box 693, 96950. Tel: 670-235-1449; 670-235-1450. Rev. Antony Kye.

Oratory—Mercedarian Missionary Sisters of Berriz, Formation House.

GARAPAN VILLAGE, DISTRICT 11, KRISTO RAI PARISH Revs. Emmanuel Alparce; Celso Magbanua.

Oratory—Maturana House of Prayer

Oratory—Navy Hill, Commonwealth Health Center Chapel

KAGMAN VILLAGE, SANTA SOLEDAD MISSION PARISH Rev. Manuel R. Corcuera.

Mailing Address: P.O. Box 500745, 96950. Tel: 670-256-4568; 670-234-3000.

SAIPAN, SAN JUDE PARISH Rev. Charlito A. Borja.

Rectory—P.O. Box 500745, 96950. Tel: 670-288-0007; Fax: 670-235-3002.

SAN ANTONIO VILLAGE, DISTRICT 6, SAN ANTONIO PARISH Rev. Francisco M. Santos.

Rectory—San Antonio, P.O. Box 500745, 96950. Tel: 670-235-4515.

SAN JOSE VILLAGE, DISTRICT 7, SAN JOSE PARISH Rev. Jesse T. Reyes.

Rectory—P.O. Box 500745, 96950. Tel: 670-234-6991.

SAN ROQUE VILLAGE, DISTRICT 9, SAN ROQUE PARISH Rev. Primitivo T. Lopez.

Rectory—P.O. Box 500745, 96950. Tel: 670-322-2404.

SAN VICENTE VILLAGE, DISTRICT 10, SAN VICENTE PARISH Rev. Rey Rosal.

Rectory—San Vicente, P.O. Box 500745, 96950. Tel: 670-235-8208.

Oratory—Our Lady of the Most Holy Rosary Dandan.

TANAPAG VILLAGE, DISTRICT 8, SANTA REMEDIOS PARISH Rev. Alberto Dela Cruz.

Rectory—P.O. Box 500745, 96950. Tel: 670-322-7254.

ISLAND OF ROTA

SONGSONG VILLAGE

1—SAN FRANCISCO DE BORJA PARISH Rev. Delfin Tumaca.

Rectory—San Francisco de Borja, Songsong Village, P.O. Box 542, Rota, 96951. Tel: 670-532-3522.

2—SAN ISIDRO PARISH (Sinapalo) Rev. Msgr. Louis Antonelli.

Rectory—Sinapalo Village, P.O. Box 590, Rota, 96951. Tel: 670-532-0720.

ISLAND OF TINIAN

SAN JOSE VILLAGE, SAN JOSE Rev. Isidro T. Ogumoro.

Catholic Rectory, San Jose Village—Tinian, 96952. Tel: 670-433-3000.

School—St. Joseph Catholic School, (Grades K-6), P.O. Box 282, Tinian, 96952. Tel: 670-433-7527; Fax: 670-433-7527. Sr. Lucia Aniban, S.I.H.M., Admin. & Prin.

DIOCESAN MISSIONS

San Ignacio Chapel (Island of Pagan) San Jose Chapel (Island of Anatahan) Santa Cruz Chapel (Island of Alamagan)Santa Cruz Chapel (Island of Agrihan)

INSTITUTIONS LOCATED IN THE DIOCESE

[A] ELEMENTARY AND HIGH SCHOOLS

TINIAN. *St. Joseph Catholic School*, (Grades K-6), P.O. Box 282, 96952. Tel: 670-433-7527; Fax: 670-433-7527. Sr. Lucia Aniban, S.I.H.M., Admin. & Prin.

[B] RESIDENCES OF SISTERS

SAIPAN. *Chalan Kanoa Formation House*, P.O. Box 500136, 96950. Tel: 670-234-6214. Sr. Asuncion Demapan, M.M.B., Local Coord. Sisters 4; Juniors 2.

MMB Maturana Community, P.O. Box 501178-CK, 96950. Tel: 670-322-9713. Email: mmbmaturana@pticom.com. Web: www.mmberriz.com. Sr. M. Pilar Latasa, M.M.B., Local Coord. Sisters 12.

Pastorelle Sisters Convent (San Antonio Parish), P.O. Box 745, 96950. Tel: 670-234-1213. Sisters Estela Altea, S.G.B.P., Local Coord.; Vilana Laluan, S.G.B.P., Local Coord.

RELIGIOUS INSTITUTES OF MEN REPRESENTED IN THE DIOCESE

For further details refer to the corresponding bracketed number in the Religious Institutes of Men or Women section.

[0690]—*The Society of Jesus*—S.J.

RELIGIOUS INSTITUTES OF WOMEN REPRESENTED IN THE DIOCESE

[2510]—*Mercedarian Missionaries of Berriz*—M.M.B.

[]—*Pastorelle Sisters*

[]—*Religious of the Virgin Mary*—R.V.M.

[]—*Sacred of Immaculate Heart of Mary*—S.I.H.M.

[1830]—*Sisters of the Good Shepherd*—R.G.S.

NECROLOGY

(No Deaths)

An asterisk (*) denotes an organization that has established tax-exempt status directly with the IRS and is not covered by the USCCB Group Ruling.

Diocese of Fajardo-Humacao, Puerto Rico

(Dioecesis Faiardensis-Humacaensi)

Most Reverend

EUSEBIO RAMOS MORALES

Bishop of Fajardo-Humacao; ordained December 15, 1983; appointed Bishop of Fajardo-Humacao March 11, 2008; consecrated May 31, 2008.

Bishop House: Carr #987 Km. 0.2 Santa Isidra I #206, Fajardo, PR 00738. Mailing Address: Apartado 888, Fajardo, PR 00738. Tel: 787-801-5700; 787-801-5800; Fax: 787-801-2600.

Email: diocesisfajardohumacao@gmail.com

ESTABLISHED JUNE 1, 2008

Comprises southeast municipalies of Puerto Rico: Humacao, Naguabo; east municipalies of Puerto Rico: Ceiba, Fajardo, Luquillo, northeast municipalies of Puerto Rico Rio Grande, Loiza, Canovanas and the Islands Municipalies of Culebra and Vieques.

Patroness of the Diocese: Nuestra Senora del Carmen and Santiago Apostol (extra-official).

STATISTICAL OVERVIEW

Personnel	
Bishop	1
Priests: Diocesan Active in Diocese	19
Number of Diocesan Priests	19
Religious Priests in Diocese	10
Total Priests in Diocese	29
Extern Priests in Diocese	3
Ordinations:	
Diocesan Priests	1
Permanent Deacons	4
Permanent Deacons in Diocese	26
Total Brothers	6
Total Sisters	27
Parishes	
Parishes	21
With Resident Pastor:	
Resident Diocesan Priests	19
Resident Religious Priests	3
Without Resident Pastor:	
Administered by Priests	21
Welfare	
Day Care Centers	1
Total Assisted	35
Special Centers for Social Services	1
Total Assisted	31
Educational	
Diocesan Students in Other Seminaries	1
Total Seminarians	1
High Schools, Diocesan and Parish	6
Total Students	1,599
Elementary Schools, Diocesan and Parish	5
Total Students	1,171
Total Students under Catholic Instruction	2,771
Vital Statistics	
Receptions into the Church:	
Infant Baptism Totals	618
Adult Baptism Totals	138
First Communions	606
Confirmations	434
Marriages:	
Catholic	115
Interfaith	17
Total Marriages	132
Deaths	350
Total Catholic Population	97,869
Total Population	293,000

Vicar General—Rev. VICENTE PARQUALETTO, S.T.

Sec. Chancellor—Rev. MIGUEL A. MERCED REYES.

Diocesan Offices and Directors

Economic Administrator—Mrs. LINDA LUGO, Mailing Address: P.O. Box 888, Fajardo, 00738. Tel: 787-801-5700; 787-801-5800; Fax: 787-801-2600.

Movimientos y Organizaciones Diocesanas—

Cursillos de Cristiandad—VACANT.

Legion de Maria—VACANT.

Renovacion Carismatica—VACANT.

Juan XXIII—VACANT.

Caballeros de Colon—VACANT.

Vicentinos—VACANT.

Talleres de Oracion y Vida—VACANT.

Catechetical Vicar—Rev. ANGEL LUIS CINTRON.

Master of Ceremonies—Rev. JOSE A. AROCHO, Mailing Address: P.O. Box 888, Fajardo, 00738.

Pastoral Vicar—Rev. OSCAR SANCHEZ, Mailing Address: P.O. Box 888, Fajardo, 00738.

Vocations—Rev. FLOYD MERCADO VIDVO.

CLERGY, PARISHES, MISSIONS AND PAROCHIAL SCHOOLS

CITY OF FAJARDO

1—CATHEDRAL SANTIAGO APOSTOL (1766) Revs. Angel L. Cintron Ortiz, Rector; Luis A. Alicea Rivera.
Res.: 16 Garrido Morales St., P.O. Box 806, 00738. Tel: 787-863-2365; Fax: 787-860-1837.
Catechesis/Religious Program—Students 55.
Chapel—Bo. Florencio, Santa Elena (1962)
Chapel—Bo. Quebrada Vueltas, Perpetuo Socorro (1965)
Chapel—La Milagrosa (1978)
Chapel—Santa Isidra, Santiago Apostol

2—SANTISIMO REDENTOR (1993) Rev. Miguel A. Merced.
Res.: Urb. Monte Brisas, Calle C-V-19, 00738. Tel: 787-863-5227; Fax: 787-860-0560.
Catechesis/Religious Program—Students 140.
Chapel—Puerto Real, Ntra. Sra. de Carmen
Chapel—Sardinera, San Juan Bautista
Chapel—Las Croabas, Maria, Madre del Senor
Chapel—Fajardo Gardens, Maria, Madre de la Providencia

CITY OF HUMACAO

3—CONCATHEDRAL DULCE NOMBRE DE JESUS (Pueblo) (1763) [CEM 3] [JC] Revs. Floyd Mercado, Rector; Raguiel Rodriguez Leon; Deacon Angel Cruz Cruz.
Res.: 3 Font Martelo St., Box 9087, Humacao, 00791. Tel: 787-852-0868; Fax: 787-850-6448.
Catechesis/Religious Program—Students 380.
Chapel—San Agustin (1955) Parcela No. 44, Bo. Anton Ruiz, Humacao, 00792.
Chapel—Nuestra Senora de la Candelaria (1956) Parcela No. 30, Candelero Arriba, Humacao, 00791.
Chapel—San Jose (1957) Carr. 922 Cotto Mabu, Humacao, 00791.
Chapel—Nuestra Senora de Fatima (1962) Bo. Juniquito, Humacao, 00791.
Chapel—Santa Teresita (1965) Bo. Candelero Abajo, Humacao, 00791.
Chapel—Nuestra Senora de la Providencia (2000) Bo. Catano, Humacao, 00791.
Chapel—Perpetuo Socorro (1944) Bo. Buena Vista, Humacao, 00791.
Chapel—Inmaculada Concepcion (1996) Urbanizacion Villa, Humacao, 00791.
Chapel—Maria Auxiliadora (1999) Bo. Candelero Abajo, Parcelas Martinez.

4—MARIA REINA DE LA PAZ (Pueblo) (1989) Revs. Kharlosg Lopez; Felix Rivera; Deacons Rafael Ulfret; Jose L. Ortiz.
Res.: Urb. Villa Universitaria, Calle 4 A-20, Humacao, 00791. Tel: 787-850-3081; 787-285-0351; Fax: 787-850-3080. Email: mariapaz@libertypr.net.
Catechesis/Religious Program—Students 210.
Chapel—Sagrado Corazon de Jesus (1940)
Chapel—San Martin de Porres (1962)
Chapel—Buen Pastor (1970)
Chapel—Bo. Tejas, Cristo Rey (1976)
Chapel—Bo. Mariana II, Santa Rosa de Lima (1978)
Chapel—Comunidad Vista Hermosa

OUTSIDE THE CITIES OF FAJARDO AND HUMACAO

CANOVANAS

1—NUESTRA SENORA DEL PILAR (1960) Rev. Fabio Moncada (Colombia); Deacon Jose R. Rivera.
P.O. Box 1615, 00729-1615.
Res.: Luis Hernaiz St., #3, 00729. Tel: 787-876-2655; 787-876-3002; Fax: 787-256-5767.
School—3 Luis Hernaiz St., 00729. Iris Del Valle, Dir. Lay Teachers 50; Students 900.
Catechesis/Religious Program—Raquel Ortiz, D.R.E. Students 11.
Mission—San Francisco Javier Bo. Camabalache, 00729.

2—RESURRECCION DEL SEÑOR (1978) Revs. Luis H. Quinones Murillo; Alfredo Martínez Veliz; Deacons Pedro Flores; Miguel Roman.
Mailing Address: P.O. Box 896, 00729-0896.
Res.: Las Parcelas de San Isidro, Carret. 188 Km. 2.0, 00729. Tel: 787-876-3917; Fax: 787-256-4836.
Mission—Ntra. Sra. de la Providencia Villas De Loiza.

3—SAGRADO CORAZON DE JESUS (1991) Rev. Fabian Rodriguez, S.J.; Deacon Anthony Calderon.
PMB 20147, P.O. Box 35000, 00729-0014.
Res.: Bo. Cubuy, Carretera 186 Km. 77, 00729. Tel: 787-876-1355; Fax: 787-886-3668.
Mission—La Milagrosa Bo. Cuatrocientas, 00729.
Mission—San Pedro Apostol Bo. Lomas, PR.

4—SAN JOSE (1971) Rev. Oscar Alberto Sanchez-Lopez; Deacon Felipe Rivera.
P.O. Box 807, 00729-0807.
Res.: Bo. Campo Rico, Carretera 185, 00729. Tel: 787-876-7167.
Mission—Ntra. Sra. de la Asuncion Carrt. 957 Km. 6.8, Palma Sola.
Mission—Ntra. Sra. del Carmen Carrt. 185 Km. 5.3, Alturas de Campo Rico.

5—SANTA MARIA MADRE DE DIOS (1971) Rev. Jose A. Rivera Maldonado; Deacon Jose L. Casaigne.
Res.: Urb. Loiza Valley, Calle Girasol E189, 00729. Tel: 787-876-0827; Fax: 787-876-0827.
Catechesis/Religious Program—Sr. Gloria Mercedes Gonzalez, M.S.B.T., D.R.E. Students 58.
Mission—Capilla Cristo Salvador Sector Pueblo Indio.
Mission—Iglesia Santa Maria Madre De Dios Carr. 8874-Bo. La Central. Tel: 787-876-1490; Fax: 787-876-1490.

CEIBA, CEIBA CO., SAN ANTONIO DE PADUA (1840) Rev. Adrian Alicea Rivera, Admin.
Res.: 561 Escolastico Lopez St., P.O. Box 77, 00735. Tel: 787-885-2530; Fax: 787-885-2218.
Mission—Sagrado Corazon de Jesus Parcelas Aguas Claras, 00735.
Mission—N.S. del Perpetuo Socorro Bo. Rio Abajo, Ceiba Co. 00735.
Chapel—Nuestra Senora de Fatima (1968) Bo. Daguao, 00735.
Catechesis/Religious Program—Students 112.

HUMACAO PLAYA, HUMACAO CO., NUESTRA SENORA DEL CARMEN (Punta Santiago) (1970) Rev. Ramon Santana.
Res.: P.O. Box 91, Punta Santiago, 00741. Tel: 787-850-2125; Fax: 787-850-2125.
Catechesis/Religious Program—Calle 5, #103 Verde Mar, P.O. Box 91, Punta Santiago, 00741. Tel: 787-852-3882. Students 125.
Chapel—Bo. Pasto Viejo, Sector El batey, Nuestra Senora del Perpetuo Socorro (1937; 1986)Tel: 787-852-4421.

LOIZA
1—SAN PATRICIO (1719) Rev. Raul Morales; Deacons Santiago Acosta; Marcos Penaloza; Pastor Perez.
Box 504, 00772-0504.
Res.: Calle Espiritu Santo #10, 00772. Tel: 787-886-1539; Fax: 787-876-7828.
Catechesis/Religious Program—Glorivee Davila, D.R.E. Students 79.
Mission—Santa Rosa Bo. Pinones.
Mission—Ntra. Sra. del Perpetuo Socorro Bo. La Torre.
Mission—Santisima Trinidad Bo. Mediana Baja.
Mission—San Antonio Bo. Las Cuevas, 00772.
Mission—Ntra. Sra. de Fatima Villa Canona, 00772.
Mission—San Rafael Villa Alvarez, 00772.
2—SANTIAGO APOSTOL, EL MAYOR (1971) Revs. Francisco Conkle-Ryan, S.T.; Jesus Palomanes-Vega, S.T. (Mexico); Bro. Luis Fernando Diaz-Betancur, S.T. (Colombia).
P.O. Box 118, 00772-0118.
Res.: Carretera 187 Km. 6.1 Bo. Mediania Alta, 00772-0118. Tel: 787-876-1879.
Catechesis/Religious Program—Students 70.
Mission—Ntra. Sra. Perpetuo Socorro Parcelas Suarez.
Mission—La Milagrosa Bo. El Jobos.
Mission—La Providencia Bo. Mini Mine.
Mission—N. Sra. De Fatima Parcelas Vieques.

LUQUILLO
1—MADRE DEL REDENTOR (1997) Rev. Jose A. Arocho; Deacon Frank Rivera.
P.O. Box 591, 00773-0591.
Res.: Barrio Pitaya, Sector Casablanca, Carr. 173, Km. 1.5, 00773. Tel: 787-889-0733; Fax: 787-889-0733.
Catechesis/Religious Program—Students 35.
Mission—N. Sra. del Carmen Carr. 983 K.2 H.0, Bo. Pitahaya.
Mission—N. Sra. Milagrosa Carr. 983 K.6 H.3, Bo. Sabana.
Mission—S. Vicente de Paul Carr. 3H 43 H.9.
Mission—N. Sra. del Perpetuo Socorro Carr. 984 K.2 H.2, San Martin.
2—SAN JOSE (1797) Revs. Vicente Pasqualetto, S.T.; Mariano Fernandez-Diaz, S.T. (Colombia); Deacon Jesus Ramos.
P.O. Box 493, 00773-0493.
Res.: Calle Soledad No. 15, fronte a Plaza de Recreo, 00773. Tel: 787-889-2590; Fax: 787-889-2590.
Mission—San Judas Bo. Mata de Platano.
Mission—Ntra. Sra. del Cobre Parcelas Fortuna.

NAGUABO, NAGUABO CO., NUESTRA SENORA DEL ROSARIO (1794), (Hispanic), [CEM 2] [JC] Rev. Leonardo Rodriguez Ochoa.
Res.: Box 655, 00718. Tel: 787-874-2235; Fax: 787-874-0150. Email: pvrosario@hotmail.com.
Chapel—Nuestra Senora del Perpetuo Socorro (1946)
Chapel—Bo. Maizales, Nuestra Senora de la Altagracia (1963)
Chapel—Bo. Duque, Nuestra Senora de Fatima (1965)
Chapel—Bo. Florida, Nuestra Senora del Perpetuo Socorro (1942)
Chapel—Nuestra Senora del Carmen Playa Hucares (1920)
Chapel—Bo. Mariana, Nuestra Senora de la Providencia (1965)
Chapel—Bo. Santiago y Lima (Botija), Santa Rosa de Lima (1975)
Mission— Barrio Rio, Sector Brazo Seco.
Mission— Barrio Cecilia, Sector La Fe.

RIO GRANDE
1—SAN FRANCISCO DE ASIS (1986) Rev. Juan B. Medina; Deacon Manuel Llanos.
Bo. Malpica, P.O. Box 1449, 00745-1449.
Res.: Barrio Malpica, 00745. Tel: 787-888-5302; Fax: 787-888-5302.
2—CRISTO REY (1970) Rev. Emerito Gomez Ortiz; Deacon Pedro J. Rivera Viera.
P.O. Box 382, Palmer, 00721-0382.
Res.: Calle Principal, #50, Palmer, 00721. Tel: 787-887-3552. Email: pcristorey@libertypr.net.
Mission—La Milagrosa Palmer. Parcela 69 Hato Rio Grande, Bo. Carola, 00721.
Mission—Ntra. Sra. de la Providencia Bloque S-1 #7, Palmer, 00721.
3—NUESTRA SENORA DEL CARMEN (1840) Rev. Manuel Villamor; Deacons Jose Carrasquillo; Vidal Diaz; Juan Rodriguez.
P.O. Box 845, 00745. Tel: 787-887-2365; Fax: 787-887-2365.
Res.: No. 9 del Carmen St., Apartado 845, 00745. Tel: 787-888-3991. Email: delcarmen_9@yahoo.com.
School—Calle 14 Urb. Alturas de Rio Grande, Apartado 1389, P.O. Box 818, 00745. Tel: 787-887-4099; Fax: 787-887-0872. Email: cnscrg@yahoo.com. Raquel Ortiz, Prin.
Catechesis/Religious Program—Students 95.
Mission—Nuestra Senora de Fatima Bo. El Verde.
Mission—Ntra. Sra. de Guadalupe Jardines de Rio Grande, 00745.
Mission—San Pedro Bo. Bartolo.
Mission—La Milagrosa Calle 14, Alturas de Rio Grande, 00745.
Mission—Sagrado Corazon de Jesus Coco Beach, 00745.

OUTSIDE THE MAIN ISLAND OF PUERTO RICO, THE SMALL ISLANDS

CULEBRA, CULEBRA CO., NUESTRA SENORA DEL CARMEN (1889; 1990) Rev. Luis M. Ruiz.
Mailing Address: P.O. Box 236, 00775. Tel: 787-742-0133.

VIEQUES, VIEQUES CO., INMACULADA CONCEPCION (1844), (Hispanic), Rev. Nelson Lopez Aponte; Deacon Justino Lopez Ortiz.
Res.: 442 Lebrum St., 00765. Tel: 787-741-2241; Fax: 787-741-2241.
Chapel—Bo. Puerto Real, Sagrado Corazon de Jesus (1949)
Chapel—Bo. Esperanza, San Gerardo (1952)
Chapel—Bo. Monte Santo, Nuestra Senora del Perpetuo Socorro (1945)
Chapel—Bo. Santa Maria, Virgen del Carmen (1942)
Chapel—Bo. Destino, Nuestra Senora de Fatima (1950)

Permanent Deacons::

Otero Lugo, Jose
Rivera Viera, Pedro J.

INSTITUTIONS LOCATED IN THE DIOCESE

[A] PAROCHIAL SCHOOLS

FAJARDO. *Colegio Santiago Apostol*, (Grades K-12), Call Box 70007, 00738. Tel: 787-863-0445; Fax: 787-860-6655. Email: santiagoapostolprl@yahoo.com. Web: www.csa-sec.org. Rev. Luis A. Alicea Rivera, Educ. Vicar; Mr. Daniel Ruben Ortiz, Prin.

HUMACAO. *Colegio Nuestra Senora del Perpetuo Socorro de Humacao, Inc.* (1984) P.O. Box 9107, 00792. Tel: 787-852-0845; Fax: 787-852-8706. Email: nuestrasocorro@gmail.com. Mrs. Mercedes M. De Arroyo, Prin.; Miss Diana Ortiz Salcedo, Librarian. Lay Teachers 26; Students 470.
Colegio San Antonio Abad (Benedictines), P.O. Box 729, 00792. Tel: 787-852-1616; Fax: 787-852-1920. Email: santabad@east-net.net. Glenda Bermudez, Prin. Brothers 3; Priests 3; Lay Teachers 29; Students 441.
Colegio San Benito (1963) P.O. Box 728, 00792. Tel: 787-850-7075; Fax: 787-285-8137. Sisters Mary Ruth Santana, Prin. (K-6); Myriam Pacheco, Dir.; Mrs. Isabel Sandel, Librarian. Sisters 6; Lay Teachers 43; Students 740.

[B] MONASTERIES AND RESIDENCES OF PRIESTS

HUMACAO. *San Antonio Abad Abbey of the Order of St. Benedict*, P.O. Box 729, 00792. Tel: 787-852-1616; Fax: 787-852-1920. Email: santabad@east-net.com. Rt. Rev. Oscar Rivera, O.S.B., Abbot; Revs. Rafael Perez, O.S.B.; Jaime Reyes, O.S.B.; Eric Buermann, O.S.B.; Mauro Simpson, O.S.B.; Ignacio Aguirre, O.S.B.; Bros. Aristedes Pacheco, Subprior; Felix Neussendorfer; Tarcisio Medina; Gregorio Valentin; Randolph Perkins; Antonio Hernandez. Brothers 8; Novices 2.

[C] HOMES AND RESIDENCES

CANOVANAS. *Hogar Teresa Toda* (1993) (For Girls), P.O. Box 868, 00729. Tel: 787-886-2060; Fax: 787-886-2075. Email: hteresatoda@aol.com; teresatoda@prtc.net. Web: www.teresatodapr.org. Calle 5-A, R-14, Villa De Loiza, Loiza, 00729. Tel: 787-886-2060; Fax: 787-886-2075. Sr. Ines Pena, Dir. Bed Capacity 28; Total Assisted Annually 60; Total Staff 15.

[D] MISCELLANEOUS

LOIZA. *Centro Esperanza, Inc.*, Calle 1, Esquina 4, Paracelas Vieques, 00772. Tel: 787-876-1545; Fax: 787-876-3389. Email: cesperanza@coqui.net. P.O. Box 482, 00772-0482. Sr. Carmen Gloria Alayon, H.C., Dir. & Contact Person. Sponsored by: Sisters of Charity, Saint Vincent de Paul.
Centro Providencia, 2 #175 Parcelas Suarez, 00772. Tel: 787-256-2320; Fax: 787-256-2320. Mailing Address: P.O. Box 482, 00772. Jose Alayon Martinez, Admin. Asst.

RELIGIOUS INSTITUTES OF WOMEN REPRESENTED IN THE DIOCESE

For further details refer to the corresponding bracketed number in the Religious Institutes of Men or Women section.

[]—*Carmelitas Teresas de San Jose*

[]—*Cenaculo Misionero Rafael Cordero*

[]—*Hermanas de Nazareth*

[]—*Hermanas Dominicas de la Santa Cruz*

[]—*Hijas de la Caridad de San Vicente de Paul*

[]—*Hijas del Corazon de Maria*

[]—*Monasterio Santa Escolastica*

NECROLOGY

(No Deaths)

Prefecture Apostolic of the Marshall Islands

Reverend Monsignor

RAYMUNDO T. SABIO, M.S.C.

Second Prefect Apostolic of the Marshall Islands; ordained December 20, 1971; appointed December 21, 2007; installed January 6, 2008. *Res.: Cathedral of the Assumption, P.O. Box 8, Majuro, MH 96960.* Tel: 692-625-6675; Fax: 692-625-5520.

Mailing Address: Assumption, Uliga, Majuro, P.O. Box 8, Majuro, MH 96960. Tel: 692-625-6675; Fax: 692-625-5520.

Email: prefecture.marshalls@gmail.com

Square Miles 500,000.

Total Population (est.) 59,000.

Prefecture Apostolic of the Marshall Islands divided from the Diocese of the Carolines-Marshall Islands and erected on August 15, 1993 and committed to the Society of Jesus, New York Province; and on January 6, 2008 committed to the Missionaries of the Sacred Heart. Area is that of the Republic of the Marshall Islands which is related by Compact of Free Association to the United States.

STATISTICAL OVERVIEW

Personnel	
Religious Priests in Diocese	4
Total Priests in Diocese	4
Ordinations:	
Permanent Deacons	1
Permanent Deacons in Diocese	1
Total Sisters	6
Parishes	
Parishes	4
With Resident Pastor:	
Resident Religious Priests	3
Without Resident Pastor:	
Administered by Priests	1
Missions	7
Professional Ministry Personnel:	
Sisters	6
Lay Ministers	32
Welfare	
Other Institutions	1
Total Assisted	400
Educational	
Diocesan Students in Other Seminaries	2
Seminaries, Religious	1
Total Seminarians	2
High Schools, Diocesan and Parish	2
Total Students	207
Elementary Schools, Diocesan and Parish	3
Total Students	623
Catechesis/Religious Education:	
High School Students	50
Elementary Students	320
Total Students under Catholic Instruction	1,202
Teachers in the Diocese:	
Sisters	4
Lay Teachers	65
Vital Statistics	
Receptions into the Church:	
Infant Baptism Totals	84
Minor Baptism Totals	13
Adult Baptism Totals	13
First Communions	149
Confirmations	48
Marriages:	
Catholic	4
Interfaith	6
Total Marriages	10
Deaths	17
Total Catholic Population	4,875
Total Population	59,000

Former Prelate—Rev. Msgr. JAMES C. GOULD, S.J., ord. May 4, 1974; appt. First Prefect Apostolic of the Marshall Islands April 23, 1993; installed Aug. 15, 1993; resigned Jan. 5, 2008.

Prefecture Consultors—Revs. YOHANES SUJONO, M.S.C.; ARIEL GALIDO, M.S.C.; AMANDUS REYAAN, M.S.C.; Deacon ALFRED CAPELLE.

Finance Committee—Mr. ALAN FOWLER; Mr. DENNIS MOMOTARO.

Secretary—Mrs. VERONICA KILUWE, Assumption, P.O. Box 8, Majuro, 96960.

Education Consultor—Sr. DOROTHY NOOK, M.M.B.

Catechetics Coordinator—Mrs. ROSITA CAPELLE.

Vocations—Rev. Msgr. RAYMUNDO T. SABIO, M.S.C.

CLERGY, PARISHES, MISSIONS AND PAROCHIAL SCHOOLS

MARSHALL ISLANDS

Mailing Address for the Marshalls: P.O. Box 8, Majuro, MH 96960. Tel: (011) 962-625-6675; Fax: (011) 962-625-5520, unless otherwise noted.

MAJURO, CATHEDRAL OF THE ASSUMPTION Rev. Ariel Galido, M.S.C.; Rev. Msgr. Raymundo T. Sabio, M.S.C.
Tel: 692-625-8307; Fax: 692-625-6507.
School—(Grades K-8) Ms. Sandy Dismas, Prin.; Mr. Luke Roverove, Asst. Prin.; Ms. Cathy Kiluwe, Librarian. Lay Teachers 23; Students 325.
High School—Ms. Sandy Dismas, Prin.; Mr. Richard David, Asst. Prin. Sisters 2; Lay Teachers 14; Students 108.
Mission—Laura Majuro Atoll.

EBEYE, QUEEN OF PEACE Rev. Yohanes Sujono, M.S.C. Mailing Address: P.O. Box 5065, Marshall Islands, 96960. Tel: 692-329-3828.
School—(Grades K-8) Mr. Gary Elaisha, Dir.; Nolan deBrum, Prin.; Mrs. Mary Peter, Librarian. Lay Teachers 16; Students 220.
High School—Mr. Terry Hazzard, Prin. Lay Teachers 8; Students 99.
Mission—Santo Gugeegue, MH.

JALUIT, SACRED HEART OF JESUS Rev. Amandus Reyaan, M.S.C. Cell: 692-455-1223; Sr. Lumine Beckmann, M.S.C., Pastoral Coord.
Jabor, Jaluit, MI. Mailing Address: P.O. Box 8, 96960.
School—Ms. Moten Naisher, Prin. Sisters 1; Lay Teachers 5; Students 78.
Mission—Namdrik

KWAJALEIN
1—BLESSED SACRAMENT, Unassigned.
2—OUTER ISLAND PARISH Rev. Msgr. Raymundo T. Sabio, M.S.C.
Mission—Arno
Mission—Wotje
Mission—Likiep
Mission—Ailinglaplap: Buoj, Woja

INSTITUTIONS LOCATED IN THE DIOCESE

[A] MISCELLANEOUS

MAJURO. *Catholic Pastoral Center: Ajeltake*, P.O. Box 8, 96960. Tel: (011) 692-247-7762; (011) 692-247-7797. Mrs. Adella Hone, Contact Person.

NECROLOGY

(No Deaths)

An asterisk (*) denotes an organization that has established tax-exempt status directly with the IRS and is not covered by the USCCB Group Ruling.

Diocese of Mayaguez, Puerto Rico

(Dioecesis Maiaguezensis)

Most Reverend

ULISES AURELIO CASIANO VARGAS, D.D.

Bishop of Mayaguez; ordained May 30, 1967; appointed Bishop March 4, 1976; ordained April 30, 1976. *Res.: P.O. Box 2272, Mayaguez, PR 00681.* Tel: 787-831-2942; 787-833-5411 (Office).

Erected by the Bull "Qui arcano Dei" on March 1, 1976 by Pope Paul VI.

Comprises a portion of the southwest of the Island.

STATISTICAL OVERVIEW

Personnel	
Bishop	1
Priests: Diocesan Active in Diocese	40
Priests: Diocesan Active Outside Diocese	5
Priests: Retired, Sick or Absent	2
Number of Diocesan Priests	47
Religious Priests in Diocese	23
Total Priests in Diocese	70
Extern Priests in Diocese	1
Ordinations:	
Diocesan Priests	2
Permanent Deacons in Diocese	22
Total Brothers	6
Total Sisters	106
Parishes	
Parishes	29
With Resident Pastor:	
Resident Diocesan Priests	22
Resident Religious Priests	7
Professional Ministry Personnel:	
Lay Ministers	768
Welfare	
Catholic Hospitals	1
Total Assisted	39,771
Homes for the Aged	3
Total Assisted	287
Specialized Homes	1
Total Assisted	240
Special Centers for Social Services	1
Total Assisted	15,000
Other Institutions	5
Total Assisted	156
Educational	
Diocesan Students in Other Seminaries	7
Total Seminarians	7
Colleges and Universities	1
Total Students	1,888
High Schools, Diocesan and Parish	4
Total Students	658
High Schools, Private	4
Total Students	890
Elementary Schools, Diocesan and Parish	5
Total Students	860
Elementary Schools, Private	6
Total Students	1,193
Catechesis/Religious Education:	
High School Students	426
Elementary Students	12,963
Total Students under Catholic Instruction	18,885
Teachers in the Diocese:	
Brothers	5
Sisters	2
Lay Teachers	325
Vital Statistics	
Receptions into the Church:	
Infant Baptism Totals	3,345
Minor Baptism Totals	198
Adult Baptism Totals	178
Received into Full Communion	62
First Communions	2,611
Confirmations	2,282
Marriages:	
Catholic	315
Interfaith	22
Total Marriages	337
Deaths	2,203
Total Catholic Population	402,010
Total Population	502,515

Vicar General—Rev. Msgr. GONZALO DIAZ.

Episcopal Vicars—

For Pastoral—Rev. Msgr. ROGELIO MUR, O.Carm.

For Diocesan Administration—Rev. Msgr. HECTOR E. RIVERA.

Chancery Office—Mailing Address: P.O. Box 2272, Mayaguez, 00681. Tel: 787-833-5411.

Chancellor—Rev. Msgr. HECTOR E. RIVERA.

Diocesan Consultors—Rev. Msgrs. GONZALO DIAZ; ROGELIO MUR, O.Carm.; Rev. JOSE L. DIEZ, O.S.A.; Rev. Msgr. HUMBERTO LOPEZ.

Diocesan Board of Administration—Rev. Msgrs. GONZALO DIAZ HERNANDEZ; ROGELIO MUR, O.Carm.; Rev. ALBERTO CASTRO, P.D.

Administrator—Mr. ALBERTO RODRIGUEZ.

Censor Librorum—Revs. JULIO FERNANDEZ; ISAIAS REVILLA, O.S.A.

Parish Priests Consultors—Rev. Msgrs. GONZALO DIAZ HERNANDEZ; ROGELIO MUR, O.Carm.; HECTOR RIVERA RAMOS.

Diocesan Offices and Directors

Youth Apostolate—VACANT.

Communications Media—Rev. JOSE JUAN CARDONA DIAZ.

Cursillos de Cristiandad—Rev. EDGARDO ACOSTA OCASRO.

Holy Childhood—Most Rev. HERMIN NEGRON.

Legion of Mary—Rev. Msgr. HECTOR E. RIVERA.

Superintendent of Schools—YOLANDA PAGAN.

Religious Consultor—Rev. JULIO FERNANDEZ.

Catechetics—VACANT.

Christian Family Movement—Rev. DELROY THOMAS SCOTT.

Religious Coordinator—Rev. JULIO FERNANDEZ.

Development and Planification—Rev. Msgr. ROGELIO MUR, O.Carm.

Vocations—Revs. ORLANDO ROSAS; DELROY THOMAS SCOTT; EDGAR CARLO.

Catholic Social Services—Sr. LOURDES T. TORO, M.S.B.T., Dir., Carr. 108 Km. 2.8 Int., Calle Obispado Final, Bo. Miradero, Mayaguez, 00681. Tel: 787-833-3627; 787-833-3638; Fax: 787-833-3627. Email: sscdmaya@caribe.net.

Seasonal Head Start Program—Calle Dr. Veve #44, San German, 00683. Tel: 787-892-3800; Fax: 787-892-3866.

CLERGY, PARISHES, MISSIONS AND PAROCHIAL SCHOOLS

CITY OF MAYAGUEZ

1—CATHEDRAL OF OUR LADY OF PURIFICATION (1763) Rev. Msgr. Hector E. Rivera Ramos, Rector; Revs. Nomar Jose Calero Gómez; Rafael Sastre Servera; Deacon Israel Valentin.

Res.: P.O. Box 220, 00681-0220. Tel: 787-831-2444; Fax: 787-831-2444.

School—Academy of the Immaculate Conception, Tel: 787-834-5400; 787-834-7824 (High School). Limary Negron, Elementary Prin.; Mr. Rene Torres, High School Prin. Lay Teachers 42; Elementary Students 300; High School Students 302.

School—Colegio La Milagrosa, Tel: 787-834-0350. Sr. Delma Morales, Prin. Sisters of Charity 6; Lay Teachers 27; Elementary Students 272; High School Students 151.

Mission—Maria Socorro de los Cristianos Barrio Leguisamo.

Mission—Santa Ana Quebrada Grande.

Catechesis/Religious Program—Students 143.

2—ASCENSION (1968) Rev. Santiago Rivera Allende; Deacon Gilberto Martinez.

Res.: Salud Sta., Box 4361, 00681-4361. Tel: 787-832-0766; Fax: 787-832-0766.

Mission—St. Teresita Bo. Limon.

Mission—Our Lady of Perpetual Help Bo. Las Vegas.

Mission—Ntra. Sra. de la Providencia (Rep. Masias) Bo. El Porvenir.

Catechesis/Religious Program—Students 160.

3—CHURCH DE EL BUEN PASTOR (1986) Revs. Jose Aponte, S.J.; Jorge Ferrer, S.J.

Res.: Urb. Mayaguez Ter., 5000 Calle San Gerardo, 00682-6627. Tel: 787-833-8800; Fax: 787-805-3660. Email: elpastor_bueno@yahoo.com.

Catechesis/Religious Program—Students 140.

Mission—El Senor de Los Milagros Alturas de Mayaguez. Tel: 787-265-5936.

Mission—Sta. Teresita Parcelas Soledad.

4—CHURCH OF THE RESURRECTION (1988) Rev. Daniel Enrique Hernandez Velez, Admin.; Deacon Jose Luis Rodriguez.

Res.: Balboa 285, 00680. Tel: 787-831-6180.

Catechesis/Religious Program—Students 46.

Chapel—Consumo, Jesus Redentor

Chapel—Rio Canas, Nuestra Senora del Perpetuo Socorro

Chapel—Barrio Quemado, Nuestra Senor del Carmen

5—NUESTRA SENORA DE FATIMA (1986) [JC] Rev. Edwin Lugo Silva, Admin.

Res.: Parcelas Castillo C-2, 00680. Tel: 787-833-0794.

Catechesis/Religious Program—Students 101.

Mission—Cristo Rey Andalucia St., Sultana, 00680.

Mission—Espiritu Santo Sagitario St., Villa del Oeste, Sabalos, 00680.

Mission—Corpus Christi Urb. Vista Verde, 00680.

6—OUR LADY OF MT. CARMEL (1957) Revs. Carlos González, S.F.M., Admin.; William Saltar.

Res.: Box 3166, 00681. Tel: 787-832-2203; 787-832-2036 (Office); Fax: 787-834-2777.

Mission—Infant of Prague Mani.

Mission—Perpetuo Socorro Jardines del Caribe.

Catechesis/Religious Program—Students 207.

7—SACRED HEART (1959) Revs. P. Angel Luis Rios Matos; Wilson Montes Rodríguez.

Res.: *Marina Station,* R.F.D., P.O. Box 3626, 00681-3626. Tel: 939-248-5224.

School—St. Benedict, Tel: 787-832-9626. Lay

Teachers 31; Elementary Students 342; High School Students 225.
Catechesis/Religious Program—Students 320.
Mission—San Jose Rosario.
Mission—San Carlos y San Antonio Rio Hondo.
Mission—La Milagrosa Bo. Malezas.

8—San Vicente (1965) [JC] Revs. Manuel Aznar Bello, C.M.; Prudencio Sanchez, C.M.; Tomàs de la Puebla, C.M. (Retired).
Res.: Ave. Guanajibo, No. 401, 00680. Tel: 787-832-8874. Email: mazivarbe@hotmail.com.
Catechesis/Religious Program—Students 63.

9—Santa Teresita (1970) Rev. Jose Juan Cardona Diaz, Admin.
Res.: Principe St., 203 Bo. Colombia, 00680. Tel: 787-806-0881; Fax: 787-806-0881.
Catechesis/Religious Program—Students 88.

OUTSIDE THE CITY OF MAYAGUEZ

Aguada

1—St. Francis of Assisi (1692) Revs. Jose Luis Diez Gabela, O.S.A. (Spain); German Lombo, O.S.A. (Spain); Isaias Revilla, O.S.A. (Spain); Ildefonso Blanco, O.S.A. (Spain); Antonio Then, O.S.A.; Deacons Hector Vargas; Benjamin Echevarria; Jorge Lopez; Wilfredo Valle.
Mailing Address: P.O. Box 608, 00602.
Res.: Calle Paz #225, 00602. Tel: 787-868-2630; Fax: 787-868-8561. Email: psfcoaguada@hotmail.com. Web: www.psfcoaguada.tripod.com.
Catechesis/Religious Program—Students 2,124.
Convent—Hermanas de la Caridad del Cardenal Sancha, Calle Jose Hernandez, Box 1136, 00602. Tel: 787-868-8257; Fax: 787-868-8257.
Mission—San Jose Sabana.
Mission—Santa Rita Laguna.
Mission—Santa Monica Cruces.
Mission—Santo Tomas de Villanueva Galicia-Columbani.
Mission—San Augustin Jaguey Chiquito.
Mission—Perpetuo Socorro Rio Grande.
Mission—Ntra. Madre de la Consolacion Naranjo Militar.
Mission—Ntra. Sra. de Altagracia Atalaya.
Mission—San Pablo Naranjo-Guanabanas.
Mission—Asuncion de Maria Marias.
Mission—Buen Consejo Cerro Gordo.
Mission—Perpetuo Socorro Mamey.
Mission—Ntra. Sra. del Carmen Guaniquilla.
Mission—Centro de Espintualidad, Madre de la Consolacion Piedras Blancas, Puerto Rico.
Mission—Ntra. Sra. de las Mercedes Carrizales.
Mission—Immaculada Concepcion Malpaso-Cesar Ruiz.
Mission—Sagrada Familia Bajio.
Mission—Sgdo. Corazon de Jesus Quebrada Larga.
Mission—Ntra. Sra. del Carmen Rio Grande-Playa.
Mission—El Buen Pastor Guayabo.
Mission—Ntra. Sra. Reina de la Paz Piedras Blancas.

2—Santuario Protomartires de la Concepcion (1524) Rev. Roberto Soler; Deacon Carlos Valentin.
Res.: Bo. Espinar, Buzon 1162, 00602. Tel: 787-891-2889.
Chapel—Bo. Palmar, El Buen Pastor
Chapel—Bò. Tablonar, El Nino Jesus
Catechesis/Religious Program—Students 88.

Aguadilla

1—St. Charles Borromeo (1780) [CEM] Revs. Edgar A. Carlo Rodriguez, Admin.; P. Harry Lopez; Deacons Samuel Caban; Victor M. Morales.
Res.: P.O. Box 238, 00605. Tel: 787-891-0575; Fax: 787-891-3622.
School—Tel: 787-891-1445; Fax: 787-882-3270. Mr. Raymond Pérez, Prin. Lay Teachers 30; Elementary Students 168; High School Students 204.
Catechesis/Religious Program—Students 425.
Convent—Tel: 787-882-3629. Sr. Ady Carmelina Sanchez, Supr. Salesian Sisters 4.
Convent—Tel: 787-891-7496. Sr. Nisha Maria, M.C. Missionaries of Charity 4.
Chapel—Bo. Corrales, Our Lady of Perpetual Help
Chapel—Caimital Alto, St. John Baptist
Chapel—Victoria-Nuestra, Senora de la Victoria
Chapel—Esteves, N. S. del Rosario
Chapel—Bda. Caban, Ntra. Sra. de la Sagrada Familia

2—La Milagrosa (1974) Revs. Ramon E. Albino; Perfecto Pérez; Deacons Jorge Casanova; Herminio Blas.
Res.: Urb. Marbella, Calle 1 Num. 379, 00603. Tel: 787-891-7014; Fax: 787-891-7014.
School—Corpus Christi, Tel: 787-882-8433. Damaris Gonzàlez Rosa, Prin. Students 239.
Catechesis/Religious Program—Students 209.
Mission—Our Lady of Victory Borinquen.
Mission—Our Lady of Fatima Camaseyes.
Mission—San Judas Tadeo Playuela, Puerto Rico.

3—San Jose Obrero (1975) Revs. Franklin Santana; Ramon E. Quezada, S.D.B.; Juan J. Gregorio, S.D.B.
Res.: P.O. Box 787, San Antonio, 00690-0787. Tel: 787-890-2449; Fax: 787-890-0436.
Catechesis/Religious Program—Students 200.
Mission—La Providencia Bo. Guerrero.
Mission—Los Santos Reyes Ramey-Maleza.

Anasco, St. Anthony Abbot (1730) Revs. Rogelio Mur Aguilar, O.Carm.; Pedro Rodriguez, O.Carm.; Hector Garcia, O.Carm.; Deacons Victor M. Rosado Cortes; Edwin Gonzalez Carrero.
Res.: Box 392, 00610. Tel: 787-826-2215. Email: antabad@coqui.net.
School—LaSalle, Tel: 787-826-6071. Bro. Angel Suarez, F.S.C., Prin. Students 264.
Catechesis/Religious Program—Students 450.
Mission—Chapel of Our Lady of Perpetual Help Miraflores.
Mission—Our Lady of Carmel La Playa.
Mission—St. Lawrence Martyr Bo. Espino.
Mission—La Immaculade Bo. Pinales.
Mission—La Providencia Bo. Carreras.
Mission—Our Lady of Monserrat Bo. Cerro Gordo.
Mission—St. Rita Bo. Marias.
Mission—Cristo Redentor Bo. Oveja.
Mission—Santa Rosa de Lima Bo. Pozo Hondo.
Jesus Maestro Casa de Formaction—

Cabo Rojo, St. Michael (1783) Revs. Angel Ortiz, Admin.; Jose R. Linares; Luis Pena.
Res.: Box 625, 00623. Tel: 787-851-1283; Fax: 787-851-1970.
School—San Agustin Email: colegiosanagustin@hotmail.com. Miss Madeline Ortiz, Dir. Sisters 2; Lay Teachers 38; Students: High School 302; Elementary 304.
Catechesis/Religious Program—Students 621.
Mission—Our Lady of Mt. Carmel Puerto Real.
Mission—St. John the Baptist Joyuda.
Mission—St. Joseph Boqueron.
Mission—Our Lady of Good Counsel Llanos Tunas.
Mission—St. Rita Las Palmas.
Mission—St. Jude Thaddeus Monte Grande.
Mission—Cristo Rey El Corozo.
Mission—Our Lady of Fatima Betances.
Mission—St. Martin de Porres Conde Avila.
Mission—Ntro. Sra. de la Providencia Bo. Miradero.

Hormigueros

1—El Salvador (1969) Rev. P. Angel Luis Rios Matos.
Res.: Box 567, 00660. Tel: 787-834-1993.
Catechesis/Religious Program—Students 80.
Chapel—Valle Hermoso Arriba, San Judas Tadeo
Chapel—Parcelas S. Romualdo, Sta. Teresita

2—Shrine of Our Lady of Monserrate (1874) Rev. Msgr. Gonzalo Diaz Hernandez; Rev. Floyd McCoy Jordain; Deacon Gilberto H. Rodriguez.
Res.: Box 24, 00660. Tel: 787-849-2260. Web: www.santuariolamonserrate.org.
Convent—Box 185, 00660. Tel: 787-849-2055; Fax: 787-849-2035. Sr. Maria Rita Cardona, O.P. Sisters of Fatima for Social Work 3.
Mission—Sagrado Corazon de Jesus Bo. Lavadero.
Mission—Ntra. Sra. de la Paz Bo. Jaquitas.
Mission—La Asuncion Bo. Carretera Nueva.
Mission—San Martin de Porres Bo. Guanajibo.
Mission—Santa Rosa de Lima Bo. El Hoyo.

Lajas

1—De la Merced Parish (1971) Rev. Urian Pèrez Zapata, Admin.; Deacon Ramon Cardona, P.D.
Res.: Calle Violeta #113, P.O. Box 1023, 00667-1023. Tel: 787-899-1910.
Catechesis/Religious Program—Students 110.
Mission—Ntra. Sra. de la Monserrate Carr. 101 Ramal 303 K.2.4, Bo. Maguayo, 00667.
Mission—San Pedro Carr. 304 Calle Principal, Bo. Parguera, 00667.
Mission—Ntra. Sra. de Monserrate Carr. 116 Parcellas Cuesta Blanca #264, Bo. Cuesta Blanca, 00667.
Mission—Ntra. Sra. del Carmen Carr. 324 K. 5.6, Bo. Salinas, 00667.
Mission—Ntra Sra. del Perpetuo Socorro Carr. 306, Bo. Paris, 00667.

2—Our Lady of the Purification (1883) Revs. Rafael Mendez, Admin.; Gerardo E. Caraballo Galindo.
Res.: Box 425, 00667. Tel: 787-899-1911; Fax: 787-899-2455.
School—St. Louis Academy Sisters of St. Joseph, Tel: 787-899-4080; Fax: 787-899-4080. Sr. Teresita Alicea, C.S.J., Prin. (Brooklyn) Sisters 2; Lay Teachers 30; Elementary Students 143; High School Students 140.
Catechesis/Religious Program—Students 283.
Convent—La Providencia, Tel: 787-899-5180.
Mission—Sagrado Corazon de Jesus Parcelas #201, Bo. La Plata, 00667.
Mission—Ntra. Sra. del Perpetuo Socorro Carretera 118 Km 0, Bo. Lajas Arriba (La Tea), 00667.
Mission—San Pablo Parcelas #48, Bo. Lajas Arriba (Parcelas), 00667.
Mission—Santa Rosa de Lima Comunidad Sta. Rosa #35, Bo. Parcelas Santa Rosa, 00667.
Mission—San Judas Tadeo Parcelas #172, Bo. Parcelas Palmarejo, 00667.
Mission—San Juan Bautista Parcela #80, Bo. Palmarejo II, 00667.
Mission—Santa Rosa de Lima Bo. La Haya.

Las Marias, Immaculate Heart of Mary (1863) Rev. Edward Acevedo, Admin.
Res.: Box 126, 00670. Tel: 787-827-3300.
Catechesis/Religious Program—Students 177.
Mission—San Jose Carr. 406, Km. 3.9, Anones, 00607.
Mission—La Milagrosa Carr. 124, R. 370, Km. 6.8 Int Buena Vista, Buena Vista, 00670.
Mission—N.S. de Fatima Palma Escrita.

Maricao, St. John the Baptist (1864) Rev. Orlando Rosas Muniz, Admin.
Res.: Box 453, 00606. Tel: 787-838-2014.
Catechesis/Religious Program—Students 142.
Mission—Sagrado Corazon Bucarabones.
Mission—Santa Rosa Indiera Fria.
Chapel—Montoso, Immaculado Corazon de Maria, Tel: 787-838-2272. Sr. Angeles Marie Pacheco, O.P., Supr. Dominican Sisters of Our Lady of Fatima 6.

Moca, Our Lady of Monserrate (1772) Revs. David Perez; Carlos F. Mendez Laracuente; Juan Bautista Morales; Rev. Msgr. Angel Latre; Revs. Enrique Ascencio; Julio A. Vera Gonzalez; Deacons Domingo Cerenzo; Norberto Perez; Germain Colon.
Res.: P.O. Box 435, 00676. Tel: 787-877-2765; Fax: 787-877-7795. Web: www.iglesiamonserrate.com.
School—Colegio Ntra. Sra. de La Monserrate Carmen O. Soto, Prin.; Hebe Mabel Saavedra, Librarian. Students 163.
Catechesis/Religious Program—Carmen A. Lorenzo, D.R.E. Students 1,257.
Mission—San Judas Tadeo Bo. Plata.
Mission—Espiritu Santo Bo. Voladoras Lomas.
Mission—Sagrada Familia Bo. Voladoras Parcelas.
Mission—Sagrado Corazon de Jesus Bo. Naranjo.
Mission—Santos Guillermo Abad y San Mateo Bo. Cuchillas La Salle.
Mission—Inmaculado Corazon de Maria Bo. Chucillas Sabana.
Mission—Virgen del Perpetuo Socorro Bo. Limon.
Mission—Cristo Rey Bo. Cuchillas Loperena.
Mission—Virgen de la Monserrate Bo. Cuchillas Cordero.
Mission—Virgen de La Providencia Bo. Rocha Magueyes.
Mission—San Pedro Apostol Bo. Rocha Sec. Lassalle.
Mission—Virgen del Rosario Bo. Capa Barreto.
Mission—Corpus Christi Bo. Capa Bosque.
Mission—El Buen Pastor Bo. Cerro Gordo.
Mission—San Martin de Porres Bo. Aceituna.

Rincon, St. Rose of Lima (1789) Revs. Delroy Thomas Scott, Admin.; Angel Roman Ramos; Deacons Heriberto Santana; Gilberto Medina Agron.
Res.: Box 128, 00677. Tel: 787-823-2650; Fax: 787-823-4400.
Catechesis/Religious Program—Students 600.
Mission—Santa Rosa Bo. Calvache.
Mission—El Cristo de la Reconciliacion Bo. Atalaya.
Mission—La Milagrosa Bo. Corcega.
Mission—La Virgin de Guadalupe Bo. Rio Grande.
Mission—Sagrado Corazon de Jesus Bo. Cruces.
Mission—Nuestra Senora del Carmen Bo. Puntas.
Mission—San Jose Bo. Jaguey.

Rosario, Our Lady of Rosary (1831) Rev. Angel Valle Nieves.
Res.: 348 St., 7.5 Kilometer, Box 692, 00636. Tel: 787-831-7232.
Mission—Nuestra Senora del Rosario
Mission—La Milagrosa Bo. Rosario Alto.
Mission—La Monseirate Bo. Rosario Penon, 00680.
Catechesis/Religious Program—Students 628.

Sabana Grande, Church of San Isidro (1813) Revs. Jorge L. Caro Morales; Edgardo Acosta Ocasro; Angel Mendez Mendez; Deacon Roberto De Jesus.
Res.: Box 817, 00637. Tel: 787-873-4475; Fax: 787-804-0327.
Catechesis/Religious Program—Students 889.
Convent—Tel: 787-873-2750. Sr. Maria Concepcion, O.P., Supr. Sisters 4.
Mission—Cristo Rey Carr.368 R.367 KM.2.0, El Papayo, 00637.
Mission—La Resurreccion Carr.121 Calle Azucena, Susua, 00637.
Mission—Sagrado Corazon de Jesus Calle Rable #44-Carr.121 K. 5.0, Bo. Maginas, 00637.
Mission—San Jose Carr.121 Km. 4.1, Bo. La Pica, 00637.
Mission—San Francisco de Asis Carr.369 Km.1.4, Bo. Cerro Gordo, 00637.
Mission—Ntra. Sra. de Monserrate Carr.2 R.365 Km.2.8 Int., Bo. Molinas, 00637.
Mission—Ntra. Sra. de Fatima Carr.328 Km.3.6, Bo. Guaras, 00637.
Mission—Santa Catalina de Siena Carr.388 Km.5.9 Int., Bo. La Torre, 00637.
Mission—Santa Ana Carr.114 R.363 Km.2.4, Bo.

La Maquina, 00637.
Mission—Ntra. Sra. del Rosario Carr.120 Km.6, Bo. Santana Pichel, 00637.
Mission—La Virgen Milagrosa Carr.364 Km.7 Interior, Bo. El Hoyo, 00637.
Mission—San Judas Tadeo Carr.117 Km.10.7, Bo. Rayo Plata, 00637.
Mission—Divino Nino Jesus Carr. 102 Km 38.1, Int. Bo. Rayo, Sector David Mendez, Sab. Gde, P.R.
Mission—Sta Lucia Carr.120 Km.3.1, Bo. Sta. Ana Moreno, 00637.

SAN GERMAN

1—ST. ROSE OF LIMA (1967) Revs. Urbano Saenz, O.S.A.; Francisco Larran, O.S.A.; Abdon Atienza, O.S.A.
Res.: Box 364, 00683. Tel: 787-892-1276; Fax: 787-892-1276. Email: rosalima@prtc.net. Web: www.mysantarosa.org.
Catechesis/Religious Program—Students 542.
Mission—N. Sra. de la Consolacion Bo. Guama.
Mission—Perpetuo Socorro Bo. Minillas Carretera.
Mission—Santa Rita Bo. Retiro Tea.
Mission—Santa Monica Bo. Minillas Valle.
Mission—St. Martin de Porres Bo. Cain.

2—SAN GERMAN DE AUXERRE Rev. Msgr. Humberto Lopez; Revs. Javier Aquino Florenciani, (Hospital Chap.); Angel L. Soto Barreto.
Mailing Address: Box 305, 00683.
Res.: 2 Jose J. Acosta St., 00683. Tel: 787-892-1027. Web: www.sangermanauxerre.com.
School—Colegio San Jose, Tel: 787-892-1009; Fax: 787-892-2275. Mrs. Glenis Mulet, Prin. Lay Teachers 27; Elementary Students 217; High School Students 111.
Catechesis/Religious Program—Students 425.
Mission—Chapel of St. Augustin Duey.
Mission—Chapel of St. Joseph Hoconuco.
Mission—Gruta de Lourdes Maresua.
Mission—Our Lady of Fatima Cotuy.
Mission—San Judas Tadeo Sabana Eneas.

SAN SEBASTIAN, SAN SEBASTIAN MARTIR (1752) Revs. Angel Antonio Perez, C.P.; Jose Lizarralde, C.P.; Ruben Beaskoa; Deacons Miguel Angel San Martin; Bernardino Medina; Nestor F. Gonzalez.
Res.: P.O. Box 801, 00685. Tel: 787-896-1028.
School—San Sebastian Martir, Tel: 787-896-5728; Fax: 787-280-6521. Nia K. Méndez, Prin. Lay Teachers 30; Elementary Students 224; High School Students 112.
Catechesis/Religious Program—Students 1,010.
Mission—Cristo Rey Bo. Perchas I.
Mission—La Pasion del Señor Bo. Perchas II.
Mission—San Gabriel de la Dolorosa Bo. Calabazas.
Mission—La Immaculada Concepcion Bo. La Lechuza.
Mission—Santa Teresita del Nino Jesus Bo. Juncal.
Mission—Ntra. Sra. del Carmen Bo. Aibonito Guerrero.
Mission—San Judas Tadeo Bo. Saltos.
Mission—San Patricio Bo. Hato Arriba.
Mission—San Pablo de la Cruz Bo. Hato Arriba (Parcelas).
Mission—Ntra. Sra. de Fatima Bo. Altozano.
Mission—Sagrado Corazon de Jesus Bo. Robles.
Mission—San Jose Obrero Bo. Hoyamala.
Mission—Santa Cruz Bo. Parcelas Guacio (Parcelas).
Mission—Espiritu Santo Bo. Culebrinas.
Mission—Cristo Resucitado Bo. Sonador.
Mission—Ntra. Senora de la Providencia Bo. Eneas.
Mission—Sagrada Familia Bo. Pozas.

On Special Assignment:
Rev.—
Diaz, Gonzalo, Chancellor & Vicar Gen., Box 24, Hormingueros.

INSTITUTIONS LOCATED IN THE DIOCESE

[A] COLLEGES AND UNIVERSITIES

ANASCO. *De La Salle Catholic College*, Apartado 61, 00610. Tel: 787-826-6071; Fax: 787-826-5185. Rene Hernandez Perez, Contact Person.

AQUADILLA. *Corpus Christi College*, Apartado 4021, 00605-4021. Tel: 787-882-8433; Fax: 787-891-4555. Email: colegiocorpuschristi@yahoo.com. Rev. Ramon E. Albino.

MOCA. *Nuestra Senora de la Monserrate College*, Apartado 435, 00676. Tel: 787-877-2765; Fax: 787-877-7795. Hilda Perez, Prin.

[B] HOSPITALS

SAN GERMAN. *Hospital of the Immaculate Conception*, Box 285, 00683. Tel: 787-892-1860; Fax: 787-264-7908. Web: www.hospconcepcion.org. Sr. Juanita Flores, H.C.; Rev. Angel Leonides Soto, Chap. Sisters of Charity. Sisters 7; Bed Capacity 167; Total Staff 735; Patients Assisted Annually (Admissions) 9,043; Emergency Visits 39,771.

[C] INSTITUTIONS

MAYAGUEZ. *Asylum for the Poor and Aged*, Calle Ramon E. Betances 162 Sur., 00680. Sisters of Charity (Spanish). Sisters 4; Bed Capacity 68; Residents 68.

Comunidad Belen, c/o P.O. Box 2272, 00681. Rev. P. Carlos Gonzalez, Contact Person.

Convent of the Servants of Mary, Hostos Ave., 401, 00680. Tel: 787-832-0391; Fax: 787-805-6160. Sr. Aurea Fernandez Fontan, Supr. Sisters care for the sick in their homes and hospital. Sisters 13.

HORMIGUEROS. *Residence for the Aged, San Jose*, Valle Hermoso, 00660. Tel: 787-832-4243; Fax: 787-833-4529. Sr. Hilda M. Rodriquez, Supr. Sisters 13; Residents 145.

[D] PERSONAL PRELATURES

MAYAGUEZ. *Opus Dei (Prelature of the Holy Cross and Opus Dei)*, 69 Orquideas St., Ensanche Martinez, 00680. Tel: 787-833-6461. Rev. Andres Eiroa.

RELIGIOUS INSTITUTES OF MEN REPRESENTED IN THE DIOCESE

For further details refer to the corresponding bracketed number in the Religious Institutes of Men or Women section.

[]—*Acies Christi* (Spain)
[0140]—*Augustinians*—O.S.A.
[0200]—*Benedictine Monks* Spain—O.S.B.
[0270]—*Carmelite Fathers and Brothers* (Spain)—O.Carm.
[1330]—*Congregation of the Mission* (Vice Province of Puerto Rico)—C.M.
[1000]—*Congregation of the Passion*—C.P.
[]—*Salesian Fathers*

RELIGIOUS INSTITUTES OF WOMEN REPRESENTED IN THE DIOCESE

[]—*Acies Christi* (Spain)
[]—*Carmelitas de Clausura* (Spain)
[]—*Hermanas de la Caridad*
[]—*Hermanas Salesianas* (Spain)
[]—*Hermanas Teatinas* (Spain)
[2340]—*Little Sisters of the Poor*—L.S.P.
[2790]—*Missionary Servants of the Most Blessed Trinity*—M.S.B.T.
[]—*Monasterio Santa Maria del Monte Carmelo*
[3580]—*Servants of Mary* (Spain)—O.S.M.
[0650]—*Sisters of Charity of St. Vincent de Paul* (Spanish)—S.C.
[]—*Sisters of Fatima* (Puerto Rico)
[]—*Sisters of Schoenstatt* (Germany)
[]—*Sisters of St. Joseph* (Brooklyn)

NECROLOGY

(No Deaths)

An asterisk (*) denotes an organization that has established tax-exempt status directly with the IRS and is not covered by the USCCB Group Ruling.

Diocese of Ponce, Puerto Rico

(Dioecesis Poncensis)

Most Reverend

FELIX LAZARO, SCH.P.

Bishop of Ponce; ordained April 9, 1961; appointed Coadjutor Bishop of Ponce March 20, 2002; consecrated April 25, 2002; appointed Bishop of Ponce June 11, 2003. *Res.: Bishop's House, P.O. Box 32205, Ponce, PR 00732-2205.* Tel: 787-848-5265; Fax: 787-841-1778.

Most Reverend

FREMIOT TORRES OLIVER, D.D.

Bishop Emeritus of Ponce; ordained April 10, 1950; appointed Bishop November 4, 1964; consecrated December 21, 1964; retired November 10, 2000. *Res.: C. Marques de Mondejar 24, 3B, Madrid 28028 Spain* Web: www.pucpr.edu. Email: jespona@telefonica.net.

ESTABLISHED NOVEMBER 21, 1924.

Square Miles 830.

Comprises the south portion of the Island of Puerto Rico and is in the Ecclesiastical Province of Puerto Rico.

Email: obispadoponce@direcway.com

flazaro@direcway.com

STATISTICAL OVERVIEW

Personnel	
Bishop	1
Retired Bishops	1
Priests: Diocesan Active in Diocese	51
Priests: Diocesan Active Outside Diocese	1
Priests: Diocesan in Foreign Missions	15
Priests: Retired, Sick or Absent	11
Number of Diocesan Priests	78
Religious Priests in Diocese	50
Total Priests in Diocese	128
Ordinations:	
Transitional Deacons	1
Permanent Deacons in Diocese	82
Total Brothers	7
Total Sisters	181
Parishes	
Parishes	43
With Resident Pastor:	
Resident Diocesan Priests	29
Resident Religious Priests	14
Pastoral Centers	186
Closed Parishes	2
Professional Ministry Personnel:	
Brothers	7
Sisters	181
Lay Ministers	1,154
Welfare	
Health Care Centers	7
Total Assisted	336,690
Homes for the Aged	2
Total Assisted	171
Residential Care of Children	1
Total Assisted	22
Day Care Centers	2
Total Assisted	10,052
Specialized Homes	10
Total Assisted	325,117
Special Centers for Social Services	4
Total Assisted	52,823
Educational	
Seminaries, Diocesan	1
Students from This Diocese	10
Students from Other Diocese	12
Diocesan Students in Other Seminaries	1
Seminaries, Religious	2
Students Religious	9
Total Seminarians	20
Colleges and Universities	1
Total Students	9,679
High Schools, Diocesan and Parish	12
Total Students	1,558
High Schools, Private	5
Total Students	806
Elementary Schools, Diocesan and Parish	17
Total Students	5,046
Elementary Schools, Private	4
Total Students	1,762
Catechesis/Religious Education:	
High School Students	2,469
Elementary Students	7,606
Total Students under Catholic Instruction	28,946
Teachers in the Diocese:	
Priests	18
Brothers	3
Sisters	16
Lay Teachers	946
Vital Statistics	
Receptions into the Church:	
Infant Baptism Totals	3,126
Minor Baptism Totals	1,836
Adult Baptism Totals	515
Received into Full Communion	5,477
First Communions	4,190
Confirmations	3,997
Marriages:	
Catholic	681
Interfaith	26
Total Marriages	707
Total Catholic Population	445,053
Total Population	593,388

Former Bishops—Most Revs. EDWIN V. BYRNE, D.D., cons. in Philadelphia, Nov. 30, 1925; transferred to San Juan, PR; promoted to Archbishop of Santa Fe, NM, June 15, 1943; died July 25, 1963; ALOYSIUS J. WILLINGER, C.Ss.R., D.D., ord. July 2, 1911; appt. Bishop of Ponce March 8, 1929; cons. Oct. 28, 1929; appt. Titular Bishop of Bida and Coadjuctor of Monterey-Fresno (cum jure successionis), Dec. 12, 1946; installed Bishop of Monterey-Fresno, Jan. 3, 1953; resigned Oct. 25, 1967; died July 25, 1973; JAMES E. MCMANUS, C.Ss.R., D.D., J.C.D., transferred to the Archdiocese of New York, Nov. 18, 1963; died July 1, 1976; His Eminence LUIS CARDINAL APONTE MARTINEZ, D.D., ord. April 10, 1950; appt. Titular Bishop of Lares and Auxiliary of Ponce, July 23, 1960; cons. Oct. 12, 1960; appt. Coadjuctor Bishop of Ponce, April 16, 1963; appt. Bishop of Ponce, Nov. 18, 1963; installed Feb. 20, 1964; promoted to Archbishop of San Juan, Nov. 4, 1964; installed Jan. 15, 1965; created Cardinal, March 5, 1973; resigned May 8, 1999; Most Revs. FREMIOT TORRES OLIVER, D.D., ord. April 10, 1950; appt. Bishop Nov. 4, 1964; cons. Dec. 21, 1964; retired Nov. 10, 2000; RICARDO SURINACH CARRERAS, D.D., ord. April 13, 1957; appt. Auxiliary Bishop of Ponce May 26, 1975; cons. July 25, 1975; appt. Bishop of Ponce Nov. 10, 2000; installed Nov. 30, 2000; retired June 11, 2003; died Jan. 19, 2005.

Vicar General—Rev. Msgr. ROBERTO GARCIA BLAY.

Pro-Vicar General—VACANT.

Chancellor—Rev. Msgr. HERMINIO DE JESUS.

Episcopal Vicar for Diocesan Administration—Rev. Msgr. ROBERTO GARCIA BLAY.

Episcopal Vicar for Pastoral Coordination—Rev. Msgr. JUAN RODRIGUEZ ORENGO.

Episcopal Vicar for Religious—Rev. MARIO MASTRANGELO, O.F.M.Cap.

Episcopal Vicar for Education—VACANT.

Episcopal Vicar for Sick—Rev. DARIO H. ARBOLEDA, O.SS.T.

Tribunal Interdiocesano de Puerto Rico—Calle Isabel No. 31, P.O. Box 32229, Ponce, 00732-2229. Tel: 787-843-4630; Fax: 787-841-7483. First instance for the Dioceses of Mayaguez and Ponce. Second Instance for the Archdiocese of San Juan.

Judicial Vicar—Rev. Msgr. ELIAS S. MORALES.

Associate Judicial Vicars—Rev. MANUEL SANTIAGO.

Moderator—Most Rev. FELIX LAZARO, Sch.P.

Judge—Mayaguez: Rev. Msgr. GONZALO DIAZ.

Diocesan Consultors—Rev. Msgrs. ROBERTO GARCIA BLAY; HERMINIO DE JESUS; MARCOS A. PANCORBO; JESÚS R. DIEZ ANTOÑANZAS; ELIAS S. MORALES; JOSE LOZANO; JUAN RODRIGUEZ ORENGO.

Diocesan Board of Administration—Rev. Msgrs. ROBERTO GARCIA BLAY; MARCOS A. PANCORBO; Deacon ALBERTO CASTRO; Mr. SANTIAGO RAMOS; Mr. JAIME SANTIAGO CANET; FELIX NEGRON MARTINEZ.

Parish Priests Consultors—Rev. Msgr. MARCOS A. PANCORBO; Rev. JOSE DIEGO RODRIGUEZ; Rev. Msgrs. JUAN RODRIGUEZ ORENGO; JOSE LOZANO.

Notaries—Mrs. LUZ DELIA MEDINA; Miss NANCY MENDEZ GARCIA.

Censores Librorum—Rev. ADALIN RIVERA.

Administrator—Rev. Msgr. ROBERTO GARCIA BLAY.

Diocesan Offices and Directors

Catechesis—Sr. LETICIA MARTINEZ, O.P.

Catholic Youth Organization—Rev. MANUEL SANTIAGO HERNANDEZ.

Children of Mary—Rev. Msgr. JUAN RODRIGUEZ ORENGO.

Committee for Community Planning—Rev. Msgr. ROBERTO GARCIA BLAY.

Communications—Sr. Socorro Bonillà, O.P., Mailing Address: P.O. Box 330986, Ponce, 00733-0986. Tel: 787-843-1548.

Cursillos de Cristiandad—Revs. Gerardo Ramirez, 4072 Ave. Tito Castro, Ste. 201, Ponce, 00716-4702; Samuel Santiago, Parroquia Santa Maria Reina, P.O. Box 32101, Ponce, 00732-2101.

Ecumenism—Rev. Msgr. Juan Rodriguez Orengo, Mailing Address: P.O. Box 32205, Ponce, 00732-2205.

Legion of Mary—Rev. Msgr. Juan Rodriguez Orengo, Mailing Address: P.O. Box 32205, Ponce, 00732-2205.

Liturgical Commission—Most Rev. Felix Lazaro Martinez, Sch.P., Mailing Address: P.O. Box 32205, Ponce, 00732-2205.

Sacred Music Commission—Rev. Msgr. Abel A. DiMarco.

St. Vincent de Paul Conferences—Mr. Ibrahim Maldonado, Cristo Rey Parish, Urb La Rambla, 2933 Calle Valladolid, Ponce, 00730-4011.

Superintendent of Schools—Mrs. Nancy Ghigliotti, Mailing Address: P.O. Box 32552, Ponce, 00732-2552. Tel: 787-848-4020; Fax: 787-844-5987.

Vigilance for the Faith—Most Rev. Felix Lazaro Martinez, Sch.P.

Vocations—Rev. Msgr. Elias S. Morales, Mailing Address: P.O. Box 32110, Ponce, 00732-2110. Tel: 787-848-4380; Fax: 787-848-4380.

Institute of Family Orientation—Deacon Francisco Lugo, Mailing Address: P.O. Box 32214, Ponce, 00732-2214. Tel: 787-840-6018; Fax: 787-848-4523.

CLERGY, PARISHES, MISSIONS AND PAROCHIAL SCHOOLS

CITY OF PONCE

1—Cathedral of Our Lady of Guadalupe (1692) Rev. Msgr. Marcos A. Pancorbo; Rev. Pedro Alejandro Moscoso Isaza; Deacons Jose Ramon Mercado; Carlos J. Rodriguez.
Res.: 32 Cristina St., Box 32210, 00732-2210. Tel: 787-842-0134; Fax: 787-848-9104.
Chapel—Church of Our Lady of Miraculous Medal P.O. Box 32210, 00732-2210.

2—Christ the King (1964) Rev. Msgr. Juan Rodriguez Orengo; Rev. Omar J. Martinez Medina, O.P.; Deacons Anibal Rosario; Eduardo A. Dosal; Manuel Roman Perez.
Res.: Urb La Rambla, 2933 Calle Valladolid, 00730-4011. Tel: 787-843-3028; Fax: 787-848-1861.
Catechesis/Religious Program—Sr. Socorro Rosario, S.S.N.D., D.R.E. Students 617.
Mission—Santa Teresita Santa Luisa, Ponce Co. 00730.
Mission—Nino Jesus de Praga Bo. Los Claves, Rio Chiquito, Ponce Co.
Mission—La Dolorosa Villa Ponce - Rambla, Calle Castellana Final, Ponce Co. 00730-4011. Tel: 787-840-8380.

3—Church of the Resurrection (1967) Rev. Msgr. Roberto Garcia Blay; Revs. Esteban Santaella; Gerardo Ramirez; Deacons Rafael Castro; Edwin Figueroa.
Glenview Gardens—PMB-98, P.O. Box 2000, Mercedita, 00715. Tel: 787-842-7167; Fax: 787-841-8718.
Mission—Immaculate Heart of Mary Bo. La Yuca, Ponce Co.
Mission—Our Lady of Monserrate Bo. Collado, Ponce Co.
Mission—San Lucas Bo. Las Vallas, Ponce Co.
Mission—Saint Joseph Bo. La Yuca, Ponce Co.
Mission—Our Lady of Carmel Bo. Carmelita, Ponce Co.

4—Church of the Sacred Heart (1969) Rev. Jose M. Galan; Deacon Reinaldo Rivera.
Res.: P.O. Box 577, Mercedita, 00715-0577. Tel: 787-843-4891; Fax: 787-848-9212.
Catechesis/Religious Program—Students 100.

5—Church Santisimo Sacramento (1984) Rev. Roberto Maldonado, L.D.
Res.: Urb. Vistas del Mar, 2238 Calle Marlin, 00716-0834. Tel: 787-843-0245; Fax: 787-284-1032.

6—Good Shepherd Parish (1968) Rev. Winston R. Mendez; Deacons Rafael D. Ruiz; Luis Gonzalez.
Res.: Calle 40-NN25, Jardines del Caribe, 00728-2675. Tel: 787-843-6202; Fax: 787-843-4422. Email: pastorbonus@prw.net. Web: www.elbuenpastorponce.parroquia.org.
Catechesis/Religious Program—Students 89.
Mission—La Milagrosa Calle 5 #69, Bo. Quebrado del Agua, Ponce, Ponce Co. 00731. Tel: 787-843-6202.

7—La Merced (1928) Revs. P. Ramón Conde Ocampo, O.de.M.; Jesus Saez Castrillo, O.de.M., Vicar; Deacons Carlos M. Rodriguez-Guilbe; José D. Ruiz; Victor Fabre.
Res.: 4632 Luna St., 00717-2000. Tel: 787-842-0069; Fax: 787-842-0603.

8—La Milagrosa (1928) Revs. Juan Lamela, C.M.; Manuel Prado, C.M.; Deacons Ramon L. Vazquez; Carlos Burgos.
Res.: Guadalupe No. 2, 00730-3110. Tel: 787-842-3188; Fax: 787-284-1100. Email: parmilagrosa@rsisp.net.
School—Tel: 787-842-6349; Fax: 787-284-1100. Liz Marie Santiago, Prin.
Catechesis/Religious Program—Students 500.

9—La Santisima Trinidad (1971) Revs. Javier Elorriaga, O.SS.T.; Guillermo Palacio, O.SS.T., Vicar; Dario H. Arboleda, O.SS.T., Vicar; Deacons Francisco Lugo; Nestor Rentas; Jose Rodriguez.
Las Delicias—Box 8226, 00732. Tel: 787-842-6073; Fax: 787-842-6073.
Catechesis/Religious Program—Students 171.
Mission—San Juan de Mata Box 8226, Bo. Magueyes, Ponce Co. 00732.
Mission—San Andres Bo. Guaragoa, Ponce Co. 00732.
Mission—Santa Ana Bo. Guaragoa, Arriba, Ponce Co. 00732.
Mission—N.S. Fatima Bo. Marueno, Arriba, Ponce Co. 00732.
Mission—San Antonio de Padua Parcelas de Marueno, Ponce Co. 00732.
Mission—N.S. del Rosario Bo. Madrigal, Ponce Co. 00732.
Mission—Inmaculada Bo. Pastillo, Ponce Co. 00732.
Mission—Cristo Rey Bo. Corral Viejo, Ponce Co. 00732.
Mission—San Miguel de los Santos Las Delicias 11, Ponce Co. 00732.
Mission—Resurreccion Bo. Santas Pascuas, Ponce Co. 00732.

10—Our Lady of Mt. Carmel (1883) Revs. Miguel Alvarez, Sch.P.; Augustin Lopez, Sch.P.; Francisco Aisa, Sch.P.; Deacon Jose Rivera Saez.
Res.: P.O. Box 7760, 00732-7760. Tel: 787-842-1333; Fax: 787-841-6861.
School—Tel: 787-842-5018; Fax: 787-842-5018. Mrs. Paquita Alvarado, Prin.
Mission—San Martin de Porres Constancia Ave., Villa del Carmen, Ponce Co. 00734. Tel: 787-848-4355.
Mission—Santa Marta c/o Santa Marta #8, Bo. Salistral, Ponce Co. 00732.

11—Our Lady of Mt. Carmel (1973) Rev. Jose Antonio Lopez Vega; Rev. Msgr. Jesùs R. Diez Antoñanzas, Vicar; Deacon Juan Altori Vargas.
Res.: P.O. Box 800187, Coto Laurel, 00780. Tel: 787-848-2030.
Mission—Santa Maria Virgen Bo. Hoyos, Ponce Co. 00780.
Mission—Sagrado Corazon de Jesus Carr. 511 K. 15, Bo. Las Raices, Ponce Co. 00780.
Mission—San Mateo Bo. Real Anon Abajo, Ponce Co. 00780.
Mission—San Martin de Porres Bo. Real Anon Arriba, Ponce Co. 00780.

12—San Conrado (1948) Rev. Jose R. Alvarado de Jesus; Deacons Emerito Lopez Cosme; Joseph Burgos.
Res.: Box 7362, 00732. Tel: 787-843-0560; Fax: 787-843-0600. Email: psconrado@prw.net. Web: psconrado.web.prw.net.
School—P.O. Box 7111, 00732. Tel: 787-843-1405; 787-842-2293; Fax: 787-841-7303. Email: sanconrado@coqui.net. Sr. Nildred Rodriguez, C.S.J., Prin.
Catechesis/Religious Program—Students 712.

13—San Jose (1965) Revs. Orlando Ramos, O.C.D.; Jacinto Rosario, O.C.D.; Mariano Fraile, O.C.D.; Alexio Jose de Armas, O.C.D.; Deacons Benjamin Pagan Diaz; Edgardo Muniz; Arnaldo Gierbolini.
Res.: Urb. San Jose, 416 Calle Beato Francisco Palau, Box 8414, 00728-1905. Tel: 787-843-3910; Fax: 787-843-1994. Email: carmelitasponce@yahoo.com.

14—San Jose Obrero (1979) Rev. Manuel Santiago; Deacon Vicente Aponte Arroyo.
Res.: *Parcelas El Tuque*, Calle Ramos Antonini #632, P.O. Box 8027, 00732-8027. Tel: 787-843-9072; Fax: 787-290-5339. Email: psjoseobrero@yahoo.com.
Mission—Ntra. Sra. del Pilar 616 M #7, Punto Oro, Ponce Co. 00728.
Mission—Cristo de la Misericordia Nueva Vida Calle J D-9.
Mission—Inmaculado Corazon de Maria Calle Lorencita Ferre, Brisas del Caribe.
Mission—Natra. Sra. de la Medalla Milagrosa Punta Diamante. (Encargada - Sor Deborah, O.P.)

15—San Vicente-Cantera (1964) Revs. Osner Domond, C.M., Admin.; Francisco Javier Ramirez, C.M., Vicar; Jean Claude Jean Philippe, C.M., Vicar; Deacons Jorge Almodovar Capielo; Hector Luis Santiago.
Res.: Paseo La Cantera No. 67, 00730-3026. Tel: 787-843-1976; Fax: 787-812-0212. Email: poncecm@hotmail.com.
Catechesis/Religious Program—Students 100.
Mission—San Vicente Rio Chiquito, Ponce Co.
Mission—Santos Reyes Bo. La Mocha, Ponce Co.
Mission—Santa Luisa Bo. Nuevo Mameyes, Ponce Co.
Mission—La Inmaculada Sector San Patricio, Ponce Co.

16—Santa Maria Reina (1952) Rev. Samuel Santiago; Deacon David Ramos.
Res.: P.O. Box 32101, 00732-2101. Tel: 787-848-5370; 787-848-3313; Fax: 787-290-4189.
School—Tel: 787-842-1164; Fax: 787-843-6755 (Elem.); 787-290-3711 (H.S.). Lydia Otero, Prin., Elem.; Carmen Ojeda, Prin., H.S.

17—Santa Teresita (1930) Bro. Luis Anibal Rosario, O.F.M.Cap.; Rev. Mario Mastrangelo, O.F.M.Cap., Vicar; Bro. Alberto A. Figueroa, O.F.M.Cap., Vicar; Deacons Casildo Rodriguez; Ildefonso Gonzalez Plaza; Luis A. Lopez Quirindongo.
Res.: 342 Victoria St., Box 7244, 00732. Tel: 787-842-3137; 787-842-5055 (Friary); Fax: 787-844-7267.
School—342 Victoria St., 00732. Tel: 787-842-4110; Fax: 787-842-4300. Helen Pérez, Prin.

18—Santuario San Judas Tadeo (1964) Revs. Angel Cuadrado, O.de.M.; Antonio Garcia, O.de.M.; Vicente Salas Avello, O.de.M.
Res.: Constancia 2518, Urb Constancia P.O. Box 7046, 00732-7046. Tel: 787-843-0572; Fax: 787-842-0148.
School—San Judas Tadeo, Tel: 787-844-2610; Fax: 787-843-3802. Nancy Arroyo, Prin.; Rev. Ramon Conde, Dir.
Catechesis/Religious Program—Urb. Constancia Calle Coloso 2929. Students 620.

Parishes in Formation

1—Church San Patricio, Closed. Now a Mission of Our Lady of Monserrate.

OUTSIDE THE CITY OF PONCE

Adjuntas, Adjuntas Co., St. Joachim (1815) Revs. Carlos Reynoso Valdez, O.R.C.; Rosalino Aguirre, O.R.C.; Deacons Samuel Sepulveda; Radames Marcucci.
Res.: 14 Rius Rivera St., 00601. Tel: 787-829-3145.
School—San Joaquin Elementary and Intermediate, 12 Primo Delgado St., 00601. Tel: 787-829-3040; Fax: 787-829-3040. Mrs. Carmen Zelideth Ortiz Reyes, Prin.
Catechesis/Religious Program—Students 144.
Mission—San Francisco Garzas, Adjuntas Co.
Mission—Sta. Ana Vegas Arriba, Adjuntas Co.
Mission—Santa Teresita Tres de Jayuya, Adjuntas Co.
Mission—Santa Rosa Pellejas, Adjuntas Co.
Mission—Virgen del Carmen Yahuecas, Adjuntas Co.
Mission—Sagrado Corazon Tanama, Adjuntas Co.
Mission—San Antonio Guilarte, Adjuntas Co.
Mission—La Milagrosa Vegas Abajo, Adjuntas Co.
Mission—Ntra Sra Fátima Juan González formerly Inm. Corazon de Maria Limani, Adjuntas Co.

Aguirre, Salinas Co., Sacred Heart (1946) Revs. Pedro Faustino Echeverria; Benjamin Lopez.
Res.: Box 260, 00704-0260. Tel: 787-853-3620; Fax: 787-853-2131.
School—Perpetuo Socorro, Street 3 Km 151, 00704-2499. Tel: 787-853-2270. Sr. Aurea E. Fuentes, R.A., Prin. Students 426.
Mission—St. Judas Las Mareas, Salinas Co.
Mission—Our Lady of Perpetual Help Coqui, Salinas Co.
Mission—St. Martin de Porres San Felipe, Salinas Co.
Mission—La Milagrosa, Salinas Co.

Arroyo, Arroyo Co., Our Lady of Mt. Carmel (1855) Revs. Juan Jose Saliva Gonzalez; Alonso Escobar Giraldo; Deacons Jacinto Rodriguez; Esteban Rivera.
Res.: General Brooke No. 18, Box 388, 00714. Tel: 787-839-3465; Fax: 787-839-1552. Email: parroquia_carmen@hotmail.com. Web: www.yaucoweb.com/parroquiadelcarmen.
Mission—Ntra Sra. del Carmen Bo. Pitahaya Carr. 3 K.43.
Mission—La Milagrosa Carr. 3 Bda. Marin, Arroyo Co.
Mission—San Jose Sector Palmarejo - Carr 3 K 6 H 3.
Mission—Ntra Sra. de Fatima Bo. Palmas Parcela 526, Arroyo Co.
Mission—San Martin Sector Santa Clara Carr. 3, Arroyo Co.

CASTAÑER, LARES CO., OUR LADY OF THE MIRACULOUS MEDAL (1969) Rev. Rosalino Aguirre Bahena, O.R.C.; Deacons Wilfredo Torres Maldonado; William Ramos.
Res.: Box 1006, Castaner, 00631. Tel: 787-829-6389.
Catechesis/Religious Program—Tel: 787-829-6389.
Chapel—La Milagrosa Chapel Bartolo, Rio Grande Co. 00669.
Chapel—La Milagrosa Chapel Bo. Mirasol, Lares Co. 00669.
Chapel—La Milagrosa Chapel Bo. Rio Prieto, Lares Co. 00669.

COAMO, COAMO CO.

1—ST. BLASE (1616) Revs. Jose Diego Rodriguez; Vicente Perez Roig; Cristobal Reilly, S.T.; Deacons Angel A. Negron; Orlando Martinez; Jaime Ortiz; Alfredo Rivera Cardona.
Res.: Box 196, 00769. Tel: 787-825-1122; Fax: 787-825-7006. Email: psblas@hotmail.com.
School—Ntra. Sra. de Valvanera, Box 1903, 00769. Tel: 787-825-1145; Fax: 787-825-1145. Ada Pedrogo, Prin.
Mission—Immaculate Heart of Mary Palmarejo, Coamo Co. 00769.
Mission—Christ the King Pulguillas, Coamo Co. 00769.
Mission—Our Lady of Mt. Carmel Hayales, Coamo Co. 00769.
Mission—Miraculous Virgin Descalabrado, Coamo Co. 00769.
Mission—Sacred Heart Santa Catalina, Coama Co. 00769.
Mission—Saint James Cilantro, Coamo Co. 00769. Fax: 787-825-1122.
Mission—Miraculous Virgin Pedro Garcia, Coamo Co. 00769.
Mission—Santa Ana Santa Ana, Coamo Co. 00769.
Mission—San Diego San Diego, Coamo Co. 00769.
Mission—Holy Family Emanueli, Coamo Co. 00769.
Mission—Our Lady of Providence Melendez, Coamo Co. 00769. Fax: 787-825-1122.
Mission—Our Lady of Fatima Bo. Cuyon.
Mission—Sacred Heart of Jesus Coamo Arriba.

2—SAN ANTONIO DE PADUA (2002) Rev. Emiliano Alamo; Deacon Pedro Garcia.
Res.: 545. Km2, Hec 2 Barrio Los Llanos, P.O. Box 2227, 00769. Tel: 787-803-4801.
Catechesis/Religious Program—Students 93.
Mission—San Martin Las Flores, Coamo, Coamo Co. 00769.
Mission—Our Lady of Lourdes Rio Jueyes, Coamo, Coamo Co. 00769.

ENSENADA, GUANICA CO., SACRED HEART (1963) Rev. Jery Rivera Martinez; Deacon Wallis S. Sanchez.
Res.: Box 179, 00647. Tel: 787-821-2857.
Mission—Divina Providencia Salinas-Providencia, Guanica Co.
Mission—Monserrate Bo. Fuig., Guanica Co.
Mission—Virgen del Rosario Bo. Guaypao, Guanica Co.

GUANICA, GUANICA CO., ST. ANTHONY ABBOT (1888) Rev. Jose Carlos Vargas; Deacon Reinaldo Galarza.
Res.: Box 804, 00653. Tel: 787-821-2147; Fax: 787-821-8896.
School—Blessed Imelda, Dr. Veve Str. 26, 00653. Tel: 787-821-2714; Fax: 787-821-2714. Students 117.
Mission—Cristo Rey Bo. Belgica, Guanica Co.
Mission—N. Sra. Rosario Bo. Santa Juanita, Guanica Co.
Mission—San Judas Bo. La Laguna, Guanica Co.
Mission—N. Sra Fatima Bo. La Luna, Guanica Co.
Mission—La Providencia Bda. Esperanza, Guanica Co.

GUAYAMA, GUAYAMA CO., ST. ANTHONY OF PADUA (1736) Revs. José J. Rached, C.Ss.R.; Terry Tull, C.Ss.R.; Henry Beauchamp, C.Ss.R.; Deacons Genaro Rivera Alicea; Francisco Carrasquillo; Juan B. Garcia.
Res.: Box 2820, 00785. Tel: 787-864-4100; Fax: 787-864-5494.
School—St. Anthony, Box 777, 00785. Tel: 787-864-2062; Fax: 787-864-1450. Wanda Pomales, Prin.
Catechesis/Religious Program—Evelyn Diaz, D.R.E. Students 437.
Mission—Our Lady of Perpetual Help Caimital, Guayama Co.
Mission—San José Obrero Branderi - Guayama, Puerto Rico.
Mission—St. Gerard Palmas, Guayama Co.
Mission—Our Lady of Mt. Carmel Pueblito del Carmen, PR.
Mission—Cristo Rey Bo. Olimpo, Guayama Co.
Mission—La Candelaria Bo. Corazon, Guayama Co.
Mission—Sgdo. Corazon Bo. Guamani, Guayama Co.
Mission—San Martin Bo. Carite, Guayama Co.

GUAYANILLA, GUAYANILLA CO., IMMACULATE CONCEPTION (1841) Revs. Raymond L. Rivera; Carlos Manuel Grullon; Deacon Miguel Sepuelveda.
Res.: P.O. Box 560573, 00656-0573. Tel: 787-835-3035; Fax: 787-835-3082. Email: inmaculada@caribe.net.
School—Immaculate Conception, P.O. Box 560573, 00656-0573. Tel: 787-835-2230. Email: info@inmaculadapr.org. Web: inmaculadapr.org. Rafael Ortiz Rodriguez, Prin.
Catechesis/Religious Program—Tel: 787-835-2230. Students 212.
Mission—Our Lady of Mt. Carmel Barrio Sierra Baja, Guayanilla Co.
Mission—Perpetuo Socorro Magas Arriba, Guayanilla Co.
Mission—San Francisco de Asis Quebradas, Guayanilla Co.
Mission—San Juan Bosco Barrio Indios, Guayanilla Co.
Mission—La Monserrate Consejo Alto, Guayanilla Co.
Mission—Virgen de Fatima Macana Rio, Guayanilla Co.
Mission—Nuestra Senora La Milagrosa Quebrada Honda, Guayanilla Co.
Mission—San Martin de Porres Macana Parcelas, Guayanilla Co.

JAYUYA, JAYUYA CO., OUR LADY OF MONSERRATE (1883) Revs. Oran de Jesus Ramirez; Jaime Rojas; Hector Zayas (ARE) (Retired); Deacons Luis Rosario; Carlos Orama; Jose A. Perez Santos.
Res.: Calle Figueras 13, 00664. Tel: 787-828-6350; Fax: 787-828-5062. Web: www.monserratejayuya.com.
Mission—Ntra Sra del Carmen Bo. Santa Clara - Jayuya, Puerto Rico.
Mission—Bo. Veguita Fama Puerto Rico.
Mission—Divino Niño Jesús Bo. Salientito - Jayuya, Puerto Rico.
Mission—Cristo Rey Bo. Collores - Jayuya.
Mission—San Jorge Bo. Coabey - Jayuya, Jayuya Co. 00664.
Mission—La Milagrosa Bo. Canalizo - Jayuya, Jayuya Co. 00664.
Mission—Buen Pastor Bo. Gripinas - Jayuya, Jayuya Co. 00664.
Mission—Santa Cecila Bo. Zama - Jayuya, Jayuya Co. 00664.
Mission—Ntra Sra de la Divina Providencia Bo. Hoyo Planes - Jayuya, Jayuya Co. 00664.
Mission—S. Antonio Bo. Mameyes - Jayuya, Jayuya Co. 00664.
Mission—Santos Reyes Bo. El Salto - Jayuya.
Mission—San Francisco Bo. Saliente - Jayuya, Jayuya Co. 00664.
Mission—San Juan Evangelista Bo. Puerto Plata - Jayuya.
Mission—San Patricio Bo. La Pica - Jayuya, San Patricio Co. 00664.
Mission—San Jose de la Montaña Bo. Hogares Seguros - Jayuya, San Antonio Co. 00664.
Mission—San Patricio La Pica Cr. Buzon 234-B, Ponce Co. 00730.

JUANA DIAZ, JUANA DIAZ CO.

1—NUESTRA SENORA DE LOURDES (Aguilita) (1984) Deacons Cirilo Carmona; Jaime Velez; Fernando Perez De La Cruz; Marcelino Lebron Romero.
Res.: P.O. Box 1824, 00795. Tel: 787-837-1097.
Mission—Virgen del Carmen Bo. Tiburones, Juana Diaz Co. 00795.
Mission—Sagrado Corazon Bo. Buyones, Juana Diaz Co. 00795.
Mission—San Pedro Nolasco Bo. La Cuarta, 00795.

2—ST. RAYMOND NONATO (1798) Rev. Msgr. Jose Lozano; Rev. Santiago Solla; Rev. Msgr. Andres Guerrero; Deacons Narciso Ortiz Negron; Norberto Santiago; William Santiago Figueroa.
Res.: Munoz Rivera 48, Box 1426, 00795. Tel: 787-837-2390; Fax: 787-837-2390. Email: parroco@juanadiaz.org. Web: www.juanadiaz.org/parroquia.
Mission—San Judas Rio Canas Abajo, Juana Diaz Co.
Mission—N.S. de Fatima Bo. Jacaquas, Juana Diaz Co.
Mission—La Milagrosa Bo. Jacaguas. Collores, Juana Diaz Co.
Mission—Santiago, Ap. Las Margaritas, Bo. Collores, Bo. Collores Arriba.
Mission—Our Lady of the Rosary Bo. Cayabo, Juana Diaz Co.
Mission—San Ramon Callabo, Bo. Callabo.
Mission—La Merced Bo. Rio Cana Arriba, Juana Diaz Co.

3—SANTA TERESITA DEL NINO JESUS (Arus) (1984) Rev. Orlando Rivera-Soto; Deacon David Rodriguez.
Barrio Arus carr., 1 Km 190 Hm. 7, 00795-1620.
Res.: P.O. Box 1620, 00795-1620. Tel: 787-214-8083.
Mission—San Martin de Porres, (Singapur)
Mission—Ntra Sra de la Monserrate, Juana Diaz Co. (Galicia)
Chapel—Chapel Divine Mercy (Piedra Aguza), Juana Diaz Co.

PATILLAS, PATILLAS CO., INMACULADO CORAZON DE MARIA (1811) Revs. Patricio Gallego Cifuentes; Nicolas Perez, Vicar; Deacons Ruben Pabon; Luis Melendez Ortiz.
Res.: Cristo #1, Box 635, 00723. Tel: 787-839-5333; Fax: 787-839-5525.
Mission—Perpetuo Socorro Bo. Marin Alto, Patillas, Patillas Co.
Mission—Madre Cabrini Bo. Guarderraya, Patillas, Patillas Co.
Mission—Sto. Cristo de Los Milagros Bo. Recio, Patillas, Patillas Co.
Mission—Nuestra Senora del Carmen Bo. Jacaboa, Patillas, Patillas Co.
Mission—Cristo Rey Bo. El Bajo, Patillas, Patillas Co.
Mission—Ntra Sra de la Providencia Bo. Providencia, Patillas, Patillas Co.
Mission—Santa Rosa de Lima Bo. Los Pollos, Patillas, Patillas Co.
Mission—S. Juan Evangelista Bo. Los Barros, Patillas, Patillas Co.
Mission—San Guillermo Bo. El Real, Patillas, Patillas Co.
Mission—Nuestra Senora del Carmen Bo. Jagual, Patillas, Patillas Co.

PENUELAS, PENUELAS CO.

1—ST. JOSEPH (1793) Revs. Octavio Gonzalez, Admin.; Francesco Donnarumma, Vicar; Deacons Carmelo Vazquez; Jose E. Gelpi Ortiz; Glidden R. Perez; Jose Torres Santiago; Joaquin Massoller.
Res.: Dr Loyola #603, P.O. Box 25, 00624. Tel: 787-836-1038; Fax: 787-836-0167.
Catechesis/Religious Program—Students 347.
Mission—La Milagrosa Carr. #132 R 391 K. 5 Sec Pueblito, El Rucio, Penuelas Co. 00624.
Mission—San Antonio de Padua Carr. #132 K-16 H 9, Bo. Pastillo - Penuelas, Penuelas Co. 00624.
Mission—Ntra. Sra. de Fatima Carr. #131 Km 5 Sect, La Vega, Bo. Macana, Penuelas Co. 00624.
Mission—Santa Ana Carr. #132 K 14. 7, Bo. Tallaboa Alta, Penuelas Co. 00624.
Mission—Santa Cruz Carr. #132 Rte. 386 Km 6. H-7, Sector Felipe Quinones Barreal, Penuelas Co. 00624.
Mission—La Milagrosa Carr. #387, Sector la Gelpa - Quebrada Ceiba, Penuelas Co. 00624.
Mission—Ntra Sra del Carmen Carr. #132 K. 7 H. 9, Bo. Santo Domingo, Penuelas Co. 00624.
Mission—San Judas Tadeo Carr. #132, Bo. Coto el Mato, Penuelas Co. 00624.
Mission—San Martin de Porres 996 Com. Caracoles III, Penuelas Co. 00624.
Mission—Divino Nino 363 Bo Tallaboa Alta III, Penuelas Co. 00624.

2—SACRED HEART (Tallaboa) (1928) Rev. Christopher De Herrera, O.S., Penuelas, PR Sacred Heart of Jesus Parish.
Res.: HC 03, P.O. Box 13063, 00624. Tel: 787-836-1164.
Catechesis/Religious Program—Students 63.
Mission—Corazon de Maria Bo. Juncos, PR.

PUENTE JOBOS, GUAYAMA CO., SS. PETER AND PAUL (2003) Rev. Manuel I. Sala.
Mailing Address: P.O. Box 837, Guayama, 00785-0837. Tel: 787-864-2912; 787-864-3301. Email: parroquiapedroypablo@yahoo.es. Web: es.geocities.com/estacionmisionera. 430 Carr. 707 Bo Puente de Jobos, Guayama, 00785-0837.

SALINAS, SALINAS CO., OUR LADY OF MONSERRAT (1854) Revs. Alberto Muniz; Mario Genaro Isla Chavez; Deacon Pablo Miranti.
Res.: Box 1172, 00751. Tel: 787-824-2215.
Mission—San Jose Plena, Salinas Co.
Mission—Santa Ana Coco, Salinas Co.
Mission—Esp. Santo Parcelas Vazquez, Salinas Co.
Mission—Virg. del Carmen Bo. Las Palmas, Salinas Co.
Mission—Santa Marta Naranjo, Salinas Co.
Mission—Inmaculada Concepcion Las Ochenta, Salinas Co.
Mission—Virgen Milagrosa Bo. Playita, Salinas Co.
Mission—Carmen Bo. Playa, Salinas Co.
Mission—Perpetuo Socorro Sabana Llana, Salinas Co.

SANTA ISABEL, SANTA ISABEL CO., ST. JAMES (1854) Revs. Juan Alberto Torres Reyes; Angel Berrios, Vicar; Deacon Jaime Martinez.
Res.: Hostos - #2, Box 137, 00757. Tel: 787-845-2450; Fax: 787-845-2485.
Catechesis/Religious Program—Students 160.
Mission—San Patricio Bo. Playita Cortada - Santa Isabel, PR.

Mission—Virgen del Rosario Bo. Penuelas Santa Isabel.
Mission—Virgen del Perpetuo Socorro
Mission—Ntra. Sra. del Carmen Bo. Playa.
Mission—Virgen de Monserrate Bo. Ollas - Santa Isabel, Santa Isabel Co.
Mission—San Ignacio de Loyola Bo. Jauca - Santa Isabel, Santa Isabel Co.

VILLALBA, VILLALBA CO.

1—OUR LADY MOTHER OF DIVINE PROVIDENCE (Mission Noell) (1962) Rev. P. Eliud Aponte Rivera.
Res.: Bo Cacao Carr. 157, Orocovis, 00720. Tel: 787-867-2052.
Catechesis/Religious Program—
Mission—Our Lady of Mt. Carmel Bo. Alturita Carr 157, Orocovis, Cacao Co.
Mission—Imm. Concepcion Bo. Cacao Carr 157, Orocovis, Cacao Co.
Mission—Nino de Praga Bo. El Frio carra 143, Orocovis, Ala de La Piedra Co.
Mission—Santa Ana Bo. Guineo Carr 143, Orocovis, Ala de La Piedra Co.
Mission—N.S. del Rosario Bo. Bauta Carr 590, Orocovis, Bauta Abajo Co.
Mission—N.S. del Pilar Bo. Damian Abajo Carr 157, Orocovis, Damian Abajo Co.
Mission—N.S. Monserrate Bo. Pozas Carr 615, Orocovis, Damian Abajo Co.
Mission—O.L. of Perp. Help Bo. La Piedra Carr 149, Orocovis, Ala de La Piedra Co.
Mission—Sacred Heart of Jesus Bo. Matrullas Carr 564, Orocovis.
Mission—San Mateo Bo. Ortiga Carr 143, Orocovis, Bauta Abajo Co.

2—OUR LADY OF MT. CARMEL (1917) Revs. Angel Sanchez; Cruz Cruz Ferdinand; Deacons Javier Gonzalez; Ramon A. Resto; Jose A. Pagan.
Res.: Box 432, 00766. Tel: 787-847-0695; Fax: 787-847-8137.
*School—*Box 1033, 00766. Tel: 787-847-2875.
Mission—Sagrado Corazon HC01 Box 5081, Romero, Villalba Co. 00766. Tel: 787-847-1591.
Mission—Jesus Crucificado Bo. Vista Alegre, Villalba Co. 00766.
Mission—Santisima Trinidad Bo. Mogote, Villalba Co. 00766.
Mission—Espiritu Santo Bo. Cerro Gordo, Villalba Co. 00766.
Mission—La Milagrosa, Villalba Co. 00766.
Mission—San Pedro Bo. Corillo, Villalba Co. 00766.
Mission—San Jose Bo. Palmarejo, Villalba Co. 00766.
Mission—Santisimo Sacramento Bo. Higuero, Villalba Co. 00766.
Mission—Jesus Crucificado Bo. Camarones, Villalba Co. 00766.
Mission—Maria Madre de la Iglesia Bo. Canonilla Abajo, Villalba Co. 00766.
Mission—Cristo de la Salud Bo. Sierrita Caonillas, Villalba Co. 00766.
Mission—Madre Cabrini Barrio Jaguey, Villalba Co. 00766.
Mission—Santa Cecilia Barrio Semil, Villalba Co. 00766.
Mission—San Alfonso Barrio Apeadero, Villalba Co. 00766.
Mission—Sagrada Familia Barrio Hatillo, Villalba Co. 00766.
Mission—San Antonio Bo. Camarones-Los Robles, Villalba Co. 00766.
Mission—La Milagrosa Bo. Hatillo Viejo, Villalba Co. 00766.
Mission—La Asuncion Bo. Cuchilla del Limon, Villalba Co. 00766.
Mission—Virgen de la Amargura Bo. Limon, Villalba Co. 00766.
Mission—N.S. del Carmen Bo. Dajas, Villalba Co. 00766.
Mission—San Francisco de Asis Bo. La Sierrita de Vacas, Villalba 00766.
Mission—La Milagrosa Bo. El Pino, Villalba 00766.
Mission—San Juan Evangelista Bo. Chichon, Villalba 00766.

YAUCO, YAUCO CO.

1—HOLY ROSARY (1756) Revs. Juan Burgos Acevedo, O.P.; Victor Perez Aviles, O.P.; Ismael Fernandez, O.P.; Deacon Jesus Vazquez Orengo.
Res.: Box 46, 00698. Tel: 787-856-1222; Fax: 787-856-6845.
*School—*Box 26, 00698. Tel: 787-856-1001; Fax: 787-267-1238. Mrs. Judith Negron, Prin.
*Catechesis/Religious Program—*Tel: 787-856-1573. Students 545.
Convent—Sisters of Fatima for Social Work, Tel: 787-856-1573. Sr. Cecilia Perez Crespo, Supr. Sisters 4.
Mission—Virgin of Mt. Carmel Duey, Yauco Co.
Mission—St. James Barinas, Yauco Co.
Mission—Our Lady of Perpetual Help Cambalaches, Yauco Co.
Mission—Our Lady of Montserrat Carrizales, Hatillo Co.
Mission—St. Lucy Sierra Alta, Yauco Co.
Mission—St. Anthony Naranjo, Yauco Co.
Mission—St. Anthony Diego Hdez, Yauco Co.
Mission—Sacred Heart Quebradas, Yauco Co.
Mission—La Milagrosa formerly St. Martin Mogotes, Puerto Rico.

2—ST. MARTIN DE PORRES (1969) Rev. Segismundo Cintron.
Res.: Las Palomas, Box 2005, 00698. Tel: 787-856-3617.
Convent—Sisters of Fatima-Motherhouse, P.O. Box 62, Santa Rita, 00698. Tel: 787-856-1476; Fax: 787-821-2439. Sr. Celeste Ortiz, O.P., Mother Gen. Sisters 126; Novices 3; Postulants 3.
Mission—Ntra. Sra. de Lourdes Bo. Susua, PR, Guanica Co.
Mission—N.S. de La Providencia Bo. Susa, Guanica Co.
Mission—S. Martin de Porres Bo. Arenas de Guancia, Guanica Co.
Mission—S. Francisco de Asis Bo. Susa, Yauco Co.
Mission—N.S. de La Monserrate Bo. Susa, Yauco Co.

3—SANTO DOMINGO DE GUZMAN (2001) Revs. Melvin Diaz Aponte; Francisco Santiago Torres, Vicar.
Mailing Address: P.O. Box 3036, 00698-3036. Tel: 787-856-8212; Fax: 787-856-8212.
Mission—Sacred Heart Bo. Collores - Yauco, Yauco.
Mission—Sta. Teresita Bo. Las Vegas - Yauco, Yauco.
Mission—St. Joseph Bo. Lluberas Yauco, Yauco.
Mission—Our Lady of Fatima Bo. Algarrobos - Yauco, Yauco.
Mission—St. Martin de Porres Bo. Almacigo Bajo - Yauco, Yauco.
Mission—St. Juan Macias Bo. Almacigo Alto - Yauco, Yauco.
Mission—Our Lady of Montserrat Bo. Rio Loco - Yauco, Yauco.
Mission—St. Rosa de Lima Bo. El Cafetal - Yauco, Yauco.

On Duty Outside the Diocese:
Revs.—
Alvarez, Pablo D., F.S.S.P., 13780 S.W. 17 Ter., Miami, FL 33175.
Barrett, Kevin S., Chap., Apostolate of Family Consecration, P.O. Box 151, Bloomingdale, OH 43910-0151.
Colon, Jose E., Colinas Montecarlo, Bldg. D-35, San Juan, 00927.
Espona Jimenez, Juan, Madrid, Spain.
Fletcher, Patrick, 62 AW/Chapel, 746 Main St., McChord AFB, WA 98438.
Gusiora, Alphonsus, P.O. Box 61, Enugwu-Ukwu (Anambra State), Nigeria.
Harrison, Brian W., O.S., P.O. Box 13230, Saint Louis, MO 63157.
Kelty, Edward J., O.S., Associazione SACRI, Via Antonio Zanoni, 44, Roma (Castel di Leva) 00134 Italy.
MacIssac, Charles, O.S., St. Joseph's Home, 140 Shepherd Ln., Totowa, NJ 07512.
Malachowski, Christopher, O.S., Bethlehem-Domus Panis Vital, Nadliwe 05-281 Urle Poland.
Medina, George, P.O. Box 286, East Boston, MA 02128.
Mezquida, Ramon, San Jose 4, Alqueria Condesa 46715, Valencia, Spain.
Morales, Francisco, P.O. Box 9023477, Viejo San Juan, 00902.
Munoz, Rafael, P.O. Box 187, Barceloneta, 00657.
Nieves, Carlos, HC763, Buzon 4240, Patillas, 00723.
Nischan, James R., 1625 Mayo Ave., Owensboro, KY 42301.
Quinones, Leoncio, Urb. Apolo, Guaynabo, 00657.
Roman, Carlos, St. Cecilia Church, 5418 Louisiana Ave., Saint Louis, MO 63111.
Sancho Piquer, Enrique, Calvario 49, 2, 4, Pafelbunoli, Valencia, Spain.
Serrano, Dionisio, Maestro Ripoll 14, 28006 Madrid, Spain.
Sirvent, Francisco, Capitan Cortes 8-2, Valencia, Spain.
Weslin, Norman V., O.S., c/o Gene and Kathy Plourdes, 19361 Mynster Springs Rd., Council Bluffs, IA 51503.
Zayas, Antonio, Naranjito, 00719.

Awaiting Assignment:
Rev.—
Capellan, Carlos Manuel Grullon

Retired:
Most Rev.—
Oliver, Fremiot Torres, D.D., C. Marquez de Mondejar 24, 3 B, 28028 Madrid, Spain. Tel: 91-726-0008 (34)
Rev. Msgrs.—
Ballester Torres, Pedro
Colon, Jose, Box 242, Merceditas, 00715.
Rev.—
Garcia Echevarria, Roberto, Bo. Real Anon, Coto Laurel, 00780.

Permanent Deacons:
Almodovar Capielo, Jorge
Altori Vargas, Juan
Aponte Arroyo, Vicente
Burgos Roca, Joseph
Carmona Cruz, Cirilo
Carrasquillo, Francisco
Castro Belen, Rafael
Castro Toro, Alberto
Dosal Lines, Eduardo
Figueroa Santana, Edwin
Galarza, Reinaldo
Garcia Malavet, Pedro
Garcia Rivera, Juan B.
Gelpi Ortiz, Jose E.
Gierbolini Rodriguez, Arnaldo
Gonzalez, Javier
Gonzalez Plaza, Ildefonso
Lebron Romero, Marcelino
Lopez Cosme, Emerito
Lopez Quirindongo, Luis A.
Lopez Sanchez, Benjamin
Lugo, Francisco
Marcucci, Radames
Martinez, Jaime
Masollet, Joaquin
Melendez Ortiz, Luis
Mendez Molina, Angel
Mendez Purcell, Jose M.
Mercado, Jose Ramon
Miranti, Pablo
Montanez, Alberto
Morales Colon, Angel R.
Muniz Rivera, Edgardo
Negron Ortiz, Angel
Niewiadonski, Arthur
Oquendo, Angel O.
Oramas, Carlos
Orsini, Pablo
Ortiz Negron, Narciso
Pabon Gonzalez, Ruben
Pagan Diaz, Benjamin
Pagan Rivera, Jose E.
Perez De La Cruz, Fernando
Perez Nieves, Glidden
Perez Santos, Jose A.
Ramos Rivera, William
Ramos Torres, David
Rentas, Nestor
Resto, Ramon
Reyes, Ruperto
Rivera, Juan Esteban
Rivera, Reinaldo
Rivera Alicea, Genaro
Rivera Burgos, Pedro
Rivera Cardona, Alfredo
Rivera Saez, Jose
Rodriguez, Casildo
Rodriguez, David
Rodriguez, Feliz
Rodriguez, Jacinto
Rodriguez, Jose
Rodriguez Guilbe, Carlos
Roman Perez, Manuel
Rosario, Anibal
Rosario, Luis
Rosario Colon, Jose
Ruiz, Jose D.
Ruiz, Rafael
Sanchez, Carlos Rodriguez
Sanchez, Wallis
Sanchez Muniz, Victor
Santiago, Hector Luis
Santiago, William
Santiago Negron, Norberto
Sepulveda, Miguel
Sepulveda, Samuel
Torres, Antonio Victor Fabre
Torres Maldonado, Wilfredo
Torres Santiago, Jose
Vazquez, Carmelo
Vazquez, Ramon
Vazquez Orengo, Jesus
Velez, Jaime

INSTITUTIONS LOCATED IN THE DIOCESE

[A] SEMINARIES

PONCE. *Diocesan Seminary* (Major), P.O. Box 32110, 00732-2110. Tel: 787-848-4380; 787-812-3024; Fax: 787-848-4380. Email: meliasalvador@hotmail.com. Rev. Msgr. Elias S. Morales, Rector; Rev. Julio A. Rolon Torres, Spiritual. Dir. Priests 2; Lay Staff 5; Seminarians 22.

[B] COLLEGES & UNIVERSITIES

PONCE. *The Pontifical Catholic University of Puerto Rico*, 2250 Avenida de las Americas, 00717-9997. Tel: 787-841-2000; Fax: 787-651-2034. Web: www.pucpr.edu. The University is composed of the following: College of Arts and Humanities and Graduate Studies in Hispanic Studies; College of Business Administration and Graduate Studies; College of Education and Graduate Studies; College of Science and Graduate Studies; School of Law; College of Graduate Studies in Behavioral Science and Community Affairs; Institute of Social Doctrine of the Church; Student Support Services; Post-Baccalaureate Achievement Program; Upward Bound Program. Priests 41; Sisters 2; School of Law 37; Lay Teachers 598; Students 9,815.

Administration: Most Revs. Felix Lazaro, Sch.P., Grand Chancellor; Ulises Casiano, Chm. Bd. Trustees; Dr. Jorge Velez Arocho, Pres.; Dr. Juan A. Quintana Lugo, Interim Vice Pres. Academic Affairs; Mrs. Irma Rodriguez, Vice Pres. Fin. Affairs; Mr. Freddie Martinez Sotomayor, Interim Vice Pres. Student Affairs; Mrs. Milagros G. Mayoral Penne, Dir. Continuing Education; Dr. Felix M. Cortes Morales, Interim Dir. Institute Devel., Research & Planning; Mr. Alfonso Santiago, Dean College of Arts and Humanities; Dr. Jaime Santiago Canet, Dean College of Business Admin.; Dr. Lillian Negron, Dean College of Education; Ms. Carmen L. Velazquez, Dean College of Science; Angel Gonzalez Roman, Dean School of Law; Mr. Ivan E. Davila, Registrar; Dr. Ana Bonilla de Sanchez, Dir. Admissions; Ms. Carmen Gonzalez, Dir. Guidance Center; Mrs. Magda I. Vargas Rodriguez, Interim Dir. Libraries; Mrs. Noelia Padua, Esq., Dir. Law Library; Dr. Herman A. Vera, Dean of College Graduate Studies; Ms. Gilda Rivera, Exec. Dir. Information Technology & Telecommunications.

Faculty: Rev. Msgrs. Herminio De Jesus; Roberto Garcia; Abel A. DiMarco; Juan Rodriguez Orengo, Dept. Teologia y Filosofia; Revs. José D. Rodriguez Martino, Dept. Teologia y Filosofia; Edwin Vazquez Vega, Chap.; Perfecto Alvarez, O.S.A.; Sr. Iris E. Rivera Cintron, C.a.Ch., Graduate Studies in Educ.; Revs. Adalin Rivera; Mario Mastrangelo, O.F.M-.Cap.; Segismundo Cintron, Lecturer in Theology; Alvaro Huerga Teruela.

Mayaguez: Edgardo Acosta Ocasio, Lecture in Theology; Revs. Jose R. Linares Pagan, Lecturer in Theology; Luis A. Rodriguez Vientos, Chap. Precinct Mayaguez, Dept. Teologia y Filosofia.

Ponce: Rev. Julio A. Rolon Torres; Jesus Diez Antonanzas, Lecturer in Theology; Rev. Msgr. Elias S. Morales Rodriguez, Lecturer in Theology; Revs. Antonio Portalatin Rodriguez, Theology; Francisco Medina Santos-Lecturer, Lecturer in Theology.

Recinto De Arecibo: Rev. Omar Bedoya Gaviria, Chap.; Victor Rojas Rodriguez, Lecture in Graduate Studies.

Extension De Coamo: Emiliano Alamo Hernando, Lecturer in Theology.

[C] SCHOOLS - INSTITUTES OF EDUCATION

PONCE. *Academia Cristo Rey Inc.*, Urb. La Rambla, c/o San Judas 3011, 00730-4091. Miss Gicela Bonilla, Prin. Students 617.

Centro San Francisco, Box 10479, 00732. Tel: 787-842-2776; 787-432-5977; Fax: 787-842-2776. Email: csfinc@aol.com. Web: www.csfinc.aol.com. Sr. Lourdes Perez Rivera, Prin.; Ms. Emma Martinez Reyes, Librarian; Mrs. Mariselly Santiago O'Conner, Librarian. Sisters of St. Joseph. Lay Teachers 28; Librarians 2; Social Workers 1; Counselors 1.

Colegio Del Sagrado Corazon De Jesus (1916) 2511 Calle Obispado, 00716-3836. Tel: 787-842-0339; Fax: 787-843-0250. Email: sagrado@coqui.net. Web: www.home.coqui.net/sagrado. Mrs. Maria Serrano, Prin.; Miss Lydia Mendez, Librarian. Religious of the Sacred Heart. Priests 1; Lay Teachers 55; Total Staff 82.

Colegio El Ave Maria, 4506 Dr. Bartolomei, Reparto Valle Alegre, 00728-3151. Tel: 787-284-2453; Fax: 787-284-2953. Email: avemaria@pucpr.edu. Sr. Milagros Pizarro, O.D.M., Dir. & Prin. Operarias del Divino Maestro (Avemarianas). Sisters 5; Lay Teachers 13; Total Staff 18; Total Enrollment 13.

Holy Family School (1913) 1270 Ave. Hostos, 00717-0928. Tel: 787-842-3208; Fax: 787-844-6773. Email: sagradafamilia1270@yahoo.com. Sr. Cecilia Serrano Guzman, H.C., Prin.; Ms. Marina Aviles, Librarian. Sisters of Charity - Saint Vincent de Paul. Sisters 2; Lay Teachers 24; Total Staff 26; Students 327.

COTO LAUREL. *Colegio Ponceno* (Day School), 1900 Carr. 14, 00780-2147. Tel: 787-848-2525; Fax: 787-259-4282. Email: colegio@copin.net. Web: www.copin.net. Revs. Hector Cruz, Sch.P., Chap. & Teacher; P. Jesus Romero, Sch.P., Teacher; Very Rev. Fernando Torres, Sch.P., Dir.; Luis de Leon, Supr.; Carmen Rizzo, Prin. (Elementary); Milagros Carmona, Librarian. Piarist Fathers. Priests 3; Deacons 2; Lay Teachers 67; Total Enrollment 965; Total Staff 75.

PLAYA PONCE. *Centros Sor Isolina Ferre, Inc.* (1969) Vocational School, P.O. Box 7282, 00732-7282. Tel: 787-843-1910; 787-842-0000; Fax: 787-844-7665; 787-540-5020. Email: mperez@csifpr.org. Web: www.csifpr.org. Sr. Rosita M. Bauza, M.S.B.T., Custodian of the Mission - Assoc. Missionary Servants of the Most Blessed Trinity., Multiservice center that promotes the integral development of children, youth and adults in all areas: health, education, arts, culture, values, spiritual development, strategies of intercessors and community empowerment. Priests 1; Sisters 5; Total Staff 400.

[D] HOMES FOR THE AGED

PONCE. *Residencia Santa Marta* Home for Aged and Infirm, Barrio Sabanetas, P.O. Box 242, Mercedita, 00715-0242. Tel: 787-840-7575; Fax: 787-651-1080. Email: rsmarta@hotmail.com. Maria Paz Troiteiro, Supr.; Rev. Jose Esteves, O.deM., Chap.; Sr. Nilda M. Rodriguez. Bed Capacity 215; Total Assisted Annually 175; Total Staff (Religious) 16; Residents 196.

[E] MONASTERIES AND RESIDENCES OF PRIESTS AND BROTHERS

PONCE. *Fraternidad Santa Teresita, Frailes Capuchinos* (Postulantado), 342 Victoria St., Box 7244, 00732. Tel: 787-842-5055; Fax: 787-844-7267. Email: jose.torres@email.pucpr.edu. Revs. Jose Angel Torres, O.F.M.Cap., Guardian & Dir. Postulantado; Mario Mastrangelo, O.F.M.Cap., Prof. at P.U.C.P.R.; Francisco Garcia, O.F.M.Cap.; Jose R. Gonzalez, O.F.M.Cap. Postulants 3.

[F] CONVENTS & RESIDENCES OF SISTERS

PONCE. *Blessed Trinity Missionary Cenacle* (1950) P.O. Box 7282, 00732-7282. Tel: 787-844-1627; Fax: 787-842-6745. Email: msbtponce@coqui.net. Web: www.msbt.org. Sr. Rosita M. Bauza, M.S.B.T., Historian. Sisters 5.

Convent of Servants of Mary (1891) Urb. La Rambla, 1703 Calle Siervas de Maria, 00730-4027. Tel: 787-842-2336; Fax: 787-844-5449. Sr. Elena Rolon Rosado, S. de M., Supr. Religious 21; Novices 6; Administered in the home 2,300; Aspirants 3.

Religiosas del Apostolado del Sagrado Corazon de Jesus (1891) P.O. Box 8300, 00732-8300. Tel: 787-842-4340; Fax: 787-813-2066. Sisters Apostolate of the Sacred Heart of Jesus 22.

Colegio Perpetuo Socorro, Bo. Coqui, Aguirre - Salinas, PR 00704. Tel: 787-853-2270; Fax: 787-853-2531. Sr. Aurea E. Fuentes, R.A., Supr., Delegada Regl. Representante de la Superiora Gen.

YAUCO. *Hermanas Dominicas de Fatima, Casa Generalicia*, P.O. Box 62, 00698-0062. Tel: 787-856-4256; 787-856-4330; Fax: 787-821-2439.

[G] PERSONAL PRELATURES

PONCE. *Prelature of the Holy Cross and Opus Dei*, Urb. Alhambra, 1814 calle Alcazar, 00716-3829. Tel: 787-844-2661; Fax: 787-844-2661. Email: pricoinf@coqui.net. Web: opusdei.org.pr. Revs. Ramon Alvarez; Jaime Bermudez Onopa; Pablo Concepcion.

[H] MISCELLANEOUS

PONCE. *Albergue La Providencia para El Bienestar Social, Inc.*, P.O. Box 10142, 00732. Tel: 787-841-2119; Fax: 787-840-6642. Email: albergueprovi@gmail.com. Web: www.laprovidencia.org. Rev. Francisco Garcia, O.F.M.Cap., Dir. Refuge Center for AIDS patients. Total Assisted 7; Total Staff 8.

Casa de Formacion Residencia Asis, c/o Chancery, P.O. Box 32205, 00732-2205.

Centro Calasanz

Centro Madre Dominga, Casa Belen (2000) Urb. San Jorge, 3504 Calle Andino Apt. 2, 00717-0777. Tel: 787-290-3627; Fax: 787-844-3240. Email: centromadredominga@hotmail.com. Sr. Elena Santana, O.P., Dir.

Fundacion Surinach, P.O. Box 32205, 00732-2205.

Institucion Magdalena Aulina - Operarias Parroquiales (Secular Institute), Simon de la Torre 43, 00730. Tel: 787-842-7209. Email: jiaulina@hotmail.com.

Jardin Infantil Aulina I and II, (I) Calle Simon de la Torre #43; (II) Calle Torre #48, Esq. Juan Seix, 00730. Grades: (I) 0-18 months; (II) 19 months-4 years

Instituto Santa Ana, P.O. Box 554, Adjuntas, 00601. Tel: 787-829-2504; Fax: 787-829-2504.

Jardin Infantil Amor De Dios, Urb. Constancia, 2456 Calle Eureka, 00717-2218. Tel: 787-842-5079; Fax: 787-984-5254. Sr. Martina Barreira, R.A.D., Dir.

Memores Domini, P.O. Box 32197, 00732-2197. Tel: 787-515-6464. Email: zaffagiu@yahoo.com.

Missionaries of Charity (1989) Mailing Address: P.O. Box 32177, 00732-2177. Tel: 787-841-5443. *Hna. Selma M.C. (D) Home for the Aged*, 683 Ramos Antonini, El Tuque, 00728. Sr. M. Violetta Neduvely, M.C., Supr. Missionaries of Charity (Mother Theresa of Calcutta). Sisters 6; Residents 44; Bed Capacity 46; Total Assisted 72; Total Staff 22.

Pastoral Care of the Sick (1982) Parroquia Santisima Trinidad, Ave Ponce de Leon 985, Urb Las Delicias, P.O. Box 8226, 00732-8226. Tel: 787-848-5600, Ext. 3202; 787-842-6073 (Parish Private); 787-651-5522 (Office Hospital - Dr. Pila); Fax: 787-290-0693. Rev. Dairo Hernando Arboleda Ibarra, O.SS.T., Dir.

Santuario Nuestra Senora del Encuentro con Dios Hilasterio Femenino, Urb Mariani 2322 Calle Dr. Santaella, P.O. Box 32212, 00732-2212. Tel: 787-848-1613. Rev. Roberto Maldonado, L.D.

COTO LAUREL. *Diocesan Fathers of Schoenstatt-Santuary of Schoenstatt*, P.O. Box 800371, 00780-0371. Tel: 787-526-6362. Rev. Ramon Fco. Garcia Lantigua, Rector.

OROCOVIS. *Santuario Nuestra Senora del Encuentro con Dios - Hilasterio Masculino*, HC-01, Box 6267, 00720. Tel: 787-867-1801; Fax: 787-867-0773. Email: orocovis_hm@lumendei.org. Rev. Roberto Maldonado, L.D.

Santuario Senora del Encuentro Con Dios Hilasterio Femenino, HC-01, Box 6267, OR 00720. Tel: 787-867-1801; Fax: 787-867-5262. Email: orocovis_hf@lumendei.org.

PENUELAS. *Congregacion San Juan Evangelista*, P.O. Box 118, 00624. Tel: 787-836-1512; Fax: 787-836-1512. Rev. Msgr. Marcos A. Pancorbo, Dir.; Bro. Arturo Ramos Ruiz, Pres. Brothers 138.

Oblates of Wisdom (1979) *Sagrado Corazon Parish*, HC-03 Box 13063, 00624-9717. Tel: 787-836-1164; 787-605-1195. Web: www.rtforum.org. Rev. Christopher De Herrera, O.S.

YAUCO. *Instituto Especial para el Desarrollo Integral del Individuo, la Familia y la Communidad, Inc.*, P.O. Box 1241, 00968-1241. Tel: 787-856-3798; Fax: 787-856-4192. Email: instyco@coqui.net. Calle Madre Dominga #66, 00968-1241. Tel: 787-856-3798; 787-856-1573; Fax: 787-856-4192. Sr. Lizandra Rosa Pagan, Dir. Sisters 2; Total Assisted 1,675; Staff 36.

RELIGIOUS INSTITUTES OF MEN REPRESENTED IN THE DIOCESE

For further details refer to the corresponding bracketed number in the Religious Institutes of Men or Women section.

[0470]—*The Capuchin Friars (Vice Province of Puerto Rico)*—O.F.M.Cap.

[0270]—*Carmelite Fathers & Brothers*—O.Carm.

[1330]—*Congregation of the Mission*—C.M.

[0650]—*Holy Ghost Fathers* (Eastern Prov.)—C.S.Sp.

[]—*Lumen Dei*—L.D.

[]—*Mercedarian Fathers*—O.deM.

[]—*Oblates of Wisdom*

[]—*Operarios Del Reino De Cristo*—O.R.C.

[0430]—*Order of Preachers-Dominicans* (Holland Prov.)—O.P.

[1310]—*Order of the Holy Trinity* (Spain)—O.SS.T.

[1040]—*Piarist Fathers* (Spain)—Sch.P.

[1070]—*Redemptorist Fathers* (San Juan Prov.)—C.SS.R.

[]—*Santuario Nuestra Senora Del Encuentro Con Dios Hislaterio Masculino Lumen Dei*

RELIGIOUS INSTITUTES OF WOMEN REPRESENTED IN THE DIOCESE

[0130]—*Apostles of the Sacred Heart of Jesus*—A.S.C.J.

[0340]—*Carmelite Sisters of Charity*—C.a.Ch.

[1070-05]—*Dominican Sisters*—O.P.

[]—*Hermanas de los Ancianos Desamparados*

[]—*Hermanas del Servicio Social*

[]—*Hermanas Del-Amor De Dios*

[]—*Hermanas Dominicas de Fatima*—O.P.
[]—*Hermanas Ntra. Sra. del Perpetuo Socorro* Juana Diaz, Ponce—N.S.P.S.
[]—*Hnas. Clarisas*—O.S.C.
[2340]—*Little Sisters of the Poor*—L.S.P.
[2710]—*Missionaries of Charity*—M.C.
[2790]—*Missionary Servants of the Most Blessed Trinity*—M.S.B.T.
[]—*Operarias del Divino Maestro (Avemarianas)*
[]—*Operarias Parroquiales*
[]—*Religious de los Santos Angeles Custodios (Adjuntas, Ponce)*—R.A.C.
[]—*Santuario Nuestra Senora Del Encuentro Con Dios Hislaterio Femenino Lumen Dei*
[]—*School Sisters of Notre Dame*—S.S.N.D.
[3580]—*Servants of Mary*—O.S.M.
[]—*Sisters of Charity of St. Vincent de Paul*—H.C.
[]—*Sisters of Perpetual Socorro*—N.S.P.S.
[]—*Sisters of St. Joseph*—S.S.J.
[2150]—*Sisters, Servants of the Immaculate Heart of Mary*—I.H.M.

NECROLOGY

† Cano, Emilio, (Retired)—Died Feb. 8, 2008
† Pacho, Jesus, (Retired)—Died May 10, 2009

An asterisk (*) denotes an organization that has established tax-exempt status directly with the IRS and is not covered by the USCCB Group Ruling.

Diocese of St. Thomas in the Virgin Islands

Most Reverend

HERBERT A. BEVARD

Bishop of St. Thomas in the Virgin Islands; ordained May 20, 1972; appointed Bishop of St. Thomas in the Virgin Islands July 7, 2008; ordained and installed September 3, 2008.

SUB TUUM PRÆSIDIUM

Chancery Office: P.O. Box 301825, Charlotte Amalie, VI 00803. Tel: 340-774-3166; Fax: 340-774-5816.

Web: www.catholicvi.com

Email: vichancery@vipowernet.net

ESTABLISHED AS PRELATURE OF VI, JULY 23, 1960.

Established as Diocese of St. Thomas in the Virgin Islands April 20, 1977.

Comprises the Islands of St. Thomas, St. Croix, St. John and Water Island.

STATISTICAL OVERVIEW

Personnel	
Bishop	1
Retired Bishops	1
Priests: Diocesan Active in Diocese	9
Priests: Diocesan Active Outside Diocese	4
Number of Diocesan Priests	13
Religious Priests in Diocese	4
Total Priests in Diocese	17
Extern Priests in Diocese	2
Ordinations:	
Transitional Deacons	1
Permanent Deacons	2
Permanent Deacons in Diocese	29
Total Brothers	2
Total Sisters	23
Parishes	
Parishes	8
With Resident Pastor:	
Resident Diocesan Priests	6
Resident Religious Priests	2
Missions	1
Welfare	
Special Centers for Social Services	3
Total Assisted	700
Other Institutions	2
Total Assisted	126
Educational	
Diocesan Students in Other Seminaries	1
Total Seminarians	1
High Schools, Diocesan and Parish	2
Total Students	197
Elementary Schools, Diocesan and Parish	3
Total Students	526
Catechesis/Religious Education:	
High School Students	139
Elementary Students	389
Total Students under Catholic Instruction	1,252
Teachers in the Diocese:	
Priests	1
Brothers	1
Lay Teachers	75
Vital Statistics	
Receptions into the Church:	
Infant Baptism Totals	234
Minor Baptism Totals	41
Adult Baptism Totals	10
Received into Full Communion	16
First Communions	212
Confirmations	132
Marriages:	
Catholic	46
Interfaith	20
Total Marriages	66
Deaths	169
Total Catholic Population	30,000
Total Population	120,917

Former Bishops—Most Revs. EDWARD J. HARPER, C.Ss.R., D.D., ord. June 18, 1939; appt. July 23, 1960; cons. Oct. 6, 1960; named first residential bishop of Diocese of St. Thomas in the Virgin Islands, April 20, 1977; retired Oct. 15, 1985; died Dec. 2, 1990; SEAN P. O'MALLEY, O.F.M.Cap., ord. Aug. 29, 1970; named coadjutor, May 30, 1984; ord. Bishop, Aug. 2, 1984; installed Oct. 16, 1985; transferred to Fall River Aug. 11, 1992; ELLIOTT G. THOMAS, D.D. (Retired), ord. June 6, 1986; cons. and installed as Bishop Dec. 12, 1993; retired June 30, 1999; GEORGE V. MURRY, S.J., ord. June 9, 1979; appt. May 5, 1998; installed June 30, 1999; appt. Bishop of Youngstown Jan. 30, 2007.

Chancery Office—Mailing Address: P.O. Box 301825, Charlotte Amalie, 00803. Tel: 340-774-3166; Fax: 340-774-5816.

Chancellor—Rev. NEIL SCANTLEBURY. Tel: 340-774-3166; Fax: 340-774-5816.

Fiscal Officer—VACANT.

Diocesan Consultors—Rev. E. PATRICK LYNCH, C.Ss.R.; Rev. Msgrs. JEROME FEUDJIO; MICHAEL F. KOSAK; Revs. NEIL SCANTLEBURY; GEORGE FRANKLIN, Ph.D.

Hispanic Ministry—Revs. CHARLES CRESPO, Mailing Address: P.O. Box 301767, St. Thomas, 00803. Tel: 340-774-0201; Fax: 340-776-9586; LOUIS KEMAYOU, Mailing Address: P.O. Box 2150, St. Croix, 00851. Tel: 340-692-2005; Fax: 340-692-2748.

Catholic Charities of the Virgin Islands, Inc.—Mr. MICHAEL AKIN, Exec. Dir., Mailing Address: P.O. Box 10736, Charlotte Amalie, 00801. Tel: 340-777-8518; Fax: 340-777-4875.

Catholic Schools Office—Rev. E. PATRICK LYNCH, C.Ss.R., Supt., 416 Custom House St., Frederiksted, 00840. Tel: 340-772-0138; Fax: 340-772-0142.

Vocations—Rev. Msgr. JEROME FEUDJIO, Mailing Address: P.O. Box 301767, St. Thomas, 00803. Tel: 340-774-0201; Fax: 340-776-9586.

Charismatic Movement—Sr. PATRICIA ALEXANDER, W.I.F., St. Croix, VI; Rev. ANTHONY ABRAHAM, Dir., Mailing Address: P.O. Box 502218, St. Thomas, 00805. Tel: 340-775-1650; Fax: 340-775-1750.

Caribbean Catholic Network (CCN)— Channel 7, Rev. Msgr. MICHAEL F. KOSAK, Gen. Mgr., P.O. Box 1160, Kingshill, 00851. Tel: 340-779-3000; Fax: 340-779-3151.

Catholic Television Network (CTN)— Channel 16, Rev. Msgr. JEROME FEUDJIO, Mailing Address: P.O. Box 301825, Charlotte Amalie, 00803. Tel: 340-774-3166; Fax: 340-774-5816.

Diocesan Newspaper— "The Catholic Islander" Rev. CHARLES CRESPO, Editor, Mailing Address: P.O. Box 301825, St. Thomas, 00803. Tel: 340-774-3166; Fax: 340-774-5816.

Communications Coordinator—Rev. Msgr. MICHAEL F. KOSAK, Mailing Address: P.O. Box 1160, Kingshill, 00851. Tel: 340-778-0484; Fax: 340-779-3151.

Prison Ministry—Rev. Msgr. JEROME FEUDJIO, St. Thomas. Tel: 340-774-3166; Fax: 340-774-5816.

Permanent Diaconate—Rev. JOHN K. MARK, Dir. Tel: 340-774-0201; Fax: 340-776-9586.

Shelters for the Homeless—Mr. MICHAEL AKIN, Exec. Dir., Mailing Address: Bethlehem House, P.O. Box 10736, Charlotte Amalie, 00801. Tel: 340-774-4663. St. Croix. Tel: 340-778-1227. Administration. Tel: 340-777-8518; Fax: 340-777-4475.

Vicar for Clergy and Religious—Rev. Msgr. JEROME FEUDJIO, Mailing Address: P.O. Box 301825, St. Thomas, 00803-1825. Tel: 340-774-3166; Fax: 340-774-5816.

CLERGY, PARISHES, MISSIONS AND PAROCHIAL SCHOOLS

ISLAND OF ST. THOMAS

(CATHOLIC POPULATION, 12,500)

1—CATHEDRAL OF STS. PETER AND PAUL (1773), (West Indian), Rev. Msgr. Jerome Feudjio, Rector; Revs. Charles Crespo; Janvier Sedjeu, Parochial Vicar; Deacons Jose Vasquez; William Kenny; Wilfredo Acosta; Clement Danet.
Mailing Address: P.O. Box 301767, 00803. Tel: 340-774-0201; 340-776-7384; Fax: 340-776-9586. Web: www.catholicvi.com.
Res.: 22A Kronprindsens Gade (Main St.), 00803. Tel: 340-774-0201; Fax: 340-776-9586.
School—Sts. Peter and Paul School, (Grades PreK-12), P.O. Box 301706, St. Thomas, 00803. Tel: 340-774-5662; 340-774-2199; Fax: 340-777-5355. Lay Teachers 14; Students 260.
School—Richard Pukenas, Prin.; Austin Walters, Vice Prin. Staff 46; Students 250.
Catechesis/Religious Program—Students 59.
Convent—Sisters of Charity of St. Elizabeth, 31 A Prindcesse Gade, P.O. Box 303785, 00803. Tel: 340-774-0248; Fax: 340-776-9586.
Mission—Chapel of St. Anne P.O. Box 306810, Carenage, 00803. Tel: 340-714-1101; Fax: 340-714-5231. Deacon Bernard Gibs.

2—HOLY FAMILY PARISH (1969), (West Indian), [JC] Revs. Neil Scantlebury; Anthony Abraham, Parochial Vicar; Deacons Roy Bruney; Austin Medina.
Res.: *213 Anna's Retreat*, P.O. Box 502218, St. Thomas, 00805. Tel: 340-775-1650; Fax: 340-775-1750. Email: holyfamilyvi@msn.com. Web: www.holyfamilyvi.com.
Catechesis/Religious Program—Students 74.

3—OUR LADY OF PERPETUAL HELP (1926), (West Indian), [CEM] Rev. John K. Mark.
Mailing Address: P.O. Box 304983, 00803. Tel: 340-774-0885; Fax: 340-774-5896. Email: olphmafolie@yahoo.com.
Catechesis/Religious Program—Students 57.

ISLAND OF ST. JOHN

(CATHOLIC POPULATION 300), OUR LADY OF MT. CARMEL PARISH (1962) Rev. Msgr. Antonio Verzosa.
Res.: P.O. Box 241, St. John, 00831. Tel: 340-776-6339 (Res. & Office); Fax: 340-693-7685. Email: olmc@hotmail.com.
Catechesis/Religious Program—Ms. Angela LaPlace, D.R.E. Students 33.

ISLAND OF ST. CROIX

(CATHOLIC POPULATION, APPROX. 17,200)
1—CHURCH OF ST. JOSEPH (1947) [JC] Rev. Louis Kemayou; Deacons Conrad Williams; Neville Charles; Raymond Leonce; Guillermo Huertas.
Mailing Address: P.O. Box 2150, Kingshill, 00851-2150. Tel: 340-692-2005; Fax: 340-692-2748.
In Res., Bro. James A. Petrait, O.S.F.S.
Res.: Mt. Pleasant #1, Frederiksted, Frederiksted, 00840.
Catechesis/Religious Program—Students 60.
2—CHURCH OF ST. PATRICK (1846), (African-Caribbean), Rev. E. Patrick Lynch, C.Ss.R.; Deacons Ed Cave; Emith Fludd; Lambert Heyliger; Louis Soto Jr.
Mailing Address: 416 Custom House St., Frederiksted, 00840. Tel: 340-772-0138; Fax: 340-772-0142. Email: stpatrick@catholicvi.org. In Res., Rev. Kevin MacDonald.
School—P.O. Box 988, Frederiksted, St. Croix, 00841. Tel: 340-772-5052; Fax: 340-772-4488. Sheryl R. Calton, Prin. Lay Teachers 12; Students 140.
Catechesis/Religious Program—Sr. Florine Bailey, I.C.M., D.R.E. Students 30.
Convent—Missionary Sisters of the Immaculate Heart of MaryCaribbean Center, P.O. Box 95, Frederiksted, St. Croix, 00841. Tel: 340-772-0341; Fax: 340-772-4908.
DeMeester Residence—P.O. Box 52, St. Croix, 00841. Tel: 340-772-0132.
Light of Christ Retreat Center—310 New St., P.O. Box 52, Kingshill, 00851. Tel: 340-772-4782; Fax: 340-772-4385.
3—CHURCH OF THE HOLY CROSS (1755), (West Indian), [CEM 3] [JC] Revs. Kenneth F. Gaddy, C.Ss.R.; Andrzej Szorc, C.Ss.R.; Bro. George Armoogam, C.Ss.R.; Deacons Ulric Benjamin; David Capriola; Vincent Colianni; Hector Rivera; Angel Maldonado.
Res.: 2182 Queen St., Christiansted, 00820. Tel: 340-773-7564; Fax: 340-713-9149.
School—St. Mary's, P.O. Box 224620, Christiansted, 00822. Tel: 340-773-0117; Fax: 340-773-1166. Mr. Terry Johnson, Prin. Lay Teachers 22; Students 207.
Catechesis/Religious Program—Tel: 340-773-7564; Fax: 340-713-9149. Rev. David Capriola, Coord. Students 68.
Mission—Sacred Heart Chapel Christiansted, U.S.V.I. 00820. Tel: 340-773-7564; Fax: 340-713-9149.
Blessed Peter Donder's Formation Residence—P.O. Box 24839, Gallows Bay, Christiansted, St. Croix, 00824-0839. Tel: 340-692-9999; Fax: 340-692-9997. Rev. Kenneth F. Gaddy, C.Ss.R., Dir.
Res.: 20 Prince St., Christiansted, 00820. Tel: 340-692-9999; Fax: 340-692-9997. Email: donders@vipowernet.com.
Convent—Missionaries of Charity, P.O. Box 3058, Christiansted, 00821. Tel: 340-773-1950; Fax: 340-713-9149.
Convent—Sisters of the Good Shepherd, P.O. Box 222984, Christiansted, 00822. Tel: 340-713-8724.
Convent—Dominican Sisters of the Immaculate Mother, O.P., Christiansted, 00820. Tel: 340-719-7299.
4—CHURCH ST. ANN (1823), (Caribbean), Rev. Msgr. Michael F. Kosak; Rev. Simon Peter Opira; Deacons Arnold Helenese; Joseph Mark; Norbert Xavier; Denis Griffith; Eugene Thompson; Hyacinthe George.
Mailing Address: 42 Barrenspot Hill, P.O. Box 1160, Kingshill, 00851-1160. Tel: 340-778-0484; Fax: 340-779-3151. Email: stannbarrenspot@yahoo.com. Web: www.catholicvi.com.
Catechesis/Religious Program—Students 147.
Chaplaincy—Herbert Grigg Home for the Aged, Kingshill, 00851. Tel: 340-778-0708.
Shrine—Our Lady of Barrenspot Hill

Chaplaincies

These chaplaincies only pertain to the Island of St. Thomas.

ST. THOMAS. *Lucinda Millin Home for the Aged.*
Queen Louise Home for the Aged.
Seaview Nursing and Rehabilitation Center.
St. Thomas Hospital and Community Health Center.

On Duty Outside the Diocese:
Revs.—
Corneille, Cecil
Herrera, Jose
Obeng, Simon
Sanchez, Alejandro

Permanent Deacons:
Acosta, Wilfredo
Benjamin, Ulric
Bruney, Roy
Capriola, David
Cave, Edward
Charles, Neville
Colianni, Vincent
Danet, Clement
Fludd, Emith
George, Hyacinthe
Gibs, Bernard
Griffith, Denis
Helenese, Arnold
Heyliger, Lambert
Huertas, Guillermo
Kenny, William
Leonce, Raymond
Maldonado, Angel
Mark, Joseph T.
Matthew, James
Medina, Austin
Monsanto, Leonard
Rivera, Hector
Soto, Louis, Jr.
Summer, William, (On Leave)
Thompson, Eugene
Vazquez, Jose
Verhoff, James, (On Leave)
Williams, Conrad
Xavier, Norbert

INSTITUTIONS LOCATED IN THE DIOCESE

[A] INTERPAROCHIAL HIGH SCHOOLS

ST. CROIX. *St. Joseph High School* (1964) 3 Mt. Pleasant, Rte. 2, Frederiksted, 00840. Tel: 340-692-2455; Fax: 340-692-2458. Email: sjhs@islands.vi. Web: www.islands.vi/~sjhs. Mrs. Deborah M. Skalkos, Head of School; Lily Alvarez, Librarian. Brothers 1; Lay Teachers 11; Students 124.

[B] ORGANIZATIONS IN THE DIOCESE

ST. THOMAS. *Miscellaneous Organizations* (For further information contact the Chancery Office), Box 301825, 00803-1825. Tel: 340-774-3166; Fax: 340-774-5816. Email: vichancery@vipowernet.net.
Catholic Charismatic Renewal Tel: 340-775-1650; Fax: 340-775-1750. Rev. Anthony Abraham, Dir.; Sr. Patricia Alexander, W.I.F., Asst. Dir.
Catholic Daughters of the Americas Tel: 340-775-7846; Fax: 340-775-1750. Ms. Alicia Doute, Regent.
Children of Mary Tel: 340-775-2890; Fax: 340-775-1750. Wende Rouse, Pres. Tel: 340-775-1351; Fax: 340-775-1750.
Gabriel Project/Rachel Project/Good Shepherd Center Tel: 340-719-0264; Fax: 340-713-9149. Sr. Digna Maria Rivas, R.G.S., Dir.
Hispanic Ministry, St. Croix. Tel: 340-692-2005; Fax: 340-692-2748. Rev. Louis Kemayou.
Knights of Columbus Council 6482, St. Croix. Tel: 340-513-8172. Michael Ciarrocca, Grand Knight.
Knights of Columbus Council 6187 Tel: 340-775-3537; Fax: 340-776-9586. Anthony Francis, Grand Knight.
Legion of Mary, St. Croix. Tel: 340-773-7564; Fax: 340-713-9149. Betty Schnieder, Pres. Tel: 340-778-1670.
Legion of Mary (St. John), St. John, 00831. Tel: 340-776-6054; Fax: 340-693-7685. Maggie Metor.
Legion of Mary, St. Thomas Tel: 340-775-3503; Fax: 340-775-1750. Eubald Rene, Pres. Tel: 340-775-3503.
Lumen 2000/Caribbean Region Tel: 340-778-0484; Fax: 340-779-3151. Rev. Msgr. Michael F. Kosak. Tel: 340-778-0484; Fax: 340-779-3151.
Magnificat Ministry Tel: 340-774-2319; Fax: 340-776-9586. Irene Acosta, Coord. Tel: 340-775-5369.
Secular Franciscans Sr. Patricia Alexander, W.I.F., Spiritual Asst. Tel: 340-778-5773; Fax: 340-719-3037.
Fraternity Our Lady of the Angels Deacon Raymond Leonce. Tel: 340-772-9131; Mrs. Cleo Hobson, Min. Tel: 340-775-0666.
Fraternity of Lady Clare of Assisi Tel: 340-779-1221; Fax: 340-775-1750. Email: hfc@holyfamilyvi.com. Ms. Diana Maguire, Min.
St. Vincent de Paul Society, St.Thomas. Tel: 340-774-3320. Ms. Nellie Gumbs, Pres. Tel: 340-775-0839.
Catholic Charities of the Virgin Islands Tel: 340-777-8518; Fax: 340-777-4475. Mr. Michael Akin, Exec. Dir.
St. Joseph Workers Tel: 340-775-2890; 340-775-1351; Fax: 340-775-1750. Web: www.holyfamilyvi.com. Orville Rouse, Pres. Tel: 340-775-1351.
Secular Order Discalced Carmelites, St. Croix. Tel: 340-778-8386. Rita M. Schuster, Dir. Tel: 340-778-8386.
Men's Fellowship, St. Ann-Barrenspot, St. Croix, 00824. Tel: 340-778-0484; Fax: 340-779-3151.
Cursillo Movement, St. Croix. Tel: 340-692-2005; Fax: 340-692-2748. Petra Arroyo.
Hispanic Ministry, P.O. Box 301767, 00803. Tel: 340-774-0201; Fax: 340-776-9586. Rev. Charles Crespo, Contact Person.
New Catechumenal Way, St. Croix. Tel: 340-692-2005; Fax: 340-692-2748. Deacons Conrad Williams, Contact Person; Neville Charles, Contact Person.

ST. CROIX. *Miscellaneous Organizations*
St. Ann's Youth Group, P.O. Box 1160, Kingshill, 00851-1160. Tel: 340-778-0484; Fax: 340-779-3151. Maudiana Jn. Baptiste, Youth Coord.
Magnificat Organization, P.O. Box 1847, Kingshill, 00851-1160. Tel: 340-778-5773; 340-719-3037. Jeanne Garcia, Coord.; Sr. Patricia Alexander, W.I.F., Spiritual Advisor.

RELIGIOUS INSTITUTES OF MEN REPRESENTED IN THE DIOCESE

For further details refer to the corresponding bracketed number in the Religious Institutes of Men or Women section.
[0920]—*Oblates of St. Francis De Sales*—O.S.F.S.
[1070]—*Redemptorist Fathers*—C.SS.R.

RELIGIOUS INSTITUTES OF WOMEN REPRESENTED IN THE DIOCESE

[]—*Association of West Indian Franciscans*—W.I.F.
[]—*Dominican Sisters of the Immaculate Mother* (Philippines)—O.P.
[2710]—*Missionaries of Charity*—M.C.
[2750]—*Missionary Sisters of the Immaculate Heart of Mary*—I.C.M.
[0590]—*Sisters of Charity of Saint Elizabeth (Convent Station)*—S.C.
[1830]—*Sisters of the Good Shepherd*—R.G.S.

NECROLOGY

† Campbell, Rev. Msgr. Bernard Kingshill, VI St. Ann—Died Jan. 23, 2009

An asterisk (*) denotes an organization that has established tax-exempt status directly with the IRS and is not covered by the USCCB Group Ruling.

Diocese of Samoa-Pago Pago

Most Reverend

JOHN QUINN WEITZEL, M.M.

Bishop of Samoa-Pago Pago; ordained June 11, 1955; appointed First Bishop of Samoa-Pago Pago June 9, 1986; ordained October 29, 1986. *Fatuoaiga: P.O. Box 596, Pago Pago, AS 96799.* Tel: 684-699-1402; Fax: 684-699-1459. Email: quinn@samoatelco.com.

CREATED A DIOCESE NOVEMBER, 1982.

The Diocese of Samoa-Pago Pago includes the islands of Tutuila; Swains; Manu'a Is., Ofu, Olosega & Ta'u; Aunu'u and Rose Island.

STATISTICAL OVERVIEW

Personnel	
Bishop	1
Priests: Diocesan Active in Diocese	14
Priests: Retired, Sick or Absent	1
Number of Diocesan Priests	15
Religious Priests in Diocese	2
Total Priests in Diocese	17
Ordinations:	
Diocesan Priests	1
Permanent Deacons in Diocese	31
Total Sisters	11
Parishes	
Parishes	16
With Resident Pastor:	
Resident Diocesan Priests	10
Resident Religious Priests	1
Without Resident Pastor:	
Administered by Priests	5
Pastoral Centers	1
Professional Ministry Personnel:	
Sisters	11
Lay Ministers	55
Welfare	
Homes for the Aged	1
Total Assisted	20
Day Care Centers	1
Total Assisted	40
Special Centers for Social Services	1
Total Assisted	84
Educational	
Diocesan Students in Other Seminaries	3
Total Seminarians	3
High Schools, Diocesan and Parish	1
Total Students	225
Elementary Schools, Diocesan and Parish	2
Total Students	313
Catechesis/Religious Education:	
High School Students	830
Elementary Students	2,443
Total Students under Catholic Instruction	3,814
Teachers in the Diocese:	
Priests	4
Sisters	7
Lay Teachers	62
Vital Statistics	
Receptions into the Church:	
Infant Baptism Totals	244
Minor Baptism Totals	66
Adult Baptism Totals	80
Received into Full Communion	48
First Communions	305
Confirmations	322
Marriages:	
Catholic	28
Interfaith	26
Total Marriages	54
Deaths	61
Total Catholic Population	14,600
Total Population	68,000

Vicar General of Diocese—Rev. VIANE ETUALE, V.G., M.A., M.Ed.

Chancellor—Mrs. IVONA T. MAUGA.

Diocesan Consultors—Most Rev. J. QUINN WEITZEL, M.M., D.D.; Revs. VIANE ETUALE, V.G., M.A., M.Ed.; KELEMETE PUA'AULI; ANDREW ATONIO, M.F.; KOLIO ETUALE, M.Div.; Rev. Msgr. ETUALE LEALOFI, J.C.D.

Diocesan Pastoral Council—Rev. VIANE ETUALE, V.G., M.A., M.Ed., Chm.

Fatuoaiga Multipurpose Cultural and Pastoral Center—Rev. Msgr. ETUALE LEALOFI, J.C.D. Faculty Members: Revs. VIANE ETUALE, V.G., M.A., M.Ed.; KELEMETE PUA'AULI; FALANIKO ATONIO; KOLIO ETUALE, M.Div.

St. Anne Society—Mrs. MALIA TALATAU PEPE, Pres.; Mrs. PASELIKA T. SOLIMALO, Vice Pres.; Mrs. AKENESE TARANGI, Treas.; Mrs. VAELA'A TALO, Sec.

Sacred Heart Society—Mrs. SUNI FELISE, Pres.; Mrs. RUFO TUITELELEAPAGA, Vice Pres.; Mrs. JOANNE KIMOTO, Treas.; Mrs. PALU VITALE, Sec.

Legion of Mary—

Children of Mary—Miss KERESESIA PUAILOA, Pres.; VACANT, Vice Pres.; Miss ADRIENNE FEAGAI, Treas.; Miss KAREN FA'ASAVALU, Sec.

Divine Mercy—Mrs. THERESA BURGOS, Pres.

Youth—Deacon MALAKI TIMU, F.K., Pres.

Women's Organization—Mrs. SALA VITALIANO, Pres.; Mrs. MATALENA KITIONA; Mrs. PALU VITALE, Treas.; Mrs. VAELA'A TALO, Sec.

Rosary Society—

Matrimonial Tribunal—

Judicial Vicar—Most Rev. J. QUINN WEITZEL, M.M., D.D.

Adjunct Judicial Vicar—Rev. Msgr. ETUALE LEALOFI, J.C.D.

Judges—Rev. Msgr. SCOTT L. MARCZUK, J.C.L.; Revs. JAMES SHIFFER, S.S.C., J.C.L.; VIANE ETUALE, V.G., M.A., M.Ed.

Defender of the Bond—VACANT.

Auditors—Revs. SETEFANO T. LUAMANU; KELEMETE PUA'AULI; Deacon FRANCIS LEASIOLAGI; Revs. KOLIO ETUALE, M.Div.; HILDRITHO RANOLA, M.A., M.Ed., M.Div.; Mrs. IVONA T. MAUGA.

Tribunal Administrator—Mrs. IVONA T. MAUGA.

Ecclesiastical Notaries—Mrs. IVONA T. MAUGA; Mrs. THERESA H. SILAO.

Vicar for Diocesan Youth—Deacon MALAKI TIMU, F.K., Dir.

Director of Vocations—Rev. KOLIO ETUALE, M.Div.

Port Chaplain—Deacon TAVITA PEREIRA.

Prison Chaplain—Deacon AUGUST GABRIEL.

Director of Propagation of the Faith—Rev. ETUALE TO'ALEPAI, M.F.

Hospital Chaplain—Deacon PENITITO LEMANA.

CLERGY, PARISHES, MISSIONS AND PAROCHIAL SCHOOLS

SAMOA-PAGO PAGO

1—CATHEDRAL OF THE HOLY FAMILY (1986) Most Rev. John Quinn Weitzel, M.M.; Revs. Asalemo Asalemo Jr. (SP), Rector; Hildritho Ranola; Deacons Francis Leasiolagi; Iosefo Vitaliano; August Gabriel; Avaletalia Hunkin.
Mailing Address: *Fatuoaiga*, P.O. Box 3594, AS 96799-3594. Tel: 684-699-1446; Fax: 684-699-1459.
Catechesis/Religious Program—Tel: 684-699-2209. Mrs. Cecilia Solofa, D.R.E.; Miss Christina Iosefo, D.R.E.; Iosefo Vitaliano, D.R.E.; Paunga Lolesio, D.R.E. Students 470.
Mission—Mary, Star of the Sea Manu'a Island, AS. Tel: 684-677-3103.

2—CHRIST THE KING (Amanave) Rev. Teofilo Schmidt, Admin.; Deacon Samuelu Aoelua.
Mailing Address: P.O. Box 5408, AS 96799. Tel: 684-688-1542.
Catechesis/Religious Program—Students 65.

3—CHRIST THE KING (Malaeloa) (1997) Rev. Iosefo Vaitele Tupuola.
Mailing Address: P.O. Box 596, AS 96799. Tel: 684-688-2438; Fax: 684-699-1459.
Catechesis/Religious Program—Meaalofa Lotomau, Catachetical Leader. Students 90.

4—CHRIST THE KING (Nu'uuli) (1983) Rev. Viane Etuale, Admin.; Deacon Niuatoa Andy Puletasi.
Mailing Address: P.O. Box 596, AS 96799. Fax: 684-699-1459.
Catechesis/Religious Program—Ameto Lemana, D.R.E. Students 105.

5—CHURCH OF SACRED HEART (Alao) (1989) Rev. Falaniko Atonio.
Mailing Address: *Alao*, P.O. Box 4175, AS 96799. Tel: 684-622-7029; Fax: 684-699-1459.
Catechesis/Religious Program—Nu'u Ituau, Catechist. Students 195.
Mission— Aoa, AS. Tel: 684-622-7416. Tumaai Solimalo, F.K., Catechist.
Mission— Amouli, AS. Tel: 684-622-7613. Esitio Savelio, Catechetical Leader.

6—CHURCH OF ST. PETER AND PAUL (Lauli'i) (1969) Rev. Vaiula Iulio; Deacons Setefano Lesa; Isidore Taaga; Moli Toilolo.
Mailing Address: P.O. Box 985, AS 96799. Tel: 684-644-5581.
Catechesis/Religious Program—Tel: 684-644-4697. Students 190.

7—CHURCH OF THE HOLY CROSS (Leone) (1861) Rev. Msgr. Etuale Lealofi; Deacon Toetofi Tavale.
Mailing Address: *Leone*, P.O. Box 1206, AS 96799. Tel: 684-688-7663; Fax: 684-699-1459.
Catechesis/Religious Program—Students 190.

8—CHURCH OF THE IMMACULATE CONCEPTION (Lepua) (1867) Rev. Andrew Atonio, M.F., Admin.; Deacon Iosefo Tarangi.
Mailing Address: *Lepua*, P.O. Box 398, AS 96799. Tel: 684-644-5512.
Catechesis/Religious Program—Tel: 684-644-2411. Leafa Gasio, D.R.E. Students 135.
Mission— Afono, AS. Tel: 684-644-4797.

9—CO-CATHEDRAL OF ST. JOSEPH THE WORKER (Fagatogo) (1974) Revs. Kelemete Pua'auli; Eneliko Auva'a, Rector; Deacons Lutia Timoteo; Iosefo Tanuvasa.
Mailing Address: *Fagatogo*, P.O. Box AA, AS 96799. Tel: 684-633-1548.
Catechesis/Religious Program—Students 270.
Mission— Utulei, AS. Deacon Iosefo Tanuvasa.

Mission— Faga'alu, AS. Tel: 684-633-2560.

10—ST. JOSEPH THE WORKER FUTIGA (2006) Rev. Kolio Etuale.
Mailing Address: P.O. Box 596, AS 96799. Tel: 684-688-7765.
Catechesis/Religious Program—Kelekolio Iosefo, Catechetical Leader. Students 63.

11—OUR LADY OF FATIMA (2002) Rev. Etuale To'alepai, M.F.
Mailing Address: *Aua Parish*, P.O. Box 4052, AS 96799. Tel: 684-644-5826; Fax: 684-699-1459.
Catechesis/Religious Program—John Pereira, D.R.E. Students 165.

12—ST. PAUL (Ili'ili) (1974) Rev. Kolio Etuale; Deacons Iosefo Toilolo; Sauileone Aigofie; Sanele Paselio.
Mailing Address: *Ili'ili*, P.O. Box 2004, AS 96799. Tel: 684-699-7572; Fax: 684-699-1459.
Office: Fatuoaiga, P.O. Box 596, AS 96799. Tel: 684-699-7575.
Catechesis/Religious Program—Lutovi'o Uti, Catechist. Students 375.
Mission— Faleniu, AS.
Mission— Pava'ia'i, AS. Tel: 684-699-7613.
Mission— Aasu/Aoloau, AS. Tel: 684-699-9766.

13—STS. PETER & PAUL, (Asili) Rev. Pale Teofilo Schmidt, Admin.
Mailing Address: P.O. Box 7286, AS 96799. Tel: 684-688-7236.
Catechesis/Religious Program—Students 97.
Mission—Amaluia

14—ST. PETER CHANEL-SA'ILELE Rev. Vaiula Iulio, Admin.
Mailing Address: P.O. Box 596, AS 96799. Tel: 684-622-7512.
Catechesis/Religious Program—Moe Sagote, Catechetical Leader; Faleagafulu Filipo, Catechist. Students 57.
Mission— Masefau, AS. Tel: 684-622-7131.
Mission— Faga'itua, AS. Tel: 684-622-7130.

15—SACRED HEART OF JESUS PARISH, VAILOA (2003) Rev. Tagaloa Timoteo Tatino; Deacon Felise Toilolo.
Mailing Address: P.O. Box 596, AS 96799. Tel: 684-688-1243.
Catechesis/Religious Program—Students 98.

16—SACRED HEART PARISH-PAGO PAGO (2001) Rev. Setefano T. Luamanu.
Res.: P.O. Box 596, AS 96799. Tel: 684-633-4035.
Catechesis/Religious Program—Taumaoe Ioane, Catechist. Total Enrollment 170.
Mission— Fagasa, AS. Tel: 684-633-1352. Ioane Afoa, Catechist.

Permanent Deacons:
Aigofie, Sauileone, F.K.
Aoelua, Samuelu
Auelua, Uikirifi
Auva'a, Lino
Carnecer, Edgar
Gabriel, August, Chap. Pago-Pago Intl. Airport
Hunkin, Avaletalia
Lafaele, Setefano
Laulu, Teofilo
Leasiolagi, Francis
Lemana, Penitito
Leo, Tavai
Mana'o, Lavekava
Paselio, Sanele
Pepe, Anitele'a Tolu
Pereira, Tavita
Puletasi, Andy Niuatoa
Sipiliano, Nua
Taaga, Isidore
Tanuvasa, Iosefo
Tarangi, Iosefo
Tavale, Toetofi
Tia, Vaipuna
Timoteo, Lutia Laupapa
Timu, Malaki, F.K.
Toilolo, Felise
Toilolo, Filipo
Toilolo, Iosefo
Toilolo, Moli
Uelese, Alefosio
Maugaotega, Tavete

INSTITUTIONS LOCATED IN THE DIOCESE

[A] PRESCHOOLS

PAGO PAGO. *Mary The Mother Montessori Early Education Center, c/o Diocese of Samoa-Pago Pago*, Fatuoaiga, P.O. Box 596, AS 96799. Tel: 684-644-1311; Fax: 684-699-1459. Sr. Marilyn Evans, M.M., Prin. & Supr. Sisters 1; Lay Teachers 8; Students 57.

[B] ELEMENTARY SCHOOLS, PAROCHIAL

LEONE. *St. Theresa*, P.O. Box 883, AS 96799-0596. Tel: 684-688-1105; Fax: 684-688-1114. Maria Pepe, Prin. Sisters 2; Lay Teachers 12; Students 171.

LEPUA. *Marist St. Francis*, Fatuoaiga, P.O. Box 429, AS 96799-0429. Fax: 684-699-1459. Sr. Carol Tevaga, F.M.A., Prin.; Mr. Sililo Asalemo, Librarian. Priests 2; Sisters 3; Lay Teachers 12; Students 142.

[C] HIGH SCHOOLS, PAROCHIAL

LEPUAPUA. *Faasao Marist College Preparatory School*, P.O. Box 729, AS 96799. Tel: 684-688-7731; Fax: 684-688-2055. Email: courgars@faasao.com. Mr. Victor Langkilde, Prin.; Mrs. Joanne Roles, Librarian. Priests 1; Sisters 1; Deacons 2; Students 225.

[D] HOMES FOR AGED & SPECIAL CARE FOR CHILDREN

PAGO PAGO. *Hope House*, P.O. Box 596, AS 96799. Tel: 684-699-2101; Fax: 684-699-6051. Sr. Elsa O. Sintilias, O.P., Admin. Aged Residents 11; Special Care Children 9; Montessori Early Education 70; Day Care Center 40; Total Staff 26.

[E] MISCELLANEOUS

PAGO PAGO. *Catholic Social Services, Inc.*, P.O. Box 596, AS 96799. Tel: 684-699-5683; Fax: 684-699-1340. Email: ccs1@samoatelco.com. Total Staff 3.

Diocesan Eucharistic League, P.O. Box 596, AS 96799. Tel: 684-699-1402; Fax: 684-699-1459. Email: ivonamauga@yahoo.com. Mrs. Ivona T. Mauga, Pres.

Knights of Columbus, 66-Aiga Paia Knights Council #14808, Box 596, AS 96799.

RELIGIOUS INSTITUTES OF MEN REPRESENTED IN THE DIOCESE

For further details refer to the corresponding bracketed number in the Religious Institutes of Men or Women section.

[0800]—*Maryknoll*—M.M.

[]—*Missionaries of the Faith*—M.F.

RELIGIOUS INSTITUTES OF WOMEN REPRESENTED IN THE DIOCESE

[]—*Dominican Sisters of the Holy Trinity*—O.P.

[2470]—*Maryknoll Sisters of St. Dominic*—M.M.

[]—*Religious Sisters of the Virgin Mary*—R.V.M.

[]—*Salesian Sisters (Daughters of Mary Help of Christians)*—F.M.A.

NECROLOGY

† Tavai, Van Camp, Pago Pago, AS Immaculate Conception—Died April 30, 2009

An asterisk (*) denotes an organization that has established tax-exempt status directly with the IRS and is not covered by the USCCB Group Ruling.

Archdiocese of San Juan, Puerto Rico

(Sancti Joannis Portoricensis)

His Eminence

LUIS CARDINAL APONTE MARTINEZ, D.D.

Retired Archbishop of San Juan; ordained April 10, 1950; appointed Titular Bishop of Lares and Auxiliary of Ponce July 23, 1960; consecrated October 12, 1960; appointed Coadjutor Bishop of Ponce April 16, 1963; appointed Bishop of Ponce November 18, 1963; installed February 22, 1964; promoted to Archbishop of San Juan November 4, 1964; installed January 15, 1965; Created Cardinal March 5, 1973; retired March 26, 1999.

Most Reverend

HECTOR M. RIVERA, D.D.

Retired Auxiliary Bishop of San Juan PR; ordained June 12, 1966; appointed Titular Bishop of Tubune in Numidia and Auxiliary Bishop of San Juan PR June 11, 1979; consecrated August 17, 1979; retired October 31, 2009. *Res.: Valle Arriba Heights, Calle Alamo, BF #20, Carolina, PR 00983.* Tel: 787-276-1413. *Mailing Address: P.O. Box 31155, San Juan, PR 00929-2155.*

Most Reverend

ROBERTO O. GONZALEZ NIEVES, O.F.M.

Archbishop of San Juan; ordained May 8, 1977; appointed Titular Bishop of Ursona and Auxiliary Bishop of Boston July 19, 1988; consecrated October 3, 1988; appointed Coadjutor Bishop of Corpus Christi May 16, 1995; transferred to Corpus Christi June 26, 1995; succeeded to See April 1, 1997; appointed Archbishop of San Juan March 26, 1999; installed May 8, 1999.

Chancery Office: P.O. Box 9021967, San Juan, PR 00902-1967. Tel: 787-727-7373; Fax: 787-726-8280.

Most Reverend

HERMIN NEGRON SANTANA, D.D.

Auxiliary Bishop of San Juan, PR; ordained May 30, 1969; appointed Titular Bishop of Gegi, North Africa and Auxiliary Bishop of San Juan, PR June 30, 1981; consecrated September 7, 1981. *Res.: Urb. Caparra Heights, 1562 C. Encarnacion, San Juan, PR 00920.* Tel: 787-277-5680.

Most Reverend

DANIEL FERNANDEZ TORRES

Auxiliary Bishop of San Juan, PR; ordained January 7, 1995; appointed Titular Bishop of Sufes and Auxiliary Bishop of San Juan, PR February 14, 2007; ordained April 21, 2007.

ERECTED AUGUST 8, 1511.

Square Miles 353.

Erected an Archdiocese April 30, 1960.

Comprises the northeast portion of the Island of Puerto Rico, with a Total Population of 1,451,146

STATISTICAL OVERVIEW

Personnel	
Retired Cardinals	1
Archbishops	1
Auxiliary Bishops	2
Retired Bishops	1
Priests: Diocesan Active in Diocese	56
Priests: Diocesan Active Outside Diocese	7
Priests: Retired, Sick or Absent	26
Number of Diocesan Priests	89
Religious Priests in Diocese	166
Total Priests in Diocese	255
Extern Priests in Diocese	31
Ordinations:	
Diocesan Priests	1
Religious Priests	2
Transitional Deacons	1
Permanent Deacons in Diocese	165
Total Brothers	18
Total Sisters	459
Parishes	
Parishes	143
With Resident Pastor:	
Resident Diocesan Priests	94
Resident Religious Priests	48
Missions	143
Professional Ministry Personnel:	
Brothers	18
Sisters	459
Lay Ministers	2,159
Welfare	
Catholic Hospitals	5
Total Assisted	33,641
Health Care Centers	4
Total Assisted	76,944
Homes for the Aged	5
Total Assisted	669
Residential Care of Children	8
Total Assisted	936
Day Care Centers	1
Total Assisted	20
Specialized Homes	5
Total Assisted	36,974
Special Centers for Social Services	10
Total Assisted	33,062
Educational	
Seminaries, Diocesan	1
Students from This Diocese	15
Students from Other Diocese	6
Diocesan Students in Other Seminaries	5
Seminaries, Religious	4
Students Religious	14
Total Seminarians	34
Colleges and Universities	2
Total Students	9,284
High Schools, Diocesan and Parish	20
Total Students	4,095
High Schools, Private	28
Total Students	6,904
Elementary Schools, Diocesan and Parish	28
Total Students	8,393
Elementary Schools, Private	41
Total Students	13,498
Non-residential Schools for the Disabled	1
Total Students	120
Catechesis/Religious Education:	
High School Students	10,999
Elementary Students	25,223
Total Students under Catholic Instruction	78,550
Teachers in the Diocese:	
Priests	41
Scholastics	76
Brothers	18
Sisters	459
Lay Teachers	2,257
Vital Statistics	
Receptions into the Church:	
Infant Baptism Totals	6,221
Minor Baptism Totals	951
Received into Full Communion	6
First Communions	4,895
Confirmations	4,166
Marriages:	
Catholic	1,045
Interfaith	94
Total Marriages	1,139
Total Catholic Population	944,508
Total Population	1,259,344

Former Bishops—Most Revs. ALONSO MANSO, D.D., appt. May 1511; JAMES H. BLENK, S.M.D.D., appt. Bishop of Puerto Rico, June 12, 1899; died April 20, 1917; WILLIAM A. JONES, O.S.A., cons. Feb. 24, 1907; died Jan. 1921; GEORGE J. CARUANA, D.D., appt. Bishop 1921; promoted to the Apostolic Delegation of Mexico, 1925; promoted to Nunciature Apostolic of Cuba, 1927; EDWIN VINCENT BYRNE, D.D., former Bishop of Ponce, Puerto Rico; cons. Nov. 30, 1925; appt. March 1929; promoted to Archdiocese of Santa Fe, June 15, 1943; died July 25, 1963; JAMES PETER DAVIS (Retired), appt. 1943; cons. Oct. 9, 1943; transferred to Archdiocese of Santa Fe, June, 1963; installed Feb. 25, 1964; retired Oct. 1974; His Eminence LUIS CARDINAL APONTE MARTINEZ, D.D. (Retired), appt. Auxiliary Bishop of Ponce July 23, 1960; cons. Oct. 12, 1960; appt. Coadjutor Bishop of Ponce April 16, 1963; succeeded to Nov. 18, 1963; installed Feb. 22, 1964; appt. Archbishop of San Juan Nov. 4, 1964; installed Jan. 15, 1965; created Cardinal March 5, 1973; retired March 26, 1999.

Vicars General—Most Revs. HECTOR RIVERA, D.D.; HERMIN NEGRON SANTANA, D.D.; Rev. Msgr. LEONARDO J. RODRIGUEZ-JIMENES.

Episcopal Moderator—

for Administration of Temporalities—Rev. Msgr. LEONARDO J. RODRIGUEZ-JIMENES, Moderator.

for Education—VACANT. Web: www.escueloscatolicos-sj.org.

for Pastoral Affairs—Rev. ALBERTO LOPEZ-FIGUEROA.

for Geographic-Pastoral Zones—San Juan-Santurce: Rev. TARSICIO GOTAY FIGAREDO, O.Carm. Bayamon: Rev. ANGEL PAGAN TORRES. Carolina: Rev. NESTOR YULFO-HOFFMAN. Rio Piedras: Rev. JOAQUIN MAYORGA-FONSECA. Guaynabo-Puerto Nuevo: Rev. WALTER GOMEZ-BACA.

Chancery Office—Mailing Address: P.O. Box 9021967, San Juan, 00902-1967. Web: www.arqsj.org.

Chancery Affairs—Miss LUCIA GUZMAN ORTA, Chancellor. Email: luciagu@arqsj.org.

Vice Chancellor—VACANT.

Metropolitan Curia—

Moderator—Rev. Msgr. LEONARDO J. RODRIGUEZ-JIMENES.

Secretary to the Archbishop—Rev. ALFONSO GUZMAN ALFARO, O.F.M. Tel: 787-725-4975; 787-977-0672.

Executive Assistant to the Archbishop—Mr. SAMUEL SOTO-ALONSO. Tel: 787-725-4975; 787-977-0672.

Assistant to the Archbishop and Secretary to the Cardinal—Miss MIRIAM RAMOS. Tel: 787-725-4975; 787-977-0672.

Judicial Vicar—Rev. PEDRO L. REYES LEBRÓN.

Adjunct Vicar—Rev. LUIS NORBERTO CORREA-GARCIA.

Judges—Miss MARIA LUCIA SANCHEZ; Revs. LUIS NORBERTO CORREA-GARCIA; JORGE AMBERT-RIVERA.

Defender of the Bond—MARIA DEL ROSARIO RINCON-BECERRA.

Instructors—Mr. RIGOBERTO HIRALDO RIOS; Mr. JOSE GARCIA FERNANDEZ; Mr. ROLANDO QUEVEDO DEL RIO; Revs. JOSE A. LANDRAU-ROMAN; CARMELO SOTO TANON; ALBITA DARILA; Mrs. CARMEN J. ACOSTA; Mrs. ANGELA GARCIA. Email: tribunal@arqsj.org.

Lawyers—ORLANDO DURAN; MILAGROS GONZALEZ-RODRIQUEZ; XAVIER HIRALDO-SANCHEZ; MARJORIE STEWART.

Diocesan Consultors—Most Revs. HERMIN NEGRON SANTANA, D.D.; HECTOR RIVERA-PEREZ, D.D.; DANIEL FERNANDEZ-TORRES; Rev. Msgrs. LEONARDO J. RODRIGUEZ JIMENES; ALBERTO LOPEZ FIGUEROA; JOSE E. CUMMINGS-ESPADA; Revs. ANGEL L. CIAPPI-AZCORRA; MILTON AGUSTIN RIVERA-VIGO; MARCO ANTONIO RIVERA PEREZ; PEDRO L. REYES LEBRÓN.

Censor Librorum—Rev. Msgr. FERNANDO B. FELICES-SANCHEZ.

Vicar of Social Communication—Rev. MILTON AGUSTIN RIVERA-VIGO.

Auxiliary Vicar of Social Communication—VACANT.

Vicar of Cultural Affairs—Rev. Msgr. EFRAIN RODRIGUEZ-OTERO.

Vicar of Development—Rev. ANGEL L. CIAPPI-AZCORRA.

Vicar of Economic Affairs—Rev. ANGEL L. CIAPPI-AZCORRA; Mrs. SANDRA RODRIGUEZ, Asst. to Vicar.

Vicar of Ecumenism—Rev. WILLIAM TORRES-PAGAN.

Vicar of Family Affairs—Rev. Msgr. WILFREDO PENA-MOREDO.

Vicar for Pastoral Affairs—Rev. Msgr. ALBERTO LOPEZ FIGUEROA.

Vicar for Education—VACANT.

Vicar of Religious—Rev. ALFONSO GUZMAN ALFARO, O.F.M.

Examinatores Cleri—VACANT.

Vicar for Vocations—Rev. EDWIN ALBERIO LONDONO ZULUAGA.

Pro-Synodal Examiner—VACANT.

Vicar for Priests—Rev. JOSE FRANCISCO QUINTERO-ANGUEIRA.

Vicar for Youth—Rev. RAMON HIRAM NEGRON, O.F.M.Cap.

Archdiocesan Offices and Directors

Boy Scouts—VACANT.

Catechetics—Most Rev. DANIEL FERNANDEZ-TORRES, Archdiocesan Coord., Calle San Jorge 201, Santurce, 00914.

Catechetics Center—Sr. MERCEDES CADENAS, Mailing Address: San Juan-Santurce, P.O. Box 9021967, San Juan, 00902-1967. Tel: 787-727-7373. Bayamon: Sr. IMELDA MORALES, M.SS.S., Mailing Address: P.O. Box 4152, Bayamon, 00958. Tel: 787-780-1173. Rio Piedras: Sr. ISABEL SOTO, M.SS.S., Mailing Address: P.O. Box 20884, San Juan, 00920. Tel: 787-761-4280. Guaynabo-PtoNuevo: Sr. ROSE MORALES, M.S.B.T., Mailing Address: P.O. Box 9021967, San Juan, 00902-1967. Tel: 787-731-6100.

Catholic Charities—Rev. ENRIQUE MANUEL CAMACHO-MONSERRATE, Mailing Address: P.O. Box 8812, San Juan, 00910-0812. Tel: 787-727-7373; Fax: 787-728-4100. Email: ssc@arqsj.org.

"El Visitante"— Weekly Catholic Paper for All Dioceses (Interdiocesan). Published By The P.R., Episcopal Conference. Revs. RUBEN GONZALEZ-MEDINA, C.M.F., Pres.; EFRAIN ZABALA, Editor; JAIME TORRES TORRES, Dir., Mailing Address: P.O. Box 41305, Minillas Sta., San Juan, 00940-1305. Tel: 787-728-3710; Fax: 787-268-1748. Offices, Pumarada St. 1704, Santurce, 00914.

Radio Stations— WORO-FM and WKVM-AM 81, Mr. ALAN CORALES, Dir., Urb. Baldrich, 415 Calle Ingeniero Carbonell, San Juan, 00918. Mailing Address: P.O. Box 9021967, San Juan, 00902-1967. Tel: 787-731-1380; 787-751-1018; Fax: 787-758-9967. Email: radiooro@arqsj.org.

Television Station— WPRV-TV CHANNEL 13, Tele Oro, Rev. MILTON AGUSTIN RIVERA-VIGO, Exec. Dir.; Mr. JUAN M. MUNIZ, Gen. Mgr., Ave Iturregui Esq. Marginal, Baldorioty De Castro Ave., Carolina, 00982. Tel: 787-276-1300; Fax: 787-276-1307. Mailing Address: P.O. Box 9021967, San Juan, 00902-1967.

Commission for Sacred Liturgy and Popular Piety—Rev. Msgr. LEONARDO J. RODRIGUEZ-JIMENES.

Subcommission for Sacred Art—Rev. Msgr. LEONARDO J. RODRIGUEZ JIMENES; Rev. RODOLFO LAMAS; Dr. ARTURO DAVILA, Urb. Baldrich, Calle Rossy #202, San Juan, 00918. Tel: 787-763-9154; Dr. TERESA TIO; FRANCISCO JAVIER BLANCO; HECTOR BALVANERA; Rev. Msgr. JOSE E. CUMMINGS-ESPADA.

Subcommission for Sacred Music—Rev. MIGUEL TRINIDAD.

Subcommission for Popular Piety—Rev. TARSICIO GOTAY FIGAREDO, O.Carm.

Subcommission for Ministries—Rev. Msgr. LEONARDO J. RODRIGUEZ-JIMENES.

Clergy Social Security (Prevision Social del Clero)—VACANT, Pres.; Revs. RICARDO HERNANDEZ, Treas.; ALBERTO DIAZ; ANGEL MENDEZ; VACANT, Sec., Mailing Address: CEP, P.O. Box 4682, San Juan, 00940-0682. Tel: 787-728-1650; Fax: 787-728-1654.

Istepa—Rev. Msgr. FRANCISCO MEDINA, Camino Alejandrino KM 3.4, Antiguo, Guaynabo, 00969. Mailing Address: Edificio 2021, Carretera #177, Guaynabo, 00969-5140. Tel: 787-731-6100; Fax: 787-731-0000.

San Juan Bautista Regional Seminary—Rev. JUAN LUIS NEGRON, Rector; Rev. Msgr. IVAN L. HUERTAS-COLON, Vice Rector; Rev. MARIO MESA, O.F.M.Cap., Dean of Studies. Spiritual Directors: Revs. PEDRO L. REYES, Mailing Address: P.O. Box 11714, San Juan, 00922-1714. Tel: 787-783-0645; 787-273-8090; Fax: 787-783-0645. Ave. De Diego 930, Urb. La Riviera, Rio Piedras, 00921. Email: seminary@coqui.net; JOSE VICENTE MARTINEZ, C.M.F.; EDWIN ALBERIO LONDONO ZULUAGA.

Serra Club—VACANT.

Vocations Promoter—Rev. EDWIN ALBERIO LONDONO ZULUAGA, Mailing Address: P.O. Box 11714, San Juan, 00922-1714. Tel: 787-706-9455; 787-273-8090.

Superintendent of Schools—Mrs. ANA CORTES, Supt.; Mrs. CARMEN RIVERA, Asst.; VACANT, Rel. Prog. Dir., Mailing Address: Edificio 2021, Carretera 177, Guaynabo, 00969-5140. Tel: 787-731-6100; Fax: 787-731-0000. Web: www.esculelascatolicas-sj.org.

Archdiocesan Historical Archive—Mrs. ELSE ZAYAS LEON, Calle San Sebastian 5-N, San Juan, 00902. Mailing Address: P.O. Box 9021967, San Juan, 00902-1967. Tel: 787-977-1447.

Youth Ministries—Rev. RAMON HIRAM NEGRON, O.F.M.Cap., Ext. Villamar, Calle Marginal AB #1, Isla Verde, 00979.

Police Chaplains—Rev. Msgrs. BAUDILIO MERINO. Tel: 787-767-6552; VALERIANO MIGUÉLEZ. Tel: 787-754-0570; Rev. ANTONIO GARCIA CASTEJON. Tel: 787-757-4454; Deacon JOSE PENA GONZALEZ. Tel: 787-786-5309.

Society for the Protection of Children—Most Rev. ROBERTO OCTAVIO GONZÁLEZ NIEVES, O.F.M., Mailing Address: P.O. Box 9021967, San Juan, 00902-1967. Tel: 787-727-7373.

United Against Hunger (Unidos Contra El Hambre)—Deacon HECTOR CRUZ DECHOUDENS, San Jorge St., No. 201, Santurce, 00914. Mailing Address: P.O. Box 11547, San Juan, 00910-2647. Tel: 787-727-7373, Ext. 240; Fax: 787-727-7938. Email: uch@arqsj.org.

Propagation of the Faith—Rev. JOSE ORLANDO CAMACHO-TORRES, C.S.Sp., 106 Ruiz Belvis St., P.O. Box 191882, Floral Park, San Juan, 00919.

Pius Union of the Clergy—VACANT, Mailing Address: P.O. Box 9021967, San Juan, 00902-1967. Tel: 787-727-7373.

Catholic Charismatic Renewal—Rev. Msgr. BAUDILIO MERINO MERINO, Dir., Arzobispado de San Juan. Tel: 787-765-6240; 787-727-7373.

Master of Ceremonies to the Archbishop—Mr. LUIS DACOSTA-DEJESUS.

Pre Cana Conferences—VACANT, Dir., Parroquia Santa Rosa Lima, 1765 Calle Lesbos, San Juan, 00926. Tel: 787-761-6586; Mr. MANUEL SANCHEZ, Urb. Country Club, 1031 Calle Genoveva De Lugo, San Juan, 00924. Tel: 787-769-3565.

Caritas of Puerto Rico—Rev. ENRIQUE MANUEL CAMACHO-MONSERRATE, Exec. Dir., Mailing Address: P.O. Box 8812, San Juan, 00910-0812. Tel: 787-727-7373; Fax: 787-728-4100.

Cursillos De Cristiandad—Revs. TOMAS GONZALEZ-GONZALEZ; VICENTE FERNANDEZ-MARINO, Mailing Address: P.O. Box 361809, San Juan, 00936-1809. Tel: 787-789-7596; Fax: 787-790-7596.

Immigrant Aid—Mrs. CANDIDA ROSA MATOS, Mailing Address: Catholic Social Services, P.O. Box 9021967, San Juan, 00902-1967. Tel: 787-727-7373.

Holy Childhood Association—Rev. JOSE ORLANDO CAMACHO-TORRES, C.S.Sp.

Holy Name Society—Mr. MIGUEL A. RODRIGUEZ, Archdiocesan Dir., Mailing Address: P.O. Box 31164, San Juan, 00929. Tel: 787-276-2212; 787-764-4813; Mr. FRANCISCO FIGUEROA, Sec. Tel: 787-768-4787.

Renovacion Conyugal (Fundacion Fernando Martinez Calle, Inc.)—Rev. BAUDILIO GUZMÁN, S.J., Dir., Urb. Ext. Roosevelt, 576 Calle Eddie Gracia, San Juan, 00918. Tel: 787-751-6001; 787-766-1363. Email: ambertsj@aol.com. Web: www.renovacion.net.

Legion of Mary—Mrs. ROSITA SANTANA, Pres.; Rev. ANGEL L. CIAPPI-AZCORRA, Spiritual Dir., Urb. Munoz Rivera, C. Betania #34, Guaynabo, 00969. Tel: 787-360-0508.

Marriage Encounter—Mr. RICARDO PACHECO; Mrs. RICARDO PACHECO, Mansiones De Rio Piedras, 1795 C. Gardenia, San Juan, 00926-7212. Tel: 787-761-1868.

Spiritual Director—VACANT.

Catholic Daughters of America—Mrs. IRMA BONILLA, c/o Julio Bonilla #50, Isabela, 00662. Tel: 787-872-6831.

Spiritual Director—Rev. Msgr. INAKI MAYONA, C.P.

Knights of Columbus—Mr. JUAN R. NIEVES-BONILLA; VACANT, Chap., P.O. Box 40175, San Juan, 00940-0175. Tel: 787-728-2690; 787-630-1167.

Movimiento "Por Un Mundo Mejor"—Rev. JUAN J. GENOVARD, M.SS.CC., Calle Duke 211, University Gardens, Rio Piedras, 00927. Tel: 787-282-9062; 787-282-0501; Fax: 787-282-9063.

Nocturnal Adoration—Mr. ANGEL PAGAN, Pres., Mailing Address: P.O. Box 190199, San Juan, 00919-0199. Tel: 787-749-0502.

Spiritual Director—Rev. RICARDO HERNANDEZ MORALES.

Talleres De Oracion y Vida P. Larranaga—Mrs. MARTA ALVAREZ, Dir., Mailing Address: P.O. Box 800140, Coto Laurel, 00780-0140. Tel: 787-848-2111; 787-948-8418.

Tourism and Apostleship of the Sea—

Casamar—VACANT.

UPR Catholic Student Center—Rev. RAFAEL RODRÍGUEZ, S.J., Mariana Bracetti 10, Rio Piedras, 00925-2201. Tel: 787-767-3348; Fax: 787-758-4145.

San Juan International Airport Chapel—Deacon EDUARDO GONZALEZ.

Carmelite Third Order—Rev. LUIS MIRANDA, O.Carm. Tel: 787-726-2631.

Casa San Clemente—

Psychological and Pastoral Counseling—257 Ponce De Leon, San Juan, 00906. Tel: 787-723-6915.

Couple to Couple League—Mr. TONY FEBLES; Mrs. TONY FEBLES, 5 C. Arzuaga, Ste. 333, San Juan, 00925-3701. Tel: 787-276-4951.

Pro-Life Center (Human Life International)—VACANT.

Pro-Life Pharmacists International—Miss SANDRA FABREGAS, Dir.

Consejo De Accion Social Arquidiocesano—Most Rev. HECTOR RIVERA, Dir., Mailing Address: P.O. Box 31155, San Juan, 00929-2155. Tel: 787-276-1413; Mrs. IDIS OTERO, Coord.

Servicios Pastorales Paules—Rev. SANTIAGO ARRIBAS, C.M., Dir., 1650, Ave. Fernandez Juncos, San Juan, 00910-0118. Tel: 787-728-0670; Fax: 787-728-0670. Mailing Address: P.O. Box 19118, San Juan, 00910-9118.

Franciscan Third Order (Secular Franciscan Order)—Rev. ROY MARTINEZ, O.F.M.Cap., Spiritual Dir.; Mrs. AWILDA VASQUEZ, Natl. Minister, Mailing Address: P.O. Box 3915, Carolina, 00984. Tel: 787-752-7363.

Focolares—LUIS NOEL SOTO, Dir., Q2 Calle 21, Ciudad Universitaria, Trujillo Alto, 00976. Tel: 787-761-5721; 787-767-2346; Fax: 787-761-5721.

Secretariado Sagrado Corazon—Most Rev. HECTOR M. RIVERA, Spiritual Dir.; Mrs. ANA M. BONET, Pres., Urb. Prado Alto, C6 Calle 4, Guaynabo, 00966. Tel: 787-781-6295.

Grupo Reina De La Paz—Miss IVETTE PACHECO, Pres., PMB 258, Ste. 2, Ave. Esmeralda 405, Guaynabo, 00969. Tel: 787-644-8256; Fax: 787-731-8256; Mrs. IVONNE MELENDEZ, Sec. Tel: 787-754-8383; VACANT, Spiritual Dir.

Union Eucaristica Reparadora (UNER)—Rev. VICTORIANO RAMOS, Spiritual Dir. (Retired); Mrs. MARIA MERCEDES MAIZ, Dir., Cond. El Paraiso, 7-D Calle Parania 1560, San Juan, 00926. Tel: 787-751-1821; Mrs. ESTHER VARGAS, Urb. Ponce de Leon, Calle 23 #250, Guaynabo, 00969. Tel: 787-789-6660; DOLLIE MORALES; MARIZA BELARANA; LUIGUI BENITEZ; SONIA RENIOS.

Sociedad San Vicente De Paul—Mrs. PETRIN, Pres., 938 Calle Azabache, San Juan, 00924.

Maranatha House of Prayer—SILVIA SAAVEDRA DE BADIA, Dir., Urb. La Arboleda, Calle Alameda B #13, Guaynabo, 00966. Tel: 787-731-1415; Rev. BANDILIO GUZMAN, S.J., Dir. Esp.

Juventud Mariana Vicenciana (JMV)—VACANT, Dir., Seminario San Vicente De Paul; Sr. MILAGROS OLIVENCIA, H.C., Archdiocesan Representative, Hospital Auxilio Mutuo.

Hermandad N. Sra. De La Caridad—CALLE S. PEDRO MARTIR. Tel: 787-720-2361; Rev. Msgr. MARIO GUIJARRO, Dir. Espiritual; VACANT, Dir., Mailing Address: P.O. Box 10151, San Juan, 00922-0151. Tel: 787-783-3522.

Movimiento Juan XXIII—Mr. ANGEL L. RIOS, Pres., Villa Contessa, F35 Calle Aragon, Bayamon, 00976. Tel: 787-787-5984; Fax: 787-785-1024.

Movimiento De Schoenstatt—Mr. CARLOS A. FALCON, Urb. Paseo Real, Calle B, D-2, San Juan, 00926. Tel: 787-748-7436.

World Apostolate of Fatima—Prof. AMERICO LOPEZ-ORTIZ, Intl. Pres., Mailing Address: P.O. Box 1968, Fernandez Juncos Sta., Mayaguez, 00681-1968. Tel: 787-833-0509; 787-487-5383.

Neocatecumenal Way—Deacon JULIO ALVAREZ, Dir., Urb. Lago Alto, F81 Calle Loiza, Trujillo Alto, 00976. Tel: 787-755-4320.
Our Lady of Providence Association—VACANT.
Perpetual Adoration—Mrs. VIRGINIA ALVAREZ, Asst., Mailing Address: Box S-763, San Juan, 00902. Tel: 787-725-7734.
Padre Nuestro—Mr. SAMUEL VALENTIN, Pres., Urb. Las Colinas, Calle 6, F. 35, Toa Baja, 00949. Tel: 787-368-3810.
Movimiento De Seglares Claretianos—Mrs. CARMEN SANCHEZ, Dir., San Antonio Maria Claret Parish. Tel: 787-797-3337.
Apostolado Del Cenaculo Misionero—Rev. VICENTE PASQUALETTO, S.T., Spiritual Dir.; Mrs. ALMA ROBLES, Urb. Los Colobos, Calle Robles #516, Carolina, 00987. Tel: 787-752-9327; 787-876-0827.
Conferencia Mariana De Puerto Rico—Mr. RICARDO HERNANDEZ; Mrs. RICARDO HERNANDEZ. Spiritual Directors: Rev. Msgr. FERNANDO B. FELICES-SANCHEZ; Rev. RICARDO HERNANDEZ MORALES.

CLERGY, PARISHES, MISSIONS AND PAROCHIAL SCHOOLS

CITY OF SAN JUAN

1—CATEDRAL DE SAN JUAN BAUTISTA (1522), (Nuestra Sra. de los Remedios). Rev. Jose Emilio Cummings, Rector; Deacons Louis Marin; Rafael Morales; Luis Echegaray Martinez.
Res.: 151 Cristo St., Box 9022145, 00902-2145. Tel: 787-722-0861; Fax: 787-722-0861.
Chapel—Santo Cristo
Chapel—San Jose, Tel: 787-725-7501.
Chapel—Santa Ana

2—ASUNCION DE LA VIRGEN (1972) Rev. José Ramón Fernández Mendez.
Res.: Calle Calve No. 1484, Urb. Antonsanti, Rio Piedras, 00927. Tel: 787-250-6771; Fax: 787-463-0894.

3—CORPUS CHRISTI (1972) Rev. Pablo Valenzuela (Spain); Deacons Francisco Gierbolini; Miguel Mendez; Juan Figueroa; Reinaldo Del Valle; Jose Perez; Casiano Lugo; Luis Fernando Amador; Luis A. Aparicio Amengual.
Res. & Mailing Address: Calle Jose Abad, 1224 Urb. Club Manor, 00924. Tel: 787-757-5821; Fax: 787-257-2741.
Mission—Santo Domingo de Guzman Carretera 849 Km. 8.7, Sector Santo Domingo, Penuelas CoEmail: pvalenzuelaz@onelinkpr.net.

4—CRISTO REDENTOR (1971) Rev. Damian Carvajal (Spain).
Res. & Mailing Address: Calle Ganges 140, Urb. El Paraiso, 00926. Tel: 787-764-1583.

5—CRISTO REY (1956) Rev. Perfecto Fondevila Penas (Spain); Deacons Victor Reyes; Miguel Roman Del Valle.
Mailing Address: 65 Inf. Sta., P.O. Box 29695, 00929-0695.
Res.: Calle Jaime Drew, No. 789, Urb. Los Maestros, Rio Piedras, 00923. Tel: 787-767-3289.

6—ESPIRITU SANTO (1941) Rev. Msgr. Valeriano Miguélez (Spain); Deacon David Henriquez.
Mailing Address: P.O. Box 190259, 00919-0259. Calle Pachin Marin, Esq. Suiza, Hato Rey, 00919.
Res.: 75 Ruiz Belvis St., Floral Park, Hato Rey, 00919. Tel: 787-754-0570.
School—P.O. Box 191715, 00917. Tel: 787-754-0490; 787-754-0555; Fax: 787-754-7154. Olga Iris Torres, Assoc. Prin. Priests 1; Lay Teachers 46; Students 756.

7—FRANCISCA JAVIERA CABRINI (1968), (Mother Cabrini) Rev. Prisciliano Cardenas.
Res.: 1564 Encarnacion St., 00920. Tel: 787-783-7447; Fax: 787-706-2073.
Catechesis/Religious Program—Students 90.

8—INMACULADO CORAZON DE MARIA (1961) Rev. Felipe Nunez-Carrion; Deacons Jose Rodriguez; Israel Suarez; Benjamin Totti Lugo.
Urb. Santiago Iglesias, #1740 Calle Rodriguez Vera, Rio Piedras, 00921. Tel: 787-782-0245; Fax: 787-782-4176. Email: corazondemaria1704@hotmail.com. Web: inmaculadocorazon.tripod.com.
Res.: Rodriguez Vera y Ferrer St., Urb. Santiago Iglesias, 00922.
Catechesis/Religious Program—Students 60.
Mission—Monacillos San Fernando, San Juan Co.
Chapel—N. Sra. del Camino, Metropolitan Hospital [JC]

9—JESUS MAESTRO (1969) Revs. Basilio Roldan, C.M. (Spain); Santiago Arribas, C.M.; Manuel Araujo, C.P.; Deacon Rafael Velazquez.
Res.: Segre 1725 Urb. Rio Piedras Heights, 00926. Tel: 787-763-8291; Fax: 787-763-8291.
Mission—Jesus Nazareno Calle Guadiana #1666, Urb. El Cerezal, 00926.

10—JESUS MEDIADOR (1988) Rev. Luis Cruez; Deacons Candido Martinez; Edwin Rivera.
Res. & Mailing Address: Calle Demetrio O'Daly 1000, Urb. Country Club, 00924. Tel: 787-752-2410; Fax: 787-752-2410.

11—MARIA AUXILIADORA (1962) Revs. Nicolas Navarro, S.D.B.; Andres Rivera, S.D.B.; Antonio Polo, S.D.B.; Bro. Jose Cabo.
Mailing Address: P.O. Box 14367, 00916.
Res.: C. Constitucion Esq. Sta. Elena, Cantera, 00916. Tel: 787-727-5346; 787-726-1995, Ext. 267.
Catechesis/Religious Program—Students 300.
Mission—Sagrado Corazon, Sector Buenavista.
Mission—Nra. Sra. del Altagracia, Sector Buenavista.
Mission—Ntra. Sra. de Fatima, Sector Ultimo Chance-Cerro.
Mission—Santisima Trinidad Ave. Borinquen Final.

12—MARIA MADRE DE LA IGLESIA (1967) Rev. Edgardo Sanabria Santaliz; Deacons George Gonzalez; Eugenio Torres Diaz.
Res.: 1120 Calle 5, Urb. Villa Nevarez, 00927. Tel: 787-765-0600.

13—MARIA REINA DEL MUNDO (1971) Rev. Mariano Martínez Galvez, O.M.I.
Mailing Address: G.P.O. Box 3828, 00936-3828. Tel: 787-781-0303.
Res.: Caserio Nemesio Canales, Roosevelt Ave. Puerto Nuevo, Rio Piedras, 00936.
Catechesis/Religious Program—Students 20.

14—NTR. SRA. DE LA CARIDAD DEL COBRE (1969) Rev. Wilfredo Echevarria Lopez.
Res.: Urb. Buena Vista, Calle 5, No. 124, 00917. Tel: 787-689-4804.
Mission—Sma. Trinidad Calle Buenos Aires, No. 25, Parada 27, Hato Rey, San Juan Co. 00919.

15—NTRA. SRA. DE FATIMA (1967) Revs. Jose Reeyes-Garcia, O.de.M.; Martin Garamendi, O.M. (Spain); Jose M. Gallego, O.M. (Spain); Antonio Garcia-Martinez, O.M. (Spain).
Mailing Address: P.O. Box 190396, 00919-0396. Tel: 787-753-6334; Fax: 787-764-3571.
Res.: 608 Munoz Rivera Ave., Stop 34, Urb. Baldrich, Hato Rey, 00919.
School—La Merced (1949) P.O. Box 364048, 00936-4048. Tel: 787-765-7342; 787-754-1162; Fax: 787-765-3970. Mrs. Rosa M. Figueroa, Prin. Lay Teachers 36; Students 485.
Mission—Egida del Maestro

16—NTRA. SRA. DE LA MEDALLA MILAGROSA (1957) Rev. Carlos Verdia Nay; Deacon De Jesús Robles Filiberty.
Mailing Address: Urb. Perez Moris, Calle Mayaguez 209, 00917.
Res.: 209 Mayaguez St., 00917. Tel: 787-751-2335; Fax: 787-274-0939.

17—NTRA. SRA. DE LA MONSERRATE (1916) Rev. Oscar Jimenez Portes, O.S.A.
Mailing Address: P.O. Box 13726, 00908-3726.
Res.: 1058 Fernandez Juncos Ave., 00907. Tel: 787-722-3134; Fax: 787-723-7838. Email: oscarjp@msn.com.
School—Santa Monica, Tel: 787-723-2573 (Elem.); 787-723-3845 (H.S.); Fax: 787-723-3992. Lay Teachers 39; Students 495.
Catechesis/Religious Program—Students 35.
Mission—Trastalleres Santa Ana, San Juan Co.

18—NTRA. SRA. DEL PERPETUO SOCORRO (1941) Rev. Msgr. Carlos Quintana-Puente.
Res.: Calle Marti 704, Miramar, Santurce, 00907-3227. Tel: 787-721-1015; 787-721-1016.
School—Jose Marti St. 704, 00907. Tel: 787-724-1447; 787-721-4540; Fax: 787-725-8104 (Elem.); 787-723-4550 (H.S.). Marie Ellen Gemel, Prin. Priests 1; Lay Teachers 102; Students 1,312.

19—NUESTRA SENORA DE BELEN (1960) Rev. Reinaldo Sagardia.
Mailing Address: P.O. Box 10845, 00922-0845. Tel: 787-793-2485; Fax: 787-792-8541.
Res.: Calle Jacinto Galib Final, Ave. San Patricio, Guaynabo.

20—NUESTRA SENORA DE LA ALTAGRACIA (1958) Rev. Gabriel Voores Rivera; Deacons Ildefonso Lugo; Rafael Colon; Euripides Lugo Lugo.
Mailing Address: Apartado 29493, 00929-0493. Tel: 787-765-0281.
Res.: Calle Felipe Gutierrez 672, Urb. Villa Prades, Rio Piedras, 00924. Tel: 787-765-0281.
Catechesis/Religious Program—Tel: 787-764-0614. Students 376.

21—NUESTRA SENORA DE LA CARIDAD DEL COBRE Rev. Pedro Luis Zaballa.
Res.: Urb. La Riviera, Calle 3 S.O. 1027, 00921-2517. Tel: 787-268-1325.

22—NUESTRA SENORA DE LA ESPERANZA (1962) Rev. Carlos D. Cruz-Davila.
Mailing Address: P.O. Box 8532, 00910-8532.
Res.: Calle Republica No. 864, Urb. Hipodromo, Parada 20, Santurce, 00910. Tel: 787-723-5998; Fax: 787-723-5998.
Mission—Ntra. Sra. de la Providencia Barriada Figueroa.
Chapel—Doctors Hospital, Tel: 787-723-2950; Fax: 787-721-3155.

23—NUESTRA SENORA DE LA MERCED (1940) Revs. Javier Fernandez; Jose Benito Osorio Mourino, O.de.M. (Spain); Javier Errecalde, O.de.M. (Spain).
Mailing Address: P.O. Box 364133, 00936-4133.
Res.: C/Pedro Espada 430, Urb. Roosevelt, Hato Rey, 00919. Tel: 787-763-3657.
Catechesis/Religious Program—Students 50.

24—NUESTRA SENORA DE LA PIEDAD (1956) Revs. Moises Rios Ruiz; Manuel Elejalde, C.P.; Jesús Etxeandia Ormaetzea, C.P., Supr.; Florencio Landa, C.P. (Spain).
Mailing Address: P.O. Box 79520, Carolina, 00984. Email: lapiedad_cp@yahoo.com.
Res.: 1001 Marginal, Villamar, Carolina, 00979. Tel: 787-726-2880; 787-726-2794; Fax: 787-982-2155.
School—Tel: 787-727-7585 (H.S.); 787-727-2460 (Elem.); Fax: 787-268-0664 (H.S.); 787-728-0125 (Elem.). Mrs. Lizette Matos, Prin.; Rev. Florencio Landa, C.P. (Spain), Dir. Priests 1; Lay Teachers 77; Students 685.

25—NUESTRA SENORA DE LA PROVIDENCIA (1959) Rev. Msgr. Baudilio Merino (Spain); Deacons Luis Vazquez; Ricardo Martinez.
Res. & Mailing Address: Santa Agueda St., No. 1730, Urb. San Gerardo, Rio Piedras, 00926. Tel: 787-765-6240; 787-765-8613; Fax: 787-765-4821.
School—Carretera #176, Km. 2.7, Calle Santa Agueda 1733, Urb. San Gerardo, Rio Piedras, 00926. Tel: 787-767-6552; 787-767-6755; Fax: 787-765-4821. Yolanda I. Martínez, Prin. Lay Teachers 35; Students 450.
Catechesis/Religious Program—Students 450.

26—NUESTRA SENORA DE LA PROVIDENCIA (1973) Rev. Hermenegildo Vicedo (Spain).
Res. & Mailing Address: 219 Aponte St., 00912. Tel: 787-727-1878.

27—NUESTRA SENORA DE LOURDES (1969) Rev. Angel L. Morales Figueroa.
Mailing Address: Bo. Obrero Sta., P.O. Box 14452, 00916.
Res.: Gilberto Monroig Ave., Cor. of Colton St., 288, 00916. Tel: 787-726-4643; Fax: 787-268-5255.

28—NUESTRA SENORA DEL CARMEN (1923) Rev. Jorge Ambert, S.J.
Mailing Address: P.O. Box 7275, 00916-7275. Tel: 787-727-0737; Fax: 787-728-4860.
Res.: Ave., Borinquen, Esq., Calle Tapia, Barrio Obrero, Santurce, 00916-7275.
School—Colegio Padre Berrios, (Grades K-9), P.O. Box 7717, 00916. Tel: 787-726-4851; Fax: 787-728-4860. Sr. Nilsa Cruz, H.C.C.S., Prin. Sisters 4; Lay Teachers 11; Students 160.
Catechesis/Religious Program—Sr. Tercida Y. De Leon, H.C.C.S., D.R.E. Students 56.
Mission—San Martin de Porres Calle: Tito Rodriguez #719 Barrio Obrero, Barrio Obrero, 00916.

29—NUESTRA SENORA DEL PILAR (1714) Revs. Ricardo Fernandez, C.M.; Maximiano Santos, C.M. (Spain); Teodoro Calzada, C.M. (Spain); Deacon Jose L. Velazquez; Bro. Jose Antonio Vaicarcel.
Mailing Address: Box 21134, 00928-1134.
Res.: Plaza de Recreo, Rio Piedras, 00928. Tel: 787-764-5088; 787-763-3161.
Mission—Santa Teresita de Nino Jesus Calle, Tanque #37, Barriada Venezuela, Rio Piedras, San Juan Co. 00925.
Chapel—Colegio La Milagrosa De Diego St. 107, Rio Piedras, 00936. Tel: 787-765-6114.
Chapel—Hogar Crea Barriada Venezuela. Tel: 787-751-5640.

30—NUESTRA SRA. DE GUADALUPE (1951) Rev. Neil Macaulay, O.M.I. (Canada).
Mailing Address: G.P.O. Box 4125, 00936-4125. Tel: 787-782-0016; Fax: 787-782-0016. In Res., Revs. Mariano Martínez Galvez, O.M.I.; Jaime Cereceda, O.M.I.
Res.: Calle 19 N.E. No. 1, Puerto Nuevo, 00920.
School—Tel: 787-782-0330; Fax: 787-782-0454. Mrs. Genevieve Zayas, Prin. Lay Teachers 37; Students 676.
Catechesis/Religious Program—Students 85.

31—RESURRECCION DEL SENOR (1968) Revs. Esteban Weliams-Figueredo; Mariano Errosti, O.F.M.
Res. & Mailing Address: Calle 31, S.O. #797, Urb. Las Lomas, 00921-1205. Tel: 787-792-1416; 787-792-5939; Fax: 787-792-1416.

32—SAGRADA FAMILIA (1971) Rev. Joaquin Mayorga-Fonseca.
Mailing Address: P.O. Box 29311, 00929.
Res.: Ave 65 de Inf., Esquina Calle 7, No. 112, Hills Brothers, Sabana Llana, 00924. Tel: 787-767-1723.
Catechesis/Religious Program—Students 2.

33—SAGRADO CORAZON DE JESUS (1971) Revs. Jaime Vergara, C.M. (Spain); Jose Yanez, C.M. (Spain);

Eugenio Villafranca Guerrero, C.M. (Spain).
Res. & Mailing Address: Calle Oxford 251, Esq. Howard Urb. University Gardens, 00927. Tel: 787-765-4798; Fax: 787-765-5456.
School—Esq. Iteramericana y Palma Real: Urb. University Gardens, Rio Piedras, 00927-4826. Tel: 787-765-9430; Fax: 787-765-5267. Mary Andreen, O.S.F., Prin.
Catechesis/Religious Program—Students 37.

34—SAGRADO CORAZON DE JESUS (1909) Rev. Ovidio Ortega Lemus (Cuba); Deacon Pedro Nel Trevalo.
Mailing Address: F. Juncos Sta., Box 8312, 00910-8312.
Res.: Ponce de Leon Ave., #1308, Stop 19, Santurce, 00910. Tel: 787-722-0235; Fax: 787-722-4845.

35—SAN AGUSTIN (1889) Revs. Miguel A. Garcia, C.Ss.R.; Gerardo Compbell, C.Ss.R.
Mailing Address: 265 Ave. Constitucion, P.O. Box 9066557, 00906-6557. In Res., Revs. Alfonso Amador, C.Ss.R. (Retired); Felipe Santiago Beugos, C.Ss.R.; Jorge Colon, C.Ss.R.
Res.: 265 Ave. Constitución, Pta. de Tierra, 00906. Tel: 787-722-4289; Fax: 787-725-7737.
School—Colegio San Agustin, 255 Constitution Ave., Box 9066547, 00906. Tel: 787-722-4544; Fax: 787-977-1700. Marie Benitez Alonso, Prin. Lay Teachers 17; Students 269.
Catechesis/Religious Program—Students 10.

36—SAN ANTONIO (1908) [JC] Rev. Roy F. Martínez, O.F.M.Cap.; Bro. Luis O. Padilla, O.F.M.Cap.; Rev. Roberto Martinez, O.F.M.Cap.
Res.: Calle Arzuaga #218, Esq. Frailes Capuchinos, Apartado 25177, 00928. Tel: 787-765-0606; Fax: 787-765-1180.
School—Tel: 787-764-0090; Fax: 787-763-7592. Minerva Feliciano, Elementary Prin.; Rev. Fray Jorge Macias, O.F.M.Cap., School Dir.; Miguel Rosa, Prin. (Intermediate & High School). Sisters 3; Lay Teachers 102; Students 1,411.
Catechesis/Religious Program—Students 51.
Mission—Nuestra Senora del Buen Consejo Calle Alto, 00926.

37—SAN FRANCISCO DE ASIS (1858) Revs. Ramon H. Negron, O.F.M.Cap.; Ramon Lopez, O.F.M.Cap.; Bros. Jaime Perez Munoz, O.F.M.Cap.; Juan Rolando Gonzalez, O.F.M.Cap.
Res.: 301 San Francisco St., Box 9024231, 00902-4231. Tel: 787-724-1131; Fax: 787-721-4616.
Catechesis/Religious Program—Students 12.
Mission—Capilla San Conrado Bo. La Perla, 00902.

38—SAN FRANCISCO DE MONTE ALVERNIA (1985) Rev. Jose Antonio Landrau Roman; Deacon Juan Bautista Perez.
Res.: Calle 10, #15 Ext. San Agustin, 00926. Tel: 787-765-8824.

39—SAN FRANCISCO JAVIER (1967) Rev. Marco Antonio Rivera Perez; Deacons Abel De Varona; Jose Hernandez.
Res.: Calle 19, G46. Urb. Fair View, 00926. Tel: 787-761-2115; Fax: 787-761-2115. Email: santj@onelinkpr.net.
Catechesis/Religious Program—Students 48.

40—SAN IGNACIO DE LOYOLA (1956) Revs. Baudilio Guzmán, S.J.; Donald M. Vega, S.J.; Deacon Carmelo Rivera.
Res. & Mailing Address: Calle Narciso 1904, 00927-6706. Tel: 787-293-7960; 787-751-7512; Fax: 787-751-7000. Email: psi@coqui.net; parroquiasanignaciopr@hotmail.com.
School—Academia San Ignacio de Loyola, 1908 Calle Narcisco, Rio Piedras, 00936. Tel: 787-765-8190; Fax: 787-765-3635. Glorimar Soegaard, Prin.; Rev. Bandilio Guzman, S.J., Dir. Students 631.
Chapel—Cond. Jardines de San Francisco

41—SAN JORGE (1965) Rev. Jesus A. Garcia (Venezuela).
Mailing Address: Loiza Sta., P.O. Box 6427, 00914-6427.
Res.: Calle San Jorge 157, Santurce, 00914. Tel: 787-724-7780.

42—SAN JOSE (Villa Caparra) (1948) Rev. Ricardo Hernandez Morales; Deacons Luis Cordero; Ramon Rodriguez.
Res.: Urb. Villa Caparra, Bloque ZM 215, Guaynabo, 00966. Tel: 787-781-1155; Fax: 787-774-8985. Email: acadparrsj@prtc.net. Web: www.parroquiasanjosevcpr.org.
School—Calle Josemaria Escriva 32, Guaynabo (Villa Caparra), 00966-2209. Tel: 787-783-1995 (H.S.); 787-792-7489 (Elem.); Fax: 787-792-7440 (Elem.); 787-781-3029 (H.S.). Sisters Catherine Ortiz, O.P., Prin. (Elementary); John Christian, Prin. (High School). Priests 1; Sisters 3; Lay Teachers 90; Students 800.

43—SAN JOSE OBRERO (1956) Rev. Angel Miguel Esquerro; Deacons Eugenio Rivera; J. Francisco Ubarri-Mestres.
Mailing Address: Calle Belmonte 470, 00923. Tel: 787-767-1448; Fax: 787-753-5392.
Res.: Urb. San Jose, Calle Belmonte 470, Rio Piedras, 00923.
Catechesis/Religious Program—Students 65.
Mission—San Antonio Ma. Claret, Embalse Sector.
Mission—San Martin de Porres, Bitumul 435 Carrillas St., 00923.

44—SAN JUAN BOSCO (1945) Revs. José Luis Gómez, S.D.B.; Miguel Rivera, S.D.B.; Lorenzo Ruiz.
Mailing Address: Barrio Obrero Sta., P.O. Box 14125, 00915.
Res.: 370 Lutz St., Villa Palmeras, 00915. Tel: 787-726-7317; Fax: 787-726-1420.
Mission—La Milagrosa Villa Palmeras, C. Lutz 300 Final, Santurce, Mayaguez Co. 00915. Tel: 787-728-2175; Fax: 787-726-7313.
Mission—Ntra. Sra. del Rosario Fajardo St., 00915.
Mission—San Martin de Porres Union St. #58, Playita, Yabucoa Co. 00915.

45—SAN JUAN DE LA CRUZ (1990) Rev. Mario Mesa, O.F.M.Cap. (Spain); Deacons Jorge Colon Velez; Luis Francisco Hernandez; Omar Santamarina.
Mailing Address: MSC 216, Urb. La Cumbre, Emiliano Pol Sta., 00926.
Res.: Urb. La Cumbre, Calle Julio Ruedas #1925, Borinquen Gardens, Rio Piedras, 00926. Tel: 787-731-2016; Fax: 787-708-0812.

46—SAN JUAN M. VIANNEY (1972), (Santo Cura de Ars) Revs. Victor Hugo Uira Alvarez, SS.CC.; Victoriano Gonzalez, SS.CC.; Eli Perdomo-Peidomo, SS.C.C.; Deacon Manuel Caban.
Res. & Mailing Address: Calle 2, F-14, Urb. Hillside, 00926. Tel: 787-790-2014.
Mission—La Milagrosa, San Juan Co.
Mission—Cristo del Perdon Parcelas Canejas, Bo. Caimito Bajo.
Mission—Dulce Nombre de Maria Bo. Dulce, Caimito Bajo.
Mission—Ntra. Sra. del Carmen Calle Fidalgo, Sector Corea, Bo. Caimito Bajo.

47—SAN LUCAS (1972) Rev. Ramon Orlando Tirado; Deacons Jose Rodriguez; Hector Cruz DeChoudens.
Mailing Address: Urb. El Senorial, Calle Pio Baroja 380, 00926. Web: psanlucas.org; www.parroquiasanlucas.org.
Res.: Pio Baroja St., No. 380, Urb. El Senorial, 00926. Tel: 787-761-5476; Fax: 787-761-5476.
Catechesis/Religious Program—Students 72.

48—SAN LUIS GONZAGA (1965) Rev. Eddie Rivera Marzan.
Res. & Mailing Address: Calle Ronda A-17, Urb. Villa Andalucia, 00926. Tel: 787-761-9438; Fax: 787-761-9438.

49—SAN LUIS REY (1968) Rev. Msgr. Manuel Garcia Perez.
Mailing Address: Ste. #65, P.O. Box 71325, 00936-8425.
Res.: Calle 43 S.E. Final, Urb. Reparto Metropolitano, Rio Piedras, 00921. Tel: 787-767-6235.
School—Calle 43 S.E. #869, Reparto Metropolitano, Rio Piedras, 00921. Tel: 787-767-4006; Fax: 787-767-6235. Silvia Almenas, Prin. Sisters 1; Lay Teachers 10; Students 213.

50—SAN MATEO (1773) Rev. Olin Pierre Louis.
Mailing Address: P.O. Box 6081, 00914-6081.
Res.: Calle San Mateo, Esq. San Jorge, Stop 25, Santurce, 00912. Tel: 787-722-4158; Fax: 787-722-4158.

51—SAN PABLO (1965) Rev. Jose Miguel Cardona Matta; Deacon Tomas Ramirez.
Res.: Duero St., No. 370, Urb. Villa Borinquen, Puerto Nuevo, 00920. Tel: 787-706-0412; Fax: 787-706-0412.
Mission—Ntra. Sra. de la Caridad Del Cobre Borinquen Towers, Puerto Nuevo, San Juan Co. 00920.

52—SAN VICENTE DE PAUL (1940) [CEM] Revs. Anulfo del Rosario Sosa, C.M.; Evaristo Oliveras, C.M.; Bro. Wilfredo Acevedo, C.M.
Mailing Address: P.O. Box 19118, 00910-0118.
Res.: 1650 Ave Fernandez Juncos, Stop 24, Santurce, 00910. Tel: 787-727-3963; Fax: 787-726-7986.
School—709 Bolivar St., Box 8699, 00910. Tel: 787-727-4273; Fax: 787-728-2263. Isabel Casanas, Prin. Lay Teachers 31; Students 539.
Catechesis/Religious Program—Students 80.

53—SANTA BERNARDITA SOUBIROUS (1982) Rev. Msgr. Wilfredo Pena-Moredo; Deacon Ismael Colon.
Mailing Address: 65 Infanteria Sta., P.O. Box 29826, 00929-0826. Tel: 787-762-0375; 787-257-7643; Fax: 787-757-6642. Email: santabernardita@yahoo.com. Web: www.parroquiasantabernardita.org.
Res.: Calle Espioncela, Esquina Calle Torcaza, Country Club, Rio Piedras, 00924.

54—SANTA CATALINA LABOURE (1977) Rev. Eusebio C. Fernandez Salazar (Colombia); Deacon Jacinto Ortiz.
Mailing Address: Urb. La Cumbre 497, PMB 507, Emiliano Pol, 00926-5636. Tel: 787-720-0303; Fax: 787-731-7166.
Res.: Carretera 842 Km. 3.6 Barrio Caimito, Rio Piedras, 00936.
Mission—Medalla Milagrosa Barrio Los Romeros, Bo. Caimito 00926-5636. Tel: 787-720-2215.
Mission—San Pablo Carretera 842, Bo. Caimito 00926.

55—SANTA CECILIA (1969) Rev. Danilo Martinez; Deacon Victor Merced de la Paz.
Mailing Address: El Senorial Sta., P.O. Box 415, 00926-0415.
Res.: Avenida Ceciliana #1, Urb. Rivieras de Cupey, Rio Piedras, 00936. Tel: 787-755-8670; 787-761-5461 (Parish House).
Catechesis/Religious Program—Students 33.
Chapel—Hogar Santa Teresa Jornet, Tel: 787-761-5805; Fax: 787-755-5575.
Chapel—Capilla San Agustin Carretera 844, Cupey Bajo.

56—SANTA LUISA DE MARILLAC (1962) Rev. Yesid Ricardo Castellanos Ruiz (Colombia); Deacon Francisco Colon.
Mailing Address: Urb. La Cumbre Ave., Emiliano Pol Sta. 497, Ste. #17, 00926-5636.
Res.: Ave. Emiliano Pol, Urb. La Cumbre, Rio Piedras, 00926. Tel: 787-720-3150; Fax: 787-720-8779.

57—SANTA MARIA DE LOS ANGELES (1954) Rev. Luis Norberto Correa-Garcia; Deacons Rafael Reyes Crespo; Ramon Luis Rivera.
Mailing Address: Box 10716, 00922-0716. Tel: 787-792-2640; Fax: 787-792-2640.
Res.: De Diego Ave., No. 930, Urb. La Rivera, Rio Piedras, 00936.

58—SANTA ROSA DE LIMA (1971) Rev. Carlos Perez Toro; Deacon Pedro Costa.
Res. & Mailing Address: Calle Lesbos No. 1765, Urb. Venus Gardens, 00926. Tel: 787-761-6586; Fax: 787-761-6586.

59—SANTA TERESA JORNET (1985) Rev. Ivan Serrano Rivera; Deacons Vicente Lasanta; Martin Cuevas.
Mailing Address: Aptdo. 415, El Senorial Mail Sta., 00926-0415.
Res.: Carr. 176 Camino el Mudo, Km. 10.0 Cupey Alto, 00926. Tel: 787-748-2978.
Mission—San Martin de Porres Camino El Mudo. Cupey, Alto, 00926.
Mission—Virgen de la Salud Camino Guayabos Carr. 176, Km. 9.5, Cupey, Alto, 00926.
Mission—Ermita N. Sra. Providencia [CEM] Camino Los Gonzalez, Km. 5.3. Tel: 787-760-8376.

60—SANTA TERESITA DEL NINO JESUS (1930) Revs. Tarsicio Gotay Figaredo, O.Carm.; Luis M. Miranda Rivera, O.Carm.; Salvador Rodrigo, O.Carm. (Spain).
Res.: 2059 Loiza St., 00911-1799. Tel: 787-727-0181; 787-727-0030; Fax: 787-728-0056. Email: tmgf@prmail.net. Web: www.parroquiasantateresita.com.
School—Tel: 787-727-4260; 787-727-4317; 787-727-4358. Ana R. Castro, Prin. Priests 1; Sisters 1; Lay Teachers 47; Students 360.
Mission—Sagrada Familia Residencial, Luis Llorens Torres, San Juan Co. 00913. Tel: 809-726-0570.

61—SANTISIMO SALVADOR (1966) Revs. Jesus Marques, Sch.P. (Spain); Rafael Capo, Sch.P., Supr.; Cecilio LaCruz, Sch.P. (Spain); Francisco Javier Lopez, Sch.P. (Spain); Juan L. Cabrerizo, Sch.P. (Spain); Deacons Luis A. Medina; Luis O. del Rio.
Res.: Niza St., 575, Urb. Villa Capri, 00924. Tel: 787-761-3314; Fax: 787-755-1595.
School—Calasanz (1968) Ave. Montecarlo, Esq. Z, Urb. Montecarlo, P.O. Box 29067, 00929-0067. Tel: 787-750-2500; Fax: 787-257-0450. Ana Celia Santos, High School Prin.; Maria Esquilin, Elementary School Prin. Priests 4; Lay Teachers 28; Students 445.
Catechesis/Religious Program—Students 65.
Mission—N. Sra. Reina de la Paz Calle #1 Esq. C-8 Urb. Berwind States, Rio Piedras, San Juan Co. 00924.
Mission—San Jose de Calasanz Calle #23 408, Parc. Hills Brothers, Rio Piedras, San Juan Co. 00924.

62—SANTISIMO SACRAMENTO (1967) Rev. Segundo Manuel Noriega Puga (Ecuador).
Res.: 500 Jerusalem St., Urb. Matienzo Cintron, Rio Piedras, 00923. Tel: 787-764-3448.
Catechesis/Religious Program—Students 40.

63—SANTOS PEDRO Y PABLO LOS APOSTOLES (1980) Rev. Joaquin Mayorqa Fonscea.
Mailing Address: Las Teresas II Apt. 7F, Calle Azabache 905, 00924-3244.
Res.: Urb. Jardines De Berwind, Calle Las Casitas, Lote K, 65 Infanteria, Rio Piedras, 00929. Tel: 787-768-1424.

64—STELLA MARIS (1965) Rev. Msgr. Antonio Jose Vazquez Colon.
Res.: 69 Cervantes St., Condado, San Juan, 00907-1947. Tel: 787-723-2240; 787-723-2359; Fax: 787-722-3200.

OUTSIDE THE CITY OF SAN JUAN

BAYAMON

1—ASCENSION DEL SENOR (1984) Revs. Pedro Gorena, O.SS.T. (Spain); Rodrigo Dallos Garcia, O.SS.T.; Deacon Juan Perez del Valle.

Mailing Address: P.O. Box 3367, 00958-3367. Tel: 787-799-6120; Fax: 787-730-7389.
Res.: Calle 31, Final, Urb. Rexville, 00957.

2—Catalina de Siena (1963) Rev. Oscar Morales Cruz, O.P.; Deacons Francisco Cruz; Antonio Santiago; Jose Rios; Agapito Diaz; Nicomedes Cosme.
Mailing Address: P.O. Box 4188, 00959-4188.
Res.: Urb. Hermanas Davila, Calle 10, Q-3, 00959. Tel: 787-785-2381; Fax: 787-269-5065.
Catechesis/Religious Program—Students 145.

3—Cristo Salvador (1998) Rev. Luis Felipe Rodriguez Guarnica.
Mailing Address: PMB 464, P.O. Box 7891, Guaynabo, 00970-7891.
Church: Parroquia Cristo Salvador, Guaynabo, 00970. Tel: 787-720-6596; 787-309-2448; Fax: 787-720-6596. Email: cristosalvador08@hotmail.com.

4—Espiritu Santo (2002) Rev. José A. Santiago, O.SS.T.
Res. & Mailing Address: Urb. Bella Vista Gardens, Calle 24, Y-300, 00957. Tel: 787-222-0935.

5—Invencion de la Santa Cruz (1772) Rev. Jose Fernando Osorio, O.P.
Res.: 12 Degetau St., 00961. Tel: 787-785-2134.

6—La Resurreccion del Senor (1987) Deacon Nicanor Mercado.
Res. & Mailing Address: Calle 12 F-1, Urb. Royal Town, 00956. Tel: 787-730-4310.
Catechesis/Religious Program—Students 60.

7—Ntra. Sra. de la Monserrate (1985) Revs. Mario Gonzalez, O.S.A. (Spain); Perfecto Alvarez, O.S.A.; Carlos Cordero, O.S.A.
Mailing Address: P.O. Box 3948, 00958-3948.
Res.: Carr. 829, Km. 6.2, Bo. Santa Olaya, Bayamon Gardens, 00958. Tel: 787-797-0708; 787-799-7340; Fax: 787-797-9953.
Mission—Cristo Rey Bo. Guaraguao, Sector La Morenita.
Mission—Santa Monica Bo. Guaraguao, Sector Pena, Bayamon Co. 00619.

8—Nuestra Senora de la Milagrosa (1968) Rev. Edgaro Pinto (Peru).
Mailing Address: P.O. Box 2104, 00960-2104.
Res.: Carr. 864, No. 82, Bo. Hato Tejas, 00960. Tel: 787-785-6620.

9—Nuestra Senora del Perpetuo Socorro (1976) Rev. Silvestre Gomez, O.P.; Deacons Ramon L. Ramon; Miguel Velez; Rafael Ortiz.
Res. & Mailing Address: Comerio St. No. 190, 00956. Tel: 787-785-2381; 787-780-4367; Fax: 787-785-2134.

10—Nuestra Senora del Rosario (1971) Rev. Miguel Angel Trinidad-Fonseca; Deacon Luis A. Navedo.
Res.: Calle Zaragoza, Bloque, B No. 34, Esq. Calle Vizcaya, Urb. Villa Espana, 00961. Tel: 787-787-0418; Fax: 787-787-0418.
Mission—Minillas San Jose.
Mission—N. Sra. del Carmen Bella Vista.
Mission—Sagrado Corazon de Jesus

11—Nuestra Sra. de los Dolores (1976) Rev. Jose Francisco Quintero Angueira; Deacon Francisco Hernandez.
Res. & Mailing Address: 18th St., Urb. Alturas de Flamboyan, Bloque DD-25, 00957. Tel: 787-786-7494.
Catechesis/Religious Program—Students 12.

12—Nuestra Sra. del Rosario (1993) Rev. Abelavido Mojica Paez; Deacon Hector Rivera.
Mailing Address: Box 3917, 00958.
Res.: Carr. 816 Km. 5.6, Barrio Nuevo, 00961. Tel: 787-730-6000; Fax: 787-730-6000.
Mission—San Juan Bautista, Montellano Co.
Mission—Jesus Maestro, Dajaos Co.
Mission—La Providencia, Dajaos Co.

13—Sagrada Familia (1976) Rev. Msgr. Leonardo J. Rodriguez-Jimenes; Deacons Americo Arroyo; Angel L. Oyola-Figueroa; Ramon L. Ortiz.
Mailing Address: P.O. Box 8478, 00959-8478. Email: sagfamilia@coqui.net.
Res.: #A-468 Cuba St., Urb. Ext. Forest Hills, 00960. Tel: 787-798-2010; Fax: 787-798-2010. Email: sagradafamilia@coqui.net.
Catechesis/Religious Program—Students 170.

14—San Agustin (1964) Revs. Felipe Fernandez, O.S.A. (Spain); Gonzalo Gonzalez, O.S.A. (Spain); Jose Ortiz (Dominican Republic); Deacons Ignacio Perez; Cristobal Rivera.
Mailing Address: Bayamon Gardens Sta., P.O. Box 4263, 00958-4283. Email: bayamonsanagustin@hotmail.com.
Res.: Urb. Lomas Verdes, Calle Duende, Bloque 2, E #21, 00956. Tel: 787-785-8611; Fax: 787-786-7631.
School—(1964) Box 4263, Bayamon Gardens Sta., 00958. Tel: 787-786-8055. Mrs. S. Morales, Prin. Lay Teachers 28; Students 406.
Mission—San Martin de Porres c/1 Barrio Juan Sanchez, Bayamon Co. 00959.
Mission—N. Sra. del Buen Consejo Villas de San Agustin, Bayamon Co. 00959.

15—San Antonio Maria Claret (1966) Revs. Jose Nieto, C.M.F.; Romualdo Fernandez, C.M.F. (Spain); Deacon Jose Dolores Rivera.
Mailing Address: P.O. Box 3292, 00958-3292.
Res.: D-24 Castiglioni Ave., Urb. Bayamon Gardens, 00957. Tel: 787-797-3337.
Catechesis/Religious Program—Students 250.

16—San Jose (1964) [CEM] Revs. Hector F. Cuadrado, C.M.F.; Jose Armengol, C.M.F. (Spain); Camilo Riano, C.M.F. (Spain); Severiano Garcia, C.M.F. (Spain); Romualdo Fernandez, C.M.F. (Spain).
Res. & Mailing Address: Dakar, F-169, Forest View, 00956. Tel: 787-785-6675; Fax: 787-785-0670.
School—Academia Claret, Tel: 787-787-6685; 787-786-7976. Israel Irizarry, Prin. Priests 3; Lay Teachers 30; Students 444.

17—San Juan Bautista de la Salle (1979) Revs. James Gil de la Madrid, M.SS.CC.; Jose M. Garcia Bastan, O.S.A. (Spain); Deacons Francisco Ortiz; Jose Vega; Jorge Rivera.
Res. & Mailing Address: A-19 Rio Cialitos St., 1ra. Secc. Estancias de Rio Hondo, 00961. Tel: 787-787-9567; Fax: 787-798-5071.

18—San Miguel Arcangel (1962) Rev. Ysidro Valero Castillo.
Mailing Address: P.O. Box 361714, 00936-1714. Tel: 787-787-4459; Fax: 787-787-4459.
Res.: Urb. Jardines de Caparra, Calle 12A Bloque AB., No. 32, 00959.
Mission—San Miguel Barriada San Miguel, Guaynabo, Guaynabo Co. 00657.

19—Santa Elena (1978) Rev. Jesus Gonzalez.
Mailing Address: P.O. Box 366, 00960-0366.
Res.: Calle 6, H-14, Urb. Sta. Elena, 00957. Tel: 787-785-6604; Fax: 787-785-6604.

20—Santa Maria (1984) Revs. Norberto Padilla; Pedro Lopez Moran, C.M.F. (Spain); Vicente Penalba, C.M.F. (Spain); Romualdo Fernandez, C.M.F. (Spain); Deacons Jose Ramon Cruz; Rafael Araya.
Mailing Address: Urb. Cana, Calle 24 #II-1, 00957.
Res.: Calle 24, Esq. 23, Urb. Cana, 00957. Tel: 787-797-7248; 787-797-8230; Fax: 787-279-5292.
Mission—San Gerardo Mayela Bo. Buena Vista, Bayamon Co. 00957.
Mission—Sagrado Corazon Bo. Cerro Gordo, Bayamon Co. 00956.

21—Santa Rita de Casia (1967) Revs. Domingo Aller, O.S.A. (Spain); Benigno Palomo, O.S.A. (Spain); Gonzalo Gonzalez, O.S.A. (Spain); Bro. Agustin Sanchez, O.S.A; Deacons Eliezer Toro; Ramon Luis Rivera; Noel Vasquez.
Res. & Mailing Address: Ave. Hostos NS-8, Urb. Santa Juanita, 00956. Tel: 787-786-3971; Fax: 787-778-3806.
Retired House—Ntra. Sra. del Buen Consejo, 00956.
Mission—San Jose Carretera 831, Bo. Minillas, Bayamon Co. 00619.
Mission—N. Sra. Del Carmen Calle Reno P-54, Urb. Vista Bella, Bayamon Co. 00619.
Mission—Sagrado Corazon De Jesus

22—Santa Rosa de Lima (1976) Rev. Virgilio Martinez (Spain); Deacon Ricardo Longueira.
Mailing Address: Calle 12, Bloque No. 28 No. 9, Urb. Santa Rosa, 00959. Tel: 787-798-2300; 787-787-1676; Fax: 787-780-3680. Email: santarosab@prtc.net. Web: www.ase-bay.org.
Res.: Urb. Sta. Rosa, Av. Main, Calles 11, 12, 13, 00959. Tel: 787-798-2300; Fax: 787-780-3680.
School—Ave. Main, Urb. Santa Rosa. Tel: 787-798-2829; 787-798-2539; Fax: 787-780-3680; 787-288-4996. Lorrie M. Cuevas Torres, Prin. Sisters 3; Lay Teachers 31; Students 672.
Catechesis/Religious Program—Students 788.

23—Santa Teresa de Jesus (1983) Rev. Edwin Londono Zuluaga; Deacon Eugenio Torres Diaz.
Mailing Address: P.O. Box 9204, 00960-9204. Email: paroteresa@gmail.com.
Res.: Calle 12 F #10, Urb. Teresita, 00960. Tel: 787-269-6749; Fax: 787-269-6749.
Mission—San Martin de Porres Rio Plantation Urb., 00961. Tel: 787-269-6749; Fax: 787-269-6749.
Mission—Convento Missioneras de La Caridad Sector Punta Brava. Tel: 787-269-0207.

24—Santiago Apostol (1966) [CEM] Revs. Julio Cesar Taveras Reymoso, M.SS.CC.; Jesus M. Ciriza, M.SS.CC. (Spain); Deacon Angel Pabon.
Res.: Urb. Sierra Bayamon, Calle 23, Bloque 23, Num. 17, 00961. Tel: 787-786-9679; 787-288-1966; Fax: 787-269-3965.
School—Tel: 787-786-9179; Fax: 787-269-3965. Mrs. Zoraida N. de Alonso, Prin. Priests 2; Lay Teachers 21; Students 359.
Catechesis/Religious Program—Students 359.

25—Santo Domingo de Guzman (1976) Rev. Silvestre Gomez, O.P.; Deacons Hèctor Negrón; Rubén González.
Mailing Address: Ext: La Milagrosa Calle 2, 00959.
Res.: Ext. La Milagrosa Calle 2, 00959. Tel: 787-786-8592.
Catechesis/Religious Program—

26—Santo Domingo De Guzman (1984) Rev. Rafael Mendez Hernandez; Deacons Virgilio Andino; Ramon Ramos.
Mailing Address: P.O. Box 3342, 00958-3342.
Res.: Parcelas Van Scoy, Calle Principal Esquina Calle, #3, 00957. Tel: 787-797-5510; 787-799-2377.
Catechesis/Religious Program—Students 173.
Mission—Santisima Trinidad Carretera 167 Km. 10, Bo. Ortiz, Corozal Co.
Mission—N. Sra. de la Providencia Urb. Los Dominicos, 00958.

Carolina

1—Cristo Rey (1971) Rev. Rafael Diaz Delgado, O.P.
Mailing Address: P.O. Box 1215, 00986-1215.
Res.: Urb. Parque Ecuestre, Calle Dulce Sueno U-8, 00987. Tel: 787-757-8712.
Mission—S. Francisco de Asis Entre las calles Tinajero y Dulce Sueno, Parque Encuestre.
Mission—Maria Auxiliadora Carrt. 857 Km. 3.6, Bo. Canovanillas.
Mission—Divino Nino Jesus Ubanizaciones: Ciudad Jardin y Colobos Park, Bo. Cambute, Carolina Co.
Mission—Cristo Rey Bo. Carruzos.

2—Epifania Del Senor (1982) Rev. Francisco Moralez Feliu; Deacon Miguel Roman.
Mailing Address & Res.: Calle Calais 425, Ext. El Comandante, 00982-3601. Tel: 787-752-1149.
Catechesis/Religious Program—Students 19.

3—Inmaculada Concepcion (1966) Rev. Hernan Berdugo (Colombia).
Mailing Address: Apartado 3562, 00984-3562. Email: pinmaccon@gmail.com.
Res.: Urb. Valle Arriba Hts., Calle Almendro A-15, 00984. Tel: 787-276-1527; Fax: 787-769-4307.
Catechesis/Religious Program—Students 58.

4—Ntra. Sra. de Fatima (1998) Rev. José Antonio Carrion Leyva; Deacon Orlando Rodriguez.
Mailing Address: Barrio Cedros, HC-3, Box 12076, 00985.
Res.: Bo. Cedros, Carr 853, Km. 13.6, 00988. Tel: 787-750-2168; Fax: 787-750-2168.
Mission—N. Sra. del Carmen Caer 853, Km. 8.0, Barrazas 00987.
Mission—Santa Teresa de Jesus Bo. Caer 853, Km. 5.0, Cacao 00987.

5—Ntra. Sra. Del Carmen (1984) Rev. Antonio Garcia (Spain); Deacons Ernie Diaz; Cesar Avila.
Mailing Address: P.O. Box 299, 00986-0299.
Res.: Urb. Lomas de Carolina, Monte Membrillo Km. 8, 00987. Tel: 787-752-8708; 787-752-4454; Fax: 787-762-6656.
School—Academia del CarmenMonte Britton:, Esq. Monte Membrillo, Lomas de Carolina, 00987. Tel: 787-757-4489; 787-757-4454. Victor Lara, Prin. Priests 1; Lay Teachers 20; Students 225.
Catechesis/Religious Program—Students 225.

6—Ntra. Sra. Reina de la Paz (1969) Rev. Angel Cuevas Rosario; Deacons Euripides Lugo; Miguel Marrero; Manuel Reyes; Efigenio Rivera.
Mailing Address: P.O. Box 3688, 00984-6388.
Res.: Calle 6, Final, Urb. Sabana Gardens, 00983. Tel: 787-752-5607; Fax: 787-762-4277.
Mission—Divino Nino Jesus

7—Ntra. Sra. Reina de Los Angeles (1960) Rev. Enrique Manuel Camacho-Monserrate; Deacon Ildefonso Berrios.
Res. & Mailing Address: Urb. Los Angeles, 29 Calle Lira, 00979-1659. Tel: 787-791-2594; Fax: 787-791-8878. Email: reinadelosangeles@catholic.org.

8—Nuestra Senora de Lourdes (1956) Rev. David Arrieta (Spain); Deacons Emilio Caceres; Nelson Soto.
Mailing Address: Urb. El Comandante, 1173 Calle Alejo Cruzado, 00924.
Res.: 1173 Alejo Cruzado, Ext. El Comandante, 00988. Tel: 787-752-3716.

9—San Andres (1982) Rev. Luis R. Velazquez-Morales; Deacons Marino Hernandez; Gilberto Mejias.
Res. & Mailing Address: MF-15 Calle 482, Urb. Country Club (4 Ta. Extension), 00982. Tel: 787-769-7076; Fax: 787-769-7076.

10—San Felipe Apostol (1971) Rev. Rodney Algarin-Rosado; Deacon Jose Rafael Vazquez.
Mailing Address: P.O. Box 1494, 00984-1494.
Res.: Calle 419, Bloque 165, No. 3, 4 Ta. Ext. Villa Carolina, 00964. Tel: 787-762-6520; Fax: 787-257-8995. Email: sanfelipepr@hotmail.com.

11—San Fernando (1851) Rev. Msgr. Efrain Rodriguez-Otero; Deacons Jose Birriel; Santiago Diaz Rosa; Prebistero Rivera.
Mailing Address: P.O. Box 128, 00986-0128.
Res.: Calle Ignacio Arzuaga #157, 00986. Tel: 787-769-0170; Fax: 787-769-5223.

12—San Francisco de Asis (1988) Rev. Frank de la Rosa Peguero (Dominican Republic).
Res. & Mailing Address: Calle 22 #0-31 A, Urb. Metropolis, 00987. Tel: 787-998-8331.

13—San Juan de Dios (1971) Rev. Julio Ortiz-Mangual; Deacons Luis R. O'Neill; Jorge Fonseca; Jose Otero Lugo.
Mailing Address: P.O. Box 3179, 00984-3179.
Res.: R-19 Canaria St., Jardines de Borinquen, 00985. Tel: 787-757-5060; Fax: 787-757-5060.
Mission—La Sagrada Familia C. Progreso A-79A,

Villa Esperanza, Carolina Co. 00985.

14—SAN VALENTIN (1971) Rev. Francisco Jose Quiceno (Colombia); Deacon Jose A. Pappaterra.
Mailing Address: P.O. Box 9382, 00988-9382.
Res.: Calle San Luis 128, Urb. Rolling Hills, 00988. Tel: 787-750-5277; Fax: 787-750-5277.
Catechesis/Religious Program—Students 66.
Mission—Jardines de Carolina Calle E, esq. Calle F, Santa Rosa, 00987. Tel: 787-750-5272.
Mission—San Antonio Urb. San Anton, Calle Tomas Ortiz, esq. Kercado, Carolina Co. 00987.

15—SANTA CLARA DE ASIS (1966) Revs. Francisco Labaka, O.F.M. (Spain); Leandro Abarrategui, O.F.M. (Spain); Luis S. Olmo, O.F.M. (Spain); Deacons Luis Del Rio Pitre; Jose A. Morales, (Retired); Luis Montes.
Mailing Address: Urb. Villa Fontana, JL-456 Via 14, 00983.
Res.: Via 14 JL No. 456 Urb. Villa Fontana, 00983. Tel: 787-768-1708; Fax: 787-750-2898.
School—(1968)Tel: 787-768-7110; Fax: 787-757-5044. Mrs. Lillivette Torres, Prin.; Rev. Leandro Abarratelegui, O.F.M., Dir. Lay Teachers 23; Students 355.
Mission—San Francisco de Asis
Mission—Parque Boliviano 5-JL Villa Fontana Park, Carolina Co. 00983.

16—SANTA GEMA GALGANI (1971) Revs. Jose R. Montanez Lopez, C.P.; Felix Barruetabena, C.P. (Spain).
Mailing Address: P.O. Box 2789, 00984-2789.
Res.: Av. Galicia Final, Urb. Vistamar, 00984. Tel: 787-769-5663; Fax: 787-750-3090.
School—Tel: 787-768-3082; 787-757-2505; Fax: 787-750-3090. Mrs. Lilia Luna de Anaya, Prin. Lay Teachers 32; Students 631.

17—SANTISIMA TRINIDAD (1982) Rev. Jose Maria Solano Uribe (Colombia); Deacons Ibrahim Suarez; Esteban Valle; Bienvenido Domenech; Gaspar Orozco.
Mailing Address: Urb. Country Club, 3 ra Ext., Ave. Campo Rico PA-16, 00982. Tel: 787-769-5665.
Res.: Avenida Campo Rico PA-16, Urb. Country Club, 00988.
Catechesis/Religious Program—Students 175.

18—SANTO CRISTO DE LA AGONIA (1971) Rev. Juan Santa Guzman; Deacons Ernesto Rivera; Miguel A. Marrero-Nieves.
Mailing Address: P.O. Box 5108, 00984-5108.
Res.: Calle Robles 29, Urb. Eduardo J. Saldana (Ceramica), 00984. Tel: 787-768-0374.
Catechesis/Religious Program—Students 60.
Mission—N. Sra. de la Esperanza Sabana Abajo, Carolina Co.

19—SANTO CRISTO DE LOS MILAGROS (1971) Rev. Nestor Yulfo-Hoffman.
Mailing Address: P.O. Box 834, 00986-0834. Fax: 787-768-3810.
Res.: Ave. Sanchez Castano, Urb. Villa Carolina, 00985. Tel: 787-768-3810.

CATANO

1—NUESTRA SENORA DEL CARMEN (1893) Revs. Roberto Arzola, O.P.; Ceferino Gómez Urias (Spain); Rafael Díaz Delgado; Deacon Angel Oquendo.
Mailing Address: P.O. Box 427, 00963-0427.
Res.: Calle Tren Num. 42, 00963. Tel: 787-275-1309.
Mission—San Martin de Porres Urb. Bayview.
Mission—San Jose Obrero

2—SAN FRANCISCO DE SALES (1969) Revs. Juan Martinez, S.D.B.; Jorge L. Gonzalez, S.D.B., Supr.
Mailing Address: P.O. Box 567, 00963-8163.
Res.: Ave. Flor del Valle Bloque BB-No. 108, Urb. Las Vegas, 00963. Tel: 787-788-5036; Fax: 787-788-8163.
Mission—Santo Domingo De Guzman Puente Blanco, Catano Co.
Mission—Maria Auxiliadora Urb. Vistas Del Morro.
Mission—San Judas Tadeo (Santuario) Parcelas Bo. Palmas.
Mission—Immaculada Concepcion Sector La Cucharilla.

DORADO

1—NTRA. SRA. DE LA SALUD (1982) Rev. Angel Pagan Torres; Deacons Hilario De Leon; Cresencio Rosario.
Mailing Address: Bo. Higuillar, P.O. Box 470, 00646-0470.
Res.: Parcela 202, Calle Principal 210, Sector San Antonio, 00646. Tel: 787-796-3418; Fax: 787-796-3418.

2—SAN ANTONIO DE PADUA (1848) Rev. Jorge Saenz Ramos; Deacons Boanerges Herrera; Benito Lugo Soto; José E. Colon; José C. Diaz.
P.O. Box 602, 00646-0602. Tel: 787-278-1416; 787-278-1154; Fax: 787-278-4759. Email: saint.antny@coqui.net.
Res.: 184 Calle Norte, P.O. Box 602, 00646. Tel: 787-278-1416.
Mission—San Martin de Porres Calle Principal Bo Mameyal, 00646.
Shrine—Christ of Reconciliation (2001) Paseo Del Cristo Lot #8, Urb. Martorell, 00646.

GUAYNABO

1—BUEN PASTOR (1965) Rev. Msgr. Francisco Medina Santos.
Res. & Mailing Address: Urb. Apolo QQIA Celle Acropolis, 00969-5014. Tel: 787-200-5308; Fax: 787-789-2653.

2—CORAZON DE JESUS (1992) Rev. Jesus Vieites, SS.CC.
Mailing Address: P.O. Box 225, 00970-0225. Tel: 787-731-0585.
Res.: Carr. 834 Km. 4.0, Bo. Sonadora, 00970.
Mission—San Juan Bosco Bo. Mamey 1.
Mission—Sagrada Familia Bo. Sonadora, Villa Jalena, Bo. Sonadora.

3—DIVINO NINO JESUS (1992) Rev. Rodolfo Lamas; Deacons Gerardo Comulada; Milton Valladares.
Mailing Address: PBM 143, HC-01, Box 29030, Caguas, 00725. Tel: 787-720-0203; Fax: 787-720-0203.
Res.: Urb. Lomas Del Sol, Calle Principal, 00971.
Mission—San Rafael Arcangel Barrio Camarones, Carr. #20, Guaynabo Co. 00970.
Mission—Jesus Nazareno Bo. Mamey, Guaynabo Co. 00970.
Mission—El Buen Pastor Carr. #1, Guaynabo Co. 00970. Tel: 787-798-9596.
Mission—N. Sra. de la Paz Bo. Quebrada Arenas, Guaynabo Co. 00971.

4—MARIA MADRE DE LA MISERICORDIA (1995) Revs. Walter Gomez-Baca; Vicente Fernandez-Marino; Carmelo Soto Tanon; Deacon Francisco Martinez.
Mailing Address: Ave. Santa Ana. #150, 00969.
Res.: Carretera 833 Km. 13.2, Bo. Santa Rosa 3, 00969. Tel: 787-789-0090; Fax: 787-790-7596.

5—MARIA MADRE DE MI SENOR (1988) Rev. Francisco Javier Quinones.
Mailing Address: P.O. Box 2150, 00970-2150. Tel: 787-789-1837; 787-720-1709.
Res.: Bo. Tortugos, Carretera 873, #1904, 00970.
Mission—Ntra. Sra. del Carmen Bo. Frailes Llanos, Sector Los Baez, Guaynabo Co. 00657.

6—NUESTRA SENORA DE LA PAZ (1992) Rev. Jose Humberto Lopez Marino; Deacons Porfirio Franco; Jose M. Castillo; Pablo Manzano.
Mailing Address: PMB 774, P.O. Box 7891, 00970-7891. Tel: 787-287-5714.
Res.: 833 Rd. LM 3.5, Bo. Guaraguao, 00970.
Mission—N. Sra. de la Divina Providencia Cantagallo, Juncos Co. 00971.
Mission—Espiritu Santo Bo. Sta. Rosa I, 00971. Tel: 787-287-2335.
Mission—Inmaculada Concepcion Bo. Camarones Centro, Ciales Co. 00971.
Mission—San Jose Obrero Bo. Sta. Rosa II, 00971.

7—SAGRADOS CORAZONES (1968) Revs. Luis Sada, SS.CC.; Mateo Mateo, SS.CC.; Eli Perdomo-Peidomo, SS.C.C.; Luis Alfonso Padilla; Deacons Ivan E. Dominguez; Ulpiano H. Rivera; Olimpio R. Zambrana Ortega.
Mailing Address: P.O. Box 3902, 00970-3902.
Res.: Urb. Ponce de Leon, 208 Ave. Esmeralda, 00969. Tel: 787-720-6151; Fax: 787-720-6151.
School—Avenue A, 00969. Tel: 787-720-2585; 787-720-6316; Fax: 787-720-6035. Email: ssccgnb@gmail.com. Edith N. Casiano, Dir. (High School & Elementary). Lay Teachers 44; Students 731.
Catechesis/Religious Program—Sr. Bibino Acevedo, D.R.E.
Mission—Virgen de la Paz Bda. Cruz Melendez, 00969.

8—SAN JUAN EVANGELISTA (1962) Rev. Rafael Suazo Martinez, Dir. School; Deacon Miguel De La Sota.
Mailing Address: P.O. Box 10151, 00922-0151. Email: psje@caribe.net; info@psje.us.
Res.: Calle Church Hill, J-5, Urb. Torrimar, 00966. Tel: 787-783-3522; Fax: 787-781-0236.
School—Tel: 787-781-5325; Fax: 787-793-8076. Rev. Rafael Suazo Martínez, Dir. Priests 1; Lay Teachers 37; Students 260.
Catechesis/Religious Program—Tafty Beuicos, D.R.E.
Mission—San Francisco de Asis [CEM] Carretera 19, La Marina, Guaynabo Co. 00966.

9—SAN PEDRO MARTIR DE VERONA (1769) Rev. Msgr. Mario A. Guijarro de Corzo (Cuba); Deacons Carlos Rivera Martinez; Humberto Reyes Anciano; Angel Loyola Zayas; Gregory A. Guijarro; Jose E. Falcon.
Mailing Address: P.O. Box 32, 00970-0032.
Res.: Calle Tapia No. 5, 00970. Tel: 787-720-2361; 787-272-6739; 787-287-1791; Fax: 787-287-2833.
School—Alpierre St. Final, Urb. Colimar, P.O. Box 2560, 00970-2560. Tel: 787-720-2219; Fax: 787-272-8770. Mrs. Ivonne D. Carlo, Prin.; Deacon Gregory A. Guijarro, Prof. & Vice Dir. Priests 2; Sisters 9; Lay Teachers 45; Students 610.
Catechesis/Religious Program—Students 267.

10—SANTA ROSA DE LIMA (1973) Rev. Jose Gregorio Guaipo; Deacon Filiberty De Jesus.
Res. & Mailing Address: 16 Parque St., Barrio Amelia, 00965. Tel: 787-781-5855; 787-783-9731; Fax: 787-781-5855; 787-783-9731.
Mission—La Milagrosa Barriada Vietnam.

TOA ALTA

1—N. SRA. DE LA PROVIDENCIA (1988) Rev. William Torres-Pagan; Deacons Gregorio Cuevas; Jose C. Pacheco.
Mailing Address: Bayamon Gardens Sta., P.O. Box 3836, Bayamon, 00958-3836. Tel: 787-797-1618.
Res.: Bo. Pinas, Carretera 861 Km. 5.6, 00954.
Mission—N. Sra. de Fatima Sector Rincon, Bo. Pinas, Comerio Co.
Mission—La Resurreccion Villa del Rio, Bo. Pinas, Comerio Co.
Mission—N. Sra. del Carmen Sector del 7.
Mission—Sagrada Familia Villa Juventud, Bo. Pinas, Comerio Co.

2—NUESTRA SENORA DE LA MEDALLA MILAGROSA Rev. Heriberto Londono (Colombia); Deacons German Hernandez; Santos Nieves.
Mailing Address: P.O. Box 335, 00954-0335.
Res.: Bo. Quebrada Cruz, Carretera 824, Km. 3.8, 00954. Tel: 787-870-4090; Fax: 787-870-8125.
Mission—Nuestra Senora del Carmen Sector El Cuco, Bo. Quebrada Cruz, Toa Alta Co. 00758.
Mission—Sagrado Corazon de Jesus Carretera 165 Km. 3.1, Quebrada Cruz, Toa Alta Co. 00758.

3—SAN ESTEBAN, PROTOMARTIR (1997) Rev. Raul Saez Munoz; Deacons Jose Ramon Perez-Bracero; Rafael Morales Figueroa.
Res. & Mailing Address: Urb. Monte Sol, Ave. Hato Tejas, Esq. Carretera 861, 00953. Tel: 787-799-2925; Fax: 787-279-8439. Email: parroquiasanesteban@prtc.net.
Catechesis/Religious Program—Students 155.
Mission—Capilla Cristo Rey Sector La Cuerda, Barrio Bucarabones, Toa Alta Co. 00953.
Mission—N. Sra. del Rosario Bo. Pajaros, RR-5, Box 4103, Bayamon, Toa Alta Co. 00956. Tel: 787-799-7950.

4—SAN FERNANDO REY (1751) [JC] Rev. Jose Angel Rodriguez Reyes; Deacons Jose Narvaez; Felipe Collazo; Pablo Irene.
Mailing Address: P.O. Box 63, 00954-0063. Email: sfdo2585@coqui.net.
Res.: Calle Jose de Diego #10, 00953. Tel: 787-870-2585.
Mission—San Antonio Rio Lajas, Dorado, Dorado Co. 00646.

5—SAN JOSE (1998) Rev. Calixto Soto (Colombia); Deacons Francisco Villamil; Enrique Laureano; Rafael Morales.
Mailing Address: P.O. Box 777, 00954-0777.
Res.: Sector Jazmin, Carretera 823, Rio Lajas, 00954. Tel: 787-870-6415.
Mission—Ntra. Sra. del Camino Bo. Espinosa, Carretera #2, Dorado, Dorado Co. 00646.
Mission—S. Francisco De Asis Bo. Maguayo, Dorado, Dorado Co. 00646.
Mission—Cristo de los Milagros
Mission—Santa Teresita Bo. Rio Lajas, Toa Alta Co. 00758.
Mission—Sagrada Familia Sector Marzan, Bo. Rio Lajas, Toa Alta Co. 00758.
Mission—Sagrado Corazon Sector Los Mudos, Bo. Quebrada Arenas, Toa Alta Co. 00758.

6—SAN JUDAS TADEO (2002) Rev. Victor Torres, O.M.I. (Panama); Deacon Luis Rivera-Albino.
Mailing Address: RP-03, Box 9169, 00954.
Res.: Carretera 804 Km. 1.2, Bo. Galateo Centro, 00954. Tel: 787-870-6643; Fax: 787-870-8018.
Mission—S. Martin de Porres Bo. Galateo.
Mission—Santa Teresa De Jesus Bo. Quebrada Cruz, Toa Alta Co. 00758.

TOA BAJA

1—ESPIRITU SANTO (1965) Revs. Lionel Pacheco Padilla, C.P.; Jose Ramon Zubizarreta Mugica, C.P. (Spain); Deacons Martin Estrada; Miguel A. Torres.
Mailing Address: Levittown Sta., P.O. Box 50272, 00950. Email: pes@coqui.net.
Res.: Paseo Damisela No. 1453, Urb. Levittown, 00949. Tel: 787-784-4805; Fax: 787-795-1248.
School—Paseo Damisela 1454, 00949. Tel: 787-784-0905; Fax: 787-795-5418. Lay Teachers 46; Students 645.
Catechesis/Religious Program—Students 195.
Mission—N. Sra. del Carmen Calle Carmen, Bo. Palo Seco, Toa Baja Co. 00759.

2—NTRA. SRA. DE LA CANDELARIA (1960) Rev. Jose Dario Martinez Tobon (Colombia); Deacons Anselmo Miranda; Roberto Rosado Ortiz; Camildo Ortiz.
Mailing Address: P.O. Box 892, 00951-0892.
Res.: Carretera No. 863, Km. 0.6, Bo. Pajaros, 00951. Tel: 787-251-0503.
Mission—Cristo Rey Calle 10, Bo. Bucarabones, Toa Alta, Toa Alta Co. 00758.
Mission—Santa Maria La Mayor Carretera #2 R.063, Bo. Macun, Bo. Macun, Toa Baja Co. 00759.
Mission—Santisima Trinidad Urb. Las Colinas, Toa Baja Co. 00759.

Mission—Buen Pastor Urb. Sta. Maria, Toa Baja Co. 00759.

3—NUESTRA SENORA DE COVADONGA (1984) Rev. Francisco Arana (Spain); Deacon Efrain Narvaez. Mailing Address: P.O. Box 9076, Bayamon, 00960-9076. Tel: 787-251-6466; Fax: 787-251-6466. Res.: Calle 13, 2-C-4, Esq. Calle 14, Urb. Covadonga, 00949.

Mission—Ntra. Sra. de Lourdes Bo. Candelaria Arenas, Toa Baja Co. 00759.

Mission—San Martin de Porres Bo. Kennedy, Toa Baja Co. 00759.

Mission—Divino Nino Jesus Urb. El Plantio, Toa Baja Co. 00759.

4—SAN JOSE OBRERO (1965) Revs. Gerardo A. Vargas Cruz, O.F.M.; Angel Dario Carrero, O.F.M., Supr.; Jesus Ponce, O.F.M.; Alfonso Guzman, O.F.M.; Deacon Ramon L. Colon.

Mailing Address: Box 173, Sabana Seca, 00952-0173. Res.: Carretera 2-R 866, Km. 3 #6, 00952. Tel: 787-784-1400; 787-795-3141; Fax: 787-784-1400.

Mission—Ntra. Sra. del Carmen

Mission—San Martin de Porres Carr. 816 PAR 1034, Villa Marisol, Sabana Seca.

5—SAN PEDRO APOSTOL (1745) Rev. Jairo Salazar Castano; Deacon Jose M. Sanchez.

Mailing Address: P.O. Box 513, 00951-0513.

Res.: 47 Las Flores St., 00949. Tel: 787-794-1327; Fax: 787-794-5967.

Catechesis/Religious Program—Students 296.

Mission—St. Teresita Calle Quintero.

Mission—Ntra. Sra. de Guadalupe Calle Crisantemo, Parcela 137-A.

Mission—San Jose Calle San Jose #303.

Mission—San Pablo Calle Universo, Parcela #9, Toaville.

Mission—La Virgen de la Providencia Bo. Villa Calma.

6—SANTISIMA TRINIDAD (1978) Rev. Juan M. Beristain (Spain); Deacons Eusebio Jaca; Justo Ortiz; Edwin Negron.

Mailing Address: Apartado 50378, Levittown, 00950-0378. Tel: 787-784-2889; Fax: 787-261-2911.

Res.: Ave. Los Dominicos, Esquina Dr. Sanchez Cardona, Levittown, 00950.

TRUJILLO ALTO

1—EXALTACION DE LA SANTA CRUZ (1801) Rev. Carlos Alberto Contreras Tribaldo; Deacons Domingo Vargas; Cesar Guiven.

Mailing Address: Box 1808, 00977-1808.

Res.: J. Diaz St., #515, frente a la Plaza de Recreo, 00977. Tel: 787-761-0507; Fax: 787-761-0507.

Catechesis/Religious Program—Students 51.

2—GRUTA DE LOURDES (1975) Rev. Msgr. Fernando Benicio Felices Sánchez; Deacon Pablo Torres.

Mailing Address: P.O. Box 1081, 00977-1081. Email: grutadelourdes1925@yahoo.com. Web: lagrutadelourdes.org.

Res.: Santuario, Gruta de Lourdes, Carretera 876 Km. 1.7, Barrio Cuevas, 00977. Tel: 787-761-0571; Fax: 787-761-0571.

3—MARIA LLENA DE GRACIA (1997) Rev. Franco Gutierrez (Spain).

Mailing Address: P.O. Box 1618, 00977-1618. Tel: 787-283-0364.

Res.: Urb. Rincon Espanol, Calle 1, Esq. Calle 4, 00977.

4—SAN BARTOLOME (1985) Rev. P. Jose Alcocer Corbaton, M.SS.CC. (Spain); Deacon Alberto Gomez.

Mailing Address & Res.: Urb. Ciudad Universitaria, X-1 Calle 16, 00976. Tel: 787-755-0120.

5—SAN FRANCISCO DE ASIS (1992) Rev. Gabriel M. Torres-Rivera; Deacons Hector Rivera; Alfredo Aponte; William Rios.

Mailing Address: P.O. Box 1316, 00977-1316.

Res.: Carr. #181 R-852, Bo.Quelseada Negrito, Quebrada Negrito, 00977. Tel: 787-305-0660.

Mission—Espiritu Santo Bo. Kennedy Hills, Carretera 181 Km. 10.

Mission—San Jose de la Montana Carretera #181 R-851, Bo. Sabana.

Mission—La Inmaculada Concepcion Bo. Talanco, Carretera #181 R-852.

6—SAN JUDAS TADEO (1980) Rev. Miguel Pons; Deacons Jose Baez; Jose Ramon Oliveras.

Mailing Address: Apartado 1535, 00977-1535.

Res.: Calle 7, Esq. 8, Urbanizacion El Conquistador, 00977-1535. Tel: 787-755-5993.

Catechesis/Religious Program—Students 75.

Mission—El Divino Pastor Carretera 844 Km. 0.2, Parcelas Carraizo, Trujillo Alto Co. 00760.

Mission—Ntra. Sra. del Carmen Carretera 175, Bo. Carraizo Alto, Trujillo Alto Co. 00760.

7—SAN PIO X (1971) Rev. Alberto Lopez; Deacons Julio Sanchez; Eduardo Carmona-Figueroa.

Mailing Address: St. Just, P.O. Box 631, 00978.

Res.: Carretera 848, K-1.4, Bo. Sain Just, 00978. Tel: 787-761-5040. Email: alfpiox2002@yahoo.com.

Mission—N. Sra. del Rosario Calle Lirio, Esq. Orquidea, Urb. Round Hill, Rio Piedras, San Juan Co. 00923.

Chaplains of Public Institutions

SANTURCE. *Ashford Presbyterian Community Hospital*, 1451 Ave. Ashford, Condado, 00940. Tel: 787-725-8820; 787-724-8320; 787-722-5765. Rev. Johnny Cruz Velazquez, O.SS.T.

Doctors Community Hospital, 1395 Calle San Rafael, 00940. Tel: 787-723-2950. Rev. Carlos D. Cruz-Davila. Tel: 787-723-5998.

Hospital Del Nino San Jorge, 255 Calle San Jorge, 00940. Tel: 787-727-1000. Vacant. Tel: 787-722-4158.

Hospital Pavia-Santurce, 1462 Calle Asia, 00940. Tel: 787-727-6060. Rev. Evaristo Oliveras, C.M. Tel: 787-727-3963.

Resident Chaplains:
Revs.—
Martinez, Danilo
Ortega, Ovidio, Hogar de Ntra. Sra. de la Providencia, Ave. Ponce de Leon, Puerta de Tierra.

On Duty Outside the Archdiocese:
Revs.—
Alecio-Rodriguez, Freddy (Sabbatical)
Del Valle, Tomas
McCoy, Floyd, Lajas, P.R.
Pierino, Vicente, U.S. Dept. of Justice, Coleman, FL.
Roldan, Juan, Caguas, P.R.
Sutil, Florencio
Torres Graciani, Ivan, Rochester, NY.

Graduate Studies:
Revs.—
Hernandez Ralat, Edwin, Rome, Italy.
Roig Lorenzo, Ricardo Augusto, Rome, Italy

Military Services:
Revs.—
Gomez-Baca, Walter, (Air Force)
Perez Vazquez, Juan De La Cruz, (Army)
Tirado, Orlando, C.M., (Air Force)

Awaiting Assignment:
Rev.—
Betancourt Ramirez, Jorge

Retired:
Rev. Msgrs.—
Cruz, Remberto
Maisonet-Ortiz, Tomas
Santoalla, Jesús Portomene
Revs.—
Candela, Rafael
Coroztieta, Jose Madoz
Cruz, Gilbert J. (Spain)
De Carlo Mena, Francisco
Diaz, Alvaro
Fuentes Rodriguez, Jose
Gonzalez, Cruz Gil
Gonzalez Chao, Luis
Quinones-Rivera, Leoncio
Ramos, Victoriano
Ribera-Ribo, Francisco J.
Sanz, Florentino (Spain)

Permanent Deacons:
Morales, Angel L.
Acosta Osorio, Santiago
Alicea Rivera, Angel L.
Amador Melendez, Luis F.
Andino Cintron, Virgilio
Andino Santos, Manuel
Aponte Diaz, Alfredo
Araya Brenes, Rafael F.
Arroyo Acevedo, Americo
Avila Rodriguez, Cesar
Baez Cotto, Pedro J.
Baez Navarro, Jose
Balasquide Vargas, Eugenio
Bermudez Martes, Jose A.
Berrios Berrios, Ildefonso
Birriel Rodriguez, Jose
Caban, Vicente
Calderon Rodriguez, Anthony
Camacho Rivera, Manuel
Carmona, Eduardo
Carrasquillo Rodriguez, Jose M.
Casaigne Ayala, Jose L.
Castillo Lopez, Jose M.
Collazo Montalvo, Felipe
Colon Andino, Gumersindo
Colon Colon, Rafael
Colon Febres, Ismael
Colon Hernandez, Ramon L.
Colon Mallen, Vicente
Colon Marrero, Miguel F.
Colon Melendez, Enrique
Colon Ramos, Luis
Colon Rivera, Francisco
Comulada Pabon, Gerardo
Cordero Mercado, Luis
Cosme Varela, Nicomedes
Costa, Pedro Tomas
Cruz De Choudens, Hector M.
Cruz Ortiz, Francisco
Cruz Trinidad, Jose Lionel
Cruz Vasquez, Ramon Jose
Cruz Vazquez, Jose R.
Cuevas Nieves, Gregorio
D'Auria, Ricardo
De Jesus Robles, Filiberty
De La Mota Pumarejo, Miguel
De Leon Sanchez, Hilario
De Varona Juarez, Abel
Del Rio del Rio, Anastasio
Del Rio Ortiz, Luis Orlando
Del Rio Ortiz, Luis Orlando
Del Rio Pitre, Luis
Del Valle Gonzalez, Reinaldo
Diaz, Miguel F.
Diaz Miranda, Ernie P.
Diaz Rivera, Jose
Diaz Rivera, Vidal
Diaz Rosa, Santiago
Diaz Sifonte, Agapito
Domenech, Bienvenido
Dominguez, Ivan
Echegaray Martinez, Luis
Encarnacion Torres, Jorge
Estrada Galarza, Martin
Falcon Matos, Jose E.
Figueroa Acevedo, Andres
Figueroa Carrasquillo, Raul
Figueroa Dominguez, Nelson
Figueroa Sanchez, Juan
Flores Torres, Pedro
Franco Torres, Porfirio
Gierbolini Santiago, Francisco
Gomez Maldonado, Alberto
Gonzalez Reyes, Ruben
Gonzalez Rosario, Pablo
Gonzalez Rosario, Pedro
Gonzalez Segarra, George
Gregorio, Ayala Garay
Guijarro del Corzo, Gregory A.
Guiven Flores, Cesar H.
Guzman Rosario, Jose A.
Henriquez Rodriguez, David A.
Hernandez, German
Hernandez Adorno, Francisco
Hernandez Hernandez, Marino
Hernandez Jorge, Jose A.
Hernandez Velez, Luis F.
Irene Vargas, Pablo
Jaca Hernandez, Eusebio
LaSanta Arroyo, Vicente
Laureano Molina, Enrique
Laureano Rivera, Juan
Llanos Calderon, Manuel Enrique
Longueira, Ricardo
Lopez, Victor Cepero
Lopez Collazo, Jesus
Lopez Echevarria, Felix
Loyola Zayas, Angel A.
Lugo Cordero, Casiano
Lugo Lugo, Euripides
Lugo Soto, Benito
Maldonado Febo, Pablo J.
Marin Mingaro, Louis
Marrero Nieves, Miguel A.
Marrero Picorneli, Jose M.
Martinez Duran, Ricardo L.
Martinez Pacini, Francisco
Martinez Santiago, Candido
Medina, Bernardino
Medina Rivera, Luis A.
Mejias Nunez, Gilberto
Melendez Lozano, Juan R.
Mendez Santiago, Miguel
Mendia Colon, Roberto
Mercado Vila, Nicanor
Merced De La Paz, Victor
Merino Raposo, Latino
Miranda Cruz, Jose
Miranda Mercado, Anselmo
Montanez, Justo
Montes Quevedo, Luis J.
Morales Gonzalez, Jose A.
Morales Maldonado, Rafael
Morales Rodriguez, Carlos R.
Narvaez Hernandez, Jose E.
Narvaez Santiago, Efrain
Navedo Rodriguez, Luis A.
Negron Morales, Gumersindo
Negron Santana, Hector
Nel Arevalo, Pedro
Nieves, Luis M.
Nieves, Martin
Nieves Carbona, Luis M.
Nieves Vazquez, Santos

Nunez, Pedro Arcadio
O'Neill Rosario, Luis R.
Ocasio Gonzalez, Domingo
Oquendo Serrano, Angel
Orlando Del Rios, Luis
Orozco Carrasquillo, Gaspar
Ortiz, Juan Rosario
Ortiz, Roberto Rosado
Ortiz Alvarado, Justo
Ortiz Collazo, Francisco
Ortiz Core, Ramon L.
Ortiz Rodriguez, Jacinto
Ortiz Rosado, Camildo
Ortiz Rosario, Feliciano
Ortiz Toro, Julio
Oyola Figueroa, Angel L.
Pabon Hernandez, Angel R.
Pabon Molina, Angel A.
Pacheco Diaz, Jose C.
Pappeterra Arthur, Jose A.
Pedro, Claudio Flores
Pena Gonzalez, Jose
Penaloza Lacen, Marcos
Perez Ayala, Edwin
Perez Bracero, Jose R.
Perez Del Valle, Juan B.
Perez Fuentes, Raul
Perez Gonzales, Ignacio
Perez Gonzalez, Luis R.
Perez Guadalupe, Jose
Perez Pizarro, Pastor
Perez Silva, Juan B.
Pizarro Davila, Angel M.
Quintana Medina, Antonio
Ramirez Abreu, Tomas
Ramos Rodriguez, Ramon L.
Ramos Torres, Jesus R.
Reyes Anciano, Humberto
Reyes Crespo, Rafael
Reyes Matos, Manuel
Reyes Torres, Victor M.
Rios Aponte, William
Rios Arroyo, Jose M.
Rivera, Enrique Velez
Rivera, Luis Marcial
Rivera, Prudencio I.
Rivera Albino, Luis
Rivera Alequin, Ulpiano H.
Rivera Archilla, Pedro
Rivera Baez, Eugenio
Rivera Collazo, Angel
Rivera De Jesus, Efigenio
Rivera Diaz, Hector R.
Rivera Estremera, Felipe
Rivera Fuentes, Jorge L.
Rivera Garcia, Edwin
Rivera Lopez, Hector M.
Rivera Martinez, Carlos
Rivera Matos, Frank
Rivera Mojica, Jose D.
Rivera Negron, Ernesto
Rivera Rios, Cristobal
Rivera Rivera, Jose R.
Rivera Rivera, Ramon L.
Rivera Rodriguez, Presbitero
Rodriguez, Luis A.
Rodriguez Acevedo, Ramon
Rodriguez Marrero, Romulo
Rodriguez Martinez, Jose
Rodriguez Melendez, Orlando
Rodriguez Perazza, Jose R.
Rodriguez Rodriguez, Jose M.
Rodriguez Rodriguez, Juan
Rodriguez Rodriguez, Wilfredo
Rodriguez Serrano, William
Roman, Luis Ramon
Roman Del Valle, Miguel A.
Roman Maldonado, Jose M.
Roman Maldonado, Miguel A.
Rosa Reo, Ramon Luis
Rosado Yambo, Martin
Sanabria Lopez, Rafael
Sanchez Acosta, Oscar
Sanchez Ortiz, Julio
Santamarina Dorta, Omar
Santiago, Ramon C.
Santiago Correa, Ramon
Santiago Rivera, Antonio
Santiago Rivera, LaTorre
Santiago Rivera, LaTorre
Santos, Juan R.
Santos Negron, Marcos A.
Soto Miranda, Nelson
Suarez, Ibrahim
Suarez Molina, Israel
Toro Toro, Obed E.
Torres Acevedo, Pablo L.
Torres Burgos, Miguel A.
Torres Diaz, Eugenio
Torres Irizarry, Jose
Torres Labauld, Jose A.
Torres Rodriguez, Dionilo
Torres Torres, Jose A.
Totti Lugo, Benjamin
Trujillo Cardona, Gerardo
Ubarri Mestres, Juan
Valladares Almodovar, Milton
Valle Valle, Esteban
Vargas Ramos, Domingo
Vazquez, Jose R.
Vazquez Garcia, Luis A.
Vazquez Rosario, Noel A.
Vega Vega, Jose P.
Veguilla Colon, Victor
Velazquez Gonzalez, Jose L.
Velazquez Reyes, Rafael
Velez Roman, Miguel
Villamil Marrero, Fco. E.

INSTITUTIONS LOCATED IN THE ARCHDIOCESE

[A] COLLEGES & UNIVERSITIES

SAN JUAN. *Sacred Heart University*, Calle Rosales esq. San Antonio, Parada 26 1/2, Santurce, 00940. P.O. Box 12383, 00914-0383. Tel: 787-728-1515. Email: jjrivera@sagrado.edu. Web: www.sagrado.edu. The University has the following Departments and Programs: Departments of Communications, Humanities, Business Administration, Education, Natural Sciences and Social Sciences. The Graduate Programs include: Masters of Business Administration in Management of Systems Information, Masters of Arts & Communications, Masters of Art & Education, Masters of Occupational Nursing, Medical Technology Certificate. Faculty 136; Total Enrollment 5,330.
Governing Board: Mr. Alberto Paraccini, Pres. Bd. of Trustees; Dr. Jose Jaime Rivera, Pres.; Dr. Lydia Espinet, Dean Academic Affairs; Mr. Jose L. Ricci Jr., Dean Admissions; Sr. Sororro Julia, Dean Devel.; Pedro Fraile, Dean Student Affairs; Dr. Isabel Yamin, Dir. Humanities; Carmen Garcia, Dir. Communications; Adalexis Rios, Dir. Educ.; Arturo Figueroa, Dir. Business Admin.; Dr. Francisco Fereer, Dir. Natural Sciences; Fernando Medina, Dir. Social Sciences; Hylsa Silva Janer, License & Legal Counsel; Ms. Mildred Pineiro, Registrar; Mr. Luis A. Quiles, Dir. Student Financial Aid; Rev. Rafael Rodríguez, S.J., Dir. Campus Ministry.

BAYAMON. *Bayamon Central University*, Avenida Zaya Verde, Bo. Hato Tejas, P.O. Box 1725, 00960-1725. Tel: 787-786-3030; Fax: 787-785-4365. Email: pbreyes@ucb.pr. Web: ucb.edu.pr. The University has the following Departments and Programs: Humanities; Business Administration; Natural Sciences; Education; Graduate Studies; Adult Education Program; Student Support Services; Upward Bound. Lay Teachers 60; Total Enrollment 3,028.
Governing Board: Rev. Mario Rodriguez-Leon, Pres. Council of Founders; C.P.A. Ismael Sanchez-Rivera, Pres. Bd. of Trustees.
Administration: Dr. Blanca Berio, Dean Academic Affairs; Mr. Mario Medina, Dean Admin. & Finances; Mr. Yanius Alvarado, Dean Student Affairs; Dr. Modesto Fernandez, Dir. Humanities; Dr. Nydia Cohen, Dir. Education; Dr. William A. Soler, Prof. & Dir. Natural Sciences; Mr. Pedro Bermudez, Dir. Institutional Devel.; Mr. Enrique Arias, Esq., Legal Counsel; Angela Ramos, Dir. Human Resources; Mr. Victor Colon, Registrar; Mrs. Christine Hernandez, Dir. Admissions; Ms. Vivian Cintron, Dir. Student Financial Aid; Ms. Ana Medina, Dir. Academic Resource Ctr.
Faculty: Revs. Felix A.P. Struik, O.P. (Holland); Luis Espinel, O.P.; Angel Diaz Caceres; Angel Dario Carrero, O.F.M.; Manuel Soler Pala, M.SS.CC.; Victor Ortiz; Antonio Gonzalez Pola.

GUAYNABO. *ISTEPA (Instituto Superior de Teologia y Pastoral)*, Edificio 2021, Carretera 177, 00969-5140. Tel: 787-731-6100; Fax: 787-731-0000. Rev. Msgr. Francisco Medina Santos, Rector. (Theology, Biblical and Pastoral courses for lay ministers and Deacons) Priests 4; Deacons 5; Lay Teachers 5; Students 994.

[B] ELEMENTARY & HIGH SCHOOLS

SAN JUAN. *Academia Perpetuo Socorro*, (Grades K-12), 704 Calle Jose Martí, 00907. Tel: 787-721-4540 (H.S.); 787-724-8104 (Elem.); Fax: 787-723-4550 (H.S.); 787-725-8104 (Elem.). Email: perpetuo@perpetuo.org. Carlos Quintana Puente, Dir.; Mr. E. Morales, Prin. (High School); Vanessa Monserrate, Prin. (Elem.); Sr. Mary Ellen Gemmell, C.S.F.N., Prin. Priests 1; Lay Teachers 102; Total Enrollment 1,312.

Academia San Ignacio de Loyola, Calle Narciso 1908, Urb. Santa Maria, 00927-6716. Tel: 787-765-8190; Fax: 787-765-3635. Email: academia@asiloyola.org. Web: www.asiloyola.org. Rev. Bandilio Guzman, S.J., Dir.; Blanca I. Esteves, Ed.D., Asst. Dir.; Glorimar Soegaard, Prin.; Adela Sabater, Librarian. Lay Teachers 53; Total Enrollment 651.

Academia Santa Monica (1996) (Grades PreK-12), Ave. Fernandez Juncos, 00908. Tel: 787-723-2573; 787-723-3845; Fax: 787-723-3992. Email: director@smonica.org. Web: www.smonica.org. P.O. Box 13726, 00908-3726. J. Oscar Jimenez, Dir.; Carmen Rodriguez, Prin. Lay Teachers 40; Students 495.

Colegio Angeles Custodios, Calle Sicilia Num. 13, San Jose, 00923. Tel: 787-763-3829; Fax: 787-764-9496. Email: cac-rpi@cac-rpi.org. Maria Aranzazu Labak, Dir.; Sr. Luis Roberto Rivera Cepeda, Prin.; Rev. Miguel Esquerro-Preciado. Students (K-8) 81; Students (9-12) 101.

Colegio Calasanz, Montecarlo Ave., 00924. Tel: 787-750-2500; Fax: 787-257-0450. Email: calasanzpr@hotmail.com. P.O. Box 29067, 00929-0067. Revs. Rafael Capo, Sch.P., Headmaster; Cecilio LaCruz, Sch.P. (Spain), Campus Min.; Maritere del Rio, Counselor; Rev. Juan L. Cabrerizo, Sch.P. (Spain), Registrar; Ana Celia Santos, Prin. (High School); Maria Esquilin, Prin. (Elementary). Priests 4; Lay Teachers 28; Total Enrollment 445.

Colegio Corazon De Maria (Archdiocesan School), Calle Ferrer y Ferrer, Urb. Santiago Igesias, 00922. Tel: 787-783-3275; Fax: 787-774-5682. PMB 266, P.O. Box 7891, Guaynabo, 00970-7891. Priests 1; Lay Teachers 18; Students 348.

Colegio Espiritu Santo, Pachín Marín Esq. Suiza St., 00917. Tel: 787-754-0490; Fax: 787-754-7154. P.O. Box 191715, 00917-1715. Rev. Msgr. Valeriano Miguélez (Spain), Dir.; Mrs. Milagros Zurkowsky, Prin.; Ms. Olga I. Torres Martínez, Asst. Prin.; Mrs. Olga D. Torres, Librarian; Mr. Edgardo Tirado, Librarian. Lay Teachers 37; Students 626.

Colegio Maria Auxiliadora, 2273 Eduardo Conde, 00915. Tel: 787-726-8288; Fax: 787-727-6497. Email: fmasanturce@hotmail.com. Sr. Margarita Foutan, F.M.A., Prin.; Elba Varela, Librarian. Sisters 8; Lay Teachers 25; Students 348.

Colegio Nuestra Senora de Guadalupe, 19 N.E. St. #1, Puerto Nuevo, 00920. Tel: 787-782-0330; Fax: 787-782-0454. P.O. Box 364125, 00936-4125. P. Neil Macaulay, Dir.; Mrs. Genevieve Zayas, Prin.; Teresita Hernández, Vice Prin.; Jackeline Wys, Librarian. Lay Teachers 35; Students 599.

Colegio Nuestra Senora de Lourdes, (Grades PreK-12), 1050 Demetrio O'Daly, Country Club, 00924. Tel: 787-769-6284; 787-769-6275; Fax: 787-750-7805; 787-757-1245. P.O. Box 29193, 65 INF Station, 00929-0193. Roxanna Vázquez, Dir. & Prin.; Melissa Carrera, Vice Prin. High School; Marisol Quinones, Librarian; Nilsa Menéndes, Librarian. Lay Teachers 45; Students 688.

Colegio Nuestra Senora Del Carmen, R.R. 2, Box 15, 00926-9701. Tel: 787-761-8010; Fax: 787-748-2505. Email: melisea@coqui.net. Sisters Arlyn Medina Vazquez, Dir.; Elizabeth Andino, Prin.; Lissette Torres, Prin.; Liliana Santiago, Prin. Sisters 8; Lay Teachers 38; Students 510.

Colegio Reina De Los Angeles, Frontera M-19 Villa Andalucia, 00926-2304. Tel: 787-761-7455; Fax: 787-761-7440. Email: colegio1972@yahoo.com. Juana F. Gomez Moya, Dir.; Ana Román, Registrar. Sisters 3; Lay Teachers 12; Students 208.

Colegio San Ignacio de Loyola, Urb. Santa Maria, 1940 Calle Sauco, 00927. Tel: 787-765-3814; Fax: 787-758-4145. Rev. Mario Alberto Torres, S.J., Dir.; Mr. Rafael Fernandez, Prin. Priests 3; Students 715.

Colegio San Vicente de Paul, 709 Bolivar St., 00910. Tel: 787-727-4271; Fax: 787-728-2263. P.O. Box 8699, Fernández Juncos Sta., 00910-8699. Rev. Evaristo Oliveras, C.M., Dir.; Isabel Casanas, Prin.; Marina Perez, Librarian; Emilio Roldan, Dean Discipline; Maria del C. Cordova, Counselor. Operated by: Congregacion de la Misión de San Vincente de Paúl, Inc. (Padres Paúles) Lay Teachers 32; Students 537.

Colegio Santo Domingo Savio, Ave. Gilberto Monroig 2278, 00916. Tel: 787-728-2175; Fax: 787-982-2903. P.O. Box 14125, Bo. Obrero Sta., 00916-4125. P. Miguel A. Rivera Borges, Dir.; P. Lorenzo Ruiz Victoria, Admin.; Maria A. Rodriguez Reyes, M.A., Prin.; Ivette Santiago Kilgore, Librarian. Lay Teachers 1; Students 214.

Nuestra Senora De Belen (Archdiocesan School), P.O. Box 10845, 00922-0845. Tel: 787-792-3115; Fax: 787-781-4920. Email: colegiobelen11@yahoo.com. Eleonor Marrero, Prin. (Elementary); Eduardo Rodríguez, Prin. (High School); Mayra

Mendez Barreto, Dir. Lay Teachers 49; Students 752.

Nuestra Senora de la Altagracia (Archdiocesan School), P.O. Box 29493, 00929-0493. Tel: 787-763-7755; Fax: 787-756-5195. Rev. Gabriel M. Torres; Mrs. Rosa M. Figueroa, Prin.; Mr. Angel Castillo, Dir. Students 375.

San Jorge (Archdiocesan School), 1701 Colon St., 00911. Tel: 787-722-3182; Fax: 787-725-4580. Email: sanjorge@iname.com. Mrs. Maritza Rosario, Prin.; Mrs. Vanesa Valdes, Dir. Lay Teachers 70; Students 681.

BAYAMON. *Academia Maria Reina*, Urb. College Park, Glasgow #1879, 00921-4899. Tel: 787-764-0690; Fax: 787-282-7556. Sr. Judith Burchyns, C.S.J., Prin.; Rita Hernández, Asst. Prin.; Lucila Aponte, Librarian. Catholic Girls School. Sisters 1; Lay Teachers 80; Students 626.

Academia Santa Maria del Camino, (Grades PreSchool-8), P.O. Box 4228, Bayamón Gardens Station, 00958-1218. Tel: 787-780-5770; Fax: 787-785-7373. Sr. Lucy del Blanco, O.S.R., Dir.; Margarita Montesinos Ortiz, Prin.; Myrha Lee Román Miró, Librarian. Sisters 1; Lay Teachers 16; Students 224.

Colegio Beato Carlos Manuel Rodriguez, Esq. Millones 2na. Ext. Lomas Verdes, 00956. Tel: 787-798-5260; 787-798-2329; 787-798-2747; Fax: 787-787-2620. Email: beato@cbcmr.org. Web: www.cbcmr.org. P.O. Box 4225, 00956. P. Luis Brioso, Dir. & Prin.; Jaime Solivan, Librarian. Students 565.

Colegio Ntra. Sra. del Rosario, Calle 5, AA-7, Repto. Valencia, 00659. Tel: 787-798-5100; Fax: 787-269-7551. Sr. Ma. Ana Jimenez Maldonado, O.P., Dir.; Elba I. Soto, Prin. Students 300.

Colegio Santa Rosa, Calle Marti 15, Estacion #1, P.O. Box 6032, 00960. Tel: 787-785-1195 (H.S.); 787-785-0381 (Elem.); Fax: 787-740-0115 (H.S.); 787-785-3791 (Elem.). Neymi A. Aponte, Prin. (High School); Mrs. Nilsa Gonzales, Prin. (Elementary). Priests 1; Lay Teachers 30; Total Enrollment 976.

Santo Tomas de Aquino, P.O. Box 1557, 00960-1557. Tel: 787-786-5015 (High School); 787-785-3838 (Elementary); Fax: 787-786-5015 (H.S.); 787-798-0180 (Elem.). Lay Teachers 50; Students 1,311.

P.O. Box 4098, 00958-1098. Mrs. Carmen J. Acosta, Elementary Prin.; Miss Micaela Hurtado, High School Prin.

CAROLINA. *Academia Del Carmen*, Monte Membrillo esq., Monte Britton, Lomas de Carolina, 00987. Tel: 787-757-4454; Fax: 787-762-6656. Email: academiadelcarmen@gmail.com. Web: academiadelcarmen.com. P.O. Box 299, 00986-0299. Aitza Vázquez, Subdirector (Elem. & High School); Mrs. Gladymir Montanez, Librarian. Priests 1; Lay Teachers 19; Total Enrollment 20.

Colegio Maria Auxiliadora, Box 797, 00986-0797. Tel: 787-762-0350; 787-768-6924; Fax: 787-257-3760. Web: cma-car.org. Rosa Perez, Dir. Priests 1; Lay Teachers 75; Students 962.

Colegio Santa Gema, Galicia Ave., Vistamar, 00983. Tel: 787-768-3082; Fax: 787-750-3090. P.O. Box 2789, 00984-2789. Mrs. Lilia Luna de Anaya, Prin.; Wanda Sánchez, Librarian. Lay Teachers 50; Students 895.

GUAYNABO. *Colegio Marista*, Alturas de Torrimar, 00969. Tel: 787-720-2186; 787-720-2187; Fax: 787-720-7020. Email: marista1@prtc.net. Bro. Ricardo Herrero, Dir.; Luz D. Romero, Prin.; Awilda Díaz, Librarian. Priests 1; Brothers 7; Lay Teachers 70; Students 1,215.

Colegio Ntra. Sra. De La Caridad, Ave. Luis Vigoreaux 19X-19, Villa Caparra., 00966. Tel: 787-781-8835; 787-781-1744; Fax: 787-781-8835. Email: caridad@coqui.net. P.O. Box 11164, 00922-1164. Sr. María Luisa Sónehezy Ramírez, Prin. St. Joseph of the Mountain Sisters. Sisters 8.

Colegio Sagrados Corazones, P.O. Box 3902, 00970-3902. Tel: 787-720-2585; Fax: 787-720-6035. Edith N. Casiano, Dir. Lay Teachers 43; Students 669.

Colegio San Pedro Martir, Alpierre (Final), 00969. Tel: 787-720-2219; Fax: 787-272-8770. P.O. Box 2560, 00970-2560. Rev. Msgr. Mario Guijarro, Dir.; Mrs. Ivonne D. Carlo, Prin. Sisters 1; Lay Teachers 28; Students 357.

Preescolar San Juan Evangelista, (Grades PreSchool), Urb. Torrimar, J 5 Calle Church HL, 00966-3109. Tel: 787-781-5325; Fax: 787-793-8076. Lourdes Rodriguez, Administrative Dir.; Flor María Lugo, Prin. Lay Teachers 33; Students 270.

HATO REY. *Colegio Lourdes*, 87 Mayaguez St., 00917. Tel: 787-767-6106; 787-756-5436; Fax: 787-767-5282. Email: clourdes@coqui.net. Web: colegiolourdes.net. P.O. Box 190847, 00919-0847. Sr. Maria Paz Asiain, O.P., Dir.; Thalia Lopez, Prin.; Josefina Arce, Librarian. Sisters 5; Lay Teachers 45; Students 898.

Colegio Nuestra Senora de La Merced, Calle Sargento Luis Medina #374, 00936. Tel: 787-765-7342; 787-754-1162; Fax: 787-765-3970. P.O. Box 364048, 00936-4048. William Súarez, Dir.; Mrs. Coville Auoyo, Prin.; Marina Azofra, Librarian. Lay Teachers 35; Students 376.

RIO PIEDRAS. *Colegio Mater Salvatoris*, Carretera 838 Km 4.8 de Rio Piedrasa Caguas, 00926-9690. Tel: 787-765-0130; Fax: 787-765-8161. R.R. 37 Box 3080, 00926-9601. Sisters 6; Lay Teachers 52; Students 905.

Colegio Nuestra Senora De La Providencia (Girls), Ave. San Ignacio #1358, Urb. Altamesa, 00921. Tel: 787-781-7506; 787-782-6344; Fax: 787-792-7888. Email: zegri@coqui.net. Sr. Lourdes Martínez, Prin. Mercedarian Sisters. Priests 1; Sisters 4; Lay Teachers 48; Students 950.

Colegio Sagrado Corazon de Jesus, (Grades PreK-8), Calle Palma Real 215, University Gardens, Rio Piedras, 00927. Tel: 787-765-9430; Fax: 787-765-5267. Rev. Jaime Vergara, C.M. (Spain), Dir.; Sr. Mary Andreen Rusin, O.S.F., Prin.; Rev. Jose Yanez, C.M. (Spain), Religion Dir. Students 793.

Colegio San Jose, (Grades 7-12), Box 21300, 00928-1300. Tel: 787-751-8177; Fax: 787-767-1746. Email: sanjose.mail@csj-pr.org. Web: www.csj-pr.org. Calle Paz Esq. Los Marianistas, 00925. Bro. Francisco T. Gonzalez, S.M., M.D., Dir. & Prin.; Alma Flores, Librarian. Priests 1; Brothers 2; Lay Teachers 43; Students 557.

SANTURCE. *Academia Sagrado Corazon, Fernandez Juncos Sta.*, Box 11368, 00910. Tel: 787-721-3300; Fax: 787-725-1865. Email: nowita@prtc.net. Rev. Francisco Javier Quinones, Spiritual Dir.; Mrs. Gladys Vélez, Prin.; Paulina Quintero, Librarian. Priests 1; Lay Teachers 25; Students 294.

Colegio de La Inmaculada, Stop 26, Ave. Ponce de Leon #1711, 00909-1997. Tel: 787-727-6673; Fax: 787-728-7768. Mrs. María Rivera de Modesto, Dir.; Mr. Jose Acevedo, Prin.; Maria Tosta Perez, Librarian. Sisters 5; Lay Teachers 30; Students 440.

Colegio Sagrada Familia (Archdiocesan School), Urb. Llorens Torres, Calle Loiza #2059, 00911. Tel: 787-726-1742; Fax: 787-726-0718. Ines Y. Elias, Prin.; Vanessa Valdes, Dir. Lay Teachers 6; Students 164.

Colegio San Juan Bosco, Carpenter Rd., Constitucion Santos Elena, 00915. Tel: 787-726-1995; Fax: 787-268-1869. Rev. Nicolas Navarro, S.D.B., Dir.; Mrs. Lissette M. Ruiz. Priests 2; Religious 15; Lay Teachers 12; Students 288.

TRUJILLO ALTO. *Santa Cruz* (Archdiocesan School), Dr. Fernandez St., #203, 00977. Tel: 787-761-1100; Fax: 787-755-3065. Box 1809, 00977-1809. Rev. Carlos Alberto Contreras Tribaldo, Dir.; Mrs. Ana L. Monzon de Matos, Prin. Sisters 1; Lay Teachers 25; Students 371.

[C] SPECIAL SCHOOLS AND SEMINARIES

SAN JUAN. *Instituto Psicopedagogico De P.R.*, P.O. Box 363744, 00936-3744. Tel: 787-783-3678; 787-783-5431; Fax: 787-792-3610. Email: ippr@coqui.net. Mr. Roberto Vazquez, Prin. Bed Capacity 134; Patients Assisted Annually 134.

BAYAMON. *Casa Mision Claret* (Claretians), Urb. Cana, Calle 24 esq. Calle 23, 00957. Tel: 787-797-8230.

Convento Ntra-Sra del Rosario (Dominicans), Calle Capitan Correa N-27, Reparto Flamingo, P.O. Box 1968, 00960. Tel: 787-785-6542; 787-786-4508; Fax: 787-798-2712. Web: dominicospr.com. P.O. Box 1968, 00960-1968.

Seminario Agustiniano Sto. Tomas De Villanueva, Carretera 830 km 5.1, Camino Los Muleros, Barrio Santaolaya, 00961. P.O. Box 3948, 00958. Tel: 787-797-0708; Fax: 787-797-9953. Email: tomasdevillanuevapr@yahoo.es. Revs. Mario Gonzalez, O.S.A. (Spain), Prior; Carlos Cordero, O.S.A. (Augustinians) Priests 3; Brothers 1.

Seminario Misionero del Espiritu Santo (Holy Spirit Fathers), Calle Zaya Verde #44-A, Hato Tejas, 00959. Tel: 787-786-8231; Fax: 787-787-2398. Email: opgcssp@caribe.net. Rev. Osvaldo Perez Gonzalez, C.S.Sp., M.Div., Prin. Supr.

CATANO. *Prenoviciado Salesiano* (Don Bosco Salesians), Ave. Flor Del Valle, Bloque BB #108, Urb. Las Vegas, 00962. Tel: 787-275-1921; Fax: 787-788-8163. Email: sanfasal@coqui.net. P.O. Box 567, 00963-8163. Rev. Adan Marrero, S.D.B.

DORADO. *Estudiantado Pasionista* (Passionists), Carretera 695 km. 3.3, Sector Los Puertos, Barrio Higuillar, 00646. Tel: 787-278-0517. P.O. Box 593, 00646-0593. Rev. Ramon Gurtubay, C.P. (Spain), Supr. Priests 2; Students 6.

RIO PIEDRAS. *Colegio San Antonio*, P.O. Box 21350, 00928-1350. Tel: 787-764-0090; Fax: 787-763-7592. Email: csa.riopiedras@gmail.com. Bro. Jorge M. Macias, O.F.M.Cap., Dir.; Miguel Rosa, Prin. (Intermediate & High School); Minerva Feliciano, Prin. (Elementary School); Nayda Jimenez, Librarian (Intermediate & High School); Annie Rivera, Librarian (Elementary School). Priests 2; Brothers 1; Sisters 3; Lay Teachers 94.

Fraternidad San Antonio (Capuchin Postnovitiate) , Calle Arzuaga #216, 00928. Tel: 787-765-8247; Fax: 787-763-9832. Web: www.capuchinspr.org. P.O. Box 25177, 00928. Revs. Roy F. Martínez, O.F.M.Cap.; Roberto Martinez, O.F.M.Cap., Guardian; Bros. Luis O. Padilla, O.F.M.Cap., Vicar; Cecilio Figueroa; German Quinones; Orlando Reyes; Elmig M. Soto, O.F.M.Cap. Priests 4; Brothers 4. In Res. Rev. Malachy Clune, O.P. (Ireland).

Fraternidad Santa Maria de Los Angeles (Centro Capuchins), Care.877 Km.1 Hm 6, 00936. Tel: 787-761-8060; 787-761-8410; Fax: 787-293-1682. Aptdo. 29882, 00929-0882. Rev. Jose Fernando Irizzary, O.F.M.Cap., Dir.; Bro. Jaime Perez Munoz, O.F.M.Cap.

Seminario Mayor Regional San Juan Bautista (Diocesan), Ave. De Diego No. 930, Urb. La Riviera, 00922-1714. Tel: 787-273-8090; 787-783-0645; Fax: 787-783-0645. Email: seminary@coqui.net. P.O. Box 11714, 00922-1714. Rev. Juan Luis Negron, Rector; Rev. Msgr. Ivan L. Huertas-Colon, Vice Rector; Revs. Pedro L. Reyes Lebrón; Tomas Gonzalez. Priests 9; Brothers 1; Lay Teachers 7; Total Staff 17.

SANTUCE. *Seminario San Vicente De Paul* (Vincentians) , C. Victoria 1658, Pda. 24, Santurce, 00940. Tel: 787-727-4110. P.O. Box 19119, 00910. Priests 3; Brothers 4.

TOA BAJA. *Post-Noviciado San Jose Obrero* (Franciscans), Carretera 866 Km. 3.4, Sabana Seca, Sabana Seca, 00952. Tel: 787-795-3141. P.O. Box 173, Sabana Seca, 00952. Rev. Eddie Caro, O.F.M., Rector.

[D] SPECIAL CENTERS

SAN JUAN. *Renovacion Conyugal dba Fundacion Fernando Martinez* 573 Calle Alverio, 00918. Tel: 787-751-6001; Fax: 787-766-1363. Email: renovacionpr@yahoo.com. Web: geocities.com/renovacionpr. Rev. Baudilio Guzmán, S.J., Dir.

Santa Ana Chapel Perpetual Adoration, Calle Tetuan 203, Box 763, 00902. Tel: 787-725-7734. Rev. Jose Emilio Cummings, Rector.

PUERTO NUEVO. *San Gabriel School For The Deaf*, Prolongacion Calle 19 NE, 00920. Tel: 787-783-3455; Fax: 787-781-3770. P.O. 360347, 00936-0347. Sr. Amparo Blasco, Dir.

RIO PIEDRAS. *Centro De Espiritualidad Ignaciana Pedro Arrupe (CEIPA)*, R.R. 10, Buzon 5348, 00926. Tel: 787-790-3557; Fax: 787-790-3162. Email: ceipapr@gmail.com. Web: geocites.com/ceipasj. Rev. Lawrence P. Searles, S.J., Dir.

Centro Universitario Catolico, 10 Mariana Bracetti St., 00925-2201. Tel: 787-763-5432; 787-767-3348; Fax: 787-296-3068. Email: elcuc2003@hotmail.com. Revs. Rafael Rodríguez, S.J., Dir.; Juan José Santiago, S.J., Coop.

[E] CLINICS, HEALTH CENTERS

SAN JUAN. *Casa La Providencia, Inc.* Drug Rehabilitation Center, P.O. Box 9020614, 00902-0614. Tel: 787-725-5358; Fax: 787-725-0058. Email: casalaprovidencia@hotmail.com. Web: casalaprovidencia.org. Sr. Adela Dominguez, Dir. Sisters Oblates of the Most Holy Redeemer 4; Bed Capacity 32; Total Assisted Annually 110; Total Staff 23.

Centro Medico de P.R., Calle 10 #1030, Puerto Nuevo, 00920. Apdo. 347, 00936. Tel: 787-763-7272. Revs. Antonio Jose Vazquez Colon (ARE), Vicario. Tel: 787-751-2335; Cell: 787-562-4065; Francisco Arana (Spain), Chap., Hospital Oncologico. Tel: 787-251-6466; Pedro Luis Zaballa, Chap., Hospital Universitario; Manuel Garcia (Spain), Chap. Hospital Municipal. Tel: 787-796-3418; Bartolome Vanrell, Chap., Hospital Cardiovascular. Tel: 787-740-3425; Evaristo Oliveras, C.M., Hosp. Pavia, Santurce. Tel: 787-727-3963; Carlos D. Cruz-Davila, Doctor's Hosp. Tel: 787-723-5998; Eugenio Villafranca, C.M. (Spain), Hosp. Auxilio Mutuo. Tel: 787-758-2000, Ext. 3024; Rev. Msgr. Valeriano Miguélez (Spain), Hosp. Pavia, Hato Rey. Tel: 787-754-0570; Revs. Hector Diaz, Hosp. Veteranos. Tel: 787-641-7582, Ext. 3350; Eddie Rivera Marzan; Philip Nunez, Hosp. Metropolitano. Tel: 787-782-4176; Carlos Cordero, O.S.A., Hosp. Regional, Bayamon. Tel: 787-786-8611; Deacons Jose R. Rivera, Hosp. Pediatrico. Tel: 787-475-7849; Andres Figueroa, Hosp. Pediatrico. Tel: 787-505-9973; Carlos Morales, Hosp. San Juan Capestrano. Tel: 787-757-2114; Hèctor Negrón, Hosp. San Pablo. Tel: 787-785-6874.

VA Medical Center, 10 Calle Casia, 00921-3200. Tel: 787-641-7582; 787-641-7575. Email: hrd198254@yahoo.com. Revs. Hector Diaz Estrada, Chap.; Eddie Rivera-Marzan, Chap. Bed Capacity 535.

BAYAMON. *Hospital Hermanos Melendez, Oficina de Administracion*, P.O. Box 306, 00960-0306. Tel: 787-785-6542. Email: normanchd@gmail.com. Rev. Carlos Pijnenburg, O.P., Chap.

Hospital Matilde Brenes, Oficina de Administracion, P.O. Box 2957, 00960-2957. Tel: 787-785-2381.

Hospital San Pablo 00959. Tel: 787-785-2134. *Oficina de Administracion*, P.O. Box 236, 00959-0236. Deacon Hèctor Negrón, Chap. Tel: 787-785-6874.

Hospital Universitario, Oficina de Administracion, Ave. Laurell, 00956. Tel: 787-785-8611. Dr. Ramon Ruiz Arnau, Dir.; Rev. Gonzalo Gonzalez, O.S.A. (Spain), Chap.

CAROLINA. *Hospital Universitario de Carolina, Oficina de Administracion*, P.O. Box 6021, 00984. Tel: 787-757-1800; Fax: 787-276-2205. Web: hospitalupr.org. Rev. Frank de la Rosa, Chap.

HATO REY. *Hospital Auxilio Mutuo* Tel: 787-758-2000, Ext. 3070; Fax: 787-771-7960. Web: www.auxiliomutuo.com. P.O. Box 1277, 00919. Rev. Eugenio Villafranca, C.M. (Spain), Chap. Bed Capacity 591; Total Staff 1,230.

Hospital Pavia, Ave. Pone De Leon, 00917. Tel: 787-754-0570. *Oficina de Administracion*, P.O. Box 190828, 00919-0828. Rev. Msgr. Valeriano Miguélez (Spain).

RIO PIEDRAS. *Hospital del Maestro*, Calle Flamboyanes #218, Hyde Park, 00929. Tel: 787-763-8383.

Hospital San Francisco 00926. Tel: 787-765-0606. *Oficina de Administracion*, P.O. Box 29025, 00929-0025. Rev. Roy F. Martínez, O.F.M.Cap., Chap.

SANTURCE. *Doctor's Community Hospital* 00909. Tel: 787-999-7620; Fax: 787-725-2124. Email: echevarria@dchpr.com. *Oficina de Administracion*, P.O. Box 11338, 00910. Rev. Carlos D. Cruz-Davila, Chap.

Hospital Pavia 00912. Tel: 787-727-3963. *Oficina de Administracion*, P.O. Box 11137, 00910-1137. Vincentian Fathers (Chaplains).

Hospital San Juan Capestrano, Rio Piedras, 00926. Tel: 787-625-2900; Fax: 787-760-6875. Email: carmo43@prw.net. Web: sjcapestrano.com. *Oficina de Administracion*, RR2 Box 11, 00926. Deacon Carlos Morales, Chap. Total Staff 230; Total Assisted Annually 5,000; Bed Capacity 108.

San Jorge's Children Hospital 00912. Tel: 787-727-1000; Fax: 787-268-3610. Email: cruz.vivaldi@sanjorgechildrenhospital.com. Web: www.sanjorgechildrenhospital.com. *Oficina de Administracion*, P.O. Box 6308, 00914-6308. Bed Capacity 125.

[F] HOMES AND RESIDENCES

SAN JUAN. *Casa La Providencia* (Drug Addicted Women), Calle Norzagaray #200, 00901. Tel: 787-725-5358; Fax: 787-725-0058. Email: casalaprovidencia@hotmail.com. P.O. Box 9020614, 00902-0614. Sr. Adela Dominguez, Dir. Total Staff 18; Patients Assisted Annually 71; Bed Capacity 32.

Centro De Orientacion Vocacional Nuestra Senora del Consuelo (Teenagers/Single Mothers), Floral Park, 20 C. Matienzo Citron, 00919. Tel: 787-250-6323; Fax: 787-250-6323. Email: oblahchr@prte.net. Total Assisted Annually 60; Total Staff 8.

BAYAMON. *Hogar Del Nino "El Ave Maria"* (For Abused Children), Carretera 861, km 2.0, Bo. Pajaros Americanos, 00957. Tel: 787-797-2382; 787-279-3003; Fax: 787-797-2382. Mailing Address: PMS 239, P.O. Box 607061, 00960-7061. Sr. Florencia Santos, Dir.

Hogar Escuela Sor Maria Rafaela (Girls with Problems), Carretera 871, km 1.0, Bo. El Volcan, Hato Tejas, 00961. Tel: 787-785-9517; 787-785-1125; Fax: 787-787-5324; 787-779-0449. Email: hogar.sormaria@gmail.com. P.O. Box 3024, PR 00960. Sr. Nelida Gonzalez, Dir.

Hogar Fatima (Girls), Ave. Santa Juanita Final, Camino Esteban Cruz, 00961. Fax: 787-780-9763. Email: fatima001@prttc.net. Web: www.osrhogarfatimainc.com. P.O. Box 4228, Bayamon Garden Sta., Bayamon, 00958-4228. Tel: 787-787-2580. Sr. Maria Saez, Dir. Patients Assisted Annually 53; Staff 17.

DORADO. *Santuario del Espiritu Santo*, Box 187, 00646-0187. Tel: 787-796-2798; Fax: 787-796-1359. Email: espiritanospr@gmail.com. Web: www.espiritanos.com. Revs. Cornelius T. McQuillan, C.S.Sp., Dir.; Eduardo Caron, C.S.Sp.; Jose Orlando Camacho-Torres, C.S.Sp.

PUERTA DE TIERRA. *Asylum For The Aged and Infirm* (Hogar de la Providencia), Stop 5, Edif. 205, 00906-6571. Tel: 787-722-1331; 787-723-2419; 787-724-3574; Fax: 787-725-4308. P.O. Box 9066571, 00906-6571. Sr. Mariá Antonia Gago González, Supr.; Revs. Ovidio Ortega, Chap.; Efrain Lopez, Chap. Sisters of the Poor. Sisters 12; Patients Assisted Annually 207.

RIO PIEDRAS. *Asylum For Orphan Girls*, 107 Jose de Diego St., 00925. Tel: 787-765-6114. Sr. Virginia Torres, H.C., Supr. Daughters of Charity. Sisters 15; Bed Capacity 70.

Centro N. Sra. de la Providencia Sisters of Notre Dame., R.F.D. #2, Box 16T, 00928. Tel: 787-761-0273.

Centro Santa Luisa (1972) (Services for the Elderly), Carretera 842, Camino Los Romeros km 1.5, Bo. Caimito, 00926. Tel: 787-720-2764; Fax: 787-731-7795. Email: centrosantaluisa@yahoo.com. Web: www.geocities.com/centrosantaluisa. Mailing Address: R.R. 6 Box 9492, 00926-9492. Sr. Glenda Y. Rios, H.C., Dir. Patients Assisted Annually 100; Total Staff 9.

Hogar Carmelitano Julian Bengochea Final (Elderly Retirement Hospice), Calle Julian Bengoechea Final, 00924. Tel: 787-769-6510; 787-769-3110; Fax: 787-768-1240. Sr. Maribelle Mejias Muniz, Admin. Carmelite Sisters (Spain). Bed Capacity 224; Patients Assisted Annually 160; Total Staff 76.

Hogar Santa Teresa Jornet for the Aged, Cupey Alto, Ave. Las cumbres, Km. 3, Hm. 8, 00926. Tel: 787-761-5805; Fax: 787-755-5575. P.O. Box 21012, 00928. Sr. Gladys Rosario Gomez, Mother Supr.; Revs. Danilo Martinez Duarte, Chap.; Cecilio de la Cruz. Sisters of the Poor. Sisters 18; Bed Capacity 200; Residents 200; Total Staff 80.

Hogares Rafaela Ibarra (Orphan or Abused Girls), Calle Torrelaguna 432, 00923. Tel: 787-763-1204; Fax: 787-763-6266. Web: www.hogaresrafaelaybarra.com. 432 Calle Torrelaguna, 00923-1773. Sr. Julia Jose, Dir. Patients Assisted Annually 40; Staff 14.

SANTURCE. *Casa de Ninos Manuel Fernandez Juncos* (Orphans and Abused Boys), Calle Villa Verde Esq. Refugio, Pda 11, Miramar, 00940. Tel: 787-724-2904; 787-725-6328; Fax: 787-724-0980. P.O. Box 9020163, 00902-0163. Revs. Candido Lizarraga, RR.T.C.; Francisco J. Arizcuren Rey; Deacon Pablo Osorio Carmona; Bros. Eliecer Balladares; Juan Manual González Fzgvieedo; Abner Irom Picon. Total Staff 22.

Politecnico Amigo (For School Dropout Boys), Calle Refugio #960, Pda II, 00940. Tel: 787-725-2059; Fax: 787-722-3436. Email: polam@prtc.net. P.O. Box 13204, 00908.

TOA ALTA. *Hogar Santisima Trinidad* (Drug Addiction Rehabilitation Home), Lote A y Lote B, km 7.0, Bo Mucarabones, Carr. 861, 00954. Tel: 787-799-6208; Fax: 787-799-1977. Email: trinita@prtc.net. PMB 326, P.O. Box 607061, Bayamon, 00960-7061. Rev. Pedro Gorena, O.SS.T. (Spain). Patients Assisted Annually 75; Total Staff 15.

TOA BAJA. *Hogar Divino Nino Jesus (Drug Addict Rehabilitation)*, Carretera 854, Km. 3.5, 00949. Tel: 787-794-0020; Fax: 787-794-0020. Email: divinoninojesus@yahoo.es. P.O. Box 2464, 00951. Julio Pacheco, Dir.

[G] PERSONAL PRELATURES

GUAYNABO. *Opus Dei* (Prelature of the Holy Cross and Opus Dei), Region of Puerto Rico of the Prelature, Urb. Villa Caparra, #35 Calle A, 00966-2211. Tel: 787-783-6206; Fax: 787-783-1201. Email: pricoinf@coqui.net. Web: www.opusdei.org.pr. Rev. Msgr. Vicente Ariza, Ph.D., J.C.D., Regl. Vicar; Revs. Alfredo Gastalver; Gonzalo Diaz; Martin Llambias; Juan Aramendi; Pablo J. Concepcion; Javier Bernaola; Justiniano Garcia.

[H] MONASTERIES AND RESIDENCES FOR PRIESTS AND BROTHERS

SAN JUAN. *The Capuchin Formation Trust of Puerto Rico*, c/o P.O. Box 9021967, 00902-1967.

Capuchin Health and Retirement Trust of Puerto Rico

Asociacion Frailes Capuchinos, Inc.

Comunidad Jesuita, Colegio San Ignacio, Urb. Santa Maria, 1940 Calle Sauco, 00927-6718. Tel: 787-758-1717, Ext. 1721; Fax: 787-750-8640. Revs. Baudilio Guzmán, S.J., Supr.; Jose A. Borges, S.J.; Mario Alberto Torres, S.J.; Donald M. Vega, S.J.

The Viceprovince of Saint John the Baptist, Puerto Rico, of the Order Friars Minor Capuchin (1905) 216 Arzuaga St., P.O. Box 21350, 00928-1350. Tel: 787-764-3090; Fax: 787-764-4070. Web: www.capuchinospr.org. Bros. Francisco Garcia Cervero, O.F.M.Cap., Vice Prov. Min.; Jorge M. Macias, O.F.M.Cap., First Councillor; Jose F. Irizarry, O.F.M.Cap., Second Councillor; Luis O. Padilla, O.F.M.Cap., Vice Prov. Sec. & Treas. & Dir. Capuchin Mass Assoc.; Elmig M. Soto, O.F.M.Cap., Dir. Capuchin Mass Assoc.; Roberto Martinez, O.F.M.Cap., Vice Provincial Treas.

Asociacion De Frailes Capuchinos, Inc.; Asociacion Misionera Capuchina; Capuchin Formation Trust of Puerto Rico; Capuchin Health and Retirement Trust of Puerto Rico Friars 28; Postulants 2; Novices 3.

HATO REY. *Jesuit Community - Casa Claver*, 398 Francisco Sein, 00917. Tel: 787-759-7654; Fax: 787-790-3162. Apto. 22634 U.P.R. Sta., 00931-2634. Rev. Fernando Pico, S.J. *Casa Spinola De Angelis* Urb. Baldrich, 580 Hostos Ave., 00902. Tel: 787-282-8522; Fax: 787-282-6087. Revs. Juan José Santiago, S.J.; Rafael Rodríguez, S.J.

TRUJILLO ALTO. *Carmelite Monastery of St. Joseph* (1651) (Monasterio Carmelita De San Jose), 00977-0568. Tel: 787-761-9548; Fax: 787-283-7235. Email: mcsjose@prdigital.com. P.O. Box 568, 00977-0568. Sr. Lutgarda Maria Reyes, O.Carm., Prioress.

[I] MISCELLANEOUS

SAN JUAN. *Caritas de Puerto Rico, Inc.*, 201 San Jorge St., 00910-0812. Tel: 787-727-7373, Ext. 1156; 787-727-7373, Ext. 1105; Fax: 787-728-4100; Tel: 787-300-4953, Ext. 1156; 787-300-4953, Ext. 1110; 787-728-3207. Email: ssc@rqsj.org. Web: www.sscpr.org. Mailing Address: P.O. Box 8812, 00910-8812. Rev. Enrique Manuel Camacho-Monserrate.

Casa San Clemente (Spiritual, Personal, Pastoral, and Psychological Counseling), Ave. Ponce De Leon 257, Puerta De Tierra, 00901. Tel: 787-723-6915; Fax: 787-977-8156. P.O. Box 9066315, 00906-6315. Rev. Terence Damian Wall, C.Ss.R., S.T.D., Exec. Dir.; Bro. Mateo Perez, C.Ss.R., Ph.D.; Ms. Ela Iglesias, Exec. Dir.

Centro Sor Isolina, Box 9511, 00926. Tel: 787-731-5700; Fax: 787-272-3390. Email: sister@prtc.net; lortiz@csifpr.org. Mrs. Lourdes M. Ortiz, M.T.S. (Social Improvement of the Poor).

El Hogar del Niño, Inc., Carr. 176 Km. 4.2 Bo. Cupey Alto, 00926. Tel: 787-761-2805; Fax: 787-283-1345. Email: elhogardelnino@prtc.net. Web: www.elhogardelninopr.org. Mailing Address: P.O. Box 20667, 00928-0667. Employees 15.

Hogar Del Buen Pastor formerly Hogar Buen Pastor (Homeless Shelter), Constitucion #250, Puerta de Tierra, 00901. Tel: 787-721-8579. P.O. Box 9066547, 00906-6547. Sr. Rosemarie Gonzalez, S.S.N.D.

Hogar Padre Venard, Inc., Calle San Francisco 305, 00901. Tel: 787-724-1131; Fax: 787-727-4616. Mailing Address: Apartado Postal 9020274, 00902-0274.

R. R. Siervas de Maria Ministras de los Enfermos, 1 Calle Fortaleza, 00901-1599. Tel: 787-723-4558; 787-724-2228; Fax: 787-721-0140. Sr. Aurea Fernandez Fontan, Supr.

RIO PIEDRAS. *Paulinas Multimedia* (Books, Cassettes and Catholic Publications), Calle Arzuaga #164, 00925-3322. Tel: 787-764-4885; 787-765-4390; Fax: 787-767-6214. Email: paulinas@yunque.net. Web: www.paulinas.org.

SANTURCE. *Beth Yash'ah* (Spiritual and Psychological Counseling), 1708 Calle Pumarada, 00912. Tel: 787-763-6708; 787-268-2661; 787-727-4100; Fax: 787-268-2661. Dr. Lucy Lopez-Roig, Dir.; Dr. Cecilia Arias.

Fondita De Jesus (Supportive, spiritual and psychosocial services and transitional/permanent housing), Calle Monserrate 704, PDA 16 1/2, 00909. Tel: 787-724-4051; Fax: 787-722-0992. Email: cartas@lafonditadejesus.org. P.O. Box 19384, 00910-1384. Tel: 787-725-0660; Fax: 787-722-0992. Socorro Rivera Rosa, Exec. Dir. Personnel 48; Total Assisted 3,100.

Servicios Pastorales Paules (Books, Leaflets and Catholic Publications), P.O. Box 19118, 00910. Tel: 787-728-0670. Rev. Santiago Arribas, C.M., Dir. Res.: 1650 Fernández Juneos, Santurce, 00910-9118. Email: centrosp@onelinkpr.net. Web: www-.padaespaulespr.org.

RELIGIOUS INSTITUTES OF MEN REPRESENTED IN THE ARCHDIOCESE

For further details refer to the corresponding bracketed number in the Religious Institutes of Men or Women section.

[0140]—*Augustinian Friars* (Spain)—O.S.A.

[0470]—*The Capuchin Friars* (Vice Prov. of Puerto Rico)—O.F.M.Cap.

[0270]—*Carmelite Fathers & Brothers* (Prov. of Aragon, Valentina, Spain)—O.Carm.

[0360]—*Claretian Missionaries* (Spain)—C.M.F.

[0310]—*Congregation of Christian Brothers* (Antilles Prov.)—C.F.C.

[0820]—*Congregation of the Fathers of Mercy* (Madrid, Spain)—C.P.M.

[1330]—*Congregation of the Mission* (Prov. of Puerto Rico)—C.M.

[1000]—*Congregation of the Passion* (Bilbao)—C.P.
[]—*Congregation of the Sacred Heart* (Spain)—C.SS.CC.
[]—*Congregation of the Terciarios Capuchinos Ntra. Sra. de los Dolores* (Spain)—T.C.
[0520]—*Franciscan Friars* (Spain)—O.F.M.
[0650]—*Holy Ghost Fathers* (American Prov.)—C.S.Sp.
[0690]—*Jesuit Fathers and Brothers* (Prov. of Puerto Rico)—S.J.
[0740]—*Marian Fathers*—M.I.C.
[0770]—*The Marist Brothers*—F.M.S.
[]—*Misioneros Contemplativos Ad-Gentes*
[1120]—*Missionaries of the Sacred Hearts of Jesus and Mary* (Spain)—M.SS.CC.
[0840]—*Missionary Servants of the Most Holy Trinity*—S.T.
[0910]—*Oblates of Mary Immaculate* (Peru Prov.)—O.M.I.
[0430]—*Order of Preachers-Dominicans* (Gen. Vicariate of P.R.)—O.P.
[1310]—*Order of the Holy Trinity* (Spain)—O.SS.T.
[1040]—*Piarist Fathers* (Spain)—Sch.P.
[1070]—*Redemptorist Fathers* (San Juan Prov.)—C.SS.R.
[1190]—*Salesians of Don Bosco* (Antilles Prov.)—S.D.B.
[0760]—*Society of Mary* (New York Prov.)—S.M.

RELIGIOUS INSTITUTES OF WOMEN REPRESENTED IN THE ARCHDIOCESE

[]—*Custodia Franciscana del Caribe "Santa Maria de la Esperanza"* (Frailes Franciscanos)
[1070-05]—*Dominican Sisters*—O.P.
[1070-06]—*Dominican Sisters*—O.P.
[1070-13]—*Dominican Sisters*—O.P.
[]—*Dominicanas Terciarias del Santisimo Sacramento* (Cadiz, Spain)
[]—*Hermanas Carmelitas de la Caridad* (Rome, Italy)—C.ach.
[]—*Hermanas Carmelitas de Madre Candelaria (Venezuela)*
[]—*Hermanas Carmelitas Teresas de San Jose (Barcelona, Spain)*
[]—*Hermanas de la Amistad Misionera en Cristo Obrero* (Amico and Madrid, Spain)
[]—*Hermanas de la B.V. Maria del Monte Carmelo* (Madrid, Spain)—H.Carm.
[]—*Hermanas de la Caridad del Cardenal Sancha* (San Domingo)—H.C.C.S.
[]—*Hermanas de la Caridad Del Sagrado Corazon De Jesus* (Madrid, Spain)
[]—*Hermanas de la Compania del Salvador* (Spain)
[]—*Hermanas De La Divina Providencia* (Rome, Italy)—CDP
[]—*Hermanas de Santos Angeles Custodios* (Bilbao, Spain)
[]—*Hermanas Dominicas de la Presentacion* (Tours, France; Colombia)
[]—*Hermanas Dominicas de Nuestra Senora del Rosario de Fatima* (Yauco)
[]—*Hermanas Franciscanas de Los Sagrados*—HH.FF.SSCC.
[]—*Hermanas Hospitalarias de Jesus Nazareno* (Cordoba, Spain)
[]—*Hermanas Mercedarias de la Caridad* (Madrid, Spain)
[]—*Hermanas Misioneras de la Madre Dolorosa y San Francisco de Asis* (Buga, Colombia)
[]—*Hermanas Misioneras de los Sagrados Corazones* (Palma de Mallorca, Spain)
[]—*Hermanitas de los Ancianos Desamparados* (Valencia, Spain)
[]—*Hijas de Maria Auxiliadora* (Torino, Italy)
[]—*Hijas Del Corazon Misericordioso De Maria* (Bogota, Colombia)
[0950]—*Instituto Misionero Hijas de San Pablo* (Rome, Italy)
[]—*Instituto Santa Mariana de Jesus (Hermanas Marianitas)* (Ecuador)—R.M.
[]—*Lumen Dei* (Madrid, Spain)—U.L.D.
[]—*Madres de Desamparados y San Jose de la Montana* (Valencia, Spain)
[]—*Madres Escolapias* (Rome)
[]—*Misioneras de Cristo Salvador*
[2710]—*Misioneras De La Caridad* (Calcutta, India)—M.C.
[]—*Misioneras del Buen Pastor* (San Juan)
[]—*Misioneras del Santisimo Sacramento y Maria Inmaculada* (Spain)
[]—*Misioneras Dominicas del Santisimo Rosario* (Madrid, Spain)
[]—*Misioneros Contemplativos Ad-Gentes*
[2720]—*Mission Helpers of the Sacred Heart*—M.H.S.H.
[2790]—*Missionary Servants of the Most Blessed Trinity* (Philadelphia, PA)—M.S.B.T.
[]—*Monjas de la Orden de la Bienventurada Virgen Maria de Monte Carmelo*—O.Carm.
[]—*Oblatas De La Santisima Trinidad* (Spain)
[]—*Oblatas del Santisimo Redentor* (Madrid, Spain)
[]—*Operarias Del Divino Maestro* (Valenzia, Spain)
[]—*Religiosas del Sagrado Corazon* (Rome, Italy)
[]—*Religiosas Oblatas del Divino Amor*
[]—*Religiosas Teatinas de la Inmaculada Concepcion* (Rome)—R.T.
[]—*Religiosas Terciarias de San Francisco de Asis y de la Inmaculada Concepcion* (Valencia, Spain)
[2970]—*School Sisters of Notre Dame* (Wilton, CT)—S.S.N.D.
[]—*Siervas De La Verdad* (Bayamon, Puerto Rico)
[3600]—*Siervas de Maria y Ministras de los Enfermos* (Rome, Italy)—S.M.
[2570]—*Sisters of Mercy* (Pittsburgh, PA)—R.S.M.
[]—*Sisters of Nazareth*
[1620]—*Sisters of Saint Francis of Millvale, Pennsylvania*—O.S.F.
[1650]—*Sisters of St. Francis of Philadelphia*—O.S.F.
[1800]—*Sisters of St. Francis of the Third Order Regular* (Williamsville, New York)—O.S.F.
[3830]—*Sisters of St. Joseph* (Brentwood)—C.S.J.
[3930]—*Sisters of St. Joseph of the Third Order of St. Francis*—S.S.J.-T.O.S.F.
[1970]—*Sisters of the Holy Family of Nazareth*—C.S.F.N.
[1490]—*Sisters of the Third Franciscan Order*—O.S.F.
[2150]—*Sisters, Servants of the Immaculate Heart of Mary*—I.H.M.
[]—*Terciarias Franciscanas de la Purisima* (Murcia, Spain)

NECROLOGY

† Soto, Rev. Msgr. Rafael Fontanez—Died Feb. 3, 2009
† Su Chao, Rev. Msgr. Tomas, San Juan, PR Segrada Familia—Died June 4, 2009
† Arango, Heriberto Londono—Died June 4, 2009
† Gray, Theodoro—Died Sept. 13, 2009
† Solozabal, Vincente Egurola—Died July 8, 2009

An asterisk (*) denotes an organization that has established tax-exempt status directly with the IRS and is not covered by the USCCB Group Ruling.

American Foreign Missions

AUGUSTINIAN MISSIONS (O.S.A.)

Foreign Missions of the Midwestern Province of the Order of St. Augustine

Foreign Missions Provincial Headquarters Province of Our Mother of Good Counsel (Midwestern): *Tolentine Center* 20300 Governors Hwy., Olympia Fields, IL 60461-1081. Phone: 708-748-5435; Fax: 708-481-2090. Very Rev. William E. Lego, O.S.A. Ord: '83, Prov.; Rev. Christopher C. Steinle, O.S.A. Ord: '98, Mission Procurator.

Midwestern Augustinian Religious serving in Foreign Missions: Most Rev. Daniel T. Turley, O.S.A. Ord: '68, Peru; Rev. Alfred M. Burke, O.S.A. Ord: '57, Japan; Rev. Charles J. Bodden, O.S.A. Ord: '78, Peru; Rev. John J. Dowling, O.S.A. Ord: '68, Peru; Rev. Richard Palmer, O.S.A. Ord: '87, Peru; Rev. John P. Tasto, O.S.A. Ord: '67, Mexico; Rev. John A. Tyma, O.S.A. Ord: '59, Peru.

Province of St. Thomas of Villanova (Eastern): P.O. Box 340, Villanova, PA 19085-0340. Phone: 610-527-3330; Fax: 610-520-0618. Very Rev. Donald F. Reilly, O.S.A. Ord: '74, Prior Prov.; Rev. Anthony P. Burrascano, O.S.A. Ord: '79, Dir. Missions; Rev. William A. McGuire, O.S.A. Ord: '65, Mission Procurator.

U.S. Religious Serving in Foreign Missions: Rev. Arthur P. Purcaro, O.S.A. Ord: '75, Peru; Rev. Francis J. Doyle, O.S.A. Ord: '70, South Africa; Rev. William R. Faix, O.S.A. Ord: '63, Czech Republic; Rev. Maurice J. Mahoney, O.S.A. Ord: '60, Japan; Rev. Thomas P. Dwyer, O.S.A. Ord: '53, Japan; Rev. Aquilino D. Gonzalez, O.S.A. Ord: '72, Peru; Rev. Michael J. Hilden, O.S.A. Ord: '73, Japan; Rev. John F. McAtee, O.S.A. Ord: '66.

AMERICAN BENEDICTINE FOREIGN MISSIONS (O.S.B.)

American Cassinese Congregation Foreign Missions

St. Vincent Archabbey: 300 Fraser Purchase Rd., Latrobe, PA 15650-2690. Phone: 724-532-6600. Arch Abbot (US) Douglas R. Nowicki, O.S.B. Ord: '72, Archabbot; Rev. Noel H. Rothrauff, O.S.B. Ord: '54, Mission Dir.

U.S. Religious serving in Taiwan: Bro. Nicholas Koss, O.S.B., Prior.

St. John's Abbey: Box 2015, Collegeville, MN 56321-2015. Fax: 320-363-3082. Rt. Rev. John Klassen, O.S.B. Ord: '77.

U.S. Religious serving Abroad: Rev. Kieran Nolan, O.S.B. Ord: '59, Japan; Rev. Neal Henry Lawrence, O.S.B. Ord: '60, Japan; Rev. Fintan Bromenshenkel, O.S.B. Ord: '45, Nassau; Rev. George Wolf, O.S.B. Ord: '44, Nassau; Very Rev. Thomas Wahl, O.S.B. Ord: '58, Japan; Rev. Cyprian Weaver, O.S.B. Ord: '72, Taiwan.

St. Benedict's Abbey: Atchison, KS 66002. Phone: 913-367-7853; Fax: 913-367-6230. Rt. Rev. Barnabas Senecal, O.S.B. Ord: '64, Abbot.

U.S. Religious serving in Brazil: Most Rev. Herbert Hermes; Rev. Kieran McInerney, O.S.B. Ord: '52; Rev. Denis Meade, O.S.B. Ord: '55; Rev. Duane Roy, O.S.B. Ord: '67.

St. Procopius Abbey: 5601 College Rd., Lisle, IL 60532. Phone: 630-969-6410; Fax: 630-969-6426. Rt. Rev. Dismas B. Kalcic, O.S.B. Ord: '61, Prior.

Assumption Abbey: P.O. Box A, Richardton, ND 58652. Phone: 701-974-3315; Fax: 701-974-3317. Rt. Rev. Brian Wangler, O.S.B. Ord: '69.

U.S. Religious serving in South America: Very Rev. Philip Vanderlin, O.S.B. Ord: '80, Prior; Rev. Gonzalo Blanco, O.S.B. Ord: '92, Subprior; Rev. Efraim Villegas, O.S.B. Ord: '88; Rev. Carlos Suarez, O.S.B. Ord: '86; Rev. Francis Wehri, O.S.B. Ord: '61; Rev. Nicolas Cano, O.S.B. Ord: '97; Bro. Fabio Mejia; Bro. Manuel Cely; Bro. Roberto Duarte.

St. Paul's Abbey: Newton, NJ 07860-0007. Phone: 973-383-2470; Fax: 973-383-5782. Very Rev. John Bosco Kim, O.S.B.

U.S. Religious serving Abroad: Rev. Damian Milliken, O.S.B. Ord: '58, Tanzania; Rev. Peter W. Blue, O.S.B. Ord: '70, Namibia.

Swiss-American Foreign Missions

Blue Cloud Abbey: Marvin, SD 57251. Phone: 605-398-9200; Fax: 605-398-9201. Rt. Rev. Thomas Hillenbrand Ord: '65, Mission Dir.

U.S. Religious serving in Guatemala: Rev. Basil Dilger, O.S.B. Ord: '61; Rev. Cletus Miller, O.S.B. Ord: '44; Rev. Bernardine Ness, O.S.B. Ord: '64.

Mount Angel Abbey: 1 Abbey Dr, Saint Benedict, OR 97373. Saint Benedict, OR 97373. Phone: 503-845-3030; Fax: 503-845-3594. Rt. Rev. Nathan Zodrow, O.S.B. Ord: '88.

U.S. Religious serving in Mexico: Very Rev. Konrad Shaefer, O.S.B. Ord: '80; Bro. James Bartos, O.S.B.

Marmion Abbey: 850 Butterfield Rd., Aurora, IL 60502. Phone: 630-897-7215; Fax: 630-897-0393. Rt. Rev. Vincent De Paul Bataille, O.S.B. Ord: '65.

AMERICAN CAPUCHIN MISSIONS (O.F.M.CAP.)

Missions of the American Provinces of the Order of Friars Capuchin (The Capuchin Friars) in the United States and other countries.

General Headquarters Via Piemonte, 70, Rome, Italy, 00187, Web: www.ofmcap.org. Very Rev. Mauro Johri, O.F.M.Cap., Gen. Min.; Rev. Helmut Rakowski, O.F.M.Cap., Sec. Gen. for the Missions.

American Capuchin Missions

Provincial Headquarters

Capuchin Foreign Missions

Province of St. Joseph: Office of Overseas Missions, 1820 Mt. Elliott St., Detroit, MI 48207. Fax: 313-579-2275. Very Rev. John Celichowski, O.F.M.Cap. Ord: '93, Prov. Min.; Bro. Campion Baer, O.F.M.Cap., Mission Sec.

U.S Religious serving Abroad: Rev. Kevin Heagerty, O.F.M.Cap. Ord: '61, Panama; Rev. Glenn Gessner, O.F.M.Cap. Ord: '60, Nicaragua; Rev. Benjamin Markwell, O.F.M.Cap. Ord: '66, Middle East; Rev. Paul Craig, O.F.M.Cap. Ord: '66, Middle East; Rev. Paul Koenig, O.F.M.Cap. Ord: '93, Middle East; Rev. Carmel Flora, O.F.M.Cap. Ord: '53, Australia; Rev. Walter Kasuboski, O.F.M-.Cap. Ord: '74, Panama; Rev. Jozef Timmers, O.F.M.Cap. Ord: '00, Panama; Rev. Andre Weller, O.F.M.Cap. Ord: '63, Panama.

Province of Mid-America: 3613 Wyandot St., Denver, CO 80211-2950. Phone: 303-477-5436; Fax: 303-477-6925. Rev. Charles Polifka, O.F.M-.Cap. Ord: '71, Prov. Min.; Stephanie Pedersen, Mission Sec.

U.S. Religious serving in Papua, New Guinea: (St. Michael the Archangel Vice Province of Papua, New Guinea and the Solomon Islands): Most Rev. Stephen Reichert, O.F.M.Cap. Ord: '69, Bishop of Mendi; Rev. Peter Meis, O.F.M.Cap. Ord: '67; Rev. Donald Debes, O.F.M.Cap. Ord: '70.

U.S. Religious serving in Mexico: Rev. William Kraus, O.F.M.Cap. Ord: '73.

Province of St. Augustine: 220 37th St., Pittsburgh, PA 15201. Phone: 412-682-6011; Fax: 412-682-0506. Very Rev. John Pavlik, O.F.M.Cap. Ord: '78, Prov. Min.; Rev. Francis Fugini, O.F.M-.Cap. Ord: '54, Coord. of Missions.

U.S. Religious serving in Papua New Guinea (St. Michael the Archangel Vice Province of Papua, New Guinea and the Solomon Islands): Rev. William Fey, O.F.M.Cap. Ord: '68, Vice Prov.; Rev. Samuel Driscoll, O.F.M.Cap. Ord: '59; Rev. Donald Lippert, O.F.M.Cap. Ord: '85; Rev. Benjamin Madden, O.F.M.Cap. Ord: '58; Rev. Brian Newman, O.F.M.Cap. Ord: '61; Rev. Cyril Repko, O.F.M.Cap. Ord: '62; Rev. Colman Studeny, O.F.M.Cap. Ord: '61; Rev. William Talentino, O.F.M.Cap. Ord: '67; Rev. Allan Wasiecko, O.F.M-.Cap. Ord: '68; Rev. Jonathan Williams, O.F.M-.Cap. Ord: '71; Bro. Raymond Ronan, O.F.M.Cap.

U.S. Religious serving in Puerto Rico (St. John the Baptist Vice Province): Rev. Mario Mastrangelo, O.F.M.Cap. Ord: '58.

Province of St. Mary: 30 Gedney Park Dr., White Plains, NY 10605. Phone: 914-761-3008.

The Capuchin Foreign Missions described here are a ministry of: The Province of St. Mary of the Capuchin Order
Rev. John Gallagher, O.F.M.Cap. Ord: '78, Prov.; Rev. Francis Gasparik, O.F.M.Cap. Ord: '86, Mission Sec.

U.S. Religious serving in Guam: Rev. George Maddock, O.F.M.Cap. Ord: '64; Rev. Randolph Nowak, O.F.M.Cap. Ord: '52; Bro. Brian Champoux, O.F.M.Cap.

U.S. Religious serving in Japan: Rev. Wayne Berndt, O.F.M.Cap. Ord: '83; Rev. Louis Chiusano, O.F.M.Cap. Ord: '57; Rev. Roland Daigle, O.F.M.Cap. Ord: '84; Rev. Peter Von Essen, O.F.M.Cap. Ord: '56; Rev. LaSalle Parsons, O.F.M-.Cap. Ord: '57; Rev. Patrick Sullivan, O.F.M.Cap. Ord: '71; Bro. Martin de Porres Schmitt, O.F.M.Cap.

U.S. Religious serving in Central America: Rev. John Clermont, O.F.M.Cap. Ord: '53, Honduras; Rev. Raymond Richard, O.F.M.Cap. Ord: '72, Honduras; Bro. James Donegan, O.F.M.Cap., Honduras.

The Seraphic Mass Association-Capuchin Mission Association: *St. Mary's Province* 210 W. 31st St., New York, NY 10001-2876.

This Association supports the Capuchin Foreign Mission.

AMERICAN CARMELITE MISSIONS (O.CARM.)

Carmelite Foreign Missions

Foreign Missions of the American Province of the Most Pure Heart of Mary

Provincial Headquarters, Carmelite Provincial Office: 1317 Frontage Rd., Darien, IL 60561. Fax: 630-971-0195. Very Rev. John F. Welch, O.Carm. Ord: '65, Prov.

Mission Office, Carmelite Missions: 8501 Bailey Rd., Darien, IL 60561-8418. Phone: 630-969-5220; Fax: 630-969-5266. Very Rev. John Malley, O.Carm. Ord: '56, Mission Dir.

U.S. Religious serving in Peru: Rev. Edward Adelmann, O.Carm. Ord: '75; Rev. James Geaney, O.Carm. Ord: '59; Most Rev. Michael LaFay, O.Carm. Ord: '60; Rev. Gerald Payea, O.Carm. Ord: '70; Rev. Michael Sgarioto, O.Carm. Ord: '85.

U.S. Religious serving in Mexico: Rev. Peter Hinde, O.Carm. Ord: '52; Rev. Thomas Jordan, O.Carm. Ord: '70.

COMBONI MISSIONARIES (VERONA FATHERS) (M.C.C.J.)

Comboni Foreign Missions

Legal Title: *Comboni Missionaries of the Heart of Jesus, Inc.*

U.S. Headquarters, Comboni Mission Center: 1318 Nagel Rd., Cincinnati, OH 45255-3120. Phone: 513-474-4997; Fax: 513-474-0382; Email: info@combonimissionaries.org. Rev. Louis Gasparini, M.C.C.J. Ord: '66, Prov. Supr.; Rev. Peter Ciuciulla, M.C.C.J. Ord: '92, Mission Dir.

U.S. Religious serving Abroad: Rev. Albert Anichini, M.C.C.J. Ord: '62, Uganda; Rev. David Baltz, M.C.C.J. Ord: '67, Uganda; Rev. Michael Barton, M.C.C.J. Ord: '75, Sudan; Rev. James Francez, M.C.C.J. Ord: '57, Mexico; Rev. John Converset, M.C.C.J. Ord: '71, South Africa.

AMERICAN CONVENTUAL FRANCISCAN MISSIONS (O.F.M.CONV.)

Conventual Franciscan Foreign Missions

General Headquarters Convento SS. XII Apostoli Piazza, SS Apostoli 51, Rome, Italy, 00187, Rev. Jaroslaw Wysoczanski, O.F.M.Conv., Sec. Gen. for the Missions; Very Rev. Justin A. Biase, O.F.M.Conv. Ord: '70, Prov. & Mission Dir.

Provincial Headquarters

Province of the Immaculate Conception: 77 St. Francis Pl., P.O. Box 629, Rensselaer, NY 12144. Phone: 518-472-1000.

U.S. Religious serving Abroad: Rev. Maury Marhafer, O.F.M.Conv. Ord: '54; Most Rev. Elias Manning, O.F.M.Conv., Bishop of Valenca, Brazil.

Province of Saint Anthony of Padua: Provincial House & Office of Mission Procurator, 12300 Folly Quarter Rd., Ellicott City, MD 21042-1419. Phone: 410-531-9200; Fax: 410-531-4881. Very Rev. Michael Kolodziej, O.F.M.Conv. Ord: '70, Minister Prov.; Joseph Hamilton, Mission Procurator.

Franciscan Mission Association: 12300 Folly Quarter Rd., Ellicott City, MD 21042. Rev. Raymond Borkowski, O.F.M.Conv. Ord: '61, Mission Animator.

U.S. Religious serving Abroad: Bro. Michael Duffy, O.F.M.Conv., Jamaica; Rev. Vincent Lachendro, O.F.M.Conv. Ord: '63, Japan; Rev. Michael Heine, O.F.M.Conv. Ord: '90, Jamaica; Rev. Brad Heckathorne, O.F.M.Conv. Ord: '81, Jamaica; Rev. James McCurry, O.F.M.Conv. Ord: '77, England;

Rev. Giles Zakowicz, O.F.M.Conv. Ord: '75, Kenya.

Province of Our Lady of Consolation: Provincial Office, 101 St. Anthony Dr., Mount Saint Francis, IN 47146. Rev. James Kent, O.F.M.Conv. Ord: '91, Minister Prov.

Religious serving Abroad: Rev. Juniper Cummings, O.F.M.Conv. Ord: '50, Vicar Custos; Rev. Terence Tobin, O.F.M.Conv. Ord: '55, Zambia; Bro. Joseph Weissling, O.F.M.Conv., Guardian; Bro. Anthony Droll, O.F.M.Conv., Zambia.

Province of Saint Bonaventure: Provincial Office, 6107 N. Kenmore Ave., Chicago, IL 60660-2797. Phone: 773-274-7681; Fax: 773-274-9751. Very Rev. Patrick Greenough, O.F.M.Conv. Ord: '87, Minister Prov.

U.S. Religious serving Abroad: Rev. John Calgaro, O.F.M.Conv. Ord: '74, Mexico; Rev. Abraham Crisostomo, O.F.M.Conv. Ord: '96; Bro. Paschal Metzger, O.F.M.Conv., Mexico; Bro. Stanislaus Zabkiewicz, O.F.M.Conv., Zambia.

CROSIER FATHERS MISSIONS (O.S.C.)

Crosier Foreign Missions

Crosier Fathers and Brothers: (Canons Regular of the Order of the Holy Cross)

U.S. Address: Crosier Province Headquarters:, 4332 N. 24th St., Phoenix, AZ 85016-6259. Phone: 602-443-7100; Fax: 602-443-7101; Email: athompson@crosier.org. Very Rev. Thomas Carkhuff, O.S.C. Ord: '76, Prov.; Bro. Albert Becker, O.S.C., Mission Dir.

U.S. Religious serving Abroad: Rev. Virgil Petermeier, O.S.C. Ord: '77, Indonesia.

AMERICAN DIVINE WORD MISSIONARIES (S.V.D.)

Society of the Divine Word Foreign Missions

Missions of the American Provinces of the Society of the Divine Word (S.V.D.), commonly known as Divine Word Missionaries

Latin: Societas Verbi Divini

Provincial Headquarters in the U.S.A.

Chicago Province: Society of the Divine Word - Province of Saint Joseph Freinademetz, S.V.D., 1985 Waukegan Rd., P.O. Box 6038, Techny, IL 60082-6038. Phone: 847-272-2700; Fax: 847-272-2517.

Publications: Divine Word Missionaries.

Very Rev. Mark Weber, S.V.D. Ord: '82, Prov. Supr.; Bro. Dennis Newton, S.V.D., Mission Dir. for all three Provinces.

Southern Province: Society of the Divine Word Province - Province of St. Augustine, 199 Seminary Dr., Bay Saint Louis, MS 39520-4638. Phone: 228-467-4322. Very Rev. James Pawlicki, S.V.D. Ord: '73, Prov. Supr. *Divine Word Missionaries Office* 1835 Waukegan Rd., Techny, IL 60082.

American Divine Word Missionaries in Overseas Missions: Rev. Daniel Bauer, S.V.D. Ord: '74, Taiwan; Rev. Joseph Bisson, S.V.D. Ord: '63, Papua, New Guinea; Archbishop Michael Blume, S.V.D. Ord: '72, Apostolic Nuncio to Togo & Benin; Rev. Francis Budenholzer, S.V.D. Ord: '72, Taiwan; Rev. Francis Bures, S.V.D. Ord: '53, Japan; Rev. Vincent Burke, S.V.D. Ord: '61, Ghana; Rev. Dennis Callan, S.V.D. Ord: '87, Korea; Rev. Ba Thai Dai, S.V.D. Ord: '05, Vietnam; Rev. Richard Daschbach, S.V.D. Ord: '64, East Timor; Rev. Anthony Dugay, S.V.D. Ord: '62, Ghana; Rev. Lloyd Fiedler, S.V.D. Ord: '70, Philippines; Bro. Ronald Fratzke, S.V.D., Thailand; Rev. Paul Gootee, S.V.D. Ord: '55, Indonesia; Rev. Lawrence Hambach, S.V.D. Ord: '61, Indonesia; Rev. James Heisig, S.V.D. Ord: '69, Japan; Rev. Xuan Ho, S.V.D. Ord: '03, St. Kitts, West Indies (Caribbean); Rev. Robert Johnson, S.V.D. Ord: '92, St. Maarten, Netherand Antilles (Caribbean); Bro. Lawrence Kieffer, S.V.D., Papua New Guinea; Rev. Robert Kisala, S.V.D. Ord: '85, Italy; Rev. Thomas Krosnicki, S.V.D. Ord: '66, St. Maarten (Caribbean); Rev. Ronald Lange, S.V.D. Ord: '71, Ghana; Rev. Anthony Duc Le, S.V.D. Ord: '06, Australia; Rev. John Hung Le, S.V.D. Ord: '04, Papua New Guinea; Rev. Timothy Lenchak, S.V.D. Ord: '75, Italy; Rev. James Liebner, S.V.D. Ord: '85, China; Rev. Michael Lindstrom, S.V.D. Ord: '82, Philippines; Bro. Damien Lunders, S.V.D., Thailand; Rev. David Mayer, S.V.D. Ord: '66, Japan; Rev. Walter Mendonca, S.V.D. Ord: '76, British Virgin Islands (Caribbean); Rev. Peter Michael, S.V.D. Ord: '40, Philippines; Rev. Theodore Murnane, S.V.D. Ord: '59, Philippines; Rev. Paul Nadolny, S.V.D. Ord: '89, Mozambique; Rev. Lawrence Nemer, S.V.D. Ord: '60, Australia; Rev. Joseph Trong Nguyen, S.V.D. Ord: '91, Vietnam; Rev. Long Phi Nguyen, S.V.D. Ord: '07, Chile; Rev. Michael Quang Nguyen, S.V.D. Ord: '02, Australia; Rev. Peter Sam Cao Nguyen, S.V.D. Ord: '86, Korea; Rev. Phong Cao Nguyen, S.V.D. Ord: '06, Brazil; Rev. Van Hiep Nguyen, S.V.D. Ord: '99, Ecuador; Rev. Vinh Daniel Nguyen, S.V.D. Ord: '07, Mexico; Rev. Joseph Minh Vu Nguyen, S.V.D. Ord: '96, Australia; Rev. Thi Pham, S.V.D. Ord: '02, Italy; Rev. Frank Power, S.V.D. Ord: '73, Jamaica; Rev. Robert Riemer, S.V.D. Ord: '60, Japan; Rev. Bartley Schmitz, S.V.D. Ord: '44, Taiwan; Rev. John Seland, S.V.D. Ord: '68, Japan; Bro. Bernard Spitzley, S.V.D., Jamaica; Rev. Arnold Steffen, S.V.D. Ord: '57, Papua New Guinea; Rev. Victor Stevko, S.V.D. Ord: '57, Australia; Rev. Nicholas Strawn, S.V.D. Ord: '62, Indonesia; Rev. David Streit, S.V.D. Ord: '69, Rome; Rev. Richard Szippl, S.V.D. Ord: '81, Japan; Rev. Gerald Theis, S.V.D. Ord: '80, Papua New Guinea; Rev. Richard Thibeau, S.V.D. Ord: '57, Mexico; Rev. Frederick Timp, S.V.D. Ord: '71, Ghana; Rev. Cong Bang Tran, S.V.D. Ord: '00, Togo; Rev. Joseph Huynh Tran, S.V.D. Ord: '03, Vietnam; Rev. Peter Tam Tran, S.V.D. Ord: '98, Australia; Rev. Vinh The Trinh, S.V.D. Ord: '07, Columbia; Rev. Andy Dinh Vu, S.V.D. Ord: '07, Ecuador; Rev. Joseph Tri Van Vu, S.V.D. Ord: '85, Vietnam; Rev. Toan Quoc Vu, S.V.D. Ord: '06, Ecuador; Rev. James Vorwek, S.V.D. Ord: '69, Argentina.

AMERICAN DOMINICAN MISSIONS (O.P.)

Dominican-Order of Preachers Foreign Missions

Foreign Missions of the American Provinces of the Order of Preachers

Provincial Headquarters

Province of St. Joseph (Eastern): 141 E. 65th St., New York, NY 10021. Phone: 212-861-3776. Very Rev. D. Dominic Izzo, O.P. Ord: '94, Prov.; Very Rev. Joseph P. Allen, O.P. Ord: '67, Mission Sec.

U.S. Religious serving in Pakistan: Rev. J. Nuttall, O.P. Ord: '69; Rev. G. L. Sukovaty, O.P. Ord: '51.

U.S. Religious serving Elsewhere: Rev. D. G. Doherty, O.P. Ord: '57, Philippines; Most Rev. Christopher Cardone, O.P. Ord: '86, Auxiliary Bishop -Solomon Islands.

U.S. Religious serving in Kenya: Very Rev. David Adeletta, O.P. Ord: '98, Vicar Prov.; Rev. M. B. Schepers, O.P. Ord: '56; Rev. Vincent Wiseman, O.P. Ord: '71; Rev. Kenneth Andrew Hofer, O.P. Ord: '02; Rev. Leon Martin A. Martiny, O.P. Ord: '98; Rev. Lewis M. Shea, O.P. Ord: '52; Rev. Thomas R. Heath, O.P. Ord: '50; Rev. John B. Croell, O.P. Ord: '98; Rev. Thomas Kraft, O.P. Ord: '84.

Province of St. Albert the Great (Central): 1909 S. Ashland Ave., Chicago, IL 60608-2994. Fax: 312-829-8471. Very Rev. Michael A. Mascari, O.P. Ord: '87, Prov.; Bro. Edward Van Merrienboer, O.P., Dir., St. Dominic Mission Society.

U.S. Religious serving in Kenya: Rev. Lewis M. Shea, O.P. Ord: '52.

U.S. Religious serving in Nigeria: Rev. Peter Otillio, O.P. Ord: '57; Rev. Joseph H. Kenny, O.P. Ord: '50; Rev. Justus Pokrzewinski, O.P. Ord: '60; Rev. Edward H. Riley, O.P. Ord: '60; Rev. Gilbert Thesing, O.P. Ord: '75; Bro. Stephen D. Lucas, O.P.

U.S. Religious serving in Bolivia: Rev. Daniel Roach, O.P. Ord: '56.

Province of the Holy Name (Western Dominican Province): 5877 Birch Ct., Oakland, CA 94618. Very Rev. Emmerich W. Vogt, O.P. Ord: '78, Prov.

U.S. Religious serving in Latin America: Rev. David Bello, O.P. Ord: '81, Mexico; Rev. Timothy Conlan, O.P. Ord: '67, Guatemala; Rev. Bartholomew de la Torre, O.P. Ord: '67, Mexico; Rev. Martin de Porres Walsh, O.P. Ord: '69, Mexico; Rev. Miguel Rolland, O.P. Ord: '88, Mexico.

U.S. Religious Serving in Kenya: Bro. Daniel Thomas, O.P.

St. Martin de Porres Province (Southern Dominican Province): 1421 N. Causeway Blvd., Ste. 200, Metairie, LA 70001-4144. Phone: 504-837-2129; Fax: 504-837-6604. Very Rev. Martin J. Gleeson, O.P. Ord: '98, Prov.

U.S. Religious serving Abroad: Rev. Jose D. Padilla, O.P. Ord: '04, Italy; Rev. Leobardo Almazan Estevez, O.P. Ord: '05, Italy; Rev. James L. Dolan, O.P. Ord: '60, Peru; Rev. Brian J. Pierce, O.P. Ord: '83, Rome; Rev. Rafael Proenza, O.P. Ord: '96, Cuba; Rev. Alfred W. Wilder, O.P. Ord: '65, Italy; Rev. Marcelo Solorzano, O.P. Ord: '95, Italy; Rev. Christopher T. Eggleton, O.P. Ord: '88, Ecuador; Rev. Charles Johnson, O.P. Ord: '06, Ecuador; Rev. David Seid, O.P. Ord: '08, China; Rev. Marcos Ramos, O.P. Ord: '01, Canada; Rev. Philip Powell, O.P. Ord: '05, Italy; Bro. Angel Mendez, O.P., Mexico.

AMERICAN FRANCISCAN MISSIONS (O.F.M.)

Franciscan Foreign Missions

Missions of the American Provinces of the Order of Friars Minor (Franciscan)in the United States and other countries

Holy Name Province: 135 W. 31st St., New York, NY 10001-3439. Phone: 973-778-1915; Phone: 888-372-6478; Fax: 973-777-5687; Web: www.hnp.org. Rev. Russell C. Becker, O.F.M. Ord: '72, Prov. Promoter of the Missions Sec. Missionary Evangelization; Bro. Thomas J. Cole, O.F.M., Mission Promoter.

U.S. Religious serving in Africa: Rev. Joseph B. Ehrhardt, O.F.M. Ord: '67.

U.S. Religious serving in Bolivia: Rev. Ignatius Harding, O.F.M. Ord: '72; Rev. William R. Keenan, O.F.M. Ord: '56; Rev. Thomas J. Kornacki, O.F.M. Ord: '77; Rev. Clement Comesky, O.F.M. Ord: '55; Bro. James McIntosh, O.F.M.

U.S. Religious serving in Brazil: Most Rev. Capistran F. Heim, O.F.M. Ord: '65; Rev. David J. Babcock, O.F.M. Ord: '53; Rev. Donald J. Chin, O.F.M. Ord: '67; Rev. Berard J. Hanlon, O.F.M. Ord: '63; Rev. Thomas P. Jones, O.F.M. Ord: '59; Rev. Juvenal F. Leahy, O.F.M. Ord: '58; Rev. Ignatius J. McGeady, O.F.M. Ord: '58; Rev. Paul J. Osborne, O.F.M. Ord: '64.

U.S. Religious serving in Japan: Rev. Bede Fitzpatrick, O.F.M. Ord: '55; Rev. Bartholomew McMahon, O.F.M. Ord: '62; Rev. Donnon P. Murray, O.F.M. Ord: '56; Rev. Callistus Sweeney, O.F.M. Ord: '53; Rev. Stanislaus Widomski, O.F.M. Ord: '62.

U.S. Religious serving in Peru: Rev. Mariano Gagnon, O.F.M. Ord: '57; Rev. Christopher J. Dunn, O.F.M. Ord: '82; Rev. Anthony Wilson, O.F.M. Ord: '87; Rev. Paul Breslin, O.F.M. Ord: '88; Rev. Carlos Sarmiento-Diaz, O.F.M. Ord: '99.

U.S. Religious serving in Puerto Rico: Most Rev. Roberto O. Gonzalez, O.F.M. Ord: '77; Rev. Alfonso Guzman Alfaro, O.F.M. Ord: '71.

U.S. Religious serving in Taiwan: Rev. Pius Liu, O.F.M. Ord: '53.

U.S. Religious serving in Vietnam: Rev. Khoa Nguyen, O.F.M. Ord: '94.

Franciscan Province of the Immaculate Conception: 125 Thompson St., New York, NY 10012. Rev. James Goode, O.F.M. Ord: '72, Sec./Missionary Evangelization & Franciscan Missionary Union.

Province-affiliated Religious serving in Honduras: Most Rev. Maurus Muldoon, O.F.M.; Most Rev Roberto Camilleri, O.F.M. Ord: '75; Rev. Albert Gauci, O.F.M. Ord: '71; Rev. Angelo Falzon, O.F.M. Ord: '84; Rev. Joseph Bonello, O.F.M. Ord: '85; Rev. Donald Salazar, O.F.M. Ord: '67; Rev. Nery Aguirre, O.F.M. Ord: '74.

Province-affiliated Religious serving in El Salvador: Rev. Flavian Mucci, O.F.M. Ord: '63; Rev. Guy Vellardita, O.F.M. Ord: '58, San Pedro; Rev. Rafael Fernandez, O.F.M. Ord: '87.

Province-affiliated Religious serving in Guatemala: Rev. Rocco Famiglietti, O.F.M. Ord: '47; Rev. Ottaviano Battolini, O.F.M. Ord: '43; Rev. Roberto Siguere, O.F.M. Ord: '65; Rev. Michael Della Penna, O.F.M. Ord: '99.

Sacred Heart Province: 3140 Meramec St., Saint Louis, MO 63118. Phone: 314-353-3421; Phone: 314-353-7470. *Franciscan Missionary Union* Phone: 314-353-7729. Rev. William Spencer, O.F.M. Ord: '74, Prov.; Rev. Michael Jennrich, O.F.M. Ord: '87, Prov. Vicar; Bro. Joseph Rogenski, O.F.M., Promoter of the Missions, Holy Land Commissariat, Secretariat for Missionary Evangelization. Rev. Jesus Aguirre-Garza, O.F.M. Ord: '96, Democratic Republic of Congo; Rev. Kenneth Capalbo, O.F.M. Ord: '74, Vietnam; Rev. Joseph Tan Doan Nguyen, O.F.M. Ord: '86, Vietnam; Bro. Jeffery Haller, O.F.M., Democratic Republic of the Congo.

U.S. Religious serving in Alaska: Rev. Joseph Hemmer, O.F.M. Ord: '54; Bro. Robert J. Ruzicka, O.F.M.; Bro. R. Justin Huber, O.F.M.

U.S. Religious serving in Brazil: Rev. Nestor Windolph, O.F.M. Ord: '55; Rev. Richard Duffy, O.F.M. Ord: '58.

St. Barbara Province: 1500 34th Ave., Oakland, CA 94601. Fax: 510-536-3970.

U.S. Religious serving Overseas: Rev. Garret Edmunds, O.F.M. Ord: '82, Israel; Rev. David Gaa, O.F.M. Ord: '98, Kazakhstan; Rev. Elias Galvez, O.F.M. Ord: '56, Mexico; Rev. John Gibbons,

O.F.M. Ord: '01, Russia; Rev. Thomas King, O.F.M. Ord: '93, Peru; Rev. Sergio Santos, O.F.M. Ord: '85, Philippines; Bro. Leo Gonzalez, O.F.M., Israel; Bro. Gerard Saunders, O.F.M., Peru; Bro. Ivo Toneck, O.F.M., Mexico.

COMMISSARIAT OF THE HOLY LAND

Franciscan Monastery, 1400 Quincy St., N.E., Washington, DC 20017. Phone: 202-526-6800; Fax: 202-529-9889; Email: secretariatusa@myfranciscan.com; Web: www.myfranciscan.com. Very Rev. Jeremy Harrington, O.F.M. Ord: '59, Guardian; Rev. David Wathen, O.F.M. Ord: '99, Vocation Dir.; Rev. James Paul Brabandt, O.F.M. Ord: '95, Mass Office; Rev. Garrett Edmunds, O.F.M. Ord: '82, Vice Commissary; Friar Fadi Azar, O.F.M.; Friar Thomas Courtney, O.F.M.; Friar-Deacon John-Sebastian Laird-Hammond, O.F.M. Ord: '91, Secretariat to the Franciscan Monastery.

Commissary Custody of the Holy Land: Jordan, Israel, Lebanon, Syria, Cyprus, Egypt, and Rhodes.

U.S. Religious serving Abroad: Rev. Fergus Clarke, O.F.M. Ord: '73, Jerusalem, Israel; Rev. David Jaeger, O.F.M. Ord: '86, Jerusalem, Israel; Rev. George Lewett, O.F.M. Ord: '88, Bethlehem, Israel; Rev. Athanasius Macora, O.F.M. Ord: '92, Jerusalem, Israel; Rev. Matthias Rendon, O.F.M. Ord: '92, Jerusalem, Israel; Rev. Danielmose Shroeder, O.F.M. Ord: '91, Jerusalem, Israel; Rev. Peter Vasko, O.F.M. Ord: '87, Jerusalem, Israel; Bro. Leo Gonzales, O.F.M., Mt. Tabor, Israel; Bro. Angel Beda Ison, O.F.M., Jerusalem, Israel; Bro. Michael Raum, O.F.M., Jerusalem, Israel; Bro. Lawrence Bode, O.F.M., Jerusalem, Israel; Bro. Gregory Giannoni, O.F.M., Jerusalem, Israel; Bro. John Savage, O.F.M., Jerusalem, Israel.

FRANCISCAN FRIARS OF THE ATONEMENT (S.A.)

General Headquarters: Graymoor:, P.O. Box 300, Garrison, NY 10524-0300. Phone: 845-424-3671; Fax: 845-424-2166.

For detailed information on the U.S. Religious working in foreign missions, please refer to the listings under the Archdiocese of New York section entitled "Monasteries and Residences of Priests and Brothers," Graymoor, Garrison, NY.

HOLY CROSS MISSION CENTER (C.S.C.)

U.S. Headquarters and Procure: Holy Cross Mission Center:, P.O. Box 543, Notre Dame, IN 46556. Phone: 574-631-5477; Fax: 574-631-6813. Rev. Thomas W. Smith, C.S.C. Ord: '72, Dir.

Legal Title: *Holy Cross Foreign Mission Society, Inc.*

Holy Cross Mission Center

Holy Cross Foreign Missions

Indiana Province: Congregation of the Holy Cross, P.O. Box 1064, Notre Dame, IN 46556-1064.

Midwest Province of Brothers: Congregation of the Holy Cross, P.O. Box 460, Notre Dame, IN 46556-0460.

Eastern Province of Priests: Congregation of the Holy Cross, 835 Clinton Ave., Bridgeport, CT 06604-2393.

South-West Province of Brothers: Congregation of the Holy Cross, 1101 St. Edward's Dr., Austin, TX 78704-6512.

Eastern Brothers Province: Congregation of the Holy Cross, 85 Overlook Cir., New Rochelle, NY 10804-4501.

U.S. Religious serving in Foreign Missions: Rev. Robert R. Baker, C.S.C. Ord: '70, Peru; Rev. James T. Banas, C.S.C. Ord: '57, Bangladesh; Rev. Gerald R. Barmasse, C.S.C. Ord: '76, Chile; Rev. David B. Burrell, C.S.C. Ord: '59, Uganda; Rev. Charles A. Delaney, C.S.C. Ord: '49, Chile; Rev. Michael M. DeLaney, C.S.C. Ord: '87, Chile; Rev. Philip T. Devlin, C.S.C. Ord: '56, Peru; Rev. Joseph A. Dorsey, C.S.C. Ord: '57, Chile; Rev. David E. Farrell, C.S.C. Ord: '68, Peru; Rev. Donald G. Fetters, C.S.C. Ord: '76, Peru; Rev. Robert Gilbo, C.S.C. Ord: '67, Chile; Rev. Robert G. Gilmour, C.S.C. Ord: '68, Ghana; Rev. Eugene Homrich, C.S.C. Ord: '55, Bangladesh; Rev. L. Peter Logsdon, C.S.C. Ord: '68, Mexico; Rev. H. Thomas McDermott, C.S.C. Ord: '79, Bangladesh; Rev. Russell K. McDougall, C.S.C. Ord: '91, Rome; Rev. Aaron J. Michka, Mexico; Rev. Daniel A. Panchot, C.S.C. Ord: '65, Mexico; Rev. Gerald T. Papen, C.S.C. Ord: '63, Chile; Rev. Joseph Peixotto, C.S.C. Ord: '61, Bangladesh; Rev. Claude Pomerleau, C.S.C. Ord: '65, Uganda; Rev. George F. Pope, C.S.C. Ord: '58, Bangladesh; Rev. Richard L. Potthast, C.S.C. Ord: '67, Uganda; Rev. Frank J. Quinlivan, C.S.C. Ord: '70, Bangladesh; Rev. Robert G. Simon, C.S.C. Ord: '61, Chile; Rev. Richard E. Stout, C.S.C. Ord: '71, Uganda; Rev. Richard W. Timm, C.S.C. Ord: '49, Bangladesh; Rev. Thomas Zurcher, C.S.C. Ord: '72, Mexico; Rev. Mark Ghyselinck, C.S.C. Ord: '88, Uganda; Bro. Donald Becker, C.S.C., Bangladesh; Bro. John Benesh, C.S.C., Peru; Bro. Thomas Dillman, C.S.C., Ghana; Bro. Ronald Drahozal, C.S.C., Bangladesh; Bro. John Flood, C.S.C., Uganda; Bro. William Gates, C.S.C., Ghana; Bro. Vincent Gross, C.S.C., Ghana; Bro. Thomas Giumenta, C.S.C., Peru; Bro. Alan Harrod, C.S.C., Uganda; Bro. Ronald Hein, C.S.C., Brazil; Bro. Bernard Klim, C.S.C., Uganda; Bro. Donald E. Kuchenmeister, C.S.C., Chile; Bro. Alfred Ledet, C.S.C., Brazil; Bro. Dismas Lenzi, C.S.C., Brazil; Bro. Norbert Lengerich, C.S.C., Brazil; Bro. Matthew Lyons, C.S.C., Chile; Bro. Matthew McKenna, C.S.C., Chile; Bro. Harold Naudet, C.S.C., Brazil; Bro. James Nichols, C.S.C., Uganda; Bro. Leonard Reeson, C.S.C., Brazil; Bro. Frank Robinson, C.S.C., Brazil; Bro. Paul Schaefer, C.S.C., Brazil; Bro. Sergio Stolf, C.S.C., Brazil; Bro. J. Rodney Struble, C.S.C., Bangladesh; Bro. Nicholas Thielman, C.S.C., Bangladesh; Bro. Ernest Turk, C.S.C., Brazil; Bro. Robert Weinmann, C.S.C., Brazil.

JESUIT MISSIONS (S.J.)

Jesuit Foreign Missions

Jesuit Mission Inc. An official missionary organization of the Provinces of the United States Assistancy of the Society of Jesus.

National Headquarters: Jesuit Missions, 1016 16th St., N.W., #400, Washington, DC 20036. Phone: 202-462-0400; Fax: 202-328-9212. Rev. Thomas H. Smolich, S.J. Ord: '86, Pres.; Rev. Thomas P. Greene, S.J. Ord: '07, Vice Pres.; Rev. James M. Shea, S.J. Ord: '75, Treas.; Very Rev. Myles Sheehan, S.J. Ord: '94, Sec.

Provinces

Society of Jesus: California Province, 300 College Ave., Los Gatos, CA 95030. Very Rev. John P. McGarry, S.J. Ord: '93, Prov.; Rev. Theodore E. Gabrielli, S.J. Ord: '96, Mission Dir.

Legal Title: *California Jesuit Missionaries*

U.S. Religious serving in Foreign Missions: Rev. Louis G. Aldrich, S.J. Ord: '86, Republic of China; Rev. Ferdinand T. Azevedo, S.J. Ord: '70, Brazil; Rev. Robert R. Becka, S.J. Ord: '60, Japan; Rev. Walter G. Brennan, S.J. Ord: '60, Japan; Rev. Robert E. Chiesa, S.J. Ord: '68, Japan; Rev. Robert W. Cunningham, S.J. Ord: '55, Philippines; Rev. John A. Donahue, S.J. Ord: '79, Honduras; Rev. John R. Donald, S.J. Ord: '72, Honduras; Rev. Gustavo D. Fernandez, S.J. Ord: '67, Guatemala; Rev. Robert Glynn, S.J. Ord: '91, Zambia; Rev. Fred J. Green, S.J. Ord: '58, Peru; Rev. Robert B. Grimaldi, S.J. Ord: '68, Honduras; Rev. Kieth Barry Martinson, S.J. Ord: '75, Republic of China; Rev. George G. Martinson, S.J. Ord: '73, Republic of China; Rev. Paul E. Pollock, S.J. Ord: '73, Thailand; Rev. Daniel J. Ross, S.J. Ord: '66, Republic of China; Rev. Richard J. Schneck, S.J. Ord: '72, Ecuador; Rev. Augustine H. Tsang, S.J. Ord: '94, Republic of China; Rev. Edward J. Thylstrup, S.J. Ord: '67, Republic of China; Rev. Charles A. Welsh, S.J. Ord: '72, Republic of China; Bro. Richard J. Devine, S.J., Japan.

Residing in other provinces: Phone: 39 06 68977 703; Cell: 39 3314350589. Phone: 39 06 69526 6112; Fax: 39 06 69526 6151. Rev. Ernest R. Martinez, S.J. Ord: '62, Supr. & Prof. Emeritus New Testament Spirituality; Phone: 39 06 68977 703; Cell: 39 3314350589. Rev. Stephen Pisano, S.J. Ord: '75, Rector & Prof. Old Testament exegesis and criticism; Phone: 39 06 69526 6112; Fax: 39 06 69526 6151.

Priests: 22; Brothers: 1

Society of Jesus: Chicago Province, 2050 N. Clark St., Chicago, IL 60614. Phone: 773-975-6363. Very Rev. Timothy P. Kesicki, S.J. Ord: '94, Prov.; Rev. Walter C. Deye, S.J. Ord: '75, Socius.

Legal Title: *Jesuit International Missions, (Formerly, Jesuits in Peru, Chicago Province, and Patna Jesuit Mission Society).*

U.S. Religious serving in Foreign Missions: Rev. Richard J. Baumann, S.J. Ord: '75, Zimbabwe; Rev. Theodore B. Bowling, S.J. Ord: '53, India; Rev. Patrick M. Casey, S.J. Ord: '72, Peru; Rev. Francis P. Chamberlain, S.J. Ord: '68, Peru; Rev. Terrence P. Charlton, S.J. Ord: '76, Kenya; Rev. Martin P. Coyne, S.J. Ord: '66, Nepal; Rev. Edwin J. Daly, S.J. Ord: '59, India; Rev. Robert M. Deiters, S.J. Ord: '58, Japan; Rev. Robert L. Dolan, S.J. Ord: '73, Peru; Rev. Jerome F. Durack, S.J. Ord: '60, India; Rev. Kevin H. Flaherty, S.J. Ord: '83, Peru; Rev. John J. Kenealy, S.J. Ord: '58, India; Rev. Roman B. Lewicki, S.J. Ord: '65, India; Rev. Jeffrey L. Klaiber, S.J. Ord: '74; Rev. Lewis Charles, S.J., Peru; Rev. James M. O'Leary, S.J. Ord: '91, Spain; Rev. John L. O'Malley, S.J. Ord: '63, Japan; Rev. Edward P. Schmidt, S.J. Ord: '71, Peru; Rev. John R. Sima, S.J. Ord: '71, Peru; Rev. George Wuest, S.J. Ord: '58; Rev. Patrick M. Casey, S.J. Ord: '72, Peru; Rev. T. Mattingly Garr, S.J. Ord: '75, Peru; Rev. Sebastian J. Carri, S.J. Ord: '67, India; Rev. Anthony Chelakat, S.J. Ord: '67, India.

Priests: 24

Detroit Province: 7303 W. Seven Mile Rd., Detroit, MI 48221-2121. Phone: 313-861-7500. Very Rev. Timothy P. Kesicki, S.J. Ord: '94, Prov.; Ms. Carrie Nantas, Provincial Asst. International Missions.

Legal Title: *Jesuit International Missions, (Formerly, Patna Jesuit Mission Society)*

U.S. Religious serving in Foreign Missions: Rev. Richard W. Cherry, S.J. Ord: '69, Sudan; Rev. Gerald A. Drinane, S.J. Ord: '62, India; Rev. Michael A. Evans, S.J. Ord: '83, Kenya; Rev. William G. Goudreau, S.J. Ord: '52, India; Rev. Eugene F. Hattie, S.J. Ord: '53, Uganda; Rev. Paul S. Kehres, S.J. Ord: '51, India; Rev. Casper J. Miller, S.J. Ord: '64, Nepal; Rev. Joseph E. Mulligan, S.J. Ord: '73, Nicaragua; Rev. James J. Regan, S.J. Ord: '67, Peru; Rev. Robert H. Schmidt, S.J. Ord: '69, India; Rev. Thomas F. Tobin, S.J. Ord: '65, India; Rev. Theodore W. Walters, S.J. Ord: '56, Tanzania; Rev. Martin T. Connell, S.J. Ord: '94, Tanzania; Bro. Richard L. Cure, S.J., Japan; Bro. James J. Boynton, S.J., Haiti.

Priests: 13; Brothers: 1

Society of Jesus: Maryland Province, 8600 LaSalle Rd., Ste. 620, Towson, MD 21286-2014. Phone: 443-921-1310; Fax: 443-921-1313. Very Rev. James M. Shea, S.J. Ord: '75, Prov.

Legal Title: *Jesuit Mission Inc., an official missionary organization of the Provinces of the United States Assistancy of the Society of Jesus.*

U.S. Religious serving in Foreign Missions: Rev. Eugene J. Barber, S.J. Ord: '63, Chile; Rev. Vincent J. Capuano, S.J. Ord: '98, Argentina; Rev. Jeffrey G.L. Chang, S.J. Ord: '99, Philippines; Rev. Edgar J. Debany, S.J. Ord: '84, Nigeria; Rev. James M. Desjardins, S.J. Ord: '77, Russia; Rev. Robert E. Hamm, S.J. Ord: '68, Nigeria; Rev. Eugene M. Rooney, S.J. Ord: '57, Chile; Rev. Dominic J. Totaro, S.J. Ord: '67, Nigeria; Rev. Eugene M. Geinzer, S.J. Ord: '74, China; Rev. Michael J. Lynch, S.J. Ord: '93, China.

Priests: 10

Society of Jesus: Missouri Province, 4511 W. Pine Blvd., St. Louis, MO 63108. Phone: 314-361-7765; Fax: 314-758-7164. Rev. Douglas W. Marcouiller, S.J. Ord: '86, Prov.

Legal Title: *The Jesuits of the Missouri Province*

U.S. Religious serving in Foreign Missions: Rev. Joseph Damhorst, S.J. Ord: '68, Belize; Rev. Yoshio Ignatius Futo, S.J. Ord: '81, China; Rev. Mauricio Gaborit, S.J. Ord: '78, El Salvador; Rev. Jeffrey D. Harrison, S.J. Ord: '87, Belize; Rev. Steven B. Hawkes-Teeples, S.J. Ord: '93, Italy, Prof. Pontifical Oriental Institute; Rev. John L. Maher, S.J. Ord: '74, Belize; Rev. Maurice M. Murray, S.J. Ord: '66, Belize; Rev. Lammert B. Otten, S.J. Ord: '65, Zambia; Rev. William T. Oulvey, S.J. Ord: '85, Italy; Rev. Raymond A. Pease, S.J. Ord: '68, Honduras; Rev. Richard D. Perl, S.J. Ord: '78, Belize; Rev. Jesus R. Riveroll, S.J. Ord: '88, Belize; Rev. William J. Snyders, S.J. Ord: '66, Belize; Rev. Ricardo Steinmetz, S.J. Ord: '55, Mexico; Rev. John J. Stochl, S.J. Ord: '54, Belize; Rev. James H. Swetnam, S.J. Ord: '58, Italy; Rev. J. Timothy Thompson, S.J. Ord: '70, Belize; Rev. Jose Antonio Vega, S.J. Ord: '00, Belize; Rev. Robert D. Voss, S.J. Ord: '72, Honduras; Rev. Jarrell D. Wade, S.J. Ord: '65, Honduras; Rev. John B. Warner, S.J. Ord: '74, Honduras; Rev. Robert A. White, S.J. Ord: '62, Tanzania; Rev. John H. Willmering, S.J. Ord: '68, Honduras; Bro. Karl D. Swift, S.J., Belize; Bro. Harold A. Teel, S.J., Belize; Bro. N. Aloysius Vogt, S.J., Belize; Bro. E. Glenn Kerfoot, S.J., Belize; Rev. Brian J. Christopher, S.J., Belize.

Priests: 24; Brothers: 4

Society of Jesus: New England Province, 85 School St., Watertown, MA 02472-4251. Phone: 617-607-2800; Fax: 617-607-2888. Very Rev. Myles N. Sheehan, S.J. Ord: '94, Prov.; Rev. Michael J. Linden, S.J. Ord: '80, Prov. Asst. International Ministries.

Legal Title: *The Society of Jesus of New England*

U.S. Religious serving in Foreign Missions: Rev.

John A. Carty, S.J. Ord: '59, Egypt; Rev. John J. Donohue, S.J. Ord: '59, Lebanon; Rev. Thomas J. Frink, S.J. Ord: '05, Jamaica; Rev. Louis L. Grenier, S.J. Ord: '49, Jamaica; Rev. Richard P. Guerrera, S.J. Ord: '73, Mozambique; Rev. Alfred J. Hicks, S.J. Ord: '66, Jordan; Rev. Joseph A. MacWade, S.J. Ord: '61, Jamaica; Rev. Martin F. McDermott, S.J. Ord: '64, Lebanon; Rev. Gerald L. McLaughlin, S.J. Ord: '59, Jamaica; Rev. Perard C. Monestime, S.J. Ord: '85, Haiti; Rev. Oliver E. Nickerson, S.J. Ord: '54, Jamaica; Rev. Kevin G. O'Connell, S.J. Ord: '69, Jordan; Rev. Francis J. Ryan, S.J. Ord: '56, Jamaica; Rev. Paul A. Schweitzer, S.J. Ord: '70, Brazil; Rev. Gregory C. Sharkey, S.J. Ord: '88, Nepal; Rev. David A. Skelskey, S.J. Ord: '80, Philippines.

Priests: 16

Society of Jesus: New York Province, 39 E. 83rd St., New York, NY 10028. Phone: 212-774-5500. Very Rev. David S. Ciancimino, S.J. Ord: '88, Prov.; Rev. Thomas R. Slon, S.J. Ord: '90, Exec. Asst. to the Prov./Socius; Rev. Ramon A. Salomone, S.J. Ord: '65, Asst. Prov. International Apostolates.

U.S. Religious serving in Foreign Missions: Rev. John S. Hagileiram, S.J. Ord: '85, Supr., Micronesia; Rev. William M. Abbott, S.J. Ord: '72, Philippines; Rev. Gerald W. Aman, S.J. Ord: '73, Nigeria; Rev. J. Dean Brackley, S.J. Ord: '76, El Salvador; Rev. John J. Carroll, S.J. Ord: '55, Philippines; Rev. Matthew J. Cassidy, S.J. Ord: '99, Ghana; Rev. Joseph A. Cavanagh, S.J. Ord: '62, Micronesia; Rev. James P. Croghan, S.J. Ord: '85, Micronesia; Rev. John F. Curran, S.J. Ord: '59, Micronesia; Rev. Joseph A. Galdon, S.J. Ord: '59, Philippines; Rev. Pasquale T. Giordano, S.J. Ord: '72, Philippines; Rev. Francis N. Glover, S.J. Ord: '58, Philippines; Very Rev. James C. Gould, S.J. Ord: '74, Micronesia; Rev. George R. Graziano, S.J. Ord: '59, Japan; Rev. John J. Halligan, S.J. Ord: '61, Ecuador; Rev. Donald J. Hinfey, S.J. Ord: '63, North-West Africa; Rev. Victor J. Helly, S.J. Ord: '54, Philippines; Rev. Francis X. Hezel, S.J. Ord: '69, Micronesia; Rev. Kenneth J. Hezel, S.J. Ord: '66; Rev. Robert C. Hogan, S.J. Ord: '64, Philippines; Rev. Raymond T. Holscher, S.J. Ord: '72, Philippines; Rev. Paul L. Horgan, S.J. Ord: '68, Micronesia; Rev. William P. Klintworth, S.J. Ord: '61, Philippines; Rev. William H. Kreutz, S.J. Ord: '69, Philippines; Rev. Dennis M. Leder, S.J. Ord: '76, Guatemala; Rev. William J. Malley, S.J. Ord: '64, Philippines; Rev. R. Richard McAuliff, S.J. Ord: '92, Micronesia; Rev. William J. McGarry, S.J. Ord: '58, Philippines; Rev. Thomas B. McGrath, S.J. Ord: '64, Guam; Rev. James A. McKeough, S.J. Ord: '54, Philippines; Rev. Daniel J. McNamara, S.J. Ord: '80, Philippines; Rev. James T. Meehan, S.J. Ord: '63, Philippines; Rev. Michael D. Moga, S.J. Ord: '64, Philippines; Rev. Gregory F. Muckenhaupt, S.J. Ord: '88, Micronesia; Rev. James A. O'Donnell, S.J. Ord: '61, Philippines; Rev. Thomas H. O'Gorman, S.J. Ord: '63, Philippines; Rev. Calvin H. Poulin, S.J. Ord: '62, Philippines; Rev. James B. Reuter, S.J. Ord: '46, Philippines; Rev. Robert A. Rice, S.J. Ord: '53, Philippines; Rev. Joseph L. Roche, S.J. Ord: '58, Philippines; Rev. Herbert Schneider, S.J. Ord: '70, Philippines; Rev. John N. Schumacher, S.J. Ord: '57, Philippines; Rev. John J. Shea, S.J. Ord: '75, Thailand; Rev. Joseph J. Smith, S.J. Ord: '57, Philippines; Rev. Thomas B. Steinbugler, S.J. Ord: '61, Philippines; Rev. Robert J. Suchan, S.J. Ord: '56, Philippines; Rev. Juan C. Villegas, S.J. Ord: '75, Colombia; Bro. David Antonelli, Micronesia.

Society of Jesus: Oregon Province, 3215 S.E. 45th Ave., P.O. Box 86010, Portland, OR 97286-0010. Phone: 503-226-6977. Rev. Patrick J. Lee, S.J. Ord: '78, Prov.; Rev. John C. Bentz, S.J. Ord: '04, Prov. Rep. for Intl. Ministries.

Legal Title: *American Jesuits in Africa*

U.S Religious serving in Foreign Missions: Rev. Joseph B. Danel, S.J. Ord: '52, Zambia; Rev. Peter J. Henriot, S.J. Ord: '70, Zambia; Rev. Ronald E. Hidaka, S.J. Ord: '74, Zambia; Rev. James P. McGloin, S.J. Ord: '74, Zambia; Rev. Bartholomew J. Murphy, S.J. Ord: '72, Tanzania; Rev. Gary N. Smith, S.J. Ord: '71, South Africa; Rev. Roy W. Thaden, S.J. Ord: '73, Zambia; Rev. Peter R. Titland, S.J. Ord: '70, Zambia.

Priests: 8

Society of Jesus: Wisconsin Province, 3400 W. Wisconsin Ave., P.O. Box 080288, Milwaukee, WI 53208-0288. Phone: 414-937-6949; Fax: 414-937-6950. Very Rev. G. Thomas Krettek, S.J. Ord: '82, Prov.; Rev. Luis Rodriguez, S.J. Ord: '65, Socius.

U.S. Religious serving in Foreign Missions: Rev. Francis X. Buchmeier, S.J. Ord: '73, Korea; Rev. John V. Daly, S.J. Ord: '66, Korea; Rev. Emil J. Denemark, S.J. Ord: '81, East Timor; Rev. Robert W. Dundon, S.J. Ord: '69, Nigeria; Rev. Jonathan Haschka, S.J. Ord: '75, Tanzania; Rev. John D. Mace, S.J. Ord: '68, East Timor; Rev. H. Francis Mathy, S.J. Ord: '58, Japan; Rev. Robert K. McIntosh, S.J. Ord: '72, Korea; Rev. John R. Schak, S.J. Ord: '61, Argentina; Rev. Nicholas E. Schiel, S.J. Ord: '55, Honduras; Rev. Christopher A. Spalatin, S.J. Ord: '71, Korea; Rev. James J. Strzok, S.J. Ord: '70, Kenya; Rev. Anthony J. Wach, S.J. Ord: '72, Uganda.

Priests: 15

CONGREGATION OF THE HOLY SPIRIT (C.S.Sp.)

Holy Spirit Foreign Missions

U.S.A. - East Province, Spiritans, 6230 Brush Run Rd., Bethel Park, PA 15102. Fax: 412-831-0970. Very Rev. Jeffrey T. Duaime, C.S.Sp. Ord: '86, Prov.

U.S. Religious serving Abroad: Rev. Remo J. Bonifazi, C.S.Sp. Ord: '45, Republic of South Africa; Rev. Paul M. Flamm, C.S.Sp. Ord: '99, Kasulu-Kigoma; Rev. Adrien T. Hebert, C.S.Sp. Ord: '58, Pomeroy, RSA; Rev. Joseph M. Herzstein, C.S.Sp. Ord: '63, Arusha; Rev. Edward T. Marchessault, C.S.Sp. Ord: '64, Arusha, Tanzania; Rev. James P. McCloskey, C.S.Sp. Ord: '80, Rome, Italy; Rev. Donald J. McEachin, C.S.Sp. Ord: '81, The Dominican Republic; Rev. Josaphat Msongore, C.S.Sp. Ord: '63, Arusha, Tanzania; Rev. Patrick A. Patten, C.S.Sp. Ord: '78, Arusha, Tanzania; Rev. Vincent G. Stegman, C.S.Sp. Ord: '62, Ethiopia; Bro. Francis Sullivan, C.S.Sp., Arusha, Tanzania; Rev. William H. Christy, C.S.Sp. Ord: '92, Beagle Bay, Australia.

JESUIT VOLUNTEERS INTERNATIONAL (S.J.)

U.S. Headquarters: Jesuit Volunteers International:, 1016 16th St. N.W., Ste. 400, Washington, DC 20036. Phone: 202-462-5200; Fax: 202-328-9212. Meghan Romey, Exec. Dir.

Selected college graduates improve education and promote human welfare, faith communities and social justice through a two-year commitment to impoverished local communities in seven developing nations.

MARYKNOLL (M.M.)

A community of American secular priests and brothers. Established in 1911 by action of the United States Hierarchy. Authorized by Pope Pius X, with later approvals by Pope Benedict XV and Pope Pius XI.

U.S Foundation Maryknoll Society Center & Administrative Offices Catholic Foreign Mission Society of America:, P.O. Box 303, Maryknoll, NY 10545-0303. Phone: 914-941-7590; Fax: 914-944-3600. Rev. Edward M. Dougherty, M.M. Ord: '79, Supr. Gen. & Pres.; Rev. Jose A. Aramburu, M.M. Ord: '84, Vicar Gen. & Vice Pres.; Rev. Edward J. McGovern, M.M. Ord: '04, Asst. Gen.; Rev. Paul R. Masson, M.M. Ord: '72, Asst. Gen.

The Society is incorporated in New York, under the Legal Title: Catholic Foreign Mission Society of America, Incorporated. It is also incorporated in California, Hawaii, Illinois, Massachusetts, Minnesota, and Missouri.

For detailed information regarding statistics, activities in the Archdioceses and Dioceses in the United States, Properties owned or sponsored and Houses in the United States, and the placement of the Maryknollers in the various Archdioceses and Dioceses, please refer to the sections for Religious Institutes of Men and the designated Archdioceses and Dioceses.

Maryknoll Foreign Missions

Maryknollers serving Overseas: Province Office:

Religious serving in Bangladesh: Rev. Robert T. McCahill, M.M. Ord: '64; Rev. William J. McIntire, M.M. Ord: '67; Rev. Douglas F. Venne, M.M. Ord: '59.

Priests 3.

Religious serving in Bolivia: Rev. Denis P. Browne, M.M. Ord: '47; Rev. Raymond J. Finch, M.M. Ord: '76; Rev. Timothy G. Graff Ord: '85; Rev. John F. Gorski, M.M. Ord: '63; Rev. Michael A. Gould, M.M. Ord: '54; Rev. Thomas P. Henehan, M.M. Ord: '65; Rev. Francis B. Higdon, M.M. Ord: '67; Rev. Sigmund S. Jamroz, M.M. Ord: '66; Rev. Stephen P. Judd, M.M. Ord: '78; Rev. Francis T. McGourn, M.M. Ord: '64; Rev. Kenneth J. Moody, M.M. Ord: '70; Rev. John J. Ogurchock, M.M. Ord: '54; Rev. Arthur J. Prall, M.M. Ord: '52; Rev. Paul M. Sykora, M.M. Ord: '76; Rev. Eugene W. Toland, M.M. Ord: '64.

Priests 13; Priest Associates 1; Brothers 4.

Religious serving in Brazil: Rev. Daniel F. McLaughlin, M.M. Ord: '61.

Priests 1.

Religious serving in Cambodia: Rev. Charles R. Dittmeier Ord: '70; Rev. John C. Barth, M.M. Ord: '91; Rev. Kevin M. Conroy Ord: '68; Rev. Robert F. Wynne, M.M. Ord: '74.

Priests 2; Priest Associates 2; Seminarians 1.

Religious serving in Chile: Rev. Dale F. Barron, M.M. Ord: '65; Rev. J. Lawrence Schanberger, M.M. Ord: '49.

Priests 2; Brothers 1.

Religious serving in El Salvador: Rev. Gerald J. Persha, M.M. Ord: '70; Rev. John H. Spain, M.M. Ord: '70.

Priests 2.

Religious serving in Ethiopia: Rev. Richard M. Baker, M.M. Ord: '71.

Priests 1.

Religious serving in Guatemala: Rev. Thomas F. Goekler, M.M. Ord: '67; Rev. William F. Mullan, M.M. Ord: '62; Rev. Robert F. Crohan, M.M. Ord: '62; Rev. Joseph W. Halpin, M.M. Ord: '52; Rev. Kevin A. Lynch, M.M. Ord: '61; Rev. John J. McGovern, M.M. Ord: '54; Rev. James M. Lynch, M.M. Ord: '74; Rev. John C. Moynihan, M.M. Ord: '67; Rev. Edward O. Custer, M.M. Ord: '72.

Priests 9; Brothers 1.

Religious serving in Honduras: Rev. Robert F. Coyne, M.M. Ord: '83; Rev. Richard C. Frank, M.M. Ord: '53.

Priests 2.

Religious serving in Hong Kong: Rev. John F. Ahearn, M.M. Ord: '73; Rev. Robert F. Astorino, M.M. Ord: '70; Rev. Peter J. Barry, M.M. Ord: '65; Rev. Anthony V. Brennan, M.M. Ord: '61; Rev. John A. Cioppa, M.M. Ord: '59; Rev. Vincent F. Corbelli, M.M. Ord: '60; Rev. John P. Cuff, M.M. Ord: '69; Rev. Thomas E. Danaher, M.M. Ord: '62; Rev. Thomas R. Egan, M.M. Ord: '74; Rev. Richard R. Fries, M.M. Ord: '76; Rev. William J. Galvin, M.M. Ord: '56; Rev. John E. Geitner, M.M. Ord: '53; Rev. Adam B. Gudalefsky, M.M. Ord: '59; Rev. Timothy Kilkelly, M.M. Ord: '90; Rev. Denis J. Hanly, M.M. Ord: '59; Rev. Scott T. Harris, M.M. Ord: '78; Rev. John J. McAuley, M.M. Ord: '81; Rev. Thomas A. Peyton, M.M. Ord: '58; Rev. Ronald R. Saucci, M.M. Ord: '65; Rev. Michael J. Sloboda, M.M. Ord: '85; Rev. Elmer P. Wurth, M.M. Ord: '56.

Priests 21; Brothers 3.

Religious serving in Indonesia: Rev. Vincent P. Cole, M.M. Ord: '71.

Priests 1.

Religious serving in Italy: Rev. Clyde Phillips, M.M. Ord: '78, Procurator Gen.

Priests 1.

Religious serving in Jamaica: Rev. Leo B. Shea, M.M. Ord: '66.

Priests 1.

Religious serving in Japan: Rev. John T. Brinkman, M.M. Ord: '71; Rev. Richard S. Czajkowski, M.M. Ord: '61; Rev. LoXuan Dam, M.M. Ord: '00; Rev. Emile E. Dumas, M.M. Ord: '67; Rev. Regis B. Ging, M.M. Ord: '66; Rev. William J. Grimm, M.M. Ord: '77; Rev. Joseph L. Hamel, M.M. Ord: '85; Rev. Joseph H. Hermes, M.M. Ord: '62; Rev. James R. Jackson, M.M. Ord: '58; Rev. James J. Mylet, M.M. Ord: '75; Rev. Robert V. Nehrig, M.M. Ord: '54; Rev. Bryce T. Nishimura, M.M. Ord: '56; Rev. Francis A. Riha, M.M. Ord: '68; Rev. Roberto Rodriguez, M.M. Ord: '95; Rev. Kenneth C. Sleyman, M.M. Ord: '90.

Priests 16.

Religious serving in Kenya: Rev. John E. Conway, M.M. Ord: '73; Rev. Edward V. Davis, M.M. Ord: '61; Rev. William Fryda, M.M. Ord: '88; Rev. Joseph G. Healey, M.M. Ord: '66; Rev. Michael C. Kirwen, M.M. Ord: '63; Rev. John J. Lange, M.M. Ord: '58; Rev. Douglas E. May, M.M. Ord: '86; Rev. Lance P. Nadeau, M.M. Ord: '90; Rev. Richard J. Quinn, M.M. Ord: '54; Rev. Richard P. Smith, M.M. Ord: '76; Rev. Kenneth F. Thesing, M.M. Ord: '69; Rev. Thomas A. Tiscornia, M.M. Ord: '73.

Priests 12; Brothers 2.

Religious serving in Korea: Rev. Edward J. Whalen, M.M. Ord: '61; Rev. Richard Agustin, M.M. Ord: '85; Rev. Francis H. Beninati, M.M. Ord: '55; Rev. Carl A. Costa, M.M. Ord: '71; Rev. Gerald J. Farrell, M.M. Ord: '57; Rev. Russell J. Feldmeier, M.M. Ord: '80; Rev. Alfred J. Fleming, M.M. Ord: '60; Rev. Gerard E. Hammond, M.M. Ord: '60; Rev. Robert M. Lilly, M.M. Ord: '60; Rev. Philip W. Mares, M.M. Ord: '86; Rev. James T. Najmowski, M.M. Ord: '76; Rev. Gerald P. O'Connor, M.M. Ord: '69; Rev. Robert R. Pellini, M.M. Ord: '59; Rev. David L. Pfeiffer, M.M. Ord: '66; Rev. Richard S. Rolewicz, M.M. Ord: '65; Rev. Joseph

A. Slaby, M.M. Ord: '66; Rev. James P. Sinnott, M.M. Ord: '60.

Priests 17.

Religious serving in Mexico: Rev. Richard L. Clifford, M.M. Ord: '53; Rev. John P. Martin, M.M. Ord: '66; Rev. Eugene A. Theisen, M.M. Ord: '53; Rev. Robert V. Tobin, M.M. Ord: '57.

Priests 4.

Religious serving in Namibia: Rev. Richard P. Albertine, M.M. Ord: '66; Rev. Richard W. Bauer, M.M. Ord: '85; Rev. Edward D. Shellito, M.M. Ord: '90; Rev. Wayne T. Weinlader, M.M. Ord: '68.

Priests 4; Brothers 2.

Religious serving in Nepal: Rev. John J. Corcoran, M.M. Ord: '63; Rev. Joseph L. Thaler, M.M. Ord: '77.

Priests 2.

Religious serving in the Philippine Islands: Rev. James H. Kroeger, M.M. Ord: '75; Rev. Jeremiah R. Burr, M.M. Ord: '67; Rev. Francis J. Felter, M.M. Ord: '69; Rev. James T. Ferry, M.M. Ord: '56; Rev. Ralph S. Kroes, M.M. Ord: '58; Rev. William J. LaRousse, M.M. Ord: '80; Rev. James D. McAuley, M.M. Ord: '80; Rev. John D. Walsh, M.M. Ord: '56.

Priests 8.

Religious serving in Peoples Republic of China: Rev. Brian Barrons, M.M. Ord: '84; Rev. Lawrence D. Radice, M.M. Ord: '85; Rev. John E. Vesey Ord: '68.

Priests 2; Associates 1.

Religious serving in Peru: Rev. Thomas J. Burns, M.M. Ord: '69; Rev. Michael J. Briggs, M.M. Ord: '76; Rev. Edmund L. Cookson, M.M. Ord: '65; Rev. Joseph Fedora, M.M. Ord: '84; Rev. James J. Madden, M.M. Ord: '60; Rev. Philip N. Erbland, M.M. Ord: '66; Rev. Robert E. Hoffman, M.M. Ord: '60; Rev. Kyungsu Son, M.M. Ord: '79.

Priests 8.

Religious serving in Samoa: Most Rev. J. Quinn Weitzel, M.M. Ord: '55.

Bishops 1.

Religious serving in Taiwan: Rev. Kurt J. Anderson, M.M. Ord: '72; Rev. Paul J. Brien, M.M. Ord: '60; Rev. Peter C. Brien, M.M. Ord: '60; Rev. Robert F. Crawford, M.M. Ord: '61; Rev. Alan T. Doyle, M.M. Ord: '64; Rev. Paul J. Duffy, M.M. Ord: '79; Rev. Clarence A. Engler, M.M. Ord: '59; Rev. Delos A. Humphrey, M.M. Ord: '54; Rev. Raymond H. Kelley, M.M. Ord: '58; Rev. John F. Kennedy, M.M. Ord: '55; Rev. Alfonso Kim, M.M. Ord: '97; Rev. J. Donald McGinnis, M.M. Ord: '53; Rev. Leonard J. Marron, M.M. Ord: '57; Rev. Eugene M. Murray, M.M. Ord: '58; Rev. Cuong H. Nguyen, M.M. Ord: '98; Rev. Nhuan D. Nguyen, M.M. Ord: '93; Rev. Brendan M. O'Connell, M.M. Ord: '63; Rev. Norbert A. Pacheco, M.M. Ord: '79; Rev. Anthony V. Polyak, M.M. Ord: '62; Rev. Louis B. Rost, M.M. Ord: '55; Rev. Francis F. Schexnayder, M.M. Ord: '64; Rev. R. Joyalito F. Tajonera, M.M. Ord: '02; Rev. Peter A. Wu, M.M. Ord: '61.

Priests 23; Brothers 1.

Religious serving in Tanzania: Rev. Michael Bassano, M.M. Ord: '75; Rev. James A. Conard, M.M. Ord: '56; Rev. James E. Eble, M.M. Ord: '88; Rev. Edward A. Hayes, M.M. Ord: '59; Rev. Ramon J. McCabe, M.M. Ord: '56; Rev. Daniel F. Ohmann, M.M. Ord: '55; Rev. David A. Smith, M.M. Ord: '85; Rev. Michael J. Snyder, M.M. Ord: '79; Rev. Kenneth J. Sullivan, M.M. Ord: '57; Rev. Donald F. Sybertz, M.M. Ord: '55; Rev. John W. Waldrep, M.M. Ord: '90.

Priests 12; Brothers 1.

Religious serving in Thailand: Rev. Thomas J. Dunleavy, M.M. Ord: '75; Rev. James W. Kofski, M.M. Ord: '91.

Priests 2; Brothers 1.

Religious serving in Vietnam: Rev. Thomas J. O'Brien, M.M. Ord: '74.

MISSIONARIES OF AFRICA (M.AFR.)

Missionaries of Africa Foreign Missions

U.S. Headquarters: Province of North America: 1624 21st St., N.W., Washington, DC 20009-1003. Phone: 202-232-5154; Fax: 202-332-8640. Rev. John Lynch, M.Afr. Ord: '62, Office of Devel. and Planned Giving; Rev. George Markwell, M.Afr. Ord: '65, Hospital Chap.; Rev. Sjef Donders, M.Afr. Ord: '57, Prof. Emeritus W.T.U.; Rev. Jimmy McTiernan, M.Afr. Ord: '71, Guestmaster; Rev. Thomas Reilly, M.Afr. Ord: '78; Rev. Jean-Claude Robitaille, M.Afr. Ord: '73, Delegate Supr.; Rev. Richard Roy, M.Afr. Ord: '71; Rev. Diego Ramon Sario Cucarella, M.Afr. Ord: '01, Studies at G.U.; Rev. Brian Denis Starkey, M.Afr. Ord: '77, Treas.; Bro. James Heintz, M.Afr., Bursar.

U.S. Religious serving in Africa: Rev. William Curran, M.Afr. Ord: '66, Ghana-West Africa; Rev. Roger A. LaBonte, M.Afr. Ord: '62, Uganda-East Africa; Rev. William Moroney, M.Afr. Ord: '61, Kenya-East Africa.

U.S. Religious serving in Great Britain: Rev. David Goergen, M.Afr. Ord: '69.

U.S. Religious serving in Spain: Rev. Rene Dionne, M.Afr. Ord: '61, Spain.

MISSIONARIES OF THE SACRED HEART (M.S.C.)

Missionaries of the Sacred Heart Foreign Missions

Missionaries of the Sacred Heart, 305 S. Lake St., P.O. Box 270, Aurora, IL 60507. Phone: 630-892-2371; Phone: 630-892-8400; Fax: 630-892-1678; Web: www.misacor-usa.org. Very Rev. Raymond Diesbourg, M.S.C. Ord: '74, Prov. Supr.; Bro. James Miller, M.S.C., Treas.

Publication(s): A New Heart for a New World

Religious serving in Papua New Guinea: Rev. Leon Weisenberger, M.S.C. Ord: '59, Local Supr.

Religious serving in Colombia, South America: Very Rev. Luis Alfonso Segura, M.S.C. Ord: '99, Section Supr.; Very Rev. German Barona Monsalve, M.S.C. Ord: '86; Rev. Tito Abdenago Medina Mora, M.S.C. Ord: '92; Rev. Hector Eduardo Mejia Arciniegas, M.S.C. Ord: '06; Rev. Dario Moreno Enciso, M.S.C. Ord: '04, Prenovitiate Dir.; Deacon Eduard Riascos, M.S.C.; Bro. Favio Castro Andino, M.S.C.; Bro. Juan Pablo Romero Contreras; Bro. Jesús Adrian Benevides Hernandez; Bro. William Tamayo; Bro. Faiber Antonio Vargas; Bro. Guillermo Cuarán Yandún; Bro. Ernesto Odilio Caicedo, M.S.C.; Bro. William Andres Tovar, M.S.C.; Bro. Jesus Felipe Trejo, M.S.C.

Religious serving in Italy: Very Rev. Mark McDonald, M.S.C. Ord: '68, Supr. Gen.

OBLATES OF ST. FRANCIS DE SALES MISSIONS (O.S.F.S.)

Oblates of St. Francis de Sales Foreign Missions

U.S. Mission Headquarters Office of the Mission Procurato Oblates of St. Francis de Sales:, 1600 Brinckle Ave., Wilmington, DE 19806-1123. Rev. John J. Hurley, O.S.F.S. Ord: '68, Mission Procurator.

U.S. Religious serving in Africa, Asia, Europe & South America: Rev. Leon V. Bonikowski, O.S.F.S. Ord: '65; Rev. Walter DeSa, O.S.F.S. Ord: '65; Rev. William R. Gore, O.S.F.S. Ord: '69; Rev. Thomas Hagan, O.S.F.S. Ord: '69; Rev. Robert J. Hindley, O.S.F.S. Ord: '58; Rev. John A. Kowalewski, O.S.F.S. Ord: '77; Rev. Michael Moore, O.S.F.S. Ord: '68; Rev. Harry J. Schlight, O.S.F.S. Ord: '44; Rev. Alfred J. Smuda, O.S.F.S. Ord: '66; Bro. James A. Petrait, O.S.F.S.; Rev. Thomas Moore, O.S.F.S. Ord: '66.

AMERICAN PASSIONIST MISSIONS (C.P.)

Passionist Foreign Missions

Home and Foreign Missions of the American Provinces of the Congregation of the Passion.

General Motherhouse: St. Giovanni e Paolo 13, Rome, Italy, 00184, Most Rev. Ottaviano D'Egidio, C.P., Supr. Gen.

Provincial Headquarters U.S.A.

St. Paul of the Cross Province: Province Pastoral Center, 80 David St., South River, NJ 08882. Phone: 732-257-7177. Very Rev. Joseph R. Jones, C.P. Ord: '65, Prov. Supr.; Very Rev. James A. Price, C.P. Ord: '94, Vice Prov. & Consultor; Very Rev. James O'Shea, C.P. Ord: '89, Consultor & Mission Procurator; Rev. John Douglas Ord: '81, Prov. Sec.

U.S. Religious serving Abroad: Rev. Richard Award, C.P. Ord: '81, West Indies; Rev. Thomas Brislin, C.P. Ord: '68, Nassau, The Bahamas; Rev. Richard Frechette, C.P. Ord: '79, Haiti; Rev. Aelred Lacomara, C.P. Ord: '57, Africa; Rev. Gaston Nsongolo, C.P., West Indies; Rev. Lawrence Rywalt, C.P. Ord: '92, Rome; Rev. Francis Finnigan, C.P., France; Rev. Hilarion Walters, C.P. Ord: '47, Philippines; Rev. Paul Ruttle, C.P., Jamaica, West Indies; Bro. Robert McKenna, C.P., Philippines; Bro. Michael Stomber, C.P., West Indies.

Mission Procurators

Eastern: Very Rev. James Price, C.P. Ord: '94; 80 David St., South River, NJ 08882. Very Rev. James O'Shea, C.P. Ord: '89; Bro. Leo DiFiore, C.P., Passionist.

Overseas Missions: 5 Grandview Ave., Pittsburgh, PA 15211.

Canada: 2102 Kipling Ave., Rexdale, Canada, M9W 4K5,

Philippines: Makati, Metro Manilla, Philippines, 1252.

Holy Cross Province (Western): 5700 N. Harlem Ave., Chicago, IL 60631. Phone: 773-631-6336; Fax: 773-631-8059. Very Rev. Donald Webber, C.P. Ord: '73, Prov.; Rev. James Strommer, C.P. Ord: '70, Consultor, Sec., & Asst. Prov.; Rev. Arthur Carrillo, C.P. Ord: '70.

Mission Appeals

Japan: Rev. Leonard Kosatka, C.P. Ord: '59.

U.S. Religious serving Abroad: Rev. Robert Coward, C.P. Ord: '68, Rome; Rev. Leonard Kosatka, C.P. Ord: '59, Japan; Rev. Denis McGowan, C.P. Ord: '55, Japan; Rev. Joseph Van Leeuwen, C.P. Ord: '64, India; Rev. John B. Ormechea, C.P. Ord: '65, Rome.

Priests: 9; Brothers: 2

AMERICAN REDEMPTORIST FATHERS (C.SS.R.)

Mission of the Provinces and Vice-Provinces in the United States and other countries and lands

Redemptorist Foreign Missions

Baltimore Province: Redemptorist Fathers of New York:, 7509 Shore Rd., Brooklyn, NY 11209. Phone: 718-833-1900; Fax: 718-630-5666. Very Rev. Patrick F. Woods, C.Ss.R. Ord: '75, Prov. Supr.

U.S. Religious serving in Dominica, WI: Rev. Michael Houston, C.Ss.R. Ord: '98.

U.S. Religious serving in Paraguay: Rev. Antonio Cannoles, C.Ss.R. Ord: '69.

U.S. Religious serving in Trinidad & Tobago: Archbishop Edward Joseph Gilbert, C.Ss.R. Ord: '64; Rev. Rodney J. Olive, C.Ss.R. Ord: '86.

Baltimore Province:

U.S. Religious serving in Brazil: Rev. Richard Blissert, C.Ss.R. Ord: '56; Rev. Karl Esker, C.Ss.R. Ord: '76; Rev. Giles Gardner, C.Ss.R. Ord: '39; Rev. Lawrence Kearns, C.Ss.R. Ord: '65; Rev. Clement Krug, C.Ss.R. Ord: '65; Rev. Patrick McGillicuddy, C.Ss.R. Ord: '79; Rev. Edward Moriarty, C.Ss.R. Ord: '42; Rev. Donald Roth, C.Ss.R. Ord: '75; Rev. John Roche, C.Ss.R. Ord: '63; Rev. William Tracey, C.Ss.R. Ord: '55; Rev. Stephen Vanyo, C.Ss.R. Ord: '62.

U.S. Religious serving in Lebanon: Rev. Charles Coury, C.Ss.R. Ord: '76.

U.S. Religious serving in St. Lucia, V.I.: Rev. Joseph F. Krastel, C.Ss.R. Ord: '64.

U.S. Religious serving in St. Croix, V.I.: Rev. Kenneth F. Gaddy, C.Ss.R. Ord: '88; Rev. E. Patrick Lynch, C.Ss.R Ord: '69; Rev. Kevin M. MacDonald, C.Ss.R. Ord: '91.

Denver Province: 1230 Parker Rd., Denver, CO 80231. Phone: 303-370-0035; Fax: 303-370-0036. Very Rev. Thomas Picton, C.Ss.R. Ord: '71, Provincial Supr.

U.S. Religious serving in Brazil: Most Rev. Gutemberg Regis, C.Ss.R., Bishop of Coari; Most Rev. Alfred Novak, C.Ss.R. Ord: '49, Bishop of Paranagua, Brazil; Rev. William Fitzgerald, C.Ss.R. Ord: '43; Rev. John Gouger, C.Ss.R. Ord: '65; Rev. Donnell Kirchner, C.Ss.R. Ord: '66; Rev. John McCarthy, C.Ss.R. Ord: '62; Rev. Thomas McIntosh, C.Ss.R. Ord: '66; Rev. William H. (Carlos) Steiner, C.Ss.R. Ord: '54; Bro. Leo Patin, C.Ss.R.

U.S. Religious serving in Nigeria: Rev. Richard Thiele, C.Ss.R. Ord: '54.

U.S. Religious serving in Thailand: Most Rev. George Yod Phimphisan, C.Ss.R. Ord: '58, Bishop of Udon Thani; Rev. Charles Cotant, C.Ss.R. Ord: '41; Rev. Francis Gautreaux, C.Ss.R. Ord: '50; Rev. Joseph Maier, C.Ss.R. Ord: '65; Rev. Robert Martin, C.Ss.R. Ord: '50; Rev. Lawrence Patin, C.Ss.R. Ord: '63; Rev. Michael Shea, C.Ss.R. Ord: '64; Rev. Leo Travis, C.Ss.R. Ord: '54; Rev. William Wright, C.Ss.R. Ord: '60.

ST. COLUMBAN'S FOREIGN MISSION SOCIETY (S.S.C.)

(The Columban Fathers)

Founded in 1918 with the approval of Pope Benedict XV. Placed under the patronage of St. Columban and made a Pontifical Society by Pope Pius XI.

PO Box 10, St Columbans, NE 68056. *Generalate*

Missionary Society of St. Columban:, 504 Tower 1, Silvercord, 30 Canton Rd. TST, Kowloon, Hong Kong, Very Rev. Tommy Murphy, S.S.C., Supr. Gen.

U.S. Foundation & Administration: Columban Fathers, St Columbans, NE 68056. Phone: 402-291-1920.

The Society is incorporated in California, Florida, Illinois, Massachusetts, Nebraska, New York, Rhode Island, and Texas and registered in Pennsylvania.

Publication: Columban Mission
Very Rev. John Burger, S.S.C. Ord: '73, Dir.; Rev. Thomas P. Reynolds, S.S.C. Ord: '61, Vice Dir.

Legal Title: *Missionary Society of St. Columban a/k/a St. Columban's Foreign Mission Society*

Publication(s): Columban Mission

St. Columban's Foreign Mission

House of Post-Graduate Studies: PO Box 10, St Columbans, NE 68056. **Collegio San Colombano,** Corso Trieste, 57, Rome, Italy, 00198, Rev. Padhraic O'Loughlin, S.S.C. Ord: '57, Procurator Gen.

U.S. Religious serving Overseas: Very Rev. Brendan O'Sullivan, S.S.C. Ord: '70, Ireland; Rev. Vincent J. Busch, S.S.C. Ord: '74, Philippines; Rev. Francis P. Carroll, S.S.C. Ord: '62, Japan; Rev. David J. Clay, S.S.C., Philippines; Rev. John Comisky, C.S.C. Ord: '68, Philippines; Rev. Neil Boyle, S.S.C. Ord: '43, Ireland; Rev. Otto Imholte, S.S.C. Ord: '63, Ireland; Rev. Michael Hoban, S.S.C. Ord: '70, Chile; Rev. David Padrnos, S.S.C. Ord: '71, Japan; Rev. Ronald Kelso, S.S.C. Ord: '73; Rev. Donald Kill, S.S.C. Ord: '72, Philippines; Rev. Joseph McSweeny, S.S.C. Ord: '90, Taiwan; Rev. John P. Moran, S.S.C. Ord: '50, Philippines; Rev. William Morton, S.S.C. Ord: '60, Mexico; Rev. Robert Mosher, S.S.C. Ord: '82, Chile; Rev. Richard L. Pankratz, S.S.C. Ord: '74; Rev. Desmond Quinn, S.S.C. Ord: '54, Ireland; Rev. Edward Quinn, S.S.C. Ord: '55, Fiji; Rev. Paul Richardson, S.S.C. Ord: '54, Philippines; Rev. Christopher Saenz, S.S.C. Ord: '00, Chile; Rev. John Wanaurny, S.S.C. Ord: '59, Mexico; Rev. Vincent J. Youngkamp, S.S.C. Ord: '59, Japan.

Priests: 29

BROTHERS OF THE SACRED HEART (S.C.)

Brothers of the Sacred Heart Foreign Missions

Provincial House, 685 Steere Farm Rd., Pascoag, RI 02859-4601. Phone: 401-568-3361; Fax: 401-568-1450. Bro. Robert Croteau, S.C., Prov. Supr.; Bro. Paul J. Hebert, S.C., Mission Procurator.

Brothers: 70; Brothers in Africa: 59

The Brothers of the Sacred Heart have mission schools and other establishments in Kenya, Lesotho, Uganda, Zambia, and Zimbabwe.

SALESIANS OF DON BOSCO (S.D.B.)

Salesians of Don Bosco Foreign Missions

Salesian Provincial House, 148 Main St., Box 639, New Rochelle, NY 10802-0639. Phone: 914-636-4225. Very Rev. Thomas Dunne, S.D.B. Ord: '72, Prov.; Rev. Mark Hyde, S.D.B. Ord: '81, Procurator.

U.S. Religious serving Abroad: Rev. Henry Bonetti, S.D.B. Ord: '73, Korea; Rev. Robert Falk, S.D.B. Ord: '63, Korea; Rev. Lawrence Gilmore, S.D.B. Ord: '84, Liberia; Rev. Harry Peterson, S.D.B. Ord: '61, Chile; Rev. John Thompson, S.D.B. Ord: '79, Swaziland; Rev. John Trisolini, S.D.B. Ord: '67, Korea; Bro. Sean McEwen, S.D.B., Ivory Coast.

Salesian Provincial House: 1100 Franklin St., San Francisco, CA 94109. Phone: 415-441-7144; Fax: 415-441-7155. Very Rev. Timothy Ploch, S.D.B. Ord: '76, Prov.

U.S. Religious serving Abroad: Bro. Joseph Reza, S.D.B., Ethiopia; Bro. William Regner, S.D.B., Sierra Leone.

SALVATORIAN MISSIONS (S.D.S.)

Salvatorian Foreign Missions

U.S.A. Provincial Headquarters: Salvatorian Provincial Offices:, 1735 N. Hi-Mount Blvd., Milwaukee, WI 53208-1720. Phone: 414-258-1735. Very Rev. David Bergner, S.D.S. Ord: '76, Prov.

Publication(s): The Salvatorian Newsletter

U.S.A. Procurator: 4033 Bacopa Pl., Lexington, KY 40509. Phone: 859-264-8058. Rev. Thomas Tureman, S.D.S. Ord: '88, Mission Dir.

U.S. Religious serving in Tanzania: Rev. Carl Gleason, S.D.S. Ord: '56; Rev. James Weyker, S.D.S. Ord: '69.

SOCIETY OF AFRICAN MISSIONS (S.M.A.)

Society of African Missions

U.S. Provincial Headquarters: 23 Bliss Ave., Tenafly, NJ 07670. Phone: 201-567-0450; Phone: 201-567-9085; Fax: 800-670-8328; Fax: 201-541-1280. Very Rev. Michael P. Moran, S.M.A. Ord: '81, Prov. Supr.

U.S. Religious serving Abroad: Rev. Ted Hayden, S.M.A. Ord: '58, Liberia.

SOCIETY OF ST. EDMUND (S.S.E.)

Edmundite Foreign Missions

U.S. Foundation: 270 Winooski Park, Colchester, VT 05439. Phone: 802-654-3400; Fax: 802-654-3409. Very Rev. Michael P. Cronogue, S.S.E. Ord: '77, Supr. Gen.

U.S. Religious serving Abroad: Rev. Edward J. Dubriske, S.S.E. Ord: '64, Venezuela; Rev. Philippe Simonnet, S.S.E. Ord: '52, France.

SOCIETY OF ST. JAMES THE APOSTLE

St. James the Apostle, Inc: 24 Clark St., Boston, MA 02109. Phone: 617-742-4715; Fax: 617-723-7389.

Founded by His Eminence Richard Cardinal Cushing, in 1958 to recruit Diocesan priest volunteers for South America.
Rev. Kevin Hays Ord: '77, Dir.; Rev. Patrick Universal Ord: '75.

Serving in Ecuador: Rev. Msgr. Desmond Dalton Ord: '70; Rev. Colm Hogan Ord: '98; Rev. Frank Jones Ord: '86; Rev. Martin Kelly Ord: '65; Rev. Cornelius Kiely Ord: '67; Rev. Colin MacInnes Ord: '70; Rev. Patrick McIntyre Ord: '60; Rev. Thomas Oates Ord: '63; Rev. Msgr. Finbarr O'Leary Ord: '60; Rev. Liam Reilly Ord: '00; Rev. Robert Thomas Ord: '61; Rev. Edward Veasey Ord: '62.

Serving in Peru: Rev. Geoffrey Adolfo Ord: '00; Rev. Ruel Arcega Ord: '95; Rev. Simon Cadwallader Ord: '97; Rev. David Costello Ord: '95; Rev. George Flynn Ord: '56; Rev. Jonathan Hart Ord: '96; Rev. Derek Leonard Ord: '96; Rev. Joseph I. Martin Ord: '56; Rev. J. Joseph McCarthy Ord: '66; Rev. John O'Leary Ord: '67; Rev. Gerard O'Meara Ord: '56; Rev. Daniel O'Sullivan Ord: '70; Rev. Raymond S. O'Sullivan Ord: '68; Rev. Denis Parry Ord: '94; Rev. John J. Pashby Ord: '60; Rev. Msgr. Jules Roos Ord: '56; Rev. Desmond A. Tynan Ord: '67.

THE SOCIETY OF MARY (S.M.)

MARIST FATHERS

Marist Foreign Missions

General Motherhouse: Via Alesandro Poerio, 63, Rome, Italy, 00152, Very Rev. John Hannan, S.M. Ord: '68, Supr. Gen.; Very Rev. Lawrence, S.M. Ord: '75, Vicar Gen.

U.S. Mission Promoter: Marist Missions, 27 Isabella St., Boston, MA 02116-5216. Phone: 617-482-0832; Fax: 617-426-1884. Rev. John Harhager, S.M. Ord: '79, Mission Promoter.

U.S. Religious serving Abroad: Rev. John Bolduc, S.M. Ord: '70, Jamaica; Rev. Paul Frechette, S.M. Ord: '76, Italy; Rev. John Galvin, S.M. Ord: '63, Solomon Islands; Rev. Joseph J. McLaughlin, S.M. Ord: '72, Philippines; Rev. Louis Morosini, S.M. Ord: '56, Solomon Islands; Rev. Alfred Puccinelli, S.M. Ord: '66, Brazil; Rev. Neil Soucy, S.M. Ord: '62, New Caldonia.

THIRD ORDER REGULAR MISSIONS (T.O.R.)

THIRD ORDER REGULAR OF ST. FRANCIS

T.O.R. Foreign Missions

Provincial Residence: Province of the Most Sacred Heart of Jesus:, P.O. Box 137, Loretto, PA 15940. Phone: 814-693-2890. Rev. Christian R. Oravec, T.O.R. Ord: '64, Minister Prov.

U.S. Religious serving Abroad: Rev. Gerald J. King, T.O.R. Ord: '71, Brazil; Rev. Paul R. Pavlik, T.O.R. Ord: '59, Brazil.

MISSIONARY SERVANTS OF THE MOST HOLY TRINITY (S.T.)

Trinity Missions

International Headquarters

Generalate, 9001 New Hampshire Ave., Ste. 300, Silver Spring, MD 20903-3626. Phone: 301-434-0092; Fax: 301-434-0255. Rev. John S. Edmunds, S.T. Ord: '76, Gen. Custodian; Bro. Steven Vesely, S.T., Sec. Gen.

U.S. Religious serving Abroad: Rev. Charles Gordon, S.T. Ord: '67, Colombia; Rev. Victor Santiago Mateo, S.T. Ord: '82, Colombia; Rev. Raymond Riding, S.T. Ord: '75, Mexico; Rev. Bruce Ward, S.T. Ord: '60, Mexico.

AMERICAN VINCENTIAN MISSIONS (C.M.)

Provincial Headquarters

Vincentian Foreign Missions

Eastern Province: St. Vincent's Seminary, 500 E. Chelten Ave., Philadelphia, PA 19144. Phone: 215-713-2400; Fax: 215-844-2085; Email: cmphila88@aol.com. Very Rev. Michael J. Carroll, C.M. Ord: '77, Prov.; Rev. Charles P. Strollo, C.M. Ord: '73, Asst. Prov.

U.S. Religious serving Abroad: Rev. Osvaldo Ayala, C.M. Ord: '01, Colon, Panama; Rev. Gilberto Caballero, C.M. Ord: '03, Panama City, Panama; Rev. John J. Carney, C.M. Ord: '82, Balboa, Panama; Rev. Jose Manuel Delgado, C.M. Ord: '04, Panama City, Panama; Rev. Edison Famania, C.M. Ord: '94, Concepcion, Panama; Rev. Joseph Fitzgerald, C.M. Ord: '05, Soloy, Panama; Very Rev. G. Gregory Gay, C.M. Ord: '80, Rome, Italy; Rev. John W. Gouldrick, C.M. Ord: '69, Rome, Italy; Rev. Alcibiades Guerra, C.M. Ord: '90, Colon, Panama; Rev. Jose Pio Jimenez, C.M. Ord: '68, Panama City, Panama; Rev. Teodoro Justavino, C.M. Ord: '90, Puerto Armuelles, Panama; Rev. John J. MacGillivray, C.M. Ord: '76, Volcan, Panama; Rev. Rolando Molina, C.M. Ord: '07, Concepcion, Panama; Rev. Geovany Morales, C.M. Ord: '01, Volcan, Panama; Rev. John P. Prager, C.M. Ord: '82, Puerto Armuelles, Panama; Rev. Teodoro A. Rios, C.M. Ord: '76, Puerto Armuelles, Panama; Rev. Secundino Rios, C.M. Ord: '01, Puerto Armuelles, Panama; Rev. Charles G. Schuster, C.M. Ord: '55, Soloy, Panama; Rev. Thomas Sendlein, C.M. Ord: '72, Taipei, Taiwan, Republic of China; Bro. G. Edgardo Lopez, C.M., Concepcion, Panama; Bro. Crecensio Tenorio A., C.M., Puerto Armuelles, Panama.

Western Province: Vincentian Fathers and Brothers, 13663 Rider Tr. N., Earth City, MO 63045-1512. Phone: 314-344-1184; Fax: 314-344-2989. Very Rev. Perry Henry, C.M. Ord: '83, Prov.

U.S Religious serving in Foreign Missions: Bro. James E. Donlevy, C.M., Supr.; Rev. W. Barry Moriarty, C.M. Ord: '67, Kenya; Rev. Thomas E. Esselman, C.M. Ord: '80; Rev. Stephen Gallegos, C.M. Ord: '88, Taiwan; Very Rev. Robert Wood, C.M. Ord: '56; Rev. John T. Richardson, C.M. Ord: '49; Rev. Robert W. Chap, C.M. Ord: '66, Taiwan (Province of China); Rev. Richard Preuss, C.M. Ord: '73, Taiwan (Province of China); Rev. Richard Wehrmeyer, C.M. Ord: '91; Rev. Francis H. Agnew, C.M. Ord: '60; Rev. Gilbert R. Walker, C.M. Ord: '87, Havana, Cuba; Rev. Lawrence F. Asma, C.M. Ord: '83, Trinidad & Tobago; Bro. Timothy Opferman, C.M.

XAVERIAN MISSIONARY FATHERS (S.X.)

Xaverian Foreign Missions

U.S. Foundation: Xaverian Missionary Fathers:, 12 Helene Ct., Wayne, NJ 07470. Phone: 201-942-2975; Fax: 201-942-5012. Rev. Carl S. Chudy, S.X. Ord: '86, Prov. Supr.; Rev. Frank B. Grappoli, S.X. Ord: '63, Local Superior & Treas. and Prov. Treas. & Mission Procurator.

Legal Title: *St. Francis Xavier Foreign Mission Society, Inc.*

Religious serving in Brazil: Rev. Francis Gugliotta, S.X. Ord: '52; Rev. Danilo Lago, S.X. Ord: '77; Rev. Gino Nasini, S.X. Ord: '65.

Religious serving in Cameroon: Rev. Rene Lovat, S.X. Ord: '57; Rev. Pierino Zoni, S.X. Ord: '61; Rev. Fernandes de Araujo Herondi, S.X. Ord: '76.

U.S. Religious serving in Colombia: Rev. Mark Marangone, S.X. Ord: '84; Rev. Mauro Loda, S.X. Ord: '99.

U.S. Religious serving in Indonesia: Rev. Bruno Orru, S.X. Ord: '63; Rev. Franco Qualizza, S.X. Ord: '71.

U.S. Religious serving in Japan: Rev. Renato Filippini, S.X. Ord: '97; Rev. Frank Sottocornola, S.X. Ord: '69.

U.S. Religious serving in Mexico: Rev. Dan Boschetto, S.X. Ord: '70; Rev. Ramon Cerratos, S.X. Ord: '99; Rev. Pablo Nieves, S.X. Ord: '99.

U.S. Religious serving in Mozambique: Rev. Dario Maso, S.X. Ord: '82; Rev. Horacio Perez, S.X. Ord: '03.

U.S. Religious serving in Sierra Leone: Most Rev. George Biguzzi, S.X.; Rev. Luciano Peterlini, S.X.

Ord: '63; Rev. Luigi Brioni, S.X. Ord: '61; Rev. Eugene Montesi, S.X. Ord: '62.

U.S Religious serving in Taiwan: Rev. Joe Vignato, S.X. Ord: '93; Rev. Martino Roia, S.X. Ord: '82; Rev. Edi Foschiatto, S.X. Ord: '81.

MISSIONHURST (C.I.C.M.)

Missionhurst Foreign Missions

American Headquarters (1946): Congregation of the Immaculate Heart of Mary:, 4651 N. 25th St., Arlington, VA 22207. Phone: 703-528-3800; Fax: 703-528-5355; Email: provincial@missionhurst.org. Very Rev. Anselme Malonda Nkuanga, C.I.C.M. Ord: '92, Prov. Supr.

Publication(s): Missionhurst Magazine

U.S Religious serving Abroad: Rev. Timothy Atkin, C.I.C.M. Ord: '74, General Councillor, Rome; Rev. Paul Delaere, C.I.C.M. Ord: '43, Belgium; Rev. Clement DeMeersman, C.I.C.M. Ord: '52, Belgium; Rev. William Missinne, C.I.C.M. Ord: '54, Belgium; Rev. Luke Moortgat, C.I.C.M. Ord: '65, Philippines; Rev. Gerard Rogmans, C.I.C.M. Ord: '55, Belgium; Rev. Roy Shea, C.I.C.M. Ord: '86, Brazil; Rev. Stanley Szarwark, C.I.C.M. Ord: '64, Dominican Republic; Bro. Leon Delanoy, C.I.C.M., Dominican Republic; Bro. Robert Dixon, C.I.C.M., Brazil.

AMERICAN OBLATE MISSIONS (O.M.I.)

Home and Foreign Missions of the United States Province of the Missionary Oblates of Mary Immaculate.

United States Province, 391 Michigan Ave., N.E., Washington, DC 20017. Phone: 202-529-4505; Fax: 202-529-4572. Rev. Louis Lougen, O.M.I. Ord: '79, Prov.

Religious in Scandinavian Missions: Rev. Michael Bradley, O.M.I. Ord: '66; Rev. Allen Courteau, O.M.I. Ord: '76; Rev. Leo Kertz, O.M.I. Ord: '63; Rev. Paul Marx, O.M.I. Ord: '65; Rev. Carroll Parker, O.M.I. Ord: '61; Rev. Clyde Rausch, O.M.I. Ord: '68.

U.S. Religious serving in Brazil: Rev. James Gibbons, O.M.I. Ord: '69; Rev. Thomas Brown, O.M.I. Ord: '55; Rev. Peter Curran, O.M.I. Ord: '71; Rev. Thomas Delaney, O.M.I. Ord: '60; Rev. John Drexel, O.M.I. Ord: '62; Rev. Edward Figueroa, O.M.I. Ord: '60; Rev. Robert Fitzpatrick, O.M.I. Ord: '71; Rev. Edmund Leising, O.M.I. Ord: '46; Rev. Paul Medeiros, O.M.I. Ord: '64; Rev. Robert Mayer, O.M.I. Ord: '67; Rev. David O'Brien, O.M.I. Ord: '59; Rev. Thomas O'Brien, O.M.I. Ord: '55; Rev. William Reinhard, O.M.I. Ord: '61; Rev. Anthony Rendon, O.M.I. Ord: '67; Rev. Charles Tierney, O.M.I. Ord: '73.

U.S. Religious serving in Canada: Rev. Normand Bonneau, O.M.I. Ord: '76; Rev. Dale Schlitt, O.M.I. Ord: '69; Rev. Ronald W. Young, O.M.I. Ord: '88.

U.S. Religious serving in Haiti: Rev. Alfred Charpentier, O.M.I. Ord: '71; Rev. Real Corriveau, O.M.I. Ord: '61; Rev. John Henault, O.M.I. Ord: '63; Rev. Charles Heon, O.M.I. Ord: '64; Rev. Joseph Vaillancourt, O.M.I. Ord: '46; Rev. Marc Boisvert, O.M.I. Ord: '84; Rev. John St. Cyr, O.M.I. Ord: '61.

U.S. Religious serving in Japan: Rev. Raymond Bourgoin, O.M.I. Ord: '66; Rev. John Deely, O.M.I. Ord: '70; Rev. Francis Hahn, O.M.I. Ord: '72; Rev. Thomas Maher, O.M.I. Ord: '57; Rev. William Maher, O.M.I. Ord: '66; Rev. Jerome Novotny, O.M.I. Ord: '68; Rev. Angelo Siani, O.M.I. Ord: '65; Rev. Bertram Silver, O.M.I. Ord: '54; Rev. Edward Williams, O.M.I. Ord: '57.

U.S. Religious serving in Mexico: Rev. John M. Curran, O.M.I. Ord: '78; Rev. James G. Dukowski, O.M.I. Ord: '67; Rev. Daniel Gagnon, O.M.I. Ord: '87; Rev. Francisco Gomez, O.M.I. Ord: '07; Rev. Robert Hickl, O.M.I. Ord: '79; Rev. Richard Junius, O.M.I. Ord: '56; Rev. Charles Krzewinski, O.M.I. Ord: '52; Rev. James Lyons, O.M.I. Ord: '61; Rev. Augustine Petru, O.M.I. Ord: '53; Rev. Francis Pfeifer, O.M.I. Ord: '59; Rev. Gilberto Pinon, O.M.I. Ord: '71; Rev. Thomas Rush, O.M.I. Ord: '73; Rev. Paul W. Wilhelm, O.M.I. Ord: '68; Rev. Gerald Kapustka, O.M.I. Ord: '65, Guatemala.

U.S. Religious serving in other countries: Rev. Robert Durette, O.M.I. Ord: '60, Bolivia; Rev. Ruben Elizondo, O.M.I. Ord: '62, Guatemala; Rev. Roger Hallee, O.M.I. Ord: '63, Colombia; Rev. Leo Guilmette, O.M.I. Ord: '63, Paraguay; Rev. David Ullrich, O.M.I. Ord: '71, Hong Kong.

U.S. Religious serving in the Philippine Islands: Rev. Armand Carignan, O.M.I. Ord: '53; Rev. Maurice Hemann, O.M.I. Ord: '50; Rev. Richard Pommier, O.M.I. Ord: '66; Rev. Richard Weixelman, O.M.I. Ord: '65.

U.S. Religious serving in Zambia: Most Rev. Paul Duffy, O.M.I., Archbishop of Mongu; Rev. James Chambers, O.M.I. Ord: '06; Rev. Patrick Gitzen, O.M.I. Ord: '75; Rev. Ronald Walker, O.M.I. Ord: '61;.

Missionary Activities

RELIGIOUS SOCIETIES ENGAGED IN MISSIONARY WORK

Augustinian Recollect Fathers: *Province of St. Nicholas Tolentine U.S. Delegation*, 3021 Frutas Ave., El Paso, TX 79905. Rev. Antonio Lasheras, O.A.R., Prov. Delegate.

Engaged in missionary work among Spanish-speaking people. Sustains mission personnel in the Archdioceses of New York and Newark, and in the Dioceses of Las Cruces and El Paso.

Congregation of the Blessed Sacrament: *Province of St. Ann*, 5384 Wilson Mills Rd., Cleveland, OH 44143.

Brothers of the Christian Schools: *U.S.A. & Toronto Regional Office of the De La Salle Christian Brothers Conference*, 3025 Fourth St., NE, Hecker Center, Ste. 300, Washington, DC 20017-1102. Phone: 202-529-0047; Web: www.lasallian.info.

The De La Salle Christian Brothers serve in 82 countries. The U.S.A./Toronto region has historic responsibilities in the Holy Land, English-speaking Africa, Central America and the Phillipines.

***Christian Foundation for Children and Aging:** One Elmwood Ave., Kansas City, KS 66103. Phone: 913-384-6500; Phone: 800-875-6564; Web: www.cfcausa.org. Robert K. Hentzen, Pres.; Paco Wertin, CEO; Larry Livingston, Contact Person.

Christian Foundation for Children and Aging (CFCA) is rooted in the Catholic social tradition of building a just society, one which proclaims that human life is sacred and that each of us is called to grow in community. As members of an interdependent global community, we learn to live in solidarity with our brothers and sisters around the world. CFCA strives to create a community of compassion by linking individual sponsors in the United States with a child, youth or aging person at project sites in 24 economically developing countries. Through sponsorship, more than 308,000 children, youth and aging persons are provided a variety of benefits including nutrition, educational assistance, clothing, medical care, spiritual development and livelihood programs for families. Founded by Catholic lay people in 1981, CFCA works with people of all faiths.

Claretian Missionaries: *Headquarters of Western Province*, 414 S. Mission Dr., San Gabriel, CA 91776. Phone: 626-289-2009; Fax: 626-289-2222. Very Rev. Richard H. DeTore, C.M.F., Prov.

Headquarters of Eastern Province, 400 N. Euclid Ave., Oak Park, IL 60302. Phone: 708-848-2076. Very Rev. Eddie DeLeon, C.M.F., Prov.

Please refer to the Religious Institutes of Men section for activities and representation in the United States.

Claret Center, 5536 S. Everett Ave., Chicago, IL 60637.

Resources for Counseling and Spiritual Directions. Chicago, IL.

Missions outside the United States entrusted to the Claretians: Guatemala, Cameroons, Mexico.

Publications: monthly magazine, U.S. Catholic; extensive line of Pamphlets and Paperback Books; bi-monthly Newsletter; Fides-Claretian.

Comboni Missionaries of the Heart of Jesus, Inc. (Verona Fathers): *Provincial Headquarters: Comboni Mission Center*, 1318 Nagel Rd., Cincinnati, OH 45255-3120. Phone: 513-474-4997; Email: info@combonimissionaries.org; Web: www.combonimissionaries.org. Rev. Louis Gasparini, M.C.C.J., Prov. Supr.; Rev. Joseph Bragotti, M.C.C.J., Mission Dir.; Rev. Paul Donohue, M.C.C.J., Communications Dir.

Foreign mission society, both priests and brothers, founded by Saint Daniel Comboni, Vicar Apostolic of Central Africa.

Active in the Archdioceses of Chicago, Cincinnati, Los Angeles and Newark.

Comboni Missionaries work with local churches in: Africa--Benin, Central African Republic, Egypt, Eritrea, Ethiopia, Ghana, Kenya, Malawi, Mozambique, South Africa, Sudan, Chad, Togo, Uganda, Zambia and Democratic Republic of Congo; Asia--Philippines, China; Latin America--Brazil, Chile, Colombia, Costa Rica, Ecuador, El Salvador, Guatemala, Mexico, Nicaragua, and Peru; North America--Canada and the United States.

Training Centers: Africa--Eritrea, Ethiopia, Kenya, Malawi, Mozambique, South Africa, Togo, Egypt, Sudan, Uganda, Democratic Republic of the Congo; Asia--Philippines; Europe--Austria, England, France, Germany, Italy, Poland, Portugal, and Spain; Latin America--Brazil, Colombia, Costa Rica, Ecuador, Mexico and Peru; North America--United States.

Publications: Comboni Press Network Newsletter; Comboni Press Feature Service; Comboni Mission Newsletter.

Comboni Missionary Sisters: *American Headquarters*, 1307 Lakeside Ave., Richmond, VA 23228-4710. Phone: 804-262-8827; Fax: 804-264-2906; Email: cmusaprov@verizon.net; Web: www.combonisrs.com. Sr. Maria de la Luz Aguilera, C.M.S., Prov. Supr.

An international congregation of 1,470 sisters founded by Bishop St. Daniel Comboni in 1872 in Verona, Italy. Engaged in pastoral and catechetical work; education; social services; health services; building Christian communities; commited to justice and peace making and care for creation; training local church leaders in Africa, America, Europe, and the Middle East.

The American Province recruits and trains sisters for the foreign mission, mission education, fundraising for missions, and pastoral ministry among the poor.

Congregation of Alexian Brothers: *Immaculate Conception Province, U.S. Provincial Headquarters*, 3040 Salt Creek Ln., Arlington Heights, IL 60005. Bro. James Classon, C.F.A., Prov.

Missionary healthcare work in Davao City, Philippines & Györ, Hungary directed by Alexian Brothers. Please refer to the Religious Institutes of Men section for activities and representation in the United States.

Congregation of Christian Brothers: *Business Offices: Edmund Rice Christian Brothers North America*, 21 Pryer Ter., New Rochelle, NY 10804-4418. Bro. Hugh B. O'Neill, C.F.C., Prov. Leader; Bro. Kevin M. Griffith, C.F.C., Deputy Prov. Leader; Bro. John J. Casey, C.F.C., Latin America Region Leader; Bro. Kevin F. Bernard, C.F.C., Latin America Deputy Region Leader.

Missionary and educational work in Central and South America and in Africa.

Congregation of the Holy Spirit and of the Immaculate Heart of Mary (1872): 6230 Brush Run Rd., Bethel Park, PA 15102. Phone: 412-831-0302; Fax: 412-831-0970. Holy Spirit Fathers and Brothers (C.S.Sp.) Eastern Province, Very Rev. Jeffrey T. Duaime, C.S.Sp., Prov. Western Province (1963), Very Rev. Daniel L. Walsh, C.S.Sp.1700 W. Alabama St. Houston TX 77098-2808 Phone: 713-522-2667; 713-522-2882 Fax: 713-522-8063.

Missionary work among the abandoned, including first evangelization, teaching, care of homeless children, and pastoral ministry.

Missionaries serve in 17 (Arch)Dioceses in the United States: the Archdiocese of San Juan and the Diocese of Arecibo in Puerto Rico; the Dioceses of Ciudad Valles, Tampico, and the Archdiocese of San Luis Potosi in Mexico; Archdiocese of Arusha, and Dioceses of Mbulu and Zanzibar in Tanzania; Nairobi in Kenya; Bethlehem in South Africa; and Awasa in Ethiopia. Other establishments in North and South America, Europe, Africa, Australia and the Dominican Republic; also the Phillipines and Taiwan.

Missionaries of Our Lady of La Salette: *Province of Mary, Mother of the Americas*, 915 Maple Ave., Hartford, CT 06114-2330. Phone: 860-956-8870; Fax: 860-956-8849. Very Rev. Joseph G. Bachand, M.S., Prov. Supr.; Rev. John R. Nuelle, M.S., Procurator.
4650 S. Broadway, Saint Louis, MO 63111-1398. Phone: 314-352-0064; Fax: 314-352-3737.

Active in Archdioceses of Buenos Aires, Argentina; Cochabamba, Bolivia; Cordoba, Argentina; and Diocese of Santiago del Estero, Argentina.

Please refer to the Religious Institutes of Men section for activities and representation in the United States.

Congregation of the Priests of the Sacred Heart, The: *U.S. Provincialate Offices*, P.O. Box 289, Hales Corners, WI 53130-0289. Phone: 414-425-6910. Very Rev. Thomas P. Cassidy, S.C.J., Prov. Supr.

Please refer to the Religious Institutes of Men section for other activities and representation in the United States.

Missionary work in the home and foreign missions; educational activities; welfare work, especially in industrial centers. Home Missions: Lower Brule and Crow Creek Indian Reservation, South Dakota; Black Missions, Diocese of Jackson, Mississippi; Spanish-speaking Apostolate, Archdiocese of Galveston-Houston and Diocese of Brownsville.

Foreign Missions: Zaire, Cameroon, Mozambique, South Africa, Brazil, Argentina, Uruguay, Chile, Venezuela, India, Indonesia and Finland.

Congregation of the Resurrection: *Resurrection Catholic Missions of the South, Inc.*, 2815 Forbes Dr., Montgomery, AL 36110. Phone: 334-263-4221; Fax: 334-263-4999.

The Resurrection Catholic Missions ministries includes a home for handicapped and severely mentally retarded children, an early childhood development facility for preschoolers, a church and elementary school, as well as an outreach program to homebound elders.

Please refer to the Religious Institutes of Men section for activities and representation in the United States. Active also in Australia, Brazil, Bolivia, Bulgaria, Canada, Germany, Jamaica, Mexico, Poland and Tanzania.

Consolata Missionaries (1901): *Provincial Headquarters (1964)*, 2301 Hwy. 27, P.O. Box 5550, Somerset, NJ 08875-5550. Phone: 732-297-9191; Fax: 732-940-3121. Rev. Charles Bonelli, I.M.C., Reg. Supr.

Legal Title: *Consolata Society for Foreign Missions.*

Serving in 26 countries around the world including the United States.

Publication: Consolata Missionaries.

Consolata Missionary Sisters (1910): 6801 Belmont Ave., N.E., P.O. Box 371, Belmont, MI 49306. Phone: 616-361-2072; Fax: 616-361-2049. Sr. Zelita M. Bragagnolo, M.C., Supr.

The congregation is committed to all types of missionary apostolate, primarily in African and South American countries.

Crosier Fathers and Brothers: *Crosier Missions*, 4332 N. 24th St., Phoenix, AZ 85016-6259. Phone: 602-443-7100; Fax: 602-443-7101. Bro. Albert Becker, O.S.C., Mission Coord. & Dir. Devel.

Legal Title: *Canons Regular of the Order of the Holy Cross.*

Missionary work among the Asmat tribes of Irian Jaya Indonesia, since 1958.

Publication: quarterly, Crossview.

Daughters of Mary Help of Christians: *St. Philip Apostle Province*, 655 Belmont Ave., Haledon, NJ 07508. Mother Phyllis Neves, F.M.A., Prov.

Legal Title: *Missionary Society of the Salesian Sisters, Inc.*

Missionary work in home and foreign countries; catechetical, educational and training centers; social services; hostels, hospitals, clinics and dispensaries; mission centers, and youth centers.

Active in U.S. within the Archdioceses of Miami, Newark, New Orleans, and New York, and the Dioceses of Paterson, Rockford, and St. Petersburg.

Eucharistic Missionaries of St. Dominic: 2645 Bardstown Rd., Saint Catharine, KY 40061-9435. Phone: 859-336-9303; Fax: 859-336-9306. Sr. Dorothy Troclair, O.P., Pres.

Missionary work and ministry in religious education; forensic social work; pastoral associates; social service; spirituality-retreat center; home & clinic nursing; hospital chaplaincy; counseling; pastoral care of the sick in homes; literacy ministry to Mayan immigrants, mental health and detention center chaplain.

Franciscan Friars of the Atonement - Generalate: *Graymoor*, P.O. Box 300, Garrison, NY 10524-0300. Phone: 845-424-2113; Fax: 845-424-2166. General Council:; Very Rev. James F. Puglisi, S.A., Min. Gen.; Rev. Timothy I. MacDonald, S.A., 1st Councilor & Vicar Gen.;

Rev. Elias D. Mallon, S.A., 2nd Councilor; Bro. Kevin Goss, S.A., 3rd Councilor & Sec. Gen.; Rev. V. Paul Ojibway, S.A., 4th Councilor.

Mission activities outside of the U.S: Japan. Also staff parishes in Canada, England, Italy and the United States. The Friars mission of reconciliation is promoted through preaching of the Gospel, ecumenism and inter-religious activity and missionary activity.

Please refer to the Religious Institutes of Men section for activities and representation in the United States.

Franciscan Missionaries of Mary, The: *U.S. Provincial House*, 3305 Wallace Ave., Bronx, NY 10467. Phone: 718-547-4693; Fax: 718-325-5102. Sr. Lois Ann Pereira, F.M.M., Prov.

The Franciscan Missionaries of Mary, founded in India in 1877 by Bl. Mary of the Passion, for Eucharistic contemplation and the work of Evangelization, is dedicated to Universal Mission. It is an international Religious Institute of Pontifical Right.

This international congregation serves 831 missions in 50 provinces and 2 delegations.

Missionary work of evangelization and development, catechetics; social work; nursing; community development programs; educational and public health programs; pastoral activity and various forms of ministry and service; immigration and prison ministries.

Franciscan Missionary Sisters for Africa: *American Headquarters Center for Promotion and Formation*, 172 Foster St., Box 35095, Brighton, MA 02135. Phone: 617-254-4343; Fax: 617-787-8007; Email: brightonsisters172@yahoo.com. Sr. Miriam Duggan, F.M.S.A., Supr. Gen.

Missions in Kenya, Uganda, South Africa, Zambia and Zimbabwe.

Publication: The Daystar.

Franciscan Mission Association: *Franciscan Mission House*, 517 Washington Ave., Rensselaer, NY 12144. Phone: 518-465-0062; Fax: 518-465-3673; Web: www.thefma.org; Web: www.franciscanseast.org. Rev. Raynald Yudin, O.F.M.Conv., Dir.

The American branch of the Franciscan Mission Crusade founded in 1924, approved by Pope Pius XI to further the work of the Conventual Franciscan Missionary Apostolate. The purpose is to aid the Mission of the Order in every possible way. The revenues of the Association accrue from the annual and perpetual enrollments in the Association, bequests, other free-will offerings and donations, membership in monthly mission club appeal.

Franciscan Mission Association (1953): *Franciscan Missions*, 322 West St., Carey, OH 43316. Phone: 419-396-6455. Bro. Bryan Hoban, O.F.M.Conv., Dir.

The purpose of the association, which is part of the Province of Our Lady of Consolation, is to give financial and other material aid to the missionaries of Africa: the Dioceses of Ndola and Solwezi, Zambia; missionaries in the Dioceses of Olancho, Tegucigalpa and Comayagua in Honduras and San Jose in Costa Rica; and missionaries of the Southwestern United States. Both living and deceased may be enrolled as members. Members of the laity have an active part in promoting the growth of the association as outlined in Vatican II.

Franciscan Mission Association, Inc.: *Province of St. Anthony of Padua*, 12300 Folly Quarter Rd., Ellicott City, MD 21042. Phone: 410-531-3695; Fax: 410-531-4881; Email: info@companionsofstanthony.org. Rev. Joseph Benicewicz, O.F.M.Conv., Dir.

Founded to support the domestic and foreign missions of the Conventual Franciscans of St. Anthony Province.

Franciscan Sisters of Allegany: *St. Elizabeth Motherhouse*, 115 E. Main St., Allegany, NY 14706. Sr. Maureen Avril Chin Fatt, O.S.F., Congregational Min.; Sr. Chris Doherty, O.S.F., Mission Society Dir.

Sisters serve in areas of education; health-care; pastoral ministry; social ministries; and other missionary work in the Archdiocese of Kingston; the Archdioceses of Goiania and Palmas, Brazil; Prelacy of Cristalandia, Brazil; Dioceses of Anapolis, Ipameri, Goias, Rui Barbosa, Miracema do Tocantins and Jatai, Brazil. Archdiocese of La Paz and Dioceses of Cochabamba, Bolivia.

Congregation 301; foreign missions 75.

Publication: Zeal.

Franciscan Sisters, Daughters of the Sacred Hearts of Jesus and Mary: *Province of St. Clara*, P.O. Box 667, Wheaton, IL 60187-0667. Phone: 630-462-7422; Fax: 630-462-7148. Sr. Beatrice Hernandez, O.S.F., Prov. Dir.

Active in the United States ministering in sponsorship of Catholic hospitals; counseling, housing; education; pastoral ministry; care of elderly; wellness; long-term care; social services; spiritual direction and retreats in Archdioceses of Milwaukee, and Chicago; in Dioceses of Joliet, Green Bay, and Springfield-Cape Girardeau; outside the U.S: Brazil and Italy.

Franciscan Sisters of Little Falls, MN: *Motherhouse*, 116 8th Ave. S.E., Little Falls, MN 56345. Phone: 320-632-2981. Sr. Mary C. Obowa, O.S.F., Pres.

Serving Catholic and non-sectarian hospitals; Catholic and non-sectarian nursing homes; group homes; apartments for the elderly; home health nursing; public health nursing; Hospice Care; Catholic high schools; Catholic elementary schools; special education; Spirituality Farm, Native Americans; community colleges; state colleges and universities; religious education; parish ministry; liturgical music ministry; music center; health and recreation center; retreat ministry; counseling; spiritual direction; social service; ministry to the poor; ministry to the migrants; consultant for healthcare & related organizations; art therapist; Hispanic Ministry; pastoral ministry; in the US and in education, health, social services in Quito, Ecuador, S.A., San Rafael, Linares, Mexico.

Franciscan Sisters of the Poor: *Congregational Office*, 133 Remsen St., Brooklyn, NY 11201. Phone: 718-643-1919; Fax: 718-643-9710. Sr. Tiziana Merletti, S.F.P., Pres.

Sisters serve in healing ministry; health care; social welfare; pastoral ministry in the U.S.; pastoral ministry and health care in the Dioceses of Assisi, Frascati, Pistoia, Rome, Padua and Messina in Italy. Mission ministry is represented in the Archdiocese of Goiania and in the Dioceses of Jatai, Ipameri & Pires Do Rio in Brazil, in the Dioceses of Dakar, Kaolack, Kolda in Senegal, West Africa, and also in the Diocese of Dumaguete in the Philippines.

Number in Congregation 138; Mission Ministry 27.

Glenmary Home Missioners (1939): *National Headquarters*, P.O. Box 465618, Cincinnati, OH 45246. Phone: 513-874-8900; Web: www.glenmary.org. Rev. Dan Dorsey, G.H.M., Pres.

Glenmary is an apostolic society of priests and brothers who, along with lay coworkers, establish the Catholic Church in small-town and rural America. Glenmary is the only religious community dedicated exclusively to serving the spiritually and materially poor in Appalachia, the rural South and Southwest. Glenmary missioners serve in areas where less than three percent of the population is Catholic, a significant percent have no church affiliation, and the poverty rate is almost twice the national average. Their missionary activities include nurturing Catholic communities, fostering ecumenism, evangelizing the unchurched, working for justice and social outreach. Glenmary staffs over 40 missions and ministries, including a pastoral center, a research center, a group volunteer program at the Glenmary Farm and commissions on evangelization and justice.

Please refer to the Religious Institutes of Men section for activities and representation in the United States.

Publication: Glenmary Challenge

Glenmary Home Mission Sisters of America (1941): *Glenmary Sisters*, P.O. Box 22264, Owensboro, KY 42304-2264. Fax: 270-686-8759. Sr. Sharon Miller, Pres.

Glenmary is a community of women religious of diocesan right - a home mission community dedicated to bringing mission presence and activity to the rural, small town areas of the United States. The sisters live and work among the poor, the sick, the oppressed and unchurched in Appalachia and the South in areas where less than 2% of the total population is Catholic. When possible the sisters work in collaboration with the Glenmary Priests and Brothers. The Glenmary Sisters believe in a holistic approach to mission - the caring of the whole person - through their ministries of evangelization, pastoral outreach, religious education, home visitation and a wide variety of social services for the poor.

Please refer to the Religious Institutes of Women section for activities in the United States.

Publications: Kinship; Kinship for Kids; Kinship for Teens.

Institute of Charity (Rosminian Fathers): *Rosmini House*, 2327 W. Heading Ave., Peoria, IL 61604.

Active in the Dioceses of Peoria and St. Petersburg.

Missions and missionary work in Tanga, Tanzania; New Zealand; Venezuela; and Kerala, India.

Jesuit Volunteers International: P.O. Box 3756, Washington, DC 20027-0256. Phone: 202-687-1132; Fax: 202-687-5082. Meghan Romey, Exec. Dir.

Selected college graduates improve education and promote human welfare, faith communities and social justice through a two-year commitment to impoverished local communities in seven developing nations.

Mariannhill, Congregation of Missionaries of (1882): 23715 Ann Arbor Tr., Dearborn Heights, MI 48127-1449. Rev. Alain Rodrigue, C.M.M., Prov. Supr.

The American-Canadian province recruits and trains young men as priests and lay brothers for foreign missions, secures funds for the foreign missions, and does a limited amount of pastoral work at home.

Active in the Archdiocese of Detroit.

Outside the U.S: Austria, Botswana, Canada, Columbia, Germany, Italy, Kenya, Mozambique, Netherlands, New Guinea, Papue, Poland, South Africa, Spain, Switzerland, Zambia and Zimbabwe.

Worldwide membership: Bishops 4; Priests 211; Brothers 88; Seminarians Professed 73; Total Members 376.

Publication: Leaves.

Marist Missionary Sisters: *North American Provincial Office:* 349 Grove St., Waltham, MA 02453. Phone: 781-893-0149; Fax: 781-894-7610; Web: www.maristmissionarysmsm.org. Sr. Judith Sheridan, S.M.S.M., Prov.; Sr. Pauline St. Pierre, Mission Promotor; Sr. Claire Rheaume, S.M.S.M., Vocation Directress.

Legal Title: *Missionary Sisters of the Society of Mary, Inc.*

Founded in France in 1845 for mission in the South Pacific, today, the International Missionary Congregation consist of 509 sisters (in seven provinces), serving the people of God in 29 countries around the world. The American Province has 105 sisters working in Massachusetts, Tennessee, Florida, California, and Jamaica, W.I. The mission is to bring the good news of God's love through spiritual and corporal works of mercy; catechetical, medical, educational and social services; pastoral ministry; formation of laity for leadership and a great concern for the poorest and most neglected. Working by preference among people of different cultures and languages, to bring about greater understanding, dignity and mutual respect.

Formation is international with a French-speaking novitiate in Senegal, an English-speaking novitiate in New Zealand and a Spanish-speaking novitiate in Peru.

Province headquarters are in the United States, Australia, France, Italy, New Caledonia, New Zealand, and Peru.

Please refer to the Religious Institutes of Women section for activities and representation in the United States.

Maryknoll Sisters of St. Dominic, Inc.: P.O. Box 311, Maryknoll, NY 10545-3011. Sr. Janice McLaughlin, M.M., Community Pres.; Sr. Rebecca Macugay, M.M., Vice Pres.; Sr. Ann Hayden, M.M., Gen. Sec.; Sr. Bitrina Kirway, M.M., Team Member.

A Pontifical Institute under the jurisdiction of the Congregation for the Institutes of Consecrated Life. The purpose of the Maryknoll Sisters Congregation is to participate in the mission presence and activity of the universal Church so that God's reign of peace, justice and love may be proclaimed and witnessed to throughout the world. The Maryknoll Sisters embrace a plurality of ministries while giving a clear sign of Christian community; faith-sharing; self-gift in service through pastoral and catechetical work; basic ecclesial communities; education; social services; medical and health promotion work; services through hostels; services to refugees; and ministries that promote human rights, social justice and the dignity and equality of women.

Please refer to the Religious Institutes of Women section for activities in the United States.

Active in Bangladesh, Bolivia, Brazil, Cambodia, Central Pacific, Chile, China, East Timor, Ecuador, El Salvador, Guatemala, Japan, Kenya, Korea, Micronesia, Mexico, Namibia, Panama, Peru, Philippines, Sudan, Taiwan, Tanzania, Thailand, USA and Zimbabwe.

Medical Missionaries of Mary: 563 Minneford Ave., Bronx, NY 10464-1118. Phone: 718-885-0945; Fax: 718-885-0010; Email: minniefordmmm@verizon.net; Web: www.mmmusa.org. Sr. Margaret Quinn, M.M.M., Congregational Ldr.; Sr. Siobhan Corkery, M.M.M., Zonal Coord.; Sr. Therese McDonough, M.M.M., Area Leader USA.

Missionary work in hospitals, clinics and leprosy treatment; public health and pastoral ministry centers in Africa, South America and Clinchco, VA.

Please refer to the Religious Institutes of Women section for activities and representation in the United States.

Active also in Angola, Benin, Rwanda, Nigeria, Uganda, Tanzania, Honduras, Kenya, Malawi, Ethiopia, England, Ireland and Brazil.

Publication: quarterly, The Mini MMM.

Medical Mission Sisters: *North American Headquarters*, 8400 Pine Rd., Philadelphia, PA 19111. Fax: 215-342-3948. Sr. Agnes Lanfermann, M.M.S., Society Coord. Elect; Sr. Rosemary Ryan, M.M.S., North American Sector Coord.; Monica M. McGinley, Pub. Rels. Dir.

Legal Title: *Society of Catholic Medical Missionaries, Inc.; Society of Catholic Medical Missionaries Generalate, Inc., (effective 1991).*

Medical Mission Sisters have the special call in the Church of "being a healing presence at the heart of a wounded world." Members commit themselves "to promote healing and wholeness in all aspects of life" in the spirit of Jesus. They share life with those who are sick and have been made poor, trying to help them to live fully as human beings. Medical Mission Sisters' healing presence today involves a full range of preventitive, curative and promotive health services; health training programs; and development and social justice activities in Ghana, Uganda, Kenya, Ethiopia, Malawi, Pakistan, India, Belgium, Venezuela, Brazil, Peru, Indonesia, Philippines, Italy, Holland, Germany, England and the United States.

Medical Mission Houses in the United States are listed under the Religious Institutes of Women Section.

Publication: Medical Mission Sisters News.

Mill Hill Missionaries: *St. Joseph's Missionary Society:* 222 W. Hartsdale Ave., Hartsdale, NY 10530. Phone: 914-682-0645; Fax: 914-682-0862; Email: mhmnar@aol.com. Rev. Bartholomew Daly, M.H.M., Reg. Rep; Rev. Terence J. Lee, M.H.M., Counselor; Rev. Emile Frische, M.H.M., Counselor; Rev. Matthew Grier, M.H.M., Bursar.

An international society of priests, brothers and associates, founded in 1866 by Herbert Vaughan, devoted entirely to the missionary needs of the Church.

Active in the U.S. in the Archdiocese of New York and in the Diocese of Phoenix.

Active outside the United States. Canada: Diocese of Kingston, ONT. Cameroon: the Archdiocese of Bamenda and the Dioceses of Buea, Kumbo, Mamfe and Ngaoundere. Congo: Diocese of Basankusu. Kenya: Archdioceses of Kisumu, Nairobi, and the Dioceses of Bungoma, Kakamega, Kisii, Malindi, Nakuru, Ngong and Homa Bay. Uganda: Archdioceses of Kampala, Tororo and the Dioceses of Jinja, Soroti, Kotido and Lugazi. South Africa: Diocese of Kroonstad, Rustenburg. Sudan: Archdiocese of Khartoum, and the Diocese of Malakal. China: Diocese of Hong Kong. India: Archdioceses of Hyderabad, and the Dioceses of Jammu-Srinagar, Varanasi and Warangal. Pakistan: Dioceses of Islamabad-Rawalpindi and Hyderabad. Malaysia: Archdiocese of Kuching, and the Dioceses of Kota Kinabalu and Sibu. Brunei: Prefecture Apostolic of Brunei. Philippines: Archdioceses of Manila, Jaro, and the Diocese of San Jose. New Zealand: Dioceses of Aukland and Hamilton. Brazil: Dioceses of Governador Valadares and Itaquai. Also Ecaudor: Archdiocese of Guayaquil. Bolivia: Archdiocese of Cochabamba.

Mission Helpers of the Sacred Heart: 1001 W. Joppa Rd., Baltimore, MD 21204. Phone: 410-823-8585; Fax: 410-825-6355. Sr. Loretta Cornell, M.H.S.H., Pres.

A Pontifical, missionary congregation with principal work of evangelization and catechesis; adult religious education; instruction of youth and children; D.R.E. programs; pastoral ministers; pastoral associates; pastoral social ministers; special ministers of the Eucharist; ministry in homes and institutions; ministry to the elderly and infirm; catechesis of blind, deaf, retarded; campus ministry; Hispanic pastoral ministry to adults and youth; spiritual direction and retreat work.

Please refer to the Religious Institutes of Women for activities and representation in the United States.

Activities also in the Archdioceses of Barquisimeto, Venezuela, and San Juan.

Publication: 2 times yearly, The Mission Helper.

Mission International, Inc.: 2301 Hwy. 27, Somerset, NJ 08873. Phone: 732-297-9191; Fax: 732-940-3121. Rev. Giuseppe Sesana, I.M.C., Chm.

Missionaries of Africa (M.Afr.): *U.S. Province of North America Headquarters:* 1624 21st St., N.W., Washington, DC 20009-1003. Fax: 202-332-8640.

International and interracial missionary society of priests and brothers working in teams almost exclusively in Africa.

Active in the Archdiocese of Washington, D.C. and the Diocese of St. Petersburg.

Training centers in Burkina Faso, Ivory Coast, Kenya, D.R. Congo, Zambia and Jerusalem.

Missionary work in Algeria, Burundi, Ethiopia, Ghana, Kenya, Malawi, Mali, Mozambique, Nigeria, Rwanda, Sudan, Tanzania, Tunisia, Uganda, Burkina Faso, Democratic Republic of Congo, Zambia, South Africa, Ivory Coast, Niger and Mauritania.

Publication: newsletter, Missionaries of Africa Report.

Missionaries of the Holy Apostles, Society of the: 22 Prospect Hill Rd., Cromwell, CT 06416. Phone: 860-632-3039; Fax: 860-635-4823. Very Rev. Addison Hallock, M.S.A., Prov. Animator.

Apostolic works consist of the promotion and formation of adult candidates for the diocesan and religious priesthood and preparation of the laity for Christian leadership.

Please refer to the Religious Institutes of Men section for activities and representation in the United States.

Activities also in Brazil, Venezuela, Cameroon, Colombia, Canada, Peru, Italy, and France.

Missionary Benedictine Sisters: *Provincial Motherhouse & Novitiate-Immaculata Monastery:* 300 N. 18th St., Norfolk, NE 68701-3687. Phone: 402-371-3438; Fax: 402-379-2877. Sr. Kevin Hermsen, O.S.B., Prioress.

Missionary work in elementary schools; catechetical programs; pastoral ministry; nursing home; hospital in the Archdiocese of Omaha and Diocese of New Ulm, Minnesota; Indian Mission, Northeast Nebraska; Hispanic ministry .

Missionary work outside the U.S. the Philippine Islands, Korea, Brazil, Argentina, Australia, China, India, Tanzania, Namibia, Kenya, Angola, Portugal, Germany, Italy, Spain, Switzerland, Bulgaria and Uganda.

Missionary Servants of the Most Blessed Trinity: *Motherhouse, Novitiate and Generalate:* 3501 Solly Ave., Philadelphia, PA 19136. Fax: 215-332-7559. Sr. Joan Marie Keller, M.S.B.T., Gen. Custodian.

The congregation's mission is the preservation of the faith. This involves nourishing the faithlife of those of the Roman Catholic tradition, cooperating in ecumenical endeavors, strengthening life-giving faith among all people, evangelization, actively promoting human development and social justice. The special apostolic intent is to advance and support the ministry of the laity in the mission of the Church, accomplished through the ministries of education, social work and health care on parish and diocesan levels.

Please refer to the Religious Institutes of Women section for activities and representation in the United States.

Active also in the Archdioceses of Kingston, San Juan and Mexico City and the Dioceses of Ponce and Mayaguez in Puerto Rico as well as the Diocese of Texcoco in Mexico.

Missionary Servants of the Most Holy Trinity (Trinity Missions): *The Generalate*, 9001 New Hampshire Ave., Ste. 300, Silver Spring, MD 20903-3626. Phone: 301-434-0092; Fax: 301-434-0255; Email: generalate@trinitymissions.org. Rev. John S. Edmunds, S.T., Gen. Custodian; Bro. Steven Vesely, S.T., Sec. Gen.; Rev. Jordan Baxter, S.T., Treas. Gen.; Rev. Domingo Rodriguez, S.T., Mission Procurator.

A clerical congregation of Pontifical Right founded for the preservation of the faith and missionary work wherever the Church directs. The major fields are the missionary areas of the southern United States and the Spanish-speaking people in the United States, Puerto Rico, Colombia, Costa Rica and Mexico. The principal work is the development of Catholic lay leaders. There is also training for the missionary priesthood and brotherhood of the congregation.

Please refer to the Religious Institutes of Men section for activities and representation in the United States.

Publication: Trinity Missions.

Missionary Sisters of St. Columban (1922): 73 Mapleton St., Brighton, MA 02135. Phone: 617-782-5683; Fax: 617-789-3569. Sr. Margaret Holleran, S.C.C., U.S. Area Coord.

The Missionary Sisters of Saint Columban are also known as the Columban Sisters. The Columban Sisters are religious women called to bring the good and the oppressed and those who have not yet had the Gospel proclaimed to them. The congregation strives to respond to the needs of the people by dedication to the work of evangelization through pastoral, educational, medical and social ministries, and supporting the efforts of the local church where its members are sent. The congregation also endeavors, through programs of mission education and animation, to deepen an awareness of global vision and world justice.

Active in the U.S. in the Archdioceses of Boston, and Los Angeles and in the Diocese of Buffalo.

Active outside the U.S. in Ireland, Myanmar, China, England, Scotland, Hong Kong, Korea, Philippines, Peru, Chile and Pakistan.

Missionary Sisters of Our Lady of Africa: *American Headquarters:* 47 W. Spring St., Winooski, VT 05404. Sr. Marie Heintz, Contact Person.

Missionary activities in Africa: catechetical, pastoral ministry, social work, education and health programs, and working with African Religious Congregations.

Missionary Sisters of the Immaculate Conception of the Mother of God: *Generalate:* 47 Garden Ave., West Paterson, NJ 07424-3337. Phone: 973-279-1484; Fax: 973-279-2991. Sr. Veronica Lee, S.M.I.C., Coord. Gen.

Missionary work in catechetical and social service centers, schools, dispensaries and hospitals.

Active in the U.S. in the Archdioceses of Galveston-Houston and Newark, and the Dioceses of Austin, Paterson, Portland, San Bernardino and Santa Fe.

Active outside the U.S. in Angola, Brazil, Germany, Namibia, Philippines and Taiwan.

Missionary Sisters of St. Peter Claver (1894): *American Headquarters:* 265 Century Ave., S., Saint Paul, MN 55125-1155. Phone: 651-738-9704. Sr. Genevieve Kudlik.

Legal Title: *The Sodality of St. Peter Claver for the African Missions.*

The congregation is of Pontifical Jurisdiction, fostering interest in and obtaining funds and requisites for the missions. Apostolate of the press in Africa

Publications: monthly magazine, Echo from Africa, annual, Claver Almanac.

Missionary Sisters of Our Lady of the Holy Rosary: 741 Polo Rd., Bryn Mawr, PA 19010. Phone: 610-520-1974. Sr. Maureen O'Malley, Congregational Ldr.; Sr. Helena McNeill, Reg. Ldr.

Founded for the evangelization of people in Africa and Latin America through educational, medical, social, pastoral and catechetical work.

Active in the U.S. in the Archdiocese of Philadelphia.

Active outside the U.S. in England, Ireland, Nigeria, Sierra Leone, Cameroon, Ethiopia, Kenya, Liberia, South Africa, Zambia, Ghana, Mexico and Brazil.

Missionary Sisters of the Immaculate Heart of Mary (1919): 238 E. 15th St.,# 5, New York, NY 10003. Phone: 212-677-2959. Sr. Flotilda

Lape, I.C.M., District Leader.

Please refer to the Religious Institutes of Women section for further details.

Missionary Sisters Servants of the Holy Spirit (1901): Techny, IL 60082-6026. Fax: 847-441-5587. Sr. Carol Welp, S.Sp.S., Prov. Supr.; Sr. Leonette Kaluzny, S.Sp.S., Supr.

Home and foreign missions including teaching, nursing and social work.

Please refer to the Religious Institutes of Women section for activities and representation in the United States.

Also active in Africa, Antigua, Australia, China, Cuba, Europe, India, Indonesia, Japan, Korea, Mexico, New Guinea, Philippine Islands, Russia, South America, and Taiwan.

Publication: SSpS Mission.

Our Lady of Victory Missionary Sisters: *Victory-Noll*, P.O. Box 109, Huntington, IN 46750-0109. Phone: 260-356-0628. Sr. Beatrice Haines, O.L.V.M., Pres.; Sr. Elizabeth Anderson, O.L.V.M., Gen. Sec.

Legal Title: *Our Lady of Victory Missionary Sisters, Inc.*

A Marian congregation proclaiming the Gospel in a personal, non-institutional way through pastoral ministry, religious education, social service and health-care programs in favor of the poor and oppressed.

Please refer to the Religious Institutes of Women section for activities and representation in the United States.

Order of Augustinian Recollects (1943): *Province of St. Augustine*, 29 Ridgeway Ave., West Orange, NJ 07052. Rev. Joseph J. Gallardo, O.A.R., Prior Prov.

Missionary work among Spanish-speaking people in the U.S., including cursillo and retreat ministry in the Archdiocese of New York.

Parish Visitors of Mary Immaculate: *Motherhouse Generalate and Novitiate-Marycrest:* P.O. Box 658, Monroe, NY 10949-0658. Phone: 845-783-2251. Sr. Carole Marie Troskowski, Gen. Supr.; Sr. Maria Catherine, Novice Dir.

Founded for the missionary visitation of families and individuals in the parish and for religious instruction of children and adults; assists parish priests in their ministry of evangelization, catechetical programs, spiritual surveys, census, follow-up religious counseling, religious social services, training laity.

Please refer to the Religious Institutes of Women section for activities and representation in the United States and overseas.

Publication: The Parish Visitor.

Passionist Sisters (1924): *Sisters of the Cross and Passion American Provincialate: Holy Family Convent*, One Wright Lane, North Kingstown, RI 02852. Sr. Theresina Scully, C.P., Province Leader.

Diversified apostolic works according to the needs of the Church; catechetical, pastoral and social work; educational functions; retreats; missionary work in the United States and Africa, Argentina, Australia, Bosnia, Botswana, Chile, England, Europe, Ireland, Jamaica, Papua New Guinea, Peru, Scotland, and Wales.

Please refer to the Religious Institutes of Women section for activities and representation in the United States.

Pontifical Institute for Foreign Missions, P.I.M.E., Inc.: *North American Region:* 17330 Quincy Ave., Detroit, MI 48221. Phone: 313-342-4066; Fax: 313-342-6816. Very Rev. Kenneth Mazur, P.I.M.E., North American Reg. Supr.

Legal Title: *Pontifical Institute for Foreign Missions (P.I.M.E.), Inc.*

The U.S. Region focuses its efforts by being at the service of the Church, both locally and globally. Its members minister in local parishes sharing their missionary vocation. It strives to raise mission awareness, foster vocations and provide financial assistance to PIME's missions and missionaries in developing countries.

Active in the Archdiocese of Detroit and the Dioceses of Columbus, Lansing, Palm Beach, and Paterson.

Outside the U.S.-Bangladesh, Brazil, Cambodia, Cameroon, Guinea-Bissau, Hong Kong/China, India, Ivory Coast, Japan, Mexico, Mayanmar (Burma), Papua New Guinea, Philippines, and Thailand.

Publication: national magazine, PIME World.

St. Joseph's Society of the Sacred Heart (Josephites): *Headquarters:* 1130 North Calvert St., Baltimore, MD 21202. Phone: 410-727-3386; Fax: 410-727-1006; Web: www.josephite-.com. Very Rev. Edward J. Chiffriller, S.S.J., Supr. Gen.

An organization of priests and brothers doing missionary work in the African American community of the United States.

Publication: The Josephite Harvest.

St. Patrick's Missionary Society: 70 Edgewater Rd, P.O Box 3080, Cliffside Park, NJ 07010-4080. Phone: 201-943-6575; Fax: 201-943-2946. Rev. Michael E. Morris, S.P.S., Supr.; Rev. Karl Langsdorf, U.S. Supr.; Rev. Michael Moore, Supr.

A society of secular priests devoted entirely to the missionary needs of the Church.

Activities in the Archdioceses of Newark, and Chicago and the Dioceses of Paterson, and San Jose.

Outside the U.S. in Nigeria-Archdiocese of Lagos, Dioceses of Abakaliki, Calabar, Abuja, Minna, Ogoja, Warri, Port Harcourt and Missio Sui Juris Bomadi. Kenya-Archdiocese of Nairobi, Dioceses of Eldoret, Kitui, Lodwar and Nakuru. Sudan-Diocese of Torit. Malawi-Dioceses of Lilongwe, Chikwawa, Zomba and Mzuzu. Zambia-Archdiocese of Lusaka, Diocese of Chipata. Brazil-Archdioceses of Sao Paulo, Dioceses of Campo Limpo, Osasco, Santo Amaro, Sao Miguel Paulista and Campina Grande. Grenada-Diocese of St. George's. South Africa-Dioceses of Tzaneen and Witbank. Zimbabwe-Archdiocese of Harare and Diocese of Mutare. Cameroon-Archdiocese of Bamenda.

Publication: Africa, St. Patrick's Mission.

Salesian Missions: 2 Lefevre Ln., New Rochelle, NY 10801. Phone: 914-633-8344.

The Salesians were founded to help bring the Faith to all people, and contribute to their social and economic development through education, especially in trade and agricultural schools. The purpose of the society is the recruitment and preparation of vocations for the missions and the education of the American public on the needs of other people through lectures, mass media, direct mail and the magazine, Salesian. It is also the purpose of the society to educate the American public on the unique system of education developed by the society's founder, St. John Bosco, as well as to spread knowledge of his life and accomplishments. Funds are raised to implement the religious, educational and technical assistance projects of the society.

Please refer to the Religious Institutes of Men section for activities and representation in the United States. Represented in over 130 countries throughout the world.

Publication: Salesian.

School Sisters of Notre Dame: *Milwaukee Province:* 13105 Watertown Plank Rd., Elm Grove, WI 53122-2291. Phone: 262-782-9850; Fax: 262-782-5725. Sr. Debra Marie Sciano, S.S.N.D., Prov. Leader.

Please refer to the Religious Institutes of Women section I.D.# [2970] for provinces, activities and representations in the United States and overseas.

Sisters of the Blessed Sacrament for Indians and Colored People (1891): *Sisters of the Blessed Sacrament:* Bensalem, PA 19020-5796. Phone: 215-244-9900; Fax: 215-244-8174. Sr. Patricia Suchalski, Pres.

Missionary work in the educational, catechetical and social services among Black and Native Americans in the U.S. and Haiti.

Please refer to the Religious Institutes of Women section for activities and representation in the United States.

Publication: Mission.

Society of African Missions: *SMA Fathers American Province*, 23 Bliss Ave., Tenafly, NJ 07670. Phone: 201-567-9085; Phone: 201-567-0450; Fax: 800-670-8328; Fax: 201-541-1280. Very Rev. Michael P. Moran, S.M.A., Prov.

Please refer to the Religious Institutes of Men section for activities and representation in the United States.

Active also in: Liberia-Diocese of Cape Palmas, Archdiocese of Monrovia, Diocese of Gbarnga; Ivory Coast-Archdiocese of Abidjan; Dioceses of Abengourou, Bondoukou, Bouake, Daloa, Gagnoa, Katiola, Grand-Bassam, Korhogo, Odienne, Man, San Pedro, Yamoussoukro, and Yopougon; Ghana-Archdiocese of Cape Coast; Dioceses of Accra, Konongo-Mampong, Keta-Akatsi, Kumasi, Sekondi-Takoradi, Obuasi; Togo-Archdiocese of Lome; Dioceses of Kara, and Sokode; Benin-Archdiocese of Cotonou & Parakou; Dioceses of Abomey, Kandi, Djougou, Natitingou, Dassa-Zoume and Porto-Novo; Nigeria-Archdioceses of Kaduna, Abuja (Benin City) Jos, Lagos, Ibadan; Dioceses of Abeokuha, Bauchi, Ilorin, Issele-Uku, Kafanchan, Kano, Kontagor, Makurdi, Ondo and Warri; Niger-Diocese of Niamey; Central African Republic-Archdiocese of Bangui; Dioceses of Berberati. Zambia-Archdiocese of Lusaka, Dioceses of Ndola, Solwezi. Egypt-Vicarate Apostolic of Alexandria Morocco-Rabat; Congo-Kinshasa, Kikwit. Tanzania-Dioceses of Mwanza and Shinyanga. Kenya-Archdiocese of Nairobi; Diocese of Ngong & Lodwar. Argentina-Archdiocese of Cordoba. Australia-Archdiocese of Perth. South Africa-Diocese of Rustenburg, Archdiocese of Pretoria. Philippines-Archdiocese of Manila. South India: Tamilnadu. Poland-Warsaw.

Society of Mary: *Marianist Province of the United States (Society of Mary):* 4425 W. Pine Blvd., Saint Louis, MO 63108. Phone: 314-533-1207; Fax: 314-533-0778. Bro. Stephen Glodek, S.M., Prov.

Educational, parish, and development work in the following territories: (Puerto Rico) Archdiocese of San Juan, Puerto Rico; (Placements in Africa) Nairobi, Kenya; Kitale, Kenya; Limuru, Kenya; Mombassa, Kenya; Karonga, Malawi; Lusaka, Zambia; (Placements in India) Ranchi, India; Bangalore, India; Patna, India; Orissa, India; (Nepal) East Nepal, Nepal; (Placements in Mexico) Coatzacoalcos, Mexico; Queretaro, Mexico; Puebla, Mexico; La Chinantla, Mexico; (Bangladesh) Dhaka, Bangladesh; (Central America) Guatemala; (South America); Davao City (The Philippines); Japan.

Society of St. Edmund: *Edmundite Generalate:* 270 Winooski Park, Colchester, VT 05439. Phone: 802-654-3400; Fax: 802-654-3409. Very Rev. Michael P. Cronogue, S.S.E., Supr. Gen.

Legal Title: *Society of St. Edmund, Inc.*

Major missionary endeavors in the United States are in Selma, Alabama and surrounding areas, and in the inner city of New Orleans (LA).

See the Foreign Mission section for the list of priests serving abroad.

Publications: Edmundite Missions.

Society of the Precious Blood: *Cincinnati Province:* 431 E. Second St., Dayton, OH 45402. Fax: 937-228-6878. Very Rev. Angelo Anthony, C.PP.S., Prov. Dir.; Rev. Larry Hemmelgarn, C.PP.S, Prov. Sec. & Mission Coord.; Bro. Joseph J. Fisher, C.PP.S., Mission Procurator.

Priests, brothers and deacons in foreign missions: 35.

Mission activities outside the U.S. in Chile, Peru, Bogota, Colombia, South America, Guatemala, Central America; Missions in La Tinta, Tucuru, Santiago, Purranque, Valdivia, LaOroya, Lima, Guatemala City, La Labor.

Publication: C.PP.S. Today.

Sons of Mary Missionary Society (1952): 567 Salem End Rd., Framingham, MA 01702-5599. Phone: 508-879-2541; Email: sonsboston@verizon.net; Web: www.sonsofmary-.com. Rev. John Murphy, F.M.S.I., Coord.; Bro. Kevin Courtney, F.M.S.I., Finance Coord.; Rev. John Coss, F.M.S.I., Councilor.

Legal Title: *Sons of Mary, Health of the Sick, Inc.*

Dedicated to the ministry of healing: medical, catechetical and social apostolates in the home and foreign missions.

Third Order Regular of St. Francis: *Province of the Most Sacred Heart of Jesus: Franciscan T.O.R. Missions*, P.O. Box 188, Loretto, PA 15940. Phone: 814-472-3348. Bro. Mark McBride, T.O.R., Prov. Dir. of Foreign Missions; Very Rev. Christian R. Oravec, T.O.R., Minister Prov-.Phone: 814-693-2890.

Secures missionaries and material aid to missions.

Active in the Archdioceses of Manaus and Sao Paulo; the Prelacy of Borba, Brazil; the Diocese of Bhagalpur, Bihar, India; and Diocese of Vice Province of Saint Joseph, Republic of South Africa.

Xaverian Missionary Fathers: *Provincial Headquarters:* 12 Helene Ct., Wayne, NJ 07470-2813. Phone: 973-942-2975; Fax: 973-942-5012. Very Rev. Carl S. Chudy, S.X.

A religious society of priests and brothers dedicated exclusively to foreign mission work and the training of candidates for missionary life.

Active in Brazil, Democratic Republic of Congo, Burundi, Chad, Cameroon, Bangladesh, Indonesia, Japan, Mexico, Sierra Leone, Colombia, Philippines, Mozambique, Taiwan, Italy, Spain, Great Britain and the United States of America.

Please refer to the Religious Institutes of Men section for activities and representation in the United States.

Publication: Xaverian Mission Newsletter.

Pontifical Mission Societies

A. The Pontifical Society for the Propagation of the Faith (1822): *National Office:* 70 W. 36th St., 8th Fl., New York, NY 10018. Phone: 212-563-8700; Fax: 212-563-8725; Email: pmsusa@propfaith.org; Web: www.onefamilyinmission.org. Rev. Msgr. John E. Kozar, Natl. Dir. & Pres.; Rev. Msgr. James A. Moloney, Vice. Pres.; Rev. Robert F. Sharman, Treas.; Rev. Msgr. Richard L. Tofani, Asst. Treas.; Rev. Msgr. Francis X. Blood, Sec.; Mr. Raymond Schroeck, Asst. Sec.

International Officers: His Eminence Ivan Dias, Prefect of the Congregation for Evangelization of Peoples; Rev. Timothy Lehane, S.V.D., Sec. Gen., Vatican City.

The Propagation of the Faith, under the direction of the Congregation for the Evangelization of Peoples, is established in every country where the Church is free to operate; it has a two-fold goal of promoting a universal missionary spirit and encouraging prayer and financial support for the local churches of the missions.

Each diocese in the United States has a director appointed by the Ordinary to promote the work of the Society through programs such as World Mission Sunday (the next-to-last Sunday in October) and Membership, presentations in seminaries, lesson plans and materials for mission animation in schools (grades 9-12) and parishes, news media and personal contact with parishes and diocesan organizations.

Offerings received by the Propagation of the Faith in the United States are joined with offerings from all other countries and distributed annually to more than 1,150 mission Dioceses and Vicariates.

Publication: Mission, Rev. Msgr. John E. Kozar, Publisher.

B. The Society of St. Peter Apostle (1889): *National Office:* 70 W. 26th St., 8th Fl., New York, NY 10018. Phone: 212-563-8700. Rev. Msgr. John E. Kozar, Natl. Dir. & Pres.; Rev. Msgr. Jan Dumon, Sec. Gen.

International Officers: His Eminence Ivan Dias, Prefect of the Congregation for Evangelization of Peoples; Rev. Msgr. Jan Dumon, Sec. Gen., Vatican City.

The Society of St. Peter Apostle, under the direction of the Congregation for the Evangelization of Peoples, is established for the support of seminarians and novices in the missions. During 2008, there were 26,792 major seminarians 50,315 minor seminarians and 9,099 novices receiving assistance from the Society of St. Peter Apostle. The Society also helps support local religious communities and retired native clergy. Each diocese in the United States has a local director who is also the Director of the Propagation of the Faith.

C. The Pontifical Missionary Union (1916): *National Office:* 70 W. 26th St., 8th Fl., New York, NY 10018. Phone: 212-563-8700. Rev. Msgr. John E. Kozar, Natl. Dir. & Pres.

International Officers: His Eminence Ivan Dias, Prefect of the Congregation for Evangelization of Peoples; Rev. Vito Del Prete, P.I.M.E., Sec. Gen., Vatican City.

The Missionary Union, under the direction of the Congregation for the Evangelization of Peoples, is established to inspire, deepen and sustain a mission spirit among priests, deacons, religious, seminarians, candidates for the religious life and others in the pastoral ministry of the Church. The director in each diocese is also the Director of the Propagation of the Faith.

D. Holy Childhood Association: *National Office:* 70 W. 36th St., 8th Fl., New York, NY 10018. Phone: 212-563-8700; Fax: 212-994-8569. Rev. Msgr. John E. Kozar, Natl. Dir. & Pres.

International Officers: His Eminence Ivan Dias, Prefect of the Congregation for Evangelization of Peoples.

The Holy Childhood Association (HCA) is one of four Pontifical Mission Societies active in some 110 countries throughout the world. Founded in France in 1843 by Bishop Charles de Forbin-Janson, HCA helps to animate the young faithful to a universal missionary spirit and to gather support from these children for the service of the local churches of Africa, Asia, remote regions of Latin America and the Pacific Islands among the poorest of the world's children.

Annually, more than two million young people, kindergarten through eighth grade, participate in HCA-sponsored programs in the United States through Catholic schools and parish religious education programs.

HCA is unique to other organizations that assist children in the Developing World in that its primary aim is to encourage children to share their faith with children in the Developing World through their prayers, personal sacrifices and financial offerings.

Contributions to HCA are allocated to mission dioceses throughout the world according to need. This system of allocating funds helps ensure that aid is distributed fairly and that those who are most desperately in need receive enough support. HCA funds are distributed to help children in 110 countries throughout the world.

More than 80% of HCA's annual funding in the United States is used for the Church's service among children in the Developing World and to provide mission education materials to children in the United States.

Parents, guardians, parish priests, religious brothers and sisters and lay people, especially teachers and catechists, play a vital role in HCA's mission. With support from these people, children can learn about children in other countries through HCA programs and learn too the message of HCA-that children are and can be missionaries today, called to share their faith and their love, in prayer and sacrifice, with the poorest of the world's children. In addition, financial contributions from adults help to underwrite the cost of education materials for children in the United States and also help support the Church's service to children in the Developing World.

Committee on the Home Missions: *U.S. Conference of Catholic Bishops*, 3211 Fourth St. N.E., Washington, DC 20017. Phone: 202-541-3011; Phone: 202-541-5400; Fax: 202-722-8752; Fax: 202-541-3473. Most Rev. Michael William Warfel, Chm.; Dr. David J. Suley, Dir.; Mr. Ken Q. Ong, Grants Specialist.

A Subcommittee of the U.S. Conference of Catholic Bishops dedicated to support of the home missions. Catholic Home Missions (CHM) makes grants to extend the Church's presence as a means of salvation and to strengthen the Church's presence in rural, remote, and poor areas within the United States. Grantees include dioceses, religious institutes, and national, regional, and interdiocesan Catholic organizations in the United States and its island territories. The CHM funds a wide range of mission and evangelization activities; examples include parish support, seminary formation, lay ministry training, religious education, and ministry with culturally diverse groups. Application materials are available January 1 of each year; the deadline for submission of completed applications is April 1. The CHM makes grant decisions once a year in September, and grants are disbursed in quarterly payments January through October. The CHM's funds come from the annual Catholic Home Missions Appeal.

Publication: quarterly newsletter, Neighbors Subheading - No data found in Sub Instituion: 329800-American Conventual Franciscan Missions

Refer to the American Foreign Mission section of the Directory and the Religious Institutes of Men section I.D. #[0480] for detailed information on provinces and activities.

Bureau of Catholic Indian Missions (1874): 2021 H St., N.W., Washington, DC 20006-4207. Phone: 202-331-8542; Fax: 202-331-8544. Board of Directors:, His Eminence Justin Cardinal Rigali, Pres.; Most Rev. Edwin F. O'Brien; Most Rev. Timothy M. Dolan; Rev. Wayne C. Paysse, Exec. Dir.; Patricia L. O'Rourke, Asst. Sec. & Treas.

Collecting and distribution of funds for the support of American Indian missions. The Bureau represents the missions in Government relations, specifically in Washington, DC.

Active throughout the United States, where American Indian, Eskimo and Aleute missions are present.

Office of Vice Postulator for the Cause of Blessed Kateri Tekakwitha Rev Msgr. Paul A. Lenz, P.A., Vice Postulator. Promotes cause for canonization of Blessed Kateria Tekakwitha.

Publications: bi-monthly newsletter; monthly Kateri Circle Agenda.

Catholic Missionary Union: 86-11 Midland Pkwy., Jamaica, NY 11432. Phone: 973-868-0461. His Eminence Edward Cardinal Egan, Pres.; Rev. John J. Foley, C.S.P., Sec. & Treas.

The corporation subsidizes Evangelization activities.

Catholic Church Extension Society of the United States of America, The (1905): 150 S. Wacker Dr.-20th Flr., Chicago, IL 60606-4200. Phone: 800-842-7804; Fax: 312-236-5276; Web: www.catholicextension.org. His Eminence Francis E. George, O.M.I., Chancellor; Rev. John J. Wall, Pres.; Mr. Thomas E. Gordon, COO; Ms. Julie Turley, Vice Pres. Devel.; Mr. Kevin P. McGowan, CFO.

Catholic Extension is a Papal society with a mission to strengthen the Church's presence and mission in under-resourced and isolated communities across the United States. Catholic Extension raises money through charitable contributions, gift annuities, trusts, and will bequests to support missionary work in America.

Requests for funds are submitted by bishops in designated American mission dioceses. Funding is for religious purposes: contruction of chapels and other mission buildings; salary subsidies for priests, religious, and lay people working for missions; seminarian education; campus ministry; pastoral and social ministry; emergency and disaster relief; chapel furnishings; evangelization, and religious education, including sponsorship of parish calendars.

Publications: EXTENSION Magazine; Catholic Extension Parish Calendars.

Catholic Near East Welfare Association (1926): 1011 First Ave., New York, NY 10022. Most Rev. Timothy M. Dolan, Pres. & Treas.; His Eminence Marc Quellet, P.S.S., Vice Pres.; Rev. Msgr. Robert L. Stern, Sec. Gen.

A papal agency for humanitarian and pastoral support established by Pope Pius XI in 1926. It promotes awareness of the condition and the needs of the churches, institutions and persons under the jurisdiction of the Congregation for the Eastern Churches and the Permanent Interdiscasterial Commission for the Church on Eastern Europe. It raises and distributes funds to help meet the material and spiritual needs of the people it serves.

The Association works for people in those lands in which from ancient times the majority of Christians have been members of the various Eastern churches. Its mandate extends to the churches and peoples of the Middle East, Northeast Africa, India and Eastern Europe. It encourages and provides assistance to projects and programs of pastoral support, humanitarian assistance, interfaith communication and public awareness.

Publication: ONE magazine

Catholic Negro American Mission Board: 2021 H St., N.W., Washington, DC 20006-4207. Phone: 202-331-8542; Fax: 202-331-8544. Board of Directors:, His Eminence Justin Cardinal Rigali, Pres.; Most Rev. Edwin F. O'Brien, Pres.; Most Rev. Timothy M. Dolan; Rev. Wayne C. Paysse, Exec. Dir.; Patricia L. O'Rourke, Asst. Sec./ Treas.

Engaged in the support of priests and sisters throughout the states below Mason and Dixon Line, especially support in poor black schools.

Active in the United States, particularly all states in the South.

Commissariat of the Holy Land: 3140 Meramec St., Saint Louis, MO 63118-4339. Phone: 314-353-7729; Fax: 314-655-0563. Bro. Joseph Rogenski, O.F.M., Commissary.

Established for collecting and distributing funds for the support of the sacred places in the Holy Land. Regional Commissariat for the Ecclesiastical Provinces of Chicago, Cincinnati, Detroit, Dubuque, Indianapolis, Kansas City, Louisville, Milwaukee, Mobile, New Orleans, Oklahoma City, Omaha, St. Louis, St. Paul-Minneapolis and San Antonio.

Commissariat of the Holy Land: P.O. Box 127, Malibu, CA 90265. Rev. Warren J. Rouse, O.F.M., Commissary Email: frwarren@serraretreat.com.

Established to collect and distribute funds for

support of the Sacred Shrines and educational and charitable institutions in the Holy Land. Assigned Territory: Ecclesiastical Provinces of Denver, Los Angeles, Portland (OR), San Francisco, Santa Fe and Seattle.

Commission for Catholic Missions Among the Colored People and the Indians (Black and Indian Mission Office) (1884): 2021 H St., N.W., Washington, DC 20006-4207. Phone: 202-331-8542; Fax: 202-331-8544. Board of Directors:, His Eminence Justin Cardinal Rigali, Pres.; Most Rev. Edwin F. O'Brien; Most Rev. Timothy M. Dolan; Rev. Wayne C. Paysse, Exec. Dir.; Patricia L. O'Rourke, Asst. Sec./Treas.

Organized by the Third Plenary Council as trustee of the funds collected in the churches for support of Black, Indian, Eskimo and Aleute evangelization programs in the United States. Grant applications are sent to Ordinaries each year and grant disbursements made in January and June.

Publication: annual, Annual Report.

Commissariat of the Holy Land: *Franciscan Monastery:* 1400 Quincy St. N.E., Washington, DC 20017. Phone: 202-526-6800 ext 887; Fax: 202-529-9850; Email: commissarywdcusa@myfranciscan.com; Email: secretariatusa@myfranciscan.com; Web: www.myfranciscan.com. Rev. Jeremy Harrington, O.F.M., Commissary; Rev. Garrett Edmunds, O.F.M., Vice Commissary; Friar John-Sebastian Laird-Hammond, O.F.M., Secretariat to the Commissariat.

Administering the "Pontifical Good Friday Collection" in the United States; to promote vocations for the Holy Land Missions; to bring to light the needs of the people, especially the Christian Community in the Holy Land, and to address those needs.

Dominican Mission Secretariate: 141 E. 65th St., New York, NY 10021-6607. Phone: 212-861-3776; Fax: 212-639-9823. Very Rev. Joseph P. Allen, O.P., Dir.

Legal Title: *St. Jude Dominican Foreign Missions, Inc. (formerly Rosary Foreign Mission Society, Inc.).*

Founded by the Order of Preachers (Dominican Friars), Province of St. Joseph for the purpose of promoting American Dominican activity in the foreign missions throughout the world. Presently the Mission Office aids and supports work in the Archdioceses of Karachi and Lahore, the Dioceses of Multan, Faisalabad and Islamabad-Rawalpindi in Pakistan. The Archdioceses of Nairobi and Kisumu in Kenya; Calayan Island, Philippines, and the Solomon Islands.

Assumption B.V.M. Province: *Holy Dormition Friary,* P.O. Box 270, Sybertsville, PA 18251. Fax: 570-788-2431. Rev. Jerome J. Wolbert, O.F.M.; Rev. Anthony Skurla, O.F.M.; Rev. Paul Guthrie, O.F.M.; Rev. Laurian Janicki, O.F.M., Guardian; Bro. Augustine Paulik, O.F.M.

Preparing missionaries to work among the people in the Byzantine Church.

General Secretariat of the Franciscan Missions, Inc.: P.O. Box 130, Waterford, WI 53185. Phone: 262-534-5470; Fax: 262-534-4342; Email: framis@wi.net; Web: www.franciscanmissions.org. Rev. Sereno Baiardi, O.F.M., Dir.; Rev. Sante De Angelis, O.F.M., Assoc. Dir.; Rev. Ponciano Macabalo, O.F.M.

General American office for assistance to Franciscan Missions under the auspices of the General Minister of the Order of Friars Minor.

Catholic Network Of Volunteer Service: 6930 Carroll Ave., Ste. 820, Takoma Park, MD 20912-4423. Phone: 301-270-0900; Fax: 301-270-0901. Most Rev. Oscar A. Solis, Episcopal Advisor; James G. Lindsay, Exec. Dir.

Catholic Network of Volunteer Service promotes, recruits and refers volunteers to missions in the United States and overseas. We represent nearly 200 faith-based volunteer programs worldwide and work with the U.S. Dioceses, religious communities and the private sector to determine their needs for help. Catholic Network of Volunteer Service (CNVS) is committed to the goal that every Catholic man and woman be invited to consider a period of service in the missions, as a vital and important manifestation of the baptismal call of all Catholic people. Currently, over 13,000 men and women are serving in CNVS member mission programs offering their gifts and abilities in full-time service to people in need and living their Catholic faith more fully. These volunteers are serving domestically for a summer, six months, a year or more, and they are serving internationally for two or more years at a time. They are single and married, recent college graduates and early retirees, doctors and teachers, parish ministers and social workers, community organizers, computer programmers, legal aides and more.

Gatherings: Annual Conference; Formation Workshops, Training Seminars.

Awards: The Father George Mader Award, given annually to honor organizations and individuals who promote the value of lay mission service. The Bishop Joseph A. Francis Award to honor organizations and individuals who promote community service.

Publications: annual, Response: Directory of Volunteer Opportunities; monthly, How Can I Help?; quarterly, FaithWorks.

Missionary Association of Catholic Women (1916): *National Office:* 1501 S. Layton Blvd., Box 3087, Milwaukee, WI 53203-3087. Phone: 414-758-2281; Email: wmo@archmil.org. Sr. Frances P. Cunningham, O.S.F., Contact Person.

Association providing material and financial aid to home and foreign missions.

MIVA-America Missionary Vehicle Association Inc.: *National Office:* 1400 Michigan Ave., N.E., Washington, DC 20017. Phone: 202-635-3444; Fax: 202-526-0830; Web: www.miva.org. Rev. Philip DeRea, M.S.C., Natl. Dir.; Larry Nigh, Office Admin.; Michele Marth, M.S.C., Appeal Coord.

The Missionary Vehicle Association (MIVA America) is a nonprofit organization whose sole purpose is to raise money to fund the purchase of reliable transportation for American missionaries working around the world. Without dependable transportation, missionaries are often unable to reach the people that most need their help. MIVA America's funds allow American Missionaries to purchase cars, trucks, jeeps, bicycles, motorcycles, boats, buses and ambulances.

Oblates of St. Francis de Sales (O.S.F.S.) (1906): *Wilmington-Philadelphia Province:* 2200 Kentmere Pkwy., Wilmington, DE 19806. Phone: 302-656-8529; Fax: 302-658-8052. Very Rev. James J. Greenfield, O.S.F.S., Prov.; Rev. David Whalen, O.S.F.S., Prov. & American Mission Dir.

Missionary work in Republic of South Africa, Diocese of Keimeos; Nambia, Diocese of Keetmamshoop; South America—Uruguay, Archdiocese of Montevideo; Brazil, Archdioceses of Rio de Janeiro and Porto Alegre (Rio Grande de Sol), Dioceses of Bage (RGS), Cruz Alta (RGS), Frederico Westphalen (RGS), and Senhor do Bofim (Bahia); India, Archdiocese of Bangalore (province of Karnataka); Haiti—Diocese of Les Gonaives; Mexico—Archdiocese of Merida.

Please refer to the Religious Institutes of Men section for activities and representation in the United States.

Provinces outside the United States: France, German-speaking, Italy, Netherlands, South America.

Pontifical Mission for Palestine (1949): 1011 First Ave., New York, NY 10022. Phone: 212-826-1480. Rev. Msgr. Robert L. Stern, Pres.; Mr. Emanuele Latini, Admin.-Vatican Office; Mr. Issam Bishara, Dir.-Beirut Office; Mr. Sami El-Yousef, Dir.-Jerusalem Office; Mr. Ra'ed Bahou, Dir.-Amman Office.

A papal agency for humanitarian and charitable assistance established by Pope Pius XII in 1949. Its mission is to assist, without regard to nationality or religion, all who suffer as a result of the repeated conflicts that have devastated Palestine and neighboring regions of the Middle East.

It encourages and supports projects and programs of relief, rehabilitation, development; collaboration with other agencies; and education.

St. Paul's Guild, Inc.: 1011 First Ave., Rm. 1940, New York, NY 10022.

Formerly National Catholic Converts' League, now interested in assisting former Protestant clergymen and former Protestant religious.

Tekakwitha Conference (1939): *National Center,* P.O. Box 6768, Great Falls, MT 59406. Phone: 406-727-0147; Phone: 800-842-9635; Fax: 406-452-9845; Email: tekconf@gmail.com; Web: www.tekconf.org.

Nonprofit organization established for evangelization within the Catholic Church with American Indians, Eskimos and missionaries working together at a national level to develop a Native American identity voice and presence in the Catholic Church. Catechesis, liturgy, youth ministry, inculturation and related areas within the Catholic Church are goals of the Conference.

Publication: 4 issues annually, Cross & Feathers.

Catholic Medical Mission Board, Inc. (1928): 10 W. 17th St., New York, NY 10011-5765. Members of the Board:, Rev. Msgr. Ferdinando D. Berardi; Rev. William J. Scanlan, S.J.; John A. Donnelly; Sr. Marilyn Fischer, S.F.P.; Rev. Msgr. Robert J. Fuhrman; Dr. Thomas G. Flynn; Dr. Patricia Smith; Mr. Thomas P. Melady; Most Rev. William Skylstad; Sr. Peggy Egan, O.S.F.; James A. Cunningham; Terry Kirch; Mr. Charles J. Casamento.

The Catholic Medical Mission Board (CMMB), founded in 1928, provides pharmaceuticals and health care supplies for organizations and clinical facilities that make health care available to the world's needy. In addition to its schedule of shipments, CMMB responds to health care emergencies. In 1999, over $43 million in medicines and related supplies were shipped to clinical faciltites in 52 countries. Financial aid is also granted to students in accredited health care training programs. CMMB's Medical Volunteer Program places health providers interested in volunteering for short-term and long-term tours of service at selected clinical sites around the world. Catholic Medical Mission Board publishes "Medical Mission News," a quarterly journal magazine which provides in-depth information on its programs.

United States Conference of Secular Institutes

U.S.C.S.I. Attn: Rev. George F. Hazler, Pres. 2104 Eagle Pointe, Bloomfield Hills, MI 48304. Members of the U.S.C.S.I. are Secular Institutes of Diocesan or Pontifical Right, canonically erected since 1947, following the promulgation of the Apostolic Constitution, "Provida Mater Ecclesia," by Pope Pius XII. The Institutes are listed on this page by the Congregation for the Institutes of Consecrated Life and for Societies of Apostolic Life. The purpose of the U.S.C.S.I., canonically erected by the Congregation as of its 1976 statutes, is to offer the Institutes an opportunity to exchange experiences, conduct research, and promote ways to make the vocation and Institutes known.

Company of St. Paul (Lay People and Priests): 52 Davis Ave., White Plains, NY 10605. Rev. Stuart Sandberg, Contact Person.
Founded in Milan, Italy November 17, 1920, under the auspices of Cardinal Andrew Ferrari; approved as a Secular Institute of Pontifical Right on June 30, 1950.
Aim: The practices of evangelical counsels is the expression of consecration to God. Professional work becomes the main means of the apostolate.

Diocesan Laborer Priests: 3706 15th St., N.E., Washington, DC 20017. Phone: 202-832-4217 Fax: 202-526-5692 Rev. Juan A. Puigbo, Delegate.
A Secular Institute of Pontifical Right founded in Spain in 1883.
The aim of the Institute is the promotion, sustenance and cultivation of apostolic, religious and priestly vocations.

Don Bosco Volunteers: P.O. Box 588, Hawthorne, NJ 07507-0588. Cathy Sylvester, Contact Person.
Founded as a Secular Institute for Women by Blessed Philip Rinaldi, S.D.B., in Turin, Italy in 1917.
Approved as an Institute of Pontifical Right in 1978. Existing in 35 countries, with over 1,200 members.
Aim: to live in the spirit of St. John Bosco, in a wide variety of apostolates in one's own environment, and in the service of the local church, particularly on behalf of youth. An Institute for Men was founded in Rome in November, 1994. For information, see address above.

Missionaries of the Kingship of Christ: P.O. Box 34513, West Bethesda, MD 20827. Phone: 301-990-8630
Under this title are included two distinct and juridically separate institutes following the spirituality of St. Francis of Assisi.

Women Missionaries of the Kingship of Christ:
Founded in Italy in 1919 and approved as an Institute of Pontifical Right in 1948. Existing in thirty-two countries, the American branch began in 1950 and has spread to 25 states. Through a consecrated life in the world they give witness to Gospel values in work, family, church, civic and social environments by living the spirit of St. Francis and the beatitudes.
Rev. Gene B. Pistacchio, O.F.M., Ecclesiastical Asst.

Men Missionaries of the Kingship of Christ:
Founded in Italy in 1928 and approved as an institute of Pontifical Right in 1998. It was established in the United States in 1962. Their purpose is spreading the social reign of Christ through individual professions and occupations.

Oblate Missionaries of Mary Immaculate: 56 Brookfield St., Lawrence, MA 01843. Women: P.O. Box 764, Lowell, MA 01853.
Founded in Canada on July 2, 1952. Approved of Pontifical Right March 24, 1984.
International Membership: The members profess the evangelical counsels. Unique spirituality based on five attitudes of life: presence of God, absence of criticism and complaints, service and Charism.
Aim: A constant availability to the will of the Father to live everywhere the charity of Christ, through service, with the help of Mary.

Opus Spiritus Sancti: 301 E. 4th St., Auburn, IA 51433. Phone: 712-688-2253 Rev. James D. McCormick, Regional Coord. Phone: 712-688-2253
Founded in Mammolshain-Koenigstein, Germany in 1950.
Approved as a Secular Institute of Diocesan Right on Dec. 8, 1959.
Aim: The general end is the perfection of its members. The members strive to achieve this aim through the effective practice in the world of the three evangelical counsels of perfection, and by making the promise to dedicate themselves totally to the particular apostolate of the Institute. The Institute also admits married or unmarried men as associate members.

Secular Institute of Schoenstatt Fathers: W284 N746 Cherry Ln., Waukesha, WI 53188. Rev. Christian Christensen, Supr.
Founded by Father Joseph Kentenich in 1965, approved as a Secular Institute of Pontifical Right, June 24, 1988.
Aim: To aid the moral and religious renewal of society and the realization of the post-Vatican II mission of the Church, especially through priestly service to the International Schoenstatt Movement. In 2009, 315 ordained members in 25 nations worldwide.

Secular Institute of Schoenstatt Sisters of Mary (Women): W284 N404 Cherry Ln., Waukesha, WI 53188-9416. Phone: 262-522-4200 Fax: 262-522-4201 Email: schoenstattsisters@schsrsmary.org
Founded in Germany in 1926 by Father Joseph Kentenich; approved as a Secular Institute of Pontifical Right in 1948.
Aim: The moral and religious renewal of society. The members practice a Marian lay asceticism as a means of growing in love for God, and consecrating the world to Him. They are active within the Schoenstatt Movement and in a wide variety of professional spheres.

Servitum Christi (Women): Mailing Address: 1209 Greenwood Ave., Pueblo, CO 81003. 184 E. 76th St., New York, NY 10021. Elaine Kozlowski, Contact Person.
Founded Origin inspired by St. Peter Julian Eymard (1868), founder of the Congregation of the Blessed Sacrament. Founded in Holland, 1952; approved as a Secular Institute of Diocesan Right May 8, 1963.
Aim: To live the mystery of the Eucharist fully as consecrated lay persons and to make known its meaning so that the reign of Christ may come and the glory of God be revealed to the world.

Society of Our Lady of the Way: 2339 N. Catalina St., Los Angeles, CA 90027.
Additional members in Cleveland, OH; Daly City & Simi Valley, CA; Bridgeport, CT; Green Bay, WI; Jersey City, NJ; New Orleans, LA; Vancouver, B.C., Canada; Tokyo, Japan.
Founded in Vienna, Austria in 1936; approved as a Secular Institute of Pontifical Right in 1953. To Christianize the secular order members are consecrated to God through the vows of chastity, obdience and poverty. They pursue individual apostolates, seeking to manifest Christ in all the circumstances of their life and work. Spirituality is Marian and Ignatian.

Voluntas Dei Institute (1958): 2104 Eagle Pointe, Bloomfield Hills, MI 48304. Email: Director@voluntasdeiusa.org Rev. George F. Hazler, Contact Person.
Approved as a Secular Institute of Pontifical Right in 1987.
The Institute assembles together within a common apostolic project both clerics and celibate laymen. The Institute directs its members to discover the will of God, adhere to it and cherish it through the profession of the vows of poverty, chastity and obedience. The Institute also includes married couples as Associate Members. These commit themselves to live according to their state in life the same ideal and apostolic project as the clerics and celibate laymen, through committment to living poverty, chastity and apostolic obedience. Members of the Institute regularly gather as a team which is the place for listening to the Word and discerning the Will of God.

Alphabetical Listing of Mission Churches in the United States

A

Aasu/Aoloau, AS, c/o Pago Pago, AS, St. Paul. (SPP)
Abbeville, LA, St. James, c/o Erath, LA, St. John. (LAF)
Abernathy, TX, Hale Co., St. Isidore, c/o Petersburg, TX, Sacred Heart. (LUB)
Abeytas, NM, Socorro Co., San Antonio, c/o La Joya, NM, Our Lady of Sorrows. (SFE)
Abie, NE, Butler Co., SS. Peter and Paul, c/o Bruno, NE, St. Anthony. (LIN)
Abilene, TX, Sacred Heart Perpetual Adoration Chapel, c/o Abilene, TX, Sacred Heart. (SAN)
Abingdon, MD, Harford Co., St. Francis, c/o Baltimore, MD, Patronage of the Mother of God. (PSC)
Abo, NM, Torrance Co., c/o Mountainair, NM, St. Alice. (SFE)
Abram, TX, Hidalgo Co., St. Mary Magdalene, c/o La Joya, TX, Our Lady, Queen of Angels. (BWN)
Absarokee, MT, Stillwater Co., St. Michael, c/o Columbus, MT, St. Mary. (GF)
Absecon, NJ, St. Andrew Kim Korean Catholic Mission, Inc., c/o Absecon, NJ, Church of Saint Elizabeth Ann Seton, Absecon, N.J. (CAM)
Absarokee, MT, Stillwater Co., St. Michael, c/o Columbus, MT, St. Mary. (GF)
Acomita, NM, Cibola Co., St. Anne, c/o Pueblo of Acoma, NM, San Esteban, Acoma Catholic Indian Mission. (GLP)
Adel, GA, Cook Co., St. Margaret Mary, c/o Adel, GA, Queen of Peace. (SAV)
Adel, OR, Lake Co., St. Richard, c/o Lakeview, OR, St. Patrick. (BAK)
Adona, AR, Conway Co., St. Elizabeth, c/o Bigelow, AR, St. Boniface. (LR)
Afono, AS, c/o Pago Pago, AS, Church of the Immaculate Conception. (SPP)
Afton, NY, Chenango Co., St. Agnes, c/o Bainbridge, NY, St. John the Evangelist. (SY)
Afton, WY, Lincoln Co., Holy Family, c/o Jackson, WY, Our Lady of the Mountains. (CHY)
Aguila, AZ, Maricopa Co., Our Lady of Guadalupe, c/o Wickenburg, AZ, St. Anthony of Padua Roman Catholic Parish. (PHX)
Aguirre, PR, Salinas Co., La Milagrosa, c/o Aguirre, PR, Sacred Heart. (PCE)
Alamillo, NM, Socorro Co., c/o Socorro, NM, San Miguel. (SFE)
Alapaha, GA, Berrien Co., St. Ann, c/o Tifton, GA, Our Divine Saviour. (SAV)
Alberton, MT, Mineral Co., St. Albert the Great, c/o Frenchtown, MT, St. John the Baptist. (HEL)
Albertville, AL, Marshall Co., Chapel of the Holy Cross, c/o Guntersville, AL, St. William. (BIR)
Albin, WY, Laramie Co., St. Joseph, c/o Pine Bluffs, WY, St. Paul's. (CHY)
Albion, NY, St. Mary Assumption, c/o Albion, NY, Holy Family. (BUF)
Albuquerque, NM, Bernalillo Co., Morada de San Jose, c/o Albuquerque, NM, St. Anne. (SFE)
Albuquerque, NM, Bernalillo Co., Our Lady of Mount Carmel, c/o Albuquerque, NM, Nativity of the Blessed Virgin Mary. (SFE)
Albuquerque, NM, Bernalillo Co., San Jose de los Duranes, c/o Albuquerque, NM, San Felipe de Neri. (SFE)
Alcalde, NM, Rio Arriba Co., c/o Ohkay Owingeh, NM, St. John the Baptist. (SFE)
Alderson, WV, Greenbrier Co., St. Mary of the Greenbrier, c/o Hinton, WV, St. Patrick. (WH)
Alexandria, NE, Thayer Co., St. Mary's, c/o Fairbury, NE, St. Michael's. (LIN)
Alger, MI, Arenac Co., St. Joseph, c/o Standish, MI, Resurrection of the Lord. (SAG)
Algodones, NM, Sandoval Co., c/o Bernalillo, NM, Our Lady of Sorrows. (SFE)
Aliquippa, PA, Beaver Co., Maronite Mission of Aliquippa, c/o Carnegie, PA, Our Lady of Victory. (SAM)
Allegan, MI, Sacred Heart, c/o Allegan, MI, Blessed Sacrament. (KAL)
Allen, SD, Bennett Co., St. John of the Cross, c/o Pine Ridge, SD, Our Lady of Sorrows. (RC)
Allendale, SC, Barnwell Co., St. Mary, c/o Orangeburg, SC, Holy Trinity. (CHR)
Alpaugh, CA, Tulare Co., Sacred Heart, c/o Corcoran, CA, Our Lady of Lourdes. (FRS)
Alpine, CA, San Diego Co., Nativity of BVM, c/o Lakeside, CA, Blessed Kateri Tekakwitha. (SD)
Alto, TN, Franklin Co., St. Margaret Mary, c/o Decherd, TN, Good Shepherd. (NSH)
Alto, TX, Venerable Antonio Margil, c/o Jacksonville, TX, Our Lady of Sorrows. (TYL)
Altoona, PA, Blair Co., Our Lady of the Assumption, c/o Altoona, PA, Our Lady of Mt. Carmel. (ALT)
Alturas de Campo Rico, PR, Ntra. Sra. del Carmen, c/o Canovanas, PR, San Jose. (FAJ)
Alturas de Mayaguez, PR, El Senor de Los Milagros, c/o Mayaguez, PR, Church De El Buen Pastor. (MGZ)
Alvord, IA, Lyon Co., Sacred Heart, c/o Rock Valley, IA, St. Mary's. (SC)
Amado, AZ, Santa Cruz Co., Assumption Chapel, c/o Tubac, AZ, Saint Ann's Roman Catholic Parish and Missions – Tubac. (TUC)
Amagansett, NY, Suffolk Co., St. Peter the Apostle, c/o East Hampton, NY, Most Holy Trinity. (RVC)
Amalia, NM, Taos Co., c/o Questa, NM, St. Anthony. (SFE)
Ambia, IN, St. Mary's Church, c/o Fowler, IN, Sacred Heart of Jesus. (LFT)
Amelia, NE, Holt Co., St. Joseph, c/o O'Neill, NE, St. Patrick. (OM)
Amherst, NE, Buffalo Co., St. John Capistran, c/o Elm Creek, NE, Immaculate Conception. (GI)
Amouli, AS, c/o Pago Pago, AS, Church of Sacred Heart. (SPP)
Anaheim, CA, Orange Co., Sacred Heart, c/o Anaheim, CA, St. Justin Martyr. (ORG)
Andes, NY, Delaware Co., St. Ann, c/o Margaretville, NY, Sacred Heart. (ALB)
Andover, NH, Merrimack Co., Immaculate Conception, c/o New London, NH, Our Lady of Fatima. (MAN)
Angel Fire, NM, Holy Angels, c/o Cimarron, NM, Immaculate Conception Church. (SFE)
Anguilla, MS, Sharkey Co., Our Mother of Mercy, c/o Leland, MS, St. James. (JKS)
Annapolis, MD, Anne Arundel Co., St. John Neuman, c/o Annapolis, MD, St. Mary. (BAL)
Anones, PR, San Jose, c/o Las Marias, PR, Immaculate Heart of Mary. (MGZ)
Anselmo, NE, Custer Co., St. Anselm's, c/o Broken Bow, NE, St. Joseph's. (GI)
Anton, TX, Hockley, Co., St. Anthony of Padua, c/o Shallowater, TX, St. Philip Benizi. (LUB)
Antonito, CO, St. Augustine, c/o Antonito, CO, Our Lady of Guadalupe. (PBL)
Antwerp, NY, Jefferson Co., St. Michael, c/o Evans Mills, NY, St. Mary. (OG)
Aoa, AS, c/o Pago Pago, AS, Church of Sacred Heart. (SPP)
Apache, OK, Caddo Co., Mother of Sorrows, c/o Elgin, OK, St. Ann. (OKL)
Aquasco, MD, Prince Georges Co., St. Dominic's, c/o Brandywine, MD, St. Michael. (WDC)
Aquin, OH, Haiti Parish Twinning Program (Saint Thomas d' Aquin), c/o Marysville, OH, Our Lady of Lourdes. (COL)
Arago, NE, Richardson Co., St. Mary's, c/o Rulo, NE, Immaculate Conception. (LIN)
Arapahoe, NE, Furnas Co., St. Germanus, c/o Cambridge, NE, St. John's. (LIN)
Arboles, CO, Archuleta Co., SS. Peter & Rose, c/o Ignacio, CO, St. Ignatius Parish. (PBL)
Arbuckle, CA, Colusa Co., Holy Cross, c/o Williams, CA, Sacred Heart. (SAC)
Argyle, MN, Marshall Co., St. Rose of Lima, c/o Stephen, MN, St. Stephen's. (CR)
Arivaca, AZ, Pima Co., St. Ferdinand, c/o Tubac, AZ, Saint Ann's Roman Catholic Parish and Missions – Tubac. (TUC)
Arlee, MT, Lake Co., Sacred Heart, c/o St. Ignatius, MT, St. Ignatius Mission. (HEL)
Armagh, MO, Franklin Co., St. Patrick, c/o Catawissa, MO, St. James. (STL)
Arnold, CA, Arnold Co., Our Lady of the Sierra, c/o Angels Camp, CA, St. Patrick Church of Angels Camp (Pastor of). (STO)
Arnold, NE, Custer Co., St. Agnes, c/o Stapleton, NE, St. John the Evangelist. (GI)
Arock, OR, Malheur Co., Holy Family, c/o Jordan Valley, OR, St. Bernard. (BAK)
Arrey, NM, Sierra Co., San Jose, c/o Garfield, NM, San Isidro. (LSC)
Arroyo, PR, Arroyo Co., La Milagrosa, c/o Arroyo, PR, Our Lady of Mt. Carmel. (PCE)
Arroyo, PR, Arroyo Co., Ntra Sra. de Fatima, c/o Arroyo, PR, Our Lady of Mt. Carmel. (PCE)
Arroyo, PR, San Jose, c/o Arroyo, PR, Our Lady of Mt. Carmel. (PCE)
Arroyo, PR, Arroyo Co., San Martin, c/o Arroyo, PR, Our Lady of Mt. Carmel. (PCE)
Arroyo Hondo, NM, Taos Co., Nuestra Senora de Dolores, c/o Arroyo Seco, NM, La Santisima Trinidad. (SFE)
Ashdown, AR, Little River Co., St. Elizabeth Ann Seton, c/o Texarkana, AR, St. Edward. (LR)
Ashland, AL, Clay Co., St. Mark, c/o Alexander City, AL, St. John the Apostle. (BIR)
Ashland, NY, Greene Co., St. Joseph's Chapel, c/o Windham, NY, St. Theresa of Child Jesus. (ALB)
Ashtabula, OH, Ashtabula Co., Our Lady of Miracles (St. Joseph Mission), c/o Ashtabula, OH, St. Joseph. (Y)
Aspermont, TX, Stonewall Co., St. Mary, c/o Rotan, TX, St. Joseph. (LUB)
Asti, CA, Our Lady of Mt. Carmel, c/o Cloverdale, CA, St. Peter's. (SR)
Astor, FL, Lake Co., St. Hubert of the Forest, c/o Ocala, FL, Our Lady of the Springs. (ORL)
Atalaya, PR, Ntra. Sra. de Altagracia, c/o Aguada, PR, St. Francis of Assisi. (MGZ)
Athena, OR, Umatilla Co., Sacred Heart, c/o Milton Freewater, OR, St. Francis of Assisi. (BAK)
Atlanta, GA, Fulton Co., Centro Catolico del Espiritu Santo, c/o Atlanta, GA, Holy Spirit. (ATL)
Atlanta, IL, Logan Co., St. Mary's, c/o Lincoln, IL, Holy Family. (PEO)
Atlantic Mine, MI, Houghton Co., St. Mary, c/o Houghton, MI, St. Ignatius Loyola. (MAR)
Atoka, OK, Atoka Co., St. Patrick Church, c/o Durant, OK, St. William. (TLS)
Atwood, CA, Orange Co., Santa Teresita, c/o Placentia, CA, St. Joseph. (ORG)
Augusta, MT, Lewis and Clark Co., St. Matthias, c/o Fairfield, MT, St. John the Evangelist. (HEL)
Aurora, NM, San Miguel Co., c/o Villanueva, NM, Our Lady of Guadalupe. (SFE)
Austin, PA, Potter Co., St. Augustine, c/o Galeton, PA, St. Bibiana. (E)
Austwell, TX, Refugio Co., St. Anthony of Padua, c/o Tivoli, TX, Our Lady of Guadalupe. (CC)
Autrain, MI, Alger Co., St. Therese, c/o Munising, MI, Sacred Heart of Jesus. (MAR)
Ava, MO, Douglas Co., St. Leo the Great, c/o Ava, MO, Immaculate Heart of Mary. (SPC)
Avoca, NE, Cass Co., Holy Trinity, c/o Syracuse, NE, St. Paulinus. (LIN)
Avon, MT, Powell Co., St. Theodore, c/o Helena, MT, Cathedral of St. Helena. (HEL)
Avondale, LA, Jefferson Civil Parish, Assumption of Mary, c/o Marrero, LA, St. Agnes Le Thi Thanh. (NO)
Avondale, PA, Chester Co., Santa Maria, Madra de Dios, c/o West Grove, PA, Assumption B.V.M. (PH)
Ayrshire, IA, Palo Alto Co., Sacred Heart, c/o Ruthven, IA, Sacred Heart. (SC)
Azle, TX, Tarrant Co., Holy Trinity, c/o Fort Worth, TX, St. Thomas. (FWT)

B

Babb, MT, Glacier Co., St. Mary, Queen of the World, c/o Browning, MT, Church of the Little Flower. (HEL)
Badger, MN, Roseau Co., St. Mary's, c/o Roseau, MN, Sacred Heart. (CR)
Baggs, WY, Carbon Co., Our Lady of the Sage, c/o Rawlins, WY, St. Joseph's. (CHY)
Bahner, MO, Pettis Co., St. John, c/o Sedalia, MO, Sacred Heart. (JC)
Bainville, MT, Roosevelt Co., Sacred Heart, c/o Poplar, MT, Our Lady of Lourdes. (GF)
Bajio, PR, Sagrada Familia, c/o Aguada, PR, St. Francis of Assisi. (MGZ)
Baker, CA, San Bernardino Co., Our Lady of the Desert, c/o Barstow, CA, St. Joseph. (SB)
Bakersfield, CA, Kern Co., Holy Spirit, c/o Bakersfield, CA, Our Lady of Guadalupe. (FRS)
Bakersfield, CA, Kern Co., St. Jude, c/o Bakersfield, CA, Our Lady of Guadalupe. (FRS)

Bald Knob, AR, White Co., St. Richard, c/o Searcy, AR, St. James. (LR)
Billings, MT, Yellowstone Co., Sts. Cyril & Methodius, c/o Billings, MT, St. Bernard. (GF)
Ballardville, MA, St. Joseph's, c/o Andover, MA, St. Augustine. (BO)
Bancroft, WV, Putnam Co., St. Patrick, c/o Nitro, WV, Holy Trinity. (WH)
Barberville, FL, Volusia Co., San Jose Mission, c/o DeLand, FL, St. Peter's Church. (ORL)
Barinas, PR, Yauco Co., St. James, c/o Yauco, PR, Holy Rosary. (PCE)
Barneston, NE, Gage Co., St. Joseph's, c/o Wymore, NE, St. Mary's. (LIN)
Barnsdall, OK, Osage Co., St. Mary, c/o Pawhuska, OK, Immaculate Conception. (TLS)
Barriada Vietnam, PR, La Milagrosa, c/o Guaynabo, PR, Santa Rosa de Lima. (SJN)
Barrington, NH, Strafford Co., Chapel of the Nativity, c/o Dover, NH, Parish of the Assumption. (MAN)
Barrio Apeadero, PR, Villalba Co., San Alfonso, c/o Villalba, PR, Our Lady of Mt. Carmel. (PCE)
Barrio Hatillo, PR, Villalba Co., Sagrada Familia, c/o Villalba, PR, Our Lady of Mt. Carmel. (PCE)
Barrio Indios, PR, Guayanilla Co., San Juan Bosco, c/o Guayanilla, PR, Immaculate Conception. (PCE)
Barrio Jaguey, PR, Villalba Co., Madre Cabrini, c/o Villalba, PR, Our Lady of Mt. Carmel. (PCE)
Barrio La Plata, Amoldadero, PR, Barrio Algarrobo, c/o Aibonito, PR, Church of St. Joseph. (CGS)
Barrio Obrero, PR, San Martin de Porres, c/o San Juan, PR, Nuestra Senora del Carmen. (SJN)
Barrio Semil, PR, Villalba Co., Santa Cecilia, c/o Villalba, PR, Our Lady of Mt. Carmel. (PCE)
Barrio Sierra Baja, PR, Guayanilla Co., Our Lady of Mt. Carmel, c/o Guayanilla, PR, Immaculate Conception. (PCE)
Barstow, TX, Ward Co., Our Lady of Refuge, c/o Pecos, TX, Santa Rosa de Lima. (ELP)
Westernport, MD, Allegany Co., St. Gabriel, c/o Westernport, MD, St. Peter. (BAL)
Bartow, WV, Pocahontas Co., St. Mark the Evangelist, c/o Marlinton, WV, St. John Neumann. (WH)
Basile, LA, Evangeline Parish, Assumption, c/o Basile, LA, St. Augustine. (LAF)
Basin, WY, Big Horn Co., St. Philip, c/o Greybull, WY, Sacred Heart. (CHY)
Bass Lake, CA, Madera Co., St. Dominic Savio, c/o Oakhurst, CA, Our Lady of the Sierra. (FRS)
Bassett, NE, Rock Co., Holy Cross, c/o Ainsworth, NE, St. Pius X. (GI)
Basye, VA, Shenandoah Co., Our Lady of the Shenandoah, c/o Woodstock, VA, St. John Bosco. (ARL)
Batesville, TX, Zavala Co., St. Patrick, c/o La Pryor, TX, St. Joseph. (LAR)
Baxley, GA, Appling Co., St. Raymond, c/o Baxley, GA, Good Shepherd. (SAV)
Baxley, GA, Appling Co., St. Rose of Lima, c/o Baxley, GA, Good Shepherd. (SAV)
Bay Mills, MI, Chippewa Co., Blessed Kateri Tekakwitha, c/o Brimley, MI, St. Francis Xavier. (MAR)
Bayamon, PR, Bayamon Co., N. Sra. Del Carmen, c/o Bayamon, PR, Santa Rita de Casia. (SJN)
Bayamon, PR, N. Sra. de la Providencia, c/o Bayamon, PR, Santo Domingo De Guzman. (SJN)
Bayamon, PR, Bayamon Co., N. Sra. del Buen Consejo, c/o Bayamon, PR, San Agustin. (SJN)
Bayamon, PR, Toa Alta Co., N. Sra. del Rosario, c/o Toa Alta, PR, San Esteban, Protomartir. (SJN)
Bayamon, PR, Bayamon Co., Sagrado Corazon, c/o Bayamon, PR, Santa Maria. (SJN)
Bayamon, PR, Bayamon Co., San Gerardo Mayela, c/o Bayamon, PR, Santa Maria. (SJN)
Bayamon, PR, Bayamon Co., San Jose, c/o Bayamon, PR, Santa Rita de Casia. (SJN)
Bayamon, PR, Bayamon Co., San Martin de Porres, c/o Bayamon, PR, San Agustin. (SJN)
Bayamon, PR, San Martin de Porres, c/o Bayamon, PR, Santa Teresa de Jesus. (SJN)
Bayamon, PR, Bayamon Co., Santa Monica, c/o Bayamon, PR, Ntra. Sra. de la Monserrate. (SJN)
Bayard, NE, Morrill Co., Sacred Heart, c/o Bridgeport, NE, All Souls. (GI)
Bayside, TX, Refugio Co., St. Mary, c/o Woodsboro, TX, St. Therese, The Little Flower. (CC)
Bda. Esperanza, PR, Guanica Co., La Providencia, c/o Guanica, PR, St. Anthony Abbot. (PCE)
Beach Haven, NJ, Ocean Co., St. Thomas Aquinas, c/o Brant Beach, NJ, St. Francis of Assisi. (TR)
Beaulieu, MN, Mahnomen Co., St. Joseph, c/o Mahnomen, MN, St. Michael's Parish. (CR)
Beaver, OK, Beaver Co., St. Frances Cabrini, c/o Guymon, OK, St. Peter's. (OKL)
Beaverton, OR, Washington Co., Mission of the Atonement, c/o Tigard, OR, St. Anthony. (P)
Beaverton, OR, Washington Co., St. Andrew Dung Lac, c/o Portland, OR, Southeast Asian Vicariate. (P)
Beaverton, OR, Washington Co., St. Andrew Dung–Lac, c/o Portland, OR, Our Lady of Lavang. (P)
Bedford Hills, NY, Westchester Co., St. Matthias, c/o Katonah, NY, St. Mary of the Assumption. (NY)
Bee, NE, Seward Co., St. Wenceslaus, c/o Dwight, NE, Assumption. (LIN)
Beech Bottom, WV, Brooke Co., Holy Family, c/o Wellsburg, WV, St. John The Evangelist. (WH)
Beemer, NE, Cuming Co., Holy Cross, c/o Wisner, NE, St. Joseph. (OM)
Bel Air, MD, Harford Co., St. Mary Magdalen, c/o Bel Air, MD, St. Margaret. (BAL)
Belfair, WA, Mason Co., Prince of Peace, c/o Port Orchard, WA, St. Gabriel. (SEA)
Belgrade, MT, Gallatin Co., Valley of Flowers, c/o Three Forks, MT, Holy Family. (HEL)
Bellflower, IL, McLean Co., St. John, c/o Farmer City, IL, Sacred Heart. (PEO)
Bellwood, NE, Butler Co., St. Joseph's, c/o Bellwood, NE, St. Peter's. (LIN)
Bemidji, MN, Beltrami Co., Holy Spirit Newman Center, c/o Bemidji, MN, St. Philip's. (CR)
Bennettsville, SC, Marlboro Co., St. Denis, c/o Cheraw, SC, St. Peter. (CHR)
Bent, NM, Otero Co., Our Lady of Guadalupe, c/o Mescalero, NM, St. Joseph. (LSC)
Benton, LA, Bossier Parish, Mary, Queen of Heaven, c/o Bossier City, LA, St. Jude. (SHP)
Benton, PA, Columbia Co., Christ the King, c/o Bloomsburg, PA, St. Columba. (HBG)
Bergland, MI, Ontonagon Co., St. Ann, c/o Ewen, MI, Sacred Heart. (MAR)
Berino, NM, Dona Ana Co., Immaculate Conception, c/o Anthony, NM, St. Anthony's. (LSC)
Berlin, NJ, Camden Co., Mater Ecclesiae Church, c/o Bellmawr, NJ, The Church of the Annunciation BVM, Bellmawr, N.J. (CAM)
Berlin, PA, Somerset Co., St. Gregory, c/o Meyersdale, PA, SS. Philip and James. (ALT)
Bermuda, LA, Natchitoches Parish, St. Charles, c/o Natchez, LA, St. Augustine's. (ALX)
Berne, NY, Albany Co., St. Bernadette, c/o Altamont, NY, St. Lucy. (ALB)
Berrien Springs, MI, Berrien Co., St. Gabriel Mission Church, c/o Bridgman, MI, Our Lady Queen of Peace. (KAL)
Berryville, AR, St. Anne, c/o Eureka Springs, AR, St. Elizabeth of Hungary. (LR)
Berryville, VA, Clarke Co., St. Bridget of Ireland, c/o Winchester, VA, Sacred Heart of Jesus. (ARL)
Bertram, TX, Burnet Co., Holy Cross, c/o Burnet, TX, Our Mother of Sorrows. (AUS)
Beryl, UT, Iron Co., San Pablo, c/o St. George, UT, St. George LLC 223. (SLC)
Betances, PR, Our Lady of Fatima, c/o Cabo Rojo, PR, St. Michael. (MGZ)
Beulah, CO, Pueblo Co., Our Lady of Lourdes, c/o Pueblo, CO, St. Francis Xavier. (PBL)
Beulaville, NC, Duplin Co., St. Teresa del Nino Jesus, c/o Kenansville, NC, Maria, Reina De Las Americas. (R)
Bevier, MO, Macon Co., Sacred Heart, c/o Macon, MO, Immaculate Conception. (JC)
Bibo, NM, Cibola Co., Our Lady of Loretto, c/o Seboyeta, NM, Our Lady of Sorrows. (GLP)
Bieber, CA, Lassen Co., St. Stephen, c/o Burney, CA, St. Francis of Assisi. (SAC)
Big Bay, MI, Marquette Co., St. Mary, c/o Marquette, MI, St. Peter Cathedral. (MAR)
Big Elbow Lake, MN, Becker Co., St. Frances Cabrini, c/o Waubun, MN, St. Ann. (CR)
Big Oak Flat, CA, Tuolumne Co., Our Lady of Mt. Carmel, c/o Sonora, CA, St. Patrick Church of Sonora (Pastor of). (STO)
Big Pine, CA, Inyo Co., St. Stephen, c/o Bishop, CA, Our Lady of Perpetual Help. (FRS)
Big Piney, WY, Sublette Co., St. Anne, c/o Pinedale, WY, Our Lady of Peace. (CHY)
Big Sky, MT, Gallatin Co., St. Joseph of Big Sky, c/o West Yellowstone, MT, Our Lady of the Pines. (HEL)
Big Sur, CA, Monterey Co., St. Francis of the Redwoods, c/o Carmel, CA, San Carlos Borromeo Basilica. (MRY)
Big Wells, TX, Dimmit Co., St. Michael, c/o Asherton, TX, Immaculate Conception. (LAR)
Bigfoot, TX, Frio Co., Our Lady of Mt. Carmel, c/o Devine, TX, St. Joseph's. (SAT)
Billings, MT, Yellowstone Co., Sts. Cyril & Methodius, c/o Billings, MT, St. Bernard. (GF)
Billings, OK, Noble Co., Sacred Heart, c/o Perry, OK, St. Rose of Lima. (OKL)
Binger, OK, Caddo Co., Our Lady of the Most Holy Rosary, c/o Anadarko, OK, St. Patrick's. (OKL)
Bird City, KS, Cheyenne Co., St. Joseph's, c/o St. Francis, KS, St. Francis of Assisi Parish. (SAL)
Birmingham, AL, Jefferson Co., St. Stephen the Martyr and Campus Center, c/o Birmingham, AL, St. Paul's Cathedral. (BIR)
Bismarck, MO, St. Francois Co., St. John, c/o Park Hills, MO, Immaculate Conception. (STL)
Bison, OK, Garfield Co., St. Joseph, c/o Hennessey, OK, St. Joseph's. (OKL)
Bison, SD, Perkins Co., Blessed Sacrament, c/o Lemmon, SD, St. Mary's. (RC)
Black Lake, LA, Natchitoches Parish, Our Lady of the Holy Rosary, c/o Campti, LA, Nativity of The Blessed Virgin Mary. (ALX)
Black Lake, NM, Colfax Co., St. Anthony, c/o Cimarron, NM, Immaculate Conception Church. (SFE)
Blackduck, MN, Beltrami Co., St. Ann, c/o Kelliher, MN, St. Patrick. (CR)
Blackville, SC, Barnwell Co., Sacred Heart, c/o Barnwell, SC, St. Andrew. (CHR)
Blackwater, AZ, Pinal Co., Holy Family, c/o Sacaton, AZ, St. Peter's. (PHX)
Blackwell's Corner, CA, Kern Co., Nuestra Senora de la Paz, c/o Wasco, CA, St. John the Evangelist. (FRS)
Blanca, CO, Costilla Co., St. James, c/o San Luis, CO, Sangre de Cristo. (PBL)
Blencoe, IA, Monona Co., St. Bernard, c/o Onawa, IA, St. John. (SC)
Blooming Grove, PA, Good Shepherd, c/o Lords Valley, PA, St. John Neumann. (SCR)
Bloomingburg, NY, Sullivan Co., Our Lady of the Assumption, c/o Middletown, NY, Our Lady of Mt. Carmel. (NY)
Blowing Rock, NC, Epiphany, c/o Boone, NC, St. Elizabeth. (CHL)
Blue Hill, NE, Webster Co., Holy Trinity, c/o Campbell, NE, St. Anne. (LIN)
Blue Lake, CA, St. Joseph, c/o Arcata, CA, St. Mary's. (SR)
Blue Mountain Lake, NY, Hamilton Co., St. Paul, c/o Indian Lake, NY, St. Mary's. (OG)
Bluetown, TX, Cameron Co., Cristo Rey, c/o Progreso, TX, Holy Spirit. (BWN)
Bly, OR, Klamath Co., St. James the Apostle, c/o Chiloquin, OR, Our Lady of Mt. Carmel. (BAK)
Bo. Aceituna, PR, San Martin de Porres, c/o Moca, PR, Our Lady of Monserrate. (MGZ)
Bo. Aibonito Guerrero, PR, Ntra. Sra. del Carmen, c/o San Sebastian, PR, San Sebastian Martir. (MGZ)
Bo. Algarrobos – Yauco, PR, Yauco, Our Lady of Fatima, c/o Yauco, PR, Santo Domingo de Guzman. (PCE)
Bo. Almacigo Alto – Yauco, PR, Yauco, St. Juan Macias, c/o Yauco, PR, Santo Domingo de Guzman. (PCE)
Bo. Almacigo Bajo – Yauco, PR, Yauco, St. Martin de Porres, c/o Yauco, PR, Santo Domingo de Guzman. (PCE)
Bo. Altozano, PR, Ntra. Sra. de Fatima, c/o San Sebastian, PR, San Sebastian Martir. (MGZ)
Bo. Arenas de Guancia, PR, Guanica Co., S. Martin de Porres, c/o Yauco, PR, St. Martin de Porres. (PCE)
Bo. Atalaya, PR, El Cristo de la Reconciliacion, c/o Rincon, PR, St. Rose of Lima. (MGZ)
Bo. Bartolo, PR, San Pedro, c/o Rio Grande, PR, Nuestra Senora del Carmen. (FAJ)
Bo. Belgica, PR, Guanica Co., Cristo Rey, c/o Guanica, PR, St. Anthony Abbot. (PCE)
Bo. Cain, PR, St. Martin de Porres, c/o San German, PR, St. Rose of Lima. (MGZ)
Bo. Calabazas, PR, San Gabriel de la Dolorosa, c/o San Sebastian, PR, San Sebastian Martir. (MGZ)
Bo. Calvache, PR, Santa Rosa, c/o Rincon, PR, St. Rose of Lima. (MGZ)
Bo. Calzada, PR, c/o Maunabo, PR, San Isidro Labrador. (CGS)
Bo. Camarones, PR, Villalba Co., Jesus Crucificado, c/o Villalba, PR, Our Lady of Mt. Carmel. (PCE)
Bo. Camarones–Los Robles, PR, Villalba Co., San Antonio, c/o Villalba, PR, Our Lady of Mt. Carmel. (PCE)
Bo. Cambute, PR, Carolina Co., Divino Nino Jesus, c/o Carolina, PR, Cristo Rey. (SJN)
Bo. Canalizo – Jayuya, PR, Jayuya Co., La Milagrosa, c/o Jayuya, PR, Our Lady of Monserrate. (PCE)
Bo. Canonilla Abajo, PR, Villalba Co., Maria Madre de la Iglesia, c/o Villalba, PR, Our Lady of Mt. Carmel. (PCE)
Bo. Canovanillas, PR, Maria Auxiliadora, c/o Carolina, PR, Cristo Rey. (SJN)
Bo. Capa Barreto, PR, Virgen del Rosario, c/o Moca, PR, Our Lady of Monserrate. (MGZ)
Bo. Capa Bosque, PR, Corpus Christi, c/o Moca, PR, Our Lady of Monserrate. (MGZ)
Bo. Carite, PR, Guayama Co., San Martin, c/o Guayama, PR, St. Anthony of Padua. (PCE)
Bo. Carola, PR, La Milagrosa, c/o Palmer, PR, Cristo Rey. (FAJ)
Bo. Carreras, PR, La Providencia, c/o Anasco, PR, St. Anthony Abbot. (MGZ)
Bo. Carretera Nueva, PR, La Asuncion, c/o Hormigueros, PR, Shrine of Our Lady of Monserrate. (MGZ)
Bo. Cayabo, PR, Juana Diaz Co., Our Lady of the Rosary, c/o Juana Diaz, PR, St. Raymond Nonato. (PCE)
Bo. Cerro Gordo, PR, El Buen Pastor, c/o Moca, PR, Our Lady of Monserrate. (MGZ)
Bo. Cerro Gordo, PR, Villalba Co., Espiritu Santo, c/o Villalba, PR, Our Lady of Mt. Carmel. (PCE)
Bo. Cerro Gordo, PR, Our Lady of Monserrat, c/o Anasco, PR, St. Anthony Abbot. (MGZ)
Bo. Cerro Gordo, PR, San Francisco de Asis, c/o Sabana Grande, PR, Church of San Isidro. (MGZ)

Bo. Chucillas Sabana, PR, Inmaculado Corazon de Maria, c/o Moca, PR, Our Lady of Monserrate. (MGZ)
Bo. Coabey – Jayuya, PR, Jayuya Co., San Jorge, c/o Jayuya, PR, Our Lady of Monserrate. (PCE)
Bo. Collado, PR, Ponce Co., Our Lady of Monserrate, c/o Mercedita, PR, Church of the Resurrection. (PCE)
Bo. Collores – Jayuya, PR, Cristo Rey, c/o Jayuya, PR, Our Lady of Monserrate. (PCE)
Bo. Collores – Yauco, PR, Yauco, Sacred Heart, c/o Yauco, PR, Santo Domingo de Guzman. (PCE)
Bo. Corazon, PR, Guayama Co., La Candelaria, c/o Guayama, PR, St. Anthony of Padua. (PCE)
Bo. Corcega, PR, La Milagrosa, c/o Rincon, PR, St. Rose of Lima. (MGZ)
Bo. Corillo, PR, Villalba Co., San Pedro, c/o Villalba, PR, Our Lady of Mt. Carmel. (PCE)
Bo. Corral Viejo, PR, Ponce Co., Cristo Rey, c/o Ponce, PR, La Santisima Trinidad. (PCE)
Bo. Coto el Mato, PR, Penuelas Co., San Judas Tadeo, c/o Penuelas, PR, St. Joseph. (PCE)
Bo. Cruces, PR, Sagrado Corazon de Jesus, c/o Rincon, PR, St. Rose of Lima. (MGZ)
Bo. Cuchilla del Limon, PR, Villalba Co., La Asuncion, c/o Villalba, PR, Our Lady of Mt. Carmel. (PCE)
Bo. Cuchillas Cordero, PR, Virgen de la Monserrate, c/o Moca, PR, Our Lady of Monserrate. (MGZ)
Bo. Cuchillas La Salle, PR, Santos Guillermo Abad y San Mateo, c/o Moca, PR, Our Lady of Monserrate. (MGZ)
Bo. Cuchillas Loperena, PR, Cristo Rey, c/o Moca, PR, Our Lady of Monserrate. (MGZ)
Bo. Cuesta Blanca, PR, Ntra. Sra. de Monserrate, c/o Lajas, PR, De la Merced Parish. (MGZ)
Bo. Culebrinas, PR, Espiritu Santo, c/o San Sebastian, PR, San Sebastian Martir. (MGZ)
Bo. Cuyon, Our Lady of Fatima, c/o Coamo, PR, St. Blase. (PCE)
Bo. Dajas, PR, Villalba Co., N.S. del Carmen, c/o Villalba, PR, Our Lady of Mt. Carmel. (PCE)
Bo. El Bajo, Patillas, PR, Patillas Co., Cristo Rey, c/o Patillas, PR, Inmaculado Corazon de Maria. (PCE)
Bo. El Cafetal – Yauco, PR, Yauco, St. Rosa de Lima, c/o Yauco, PR, Santo Domingo de Guzman. (PCE)
Bo. El Hoyo, PR, La Virgen Milagrosa, c/o Sabana Grande, PR, Church of San Isidro. (MGZ)
Bo. El Hoyo, PR, Santa Rosa de Lima, c/o Hormigueros, PR, Shrine of Our Lady of Monserrate. (MGZ)
Bo. El Jobos, PR, La Milagrosa, c/o Loiza, PR, Santiago Apostol, El Mayor. (FAJ)
Bo. El Porvenir, PR, Ntra. Sra. de la Providencia (Rep. Masias), c/o Mayaguez, PR, Ascension. (MGZ)
Bo. El Real, Patillas, PR, Patillas Co., San Guillermo, c/o Patillas, PR, Inmaculado Corazon de Maria. (PCE)
Bo. El Salto – Jayuya, PR, Santos Reyes, c/o Jayuya, PR, Our Lady of Monserrate. (PCE)
Bo. El Verde, PR, Nuestra Senora de Fatima, c/o Rio Grande, PR, Nuestra Senora del Carmen. (FAJ)
Bo. Eneas, PR, Ntra. Senora de la Providencia, c/o San Sebastian, PR, San Sebastian Martir. (MGZ)
Bo. Espino, PR, St. Lawrence Martyr, c/o Anasco, PR, St. Anthony Abbot. (MGZ)
Bo. Fuig., PR, Guanica Co., Monserrate, c/o Ensenada, PR, Sacred Heart. (PCE)
Bo. Gripinas – Jayuya, PR, Jayuya Co., Buen Pastor, c/o Jayuya, PR, Our Lady of Monserrate. (PCE)
Bo. Guama, PR, N. Sra. de la Consolacion, c/o San German, PR, St. Rose of Lima. (MGZ)
Bo. Guamani, PR, Guayama Co., Sgdo. Corazon, c/o Guayama, PR, St. Anthony of Padua. (PCE)
Bo. Guanajibo, PR, San Martin de Porres, c/o Hormigueros, PR, Shrine of Our Lady of Monserrate. (MGZ)
Bo. Guaragoa, PR, Ponce Co., San Andres, c/o Ponce, PR, La Santisima Trinidad. (PCE)
Bo. Guaragoa, Arriba, PR, Ponce Co., Santa Ana, c/o Ponce, PR, La Santisima Trinidad. (PCE)
Bo. Guaras, PR, Ntra. Sra. de Fatima, c/o Sabana Grande, PR, Church of San Isidro. (MGZ)
Bo. Guarderraya, Patillas, PR, Patillas Co., Madre Cabrini, c/o Patillas, PR, Inmaculado Corazon de Maria. (PCE)
Bo. Guaypao, PR, Guanica Co., Virgen del Rosario, c/o Ensenada, PR, Sacred Heart. (PCE)
Bo. Guerrero, PR, La Providencia, c/o San Antonio, PR, San Jose Obrero. (MGZ)
Bo. Hatillo Viejo, PR, Villalba Co., La Milagrosa, c/o Villalba, PR, Our Lady of Mt. Carmel. (PCE)
Bo. Hato Arriba, PR, San Patricio, c/o San Sebastian, PR, San Sebastian Martir. (MGZ)
Bo. Hato Arriba (Parcelas), PR, San Pablo de la Cruz, c/o San Sebastian, PR, San Sebastian Martir. (MGZ)
Bo. Higuero, PR, Villalba Co., Santisimo Sacramento, c/o Villalba, PR, Our Lady of Mt. Carmel. (PCE)
Bo. Hogares Seguros – Jayuya, PR, San Antonio Co., San Jose de la Montaña, c/o Jayuya, PR, Our Lady of Monserrate. (PCE)
Bo. Hoyamala, PR, San Jose Obrero, c/o San Sebastian, PR, San Sebastian Martir. (MGZ)
Bo. Hoyo Planes – Jayuya, PR, Jayuya Co., Ntra Sra de la Divina Providencia, c/o Jayuya, PR, Our Lady of Monserrate. (PCE)
Bo. Hoyos, PR, Ponce Co., Santa Maria Virgen, c/o Coto Laurel, PR, Our Lady of Mt. Carmel. (PCE)
Bo. Jacaboa, Patillas, PR, Patillas Co., Nuestra Senora del Carmen, c/o Patillas, PR, Inmaculado Corazon de Maria. (PCE)
Bo. Jacaquas, PR, Juana Diaz Co., N.S. de Fatima, c/o Juana Diaz, PR, St. Raymond Nonato. (PCE)
Bo. Jagual, Patillas, PR, Patillas Co., Nuestra Senora del Carmen, c/o Patillas, PR, Inmaculado Corazon de Maria. (PCE)
Bo. Jaguey, PR, San Jose, c/o Rincon, PR, St. Rose of Lima. (MGZ)
Bo. Jaquitas, PR, Ntra. Sra. de la Paz, c/o Hormigueros, PR, Shrine of Our Lady of Monserrate. (MGZ)
Bo. Jauca – Santa Isabel, PR, Santa Isabel Co., San Ignacio de Loyola, c/o Santa Isabel, PR, St. James. (PCE)
Bo. Juncal, PR, Santa Teresita del Nino Jesus, c/o San Sebastian, PR, San Sebastian Martir. (MGZ)
Bo. Juncos, PR, Corazon de Maria, c/o Penuelas, PR, Sacred Heart. (PCE)
Bo. La Haya, PR, Santa Rosa de Lima, c/o Lajas, PR, Our Lady of the Purification. (MGZ)
Bo. La Laguna, PR, Guanica Co., San Judas, c/o Guanica, PR, St. Anthony Abbot. (PCE)
Bo. La Lechuza, PR, La Immaculada Concepcion, c/o San Sebastian, PR, San Sebastian Martir. (MGZ)
Bo. La Luna, PR, Guanica Co., N. Sra Fatima, c/o Guanica, PR, St. Anthony Abbot. (PCE)
Bo. La Maquina, PR, Santa Ana, c/o Sabana Grande, PR, Church of San Isidro. (MGZ)
Bo. La Mocha, PR, Ponce Co., Santos Reyes, c/o Ponce, PR, San Vicente–Cantera. (PCE)
Bo. La Pica, PR, San Jose, c/o Sabana Grande, PR, Church of San Isidro. (MGZ)
Bo. La Pica – Jayuya, PR, San Patricio Co., San Patricio, c/o Jayuya, PR, Our Lady of Monserrate. (PCE)
Bo. La Plata, PR, Sagrado Corazon de Jesus, c/o Lajas, PR, Our Lady of the Purification. (MGZ)
Bo. La Torre, PR, Ntra. Sra. del Perpetuo Socorro, c/o Loiza, PR, San Patricio. (FAJ)
Bo. La Torre, PR, Santa Catalina de Siena, c/o Sabana Grande, PR, Church of San Isidro. (MGZ)
Bo. La Yuca, PR, Ponce Co., Immaculate Heart of Mary, c/o Mercedita, PR, Church of the Resurrection. (PCE)
Bo. Lajas Arriba (La Tea), PR, Ntra. Sra. del Perpetuo Socorro, c/o Lajas, PR, Our Lady of the Purification. (MGZ)
Bo. Lajas Arriba (Parcelas), PR, San Pablo, c/o Lajas, PR, Our Lady of the Purification. (MGZ)
Bo. Las Palmas, PR, Salinas Co., Virg. del Carmen, c/o Salinas, PR, Our Lady of Monserrat. (PCE)
Bo. Las Raices, PR, Ponce Co., Sagrado Corazon de Jesus, c/o Coto Laurel, PR, Our Lady of Mt. Carmel. (PCE)
Bo. Las Vallas, PR, Ponce Co., San Lucas, c/o Mercedita, PR, Church of the Resurrection. (PCE)
Bo. Las Vegas, PR, Our Lady of Perpetual Help, c/o Mayaguez, PR, Ascension. (MGZ)
Bo. Las Vegas – Yauco, PR, Yauco, Sta. Teresita, c/o Yauco, PR, Santo Domingo de Guzman. (PCE)
Bo. Lavadero, PR, Sagrado Corazon de Jesus, c/o Hormigueros, PR, Shrine of Our Lady of Monserrate. (MGZ)
Bo. Limon, PR, St. Teresita, c/o Mayaguez, PR, Ascension. (MGZ)
Bo. Limon, PR, Villalba Co., Virgen de la Amargura, c/o Villalba, PR, Our Lady of Mt. Carmel. (PCE)
Bo. Limon, PR, Virgen del Perpetuo Socorro, c/o Moca, PR, Our Lady of Monserrate. (MGZ)
Bo. Lizas, PR, c/o Maunabo, PR, San Isidro Labrador. (CGS)
Bo. Lluberas Yauco, PR, Yauco, St. Joseph, c/o Yauco, PR, Santo Domingo de Guzman. (PCE)
Bo. Lomas, PR, San Pedro Apostol, c/o Canovanas, PR, Sagrado Corazon de Jesus. (FAJ)
Bo. Los Barros, Patillas, PR, Patillas Co., S. Juan Evangelista, c/o Patillas, PR, Inmaculado Corazon de Maria. (PCE)
Bo. Los Pollos, Patillas, PR, Patillas Co., Santa Rosa de Lima, c/o Patillas, PR, Inmaculado Corazon de Maria. (PCE)
Bo. Macana, PR, Penuelas Co., Ntra. Sra. de Fatima, c/o Penuelas, PR, St. Joseph. (PCE)
Bo. Macun, PR, Toa Baja Co., Santa Maria La Mayor, c/o Toa Baja, PR, Ntra. Sra. de la Candelaria. (SJN)
Bo. Madrigal, PR, Ponce Co., N.S. del Rosario, c/o Ponce, PR, La Santisima Trinidad. (PCE)
Bo. Maginas, PR, Sagrado Corazon de Jesus, c/o Sabana Grande, PR, Church of San Isidro. (MGZ)
Bo. Maguayo, PR, Ntra. Sra. de la Monserrate, c/o Lajas, PR, De la Merced Parish. (MGZ)
Bo. Magueyes, PR, Ponce Co., San Juan de Mata, c/o Ponce, PR, La Santisima Trinidad. (PCE)
Bo. Malezas, PR, La Milagrosa, c/o Mayaguez, PR, Sacred Heart. (MGZ)
Bo. Mameyes – Jayuya, PR, Jayuya Co., S. Antonio, c/o Jayuya, PR, Our Lady of Monserrate. (PCE)
Bo. Marias, PR, St. Rita, c/o Anasco, PR, St. Anthony Abbot. (MGZ)
Bo. Marin Alto, Patillas, PR, Patillas Co., Perpetuo Socorro, c/o Patillas, PR, Inmaculado Corazon de Maria. (PCE)
Bo. Marueno, Arriba, PR, Ponce Co., N.S. Fatima, c/o Ponce, PR, La Santisima Trinidad. (PCE)
Bo. Mediana Baja, PR, Santisima Trinidad, c/o Loiza, PR, San Patricio. (FAJ)
Bo. Mini Mine, PR, La Providencia, c/o Loiza, PR, Santiago Apostol, El Mayor. (FAJ)
Bo. Minillas Carretera, PR, Perpetuo Socorro, c/o San German, PR, St. Rose of Lima. (MGZ)
Bo. Minillas Valle, PR, Santa Monica, c/o San German, PR, St. Rose of Lima. (MGZ)
Bo. Miradero, PR, Ntro. Sra. de la Providencia, c/o Cabo Rojo, PR, St. Michael. (MGZ)
Bo. Mogote, PR, Villalba Co., Santisima Trinidad, c/o Villalba, PR, Our Lady of Mt. Carmel. (PCE)
Bo. Molinas, PR, Ntra. Sra. de Monserrate, c/o Sabana Grande, PR, Church of San Isidro. (MGZ)
Bo. Naranjo, PR, Sagrado Corazon de Jesus, c/o Moca, PR, Our Lady of Monserrate. (MGZ)
Bo. Nuevo Mameyes, PR, Ponce Co., Santa Luisa, c/o Ponce, PR, San Vicente–Cantera. (PCE)
Bo. Olimpo, PR, Guayama Co., Cristo Rey, c/o Guayama, PR, St. Anthony of Padua. (PCE)
Bo. Ollas – Santa Isabel, PR, Santa Isabel Co., Virgen de Monserrate, c/o Santa Isabel, PR, St. James. (PCE)
Bo. Ortiz, PR, Corozal Co., Santisima Trinidad, c/o Bayamon, PR, Santo Domingo De Guzman. (SJN)
Bo. Oveja, PR, Cristo Redentor, c/o Anasco, PR, St. Anthony Abbot. (MGZ)
Bo. Palmarejo, PR, Villalba Co., San Jose, c/o Villalba, PR, Our Lady of Mt. Carmel. (PCE)
Bo. Palmarejo II, PR, San Juan Bautista, c/o Lajas, PR, Our Lady of the Purification. (MGZ)
Bo. Paloseco, PR, c/o Maunabo, PR, San Isidro Labrador. (CGS)
Bo. Parcelas Guacio (Parcelas), PR, Santa Cruz, c/o San Sebastian, PR, San Sebastian Martir. (MGZ)
Bo. Parcelas Palmarejo, PR, San Judas Tadeo, c/o Lajas, PR, Our Lady of the Purification. (MGZ)
Bo. Parcelas Santa Rosa, PR, Santa Rosa de Lima, c/o Lajas, PR, Our Lady of the Purification. (MGZ)
Bo. Parguera, PR, San Pedro, c/o Lajas, PR, De la Merced Parish. (MGZ)
Bo. Paris, PR, Ntra Sra. del Perpetuo Socorro, c/o Lajas, PR, De la Merced Parish. (MGZ)
Bo. Pastillo, PR, Ponce Co., Inmaculada, c/o Ponce, PR, La Santisima Trinidad. (PCE)
Bo. Pastillo – Penuelas, PR, Penuelas Co., San Antonio de Padua, c/o Penuelas, PR, St. Joseph. (PCE)
Bo. Penuelas Santa Isabel, PR, Virgen del Rosario, c/o Santa Isabel, PR, St. James. (PCE)
Bo. Perchas I, PR, Cristo Rey, c/o San Sebastian, PR, San Sebastian Martir. (MGZ)
Bo. Perchas II, PR, La Pasion del Señor, c/o San Sebastian, PR, San Sebastian Martir. (MGZ)
Bo. Pinales, PR, La Immaculade, c/o Anasco, PR, St. Anthony Abbot. (MGZ)
Bo. Pinas, PR, Comerio Co., La Resurreccion, c/o Bayamon, PR, N. Sra. de la Providencia. (SJN)
Bo. Pinas, PR, Comerio Co., N. Sra. de Fatima, c/o Bayamon, PR, N. Sra. de la Providencia. (SJN)
Bo. Pinas, PR, Comerio Co., Sagrada Familia, c/o Bayamon, PR, N. Sra. de la Providencia. (SJN)
Bo. Pinones, PR, Santa Rosa, c/o Loiza, PR, San Patricio. (FAJ)
Bo. Pitahaya, PR, N. Sra. del Carmen, c/o Luquillo, PR, Madre del Redentor. (FAJ)
Bo. Pitahaya Carr. 3 K.43, PR, Ntra Sra. del Carmen, c/o Arroyo, PR, Our Lady of Mt. Carmel. (PCE)
Bo. Plata, PR, San Judas Tadeo, c/o Moca, PR, Our Lady of Monserrate. (MGZ)
Bo. Playa, PR, Salinas Co., Carmen, c/o Salinas, PR, Our Lady of Monserrat. (PCE)
Bo. Playita, PR, Salinas Co., Virgen Milagrosa, c/o Salinas, PR, Our Lady of Monserrat. (PCE)
Bo. Playita Cortada – Santa Isabel, PR, San Patricio, c/o Santa Isabel, PR, St. James. (PCE)
Bo. Pozas, PR, Sagrada Familia, c/o San Sebastian, PR, San Sebastian Martir. (MGZ)
Bo. Pozo Hondo, PR, Santa Rosa de Lima, c/o Anasco, PR, St. Anthony Abbot. (MGZ)
Bo. Providencia, Patillas, PR, Patillas Co., Ntra Sra de la Providencia, c/o Patillas, PR, Inmaculado Corazon de Maria. (PCE)
Bo. Puerto Plata – Jayuya, PR, San Juan Evangelista, c/o Jayuya, PR, Our Lady of Monserrate. (PCE)
Bo. Puntas, PR, Nuestra Senora del Carmen, c/o Rincon, PR, St. Rose of Lima. (MGZ)
Bo. Quebrada Arenas, PR, c/o Maunabo, PR, San Isidro Labrador. (CGS)
Bo. Quebrado del Agua, Ponce, PR, Ponce Co., La Milagrosa, c/o Ponce, PR, Good Shepherd Parish. (PCE)
Bo. Rayo Plata, PR, San Judas Tadeo, c/o Sabana Grande, PR, Church of San Isidro. (MGZ)

Bo. Real Anon Abajo, PR, Ponce Co., San Mateo, c/o Coto Laurel, PR, Our Lady of Mt. Carmel. (PCE)
Bo. Real Anon Arriba, PR, Ponce Co., San Martin de Porres, c/o Coto Laurel, PR, Our Lady of Mt. Carmel. (PCE)
Bo. Recio, Patillas, PR, Patillas Co., Sto. Cristo de Los Milagros, c/o Patillas, PR, Inmaculado Corazon de Maria. (PCE)
Bo. Retiro Tea, PR, Santa Rita, c/o San German, PR, St. Rose of Lima. (MGZ)
Bo. Rio Cana Arriba, PR, Juana Diaz Co., La Merced, c/o Juana Diaz, PR, St. Raymond Nonato. (PCE)
Bo. Rio Grande, PR, La Virgin de Guadalupe, c/o Rincon, PR, St. Rose of Lima. (MGZ)
Bo. Rio Loco – Yauco, PR, Yauco, Our Lady of Montserrat, c/o Yauco, PR, Santo Domingo de Guzman. (PCE)
Bo. Robles, PR, Sagrado Corazon de Jesus, c/o San Sebastian, PR, San Sebastian Martir. (MGZ)
Bo. Rocha Magueyes, PR, Virgen de La Providencia, c/o Moca, PR, Our Lady of Monserrate. (MGZ)
Bo. Rocha Sec. Lassalle, PR, San Pedro Apostol, c/o Moca, PR, Our Lady of Monserrate. (MGZ)
Bo. Rosario Alto, PR, La Milagrosa, c/o Rosario, PR, Our Lady of Rosary. (MGZ)
Bo. Rosario Penon, PR, La Monseirate, c/o Rosario, PR, Our Lady of Rosary. (MGZ)
Bo. Sabana, PR, N. Sra. Milagrosa, c/o Luquillo, PR, Madre del Redentor. (FAJ)
Bo. Sabana, PR, San Jose de la Montana, c/o Trujillo Alto, PR, San Francisco de Asis. (SJN)
Bo. Saliente – Jayuya, PR, Jayuya Co., San Francisco, c/o Jayuya, PR, Our Lady of Monserrate. (PCE)
Bo. Salientito – Jayuya, Divino Niño Jesús, c/o Jayuya, PR, Our Lady of Monserrate. (PCE)
Bo. Salinas, PR, Ntra. Sra. del Carmen, c/o Lajas, PR, De la Merced Parish. (MGZ)
Bo. Salistral, PR, Ponce Co., Santa Marta, c/o Ponce, PR, Our Lady of Mt. Carmel. (PCE)
Bo. Saltos, PR, San Judas Tadeo, c/o San Sebastian, PR, San Sebastian Martir. (MGZ)
Bo. Santa Clara – Jayuya, Ntra Sra del Carmen, c/o Jayuya, PR, Our Lady of Monserrate. (PCE)
Bo. Santa Juanita, PR, Guanica Co., N. Sra. Rosario, c/o Guanica, PR, St. Anthony Abbot. (PCE)
Bo. Santana Pichel, PR, Ntra. Sra. del Rosario, c/o Sabana Grande, PR, Church of San Isidro. (MGZ)
Bo. Santas Pascuas, PR, Ponce Co., Resurreccion, c/o Ponce, PR, La Santisima Trinidad. (PCE)
Bo. Santo Domingo, PR, Penuelas Co., Ntra Sra del Carmen, c/o Penuelas, PR, St. Joseph. (PCE)
Bo. Sierrita Caonillas, PR, Villalba Co., Cristo de la Salud, c/o Villalba, PR, Our Lady of Mt. Carmel. (PCE)
Bo. Sonador, PR, Cristo Resucitado, c/o San Sebastian, PR, San Sebastian Martir. (MGZ)
Bo. Sonadora, PR, Sagrada Familia, c/o Guaynabo, PR, Corazon de Jesus. (SJN)
Bo. Sta. Ana Moreno, PR, Sta Lucia, c/o Sabana Grande, PR, Church of San Isidro. (MGZ)
Bo. Susa, PR, Yauco Co., N.S. de La Monserrate, c/o Yauco, PR, St. Martin de Porres. (PCE)
Bo. Susa, PR, Guanica Co., N.S. de La Providencia, c/o Yauco, PR, St. Martin de Porres. (PCE)
Bo. Susa, PR, Yauco Co., S. Francisco de Asis, c/o Yauco, PR, St. Martin de Porres. (PCE)
Bo. Susua, PR, Guanica Co., Ntra. Sra. de Lourdes, c/o Yauco, PR, St. Martin de Porres. (PCE)
Bo. Talante (La Pica), PR, c/o Maunabo, PR, San Isidro Labrador. (CGS)
Bo. Tallaboa Alta, PR, Penuelas Co., Santa Ana, c/o Penuelas, PR, St. Joseph. (PCE)
Bo. Vista Alegre, PR, Villalba Co., Jesus Crucificado, c/o Villalba, PR, Our Lady of Mt. Carmel. (PCE)
Bo. Voladoras Lomas, PR, Espiritu Santo, c/o Moca, PR, Our Lady of Monserrate. (MGZ)
Bo. Voladoras Parcelas, PR, Sagrada Familia, c/o Moca, PR, Our Lady of Monserrate. (MGZ)
Bo. Zama – Jayuya, PR, Jayuya Co., Santa Cecila, c/o Jayuya, PR, Our Lady of Monserrate. (PCE)
Bodega, CA, St. Teresa, c/o Occidental, CA, St. Philip. (SR)
Boise City, OK, Cimarron Co., Good Shepherd, c/o Guymon, OK, St. Peter's. (OKL)
Boles Acres, NM, Otero Co., Our Lady of the Desert, c/o Alamogordo, NM, Immaculate Conception. (LSC)
Bolinas, CA, Marin Co., St. Mary Magdalene, c/o Olema, CA, Sacred Heart. (SFR)
Boling, TX, Wharton Co., St. Joseph, c/o Wharton, TX, Holy Family. (VIC)
Bon Secour, AL, Baldwin Co., Our Lady of Bon Secour, c/o Magnolia Springs, AL, St. John the Baptist. (MOB)
Bonanza, OR, Klamath Co., St. Frances Cabrini, c/o Merrill, OR, St. Augustine. (BAK)
Bongard, IL, Champaign Co., Immaculate Conception, c/o Philo, IL, St. Thomas. (PEO)
Bonneau, SC, Berkeley Co., Our Lady of Peace, c/o Moncks Corner, SC, St. Philip Benizi. (CHR)
Booker, TX, Lipscomb Co., St. Peter, c/o Perryton, TX, Immaculate Conception. (AMA)
Booneville, KY, Owsley Co., Booneville Catholic Church of the Holy Family, c/o Beattyville, KY, Queen of All Saints. (LEX)
Boonville, CA, Mendocino Co., St. Elizabeth Seton, c/o Ukiah, CA, St. Mary of the Angels. (SR)
Boqueron, PR, St. Joseph, c/o Cabo Rojo, PR, St. Michael. (MGZ)
Borica, NM, Guadalupe Co., c/o Santa Rosa, NM, St. Rose of Lima. (SFE)
Borinquen, PR, Our Lady of Victory, c/o Aguadilla, PR, La Milagrosa. (MGZ)
Bosque, NM, Valencia Co., c/o Belen, NM, Our Lady of Belen. (SFE)
Boswell, OK, Choctaw Co., St. Jude, c/o Hugo, OK, Immaculate Conception. (TLS)
Boulder Valley, MT, Jefferson Co., St. John the Evangelist, c/o Boulder, MT, St. Catherine. (HEL)
Bowie, AZ, Our Lady of Guadalupe, c/o Willcox, AZ, Sacred Heart of Jesus Roman Catholic Church – Willcox. (TUC)
Bowling Green, FL, Hardee Co., Holy Child, c/o Wauchula, FL, St. Michael. (VEN)
Box Elder, MT, Hill Co., St. Anthony, c/o Box Elder, MT, St. Margaret Mary. (GF)
Rocky Boys Indian Reservation, MT, Hill Co., St. Mary, c/o Box Elder, MT, St. Margaret Mary. (GF)
Bozrah, CT, New London Co., St. John, c/o Norwichtown, CT, Sacred Heart. (NOR)
Bradley, CA, Monterey Co., Our Lady of Guadalupe, c/o San Miguel, CA, San Miguel. (MRY)
Brainardsville, NY, Franklin Co., St. Jude, c/o Chateaugay, NY, Catholic Community of Burke and Chateaugay. (OG)
Braithwaite, LA, Plaquemines Parish, Assumption of Our Lady, c/o Braithwaite, LA, St. Thomas. (NO)
Branch, LA, Acadia Parish, St. Edmund Chapel, c/o Rayne, LA, St. Leo IV. (LAF)
Branderi – Guayama, San José Obrero, c/o Guayama, PR, St. Anthony of Padua. (PCE)
Branford, FL, Suwannee Co., San Juan, c/o High Springs, FL, St. Madeleine Sophie Parish. (STA)
Brewster, MA, Barnstable Co., Immaculate Conception, c/o Brewster, MA, Our Lady of the Cape. (FR)
Bridge City, LA, Jefferson Parish, Holy Guardian Angels Mission, c/o Westwego, LA, Our Lady of Prompt Succor. (NO)
Bridgeport, CA, Mono Co., Infant of Prague Mission Church, c/o Mammoth Lakes, CA, St. Joseph Church of Mammoth Lakes. (STO)
Bridger, SD, Ziebach Co., Immaculate Conception, c/o Eagle Butte, SD, All Saints. (RC)
Brier Hill, NY, St. Lawrence Co., Our Lady of Grace, c/o Morristown, NY, The Roman Catholic Community of Morristown, Hammond and Rossie. (OG)
Brisas del Caribe, PR, Inmaculado Corazon de Maria, c/o Ponce, PR, San Jose Obrero. (PCE)
Brisbane, CA, San Mateo Co., Our Lady of Guadalupe, c/o San Francisco, CA, Visitacion, Church of the. (SFR)
Bristol, CO, Prowers Co., St. Mary, c/o Holly, CO, St. Frances of Rome. (PBL)
Bristol, NH, Our Lady of Grace, c/o Plymouth, NH, Holy Trinity Parish. (MAN)
Bristow, OK, Creek Co., St. Joseph, c/o Tulsa, OK, St. Catherine. (TLS)
Broadview, MT, Yellowstone Co., St. Theresa the Little Flower, c/o Roundup, MT, St. Benedict. (GF)
Brockton, MT, Roosevelt Co., St. Thomas, c/o Poplar, MT, Our Lady of Lourdes. (GF)
Bronte, TX, Coke Co., St. James, c/o Ballinger, TX, St. Mary Star of the Sea. (SAN)
Bronx, NY, St. Anthony, c/o Bronx, NY, St. Frances of Rome. (NY)
Bronx, NY, St. Francis of Assisi, c/o Bronx, NY, St. Frances of Rome. (NY)
Bronx, NY, St. Francis of Assisi, c/o Bronx, NY, Sacred Heart. (NY)
Brooklyn, NY, Kings Co., Regina Pacis Votive Shrine, c/o Brooklyn, NY, St. Rosalia–Regina Pacis. (BRK)
Brooks, MN, Red Lake Co., St. Joseph, c/o Red Lake Falls, MN, St. Joseph's. (CR)
Brookville, IN, SS. Philomena and Cecilia, c/o Batesville, IN, St. Mary–of–the–Rock. (IND)
Brown City, MI, Sanilac Co., c/o Yale, MI, Sacred Heart. (DET)
Brownstown, IN, Jackson Co., Our Lady of Providence, c/o Seymour, IN, St. Ambrose. (IND)
Brownsville, OR, Linn Co., Holy Trinity, c/o Sweet Home, OR, St. Helen Catholic Church. (P)
Brownsville, TN, Haywood Co., St. John Church, c/o Jackson, TN, St. Mary Church. (MEM)
Brownsville, TX, Cameron Co., Sacred Heart, c/o Brownsville, TX, Immaculate Conception Cathedral. (BWN)
Brownsville, TX, Cameron Co., St. Thomas, c/o Brownsville, TX, Immaculate Conception Cathedral. (BWN)
Bruceton Mills, WV, Preston Co., Mary Help of Christians, c/o Morgantown, WV, St. Luke the Evangelist. (WH)
Bruni, TX, Jim Hogg Co., Sacred Heart, c/o Hebbronville, TX, Our Lady of Guadalupe. (LAR)
Brunswick, NE, Antelope Co., St. Ignatius, c/o Creighton, NE, St. Ludger. (OM)
Bryan, TX, Brazos Co., San Salvador, c/o Bryan, TX, St. Anthony. (AUS)
Bucarabones, PR, Sagrado Corazon, c/o Maricao, PR, St. John the Baptist. (MGZ)
Buckhorn, CA, Amador Co., Our Lady of the Pines, c/o Jackson, CA, St. Patrick's. (SAC)
Buena Vista, GA, Marion Co., St. Mary Magdalen, c/o Columbus, GA, Our Lady of Lourdes. (SAV)
Buena Vista, PR, La Milagrosa, c/o Las Marias, PR, Immaculate Heart of Mary. (MGZ)
Buenavista, NM, Mora Co., c/o Mora, NM, St. Gertrude. (SFE)
Bueyeros, NM, Harding Co., c/o Roy, NM, Holy Family–St. Joseph. (SFE)
Buffalo, OK, Harper Co., St. Joseph, c/o Woodward, OK, St. Peter's. (OKL)
Buffalo Creek, CO, Jefferson Co., St. Elizabeth, c/o Conifer, CO, Our Lady of The Pines. (DEN)
Buffalo Twp., WI, WI, St. Andrew, c/o Pardeeville, WI, St. Mary of the Most Holy Rosary. (MAD)
Buhach, CA, Merced Co., Immaculate Conception, c/o Atwater, CA, St. Anthony. (FRS)
Bullhead, SD, Corson Co., St. Aloysius, c/o McLaughlin, SD, St. Bernard. (RC)
Bullhead, SD, Corson Co., St. Aloysius, c/o McLaughlin, SD, Standing Rock Reservation. (RC)
Bullville, NY, Orange Co., St. Paul, c/o Middletown, NY, Our Lady of Mt. Carmel. (NY)
Bunker, MO, Reynolds Co., Christ the King, c/o Salem, MO, Sacred Heart. (SPC)
Burchard, NE, Pawnee Co., Sacred Heart, c/o Steinauer, NE, St. Anthony. (LIN)
Burkesville, KY, Cumberland Co., Holy Cross Catholic, c/o Albany, KY, Emmanuel Catholic. (L)
Burlington, TX, St. Michael, c/o Burlington, TX, St. Ann. (AUS)
Burlington Junction, MO, Nodaway Co., St. Benedict Catholic Church, c/o Tarkio, MO, St. Paul the Apostle. (KC)
Burwell, NE, Garfield Co., Sacred Heart, c/o Ord, NE, Our Lady of Perpetual Help. (GI)
Busby, MT, Big Horn Co., Christ the King, c/o Lame Deer, MT, Blessed Sacrament. (GF)
Bush, LA, St. Tammany Parish, St. Michael the Archangel, c/o Abita Springs, LA, St. Jane de Chantal. (NO)
Butler, AL, Washington Co., St. Paul, c/o Butler, AL, St. John The Evangelist. (MOB)
Butte La Rose, LA, St. Martin Parish, Sacred Heart, c/o Breaux Bridge, LA, Our Lady of Mercy. (LAF)
Bylas, AZ, Blessed Kateri Tekakwitha, c/o San Carlos, AZ, San Carlos Apache Roman Catholic Community – San Carlos. (TUC)

C

Cabezon, NM, Sandoval Co., San Jose, c/o Cuba, NM, Immaculate Conception. (GLP)
Cabool, MO, Texas Co., St. Michael, c/o Mountain Grove, MO, Sacred Heart. (SPC)
Cactus, TX, Sherman Co., Our Lady of Guadalupe, c/o Stratford, TX, St. Joseph's. (AMA)
Cade, LA, St. Martin Parish, St. Anthony, c/o Broussard, LA, St. Joseph. (LAF)
Caimital, PR, Guayama Co., Our Lady of Perpetual Help, c/o Guayama, PR, St. Anthony of Padua. (PCE)
Cairo, GA, Grady Co., St. Elizabeth Ann Seton, c/o Thomasville, GA, St. Augustine. (SAV)
Caldwell, TX, Burleson Co., Holy Rosary, c/o Caldwell, TX, St. Mary. (AUS)
California City, CA, Kern Co., St. Joseph, c/o California City, CA, Our Lady of Lourdes. (FRS)
Callabo, PR, Bo. Callabo, San Ramon, c/o Juana Diaz, PR, St. Raymond Nonato. (PCE)
Callaway, MN, Becker Co., Assumption, c/o Frazee, MN, Sacred Heart. (CR)
Callaway, NE, Logan Co., St. Boniface, c/o Stapleton, NE, St. John the Evangelist. (GI)
Calumet, OK, Canadian Co., Immaculate Heart of Mary, c/o Okarche, OK, Holy Trinity. (OKL)
Calvert, TX, Robertson Co., St. Mary, Calvert, c/o Hearne, TX, St. Mary. (AUS)
Camaseyes, PR, Our Lady of Fatima, c/o Aguadilla, PR, La Milagrosa. (MGZ)
Cambalaches, PR, Yauco Co., Our Lady of Perpetual Help, c/o Yauco, PR, Holy Rosary. (PCE)
Cambridge, IL, Henry Co., St. John Vianney, c/o Woodhull, IL, St. John's. (PEO)
Camden, AL, Wilcox Co., St. Joseph, c/o Monroeville, AL, Annunciation. (MOB)
Camilla, GA, Mitchell Co., St. John Vianney, c/o Moultrie, GA, Immaculate Conception. (SAV)
Camp Sacramento, CA, El Dorado Co., Our Lady of the Sierra, c/o South Lake Tahoe, CA, St. Theresa. (SAC)
Camp Wood, TX, Real Co., St. Mary Magdalen, c/o Rocksprings, TX, Sacred Heart of Mary. (SAT)

Campbell, NY, Steuben Co., St. Joseph, c/o Addison, NY, St. Stanislaus. (ROC)
Campbellton, TX, Atascosa Co., Sacred Heart, c/o Pleasanton, TX, St. Andrew. (SAT)
Campton, KY, Wolfe Co., Catholic Church of the Good Shepherd, c/o Jackson, KY, Holy Cross. (LEX)
Campus, IL, Sacred Heart, c/o Odell, IL, St. Paul's. (PEO)
Canaan, NH, Grafton Co., St. Mary, c/o Enfield, NH, St. Helena. (MAN)
Canadohta Lake, PA, Crawford Co., Our Lady of Fatima, c/o Union City, PA, St. Teresa of Avila. (E)
Candelaria, TX, Presidio Co., Our Lady of Peace, c/o Presidio, TX, Santa Teresa de Jesus. (ELP)
Canjilon, NM, Rio Arriba Co., San Juan Nepumoceno, c/o Chama, NM, St. Patrick. (SFE)
Canon, NM, Sandoval Co., c/o Jemez Pueblo, NM, San Diego Indian Missions. (SFE)
Canon de Vallecitos, NM, Rio Arriba Co., c/o El Rito, NM, San Juan Nepomuceno. (SFE)
Canoncito, NM, Mora Co., c/o Mora, NM, St. Gertrude. (SFE)
Canoncito, NM, Santa Fe Co., c/o Pecos, NM, St. Anthony of Padua. (SFE)
Canoncito, NM, Bernalillo Co., c/o Tijeras, NM, Holy Child. (SFE)
Canones, NM, Rio Arriba Co., c/o Abiquiu, NM, St. Thomas Apostle. (SFE)
Canovanas, PR, La Milagrosa, c/o Canovanas, PR, Sagrado Corazon de Jesus. (FAJ)
Canovanas, PR, San Francisco Javier, c/o Canovanas, PR, Nuestra Senora del Pilar. (FAJ)
Canton, NC, Haywood Co., Immaculate Conception, c/o Waynesville, NC, St. John the Evangelist. (CHL)
Cantonment, FL, Escambia Co., St. Elizabeth of Hungary, c/o Cantonment, FL, St. Jude Thaddeus. (PT)
Cantwell, AK, c/o Healy, AK, Holy Mary of Guadalupe Catholic Church Healy. (FBK)
Canyon Ferry, MT, Lewis and Clark Co., Our Lady of the Lake, c/o East Helena, MT, SS. Cyril and Methodius. (HEL)
Capitan, NM, Lincoln Co., Sacred Heart, c/o Carrizozo, NM, St. Rita. (LSC)
Capulin, NM, Rio Arriba Co., c/o Abiquiu, NM, St. Thomas Apostle. (SFE)
Carbondale, CO, Garfield Co., St. Mary of the Crown, c/o Carbondale, CO, St. Vincent de Paul. (DEN)
Carenage, VI, Chapel of St. Anne, c/o Charlotte Amalie, VI, Cathedral of Sts. Peter and Paul. (STV)
Carnation, WA, King Co., St. Anthony, c/o Snoqualmie, WA, Our Lady of Sorrows. (SEA)
Carnegie, OK, Caddo Co., St. Richard, c/o Anadarko, OK, St. Patrick's. (OKL)
Carnuel, NM, Bernalillo Co., Holy Child, c/o Tijeras, NM, Holy Child. (SFE)
Carolina, PR, Barrazas, N. Sra. del Carmen, c/o Carolina, PR, Ntra. Sra. de Fatima. (SJN)
Carolina, PR, Carolina Co., Parque Boliviano 5–JL, c/o Carolina, PR, Santa Clara de Asis. (SJN)
Carolina, PR, Carolina Co., San Antonio, c/o Carolina, PR, San Valentin. (SJN)
Carolina, PR, Cacao, Santa Teresa de Jesus, c/o Carolina, PR, Ntra. Sra. de Fatima. (SJN)
Carpenter, WY, Laramie Co., St. Peter, c/o Pine Bluffs, WY, St. Paul's. (CHY)
Carrissa Plains, CA, San Luis Obispo Co., St. James Mission, c/o Santa Margarita, CA, Santa Margarita de Cortona. (MRY)
Carrizales, PR, Ntra. Sra. de las Mercedes, c/o Aguada, PR, St. Francis of Assisi. (MGZ)
Carrizales, PR, Hatillo Co., Our Lady of Montserrat, c/o Yauco, PR, Holy Rosary. (PCE)
Carroll, NH, Coos Co., St. Patrick, c/o Lancaster, NH, Gate of Heaven. (MAN)
Caruthers, CA, Fresno Co., Our Lady of the Assumption, c/o Easton, CA, St. Jude. (FRS)
Casa Colorada, NM, Valencia Co., c/o Tome, NM, Immaculate Conception. (SFE)
Cascade, CO, El Paso Co., Holy Rosary, c/o Colorado Springs, CO, Sacred Heart. (COS)
Cascade, MT, Cascade Co., Sacred Heart, c/o Fort Shaw, MT, St. Ann. (GF)
Cascade, PA, Lycoming Co., Assumption of the B.V.M., c/o Williamsport, PA, St. Ann's. (SCR)
Cascade, WI, Sheboygan Co., St. Michael Chapel, c/o Eden, WI, Shepherd of the Hills (Good Shepherd). (MIL)
Catarina, TX, Dimmit Co., St. Henry, c/o Asherton, TX, Immaculate Conception. (LAR)
Cathlamet, WA, Wahkiakum Co., St. Catherine, c/o Longview, WA, St. Rose de Viterbo. (SEA)
Cave Junction, OR, Josephine Co., St. Patrick of the Forest, c/o Grants Pass, OR, St. Anne. (P)
Cawker City, KS, Mitchell Co., SS. Peter & Paul, c/o Tipton, KS, St. Boniface Parish. (SAL)
Cazadero, CA, St. Colman, c/o Guerneville, CA, St. Elizabeth. (SR)
Cebolla, NM, Rio Arriba Co., Santo Nino, c/o Chama, NM, St. Patrick. (SFE)
Cedar Bluffs, NE, Saunders Co., St. Mary, c/o Colon, NE, St. Joseph's. (LIN)
Cedar City, UT, Iron Co., St. Gertrude, c/o Cedar City, UT, Christ the King LLC 203. (SLC)
Cedar Creek, AZ, Gila Co., St. Anthony, c/o Cibecue, AZ, St. Catherine. (GLP)
Cedar Hill, NE, Saunders Co., Sacred Heart, c/o Morse Bluff, NE, St. George. (LIN)
Cedar Hill, TN, Robertson Co., St. Michael, c/o Springfield, TN, Our Lady of Lourdes. (NSH)
Cedaredge, CO, Delta Co., St. Philip Benizi, c/o Delta, CO, St. Michael. (PBL)
Cedarville, CA, Modoc Co., St. James, c/o Alturas, CA, Sacred Heart. (SAC)
Ceiba, PR, Ceiba Co., N.S. del Perpetuo Socorro, c/o Ceiba, PR, San Antonio de Padua. (FAJ)
Ceiba, PR, Sagrado Corazon de Jesus, c/o Ceiba, PR, San Antonio de Padua. (FAJ)
Celina, TN, Clay Co., Divine Savior, c/o Cookeville, TN, St. Thomas Aquinas. (NSH)
Center, MO, Ralls Co., St. Paul (Historic Church), c/o Perry, MO, St. William. (JC)
Centermoreland, PA, Luzerne Co., Blessed Sacrament, c/o Wyoming, PA, St. Frances Cabrini. (SCR)
Centerville, MT, Cascade Co., Holy Trinity, c/o Belt, MT, St. Mark the Evangelist. (GF)
Centerville, TX, Leon Co., St. Leo the Great, c/o Crockett, TX, St. Francis of the Tejas. (TYL)
Centreville, MI, St. Joseph Co., St. Clare, c/o Three Rivers, MI, Immaculate Conception. (KAL)
Cerrito, NM, San Miguel Co., c/o Villanueva, NM, Our Lady of Guadalupe. (SFE)
Cerro, NM, Taos Co., c/o Questa, NM, St. Anthony. (SFE)
Cerro Gordo, PR, Buen Consejo, c/o Aguada, PR, St. Francis of Assisi. (MGZ)
Chacon, NM, Mora Co., c/o Mora, NM, St. Gertrude. (SFE)
Chalmette, LA, St. Bernard Parish, Chapel of St. Lawrence, c/o Chalmette, LA, Our Lady of Prompt Succor. (NO)
Chama, CO, Costilla Co., Immaculate Conception, c/o San Luis, CO, Sangre de Cristo. (PBL)
Chamisal, NM, Taos Co., Santa Cruz Mission, c/o Penasco, NM, San Antonio de Padua. (SFE)
Chamita, NM, Rio Arriba Co., c/o Ohkay Owingeh, NM, St. John the Baptist. (SFE)
Chandler, TX, Van Sand Co., St. Boniface, c/o Athens, TX, St. Edward Church. (TYL)
Chantilly, VA, Corpus Christi Mission, c/o Middleburg, VA, St. Stephen the Martyr. (ARL)
Charlemont, MA, Franklin Co., St. Christopher, c/o Shelburne Falls, MA, St. Joseph's. (SPR)
Charlestown, RI, Washington Co., St. James, c/o Carolina, RI, St. Mary. (PRO)
Charley Creek, MT, Richland Co., St. Bernard, c/o Sidney, MT, St. Matthew. (GF)
Charlo, MT, Lake Co., St. Joseph's, c/o Ronan, MT, Sacred Heart. (HEL)
Cherokee, NC, Swain Co., Our Lady of Guadalupe, c/o Bryson City, NC, St. Joseph. (CHL)
Cherokee, OK, Alfalfa Co., St. Cornelius, c/o Alva, OK, Sacred Heart. (OKL)
Cherry Creek, SD, Ziebach Co., St. Joseph, c/o Eagle Butte, SD, All Saints. (RC)
Cherry Hill, NJ, Camden Co., St. Yi Yun Il John Korean Catholic Mission, c/o Cherry Hill, NJ, Holy Eucharist Parish, Cherry Hill, N.J. (CAM)
Chesapeake City, MD, Cecil Co., St. Rose of Lima, c/o Middletown, DE, St. Joseph. (WIL)
Chester, CA, Plumas Co., Christ the King, c/o Westwood, CA, Our Lady of the Snows. (SAC)
Chester, MA, Hampden Co., St. John, c/o Huntington, MA, St. Thomas. (SPR)
Chester, PA, Delaware Co., St. Hedwig Chapel, c/o Clifton Heights, PA, Sacred Heart. (PH)
Chicago, IL, Angel Guardian Croatian Catholic Mission, c/o Chicago, IL, Archdiocese of Chicago's Joseph Cardinal Bernardin Archives and Records Center. (CHI)
Chicago, IL, Our Lady of Fatima Mission, c/o Chicago, IL, Archdiocese of Chicago's Joseph Cardinal Bernardin Archives and Records Center. (CHI)
Chicago, IL, Our Lady of the Cross Mission Chapel, c/o Chicago, IL, Archdiocese of Chicago's Joseph Cardinal Bernardin Archives and Records Center. (CHI)
Chicago, IL, Cook Co., Sacred Heart, c/o Chicago, IL, Holy Name of Mary. (CHI)
Chicago, IL, San Marcello Mission, c/o Chicago, IL, Archdiocese of Chicago's Joseph Cardinal Bernardin Archives and Records Center. (CHI)
Chicago, IL, Santa Lucia Mission, c/o Chicago, IL, Archdiocese of Chicago's Joseph Cardinal Bernardin Archives and Records Center. (CHI)
Chicago, IL, St. Florian Mission, c/o Chicago, IL, Archdiocese of Chicago's Joseph Cardinal Bernardin Archives and Records Center. (CHI)
Chicago, IL, St. Hedwig Mission, c/o Chicago, IL, Archdiocese of Chicago's Joseph Cardinal Bernardin Archives and Records Center. (CHI)
Chicago, IL, St. Hyacinth Mission, c/o Chicago, IL, Archdiocese of Chicago's Joseph Cardinal Bernardin Archives and Records Center. (CHI)
Childersburg, AL, Talladega Co., Holy Name of Jesus, c/o Sylacauga, AL, St. Jude. (BIR)
Chili, NM, Bernalillo Co., San Juan de Nepumoceno, c/o Tijeras, NM, Holy Child. (SFE)
China Spring, TX, McLennan Co., St. Philip, c/o McGregor, TX, St. Eugene Catholic Church – McGregor, Texas. (AUS)
Chippewa Lake, OH, Medina Co., Jesus Divine Redeemer, c/o Litchfield, OH, Our Lady Help of Christians Parish. (CLV)
Chireno, TX, Nacogdoches Co., Our Lady of Lourdes, c/o Nacogdoches, TX, Sacred Heart. (TYL)
Chittenden, VT, Rutland Co., St. Robert, c/o Pittsford, VT, St. Alphonsus Liguori. (BUR)
Choctaw, LA, Lafourche Parish, St. James, c/o Thibodaux, LA, St. Lawrence the Martyr. (HT)
Christiansted, VI, U.S.V.I., Sacred Heart Chapel, c/o Christiansted, VI, Church of the Holy Cross. (STV)
Christine, TX, Atascosa Co., St. Ignatius, c/o Jourdanton, TX, St. Matthew's. (SAT)
Christmas Valley, OR, Lake Co., Holy Family, c/o La Pine, OR, Holy Redeemer. (BAK)
Chualar, CA, Monterey Co., Chualar Mission, c/o Gonzales, CA, St. Theodore. (MRY)
Chugwater, WY, Platte Co., Mary Queen of Heaven, c/o Wheatland, WY, St. Patrick's. (CHY)
Cilantro, PR, Coamo Co., Saint James, c/o Coamo, PR, St. Blase. (PCE)
Cincinnatus, NY, Cortland Co., Our Lady of Perpetual Help, c/o Marathon, NY, St. Stephen. (SY)
Cincinnatus, NY, Cortland Co., Our Lady of Perpetual Help, c/o Whitney Point, NY, The Catholic Community of St. Stephen–St. Patrick. (SY)
Citra, FL, Christ the King, c/o Ocala, FL, Blessed Trinity. (ORL)
Clallam Bay, WA, Clallam Co., St. Thomas the Apostle, c/o Forks, WA, St. Anne Parish. (SEA)
Clancy, MT, Jefferson Co., St. John's, c/o East Helena, MT, SS. Cyril and Methodius. (HEL)
Claremont, NH, Sullivan Co., Old St. Mary, c/o Claremont, NH, St. Mary. (MAN)
Clark, WY, Park Co., Our Lady of the Valley, c/o Powell, WY, St. Barbara. (CHY)
Clarkdale, AZ, Yavapai Co., St. Cecilia, c/o Cottonwood, AZ, Immaculate Conception Roman Catholic Parish. (PHX)
Clarks, NE, Merrick Co., c/o Fullerton, NE, St. Peter. (OM)
Clarkson, NE, Colfax Co., Holy Trinity, c/o Howells, NE, SS. Peter and Paul. (OM)
Clarksville, MO, Pike Co., Mary Queen of Peace, c/o Louisiana, MO, St. Joseph. (JC)
Clatskanie, OR, Columbia Co., St. John the Baptist, c/o Rainier, OR, Nativity B.V.M. (P)
Claypool, AZ, Gila Co., St. Joseph, c/o Miami, AZ, Our Lady of the Blessed Sacrament Roman Catholic Church – Miami. (TUC)
Clayton, AL, Barbour Co., Ventress Correctional Facility, c/o Eufaula, AL, Holy Redeemer. (MOB)
Clayton, GA, Rabun Co., St. Helena, c/o Clarkesville, GA, St. Mark. (ATL)
Clayton, OK, Pushmataha Co., Holy Trinity, c/o Wilburton, OK, Sacred Heart. (TLS)
Clear Spring, MD, Washington Co., St. Michael, c/o Hagerstown, MD, St. Mary. (BAL)
Clearmont, WY, Johnson Co., St. Mary, c/o Buffalo, WY, St. John the Baptist. (CHY)
Clearwater, NE, Mission of St. Theresa of Avila, Clearwater, NE, c/o Ewing, NE, St. Peter de Alcantara. (OM)
Clendenin, WV, Kanawha Co., St. Anne, c/o Elkview, WV, Our Lady of the Hills. (WH)
Cleveland, NM, Mora Co., c/o Mora, NM, St. Gertrude. (SFE)
Cleveland, OH, c/o Cleveland, OH, Our Lady of Mount Carmel. (CLV)
Cleveland, OK, Pawnee Co., St. Joseph, c/o Fairfax, OK, Sacred Heart. (TLS)
Clewiston, FL, Hendry Co., Santa Rosa de Lima, c/o Clewiston, FL, St. Margaret. (VEN)
Clifton, AZ, Greenlee Co., St. Mary, c/o Clifton, AZ, Sacred Heart Roman Catholic Church and St. Mary's Mission – Clifton. (TUC)
Clinton, AR, Van Buren Co., St. Jude, c/o Fairfield Bay, AR, St. Francis Assisi. (LR)
Clinton Corners, NY, Dutchess Co., c/o Millbrook, NY, St. Joseph. (NY)
Cloudcroft, NM, Otero Co., Sacred Heart, c/o Alamogordo, NM, Immaculate Conception. (LSC)
Cloverdale, OR, Tillamook Co., St. Joseph, c/o Tillamook, OR, Sacred Heart. (P)
Clyde, TX, Callahan Co., Sts. Joachim and Ann, c/o Abilene, TX, Sacred Heart. (SAN)
Clyde Park, MT, Park Co., St. Margaret, c/o Livingston, MT, St. Mary. (GF)
Coal Mine, TX, Atascosa Co., Immaculate Conception, c/o Lytle, TX, St. Andrew. (SAT)
Coalburg, WV, Kanawha Co., Good Shepherd, c/o Belle, WV, St. John. (WH)
Coamo Arriba, Sacred Heart of Jesus, c/o Coamo, PR, St. Blase. (PCE)

Cochiti, NM, Sandoval Co., St. Bonaventure, c/o Pena Blanca, NM, Nuestra Senora De Guadalupe. (SFE)
Cochranton, PA, Crawford Co., Our Lady of Lourdes, c/o Guys Mills, PA, St. Hippolyte. (E)
Cochranville, PA, Chester Co., St. Malachy, c/o Parkesburg, PA, Our Lady of Consolation. (PH)
Coco, PR, Salinas Co., Santa Ana, c/o Salinas, PR, Our Lady of Monserrat. (PCE)
Coffman Cove, AK, c/o Craig, AK, St. John by the Sea. (JUN)
Cole Camp, MO, Benton Co., SS. Peter & Paul, c/o Warsaw, MO, St. Ann. (JC)
Collegeville, AL, Jefferson Co., Sacred Heart, c/o Birmingham, AL, Our Lady Queen of the Universe. (BIR)
Collores, PR, Juana Diaz Co., La Milagrosa, c/o Juana Diaz, PR, St. Raymond Nonato. (PCE)
Colon, MI, St. Joseph Co., St. Barbara, c/o Bronson, MI, St. Mary's. (KAL)
Colonia Nueva, TX, Hidalgo Co., Christ the King, c/o Donna, TX, St. Joseph. (BWN)
Colonial Beach, VA, Westmoreland Co., St. Anthony's, c/o Colonial Beach, VA, St. Elizabeth of Hungary. (ARL)
Colonias, NM, Guadalupe Co., c/o Santa Rosa, NM, St. Rose of Lima. (SFE)
Colrain, MA, Franklin Co., St. John the Baptist, c/o Shelburne Falls, MA, St. Joseph's. (SPR)
Columbia, CA, Tuolumne Co., St. Anne, c/o Sonora, CA, St. Patrick Church of Sonora (Pastor of). (STO)
Columbia, KY, Adair Co., Good Shepherd, c/o Jamestown, KY, Holy Spirit. (L)
Columbia, LA, Caldwell Parish, St. John, c/o Winnsboro, LA, St. Mary. (ALX)
Columbia, NC, Tyrrell Co., All Souls, c/o Edenton, NC, St. Anne. (R)
Columbus, NM, Luna Co., c/o Deming, NM, Holy Family. (LSC)
Comal, TX, Comal Co., St. Joseph, c/o New Braunfels, TX, SS. Peter and Paul. (SAT)
Comstock, TX, Valverde Co., Mary, Queen of the Universe, c/o Del Rio, TX, Sacred Heart. (SAT)
Concepcion, TX, Duval Co., Immaculate Conception, c/o Premont, TX, St. Theresa of the Infant Jesus. (CC)
Concrete, WA, Skagit Co., St. Catherine, c/o Sedro Woolley, WA, Immaculate Heart of Mary. (SEA)
Conde Avila, PR, St. Martin de Porres, c/o Cabo Rojo, PR, St. Michael. (MGZ)
Conehatta, MS, Newton Co., St. Catherine, c/o Philadelphia, MS, Holy Rosary. (JKS)
Congress, AZ, Yavapai Co., Good Shepherd of the Desert, c/o Wickenburg, AZ, St. Anthony of Padua Roman Catholic Parish. (PHX)
Conowingo, MD, Cecil Co., St. Patrick, c/o Perryville, MD, Church of the Good Shepherd. (WIL)
Consejo Alto, PR, Guayanilla Co., La Monserrate, c/o Guayanilla, PR, Immaculate Conception. (PCE)
Constantia, NY, Oswego Co., St. Bernadette, c/o Cleveland, NY, St. Mary of the Assumption. (SY)
Contreras, NM, Socorro Co., San Jose, c/o La Joya, NM, Our Lady of Sorrows. (SFE)
Cookson, OK, Cherokee Co., St. John the Evangelist, c/o Sallisaw, OK, St. Francis Xavier. (TLS)
Cooper, TX, Delta Co., St. Clare Mission, c/o Sulphur Springs, TX, St. James. (TYL)
Cooper Landing, AK, St. John Neumann Church, c/o Seward, AK, Sacred Heart. (ANC)
Copper Harbor, MI, Keweenaw Co., Our Lady of the Pines, c/o Calumet, MI, Our Lady of Peace. (MAR)
Coqui, PR, Salinas Co., Our Lady of Perpetual Help, c/o Aguirre, PR, Sacred Heart. (PCE)
Coral, MI, Montcalm Co., St. Clara, c/o Sand Lake, MI, Mary Queen of Apostles. (GR)
Cordell, OK, Washita Co., St. Anne, c/o Clinton, OK, St. Mary's. (OKL)
Cordova, MD, Talbot Co., St. Joseph, c/o Easton, MD, SS. Peter and Paul. (WIL)
Cordova, NM, Rio Arriba Co., San Antonio, c/o Chimayo, NM, Holy Family. (SFE)
Corning, AR, Clay Co., St. Joseph the Worker, c/o Paragould, AR, St. Mary. (LR)
Corona, NM, Lincoln Co., St. Therese of the Little Flower, c/o Carrizozo, NM, St. Rita. (LSC)
Corona, NY, Queens Co., Our Lady of Mount Carmel, c/o Corona, NY, St. Leo. (BRK)
Corpus Christi, TX, Nueces Co., St. Mary, c/o Corpus Christi, TX, St. Peter Prince of Apostles. (CC)
Cortez, CO, Montezuma, Co., Our Lady of Victory Church, c/o Cortez, CO, St. Rita. (PBL)
Costilla, NM, Taos Co., c/o Questa, NM, St. Anthony. (SFE)
Cotton City, NM, Hidalgo Co., St. Jude, c/o Lordsburg, NM, St. Joseph. (LSC)
Cottonwood, CA, Shasta Co., St. Anne, c/o Anderson, CA, Sacred Heart. (SAC)
Cotuy, PR, Our Lady of Fatima, c/o San German, PR, San German de Auxerre. (MGZ)
Coupeville, WA, Island Co., St. Mary, c/o Oak Harbor, WA, St. Augustine. (SEA)
Coushatta, LA, Red River Parish, St. George, c/o Bossier City, LA, Mary, Queen of Peace. (SHP)
Covelo, CA, Mendocino Co., Our Lady, Queen of Peace, c/o Willits, CA, St. Anthony of Padua. (SR)
Covina, CA, Annunciation Mission, c/o North Hollywood, CA, St. Anne. (NTN)
Covington, KY, Kenton Co., St. Ann, c/o Covington, KY, St. John. (COV)
Cox, SD, Harding Co., St. Agnes, c/o Buffalo, SD, St. Anthony. (RC)
Coyanosa, TX, Pecos Co., St. Isidore, c/o Crane, TX, Good Shepherd. (SAN)
Coyote, NM, Rio Arriba Co., c/o Abiquiu, NM, St. Thomas Apostle. (SFE)
Crane, OR, Harney Co., St. Thomas, c/o Burns, OR, Holy Family. (BAK)
Cranfield, MS, Adams Co., St. John the Baptist, c/o Natchez, MS, Holy Family. (JKS)
Crates, PA, Clarion Co., St. Nicholas, c/o New Bethlehem, PA, St. Charles. (E)
Crawfordsville, AR, Crittenden Co., Sacred Heart, c/o West Memphis, AR, St. Michael. (LR)
Creede, CO, Mineral Co., Immaculate Conception, c/o Del Norte, CO, Holy Name of Mary. (PBL)
Crescent, OK, Logan Co., St. Margaret Mary, c/o Guthrie, OK, St. Mary's. (OKL)
Crescent City, IL, Iroquois Co., St. Joseph, c/o Watseka, IL, St. Edmund. (JOL)
Creswell, OR, Lane Co., St. Philip Benizi, c/o Cottage Grove, OR, Our Lady of Perpetual Help. (P)
Cripple Creek, CO, Teller Co., St. Peter's, c/o Woodland Park, CO, Our Lady of the Woods. (COS)
Cristo Rey, TX, Starr Co., Cristo Rey, c/o Grulla, TX, Holy Family. (BWN)
Cross City, FL, Holy Cross, c/o Chiefland, FL, St. John the Evangelist. (STA)
Crosstown, MO, Perry Co., St. James, c/o Perryville, MO, St. Vincent De Paul. (STL)
Crown Point, LA, St. Pius, c/o Lafitte, LA, St. Anthony. (NO)
Crows Landing, CA, Stanislaus Co., Immaculate Heart of Mary, c/o Patterson, CA, Sacred Heart Church of Patterson (Pastor of). (STO)
Cruces, PR, Santa Monica, c/o Aguada, PR, St. Francis of Assisi. (MGZ)
Crucible, PA, Greene Co., St. Mary, c/o Carmichael, PA, Our Lady of Consolation. (PIT)
Cuadrilla, TX, El Paso Co., San Jose, c/o Fabens, TX, Our Lady of Guadalupe. (ELP)
Cubero, NM, Cibola Co., Our Lady of Light, c/o Seboyeta, NM, Our Lady of Sorrows. (GLP)
Cuchillo, NM, Sierra Co., St. Joseph, c/o Truth or Consequences, NM, Our Lady of Perpetual Help. (LSC)
Cuervo, NM, Guadalupe Co., c/o Santa Rosa, NM, St. Rose of Lima. (SFE)
Culbertson, MT, Roosevelt Co., St. Anthony, c/o Poplar, MT, Our Lady of Lourdes. (GF)
Cullman, AL, Cullman Co., St. Boniface, c/o Cullman, AL, Sacred Heart. (BIR)
Cundiyo, NM, Rio Arriba Co., Santo Domingo, c/o Chimayo, NM, Holy Family. (SFE)
Cuny Table, SD, Shannon Co., St. Joseph, c/o Pine Ridge, SD, Holy Rosary. (RC)
Curtis, MI, Mackinac Co., St. Timothy, c/o Grand Marais, MI, Holy Rosary Church. (MAR)
Custer, MT, Yellowstone Co., St. Mary, c/o Hardin, MT, St. Joseph. (GF)
Cuthbert, GA, Randolph Co., St. Luke, c/o Blakely, GA, Holy Family. (SAV)

D

Dahlia, NM, Guadalupe Co., c/o Anton Chico, NM, San Jose. (SFE)
Dallas City, IL, Hancock Co., Sacred Heart, c/o Nauvoo, IL, SS. Peter and Paul. (PEO)
Dalton, NE, Cheyenne Co., St. Mary, c/o Bridgeport, NE, All Souls. (GI)
Dandan, Our Lady of the Most Holy Rosary, c/o Saipan, MP, San Vicente Parish. (CHK)
Danforth, ME, Washington Co., St. Ann, c/o Lincoln, ME, St. Mary. (PRT)
Danville, AR, Yell Co., St. Andrew, c/o Waldron, AR, St. Jude Thaddeus Church. (LR)
Danville, VT, Caledonia Co., Our Lady Queen of Peace, c/o Saint Johnsbury, VT, St. Elizabeth. (BUR)
Darby, MT, Ravalli Co., St. Philip Benizi, c/o Hamilton, MT, St. Francis. (HEL)
Darien, GA, McIntosh Co., Nativity of Our Lady, c/o Brunswick, GA, St. Francis Xavier. (SAV)
Darlington, SC, Darlington Co., St. Joseph the Worker, c/o Hartsville, SC, St. Mary the Virgin Mother. (CHR)
Darrington, WA, Snohomish Co., St. John Mary Vianney, c/o Arlington, WA, Immaculate Conception. (SEA)
Datil, NM, Catron Co., Nativity of the Blessed Virgin Mary, c/o Reserve, NM, Santo Nino. (GLP)
David City, NE, Butler Co., Assumption, c/o David City, NE, St. Mary's. (LIN)
Dayton, OR, Yamhill Co., St. Martin de Porres, c/o McMinnville, OR, St. James. (P)
De Bruce, NY, Sullivan Co., Sacred Heart, c/o Livingston Manor, NY, St. Aloysius. (NY)
De Ruyter, NY, Madison Co., St. Lawrence, c/o Truxton, NY, St. Patrick. (SY)
Decatur, NE, Burt Co., Holy Family, c/o Tekamah, NE, St. Patrick. (OM)
Deep Creek Lake, MD, Garrett Co., St. Peter at the Lake, c/o Oakland, MD, St. Peter the Apostle. (BAL)
Del City, OK, Mission Co., c/o Del City, OK, St. Paul, Apostle. (OKL)
Del Rio, TX, Valverde Co., San Juan Diego Chapel, c/o Del Rio, TX, Our Lady of Guadalupe. (SAT)
Del Valle, TX, Travis Co., San Juan Diego, c/o Austin, TX, San Francisco. (AUS)
Delancey, PA, St. Adrian, c/o Punxsutawney, PA, St. Anthony of Padua. (E)
Delhi, CA, Merced Co., Blessed Teresa of Calcutta, c/o Livingston, CA, St. Jude Thaddeus. (FRS)
Delhi, LA, Richland Parish, St. Theresa, c/o Rayville, LA, Sacred Heart. (SHP)
Dell City, TX, Hudspeth Co., San Isidro, c/o Van Horn, TX, Our Lady of Fatima. (ELP)
Delmar, MD, Wicomico Co., Holy Redeemer, c/o Salisbury, MD, St. Francis De Sales. (WIL)
Delmas Dedeaux, MS, Harrison Co., Our Lady of Chartres, c/o Gulfport, MS, St. Ann. (BLX)
Delta, UT, Millard Co., St. John Bosco, c/o Milford, UT, Saint Bridget LLC 217. (SLC)
Deming, WA, Whatcom Co., St. Peter, c/o Lynden, WA, St. Joseph. (SEA)
Dennis Port, MA, Barnstable Co., Our Lady of the Annunciation, c/o West Harwich, MA, Holy Trinity. (FR)
Denton, MD, Caroline Co., St. Elizabeth of Hungary, c/o Ridgely, MD, St. Benedict. (WIL)
Denton, MT, Fergus Co., St. Anthony, c/o Stanford, MT, St. Rose of Lima. (GF)
Denver, CO, Our Lady of Visitation, c/o Westminster, CO, Holy Trinity. (DEN)
Depew, NY, St. Augustine, c/o Depew, NY, St. James. (BUF)
Des Moines, NM, Union Co., Our Lady of Guadalupe, c/o Clayton, NM, St. Francis Xavier. (SFE)
Descalabrado, PR, Coamo Co., Miraculous Virgin, c/o Coamo, PR, St. Blase. (PCE)
Detroit, OR, St. Christopher, c/o Sublimity, OR, St. Boniface. (P)
Deweese, NE, Clay Co., Assumption, c/o Lawrence, NE, Sacred Heart. (LIN)
Dexter, OR, Lane Co., St. Henry, c/o Oakridge, OR, St. Michael. (P)
Diego Hdez, PR, Yauco Co., St. Anthony, c/o Yauco, PR, Holy Rosary. (PCE)
Diener Ranch At Five Points, CA, Fresno Co., Holy Family Chapel, c/o Riverdale, CA, St. Ann. (FRS)
Dilia, NM, Guadalupe Co., c/o Anton Chico, NM, San Jose. (SFE)
Dilley, TX, Frio Co., St. Mary, c/o Dilley, TX, St. Joseph's. (SAT)
Dillon, CO, Summit Co., Our Lady of Peace, c/o Frisco, CO, St. Mary. (DEN)
Dividing Ridge, KY, Pendleton Co., St. John's, c/o Williamstown, KY, St. William. (COV)
Dixon, NE, Dixon Co., St. Anne, c/o Laurel, NE, St. Mary. (OM)
Dobbins, CA, Yuba Co., Sacred Heart Church, c/o Marysville, CA, St. Joseph. (SAC)
Dodson, MT, Phillips Co., Sacred Heart, c/o Malta, MT, St. Mary. (GF)
Dolan Springs, AZ, Mohave Co., Our Lady of the Desert, c/o Kingman, AZ, St. Mary Roman Catholic Parish. (PHX)
Dollar Bay, MI, Houghton Co., St. Francis of Assisi, c/o Hancock, MI, Resurrection. (MAR)
Donaldson, IN, Maria Center, c/o Donaldson, IN, Convent Ancilla Domini. (FTW)
Donalsonville, GA, Seminole Co., Church of the Incarnation, c/o Bainbridge, GA, St. Joseph's. (SAV)
Doniphan, KS, Doniphan Co., St. John the Baptist, c/o Atchison, KS, St. Benedict's. (KCK)
Donken, MI, Houghton Co., Immaculate Heart of Mary, c/o Chassell, MI, St. Anne. (MAR)
Dorado, PR, Dorado Co., Ntra. Sra. del Camino, c/o Toa Alta, PR, San Jose. (SJN)
Dorado, PR, Dorado Co., S. Francisco De Asis, c/o Toa Alta, PR, San Jose. (SJN)
Dorado, PR, Dorado Co., San Antonio, c/o Toa Alta, PR, San Fernando Rey. (SJN)
Dorado, PR, San Martin de Porres, c/o Dorado, PR, San Antonio de Padua. (SJN)
Dorothy, NJ, Atlantic Co., St. Bernard, c/o Mays Landing, NJ, Church of St. Vincent de Paul, Mays Landing, N.J. (CAM)
Dorrance, KS, Russell Co., St. Joseph, c/o Wilson, KS, St. Wenceslaus Parish. (SAL)
Dorris, CA, Siskiyou Co., Our Lady of Good Counsel, c/o Tulelake, CA, Holy Cross. (SAC)
Douglas, NE, Otoe Co., St. Martin's, c/o Palmyra, NE, St. Leo's. (LIN)
Dove Creek, CO, Dolores Co., St. Jude, c/o Cortez, CO, St. Margaret Mary. (PBL)

Downey, CA, Los Angeles Co., Los Padrinos Juvenile Hall, c/o Downey, CA, St. Raymond. (LA)
Downey, CA, Los Angeles Co., Rancho Los Amigos Hospital, c/o Downey, CA, St. Raymond. (LA)
Downs, KS, Osborne Co., St. Mary's, c/o Osborne, KS, St. Aloysius Gonzaga Parish. (SAL)
Downsville, NY, Delaware Co., Holy Family, c/o Walton, NY, St. John the Baptist. (ALB)
Doylesburg, PA, Franklin Co., Our Lady of Refuge, c/o Chambersburg, PA, Corpus Christi. (HBG)
Draper, SD, Jones Co., St. Anthony of Padua, c/o Presho, SD, Christ the King. (RC)
Drewsey, OR, Harney Co., Our Lady of Loretto, c/o Burns, OR, Holy Family. (BAK)
Drifting, PA, Clearfield Co., St. Severin, c/o Frenchville, PA, St. Mary of the Assumption. (E)
Driftwood, PA, Cameron Co., St. James, c/o Emporium, PA, St. Mark. (E)
Driscoll, TX, Nueces Co., St. James, c/o Bishop, TX, St. James. (CC)
Drummond Island, MI, Chippewa Co., St. Florence, c/o DeTour, MI, Sacred Heart. (MAR)
Drumright, OK, Creek Co., St. Mary, c/o Cushing, OK, SS. Peter and Paul. (TLS)
Dubina, TX, Fayette Co., SS. Cyril and Methodius, c/o Weimar, TX, St. Michael. (VIC)
Dubois, WY, Fremont Co., Our Lady of the Woods, c/o Riverton, WY, St. Margaret's. (CHY)
Dubuisson, MS, Harrison Co., St. Ann, c/o Pass Christian, MS, St. Stephen. (BLX)
Duchesne, UT, Duchesne Co., Holy Spirit, c/o Roosevelt, UT, Saint Helen LLC 224. (SLC)
Duey, PR, Chapel of St. Augustin, c/o San German, PR, San German de Auxerre. (MGZ)
Duey, PR, Yauco Co., Virgin of Mt. Carmel, c/o Yauco, PR, Holy Rosary. (PCE)
Dulce, NM, Rio Arriba Co., St. Anthony, c/o Dulce, NM, St. Francis of Assisi. (GLP)
Duluth, GA, Gwinnett Co., Mision del Divino Nino Jesus, c/o Johns Creek, GA, St. Benedict. (ATL)
Dumas, AR, Desha Co., Holy Child, c/o Monticello, AR, St. Mark. (LR)
Duncan, OK, Stephens Co., St. Thomas Aquinas Chapel, c/o Duncan, OK, Assumption. (OKL)
Duncannon, PA, Perry Co., St. Bernadette, c/o Marysville, PA, Our Lady of Good Counsel. (HBG)
Dundee, NY, Yates Co., St. Andrew, c/o Penn Yan, NY, St. Michael. (ROC)
Dupree, SD, Ziebach Co., Sacred Heart, c/o Eagle Butte, SD, All Saints. (RC)
Dupuyer, MT, Pondera Co., Holy Cross, c/o Valier, MT, St. Francis. (HEL)
Duran, NM, Torrance Co., c/o Vaughn, NM, St. Mary. (SFE)
Durham, CA, Butte Co., St. James, c/o Chico, CA, St. John the Baptist. (SAC)
Dyer, NV, Esmeralda Co., Our Lady of Guadalupe, c/o Tonopah, NV, St. Patrick. (LAV)

E

Eagle, AK, c/o Delta Junction, AK, Our Lady of Sorrows Catholic Church Delta Junction. (FBK)
Eagle, CO, Eagle Co., St. Mary Church, c/o Edwards, CO, St. Clare of Assisi. (DEN)
Eagle Harbor, MI, Keweenaw Co., Holy Redeemer, c/o Calumet, MI, Our Lady of Peace. (MAR)
Eagle Nest, NM, Colfax Co., St. Mel, c/o Cimarron, NM, Immaculate Conception Church. (SFE)
Eagles Mere, PA, Sullivan Co., St. Francis of Assisi, c/o Dushore, PA, St. Basil's. (SCR)
Eagleville, CT, Tolland Co., St. Joseph, c/o Coventry, CT, St. Mary. (NOR)
Easley, SC, Anderson Co., St. Luke, c/o Pickens, SC, Holy Cross. (CHR)
East Barre, VT, Washington Co., St. Cecilia & St. Frances Cabrini, c/o Graniteville, VT, St. Sylvester. (BUR)
East Berkshire, VT, Franklin Co., Our Lady of Lourdes, c/o Richford, VT, All Saints. (BUR)
East Durham, NY, Greene Co., St. Mary, c/o Cairo, NY, Sacred Heart. (ALB)
East Eden, NY, Erie Co., St. Mary, c/o Boston, NY, St. John the Baptist. (BUF)
East Fairfield, VT, Franklin Co., St. Anthony–St. George, c/o Fairfield, VT, St. Patrick. (BUR)
East Glacier, MT, Glacier Co., Chapel of the Ascension, c/o Browning, MT, Church of the Little Flower. (HEL)
East Highlands, CA, San Bernardino Co., St. John Bosco, c/o Highland, CA, St. Adelaide. (SB)
East Quogue, NY, Suffolk Co., c/o Hampton Bays, NY, St. Rosalie's. (RVC)
East Sebago, ME, Cumberland Co., Our Lady of Sebago, c/o Gorham, ME, St. Anne. (PRT)
Eatonville, WA, Pierce Co., Our Lady of Good Counsel, c/o Puyallup, WA, Holy Disciples. (SEA)
La Villa, TX, Hidalgo Co., Our Lady of Guadalupe, c/o Edcouch, TX, St. Theresa of the Infant Jesus. (BWN)
Eden, WY, Sweetwater Co., St. Christopher, c/o Rock Springs, WY, Holy Spirit Catholic Community. (CHY)
Edenville, MI, Gladwin Co., St. Anne, c/o Coleman, MI, St. Philip Neri. (SAG)
Edgemont, SD, Fall River Co., St. James the Apostle, c/o Hot Springs, SD, St. Anthony of Padua. (RC)
Edgewater, FL, Volusia Co., St. Gerard, c/o New Smyrna Beach, FL, Sacred Heart. (ORL)
Edgewood, NM, St. Elizabeth Ann Seton, c/o Moriarty, NM, Estancia Valley Catholic Parish. (SFE)
Edinburg, TX, Hidalgo Co., Capilla de San Jose, c/o Edinburg, TX, Sacred Heart. (BWN)
Edison, NJ, Middlesex Co., St. Margaret Mary Alacoque, c/o Edison, NJ, Guardian Angels. (MET)
Edison, NJ, St. Theresa of the Infant Jesus, c/o New Brunswick, NJ, St. Mary of Mount Virgin. (MET)
Edisto Island, SC, Charleston Co., SS. Frederick & Stephen, c/o Yonges Island, SC, St. Mary. (CHR)
Effie, LA, Avoyelles Parish, St. Winifred, c/o Deville, LA, St. John the Baptist. (ALX)
Egan, LA, Acadia Parish, St. Michael, c/o Iota, LA, St. Joseph. (LAF)
Ekalaka, MT, Carter Co., St. Joan of Arc, c/o Baker, MT, St. John the Evangelist. (GF)
El Cajon, CA, San Diego Co., Immaculate Conception of BVM, c/o Lakeside, CA, Blessed Kateri Tekakwitha. (SD)
El Carmen, NM, Mora Co., c/o Mora, NM, St. Gertrude. (SFE)
El Corozo, PR, Cristo Rey, c/o Cabo Rojo, PR, St. Michael. (MGZ)
El Duende, NM, Rio Arriba Co., c/o Espanola, NM, Sacred Heart. (SFE)
El Flaco, Hidalgo Co., TX, Centro Catolico San Juan Diego, c/o Alton, TX, San Martin de Porres. (BWN)
El Guache, NM, Rio Arriba Co., c/o Espanola, NM, Sacred Heart. (SFE)
El Guique, NM, Rio Arriba Co., c/o Ohkay Owingeh, NM, St. John the Baptist. (SFE)
El Indio, TX, Maverick Co., Our Lady of San Juan, c/o Eagle Pass, TX, Sacred Heart. (LAR)
El Macho, NM, San Miguel Co., c/o Pecos, NM, St. Anthony of Padua. (SFE)
El Nido, CA, St. George, c/o Chowchilla, CA, St. Columba. (FRS)
El Papayo, PR, Cristo Rey, c/o Sabana Grande, PR, Church of San Isidro. (MGZ)
El Paso, TX, El Paso Co., La Resurreccion Mission, c/o El Paso, TX, El Buen Pastor Mission. (ELP)
El Paso, TX, El Paso Co., Santa Teresita, c/o El Paso, TX, San Judas Tadeo. (ELP)
El Pueblo, NM, San Miguel Co., San Antonio de Padua, c/o Ribera, NM, San Miguel Del Vado. (SFE)
El Rancho, NM, Santa Fe Co., c/o Santa Fe, NM, N.S. de Guadalupe del Valle de Pojoaque. (SFE)
El Rio, CA, Ventura Co., Santa Clara Chapel, c/o Oxnard, CA, Santa Clara. (LA)
El Rucio, PR, Penuelas Co., La Milagrosa, c/o Penuelas, PR, St. Joseph. (PCE)
El Sauz, TX, Starr Co., Our Lady of Guadalupe, c/o Roma, TX, Sacred Heart. (BWN)
El Valle, NM, Taos Co., San Miguel Archangel, c/o Chimayo, NM, Holy Family. (SFE)
Elba, NE, Howard Co., St. Joseph, c/o St. Paul, NE, SS. Peter and Paul. (GI)
Elberta, UT, Utah Co., Mission San Isidro, c/o Orem, UT, St. Francis of Assisi LLC 221. (SLC)
Elbridge, MI, Oceana Co., Kateri Tekawitha Native American Center & St. Joseph Center, c/o Hart, MI, St. Gregory's. (GR)
Eleele, HI, Kauai Co., Sacred Heart, c/o Kalaheo, HI, Holy Cross. (HON)
Elfin Cove, AK, c/o Yakutat, AK, St. Ann. (JUN)
Elizabeth, IN, Harrison Co., St. Peter, c/o Corydon, IN, St. Joseph. (IND)
Elizabeth, LA, Allen Parish, St. Frances, c/o Oakdale, LA, Sacred Heart. (LKC)
Elizabeth, WV, Wirt Co., St. Elizabeth of Hungary, c/o Spencer, WV, Holy Redeemer. (WH)
Elizabethtown, NC, Bladen Co., Our Lady of the Snows, c/o Whiteville, NC, Sacred Heart. (R)
Elk, CA, Blessed Sacrament, c/o Mendocino, CA, St. Anthony. (SR)
Elk, TX, McLennon Co., St. Joseph, c/o West, TX, St. Martin. (AUS)
Elkhorn City, KY, Pike Co., St. Joseph the Worker, c/o Pikeville, KY, St. Francis of Assisi. (LEX)
Elkin, NC, Surry Co., St. Stephen, c/o North Wilkesboro, NC, St. John Baptist de LaSalle. (CHL)
Ellinger/Hostyn Hill, TX, Fayette Co., St. Mary, c/o Fayetteville, TX, St. John the Baptist. (AUS)
Elmer, LA, Rapides Parish, St. Peter, c/o Glenmora, LA, St. Louis. (ALX)
Elmwood, NE, Cass Co., St. Mary's, c/o Manley, NE, St. Patrick's. (LIN)
Elsie, NE, Perkins Co., Resurrection of Our Lord, c/o Wallace, NE, St. Mary's. (LIN)
Emanueli, PR, Coamo Co., Holy Family, c/o Coamo, PR, St. Blase. (PCE)
Eminence, KY, Henry Co., St. John Chrysostom, c/o Shelbyville, KY, Annunciation of the Blessed Virgin Mary. (L)
Eminence, MO, Shannon Co., St. Sylvester, c/o Mountain View, MO, St. John Vianney. (SPC)
Emmanuel, LA, Natchitoches Parish, Holy Rosary, c/o Cloutierville, LA, St. John the Baptist. (ALX)
Emory, TX, Rains Co., St. John the Evangelist Church, c/o Mineola, TX, St. Peter the Apostle. (TYL)
Empire, NV, Washoe Co., St. Joseph the Worker, c/o Fernley, NV, St. Robert Bellarmine. (RNO)
Encinal, NM, Valencia Co., Nativity of the Blessed Virgin Mary, c/o Laguna, NM, St. Joseph. (GLP)
Encino, NM, Torrance Co., c/o Vaughn, NM, St. Mary. (SFE)
Encino, TX, Brooks Co., St. Ann, c/o Falfurrias, TX, Sacred Heart. (CC)
England, AR, Lonoke Co., Holy Trinity, c/o Carlisle, AR, St. Rose of Lima Church. (LR)
Ephraim, UT, Sanpete Co., St. Jude, c/o Central Valley, UT, Saint Elizabeth LLC 220. (SLC)
Ericson, NE, St. Theresa of the Child Jesus, c/o Spalding, NE, St. Michael's. (GI)
Erie, CO, Weld Co., St. Scholastica, c/o Northglenn, CO, Immaculate Heart of Mary. (DEN)
Erie, IL, Whiteside Co., St. Ambrose, c/o Prophetstown, IL, St. Catherine. (RCK)
Errol, NH, St. Pius the Tenth, c/o Colebrook, NH, North American Martyrs Parish. (MAN)
Escalante, UT, Garfield Co., St. Sylvester, c/o Cedar City, UT, Christ the King LLC 203. (SLC)
Escobosa, NM, Bernalillo Co., San Isidro, c/o Tijeras, NM, Holy Child. (SFE)
Esopus, NY, Ulster Co., Sacred Heart, c/o Port Ewen, NY, Presentation of the Blessed Virgin Mary. (NY)
Esparto, CA, Yolo Co., St. Martin, c/o Winters, CA, St. Anthony. (SAC)
Essex, IL, Kankakee Co., St. Lawrence O'Toole, c/o Braidwood, IL, Immaculate Conception. (JOL)
Estaca, NM, Rio Arriba Co., c/o Ohkay Owingeh, NM, St. John the Baptist. (SFE)
Estancia, NM, Torrance Co., Sts. Peter & Paul, c/o Moriarty, NM, Estancia Valley Catholic Parish. (SFE)
Estherwood, LA, Acadia Parish, St. Margaret, c/o Mermentau, LA, St. John the Evangelist. (LAF)
Ethete, WY, Fremont Co., St. Joseph, c/o Saint Stephens, WY, St. Stephen's. (CHY)
Etna, CA, Siskiyou Co., St. Mary's, c/o Fort Jones, CA, Sacred Heart. (SAC)
Ettal, FM, c/o Chuuk, FM, Mortlock. (CI)
Euclid, MN, Polk Co., St. Mary, c/o Warren, MN, SS. Peter and Paul. (CR)
Eufaula, OK, McIntosh Co., St. Paul's, c/o Krebs, OK, St. Joseph's. (TLS)
Eureka, CA, St. Joseph, c/o Eureka, CA, St. Bernard. (SR)
Eutaw, AL, Greene Co., St. Mary, c/o Demopolis, AL, St. Leo. (BIR)
Everglades City, FL, Collier Co., Holy Family, c/o Marco Island, FL, San Marco. (VEN)
Excursion Inlet, AK, c/o Yakutat, AK, St. Ann. (JUN)
Expressway Heights, TX, Hidalgo Co., Nuestra Senora de Guadalupe, c/o Weslaco, TX, San Martin de Porres. (BWN)

F

Faga'alu, AS, c/o Pago Pago, AS, Co–Cathedral of St. Joseph the Worker. (SPP)
Faga'itua, AS, c/o Pago Pago, AS, St. Peter Chanel–Sa'ilele. (SPP)
Fagasa, AS, c/o Pago Pago, AS, Sacred Heart Parish–Pago Pago. (SPP)
Fairacres, NM, Dona Ana Co., San Jose Mission, c/o Mesilla, NM, Basilica of San Albino. (LSC)
Fairfield, AL, Jefferson Co., St. Mary's, c/o Birmingham, AL, Holy Family. (BIR)
Fairford, AL, Washington Co., Our Lady of Sorrows, c/o Mount Vernon, AL, St. Peter the Apostle. (MOB)
Fairplay, CO, Park Co., St. Joseph, c/o Buena Vista, CO, St. Rose of Lima. (COS)
Fairview, MT, Richland Co., St. Catherine, c/o Sidney, MT, St. Matthew. (GF)
Fairview, OK, Major Co., St. Ann, c/o Okeene, OK, St. Anthony's. (OKL)
Falcon, TX, Zapata Co., Santa Ana, c/o Zapata, TX, Our Lady of Lourdes. (LAR)
Falcon Heights, TX, Starr Co., Holy Trinity, c/o Roma, TX, Our Lady of Refuge. (BWN)
Faleniu, AS, c/o Pago Pago, AS, St. Paul. (SPP)
Fall River Mills, CA, Shasta Co., Our Lady of the Valley, c/o Burney, CA, St. Francis of Assisi. (SAC)
Falun, MN, Roseau Co., St. Philip, c/o Roseau, MN, Sacred Heart. (CR)
Farmersville, CA, Tulare Co., St. Anthony of Egypt, c/o Exeter, CA, Sacred Heart. (FRS)
Farmerville, LA, Union Parish, Our Lady of Perpetual Help, c/o West Monroe, LA, St. Paschal. (SHP)
Farnam, NE, Dawson Co., St. Joseph's, c/o Curtis, NE, St. James. (LIN)
Farwell, NE, Howard Co., St. Anthony of Padua, c/o St. Paul, NE, SS. Peter and Paul. (GI)

Fashing, TX, Atascosa Co., St. Elizabeth, c/o Karnes City, TX, St. Cornelius. (SAT)
Fayette, AL, Fayette Co., Holy Family, c/o Winfield, AL, Holy Spirit. (BIR)
Faysville, TX, Hidalgo Co., St. Theresa Faysville, c/o Edinburg, TX, St. Joseph the Worker. (BWN)
Faywood, NM, Luna Co., San Jose, c/o Hurley, NM, Infant Jesus. (LSC)
Fellsmere, FL, Indian River Co., c/o Fellsmere, FL, Our Lady of Guadalupe Mission. (PMB)
Fence Lake, NM, Valencia Co., El Morro, c/o Ramah, NM, San Lorenzo. (GLP)
Fillmore, UT, Millard Co., Holy Family, c/o Milford, UT, Saint Bridget LLC 217. (SLC)
Fine, NY, St. Lawrence Co., St. Michael, c/o Star Lake, NY, St. Hubert. (OG)
Fisher, MN, Polk Co., St. Francis, c/o East Grand Forks, MN, Sacred Heart. (CR)
Fishville, LA, Grant Parish, St. Edward, c/o Jena, LA, St. Mary. (ALX)
Fitzgerald, GA, Ben Hill Co., St. William, c/o Douglas, GA, St. Paul's. (SAV)
Flagler, CO, Kit Carson Co., St. Mary, c/o Limon, CO, Our Lady of Victory. (COS)
Flagstaff, AZ, Flagstaff Mission, c/o Phoenix, AZ, Assumption of B.V.M. (STN)
Flanagan, IL, Livingston Co., St. Joseph, c/o Pontiac, IL, St. Mary's. (PEO)
Flatwoods, LA, Rapides Parish, St. Cyril, c/o Boyce, LA, St. Margaret. (ALX)
Fleming, CO, Logan Co., St. Peter the Apostle, c/o Holyoke, CO, St. Patrick. (DEN)
Florence, MT, Ravalli Co., St. Joseph, c/o Stevensville, MT, St. Mary. (HEL)
Florian, MN, Marshall Co., Assumption Church of Florian, c/o Stephen, MN, St. Stephen's. (CR)
Floyd, VA, Floyd Co., Church of All Saints, c/o Woodlawn, VA, St. Joseph's. (RIC)
Folkston, GA, Charlton Co., St. Francis of Assisi, c/o St. Marys, GA, Our Lady Star of the Sea. (SAV)
Folsom, NM, Union Co., St. Joseph, c/o Clayton, NM, St. Francis Xavier. (SFE)
Foreman, AR, Little River Co., Sacred Heart, c/o Texarkana, AR, St. Edward. (LR)
Forest City, MO, Holt Co., St. Patrick, c/o Savannah, MO, St. Rose of Lima. (KC)
Forest Hill, LA, Rapides Parish, Our Lady of Guadalupe, c/o Lecompte, LA, St. Martin. (ALX)
Forest Park, GA, Clayton Co., San Felipe de Jesus, c/o Atlanta, GA, Sacred Heart of Jesus. (ATL)
Foresthill, CA, Placer Co., St. Joseph of Foresthill, c/o Auburn, CA, St. Joseph. (SAC)
Forestville, MI, Sanilac Co., St. John Chrysostom, c/o Port Sanilac, MI, St. Mary. (SAG)
Forestville, PA, Butler Co., St. Anthony Church, c/o Slippery Rock, PA, St. Peter. (PIT)
Forrest, IL, Livingston Co., St. James, c/o Chatsworth, IL, SS. Peter and Paul. (PEO)
Forrest City, St. Francis of Assisi, c/o Brinkley, AR, St. John the Baptist. (LR)
Fort Adams, MS, Wilkinson Co., St. Patrick, c/o Woodville, MS, St. Joseph. (JKS)
Fort Bridger, WY, Uinta Co., St. Helen, c/o Evanston, WY, St. Mary Magdalen. (CHY)
Fort Duchesne, UT, Uintah Co., Blessed Kateri Tekakwitha, c/o Roosevelt, UT, Saint Helen LLC 224. (SLC)
Fort Garland, CO, Costilla Co., Holy Family, c/o San Luis, CO, Sangre de Cristo. (PBL)
Fort Montgomery, NY, Orange Co., Blessed Sacrament, c/o Highland Falls, NY, Sacred Heart of Jesus. (NY)
Fort Stanton, NM, Lincoln Co., Sacred Heart, c/o Ruidoso, NM, St. Eleanor. (LSC)
Fort Valley, GA, Peach Co., St. Juliana, c/o Kathleen, GA, St. Patrick. (SAV)
Fossil, OR, Wheeler Co., St. Catherine, c/o Condon, OR, St. John. (BAK)
Foster City, MI, Dickinson Co., St. Joseph, c/o Bark River, MI, St. Elizabeth Ann Seton. (MAR)
Fountain, FL, Bay Co., Our Lady Queen of Peace, c/o Panama City, FL, Our Lady of the Rosary. (PT)
Fowler, CO, Otero Co., Mary Queen of Heaven, c/o Rocky Ford, CO, St. Peter. (PBL)
Frances, CO, Archuleta Co., St. Francis, c/o Pagosa Springs, CO, Immaculate Heart of Mary. (PBL)
Frances, WA, Pacific Co., Holy Family, c/o Pe Ell, WA, St. Joseph. (SEA)
Franconia, NH, Grafton Co., Our Lady of the Snows, c/o Littleton, NH, St. Rose of Lima. (MAN)
Frankford, DE, Sussex Co., Our Lady of Guadalupe, c/o Bethany Beach, DE, St. Ann. (WIL)
Franklin, NE, Franklin Co., St. Kathrine Drexel, c/o Red Cloud, NE, Sacred Heart. (LIN)
Franklin, NY, Delaware Co., St. Paul, c/o Sidney, NY, Sacred Heart. (ALB)
Franklin, VT, Franklin Co., St. Mary, c/o Sheldon Springs, VT, St. Anthony. (BUR)
Frankston, TX, Anderson Co., St. Charles Borromeo, c/o Palestine, TX, Sacred Heart. (TYL)
Frazer, MT, Valley Co., St. Joseph, c/o Wolf Point, MT, Immaculate Conception. (GF)
Frederick, OK, St. Helen Church, c/o Altus, OK, Prince of Peace. (OKL)
Fredericksburg, TX, Gillespie Co., Our Lady of Guadalupe, c/o Fredericksburg, TX, St. Mary's. (SAT)
Freeport, FL, Walton Co., Christ the King Catholic Mission, c/o Santa Rosa Beach, FL, St. Rita. (PT)
Freeport, ME, Cumberland Co., St. Jude's, c/o Yarmouth, ME, Sacred Heart. (PRT)
French Camp, CA, San Joaquin Co., Good Shepherd, c/o Stockton, CA, St. George Church (Pastor of). (STO)
French Village, MO, St. Francois Co., St. Anne, c/o Bonne Terre, MO, St. Joseph's. (STL)
Fresno, CA, Fresno Co., St. Francis, c/o Fresno, CA, St. John Cathedral. (FRS)
Frewsburg, NY, Our Lady of Victory, c/o Jamestown, NY, St. James. (BUF)
Frieburg, MI, Sanilac Co., St. Ignatius, c/o Argyle, MI, St. Joseph. (SAG)
Frilot Cove, LA, Evangeline Parish, St. Ann, c/o Opelousas, LA, St. Joseph. (LAF)
Fromberg, MT, Carbon Co., St. Joseph, c/o Bridger, MT, Sacred Heart. (GF)
Fronton, TX, Starr Co., Lamb of God, c/o Roma, TX, Our Lady of Refuge. (BWN)
Fryeburg, ME, Oxford Co., St. Elizabeth Ann Seton, c/o Bridgton, ME, St. Joseph. (PRT)
Fulton, MS, Itawamba Co., Christ the King, c/o Tupelo, MS, St. James. (JKS)

G

Gabriels, NY, Franklin Co., Assumption of the B.V.M., c/o Bloomingdale, NY, St. Paul. (OG)
Gainesville, MO, Ozark Co., St. William, c/o Ava, MO, Immaculate Heart of Mary. (SPC)
Gainesville, VA, Prince William Co., St. Katharine Drexel Mission, c/o Middleburg, VA, St. Stephen the Martyr. (ARL)
Gaithersburg, MD, Mother of God Community School, c/o Annandale, VA, Epiphany of Our Lord. (PSC)
Galicia–Columbani, PR, Santo Tomas de Villanueva, c/o Aguada, PR, St. Francis of Assisi. (MGZ)
Galisteo, NM, Santa Fe Co., c/o Cerrillos, NM, St. Joseph. (SFE)
Gallatin, MO, Daviess Co., Mary Immaculate, c/o Hamilton, MO, Sacred Heart. (KC)
Gallegos, NM, Harding Co., c/o Roy, NM, Holy Family–St. Joseph. (SFE)
Gallina, NM, Rio Arriba Co., c/o Abiquiu, NM, St. Thomas Apostle. (SFE)
Gallinas, NM, San Miguel Co., Santo Nino, c/o Las Vegas, NM, Our Lady of Sorrows Church. (SFE)
Gallitzin, PA, Cambria Co., c/o Gallitzin, PA, St. Demetrius. (ALT)
Galway, NY, Saratoga Co., St. Mary's, c/o Hagaman, NY, St. Stephen. (ALB)
Ganado, AZ, Apache Co., St. Anne, c/o Ganado, AZ, All Saints. (GLP)
Garcia, CO, Costilla Co., Sacred Heart of Jesus, c/o San Luis, CO, Sangre de Cristo. (PBL)
Garden Plain, KS, Immaculate Conception, c/o Garden Plain, KS, St. Anthony. (WCH)
Gardena, CA, Los Angeles Co., St. Francis Korean Catholic Center, c/o Gardena, CA, St. Anthony of Padua. (LA)
Gardiner, MT, Park Co., St. William, c/o Livingston, MT, St. Mary. (GF)
Gardner, CO, Huerfano Co., Sacred Heart, c/o Walsenburg, CO, St. Mary. (PBL)
Garrison, NY, Putnam Co., St. Joseph's Chapel, c/o Cold Spring, NY, Our Lady of Loretto. (NY)
Garzas, PR, Adjuntas Co., San Francisco, c/o Adjuntas, PR, St. Joachim. (PCE)
Genesee, PA, Potter Co., Sacred Heart, c/o Galeton, PA, St. Bibiana. (E)
Geneva, AL, Geneva Co., St. Mary, c/o Enterprise, AL, St. John. (MOB)
Gentilly, MN, Polk Co., St. Peter, c/o Crookston, MN, Cathedral of the Immaculate Conception. (CR)
George West, TX, Live Oak Co., c/o George West, TX, St. George. (CC)
Georgetown, CA, El Dorado Co., St. James, c/o Placerville, CA, St. Patrick's. (SAC)
Georgetown, CO, Clear Creek Co., Our Lady of Lourdes, c/o Idaho Springs, CO, St. Paul. (DEN)
Georgetown, MN, Clay Co., St. John, c/o Moorhead, MN, St. Francis de Sales. (CR)
Georgia, VT, Franklin Co., Ascension, c/o St. Albans, VT, Holy Angels. (BUR)
Geraldine, MT, Chouteau Co., St. Margaret, c/o Fort Benton, MT, Immaculate Conception. (GF)
Germfask, MI, Schoolcraft Co., St. Therese, c/o Grand Marais, MI, Holy Rosary Church. (MAR)
Geyser, MT, Judith Basin Co., St. Cyril, c/o Stanford, MT, St. Rose of Lima. (GF)
Gila, NM, Grant Co., St. Isidore, c/o Silver City, NM, St. Vincent de Paul. (LSC)
Gilchrist, OR, Klamath Co., Our Lady of the Snows, c/o La Pine, OR, Holy Redeemer. (BAK)
Giltner, NE, Hamilton Co., St. Joseph's, c/o Aurora, NE, St. Mary's. (LIN)
Girdwood, AK, Our Lady of the Snows, c/o Anchorage, AK, St. Elizabeth Ann Seton. (ANC)
Glasgo, CT, New London Co., St. Anne, c/o Voluntown, CT, St. Thomas the Apostle. (NOR)
Glencoe, LA, St. Mary Parish, St. Joan of Arc, c/o Baldwin, LA, St. Peter the Apostle. (LAF)
Glencoe, NM, Lincoln Co., San Ysidro, c/o Ruidoso, NM, St. Eleanor. (LSC)
Glendale, OR, Douglas Co., Holy Family, c/o Myrtle Creek, OR, All Souls. (P)
Glendale, RI, Providence Co., St. Louis Chapel, c/o Harrisville, RI, St. Patrick. (PRO)
Glennon, MO, Bollinger Co., St. Anthony, c/o Leopold, MO, St. John. (SPC)
Glennville, GA, Tattnall Co., St. Jude, c/o Claxton, GA, St. Christopher. (SAV)
Glentana, MT, Valley Co., Holy Family, c/o Glasgow, MT, St. Raphael. (GF)
Glenwood, AR, Pike Co., Our Lady of Guadalupe, c/o Mena, AR, St. Agnes. (LR)
Glenwood, NM, Catron Co., Santo Nino, c/o Alpine, AZ, St. Helena. (GLP)
Glidden, IA, Carroll Co., St. Elizabeth Seton Church, c/o Lidderdale, IA, Holy Family. (SC)
Glorieta, NM, Santa Fe Co., c/o Pecos, NM, St. Anthony of Padua. (SFE)
Gloster, MS, Amite Co., Holy Family, c/o Woodville, MS, St. Joseph. (JKS)
Gobles, MI, Van Buren Co., St. Jude's Church, c/o Paw Paw, MI, St. Mary. (KAL)
Gold Beach, OR, Curry Co., St. Charles Borromeo, c/o Brookings, OR, Star of the Sea. (P)
Gold Hill, OR, Jackson Co., Our Lady of the River Mission, c/o Grants Pass, OR, St. Anne. (P)
Goldcreek, MT, Powell Co., St. Mary, c/o Drummond, MT, St. Michael. (HEL)
Golden, NM, Santa Fe Co., c/o Cerrillos, NM, St. Joseph. (SFE)
Golden Hill, MD, Dorchester Co., St. Mary, Star of the Sea, c/o Cambridge, MD, St. Mary Refuge of Sinners. (WIL)
Goldens Bridge, NY, Westchester Co., St. Michael, c/o Croton Falls, NY, St. Joseph. (NY)
Golondrinas, NM, Mora Co., c/o Mora, NM, St. Gertrude. (SFE)
Goltry, OK, Alfalfa Co., St. Michael, c/o Enid, OK, St. Gregory the Great. (OKL)
Gonzales, TX, Gonzales Co., Sacred Heart, c/o Gonzales, TX, St. James. (SAT)
Gonzales Ranch, NM, San Miguel Co., c/o Villanueva, NM, Our Lady of Guadalupe. (SFE)
Goodhue, MN, Goodhue Co., Holy Trinity, c/o Goodhue, MN, St. Columbkill. (STP)
Goodridge, MN, Pennington Co., St. Anne, c/o Oklee, MN, St. Francis Xavier's. (CR)
Gorum, LA, Natchitoches Parish, St. Margaret Mary, c/o Boyce, LA, St. Margaret. (ALX)
Goshen, NJ, Cape May Co., St. Elizabeth, c/o Woodbine, NJ, St. Casimir's R.C. Church, Woodbine, N.J. (CAM)
Gothenburg, NE, Dawson Co., Our Lady of Good Counsel, c/o Cozad, NE, Christ the King. (GI)
Goudeau, LA, Avoyelles Parish, St. Charles, c/o Evergreen, LA, Little Flower. (ALX)
Grady, AR, Lincoln Co., Blessed Sacrament, c/o Star City, AR, St. Justin. (LR)
Grafton, NE, Fillmore Co., St. Helena's, c/o Sutton, NE, St. Mary's. (LIN)
Granby, CO, Grand Co., Our Lady of the Snow, c/o Granby, CO, St. Anne. (DEN)
Grand Isle, VT, Grand Isle Co., St. Joseph, c/o South Hero, VT, St. Rose of Lima. (BUR)
Grand Junction, IA, Greene Co., St. Brigid, c/o Jefferson, IA, St. Joseph's. (SC)
Grand Ridge, IL, La Salle Co., St. Mary's, c/o Ottawa, IL, St. Columba. (PEO)
Grand Saline, TX, Van Zandt Co., St. Celestine, c/o Mineola, TX, St. Peter the Apostle. (TYL)
Grandfalls, TX, Ward Co., St. Gertrude, c/o Monahans, TX, St. John the Apostle and Evangelist. (ELP)
Grant, MI, Newaygo Co., Our Lady of Guadalupe Church, c/o Newaygo, MI, St. Bartholomew's. (GR)
Grass Valley, OR, Sherman Co., St. John the Baptist, c/o Wasco, OR, St. Mary. (BAK)
Grassflat, PA, Clearfield Co., SS. Peter & Paul, c/o Frenchville, PA, St. Mary of the Assumption. (E)
Greasewood, AZ, Navajo Co., Our Lady of the Rosary, c/o Ganado, AZ, All Saints. (GLP)
Great Falls, SC, Chester Co., St. Michael, c/o Lancaster, SC, St. Catherine. (CHR)
Greeley, PA, Pike Co., Sacred Heart of Jesus, c/o Shohola, PA, St. Ann's. (SCR)
Green Lake, ME, Hancock Co., Our Lady of the Lake, c/o Ellsworth, ME, St. Joseph. (PRT)
Green River, UT, Emery Co., St. Michael, c/o East Carbon, UT, Good Shepherd LLC 204. (SLC)
Greene, ME, Androscoggin Co., St. Francis, c/o Sabattus, ME, Our Lady of the Rosary. (PRT)
Greenfield, MO, Dade Co., St. Patrick, c/o Mount Vernon, MO, St. Susanne. (SPC)

ooro, AL, Hale Co., Our Lady of Lourdes, c/o nopolis, AL, St. Leo. (BIR)
enup, KY, St. Lawrence, c/o Ashland, KY, Holy Family. (LEX)
reenville, CA, Plumas Co., St. Anthony, c/o Quincy, CA, St. John. (SAC)
Greenwood, NE, Cass Co., St. Joseph's, c/o Ashland, NE, St. Mary's. (LIN)
Greig, NY, Lewis Co., St. Thomas, c/o Lowville, NY, St. Mary. (OG)
Gretna, LA, Jefferson Parish, St. Anthony Mission, c/o Gretna, LA, St. Joseph. (NO)
Groveton, TX, c/o Trinity, TX, Most Holy Trinity. (TYL)
Gruver, TX, Hansford Co., Cristo Redentor, c/o Spearman, TX, Sacred Heart. (AMA)
Grygla, MN, Marshall Co., St. Clement, c/o Oklee, MN, St. Francis Xavier's. (CR)
Guachupanque, NM, Rio Arriba Co., c/o Espanola, NM, Sacred Heart. (SFE)
Guadalupita, NM, Mora Co., c/o Mora, NM, St. Gertrude. (SFE)
Gualala, CA, Mary, Star of the Sea, c/o Point Arena, CA, St. Aloysius. (SR)
Guaniquilla, PR, Ntra. Sra. del Carmen, c/o Aguada, PR, St. Francis of Assisi. (MGZ)
Guayabo, PR, El Buen Pastor, c/o Aguada, PR, St. Francis of Assisi. (MGZ)
Guaynabo, PR, Guaynabo Co., El Buen Pastor, c/o Caguas, PR, Divino Nino Jesus. (SJN)
Guaynabo, PR, Espiritu Santo, c/o Guaynabo, PR, Nuestra Senora de la Paz. (SJN)
Guaynabo, PR, Ciales Co., Inmaculada Concepcion, c/o Guaynabo, PR, Nuestra Senora de la Paz. (SJN)
Guaynabo, PR, Guaynabo Co., Jesus Nazareno, c/o Caguas, PR, Divino Nino Jesus. (SJN)
Guaynabo, PR, Juncos Co., N. Sra. de la Divina Providencia, c/o Guaynabo, PR, Nuestra Senora de la Paz. (SJN)
Guaynabo, PR, Guaynabo Co., N. Sra. de la Paz, c/o Caguas, PR, Divino Nino Jesus. (SJN)
Guaynabo, PR, Guaynabo Co., Ntra. Sra. del Carmen, c/o Guaynabo, PR, Maria Madre de Mi Senor. (SJN)
Guaynabo, PR, San Jose Obrero, c/o Guaynabo, PR, Nuestra Senora de la Paz. (SJN)
Guaynabo, PR, Guaynabo Co., San Miguel, c/o San Juan, PR, San Miguel Arcangel. (SJN)
Guaynabo, PR, Guaynabo Co., San Rafael Arcangel, c/o Caguas, PR, Divino Nino Jesus. (SJN)
Guaynabo, PR, Virgen de la Paz, c/o Guaynabo, PR, Sagrados Corazones. (SJN)
Gugeegue, MH, MH, Santo, c/o Marshall Islands, MH, Queen of Peace. (MI)
Guilarte, PR, Adjuntas Co., San Antonio, c/o Adjuntas, PR, St. Joachim. (PCE)
Gulf Breeze, FL, Santa Rosa Co., Our Lady of the Assumption, c/o Gulf Breeze, FL, St. Ann. (PT)
Gulliver, MI, Schoolcraft Co., Divine Infant of Prague, c/o Manistique, MI, St. Francis de Sales. (MAR)
Gunnison, UT, Sanpete Co., San Juan Diego Mission, c/o Central Valley, UT, Saint Elizabeth LLC 220. (SLC)
Gussetville, TX, Live Oak Co., St. Joseph, c/o George West, TX, St. George. (CC)
Gustavus, AK, c/o Yakutat, AK, St. Ann. (JUN)
Gypsum, KS, Saline Co., St. Patricks, c/o Solomon, KS, Immaculate Conception of the Blessed Virgin Mary Parish. (SAL)

H

Hachita, NM, Grant Co., St. Catherine, c/o Lordsburg, NM, St. Joseph. (LSC)
Hagerman, NM, Chavez Co., St. Catherine, c/o Dexter, NM, Immaculate Conception. (LSC)
Hagerstown, MD, Washington Co., St. Ann's, c/o Baltimore, MD, Patronage of the Mother of God. (PSC)
Haleyville, AL, Winston Co., Our Lady of Guadalupe, c/o Winfield, AL, Holy Spirit. (BIR)
Halfway, OR, Baker Co., St. Therese, c/o Baker, OR, Cathedral of St. Francis De Sales. (BAK)
Hallettsville, TX, Lavaca Co., Ascension of Our Lord, c/o Hallettsville, TX, St. John the Baptist. (VIC)
Hallsville, TX, Harrison Co., Our Lady of Grace, c/o Longview, TX, St. Mary. (TYL)
Halstad, MN, Norman Co., Holy Family, c/o Ada, MN, St. Joseph's. (CR)
Hamburg, AR, Ashley Co., Holy Spirit, c/o Lake Village, AR, Our Lady of the Lake. (LR)
Hamilton, IL, Hancock Co., St. Mary, c/o Warsaw, IL, Sacred Heart. (PEO)
Hamilton, KS, Greenwood Co., St. John, c/o Eureka, KS, Sacred Heart. (WCH)
Hamilton City, CA, Glenn Co., St. Mary, c/o Orland, CA, St. Dominic. (SAC)
Hamlin, TX, Jones Co., Holy Trinity, c/o Anson, TX, St. Michael. (LUB)
Hammond, OR, Clatsop Co., St. Francis de Sales, c/o Astoria, OR, St. Mary, Star of the Sea. (P)
Hampton, CT, Windham Co., Our Lady of Lourdes, c/o Brooklyn, CT, Our Lady of La Salette. (NOR)
Hampton, IL, Rock Island Co., St. Mary, c/o Rapids City, IL, St. John the Baptist. (PEO)
Hampton, SC, Hampton Co., St. Mary, c/o Ridgeland, SC, St. Anthony. (CHR)
Hanalei, HI, Kauai Co., St. William, c/o Kapaa, HI, St. Catherine. (HON)
Hanna, WY, Carbon Co., St. Joseph, c/o Saratoga, WY, St. Ann's. (CHY)
Hanover, NM, Grant Co., Holy Family, c/o Bayard, NM, Our Lady of Fatima. (LSC)
Happy Camp, CA, Siskiyou Co., All Saints, c/o Fort Jones, CA, Sacred Heart. (SAC)
Hardeeville, SC, Jasper Co., St. Anthony, c/o Ridgeland, SC, St. Anthony. (CHR)
Hargill, TX, Hidalgo Co., St. Frances Xavier Cabrini, c/o Raymondville, TX, Our Lady of Guadalupe. (BWN)
Harlem, MT, Blaine Co., Sacred Heart, Fort Belknap, c/o Hays, MT, St. Paul's Indian Mission. (GF)
Harlem, MT, Blaine Co., St. Thomas the Apostle, c/o Chinook, MT, St. Gabriel. (GF)
Harmon, NY, Westchester Co., Church of the Good Shepherd, c/o Croton–on–Hudson, NY, Holy Name of Mary. (NY)
Harmony, WA, Lewis Co., St. Yves, c/o Morton, WA, Sacred Heart. (SEA)
Harrah, OK, Oklahoma Co., St. Teresa of Avila, c/o McLoud, OK, St. Vincent de Paul. (OKL)
Harrington, DE, Kent Co., St. Bernadette, c/o Milford, DE, St. John the Apostle. (WIL)
Harrison, NE, Sioux Co., Church of the Nativity of the Blessed Virgin Mary, c/o Crawford, NE, St. John the Baptist. (GI)
Hart, TX, Castro Co., St. John's, c/o Dimmitt, TX, Immaculate Conception. (AMA)
Hartford, AR, Sebastian Co., St. Leo's, c/o Fort Smith, AR, Immaculate Conception. (LR)
Harvard, MI, Kent Co., St. Margaret, c/o Greenville, MI, St. Charles Borromeo. (GR)
Harvey, LA, Jefferson Parish, Infant Jesus of Prague, c/o Harvey, LA, St. Martha. (NO)
Haskell, TX, Haskell Co., St. George, c/o Stamford, TX, St. Ann. (LUB)
Hato Rey, PR, San Juan Co., Sma. Trinidad, c/o San Juan, PR, Ntr. Sra. de la Caridad del Cobre. (SJN)
Hawk Run, PA, Clearfield Co., SS. Peter & Paul, c/o Morrisdale, PA, St. Agnes. (E)
Hawkinsville, CA, Siskiyou Co., Immaculate Conception, c/o Yreka, CA, St. Joseph. (SAC)
Hawley, MN, Clay Co., St. Andrew, c/o Dilworth, MN, St. Elizabeth. (CR)
Hawthorne, FL, Alachua Co., St. Philip Neri, c/o Gainesville, FL, St. Patrick Church. (STA)
Haxtun, CO, Phillips Co., Christ the King, c/o Holyoke, CO, St. Patrick. (DEN)
Hay Springs, NE, Sheridan Co., St. Columbkille, c/o Gordon, NE, St. Leo's. (GI)
Hayales, PR, Coamo Co., Our Lady of Mt. Carmel, c/o Coamo, PR, St. Blase. (PCE)
Hayden, NM, Quay Co., Holy Trinity, c/o Clayton, NM, St. Francis Xavier. (SFE)
Hayesville, NC, Clay Co., Immaculate Heart of Mary, c/o Murphy, NC, St. William. (CHL)
Hayfork, CA, Trinity Co., Holy Trinity, c/o Weaverville, CA, St. Patrick. (SAC)
Hazard, NE, Sherman Co., St. Gabriel, c/o Loup City, NE, St. Josaphat's. (GI)
Hazlehurst, MS, Copiah Co., St. Martin, c/o Crystal Springs, MS, St. John the Evangelist. (JKS)
Hazleton, PA, Luzerne Co., St. Ladislaus, c/o Hazleton, PA, SS. Cyril & Methodius, Hazleton. (SCR)
Healdton, OK, Carter Co., St. Cecilia, c/o Ardmore, OK, St. Mary. (OKL)
Heart Butte, MT, Glacier Co., Holy Family Mission, c/o Heart Butte, MT, St. Anne (Blackfeet Reservation). (HEL)
Heartwell, NE, Kearney Co., Holy Family, c/o Minden, NE, St. John the Baptist. (LIN)
Heber, CA, Imperial Co., Sacred Heart, c/o El Centro, CA, Our Lady of Guadalupe. (SD)
Heber City, UT, Wasatch Co., St. Lawrence, c/o Park City, UT, Saint Mary of the Assumption LLC 238. (SLC)
Heber Springs, AR, Cleburne Co., St. Albert, c/o Searcy, AR, St. James. (LR)
Hedgesville, WV, Berkeley Co., St. Bernadette, c/o Martinsburg, WV, St. Joseph's. (WH)
Heidelberg, KY, Lee Co., St. Therese, c/o Beattyville, KY, Queen of All Saints. (LEX)
Helena, TX, Karnes Co., St. Helena, c/o Panna Maria, TX, Immaculate Conception of the Blessed Virgin Mary. (SAT)
Hemingford, NE, Box Butte Co., St. Bridget, c/o Alliance, NE, Holy Rosary. (GI)
Henderson, NY, Jefferson Co., Queen of Heaven, c/o Adams, NY, St. Cecilia. (OG)
Hermleigh, TX, Scurry Co., St. John, c/o Snyder, TX, St. Elizabeth's. (LUB)
Hermosa, SD, Custer Co., St. Michael's, c/o Rapid City, SD, Cathedral of Our Lady of Perpetual Help. (RC)
Hernandez, NM, Rio Arriba Co., c/o Espanola, NM, Sacred Heart. (SFE)
Hesperia, MI, Oceana Co., Christ the King, c/o Fremont, MI, St. Michael. (GR)
Hessel, MI, Mackinac Co., Our Lady of the Snows, c/o Goetzville, MI, St. Stanislaus Kostka. (MAR)
High Falls, NY, Ulster Co., Our Lady Help of Christians, c/o Rosendale, NY, St. Peter. (NY)
Highland, MO, Perry Co., St. Joseph, c/o Perryville, MO, St. Vincent De Paul. (STL)
Highlands, NC, Macon Co., Our Lady of the Mountains, c/o Franklin, NC, St. Francis of Assisi. (CHL)
Hill City, SD, Pennington Co., St. Rose of Lima, c/o Rapid City, SD, Blessed Sacrament. (RC)
Hillsboro, NM, Sierra Co., Our Lady of Guadalupe, c/o Garfield, NM, San Isidro. (LSC)
Hinsdale, MT, Valley Co., St. Albert, c/o Glasgow, MT, St. Raphael. (GF)
Hinton, OK, Caddo Co., Sacred Heart, c/o Weatherford, OK, St. Eugene's. (OKL)
Hobart, OK, Kiewa Co., Sts. Peter and Paul, c/o Mangum, OK, Sacred Heart. (OKL)
Hobson, MT, Judith Basin Co., Sacred Heart, c/o Stanford, MT, St. Rose of Lima. (GF)
Hochheim, TX, DeWitt Co., St. Ann, c/o Yoakum, TX, St. Joseph. (VIC)
Hoconuco, PR, Chapel of St. Joseph, c/o San German, PR, San German de Auxerre. (MGZ)
Hode, KY, Martin Co., St. John Neumann, c/o Louisa, KY, St. Jude. (LEX)
Hogeland, MT, Blaine Co., St. Thomas Aquinas, c/o Chinook, MT, St. Gabriel. (GF)
Hollandale, MS, Washington Co., Immaculate Conception, c/o Leland, MS, St. James. (JKS)
Hollis, AK, c/o Craig, AK, St. John by the Sea. (JUN)
Hollis, OK, Harmon Co., Our Lady of Guadalupe, c/o Mangum, OK, Sacred Heart. (OKL)
Holly Lake Rach, TX, Sulphur Co., Holy Spirit Church, c/o Gilmer, TX, St. Francis of Assisi. (TYL)
Holman, NM, Mora Co., c/o Mora, NM, St. Gertrude. (SFE)
Holman, TX, Fayette Co., St. Wenceslaus, c/o Schulenburg, TX, St. John The Baptist. (VIC)
Holton, IN, Ripley Co., St. Mary Magdalen, c/o Osgood, IN, St. John. (IND)
Holualoa, HI, Hawaii Co., Immaculate Conception, c/o Kailua–Kona, HI, St. Michael The Archangel. (HON)
Holyoke, MA, Hampden Co., Holyoke Soldier's Home Chapel, c/o Holyoke, MA, Blessed Sacrament. (SPR)
Holyrood, KS, Ellsworth Co., St. Mary Parish, c/o Wilson, KS, St. Wenceslaus Parish. (SAL)
Homer, IL, Champaign Co., St. Charles Borromeo, c/o Penfield, IL, St. Lawrence's. (PEO)
Homer, LA, Claiborne Parish, St. Margaret, c/o Minden, LA, St. Paul. (SHP)
Homer, NE, Dakota Co., St. Cornelius, c/o Winnebago, NE, St. Augustine's. (OM)
Hominy, OK, Osage Co., c/o Fairfax, OK, Sacred Heart. (TLS)
Honalo, HI, Hawaii Co., St. Paul, c/o Kailua–Kona, HI, St. Michael The Archangel. (HON)
Honokahua (Kapalua), HI, Maui Co., Sacred Hearts of Jesus and Mary, c/o Lahaina, HI, Maria Lanakila. (HON)
Honomu, HI, Hawaii Co., Good Shepherd, c/o Papaikou, HI, Immaculate Heart of Mary. (HON)
Hooker, OK, Texas Co., Sacred Heart, c/o Guymon, OK, St. Peter's. (OKL)
Hoonah, AK, c/o Yakutat, AK, St. Ann. (JUN)
Hooppole, IL, Henry Co., St. Mary's, c/o Annawan, IL, Sacred Heart. (PEO)
Hopedale, IL, Tazewell Co., St. Joseph's, c/o Delavan, IL, St. Mary's. (PEO)
Hopkins Park, IL, Kankakee Co., Sacred Heart, c/o Momence, IL, St. Patrick. (JOL)
Hopland, CA, St. Francis Mission, c/o Ukiah, CA, St. Mary of the Angels. (SR)
Hornitos, CA, Mariposa Co., St. Catherine of Siena, c/o Mariposa, CA, St. Joseph. (FRS)
Horse Cave, KY, Hart Co., Our Lady of the Caves Church, c/o Glasgow, KY, St. Helen. (L)
Horse Springs, NM, Catron Co., St. Anne, c/o Reserve, NM, Santo Nino. (GLP)
Horseshoe Bay, TX, Burnet Co., Our Lady of the Lake (Sunrise Beach), c/o Kingsland, TX, St. Charles Borromeo Catholic Church – Kingsland, Texas. (AUS)
Horseshoe Bend, AR, Izard Co., St. Mary of the Mount Church, c/o Cherokee Village, AR, St. Michael. (LR)
Horseshoe Lake, AR, Crittenden Co., St. Mary of the Lake, c/o Brinkley, AR, St. John the Baptist. (LR)
Hot Springs, MT, Sanders Co., Sacred Heart, c/o Plains, MT, St. James. (HEL)
Hotchkiss, CO, Delta Co., St. Margaret Mary, c/o Paonia, CO, Sacred Heart. (PBL)
Houston, MS, Chickasaw Co., Immaculate Heart of Mary, c/o Aberdeen, MS, St. Francis of Assisi. (JKS)
Hubbard, NE, Dakota Co., St. Mary, c/o Jackson, NE, St. Patrick. (OM)
Hubbard, OR, Marion Co., St. Agnes, c/o Woodburn, OR, St. Luke. (P)

Hudson, IN, Steuben Co., St. Mary of the Angels, c/o Waterloo, IN, St. Michael the Archangel. (FTW)
Hugo, CO, Lincoln Co., St. Anthony of Padua, c/o Limon, CO, Our Lady of Victory. (COS)
Hulett, WY, Crook Co., St. Matthew's, c/o Newcastle, WY, Corpus Christi. (CHY)
Humansville, MO, Polk Co., St. Catherine, c/o Bolivar, MO, Sacred Heart. (SPC)
Hume, IL, Edgar Co., St. Michael's, c/o Villa Grove, IL, Sacred Heart. (SFD)
Humphrey, NY, Cattaraugus Co., St. Pacificus, c/o Ellicottville, NY, Holy Name of Mary. (BUF)
Hunter, NY, St. Mary's Church, c/o Haines Falls, NY, Sacred Heart–Immaculate Conception Church. (ALB)
Huntingdon, TN, Carroll Co., Holy Family Church, c/o Camden, TN, St. Mary Church. (MEM)
Huntington, UT, Emery Co., San Rafael, c/o Price, UT, Notre Dame de Lourdes LLC 207. (SLC)
Huntsville, OH, Logan Co., St. George Chapel Marianists of Ohio, c/o Russells Point, OH, St. Mary of the Woods. (CIN)
Huntsville, UT, Weber Co., St. Florence, c/o Ogden, UT, Saint Joseph LLC 230. (SLC)
Hurley, MS, Jackson Co., St. Ann, c/o Moss Point, MS, St. Joseph. (BLX)
Hurley, NY, Msgr. O'Reilly Chapel, c/o Kingston, NY, St. Joseph. (NY)
Hurtsboro, AL, Russell Co., John XXIII Center, c/o Fort Mitchell, AL, St. Joseph. (MOB)
Hyannis, NE, Grant Co., All Saint's, c/o Mullen, NE, St. Mary's. (GI)
Hydaburg, AK, c/o Craig, AK, St. John by the Sea. (JUN)
Hysham, MT, Treasure Co., St. Joseph, c/o Forsyth, MT, Immaculate Conception. (GF)

I

Imperial, TX, Pecos Co., Our Lady of Lourdes, c/o Crane, TX, Good Shepherd. (SAN)
Independence, CA, Inyo Co., St. Vivian, c/o Lone Pine, CA, Santa Rosa. (FRS)
Indian Land, SC, Our Lady of Grace, c/o Fort Mill, SC, St. Philip Neri. (CHR)
Indiera Fria, PR, Santa Rosa, c/o Maricao, PR, St. John the Baptist. (MGZ)
Industry, TX, Austin Co., Immaculate Conception, c/o Bellville, TX, Sts. Peter & Paul. (GAL)
Inglis, FL, Levy Co., St. Anthony the Abbot, c/o Williston, FL, Holy Family. (STA)
Ingold, NC, Sampson Co., San Juan, c/o Clinton, NC, Immaculate Conception. (R)
Interior, SD, Jackson Co., Holy Rosary, c/o Wall, SD, St. Patrick's. (RC)
Inverness, MT, Hill Co., Sacred Heart, c/o Chester, MT, Our Lady of Ransom. (GF)
Ione, CA, Amador Co., Mule Creek State Prison, c/o Ione, CA, Sacred Heart of Jesus. (SAC)
Ione, CA, Amador Co., Preston California Youth Facility, Ione, c/o Ione, CA, Sacred Heart of Jesus. (SAC)
Iowa, LA, Calcasieu Parish, St. Peter Claver, c/o Welsh, LA, St. Joseph. (LKC)
Iraan, TX, Pecos Co., St. Francis, c/o Big Lake, TX, St. Margaret of Cortona. (SAN)
Irish Grove Rd., IL, Stephenson Co., St. Patrick, c/o Durand, IL, St. Mary. (RCK)
Irishtown, MI, Gratiot Co., St. Patrick, c/o Shepherd, MI, St. Vincent De Paul. (SAG)
Isabel, SD, Dewey Co., St. Mary, c/o Timber Lake, SD, Holy Cross. (RC)
Island Heights, NJ, Ocean Co., St. Gertrude, c/o Toms River, NJ, St. Joseph. (TR)
Isle La Motte, VT, Grand Isle Co., St. Joseph, c/o Alburgh, VT, St. Amadeus. (BUR)
Isle of Hope, GA, Chatham Co., Our Lady of Good Hope, c/o Savannah, GA, St. James. (SAV)
Islesford, ME, Hancock Co., Our Lady Star of the Sea, c/o Bar Harbor, ME, St. Ignatius. (PRT)
Iuka, MS, Tishomingo Co., St. Mary, c/o Booneville, MS, St. Francis of Assisi. (JKS)
Ivanhoe, CA, Tulare Co., San Felipe de Jesus, c/o Visalia, CA, Holy Family. (FRS)

J

Jackpot, NV, Elko Co., Our Lady of Guadalupe, c/o Elko, NV, St. Joseph's. (RNO)
Jackson, AL, Clarke Co., Visitation, c/o Grove Hill, AL, Sacred Heart. (MOB)
Jackson, MI, St. Stanislaus Kosta, c/o Jackson, MI, St. Mary Star of the Sea. (LAN)
Jacksonville, FL, Duval Co., St. Peter, c/o Jacksonville Beach, FL, St. Paul's. (STA)
Jacksonville, OR, Jackson Co., St. Joseph, c/o Medford, OR, Sacred Heart of Jesus. (P)
Jacksonville, TX, Cherokee Co., Our Lady of Guadalupe, c/o Jacksonville, TX, Our Lady of Sorrows. (TYL)
Jacumba, CA, San Diego Co., St. Mary Magdalene, c/o Campo, CA, St. Adelaide of Burgundy Parish. (SD)
Jaguey Chiquito, PR, San Augustin, c/o Aguada, PR, St. Francis of Assisi. (MGZ)
Jamestown, PA, Mercer Co., St. Margaret, c/o Greenville, PA, St. Michael. (E)
Jamestown, TN, Saint Christopher, c/o Harriman, TN, Blessed Sacrament. (KNX)
Jarales, NM, Valencia Co., c/o Belen, NM, Our Lady of Belen. (SFE)
Jardines del Caribe, PR, Perpetuo Socorro, c/o Mayaguez, PR, Our Lady of Mt. Carmel. (MGZ)
Jasper, FL, Hamilton Co., St. Therese of the Child Jesus, c/o Live Oak, FL, St. Francis Xavier. (STA)
Java Center, NY, St. Patrick, c/o Strykersville, NY, St. John Neumann. (BUF)
Jayton, TX, Kent Co., Epiphany, c/o Spur, TX, St. Mary. (LUB)
Jayuya, Bo. Veguita Fama, c/o Jayuya, PR, Our Lady of Monserrate. (PCE)
Jefferson, GA, Jackson Co., St. Catherine Laboure, c/o Toccoa, GA, St. Mary. (ATL)
Jefferson, NH, Coos Co., St. Agnes, c/o Lancaster, NH, Gate of Heaven. (MAN)
Jefferson, OR, Marion Co., St. Thomas, c/o Scio, OR, St. Bernard. (P)
Jefferson, TX, St. Paul of Tarsus Mission, c/o Jefferson, TX, Immaculate Conception. (TYL)
Jeffrey City, WY, Freemont Co., St. Brendan, c/o Lander, WY, Holy Rosary. (CHY)
Jenny Lind, AR, SS. Sabina & Mary Church, c/o Barling, AR, Sacred Heart of Mary. (LR)
Jerome, AZ, Yavapai Co., Holy Family, c/o Cottonwood, AZ, Immaculate Conception Roman Catholic Parish. (PHX)
Jersey City, NJ, Hudson Co., c/o Jersey City, NJ, St. Ann's. (NEW)
Jocko, MT, Lake Co., St. John Berchman's, c/o St. Ignatius, MT, St. Ignatius Mission. (HEL)
Johnson City, TX, Blanco Co., Good Shepherd, c/o Blanco, TX, St. Ferdinand. (AUS)
Johnsonville, SC, Florence Co., St. Patrick the Apostle, c/o Lake City, SC, St. Philip the Apostle. (CHR)
Joliet, MT, Carbon Co., St. John, c/o Bridger, MT, Sacred Heart. (GF)
Jonestown, PA, Lebanon Co., Our Lady of Fatima, c/o Lebanon, PA, Assumption of the Blessed Virgin Mary. (HBG)
Jonesville, LA, Catahoula Parish, St. Gerard, c/o Ferriday, LA, St. Patrick. (ALX)
Jordan, MN, Scott Co., St. Catherine of Spring Lake Township, c/o Jordan, MN, St. Patrick of Cedar Lake Township. (STP)
Jordan, MT, Garfield Co., St. John the Baptist, c/o Circle, MT, St. Francis Xavier. (GF)
Joyuda, PR, St. John the Baptist, c/o Cabo Rojo, PR, St. Michael. (MGZ)
Juana Diaz, PR, Juana Diaz Co., Ntra Sra de la Monserrate, c/o Juana Diaz, PR, Santa Teresita del Nino Jesus. (PCE)
Juana Diaz, PR, Juana Diaz Co., Sagrado Corazon, c/o Juana Diaz, PR, Nuestra Senora de Lourdes. (PCE)
Juana Diaz, PR, San Pedro Nolasco, c/o Juana Diaz, PR, Nuestra Senora de Lourdes. (PCE)
Juana Diaz, PR, Juana Diaz Co., Virgen del Carmen, c/o Juana Diaz, PR, Nuestra Senora de Lourdes. (PCE)
Judith Gap, MT, Wheatland Co., Immaculate Conception, c/o Harlowton, MT, St. Joseph. (HEL)
Julian, NE, Nemaha Co., St. Bernard's, c/o Nebraska City, NE, St. Joseph's. (LIN)
Junction, TX, Kimble Co., St. Theresa Church, c/o Menard, TX, Sacred Heart. (SAN)
Juniata, NE, Adams Co., Assumption, c/o Roseland, NE, Sacred Heart. (LIN)
Juntura, OR, Malheur Co., St. Charles, c/o Burns, OR, Holy Family. (BAK)

K

Kahakuloa, HI, Maui Co., St. Francis Xavier, c/o Waihee, HI, St. Ann. (HON)
Kahaluu, HI, Hawaii Co., St. Peter by the Sea, c/o Kailua-Kona, HI, St. Michael The Archangel. (HON)
Kahuku, HI, Honolulu Co., St. Joachim, c/o Kahuku, HI, St. Roch. (HON)
Kake, AK, c/o Yakutat, AK, St. Ann. (JUN)
Kake, AK, c/o Sitka, AK, St. Gregory of Nazianzen. (JUN)
Kalama, WA, Cowlitz Co., St. Joseph, c/o Woodland, WA, St. Philip. (SEA)
Kalaoa, HI, Hawaii Co., Holy Rosary, c/o Kailua-Kona, HI, St. Michael The Archangel. (HON)
Kaplan, LA, Vermilion Parish, St. Frances Xavier Cabrini, c/o Kaplan, LA, Our Lady of the Holy Rosary. (LAF)
Karlstad, MN, Marshall Co., St. Edward, c/o Greenbush, MN, Blessed Sacrament. (CR)
Kaupo, HI, Maui Co., St. Joseph, c/o Hana, HI, St. Mary. (HON)
Kaycee, WY, Johnson Co., St. Hubert, c/o Buffalo, WY, St. John the Baptist. (CHY)
Keaau, HI, Hawaii Co., Holy Rosary, c/o Mountain View, HI, St. Theresa. (HON)
Kealakekua, HI, Hawaii Co., St. John the Baptist, c/o Captain Cook, HI, St. Benedict. (HON)
Kelly, NM, Socorro Co., c/o Socorro, NM, San Miguel. (SFE)
Kelseyville, CA, St. Peter, c/o Lakeport, CA, St. Mary. (SR)
Kenel, SD, Corson Co., Assumption of the Blessed Virgin Mary Church, c/o McLaughlin, SD, Standing Rock Reservation. (RC)
Kenel, SD, Corson Co., Our Lady of the Assumption Parish, c/o McLaughlin, SD, St. Bernard. (RC)
Kerhonkson, NY, Ulster Co., Our Lady of Lourdes, c/o Ellenville, NY, St. Mary and St. Andrew. (NY)
Kettleman City, CA, Kings Co., St. Cecilia, c/o Avenal, CA, St. Joseph. (FRS)
Kewanna, IN, Fulton Co., St. Ann, c/o Rochester, IN, St. Joseph. (LFT)
Key West, FL, Monroe Co., St. Mary, Star of the Sea Outreach Mission, c/o Key West, FL, St. Mary, Star of the Sea. (MIA)
Keyapaha, SD, Tripp Co., St. Ann, c/o Winner, SD, Immaculate Conception. (RC)
Keystone, SD, Pennington Co., Our Lady of Mt. Carmel, c/o Rapid City, SD, Blessed Sacrament. (RC)
Kilauea, HI, Kauai Co., St. Sylvester, c/o Kapaa, HI, St. Catherine. (HON)
Kilkenny, MN, Le Sueur Co., St. Canice, c/o Montgomery, MN, Most Holy Redeemer. (STP)
Killington, VT, Rutland Co., Our Lady of the Mountains, c/o Woodstock, VT, Our Lady of the Snows. (BUR)
King, NC, Stokes Co., Good Shepherd, c/o Winston-Salem, NC, St. Benedict the Moor. (CHL)
King Ranch, TX, Kleberg Co., Christ the King, c/o Kingsville, TX, St. Martin. (CC)
Kingman, ME, Penobscot Co., St. James, c/o Lincoln, ME, St. Mary. (PRT)
Kings Beach, CA, Placer Co., Our Lady of the Lake, c/o Truckee, CA, Assumption of the Blessed Virgin Mary. (SAC)
Kings Mountain, NC, Cleveland Co., Christ the King, c/o Shelby, NC, St. Mary's. (CHL)
Kingston, WI, Green Lake Co., St. Mary, c/o Markesan, WI, St. Joseph. (MAD)
Kingsville, TX, Kleberg Co., St. Thomas Aquinas Catholic Campus Center – Texas A & M, c/o Kingsville, TX, St. Gertrude. (CC)
Kinnear, WY, Fremont Co., St. Edward, c/o Riverton, WY, St. Margaret's. (CHY)
Kipahulu, HI, Maui Co., St. Paul, c/o Hana, HI, St. Mary. (HON)
Kirtland, NM, San Juan Co., San Juan Catholic Center, c/o Waterflow, NM, Sacred Heart. (GLP)
Kit Carson, CO, Cheyenne Co., St. Augustine, c/o Cheyenne Wells, CO, Sacred Heart. (COS)
Klamath, CA, St. Robert and Ann, c/o Crescent City, CA, St. Joseph. (SR)
Kluckwan, AK, c/o Haines, AK, Sacred Heart. (JUN)
Knickerbocker, TX, Tom Green Co., Immaculate Conception, c/o Eldorado, TX, Our Lady of Guadalupe. (SAN)
Knippa, TX, Uvalde Co., St. Joseph, c/o Sabinal, TX, St. Patrick's. (SAT)
Koeltztown, MO, St. Boniface, c/o Argyle, MO, St. Aloysius. (JC)
Kolin, LA, Rapides Parish, Sts. Francis and Anne, c/o Deville, LA, St. John the Baptist. (ALX)
Kovar, TX, Bastrop Co., Sts. Peter and Paul, c/o Smithville, TX, St. Paul the Apostle. (AUS)
Kress, TX, Swisher Co., St. Paul the Apostle, c/o Tulia, TX, Church of the Holy Spirit. (AMA)
Kuttu, FM, c/o Chuuk, FM, Mortlock. (CI)

L

L'Erable, IL, Iroquois Co., St. John the Baptist, c/o Ashkum, IL, Assumption of the Blessed Virgin Mary. (JOL)
La Bajada, NM, Sandoval Co., San Miguel, c/o Pena Blanca, NM, Nuestra Senora De Guadalupe. (SFE)
La Casita, TX, Starr Co., Our Lady of the Peace, c/o Grulla, TX, Holy Family. (BWN)
La Cienega, NM, Santa Fe Co., San Jose, c/o Santa Fe, NM, San Isidro. (SFE)
La Cueva, NM, Mora Co., c/o Mora, NM, St. Gertrude. (SFE)
La Grange, CA, Stanislaus Co., St. Louis, c/o Hughson, CA, St. Anthony Church of Hughson (Pastor of). (STO)
La Grange, MO, Lewis Co., Notre Dame, c/o Canton, MO, St. Joseph. (JC)
La Honda, CA, San Mateo Co., Our Lady of Refuge, c/o Half Moon Bay, CA, Our Lady of the Pillar. (SFR)
La Isla, TX, El Paso Co., San Luis, c/o Fabens, TX, Our Lady of Guadalupe. (ELP)

La Jara, CO, Conejos Co., Our Lady of the Valley, c/o Capulin, CO, St. Joseph. (PBL)
La Jara, NM, Sandoval Co., Santo Nino, c/o Cuba, NM, Immaculate Conception. (GLP)
La Lagunita, NM, San Miguel Co., c/o Ribera, NM, San Miguel Del Vado. (SFE)
La Luz, NM, Otero Co., Our Lady of the Light, c/o Alamogordo, NM, Immaculate Conception. (LSC)
La Madera, NM, Rio Arriba Co., c/o El Rito, NM, San Juan Nepomuceno. (SFE)
La Marina, PR, Guaynabo Co., San Francisco de Asis, c/o San Juan, PR, San Juan Evangelista. (SJN)
La Mesa, NM, Dona Ana Co., San Pedro (Del Cerro), c/o La Mesa, NM, San Jose. (LSC)
La Paloma, TX, Cameron Co., Our Lady of Lourdes, c/o San Benito, TX, St. Ignatius. (BWN)
La Playa, PR, Our Lady of Carmel, c/o Anasco, PR, St. Anthony Abbot. (MGZ)
La Salle, TX, Jackson Co., St. Theresa, c/o Vanderbilt, TX, St. John Bosco. (VIC)
La Union, NM, Dona Ana Co., Our Lady of Refuge, c/o Anthony, NM, St. Anthony's. (LSC)
La Veta, CO, Huerfano Co., Christ the King, c/o Walsenburg, CO, St. Mary. (PBL)
La Villa, TX, Hidalgo Co., Our Lady of Guadalupe, c/o Edcouch, TX, St. Theresa of the Infant Jesus. (BWN)
LaCrosse, IN, LaPorte Co., St. Martin, c/o Wanatah, IN, Sacred Heart. (GRY)
LaSal, UT, San Juan Co., Sacred Heart, c/o Moab, UT, Saint Pius X LLC 244. (SLC)
Labelle, FL, Hendry Co., Holy Martyrs Mission, c/o LaBelle, FL, Our Lady Queen of Heaven. (VEN)
Lacassine, LA, Jefferson Davis Parish, St. John the Evangelist, c/o Fenton, LA, St. Charles Borromeo. (LKC)
Lacey, MI, Barry Co., Our Lady of Great Oak, c/o Delton, MI, St. Ambrose. (KAL)
Lackawaxen, PA, Pike Co., St. Mary of the Assumption, c/o Shohola, PA, St. Ann's. (SCR)
Laddonia, MO, Audrain Co., St. John, c/o Vandalia, MO, Sacred Heart. (JC)
Lafayette, LA, Lafayette Parish, Gift of Mary Chapel, c/o Lafayette, LA, St. Genevieve. (LAF)
Lafayette, LA, Lafayette Parish, Our Lady of Good Hope, c/o Lafayette, LA, St. Paul The Apostle. (LAF)
Laguna, PR, Santa Rita, c/o Aguada, PR, St. Francis of Assisi. (MGZ)
Laguna Heights, TX, Cameron Co., Laguna Heights Chapel, c/o Port Isabel, TX, Our Lady Star of the Sea. (BWN)
Lajitas, TX, Brewster Co., Lajitas Mission, c/o Presidio, TX, Santa Teresa de Jesus. (ELP)
Lake Arthur, NM, Chavez Co., Our Lady of Guadalupe, c/o Dexter, NM, Immaculate Conception. (LSC)
Lake Bonaparte, NY, St. Rita, c/o Harrisville, NY, St. Francis Solanus. (OG)
Lake Carmel, NY, Putnam Co., Our Lady of the Lake/Mt. Carmel, c/o Carmel, NY, St. James the Apostle. (NY)
Lake Charles, LA, Calcasieu Parish, Our Lady of Fatima Chapel, c/o Lake Charles, LA, Immaculate Heart of Mary. (LKC)
Lake Hughes, CA, Los Angeles Co., St. Elizabeth, c/o Lancaster, CA, Blessed Junipero Serra. (LA)
Lake Huntington, NY, Sullivan Co., Our Lady of the Lake, c/o Narrowsburg, NY, St. Francis Xavier. (NY)
Lake Park, MN, Becker Co., St. Francis Xavier, c/o Detroit Lakes, MN, St. Mary of the Lakes. (CR)
Lake Titus, NY, Franklin Co., St. Mary, c/o Malone, NY, St. Helen. (OG)
Lake Wallenpaupack, PA, Pike Co., St. Veronica, c/o Hawley, PA, Blessed Virgin Mary, Queen of Peace. (SCR)
Lake Wylie, SC, York Co., All Saints, c/o York, SC, Divine Saviour. (CHR)
Lakehills, TX, Bandera Co., St. Victor's Chapel, c/o Bandera, TX, St. Stanislaus. (SAT)
Lakeside, SD, Meade Co., St. Margaret, c/o Wall, SD, St. Patrick's. (RC)
Lakeview, MI, Montcalm Co., St. Frances de Sales, c/o Howard City, MI, Christ the King. (GR)
Lakewood, NJ, Ocean Co., Holy Family Church, c/o Lakewood, NJ, St. Mary of the Lake. (TR)
Lambert, MT, Richland Co., St. Theresa, c/o Sidney, MT, St. Matthew. (GF)
Lamesa, TX, Dawson Co., Our Lady of Guadalupe, c/o Lamesa, TX, St. Margaret Mary. (LUB)
Lancaster, MN, Kittson Co., Holy Rosary, c/o Hallock, MN, St. Patrick's. (CR)
Langley Park, MD, Prince George's Co., Catholic Community of Langley Park, c/o Silver Spring, MD, St. Camillus. (WDC)
Lantana, FL, Palm Beach Co., c/o Miami, FL, Assumption of B.V.M. (SJP)
Laporte, MN, Hubbard Co., St. Theodore, c/o Nevis, MN, Our Lady of the Pines. (CR)
Laredo, TX, Webb Co., Santa Cruz, c/o Laredo, TX, Holy Redeemer. (LAR)
Largo, FL, Pinellas Co., Holy Martyrs of Vietnam, c/o Largo, FL, St. Matthew. (SP)
Las Colonias, NM, Taos Co., Santo Nino de Atocha, c/o Arroyo Seco, NM, La Santisima Trinidad. (SFE)
Las Colonias, NM, San Miguel Co., c/o Pecos, NM, St. Anthony of Padua. (SFE)
Las Flores, Coamo, PR, Coamo Co., San Martin, c/o Coamo, PR, San Antonio de Padua. (PCE)
Las Mareas, PR, Salinas Co., St. Judas, c/o Aguirre, PR, Sacred Heart. (PCE)
Las Margaritas, Bo. Collores, PR, Bo. Collores Arriba, Santiago, Ap., c/o Juana Diaz, PR, St. Raymond Nonato. (PCE)
Las Mesitas, CO, Conejos Co., San Isidro Brador, c/o Antonito, CO, Our Lady of Guadalupe. (PBL)
Las Nutrias, NM, Socorro Co., San Isidro, c/o La Joya, NM, Our Lady of Sorrows. (SFE)
Las Ochenta, PR, Salinas Co., Inmaculada Concepcion, c/o Salinas, PR, Our Lady of Monserrat. (PCE)
Las Palmas, PR, St. Rita, c/o Cabo Rojo, PR, St. Michael. (MGZ)
Las Palomas, NM, Sierra Co., San Ysidro, c/o Truth or Consequences, NM, Our Lady of Perpetual Help. (LSC)
Las Rucias, TX, Cameron Co., Sacred Heart, c/o San Benito, TX, St. Ignatius. (BWN)
Las Tablas, NM, Taos Co., c/o El Rito, NM, San Juan Nepomuceno. (SFE)
Lasara, TX, Willacy Co., St. Patrick, c/o Raymondville, TX, Our Lady of Guadalupe. (BWN)
Latimer, MS, Jackson Co., Christ the King, c/o Vancleave, MS, Holy Spirit Catholic Church. (BLX)
Laurens, SC, Laurens Co., Holy Spirit, c/o Joanna, SC, St. Boniface. (CHR)
Lawrence, NE, Nuckolls Co., St. Stephen's, c/o Lawrence, NE, Sacred Heart. (LIN)
Le Bleu Settlement, LA, Calcasieu Parish, St. Joseph, c/o Iowa, LA, St. Raphael. (LKC)
Le Doux, NM, Mora Co., c/o Mora, NM, St. Gertrude. (SFE)
LeGrand, CA, Merced Co., Our Lady of Lourdes, c/o Planada, CA, Sacred Heart. (FRS)
LeRoy, NY, St. Joseph, c/o LeRoy, NY, Our Lady of Mercy. (BUF)
Leakesville, MS, Perry Co., Holy Trinity, c/o Waynesboro, MS, St. Bernadette. (BLX)
Leakey, TX, Real Co., St. Raymond of Pennafort, c/o Rocksprings, TX, Sacred Heart of Mary. (SAT)
Leavenworth, KS, Kickapoo Twp., Sacred Heart, c/o Leavenworth, KS, Immaculate Conception–St. Joseph. (KCK)
Lebanon, OH, c/o Lebanon, OH, St. Francis de Sales. (CIN)
Ledgedale, PA, Wayne Co., St. Mary, c/o Lake Ariel, PA, St. Thomas More. (SCR)
Lee Vining, CA, Mono Co., Our Savior of the Mountains, c/o Mammoth Lakes, CA, St. Joseph Church of Mammoth Lakes. (STO)
Leicester, VT, Addison Co., St. Agnes, c/o Brandon, VT, St. Mary's. (BUR)
Leming, TX, Loire Co., Our Lady of Guadalupe, c/o Pleasanton, TX, St. Luke–Loire. (SAT)
Lemitar, NM, Socorro Co., c/o Socorro, NM, San Miguel. (SFE)
Lemoore, CA, Kings Co., St. Joseph, c/o Lemoore, CA, St. Peter Prince of Apostles. (FRS)
Lenorah, TX, Martin Co., St. Isidore, c/o Stanton, TX, St. Joseph's. (SAN)
Lesterville, MO, Reynolds Co., Our Lady of Sorrows, c/o Ironton, MO, Ste. Marie Du Lac. (SPC)
Lewiston, CA, Trinity Co., St. Gilbert, c/o Weaverville, CA, St. Patrick. (SAC)
Lexington, IL, McLean Co., St. Mary, c/o Chenoa, IL, St. Joseph's. (PEO)
Lexington, TX, Lee Co., Holy Family, c/o Dime Box, TX, St. Joseph. (AUS)
Leyba, NM, San Miguel Co., c/o Villanueva, NM, Our Lady of Guadalupe. (SFE)
Liberty, KY, Casey Co., Sacred Heart, c/o Liberty, KY, St. Bernard. (L)
Licking, MO, Texas Co., St. John The Baptist, c/o Houston, MO, St. Mark. (SPC)
Lilburn, GA, Gwinnet Co., Our Lady of the Americas, c/o Norcross, GA, Saint Patrick. (ATL)
Limani, PR, Adjuntas Co., Ntra Sra Fátima Juan González, c/o Adjuntas, PR, St. Joachim. (PCE)
Lincoln, MA, Middlesex Co., St. Joseph, c/o Weston, MA, St. Julia. (BO)
Lincoln, MT, Lewis and Clark Co., St. Jude's, c/o Helmville, MT, St. Thomas. (HEL)
Lincoln, NM, Lincoln Co., San Juan, c/o Ruidoso, NM, St. Eleanor. (LSC)
Lindsay, OK, Garvin Co., St. Peter's, c/o Pauls Valley, OK, St. Catherine of Siena. (OKL)
Lindsborg, KS, McPherson Co., St. Bridget of Sweden, c/o McPherson, KS, St. Joseph. (WCH)
Linlithgo, NY, Columbia Co., Nativity, c/o Hudson, NY, Parish of the Holy Trinity. (ALB)
Linville, NC, Avery Co., St. Bernadette, c/o Spruce Pine, NC, St. Lucien. (CHL)
Lisco, NE, Garden Co., St. Gall, c/o Chappell, NE, St. Joseph's. (GI)
Litchfield, OH, Medina Co., Jesus the Christ Child, c/o Litchfield, OH, Our Lady Help of Christians Parish. (CLV)
Little Diomede, AK, Nome Census Area, St. Jude Catholic Church Little Diomede, c/o Nome, AK, St. Joseph Catholic Church Nome. (FBK)
Little Italy, AR, Pulaski Co., St. Francis of Assisi, c/o Bigelow, AR, St. Boniface. (LR)
Little Orleans, MD, Allegany Co., St. Patrick's, c/o Hancock, MD, St. Peter's. (BAL)
Littlerock, CA, Los Angeles Co., Our Lady of the Desert, c/o Palmdale, CA, St. Mary. (LA)
Littleton, WV, Wetzel Co., Assumption of the Blessed Virgin Mary, c/o Mannington, WV, St. Patrick's. (WH)
Live Oak, CA, Sutter Co., Our Lady of Guadalupe, c/o Gridley, CA, Sacred Heart. (SAC)
Llano Quemado, NM, Taos Co., N.S. del Carmel, c/o Ranchos De Taos, NM, San Francisco de Asis. (SFE)
Llano San Juan, NM, Taos Co., San Juan Nepomuceno Mission, c/o Penasco, NM, San Antonio de Padua. (SFE)
Llanos Tunas, PR, Our Lady of Good Counsel, c/o Cabo Rojo, PR, St. Michael. (MGZ)
Lobatos, CO, Conejos Co., Sagrada Familia, c/o Antonito, CO, Our Lady of Guadalupe. (PBL)
Loch Lomond, CA, Our Lady of the Lake, c/o Middletown, CA, St. Joseph. (SR)
Lockney, TX, Floyd Co., San Jose, c/o Plainview, TX, St. Alice. (LUB)
Lockport, NY, St. Joseph, c/o Lockport, NY, All Saints. (BUF)
Lodgepole, MT, Blaine Co., St. Thomas, c/o Hays, MT, St. Paul's Indian Mission. (GF)
Lodi, OH, Medina Co., Jesus Our Teacher, c/o Litchfield, OH, Our Lady Help of Christians Parish. (CLV)
Logan, KS, Phillips Co., St. John the Evangelist, c/o Phillipsburg, KS, Saints Philip and James Parish. (SAL)
Logan, NM, Quay Co., San Antonio, c/o Tucumcari, NM, St. Anne. (SFE)
Logan, UT, Cache Co., Utah State University, c/o Hyde Park, UT, Saint Thomas Aquinas LLC 247. (SLC)
Loiza, PR, Ntra. Sra. de Fatima, c/o Loiza, PR, San Patricio. (FAJ)
Loiza, PR, San Antonio, c/o Loiza, PR, San Patricio. (FAJ)
Loiza, PR, San Rafael, c/o Loiza, PR, San Patricio. (FAJ)
Loleta, CA, St. Patrick, c/o Fortuna, CA, St. Joseph. (SR)
Lolo, MT, Missoula Co., Spirit of Christ, c/o Missoula, MT, Blessed Trinity Parish. (HEL)
Lometa, TX, Lampasas Co., Good Shepherd Catholic Church, c/o Lampasas, TX, St. Mary of the Immaculate Conception. (AUS)
London, CA, Tulare Co., Santa Cruz, c/o Kingsburg, CA, Holy Family. (FRS)
Long Beach, CA, Los Angeles Co., Our Lady of Mt. Carmel Cambodian Catholic Center, c/o Long Beach, CA, St. Anthony. (LA)
Long Creek, OR, Grant Co., St. Katherine, c/o John Day, OR, St. Elizabeth. (BAK)
Long Eddy, NY, St. Patrick, c/o Callicoon, NY, Holy Cross. (NY)
Long Island, ME, Cumberland Co., c/o Portland, ME, St. Christopher's. (PRT)
Lopeno, TX, Zapata Co., San Pedro, c/o Zapata, TX, Our Lady of Lourdes. (LAR)
Lopezville, TX, Hidalgo Co., Immaculate Conception, c/o San Juan, TX, St. John the Baptist. (BWN)
Loraine, TX, Mitchell Co., St. Joseph, c/o Colorado City, TX, St. Ann's. (SAN)
Lorenzo, TX, Crosby Co., San Lorenzo, c/o Idalou, TX, St. Philip Benizi. (LUB)
Loris, SC, Horry Co., Catholic Church of the Resurrection, c/o Conway, SC, St. James. (CHR)
Los Alamos, CA, St. Anthony's Church, c/o Santa Maria, CA, St. Louis de Montfort. (LA)
Los Angeles, CA, Old Co., Assumption, c/o Los Angeles, CA, Assumption. (LA)
Los Angeles, CA, Los Angeles Co., Blessed Alphonsa Catholic Mission, c/o Chatsworth, CA, St. John Eudes. (LA)
Los Angeles, CA, Hermanas Misioneras Servidoras de la Palabra, c/o Los Angeles, CA, Santa Isabel. (LA)
Los Angeles, CA, Los Angeles Co., La Purisima Chapel, c/o Los Angeles, CA, Our Lady of the Rosary of Talpa. (LA)
Los Angeles, CA, Los Angeles Co., San Conrado, c/o Los Angeles, CA, St. Peter. (LA)
Los Angeles, CA, Los Angeles Co., San Felipe, c/o Los Angeles, CA, Our Lady of Guadalupe. (LA)
Los Angeles, CA, Los Angeles Co., Santo Nino, c/o Los Angeles, CA, St. Vincent De Paul. (LA)
Los Angeles, CA, Los Angeles Co., St. John Bosco, c/o Los Angeles, CA, St. Odilia. (LA)
Los Angeles, CA, Los Angeles Co., St. Turibius, c/o Los Angeles, CA, St. Joseph. (LA)

Los Chavez, NM, Valencia Co., c/o Belen, NM, Our Lady of Belen. (SFE)
Los Cordovas, NM, Taos Co., San Isidro, c/o Ranchos De Taos, NM, San Francisco de Asis. (SFE)
Los Ebanos, TX, Hidalgo Co., St. Michael, c/o La Joya, TX, Our Lady, Queen of Angels. (BWN)
Los Garcias Ranch, TX, Starr Co., Sacred Heart, c/o Rio Grande City, TX, Immaculate Conception. (BWN)
Los Hueros, NM, Mora Co., c/o Wagon Mound, NM, Santa Clara. (SFE)
Los Le Febres, NM, Mora Co., c/o Wagon Mound, NM, Santa Clara. (SFE)
Los Lentes, NM, Valencia Co., San Antonio, c/o Los Lunas, NM, San Clemente. (SFE)
Los Lunas, NM, San Juan Diego, c/o Los Lunas, NM, San Clemente. (SFE)
Los Martinez, NM, San Juan Co., Our Lady of Guadalupe, c/o Bloomfield, NM, St. Rose of Lima. (GLP)
Los Saenz, TX, Starr Co., Holy Family, c/o Roma, TX, Our Lady of Refuge. (BWN)
Los Sauces, CO, Conejos Co., St. Anthony, c/o Capulin, CO, St. Joseph. (PBL)
Los Valdeses, CO, Rio Grande Co., St. Francis of Assisi, c/o Del Norte, CO, Holy Name of Mary. (PBL)
Losap, FM, c/o Chuuk, FM, Mortlock. (CI)
Lott, TX, Falls Co., Sacred Heart, c/o Marlin, TX, St. Joseph. (AUS)
Louise, TX, Wharton Co., St. Procopius, c/o El Campo, TX, St. Andrew. (VIC)
Louisville, GA, Jefferson Co., St. Joan of Arc, c/o Waynesboro, GA, Sacred Heart. (SAV)
Loveladies, NJ, Ocean Co., St. Clare, c/o Brant Beach, NJ, St. Francis of Assisi. (TR)
Lowell, VT, Orleans Co., St. Ignatius Loyola, c/o Troy, VT, Sacred Heart of Jesus. (BUR)
Lower San Francisco, NM, Catron Co., San Isidro, c/o Reserve, NM, Santo Nino. (GLP)
Loyalton, CA, Sierra Co., Holy Rosary, c/o Portola, CA, Holy Family. (SAC)
Lozano, TX, Cameron Co., St. Vincent de Paul, c/o Rio Hondo, TX, St. Helen. (BWN)
Lucedale, MS, George Co., St. Lucy, c/o Wiggins, MS, St. Francis Xavier. (BLX)
Lucerne, CA, Queen of the Rosary, c/o Clearlake, CA, Our Lady, Queen of Peace. (SR)
Lucero, NM, Mora Co., c/o Mora, NM, St. Gertrude. (SFE)
Luis Llorens Torres, PR, San Juan Co., Sagrada Familia, c/o San Juan, PR, Santa Teresita Del Nino Jesus. (SJN)
Luis Lopez, NM, Socorro Co., c/o Socorro, NM, San Miguel. (SFE)
Lukunor, FM, c/o Chuuk, FM, Mortlock. (CI)
Lummi, WA, Whatcom Co., St. Joachim (Indian Reservation), c/o Ferndale, WA, St. Joseph. (SEA)
Lunenburg, VT, Orleans Co., St. Leo, c/o St. Johnsbury, VT, St. John the Evangelist. (BUR)
Luther, MI, Lake Co., St. Ignatius, c/o Baldwin, MI, St. Ann's. (GR)
Lyden, NM, Rio Arriba Co., San Jose, c/o Dixon, NM, St. Anthony. (SFE)
Lyman, NE, Scotts Bluff Co., Sacred Heart, c/o Mitchell, NE, St. Theresa's. (GI)
Lyons, OR, Linn Co., St. Patrick, c/o Scio, OR, Our Lady of Lourdes. (P)
Lyons Falls, NY, Lewis Co., St. John, c/o Port Leyden, NY, St. Martin. (OG)

M

Macana Parcelas, PR, Guayanilla Co., San Martin de Porres, c/o Guayanilla, PR, Immaculate Conception. (PCE)
Macana Rio, PR, Guayanilla Co., Virgen de Fatima, c/o Guayanilla, PR, Immaculate Conception. (PCE)
Macon, MS, Noxubee Co., Corpus Christi, c/o Starkville, MS, St. Joseph. (JKS)
Macy, NE, Thurston Co., Our Lady of Fatima, c/o Winnebago, NE, St. Joseph. (OM)
Madawaska, ME, Aroostook Co., St. Michael's Chapel, c/o St. Agatha, ME, Our Lady of the Valley. (PRT)
Madera, CA, Madera Co., St. Agnes, c/o Madera, CA, St. Joachim. (FRS)
Madera, PA, Clearfield Co., Immaculate Conception, c/o Houtzdale, PA, Christ the King. (E)
Madison, GA, Morgan Co., St. James, c/o Covington, GA, St. Augustine of Hippo. (ATL)
Madison, KS, Greenwood Co., St. Teresa Of Avila, c/o Eureka, KS, Sacred Heart. (WCH)
Magas Arriba, PR, Guayanilla Co., Perpetuo Socorro, c/o Guayanilla, PR, Immaculate Conception. (PCE)
Magdalena, NM, Socorro Co., c/o Socorro, NM, San Miguel. (SFE)
Mageetown, PA, Crawford Co., Immaculate Conception, c/o Titusville, PA, St. Titus. (E)
Magnolia, AR, Columbia Co., Immaculate Heart of Mary, c/o Camden, AR, St. Louis. (LR)
Magnolia, MS, Pike Co., St. James, c/o Chatawa, MS, St. Teresa. (JKS)
Majuro Atoll, MH, Laura, c/o Majuro, MH, Cathedral of the Assumption. (MI)
Malaga, CA, Fresno Co., Christ the King, c/o Fresno, CA, St. Anthony Claret. (FRS)
Malaga, NM, Eddy Co., Cristo Rey, c/o Loving, NM, Our Lady of Grace. (LSC)
Malpaso–Cesar Ruiz, PR, Immaculada Concepcion, c/o Aguada, PR, St. Francis of Assisi. (MGZ)
Mamey, PR, Perpetuo Socorro, c/o Aguada, PR, St. Francis of Assisi. (MGZ)
Manahawkin, NJ, Ocean Co., St. Mary of the Pines, c/o Barnegat, NJ, St. Mary. (TR)
Manassa, CO, Conejos Co., St. Therese of the Child Jesus, c/o Capulin, CO, St. Joseph. (PBL)
Manchester, KY, Clay Co., St. Ann, c/o London, KY, St. William. (LEX)
Manderson, SD, Shannon Co., Sacred Heart, (Wounded Knee), c/o Manderson, SD, St. Agnes. (RC)
Mani, PR, Infant of Prague, c/o Mayaguez, PR, Our Lady of Mt. Carmel. (MGZ)
Manito, IL, Mason Co., Immaculate Conception, c/o Havana, IL, St. Patrick's. (PEO)
Manitou Springs, CO, El Paso Co., Our Lady of Perpetual Help, c/o Colorado Springs, CO, Sacred Heart. (COS)
Mannford, OK, Creek Co., Our Lady of the Lake, c/o Sand Springs, OK, St. Patrick's. (TLS)
Manning, SC, Clarendon Co., Our Lady of Hope Mission, c/o Summerton, SC, St. Mary. (CHR)
Manset, ME, Hancock Co., St. Peter's, c/o Bar Harbor, ME, St. Ignatius. (PRT)
Mansfield, WA, Douglas Co., St. Mary, c/o Chelan, WA, St. Anne's. (YAK)
Manu'a Island, AS, Mary, Star of the Sea, c/o Pago Pago, AS, Cathedral of the Holy Family. (SPP)
Many, LA, Sabine Parish, St. Terence, c/o Many, LA, St. John the Baptist. (SHP)
Many Farms, AZ, Apache Co., St. Anthony, c/o Chinle, AZ, Our Lady of Fatima. (GLP)
Manzano, NM, Torrance Co., c/o Mountainair, NM, St. Alice. (SFE)
Maple, NC, Currituck Co., St. Katharine Drexel, c/o Elizabeth City, NC, Holy Family. (R)
Marak, TX, Milam Co., Ss. Cyril & Methodius, c/o Burlington, TX, St. Joseph. (AUS)
Marana, AZ, Pima Co., San Juan Bautista, c/o Tucson, AZ, Blessed Kateri Tekakwitha Roman Catholic Missions Parish – Tucson. (TUC)
Marathon, TX, Brewster Co., St. Mary, c/o Alpine, TX, Our Lady of Peace. (ELP)
Marcellus, MI, Cass Co., St. Margaret Mary, c/o Mattawan, MI, St. John Bosco. (KAL)
Marengo, IN, Crawford Co., St. Joseph, c/o Depauw, IN, St. Bernard. (IND)
Marenisco, MI, Gogebic Co., St. Catherine, c/o Wakefield, MI, Immaculate Conception of the Blessed Virgin Mary. (MAR)
Maresua, PR, Gruta de Lourdes, c/o San German, PR, San German de Auxerre. (MGZ)
Marianna, AR, Lee Co., St. Andrew, c/o Helena, AR, St. Mary. (LR)
Marias, PR, Asuncion de Maria, c/o Aguada, PR, St. Francis of Assisi. (MGZ)
Maricopa, AZ, Pinal Co., San Lucy, c/o Laveen, AZ, St. John The Baptist. (PHX)
Maricopa, AZ, Pinal Co., St. Francis, c/o Sacaton, AZ, St. Peter's. (PHX)
Marienville, PA, Forest Co., St. Anne, c/o Crown, PA, St. Mary. (E)
Marietta, OK, Good Shepherd, c/o Madill, OK, Holy Cross Church. (OKL)
Marion, NC, McDowell Co., Our Lady of the Angels, c/o Morganton, NC, St. Charles Borromeo. (CHL)
Marion, SC, Marion Co., Infant Jesus, c/o Dillon, SC, St. Louis. (CHR)
Marion, TX, Guadalupe Co., Immaculate Conception, c/o Schertz, TX, Church of the Good Shepherd. (SAT)
Marked Tree, AR, St. Norbert, c/o Jonesboro, AR, Blessed Sacrament. (LR)
Markham, TX, Matagorda Co., St. Robert, c/o Blessing, TX, St. Peter's. (VIC)
Marksville, LA, Avoyelles Parish, St. Richard, c/o Marksville, LA, Holy Ghost. (ALX)
Marlow, OK, Stephens Co., Immaculate Conception, c/o Duncan, OK, Assumption. (OKL)
Marshall, MN, St. Clotilde, c/o Marshall, MN, Holy Redeemer. (NU)
Marshfield, MA, Plymouth Co., St. Theresa's, c/o Marshfield, MA, St. Christine. (BO)
Marshfield, VT, Washington Co., North American Martyrs, c/o Montpelier, VT, St. Augustine. (BUR)
Mascotte, FL, Mission Outreach – Santo Toribio Romo, c/o Clermont, FL, Blessed Sacrament. (ORL)
Masefau, AS, c/o Pago Pago, AS, St. Peter Chanel–Sa'ilele. (SPP)
Mason, TX, Mason Co., St. Joseph, c/o Llano, TX, Holy Trinity Catholic Church – Llano, Texas. (AUS)
Mason, WV, Mason Co., St. Joseph, c/o Point Pleasant, WV, Sacred Heart. (WH)
Matador, TX, Motley Co., Our Lady of Guadalupe, c/o Floydada, TX, St. Mary Magdalen. (LUB)
Mattituck, NY, Suffolk Co., Our Lady of Good Counsel, c/o Cutchogue, NY, Sacred Heart. (RVC)
Maupin, OR, Wasco Co., St. Mary, c/o Dufur, OR, St. Alphonsus. (BAK)
Maxwell, NM, Colfax Co., c/o Springer, NM, St. Joseph. (SFE)
Mayaguez, PR, Corpus Christi, c/o Mayaguez, PR, Nuestra Senora De Fatima. (MGZ)
Mayaguez, PR, Cristo Rey, c/o Mayaguez, PR, Nuestra Senora De Fatima. (MGZ)
Mayaguez, PR, Espiritu Santo, c/o Mayaguez, PR, Nuestra Senora De Fatima. (MGZ)
Mayaguez, PR, Maria Socorro de los Cristianos, c/o Mayaguez, PR, Cathedral of Our Lady of Purification. (MGZ)
Mayaguez, PR, Santa Ana, c/o Mayaguez, PR, Cathedral of Our Lady of Purification. (MGZ)
Mayetta, KS, Jackson Co., Our Lady of the Snows Shrine, c/o Holton, KS, St. Dominic. (KCK)
Maysville, MO, DeKalb Co., St. Aloysius, c/o Cameron, MO, St. Munchin. (KC)
Mc Cool Junction, NE, York Co., St. Patrick's, c/o Exeter, NE, St. Stephen's. (LIN)
McCartys, NM, Cibola Co., Santa Maria de Acoma, c/o Pueblo of Acoma, NM, San Esteban, Acoma Catholic Indian Mission. (GLP)
McCook, NE, Red Willow Co., Sacred Heart, c/o McCook, NE, St. Patrick. (LIN)
McCook, NE, Red Willow Co., St. Ann's, c/o McCook, NE, St. Patrick. (LIN)
McCormick, SC, McCormick Co., Good Shepherd, c/o Abbeville, SC, Sacred Heart. (CHR)
McCrory, AR, Woodruff Co., St. Mary, c/o Wynne, AR, St. Peter. (LR)
McDermitt, NV, Humboldt Co., Sacred Heart, c/o Winnemucca, NV, St. Paul. (RNO)
McKee, KY, Jackson Co., St. Paul, c/o Berea, KY, St. Clare. (LEX)
McRoberts, KY, Letcher Co., Holy Angels, c/o Jenkins, KY, St. George. (LEX)
Mead, CO, Weld Co., Guardian Angels, c/o Northglenn, CO, Immaculate Heart of Mary. (DEN)
Meadville, MS, Franklin Co., St. Ann, c/o Brookhaven, MS, St. Francis. (JKS)
Medanales, NM, Rio Arriba Co., c/o Abiquiu, NM, St. Thomas Apostle. (SFE)
Medicine Lake, MT, Sheridan Co., St. Patrick, c/o Plentywood, MT, St. Joseph. (GF)
Medicine Root, SD, Shannon Co., St. Stephens, c/o Pine Ridge, SD, Our Lady of Sorrows. (RC)
Medina, NY, Sacred Heart, c/o Medina, NY, Holy Trinity. (BUF)
Meeker, OK, Lincoln Co., St. Michael, c/o Prague, OK, St. Wenceslaus, National Shrine of the Infant Jesus of Prague. (OKL)
Meeteetse, WY, Park Co., St. Therese, c/o Cody, WY, St. Anthony. (CHY)
Melendez, PR, Coamo Co., Our Lady of Providence, c/o Coamo, PR, St. Blase. (PCE)
Melrose, MT, Silver Bow Co., St. John The Apostle, c/o Dillon, MT, St. Rose of Lima. (HEL)
Melrose, NM, Curry Co., c/o Clovis, NM, Sacred Heart. (SFE)
Melstone, MT, Musselshell Co., Our Lady of Mercy, c/o Roundup, MT, St. Benedict. (GF)
Melvin, IL, Ford Co., St. George, c/o Gibson City, IL, Our Lady of Lourdes. (JOL)
Melvin, TX, McCullogh Co., St. Francis Xavier, c/o Brady, TX, St. Patrick's. (SAN)
Mercersburg, PA, Franklin Co., St. Luke the Evangelist, c/o Greencastle, PA, St. Mark the Evangelist. (HBG)
Mereta, TX, Tom Green Co., Holy Family, c/o Wall, TX, St. Ambrose. (SAN)
Merkel, TX, Taylor Co., Our Mother of Mercy, c/o Abilene, TX, St. Vincent Pallotti. (SAN)
Merrill, IA, Plymouth Co., St. Joseph at Ellendale, c/o Merrill, IA, Assumption Church. (SC)
Mertzon, TX, Irion Co., St. Peter's, c/o Eldorado, TX, Our Lady of Guadalupe. (SAN)
Mesa de Poleo, NM, Rio Arriba Co., c/o Abiquiu, NM, St. Thomas Apostle. (SFE)
Mesita, NM, Valencia Co., Sacred Heart, c/o Laguna, NM, St. Joseph. (GLP)
Mesquite, NM, Dona Ana Co., Our Lady of Perpetual Help, c/o San Miguel, NM, San Miguel. (LSC)
Metter, GA, Candler Co., Holy Family, c/o Swainsboro, GA, Holy Trinity. (SAV)
Meyers Chuck, AK, c/o Craig, AK, St. John by the Sea. (JUN)
Miami, FL, La Milagrosa, c/o Miami, FL, Corpus Christi. (MIA)
Miami, FL, Nuestra Senora de Altagracia, c/o Miami, FL, Corpus Christi. (MIA)
Miami, FL, San Francisco y Santa Clara, c/o Miami, FL, Corpus Christi. (MIA)
Miami, FL, San Juan Bautista, c/o Miami, FL, Corpus Christi. (MIA)
Michigan City, IN, La Porte Co., Maronite Catholic Community, c/o Lombard, IL, Our Lady of Lebanon Maronite Catholic Church. (OLL)

Michigan City, IN, Sacred Heart, c/o Michigan City, IN, St. Mary of the Immaculate Conception. (GRY)
Mico, TX, Medina Co., St. Francis of Assisi (Medina Lake Chapel), c/o Castroville, TX, St. Louis. (SAT)
Middle River, MN, Marshall Co., St. Joseph, c/o Greenbush, MN, Blessed Sacrament. (CR)
Middlebourne, WV, Tyler Co., St. Lawrence, c/o Paden City, WV, Mater Dolorosa. (WH)
Middletown, PA, Susquehanna Co., St. Patrick, c/o Friendsville, PA, St. Francis Xavier. (SCR)
Middleville, NY, Herkimer Co., St. Mary of the Assumption, c/o Newport, NY, St. John the Baptist. (ALB)
Midkiff, TX, Upton Co., St. Thomas, c/o Garden City, TX, St. Lawrence. (SAN)
Midland, LA, St. Aloysius, c/o Morse, LA, Immaculate Conception. (LAF)
Mifflinburg, PA, Union Co., Saint George Church, c/o Lewisburg, PA, Sacred Heart of Jesus. (HBG)
Milagro, NM, Guadalupe Co., c/o Santa Rosa, NM, St. Rose of Lima. (SFE)
Milan, TN, Northern Gibson Co., c/o Humboldt, TN, Sacred Heart. (MEM)
Mildred, PA, Sullivan Co., St. Francis of Assisi, c/o Dushore, PA, St. Basil's. (SCR)
Milesville, SD, Haakon Co., St. Mary, c/o Philip, SD, Sacred Heart. (RC)
Milford Center, OH, Union Co., Sacred Heart, c/o Plain City, OH, St. Joseph. (COL)
Mill City, OR, St. Catherine of Siena, c/o Sublimity, OR, St. Boniface. (P)
Mill Rift, PA, Pike Co., Holy Family, c/o Matamoras, PA, St. Joseph. (SCR)
Mill River, MA, Berkshire Co., Immaculate Conception, c/o Sheffield, MA, Our Lady of the Valley. (SPR)
Millen, GA, Jenkins Co., St. Bernadette, c/o Sylvania, GA, Our Lady of the Assumption. (SAV)
Millersview, TX, Concho C., Our Lady of Guadalupe, c/o Eden, TX, St. Charles. (SAN)
Millerton, NY, Dutchess Co., St. Patrick, c/o Amenia, NY, Immaculate Conception. (NY)
Milligan, NE, Fillmore Co., St. Wenceslaus, c/o Friend, NE, St. Joseph's. (LIN)
Millington, MI, Tuscola Co., St. Bernard, c/o Vassar, MI, St. Frances Xavier Cabrini. (SAG)
Millsboro, DE, Sussex Co., Mary Mother of Peace, c/o Georgetown, DE, St. Michael the Archangel. (WIL)
Millwood, NY, Westchester Co., Our Lady of the Wayside, c/o Briarcliff Manor, NY, St. Theresa. (NY)
Milolii, HI, Honaunau Co., St. Peter, c/o Captain Cook, HI, St. Benedict. (HON)
Milwaukee, WI, Milwaukee Co., St. John's Chapel, c/o Milwaukee, WI, All Saints. (MIL)
Minerva, KY, Mason Co., St. James, c/o Brooksville, KY, St. James. (COV)
Minot, ND, Ward Co., St. Michael, c/o Wilton, ND, SS. Peter and Paul. (STN)
Miraflores, PR, Chapel of Our Lady of Perpetual Help, c/o Anasco, PR, St. Anthony Abbot. (MGZ)
Mirando City, TX, Jim Hogg Co., St. Agnes, c/o Hebbronville, TX, Our Lady of Guadalupe. (LAR)
Mission, SD, Todd Co., St. Thomas, c/o St. Francis, SD, St. Francis Mission/Rosebud Educational Society. (RC)
Mission, TX, Hidalgo Co., Our Lady of Fatima, c/o Mission, TX, San Cristobal Magallanes & Companions. (BWN)
Mission, TX, Hidalgo Co., Our Lady of Lourdes, c/o Mission, TX, San Cristobal Magallanes & Companions. (BWN)
Moch, FM, c/o Chuuk, FM, Mortlock. (CI)
Modesto, CA, Stanislaus Co., Ntra. Senora de Guadalupe, c/o Ceres, CA, St. Jude Church (Pastor of). (STO)
Mogotes, La Milagrosa, c/o Yauco, PR, Holy Rosary. (PCE)
Mokelumne Hill, CA, Calaveras Co., St. Thomas Aquinas, c/o San Andreas, CA, St. Andrew Church of San Andreas (Pastor of). (STO)
Monarch, MT, Cascade Co., St. Clement, c/o Belt, MT, St. Mark the Evangelist. (GF)
Moncla, LA, Avoyelles Parish, St. John the Baptist, c/o Marksville, LA, Our Lady of Lourdes. (ALX)
Monet Ferry, LA, Natchitoches Parish, Holy Family, c/o Cloutierville, LA, St. John the Baptist. (ALX)
Mongaup Valley, NY, Sullivan Co., St. Joseph, c/o Monticello, NY, St. Peter. (NY)
Monroe, NY, Sacred Heart Chapel, c/o Monroe, NY, Sacred Heart Church. (NY)
Monroeville, AL, Wilcox Co., Mission of Annunciation Parish, c/o Monroeville, AL, St. Joseph. (MOB)
Montague, MI, Muskegon Co., St John, c/o Shelby, MI, Our Lady of Fatima. (GR)
Monte Alto, TX, Hidalgo Co., Christ the King, c/o Elsa, TX, Sacred Heart. (BWN)
Monte Aplanado, NM, Mora Co., c/o Mora, NM, St. Gertrude. (SFE)
Monte Cristo, Hidalgo Co., TX, Capilla Santa Cecilia, c/o Alton, TX, San Martin de Porres. (BWN)
Monte Grande, PR, St. Jude Thaddeus, c/o Cabo Rojo, PR, St. Michael. (MGZ)
Monte Rio, CA, St. Catherine, c/o Guerneville, CA, St. Elizabeth. (SR)
Montecello, NM, Sierra Co., St. Ignatius, c/o Truth or Consequences, NM, Our Lady of Perpetual Help. (LSC)
Monterey, MA, Berkshire Co., Our Lady of the Hills, c/o Sheffield, MA, Our Lady of the Valley. (SPR)
Montesano, WA, Grays Harbor Co., St. John, c/o Elma, WA, St. Joseph. (SEA)
Montezuma, GA, Macon Co., St. Michael, c/o Cordele, GA, St. Theresa. (SAV)
Montgomery, AL, Montgomery Co., Resurrection Catholic Mission, c/o Montgomery, AL, Resurrection Catholic Church. (MOB)
Montgomery, LA, Grant Parish, St. Patrick, c/o Colfax, LA, St. Joseph. (ALX)
Montgomery Center, VT, Franklin Co., St. Isidore, c/o Richford, VT, All Saints. (BUR)
Monticello, MS, Lawrence Co., St. Lawrence, c/o Bassfield, MS, St. Peter. (BLX)
Monument, OR, Grant Co., St. Anne, c/o John Day, OR, St. Elizabeth. (BAK)
Moody, TX, McLennan Co., Our Lady of San Juan, c/o McGregor, TX, St. Eugene Catholic Church – McGregor, Texas. (AUS)
Moorcroft, WY, Crook Co., St. Patrick, c/o Gillette, WY, St. Matthew's. (CHY)
Moore, MT, Fergus Co., St. Mathias, c/o Stanford, MT, St. Rose of Lima. (GF)
Moore, TX, Frio Co., St. Augustine, c/o Devine, TX, St. Joseph's. (SAT)
Mooreland, OK, Woodward Co., Sacred Heart, c/o Woodward, OK, St. Peter's. (OKL)
Moorhead, MN, Clay Co., St. Thomas Newman Center, c/o Moorhead, MN, St. Joseph's. (CR)
Moquino, NM, Valencia Co., Santa Rosalia, c/o Seboyeta, NM, Our Lady of Sorrows. (GLP)
Moretown, VT, Washington Co., St. Patrick, c/o Waterbury, VT, St. Andrew. (BUR)
Morgan City, LA, St. Mary Parish, St. Rosalie, c/o Morgan City, LA, Holy Cross. (HT)
Morning View, KY, Kenton Co., Assumption of the Blessed Virgin, c/o Kenton, KY, St. Matthew. (COV)
Morrill, NE, Scotts Bluff Co., St. Ann, c/o Mitchell, NE, St. Theresa's. (GI)
Morrison Bluff, AR, Logan Co., SS. Peter & Paul Church, c/o Scranton, AR, St. Ignatius. (LR)
Morristown, SD, Corson Co., Sacred Heart, c/o Lemmon, SD, St. Mary's. (RC)
Moses, NM, Union Co., Sacred Heart, c/o Clayton, NM, St. Francis Xavier. (SFE)
Mount Ida, AR, Montgomery Co., All Saints, c/o Mena, AR, St. Agnes. (LR)
Mount Pulaski, IL, Logan Co., St. Thomas Aquinas, c/o Elkhart, IL, St. Patrick. (PEO)
Mount Vernon, AL, Mobile Co., St. Theresa, c/o Citronelle, AL, St. Thomas. (MOB)
Mountain View, AR, Stone Co., St. Mary Church, c/o Mountain Home, AR, St. Peter the Fisherman. (LR)
Moxham, PA, Cambria Co., St. Anne's, c/o Johnstown, PA, St. Therese of the Child Jesus. (ALT)
Mt. Palatine, IL, La Salle Co., Immaculate Conception, c/o Wenona, IL, St. Mary's. (PEO)
Mt. Vernon, KY, Rockcastle Co., Our Lady of Mt. Vernon, c/o Berea, KY, St. Clare. (LEX)
Mud Butte, SD, Meade Co., St. Joseph, c/o Faith, SD, St. Joseph. (RC)
Mukilteo, WA, Snohomish Co., St. John, c/o Everett, WA, St. Mary Magdalen. (SEA)
Mulvey, LA, Vermilion Parish, St. David, c/o Gueydan, LA, St. Peter the Apostle. (LAF)
Mumford, NY, Monroe Co., St. Patrick, c/o Caledonia, NY, St. Columba. (ROC)
Murphys, CA, Murphys Co., St. Patrick, c/o Angels Camp, CA, St. Patrick Church of Angels Camp (Pastor of). (STO)
Myrtle Point, OR, Coos Co., Sts. Ann and Michael, c/o Coquille, OR, Holy Name. (P)

N

Naco, AZ, Cochise Co., St. Michael, c/o Bisbee, AZ, Saint Patrick Roman Catholic Parish – Bisbee. (TUC)
Nacogdoches, TX, Nacogdoches Co., Immaculate Conception – Moral, c/o Nacogdoches, TX, Sacred Heart. (TYL)
Nacogdoches, TX, Nacogdoches Co., Our Lady of Guadalupe, c/o Nacogdoches, TX, Sacred Heart. (TYL)
Nags Head, NC, Dare Co., Holy Trinity by the Sea Catholic, c/o Kitty Hawk, NC, Holy Redeemer by the Sea. (R)
Naknek, AK, Bristol Bay Borough, St. Theresa, c/o Dillingham, AK, Holy Rosary. (ANC)
Nalcrest, FL, Polk Co., St. Leo the Great, c/o Lake Wales, FL, Holy Spirit. (ORL)
Nama, FM, c/o Chuuk, FM, Mortlock. (CI)
Nambe, NM, Santa Fe Co., c/o Santa Fe, NM, N.S. de Guadalupe del Valle de Pojoaque. (SFE)
Nambe Indian Pueblo, NM, Santa Fe Co., c/o Santa Fe, NM, N.S. de Guadalupe del Valle de Pojoaque. (SFE)
Namoluk, FM, c/o Chuuk, FM, Mortlock. (CI)
Nanuet, NY, Rockland Co., St. Anthony Shrine Church, c/o Nanuet, NY, St. Anthony. (NY)
Naples, FL, Collier Co., St. Finbarr, c/o Marco Island, FL, San Marco. (VEN)
Nara Visa, NM, Quay Co., Sacred Heart, c/o Tucumcari, NM, St. Anne. (SFE)
Naranjo, PR, Salinas Co., Santa Marta, c/o Salinas, PR, Our Lady of Monserrat. (PCE)
Naranjo, PR, Yauco Co., St. Anthony, c/o Yauco, PR, Holy Rosary. (PCE)
Naranjo Militar, PR, Ntra. Madre de la Consolacion, c/o Aguada, PR, St. Francis of Assisi. (MGZ)
Naranjo–Guanabanas, PR, San Pablo, c/o Aguada, PR, St. Francis of Assisi. (MGZ)
Naschitti, NM, San Juan Co., St. Anthony, c/o Tohatchi, NM, St. Mary Church. (GLP)
Nashport, OH, Muskingum Co., St. Mary, c/o Dresden, OH, St. Ann's. (COL)
Nashua, MT, Valley Co., Queen of the Angels, c/o Glasgow, MT, St. Raphael. (GF)
Nashville, GA, Berrien Co., St. Mary, c/o Adel, GA, Queen of Peace. (SAV)
Nashville, MI, Barry Co., St. Cyril, c/o Hastings, MI, St. Rose of Lima. (KAL)
Natalia, TX, Medina Co., St. John Bosco, c/o Lytle, TX, St. Andrew. (SAT)
Natural Bridge, NY, Jefferson Co., St. Henry, c/o Harrisville, NY, St. Francis Solanus. (OG)
Naubinway, MI, Mackinac Co., St. Stephen, c/o Newberry, MI, St. Gregory. (MAR)
Naukati, AK, c/o Craig, AK, St. John by the Sea. (JUN)
Naytahwaush, MN, Mahnomen Co., St. Anne, c/o Waubun, MN, St. Ann. (CR)
Nebish, MN, Beltrami Co., St. John, c/o Kelliher, MN, St. Patrick. (CR)
Nederland, CO, Boulder Co., St. Rita, c/o Boulder, CO, Sacred Heart of Jesus. (DEN)
Nelson, NE, Nuckolls Co., Sacred Heart, c/o Superior, NE, St. Joseph's. (LIN)
Nenzel, NE, Cherry Co., St. Mary, c/o Valentine, NE, St. Nicholas. (GI)
New Almelo, KS, Norton Co., St. Joseph's Church, c/o Norton, KS, St. Francis of Assisi Parish. (SAL)
New Braunfels, TX, Comal Co., St. John, c/o New Braunfels, TX, Our Lady of Perpetual Help. (SAT)
New Castle, VA, Craig Co., St. John the Evangelist, c/o Fincastle, VA, Church of the Transfiguration. (RIC)
New Deal, TX, Lubbock Co., Our Lady Queen of Apostles, c/o Lubbock, TX, St. Patrick. (LUB)
New Dorp Beach, NY, Richmond Co., Our Lady of Lourdes, c/o Staten Island, NY, Our Lady, Queen of Peace. (NY)
New Germany, PA, Cambria Co., Immaculate Conception, c/o Summerhill, PA, St. John. (ALT)
New Haven, MO, Franklin Co., St. Gerald, c/o New Haven, MO, Holy Family. (STL)
New Hope, TN, Marion Co., Virgin of the Poor Shrine, c/o South Pittsburg, TN, Our Lady of Lourdes. (KNX)
New Iberia, LA, Iberia Parish, St. Jude, c/o New Iberia, LA, St. Edward. (LAF)
New Middletown, IN, Harrison Co., Most Precious Blood, c/o Corydon, IN, St. Joseph. (IND)
New Milford, PA, Susquehanna Co., St. John the Apostle, c/o Great Bend, PA, St. Lawrence. (SCR)
New Orleans, LA, Orleans Civil Parish, Our Lady of Guadalupe, c/o New Orleans, LA, St. Louis Cathedral. (NO)
New Orleans, LA, Orleans Civil Parish, Our Lady of La Vang, c/o New Orleans, LA, Mary, Queen of Vietnam. (NO)
New Orleans, LA, Orleans Civil Parish, St. Joseph, c/o Marrero, LA, St. Agnes Le Thi Thanh. (NO)
New River, AZ, Catholic Community of the Good Shepherd, A Quasi–Parish, c/o Anthem, AZ, St. Rose Philippine Duchesne Roman Catholic Parish. (PHX)
New Village, NJ, Warren Co., St. Christopher, c/o Phillipsburg, NJ, St. Philip & St. James. (MET)
New York, NY, Chapel of the Resurrection, c/o New York, NY, Church of the Resurrection. (NY)
New York, NY, Richmond Co., Christ the King, c/o Staten Island, NY, St. Mary of the Assumption. (NY)
New York, NY, New York Co., Resurrection, c/o New York, NY, St. Charles Borromeo. (NY)
New York, NY, New York Co., Sacred Hearts of Jesus and Mary, c/o New York, NY, Our Lady of the Scapular and St. Stephen. (NY)
New York, NY, New York Co., St. Monica, c/o New York, NY, Our Lady of Guadalupe at St. Bernard's. (NY)
Newburgh/Roseton, NY, Orange Co., Our Lady of Mercy, c/o Marlboro, NY, St. Mary. (NY)
Newfoundland, PA, Wayne Co., St. Anthony of Padua, c/o Gouldsboro, PA, St. Rita. (SCR)
Newport, AR, Jackson Co., St. Cecilia, c/o Batesville, AR, St. Mary. (LR)
Newton, MS, Newton Co., St. Anne, c/o Forest, MS, St. Michael. (JKS)

Newton, PA, Lackawanna Co., St. Benedict, c/o Clarks Summit, PA, Our Lady of the Snows. (SCR)
Newton Falls, NY, St. Lawrence Co., St. Anthony of Padua, c/o Star Lake, NY, St. Hubert. (OG)
Ngcheangl, FM, c/o Palau, PW, Sacred Heart. (CI)
Ngulu, FM, c/o Yap, FM, Queen of Heaven. (CI)
Nicasio, CA, Marin Co., St. Mary, c/o Lagunitas, CA, St. Cecilia. (SFR)
Nicolaus, CA, Sutter Co., St. Boniface, c/o Lincoln, CA, St. Joseph. (SAC)
Niland, CA, Immaculate Heart of Mary, c/o Calipatria, CA, St. Patrick. (SD)
Ninilchik, AK, St. Peter the Apostle, c/o Homer, AK, St. John the Baptist. (ANC)
No Water, SD, Shannon Co., Our Lady of Good Counsel, c/o Pine Ridge, SD, Holy Rosary. (RC)
Noble, LA, Sabine Parish, St. Ann, c/o Zwolle, LA, St. Joseph. (SHP)
Nocatee, FL, De Soto Co., Blessed Juan Diego, c/o Arcadia, FL, St. Paul. (VEN)
Noel, MO, McDonald Co., Nativity of Our Lord, c/o Neosho, MO, St. Canera. (SPC)
Norborne, MO, Carroll Co., Sacred Heart, c/o Carrollton, MO, St. Mary's. (KC)
Nordheim, TX, DeWitt Co., St. Ann's, c/o Yorktown, TX, Holy Cross. (VIC)
Norias Ranch, TX, Kenedy Co., Santa Elena, c/o Sarita, TX, Our Lady of Guadalupe. (CC)
North East, MD, Cecil Co., St. Jude, c/o Elkton, MD, Immaculate Conception. (WIL)
North Eastham, MA, Barnstable Co., Visitation Church, c/o Wellfleet, MA, Our Lady of Lourdes. (FR)
North Fork, CA, Madera Co., St. Joseph the Worker, c/o Oakhurst, CA, Our Lady of the Sierra. (FRS)
North Fort Myers, FL, Lee Co., St. Therese, c/o Fort Myers, FL, St. Francis Xavier. (VEN)
North Greenbush, NY, Rensselaer Co., Van Rensselaer Manor, County Nursing Home, c/o Troy, NY, St. Michael the Archangel. (ALB)
North Hollywood, CA, Los Angeles Co., Our Lady of Zapopan, c/o Sun Valley, CA, Our Lady of the Holy Rosary. (LA)
North Powder, OR, Union Co., St. Anthony, c/o La Grande, OR, Our Lady of the Valley. (BAK)
North Pownal, VT, Bennington Co., Our Lady of Lourdes, c/o Bennington, VT, Sacred Heart St. Francis de Sales. (BUR)
North Salem, NY, Westchester Co., St. John, c/o Croton Falls, NY, St. Joseph. (NY)
North San Juan, CA, Nevada Co., St. John, c/o Downieville, CA, Immaculate Conception. (SAC)
Northbrook, IL, Mission of the Holy Ghost, c/o Chicago, IL, Archdiocese of Chicago's Joseph Cardinal Bernardin Archives and Records Center. (CHI)
Northland, MI, Marquette Co., St. Joseph, c/o Gwinn, MI, St. Anthony. (MAR)
Northwood, NH, Rockingham Co., St. Joseph, c/o Pittsfield, NH, Our Lady of Lourdes. (MAN)
Norton, VT, Essex Co., St. Bernard, c/o Island Pond, VT, St. James the Greater. (BUR)
Norwich, VT, Windsor Co., St. Francis of Assisi, c/o Bradford, VT, Our Lady of Perpetual Help. (BUR)
Nova–Savannah, OH, Medina Co., Jesus the Good Shepherd, c/o Litchfield, OH, Our Lady Help of Christians Parish. (CLV)
Novinger, MO, Adair Co., St. Rose of Lima, c/o Kirksville, MO, Mary Immaculate. (JC)
Nowata, OK, Nowata Co., St. Catherine, c/o Dewey, OK, Our Lady of Guadalupe. (TLS)
Noxon, MT, c/o Thompson Falls, MT, St. William. (HEL)
Nucla, CO, Montrose Co., Our Lady of Sorrows, c/o Telluride, CO, St. Patrick. (PBL)
Nunam Iqua, AK, St. Peter Catholic Church Nunam Iqua, c/o Alakanuk, AK, St. Ignatius Catholic Church Alakanuk. (FBK)
Nuremberg, PA, Luzerne Co., St. Joseph, c/o Weston, PA, Sacred Heart. (SCR)

O

O'Connor Ranch, TX, Refugio Co., St. Dennis, c/o Tivoli, TX, Our Lady of Guadalupe. (CC)
Oak Beach, NY, Suffolk Co., c/o Babylon, NY, St. Joseph. (RVC)
Oak Creek, CO, Routt Co., St. Martin of Tours, c/o Steamboat Springs, CO, Holy Name. (DEN)
Oak Grove, MO, Jackson Co., St. Jude the Apostle, c/o Odessa, MO, St. George. (KC)
Ocala National Forest, FL, Marion Co., St. Joseph of the Forest, c/o Ocala, FL, Our Lady of the Springs. (ORL)
Ocate, NM, Mora Co., c/o Wagon Mound, NM, Santa Clara. (SFE)
Ocean City, MD, Worcester Co., Holy Savior, c/o Ocean City, MD, St. Mary, Star of the Sea. (WIL)
Oceano, CA, San Luis Obispo Co., St. Francis of Assisi, c/o Arroyo Grande, CA, St. Patrick. (MRY)
Odell, NE, Gage Co., St. Mary's, c/o Wymore, NE, St. Mary's. (LIN)
Odessa, TX, Ector Co., Our Lady of San Juan, c/o Odessa, TX, St. Elizabeth Ann Seton. (SAN)
Odessa, TX, Ector Co., St. Martin de Porres, c/o Odessa, TX, St. Joseph. (SAN)
Oglala, SD, Shannon Co., Our Lady of Sioux, c/o Pine Ridge, SD, Holy Rosary. (RC)
Ogunquit, ME, All Saints Church, c/o Wells, ME, Holy Spirit Parish. (PRT)
Oilton, TX, Jim Hogg Co., St. Bridget, c/o Hebbronville, TX, Our Lady of Guadalupe. (LAR)
Ojo Armarillo, NM, San Juan Co., Sacred Heart Missionary Cenacle, c/o Waterflow, NM, Sacred Heart. (GLP)
Ojo Caliente, NM, Rio Arriba Co., c/o El Rito, NM, San Juan Nepomuceno. (SFE)
Ojo Feliz, NM, Mora Co., c/o Mora, NM, St. Gertrude. (SFE)
Ojo Sarco, NM, Rio Arriba Co., Santo Tomas, c/o Chimayo, NM, Holy Family. (SFE)
Okeechobee, FL, Okeechobee Co., St. Theresa of the Child Jesus, c/o Moore Haven, FL, St. Joseph the Worker. (VEN)
Okemah, OK, Okfuskee Co., St. Teresa, c/o Henryetta, OK, St. Stephen's. (TLS)
Okmulgee, OK, Okmulgee Co., Uganda Martyrs, c/o Okmulgee, OK, St. Anthony's. (TLS)
Okolona, MS, Chickasaw Co., St. Theresa, c/o Aberdeen, MS, St. Francis of Assisi. (JKS)
Okreek, SD, Todd Co., St. Peter, c/o St. Francis, SD, St. Francis Mission/Rosebud Educational Society. (RC)
Okreek, SD, Todd Co., St. Peter's, c/o Mission, SD, St. Thomas the Apostle. (RC)
Olcott, NY, St. Charles Borromeo, c/o Newfane, NY, St. Brendan on the Lake. (BUF)
Old River, LA, Natchitoches Parish, St. Anne, c/o Natchez, LA, St. Augustine's. (ALX)
Old Washington, TX, Washington Co., Blessed Virgin Mary Chapel, c/o Somerville, TX, St. Ann. (AUS)
Olean, NE, Colfax Co., Sacred Heart, c/o Dodge, NE, St. Wenceslaus. (OM)
Olean, NY, Cattaraugus Co., Transfiguration, c/o Olean, NY, St. John. (BUF)
Olla, LA, La Salle Parish, St. William, c/o Winnfield, LA, Our Lady of Lourdes. (ALX)
Olmito, TX, Cameron Co., Our Heavenly Father, c/o Brownsville, TX, The Parish of the Lord of Divine Mercy. (BWN)
Olton, TX, Lamb Co., St. Peter, Apostle, c/o Hale Center, TX, St. Theresa's. (LUB)
Olympic Valley, CA, Placer Co., Queen of the Snows, c/o Tahoe City, CA, Corpus Christi. (SAC)
Oneida, PA, Schuykill Co., St. John the Baptist, c/o Sheppton, PA, St. Joseph. (ALN)
Oneop, FM, c/o Chuuk, FM, Mortlock. (CI)
Onset, MA, Plymouth Co., St. Mary Star of the Sea, c/o Buzzards Bay, MA, St. Margaret. (FR)
Opelousas, LA, St. Landry Parish, Christ the King, c/o Grand Coteau, LA, St. Charles Borromeo. (LAF)
Oracle, AZ, Pinal Co., St. Helen, c/o San Manuel, AZ, Saint Bartholomew Roman Catholic Parish – San Manuel. (TUC)
Orange Lake, NY, Orange Co., Our Lady of the Lake, c/o Newburgh, NY, St. Patrick. (NY)
Orange Park, FL, Clay Co., Moosehaven Chapel, c/o Orange Park, FL, St. Catherine's. (STA)
Ordway, CO, Crowley Co., St. Peter Chapel, c/o Rocky Ford, CO, St. Peter. (PBL)
Orlando, FL, Orange Co., St. Ignatius Kim Korean Mission, c/o Orlando, FL, St. James Cathedral. (ORL)
Orocovis, PR, Cacao Co., Imm. Concepcion, c/o Orocovis, PR, Our Lady Mother of Divine Providence. (PCE)
Orocovis, PR, Damian Abajo Co., N.S. Monserrate, c/o Orocovis, PR, Our Lady Mother of Divine Providence. (PCE)
Orocovis, PR, Damian Abajo Co., N.S. del Pilar, c/o Orocovis, PR, Our Lady Mother of Divine Providence. (PCE)
Orocovis, PR, Bauta Abajo Co., N.S. del Rosario, c/o Orocovis, PR, Our Lady Mother of Divine Providence. (PCE)
Orocovis, PR, Ala de La Piedra Co., Nino de Praga, c/o Orocovis, PR, Our Lady Mother of Divine Providence. (PCE)
Orocovis, PR, Ala de La Piedra Co., O.L. of Perp. Help, c/o Orocovis, PR, Our Lady Mother of Divine Providence. (PCE)
Orocovis, PR, Cacao Co., Our Lady of Mt. Carmel, c/o Orocovis, PR, Our Lady Mother of Divine Providence. (PCE)
Orocovis, PR, Sacred Heart of Jesus, c/o Orocovis, PR, Our Lady Mother of Divine Providence. (PCE)
Orocovis, PR, Bauta Abajo Co., San Mateo, c/o Orocovis, PR, Our Lady Mother of Divine Providence. (PCE)
Orocovis, PR, Ala de La Piedra Co., Santa Ana, c/o Orocovis, PR, Our Lady Mother of Divine Providence. (PCE)
Orting, WA, Pierce Co., SS. Cosmas and Damian, c/o Sumner, WA, St. Andrew. (SEA)
Ortiz, CO, Conejos Co., San Juan Nepomuceno y San Cayetano, c/o Antonito, CO, Our Lady of Guadalupe. (PBL)
Osceola, AR, Mississippi Co., St. Matthew, c/o Blytheville, AR, Immaculate Conception. (LR)
Osceola, MO, St. Clair Co., St. Catherine's, c/o Clinton, MO, Holy Rosary. (KC)
Osceola, NE, Polk Co., St. Mary's, c/o Osceola, NE, St. Vincent Ferrer. (LIN)
Oshkosh, NE, Garden Co., St. Elizabeth, c/o Chappell, NE, St. Joseph's. (GI)
Oslo, MN, Marshall Co., St. Joseph, c/o Warren, MN, SS. Peter and Paul. (CR)
Otis, MA, Berkshire Co., St. Mary of the Lakes, c/o Lee, MA, St. Mary's. (SPR)
Oto, IA, Woodbury Co., St. Mary's, c/o Mapleton, IA, St. Mary's. (SC)
Otter Lake, NY, Oneida Co., St. Mary of the Snows, c/o Forestport, NY, St. Patrick. (SY)
Otter River, MA, St. Martin, c/o East Templeton, MA, Holy Cross. (WOR)
Overton, NE, Dawson Co., Holy Rosary, c/o Elm Creek, NE, Immaculate Conception. (GI)
Overton, TX, Rusk Co., Our Lady Queen of Angels, c/o Kilgore, TX, Christ the King. (TYL)
Owasco, NY, Cayuga Co., St. Ann, c/o Auburn, NY, Sacred Heart. (ROC)
Owensboro, KY, Daviess Co., Good Samaritan Refugee Home, c/o Owensboro, KY, SS. Joseph and Paul. (OWN)
Owenton, KY, Owen Co., St. Edward, c/o Warsaw, KY, St. Joseph. (COV)
Owingsville, KY, Bath Co., St. Julie Catholic Church, c/o West Liberty, KY, Prince of Peace. (LEX)
Owl's Head, NY, Franklin Co., St. Joseph, c/o Malone, NY, St. Helen. (OG)
Oxford, NE, Furnas Co., St. Michael's, c/o Orleans, NE, St. Mary's. (LIN)
Oxnard, CA, Ventura Co., Christ the King, c/o Oxnard, CA, Our Lady of Guadalupe Parish. (LA)

P

Paducah, TX, Cottle Co., St. Elizabeth, c/o Floydada, TX, St. Mary Magdalen. (LUB)
Pageland, SC, Chesterfield Co., St. Ernest, c/o Cheraw, SC, St. Peter. (CHR)
Pagosa Junction, CO, Archuleta Co., St. John Baptist, c/o Pagosa Springs, CO, Immaculate Heart of Mary. (PBL)
Paguate, NM, Valencia Co., St. Elizabeth of Hungary, c/o Laguna, NM, St. Joseph. (GLP)
Painesdale, MI, Houghton Co., Sacred Heart, c/o Chassell, MI, St. Anne. (MAR)
Paisley, OR, Lake Co., St. John the Apostle, c/o Lakeview, OR, St. Patrick. (BAK)
Palisade, CO, Mesa Co., St. Ann, c/o Grand Junction, CO, Immaculate Heart of Mary. (PBL)
Palisade, NE, Hitchcock Co., Holy Family, c/o Trenton, NE, St. James. (LIN)
Palito Blanco, TX, Jim Wells Co., St. Joseph, c/o San Diego, TX, St. Francis de Paula. (CC)
Palma Escrita, PR, N.S. de Fatima, c/o Las Marias, PR, Immaculate Heart of Mary. (MGZ)
Palma Sola, PR, Ntra. Sra. de la Asuncion, c/o Canovanas, PR, San Jose. (FAJ)
Palmarejo, PR, Coamo Co., Immaculate Heart of Mary, c/o Coamo, PR, St. Blase. (PCE)
Palmas, PR, Guayama Co., St. Gerard, c/o Guayama, PR, St. Anthony of Padua. (PCE)
Palmer, MI, Marquette Co., Our Lady Perpetual Help, c/o Negaunee, MI, St. Paul. (MAR)
Palmer, PR, Ntra. Sra. de la Providencia, c/o Palmer, PR, Cristo Rey. (FAJ)
Palmetto, LA, St. Landry Parish, St. Thomas, the Apostle, c/o Melville, LA, St. John the Evangelist. (LAF)
Palo Blanco, NM, Colfax Co., c/o Springer, NM, St. Joseph. (SFE)
Paoli, IN, Orange Co., Our Lord Jesus Christ the King, c/o French Lick, IN, Our Lady of the Springs. (IND)
Parachute, CO, Garfield Co., St. Brendan, c/o Rifle, CO, St. Mary. (DEN)
Paradise, MI, Chippewa Co., Our Lady of Victory, c/o Newberry, MI, St. Gregory. (MAR)
Paradise Valley, NV, Humboldt Co., St. Alphonsus, c/o Winnemucca, NV, St. Paul. (RNO)
Paraje, NM, Valencia Co., St. Margaret Mary, c/o Laguna, NM, St. Joseph. (GLP)
Parcelas Fortuna, PR, Ntra. Sra. del Cobre, c/o Luquillo, PR, San Jose. (FAJ)
Parcelas Soledad, PR, Sta. Teresita, c/o Mayaguez, PR, Church De El Buen Pastor. (MGZ)
Parcelas Suarez, PR, Ntra. Sra. Perpetuo Socorro, c/o Loiza, PR, Santiago Apostol, El Mayor. (FAJ)
Parcelas Vazquez, PR, Salinas Co., Esp. Santo, c/o Salinas, PR, Our Lady of Monserrat. (PCE)
Parcelas Vieques, PR, N. Sra. De Fatima, c/o Loiza, PR, Santiago Apostol, El Mayor. (FAJ)
Parcelas de Marueno, PR, Ponce Co., San Antonio de Padua, c/o Ponce, PR, La Santisima Trinidad. (PCE)
Parem, FM, c/o Chuuk, FM, Sacred Heart. (CI)

Paris, MI, Mecosta Co., St. Anne, c/o Reed City, MI, St. Philip Neri. (GR)
Paris, MO, Monroe Co., St. Frances Cabrini, c/o Perry, MO, St. William. (JC)
Parishville, NY, St. Lawrence Co., St. Michael, c/o Colton, NY, St. Patrick. (OG)
Parks, LA, St. Louis, c/o Parks, LA, St. Joseph. (LAF)
Parmelee, SD, Todd Co., St. Agnes, c/o St. Francis, SD, St. Francis Mission/Rosebud Educational Society. (RC)
Parque Encuestre, PR, S. Francisco de Asis, c/o Carolina, PR, Cristo Rey. (SJN)
Parsons, TN, Decatur Co., St. Regina, c/o Lexington, TN, St. Andrew the Apostle. (MEM)
Pastura, NM, Guadalupe Co., c/o Vaughn, NM, St. Mary. (SFE)
Patch Grove, WI, Grant Co., St. John Parish, c/o Bloomington, WI, St. Mary. (MAD)
Patrick Springs, VA, Patrick, Church of the Risen Lord, c/o Woodlawn, VA, St. Joseph's. (RIC)
Patten, ME, Penobscot Co., St. Paul, c/o Houlton, ME, St. Agnes. (PRT)
Paul Smiths, NY, Franklin Co., St. Gabriel, c/o Lake Clear, NY, St. John in the Wilderness. (OG)
Pava'ia'i, AS, c/o Pago Pago, AS, St. Paul. (SPP)
Pawnee, OK, Pawnee Co., St. John, c/o Cushing, OK, SS. Peter and Paul. (TLS)
Pawnee, TX, Bee Co., Our Lady of Guadalupe, c/o Three Rivers, TX, Sacred Heart. (CC)
Paxton, NE, Keith Co., St. Patrick's Church, c/o Ogallala, NE, St. Luke's. (GI)
Peapack, NJ, St. Brigid, c/o Far Hills, NJ, St. Elizabeth. (MET)
Pearce, AZ, Cochise Co., St. Francis of Assisi, c/o Pearce, AZ, Saint Jude Thaddeus Roman Catholic Parish – Pearce Sunsites. (TUC)
Pecan Island, LA, Vermilion Parish, Sacred Heart, c/o Abbeville, LA, St. Anne. (LAF)
Peck, MI, Sanilac Co., St. John, c/o Sandusky, MI, St. Joseph. (SAG)
Pedro Garcia, PR, Coamo Co., Miraculous Virgin, c/o Coamo, PR, St. Blase. (PCE)
Pelican, AK, c/o Yakutat, AK, St. Ann. (JUN)
Pellejas, PR, Adjuntas Co., Santa Rosa, c/o Adjuntas, PR, St. Joachim. (PCE)
Pembroke, GA, Bryan Co., Holy Cross, c/o Claxton, GA, St. Christopher. (SAV)
Penitas, TX, Hidalgo Co., St. Anthony, c/o La Joya, TX, Our Lady, Queen of Angels. (BWN)
Pennington, MN, Beltrami Co., St. Charles, c/o Bemidji, MN, St. Philip's. (CR)
Pensacola, FL, Escambia Co., Church of Our Savior, c/o Pensacola, FL, St. Paul. (PT)
Pentwater, MI, Oceana Co., St. Vincent, c/o Hart, MI, St. Joseph's. (GR)
Penuelas, PR, Penuelas Co., Divino Nino, c/o Penuelas, PR, St. Joseph. (PCE)
Penuelas, PR, Penuelas Co., San Martin de Porres, c/o Penuelas, PR, St. Joseph. (PCE)
Pep, TX, Hockley Co., St. Philip Neri, c/o Morton, TX, St. Ann. (LUB)
Perrinton, MI, Gratiot Co., St. Martin De Porres, c/o Ithaca, MI, St. Paul the Apostle. (SAG)
Perry Park, KY, Owen Co., Transfiguration, c/o Carrollton, KY, St. John the Evangelist. (COV)
Perryville, KY, Boyle Co., St. Mary, c/o Harrodsburg, KY, St. Andrew. (LEX)
Peru, NE, Nemaha Co., St. Clara, c/o Auburn, NE, St. Joseph's. (LIN)
Petaca, NM, Taos Co., c/o El Rito, NM, San Juan Nepomuceno. (SFE)
Petersville, MD, Frederick Co., St. Mary's, c/o Brunswick, MD, St. Francis of Assisi. (BAL)
Petrolia, CA, St. Patrick, c/o Ferndale, CA, Church of the Assumption. (SR)
Phelps, KY, Pike Co., Jesus of the Mountains Catholic Church, c/o Pikeville, KY, St. Francis of Assisi. (LEX)
Philadelphia, MS, Neshoba Co., St. Theresa, c/o Philadelphia, MS, Holy Rosary. (JKS)
Philadelphia, NY, Jefferson Co., St. Joseph, c/o Evans Mills, NY, St. Mary. (OG)
Philadelphia, PA, Philadelphia Co., Holy Redeemer Chinese Church, c/o Philadelphia, PA, St. John the Evangelist. (PH)
Philadelphia, PA, Philadelphia Co., St. Nicholas, c/o Philadelphia, PA, Immaculate Conception of Blessed Virgin Mary, Cathedral. (PHU)
Philadelphia, PA, c/o Philadelphia, PA, St. Francis Xavier. (PH)
Phillipsburg, KY, Marion Co., Our Lady of Fatima, c/o Campbellsville, KY, Our Lady of Perpetual Help. (L)
Phoenix, AZ, Maricopa Co., Our Lady of Fatima, c/o Phoenix, AZ, St. Anthony Roman Catholic Parish. (PHX)
Picacho, NM, Lincoln Co., St. Joseph, c/o Ruidoso, NM, St. Eleanor. (LSC)
Pickens, WV, Randolph Co., Sacred Heart, c/o Buckhannon, WV, Holy Rosary. (WH)
Pickwick Dam, TN, Hardin Co., Our Lady of the Lake, c/o Savannah, TN, St. Mary Church. (MEM)
Picuris Indian Pueblo, NM, Taos Co., San Lorenzo Mission, c/o Penasco, NM, San Antonio de Padua. (SFE)
Piedmont, AL, Calhoun Co., St. Joachim, c/o Jacksonville, AL, St. Charles. (BIR)
Piedras Blancas, PR, Ntra. Sra. Reina de la Paz, c/o Aguada, PR, St. Francis of Assisi. (MGZ)
Piedras Blancas, Centro de Espintualidad, Madre de la Consolacion, c/o Aguada, PR, St. Francis of Assisi. (MGZ)
Piis, FM, c/o Chuuk, FM, Mortlock. (CI)
Pilar, NM, Taos Co., Nuestra Senora de los Dolores, c/o Dixon, NM, St. Anthony. (SFE)
Pima, AZ, Graham Co., Pima Mission, c/o Safford, AZ, Saint Rose of Lima Roman Catholic Parish – Safford. (TUC)
Pin Oak, TX, Bastrop Co., St. Mary's in Pin Oak, c/o Giddings, TX, St. Margaret. (AUS)
Pine Bluff, AR, Jefferson Co., St. Mary Plum Bayou, c/o Pine Bluff, AR, St. Joseph. (LR)
Pine Bluff, AR, Jefferson Co., St. Raphael, c/o Pine Bluff, AR, St. Peter. (LR)
Pine Island, NY, Orange Co., St. Stanislaus, c/o Florida, NY, St. Joseph. (NY)
Pine Springs, AZ, Apache Co., St. Rose, c/o Houck, AZ, St. John the Evangelist. (GLP)
Pinedale, CA, Fresno Co., St. Agnes, c/o Fresno, CA, St. Anthony of Padua. (FRS)
Pineville, KY, Bell Co., St. Anthony, c/o Middlesboro, KY, St. Julian. (LEX)
Pineville, WV, Wyoming Co., Holy Cross, c/o Mullens, WV, St. John the Evangelist. (WH)
Pinon, AZ, Navajo Co., St. Mary of the Rosary, c/o Chinle, AZ, Our Lady of Fatima. (GLP)
Pinos Altos, NM, Grant Co., Holy Cross, c/o Silver City, NM, St. Vincent de Paul. (LSC)
Pinos Wells, NM, Torrance Co., c/o Vaughn, NM, St. Mary. (SFE)
Pintada, NM, Guadalupe Co., c/o Santa Rosa, NM, St. Rose of Lima. (SFE)
Piqua, KS, Woodson Co., St. Martin, c/o Iola, KS, St. John. (WCH)
Piru, CA, Ventura Co., San Salvador, c/o Fillmore, CA, St. Francis of Assisi. (LA)
Placita, NM, Taos Co., Nuestra Senora de la Asuncion Mission, c/o Penasco, NM, San Antonio de Padua. (SFE)
Placitas, NM, Sierra Co., San Lorenzo, c/o Truth or Consequences, NM, Our Lady of Perpetual Help. (LSC)
Placitas, NM, Sandoval Co., c/o Bernalillo, NM, Our Lady of Sorrows. (SFE)
Placitas, NM, Rio Arriba Co., c/o El Rito, NM, San Juan Nepomuceno. (SFE)
Plains, TX, Yoakum Co., Sacred Heart, c/o Denver City, TX, St. William. (LUB)
Plainview, SD, Meade Co., Our Lady of Victory, c/o Faith, SD, St. Joseph. (RC)
Plasi, NE, Saunders Co., SS. Cyril and Methodius, c/o Prague, NE, St. John's. (LIN)
Playas, NM, Hidalgo Co., St. Augustine, c/o Lordsburg, NM, St. Joseph. (LSC)
Playita, PR, Yabucoa Co., San Martin de Porres, c/o San Juan, PR, San Juan Bosco. (SJN)
Playuela, San Judas Tadeo, c/o Aguadilla, PR, La Milagrosa. (MGZ)
Pleasanton, NE, Buffalo Co., St. Mary's, c/o Ravenna, NE, Our Lady of Lourdes. (GI)
Pleasantville, NJ, Atlantic Co., Our Lady Star of the East, c/o Somerset, NJ, St. Sharbel. (SAM)
Pleasantville Park, NY, Westchester Co., Our Lady of Pompeii, c/o Pleasantville, NY, Holy Innocents. (NY)
Plena, PR, Salinas Co., San Jose, c/o Salinas, PR, Our Lady of Monserrat. (PCE)
Plevna, MT, Fallon Co., St. Anthony, c/o Baker, MT, St. John the Evangelist. (GF)
Plum Island, MA, St. James, c/o Newburyport, MA, Immaculate Conception. (BO)
Plush, OR, Lake Co., St. Thomas, c/o Lakeview, OR, St. Patrick. (BAK)
Plymouth, CA, Amador Co., St. Mary of the Mountains, c/o Sutter Creek, CA, Immaculate Conception. (SAC)
Plymouth Meeting, PA, Montgomery Co., Our Lady of Mount Carmel, c/o Norristown, PA, Holy Saviour. (PH)
Pocahontas, PA, Somerset Co., St. Mary's, c/o West Salisbury, PA, St. Michael's. (ALT)
Pohnpei, FM, c/o Pohnpei, FM, Sacred Heart. (CI)
Point Comfort, TX, Calhoun Co., St. Ann, c/o Port Lavaca, TX, Our Lady of the Gulf. (VIC)
Pointblank, TX, San Jacinto Co., St. Stephen the Martyr, c/o New Waverly, TX, St. Joseph. (GAL)
Polvadera, NM, Socorro Co., c/o Socorro, NM, San Miguel. (SFE)
Ponce, PR, Cristo de la Misericordia, c/o Ponce, PR, San Jose Obrero. (PCE)
Ponce, PR, Ponce Co., La Dolorosa, c/o Ponce, PR, Christ the King. (PCE)
Ponce, PR, Natra. Sra. de la Medalla Milagrosa, c/o Ponce, PR, San Jose Obrero. (PCE)
Ponce, PR, Ponce Co., Our Lady of Carmel, c/o Mercedita, PR, Church of the Resurrection. (PCE)
Ponce, PR, Ponce Co., Saint Joseph, c/o Mercedita, PR, Church of the Resurrection. (PCE)
Ponce, PR, Ponce Co., San Miguel de los Santos, c/o Ponce, PR, La Santisima Trinidad. (PCE)
Ponce, PR, Ponce Co., San Patricio, c/o Jayuya, PR, Our Lady of Monserrate. (PCE)
Ponce, PR, Ponce Co., Santa Teresita, c/o Ponce, PR, Christ the King. (PCE)
Pond Creek, OH, Scioto Co., Holy Trinity, c/o West Portsmouth, OH, Our Lady of Sorrows. (COL)
Pond Creek, OK, Grant Co., St. Joseph's, c/o Medford, OK, St. Mary's. (OKL)
Pond Eddy, NY, Sullivan Co., Sacred Heart, c/o Yulan, NY, St. Anthony of Padua. (NY)
Ponderosa, NM, Sandoval Co., c/o Jemez Pueblo, NM, San Diego Indian Missions. (SFE)
Ponsford, MN, Becker Co., St. Theodore, c/o Ogema, MN, Most Holy Redeemer. (CR)
Pontotoc, MS, Pontotoc Co., St. Christopher, c/o New Albany, MS, St. Francis of Assisi. (JKS)
Poplarville, MS, Pearl River Co., St. Joseph, c/o Lumberton, MS, Our Lady of Perpetual Help. (BLX)
Porcupine, SD, Shannon Co., St. Paul, Sharpes Corner, c/o Porcupine, SD, Church of Christ the King. (RC)
Port Costa, CA, Contra Costa Co., St. Patrick, c/o Crockett, CA, St. Rose of Lima. (OAK)
Port Deposit, MD, Cecil Co., St. Teresa, c/o Perryville, MD, Church of the Good Shepherd. (WIL)
Port Huron, MI, St. Clair Co., Our Lady of Guadalupe Mission, c/o Port Huron, MI, Holy Trinity. (DET)
Port Norris, NJ, Cumberland Co., St. Anthony, c/o Cedarville, NJ, St. Michael's Roman Catholic Church. (CAM)
Port O'Connor, TX, Calhoun Co., St. Joseph, c/o Port Lavaca, TX, Our Lady of the Gulf. (VIC)
Port Orford, OR, Curry Co., St. John the Baptist, c/o Bandon, OR, Holy Trinity. (P)
Port St. Joe, FL, Gulf Co., San Blas Catholic Mission, c/o Port St. Joe, FL, St. Joseph. (PT)
Portage Des Sioux, MO, St. Charles Co., Immaculate Conception, c/o Portage Des Sioux, MO, St. Francis of Assisi. (STL)
Portales, NM, Roosevelt Co., Thomas More Center, c/o Portales, NM, St. Helen. (SFE)
Portland, PA, Northampton Co., St. Vincent de Paul, c/o Bangor, PA, Our Lady of Good Counsel. (ALN)
Portola Valley, CA, San Mateo Co., Our Lady of the Wayside, c/o Menlo Park, CA, St. Denis. (SFR)
Portville, NY, Oratory of the Sacred Heart, c/o Olean, NY, St. Mary of the Angels. (BUF)
Poston, AZ, Kateri Tekakwitha Indian Mission, c/o Parker, AZ, Sacred Heart Roman Catholic Parish – Parker. (TUC)
Potato Creek, SD, Jackson Co., St. Henry, c/o Pine Ridge, SD, Saint Ignatius Loyola. (RC)
Poughkeepsie, NY, Our Lady of the Rosary, c/o Poughkeepsie, NY, St. Peter. (NY)
Power, MT, Teton Co., Guardian Angel, c/o Dutton, MT, St. William. (HEL)
Prairie Laurent, LA, St. Landry Parish, St. Jules, c/o Leonville, LA, St. Catherine. (LAF)
Prairie Ronde, LA, St. Landry Parish, Sacred Heart, c/o Lawtell, LA, St. Bridget. (LAF)
Prairie View, AR, Logan Co., St. Meinrad, c/o Scranton, AR, St. Ignatius. (LR)
Prentiss, MS, Jefferson Davis Co., St. Mary's, c/o Bassfield, MS, St. Peter. (BLX)
Primrose, NE, Boone Co., St. Mary, c/o Cedar Rapids, NE, St. Anthony. (OM)
Princeton, CA, Colusa Co., St. Joseph, c/o Colusa, CA, Our Lady of Lourdes. (SAC)
Princeton, MO, Mercer Co., Immaculate Heart of Mary Church, c/o Trenton, MO, St. Joseph's. (KC)
Proctorsville, VT, Windsor Co., Holy Name of Mary, c/o Ludlow, VT, Annunciation of the Blessed Virgin Mary. (BUR)
Promise, SD, Dewey Co., St. Catherine, c/o Eagle Butte, SD, All Saints. (RC)
Promised Land, PA, Monroe Co., Our Lady of Fatima, c/o Canadensis, PA, St. Bernadette. (SCR)
Prudence Island, RI, Newport Co., Our Lady of Prudence, c/o Bristol, RI, St. Mary. (PRO)
Puako, HI, Hawaii Co., Church of the Ascension, Puako, c/o Kamuela, HI, Church of the Annunciation. (HON)
Pueblito del Carmen, PR, Our Lady of Mt. Carmel, c/o Guayama, PR, St. Anthony of Padua. (PCE)
Pueblitos, NM, Valencia Co., c/o Belen, NM, Our Lady of Belen. (SFE)
Puente Blanco, PR, Catano Co., Santo Domingo De Guzman, c/o Catano, PR, San Francisco de Sales. (SJN)
Puerto Nuevo, PR, San Juan Co., Ntra. Sra. de la Caridad, c/o Puerto Nuevo, PR, San Pablo. (SJN)
Puerto Real, PR, Our Lady of Mt. Carmel, c/o Cabo Rojo, PR, St. Michael. (MGZ)
Puerto de Luna, NM, Guadalupe Co., c/o Santa Rosa, NM, St. Rose of Lima. (SFE)

Pulaski, VA, Davis Co., St. Edward, c/o Wytheville, VA, St. Mary the Mother of God. (RIC)
Pulguillas, PR, Coamo Co., Christ the King, c/o Coamo, PR, St. Blase. (PCE)
Punta de Agua, NM, Torrance Co., c/o Mountainair, NM, St. Alice. (SFE)
Punto Oro, PR, Ponce Co., Ntra. Sra. del Pilar, c/o Ponce, PR, San Jose Obrero. (PCE)
Putnam Valley, NY, Putnam Co., North American Martyrs, c/o Cortlandt Manor, NY, St. Columbanus. (NY)
Puuiki, HI, Maui Co., St. Peter, c/o Hana, HI, St. Mary. (HON)

Q

Quartzsite, AZ, Queen of Peace, c/o Parker, AZ, Sacred Heart Roman Catholic Parish – Parker. (TUC)
Quebrada Honda, PR, Guayanilla Co., Nuestra Senora La Milagrosa, c/o Guayanilla, PR, Immaculate Conception. (PCE)
Quebrada Larga, PR, Sgdo. Corazon de Jesus, c/o Aguada, PR, St. Francis of Assisi. (MGZ)
Quebradas, PR, Yauco Co., Sacred Heart, c/o Yauco, PR, Holy Rosary. (PCE)
Quebradas, PR, Guayanilla Co., San Francisco de Asis, c/o Guayanilla, PR, Immaculate Conception. (PCE)
Queensbury, NY, Warren Co., Our Lady of the Assumption, c/o Lake George, NY, Sacred Heart. (ALB)
Queenstown, MD, Queen Anne Co., St. Peter, c/o Centreville, MD, Our Mother of Sorrows. (WIL)
Quemado, TX, Maverick Co., Our Lady of Guadalupe, c/o Eagle Pass, TX, Our Lady of Refuge. (LAR)

R

Ragley, LA, St. Pius X Mission, c/o Lake Charles, LA, St. Theodore. (LKC)
Rainsville, NM, Mora Co., c/o Mora, NM, St. Gertrude. (SFE)
Ralls, TX, Crosby Co., St. Joseph, c/o Ralls, TX, St. Michael. (LUB)
Ralph, SD, Harding Co., St. Isidore, c/o Buffalo, SD, St. Anthony. (RC)
Ralston, PA, Lycoming Co., St. Aloysius, c/o Canton, PA, St. Michael. (SCR)
Ramey–Maleza, PR, Los Santos Reyes, c/o San Antonio, PR, San Jose Obrero. (MGZ)
Ramirez, TX, Duval Co., Our Lady of Guadalupe, c/o Premont, TX, St. Theresa of the Infant Jesus. (CC)
Ranchester, WY, Sheridan Co., St. Edmund, c/o Sheridan, WY, Holy Name. (CHY)
Ranchito, TX, Fisher Co., Sacred Heart, c/o Rotan, TX, St. Joseph. (LUB)
Ranchitos, NM, Rio Arriba Co., c/o Ohkay Owingeh, NM, St. John the Baptist. (SFE)
Rancho Murieta, CA, Sacramento Co., c/o Elk Grove, CA, St. Joseph. (SAC)
Randsburg, CA, Kern Co., Santa Barbara, c/o Ridgecrest, CA, St. Ann. (FRS)
Rangeley, ME, Franklin Co., St. Luke, c/o Oquossoc, ME, Our Lady of the Lakes. (PRT)
Rankin, TX, St. Thomas, c/o Big Lake, TX, St. Margaret of Cortona. (SAN)
Rapid City, SD, Pennington Co., Indian Health Service, Sioux San Hospital and Pennington County Jail, c/o Rapid City, SD, St. Isaac Jogues. (RC)
Raymond, CA, Madera Co., St. Anne, c/o Madera, CA, St. Joachim. (FRS)
Raymond, ME, Cumberland Co., St. Raymond Chapel, c/o Windham, ME, Our Lady of Perpetual Help. (PRT)
Raymond, MS, Hinds Co., Immaculate Conception, c/o Clinton, MS, Holy Savior. (JKS)
Raynesford, MT, Judith Basin Co., St. Mary, c/o Belt, MT, St. Mark the Evangelist. (GF)
Reading, PA, Berks Co., Holy Rosary Chapel, c/o Reading, PA, Holy Rosary. (ALN)
Red Cliff, CO, Eagle Co., Our Lady of Mt. Carmel, c/o Minturn, CO, St. Patrick. (DEN)
Red Feather Lakes, CO, Larimer Co., Our Lady of the Lakes, c/o Fort Collins, CO, St. Joseph. (DEN)
Red Owl, SD, Meade Co., St. Anthony, c/o Faith, SD, St. Joseph. (RC)
Red River, NM, Taos Co., c/o Questa, NM, St. Anthony. (SFE)
Red Scaffold, SD, Ziebach Co., Sacred Heart, c/o Eagle Butte, SD, All Saints. (RC)
Red Shirt Table, SD, Shannon Co., St. Bernard, c/o Pine Ridge, SD, Holy Rosary. (RC)
Reddick, IL, Kankakee Co., St. Mary, c/o Cabery, IL, St. Joseph. (JOL)
Redford, TX, Presidio Co., San Jose, c/o Presidio, TX, Santa Teresa de Jesus. (ELP)
Redwood, TX, Guadalupe Co., St. Joseph, c/o Seguin, TX, Our Lady of Guadalupe. (SAT)
Redwood City, CA, San Mateo Co., San Jose Obrero, c/o Menlo Park, CA, St. Anthony. (SFR)
Reform, AL, Pickens Co., St. Robert, c/o Tuscaloosa, AL, St. Francis of Assisi University Parish. (BIR)
Reidsville, GA, St. Andrew the Apostle, c/o Vidalia, GA, Sacred Heart. (SAV)
Reserve, NM, Catron Co., St. Francis, c/o Reserve, NM, Santo Nino. (GLP)
Reva, SD, Harding Co., Our Lady of the Prairie, c/o Buffalo, SD, St. Anthony. (RC)
Rhinecliff, NY, Dutchess Co., St. Joseph, c/o Rhinebeck, NY, The Good Shepherd. (NY)
Ricardo, TX, Kleberg Co., Sacred Heart, c/o Riviera, TX, Our Lady of Consolation. (CC)
Rices Landing, PA, Greene Co., Sacred Heart, c/o Carmichael, PA, Our Lady of Consolation. (PIT)
Rich Hill, MO, Bates Co., St. Bridget's, c/o Nevada, MO, St. Mary. (KC)
Richey, MT, Dawson Co., St. Francis de Sales, c/o Circle, MT, St. Francis Xavier. (GF)
Richgrove, CA, Tulare Co., St. Vincent, c/o Delano, CA, St. Mary of the Miraculous Medal. (FRS)
Richmond, KY, Madison Co., St. Stephen the Martyr, c/o Richmond, KY, St. Mark. (LEX)
Rico, CO, Dolores Co., Immaculate Heart of Mary Chapel, c/o Cortez, CO, St. Rita. (PBL)
Ridgefield, WA, Clark Co., St. Mary of Guadalupe, c/o Battle Ground, WA, Sacred Heart. (SEA)
Ridgeview, SD, Dewey Co., St. Joseph, c/o Eagle Butte, SD, All Saints. (RC)
Riegelwood, NC, Columbus Co., Christ the King, c/o Wilmington, NC, St. Mark. (R)
Riley, NM, Socorro Co., c/o Socorro, NM, San Miguel. (SFE)
Rileyville, PA, Wayne Co., St. Joseph, c/o Honesdale, PA, St. John the Evangelist. (SCR)
Rimersburg, PA, Clarion Co., St. Richard, c/o East Brady, PA, St. Eusebius. (E)
Rincon, NM, Dona Ana Co., Our Lady of All Nations, c/o Hatch, NM, Our Lord of Mercy. (LSC)
Ringgold, LA, Bienville Parish, Blessed Sacrament, c/o Minden, LA, St. Paul. (SHP)
Rio Bravo, TX, Webb Co., Santa Monica Mission, c/o Rio Bravo, TX, Santa Rita de Casia Independent Mission. (LAR)
Rio Canas Abajo, PR, Juana Diaz Co., San Judas, c/o Juana Diaz, PR, St. Raymond Nonato. (PCE)
Rio Chiquito, NM, Rio Arriba Co., Sagrado Corazon, c/o Chimayo, NM, Holy Family. (SFE)
Rio Chiquito, PR, Ponce Co., Nino Jesus de Praga, c/o Ponce, PR, Christ the King. (PCE)
Rio Chiquito, PR, Ponce Co., San Vicente, c/o Ponce, PR, San Vicente–Cantera. (PCE)
Rio Grande, PR, La Milagrosa, c/o Rio Grande, PR, Nuestra Senora del Carmen. (FAJ)
Rio Grande, PR, Ntra. Sra. de Guadalupe, c/o Rio Grande, PR, Nuestra Senora del Carmen. (FAJ)
Rio Grande, PR, Perpetuo Socorro, c/o Aguada, PR, St. Francis of Assisi. (MGZ)
Rio Grande, PR, Sagrado Corazon de Jesus, c/o Rio Grande, PR, Nuestra Senora del Carmen. (FAJ)
Rio Grande–Playa, PR, Ntra. Sra. del Carmen, c/o Aguada, PR, St. Francis of Assisi. (MGZ)
Rio Hondo, PR, San Carlos y San Antonio, c/o Mayaguez, PR, Sacred Heart. (MGZ)
Rio Jueyes, Coamo, PR, Coamo Co., Our Lady of Lourdes, c/o Coamo, PR, San Antonio de Padua. (PCE)
Rio Lucio, NM, Taos Co., Sagrado Corazon Mission, c/o Penasco, NM, San Antonio de Padua. (SFE)
Rio Piedras, PR, San Juan Co., N. Sra. Reina de la Paz, c/o San Juan, PR, Santisimo Salvador. (SJN)
Rio Piedras, PR, San Juan Co., N. Sra. del Rosario, c/o Trujillo Alto, PR, San Pio X. (SJN)
Rio Piedras, PR, San Juan Co., San Jose de Calasanz, c/o San Juan, PR, Santisimo Salvador. (SJN)
Rio Piedras, PR, San Juan Co., Santa Teresita de Nino Jesus, c/o San Juan, PR, Nuestra Senora del Pilar. (SJN)
Rio Rancho, NM, Sandoval Co., St. John Vianney, c/o Rio Rancho, NM, St. Thomas Aquinas. (SFE)
Rio Verde, AZ, Maricopa Co., St. Dominic, c/o Fountain Hills, AZ, Ascension Roman Catholic Parish. (PHX)
Rio en Medio, NM, Sante Fe Co., Our Lady of Sorrows, c/o Santa Fe, NM, Our Lady of Guadalupe. (SFE)
Rios, TX, Duval Co., St. Francis of Assisi, c/o Premont, TX, St. Theresa of the Infant Jesus. (CC)
Ripley, TN, Lauderdale Co., Ave Maria, c/o Covington, TN, St. Alphonsus Church. (MEM)
Rising Sun, MD, Cecil Co., St. Agnes, c/o Perryville, MD, Church of the Good Shepherd. (WIL)
River Forest, IL, St. Thomas Mission, c/o Chicago, IL, Archdiocese of Chicago's Joseph Cardinal Bernardin Archives and Records Center. (CHI)
Riverside, CA, Riverside Co., Our Lady of Guadalupe, c/o Riverside, CA, St. John the Evangelist. (SB)
Riviera, TX, Kleberg Co., Our Lady of Guadalupe, c/o Riviera, TX, Our Lady of Consolation. (CC)
Roanoke, AL, Randolph Co., Immaculate Conception, c/o Lanett, AL, Holy Family. (BIR)
Robbins, IL, Cook Co., St. Peter Claver, c/o Blue Island, IL, St. Benedict. (CHI)
Robbins, NC, Moore Co., Saint Juan Diego, c/o Pinehurst, NC, Sacred Heart. (R)
Robbinsville, NC, Graham Co., Prince of Peace, c/o Andrews, NC, Holy Redeemer. (CHL)
Robert Lee, TX, Coke Co., Our Lady of Guadalupe, c/o Ballinger, TX, St. Mary Star of the Sea. (SAN)
Roberts, IL, Ford Co., Immaculate Conception, c/o Piper City, IL, St. Peter. (JOL)
Roberts, IL, Immaculate Conception, c/o Gibson City, IL, Our Lady of Lourdes. (JOL)
Robinson Township, MI, Ottawa Co., St. Anthony, c/o Grand Haven, MI, St. Patrick's. (GR)
Robstown, TX, Nueces Co., St. Mary, c/o Robstown, TX, St. Anthony. (CC)
Robstown, TX, St. Vivian, c/o Corpus Christi, TX, Our Lady of Mount Carmel. (CC)
Roby, MO, Texas Co., St. Vincent de Paul, c/o Houston, MO, St. Mark. (SPC)
Rochester, VT, Windsor Co., St. Elizabeth, c/o Bethel, VT, St. Anthony. (BUR)
Rociada Abajo, NM, San Miguel Co., Santo Nino, c/o Las Vegas, NM, Our Lady of Sorrows Church. (SFE)
Rock City Falls, NY, Saratoga Co., St. Paul, c/o Greenfield Center, NY, St. Joseph. (ALB)
Rock Hall, MD, Kent Co., St. John, c/o Chestertown, MD, Sacred Heart. (WIL)
Rock Point, MD, Charles Co., St. Francis de Sales, c/o Newburg, MD, Holy Ghost. (WDC)
Rockvale, CO, Fremont Co., St. Patrick, c/o Florence, CO, St. Benedict. (PBL)
Rockville, NE, Sherman Co., St. Mary's, c/o Ravenna, NE, Our Lady of Lourdes. (GI)
Rockwood, ME, Somerset Co., St. Joseph's, c/o Greenville, ME, Holy Family. (PRT)
Rocky Boys Indian Reservation, MT, Hill Co., St. Mary, c/o Box Elder, MT, St. Margaret Mary. (GF)
Rocky Mount, NC, Nash & Edgecombe Cos., Immaculate Conception, c/o Rocky Mount, NC, Our Lady of Perpetual Help. (R)
Rodarte, NM, Taos Co., Santa Barbara Mission, c/o Penasco, NM, San Antonio de Padua. (SFE)
Rodeo, NM, Hidalgo Co., San Felipe, c/o Lordsburg, NM, St. Joseph. (LSC)
Roland, OK, Sequoyah Co., Blessed Kateri Tekakwitha, c/o Sallisaw, OK, St. Francis Xavier. (TLS)
Romanum, FM, St. Joseph, c/o Chuuk, FM, St. Francis Assisi. (CI)
Romeo, CO, Conejos Co., Our Lady of the Immaculate Conception, c/o Capulin, CO, St. Joseph. (PBL)
Romero, PR, Villalba Co., Sagrado Corazon, c/o Villalba, PR, Our Lady of Mt. Carmel. (PCE)
Roosevelt Lake, AZ, Gila Co., St. Theresa, c/o Miami, AZ, Our Lady of the Blessed Sacrament Roman Catholic Church – Miami. (TUC)
Ropesville, TX, Hockley Co., San Francisco de Asis, c/o Brownfield, TX, St. Anthony's. (LUB)
Rosario, PR, Nuestra Senora del Rosario, c/o Rosario, PR, Our Lady of Rosary. (MGZ)
Rosario, PR, San Jose, c/o Mayaguez, PR, Sacred Heart. (MGZ)
Roscoe, IL, Winnebago Co., Church of the Holy Spirit, c/o South Beloit, IL, St. Peter. (RCK)
Roscoe, NY, Sullivan Co., Gate of Heaven, c/o Livingston Manor, NY, St. Aloysius. (NY)
Roscoe, TX, Nolan Co., St. Albert the Great, c/o Sweetwater, TX, Immaculate Heart of Mary. (SAN)
Rosebud, SD, Todd Co., St. Bridget, c/o St. Francis, SD, St. Francis Mission/Rosebud Educational Society. (RC)
Rosita, TX, Starr Co., Santa Rosa de Lima, c/o Roma, TX, Sacred Heart. (BWN)
Rotten Bayou, MS, Harrison Co., St. William, c/o Pass Christian, MS, St. Stephen. (BLX)
Roulette, PA, Potter Co., St. Mary, c/o Port Allegany, PA, St. Gabriel the Archangel. (E)
Round Mountain, NV, St. Barbara, c/o Tonopah, NV, St. Patrick. (LAV)
Round Rock, AZ, Apache Co., Our Lady of Guadalupe, c/o Lukachukai, AZ, St. Isabel. (GLP)
Rowe, NM, San Miguel Co., c/o Pecos, NM, St. Anthony of Padua. (SFE)
Roxbury, CT, Litchfield Co., St. Patrick's, c/o Washington Depot, CT, Our Lady of Perpetual Help. (HRT)
Roxbury, NY, Delaware Co., Our Lady of Good Counsel, c/o Margaretville, NY, Sacred Heart. (ALB)
Rushville, NE, Sheridan Co., Immaculate Conception, c/o Gordon, NE, St. Leo's. (GI)
Rushville, NY, Ontario Co., St. Mary, c/o Penn Yan, NY, St. Theresa. (ROC)
Rusk, TX, Cherokee Co., Sacred Heart, c/o Jacksonville, TX, Our Lady of Sorrows. (TYL)
Russell, NY, St. Lawrence Co., St. Paul–Pyrites, c/o Canton, NY, St. Mary. (OG)
Russian Mission, AK, Wade Hampton Co., Our Lady of Guadalupe Catholic Church Russian Mission, c/o Marshall, AK, Immaculate Heart of Mary Catholic Church Marshall. (FBK)
Rutherford, CA, Holy Family, c/o Yountville, CA, St. Joan of Arc. (SR)
Rutland, IL, La Salle Co., Sacred Heart, c/o Toluca, IL, St. Ann's. (PEO)
Ryan, OK, Jefferson Co., San Jose, c/o Duncan, OK, Assumption. (OKL)

Rye, CO, Pueblo Co., St. Aloysius, c/o Pueblo, CO, Holy Family. (PBL)
Ryegate, MT, Golden Valley Co., St Mathias, c/o Roundup, MT, St. Benedict. (GF)

S

Sab. Gde, P.R., Divino Nino Jesus, c/o Sabana Grande, PR, Church of San Isidro. (MGZ)
Sabana, PR, San Jose, c/o Aguada, PR, St. Francis of Assisi. (MGZ)
Sabana Eneas, PR, San Judas Tadeo, c/o San German, PR, San German de Auxerre. (MGZ)
Sabana Llana, PR, Salinas Co., Perpetuo Socorro, c/o Salinas, PR, Our Lady of Monserrat. (PCE)
Sabana Seca, PR, San Martin de Porres, c/o Sabana Seca, PR, San Jose Obrero. (SJN)
Sabin, MN, Clay Co., St. Cecilia, c/o Barnesville, MN, Assumption. (CR)
Sabinal, NM, Socorro Co., San Antonio, c/o La Joya, NM, Our Lady of Sorrows. (SFE)
Sabinoso, NM, San Miguel Co., c/o Roy, NM, Holy Family–St. Joseph. (SFE)
Sacaton, AZ, Pinal Co., St. Anthony, c/o Sacaton, AZ, St. Peter's. (PHX)
Sacaton Flats, AZ, Pinal Co., Our Lady of Victory, c/o Sacaton, AZ, St. Peter's. (PHX)
Saco, MT, Phillips Co., St. Francis of Assisi, c/o Malta, MT, St. Mary. (GF)
Saegertown, PA, Crawford Co., St. Bernadette, c/o Meadville, PA, St. Agatha. (E)
Sagamore, MA, Barnstable Co., St. Theresa, c/o East Sandwich, MA, Corpus Christi. (FR)
Saipan, MP, Korean Catholic Community, c/o Saipan, MP, Cathedral of Our Lady of Mt. Carmel. (CHK)
Salem, IN, Washington Co., St. Patrick, c/o Scottsburg, IN, American Martyrs. (IND)
Salem, MI, Holy Ascension, c/o Dearborn, MI, St. Michael's. (STN)
Salida, CA, Stanislaus Co., Our Lady of San Juan de los Lagos, c/o Modesto, CA, Holy Family Church (Pastor of). (STO)
Salinas–Providencia, PR, Guanica Co., Divina Providencia, c/o Ensenada, PR, Sacred Heart. (PCE)
Salineno, TX, Starr Co., St. Joseph, c/o Roma, TX, Our Lady of Refuge. (BWN)
Salon Usos Multiples–Urb. April Gardens, PR, Las Piedras, c/o Las Piedras, PR, Inmaculada Concepcion. (CGS)
Saltillo, MS, Lee Co., St. Thomas Aquinas, c/o Tupelo, MS, St. James. (JKS)
Salton City, CA, Imperial Co., c/o Borrego Springs, CA, St. Richard. (SD)
San Acacio, CO, Costilla Co., San Acacio, c/o San Luis, CO, Sangre de Cristo. (PBL)
San Antonio, CO, Conejos Co., San Antonio de Padua, c/o Antonito, CO, Our Lady of Guadalupe. (PBL)
San Antonio, NM, San Miguel Co., Los Vigiles (Our Lady of Refuge), c/o Las Vegas, NM, Immaculate Conception. (SFE)
San Antonio, NM, Socorro Co., c/o Socorro, NM, San Miguel. (SFE)
San Antonio, NM, Bernalillo Co., c/o Tijeras, NM, Holy Child. (SFE)
San Antonio, TX, Bexar Co., Purisima Concepcion, c/o San Antonio, TX, St. Cecilia. (SAT)
San Antonio, TX, Bexar Co., San Francesco di Paola (Italian), c/o San Antonio, TX, Cathedral of San Fernando. (SAT)
San Antonio, TX, Bexar Co., Santa Maria Goretti, c/o San Antonio, TX, St. Jude. (SAT)
San Antonio, TX, Bexar Co., St. Catherine, c/o San Antonio, TX, St. Margaret Mary. (SAT)
San Antonio, TX, Bexar Co., St. Frances Cabrini, c/o San Antonio, TX, San Francisco de la Espada. (SAT)
San Antonio, TX, Bexar Co., St. John Vianney, c/o LaCoste, TX, Our Lady of Grace. (SAT)
San Antonito, NM, Senor de Mapimi, c/o Tijeras, NM, Holy Child. (SFE)
San Ardo, CA, Monterey Co., Our Lady of Ransom, c/o San Miguel, CA, San Miguel. (MRY)
San Benito, TX, Cameron Co., St. Joseph, c/o San Benito, TX, Our Lady, Queen of the Universe. (BWN)
San Cristobal, NM, Taos Co., San Cristobal, c/o Arroyo Seco, NM, La Santisima Trinidad. (SFE)
San Diego, CA, San Diego Co., SDSU Newman Center, c/o San Diego, CA, Blessed Sacrament. (SD)
San Diego, PR, Coamo Co., San Diego, c/o Coamo, PR, St. Blase. (PCE)
San Felipe, NM, Sandoval Co., San Felipe, c/o Pena Blanca, NM, Nuestra Senora De Guadalupe. (SFE)
San Felipe, PR, Salinas Co., St. Martin de Porres, c/o Aguirre, PR, Sacred Heart. (PCE)
San Felipe, TX, Cameron Co., San Felipe, c/o Harlingen, TX, Our Lady of the Assumption. (BWN)
San Fernando, PR, San Juan Co., Monacillos, c/o Rio Piedras, PR, Inmaculado Corazon de Maria. (SJN)
San Francisco, CA, San Francisco Co., All Hallows Chapel, c/o San Francisco, CA, Our Lady of Lourdes. (SFR)
San Francisco, CA, San Francisco Co., Dominican Sisters of Mission San Jose, c/o San Francisco, CA, St. James. (SFR)
San Francisco, CO, Costilla Co., St. Francis of Assisi, c/o San Luis, CO, Sangre de Cristo. (PBL)
San Ignacio, NM, Guadalupe Co., c/o Santa Rosa, NM, St. Rose of Lima. (SFE)
San Ignacio, TX, Zapata Co., Our Lady of Refuge, c/o Zapata, TX, Our Lady of Lourdes. (LAR)
San Isidro, CO, Costilla Co., St. Isidro, c/o San Luis, CO, Sangre de Cristo. (PBL)
San Isidro, NM, Dona Ana Co., San Isidro, c/o Dona Ana, NM, Our Lady of the Purification. (LSC)
San Isidro Norte, NM, San Miguel Co., c/o Ribera, NM, San Miguel Del Vado. (SFE)
San Isidro Sur, NM, San Miguel Co., c/o Ribera, NM, San Miguel Del Vado. (SFE)
San Joaquin, CA, Fresno Co., St. Vincent de Paul, c/o Tranquillity, CA, St. Paul. (FRS)
San Jon, NM, Quay Co., Our Lady of Guadalupe, c/o Tucumcari, NM, St. Anne. (SFE)
San Jose, AZ, Graham Co., San Jose, c/o Solomon, AZ, Our Lady of Guadalupe Roman Catholic Parish – Solomon. (TUC)
San Jose, CA, Santa Clara Co., Santee Mission, c/o San Jose, CA, St. Maria Goretti. (SJ)
San Jose, NM, San Miguel Co., c/o Ribera, NM, San Miguel Del Vado. (SFE)
San Jose, PR, Minillas, c/o Bayamon, PR, Nuestra Senora del Rosario. (SJN)
San Jose Ranch, TX, Duval Co., St. Joseph, c/o Benavides, TX, Santa Rosa de Lima. (CC)
San Juan, NM, Grant Co., San Juan, c/o Hurley, NM, Infant Jesus. (LSC)
San Juan, NM, San Miguel Co., c/o Ribera, NM, San Miguel Del Vado. (SFE)
San Juan, PR, Capilla San Conrado, c/o San Juan, PR, San Francisco de Asis. (SJN)
San Juan, PR, Jesus Nazareno, c/o San Juan, PR, Jesus Maestro. (SJN)
San Juan, PR, San Juan Co., La Milagrosa, c/o San Juan, PR, San Juan M. Vianney. (SJN)
San Juan, PR, Bo. Caimito, Medalla Milagrosa, c/o San Juan, PR, Santa Catalina Laboure. (SJN)
San Juan, PR, Ntra. Sra. del Rosario, c/o San Juan, PR, San Juan Bosco. (SJN)
San Juan, PR, Nuestra Senora del Buen Consejo, c/o San Juan, PR, San Antonio. (SJN)
San Juan, PR, San Martin de Porres, c/o San Juan, PR, Santa Teresa Jornet. (SJN)
San Juan, PR, San Martin de Porres, Bitumul, c/o San Juan, PR, San Jose Obrero. (SJN)
San Juan, PR, Bo. Caimito, San Pablo, c/o San Juan, PR, Santa Catalina Laboure. (SJN)
San Juan, PR, Virgen de la Salud, c/o San Juan, PR, Santa Teresa Jornet. (SJN)
San Lorenzo, NM, Grant Co., San Lorenzo–Black Range Station, c/o Bayard, NM, Our Lady of Fatima. (LSC)
San Lucas, CA, Monterey Co., St. Luke, c/o King City, CA, St. John the Baptist. (MRY)
San Luis, NM, Sandoval Co., Saint Aloysius Gonzaga, c/o Cuba, NM, Immaculate Conception. (GLP)
San Manuel, TX, Hidalgo Co., St. Anne San Manuel, c/o Edinburg, TX, St. Joseph the Worker. (BWN)
San Marcos, CA, San Diego Co., c/o San Marcos, CA, St. Mark. (SD)
San Marcos, TX, Hays Co., Guadalupe Chapel, c/o San Marcos, TX, St. John the Evangelist. (AUS)
San Martin, PR, N. Sra. del Perpetuo Socorro, c/o Luquillo, PR, Madre del Redentor. (FAJ)
San Patricio, NM, Lincoln Co., St. Jude Thaddeus, c/o Ruidoso, NM, St. Eleanor. (LSC)
San Pedro, CO, Costilla Co., SS. Peter and Paul, c/o San Luis, CO, Sangre de Cristo. (PBL)
San Pedro, TX, Cameron Co., San Pedro, c/o Brownsville, TX, The Parish of the Lord of Divine Mercy. (BWN)
San Perlita, TX, Hidalgo Co., St. Anne, Mother of Mary, c/o Raymondville, TX, Our Lady of Guadalupe. (BWN)
San Rafael, CA, Marin Co., St. Sylvester, c/o San Rafael, CA, St. Raphael. (SFR)
San Rafael, CO, Conejos Co., San Pedro y San Rafael, c/o Antonito, CO, Our Lady of Guadalupe. (PBL)
San Simon, AZ, Our Lady of Perpetual Help, c/o Willcox, AZ, Sacred Heart of Jesus Roman Catholic Church – Willcox. (TUC)
San Ysidro, NM, Sandoval Co., c/o Jemez Pueblo, NM, San Diego Indian Missions. (SFE)
Sand Hill, GA, Our Lady of Guadalupe, c/o Claxton, GA, St. Christopher. (SAV)
Sanderson, TX, St. James, c/o Fort Stockton, TX, St. Joseph's. (SAN)
Sandersville, GA, Washington Co., St. William, c/o Dublin, GA, Immaculate Conception. (SAV)
Sandia, TX, St. Francis of Assisi Mission, c/o Orange Grove, TX, St. John of the Cross. (CC)
Sandia Indian Pueblo, NM, Sandoval Co., c/o Bernalillo, NM, Our Lady of Sorrows. (SFE)
Sandy Valley, NV, Clark Co., St. Catherine of Siena, c/o Las Vegas, NV, Christ the King. (LAV)
Santa Ana, NM, Sandoval Co., c/o Jemez Pueblo, NM, San Diego Indian Missions. (SFE)
Santa Ana, PR, Coamo Co., Santa Ana, c/o Coamo, PR, St. Blase. (PCE)
Santa Ana, PR, San Juan Co., Trastalleres, c/o San Juan, PR, Ntra. Sra. de la Monserrate. (SJN)
Santa Catalina, PR, Coama Co., Sacred Heart, c/o Coamo, PR, St. Blase. (PCE)
Santa Clara, NY, St. Peter, c/o St. Regis Falls, NY, St. Ann. (OG)
Santa Cruz, AZ, Pinal Co., St. Catherine, c/o Laveen, AZ, St. John The Baptist. (PHX)
Santa Cruz, CA, Santa Cruz Co., Mision Galeria, c/o Santa Cruz, CA, Holy Cross. (MRY)
Santa Fe, NM, Santa Fe Co., Our Lady of Guadalupe, c/o Santa Fe, NM, Cristo Rey. (SFE)
Santa Isabel, PR, Ntra. Sra. del Carmen, c/o Santa Isabel, PR, St. James. (PCE)
Santa Maria, TX, Cameron Co., St. Margaret Ann, c/o Progreso, TX, Holy Spirit. (BWN)
Santa Monica, TX, Willacy Co., Santa Monica, c/o Lyford, TX, Prince of Peace. (BWN)
Santa Rita, NM, San Miguel Co., c/o Ribera, NM, San Miguel Del Vado. (SFE)
Santa Rosa, PR, Jardines de Carolina, c/o Carolina, PR, San Valentin. (SJN)
Santa Teresa, NM, Dona Ana Co, Santa Teresa de Avila, c/o Sunland Park, NM, St. Martin de Porres. (LSC)
Santan, AZ, Pinal Co., St. Anne, c/o Sacaton, AZ, St. Peter's. (PHX)
Santiago–Talco, NM, Mora Co., c/o Mora, NM, St. Gertrude. (SFE)
Santo Domingo, NM, Sandoval Co., Santo Domingo, c/o Pena Blanca, NM, Nuestra Senora De Guadalupe. (SFE)
Santurce, PR, Mayaguez Co., La Milagrosa, c/o San Juan, PR, San Juan Bosco. (SJN)
Sapello, NM, San Miguel Co., Our Lady of Guadalupe, c/o Las Vegas, NM, Our Lady of Sorrows Church. (SFE)
Sapphire, NC, St. Jude, c/o Brevard, NC, Sacred Heart. (CHL)
Saragosa, TX, Reeves Co., Our Lady of Guadalupe, c/o Balmorhea, TX, Christ the King. (ELP)
Saratoga Lake, NY, Saratoga Co., St. Isaac Jogues, c/o Stillwater, NY, St. Peter the Apostle. (ALB)
Sardis, MS, Panola Co., St. John the Baptist, c/o Batesville, MS, St. Mary. (JKS)
Sargent, NE, Cluster Co., Assumption of the Blessed Virgin Mary, c/o Broken Bow, NE, St. Joseph's. (GI)
Sartwell, PA, McKean Co., St. Mary, c/o Eldred, PA, St. Raphael. (E)
Saspamco, TX, Bexar Co., Our Lady of Perpetual Help, c/o Elmendorf, TX, St. Anthony. (SAT)
Satin, TX, Satin Falls Co., Santa Rita, c/o Waco, TX, St. Francis on the Brazos. (AUS)
Satowan, FM, c/o Chuuk, FM, Mortlock. (CI)
Savage, MT, Richland Co., St. Michael, c/o Sidney, MT, St. Matthew. (GF)
Savannah, NY, Wayne Co., St. Patrick, c/o Clyde, NY, St. John the Evangelist. (ROC)
Savoy, LA, St. Landry Parish, St. Thomas, c/o Church Point, LA, St. Edward. (LAF)
Sawmill, AZ, Apache Co., St. Francis Mission, c/o Navajo, NM, St. Berard. (GLP)
Sawyer, MI, Berrien Co., St. Agnes, c/o Three Oaks, MI, St. Mary of the Assumption. (KAL)
Sawyer's Bar, CA, Siskiyou Co., St. Joseph, c/o Fort Jones, CA, Sacred Heart. (SAC)
Saxtons River, VT, Windham Co., St. Edmund of Canterbury, c/o Putney, VT, Our Lady of Mercy. (BUR)
Sayre, OK, Beckham Co., Queen of All Saints, c/o Elk City, OK, St. Matthew's. (OKL)
Scenic, AZ, Mohave Co., La Santisima Trinidad Catholic Mission A Quasi–Parish, c/o Kingman, AZ, St. Mary Roman Catholic Parish. (PHX)
Schenevus, NY, Otsego Co., St. Mary, c/o Worcester, NY, St. Joseph. (ALB)
Schoolcraft, NE, Madison Co., St. Francis de Sales, c/o Battle Creek, NE, St. Patrick's. (OM)
Scio, NY, Allegany Co., St. Joseph, c/o Belmont, NY, Holy Family of Jesus, Mary & Joseph. (BUF)
Scotland, CT, Windham Co., St. Margaret, c/o Willimantic, CT, St. Joseph. (NOR)
Scotland Neck, NC, Halifax Co., St. Anne, c/o Ahoskie, NC, St. Charles Borromeo. (R)
Scotts Mills, OR, Marion Co., Holy Rosary, c/o Mt. Angel, OR, St. Mary. (P)
Scottsville, VA, Albemarle Co., St. George's, c/o Charlottesville, VA, Church of the Holy Comforter. (RIC)
Scriba, NY, Oswego Co., Sacred Heart, c/o Oswego, NY, St. Peter. (SY)
Scribner, NE, Dodge Co., St. Lawrence, c/o Hooper, NE, St. Rose of Lima. (OM)
Seabrook, NH, Rockingham Co., St. Elizabeth of Hungary, c/o Hampton, NH, Our Lady of the Miraculous Medal. (MAN)

Seadrift, TX, Calhoun Co., St. Patrick, c/o Port Lavaca, TX, Our Lady of the Gulf. (VIC)
Seagraves, TX, Gaines Co., St. Paul's, c/o Seminole, TX, St. James. (LUB)
Seama, NM, Valencia Co., St. Anne, c/o Laguna, NM, St. Joseph. (GLP)
Seaside, CA, Seaside, Monterey Co., c/o Seaside, CA, St. Francis Xavier. (MRY)
Sebastian, TX, Willacy Co., St. Martin, c/o Lyford, TX, Prince of Peace. (BWN)
Seco Mines, TX, Maverick Co., Our Lady of Lourdes, c/o Eagle Pass, TX, Our Lady of Refuge. (LAR)
Sector Brazo Seco, PR, c/o Naguabo, PR, Nuestra Senora del Rosario. (FAJ)
Sector Felipe Quinones Barreal, PR, Penuelas Co., Santa Cruz, c/o Penuelas, PR, St. Joseph. (PCE)
Sector La Cucharilla, PR, Immaculada Concepcion, c/o Catano, PR, San Francisco de Sales. (SJN)
Sector La Fe, PR, c/o Naguabo, PR, Nuestra Senora del Rosario. (FAJ)
Sector Punta Brava, PR, Convento Missioneras de La Caridad, c/o Bayamon, PR, Santa Teresa de Jesus. (SJN)
Sector San Patricio, PR, Ponce Co., La Inmaculada, c/o Ponce, PR, San Vicente–Cantera. (PCE)
Sector Santo Domingo, PR, Penuelas Co., Santo Domingo de Guzman, c/o San Juan, PR, Corpus Christi. (SJN)
Sector la Gelpa – Quebrada Ceiba, PR, Penuelas Co., La Milagrosa, c/o Penuelas, PR, St. Joseph. (PCE)
Sedillo, NM, Bernalillo Co., San Isidro, c/o Tijeras, NM, Holy Child. (SFE)
Seeley Lake, MT, Missoula Co., Living Water, c/o Bonner, MT, St. Ann. (HEL)
Segundo, CO, Las Animas Co., St. Ignatius, c/o Trinidad, CO, Most Holy Trinity, Trinidad Area Catholic Community (Trinidad Cluster). (PBL)
Seiling, OK, Dewey Co., St. Thomas, c/o Okeene, OK, St. Anthony's. (OKL)
Selinsgrove, PA, Snyder Co., Selinsgrove Center, c/o Selinsgrove, PA, St. Pius X. (HBG)
Selinsgrove, PA, Snyder Co., Snyder County Prison, c/o Selinsgrove, PA, St. Pius X. (HBG)
Selinsgrove, PA, Snyder Co., Susquehanna University, c/o Selinsgrove, PA, St. Pius X. (HBG)
Sena, NM, San Miguel Co., c/o Villanueva, NM, Our Lady of Guadalupe. (SFE)
Seneca, OR, Grant Co., St. Charles, c/o John Day, OR, St. Elizabeth. (BAK)
Seneca, SC, Oconee Co., St. Paul the Apostle, c/o Clemson, SC, St. Andrew. (CHR)
Servilleta, NM, Taos Co., c/o El Rito, NM, San Juan Nepomuceno. (SFE)
Seville–Creston, OH, Medina Co., Jesus Emmanuel, c/o Litchfield, OH, Our Lady Help of Christians Parish. (CLV)
Shafer, MN, Chisago Co., St. Francis Xavier, c/o Taylors Falls, MN, St. Joseph's. (STP)
Shafter, TX, Presidio Co., Sgdo. Corazon de Jesus, c/o Presidio, TX, Santa Teresa de Jesus. (ELP)
Shamrock, TX, Wheeler Co., St. Patrick, c/o Wellington, TX, Our Mother of Mercy. (AMA)
Sharon, GA, Talifero Co., Purification, c/o Washington, GA, St. Joseph. (ATL)
Shasta Lake City, CA, Shasta Co., St. Michael, c/o Redding, CA, St. Joseph. (SAC)
Shattuck, OK, Ellis Co., Holy Name, c/o Woodward, OK, St. Peter's. (OKL)
Shawmut, MT, Wheatland Co., Blessed Sacrament, c/o Harlowton, MT, St. Joseph. (HEL)
Sheffield, TX, Pecos Co., Good Shepherd, c/o Ozona, TX, Our Lady of Perpetual Help. (SAN)
Shelton, NE, Buffalo Co., Sacred Heart, c/o Wood River, NE, St. Mary's. (GI)
Shickley, NE, Fillmore Co., St. Mary, c/o Geneva, NE, St. Joseph's. (LIN)
Shidler, OK, Osage Co., St. Ann, c/o Pawhuska, OK, Immaculate Conception. (TLS)
Shingletown, CA, Shasta Co., Mary Queen of Peace, c/o Redding, CA, Our Lady of Mercy. (SAC)
Shoreham, VT, Addison Co., St. Bernadette/St. Genevieve, c/o Middlebury, VT, Assumption of the Blessed Virgin Mary. (BUR)
Shoshone–Tecopa, CA, CA, St. John the Baptist, c/o Lone Pine, CA, Santa Rosa. (FRS)
Shoshoni, WY, Fremont Co., St. Joseph, c/o Riverton, WY, St. Margaret's. (CHY)
Shreveport, LA, Caddo Parish, St. Catherine of Siena, c/o Shreveport, LA, St. John Berchmans Cathedral. (SHP)
Shubert, NE, Richardson Co., St. Anne's, c/o Dawson, NE, St. Mary's. (LIN)
Sieper, LA, Rapides Parish, St. Jude, c/o Glenmora, LA, St. Louis. (ALX)
Sierra Alta, PR, Yauco Co., St. Lucy, c/o Yauco, PR, Holy Rosary. (PCE)
Sierra Blanca, TX, Hudspeth Co., Our Lady of Miracles, c/o Van Horn, TX, Our Lady of Fatima. (ELP)
Sigel, PA, Jefferson Co., St. Dominic, c/o Brookville, PA, Immaculate Conception. (E)
Sile, NM, Sandoval Co., Santa Barbara, c/o Pena Blanca, NM, Nuestra Senora De Guadalupe. (SFE)
Siletz, OR, Lincoln Co., St. Mary, c/o Newport, OR, Sacred Heart Parish. (P)
Silver Lake, PA, Susquehanna Co., St. Augustine, c/o Friendsville, PA, St. Joseph. (SCR)
Silverton, CO, San Juan Co., St. Patrick, c/o Ouray, CO, St. Daniel the Prophet. (PBL)
Skagway, AK, St. Therese of the Child Jesus, c/o Haines, AK, Sacred Heart. (JUN)
Slidell, LA, Edolia Barros, c/o Slidell, LA, St. Genevieve. (NO)
Smith, NV, Lyon Co., St. John the Baptist, c/o Yerington, NV, Holy Family. (RNO)
Smithfield, NE, Gosper Co., St. John's, c/o Holdrege, NE, All Saints. (LIN)
Smiths Corners, MI, Huron Co., Most Holy Trinity, c/o Rapson, MI, St. Joseph. (SAG)
Snow Shoe, PA, Centre Co., c/o Clarence, PA, Queen of Archangels. (ALT)
Snowmass Village, CO, Pitkin Co., Snowmass Chapel, c/o Aspen, CO, St. Mary. (DEN)
Solana Beach, CA, San Diego Co., St. Leo, c/o Solana Beach, CA, St. James. (SD)
Soledad, CA, Monterey Co., Nuestra Senora de la Soledad, c/o Soledad, CA, Our Lady of Solitude. (MRY)
Sonoita, AZ, Santa Cruz Co., Our Lady of Angels, c/o Patagonia, AZ, Saint Therese of Lisieux Roman Catholic Parish – Patagonia. (TUC)
Sonsorol, FM, c/o Palau, PW, Sacred Heart. (CI)
South Colton, NY, St. Lawrence Co., St. Paul, c/o Colton, NY, St. Patrick. (OG)
South Fork, CO, Rio Grande Co., Holy Family, c/o Del Norte, CO, Holy Name of Mary. (PBL)
South Royalston, MA, Worcester Co., Our Lady Queen of Heaven, c/o Athol, MA, Our Lady Immaculate. (WOR)
South Salem, NY, Westchester Co., The White Church, c/o Katonah, NY, St. Mary of the Assumption. (NY)
South Strafford, VT, Orange Co., Our Lady of Light, c/o Bradford, VT, Our Lady of Perpetual Help. (BUR)
South Tucson, AZ, Pima Co., Blessed Kateri Tekakwitha Parish Center, c/o Tucson, AZ, Blessed Kateri Tekakwitha Roman Catholic Missions Parish – Tucson. (TUC)
Southton, TX, Bexar Co., St. Ann, c/o San Antonio, TX, San Juan Capistrano. (SAT)
Southwest Oswego, NY, Oswego Co., St. Joseph, c/o Hannibal, NY, Our Lady of the Rosary. (SY)
Spanish Lake, LA, Natchitoches Parish, St. Anne, c/o Powhatan, LA, St. Francis of Assisi. (ALX)
Sparta, NC, St. Frances of Rome, c/o Jefferson, NC, St. Francis of Assisi. (CHL)
Spelter, WV, Harrison Co., Holy Family, c/o Shinnston, WV, St. Ann's. (WH)
Spencer, OH, Medina Co., Jesus Our Savior, c/o Litchfield, OH, Our Lady Help of Christians Parish. (CLV)
Spencer Mountain, NC, Gaston Co., St. Helen, c/o Charlotte, NC, Our Lady of Consolation. (CHL)
Spencerville, OH, Allen Co., St. Patrick, c/o Delphos, OH, St. John the Baptist. (TOL)
Spiro, OK, Leflore Co., St. Elizabeth Seton, c/o Poteau, OK, Immaculate Conception. (TLS)
Spofford Junction, TX, Kinney Co., St. Blaise, c/o Brackettville, TX, St. Mary Magdalen. (SAT)
Spring Creek, SD, Todd Co., St. Patrick, c/o St. Francis, SD, St. Charles Borromeo. (RC)
Spring Creek, SD, Todd Co., St. Patrick, c/o St. Francis, SD, St. Francis Mission/Rosebud Educational Society. (RC)
Spring Lake, NJ, Monmouth Co., St. Margaret, c/o Spring Lake, NJ, St. Catharine. (TR)
Springfield, KY, Washington Co., Holy Rosary–Manton, c/o Springfield, KY, Holy Trinity. (L)
Springfield, MA, Hampdon Co., St. Francis Chapel, c/o Springfield, MA, St. Michael's Cathedral. (SPR)
Springfield, SC, Orangeburg Co., St. Theresa, c/o Barnwell, SC, St. Andrew. (CHR)
Springhill, LA, Webster Parish, Sacred Heart, c/o Minden, LA, St. Paul. (SHP)
Squaw Valley, CA, Fresno Co., St. Rita, c/o Orange Cove, CA, St. Isidore the Farmer. (FRS)
St. Augustine, FL, St. Johns Co., Prince of Peace, c/o St. Augustine, FL, Cathedral – Basilica of St. Augustine. (STA)
St. Augustine, FL, St. Johns Co., St. Benedict the Moor, c/o St. Augustine, FL, Cathedral – Basilica of St. Augustine. (STA)
St. Boniface, PA, Cambria Co., St. Boniface Chapel, c/o Hastings, PA, St. Bernard. (ALT)
St. David, IL, Fulton Co., St. Michael, c/o Lewistown, IL, St. Mary's. (PEO)
St. Denis, IN, Jennings Co., St. Denis, c/o Greensburg, IN, Immaculate Conception. (IND)
St. Elmo, IL, Fayette Co., St. Mary, c/o Altamont, IL, St. Clare. (SFD)
St. Francis, SD, Todd Co., St. Charles, c/o St. Francis, SD, St. Francis Mission/Rosebud Educational Society. (RC)
St. Helena Island, SC, Beaufort Co., Holy Cross, c/o Beaufort, SC, St. Peter. (CHR)
St. Mary, NE, Johnson Co., St. Mary's, c/o Tecumseh, NE, St. Andrew's. (LIN)
St. Michaels, AZ, Apache Co., St. Michael's Mission for Navajo Indians, c/o St. Michaels, AZ, St. Michael. (GLP)
St. Michaels, MD, Talbot Co., St. Michael, c/o Easton, MD, SS. Peter and Paul. (WIL)
St. Paul, TX, San Patricio Co., St. Paul, c/o Sinton, TX, Sacred Heart. (CC)
St. Pete Beach, FL, Pinellas Co., St. Casimir Lithuanian Mission, c/o Gulfport, FL, Most Holy Name of Jesus. (SP)
St. Petersburg, FL, Pinellas Co., The Mercy of God Polish Mission, c/o St. Petersburg, FL, St. Paul. (SP)
St. Xavier, MT, Big Horn Co., St. Francis Xavier, c/o Crow Agency, MT, St. Dennis. (GF)
Staatsburg, NY, Dutchess Co., St. Paul, c/o Hyde Park, NY, Regina Coeli. (NY)
Stamford, VT, Bennington Co., St. John Bosco, c/o Readsboro, VT, St. Joachim. (BUR)
Standish, NY, Clinton Co., St. Michael, c/o Lyon Mountain, NY, St. Bernard. (OG)
Stanfield, AZ, Pinal Co., St. Mary Mission, c/o Casa Grande, AZ, Saint Anthony of Padua Roman Catholic Parish – Casa Grande. (TUC)
Starr School, MT, Sacred Heart, c/o Browning, MT, Church of the Little Flower. (HEL)
Starrucca, PA, Wayne Co., St. Paul, c/o Jackson, PA, St. Martin of Tours. (SCR)
Staten Island, NY, Holy Rosary, c/o Staten Island, NY, Holy Rosary. (NY)
Staten Island, NY, Staten Island Co., St. Nicholas, c/o Staten Island, NY, St. Teresa. (NY)
Stedman, NC, Cumberland Co., St. Isidore, c/o Hope Mills, NC, Good Shepherd. (R)
Steilacoom, WA, Pierce Co., Immaculate Conception, c/o Lakewood, WA, St. John Bosco. (SEA)
Stephentown, NY, Rensselaer Co., St. Joseph's, c/o New Lebanon, NY, Immaculate Conception. (ALB)
Stepstone, KY, Pendleton Co., Immaculate Conception, c/o California, KY, Sts. Peter and Paul. (COV)
Sterling, OK, Comanche Co., Our Lady of Perpetual Help, c/o Elgin, OK, St. Ann. (OKL)
Stevenson, WA, Skamania Co., Star of the Sea, c/o Camas, WA, St. Thomas Aquinas. (SEA)
Stevinson, CA, Merced Co., St. Mary, c/o Hilmar, CA, Holy Rosary. (FRS)
Stigler, OK, Haskell Co., St. Joseph, c/o Poteau, OK, Immaculate Conception. (TLS)
Stilwell, OK, Adair Co., San Juan Mission, c/o Tahlequah, OK, St. Brigid. (TLS)
Stinnett, TX, Hutchinson Co., St. Ann's, c/o Borger, TX, St. John the Evangelist. (AMA)
Stockbridge, MA, Berkshire Co., Saint Joseph, c/o Lee, MA, St. Mary's. (SPR)
Stockton, CA, San Joaquin Co., St. Sharbel Maronite Catholic Mission, c/o Millbrae, CA, Our Lady of Lebanon Maronite Catholic Church. (OLL)
Stockton, MO, Cedar Co., St. Peter the Apostle, c/o El Dorado Springs, MO, St. Elizabeth of Hungary. (SPC)
Stockton, NJ, St. Agnes, c/o Lambertville, NJ, St. John the Evangelist. (MET)
Stoneham, TX, Grimes Co., St. Joseph, c/o Plantersville, TX, St. Mary. (GAL)
Stonewall, LA, DeSoto Parish, St. Ann's Chapel, c/o Mansfield, LA, St. Joseph. (SHP)
Stonyford, CA, Colusa Co., St. Mary of the Mountain, c/o Williams, CA, Sacred Heart. (SAC)
Story, WY, Sheridan Co., Our Lady of the Pines, c/o Sheridan, WY, Holy Name. (CHY)
Strathmore, CA, Tulare Co., St. James Catholic Church, c/o Lindsay, CA, Sacred Heart. (FRS)
Stratton, ME, Franklin Co., St. John, c/o Oquossoc, ME, Our Lady of the Lakes. (PRT)
Stratton, NE, Hitchcock Co., St. Joseph's, c/o Benkelman, NE, St. Joseph's. (LIN)
Stratton Mountain, VT, Windham Co., Chapel of the Snows, c/o Putney, VT, Our Lady of Mercy. (BUR)
Strawn, IL, Livingston Co., St. Rose, c/o Fairbury, IL, St. John the Baptist. (PEO)
String Prairie, TX, Bastrop Co., Assumption of the Blessed Virgin Mary, c/o Bastrop, TX, Sacred Heart. (AUS)
Stroud, OK, Lincoln Co., St. Louis, c/o Chandler, OK, Our Lady of Sorrows. (OKL)
Sturgeon Bay, WI, c/o Sturgeon Bay, WI, Corpus Christi. (GB)
Sugar Island, MI, Chippewa Co., Sacred Heart, c/o Sault Sainte Marie, MI, Holy Name of Mary. (MAR)
Sugarloaf Shores, FL, Sugarloaf Firehouse, c/o Big Pine Key, FL, St. Peter. (MIA)
Sugarloaf U.S.A., ME, Franklin Co., Richard H. Bell Memorial Chapel, c/o Oquossoc, ME, Our Lady of the Lakes. (PRT)
Sullivan City, TX, Hidalgo Co., St. William, c/o La Joya, TX, Our Lady, Queen of Angels. (BWN)
Sulphur, OK, Murray Co., St. Francis Xavier, c/o Ada, OK, St. Joseph. (OKL)

T, St. Thomas Aquinas, c/o Shelby, MT, St.
...n. (HEL)
...nce, WY, Crook Co., St. Paul, c/o Newcastle, WY,
...orpus Christi. (CHY)
...undown, TX, Hockley Co., San Isidro, c/o Levelland, TX, St. Michael's. (LUB)
Sunray, TX, Moore Co., Christ the King, c/o Dumas, TX, SS. Peter and Paul. (AMA)
Sunriver, OR, Deschutes Co., Holy Trinity, c/o La Pine, OR, Holy Redeemer. (BAK)
Superior, MT, Mineral Co., St. Mary Queen of Heaven, c/o Frenchtown, MT, St. John the Baptist. (HEL)
Superior, WY, Sweetwater Co., St. Vivian, c/o Rock Springs, WY, Holy Spirit Catholic Community. (CHY)
Suquamish, WA, Kitsap Co., St. Peter, c/o Poulsbo, WA, St. Olaf. (SEA)
Surf City, NC, Pender Co., St. Mary, Gate of Heaven, c/o Hampstead, NC, St. Jude the Apostle. (R)
Surf City, NJ, Ocean Co., St. Thomas of Villanova, c/o Brant Beach, NJ, St. Francis of Assisi. (TR)
Susua, PR, La Resurreccion, c/o Sabana Grande, PR, Church of San Isidro. (MGZ)
Swartz, LA, Ouachita Parish, St. Lawrence, c/o Monroe, LA, Our Lady of Fatima. (SHP)
Sweet Lake, LA, Cameron Parish, St. Patrick's, c/o Big Lake, LA, St. Mary of the Lake. (LKC)
Sweet Springs, MO, Saline Co., Holy Family, c/o Marshall, MO, St. Peter. (JC)

T

Ta, FM, c/o Chuuk, FM, Mortlock. (CI)
Tabor, MN, Polk Co., Holy Trinity, c/o East Grand Forks, MN, Sacred Heart. (CR)
Tache Indian Reservation, CA, Kings Co., Santa Rosa, c/o Lemoore, CA, St. Peter Prince of Apostles. (FRS)
Tajique, NM, San Antonio, c/o Moriarty, NM, Estancia Valley Catholic Parish. (SFE)
Talihina, OK, Leflore Co., St. Catherine of Siena, c/o Wilburton, OK, Sacred Heart. (TLS)
Talpa, NM, Taos Co., N.S. de San Juan de Los Lagos, c/o Ranchos De Taos, NM, San Francisco de Asis. (SFE)
Tampa, FL, Hillsborough Co., Immaculate Conception Haitian Catholic Mission, c/o Tampa, FL, Epiphany of Our Lord. (SP)
Tampa, FL, Santa Maria, c/o Tampa, FL, St. Mary. (SP)
Tampa, FL, Hillsborough Co., St. Joseph Vietnamese Mission, c/o Tampa, FL, Epiphany of Our Lord. (SP)
Tampa, KS, Holy Redemer Church, c/o Marion, KS, Holy Family. (WCH)
Tanama, PR, Adjuntas Co., Sagrado Corazon, c/o Adjuntas, PR, St. Joachim. (PCE)
Taos, NM, Taos Co., St. Jerome, c/o Taos, NM, Nuestra Senora De Guadalupe. (SFE)
Tatum, NM, Lea Co., Our Lady of the Holy Rosary, c/o Lovington, NM, St. Thomas Aquinas. (LSC)
Tatum, TX, Panola Co., San Pedro the Fisherman, c/o Marshall, TX, St. Joseph. (TYL)
Taylorsville, KY, Spencer Co., All Saints Church, c/o Mount Washington, KY, St. Francis Xavier. (L)
Taylorsville, NC, Alexander Co., Holy Trinity, c/o Statesville, NC, St. Philip the Apostle. (CHL)
Teague, TX, Freestone Co., St. Mary, c/o Fairfield, TX, St. Bernard of Clairvaux. (TYL)
Tecolotito, NM, San Miguel Co., c/o Anton Chico, NM, San Jose. (SFE)
Tehama, CA, Tehama Co., St. Stanislaus, c/o Corning, CA, Immaculate Conception. (SAC)
Tenakee Springs, AK, c/o Yakutat, AK, St. Ann. (JUN)
Tenino, WA, Thurston Co., St. Peter, c/o Yelm, WA, St. Columban. (SEA)
Tennessee, IL, McDonough Co., Sacred Heart, c/o Macomb, IL, St. Paul's. (PEO)
Terra Alta, WV, Preston Co., St. Edward, c/o Kingwood, WV, St. Sebastian's. (WH)
Terra Bella, CA, Tulare Co., Blessed Miguel Agustin Pro, c/o Porterville, CA, St. Anne. (FRS)
Terry, MT, Prairie Co., Sacred Heart, c/o Miles City, MT, Sacred Heart. (GF)
Tesuque, NM, Santa Fe Co., San Ysidro, c/o Santa Fe, NM, Our Lady of Guadalupe. (SFE)
Texico, NM, Curry Co., c/o Clovis, NM, Our Lady of Guadalupe. (SFE)
Texline, TX, Dallum Co., St. Mary's, c/o Dalhart, TX, St. Anthony of Padua. (AMA)
Thatcher, AZ, Graham Co., Newman Center, c/o Safford, AZ, Saint Rose of Lima Roman Catholic Parish – Safford. (TUC)
Thayer, MO, Oregon Co., Sacred Heart, c/o West Plains, MO, St. Mary. (SPC)
Thedford, NE, Thomas Co., St. Thomas of Canterbury, c/o Mullen, NE, St. Mary's. (GI)
Theresa, NY, Jefferson Co., St. Theresa of Avila, c/o Evans Mills, NY, St. Mary. (OG)
Thermal, CA, Riverside Co., El Senor de la Misericordia, c/o San Jacinto, CA, St. Joseph Mission. (SB)
Thermal, CA, Riverside Co., Sacred Heart of Mary & Jesus, c/o Coachella, CA, Our Lady of Soledad. (SB)
Thermal, CA, Riverside Co., San Felipe de Jesus, c/o Coachella, CA, Our Lady of Soledad. (SB)
Thomas, OK, Custer Co., Blessed Sacrament, c/o Weatherford, OK, St. Eugene's. (OKL)
Thomasville, AL, Clarke Co., St. Joseph, c/o Grove Hill, AL, Sacred Heart. (MOB)
Thoreau, NM, Risen Savior, c/o Crownpoint, NM, St. Paul. (GLP)
Thorne Bay, AK, c/o Craig, AK, St. John by the Sea. (JUN)
Thornhurst, PA, Luzerne Co., St. Mark, c/o Bear Creek, PA, St. Elizabeth. (SCR)
Thornton, CA, San Joaquin Co., Mater Ecclesiae, c/o Lodi, CA, St. Anne Church (Pastor of). (STO)
Three Rivers, CA, Tulare Co., St. Clair, c/o Woodlake, CA, St. Frances Cabrini. (FRS)
Three Rivers, NM, Otero Co., St. Patrick, c/o Mescalero, NM, St. Joseph. (LSC)
Three Rocks, CA, Fresno Co., Our Lady of Lourdes, c/o Mendota, CA, Our Lady of Guadalupe. (FRS)
Thunder Butte, SD, Ziebach Co., St. Luke, c/o Eagle Butte, SD, All Saints. (RC)
Tijeras, NM, Bernalillo Co., c/o Tijeras, NM, Holy Child. (SFE)
Tilden, TX, McMullen Co., St. Joseph, c/o Charlotte, TX, St. Rose of Lima. (SAT)
Timpson, TX, Shelby Co., Epiphany, c/o Center, TX, St. Therese. (TYL)
Tinaja, NM, Colfax Co., c/o Springer, NM, St. Joseph. (SFE)
Tioga, PA, Tioga Co., St. Mary, c/o Mansfield, PA, Holy Child. (SCR)
Tionesta, PA, Forest Co., St. Anthony, c/o Tidioute, PA, St. John. (E)
Tishomingo, OK, Johnston Co., St. Anthony, c/o Ardmore, OK, St. Mary. (OKL)
Tiskilwa, IL, Bureau Co., St. Mary, c/o DePue, IL, St. Mary's. (PEO)
Toa Alta, PR, Toa Alta Co., Capilla Cristo Rey, c/o Toa Alta, PR, San Esteban, Protomartir. (SJN)
Toa Alta, PR, Toa Alta Co., Cristo Rey, c/o Toa Baja, PR, Ntra. Sra. de la Candelaria. (SJN)
Toa Alta, PR, Toa Alta Co., Nuestra Senora del Carmen, c/o Toa Alta, PR, Nuestra Senora de la Medalla Milagrosa. (SJN)
Toa Alta, PR, Toa Alta Co., Sagrada Familia, c/o Toa Alta, PR, San Jose. (SJN)
Toa Alta, PR, Toa Alta Co., Sagrado Corazon, c/o Toa Alta, PR, San Jose. (SJN)
Toa Alta, PR, Toa Alta Co., Sagrado Corazon de Jesus, c/o Toa Alta, PR, Nuestra Senora de la Medalla Milagrosa. (SJN)
Toa Alta, PR, Toa Alta Co., Santa Teresa De Jesus, c/o Toa Alta, PR, San Judas Tadeo. (SJN)
Toa Alta, PR, Toa Alta Co., Santa Teresita, c/o Toa Alta, PR, San Jose. (SJN)
Toa Baja, PR, Toa Baja Co., Buen Pastor, c/o Toa Baja, PR, Ntra. Sra. de la Candelaria. (SJN)
Toa Baja, PR, Toa Baja Co., Divino Nino Jesus, c/o Bayamon, PR, Nuestra Senora de Covadonga. (SJN)
Toa Baja, PR, Toa Baja Co., N. Sra. del Carmen, c/o Toa Baja, PR, Espiritu Santo. (SJN)
Toa Baja, PR, Toa Baja Co., Ntra. Sra. de Lourdes, c/o Bayamon, PR, Nuestra Senora de Covadonga. (SJN)
Toa Baja, PR, Toa Baja Co., San Martin de Porres, c/o Bayamon, PR, Nuestra Senora de Covadonga. (SJN)
Toa Baja, PR, Toa Baja Co., Santisima Trinidad, c/o Toa Baja, PR, Ntra. Sra. de la Candelaria. (SJN)
Tobias, NE, Saline Co., St. Joseph's, c/o Wilber, NE, St. Wenceslaus. (LIN)
Tollhouse, CA, Fresno Co., Infant Jesus of Prague, c/o Fresno, CA, Holy Spirit. (FRS)
Tomales, CA, Marin Co., St. Helen, c/o Tomales, CA, Church of the Assumption. (SFR)
Tomkins Cove, NY, Rockland Co., Immaculate Conception, c/o Stony Point, NY, Immaculate Conception. (NY)
Tompkinsville, KY, Monroe Co., Christ the King, c/o Edmonton, KY, Christ the Healer. (L)
Tonawanda, NY, Erie Co., St. Andrew Kim, c/o Kenmore, NY, St. Andrew. (BUF)
Tonto Basin, AZ, Tonto Basin/Punkin Center, c/o Payson, AZ, Saint Philip the Apostle Roman Catholic Church – Payson. (TUC)
Tonyville, CA, Tulare Co., St. Anthony Church, c/o Lindsay, CA, Sacred Heart. (FRS)
Tornillo, TX, El Paso Co., Santa Rita, c/o Fabens, TX, Our Lady of Guadalupe. (ELP)
Torreon, NM, Torrance Co., c/o Mountainair, NM, St. Alice. (SFE)
Torrey, UT, Wayne Co., St. Anthony of the Desert, c/o Central Valley, UT, Saint Elizabeth LLC 220. (SLC)
Touhy, NE, Saunders Co., St. Vitus, c/o Weston, NE, St. John Nepomucene. (LIN)
Townsend, TN, Blount Co., St. Francis of Assisi, c/o Alcoa, TN, Our Lady of Fatima. (KNX)
Townshend, VT, Windham Co., Our Lady of the Valley, c/o Putney, VT, Our Lady of Mercy. (BUR)
Toyah, TX, Reeves Co., St. Emily, c/o Pecos, TX, St. Catherine. (ELP)
Trail City, SD, Corson Co., Holy Rosary, c/o Timber Lake, SD, Holy Cross. (RC)
Trampas, NM, Taos Co., San Jose de Gracia, c/o Chimayo, NM, Holy Family. (SFE)
Trapper Creek, AK, St. Philip Benizi, c/o Talkeetna, AK, St. Bernard. (ANC)
Traver, CA, Tulare Co., St. John the Baptist Educational Center, c/o Kingsburg, CA, Holy Family. (FRS)
Tremonton, UT, Box Elder Co., Santa Ana, c/o Brigham City, UT, Saint Henry LLC 225. (SLC)
Trenton, GA, Dade Co., St. Katherine Drexel, c/o Lookout Mountain, GA, Our Lady of the Mount. (ATL)
Tres Piedras, NM, Taos Co., c/o El Rito, NM, San Juan Nepomuceno. (SFE)
Tres de Jayuya, PR, Adjuntas Co., Santa Teresita, c/o Adjuntas, PR, St. Joachim. (PCE)
Triadelphia, WV, Ohio Co., Our Lady of Seven Dolors, c/o Wheeling, WV, St. Vincent de Paul. (WH)
Trichel, LA, Natchitoches Parish, St. Joseph, c/o Campti, LA, Nativity of The Blessed Virgin Mary. (ALX)
Trinidad, CA, Holy Trinity, c/o McKinleyville, CA, Christ the King. (SR)
Trout Lake, MI, Chippewa Co., St. Mary, c/o Rudyard, MI, St. Joseph. (MAR)
Troy, MT, Lincoln Co., Immaculate Conception, c/o Libby, MT, St. Joseph. (HEL)
Troy, NY, Rensselaer Co., The Springs Nursing Home, c/o Troy, NY, St. Michael the Archangel. (ALB)
Troy, PA, Bradford Co., St. John Nepomucene, c/o Canton, PA, St. Michael. (SCR)
Truchas, NM, Rio Arriba Co., Holy Rosary, c/o Chimayo, NM, Holy Family. (SFE)
Trujillo, CO, Archuleta Co., St. James, c/o Pagosa Springs, CO, Immaculate Heart of Mary. (PBL)
Trujillo, NM, San Miguel Co., San Isidro, c/o Las Vegas, NM, Our Lady of Sorrows Church. (SFE)
Trujillo Alto, PR, Trujillo Alto Co., El Divino Pastor, c/o Trujillo Alto, PR, San Judas Tadeo. (SJN)
Trujillo Alto, PR, Trujillo Alto Co., Ntra. Sra. del Carmen, c/o Trujillo Alto, PR, San Judas Tadeo. (SJN)
Tsaile, AZ, Apache Co., St. Ann, c/o Lukachukai, AZ, St. Isabel. (GLP)
Tucson, AZ, Pima Co., Cristo Rey, c/o Tucson, AZ, Blessed Kateri Tekakwitha Roman Catholic Missions Parish – Tucson. (TUC)
Tucson, AZ, Pima Co., El Senor de los Milagros, c/o Tucson, AZ, Blessed Kateri Tekakwitha Roman Catholic Missions Parish – Tucson. (TUC)
Tucson, AZ, Pima Co., Our Lady of Guadalupe Capilla, c/o Tucson, AZ, Santa Cruz Roman Catholic Parish – Tucson. (TUC)
Tucson, AZ, San Cosme, c/o Tucson, AZ, Saint Augustine Cathedral Roman Catholic Parish – Tucson. (TUC)
Tucson, AZ, Pima Co., San Ignacio de Loyola, c/o Tucson, AZ, Blessed Kateri Tekakwitha Roman Catholic Missions Parish – Tucson. (TUC)
Tucson, AZ, Pima Co., San Martin, c/o Tucson, AZ, Blessed Kateri Tekakwitha Roman Catholic Missions Parish – Tucson. (TUC)
Tucson, AZ, Pima Co., Santa Rosa, c/o Tucson, AZ, Blessed Kateri Tekakwitha Roman Catholic Missions Parish – Tucson. (TUC)
Tucson, AZ, Pima Co., St. Anthony's Catholic Instruction Center and Capilla, c/o Tucson, AZ, Santa Cruz Roman Catholic Parish – Tucson. (TUC)
Tucson, AZ, Pima Co., St. Mary of the Desert, c/o Tucson, AZ, Our Lady of Fatima Roman Catholic Parish – Tucson. (TUC)
Tulalip, WA, Snohomish Co., Tulalip Indian Reservation, St. Anne, c/o Marysville, WA, St. Mary. (SEA)
Tule Indian Reservation, CA, Tulare Co., Mater Dolorosa, c/o Porterville, CA, St. Anne. (FRS)
Tullytown, PA, Bucks Co., Sacred Heart of Jesus, c/o Bristol, PA, St. Ann. (PH)
Tuolumne, CA, Tuolumne Co., St. Joseph, c/o Twain Harte, CA, All Saints Church (Pastor of). (STO)
Turquillo, NM, Mora Co., c/o Mora, NM, St. Gertrude. (SFE)
Tuscaloosa, AL, Tuscaloosa Co., St. John, c/o Tuscaloosa, AL, Holy Spirit. (BIR)
Twin Bridges, MT, Jefferson Co., Notre Dame, c/o Whitehall, MT, St. Teresa of Avila. (HEL)
Twin Lakes, GA, Lowndes Co., St. Jose, c/o Adel, GA, Queen of Peace. (SAV)
Twin Rocks, PA, Cambria Co., SS. Timothy & Mark Chapel, c/o Twin Rocks, PA, SS. Timothy & Mark. (ALT)
Twin Sisters, TX, Blanco Co., St. Mary's Help of Christians, c/o Blanco, TX, St. Ferdinand. (AUS)
Twin Valley, MN, Norman Co., St. William, c/o Ada, MN, St. Joseph's. (CR)
Tyler, TX, St. Joseph the Worker Mission, c/o Tyler, TX, Cathedral of the Immaculate Conception. (TYL)
Tylertown, MS, Walthall Co., St. Paul the Apostle, c/o Columbia, MS, Most Holy Trinity. (BLX)
Tynan, TX, Bee Co., St. Francis Xavier, c/o Skidmore, TX, Immaculate Conception. (CC)

U

Ulupalakua, HI, Maui Co., St. James the Less, c/o Kula, HI, Our Lady Queen of the Angels. (HON)
Unadilla, NY, Otsego Co., St. Ambrose, c/o Sidney, NY, Sacred Heart. (ALB)
Union City, MI, Branch Co., Our Lady of Fatima, c/o Coldwater, MI, St. Charles Borromeo. (KAL)
Union Springs, AL, Bullock Co., Bullock County Correctional Facility, c/o Eufaula, AL, Holy Redeemer. (MOB)
Union Springs, AL, Bullock Co., St. Pius X, c/o Eufaula, AL, Holy Redeemer. (MOB)
Unionville, MO, Putnam Co., St. Mary, c/o Milan, MO, St. Mary. (JC)
Unionville, NY, Orange Co., Our Lady of the Scapular, c/o Middletown, NY, Holy Cross. (NY)
Unity, OR, Baker Co., St. Joseph, c/o Vale, OR, St. Patrick. (BAK)
Universal, IN, Vermillion Co., St. Joseph, c/o Clinton, IN, Sacred Heart. (IND)
Upton, WY, Weston Co., St. Anthony, c/o Newcastle, WY, Corpus Christi. (CHY)
Urich, MO, Henry Co., Holy Trinity, c/o Holden, MO, St. Patrick's. (KC)
Ute, IA, Monona Co., St. Mary's, c/o Dow City, IA, St. Boniface. (SC)
Utica, NE, Seward Co., St. Patrick's, c/o Beaver Crossing, NE, Sacred Heart. (LIN)
Utulei, AS, c/o Pago Pago, AS, Co–Cathedral of St. Joseph the Worker. (SPP)

V

Vadito, NM, Taos Co., Nuestra Senora de los Dolores Mission, c/o Penasco, NM, San Antonio de Padua. (SFE)
Valdez, NM, Taos Co., San Antonio de Padua, c/o Arroyo Seco, NM, La Santisima Trinidad. (SFE)
Valencia, NM, Valencia Co., Sangre de Cristo, c/o Peralta, NM, Our Lady of Guadalupe. (SFE)
Valentine, TX, Jeff Davis Co., Sacred Heart, c/o Van Horn, TX, Our Lady of Fatima. (ELP)
Valeria, IA, Jasper Co., Sacred Heart, c/o Colfax, IA, Immaculate Conception. (DAV)
Vallecitos, NM, Rio Arriba Co., c/o El Rito, NM, San Juan Nepomuceno. (SFE)
Van Buren, MO, Carter Co., St. George, c/o Piedmont, MO, St. Catherine of Siena. (SPC)
Vanceboro, ME, Washington Co., Guardian Angel, c/o Lincoln, ME, St. Mary. (PRT)
Vandalia, NY, Cattaraugus Co., St. John the Baptist, c/o Allegany, NY, St. Bonaventure. (BUF)
Vanderpool, TX, Bandera Co., St. Mary, c/o Sabinal, TX, St. Patrick's. (SAT)
Variadero, NM, San Miguel Co., Holy Family, c/o Las Vegas, NM, Our Lady of Sorrows Church. (SFE)
Vegas Abajo, PR, Adjuntas Co., La Milagrosa, c/o Adjuntas, PR, St. Joachim. (PCE)
Vegas Arriba, PR, Adjuntas Co., Sta. Ana, c/o Adjuntas, PR, St. Joachim. (PCE)
Veguita, NM, Socorro Co., San Juan, c/o La Joya, NM, Our Lady of Sorrows. (SFE)
Velarde, NM, Rio Arriba Co., Nuestra Senora de Guadalupe, c/o Dixon, NM, St. Anthony. (SFE)
Verdigre, NE, Knox Co., St. William, c/o Verdigre, NE, St. Wenceslaus. (OM)
Verdunville, LA, St. Mary Parish, Immaculate Conception, c/o Franklin, LA, St. Jules. (LAF)
Verona Beach, NY, Oneida Co., St. Mary, c/o North Bay, NY, St. John. (SY)
Versailles, MO, Morgan Co., St. Philip Benizi, c/o Laurie, MO, Shrine of St. Patrick. (JC)
Viburnum, MO, Iron Co., St. Philip Benizi, c/o Ironton, MO, Ste. Marie Du Lac. (SPC)
Victor, CO, Teller Co., St. Victor's, c/o Woodland Park, CO, Our Lady of the Woods. (COS)
Victoria, TX, Victoria Co., Holy Trinity, c/o Victoria, TX, Our Lady of Sorrows. (VIC)
Vida, MT, McCone Co., St. Ann, c/o Wolf Point, MT, Immaculate Conception. (GF)
Vigil, CO, Las Animas Co., St. Isidore, c/o Trinidad, CO, Most Holy Trinity, Trinidad Area Catholic Community (Trinidad Cluster). (PBL)
Villa Esperanza, PR, Carolina Co., La Sagrada Familia, c/o Carolina, PR, San Juan de Dios. (SJN)
Villa del Carmen, PR, Ponce Co., San Martin de Porres, c/o Ponce, PR, Our Lady of Mt. Carmel. (PCE)
Villalba, PR, Villalba Co., La Milagrosa, c/o Villalba, PR, Our Lady of Mt. Carmel. (PCE)
Villalba, PR, Villalba, La Milagrosa, c/o Villalba, PR, Our Lady of Mt. Carmel. (PCE)
Villalba, PR, Villalba, San Francisco de Asis, c/o Villalba, PR, Our Lady of Mt. Carmel. (PCE)
Villalba, PR, Villalba, San Juan Evangelista, c/o Villalba, PR, Our Lady of Mt. Carmel. (PCE)
Villas De Loiza, PR, Ntra. Sra. de la Providencia, c/o Canovanas, PR, Resurreccion del Señor. (FAJ)
Viola, IL, Mercer Co., St. John, c/o Aledo, IL, St. Anthony's Church. (PEO)
Virginia Beach, VA, Virginia Beach Co., Our Lady of Perpetual Help, c/o Williamsburg, VA, Ascension of Our Lord. (PSC)
Volcano, CA, Amador Co., St. Bernard, c/o Jackson, CA, St. Patrick's. (SAC)

W

Wa Keeney, KS, Trego Co., St. Michael, c/o WaKeeney, KS, Christ the King Parish. (SAL)
Wadesboro, NC, Anson Co., Sacred Heart, c/o Hamlet, NC, St. James. (CHL)
Wadsworth, TX, Matagorda Co., Sacred Heart, c/o Bay City, TX, Holy Cross. (VIC)
Waelder, TX, Gonzales Co., St. Patrick, c/o Gonzales, TX, St. James. (SAT)
Wahneta, FL, Polk Co., Our Lady of Guadalupe, c/o Bartow, FL, St. Thomas Aquinas. (ORL)
Waiakoa, HI, Maui Co., Holy Ghost, c/o Kula, HI, Our Lady Queen of the Angels. (HON)
Waialua, HI, Honolulu Co., SS. Peter and Paul, c/o Waialua, HI, St. Michael. (HON)
Waikapu, HI, Maui Co., St. Joseph, c/o Waihee, HI, St. Ann. (HON)
Waimea, HI, Kauai Co., Sacred Hearts of Jesus & Mary, c/o Kekaha, HI, St. Theresa. (HON)
Waitsfield, VT, Washington Co., Our Lady of the Snows, c/o Waterbury, VT, St. Andrew. (BUR)
Wakefield, VA, Southampton Co., Infant of Prague, c/o Franklin, VA, St. Jude. (RIC)
Wakita, OK, Grant Co., St. Mary's Assumption, c/o Medford, OK, St. Mary's. (OKL)
Wakpala, SD, Corson Co., St. Bede, c/o McLaughlin, SD, St. Bernard. (RC)
Wakpala, SD, Corson Co., St. Bede, c/o McLaughlin, SD, Standing Rock Reservation. (RC)
Walden, CO, Jackson Co., St. Ignatius, c/o Kremmling, CO, St. Peter. (DEN)
Wales, MA, Hampden Co., St. Monica, c/o Brimfield, MA, St. Christopher's. (SPR)
Walhalla, SC, Oconee Co., St. Francis of Assisi, c/o Clemson, SC, St. Andrew. (CHR)
Walker Valley, NY, Ulster Co., Our Lady of the Valley, c/o Pine Bush, NY, The Infant Saviour. (NY)
Wallace, NC, Duplin Co., Transfiguration, c/o Burgaw, NC, St. Joseph. (R)
Wallkill, NY, Ulster Co., St. Benedict, c/o Walden, NY, Most Precious Blood. (NY)
Wallowa, OR, Wallowa Co., St. Pius X, c/o Enterprise, OR, St. Katherine's. (BAK)
Walls, MS, DeSoto Co., Sacred Heart, c/o Walls, MS, Sacred Heart. (JKS)
Walls, MS, DeSoto Co., Sacred Heart, c/o Robinsonville, MS, Good Shepherd Catholic Church. (JKS)
Walpole, NH, St. Joseph, c/o Charlestown, NH, All Saints Parish. (MAN)
Walterboro, SC, Colleton Co., St. James the Greater, c/o Walterboro, SC, St. Anthony. (CHR)
Walters, OK, Cotton Co., St. Patrick Church, c/o Duncan, OK, Assumption. (OKL)
Wamsutter, WY, Sweetwater Co., St. Anthony, c/o Rock Springs, WY, Holy Spirit Catholic Community. (CHY)
Wanette, OK, Pottawatomie Co., St. Mary, c/o Konawa, OK, Sacred Heart. (OKL)
Wareham, MA, Plymouth Co., St. Anthony, c/o Wareham, MA, St. Patrick's. (FR)
Warm Springs, GA, Meriwether Co., St. Elizabeth Seton, c/o LaGrange, GA, St. Peter. (ATL)
Warm Springs, OR, Jefferson Co., Blessed Kateri Tekakwitha, c/o Madras, OR, St. Patrick. (BAK)
Warner Springs, CA, San Diego Co., St. Francis of Assisi, c/o Santa Ysabel, CA, Santa Ysabel Indian Mission. (SD)
Warren, AR, Bradley Co., St. Luke, c/o Monticello, AR, St. Mark. (LR)
Warrenton, NC, Warren Co., St. Joseph, c/o Henderson, NC, St. James. (R)
Warrenton, TX, Fayette Co., St. Martin, c/o Fayetteville, TX, St. John the Baptist. (AUS)
Warrior, AL, Jefferson Co., St. Henry, c/o Gardendale, AL, St. Elizabeth Ann Seton. (BIR)
Washburn, IL, Woodford Co., St. Elizabeth, c/o Metamora, IL, St. Mary's. (PEO)
Washington, DC, c/o Washington, DC, St. Ann. (WDC)
Washington, GA, Elbert Co., St. Mary's, c/o Washington, GA, St. Joseph. (ATL)
Washoe Valley, NV, Washoe Co., Holy Spirit, c/o Reno, NV, St. Rose of Lima. (RNO)
Waskom, TX, Harrison Co., St. Lawrence Brindisi, c/o Jefferson, TX, Immaculate Conception. (TYL)
Watauga, SD, Corson Co., St. Michael, c/o McLaughlin, SD, Standing Rock Reservation. (RC)
Waterproof, LA, Tensas Parish, St. Francis of Assisi, c/o St. Joseph, LA, St. Joseph. (ALX)
Watonga, OK, Blaine Co., St. Rose of Lima, c/o Kingfisher, OK, SS. Peter and Paul. (OKL)
Watrous, NM, Mora Co., c/o Wagon Mound, NM, Santa Clara. (SFE)
Wattenburg, CO, Weld Co., Our Lady of Grace, c/o Fort Lupton, CO, St. William. (DEN)
Wauneta, NE, Chase Co., St. John's, c/o Trenton, NE, St. James. (LIN)
Wayland, MO, Clark Co., St. Martha, c/o Kahoka, MO, St. Michael the Archangel. (JC)
Waynoka, OK, Woods Co., Our Mother of Mercy, c/o Alva, OK, Sacred Heart. (OKL)
Webbers Falls, OK, Muskogee Co., St. Joseph, c/o Sallisaw, OK, St. Francis Xavier. (TLS)
Weirs Beach, NH, Belknap Co., St. Helena, c/o Lakeport, NH, Our Lady of the Lakes. (MAN)
Welch, OK, Craig Co., St. Ann, c/o Miami, OK, Sacred Heart. (TLS)
Weldona, CO, Morgan Co., St. Francis of Assisi, c/o Fort Morgan, CO, St. Helena. (DEN)
Wellfleet, NE, Lincoln Co., St. William's, c/o Curtis, NE, St. James. (LIN)
Wells River, VT, Orange Co., St. Eugene, c/o Bradford, VT, Our Lady of Perpetual Help. (BUR)
Wenden, AZ, St. John the Baptist, c/o Parker, AZ, Sacred Heart Roman Catholic Parish – Parker. (TUC)
Weslaco, TX, Hidalgo Co., St. Jude Chapel, c/o Weslaco, TX, San Martin de Porres. (BWN)
West Barnstable, MA, Barnstable Co., Our Lady of Hope, c/o Centerville, MA, Our Lady of Victory. (FR)
West Castleton, VT, Rutland Co., St. Matthew of Avalon, c/o Fair Haven, VT, Our Lady of Seven Dolors. (BUR)
West Charleston, VT, Orleans Co., St. Benedict Labre, c/o Derby Line, VT, St. Edward. (BUR)
West Columbia, TX, Brazoria Co., St. John the Apostle, c/o Sweeny, TX, Our Lady of Perpetual Help. (GAL)
West Covina, CA, Los Angeles Co., St. Christopher Korean Catholic Community, c/o West Covina, CA, St. Christopher. (LA)
West Dundee, IL, Kane Co., St. Mary, c/o Dundee, IL, St. Catherine of Siena. (RCK)
West Gilgo Beach, NY, Suffolk Co., c/o Babylon, NY, St. Joseph. (RVC)
West Glacier, MT, Flathead Co., c/o Columbia Falls, MT, St. Richard. (HEL)
West Hempstead, NY, Nassau Co., Chapel, c/o West Hempstead, NY, St. Thomas, the Apostle. (RVC)
West Pawlet, VT, Rutland Co., St. Frances Cabrini, c/o Fair Haven, VT, Our Lady of Seven Dolors. (BUR)
West Peru, NY, Clinton Co., St. Patrick, c/o Peru, NY, St. Augustine. (OG)
West Point, CA, Calaveras Co., Our Lady of Fatima, c/o San Andreas, CA, St. Andrew Church of San Andreas (Pastor of). (STO)
West Shokan, NY, Ulster Co., St. Augustine, c/o Woodstock, NY, St. John. (NY)
Westernport, MD, Allegany Co., St. Gabriel, c/o Westernport, MD, St. Peter. (BAL)
Westfield, PA, Tioga Co., St. Catherine, c/o Elkland, PA, St. Thomas the Apostle. (SCR)
Westfield, WI, Marquette Co., Good Shepherd, c/o Montello, WI, St. John the Baptist. (MAD)
Westhoff, TX, DeWitt Co., St. Aloysius, c/o Meyersville, TX, SS. Peter & Paul. (VIC)
Westover, MD, Somerset Co., St. Elizabeth, c/o Pocomoke City, MD, Holy Name of Jesus. (WIL)
Westport, WA, Grays Harbor Co., St. Paul, c/o Aberdeen, WA, St. Mary. (SEA)
Westville, NY, Franklin Co., c/o Constable, NY, The Catholic Community of Constable, Westville and Trout River. (OG)
Westway, TX, El Paso Co., Immaculate Heart of Mary, c/o Canutillo, TX, St. Patrick. (ELP)
Wewahitchka, FL, Gulf Co., St. Lawrence Mission, c/o Port St. Joe, FL, St. Joseph. (PT)
Wheatfields, AZ, Apache Co., Our Lady of the Lake, c/o Lukachukai, AZ, St. Isabel. (GLP)
Wheatland, CA, Yuba Co., St. Daniel, c/o Lincoln, CA, St. Joseph. (SAC)
Wheatville, NY, Genesee Co., St. Patrick, c/o Oakfield, NY, St. Padre Pio. (BUF)
Wheelwright, MA, Hardwick Co., St. Augustine, c/o Gilbertville, MA, St. Aloysius. (WOR)
Whetstone, AZ, Cochise Co., Good Shepherd, c/o Sierra Vista, AZ, Saint Andrew the Apostle Roman Catholic Parish – Sierra Vista. (TUC)
White Church, MO, Howell Co., St. Joseph, c/o Willow Springs, MO, Sacred Heart. (SPC)
White Earth, MN, Becker Co., St. Benedict, c/o Ogema, MN, Most Holy Redeemer. (CR)
White Horse, SD, Dewey Co., St. Therese, c/o Eagle Butte, SD, All Saints. (RC)
White Horse Beach, MA, St. Catherine's Chapel, c/o Manomet, MA, St. Bonaventure. (BO)
White Lake, NY, Sullivan Co., St. Anne, c/o Monticello, NY, St. Peter. (NY)
White Pigeon, MI, St. Joseph Co., St. Joseph, c/o Sturgis, MI, Holy Angels. (KAL)
White River, SD, Mellette Co., Sacred Heart, c/o St. Francis, SD, St. Francis Mission/Rosebud Educational Society. (RC)
White River, SD, Mellette Co., St. Ignatius, c/o St. Francis, SD, St. Francis Mission/Rosebud Educational Society. (RC)

White Rock, NM, Los Alamos Co., St. Joseph, c/o Los Alamos, NM, Immaculate Heart of Mary. (SFE)
Whiteville, LA, Resurrection, c/o Morrow, LA, St. Peter. (LAF)
Wibaux, MT, Wibaux Co., St. Peter, c/o Glendive, MT, Sacred Heart. (GF)
Wibaux, MT, Wibaux Co., St. Philip, c/o Glendive, MT, Sacred Heart. (GF)
Wilkeson, WA, Pierce Co., Our Lady of Lourdes, c/o Buckley, WA, St. Aloysius. (SEA)
Willacoochee, GA, Atkinson Co., Holy Family, c/o Douglas, GA, St. Paul's. (SAV)
Willard, NM, Torrance Co., c/o Mountainair, NM, St. Alice. (SFE)
Williams, CA, Colusa Co., Annunciation, c/o Williams, CA, Sacred Heart. (SAC)
Williams, MN, Lake of the Woods Co., St. Joseph, c/o Baudette, MN, Sacred Heart. (CR)
Williamsfield, IL, Knox Co., St. James, c/o Brimfield, IL, St. Joseph's. (PEO)
Williamstown, PA, Dauphin Co., Sacred Heart of Jesus, c/o Lykens, PA, Our Lady Help of Christians. (HBG)
Williamstown, VT, Orange Co., St. Edward, c/o Northfield, VT, St. John the Evangelist. (BUR)
Williamsville, MO, Wayne Co., Our Lady of Sorrows, c/o Piedmont, MO, St. Catherine of Siena. (SPC)
Willow, AK, St. Christopher, c/o Big Lake, AK, Corp. of Our Lady of the Lake Church. (ANC)
Wills Point, TX, Van Zandt Co., St. Luke, c/o Canton, TX, St. Therese. (TYL)
Wilson, TX, Lynn Co., Blessed Sacrament, c/o Post, TX, Holy Cross. (LUB)
Wilton, MN, Beltrami Co., Sacred Heart, c/o Red Lake, MN, St. Mary's Mission Church. (CR)
Wimauma, FL, Hillsborough, Our Lady of Guadalupe Mission, c/o Sun City Center, FL, Prince of Peace. (SP)
Windsor, MO, Henry Co., St. Bartholomew, c/o Clinton, MO, Holy Rosary. (KC)
Wingdale, NY, Dutchess Co., Our Lady of Solace Mission, c/o Dover Plains, NY, St. Charles Borromeo. (NY)
Winifred, MT, Fergus Co., Holy Family, c/o Lewistown, MT, St. Leo. (GF)
Winn, ME, Penobscot Co., Sacred Heart, c/o Lincoln, ME, St. Mary. (PRT)
Winn, MI, Isabella Co., St. Leo, c/o Shepherd, MI, St. Vincent De Paul. (SAG)
Winnett, MT, Petroleum Co., St. Aloysius, c/o Roundup, MT, St. Benedict. (GF)
Winnsboro, SC, Fairfield Co., St. Theresa, c/o Blythewood, SC, Transfiguration. (CHR)
Winona, MS, Montgomery Co., Sacred Heart, c/o Lexington, MS, St. Thomas. (JKS)
Winston–Salem, NC, Forsyth Co., Our Lady of Fatima, c/o Winston–Salem, NC, Our Lady of Mercy. (CHL)
Winter Harbor, ME, Hancock Co., St. Margaret, c/o Ellsworth, ME, St. Joseph. (PRT)
Winter Park, CO, Grand Co., St. Bernard of Montjoux, c/o Granby, CO, St. Anne. (DEN)
Wisdom, MT, Beaverhead Co., Our Lady of Wisdom, c/o Dillon, MT, St. Rose of Lima. (HEL)
Wolf Creek, MT, Lewis and Clark Co., Sacred Heart, c/o Helena, MT, Our Lady of the Valley. (HEL)
Wolfforth, TX, Lubbock Co., St. Francis of Assisi, c/o Lubbock, TX, San Ramon. (LUB)
Wood, SD, Melette Co., Our Lady of Good Counsel, c/o White River, SD, St. Ignatius. (RC)
Wood, SD, Mellette Co., Our Lady of Good Counsel, c/o St. Francis, SD, St. Francis Mission/Rosebud Educational Society. (RC)
Woodland, WI, Dodge Co., St. Mary, c/o Neosho, WI, St. Matthew. (MIL)
Woodville, CA, Tulare Co., St. Francis of Assisi, c/o Tipton, CA, St. John The Evangelist. (FRS)
Woodville, FL, Leon Co., St. Stephen the Protomartyr, c/o Crawfordville, FL, St. Elizabeth Ann Seton. (PT)
Woodward, IA, St. John of God, c/o Madrid, IA, St. Malachy's. (SC)
Worcester, MA, St. Andrew the Apostle Mission, c/o Worcester, MA, St. Peter. (WOR)
Wright, WY, Campbell Co., Blessed Sacrament, c/o Gillette, WY, St. Matthew's. (CHY)
Wyola, MT, Big Horn Co., Blessed Kateri Tekakwitha, c/o Lodge Grass, MT, Our Lady of Loretto. (GF)

Y

Yacolt, WA, Clark Co., St. Joseph the Workman, c/o Battle Ground, WA, Sacred Heart. (SEA)
Yahuecas, PR, Adjuntas Co., Virgen del Carmen, c/o Adjuntas, PR, St. Joachim. (PCE)
Yakima, WA, Yakima Co., St. Joseph Mission at the Ahtanum, c/o Yakima, WA, Holy Family. (YAK)
Yancey, TX, Medina Co., Immaculate Heart of Mary, c/o D'Hanis, TX, Holy Cross. (SAT)
Yarmouth Port, MA, Barnstable Co., Sacred Heart Chapel, c/o Hyannis, MA, St. Francis Xavier's. (FR)
Yarnell, AZ, Yavapai Co., St. Mary Mediatrix, A Quasi Parish, c/o Bagdad, AZ, St. Francis of Assisi Roman Catholic Parish. (PHX)
Yellville, AR, Marion Co., St Andrews Catholic Church, c/o Harrison, AR, Mary, Mother of God. (LR)
Yolo, CA, Yolo Co., Our Lady of Guadalupe, c/o Woodland, CA, Holy Rosary. (SAC)
York Beach, ME, York Co., Star of the Sea, c/o York, ME, St. Christopher–by–the–Sea. (PRT)
Yorktown, TX, DeWitt Co., San Luis, c/o Yorktown, TX, Holy Cross. (VIC)
Young, AZ, Gila Co., St. Benedict Mission, c/o Payson, AZ, Saint Philip the Apostle Roman Catholic Church – Payson. (TUC)
Youngsville, NM, Rio Arriba Co., c/o Abiquiu, NM, St. Thomas Apostle. (SFE)
Youngsville, NY, Sullivan Co., St. Francis of Assisi, c/o Jeffersonville, NY, St. George–St. Francis. (NY)
Yuma, AZ, Yuma Co., Our Lady of Guadalupe, c/o Yuma, AZ, Immaculate Conception Roman Catholic Parish & Guadalupe Mission – Yuma. (TUC)

Z

Zamora, CA, Yolo Co., St. Agnes, c/o Knights Landing, CA, St. Paul. (SAC)
Zapata, TX, Zapata Co., Ntra. Sra. De Lourdes, c/o Zapata, TX, Our Lady of Lourdes. (LAR)
Zia, NM, Sandoval Co., c/o Jemez Pueblo, NM, San Diego Indian Missions. (SFE)
Zolfo Springs, FL, Hardee Co., San Alfonso Catholic Center, c/o Wauchula, FL, St. Michael. (VEN)
Zortman, MT, Phillips Co., St. Joseph, c/o Hays, MT, St. Paul's Indian Mission. (GF)

MINISTRIES OF PRIESTS FOR LIFE

Rachel's Vineyard

Kevin & Theresa Burke

Rachel's Vineyard is the world's largest ministry of healing after abortion. Founded by Dr. Theresa and Kevin Burke, it became a ministry of Priests for Life several years ago. It is a retreat model based on trauma theory and offering, in both Catholic and interdenominational formats, an opportunity for women and men who have lost children to abortion to process their grief and begin the road to healing.

The retreats are rooted in Scripture and the sacraments and utilize the services of clergy and professional counselors. Over 650 retreats were offered worldwide in the past year at 195 Rachel's Vineyard retreat sites, 84 of which are run by local dioceses. Along with the retreats, Rachel's Vineyard facilitates personal follow-up and ongoing care as the journey of healing continues through life.

Rachel's Vineyard
is a ministry of Priests For Life.

www.RachelsVineyard.org

Silent No More Awareness Campaign

Janet Morana, Georgette Forney, Fr. Frank Pavone

The Silent No More Awareness Campaign is the world's largest mobilization of women and men who have lost children to abortion and are sharing their testimony. Founded by Janet Morana of Priests for Life and Georgette Forney of Anglicans for Life, this campaign seeks to bring post-abortion healing to those who need it, to educate the public about the harm abortion does, and to use the power of personal testimony to expose the harm of abortion and the healing power of Jesus Christ.

Members of the campaign share their testimony at public rallies, in Churches, in the media, in legislative assemblies, and in one-to-one encounters. Those who want to express their regret for abortion but remain anonymous can also do so through this campaign.

Silent No More Awareness Campaign
is a project of Priests For Life
and Anglicans For Life..

www.SilentNoMoreAwareness.org

African-American Outreach

Dr. Alveda C. King

The African-American Outreach of Priests for Life seeks to foster within the African-American community a sense of ownership within the pro-life movement, which transcends any single ethnic, religious, or political group. Sadly, African Americans, though comprising only about 13% of the population, have roughly 33% of the abortions.

Dr. Alveda King, full-time Pastoral Associate of Priests for Life, is the niece of Dr. Martin Luther King, Jr. and coordinates our African-American Outreach. Through media appearances, an extensive speaking schedule, and coordinated efforts with other African-American leaders, Dr. King works to advance what she calls "the civil rights movement of our day."

African-American Outreach
is a project of Priests For Life.

www.AfricanAmericanOutreach.org

These are three of the many ministries of Priests for Life; others include our Lay Missionaries of the Gospel of Life, Deacons for Life, Seminarians for Life, Hispanic Outreach, Life on the Line, and Gospel of Life Ministries.

Priests For Life

PO Box 141172 • Staten Island, NY 10314
888-735-3448 • 718-980-4400
Fax 718-980-6515 • mail@priestsforlife.org

www.priestsforlife.org

Religious Institutes

Index for Religious Institutes of Men

Religious Order Initials for Men

Initials	Order	Code
A.A.	Assumptionists	[0130]
B.G.S.	Little Brothers of the Good Shepherd	[0580]
B.S.O.	Basilian Salvatorian Fathers	[0190]
C.F.A.	Alexian Brothers	[0120]
C.F.C.	Congregation of Christian Brothers	[0310]
C.F.M.M.	Brothers of Our Lady, Mother of Mercy	[0980]
C.F.P.	Brothers of the Poor of St. Francis	[0460]
C.F.R.	Franciscan Friars of the Renewal	[0535]
C.F.X.	Brothers of St. Francis Xavier	[1350]
C.I.C.M.	Missionhurst Congregation of the Immaculate Heart of Mary	[0860]
C.J.	Josephite Fathers	[0710]
C.M.	Congregation of the Mission	[1330]
C.M.C.	Congregation of Mother Coredemptrix	[0865]
C.M.F.	Claretian Missionaries	[0360]
C.M.I.	Carmelites of Mary Immaculate	[0275]
C.M.L.M.	The Congregation of Maronite Lebanese Missionaries	[0785]
C.M.M.	Congregation of Mariannhill Missionaries, Marianhill Fathers & Brothers	[0750]
C.O.	Oratorians	[0950]
C.P.	Congregation of the Passion	[1000]
C.P.M.	Congregation of the Fathers of Mercy	[0820]
C.PP.S.	Society of the Precious Blood	[1060]
C.R.	Congregation of the Resurrection	[1080]
C.R.	Theatine Fathers	[1300]
C.R.L.	Canons Regular of the Lateran	[0250]
C.R.M.	Adorno Fathers	[0100]
C.R.S.	Somascan Fathers	[1250]
C.R.S.P.	Clerics Regular of St. Paul	[0160]
C.S.	Missionaries of St. Charles-Scalabrinians	[1210]
C.S.C.	Brothers of the Congregation of Holy Cross	[0600]
C.S.C.	Priests of the Congregation of Holy Cross	[0610]
C.S.J.	Congregation of St. Joseph	[1150]
C.S.P.	Paulist Fathers	[1030]
C.S.P.X.	Brothers of Saint Pius X	[1180]
C.S.S.	Stigmatine Fathers and Brothers.	[1280]
C.S.Sp.	Congregation of the Holy Spirit	[0650]
C.Ss.R.	Redemptorist Fathers	[1070]
C.S.V.	Clerics of St. Viator	[1320]
Er.Cam.	Camaldolese Hermits of the Congregation of Monte Corona	[0230]
F.C.	Brothers of Charity	[0290]
F.D.P.	Sons of Divine Providence	[0410]
F.F.I.	Franciscan Friars of the Immaculate	[0533]
F.F.S.C.	Franciscan Brothers of the Holy Cross	[0510]
F.I.C.	Brothers of Christian Instruction	[0320]
F.M.M.	Brothers of Mercy	[0810]
F.M.M.	Missionary Fraternity of Mary	[0855]
F.M.S.	The Marist Brothers	[0770]
F.M.S.I.	Sons of Mary Missionary Society	[1270]
F.S.C.	Brothers of the Christian Schools	[0330]
F.S.C.B.	Priestly Fraternity of the Missionaries of St. Charles Borromeo	[1205]
F.S.E.	Brothers of the Holy Eucharist	[0620]
F.S.P.	Brothers of St. Patrick	[1160]
F.S.R.	Brothers of the Congregation of Our Lady of the Holy Rosary	[0960]
F.S.S.P.	Priestly Fraternity of St. Peter	[1065]
G.H.M.	The Glenmary Home Missioners	[0570]
H.G.N.	Heralds of Good News	[0585]
I.C.	Institute of Charity	[0300]
I.C.	Institute of Christ the King - Sovereign Priest	[0305]
I.H.M.	Brothers of the Immaculate Heart of Mary	[0680]
I.M.C.	Consolata Missionaries	[0390]
L.B.S.F.	Little Brothers of Saint Francis	[1144]
L.C.	Legionaries of Christ	[0730]
M.Afr.	Missionaries of Africa	[0850]
M.C.C.J.	Comboni Missionaries of the Heart of Jesus (Verona)	[0380]
M.E.P.	Paris Foreign Mission Society	[0897]
M.H.M.	Mill Hill Missionaries	[0830]
M.I.C.	Congregation of Marians of the Immaculate Conception	[0740]
M.M.	Maryknoll	[0800]
M.S.	The Missionaries of Our Lady of La Salette	[0720]
M.S.A.	Society of the Missionaries of the Holy Apostles	[0590]
M.S.C.	Missionaries of the Sacred Heart	[1110]
M.S.F.	Congregation of the Missionaries of the Holy Family	[0630]
M.S.F.S.	Missionaries of St. Francis de Sales	[0485]
M.S.P.	Missionary Society of St. Paul of Nigeria	[0854]
M.Sp.S.	Missionaries of the Holy Spirit	[0660]
M.S.S.	Missionaries of the Blessed Sacrament	[0825]
M.SS.CC.	Missionaries of the Sacred Hearts of Jesus and Mary	[1120]
O.A.R.	Order of Augustinian Recollects	[0150]
O.Carm.	Carmelite Fathers and Brothers	[0270]
O.Cart.	Order of Carthusians	[0280]
O.C.D.	Discalced Carmelite Friars	[0260]
O.Cist.	Cistercian Fathers	[0340]
O.C.S.O.	The Cistercian Order of the Strict Observance (Trappists)	[0350]
O.de.M.	Order of Our Lady of Mercy	[0970]
O.F.M.	Franciscan Friars	[0520]
O.F.M.Cap.	The Capuchin Franciscan Friars	[0470]
O.F.M.Conv.	Conventual Franciscans	[0480]
O.H.	Hospitaller Brothers of St. John of God	[0670]
O.M.	Minim Fathers	[0835]
O.Mar.	Maronite Monks of Adoration	[0790]
O.M.I.	Oblates of Mary Immaculate	[0910]
O.M.M.	Maronite Order of the Blessed Virgin Mary	[0782]
O.M.V.	Oblates of the Virgin Mary	[0940]
O.P.	Order of Preachers (Dominicans)	[0430]
O.Praem.	Canons Regular of Premontre	[0900]
O.S.A.	The Augustinians	[0140]
O.S.B.	Benedictine Monks	[0200]
O S.B.M.	Order of St. Basil the Great	[018
O.S.C.	Canons Regular of the Order of the Holy Cross	[040
O.S.Cam.	Camillian Fathers and Brothers	[024
O.S.F.	Congregation of the Religious Brothers of the Third Order Regular of St. Francis	[049
O.S.F.	Franciscan Brothers of the Third Order Regular	[051
O.S.F.	Franciscan Missionary Brothers of the Sacred Heart of Jesus	[054
O.S.F.S.	Oblates of St. Francis de Sales	[092
O.S.J.	Oblates of St. Joseph	[093
O.S.M.	Servites	[124
O.S.P.P.E.	Pauline Fathers	[101
O.Ss.S.	Brigittine Monks	[089
O.SS.T.	Order of the Most Holy Trinity	[131
P.I.M.E.	Pontifical Institute for Foreign Missions	[105
R.C.J.	Rogationist Fathers	[109
S.A.	Franciscan Friars of the Atonement	[053
S.A.C.	Society of the Catholic Apostolate	[099
S.C.	Brothers of the Sacred Heart	[110
S.C.	Servants of Charity	[122
S.Ch.	Society of Christ	[126
Sch.P.	Piarist Fathers.	[104
S.C.J.	Congregation of the Priests of the Sacred Heart	[113
S.D.B.	Salesians of Don Bosco	[119
S.D.S.	Society of the Divine Savior	[120
S.D.V.	Vocationist Fathers	[134
S.F.	Sons of the Holy Family	[064
S.J.	Jesuit Fathers and Brothers	[069
S.M.	Society of Mary (Marianists)	[076
S.M.	Marist Fathers	[078
S.M.A.	Society of African Missions	[011
S.M.M.	Montfort Missionaries	[087
S.O.L.T.	Society of Our Lady of the Most Holy Trinity	[097
s.P.	Servants of the Paraclete	[123
S.P.S.	St. Patrick's Missionary Society	[117
S.S.	Society of the Priests of Saint Sulpice	[129
S.S.C.	Society of St. Columban	[037
SS.CC.	Congregation of the Sacred Hearts of Jesus and Mary	[114
S.S.E.	Society of Saint Edmund	[044
S.S.J.	St. Joseph's Society of the Sacred Heart	[070
S.S.P.	Pauline Fathers and Brothers	[102
S.S.S.	Congregation of the Blessed Sacrament	[022
S.T.	Missionary Servants of the Most Holy Trinity	[084
S.X.	Xaverian Missionary Fathers	[136
S.V.D.	Society of the Divine Word	[042
V.C.	Vincentian Congregation (India)	[042
T.O.R.	Third Order Regular of Saint Francis	[056

Religious Institutes of Men

The Conference of Major Religious Superiors of Men, U.S.A., 8808 Cameron St., Silver Spring, MD 20910. Tel: 301-588-4030; Fax: 301-587-4575; Website: cmsm.org. A canonical conference of the major superiors of religious communities and institutes of men for the purpose of promoting the spiritual and apostolic welfare of Priests and Brothers. Rev. Paul Lininger, O.F.M.Conv., Exec. Dir.; Very Rev. Thomas P. Cassidy, S.C.J., Pres.; Very Rev. Thomas Smolich, S.J., Vice Pres.; Bro. Francis Carr, F.S.C., Sec. & Treas.

[0100] (C.R.M.)—ADORNO FATHERS
(Clerics Regular Minor)

General Motherhouse: *Via Alpi Apuane 1*, 00141, Rome, Italy, Very Rev. Raffaele Mandolesi, C.R.M., Supr. Gen.

U.S. Foundation (1936): *St. Michael's Seminary*, 575 Darlington Ave., Ramsey, NJ 07446. Tel: 201-327-7375; Fax: 201-327-8131. Rev. Hector DiNardo, C.R.M., U.S. Delegate; Rev. Nicholas Capetola, C.R.M., Supr./Rector.

Priests: 10; Brothers: 5

Represented in the Archdiocese of Newark and in the Diocese of Charleston.

[0110] (S.M.A.)—SOCIETY OF AFRICAN MISSIONS
(Societas Missionum ad Afros)

Founded Dec. 8, 1856 with the approval of Pope Pius IX. A clerical society of apostolic life.

Generalate: Via della Nocetta 111, 00164, Rome, Italy, Very Rev. Kieran O'Reilly, S.M.A., Supr. Gen; Very Rev. Jean-Marie Guillaume, S.M.A., Vicar Gen; Rev. Thomas M. Wright, S.M.A., Gen. Councilor; Rev. Paul Ennin, S.M.A., Gen. Councilor.

American Province (1941): 23 Bliss Ave., Tenafly, NJ 07670. Tel: 201-567-9085; Fax: 800-670-8328. Very Rev. Michael P. Moran, S.M.A., Prov. Supr; Rev. Brendan Darcy, S.M.A., Vice Prov; Rev. Frank Allen Wright, S.M.A., Councilor.

Legal Title: Society of African Missions, Inc. NJ.

Priests: 26; Lay Missionary in temporary commitment: 4; Lay Missionary in permanent commitment: 1; Priest Associates: 1

Represented in the Archdioceses of Boston, Newark and Washington.

[0120] (C.F.A.)—ALEXIAN BROTHERS
(Congregatio Fratrum Cellitarum seu Alexianorum)

Generalate: Signal Mountain, TN 37377. Tel: 423-886-0212. Bro. Edward Walsh, Supr. Gen; Bro. Warren Longo, Asst. Supr. Gen; Bro. Nikolaus Hahn, Gen. Councilor 52001, Aachen, Germany, Bro. Dominiek Champagne, C.F.A., Gen. Councilor B-2530, Boechout, Belgium,

General Motherhouse: *Congregation of Alexian Brothers*, No. 198 James Blvd., Signal Mountain, TN 37377. Tel: 423-886-0212; Fax: 423-886-0208.

United States Province: 3040 W. Salt Creek Ln., Arlington Heights, IL 60005. Tel: 847-385-7147; Fax: 847-483-7036. Councilors: Bro. James Classon, C.F.A., Prov; Bro. Theodore Loucks, C.F.A; Bro. John Howard, C.F.A; Bro. Richard Lowe, C.F.A; Bro. Lawrence Krueger, C.F.A., Vicar Prov.

Professed Brothers: 33; Novice Brothers: 1

Properties owned or sponsored: General Hospitals 4; Continuing Care Retirement Communities 2; Alzheimers Assisted Living Facility 1; Novitiates 2; Nursing Homes 2; Residential AIDS Facility 2; HUD Housing 2; Pace 2; Mobile Clinic & Wellness Center (Davo City, Philipppines) 1; Independent Living facility 1; Senior Center 1.

Represented in the Archdioceses of Chicago, Milwaukee and St. Louis and in the Diocese of Knoxville. Also in Davao City, Philippines and Györ, Hungary.

[0130] (A.A.)—ASSUMPTIONISTS
(Augustinians of the Assumption)

General House: via San Pio V, 55, 00165, Rome, Italy, Very Rev. Richard Lamoureux, A.A., Supr. Gen.

Province of North America (1946): 330 Market St., Brighton, MA 02135. Tel: 617-783-0400. Rev. Marcel Poirier, A.A., Prov. Supr. Councilors: Rev. Miguel Diaz Ayllon, A.A; Rev. Dennis Gallagher, A.A; Rev. Donald Espinosa, A.A., Prov. Treas.

Priests: 45; Brothers: 10; Parishes: 1; Shrines: 1; Colleges: 1; Formation Centers: 1; Novitiates: 1; Residences: 8

Represented in the Archdioceses of Boston and New York and in the Dioceses of Nashville and Worcester. Also in Korea, Philippines, Kenya, Mexico, Tanzania, Italy and Canada.

[0140] (O.S.A.)—THE AUGUSTINIANS
(Ordo Sancti Augustini)

Founded in 1244, first American foundation 1796.

Generalate: *Via Paolo VI - 25*, 00193, Rome, Italy, Very Rev. Robert F. Prevost, O.S.A., Gen.

Province of St. Thomas of Villanova (1796): *Saint Augustine Friary*, 214 Ashwood Rd., P.O. Box 340, Villanova, PA 19085-0340. Tel: 610-527-3330. Counselors: Very Rev. Donald F. Reilly, O.S.A., Prior Prov; Rev. John R. Flynn, O.S.A., Prov. Sec; Rev. William A. McGuire, O.S.A., Prov. Treas; Rev. William J. Donnelly, O.S.A; Rev. William T. Garland, O.S.A; Rev. Joseph A. Genito, O.S.A; Rev. Anthony M. Genovese, O.S.A; Rev. James M. Paradis, O.S.A; Rev. Jorge A. Reyes, O.S.A; Rev. Kevin DePrinzio, O.S.A., Dir. Vocations; Rev. Joseph S. Mostardi, O.S.A., Dir. Augustinian Volunteers; Rev. Anthony P. Burrascano, O.S.A., Dir. Mission Office; Rev. John J. Sheridan, O.S.A., Archivist; Rev. John E. Deegan, O.S.A., Dir. Augustinian Justice & Peace Office; Rev. Gary N. McCloskey, O.S.A., Dir. "Augustinian Friends"; Bro. Robert Thornton, O.S.A., Coord. Abuse Prevention & Educ; Rev. Gordon E. Marcellus, O.S.A., Devel. Office; Rev. William M. Cleary, O.S.A., Devel. Office.

Legal Title: The Brothers of the Order of Hermits of Saint Augustine (The Brothers of the Order of Hermits of St. Augustine, a corporation in the state of Pennsylvania 1804).

Priests: 190; Students of Theology: 1; Brothers: 4; Permanent Deacons: 1; Parishes (USA 15, Japan 4; South Africa 1): 20; Major Seminaries: 1; Colleges: 1; Universities: 1; Preparatory Schools and High Schools & Foreign Missions: 5

Represented in the Archdioceses of Boston, Miami, New York and Philadelphia and in the Dioceses of Albany, Charlotte and Venice.

Province of Our Mother of Good Counsel (Order of St. Augustine) (1941): *Tolentine College & Center*, 20300 Governors Hwy., Olympia Fields, IL 60461-1081. Tel: 708-748-9500; Fax: 708-481-2090; Web: www.MidwestAugustinians.org. Very Rev. William E. Lego, O.S.A., Prior Prov; Rev. G. Jerome Knies, O.S.A., Vicar Prov. & Personnel Dir; Bro. Thomas P. Taylor, O.S.A., Prov. Sec; Rev. Michael J. Slattery, O.S.A., Prov. Treas; Rev. Thomas R. McCarthy, O.S.A., Vocation Dir.

Fathers: 77; Bishops: 2; Professed Brothers: 15; Parishes: 7; High Schools: 3; Retreat Centers: 1; Residences: 4

Represented in the Archdioceses of Chicago, Detroit and Milwaukee and in the Dioceses of Joliet, Kalamazoo, Lansing and Tulsa. Also in Peru, South America.

Province of St. Augustine: 1605 28th St., San Diego, CA 92102. Tel: 619-235-0247. Rev. Gary E. Sanders, O.S.A., Prov. Counselors: Rev. James P. Retzner, O.S.A., Sec; Rev. Robert W. Gavotto, O.S.A; Rev. John D. Keller, O.S.A; Rev. Gregory D. Heidenblut, O.S.A; Rev. Richard S. Hardick, O.S.A.

Priests: 24; Deacons: 2; Brothers: 5; Parishes: 5; High Schools: 2; Orphanages: 1

Legal Holdings or Titles: St. Augustine High School, San Diego, CA; Monica House, San Diego, CA; Tierra del Sol, Boulevard, CA; St. Rita House, San Francisco, CA; Villanova Preparatory School, Ojai, CA; Austin House, San Diego, CA.

Represented in the Archdioceses of Los Angeles and Portland in Oregon and in the Dioceses of Oakland and San Diego.

St. Augustine Monastery: 611 Cedar Ave., P.O. Box 279, Richland, NJ 08350. Tel: 856-697-2600; Fax: 856-697-8389. Rev. Paul Galetto, O.S.A., Pres; Rev. Ronald A. Hamaday, O.S.A., Prior; Rev. Francis J. Horn, O.S.A., Headmaster & Treas; Rev. Keith Hollis, O.S.A., Campus Min; Rev. Stephen M. Curry, O.S.A.

Represented in the Archdiocese of Philadelphia and in the Diocese of Camden.

Region U.S.A. (1993): *Cristo Rey Church*, 767 Ave. A, Beaumont, TX 77701. Tel: 409-835-7788. Rev. Luis Urriza, O.S.A.

Fathers: 4

Represented in the Archdiocese of San Antonio and in the Diocese of Beaumont.

[0150] (O.A.R.)—ORDER OF AUGUSTINIAN RECOLLECTS
(Ordo Augustinianorum Recollectorum)

General Motherhouse: Viale dell' Astronomia, 27, Casella Postale 10760, 00144, Rome, Italy, Very Rev. Javier Guerra, O.A.R., Prior Gen.

Province of St. Augustine (1943): *Augustinian Recollects*, 29 Ridgeway Ave., West Orange, NJ 07052-3297. Tel: 973-731-0616; Fax: 973-731-1033. Rev. Joseph J. Gallardo, O.A.R., Prior Prov; Rev. Domingos A. Machado, O.A.R., 1st Councilor, Vicar of Prov; Rev. Fidel Hernandez, 2nd Councilor; Rev. J. Michael Rafferty, O.A.R., 3rd Councilor; Rev. Eliseo Gonzalez, O.A.R., 4th Councilor.

Bishops: 1; Priests: 35; Brothers: 4; Professed Clerics: 6; Postulants: 2; Permanent Deacons: 3

Represented in the Archdioceses of Los Angeles, Newark and New York and in the Diocese of Orange. Also in Mexico.

Province of St. Nicholas of Tolentine (U.S.A. Delegation): 3021 Frutas Ave., El Paso, TX 79905. Rev. Antonio Lasheras, O.A.R., Prov. Delegate.

Priests: 21

Represented in the Archdioceses of Newark and New York and in the Dioceses of El Paso and Las Cruces.

[0160] (C.R.S.P.)—CLERICS REGULAR OF ST. PAUL
(Barnabite Fathers)

(Ordo Clericorum Regularium Sancti Pauli)

Founded in Milan, Italy in 1533. First foundation in the United States in 1952 in Buffalo, NY.

Historical Motherhouse Church of St. Barnabas, Milan, since 1545.

General Motherhouse: Via Giacomo Medici, 15, Rome, Italy, Most Rev. Giovanni M. Villa, C.R.S.P., Supr. Gen.

North American Province: 981 Swann Rd., P.O. Box 167, Youngstown, NY 14174-0167. Tel: 716-754-7489. Very Rev. Gabriel M. Patil, C.R.S.P., Prov.

Legal Title: Barnabite Fathers, Inc.

Priests: 15

Fathers staff and serve: Parishes; Marian Shrine; Colleges; Spiritual Centers.

Properties Owned or Sponsored: Our Lady of Fatima Shrine and Barnabite Fathers Seminary, Youngstown, NY; Barnabite Spiritual Center, Bethlehem, PA; St. Anthony M. Zaccaria Seminary.

Represented in the Dioceses of Allentown, Buffalo, and San Diego. Also in Hamilton, Ontario, Canada.

[0180] (O.S.B.M.)—ORDER OF ST. BASIL THE GREAT
(Ordo Sancti Basilii Magni)

General Superior "Protoarchimandrita": Via San Giosafat 8, (Aventino), 00153, Rome, Italy, Rev. Basilio Koubetch, O.S.B.M.

American Province (1948): 29 Peacock Ln., Locust Valley, NY 11560. Tel: 516-609-3262; Fax: 516-609-3264. Very Rev. Philip Sandrick, O.S.B.M., Prov.

Fathers: 24; Brothers: 3; Parishes: 6; Community Houses: 6; Novitiates: 1; Monasteries: 3; Retreat Houses: 1; Libraries: 1

Represented in the Byzantine Rite Archdiocese of Philadelphia and in the Byzantine Rite Dioceses of Chicago, Parma, Passaic and Stamford.

[0190] (B.S.O.)—BASILIAN SALVATORIAN FATHERS

General Motherhouse: *Holy Savior Monastery*, Saida, Lebanon, Archimandrite Sleyman Abouzeid, B.S.O., Supr. Gen.

American Headquarters: *Basilian Salvatorian Fathers*, 30 East St., Methuen, MA 01844. Rt. Rev. John Faraj, B.S.O., Prov. Supr; Rt. Rev. Simon Hage, B.S.O; Rev. Lawrence Tumminelli, B.S.O; Rt. Rev. Archimandrite John Jadaa, B.S.O; Rev. Youssef Aziz, B.S.O; Rt. Rev. George Dagher, B.S.O; Rev. Eugene Mitchell, B.S.O., General Economos; Rev. Martin A. Hyatt, B.S.O., Local Supr; Rev. Antoine Rizk, B.S.O.

Fathers in American Region: 22

Novitiate and House of Studies: St. Basils Seminary; Methuen, MA.

Parishes: Canada 4; U.S.A. 7.

Represented in the Archdioceses of Boston and Miami, the Dioceses of Cleveland, Manchester and Norwich and the Eparchy of Newton.

[0200] (O.S.B.)—BENEDICTINE MONKS
(Ordo Sancti Benedicti)

American Cassinese Congregation of the Order of Saint Benedict (Established by Pope Pius IX, August 24, 1855.)

Headquarters: *Saint John's Abbey*, 31802 County Rd. 159, P.O. Box 2015, Collegeville, MN 56321-2015. Tel: 320-363-3935; Fax: 320-363-3082. Rt. Rev. Timothy Kelly, O.S.B., Abbot & Pres. President's Council: Rt. Rev. Hugh R. Anderson, O.S.B St. Procopius Abbey: Rt. Rev. Douglas R. Nowicki, O.S.B Saint Vincent Archabbey: Rt. Rev. Claude J. Peifer, O.S.B Saint Bede Abbey: Rev. Thomas Acklin, O.S.B Saint Vincent Archabbey: Rev. Daniel Ward, O.S.B Saint John Abbey: The Abbeys and Priories belonging to this Congregation are as follows:

Saint Vincent Archabbey: 300 Fraser Purchase Rd., Latrobe, PA 15650-2690. Tel: 724-532-6600. Rt. Rev. Douglas R. Nowicki, O.S.B., Archabbot; Rt. Rev. Paul R. Maher, O.S.B., Archabbot (Resigned); Most Rev. Rembert G. Weakland, O.S.B., Resigned Archbishop of Milwaukee.
Legal Title: The Benedictine Society of Westmoreland County; Saint Vincent College Corporation; The Wimmer Corporation; The Saint Vincent Cemetery Corporation.
Priests: 115; Deacons: 3; Solemn Professed Choir-Monks: 34; Junior Professed Monks: 9; Brothers: 2; Choir Novices: 5
Represented in the Archdiocese of Baltimore and in the Dioceses of Altoona-Johnstown, Erie, Greensburg, Harrisburg, Pittsburgh, Richmond, Savannah and Wheeling-Charleston.

American Cassinese Congregations

St. John's Abbey: 31802 County Rd 159, P.O. Box 2015, Collegeville, MN 56321-2015. Tel: 320-363-2011; Fax: 320-363-3082. Rt. Rev. John Klassen, O.S.B., Abbot; Very Rev. Thomas Andert, O.S.B., Prior; Very Rev. Jonathan Licari, O.S.B., Subprior.
Fathers: 99; Professed Brothers: 50; Novices: 6; Abbeys: 1; Dependent Priories: 1; Parishes: 13; Chaplaincies: 8; Japanese Residences: 1; Schools of Theology: 1; Universities: 1; High Schools: 1; Novitiates: 1
Monastery founded in 1856 and raised to an Abbey in 1866.
Legal Holdings: Saint John's Seminary; Saint John's University; Saint John's Preparatory School; Saint John's Abbey.
Represented in the Archdiocese of St. Paul-Minneapolis and in the Dioceses of New Ulm, St. Cloud and San Bernardino. Also in Japan, The Bahamas and Republic of China.

St. Benedict's Abbey: 1020 North Second St., Atchison, KS 66002-1499. Tel: 913-367-7853; Fax: 913-367-6230. Rt. Rev. Barnabas Senecal, O.S.B; Rt. Rev. Owen Purcell, O.S.B., Retired Abbot; Rt. Rev. Ralph Koehler, O.S.B., Retired Abbot; Very Rev. James R. Albers, O.S.B., Prior; Rev. Meinrad Miller, O.S.B., Subprior.
Bishops: 1; Fathers: 35; Brothers Professed: 14; Abbeys: 1; Parishes: 12; Missions: 1; Chaplaincies: 4; Colleges: 1; High Schools: 1
Founded in 1857 and raised to an Abbey in 1876.
Represented in the Archdiocese of Kansas City in Kansas. Also in Brazil.

St. Mary's Abbey: *Delbarton*, 230 Mendham Rd., Morristown, NJ 07960. Tel: 973-538-3231; Fax: 973-538-7109; Web: www.osbmonks.org. Rt. Rev. Giles P. Hayes, O.S.B., Abbot; Very Rev. Bruno A. Ugliano, O.S.B., Prior; Rev. Luke L. Travers, O.S.B., Subprior.
Priests: 36; Brothers: 6; Deacons: 2; Juniors: 1; Parishes: 2; Preparatory Schools: 1; Retreat Centers: 1
Monastery founded in 1857 and raised to an Abbey in 1884.
Represented in the Archdiocese of Newark and in the Dioceses of Metuchen, Paterson and Trenton.

Newark Abbey: 528 Dr. Martin Luther King, Jr. Blvd., Newark, NJ 07102. Tel: 973-792-5800; Fax: 973-643-6922. Rt. Rev. Melvin J. Valvano, O.S.B., Abbot; Very Rev. Mark M. Payne, O.S.B., Prior; Very Rev. Matthew S. Wotelko, O.S.B., Subprior.
Priests: 12; Brothers: 5; Abbeys: 1; Parishes: 1; Preparatory (High) Schools: 1
Priory founded 1857; Abbey in 1884; title transferred from Newark to Morristown, N.J. in 1956; became Abbey again in 1968 and known as Newark Abbey under the patronage of the Immaculate Conception.
Legal Holding: St. Benedict Preparatory School, Newark, NJ.
Represented in the Archdioceses of Indianapolis and Newark.

Belmont Abbey: 100 Belmont-Mount Holly Rd., Belmont, NC 28012-1802. Tel: 704-825-6675; Fax: 704-825-6242. Rt. Rev. Placid D. Solari, O.S.B., Abbot; Rt. Rev. Oscar C. Burnett, O.S.B., Retired Abbot; Very Rev. David G. Brown, O.S.B., Prior.
Legal Title: Southern Benedictine Society of North Carolina, Incorporated.
Priests: 13; Brothers: 5
Monastery founded in 1876, raised to an Abbey in 1884 and erected into an Abbey Nullius in 1910; Abbey Nullius suppressed January 1, 1977 and incorporated into Diocese of Charlotte.
Properties owned or sponsored: Belmont Abbey College, Belmont, NC.

St. Bernard Abbey (1891): Cullman, AL 35055. Tel: 256-734-8291; Fax: 256-734-3885. Rt. Rev. Cletus D. Meagher, O.S.B., Abbot; Very Rev. Kevin D. McGrath, O.S.B., Prior & Novice Master; Ven. Bro. Leo Borelli, O.S.B., Subprior.
Legal Title: St. Benedictine Society of Alabama, Inc.
Priests: 13; Brothers: 17
Represented in the Archdiocese of Mobile and in the Diocese of Birmingham.

St. Procopius Abbey: 5601 College Rd., Lisle, IL 60532. Tel: 630-969-6410; Fax: 630-969-6426. Rt. Rev. Dismas B. Kalcic, O.S.B., Abbot; Very Rev. Anthony J. Jacob, O.S.B., Prior & Procurator; Very Ven. Columban Trojan, O.S.B., Subprior & Business Mgr; Rev. James Flint, O.S.B., Treas.
Archbishops: 1; Priests: 21; Brothers: 11; Oblates: 1
Monastery founded in 1885 and raised to an Abbey in 1894.
Legal Holdings or Titles: Benedictine University, Lisle, IL; Benet Academy, Lisle, IL; Benedictine Chinese Mission, Lisle, IL; Slav Mission, Lisle, IL; St. Procopius Abbey Endowment, Lisle, IL.
Represented in the Diocese of Joliet. Also in Taiwan.

St. Gregory's Abbey: 1900 W. MacArthur St., Shawnee, OK 74804. Tel: 405-878-5491; Fax: 405-878-5189. Rt. Rev. Lawrence Stasyszen, O.S.B., Abbot; Rt. Rev. Adrian Vorderlandwehr, O.S.B., Resigned; Rt. Rev. Charles Massoth, O.S.B., Resigned; Rt. Rev. Martin Lugo, O.S.B., Resigned; Very Rev. Louis Vanderley, O.S.B., Prior; Rev. Joachim Spexarth, O.S.B., Subprior.
Legal Titles: Benedictine Fathers of Sacred Heart Mission, Inc.; St. Gregory's University, Endowment Foundation, Inc., Shawnee, OK; Saint Gregory's Abbey Benefit Trust.
Priests: 17; Brothers: 8
Monastery founded in 1875 and raised to an Abbey in 1896.
Ministries in 3 Parishes and 2 military installations.
Represented in the Archdiocese of Oklahoma City and in the Diocese of Tulsa.
Properties owned or sponsored: Mabee-Gerrer Museum of Art, Shawnee, OK; St. Gregory's University, Shawnee, OK.

Saint Leo Abbey: 33601 SR 52, P.O. Box 2350, Saint Leo, FL 33574. Tel: 352-588-8624; Fax: 352-588-5217; Email: abbey@saintleo.edu; Web: www.saintleoabbey.org. Rt. Rev. Isaac Camacho, O.S.B., Abbot.
Legal Title: Order of St. Benedict of Florida, Inc.
Fathers: 9; Brothers: 12; Internal Oblates: 1
Founded in 1889 and raised to an Abbey in 1902.
Represented in the Diocese of St. Petersburg.

Assumption Abbey: P.O. Box A, Richardton, ND 58652. Tel: 701-974-3315. Rt. Rev. Brian Wangler, O.S.B., Abbot; Rt. Rev. Patrick Moore, O.S.B., Resigned Abbot; Bro. Basil Kirsch, O.S.B., Prior; Rev. Sebastian Schmidt, O.S.B., Subprior.
Priests: 32; Brothers: 20
Founded in 1893 and raised to an Abbey in 1903.
Represented in the Dioceses of Bismarck, Cheyenne, Fargo and Indianapolis. Also in Colombia.
Properties owned or sponsored: Abbey; Dependent Priory; Parishes 4; Chaplaincies 5; Indian Mission.

St. Bede Abbey: 24 W. U.S. Hwy. 6, Peru, IL 61354. Tel: 815-223-3140. Rt. Rev. Marion E. Balsavich, O.S.B., Resigned Abbot; Rt. Rev. Roger F. Corpus, O.S.B., Resigned Abbot; Rt. Rev. Claude J. Peifer, O.S.B., Abbot; Bro. Anthony Shaughnessy, O.S.B., Prior; Very Rev. Dominic M. Garramone, O.S.B., Subprior.
Legal Title: The Benedictine Society of Saint Bede.
Priests: 20; Brothers: 6
Monastery founded in 1891 and raised to an Abbey in 1910.
Represented in the Diocese of Peoria.
Properties owned or sponsored: Parishes 1.

St. Martin's Abbey: 5300 Pacific Ave. S.E., Lacey, WA 98503-7500. Rt. Rev. Neal G. Roth, O.S.B; Rt. Rev. Conrad R. Rausch, O.S.B., Resigned Abbot; Rt. Rev. Adrian Parcher, O.S.B., Resigned Abbot; Very Rev. Alfred J. Hulscher, O.S.B., Prior; Very Rev. Clement Pangratz, O.S.B., Subprior.
Priests: 19; Brothers: 13
Monastery founded in 1895 and raised to an Abbey in 1914.
Legal Holdings or Titles: St. Martin's Abbey; St. Martin's University.
Represented in the Archdiocese of Seattle and in the Diocese of Spokane.

Holy Cross Abbey: 2951 E. Hwy. 50, Canon City, CO 81212. Tel: 719-275-8631. Very Rev. Maurice C. Haefling, O.S.B., Vicar Admin; Rt. Rev. Warren J. Heidgen, O.S.B., Retired Abbot; Rt. Rev. Kenneth C. Hein, O.S.B., Retired Abbot.
Fathers: 3; Oblates: 1
Founded in 1886 and raised to an Abbey in 1925.
Represented in the Archdiocese of Denver and in the Diocese of Pueblo.

St. Anselm Abbey: 100 St. Anselm Dr., Manchester, NH 03102-1310. Tel: 603-641-7000; Fax: 603-641-7267. Rt. Rev. Matthew K. Leavy, O.S.B., Abbot; Most Rev. Joseph John Gerry, O.S.B., 3rd Abbot, Tenth Bishop of Portland, ME; Bro. Isaac Murphy, O.S.B., Prior; Very Rev. Peter J. Guerin, O.S.B., Subprior.
Legal Title: Order of Saint Benedict of New Hampshire.
Bishops: 1; Abbots: 1; Fathers: 21; Brothers: 4
Monastery founded in 1889 and raised to an Abbey in 1927.
Represented in the Archdiocese of San Francisco and in the Diocese of Manchester.

St. Andrew Abbey: 10510 Buckeye Rd., Cleveland, OH 44104. Tel: 216-721-5300. Rt. Rev. Christopher Schwartz, O.S.B., Abbot; Very Rev. Gary Hoover, O.S.B., Prior; Very Rev. Albert Marflak, O.S.B., Subprior.
Bishops: 1; Abbots: 1; Brothers: 10; Abbeys: 1; Parishes: 2; High Schools: 1; Chaplaincies: 2; Novices: 1
Founded in 1922 and raised to an Abbey in 1934.
Legal Holdings or Titles: Benedictine Order of Cleveland; Benedictine High School.
Represented in the Dioceses of Cleveland and Great Falls-Billings.

Holy Trinity Monastery: P.O. Box 990, Butler, PA 16003-0990. Tel: 724-287-4461; Fax: 724-287-6160; Email: hegumenleo@aol.com. Rt. Rev. Leo R. Schlosser, Hegumen; Rev. Anselm Orlosky; Bro. James Merva; Bro. Michael Zetzer.
Priests: 3; Brothers: 2
Represented in the Byzantine Archeparchy of Pittsburgh.

Benedictine Priory: 6502 Seawright Dr., Savannah, GA 31406. Tel: 912-356-3520; Fax: 912-356-3527. Very Rev. Frank E. Ziemkiewicz, O.S.B., Prior.
Priests: 4; Brothers: 1; High Schools: 1
Founded 1877, dependent priory of St. Vincent Archabbey, Latrobe, PA.
Represented in the Diocese of Savannah.

Woodside Priory: 302 Portola Rd., Portola Valley, CA 94028. Tel: 650-851-8220. Very Rev. Martin J. Mager, O.S.B., Supr.
Legal Title: Benedictine Fathers of the Priory, Inc.
Priests: 3; Brothers: 1; High Schools: 1; Middle Schools: 1
Founded in 1956, erected as Conventual Priory 1958, became a dependent Priory upon St. Anselm's Abbey, Manchester, NH, 1976.
Represented in the Archdiocese of San Francisco.

Abadia Benedictine-de San Antonio Abad: P.O. Box 729, Humacao, PR 00792. Tel: 787-852-1616; Tel: 787-852-1766; Fax: 787-852-1920. Rt. Rev. Oscar Rivera, O.S.B., Abbot; Rev. Eduardo Torrellas, O.S.B., Prior; Bro. Aristedes Pacheco, Subprior.
Priests: 7; Brothers: 7
Monastery founded in 1947 and became an abbey in 1984.

Mary Mother of the Church Abbey: 12829 River Rd., Richmond, VA 23238-7206. Tel: 804-784-3508; Fax: 804-784-2214. Rt. Rev. Patrick Moore, O.S.B., Admin; Rev. Donald F. Scales, O.S.B., Prior.
Priests: 9; Brothers: 4; Abbeys: 1; Chaplaincies: 3; High Schools: 1
Community founded in 1911 and became an Abbey in 1989.
Legal Holdings: Benedictine High School of Richmond; Mary Mother of the Church Abbey.
Represented in the Diocese of Richmond.

Swiss-American Congregations

St. Meinrad Archabbey: No. 100 Hill Dr., Saint Meinrad, IN 47577. Rev. Gabriel Hodges, O.S.B., Program Coord., Institute for Priests and Presbyterates.
Founded by Pope Pius IX, 1870, and Pope Leo XIII, April 5, 1881.
The Abbeys and Priories belonging to this Federation are as follows:

St. Meinrad Archabbey: No. 100 Hill Dr., Saint Meinrad, IN 47577. Tel: 812-357-6611; Fax: 812-357-6551. Rt. Rev. Justin DuVall, O.S.B., Archabbot; Rt. Rev. Lambert Reilly, O.S.B., Resigned Archabbot; Rt. Rev. Bonaventure Knaebel, O.S.B., Retired Archabbot; Rev. Tobias Colgan, O.S.B., Prior.
Archbishops: 1; Priests: 67; Brothers: 24; Parishes: 19; Schools of Theology: 1; Chaplaincies: 7
Founded 1854; raised to an Abbey in 1870.
Represented in the Archdioceses of Chicago, Hartford, Indianapolis and Washington and in the Dioceses of Charleston, Evansville, Gary, Owensboro and Sioux Falls.

Conception Abbey: 37174 State Hwy. VV, Conception, MO 64433. Tel: 660-944-3100; Fax: 660-944-2800. Rt. Rev. Gregory Polan, O.S.B., Abbot; Rev. Daniel Petsche, O.S.B., Prior; Bro. Bernard Montgomery, O.S.B., Subprior.
Legal Title: Conception Abbey, Inc.
Archbishops: 1; Fathers: 35; Brothers: 23; Parishes: 8; Seminary College: 1; Chaplaincies: 6
Founded December 8, 1873; Abbey April 5, 1881.
Represented in the Archdioceses of Kansas City in Kansas and Omaha and in the Dioceses of Dodge City, Jefferson City, Kansas City-St. Joseph, Little Rock, Springfield-Cape Girardeau and Tulsa.

Mount Michael Abbey: 22520 Mount Michael Rd., Elkhorn, NE 68022-3400. Tel: 402-289-2541; Fax: 402-289-4539. Rt. Rev. Michael Liebl, O.S.B., Abbot; Rev. Richard Thell, O.S.B., Prior; Rev. Louis L. Sojka, O.S.B., Subprior.
Fathers: 11; Brothers: 13
Legal Holdings & Titles: Mount Michael Benedictine Abbey; Mount Michael Benedictine School; Mount Michael Foundation.
Monks serve and staff: Parishes 2.
Represented in the Archdiocese of Omaha and in the Diocese of Pueblo.

Subiaco Abbey: Subiaco, AR 72865. Tel: 479-934-1000; Fax: 479-934-4328. Rt. Rev. Jerome Kodell, O.S.B., Abbot; Rev. David Bellinghausen, O.S.B., Prior; Bro. Ephrem O'Bryan, O.S.B., Subprior.
Fathers: 22; Perpetually Professed Brothers: 19; Temporarily Professed Brothers: 1; Oblates: 1
Properties staffed or sponsored: Parishes 7; High School 1.
Represented in the Diocese of Little Rock.

St. Joseph Abbey: Saint Benedict, LA 70457. Tel: 985-892-1800; Fax: 985-867-2270; Web: www.sjasc.edu. Rt. Rev. Patrick Regan, O.S.B., Retired Abbot; Rt. Rev. Justin Brown, O.S.B., Abbot; Bro. Brian Harrington, O.S.B., Prior.
Fathers: 22; Brothers: 15; Parishes: 3; Novitiates: 1; Seminary College: 1
Legal Holdings: St. Joseph Seminary College, St. Benedict, LA.
Represented in the Archdiocese of New Orleans.

Mt. Angel Abbey: *St. Benedict*, Mt. Angel Abbey & Seminary, One Abbey Dr., Saint Benedict, OR 97373. Tel: 503-845-3030; Fax: 503-845-3594. Rt. Rev. Gregory Duerr, O.S.B., Admin; Rev. Joseph Nguyen, O.S.B., Subprior.
Finally Professed Monks (Priests): 32; Finally Professed

Monks (Brothers): 18; Temporarily Professed Monks (Brothers): 5
Founded on Oct. 30, 1882, from Engelberg in Switzerland and raised to an abbey on March 24, 1904.
Legal Holdings or Titles: Monastery of Our Lady of the Angels, Cuernavaca, Morelos, Mexico.

Marmion Abbey: 850 Butterfield Rd., Aurora, IL 60502. Tel: 630-897-7215. Rt. Rev. Vincent De Paul Bataille, O.S.B., Abbot; Rt. Rev. Gerald Benkert, O.S.B., Abbot Emeritus; Rt. Rev. David J. Cyr, O.S.B., Abbot Emeritus; Very Rev. Basil Yender, O.S.B., Prior; Rev. Kenneth Theisen, O.S.B., Subprior.
Priests: 28; Brothers: 11
Founded as Dependent Priory of St. Meinrad's Abbey, June 20, 1943; Abbey since March 21, 1947.
Represented in the Diocese of Rockford. Also in Quetzaltenango, Guatemala.
Properties staffed or sponsored: Parishes 1; High Schools 2.

St. Benedict's Abbey: 12605 224th Ave., Benet Lake, WI 53102. Tel: 262-396-4311; Fax: 262-396-4365; Email: benedictines@msn.com. Rt. Rev. Edmund J. Boyce, O.S.B., Abbot; Rt. Rev. Andrew V. Garber, O.S.B., Abbot Resigned & Prior; Rt. Rev. Robert C. Schoofs, O.S.B., Abbot Resigned; Rt. Rev. Leo M. Ryska, O.S.B., Abbot Resigned; Very Rev. Henry V. Nurre, O.S.B., Subprior.
Legal Titles: Benedictine Monks, Inc.; St Benedict's Home Missionary Society.
Priests: 9; Brothers: 11
Monastery founded in 1945 and raised to an Abbey in 1952.
Represented in the Archdiocese of Milwaukee.

Glastonbury Abbey: 16 Hull St., Hingham, MA 02043. Tel: 781-749-2155; Fax: 781-749-7236. Very Rev. Mark F. Serna, Prior Admin.
Monks in Solemn Vows: 10
Property owned: Lincoln School Apartments for the Elderly and Handicapped, Hingham, MA.
Represented in the Archdiocese of Boston.

Blue Cloud Abbey: P.O. Box 98, Marvin, SD 57251-0098. Tel: 605-398-9200; Fax: 605-398-9201. Rt. Rev. Denis Quinkert, O.S.B., Abbot; Bro. Benet Tvedten, O.S.B., Prior. Retired Abbots: Rt. Rev. Alan Berndt, O.S.B; Rt. Rev. Thomas Hillenbrand, O.S.B.
Legal Title: Blue Cloud Abbey, Inc.
Priests: 15; Brothers: 14
Monastery founded June 24, 1950; raised to a Priory August 5, 1952; raised to an Abbey March 21, 1954.
Represented in the Diocese of Sioux Falls. Also in Guatemala.

Corpus Christi Abbey: 101 S. Vista Dr., Sandia, TX 78383. Tel: 503-845-3304; Fax: 503-845-3202; Email: abbotp@mtangel.edu. Rt. Rev. Peter Eberle, O.S.B., Abbot; Bro. Simon Huggins, O.S.B., Prior.
Fathers: 4; Professed Brothers: 4
Property owned: Benedictine Retreat Center, Sandia, TX.
Represented in the Diocese of Corpus Christi.

Prince of Peace Abbey: 650 Benet Hill Rd., Oceanside, CA 92054. Tel: 760-967-4200; Email: princeabby@aol.com; Web: www.princeofpeaceabbey.org. Rt. Rev. Charles Wright, O.S.B., Abbot; Very Rev. Sharbel Ewen, O.S.B., Prior.
Fathers: 7; Brothers: 18

St. Benedict Abbey: 252 Still River Rd., P.O. Box 67, Still River, MA 01467. Tel: 978-456-3221; Fax: 978-456-8181; Email: saintbenedict@abbey.org. Rt. Rev. Gabriel Gibbs, O.S.B., Abbot; Very Rev. Xavier Connelly, O.S.B., Prior.
Priests: 8; Brothers: 6; Oblates: 1
Represented in the Diocese of Worcester.

Congregation of St. Ottilien for Foreign Missions

St. Paul's Abbey: 289 Rt. 206 South, P.O. Box 7, Newton, NJ 07860-0007. Tel: 973-383-2470; Fax: 973-383-5782. Rt. Rev. Joel P. Macul, O.S.B., Abbot; Rt. Rev. Justin E. Dzikowicz, O.S.B., Resigned Abbot; Rt. Rev. Augustine J. Hinches, O.S.B., Resigned Abbot; Very Rev. Samuel Kim, O.S.B., Prior.
Solemnly Professed Monks (Priests 8): 14
(Benedictine Missionaries)
Monastery established March 15, 1924; elevated to an Abbey June 9, 1947.
Represented in the Diocese of Paterson.

Christ the King Priory (1985) - Benedictine Mission House (1935): Benedictine Mission House was founded in 1935 and raised to the rank of Priory in 1985. P.O. Box 528, Schuyler, NE 68661. Tel: 402-352-2177; Fax: 402-352-2176. Rev. Germar Neubert, O.S.B., Prior; Rev. Volker Futter, O.S.B; Rev. Thomas Leitner, O.S.B; Rev. Paul L. Kasun, O.S.B.
Fathers: 4; Brothers: 4
Represented in the Archdiocese of Omaha.

Congregation of the Annunciation

St. Andrew's Abbey: P.O. Box 40, Valyermo, CA 93563. Tel: 661-944-2178. Very Rev. Damien Toilolo, O.S.B., Prior; Rev. Joseph Brennan, O.S.B., Subprior.
Monks in Solemn Vows: 19; Simple Vows: 4
Represented in the Archdiocese of Los Angeles.

Houses Not In Congregations

Mount Saviour Monastery: 231 Monastery Rd., Pine City, NY 14871-9787. Tel: 607-734-1688; Fax: 607-734-1689; Email: info@msaviour.org. Very Rev. Martin Boler, O.S.B; Rev. James Cronin, O.S.B., Prior.
Professed Monks: 12
Monastery founded in 1950, raised to Independent Priory 1957.
Represented in the Diocese of Rochester.

Weston Priory (1953): 58 Priory Hill Rd., Weston, VT 05161. Tel: 802-824-5409; Fax: 802-824-3573. Very Rev. Richard Iaquinto, O.S.B., Prior.
Monks: 15
Represented in the Diocese of Burlington.

Camaldolese Benedictine Congregation (Congregatio Camaldulensis Ordinis Sancti Benedicti)

U.S. Foundation (1958): *New Camaldoli Hermitage*, 62485 Hwy. 1, Big Sur, CA 93920. Tel: 831-667-2456. Very Rev. Raniero Hoffman, O.S.B.Cam., Prior.
Fathers: 13; Professed Brothers: 7
Represented in the Dioceses of Monterey and Oakland.

English Benedictine Congregation

St. Anselm's Abbey: 4501 S. Dakota Ave. N.E., Washington, DC 20017. Tel: 202-269-2300; Fax: 202-269-2312. Rev. Dom McGurk, Prior & Admin.
Legal Title: Benedictine Foundation at Washington DC.
Solemnly Professed Monks: 19

Abbey of St. Gregory the Great: 285 Cory's Ln., Portsmouth, RI 02871. Tel: 401-683-2000; Fax: 401-683-5888. Rt. Rev. Caedmon Holmes, O.S.B., Abbot.
Choir Religious: 15

Abbey of St. Mary and St. Louis: 500 S. Mason Rd., Saint Louis, MO 63141-8500. Tel: 314-434-3690; Fax: 314-434-0795. Rt. Rev. Thomas Frerking, O.S.B., Abbot.
Solemnly Professed Monks (Priests 15): 22; Simply Professed Monks: 6; Oblates: 1
Founded as a dependent Priory 1955, granted independence 1973, raised to status of Abbey 1989.

Sylvestrine Benedictine Congregation (Monachorum Silvestrinorum, O.S.B.)

Foundations in the U.S. (1910): *Saint Benedict Priory*, 2711 E. Drahner Rd., Oxford, MI 48370. Tel: 248-628-2249. Very Rev. Daniel Homan, O.S.B., Conventual Prior.
Brothers: 4; Priests: 6; Regular Oblates: 3
Represented in the Archdiocese of Detroit and in the Diocese of Paterson.

Olivetan Benedictines (Congregatio Sanctae Mariae Montis Oliveti Ordinis Sancti Benedicti)

General Motherhouse: *St. Sylvester Monastery*, Fabriano, Italy, Very Rev. Michael Kelly, O.S.B., Abbot Gen.

U.S. Foundations: *Holy Trinity Monastery*, P.O. Box 298, Saint David, AZ 85630. Tel: 520-720-4642; Fax: 520-720-4202. Rev. Henri Capdeville, O.S.B., Prior; Rev. Benedict Lemekt, O.S.B.
Solemnly Professed: 6; Postulants: 1
Represented in the Diocese of Tucson.

Our Lady of Guadalupe Abbey: P.O. Box 1080, Pecos, NM 87552-1080. Tel: 505-757-6415. Rev. Christopher Zielenski, O.S.B., Abbot; Bro. James Marron, Claustral Prior.
Priests: 6; Brothers: 6
Represented in the Archdiocese of Santa Fe.

Benedictine Monastery of Hawaii: 67-290 Farrington Hwy., P.O. Box 490, Waialua, HI 96791. Tel: 808-637-7887; Fax: 808-637-8601; Email: monastery@hawaiibenedictines.org; Web: www.hawaiibenedictines.org. Rev. David Barfknecht, O.S.B., Supr.
Priests: 3; Brothers: 2

Subiaco Benedictine Congregation

Monastery of Christ in the Desert (1964): Abiquiu, NM 87510. Tel: 801-545-8567. Rt. Rev. Philip Lawrence, O.S.B., Abbot.
Monks: 72
Independent 1983; Abbey 1996.
Represented in the Archdioceses of Chicago, Santa Fe, and Dallas. Also in Mexico and South Africa.

Saint Mary's Monastery: P.O. Box 345, Petersham, MA 01366. Tel: 978-724-3350. Rev. Dom Anselm Atkinson, O.S.B., Supr.
Monks: 7
Dependent Monastery 1987.
Represented in the Diocese of Worcester.

Solesmes Congregation

Benedictine Monks, Solesmes Congregation: *Our Lady of Clear Creek Monastery*, 5804 W. Monastery Rd., Hulbert, OK 74441. Tel: 918-772-2454. Rev. Philip Anderson, O.S.B., Prior.
Legal Title: Foundation for the Annunciation Monastery of Clear Creek.

[0220] (S.S.S.)—CONGREGATION OF THE BLESSED SACRAMENT
(Congregatio Sanctissimi Sacramenti)

Generalate: 46 Via Giovanni Battista de Rossi, 00161, Rome, Italy, Very Rev. Fiorenzo Salvi, S.S.S., Supr.

Province of St. Ann (1931): 5384 Wilson Mills Rd., Cleveland, OH 44143. Tel: 440-442-6311. Very Rev. Norman B. Pelletier, S.S.S., Prov; Rev. Michael Arkins, S.S.S., Vicar Prov; Rev. Dana Pelotte, S.S.S., Consultor & Prov. Treas. Consultors: Rev. John Thomas Lane, S.S.S., Consultor for Formation; Rev. John Keenan, S.S.S.
Bishops: 1; Priests: 37; Permanent Deacons: 1; Brothers: 13
Properties staffed or owned: Parishes 7; Seminary 1; Community Houses 9; Novitiate 1.
Represented in the Archdioceses of Galveston-Houston, New York and San Antonio and in the Dioceses of Cleveland, Chicago, and St. Petersburg.

[0230] (ER. CAM.)—CAMALDOLESE HERMITS OF THE CONGREGATION OF MONTECORONA
(Eremitae Camaldulenses Congregationis Montis Coronae)

General Motherhouse: *Sacro Eremo*, Via del Tuscolo 45, 00040 Monte Porzio Catone, Rome, Italy, Rt. Rev. Lanfranco Longhi, Er.Cam., Father Major.

U.S. Foundation (1959): *Holy Family Hermitage*, 1501 Fairplay Rd., Bloomingdale, OH 43910-7971. Tel: 740-765-4511. Very Rev. Basil Corriere, Er.Cam., Prior.
Hermit Priests: 4; Professed: 3
Represented in the Diocese of Steubenville.

[0240] (M.I.)—CAMILLIAN FATHERS AND BROTHERS OR ORDER OF ST. CAMILLUS
(Ministers of the Infirm or Sick)
(Ministri degli Infermi)

General Motherhouse: *Casa Generalizia*, Ministri degli Infermi, Piazza della Maddalena 53, 00186, Rome, Italy, Very Rev. Renato Salvatore, M.I., Supr. Gen; Rev. Jesus Ruiz, M.I., Vicar Gen; Bro. Luca Perletti, M.I., Sec. Gen. & Sec. of Formation; Rev. Paulo Guarise, M.I., Sec. of Ministry; Rev. Babychan Pazhanilath, M.I., Sec. of Missions.

North American Province (1923): *Provincialate*, 3345 S. 10th St., Milwaukee, WI 53215. Tel: 414-481-3696; Fax: 414-481-8044. Very Rev. Richard O'Donnell, M.I., Prov; Rev. Louis Lussier, M.I., Vicar Prov; Rev. Joseph L. Bisoffi, M.I; Rev. Albert Schempp, M.I; Bro. Mario Crivello, M.I.
Fathers: 11; Professed Brothers: 3
Legal Titles: St. Camillus Health Center Inc., Wauwatosa, WI; St. Camillus Health System, Wauwatosa, WI; San Camillo, Inc., Wauwatosa, WI; St. Camillus Ministries Inc., Wauwatosa, WI; St. Camillus Communities Inc., Wauwatosa, WI; Order of St. Camillus Foundation, Wauwatosa, WI.
Represented in the Archdiocese of Milwaukee and in the Dioceses of Savannah and Worcester.

[0250] (C.R.L.)—CANONS REGULAR OF THE LATERAN
(Ordo Canonicorum Regularium S. Augustini Congregations Ss. Salvatoris Lateranensis)

General House: *Curia Generalizia dei Canonicio Regolari Lateranensi*, Piazza S. Pietro in Vincoli, 4A, 00184, Roma, Italy,

United States: *Canons Regular of the Lateran*, 2317 Washington Ave., Bronx, NY 10458. Tel: 212-295-9600. Rev. Jose L. Biain, C.R.L., Supr.
Priests: 6; Brothers: 4
Represented in the Archdiocese of New York and in the Diocese of Arecibo (PR).

[0260] (O.C.D.)—DISCALCED CARMELITE FRIARS
(Ordo Carmelitarum Discalceatorum)

Founded Mt. Carmel, Palestine in the 13th Century.

Generalate: *Carmelitani Scalzi*, Corso d'Italia, 38, 00198, Rome, Italy, Very Rev. Luis Arostegui Gamboa, O.C.D., Supr. Gen.

California-Arizona Province (1983): 926 E. Highland Ave., P.O. Box 2178, Redlands, CA 92373. Tel: 909-793-0424; Fax: 909-335-1304. Very Rev. Gerald Werner, O.C.D., Prov.
Legal Title: Discalced Carmelite Province of California.
Fathers: 32; Brothers: 2; Students: 13; Postulants: 2; Novices: 2
Represented in the Archdioceses of Los Angeles, Portland and Seattle and in the Dioceses of San Jose, San Bernardino, Santa Rosa and Tucson. Also in Uganda.
Properties owned, staffed or sponsored: Parishes 4; Retreat House; Novitiate; House of Studies; House of Prayer; Institute of Spirituality.

Province of St. Therese of Oklahoma (1935): *Provincial House*, 906 Kentucky Ave., San Antonio, TX 78201. Tel: 201-735-9127. Very Rev. Ralph Reyes, O.C.D., Prov.
Fathers: 21; Brothers: 1; Students of Philosophy: 1; Students of Theology: 2
Represented in the Archdioceses of New Orleans, Oklahoma City and San Antonio and in the Dioceses of Dallas and Little Rock.
Properties staffed or sponsored: Parishes 3; Community Houses 1; Novitiate 1; Student House 1.

Washington Province of the Immaculate Heart of Mary (1947): *Discalced Carmelites-Prov. Office*, 1233 S. 45th St., Milwaukee, WI 53214-3693. Tel: 414-672-7212; Fax: 414-672-3138. Very Rev. John Sullivan,

...C.D., Prov.
...athers: 57; Deacons: 1; Brothers: 11; Temporary Professed Brothers: 6; Bishops: 1; Novices: 2; Postulants: 1
Represented in the Archdioceses of Boston, Milwaukee and Washington and in the Diocese of Wheeling-Charleston. Also in Nairobi, Kenya.
Properties owned or sponsored: Community Houses 6.

Polish Province of the Holy Spirit, Poland (1949): *Monastery of Our Lady of Mt. Carmel*, 1628 Ridge Rd., Munster, IN 46321. Tel: 219-838-7111; Fax: 219-838-7214; Email: carmelmunster@yahoo.com. Rev. Jacek Palica, O.C.D., Prior.
Priests: 11; Brothers: 2
Represented in the Diocese of Gary.

[0270] (O.CARM.)—CARMELITE FATHERS & BROTHERS
(Ordo Fratrum Beatissimae Virginis Mariae de Monte Carmelo)

General Curia: Via Giovanni Lanza, 138, 00184, Rome, Italy, Most Rev. Fernando Millan Romeral, O.Carm., Prior Gen.

Province of the Most Pure Heart of Mary (1864): *Carmelite Provincial Office*, 1317 Frontage Rd., Darien, IL 60561. Tel: 630-971-0050; Fax: 630-971-0195. Very Rev. John F. Welch, O.Carm., Prior Prov; Rev. Bernhard Bauerle, O.Carm., Officer & Treas. Commissary Provincials: Rev. James Boyce, O.Carm., Prov. Eastern Commissary; Rev. David L. Simpson, O.Carm., Prov. Midwest Commissary; Rev. William Harry, O.Carm., Prov. Western Commissary; Rev. Enrique Laguna Yargas, O.Carm., Prov. Peru Commissary. Councilors: Rev. Bernhard Bauerle, O.Carm; Rev. Gregory Houck, O.Carm; Rev. Ronald Oakham, O.Carm; Rev. Quinn Conners, O.Carm; Rev. Robert E. Colaresi, O.Carm., Dir. Little Flower Society; Rev. John Malley, O.Carm., Dir.-Carmelite Mission Office; Sr. Mary Martin, Delegate to Lay Carmelites.
Priests: 164; Clerics: 5; Pre-Novitiates: 6; Novices: 2; Brothers: 29
Ministries in 31 Parishes.
Properties owned: Spiritual Centers 3; Shopping-center Chapels 2; Carefree Village, residence for senior citizens, Darien, IL; High Schools 6; Community Houses 48; House of Study 7; Cemetery 1; Shrine 2.
Represented in the Archdioceses of Boston, Chicago, Galveston-Houston, Kansas City in Kansas, Los Angeles, Louisville, Newark and Washington and in the Dioceses of Joliet, Pittsburgh, Phoenix, Sacramento, Tucson and Venice. Also in Canada, Peru and Mexico.

Province of the Most Pure Heart of Mary: *St. Therese Priory*, 75 E. Mariposa St., Phoenix, AZ 85012-1631. Rev. Charles Kurgan, O.Carm; Rev. Valentine Boyle, O.Carm.

Province of St. Elias (1931): P.O. Box 3079, Middletown, NY 10940-0890. Tel: 845-344-2223. Rev. Mario Esposito, O.Carm., Prov.
Fathers: 51; Brothers: 5; Novices: 4; Pre-Novices: 3; Professed Students: 10
Legal Holdings or Titles: The Missionary Society of Our Lady of Mt. Carmel of the State of New York; The Carmelite Fathers, Inc. of New York; Carmelite Fathers, Inc. of the Commonwealth of Massachusetts; Mt. Carmel Hermitage; Order of Carmelites of Palm Beach, Inc.; National Shrine of Our Lady of Mount Carmel, Inc.
Represented in the Archdioceses of New York, Miami, Newark and Washington and in the Dioceses of Albany, Dodge City, Greensburg, Palm Beach, Rochester, Sioux Falls, and Trenton. Also in Trinidad & Vietnam.
Properties staffed, owned or sponsored: Parishes 7; Priories 17; Houses of Study 2; Retreat Houses 1; Novitiate 1; Hermitages 1; Shrines 1.

Mt. Carmel Hermitage: 244 Baileys Rd., Bolivar, PA 15923. Tel: 724-238-0423; Fax: 724-238-0423. Rev. Bede J.K. Mulligan, O.Carm; Rev. Simeon D. Marro, O.Carm.
Fathers: 2; Brothers: 1
Founded in 1970, became dependent upon St. Elias Province in 1995.
Represented in the Diocese of Greensburg.

Carmelite Hermitage of the Blessed Virgin Mary (O.Carm): 8249 de Montreville Tr. N., Lake Elmo, MN 55042-9545. Tel: 651-779-7351; Fax: 651-779-7351; Email: carmelus@earthlink.net; Web: www.decorcarmeli.com. Rev. John M. Burns, O.Carm., Prior; Rev. Joseph V. Vaccaro, O.Carm; Rev. Patrick Peter Peach, O.Carm.
Fathers: 3; Brothers: 4

[0275] (C.M.I.)—CARMELITES OF MARY IMMACULATE
(Congregatio Fratrum Carmelitarum B.V. Mariae Immaculatae)

Founded by Blessed Kuriakose Elias Chavara and Companions at Mannanam, Kerala, India in 1831.

Generalate: *CMI Generalate Chavara Hills*, P.B. No. 3105, Kakkanad P.O., 682030, Kochi, India, Tel: 484-378-137; Fax: 484-378-363. Very Rev. Antony Kariyil, C.M.I., Prior Gen.

North American Headquarters: 21 Nassau Ave., Brooklyn, NY 11222. Tel: 718-388-4866. Rev. Jose Panthaplamthottiyil, C.M.I., Coord. Gen; Rev. Walter Thelapilly, C.M.I., Procurator Missions.
Legal Title: Carmelites of Mary Immaculate, Inc.
Priests in the United States and in Canada: 106
Ministries in Parishes; Hospitals; Universities; Prisons; Mission to the Syro-Malabar Catholics.
Represented in the Archdioceses of Boston, Hartford, Los Angeles, New York and Philadelphia and in the Dioceses of Alexandria, Amarillo, Beaumont, Brooklyn, Camden, Charleston, Covington, Joliet, Lafayette, Lake Charles, Metuchen, Nashville, New Ulm, Rockville Centre, St. Augustine, St. Paul & Minneapolis, Salina, San Angelo, Shreveport, Sioux Falls, Syracuse, Toledo, Tulsa, Tyler and Victoria. Also in Canada.

[0280] (O.CART.)—ORDER OF CARTHUSIANS
(Ordo Cartusianorum)

Motherhouse: *Grande Chartreuse*, St. Pierre de Chartreuse (Isere), France, Rev. Marcellin Theeuwes, Supr. Gen.

U.S. Charterhouse of the Transfiguration (1951): *Carthusian Monastery*, 1084 Ave Maria Way, Arlington, VT 05250. Tel: 802-362-2550; Fax: 802-362-3584; Email: carthusians_in_america@chartreuse.info; Web: www.chartreux.org; Web: transfiguration.chartreux.org. Rev. Lorenzo Maria T. De La Rosa Jr., O.Cart., Prior.
Total in Community: 15
Legal Titles: Carthusian Foundation in America, Inc.; Carthusian Foundation, Association Fraternelle Romande.
Represented in the Diocese of Burlington.

[0290] (F.C.)—BROTHERS OF CHARITY
(Congregatio Fratrum Caritate)

General Motherhouse (1807): Via G.B. Pagano 35, 00167, Rome, Italy, Bro. Rene Stockman, F.C., Supr. Gen.

American Region (1963) (1963): *Region of Our Lady of Charity*, 7720 Doe Ln., Glenside, PA 19038. Bro. John Fitzgerald, F.C., Regional Supr. for U.S.
Represented in the Archdioceses of Philadelphia and Washington D.C.

[0300] (I.C.)—INSTITUTE OF CHARITY
Rosminians Institutum Charitatis

General Motherhouse: *Collegio Rosmini Via Porta*, Latina 17, Rome, Italy, Very Rev. James Flynn, I.C., Supr. Gen.

U.S. Foundation (1877): 2327 W. Heading Ave., Peoria, IL 61604. Tel: 309-676-6341. Rev. William T. Miller, I.C., Prov.
Fathers in the U.S: 11; Parishes: 8
Represented in the Dioceses of Peoria and St. Petersburg.

[0305] (I.C.)—INSTITUTE OF CHRIST THE KING-SOVEREIGN PRIEST
Institute of Christ the King-Sovereign Priest
Institutum Christi Regis Summi Sacerdotis

General Motherhouse and House of Formation: *Villa Martelli*,, Via di Gricigliano 52, 50065, Sieci, Italy, Rev. Msgr. Gilles Wach, Prior Gen.

U.S. Mailing Address: *Institute of Christ the King-Sovereign Priest*, 6415 S. Woodlawn Ave., Chicago, IL 60637.

American Headquarters: *Shrine of Christ the King Sovereign Priest*, 6415 S. Woodlawn Ave., Chicago, IL 60637. Tel: 773-363-7409; Fax: 773-363-7824; Email: info@institute-christ-king.org. Rev. Msgr. R. Michael Schmitz, Prov. Supr. & Vicar Gen; Rev. Matthew L. Talarico, Vice Rector & Vice Prov.

[0310] (C.F.C.)—CONGREGATION OF CHRISTIAN BROTHERS

Founded in Ireland in 1802. First foundation in the United States in 1906.

Congregation Center: Rome, Italy, Bro. Joseph P. Pinto, C.F.C., Congregation Leader.
Bro. Hugh B. O'Neill, C.F.C., Prov. Leader; Bro. Kevin M. Griffith, C.F.C., Dept. Prov. Leader. Councilors: Bro. Daniel J. Casey, C.F.C; Bro. J. Barry Lynch, C.F.C; Bro. Anthony M. Murphy, C.F.C; Bro. Raymond Vercruysse, C.F.C.
Legal Title: The Christian Brothers Institute, Inc.; Christian Brothers of Ireland, Inc.; Mount Sion Community, Inc.
Brothers: 250
Represented in the Archdioceses of Boston, Chicago, Detroit, Miami, New Orleans, New York, Newark, and Seattle and in the Dioceses of Brooklyn, Brownsville, Charleston, Helena, Honolulu, Jackson, Joliet, Lafayette, Monterey, Orlando, Phoenix, Providence, Rochester, Spokane, St. Petersburg and Venice. Also in Canada and West Indies.
Ministries: Colleges 1; High Schools 23; Grade Schools 4; Houses of Formation 2; Migrant Education Centers 2; Care Center; Parishes 2; Retreat House; Learning Centers 2.

Development Office: Christian Brothers Association: P.O. Box 42903, Evergreen Park, IL 60805-0903. Tel: 773-233-2949. Bro. Donald F. McGovern, C.F.C., Dir.

[0320] (F.I.C.)—BROTHERS OF CHRISTIAN INSTRUCTION
/La Mennais Brothers
(Institutum Fratrum Instructionis Christianae)

General Motherhouse: *Casa Generalizia*, Via della Divina Provvidenza, 44 00166, Rome, Italy, Tel: 66-41-5618; Fax: 66-51-0242. Bro. Yannick Houssay, Supr. Gen.

American Province (1946): *Notre Dame Province-Notre Dame Institute*, P.O. Box 159, Alfred, ME 04002. Tel: 207-324-0067. Bro. Daniel Caron, F.I.C., Prov.
Brothers: 32; Colleges: 1; High Schools: 2; Retreat Centers: 1
Represented in the Dioceses of Fall River, Ogdensburg, Portland (In Maine) and Youngstown.

[0330] (F.S.C.)—BROTHERS OF THE CHRISTIAN SCHOOLS
(Fratres Scholarum Christianarum)

General Motherhouse: *Casa Generalizia*, Via Aurelia 476, CP 9099 00100, Rome, Italy, Bro. Alvaro Rodriquez Echeverria, F.S.C., Supr. Gen; Bro. Thomas Johnson, F.S.C., Vicar Gen.

Christian Brothers Conference: *USA/Toronto Region*, Hecker Center, 3025 Fourth St. N.E., Ste. 300, Washington, DC 20017-1102. Tel: 202-529-0047; Web: www.lasallian.info. Bro. Robert Schieler, F.S.C., Gen. Councilor; Bro. Gerard J. Frendreis, F.S.C., Dir. Admin. & Finance.
Organizations served by this office: Regional Conference of USA-Toronto Brother Provincials; Regional F.S.C. Education Board; Regional F.S.C. Finance Board; Regional F.S.C. Vocation and Formation Board; F.S.C.; Lasallian Volunteers, Lasallian Association of Miguel Schools, Regional Mission Formation Board; Lasallian Association of College and University Presidents; Chief Administrators of Lasallian Secondary Schools; Huether Lasallian Conference; Buttimer Institute of Lasallian Studies; Lasallian Leadership Institute; Lasallian Social Justice Institute.
Organizations associated with this office: Christian Brothers Major Superiors.
Properties owned and or sponsored: Bethlehem University of the Holy Land, P.O. Box 9, Bethlehem, via Israel (Incorporated in the State of New Jersey); Christian Brother Conference Community, Hyattsville, MD; Sangre de Cristo Center, Santa Fe, NM.

The Provincialate (1845): Box 29, Adamstown, MD 21710. Tel: 301-874-5188; Fax: 301-874-5674. Bro. Dennis M. Malloy, F.S.C., Prov., Visitor; Bro. Timothy J. Froehlich, F.S.C., Dir. Finance; Bro. Kevin Stanton, F.S.C., Dir. Devel. & St. LaSalle Auxiliary; Bro. James Dries, F.S.C., Dir. Vocations; Bro. Charles Mrozinski, F.S.C., Sec.
Brothers: 171
Legal Holdings or Titles: Christian Brothers of Frederick, Inc.; Ammendale Normal Institute of Prince George's County, Inc.; Christian Brothers Community Support Charitable Trust.
Represented in the Archdioceses of Baltimore, Newark, Philadelphia and Washington and in the Dioceses of Camden and Pittsburgh.

Brothers of the Christian Schools (Midwest Province): 7650 S. Country Line Rd., Burr Ridge, IL 60527-7959. Tel: 630-323-3725; Fax: 630-323-3779; Email: info@cbmidwest.org. Bro. Francis Carr, F.S.C., Visitor; Bro. Larry Schatz, F.S.C., Aux. Visitor; Bro. Thomas Hetland, F.S.C., Dir. Devel; Bro. Joseph Saurbier, F.S.C., Dir. Finance; Bro. Patrick Conway, F.S.C., Dir. Vocations/Formation; Bro. Nicholas Schumer, F.S.C., Dir. St. LaSalle Auxiliary; Bro. William Clarey, F.S.C., Dir.-Senior Brothers; Ms. Tina Bonacci, Dir. Formation & Accompaniment; Bro. Kevin Convey, F.S.C., Dir. Educ. & Mission.
Brothers: 170
Legal Titles: The Christian Brothers of the Midwest, Inc.; The Christian Brothers of Illinois; Brothers of the Christian Schools of the St. Louis District; The Christian Brothers of Minnesota.
Represented in the Archdioceses of Chicago, Cincinnati, Milwaukee, St. Louis and St. Paul-Minneapolis and the Dioceses of Green Bay, Helena, Jefferson City, Joliet, Kansas City-St. Joseph, Memphis, Omaha, Tulsa and Winona.
Properties owned, staffed or sponsored: Communities 31; Universities 3; High Schools 17; Middle Schools 7; Elementary Schools 1; Retreat Houses 3; Publishing House 1.

LaSalle Provincialate Inc. (1848): 800 Newman Springs Rd., Lincroft, NJ 07738. Tel: 732-842-7420; Fax: 732-530-3504. Bro. Frank Byrne, F.S.C., Chm. Bd; Bro. Michael Corry, F.S.C; Bro. Joseph Jozwiak, F.S.C., Vice Pres; Bro. Gerard Conforti, F.S.C., Treas; Bro. William Martin, F.S.C., Dir. Devel St. La Salle Auxiliary: P.O. Box 238, Lincroft, NJ 07738
Brothers: 162
Represented in the Archdioceses of Detroit, Newark and New York and in the Dioceses of Albany, Buffalo, Syracuse and Trenton.
Properties owned, staffed or sponsored: Colleges 1; High Schools 10; Elementary Schools 1; Welfare Schools 1; Community Houses 17.

Christian Brothers' Center-Provincial Offices (1957): St. LaSalle Auxiliary and Office of Public Information and Development, No. 635 Ocean Rd., Narragansett, RI 02882-1314. Tel: 401-789-0244; Fax: 401-783-5303. Bro. Edmond Precourt, F.S.C., Dir; Bro. Vincent Pelletier, F.S.C., Dir. Formation; Bro. Frederick Del

Antonio, F.S.C., Assoc. Finance Dir; Mrs. Mary Yakey, Health Care Coord.
Brothers: 70
Legal Titles: Brothers of the Christian Schools; District of Eastern North America (Trenton, NJ)
Represented in the Dioceses of Brooklyn, Providence, Rockville Centre, and Trenton.
Properties owned, staffed or sponsored: High Schools 5; Elementary Schools 2; Community Houses 10.

Province of San Francisco (1868): *Brothers of the Christian Schools Provincial Office*, P.O. Box 3720, Napa, CA 94558-0372. Tel: 707-252-0222. Bro. Stanislaus Campbell, F.S.C., Prov.
Brothers: 94
Represented in the Archdioceses of Los Angeles, Portland in Oregon and San Francisco and the Dioceses of Oakland, Orange, Sacramento, Santa Rosa, Tucson and Yakima. Also in Israel, Mexico, England, Ethiopia, Singapore, and Vietnam.
Properties owned, staffed or sponsored: Colleges 1; High Schools 11; Middle and Elementary Schools 1; Community Houses 14; Retreat & Conference Center 1.

Province of New Orleans-Santa Fe (1921): *De La Salle-Christian Brothers Provincialate*, 1522 Carmel Dr., Lafayette, LA 70501. Tel: 337-234-1973. Bro. Timothy Coldwell, F.S.C., Prov; Bro. Clarence Fioke, F.S.C., Finance Dir; Bro. David Sinitiere, Auxiliary Prov.
Brothers: 64
Legal Holdings or Titles: NOSF, Inc.; St. La Salle Auxiliary; Brothers of the Christian Schools of Lafayette Retirement Trust; The Christian Brothers Foundation; Christian Brothers Charitable Trust; De La Salle Christian Brothers, Lafayette, LA; Come Lord Jesus, Lafayette, LA; Community of Jesus Crucified, Lafayette, LA; St. La Salle Auxiliary, Lafayette, LA; Magnolia Lafayette, Inc.
Properties owned, staffed or sponsored: College; High Schools 7; Elementary Schools 2.
Represented in the Archdioceses of Denver, New Orleans and Santa Fe and in the Dioceses of El Paso and Lafayette (LA).

[0340] (O.CIST.)—CISTERCIAN ABBEY
(Ordo Cisterciensis)

Headquarters: *Piazza del Tempio di Diana*, 14 I-00153, Rome, Italy, Rt. Rev. Maurus Esteva, O.Cist., Abbot Gen.

Cistercian Abbey: *Our Lady of Spring Bank*, 17304 Havenwood Rd., Sparta, WI 54656. Tel: 608-269-8138; Fax: 608-269-1992; Email: porter@MonksOnline.org; Web: www.MonksOnline.org. Very Rev. Bernard McCoy, O.Cist., Prior; Rev. Robert Keffer, O.Cist., Subprior.
Solemnly Professed: 6

Cistercian Monastery: *Our Lady of Dallas*, 3550 Cistercian Rd., Irving, TX 75039. Tel: 972-438-2044. Rt. Rev. Denis M. Farkasfalvy, O.Cist., Abbot; Rev. Peter Verhalen, O.Cist., Prior; Rev. Bernard Marton, O.Cist., Subprior.
Priests: 18; Junior Monks: 11
Staff: Universities 2; Preparatory School 1; Novitiate 1; Chaplaincies 1.
Properties owned: Abbey and Preparatory School.
Represented in the Dioceses of Dallas and Fort Worth.

Cistercian Monastery of Our Lady of Fatima: 564 Walton Ave., Mount Laurel, NJ 08054. Tel: 856-235-1330. Rev. Lino S. Parente, O.Cist., Prior; Rev. Maurizio Nicoletti, O.Cist; Rev. Awte Weldu, O.Cist.
Established in 1961 as a dependent Monastery of the Congregation of Casamari (Italy).
Property owned: Fatima House and the Monastery.

Cistercian Conventual Priory: *St. Mary's Priory*, 70 Schuylkill Rd., New Ringgold, PA 17960. Tel: 570-943-2645; Fax: 570-943-3035. Very Rev. Luke Anderson, S.O.Cist., Ph.D, Prior.
Legal Title: The Cistercian Monastery of Pennsylvania.
Monks: 2

[0350] (O.C.S.O.)—THE CISTERCIAN ORDER OF THE STRICT OBSERVANCE
(TRAPPISTS)
(Ordo Cisterciensium Strictioris Observantiae)

Generalate: *Casa Generalizia*, O.C.S.O., 33 Viale Africa, 00144, Rome, Italy, Rt. Rev. Dom Eamon Fitzgerald, O.C.S.O., Abbot Gen.

Abbey of Gethsemani (1848): No. 3642 Monks Rd., Trappist, KY 40051. Tel: 502-549-3117. Rt. Rev. Elias Dietz, O.C.S.O., Abbot.
Priests: 17; Brothers: 52

Abbey of Our Lady of New Melleray (1849): 6632 Melleray Cir., Peosta, IA 52068. Tel: 563-588-2319. Rt. Rev. Brendan J. Freeman, O.C.S.O., Abbot; Rev. Neil Paquette, O.C.S.O., Prior; Rev. Stephen Verbest, O.C.S.O., Novice Dir. & Vocation Dir. & Sub-Prior.
Professed Monks 34 (Priests 19)

St. Joseph's Abbey (1825): 167 N. Spencer Rd., Spencer, MA 01562-1233. Tel: 508-885-8700; Fax: 508-885-8701. Rt. Rev. Damian Carr, O.C.S.O., Abbot.
Legal Title: Cistercian Abbey of Spencer, Inc.
Total in Community: 71; Priests: 27; Solemnly Professed: 66; Simply Professed: 1; Novices: 2

Monastery of the Holy Spirit, Inc. (1944): 2625 Hwy. 212 S.W., Conyers, GA 30094. Tel: 770-483-8705; Fax: 770-760-0989. Rev. Francis Michael Stiteler, O.C.S.O., Abbot.
Professed Monks: 38; Priests: 20
Represented in the Archdiocese of Atlanta.

Abbey of Our Lady of Guadalupe (1948): P.O. Box 97, Lafayette, OR 97127. Tel: 503-852-7174; Fax: 503-852-7748. Rt. Rev. Peter McCarthy, O.C.S.O., Abbot; Very Rev. Dismas Gannon, O.C.S.O., Prior; Bro. Phillip Wertman, O.C.S.O., Subprior.
Solemnly Professed: 30; Priests: 12; Simply Professed: 2

Abbey of Our Lady of the Holy Trinity (1947): 1250 S. 9500 E., Huntsville, UT 84317. Tel: 801-745-3784. Rev. David Altman, O.C.S.O., Abbot.
Priests: 10; Brothers: 8; Oblates: 1

Abbey of the Genesee (1951): 3258 River Rd., P.O. Box 900, Piffard, NY 14533. Tel: 585-243-0660. Rt. Rev. John Denburger, O.C.S.O., Abbot; Rt. Rev. John Eudes Bamberger, O.C.S.O., Abbot Emeritus; Rev. Jerome J. Machar, O.C.S.O., Prior & Guest Master; Rev. Gerard D'Souza, O.C.S.O., Novice Master Retreat House.
Solemnly Professed: 33; Professed Priests: 12

Mepkin Abbey (1949): 1098 Mepkin Abbey Rd., Moncks Corner, SC 29461. Tel: 843-761-8509; Fax: 843-761-6719. Rev. Kevin V. Walsh, O.C.S.O., Novice Master & Prior; Rt. Rev. Stan Gumula, O.S.C.O., Abbot; Bro. John Corrigan, Business Mgr; Bro. Edward Shivell; Rt. Rev. Christian Aidan Carr, O.C.S.O.
Priests: 9; Monks in Community: 20

Abbey of Our Lady of the Holy Cross (1950): 901 Cool Spring Ln., Berryville, VA 22611-2700. Tel: 540-955-1425; Fax: 540-955-1356. Rt. Rev. Robert T. Barnes, O.C.S.O., Abbot.
Legal Title: Community of Cistercians of the Strict Observance, Inc.
Solemnly Professed: 22; Priests: 11

Assumption Abbey: Rte. 5, Box 1056, Ava, MO 65608. Tel: 417-683-5110; Fax: 417-683-5658. Rt. Rev. Robert Matter, O.C.S.O., Abbot (Retired); Rt. Rev. Cyprian Harrison, O.C.S.O., Abbot (Retired), Supr.
Priests: 5; Professed: 9

Abbey of New Clairvaux (1955): *Trappist-Cistercian Abbey*, Vina, CA 96092. Tel: 530-839-2161. Rt. Rev. Paul Mark Schwan, O.C.S.O., Abbot.
Legal Title: Abbey of New Clairvaux, Inc.
Solemn Vows: 16; Simple Vows: 5; Novices: 1; Postulants: 1

St. Benedict's Monastery (1956): 1012 Monastery Rd., Snowmass, CO 81654. Tel: 970-927-3311. Rt. Rev. Joseph Boyle, O.C.S.O., Abbot; Bro. Raymond Roberts, O.C.S.O., Prior; Rev. Charles Albanese, O.C.S.O., Subprior.
Professed Monks: 12

[0360] (C.M.F.)—CLARETIAN MISSIONARIES
(Missionary Sons of the Immaculate Heart of Mary)
(Congregatio Missionariorum Filiorum Immaculati Cordis Beatae Mariae Virginis.)

General Headquarters: Via Sacro Cuore di Maria 5, Rome, Italy, Very Rev. Joseph Abella, C.M.F., Supr. Gen.

Western Province: *Provincial Headquarters*, 414 S. Mission Dr., San Gabriel, CA 91776. Tel: 626-289-2009; Fax: 626-289-2222. Very Rev. Richard H. DeTore, C.M.F; Rev. Daryl Olds, C.M.F; Rev. Jose L. Sanchez, C.M.F; Rev. Paul J. Keller, C.M.F; Bro. Rene LePage, C.M.F.
Legal Title: Claretian Missionaries-Western Province, Inc. A not-for-profit corporation under the laws of the State of California having as its purpose the support of any Roman Catholic benevolent, charitable, educational or missionary undertakings of the Claretian Missionaries - Western Province, Inc. Other Corporations: Dominguez Seminary, Inc., Compton, CA; Claretian Educational and Renewal Center, Inc., Los Angeles, CA; Claretian Tape Ministry Inc., Los Angeles, CA.
Fathers: 59; Brothers: 6; Students: 4
Ministries in the following areas: Parishes; Novitiate; House of Study; Centers for Spanish Speaking; Renewal Centers; Education; Spiritual Direction.
Represented in the Archdioceses of Los Angeles and San Antonio and in the Dioceses of Fresno and Phoenix.

Eastern Province: *Claretian Missionary Headquarters*, 400 N. Euclid Ave., Oak Park, IL 60302. Tel: 708-848-2076; Fax: 708-848-2069. Very Rev. Eddie DeLeon, C.M.F., Prov. Supr; Rev. Mark J. Brummel, C.M.F., Treas. & Consultor; Rev. Carl J. Quebedeaux, C.M.F., Sec. & Consultor; Rev. Ronald Stua, C.M.F., Vicar & Consultor; Rev. Bruce L. Wellems, C.M.F., Consultor.
Fathers: 36; Brothers: 6; Scholastics: 10; House of Study: 1
Legal Holdings or Titles: The Congregation of Sons of the Immaculate Heart of Mary of the Eastern Province, Inc.; Claret Center, Chicago, IL; Claretian Volunteer Program, Chicago, IL; Claretian Associates, Chicago, IL; Claretians, Inc.; St. Jude League, Inc.; St. Jude Seminary, Inc.
Represented in the Archdioceses of Atlanta and Chicago and in the Dioceses of Metuchen and Springfield-Cape Girardeau.

[0370] (S.S.C.)—SOCIETY OF ST. COLUMBAN
(Societas Sancti Columbani pro missionibus ad Exteros)

Central Administration (1918): *Missionary Society of St. Columban*, 504 Tower 1, Silvercord, 30 Canton Rd. TST, Kowloon, Hong Kong, Very Rev. Tommy Murphy, S.S.C., Supr.
Members: 575

Region in the United States: *Society of St. Columban*, P.O Box 10, St Columbans, NE 68056. Tel: 402-291-1920. Very Rev. Arturo Aguilar, S.S.C., Regl. Dir; Rev. William Morton, S.S.C., Vice Dir. Council: Rev. Thomas Shaughnessy, S.S.C; Rev. Kevin Mullins, S.S.C; Rev. Charles Duster, S.S.C; Rev. Peter Kenny, S.S.C.
Fathers: 82
Legal Titles: St. Columban's Foreign Mission Society; The Columban Fathers; Missionary Society of St. Columban.
Represented in the Archdioceses of Chicago, Los Angeles, Omaha and Washington D.C. and in the Dioceses of Buffalo, El Paso, Orange, Providence and San Bernardino.

[0380] (M.C.C.J.)—COMBONI MISSIONARIES OF THE HEART OF JESUS
(Verona Fathers) Missionarii Comboniani Cordis Jesu
(A Pontifical World Missionary Congregation Of Priests And Brothers)

Founded by Saint Daniel Comboni in 1867, First foundation in the United States in 1939.

General Motherhouse: *Missionari Comboniani*, Via Luigi Lilio 80, 00142, Rome, Italy, Very Rev. Teresino Serra, M.C.C.J., Supr. Gen.

North American Province (1950): *Comboni Mission Center*, 1318 Nagel Rd., Cincinnati, OH 45255-3120. Tel: 513-474-4997; Fax: 513-474-0382; Email: info@ComboniMissionaries.org; Web: www.ComboniMissionaries.org. Rev. Louis Gasparini, M.C.C.J., Prov; Rev. Peter Ciuciulla, M.C.C.J., Mission Office Dir.
Legal Title: Comboni Missionaries of the Heart of Jesus, Inc.
Priests: 31; Brothers: 1; Scholastics: 2; Home Mission Parishes: 4; Mission Centers: 4
Represented in the Archdioceses of Chicago, Cincinnati, Los Angeles and Newark.

[0390] (I.M.C.)—CONSOLATA MISSIONARIES
(Institutum Missionum a Consolata)

General Motherhouse: Viale delle Mura Aurelie 11, Rome, Italy, Very Rev. Aquileo Fiorentini, Supr. Gen.

Headquarters in the U.S: 2301 Rte. 27, P.O. Box 5550, Somerset, NJ 08875-5550. Tel: 732-297-9191; Fax: 732-940-3121. Rev. Charles Bonelli, I.M.C., Regl. Supr.
Legal Title: Consolata Society for Foreign Missions.
Priests: 14
Properties owned: Mission Community House 2.
Represented in the Dioceses of Buffalo, Metuchen and San Bernardino.

[0400] (O.S.C.)—CANONS REGULAR OF THE ORDER OF THE HOLY CROSS
(Crosier Fathers and Brothers)
Canonici Regulares Ordinis Sanctae Crucis (Cruciferi)

Generalate: *Generalatus Ordinis S. Crucis*, Via del Velabro 19, 00186, Rome, Italy, Very Rev. Glen Lewandowski, O.S.C., Master Gen.

United States Province: *Province of St. Odilia, Crosier National Headquarters*, 4332 W. 24th St., Phoenix, AZ 85016-6259. Tel: 602-443-7100; Fax: 602-443-7101. Very Rev. Thomas R. Carkhuff, O.S.C., Prov. Provincial Councilors: Very Rev. Steven Henrich, O.S.C; Rev. Kermit Holl, O.S.C; Rev. Thomas A. Enneking, O.S.C; Bro. Jeffrey Breer, O.S.C.
Bishops: 1; Fathers: 45; Brothers: 16
Legal Titles: Crosier Fathers and Brothers Province, Inc.; Canons Regular of the Order of the Holy Cross.
Represented in the Archdioceses of Baltimore, Detroit and St. Paul-Minneapolis and in the Dioceses of Duluth, Phoenix and St. Cloud. Also in Indonesia.
Properties owned, sponsored or staffed: Houses 2; Novitiates 1; Parishes 8; Foreign Mission 1.

[0410] (F.D.P.)—SONS OF DIVINE PROVIDENCE
(Filiorum Divinae Providentiae)

General Motherhouse: Via Etruria 6, 00183, Rome, Italy, Very Rev. Flavio Peloso, F.D.P., Supr. Gen.
Founded in 1893 by St. Don Louis Orione.

Missionary Delegation-Our Lady Mother of the Church-U.S. Foundation: III Orient Ave., East Boston, MA 02128. Tel: 617-569-2100; Fax: 617-561-1138. Rev. John Kilmartin, F.D.P., Reg. Supr.
Priests: 10
Properties staffed or owned: Parishes 3; Nursing Home 2; Shrine 1.
Represented in the Archdioceses of Boston and New York and in the Diocese of Evansville.

[0420] (S.V.D.)—SOCIETY OF THE DIVINE WORD
(Societas Verbi Divini)

General Motherhouse: *Collegio del Verbo Divino*, Via dei Verbiti 1, 00154, Rome, Italy, Very Rev. Antonio Pernia, S.V.D., Supr. Gen.
Founded 1875, in Steyl, Netherlands; First U.S.A. province erected in 1897 with Headquarters at St. Mary's Mission House (Divine Word Seminary) Techny, Illinois; later separating into four provinces. In 1985 the Eastern and Northern Provinces combined.

Chicago Province (1985): *Province of Saint Joseph Freinademetz, S.V.D. Province Center*, 1985 Waukegan

P.O. Box 6038, Techny, IL 60082-6038. Tel: 847-272-2700; Fax: 847-272-2517. Very Rev. Mark Weber, S.V.D., Prov; Rev. Thomas J. Ascheman, S.V.D., Vice Prov; Rev. Dariusz Garbaciak, S.V.D., Treas; Rev. Guilherme A. Andrino, S.V.D; Rev. Chien Dinh, S.V.D; Rev. Joseph Chau Nguyen, S.V.D; Rev. Khoa Quang Nguyen, S.V.D.

Legal Titles: Society of the Divine Word; Divine Word Funds, Inc.; Divine Word International; Techny Towers Conference and Retreat Center; Blessed Arnold Charitable Trust; DWTCRE Charitable Trust; S.V.D. Funds, Inc.

Archbishops 1; Bishops 1; Priests 175; Brothers 34; Theologians 27; Brothers in Temporary Vows 4.

Minor Seminarians: Colleges 34; Novices 4; Associates 1.

Properties owned: Theologate; College; 3 Retreat Houses; House of Studies; Conference Center; 3 Retirement Houses.

Represented in the Archdioceses of Boston, Chicago, Dubuque, Indianapolis, Milwaukee, St. Louis and Washington and in the Dioceses of Memphis, Pittsburgh, Trenton and Wheeling-Charleston. Also in Canada, Jamaica, Netherland Antilles, British Virgin Islands, and the West Indies.

Divine Word Missionaries: 1835 Waukegan Rd., P.O. Box 6099, Techny, IL 60082-6099. Bro. Dennis Newton, S.V.D., Pres.

Divine Word Missionaries is within the territory of the Chicago Province but assists members of all three United States SVD Provinces serving overseas and reports directly to Rome regarding its international fundraising activities.

Legal Titles: Divine Word Missionaries, Inc.; S.V.D. Catholic Universities.

Eastern Province: Amalgamated with Northern Province. See Chicago Province.: Amalgamated with Northern Province. See Chicago Province.

Southern Province: *Southern Province of St. Augustine*, 199 Seminary Dr., Bay Saint Louis, MS 39520. Tel: 228-467-4322; Tel: 228-467-3815; Email: pawlicki@inaword.com. Very Rev. James Pawlicki, S.V.D., Prov; Rev. Paul Kahan, S.V.D., Vice Prov; Rev. George Gormley, S.V.D., Treas.

Fathers: 60; Brothers: 4; Parishes: 26; Mission Stations: 3; Elementary Schools: 5

Address applications for Retreats and Missions to: Rev. William J. Kelley, S.V.D., Retreat Center.

Represented in the Archdioceses of Galveston-Houston and New Orleans and in the Dioceses of Baton Rouge, Beaumont, Biloxi, Fort Worth, Jackson, Lafayette (LA), Little Rock, and Lake Charles.

Western Province (1964): *Province of St. Therese of the Child Jesus*, 11316 Cypress Ave, Riverside, CA 92505. Tel: 951-687-7600; Fax: 951-687-3158. Very Rev. Briccio Tamoro, S.V.D., Prov; Rev. Michael Manning, S.V.D., Vice Prov; Rev. Henry Noga, S.V.D., Prov. Treas.

Fathers: 53; Brothers: 6

Represented in the Archdiocese of Los Angeles and in the Dioceses of Oakland, Orange, San Bernardino and San Diego.

Properties staffed, sponsored or owned: High Schools 1; Parishes 13; Hospitals 3; Prisons 2; Retreat Centers 1.

[0430] (O.P.)—ORDER OF PREACHERS

Dominicans Fratres Sacri Ordinis Praedicatorum

Generalitia: *Convento Santa Sabina*, Piazza Pietro d'Illiria, Aventino 00153, Rome, Italy, Most Rev. Carlos A. Azpiroz Costa, O.P., 86th Master of the Order; Very Rev. Edward M. Ruane, O.P., Vicar of the Mastery of Orders & Asst for U.S.A. Provinces; Very Rev. Robert Ombres, O.P., Procurator Gen.

Province of St. Joseph-Eastern Dominican Province (1805): *Dominican Provincial Offices*, 141 E. 65th St., New York, NY 10065-6618. Tel: 212-737-5757; Fax: 212-861-4216. Very Rev. David Dominic Izzo, O.P., Prior Prov; Rev. Brian Mulcahy, O.P., Socius and Vicar Provincial; Rev. Kenneth Sicard, O.P., Prov. Econ. Admin; Rev. John C. Vidmar, O.P., Archivist; Rev. Terence S. Keegen, O.P., Regent of Studies; Rev. Jon S. McPhail, Dir. Continuing Formation; Ms. Janice T. Brown, Dir.-Health Services; Rev. John A. McMahon, O.P., Dir.-Center for Assisted Living; Rev. Peter John Cameron, O.P., Dir. Preaching; Rev. William P. Garrott, O.P., Dir.-Vocations; Rev. Mario Juan Diego Brunetta, O.P., Dir. Dominican Laity & Clerical Fraternities; Very Rev. Joseph P. Allen, O.P., Sec.-Missions & Dir.-Dominican Foreign Missions; Rev. Elias A. Henritzy, O.P., Promoter-Social Justice; Rev. Scott Matthew Erickson, O.P., Promoter-Holy Name Society; Rev. Andre-Joseph LaCasse, O.P., Promoter-Rosary; Rev. Raymond F. Halligan, O.P., Dir. Rosary Shrine of St. Jude (Washington); Rev. John Farren, O.P., Vicar Provincial for Advancement, Deserving Poor Boys Priesthood Assoc., Inc.; St. Jude Dominican Missions, Inc.; St. Martin de Porres Guild, Inc.; Rosary Apostolate, Inc.Very Rev. Steven C. Boguslawski, O.P., Pres., Pontifical Faculty of the Immaculate Conception (Washington, D.C.); Rev. Michael Detemple, O.P., Promoter of the Dominican Family.

Corporate Title: Dominican Fathers Province of St. Joseph.

Legal Titles: Retirement Plan and Pension Plan; Dominican Fathers, Province of St. Joseph; Dominican Friars' Guilds, Inc.; Deserving Poor Boys Priesthood Association, Inc.; St. Jude Dominican Missions, Inc.; St. Martin de Porres Guild, Inc.; Dominican Foreign Missions; Handicapped Children's Fund, Peru; Rosary Shrine of St. Jude, (Washington, DC); Rosary Apostolate.

Represented in the Archdioceses of Boston, Chicago, Cincinnati, Detroit, Hartford, Louisville, Miami, Newark, New York and Washington and in the Dioceses of Buffalo, Camden, Fort Wayne-South Bend, Columbus, Grand Rapids, Harrisburg, Manchester, Providence, Richmond, Rochester, Rockville Centre, Springfield, Steubenville, Wilmington and Youngstown.

Properties owned, staffed or sponsored: Priories 10; Houses 10; Parishes 17; Campus Ministries 7; Colleges 1; Houses of Study 2; Novitiates 2; Mission Abroad 1; Health Care Ministry 1; Health Care Facility 1.

Province of the Most Holy Name of Jesus-Western Dominican Province (1912): 5877 Birch Ct., Oakland, CA 94618-1626. Tel: 510-658-8722; Fax: 510-658-1061; Email: WDP@opwest.org. Very Rev. Emmerich W. Vogt, O.P., Prior Prov; Rev. Mark Padrez, O.P., Vicar Prov. & Socius; Rev. Martin Walsh, O.P., Dir. Mission Foundation; Rev. Richard Schenk, O.P., Regent of Studies; Rev. Dominic DeDomenico, O.P., Treas; Rev. Jerome Cudden, O.P., Dir. Devel; Rev. Steven Maekawa, O.P., Dir. Vocations; Rev. Jude Eli, O.P., Dir.-Preaching; Bro. Raymond Bertheaux, O.P., Archivist.

Legal Title: Province of the Holy Name, Inc.

Fathers: 120; Brothers: 6; Professed Clerics: 21; Novices: 3; Donatus: 1; Parishes: 9; Newman Centers/ Personal Parishes: 10; Retreat Houses: 1; Houses of Study: 1; Novitiates: 1

Represented in the Archdioceses of Anchorage, Los Angeles, Portland in Oregon, San Francisco, Seattle, St. Louis and Washington and in the Dioceses of Fall River, Las Vegas, Oakland, Phoenix, Providence, Sacramento, Salt Lake City, San Bernardino, San Diego, San Jose and Tucson. Also in Australia, Guatemala, Mexico, Kenya, Switzerland, Italy and Lithuania and Jerusalem.

Province of St. Albert the Great-Central Dominican Province (1939): 1909 S. Ashland Ave., Chicago, IL 60608. Tel: 312-666-3244; Fax: 312-829-8471. Very Rev. Michael A. Mascari, O.P., Prov; Rev. John J. Meany, O.P., Socius, Vicar Prov. & Economic Admin; Rev. David F. Wright, O.P., Archivist; Rev. Andrew-Carl Wisdom, O.P., Promoter of Vocations & Dir.-Society Vocational Support; Rev. Donald J. Goergen, O.P., Promoter of Social Justice; Rev. Jay Harrington, O.P., Regent; Rev. Robert J. Botthof, O.P., Dir., Shrine of St. Jude; Bro. Edward Van Merrienboer, O.P., Vicar for Ministry, Vicar for Mission Devel. & Dir. St. Dominic Mission Society.

Fathers: 158; Professed Clerics: 17; Novices: 7; Brothers: 15

Legal Titles: Dominicans, Province of St. Albert the Great, U.S.A.; Shrine of St. Jude Thaddeus, Inc.; Society for Vocational Support, Inc.; St. Dominic Mission Society; Dominican Social Action Fund; Dominican Laity; Dominican Central Productions; The Bolivian Trust of the Dominicans, Office for Mission Advancement.

Represented in the Archdioceses of Chicago, Denver, Detroit, Indianapolis, St. Louis, St. Paul-Minneapolis and Santa Fe and in the Dioceses of Colorado Springs, Des Moines, Grand Rapids, Jefferson City, Joliet, Lafayette in Indiana, Madison, Springfield in Illinois, Superior and Winona.

Properties owned, staffed or sponsored: Parishes 9; Convents 8; Houses 11; Houses of Studies 2; Novitiate; High Schools 1.

Southern Dominican Province of St. Martin de Porres (1979): 1421 N. Causeway Blvd., Ste. 200, Metairie, LA 70001-4144. Tel: 504-837-2129; Fax: 504-837-6604. Very Rev. Martin J. Gleeson, O.P., Prov; Very Rev. Emiliano Zapata, O.P., Vicar Prov; Rev. Charles Luke Latour, O.P., Econ. Admin. & Promoter of Vocations; Very Rev. Robert U. Perry, O.P., Promoter for Permanent Formation; Very Rev. Wayne A. Cavalier, O.P., Regent of Studies; Rev. David G. Caron, O.P., Asst. Promoter of Vocations.

Fathers: 104; Professed Clerics: 12; Brothers: 7; Novices: 4; Deacons: 1

Legal Holdings or Titles: Southern Dominican Foundation; Retirement and Community Support Plan, Southern Dominican Province, U.S.A.; Shrine of St. Martin de Porres; DePorres Property.

Represented in the Archdioceses of Chicago, Galveston-Houston, Louisville, Miami, New Orleans, San Antonio and St. Louis and in the Dioceses of Austin, Baton Rouge, Columbus, Dallas, Fort Worth, Memphis, Raleigh, Tucson, Tyler and Venice.

Properties owned, staffed or sponsored: Parishes 12; Priories 8; Houses 5; Shrines 1; Provincial Offices 1.

U.S. Foundation (1926): *Province of Spain*, P.O. Box 279, San Diego, TX 78384. Tel: 361-279-3596. Rev. Benito Retortillo, O.P; Rev. Epifanio Rodriguez, O.P.

Priests: 2

Represented in the Diocese of Corpus Christi.

[0440] (S.S.E.)—SOCIETY OF SAINT EDMUND

(Societas Sancti Edmundi)

General Motherhouse: *Edmundite Generalate*, 270 Winooski Park, Colchester, VT 05439. Tel: 802-654-3400; Fax: 802-654-3409. Very Rev. Michael P. Cronogue, S.S.E., Supr. Gen. Councilors: Rev. Stephen W. Hornat, S.S.E; Rev. Carroll W. Plourde, S.S.E; Rev. Stanley Deresienski, S.S.E; Rev. Brian J. Cummings, S.S.E.

Legal Title: Society of St. Edmund, Inc.

Bishops: 1; Fathers: 31; Brothers: 4

Represented in the Archdioceses of Detroit, Mobile and New Orleans and in the Dioceses of Burlington, Norwich and Venice. Also Venezuela and France.

Properties owned, staffed or sponsored: Parishes 13; College 1; Shrine; Novitiate.

[0460] (C.F.P.)—BROTHERS OF THE POOR OF ST. FRANCIS

(Congregatio Fratrum Pauperum)

Motherhouse: Aachen, Germany, Bro. Mark Gastel, C.F.P., Min. Gen.

USA Community of St. Joseph: P.O. Box 30359, Cincinnati, OH 45230-0359. Tel: 513-924-0111; Fax: 513-321-3777. Bro. Joel Stern, C.F.P., U.S.A Community Admin.

Professed Brothers: 16

Brothers serve and staff: Development Office; High School; Elementary School.

Brothers' Special Mission: Care and education of neglected youth; elementary & secondary education; human services.

Represented in the Archdioceses of Cincinnati and Newark and in the Dioceses of Covington, Davenport, El Paso and Little Rock.

[0470] (O.F.M.CAP.)—THE CAPUCHIN FRANCISCAN FRIARS

(Ordo Fratrum Minorum Capuccinorum)

Generalate: *Curia Generale dei Cappuccini*, Via Piemonte 70, 00187, Rome, Italy, Web: www.ofmcap.org. Bro. Mauro Johri, O.F.M.Cap., Gen. Min.

Province of St. Joseph (1857) (1857): *Calvary Province*, 1820 Mt. Elliott St., Detroit, MI 48207-3496. Tel: 313-579-2100; Fax: 313-579-2275. Very Rev. John Celichowski, O.F.M.Cap., Prov. Min; Bro. Robert Smith, O.F.M.Cap., Prov. Vicar; Bro. Randolph Graczyk, O.F.M.Cap., Sec.-Religious Affairs; Bro. T.L. Michael Auman, O.F.M.Cap., Dir.-Communications; Rev. Edward Foley, O.F.M.Cap., Dir.-Continuing Education; Rev. Richard Hart, O.F.M.Cap., Dir.-Preachers; Rev. James Zelinski, O.F.M.Cap., Dir.-JPE; Rev. Campion Baer, O.F.M.Cap., Overseas Missions; Rev. Lester Bach, O.F.M.Cap., Prov. Asst.-Secular Franciscan Order; Bro. Richard Merling, O.F.M.Cap., Dir.-Solanus Guild; Bro. Leo Wollenweber, O.F.M.Cap., Vice Postulator-Cause of Ven. Solanus Casey; Rev. Patrick McSherry, O.F.M.Cap., Archivist; Rev. Michael Crosby, O.F.M.Cap., Corp. Responsibility Agent; Mr. Harlan Swift, Corp. Sec./Treas; Ms. Judy Gilleran, Admin. Asst; Rev. William Cieslak, O.F.M.Cap., Prov. Devel; Mr. Jeff Parrish, Dir., Human Resources; Bro. Mark Carrico, O.F.M.Cap., Office of Pastoral Care & Conciliation; Ms. Colleen Crane, Dir. Public Rels; Ms. Mary Hague, Dir. Wellness; Shelly Roder, Dir. Cap Corps. Councilors: Rev. Mark Joseph Costello, O.F.M.Cap; Rev. Francis Voris, O.F.M.Cap; Bro. Mark Carrico, O.F.M.Cap.

Legal Title: Province of St. Joseph of the Capuchin Order, Inc.

Priests: 135; Perpetually Professed Lay Friars: 38

Parishes, Hospitals, Nursing Homes, Hospices, Prisons, Retreat Centers, Soup Kitchens; Direct Services to the Poor; Educational Institutions; Home and Foreign Missions.

Represented in the Archdioceses of Chicago, Detroit, Los Angeles, Milwaukee, and St. Paul-Minneapolis, and in the Dioceses of Fort Wayne-South Bend, Great Falls-Billings, Green Bay, LaCrosse, Las Cruces, Madison, Marquette, Saginaw, San Diego, Superior, Tucson, and Winnipeg. Also the vicariate of Bluefields, Nicaragua and in Dioceses of Managua, Panama and Australia.

Province of St. Augustine (1873): *Provincial Office*, 220 37th St., Pittsburgh, PA 15201. Tel: 412-682-6011; Fax: 412-682-0506. Very Rev. John Pavlik, O.F.M-.Cap., Prov. Min; Rev. John Pfannenstiel, O.F.M.Cap., Vicar Prov; Bro. Robert Toomey, O.F.M.Cap. Definitors: Rev. Thomas Betz, O.F.M.Cap; Rev. W. David Nestler, O.F.M.Cap; Rev. John Bednarik, O.F.M.Cap; Mr. R. Joseph Kusnir, CFO. Vocations Co-Directors: Rev. Thomas Betz, O.F.M.Cap., Vocation Min; Rev. Moises Villalta, O.F.M.Cap., Vocation Min.

Cardinals: 1; Priests: 122; Brothers: 34; Professed in Formation: 30; Novices: 8; Postulants: 8

Legal Titles: Province of St. Augustine of the Capuchin Order; Headquarters of Capuchin Franciscan Volunteer Corps., Inc.; Augustine Province of the Capuchin Order; National Headquarters of Archconfraternity of Christian Mothers; Mission Office of Seraphic Mass Association; Secular Franciscan Order of St. Augustine, Province; Capuchin Friars Sick and Elderly Trust Fund; St. Fidelis, Inc.; Capuchin Friars Formation and Education Trust Fund.

Represented in the Archdioceses of Baltimore, Philadelphia and Washington and in the Dioceses of Altoona-Johnstown, Cleveland, Greensburg, Harrisburg, Pittsburgh and Wheeling-Charleston. Also in Papua New Guinea and Puerto Rico.

Properties owned, staffed or sponsored: Parishes 19; Formation Houses 3; Novitiate 1; Friaries 18; Postulancy Houses 1; Hospital Chaplain 7; Military Chaplain 1; Foreign Missions 2.

Province of St. Mary: *St. Conrad Friary*, 30 Gedney Park Dr., White Plains, NY 10605. Tel: 914-761-3008; Fax: 914-948-6429. Rev. John Gallagher, O.F.M.Cap., Minister Prov. Definitors: Rev. John McHugh, O.F.M-.Cap., Vicar Prov; Rev. Francis Gasparik, O.F.M.Cap;

Bro. Timothy Jones, O.F.M.Cap; Bro. Celestino Arias, O.F.M.Cap.
Legal Title: The Province of St. Mary of the Capuchin Order; Capuchin Friars International, Inc.; St. Francis of Assisi Foundation; Capuchin Friars of North America.
Bishops: 2; Priests: 106; Professed Clerical Brothers: 4; Professed Lay Brothers: 37; Novices: 3; Postulants: 3
Represented in the Archdioceses of Agana, Boston and New York and in the Dioceses of Bridgeport, Brooklyn, Burlington, Honolulu, Manchester, Norwich, Portland (In Maine), Rochester, Rockville Centre and St. Petersburg. Also in Japan.
Properties staffed or sponsored: Parishes 13; Chaplaincies 15; Novitiate 1; Foreign Missions 3.

Development Office: *St. John's Friary*, 210 W. 31st St., New York, NY 10001.

Province of the Sacred Stigmata of St. Francis: *Our Lady Guadalupe Friary*, 319 - 36th St., P.O. Box 809, Union City, NJ 07087. Tel: 201-865-0611; Fax: 201-866-7035. Very Rev. Brian Tomlinson, O.F.M.Cap., Prov. Min; Rev. Nicholas A. Mormando, O.F.M.Cap., Prov. Vicar. Definitors: Rev. Ronald Giannone, O.F.M.Cap; Rev. John LoSasso, O.F.M.Cap; Bro. John Paul Russo, O.F.M.Cap.
Priests: 33; Brothers: 13; Temporary Professed: 1; Parishes: 8; Friaries: 4; Retreat Houses: 1; Hospital Chaplaincies: 1
Represented in the Archdioceses of Newark and New York and in the Dioceses of Charlotte, Paterson, St. Petersburg and Wilmington.

Our Lady of Angels, Western America Province: 1345 Cortez Ave., Burlingame, CA 94010. Rev. Matthew Elshoff, O.F.M.Cap., Prov. Definitors: Rev. Camillus MacRory, O.F.M.Cap., Spiritual Asst.-Secular Franciscans; Rev. Donal Burke, O.F.M.Cap., Dir.-Devel./Finances; Rev. Miguel Angel Ortiz, O.F.M.Cap., Dir.-Foreign Missions, Sec; Rev. Jesus Vela, O.F.M.Cap., Vicar; Rev. Peter Banks, O.F.M.Cap; Rev. Michael Mahoney, O.F.M.Cap; Rev. Robert A. Barbato, O.F.M.Cap.
Priests: 40; Brothers: 12; Brothers in Formation: 11; Novices: 4; Postulants: 10
Ministries in Parishes, High Schools, Novitiates, Chaplaincies, House of Study, Retreats, Foreign Missions, Campus Ministry, Prison Chaplaincy and Hospital Chaplaincy.
Represented in the Archdioceses of Los Angeles and San Francisco and in the Dioceses of Oakland and San Bernardino. Also in Mexico.

Province of SS. Stanislaus and Adalbert (1948): *St. Stanislaus Friary*, 2 Manor Dr., Oak Ridge, NJ 07438. Tel: 973-697-7757. Rev. Marek Przeczewski, O.F.M.Cap., Prov. Minister; Rev. Krzysztof Lewandowski, O.F.M.Cap., Provincial Vicar; Deacon Jerzy Krzyskow, Admin.
Fathers: 4
Represented in the Dioceses of Metuchen and Paterson.

Vice Province of Our Lady of Guadalupe: *Capuchin Franciscan Friars of Texas*, 5605 Bernal Dr., Dallas, TX 75212. Tel: 214-500-8595; Tel: 214-637-6673; Fax: 214-637-2454. Rev. Mario Garcia, O.F.M.Cap., Vice Prov.
Fathers: 10; Brothers: 2
Members serve and staff: Parishes 3; Mission 1; Cursillo Centers 2.
Represented in the Dioceses of Dallas and Fort Worth.

Province of Mid-America (1977): 3613 Wyandot St., Denver, CO 80211-2950. Tel: 303-477-5436; Fax: 303-477-6925; Web: www.midamcaps.org. Rev. Charles Polifka, O.F.M.Cap., Prov. Min; Rev. James Moster, O.F.M.Cap., Prov. Vicar; Rev. Gene Emrisek, O.F.M.Cap., Initial Formation Dir; Rev. Blaine Burkey, O.F.M.Cap., Communications Dir. & Archivist; Rev. John Lager, O.F.M.Cap., Vocation Dir; Stephanie Pedersen, Dir. Devel. & Missionary Activities; Rev. Francis X. Grinko, O.F.M.Cap., Councilor; Rev. Christopher Popravak, O.F.M.Cap., Councilor; Rev. John Schmeidler, O.F.M.Cap., Councilor.
Bishops: 2; Priests: 39; Students: 5; Lay Brothers: 8; Temporary Professed Brothers: 3; Novices: 1; Postulants: 4
Legal Titles: Capuchin Province of Mid-America, Inc.; St. Francis Seminary Endowment Foundation, Inc.
Represented in the Archdioceses of Denver, Kansas City in Kansas and St. Louis and in the Dioceses of Colorado Springs, Pueblo, and Salina.

Vice Province of St. John the Baptist (1905): *Vice Provincial Offices*, 216 Arzuaga St., P.O. Box 21350, Rio Piedras, PR 00928-1350. Tel: 787-764-3090; Fax: 787-764-4070; Email: jorge.macias@capuchinospr.org; Web: www.capuchinospr.org. Bro. Francisco Garcia, O.F.M.Cap., Vice Prov. Min; Bro. Jorge M. Macias, O.F.M.Cap., First Councilor; Bro. Fernando Irizarry, O.F.M.Cap., Second Councilor; Bro. Jorge Macias de Cespedes, O.F.M.Cap., Vice Prov. Sec./Treas. & Dir. Capuchin Mass Assoc. (Asociacion Misionera Capuchina).
Friars: 25; Postulants: 5
Legal Titles: Asociacion de Frailes Capuchinos, Inc.; Asociacion Misionera Capuchina; Capuchin Formation Trust of Puerto Rico; Capuchin Health and Retirement Trust of Puerto Rico.
Represented in the Archdiocese of San Juan and in the Dioceses of Arecibo, Caguas and Ponce.
Properties owned, staffed and sponsored: Formation Fraternites 3; Parishes 4; Retreat Center 1; Friaries 6; Mission Office 1.

[0480] (O.F.M.CONV.)—CONVENTUAL FRANCISCANS

(Friars Minor Conventual)
(Ordo Fratrum Minorum S. Francisci Conventualium)

General Curia: Piazza SS. Apostoli, 51, 00187, Rome, Italy, Most Rev. Marco Tasca, O.F.M.Conv., Min. Gen; Very Rev. John Joseph Dolan, O.F.M.Conv., Asst. Gen.

Province of the Immaculate Conception B.V.M. (1852): *Provincial Office*, P.O. Box 629, Rensselaer, NY 12144. Tel: 518-472-1000; Fax: 518-472-1013; Web: www.franciscanseast.org. Very Rev. Justin A. Biase, O.F.M.Conv., Min. Prov; Rev. Brad A. Milunski, O.F.M.Conv., Vicar Prov; Bro. Edward Falsey, O.F.M.Conv., Province Sec; Bro. Raymond Sobocinski, O.F.M.Conv., Province Treas; Rev. John Burkhard, O.F.M.Conv., Province Definitor; Rev. William Robinson, O.F.M.Conv., Province Definitor.
Fathers: 75; Professed Brothers: 28; Parishes: 20; Friaries: 17; Chaplaincies: 5; Filial Houses: 1
Legal Titles: Order of Friars Minor Conventual Immaculate Conception; Province Charitable Trust; Franciscorps, Inc., Rensselaer, NY; The Franciscan Center for Spirituality, Inc., Albany, NY; Franciscans in Collaborative Ministry, Inc., Rensselaer, NY.
Represented in the Archdioceses of New York and Washington and in the Dioceses of Albany, Charlotte, Raleigh, Syracuse and Trenton. Also in Canada and Costa Rica.

Province of St. Anthony of Padua (1906): *Provincial House*, 12300 Folly Quarter Rd., Ellicott City, MD 21042-1419. Tel: 410-531-1400; Fax: 410-531-4881. Very Rev. Michael Kolodziej, O.F.M.Conv., Minister Prov; Rev. Mark Szayni, O.F.M.Conv., Vicar Prov; Rev. Joseph Benicewicz, O.F.M.Conv., Treas; Rev. Thomas Lavin, O.F.M.Conv., Sec. Definitors: Rev. Romuald Meogrossi, O.F.M.Conv; Rev. Jude Surowiec, O.F.M.Conv; Rev. Jude Michael Krill, O.F.M.Conv; Rev. Timothy Kulbicki, O.F.M.Conv.
Priests: 111; Brothers in Solemn Vows: 14; Clerics in Temporary Vows: 3; Novices: 1; Candidates: 5; Friaries: 25; Filial Houses: 8
Legal Titles: St. Francis High School of Athol Springs, NY, Inc.; The Father Justin Rosary Hour, Inc.; Franciscan Fathers Minor Conventuals of Buffalo, NY, Inc.; The Franciscan Center, Inc.; St. Anthony of Padua Province, Franciscan Fathers Minor Conventual, U.S.A., Inc.; Order of Friars Minor Conventual, Inc.; Conventual Franciscan Friars, St. Anthony of Padua Province, Franciscan Mission Association, Inc.; Franciscan Fathers Minor Conventual, St. Anthony of Padua Province U.S.A., MA. Inc.; Franciscan Friars, St. Anthony of Padua Province, Education Fund, Inc.; Franciscan Friars, St. Anthony of Padua Province, Fund for the Aged and Infirm, Inc.; Franciscan Minor Conventuals of Maryland, of Ellicott City, MD, Inc.; The Franciscan Fathers, Minor Conventuals of St. Stanislaus Church of Baltimore City, MD, Inc.; St. Francis of Assisi Community, Inc.; Order of Friars Minor Conventual, St. Anthony of Padua Province, U.S.A., Inc.; St. Stanislaus Cemetery, Inc.; Anthony-Corps, Inc.; Fr. Justin Ministry Fund, Inc.
Represented in the Archdioceses of Atlanta, Baltimore, Boston and Hartford and in the Dioceses of Altoona-Johnstown, Bridgeport, Brooklyn, Buffalo, Fall River, Harrisburg, Norwich, Palm Beach, Paterson, Springfield in Massachusetts and Trenton.
Apostolates owned, staffed or sponsored: Novitiates 1; House of Study 1; Parishes 28; Campus Ministries 4; High Schools 2; Youth-Crisis Shelter 1; Sisters' Chaplaincies 1; Hospital-Nursing Home Chaplaincies 3; Apostolates Radio Apostolate; Healing Ministry; Preaching Apostolate; Foreign Missions 3; Candidate House; Youth Ministry.

St. Bonaventure Province (1939): 6107 N. Kenmore Ave., Chicago, IL 60660-2797. Tel: 773-274-7681; Fax: 773-274-9751. Very Rev. Patrick Greenough, O.F.M.Conv., Min. Prov; Bro. George Searles, Treas. Definitors: Rev. Steve McKinley, O.F.M.Conv., Vicar Prov; Bro. Juniper Kriss, O.F.M.Conv; Rev. Robert Joseph Switanowski, O.F.M.Conv; Rev. James Jankowski, O.F.M.Conv; Bro. Joseph Wood, O.F.M.Conv., Sec.
Fathers: 26; Professed Clerics: 8; Brothers: 19
Legal Titles: Conventual Franciscans of St. Bonaventure Province; Franciscan Friars Educational Corp.; Conventual Franciscan Friars of Marytown; Shrine of St. Maximillian Kolbe; St. Hedwig Cemetery and Mausoleum; The Conventual Franciscans of Saint Bonaventure Province Charitable Continuing Care Trust Fund.
Represented in the Archdioceses of Chicago, Detroit and Milwaukee and in the Dioceses of Peoria and Rockford. Also in Mexico.
Properties owned or sponsored: Parishes 5; Chaplaincies; Marian Center; Shrine.

Province of Our Lady of Consolation (1926): 101 Anthony Dr., Mount Saint Francis, IN 47146. Tel: 812-923-8444. Very Rev. James Kent, Min. Prov; Bro. Robert Baxter, O.F.M.Conv., Sec.
Fathers: 78; Brothers: 27; Professed Clerics: 3; Candidates: 4; Novices: 2; Friaries: 20; Parishes: 22; Houses of Formation: 3; Retreat-Renewal Centers: 3; Missions: 15; Chaplaincies: 4

Development Office: 103 St. Francis Blvd., Mount Saint Francis, IN 47146. Tel: 812-923-5250.

Province of St. Joseph of Cupertino (1981): *St. Joseph of Cupertino Friary*, P.O. Box 820, Arroyo Grande, CA 93421-0820. Tel: 805-489-1012; Tel: 805-473-2256; Fax: 805-489-8303. Rev. Christopher Deitz, O.F.M.Conv., Min. Prov; Very Rev. Gary Klauer, O.F.M.Conv., Vicar; Rev. Raymond Mallett, O.F.M.Conv., Definitor; Rev. Paul Gawlowski, O.F.M.Conv., Definitor; Bro. George Cherrie, O.F.M.Conv., Definitor & Sec.
Legal Title: Conventual Franciscans of California, Inc.
Priests: 33; Brothers: 11; Clerics (Professed Seminarians): 5
Represented in the Archdioceses of Los Angeles, Military and San Francisco and in the Dioceses of Fresno, Monterey, Oakland and Reno.
Properties owned, staffed or sponsored: Parishes 6; Chaplaincies 3; High Schools 1; Houses of Formation 2.

[0485] (M.S.F.S.)—MISSIONARIES OF ST. FRANCIS DE SALES

(Missionariorum Sancti Francisci Salesi)
Founded in Annecy, France 1838. Established in the United States of America as a region on July 3, 2007.

Motherhouse: Chemin de Proupeine, F-74000, Annecy, France,

American Mission: *Villa Luyet*, 109 Johnson Rd., Lawrenceville, GA 30045-5521. Rev. Martin Kopchik, M.S.F.S., Mission Supr; Rev. John F. Tiernan III, M.S.F.S; Rev. John C. DeVore, M.S.F.S; Rev. Joseph Mullakkara, M.S.F.S; Rev. Abrama Mullenkuzhy, M.S.F.S; Rev. Augustine Tharappel, M.S.F.S.
Legal Title: Missionaries of St. Francis de Sales, Inc.
Fathers: 6; Fathers from provinces outside U.S: 15
Properties Staffed: Parishes 2; Convents 1.
Properties Owned: Villa Luyet Mission Residence, Lawrenceville, GA; Wellspring House of Spirituality, Tyler, TX.
Represented in the Archdioceses of Atlanta, Chicago, Galveston-Houston and Mobile and in the Dioceses of Alexandria, Birmingham in Alabama, Cleveland, Lansing, Nashville, St. Augustine and Tyler.

[0490] (O.S.F.)—CONGREGATION OF THE RELIGIOUS BROTHERS OF THE THIRD ORDER REGULAR OF ST. FRANCIS

Franciscan Brothers of Brooklyn

Generalate (1858): *St. Francis Monastery*, 135 Remsen St., Brooklyn, NY 11201-4212. Tel: 212-858-8217; Fax: 718-858-8306. Bro. William Boslet, O.S.F., Supr. Gen. Councilors: Bro. Thomas Grady, O.S.F; Bro. Joshua DiMauro, O.S.F; Bro. Gabriel O'Brien, O.S.F; Bro. Richard Contino, O.S.F.
Brothers: 78
Legal Titles and Holdings: St. Francis Monastery; Franciscan Brothers' Generalate; Franciscan Brothers, Inc., Brooklyn, NY; Mount Alvernia, Inc.; St. Francis Center, Inc., Rockville Centre, NY.
Ministries in the field of Education at all levels; Pastoral Ministries, Social Services; Spirituality Centers.
Represented in the Dioceses of Brooklyn, Rockville Centre and Springfield-Cape Girardeau.

[0510] (F.F.S.C.)—FRANCISCAN BROTHERS OF THE HOLY CROSS

Generalate: *St. Josefshaus*, 53547 Hausen/Wied, Linz Rhein, Germany, Bro. Ulrich Schmitz, F.F.S.C., Supr. Gen.

American Region (1924): 2500 St. James Rd., Springfield, IL 62707. Tel: 217-528-4757; Fax: 217-528-4824. Bro. John Francis Tyrrell, F.F.S.C., Pres./Supr; Bro. Stephen Bissler, F.F.S.C., Treas; Bro. Christian Guertin, F.F.S.C., Vice Pres./Vicar; Bro. Ulrich Schmitz, F.F.S.C; Bro. Joel Mark Rousseau, F.F.S.C., Sec.
Brothers: 12
Represented in the Archdiocese of St. Louis and in the Dioceses of Madison and Springfield in Illinois.
Properties owned, staffed or sponsored: Home for Mentally Handicapped; Adult Training Center for Mentally Handicapped; Secretarial; Chaplaincy; Novitiate; Community Living Facility; Pastoral leadership.

[0515] (O.S.F.)—FRANCISCAN BROTHERS OF THE THIRD ORDER REGULAR

Generalate: *Franciscan Brothers' Generalate*, Mountbellow, Ireland,

United States Region: 4522 Gainsborough Ave., Los Angeles, CA 90027. Tel: 323-644-2740; Fax: 323-644-2977. Bro. Paulinus Horkan, O.S.F., Reg. Supr.
Brothers: 7
Ministries in the field of secondary education.
Represented in the Archdiocese of Los Angeles.

[0520] (O.F.M.)—FRANCISCAN FRIARS

(Ordinis Fratrum Minorum)

General Headquarters: *Curia Generalizia dei Frati Minori*, Via S. Maria Mediatrice, 25, 00165, Rome, Italy, Rev. Jose R. Carballo, O.F.M., Min. Gen; Very Rev. Finian McGinn, O.F.M., English-Speaking General Definitor.

Order of Friars Minor: *English-Speaking Conference*, 48 Old Park Ln., New Milford, CT 06776. Tel: 860-350-1611; Fax: 860-350-3214. Rev. Thomas Washburn, O.F.M., Exec. Sec; Very Rev. John F. O'Connor, O.F.M., Pres; Very Rev. Caoimhin O. Laoide, O.F.M., Vice Pres; Very Rev. Finian McGinn, O.F.M., Gen. Definitor.
Includes: Order of Friars Minor Provinces 12; Custodies

the United States, Canada, England, Ireland and Malta.

Province of St. John the Baptist (1844): 1615 Vine St., Cincinnati, OH 45202-6400. Tel: 513-721-4700; Fax: 513-421-9672. Rev. Jeffrey Scheeler, O.F.M., Prov. Min; Rev. Donald Miller, O.F.M., Vocation Dir; Rev. Arthur Espelage, O.F.M., Prov. Canonist. Councillors: Rev. Dennet Jung, O.F.M; Rev. Mark Soehner, O.F.M; Bro. Michael Dubec, O.F.M., Dir.-Devel; Rev. William Farris, O.F.M; Bro. Gene Mayer, O.F.M., Prov. Sec; Rev. Kenan Freson, O.F.M., Prov. Liaison to Sponsored Ministries; Rev. Maynard Tetreault, O.F.M., Bldg. Coord; Rev. Page Polk, O.F.M., Dir.-Continuing Educ./Formation; Sr. Donna Graham, O.S.F., Dir.-Office of Peace, Justice & Integrity of Creation; Bro. Vincent Delorenzo, O.F.M., Dir. Franciscan Mission Office; Bro. David Crank, O.F.M., Dir.-Office of Senior Friars; Rev. Daniel J. Anderson, O.F.M., Admin. Asst. to Prov. Min; Bro. Juniper Crouch, O.F.M., Prov. Spiritual Asst. for Secular Order; Bro. Timothy Lamb, O.F.M., Personnel Advr; Rev. Frank J. Jasper, O.F.M., Prov. Vicar & Treas; Mr. David O'Brien, CFO; Bro. Brian Maloney, O.F.M., Dir.-Friar Works/Franciscan Mission & Ministry; Ms. Toni Cashnelli, Dir.-Office of Communications; Bro. Allan Schmitz, O.F.M., Prov. Archivist; Rev. James Van Vurst, O.F.M, Spec. Delegate for Child Protection.

Priests: 112; Temporary Professed: 6; Novices: 2; Brothers: 54

Represented in the Archdioceses of Chicago, Cincinnati, Detroit, Galveston-Houston, Indianapolis, Los Angeles, New Orleans, Santa Fe and Washington and in the Dioceses of Allentown, Alexandria, Austin, El Paso, Gallup, Gary, Greensburg, Houma-Thibodaux, Lafayette, Las Cruces, Lexington, Peoria, Phoenix, Pittsburgh, Shreveport, Springfield-Gape Girardeau, Springfield-Cape Girardeau, St. Petersburg, and Venice. Also in Military Services.

Province of The Sacred Heart (1858): 3140 Meramec St., Saint Louis, MO 63118. Tel: 314-353-3421. Rev. William Spencer, O.F.M., Prov. Min; Rev. Michael Jennrich, O.F.M., Prov. Vicar; Bro. Christopher Lambert, O.F.M., Prov. Sec; Rev. Michael Hill, O.F.M., Prov. Treas; Bro. Joseph Rogenski, Prov. Promoter of the Missions, Commissary of the Holy Land, Secretariat Missionary Evangelization. Councilors: Rev. Ralph Parthie, O.F.M; Rev. Tony Posadas, O.F.M; Rev. James Lause, O.F.M; Rev. John Dombrowski, O.F.M; Rev. Edward Shea, O.F.M.

Legal Titles: Franciscan Fathers of the State of Missouri; Franciscan Fathers of the State of Illinois; Franciscan Press; Franciscan Tertiary Province of the Sacred Heart, Incorporated; Mayslake Village; Franciscan Mayslake Village; Cloister Courts; Employees of the Franciscan Orders.

Solemnly Professed: Priests 164; Brothers 62; Simply Professed: Brothers 12; Permanent Deacons 1.

Represented in the Archdioceses of Chicago, Indianapolis, Military Services, St. Louis, St. Paul-Minneapolis and San Antonio and the Dioceses of Belleville, Cleveland, Evansville, Fairbanks, Fort Worth, Gaylord, Joliet, Knoxville, Nashville, Shreveport, Springfield in Illinois, Springfield-Cape Girardeau and Superior.

Properties owned, sponsored or staffed: Friaries 31; Parishes 40; Missions 14; Institutional Chaplaincies 16; Chaplaincies for Religious 5; Formation Houses 2; Novitiates 1; Colleges 1; High Schools 2.

Province of the Assumption of the Blessed Virgin Mary, Inc. (1887): *Provincial Office*, 9230 W. Highland Park Ave., Franklin, WI 53132. Tel: 414-525-9253; Fax: 414-525-9289; Email: province@ofm-abvm.org; Web: ofm-abvm.org. Very Rev. Leslie J. Hoppe, O.F.M., Prov; Rev. John Puodziunas, O.F.M., Vicar. Provincial Councilors: Rev. Francis Berna, O.F.M; Rev. Edward G. Tlucek, O.F.M; Rev. Bernard Kennedy, O.F.M; Bro. Craig Wilking, O.F.M; Bro. Andrew Brophy, O.F.M; Rev. Laurian Janicki, O.F.M., Dir. of Evangelization Center; Rev. Roch Niemier, O.F.M., Prov. Spiritual Asst. of Secular Franciscan Order; Rev. John Puodziunas, O.F.M., Prov. Dir. of Vocations.

Priests: 91; Professed Clerics: 3; Professed Brothers: 39; Deacons: 3

Legal Holdings or Titles: St. Mary of the Angels Friary, Green Bay, WI; Queen of Peace Friary, Burlington, WI; Our Lady of Lourdes Friary, Cedar Lake, IN; San Damiano Friary, Cedar Lake, IN; St. Stanislaus Friary, Cleveland, OH; St. Francis of Assisi School, Greenwood, MS; Francis and Clare Friary, Franklin, WI; Franciscan Pilgrimage Programs, Inc., Franklin, WI; Holy Dormition Friary, Sybertsville, PA; Holy Name Friary, Chicago, IL; St. Francis of Assisi Friary, Greenwood, MS; Assumption BVM Friary, Pulaski, WI; St. Anthony Friary, Milwaukee, WI; Sacred Heart Friary, McAllen, TX.

Properties owned or staffed: Parishes 16; Friaries 12.

Represented in the Archdioceses of Chicago, Detroit, Milwaukee, Newark, New York, Philadelphia, Philadelphia Ukrainian and Pittsburgh Byzantine and in the Dioceses of Brownsville, Cleveland, Gary, Gaylord, Green Bay, Jackson, Las Vegas, Parma and Rochester.

Province of Our Lady of Guadalupe (1985): *Curia Juan Diego*, 1204 Stinson St., SW, Albuquerque, NM 87121-3440. Tel: 505-831-9199; Fax: 505-831-9577. Rev. Gino Correa, O.F.M., Min. Prov; Rev. Ron Walters, O.F.M., Vicar Prov. & Sec. Formation. Councilors: Rev. Gonzalo Moreno, O.F.M., Vocation Dir; Rev. Sean Murnan, O.F.M; Bro. Duane Torisky, O.F.M., Sec., Province Notary Council Member; Rev. Ron Walters, O.F.M., Treas; Bro. Jose Rodriguez, O.F.M.

Priests: 39; Brothers: 16; Postulants: 3

Legal Titles: The Province of Our Lady of Guadalupe of the Order of Friars Minor, Inc.

Represented in the Archdioceses of San Antonio and Santa Fe and in the Dioceses of Gallup and Las Cruces.

Province of the Most Holy Name (1901): 129 W. 31st. St., 2nd Fl., New York, NY 10001-3403. Tel: 646-473-0265; Fax: 800-420-1078; Email: hnp@hnp.org. Very Rev. John F. O'Connor, O.F.M., Prov. Minister; Very Rev. Dominic Monti, O.F.M., Prov. Vicar. Provincial Councilors: Rev. Kevin J. Mullen, O.F.M; Rev. Thomas Conway, O.F.M., Prov. Councilor; Rev. Francis J. DiSpigno, O.F.M., Prov. Councilor; Rev. Daniel P. Dwyer, O.F.M., Prov. Councilor; Rev. Christopher A. Coccia, O.F.M., Prov. Councilor; Bro. Francis Edward Coughlin, O.F.M., Prov. Councilor; Bro. Michael Harlan, O.F.M., Prov. Sec; Rev. Vincent B. Grogan, O.F.M., Canonical Counsel; Ms. Jocelyn Thomas, Dir. Communications; Rev. Joseph M. Hertel, O.F.M., Dir; Rev. Dennis Wilson, O.F.M., Treas; Rev. Russell C. Becker, O.F.M., Promoter of the Missions & Sec.-Missionary Evangelization; Rev. Brian E. Smail, O.F.M., Dir. Vocations; Rev. Richard Trezza, O.F.M., Prov. Spiritual Asst.

Solemn Profession: Archbishop 1; Priests 273; Brothers 68; Permanent Deacons 3; Temporary Profession: Brothers 4; Clerics 13; Novices 3.

Represented in the Archdioceses of Atlanta, Baltimore, Boston, Hartford, Miami, Newark, New York, Philadelphia, San Juan and Washington and in the Dioceses of Albany, Arlington, Altoona-Johnstown, Buffalo, Camden, Charleston, Charlotte, Fall River, Ft. Wayne-South Bend, Paterson, Providence, Raleigh, Salt Lake City, San Diego, St. Petersburg, Steubenville, Trenton and Wilmington. Also in Lima, Peru.

Properties owned or sponsored: Province Parishes 28; Missions 1; School of Theology 1; Retreat Centers 2; University 1; Colleges 1; Community Houses-Residences 45; Houses of Formation 3; Shrine Churches 3; Campus Ministry 1.

Province of St. Barbara (1915): *The Franciscan Friars of California (1900)*, 1500 34th Ave., Oakland, CA 94601. Tel: 510-536-3722; Fax: 510-536-3970. Rev. John S. Harow, O.F.M., Prov. Minister; Rev. Kenneth J. Laverone, O.F.M., Vicar Prov. Definitors: Rev. Charles Talley, O.F.M; Rev. Oscar Mendez Guzman, O.F.M; Rev. Franklin Fong, O.F.M; Rev. Michael Doherty, O.F.M; Rev. Joe Schwab, O.F.M; Bro. Robert Rodriguez, O.F.M; Bro. Peter Boegel, O.F.M., Prov. Sec.

Priests: 126; Solemnly Professed Lay Brothers: 61; Simply Professed Brothers: 9; Novices: 3; Pre-Novitiates: 5

Legal Titles: Franciscan Friars of California; Franciscan Friars of Arizona; Franciscan Friars of Oregon.

Represented in the Archdioceses of Los Angeles, Milwaukee, Portland in Oregon and San Francisco and in the Dioceses of Fresno, Las Cruces, Monterey, Oakland, Orange, Pensacola-Tallahassee, Phoenix, Sacramento, San Diego, San Jose, Santa Rosa, Spokane and Tucson.

Province of the Immaculate Conception (Friars Minor of the Order of St. Francis): 125 Thompson St., New York, NY 10012. Tel: 212-674-4388. Rev. Robert M. Campagna, O.F.M., Prov. Min; Rev. Patrick Boyle, O.F.M., Vicar Prov. Definitors: Rev. Ralph Paonessa, O.F.M; Bro. Charles Gingerich, O.F.M; Rev. Dennis Wheatley, O.F.M; Rev. Joseph F. Lorenzo, O.F.M; Rev. Antonio Nardoianni, O.F.M; Bro. Ronald Bolfeta, O.F.M., Prov. Sec. & Treas; Rev. Vit Fiala, O.F.M., SFO Prov. Spiritual Asst; Rev. James Goode, O.F.M., Promoter of the Franciscan Missions; Ms. Madeline Bonnici, Exec. Dir. Franciscan Mission Associates 274-280 W. Lincoln Ave., Mount Vernon, NY 10550.Rev. Robert M. Campagna, O.F.M., Pius League of St. Anthony.

Fathers: 122; Bishops: 3; Brothers: 22; Permanent Deacons: 2

Properties owned or staffed: Parishes 31; Residences 21.

Represented in the Archdioceses of Boston, Hartford and New York and in the Dioceses of Albany, Bridgeport, Brooklyn, Fall River, Manchester, Pittsburgh, St. Petersburg, Wheeling-Charleston and Youngstown. Also in Central America, Toronto and Italy.

Commissariat of The Holy Cross (1912): 14246 Main St., P.O. Box 608, Lemont, IL 60439. Tel: 630-257-2494; Fax: 630-257-6432. Rev. Blase Chemazar, O.F.M., Pres. Councilors: Rev. Athanasius Lovrencic, O.F.M; Rev. Bernard Karmanocky, O.F.M; Rev. Krizolog Cimerman, O.F.M.

Fathers: 7; Monasteries: 1; Retreat Houses: 1; Mission Centers: 1

Legal Titles: The Slovene Franciscan Fathers, Order of Friars Minor, Commissariat of the Holy Cross, Lemont, IL; St. Mary's Retreat House, Lemont, IL.

Represented in the Archdioceses of Chicago and New York and in the Diocese of Altoona-Johnstown.

Holy Family Friary: 232 S. Home Ave., Pittsburgh, PA 15202-2899. Tel: 412-761-2550. Rev. David Moczulski, O.F.M., Evangelization/Sacramental Ministry & Chap. Sisters of the Holy Family of Nazareth, Secular FranciscansRev. Michael Lenz, O.F.M., Vicar/Sacramental Ministry/Byzantine Rite Ministry, Guardian; Bro. Paschal Dierks, O.F.M., (Retired).

Franciscan Friars: *Mt. Alverna Friary*, 517 S. Belle Vista Ave., Youngstown, OH 44509. Tel: 330-799-1888. Rev. Jules Wong, O.F.M; Rev. Vit Fiala, O.F.M., Guardian.

Represented in the Diocese of Youngstown.

Croatian Franciscan Custody of the Holy Family of U.S. & Canada (1926): 4851 S. Drexel Blvd., Chicago, IL 60615-1703. Tel: 773-536-0552; Fax: 773-536-2094; Email: custody@sbcqlobal.net. Rev. Marko Puljic, O.F.M., Custos. Councilors: Rev. Stjepan Pandzic, O.F.M; Rev. Paul Maslach, O.F.M; Rev. Jozo Grbes, O.F.M; Rev. Nikola Pasalic, O.F.M.

Fathers: 29; Friaries: 1; Parishes: 8; Missions in Canada: 6

Represented in the Archdioceses of Chicago, Detroit, Milwaukee, New York and St. Louis. Also in Canada.

Lithuanian Franciscan Province of St. Casimir: 28 Beach Ave., P.O. Box 980, Kennebunkport, ME 04046-0980. Tel: 207-967-2011; Fax: 207-967-5721; Email: johnbac@roadrunner.com; Web: www.framon.net. Rev. Aurelijus Gricius, O.F.M., Guardian; Rev. John J. Bacevicius, O.F.M., Vicar of Friary; Rev. Raimudas Bukauskas, O.F.M., Treas. of Friary; Rev. Placid Barius, O.F.M., Province Delegate; Rev. Gabriel Baltrusaitis, O.F.M; Rev. Andrew R. Bisson, O.F.M; Rev. Francis Giedgaudas, O.F.M.

Bishops: 1; Fathers: 8

Properties owned or sponsored: Friaries 3; Parishes 1; Summer Camps 1; Guest House 1.

Represented in the Dioceses of Portland (In Maine) and St. Petersburg. Also in Toronto, Canada.

U.S. Foundation (1940): *Province of the Holy Gospel Roger Bacon College*, 2400 Marr St., El Paso, TX 79903. Rev. Francisco Javier Camargo, O.F.M.

Priests: 3; Brothers: 1

Represented in the Diocese of El Paso.

Franciscan Monastery: 1400 Quincy St., N.E., Washington, DC 20017. Tel: 202-526-6800; Fax: 202-529-9889; Email: secretariatusa@myfrancsican.com; Web: www.myfranciscan.com. Rev. Jeremy Harrington, O.F.M., Commissary; Rev. Garrett Edmunds, O.F.M., Vice Commissary; Friar Fadi Azar, O.F.M; Rev. James Paul Brabandt, O.F.M; Friar Thomas Courtney, O.F.M; Friar Aloysius Florio, O.F.M., Vicar; Rev. Romuald Green, O.F.M; Friar-Deacon John-Sebastian Laird-Hammond, O.F.M., Sec. to the Commissary/Guardian; Friar Simon McKay, O.F.M; Friar Roger Petras, O.F.M; Rev. Stephen F. Sabbagh, O.F.M; Rev. Francisco Sihuay, O.F.M; Rev. Jacob-Matthew Smith, O.F.M; Rev. Kevin Treston, O.F.M; Rev. David Wathen, O.F.M., Dir. Holy Land Pilgrimage; Friar Maximilian Wojciechowski, O.F.M; Rev. Manuel Ybarra, O.F.M., Treas; Friar Callistus Welch, O.F.M; Rev. Edward Flanagan, O.F.M.

Priests: 11; Brothers: 8; Permanent Deacons: 1; Solemnly Professed: 20

Represented in the Archdiocese of Washington.

Academy of American Franciscan History: 1712 Euclid Ave., Berkeley, CA 94709. Dr. Jeffrey M. Burns, Dir.

Legal Title: Academy of American Franciscan History.

Franciscan Vocational Office (F.V.C.) (1944): *Franciscan Vocation Ministry of Holy Name Province*, 129 W. 31st St., 2nd Fl., New York, NY 10001. Web: www.beafranciscan.org. Rev. Brian E. Smail, O.F.M., Vocation Dir.

Franciscan Society organized nationally to promote cooperative and unified vocational effort in the Franciscan Provinces, Vice-Provinces and Custodies of the U.S.A.

National Fraternity of the Secular Franciscan Order, U.S.A: (formerly North American Federation, Third Order of St. Francis), 1645 35th St., Oak Brook, IL 60523. Tel: 1-800-FRANCIS; Web: www.nafra-sfo.org. Rev. Patrick Mendés, S.F.O., Nat'l Min.

Founded by St. Francis of Assisi in 1209, to give laity and diocesan clergy an opportunity to live the Gospel intently. There are approximately 15,000 members in nearly 741 fraternities located in 30 geographic regions.

[0530] (S.A.)—FRANCISCAN FRIARS OF THE ATONEMENT

(Societas Adunationis T.O.R.)

Motherhouse: *St. Paul's Friary*, New York Office of the Minister General P.O. Box 300, Garrison, NY 10524-0300. Tel: 845-424-2113; Fax: 845-424-2166.

Priests: 68; Professed Seminarians: 1; Professed Brothers: 36; Friaries: 13; Parishes (U.S. and Canada): 6; Overseas Ministries: England, Italy, and Japan: 1; Ecumenical Institute: 1; Pastoral Center: 1; Campus Ministries: 1; Retreat and Conference Center: 1; Rehabilitation Center for Alcoholics: 2; Shelter for Homeless Men: 1; Military Chaplaincies: 1

Legal Titles: St. Christopher's Inn; St. James Friary; St. Paul's Friary; St. Francis of Assisi Novitiate; St. Joseph's Rehabilitation Center.

Represented in the Archdioceses of Boston, Hartford, Los Angeles, New York and Washington and in the Dioceses of Albany, Arlington, Brooklyn, Buffalo, Charlotte, Ogdensburg, Raleigh and Steubenville.

[0533] (F.F.I.)—FRANCISCAN FRIARS OF THE IMMACULATE

General Motherhouse: Founded 1990. Benevento, Italy,

American Motherhouse: *Marian Friary of Our Lady of Guadalupe*, 199 Colonel Brown Rd., Griswold, CT 06351. Tel: 860-376-6840. Rev. Angelo Mary Geiger, F.I., American Supr.

Legal Title: Marian Friary of Our Lady of Guadalupe.

Represented in the Archdiocese of Indianapolis and in the Dioceses of Fall River, La Crosse, Norwich and

Syracuse.

[0535] (C.F.R.)—FRANCISCAN FRIARS OF THE RENEWAL

Central House: *Saint Crispin Friary*, 420 E. 156th St., Bronx, NY 10455. Tel: 718-665-2441. Rev. Bernard Marie Murphy, C.F.R., Community Servant; Rev. Anthony Marie Baetzold, C.F.R., Vicar. Counselors: Rev. Benedict J. Groeschel, C.F.R; Rev. Mariusz C. Koch, C.F.R; Rev. Richard Roemer, C.F.R; Rev. Luke Fletcher, C.F.R.

Represented in the Archdioceses of Newark, New York and Santa Fe and in the Diocese of Fort Worth.

[0540] (O.S.F.)—FRANCISCAN MISSIONARY BROTHERS OF THE SACRED HEART OF JESUS

(Fratres Missionarii sti Francisci de Sso. Corde Jesu)

Bro. John A. Spila, O.S.F., Dir. Gen.

Brothers: 8

Legal Holdings or Titles: The Black Madonna Shrine and Grottos (Our Lady of Czestochowa); St. Joseph Hill Infirmary, Inc.; Price Memorial, Eureka, MO; Merkle-Knipprath Nursing Home and Apartment Community, Clifton, MO.

Represented in the Archdiocese of St. Louis and in the Diocese of Joliet.

[0560] (T.O.R.)—THIRD ORDER REGULAR OF SAINT FRANCIS

(Tertius Ordo Regularis de Poenitentia)

General Motherhouse: *SS. Cosmas and Damian*, Via dei Fori Imperiali, 1, Rome, Italy, Very Rev. Michael J. Higgins, T.O.R; Rev. John Kochuchira, T.O.R. Counselors: Rev. Bernat Nebot Llinás, T.O.R; Rev. Amando Trujillo Cano, T.O.R; Rev. Francesco Masseria, T.O.R.

Province of the Most Sacred Heart of Jesus (1910): *Provincial Office*, P.O. Box 137, Loretto, PA 15940. Tel: 814-693-2890; Fax: 814-472-8992. Very Rev. Christian R. Oravec, T.O.R., Minister Prov; Rev. Nicholas Polichnowski, T.O.R., Vicar Prov. Councilors: Rev. Peter A. Lyons, T.O.R; Rev. Gabriel Zeis, T.O.R; Rev. Richard L. Davis, T.O.R; Bro. John Paul McMahon, T.O.R., Prov. Sec; Bro. Richard Gates, T.O.R., Assoc. Dir. Vocations; Rev. Jonathan St. Andre, T.O.R., Dir. Vocations; Rev. David Morrier, T.O.R., Secular Franciscans Prov. Spiritual Asst; Rev. Bernard Tickerhoof, T.O.R.

Legal Title: Province of the Most Sacred Heart of Jesus, Third Order Regular of Saint Francis (USA), Loretto, PA.

Fathers: 103; Professed Clerics: 9; Brothers: 24; Novices: 1; Postulants: 6

Ministries in Parishes; Universities and Colleges; High Schools; Chaplaincies; House of Study 1; Novitiates 1; Laymen's Retreat League.

Represented in the Archdioceses of Baltimore, Philadelphia and Washington and in the Dioceses of Altoona-Johnstown, Arlington, Charlotte, Dallas, Fort Worth, La Crosse, Pittsburgh, Rockville Centre, St. Petersburg, Sioux Falls, Steubenville, Venice, Wilmington and Wheeling-Charleston.

Province of the Immaculate Conception: *Saint Bridget Church*, 3811 Emerson Ave., N., Minneapolis, MN 55412-2038. Tel: 612-529-7779; Fax: 612-529-8451. Very Rev. Anthony M. Criscitelli, T.O.R., Min. Prov. Councilors: Very Rev. J. Patrick Quinn, T.O.R., Vicar Prov; Very Rev. William P. Linhares, T.O.R; Rev. Bradley Baldwin, T.O.R; Rev. Carl Vacek, T.O.R; Bro. David Liedl, T.O.R.

Legal Title: Third Order Regular of St. Francis, Province of the Immaculate Conception (USA).

Priests: 40; Brothers: 5

Represented in the Archdioceses of St. Paul-Minneapolis and Washington and in the Dioceses of Altoona-Johnstown, Arlington, Fort Worth, Orlando and Wheeling-Charleston.

U.S.A. Franciscan Vice Province of Our Lady of Guadalupe - T.O.R: 301 Jefferson Ave., Waco, TX 76701. Very Rev. David Gutierrez, T.O.R., Prov. Delegate; Very Rev. Esteban Jasso, T.O.R; Very Rev. Angel Infante, T.O.R; Very Rev. Juan Carlos Bello, T.O.R; Very Rev. Florenco Rodriguez, T.O.R; Very Rev. Roman Burgos, T.O.R; Very Rev. Lorenzo Soler, T.O.R.

Fathers: 8

Represented in the Archdiocese of San Antonio and in the Dioceses of Austin and Fort Worth.

[0570] (G.H.M.)—THE GLENMARY HOME MISSIONERS

(Societas Missionariorum Domesticorum Americas)
(The Home Missioners of America)

General Headquarters: P.O. Box 465618, Cincinnati, OH 45246. Tel: 513-874-8900; Web: www.glenmary-.org. Rev. Dan Dorsey, G.H.M., Pres; Rev. Dominic R. Duggins, G.H.M., 1st Vice Pres. & Dir. Devel; Rev. Mike Kerin, G.H.M., 2nd Vice Pres; Sandra M. Wissel, Treas; Bro. Dennis Craig, G.H.M., House Dir; Rev. Steve Pawelk, G.H.M., Dir.-Vocation Office.

Houses of Formation: *Candidacy*, 300 Peach Alley, Hartford, KY 42347. Tel: 270-298-9886. Rev. Victor Subb, Dir.-Candidates; Bro. Tom Sheehy, Co-Dir; Rev. Dave Glockner, Dir.-Novices; Rev. Tom Kirkendoll, G.H.M., Co-Dir. Novices; Bro. Jose Grosek, Dir. Volunteer Programs P.O. Box 7, Vanceburg, KY 41179.Rev. Jay Gilchrist, Dir.- Pastoral Coord. Program; Rev. Peter Richardson, G.H.M., Dir.-Dept. of Pastoral Services; Dr. Kenneth Sanchagrin, Dir.-Glenmary Research Center.

Fathers: 54; Candidates: 7; Professed Brothers: 16; Novices: 4

Represented in the Archdiocese of Cincinnati and in the Dioceses of Birmingham, Covington, Jackson, Knoxville, Lexington, Little Rock, Nashville, Owensboro, Raleigh, Richmond, Savannah, Tulsa and Wheeling-Charleston.

Properties owned, sponsored or staffed: Missions 60; Houses of Study 2; Pastoral and Research Centers 2; Volunteer Center.

[0580] (B.G.S.)—LITTLE BROTHERS OF THE GOOD SHEPHERD

Villa Mathias: 901 Bro. Mathias Pl., N.W., P.O. Box 389, Albuquerque, NM 87102. Tel: 505-243-4238; Fax: 505-764-9721.

General Headquarters: 82 Stinson St., P.O. Box 1003, L8N 3R1, Hamilton, Canada, Tel: 416-869-3619. Bro. Justin Howson, B.G.S., Supr. Gen; Bro. David Lynch, B.G.S., Vicar Gen; Bro. Raphael Mieszala, B.G.S., Sec. Gen; Bro. Richard MacPhee, B.G.S., Treas. Gen; Bro. Gerard Sullivan, B.G.S., Councillor; Bro. Charles Searson, B.G.S., Dir., Novices.

Professed Brothers: 29

Legal Holdings and Titles: Caritas Deus, Inc. of New Mexico; Camillus House Inc. of Florida; Camillus Health Concern Inc. of Florida; Charity Unlimited, Inc. of New Mexico; BGS Charitable of Illinois; Brother Mathias Barrett Inc. of Illinois; Brother Mathias Barrett Inc. of New Mexico; Brothers of Good Shepherd Inc. of Florida; Brothers of The Good Shepherd Inc. of New Mexico; Brother Mathias Barrett Inc. of New Mexico; Good Shepherd Center Inc. of New Mexico; Good Shepherd Manor, Inc., Momence, IL; Little Brothers of Good Shepherd Inc.of Illinois; Villa Mathia, Inc. of New Mexico; Brothers of the Good Shepherd Inc. of California, Los Angeles, CA; Charity Unlimited Inc. of Florida.

Represented in the Archdioceses of Miami and Santa Fe and in the Diocese of Joliet.

Properties owned and /or sponsored: temporary shelters for marginalized men and women 14; shelter for battered women & children 3; residences for persons with AIDS 1.

[0585] (H.G.N.)—HERALDS OF GOOD NEWS

Founded on Oct. 14, 1984 at Eluru, Andhra Pradesh, India. Missionary Society of Apostolic Life of Pontifical Right.

Generalate: Heralds of Good News: R.S. Post, W.G. Dt., 534005, Eluru, India, Tel: 91-88-12-235973; Fax: 91-88-12-230256.

U.S. Address: Heralds of Good News: 118 E. Chester Ave., Middlesboro, KY 40965. Tel: 606-248-2068; Fax: 606-248-2207. Rev. C. Amalanathn, Mission Representative.

Legal Title: Heralds of Good News Missionary Society, Inc.

Priests in the U.S: 25

Represented in the Dioceses of Biloxi, Fort Worth, Gallup, Lexington, Owensboro, Portland, and Wheeling-Charleston. Also represented in India.

[0590] (M.S.A.)—SOCIETY OF THE MISSIONARIES OF THE HOLY APOSTLES

General Administration: *Society of the Missionaries of the Holy Apostles*, 8594 rue Berri, H2P 2G4, Montreal, Canada, Tel: 514-387-2222; Fax: 514-387-0863. Very Rev. Isaac M. Chuquizana, M.S.A., Supr. Gen. Animator.

Society of Missionaries of Holy Apostles: *Provincial Administration Headquarters*, 22 Prospect Hill Rd., Cromwell, CT 06416. Tel: 866-344-8134; Fax: 860-635-4823. Very Rev. Addison Hallock, M.S.A., Prov. Animator.

Priests: 39; Brothers: 5

Represented in the Archdioceses of Hartford, Los Angeles, New York and Washington and in the Dioceses of Norwich, Pennsacola-Tallahassee, Richmond (with US Navy), Wheeling-Charleston, Wilmington and Venice.

Properties owned, staffed or sponsored: Holy Apostles College and Seminary; 8 Parishes; Hermitage; Hospital Chaplaincies; Retreat House.

[0600] (C.S.C.)—BROTHERS OF THE CONGREGATION OF HOLY CROSS

(Congregatio A Sancta Cruce)

Generalate: *Congregazione di Santa Croce*, Via Framura 85, 00168, Rome, Italy, Rev. Hugh W. Cleary, C.S.C., Supr. Gen; Bro. John Paige, C.S.C., First Asst. & Vicar; Rev. Mario Lachapelle, C.S.C., Second Asst; Bro. Joseph Kofi Tsiquaye, C.S.C., Third Asst; Rev. Richard Warner, C.S.C., Fourth Asst; Rev. Harold Bijoy Rodrigues, C.S.C., Fifth Asst; Rev. Eric Jasmin, C.S.C., Sixth Asst.

Midwest Province of the Brothers of Holy Cross (1841): 54515 State Rd. 933 N., P.O. Box 460, Notre Dame, IN 46556. Tel: 574-631-4000; Fax: 574-631-2999; Web: www.brothersofholycross.com. Bro. Chester Freel, C.S.C., Prov. Supr; Bro. Raymond Papenfuss, C.S.C., Asst. Prov. & Vicar; Bro. Thomas Minta, C.S.C., Sec; Bro. Kenneth Haders, C.S.C., Steward & Treas; Bro. Lewis T. Brazil, C.S.C., Councilor; Bro. Robert Lavelle, C.S.C., Councilor; Bro. Richard Gilman, C.S.C., Councilor.

Legal Title: Notre Dame, Ind. Brothers of Holy Cross, Inc.

Professed Brothers: 176

Properties owned, staffed or sponsored: Community Houses 2; Colleges 1; High Schools 5; Scholasticates 2; Foreign Mission Schools 3.

Represented in the Archdioceses of Chicago, Detroit, Los Angeles, Portland in Oregon and San Antonio and in the Dioceses of Austin, Cleveland, Colorado Springs, Fort Wayne-South Bend, Lansing, Oakland, Peoria, Phoenix, St. Petersburg and Venice. Also in West Africa, Chile, Peru, and Vancouver.

South-West Province of the Brothers of Holy Cross: *Brother John Baptist Province Center, St. Edward University*, 1101 St. Edwards Dr., Austin, TX 78704. Tel: 512-442-7856. Bro. Donald Blauvelt, C.S.C., Prov. Supr; Bro. William Nick, C.S.C., Asst. Prov; Bro. Joel Giallanza, C.S.C., Sec; Bro. Harold Ehlinger, C.S.C., Steward. Councilors: Bro. Richard Daly, C.S.C; Bro. Michael Winslow, C.S.C; Bro. Stephen Walsh, C.S.C.

Legal Title: Brothers of Holy Cross of Texas, Inc.

Professed Brothers: 92; Temporarily Professed: 6

Represented in the Archdioceses of Los Angeles, Miami, New Orleans, Portland in Oregon and San Antonio and in the Dioceses of Austin, Beaumont, Cheyenne, Fort Wayne-South Bend, Knoxville, Oakland and San Jose.

Properties owned, staffed, or sponsored: Colleges 1; High Schools 5; Middle Schools 1; Home for Boys 1; Schools Foreign Mission Schools 2.

Eastern Province of the Brothers of Holy Cross: 85 Overlook Cir., New Rochelle, NY 10804. Tel: 914-632-4468; Tel: 914-632-4469; Fax: 914-632-2490. Bro. Thomas A. Dziekan, C.S.C., Prov; Bro. William Zaydak, C.S.C., Vicar; Bro. George C. Schmitz, C.S.C., Steward. Councilors: Bro. Jerome Donnelly, C.S.C; Bro. Mark Knightly, C.S.C., Sec; Bro. Jonathan Beebe, C.S.C; Bro. Edward Boyer, C.S.C; Bro. James J. Branigan, C.S.C; Bro. Stephen J. LaMendola, C.S.C. In Res. Bro. James Rio, C.S.C; Bro. Robert Russo, C.S.C., Dir.

Legal Title: Brothers of Holy Cross of the Eastern Province of the United States of America, Inc.

Professed Brothers: 100; Temporarily Professed: 5

Properties owned, staffed or sponsored: High Schools 4; Foreign Mission Houses 6; Middle School; Spiritual Life Center; Provincial Residence.

Represented in the Archdioceses of Hartford, New York and Washington and in the Dioceses of Albany, Brooklyn and Wilmington.

[0610] (C.S.C.)—PRIESTS OF THE CONGREGATION OF HOLY CROSS

Congregatio a Sancta Cruce

Generalate: *Curia Generalizia di Santa Croce*, Via Framura 85, 00168, Rome, Italy, Rev. Hugh W. Cleary, C.S.C., Supr. Gen; Bro. John Paige, C.S.C., First Asst. & Vicar; Rev. Mario Lachapelle, C.S.C., Second Asst; Bro. Joseph Kofi Tsiquaye, C.S.C., Third Asst; Rev. Richard V. Warner, C.S.C., Fourth Asst; Rev. Harold Bijoy Rodrigues, C.S.C., Fifth Asst; Rev. Fritz Louis, C.S.C., Sixth Asst; Rev. Carl F. Ebey, C.S.C., Gen. Steward; Rev. Paul LeBlanc, C.S.C., Procurator.

Rev. David T. Tyson, C.S.C., Prov. Supr; Rev. Kenneth M. Molinaro, C.S.C., First Asst. Prov. & Vicar; Rev. Anthony V. Szakaly, C.S.C., Second Asst. Prov; Rev. Edwin H. Obermiller, C.S.C., Third Asst. Prov. Provincial Councilors: Rev. William Beauchamp, C.S.C; Rev. Thomas E. Blantz, C.S.C; Rev. Peter A. Jarret, C.S.C; Rev. Charles W. Kohlerman, C.S.C; Rev. Patrick M. Neary, C.S.C; Rev. William M. Lies, C.S.C; Rev. Michael C. Mathews, C.S.C; Rev. James E. McDonald, C.S.C; Rev. Francis J. Murphy, C.S.C; Rev. Neil F. Wack, C.S.C.

Legal Title: Priests of Holy Cross, Indiana Province, Inc.

Fathers: 288; Professed Clerics: 4; Temporary Professed Clerics: 32; Novices: 9; Candidates: 55; Professed Brothers: 14

Represented in the Archdioceses of Anchorage, Baltimore, Chicago, Detroit, Los Angeles, Military Service, USA, New Orleans, New York, Portland in Oregon, San Antonio, San Francisco and Washington and in the Dioceses of Bridgeport, Cleveland, Colorado Springs, Erie, Fall River, Fort Wayne-South Bend, Gary, Kalamazoo, Monterey, Oakland, Phoenix, San Bernardino and San Jose.

Properties owned, sponsored or staffed: College Seminary; Theological Seminary; Novitiate; Mission Center; Provincial House; Postulate; Universities 2; High Schools 1; Parishes 12; Chaplaincies 17; Publishing House; Retreat House.

Holy Cross Oversea Lay Missionary Program: P.O. Box 668, Notre Dame, IN 46556. Rev. Thomas W. Smith, C.S.C., Dir.

Holy Cross Association: Box K, Notre Dame, IN 46556. Rev. Herbert C. Yost, C.S.C., Dir.

Represented in the Archdioceses of Anchorage, Baltimore, Chicago, Detroit, Los Angeles, Military Services, USA, New Orleans, New York, Portland in Oregon, San Antonio, San Francisco and Washington and in the Dioceses of Bridgeport, Cleveland, Colorado Springs, Erie, Fall River, Fort Wayne-South Bend, Gary, Kalamazoo, Monterey, Oakland, Phoenix, San Bernardino and San Jose.

Congregation of Holy Cross-Eastern Province, Inc:

Provincial Headquarters, 835 Clinton Ave., Bridgeport, CT 06604. Tel: 203-367-7252; Tel: 203-367-1152; Fax: 203-366-7886. Rev. Thomas P. Looney, C.S.C., Prov. Supr; Rev. Thomas C. Bertone, C.S.C., Asst. Prov. & Vicar; Rev. James Lackenmier, C.S.C., Treas. & Steward. Prov. Councilors: Rev. Mark T. Cregan, C.S.C; Rev. John Denning, C.S.C; Bro. Patrick Lynch, C.S.C; Rev. Thomas J. O'Hara, C.S.C; Rev. John P. Phalen, C.S.C; Rev. John J. Ryan, C.S.C.
Fathers: 104; Temporarily Professed Clerics: 4; Candidates: 3; Brothers Professed: 8
Represented in the Archdioceses of Boston, Hartford, Los Angeles, New Orleans, New York and San Francisco and in the Dioceses of Albany, Austin, Bridgeport, Burlington, Fall River, Fort Wayne-South Bend, Manchester, Orlando, Palm Beach, Rochester, Scranton and St. Petersburg.
Properties owned, sponsored or staffed: Colleges 2; Parishes 7; Retreat House; Chaplaincies 4; Campus Ministry 5; Family Rosary Crusade; Family Theater.

Holy Cross Southern Province (1968): *Provincial House*, 2111 Brackenridge St., Austin, TX 78704. Tel: 512-443-3886; Fax: 512-416-1216. Rev. David T. Tyson, C.S.C., Prov. Supr; Rev. Kenneth M. Molinaro, C.S.C., Asst. Prov. & Vicar; Rev. Anthony V. Szakaly, C.S.C., Asst. Prov. & Steward. Members Rev. Jeffrey L. Allison, C.S.C; Rev. E. William Beauchamps, C.S.C; Rev. Thomas E. Chambers, C.S.C; Rev. Robert A. Dowd, C.S.C; Rev. Peter A. Jarret, C.S.C; Rev. Michael C. Mathews, C.S.C; Rev. James E. McDonald, C.S.C; Rev. Patrick M. Neary, C.S.C; Bro. Edward C. Luther, C.S.C.
Legal Title: Congregation of Holy Cross, Southern Province, Inc.
Fathers: 22; Professed Brothers: 2; Temporary Professed: 7
Ministries in Parishes; Foreign Missions; Chaplaincies; Social Service; Schools.
Represented in the Archdioceses of New Orleans and San Antonio and in the Dioceses of Austin, Fort Wayne-South Bend, Lafayette (LA) and Las Cruces.

[0620] (F.S.E.)—BROTHERS OF THE HOLY EUCHARIST

Founded in the United States 1957.

General Motherhouse and Novitiate: P.O. Box 25, Plaucheville, LA 71362. Tel: 318-922-3630; Tel: 318-922-3401. Bro. Andre M. Lucia, F.S.E., Supr. Gen.
Represented in the Dioceses of Alexandria and Baton Rouge.

[0630] (M.S.F.)—CONGREGATION OF THE MISSIONARIES OF THE HOLY FAMILY

(Congregatio Missionariorum a Sacra Familia)

General Motherhouse: Via Odoado Beccari, 41 00154, Rome, Italy, Tel: 011-39-0657-5519; Fax: 011-39-0657-55208. Very Rev. Edmund Michalski, M.S.F., Supr. Gen.

MSF Center: *Provincialate USA of the Missionaries of the Holy Family, Office*, 3014 Oregon Ave., Saint Louis, MO 63118. Tel: 314-577-6300; Fax: 314-577-6301. Rev. Philip Sosa, M.S.F., Prov. Supr.
Fathers: 26; Theology Students: 1; Brothers: 3
Ministries in House of Study 2; Parishes 8; Chaplaincies 2.
Represented in the Archdioceses of Louisville, St. Louis and San Antonio and in the Dioceses of Brownsville, Corpus Christi, Duluth, and Richmond. Also in Canada.

General Mission Office - M.S.F., Inc: 260 W. Euclid Blvd., P.O. Box 918, West Point, VA 23181. Tel: 804-843-2622; Fax: 804-843-3182. Rev. John Brieffies, M.S.F., Exec. Dir.

MSF Provincial Residence: 3582 Pearson Pointe Ct., Saint Louis, MO 63139. Tel: 314-416-0299.

[0640] (S.F.)—SONS OF THE HOLY FAMILY

(Congregatio Filiorum Sacrae Familiae)

General Motherhouse: Entenza 301, 08029, Barcelona, Spain, Very Rev. Luis Picazo, S.F., Gen. Supr.

U.S. Foundation (1920): 401 Randolph Rd., P.O. Box 4138, Silver Spring, MD 20914-4138. Tel: 301-622-1184. Rev. Miguel Mateo, S.F., Vice Prov.
Fathers: 13
Represented in the Archdioceses of Santa Fe and Washington.

[0650] (C.S.SP.)—CONGREGATION OF THE HOLY SPIRIT

(Congregation of the Holy Spirit under the protection of the Immaculate Heart of Mary, Spiritans.)
(Congregatio Sancti Spiritus sub tutela Immaculati Cordis Beatissimae Virginis Mariae)

Generalate: Clivo di Cinna 195, 00136, Rome, Italy, Very Rev. Jean-Paul Hoch, C.S.Sp.

Eastern Province of the United States (1872): 6230 Brush Run Rd., Bethel Park, PA 15102. Tel: 412-831-0302; Fax: 412-831-0970. Very Rev. Jeffrey T. Duaime, C.S.Sp., Prov. Supr. Councilors: Rev. Timothy Hickey, C.S.Sp; Very Rev. John Fogarty, C.S.Sp; Rev. Christopher H. McDermott, C.S.Sp; Rev. John A. Sawicki, C.S.Sp., Prov. Treas. & Councilor; Rev. Freddy J. Washington, C.S.Sp.
Fathers in the U.S: 56; Professed Brothers: 1
Legal Holdings: Archconfraternity of the Holy Ghost; Provincial Residence; Duquesne University; Laval House; Holy Ghost Preparatory School; Bethel Holy Spirit Animation Center.
Represented in the Archdioceses of Baltimore, Chicago, Cincinnati, Detroit, New York, Philadelphia and Washington and in the Dioceses of Arlington, Pittsburgh, Providence and Venice. Also in Puerto Rico and the Dominican Republic.
Properties owned, sponsored or staffed: Parishes 9; Retirement Residences 2.

Western Province of the United States (1964): *Congregation of the Holy Spirit*, 1700 W. Alabama St., Houston, TX 77098-2808. Tel: 713-522-2882; Fax: 713-522-8063; Web: www.spiritans.org. Rev. Joseph B. Gaglione, C.S.Sp., Council Member. Prov. Councilors: Very Rev. Daniel L. Walsh, C.S.Sp., Prov. Supr; Bro. Michael E. Suazo, C.S.Sp., Prov. Sec., Dir. Vocations & Bursar; Rev. Phillip R. Howard, C.S.Sp; Rev. Huy Q. Dinh; Rev. Michael T. White, C.S.Sp., First Asst.
Priests: 32; Professed Brothers: 1; Candidates: 2; Scholastics: 7; Lay Spiritans: 16
Staff: Parishes 5; Training Centers 1.
Represented in the Archdiocese of Galveston-Houston and in the Dioceses of Baton Rouge, Little Rock, Phoenix, San Bernardino, and San Diego. Also in Mexico, Taiwan, and the Philippines.
Properties owned, sponsored or staffed: Holy Spirit Provincialate, Houston, TX; Casa Laval, Hemet, CA; Properties in Mexico: Iglesia de Santa Ana; Mission San Juan Bautista.

Holy Ghost Fathers of Ireland (1971): 4849 37th St., Long Island City, NY 11101. Tel: 718-729-5273; Fax: 718-729-6949. Very Rev. Thomas Basquel, C.S.Sp., Prov. Delegate U.S.A. East; Rev. Joseph Glynn, C.S.Sp., Prov. Delegate U.S.A. West. Councilors: Very Rev. Thomas Basquel, C.S.Sp; Rev. Edmond B. Duggan, C.S.Sp; Rev. Noel P. O'Meara, C.S.Sp; Rev. Jerry Kirwin, C.S.Sp.
Fathers: 31
Represented in the Archdioceses of Boston, Miami, and San Francisco and in the Dioceses of Brooklyn, Fargo, Palm Beach, Peoria and St. Augustine.

[0660] (M.SP.S.)—MISSIONARIES OF THE HOLY SPIRIT

General Motherhouse: Av. Universidad 1702 04010, Mexico, D.F., Mexico, Tel: 5-658-74-33; Tel: 5-658-7851. Very Rev. Domenico Di Raimundo, Supr. Gen.

American Headquarters: 9792 Oma, Garden Grove, CA 92841. Tel: 714-534-5476.
Priests: 23; Professed: 19; Novices: 4; Parishes: 4; Houses of Study: 1; Novitiates: 1; Theologates: 1
Represented in the Archdioceses of Los Angeles and Portland in Oregon and in the Dioceses of Orange and Seattle.

[0670] (O.H.)—HOSPITALLER BROTHERS OF ST. JOHN OF GOD

General Motherhouse: *Hospitaller Brothers of St. John of God*, Order Founded by St. John of God at Granada, Spain, in 1537. via della Nocetta 263, 00164, Rome, Italy, Rev. Donatus Forkan, O.H., Prior Gen.

American Province of Our Lady Queen of Angels (1970): *Villa Maria-Provincial Curia*, 2425 S. Western Ave., Los Angeles, CA 90018. Tel: 323-734-0233; Fax: 323-731-5987; Email: usaprov-office@sbcglobal.net. Bro. Pablo Lopez, O.H., Prov.
Brothers: 24; Solemnly Professed: 24; Priests: 3
Legal Holdings: St. John of God Retirement and Care Center, Los Angeles, CA; St. Joseph Health and Retirement Center, Ojai, CA; St. John of God Health Care Services, Victorville, CA.
Represented in the Archdiocese of Los Angeles and in the Diocese of San Bernardino.

[0680] I.H.M.—BROTHERS OF THE IMMACULATE HEART OF MARY

General Motherhouse (1948): 609 N. 7th St., Steubenville, OH 43952. Tel: 740-283-2462. Bro. Dominic Carroll, I.H.M., Supr. Gen; Bro. Anthony Motto, I.H.M., Novice Master; Bro. Patrick Geary, I.H.M., Vocation Dir.
Professed Brothers: 4
Ministries in: Novitiate; Bishop's Residence; CCD Center; Pastoral Associates 3.
Represented in the Diocese of Steubenville.

[0690] S.J.—JESUIT FATHERS AND BROTHERS

(Societas Jesu)

Generalate: Borgo S. Spirito 4, 00193, Rome, Italy, Rev. Adolfo Nicolas, S.J., Gen; Rev. Ignacio Echarte, S.J., Sec; Rev. James E. Grummer, S.J., U.S. Asst.

Jesuit Conference: *The Society of Jesus in the United States National Offices*, 1016 16th St., N.W., Ste. 400, Washington, DC 20036. Tel: 202-462-0400; Fax: 202-328-9212. Rev. Thomas H. Smolich, S.J., Pres; Rev. Thomas P. Gaunt, S.J., Exec. Sec; Rev. Steven C. Dillard, S.J., Sec. Formation; Rev. Thomas P. Greene, S.J., Sec.-Social Intl. Ministries; Rev. Paul B. Macke, S.J., Sec.-Pastoral Ministries & Jesuit Life; Rev. Charles F. Kelley, S.J., Dir. Assistancy Planning; Mr. James L. Rogers, Sec. Communications; Rev. Albert J. DiUlio, S.J., Sec. Finance & Higher Educ.

Maryland Province of the Society of Jesus (1833) (1833): 8600 LaSalle Rd., Ste. 620, Towson, MD 21286-2014. Tel: 443-921-1310; Fax: 443-921-1313. Very Rev. James M. Shea, S.J., Prov; Rev. James A. Casciotti, S.J., Socius; Ms. Rose Ann D'Alesandro, Asst. Treas; Rev. Ronald J. Amiot, S.J., Asst. Healthcare Planning; Mrs. Deirdre Elmore Banscher, Health Care Coord; Rev. James L. Connor, S.J., Asst. Prov. for Mission & Continuing Renewal; Rev. Charles A. Frederico, S.J., Vocations Dir; Rev. Thomas H. Feely, S.J., Asst. for Formation; Rev. Gerald P. Fogarty, S.J., Archivist; Rev. Liborio J. LaMartina, S.J., Resident Archivist; Rev. Joseph E. Lingan, S.J., Novice Dir; Ms. Maureen Locher, Special Case Coord; Rev. Brian O. McDermott, S.J., Tertian Instructor; Rev. James A. O'Brien, S.J., Promoter, Christian Life Communities; Ms. Mary Tilghman, Acting Dir. Communications; Mr. Edward F. Plocha, Dir. Advancement; Rev. William C. Rickle, S.J., Asst. for Latino Ministries; Rev. William P. Ryan, S.J., Treas; Rev. David A. Sauter, S.J., Asst. for Schools.
Legal Title: Corporation of the Roman Catholic Clergymen, Maryland.
Fathers: 314; Scholastics: 25; Brothers: 12
Represented in the Archdioceses of Baltimore, Philadelphia and Washington and in the Dioceses of Allentown, Charlotte, Raleigh, Richmond, Scranton and Wheeling-Charleston.
Properties owned, sponsored or staffed: Parishes 14; Universities 5; High Schools 5; Middle and Grammar Schools 7; Houses of Retreats 3; Residences 26.

Province of New York (1943): 39 E. 83rd St., New York, NY 10028. Tel: 212-774-5500; Fax: 212-794-1036. Very Rev. David S. Ciancimino, S.J., Prov; Rev. Thomas R. Slon, S.J., Socius & Exec. Asst. to the Prov; Rev. Walter F. Modrys, S.J., Prov. Treas; Rev. Thomas H. Feely, S.J., Asst. for Formation-Maryland & New York Provs; Rev. Ramon A. Salomone, S.J., Asst. for Int'l Apostolate; Rev. Charles A. Frederico, S.J., Dir. of Vocations, Maryland & New York Provs; Rev. James F. Keenan, S.J., Dir. of Province Devel. Office; Rev. James J. Yannarell, S.J., Prov. Health Care Coord; Rev. Mark C. Hallinan, S.J., Asst. for Social Ministries; Rev. Vincent L. Biagi, S.J., Asst. for Sec. & Pre-Sec. Education & Lay Formation; Rev. Edward J. Quinnan, S.J., Asst. for Pastoral Ministry & Province Representative to the Jesuit Collaborative.
Legal Title: The New York Province of the Society of Jesus, New York, NY.
Fathers: 372; Scholastics: 11; Brothers: 17
Represented in the Archdioceses of Newark and New York and in the Dioceses of Albany, Brooklyn, Buffalo, Paterson, Rochester, Rockville Centre and Syracuse. Also in Guam, the Caroline Islands, Chalan Kanoa and the Prefecture Apostolic of Marshall Islands, West Africa - Nigeria & Ghana.
Properties owned, sponsored or staffed: Parishes 8; Universities 1; Colleges 3; High Schools 8; Houses for Laymen's Retreats 3; House of Study 1; Novitiates 1; Community Houses 4.

The Jesuits of the Missouri Province (Missouri Province of the Society of Jesus): *Province Offices*, 4511 W. Pine Blvd., Saint Louis, MO 63108-2191. Tel: 314-361-7765; Fax: 314-758-7164. Rev. Douglas W. Marcouiller, S.J., Prov; Rev. Michael G. Harter, S.J., Socius; Rev. David J. Suwalsky, S.J., Treas; Rev. John F. Armstrong, S.J., Asst. for Formation; Rev. Louis J. McCabe, S.J., Asst. for Vocations & Planning; Mr. Sean Agniel, Asst. for Social Ministries; Rev. Robert F. Weiss, S.J., Delegate for Higher Education & Assoc. Dir. Jesuit Advancement Office; Rev. L. Gene Martens, S.J., Assoc. Dir. Jesuit Advancement Office; Rev. David L. Fleming, S.J., Editor Of Jesuit Bulletin, Publication: The Jesuit BulletinDr. David P. Miros, Archivist; Rev. William B. Faherty, S.J., Archivist Emeritus; Mr. Arthur G. Zinselmeyer, Asst. for Secondary & Pre-Secondary Education; Rev. Richard O. Buhler, S.J., Asst. for Pastoral & Spiritual Ministries; Mr. Thom Digman, Asst. for Advancement.
Fathers: 205; Students in Major Seminary: 25; Novices: 6; Brothers: 16
Legal Titles: Regis Jesuit High School Corporation, Aurora, CO; Regis University, Denver, CO; Rockhurst University; Rockhurst High School, Kansas City, MO; The Province-The Jesuits of the Missouri Province; Bellarmine House of Studies - The Jesuits of the Missouri Province; Fusz Pavilion - The Jesuits of the Missouri Province; Institute of Jesuit Sources - The Jesuits of the Missouri Province; Jesuit Mission Bureau - The Jesuits of the Missouri Province; Review for Religious - The Jesuits of the Missouri Province; DeSmet Jesuit High School; Jesuit Community Corporation at Saint Louis University; Saint Louis University; St. Louis University High School; White House Retreat, Inc.; Loyola Academy, St. Louis, MO; Arrupe Jesuit High School, Denver, CO; Society of Jesus in Belize, Inc., Belize; Jesuit Retreat House, Sedalia,CO.
Ministries in Parishes; Universities; High Schools; Middle Schools; Novitiate; First Studies House; Curia; Retreat Houses.
Represented in the Archdioceses of Denver, Kansas City in Kansas and St. Louis and in the Diocese of Kansas City-St. Joseph. Also in Belize.

New Orleans Province (1907) (1907): 710 Baronne St., Ste. B, New Orleans, LA 70113-1064. Tel: 504-571-1055; Fax: 504-571-1744; Email: noprovsj@norprov.org; Web: www.norprov.org. Very Rev. Mark Lewis, S.J., Provincial; Rev. John F. Armstrong, S.J., Asst. for Formation; Mary Baudouin, Asst. for Social Ministries; Rev. Michael D. Dooley, S.J., Asst. for Secondary Education; Rev. Warren J. Broussard, S.J., Asst. for Pastoral Ministry & Retreat Ministry; Bro. Lawrence J. Lundin, S.J., Treas; Rev. George F. Lundy, S.J., Asst.

for Higher Education; Rev. Stephen C. Rowntree, S.J., Asst. for International Ministries; Rev. Raymond Fitzgerald, S.J., Socius; Mike Bourg, Dir. Devel.
Legal Title: Catholic Society of Religious and Literary Education, A Louisiana Corporation.
Fathers: 163; Students in Major Seminary: 35; Novices: 8; Brothers: 16
Represented in the Archdioceses of Atlanta, Galveston-Houston, New Orleans, San Antonio and Santa Fe and in the Dioceses of Austin, Baton Rouge, Birmingham, Dallas, El Paso, Fort Worth, Lafayette (LA), Las Cruces, Mobile, St. Augustine, St. Petersburg, Tyler and Venice.
Properties owned, sponsored or staffed: Parishes 8; Universities 1; Colleges 1; High Schools 5; Elementary Schools 1; Novitiate 1; Houses of Retreat 5.

California Province (1909): 300 College Ave., P.O. Box 519, Los Gatos, CA 95031-0519. Tel: 408-884-1600. Very Rev. John P. McGarry, S.J., Prov; Rev. Alfred E. Naucke, S.J., Exec. Asst; Rev. Edwin B. Harris, S.J., Asst. for Secondary Education; Rev. Chi Ngo, S.J., Asst. Formation; Bro. James Siwicki, S.J., Dir. Vocations; Rev. Gerdenio M. Manuel, S.J., Asst. for Higher Educ. & Dir. Studies; Rev. Theodore E. Gabrielli, S.J., Asst. for Intl. Min. & Dir., California Jesuit Missionaries; Rev. Dennis R. Parnell, S.J., Prov. Treas; Mr. Joseph B. Naylor, Prov. Dir. Advancement; Bro. Daniel J. Peterson, S.J., Prov. Archivist; Rev. John D. Murphy, S.J., Tertian Instructor; Rev. Doan T. Hoang, S.J., Apostleship of Prayer; Rev. William J. Kelley, S.J., Asst. for Pastoral Ministries; Rev. Charles J. Tilley, S.J., Special Projects Mgr.
Legal Title: The California Province of the Society of Jesus.
Fathers: 313; Brothers: 25; Scholastics: 32; Scholastic Novices: 17
Represented in the Archdioceses of Los Angeles and San Francisco and in the Dioceses of Fresno, Honolulu, Oakland, Orange, Phoenix, Sacramento, Salt Lake City, San Diego, San Jose, Stockton and Tucson.
Properties owned, sponsored or staffed: Parishes 12; Universities 3; High Schools 7; Novitiates 1; Retreat Center 2.

New England Province (1926): 85 School St., Watertown, MA 02472-4251. Tel: 617-607-2800; Fax: 617-607-2888. Very Rev. Myles N. Sheehan, S.J., Prov; Rev. John J. Higgins, S.J., Exec. Asst; Rev. Dennis J. Yesalonia, S.J., Prov. Treas; Rev. Thomas H. Feely, S.J., Prov. Asst. Formation; Rev. John T. Butler, S.J., Dir. Vocations; Rev. Michael J. Linden, S.J., Prov. Asst. for Pastoral Social & Int'l Ministries; Rev. George T. Williams, S.J., Prov. Coord.-Criminal Justice Ministry; Rev. Robert J. Daly, S.J., Prov. Asst. Higher Educ; Rev. James M. Shaughnessy, S.J., Liaison Hospital Chaplaincy Ministry.
Legal Title: The Society of Jesus of New England.
Fathers: 273; Scholastics: 25; Brothers: 13; Parishes: 6; Universities: 2; Colleges: 1; High Schools: 3; Houses of Retreat: 2; Seminaries: 1
Represented in the Archdioceses of Baltimore, Boston, Chicago, Los Angeles, Milwaukee, New Orleans, New York, St. Louis, Seattle and Washington and in the Dioceses of Baton Rouge, Bridgeport, Brooklyn, Buffalo, Burlington, Fairbanks, Fall River, Fort Wayne-South Bend, Honolulu, Manchester, Norwich, Oakland, Portland (In Maine), Providence, Rapid City, St. Augustine, San Diego, San Jose, Scranton, Spokane, Syracuse, Tucson, and Worcester.

Chicago Province - Society of Jesus (S.J.) (1928): 2050 N. Clark St., Chicago, IL 60614. Tel: 773-975-6363; Fax: 773-975-0230. Very Rev. Timothy P. Kesicki, S.J., Prov; Rev. Walter C. Deye, S.J., Socius; Rev. Raymond P. Guaio, S.J., Asst. for Formation; Rev. Theodore G. Munz, S.J., Prov. Treas. and Asst. for Business and Fin; Rev. James S. Prehn, S.J., Asst. for Secondary Educ; Rev. Patrick A. Fairbanks, S.J., Asst. for Vocations; Rev. Paul V. Robb, S.J., Asst. Treas; Rev. Paul J. Faulstich, S.J., Asst. for Records & Research.
Legal Title: Chicago Province of the Society of Jesus.
Fathers: 174; Scholastics: 21; Brothers: 12; Scholastic Novices: 4
Quarterly Publication: Company Magazine. Offices, 1400 W. Devon Ave.-#511, Chicago, IL 60660-1312. Tel: 773-761-9432. Fax: 773-761-9443.
Represented in the Archdioceses of Chicago, Cincinnati, Indianapolis and Louisville and in the Dioceses of Covington, Fort Wayne-South Bend, Gary, Joliet, Lafayette in Indiana and Lexington.
Properties Sponsored: Parishes 3; Universities 2; High Schools 6; Retreat Houses 2; Diocesan Major Seminary 1; Residences 20; House of Writers 1.

Oregon Province - Society of Jesus (1932): 3215 S.E. 45th Ave, P.O. Box 86010, Portland, OR 97286-0010. Tel: 503-226-6977. Rev. Patrick J. Lee, S.J., Prov; Rev. Thomas Lankenau, S.J., Socius; Rev. John C. Bentz, S.J., Asst. International Ministries & Asst. Vocations; Rev. William M. Watson, S.J., Province Representative Intl. Ministries; Rev. Michael A. Tyrrell, S.J., Prov. Treas; Rev. Patrick J. Twohy, S.J., Asst. for Native Ministries; Rev. Patrick J. Conroy, S.J., Asst. for Formation; Rev. Peter D. Byrne, S.J., Asst. for Parishes & Spiritual Ministries.
Fathers: 191; Scholastics: 32; Brothers: 7
Legal Titles: Society of Jesus, Oregon Province, Portland, OR; The Pioneer Educational Society, Spokane, WA; Montana Catholic Missions, SJ; The Society of Jesus, Alaska.
Represented in the Archdioceses of Anchorage, Portland in Oregon and Seattle and in the Dioceses of Baker, Boise, Fairbanks, Great Falls-Billings, Helena, Spokane and Yakima.
Properties owned, sponsored or staffed: Parishes 7; Universities 2; High Schools 4; Middle Schools 1; House of Study 1; Novitiates 1.

Detroit Province - Society of Jesus (S.J.) (1955): 7303 W. Seven Mile Rd., Detroit, MI 48221. Tel: 313-861-7500; Fax: 313-861-4230. Very Rev. Timothy P. Kesicki, S.J., Prov. Supr; Rev. Walter C. Deye, S.J., Exec. Asst; Rev. Theodore G. Munz, S.J., Treas; Ms. Carrie Nantais, Asst. for Social & International Ministries; Rev. Raymond P. Guiao, S.J., Asst. Formation; Ms. Jenene M. Francis, Asst. Pastoral Ministries; Rev. Patrick A. Fairbanks, S.J., Asst. Vocation Promotion; Rev. James S. Prehn, S.J., Asst. Secondary Educ; Mr. Timothy J. Freeman, Asst. Devel; Mr. Jeremy W. Langford, Asst. Communications.
Fathers: 118; Scholastics: 20; Brothers: 16
Legal Titles: Detroit Province of the Society of Jesus; Colombiere Center, Clarkston, MI; Jesuit Retreat House of Cleveland, Ohio; Jesuit Seminary Association; Jesuit International Missions; John Carroll University of Cleveland, Ohio; John Carroll Jesuit Community Corporation; Loyola High School, Detroit, MI; Loyola of the Lakes Jesuit Retreat House, Inc.; Manresa Jesuit Retreat House; Patna Jesuit Mission Society, Inc.; St. Ignatius High School of Cleveland, Ohio; St. John's Jesuit High School of Toledo, Ohio; University of Detroit Mercy; The Jesuit Community Corporation at the University of Detroit; University of Detroit Jesuit High School and Academy; Walsh Jesuit High School.
Represented in the Archdioceses of Baltimore, Boston, Chicago, Detroit, Los Angeles, Military Services, Mobile, New Orleans, New York and Washington and in the Dioceses of Charlotte, Cleveland, Columbus, Gaylord, Lansing, Lexington, Marquette, Oakland, Saginaw, Toledo, Wheeling-Charleston, Winona, and Worcester.
Properties owned, sponsored or staffed: Parishes 4; Universities 2; High Schools 5; Retreat Houses 2.

Wisconsin Province - Society of Jesus (S.J.) (1955): 3400 W. Wisconsin Ave., P.O. Box 080288, Milwaukee, WI 53208-0288. Tel: 414-937-6949; Fax: 414-937-6950. Very Rev. G. Thomas Krettek, S.J., Prov; Rev. Luis Rodriguez, S.J., Asst. Prov. Pastoral Ministries; Rev. John M. Paul, S.J., Dir. Formation; Rev. James J. Gladstone, S.J., Prov. Asst., Personnel & Retreat Ministry; Rev. Thomas A. Lawler, S.J., Vocation Dir; Rev. Eugene M. Dutkiewicz, S.J., Prov. Asst. Finance; Rev. John L. Treloar, S.J., Prov. Asst. Higher Educ; Rev. Patrick Burns, S.J., Dir. Planning & Implementation for Province Reconfiguration; Rev. Frank A. Majka, S.J., Prov. Asst. for Secondary Education.
Legal Title: Wisconsin Province of the Society of Jesus.
Fathers: 228; Novices: 8; Brothers: 17; Scholastics: 24
Represented in the Archdioceses of Milwaukee, Omaha and St. Paul-Minneapolis and in the Dioceses of Des Moines, Green Bay, Rapid City, Winona and Cheyenne.
Properties owned, sponsored or staffed: Parishes 7; Universities 2; High Schools 4; Middle Schools 2; Elementary Schools 2; Community Houses 17; Novitiate; Native American Missions 3; Retreat Houses 4.

U.S. Address: 12725 S.W. 6th St., Miami, FL 33184. Tel: 786-621-4595; Fax: 305-559-3160. Rev. Felix F. Polanco, S.J., Prov; Rev. Francisco Perez Lerena, S.J., Miami Reg. Supr.
Fathers: 99; Scholastics: 34; Brothers: 11
Represented in the Archdiocese of Miami. Also in Santo Domingo.
Properties owned, staffed or sponsored: High Schools: Loyola in Dominican Republic, Belen Jesuit Prep in Miami; Novitiate 1; House of Retreat 3 in Santo Domingo; Juan Pablo II in Miami; Residences 2.
Rev. Mario A. Torres, S.J., Reg. Supr; Rev. John F. Talbot, S.J., Exec. Asst. to Reg. Supr; Rev. Baudillo Guzman, S.J., Exec. Treas; Rev. Alvaro Velez, S.J., Auditor.
Fathers: 17; Scholastics: 7
Represented in the Archdiocese of San Juan and in the Dioceses of Fajardo-Humacao, Mayaguez, and Palm Beach.
Properties owned, sponsored or staffed: Parishes 3; High Schools 1; Residences 2; Campus Ministry Centers 1.

[0700] (S.S.J.)—ST. JOSEPH'S SOCIETY OF THE SACRED HEART

(The Josephites)
(Societas Sancti Joseph SSmi Cordis)

Central House Administration: 1130 N. Calvert St., Baltimore, MD 21202. Tel: 410-727-3386; Fax: 410-727-1006; Email: superiorgeneral@josephite.com; Web: www.josephite.com. Very Rev. Edward J. Chiffriller, S.S.J., Supr. Gen.
Fathers: 72; Brothers: 6; Seminarians: 18; Novices: 4
Legal Titles: St. Joseph's Society of the Sacred Heart, Inc.; St. Joseph Manor Foundation, Inc.; The Josephite Retirement and Disability Benefits Trust; The Josephite Seminarian Education Trust.
Represented in the Archdioceses of Baltimore, Galveston-Houston, Los Angeles, Mobile, New Orleans and Washington and in the Dioceses of Arlington, Baton Rouge, Beaumont, Biloxi, Birmingham, Jackson and Lafayette (LA). Also in Nigeria.
Properties owned, staffed or sponsored: Parishes 40; Elementary Schools 9; High School; House of Study; Major Seminary; Novitiate; Nigerian Formation House.

[0710] (C.J.)—JOSEPHITE FATHERS

(Institutum Josephitarum Gerardimontensium)

General Motherhouse: Geraardsbergen (Ghent), Belgium, Most Rev. Robert Hamilton, C.J., Supr. Gen.

U.S. Foundation: *St. Joseph Seminary, Provincialate and Novitiate*, 180 Patterson Rd., Santa Maria, CA 93455. Tel: 805-937-5378; Fax: 805-937-5759. Very Rev. Charles Hofschulte, C.J., Prov. Supr.
Fathers: 8
Ministry to: Parishes; Academic Education.
Represented in the Archdiocese of Los Angeles.

[0720] (M.S.)—THE MISSIONARIES OF OUR LADY OF LA SALETTE

(Congregatio Missionariorum Vulgo "De la Salette")

General House: Piazza Madonna Della Salette 3, 00152, Rome, Italy, Very Rev. Dennis J. Loomis, M.S., Supr. Gen.
American Region was established in 1892; Canonically erected 1934; Divided into other Provinces in 1945, 1958, 1967 and restructured into one Province in 2000.

Province of Mary, Mother of the Americas (2000): 915 Maple Ave., Hartford, CT 06114-2330. Tel: 860-956-8870. Very Rev. Joseph G. Bachand, M.S., Prov. Supr; Rev. James H. Kuczynski, M.S., Vicar; Rev. William Kaliyadan, M.S., Asst; Rev. Brian Schloth, M.S., Prov. Treas.
Legal Title: Missionaries of LaSalette Corp.; MLS Religious Trust.
Priests: 123; Brothers: 29; Oblate Brothers: 3; Scholastics: 1
Represented in the Archdioceses of Atlanta, Boston, Galveston-Houston Hartford, Milwaukee, Brooklyn, St. Louis and Washington and in the Dioceses of Albany, Beaumont, Fall River, Jefferson City, Lake Charles, Manchester, Norwich, Orlando, Peoria, Providence, Raleigh, Rockville Centre, Springfield in Massachusetts, Tucson, Tyler, Venice and Worcester. Also in Canada.

[0730] (L.C.)—LEGIONARIES OF CHRIST

Founded in Mexico in 1941, first foundation in United States 1965.

General Headquarters: Via Aurelia 677, Rome, Italy, Tel: 011-39-06-664991; Fax: 011-39-06-66499372. Very Rev. Alvaro Corcuera, L.C., Gen. Dir.

New York Territory Headquarters: 590 Columbus Ave., P.O. Box 205, Thornwood, NY 10594. Tel: 914-495-9000; Fax: 914-495-9050. Very Rev. Julio Marti, L.C., Territorial Dir; Rev. Anthony Bannon, L.C., Nat'l. Dir. Novitiate and Juniorate 475 Oak Ave., Cheshire, CT 06410.Rev. Christopher Brackett, L.C., Rector.
Priests: 61; Religious: 234; Novices: 79
Represented in the Archdioceses of Hartford, New York, Philadelphia and Washington and in the Dioceses of Manchester and Providence.

Atlanta Territory Headquarters: 4040 Gunnin Rd., Norcross, GA 30092. Tel: 770-671-8778; Fax: 678-916-7543.
Priests: 67; Religious: 3
Represented in the Archdioceses of Atlanta, Chicago, Denver, Detroit, Galveston-Houston, Los Angeles and St. Louis and in the Dioceses of Dallas, Gary, Lincoln, Madison, Phoenix, Sacramento and San Jose.

[0740] (M.I.C.)—CONGREGATION OF MARIANS OF THE IMMACULATE CONCEPTION

(Congregatio Clericorum Marianorum sub titulo Immaculatae Conceptionis Beatae Mariae Virginis)

General Motherhouse: Via Corsica 1, 00198, Rome, Italy, Tel: 011-39-06-853-7031; Fax: 011-39-06-853-7032. Very Rev. Jan Rokosz, M.I.C., Gen. Supr; Very Rev. Marek Szczepaniak, M.I.C., Vicar Gen; Rev. Joseph Roesch, M.I.C., 2nd Gen. Councilor; Rev. Andrzej Pakula, M.I.C., 3rd Gen. Councilor; Rev. Andzrej Szostek, M.I.C., 4th Gen. Councilor.

Blessed Virgin Mary, Mother of Mercy Province: 2 Prospect Hill Rd., Stockbridge, MA 01262-0951. Tel: 413-298-3931; Fax: 413-298-0207; Email: provincial@marian.org; Web: www.marian.org; Web: www.thedivinemercy.org. Very Rev. Daniel Cambra, M.I.C., Prov. Supr. Provincial Councilors: Very Rev. Kazimierz Chwalek, M.I.C., Vicar Prov; Rev. Timothy Roth, M.I.C., 2nd Councilor; Rev. Donald Calloway, M.I.C., 3rd Councilor; Bro. Brian Manian, M.I.C., 4th Councilor; Bro. Donald Schaefer, M.I.C., Prov. Treas.
Fathers: 49; Brothers: 7; Seminarians: 18; Novices: 8; Postulants: 4
Legal Holdings: Marian Fathers of the Immaculate Conception of the B.V.M., Inc., 2 Prospect Hill Rd., Stockbridge, MA 01262; Congregation of Marians of the Immaculate Conception; Congregation of Marian Fathers of the Immaculate Conception of the Most Blessed Virgin Mary; Association of Marian Helpers; Marian Service Corporation; Marian Helpers Corporation; Eucharistic Apostles of the Divine Mercy (EADM); Healthcare Professionals-Nurses and Doctors-for Divine Mercy; John Paul II Institute of Divine Mercy; Marian Helpers Center; Marian House of Studies; Marian Scholasticate; Marianpolis Preparatory School; Mother of Mercy Messengers (MOMM); National Shrine of the Divine Mercy.
Represented in the Archdioceses of Chicago, Milwaukee

and Washington, DC and in the Dioceses of Fairbanks, Joliet, Norwich, Portland, Springfield in Massachusetts and Steubenville. Also in Argentina.

Properties owned, staffed or sponsored: 7 Religious Houses; 3 Residences; 6 Parishes; 1 High School. In Argentine Vicariate: 2 Religious Houses; 2 Parishes; 2 Grade Schools.

[0750] (C.M.M.)—CONGREGATION OF MARIANNHILL MISSIONARIES, MARIANNHILL FATHERS AND BROTHERS

(Congregatio Missionariorum de Mariannhill)

Generalate: Via S. Giovanni Eudes 91, 00163, Rome, Italy, Very Rev. Damian Weber, C.M.M., Supr. Gen.

American-Canadian Province (1938): *Our Lady of Grace Monastery*, 23715 Ann Arbor Trail, Dearborn Heights, MI 48127-1449. Tel: 313-561-7140; Fax: 313-561-9486. Rev. Thomas Heier, C.M.M., American Reg; Rev. Thomas Szura, C.M.M., Procurator.

Fathers: 6; Brothers: 3

Legal Holdings: Mariannhill Retreat Center, Dearborn Heights, MI.

Represented in the Archdiocese of Detroit.

[0760] (S.M.)—SOCIETY OF MARY

(Marianists)
(Societas Mariae--Marianistae)

General Motherhouse: Via Latina 22, 00179, Rome, Italy, Very Rev. Manuel Cortes, S.M., Supr. Gen.

The Province of Cincinnati (1849); Province of the Pacific (1948); Province of St. Louis (1908) and the Province of New York (1961) have merged June 30th, 2002 to form the Marianist Province of the United States.

Marianist Province of the United States (Society of Mary) (2002): 4425 W. Pine, Saint Louis, MO 63108-2301. Tel: 314-533-1207; Fax: 314-533-0778. Bro. Stephen Glodek, S.M., Prov; Rev. James Fitz, S.M., Asst. Prov. Councilors: Rev. George Cerniglia, S.M; Rev. Joseph Lackner, S.M; Rev. Stephen Tutas, S.M; Rev. Oscar Vasquez, S.M; Bro. Edward Brink, S.M; Bro. Joseph Markel, S.M; Bro. Jack Ventura, S.M.

Fathers: 146; Brothers: 400; Brothers Perpetual Professed: 349; Novices: 33; Aspirants: 40

Legal Titles and Holdings - Properties owned: Marianist Provincial Office, St. Louis, MO; St. Mary's University, San Antonio, TX; Central Catholic Marianist High School, San Antonio, TX; Tecaboca: Marianist Center for Spiritual Renewal, Ingram, TX; Chaminade Preparatory, St. Louis, MO; St. John Vianney High School, St. Louis, MO; Marianist Galleries, St. Louis, MO; Marianist Retreat & Conference Center, Eureka, MO; Marianist Community, St. Louis; Mount St. John; Bergamo Center; University of Dayton; Chaminade-Julienne High School; Marianist Mission, Dayton OH; Governor's Island, Huntsville, OH; Marianist Communities in: Cleveland, OH; Cincinnati, OH; Dayton, OH; Marianist Community, Baltimore, MD; Marianist Family Center, Cape May Point, NJ; Marianist Community Residence, Vernon, CT; Marianist Community Residences, Hollywood, FL; Chaminade/Madonna High School, Hollywood, FL; Colegio San Jose, Rio Piedras, PR; Chaminade University, Honolulu, HI; St. Louis School, Honolulu, HI; Marianist Center, Honolulu, HI; Marianist Communities, Honolulu, HI; Marianist Residence, Maui, HI.

Members serve and staff: Parishes; Universities, High Schools, Middle Schools and Elementary Schools; Retreat Houses; Apostolic Centers; Missions in India, Kenya, Malawi, Mexico, Philippines & Zambia.

Represented in the Archdioceses of Baltimore, Boston, Cincinnati, Hartford, Los Angeles, Miami, Philadelphia, St. Louis, San Antonio, San Francisco and San Juan and in the Dioceses of Belleville, Brooklyn, Camden, Cleveland, Columbus, Fort Wayne-South Bend, Fort Worth, Honolulu, Norwich, Orange, Oakland, Rockville Centre and San Jose. Also in Ireland.

Province of Meribah (1976): *Marianist Provincial Residence*, 240 Emory Rd., Mineola, NY 11501. Tel: 516-742-5555. Bro. Thomas J. Cleary, S.M., Prov. Asst. for Education; Rev. Garrett J. Long, S.M., Asst. Prov. & Asst. for Religious Life; Bro. James W. Conway, S.M., Asst for Temporalities. Councilors: Bro. Timothy S. Driscoll, S.M; Rev. Thomas A. Cardone, S.M.

Legal Holdings: Chaminade High School, Mineola, NY; Kellenberg Memorial High School, Uniondale, NY; Marianist Residence, Accord, NY.

[0770] (F.M.S.)—THE MARIST BROTHERS

(Fratres Maristae a Scholis)

Generalate: Rome, Italy, Rev. Bro. Emili Turu, F.M.S., Supr. Gen; Rev. Bro. Joseph McKee, F.M.S., Vicar Gen.

Province of the United States of America (2003): *Provincial Office*, 1241 Kennedy Blvd., Bayonne, NJ 07002. Tel: 201-823-1115; Fax: 201-823-2232. Bro. James McKnight, F.M.S., Dir. Marist Foreign Missions; Bro. Hugh Turley, F.M.S., Devel; Mr. Frank Pellegrino, C.F.O. Councilors: Bro. Ben Consigli, F.M.S., Prov; Bro. Roy George, F.M.S., Asst. Prov; Bro. Stephen Schlitte, F.M.S; Bro. Hank Hammer, F.M.S., Academic Dean; Bro. Kevin Handibode, F.M.S; Bro. Ken Hogan, F.M.S; Bro. James Kearney, F.M.S; Rev. Bro. Sean D. Sammon, F.M.S.

Brothers: 185

Legal Titles: Marist Brothers of the Schools, Inc.; The Marist Brothers.

Represented in the Archdioceses of Boston, Chicago, Miami, Newark and New York and in the Dioceses of Albany, Brooklyn, Brownsville, Laredo, Rockville Centre and Wheeling-Charleston.

Properties owned, staffed or sponsored; High Schools 15; community houses 32; junior high school 2; community school in Japan 1.

[0780] (S.M.)—MARIST FATHERS

(Societas Mariae)

General Motherhouse: *via Alessandro Poerio 63*, Rome, Italy, Very Rev. Jan Hulshof, S.M., Supr. Gen; Rev. John Harhager, S.M., Treas. Gen.

The first Marist foundation in the United States was in 1863, St. Michael's in Convent, Louisiana. The first Marist Province in the United States was established in 1889 under the name of American Province. This Province was subdivided in 1924 into the Washington Province and the Boston Province; On January 1, 1962, the San Francisco Province was established. On January 1, 2000 the San Francisco and Washington Provinces merged. On September 8, 2000 the merged entity became officially known as the Atlanta Province. The Boston Province continues as a separate province.

Atlanta Province (2000): P.O. Box 81144, Atlanta, GA 30366-1144. Tel: 770-458-1435. Very Rev. Timothy G. Keating, S.M., Prov; Rev. Rene J. Iturbe, S.M., Vicar Prov. & Councilor; Bro. Matthew F. Wade, S.M., Prov. Treas; Rev. Francis H. Springer, S.M., Mission Promoter; Rev. William F. Rowland, S.M., Dir. Vocations; Rev. Charles Girard, S.M., Archivist; Rev. Edwin L. Keel, S.M., Promoter of Marist Laity; Rev. Peter R. Blanchard, S.M., Promoter of Marist Laity; Rev. J. Michael Seifert, S.M., Prov. Council; Rev. John Harhager, S.M., Prov. Council; Bro. Randy T. Hoover, S.M., Prov. Council; Rev. Bruce Lery, S.M., Prov. Council.

Fathers: 71; Brothers: 14

Legal Holdings & Titles: Marist Society, Inc.; Marist College and Marist Center, Washington, DC; Marist Society of GA; Marist School, Atlanta, GA; Marist Society of OH; Marist Society of LA; Marist Community, New Orleans, LA; Marist Society of PA

Properties owned, sponsored or staffed: Community Houses 7; Parishes 8; Seminaries/Houses of Study 2; High School 1.

Represented in the Archdioceses of Atlanta, Chicago, Los Angeles, Miami, Military Services, USA, New Orleans, Philadelphia, San Francisco, St. Paul-Minneapolis and Washington and in the Dioceses of Baton Rouge, Brooklyn, Brownsville, Cleveland, Monterey, Oakland, Orange, San Bernardino, Savannah, St. Petersburg and Wheeling-Charleston

Boston Province (Marist Fathers) (1924): *Marist Provincial House*, 27 Isabella St., Boston, MA 02116-5216. Tel: 617-426-5297; Fax: 617-848-3767. Very Rev. Roland A. Lajoie, S.M., Prov; Rev. Albert DiIanni, S.M., Prov. Dir. of Third Order of Mary, Vocation Dir. & Prov. Council; Rev. Raymond E. Coolong, S.M., Vicar & Council Prov; Rev. Walter Gaudreau, S.M., Prov. Council; Rev. Joseph Hindelang, S.M., Prov. Council; Rev. James Strasz, S.M., Prov. Council; Rev. Andrew Albert, S.M., Prov. Treas; Rev. Robert Graham, S.M., Prov. Archivist; Rev. Normand J. Martin, S.M., Dir. Lourdes Center.

Legal Titles: Marist Fathers of Boston; Marist Fathers of Detroit, Inc.; Marist Fathers of New York.

Fathers: 61; Brothers: 6; Seminarians: 1

Properties owned, sponsored or staffed: Community Houses 5; Parishes 5; High Schools 1; Retreat House 1.

Represented in the Archdioceses of Boston, Hartford and Detroit, and in the Dioceses of Brooklyn, Burlington and Portland (In Maine).

[0782] (O.M.M.)—MARONITE ORDER OF THE BLESSED VIRGIN MARY

Maronite Order of the Blessed Virgin Mary: 4405 Earhart Rd., Ann Arbor, MI 48105. Tel: 734-662-4822; Fax: 734-662-4822. Rev. Joseph Khalil, O.M.M; Rev. Ziad Antoun, O.M.M; Rev. Hanna Tayar, O.M.M; Rev. Paul Tarabay, O.M.M; Rev. Nabil Habchi, O.M.M.

[0785] (C.M.L.M.)—THE CONGREGATION OF MARONITE LEBANESE MISSIONARIES

Founded at the Monastery of Kreim-Ghosta (Mountain of Lebanon), in the year 1865. Established in the United States March of 1991: Agreement between Archbishop Zayek of the Diocese of St. Maron and the Congregation to serve the parishes of San Antonio, Dallas and Houston.

U.S. Headquarters: *Our Lady of the Cedars Maronite Mission*, 11935 Bellfort Village, Houston, TX 77031. Tel: 281-568-6800; Fax: 281-564-6961. Rev. Abdallah Zaidan, C.M.L.M., Supr.

Bishops: 1; Priests: 95; Seminarians: 14; Postulants: 1; Novices: 9

Represented in the Dioceses of Our Lady of Lebanon and the Eparchy of St. Maron.

Our Lady of Mt. Lebanon: *St. Peter Cathedral*, 333 S. San Vicente Blvd., Los Angeles, CA 90048. Tel: 310-275-6634; Fax: 310-858-0856.

[0790] (M.M.A.)—MARONITE MONKS OF ADORATION

Monastery of the Most Holy Trinity: 67 Dugway Rd., Petersham, MA 01366-9725. Tel: 978-724-3347. Rt. Rev. William J. Driscoll, M.M.A., Abbot; Very Rev. Louis Marie Dauphinais, M.M.A., Prior.

Priests: 9; Brothers: 9; Monks in Community: 18

[0800] (M.M.)—MARYKNOLL

Catholic Foreign Mission Society of America, Inc.

U.S. Foundation (1911): *Maryknoll Society Center & Admin. Offices*, Maryknoll, NY 10545-0305. Tel: 914-941-7590; Fax: 914-944-3605. Rev. Edward M. Dougherty, M.M., Supr. Gen. & Pres; Rev. Jose A. Aramburu, M.M., Vicar Gen. & Vice Pres; Rev. Edward J. McGovern, M.M., Asst. Gen; Rev. Paul R. Masson, M.M., Asst. Gen. & Sec.

Legal Title: Catholic Foreign Mission Society of America Incorporated, Training Center; Maryknoll Society Center, Maryknoll, NY 10545.

Houses in Archdioceses and Dioceses:

Buffalo: *Maryknoll Fathers and Brothers*, 127 Chadduck Ave., Buffalo, NY 14207. Tel: 716-875-0005; Fax: 716-875-2322.

Chicago: *Maryknoll Fathers and Brothers*, 5128 S. Hyde Park Blvd., Chicago, IL 60615-4217. Tel: 773-493-3367; Fax: 773-493-3427; Email: chicago@maryknoll.org; Web: www.maryknoll.org/society. Rev. John W. Eybel, M.M., Rector; Rev. William J. Donnelly, M.M; Rev. Herman W. Cisek, M.M; Bro. Joseph Bruener, M.M; Bro. Adrian R. Mazuchowski, M.M; Gregory Darr, Regl. Dir; Mr. Jay Weingarten, Major Gift Officer.

Cincinnati: *Maryknoll Fathers and Brothers*, 6930 Greenfield Dr., Cincinnati, OH 45224. Tel: 513-681-7888.

Cleveland: *Maryknoll Fathers and Brothers*, 10309 Edgewater Dr., Cleveland, OH 44102. Tel: 216-651-2121; Fax: 216-651-8242. Rev. James H. Huvane, M.M; Rev. Richard S. Kardian, M.M St. Theresa's Res: P.O. Box 321, Maryknoll, NY 10545-0321

Denver: *Maryknoll Fathers and Brothers*, 3554 Marion St., Denver, CO 80205. Tel: 303-296-1196; Fax: 303-296-1196.

Galveston-Houston: *Maryknoll Fathers and Brothers*, 2360 Rice Blvd., Houston, TX 77005. Tel: 713-529-1912; Fax: 713-529-0372; Email: mklhouston@maryknoll.org.

Los Angeles: *Maryknoll Fathers and Brothers*, 745 W. Adams Blvd., Los Angeles, CA 90007. Tel: 213-747-9676; Fax: 213-747-8923.

St. Paul: *Maryknoll Fathers and Brothers*, P.O. Box 20626, Minneapolis, MN 55420. Tel: 952-884-1024; Fax: 952-884-1371; Email: minneapolis@maryknoll.org; Web: www.maryknoll.org.

San Jose: *Maryknoll Residence*, 23000 Cristo Rey Dr., Los Altos, CA 94024-7499. Tel: 650-967-3822; Fax: 650-965-3473.

Seattle: *Maryknoll Fathers and Brothers*, 958 16th Ave., E., Seattle, WA 98112. Tel: 206-322-8831; Fax: 206-324-6909.

Washington: *Maryknoll Fathers and Brothers*, 4834 16th St., N.W., Washington, DC 20011. Tel: 202-726-4252; Tel: 202-726-4281; Fax: 202-726-0466.

Priests: 449; Students of Theology: 13; Brothers: 62; Priest Associates: 4

Properties owned or sponsored: Major Society Center; House of Formation; U.S. Community Houses 22.

Represented in the Archdioceses of Boston, Chicago, Cincinnati, Denver, Detroit, Galveston-Houston, Los Angeles, New York, St. Louis, St. Paul-Minneapolis, San Francisco, Seattle and Washington and in the Dioceses of Buffalo, Cleveland, and San Jose.

[0810] (F.M.M.)—BROTHERS OF MERCY

General Motherhouse: D-56412, Montabaur, Germany, Bro. Stephan Geissler, F.M.M., Supr. Gen.

American Region: 4520 Ransom Rd., Clarence, NY 14031. Tel: 716-759-8341; Fax: 716-759-7243. Bro. Jude Holzfoerster, F.M.M., Regional Supr. Assistants Bro. Terrence Mansfield, F.M.M; Bro. Edward Lewis, F.M.M.

Brothers: 12

Legal Holdings or Titles: Brothers of Mercy Nursing Home Co., Inc.; Brothers of Mercy Housing Co., Inc.; Brothers of Mercy Sacred Heart Home, Inc.

Represented in the Diocese of Buffalo.

[0820] (C.P.M.)—CONGREGATION OF THE FATHERS OF MERCY

(Congregatio Presbyterorum a Misericordia)

Generalate and Novitiate (1808): 806 Shaker Museum Rd., Auburn, KY 42206. Tel: 270-542-4146; Fax: 270-542-4147; Web: www.fathersofmercy.com. Rev. David Wilton, C.P.M., Supr. Gen; Rev. Ben Cameron, C.P.M., Asst. Gen; Very Rev. William Casey, C.P.M., Consultor; Rev. Anthony M. Stephens, C.P.M., Consultor; Rev. Thomas Sullivan, C.P.M., Consultor; Rev. Louis Caporiccio, C.P.M., Sec. Gen; Rev. Charles Zmudzinski, C.P.M., Treas.Gen.

Priests: 25; Novices: 1; Students: 9

Represented in the Archdiocese of Louisville and in the Dioceses of Columbus, Cheyenne, Lexington, Marquette, and Owensboro.

[0825] (M.S.S.)—MISSIONARIES OF THE BLESSED SACRAMENT
Missionaries of the Blessed Sacrament

Regional Headquarters: 2933 Street Rd., Bensalem, PA 19020. Tel: 215-244-9211; Fax: 215-244-9211. Rev. Victor P. Warkulwiz, M.S.S., Supr.
Fathers: 2
Ministries in Special Apostolate: Promotion of perpetual Eucharistic adoration.
Represented in the Archdiocese of Philadelphia and in the Diocese of Lafayette.

[0830] (M.H.M.)—MILL HILL MISSIONARIES
St. Joseph's Missionary Society of Mill Hill

International Headquarters: *St. Joseph's Missionary Society*, P.O. Box 3608, SL6 7UX, Maidenhead, England, Web: millhillmissionaries.com. Very Rev. Anthony Chantry, M.H.M., Gen. Supr.

American Headquarters: *Mill Hill Missionaries*, 222 W. Hartsdale Ave., Hartsdale, NY 10530-1667. Tel: 914-682-0645; Fax: 914-682-0862; Email: MHMNAR@aol.com. Rev. Bartholomew Daly, M.H.M., Reg. Rep.
Legal Title: Mill Hill Fathers, Inc.
Fathers: 10; Brothers: 1; Associates: 1
Represented in the Archdiocese of New York and Diocese of Phoenix.

[0835] (O.M.)—MINIM FATHERS

General Motherhouse: Piazza San Francesco di Paola, 10 00184, Rome, Italy, Tel: 011-39-6-4882613; Fax: 011-39-6-4882613. Very Rev. Francesco Marinelli, O.M., Supr. Gen.

North American Delegation (1970): 3431 Portola Ave., Los Angeles, CA 90032. Tel: 323-223-1101. Rev. Mario Pisano, O.M., Delegate Gen.
Legal Title: Minim Fathers.
Priests: 3
Vocation Center, 6043 N. Barranca Ave., Azusa, CA 91702.
Represented in the Archdiocese of Los Angeles.

[0840] (S.T.)—MISSIONARY SERVANTS OF THE MOST HOLY TRINITY
(Missionarii Servi Sanctissimae Trinitatis)
(Trinity Missions)

Generalate-Missionary Servants of the Most Holy Trinity: 9001 New Hampshire Ave., Ste. 300, Silver Spring, MD 20903-3626. Tel: 301-434-0092; Fax: 301-434-0255. Rev. John S. Edmunds, S.T., Gen. Custodian; Rev. Michael Barth, S.T., Vicar Gen; Rev. Dennis M. Berry, S.T., Gen. Councilor; Rev. Francisco Gomez, S.T., Gen. Councilor; Bro. Steven Vesely, S.T., Sec. Gen. & Gen. Councilor; Bro. Jordan Baxter, S.T., Treas. Gen.
Legal Title: Missionary Servants of the Most Holy Trinity (aka) Trinity Missions; Missionary Servants Charitable Trust; Father Judge Charitable Trust.
Priests: 90; Brothers: 24; Student Brothers: 15; Candidates: 59; Deacons: 3; Novices: 10
Ministry in the following areas: Missionary Cenacles; Parishes; Missions; Stations and Specialized Apostolates; Lay Apostolate Secretariat; Counseling Centers; Hospitals and Rest Home Chaplains; AA Programs; Protective Institutions; Prison Chaplains; Community Centers
Properties owned and or sponsored: Generalate, Silver Spring, MD; Parish, rectory and school, Holy Trinity, AL; Philadelphia, PA; School Buildings, Camden, MS; St. Joseph Shrine, Stirling, NJ; Former minor seminary building, Monroe, VA; Residences: Harpers Ferry, WV; Senior Ministry Residence, Adelphi, MD and University Park, MD.
Represented in the Archdioceses of Baltimore, Los Angeles, Mobile, Newark, and Washington and in the Dioceses of Biloxi, Boise, Jackson, Knoxville, Paterson, Pensacola-Tallahassee, San Bernardino, San Diego, Savannah and Tucson. Also in Mexico, Puerto Rico, Colombia and Costa Rica.

[0850] (M.AFR.)—MISSIONARIES OF AFRICA
(Societas Missionariorum Africae)

Generalate: 269 via Aurelia, C.P. 9078 I-00165, Rome, Italy, Rev. Gerard Chabanon, M.Afr., Supr. Gen.

Province of North America: 1624 21st. St. N.W., Washington, DC 20009-1003. Tel: 202-232-5154; Fax: 202-332-8640. Rev. George Markwell, M.Afr., Hospital Chap; Rev. John Lynch, M.Afr., Office of Planned Giving; Rev. Sjef Donders, M.Afr., Prof. Emeritus; Bro. James Heintz, M.Afr., Bursar; Rev. Jimmy McTiernan, M.Afr., Guestmaster; Rev. Thomas Reilly, M.Afr; Rev. Jean-Claude Robitaille, M.Afr., Delegate Supr; Rev. Richard Roy, M.Afr; Rev. Diego Ramon Sario Cucarella, M.Afr., Studies at G.U; Rev. Brian Denis Starkey, M.Afr., Treas.
Priests: 25; Brothers: 4
Represented in the Archdiocese of Washington and in the Diocese of St. Petersburg.

[0854] (M.S.P.)—MISSIONARY SOCIETY OF ST. PAUL OF NIGERIA

Generalate: *Gwagwalada*, P.O. Box 23, Abuja, Nigeria, Very Rev. Anselm Umoren, M.S.P., Supr. Gen.

U.S. Region: *Missionary Society of St. Paul, Inc.*, 3607 Meriburr Ln., P.O. Box 300145, Houston, TX 77230-0145. Tel: 713-842-6090; Fax: 713-747-4263; Web: www.mspamericanregion.org. Very Rev. Desmond Ohankwere, M.S.P., Local Supr.
Legal Title: Missionary Society of St. Paul, Inc., Houston, TX.
Universal number of Priests: 210; Priests in U.S: 36
Represented in the Archdiocese of Galveston-Houston.

[0855] (F.M.M.)—MISSIONARY FRATERNITY OF MARY

General Headquarters: 6A Calle 48-98, Zona 7-Apartado Postal 623-I, Zona 7, Guatemala, Rev. Msgr. Eduardo Aguirre-Oestmann, Gen. Moderator.

U.S. Foundation (1991): 340 Pine St., Seaford, DE 19973. Tel: 302-629-5115. Rev. Ruben A. Soto, F.M.M., Regional Vicar; Rev. Juan Vicente Hidalgo.
Represented in the Diocese of Wilmington.

[0860] (C.I.C.M.)—MISSIONHURST CONGREGATION OF THE IMMACULATE HEART OF MARY
(Congregatio Immaculati Cordis Mariae)
Foreign and Home missions.

Generalate: *Casa Generalizia C.I.C.M.*, Via S. Giovanni Eudes, 95, 00163, Rome, Italy, Very Rev. Edouard Tsimba, C.I.C.M., Supr. Gen.

U.S. Province (1946): *Missionhurst*, 4651 N. 25th St., Arlington, VA 22207. Tel: 703-528-3800; Fax: 703-528-5355. Very Rev. Anselme Malonda Nkuanga, C.I.C.M.
Legal Title: American I.H.M. Province, Inc.; Immaculate Heart Missions, Inc.; Missionhurst, Inc.
Fathers: 39; Students: 1
Ministries in Parishes; Prison Ministry; Campus Ministry; Hospital Pastoral Work.
Represented in the Archdioceses of Boston, New York, Philadelphia and San Antonio and in the Dioceses of Arlington, Brownsville and Raleigh.

[0865] (C.M.C.)—CONGREGATION OF THE MOTHER COREDEMPTRIX
Founded in the United States 1975.

U.S. Assumption Province: *Congregation of the Mother Coredemptrix*, 1900 Grand Ave., Carthage, MO 64836-3500. Tel: 417-358-7787; Fax: 417-358-9508; Email: cmc@dongcong.net. Very Rev. Michael M. Tran Mai, C.M.C., Prov. Supr.
Priests: 63; Brothers: 51; Novices: 3; Candidates: 2
Represented in the Diocese of Springfield-Cape Girardeau.

[0870] (S.M.M.)—MONTFORT MISSIONARIES
(Missionaries of the Company of Mary)
(Societas Mariae Montfortana)

Generalate: Viale Dei Monfortani 65, 00135, Rome, Italy, Very Rev. Santino Brembilla, S.M.M.

United States Province (1948): *Montfort Missionaries*, 101-18 104th St., Ozone Park, NY 11416. Tel: 718-849-5885; Fax: 718-849-7518. Very Rev. Matthew J. Considine, S.M.M. Counselors: Rev. Thomas Poth, S.M.M; Rev. George J. Werner, S.M.M; Rev. William Considine, S.M.M; Rev. Gerald Fitzsimmons, S.M.M.
Legal Title: Missionaries of the Company of Mary.
Fathers: 25; Brothers: 2; Parishes: 2; Community Houses: 6; Scholastics: 1
Represented in the Archdiocese of Hartford and in the Dioceses of Brooklyn and Rockville Centre.

[0895] (O.SS.S.)—BRIGITTINE MONKS
(The Order of the Most Holy Savior)

Priory of Our Lady of Consolation: 23300 Walker Ln., Amity, OR 97101. Tel: 503-835-8080; Fax: 503-835-9662; Email: monks@brigittine.org; Web: www.brigittine.org. Bro. Bernard Ner Suguitan, O.Ss.S., Prior.
Professed Monks: 8
Represented in the Archdiocese of Portland in Oregon.

[0897] (M.E.P.)—PARIS FOREIGN MISSION SOCIETY
(Societas Parisiensis Missionum Ad Exteros)
Society of secular priests, without vows, of Pontifical Right.

Headquarters: 128 Rue du Bac, Paris, France, Very Rev. Jean-Baptiste Etcharren, M.E.P., Supr. Gen.

U.S. Establishment: *Paris Foreign Mission Society*, 930 Ashbury St., San Francisco, CA 94117. Tel: 415-664-6747. Rev. Jacques R. Didier, M.E.P., Dir.
Legal Title: American Auxiliary of Paris Foreign Missions, Inc.
Priests: 2
Represented in the Archdiocese of San Francisco.

[0900] (O.PRAEM.)—CANONS REGULAR OF PREMONTRE
(Norbertines, Order of St. Norbert, Premonstratensians)
(Ordo Canonicorum Regularium Praemonstratensium)
Founded in France in the 12th century. First foundation in the United States in 1893.
Most Rev. Thomas A. Handgratinger, O.Praem., Abbot Gen.

Norbertine Generalate: 27 Viale Giotto, 00153, Rome, Italy, Tel: 011-39-06-571-766-1; Tel: 571-766-212; Fax: 011-39-06-57-80906.

United States: *St. Norbert Abbey*, 1016 N. Broadway, De Pere, WI 54115-2697. Tel: 920-337-4300; Fax: 920-337-4328. Rt. Rev. Gary J. Neville, O.Praem., Abbot; Rt. Rev. E. Thomas De Wane, O.Praem., Abbot Emeritus; Rt. Rev. Jerome G. Tremel, O.Praem., Abbot Emeritus; Very Rev. James B. Herring, O.Praem., Prior; Rev. John M. Tourangeau, O.Praem., Vocation Coord; Rev. John P. Kastenholz, O.Praem., Sec. Treas; Rev. Conrad J. Kratz, O.Praem., Dir. Norbertine Center for Spirituality; Very Rev. David M. Komatz, O.Praem., Dir. of Formation/St. Norbert Abbey.
Legal Title: The Premonstratensian Fathers; NORBERT & CO., a nominee of The Premonstratensian Fathers; Norbertine Fathers; St. Norbert Abbey, Inc.; The Walnut Markets, Inc.; Los Amigos del Peru, Inc.; Norbertine Generalate, Inc.
Fathers: 65; Brothers: 4; Novices: 3
Properties owned, staffed or sponsored: Dependent Priories 4; House of Studies 1; Colleges 1; Chaplaincies 5; Parishes 12.
Represented in the Archdioceses of Chicago, Military Services, USA and Santa Fe and in the Dioceses of Green Bay, Jackson, Madison. Also in Peru.

Daylesford Abbey: *Norbertine Fathers and Brothers*, 220 S. Valley Rd., Paoli, PA 19301-1900. Tel: 610-647-2530; Fax: 610-651-0219. Rt. Rev. Richard J. Antonucci, O.Praem., Abbot; Rt. Rev. Ronald J. Rossi, O.Praem., Abbot Emeritus; Very Rev. John Joseph Novielli, O.Praem., Vocation Dir; Very Rev. Andrew D. Ciferni, O.Praem., Prior; Rev. Joseph A. Serano, O.Praem., Treas.
Legal Title: Nobertine Fathers, Inc.
Fathers: 26; Brothers: 6; Properties Owned, Staffed or Sponsored: Chaplaincies: 1; Seminaries: 1; Parishes: 3
Represented in the Archdiocese of Philadelphia. Also in Peru.

St. Michael's Abbey: 19292 El Toro Rd., Silverado, CA 92676. Tel: 949-858-0222; Fax: 949-858-4583. Rt. Rev. Eugene J. Hayes, O.Praem., Abbot; Very Rev. Hugh C. Barbour, O.Praem., Prior P.O. Box 819, El Toro, CA 92630
Legal Title: The Norbertine Fathers of Orange, Inc.
Priests: 49; Juniors: 14; Postulants: 5; Novices: 1; Deacons: 1
Properties owned: St. Michael's College Preparatory High School, Orange, CA: Summer Camp, Orange, CA.
Represented in the Archdiocese of Los Angeles and in the Diocese of Orange.

[0910] (O.M.I.)—OBLATES OF MARY IMMACULATE

General House: *Oblati di Maria Immacolata*, C.P. 9061, 00100, Roma-Aurelio, Italy, Very Rev. Wilhelm Steckling, O.M.I., Supr. Gen; Very Rev. Eugene King, O.M.I., Vicar Gen.

United States Province (1999): *Missionary Oblates of Mary Immaculate, Provincial Admin. Office*, 391 Michigan Ave., N.E., Washington, DC 20017-1516. Tel: 202-529-4505; Fax: 202-529-4572. Very Rev. Louis Lougen, O.M.I., Provincial. Councilors: Rev. William O'Donnell, O.M.I., Personnel Dir; Rev. Richard Sudlik, O.M.I., Area Councilor-Northeast/Southeast Areas 60 Wyman St., Lowell, MA 01852-2841.Rev. Allen Maes, O.M.I., Area Councilor-North Central/South Central Areas 224 S. Demazenod Dr., Belleville, IL 62223-1035.Rev. Joseph H. Hitpas, O.M.I., Treas; Very Rev. J. William Morell, O.M.I., Vicar Prov; Rev. Thomas Ovalle, O.M.I., Area Councilor-Southwest Area 327 Oblate Dr., San Antonio, TX 78216-6602.Rev. William Antone, O.M.I., Area Councilor-Pacific Area 1329 Griffith St., San Fernando, CA 91340-3905.Rev. Warren Brown, O.M.I., Councilor-At-Large; Bro. William Johnson, O.M.I., Councilor-At-Large.
Fathers: 313; Brothers: 24; Scholastics: 13
Ministries in Retreat Centers, Shrines, Parishes, Chaplaincies, Religious Residences and Houses, Retirement Centers and the Media.
Represented in the Archdioceses of Anchorage, Boston, Chicago, Galveston-Houston, Los Angeles, Miami, New Orleans, New York, St. Louis, St. Paul-Minneapolis, San Antonio and Washington and in the Dioceses of Austin, Belleville, Brownsville, Buffalo, Columbus, Corpus Christi, Crookston, Duluth, Indianapolis, Juneau, Laredo, Manchester, Norwich, Oakland, Palm Beach, Pensacola-Tallahassee, Portland (In Maine), Providence, San Angelo, San Diego, Santa Rosa, Sioux Falls, Springfield in Illinois, and Springfield-Cape Girardeau. Also in Brazil, Canada, Hong Kong, Mexico, and Zambia.

Northeast/Southeast Area Office: 60 Wyman St., Lowell, MA 01852-2841. Tel: 978-458-9912; Fax: 978-458-7274. Rev. Richard Sudlik, O.M.I., Area Councilor.

North/South Central Area Office: 224 S. DeMazenod Dr., Belleville, IL 62223-1035. Tel: 618-394-6985; Fax: 618-394-6987. Rev. Allen Maes, O.M.I., Area Councilor.

[0920] (O.S.F.S.)—OBLATES OF ST. FRANCIS DE SALES
(Congregatio Oblatorum Sancti Francisci Salesii)

General Motherhouse: Via Dandolo 49, Rome, Italy, In July 1966, the American Province was renamed the Wilmington/Philadelphia Province, and the Toledo/

Detroit Province was canonically established.

Wilmington-Philadelphia Province (1906): 2200 Kentmere Pkwy., Wilmington, DE 19806. Very Rev. James J. Greenfield, O.S.F.S., Prov. Provincial Councilors: Very Rev. James Dalton, O.S.F.S; Very Rev. Robert L. Bazzoli, O.S.F.S; Rev. Donald J. Heet, O.S.F.S; Rev. Mark S. Mealey, O.S.F.S. Provincial Staff: Rev. Michael C. Connolly, O.S.F.S., Prov. Canonist; Rev. William E. Davis, O.S.F.S., Dir. Senior Oblates; Rev. Michael S. Murray, O.S.F.S., Dir. De Sales Spirituality Center; Rev. Kevin M. Nadolski, O.S.F.S., Dir. Vocations & Communications; Bro. Edward F. Ogden, O.S.F.S., Dir. Formation & Pres. Prov. Conference; Rev. Barry R. Strong, O.S.F.S., Dir. Prov. Admin; Rev. Mark F. Plaushin, O.S.F.S., Dir. Planning; Mr. Patrick Kennedy, O.S.F.S., Peace & Justice Advisor; Rev. Michael J. McCue, O.S.F.S., Dir. De Sales Service Works.
Fathers: 155; Brothers: 15; Post-Novitiate: 5; Postulants: 1
Properties owned, staffed or sponsored: Parishes 22; Universities 1; Houses of Study 1; Novitiates 1; High Schools 4; Chaplaincies 13; Foreign Missions 4; Middle School 1.
Represented in the Archdioceses of Boston, Philadelphia and Washington, DC and in the Dioceses of Allentown, Arlington, Camden, Charlotte, Raleigh, Venice and Wilmington.

Toledo-Detroit Province (1966): 2043 Parkside Blvd., Toledo, OH 43607-1597. Tel: 419-724-9851; Fax: 419-724-9853. Very Rev. David Whalen, O.S.F.S., Prov; Rev. Geoff Rose, O.S.F.S; Rev. Kenneth N. McKenna, O.S.F.S., Councilor; Rev. Ronald W. E. Olszewski, O.S.F.S., Councilor & Asst. Prov.
Legal Title: Oblates of St. Francis de Sales, Inc.
Priests: 55; Brothers: 11; Scholastics: 6; Postulants: 1
Ministries in Parishes; High schools; Chaplaincies; Missionaries; Armed Forces; Senior Citizens Residence.
Properties owned, staffed or sponsored: Provincialate, Toledo, OH; St. Francis de Sales High School, Toledo, OH; Oblate Residence, Jackson, MI; Oblate Residence, Toronto, Canada.
Represented in the Archdioceses of Chicago, Detroit, Miami, Military Services, USA and Philadelphia and in the Dioceses of Buffalo, Erie, Kalamazoo, Lansing, Oakland, Palm Beach, Saginaw, Stockton and Toledo. Also in Canada, Mexico, and Virgin Islands.

[0930] (O.S.J.)—OBLATES OF ST. JOSEPH

(Congregatio Oblatorum S. Joseph)

Founded in Italy in 1878. Founder: Saint Joseph Marello (1844-1895). Cause of Beatification introduced May 28, 1948; Beatified 1993; Canonized 2001. First foundation in U.S. in 1929.

Motherhouse: Corso Alfieri 384, Asti, Italy,

General House: Via Boccea 364, Rome, Italy, Rev. Michael Piscopo, O.S.J., Supr. Gen; Very Rev. Sebastian Jacobi, O.S.J., Vicar Gen; Very Rev. Giocondo Bronzini, O.S.J., Procurator Gen.

Oblates of St. Joseph Eastern Province: 1880 Hwy. 315, Pittston, PA 18640. Tel: 570-654-7542; Fax: 570-654-8621. Very Rev. Paul A. McDonnell, O.S.J., Prov. Councilors: Rev. Gregory T. Finn, O.S.J; Rev. Joseph D. Sibilano, O.S.J.
Priests: 10
Parishes 4; Community Houses 1; Houses of Studies 1.
Properties owned: St. Joseph's Oblate Seminary, Pittston, PA.
Represented in the Diocese of Scranton.

California Province: 544 W. Cliff Dr., Santa Cruz, CA 95060. Tel: 831-457-1868; Fax: 831-457-1317. Rev. John Warburton, O.S.J., Prov. Councilors: Rev. Larry Toschi, O.S.J; Rev. Carlos Esquivel, O.S.J.
Legal Title: Oblates of St. Joseph.
Priests: 14; Brothers: 3; Students: 4
Parishes 4; Community Houses 5; Houses of Study 1; Shrines 1.
Properties owned: St. Joseph House of Studies, Berkeley, CA; Mount St. Joseph Seminary, Loomis, CA; Shrine of St. Joseph, Guardian of the Redeemer, Santa Cruz, CA; St. Joseph Marello House of Studies, Oxnard CA; St. Joseph's Villa, Soda Springs. CA.
Represented in the Archdiocese of Los Angeles and in the Dioceses of Fresno, Monterey and Sacramento.

[0940] (O.M.V.)—OBLATES OF THE VIRGIN MARY

(Congregation of the Oblates of the Virgin Mary)
(Congregatio Oblatorum Beatae Mariae Virginis)

Generalate: Viale XXX Aprile, 00153, Rome, Italy, Very Rev. Sergio Zirattu, O.M.V., Rector Major.

St. Ignatius Province: 2 Ipswich St., Boston, MA 02215-3607. Tel: 617-536-4141; Web: www.omvusa.org. Rev. William M. Brown, O.M.V., Prov.
Priests in U.S: 31; Brothers: 5
Ministries in Parishes; Hospital and Prison Chaplaincies; Retreats & Parish Missions; Novitiate; Community Houses; College Seminary Shrine Chaplaincies.
Legal Holdings: St. Clement's Eucharistic Shrine, Boston, MA; St. Joseph House, Milton, MA; St. Ignatius Province of the Oblates of the Virgin Mary, Inc., Boston, Ma.
Represented in the Archdioceses of Boston, Denver, and Los Angeles and in the Diocese Springfield in Illinois. Also in the Philippines.

[0950] (C.O.)—ORATORIANS

(Confederatio Oratorii S. Philippi Nerii)

A Confederation of Autonomous Houses first founded in Rome, 1575.

General Confederation: Via Di Parione, 33, 1-00186, Rome, Italy, Tel: (39) 06-689-25-37. Rev. Edoardo Cerrato, C.O., Procurator Gen; Rev. Felix Selden, C.O., Delegate of the Holy See Landstrasser Hauptstr, 56, Wien, Austria, A-1030,

The Oratory of Rock Hill: P.O. Box 11586, Rock Hill, SC 29731. Tel: 803-327-2097. Very Rev. Joseph A. Wahl, C.O., Father Provost.
Fathers: 13; Brothers: 5; Novices: 2
Represented in the Diocese of Charleston.

The Oratorian Community of Monterey: Monterey, CA 93942. Tel: 831-373-0476. Very Rev. Peter C. Sanders, Provost. & Major Supr; Rev. Thomas A. Kieffer, Vicar & Sec.
Total in Community: 2
Oratorian Foundation Inc., Arizona, Yarnell, AZ 85362. An outreach of the Oratorian Community in Monterey.
Represented in the Diocese of Monterey.

The Pittsburgh Oratory: *Congregation of the Oratory of St. Philip Neri*, 4450 Bayard St., Pittsburgh, PA 15213-1506. Tel: 412-681-3181. Very Rev. Drew P. Morgan, C.O., Provost; Rev. David S. Abernethy, C.O., Vicar; Rev. Michael Darcy, C.O; Bro. Paul Werley, C.O; Rev. Joshua Kibler, C.O; Rev. Stephen Lowery, C.O.
Fathers: 5; Novices: 1
Represented in the Diocese of Pittsburgh.

The Oratory of Pharr: P.O. Box 1698, Pharr, TX 78577-1630. Tel: 956-843-8217; Fax: 956-843-2946. Very Rev. Leo Francis Daniels, C.O., Provost; Rev. Mario Alberto Aviles, C.O., Treas. Deputy for Latin America & Vicar; Rev. Jose Encarnacion Losoya, C.O; Rev. Jose Juan Ortiz, C.O; Bro. Nilton Cueto, C.O.
Ministries in Parish work; Services to the poor; promotion of Mexican-American cultural services; Education at all levels; Spanish language communities.
Properties owned: Casa Maria of the Oratory, Pharr, TX; Oratory Academy-Academia Oratoriana, Pharr, TX; Oratory Athenaeum For University Preparation; Pharr Oratory of St. Philip Neri of Pontifical Right.
Represented in the Diocese of Brownsville. Also in Mexico.
Secular Oratory, Lay institute Founded by St. Philip Neri. Principal Work; Federacion Mexicana del Oratorio de San Felipe Neri, American Office, The Oratory, Rte. 4 Box 118, Pharr, TX 78577. The Pharr Oratory is a member of the Mexican Federation of Oratories and at present serves as the American office of all eleven houses.

The Oratory of St. Philip Neri: 109 Willoughby St., Brooklyn, NY 11201. Tel: 718-875-2096; Fax: 718-875-4678. Very Rev. Dennis M. Corrado, C.O., Provost.
Fathers: 5; Brothers: 1

The New Brunswick Congregation of the Oratory of St. Philip Neri: 94 Somerset St., New Brunswick, NJ 08901. Tel: 732-545-6820; Fax: 732-545-4069; Email: oratorians@nboratory.org; Web: www.nboratory.org. Very Rev. Peter R. Cebulka, C.O., Provost; Rev. Thomas A. Odorizzi, C.O., Vicar & Treas; Rev. Kevin Patrick Kelly, C.O., Sec; Deacon Jeffrey Calia, C.O; Bro. Robert Peck, C.O.
Priests: 3; Deacons: 1; Seminarians: 1

[0960] (F.S.R.)—BROTHERS OF THE CONGREGATION OF OUR LADY OF THE HOLY ROSARY

Founded in the United States in 1957.

General Motherhouse and Novitiate: 232 Sunnyside Dr., Reno, NV 89503-3510. Tel: 775-747-4441. Bro. Matthew Cunningham, F.S.R., Supr; Bro. Philip Napolitano, F.S.R., Asst. Supr.
Brothers: 3
Ministries in the field of Education and Pastoral Ministry.
Represented in the Diocese of Reno.

[0970] (O.DE.M)—ORDER OF OUR LADY OF MERCY

(Mercedarians Friars)
(Ordo de Beatae Mariae Virginis de Mercede)

Founded in Barcelona, Spain on August 10, 1218.

Generalate: *Curia Generalizia dei PP Mercedari*, Via Monte Carmelo 3 00166, Rome, Italy, Very Rev. Giovannino Tolu, O.de.M., Master Gen.

U.S.A. Provincial Headquarters: *Vicariate of Mary, Co-Redemptress*, 7758 E. Main Rd., Le Roy, NY 14482-9701. Tel: 585-768-7110. Rev. Richard S. Rasch, O.de.M., Prov. Supr.
Priests: 18; Brothers: 9
Ministries in Parishes, education, hospital and prison chaplaincies, retreats; newman campus chaplaincies; mission word.
Properties owned: St. Raymond Nonnatus Novitiate, Le Roy, NY; Monastery of Our Lady of Mercy, Philadelphia, PA; Saint Peter Nolasco Residence, St. Petersburg, FL.
Represented in the Archdiocese of Philadelphia and in the Dioceses of Buffalo, Cleveland and St. Petersburg. Also in South India.

[0975] (S.O.L.T.)—SOCIETY OF OUR LADY OF THE MOST HOLY TRINITY

International House: *Casa San Jose*, 109 W. Ave. F, P.O. Box 152, Robstown, TX 78380. Tel: 361-387-2754. Rev. Rogelio Rosalinas, S.O.L.T., Gen. Priest Servant.
Priests: 92; Deacons: 6; Novices: 7; Seminarians: 19
Pastoral Ministries: Community House; House of Study-Novitiate, Migrant Ministry.
Represented in the Archdioceses of Atlanta, Galveston-Houston, Hartford, Military Services, Milwaukee, Portland in Oregon, San Antonio, San Juan, Santa Fe and Seattle and in the Dioceses of Albany, Austin, Cheyenne, Corpus Christi, Fargo, Harrisburg, Helena, Kansas City-St. Joseph, Lafayette, Laredo, Pensacola-Tallahassee, Phoenix, Pittsburgh, Portland (In Maine), Providence, Pueblo and Wheeling-Charleston.

[0980] (C.F.M.M.)—BROTHERS OF OUR LADY, MOTHER OF MERCY

(Congregatio Fratrum Beatae Mariae Virginis, Matris Misericordiae)

Generalate: Gasthuisring 54 5041 DT, Tilburg, The Netherlands,

U.S. Region: 7140 Ramsgate Ave., Los Angeles, CA 90045. Bro. John Grever, C.F.M.M., Contact Person.
Brothers: 3
Represented in the Archdiocese of Los Angeles.

[0990] (S.A.C.)—SOCIETY OF THE CATHOLIC APOSTOLATE

(Pallottines)

Generalate: *Pallottines*, Piazza S.V. Pallotti 204 00186, Rome, Italy,

Province of the Immaculate Conception (Eastern) (1953): 204 Raymond Ave., P.O. Box 979, South Orange, NJ 07079. Tel: 201-762-2926. Very Rev. Peter T. Sticco, S.A.C., Prov; Rev. Frank S. Donio, S.A.C., 1st Consultor; Rev. Frank Gaetano, S.A.C., Bursar. Consultors: Rev. Bernard P. Carman, S.A.C; Rev. Frank Amato, S.A.C; Bro. James Beamesderfer, S.A.C.
Fathers: 13; Professed Brothers: 2
Properties owned, sponsored or staffed: Parishes 3; Seminary; High school; Novitiate; Shrine of St. Jude, Pallottine Center for Apostolic Causes.
Represented in the Archdioceses of Baltimore, Newark and Washington and in the Dioceses of Brooklyn and Camden.

Mother of God Province (1946): *Pallottine Fathers and Brothers, Inc.*, 5424 W. Blue Mound Rd., Milwaukee, WI 53208. Tel: 414-259-0688; Fax: 414-258-9314. Very Rev. Leon J. Martin, S.A.C., Prov; Rev. Joseph Koyickal, S.A.C., 1st Consultor; Bro. James Scarpace, S.A.C., Consultor.
Fathers: 9; Brothers: 1
Ministries in Parishes; Retreat House; Hospital Chaplaincies; High School.
Represented in the Archdiocese of Milwaukee.

U.S. Foundation: 3352 4th St., P.O. Box 249, Wyandotte, MI 48192. Rev. Gerard Frawley, S.A.C., Prov. Delegate.
Fathers: 12; Brothers: 1
Parishes 4; Missions 3.
Represented in the Archdioceses of Detroit, New York and San Francisco and in the Diocese of Fort Worth.

Irish Province (1909): Homestead, Sandyford Rd., Dundrum, Dublin 16, Ireland, Rev. Eamonn Monson, S.C.A., Prov.

Queen of the Apostles Province (1909): Via Giuseppe Ferrari, 1-Rome, Italy, Very Rev. Gaetano Ianni, S.A.C., Prov.

U.S. Foundation: *Our Lady of Mt. Carmel Shrine and Church*, 448 E. 116th, New York, NY 10029. Tel: 212-534-0681.
Fathers: 7
Parishes 3.
Represented in the Archdiocese of New York and in the Dioceses of Albany and Pensacola-Tallahassee.

Infant Jesus Delegature of Christ The King Province: *Mission House and Infant Jesus Shrine*, 3452 Niagara Falls Blvd., North Tonawanda, NY 14120-0563. Rev. John Posiewala, S.A.C., Supr. & Prov. Delegate.
Priests: 11
Represented in the Dioceses of Brooklyn and Buffalo.

[1000] (C.P.)—CONGREGATION OF THE PASSION

(Congregatio Passionis Jesu Christi)

Founded in Italy in 1720 by St. Paul of the Cross. First foundation in United States in 1852.

General Motherhouse: *SS. Giovanni e Paolo Monastery*, Rome 00184, Italy, Most Rev. Ottaviano D'Egidio, C.P., Supr. Gen.

Eastern Province, Province of St. Paul of the Cross (1852): *Province Pastoral Center*, 80 David St., South River, NJ 08882. Tel: 732-257-7177. Very Rev. Joseph R. Jones, C.P., Prov; Very Rev. James A. Price, C.P., 1st Consultor; Very Rev. James O'Shea, C.P., 2nd Consultor.
Legal Title: St. Paul's Benevolent, Educational and Missionary Institute of West Hoboken, New Jersey; Passionist Missions, Inc.; Passionist Missionaries, Inc.
Fathers: 134; Professed Clerics: 2; Brothers: 23
Properties owned, sponsored or staffed: Parishes 9; Community Houses 21; House of Study 1.

Represented in the Archdioceses of Atlanta, Baltimore, Hartford, Newark and New York and in the Dioceses of Altoona-Johnstown, Brooklyn, Metuchen, Palm Beach, Pittsburgh, Raleigh, Rockville Centre, Scranton, Springfield in Massachusetts, Wheeling-Charleston and Worcester. Also in Canada.

Western Province, Holy Cross Province: *Passionist Provincial Office*, 5700 N. Harlem Ave., Chicago, IL 60631. Tel: 773-631-6336. Very Rev. Donald Webber, C.P., Prov. Consultors: Rev. James Strommer, C.P., Asst. Prov. Consultor; Rev. Joseph Moons, C.P., Prov. Consultor; Rev. John Schork, C.P., Consultor; Rev. Philip Paxton, C.P., Consultor.

Legal Title: Congregation of the Passion, Holy Cross Province.

Fathers: 60; Brothers: 8

Properties owned or sponsored: Passionist Provincial Office; Stauros International; Immaculate Conception Monastery; St. Vincent Strambi Passionist Community, Chicago, IL; Immaculate Conception Parish, Chicago, IL.

Represented in the Archdioceses of Chicago, Detroit, Galveston-Houston, Los Angeles, Louisville and San Antonio and in the Dioceses of Birmingham and Sacramento.

[1010] (O.S.P.P.E.)—PAULINE FATHERS

(Ordo Sancti Pauli Primi Eremitae)

Founded in Hungary in the 13th Century. First foundation in the United States in 1953.

General Motherhouse: *Ojcowie Paulini - Jasna Gora*, ul. Kordeckiego 2 42-225, Czestochowa, Poland, Rev. Izdydor Matuszewski, O.S.P.P.E., Gen. Supr.

American Provincial Motherhouse (1984): *Shrine of Our Lady of Czestochowa, Pauline Fathers Monastery*, Beacon Hill, P.O. Box 2049, 654 Ferry Rd., Doylestown, PA 18901. Tel: 215-345-0607; Fax: 215-348-2148. Very Rev. Krzysztof Wieliczko, O.S.P.P.E., Prov. & Prior; Rev. Jan Kolmaga, O.S.P.P.E., Shrine Dir.

Priests in U.S: 24; Brothers: 5

Represented in the Archdioceses of Chicago, New York and Philadelphia and in the Dioceses of Greensburg and Norwich.

[1020] (S.S.P.)—PAULINE FATHERS AND BROTHERS

Society of St. Paul for the Apostolate of Communications

Corporate Name: Pious Society of St. Paul

General Motherhouse: Via Alessandro Severo, 58 00145, Rome, Italy, Very Rev. Silvio Sassi, S.S.P., Supr. Gen; Very Rev. Jose Pottayil, S.S.P., Vicar Gen.

United States Province (1932): *Pious Society of St. Paul*, 2187 Victory Blvd., Staten Island, NY 10314. Tel: 718-761-0047. Very Rev. Ernesto Tigreros, S.S.P., Prov. Supr; Rev. Edmund C. Lane, S.S.P., Vicar Prov; Rev. Joseph Eruppakkatt, S.S.P., Dir., ST PAULS/Alba House Communications; Rev. Joseph Javillo, S.S.P., Prov. Bursar; Bro. Richard Brunner, S.S.P., Vocation Dir; Bro. Dismas Beique, S.S.P., Prov. Councillor; Bro. Dominic Calabro, S.S.P., Prov. Councillor; Bro. Edward Donaher, S.S.P., Prov. Councillor.

Legal Title: Pious Society of St. Paul, Inc.

Priests: 13; Brothers: 22

Represented in the Archdioceses of Detroit and New York and in the Diocese of Youngstown.

Los Angeles Province: 112 S. Herbert Ave., Los Angeles, CA 90063. Tel: 323-269-5010; Fax: 323-268-4583. Rev. Marco Antonio Vences, S.S.P., Supr; Rev. Francisco M. Rosas Zevada, S.S.P; Rev. Valeriano Giachino, S.S.P; Rev. Tomas Martinez, S.S.P.

Priests: 5

Miami Province: *Society of St. Paul*, 8455 SW 2nd St., Miami, FL 33144. Tel: 305-480-5377. Rev. Carlos Sabugo Barradas, S.S.P., Supr.

Priests: 2; Clerics: 1

[1030] (C.S.P.)—PAULIST FATHERS

(Societas Missionaria a S. Paulo Apostolo)

Paulist Fathers Motherhouse (1858): 86-11 Midland Pkwy., Jamaica, NY 11432. Tel: 718-291-5995. Very Rev. John F. Duffy, C.S.P., Pres.

Legal Title: Missionary Society of St. Paul the Apostle in the State of New York.

Fathers: 138; Students in Major Seminary: 7; Novices: 3

Properties owned or sponsored: Newman Campus Chaplaincies; Information Centers; Paulist Press; Paulist Radio-TV-Film Communications Svcs.; Paulist National Catholic Evangelization Association; House of Study; Novitiate.

Represented in the Archdioceses of Boston, Chicago, Los Angeles, New York, Portland in Oregon, St. Paul-Minneapolis, San Francisco and Washington and in the Dioceses of Austin, Brooklyn, Columbus, Grand Rapids, Knoxville, Memphis, Oakland and Paterson.

[1040] (SCH.P.)—PIARIST FATHERS

(Ordo Clericorum Regularum Pauperum Matris Dei Scholarum Piarum)

General Motherhouse: *San Pantaleo*, Piazza De Massimi, 00186, 4, Rome, Italy, Very Rev. Joseph Lecea, Sch.P., Supr. Gen.

USA Province (1975): *Piarist Fathers-USA Province*, 1339 Monroe St., N.E., Washington, DC 20017-2510. Tel: 305-279-2333; Fax: 305-279-0925; Email: provinceusa@yahoo.com. Rev. Mario B. Vizcaino, Sch.P., Prov. Supr.

Priests: 16; Professed Seminarians: 10; Novices: 4; Pre-Novices: 4

Legal Titles and Holdings: Piarist Fathers-USA Province, Inc; Piarist Fathers, Inc.; Order of the Pious Schools, Inc.; Piarist Fathers House of Studies, Washington, DC; Piarist Fathers, Queen of Pious Schools, Inc., Washington, D.C.; The Piarist School, Martin, KY; Piarist Fathers Residence, Martin, KY; Devon Preparatory School, Devon, PA.

Represented in the Archdioceses of Miami, Philadelphia and Washington and in the Diocese of Lexington.

New York-Puerto Rico Vice Province: 1900 Road 14, Coto Laurel, PR 00780-2147. Tel: 787-848-1592; Fax: 787-841-5173. Very Rev. Fernando Torres, Sch.P., Vice Prov.

Bishops: 1; Priests: 18; Deacons: 1; Juniors: 2

Houses 4; House of Formation 2; Parishes 3; High Schools 2; Schools 4.

Represented in the Archdioceses of New York and San Juan and in the Diocese of Ponce. Also Calasanzian Fathers and Padres Escolapios de P.R.

California's Vice Province Piarist Fathers: *Piarist Fathers*, 3940 Perry St., Los Angeles, CA 90063-1174. Tel: 323-708-5864; Fax: 323-266-4907. Rev. Miguel Mascorro, Sch.P., Vice Prov.

Priests: 19; Pre-Novices: 4; Seminarians: 4

Properties owned, staffed or sponsored: Parishes 6; Grammar Schools 2; House of Formation 2.

Represented in the Archdiocese of Los Angeles.

[1050] (P.I.M.E.)—PONTIFICAL INSTITUTE FOR FOREIGN MISSIONS, INC.

General Motherhouse: Via F. D. Guerrazzi 11, 00152, Rome, Italy, Very Rev. Gian Battostа Zanchi, P.I.M.E., Supr. Gen.

North American Region: 17330 Quincy Ave., Detroit, MI 48221. Tel: 313-342-4066; Fax: 313-342-6816. Very Rev. Ken Mazur, P.I.M.E., Reg. Supr.

Fathers: 21

Legal Titles and Holdings: PIME Missionaries - PIME Mission Center; PIME College Community, Detroit, MI; PIME Missionaries, Wayne, NJ & Tequesta, FL.

Formation Communities 1; Mission Houses 4.

Represented in the Archdiocese of Detroit and in the Dioceses of Paterson, Columbus and Palm Beach.

[1060] (C.PP.S.)—SOCIETY OF THE PRECIOUS BLOOD

(Congregatio Missionariorum Pretiosissimi Sanguinis Domini Nostri Jesu Christi)

General Motherhouse: Viale di Porta Ardeatina 66, 1-00154 Rome, Italy, Very Rev. Francesco Bartoloni, C.PP.S., Moderator.

Cincinnati Province: 431 E. Second St., Dayton, OH 45402. Tel: 937-228-9263. Very Rev. Angelo Anthony, C.PP.S., Prov. Dir. Provincial Council: Rev. Kenneth Schnipke, C.PP.S; Rev. Larry Hemmelgarn, C.PP.S; Rev. Thomas Hemm, C.PP.S; Rev. Clarence E. Williams, C.PP.S; Bro. Joseph J. Fisher, C.PP.S., Treas. & Mission Procurator; Rev. Kenneth Schroeder, C.PP.S.

Fathers: 139; Brothers: 28; Students in Major Seminaries: 18; Students in Preparatory Seminary: 12

Ministries in Parishes; Missions; Chaplaincies; Shrine; Education; Retreat Preaching; Community Houses; Houses of Study; Military Chaplains; Precious Blood Ministry of Reconciliation.

Represented in the Archdioceses of Chicago, Cincinnati and Military Services, USA and in the Dioceses of Cleveland, Columbus, Fort Wayne-South Bend, Gary, Harrisburg, Lafayette in Indiana, Orange, Orlando and Toledo.

Kansas City Province: *Precious Blood Society Provincial Office*, P.O. Box 339, Liberty, MO 64069-0339. Tel: 816-781-4344; Fax: 816-781-3639. Rev. James A. Urbanic, C.PP.S., Prov. Dir; Rev. Joseph Nassal, C.PP.S., 1st Consultor; Rev. Richard Bayuk, C.PP.S., 2nd Consultor & Prov. Treas; Rev. Aloys Ebach, C.PP.S., 3rd Consultor & Prov. Sec; Rev. Garry Richmeier, C.PP.S., 4th Consultor.

Bishops: 1; Fathers: 48; Brothers: 3

Ministries in Parishes; Missions; Houses of Study; Community House; Chaplaincies.

Represented in the Archdioceses of Chicago, Cincinnati, Denver, Dubuque, Kansas City in Kansas and Los Angeles and in the Dioceses of Davenport, Jefferson City, Joliet in Illinois, Kansas City-St. Joseph, Oakland, San Angelo and Wichita.

Atlantic Province: *Society of the Precious Blood, Provincial House*, 13313 Niagara Pkwy., L2E 6S6, Niagara Falls, Canada, Tel: 905-382-1118. Very Rev. Peter Nobili, C.PP.S., Prov; Rev. Sam D'Agelo, C.PP.S., Sec.

Priests in the U.S: 3

Represented in the Archdiocese of Miami and in the Dioceses of Buffalo and Rochester. Also in Canada.

[1065] (F.S.S.P.)—PRIESTLY FRATERNITY OF ST. PETER

Founded in Switzerland in 1988. First foundation in United States in 1991.

General Motherhouse: *Fraternitas Sacerdotalis Sancti Petri*, Maison St. Pierre Canisius, Chemin du Schoenberg 8, CH-1700 Fribourg, Switzerland, Tel: 41-26-488-0037; Fax: 41-26-488-0038. Rev. John Berg, F.S.S.P., Supr. Gen.

International Seminary: *Priesterseminar Sankt Petrus,*, Kirchstrasse 16, D-88145, Opfenbach-Wigratzbad, Germany, Tel: 49-8385 9221 0; Fax: 49-8385 9221 33. Rev. Franz Karl Banauch, F.S.S.P., Rector.

U.S. Headquarters: *Priestly Fraternity of St. Peter-North American District Headquarters*, Griffin Rd., P.O. Box 196, Elmhurst, PA 18416. Tel: 570-842-4000; Fax: 570-842-4001. Rev. Eric Flood, F.S.S.P., Dist. Supr; Rev. Gregory Pendergraft, F.S.S.P., Dir.-Devel; Rev. Carl N. Gismondi, F.S.S.P., Dist. Bursar.

House of Formation: *Our Lady of Guadalupe Seminary*, 7880 W. Denton Rd., P.O. Box 147, Denton, NE 68339. Tel: 402-797-7700; Fax: 402-797-7705. Very Rev. Josef Bisig, F.S.S.P., Rector; Rev. James B. Buckley, F.S.S.P; Rev. Robert Ferguson, F.S.S.P; Rev. Robert Fromageot, F.S.S.P; Rev. Calvin R. Goodwin, F.S.S.P; Rev. Joseph Portzer, F.S.S.P; Rev. Charles Ryan, F.S.S.P; Rev. Charles Van Vliet, F.S.S.P.

Priests: 8; Seminarians: 75

Properties owned or sponsored: Houses 29; High Schools 1.

Represented in the Archdioceses of Atlanta, Denver, Indianapolis, Kansas City, Oklahoma City and Omaha and in the Dioceses of Boise, Charleston, Colorado Springs, Corpus Christi, Dallas, Fort Worth, Harrisburg, Lafayette in Indiana, Lexington, Lincoln, Little Rock, Paterson, Phoenix, Rapid City, Sacramento, Scranton, Tulsa, Tyler and Youngstown. Also Canada.

[1070] (C.SS.R.)—REDEMPTORIST FATHERS

(Congregatio Sanctissimi Redemptoris-Redemptorist)

Generalate: *Sant' Alfonso*, Via Merulana 31. C.P. 2458 I-00100, Rome, Italy, Very Rev. Joseph Tobin, C.Ss.R., Supr. Gen; Very Rev. Serafino Fiore, C.Ss.R., Vicar Gen; Rev. Jose Sousa, C.Ss.R., Proc. Gen.

Province of Baltimore (1850): *Provincial Residence*, 7509 Shore Rd., Brooklyn, NY 11209-2807. Tel: 718-833-1900; Fax: 718-630-5666. Very Rev. Patrick F. Woods, C.Ss.R., Prov. Supr; Rev. Alfred E. Bradley, C.Ss.R., Prov. Vicar; Rev. Edmund J. Faliskie, C.Ss.R., Prov. Procurator & Consultor; Rev. Carl W. Hoegerl, C.Ss.R., Prov. Archivist; Rev. Robert Pagliari, C.Ss.R., Asst. Procurator & Sec. to Province; Rev. Lawrence E. Lover, C.Ss.R., Canonical Consultor.

Bishops: 2; Priests: 145; Brothers: 14; Novices: 1; Postulants: 13

Properties owned, staffed or sponsored: Parishes 18; Residences 3; Retreat Houses 3; Community Houses 24.

Represented in the Archdioceses of Baltimore, Boston, New York, Philadelphia and Washington and in the Dioceses of Albany, Brooklyn, Harrisburg, Rockville Centre, Springfield, Toledo, Trenton and Wilmington. Also in the West Indies.

Richmond Vice Province (1942): *Vice Provincial Hqtrs.*, 313 Hillman St., P.O. Box 1529, New Smyrna Beach, FL 32170. Tel: 386-427-3094. Very Rev. Jerome L. Chavarria, C.Ss.R., Vice Prov; Rev. Peter E. Sousa, C.Ss.R., Vicar. Consultors: Deacon Darrell Cevasco, C.Ss.R., Vocation Dir; Rev. Glenn D. Parker, C.Ss.R., Cons.

Legal Title: Congregation of the Most Holy Redeemer; Redemptorist Fathers of Florida, Inc; Redemptorists Fathers of South Carolina; Redemptorists Fathers of North Carolina, Inc; Redemptorists Fathers of Virginia, Incorporated; Redemptorists Fathers of Georgia, Incorporated.

Priests: 26; Brothers: 3; Deacons: 1

Properties owned, staffed or sponsored: Parishes 6; Retreat Houses 1; Retirement Home 1; Residences 1; Missions 3.

Represented in the Dioceses of Charleston, Charlotte, Orlando and Richmond.

The Redemptorists Denver Province (1996): *The Redemptorist Provincial Residence*, 1230 S. Parker Rd., Denver, CO 80231-7556. Tel: 303-370-0035; Tel: 303-565-5450; Tel: 303-565-5409; Fax: 303-370-0036; Web: www.redemptoristsdenver.org. Very Rev. Thomas D. Picton, C.Ss.R., Prov. Supr; Rev. Robert Halter, C.Ss.R., Prov. Consultor; Rev. Richard Mevissen, C.Ss.R., Vicar; Rev. Allan Weinert, C.Ss.R., Treas.

Legal Titles: The Redemptorists/Denver Province; The Redemptorists of Denver, Colorado; The Redemptorists of Greeley, Colorado, Inc., Denver, CO; Redemptorist Fathers (Boise, ID), Denver, CO; Redemptorists Society of Oregon (Portland, OR), Denver, CO; The Society of the Redemptorists of the City Grand Rapids, Michigan, Denver, CO; The Redemptorists of Nebraska (Omaha, NE), Denver, CO; Redemptorists of Hamtrack, Denver, CO; The Redemptorist Fathers of Hennepin County (St.Paul-Minneapolis, MN), Denver, CO; Redemptorist Fathers (St. Louis, MO), Denver, CO; The Redemptorist Fathers of Kansas City, Missouri, The Redemptorists of Blessed Sacrament - The Redemptorist Fathers of Chicago (Chicago, IL), Denver, CO; Redemptorist Society of Alaska (Anchorage, AK), Denver, CO; The Redemptorist Society of Arizona (Tucson, AZ), Denver, CO; The Redemptorists Society of Washington, Palisades Retreat Association, A School of Christian Living (Seattle, WA), Denver, CO; The Redemptorist Community of Wichita, Kansas, Inc., Society of the Redemptorist Fathers of Wichita, Kansas, Denver, CO.; Redemptorist Fathers of St. Alphonsus Parish (Chicago, IL), Denver, CO.; Redemptorist Fathers of Iowa; Redemptorists of Berkeley; Redemptorists of Oakland; Redemptorists of Whittier; The Redemptorists (Glenview, IL) Denver, CO.; Redemptorist Fathers, d/b/a Liguori Publications; Holy

Redeemer Center; Redemptorist Society of California; Redemptorist Theology Residence; Redemptorist Hispanic Ministry, Inc.; Liguori Mission House/ Redemptorists: St. Clement Health Care Center; St. John Neumann House; Our Mother of Perpetual Help Retreat House of Oconomowoc, Wisc. Inc., d/b/a/ Redemptorist Retreat Center; Redemptorist Social Services Center, Inc.; Redemptorists of Mattese; Redemptorist Fathers of Bellaire, Texas; The Redemptorists/San Antonio; The Society of Redemptorists; Redemptorist Vice-Provincialate of New Orleans; Redemptorist Fathers of Baton Rouge, Inc.; The Redemptorists of the South Endowment Fund, Inc.; The Redemptorist Education and Formation Foundation, Inc.; Redemptorists of Tennessee; Redemptorist Vietnamese Ministry; Redemptorists of Mississippi
Properties owned, sponsored or staffed: Parishes 16; Retreat Houses 4; Residences 7; Community Houses 13.
Represented in the Archdioceses of Chicago, Denver, Detroit, Los Angeles, Milwaukee, New Orleans, New York, San Antonio, St. Louis, St. Paul-Minneapolis and Seattle and in the Dioceses of Baton Rouge, Biloxi, Grand Rapids, Kansas City-St. Joseph Oakland, Tucson and Wichita. Also in Foreign Missions.

Bangkok Vice-Province: *Redemptorist*, St. John Neumann, 6 Ramkauhaeng 184, Minburi, Bangkok, 10510, Thailand, Very Rev. John Somphong Teowtrakul, C.Ss.R., Vice Prov.

Manaus Vice-Province: *Redentoristas*, Caixa Postal 217, 69011-970 Manaus, Amazonas South America, Brazil, Very Rev. Manuel Soares, C.Ss.R., Vice Prov Region of Nigeria: P.O. Box 29585, Secretariat, Bodija, Ibadan, Oyo State, Nigeria,Very Rev. Callistus Nwachukwu, Vice-Prov.

[1080] (C.R.)—CONGREGATION OF THE RESURRECTION

(Congregatio a Resurrectione Domini Nostri Jesu Christi)

Generalate: Via San Sebastianello 11 00187, Rome, Italy, Very Rev. Norbert W. Raszeja, C.R., Supr. Gen.

U.S. of America Province: 7050 N. Oakley Ave., Chicago, IL 60645. Tel: 773-465-8320. Very Rev. Michael Danek, C.R., Prov. Supr; Rev. Leonard Krzywda, C.R. Councilors: Rev. Anthony Dziorek, C.R; Rev. Joseph Glab, C.R; Rev. Gary Hogan, C.R.
Fathers: 53; Brothers: 4
Ministries in Parishes; Missions; High School; Chaplaincies.
Represented in the Archdioceses of Chicago, Mobile and St. Louis and in the Dioceses of Kalamazoo, Pensacola-Tallahassee, Rockford and San Bernardino. Also in Bermuda.

Ontario Kentucky Province U.S. Address: *St. Cecila - Villa Pacis House*, 515 D S. Shelby St., Louisville, KY 40202. Tel: 502-589-6113; Fax: 502-589-6116. Rev. Daniel Lobsinger, C.R; Rev. Raymond Hofmann, C.R; Rev. John Lesousky, C.R; Rev. John Miles, C.R; Rev. Charles Schoenbaechler, C.R; Deacon Brian Karley, C.R., Supr; Deacon Philip Tremblay, C.R.
Members of Province in U.S.A: 12
Properties owned, sponsored or staffed: Parishes 1; Community Houses 4; University 1.
Represented in the Archdiocese of Louisville.

4252 W. Pine Blvd., Saint Louis, MO 63108. Tel: 314-652-8814. Rev. Gary Hogan, C.R., Rector; Rev. Stephen Gira, C.R., Supr.

[1090] (R.C.J.)—ROGATIONIST FATHERS

(Congregatio Rogationis-a-Corde-Jesu)

Generalate: via Tuscolana 167 00182, Rome, Italy, Very Rev. George Nalin, R.C.J., Supr. Gen.

U.S.A. Delegation: 2688 S. Newmark Ave., Box 37, Sanger, CA 93657. Tel: 559-875-5808; Tel: 559-875-2025; Fax: 559-875-1281. Rev. F. Antonio Carlucci, R.C.J., Delegation Supr.

U.S. Foundations: *St. Mary's Church*, 828 O St., P.O. Box 335, Sanger, CA 93657. Tel: 559-875-2025. Rev. Salvatore Ciranni, R.C.J; Rev. Philip Puntrello, R.C.J; Rev. Antonio Carlucci, R.C.J; Rev. Jupiter Quinto, R.C.J.
Legal Title: Congregation of Rogationists, Inc.
Priests: 6
Ministries in Parishes; Vocation Center; Formation House; Social Service Center.
Represented in the Archdiocese of Los Angeles and in the Diocese of Fresno.

[1100] (S.C.)—BROTHERS OF THE SACRED HEART

(Societas Fratrum Sacris Cordis)

Founded in Lyons, France in 1821. First foundation in the United States in Mobile in 1847.

Generalate: Piazza Sacro Cuore, No. 3, 00151, Rome, Italy, Bro. Jose Ignacio Carmonia, S.C., Supr. Gen.

New Orleans Province (1847): *Provincial Office*, 4600 Elysian Fields Ave., New Orleans, LA 70122. Tel: 504-301-4758; Fax: 504-301-4843. Bro. Ronald Talbot, S.C., Prov. Provincial Councilors: Bro. Ronald Hingle, S.C; Bro. Francis David, S.C; Bro. Ivy LeBlanc, S.C., Treas; Bro. Bernard Couvillion, S.C.
Legal Title: Brothers of the Sacred Heart, (a Louisiana Corporation); Brothers of the Sacred Heart Foundation of the New Orleans Province, Inc.
Perpetual Professed: 51; Ordained Brothers: 4
Incorporated Schools: Brother Martin High School, New Orleans, LA; Catholic High School, Baton Rouge, LA; Saint Stanislaus College, Bay St. Louis, MS.
Represented in the Archdioceses of Mobile and New Orleans and in the Dioceses of Baton Rouge, Biloxi, Gallup and Houma-Thibodaux.

New England Province (1945): *Provincial House - Brothers of the Sacred Heart*, 685 Steere Farm Rd., Pascoag, RI 02859-4601. Tel: 401-568-3361; Fax: 401-568-1450. Bro. Robert Croteau, S.C., Prov. Supr. Councilors: Bro. Mark E. Hilton, S.C; Bro. Raymond Hetu, S.C; Bro. Clifford King, S.C; Bro. Willie A. Morin, S.C., Prov. Sec; Bro. Robert T. Gagne, S.C., Accts. Mgr; Bro. Daniel St. Jacques, S.C.
Brothers: 66
Properties owned: Brothers of the Sacred Heart Provincial House, Pascoag, RI; Mt. St. Charles Academy, Woonsocket, RI; Bishop Guertin High School, Nashua, NH; St. John Residence, Woonsocket, RI; Brothers of the Sacred Heart Residence Nashua, NH
Represented in the Archdiocese of Hartford and in the Dioceses of Manchester and Providence. Also in England.

Province of New York (1960): *Brothers of the Sacred Heart Provincial House*, 141-11 123 Ave., South Ozone Park, NY 11436-1426. Tel: 718-322-3309; Fax: 718-529-6004. Bro. Joseph Rocco, S.C., Prov.
Final Professed Brothers: 49
Ministries in the field of Education; Spiritual Centers; Kenya Missions; Philippines Delegation.
Properties owned: Sacred Heart Center, Belvidere, NJ; Msgr. McClancy High School, East Elmhurst, NY; St. Joseph High School, Metuchen, NJ.
Represented in the Dioceses of Brooklyn, Metuchen, and Trenton. Also in Kenya and the Philippines.

[1110] (M.S.C.)—MISSIONARIES OF THE SACRED HEART

(Societas Missionarii Sacratissimi Cordis Jesu)

General Motherhouse: Via Asmara 11 00199, Rome, Italy, Very Rev. Mark McDonald, M.S.C., Supr. Gen.

United States Province (1939): 305 S. Lake St., P.O. Box 270, Aurora, IL 60507. Tel: 630-892-8400; Tel: 630-892-2371; Fax: 630-892-3071. Very Rev. Raymond Diesbourg, M.S.C., Prov. Supr. Consultors: Rev. David Foxen, M.S.C., Vice Prov; Bro. James Miller, M.S.C; Rev. Pierre Aubin, M.S.C; Rev. Earl Henley, M.S.C; Rev. Michael Camilli, M.S.C; Very Rev. Luis Alfonso Segura, M.S.C.
Legal Title: Society of the Missionaries of the Sacred Heart.
Fathers: 48; Brothers: 15; Foreign Missionaries: 1; Professed Students: 11
Properties owned, staffed or sponsored: Residential Houses 3; Parishes 14; Chaplaincies 2; Foreign Missions 1.
Represented in the Archdioceses of Chicago and Philadelphia and in the Dioceses of Allentown, Ogdensburg, Orange in California, Pensacola-Tallahassee, Rockford and San Bernardino. Also in Colombia, Dominican Republic, Italy and Papua New Guinea.

U.S. Section of the Irish Province for California and Southern States: *Sectional Hqtrs*, 123 W. Laurel, San Antonio, TX 78212-2916. Tel: 210-226-5514; Fax: 210-226-5725. Sectional Leadership Team Rev. William Collins, M.S.C., Supr; Rev. James Dudley, M.S.C; Rev. Michael Fitzgibbon, M.S.C.
Priests: 20
Represented in the Archdioceses of Los Angeles and San Antonio and in the Dioceses of Beaumont, Charleston, Corpus Christi, Dallas, San Angelo and Tyler.

[1120] (M.SS.CC.)—MISSIONARIES OF THE SACRED HEARTS OF JESUS AND MARY

(Missionarii a Sacris Cordibus Jesus et Mariae)

Founded in Italy in 1833.

General Motherhouse: Via dei Falegnami 23, Rome, Italy, Very Rev. Salvatore Izzo, M.SS.CC., Supr. Gen.

American Headquarters: 2249 Shore Rd., Linwood, NJ 08221. Tel: 609-927-5600; Fax: 609-927-5262. Rev. Peter DiTomasso, M.SS.CC., Mission Procurator; Rev. Malcolm MacLeod, M.SS.CC., Reg. Supr; Rev. John Perdue, M.SS.CC., Vice-Rector.
Legal Title: Missionaries of the Sacred Heart of Jesus and Mary.
Priests: 9; Brothers: 2
Represented in the Dioceses of Camden and Harrisburg.

[1130] (S.C.J.)—CONGREGATION OF THE PRIESTS OF THE SACRED HEART

(Priests of the Sacred Heart)
(Congregatio Sacerdotum a Corde Jesu)

General Motherhouse: *Curia Generalizia, S.C.J.*, Via Casale S. Pio v, no. 20 00165, Rome, Italy, Very Rev. Jose Ornelas Carvalho, S.C.J., Supr. Gen.

United States Province (1933): *Provincialate Offices*, P.O. Box 289, Hales Corners, WI 53130-0289. Tel: 414-425-6910. Very Rev. Thomas P. Cassidy, S.C.J., Prov. Supr.
Bishops: 1; Priests: 74; Clerics: 2; Brothers: 15; Deacons: 1; Novices: 3
Represented in the Archdioceses of Chicago, Galveston-Houston, Milwaukee and San Antonio and in the Dioceses of Brownsville, Green Bay, Jackson, Rapid City, St. Petersburg and Sioux Falls.

[1140] (SS.CC.)—CONGREGATION OF THE SACRED HEARTS OF JESUS AND MARY

(Congregatio Sacrorum Cordium)

General Motherhouse: *Casa Generalizia-Padri Dei Sacri Cuori-Via*, Rivarone 85 00166, Rome, Italy, Very Rev. Javier Alvarez-Ossorio, SS.CC., Supr. Gen.
Legal Title: Congregation of the Sacred Hearts of Jesus and Mary.

Eastern Province (1946): *Provincial House*, 77 Adams St., Box 111, Fairhaven, MA 02719-0111. Tel: 508-993-2442; Fax: 508-996-5499. Rev. William F. Petrie, SS.CC., Prov; Rev. Thomas McElroy, SS.CC., Vicar Prov. Councilors: Bro. Paul R. Alves, SS.CC; Rev. Fintan Sheeran, SS.CC; Rev. Robert Charlton, SS.CC.
Priests: 61; Brothers: 3; Novices: 6
Properties owned or staffed: Parishes 11; Community Houses 5; House of Studies 1; Houses of Formation 2.
Represented in the Archdiocese of Washington and in the Dioceses of Brownsville, Fall River and Las Cruces. Also in Bahamas, India, and Mexico.

Western United States Province (1970): *Congregation of the Sacred Hearts of Jesus and Mary*, 2150 Damien Ave., La Verne, CA 91750. Tel: 909-593-5441; Fax: 909-593-3971. Very Rev. Donal McCarthy, SS.CC., Prov. Supr.
Priests: 22
Ministries in the field of Religious and Academic Education; Parishes; Chaplaincies.
Represented in the Archdiocese of Los Angeles and in the Dioceses of Orange and San Bernardino.

Hawaii Province: *Sacred Hearts Center*, Box 1365, Kaneohe, Oahu, HI 96744. Tel: 808-247-5035; Fax: 808-235-8849. Very Rev. Christopher Keahi, SS.CC., Prov.
Fathers: 17; Brothers: 6
Properties owned, staffed or sponsored: Churches 6; Mission 1; Chaplaincies 1.

[1144] (L.B.S.F.)—LITTLE BROTHERS OF SAINT FRANCIS

Founded in the United States in 1970 by Bro. James Curran, L.B.S.F.

Regional Fraternity and Novitiate (1970): 785-789 Parker St., Roxbury, MA 02120. Tel: 617-442-2556; Web: www.littlebrothersofstfrancis.org.
Legal Title: Little Brothers of Saint Francis - Franciscan Fraternity of Peace and Love, Inc.
Professed Brothers: 7
Represented in the Archdiocese of Boston.

[1150] (C.S.J.)—CONGREGATION OF ST. JOSEPH

(Congregatio Sancti Joseph)

Founded in Turin, Italy in 1873. First foundation in United States in 1951.

General Motherhouse: Via Belvedere Montello 77 00166, Rome, Italy, Rev. Mario Aldegani, C.S.J., Supr. Gen.

U.S. and Mexico Vice Province: *St. Leonard House*, 4076 Case Rd., Avon, OH 44011. Tel: 440-934-6270. Rev. Giuseppe Rainone, C.S.J., Prov. Supr.
Priests: 23; Brothers: 1; Scholastics: 7
Properties owned, staffed or sponsored: Parishes 5; High Schools 1; Youth Retreat Center.
Properties owned: St. Leonard House, Avon, OH.
Represented in the Archdiocese of Los Angeles and in the Diocese of Cleveland. Also in Mexico.

[1160] (F.S.P.)—BROTHERS OF ST. PATRICK

(Patrician Brothers)

Founded in Ireland 1808 by Bishop Daniel Delaney.

U.S. Foundation (1948): *St. Patrick's Novitiate*, 7820 Bolsa Ave., Midway City, CA 92655. Tel: 714-897-8181; Fax: 714-898-9020. Bro. Philip Shepler, F.S.P., Pres.
Brothers: 6
Represented in the Archdiocese of Los Angeles and Diocese of Orange.

[1170] (S.P.S.)—ST. PATRICK'S MISSIONARY SOCIETY

(St. Patrick Fathers)

Founded March 17, 1932 with the approval of Pope Pius XI. A Pontifical Society of secular priests devoted entirely to the missionary needs of the Church.

International Headquarters: St. Patrick's, Kiltegan, Wicklow, Ireland, Very Rev. Seamus O'Neill, S.P.S., Supr. Gen; Rev. David Walsh, S.P.S., Vicar Gen; Rev. Brendan Cooney, S.P.S., Proc. Gen.-Rome; Rev. Karl Langsdorf, S.P.S., Supr. for North America.
Total number of Priests: 308; Priests in the U.S: 10

U.S. Foundations (1965): *St. Patrick's (1967)*, 19536 Eric Dr., Saratoga, CA 95070. Tel: 408-253-3135; Fax: 408-253-5433. Rev. Michael Moore, S.P.S., Supr; Rev. Michael E. Morris, S.P.S., Supr St. Patrick's (1965): 70 Edgewater Rd., Box 3080, Cliffside Park, NJ 07010.Rev. Karl Langsdorf, S.P.S., Supr., North America St. Patrick's (1968): 1347 W. Granville Ave., Chicago, IL 60660
Legal Title: St. Patrick's Missionary Society, Camden, NJ.
Represented in the Archdioceses of Chicago and Newark and in the Dioceses of Paterson, San Bernardino

and San Jose.

[1180] (C.S.P.X.)—BROTHERS OF SAINT PIUS X

Founded in the United States in 1952.

Motherhouse: P.O. Box 284, Spring Valley, WI 54767. Tel: 715-778-4999. Bro. Charles Bisenius, Dir.

Ministries in the field of Religious and Academic Education; Health Care; Community services and Administration.

Represented in the Diocese of La Crosse.

[1190] (S.D.B.)—SALESIANS OF DON BOSCO

(Societas Sancti Francisci Salesii)

Generalate: *Salesian Don Bosco*, via Della Pisana, 1111, C.P.18333, 00163 Roma-Bravetta, Italy, Very Rev. Pascual Chavez, S.D.B., Rector Major.

Province of St. Philip the Apostle (1902): 148 Main St., New Rochelle, NY 10801. Tel: 914-636-4225. Very Rev. Thomas Dunne, S.D.B., Prov; Rev. Steven Dumais, S.D.B., Vice Prov; Bro. Thomas Dion, S.D.B., Prov. Economer & Councilor; Rev. William F. Keane, S.D.B., Dir. Formation & Councilor; Bro. Bernard Dube, S.D.B., Councilor; Rev. Stephen Ryan, S.D.B., Dir. of Youth Ministry & Councilor.

Legal Title: Salesian Society, Inc., New Rochelle, NY.

Fathers: 138; Professed Clerics: 13; Students in Major Seminaries: 5; Coadjutor-Brothers: 35

Ministries in: Parishes; High Schools; Boys and Girls Clubs; Camps; Shrine; Retreat Center.

Represented in the Archdioceses of Boston, Chicago, Newark, New Orleans, New York and Washington and in the Dioceses of Birmingham, Passaic, St. Petersburg and Scranton. Also in Canada.

San Francisco Province (1926): *Salesian Society - San Francisco*, 1100 Franklin St., San Francisco, CA 94109. Tel: 415-441-7144; Fax: 415-441-7155. Very Rev. Timothy Ploch, S.D.B., Prov; Rev. Thomas Prendiville, S.D.B., Vice. Prov. Councilors: Bro. Michael Touchstone, S.D.B., Treas; Rev. Mel Trinidad, S.D.B; Bro. Alphonse Vu, S.D.B.

Priests: 74; Professed Brothers: 22; Seminarians: 5

Ministries in Parishes; High Schools; Retreat House; Youth Centers.

Represented in the Archdioceses of Los Angeles and San Francisco and in the Dioceses of Laredo, Monterey, Oakland, Santa Rosa and Stockton.

[1200] (S.D.S.)—SOCIETY OF THE DIVINE SAVIOR

(Salvatorian Fathers and Brothers)
(Salvatorians - Societas Divini Salvatoris)

General Motherhouse: *Curia Generalizia dei Salvatoriani*, Via Conciliazione 51, I-00193, Rome, Italy, Very Rev. Andrew Urbanski, S.D.S., Supr. Gen.

U.S.A. Province (1892): *Salvatorian Provincial Offices*, 1735 N. Hi-Mount Blvd., Milwaukee, WI 53208-1720. Tel: 414-258-1735; Fax: 414-258-1934. Rev. David Bergner, S.D.S., Prov; Rev. Jeffrey Wocken, S.D.S., Vicar; Rev. Scott Wallenfelsz, S.D.S., Treas. Consultors: Rev. Scott Jones, S.D.S; Bro. Sean McLaughlin, S.D.S; Rev. Robert Marsicek, S.D.S; Rev. Dennis Thiessen, S.D.S.

Fathers: 76; Brothers: 28; Clerics: 2; Total: 106

Legal Titles: Society of the Divine Savior; Society of the Divine Savior Ongoing Community Support Trust; Camp St. Charles, Inc.; Lay Salvatorians Inc.; Salvatorian Institute of Philosophy and Theology Inc.; Fund Raising and Public Relations Center; Salvatorian Center, New Holstein, WI 53061.

Properties owned, staffed or sponsored: Parishes 16; Houses of Study and Formation 2.

Represented in the Archdioceses of Milwaukee, New York, Portland in Oregon and Washington and in the Dioceses of Birmingham, Bismarck, Brooklyn, Green Bay, Harrisburg, LaCrosse, Lexington, Madison, Nashville, Oakland, Orlando, Phoenix, Sacramento, Santa Rosa, Savannah, Seattle, St. Cloud, Tucson, Venice, Wheeling-Charleston and Wilmington.

[1205] F.S.C.B.—PRIESTLY FRATERNITY OF THE MISSIONARIES OF ST. CHARLES BORROMEO

(Sacerdotalis Fraternitas Missionarium a Sancti Carolo Borromeo)

General Motherhouse: Via Boccea 761, 00166, Rome, Italy, Rev. Massimo Camisasca, F.S.C.B., Supr. Gen; Rev. Paolo Sottopietra, F.S.C.B; Rev. Gianluca Attanasio, F.S.C.B., Gen. Sec.

North American Regional Delegation: *Priestly Fraternity of the Missionaries of St. Charles Borromeo, Inc.*, 21 Follen Rd., Lexington, MA 02421-5921. Tel: 617-304-4324; Tel: 781-538-6181; Web: www.fraternityofsaintcharles.org. Rev. Antonio Lopez, F.S.C.B., Contact Person; Rev. Jose Medina, F.S.C.B; Rev. Stefano Colombo, F.S.C.B; Rev. Luca Brancolini, F.S.C.B.

Legal Title: Priestly Fraternity of the Missionaries of St. Charles Borromeo, Inc.

Priests: 9

Properties owned: House of Formation 1; Parishes staffed: 1

Represented in the Archdioceses of Boston, Denver and Washington.

[1210] (C.S.)—MISSIONARIES OF ST. CHARLES-SCALABRINIANS

(Congregatio Missionariorum A Sancto Carolo)

General Motherhouse: Via Calandrelli 42, 00153, Rome, Italy, Very Rev. Sergio Geremia, C.S., Supr. Gen.

Province of St. Charles Borromeo (188): *Scalabrinians Provincial Curia*, 209 Flagg Pl., Staten Island, NY 10304. Tel: 718-351-8808; Fax: 718-667-4598. Rev. Matthew Didone, C.S., Prov. Supr; Rev. Rinaldo Vecchiato, C.S., Treas.

Legal Title: The Pious Society of the Missionaries of St. Charles Borromeo, Inc.

Fathers: 95; Brothers: 2

Properties staffed or owned: Parishes 30; Missions 7; Homes for Aged 2; Seminaries 4; Center for Migration Studies.

Represented in the Archdioceses of Atlanta, Boston, Miami, New York and Washington and in the Dioceses of Brooklyn, Buffalo, Orlando, Palm Beach, Providence and Venice. Also in Eastern Canada, Venezuela, Colombia, the Dominican Republic and Haiti.

Province of St. John Baptist (1903): *Missionaries of St. Charles - Fathers of St. Charles*, 546 N. East Ave., Oak Park, IL 60302. Tel: 708-386-4430; Fax: 708-386-4457. Rev. Adilso Balen, C.S., Prov. Supr.

Fathers: 63; Brothers: 2

Legal Titles: The Fathers of Saint Charles; Scalabrinian Community Support Corp.; Scalabrinian Community Formation Corp.

Ministries in 20 Parishes; 2 Homes for the Aged; 3 Missions; 6 Seminaries; 6 Centers for Migrants and Refugees; 2 Diocesan office for Hispanic Ministry.

Represented in the Archdioceses of Chicago, Cincinnati, Galveston-Houston, Kansas City in Kansas and Los Angeles and in the Dioceses of Dallas, Kansas City-St. Joseph and San Jose. Also in Canada, Guatemala and Mexico.

[1220] (S.C.)—SERVANTS OF CHARITY

(Guanellians)
(Congregatio Servorum a Charitate)

General Motherhouse: Vicolo Clementi 41, Rome, Italy, Very Rev. Alfonso Crippa, S.C., Supr. Gen.

U.S. Headquarters: *Servants of Charity*, 1795 S. Sproul Rd., Springfield, PA 19064. Tel: 610-328-3406; Fax: 610-328-1019. Rev. Luigi De Giambattista, S.C., Prov., Divine Providence Province.

Legal Title: Pious Union of St. Joseph.

Priests: 9

Publication: The Voice of Providence.

Ministry for the suffering and dying: Schools for mentally handicapped boys 2; Residences for mentally handicapped adults 2; Parishes 1; House of Formation 1; Chaplaincies 1.

Represented in the Archdiocese of Philadelphia and in the Dioceses of Lansing and Providence.

[1230] (S.P.)—SERVANTS OF THE PARACLETE

Generalate: P.O. Box 539, Cedar Hill, MO 63016-0539. Tel: 636-274-1979; Fax: 636-274-1430; Web: www.theservants.org. Very Rev. Peter Lechner, s.P., Servant Gen; Rev. Philip Taylor, s.P., Sec. Gen; Rev. Benedict Livingstone, Asst. for the Apostolate; Very Rev. Liam Hoare, s.P., Vicar Gen; Rev. Paul Valley, s.P., Treas. Gen.

Legal Titles: Servants of the Paraclete Generalate: A New Mexico Corporation.; Servants of the Paraclete: A New Mexico Corporation.; Servants of the Paraclete, A Missouri Corporation.; Development Office.

Represented in the Archdioceses of St. Louis and Santa Fe.

U.S. Motherhouse (1952): *Servants of the Paraclete*, P.O. Box 10, Jemez Springs, NM 87025-0010. Tel: 505-829-3586; Fax: 505-829-3706; Email: paulsp1000@yahoo.com. Rev. Paul Valley, s.P.

[1240] (O.S.M.)—SERVITES

(Order of Friar Servants of Mary)
(Ordo Fratrum Servorum Beatae Virginis Mariae)

Generalate: *Curia Generalizia dei Servi di Maria*, Convento San Marcello Piazza San Marcello al Corso, 5, 00187, Rome, Italy,

Servite Friars (1999): *United States of America Province Servite Provincial Center*, 3121 W. Jackson Blvd., Chicago, IL 60612-2729. Tel: 773-533-0360; Fax: 773-533-8307. Very Rev. John M. Fontana, O.S.M., Prior Prov; Rev. Luke M. Stano, O.S.M., Asst. Prov; Rev. Frank M. Falco, O.S.M., Prov. Councilor; Rev. Gerald M. Horan, O.S.M., Prov. Councilor; Rev. Michael M. Pontarelli, O.S.M., Prov. Councilor & Prov. Vocation Team Coord 31520 Camino Capistrano, San Juan Capistrano, CA 92675.Bro. Edmund M. Baran, O.S.M., Prov. Treas; Bro. Michael M. Callary, O.S.M., Prov./Corp. Sec. & Province Mission Procurator; Rev. Conrad M. Borntrager, O.S.M., Archivist & Historian; Rev. Christopher M. Krymski, O.S.M., Dir. National Shrine of St. Peregrine; Rev. Lawrence M. Choate, O.S.M., Dir. Prov. Devel; Rev. Vidal M. Martinez, O.S.M., Natl. Asst. Servite Secular Order; Rev. John M. Topper, O.S.M., Dir. Sanctuary of Our Sorrowful Mother; Rev. Robert M. Warsey, O.S.M., Dir. Marian Center & Dir. National Shrine of Our Lady of Sorrows.

Priests: 71; Professed Brothers: 12; Temporary Professed Friars: 3; Novices: 2

Legal Titles: The Order of Friar Servants of Mary-United States of America Province, Inc., 3121 W. Jackson Blvd., Chicago, IL, Tel: 773-533-0360; Fax: 773-533-8307; Retirement Plan of the Order of Friar Servants of Mary-United States of America Province, Inc., 3121 W. Jackson Blvd., Chicago, IL 60612-2729, Tel: 773-533-0360; Fax: 773-533-8307; Charitable Trust of the Order of Friar Servants of Mary-United States of America Province, Inc., 3121 W. Jackson Blvd., Chicago, IL 60612-2729, Tel: 773-533-0360; Fax: 773-533-8307; Servite High School, Anaheim, CA, A California Corporation, 1952 W. La Palma Ave., Anaheim, CA 92801, Tel: 714-774-7575; Fax: 714-774-1404; Sanctuary of Our Sorrowful Mother, Inc., P.O. Box 20008, Portland, OR 97294-0008, Tel: 503-254-7371; Fax: 503-254-9682.

Properties Owned, Staffed and Sponsored: Parishes 2 owned, 7 staffed; High Schools 1; Shrines 3; Residences 6; Hospital Chaplaincies 1; Sister Chaplaincies 1.

Represented in the Archdioceses of Chicago, Denver, Hartford, Portland in Oregon and St. Louis and in the Dioceses of Oakland, Orange and Springfield-Cape Girardeau. Also in Australia, Ireland and South Africa.

[1250] (C.R.S.)—SOMASCAN FATHERS

(Clericorum Regularium Somaschensium)
(Order of St. Jerome Aemilian)

General Motherhouse: Via Casal Morena, 8 00040, Morena - Rome, Italy, Rev. Franco Moscone, C.R.S., Father Gen.

U.S. Foundation: *Pine Haven Boys Center*, 133 River Rd., P.O. Box 162, Suncook, NH 03275. Tel: 603-485-7141. Rev. John B. Vitali, C.R.S., Supr.

Priests: 9

Represented in the Archdiocese of Galveston-Houston and Diocese of Manchester.

[1260] (S.CH.)—SOCIETY OF CHRIST

(Societas Christi Pro Emigrantibus Polonis)

General Motherhouse: 60-962 Poznan Ulica Panny Marii 4, Poland, Very Rev. Tomasz Sielicki, S.Ch., Supr. Gen; Rev. Andrzej Duczkowski, S.Ch., Procurator Gen Via Pietro Cavallini 38, Rome, Italy, 00193,

American-Canadian Province: *Provincial House*, 786 W. Sunset Ave., Lombard, IL 60148. Tel: 630-424-0401; Fax: 630-424-0409. Rev. Pawel Bandurski, S.Ch., Prov; Rev. Jacek Walkiewicz, S.Ch., Vice Prov; Rev. Zygmunt Ostrwoski, S.Ch., Treas.

Priests: 53; Seminarians: 4

Represented in the Archdioceses of Atlanta; Baltimore, Chicago, Detroit, Galveston- Houston, Los Angeles, Milwaukee, New York, Portland in Oregon, St. Paul-Minneapolis, San Francisco, Seattle and Washington and in the Dioceses of Dallas, Joliet, Phoenix, San Diego, San Jose and Toledo. Also in Canada.

[1270] (F.M.S.I.)—SONS OF MARY MISSIONARY SOCIETY

(Sons of Mary, Health of the Sick)
(Filii Mariae Salutis Infirmorum)

General Headquarters: 567 Salem End Rd., Framingham, MA 01702-5599. Tel: 508-879-2541; Fax: 508-879-7667; Email: sonsboston@verizon.net; Web: www.sonsofmary.com. Rev. John Murphy, F.M.S.I., Coord; Bro. Kevin Courtney, F.M.S.I., Fin. Coord; Rev. John Coss, F.M.S.I., Councilor.

Professed: 12

Represented in the Archdiocese of Boston. Also in the Philippines.

[1280] (C.S.S.)—STIGMATINE FATHERS AND BROTHERS

(Congregation of the Sacred Stigmata)

General Motherhouse: Via Mazzarino No. 16, Rome, Italy, Very Rev. Andrea Meschi, C.S.S., Supr. Gen.

North American Province (1940): 554 Lexington St., Waltham, MA 02452. Tel: 781-209-3100; Fax: 781-894-9785. Rev. Robert S. White, C.S.S., Prov. Supr.

Legal Title: Stigmatine Fathers & Brother, Inc.

Priests: 17

Properties owned, staffed or sponsored: Parishes 3; Retreat & Conference Center.

Represented in the Archdioceses of Boston and New York and in the Dioceses of Springfield in Massachusetts and Worcester.

[1290] (S.S.)—SOCIETY OF THE PRIESTS OF SAINT SULPICE

(Societas Presbyterorum a S. Sulpitio)

General Motherhouse: 6 rue du Regard, Paris 75006, France, Very Rev. Ronald D. Witherup, S.S., Supr. Gen.

U.S. Provincial House: 5408 Roland Ave., Baltimore, MD 21210. Tel: 410-323-5070; Fax: 410-433-6524. Very Rev. Thomas R. Ulshafer, S.S., Prov; Judith A. Mohan, Exec. Asst. to Prov; Rev. Gerald D. McBrearity, S.S., Dir.-Formation and Personnel; Rev. Michael L. Barre, S.S., Prov. Treas.

Legal Title: The Associated Sulpicians of the United States, Inc.

Fathers: 69

Represented in the Archdioceses of Baltimore, Hartford,

Los Angeles, San Antonio, San Francisco and Washington D.C. and in the Dioceses of Bridgeport, Lansing, Monterey, Oakland, San Jose and Scranton.

[1300] (C.R.)—THEATINE FATHERS
(Congregatio Clericorum Regularium)

General Motherhouse: *Sant' Andrea della Valle*, Piazza Vidoni, 6 00186, Rome, Italy, Very Rev. Valentin Arteaga, C.R.

U.S. Headquarters: 1050 S. Birch St., Denver, CO 80222. Tel: 303-756-5522. Very Rev. Joseph L. Gallegos, C.R.
Fathers: 17; Clerics: 5
Parishes 9; House of Formation 1; Provincial House 1.
Represented in the Archdioceses of Denver and New York and in the Diocese of Pueblo.

[1310] (O.SS.T.)—ORDER OF THE MOST HOLY TRINITY
(Holy Trinity Fathers, Inc.)
(Ordo Sanctissimae Trinitatis; The Trinitarians)
Founded in France in 1198 by St. John De Matha for the ransom of Christian slaves. First settlement in the United States in 1911.

General Curia: Via Massimi, 114/C 00136, 00136, Rome, Italy, Most Rev. Jose Narlaly, O.SS.T., Min. Gen.

U.S.A. Province (1950): *Province of the Immaculate Heart of Mary*, P.O. Box 5719, Baltimore, MD 21282-0742. Tel: 410-486-5171. Very Rev. Victor Scocco, O.SS.T., Min. Prov; Very Rev. Thomas N. Cerulo, O.SS.T., Vicar Prov. Councilors: Rev. Kurt J. Klismet, O.SS.T., Prov. Treas; Rev. Thomas J. Burke, O.SS.T; Very Rev. James R. Day, O.SS.T; Very Rev. J. Edward Owens, O.SS.T; Rev. Kurt J. Klismet, O.SS.T., Treas. Prov. & Sec. Prov. On Assignment Outside the USA: Rev. Michael J. Conway, O.SS.T Trinitarian Community: Cairo, Egypt,
Trinitarian Communities in the U.S: 14; Fathers: 43; Brothers: 3
Ministries in 9 parishes; Seminary Facility Positions; High Schools; Prison Chaplaincies; Hospital Chaplaincies; India Foundation; Mission for Persecuted Christians.
Properties owned: DeMatha Catholic High School, Hyattsville, MD; Holy Trinity Monastery, Pikesville, MD; Trinity House, Victoria, TX; Trinitarian Residence, Ellicott, MD; Trinitarian Residence, Adelphi, MD.
Represented in the Archdioceses of Baltimore, Los Angeles, Philadelphia and Washington and in the Dioceses of Dallas, Trenton and Victoria. Also in Egypt and India.

[1320] (C.S.V.)—CLERICS OF ST. VIATOR
(Congregatio Clericorum Sancti Viatoris)

General Motherhouse: *Chierici di San Viatore*, Via Padre Angelo Paoli, 41, Casella Postale 10793 00144, Rome, Italy, Very Rev. Mark R. Francis, C.S.V., Supr. Gen.

Province of Chicago (1882): 1212 E. Euclid Ave., Arlington Heights, IL 60004. Tel: 847-398-1354. Rev. Thomas R. von Behren, C.S.V., Prov; Bro. Michael T. Gosch, C.S.V., Asst. Prov; Rev. Corey D. Brost, C.S.V., Councilor; Rev. William L. Carpenter, C.S.V., Councilor; Rev. Richard J. Pighini, C.S.V., Councilor.
Fathers: 64; Brothers: 16
Properties owned, staffed or sponsored: Parishes 11; High Schools 4; Formation Houses 3.
Represented in the Archdiocese of Chicago and in the Dioceses of Fort Wayne-South Bend, Joliet, Kansas City, Las Vegas, Little Rock, Peoria, Rockford, San Bernadino, and Tucson. Also in Belize, Colombia and Italy.

[1330] (C.M.)—CONGREGATION OF THE MISSION
(Vincentians)
(Congregatio Missionis Sti. Vincentii a Paulo)
Founded in France in 1625. First foundation in the United States in 1818.

General Motherhouse: *Curia Generalizia*, Via dei Capasso, 30 00164, Roma, Italy, Very Rev. G. Gregory Gay, C.M., Supr. Gen; Rev. John W. Gouldrick, C.M., Econome Gen.

Eastern Province of the U.S.A. (1888): *St. Vincent's Seminary*, 500 E. Chelten Ave., Philadelphia, PA 19144. Tel: 215-713-2400; Fax: 215-844-2085. Very Rev. Michael J. Carroll, C.M., Prov; Rev. Charles P. Strollo, C.M., Asst. Prov; Rev. Elmer Bauer III, C.M., Prov. Treas; Mr. Allen Andrews, Exec. Dir. Finance. Consultors: Rev. David M. O'Connell, C.M; Rev. Michael Manh Nguyen, C.M; Rev. Emmet J. Nolan, C.M.
Legal Title: Congregation of the Mission of St. Vincent de Paul in Germantown, Inc.
Fathers: 135; Brothers: 10; Students in Major Seminaries: 2; College Seminarians: 4
Properties owned, sponsored or staffed: Parishes 15; Missions in Republic of Panama 8; Universities 2; Major Seminary Residences 1; Novitiates 1; Retreat Houses 1.
Represented in the Archdioceses of Baltimore, Mobile, New York, Philadelphia and Washington and in the Dioceses of Albany, Allentown, Birmingham, Brooklyn, Buffalo, Charlotte, Grand Rapids, Metuchen and Rockville Centre.

Western Province of the U.S.A. (1888): 13663 Rider Trail N., Earth City, MO 63045-1512. Tel: 314-344-1184; Fax: 314-344-2989. Very Rev. Perry Henry, C.M., Prov; Rev. Mark S. Pranaitis, C.M., Asst. Prov; Mr. Thomas Beck, Prov. Treas.
Legal Title: Congregation of the Mission Western Province; Congregation of the Mission Western Province, Texas; Congregation of the Mission Western Province, Louisiana; Congregation of the Mission Western Province, California.
Priests: 142; Brothers: 19
Serving in 19 U.S. (arch)dioceses; Universities; Foreign Mission Stations; Houses of Apostolic Activity; Parishes; Home Mission Parishes; Seminaries; Retreat/ Evangelization Centers.
Represented in the Archdioceses of Chicago, Denver, Los Angeles, Milwaukee, New Orleans, Saint Louis, and San Antonio and in the Dioceses of Belleville, Cheyenne, Dallas, Evansville, Gallup, Jefferson City, Kansas City-St. Joseph, Joliet, Little Rock, Memphis, Phoenix, Pueblo, Springfield-Cape Girardeau, and Stockton. Also in the Archdioceses of Nairobi, Kenya, Nyeri, Port of Spain, Trinidad & Tobago, and Havana, Cuba.

The New England Province of the Vincentian Fathers (1975): *DePaul Vincentian Provincial Residence*, 234 Keeney St., Manchester, CT 06040-7048. Tel: 860-643-2828; Fax: 860-533-9462. Very Rev. Andrzej Rafal Kopystynski, C.M., Prov.
Fathers: 26; Brothers: 1
Legal Title: New England Province of the Congregation of the Mission, Inc.; Charitable Trust of the New England Province of the Congregation of the Mission.
Represented in the Archdiocese of Hartford and in the Dioceses of Bridgeport, Brooklyn and Manchester.

American Italian Branch (Naples, Italy) (1922): *Our Lady of Pompei Church*, 3600 Claremont St., Baltimore, MD 21224. Tel: 410-675-7790. Rev. Luigi Esposito, Supr.
Legal Title: Vincentian Fathers of the Neapolitan Province of Maryland Charities, Inc.
Represented in the Archdiocese of Baltimore.

American Spanish Branch (Zaragoza, Spain) (1926): *Holy Agony Church*, 1834 3rd Ave., New York, NY 10029. Tel: 212-289-5589; Fax: 212-289-8321. Rev. Victor Elia, C.M; Rev. Candido Arrizurieta, C.M; Rev. Jesus Eguaras, C.M; Rev. Jesus Arellano, C.M.
Legal Title: Padres Paules Community - Vincentians Inc.
Fathers: 4
Represented in the Archdioceses of Los Angeles and New York.

[1335] (V.C.)—VINCENTIAN CONGREGATION
(Vincentians)
Founded by Rev. Fr. Varkey Kattarath at Thottakom, Kerala, India in 1904.

Generalate: *Vincentian Generalate*, P.O. Box No. 2250 - Edappally Kochi 682 024, Kerala, India, Very Rev. Varghese Parapuram, V.C., Supr. Gen.

St. Joseph Province: *Vincentian Provincial House*, S.H. Mount P.O. Kottayam 686 006, Kerala, India, Tel: 481-256-3559. Very Rev. George Arackal, V.C., Prov. Supr.

North American Headquarters: *Vincentian House*, 210 5th Ave., S.E., Saint Cloud, MN 56304. Tel: 320-229-7759. Rev. Jose Edyadiyil, V.C., Reg. Coord; Rev. Joseph J. Arackal, V.C., Mission Procurator.
Fathers: 7
Represented in the Archdiocese of St. Paul and Minneapolis and in the Dioceses of Sioux Falls, St. Cloud and Trenton.

[1340] (S.D.V.)—VOCATIONIST FATHERS
(The Society of Divine Vocations)

Generali: Via Cortina D'Ampezzo, 140 00135, Rome, Italy, Tel: 011 39 06 33 12725; Fax: 011 39 06 33 12758. Very Rev. Louis Caputo, S.D.V., Supr. Gen.

American Headquarters: 90 Brooklake Rd., Florham Park, NJ 07932. Tel: 973-966-6262; Fax: 973-593-8381. Rev. Ignatius Okoroji, S.D.V., Rel. Supr. & Master of Novices; Rev. Vernon Kohlmann, S.D.V., Vice Supr. & Vocation Dir; Rev. Mario Muccitelli, S.D.V., Delegate Emeritus.

U.S. Foundations: *Our Lady of Perpetual Help Center*, 90 Brooklake Rd., Florham Park, NJ 07932. Tel: 973-966-6262; Fax: 973-593-8381. Rev. Ignatius Okorgi, S.D.V; Rev. Vernon Kohlmann, S.D.V.
Represented in the Archdiocese of Newark and in the Diocese of Paterson.

[1350] (C.F.X.)—BROTHERS OF ST. FRANCIS XAVIER
(Congregatio Fratrum Xaverianorum)

Generalate - Xaverian Brothers: 4409 Frederick Ave., Baltimore, MD 21229. Tel: 410-644-0034; Fax: 410-644-2762. Bro. Lawrence Harvey, C.F.X., Gen. Supr.; Bro. Daniel Skala, C.F.X., Vicar; Bro. Cornelius Hubbuch, C.F.X., Pastoral Care; Bro. Paul Murray, C.F.X., Gen. Councilor for the U.S; Bro. James Connolly, C.F.X., Dir. Volunteers & Vocation; Bro. Jerimiah O'Leary, C.F.X., Coord. Peace & Justice; Ms. Alice Hession, Dir. Xaverian Sponsored Schools; Bro. Peter Campbell, C.F.X., Congregational Treas; Mr. Richard Costello, Dir. Devel.
Brothers: 241
Legal Titles: Xaverian Brothers USA Inc.; Isidore Charitable Trust; Paul van Gerwen Religious & Charitable Trust.
Ministries in the field of: Religious and Academic Education at all levels; Diocesan Offices; Pastoral Ministry; Mission Schools; Communities; Houses and House of Formation.
Represented in the Archdioceses of Baltimore, Boston, Chicago, Los Angeles, Louisville, Milwaukee, New York and Washington and in the Dioceses of Arlington, Brooklyn, Charleston, Norwich, Richmond, Venice, Wilmington and Worcester. Also in Bolivia, Belgium, Congo, England, Haiti, Kenya and Lithuania.

[1360] (S.X.)—XAVERIAN MISSIONARY FATHERS
(Saint Francis Xavier Foreign Mission Society)
(Pia Societas Sancti Francisci Xaverii pro Exteris Missionibus)

General Motherhouse: *Istituto Saveriano Missioni Estere*, Viale Vaticano 40 00165, Rome, Italy, Very Rev. Rino Benzoni, S.X., Supr. Gen.

U.S. Province: *Xaverian Missionary Fathers*, 12 Helene Ct., Wayne, NJ 07470. Tel: 973-942-2975; Fax: 973-942-5012. Very Rev. Carl S. Chudy, S.X., Prov.
Fathers: 17 ; Seminarians: 6
Mission Houses 2; Houses of Formation 2.
Represented in the Archdioceses of Boston, Chicago and Milwaukee and in the Diocese of Paterson.

Index for Religious Institutes of Women

(The initial D or P indicates Diocesan or Pontifical Jurisdiction.)

Religious Order Initials for Women

Initials	Order	Code
A.B.S.	Auxiliaries of the Blessed Sacrament	[]
A.C.J.	Handmaids of the Sacred Heart of Jesus	[1870]
A.D.	Sisters of the Lamb of God	[2260]
A.I.M.	Association of Mary Immaculate	[]
A.N.G.	A New Genesis	[]
A.P.	Nuns of Perpetual Adoration of Blessed Sacrament	[3190]
A.P.B.	Adorers of the Precious Blood	[0110]
A.P.G.	Sisters of Perpetual Adoration	[3195]
A.R.	Handmaids of the Sacred Heart of Jesus for Reparation	[1880]
A.R.	Augustinian Recollects	[]
A.S.C.	Adorers of the Blood of Christ	[0100]
A.S.C.J.	Apostles of the Sacred Heart of Jesus	[0130]
B.C.	Notre Dame du Bon Conseil (Quebec)	[]
Bethl.	Bethlemita Daughters of the Sacred Heart of Jesus	[0910]
B.V.M.	Sisters of Charity of Blessed Virgin Mary	[0430]
B.V.M.C.	Blessed Virgin Missionaries of Carmel	[]
C.a.Ch.	Carmeilte Sisters of Charity	[0340]
Carmel.D.C.J.	Carmelite Sisters of the Divine Heart of Jesus	[0360]
C.B.S.	Congregation of Bon Secours	[0270]
C.C.	Carmel Community	[0310]
C.C.V.I.	Sisters of Charity of Incarnate Word	[0460]
CCVI	Sisters of Charity of Incarnate Word (Houston, TX)	[0470]
C.C.W.	Carmeiite Community of the Word	[0315]
C.D.P.	Sisters of Divine Providence	[0990]
C.D.P.	Sisters of Divine Providence of Melbourne, Kentucky	[1000]
C.D.P.	Sisters of Divine Providence of San Antonio, TX	[1010]
C.D.P.	Capuchin Sisters (Spain)	[]
C.D.S.	Congregation of Divine Spirit	[1040]
C.F.M.M.	Minim Daughters of Mary Immaculate	[2675]
C.F.P.	Feminine Congregation of the Passion	[]
C.F.P.	Mexican Passionist Sisters	[]
C.G.S.	Contemplatives of Good Shepherd	[1830]
C.H.F.	Sisters of Holy Faith	[1940]
C H.M.	Congregation of Humility of Mary	[2100]
C.H.S.	Community of the Holy Spirit	[2020]
C.I.C.	Sisters of Immaculate Conception	[2120]
C.I.J.	Congregation of Infant Jesus	[2230]
C.J.C.	Poor Sisters of Jesus Crucified and Sorrowful Mother	[3240]
C.K.	School Sisters of Christ the King	[]
C.L.H.C.	Congregation of Our Lady Help of the Clergy	[3090]
C.M.C.	Congregation of Mother of Carmel	[]
C.M.R.	Congregation of Mary Queen	[0397]
C.M.S.	Comboni Missionary Sisters	[0690]
C.M.S.	Cashel Mercy Sisters	[2515]
C.M.S.T.	Missionary Carmelites of St. Teresa	[0390]
C.N.D.	Congregation of Notre Dame	[2980]
C.O.C.	Companions of Christ	[]
C.P.	Religious of the Passion of Jesus Christ	[3170]
C.P.	Sisters of the Cross and Passion	[3180]
C.P.C.	Capuchin Poor Clares	[]
C.P.C.	St. Clare Capuchin Sisters	[]
C.P.P.S.	Sisters of the Precious Blood Dayton, Ohio	[3260]
C.P.P.S.	Sisters of the Most Precious Blood, (O'Fallon, MO)	[3270]
C.P.S.	Missionary Sisters of the Precious Blood	[2850]
C.R.	Sisters of the Resurrection	[3480]
C.S.	Company of the Savior	[0710]
C.S.	The Christian Sisters (Pious Union)	[]
C.S.A.	Sisters of Charity of St. Augustine	[0580]
C.S.A.	Sisters of St. Agnes	[3710]
C.S.A.	Albertine Sisters (Krakow, Poland)	[]
C.S.A.C.	Sisters of the Catholic Apostolate (Pallottine)	[3140]
C.S.B.	Congregation of St. Brigid	[3735]
C.S.C.	Congregation of Sisters of Holy Cross	[1920]
C.S.C.	Sisters of Holy Cross	[1930]
C.S.C.	Sisters of Holy Cross and Seven Dolors	[]
C.S.E.	Carmelite Sisters of the Eucharist	[]
C.S.F.N.	Sisters of Holy Family of Nazareth	[1970]
C.S.J.	Hermanas Carmelitas de San Jose	[1895]
C.S.J.	Sisters of St. Joseph (Boston, Brighton)	[3830-01]
C.S.J.	Sisters of St. Joseph (Orange)	[3830-03]
C.S.J.	Sisters of St. Joseph (Rockville Centre, Brentwood)	[3830-05]
C.S.J.	Sisters of St. Joseph (Pittsburgh, Baden)	[3830-13]
C.S.J.	Sisters of St. Joseph (Salina, Concordia)	[3830-15]
C.S.J.	Sisters of St. Joseph (Wichita)	[3830-18]
C.S.J.	Congregation of the Sisters of St. Joseph	[3832]
C.S.J.	Sisters of St. Joseph of Carondelet	[3840]
C.S.J.	Sisters of St. Joseph of Chambery	[3850]
C.S.J.	Sisters of St. Joseph (Lyons, France)	[3870]
C.S.J.	Sisters of St. Joseph of Medaille	[3880]
C.S.JB.	Sisters of St. John the Baptist	[3820]
C.S.J.P.	Sisters of St. Joseph of Peace	[3890]
C.S.M.	Sisters of St. Martha of Antigonish N.S	[3937]
C.S.N.	Congregation of Sisters of Nazareth	[]
C.S.R.	Sisters of Holy Redeemer	[2000]
C.S.S.F.	Felician Sisters	[1170]
C.S.Sp.	Sisters of Holy Spirit	[2030]
C.S.S.T.	Carmelite Sisters of St. Teresa	[]
C.S.T.	Carmelite Sisters of St. Therese of Infant Jesus	[0380]
C.V.D.	Sisters of Bethany	[0250]
C.V.I.	Congregation of Incarnate Word and Blessed Sacrament	[2190]
C.V.I.	Religious of the Incarnate Word	[3449]
D.C.	Daughters of Charity of St. Vincent de Paul	[0760]
D.C.	Daughters of the Cross	[0770]
D.C.M.	Diocesan Carmelites of Maine	[]
D.C.P.B.	Daughters of Charity of Most Precious Blood	[0740]
D.D.L.	Daughters of Divine Love	[0793]
D.H.M.	Daughters of Heart of Mary	[0810]
D.H.S.	Daughters of the Holy Spirit	[0820]
D.L.F.	Daughters of Our Lady of Fatima	[]
D.L.J.C.	Disciples of the Lord Jesus Christ	[0965]
D.M.	Daughters of Mary of the Immaculate Conception	[0860]
D.M.	Daughters of Our Lady of Mercy	[0890]
D.M.I.	Daughters of Mary Immaculate (Chaldean)	[]
D.M.J.	Daughters of Mary and Joseph	[0880]
D.O.M.	Daughters of Mercy (Croatian)	[]
D.S.F.	Daughters of St. Francis of Assisi	[0920]
D.S.M.P.	Daughters of St. Mary of Providence	[0940]
D.W.	Daughters of Wisdom	[0960]
E.F.M.S.	Eucharistic Franciscan Missionary Sisters	[1150]
E.I.N.	Servants of the Immaculate Child Mary	[3615]
E.M.S.	Eucharistic Missionary Society	
F.A.S.	Franciscan Apostolic Sisters	
F.C.	Daughters of the Cross of Liege	[0
F.C.J.	Society of Sisters Faithful Companions of Jesus	[4
F.C.S.C.J.	Daughters of Charity of the Sacred Heart of Jesus	[0
F.D.C.	Daughters of Divine Charity	[0
Fd.CC.	Canossian Daughters of Charity	[0
F.D.L.P.	Daughters of Providence	
F.D.N.S.C.	Daughters of Our Lady of the Sacred Heart	[0
F.D.P.	Daughters of Divine Providence	[08
F.D.Z.	Daughters of Divine Zeal	[07
F.H.I.C.	Franciscan Hospitaller Sisters of the Immaculate Conception	[12
F.H.M.	Franciscan Handmaids of the Most Pure Heart of Mary	[12
F.H.M.	Franciscan Sisters Daughters of Mercy	[12
F.J.	Congregation of the Daughters of Jesus	[08
F.L.G.	Franciscan Sisters of Our Lady of Grace	
F.M.A.	Daughters of Mary Help of Christians	[08
F.M.I.	Congregation of the Daughters of Mary Immaculate (Marianist Sisters)	[08
F.M.I.	Franciscan Sisters of Mary Immaculate of the Third Order of St. Francis of Assisi	[15
F.M.I.J.	Franciscan Missionaries of the Infant Jesus	[13
F.M.M.	The Franciscan Missionaries of Mary	[13
F.M.S.A.	Franciscan Missionary Sisters for Africa	[13
F.M.S.C.	Franciscan Missionary Sisters of the Sacred Heart	[14
F.M.S.J.	Mill Hill Sisters	[14
F.M.S.R.	Daughters of Our Lady of Holy Rosary	[08
F.N.S.S.C.	Franciscan Sisters of Our Lady of the Sacred Heart	
F.S.E.	The Institute of the Franciscan Sisters of the Eucharist	[12
F.S.G.M.	Sisters of St. Francis of the Martyr St. George	[16
F.S.J.	Religious Daughters of St. Joseph	[09
F.S.M.	Franciscan Sisters of Mary	[14
F.S.O.L.	Franciscan Sisters of Our Lady	
F.S.P.	Pious Society Daughters of St. Paul	[09
F.S.P.	Franciscan Sisters of Peace	[14
F.S.P.A.	Congregation of the Sisters of the Third Order of St. Francis of Perpetual Adoration	[17
F.S.R.	Franciscan Sisters of Ringwood	[14
F.S.S.C.	Franciscan Sisters of St. Clare (Pious Union)	
F.S.S.E.	Franciscan Sisters of St. Elizabeth	[14
F.S.S.J.	Franciscan Sisters of St. Joseph	[14
F S.S.M.	Franciscan Sisters of the Sorrowful Mother	
F.S.Sp.J.	Franciscan Sisters of the Spirit of Jesus	
G.H.M.S.	Home Mission Sisters of America (Glenmary)	[20
G.N.S.H.	Grey Nuns of the Sacred Heart	[18
H.B.S.	Hermanas Contemplativas del Buen Pastor	
H.C.G.	Hermanas Catequistas Guadalupanas	[19
H.F.deS.J.	Franciscan Sisters of St. Joseph (Mexico City)	

.S.J.	Franciscan Sisters of St. Joseph	[1480]
.S.	Congregation de Hermanas Guadalupanas de la Salle	[]
.C.J.	Congregation of the Handmaids of the Holy Child Jesus	[1855]
.S.	Society of Helpers	[1890]
.	Hermanas Josefinas	[1910]
.D.	Las Hermanas de Juan Diego	[]
.	Sisters of the Humility of Mary	[2110]
.C.	Hermits of Mount Carmel	[]
.S.S.	Mercedarian Sisters of the Blessed Sacrament	[2590]
.S.S.	Religious Sisters of the Apostolate of the Blessed Sacrament	[3370]
.Carm.	Hermits of Our Lady of Mt. Carmel	[]
.B.	Congregation of the Handmaids of the Precious Blood	[1860]
.F.	Sisters of the Holy Rosary of Fatima (Mexico)	[]
.H.	Handmaids of the Sacred Heart of Pohang	[]
.M.	Hermit Sisters of Mary	[]
p.S.	Daughters of the Holy Spirit Nazareth of the Good Shepherd	[]
.S.	Hermanas del Servicio Social	[]
.S.R.	Hermit Sisters of Romuald	[]
.	Handmaids of the Most Holy Trinity	[]
.M.	Sisters, Home Visitors of Mary	[2090]
.V.M.	Institute of the Blessed Virgin Mary (Loretto Sisters)	[2370]
.V.M.	Institute of the Blessed Virgin Mary (Loretto Sisters)	[2380]
.	Vietnamese Sisters Incarnational Consecration	[]
.M.	Incarnatio-Consecratio-Missio	[2187]
.M.	Missionary Sisters of the Immaculate Heart of Mary	[2750]
.M.	Sisters of the Immaculate Heart of Mary at Mirinae	[2182]
.M.	Sisters of the Immaculate Heart of Mary Mother of Christ	[2183]
.M.	Sisters Servants of the Immaculate Heart of Mary	[2150]
.M.	Sisters Servants of the Immaculate Heart of Mary	[2160]
.M.	Sisters Servants of the Immaculate Heart of Mary	[2170]
.M.	Sisters Servants of the Immaculate Heart of Mary	[2180]
.M.	The California Institute of the Sisters of the Most Holy and Immaculate Heart of the Blessed Virgin Mary	[2930]
.M.	Sisters of the Immaculate Heart of Mary of Wichita	[2185]
.	Sisters of the Infant Jesus	[2240]
.	Sisters of Charity of the Infant Mary	[]
.S.M.	Secular Institute of Schoenstatt Sisters of Mary	[]
.B.S.	Congregation of the Incarnate Word and Blessed Sacrament	[2200]
.B.S.	Congregation of the Incarnate Word and Blessed Sacrament	[2205]
S.O.P.	Dominican Oblates of Jesus (Spain)	[]
B.	Ladies of Bethany	[]
C.M.	Sisters of the Little Company of Mary	[2270]
H.C.N.T.	Lovers of the Holy Cross Nha Trang	[2385]
H.C.	Lovers of the Holy Cross Sisters	[2390]
H.C.	Lovers of the Holy Cross Sisters	[2392]
M.S.C.	Little Missionary Sisters of Charity	[2290]
S.	Lasallian Sisters (Vietnam)	[]
S.A.	Little Sisters of the Assumption	[2310]
S.G.	Little Sisters of the Gospel (France)	[]
S.I.C.	Little Servant Sisters of the Immaculate Conception	[2300]
S.J.	Little Sisters of Jesus	[2330]
S.J.M.	Little Sisters of Jesus and Mary	[2331]
S.P.	Little Sisters of the Poor	[2340]
M.C.	Consolata Missionary Sisters	[0720]
M.C.	Missionaries of Charity	[2710]
M.C.	Poor Clare Missionary Sisters	[2840]
M.C.D.P.	Missionary Catechists of Divine Providence, San Antonio, TX	[2690]
M.C.M.	Cordi Marian Sisters	[]
M.C.P.	Missioneras Catequestas de los Pobres	[]
M.C.S.	Missionary Sisters of the Sacred Side	[]
M.C.S.J.M.	Congregation of Missionary Catechists of the Sacred Heart of Jesus and Mary	[]
M.D.	Mothers of the Helpless	[]
M.D.P.V.M.	Missionary Daughters of the Most Pure Virgin Mary	[]
M.E.	Missionary Ecumenical (Rome)	[]
M.C.SS.CC.J.M.	Missionary Catechists of the Sacred Hearts of Jesus and Mary	[2700]
M.E.S.S.T.	Eucharistic Missionaries of the Most Holy Trinity	[]
M.E.S.T.	Eucharistic Missionaries of St. Theresa (Mexico)	[]
M.F.P.	Franciscan Missionaries Our Lady of Peace	[]
M.G.Sp.S.	Guadalupan Missionaries of the Holy Spirit	[1845]
M.H.S.	Sisters of the Most Holy Sacrament	[2940]
M.H.S.H.	Mission Helpers of the Sacred Heart	[2720]
M.I.C.	Missionary Sisters of the Immaculate Conception (Canada)	[]
M.J.	Missionary Sisters of Jesus	[]
M.J.M.J.	Missionaries of Jesus, Mary and Joseph	[2770]
M.M.	Maryknoll Sisters of St. Dominic	[2470]
M.M.B.	Mercedarian Missionaries of Berriz	[2510]
M.M.D.	Servite Missionary Sisters of the Sorrowful Mother	[]
M.M.M.	Medical Missionaries of Mary	[2480]
M.M.S.	Medical Mission Sisters	[2490]
M.O.M.	Missionary Sisters of Our Lady of Mercy	[2830]
M.P.F.	Religious Teachers Filippini	[3430]
M.P.H.	Missionary Sisters of Our Lady of Perpetual Help	[]
M.P.S.	Misioneras del Perpetual Socorro	[]
M.P.S.	Missionary Sisters of Our Lady of Perpetual Help	[]
M.P.V.	Religious Venerini Sisters	[4180]
M.R.	Marianist Sisters	[]
M.S.	Marian Sisters of the Diocese of Lincoln	[2400]
M.S.B.T.	Missionary Servants of the Most Blessed Trinity	[2790]
M.S.C.	Congregation of the Marianites of the Holy Cross	[2410]
M.S.C.	Missionary Sisters of the Most Sacred Heart of Jesus of Hiltrup	[2800]
M.S.C.	Missionary Sisters of the Sacred Heart	[2860]
M.S.C.Gpe.	Missionaries of the Sacred Heart of Jesus and of Our Lady of Guadalupe	[2865]
M.S.C.K.	Missionary Sisters of Christ the King	[2715]
M.S.E.	Missionary Sisters of the Eucharist	[2527]
M.S.F.	Missionary Sisters of the Holy Family	[]
M.S.H.F.	Missionary Sisters of the Holy Family (Poland)	[]
M.S.H.R.	Missionary Sisters of the Holy Rosary	[2730]
M.S.J.	Medical Sisters of St. Joseph	[2500]
M.S.K.C.P.	Missionary Sisters of Christ the King of Polonia	[]
M.S.M.G.	Missionary Sisters of Mother of God	[2810]
M.S.O.L.A.	Missionary Sisters of Our Lady of Africa	[2820]
M.S.S.A.	Missionary Servants of St. Anthony	[2890]
M.S.S.C.B.	Missionary Sisters of St. Charles Borromeo	[2900]
M.S.S.J.	Missionary Servants of St. Joseph (Spain)	[]
M.S.Sp.	Mission Sisters of the Holy Spirit	[2740]
M.SS.S.	Missionary Sisters of the Most Blessed Sacrament	[2780]
M.T.G.	Adorers of the Holy Cross	[4155]
M.X.Y.	The Yarumal Foreign Mission Institute (Colombia)	[]
N.A.U.-O.L.C.	North American Unions of Sisters of Our Lady of Charity	[3070]
N.D.	Notre Dame Sisters	[2960]
N.D.S.	Congregation of Notre Dame de Sion	[2950]
O.A.R.	Augustinian Recollect Sisters	[]
O.B.T.	Sisters Oblates to the Blessed Trinity	[3020]
O.C.A.	Carmelite Vietnamese of Our Lady of Mt. Carmel	[]
O.Carm.	Calced Carmelites	[0300]
O.Carm.	Carmelite Nuns of the Ancient Observance	[0320]
O.Carm.	Carmelite Sisters for Aged and Infirm	[0330]
O.Carm.	Carmelite Sisters (Corpus Christi)	[0350]
O.Carm.	Congregation of Our Lady of Mt. Carmel	[0400]
O.Carm.	Institute of the Sisters of Our Lady of Mt. Carmel	[0410]
O.C.D.	Carmelite Sisters of the Most Sacred Heart of Los Angeles	[0370]
O.C.D.	Discalced Carmelite Nuns	[0420]
O.C.D.	Carmelitas del Sagrado Corazon	[]
O.Cist.	Cistercian Nuns	[0680]
O.C.S.O.	Cistercian Nuns of the Strict Observance	[0670]
O.D.N.	Company of Mary	[0700]
O.L.C.	Sisters of Our Lady of Charity	[3071]
O.L.C.	Sisters of Our Lady of Charity	[3073]
O.L.G.	Sisters of Our Lady of the Garden	[]
O.L.L.	Sisters of Our Lady of Lourdes	[]
O.L.M.	Sisters of Charity of Our Lady of Mercy	[0510]
O.L.S.	Sisters of Our Lady of Sorrows	[3120]
O.L.V.M.	Our Lady of Victory Missionary Sisters	[3130]
O.M.M.I.	Oblate Missionaries of Mary Immaculate	[]
O.M.O.	Oblates of the Mother of Orphans	[3035]
O.P.	Dominican Contemplative Nuns (Cloistered)	[1050]
O.P.	Dominican Contemplative Sisters (Cloistered)	[1060]
O.P.	Dominican Sisters (St. Catharine, KY)	[1070-01]
O.P.	Dominican Sisters (Columbus, OH)	[1070-02]
O.P.	Dominican Sisters (Sinsinawa, WI)	[1070-03]
O.P.	Dominican Sisters (San Rafael, CA)	[1070-04]
O.P.	Dominican Sisters (Amityville, NY)	[1070-05]
O.P.	Dominican Sisters (Newburgh, NY)	[1070-06]
O.P.	Dominican Sisters (Nashville, TN)	[1070-07]
O.P.	Dominican Sisters (New Orleans, LA)	[1070-08]
O.P.	Dominican Sisters (Racine, WI)	[1070-09]
O.P.	Dominican Sisters (Springfield, IL)	[1070-10]
O.P.	Dominican Sisters (Sparkill, NY)	[1070-11]
O.P.	Dominican Sisters (San Jose, CA)	[1070-12]

O.P.	Dominican Sisters (Adrian, MI)	[1070-13]
O.P.	Dominican Sisters (Grand Rapids, MI)	[1070-14]
O.P.	Dominican Sisters (Blauvelt, NY)	[1070-15]
O.P.	Dominican Sisters (Ossining, NY)	[1070-16]
O.P.	Dominican Sisters (Elkins Park, PA)	[1070-17]
O.P.	Dominican Sisters (Caldwell, PA)	[1070-18]
O.P.	Dominican Sisters (Houston, TX)	[1070-19]
O.P.	Dominican Sisters (Tacoma, WA)	[1070-20]
O.P.	Dominican Sisters (Edmonds, WA)	[1070-21]
O.P.	Dominican Sisters (Fall River, MA)	[1070-22]
O.P.	Dominican Sisters (Hawthorne, NY)	[1070-23]
O.P.	Dominican Sisters (Great Bend, KS)	[1070-24]
O P.	Dominican Sisters (Kenosha, WI)	[1070-25]
O.P.	Dominican Sisters (Oxford, MI)	[1070-26]
O.P.	Dominican Sisters (Justice, IL)	[1070-27]
O.P.	Dominican Sisters (Akron, OH)	[1070-28]
O.P.	Dominican Sisters (Spokane, WA)	[1070-29]
O.P.	Dominican Sisters (Oxford, South Africa)	[1070-30]
O.P.	Marian Society of Dominican Catechists	[1090]
O.P.	Dominican Sisters of Charity of the Presentation of the Blessed Virgin	[1100]
O.P.	Dominican Sisters of Hope	[1105]
O.P.	Dominican Sisters of Our Lady of the Rosary and of Saint Catherine of Siena, Cabra	[1110]
O.P.	Dominican Sisters of Peace	[1115]
O.P.	Dominican Sisters of the Roman Congregation	[1120]
O.P.	Dominican Rural Missionaries	[1130]
O.P.	Eucharistic Missionaries of St. Dominic	[1140]
O.P.	Dominican Sisters of Carondelet	[]
O.P.	Religious Missionaries of St. Dominic (Spanish Prov.)	[]
O.P.	Dominican Sisters of Mt. Thabor	[]
O.P.	Dominican Sisters of Our Lady of the Most Holy Rosary	[]
O.P.	Dominican Sisters (Vietnam)	[]
O.P.	Dominican Contemplative Sisters	[]
O.P.	Dominican Sisters (Colombia)	[]
O.P.	Dominican Sisters (Ecuador)	[]
O.P.	Hermanas Dominicanas de la Doctrine Cristiana	[]
O.S.A.	Augustinian Nuns of Contemplative Life	[0160]
O.S.A.	Congregation of Augustinian Sisters Servants of Jesus and Mary	[2145]
O.S.A.	Sisters of St. Rita	[4010]
O.S.A.	Sisters of St. Augustine	[]
O.S.A.	Augustinian Sisters of Our Lady of Consolation	[]
O.S.B.	Benedictine Nuns of the Congregation of Solesmes	[0170]
O.S.B.	Benedictine Nuns of the Primitive Observance	[0180]
O.S.B.	Benedictine Nuns	[0190]
O.S.B.	Benedictine Sisters	[0200]
O.S.B.	Missionary Benedictine Sisters	[0210]
O.S.B.	Congregation of the Benedictine Sisters of Perpetual Adoration of Pontifical Jurisdiction	[0220]
O.S.B.	Benedictine Sisters of Pontifical Jurisdiction	[0230]
O.S.B.	Benedictine Nuns	[0233]
O.S.B.	Olivetan Benedictine Sisters	[0240]
O.S.B.	Congregation of Jesus Crucified	[2250]
O.S.B.	Benedictine Congregation of Our Lady of Monte	[]
O.S.B.	Benedictine Sisters of Sacred Heart	[]
O.S.B.	Contemplative Sisters of St. Benedict	[]
O.S.B.	Benedictine Sisters of Liberty	[]
O.S.B.	Congregation of the Benedictine Sisters of the Sacred Heart	[]
O.S.B.Cam.	Camaldolese Benedictine Sisters	[]
O.S.B.M.	Sisters of the Order of St. Basil the Great	[3730]
O.S.B.S.	Oblate Sisters of the Blessed Sacrament	[3010]
O.S.C.	Order of St. Clare	[3760]
O.S.C.Cap.	Capuchin Poor Clares	[3765]
O.S.F.	Franciscan Sisters of Allegany New York	[1180]
O.S.F.	The Franciscan Sisters of Baltimore	[1200]
O.S.F.	Franciscan Sisters of Chicago	[1210]
O.S.F.	Franciscan Sisters of Christian Charity	[1230]
O.S.F.	Franciscan Sister, Daughters of the Sacred Hearts of Jesus and Mary	[1240]
O.S.F.	Franciscan Sisters of the Immaculate Conception	[1280]
O.S.F.	Franciscan Sisters of the Immaculate Conception and St. Joseph for the Dying	[1300]
O S.F.	Franciscan Sisters of Little Falls, Minnesota	[1310]
O.S.F.	Franciscan Missionary Sisters of the Immaculate Conception	[1350]
O.S.F.	Missionary Franciscan Sisters of the Immaculate Conception	[1360]
O.S.F.	Franciscan Missionaries of Our Lady	[1380]
O.S.F.	Franciscan Missionary Sisters of Our Lady of Sorrows	[1390]
O.S.F.	Franciscan Sisters of Our Lady of Perpetual Help	[1430]
O.S.F.	Franciscan Sisters of the Sacred Heart	[1450]
O.S.F.	Franciscan Sisters of St. Paul	[1485]
O.S.F.	Sisters of the Third Franciscan Order	[1490]
O.S.F.	St. Francis Mission Community	[1505]
O.S.F.	Sisters of St. Francis	[1510]
O.S.F.	Sisters of St. Francis of Christ the King	[1520]
O.S.F.	Sisters of St. Francis of the Congregation of Our Lady of Lourdes, Sylvania, Ohio	[1530]
O.S.F.	Sisters of Saint Francis, Clinton, Iowa	[1540]
O.S.F.	Sisters of St. Francis of the Holy Cross	[1550]
O.S.F.	Sisters of St. Francis of the Holy Eucharist	[1560]
O.S.F.	Sisters of St. Francis of the Holy Family	[1570]
O.S.F.	Sisters of St. Francis of the Immaculate Conception	[1580]
O.S.F.	Sisters of St. Francis of the Immaculate Heart of Mary (Hankinson, North Dakota)	[1590]
O.S.F.	Sisters of Saint Francis of Millvale, Pennsylvania	[1620]
O.S.F.	Sisters of St. Francis of Penance and Christian Charity	[1630]
O.S.F.	Sisters of St. Francis of Perpetual Adoration	[1640]
O.S.F.	Sisters of St. Francis of the Neumann Communities	[1805]
O.S.F.	The Sisters of St. Francis of Philadelphia	[1650]
O.S.F.	Sisters of Saint Francis of the Providence of God	[1660]
O.S.F.	Sisters of St. Francis of Savannah, MO	[1670]
O.S.F.	School Sisters of St. Francis	[1680]
O.S.F.	School Sisters of the Third Order of St. Francis (Pittsburgh, PA)	[1690]
O.S.F.	School Sisters of the Third Order of St. Francis (Panhandle, TX)	[1695]
O.S.F.	School Sisters of the Third Order of St. Francis (Bethlehem, PA)	[1700]
O.S F.	The Sisters of St. Francis of Assisi	[1705]
O.S.F.	Congregation of the Third Order of St. Francis of Mary Immaculate (Joliet, IL)	[1710]
O.S.F.	Sisters of the Third Order Regular of St. Francis of the Congregation of Our Lady of Lourdes	[1720]
O.S.F.	Congregation of the Sisters of the Third Order of St. Francis (Oldenburg, IN)	[1730]
O.S.F.	Sisters of the Third Order of St. Francis of Penance and Charity	[1760]
O.S.F.	Sisters of the Third Order of St. Francis (Peoria, IL)	[1770]
O.S.F.	Sisters of St. Francis of the Third Order Regular (Williamsville, New York)	[1800]
O.S.F.	Bernardine Sisters of the Third Order of St. Francis	[181
O.S.F.	Hospital Sisters of the Third Order of St. Francis	[182
O.S.F.	Servants of the Holy Infancy of Jesus	[198
O.S.F.	Consolation Sisters (Highland, CA)	
O.S.F.	Franciscan Sisters of Christ the Divine Teacher	
O.S.F.	St. Francis Mission Community	
O.S.F.S.	Oblate Sisters of St. Francis de Sales	[306
O.S.H.J.	Oblate Sisters of the Sacred Heart of Jesus	[305
O.S.M.	Mantellate Sisters, Servants of Mary of Blue Island	[357
O.S.M.	Mantellate Sisters, Servants of Mary of Plainfield	[357
O.S.M.	Servants of Mary	[358
O.S.M.	Servants of Mary (Servite Sisters)	[359
O.S.M.	Oblates of St. Martha	
O.S.P.	Oblate Sisters of Providence	[304
O.S.S.	Sacramentine Nuns	[349
O.SS.R.	Order of the Most Holy Redeemer	[201
O.SS.R.	Oblates of the Most Holy Redeemer	[303
O.SS.S.	The Brigittine Sisters	[028
O.SS.T.	Sisters of the Most Holy Trinity	[026
O.S.U.	Ursuline Nuns (Roman Union)	[411
O.S.U.	Ursuline Nuns of the Congregation of Paris (St. Martin, OH)	[412
O.S.U.	Ursuline Nuns of the Congregation of Paris (Cincinnati, OH)	[4120-0
O.S.U.	Ursuline Nuns of the Congregation of Paris (Kansas City, KS)	[4120-0
O.S.U.	Ursuline Nuns of the Congregation of Paris (Louisville, KY)	[4120-0
O.S.U.	Ursuline Nuns of the Congregation of Paris (Cleveland, OH)	[4120-0
O.S.U.	Ursuline Nuns of the Congregation of Paris (Owensboro, KY)	[4120-0
O.S.U.	Ursuline Nuns of the Congregation of Paris (Toledo, OH)	[4120-0
O.S.U.	Ursuline Nuns of the Congregation of Paris (Youngstown, OH)	[4120-0
O.S.U.	Ursuline Sisters of the Congregation of Tildonk, Belgium	[413
O.S.U.	Irish Ursuline Union	[415
P.B.V.M.	Presentation of the Blessed Virgin Mary Sisters	[328
P.B.V.M.	Sisters of the Presentation of the B.V.M	[332
P B.V.M.	Union of the Sisters of the Presentation of the Blessed Virgin Mary	[333
P.C.C.	Order of St. Clare	[376
P.C.I.	Pax Christi Institute	
P.C.J.	Sisters of the Poor Child Jesus	[322
P.C.P.A.	Poor Clares of Perpetual Adoration	[321
P.D.D.M.	Pious Disciples of the Divine Master	[098
P.F.M.	Franciscans of Mary	[228
P.H.J.C.	Poor Handmaids of Jesus Christ	[323
P.M.	Sisters of the Presentation of Mary	[331
P.O.S.C.	Little Workers of the Sacred Heart	[234
P.S.N.	Poor Sisters of Nazareth	[3242
P.S.S.F.	The Little Sisters of the Holy Family	[2320
P.S.S.J.	Poor Sisters of St. Joseph	[325
P.V.M.I.	The Parish Visitors of Mary Immaculate	[3160
Q.M.H.C.	Quinhon Missionary Sisters of the Holy Cross	[
R.A.	Religious of the Apostolate of the Sacred Heart	[3380
R.A.	Religious of the Assumption	[3390
R.A.	Antonine Sisters	[
R.A.D.	Sisters of the Love of God	[
R.C.	Congregation of Our Lady of Retreat in the Cenacle	[3110
R.C.D.	Sisters of Our Lady of Christian Doctrine	[3080
R.C.E.	Religious of Christian Education	[3410
R.C.M.	Sisters of the Immaculate Conception	[2130
R.C.S.C.J.	Sisters of the Cross of the Sacred Heart of Jesus (Mexico)	[
R.D.C.	Sisters of the Divine Compassion	[0970
R.F.	Sisters of St. Philip Neri Missionary Teachers	[

.R.	Sisters of Our Lady of Refuge	[]
.S.	The Sisters of the Good Shepherd	[1830]
.S.J.	Religious Hospitallers of Saint Joseph	[3440]
.M.	Religious of Jesus and Mary	[3450]
I.	Marianitas	[]
I.I.	Claretian Missionary Sisters	[0685]
.I.	Religious of Mary Immaculate	[3460]
I.M.	Mercedarian Sisters	[]
.D.A.	Sisters Oblates to Divine Love	[]
.L.C.	Our Lady of Charity of Refuge	[3072]
.C.	Religious Sisters of Charity	[3400]
.C.J.	Society of the Sacred Heart	[4070]
.H.M.	Religious of the Sacred Heart of Mary	[3465]
.J.	Religious of St. Joseph of Australia	[]
.M.	Religious Sisters of Mercy of Alma, Michigan	[2519]
.M.	Sisters of Mercy	[2520]
.M.	Sisters of Mercy of Ardagh & Clonmacnois	[2523]
.M.	Sisters of Mercy (Galway)	[2535]
.M.	Sisters of Mercy	[2540]
.M.	Sisters of Mercy (Sligo)	[2549]
.M.	Sisters of Mercy	[2550]
.M.	Sisters of Mercy of the Americas	[2575]
.M.	Sisters of Mercy (Ballyshannon, Ireland)	[]
.M.	Sisters of Mercy (Mayo, Ireland)	[]
.M.	Sisters of Mercy of Mississippi, Inc.	[]
.M.	Sisters of Mercy of Portland	[2655]
.M.	Diocesan Sisters of Mercy	[]
.R.	Congregation of Our Lady of the Holy Rosary	[3100]
T.	Theatine Sisters of the Immaculate Conception	[]
V.M.	Religious of the Blessed Virgin Mary	[]
A.	Franciscan Sisters of the Atonement	[1190]
A.A.	Sisters Auxillaries of the Apostolate	[0140]
A.B.	Sisters of St. Anne Bangalone	[]
A.C.	Sisters of the Guardian Angel	[1850]
A.C.	Pallottine Missionary Sisters Queen of Apostles Prov	[3150]
A.S.V.	Sisters of the Assumption	[0150]
B.S.	The Sisters of the Blessed Sacrament for Indians and Colored People	[0260]
C.	Sisters of Charity of Cincinnati, Ohio	[0440]
C.	Sisters of Charity of Seton Hill, Greensburg, PA	[0570]
C.	Sisters of St. Elizabeth, Convent Station	[0590]
C.	Sisters of Charity of St. Vincent de Paul, Halifax	[0640]
C.	Sisters of Charity of St. Vincent de Paul, New York	[0650]
C.C.	Sisters of Christian Charity	[0660]
h.P.	Sisters of the Pious Schools	[3200]
C.I.C.	Sisters of Charity of the Immaculate Conception of Ivrea	[0450]
C.I.M.	Servants of the Immaculate Heart of Mary	[3550]
C.K.	Sisters of Christ the King	[]
C.L.	Sisters of Charity of Leavenworth, Kansas	[0480]
C.M.C.	Sisters of Charity of Our Lady, Mother of the Church	[0530]
C.M.M.	Sisters of Charity of Our Lady Mother of Mercy	[0520]
C.M.M.	Medical Mission Sisters	[2490]
C.N.	Sisters of Charity of Nazareth	[0500]
C.O.	Sisters of Charity of Ottawa (Grey Nuns of the Cross)	[0540]
C.O.	Sisters of Charity of Quebec (Grey Nuns)	[0560]
C.R.H.	Sisters of Charity of Rolling Meadows	[]
C.S.C.	Sisters of Mercy of the Holy Cross	[2630]
C.S.J.A.	Sisters of Charity of St. Joan Antida	[0600]
C.S.L.	Sisters of Charity of St. Louis	[0620]
C.S.H.	Sisters of Charity of St. Hyacinthe (Grey Nuns)	[0610]
C.V.	Sisters of Charity of St. Vincent de Paul of Suwon	[0655]
deP.	Sister Servants of the Poor	[]
S.D.R.	Sisters of the Divine Redeemer	[1020]
S.D.S.	Sisters of the Divine Saviour	[1030]
S.D.S.H.	Sisters of the Society Devoted to the Sacred Heart	[4050]
S.D.V.	Vocationist Sisters	[4210]
S.E.	Sisters of Emanuel	[]
S.E.C.	Sisters of the Eucharistic Covenant	[]
S.F.C.C.	Sisters for Christian Community	[]
S.F.M.A.	Franciscan Missionary Sisters of Assisi	[1330]
S.F.p.	Franciscan Sisters of the Poor	[1440]
S.G.M.	Sisters of Charity of Montreal (Grey Nuns)	[0490]
S.G.S.	Hermanas del Buen Pastor	[]
S.H.C.J.	Society of the Holy Child Jesus	[4060]
S.H.F.	Sisters of the Holy Family	[1960]
S.H.J.M.	Sisters of the Sacred Hearts of Jesus and Mary	[3680]
S.H.S.	Sisters of the Holy Spirit	[2040]
S.H.Sp.	Sisters of the Holy Spirit and Mary Immaculate	[2050]
S.I.M.	Missionaries of the Kingship of Chnst	[]
S.I.W.	Sisters of the Incarnate Word and the Blessed Sacrament	[2210]
S.J.	Servants of Jesus	[3560]
S.J.A.	Sisters of Ste. Jeanne D'Arc	[3815]
S.J.B.	Sisters of St. John Bosco (Taylor, TX)	[]
S.J.C.	Sisters of St. Joseph of Cluny	[3860]
S.J.S.	Servants of the Blessed Sacrament	[3499]
S.J.S.	Sisters of Jesus the Savior	[2245]
S.J.S M.	Sisters of St. Joseph of St. Mark	[3910]
S.J.W.	Sisters of St. Joseph the Worker	[3920]
S.L.	Sisters of Loretto at the Foot of the Cross	[2360]
S.L.T.	Pious Society of Our Lady of the Most Holy Trinity	[]
S.L.W.	Sisters of the Living Word	[2350]
S.M.	Marist Sisters Congregation of Mary	[2430]
S.M.	Sisters of Mercy	[2516]
S.M.	Sisters of Mercy	[2518]
S.M.	Sisters of Mercy	[2570]
S.M.	Sisters of Mercy (Cork and Ross)	[2600]
S.M.	Misericordia Sisters	[2680]
S.M.	Sisters Servants of Mary	[3600]
S.M.	Sisters of Mercy (Loughrea, Ireland)	[]
S.M.	Sisters of Mercy of Tralee	[]
S.M.G.	Poor Servants of the Mother of God	[3640]
S.M.I.	Sisters of Mary Immaculate	[2440]
S.M.I.C.	Missionary Sisters of the Immaculate Conception of the Mother of God	[2760]
S.M.M.G.	Sisters of Mary, Mother of God	[]
S.M.M.I.	Sisters Minor of the Mary Immaculate	[]
S.M.M.S.	Society of Mary Missionary Sisters	[]
S.M.P.	Sisters of Mary of the Presentation	[2450]
S.M.P.	Daughters of Our Mother of Peace	[]
S.M.P.	Society of Our Mother of Peace	[]
S.M.R.	Society of Mary Reparatrix	[2560]
S.M.S.H.	Sisters of Saint Marthe (of St. Hyacinthe)	[3940]
S.M.S.M.	Marist Missionary Sisters	[2420]
S.N.D.	Sisters of Notre Dame	[2990]
S.N.D.deN.	Sisters of Notre Dame de Namur	[3000]
S.N.J.M.	Sisters of the Holy Names of Jesus and Mary	[1990]
S.O.L.M.	Sisters of Our Lady of Mercy	[2670]
S.O.L.P.H.	Sisters of Our Lady of Perpetual Help	[]
S.O.L.T.	Sisters of the Society of Our Lady of the Most Holy Trinity	[3105]
S.P.	Sisters of Providence	[3340]
S.P.	Sisters of Providence	[3350]
S.P.	Sisters of Providence of Saint Mary-of-the-Woods, IN	[3360]
S.P.C.	Sisters of St. Paul of Chartres	[3980]
S.R.	Sisters of Reparation of the Sacred Wounds of Jesus	[3475]
S.R.C.	Servants of Our Lady, Queen of Clergy	[3650]
S.R.C.M.	Sisters of Reparation of the Congregation of Mary	[3470]
S.S.A.	Sisters of St. Ann	[3718]
S.S.A.	Sisters of St. Anne	[3720]
S.S.C.	Missionary Sisters of St. Columban	[2880]
S.S.C.	Sisters of St. Casimir	[3740]
S.S.C.	Society of the Sisters of the Church	[]
SS.CC.	Congregation of the Sacred Hearts and of Perpetual Adoration	[3690]
S.S.Ch.	Sisters of St. Chretienne	[3750]
S.S.C.J.	Servants of the Most Sacred Heart of Jesus	[3630]
S.S.C.J.	Sisters of the Sacred Heart of Jesus of Saint Jacut	[3670]
S.S.C.M.	Servants of the Holy Heart of Mary	[3520]
SS.C.M.	Sisters of Saints Cyril and Methodius	[3780]
S.S.D.	Institute of the Sisters of St. Dorothy	[3790]
S.S.E.	Sisters of St. Elizabeth	[3800]
S.S.F.	Congregation of the Sisters of the Holy Family	[1950]
S.S.H.	Sisters Servants of the Most Sacred Heart	[]
S.S.H.J.	Sisters of the Sacred Heart of Jesus	[3658]
S.S.H.J.P.	Servants of the Sacred Heart of Jesus and of the Poor	[3660]
S.S.J.	Servants of St. Joseph	[3595]
S.S.J.	Sisters of St. Joseph (Buffalo)	[3830-06]
S.S.J.	Sisters of St. Joseph (Burlington)	[3830-07]
S.S.J.	Sisters of St. Joseph (Erie)	[3830-09]
S.S.J.	Sisters of St. Joseph (Kalamazoo, Nazareth)	[3830-11]
S.S.J.	Sisters of St. Joseph (Ogdensburg)	[3830-12]
S.S.J.	Sisters of St. Joseph (Rochester)	[3830-14]
S.S.J.	Sisters of St. Joseph, (Springfield, MA)	[3830-16]
S.S.J.	Sisters of St. Joseph (Wheeling, Eng)	[3830-17]
S.S.J.	Sisters of Saint Joseph of Chestnut Hill, Philadelphia	[3893]
S.S.J.	Sisters of St. Joseph of St. Augustine, Florida	[3900]
S.S.J.C.	Sisters of St. Joseph Benedict Cottolengo	[]
S.S.J.-T.O.S.F.	Sisters of St. Joseph of the Third Order of St. Francis	[3930]
S.S.L.	Congregation of the Sisters of St. Louis, Juilly-Monaghan	[3935]
S.S.LOG.	Seton Sisters of Our Lady of Guadalupe, Tucson	[]
S.S.M.	Sisters of the Sorrowful Mother (Third Order of St. Francis)	[4100]
S.S.M.I.	Sisters Servants of Mary Immaculate	[3510]
S.S.M.I.	Sisters Servants of Mary Immaculate	[3610]
S.S.M.I.	Sisters Servants of Mary Immaculate	[3620]
S.S.M.N.	Sisters of Saint Mary of Namur	[3950]
S.S.M.O.	Sisters of St. Mary of Oregon	[3960]
S.S.N.D.	School Sisters of Notre Dame	[2970]
S.S.P.C.	Missionary Sisters of St. Peter Claver	[3990]
S.Sp.S.	Missionary Sisters Servants of the Holy Spirit	[3530]
S.Sp.S.deA.P.	Sister Servants of the Holy Spirit of Perpetual Adoration	[3540]
S.S.S.	Servants of the Blessed Sacrament	[3500]
S.S.S.	Sisters of Social Service of Los Angeles, Inc.	[4080]
S.S.S.	Sisters of Social Service	[4090]
S.S.S.F.	School Sisters of St. Francis	[1680]
S.S.T.V.	Congregation of Sisters of St. Thomas of Villanova	[4030]
S.T.J.	Society of St. Teresa of Jesus	[4020]
S.U.	Society of St. Ursula	[4040]
S.U.S.C.	Sisters of the Holy Union	[2070]
S.V.	Sisters of Life	[2265]
S.V.M.	Sisters of the Visitation of the Congregation of the Immaculate Heart of Mary	[4200]
V.D.C.	Verbum Dei Community	[]
V.H.M.	Visitation Nuns	[4190]
V.S.	Vestiarski Sisters	[]
V.S.C.	Vincentian Sisters of Charity	[4160]
V.S.C.	Vincentian Sisters of Charity	[4170]

V.Z. Sisters of Charity of St. Vincent de Paul .... [0630]

X.M.M. Xaverian Missionary Society of Mary, Inc. .... [4230]

X.S. Catholic Mission Sisters of St. Francis Xavier .... [3810]

Religious Institutes of Women

Women Leadership Conference of Women Religious of the United States of America—National Office: 8808 Cameron St., Silver Spring, MD 20910. Tel: 301-588-4955; Fax: 301-587-4575; Website: www.lcwr.org. Sr. Marlene Weisenbeck, F.S.P.A, Pres.; Sr. Mary Hughes, O.P., Pres. Elect; Sr. J. Lora Dambroski, O.S.F., Past Pres.; Sr. Ellen Dauwer, S.C., Sec.; Sr. Elizabeth Ney, C.S.J., Treas.; Sr. Jane Burke, S.S.N.D., Exec. Dir. Council of Major Superiors of Women Religious in the United States of America—1211 Lawrence St., N.E., P.O. Box 4467, Washington, DC 20017-0467. Tel: 202-832-2575; Fax: 202-832-6325. Mother Mary Quentin Sheridan, R.S.M., Chm.

(The initial (D) or (P) indicates Diocesan or Pontifical Jurisdiction.)

[0100] (A.S.C.)—ADORERS OF THE BLOOD OF CHRIST (P)

Founded in Acuto, Italy, in 1834. First foundation in the United States in 1870.

General Motherhouse: Via Beata Maria De Mattias 10, Rome, Italy, 00183. Sr. Bernarda Kristic, A.S.C., Supr. Gen.

Regional Offices - United States Region: *Adorers of the Blood of Christ*, 4233 Sulphur Ave., Saint Louis, MO 63109. Tel: 314-351-6294; Fax: 314-351-6789. Sr. Jan Renz, A.S.C., Regional Leader.

Professed Sisters: 316.

Properties owned and/or sponsored: Villa Maria, Mulvane, KS; Newman University, Wichita, KS; St. Joseph Villa, David City, NE; St. Joseph Convent-Provincial House; Precious Blood Spiritual Center; St. Anne's Retirement Community, Inc.; De Matias Residence; St. Anne's Independent Living Retirement Village, Columbia PA.

Legal Title: *Adorers of the Blood of Christ.*

Sisters serve and staff: Colleges; Secondary & Elementary Schools; Special & Religious Education; Hospitals; Pastoral Care; Nursing Homes; Domestic Service in Communities & Institutions; Administration in Religious Orders & Parishes; Prayer Ministry; Retreat Ministry; Social Service; Pastoral & Chaplaincy Ministry; Prison & Minority Ministries; Ministry to the Homeless; Diocesan Offices; Homes for the Aged & Home Nursing; Foreign Missions.

Represented in the Archdioceses of Chicago, Detroit, Kansas City in Kansas, Newark, New York, Oklahoma City, Philadelphia, St. Louis, San Antonio, San Francisco and Washington and in the Dioceses of Alexandria, Arlington, Belleville, Dodge City, El Paso, Fort Worth, Gallup, Harrisburg, Jefferson City, Kansas City, Lexington, Lincoln, Oakland, Salina, San Diego, Springfield-Cape Girardeau, Springfield in Illinois, Tucson, Wilmington, Wichita and Youngstown. Also in Bolivia, Guatemala, Korea and Rome.

Ruma Center(1876): 2 Pioneer Ln., Red Bud, IL 62278. Tel: 618-282-3848.

Wichita Center(1929): 1165 Southwest Blvd., Wichita, KS 67213-1394. Tel: 316-942-2201.

Columbia Center(1925): 3950 Columbia Ave., Columbia, PA 17512-9714. Tel: 717-285-4536.

[0110] A.P.B.—THE SISTERS ADORERS OF THE PRECIOUS BLOOD (P)
(Cloistered Contemplative Order)

American Federation: Consisting of Five Autonomous Monasteries: 400 Pratt St., Watertown, NY 13601-4238. Tel: 315-788-1669. Sr. Mary Jo Divney, A.P.B., Pres. American Federation.

Professed Sisters: 75; Novices: 8; Postulants: 2.

Represented in the Dioceses of Brooklyn, Manchester, Ogdensburg and Portland (In Maine).

New York: 5400 Ft. Hamilton Pkwy., Brooklyn, NY 11219. Tel: 718-438-6371.

New Hampshire: 700 Bridge St., Manchester, NH 03104. Tel: 603-623-4264.

New York: 400 Pratt St., Watertown, NY 13601. Tel: 315-788-1669.

Maine: 166 State St., Portland, ME 04101. Tel: 207-774-0861.

Canada: 9415 165th St., Edmonton, Canada, T5R 2S5. Tel: 403-484-6691.

[0130] (A.S.C.J.)—APOSTLES OF THE SACRED HEART OF JESUS (P)

Founded in Italy in 1894. First Foundation in United States 1902.

General Motherhouse: *Apostole del Sacro Cuore di Gesu*, Via Germano Sommeiller 38, Rome, Italy, 00185. Mother Clare Millea, A.S.C.J., Supr. Gen.; Sr. Chiara Cervato, Sec.

U.S. Provincial Motherhouse: *Mt. Sacred Heart*, 295 Benham St., Hamden, CT 06514. Tel: 203-248-4225; Fax: 203-230-8341.

Professed Sisters: 132.

Properties owned and/or sponsored: Clelian House Convent, St. Louis, MO; Our Lady of Hope Convent, St. Louis, MO; Mary, Mother of the Church Convent, Hamden, CT; Mount Sacred Heart College for Sisters; Sacred Heart Academy; Sacred Heart Manor; Sacred Heart Manor Nursery and Kindergarten; Clelian Adult Day Care, Hamden, CT; Sacred Heart on the Lake, Higganum, CT; Cor Jesu Academy, St. Louis, MO; Sacred Heart Villa Nursery, St. Louis, MO; Our Lady Queen of Apostles (Convent & Retreat and Spirituality Center), Imperial, MO; Clelian Heights School for Exceptional Children, Greensburg, PA; Sacred Heart Private Elementary School, Bronx, NY.

Ministry in the fields of Education, Health Care, Parishes, Adult Day Care and Immigrant Services.

Represented in the Archdioceses of Hartford, New York and St. Louis and in the Dioceses of Bridgeport, Greensburg, Norwich and Pensacola-Tallahassee. Also in Rome and Taiwan.

[0150] S.A.S.V.—SISTERS OF THE ASSUMPTION (P)

Founded in Saint-Gregoire, P.Q., Canada in 1853. First foundation in the United States in 1891.

General Motherhouse: Nicolet, Canada Sr. Denise Brochu, S.A.S.V., Supr. Gen.

United States Region: *Regional Office*, 316 Lincoln St., Worcester, MA 01605. Tel: 508-856-9383. Sr. Lorraine Normand, S.A.S.V., Reg. Treas.

Total in Region and Professed: 72.

Legal Holdings: Assumption Residence of the Sisters of the Assumption of the Blessed Virgin, Petersham, MA; Harper Residence, Worcester, MA.

Ministry in all levels of education.

Missions in Japan, Brazil and Ecuador.

Represented in the Archdiocese of Boston and in the Dioceses of Albany, Fall River, Portland (In Maine), Providence, Springfield in Massachusetts and Worcester.

[0160] (O.S.A.)—AUGUSTINIAN NUNS OF CONTEMPLATIVE LIFE (P)

Augustinian Contemplative Nuns: *Mother of Good Counsel Convent*, 440 N. Marley Rd., New Lenox, IL 60451. Sr. Mary Villar, O.S.A., Prioress.

Total in Community: 5.

Legal Title: *Augustinian Cloistered Nuns, Inc.*

Represented in the Diocese of Joliet.

[0170] (O.S.B.)—BENEDICTINE NUNS OF THE CONGREGATION OF SOLESMES (P)

Order originated in Italy, c.529. Congregation of Solesmes formed in France in 1837.

U.S. Establishment (1981): *Monastery of the Immaculate Heart of Mary*, 4103 VT Rte. 100, Westfield, VT 05874. Tel: 802-744-6525; Fax: 802-744-6236. Rev. Mother Laurence Couture, O.S.B., Prioress.

Total in Congregation : 916; Total in Community: 16.

Represented in the Diocese of Burlington.

[0180] (O.S.B.)—BENEDICTINE NUNS OF THE PRIMITIVE OBSERVANCE (P)

First founded in Italy in about c.529. First United States establishment in 1948.

Abbey of Regina Laudis: 273 Flanders Rd., Bethlehem, CT 06751. Tel: 203-266-7727; Fax: 203-266-5915. Rt. Rev. Mother David Serna, O.S.B., Abbess.

Professed Nuns: 29; Sisters in First Vows: 5; Novices: 3.

[0190] (O.S.B.)—BENEDICTINE NUNS (P)

First founded in Italy in c.529. Founded in the United States in 1931 from St. Walburg Abbey, Eichstatt, Bavaria, Germany.

The Sisters of St. Benedict of Westmoreland County: *St. Emma Monastery*, 1001 Harvey Ave., Greensburg, PA 15601-1491. Tel: 724-834-3060; Fax: 724-834-5772; Email: benedictinenuns@stemma.org. Mother Mary Anne Noll, O.S.B., Prioress.

Professed Nuns: 11; Novices: 1.

Ministry in Monastic Life; Benedictine hospitality extended through adjacent St. Emma Retreat House; Monastic Guest House.

Represented in the Diocese of Greensburg.

Benedictine Nuns: *Abbey of St. Walburga*, 1029 Benedictine Way, Virginia Dale, CO 80536. Tel: 970-472-0612; Fax: 970-484-4342; Email: abbey@walburga.org. Mother Maria Michael Newe, O.S.B., Abbess; Mother Maria-Thomas Beil, O.S.B., Retired Abbess.

Sisters: 19; Novices: 3; Claustral Oblate: 1.

Represented in the Archdiocese of Denver.

[0210] (O.S.B.)—MISSIONARY BENEDICTINE SISTERS (P)

The Congregation of Missionary Benedictine Sisters is of Pontifical Jurisdiction. Its Constitutions were approved by Rome on June 25, 1934; Revised approval June 29, 1983.

Generalate: Rome, Italy

Provincial Motherhouse and Novitiate: *Immaculata Monastery (1923)*, 300 N. 18th St., Norfolk, NE 68701-3687. Tel: 402-371-3438; Fax: 402-379-2877. Sr. Kevin Hermsen, O.S.B., Prioress.

Professed Sisters: 35; Junior Sisters: 1.

Legal Holdings or Titles: Missionary Benedictine Sisters, Inc., Norfolk, NE; Providence Medical Center, Inc., Wayne, NE; Graceville Missionary Benedictine Sisters, Inc., dba Holy Trinity Hospital - Grace Home, Graceville, MN.

Ministry in the fields of Education; Health & Hospitals; Social Services with Hispanics; Nursing Homes.

Represented in the Archdiocese of Omaha and in the Diocese of New Ulm.

[0220] (O.S.B.)—CONGREGATION OF THE BENEDICTINE SISTERS OF PERPETUAL ADORATION OF PONTIFICAL JURISDICTION (P)

Founded from Maria Rickenbach, Switzerland in 1874 with first monastery at Clyde, MO. Congregation erected by decree of the Holy See on June 16, 1936.

General Motherhouse: *Benedictine Convent of Perpetual Adoration*, 31970 State Hwy. P, Clyde, MO 64432. Tel: 660-944-2221; Fax: 660-944-2152. Sr. Patricia Nyquist, Prioress Gen.

Total in Community: 60; Total in Congregation : 86; Novices: 2; Postulants: 1.

San Benito Monastery: Box 510, Dayton, WY 82836.

Interdependent Monasteries: 800 N. Country Club Rd., Tucson, AZ 85716.

Ministry in Monastic/Contemplative/Eucharistic Apostolate of Prayer; Liturgy of the Hours four times daily in Choir; Contemplative Prayer and Monastic Atmosphere Shared with Others; Prayer Days and Retreats for Sisters; Editing and Publishing Bimonthly Magazine: Spirit & Life; Production and Distribution of Altar Breads; Liturgical Vestments; Correspondence.

Represented in the Dioceses of Cheyenne, Kansas City-St. Joseph and Tucson.

[0230] (O.S.B.)—BENEDICTINE SISTERS OF PONTIFICAL JURISDICTION (P)

(I) The Federation of St. Scholastica

Erected by Decree of the Holy See, February 25, 1922, with final approbation by Decree of June 10, 1930. Nineteen Monasteries in the United States and two in Mexico. Total number in the Federation 891. Sr. Esther Fangman, O.S.B., Federation Pres., residing at: Benedictines of Pontifical Jurisdiction, 3741 Forest Ave., Kansas City, MO 64109. Phone: 816-753-2514.

Benedictine Sisters of Baltimore, Inc: *Emmanuel Monastery*, 2229 W. Joppa Rd., Lutherville Timonium, MD 21093. Tel: 410-821-5792; Fax: 410-296-9560; Email: bensrs@emmanuelosb.org; Web: www.emmanuelosb.org. Sr. Kathleen White, O.S.B., Prioress.

Total in Community: 14.

Ministry in the field of Education; Parish Ministry; Retreats and Spiritual Direction; Justice Ministry; Social Services; Administrative Services; Hospital Service Ministry and Hospice Chaplaincy.

Represented in the Archdioceses of Baltimore and Newark.

Benedictine Sisters of the Byzantine Rite (1969): *Queen of Heaven Monastery*, 8640 Squires Ln., N.E., Warren, OH 44484. Tel: 330-856-1813. Sr. Margaret Mary Schima, O.S.B., Prioress.

Professed Sisters: 7.

Ministry in Religious and Academic Education; Pastoral Ministry; Administration.

Represented in the Archdiocese of Pittsburgh Byzantine Rite.

Mount St. Scholastica Inc. (1863): *Motherhouse of the Sisters of St. Benedict*, 801 S. Eighth St., Atchison, KS 66002-2778. Tel: 913-360-6200; Fax: 913-360-6190; Web: www.mountosb.org. Sr. Anne Shepard, O.S.B., Prioress.

Professed Sisters: 162; Novices: 1; Postulants: 1.

Legal Holdings: Dooley Center, Inc.; Mount St. Scholastica, Inc., Atchison, KS.

Ministry in the field of Academic Education at all levels; Counseling; Retreats; Spirituality Center; Spiritual Direction; Social Services; Hospitality; Music Conservatory; Pastoral Ministry; Ministry to women of all ages; Missionary Work in Brazil.

Represented in the Archdioceses of Kansas City in Kansas, Oklahoma City, and St. Louis and in the Dioceses of Des Moines, Lincoln and Kansas City-St. Joseph. Also in Brazil.

Benedictine Sisters of Elk Co. (1852): *St. Joseph*

Monastery, St. Marys, PA 15857. Tel: 814-834-2267; Fax: 814-834-3270. Sr. Jacinta Conklin, O.S.B., Prioress.
Professed Sisters: 18.
Ministry in the fields of Academic and Religious Education; Pastoral Ministry; Retreats.

Benedictine Sisters (1998): *Transfiguration Monastery*, 526 Fairview St., Emmaus, PA 18049-3837. Tel: 610-965-6818. Sr. Martina Revak, O.S.B., Supr.
Professed Sisters: 3.
Legal Title: *Benedictine Sisters of Emmaus.*
Ministry in the fields of Education; Pastoral Ministry; Hospitality and Spirituality.
Represented in the Diocese of Allentown.

Benedictine Sisters of Erie (1856): *Mt. St. Benedict Monastery*, 6101 East Lake Rd., Erie, PA 16511. Tel: 814-899-0614; Fax: 814-898-4004. Sr. Christine Vladimiroff, O.S.B., Prioress.
Total in Congregation : 105; Professed Sisters: 105.
Properties owned and/or sponsored: Mount Saint Benedict Monastery; Glinodo Center; St. Benedict Education Center; Benet Center; 8 Community Houses.
Sisters serve and staff: High Schools; Elementary Schools; Colleges; Day Care Centers; Residence for Elderly and Handicapped; Hospitals; Social Services; Diocesan Offices; Pastoral Ministry; Religious Education.
Represented in the Dioceses of Cleveland, Erie, and Wilmington.

Benedictine Sisters of Chicago O.S.B. (1861): *St. Scholastica Monastery*, 7430 N. Ridge Blvd., Chicago, IL 60645. Tel: 773-764-2413. Sr. Patricia Crowley, O.S.B., Prioress; Sr. Vivian Ivantic, Community Archivist.
Professed Sisters: 52.
Properties owned and/or sponsored: St. Scholastica Monastery, Chicago, IL; St. Scholastica Academy, Chicago, IL.
Ministry in High Schools; Parish Ministry; Education Administration; Religious Education; Management Consultant; Spiritual Direction; Shelter Ministry; Community Center Work; Social Service Counseling; Music; Massage Therapy; Group Facilitation; Preschool; Psychiatric Social Work; Pastoral Psychotherapy.
Represented in the Archdiocese of Chicago and in the Diocese of Pueblo.

Benedictine Sisters of the Sacred Heart O.S.B. (1895): *Sacred Heart Monastery*, 1910 Maple Ave., Lisle, IL 60532-2164. Tel: 630-725-6000. Sr. Judith Ann Heble, O.S.B., Prioress.
Professed Sisters: 29.
Legal Title: *Benedictine Sisters of the Sacred Heart Charitable Trust.*
Sisters serve and staff: High Schools; Elementary Schools; Colleges; Villa St. Benedict; Religious Education; Pastoral Ministry; Nurses Administration; Independent Positions involving Secretarial, Counseling, Liturgical Works, Occupational Therapy.
Represented in the Diocese of Joliet.

Sisters of Benedict of Colorado, Inc: 4264 W. Ponds View Dr., Littleton, CO 80123. Tel: 303-795-2378. Sr. Judith Elms, O.S.B., Supr.

Benedictine Sisters of Elizabeth, NJ O.S.B. (1868): *St. Walburga Monastery and Novitiate*, 851 N. Broad St., Elizabeth, NJ 07208. Tel: 908-352-4278. Sr. Sharon McHugh, O.S.B., Prioress; Sr. Cynthia Cunningham, O.S.B., Sub Prioress.
Professed Sisters: 44.
Legal Holdings and Titles: Benedictine Hospital, Kingston, NY; Benedictine Academy, Elizabeth, NJ.
Represented in the Archdioceses of New York and Newark.

Benedictine Sisters of Pittsburgh, PA O.S.B. (1870): *St. Benedict Monastery*, 4530 Perrysville Ave., Pittsburgh, PA 15229-2296. Tel: 412-931-2844. Sr. Benita DeMatteis, O.S.B., Prioress.
Professed Sisters: 55.
Ministry in the field of Education in all levels; Religious and Special Education; Pastoral Ministry; Childcare; Social Service; Campus Ministry; Hospital Chaplaincy; Art Education; Ministry Resource; Outreach with Poor; Benedictine Center for Senior Citizens.
Represented in the Dioceses of Greensburg, Pittsburgh and Lexington.

Sisters of Benedict O.S.B. (1968): *Red Plains Spirituality Center*, 728 Richland Rd., S.W., Piedmont, OK 73078-9324. Tel: 405-373-4565; Fax: 405-373-3392. Sr. Anne Shepard, O.S.B., Prioress.
Professed Sisters: 9.
Properties owned and/or sponsored: Red Plains Spirituality Center, Piedmont, OK.
Ministry in the fields of Education, CCD and Adult Religious Education; Spiritual Formation; Spiritual Direction; Retreats.
Represented in the Archdiocese of Oklahoma City.

Benedictine Sisters O.S.B. (1879): *St. Joseph Monastery*, 2200 S. Lewis, Tulsa, OK 74114-3100. Tel: 918-742-4989; Fax: 918-744-1374. Sr. Christine Ereiser, O.S.B., Prioress.
Professed Sisters: 22.
Legal Holdings and Titles: Congregation of the Benedictine Sisters of the Sacred Hearts; Monte Cassino School.
Ministry in the field of Academic Education; Catechetics; Evangelization; Social Work; Pastoral Ministry; Counseling & Spiritual Direction; Prison Ministry; Religious Education & Religious Formation.
Represented in the Archdiocese of Oklahoma City and in the Dioceses of Lincoln and Tulsa.

Benedictine Sisters of Pontifical Jurisdiction O.S.B. (1857): *St. Gertrude Monastery*, 14259 Benedictine Ln., Ridgely, MD 21660-1434. Tel: 410-634-2497. Sr. Catherine Higley, O.S.B., Prioress.
Professed Sisters: 26.
Legal Holdings and Titles: The Benedictine School for Exceptional Children; Berg Retreat Facility; St. Martin's Barn; St. Martin House, Ridgely, MD; St. Benedict, Wilmington, DE.
Ministry in Special Schools and Secondary Education; Ministry to the poor and homeless; Ministry to Hospice.
Represented in the Diocese of Wilmington.

St. Walburg Monastery of Benedictine Sisters of Covington, KY O.S.B. (1859): *St. Walburg Monastery*, 2500 Amsterdam Rd., Villa Hills, KY 41017-5316. Tel: 859-331-6324; Fax: 859-331-2136. Sr. Mary Catherine Wenstrup, O.S.B., Prioress; Sr. Betty Cahill, O.S.B., Community Archivist; Sr. Margaret Mary Gough, O.S.B., Community Archivist.
Professed Sisters: 70.
Legal Titles and Holdings: Villa Madonna Montessori School; Villa Madonna Academy; Villa Madonna Center - Spirituality Center.
Sisters serve and staff: Diocesan Offices; Pastoral and Social Ministry; Public Health Care; all levels of academic education (elementary and high school).
Represented in the Archdiocese of Cincinnati and in the Dioceses of Covington, Lexington and Pueblo.

Benedictine Sisters (1902): *Sacred Heart Monastery*, 916 Convent Rd., Cullman, AL 35055. Tel: 256-734-2199; Fax: 256-734-7592. Sr. Janet Marie Flemming, O.S.B., Prioress; Sr. Mary Ruth Coffman, O.S.B., Community Archivist.
Professed Sisters: 48.
Properties owned and/or sponsored: Benedictine Spirituality and Conference Center; Benedictine Manor Retirement Home; Sacred Heart Monastery of Cullman, AL Foundation.
Sisters serve and staff: all levels of Academic Education; Pastoral Ministry; Diocesan Offices; Retirement Homes; Conference Centers; Rural Health Center (Doctor); Nurses; Lawyer.
Represented in the Diocese of Birmingham.

Benedictine Sisters of Virginia O.S.B. (1868): *St. Benedict Monastery*, 4535 Linton Hall Rd., Bristow, VA 20136-1217. Tel: 703-361-0106. Sr. Cecilia Dwyer, O.S.B., Prioress.
Total Professed Sisters: 36.
Legal Holdings and Titles: Benedictine Sisters of Virginia, Inc.; St. Gertrude High School, Richmond, VA; Linton Hall School; Benedictine Pastoral Center; Benedictine Counseling Services, Bristow, VA; B.E.A-.C.O.N., Bristow, VA.
Represented in the Dioceses of Arlington and Richmond.

Benedictine Sisters (1911): *St. Scholastica's Monastery and Novitiate*, 416 W. Highland Dr., Boerne, TX 78006. Tel: 830-249-2645; Fax: 830-249-1365. Sr. Bernadine Reyes, O.S.B., Prioress.
Total in Community: 18.
Properties owned and/or sponsored: St. Scholastica Monastery; Benedictine Sisters Charitable Trust I; Benedictine Sisters Charitable Trust II.
Represented in the Archdiocese of San Antonio and in the Diocese of Laredo.

Benedictine Sisters of St. Lucy's Priory Inc. O.S.B. (1956): *St. Lucy's Priory*, 19045 E. Sierra Madre Ave., Glendora, CA 91741. Tel: 626-335-1682. Sr. Elizabeth Brown, O.S.B., Prioress.
Professed Sisters: 12.
Legal Holdings: St. Lucy's Priory High School; St. Lucy's Benedictine Child Development Center.
Sisters serve and staff: all levels of Academic Education; Pastoral Ministry.
Represented in the Archdiocese of Los Angeles and in the Diocese of San Diego.

Benedictine Sisters of Florida (1889): *Holy Name Monastery*, P.O. Box 2450, St. Leo, FL 33574-2450. Tel: 352-588-8320; Fax: 352-588-8319. Sr. Mary Clare Neuhofer, O.S.B., Prioress; Sr. M. Dorothy Neuhofer, O.S.B., Community Archivist.
Professed Sisters: 18.
Represented in the Diocese of St. Petersburg.

Sisters of St. Benedict (1963): *Benet Hill Monastery-Motherhouse*, 3190 Benet Ln., Colorado Springs, CO 80921-1509. Tel: 719-633-0655; Fax: 719-471-0403. Sr. Anne Stedman, O.S.B., Prioress; Sr. Diane Liston, O.S.B., Community Archivist.
Total in Community: 38.
Properties owned and/or sponsored: Benet Hill Monastery and Ministry Center.
Represented in the Archdioceses of Denver and Santa Fe and in the Diocese of Colorado Springs. Also in Jamaica.

Benedictine Sisters O.S.B. (1989): *Queen of Angels Monastery*, 23615 N.E. 100th St., Liberty, MO 64068. Tel: 816-750-4618; Fax: 816-750-4620; Web: www.libertybenedictinesisters.org. Sr. Agnes Helgenberger, O.S.B., Prioress.
Professed Sisters: 6.
Ministry in Companioning; food for the hungry; prison ministry; thrift stores; Religious education and retreats; Nursing.
Represented in the Diocese of Kansas City-St. Joseph.
Erected by Decree of the Apostolic See on April 14, 1937, with final approbation by Decree of April 4, 1950.

(II) The Federation of St. Gertrude: 802 E. 10th St., Ferdinand, IN 47532.

Federation Office: *Monastery Immaculate Conception (1867)*, 802 E. 10th St., Ferdinand, IN 47532-9239. Tel: 812-367-1411; Fax: 812-367-2313. Sr. Joella Kidwell, O.S.B., Federation Pres.
Total in Federation: 754.

Seventeen members monasteries from this Federation as follows:

Benedictine Sisters of Belcourt O.S.B: *Queen of Peace Monastery (1956)*, 802 E. 10th St., Ferdinand, IN 47532-9239. Tel: 812-367-1411 Ext. 2917; Fax: 812-367-2313; Email: khosb@thedome.org. Sr. Joella Kidwell, O.S.B., Pres. & Admin.
Community Ministry.
Represented in the Diocese of Fargo.

Benedictine Sisters O.S.B: *Our Lady of Peace Monastery*, 3710 W. Broadway, Columbia, MO 65203-0116. Tel: 573-446-2300; Fax: 573-446-2312; Email: smeek37@gmail.com; Web: www.benedictinesister.org. Sr. Sandra Meek, O.S.B., Admin.
Professed Sisters: 7.
Ministry in Religious Education; Home Health Care; Pastoral Care; Parish, Social and Nursing Ministries; Counseling.
Represented in the Dioceses of Jefferson City and Springfield Cape-Girardeau.

Monastery of St. Gertrude (1882): 465 Keuterville Rd., Cottonwood, ID 83522-5183. Tel: 208-962-3224; Fax: 208-962-7212. Sr. Clarissa Goeckner, O.S.B., Prioress; Rev. Eamonn McNerney, Chap.
Professed Sisters: 59.
Legal Title: *Idaho Corporation of Benedictine Sisters.*
Sisters serve in Education; Parish Ministry; Health Care; Retreat Ministry; Social Work; Counseling; St. Gertrude's Museum, Spirit Center Retreat House.
Represented in the Archdioceses of Los Angeles and Seattle and in the Dioceses of Boise, St. Cloud and Spokane.

Sisters of St. Benedict of Crookston O.S.B: *Mount St. Benedict Monastery (1919)*, 620 E. Summit Ave., Crookston, MN 56716-2799. Tel: 218-281-3441; Fax: 218-281-6966. Sr. Lenore Paschke, O.S.B., Prioress.
Professed Sisters: 80.
Legal Titles or Holdings: Villa St. Vincent, Crookston, MN.
Sisters serve and staff: Elementary; Colleges; Nursing Homes; Assisted Living Facilities; Religious Education Center; Adult Education; Parish Ministry; Pastoral Care; Retreat Centers & Social Services; Child Care; Nursery School.
Represented in the Dioceses of Brownsville, Crookston and New Ulm.

Benedictine Sisters O.S.B. (1867): *Monastery Immaculate Conception*, 802 E. 10th St., Ferdinand, IN 47532-9239. Tel: 812-367-1411; Fax: 812-367-2313. Sr. Kristine Anne Harpenau, O.S.B., Prioress.
Professed Sisters: 168; Perpetually Professed: 162; Temporary Commitment: 6.
Legal Title: *Sisters of St. Benedict of Ferdinand, Indiana, Inc.*
Sisters sponsor: Kordes Retreat Center, Ferdinand, IN.
Sisters serve and staff: on all levels of Academic Education; Religious Education; Parish Ministry; Hospitals; Public Health-Social Service Agencies; Diocesan Offices; Foreign Missions; Hispanic Ministries; Retreat House; Community Ministry; Psychology and Counseling Agencies.
Represented in the Archdioceses of Indianapolis, and Louisville and in the Dioceses of Evansville, Joliet and Owensboro. Also in Rome and Peru.

Benedictine Sisters, O.S.B. of St. Scholastica Monastery (1879): *St. Scholastica Monastery*, P.O. Box 3849, Fort Smith, AR 72913-3489. Tel: 479-783-4147; Fax: 479-782-4352. Sr. Maria Goretti DeAngeli, O.S.B., Prioress.
Professed Sisters: 63.
Ministry in the fields of Religious Education; Retreat Center; Parish Ministry; Hospital Chaplaincy; House of Prayer; Retreat Ministry; Counseling; Spiritual Direction.

Sisters of St. Benedict of Riverside, California, Inc., (1972): *Holy Spirit Monastery*, 22791 Pico St., Grand Terrace, CA 92313-5725. Tel: 909-783-4446; Fax: 909-783-3525. Sr. Mary Ann Schepers, O.S.B., Prioress.
Professed Sisters: 6.
Ministry in Religious Education; Parish Ministry; Spritual Guidance; Retreat Ministry; Educating Mentally Challenged Children.
Represented in the Diocese of San Bernardino.

Monastery of St. Benedict Center (1902): P.O. Box 5070, Madison, WI 53705-0070. Tel: 608-836-1631; Fax: 608-836-5586. Sr. Joella Kidwell, O.S.B., Pres. & Admin.
Professed Sisters: 1.
Legal Titles: Sisters of St. Benedict, Sioux City, Iowa, Inc.; Sisters of St. Benedict of Madison, Wisconsin, Inc.
Sisters Serve: Community Building, Prayer.
Represented in the Diocese of Sioux City.

Benedictine Sisters of Mt. Angel, Oregon (1882): *Queen of Angels Monastery*, 840 S. Main St., Mount Angel, OR 97362-9527. Tel: 503-845-6141; Fax: 503-845-6585; Email: qamosb@yahoo.com; Web:

www.benedictine-srs.org. Sr. Donna Marie Chartraw, O.S.B., Prioress.
Professed Sisters: 38.
Corporate Ministries: Shalom Prayer Center; St. Joseph's Shelter, Mt. Angel, OR.
Sisters serve: High School; Seminary; Parish Ministry; Retreat and Prayer Ministry; Spiritual Direction; Work with Handicapped and Aging; Ministry to Poor and Hispanics.
Represented in the Archdiocese of Portland in Oregon.

Benedictine Convent of St. Martin (1889): *St. Martin Monastery*, 1851-C St. Martin Dr., Rapid City, SD 57702-9602. Tel: 605-343-8011; Fax: 605-399-2723. Sr. Yvette Mallow, O.S.B., Prioress.
Professed Sisters: 31.
Ministry in the fields of Religious Education; Parish and Jail Ministry; Hospital Chaplaincy; Retreat and Spiritual Direction.
Represented in the Dioceses of Cheyenne and Rapid City.

Sisters of St. Benedict of Beech Grove, Ind., Inc. (1956): *Our Lady of Grace Monastery*, 1402 Southern Ave., Beech Grove, IN 46107-1197. Tel: 317-787-3287; Fax: 317-780-2368. Sr. Juliann Babcock, O.S.B., Prioress.
Professed Sisters: 69.
Legal Titles: Sisters of St. Benedict of Beech Grove, IN, Inc.; Charitable Trust of the Monastery of Our Lady of Grace, Sisters of the Order of St. Benedict.
Ministry in Education; Parish Ministries; Retirement Home; Educational Center; Religious Education; Hospitals.
Represented in the Archdioceses of Cincinnati, Indianapolis and Louisville and in the Diocese of Evansville.
Properties owned and sponsored: Our Lady of Grace Monastery; Benedict Inn Retreat and Conference Center; St. Paul Hermitage; Regina Retreat.

Benedictine Sisters of Richardton, O.S.B. (1916): *Sacred Heart Monastery (1916)*, P.O. Box 364, Richardton, ND 58652-0364. Tel: 701-974-2121; Fax: 701-974-2124. Sr. Ruth Fox, O.S.B., Prioress.
Professed Sisters: 27.
Legal Titles or Holdings: Benedictine Sponsorship Board, Inc.; Marillac Manor, Inc.; Subiaco Manor Inc.; Sacred Heart Benedictine Foundation; Pia Tegler Foundation.
Ministry in the fields of Academic Education; Hospital Chaplaincy; Native American Ministry; Parish Ministry; Health Care.
Represented in the Diocese of Bismarck.

The Benedictine Sisters of Mother of God Monastery O.S.B: *Mother of God Monastery (1961)*, 110 28th Ave., S.E., Watertown, SD 57201-8418. Tel: 605-882-6600; Fax: 605-882-6658. Sr. Ramona Fallon, O.S.B., Prioress.
Professed Sisters: 55.
Legal Titles: The Benedictine Sisters of Mother of God Monastery, Watertown, SD; St. Ann's Corporation (includes Benet Place & Evergreen Assisted Living), Watertown, SD; Retirement Trust, Watertown, SD; Benedictine Sisters Foundation of Watertown, SD.
Sisters serve and staff: in Elementary Education; Religious Education Centers; Parish Ministry; Social Services; Hospitals and Hospices; Retreat Center; Juvenile Services; Prison Ministry; Native American Ministries; Hispanic Ministries; Libraries & Archives; and Congregate Housing for Elderly.
Represented in the Archdiocese of St. Paul-Minneapolis and in the Dioceses of Fargo, New Ulm and Sioux Falls.

St. Benedict's Monastery (1912): 225 Masters Ave., Winnipeg, Canada, R4A 2A1. Tel: 204-338-4601; Fax: 304-339-1705. Sr. Virginia Evard, O.S.B., Prioress.
Professed Sisters: 24.
Ministry in Retreat & Conference Center; Education; Health Care.
Represented in the Dioceses of Calgary, Edmonton and Winnipeg, Canada.

Benedictine Convent of the Sacred Heart: *Sacred Heart Monastery (1880)*, 1005 W. 8th St., Yankton, SD 57078-3389. Tel: 605-668-6000; Fax: 605-668-6153. Sr. Jennifer Kehrwald, O.S.B., Prioress.
Professed Sisters: 117.
Sisters serve and staff: in Health Care Institutions; all levels of Academic Education; Social Services; Parish Ministry; Pastoral Care; Diocesan Offices; Counseling & Religious Education.
Represented in the Archdiocese of Omaha and in the Dioceses of Grand Island, Lincoln, Rapid City and Sioux Falls.

Benedictine Sisters of Nanaimo: *House of Bread Monastery (1993)*, 2329 Arbot Rd., Nanaimo, Canada, V9R 5K3. Tel: 250-753-1763; Fax: 250-754-3744. Sr. Barbara Rinehart, O.S.B., Prioress.
Professed Sisters: 9.
Corporate Ministries: Bethlehem Retreat Centre; Bethlehem Counseling Centre.
Sisters serve: Counseling; Retreat and Prayer Ministry; Nursing; Artist.
Represented in the Diocese of Victoria, Canada.

(III): The Federation of St. Benedict: 2200 88th Ave., W., Rock Island, IL 61201-7649. Tel: 309-283-2124; Fax: 309-382-2200. Sr. Susan Hutchens, O.S.B., Pres.
Total number of Sisters in Federation: 623.
Legal Title: *Federation of St. Benedict.*
Erected by decree of the Holy See March 24, 1947.
Twelve monasteries form this Federation; in addition to the nine American monasteries listed, three autonomous monasteries exist: Japan, St. Benedict's Monastery (1985); Muroran, Hokkaido; Taiwan, St. Benedict Monastery (1988) Tanshui, Taipei; Bahamas, Saint Martin Monastery (1994) Nassau.

Sisters of St. Benedict (1994): *Mount Benedict Monastery*, 6000 S. 1075 E., Ogden, UT 84405-4945. Tel: 801-479-6030. Sr. Danile Knight, O.S.B., Prioress.
Professed Sisters: 8.
Sisters serve and staff: Health Care; Campus Ministry; Parish Ministry; Spiritual Direction.
Represented in the Diocese of Salt Lake City.

Sisters of the Order of Saint Benedict-O.S.B. (1857): *Monasterio Santa Escolastica*, Apartado 8526, Humacao, Puerto Rico Tel: 787-852-4222; Fax: 787-850-5279. Sr. Angela Berrios, O.S.B.
Sisters: 10; Novices: 1.
Legal Title: *Sisters of the Order of Saint Benedict, Inc.*
Ministry in the field of Education at all levels; Parish Ministry.
Represented in the Diocese of Caguas.

Sisters of the Order of Saint Benedict-O.S.B. (1857): *St. Benedict's Monastery-Motherhouse and Novitiate*, 104 Chapel Ln., St. Joseph, MN 56374-0220. Tel: 320-363-7100. Sr. Nancy Bauer, O.S.B., Prioress; Sr. Renee Rau, O.S.B., Archivist.
Total Sisters in Congregation: 270.
Legal Title: *Sisters of the Order of Saint Benedict, St. Joseph, MN.*
Ministry in the field of Education at all levels; Indian Missions; Hospitals; Nursing Homes; Individual Apostolates; Diocesan Marriage Tribunal; Parish Ministry; Social Work; Spirituality and Retreat Counseling.
Represented in the Archdioceses of Portland in Oregon and St. Paul-Minneapolis and in the Dioceses of New Ulm, St. Cloud, San Diego and Santa Rosa.

Sisters of St. Benedict - St. Scholastica Monastery O.S.B. (1892): 1001 Kenwood Ave., Duluth, MN 55811. Tel: 218-723-6555. Sr. Lois Eckes, O.S.B., Prioress; Sr. Margaret Clarke, O.S.B., Archivist.
Total in Community: 109.
Ministry in the field of Academic Education at all levels; Religious Education; Indian Ministry; Residence for Elderly; Nursing Homes; Hospitals; Pastoral Care and Parish Ministries; Prison Ministry; Peace and Justice; Retreat Center.
Properties owned and/or sponsored: Benedictine Sisters Benevolent Association, McCabe Renewal Center, Duluth, MN; College of St. Scholastica; Benedictine Health System; St. Mary's Medical Center, Duluth, MN; Benedictine Living Communities, Inc., Duluth, MN: Benedictine Living Center of Garrison, Garrison, ND; Prince of Peace Care Center & Evergreen Place, Ellendale, ND; St. Benedict's Health Center & Benedict's Court, Dickenson, ND; St. Catherine's Living Center, Wahpeton, ND; St. Rose Care Center & Rosewood Court, LaMoure, ND; Benedictine Living Communities Foundation, Bismarck, ND; Benedictine Health Center; Polinsky Rehabilitation Center, Duluth, MN; St. Joseph's Medical Center, Brainerd, MN; St. Mary's Regional Health Center, Detroit Lakes, MN; St. Francis Regional Medical Center, Shakopee, MN; St. Mary's Hospital, Cottonwood, ID; Tekakwitha Living Center, Inc., Sisseton, SD; Madonna Towers of Rochester, Inc., Rochester, MN; St. Gertrude's Health Center, Shakopee, MN; Benedictine Health Dimensions, Cambridge, MN; St. Mary's Hospital, Superior, WI; St. Anne of Winona, Winona, MN; Villa St. Benedict, Lisle, IL; Villa St. Vincent, Crookston, MN, St. Benedict's Family Medical Center, Jerome, ID; Benedictine Care Centers: St. Brigid's at Hi-Park, Red Wing, MN; St. Isidore Health Center of Greenwood Prairie, Plainview, MN; Benedictine Health Center at Innsbruck, New Brighton, MN; St. Eligius Health Center, Duluth, MN; Green Prairie Place, Plainview, MN; The Villa at Hi-Park, Red Wing, MN; Benedictine Living Community of St. Peter, St. Peter, MN; Madonna Meadows of Rochester, Rochester, MN; Living Community of St. Joseph, St. Joseph, MO; Benedictine Senior Living at Steeple Pointe, Osseo, MN; Benedictine Health Center of Minneapolis, MN; Arrowhead Senior Living Community dba St. Michael's Health and Rehabilitation Center, Virginia, MN; Arrowhead Senior Living Community dba St. Raphael's Health and Rehabilitation Center, Virginia, MN; Bridges Care Community, Ada, MN.
Represented in the Archdioceses of Chicago, Milwaukee and St. Paul-Minneapolis, and in the Dioceses of Bismarck, Boise, Crookston, Duluth, Fargo, Joliet, Kansas City-St. Joseph; New Ulm, Peoria, Phoenix, St. Cloud, Superior, Sioux Falls and Winona.

St. Bede Monastery (1948): 1190 Priory Rd., P.O. Box 66, Eau Claire, WI 54702. Tel: 715-834-3176. Sr. Michaela Hedican, O.S.B., Prioress.
Total in Community: 29.
Properties owned and sponsored: St. Bede Monastery; St. Bede Retreat and Conference Center.
Represented in the Archdioceses of Louisville and San Antonio and in the Dioceses of La Crosse and Springfield-Cape Girardeau.

Sisters of St. Benedict O.S.B. (1874): *St. Mary Monastery*, 2200 88th Ave., W., Rock Island, IL 61201-7649. Tel: 309-283-2100; Fax: 309-283-2200. Sr. Phyllis McMurray, O.S.B., Prioress; Sr. Rita Cain, Archivist.
Total in Community: 56.
Ministry in the field of Religious and Academic Education; Pastoral Care; Parish Ministry.
Represented in the Dioceses of Davenport and Peoria.

Benedictine Sisters of the Annunciation, B.M.V. (1947): *Annunciation Monastery*, 7520 University Dr., Bismarck, ND 58504-9653. Tel: 701-255-1520. Sr. Nancy Miller, O.S.B., Prioress.
Professed Sisters: 60.
Ministry in Hospitals; Parish Ministry and Catechetical Work; Education, Health Care and Spiritual Direction.
Represented in the Diocese of Bismarck.

Sisters of St. Benedict (1948): *St. Paul's Monastery*, 2675 Benet Rd., St. Paul, MN 55109. Tel: 651-777-8181; Fax: 651-777-4442. Sr. Lucia Schwickerath, D.S.B., Prioress.
Professed Sisters: 52.
Sisters serve and staff: Schools; Long term care facilities; Administration; Child care; Retreat Center; Parish Ministry; Social Service and various other apostolic work.
Represented in the Archdiocese of St. Paul-Minneapolis and in the Diocese of Great Falls.

Sisters of St. Benedict O.S.B. (1952): *St. Placid Priory*, 500 College St., NE, Lacey, WA 98516. Tel: 360-438-1771. Sr. Maureen O'Larey, O.S.B., Prioress.
Professed Sisters: 16.
Sisters serve in the field of Education; Spirituality and Pastoral Care.
Represented in the Archdioceses of Portland in Oregon and Seattle.

[0233] (O.S.B.)—BENEDICTINE NUNS (P)
Subiaco Congregation

St. Scholastica Priory, Benedictine Nuns (Cloistered): 271 N. Main St., Box 606, Petersham, MA 01366-0606. Tel: 978-724-3213; Fax: 978-724-3216. Very Rev. Mother Mary Elizabeth Kloss, O.S.B., Prioress; Sr. Mary Angela Kloss, O.S.B., Sub-Prioress.
Nuns in Solemn Vows: 9.

[0235] (O.S.B.CAM.)—CAMALDOLESE BENEDICTINE SISTERS (P)
Camaldolese Congregation

First founded in Italy in the 11th century, affiliated with monastery in Rome founded in 1722; United States foundation in 1988.

Transfiguration Monastery: *Camaldolese Benedictine Sisters*, 701 NY Rte. 79, Windsor, NY 13865. Tel: 607-655-2366. Sr. Donald Corcoran, O.S.B.Cam., Prioress.
Professed Nuns: 3.
Ministry in Monastic life and Benedictine hospitality.
Represented in the Diocese of Syracuse.

[0240] (O.S.B.)—OLIVETAN BENEDICTINE SISTERS (D)

Established in the Diocese of Little Rock in 1887.

Motherhouse and Novitiate (1887): *Holy Angels Convent*, P.O. Drawer 130, Jonesboro, AR 72403-0130. Tel: 870-935-5810; Fax: 870-935-4210. Sr. Mary Anne Nuce, O.S.B., Prioress.
Professed Sisters: 43; Postulants: 1.
Properties owned and/or sponsored: St. Bernards Healthcare, Inc., Jonesboro, AR; St. Bernards Development Foundation, Inc., Jonesboro, AR.
Sisters serve and staff: Healthcare Ministries; Grammar Schools; Diocesan Ministries; CCD Centers & Parish Services.
Represented in the Dioceses of Fort Worth and Little Rock.

[0250] (C.V.D.)—SISTERS OF BETHANY (P)

Founded in El Salvador in 1928.

General Motherhouse: *Instituto Bethania*, Santa Tecla, El Salvador Mother Dolores de Maria Zea; Mother Foundrees Madre Luz Elena Ordonez, Supr. Gen.

U.S. Address (1949): *Bethany House*, 850 N. Hobart Blvd., Los Angeles, CA 90029. Tel: 323-665-6937; Tel: 323-669-9411. Sr. Leticia Gomez, C.V.D., Supr.
Professed Sisters: 10.
Ministry in Social Service Centers; Parish Work.
Represented in the Archdiocese of Los Angeles.

[0260] (S.B.S.)—THE SISTERS OF THE BLESSED SACRAMENT FOR INDIANS AND COLORED PEOPLE (P)

Founded in the United States in 1891.

General Motherhouse: 1663 Bristol Pike, Bensalem, PA 19020-5796. Tel: 215-244-9900. Sr. Patricia Suchalski, Pres.
Professed Sisters: 149.
Sisters serve and staff in the field of Education on all levels; Catechetical Schools; Adult Education and Social Service; House of Prayer; Evangelization Center.
Represented in the Archdioceses of Boston, New Orleans, New York, Philadelphia, Portland in Oregon and Santa Fe and in the Dioceses of Birmingham, Biloxi, Evansville, Gallup, Memphis, Palm Beach, Phoenix, Richmond and Tucson. Also in Haiti.

[0270] (C.B.S.)—CONGREGATION OF BON SECOURS (P)

Founded in France in 1824. First foundation in the United States in 1881.

United States: *Provincial House and Novitiate*, 1525 Marriottsville Rd., Marriottsville, MD 21104. Tel:

410-442-1333; Fax: 410-442-1394. Sr. Rose Marie Jasinski, C.B.S., Pres. Sr. Patricia Eck, C.B.S., Congregation Leader.
Total Sisters in U.S: 35.
Sisters own and operate: Bon Secours Spiritual Center.
Represented in the Archdioceses of Baltimore, Detroit, Miami, Newark and New York and in the Dioceses of Charleston, Richmond and Venice.

[0280] (O.SS.S.)—THE BRIGITTINE SISTERS (P)

Founded in Sweden in the 14th century.

Motherhouse: Rome, Italy

Convent in U.S.A. (1957): *Convent of St. Birgitta*, 4 Runkenhage Rd., Darien, CT 06820. Tel: 203-655-1068; Fax: 203-655-3496; Email: conventsb@optonline.net. Sr. M. Eunice Kulangarathottiyil, O.SS.S., Supr.
Professed Sisters: 8.
Legal Title: *Order of the Most Holy Savior of St. Bridget.*
Monastic tradition, Semi cloister.
Represented in the Diocese of Bridgeport.

[0300] (O.CARM.)—CALCED CARMELITES (P)

Carmelite Nuns of the Ancient Observance, Strictly Cloistered, belonging in the Second Order of Carmel.
Founded in Naples, Italy in 1536. First foundation in the United States in 1931.

Carmelite Monastery of St. Therese: *Little Flower of Jesus and St. M. Magdalen De Pazzi, St. Therese's Valley*, 3551 Lanark Rd., Coopersburg, PA 18036-9324. Mother Mary Therese, O.Carm., Prioress.
Professed Sisters: 8.
Legal Title: *The Carmelite Sisters of St. Therese's Valley, Inc.*
Represented in the Dioceses of Allentown, Fargo, San Angelo and Superior.

[0315] (C.C.W.)—CARMELITE COMMUNITY OF THE WORD (D)

Motherhouse & Novitiate: *Incarnation Center (1971)*, 3904 Bem Rd., Gallitzin, PA 16641. Fax: 814-886-4098. Sr. Marilyn Welch, C.C.W., Admin. Gen.
Total in Community: 18.
Ministries in Diocesan Administration; the field of Religious and Academic Education at all levels; Pastoral Care to the Imprisoned, Institutionalized, Elderly, Mentally Handicapped, Family Life Support Groups and the Poor; Parish Ministry; Mission activity in Appalachia.
Represented in the Diocese of Altoona-Johnstown.

[0320] (O.CARM.)—CARMELITE NUNS OF THE ANCIENT OBSERVANCE (P)

Carmelite Nuns of the Ancient Observance

Strictly Cloistered, belonging to the Second Order of Carmel. Founded in Guelder, Holland, in 1453. First foundation in the United States in 1930.

Carmel of Mary (1954): 17765 78th St., S.E., Wahpeton, ND 58075. Tel: 701-642-2360. Mother Joseph Marie of the Child Jesus, O.Carm., Prioress.
Total in Community: 9.
Represented in the Diocese of Fargo.

Monastery of Our Lady of Grace (1989): 6202 CR 339 Via Maria, Christoval, TX 76935-3023. Tel: 325-853-1722; Web: carmelnet.org/christoval/christoval.htm. Sr. Mary Grace, O.Carm., Vicar Prioress.
Professed Sisters: 5; Postulants: 2.
Represented in the Diocese of San Angelo.

Carmel of the Sacred Heart (1963): 430 Laurel Ave., Hudson, WI 54016. Tel: 715-386-2156. Sr. Lucia LaMontagne, O.Carm., Prioress & Archivist.
Professed Sisters: 6.
Legal Title: *Carmelite Nuns of the Diocese of Superior, Inc.*
Represented in the Diocese of Superior.

[0330] (O.CARM.)—CARMELITE SISTERS FOR THE AGED AND INFIRM (P)

Founded in 1929 in New York, Foundress: Mother M. Angeline Teresa, O.Carm.

Motherhouse and Novitiate: *St. Teresa's Motherhouse and Novitiate*, 600 Woods Rd., Avila on the Hudson, Germantown, NY 12526. Mother M. Mark Louis, O.Carm., Supr. Gen.
Professed Sisters: 196.
Sponsored Works: Carmelite System Inc., Germantown, NY; Carmel Terrace, Framingham, MA; St. Patrick Home, Bronx, NY; St. Margaret Hall, Cincinnati, OH; Carmel Manor, Fort Thomas, KY; Kahl Home for the Aged, Davenport, IA; St. Patrick's Manor, Framingham, MA; Marian Manor, South Boston, MA; St. Patrick's Residence, Naperville, IL; Lourdes - Noreen McKeen Residence, West Palm Beach, FL; Mother Angeline McCrory Manor, Columbus, OH; Avila Institute of Gerontology; Our Lady's Manor, Dublin, Ireland.
Represented in the Archdioceses of Boston, Cincinnati and New York and in the Dioceses of Albany, Altoona-Johnstown, Brooklyn, Columbus, Covington, Davenport, Joliet, Palm Beach, Scranton and Syracuse.

[0340] (C.A.CH.)—CARMELITE SISTERS OF CHARITY (P)

Founded in 1826.

Motherhouse: Vic, Spain

Generalate: *Carlo Zucchi*, 12, Rome, Italy, 00165. Tel: 06-662-03-52.

Provincial/Formation House: *Carmelite Sisters of Charity*, 701 Beacon Rd., Silver Spring, MD 20903. Tel: 301-434-6344. Sr. Maria Pilar Chamorro, C.C.V., Prov.
Ministry in Health Clinics; Parishes; Higher Education; Immigrants, Hispanics and Homeless, Educational Centers.
Properties owned or sponsored: Mount Carmel House; Formation House.
Represented in the Archdiocese of Washington and in the Diocese of Brooklyn.

[0350] (O.CARM.)—CARMELITE SISTERS (CORPUS CHRISTI) (P)

First foundation in the United States in 1920.

General Motherhouse: Tunapuna, Trinidad, West Indies Sr. Petronilla Joseph, O.Carm., Prioress Gen.

U.S. Address: *Mount Carmel Home-Keen's Memorial*, 412 W. 18th, Kearney, NE 68847. Tel: 308-237-2287; Tel: 308-338-1263. Sr. Dorothy Cavaness, O.Carm., Supr.Gen.
Professed Sisters: 9.
Ministry in Home and foreign missions; Academic and Religious Education; Social Work.
Represented in the Dioceses of Grand Island and Providence.

[0360] (CARMEL D.C.J.)—CARMELITE SISTERS OF THE DIVINE HEART OF JESUS (P)

Founded in Germany in 1891. First Convent in the United States in 1912.

General Motherhouse: Sittard, Netherlands Antilles Mother M. Angleina, Supr. Gen.

Northern Province: 1230 Kavanaugh Pl., Milwaukee, WI 53213. Tel: 414-453-4040; Fax: 414-453-6503. Sr. Maria Giuseppe, Prov.

Central Province: 10341 Manchester Rd., St. Louis, MO 63122. Tel: 314-965-7616. Sr. Mary Joseph, Prov. Supr.

South Western Province: 4130 S. Alameda, Corpus Christi, TX 78411. Sr. M. Lydia Ann Braun, Provincial Supr.
Professed Sisters Worldwide: 457; Total Sisters in U.S: 70; Novices: 72; Postulants: 36.
Sisters minister to Homes for Children 2; Homes for the Aged 9; Day Nurseries 4; Mission work in Africa, Iceland, Nicaragua, Venezuela and Brazil.
Represented in the Archdioceses of Milwaukee, St. Louis and San Antonio and in the Dioceses of Corpus Christi, Gary, Grand Rapids, Owensboro and San Diego.

[0370] (O.C.D.)—CARMELITE SISTERS OF THE MOST SACRED HEART OF LOS ANGELES (P)

General Motherhouse & Novitiate: *Carmelite Sisters of the Most Sacred Heart of Los Angeles*, 920 E. Alhambra Rd., Alhambra, CA 91801. Tel: 626-289-1353; Fax: 626-308-1913. Mother Regina Marie Gorman, O.C.D., Supr. Gen.
Total in Community: 137.
Legal Titles: Carmelite Sisters of the Most Sacred Heart of Los Angeles; Carmelite Educational Centers, Inc.; dba Sacred Heart Retreat House, Alhambra, CA; dba Mount Carmel in the Desert Retreat House and Day Care Center, Palmdale, CA; dba St. Joseph Center, Alhambra, CA; Little Flower Center, Inc.; dba Little Flower Missionary House, Los Angeles, CA; Avila Gardens Residence for Seniors, Duarte, CA; Santa Teresita Medical Center, Duarte, CA; Maycrest Manor, Inc. Culver City, CA.
The sisters serve and staff: Religious and academic education; healthcare centers; skilled nursing facilities for the care of the aged; nursery schools with day care and kindergarten; retreat houses; ministry to the elderly, sick and convalescents; evangelization centers and ministry to the youth.
Represented in the Archdioceses of Denver, Los Angeles and Miami and in the Dioceses of Tucson and Steubenville.

[0380] (C.S.T.)—CARMELITE SISTERS OF ST. THERESE OF THE INFANT JESUS (D)

Founded in the United States in 1917 at Bentley, OK.

General Motherhouse: *Villa Teresa*, 1300 Classen Dr., Oklahoma City, OK 73103-2447. Tel: 405-232-7926. Sr. Patricia Ann Miller, Gen. Supr.
Total in Community: 20.
Legal Title: *Carmelite Sisters of St. Therese of the Infant Jesus.*
Ministry in the field of Academic Education; Religious Education and Parish Ministry.
Properties owned and sponsored: Villa Teresa School, Oklahoma City, OK; Villa Teresa Moore, Oklahoma City, OK.
Represented in the Archdiocese of Oklahoma City.

[0390] (C.M.S.T.)—MISSIONARY CARMELITES OF ST. TERESA (P)

Founded in Mexico City in 1903.

General Motherhouse: Fresno No. 150, Col. Santa Maria la Ribera, Mexico, 06400. Sr. Fidelina Herrera, Supr. Gen.

U.S. Holy Family Province (1983): 9548 Deer Trail Dr., Houston, TX 77038. Tel: 281-445-5520; Fax: 281-445-5748. Sr. Maria Isabel Torres, C.M.S.T, Prov. Supr.
Professed Sisters: 60.
Ministry in Pastoral; Hospital Chaplaincy and Retreats.
Represented in the Archdioceses of Galveston-Houston and Oklahoma City and in the Dioceses of Beaumont and Little Rock.

[0397] (C.M.R.)—CONGREGATION OF MARY, QUEEN (P)

Founded in Vietnam in 1670 by Bishop Pierre Lambert de la Motte. First foundation in the United States in 1979 in Springfield, MO.

U.S. Regional: 625 S. Jefferson Ave., Springfield, MO 65806. Tel: 417-869-9842; Fax: 417-832-0852. Sr. Marguerite A. Tran, C.M.R., Reg. Leader.
Professed Sisters: 20.
Legal Title: *Congregation of Mary Queen, American Region.*
Represented in the Archdiocese of St. Louis and in the Dioceses of Dallas, Kansas City-St. Joseph and Springfield-Cape Girardeau.

[0400] (O.CARM.)—CONGREGATION OF OUR LADY OF MOUNT CARMEL (P)

Founded in France in 1824. First foundation in the United States in 1833.

Generalate: P.O. Box 476, Lacombe, LA 70445. Tel: 504-524-2398; Tel: 985-882-7577; Fax: 504-524-5011. Sr. Elizabeth Fitzpatrick, O.Carm., Pres.; Sr. Lawrence Habetz, O.Carm., Vice Pres./Sec. & Devel. Dir.; Sr. Therese Gregoire, O.Carm., Treas./Archivist.
Professed Sisters: 86.
Ministry in the field of Education on all levels; Hospitals; Social Service; Religious Education; Pastoral Ministry and Retreat Work; Prison Education Ministry.
Represented in the Archdiocese of New Orleans and in the Dioceses of Houma-Thibodaux, Joliet in Illinois and Lafayette (LA). Also in the Philippines.

[0410] (O.CARM.)—INSTITUTE OF THE SISTERS OF OUR LADY OF MOUNT CARMEL (P)

Istituto delle Suore di Nostra Signora del Carmelo

Founded in Italy in 1854. First foundation in the United States, 1947.

General Motherhouse: *Istituto di Nostra Signora del Carmelo*, Via dei Baglioni 10, Rome, Italy

U.S. Headquarters: *Carmelite Sisters*, 5 Wheatland St., Peabody, MA 01960. Tel: 978-531-4733. Sr. Kathleen A. Bettencourt, O.Carm., Supr.
Professed Sisters: 16.
Ministry in Holy Childhood Nursery; Kindergarten; Preschools; Daycare Centers
Represented in the Archdioceses of Boston and Washington and in the Diocese of St. Augustine.

[0420] (O.C.D.)—DISCALCED CARMELITE NUNS (P)

Founded in Spain in 1562. First foundation in the United States in 1790 in Charles County, Maryland; later this monastery was moved to Baltimore.
The Monasteries listed here are strictly contemplative and belong to the Order of Discalced Carmelites.

Carmelite Monastery (1790): 1318 Dulaney Valley Rd., Baltimore, MD 21286. Tel: 410-823-7415; Email: info@baltimorecarmel.org; Web: www.baltimorecarmel.org. Sr. Colette Ackerman, O.C.D., Prioress.
Professed Sisters: 15; Simple Professed: 1.
Legal Title: *Carmelite Sisters of Baltimore.*

Carmel of St. Joseph (1863): 9150 Clayton Rd., St. Louis, MO 63124. Tel: 314-993-6899; Fax: 314-993-5093; Email: stlouiscarmel@sbcglobal.net; Web: www.stormpages.com/mtcarmel. Mother Mary Joseph, O.C.D., Prioress.
Professed Cloistered Nuns: 8; Professed Extern Sisters: 1; Postulants: 1.

Monastery of St. Joseph and St. Teresa (1877): *Discalced Carmelite Nuns*, 73530 River Rd., Covington, LA 70435-2206. Tel: 985-898-0923; Fax: 985-871-9333; Email: covingtoncarmel@yahoo.com; Web: www.covingtoncarmelite.org. Sr. Joan Monkhouse, O.C.D., Prioress.
Solemnly Professed: 7; Junior Professed: 1; Novices: 1; Postulants: 1.

Discalced Carmelite Monastery (1890): 61 Mt. Pleasant Ave., Boston, MA 02119. Tel: 617-442-1411; Fax: 617-442-0203; Email: bostoncarmel@juno.com; Web: www.carmelitesofboston.org. Sr. Eileen Mary Linden, O.C.D., Prioress.
Total in Community: 12.

Carmelite Monastery (1902): 66th Ave. and Old York

Rd., Oak Ln., Philadelphia, PA 19126. Tel: 215-424-6143; Fax: 215-424-6143; Fax: 215-424-6145. Mother Barbara of the Holy Ghost, O.C.D., Prioress.
Professed Nuns: 8.

Monastery of Our Lady of Mt. Carmel (1907): *Office of Episcopal Delegate for Religious Diocese of Brooklyn*, 310 Prospect Park W., Brooklyn, NY 11215-6214. Tel: 718-399-5900. Sr. Maryann Seton LoPiccolo, S.C., Vice Chancellor (Diocese of Brooklyn).

Monastery of Our Lady of Mt. Carmel and St. Joseph: 361 Highland Blvd., Brooklyn, NY 11207. Tel: 718-235-0422. Mother Maria Luz, O.C.D., Prioress.
Total in Community: 6.

Carmelite Monastery of the Infant Jesus (1908): 1000 Lincoln St., Santa Clara, CA 95050. Tel: 408-296-8412. Sr. Emmanuel of Bethlehem, O.C.D., Prioress.
Sisters Solemn Vows: 19; Novices: 1.

St. Joseph's Carmelite Monastery (1908): 2215 N.E. 147th, Shoreline, WA 98155. Tel: 206-363-7150; Fax: 206-365-7335. Sr. Maria Valla, O.C.D., Prioress.
Professed Sisters: 5; Novices: 2.
Legal Title: *Carmelite Monastery of Seattle.*

Carmel of the Queen of Heaven (Formerly known as Regina Coeli Monastery) (1911): 17937 250th St., Eldridge, IA 52748-9425. Tel: 563-285-8387; Fax: 563-285-7467. Sr. Lynne Elwinger, O.C.D., Prioress.
Professed Sisters: 10.

Discalced Carmelite Nuns (1930): *Monastery of Mary Immaculate and St. Joseph*, 1740 Newburg Rd., Louisville, KY 40205. Tel: 502-451-6796. Mother Francis, Prioress; Sr. Clare, Archivist.
Solemnly Professed Sisters: 10; Temporary Professed: 1; Novices: 1.
Legal Title: *Carmelite Monastery of Louisville, Inc.*

Order of Discalced Carmelites O.C.D. (1913): *Carmel of St. Teresa of Los Angeles, Inc.*, 215 E. Alhambra Rd., Alhambra, CA 91801. Tel: 626-282-2387; Fax: 626-282-2053; Email: teresacarm@aol.com. Sr. Brenda Marie, O.C.D., Prioress.
Total in Community: 17.

Carmelite Monastery (1916): 4300 Mount Carmel Dr. N.E., Ada (Parnell), MI 49301. Web: www.carmelitenuns.com. Mother Elizabeth Ann, O.C.D., Prioress.
Professed: 12; Externs: 1.

Discalced Carmelite Nuns (2000): *Carmelite Monastery*, 89 Hiddenbrooke Dr., Beacon, NY 12508-2230. Tel: 845-831-5572; Fax: 845-831-5579; Email: beaconcarmel@optonline.net; Web: www.carmelitesbeacon.org. Sr. Michaelene Devine, O.C.D., Prioress.
Total in Community: 18.

Discalced Carmelite Monastery of St. Therese of the Child Jesus (1920): 75 Carmel Rd., Buffalo, NY 14214. Tel: 716-837-6499. Mother Miriam of Jesus, O.C.D., Prioress.
Cloistered Professed Sisters: 11; Extern Professed Sisters: 2; Novices: 1.

Monastery of Discalced Carmelites (1922): 22143 Main St., P.O. Box 260, Oldenburg, IN 47036-0260. Tel: 812-932-2075. Sr. Jean Alice McGoff, O.C.D., Prioress.
Contemplative Professed Nuns: 9.
Legal Title: *Monastery of the Resurrection, Discalced Carmelites, Sisters of Our Lady of Mount Carmel Carmelite Monastery.*

Carmel of the Holy Family (1923): 3176 Fairmount Blvd., Cleveland, OH 44118-4199. Tel: 216-321-6568; Fax: 216-321-1904; Web: clevelandcarmel.org. Sr. Annamae Dannes, O.C.D., Prioress.
Contemplative Professed Nuns: 13.

Discalced Carmelites of the Order of Our Lady of Mount Carmel O.C.D. (1925): *Monastery of Our Lady and St. Therese*, 27601 Hwy. 1, Carmel, CA 93923. Tel: 831-624-3043; Fax: 831-624-5495; Email: carmelitesofcarmelca@catholic.org; Web: carmelitesistersbythesea.net. Mother Teresita of the Holy Face, O.C.D., Prioress.
Professed Sisters: 10.
Legal Title: *Carmelite Monastery of Carmel, California, Inc.*

Discalced Carmelites O.C.D. (1926): *Monastery of the Most Blessed Virgin Mary of Mount Carmel*, 189 Madison Ave., Morristown, NJ 07960. Mother Therese, O.C.D., Prioress.
Professed Sisters: 9; Novices: 1.

Order of Discalced Carmelites O.C.D. (1926): *Carmelite Monastery of the Trinity*, 5158 Hawley Blvd., San Diego, CA 92116. Tel: 619-280-5424. Sr. Yvonne Hanke, O.C.D., Prioress.
Professed Nuns: 13; Junior Professed: 1.

Monastery of St. Therese of the Child Jesus (1926): 35750 Moravian Dr., Clinton Township, MI 48035-2138. Tel: 586-790-7255. Mother Mary Elizabeth, O.C.D., Prioress.
Professed Nuns: 6; Professed Extern Sisters: 1; Novices: 1.

Carmel of St. Therese of Lisieux, Inc. (1927): *Discalced Carmelite Nuns*, P.O. Box 57, Loretto, PA 15940-0057. Tel: 814-472-8620. Mother John of the Cross, O.C.D., Prioress.
Solemn Professed Nuns: 10.

Discalced Carmelite Nuns O.C.D. (1928): *Carmelite Monastery of Cristo Rey*, 721 Parker Ave., San Francisco, CA 94118-4227. Tel: 415-387-2640.
Total in Community: 17.

Monastery of Discalced Carmelites (1928): 600 Flowers Ave., Dallas, TX 75211. Rev. Mother Mary Regina, O.C.D., Prioress.
Professed Nuns: 12.

Discalced Carmelite Nuns (1930): *Monastery of Our Lady and St. Joseph*, 1931 W. Jefferson Rd., Pittsford, NY 14534. Tel: 585-427-7094. Mother Therese Marie of Jesus Crucified, Prioress.
Professed Nuns with Solemn Vows: 13.
Legal Title: *Carmelite Monastery of Rochester.*

Monastery of Discalced Carmelites O.C.D. (1930): *Monastery of Our Lady of Mount Carmel and St. Therese of the Child Jesus*, 25 Watson Ave., Barrington, RI 02806. Tel: 401-245-3421. Sr. Susan Lumb, O.C.D., Prioress.
Total in Community: 16.

Discalced Carmelite Nuns O.C.D. (1934): *Monastery of the Infant Jesus of Prague and Our Lady of Guadalupe*, 6301 Culebra & St. Joseph Way, San Antonio, TX 78238-4909. Tel: 210-680-1834. Mother Therese Leonard, Prioress.
Total in Community: 7.

Carmel of the Holy Family and St. Therese (1935): 6981 Teresian Way, P.O. Box 4210, Georgetown, CA 95634. Tel: 530-333-1617; Web: www.CarmeliteMonastery.com. Mother Christine, Prioress.
Total in Community: 14.

Discalced Carmelite Nuns O.C.D. (1936): *Monastery of Mary, Mother of Grace*, 1250 Carmel Dr., Lafayette, LA 70501. Tel: 337-232-4651. Mother Regina Mullins, O.C.D., Prioress.
Total in Community: 15.

Discalced Carmelite Nuns O.C.D. (1939): *Carmel of St. Joseph*, 20,000 N. County Line Rd., Piedmont, OK 73078. Sr. Donna Ross, O.C.D., Prioress.
Total in Community: 11.

Discalced Carmelite Nuns of Milwaukee O.C.D. (1940): *Carmel of the Mother of God*, W267 N2517 Meadowbrook Rd., Pewaukee, WI 53072. Tel: 262-691-0336; Fax: 262-695-0143; Email: pewaukeecarmel@aol.com. Sr. Mary Agnes Kramer, O.C.D., Prioress.
Total in Community: 9.

Discalced Carmelite Nuns of Alexandria, South Dakota, Inc. O.C.D: *Monastery of Our Mother of Mercy and St. Joseph*, 221 5th St. W., P.O. Box 67, Alexandria, SD 57311-0067. Tel: 605-239-4382. Mother Marie Therese of the Child Jesus, Prioress.
Total in Community: 13.

Carmelite Monastery (1943): 716 Dauphin Island Pkwy., Mobile, AL 36606. Tel: 251-471-3991; Fax: 251-471-3991. Mother Marie Therese, Prioress.
Solemnly Professed Nuns: 4.

Discalced Carmelite Monastery (1945): 49 Mount Carmel Rd., Santa Fe, NM 87505-0352. Tel: 505-983-7232. Mother Rose Teresa, O.C.D., Prioress.
Total in Community: 9.

Discalced Carmelite Monastery (1946): 275 Pleasant St., Concord, NH 03301-2590. Tel: 603-225-5791. Sr. Claudette Blais, O.C.D., Prioress.
Solemnly Professed Nuns: 6; Novices: 3.

Sisters of Our Lady of Mount Carmel of Terre Haute: *Carmelite Monastery*, 59 Allendale, Terre Haute, IN 47802-4751. Tel: 812-299-1410; Fax: 812-299-5820; Email: carmelth@heartsawake.org. Mother Anne Brackmann, O.C.D., Prioress.
Professed Nuns: 12.

Discalced Carmelite Nuns of Colorado, Inc. (1948): *Carmel of Holy Spirit*, 6138 S. Gallup St., Littleton, CO 80120-2702. Tel: 303-798-4176. Mother Gemma Marie of the Passion of Jesus, D.C., Prioress.
Professed Nuns: 10; Professed novice: 1.

Order of Discalced Carmelites O.C.D. (1949): *Carmel of Mary Immaculate and St. Mary Magdalen*, 26 Harmony School Rd., Flemington, NJ 08822. Mother Anne of Christ, O.C.D., Prioress.
Novices: 2; Professed: 16; Total in Community: 18.

Discalced Carmelite Nuns O.C.D. (1950): *Monastery of the Infant Jesus of Prague*, 3501 Silver Lake Rd., Traverse City, MI 49684-8949. Tel: 231-946-4960. Mother Mary of Jesus Markey, O.C.D., Prioress and Archivist.
Solemnly Professed: 4; Sisters in Formation: 2.

Discalced Carmelite Nuns O.C.D. (1951): *Monastery of the Holy Cross*, N4028 N. Hwy. U.S. 2, P.O. Box 397, Iron Mountain, MI 49801. Tel: 906-774-0561. Mother Maria of Jesus, O.C.D., Prioress.
Total in Community: 21.

Discalced Carmelite Nuns O.C.D: *Monastery of the Holy Name of Jesus*, 6100 Pepper Rd., Denmark, WI 54208. Tel: 920-863-5055; Email: holynamecarmel@catholic.org. Mother Mary Elizabeth, O.C.D., Prioress.

Discalced Carmelite Nuns O.C.D. (1950): *Monastery of the Immaculate Heart of Mary*, 94 Main St., P.O. Box F, Montpelier, VT 05601-1455. Tel: 914-831-5572. Sr. Jeanne Gonyon, O.C.D., Prioress.
Total in Community: 10.

Discalced Carmelite Nuns O.C.D. (1950): *Discalced Carmelite Nuns of Little Rock*, 7201 W. 32nd St., Little Rock, AR 72204-4716. Tel: 501-565-5121. Sr. Cecilia Chun, O.C.D., Prioress.
Professed Sisters: 13.
Legal Title: *Discalced Carmelite Nuns of Little Rock.*

Discalced Carmelite Nuns O.C.D. (1951): *Monastery of Our Lady of Mount Carmel and The Little Flower*, 2155 Terry Rd., Jackson, MS 39204. Tel: 601-373-1460. Sr. Margaret Mary Flynn, O.C.D., Prioress.
Professed Nuns: 6.

Carmel of the Immaculate Heart of Mary (1952): 5714 Holladay Blvd., Salt Lake City, UT 84121-1599. Tel: 801-277-6075. Mother Maureen Goodwin, O.C.D., Prioress; Sr. Mary Ann Krajiceb, O.C.D., Archivist.
Solemn Vows: 8; Finally Professed Externs: 1.

Discalced Carmelite Nuns of St. Paul (1952): *Carmel of Our Lady of Divine Providence*, 8251 De Montreville Trail N., Lake Elmo, MN 55042-9547. Tel: 651-777-3882. Mother Marie of the Incarnation, O.C.D., Prioress.
Professed Sisters: 12; Novices: 1.

Discalced Carmelite Nuns O.C.D. (1953): 1 Maria Hall Dr., Danville, PA 17821. Tel: 570-275-4682; Fax: 570-275-4684. Sr. Joan Lundy, O.C.D., Prioress.
Professed Sisters: 12.

Discalced Carmelite Nuns O.C.D. (1954): *Monastery of Our Lady of the Mountains*, 1950 La Fond Dr., Reno, NV 89509-3099. Tel: 775-323-3236; Fax: 775-322-1532; Email: renocarmel@carmelofreno.net; Web: www.carmelofreno.com. Sr. Susan Weber, O.C.D., Prioress.
Professed Nuns: 15.

Carmel of Maria Regina O.C.D. (1957): 87609 Green Hill Rd., Eugene, OR 97402. Tel: 541-345-8649; Fax: 541-345-4857. Mother Elizabeth Mary, O.C.D., Prioress & Community Archivist.
Total in Community: 10.

Monastery of the Holy Family (1957): 510 E. Gore Rd., Erie, PA 16509. Mother Emmanuel of the Mother of God, Prioress.
Professed Sisters: 5.

Discalced Carmelite Nuns (1958): 11 W. Back St., Savannah, GA 31419-3219. Tel: 912-925-8505. Sr. Joann Gartner, O.C.D., Prioress.
Total in Community: 6; Professed Nuns: 3.

Monastery of the Most Holy Trinity (1958): 5801 Mt. Carmel Dr., Arlington, TX 76017. Tel: 817-468-1781. Mother Maria of Jesus Crucified Brinkley, O.C.D., Prioress.
Total in Community: 12.

Discalced Carmelite Nuns O.C.D. (1958): *Discalced Carmelite Nuns of New Caney, Texas*, 1100 Parthenon Pl., New Caney, TX 77357-3276. Sr. Angel Teresa Sweeney, O.C.D., Prioress; Sr. Mary Ann Harrison, O.C.D., 1st Council Sister.
Total in Community: 8.
Legal Title: *Discalced Carmelite Nuns of New Caney, TX.*

Monastery of Discalced Carmelites (1959): 1101 N. River Rd., Des Plaines, IL 60016. Tel: 847-298-4241. Mother Anne of Jesus, Prioress.
Total in Community: 15.

Order of Discalced Carmelites O.C.D. (1958): *Carmel of St. Therese*, 15 Mt. Carmel Rd., Danvers, MA 01923-3796. Tel: 978-774-3008. Sr. Anne of the Mother of God, O.C.D., Prioress.
Legal Title: *Discalced Carmelite Nuns of Danvers.*

Discalced Carmelite Nuns O.C.D. (1960): *Monastery of The Sacred Heart and St. Joseph*, 2201 W. Main St., Jefferson City, MO 65109. Tel: 573-636-3364. Mother Marie Therese, O.C.D., Prioress.
Solemnly Professed Nuns: 7; Temporarily Professed Novices: 1.

Carmel of the Assumption (1961): 5206 Center Dr., Latrobe, PA 15650-5204. Tel: 724-539-1056. Sr. Mary Wild, O.C.D., Prioress.
Professed Sisters: 13.

Discalced Carmelite Nuns, Inc. (1962): *Monastery of the Discalced Carmelite Nuns*, 2901 S. Cecelia St., Sioux City, IA 51106-3299. Tel: 712-276-1680. Mother Kateri Marie of the Eucharist, O.C.D., Prioress.
Total in Community: 7.

Carmelite Monastery of the Mother of God (1965): 530 Blackstone Dr., San Rafael, CA 94903. Tel: 415-479-6872; Fax: 415-491-4964; Email: srdol@motherofgodcarmel.org. Mother Dolores Sullivan, O.C.D., Prioress.
Total in Community: 8.

Discalced Carmelite Nuns O.C.D: *Carmel of St. Anne*, 424 E. Monastery St., Springfield, MO 65807. Tel: 573-881-2115.

Mailing Address: 2201 W. Main St., Jefferson City, MO 65109. Mother Marya, O.C.D., Prioress.
Total in Community: 3.

Carmel of the Holy Trinity: 6301 Pali Hwy., Kaneohe, HI 96744. Tel: 808-261-6542. Mother Agnes Marie Wong, O.C.D., Prioress.
Total in Community: 5.

Discalced Carmelite Nuns of the Byzantine Rite (1980): *Holy Annunciation Monastery*, 403 W. County Rd., Sugarloaf, PA 18249. Tel: 570-788-1205; Fax: 570-788-3329. Mother Marie Helen of the Cross, O.C.D., Prioress.
Professed Nuns: 12.
Represented in the Diocese of Passaic.

Carmel of Port Tobacco (1976): 5678 Mt. Carmel Rd., La Plata, MD 20646. Mother Ana of Jesus, O.C.D., Prioress.
Solemn Professed: 9; Novices: 1.

[0430] B.V.M.—SISTERS OF CHARITY OF THE BLESSED VIRGIN MARY (P)

Founded in America in 1833.

BVM Center: *Mount Carmel*, 1100 Carmel Dr., Dubuque, IA 52003-7991. Tel: 563-588-2351; Fax: 563-588-4832; Web: www.bvmcong.org. Sr. Mary Ann Zollmann, B.V.M., Pres.

Total in Congregation : 541.

Sisters serve and staff: in the field of Academic Education on all levels; Health Care Services; Religious Education; Chaplaincies; Pastoral Care and Parish Ministry; Campus Ministry; Diocesan School Offices; Diocesan Services-Administration; Social Work; Homeless Shelters; Social Justice/Advocacies.

Represented in the Archdioceses of Chicago, Denver, Dubuque, Los Angeles, Omaha, Milwaukee, Portland in Oregon, San Antonio, St. Louis, St. Paul-Minneapolis, San Francisco, Seattle and Washington and in the Dioceses of Arlington, Biloxi, Davenport, Des Moines, Fort Wayne-South Bend, Fresno, Helena, Honolulu, Jackson, Joliet, Kansas City-St. Joseph, Lafayette, Las Vegas, Lexington, Memphis, Oakland, Orange, Orlando, Peoria, Phoenix, Rockford, Rockville Centre, San Bernardino, San Jose, Santa Rosa, Sioux City, Springfield-Cape Girardeau, Venice and Winona. Also in Ecuador, Ghana and Guatemala.

[0440] (S.C.)—SISTERS OF CHARITY OF CINCINNATI, OHIO (P)

Founded by Saint Elizabeth Ann Seton, Emmitsburg, MD, 1809. The Cincinnati Community became independent in 1852, Papal approval in 1939.

General Motherhouse (1852): *Mount St. Joseph*, 5900 Delhi Rd., Mount Saint Joseph, OH 45051. Tel: 513-347-5300; Fax: 513-347-5228; Web: www.srcharitycinti.org. Sr. Barbara Hagedorn, S.C., Pres.

Professed Sisters: 439.

Legal Title: *Sisters of Charity, Cincinnati, OH.*

Sisters serve and staff: Colleges; Secondary and Elementary Schools; Parishes; Healthcare; Foreign Missions; Home for Profoundly Challenged; Senior Care Services; Social Services; Congregational Services; Marian Shrine.

Represented in the Archdioceses of Baltimore, Cincinnati, Denver, Detroit, Dubuque, Indianapolis, Louisville, Miami, Newark, New York, San Francisco, Santa Fe and Washington and in the Dioceses of Brownsville, Cleveland, Colorado Springs, Columbus, Covington, El Paso, Ft. Wayne-South Bend, Helena, Kalamazoo, Lansing, Lexington, Oakland, Paterson, Pueblo, Saginaw, St. Petersburg, Toledo, Wilmington, and Venice. Also in Guatemala and Anapra, Mexico.

[0450] (S.C.I.C.)—SISTERS OF CHARITY OF THE IMMACULATE CONCEPTION OF IVREA (P)

Founded in Italy in the 18th Century. First foundation in the United States in 1961.

General Motherhouse: Via della Renella 85, Rome, Italy Tel: 396-5818145. Sr. Palma Giuliana Porro, Supr. Gen.

Total in Congregation : 898.

U.S. Foundation (1961): *Immaculate Virgin of Miracles Convent*, 628 Prittstow Rd., Mount Pleasant, PA 15666. Tel: 412-887-0220. Sr. M. Letizia Tribuzio, S.C.I.C., Reg. Supr. Tel: 412-887-6753.

Professed Sisters in the U.S: 9.

Properties owned and/or sponsored: Verna Montessori Children's House & Elementary School; Immaculate Virgin of Miracles Convent, Mt. Pleasant, PA.

Sisters serve and staff: Kindergarten and Elementary Schools and Middle School; Parish Services; Religious Education; Pastoral Ministry.

Represented in the Diocese of Greensburg.

[0460] (C.C.V.I.)—CONGREGATION OF THE SISTERS OF CHARITY OF THE INCARNATE WORD (P)

Founded in 1869 at San Antonio, Texas.

Generalate: 4503 Broadway, San Antonio, TX 78209-6209. Tel: 210-828-2244; Fax: 210-828-9741. Sr. Yolanda Tarango, C.C.V.I., Congregational Coord.

Incarnate Word Provincialate - U.S. Province: P.O. Box 15378, San Antonio, TX 78212-8578. Tel: 210-734-8310; Fax: 210-734-8369. Sr. Bette Anne Bluhm, C.C.V.I., Prov. Coord.

Incarnate Word Retirement Community: 4707 Broadway, San Antonio, TX 78209-6215. Tel: 210-829-7561; Fax: 210-828-0020. Mr. Steven Fuller, Exec. Dir.

Universal total in Congregation: 377; U.S. Province: 202.

Properties owned and/or sponsored: Universities 1; High Schools 3; Hospitals (co-sponsored) 27; Temporary shelter for homeless women & children 2; Retirement Center 1.

Ministry in the field of Education at all levels; Hospitals and Health Service Agencies; Nursing Homes; Pastoral Ministries; Diocesan Offices; Social Service Agencies.

Represented in the Archdioceses of Chicago, New Orleans, St. Louis, and San Antonio and in the Dioceses of Amarillo, Corpus Christi, Dallas, El Paso, Fort Worth, Jefferson City, LaCrosse, WI, Spokane, and Victoria, TX. Also in Ireland, Mexico, Peru, and Zambia.

[0470] (CCVI)—CONGREGATION OF THE SISTERS OF CHARITY OF THE INCARNATE WORD, HOUSTON, TEXAS (P)

Founded in the United States in 1866, St. Mary's Infirmary Galveston, TX.

Motherhouse: *Villa de Matel*, 6510 Lawndale St., P.O. Box 230969, Houston, TX 77223-0969. Tel: 713-928-6053; Fax: 713-928-8148. Sr. Lillian Anne Healy, Congregation Leader.

Total in Congregation : 172.

Legal Titles: Incarnate Word Charitable Trust; The Congregation of the Sisters of Charity of the Incarnate Word, Houston, Texas.

Sisters serve and staff: Hospitals; Homes for Aged; Elementary Schools; Social Services; Retreat Centers.

Represented in the Archdioceses of Galveston-Houston and Los Angeles and in the Dioceses of Alexandria, Beaumont, Lake Charles, Salt Lake City, San Bernardino, Shreveport, St. Louis and Tyler. Also in Ireland, Guatemala, San Salvador and Kenya.

[0480] (S.C.L.)—SISTERS OF CHARITY OF LEAVENWORTH, KANSAS (P)

Founded in the United States in 1858.

Community Offices and Motherhouse: 4200 S. 4th St., Leavenworth, KS 66048-5054. Tel: 913-758-6501; Fax: 912-682-2128. Sr. Joan Sue Miller, S.C.L., Community Dir.; Sr. Barbara Sellers, S.C.L., Archivist.

Total in Community: 295.

Ministries to AIDS Victims; Cross-culture; Elderly; Immigrants; Prisoners, Handicapped Adults and Youth; Health Service Agencies; Mental Health; Native Americans; and Social Service Agencies.

Properties owned and sponsored: University of Saint Mary, Leavenworth, KS; Cristo Rey Kansas City High School, KCMO. Residential and Day Treatment Centers for Children: Mount St. Vincent Home, Denver, CO; Saint John's Health Center, Santa Monica, CA; Health Facilities: Sisters of Charity of Leavenworth Health System, Lenexa, KS; Saint John's Health Center, Santa Monica, CA; Saint Joseph Hospital, Denver, CO; St. Mary's Hospital & Medical Center, Grand Junction, CO; Saint John Hospital, Leavenworth, KS; St. Francis Health Center, Topeka, KS; Providence Medical Center, Kansas City, KS; Saint Vincent Healthcare, Billings, MT; St. James Healthcare, Butte, MT; Holy Rosary Healthcare, Miles City, MT; Marian Clinic, Topeka, KS; Marillac Clinic, Grand Junction, CO; Caritas Clinic, Inc., Kansas City, KS; Saint Vincent Clinic, Leavenworth, KS (Div. of Caritas Clinics); Duchesne Clinic, Kansas City, KS (Div. of Caritas Clinics).

Sisters serving in Elementary; Secondary and Higher Education; Nursing Education; Special Education; Religious Education; Ministry Training; Hospitals; Latin American Missions; Diocesan Offices; Parish Administration and Pastoral Ministry; Liturgy-Music Ministry; Campus Ministry; Spiritual Direction; Communications; Social Justice; Housing.

Represented in the Archdioceses of Denver, Kansas City in Kansas, Los Angeles, Milwaukee and Santa Fe and in the Dioceses of Charlotte, Cheyenne, Gallup, Great Falls-Billings, Helena, Jackson, Kansas City-St. Joseph, Oakland and Pueblo. Also in Peru.

[0490] (S.G.M.)—SISTERS OF CHARITY OF MONTREAL (P)

(Grey Nuns)

Founded in 1737 by Saint Marguerite d'Youville at Montreal, Canada. First foundation in the United States in 1855.

Generalate: *General Administration*, 138 Rue Saint-Pierre, Montreal, Canada, H2Y 2L7. Tel: 514-842-9411. Sr. Jacqueline St. Yves, S.G.M., Congregational Leader.

St. Joseph Area U.S.A: *Area Administration-SGM*, 10 Pelham Rd., Ste. 1000, Lexington, MA 02421-8499. Tel: 781-674-7407. Sr. Helene Georges, S.G.M., Dir.-Formation; Sr. June Ketterer, S.G.M., Area Coord.

Total in Community: 32.

Legal Title: *The Grey Nuns Charities, Inc.*

Ministry in religious education, retreat ministry, social justice, thrift shop, congregational governance & administration, housing for the elderly, hospitals, nursing homes, parish ministry, pastoral care and prayer ministry.

Represented in the Archdiocese of Boston and in the Diocese of Manchester.

[0500] (S.C.N.)—SISTERS OF CHARITY OF NAZARETH (P)

Founded in the United States in 1812.

SCN Center: P.O. Box 172, Nazareth, KY 40048. Tel: 502-348-1555; Fax: 502-348-1502. Sr. Mary Elizabeth Miller, S.C.N., Pres.

Total in Congregation : 673.

Legal Title: *Nazareth Literary & Benevolent Institution.*

Properties owned or sponsored: Camp Maria, Leonardtown, MD; Facilities for the Elderly and Handicapped; Nazareth Village I, Nazareth Village II, Nazareth, KY; Nazareth Home, Louisville, KY.

Nazareth Office: P.O. Box 187, Nazareth, KY 40048. Tel: 502-331-4072; Fax: 502-331-4076. Sr. Judy Raley, S.C.N., Prov.; Sr. Brenda Gonzales, S.C.N., Vice Prov.

Sisters serve and staff: in the field of Academic Education on all levels; Special Education Services; Social Services; Libraries; Parish Ministry; Archdiocesan Offices; Health Care Institutions; Retreat Centers; Literacy & Retirement Centers.

Represented in the Archdioceses of Boston, Indianapolis, Louisville, Miami, Mobile and Philadelphia and in the Dioceses of Charleston, Cleveland, Columbus, Covington, Greensburg, Jackson, Knoxville, Little Rock, Lexington, Madison, Memphis, Owensboro, Pittsburgh, Richmond, Scranton, St. Petersburg, Steubenville and Venice. Also in Belize and Botswana.

Louisville Office: 676 Atwood, P.O. Box 17545, Louisville, KY 40217. Tel: 502-636-0411; Fax: 502-636-0412. Sr. Adeline Fehribach, S.C.N., Vice Prov.

Eastern Province: *SCN Provincial House*, E. Boring Canal Rd., KSV Raman Ln., GPO Box 219, Patna, Bihar, India, 800 001. Tel: 011-91-612-2532-579. Sr. Sangeeta Ayithamattam, S.C.N., Prov.; Sr. Reena Theruvankunnel, S.C.N., Vice Prov.; Sr. Basanti Lakra, S.C.N., Vice Prov.

[0510] (O.L.M.)—SISTERS OF CHARITY OF OUR LADY OF MERCY (D)

Founded in Charleston, South Carolina in 1829.

Generalate and Motherhouse: *Sisters of Charity of Our Lady of Mercy*, 424 Fort Johnson Rd., P.O. Box 12410, Charleston, SC 29422. Tel: 843-795-2866; Fax: 843-795-6083. Sr. Bridget Sullivan, O.L.M., Gen. Supr.

Total in Community: 21.

Properties owned and/or sponsored: Motherhouse, May Forest, Charleston, SC; Our Lady of Mercy Convent, Johns Island, SC; Our Lady of Mercy Community Outreach Services, Inc. Johns Island, SC.

Legal Title: *Barry Charitable Trust.*

Sisters serve and staff: Parishes; Social Services.

Represented in the Diocese of Charleston.

[0520] (S.C.M.M.)—SISTERS OF CHARITY OF OUR LADY, MOTHER OF MERCY (P)

Founded in Holland 1832. First foundation in the United States in 1874.

General Motherhouse: Den Bosch, The Netherlands

Universal total in Congregation: 752.

SCMM Provincial Center: 32 Tuttle Pl., East Haven, CT 06512. Tel: 203-469-7872. Sr. Barbara Ann Valentine, S.C.M.M., Prov.

Total in Community: 14.

Represented in the Archdioceses of Chicago, Detroit, Hartford and St. Paul-Minneapolis and in the Diocese of San Diego.

[0530] (S.C.M.C.)—SISTERS OF CHARITY OF OUR LADY, MOTHER OF THE CHURCH (P)

First foundation in the United States in 1970.

General Motherhouse: Baltic, CT 06330. Tel: 860-822-8241; Fax: 860-822-9842. Mother M. Anthony Lemire, Supr. Gen.

Professed Sisters: 60; Junior Professed: 4; Novices: 3.

Properties owned, staffed or sponsored: High Schools 1; Nursing Home 1; Elementary Schools 8; Catechetical Schools 5; Shelter for the Homeless 1; Hispanic Ministry 1; Educational Tutoring Center 1; Assisted Living, CBRF 1.

Represented in the Archdioceses of Hartford and St. Paul-Minneapolis and in the Dioceses of Madison and Norwich.

[0540] (S.C.O.)—SISTERS OF CHARITY OF OTTAWA (P)

(Grey Nuns of the Cross)

Founded in Ottawa, Canada, in 1845. First foundation in the United States in 1857.

General Motherhouse: 9 Bruyere St., Ottawa, Canada, K1N 5C9. Sr. Lorraine Desjardins, S.C.O., Gen. Supr.

Total number of Sisters in Congregation based in Ottawa: 630.

American Province (1950): *St. Joseph*, 559 Fletcher St., Lowell, MA 01854-3434. Tel: 978-458-4472; Fax: 978-441-1452. Sr. Prescille Malo, S.C.O., Prov. Supr.; Sr. Pauline LeBlanc, S.C.O., Archivist.

Professed U.S. Sisters: 24.

Properties owned and/or sponsored: D'Youville Senior Care, Inc, Lowell, MA; Bachand Hall, Lowell, MA; St. Joseph Residence, Lowell, MA; Provincial House, Lowell, MA.

Legal Title: *Sisters of Charity of Ottawa.*

Sisters staff: Grammar Schools; Health Care and Pastoral Ministries; Apostolate of Aging.

Sisters sponsor: Saints Medical Center, Lowell, MA.

Represented in the Archdiocese of Boston.

[0560] (S.C.Q.)—SISTERS OF CHARITY OF QUEBEC (P)

(Grey Nuns)

Founded in Quebec in 1849. First United States foundation in 1890.

General Motherhouse: 2655 Le Pelletier St., Beauport, Canada, GIC 3X7. Tel: 418-628-8860. Sr. Morin Huguette, S.C.Q., Supr.

U.S. House (1908): *Franco-American School*, 357 Pawtucket St., Lowell, MA 01854. Tel: 508-458-1251. Sr. Lorraine Richard, S.C.Q.

U.S. House (1917): *Sacred Heart Home, Inc.*, 359 Summer St., New Bedford, MA 02740. Tel: 508-996-6751. Sr. Lorraine Richard, S.C.Q., Supr.

Professed U.S. Sisters: 4.
Sisters serve and staff: The field of education and care of the elderly; Franco American School, Lowell, MA; Sacred Heart Home, New Bedford, MA.
Represented in the Archdiocese of Boston and in the Diocese of Fall River.

[0570] (S.C.)—SISTERS OF CHARITY OF SETON HILL, GREENSBURG, PENNSYLVANIA (P)

Founded in the United States in 1870.

Motherhouse: *Caritas Christi*, 129 DePaul Center Rd, Greensburg, PA 15601. Tel: 724-853-7948; Fax: 724-838-1512.

Generalate: *Sisters of Charity of Seton Hill*, 4933 W. Patterson Ave., Chicago, IL 60641-3512. Tel: 773-205-1822; Tel: 773-205-1823; Fax: 773-205-1855; Email: marlenemondalek@hotmail.com. Sr. Marlene Mondalek, S.C., Gen. Supr.
Total in Community: 439.
Properties owned and/or sponsored: Elizabeth Seton Center, Pittsburgh, PA; Korea Province in Kwangju, Korea.
Ministry in the field of Religious and Academic Education at all levels; Special Education and Rehabilitation Services for Children and Adults with physical and mental handicaps; Social and Legal Services; Health Care; Retreat Centers; Day Care Centers for Children and Adults; Pastoral and Campus Ministry; Community Service Center, Shelters for the Homeless; Spiritual Direction; Diocesan Offices; and Art Ministry.

U.S. Province - Provincialate: *DePaul Center*, 144 DePaul Center Rd, Greensburg, PA 15601. Tel: 724-836-0406; Fax: 724-836-8280. Sr. Vivien Linkhauer, S.C., Prov. Supr.; Sr. Louise Grundish, S.C., Archivist.
Represented in the Archdioceses of Chicago and Cincinnati, and in the Dioceses of Altoona-Johnstown, Erie, Cleveland, Greensburg, Orlando, Phoenix, Pittsburgh, Tucson, Wheeling-Charleston and Youngstown. Also in Israel.

[0580] (C.S.A.)—SISTERS OF CHARITY OF ST. AUGUSTINE (D)

Founded in Cleveland, Ohio in 1851.

Motherhouse: *Mount Augustine*, 5232 Broadview Rd., Richfield, OH 44286. Sr. Miriam Erb, C.S.A., Congregational Leader; Sr. Mary Denis Maher, C.S.A., Archivist.
Total in Congregation : 62.
Properties owned and sponsored: CSA Health Network, Cleveland, OH; Providence Hospitals, Columbia, SC; Sisters of Charity of St. Augustine Health System Inc., Cleveland OH; Mercy Medical Center, Canton OH; Westlake Health Campus Association dba St. John West Shore Hospital, Westlake, OH; St. Vincent Charity Hospital, Cleveland, OH; Regina Health Center, Richfield, OH; Sisters of Charity Foundation of Cleveland; Sisters of Charity Foundation of Canton; Sisters of Charity Foundation of South Carolina.
Represented in the Dioceses of Charleston, Cleveland, Lexington and Youngstown.

[0590] (S.C.)—SISTERS OF CHARITY OF SAINT ELIZABETH, CONVENT STATION (P)

Founded in Newark, New Jersey in 1859.

General Motherhouse: *Convent of St. Elizabeth - Administration Building*, P.O. Box 476, Convent Station, NJ 07961-0476. Tel: 973-290-5000; Tel: 973-290-5450; Fax: 973-290-5335. Sr. Maureen Shaughnessy, Gen. Supr.; Sr. Elizabeth McLoughlin, Archivist; Sr. Miriam Teresa, League of Prayer.
Total in Congregation : 439.
Properties and Legal Titles: Sisters of Charity of Saint Elizabeth Academy of Saint Elizabeth, Convent Station, NJ; Saint Vincent Academy, Newark, NJ; Josephine's Place, Elizabeth, NJ.
Sisters serve and staff: Academies; High Schools; Elementary Schools; Hospitals; C.C.D.; Parish Work; Social Work; Health Services; College Teaching.
Represented in the Archdioceses of Baltimore, Boston, Hartford, Newark and New York and in the Dioceses of Charlotte, El Paso, Fairbanks, Fall River, Gallup, Jackson, Metuchen, Paterson, Palm Beach, Providence, Pensacola-Tallahassee, Raleigh, St. Petersburg, Syracuse, Trenton, Tucson, Wheeling-Charleston and Wilmington. Also in St. Thomas, Virgin Islands, San Salvador, Central America.

[0600] (S.C.S.J.A.)—SISTERS OF CHARITY OF ST. JOAN ANTIDA (P)

Founded in France in 1799 by Saint Joan Antida Thouret. First foundation in the U.S. 1932.

General Motherhouse: *Suore della Carita di Santa Giovanna Antida*, Via S. Maria in Cosmedin 5, Rome, Italy, 00153. Sr. M. Luisa Colombo, Supr. Gen.

North American Province (1976): *Regina Mundi Provincial House*, 8560 N. 76th Pl., Milwaukee, WI 53223. Tel: 414-354-9233; Fax: 414-355-6463. Sr. Anne Marie Baemmert, S.C.S.J.A., Prov.
Total in Congregation : 35.
Ministry in schools; neighborhood services and parishes.
Properties owned and sponsored: St. Joan Antida High School, Inc; Guardian Angel Learning Center, Inc.; St. Joan Antida High School Foundation, Ltd.
Represented in the Archdiocese of Milwaukee and in the Diocese of Gallup.

[0610] (S.C.S.H.)—SISTERS OF CHARITY OF ST. HYACINTHE (P)

(Grey Nuns)

Founded in 1840 in St. Hyacinthe, P.Q., Canada. First United States foundation in 1878.

General House: 16470 Avenue Bourdages, SUD, St. Hyacinthe, Canada, J2T 4J8. Sr. Diane Beaudoin, S.C.S.H., Supr. Gen.; Sr. Claudette Jacques, S.C.S.H., Gen. Sec.
Universal total in Congregation: 187.
Legal Title: *The Society of the Sisters of Charity, Lewiston, ME.*

U.S. Regional Administration: *Sisters of Charity of St. Hyacinthe*, 98 Campus Ave., Lewiston, ME 04240-6076. Tel: 207-782-0798. Sr. Diane Beaudoin, Pres.; Sr. Claudette Jacques, S.C.S.H., Sec.
Total number in U.S: 8.
Properties owned and/or sponsored: St. Peter's Home, Manchester, NH.
Represented in the Dioceses of Manchester and Portland (In Maine). Also in Canada and Haiti.

[0620] (S.C.S.L.)—SISTERS OF CHARITY OF ST. LOUIS (P)

Founded in France in 1803. First foundation in the United States in 1910.

Generalate: 5169 Avenue MacDonald, Montreal, Canada, H3X 2V9. Sr. Nicole Jégo, Supr. Gen.
Universal total in Congregation: 626.

American Sector: 4907 S. Catherine St., Plattsburgh, NY 12901. Tel: 518-563-7410; Email: p-burgh@scslnys.org. Sr. Bernadette Ducharme, Local Supr.
Total in Community: 7.
Properties owned and sponsored: Our Lady of Victory Convent, Plattsburgh, NY.
Represented in the Diocese of Ogdensburg.

[0630] (V.Z.)—SISTERS OF CHARITY OF ST. VINCENT DE PAUL OF ZAGREB (P)

Founded in Croatia (Austria-Hungary) in 1845. First U.S. foundation in 1955.

General Motherhouse: Zagreb, Croatia Mother Maria Blaga Buncuga, Supr. Gen.

U.S. Foundation: *Sisters of Charity Convent*, 171 Knox Ave., West Seneca, NY 14224. Tel: 716-825-5859. Sr. M. Stella Simetich, V.Z., Supr.
Professed Sisters: 9.
Sisters staff: CCD Centers and Parish Services; Hospital & Health Services.
Represented in the Diocese of Buffalo.

[0640] (S.C.)—SISTERS OF CHARITY OF ST. VINCENT DE PAUL, HALIFAX (P)

Founded by Saint Elizabeth Ann Seton, Emmitsburg, Maryland in 1809. Congregation at Halifax became independent in 1856, Papal approved in 1908.

Sisters of Charity Centre: 215 Seton Rd., Halifax, Canada, B3M 0C9. Tel: 902-406-8077; Fax: 902-457-3506. Sr. Donna Geernaert, Congregational Leader; Mrs. Patti Bannister, Archivist.
Total in Congregation : 476.
Legal Title: *Sisters of Charity (Halifax).*

Commonwealth of Massachusetts: *Boston Office*, 125 Oakland St., Wellesley Hills, MA 02481-5338. Tel: 781-997-1100; Fax: 781-997-1358. Sr. Sally McLaughlin, S.C., Congregational Councillor Tel: 781-997-1355; Fax: 781-997-1358; Sr. Ann Regan, S.C., Congregational Councillor Tel: 781-997-1356; Fax: 781-997-1358.
Legal Titles: Sisters of Charity (Halifax) Supporting Corporation, 125 Oakland St. Wellesley Hills, MA 02481-5338. Phone: 781-997-1110; Fax: 781-237-8152. Sr. Donna Geernaert, Congregational Leader; Sisters of Charity (Halifax) Corporate Mission, Inc., 125 Oakland St. Wellesley Hills, MA 02481-5338. Tel: 781-997-1100; Fax: 781-997-1358. Sr. Donna Geernaert, Congregational Leader.

Mount St. Vincent Retirement Community: 125 Oakland St., Wellesley Hills, MA 02481-5338. Tel: 781-997-1110; Fax: 781-237-8152. Sr. Eleanor Ballantine, S.C., Community Leadership Team Tel: 781-997-1165; Fax: 781-237-8152; Sr. Kathleen Crowley, S.C., Community Leadership Team Tel: 781-997-1165; Fax: 781-237-8152; Sr. Maureen Murphy, S.C., Community Leadership Team Tel: 781-997-1165; Fax: 781-237-8152.
Legal Titles and Holdings: Marillac Residence, Inc., Wellesley Hills, MA; Elizabeth Seton Residence, Inc., Wellesley Hills, MA.

State of New York: *New York Office*, 85-10 61st Rd., Rego Park, NY 11374. Tel: 718-651-1685; Fax: 718-651-5645; Email: scnyoffice@aol.com. Sr. Maryanne Fitzgerald, Congregational Councillor Tel: 516-622-9655; Sr. Roberta Kerins, Congregational Councillor Tel: 301-773-0208.
Ministering in education at all levels; parish ministry; spiritual direction/retreats; social services; pastoral ministry; administration.
Represented in the Archdioceses of Boston and New York and in the Dioceses of Brooklyn, Metuchen and Rockville Centre. Also in Canada, Bermuda, Dominican Republic and Peru.

[0650] (S.C.)—SISTERS OF CHARITY OF ST. VINCENT DE PAUL OF NEW YORK (D)

Founded in Emmitsburg, Maryland in 1809 by Saint Elizabeth Ann Seton.

General Motherhouse: *Sisters of Charity Center*, 6301 Riverdale Ave., Bronx, NY 10471-1093. Tel: 718-549-9200; Fax: 718-884-3013. Sr. Dorothy Metz, S.C., Pres.
Total in Congregation : 366.
Sisters serve and staff: Colleges; High Schools; Elementary Schools; General Hospitals; New York Foundling Hospital; House of Prayer; Supportive Housing for low income Elderly; Residence for Senior and Invalid Sisters; Mental Health Divisions, Rest House for Community use; Housing for Homeless; Parish Pastoral Ministry; Advocacy Programs; Outreach Pastoral Ministry; Spirituality Programs.
Represented in the Archdioceses of Miami, New York and Philadelphia and in the Dioceses of Brooklyn and Rockville Centre. Also in Guatemala.

[0655] (S.C.V.)—SISTERS OF CHARITY OF ST. VINCENT DE PAUL OF SUWON

Motherhouse is located in Suwon, Korea.
Represented in the Archdiocese of Denver.
The sisters provide service to the poor, caring for the sick poor, elderly, mentally disabled, single mothers, dying people, prisoners, and refugees from North Korea.
Total Members: 230.
Sr. Regina Park, Pres.

Motherhouse & Generalate: 93-3 Chi-Dong Paddal-Gu, Suwon City, KyoungGi Province, Korea, North Tel: 031-241-2151.

U.S. Address(1996): *St. Anna's Home*, 3147 S. Pagosa St., Aurora, CO 80013. Tel: 303-627-2986; Fax: 720-379-6308; Email: stannashome@hotmail.com.
Total Sisters in U.S: 4.

[0660] (S.C.C.)—SISTERS OF CHRISTIAN CHARITY (P)

Daughters of the Blessed Virgin Mary of the Immaculate Conception

Founded in Germany in 1849. First foundation in the United States in 1873.

Generalate: *Suore della Carita Cristiana, Casa Generalizia*, Largo XXI Aprile, 10, Rome, Italy, 00162. Tel: 011-3906-86071-35. Sr. Adalberta Mette, Supr. Gen.
Universal total in Congregation: 581.

North American Eastern Province (1927): *Mallinckrodt Convent Div. of North American Province*, 350 Bernardsville Rd., Mendham, NJ 07945. Tel: 973-543-6528. Sr. Joan Daniel Healy, S.C.C., Prov. Supr.; Sr. Mary Pierre Koesters, S.C.C., Archivist.
Professed Sisters: 218.
Ministry in Academic Education; Retreat House; Catechetical Centers; Religion Coordinators; Health care and Parish Ministry.
Properties owned and/or sponsored: Villa Pauline, Retreat House, Mendham, NJ; Divine Providence Hospital, Williamsport, PA; Holy Spirit Hospital, Camp Hill, PA; Mallinckrodt Convent Motherhouse, Mendham, NJ; Holy Family Convent, Home for Aged and Retired Sisters, Danville, PA; Muncy Valley Hospital, Muncy, PA.
Represented in the Archdioceses of Newark, New York, Philadelphia, and Washington DC and in the Dioceses of Allentown, Camden, Harrisburg, Metuchen, Paterson, Scranton, and Wilmington.

North American Western Province: *Sisters of Christian Charity - Daughters of the Blessed Virgin Mary of the Immaculate Conception*, 2041 Elmwood Ave., Wilmette, IL 60091-1431. Tel: 847-920-9341; Fax: 847-920-9346. Sr. Janice Boyer, S.C.C., Prov. Supr.; Sr. Anastasia Sanford, Archivist.
Professed Sisters: 62.
Ministry in Academic & Religious Education; Pastoral Ministry; Parish Ministry; Ministry to Aged; Prayer Ministry; Ministry to the Poor and Multi-Cultural.
Properties owned and sponsored: Maria Immaculata Convent; Sacred Heart Convent, Wilmette, IL; the Josephinum Convent and Academy, Chicago, IL.
Represented in the Archdioceses of Chicago, New Orleans and St. Louis and in the Diocese of Rapid City.

[0670] (O.C.S.O.)—CISTERCIAN NUNS OF THE STRICT OBSERVANCE (P)

Founded at Citeaux, France, in 1098. First foundation in the United States in 1949.

Generalate: Viale Africa 33, Rome, Italy, 00144.
Total universal number of Nuns in Order: 1782.
Contemplative and Monastic

U.S. Establishments:

Mount St. Mary's Abbey: 300 Arnold St., Wrentham, MA 02093-1799. Tel: 508-528-1282; Fax: 508-528-5360. Mother Maureen McCabe, O.C.S.O., Abbess.
Total in Community: 48.
Represented in the Archdiocese of Boston.

Our Lady of the Mississippi Abbey: 8400 Abbey Hill Rd., Dubuque, IA 52003. Tel: 563-582-2595; Fax: 563-582-5511. Rev. Mother Nettie Gamble, O.C.S.O., Abbess.
Total in Community: 22.
Legal Title: *Trappistine Nuns, Inc.; Iowa Cistercians of the Strict Observance.*
Represented in the Archdiocese of Dubuque.

Santa Rita Abbey: H.C. 1 Box 929, Sonoita, AZ 85637-9705. Tel: 520-455-5595. Mother Miriam Pollard, O.C.S.O., Prioress.
Total in Community: 11.
Legal Title: *Cistercian Nuns of the Strict Observance.*
Represented in the Diocese of Tucson.

Our Lady of the Redwoods Abbey: 18104 Briceland Thorn Rd., Whitethorn, CA 95589. Tel: 707-986-7419; Web: www.redwoodsabbey.org. Sr. Kathy DeVico, O.C.S.O., Abbess.
Total in Community: 11.
Represented in the Diocese of Santa Rosa.

Our Lady of the Angels Monastery: 3365 Monastery Dr., Crozet, VA 22932. Tel: 434-823-1452; Fax: 434-823-6379. Mother Marion Rissetto, O.C.S.O., Prioress.
Legal Title: *Cistercian Nuns of the Strict Observance in Virginia, Inc.*
Represented in the Diocese of Richmond.

[0680] (O.CIST.)—CISTERCIAN NUNS (P)

Founded in 1098 at Citeaux, France. It is composed of monks and nuns in independent houses.

Generalate: *Piazza del Tempio di Diana*, 14, Rome, Italy, 00153. Rt. Rev. Maurus Esteva, O.Cist., Abbot Gen.

U.S. Headquarters: *Valley of Our Lady Monastery*, E11096 Yanke Dr., Prairie Du Sac, WI 53578-9737. Tel: 608-643-3520; Fax: 608-643-2801. Rev. Mother Bernarda Seferovich, O. Cist., Prioress.
Total in Community: 20.

[0685] (R.M.I.)—CLARETIAN MISSIONARY SISTERS (P)

Religious of Mary Immaculate Claretian Missionary Sisters

Founded in Santiago de Cuba, August 25, 1855. Established in the United States in 1956.

Generalate: Via Calandelli 16, Rome, Italy, 00153. Eusebia Pizarro, Supr. Gen.

U.S. Delegation: 9600 W. Atlantic Ave., Delray Beach, FL 33446. Sr. Regina Tutzo, R.M.I., Local Supr.
Sisters in the World: 600; Sisters in Florida: 11.
Legal Title: *Claretian Missionary Sisters of Florida, Inc.*
Ministry in Religious Education; Theological Formation in Pastoral Institutes and Seminaries; Social Ministries; Parish and Diocesan Ministries.
Represented in the Archdiocese of Miami and in the Diocese of Palm Beach.

[0690] (C.M.S.)—COMBONI MISSIONARY SISTERS (P)

Founded in Italy in 1872. An international congregation of 1,470 sisters serving in the mission fields of Africa, America, Europe, and the Middle East. First United States foundation in 1950.

Generalate: Rome, Italy Sr. Adele Brambilla, C.M.S., Supr. Gen.

American Headquarters: 1307 Lakeside Ave., Richmond, VA 23228-4710. Tel: 804-262-8827; Fax: 804-264-2906; Email: cmsusaprov@verizon.net; Web: www.combonisrs.com. Sr. Maria de la Luz Aguilera, C.M.S., Prov. Supr.
Legal Titles & Holdings: Provincial House, Comboni Missionary Sisters, Inc., Richmond, VA.
Represented in the Archdiocese of Baltimore and in the Diocese of Richmond.

[0700] (O.D.N.)—COMPANY OF MARY (P)

Founded in Bordeaux, France, April 7, 1607, by St. Jeanne de Lestonnac. First foundation in the United States in 1926, in Douglas, Arizona.

General Motherhouse: Rome, Italy Sr. Beatriz Acosta, O.D.N., Supr. Gen.
Universal total in Congregation: 1798.

U.S. Motherhouse (1926): *Company of Mary Provincial House*, 16791 E. Main St., Tustin, CA 92780. Tel: 714-541-3125. Sr. Leticia Salazar, O.D.N., Prov. Supr.; Sr. Kathy Schneider, O.D.N., Community Archivist.
Professed: 45.
Properties owned and/or sponsored: Divine Providence Kindergarten & Day Nursery, Los Angeles, CA; Lestonnac Kindergarten & Day Nursery, Douglas, AZ; St. Jeanne De Lestonnac School, Tustin, CA; St. Jeanne de Lestonnac Kindergarten & Day Nursery, Los Angeles, CA; St. Jeanne de Lestonnac School, Temecula, CA; St. Joseph Residence for Women, Los Angeles, CA; Vina de Lestonnac Ministry Center-Retreat, Temecula, CA; Lestonnac Residence for Women, Tustin, CA; Lestonnac Retreat Center, Tustin, CA.
Sisters serve and staff: Pre-Schools - Kindergartens; Grammar Schools; Religious Instruction Centers; Residences; Parishes & Retreat Centers.
Represented in the Archdiocese of Los Angeles and in the Dioceses of Orange, San Bernardino and Tucson.

[0710] (C.S.)—THE COMPANY OF THE SAVIOR (D)

Founded in Spain in 1952. First United States foundation in 1962.

General Motherhouse: Tajsia de Cusariego 19, Madrid, Spain, 28023. Mother Amelia Lora-Tamayo, Supr. Gen.

U.S. Foundation: 820 Clinton Ave., Bridgeport, CT 06604. Tel: 203-368-1875.
Professed Sisters: 80; Novices: 3.
Represented in the Diocese of Bridgeport.

[0720] (M.C.)—CONSOLATA MISSIONARY SISTERS (P)

Founded in Italy in 1910. First foundation in the United States in 1954.

Motherhouse: *Istituto Suore Missionarie della Consolata*, Via Cassia Km.37-BivioUmilta, Nepi, VT, Italy, 01036. Mother Gabriella Bono, Supr. Gen.
Universal total in Congregation: 760.
Represented in the Dioceses of Birmingham, Grand Rapids and Saginaw.

U.S. Headquarters: *Consolata Missionary Sisters*, 6801 Belmont Rd., P.O. Box 371, Belmont, MI 49306. Tel: 616-361-2072; Fax: 616-361-2049. Sr. Zelita M. Bragagnolo, M.C., Supr.
Total in Community: 25.
Sisters serve and staff: Catechetical and Pastoral Work; Apostolate among Minorities; Elementary Schools.

[0725] (M.C-M.)—CORDI-MARIAN MISSIONARY SISTERS CONGREGATION (P)

Founded in Mexico City in 1921. First United States foundation in 1926.

General Motherhouse: Apdo. Postal #1109, Toluca, Mexico, 50091. Sr. Maria Cibrian, M.C.M., Supr. Gen.

U.S. Provincial House: 11624 FM 471, Apt. 501, San Antonio, TX 78253. Tel: 210-798-8220; Fax: 210-798-8225. Sr. M. Teresa Cruz, M.C.M., Prov. Supr.
Total in Congregation : 110; Total number in U.S. community: 33.
Properties owned and/or sponsored: Cordi-Marian Villa-Retreat Center and Provincial House, San Antonio, TX; East St. Louis Catholic Day Care Center and Convent, East St. Louis, IL; Formation House, San Antonio, TX.
Ministry in Catechetical Centers; Pastoral Ministry Programs; Elementary Education; Kindergarten and Day Care Centers; Retreat Center; Social Service; Rel. Articles & Book Stores; Ministry to Hispanics.
Represented in the Archdiocese of San Antonio and in the Dioceses of Belleville and Springfield-Cape Girardeau.

[0730] (FD.CC.)—CANOSSIAN DAUGHTERS OF CHARITY (P)

Canossian Sisters

Founded in Verona, Italy in 1808.

General Motherhouse: via della Stazione di Ottavia 70, Rome, Italy, 00135.

U.S. Provincial House: *Cristo Rey-Canossian Sisters*, 5625 Isleta Blvd., S.W., Albuquerque, NM 87105. Tel: 505-873-2854. Sr. Anne Bosio, Prov. Supr.
Sisters in U.S: 41.
Ministry in Evangelization; Spirituality Center, Integral Promotion of the Person; Parish Pastoral Ministry; Pastoral Care of the Sick; Intermediate Care Facility for Developmentally Disabled Children; Lay Volunteer Program.
Represented in the Archdioceses of San Francisco and Santa Fe and in the Diocese of Sacramento. Also in Canada and Mexico.

[0740] (D.C.P.B.)—DAUGHTERS OF CHARITY OF THE MOST PRECIOUS BLOOD

Founded in Pagani, Italy in 1872. First foundation in United States in 1908.

Generalate: Via Vigna Fabbri 45, Rome, Italy Sr. Alfonsa Bove, Mother Gen.

U.S. Address: *Daughters of Charity of the Most Precious Blood*, 1482 North Ave., Bridgeport, CT 06604. Tel: 203-334-7000. Sr. Alfonsa Kunnel, D.C.P.B., Supr.
Total in Community: 18.
Represented in the Dioceses of Albany, Bridgeport and Paterson.

[0750] (F.C.S.C.J.)—DAUGHTERS OF THE CHARITY OF THE SACRED HEART OF JESUS (P)

First founded in France at La Salle de Vihiers in 1823. First founded in the United States at Newport, Vermont in October 1905.

Generalate: Montgeron, France

General Motherhouse: La Salle de Vihiers, France Sr. Genevieve Penisson, Supr. Gen.

Mount Sacred Heart Provincial House: *Daughters of the Charity of the Sacred Heart of Jesus (1949)*, 226 Grove St., Littleton, NH 03561. Tel: 603-444-5346; Fax: 603-444-5348. Sr. Elaine Voyer, F.C.S.C.J., Prov.
Total number in Province: 38.
Sisters serve and staff: Elementary Schools; High Schools; Catechetical Centers; Spiritual Directors; Pastoral Ministry; Preschools; Foreign Missions.
Represented in the Archdiocese of Boston and in the Dioceses of Burlington, Fall River, Manchester and Ogdensburg.

[0760] (D.C.)—DAUGHTERS OF CHARITY OF ST. VINCENT DE PAUL (P)

Founded in France in 1633. First foundation in the United States in 1809 by Saint Elizabeth Ann Seton, Emmitsburg, MD.

General Motherhouse: Paris, France Sr. Evelyne Franc, Supr. Gen.

Emmitsburg Province (Southeast) (1809): *St. Joseph's Provincial House*, 333 South Seton Ave., Emmitsburg, MD 21727. Tel: 301-447-3121; Fax: 301-447-6038. Sr. Claire Debes, D.C., Prov.
Total number in Province: 155.
Legal Title: *Sisters of Charity of St. Joseph's.*
Sisters serve and staff: High Schools; Elementary Schools; Medical Clinics; Hospitals; Nursing Homes; Homes for unmarried Mothers; Child Caring Homes; Social Service Centers; Catholic Charities; Parish Ministries; Outreach Centers; Hispanic Ministry; Hospice; Home Health.
Represented in the Archdioceses of Baltimore and Washington and in the Dioceses of Charleston, Raleigh, Savannah, St. Augustine and Wheeling-Charleston.

West Central Province (1910): *Marillac Provincial House*, 4328 Westminster Pl., St. Louis, MO 63108. Tel: 314-533-3004. Sr. Mary Walz, D.C., Prov.
Total in Community: 176.
Ministry in the field of Religious and Academic Education at all levels; Hospitals; Psychiatric Hospitals; Parish Ministry; Health & Social Service Centers; Day Care Centers; Clinics; Homes for Children; Catholic Charities Offices; Housing; Peace and Justice; Diocesan Offices; Home Health Care; Emergency Relief Centers; Spiritual Direction and Retreats
Sponsors: Daughters of Charity Services of New Orleans; Daughters of Charity Services of San Antonio-La Mision Div., San Antonio, TX; Daughters of Charity Services of San Antonio-DePaul Div., San Antonio, TX; Daughters of Charity Community Services of El Paso (DCCS-EP); Daughters of Charity Health Services of Austin, Austin, TX; De Paul Center, Waco, TX; Providence Health Center, Waco, TX; Daughters of Charity Services of Arkansas-DePaul Health Center, Dumas, AR; St. Elizabeth Health Center, Gould, AR; Ascension Health, St. Louis, MO; Daughters of Charity Healthcare Foundation of St. Louis; Proyecto Juan Diego, Brownsville, TX.
Represented in the Archdioceses of New Orleans, St. Louis and San Antonio and in the Dioceses of Austin, Brownsville, El Paso, Kansas City-St. Joseph, Little Rock and Springfield-Cape Girardeau.

East Central Province - Evansville (1969): *Daughters of Charity of St. Vincent de Paul of Indiana, Inc.*, 9400 New Harmony Rd., Evansville, IN 47720. Tel: 812-963-3341; Fax: 812-963-7589. Sr. Honora Remes, D.C., Prov. Supr.
Total in Community: 126.
Legal Title: *Mater Dei Provincialate, Inc.*
Ministries of Insertion Religious and Academic Education at all levels; Campus Ministry; Parish Ministry; Social Services in Parishes; Catholic Charities Office; Prison Ministry; Shelters for Homeless; Hispanic Ministry.
Sponsored Works: Home for Retired Sisters; General Hospitals; Skilled Nursing Facilities; Clinics; Home Health Care; Day Care Centers and Neighborhood Services; Childrens' Residence; Services to Elderly.
Co-Sponsored Organizations: Ascension Health.
Represented in the Archdioceses of Chicago, Detroit, Indianapolis, Milwaukee and Mobile and in the Dioceses of Belleville, Birmingham, Evansville, Jackson, Lafayette (IN), Nashville and Saginaw.

Northeast Province (1969): *De Paul Provincial House*, 96 Menand Rd., Albany, NY 12204-1499. Sr. Louise Gallahue, D.C., Prov. Supr.; John Diefenderfer, Archivist.
Total in Community: 165.
Ministry in the field of Academic Education at all levels; Hospital; Specialized Hospitals; Child Caring Homes; Day Care Centers; Social Service Centers; Parish Centers.
Represented in the Archdioceses of Boston, New York and Philadelphia and in the Dioceses of Albany, Bridgeport, Brooklyn, Buffalo, Greensburg, Metuchen, Ogdensburg, Syracuse and Wilmington. Also in Canada.

Province of the West (Los Altos Hills) (1969): *Seton Provincialate*, 26000 Altamont Rd., Los Altos, CA 94022-4317. Tel: 650-941-4490; Fax: 650-949-8883. Sr. Marjory Ann Baez, D.C., Prov.
Total in Community: 126.
Properties owned and sponsored: Seton Medical Center, Daly City, CA; Seton Provincialate, Los Altos Hills, CA; St. Vincent Medical Center, Los Angeles, CA; St. Vincent's Senior Citizen Nutrition Program, Los Angeles, CA; St. Francis Medical Center, Lynwood, CA; Maryvale, Rosemead, CA; Mount St. Joseph-St. Elizabeth, San Francisco, CA; O'Connor Hospital, San Jose, CA; Villa Siena, Mountain View, CA; St. Louise Regional Hospital, Gilroy, CA; St. Vincent's, Santa Barbara, CA; Our Lady of the Rosary of Talpa School, Los Angeles, CA; Our Lady of the Miraculous Medal School, Montebello, CA; Our Lady of the Visitacion School, San Francisco, CA; St. Patrick School, San Jose, CA; St. Elizabeth Seton School, Palo Alto, CA.
Represented in the Archdioceses of Anchorage, Los Angeles and San Francisco and in the Dioceses of Gallup, Phoenix, Salt Lake City and San Jose.

[0770] (D.C.)—DAUGHTERS OF THE CROSS (D)

Founded in France in 1640. First foundation in the United States in 1855.

Motherhouse: *Daughters of the Cross Motherhouse*, 411 E. Flournoy-Lucas Rd., Shreveport, LA 71115-3901. Tel: 318-797-0887. Sr. Maria Smith, Pres.
Total in Community: 3.
Represented in the Diocese of Shreveport.

[0780] (F.C.)—DAUGHTERS OF THE CROSS OF LIEGE (P)

Founded in Liege, Belgium in 1833. First foundation in the United States in 1958.

Principal House: *St. Bernard Convent*, 165 W. Eaton Ave., Tracy, CA 95376. Sr. Maureen O'Brien, F.C., Supr.
Total in Community: 6.
Represented in the Diocese of Stockton.

[0790] (F.D.C.)—DAUGHTERS OF DIVINE CHARITY (P)

Founded in Austria on November 21, 1868 by Mother Franziska Lechner. First founded in the United States on October 8, 1913, in New York City. Established in Akron, Ohio in 1950 as St. Mary Province.

General Motherhouse: Vienna, Austria

Generalate: *Grottaferrata*, Rome, Italy

St. Joseph Province (1921): *Provincialate:*, 850 Hylan Blvd., Staten Island, NY 10305-2021. Tel: 718-981-4402; Fax: 718-556-3550; Email: sisterwilliam@gmail.com; Web: www.godslovefdc.org. Sr. M. William McGovern, F.D.C., Prov. Supr.
Professed Sisters: 28.
Properties owned and/or sponsored: St. Mary's Residence, NY; St. Joseph Hill Academy, Staten Island, NY.
Ministry in Education; Nursing; Residence for Young Women; CCD; Youth Ministry.
Represented in the Archdiocese of New York and in the Diocese of San Diego.

St. Mary Province (1950): *Provincial Motherhouse and Novitiate*, 39 N. Portage Path, Akron, OH 44303-1183. Tel: 330-867-4960. Sr. Mary Coffelt, Prov. Supr.
Total in Community: 17.
Properties owned and/or sponsored: Daughters of Divine Charity, Inc.; Leonora Hall Convent; Leonora Hall Residence; Francesca Residence.
Ministry in the field of Education; Parish Ministry; Home for the Well Elderly Men and Women: Home for Young Women; Deaf Community of New York
Represented in the Archdioceses of Milwaukee and New York and in the Diocese of Cleveland.

Holy Trinity Province (1972): *Provincial House*, 39315 N. Woodward Ave., Bloomfield Hills, MI 48304. Tel: 248-645-5318. Sr. Hyacinthe Vamos, Prov. Supr.
Professed Sisters: 15.
Ministry in Education; Foster Care Residence; Homes for the Aged.
Represented in the Archdiocese of Detroit and in the Diocese of Fort Wayne-South Bend.

[0793] (D.D.L.)—DAUGHTERS OF DIVINE LOVE (P)

Founded in Ukpor, Nigeria in 1969. First United States Foundation in 1990.

General House: Fifth Avenue, P.O. Box 546, Enugu, Nigeria Tel: 042-559071; Tel: 042-551742. Rev. Mother Ifechukwu Udorah, D.D.L., Mother Gen.
Professed Sisters in Congregation: 800.

U.S. Regional House: 2601 N. Sayer Ave., Chicago, IL 60707. Tel: 773-622-2434; Fax: 773-622-2499; Email: ddloveus@aol.com. Sr. Mary Thecla Akubue, D.D.L., Reg. Supr.
Professed Sisters in U.S: 46.
Ministry in the field of Administration; Religious and Academic Education at all levels; Special Education; Health Services; Parish and Diocesan Services; Retreat Work; Social Work.
Represented in the Archdioceses of Chicago, Galveston-Houston, Newark, New Orleans and Washington and in the Dioceses of Brooklyn, Brownsville, Portland in Oregon and Springfield in Illinois.

[0795] (F.D.Z.)—DAUGHTERS OF DIVINE ZEAL (P)

Founded in Messina, Italy in 1887 by Saint Hannibal Maria DiFrancia. First foundation in the United States in 1951.

Generalate: *Figlie Del Divino Zelo*, Circonvallazione Appia 144, Rome, Italy, 00179. Mother M. Diodata Guerrera, F.D.Z., Supr. Gen.
Universal total in Congregation: 1000.

U.S. Headquarters: *Hannibal House Spiritual Center*, 1526 Hill Rd., Reading, PA 19602. Tel: 610-375-1738; Tel: 610-375-9072; Fax: 610-374-0369; Email: srdivinezeal@aol.com. Sr. Angelie Marie Inoferio, F.D.Z., Supr.
Total in Community: 3.
Ministry in the field of Religious and Academic Education; Parish and Youth Ministry; Retreat, Vocation, Prayer and Apostolate.
Represented in the Diocese of Allentown.

[0810] (D.H.M.)—DAUGHTERS OF THE HEART OF MARY (P)

Founded in France in 1790. First United States foundation in 1851.

Generalate: 39 rue Notre Dame des Champs, Paris, France, 75006.

Provincialate: 1339 Northampton St., Holyoke, MA 01040-1958. Tel: 413-532-7406; Fax: 413-533-4217. Sr. Clare A. Thompson, D.H.M., Prov.
Professed Sisters U.S.A: 53.
Represented in the Archdioceses of Boston, Chicago, New York, Philadelphia, St. Louis and St. Paul-Minneapolis and in the Dioceses of Camden, Ogdensburg and Springfield in Massachusetts.
Properties owned or sponsored: Marian Center, Holyoke, MA; Maryhill, St. Faul, MN; Nardin Academy, Buffalo, NY; Heart of Mary Center, St. Louis, MO; St. Joseph's School for the Deaf, Bronx, NY.

[0820] (D.H.S.)—DAUGHTERS OF THE HOLY SPIRIT

Founded in France in 1706. First foundation in the U.S. in 1902.

Generalate: *Congregation des Filles du Saint Esprit*, 15 Boulevard Sebastopol, B.P. 50148, Rennes Cedex 3, France, 35101. Sr. Agnes Stephan, F.S.E., Supr. Gen.

General Motherhouse: *Maison-mere des Filles du Saint Esprit*, 20 rue des Capucins - BP 4538, Saint-Brieuc Cedex 2, France, 22045.

Provincial House: *Daughters of the Holy Spirit, Inc.*, 72 Church St., Putnam, CT 06260. Tel: 860-928-0891. Sr. Norma Bourdon, D.H.S., Prov.
Total in Community: 113.
Ministry in the field of Academic Education at all levels; Home/District Nursing; Health Care Center for Daughters of the Holy Spirit; and Various Social and Pastoral Ministries of Service.
Represented in the Archdioceses of Hartford and Mobile and in the Dioceses of Birmingham, Bridgeport, Burlington, Norwich, Ogdensburg, Providence, Richmond, Sacramento, Springfield in Massachusetts, Stockton and Worcester.

[0850] (F.M.A.)—DAUGHTERS OF MARY HELP OF CHRISTIANS (P)
Salesian Sisters of St. John Bosco

Founded in Mornese, Italy, in 1872. First foundation in the U.S. in 1908 at Paterson, NJ.

General Motherhouse: Via Ateneo Salesiano, 81, 00139, Rome, Italy Very Rev. Mother Yvonne Reungoat, F.M.A., Mother Gen.
Universal total in Congregation: 14115.

Province of St. Philip, Apostle: *Provincial House*, 655 Belmont Ave., Haledon, NJ 07508-2398. Tel: 973-790-7963. Mother Phyllis Neves, F.M.A., Prov.
Total in Community: 100.
Properties owned and/or sponsored: Provincial House, Haledon, NJ; Mary Help of Christians Academy, North Haledon, NJ; Sacred Heart Center, Newton, NJ; Villa Madonna School-Salesian Sisters of Tampa, Inc., Tampa, FL; Camp Auxilium Learning Center, Newton, NJ.
Legal Title: *Missionary Society of the Salesian Sisters, Inc.; Salesian Sisters of Tampa, Inc.*
Ministry in the field of academic and religious education at all levels; Youth Ministry.
Represented in the Archdioceses of Miami, Newark, New Orleans and New York and in the Dioceses of Paterson and St. Petersburg.

Province of Mary Immaculate: *FMA Provincial House*, 6019 Buena Vista, San Antonio, TX 78237. Tel: 210-432-0090; Fax: 210-432-4016. Sr. Sandra Neaves, F.M.A., Prov.
Total in Community: 103.
Properties owned and/or sponsored: FMA Provincial House & St. John Bosco School, San Antonio, TX; Mary Help of Christians School, Laredo, TX; Salesian Sisters School - Salesian Sisters: MHC Youth Center, Inc., Corralitos, CA; Salesian Sisters Convent, Colorado Springs, Co; Formation House, Bellflower, CA.
Legal Title: *Institute of the Daughters of Mary Help of Christians - Salesian Sisters of St. John Bosco, San Antonio, TX.*
Ministry in Education; Youth Ministry; Religious Education and Outreach to the Poor.
Represented in the Archdioceses of Los Angeles, New Orleans, San Antonio and San Francisco and in the Dioceses of Austin, Colorado Springs, Laredo, Monterey, and Phoenix.

[0860] (D.M.)—DAUGHTERS OF MARY OF THE IMMACULATE CONCEPTION (P)

Founded in New Britain in 1904.

Motherhouse - Main Headquarters: *Admin. Offices*, 314 Osgood Ave., New Britain, CT 06053.

General Motherhouse: 643 Burritt St., New Britain, CT 06053. Tel: 860-225-9406. Mother Mary Jennifer, Supr. Gen.
Total in Community: 43.
Properties owned and/or sponsored: St. Lucian's Home, New Britain, CT; Monsignor Bojnowski Manor, New Britain, CT; Motherhouse and Novitiate Comples, New Britain, CT; St. Joseph's Home, NY; St. Agnes Residence, NY; Our Lady's Guild House, Boston, MA; Santa Maria Nursing Facility, Cambridge MA.
Legal Title: *Congregation of the Daughters of Mary of the Immaculate Conception, Inc.*
Ministry in the field of Education; Home for the Aged; Homes for Working Girls and Students; Skilled Care.
Represented in the Archdioceses of Boston, Hartford and New York and in the Diocese of Springfield in Massachusetts.

[0870] (F.M.I.)—CONGREGATION OF THE DAUGHTERS OF MARY IMMACULATE (P)
Marianist Sisters

Founded in France in 1816.

Motherhouse: Rome, Italy Mother Jolle Bec, Supr. Gen.

U.S. Foundation (1949): *Marianist Sisters Residence*, 235 W. Ligustrum Dr., San Antonio, TX 78228. Tel: 210-433-5501; Fax: 210-433-0300. Sr. Evangeline Escobar, Prov. Supr.
Total in Community: 16.
Properties owned and/or sponsored: Marianist Sisters Residence, San Antonio, TX.
Represented in the Archdioceses of Cincinnati and San Antonio.

[0880] (D.M.J.)—DAUGHTERS OF MARY AND JOSEPH (P)

Founded in Belgium in 1817. First U.S. Foundation in 1926.

Generalate: Via dei Lucchesi, 3, Roma, Italy, 00187. Sr. Linda Webb, Supr. Gen.

Novitiate: 5300 Crest Rd., Rancho Palos Verdes, CA 90275-5004. Tel: 310-377-9968; Fax: 310-541-5967. Sr. Frances Fisher, Vocation Dir.; Sr. Helen Vigil, Formation Contact.

Regionalate: 5300 Crest Rd., Rancho Palos Verdes, CA 90275-5004. Tel: 310-377-9968. Sr. Nuala Briody, D.M.J., Regional Admin.
Professed Sisters: 50.
Legal Title: *Daughters of Mary and Joseph, California.*
Sisters staff: Grammar & High Schools, Parish Ministry; Health Ministry; Missionary Work; Retreat Work.
Represented in the Archdioceses of Los Angeles and San Francisco and in the Dioceses of Monterey, San Bernardino and San Diego.

[0890] (D.M.)—DAUGHTERS OF OUR LADY OF MERCY (P)

Founded in Italy in 1837 by Saint Mary Joseph Rossello. First foundation in the United States in 1919.

Generalate: Via Monte Grappa, No. 7, Savona, Italy Rev. Mother M. Beatriz Lassalle, Supr. Gen.

Provincialate and Novitiate: *Villa Rossello*, 1009 Main Rd., Newfield, NJ 08344. Tel: 856-697-2983. Sr. Daniel Marie Catherine, Prov. Supr.; Sr. Loretta Marie Stevens, D.M., Community Archivist.
Total in Community: 54.
Legal Holdings: Our Lady of Mercy Academy, Newfield, NJ.
Ministry in the field of Education; Health Services; Skilled Nursing Center; Pastoral Counseling, C.C.D. and Parish Work.
Represented in the Dioceses of Camden, Harrisburg and Scranton. Also in the West Indies.

[0895] (F.M.S.R.)—DAUGHTERS OF OUR LADY OF THE HOLY ROSARY (P)

Founded in 1946 in Trung Linh, Bui Chu, North Vietnam by Bishop Dominic Maria Ho Ngoc Can. First foundation in the United States in 1967.
Sr. M. John Bosco Dinh thi Kim Thanh, F.M.S.R.

U.S. Provincial Office: *Annunciation Convent*, 1492 Moss St., New Orleans, LA 70119-2904. Sr. Mary James Hang-Nga Thi Tran, F.M.S.R., Prov. Supr.
Total in Community: 55.
Properties owned and/or sponsored: Five residences.
Ministry in the field of Education; Health Services; Pastoral Ministry.
Represented in the Archdiocese of New Orleans and Oklahoma City and in the Dioceses of Biloxi, Charleston, Houma-Thibodaux and Shreveport.

[0900] (F.D.N.S.C.)—DAUGHTERS OF OUR LADY OF THE SACRED HEART (P)

Founded in France in 1882.

Motherhouse: Via Casale S. Pio V, 37, Rome, Italy Sr. Mary Fyfe, Supr. Gen.

U.S. Foundation (1955): *St. Francis de Sales Convent*, 424 E. Browning Rd., Bellmawr, NJ 08031. Tel: 856-931-8973; Fax: 856-931-7018.
Professed Sisters in the U.S: 11.
Represented in the Diocese of Camden.

[0910] (BETHL.)—BETHLEMITA, DAUGHTER OF THE SACRED HEART OF JESUS (P)

Founded in Guatemala in 1861. First foundation in the United States in Dallas, TX.

Motherhouse: Bogota, Colombia

U.S. Foundation: *St. Joseph Residence, Inc.*, 330 W. Pembroke St., Dallas, TX 75208. Tel: 214-948-3597. Sr. Adelaide Bocanegra, Admin.
Professed Sisters: 6.
Represented in the Diocese of Dallas.

[0920] (D.S.F.)—CONGREGATION OF THE DAUGHTERS OF ST. FRANCIS OF ASSISI

Founded in Hungary, 1894. First foundation in the United States in 1946.

Motherhouse: *American Province: St. Joseph's Convent,* 507 N. Prairie St., Lacon, IL 61540. Tel: 309-246-2175. Sr. Adriana Zdila, D.S.F., Pres.

Professed Sisters: 14.

Legal Title: *Congregation of the Daughters of St. Francis of Assisi, American Province.*

Represented in the Dioceses of Peoria and Springfield-Cape Girardeau.

[0930] (F.S.J.)—RELIGIOUS DAUGHTERS OF ST. JOSEPH (P)

Founded in Gerona, Spain in 1875.

General Motherhouse: *General Asensio Cabanillas,* 18, Madrid, Spain, 28003. Mother Ma. Benita de la Cuerda, Supr. Gen.

Universal total in Congregation: 680.

Regional House: *Calzada Ermita Istapalapa,* Mexico Sr. Maria Mendia Ajona, Prov.

U.S. Foundation: 6677 Del Rosa Ave., San Bernardino, CA 92404. Tel: 909-888-4877. Sr. Maria Belen Manso, Supr.

Total in Community: 5.

Legal Title: *Daughters of St. Joseph of California, Inc.*

Represented in the Archdiocese of Los Angeles.

[0940] (D.S.M.P.)—DAUGHTERS OF ST. MARY OF PROVIDENCE (P)

Founded in Italy in 1881. First foundation in the United States in 1913.

Generalate: Rome, Italy Mother Giustina Valicenti, D.S.M.P., Supr. Gen.

Provincialate: *Daughters of St. Mary of Providence Immaculate Conception Province,* 4200 N. Austin Ave., Chicago, IL 60634. Tel: 773-205-1313; Tel: 773-545-8300. Sr. Patricia McCafferty, Prov.

Professed Sisters: 68.

Represented in the Archdioceses of Boston, Chicago and Philadelphia and in the Dioceses of Camden, Gary, Lansing, Milwaukee, New Ulm, Providence, Sioux Falls and Syracuse.

[0950] (F.S.P.)—PIOUS SOCIETY DAUGHTERS OF ST. PAUL (P)
Missionary Sisters of the Media of Communications

Founded in Alba, Piedmont, Italy, on June 15, 1915. First founded in the United States on June 28, 1932, in New York.

General Motherhouse: Rome, Italy Sr. Maria Antonieta Bruscato, Supr. Gen.

Universal total in Congregation: 2430.

Provincial House, Novitiate, Publishing House: 50 St. Paul's Ave., Jamaica Plain, MA 02130. Tel: 617-522-8911. Sr. Mary Sophie Stewart, F.S.P., Local Supr.; Sr. Margaret Timothy Sato, F.S.P., Prov. Supr.

Total in Community: 134.

Properties owned and/or sponsored: Pauline Book and Media Centers, found in 13 locations throughout the U.S.; Provincialate, Boston, MA; St. Thecla Retreat House, Billerica, MA.

Legal Title: *Daughters of St. Paul, Inc.*

Represented in the Archdioceses of Boston, Chicago, Los Angeles, Miami, New Orleans, New York, Philadelphia, St. Louis and San Francisco and in the Dioceses of Arlington, Charleston, Honolulu, and San Diego. Also in Canada.

[0960] (D.W.)—DAUGHTERS OF WISDOM (P)

Founded in France in 1703. First foundation in the United States in 1904.

General Motherhouse: *St. Laurent-sur-Sevre,* Vendee, France

Superior General Headquarters located in Rome, Italy.

U.S. Province (1949): *Provincial House,* 385 Ocean Ave., Islip, NY 11751-4600. Tel: 631-277-2660; Fax: 631-277-3274. Sr. Ann Gray, D.W., Prov.

Professed Sisters: 100.

Properties owned and/or sponsored: Wisdom House Center for Spirituality, Litchfield, CT; Our Lady of Perpetual Help Convent (Rest Home for Sisters), Sound Beach, NY; Provincial House, Islip, NY.

Ministry in all levels of Education; Retreat House; Hospital & Health Services; Orphanage; Social Work; Pediatrics Clinic.

Represented in the Archdioceses of Hartford and Washington and in the Dioceses of Arlington, Brooklyn, Charleston, Portland (In Maine), Raleigh, Richmond, Rockville Centre, St. Petersburg and Wheeling-Charleston.

[0965] (D.L.J.C.)—DISCIPLES OF THE LORD JESUS CHRIST (P)

Founded in the United States in 1972.

Motherhouse: P.O. Box 64, Prayer Town, TX 79010. Tel: 806-534-2312; Fax: 806-534-2223; Email: sisters@dljc.org; Web: www.dljc.org. Mother Lucy Lukasiewicz, Supr. Gen.

Total in Community: 33.

Legal Holdings and Titles: Prayertown Emmanuel Retreat House, Prayer Town, TX.

Ministry in Retreat Work and Evangelization.

Represented in the Diocese of Amarillo. Also in Mexico.

[0970] (R.D.C.)—SISTERS OF THE DIVINE COMPASSION (D)

Founded in the United States in 1886.

General Motherhouse: *Good Counsel Convent,* 52 N. Broadway, White Plains, NY 10603. Tel: 914-798-1300; Fax: 914-949-5169. Sr. Susan Merritt, R.D.C., Pres.

Total in Community: 92.

Legal Holdings and Titles: Academy of Our Lady of Good Counsel High School and Elementary School, White Plains, NY; Preston High School, New York, NY; Divine Compassion Center for Spiritual Renewal, NY; Migrant Ministry, Goshen, NY; Residence, Hampton Bays, NY; RDC Center for Counseling and Human Development.

Ministry in Preschool, Elementary, Secondary, College and University Education; Religious Education; Educational Consultation; Adult Education; Special Education; Pastoral Ministry; Retreat Work and Spiritual Direction; Counseling; Social Services; Migrant Ministry; Health Services; Administration and Business Services.

Represented in the Archdiocese of New York.

[0980] (P.D.D.M.)—PIOUS DISCIPLES OF THE DIVINE MASTER (P)

Founded in 1924. First foundation in the United States in 1948.

General Motherhouse: Rome, Italy Sr. M. Regina Cesarato, Supr. Gen.

Universal total in Congregation: 1426.

U.S. Headquarters: 60 Sunset Ave., Staten Island, NY 10314. Tel: 718-494-8597; Fax: 718-494-2123. Sr. M. Nieves Salinas, P.D.D.M., Reg. Supr.

Total number in Region: 48.

Ministry is a Three Dimensional Mission: Eucharistic, Priestly, Liturgical.

Represented in the Archdioceses of Boston, Los Angeles and New York and in the Dioceses of Fresno and San Jose.

[0990] (C.D.P.)—SISTERS OF DIVINE PROVIDENCE (P)

Founded in Germany in 1851. First foundation in the United States in 1876; incorporation granted September 17, 1881.

Amended and restated articles of incorporation on December 28, 2001.

General Motherhouse: *Mother of Providence Convent,* 12 Christopher St., Wakefield, RI 02879. Tel: 401-782-1785; Fax: 401-782-6967. Sr. Janet Folkl, Gen. Supr.

Marie de la Roche Province (2001): *Providence Heights,* 9000 Babcock Blvd., Allison Park, PA 15101. Tel: 412-931-5241; Fax: 412-635-5416. Sr. Mary Francis Fletcher, C.D.P., Prov. Supr.; Sr. Claudia Ward, C.D.P., Area Asst.-Kingston, MA; Sr. Jacklyn Pritchard, C.D.P., Area Asst.-St. Louis, MO.

Total in Community: 258.

Ministry in the fields of Education; Social Services; Pastoral Ministry; and Health Care Services.

Properties owned and sponsored: La Roche College, Pittsburgh, PA; Providence Heights Alpha School, Allison Park, PA; Transfiguration House of Prayer, Butler, PA; Kearns Spirituality Center, Allison Park, PA; Providence Connections, Inc.; Providence Family Support Center, Pittsburgh, PA; Providence Villa, Gibsonia, PA; Amelia House, Clarion, PA; Sisters of Divine Providence of Allegheny County, Allison Park, PA; Divine Providence Foundation, Allison Park, PA; Sisters of Divine Providence Charitable Trust, Allison Park, PA; Providence Ministry Corporation, Bridgeton, MO; Sacred Heart High School, Kingston, MA; Sacred Heart Elementary School, Kingston, MA.

Represented in the Archdioceses of Boston, Denver, Detroit, Kansas City in Kansas, Richmond, Wheeling-Charleston, St. Louis, Santa Fe and San Juan and in the Dioceses of Arecibo (PR), Bismarck, Brownsville, Cleveland, Columbus, Erie, Greensburg, Jackson, Nashville, Orlando, Phoenix, Pittsburgh, Providence, Raleigh, Springfield-Cape Girardeau, Springfield in Illinois and Youngstown. Also in the Dominican Republic and Italy.

[1000] (C.D.P.)—CONGREGATION OF DIVINE PROVIDENCE, MELBOURNE, KENTUCKY (P)

Founded in France in 1762. First foundation in the United States in 1889.

General Motherhouse: *St. Jean de Bassel,* Fenetrange, France, 57930. Sr. Pascale Kubler, Supr. Gen.

American Provincial House (1889): *St. Anne Convent,* 1000 St. Anne Dr., Melbourne, KY 41059. Tel: 606-441-0679. Sr. Frances E. Moore, C.D.P., Prov. Supr.; Sr. Mary Joan Dohmen, C.D.P., Archivist.

Total number in Province: 147.

Ministry in the field of Academic Education at all levels; Montessori Schools; Home for Working Women; Retreat Center; Religious Education & Pastoral Ministry; Health & Social Services.

Represented in the Archdioceses of Cincinnati, Indianapolis, New York and Washington and in the Dioceses of Covington, Duluth, Lexington, Manchester, Toledo and Wheeling-Charleston. Also in West Africa.

[1010] (C.D.P.)—CONGREGATION OF DIVINE PROVIDENCE, SAN ANTONIO, TEXAS (P)

Founded in France in 1762. First foundation in the United States in 1866.

515 S.W. 24th St., San Antonio, TX 78207. Tel: 210-434-1866; Fax: 210-568-1050.

The Generalate: P.O. Box 37345, San Antonio, TX 78237. Sr. Jane Ann Slater, Supr. Gen. Councilors: Sr. Marlene Quesenberry, C.D.P.; Sr. Rosalie Karstedt, C.D.P.; Sr. Imelda Gonzalez, C.D.P.; Sr. Dianne Heinrich, C.D.P.; Sr. Charlotte Kitowski, Archivist; Sr. Madonna Sangalli, C.D.P., Treas.

Novitiate and Formation: *Formation/Vocation Office,* 515 S.W. 24th St., San Antonio, TX 78207-4600. Tel: 210-434-1866.

Properties owned and/or sponsored: Our Lady of the Lake Retirement Center, San Antonio, TX; Moye Center, Castroville, TX.

Legal Titles & Holdings: Congregation of Divine Providence, Inc.; Providence Trust, San Antonio, TX.

Ministry in all levels of Education; Catechetical Centers; Hospitals, Clinics; Diocesan Offices; Retreat Houses; Spiritual Direction-Counseling; Pastoral; Social Work; Chaplaincies in Public Institutions; Home-Health Care; Administration.

Represented in the Archdioceses of Denver, Galveston-Houston, New Orleans, San Antonio, San Francisco, Seattle and St. Louis and in the Dioceses of Alexandria, Austin, Brownsville, Dallas, Fort-Worth, Houma-Thibodaux, La Crosse, Lafayette (LA), Laredo, St. Petersburg, San Angelo, San Jose, Savannah, Victoria and Wichita. Also in Mexico.

[1020] (S.D.R.)—SISTERS OF THE DIVINE REDEEMER (P)

Founded in 1849 at Niederbronn, France. First foundation in the United States on October 6, 1912 at McKeesport.

Generalate: *Suore del Divin Redentore,* Via Casale Piombino 14, Rome, Italy, 00135. Tel: 011-39-06-305-2512. Sr. M. Julia Zarembova, Supr. Gen.

American Province (1922): *Divine Redeemer Motherhouse,* 999 Rock Run Rd., Elizabeth, PA 15037-2613. Tel: 412-751-8600; Fax: 412-751-0355. Sr. M. Monica Kosztolnyik, Archivist; Sr. Rosemary Horvath, S.D.R., Prov. Supr.

Total number in Province: 22.

Legal Titles and Holdings: Sisters of the Divine Redeemer Charitable Trust; Divine Redeemer Health Care Ministries Corp., Elizabeth, PA.

Sisters serve and staff: CCD Center; Nursing Home.

Represented in the Archdiocese of Philadelphia and in the Diocese of Pittsburgh.

[1030] (S.D.S.)—SISTERS OF THE DIVINE SAVIOR

Founded in Tivoli, Italy, in 1888. First foundation in the United States in 1895.

General Motherhouse: Viale delle Mura Gianicolensi 67, Rome, Italy Sr. Therezinha Joana Rasera, Supr. Gen.

North American Province: *Sisters of the Divine Savior,* 4311 N. 100th St., Milwaukee, WI 53222-1393. Tel: 414-466-0810; Fax: 414-466-4335. Sr. Carol Thresher, S.D.S., Prov. Supr.; Sr. Aquin Gilles, S.D.S., Archivist.

Total number in U.S. community: 88.

Ministry in all levels of Education; Pastoral and Social Services; Health Care; and Homes for the Aged.

Properties owned or sponsored: St. Anne's Home for the Elderly; Divine Savior Holy Angels High School, Milwaukee, WI; Divine Savior Healthcare, Inc., Portage, WI.

Represented in the Archdiocese of Milwaukee and in the Dioceses of Birmingham, Gallup, Green Bay, La Crosse, Madison, Monterey, Nashville, Phoenix, and Tucson.

[1040] (C.D.S.)—CONGREGATION OF THE DIVINE SPIRIT (D)

First foundation in Erie, Pennsylvania in 1956.

Motherhouse: 409 W. 6th St., Erie, PA 16507. Tel: 814-455-3590. Mother Patricia O'Connor, Supr. Gen.

Membership: 35.

Sisters serve and staff: Parochial Schools; CCD Activities; Home for Aged; Social Work.

Represented in the Dioceses of Erie and Youngstown.

[1050] (O.P.)—DOMINICAN CONTEMPLATIVE NUNS (P)
(The Nuns of the Orders of Preachers)

Founded in France in 1206. First foundation in the United States in 1880. Monastic contemplative branch of the Order of Preachers. Papal cloister.

Nuns of the Order of Preachers O.P: *Corpus Christi Monastery,* 1230 Lafayette Ave., Bronx, NY 10474. Tel: 718-328-6996; Fax: 718-328-1974. Sr. Maria Pia of the Eucharist, O.P., Prioress.

Total in Community: 12.

Monastery of the Blessed Sacrament: *Nuns of the Order of Preachers,* 29575 Middlebelt, Farmington Hills, MI 48334-2311. Tel: 248-626-8321; Tel: 248-626-8253; Fax: 248-626-8724. Sr. Mary Thomas, O.P.,

Prioress.
Cloistered Sisters: 31; Extern Sisters: 3.
Nuns of the Order of Preachers (Cloistered Dominican Nuns, Perpetual Adoration)

Monastery of the Angels: *Cloistered Dominican Nuns*, 1977 Carmen Ave., Los Angeles, CA 90068. Tel: 323-466-2186. Sr. Mary Raymond, O.P., Prioress.
Sisters: 20.
Legal Title: *The Monastery of the Angels.*

Monastery of the Angels: Karachi, Pakistan Mother Mary Rose, O.P., Prioress.
Sisters: 9.

Queen of Angels Monastery: Bocaue, Bulacan, Philippines Sr. Mary Joseph, O.P., Prioress.
Sisters: 20.

Corpus Christi Monastery: 215 Oak Grove Ave., Menlo Park, CA 94025-3272. Tel: 650-322-1801; Fax: 650-322-6816. Sr. Mary Assumpta, O.P., Prioress.
Cloistered Total Number in Community: 17.

Dominican Nuns O.P: *Monastery of the Mother of God*, 1430 Riverdale St., West Springfield, MA 01089-4698. Tel: 413-736-3639; Fax: 413-736-0850. Sr. Mary St. John, O.P., Prioress.
Total in Community: 19.

Dominican Contemplative Nuns - O.P: *Monastery of Our Lady of the Rosary*, 335 Doat St., Buffalo, NY 14211-2199. Tel: 716-892-0066; Fax: 716-897-1566. Mother Mary Gemma, O.P., Prioress.
Solemnly Professed: 22; Extern Sisters: 3; Novices: 2; Simple Vows: 1; Postulants: 1.
Legal Title: *Dominican Nuns of the Perpetual Rosary.*

Monastery of Our Lady of Grace: 11 Race Hill Rd., Guilford, CT 06437-1099. Tel: 203-457-0599. Sr. Claire, O.P., Prioress.
Total in Community: 32.
Legal Title: *Dominican Nuns of North Guilford, CT Inc.*

Monastery of the Infant Jesus: *Dominican Contemplative Nuns*, 1501 Lotus Ln., Lufkin, TX 75904. Tel: 936-634-4233; Fax: 936-634-2156. Sr. Mary John, O.P., Prioress.
Professed: 26.

Monastery of Our Lady of the Rosary (Rosary Shrine): 543 Springfield Ave., Summit, NJ 07901. Tel: 908-273-1228. Sr. Mary Martin, O.P., Prioress.
Professed Choir Sisters: 15.

Nuns of the Order of Preachers O.P: *Monastery of Mary the Queen*, 1310 W. Church St., Elmira, NY 14905. Tel: 607-734-9506; Fax: 607-734-1452. Sr. Miriam, O.P., Prioress.
Total in Community: 13.

Monastery of the Dominican Nuns of the Perpetual Rosary (Cloistered): 605 14th St. & West St., Union City, NJ 07087-3199. Tel: 201-866-7004. Mother Mary Jordan, O.P., Prioress.
Professed Sisters: 3.

Monastery of the Perpetual Rosary: 1500 Haddon Ave., Camden, NJ 08103. Mother Mary Immaculate Heart, O.P., Prioress.
Professed Nuns: 6.

St. Dominic's Monastery (Contemplative): 2636 Monastery Rd., Linden, VA 22642. Sr. Mary Paul, O.P., Prioress.
Nuns : 9.

The Dominican Nuns of the Perpetual Rosary (Cloistered-Contemplative): *Monastery of the Immaculate Heart of Mary*, 1834 Lititz Pike, Lancaster, PA 17601-6585. Tel: 717-569-2104; Fax: 717-569-1598; Email: monlanc@aol.com. Sr. Mary Albert, O.P., Prioress.
Solemnly Professed: 11.

Dominican Monastery of the Perpetual Rosary: 802 Court St., Syracuse, NY 13208. Tel: 315-471-6762. Sr. Bernadette Marie, O.P., Prioress.
Total in Community: 12.
Solemn Vows, Papal enclosure.

Dominican Monastery of St. Jude: 143 County Rd. 20 E., P.O. Box 170, Marbury, AL 36051. Tel: 205-755-1322. Mother Mary Aimee, O.P., Prioress.
Professed Nuns: 6; Novices: 1; Postulants: 1.
Legal Title: *Dominican Nuns of Perpetual Rosary and Adoration.*

[1060] (O.P.)—DOMINICAN CONTEMPLATIVE SISTERS (D)
Cloistered Contemplative

Founded in Calais, France in 1880.

Monastery of the Dominican Sisters of the Perpetual Rosary (Cloistered): 217 N. 68th St., Milwaukee, WI 53213. Tel: 414-258-0579; Email: frannl@wi.rr.com; Web: www.dsopr.org. Mother Miriam Leonard, O.P., Prioress.
Professed Sisters: 10.

[1070] (O.P.)—COLLABORATIVE DOMINICAN NOVITIATE DOMINICAN SISTERS (P)

There are seventeen Congregations of the Dominican Sisters of the Third Order of St. Dominic in the United States. The list of General Motherhouses follows in the order of seniority. If the Congregation is known under a more familiar name, that name is given under the name of the Congregation.

4928 Washington Blvd., St. Louis, MO 63108-1621. Tel: 314-454-0664.

[1070-03] —SINSINAWA DOMINICAN CONGREGATION OF THE MOST HOLY ROSARY (P)

Generalate: *Sinsinawa Dominican Congregation of the Most Holy Rosary*, 585 County Rd. Z, Sinsinawa, WI 53824-9701. Tel: 608-748-4411. Sr. Patricia Mulcahey, O.P., Prioress of the Congregation; Sr. Lois Hoh, O.P., Archivist.
Total in Community: 591.
Ministry in a variety of cultures in Preaching & Evangelization; Elementary, Secondary and Higher Education; Medical, Legal and Social Services; Adult and Religious Education; Diocesan and Parish Administration, Spiritual Direction and Counseling; Rural, Migrant and Native American Services; Writing Research.
Properties owned or Institutions sponsored: Sinsinawa Dominicans, Inc., Dominican University, River Forest, IL; Sinsinawa Housing, Inc., (Academy Apartments), Sinsinawa, WI; Bethlehem Academy, Faribault, MN; Dominican High School, Whitefish Bay, WI; Queen of Peace High School, Burbank, IL; Trinity High School, River Forest, IL; Sinsinawa Nursing, Inc., (St. Dominic Villa), Sinsinawa, WI; Dominican Motherhouse, Sinsinawa, WI; Camp We-Ha-Kee, Winter, WI; Edgewood Campus School; Edgewood High School; Edgewood College, Madison, WI.
Represented in the Archdioceses of Atlanta, Chicago, Denver, Dubuque, Los Angeles, Miami, Milwaukee, Mobile, Newark, New York, Omaha, Portland in Oregon, St. Louis, St. Paul-Minneapolis, San Antonio, San Francisco, Santa Fe, Seattle and Washington and in the Dioceses of Albany, Austin, Birmingham, Brownsville, Charleston, Cheyenne, Columbus, Dallas, Davenport, Gallup, Gaylord, Grand Rapids, Green Bay, Helena, Honolulu, Jackson, Joliet, Juneau, La Crosse, Madison, Memphis, Nashville, Oakland, Orlando, Owensboro, Palm Beach, Pensacola-Tallahassee, Peoria, Phoenix, Rockford, Sacramento, Saginaw, San Angelo, San Diego, San Jose, Santa Rosa, St. Augustine, St. Cloud, St. Petersburg, Spokane, Trenton, Tulsa, Winona and Venice. Also in Bolivia, Italy, Mexico and Trinidad.

[1070-04] —CONGREGATION OF THE MOST HOLY NAME (P)

Generalate: *Dominican Sisters of San Rafael*, 1520 Grand Ave., San Rafael, CA 94901. Tel: 415-453-8303; Fax: 415-453-8367. Sr. Maureen McInerney, O.P.
Total in Community: 121.
Legal Holdings and Titles: San Domenico School, San Anselmo, CA; Santa Sabina Retreat Center, San Rafael, CA; St. Rose Corporation, San Francisco, CA; St. Joseph's Regional Health System; St. Joseph's Housing Corporation, Stockton, CA; St. Mary's Regional Medical Center, Reno, NV; Sisters of St. Dominic, Congregation of the Most Holy Name, San Rafael, CA; Mission Holding Corporation, San Rafael, CA.
Represented in the Archdiocese San Francisco and in the Dioceses of Monterey, Oakland, Reno, Sacramento, San Jose, Santa Rosa and Stockton. Also in Mexico.

[1070-05] —CONGREGATION OF THE HOLY CROSS (D)

General Motherhouse: *Queen of the Rosary Motherhouse*, Albany Ave., Amityville, NY 11701. Tel: 631-842-6000; Fax: 631-842-0240. Sr. Mary Hughes, O.P., Prioress; Sr. Clare Patrice Farrell, O.P., Archivist.
Total in Community: 535.
Legal Title: *The Sisters of the Order of Saint Dominic.*
Sisters are engaged in the ministry of Education at all levels; Catechetical Schools; Handicapped, Adult and Continuing Education; Hospitals; Homes for the Aged; Residence for Senior Citizens; Spiritual Life Centers; Chaplaincy; Advocacy; Communications; Social Service Institutions; Shelters; Pastoral Services; Prison Ministry; Retreats; Health Services; Ministry to AIDS Victims; Environmental Education Ministry.
Represented in the Archdioceses of Hartford, Newark and New York and in the Dioceses of Albany, Brooklyn, Fort Wayne-South Bend, Kalamazoo, Providence, Rochester, Rockville Centre and Trenton. Also in Puerto Rico and Dominican Republic.

[1070-07] —CONGREGATION OF ST. CECILIA (P)

General Motherhouse: *St. Cecilia Convent*, 801 Dominican Dr., Nashville, TN 37228-1909. Tel: 615-256-5486; Fax: 615-687-3512. Mother Ann Marie Karlovic, O.P., Prioress Gen.; Sr. Marian Sartain, O.P., Archivist and Sec. Gen.
Professed Sisters in Community: 252; Novices: 13; Postulants: 23.
Ministry in the field of Academic Education at all levels.
Legal Holdings and Titles: Aquinas College, Nashville, TN.
Represented in the Archdioceses of Atlanta, Baltimore, Cincinnati, Denver, New Orleans, St. Louis, St. Paul-Minneapolis and Washington and in the Dioceses of Arlington, Birmingham, Charleston,Joliet in Illinois, Knoxville, Lafayette in Indiana, Memphis, Nashville, Providence and Richmond. Also in Sydney, Australia.

[1070-09] —CONGREGATION OF ST. CATHERINE OF SIENA (P)

General Motherhouse: *Convent of St. Catherine*, 5635 Erie St., Racine, WI 53402-1900. Tel: 262-639-4100; Fax: 262-639-9702. Sr. Sharon Simon, O.P., Pres.; Sr. Shirley Kubat, Archivist.
Total in Community: 164.
Legal Holdings and Titles: Sisters of St. Dominic, Racine, WI; Dominican College of Racine, Inc., Racine, WI; St. Catherine's High School of Racine, Inc., Racine, WI; Racine Dominican Ministries, Inc., Racine, WI; St. Catherine's Infirmary, Inc., Racine, WI.
Properties sponsored: Franciscan Sisters, Daughters of the Sacred Hearts of Jesus and Mary, Wheaton, IL and the Sisters of St. Dominic, Racine, WI; Catherine Marian Housing, Inc.
Sisters minister in the areas of Elementary, Secondary, Higher and Music-Cultural Education; Adult Education; Religious Education; Administration; Parish and Pastoral Ministry; Prison Ministry; Social Justice; Campus Ministry; Social Services, Hospital and Health Services; Writing-Research; Hospital Chaplains; Diocesan Services; Retreats-Prayer Programs; Community Services.
Represented in the Archdioceses of Chicago, Detroit, Milwaukee, St. Louis and Santa Fe and in the Dioceses of Gallup, Green Bay, Jackson, Las Cruces, Las Vegas, Madison, Oakland, Toledo and Winona.

[1070-10] —DOMINICAN SISTERS OF SPRINGFIELD, ILLINOIS (P)

General Motherhouse: *Sacred Heart Convent*, 1237 W. Monroe St., Springfield, IL 62704-1680. Tel: 217-787-0481; Fax: 217-787-8169. Sr. Rose Marie Riley, O.P., Prioress Gen.; Sr. Linda Tonellato, Archivist.
Total in Community: 247.
Legal Holdings or Titles: Dominican Sisters of Springfield, Illinois, Inc., Dominican Sisters of Springfield in Illinois Charitable Trust, Springfield, IL; Jubilee Farm, NFP, Springfield, IL; Dominican Literacy Center, Aurora, IL; Dominican Literacy Center, Chicago, IL; Marian Catholic High School, Chicago Heights, IL; Rosary High School, Aurora, IL; Sacred Heart-Griffin High School, Springfield, IL; St. Dominic-Jackson Memorial Hospital, Jackson, MS.
Ministry in Elementary, Secondary Schools and College, Religious & Academic Education; Learning Centers; Hospitals, Nursing Homes, Congregation's Infirmary and Retirement Centers; Retreat & Renewal Center; Administrative Positions in Parishes and Diocesan Offices; Parish Liturgist/Musician & Pastoral Associates; Prison Ministry; Social Services; Foreign Missions.
Represented in the Archdioceses of Chicago, Detroit, Dubuque and Washington D.C., and in the Dioceses of Belleville, Jackson, Joliet, Peoria, Rockford, Springfield in Illinois and Superior. Also in Peru.

[1070-11] —CONGREGATION OF OUR LADY OF THE ROSARY (D)

General Motherhouse and Novitiate: *Dominican Convent of Our Lady of the Rosary*, 175 Rte. 340, Sparkill, NY 10976. Tel: 845-359-4199. Sr. Maryann Summa, O.P., Pres.
Total in Community: 362.
Legal Title: *Dominican Congregation of Our Lady of the Rosary.*
Ministry in High Schools and Elementary Schools; Adult Education/Literacy; Parishes; Pastoral; Colleges; House of Prayers; Housing and Community Centers; Foreign Missions; Substance Abuse Recovery.
Properties sponsored: Aquinas High School, New York, NY; Albertus Magnus High School, Bardonia, NY; Thorpe Family Residence, Bronx, NY.
Represented in the Archdioceses of Chicago, New York and St. Louis and in the Dioceses of Bridgeport, Brooklyn, Charleston, Great Falls-Billings, Helena, Jefferson City, Oakland, Rockville Centre, San Diego, St. Petersburg, Trenton and Wilmington.

[1070-12] —CONGREGATION OF THE QUEEN OF THE HOLY ROSARY (P)

General Motherhouse: *Dominican Convent*, 43326 Mission Blvd., Fremont, CA 94539. Tel: 510-657-2468; Fax: 510-657-1734. Sr. Gloria Marie Jones, Congregational Prioress; Sr. Pauline Bouton, Congregational Sec.
Professed: 220; Novices: 2.
Legal Title: *Dominican Sisters of Mission San Jose, a Corporation, Queen of the Holy Rosary College, a Corporation, Mission San Jose, CA; St. Catherine's Military Academy, a Corporation, Anaheim, CA; Immaculate Conception Academy, a Corporation, San Francisco, CA; Flintridge Sacred Heart Academy, a Corporation, La Canada-Flintridge, CA; Pia Backes Support Trust, Fremont, CA.*
The Community is engaged in the Preaching Mission of St. Dominic through ministry in education at all levels, campus ministry, pastoral services, social justice, communications, health services, Congregational services, and full time study.
Represented in the Archdioceses of Los Angeles, San Francisco and St. Louis and in the Dioceses of Fresno, Oakland, Orange, San Bernardino, San Jose and Tucson. Also in Germany, Mexico, and Guatamala.

[1070-13] —CONGREGATION OF THE MOST

HOLY ROSARY (P)

General Motherhouse: 1257 Siena Heights Dr., Adrian, MI 49221. Tel: 517-266-3400; Fax: 517-266-3545. Sr. Donna Markham, O.P., Prioress.

Total in Congregation : 825.

Legal Holdings or Titles: Dominican Sisters of Adrian, MI, Inc., Adrian, MI; Camilla Madden Charitable Trust, Adrian, MI; Adrian Dominican Sisters Office of Development, Adrian, MI; Dominican High School, Detroit, MI; Dominican Hospital, Santa Cruz, CA; Dominican Life Center, Adrian, MI; Regina Dominican High School, Wilmette, IL; Rosarian Academy, West Palm Beach, FL; Siena Heights University, Adrian, MI; St. Joseph Academy, Adrian, MI; St. Rose Dominican Hospitals, Henderson, NV; Weber Retreat Center, Adrian, MI.

Sisters minister in the areas of Formal Education - as administrators, teachers and consultants at elementary, secondary, college, state and diocesan levels; Pastoral Ministry - parishes, hospitals and campuses; Religious Education - coordinators and teachers; Social Services - case workers, administrators, counselors, therapists, consultants, care-givers for elderly and staff for retirement centers; Health Services - administrators, nurses, therapists, doctors, physician assistants, psychologists, technologists and dietitians; Business Services - directors, accountants, secretaries, administrative assistants, typists, bookkeepers, office managers, office staff, drivers and housekeeping staff; Spiritual Direction - retreat work, formation, congregation leadership and as diocesan vicars for Religious; Social Justice - coordinators, staff and community organizers; other ministries including research, law, science, public relations, art, communications and full-time study.

Represented in the Archdioceses of Anchorage, Atlanta, Chicago, Cincinnati, Detroit, Galveston-Houston, Indianapolis, Louisville, Miami, New Orleans, New York, Oklahoma City, Philadelphia, Portland in Oregon; St. Louis, San Antonio, San Francisco, Santa Fe, Seattle and Washington and the Dioceses of Birmingham, Boise, Charleston, Cleveland, Columbus, El Paso, Fresno, Fort Wayne-South Bend, Gallup, Gary, Gaylord, Great Falls-Billings, Green Bay, Jackson, Joliet, Kalamazoo, Las Vegas, Lansing, Lexington, Madison, Marquette, Monterey, Oakland, Orange, Orlando, Palm Beach, Pensacola-Tallahassee, Peoria, Phoenix, Providence, Pueblo, Raleigh, Richmond, Rockford, Saginaw, St. Petersburg, San Bernardino, San Diego, San Jose, Savannah, Superior, Toledo, Tucson and Venice. Also in Swaziland, Canada, Italy, Dominican Republic, Mexico, and Puerto Rico.

Mission Chapters (1982):

Florida Mission Chapter: 810 N. Olive Ave., West Palm Beach, FL 33401. Tel: 561-832-6521. Sr. Anne Liam Lees, O.P., Chapter Prioress.

Adrian Crossroads Mission Chapter: 1257 Siena Heights Dr., Adrian, MI 49221. Tel: 517-266-4240. Sr. Mary Ellen Youngblood, O.P., Chapter Prioress.

Mid-Atlantic Mission Chapter: P.O. Box 501507, Atlanta, GA 31150. Tel: 678-243-5408. Sr. Mary Priniski, O.P., Chapter Prioress.

Dominican Midwest Mission Chapter: 1515 W. Ogden Ave., La Grange Park, IL 60526. Tel: 708-482-5047. Sr. Patricia Ann Dulka, O.P., Chapter Prioress.

Holy Rosary Mission Chapter: 1257 Siena Heights Dr., Adrian, MI 49221. Tel: 517-266-4107. Sr. Josephine Gaugier, O.P., Chapter Prioress.

Great Lakes Dominican Mission Chapter: 29000 W. 11 Mile Rd., Farmington, MI 48336. Tel: 248-478-4284. Sr. Frances Nadolny, O.P., Chapter Prioress.

Dominican West Mission Chapter: 3250 19th Ave., Fl. 4, San Francisco, CA 94132. Tel: 415-504-3525. Sr. Judith Benkert, O.P., Chapter Prioress.

[1070-14] —CONGREGATION OF OUR LADY OF THE SACRED HEART (P)

General Motherhouse: *Marywood*, 2025 E. Fulton St., Grand Rapids, MI 49503. Tel: 616-459-2910; Fax: 616-454-6105. Sr. Nathalie Meyer, O.P., Prioress; Sr. Rose Marie Martin, O.P., Archivist.

Total in Community: 260.

Legal Holdings or Titles: Sisters of the Order of St. Dominic of Grand Rapids; Marywood Academy; Sisters of St. Dominic of the Congregation of Our Lady of the Sacred Heart Charitable Trust.

Sisters are involved in Academic and Religious Education at all levels; Liturgy; Pastoral Ministry and Administration; Diocesan Offices; Food Service; Health Care; Congregational Services; Social Work; Sabbatical Volunteer; Public Education and Study; Foreign Missions; Justice Advocacy.

Represented in the Archdioceses of Baltimore, Chicago, Detroit, St. Louis, Santa Fe and Seattle and in the Dioceses of Brooklyn, Colorado Springs, Dallas, Dodge City, Fort Wayne-South Bend, Gaylord, Grand Rapids, Great Falls-Billings, Helena, Kalamazoo, Lansing, Lexington, Oakland, Saginaw and Shreveport. Also in Peru, Honduras, & Superior.

[1070-15] —CONGREGATION OF SAINT DOMINIC (D)

General Motherhouse: *Sisters of Saint Dominic of Blauvelt*, 496 Western Hwy., Blauvelt, NY 10913-2097. Tel: 845-359-5600; Fax: 845-359-5773. Sr. Mary Malone, O.P., Pres.; Sr. Judith Campbell, O.P., Archivist.

Total in Community: 157.

Sisters serve and staff: Elementary; Secondary; Higher Education; Special Education; Hospital Care; Pastoral Care; Parish Ministry; Retreat Work; Child Care; Neighborhood Services; Services to Migrants; Services to Chemically Dependent.

Represented in the Archdioceses of Newark and New York and in the Dioceses of Orlando, Providence, Rockville Centre, San Bernardino and Trenton.

[1070-17] —CONGREGATION OF ST. CATHERINE DE RICCI (P)

General Motherhouse: *Fanjeaux*, 1750 Ashbourne Rd., Elkins Park, PA 19027-2596. Tel: 215-635-6027. Sr. Carolyn Krebs, O.P., Pres.

Professed Sisters: 72.

Properties owned and/or sponsored: Dominican Retreat House/Convent of Our Lady of Prouille, Elkins Park, PA; St. Dominic Hall, Elkins Park, PA; Dominican Retreat, Immaculate Heart of Mary Convent, McLean, VA; Dominican Retreat House/Our Lady of Grace Convent, Niskayuna, NY; St. Catherine Hall, Elkins Park, PA.

Sisters serve and staff: Religious Education Centers and Parish Services; Hospital; Pastoral Ministry; College; Diocesan Offices; Special Services; Spiritual Direction; Counseling Center; Retreat Houses.

Represented in the Archdioceses of Cincinnati, Detroit, Philadelphia and Santa Fe and in the Dioceses of Albany, Arlington, Biloxi, Camden, Harrisburg, Orlando, Palm Beach, Providence and Raleigh.

[1070-18] —SISTERS OF ST. DOMINIC OF THE AMERICAN CONGREGATION OF THE SACRED HEART OF JESUS (D)

Dominican Motherhouse: 1 Ryerson Ave., Caldwell, NJ 07006. Tel: 973-403-3331; Fax: 973-228-9611. Sr. Arlene Antczak, O.P., Prioress; Sr. Patricia McKearney, O.P., Archivist.

Total in Community: 160.

Properties owned and/or sponsored: Caldwell College, Caldwell, NJ; Mount Saint Dominic Academy, Caldwell, NJ; St. Dominic Academy, Jersey City, NJ; Lacordaire Academy, Upper Montclair, NJ.

Legal Title: *Sisters of St. Dominic of Caldwell, NJ.*

Ministry in Education at all levels; Pastoral Ministry; Health and Human Services.

Represented in the Archdioceses of Newark and Portland in Oregon and in the Dioceses of Metuchen, Paterson, Savannah, Springfield in Illinois and Trenton. Also in the Dominican Republic.

[1070-19] —DOMINICAN SISTERS OF HOUSTON, TEXAS (CONGREGATION OF THE SACRED HEART) (P)

General Motherhouse & Novitiate: *Dominican Sisters*, 6501 Almeda Rd., Houston, TX 77021. Tel: 713-747-3310; Fax: 713-747-4707. Sr. Adrian Dover, O.P., Prioress.

Total in Community: 89.

Legal Title: *Dominican Sisters of Houston, Texas, Inc. (aka Sacred Heart Convent of Houston).*

Ministry in the field of Academic Education at all levels and parish Ministry.

Properties owned and sponsored: St. Agnes Academy, St. Agnes Academy Foundation, St. Pius X High School, St. Pius X High School Foundation, Inc., The Sacred Heart Convent Retirement Trust.

Represented in the Archdioceses of Galveston-Houston, Indianapolis, Los Angeles, San Antonio and St. Louis and in the Dioceses of Austin, Beaumont, Corpus Christi, Dallas, Houma-Thibodaux, San Bernardino, San Jose and Tyler. Also in Guatemala and Kenya.

[1070-20] —CONGREGATION OF ST. THOMAS AQUINAS (P)

Motherhouse: *Tacoma Dominican Center*, 935 Fawcett Ave. S., Tacoma, WA 98402-5605. Tel: 253-272-9688; Fax: 253-272-8790. Sr. Sharon Casey, O.P.

Total in Community: 63.

Legal Holdings and Titles: Sisters of St. Dominic, Tacoma Dominican Center; Sisters of St. Dominic - Tacoma Charitable Trust.

Ministry in a variety of missions.

Represented in the Archdiocese of Seattle and in the Dioceses of Fresno, San Diego and Yakima. Also in Canada.

[1070-23] —CONGREGATION OF ST. ROSE OF LIMA THE SERVANTS OF RELIEF FOR INCURABLE CANCER IN THE U.S. (P)

General Motherhouse: *Rosary Hill Home*, Hawthorne, NY 10532. Tel: 914-769-0114. Mother Mary Francis, O.P., Supr. Gen.

Total in Community: 59.

The work of these sisters is confined entirely to the incurable cancerous poor.

Represented in the Archdioceses of Atlanta, New York and Philadelphia. Also in Kisumu, Kenya.

[1070-25] —CONGREGATION OF THE DOMINICAN SISTERS OF ST. CATHERINE OF SIENA OF KENOSHA (P)

General Motherhouse & Novitiate: P.O. Box 1288, Kenosha, WI 53141. Tel: 262-694-2067; Fax: 262-694-6542. Sr. Susan Anne Snyder, O.P., Prioress.

Total in Community: 10.

Properties owned and/or sponsored: Our Lady of Fatima Villa, Saratoga, CA; Mercy Medical Center, Merced, CA.

Legal Title: *Dominican Sisters of St. Catherine of Siena, Inc.*

Represented in the Archdioceses of Milwaukee and Santa Fe and in the Dioceses of Baker, Columbus, Fresno and San Jose.

[1070-27] —CONGREGATION OF THE IMMACULATE CONCEPTION (D)

Provincial House: *Immaculate Conception Provincial House*, 9000 W. 81st St., Justice, IL 60458. Tel: 708-458-3040. Mother M. Natalie, O.P., Vicar Prov.

Total in Community: 31.

Represented in the Archdioceses of Chicago and Milwaukee and in the Diocese of Little Rock. Also in Canada.

[1070-30] —DOMINICAN SISTERS OF OAKFORD (P)

U.S. Regional Center: *Dominican Sisters of Oakford*, 980 Woodland Ave., San Leandro, CA 94577. Tel: 510-638-2822; Fax: 510-633-9734. Sr. Anna Oven, O.P., Reg. Prioress.

Total in Community: 19.

Properties owned and/or sponsored: 3 residences in California; Formation House, San Leandro, CA; St. Catherine's Convent, Sunnyvale, CA; Our Lady of Oakford Regional Center, San Leandro, CA.

Ministries in Teaching, Spiritual Direction; Massage Therapy; Counseling; Parish Work; Adult Education; Community Outreach; Social Work and Nursing.

Represented in the Dioceses of Oakland, San Bernardino, San Jose and Tucson.

[1100] (O.P.)—DOMINICAN SISTERS OF CHARITY OF THE PRESENTATION OF THE BLESSED VIRGIN (P)

Founded in France in 1696. First foundation in the United States in 1906.

Motherhouse: 15 Quai Portillon, Tours Cedex 2, France, 37081.

Universal total in Congregation: 2527.

Provincial House: 3012 Elm St., Dighton, MA 02715. Tel: 508-669-5425; Tel: 508-669-5433; Tel: 508-669-5023; Fax: 508-669-6521. Sr. Vimala Vadakumpadan, O.P., Major Supr.

Total number in Province: 36.

Ministry in Hospitals; Homes for the Aged; Residence for Working Women and Students; Dispensaries; Education; Pastoral Ministry.

Represented in the Archdiocese of Washington and in the Dioceses of Brownsville, Fall River and Providence. Also in India, Haiti, Honduras, Korea, Peru, Bolivia, Colombia and Mexico.

[1105] (O.P.)—DOMINICAN SISTERS OF HOPE (P)

Founded July 20, 1995, as a merging of three former Congregations: Dominican Sisters of the Congregation of the Most Holy Rosary of Newburgh, NY; Dominican Sisters of the Sick Poor of Ossining, NY and Congregation of Catherine of Siena of Fall River, MA.

General Administrative Offices: *Dominican Sisters of Hope*, 299 N. Highland Ave., Ossining, NY 10562. Tel: 914-941-4420; Fax: 914-941-1125. Sr. Lorelle Elcock, O.P., Prioress.

Total in Community: 223.

Legal Titles and Holdings: Dominican Sisters of Hope Ministry Trust. Sisters of St. Dominic Charitable Trust. Ministry in Religious & Academic Education at all levels; Health, social, community and pastoral services in low income area; Parish service, counseling, retreats and spiritual direction.

Represented in the Archdioceses of Cincinnati, Denver, Detroit, Hartford, Newark, New York, Oklahoma City and Philadelphia and in the Dioceses of Bridgeport, Brooklyn, Camden, Fall River, Gallup, Jackson, Manchester Metuchen, Ogdensburg, Palm Beach, Paterson, Providence, Richmond, Rockville Centre, San Juan, Trenton, Venice and Wheeling.

[1110] (O.P.)—DOMINICAN SISTERS OF OUR LADY OF THE ROSARY AND OF SAINT CATHERINE OF SIENA, CABRA (P)

Founded in Ireland in 1644.

General Motherhouse: *Cabra*, Dublin 7, Ireland

Region of Louisiana established in 1978.

Regional House: Dominican Sisters, Cabra: 1930 Robert E. Lee, New Orleans, LA 70122. Tel: 504-288-1593. Sr. Elizabeth Ferguson, O.P., Reg. Prioress.

Total number in local community: 11.

Ministry in Academic and Religious Education; Parish Ministry; Neighborhood Social Service Agency; Diocesan Tribunal; Prison Ministry; Adult Education; Social Apostolate; Retreats; Spiritual Direction.

Represented in the Archdiocese of New Orleans and in the Dioceses of Fort Worth and Houma-Thibodaux.

[1115] O.P.—DOMINICAN SISTERS OF PEACE (P)

Generalate: 2320 Airport Dr., Columbus, OH 43219-2098. Tel: 614-416-1900; Fax: 614-252-7435. Sr. Margaret Ormond, O.P., Prioress.
Total in Community: 690.
Legal Title: *Dominican Sisters of Peace, Inc.*
Properties Owned and/or Sponsored: Albertus Magnus College, New Haven, CT; Cedar Park Place, Great Bend, KS; Clausen Manor, Waterford, MI; Crown Point Ecology Center, Bath, OH; Crystal Spring Center for Ecology, Spirituality & Education, Plainville, MA; Dominican Academy, New York, NY; Dominican Center, Oxford, MI; Fox Manor, Waterford, MI; Heartland Center for Spirituality, Great Bend, KS; Heartland Center for Wholistic Health, Great Bend, KS; Heartland Farm, Pawnee Rock, KS; Lourdes Nursing Home & Rehabilitation Center, Waterford, MI; Martin de Porres Center, Columbus, OH
Mendelson Assisted Living Home, Waterford, MI; Mohum Health Care Center, Columbus, OH; Ohio Dominican University, Columbus, OH; Our Lady of the Elms School, Akron, OH; Rosary Academy Learning Center, Watertown, MA; Rosaryville Spirit Life Center, Ponchatoula, LA; St. Agnes Academy-St. Dominic School, Memphis, TN; St. Catharine College, St. Catharine, KY; St. Catharine Farm, St. Catharine, KY; St. Joseph Hall, Watertown, MA; St. Mary's Retreat House, Oxford, MI; St. Mary's Dominican High School, New Orleans, LA; St. Rose Spirituality House, Waterford, MI; Sansbury Care Center, St. Catharine, KY
Shepherd's Corner, Blacklick, OH.
Ministry in Diocesan Offices; the field of Academic Education at all levels; Religious Education; Adult Education Programs; Congregational Infirmary; Art and Ecological/Environment; Hospitals; Care of the Elderly; Parish Ministry; Pastoral Care; Justice and Peace Ministry; Retreat Centers and Spiritual Programs; Foreign Missions; Counseling and Canon Law Ministry; Campus Ministry; Social Work; Health Care Ministries; Ministry to Minorities; Housing.
Represented in the Archdioceses of Baltimore, Boston, Chicago, Cincinnati, Denver, Detroit, Hartford, Kansas City in Kansas, Louisville, Milwaukee, New Orleans, New York, Oklahoma City, Omaha, Philadelphia, San Antonio, Santa Fe and Seattle and in the Dioceses of Baton Rouge, Beaumont, Brooklyn, Brownsville, Cleveland, Columbus, Davenport, Dodge City, Fort Worth, Green Bay, Great Falls-Billings, Grand Island, Gallup, Gary, Houma-Thibodaux, Jackson, Kansas City-St. Joseph, Lafayette, Las Cruces, Lincoln, Memphis, Palm Beach, Paterson, Phoenix, Pittsburgh, Providence, Pueble, Saginaw, Salina, Trenton, Tucson, Wheeling-Charleston, Wichita, Worcester and Yakima. Also in Peru, Honduras and Nigeria.

[1120] (O.P.)—DOMINICAN SISTERS OF THE ROMAN CONGREGATION

Founded in France in 1621. First United States foundation in 1904.

General Motherhouse: Rome, Italy Sr. Jacqueline Provencher, Prioress Gen.
Universal total in Congregation: 450.

U.S. Provincial Office: 123 Dumont Ave., Lewiston, ME 04240-6107. Tel: 207-782-3535; Fax: 207-782-0435. Sr. Monique Belanger, O.P., Prov. Prioress.
Total in Community: 19.
Properties owned and/or sponsored: Retreat House; Residences 4.
Ministry in the field of Religious & Academic Education; Adult Education; Indian Reservation; Pastoral Ministry; Health Care; Social Work.
Represented in the Archdioceses of Chicago and New York and in the Dioceses of Davenport, Gallup, Phoenix and Portland (In Maine).

[1145] (O.P.)—RELIGIOUS MISSIONARIES OF ST. DOMINIC, INC. (P)

General Motherhouse: Via di Val Cannuta 138, Rome, Italy, 00166. Tel: 39-06-66-37-521; Email: dominicas.roma@libero.it. Sr. Elvira Diez, O.P., Prioress Gen.

U.S. Delegation Office: 2237 Waldron Rd., Corpus Christi, TX 78418. Tel: 361-939-8102; Fax: 361-939-8203. Sr. Claudia X. Ongpin, O.P., Delegate of the Supr. Gen.
Total in Congregation : 667; Sisters in the U.S: 22.
Represented in the Archdiocese of Los Angeles and in the Diocese of Corpus Christi.

[1150] (E.F.M.S.)—EUCHARISTIC FRANCISCAN MISSIONARY SISTERS (D)

Founded in Mexico in 1943. Mother Maria Gemma de Jesus Aranda, Founderess.

Motherhouse: *Our Lady's Convent*, 943 S. Soto St., Los Angeles, CA 90023. Tel: 323-264-6556.

1421 Cota Ave., Torrance, CA 90501. Tel: 310-328-6725. Mother Rose Seraphim, E.F.M.S., Supr. Gen.; Sr. Miriam Joseph, E.F.M.S., Gen. Sec.
Total in Community: 26.
Legal Title: *Eucharistic Franciscan Missionary Sisters of Los Angeles.*
Sisters serve and staff: The field of Education; Missionary Activities; Catechetics; Social Work; Diocesan and Administration offices.
Represented in the Archdiocese of Los Angeles and in the Dioceses of Stockton and Tyler.

[1170] (C.S.S.F.)—FELICIAN SISTERS (P)

(Congregation of Sisters of St. Felix of Cantalice, of the III Order of St. Francis)

Founded in Poland in 1855. First foundation in the United States in Polonia, Wisconsin in 1874.

General Motherhouse: Via del Casaletto 540, Rome, Italy, 00151. Sr. Mary Barbara Ann Bosch, C.S.S.F., Min. Gen.

Presentation of the B.V.M. Province (1874): *Motherhouse and Novitiate-Provincialate*, 36800 Schoolcraft Rd., Livonia, MI 48150. Tel: 734-591-1730; Fax: 734-591-1710. Sr. Mary Renetta Rumpz, C.S.S.F., Prov. Min.
Professed: 153; Novices: 1.
Properties owned and/or sponsored: Madonna University; Ladywood High School; Montessori Center of Our Lady, Livonia, MI; St. Mary Mercy Hospital, Livonia, MI; St. Joseph Day Care; Presentation Prayer Center, Jackson, MI; Maryville Center, Holly, MI; Angela Hospice Home Care and Inpatient Facility, Marian Professional Building, Livonia, MI; Marywood Nursing Care Center; Inpatient Facility, Marian Professional Bldg.; Marybrook Manor Assisted Living.
Ministry in the field of Academic Education at all levels; Catechetical Center; CCD Programs; Archival and Secretarial Services in Seminary; Diocesan Nursing Home; Pastoral Ministry Programs; DRE Offices; Hospital; Health Care Nursing Homes; Assisted Living; Hospice Inpatient and Home Care Program; Day care Centers; Retreat Centers; House of Prayer; Senior Clergy Residence.
Represented in the Archdiocese of Detroit and in the Dioceses of Fort Wayne-South Bend, Gaylord, Lansing and Saginaw.

Immaculate Heart of Mary Province (1900): 600 Doat St., Buffalo, NY 14211. Tel: 716-892-4141; Fax: 716-892-4177. Sr. Mary Christopher Moore, C.S.S.F., Prov. Minister; Sr. Mary Kenneth Mondrala, C.S.S.F., Prov. Archivist.
Total in Province: 172.
Properties owned and/or sponsored: Villa Maria College of Buffalo; Villa Maria Academy.
Ministry in Education on all levels; School for Mentally and Multiply Handicapped;Religious Education Programs; Outreach Centers; Parish Ministries; Social Services; Prison Ministries; Campus Ministries; Diocesan Office.
Represented in the Archdioceses of Los Angeles, Newark and New York and in the Dioceses of Buffalo, Charleston, Syracuse and Rochester. Also in Italy.

Mother of Good Counsel Province (1910): *Mother of Good Counsel Provincialate & Convent*, 3800 W. Peterson Ave., Chicago, IL 60659. Tel: 773-463-3020. Sr. Mary Andrea Chudzik, C.S.S.F., Prov. Minister; Sr. M. Alodia Stozek, C.S.S.F., Community Archivist.
Total in Community: 148.
Ministry in the field of Academic and Religious Education at all levels; Homes for Aged; Independent Living for the Elderly; Assisted Living for the Elderly; Pastoral Ministry; Social Workers; Family Therapists; Day Care Centers; Hospitals; Infirmary for Sisters.
Represented in the Archdioceses of Chicago and Milwaukee and in the Dioceses of Belleville, Green Bay, Joliet and La Crosse.

Immaculate Conception Provincial House (1913): *Motherhouse and Novitiate-Immaculate Conception Convent*, 260 S Main St., Lodi, NJ 07644-2196. Tel: 973-473-7447; Fax: 973-473-7126; Web: www.feliciansisters.org. Sr. Mary Bridget Becker, C.S.S.F., Treas.; Sr. Mary Virginia Tomasiak; Sr. Rose Marie Smiglewski, Prov. Archivist.
Total in Community: 143.
Properties sponsored: Immaculate Conception High School; Felician College; Felician College Day Care Center; Felician School for Exceptional Children, Lodi, NJ; Felician Retreat Center; Our Lady of Grace Home St. Ignatius Nursing Home.
Sisters serve and staff: Colleges; High Schools; Elementary Schools; Hospitals;Home for Aged; Infirmary for Sisters; Day Care Center; School for Exceptional Children; Religious Education; Parish Ministries.
Represented in the Archdioceses of Newark and Philadelphia and in the Dioceses of Metuchen, Paterson, and Wilmington.

Our Lady of the Sacred Heart Province (1921): *Provincial House, Felician Sisters of Pennsylvania*, 1500 Woodcrest Ave., Coraopolis, PA 15108. Tel: 412-264-2890; Fax: 412-264-7047. Sr. Mary Christopher Moore, C.S.S.F., Prov. Min.
Total number in Province: 83.
Legal Holdings and Titles: Felician Sisters of Pennsylvania; Our Lady of the Sacred Heart High School.
Ministry in the field of Academic Education at all levels; Religious Education; CCD Centers; Youth and Pastoral Ministry; Home for Mentally Challenged Children & Adults; Infirmary and Home for Aged; Missionary Work.
Represented in the Dioceses of Altoona-Johnstown, Charleston, Greensburg and Pittsburgh.

Our Lady of the Angels Province (1932): *Felician Sisters Provincial House/Novitiate, Our Lady of the Angels Convent*, 1315 Enfield St., Enfield, CT 06082-4929. Tel: 860-745-7791; Fax: 860-741-0819. Sr. Mary Bernardine Mucha, C.S.S.F., Prov. Min.
Sisters in Province: 73.
Ministry in the field of Religious and Academic Education; Pastoral Ministry; Social Services; Healthcare.
Properties owned and sponsored: Enfield Montessori School; Felician Adult Day Care, Enfield, CT; St. Joseph Hospital, Bangor, ME; St. Francis Residence, Enfield, CT.
Represented in the Archdiocese of Hartford and in the Dioceses of Albany, Manchester, Portland (In Maine), Providence, Springfield in Massachusetts and Worcester.

Assumption of the B.V.M. Province (1953): *Provincial House*, 4210 Meadowlark Ln., S.E., Rio Rancho, NM 87124-1021. Sr. Danat Marie Brysch, C.S.S.F., Prov. Min.
Total in Community: 50.
Legal Titles and Holdings: Felician Sisters of the Southwest, Inc.; St. Felix Pantry Inc.
Sisters serve and staff: High Schools; Elementary Schools; Religious Education Centers & Classes; Health Care; Pastoral Care; Food & Clothing Pantry; Youth Ministry; Adult Education; Social Work.
Represented in the Archdioceses of Los Angeles, San Antonio and Santa Fe and in the Diocese of Laredo.

[1180] (O.S.F.)—FRANCISCAN SISTERS OF ALLEGANY, NEW YORK (P)

Founded in the United States in 1859.

General Motherhouse (1859): *St. Elizabeth Motherhouse*, 115 E. Main St., Allegany, NY 14706. Tel: 716-373-0200; Fax: 716-372-5774. Sr. Maureen Avril Chin Fatt, O.S.F., Congregational Min.
Total in Community: 301.
Legal Titles and Holdings: Franciscan Sisters of Allegany, NY, Inc.; Canticle Farm, Inc., Allegany, NY; St. Elizabeth Mission Society, Inc., Allegany, NY; Dr. Lyle F. Renodin Foundation, Inc., Allegany, NY; Franciscan of Center of Tampa, FL, Inc., Tampa, FL; The Dwelling Place of NY Inc., NY.
Ministry to Evangelization in all levels of Education; Health Care; Social Services; Pastoral; Spiritual Ministries and Social Advocacy.
Represented in the Archdioceses of Boston, Miami, Newark, New York, Philadelphia and Washington and in the Dioceses of Buffalo, Camden, Gallup, Metuchen, Palm Beach, Rochester, Rockville Centre, St. Petersburg, Spokane, Springfield in Massachusetts, Syracuse, Trenton and Venice. Also in Bolivia, Brazil and Jamaica.

Jamaica: *Immaculate Conception Convent*, 152 Constant Spring Rd., Box 1654, Kingston, Jamaica Tel: 876-925-6888. Sr. Maureen Clare Hall, O.S.F., Local Min.

Brazil Region: *Convento Mae Admiravel*, C.P. 322, 75001-970 Anapolis, Goias, Brazil Tel: 011-55-62-3333-3803. Sr. Rosimeire Dias Noleto, O.S.F., Regl. Min.

[1190] (S.A.)—FRANCISCAN SISTERS OF THE ATONEMENT (P)

Founded in the United States in 1898.

Motherhouse: *St. Francis Convent-Graymoor*, 41 Old Highland Tpke., Garrison, NY 10524. Tel: 845-424-3623; Fax: 845-424-3298. Sr. Nancy Conboy, S.A., Min. Gen.; Sr. Rene Drolet, S.A., Archivist.
Total in Community: 164.
Properties owned and/or sponsored: St. Francis Convent-Complex, Garrison, NY; Mother Lurana House, Garrison, NY; Washington Retreat House, Washington, D.C.
Represented in the Archdioceses of Boston, Detroit, Newark, New York and Washington and in the Dioceses of Albany, Bridgeport, Burlington, Fresno, Las Vegas, Monterey, Norwich, Ogdensburg, Pittsburgh, Reno, Salt Lake City, Syracuse and Trenton. Also in Canada, Brazil, Ireland, Italy and Japan.

[1210] (O.S.F.)—FRANCISCAN SISTERS OF CHICAGO (P)

Founded in Chicago, Illinois in 1894 by Mother Mary Theresa (Josephine Dudzik) Venerable Servant of God.

General Motherhouse: *Our Lady of Victory Convent*, 11400 Theresa Dr., Lemont, IL 60439-2728. Tel: 630-243-3600; Fax: 630-243-3601. Sr. Diane Marie Collins, O.S.F., Gen. Min.
Total in Community: 52.
Properties owned and/or sponsored: Addolorata Villa, Wheeling, IL; St. Anthony Home, Inc., Crown Point, IN; St. Joseph Home of Chicago, Inc., Chicago, IL; St. Mary of the Woods, Avon, OH; Marian Village, Homer Glen, IL; Mount Alverna Village, Cleveland, OH; Mother Theresa Home, Inc.; Franciscan Village, Lemont, IL; St. Francis House of Prayer; Franciscan Sisters of Chicago Service Corp. Our Lady of Victory Convent, Lemont, IL; Franciscan Community Services, Crown Point, IN; Franciscan Senior Estates, Louisville, KY; St. James Senior Estates, Crete, IL; St. Jude House, Crown Point, IN; The Clare at Water Tower, Chicago, IL; Villa de San Antonio, San Antonio, TX; The Village at Victory Lakes, Lindenhurst, IL; University Place, West Lafayette, IN; Marion Village, Homer Glen, IL; St. James Senior Estates, Crete, IL; Franciscan Senior Estates, Louisville, KY; St. Jude House, Crown Point, IN; St. Mary of the Woods, Avon, OH; University Place, West Lafayette, IN; The Clare at Water Tower, Chicago, IL; The Village at Victory Lakes, Lindenhurst, IL.
Sisters serve and staff: CCD Programs.
Represented in the Archdioceses of Chicago and Louisville and in the Dioceses of Cleveland, Gary, Joliet, Lafayette and San Antonio.

[1230] (O.S.F.)—FRANCISCAN SISTERS OF CHRISTIAN CHARITY (P)

Founded in the United States in 1869.

Motherhouse: *Holy Family Convent*, 2409 S. Alverno Rd., Manitowoc, WI 54220. Tel: 920-682-7728; Fax: 920-682-4195. Sr. Louise Hembrecht, Community Dir.; Sr. Donna Marie Kessler, Community Archivist.

Total in Community: 341.

Properties owned or sponsored: Holy Family Convent, Manitowoc, WI; Holy Family Convent of Franciscan Sisters of Christian Charity, Inc., Manitowoc, WI; Holy Family Memorial, Inc., Manitowoc, WI; The Retirement Trust of the Franciscan Sisters of Christian Charity, Manitowoc, WI; St. Francis Memorial Hospital, West Point, NE; St. Paul Villa, Kaukauna, WI; St. Paul Home, Kaukauna, WI; St. Paul Manor, Kaukauna, WI; Silver Lake College, Manitowoc, WI; Franciscan Sisters of Christian Charity Health Care Ministry, Inc., Manitowoc, WI; Holy Family Conservatory of Music, Manitowoc, WI; Chiara Convent, Manitowoc, WI; St. Clare Convent, Manitowoc, WI; St. Francis Convent, Manitowoc, WI; St. Joseph Retirement Community, West Point, NE; Good Samaritan Medical Center, Zanesville, OH.

Represented in the Archdioceses of Chicago and Omaha and in the Dioceses of Columbus, Green Bay, Jackson, Lincoln, Honolulu, Marquette, Phoenix, Steubenville and Tucson.

[1235] (F.H.M.)—FRANCISCAN SISTERS DAUGHTERS OF MERCY (P)

Franciscanas Hijas de la Misericordia

Founded in Pina, Mallorca, Spain in 1856. First U.S. establishment in 1962.

General Motherhouse: Calle El Nectar, 18, Madrid, Spain, 28022. Sr. Roberta Pauline Aguirre, Supr. Gen.

Universal total in Congregation: 435.

U.S. Regional and House of Formation: 1207 Montopolis Dr., Austin, TX 78741. Tel: 512-385-5090; Tel: 512-389-3411. Sr. Rose Moreno, F.H.M., Reg. Delegate Email: rmfhm@yahoo.com.

Professed Sisters: 6.

Ministry in Catechetical work; Pastoral work; Kindergarten.

Represented in the Diocese of Austin.

[1240] (O.S.F.)—FRANCISCAN SISTERS, DAUGHTERS OF THE SACRED HEARTS OF JESUS AND MARY (P)

Founded in Germany in 1860. First foundation in the United States in 1872.

Generalate: *Via di S. Alessio 24*, Rome, Italy, 00153. Sr. Mary Lou Wirtz, O.S.F., Gen. Dir.

Universal total in Congregation: 670.

St. Clara's Province (1877): *Convent of Our Lady of the Angels, Motherhouse and Novitiate*, P.O. Box 667, Wheaton, IL 60189-0667. Tel: 630-462-7422. Sr. Beatrice Hernandez, O.S.F., Prov. Dir.

Total number in Province: 73.

Legal Holdings and Titles: *Affinity Health System, Menasha, WI; *Franciscan Ministries Community Foundation, Inc., Wheaton, IL; *Marianjoy Foundation, Inc., Wheaton, IL; *Marianjoy, Inc., Wheaton, IL; *Network Health System Inc.; Menasha, WI; *Rehabilitation Medicine Clinic Inc.; Wheaton, IL; *Sartori Health Care Foundation, Inc., Cedar Falls, IA; *Wheaton Franciscan Healthcare - Circle of Life Foundation, Inc.; *Wheaton Franciscan Healthcare - Elmbrook Memorial Foundation, Inc., Brookfield, WI; *Wheaton Franciscan Healthcare - Foundation for St. Francis, Inc.; *Wheaton Franciscan Healthcare - Marian Franciscan Center, Inc., Milwaukee, WI; *Wheaton Franciscan Healthcare - Southeast Wisconsin, Inc., Milwaukee, WI; *Wheaton Franciscan Medical Group, Inc., Milwaukee, WI; Assisi Homes - Batavia Apartments, Inc., Batavia, IL; Assisi Homes - Colony Park, Inc., Carol Stream, IL; Assisi Homes - Constitution House, Inc., Aurora, IL; Assisi Homes - Jefferson Court, Inc., Milwaukee, WI; Assisi Homes - Kenosha, Inc., Kenosha, WI; Assisi Homes - Saxony, Inc., Kenosha, WI; Assisi Homes of Gurnee, Inc., Gurnee, IL; Assisi Homes of Illinois, Inc., Wheaton, IL; Assisi Homes of Neenah, Inc., Neenah, WI; Canticle Ministries, Inc., Wheaton, IL; Canticle Place, Inc., Wheaton, IL; Catherine Marian Housing, Inc., Racine, WI; Clara Pfaender Fund, Inc., Wheaton, IL; Clare Gardens, Inc., Denver, CO; Clare of Assisi Homes - Westminister, Inc., Westminister, CO; Covenant Foundation, Inc., Waterloo, IA; Covenant Medical Center, Inc., Waterloo, IA

Dayspring Villa, Inc., Denver, CO; Francis Heights, Inc., Denver, CO; Franciscan Health and Education Corporation, Inc., Wheaton, IL; Franciscan Ministries, Inc., Wheaton, IL; Franciscan Seniors, Kenosha, Inc., Kenoshah, WI; Franciscan Sisters Charitable Fund of Colorado, Inc., Denver, CO; Marian Housing Center, Inc., Racine, WI; Marian Park, Inc., Wheaton, IL; Marianjoy Rehabilitation Auxiliary, Wheaton, IL; Marianjoy Rehabilitation Hospital & Clinics, Inc., Wheaton, IL; Mercy Hospital of Franciscan Sisters, Inc., Oelwein, IA; Mercy Medical Center of Oshkosh, Inc., Oshkosh, WI.; O.S.F. Services, Inc., Milwaukee, WI; Ridgeway Place, Inc., Waterloo, IA; Rush Oak Park Hospital, Oak Park, IL; S.E.T. Ministry, Inc., Milwaukee, WI; Sartori Memorial Hospital, Inc., Cedar Falls, IA; St. Catherine's Hospital, Inc., Kenosha, WI; St. Elizabeth Hospital Community Foundation, Inc., Appleton, WI; St. Elizabeth Hospital Inc., Appleton, WI

Starved Rock - LaSalle Manor, Inc., LaSalle, IL; Villa Maria, Inc., Westminster, CO; Villa St. Clare, Inc., Neenah, WI; Villa St. Francis, Inc., Milwaukee, WI; Wheaton Franciscan Healthcare - All Saints Foundation Inc., Racine, WI; Wheaton Franciscan Healthcare - All Saints, Inc., Racine, WI; Wheaton Franciscan Healthcare - Elmbrook Memorial Inc., Brookfield, WI.; Wheaton Franciscan Healthcare - Iowa, Inc., Waterloo, IA; Wheaton Franciscan Healthcare - St. Francis, Inc., Milwaukee, WI; Wheaton Franciscan - St. Joseph Foundation, Inc., Milwaukee, WI; Wheaton Franciscan, Inc., Milwaukee, WI; Wheaton Franciscan Healthcare - Terrace at St. Francis, Inc., Milwaukee, WI; Wheaton Franciscan Healthcare - The Wisconsin Heart Hospital, Inc.; Wheaton Franciscan Home Health & Hospice, Inc., Milwaukee, WI; Wheaton Franciscan Services, Inc., Wheaton, IL; Wheaton Franciscan Sisters Religious Charitable Trust, Wheaton, IL.

Sisters serve, sponsor and staff: Hospitals; Housing Development; Parish Ministry; Spirituality Center; Corporate Offices; System Ministries Sponsorship of Catholic Hospitals; Long-term Care; Social Services; Wellness; Spiritual Direction; Foreign Mission.

Represented in the Archdioceses of Chicago, Denver, Milwaukee and St. Louis and in the Dioceses of Gary, Green Bay, Joliet and Springfield-Cape Girardeau. Also in Brazil and Italy.

[1250] (F.S.E.)—FRANCISCAN SISTERS OF THE EUCHARIST, INC.

Founded December 2, 1973.

Motherhouse: *John Lateran Center*, 405 Allen Ave., Meriden, CT 06451. Tel: 203-238-2243. Team Members: Mother Shaun Vergauwen, F.S.E., Mother Gen.; Mother Miriam Seiferman, Vicar Gen.; Mother Suzanne Gross, F.S.E.; Mother Mary Ann Schmitz, F.S.E.; Mother Agnese Hutchinson, F.S.E.; Mother Barbara Johnson, F.S.E.

Total in Community: 82.

Legal Title: *Franciscan Sisters of the Eucharist, Inc.*

Schools and programs operated under: Franciscan Life Center Network, Incorporated.

Represented in the Archdioceses of Galveston-Houston, Hartford and Portland in Oregon and in the Dioceses of Arlington, Boise, Duluth, and Grand Rapids. Also in Israel, Italy and Kingston, Jamaica.

Generalate: 215 Goodspeed Ave., Meriden, CT 06451. Tel: 203-237-0841.

[1260] (F.H.M.)—FRANCISCAN HANDMAIDS OF THE MOST PURE HEART OF MARY (D)

Founded in the United States in 1916.

General Motherhouse: 15 W. 124th St., New York, NY 10027. Tel: 212-289-5655.

Novitiate: 444 Woodvale Ave., Staten Island, NY 10309. Sr. Maria Goretti, O.P., Congregation Min.; Sr. Loretta Theresa, Dir. Formation; Sr. Jacqueline, Community Archivist.

Total in Community: 23.

Properties owned and/or sponsored: St. Benedict Day Nursery; Camp Saint Edward; Franciscan Handmaids of Mary Novitiate; Franciscan Handmaids of Mary Motherhouse.

Ministry in the field of Education, Social Work and Pastoral Care.

Represented in the Archdiocese of New York.

[1270] (F.H.I.C.)—FRANCISCAN HOSPITALLER SISTERS OF THE IMMACULATE CONCEPTION (P)

Founded in Portugal in 1876.

General Motherhouse: Linda-a-Pastora, Portugal Sr. Maria da Conceição Galvão Ribeiro, Supr. Gen.

U.S. Foundation (1960): *St. Joseph Novitiate*, 300 S. 17th St., San Jose, CA 95112-2245. Tel: 408-998-2896; Fax: 408-998-3407. Sr. Teresa Maria Costa, F.H.I.C., Supr.

Total in Community: 18.

Sisters serve and staff: Parishes; Schools; Hospitals; Social Work.

Represented in the Dioceses of Fresno, Monterey and San Jose.

[1300] (O.S.F.)—FRANCISCAN SISTERS OF THE IMMACULATE CONCEPTION AND ST. JOSEPH FOR THE DYING (D)

Founded in the United States in December, 1919 at San Carlos Parish, Monterey, California.

General Motherhouse: *Ave Maria Convent*, 1249 Josselyn Canyon Rd, Monterey, CA 93940. Tel: 831-373-1216. Sr. Mary Angela Zwolenik.

Total in Community: 1.

Legal Holding: Ave Maria Convalescent Hospital, Monterey, CA.

Represented in the Diocese of Monterey.

[1310] (O.S.F.)—FRANCISCAN SISTERS OF LITTLE FALLS, MINNESOTA (P)

Founded in the United States in 1891.

General Motherhouse: *St. Francis' Convent*, Little Falls, MN 56345. Tel: 320-632-2981. Sr. Mary C. Obowa, O.S.F., Pres.

Total in Community: 181.

Secondary and Elementary Education; Health Care in Nursing Homes, Home Health Care; Hospice Care; Hospitals, Apartments for The Elderly, Children's Home, Clinics; Religious Education; Parish Ministry; Retreat Ministries; Liturgical Music; Music Center; Ministry to Refugees; Health and Recreation Center; Diocesan Offices; Social Services; Counseling; Spiritual Direction; Consulting; Ministry to the Poor; Ministry to Migrants; Craft Activities; Ministry in Ecology; Social Justice and Nonviolent Activities; Spirtuality Farm; Native American Ministry; Hispanic Ministry.

Properties owned or sponsored: St. Francis Music Center; St. Francis Health & Recreation Center; Clare's Well.

Represented in the Archdioceses of Chicago, Los Angeles, Milwaukee, St. Paul-Minneapolis, Santa Fe and San Francisco and in the Dioceses of Brownsville, Fargo, Jackson, Joliet, Oakland, Phoenix, Sioux Falls, St. Cloud, Stockton, Tucson and Winona. Also in Ecuador and Mexico.

[1320] (F.M.S.A.)—FRANCISCAN MISSIONARY SISTERS FOR AFRICA (P)

Generalate: *Franciscan Missionary Sisters for Africa*, 34a Gilford Rd., Sandymount, Dublin 4, Ireland Tel: 011-353-1-2838376; Fax: 011-353-1-2602049.

American Headquarters: 172 Foster St., P.O. Box 35095, Brighton, MA 02135. Tel: 617-254-4343; Fax: 617-787-8007. Sr. Nelezinha Carvalho, F.M.S.A.

Total in Community: 7.

Represented in the Archdiocese of Boston.

[1330] (S.F.M.A.)—FRANCISCAN MISSIONARY SISTERS OF ASSISI (P)

General Motherhouse: Via San Francesco, 13, Assisi, Italy, 06081. Sr. Juliana Malama, Mother Gen.

U.S. Vice Province (1961): *St. Francis Convent/Vice Provincial House and Formation House*, 1039 Northampton St., Holyoke, MA 01040. Tel: 413-532-8156; Fax: 413-534-7741. Sr. Carol Woods, Vice Prov. Supr.

Total in Community: 15.

Represented in the Archdiocese of New York and in the Diocese of Springfield in Massachusetts.

[1350] (O.S.F.)—FRANCISCAN SISTERS OF THE IMMACULATE CONCEPTION (P)

Founded in Mexico in 1874. First foundation in the United States in 1926.

Provincial House: 13367 Borden Ave., Unit A, Sylmar, CA 91342-2804. Tel: 818-364-6122; Tel: 818-364-5557; Tel: 818-364-5558; Email: provstclare@verizon.net. Sr. Leticia Rodriguez, O.S.F., Prov. Supr.; Sr. Mary Gabriel De Leon, O.S.F., Community Archivist.

Total in Community: 103.

Legal Holdings and Titles: Franciscan Missionary Sisters of the Immaculate Conception, Inc.; Poverello of Assisi Retreat House, San Fernando, CA; St. Francis Home, Santa Ana, CA; Mother Gertrude Balcazar Home, San Fernando, CA; Provincialate, Sylmar, CA; St. Clare Convent, Sylmar, CA.

Ministry in the field of Education and Religious Education to Children and Adults; Health Care in Hospitals and Home Visitation to the Sick.

Represented in the Archdiocese of Los Angeles and in the Dioceses of Gallup and Orange in California. Also in Mexico.

Novitiate: 11306 Laurel Canyon Blvd., San Fernando, CA 91340.

Novitiate: 8619 Louise Ave., Northridge, CA 91324-3417. Tel: 818-709-7523.

[1360] (M.F.I.C.)—MISSIONARY FRANCISCAN SISTERS OF THE IMMACULATE CONCEPTION (P)

Founded in the United States in 1873 in Belle Prairie, Minnesota.

General Motherhouse: Rome, Italy Sr. Elaine Morzone, M.F.I.C., Gen. Min.

Provincialate: *Immaculate Conception Province*, 790 Centre St., Newton, MA 02458-2530. Tel: 617-527-1004; Fax: 617-527-2528. Sr. Suzanne Fondini, M.F.I.C., Prov.

Total number in Province: 146.

Represented in the Archdioceses of Boston, Newark and New York and in the Dioceses of Bridgeport, Brooklyn, Providence, Savannah, Syracuse and Venice. Also in Peru and Bolivia.

[1365] (F.M.I.J.)—FRANCISCAN MISSIONARY SISTERS OF THE INFANT JESUS (P)

Founded in Aquila, Italy in 1879 by Sr. Maria Giuseppa Micarelli. First foundation in the United States in 1961.

Generalate: Piazza Nicoloso da Recco 13, Rome, Italy, 00154. Tel: 6-575-8358. Mother Teresa Ferrante, F.M.I.J., Supr. Gen.

U.S. Province and Novitiate: 1215 Kresson Rd., Cherry Hill, NJ 08003. Tel: 856-428-8834; Fax: 856-428-5599; Email: fmijusdel@yahoo.com. Sr. Angela Pia Camillotti, F.M.I.J., Delegate Supr.

Professed Sisters: 17.

Ministries of Evangelization; Education; Health Care; Social-Pastoral Services.

Represented in the Dioceses of Arlington, Camden and

Trenton.

[1370] (F.M.M.)—THE FRANCISCAN MISSIONARIES OF MARY (P)

Founded in India in 1877. First foundation in the United States in 1903.

General Motherhouse: 12 via Giusti, Rome, Italy Sr. Suzanne Phillips, F.M.M., Supr. Gen.

Franciscan Missionaries of Mary-U.S. Province (1920): 3305 Wallace Ave., Bronx, NY 10467-6599. Tel: 718-547-4693; Fax: 718-325-5102; Email: palfmm@aol.com; Web: www.fmmusa.org. Sr. Lois Ann Pereira, F.M.M., Prov.

Total in Province: 122.

Ministry in Educational Projects among Minority Group of Immigrants; Child Care Agencies; Cardiac and General Hospital; General Pediatric Hospital with Rehabilitation Specialty; Chaplaincy; Retreat Work; Day Care for Elderly; Catechetics; Mission Animation & Formation; Home Visiting & Community Development.

Represented in the Archdioceses of Boston, Chicago and New York and in the Dioceses of El Paso, Las Cruces, Providence, Rockville Centre, Savannah and St. Petersburg.

[1380] (O.S.F.)—FRANCISCAN MISSIONARIES OF OUR LADY (P)

Founded in Calais, France in 1854. First U.S. foundation in Monroe, LA, 1913.

Generalate: Paris, France

Provincial and Novitiate House: *Maryville Convent*, 4200 Essen Ln., Baton Rouge, LA 70809. Tel: 225-926-1627; Fax: 225-925-5268. Sr. Barbara Arceneaux, Supr.

Total in Community: 19.

Properties owned and sponsored: Our Lady of the Lake Regional Medical Center, Baton Rouge, LA; Ollie Steele Burden Manor, Inc., Baton Rouge, LA; Our Lady of Lourdes Regional Medical Center, Lafayette, LA; St. Francis Medical Center, Monroe, LA; FMOL Health System, Inc., Baton Rouge, LA; Haiti Mission, Inc., Baton Rouge, LA; St. Elizabeth Hospital, Gonzales, LA.

Represented in the Dioceses of Baton Rouge, Lafayette (LA) and Shreveport.

[1390] (O.S.F.)—FRANCISCAN MISSIONARY SISTERS OF OUR LADY OF SORROWS (D)

Founded in Hunan China in 1939. First United States foundation in 1950.

Community Headquarters: *Our Lady of Peace Retreat House*, 3600 S.W. 170th Ave., Beaverton, OR 97006. Tel: 503-649-7127; Fax: 503-259-9507. Sr. Mary Francis Coleman, Supr. Gen.

Total in Community: 38.

Legal Titles and Holdings: Our Lady of Peace Retreat, Beaverton, OR; St. Clare Retreat House, Soquel, CA.

Ministry in religious and academic education; retreat houses, group homes and foreign missions.

Represented in the Archdiocese of Portland in Oregon and in the Diocese of Monterey.

[1400] (F.M.S.C.)—FRANCISCAN MISSIONARY SISTERS OF THE SACRED HEART (P)

Founded in Italy in 1861. First foundation in the U.S. in New York City (1865).

General Motherhouse: Rome, Italy Sr. Emmapia Bottamedi, Supr. Gen.

St. Francis Province (1869): *Mt. St. Francis*, 250 South St., Peekskill, NY 10566. Tel: 914-737-5409; Fax: 914-736-9614. Sr. Anne James Guerin, F.M.S.C., Prov.

Universal total in Congregation: 782; Total in United States Province: 44.

Legal Title: *Missionary Sisters of the Third Order of St. Francis.*

Ministry in Religious and Academic Education; Health Care for Retired Sisters; Pastoral Ministry; Prison Apostolate; Hospital Ministry.

Represented in the Archdioceses of Newark and New York and in Diocese of Brooklyn.

[1410] (F.M.S.J.)—MILL HILL SISTERS (P)

Franciscan Missionaries of St. Joseph

Founded in 1883. First United States foundation in 1952.

Generalate: *St. Joseph's Convent*, 150 Greenleach Ln., Worsley, Manchester, England, M28 2TS. Sr. Joan O'Gorman, F.M.S.J., Supr. Gen.

American Headquarters: *Franciscan House*, 703 Derzee Ct., Delmar, NY 12054. Tel: 518-512-4362. Sr. Judith Dever, F.M.S.J., Admin.

Total in Community: 2.

Legal Title: *Mill Hill Sisters - New York Charitable Trust.*

Represented in the Dioceses of Albany and Syracuse.

[1415] (F.S.M.)—FRANCISCAN SISTERS OF MARY (P)

Founded in the United States in 1872.

Administrative Offices & Novitiate: *Franciscan Sisters of Mary*, 1100 Bellevue Ave., St. Louis, MO 63117-1826. Tel: 314-768-1824; Fax: 314-768-1880. Rose Mary Dowling, F.S.M., Pres.

Total in Community: 117.

Ministry in Hospitals; Skilled Nursing Facilities; Rehabilitation Unit; Woman's Center; Social Services; Pastoral Services; Wholistic Health Services; Consultation Services; Spiritual Direction.

Properties owned or sponsored: St. Mary of the Angels, St. Louis, MO.

Represented in the Archdioceses of Chicago, Cincinnati, Milwaukee and St. Louis and in the Dioceses of Charleston, Corpus Christi, Gallup, Jefferson City, Kansas City-St. Joseph, Madison, Springfield-Cape Girardeau and Tucson.

[1425] (F.S.P.)—FRANCISCAN SISTERS OF PEACE (D)

Sisters of St. Francis of Peace: *Congregation Center*, 20 Ridge St., Haverstraw, NY 10927-1115. Tel: 845-942-2527; Fax: 845-429-8141. Sr. Jeanne Gilligan, F.S.P., Congregation Min.

Total in Community: 72.

Legal Titles and Holdings: Cortlandt Manor, New York, NY; Congregation Center, Haverstraw, NY.

Ministry in Youth; Care for the Aged; Pastoral; Education; Nursing; Catechetical; Social Work; Prison Ministry; Ministry to Unwed Mothers; Evangelization; Social Services; Chaplaincies.

Represented in the Archdioceses of Newark, New York and San Francisco and in the Dioceses of Albany, Brooklyn, Gallup, Paterson, Rockville Centre and Tucson.

[1430] (O.S.F.)—FRANCISCAN SISTERS OF OUR LADY OF PERPETUAL HELP (P)

Founded in the United States in 1901.

Motherhouse and Novitiate: *Franciscan Sisters of Our Lady of Perpetual Help*, 335 S. Kirkwood Rd., St. Louis, MO 63122. Tel: 314-965-3700; Fax: 314-965-3710. Sr. Regina Marie Strassburger, O.S.F., Supr. Gen.

Total in Community: 100.

Legal Holdings and Titles: Villa St. Joseph Motherhouse and Novitiate, St. Louis, MO; Perpetual Help Retirement Corporation, St. Louis, MO.

Ministry in Education; Nursing Homes; Rehabilitation Hospital; Indian Missions; Parish Ministries.

Represented in the Archdioceses of Chicago, Cincinnati, Kansas City in Kansas, Milwaukee, Omaha, Santa Fe and St. Louis, and in the Dioceses of Austin, Belleville, El Paso, Grand Rapids, Jefferson City, Lafayette (IN), Las Cruces, Pueblo, Rockford, Rockville Centre, St. Petersburg, Shreveport, Springfield-Cape Girardeau, Springfield in Illinois and Toledo.

[1440] (S.F.P.)—FRANCISCAN SISTERS OF THE POOR (P)

Founded in Aachen, Germany in 1845. First foundation in the United States in 1858.

Congregational Office: 133 Remsen St., Brooklyn, NY 11201. Tel: 718-643-1919; Fax: 718-643-9710. Sr. Tiziana Merletti, S.F.P., Congregational Min.

Total in Community: 138.

U.S. Area: 60 Compton Rd., Cincinnati, OH 45215. Tel: 513-761-9040; Fax: 513-761-6703. Sr. Joanne Schuster, S.F.P., U.S. Area Councilor.

Congregation sponsors: Franciscan Sisters of the Poor Foundation, Inc.; St. Leonard Center, Centerville, OH; Franciscan Health System of Dayton, Inc.; Co-Sponsors: St. Anthony Medical Center, Inc., Columbus, OH; West Park Retirement Community, Inc., Cincinnati, OH; St. Raphael Social Service Center, Inc., Hamilton, OH; West Park II, Inc.; St. John Social Service Center, Inc.; Franciscan Health System of Cincinnati, Inc. Parent: —Subsidiaries: St. Clare Retirement Community, Inc. Parent: —Subsidiaries: Mary Black Schroder Home for the Aging, Inc., Hamilton, OH; Brazil Regional House and Frascati Complex, Italy.

Represented in the Archdioceses of Cincinnati, Detroit, Newark, New York and Philadelphia and in the Dioceses of Brooklyn, Columbus and Lansing. Also in Italy, Senegal and Brazil.

[1450] (O.S.F.)—FRANCISCAN SISTERS OF THE SACRED HEART (P)

Congregation of the Franciscan Sisters of the Sacred Heart. Founded in Germany 1866. Established in the United States in 1876.

Motherhouse, Novitiate, Postulancy & Portiuncula Center for Prayer: *St. Francis Woods*, 9201 W. St. Francis Rd., Frankfort, IL 60423-8335. Tel: 815-469-4895; Fax: 815-464-3809. Sr. Judith Plumb, Gen. Supr.

Total in Community: 94.

Legal Title: *An Association of Franciscan Sisters of the Sacred Heart; Legal Titles for Health Care entities; Provena Health; St. Anne's Maternity Home; Franciscan Foundation.*

Sisters sponsor: St. Joseph Medical Center, Joliet, IL; St. Joseph Hospital, Elgin, IL; Villa Franciscan, Joliet, IL; Sacred Heart Home, Avilla, IN; LaVerna Terrace, Avilla, IN; St. Anne's Maternity Home, Los Angeles, CA; United Samaritans Medical Center, Logan Campus-Danville, IL; United Samaritans Medical Center, Sager Campus-Danville, IL; Franciscan Foundation, Frankfort, IL.

Sisters serve and staff: Elementary Schools; High School; Religious Education Centers; Neighborhood Health Care Centers; Foreign Mission Centers; Direct Domestic Work at Retreat Houses; Canon Lawyer; Diocesan Offices; Retreat Centers; Clinics, Home Health Agencies, Health Care Systems, Hospitals, Nursing and Retirement Homes; Home for Unwed Mothers; Apartments-Well Elderly; Parish & Youth Ministry; Liturgical Ministry; Social Work; Congregate Care Facility.

Represented in the Archdioceses of Chicago and Los Angeles and in the Dioceses of Fort Wayne-South Bend, Gary, Joliet, Peoria and Rockford. Also in Brazil.

[1460] (F.S.S.E.)—FRANCISCAN SISTERS OF ST. ELIZABETH (P)

(Suore Franciscane Elisabettine)

First founded in Naples, Italy, 1865. Founded in United States in Newark, New Jersey in 1919.

General Motherhouse: Via Marsico Nuovo 35, Rome, Italy Mother Clara Capaso, Supr. Gen.

Delegate House: 499 Park Rd., Parsippany, NJ 07054. Tel: 973-539-3797. Mother Gina Maria Amico, Delegate Gen.

Total number in the U.S: 56; Total in Community: 300.

Ministry in Day Nurseries; Mission Houses; Elementary Schools and Montessori Schools.

Sister Serve Christ in the person of the poor in Schools & Day Nursery Schools; Catechetical Instruction; Hospitals; Homes for the Poor, Aged and Disabled.

Represented in the Archdiocese of Newark and in the Dioceses of Paterson and St. Petersburg, FL. Also in India, Indonesia, Italy, Panama, Philippines and Africa.

[1470] (F.S.S.J.)—FRANCISCAN SISTERS OF ST. JOSEPH (P)

Founded in the United States in 1897.

General Motherhouse: *Immaculate Conception Convent*, 5286 S. Park Ave., Hamburg, NY 14075. Tel: 716-649-1205; Fax: 716-649-5958. Sr. Judith Elaine Salzman, F.S.S.J., Gen. Min.

Total in Community: 98.

Properties owned and/or sponsored: Immaculata Academy, Hamburg, NY; Marycrest Manor, Livonia, MI.

Ministry in Education; Health Care; Parish Ministries; Social Services.

Represented in the Archdioceses of Baltimore, Detroit and Milwaukee and in the Dioceses of Allentown, Arlington, Buffalo, Springfield in Massachusetts and Trenton.

[1480] (H.F.S.J.)—FRANCISCAN SISTERS OF ST. JOSEPH (D)

Founded in Mexico.

Motherhouse: Ave. Revolucion No. 431, Delegacion, Benito Juarez, Mexico, 03801 D.F.. Tel: 515-1774. Rev. Madre Eva Juana Perez, H.F.S.J.

U.S. Address: *St. Paul's College*, 3015 4th St., N.E., Washington, DC 20017-1199. Tel: 202-832-6262; Tel: 202-269-2515. Sr. Maria de Jesus Jimenez, H.F.S.J.

Total in Community: 5.

Ministry in domestic areas.

Represented in the Archdiocese of Washington.

[1485] (O.S.F.)—FRANCISCAN SISTERS OF ST. PAUL, MN (P)

Franciscan Sisters of the Blessed Virgin Mary of the Holy Angels (Beatae Mariae Virginis Angelorum)

Founded in Germany in 1863. First foundation in the United States in St. Paul in 1923.

General Motherhouse (1863): *St. Marienhaus*, Waldbreitbach, bei Neuwied, Rhine, Germany Sr. Basina Kloos, O.S.F., Supr. Gen.

Universal total in Congregation: 360.

U.S. Foundation: *Franciscan Regional Center*, 1388 Prior Ave. S., Saint Paul, MN 55116. Tel: 651-690-1501; Fax: 651-690-2509. Sr. Mary Lucy Scheffler, O.S.F.

Total in Community: 10.

Represented in the Archdiocese of St. Paul-Minneapolis.

[1500] (F.M.I.)—FRANCISCAN SISTERS OF MARY IMMACULATE OF THE THIRD ORDER OF ST. FRANCIS OF ASSISI (P)

Founded in Switzerland in the 16th Century. First founded in the United States on Aug. 15, 1932 at Amarillo, Texas.

General House: Carrera 81 C No. 24B-20, Barrio Modelia, Bogota, Colombia Sr. Hermana Noemi Quesada, F.M.I., Supr. Gen.

Universal total in Congregation: 578.

U.S. Provincial House and Novitiate (1964): *St. Francis Convent (1932)*, 4301 N.E. 18th Ave., Amarillo, TX 79107-7220. Tel: 806-383-5769; Fax: 806-383-6545. Sr. Solangel Diaz, F.M.I., Prov. Supr.

Total in Community: 45.

Represented in the Archdiocese of Los Angeles and in the Diocese of Amarillo. Also in Central & South America.

[1505] (O.S.F.)—ST. FRANCIS MISSION

COMMUNITY (P)

Established 1981 in the United States of America in Amarillo, Texas, as an autonomous province of the Franciscan Sisters of Mary Immaculate.

General Motherhouse: *Our Lady of the Angels Convent*, 8202 CR 7700, Wolfforth, TX 79382. Tel: 806-863-4904. Sr. Charlotte Lujan, O.S.F., Prov. Min.

Professed Sisters: 18.

Ministry in the field of Religious and Academic Education at all levels; Parish Work; Pastoral Care in Hospitals.

Properties owned: La Verna Convent, Amarillo, TX; St. Francis Convent, Lubbock, TX; 43 acres of real estate.

Represented in the Archdiocese of Los Angeles and in the Dioceses of Amarillo and Lubbock. Also in Juarez, Mexico.

[1510] (O.S.F.)—SISTERS OF ST. FRANCIS (D)

Sisters of St. Francis of the Mission of the Immaculate Virgin

Founded in New York in 1893.

Canonical union in 2004 with Sisters of the Third Franciscan Order (Syracuse, NY) and Sisters of St. Francis of the Third Order Regular (Williamsville, NY). Now known as Sisters of St. Francis of the Neumann Communities.

[1520] (S.S.F.C.R.-O.S.F.)—SCHOOL SISTERS OF ST. FRANCIS OF CHRIST THE KING (D)

Founded in Maribor, Slovenia in 1869 by Sr. Margareta Pucher. First house in the United States at Kansas City, Kansas, in 1909. U.S. Province established in 1922.

Generalate: Grottaferrata, Italy Sr. Natalija Palac, Supr. Gen.

Universal total in Congregation: 1080.

North American Provincial House: 13900 Main St., Lemont, IL 60439. Tel: 630-257-7495. Sr. M. Patricia Kolenda, S.S.F.C.R., Prov. Supr.

Total in Community: 47.

Ministry in Education, Care for Seniors, Parish Ministry; Retreat Ministry.

Properties owned and sponsored: Mount Assisi Convent, Lemont, IL; Mount Assisi Academy, Lemont, IL; Alvernia Manor, Lemont, IL; Our Lady of Angels House of Prayer, Lemont, IL.

Represented in the Archdiocese of Chicago and in the Diocese of Joliet.

[1530] (O.S.F.)—SISTERS OF ST. FRANCIS OF THE CONGREGATION OF OUR LADY OF LOURDES, SYLVANIA, OHIO (P)

Founded in the United States in 1916 at Sylvania, Ohio. Foundation from Rochester, Minnesota.

General Motherhouse: *Convent*, 6832 Convent Blvd., Sylvania, OH 43560-2897. Tel: 419-882-2016; Fax: 419-885-8643; Email: premley@sistersosf.org; Web: www.sistersosf.org. Sr. Diana Lynn Eckel, O.S.F., Congregational Min.

Total number in the Congregation: 204.

Ministry in the field of Religious and Academic Education at all levels; Healthcare; Communications; Media; Producing; Counseling; Parish Ministries; Retreat Center; Social Services.

Properties owned and sponsored: Lourdes College, Sylvania, OH; Franciscan Services Corp., Sylvania, OH; Sylvania Franciscan Academy, Sylvania, OH. Sponsored Ministries: Franciscan Care Centers, Sylvania, OH; Rosary Care Center, Sylvania, OH; Madonna Manor, KY; Franciscan Properties, Sylvania, OH; Bethany House, Toledo, OH; Trinity Health System, Steubenville, OH; Sophia Center, Inc.

Represented in the Archdioceses of Cincinnati, Detroit, New Orleans and St. Paul-Minneapolis and in the Dioceses of Austin, Biloxi, Cleveland, Columbus, Fort Wayne-South Bend, Gallup, Lansing, Raleigh, Richmond, St. Cloud, Steubenville, Toledo, Tyler, and Wheeling-Charleston.

[1540] (O.S.F.)—SISTERS OF SAINT FRANCIS, CLINTON, IOWA (P)

Founded in the United States in 1866.

General Motherhouse: *Administrative Center*, 843-13th Ave. N., Clinton, IA 52732-5115. Tel: 563-242-7611; Fax: 563-243-0007. Sr. Janice Cebula, O.S.F., Pres.

Ministry in the field of Academic Education at all levels; Health Care in Centers and Homes for the Aged; Pastoral Ministry; Religious Education and Spiritual Direction; Ministry to the Poor and Disabled.

Properties and Legal Holdings: The Alverno Health Care Facility; Mount St. Clare Speech and Hearing Center; Sisters of St. Francis, Clinton, IA; Iowa Charitable Trust, Clinton, IA; The Canticle, Clinton, IA; Mount Saint Clare Education Foundation.

Represented in the Archdioceses of Chicago, Dubuque and St. Louis and in the Dioceses of Belleville, Davenport, Des Moines, Lafayette (IN), Lexington, Portland, Phoenix, Rockford, San Bernardino, San Diego and Sioux City. Also in Peru.

[1550] (O.S.F.)—SISTERS OF ST. FRANCIS OF THE HOLY CROSS (P)

Founded in Wisconsin in 1881.

Motherhouse and Novitiate: *St. Francis Convent*, 3110 Nicolet Dr., Green Bay, WI 54311-7212. Tel: 920-468-1828; Fax: 920-468-1207. Sr. Donna Koch, O.S.F., Pres.

Total in Community: 70.

Legal Title: *Sisters of St. Francis of the Holy Cross, Inc.*

Ministries in the following areas: Education; Pastoral Ministry and Religious Education; Ministry to the Elderly; Health Care; Hospital Chaplaincy; Retreat Work.

Represented in the Archdiocese of Milwaukee and in the Diocese of Green Bay.

[1560] (O.S.F.)—SISTERS OF ST. FRANCIS OF THE HOLY EUCHARIST (D)

Founded in Grimmenstein, Switzerland in 1378. First foundation in the United States in 1892.

Motherhouse, Novitiate and Prayer Center: *St. Francis Convent*, 2100 N. Noland Rd., Independence, MO 64050. Tel: 816-252-1673; Fax: 816-252-5574. Sr. M. Lucy Lang, O.S.F., Sister Servant; Sr. M. Connie Boulch, O.S.F., Vicar.

Total in Community: 17.

Legal Titles: Franciscan Prayer Center, Independence, MO; Sisters of St. Francis of the Holy Eucharist Foundation, Independence, MO.

Ministry in the following areas: Education at all levels; Retreat; Evangelization; Pastoral.

Represented in the Diocese of Kansas City-St. Joseph.

[1570] (O.S.F.)—SISTERS OF ST. FRANCIS OF THE HOLY FAMILY (P)

Founded in Germany in 1864. First foundation in the United States in 1875.

Motherhouse and Novitiate: *Mount St. Francis*, 3390 Windsor Ave., Dubuque, IA 52001-1311. Tel: 563-583-9786; Fax: 563-583-3250. Sr. Nancy Schreck, Pres.; Sr. Veronica Bagenstos, Community Archivist.

Total in Community: 315.

Ministry in the following areas: Academic and Religious Education at all levels; Spirituality and Parish Ministry; Health-Pastoral Care; Diocesan Offices; Social Service-Social Justice and Peace; Food Service-Dietary; Communication Centers; Clerical Work-Business; Administration; Campus Ministry; Music Studios; International Missions.

Properties owned and sponsored: Shalom Retreat Center, Dubuque, IA; Sisters of St. Francis of the Holy Family Charitable Trust, Dubuque, IA.

Represented in the Archdioceses of Chicago, Detroit, Dubuque, Omaha, St. Paul-Minneapolis and San Antonio and in the Dioceses of Charleston, Davenport, Des Moines, Jackson, Joliet, Madison, Manchester, New Ulm, Phoenix, Reno, Rockford, St. Petersburg, St. Lucia, Santa Rosa, Sioux City, Superior, Toronto, Tulsa, Tyler and Winona. Also in Central America.

[1580] (O.S.F.)—SISTERS OF ST. FRANCIS OF THE IMMACULATE CONCEPTION (D)

Founded in the United States in 1891.

Motherhouse: *Immaculate Conception Convent*, 2408 W. Heading Ave., West Peoria, IL 61604-5096. Tel: 309-674-6168. Sr. Paula Vasquez, Pres.; Sr. Mary Louise Hynd, Archivist.

Total in Community: 40.

Properties owned: Immaculate Conception Convent, Peoria, IL; St. Joseph's Home of Springfield in Illinois.

Represented in the Dioceses of Peoria and Springfield in Illinois.

[1590] (O.S.F.)—SISTERS OF ST. FRANCIS OF THE IMMACULATE HEART OF MARY (HANKINSON, NORTH DAKOTA) (P)

Founded in 1241 in Bavaria. First founded in the United States in 1913 at Collegeville, Minnesota.

General Motherhouse: Dillingen, Germany Sr. Ann Marie Friederichs, Supr. Gen.

Province of Hankinson (1928): *Sisters of St. Francis Motherhouse*, Hankinson, ND 58041-0447. Tel: 701-242-7195. Sr. Donna Welder, O.S.F., Prov. Supr.

Professed Sisters: 32.

Legal Holdings or Titles: St. Gerard's Community Nursing Home, Hankinson, ND; St. Anne's Guest Home, Grand Forks, ND.

Ministry in the field of Religious and Academic Education; Health Care in Hospitals; Homes for the Aged.

Represented in the Diocese of Fargo.

[1600] (F.S.G.M.)—SISTERS OF ST. FRANCIS OF THE MARTYR ST. GEORGE (P)

Founded in Thuine, Germany. First United States foundation in 1923.

General Motherhouse: Thuine, Germany Mother Margaretha Maria Brand, F.S.G.M., Supr. Gen.

Provincial Motherhouse: *St. Francis Convent and Novitiate*, 1 Franciscan Way, P.O. Box 9020, Alton, IL 62002-9020. Tel: 618-463-2750; Tel: 618-463-2755. Mother M. Regina Pacis Coury, F.S.G.M., Prov.

Worldwide Total: 1310; Total in American Province: 161.

Properties owned and sponsored: Saint Anthony's Hospital, Alton, IL; St. Francis Day Care Center, Alton, IL; Mother of Good Counsel Home, St. Louis, MO; Saint Clare Hospital, Alton, IL.

Sisters serve and staff: Hospitals; Skilled Nursing Facility; Foreign Missions; Day Care Center; Retirement Homes for the Aged; Grade & High Schools; Retirement Homes for Priests; Archdiocesan Offices.

Represented in the Archdioceses of Kansas City in Kansas, Philadelphia, St. Louis and Washington and in the Dioceses of La Crosse, Lincoln, Metuchen, Peoria, Springfield in Illinois, Steubenville and Tulsa. Also in Brazil.

[1620] (O.S.F.)—SISTERS OF SAINT FRANCIS OF MILLVALE, PENNSYLVANIA (P)

Canonical merger 2008 into Sisters of St. Francis of the Neumann Communities, Kenedy ID: 1805.

[1630] (O.S.F.)—SISTERS OF ST. FRANCIS OF PENANCE AND CHRISTIAN CHARITY (P)

(aka Sisters of St. Francis of the Holy Name Province)

Founded in Holland in 1835. First foundation in the United States in 1874.

General Motherhouse: Rome, Italy Sr. Anisia Margareta Schneider, Gen. Min.

Universal total in Congregation: 1712.

Holy Name Province (1928): *Sisters of St. Francis*, 4421 Lower River Rd., Stella Niagara, NY 14144. Tel: 716-754-4312; Fax: 716-754-7657. Sr. Dorothy Mueller, O.S.F., Prov. Minister.

Total in Community: 163.

Legal Holdings: Stella Niagara Education Park, Stella Niagara, NY; Buffalo Academy of the Sacred Heart, Buffalo, NY; Francis Center, Niagara Falls, NY; St. Francis of Holy Name Province, Inc., Stella Niagara, NY; Center of Renewal, Stella Niagara, NY.

Ministry in the field of Academic Education at all levels; Foreign Mission Work; Health and Hospital Care; Social Work; Pastoral Ministry.

Represented in the Archdioceses of Cincinnati, Louisville, Miami and Santa Fe and in the Dioceses of Buffalo, Columbus, Paterson, Steubenville, Trenton, and Wheeling-Charleston. Also in Canada.

Sacred Heart Province (1939): *Provincial Motherhouse-Marycrest*, 5314 Columbine Rd, Denver, CO 80221. Tel: 303-458-6270. Sr. Karen Crouse, Prov. Min.

Total in Community: 50.

Legal Holdings or Titles: Marycrest Motherhouse; Marycrest Franciscans Development, Inc.; Marycrest Franciscan Ministries, Denver, CO; St. Francis Home, (Home for Abused Native American Children), Manderson, SD; Marian Residence, Convent for Retired Sisters, Alliance, NE; St. Francis Convent.

Sisters serve and staff: High Schools; Parish Ministries; Apostolate of Aging; Home for Neglected Children; Retreat Ministry; Formation Programs; Administrative; Social Outreach.

Represented in the Archdioceses of Denver and Omaha, and in the Dioceses of Grand Island and Rapid City.

St. Francis Province (1939): 1330 Brewster Ave., P.O. Box 1028, Redwood City, CA 94062-1312. Tel: 650-369-1725; Fax: 650-369-0845. Sr. Carol Snyder, O.S.F., Prov. Min.

Total in Community: 72.

Legal Title: *Sisters of St. Francis of Penance and Christian Charity, OSF.*

Ministry in the following areas: Diocesan Offices; Parish Ministry; Pastoral Ministry; Services Agencies; Hospitals; Residence for Retired Men and Women; CCD Centers; ESL; Advocacy.

Represented in the Archdioceses of Los Angeles, San Francisco and Seattle and in the Dioceses of Las Vegas, Oakland, Sacramento and San Jose.

[1640] (O.S.F.)—SISTERS OF ST. FRANCIS OF PERPETUAL ADORATION (P)

Founded in Germany in 1863. First foundation in the United States in 1875.

Generalate: Olpe, Westfalen, Germany Sr. Magdalena Krol, Supr. Gen.

Universal total in Congregation: 492.

Province of the Immaculate Heart of Mary (1875): *Provincial House and Novitiate, St. Francis Convent*, P.O. Box 766, Mishawaka, IN 46546-0766. Tel: 574-259-5427. Sr. M. Angela Mellady, O.S.F., Prov.

Total in Community: 123.

Ministry in the field of Academic Education at all levels; Health Care in Hospitals; Ecclesial Ministry at parish and diocesan level.

Properties owned: Sisters of St. Francis of Perpetual Adoration, Inc.; St. Francis Convent, Mishawaka, IN; University of St. Francis, Inc., Fort Wayne, IN; Sisters of St. Francis Health Services, Inc.; Sisters of St. Francis Health Services, Inc., Corporate Office, Mishawaka, IN, owns the following: Alverno Clinical Laboratories, Inc., Hammond, IN; Corporate Office, Lafayette Home Hospital, Lafayette, IN; St. Anthony Medical Center of Crown Point, Crown Point, IN; St. Anthony Memorial Health Centers, Michigan City, IN; St. Clare Medical Center, Crawfordsville, IN; St. Elizabeth Medical Center, Lafayette, IN; St. Francis Hospital & Health Centers, Beech Grove, IN (including the Indianapolis, IN campus and Mooresville, IN campus); St. James Hospital and Health Centers, Chicago Heights, IL (including the Olympia Fields, IL campus); St. Margaret Mercy Health Care Centers, North Campus, Hammond, IN; Saint Margaret Mercy Health Care Centers, South Campus, Dyer, IN; Alverno Information Services, Beech Grove, IN.

Represented in the Archdioceses of Chicago and Indianapolis and in the Dioceses of Fort Wayne-South Bend, Gary and Lafayette in Indiana.

Province of St. Joseph (March 19, 1932): *Provincial House and Formation House-Mt. St. Francis*, 7665 Assisi Heights, Colorado Springs, CO 80919. Tel: 719-598-5486. Sr. Stephanie McReynolds, O.S.F., Prov.
Professed Sisters: 59.
Ministry in Education; Hospitals; Homes for the Aged; Parish/Pastoral Ministry; Peace & Justice; Social Ministries; Retreat Centers.
Represented in the Archdioceses of Denver, Los Angeles, Omaha and Santa Fe and in the Dioceses of Colorado Springs, Grand Island, Lincoln, Pueblo and Wichita.

[1650] (O.S.F.)—THE SISTERS OF ST. FRANCIS OF PHILADELPHIA (P)

Founded in the United States in 1855.

Congregational Motherhouse: *Our Lady of Angels Convent*, 609 S. Convent Rd., Aston, PA 19014. Tel: 610-459-4125. Sr. Esther Anderson, O.S.F., Congregational Min.; Sr. Marijane Hresko, O.S.F., Asst. Congregational Min.; Sr. Donna Desien, O.S.F., Congregational Sec.; Sr. Helen Jacobson, O.S.F., Archivist.
Total in Community: 578.
Ministry in Health Care; Eldercare; Academic and Religious Education at all Levels; Specialized Education; Parish Ministry; Social Services; Family Centers; Renewal Centers; Diocesan Offices; Retreat Ministry; National Organizations.
Properties owned: Sisters of St. Francis, Sea Isle City, NJ; Sisters of St. Francis, Aston, PA; Bay House, Tacoma, WA; Marion House, Tacoma, WA; St. Ann Convent, Tacoma, WA; Neumann College, Aston, PA; Assisi House, Aston, PA; Portiuncula Convent, Aston, PA; St. Mary Convent, Langhorne, PA; Franciscan Residence, Langhorne, PA; St. Agnes Convent, Philadelphia, PA; Neumann Convent, Reading, PA; The Catholic High School of Baltimore, Baltimore, MD; St. Joseph Counseling Center, Spokane, WA; Anna Bachmann House, Aston, PA; Sisters of St. Francis, Aston, PA; Sisters of St. Francis, Aston, PA; Sisters of St. Francis, Wilmington, DE; Sisters of St. Francis of Philadelphia, Canticle House, Philadelphia, PA; Sisters of St. Francis of Philadelphia, TAU Convent, Aston, PA; St. Clare Renewal Center, Aston, PA; Sisters of St. Francis of Philadelphia, Our Lady of the Valley, Aston, PA; Mt. Alvernia Convent, Aston, PA; St. Clare Convent, Trenton, NJ; Sisters of St. Francis of Philadelphia, Mt. St. Francis Convent, Ringwood, NJ; Franciscan Spiritual Center, Ringwood, NJ; Chaplain's Residence, Ringwood, NJ; Caretaker's Residence, Ringwood, NJ; Our Lady of Angels Convent, Ringwood, NJ; St. Clare Convent, Ringwood, NJ; St. Joseph Residence, Ringwood, NJ.
Represented in the Archdioceses of Atlanta, Baltimore, Boston, Hartford, Los Angeles, Mobile, Newark, Philadelphia, Portland in Oregon, San Francisco, San Juan, Seattle, and Washington and in the Dioceses of Allentown, Arlington, Baker, Birmingham, Caguas (PR), Camden, Charlotte, Charleston, Cheyenne, Fairbanks, Fresno, Harrisburg, Honolulu, Lexington, Manchester, Oakland, Orlando, Paterson, Pensacola-Tallahassee, Providence, Raleigh, St. Louis, San Bernardino, San Diego, Spokane, Trenton, Venice, Wilmington and Worcester. Also in Ireland, Kenya and Uganda.

[1660] (O.S.F.)—SISTERS OF SAINT FRANCIS OF THE PROVIDENCE OF GOD (P)

Founded in Pittsburgh in 1922.

Generalate: 140 Hamilton Rd., Pittsburgh, PA 15234-2364. Sr. Janet Gardner, O.S.F., Gen. Min.

Motherhouse: *St. Francis Convent*, 3603 McRoberts Rd., Pittsburgh, PA 15234-2398. Tel: 412-882-9911; Fax: 412-885-7210. Sr. J. Lora Dambroski, O.S.F., U.S.A. Prov. Min.
Total Professed: 85.
Ministry in the field of Education; Health Care; Social Service; Pastoral, Parish & Retreat Ministries; Retreat Directors; Prison Chaplains; Foreign Mission work in Brazil & Lithuania.
Properties owned and sponsored: Sisters of St. Francis of the Providence of God; Sisters of St. Francis, Mt. Vernon IL, Inc.; Sisters of St. Francis of the Providence of God Ministries Corporation; St. Francis Academy; Franciscan Child Day Care Center; Franciscan Spirit and Life Center.
Represented in the Archdiocese of Newark and in the Dioceses of Albany, Buffalo, Paterson and Pittsburgh.

[1670] (O.S.F.)—SISTERS OF ST. FRANCIS OF SAVANNAH, MO (P)

Founded in Austria in 1850. Founded in the United States, August 22, 1922.

Provincial House and Novitiate: 104 E. Park, Box 488, Savannah, MO 64485-0488. Tel: 816-324-3179; Fax: 816-324-7264; Web: www.sistersofstfrancis.org. Sr. Kathleen Reichert, Prov. Supr.
Total in Community: 12.
Legal Holdings and Titles: Sisters of St. Francis of Savannah, Inc.; Maintenance and Custodial Care Trust of the Franciscan Sisters of Savannah.
Ministry in rural life issues; Peace and Justice; Pastoral Care; Religious Education; Food Pantry.
Represented in the Diocese of Kansas City-St. Joseph.

[1680] (O.S.F.)—SCHOOL SISTERS OF ST. FRANCIS (P)

Founded in the United States in 1874.

General Motherhouse: 1501 S. Layton Blvd., Milwaukee, WI 53215. Tel: 414-384-4105; Fax: 414-944-6060. Sr. Kathleen Kluthe, O.S.F., Pres.; Sr. Patricia Baier, O.S.F., Vice Pres.; Sr. Arlene Woelfel, O.S.F., Vice Pres.; Sr. Rita Eble, O.S.F, Vice Pres.; Sr. Catherine M. Ryan, O.S.F., Treas.; Sr. Charlita Foxhoven, O.S.F., Asst. Treas.; Sr. Corrine Dais, O.S.F., Archivist.
Total in Congregation : 1036; Total in U.S: 615.
Properties owned and/or sponsored: St. Joseph Convent, Milwaukee, WI; School Sisters of St. Francis, Inc.

U.S. Province: 1515 S. Layton Blvd., Milwaukee, WI 53215. Tel: 414-384-1515. Provincial Team: Sr. Barbara Kraemer; Sr. Elizabeth Heese; Sr. Maureen McCarthy.
Properties owned and sponsored: Alverno College, Milwaukee, WI; Clement Manor, Inc., Greenfield, WI; Maryhill Manor, Niagara, WI; New Cassel, Omaha, NE; Clare Towers I, Milwaukee, WI; Telos, Inc., Milwaukee, WI; St. Clare Management, Inc., Milwaukee, WI; Sacred Heart Center, Milwaukee, WI; St. Joseph Convent, Campbellsport, WI; School Sisters of St. Francis of St. Joseph's Convent, Milwaukee, Wisconsin, Inc.
Sisters serve and staff: Universities, Colleges, Seminaries, High Schools, Grade Schools, Preschools, Adult and Special Education; National and Diocesan Offices; Hospitals and Nursing Homes; School & Parish Musicians; Retreat and Spiritual Direction; Social Ministries; Campus Ministry; Psychotherapy; Home Health Care Service; Religious Education and CCD; Pastoral Ministry; Pastoral Associate; Health Pastoral Care; Retirement Homes.
Represented in the Archdioceses of Anchorage, Chicago, Denver, Dubuque, Milwaukee, New York, Oklahoma City, Omaha, St. Paul-Minneapolis, and Washington and in the Dioceses of Charlotte, Davenport, Des Moines, El Paso, Grand Island, Green Bay, Jackson, Jefferson City, Joliet, La Crosse, Lexington, Lincoln, Madison, Nashville, New Ulm, Orange, Phoenix, Rockford, San Bernardino, Sioux City, St. Petersburg, Superior, Tucson, Wheeling-Charleston and Winona.

[1690] (O.S.F.)—SCHOOL SISTERS OF THE THIRD ORDER REGULAR OF ST. FRANCIS UNITED STATES PROVINCE (PITTSBURGH, PA) (P)

Founded in Austria in 1843. First foundation in the U.S. in 1913.

Generalate: Via Nicolo Piccolomini 27, 00165, Rome, Italy Sr. Mary Xavier Bomberger, O.S.F., Gen. Min.

Motherhouse and Novitiate: *Mount Assisi Convent*, 934 Forest Ave., Bellevue, Pittsburgh, PA 15202. Tel: 412-761-6004; Fax: 412-761-0290. Sr. Elaine Hromulak, O.S.F., Prov. Min. Tel: 412-761-2855.
Total in Community: 95.
Legal Titles: School Sisters of the Third Order Regular of St. Francis; School Sisters of the Third Order of St. Francis, of Texas.
Ministry in the following areas: the field of academic education at all levels; CCD Centers; Pastoral Ministry; Pastoral Associate; Residence Home for the Elderly; Mission Work; Hospital Ministry; Campus Ministry; Social Ministry.
Represented in the Archdioceses of Newark, Philadelphia and San Antonio and in the Dioceses of Allentown, Erie, Greensburg, Manchester, Metuchen, Phoenix, Pittsburgh, San Angelo, Springfield in Massachusetts, Trenton and Tucson. Also in South Africa and Rome, Italy.

[1695] (O.S.F.)—SCHOOL SISTERS OF THE THIRD ORDER OF ST. FRANCIS (PANHANDLE, TEXAS) (P)

Founded in Austria, 1723; The Vienna Foundation in 1845. First founded in the United States, 1931.

General Motherhouse: Vienna, Austria

American Center and Novitiate: 119 Franciscan Way, P.O. Box 906, Panhandle, TX 79068. Tel: 806-537-3182. Sr. Mary Ana Steele, O.S.F., Reg. Supr.
Total number in U.S: 24.
Ministry in the following areas: Elementary and High Schools; Faith Formation; Nursing Home; Youth Groups.
Represented in the Diocese of Amarillo.

[1700] (O.S.F.)—SCHOOL SISTERS OF THE THIRD ORDER REGULAR OF ST. FRANCIS (BETHLEHEM, PA) (P)

Founded in Austria, 1843. First founded in the United States, 1913.

General Motherhouse: Via Nicolo Piccolomini 27, Rome, Italy, 00165. Sr. Mary Xavier Bomberger, O.S.F., Gen. Min.

Bethlehem Novitiate: 395 Bridle Path Rd., Bethlehem, PA 18017-3105. Tel: 610-866-2597; Tel: 610-867-8890; Fax: 610-861-7478. Sr. Elaine Hromulak, O.S.F., Prov. Min. Tel: 412-761-2855.
Sisters: 46.
Properties owned and/or sponsored: St. Francis Center for Renewal, Bethlehem, PA.

[1705] (O.S.F.)—THE SISTERS OF ST. FRANCIS OF ASSISI (P)

(Sisters of Penance and Charity)

Founded in the United States in 1849.

General Motherhouse: *St. Francis Convent*, 3221 S. Lake Dr., St. Francis, WI 53235-3799. Tel: 414-744-1160; Fax: 414-744-7193; Web: www.lakeosfs.org. Sr. Florence Deacon, O.S.F., Dir.
Total in Community: 254.
Legal Titles: The Sisters of St. Francis of Assisi, Inc.; The Ongoing Community Support Trust of the Sisters of St. Francis, Inc.; Declaration of Trust of the Franciscan Sisters of Baltimore, Inc.
Goals of the Congregation are to bring the healing, teaching, reconciling and liberating power of Jesus into the human situations in which we live and minister; to be in solidarity with the poor through the work of justice and peace; to appreciate and affirm and to encourage the development of each community member and each community apostolate for the sake of full effectiveness in the ministry of the Church; and to work effectively toward implementing co-responsibility, subsidiary and accountability at all levels within the Congregation.
Corporate Ministries: Franciscan Youth Center, Inc., Baltimore, MD; St. Elizabeth School, Inc., Baltimore, MD; Franciscan Center, Inc., Baltimore, MD; St. Ann Center for Intergenerational Care, Inc., Milwaukee, WI; St. Mary's Academy, Inc., Milwaukee, WI; Cardinal Stritch University, Inc., Milwaukee, WI; St. Coletta's of Wisconsin, Inc., Jefferson, WI; St. Coletta Wisconsin Charitable Foundation, Inc., Jefferson Charitable Trust, Jefferson, WI; St. Coletta's of Illinois, Palos Park, IL; St. Coletta's of Illinois Foundation, Inc., Palos Park, IL; St. Coletta's of Massachusetts: Cardinal Cushing School and Training Center, Hanover, MA; Cushing Residence, Inc., Hanover, MA; Cardinal Cushing School Foundation of Hanover Charitable Trust, Hanover, MA; Cardinal Cushing Centers, Inc. Braintree Campus and Braintree St. Coletta, Braintree, MA. Services to the Elderly: Alverno Housing Corporation, Jefferson, WI; Canticle Court, Inc.; Juniper Court, Inc., St. Francis, WI.
Represented in the Archdioceses of Baltimore, Boston, Chicago, Denver, Dubuque, Milwaukee, San Antonio, Santa Fe, St. Louis and Washington and in the Dioceses of Austin, Brownsville, Cheyenne, Des Moines, Gary, Green Bay, Joliet, Kansas City-St. Joseph, La Crosse, Madison, Phoenix, San Diego, Sioux Falls, Superior, Tucson, Tulsa and Winona. Also in Ireland, Mexico and Taiwan.

[1710] (O.S.F.)—CONGREGATION OF THE THIRD ORDER OF ST. FRANCIS OF MARY IMMACULATE, JOLIET, IL (P)

Founded in the United States, Joliet, Illinois, in 1865.

Central Administration Offices: 1433 Essington Rd., Joliet, IL 60432-2873. Tel: 815-725-8735. Sr. Mary Rose Lieb, O.S.F., Pres.; Sr. Marian Voelker, O.S.F., Community Archivist.
Total in Community: 199.
Legal Titles: Congregation of the Third Order of St. Francis of Mary Immaculate, Joliet, IL; Retirement Plan Trust of the Congregation of the Third Order of St. Francis of Mary Immaculate, Joliet, IL.
Sponsored Institutions: Franciscan Learning Center, Guardian Angel Community Services, Joliet Catholic Academy, Our Lady of Angels Retirement Home, University of St. Francis.
Ministry in the following areas: School and Adult Education; Retirement Home; House of Prayer. Also engaged in Religious Education; Social Services; Spiritual Direction; Nursing and Health Services; Hospital and Parish Ministry; Prison Ministry; Hispanic Ministry; Senior Housing.
Represented in the Archdioceses of Boston, Chicago, Cincinnati, Denver, Miami, Milwaukee, Mobile and New York and in the Dioceses of Cleveland, Colorado Springs, Columbus, Fort Wayne-South Bend, Jackson, Joliet, Lansing, Palm Beach, Peoria, Phoenix, Rockford, St. Cloud, St. Petersburg, Springfield (IL), Stockton, Superior, Toledo, Tucson and Youngstown. Also in Brazil.

[1720] (O.S.F.)—SISTERS OF THE THIRD ORDER REGULAR OF ST. FRANCIS OF THE CONGREGATION OF OUR LADY OF LOURDES (P)

Founded in the United States in 1877.

Administration Center: *Assisi Heights*, 1001 14th St., N.W., Ste 100, Rochester, MN 55901. Tel: 507-282-7441; Fax: 507-282-7762. Sr. Tierney Trueman, O.S.F., Pres./Community Min. Tel: 507-280-2198; Sr. Mary Lonan Reilly, Community Archivist.
Total in Community: 264.
Ministry in the following areas: Education Services; Pastoral Concerns Development; Religious Life Development; Spiritual Life Development; Community Life Development; Social Concerns Development; Business Services; Health Care Services; Support Services.
Properties owned and sponsored: Holy Spirit Retreat Center, Janesville, MN; Assisi Heights, Rochester, MN.
Represented in the Archdioceses of Chicago, Cincinnati, Denver, Indianapolis, Milwaukee, St. Paul-Minneapolis, Santa Fe and Washington and in the Dioceses of Charleston, Columbus, Great Falls-Billings, Joliet, New Ulm, Oakland, Owensboro, Pueblo, St. Cloud, San Bernardino, San Diego, Sioux Falls, Sioux City,

Springfield-Cape Girardeau, Superior and Winona. Also in Colombia.

[1730] (O.S.F.)—CONGREGATION OF THE SISTERS OF THE THIRD ORDER OF ST. FRANCIS, OLDENBURG, IN (P)

Founded in U.S., Oldenburg, Indiana in 1851.

General Motherhouse and Novitiate: *Convent of the Immaculate Conception*, Oldenburg, IN 47036. Tel: 812-934-2475. Sr. Barbara Piller, O.S.F., Congregational Min.

Total in Community: 264.

Properties owned and/or sponsored: Marian College, Indianapolis, IN; Oldenburg Academy, Oldenburg, IN.

Sisters serve & staff: Liberal Arts College, Academy, High Schools, Elementary Schools; Navajo, Crow Indian and Cheyenne Missions; Religious Education Centers; Hospital & Parish Ministry; Apostolate of Aging; Diocesan Offices; Retreat & Counseling Ministry; Hispanic Ministry; Justice & Peace Offices; Clerical Staff; Social Services; Foreign Missions: New Guinea.

Represented in the Archdioceses of Cincinnati, Detroit, Indianapolis, Los Angeles, New Orleans and St. Louis and in the Dioceses of Buffalo, Charleston, Cheyenne, Columbus, Evansville, Gallup, Great Falls-Billings, Lexington, Peoria, Springfield (IL), and Wheeling-Charleston.

[1760] (O.S.F.)—SISTERS OF THE THIRD ORDER OF ST. FRANCIS OF PENANCE AND OF CHARITY (P)

Founded in Tiffin, Ohio in 1869.

General Motherhouse: *St. Francis Convent*, St. Francis Ave., Tiffin, OH 44883. Tel: 419-447-0435; Fax: 419-447-1612. Sr. Jacquelyn Doepker, O.S.F., Community Min.

Total in Community: 105.

Legal Title: *Sisters of St. Francis of Tiffin, OH.*

Ministry in the following areas: Parochial Schools; Ministry to the Aged; Parish Ministry; Retreat and Renewal Centers; Diocese Offices; Health Care; Health-Pastoral Care; Administration; Childcare; Social Justice Outreach.

Properties owned or sponsored: St. Francis Villas, Inc.; St. Francis Home, Inc., Tiffin, OH; Franciscan Earth Literacy Center (FELC); St. Francis Senior Ministries Day Care, Inc.; St. Francis Senior Ministries Memorial Foundation, Inc. (SFSMMF); St. Francis Spirituality Center (SFSC); St. Francis Senior Ministries, Inc.; Friedman Village at St. Francis.

Represented in the Archdiocese of Milwaukee and in the Dioceses of Columbus, Charlotte, Lansing, Lexington, Owensboro, Toledo, Wheeling-Charleston and Youngstown. Also in Mexico.

[1770] (O.S.F.)—THE SISTERS OF THE THIRD ORDER OF ST. FRANCIS (EAST PEORIA, ILLINOIS) (P)

Founded in the United States in 1877.

Motherhouse: 1175 St. Francis Ln., East Peoria, IL 61611-1299. Tel: 309-699-7215. Sr. Judith Ann Duvall, O.S.F., Major Supr.

Total in Community: 33.

Properties owned and sponsored: Saint Francis Medical Center, Peoria, IL; St. Joseph Medical Center, Bloomington, IL; St. Mary Medical Center, Galesburg, IL; St. James-John W. Albrecht Medical Center, Pontiac, IL; Saint Anthony Medical Center, Rockford, IL; St. Francis Hospital, Escanaba, MI; OSF Healthcare System, Peoria, IL; OSF Healthcare Foundation, Peoria, IL; Motherhouse, East Peoria, IL; Saint Clare Home, Peoria Heights, IL; Holy Family Medical Center, Monmouth, IL.

Represented in the Dioceses of Marquette, Peoria and Rockford.

[1780] (F.S.P.A.)—CONGREGATION OF THE SISTERS OF THIRD ORDER OF ST. FRANCIS OF PERPETUAL ADORATION (P)

(Franciscan Sisters of Perpetual Adoration)

Founded in the United States in 1849.

Generalate - Motherhouse and Novitiate: *St. Rose Convent*, 912 Market St., La Crosse, WI 54601-4782. Tel: 608-782-5610; Fax: 608-782-6301. Sr. Marlene Weisenbeck, F.S.P.A., Pres.; Sr. Mary Ann Gschwind, F.S.P.A., Archivist.

Total in Congregation : 317.

Properties owned and sponsored: St. Anthony Regional Hospital, Inc., Carroll, IA; Viterbo University, Inc., La Crosse, WI; Villa St. Joseph, La Crosse, WI; Franciscan Skemp Healthcare, La Crosse, WI; Clare Center, Spokane, WA; Franciscan Spirituality Center, La Crosse, WI; Prairiewoods - Franciscan Spirituality Center, Hiawatha, IA; Marywood - Franciscan Spirituality Center, Arbor Vitae, WI; WomanWell, St. Paul, MN.

Represented in the Archdioceses of Agana (GU), Chicago, Denver, Dubuque, Los Angeles, Milwaukee, Mobile, Portland in Oregon, Santa Fe, Seattle and St. Paul-Minneapolis and in the Dioceses of Colorado Springs, Davenport, El Paso, Gallup, Green Bay, Jackson, La Crosse, Las Vegas, Madison, Omaha, Peoria, Phoenix, Savannah, Sioux City, Spokane, Superior, Tucson and Winona. Also in Canada, Cameroon, El Salvador, Mexico and Zimbabwe.

[1805] O.S.F.—SISTERS OF ST. FRANCIS OF THE NEUMANN COMMUNITIES (P)

Congregation Offices: 2500 Grant Blvd., Ste. 3, Syracuse, NY 13208. Tel: 315-634-7000; Fax: 315-634-7023; Email: sisters@sosf.org; Web: www.sosf.org.

Total in Community: 528.

Ministry in academic education at all levels; hospitals; schools of nursing; religious education & pastoral ministry; retreat houses; rehabilitation center; home for the dying; adult & child day care; diocesan offices; social services; day nurseries; parishes

Sponsored ministries: Nazareth Day Nursery, New York, NY; Hastings Health Systems, Inc., Poughkeepsie, NY; Gingerbread House Day Care & Preschool, Syracuse, NY; St. Joseph's Hospital Health Center, Syracuse, NY; St. Elizabeth Medical Center, Utica, NY; St. Francis Social Adult Day Care Center, Syracuse, NY; Francis House, Syracuse, NY; St. Francis Healthcare System, Honolulu, HI; St. Francis School, Honolulu, HI; Mercy Health & Rehabilitation Center, Auburn, NY; Portiuncula Foundation, Millvale, PA; Mt. Alvernia Day Care & Learning Center, Millvale, PA; Mt. Alvernia High School, Millvale, PA.

Properties owned: Sisters of St. Francis Centers in Hastings-on-Hudson, Syracuse, Williamsville, Honolulu, HI, Millvale, PA; Stella Maris Retreat Center, Skaneateles, NY.

Represented in the Archdioceses of Baltimore, Boston, Los Angeles, Newark, New York, Philadelphia and Washington and in the Dioceses of Albany, Altoona-Johnstown, Buffalo, Camden, Charleston, Cleveland, Gallup, Greensburg, Harrisburg, Honolulu, Lubbock, Orange, Orlando, Pittsburgh, Richmond, Rochester, San Diego, Santa Fe, Scranton, St. Petersburg, Syracuse, Trenton and Venice. Also in Africa & Peru

[1810] (O.S.F.)—BERNARDINE FRANCISCAN SISTERS (P)

Founded in the United States in 1894.

Congregational Leadership Offices: 450 St. Bernardine St., Reading, PA 19607-1737. Tel: 484-334-6976; Fax: 484-334-6977. Sr. Madonna Marie Harvath, O.S.F., Congregational Min.

Total in Community: 375.

Total number in the United States: 267.

Ministry in the field of academic education at all levels - preschool to college; religious education of children & adults; hospitals, health & home care; retreat work; social work.

Represented in the Archdioceses of Detroit, Kansas City in Kansas, Los Angeles, Newark, Philadelphia, San Antonio, San Juan and Washington and in the Dioceses of Allentown, Bridgeport, Fall River, Metuchen, Richmond, Saginaw, Scranton, Trenton and Worcester. Also in Brazil, Dominican Republic, Liberia and Mozambique.

[1820] (O.S.F.)—HOSPITAL SISTERS OF THE THIRD ORDER REGULAR OF ST. FRANCIS (P)

Founded in Germany in 1844. First foundation in the United States in 1875.

General Motherhouse: *Muenster*, Westphalia, Germany Sr. Sherrey Murphy, O.S.F., Gen. Supr.

American Province (1875): *St. Francis Convent, Motherhouse and Novitiate*, Box 19431, Springfield, IL 62794. Tel: 217-522-3386. Sr. Jomary Trstensky, O.S.F., Prov. Supr.; Sr. Janice Schneider, O.S.F., Prov. Sec. & Contact Person.

Total in Community: 113.

Properties owned or sponsored: Residence 13; St. Francis Convent, Motherhouse, Novitiate, Springfield, IL; Hospital Sisters Services, Inc., Springfield, IL; Hospital Sisters of St. Francis Foundation, Springfield, IL; Hospital Sisters Health System, Springfield, IL; St. John's Hospital, Springfield, IL; St. John's College of Nursing, Springfield, IL; St. Mary's Hospital, Decatur, IL; St. Anthony Memorial Hospital, Effingham, IL; St. Joseph's Hospital, Highland, IL; St. Francis Hospital, Litchfield, IL; St. Elizabeth's Hospital, Belleville, IL; St. Joseph's Hospital, Breese, IL; St. Mary's Hospital Medical Center, Green Bay, WI; St. Vincent Hospital, Green Bay, WI; Sacred Heart Hospital, Eau Claire, WI; St. Francis Apartments, Eau Claire, WI; St. Nicholas Hospital, Sheboygan, WI; St. Mary's Hospital, Streator, IL; Hospital Sisters Tanzania, Springfield, IL; Hospital Sisters of St. Francis, USA, Inc.; Hospital Sisters Health Care West, Inc., Chippewa Falls, WI; St. Joseph's Hospital, Chippewa Falls, WI; L.E. Phillips Treatment Center for the Chemically Dependent, Chippewa Falls, WI; Hospital Sisters Mission Outreach, Springfield, IL; Chiara Center, Springfield, IL.

Sisters serve and staff: Hospitals; Home Health Services; Catechetical; Care of Chemically Dependent; Social Ministries; Pastoral Ministries; Overseas Missions.

Represented in the Archdioceses of Chicago and Milwaukee and in the Dioceses of Belleville, Green Bay, La Crosse, Peoria and Springfield in Illinois. Also in Tanzania, Germany and Haiti.

[1830] (R.G.S. - C.G.S.)—THE SISTERS OF THE GOOD SHEPHERD (P)

Congregation of Our Lady of Charity of the Good Shepherd

Founded in France in 1835. First foundation in the United States in Louisville, KY, 1842.

Generalate for the Provinces: *Suore del Buon Pastore*, via Raffaello Sardiello 20, Rome, Italy, 00165. Sr. Brigid Lawlor, Supr. Gen.

Province of Mid-North America (2000): *Province Center*, 7654 Natural Bridge Blvd., St. Louis, MO 63121. Tel: 314-381-3400; Fax: 314-381-7102. Sr. Mary Catherine Massei, R.G.S., Prov.

Professed Apostolic Sisters: 148; Contemplative Sisters: 47.

Legal Title: *Sisters of the Good Shepherd Province of Mid-North America; Pelletier Trust, a Charitable Trust of the Sisters of the Good Shepherd; Sisters of the Good Shepherd Province of Mid-North America Foundation.*

Properties owned and staffed: Good Shepherd Pelletier, Fort Thomas, KY; Sisters of the Good Shepherd of Detroit aka Vista Maria, Dearborn Heights, MI; Good Shepherd Corporation, Clarks Summit, PA aka Lourdesmont Good Shepherd Youth & Family Services, Clarks Summit, PA; CORA Services, Inc., Philadelphia, PA; Good Shepherd Corporation d.b.a. Good Shepherd Neighborhood House, Mediation Program, Philadelphia, PA; House of the Good Shepherd, Baltimore, MD; Good Shepherd Services, Atlanta, GA; Good Shepherd Corporation of Orlando, Inc., Orlando, FL; Good Shepherd Shelter, Los Angeles, CA; Gracenter, San Francisco, CA; Droste Residence, St. Louis, MO; House of the Good Shepherd of Memphis dba DeNeuville Learning Center, Memphis, TN; House of the Good Shepherd, Chicago, IL; Immaculate Heart Convent, St. Louis, MO; Good Shepherd Provincialate, St. Louis, MO; Home of the Good Shepherd Inc., St. Paul, MN.

Represented in the Archdioceses of Atlanta, Baltimore, Chicago, Detroit, Los Angeles, Louisville, Omaha, Portland in Oregon, Philadelphia, St. Louis, St. Paul-Minneapolis, San Francisco and Washington and in the Dioceses of Columbus, Covington, Gallup, Memphis, Orlando, Scranton and Springfield in Illinois.

Province of New York (1857): *Sisters of the Good Shepherd*, 25-30 21st. Ave., Astoria, NY 11105. Tel: 718-278-1155; Fax: 718-278-1158. Sr. Ellen Kelly, Prov.

Professed Apostolic Sisters: 58; Professed Contemplative Sisters: 34.

Legal Title: *Sisters of the Good Shepherd, Province of New York.*

Legal Holdings or Titles: Sisters of the Good Shepherd, New York, NY; Sisters of the Good Shepherd, Albany, NY; Sisters of the Good Shepherd, Huntington, NY; House of the Good Shepherd in the City of Hartford, Hartford, CT; Good Shepherd Volunteers, Astoria, NY; Madonna Hall, Marlboro, MA; Handcrafting Justice, Inc., Astoria, NY; Maria Droste Services (Madonna Hall); Sisters of the Good Shepherd, Marlboro, MA; Collier Youth Services; Sisters of the Good Shepherd of New Jersey; St. Germaine's Services.

Ministry in Counseling Centers; Social Service Agencies; Special Education Schools; Neighborhood Family Services; Adolescent Residential Programs; Human Services Workshops; Pastoral Ministry; Prison Ministry; Hospital Chaplaincy.

Programs sponsored: Good Shepherd Services, New York, NY; Maria Droste Services, New York, NY; Handcrafting Justice, Inc.; Collier Services, Wickatunk, NJ; Good Shepherd Volunteers.

Represented in the Archdioceses of Boston, Hartford and New York and in the Dioceses of Albany, Brooklyn, Fall River, Metuchen, Rockville Centre and Trenton.

[1840] (G.N.S.H.)—GREY NUNS OF THE SACRED HEART (P)

General Motherhouse (1921): 1750 Quarry Rd., Yardley, PA 19067-3998. Tel: 215-968-4236; Fax: 215-860-5612. Sr. Julia C. Lanigan, G.N.S.H., Pres.; Ms. Eileen Dickerson, Dir. Congregational Advancement Office.

Total in Community: 126.

Properties owned and/or sponsored: Holy Angels Academy, Buffalo, NY; Motherhouse Complex, Yardley, PA.

Sisters staff: College, Secondary and Elementary Education; Hospitals; Nursing Homes; Pastoral Care; Personal Care Home; CCD-Parish Services; Diocesan Offices; Campus Ministry; Prison Ministry; Homeless Housing.

Represented in the Archdioceses of Atlanta, Baltimore, New York and Philadelphia and in the Dioceses of Brooklyn, Buffalo, Ogdensburg, Rochester, Rockville Centre and Trenton. Also in Port-Au-Prince, Haiti.

[1845] (M.G.SP.S.)—GUADALUPAN MISSIONARIES OF THE HOLY SPIRIT (P)

(Misioneras Guadalupanas del Espiritu Santo)

Founded in Morelia, Michoacan, Mexico in 1930 by Rev. Felix de Jesus Rougier, M.Sp.S.

General Motherhouse: Hidalgo #7, Tlalpan 14000, Mexico, D.F., Mexico Mother Juventina Garcia, Supr. Gen.

U.S. Novitiate: 758 S. Dunsmuir Ave., Los Angeles, CA 90036-3811. Tel: 213-936-0135.

Total Sisters in U.S: 48.

Legal Title: *Missionary Guadalupanas of the Holy Spirit, Inc.*

Ministry in Religious Education; Pastoral and Parish Ministries.

Represented in the Archdioceses of Denver, Chicago, Los Angeles and Miami and in the Dioceses of Birmingham, Fall River, Harrisburg, Lincoln, Jackson, Palm Beach, Pueblo and Stockton.

[1850] (S.A.C.)—SISTERS OF THE GUARDIAN ANGEL (P)

Founded in Quillan, France in 1839.

General Motherhouse: A vda, del Valle, 42, Madrid 3, Spain Sr. Sagrario Escudero, S.A.C., Supr. Gen.

U.S. Foundation: 1245 S. Van Ness, Los Angeles, CA 90019. Tel: 213-732-7881.
Represented in the Archdiocese of Los Angeles.

[1855] (H.H.C.J.)—CONGREGATION OF THE HANDMAIDS OF THE HOLY CHILD JESUS (P)

Founded in Calabar, Nigeria in 1931 by Sister Mary Charles Magdalen Walker. Obtained Pontifical Status in 1971; first foundation in United States in 1992.

Generalate and Motherhouse: *Handmaids of the Holy Child Jesus - The Generalate, Ifuho,* P.O. Box 155, Ikot Ekpene, Nigeria Tel: 082-775-199. Sr. Leonie-Martha Okaraga, H.H.C.J., Supr. Gen.

North American Mission: *Ancilla Convent,* 3614 Englewood Dr., Pearland, TX 77584. Tel: 281-692-0098; Fax: 281-692-0049; Web: www.hhcjsisters.org. Sr. Caroline Onyeoziri, H.H.C.J., U.S. Supr.; Sr. Felicia Agibi, H.H.C.J., Devel. Dir.
Universal number of Professed Sisters: 774; Professed Sisters in the U.S. and Canada: 60.
Ministry in the field of Education at all levels; Pastoral Work; Health Care services; Women Empowerment; AIDS Education; Special Education; Youth Ministry; Clothing/Counseling Thrift Store.
Represented in the Archdioceses of Galveston-Houston, Mobile and Washington and in the Dioceses of Sacramento and St. Petersburg.

[1860] (H.P.B.)—HANDMAIDS OF THE PRECIOUS BLOOD (P)

Founded in Jemez Springs, New Mexico in 1947.

Motherhouse and Novitiate: *Cor Jesu Monastery,* P.O. Box 90, Jemez Springs, NM 87025. Tel: 575-829-3906. Rev. Mother Marietta, H.P.B., Mother Prioress.
Professed Sisters: 22; First Professed: 1.
Ministry as Contemplative, Life of Eucharistic Adoration (Perpetual) for the sanctification of priests and for the entire world.
Represented in the Archdioceses of Chicago and Santa Fe.

[1870] (A.C.J.)—THE HANDMAIDS OF THE SACRED HEART OF JESUS (P)

Founded in Spain in 1877. First foundation in the United States in 1926.

General Motherhouse: Largo dei Monti Parioli, 3, Rome, Italy, 00197. Sr. Inmaculada Fukasawa, Supr. Gen.
Universal total in Congregation: 1237.

Provincial Motherhouse: 2025 Church Rd., Wyncote, PA 19095. Tel: 215-576-6250; Fax: 215-576-8052. Sr. Dorothy Beck, A.C.J., Prov.
Total in Community: 34.
Properties owned: St. Raphaela Center, Haverford, PA; Ancillae Assumpta Academy, Wyncote, PA; Handmaids of Sacred Heart of Jesus, Philadelphia, PA; facilities in Georgia and Florida.
Sisters serve and staff: Elementary School; Retreat Center; Mission Center; Parish Ministry; CCD; Hispanic Pastoral Ministry; Vietnamese & Cambodian Pastoral Ministry; Mission work.
Represented in the Archdioceses of Atlanta, Miami and Philadelphia.

[1880] (A.R.)—HANDMAIDS OF REPARATION OF THE SACRED HEART OF JESUS (P)

Founded in Messina, Italy in 1918.

U.S. Foundation (1958): *Sacred Heart Villa,* 36 Villa Dr., Steubenville, OH 43953-7129. Tel: 740-282-3801. Sr. Mary Ernestine Vitello, A.R., Supr.
Total number in U.S: 6.
Ministry in Apostolic Work in Religious & Academic Education: Education All Levels; Religious Education; Parish and Diocesan Ministry; CCD Work; Orphanages; Missionary Work in Africa, Brazil and Poland.
Represented in the Dioceses of Arlington and Steubenville. Also in Africa, Brazil, Italy and Poland.

[1890] (H.H.S.)—SOCIETY OF HELPERS (P)

Founded in France in 1856. First foundation in the U.S. in 1892.

Generalate: 16 rue St. J. Baptiste de la Salle, Paris, France, 75006. Sr. Elizabeth Flick, Supr. Gen.

American Provincial Office (1921): 4721 J S. Woodlawn, Chicago, IL 60615. Tel: 773-548-5026. Sr. Mary Ellen Moore, S.H., Prov. Supr.
Total number in U.S. Province: 28.
Legal Title: *Society of the Helpers of the Holy Souls; Helpers of the Holy Souls; Province of the Helpers of the Holy Souls in the United States.*
Represented in the Archdioceses of Chicago, New York, St. Louis and San Francisco and in the Diocese of Charleston.

[1895] C.S.J.—HERMANAS CARMELITAS DE SAN JOSE (P)

Founded in El Salvador C.A. in 1916. First foundation in the United States in 2003.

Motherhouse: Final 14 Ave. Norte, Colonia San Antonio Las Palmeras Depto., De La Libertad, El Salvador

Regional House: 141 W. 87th Pl., Los Angeles, CA 90003. Tel: 323-758-6840; Tel: 323-752-2838. Sr. Enedina de Jesus Hernandez, C.S.J., Reg. Supr. US Community.
Total in Congregation : 201; U.S. Community: 4.
Ministry in Pastoral Care: Pastoral assistance in spiritual guidance and counseling; visitation of the sick and elderly; sacramental preparation; religious education for children, youth and/or adults; pastoral visits to the poor; faith formation.

[1900] (H.C.G.)—HERMANAS CATEQUISTAS GUADALUPANAS (P)

Founded in Saltillo, Coahuila, Mexico in 1923. First United States foundation in 1950.

Motherhouse and Novitiate: Saltillo, Coahuila, Mexico

U.S. Address: *Hermanas Catequistas Guadalupanas Convents,* 4110 S. Flores, San Antonio, TX 78214. Tel: 210-532-9344. Sr. Maria Martha Ruiz, H.C.G., Reg. Delegate.
Total number in the U.S: 14.
Represented in the Archdioceses of Oklahoma City and San Antonio and in the Diocese of Fort Worth.

[1910] (H.J.)—HERMANAS JOSEFINAS (P)

General Motherhouse: Condor 336, Col. las Aguilas, Delg. Alvaro Obregon, Mexico, 01710. Mother Isabel Vargas Huante, h.j., Gen. & Supr.

U.S. Address: *Assumption Seminary,* 2600 W. Woodlawn Ave., P.O. Box 28240, San Antonio, TX 78284. Tel: 210-734-0039.
Sisters: 10.
Represented in the Archdioceses of Chicago, Los Angeles and San Antonio and in the Diocese of Joliet in Illinois.

[1920] (C.S.C.)—CONGREGATION OF THE SISTERS OF THE HOLY CROSS (P)

Founded at Le Mans, France in 1841. First foundation in the U.S. in 1843.

General Administration: *Sisters of the Holy Cross Generalate,* 301 Bertrand Hall-Saint Mary's, Notre Dame, IN 46556-5000. Tel: 574-284-5550; Fax: 574-284-5779. Sr. Joan Marie Steadman, C.S.C., Pres.; Sr. Sharlet Ann Wagner, C.S.C., Gen. Sec.
Professed Members: 441; Temporarily Professed: 32; Novices: 8; Candidates: 15.
Legal Title: Sisters of the Holy Cross, Inc.; The Academy of the Holy Cross, Inc., MD; The Corporation of Saint Mary's College, Notre Dame, IN; Holy Cross Ministries of Utah; Society of the Congregation of the Sisters of the Holy Cross, Bangladesh.

Areas and Coordinators:
Angela Area - USA Retired, Notre Dame, IN. Tel: 574-284-5559. Sr. M. Rose Edward Goodrow, C.S.C., Coord.
Area of Africa - Ghana and Uganda Tel: 256-43-4123127. Sr. Mary Alice Bowler, C.S.C., Coord.
Area of Asia - Bangladesh and India. Tel: 880-2-912-9600. Sr. Philomena Quiah, C.S.C., Coord.
Area of North America - USA & Mexico, Austin, TX. Tel: 512-912-0243. Sr. Judith Hallock C.S.C., Coord.
Area of South America - Brazil and Peru. Tel: 51-1-328-0704. Sr. Patricia Dieringer, C.S.C., Coord.
Sisters serve and staff: Colleges; High Schools; Grade Schools; Adult Education Centers; Social Service Centers; Prayer Centers; Counseling Centers; Human Rights Centers; Women's Development Center; Hospitals and other Health Ministries, including Health Systems, Primary Health Care and Long Term Health Care; Parish Ministry; Diocesan Catechetical Services; Other Parish and Diocesan Ministries; Retirement Homes; Senior Citizen Residences; Pastoral Ministry with the Deaf; Correctional Institution.
Represented in the Archdioceses of Baltimore, Chicago, Cincinnati, Indianapolis, Los Angeles, Seattle and Washington and in the Dioceses of Arlington, Austin, Boise, Columbus, Fort Wayne-South Bend, Fresno, Gary, Joliet, Knoxville, Lafayette in Indiana, Lexington, Oakland, Orange, Palm Beach, Peoria, Raleigh, Richmond, Sacramento, St. Petersburg, Salt Lake City, and Tucson. Also in Brazil, Peru, Ghana, Uganda, Mexico, Bangladesh and India.

[1930] (C.S.C.)—SISTERS OF HOLY CROSS (P)

Founded in Le Mans, France in 1841. First foundation in Canada in 1847.

General Administration: 905 rue Basile-Moreau, St-Laurent, Montreal, Canada, H4L 4A1. Sr. Kesta Occident, C.S.C., Gen. Animator.
Universal total in Congregation: 653.

American Regional Office: *Sisters of Holy Cross,* 377 Island Pond Rd., Manchester, NH 03109-4811. Tel: 603-622-9504; Fax: 603-622-9782. Sr. Carol J. Descoteaux, C.S.C., Reg. Animator.
Total number in Region: 115.
Ministry in the field of Academic Education at all levels; Religious Education Centers; Social and Family Services; Counselor-Therapist; Parish Ministry; Sabbatical Programs; Adoption Agency; Clinical leader/nurses; Youth and Hospital Chaplaincies; Administrative Positions; Diocesan Services; Hispanic Ministry; Ministry to Abused Women and Children; Social Work and Elderly Assistance.
Properties owned: Holy Cross Early Childhood Center, Manchester, NH; St. George Manor, Manchester, NH; Londonderry House, Londonderry, NH; Sisters of the Holy Cross, 454 Island Pond Rd., Manchester, NH 03109; 136 Lynwood Ln., Manchester, NH 03109; 113 Wedgewood Ln., Manchester, NH 03109; 377 Island Pond Rd., Manchester, NH; Fairview Rd., R.R. 1, Box 191, Pittsfield, NH 03263; Four units at Crosswoods Path Condos, Merrimack, NH.
Represented in the Archdiocese of Boston and in the Dioceses of Bridgeport, Burlington, Fall River, Manchester, Norwich, and St. Petersburg. Also in Bangladesh, Cameroon, Chile, Haiti, Mali, Rome and Peru.

[1940] (C.H.F.)—CONGREGATION OF THE SISTERS OF THE HOLY FAITH (P)

Founded in Ireland in 1856. First foundation in U.S. in 1953. St. John of God School, 13817 Pioneer Blvd., Norwalk, California, 90650.

Motherhouse: Glasnevin, Dublin II, Ireland

U.S. Region: 12322 S. Paramount Blvd., Downey, CA 90242. Tel: 562-869-6092; Fax: 562-869-4609. Rev. Dolores Madden, C.H.F., Regl. Leader.
Total in Community: 31.
Represented in the Archdioceses of Los Angeles, New Orleans and San Francisco and in the Diocese of Sacramento.

[1950] (S.S.F.)—CONGREGATION OF THE SISTERS OF THE HOLY FAMILY (P)

Founded in New Orleans, Louisiana, in 1842.

Motherhouse: 6901 Chef Menteur Hwy., New Orleans, LA 70126. Tel: 504-241-3088. Sr. Eva Regina Martin, S.S.F., Supr. Gen.
Total in Community: 115.
Ministry in Secondary and Elementary Schools; Day Care Centers; Pastoral and Social Services; Nursing Home and Apartments for the Elderly, Disabled and Handicapped.
Represented in the Archdioceses of Galveston-Houston, New Orleans and Washington and in the Diocese of Lafayette (LA). Also in Belize, Central America.

[1960] (S.H.F.)—SISTERS OF THE HOLY FAMILY (P)

Founded in San Francisco, California, in 1872.

General Motherhouse: P.O. Box 3248, Fremont, CA 94539. Tel: 510-624-4500; Fax: 510-624-4537. Sr. Gladys Guenther, S.H.F., Congregational Pres.
Total in Community: 93.
Properties owned and/or sponsored: St. Elizabeth's Day Home, San Jose, CA.
Ministry in the following areas: Child Care; Developmentally Challenged; School Counseling; Religious Education and Pastoral Care; Social Service Agencies related to Child Protective Services; Hospital Chaplaincy; Parish Administration.
Represented in the Archdioceses of Anchorage, Los Angeles, and San Francisco and in the Dioceses of Fresno, Honolulu, Las Vegas, Monterey, Oakland, Reno, Sacramento, San Diego, San Jose and Stockton.

[1970] (C.S.F.N.)—SISTERS OF THE HOLY FAMILY OF NAZARETH (P)

Founded in Italy in 1875. First foundation in the United States in 1885.

General Motherhouse: Rome, Italy Sr. M. Janice Fulmer, C.S.F.N., Supr. Gen.

Holy Family Province (1885): 310 N. River Rd., Des Plaines, IL 60016-1211. Tel: 847-298-6760; Fax: 847-803-1941. Sr. Sally Marie Kiepura, C.S.F.N., Prov. Supr.; Sr. M. Gemma, C.S.F.N., Archivist.
Total number in United States: 357.
Ministry in Academic Education; Hospitals and Health Care; Social Work; Retreat Work; Religious Education; Child Care.
Co-Sponsors: Resurrection Health Care.
Represented in the Archdiocese of Chicago.

[1980] (O.S.F.)—CONGREGATION OF THE SERVANTS OF THE HOLY CHILD JESUS OF THE THIRD ORDER REGULAR OF SAINT FRANCIS (P)

Founded in Germany in 1855. First founded in the United States on April 9, 1929, at Staten Island, New York.

General Motherhouse: *Kloster Oberzell,* Wuerzburg, Germany Mother Veridiana Duerr, Supr. Gen.

Regional House: *Servants of the Holy Child Jesus-Villa Maria,* 109 Rte. 156, Yardville, NJ 08620. Tel: 609-585-4660; Fax: 609-585-2759. Sr. M. Antonia Cooper, Reg. Min.
Total in American Region: 19.
Properties owned and/or sponsored: Holy Family Regional House/Villa Maria Sanitarium, Yardville, NJ.
Ministry in Social Work; Health Care; Teaching.
Represented in the Archdiocese of Newark and Dioceses of Metuchen and Trenton.

[1990] (S.N.J.M.)—SISTERS OF THE HOLY NAMES OF JESUS AND MARY (P)

Founded by Blessed Marie Rose Durocher, in Longueuil, Quebec, Canada in 1843. First foundation in the U.S. in 1859.

Generalate: 80, rue Saint-Charles Est, Longueuil, Canada, J4H 1A9. Tel: 450-651-8104. Sr. Lorraine St-Hilaire, Supr.

An international congregation of 1,200 religious women with missions in Lesotho, Nicaragua, Peru and Brazil. Congregational sponsored works include colleges; adult centers; secondary, elementary and preschools; continuing care retirement community and health clinics.

U.S.-Ontario Province: *Provincial Administration*, Box 398, Marylhurst, OR 97036. Tel: 503-675-7100; Fax: 503-675-7136; Web: www.snjmusontario.org. Sr. Joan Saalfeld, S.N.J.M., Prov.

Total in Province: 610.

Properties owned and/or sponsored: Academy of the Holy Names, Albany, NY; Academy of the Holy Names, Tampa, FL; Convent, Marylhurst, OR; St. Mary's Academy, Portland, OR; Mary's Woods at Maryhurst, Inc., Marylhurst, OR; Provincial House, Los Gatos, CA; Holy Names University, Oakland, CA; Holy Names High School, Oakland, CA; Ramona Convent Secondary School, Alhambra, CA; Villa Maria del Mar, Santa Cruz, CA; Next Step Learning Center, Oakland, CA; Villa Holy Names, Los Gatos, CA; Convent, Spokane, WA; Holy Names Academy, Seattle, WA; Holy Names Music Center, Spokane, WA; Tutwiler Clinic; Jonestown Family Center for Education and Wellness; Holy Names Heritage Center.

Sisters ministering in works sponsored by other institutions/agencies include Formal Education in Universities, Secondary, Elementary and Preschools; Adult Basic Education/Literacy; Administration in Diocesan Offices; Campus Ministry; Pastoral Ministry; Religious Education, Health Care and Social Services.

Represented in the Archdioceses of Los Angeles, Portland in Oregon, San Francisco, Seattle and Washington, DC and in the Dioceses of Albany, Baker, Jackson, Monterey, Oakland, Orlando, Palm Beach, St. Petersburg, Spokane, Venice and Yakima.

[2000] (C.S.R.)—SISTERS OF THE HOLY REDEEMER (P)

First foundation in the United States on March 19, 1924 in Baltimore, Maryland.

American Province of the Immaculate Conception: 521 Moredon Rd., Huntingdon Valley, PA 19006. Tel: 215-914-4100; Fax: 215-914-4171. Sr. Anne Marie Haas, C.S.R., Prov. Supr.

Legal Holdings and Titles: Holy Redeemer Health Care Corporation and Foundation; Holy Redeemer Health System; Holy Redeemer Hospital and Medical Center; St. Joseph's Manor; The Lafayette-Redeemer; Holy Redeemer Active and Retirement Living Communities; Holy Redeemer Home Care; Holy Redeemer Transitional Care Unit; Holy Redeemer Physician and Ambulatory Services; Redeemer Village & Redeemer Village II; Drueding Center/Project Rainbow; HRH Management Corporation; Convents— Provincialate; Angelus Convent; Emmanuel Convent; St. Elizabeth Convent

Represented in the Archdioceses of Newark and Philadelphia and in the Dioceses of Camden, Metuchen and Trenton.

[2010] (O.SS.R.)—ORDER OF THE MOST HOLY REDEEMER (P)
(Redemptoristine Nuns)

Founded 1731 by St. Alphonsus de Liguori and Ven. Maria Celeste. (Contemplative). Rule approved 1750 by Pope Benedict XIV. First United States Monastery (1957) Esopus, New York.

Monastery of St. Alphonsus (1960): 200 Liguori Dr., Liguori, MO 63057. Tel: 636-464-1093; Fax: 636-464-9446. Sr. Janice Marie Klein, O.Ss.R., Prioress.

Total in Community: 15.

Represented in the Archdioceses of New York and St. Louis.

Mother of Perpetual Help Monastery: *Redemptoristine Nuns*, P.O. Box 220, Esopus, NY 12429-0220. Tel: 845-384-6533; Fax: 845-384-6654; Email: rednuns@juno.com. Sr. Paula Schmidt, O.SS.R., Prioress.

Total in Community: 10; Solemnly Professed Nuns: 9.

Solemn Vows, Papal Enclosure.

[2020] (C.H.S.)—COMMUNITY OF THE HOLY SPIRIT (D)

U.S. Foundation (1970): 6151 Rancho Mission Rd. - #205, San Diego, CA 92108. Tel: 619-584-0809. Sr. MaryJo Anderson, C.H.S.

Total in Community: 17.

Ministry in the field of Education; Health Care; and Social Services.

Represented in the Dioceses of Oakland, Orange, Portland in Oregon, Reno, Las Vegas, San Diego, San Jose and Wichita.

[2030] (C.S.SP.)—SISTERS OF THE HOLY SPIRIT (D)

Founded in the United States 1919; Decree of Establishment 1932.

Motherhouse and Novitiate: 10102 Granger Rd., Cleveland, OH 44125. Sr. Patricia Raelene Peters, C.S.Sp., Supr. Gen.

Total in Community: 12.

Represented in the Diocese of Cleveland.

[2040] (S.H.S.)—SISTERS OF THE HOLY SPIRIT (D)

Founded in the United States in 1913 at Donora, Pennsylvania.

Motherhouse: 5246 Clarwin Ave., Ross Township, Pittsburgh, PA 15229-2208. Tel: 412-931-1917; Fax: 412-931-3711; Email: srshs@verizon.net; Web: www.sistersoftheholyspirit.com. Sr. M. Bridget Miller, S.H.S., Gen. Supr.

Total in Community: 39.

Facilities owned and staffed: Corporation of Sisters of the Holy Spirit of Pittsburgh; Martina Spiritual Renewal Center Inc.

Sisters serve and staff: Elementary Schools; Religious Education; Health and Social Services; Retreat Services; Child Day Care; Care Facility for the Aged; Pastoral Ministry.

Represented in the Dioceses of Greensburg and Pittsburgh.

[2050] (S.H.SP.)—SISTERS OF THE HOLY SPIRIT AND MARY IMMACULATE (P)

Founded in America in 1893. Papal Approbation 1930; final Approbation, 1938.

General Motherhouse: *Convent of the Holy Spirit and Mary Immaculate*, 301 Yucca St., San Antonio, TX 78203. Tel: 210-533-5149. Sr. Miriam Mitchell, S.H.Sp., Gen. Supr.

Professed Sisters: 94.

Legal Holdings: Holy Spirit Trust; Holy Spirit Motherhouse; Healy Murphy Center, Inc., San Antonio, TX; Mother of Perpetual Help Nursing Home, Brownsville, TX.

Ministry in the following areas: Education; Health Care; Pastoral Ministry; Catechetical Ministry; Social Service; Retreats.

Represented in the Archdioceses of Galveston-Houston, New Orleans and San Antonio and in the Dioceses of Biloxi, Brownsville, Corpus Christi, Dallas, Fort Worth, Houma-Thibodaux, Jackson and Lafayette (LA). Also in Mexico and Zambia.

[2060] (O.SS.T.)—SISTERS OF THE MOST HOLY TRINITY (P)

Founded in Rome in 1198. First foundation in the United States in 1920.

General Motherhouse: Rome, Italy

Provincial House: *Immaculate Conception Province*, 21281 Chardon Rd., Euclid, OH 44117. Tel: 216-481-8232; Fax: 216-481-6577. Sr. M. Rochelle Guertal, O.SS.T., Reg. Delegate.

Total in Community: 23.

Properties owned and/or sponsored: Our Lady of Lourdes Shrine, Euclid, OH.

Represented in the Archdiocese of Philadelphia and in the Diocese of Cleveland.

[2070] (S.U.S.C.)—HOLY UNION SISTERS (P)

Founded in France in 1826. First foundation in the United States in 1886.

Generalate: Rome, Italy Sr. Carol Regan, S.U.S.C., Supr. Gen.

United States Province: 444 Centre St., P.O. Box 410, Milton, MA 02186-0006. Tel: 617-696-8765; Fax: 617-696-8571. Province Mission Team: Sr. Mary Catherine Burns, S.U.S.C.; Sr. Paula Coelho, S.U.S.C.; Sr. Maryellen Ryan, S.U.S.C.

Total in Community: 109.

Legal Title: *Holy Union Sisters, Inc.*

Sponsored Ministry: Country Day School of the Holy Union, Inc., Groton, MA.

Ministry in the field of Religious and Academic Education; Social Services; Pastoral Care; Pastoral Ministry; Spiritual Renewal; Day Care; Ministry Education; Family Ministry; Nursing; Peace & Justice; Spanish Apostolate; Ministry to the Handicapped; Ministry to Immigrants and Refugees; Clerical & Secretarial services; Diocesan Administrative services.

Represented in the Archdioceses of Baltimore, Boston, Detroit and New York and in the Dioceses of Albany, Brooklyn, Fall River, Harrisburg, Lexington, Providence, Rockville Centre, and Richmond.

[2080] (G.H.M.S.)—HOME MISSION SISTERS OF AMERICA (D)
(Glenmary Sisters)

Founded July 16, 1952.

Motherhouse: *Glenmary Sisters - Glenmary Center*, P.O. Box 22264, Owensboro, KY 42304-2264. Tel: 270-686-8401. Sr. Sharon Miller, Pres.

Total in Community: 12.

Service to Home Missions.

Represented in the Dioceses of Lexington, Owensboro, Savannah and Springfield Cape-Girardeau.

[2090] (H.V.M.)—SISTERS HOME VISITORS OF MARY (D)

Founded in Detroit, Michigan in 1949.

Motherhouse: 121 E. Boston Blvd., Detroit, MI 48202. Tel: 313-869-2160; Email: homevisitors@att.net.

Total in Community: 22.

Ministry in Urban Parishes; Senior Citizen; Schools and Preschools; Religious Education, RCIA; Clinic; Community Org.

Represented in the Archdiocese of Detroit. Also in Nigeria.

[2100] (C.H.M.)—CONGREGATION OF THE HUMILITY OF MARY (P)

Founded in France in 1854. First United States foundation in 1864.

Motherhouse: *Humility of Mary Center*, Davenport, IA 52804. Sr. Mary Rehmann, C.H.M., Pres.

Total in Community: 144.

Legal Titles: Congregation of the Humility of Mary; Humility of Mary Housing, Inc; Congregation of the Humility of Mary Charitable Trust; New Horizons of Faith: Our Lady of the Prairie Retreat; Humility of Mary Shelter, Inc.

Ministry in Schools and Colleges; Religious Education Centers; Migrant Programs; Pastoral Ministry; Social Services; Inner City Programs; Health Services and Ministry to the Elderly.

Represented in the Archdioceses of Chicago, Denver, Dubuque, Los Angeles and Seattle and in the Dioceses of Davenport, Des Moines, Great Falls-Billings, Jackson, Lexington, Peoria, Richmond, Rockford, Tulsa and Wheeling-Charleston. Also in Mexico.

[2110] (H.M.)—SISTERS OF THE HUMILITY OF MARY, INC. (P)

Founded in France in 1854. First foundation in the United States in 1864 at Villa Maria, Lawrence County, Pennsylvania, 16155.

Motherhouse: *Villa Maria Community Center*, P.O. Box 914, Villa Maria, PA 16155-0914. Tel: 724-964-8861; Fax: 724-964-8082. Sr. Susan Schorsten, H.M., Major Supr.; Sr. Joanne Gardner, H.M., Community Archivist.

Total in Community: 178.

Ministry in the field of Academic and Religious Education at all levels; Hospitals and Nursing Home, Assisted Living; Parish and Pastoral Ministries; Publishing of Education Materials; Legal Services; Social Services; Ministry to persons who are Native Americans, Migrants, Hispanics, Haitians and Rural Poor; Housing Ministry to Single Parents, Independent Elderly; Retreat Ministry; Spirituality and Counseling; Advocacy for Eco-justice; Marketing of Creative Arts.

Legal Holdings and Titles: Sisters of the Humility of Mary (Motherhouse), Villa Maria, PA; Sisters of the Humility of Mary Charitable Trust, Villa Maria, PA; Magnificat High School, Rocky River, OH; Villa Montessori Center, Cleveland, OH; The Center for Learning, Villa Maria, PA; Villa Maria Education and Spirituality Center, Villa Maria, PA; Humility of Mary Housing, Inc., Akron, OH; HM Housing Development Corporation, Akron, OH; HM Life Opportunity Services, Akron, OH; Villa Residential Services (Villa Maria Apartments), Villa Maria, PA; Heartbeats, Rocky River, OH.

Represented in the Archdioceses of Baltimore and Cincinnati and in the Dioceses of Arlington, Cleveland, Erie, Grand Island, Lansing, Lexington, Palm Beach, Pittsburgh, Richmond, Tucson, Wheeling-Charleston and Youngstown. Also in Haiti.

[2120] (R.C.M.)—SISTERS OF THE IMMACULATE CONCEPTION (P)

Founded in Spain in 1892.

General Motherhouse: Princesa 19 y 21, Madrid, Spain, 28008. Mother Maria Luz Martinez, Mother Gen.

U.S. Delegation House (1962): 2230 Franklin, San Francisco, CA 94109. Tel: 415-474-0159. Sr. Angeles Marin, Reg. Supr.

Represented in the Archdiocese of San Francisco and in the Diocese of Fresno.

[2140] —SISTERS OF THE IMMACULATE CONCEPTION OF THE BLESSED VIRGIN MARY (LITHUANIAN) (P)

Founded in Marijampole, Lithuania in 1918. First foundation in the United States in 1936.

American Headquarters: *Immaculate Conception Convent and Novitiate*, 600 Liberty Hwy., Putnam, CT 06260-2503. Tel: 860-928-7955; Fax: 860-928-1930. Sr. Igne Marijosius, Supr.

Total in Community: 16.

Legal Titles & Holdings: Immaculate Conception Convent; Matulaitis Nursing Home, Putnam, CT; Camp Neringa, Marlboro, VT.

Ministry in Nursing Homes; Retreat House; Catechetical Work in Parishes; Summer Camp for Children and Young Adults.

Represented in the Archdiocese of Chicago and in the Dioceses of Burlington and Norwich. Also in Canada.

[2145] (O.S.A.)—CONGREGATION OF AUGUSTINIAN SISTERS SERVANTS OF JESUS AND MARY (P)

Generalate: via Nomentana 514, Rome, Italy Mother Atanasia Buhagiar, Gen.

Malta Province: 208 Fleur-de-Lys, B'Kara, Malta Mother

Miriam Grech, Mother Prov.

U.S. Foundation: *St. John Convent*, 531 E. Broadway, Brandenburg, KY 40108. Sr. Lydia Falzon, Supr.
Total in Community: 4.
Represented in the Archdiocese of Louisville.

[2150] (I.H.M.)—SISTERS, SERVANTS OF THE IMMACULATE HEART OF MARY (P)

Founded in the United States in 1845.

SSIHM Leadership Council: 610 W. Elm, Monroe, MI 48162-7909. Tel: 734-240-9700; Fax: 734-240-9784. Sr. Mary Frances Gilleran, I.H.M., Pres.
Total in Congregation : 441.
Legal Titles: Marygrove College, Detroit, MI; Marian High School for Young Women, Bloomfield Hills, MI; Visitation Spirituality Center.
Ministry in Academic and Religious Education at all levels; Pastoral Ministry (parish, healthcare, campus and prison settings); Diocesan and Parish Administration; Peace and Justice; Social Service and Counseling; Spiritual Growth and Development; Overseas Ministries.
Represented in the Archdioceses of Atlanta, Boston, Chicago, Detroit, Galveston-Houston, Louisville, Miami, Milwaukee, Mobile, Oklahoma City, Philadelphia, St. Paul-Minneapolis, San Antonio, San Juan, Santa Fe and Washington D.C. and in the Dioceses of Albany, Austin, Cleveland, El Paso, Fort Wayne-South Bend, Joliet, Kalamazoo, Kansas City-St. Joseph, Lansing, Lexington, Marquette, Monterey, Oakland, Orange, Orlando, Palm Beach, Pensacola-Tallahassee, Phoenix, Portland, Raleigh, Richmond, San Diego, Saginaw, St. Augustine, Toledo Venice and Wilmington. Also in Canada, Italy, Mexico, South Africa and Uganda.

River House - IHM Spirituality Center: 805 W. Elm Ave., Monroe, MI 48162. Tel: 734-240-5494; Fax: 734-240-5495; Email: riverhouse@ihmsisters.org; Web: www.ihmsisters.org.
Sisters: 3.
Sponsorship of I.H.M. Congregation.

Visitation North Spirituality Center: 7227 Lahser Rd., Bloomfield Hills, MI 48301. Tel: 248-433-0950; Fax: 248-433-0952; Email: visitationnorth@ihmsisters.org; Web: www.visitationnorth.org.
Sisters: 4.
Sponsorship of I.H.M. Congregation.

[2160] (I.H.M.)—SISTERS, SERVANTS OF THE IMMACULATE HEART OF MARY (P)

Founded in 1845. Established in Scranton, Pennsylvania in 1871.

General Motherhouse: *Immaculate Heart of Mary Center*, 2300 Adams Ave., Scranton, PA 18509. Tel: 570-342-6850; Fax: 570-346-5439. Sr. Mary Persico, I.H.M., Pres.
Total in Community: 496.
Properties owned and/or sponsored: IHM Center; Pascucci Family Our Lady of Peace Residence; Our Lady of Grace Center; Manhasset, NY.
Ministry in the field of Academic Education; Hospitals; Early Childhood Education Centers; Spiritual Renewal Center; Directors of Religious Education; Pastoral Ministries; Social Services; Campus Ministry; Volunteer Services; Family Ministry; Drug and Alcohol Counseling; Ministry to Hispanics; Diocesan Offices.
Represented in the Archdioceses of Baltimore, Boston, Detroit, Hartford, Miami, Newark, New York, Philadelphia, Santa Fe and Washington and in the Dioceses of Albany, Allentown, Altoona-Johnstown, Boise, Bridgeport, Brooklyn, Camden, Cleveland, Fort Wayne-South Bend, Harrisburg, Jackson, Metuchen, Orlando, Paterson, Pittsburgh, Raleigh, Rochester, Rockville Centre, St. Augustine, St. Petersburg, Scranton, Springfield in Massachusetts, Syracuse, Trenton, Wheeling-Charleston and Wilmington. Also in Chile, Guatemala, Peru and Rome.

[2170] (I.H.M.)—SISTERS, SERVANTS OF THE IMMACULATE HEART OF MARY (P)

Founded in 1845. Established in West Chester, Pennsylvania in 1872.

General Motherhouse: *Villa Maria House of Studies*, 1140 King Rd., Immaculata, PA 19345. Tel: 610-647-2160; Fax: 610-889-4874. Sr. Lorraine McGrew, I.H.M., Gen. Supr.
Total in Congregation : 901.
Ministry in the field of Academic Education at all levels in the U.S. as well as Peru & Chile; Pastoral Ministry; Literacy Centers; Infirmary work.
Represented in the Archdioceses of Atlanta, Hartford, Miami and Philadelphia and in the Dioceses of Allentown, Camden, Harrisburg, Metuchen, Raleigh, Richmond, Savannah and Trenton.

[2180] (I.H.M.)—SISTERS OF THE IMMACULATE HEART OF MARY (P)

Founded in Spain in 1848. First foundation in the United States in 1871.

General Motherhouse: Girona, Spain

U.S. Province: 3820 N. Sabino Canyon Rd., Tucson, AZ 85750-6534. Tel: 520-886-4273. Sr. Alice M. Martinez, Prov. Supr.; Sr. Mary Evelyn Soto, Sec. & Community Archivist.
Total in Community: 21.
Ministry in the field of Academic and Religious Education.
Represented in the Diocese of Tucson.

[2182] (I.H.M.M.)—SISTERS OF THE IMMACULATE HEART OF MARY OF MIRINAE (P)

Founded in 1976 by Rev. Francis Haengman Tiyeng, Marinae, Diocese of Suwon, Korea, under the motto "Through the Immaculate Heart of Mary to the Most Holy Trinity."

Motherhouse: Mirinae, Korea, South

U.S. Foundation: *Immaculate Heart of Mary Pre School*, 423 South Commonwealth Ave., Los Angeles, CA 90020. Sr. Inviolata Chang, I.H.M.M., Sec.
Properties owned and/or sponsored: Sisters of the Immaculate Heart of Mary of Mirinae, Los Angeles, CA.
Ministry in retreat work, school, youth and care for the aged.
Represented in the Archdiocese of Los Angeles.

[2183] (I.H.M.)—SISTERS OF THE IMMACULATE HEART OF MARY MOTHER OF CHRIST, NIGERIA (P)

Founded in Nigeria, West Africa in 1937. Classified with the Pontifical Institute Right in 1973.

Motherhouse-Immaculate Heart Generalate: P.O. Box 1551, Anambra State, Odoakpu-Onitsha, Nigeria Tel: 234-46-026; Tel: 234-46-485. Mother Mary Dominica Odita, Mother Gen.
Total in Congregation : 827.

U.S.A. Regional House: *Immaculate Heart Convent*, 1209 South Walnut, Freeport, IL 61032. Tel: 815-297-8287. Sr. Mary Nesta Ekene Ezeanya, Reg. Supr.
Total number of Sisters in the U.S: 35.
Legal Title: *The Congregation of the Sisters of the Immaculate Heart of Mary Mother of Christ - Nigeria.*
Ministry in Education; Hospital/Clinic, Pastoral/Social Services; Care of the Aged; Diocesan House Care.
Represented in the Archdioceses of Milwaukee, Seattle and St. Paul-Minneapolis and in the Dioceses of Gallup, Rockford and Syracuse.

[2185] (I.H.M.)—SISTERS OF THE IMMACULATE HEART OF MARY OF WICHITA (D)

Founded in Olot, Spain, in 1848. First foundation in United States in 1871. Wichita foundation in 1979. Canonically established as a religious institute of Diocesan right in 2007.

Motherhouse: 145 S. Millwood St., Wichita, KS 67213. Tel: 316-722-9316. Mother Marie Bernadette Mertens, I.H.M., Gen. Supr.
Total in Community: 18.
Apostolate: Contemplation of the Word and the spread of His Message of salvation through the various works and levels of education and retreat work.
Represented in the Diocese of Wichita.

[2187] (I.C.M.)—INCARNATIO-CONSECRATIO-MISSIO (P)

Founded in Vietnam in 1969. First foundation in the United States in 1975.

Motherhouse: 403 Ta Ha, Phuong Loc Tien, Thi Xa Bao Loc, Lam Dong, Vietnam Tel: 011-84-63-862-177.

U.S. Regional House: *Incarnatio-Consecratio-Missio, Inc.*, 5185 Jetsail Dr., Orlando, FL 32812. Tel: 407-658-4124; Fax: 407-658-4124; Email: icmorlando@yahoo.com. Sr. Marie Nguyen, I.C.M., Contact Person.
Universal Membership: 102; Aspirants: 35.
Ministry in the areas of Education; Healthcare; Missionary Outreach; Parish Ministries and Pastoral Care.
Represented in the Dioceses of Baton Rouge and Orlando. Also in Vietnam.

[2190] (C.V.I.)—CONGREGATION OF THE INCARNATE WORD AND BLESSED SACRAMENT (P)

Founded in France in 1625. First foundation in the United States in 1853.

Motherhouse and Novitiate: *Incarnate Word Convent*, 3400 Bradford Pl., Houston, TX 77025-1398. Tel: 713-668-0423. Sr. Rosalia Purcell, C.V.I., Supr.; Sr. Dympna Lyons, Archivist; Sr. Brendan O'Donnell, Archivist.
Total in Community: 45.
Ministry in the field of Academic and Religious Education; Administration; Diocesan Ministry - Pastoral Care; Parish Ministry; Literacy Programs.
Represented in the Archdiocese of Galveston-Houston and in the Diocese of Beaumont.

[2200] (I.W.B.S.)—CONGREGATION OF THE INCARNATE WORD AND BLESSED SACRAMENT (P)

Founded in France in 1625. First founded in the United States in 1853.

Motherhouse and Novitiate: *Incarnate Word Convent*, 1101 N.E. Water St., Victoria, TX 77901-9233. Tel: 361-575-2266; Fax: 361-575-2165. Sr. M. Evelyn Korenek, I.W.B.S., Supr. Gen.; Sr. Mary Virginia Sheblak, I.W.B.S., Community Archivist.
Perpetually Professed: 83; Annually Professed: 1.
Legal Titles: Sisters of the Incarnate Word and Blessed Sacrament, Victoria, Texas, Inc.; Sisters of the Incarnate Word and Blessed Sacrament of Victoria, Texas Medical and Retirement Trust, Victoria, TX.
Ministry in the field of Education; CCD Centers; Hospitals; Pastoral Ministry.
Properties owned or sponsored: Nazareth Academy, Victoria, TX; Blessed Sacrament Academy, San Antonio, TX.
Represented in the Archdiocese of San Antonio and in the Dioceses of Corpus Christi, Dallas, Galveston-Houston and Victoria. Also in Africa and France.

[2205] (I.W.B.S.)—SISTERS OF THE INCARNATE WORD AND BLESSED SACRAMENT (P)

Founded in France in 1625. First founded in the United States in 1853.

Motherhouse and Novitiate: *Incarnate Word Convent*, 2930 S. Alameda St., Corpus Christi, TX 78404. Tel: 361-882-5413; Fax: 361-880-4152. Sr. Michelle Marie Kuntscher, Supr. Gen.
Sisters: 56.
Legal Titles: Convent Academy of the Incarnate Word; Incarnate Word Academy Foundation; Fannie Bluntzer Nason Renewal Center, Inc., Corpus Christi, TX.
Sisters serve and staff: Private High Schools; Private Kindergartens; Montessori; Private Middle Schools; Parochial and Private Elementary Schools; Other ministries include Religious Education; Hospital Ministry; Vocation Ministry; Prison Ministry; Social Service; Diocesan Offices; Adult Education; General Administration; Retreat Ministry; Parish Ministry.
Represented in the Archdiocese of Galveston-Houston and in the Dioceses of Brownsville, Corpus Christi and Beaumont.

[2210] (S.I.W.)—SISTERS OF THE INCARNATE WORD AND BLESSED SACRAMENT (P)

Founded in France in 1625. First foundation in the United States in 1853.

Motherhouse and Novitiate: 6618 Pearl Rd., Parma Heights, OH 44130-3808. Tel: 440-886-6440. Sr. Mary Rose Kocab, S.I.W., Congregational Leader.
Total in Community: 26.
Ministry includes Evangelization; Elementary and Religious Education; Spiritual Ministry (Retreat and Spiritual Direction); Pastoral Ministry in Parishes, Hospitals and Nursing Homes; Social Service.
Represented in the Diocese of Cleveland.

[2230] (C.I.J.)—CONGREGATION OF THE INFANT JESUS (D)

Founded in France in 1835. First foundation in the United States in 1905.

General Motherhouse: 984 North Village Ave., Rockville Centre, NY 11570. Tel: 516-823-3800; Tel: 516-823-3808; Fax: 516-594-0412. Sr. Dolores Wisniewski, C.I.J., Pres.
Total in Community: 51.
Corporate Title: Nursing Sisters of the Sick Poor Inc.
Ministry in the fields of Nursing; Social Work; Physical Therapy; Pastoral Care; Chaplains; Retreat Work; Parish Ministry; and other works related to Health Services.
Represented in the Dioceses of Brooklyn, Lexington, Portland and Rockville Centre.

[2245] (S.J.S.)—SISTERS OF JESUS THE SAVIOR (P)

Founded in Elele, Nigeria in 1985.

U.S. Foundation: *St. Bartholomew Convent*, 2291 E. Outer Dr., Detroit, MI 48234.
Professed Sisters: 4.
Ministry in Education and Social Assistance.
Represented in the Archdiocese of Detroit.

[2250] (O.S.B.)—CONGREGATION OF BENEDICTINES OF JESUS CRUCIFIED (P)

Founded in France in 1930. First foundation in the United States in Devon, PA in 1955. Second foundation in Newport, RI in 1962. Both foundations merged in Branford, CT in 2001.

General Motherhouse: Brou-sur-Chantereine, France Mother Godefrieda Bouwman, O.S.B., Prioress Gen.

U.S. Foundations: 61 Burban Dr., Branford, CT 06405-4003. Tel: 203-315-9964; Tel: 230-315-0106; Fax: 203-483-5829; Email: monasterygc@juno.com; Web: benedictinesjc.org. Sr. Marie Rita Syn, O.S.B., Prioress; Sr. Marie-Zita Wenker, O.S.B., Vocation Dir.
Total number in the U.S: 17.
Represented in the Archdiocese of Hartford.

[2260] (A.D.)—SISTERS OF THE LAMB OF GOD (D)

Founded in France 1945.

General Motherhouse: *Institute of the Lamb of God*, 85 Rt. du Vieux Saint Marc, Brest, France, 29283. Sr. Marie Francois Piriou, A.D., Supr. Gen.

U.S. Foundation (1958): *House of Formation*, 2063 Wyandotte Ave., Owensboro, KY 42301. Tel: 270-926-8656. Sr. Claire Marle, Supr.; Sr. Audrey Gold, Formation Dir.
Sisters: 11.

[2265] (S.V.)—SISTERS OF LIFE
Founded 1191.

Generalate: 586 McLean Ave., Yonkers, NY 10705. Tel: 914-968-8094; Fax: 914-968-0462. Mother Agnes Mary Donovan, S.V., Supr. Gen.
Legal Title: Sisters of Life, Inc.
Ministry: serving pregnant women vulnerable to abortion, post abortion healing retreats, general retreats, Family Life/Respect Life office of the Archdiocese of New York.
Represented in the Archdiocese of New York and in the Diocese of Bridgeport.

[2270] (L.C.M.)—SISTERS OF THE LITTLE COMPANY OF MARY (P)
Founded in England in 1877. First foundation in the United States in 1893.

Generalate: *Little Company of Mary Generalate*, 28 Trinity Crescent, Tooting Bec London, England, SW17 7AE.
Universal Total in Congregation 323: Final Professed Sisters 305; Temporary Professed Sisters 12; Novices 1; Candidates 5.

Provincial Office: *Province of the Immaculate Conception, The Little Company of Mary*, 9350 S. California Ave., Evergreen Park, IL 60805. Tel: 708-422-0130. Sr. Kathleen McIntyre, L.C.M., Province Leader.
Total in Community: 22.
Ministry in Hospitals and Health Care; Pastoral/Parish areas.
Properties owned: Little Company of Mary Hospital and Health Care Centers, Evergreen Park, IL; Memorial Hospital and Health Care Center, Jasper, IN; Little Company of Mary Health Services (Little Company of Mary Hospital, Torrance, CA and San Pedro Peninsula Hospital, San Pedro, CA).
Represented in the Archdioceses of Chicago and Los Angeles and in the Diocese of Evansville.

[2280] (P.F.M.)—LITTLE FRANCISCANS OF MARY (U.S.)
Founded in the United States in 1889.

General Motherhouse: *Baie St. Paul (Charlevoix)*, Canada Sr. Francoise Duchesne, P.F.M., Supr. Gen.

American Region: *St. Francis*, 55 Moore Ave., Worcester, MA 01602. Tel: 508-755-0878. Sr. Jacquelyn Alix, Reg. Supr.
Total number in Congregation including Canada and the United States: 185.
Represented in the Dioceses of Portland (In Maine) and Worcester.

[2300] (L.S.I.C.)—LITTLE SERVANT SISTERS OF THE IMMACULATE CONCEPTION (P)
Founded by Blessed Edmund Bojanowski in Poland on May 3, 1850. First foundation in the United States on December 8, 1926.

General Motherhouse: Stara Wies 460, 36-200 Brzozow, skr. poczt. 66, woj., Podkarpackie, Poland Mother Beata Chwistek, L.S.I.C., Supr. Gen.
Total in Congregation : 1315.

Holy Trinity Province: *Little Servants Sisters of the Immaculate Conception Provincialate-Novitiate*, 1000 Cropwell Rd., Cherry Hill, NJ 08003. Tel: 856-424-1962; Fax: 856-424-5333; Email: lsic.prov@verizon.net; Web: www.littleservantsisters.com. Mother Jadwiga Cierpinska, L.S.I.C., Supr. Prov.; Sr. M. Philomena Nowicka, L.S.I.C., Vocation Dir.; Sr. Dorota Baranowska, L.S.I.C., Vocation Dir.
Professed Sisters: 72; Novices: 1.
Legal Titles: Congregation of the Little Servant Sisters of the Blessed Virgin Mary of the Immaculate Conception (Congregatio Sororum Servularum Beatae Mariae Virginis Immaculatae Conceptae), (Properties owned) Immaculate Conception Convent: Provincialate-Novitiate, Cherry Hill, NJ; Blessed Edmund Early Childhood Education Center, Cherry Hill, NJ; Marian Residence, Cherry Hill, NJ; St. John's Retreat House, Atlantic City, NJ; St. Joseph's Convent, Woodbridge, NJ; St. Joseph's Senior Home (Assisted Living and Nursing Center), Woodbridge, NJ.
Ministry: all levels of Religious Education, Pre-school and Academic Education; Parish Work; Social Work, Hospital Pastoral Care; Visiting Home Nursing Service; Senior Residential Homes; Assisted Living; Skilled Nursing Homes; Retreat House; Prayer Groups & Youth Ministry.
Represented in the Archdioceses of Newark and Philadelphia and in the Dioceses of Camden, Metuchen and Palm Beach. Also in the Philippines.

[2310] (L.S.A.)—LITTLE SISTERS OF THE ASSUMPTION (P)
Founded in France in 1865. First foundation in the United States in 1891.

General Motherhouse: 57 rue Violet, Paris, France, 75015. Sr. Mercedes Martinez, P.C.I., Supr. Gen.

United States Province: *Little Sisters of the Assumption Provincialate*, 100 Gladstone Ave., Walden, NY 12586. Tel: 845-778-0667; Web: www.littlesisters.org. Sr. Annette Allain, L.S.A., Prov.
Total in Community: 34.
Legal Title: *Family Lifeline Volunteers, Inc., New York, NY.*
Ministry in Home Health; Community Development Supportive Family Services Located in Poverty Areas; Services are predominantly provided in the Home Setting.
Represented in the Archdioceses of Boston, New York and Philadelphia and in the Diocese of Worcester.

[2315] (L.S.G.)—LITTLE SISTERS OF THE GOSPEL (D)
Founded in 1963 in France by Rev. Rene Voillaume. First foundation in the United States in 1972 in New York.

Generalate: 31 Rue George Politzer, St. Denis, France, 93200. Tel: 1-48233228.

U.S. House: P.O. Box 541355, Mott Haven Sta., Bronx, NY 10454. Tel: 718-402-2092.
Professed Sisters: 74; Novices: 2; Postulants: 6.
Residence: 340 Willis Ave., Bronx, NY, 10454.
Ministry in Prison Ministry; Service to the Poor and Underserved.
Represented in the Archdiocese of New York.

[2330] (L.S.J.)—LITTLE SISTERS OF JESUS (P)
Founded in the Sahara in 1939. First foundation in the United States in 1952.

General Motherhouse: Rome, Italy Sr. Gertrud-Veronika Wiedmann, Prioress Gen.
Universal total in Congregation: 1235.

U.S. Regional House: 400 N. Streeper St., Baltimore, MD 21224-1230. Tel: 410-327-7823. Sr. Lynn Flear, L.S.J., Reg. Dir.
Total number in U.S: 28.
Represented in the Archdioceses of Anchorage, Baltimore, Chicago and Washington and in the Dioceses of Altoona-Johnstown, Fairbanks and Paterson.

[2331] (L.S.J.M.)—LITTLE SISTERS OF JESUS AND MARY (D)
Founded in the United States in 1974. Sr. Mary Elizabeth, Foundress.

Joseph House: P.O. Box 1755, Salisbury, MD 21802. Tel: 410-543-1645; Fax: 410-742-3390. Sr. Constance R. Ladd, L.S.J.M., Supr. Gen.
Total in Community: 7.
Represented in the Diocese of Wilmington.

[2340] (L.S.P.)—LITTLE SISTERS OF THE POOR (P)
Founded in France in 1839. First foundation in the United States in 1868.

General Motherhouse: *La Tour St. Joseph*, 35190, St. Pern, France Mother Celine de la Visitation, Supr. Gen.

Province of Brooklyn (1868): *Queen of Peace Residence*, 110-30 221st St., Queens Village, NY 11429. Mother Margaret Regina Halloran, L.S.P., Prov.
Total number in Province: 128.
Ministry in Homes for the Aged.
Represented in the Archdioceses of Boston, Hartford, Philadelphia and New York and in the Dioceses of Albany, Brooklyn, Metuchen, Paterson, Providence and Scranton. Also in Montreal.

Province of Baltimore: *Little Sisters of the Poor*, 601 Maiden Choice Ln., Catonsville, MD 21228-3698. Tel: 410-744-9367; Fax: 410-747-0601. Sr. Loraine Marie Maguire, L.S.P., Prov.
Total number in Province: 110.
Ministry in Homes for the Aged.
Represented in the Archdioceses of Baltimore, Cincinnati, Indianapolis, Mobile and Washington and in the Dioceses of Cleveland, Pittsburgh, Richmond, Toledo and Wilmington.

Province of Chicago: *Little Sisters of the Poor, Chicago Province, Inc.*, 80 W. Northwest Hwy., Palatine, IL 60067-3582. Tel: 847-358-5700; Fax: 847-934-6852. Sr. Maria Christine Lynch, Prov.
Total number in Province: 126.
Ministry in Homes for the Aged.
Represented in the Archdioceses of Chicago, Denver, Los Angeles, Louisville, St. Louis, St. Paul-Minneapolis and San Francisco and in the Dioceses of Evansville, Gallup and Kansas City-St. Joseph.

[2345] (P.O.S.C.)—LITTLE WORKERS OF THE SACRED HEARTS (P)
Founded in Italy in 1892. First foundation in the U.S. in 1948.

General House: Via dei Pamphili 3, Rome, Italy, 00152.

Motherhouse and Novitiate: *Our Lady of Grace Convent*, 635 Glenbrook Rd., Stamford, CT 06906-1409. Tel: 203-348-5531. Sr. Gesuina Gencarelli, P.O.S.C., Supr.
Ministry in Day Care; Catechetics; Preschool.
Represented in the Archdioceses of Philadelphia and Washington and in the Diocese of Bridgeport.

[2350] (S.L.W.)—SISTERS OF THE LIVING WORD (D)
Founded in the United States in 1975.

General Motherhouse: *The Living Word Center*, 800 N. Fernandez Ave. B, Arlington Heights, IL 60004-5336. Tel: 847-577-5972; Fax: 847-577-5980. Leadership Team: Sr. Lynda Rink, S.L.W.; Sr. Rita Worm, S.L.W.; Sr. Joel Curcio, S.L.W.
Total in Community: 69.
Ministry in the field of Academic and Religious Education; Health Care; Parish Ministry and Social Services.
Represented in the Archdioceses of Chicago, Detroit, New Orleans and St. Paul-Minneapolis and in the Dioceses of Alexandria, Cleveland, El Paso, Jackson, Joliet, Lansing, Memphis, Rapid City and Sioux City.

[2360] (S.L.)—SISTERS OF LORETTO AT THE FOOT OF THE CROSS (P)
Founded in America in 1812.

General Motherhouse & Novitiate: *Loretto Motherhouse and Novitiate*, Nerinx, KY 40049. Tel: 270-865-5811.

Administrative Office: 4000 S. Wadsworth Blvd, Littleton, CO 80123-1308. Tel: 303-783-0450; Fax: 303-783-0611. Sr. Catherine Mueller, S.L., Pres.
Total in Congregation : 257.
Legal Title: *Loretto Literary and Benevolent Institution.*
Ministry in the field of Academic and Religious Education at all levels; Specialized Education; Health Care-Aging; Community Administration; Pastoral Ministry; Social Justice-Social Service; Administration; Diocesan Offices; Medicine and Nursing; Prayer Retreats; Clerical Offices; Consultants; Spirituality Center.
Represented in the Archdioceses of Chicago, Denver, Galveston-Houston Indianapolis, Louisville, Mobile, New Orleans, New York, St. Louis, San Antonio, Santa Fe, Seattle and Washington and in the Dioceses of Cheyenne, Colorado Springs, El Paso, Kansas City-St. Joseph, Knoxville, Lexington, Oakland, Orange, Orlando, Portland, Pueblo, Rockford, San Diego, San Jose, Wheeling-Charleston and Worcester.

[2370] (I.B.V.M.)—INSTITUTE OF THE BLESSED VIRGIN MARY (LORETTO SISTERS) (P)
Founded in St. Omer, Belgium, 1609. First foundation in Canada in 1847; in the United States in 1880.

Generalate: *Casa Loreto*, Via Massaua 3, Rome, Italy, 00162. Sr. Marian Moriarty, I.B.V.M., Supr. Gen.
Total in Congregation : 1264.

Provincial Office United States: *Loretto Convent*, P.O. Box 508, Wheaton, IL 60189. Tel: 630-665-3814; Fax: 630-653-4886. Sr. Rosemary Lynch, I.B.V.M., Prov.
Total in Community: 88.
Sisters serve and staff: High Schools; Grammar Schools; Missionary Work; Correspondence School; University; Pastoral Ministry; Adult Education; Social Work; Retreat Ministry; Diocesan Office; Director of Religious Education.
Properties owned: Loretto Development Office; Loretto Convent, Wheaton, IL; Loretto Early Childhood Center, Wheaton, IL; Loretto Center, Wheaton, IL; Houses in California, Arizona and Illinois.
Represented in the Archdiocese of Chicago and in the Dioceses of Joliet, Marquette, Phoenix and Sacramento.

[2385] L.H.C.N.T.—LOVERS OF THE HOLY CROSS NHA TRANG (D)
Founded in Vietnam in 1950. First Foundation in the United States in 2003.

Motherhouse: HT25 Cam Hoa Cam Ranh, Khanh Hoa, Nha Trang, Vietnam

Regional House: 21618 Juan Ave., Hawaiian Gardens, CA 90716. Tel: 562-809-1570; Fax: 562-809-1570. Sr. Mary Men T. Pham, L.H.C.N.T., Rel. Supr.
Total in Congregation : 285; U.S. Community: 5.
Ministry in Pastoral Care: religious education for youth and/or adults, faith formation.

[2390] (L.H.C.)—LOVERS OF THE HOLY CROSS SISTERS (D)
Founded in 1670 in Vietnam by Bishop Pierre Lambert de la Motte. First foundation in the United States in 1976. Established as an autonomous institute of Consecrated Life of Diocesan Right in 1992.

General Motherhouse: *Holy Cross Convent*, 14700 South Van Ness Ave., Gardena, CA 90249. Tel: 310-768-1906; Tel: 310-516-0271; Fax: 310-352-6435. Sr. Anne Lanh Thi Tran, L.H.C., Supr. Gen.
Sisters: 58; Novices: 4; Postulants: 2; Aspirants: 10; Oblates: 1.
Legal Title: *Lovers of the Holy Cross Sisters, Inc.*
Represented in the Archdiocese of Los Angeles and in the Dioceses of Orange and San Bernardino.

[2392] (L.H.C.)—LOVERS OF THE HOLY CROSS SISTERS (P)
(Sisters, Lovers of the Holy Cross)
Founded in Vietnam in 1670 by Bishop Pierre Lambert de la Motte. First foundation in the United States in 1975.

U.S. Foundation: *St. Theresa Convent*, 43 Crown Ln., Westbury, NY 11590. Tel: 516-333-9464. Sr. Theresa

Nguyen, L.H.C., Supr.
Legal Title: *Sisters, Lovers of the Holy Cross, Inc.*
Represented in the Diocese of Rockville Centre.

[2400] (M.S.)—MARIAN SISTERS OF THE DIOCESE OF LINCOLN (D)

Marycrest Motherhouse: *Marian Center*, 6765 N. 112th, Waverly, NE 68462. Tel: 402-786-2750; Fax: 402-786-7256. Sr. Jacquelyn Darner, M.S., Major Supr.
Total in Community: 36.
Ministry in the field of Education; Specialized Education; Health Care; Catechetics.
Represented in the Diocese of Lincoln.

[2410] (M.S.C.)—CONGREGATION OF THE MARIANITES OF HOLY CROSS (P)

Founded in France in 1841. First foundation in the United States in 1843.

Congregational Administration Headquarters: 1011 Gallier St., New Orleans, LA 70117. Tel: 504-945-1620; Web: www.marianites.org. Sr. Suellen Tennyson, M.S.C., Congregational Leader.
Total number in North America: 138.
Ministry in Diocesan Administration and Parishes; Social & Health Services; and the field of Education.
Legal Holdings or Titles: Our Lady of Holy Cross Convent, New Orleans, LA; Our Lady of Holy Cross College, New Orleans, LA; Prompt Succor Nursing Home, Opelousas, LA; C'est la Vie (Senior Citizen Independent Living Units), Opelousas, LA; Holy Angels Congregational Center, New Orleans, LA.
Represented in the Archdiocese of New Orleans and in the Dioceses of Alexandria, Austin, Baton Rouge, Camden, Dallas, Houma-Thibodaux, Lafayette (LA), Lake Charles, Manchester, Paterson and Trenton. Also in Bangladesh, France and Canada.

[2420] (S.M.S.M.)—MARIST MISSIONARY SISTERS (MISSIONARY SISTERS OF THE SOCIETY OF MARY) INC. (P)

Founded in France in 1845-1857. First foundation in the United States in Boston, Massachusetts 1922.

Motherhouse: Via Cassia, 1243, Rome, Italy, 00189.
Universal total in Congregation: 489.

North American Province: *Provincial Office*, 349 Grove St., Waltham, MA 02453-6018. Tel: 781-893-0149; Fax: 781-894-7610. Sr. Judith Sheridan, S.M.S.M., Prov.
Represented in the Archdiocese of Boston and in the Dioceses of Brownsville, Memphis, Oakland, St. Petersburg and San Diego.

[2430] (S.M.)—MARIST SISTERS/CONGREGATION OF MARY (P)

Founded in France 1824 by Venerable John Claude Colin and Jeanne Marie Chavoin.

Generalate: Via Aurelia 292, Rome, Italy, 00165. Sr. Monica O'Brien, S.M., Congregational Leader.
Universal total in Congregation: 400.

U.S. Foundation (1956): *Marist Sisters - Congregation of Mary*, 9312 S. Kolmar Ave., Oak Lawn, IL 60454. Tel: 708-636-0259. Sr. Linda Sevcik, S.M., Sector Leader.
Total in Community: 15.
Legal Title: *Marist Sisters Inc. 16057 Hauss, Eastpointe, MI, 48021.*
Ministry in Elementary & Adult Education; Pastoral Ministry; Counseling; Pastoral Care in Hospitals; Physical Therapy; Seminary Formation; Social Ministry.
Represented in the Archdioceses of Chicago and Detroit and in the Dioceses of Laredo and Wheeling-Charleston.

[2440] (S.M.I.)—CATECHIST SISTERS OF MARY IMMACULATE HELP OF CHRISTIANS, INC. (P)

Catechist Sisters of Mary Immaculate, Help of Christians

Founded in India in 1948 by the late Bishop Louis LaRavoire Morrow, Bishop of Krishnagar, India.

General Motherhouse: *Krishnagar*, Nadia Dist., West Bengal, India, 741 101. Sr. Lisette Thuruthimattam, Supr. Gen.
Universal total in Congregation: 584.

U.S. Foundation (1981): *Sisters of Mary Immaculate*, 118 Park Rd., Leechburg, PA 15656. Tel: 724-845-2828. Sr. Jessy George Mullankuzhiyil, S.M.I., Delegation Supr.; Sr. Mercy F. Anchalakal, S.M.I., Supr.
Total in Community: 6.
Legal Holdings and Titles: Bishop Morrow Personal Care Home, Leechburg, PA

[2450] (S.M.P.)—SISTERS OF MARY OF THE PRESENTATION (P)

Founded in France. First foundation in the United States in 1903.

General Motherhouse: *Broons*, 27 Rue de la Barriere, B.P. 31, Broons, France, 22250. Sr. Annick Geffrelot, Supr. Gen.

U.S. Provincial House & Novitiate at Maryvale: 11550 River Rd., Valley City, ND 58072-9620. Tel: 701-845-2864. Sr. Carol Jean Kuntz, Supr. Prov.
Total in Community: 33.
Properties owned and/or sponsored: St. Margaret's Hospital, Spring Valley, IL; Prairieland Home Health Agency, Spring Valley, IL; St. Andrew Health Center, Bottineau, ND; St. Aloisius Medical Center, Harvey, ND; Presentation Medical Center, Rolla, ND; Ave Maria Village, Jamestown, ND; Maryhill Manor, Enderlin, ND; Rosewood on Broadway, Fargo, ND; Villa Maria, Fargo, ND; Sheyenne Care Center, Valley City, ND.
Ministry in the field of Religious and Academic Education at all levels; Parish Ministry; Hospitals and Home Health Agencies.
Represented in the Dioceses of Bismarck, Crookston, Fargo and Peoria.

[2460] (S.M.R.)—SOCIETY OF MARY REPARATRIX (P)

Founded in France in 1857. First foundation in the United States in 1908.

Generalate: *Society Di Maria Riparatrice*, Via dei Lucchesi 3, Rome, Italy, 00187. Sr. Christine Barriere, Supr. Gen.
Total International Membership: 735.

U.S. Region: 17320 Grange Rd., Riverview, MI 48193. Tel: 734-285-4510; Fax: 734-285-8147. Sr. Ann Kasparek, S.M.R., Reg.
Total in Community: 22.
Represented in the Archdioceses of Detroit, Miami and New York and in the Diocese of Brooklyn.

[2470] (M.M.)—MARYKNOLL SISTERS OF ST. DOMINIC (P)

Founded in New York 1912.

Orientation Program: *Maryknoll Sisters*, Sr. Theresa Kastner, M.M., Co-Dir.; Sr. Shu-Chen Wu, M.M., Co-Dir.

Center: Maryknoll Sisters Center, Maryknoll, NY 10545-0311. Tel: 914-941-7575. Sr. Janice McLaughlin, M.M., Community Pres.; Sr. Rebecca Macugay, M.M., Vice Pres.; Sr. Ann Hayden, M.M., Gen. Sec.; Sr. Bitrina Kirway, M.M., Team Member. Center Coordinators: Sr. Marcelline Yurkovic, M.M.; Sr. Eugenia Lorio, M.M.; Sr. Patricia Ring, M.M.; Sr. Miedal Stone, M.M.
Total in Congregation : 529.
Legal Titles and Holdings: Maryknoll Sisters of St. Dominic, Inc.; Maryknoll Mission Institute.
Represented in the Archdioceses of Baltimore, Boston, Chicago, Cincinnati, Galveston-Houston, Hartford, Los Angeles, Newark, New York, Portland in Oregon, Santa Fe, and Washington DC and in the Dioceses of Albany, Baker, Brooklyn, Charlotte, Duluth, El Paso, Gallup, Harrisburg, Honolulu, Kansas City-St. Joseph, Norwich, Oakland, Palm Beach, Phoenix, Providence, Rockville Centre, San Diego, San Jose and Tucson.

[2480] (M.M.M.)—MEDICAL MISSIONARIES OF MARY (P)

Founded in Nigeria in 1937. First United States Foundation in 1950.

Congregation Centre: *Rosemount*, Booterstown Ave., Blackrock. County Dublin, Ireland Mother Mary Martin, M.M.M., Foundress; Sr. Siobhan Corkery, M.M.M., Congregational Leader.

Medical Missionaries of Mary: 563 Minneford Ave., Bronx, NY 10464-1118. Tel: 718-885-0945; Fax: 718-885-0945; Email: minniefordmmm@verizon.net; Web: www.mmusa.org. Sr. Jean Clare Eason, M.M.M., Area Leader.
Total in Congregation : 414.
Represented in the Archdioceses of Boston, Chicago and New York and in the Dioceses of Richmond and San Diego.

[2490] (M.M.S.)—MEDICAL MISSION SISTERS (P)

Generalate: London, England Sr. Agnes Lanfermann, M.M.S., Society Coord.
Universal total in Congregation: 605.

North American Headquarters (1925): 8400 Pine Rd., Philadelphia, PA 19111. Tel: 215-742-6100; Fax: 215-342-3948. Sr. Rosemary Ryan, M.M.S., North American Coord.
Total number in North America: 119.
Legal Titles: Society of Catholic Medical Missionaries, Inc.; Society of Catholic Medical Missionaries Generalate, Inc.
Represented in the Archdioceses of Baltimore, Boston, Hartford, Louisville, Philadelphia, Santa Fe, Seattle and Washington and in the Dioceses of Camden, Gallup, Harrisburg, Las Cruces, Orange, Palm Beach, Richmond, St. Petersburg, San Diego and Tucson. Also in Mexico.

[2500] (M.S.J.)—MEDICAL SISTERS OF ST. JOSEPH (P)

Founded in Kerala, South India, 1946.

General Motherhouse: *Dharmagiri*, P.O. Kothamangalam, Kerala, India, 686691. Mother Ruth, Supr. Gen.

U.S. Foundation (1985): *Medical Sisters of Joseph*, 3435 E. Funston, Wichita, KS 67218. Tel: 316-686-4746. Sr. Rosamma Chythania Varkey, M.S.J., Supr.
Total in Congregation : 900.
Ministry as Health Care Apostolates.
Represented in the Diocese of Wichita.

[2510] (M.M.B.)—MERCEDARIAN MISSIONARIES OF BERRIZ (P)

Order originated in Berriz, Spain 1548. Transformed into a missionary institute in 1930 in Spain. First foundation in U.S. in 1946 in Kansas City, MO.
Total Number of Sisters in the Institute: 447.

Generalate: *Mercedarie Missionarie di Berriz*, Viale Polo 10, Rome, Italy, 00198. Tel: 39-068-41-3441. Sr. Amelia Kuwaji, M.M.B., Gen. Coord.

U.S. Regional House: *Mercedarian Missionaries of Berriz*, 2115 Maturanna Dr., #101B, Liberty, MO 64068-7985. Tel: 816-781-8202; Fax: 816-781-8205; Email: mmbus@sbcglobal.net; Web: mmberriz.org. Sr. Sandra Thibodeaux, M.M.B., Reg. Coord.
Total number in Region: 14; Total number in Institute: 447.
Ministries in Health, Pastoral Care and Religious Education.
Property sponsored: Our Lady of Mercy Country Home. Liberty, MO.
Represented in the Diocese of Kansas City-St. Joseph. Also in Japan, Taiwan, Philippines, Guam, Federated States of Micronesia, Republic of Palau, Commonwealth of the Northern Marianas, Peru, Ecuador, Guatemala, Nicaragua, Mexico, Democratic Republic of Congo, Zambia, Spain and Rome, Italy.

[2519] (R.S.M.)—RELIGIOUS SISTERS OF MERCY OF ALMA, MICHIGAN (P)

The Religious Sisters of Mercy of Alma was officially founded on September 1, 1973; Diocesan approval on Jan. 25, 1974; Pontifical recognition and Constitutions of Community approved June 18, 1982. Final approval of constitution May 31, 1991.

Motherhouse and Novitiate: *Religious Sisters of Mercy*, 1965 Michigan Ave., Alma, MI 48801. Tel: 989-463-6035.
Total in Community: 80.
Represented in the Archdioceses of Boston, Denver, Hartford, Portland in Oregon and Washington and in the Dioceses of Lansing, Saginaw, Tulsa and Winona. Also in Australia, Germany and Italy.

[2549] (R.S.M.)—SISTERS OF MERCY (P)

Founded in Ireland in 1831. First foundation in the United States in 1956.

General Motherhouse: *Congregation of the Sisters of Mercy*, 13/14 Moyle Park, Clondalkin, Dublin 22, Ireland Tel: 01-467-3737. Sr. Coirle McCarthy, Supr. Gen.
Total in Congregation : 2770.

U.S. Provincial House: *Sisters of Mercy*, 1075 Bermuda Dr., Redlands, CA 92374. Tel: 909-798-4747; Fax: 909-798-5300. Sr. Rosaline O'Connor, R.S.M., Prov. Supr.
Professed Sisters in U.S. Province: 84.
Legal Title: *Congregation of the Sisters of Mercy-San Bernardino.*
Ministry in the field of Religious Education; Parishes; Social Services; Diocesan Offices
Represented in the Archdioceses of Chicago, Miami and St. Louis and in the Dioceses of Biloxi, Camden, Fargo, Great Falls-Billings, Las Vegas, Memphis, Mobile, Monterey, Oakland, Orange, Orlando, Palm Beach, Providence, Rapid City, Reno, Sacramento, St. Augustine, San Diego, San Jose, Santa Rosa, San Bernardino, Sioux Falls and Venice.

Sisters of Mercy (1971): 5392 S.W. 33rd Ave., Fort Lauderdale, FL 33312. Tel: 954-989-8291. Sr. Rosaline O'Connor, R.S.M., Prov. Supr.
Total in Community: 4.
Ministry in the field of Education and Parish Work.
Represented in the Archdiocese of Miami.

U.S. Foundation: *St. Joan of Arc*, 500 S.W. 4th Ave., Boca Raton, FL 33432. Tel: 561-368-6655. Sr. Kathleen Sweeney, Communications Coord.
Professed Sisters: 4.
Represented in the Diocese of Palm Beach.

[2575] (R.S.M.)—SISTERS OF MERCY OF THE AMERICAS (P)

Catherine McAuley founded the Sisters of Mercy in Dublin, Ireland, in 1831. Ten years later, she received confirmation of the Rule by Pope Gregory XVI. In 1843 the Sisters of Mercy established their first U.S.A. foundation in Pittsburgh, followed by various amalgamations. In 1991 the members of the nine provinces of the Union and of 16 other Mercy congregations founded the Sisters of Mercy of the Americas consisting of 25 regional communities.

In 2009, the Sisters of Mercy of the Americas completed a restructuring of the 25 Regional Communities into six communities within the Institute: Caribbean, Central America, South America Community; Mid-Atlantic Community; Northeast Community; New York, Pennsylvania, Pacific West Community; and West Midwest Community. The Sisters of Mercy of the Americas are represented in: Argentina, the Bahamas, Belize, Bolivia, Canada, Chile, Guam, Guatemala, Guyana, Haiti, Honduras, Ireland, Jamaica, Panama, Peru, the Philippines, Puerto Rico, South Africa, the United States of America, and West Africa.

Institute Administrative Offices: 8380 Colesville Rd., #300, Silver Spring, MD 20910-6264. Tel: 301-587-0423; Fax: 301-587-0533.
Total in Congregation : 3973.
Legal Title: *Sisters of Mercy of the Americas, Inc.*
Mercy Action, Inc. is separately incorporated to support works directed toward systemic change.
Mercy Volunteer Corps, Inc. is separately incorporated to conduct a volunteer lay ministry program to further the works of mercy.
Conference for Mercy High Education, Inc., is separately incorporated for the purpose of support, coordination and facilitation of the ministry and educational mission of the institutions of higher education recognized by the Sisters of Mercy of the Americas.
Institute Leadership Team Sr. Mary Waskowiak, R.S.M., Pres.; Sr. Eileen Campbell, R.S.M.; Sr. Anne Curtis, R.S.M.; Sr. Patricia McDermott, R.S.M., Vice Pres.; Sr. Linda Werthman, R.S.M.

Sisters of Mercy of the Americas, CCASA (Caribbean, Central America, South America) Community: 8380 Colesville Rd., #300, Silver Spring, MD 20910-6264. Tel: 301-587-0423; Fax: 301-587-0533. Community Transition Team Sr. Dina Altamiranda, R.S.M., Pres.; Sr. Julie Matthews, R.S.M., Vice Pres.; Sr. Carolee Chanona, R.S.M.; Sr. Patricia Mulderick, R.S.M.
Total in Community: 89.
Legal Title: *Sisters of Mercy of the Americas, CCASA Community, Inc.*

Sisters of Mercy of the Americas, Northeast Community: 15 Highland View Rd., Cumberland, RI 02864-1124. Tel: 401-333-6333; Fax: 401-333-6450; Email: info@mercynortheast.org. Community Leadership Team: Sr. Ellen Kurtz, R.S.M., Pres.; Sr. Michele Aronica, R.S.M., Vice Pres.; Sr. Eileen Dooling, R.S.M.; Sr. Jacqueline Marie Kieslich, R.S.M.; Sr. Maureen McElroy, R.S.M.; Sr. Kathleen Turley, R.S.M.; Gerald Sullivan, COO; Chole Van Aken, Dir. Communications; Sr. Kathleen Pritty, R.S.M., Dir. Justice; Susan Jenkinson, Dir. Sponsorship; Nancy Bancroft, Assoc. Dir. Sponsorship; Sr. Elaine Deasy, R.S.M., Dir. Vocation & Incorporation; Sr. Dale Jarvis, R.S.M., Dir. Vocation & Incorporation; Sr. Eleanor Little, R.S.M., Archivist; Deborah Wallace, Human Resources Mgr.
Vowed Members: 794; Assoc. Members: 396.
Legal Title: *Sisters of Mercy of the Americas-Northeast Community, Inc.*
Ministry in the field of spirituality & retreat work; diocesan & pastoral services; peace & justice initiatives; parish ministry; religious & academic education at all levels; hospitals & health care services/facilities; literacy centers; hospitality houses; nursing homes; social services; counseling services; transitional houses & foreign missionary work.
Sponsored Ministries: Colleges & Universities: Maria College, Albany, NY; Marian Court College, Swampscott, MA; St. Joseph's College, Standish, ME; St. Joseph College, West Hartford, CT; Salve Regina University, Newport, RI.
Secondary Education: Catherine McAuley High School, Portland, ME; Lauralton Hall, Milford, CT; St. Mary Academy, Bay View, PreK-12, Riverside, RI.
Elementary Education: Mater Christi School, Burlington, VT; Mercymount Country Day School, Cumberland, RI; Mount Saint Mary Academy, Manchester, NH.
Hospitals & Health Care Services: St. Peter's Hospital, Albany, NY; St. Peter's Health Care, Albany, NY; St. Peter's Hospital Foundation, Albany, NY; The Community Hospice, Rensselaer, NY; Mercy Cares for Kids, Albany, NY; Our Lady of Mercy Life Center, Guilderland, NY; St. Peters Nursing and Rehabilitation Center, Albany, NY; McAuley Living Services, Albany, NY; Mercy Health System of Maine/Mercy Hospital, Portland, ME; Mercy Community Health System, West Hartford, CT; Saint Mary Home, West Hartford, CT; The McAuley, Inc., West Hartford, CT; Mercy Community Home Care Services, West Hartford, CT; Warde Health Center, Windham, NH; McAuley Residence, Portland, ME; Gary's House, Portland, ME; Visiting Nurses Association, Portland, ME; Mount Saint Rita Health Centre, Cumberland, RI.
Housing & Shelter: Mercy Housing and Shelter, Hartford, CT; Frances Warde House, Manchester, NH; McAuley Commons, Windham, NH.
Social Services: Circles of Mercy, Albany, NY; McAuley Corporation, Providence, RI; Mercy Connections, Burlington, VT.
Spirituality Centers & Retreat Houses: Mercy Center at Madison, Madison, CT; Institute for Spiritual Development, Burlington, VT.
Represented in the Archdioceses of Anchorage, Baltimore, Boston, Chicago, Hartford, Miami, Newark, New York, Omaha, Santa Fe, St. Louis, and Washington and in the Dioceses of Albany, Bridgeport, Brooklyn, Burlington, Fall River, Manchester, Norwich, Palm Beach, Pensacola-Tallahassee, Pittsburgh, Portland (ME), Providence, Richmond, St. Augustine, Springfield (MA), Syracuse and Worcester. Also in Belize, Haiti, Honduras and Guatemala.

Brooklyn (P)

Institute of the Sisters of Mercy of the Americas, Mid-Atlantic Community, Inc: 273 Willoughy Ave., Brooklyn, NY 11205. Tel: 718-622-5750. Sr. Christine McCann, R.S.M., Pres.
Total in Community: 1072.
Properties owned or sponsored: mercyFirst, Angel Guardian Campus; Mercy Home for Children; Catherine McAuley High School, Brooklyn, NY; mercyFirst, Syosset Campus; Our Lady of Mercy Academy, Syosset
Sisters serve and staff: Elementary and High Schools; Institutions of Higher Education; Child Care Institutions; Pastoral Ministry Programs and Spirituality and Retreat Programs.
Represented in the Archdioceses of Baltimore and Detroit and in the Dioceses of Brooklyn, Orlando and Rockville Centre.

Buffalo (P)

Sisters of Mercy of the Americas (New York, Pennsylvania, Pacific West Community: 625 Abbott Rd., Buffalo, NY 14220. Tel: 716-826-5051; Fax: 716-826-1518; Email: nhoff@mercynyppaw.org; Web: sistersofmercy.org.
Total in Community: 490; Associates: 410.
Legal Title: *Sisters of Mercy of the Americas - New York, Pennsylvania, Pacific West Community, Inc.*
Ministry in the fields of spirituality and retreat work, diocesan and pastoral services, peace and justice initiatives, parish ministry; religious and academic education at all levels; hospitals and health care services/facilities, literacy centers, hospitality houses, social services; counseling services; transitional houses and foreign missionary work.
Properties owned (sponsored ministries): Carlow University, Pittsburgh, PA; Mercyhurst College, Erie, PA; Trocaire College, Buffalo, NY; Our Lady of Mercy High School, Rochester, NY; Mercyhurst Preparatory School, Erie, PA; Mt. Mercy Academy, Buffalo, NY; Notre Dame High School, Elmira, NY; The Campus School of Carlow University, Pittsburgh, PA; Mercy Center of the Arts, Erie, PA; Pittsburgh Mercy Health System, Pittsburgh, PA; Holy Cross Hospital, Ft. Lauderdale, FL; Catholic Health System, Buffalo, NY; St. James Mercy Health System, Hornell, NY; Mercy Terrace Apartments, Erie, PA; Catherine McAuley Housing Inc., d.b.a Mercy Residential Services, Rochester, NY; Erie DAWN, Inc., Erie, PA; Mercy Center for Women, Erie, PA; Sisters Place, Pittsburgh, PA; Mercy Outreach Center Inc., Rochester, NY; Mercy Center on Aging, Erie, PA; Intersection, Pittsburgh, PA; Mercy Prayer Center, Rochester, NY.
Represented in the Archdioceses of Indianapolis, Miami, San Juan and Washington and in the Dioceses of Bridgeport, Buffalo, Erie, Fall River, MA, Laredo, Orlando, Palm Beach, Phoenix, Pittsburgh, Rochester and San Jose. Also in the Philippine Islands.
Community Leadership Team Sr. Nancy Hoff, R.S.M., Pres.; Sr. Patricia Prinzing, R.S.M., Vice Pres.; Sr. JoAnne Courneen, R.S.M.; Sr. Guadalupe Lumantas, R.S.M.; Sr. Geraldine Rosinski, R.S.M.

Merion (P)

Mid-Atlantic Community, Convent of Mercy: *Convent of the Sisters of Mercy,* 515 Montgomery Ave., Merion Station, PA 19066. Tel: 610-664-6650; Fax: 610-664-3429. Sr. Christine McCann, R.S.M., Pres.; Sr. Marian Francis Kelly, R.S.M., Local Coord.
Total in Community: 1109.
Legal Title: *Sisters of Mercy Mid-Atlantic Community.*
Properties owned, staffed or sponsored: Gwynedd Mercy College; McAuley Convent; Merion Mercy Academy; Waldron Mercy Academy; Gwynedd Mercy Academy; Mercy Vocational High School; Walsingham Academy; Mercy Health System.
Sisters serve and staff: Religious and academic education at all levels; Hospices; House of Prayer; Social service organizations.
Represented in the Archdioceses of Anchorage, Atlanta, Baltimore, Newark, Philadelphia, St. Louis and Washington and in the Dioceses of Allentown, Brooklyn, Camden, Laredo, Phoenix, Providence, Raleigh, Richmond, Scranton, Springfield, Trenton, Tucson, Wilmington and Worcester. Also in Bolivia, Italy, Jamaica, Peru and South Africa

New Jersey (P)

Mid-Atlantic Community: 1645 U.S. Hwy. 22, W., Watchung, NJ 07069-6587. Tel: 908-756-0994; Fax: 908-754-0164. Sr. Christine McCann, R.S.M., Pres.; Sr. Elizabeth O'Hara, R.S.M., Archivist.
Total in Community: 1071.
Legal Title: *Sisters of Mercy of Americas Mid-Atlantic Community.*
Ministry in the field of Religious and Academic Education at all levels; Health Care and Hospital Chaplaincy; Diocesan Administration; Parish and Prison Ministry; School for Special Education; Day Center for Senior Citizens; Child Day Care Center; House of Prayer; Social Service.
Properties owned or sponsored: McAuley Hall; McAuley School for the Exceptional Child, Watchung, NJ; Georgian Court University, Lakewood, NJ; Mount Saint Mary Academy, Watchung, NJ; Mount Saint Mary House of Prayer, Watchung, NJ; Mercy Center, Asbury Park, NJ.
Represented in the Archdioceses of New York, Newark, Philadelphia, St. Louis and Washington and in the Dioceses of Austin, Bridgeport, Camden, Charlotte, Metuchen, Orlando, Paterson, Rochester, Santa Rosa and Trenton.

New York (P)

Sisters of Mercy of the Americas Mid-Atlantic Community: 150 Ridge Rd., Hartsdale, NY 10530. Tel: 914-328-3200; Fax: 914-328-3761. Sr. Christine McCann, R.S.M., Pres.
Total in Community: 1071.
Legal Title: *Instittue of the Sisters of Mercy of the Americas, Mid-Atlantic Community.*
Ministry in the field of Academic Education at all levels; Health and Child care; Special Education; Social Services; Spirituality and Counseling centers; Catechetical services; Pastoral Ministry.
Properties owned and/or sponsored: Our Lady of Victory Academy, NY; St. Catharine Academy, NY; Mercy Center, Bronx, NY.
Represented in the Archdioceses of Hartford, Los Angeles and New York and in the Dioceses of Ogdensburg, Rockville Centre and Worcester.

North Carolina (P)

Sisters of Mercy of the Americas, South Central Community: 101 Mercy Dr., Belmont, NC 28012. Tel: 704-829-5260; Fax: 704-829-5267; Email: info@mercysc.org; Web: www.mercysc.org.
Total in Community: 720.
Legal Title: *Sisters of Mercy of the Americas, South Central Community, Inc.*
Ministry in the following areas: Education: Daycare and Preschool Centers; Elementary Schools; High Schools; Institutions of Higher Education; Special Education; Education Research Programs; Schools for Exceptional Children; Adult Education.
Healthcare: Hospitals; Ambulatory Health Care Center; Long Term Care; Multi-Level Long-Term Care Facility and Health Systems; Urgent Care Centers.
Social Services: Developmental Center for Handicapped Children; Social Work Centers; Care and Counseling; AIDS Ministry.
Retreat/Renewal Centers: Psycho-Spiritual Programs, Conference/Retreat Centers.
Housing: Homes for Aged; Transitional housing for women and children.
Parish Ministry: Pastoral Ministry Programs; Parish ministry; Diocesan ministry.
Properties owned, sponsored or co-sponsored: Alpha Academy, Kingston, Jamaica, WI; Alpha Boys' School, Kingston, Jamaica, WI; Alpha Infant School, Kingston, Jamaica, WI; Alpha Primary School, Kingston, Jamaica, WI; Jessie Ripoll Primary School, Kingston, Jamaica, WI; Mt. St. Joseph Prep School, Manchester, Jamaica, WI; St. John Bosco Children's Home, Manchester, Jamaica, WI; Well of Mercy, Inc. Hamptonville, NC; Holy Angels, Belmont, NC; House of Mercy, Belmont, NC; Catherine's House, Belmont, NC; Sisters of Mercy of NC Foundation, Inc., Charlotte, NC; Sisters of Mercy Services Corporation, Asheville, NC; Mercy Heights Nursery-K, Tamuning, GU; Our Lady of the Pines Retreat Center, Fremont, OH; House of Mercy, Baltimore, MD; Murphy Initiative for Justice and Peace, Baltimore, MD; Mount Saint Agnes College; Mercy Villa; Mercy High School, Baltimore, MD; Mount Saint Agnes Theological Center for Women, Baltimore, MD; St. Joseph's Health System, Atlanta (CHE), Atlanta, GA; Marian House, Baltimore, MD; Mount de Sales Academy, Macon, GA; Mercy Medical, Inc. Daphne (CHE), Daphne, AL; St. Mary's Health Care System, Inc. (CHE), Athens, GA; Sisters Academy of Baltimore, Baltimore, MD; The Savannah Institute of the Sisters of Mercy, Inc.; (St. Vincent's Academy), Savannah, GA; Mercy Health Services & (Mercy Medical Center & Stella Maris), Baltimore, MD; St. Joseph's/Candler Health System, Savannah, GA; Catholic Health East, Newtown Square, PA; Mercy Action Marianas, Ltd., Tamuning, GU; Infant of Prague Nursery-K, Mangilao, GU; Academy of Our Lady of Mercy, Inc., Louisville, KY; Assumption High School, Inc.; Louisville, KY; McAuley High School, Inc., Cincinnati, OH; Mother of Mercy High School, Inc., Cincinnati, OH; Mercy Montessori Center, Cincinnati, OH; Mercy Neighborhood Ministries, Cincinnati, OH; Sisters of Mercy of Jamaica, West Indies, Kingston, Jamaica, West Indies; House of Mercy, Inc., Nashville, TN; Catholic Healthcare Partners (CHP), Cincinnati, OH; McAuley LLC, Louisville, KY; Mercy Conference and Retreat Center, St. Louis, MO; Our Lady of Wisdom, New Orleans, LA; Mount St. Mary Academy, Little Rock, AR; Mercy Crest Housing, Inc., Barling, AR; Mount Saint Mary High School, Oklahoma City, OK; Arise - Support Center, Alamo, TX; Arise - Muniz, Edinburg, TX; Arise - Las Milpas, Pharr, TX; Arise - South Tower, Alamo, TX; Mercy Housing, Inc., Denver, CO.
Represented in the Archdioceses of Agana (GU), Atlanta, Baltimore, Cincinnati, Detroit, Louisville, Mobile, New Orleans, Oklahoma City, St. Louis, San Antonio and Washington and in the Dioceses of Arlington, Belleville, Biloxi, Birmingham, Brownsville, Caroline Islands, Charlotte, Cleveland, Fort Worth, Jackson, Knoxville, Lansing, Laredo, Las Cruces, Little Rock, Lubbock, Memphis, Metuchen, Nashville, Orlando, Owensboro, Pensacola-Tallahassee, Portland in Maine, Portland in Oregon, Richmond, Savannah, Springfield-Cape Girardeau, Toledo, Trenton, Wheeling-Charleston, Wichita and Wilmington. Also in Jamaica, West Indies, Cape Coast, Ghana and Guyana.
Leadership Team: Sr. Kathy Green, R.S.M., Pres.; Sr. Jane Mary Hotstream, R.S.M., Vice Pres.; Sr. Marie Chin, R.S.M.; Sr. Angela Perez, R.S.M.; Sr. Barbara Wheeley, R.S.M.; Sr. Paulette Williams, R.S.M.

Omaha (P)

Sisters of Mercy of the Americas, West Midwest Community: 7262 Mercy Rd., Omaha, NE 68124-2389. Tel: 402-393-8225; Fax: 402-393-8145; Email: info@mercywmw.org; Web: www.mercywest-midwest.org. Community Leadership Team: Sr. Norita Cooney, R.S.M., Pres.; Sr. Judith Frikker, R.S.M.,

Substitute for Pres. Team Members: Sr. Judith Cannon, R.S.M.; Sr. Michelle Gorman, R.S.M.; Sr. Sheila Megley, R.S.M.; Sr. Kathy Thornton, R.S.M.
Total in Community: 810; Total Number of Associates: 565.
Legal Title: *Sisters of Mercy of the Americas West Midwest Community, Inc.*
Ministry in the following areas: field of spirituality & retreat work; diocesan & pastoral services; peace & justice initiatives; parish ministry; religious & academic education at all levels; hospitals and healthcare services/facilities; literacy centers and programs; hospitality houses; nursing homes; social services; counseling services; transitional houses; foreign ministry work; prison ministry; long-term care facilities for the aged; housing for families and elderly.
Sponsored Ministries (city listed indicates central administrative location of the ministry-some ministries may have multiple locations): Colleges and Higher Education: Mount Mercy College, Cedar Rapids, IA; Saint Xavier University, Chicago, IL; University of Detroit Mercy, Detroit, MI (co-sponsor); College of Saint Mary, Omaha, NE (affiliated/historical partner). Secondary Education: Cristo Rey High School, Sacramento, CA (co-sponsor); Mercy Education Resource Center, Sacramento, CA; Mercy Education Project, Detroit, MI; Mercy High School, Burlingame, CA; Mercy High School, San Francisco, CA; Mercy High School, Detroit, MI; Mercy High School, Omaha, NE; Mother McAuley Liberal Arts High School, Chicago, IL; Catherine McAuley Center Literacy Program, Cedar Rapids, IA.
Hospitals & Healthcare Services (city listed indicates central administrative location of the ministry. Some ministries may have multiple locations): Catholic Health Initiatives, Denver, CO (co-sponsor); Catholic Health Ministries/Trinity Health, Novi, MI (participating entity); Catholic Healthcare West, San Francisco, CA (co-sponsor); Mercy Health System of Chicago, Chicago, IL; Mercy Hospital, Iowa City, IA; Mercy Medical Center, Cedar Rapids, IA; Provena Health, Chicago, IL (co-sponsor); Scripps Mercy Chula Vista Hospital, Chula Vista, CA; Scripps Mercy Hospital, San Diego, CA; Elder Care Alliance, Oakland, CA (co-sponsor); and Mercy Retirement and Care Center, Oakland, CA. Housing & Shelter: Mercy Housing, Inc., Denver, CO (co-sponsor); St. Catherine Residence, Milwaukee, WI; McAuley Apartments, Chicago, IL. Social Services: Catherine McAuley Center, Cedar Rapids, IA; Waterloo House of Mercy, Waterloo, IA. Development: Mercy Foundation Sacramento, Rancho Cordova, CA; and Mercy Foundation North, Redding, CA. Spirituality/Retreat Centers: Knowles Mercy Spirituality Center, Waterloo, NE; Mercy Center, Auburn, CA; Mercy Center, Burlingame, CA.
Represented in the Archdioceses of Baltimore, Chicago, Denver, Detroit, Dubuque, Hartford, Los Angeles, Louisville, Milwaukee, New York, Omaha, Portland in Oregon, Santa Fe, Seattle, St. Louis, St. Paul-Minneapolis, San Francisco and Washington and in the Dioceses of Boise, Charleston, Charlotte, Colorado Springs, Davenport, Des Moines, El Paso, Fresno, Gaylord, Grand Rapids, Great Falls-Billings, Helena, Joliet, Kalamazoo, Kansas City in Kansas, Kansas City-St. Joseph, Knoxville, Lansing, Laredo, Las Vegas, Lexington, Lincoln, Monterey, Oakland, Orange, Peoria, Phoenix, Pueblo, Reno, Rockford, Sacramento, Saginaw, San Diego, San Jose, Sioux City, St. Cloud, Springfield-Cape Girardeau, St. Petersburg, Stockton, Wheeling-Charleston and Winona. Also in Ireland, Peru, South Africa, Sudan, and Uganda.

[2590] (H.M.S.S.)—MERCEDARIAN SISTERS OF THE BLESSED SACRAMENT (P)
(Hermanas Mercedarias del Santisimo Sacramento)

Founded in Mexico in 1910. First foundation in the United States in 1926.

Mercedarian Sisters of the Blessed Sacrament: 227 Keller St., San Antonio, TX 78204. Tel: 210-223-5013; Fax: 210-444-0779.

General Motherhouse: Fernandez Leal #130, Coyoacan, Mexico, 04330. Sr. M. Dolores Muñoz, H.M.S.S., Regl. Supr.

Regional House: 234 W. Cevallos St., San Antonio, TX 78204. Tel: 210-222-1354.
Professed Sisters in the U.S: 31.
Represented in the Archdiocese of San Antonio and in the Dioceses of Baton Rouge, Cleveland, Corpus Christi and San Diego.

[2600] (R.S.M.)—SISTERS OF MERCY (D)

Founded in the United States in 1960.

General Motherhouse: *Congregation of the Sisters of Mercy*, 13/14 Moyle Park, Convent Rd., Clondalkin, Dublin 22, Ireland Sr. Coirle McCarthy, Supr. Gen.

U.S. Address: *Sacred Heart Convent*, 6240 105th St., Jacksonville, FL 32244. Tel: 904-771-3858. Sr. Patricia O'Hea, Contact Person.
Represented in the Diocese of St. Augustine.

[2630] (S.C.S.C.)—SISTERS OF MERCY OF THE HOLY CROSS (P)

Founded in Switzerland in 1856. First foundation in the U.S. in 1912.

General Motherhouse: Ingenbohl, Switzerland Sr. Marjia Brizar, S.C.S.C., Supr. Gen.

U.S. Provincial Office: *Holy Cross Sisters*, 1400 O'Day St., Merrill, WI 54452. Tel: 715-539-1460; Fax: 715-539-1458. Sr. Celine Goessl, S.C.S.C., Prov.
Total in Community: 37.
Legal Title: Sisters of Mercy of the Holy Cross of Merrill, WI, Inc.; Sponsored Institution: Bell Tower Residence, Inc.
Ministry in the following areas: Schools; Hospitals; Social Ministries and Parishes; Retirement Homes; Adult Education; Campus Ministries; Prison Ministry.
Represented in the Archdioceses of Cincinnati and New Orleans and in the Dioceses of Belleville, La Crosse, Lansing and Superior.

[2655] —DIOCESAN SISTERS OF MERCY OF PORTLAND (D)

Motherhouse: *Diocesan Sisters of Mercy of Portland*, 265 Cottage Rd., South Portland, ME 04106. Tel: 207-767-5804. Sr. Carol Le Tourneau, R.S.M.

[2670] (S.O.L.M.)—SISTERS OF OUR LADY OF MERCY (P)
(Mercedarians)

General Motherhouse: via Ostriana 24, Rome, Italy Mother Igina Caddori, Supr. Gen.

Brooklyn: *Most Precious Blood*, 133 27th Ave., Brooklyn, NY 11214. Sr. Doloretta, Supr.
Sisters: 6.
Represented in the Dioceses of Brooklyn and St. Petersburg.

[2675] (C.F.M.M.)—MINIM DAUGHTERS OF MARY IMMACULATE (P)

Founded in Leon, Guanajuato, Mexico 1886. Came to the United States in 1926.

U.S. Regional House: *Minim Daughters of Mary Immaculate*, 555 Patagonia Hwy., Nogales, AZ 85628. Tel: 520-287-3377; Fax: 520-287-2910. Sr. Rosa Maria Ruiz, C.F.M.M., Reg. Supr.
Total Sisters in the U.S: 17.
Properties owned and/or sponsored: Lourdes Catholic School, Nogales, AZ.
Ministry in Academic and Religious Education and Health Care.
Represented in the Diocese of Tucson.

[2677] (S.M.M.I.)—SISTERS MINOR OF MARY IMMACULATE (D)

First foundation in the United States June 13, 1989. Active- contemplative Franciscan Religious Congregation following the spirituality of St. Maximilian Mary Kolbe, O.F.M.Conv. and St. Terese of Liseux.

Central Motherhouse & Novitiate: Via Germanico 198, Rome, Italy, 00192. Tel: 011-39-06-324-2036. Maria Elisabetta Patrizi, Foundress.

American Headquarters - St. Francis Villa: 138 Brushy Hill Rd., Danbury, CT 06810-8431. Tel: 203-744-8041. Sr. Kathleen Howard, S.M.M.I., U.S. Delegate.
Legal Title: *Sisters Minor of Mary Immaculate.*
Ministry in the field of Academic and Religious Education; Health Care; Pastoral Care; Care to the elderly, youths, widows and immigrants.
Represented in the Archdiocese of Hartford, and in the Diocese of Bridgeport.

[2680] (S.M.)—MISERICORDIA SISTERS (P)

Founded in Canada in 1848. First foundation in the United States in 1887.

General Motherhouse: 12435 Misericorde Ave., Montreal, Canada, H4J 2G3. Tel: 514-332-0550. Sr. Monique Lallier, S.M., Supr.

U.S. Address: 225 Carol Ave., Pelham, NY 10803. Sr. Ellen Hunt, S.M., Supr.
Represented in the Archdiocese of New York.

[2690] (M.C.D.P.)—MISSIONARY CATECHISTS OF DIVINE PROVIDENCE, SAN ANTONIO, TEXAS (P)

Autonomy with Pontifical status granted December 12, 1989.

Administrative House: *St. Andrew's Convent*, 2318 Castroville Rd., San Antonio, TX 78237. Tel: 210-432-0113; Fax: 210-432-1709. Sr. Mary Lou Barba, Supr.
Total in Community: 40.
Properties owned or sponsored: Benitia Family Center, San Antonio, TX.
Represented in the Archdioceses of Galveston-Houston, Los Angeles, Omaha and San Antonio and in the Dioceses of Austin, Brownsville, Corpus Christi, Dallas, Fort Worth and San Jose.

[2700] (M.C.S.H.)—MISSIONARY CATECHISTS OF THE SACRED HEARTS OF JESUS AND MARY (D)

Founded in Mexico City, D.F. in 1918. U.S. foundation in 1943 in Victoria, Texas.

Central House: Mexico City, Mexico Sr. Laura M. Solano, Supr. Gen.

Immaculate Heart of Mary Province: 203 E. Sabine St., Victoria, TX 77901. Tel: 361-570-3332; Fax: 361-570-3377. Sr. Miriam Perez, M.C.S.H., Prov. Supr.
Total number in U.S. Province: 44.
Ministry in Catechetical family ministry in parishes and missions.
Represented in the Archdiocese of Galveston-Houston and in the Dioceses of Lubbock, Metuchen and Victoria.

[2710] (M.C.)—MISSIONARIES OF CHARITY (P)

Founded in India, 1950.

General Motherhouse: 54A AJC Bose Rd., Calcutta, India, 700016. Sr. M. Prema, M.C., Supr. Gen.

U.S. Foundation & Office (1971): *Missionaries of Charity*, 335 E. 145th St., Bronx, NY 10451. Tel: 718-292-0019. Sr. Leticia, M.C., Reg. Supr.
Professed Sisters in Congregation: 4900.
Legal Title: *Missionaries of Charity, Inc.*
Sisters serve and staff: Soup Kitchens; Emergency Shelters for Women; Homes for Unwed Mothers; Shelters for Unwed Mothers; Shelters for Men; Religious Education Programs; After-School and Summer Camp Programs for Children; Homes for AIDS Patients; Prison Ministry; Nursing Homes; Hospital and Shut-in Ministry; Family Counseling and Ministry; Foreign Missionary Work.
Represented in the Archdioceses of Atlanta, Baltimore, Boston, Chicago, Denver, Detroit, Galveston-Houston, Indianapolis, Los Angeles, Miami, New York, Newark, Philadelphia, San Francisco, St. Louis, St. Paul-Minneapolis and Washington and in the Dioceses of Baton Rouge, Bridgeport, Brooklyn, Charlotte, Dallas, Fall River, Gallup, Gary, Lafayette, Lexington, Little Rock, Memphis, Peoria, Phoenix, Sacramento. Spokane and Trenton. Also in Canada, Mexico, Central America and South America.

[2715] (M.CH.R.)—MISSIONARY SISTERS OF CHRIST THE KING FOR POLONIA (P)

Founded in Poland on November 21, 1959 by Father Ignacy Posadzy, TChr. First foundation in the U.S. 1978.

General Motherhouse: *Siostry Misjonarki Chrystusa Krola dla Polonii*, ul. Siostr Misjonarek 10, Poznan, 50, Poland, 61-680. Sr. Edyta Rychel, M.Ch.R., Supr. Gen.
Total in Congregation : 230.

Delegation Superior in the U.S: *Missionary Sisters of Christ the King for Polonia*, 4910 North Menard Ave., Chicago, IL 60630. Tel: 773-481-1831; Fax: 773-545-4171. Sr. Ewa Biniek, M.Ch.R., Supr.; Sr. Gertruda Szymanska, M.Ch.R., Sec.; Sr. Marta Cichon, M.Ch.R., Treas.
Total in Congregation : 198; Professed in U.S. and Canada: 40.
Legal Title: *Missionary Sisters of Christ the King for Polonia.*
Ministry among Polish immigrants and people of Polish heritage.
Represented in the Archdioceses of Chicago, Detroit and Los Angeles and in the Dioceses of Phoenix and San Jose. Also in Toronto, Brampton, Oshawa, Mississauga and Vancouver, Canada.

[2717] (M.D.P.V.M.)—MISSIONARY DAUGHTERS OF THE MOST PURE VIRGIN MARY (P)

Founded in Mexico. First foundation in the United States in the Diocese of Corpus Christi 1916.

General Motherhouse: *Heroe de Nacocariz*, 721 Sur Aguascalientes, Mexico Mother Rita Ramirez, M.D-.P.V.M., Gen. Supr.

Missionary Daughters of the Most Pure Virgin Mary: 919 N. 9th St., Kingsville, TX 78363. Tel: 361-595-1087. Sr. Consuelo Ramirez, M.D.P.V.M., Supr.; Sr. Carmen Villalpando, M.D.P.V.M., Sec.; Sr. Maximina Cruz, M.D.P.V.M., Treas.
Total in Congregation : 442; Present in U.S: 28.
Legal Title: *Missionary Daughters of the Most Pure Virgin Mary.*
Ministry in the field of Religious and Academic Education at the elementary level; Pastoral Ministry.
Represented in the Dioceses of Camden, Corpus Christi and Yakima.

[2720] (M.H.S.H.)—MISSION HELPERS OF THE SACRED HEART (P)

Founded in the United States in 1890.

Mission Helper Center: 1001 W. Joppa Rd., Baltimore, MD 21204. Tel: 410-823-8585; Fax: 410-825-6355. Sr. Loretta Cornell, M.H.S.H., Pres.
Total in Community: 75.
Legal Title: *Institute of Mission Helpers of Baltimore City.*
Represented in the Archdioceses of Baltimore, Boston, Cincinnati, Indianapolis, San Juan (PR), Seattle and Washington and in the Dioceses of Birmingham, Erie, Orlando, Pittsburgh, Rochester, and Tucson. Also in Venezuela.

[2725] (M.S.E.)—MISSIONARY SISTERS OF THE EUCHARIST

Founded in Guatemala, C.A. in 1975. First foundation in the United States in 2001.

Motherhouse: San Andres Semetabaj, Solola, Guatemala Sr. Marta Esperanza Juracan, M.S.E., Supr.

Gen.
Total in Community: 51.

Visitation Convent, Magnificat Houses: 3301 San Jacinto St., Houston, TX 77004. Tel: 713-523-8831.

Mailing Address: P.O. Box 88147, Houston, TX 77288-0147. Sr. Leocadia Otzoy, M.S.E., Local Supr.
Ministry in parishes, missionary work, health care and social services.
Represented in the Archdiocese of Galveston-Houston.

[2730] (M.S.H.R.)—MISSIONARY SISTERS OF THE HOLY ROSARY (P)

Generalate (1924): 23 Cross Ave., Blackrock County, Dublin, Ireland Sr. Maureen O'Malley, Congregational Leader.

U.S. Regional Headquarters (1954): *Missionary Sisters of the Holy Rosary,* 741 Polo Rd., Bryn Mawr, PA 19010. Tel: 610-520-1974. Sr. Helena McNeill, Reg. Leader.
Total in Community: 382.
Represented in the Archdiocese of Philadelphia.

[2740] (M.S.SP.)—MISSION SISTERS OF THE HOLY SPIRIT (D)

Motherhouse and Novitiate: 1030 N. River Rd., Saginaw, MI 48609. Tel: 989-781-0934. Sr. Margo Tafoya, Pres.
Total in Community: 7.
Legal Title: *Society of the Mission Sisters of the Holy Spirit of the Diocese of Saginaw Holy Spirit Sisters Charitable Trust, Saginaw, MI.*
Ministry in Social Services; Religious Education at all levels including Developmentally Disabled; Pastoral Ministry.
Represented in the Diocese of Saginaw.

[2750] (I.C.M.)—MISSIONARY SISTERS OF THE IMMACULATE HEART OF MARY (P)

Founded in India in 1897. First foundation in the United States in 1919.

Generalate: Via Filogaso 40, Rome, Italy, 00173. Sr. M. Josee Cleymans, I.C.M., Supr. Gen.
Universal total in Congregation: 789.

American Province: 238 E. 15th St., #5, New York, NY 10003. Tel: 212-677-2959; Tel: 212-260-8567; Fax: 212-475-7455. Sr. Flotilda Lape, I.C.M., Prov.
Total in Community: 15.
Missionaries Minister in Education; Catechetical; Pastoral and Social Ministry; Health Care; Ecology; Leprosaria; International Justice and the Promotion of Human Dignity.
Represented in the Archdioceses of Los Angeles, Newark and New York and in the Diocese of Brownsville. Also in Belgium, Brazil, Burundi, Cameroon, Guatemala, Hong Kong, India, Italy, Philippines, Taiwan, Mongolia, Caribbean Islands, Congo and South Africa.

[2760] (S.M.I.C.)—MISSIONARY SISTERS OF THE IMMACULATE CONCEPTION OF THE MOTHER OF GOD (P)

Founded in Brazil in 1910. First foundation in the United States in 1922.

Generalate: 47 Garden Ave., West Paterson, NJ 07424. Tel: 973-279-1484. Sr. Veronica Lee, S.M.I.C., Coord. Gen.

U.S. Province (1960): *Provincialate of the Immaculate Conception,* 779 Broadway, Paterson, NJ 07514. Tel: 973-279-3790. Sr. Kathryn Conti, S.M.I.C., Prov. Coord.
Professed Sisters: 38.
Legal Titles: Missionary Sisters of the Immaculate Conception, Inc.; Province of the Immaculate Conception, Inc.
Sisters serve and staff: Religious Education; Pastoral Ministries; Health and Social Work.
Represented in the Archdioceses of Galveston-Houston, Newark, Santa Fe and Washington and in the Dioceses of Austin, Gallup, Paterson, Portland (In Maine) and San Bernardino.

[2770] (M.J.M.J.)—MISSIONARY SISTERS OF JESUS, MARY AND JOSEPH (P)

Founded in Spain in 1942. First foundation in the United States in 1956. Mother Maria Dolores de la Cruz Domingo, Foundress.

Motherhouse: Plaza Inmaculada Concepcion 1, Madrid, Spain, 28019. Sr. Alicia Elizalde, M.J.M.J., Supr. Gen.

Delegation Headquarters: *Mount Thabor Convent,* 12940 Leopard St., Corpus Christi, TX 78410. Tel: 361-241-1955; Fax: 361-241-2271. Sr. Maria Margarita Bitoni, M.J.M.J., Delegation Supr.; Sr. Milagros Tormo, M.J.M.J., Local Supr.
Sisters: 25.
Properties owned and/or sponsored: St. Joseph of the Valley Preschool, El Paso, TX; The Ark Assessment Center & Emergency Shelter for Youth.
Represented in the Archdiocese of San Antonio and in the Dioceses of Corpus Christi and El Paso. Also in Mexico.

[2780] (M.SS.S.)—MISSIONARY SISTERS OF THE MOST BLESSED SACRAMENT (P)

General Motherhouse: Calle Navarro Amandi, 11, Madrid, Spain, 28033. Mother Leonor Gutierreg, Mother Gen.

U.S. Foundation: *Convent of Mary Immaculate,* 1111 Wordin Ave., Bridgeport, CT 06605. Sr. Presentacios Zabala, Prov.

[2790] (M.S.B.T.)—MISSIONARY SERVANTS OF THE MOST BLESSED TRINITY (P)

Founded in the United States in 1912.

Motherhouse-Generalate-Novitiate and Candidacy: 3501 Solly Ave., Philadelphia, PA 19136. Tel: 215-335-7550. Sr. Joan Marie Keller, M.S.B.T., Gen. Custodian.
Total in Community: 151.
Properties owned and sponsored: Blessed Trinity Mother Missionary Cenacle, Philadelphia, PA; Blessed Trinity Shrine Retreat Cenacle, Holy Trinity, AL; Trinita Ecumenical Retreat Center, New Hartford, CT; Blessed Trinity Mother Missionary Cenacle, Philadelphia, PA.
Represented in the Archdioceses of Baltimore, Boston, Hartford, Newark, Mobile, New York and Philadelphia and in the Dioceses of Birmingham, Brooklyn, Charlotte, Fall River, Gallup, Owensboro, Paterson, Rockville Centre, Tuscon and Wilmington. Also in Puerto Rico, Mexico, and Jamaica.

[2800] (M.S.C.)—MISSIONARY SISTERS OF THE MOST SACRED HEART OF JESUS (OF HILTRUP) (P)

Founded in Germany in 1899. First foundation in the United States in 1908.

Generalate: Via Martiri di Via Fani, Sutri (Viterbo), Italy Sr. Mechthild Schnieder, M.S.C.

American Province-Motherhouse (1908): *Sacred Heart Villa,* 51 Seminary Ave., Reading, PA 19605. Tel: 610-929-5751. Sr. Marie Raymond Gazo, M.S.C., Coord.
Total number in U.S. Province: 69.
Legal Title: *Missionary Sisters of the Most Sacred Heart of Jesus, Inc.*
Ministry in Education; Health Care; Home Health Care; Parish Ministry; Pastoral Ministry to people on the move; Prison Ministry; Counseling; Social Ministry; Spiritual Ministry.
Properties owned or sponsored: MSC Province Center; Chevalier House, Bethany Convent, Sacred Heart Villa, Reading, PA.
Represented in the Archdioceses of Atlanta, Galveston-Houston and Philadelphia and in the Dioceses of Allentown, Harrisburg, San Bernardino, Syracuse and Venice. Also in Mexico.

MSC Province Center: 2811 Moyers Ln., Reading, PA 19605. Tel: 610-929-5944. Sr. Lorraine Molchanow, M.S.C., Prov.

[2810] (M.S.M.G.)—MISSIONARY SISTERS OF MOTHER OF GOD (D)

(Byzantine Ukrainian Rite-Stamford)

Motherhouse: 711 N. Franklin St., Philadelphia, PA 19123. Tel: 215-627-7808.

U.S. Province: 111 W. North St., Stamford, CT 06902. Tel: 203-323-1237. Sr. Nadia Baranik, M.S.M.G., Treas.
Professed Sisters: 11.
Ministry in the field of Education.
Represented in the Ukrainian Archdiocese of Philadelphia and in the Ukrainian Diocese of Stamford.

[2820] (M.S.O.L.A.)—MISSIONARY SISTERS OF OUR LADY OF AFRICA (P)

(Sisters of Africa)

Founded in Algiers, N. Africa in 1869. First foundation in the United States in 1929.

General Motherhouse: Rome, Italy Sr. Maria del Pilar Benavente Serrano, Supr. Gen.
Universal total in Congregation: 919.

American Headquarters: 47 West Spring St., Winooski, VT 05404. Tel: 802-655-4003. Sr. Marie Heintz, Contact Person.
Total number in U.S: 15.
Represented in the Dioceses of Burlington and Springfield (MA).

[2830] (M.O.M.)—MISSIONARY SISTERS OF OUR LADY OF MERCY (D)

Founded in Piaui, Brazil in 1938. First foundation in the United States at Lackawanna, New York in 1955.

General Motherhouse: Salvador, Bahia, Brazil Mother Raquel de Novais Borges, Supr. Gen.

U.S. Headquarters: *Rainbow K,* 388 Franklin St., Buffalo, NY 14202. Tel: 716-854-5198. Sr. Mary Neves, M.O.M., Supr.
Total in Community: 2.
Represented in the Diocese of Buffalo.

[2840] (M.C.)—POOR CLARE MISSIONARY SISTERS (P)

Founded in Mexico by Mother Maria Ines Teresa Arias.

General Motherhouse: Via Cardinale Garampi 17, Pineta Sachetti, Rome, Italy Mother Julia Meijueiro Morosini, Gen. Supr.

U.S. Foundation: *Regional House and Novitiate,* 1019 N. Newhope, Santa Ana, CA 92703.
Total in Community: 42.
Ministry in Day Nurseries, Schools and Retreat House.
Represented in the Archdiocese of Los Angeles and in the Dioceses of Orange in California and Springfield-Cape Girardeau.

[2850] (C.P.S.)—MISSIONARY SISTERS OF THE PRECIOUS BLOOD (P)

Founded in South Africa on Sept. 8, 1885. First founded in the United States at Princeton, New Jersey on August 15, 1925.

Generalate: *Casa Generalizia,* Suore Missionarie del Preziosissimo Sangue Mariannhill, Via San Giovanni Eudes 93, Rome, Italy, I-00163.
Universal total in Congregation: 889.

North American Province: 1094 Welsh Rd., P.O. Box 97, Reading, PA 19607-0097. Tel: 610-777-1624. Sr. Mary William Verhoeveu, C.P.S., Prov.
Total number in Province: 60.
Represented in the Dioceses of Allentown, Brooklyn and Lexington. Also in Canada.

[2860] (M.S.C.)—MISSIONARY SISTERS OF THE SACRED HEART OF JESUS (P)

(Cabrini Sisters)

Founded in Italy in 1880, by Saint Frances Xavier Cabrini. First foundation in the United States in 1889.

Motherhouse: Viale Cortina D'Ampezzo 269, Rome, Italy, 00135. Sr. Patricia Spillane, M.S.C., Supr. Gen.

Provincial Office: 222 E. 19th St., 5B, New York, NY 10003. Sr. Pietrina Raccuglia, Prov. Supr.
Professed Sisters: 337; Total in Congregation : 362.
Ministry in the field of Education; Hospitals; Nursing Homes; Child Care; Retreat and Shrine Ministries; Parish Ministry.
Represented in the Archdioceses of Chicago, Denver, New Orleans, New York, Philadelphia and Seattle. Also in Argentina, Australia, Brazil, Central America, England, Ethiopia, France, Italy, Mexico, Paraguay, Philippines, Portugal, Siberia, Spain, Switzerland and Swaziland.

[2865] (M.S.C.GPE.)—MISSIONARIES OF THE SACRED HEART OF JESUS AND OUR LADY OF GUADALUPE (P)

National Address: 1212 E. Euclid Ave., Arlington Heights, IL 60004. Tel: 847-255-5616. Sr. Eva Perez, Local Supr.
Ministry in Schools, Nursing Homes, Seminaries and Foreign Missions.
Represented in the Archdioceses of Boston, Chicago, San Francisco and Washington and in the Diocese of Rockford.

[2880] (S.S.C.)—MISSIONARY SISTERS OF ST. COLUMBAN (P)

(Columban Sisters)

Founded in Ireland in 1922. First foundation in the United States in 1930.

General Motherhouse: Wicklow, Ireland Sr. Anne Ryan, S.S.C., Congregational Leader.

U.S. Region: 73 Mapleton St., Brighton, MA 02135-2821. Tel: 617-782-5683; Fax: 617-789-3569. Sr. Margaret Holleran, S.C.C., U.S. Area Coord.
Professed Sisters: 22.
Represented in the Archdioceses of Boston and Los Angeles and in the Diocese of Buffalo.

[2890] (M.S.S.A.)—MISSIONARY SERVANTS OF ST. ANTHONY (D)

Founded in the United States in 1929.

General Motherhouse: 100 Peter Baque Rd., San Antonio, TX 78209-1805. Tel: 210-824-4553. Sr. Mary Ann Domagalski, M.S.S.A., Supr.
Total in Community: 3.
Represented in the Archdiocese of San Antonio.

[2900] (M.S.C.S.)—MISSIONARY SISTERS OF ST. CHARLES BORROMEO (P)

(Scalabrinians)

Founded in Italy in 1895. First in the United States in 1941.

Motherhouse: Via Monte del Gallo 68, Rome, Italy, 00165. Sr. Alda Monica Malvessi, M.S.C.S., Gen. Supr.
Total in Congregation : 745.

North American Provincial House & Bishop Scalabrini Community: 1414 N. 37th Ave., Melrose Park, IL 60160. Tel: 708-343-2162; Fax: 708-343-6452. Sr. Marciana Zambiasi, M.S.C.S., Prov. Supr.
Total in Community: 64.
Ministry in the fields of Education; Pastoral Care of the Sick; Catechesis; Social Service; Pastoral Care of Migrants and Refugees.
Represented in the Archdioceses of Boston, Chicago, New York and Washington and in the Diocese of Springfield in Massachusetts. Also in Canada, Mexico, the Philippines, India and Indonesia.

[2920] (M.D.)—MOTHERS OF THE HELPLESS (D)

Founded in Malaga, Spain in 1881. Founded in the United States in 1916.

General Motherhouse: Avda. San Jose de la Montana No. 15, Valencia, Spain, 46008. Mother Maria Angeles Villar, Supr. Gen.

U.S. Address: *Sacred Heart Residence*, 432 W. 20th St., New York, NY 10011. Mother Esperanza Fernandez, Supr.
Professed Sisters in U.S: 6.
Properties owned and sponsored: Sacred Heart Residence; San Jose Day Nursery, New York, NY.
Represented in the Archdiocese of New York.

[2930] (I.H.M.)—THE CALIFORNIA INSTITUTE OF THE SISTERS OF THE MOST HOLY AND IMMACULATE HEART OF THE BLESSED VIRGIN MARY (P)

Founded in Spain in 1848. First foundation in the United States in 1871.

Generalate, Novitiate and Retreat House: 3431 Waverly Dr., Los Angeles, CA 90027. Tel: 323-664-3357 Ext. 114. Sr. Catherine Rose, I.H.M., Supr. & Treas.
Professed Sisters: 9.
Properties staffed: Grammar Schools.
Represented in the Archdiocese of Los Angeles.

[2940] (M.H.S.)—SISTERS OF THE MOST HOLY SACRAMENT (P)

Founded in France in 1851. First foundation in the United States in 1872. Pontifical Approbation 1935.

Generalate: *Sisters of the Most Holy Sacrament*, 313 Corona Dr., Lafayette, LA 70503-4757. Tel: 337-981-8475. Sr. Judine Theriot, M.H.S., Major Supr.
Total in Community: 28.
Legal Titles: St. Augustine Trust Fund, Lafayette, LA; Bethany Health Care Center, Lafayette, LA.
Ministry in the field of Education; Homes for the Aged; Pastoral Care.
Represented in the Archdiocese of New Orleans and in the Dioceses of Baton Rouge and Lafayette (LA).

[2950] (N.D.S.)—CONGREGATION OF NOTRE DAME DE SION (P)

Founded in France in 1850. First foundation in the United States in 1892.

Generalate: Rome, Italy Sr. Maureen Cusick, Supr. Gen.
Universal total in Congregation: 535.

Notre Dame de Sion: 3823 Locust St., Kansas City, MO 64109. Tel: 816-531-1374.
Represented in the Archdiocese of Chicago and in the Dioceses of Brooklyn and Kansas City-St. Joseph.

[2960] (N.D.)—NOTRE DAME SISTERS (P)

Founded in Czechoslovakia, Europe in 1853. First foundation in the United States in 1910.

General Motherhouse: Hradec Kralove, Czech Republic Mother Miriam Baumrukova, N.D., Supr. Gen.

U.S. Provincial Motherhouse: *Notre Dame Convent*, 3501 State St., Omaha, NE 68112-1709. Tel: 402-455-2994; Fax: 402-455-3974. Sr. Celeste Wobeter, N.D., Prov.
Total in Community: 50.
Sisters serve and staff: all levels of academic education; Hispanic Ministry; Pastoral Care; Housing for low income elderly; Social Work; Religious Education; Youth Ministry; Chemical Dependency Counseling; Health Care; TEC; Adult Education; Community Administration and Services.
Represented in the Archdioceses of Denver, Dubuque and Omaha and in the Dioceses of Davenport, Kansas City-St. Joseph, Lincoln, and Pueblo.

[2970] (S.S.N.D.)—SCHOOL SISTERS OF NOTRE DAME (P)

Founded in Germany in 1833. First foundation in the United States in 1847.

General Motherhouse: Rome, Italy Sr. Mary V. Maher, Supr. Gen.

Milwaukee Province (1850); Milwaukee (1983); Mequon (1959): *Milwaukee Province, Provincial Offices*, 13105 Watertown Plank Rd., Elm Grove, WI 53122-2291. Tel: 262-782-9850; Fax: 262-782-5725. Sr. Debra Marie Sciano, S.S.N.D., Prov. Leader.
Total in Community: 387.
Properties owned and/or sponsored: Mount Mary College, Milwaukee, WI; Notre Dame of Elm Grove, Elm Grove, WI; Our Lady of Mt. Carmel Convent, Mt. Calvary, WI.
Legal Titles: School Sisters of Notre Dame Milwaukee Province, Inc.; School Sisters of Notre Dame at Milwaukee, Wisconsin, Inc. Charitable Trust.
Various ministries to Women, Youth, the Poor, Sick and Elderly; all levels of Academic Education; D.R.E.'s; Pastoral Associates.
Represented in the Archdioceses of Chicago, Detroit, Milwaukee and Seattle and in the Dioceses of Austin, El Paso, Fort Wayne-South Bend, Gary, Grand Rapids, Green Bay, La Crosse, Madison, Marquette, Memphis, Palm Beach, Phoenix, Steubenville, Trenton and Wheeling-Charleston. Also in Europe and Guam.

Atlantic-Midwest Province: *School Sisters of Notre Dame*, 6401 N. Charles St., Baltimore, MD 21212-1099. Tel: 410-377-7774; Fax: 410-377-5363. Sr. Kathleen Cornell, S.S.N.D., Prov. Leader.
Total in Community: 611.
Properties Owned and Legal Titles: School Sisters of Notre Dame in the City of Baltimore; Maria Health Care Center, Inc.; Villa Assumpta-Motherhouse of Baltimore Province.
Ministries to the Needy and Elderly; Teaching and Administering in the field of Academic Education at all levels; D.R.E.'s and Pastoral Associates.
Represented in the Archdioceses of Baltimore, Boston, Chicago, Hartford, Miami, Milwaukee, Newark, New York, Philadelphia and Washington and in the Dioceses of Albany, Arlington, Bridgeport, Brooklyn, Charleston, Charlotte, Gary, Grand Rapids, Jackson, Joliet, Laredo, Lexington, Manchester, Memphis, Palm Beach, Paterson, Peoria, Phoenix, Pittsburgh, Providence, Richmond, Rochester, Rockford, Rockville Centre, St. Petersburg, Trenton, Tulsa, Venice, Wheeling-Charleston and Wilmington. Also in Honduras, Nepal, Nigeria, Puerto Rico, Rome, Sudan & Switzerland.
Sponsored Corporate Ministries: College of Notre Dame of Maryland; Notre Dame Preparatory School; Institute of Notre Dame, Baltimore, MD; Academy of the Holy Angels, Demarest, NJ; The Caroline Friess Center, Inc.' Academy of Our Lady, Chicago, Inc.; Caroline House, Inc.; School Sisters of Notre Dame Educational Center, Inc.; SisterHouse; Corazon A Corazon, NFP; Notre Dame Learning Center, Inc.
Co-Sponsored Ministries: Sisters Academy of Baltimore, Inc.; Mother Seton Academy, Inc.; Marian House, Incorporated.

St. Louis Province (1895): *School Sisters of Notre Dame*, 320 E. Ripa Ave., St. Louis, MO 63125. Tel: 314-544-0455; Fax: 314-544-6754. Sr. Joan Markus, S.S.N.D., Prov. Supr.
Total in Community: 481.
Legal Title: *The School Sisters of Notre Dame of St. Louis.*
Represented in the Archdioceses of Baltimore, Denver, Detroit, Indianapolis, Los Angeles, Milwaukee, New Orleans, Omaha, St. Louis and San Antonio and in the Dioceses of Belleville, Bismarck, Brownsville, Dallas, Davenport, Evansville, Fresno, Jackson, Jefferson City, Lafayette in Louisiana, Monterey, Oakland, Orange, Peoria, Phoenix, Providence, Rapid City, Rockford, San Diego, Springfield-Cape Girardeau, Springfield in Illinois, Tucson and Victoria. Also in Japan and Nepal.

Mankato Province (1912): *School Sisters of Notre Dame*, 170 Good Counsel Dr., Mankato, MN 56001-3138. Tel: 507-389-4200; Fax: 507-389-4125. Sr. Marjorie Klein, S.S.N.D., Prov. Leader; Sr. Mary Kay Ash, Community Archivist.
Total in Community: 318.
Legal Titles: School Sisters of Notre Dame at Mankato, Minnesota, Inc.; School Sisters of Notre Dame at Mankato, Minnesota, Inc. - Charitable Trust; School Sisters of Notre Dame Cooperative Investment Fund.
Represented in the Archdioceses of Chicago, Dubuque, New Orleans, Seattle, St. Louis, St. Paul-Minneapolis, San Francisco and Washington and in the Dioceses of Bismarck, Charlotte, Dallas, New Ulm, Phoenix, Richmond, San Jose, Superior, St. Cloud, and Winona. Also in Nigeria, Ghana, Guatemala, Kenya and Rome, Italy.

Northeast Office (1957): *School Sisters of Notre Dame*, 345 Belden Hill Rd., Wilton, CT 06897. Tel: 203-762-1220; Fax: 203-762-9434. Sr. Kathleen Cornell, S.S.N.D., Prov. Leader.
Total in Community: 279.
Legal Holdings and Titles: The Northeastern Province of the School Sisters of Notre Dame in the State of Connecticut; Motherhouse and Lourdes Health Care Center, Wilton, CT; Academy of the Holy Angels, Demarest, NJ.
Represented in the Archdioceses of Baltimore, Boston, Chicago, Hartford, Milwaukee, Newark, New York and Washington and in the Dioceses of Albany, Bridgeport, Brooklyn, Brownsville, Grand Rapids, Manchester, Norwich, Palm Beach, Paterson, Phoenix, Providence, Rochester, Rockville Centre, St. Petersburg and Springfield. Also in Chile, Switzerland, Ghana, Guatemala, Paraguay, Peru and Puerto Rico.

Dallas Province (1961): *Notre Dame of Dallas - School Sisters of Notre Dame*, P.O. Box 227275, Dallas, TX 75222. Tel: 214-330-9152; Fax: 214-330-9197. Sr. Addie Lorraine Walker, S.S.N.D., Prov.
Total in Community: 127.
Legal Title: *School Sisters of Notre Dame of Dallas Charitable Trust.*
Represented in the Archdioceses of Chicago, Galveston-Houston, New Orleans, San Antonio and St. Louis and in the Dioceses of Alexandria, Amarillo, Austin, Baton Rouge, Brownsville, Dallas, Davenport, El Paso, Fort Worth, Houma-Thibodaux, Jackson, Lafayette (LA), Little Rock.

Chicago Office: *School Sisters of Notre Dame*, 4425 N. Ozanam Ave., Norridge, IL 60706-4507. Tel: 708-583-2402. Sr. Kathleen Cornell, S.S.N.D., Prov. Leader.
Total in Community: 107; Residences: 2.
Properties owned and/or sponsored: Academy of Our Lady, Chicago, IL.
Ministry in the field of Academic, Special and Religious Education; Day Care Centers; Foreign Mission work; Nurses; Pastoral Work; Apostolate of the Aging; Vicar for Women Religious.
Represented in the Archdioceses of Baltimore, Chicago, Los Angeles, Miami, Milwaukee and Washington and in the Dioceses of Joliet, Peoria and Rockford. Also in Nepal.

[2980] (C.N.D.)—SISTERS OF THE CONGREGATION DE NOTRE DAME (P)

Founded in Canada in 1653. First Foundation in the United States in 1860. American Novitiate established at Chicago, Illinois.

Blessed Sacrament Province: 30 Highfield Rd., Wilton, CT 06897.

Generalate and Motherhouse: 2330 Sherbrooke St., W, Montreal, Canada, H3H 1G8. Sr. Josephine Badali, C.N.D., Congregational Leader.

U.S. Province (1946): *Blessed Sacrament Province*, 30 Highfield Rd., Wilton, CT 06897. Tel: 203-762-4300; Fax: 203-762-4319. Sr. Patricia McCarthy, C.N.D., Prov. Leader.
Total number in the U.S. Province: 144.
Represented in the Archdioceses of Chicago, Hartford, Newark, New York and Oklahoma City and in the Dioceses of Albany, Bridgeport, Brooklyn, Charlotte, Joliet, Providence, Rapid City, Richmond, Scranton.

[2990] (S.N.D.)—SISTERS OF NOTRE DAME (P)

Founded in Germany in 1850. First foundation in the United States in 1874.

Generalate: Rome, Italy Sr. Mary Sujita Kallupurakkathu, S.N.D., Supr. Gen.
Universal total in Congregation: 2300.

Cleveland Province (1874): *Notre Dame Educational Center - Provincial Center, Juniorate, & Novitiate*, 13000 Auburn Rd., Chardon, OH 44024-9331. Tel: 440-286-7101; Fax: 440-286-3377. Sr. Cecilia Liberatore, S.N.D., Prov. Supr.; Sr. M. Patricia Teckman, Prov. Sec.
Total in Community: 348.
Legal Titles: The Corporation of the Sisters of Notre Dame of Chardon, Ohio; The Sisters of Notre Dame Charitable Trust.
Ministry in the field of Academic Education at all levels; Special Education for Exceptional Children; Foreign Mission Work; Religious Education; Pastoral Care; Hospital Chaplaincy; Counseling Ministries; Community Service; Diocesan and National Offices; Pastoral Associate/Minister and D.R.E.; Parish Ministry; Retreat Direction; Spiritual Direction; Hispanic & Refugee Outreach; Ministry to the Sick and Elderly in Hospitals and Nursing Homes; Youth Ministry; Campus Ministry; Writing; Liturgy and Music; Public Defender for Juveniles; Hospice Work; Respite Home for Children; Art Therapy; Bereavement Ministry; Social Service Literacy.
Properties owned and sponsored: Notre Dame Cathedral Latin School, Chardon, OH; Notre Dame Elementary School, Chardon, OH; Notre Dame Pre School, Chardon, OH; Regina High School, Cleveland, OH; Julie Billiart School, Lyndhurst, OH.
Represented in the Archdioceses of Los Angeles, Miami and Washington and in the Dioceses of Arlington, Cleveland, Orlando, Raleigh, St. Petersburg, St. Augustine, Toledo, Venice and Youngstown. Also in Nicaragua, Philippines, Rome and Tanzania.

Covington Province (1924): *Provincial House and Novitiate of the Sisters of Notre Dame*, 1601 Dixie Hwy., (St. Joseph Heights), Covington, KY 41011. Tel: 859-291-2040; Fax: 859-291-1774. Sr. Marla Monahan, S.N.D., Prov.
Total in Community: 136.
Legal Title: *Sisters of Notre Dame of Covington, KY, Inc.*
Ministry in the field of Education; Hospital and Health Care Services; Child Care.
Properties sponsored and owned: Saint Claire Regional Medical Center, Morehead, KY; St. Charles Care Center and Village, Covington, KY; Notre Academy, Covington, KY; Julie Learning Center, Park Hills, KY.
Represented in the Archdiocese of Cincinnati, Covington and Lexington. Also in Hoima, Uganda and East Africa.

Province of Toledo (1924): *Notre Dame Provincial Center*, 3837 Secor Rd., Toledo, OH 43623. Tel: 419-474-5485. Sr. Mary Delores Gatliff, S.N.D., Prov. Supr.
Total in Community: 219.
Ministry in the field of Academic Education; Special Education for Exceptional Children; Foreign Mission Work; Religious Education, Pastoral Ministry, Vocational School, Health Care Ministry, Counseling Ministry, Community Service, Diocesan Offices, Spiritual Life, Hispanic and Migrant, Campus Ministries, Child Care, Care for Handicapped.
Properties owned and sponsored: Notre Dame Academy; Double ARC; Maria Early Learning Center; Mary Immaculate School; Lial Catholic School; Convent & Renewal Center, Whitehouse, OH; Holy Trinity Mission, Papua, New Guinea.
Represented in the Archdioceses of Chicago, Detroit, Indianapolis, New Orleans and Santa Fe and in the Dioceses of Brooklyn, Charleston, Cleveland, Covington, Fort Wayne-South Bend, Orange, Orlando, St. Augustine and Toledo.

Province of Los Angeles (1961): *Notre Dame Provincialate*, 1776 Hendrix Ave., Thousand Oaks, CA 91360. Tel: 805-496-3243; Fax: 805-379-3616. Sr. Mary Kristin Battles, S.N.D., Prov. Supr.
Total number in Province: 67.
Legal Titles: Corporation of the Sisters of Notre Dame of Los Angeles; Notre Dame Academy High School; Notre Dame Academy Elementary School, Los Angeles, CA; Notre Dame Center; La Reina High School, Thousand Oaks, CA; Providence House, Long Beach, CA; Notre Dame Learning Center.

Ministry in the field of Education and Parish and Social Ministry; Catechetics; Foreign Mission Work.
Represented in the Archdiocese of Los Angeles.

[3000] (S.N.D.DEN.)—SISTERS OF NOTRE DAME DE NAMUR (P)

Founded in France in 1804. First foundation in the United States in 1840.

Generalate: *Suore di Nostra Signora di Namur*, Via Raffaello Sardiello 20, Rome, Italy, 00165. Tel: 011-39-06-6641-8704. Sr. Teresita Weind, S.N.D.deN., Gen. Moderator.

U.S. Notre Dame Congregational Center: *Congregational Mission Office*, 30 Jeffreys Neck Rd., Ipswich, MA 01938. Tel: 978-356-2159; Fax: 978-356-2118. Sr. Lorraine Connell, S.N.D.deN., Treas.

Boston Province (1973): *Sisters of Notre Dame de Namur*, 351 Broadway, Everett, MA 02149. Tel: 617-387-2500; Fax: 617-387-1303. Prov. Team: Sr. Rosemary Crowley, S.N.D.deN.; Sr. Evelyn McKenna, S.N.D.deN.; Sr. Patricia McSharry, S.N.D.
Total in Community: 197.
Legal Title: *The Boston Province of the Sisters of Notre Dame de Namur, Inc.*
Ministry in the field of Academic Education at all levels; Adult Education Programs; Parish Ministries; Religious Education Programs; and Social Services.
Properties owned and sponsored: Notre Dame Academy, Worcester, MA, Notre Dame Children's Class, Wenham, MA; Notre Dame Education Center, South Boston, MA; St. Patrick School and Education Center, Lowell, MA.
Represented in the Archdioceses of Boston, Hartford, Louisville and Washington and in the Dioceses of Albany, Gallup, Manchester, Orlando, Springfield in Massachusetts and Worcester.

Ipswich Province (1973): *Sisters of Notre Dame de Namur Provincialate*, 30 Jeffrey's Neck Rd., Ipswich, MA 01938. Tel: 978-356-4381; Fax: 978-356-9759. Prov. Admin. Team: Sr. Mary Boretti, S.N.D.deN.; Sr. Mary M. Farren, S.N.D.deN.; Sr. Andrea Walsh, S.N.D.deN.
Total in Community: 167.
Legal Titles: Notre Dame Training School, Inc.; The Sisters of Notre Dame de Namur, Ipswich, MA.
Ministry in all fields of Education; Pastoral Ministry; Health, Social and Community Services; Retreat Work.
Properties owned and sponsored: Academy of Notre Dame, Tyngsboro, MA; Notre Dame Academy, Hingham, MA; Notre Dame Long Term Health Care Facility, Worcester, MA; Notre Dame Education Center, Lawrence, MA; Cuvilly Arts and Earth Center, Ipswich, MA; Notre Dame du Lac, Worcester, MA; St. Julie Billiart Residential Care Center, Ipswich, MA.
Represented in the Archdiocese of Boston and in the Dioceses of Manchester and Worcester.

Connecticut Province (1959): *The Connecticut Province of the Sisters of Notre Dame de Namur, Inc.*, Sisters of Notre Dame de Namur Province Center, 468 Poquonock Ave., Windsor, CT 06095-2473. Tel: 860-688-1832. Prov. Admin. Team: Sr. Mary Rose Crowley, S.N.D.deN.; Sr. Maureen O'Brien, S.N.D.deN.
Total in Community: 113.
Sisters serve and staff: Colleges, High Schools, Grammar Schools; Sisters Engaged in Specialized Educational Programs: Pastoral Ministry and Religious Education, Social Health and Community Services, Diocesan Offices, Spiritual Direction and Adult Basic Education.
Represented in the Archdioceses of Boston, Hartford and Washington D.C. and in the Dioceses of Bridgeport, Burlington, Norwich, Providence, Scranton, St. Augustine, Springfield (MA) and Worcester.

Baltimore Province (1934): *Sisters of Notre Dame de Namur, Maryland Province Center*, 1531 Greenspring Valley Rd., Stevenson, MD 21153. Tel: 410-486-5599.
Total in Community: 96.
Properties owned and sponsored: Maryland Province Center, Stevenson, MD; Villa Julie Residence, Stevenson, MD; Maryvale Preparatory School, Brooklandville, MD; Notre Dame Academy, Villanova, PA; Trinity School, Ellicot City, MD; Development Program, Stevenson, MD; Sisters Academy of Baltimore, Inc.
Represented in the Archdioceses of Baltimore, Philadelphia and Washington, D.C. and in the Dioceses of Atlanta, Brooklyn, Harrisburg, Portland (ME), Rockville Centre and Wilmington.
Leadership Team: Sr. Marian Schaechtel, S.N.D.deN., Prov. Moderator; Sr. Rosemary Donohue, S.N.D.deN.; Sr. Florence Maier, S.N.D.deN.; Sr. Bernadette Glodek, S.N.D.deN.

Chesapeake Province (1990): *Sisters of Notre Dame de Namur Provincial Offices*, 305 Cable St., Baltimore, MD 21210-2511. Tel: 410-243-1993; Fax: 410-243-2279. Administrative Team: Sr. Mary Donohue, S.N.D-.deN.; Sr. Edithann Kane, S.N.D.deN.
Total in Community: 67.
Represented in the Archdioceses of Baltimore, Miami, New York, Philadelphia and Washington and in the Dioceses of Arlington, Raleigh, and Wheeling-Charleston. Also in Brazil, Kenya, Mexico, and Dem. Republic of Congo.

Ohio Province (1840): *Sisters of Notre Dame de Namur Provincial House*, 701 E. Columbia Ave., Cincinnati, OH 45215. Tel: 513-761-7636. Sr. Marilyn Kerber, S.N.D.deN., Canonical Representative.
Total in Community: 175.
Legal Titles: St. Mary's Educational Institute at Cincinnati; Sisters of Notre Dame de Namur - Ohio Province; Sisters of Notre Dame de Namur, Ohio Province, Charitable Trust.
Ministry in the field of Education at all levels; Pastoral Ministry; Administration and Services; Social Services; Communication; Health Care; Community Services.
Represented in the Archdioceses of Boston, Chicago, Cincinnati and Louisville and in the Dioceses of Austin, Buffalo, Columbus, Covington, Joliet, Phoenix, and Saginaw. Also in Brazil, Kenya, Nicaragua, Nigeria, Rome and Peru.

California Province (1851): *Province Center - Sisters of Notre Dame de Namur*, 1520 Ralston Ave., Belmont, CA 94002. Provincial Team: Sr. Louise O'Reilly, S.N.D.deN.; Sr. Dolores Quigg, S.N.D.deN.; Sr. Maureen Hilliard, S.N.D.deN.
Total in Community: 130.
Legal Title: *Sisters of Notre Dame de Namur California Province.*
Ministries in the field of Academic Education at all levels; Adult Education Programs; Parish Ministries; Religious Education Programs; Social Services; Diocesan Administration; and Health.
Represented in the Archdioceses of Los Angeles, Portland in Oregon, San Francisco and Seattle and in the Dioceses of Burlington, Des Moines, Monterey, Oakland, Sacramento, San Jose and Stockton.
Properties owned or sponsored: Notre Dame de Namur University, Belmont, CA; Moreland Notre Dame Elementary, Watsonville, CA; Notre Dame Elementary, Belmont, CA; Notre Dame High School, Belmont, CA; Notre Dame High School, San Jose, CA; Cristo Rey, Sacramento, CA. (Co-sponsored with Sisters of Mercy and Jesuits).

Base Communities Province (1989): *Sisters of Notre Dame de Namur Base Communities Province Office:*, 125 Michigan Ave., N.E., Washington, DC 20017-1004. Tel: 202-884-9750. Communications Network Sr. Loreta Jordan, S.N.D.deN.; Sr. Joan Ferraro, S.N.D.deN.; Sr. Marcella Missar, S.N.D.deN.
Total in Province: 44.
Legal Title: *Sisters of Notre Dame de Namur Base Communities, Inc.*
Ministry in Formal Education; Health Care; Social Services/Community Development; Pastoral Ministry.
Represented in the Archdioceses of Baltimore, Boston, Hartford, Philadelphia and Washington and in the Dioceses of Brooklyn, Charleston, Fort Wayne-South Bend, Orlando, Richmond, Rockville Centre and Wilmington.

[3010] (O.S.B.S.)—OBLATE SISTERS OF THE BLESSED SACRAMENT (D)

Founded in 1935 by Rev. Sylvester Eisenman, O.S.B.

Motherhouse: *St. Sylvester's Convent*, 103 Church Dr., P.O. Box 217, Marty, SD 57361. Tel: 605-384-3305. Sr. Inez Jetty, O.S.B.S., Supr.

Kateri Convent: 821 Farlow Ave., Rapid City, SD 57701. Tel: 605-343-6261. Sr. Miriam Shindelar, O.S.B.S., Treas.
Total in Community: 6.
Represented in the Dioceses of Rapid City and Sioux Falls.

[3020] (O.B.T.)—SISTERS OBLATES TO THE BLESSED TRINITY (D)

Founded in Italy in 1923. First foundation in the United States in 1987.

U.S. Generalate & Novitiate: *St. Aloysius Gonzaga Novitiate*, 306 Beekman Rd., P.O. Box 98, Hopewell Junction, NY 12533. Tel: 845-226-5671; Fax: 845-226-5671; Email: Jstab35097@aol.com. Mother Gloria Castro, Supr. Gen.
Total in Community: 40.
Represented in the Archdioceses of New York and San Juan and in the Dioceses of Madison and Ponce. Also in Italy and San Salvador.

[3035] (O.M.O.)—OBLATES OF THE MOTHER OF ORPHANS (P)

Founded in Italy on September 8, 1945.

General Motherhouse: via Amundsen 10, Milano, Italy Sr. Lucilla Passoni, Gen. Supr.
Universal total in Congregation: 200.

U.S. Address: 20 E. 72nd St., New York, NY 10021. Sr. Maria Isabel Reina, O.M.O., Supr.
Total in Community: 3.
Represented in the Archdiocese of New York. Also in Cameroon, Colombia, El Salvador, Guatemala and Italy.

[3040] (O.S.P.)—OBLATE SISTERS OF PROVIDENCE (P)

Founded in the United States in 1829.

General Motherhouse: *Our Lady of Mount Providence Convent*, 701 Gun Rd., Baltimore, MD 21227. Tel: 410-242-8500. Sr. Mary Annette Beecham, O.S.P., Supr. Gen.; Sr. Mary Ricardo Maddox, O.S.P., Asst. Supr. Gen.; Sr. Mary Crescentia Proctor, O.S.P., Sec. Gen.; Sr. Mary Sharon Young, O.S.P., Treas.
Professed Sisters: 88.
Legal Title: *The Oblate Sisters of Providence of the City of Baltimore.*
Sisters serve as Pastoral Ministry-Associates; in the field of Education; Reading Centers; Day Care Centers; Teaching; Counseling; Hispanic & Migrant ministry.
Represented in the Archdioceses of Baltimore and Miami and in the Diocese of Buffalo. Also in Costa Rica.

[3050] (O.S.H.J.)—OBLATE SISTERS OF THE SACRED HEART OF JESUS (P)

Founded in 1894. First foundation in the United States in 1949.

General Motherhouse: Rome, Italy

American Headquarters: *Villa Maria Teresa*, 50 Warner Rd., Hubbard, OH 44425. Tel: 330-759-9329; Fax: 330-759-7290. Sr. Vittoria Nisi, O.S.H.J., Supr.
Total in Community: 17; Total in Congregation : 220.
Represented in the Diocese of Youngstown.

[3060] (O.S.F.S.)—OBLATE SISTERS OF ST. FRANCIS DE SALES (P)

Founded in France in 1866. First foundation in the United States in 1951.

General Motherhouse: 4 rue des Terrasses, Troyes, France

American Headquarters: *Villa Aviat Convent*, 399 Childs Rd., Childs, MD 21916. Tel: 410-398-3699. Sr. Anne Elizabeth, O.S.F.S., Supr.
Total in Community: 15.
Ministry in the field of Academic and Religious Education.
Represented in the Archdiocese of Philadelphia and in the Dioceses of Arlington and Wilmington.

[3070] (N.A.U.-O.L.C.)—NORTH AMERICAN UNION SISTERS OF OUR LADY OF CHARITY (P)

Founded in Caen, France in 1641, by St. John Eudes. First foundation in the United States in 1855; autonomous houses were federated in 1944 and in 1979 the Union was established.

General Motherhouse and Administrative Centre: 620 Roswell Rd., P.O. Box 340, Carrollton, OH 44615-0340. Tel: 330-627-1641; Fax: 330-627-5789; Email: naucenter@hotmail.com. Sr. Carol Pregno, O.L.C., Supr. Gen.
Total Sisters Membership: 77.
Legal Title: *North American Union of the Sisters of Our Lady of Charity, Inc.*
The primary ministry of the sisters is with the marginalized and wounded, especially women and children: people living with HIV/AIDS, Hispanic ministry and parish ministries, battered women, delinquent girls, nursing homes, human trafficking, both in residential and outreach programs.
Represented in the Archdiocese of New York and the Dioceses of Buffalo, Dallas, El Paso, Erie, Green Bay, Pittsburgh, San Diego, Steubenville and Wheeling-Charleston. Also in Mexico.

San Diego

North American Union Sisters of Our Lady of Charity: 1930 Illion St., San Diego, CA 92110. Tel: 619-275-0764. Sr. Zita Toto, Local Supr.

Fort Myers

North American Union Sisters of Our Lady of Charity: 2140 Cottage St., Apt. 110, Fort Myers, FL 33901. Tel: 239-337-4550; Email: olcflo@worldnet.att.net. Sr. Mary John Franey, Local Supr.

Buffalo

North American Union of the Sisters of Our Lady of Charity: 3800 Howard Rd., Hamburg, NY 14075. Tel: 716-648-4988; Fax: 716-648-3062; Email: altarbread@verizon.net. Sr. Rosemary Toth, Local Supr.
Legal Title: *Sisters of Our Lady of Charity of Refuge, Inc.*
Dallas Sr. Yolanda Martinez, Local Supr.
Total in Community: 8.
Legal Title: *Sisters of Our Lady of Charity and Refuge.*

El Paso

North American Union of Our Lady of Charity: 415 N. Glenwood Dr., El Paso, TX 79905. Tel: 915-722-0737; Fax: 915-779-2664; Email: mescobar1125@hotmail.com. Sr. Martha P. Escobar, Local Supr.
Legal Title: *North American Sisters of Our Lady of Charity, Inc.*

Erie

North American Union of the Sisters of Our Lady of Charity (1934): 4635 East Lake Rd., Erie, PA 16511. Tel: 814-899-1052; Fax: 814-899-1573; Email: srgentile@hotmail.com. Sr. Catherine Gentile, Local Supr.
Legal Titles: Gannondale Residential Center for Girls, Erie, PA; North American Union Sisters of Our Lady of Charity, Inc.

Green Bay

North American Union of the Sisters of Our Lady of Charity: 2560 Shawano Ave., P.O. Box 10357, Green Bay, WI 54307. Tel: 920-434-8208; Fax: 920-662-0047; Email: sdonna@athenet.net. Sr. Donna Truckey, Local Supr.
Legal Titles: Sisters of Our Lady of Charity of the North American Union, Inc.; McClosky Program, Inc., Green Bay, WI.

Pittsburgh

North American Union of the Sisters of Our Lady of Charity: *Nativity Convent*, 4100 Vinceton St., Pittsburgh, PA 15214. Tel: 412-931-2299; Fax: 412-931-6044. Sr. Sheila Rooney, Local Supr.
Legal Titles: North American Union Sisters of Our Lady of Charity, Inc.; Eudes Institute.

Steubenville

North American Union Sisters of Our Lady of Charity: 620 Roswell Rd., N.W., P.O. Box 158, Carrollton, OH 44615-0158. Tel: 330-627-7647; Fax: 330-627-4415; Email: nauoleoh@eohio.net. Sr. Sheila Rooney, Local Supr.
Legal Title: *North American Union Sisters of Our Lady of Charity, Inc.*

Newburgh

North American Union of the Sisters of Our Lady of Charity: 157 Liberty St., Newburgh, NY 12550. Tel: 845-561-4354; Fax: 845-561-4354; Email: marthahmolc@aol.com. Sr. Martha Hernandez, Local Supr.
Legal Title: *North American Union Sisters of Our Lady of Charity, Inc.*

Wheeling

North American Union Sisters of Our Lady of Charity: 141 Edgington Ln., Wheeling, WV 26003. Tel: 304-242-7070; Fax: 304-242-0042; Email: d.kohlman@att.net. Sr. Deana Kohlman, Local Supr.
Legal Title: *North American Union Sisters of Our Lady of Charity, Inc.*

[3072] (R.O.L.C.)—OUR LADY OF CHARITY OF REFUGE (P)

Monastery of Our Lady of Charity of Refuge: 1125 Malvern Ave., Hot Springs National Park, AR 71901. Tel: 501-623-1393; Fax: 501-623-1509. Sr. Theresa Marie Lalancette, R.O.L.C. Supr.
Total in Community: 7.

[3080] (R.C.D.)—SISTERS OF OUR LADY OF CHRISTIAN DOCTRINE (D)

Founded in New York in 1910 for the work of religious education and social service.

Central Office: *Visitation House*, 629 North Midland Ave., Nyack, NY 10960. Tel: 845-727-1011. Sr. Agnes O'Connor, R.C.D., Pres.
Total in Community: 24.
Ministry in the field of Religious Education and Spirituality; Social Work, Nursing and Counseling.
Represented in the Archdiocese of New York.

[3090] (C.L.H.C.)—CONGREGATION OF OUR LADY, HELP OF THE CLERGY (D)

Maryvale Sisters

Founded in the United States in 1961.

Motherhouse: *Maryvale Motherhouse*, 2522 June Bug Rd., Vale, NC 28168. Tel: 704-276-2626. Mother Mary Louis, Supr.
Total in Community: 5.
Represented in the Diocese of Charlotte.

[3100] (R.S.R.)—CONGREGATION OF OUR LADY OF THE HOLY ROSARY (P)

Founded in Rimouski, P.Q., Canada in 1874. First foundation in the United States in 1899.

General Motherhouse: 300 Alle du Rosaire, Rimouski, Canada, G5L 3E3. Tel: 418-724-5940. Sr. Ida Cote, R.S.R., Supr. Gen.

U.S. Address: *Our Lady of the Holy Rosary*, 20 Thomas St., Portland, ME 04102. Tel: 207-774-3756; Tel: 207-772-3130. Sr. Carole Jean Lappa, R.S.R., Reg.
Total number in the Region: 8.

Our Lady of the Holy Rosary Regional House: 25 Portland Ave., Old Orchard Beach, ME 04064. Tel: 207-934-0592. Sr. Maureen Bellerose, R.S.R., Regional Coord.
Ministry in the fields of Education, Diocesan Ministry, Retreat Ministry.
Represented in the Diocese of Portland (In Maine).

[3105] (S.O.L.T.)—SISTERS OF THE SOCIETY OF OUR LADY OF THE MOST HOLY TRINITY

Founded in 1958 in New Mexico by Fr. James H. Flanagan. The Society of Our Lady of the Most Holy Trinity is composed of priests, brothers, permanent deacons, sisters, consecrated widows and laity (both single and married). Its members serve on Ecclesial Teams made up of all vocations while living a Marian Trinitarian spirituality.

Motherhouse: P.O. Box 536, Bosque, NM 87006. Tel: 505-861-7175; Fax: 505-864-6776; Email: srannemarie@earthlink.net; Web: www.soltsisters.org. Sr. Anne Marie Walsh, Gen. Sister Servant.
Total number of Sisters in Community: 98.

U.S. Regionalate: P.O. Box 152, Robstown, TX 78380. Tel: 361-287-8090. Sr. Mary Teresa Pacheco, S.O.L.T., American Reg. Sister Servant.
Professed Sisters: 98; Novices: 12; Candidates: 20.
Represented in the Archdioceses of Santa Fe and Seattle and in the Dioceses of Corpus Christi, Fargo, Kansas City-St. Joseph and Laredo.

[3110] (R.C.)—N AMERICAN PROVINCE CONGREGATION OF OUR LADY OF THE CENACLE OF CHICAGO (P)

Founded in France in 1826. First foundation in the United States in 1892.

Generalate: Piazza Madonna del Cenacolo, 15, Rome, Italy, 00136.

North American Province (2000): *Congregation of Our Lady of the Cenacle*, 513 Fullerton Pkwy., Chicago, IL 60614-6428. Tel: 773-528-6300; Fax: 773-549-0554. Sr. Evelyn Jegen, R.C., Prov.
Total in Community: 136.
Properties owned and sponsored: Cenacle Sisters, Hoschton, GA; Cenacle of St. Regis of Flushing, Inc., Ronkonkoma, NY; Cenacle Convent, Inc., Chicago, IL; Cenacle Convent, Inc., Houston, TX; Warrenville Cenacle Retreat House, Warrenville, IL; Religious of Our Lady of the Cenacle of New Brunswick, NJ, Metuchen, NJ; Convent of Our Lady of the Cenacle, Metairie, LA; The Cenacle Convent of Palm Beach Co., Inc., Palm Beach, FL; Ronkonkoma Cenacle, Inc., Rockville Centre, NY; Cenacle Sisters, Gainesville, FL.
Represented in the Archdioceses of Atlanta, Chicago, Denver, Galveston-Houston, New Orleans, New York and St. Louis and in the Dioceses of Fort Wayne-South Bend, Green Bay, Joliet, Metuchen, Palm Beach, Paterson, Rochester, Rockville Centre, St. Augustine, St. Petersburg, and Wheeling-Charleston. Also in Canada.

[3120] (O.L.S.)—SISTERS OF OUR LADY OF SORROWS (P)

Founded in Italy in 1839. First foundation in the United States in 1947.

General Motherhouse: Viale Vaticano 90, Rome, Italy, 00165. Mother Lina Rossi, O.L.S., Supr. Gen.

American Headquarters: *Sisters of Our Lady of Sorrows Convent*, 9894 Norris Ferry Rd., Shreveport, LA 71106. Fax: 318-797-7003. Sr. Carla Bertani, O.L.S., Supr.
Total in Community: 28; Universal total in Congregation: 300.
Ministry in the field of Education; Work with people with mental retardation; Outreach to the poor; Pastoral Ministry; CCD & Adult Education; early childhood education; afterschool art & education program.
Represented in the Dioceses of Alexandria, Lafayette in Louisiana and Shreveport.

[3130] (O.L.V.M.)—OUR LADY OF VICTORY MISSIONARY SISTERS (P)

Founded in the United States in 1922.

Motherhouse: *Victory Noll*, P.O. Box 109, Huntington, IN 46750-0109. Tel: 260-356-0628; Fax: 260-358-1504; Email: victorynoll@olvm.org. Sr. Beatrice Haines, O.L.V.M., Pres.
Total in Community: 120.
Legal Holding: Victory Noll Sisters Community Support Trust.
Represented in the Archdioceses of Chicago, Denver, Dubuque, Los Angeles, Louisville, San Antonio and Santa Fe and in the Dioceses of Cheyenne, Fort Wayne-South Bend, Phoenix, Salina, Salt Lake City, San Bernardino, San Diego, Toledo and Tucson.

[3140] (C.S.A.C.)—SISTERS OF THE CATHOLIC APOSTOLATE (PALLOTTINE) (P)

Founded in Italy in 1835. First foundation in the United States in 1889.

General Motherhouse: Viale Kennedy No. 85, Grottaferrata 00046, Rome, Italy Mother M. Serena Cambiaghi, C.S.A.C., Supr. Gen.
Universal total in Congregation: 540.

Provincial Motherhouse in America: *Queen of Apostles Convent*, 98 Harriman Heights Rd., Monroe, NY 10950. Sr. Olivia Reginella, C.S.A.C., Prov. Moderator.
Total in Community: 35.
Ministry in the field of Academic and Religious Education at Elementary and Secondary Levels; Pastoral Services.
Represented in the Archdioceses of Newark and New York.

Provincial: P.O. Box 118, Harriman, NY 10926. Tel: 845-492-5080.

[3150] (S.A.C.)—PALLOTTINE MISSIONARY SISTERS - QUEEN OF APOSTLES PROVINCE (P)

(Missionary Sisters of the Catholic Apostolate)

Founded in Rome, Italy in 1838. First founded in the United States in 1912.

General Motherhouse: Rome, Italy Sr. Stella Holitz, S.A.C., Supr. Gen.

American Provincialate: *Pallottine Renewal Center*, 15270 Old Halls Ferry Rd., Florissant, MO 63034. Tel: 314-837-7100; Fax: 314-837-1041. Sr. Gail Borgmeyer, S.A.C., Prov.; Sr. Marian Ruth Creamer, S.A.C., Archivist.
Total in Community: 680.
Properties owned and/or sponsored: Pallottine Renewal Center, Florissant, MO; St. Mary's Hospital & Convent, Huntington, WV; St. Joseph's Hospital & Convent, Buckhannon, WV; St. Vincent Pallotti Convent, High School & Child Care Center, Laurel, MD.
Sisters minister in the fields of Health Care; Child Day Care; Education; Retreat and Renewal Ministry; Social Services; Parish and Pastoral Work.
Represented in the Archdioceses of St. Louis and Washington and in the Diocese of Wheeling-Charleston.

[3160] (P.V.M.I.)—PARISH VISITORS OF MARY IMMACULATE (P)

Founded in New York City in 1920 for family visitation and religious education. A contemplative-missionary community serving the Church by person-to-person evangelization.

Motherhouse and Novitiate: *Marycrest*, P.O. Box 658, Monroe, NY 10949-0658. Tel: 845-783-2251. Sr. Carole Marie Troskowski, Gen. Supr.; Sr. Maria Catherine, Novice Dir.
Total in Community: 60.
Ministry in evangelization, catechetics, & spiritual counseling; liaison for social services.
Represented in the Archdiocese of New York. Also in Nigeria and Philippines.

[3170] (C.P.)—RELIGIOUS OF THE PASSION OF JESUS CHRIST (P)

(Passionist Nuns)

Founded in Italy in 1771 by St. Paul of the Cross. First foundation in the United States in 1910.

2715 Churchview Ave., Pittsburgh, PA 15227. Tel: 412-881-1155. Mother Joyce Foga, C.P., Supr.
Perpetual Vows: 8; Temporary Vows: 2.

The Religious of the Passion of Jesus Christ (Contemplative) (1926): *St. Gabriel's Monastery*, 631 Griffin Pond Rd., Clarks Summit, PA 18411. Tel: 570-586-2791; Fax: 570-586-8210. Sr. Teresita Kho, C.P., Supr.
Professed Sisters: 7.
Sisters serve and staff: Retreats and other Programs for Women and Men of all Faiths; Clergy and Religious; Ecumenical Groups; Business and Civic Groups.
Legal Holding: St. Gabriel's Monastery and Retreat Center.

Passionist Nuns (Cloistered Contemplative) (1946): *Passionist Nuns*, 8564 Crisp Rd., Whitesville, KY 42378. Tel: 270-233-4571. Mother Catherine Marie, C.P., Supr.
Professed Nuns: 14; Temporary Vows: 2; Postulants: 1; Novices: 1.

Passionist Nuns (Contemplative) (1947): *Monastery of the Sacred Passion*, 1151 Donaldson Hwy., Erlanger, KY 41018-1000. Tel: 859-371-8568. Sr. Margaret Mary, C.P., Supr.
Total in Community: 8.
Legal Title: *Passionist Nuns of Covington, KY.*

Passionist Nuns (Cloistered) (1948): *Passionist Monastery*, 15700 Clayton Rd., Ellisville, MO 63011. Tel: 636-527-6867. Mother Mary Salvador, C.P., Supr.
Total in Community: 10.

[3180] (C.P.)—SISTERS OF THE CROSS AND PASSION (P)

(Passionist Sisters)

Founded in 1852. First foundation in the United States in 1924.

Generalate: *Parkmount*, 458 Bury New Rd., Salford, England, M7 4LH. Sr. Maria Angelica Algorta, C.P., Congregational Leader.

Motherhouse-American Provincial Office: One Wright Ln., North Kingstown, RI 02852. Tel: 401-294-3554. Sr. Theresina Scully, C.P., Prov. Leader.
Professed Sisters: 35.
Sisters minister in Retreat Houses; Elementary Education; Hospital Chaplaincy; Parish Ministry; Religious Education; Social Services; Marriage Tribunals.
Properties owned and operated: Our Lady of Calvary Retreat, Farmington, CT.
Represented in the Archdioceses of Hartford and New York and in the Dioceses of Memphis, Norwich, Providence and Rockville Centre. Also in Jamaica, West Indies.

[3190] (A.P.)—NUNS OF THE PERPETUAL ADORATION OF THE BLESSED SACRAMENT (P)

Founded in Rome in 1807. First foundation in the United States in 1925.

El Paso: *Expiatory Shrine of Christ the King and Monastery of Perpetual Adoration*, 145 N. Cotton Ave., El Paso, TX 79901. Tel: 915-533-5323; Email:

mary.guadalupe@att.net. Mother Maria Isabel, A.P., Supr.
Sisters: 14.
Represented in the Archdioceses of Anchorage and San Francisco and in the Diocese of El Paso and Sioux Falls.

San Francisco: *Monastery of Perpetual Adoration*, 771 Ashbury St., San Francisco, CA 94117. Tel: 415-566-2743. Mother Rosalba Maria, A.P., Supr.
Sisters: 13.
Represented in the Archdiocese of San Francisco. Also in Africa, Chile, Italy, Mexico and Spain.

[3195] (A.P.G.)—SISTER OF PERPETUAL ADORATION OF GUADALUPE, INC. (P)

U.S. Foundation: 2403 W. Travis, San Antonio, TX 78207. Tel: 210-227-5546. Mother Ma. Concepcion Quesada A., A.P.G., Gen. Counsel.
Total in Community: 9.

[3200] (SCH.P.)—SISTERS OF THE PIOUS SCHOOLS (P)
(Escolapias)

Founded in Figueras, Spain in 1829.
Universal total in Congregation: 675.

General Motherhouse: Via Crescenzio 77, Rome, Italy, 00193. Mother M. Divina Garcia, Sch.P., Supr. Gen.

U.S. Headquarters (1954): 17601 Nordhoff St., Northridge, CA 91325. Tel: 818-885-6265; Fax: 818-718-6752. Sr. Guadalupe Gonzalez, Sch.P.
Total in Community: 12.
Ministry in Religious Education; Parish Schools.
Represented in the Archdiocese of Los Angeles.

[3210] (P.C.P.A.)—POOR CLARES OF PERPETUAL ADORATION (P)

Founded in France, 1854. First foundation in the United States at Cleveland, Ohio, 1921. Poor Clares of Perpetual Adoration, cloistered, contemplative, solemn vows. Object: Perpetual Adoration in spirit of Praise and Thanksgiving and Gospel living. Solemn Exposition day and night. Each monastery is autonomous.

Sancta Clara Monastery (1946): 4200 N. Market Ave., Canton, OH 44714. Tel: 330-492-1171; Fax: 330-492-2227. Mother Marion Zeltmann, P.C.P.A., Abbess.
Total in Community: 11.

Saint Joseph Adoration Monastery (1956): 2311 Stockham Ln., Portsmouth, OH 45662-3049. Tel: 740-353-4713; Email: nuns@stjosephmonastery.com; Web: www.stjosephmonastery.com. Mother Dolores Marie, Abbess.
Total in Community: 10.
Legal Holdings and Titles: Poor Clares of Perpetual Adoration; St. Joseph Adoration Monastery.

Adoration Monastery (1921): 4108 Euclid Ave., Cleveland, OH 44103. Tel: 216-361-0783. Mother Mary James, P.C.P.A., Abbess.
Total in Community: 18.

Poor Clares of Perpetual Adoration (1954): *Our Lady of the Most Blessed Sacrament Monastery*, 3900 13th St., N.E., Washington, DC 20017-2699. Tel: 202-526-6808; Fax: 202-526-0678; Email: ourprayer4u@poorclareswdc.org; Web: www.poorclareswdc.org. Mother Mary Angela Perry, P.C.P.A., Abbess.
Total in Community: 7.

Our Lady of the Angels Monastery: *Shrine of the Most Blessed Sacrament*, 3222 County Rd. 548, Hanceville, AL 35077. Tel: 205-271-2917; Fax: 205-795-5702. Mother M. Angelica, P.C.P.A., Abbess & Pres.
Total in Community: 34; Novices: 4; Postulants: 7.
Legal Title: *Our Lady of the Angels Monastery, Inc.*
Represented in the Diocese of Birmingham.

[3220] (P.C.J.)—SISTERS OF THE POOR CHILD JESUS (P)

Founded on February 2, 1844 in Germany. First founded in the United States on July 2, 1924 at Parkersburg, West Virginia.

General Motherhouse: Haus Loreto, Simpleveld, Netherlands Antilles Sr. Maria del Rocio, P.C.J., Supr. Gen.
Universal total in Congregation: 500.

American Region and Novitiate: *In Mohun Health Care Center*, 2340 Airport Dr., Columbus, OH 43219. Sr. Mary Thomasina John, P.C.J., Contact Person.
Total in Community: 3.
Ministry in the field of Education.
Represented in the Dioceses of Columbus and Wheeling-Charleston.

[3230] (P.H.J.C.)—POOR HANDMAIDS OF JESUS CHRIST (P)
(The Ancilla Domini Sisters)

Founded in Germany in 1851. First foundation in the United States in 1868.

General Motherhouse: Dernbach, Westerwald, Germany Sr. Jolise May, P.H.J.C., Supr. Gen.

American Province-Provincialate: *Convent Ancilla Domini*, 9601 Union Rd., P.O. Box 1, Donaldson, IN 46513. Tel: 574-936-9936; Fax: 574-935-1785. Sr. Nora Hahn, P.H.J.C., Prov. Councilors: Sr. Virginia Kampwerth, P.H.J.C.; Sr. Kathy Haas, P.H.J.C.; Sr. Marlene Ann Lama, P.H.J.C.; Fred Arand, Treas.; Sr. Mary Josef Shingler, P.H.J.C., Dir. Devel.
Professed Sisters: 125.
Ministry in the field of Academic Education at all levels; Healthcare; Parish Ministries; Retreat Ministries; Child Care Institutions; and Retirement Homes.
Properties owned or sponsored: Ancilla Domini College; Convent Ancilla Domini; Bethany Retreat House; St. Henry Convent; Sojourner Truth House; Catherine Kasper Life Center, Inc.; Lindenwood Retreat & Ministry Center; Earthworks, Inc.; HealthVisions Midwest, East Chicago, IN; Poor Handmaids of Jesus Christ Community Support Trust, Donaldson, IN; Ancilla Systems, Inc., Hobart, IN; Ancilla Domini Convent, Milwaukee, WI; Ancilla Domini Hospitals; Self Insurance Trust; St. Catherine Convent, East Chicago, IN; Annunciation Convent, Hoffman Estates, IL; Mary Katherine Convent, Cairo, IL; Marian Convent, Fort Wayne, IN; St. Mary Convent, East St. Louis, IL; St. Joseph Community Health Foundation, Ft. Wayne, IN; Nazareth Home, East Chicago, IN.
Represented in the Archdioceses of Chicago, Cincinnati, Indianapolis and Milwaukee and in the Dioceses of Belleville, Fort Wayne-South Bend, Gary, Lafayette in Indiana, Providence, Savannah and Springfield in Illinois. Also in Africa, Brazil, Germany and Mexico.

[3240] (C.J.C.)—POOR SISTERS OF JESUS CRUCIFIED AND THE SORROWFUL MOTHER (D)

Founded in the United States in 1924.

General Motherhouse and Novitiate: *Our Lady of Sorrows Convent*, 261 Thatcher St., Brockton, MA 02302-3997. Sr. Mary Valliere, C.J.C., Gen. Supr.
Total in Community: 25.
Properties owned and/or sponsored: St. Joseph Manor Health Care, Inc; Mater Dei Adult Day Health Program; Our Lady of Sorrows Convent, Brockton, MA; St. Mary's Villa Nursing Home, Elmhurst, PA; St. Mary's Villa Residence, Elmhurst, PA.
Ministry in Nursing Homes; Education Center; Elementary Schools; Assisted Living facilities; and Pastoral Ministry.
Represented in the Archdiocese of Boston.

[3242] (C.S.N.)—THE CONGREGATION OF THE SISTERS OF NAZARETH (P)

Founded in England by Mother St. Basil.

Motherhouse: Hammersmith, London, England, W6 8DB. Sr. St. Hilary, Supr. Gen.

Regional Headquarters: *Nazareth House*, 3333 Manning Ave., Los Angeles, CA 90064. Tel: 310-839-2361. Sr. John Berchmans, Supr.
Professed Sisters: 32.
Legal Title: *The Congregation of the Sisters of Nazareth Mother House U.S.A., Inc.*
Represented in the Archdioceses of Los Angeles and San Francisco and in the Dioceses of Fresno, Madison and San Diego. Also in American Samoa.

[3250] (P.S.S.J.)—POOR SISTERS OF ST. JOSEPH (P)

Founded in Buenos Aires, Argentina in 1880.

General Motherhouse: Pte. Peron 734, 1663 Muniz, Buenos Aires, Argentina Mother Martha S. Guerrero, Mother Gen.

U.S. Foundation: *Casa Belen*, 305 E. Fourth St., Bethlehem, PA 18015. Tel: 610-867-4030.

U.S. Motherhouse: *St. Gabriel Convent*, 4319 Sano St., Alexandria, VA 22312. Tel: 703-354-0395.

Casa Nazareth: 532 Spruce St., Reading, PA 19602. Tel: 610-378-1947.
Total in Community: 11.
Represented in the Dioceses of Allentown and Arlington.

[3260] (C.PP.S.)—SISTERS OF THE PRECIOUS BLOOD (DAYTON, OHIO) (P)

Founded in Switzerland in 1834. First foundation in the United States in 1844.

Generalate: 4000 Denlinger Rd., Dayton, OH 45426. Tel: 937-837-3302; Fax: 937-837-8825. Sr. Florence Seifert, C.PP.S., Pres.; Sr. Jeanette Buehler, C.PP.S., Vice Pres., Councilor & Sec.; Sr. Marita Beumer, C.PP.S., Councilor; Sr. Madonna Ratermann, C.PP.S., Councilor; Sr. Edna Hess, C.PP.S., Treas. & Councilor; Sr. Noreen Jutte, C.PP.S., Archivist.
Total Membership: 183.
Ministry in Universities; High Schools; Elementary Schools; Diocesan Offices; Pastoral Ministry in Hospitals and Long-term Care Centers; Religious and Adult Education; Nursing Care; Homemaking Services in Homes for the Aged; Ethnic Minorities and Marginalized Peoples; Retreat and Music Ministry; Missionary and Volunteer Services.
Properties owned and sponsored: Generalate, Dayton, OH; Salem Heights Convent, Dayton, OH; Maria Stein Center, Maria Stein, OH.
Represented in the Archdioceses of Cincinnati, Denver and Philadelphia and in the Dioceses of Cleveland, Columbus, Kalamazoo, Knoxville, Lafayette in Indiana, Lansing, Lexington, Phoenix, Saginaw, San Bernardino, San Diego, and Toledo. Also in Chile and Guatemala.

[3270] (C.PP.S.)—SISTERS OF THE MOST PRECIOUS BLOOD (O'FALLON, MO.) (P)

Founded in Switzerland in 1845. First foundation in the United States in 1870.

General Motherhouse: *St. Mary's Institute of O'Fallon*, 204 N. Main St., O'Fallon, MO 63366-2299. Tel: 636-240-6010; Fax: 636-272-5031. Sr. Mary Whited, C.PP.S., Supr. Gen. General Councilors: Sr. Fran Raia, C.PP.S.; Sr. Carmen Schnyder, Treas. & Councilor; Sr. Carol Boschert; Sr. Marie Orf, C.PP.S.; Sr. Dory Obermann, Sec.; Sr. Mary Joan Dyer, Community Archivist.
Total in Community: 168.
Ministry in the field of Education; Care of the Elderly; Pastoral and Parish Ministry; Ecclesiastical Art; Foreign Missions; Social Services; Prayer/Presence.
Properties owned: St. Mary's Institute of O'Fallon, O'Fallon, MO; Charitable Trust, Sisters of the Most Precious Blood of O'Fallon, MO; St. Elizabeth Academy, St. Louis, MO; St. Elizabeth Adult Day Care Center, St. Louis, MO; Centers for Professional and Pastoral Services, O'Fallon, MO.
Represented in the Archdioceses of Anchorage, St. Louis and Washington and in the Dioceses of Jefferson City, Las Cruces, Springfield in Illinois and Wheeling-Charleston. Also in Bolivia, Peru, Estonia, Finland and Italy.

[3310] (P.M.)—SISTERS OF THE PRESENTATION OF MARY (P)

Founded in France in 1796. First foundation in the United States in 1873.

General Motherhouse: *Presentazione di Maria*, Viale PIO XI, 29 C.P. 104, Castelgandolfo, Italy, 00040. Mother Angele Dion, Supr. Gen.

Inter-Provincial Novitiate: 186 Lowell Rd., Hudson, NH 03051. Tel: 603-880-8186. Sr. Suzette Tanguay, Dir.

Manchester Province: *Provincial Administration*, 495 Mammoth Rd., Manchester, NH 03104-5494. Tel: 603-669-1080. Sr. Suzanne Bourret, P.M., Prov. Supr.
Total Number in Province: 132.
Properties owned and/or sponsored: Rivier College, Nashua, NH; Presentation of Mary Academy, Hudson, NH; Provincial House; St. Joseph Residence; St. Marie Residence, Manchester, NH; Our Lady of Hope House of Prayer, New Ipswich, NH; Bethany House, Manchester, NH; Presentation of Mary Novitiate, Hudson, NH; Emmanuel House, Woonsocket, RI; Emmaus Convent, Manchester, NH; Presentation of Mary Convent, Nashua, NH.
Represented in the Archdiocese of Galveston-Houston and in the Dioceses Manchester and Providence.

Methuen Province - Provincial Administration: *Sisters of the Presentation of Mary*, 209 Lawrence St., Methuen, MA 01844. Tel: 978-687-1369; Fax: 978-685-0980. Sr. Cecile Plasse, P.M., Prov.
Total number in Province: 103.
Properties owned and/or sponsored: Montessori Day Nurseries; Marie Joseph Spiritual Center, Biddeford, ME; Presentation of Mary Academy, Methuen, MA.
Ministry in High Schools; Elementary Schools; Montessori Day Nurseries; Religious Instruction Centers; Spiritual Retreat Center.
Represented in the Archdiocese of Boston and in the Dioceses of Portland (In Maine), Springfield in Massachusetts and Worcester.

[3320] (P.B.V.M.)—SISTERS OF THE PRESENTATION OF THE B.V.M. (P)

Founded in Ireland in 1775. First foundation in San Francisco, CA in 1854.
Represented in the United States in the following Archdioceses and Dioceses.

Dubuque (P)

Mt. Loretto Convent, Motherhouse and Novitiate: 2360 Carter Rd., Dubuque, IA 52001-2997. Tel: 563-588-2008; Fax: 563-588-4463. Sr. Jennifer Rausch, P.B.V.M., Pres.
Total in Community: 130.
Legal Title: *Sisters of the Presentation of the B.V.M., Dubuque, IA.*
Ministry in the field of Religious and Academic Education; Hospital & Prison Chaplaincy; Elder Care; Parish & Campus Ministries; South American Bolivian Mission; Diocesan/Metropolitan Offices; Retreat & Spiritual Direction; Hispanic Ministry; Peace and Justice; Social Services.
Represented in the Archdioceses of Chicago, Dubuque, Louisville, New Orleans, St. Paul-Minneapolis and Washington and in the Dioceses of Brownsville, Covington, Davenport, Fort Wayne-South Bend, Jackson, La Crosse, Madison, Omaha, Orlando, Sioux City, Sioux Falls, and Winona. Also in Bolivia.

New York (P)

Mt. St. Joseph Administration Center: *Sisters of the Presentation of the Blessed Virgin Mary*, 880 Jackson Ave., New Windsor, NY 12553. Tel: 845-564-0513; Fax: 845-567-0219. Sr. Catherine Cleary, P.B.V.M., Pres.; Sr. Margaret Muller, P.B.V.M., Community Archivist.
Total in Community: 136.
Ministry in the field of Academic Education at all levels; Pastoral Services; Health Care and Social Services.
Represented in the Archdioceses of Boston, Los Angeles, Newark, New York and Washington and in the

Dioceses of Brooklyn, Metuchen, Norwich, Paterson, Providence, Trenton and Worcester. Also in Bolivia.

Our Lady of the Presentation Motherhouse: 419 Woodrow Rd., Staten Island, NY 10312. Tel: 718-356-2121. Sr. Rosemary Ward, Congregational Leader.
Professed Sisters: 18.
Ministry in Elementary Schools; University; Campus Ministry; Pastoral Counseling; Adult Education; Healing & Parish Ministry.
Represented in the Archdioceses of New York and Philadelphia and in the Diocese of Sioux Falls.

San Francisco Presentation Congregational Offices: 281 Masonic Ave., San Francisco, CA 94118. Tel: 415-422-5001. Sr. Pamela Chiesa, P.B.V.M., Pres. Tel: 415-422-5013; Christine Doan, Archivist.
Total in Community: 97.
Legal Title: *Sisters of the Presentation.*
Ministry in the field of Religious and Academic Education at all levels; Parish Ministry; Social and Health Ministry; College and University Teaching; Retreat Work; Church Related Administrative Positions; Missionary Work; Internal Ministry.
Represented in the Archdioceses of Los Angeles and San Francisco and in the Dioceses of Fresno, Oakland, Orange and San Jose.

Albany (P)

St. Colman's Presentation Convent, Motherhouse and Novitiate: Sisters of the Presentation of the Blessed Virgin Mary P.V.B.M., 11 Haswell Rd, Watervliet, NY 12189. Tel: 518-273-4911; Fax: 518-273-3312. Mother Mary Carmel, Supr.
Total in Community: 30.
Ministry in the field of Academic Education; Day Care Center; Child Caring Institution; Resident School for Autistic & Emotionally Disturbed Children; Parish Ministry.
Represented in the Diocese of Albany.

Fargo (P)

Sacred Heart Convent, Motherhouse and Novitiate: *Sisters of Presentation of the Blessed Virgin Mary P.B.V.M.*, 1101 32nd Ave. S., Fargo, ND 58103. Tel: 701-237-4857; Email: presentationsrs@cableone.net. Sr. Mary Margaret Mooney, P.B.V.M., Pres.; Sr. Maureen Walker, Archivist.
Total in Community: 49.
Sponsored Ministries: Presentation Prayer Center, Fargo, ND; Presentation Center, Fargo, ND; Hughes, Inc., Fargo, ND; Office of Peace and Justice, ND; The Presentation Sisters Foundation, Fargo, ND; Presentation Partners in Housing; Office of Peace & Justice.
Represented in the Dioceses of Columbus, Fargo and Jackson. Also in Peru.

Sioux Falls (P)

Presentation Convent, Motherhouse and Novitiate: *Sisters of the Presentation of the Blessed Virgin Mary*, 1500 N. Second St., Aberdeen, SD 57401. Tel: 605-229-8419. Sr. Pam Donelan, P.B.V.M., Pres.; Sr. Lois Ann Sargent, Congregation Archivist.
Total in Community: 101.
Ministry in the field of Academic Education; Hospitals; Homes for the Aged; Parish Pastoral Ministry; Hispanic Ministry; Ministry in Zambia, Africa, and Guatamala.
Represented in the Diocese of Sioux Falls.

Worcester (P)

Presentation Convent of the Presentation of the B.V.M: 99 Church St., Leominster, MA 01453. Sr. Catherine Cleary, P.B.V.M., Pres.
Total in Community: 136.
Sisters staff: Elementary and High School Education; Pastoral Ministry; Social Services; Nursing.
Represented in the Archdioceses of Boston, Los Angeles, Newark, New York and Washington and in the Dioceses of Brooklyn, Metuchen, Norwich, Paterson, Providence, Trenton and Worcester. Also in Bolivia.

[3330] (P.B.V.M.)—UNION OF SISTERS OF THE PRESENTATION OF THE BLESSED VIRGIN MARY (P)

The Congregation of the Presentation was founded in Cork, Ireland, 1775. By decree of the Sacred Congregation for Religious, the Union of Sisters of the Presentation was established in Ireland in 1976. First U.S.A. Province in 1989.

Generalate: Monasterevan Co., Kildare, Ireland Tel: 045-525-335. Sr. Terry Abraham, P.B.V.M., Supr. Gen.; Sr. Antonio Heaphy, P.B.V.M., Provincial; Sr. Vera Butler, P.B.V.M., Asst. Provincial; Sr. Katherine Fennell, P.B.V.M., Treas.

Novitiate: 10843 Gorman Ave., Los Angeles, CA 90059. Tel: 714-220-2861.
Perpetual Profession: 65.
Sisters serve and staff: Elementary and Religious Education; Parish Ministry; Retreat Ministry; Health & Hospital Services; Social Services.
Represented in the Archdioceses of Los Angeles, Mobile, New Orleans, San Antonio and San Francisco and in the Dioceses of Biloxi, Jackson, Oakland, Orange, Phoenix, San Bernardino, and Tucson.

[3340] (S.P.)—SISTERS OF PROVIDENCE (D)

Founded in Kingston, Canada in 1861. First foundation in the United States in 1873. Became independent, diocesan foundation in 1892.

Providence Motherhouse: 5 Gamelin St., Holyoke, MA 01040-4081. Tel: 413-536-7511; Fax: 413-536-7917; Email: sisters@sisofprov.org. Sr. Kathleen Popko, S.P., Congregation Pres.
Professed Sisters: 55.
Legal Holdings and Titles: Sisters of Providence, Inc., Holyoke, MA; Sisters of Providence Health System, Springfield, MA; Family Services: Providence Ministries for the Needy, Holyoke, MA; Brightside for Families and Children, Inc., West Springfield, MA; Retreat Center: Genesis Spiritual Life and Conference Center, Westfield, MA; Mary's Meadow at Providence Place, Inc., Holyoke, MA; Senior Independent Living: Providence Place, Holyoke, MA; Sponsoring Congregation of Catholic Health East; Sisters of Providence Health System, Inc., Springfield, MA; Hospitals: Mercy Hospital, Springfield, MA; Providence Behavioral Health Hospital, Holyoke, MA; Sisters of Providence Care Centers, Inc., including: Beaven-Kelley Home, Holyoke, MA; Farren Care Center, Turners Falls, MA; Mount St. Vincent Nursing Home, Holyoke, MA; Providence Care Center of Lenox, Lenox, MA; St. Luke's Home, Springfield, MA; St. Joseph of the Pines, Inc., Southern Pines, NC.
Represented in the Dioceses of Springfield in Massachusetts and Worcester.

[3350] (S.P.)—SISTERS OF PROVIDENCE (P)

Founded in Montreal in 1843. First foundation in the United States in 1856.

General Motherhouse and Novitiate: 12055 rue Grenet, Montreal, Canada, H4J 2J5. Sr. Kathryn Rutan, Supr. Gen.

Mother Joseph Province (2000): *Sisters of Providence*, 1801 Lind Ave., SW, #9016, Renton, WA 98057-9016. Tel: 425-525-3355; Fax: 425-525-3984; Web: www.sistersofprovidence.net. Sr. Margaret Botch, S.P., Prov. Supr.
Total in Community: 767; Sisters in Province: 161.
Ministry in the field of Academic Education; Health Care Services; Hospitals & Skilled Nursing Facilities; Outpatient Health Care Services; Home, Health and Hospice; Retirement Homes; Children's Nursing Centers; Senior and Handicapped Housing Facilities; Shelters for Homeless Women with Children; Transitional Housing for Women; Assisted Living facilities; Health Plans; Health Care Clinics; Child and Family Services; Prison Ministry.
Properties, entities and divisions owned or operated: Sisters of Providence - Mother Joseph Province; St. Joseph Residence, Seattle, WA; Mount St. Joseph, Spokane, WA; Providence-Pariseau; Providence Hospitality House, Seattle, WA; Sojourner Place, Seattle, WA; Providence Alaska Medical Center, Anchorage, AK; Providence Extended Care Center, Anchorage, AK; Providence Health System Housing; Providence Horizon House, Anchorage, AK; Providence Home Health Care, Anchorage, AK; Providence Seward Medical Center, Seward, AK; Providence Kodiak Island Medical Center, Kodiak, AK; Providence Regional Medical Center, Everett, WA; Providence Hospice and Home Care of Snohomish County, Everett, WA; Heritage House at the Market (leased), Seattle, WA; Providence Hospice of Seattle, Seattle, WA; Providence Mount St. Vincent, Seattle, WA; Providence St. Peter Hospital, Olympia, WA; Providence Mother Joseph Care Center, Olympia, WA; Providence Marianwood, Issaquah, WA; Providence Centralia Hospital, Centralia, WA; Providence Sound HomeCare and Hospice, Olympia, WA; Providence St. Francis Association dba St. Francis House, Olympia, WA; St. Luke Association dba-Providence Place, Chehalis, WA; Providence Blanchet Association dba Providence Blanchet House, Centralia, WA; Providence Rossi Association dba Providence Rossi House, Centralia, WA; Sisters of Providence in Oregon— Oregon Regional Office; Providence St. Vincent Medical Center; Providence Portland Medical Center; Providence Child Center, Portland, OR; Providence Milwaukie Hospital, Milwaukie, OR; Providence Newberg Medical Center, Newberg, OR; Providence Seaside Hospital (leased), Seaside, OR; The Gamelin Association dba—Providence House, Yakima, WA; The Gamelin-Oregon Association dba—Emilie House, Portland, OR; The Gamelin-California Association, Oakland, CA; Providence Medford Medical Center, Medford, OR. Sisters of Providence in California-Providence High School; Providence Saint Joseph Medical Center, Burbank, CA; The Providence Housing Association dba Vincent House, Seattle, WA; Providence Health & Services, Seattle, WA.
Represented in the Archdioceses of Anchorage, Los Angeles, Portland in Oregon and Seattle and in the Dioceses of Baker, Great Falls-Billings, Helena, Oakland, Spokane and Yakima.

Novitiate House: 1016 N. Superior St., #4, Spokane, WA 99202-2096. Tel: 509-487-7644; Fax: 509-489-0964. Sr. Marilyn Charette, S.P., Novitiate Dir.

Vocation Office: 9 E. Ninth Ave., Spokane, WA 99202-1209. Tel: 509-474-2323.

Our Lady of Province: 47 W. Spring St., Winooski, VT 05404. Tel: 802-655-2395; Fax: 802-655-3888. Sr. Carmen Proulx, S.P., Coord.
Total in Community: 24.

Emilie Gamelin Province (2005): *Sisters of Providence*, 47 W. Spring St., Winooski, VT 05404. Tel: 802-655-2395; Fax: 802-655-3888. Sr. Carmen Proulx, S.P., Coord.
Total in Community: 23.

[3360] (S.P.)—SISTERS OF PROVIDENCE OF SAINT MARY-OF-THE-WOODS, INDIANA (P)

Founded in France in 1806. First foundation in the United States in 1840.

General Administration: *Sisters of Providence*, Owens Hall, Saint Mary Of The Woods, IN 47876-1007. Tel: 812-535-4193; Web: www.sistersofprovidence.org. Sr. Denise Wilkinson, S.P., Gen. Supr.; Sr. Mary Ryan, S.P., Congregation Archivist; Sr. Rosemary Schmalz, S.P., Gen. Sec.
Total number Professed Sisters: 400.
Legal Titles and Sponsored Institutions: Guerin College Preparatory High School, River Grove, IL; *Guerin Outreach Ministries, Inc., Saint Mary-of-the-Woods, IN; Saint Mary-of-the-Woods College, Saint Mary-of-the-Woods, IN; Woods Day Care/Preschool, Inc., St. Mary-of-the-Woods, IN; Providence Self Sufficiency Ministries, Inc., Georgetown, IN; Sisters of Providence Community Support Trust (1969-Foundation to provide support for the aged and infirm members of the Congregation) Indianapolis, IN; Providence Health Care, Inc., St. Mary-of-the-Woods, IN; Providence Cristo Rey High School, Indianapolis, IN.
Ministry in the fields of Education at all levels; Diocesan Offices; Parish and Pastoral Ministry; Health Care and Retirement Facilities; Congregation Administration; Social Services; Therapeutic/Rehabilitative/Mental Health Services.
Represented in the Archdioceses of Boston, Chicago, Cincinnati, Indianapolis, Louisville, Los Angeles, Oklahoma City, Omaha, Portland in Oregon, St. Paul-Minneapolis, San Antonio, San Francisco, Santa Fe and Washington and in the Dioceses of Belleville, Charlotte, Cleveland, Corpus Christi, Duluth, Evansville, Fort Wayne-South Bend, Gary, Joliet, La Crosse, Lafayette (LA), Lafayette in Indiana, Lexington, Manchester, Orange, St. Petersburg, San Bernardino, San Diego, Trenton and Venice. Also in China, Singapore and Taiwan.

Area of Taiwan: *Providence University*, 200 Chung Chi Rd., Shalu 433, Taichung County, Taiwan, Republic of China Tel: 011-886-4-2631-1182. Sr. Marilyn Baker, S.P., Area Rep.
Total in Community: 10.
Ministry in the field of Education; Elderly Care; Opportunity Center for Mentally Handicapped.
Represented in the Archdiocese of Taipei and in the Dioceses of Taichung and Tainan.

[3390] (R.A.)—RELIGIOUS OF THE ASSUMPTION (P)

Founded in France in 1839. Established in the United States in 1919.

Generalate: 17 rue de l'Assomption, Paris, France, 75016.
Universal total in Congregation: 1300.
Represented in the 34 countries through Europe, Africa, Asia, North America, Central America and South America.

Administrative Office: 1001 S. 47th St., Philadelphia, PA 19143. Tel: 215-386-2545.

North America Province: *Provincial House*, 11 Old English Rd., Worcester, MA 01609. Tel: 508-793-1954. Sr. Mary Ann Azanza, R.A., Prov. Supr.
Total number in Province: 26.
Ministry in Spiritual Formation; Counseling; Campus Ministry; Pastoral and Social Ministry; Education; Peace and Justice.
Represented in the Archdiocese of Philadelphia and in the Dioceses of Worcester and Las Cruces.

[3400] (R.S.C.)—RELIGIOUS SISTERS OF CHARITY (P)

Founded in Dublin, Ireland in 1815. Sisters in entire Congregation 505.

Motherhouse: *Caritas*, 15 Gilford Rd., Sandymount, Dublin 4, Ireland Sr. Mary Christian, Supr. Gen.

U.S. Headquarters & Novitiate (1953): *Regional Residence*, 10668 St. James Dr., Culver City, CA 90230. Tel: 310-559-0176; Fax: 310-559-3530. Sr. Marsha Moon, R.S.C., Reg. Leader.
Total in U.S. Community: 32.
Represented in the Archdiocese of Los Angeles.

[3410] (R.C.E.)—RELIGIOUS OF CHRISTIAN EDUCATION (P)

Founded in France in 1817. First foundation in the United States in 1905.

General Motherhouse: France

Provincial Residence: 444 Centre St., Milton, MA 02186. Tel: 781-894-2008; Fax: 401-349-4970. Sr. Martha Brigham, R.C.E., Pres.
Total in Community: 14.
Legal Title: *Religious of Christian Education, Inc.*
Ministry in Religious Education Centers; Pastoral Associates; Teaching; Home Care.
Represented in the Archdiocese of Boston and in the Dioceses of Fall River and Springfield in Massachusetts.

[3430] (M.P.F.)—RELIGIOUS TEACHERS FILIPPINI (P)

Founded in Italy in 1692. First foundation in the United States in 1910.

General Motherhouse: *Villa Maria Regina*, Via Stazione Ottavia, 72, Rome, Italy Sr. Nicolina Bandiera, M.P.F., Supr. Gen.

St. Lucy Filippini Province: Villa Walsh, Morristown, NJ 07960-4928. Tel: 973-538-2886. Sr. Betty Jean Takacs, M.P.F., Prov. Supr.; Sr. Mary DeBacco, M.P.F., Community Archivist.
Total in Community: 230.
Ministry in the field of Religious and Academic Education in elementary and secondary schools; Child Care Centers; Parish Ministry; Pastoral Care; Foreign Mission Work; House of Prayer; Retreat House.
Properties owned and sponsored: Villa Walsh, Morristown, NJ; Villa Victoria, Trenton, NJ; St. Joseph by The Sea, South Mantoloking, NJ.
Represented in the Archdioceses of Hartford, Newark, Philadelphia and Santa Fe, and in the Dioceses of Brooklyn, Cleveland, Camden, Metuchen, Orlando, Paterson, Pittsburgh, Providence, Scranton and Trenton.

Queen of Apostles Province: *Religious Teachers Filippini M.P.F.*, 474 East Rd., Bristol, CT 06010. Tel: 860-584-2138. Sr. Frances Stavalo, M.P.F., Prov.; Sr. Josephine Riccio, M.P.F., Community Archivist.
Total in Community: 27.
Ministry in the field of Education; Pastoral Ministry; Catechetical Centers; Youth Retreats; Foreign Mission Work.
Represented in the Archdiocese of Hartford and in the Dioceses of Bridgeport, Norwich, Orlando and Providence.

[3449] (C.V.I.)—RELIGIOUS OF THE INCARNATE WORD (P)

Founded in Lyon, France, in 1625. First foundation in the United States in 1853, in Mexico 1894.

General Motherhouse: Industria #1-Col. Toriello Guerra, Deleg., Tlalpan, Mexico, D.F. 14050. Sr. Margarita Dibildox, C.V.I., Gen. Supr.

U.S. Vice Provincial House: 153 Rainier Ct., Chula Vista, CA 91911. Tel: 619-420-0231. Sr. Camille Crabbe, C.V.I., Vice Prov.
Total in Congregation : 470.
Ministry in Parishes; Schools; Missions and Boarding for Students.
Represented in the Diocese of San Diego. Also in Africa, Argentina, El Salvador, France, Guatemala, Mexico, Spain and Uruguay.

[3450] (R.J.M.)—RELIGIOUS OF JESUS AND MARY (P)

Founded at Lyons, France, 1818. First foundation in the United States in 1877.

Motherhouse: Via Nomentana 325, Rome, Italy Rev. Sr. Angeles Alino, R.J.M., Supr. Gen.
Universal total in Congregation: 1433.

United States Province Provincialate: 125 Michigan Ave., N.E., 4th Fl., Washington, DC 20017. Tel: 202-884-9795; Fax: 202-884-9794. Sr. Eileen C. Reid, R.J.M., Prov.; Sr. Janice Farnham, R.J.M., Archivist.
Total in Community: 103.
Legal Title: *Religious of Jesus and Mary, Inc.*
Ministry in the field of Academic and Religious Education; Pastoral Ministry; Social Services; Volunteer Program.
Represented in the Archdioceses of Boston, Los Angeles, New York and Washington and in the Dioceses of Fall River, Manchester, Providence and San Diego. Also in Haiti.

[3460] (R.M.I.)—RELIGIOUS OF MARY IMMACULATE (P)

Founded in Madrid, Spain in 1876.

Mother House: Madrid, Spain

Generalate: Rome, Italy

U.S. Foundation (1954): *Villa Maria*, 719 Augusta St., San Antonio, TX 78215. Tel: 210-226-0025; Fax: 210-226-3305. Sr. Martha Ochoa, R.M.I., Local Supr.
Total in Community: 9.

Headquarters: *Centro Maria*, 539 West 54th St., New York, NY 10019. Tel: 212-581-5273. Sr. Clara Echeverria, R.M.I., Local Supr.
Total in Community: 6.
Represented in the Archdioceses of New York, San Antonio and Washington.

[3465] (R.S.H.M.)—RELIGIOUS OF THE SACRED HEART OF MARY (P)

Founded in France in 1849. First foundation in the United States in 1877.

Generalate: Via Sorelle Marchisio 41, Rome, Italy, 00168. Sr. Terezinha Cecchin, R.S.C.M., Gen. Supr.
Universal total in Congregation: 900.

Eastern American Province (1907): 50 Wilson Park Dr., Tarrytown, NY 10591. Tel: 914-631-8872. Sr. Rosamond Blanchet, R.S.H.M., Prov.
Total in Community: 193.
Legal Title: *Sisters of the Sacred Heart of Mary.*
Ministries including Education; Pastoral Ministry; Retreat and Spiritual Direction; Health Care and Social Work.
Represented in the Archdioceses of Baltimore, New York and St. Louis and in the Dioceses of Arlington, Brooklyn, Norwich, Oakland, Palm Beach, Richmond, Rockville Centre, Trenton, Venice and Winona. Also in Africa and Europe.

Western American Province (1959): *Religious of the Sacred Heart of Mary R.S.H.M. Provincial Center*, 441 N. Garfield Ave., Montebello, CA 90640-2901. Tel: 323-887-8821; Fax: 323-887-8952. Sr. Mary Genino, R.S.H.M., Prov.
Total number in Province: 68.
Legal Titles or Holdings: Religious of the Sacred Heart of Mary, Western American Province, a California nonprofit corporation, Marymount School, a California nonprofit corporation.
Ministry in the field of Academic Education at all levels; Diverse Pastoral Ministries; Prison Ministry; Justice and Peace Advocacies; Women Shelters; Youths at Risk.
Represented in the Archdioceses of Los Angeles and San Francisco and in the Dioceses of San Bernardino. Also in Mexico.

[3470] (S.R.C.M.)—SISTERS OF REPARATION OF THE CONGREGATION OF MARY, INC. (D)

St. Zita's Villa, Monsey, NY 10952. Tel: 845-356-2011. Sr. Maureen Francis, S.R.C.M.
Total in Community: 3.
Represented in the Archdiocese of New York.

[3475] (S.R.)—SISTERS OF REPARATION OF THE SACRED WOUNDS OF JESUS (D)

Founded in 1954 in New York by Mother Mary Rose Therese, S.R. Established in the Diocese of San Diego in 1959. Motherhouse and Novitiate transferred to the Archdiocese of Portland in Oregon in 1973.

General Motherhouse and Novitiate: *Sacred Wounds of Jesus Convent*, 2120 S.E. 24th Ave., Portland, OR 97214. Tel: 503-236-4207; Fax: 503-236-3400; Email: repsrs@comcast.net; Email: MMAngels@comcast.net; Web: www.reparationsisters.org. Mother Mary of the Angels, S.R., Supr.
Sisters: 2; Donne Members: 160.
Legal Title: *Sisters of Reparation of the Sacred Wounds of Jesus, Inc., Portland, OR.*
Ministry in Health Care; Education; Pastoral Animation.
Represented in the Archdiocese of Portland in Oregon.

[3480] (C.R.)—SISTERS OF THE RESURRECTION (P)

Founded in Rome, Italy, in 1891. First foundation in the United States in 1900.

General Motherhouse: Via Marcantonio Colonna 52A, Rome, Italy Rev. Mother Dolores Stepien, C.R., Supr. Gen.
Universal total in Congregation: 450.

Western Province Provincialhouse and Novitiate: 7432 Talcott Ave., Chicago, IL 60631. Tel: 773-792-6363. Sr. Virginia Ann Wanzek, C.R., Prov. Supr.
Total in Community: 46.
Properties owned or sponsored: Resurrection High School; Resurrection Health Care Corporation.
Represented in the Archdioceses of Chicago, Milwaukee and Mobile.

Eastern Province Provincialhouse and Novitiate: *Sisters of the Resurrection*, 35 Boltwood Ave., Castleton On Hudson, NY 12033. Tel: 518-732-2226; Fax: 518-732-2898; Email: crsister@resurrectionsisters.org. Sr. Cecilia Mary Berdar, C.R., Prov. Supr.
Total in Community: 39.
Legal Title: *Sisters of the Resurrection, New York, Inc.*
Ministry in Nursing Homes; Elementary Schools; Christian Doctrine Centers; High School for Girls; Preschools; Pastoral Associates.
Represented in the Archdiocese of New York and in the Dioceses of Albany and Trenton.

[3490] (O.S.S.)—RELIGIOUS OF THE ORDER OF THE BLESSED SACRAMENT AND OF OUR LADY (P)

Founded in France in 1639. First foundation in the United States in 1912. The Sisters devote their lives to the perpetual adoration of Christ in the Eucharist.

Blessed Sacrament Monastery: 86 Dromore Rd., Scarsdale, NY 10583-1706. Tel: 914-722-1657. Sr. Mary Veronica, O.S.S., Prioress.
Professed Sisters: 7.

Monastery of Perpetual Adoration (1951): 2798 U.S. 31 N., P.O. Box 86, Conway, MI 49722. Tel: 231-347-0447. Sr. Mary Rosalie, O.S.S., Prioress.
Professed Sisters: 2.
Represented in the Archdiocese of New York and in the Diocese of Gaylord.

[3499] (S.J.S.)—SISTER SERVANTS OF THE BLESSED SACRAMENT (P)

Founded in Mexico in 1904. First foundation in the United States in 1926.

General Motherhouse: Juan Bernardino 650, Guadalajara, Jalisco, Mexico, 45000. Sr. Rosa Maria Sierra Barba, S.J.S., Supr. Gen.

U.S. Province: 3173 Winnetka Dr., Bonita, CA 91902. Tel: 619-267-0720; Fax: 619-267-0920. Sr. Maria Paz Uribe, S.J.S., Prov. Supr.
Total in Community: 57.
Legal Title: *Sister Servants of the Blessed Sacrament, Inc.*
Ministry in the field of Education.
Represented in the Archdiocese of Los Angeles and in the Dioceses of Fresno, Sacramento, San Diego and Monterey.

[3500] (S.S.S.)—SERVANTS OF THE BLESSED SACRAMENT (P)

Founded in France in 1859; First foundation in the United States in 1947.

General Motherhouse: 580 Dufferin, Sherbrooke, Canada, J1H 4N1.

U.S. Address: *Blessed Sacrament Convent*, 101 Silver St., Waterville, ME 04901. Tel: 207-872-7072; Fax: 207-873-2317. Sr. Josephine Roney, S.S.S., Local/Regional Supr.
Total in Community: 13.
Represented in the Dioceses of Portland (In Maine) and Pueblo (Colorado).

[3510] (S.S.C.K.)—CONGREGATION OF SISTER SERVANTS OF CHRIST THE KING (D)

Founded in the United States in 1936.

General Motherhouse: *Loretto Convent*, N. 8114 Co. W.W. Calvary St., Mount Calvary, WI 53057. Tel: 920-753-3211. Sr. Stephen Bloesl, Supr.
Professed Sisters: 6.
Represented in the Archdiocese of Milwaukee and in the Diocese of Fargo.

[3520] (S.S.C.M.)—SERVANTS OF THE HOLY HEART OF MARY (P)

Founded in Paris, France in 1860. First foundation in the United States in 1889.

Generalate: 2029 rue Holy Cross, Montreal, Canada, H4E 2A4. Sr. Louise Payeur, S.S.C.M., Supr. Gen.

United States Region-Holy Family Province: *Provincialate*, 15 Elmwood Dr., Kankakee, IL 60901. Tel: 815-937-2380. Sr. Linda K. Hatton, S.S.C.M., Prov. Supr.
Total number in Region: 40.
Legal Title: *Servants of the Holy Heart of Mary.*
Provena Health.
Ministry in Grammar Schools; Nursing Homes; Health Care; Education; Pastoral Ministry; Parishes; Ministry to the Aged; and Home Missions.
Represented in the Archdiocese of Milwaukee and in the Dioceses of Belleville, Joliet, Peoria and Rockford.

[3530] (S.SP.S.)—MISSIONARY SISTERS SERVANTS OF THE HOLY SPIRIT (P)

Founded in Holland in 1889. First foundation in the United States in 1901.

General Motherhouse: *Convento dello Spirito Santo*, Via Cassia 645, Rome, Italy, 00189. Sr. Maria Theresia Hornemann, S.Sp.S., Supr. Gen.
Universal total in Congregation: 3391.

American Motherhouse (1901): *Convent of the Holy Spirit*, 319 Waukegan Rd., P.O. Box 6026, Techny, IL 60082-6026. Tel: 847-441-0126; Fax: 847-441-5587. Sr. Carol Welp, S.Sp.S., Prov.
Total in Community: 77.
Legal Titles: Missionary Sisters Sponsorship, Inc., Techny, IL; Arnold Janssen Foundation, Techny, IL; Helena Stollenwerk Foundation, Techny, IL.
Ministry in Schools; Catechetical Work; Parish Ministry & Administration.
Represented in the Archdioceses of Chicago and New York and in the Diocese of Memphis.

[3540] (S.SP.S.DEA.P.)—SISTER-SERVANTS OF THE HOLY SPIRIT OF PERPETUAL ADORATION (P)

Founded in Holland in 1896. First foundation in the United States in 1915. Second foundation in the United States in 1928.

Generalate: Convent of the Most Holy Trinity, Bad Driburg, Germany Sr. Mary Cecilia, S.Sp.S.deA.P., Supr. Gen.

U.S. House of Formation: *Mount Grace Convent*, 1438 E. Warne Ave., Saint Louis, MO 63107-1015. Tel: 313-381-5686. Sr. Mary Catherine, S.Sp.S.deA.P., Supr.
Professed Sisters: 24.

Convent of Divine Love: 2212 Green St., Philadelphia, PA 19130-3197. Tel: 215-567-0123. Sr. Mary Caritas, S.Sp.S.deA.P., Supr.
Professed Sisters: 23.

Blessed Sacrament Convent: 4105 Ocean Dr., Corpus Christi, TX 78411. Tel: 361-852-6212. Sr. Mary Margaret Friedl, S.Sp.S. de A.P., Supr.
Professed Sisters: 9.

Adoration Convent of Christ the King Church: 1040 S. Cotner Blvd., Lincoln, NE 68510. Tel: 402-489-0765. Sr. Mary Henrita, S.Sp.S.deA.P., Supr.
Professed Sisters: 7.
Represented in the Archdioceses of Lincoln.

[3550] (S.C.I.M.)—SERVANTS OF THE IMMACULATE HEART OF MARY (P)

Good Shepherd Sisters of Quebec

Founded in Canada in 1850. First foundation in the United States in 1882.

Generalate: 2550, rue Marie-Fitzbach, Canada Sr. Theresa Rounds, S.C.I.M., Supr. Gen.

Universal total in Congregation: 538.

Provincial Headquarters: *St. Joseph Province*, 409 Pool St., Biddeford, ME 04005. Tel: 207-282-4976; Fax: 207-282-7376. Sr. Theresa Therrien, S.C.I.M., Prov.

Total in Community: 61.

Ministry in Grammar Schools; Adoption Agency; Group Home for Unmarried Mothers; Youth (Retreat Work); Apostolate to the Elderly; High School Campus Ministry; Prison/Jail Ministry; Home for Women in Transition.

Represented in the Archdiocese of Boston and in the Diocese of Portland (In Maine).

[3560] (S.J.)—SERVANTS OF JESUS (P)

Founded in Detroit, Michigan in 1974.

Headquarters: *Servants of Jesus*, 6055 Weiss, Saginaw, MI 48603. Tel: 989-249-4940.

Total in Community: 18.

Ministries: Diocesan Offices; Parish Ministry; Religious Education; Catholic Schools; Legal Aid; Health Care.

Represented in the Archdiocese of Detroit and in the Dioceses of Grand Rapids, Gaylord and Saginaw.

[3570] (O.S.M.)—MANTELLATE SISTERS, SERVANTS OF MARY OF BLUE ISLAND (P)

Founded in Italy in 1861. First foundation in the United States in 1916.

Generalate and Novitiate: Rome, Italy

U.S. Motherhouse & Novitiate: *Convent of Our Mother of Sorrows*, 13811 S. Western Ave., Blue Island, IL 60406. Tel: 708-385-2103. Sr. M. Eleanor Carella, O.S.M., Reg. Supr.

Professed Sisters: 13.

Represented in the Archdiocese of Chicago.

[3572] (O.S.M.)—MANTELLATE SISTERS SERVANTS OF MARY OF PLAINFIELD (P)

Founded October 6, 1861 in Treppio, Italy. First founded in the United States 1916.

Universal number of Mantellate Sisters: 392.

Mantellate Sisters Servants of Mary of Plainfield (1977): 16949 S. Drauden Rd., Plainfield, IL 60586-9168. Tel: 815-436-5796. Sr. Louise Staszewski, O.S.M., Reg. Supr.

Sisters: 7.

Ministry in the field of Academic Education; Parish Ministry; Retreats; Social Work; Nursing; Homes for the Aged; Foreign Missions.

Represented in the Archdiocese of Chicago and in the Diocese of Joliet.

[3580] (O.S.M.)—SERVANTS OF MARY (P)

Founded in Italy in the 13th Century. First foundation in the United States in 1893.

General Motherhouse: *St. Joseph Priory*, Harrow Rd. W., Dorking, Surrey, England, RH43BE. Sr. Marie Therese Connor, O.S.M., Prioress Gen.

American Province (1893): *Provincial Motherhouse, Convent of Our Lady of Sorrows*, 7400 Military Ave., Omaha, NE 68134-3398. Tel: 402-571-2547; Fax: 402-573-6055; Web: osms.org. Sr. Virginia Silvestri, O.S.M., Prov.

Total in Community: 87.

Properties owned and/or sponsored: Marian High School, Omaha, NE; Our Lady of Sorrows Convent, Omaha, NE.

Ministry in the field of Religious and Academic Education at all levels; Parishes; Social Service Agencies; Diocesan Offices; Hospital Pastoral Care; Counseling Agencies; Peace and Justice Offices; Campus Ministry; Hospice; Health Care Services; Medical Research; Consulting; Spiritual Direction; Retreat Work.

Represented in the Archdioceses of Detroit, Omaha and Portland in Oregon and in the Dioceses of Des Moines, Gaylord, Grand Island, Green Bay, Ogdensburg and Tucson.

[3590] (O.S.M.)—SERVANTS OF MARY (SERVITE SISTERS) (D)

Founded in Italy in the 13th Century. First foundation in the United States in 1912.

General Motherhouse: *Servants of Mary*, 1000 College Ave. W., Ladysmith, WI 54848-2199. Tel: 715-532-3364; Fax: 715-532-9611; Web: www.servitesisters.org. Sr. Theresa H. Sandok, O.S.M., Pres.

Total in Community: 61.

Ministry in the fields of Education, Health Care, Pastoral Ministry, Parish Administration, Social Services and Law.

Represented in the Archdioceses of Boston, Chicago, Milwaukee and St. Paul-Minneapolis and in the Dioceses of Joliet, La Crosse, Phoenix, Superior and St. Petersburg.

[3595] (S.S.J.)—SERVANTS OF ST. JOSEPH (P)

Founded in Spain in 1874.

Motherhouse: Salamanca, Spain

General House: Rome, Italy Mother Josefa Somoza, Supr. Gen.

U.S. Address (1957): 203 N. Spring St., Falls Church, VA 22046. Tel: 703-533-8441; Fax: 703-534-9549. Sr. Augustina Temprano.

Total in Community: 7.

Represented in the Diocese of Arlington.

[3600] (S.DEM.)—SISTERS SERVANTS OF MARY (P)

Founded in Madrid, Spain by St. Maria Soledad Torres, August 15, 1851. First foundation in the United States in 1914.

Total Membership 1,700 Sisters.

General Motherhouse: via Antonio Musa 16, Rome, Italy, 00161. Mother Alfonsa Bellido, S.deM., Supr. Gen.

Provincial Motherhouse: 800 N. 18th St., Kansas City, KS 66102. Sr. Carmela Sanz, S.deM., Prov. Supr.; Sr. Claudia Rodriguez, S.deM., Local Supr.; Sr. Silvia Enriguez, S.deM., Community Archivist; Ema Munoz, S.de M., Treas.

Total number in Province: 249.

Represented in the Archdioceses of Kansas City in Kansas, Los Angeles, New Orleans and New York.

[3610] (S.S.M.I.)—SISTERS SERVANTS OF MARY IMMACULATE (P)

Founded in Zuzel, Ukraine on August 28, 1892. Approved by the Holy See, 1932. Arrived in the United States on August 15, 1935 at Stamford, Connecticut.

Generalate: Via Cassia Antica 104, Rome, Italy, 00191. Sr. Janice Soluk, S.S.M.I., Supr. Gen.

Sisters Servants of Mary Immaculate: *Sisters Servants Ln.*, 9 Emmanuel Dr., P.O. Box 9, Sloatsburg, NY 10974-0009. Tel: 845-753-2840. Sr. Michele Yakymovitch, S.S.M.I., Prov. Supr.

Total in Community: 33.

Properties owned and/or sponsored: Immaculate Conception Provincialate & Novitiate; St. Joseph's Home (for the aged); Saint Mary's Villa Spiritual, Cultural and Educational Center, Sloatsburg, NY.

Ministry in the field of Education; Parish and Pastoral ministry; Health Care; Administration; Retreat Ministry; Hospitality; Holy Dormition Pilgrimage; Catechetical; Seminary Library; Youth Ministry.

Represented in the Ukrainian and Byzantine Rite Catholic Dioceses of the United States.

[3615] (E.I.N.)—SERVANTS OF THE IMMACULATE CHILD MARY (ESCLAVAS DE LA INMACULADA NINA) (P)

Founded in Mexico in 1901. First foundation in the United States in 1978.

Motherhouse: *Mother Maria Reina Mula Casas*, Dr. Espina #10, 28019 Madrid, Spain

Provincial House: Matamoros #100, Tlalpan D.F., Mexico, C.P. 14000. Sr. M. Celina Luz Maria Perez Romero, E.W.

U.S. Foundation: 5135 Dartmouth Ave., Los Angeles, CA 90032. Tel: 323-225-3279. Sr. Raquel Diaz, E.I.N., Supr.; Sr. Josefina Lopez, E.I.N.; Sr. Maria del Refugio Carlos, E.I.N.; Sr. Josefina Guzman, E.I.N.

House of Formation: 350 S. Boyle Ave., Los Angeles, CA 90033. Tel: 323-269-7786. Sr. Raquel Diaz, E.I.N., Supr.; Sr. Maria Espindola, E.I.N.; Sr. Petra Lopez, E.I.N.

Total number of Sisters in the U.S: 3.

Ministry in the field of religious education and adult formation in parishes.

Represented in the Archdiocese of Los Angeles.

[3620] (S.S.M.I.)—SISTERS SERVANTS OF MARY IMMACULATE (P)

First founded in Poland in 1878.

General Motherhouse: Mariowka-Opoczynska, Poland Mother Danuta Wrobel, Mother Gen.

Total number of Sisters in the U.S: 33; Universal total in Congregation: 860.

American Province (1935): 1220 Tugwell Dr., Catonsville, MD 21228. Tel: 410-747-1353. Sr. Krystyna Mroczek, Prov. Supr.; Sr. Marianna Danko, Community Archivist.

Total in Community: 33.

Represented in the Archdioceses of Baltimore and Washington and in the Diocese of Cleveland.

[3630] (S.S.C.J.)—SERVANTS OF THE MOST SACRED HEART OF JESUS (P)

Founded in Poland in 1894.

General Motherhouse: 24 Garncarska St., Cracow, Poland Sr. Agnieszka Kijowska, Supr. Gen.

Sister Servants of the Most Sacred Heart of Jesus (1959): *Sacred Heart Province*, 866 Cambria St., Cresson, PA 16630-1713. Tel: 814-886-4223. Sr. Ryszarda Wittbrodt, S.S.C.J., Prov. Supr.

Total number in Province: 25.

Represented in the Archdiocese of Philadelphia and in the Dioceses of Altoona-Johnstown and Wilmington. Also in Mandeville, Jamaica.

[3640] (S.M.G.)—POOR SERVANTS OF THE MOTHER OF GOD (P)

Founded in London, England in 1869. First foundation in the United States in 1947.

General Motherhouse: Maryfield, Roehampton, London, England, S.W. 15. Sr. Mary Whelan, S.M.G., Supr. Gen.

American Foundation: *Maryfield Nursing Home*, 1315 Greensboro Rd., High Point, NC 27260. Tel: 336-886-2444. Sr. Teresa Twomey, S.M.G., Reg. Supr.

Total in Community: 19.

Ministry in Hospitals; Nursing Homes; Schools; Retreat House.

Represented in the Archdiocese of Philadelphia and in the Dioceses of Charlotte, Gallup, Metuchen and Richmond.

[3658] (S.S.H.J.)—SISTERS OF THE SACRED HEART OF JESUS (P)

Founded in Ragusa, Italy in 1889. First foundation in the United States in 1951.

Generalate House: *Instituto Sacro Cuore di Ragusa*, Via Cassia 1714, Rome, Italy, 00123.

Universal total in Congregation: 620.

Motherhouse: *Instituto Sacro Cuore*, Via Suor Maria Schinina 2, Ragusa, Italy, 97100.

American Headquarters: *Sacred Heart Villa School & Convent*, 5269 Lewiston Rd., Lewiston, NY 14092. Tel: 716-284-8273.

Legal Titles: Sacred Heart Villa School & Convent, Lewiston, NY; Saint Frances Cabrini Nursery and Convent, North Haven, CT.

Ministry in the field of Religious and Academic Education at all levels; Hospitals; Homes for the Aged; Orphanages; Parish Ministry; Youth Ministry; Foreign Missions; Social Services.

Represented in the Archdiocese of Hartford and in the Diocese of Buffalo.

[3660] (S.S.H.J.P.)—SERVANTS OF THE SACRED HEART OF JESUS AND OF THE POOR (P)

Founded in Leon, Gto., Mexico in 1885. First foundation in U.S. in 1907.

Motherhouse: Apartado 92, Puebla, Pue, Mexico, 72000. Tel: 01152-2222-42-18-69. Mother Magdalena Sofia Juarez, Gen. Supr.

U.S. Address: *Sacred Heart Children's Home Convent*, 3310 S. Zapata Hwy., Laredo, TX 78046. Tel: 956-723-3343; Fax: 956-723-3409. Mother Maria Yolanda Fernandez, S.S.H.J.P., Major Supr.; Mother Maria Teresa Grajeda, S.S.H.J.P., Supr.; Sr. Maria Isidra Valdez, S.S.H.J.P., Admin.

Professed Sisters in U.S: 35.

Ministry in academic and religious education at all levels; Children's Home.

Represented in the Dioceses of Laredo and El Paso.

[3670] (S.S.C.J.)—SISTERS OF THE SACRED HEART OF JESUS OF SAINT JACUT (P)

Founded in France in 1816. First foundation in the United States in 1903.

Generalate: *Villa des Otages*, No. 8 85 rue Haxo, Paris, France, 75020.

Motherhouse: St. Jacut les Pins, Brittany, France, 56220.

USA/Mexico Province (1916): *Provincialate Offices*, 11931 Radium St., San Antonio, TX 78216. Tel: 210-344-7203; Fax: 210-341-0721. Sr. Cecilia Rodriguez, S.S.C.J., Prov.

Total in Community: 46.

Ministry in Education; Pastoral Work; Schools of Religion; Health Care; Mexico Missions.

Properties owned or sponsored: Mount Sacred Heart School, San Antonio, TX; Casa Angelique; Holy Spirit Convent, San Antonio, TX; Santa Maria Community, San Antonio, TX; St. Joseph's Community, San Antonio, TX; Beth Rachamim Community, San Antonio, TX; Sacred Heart Community, San Antonio, TX; Casa Ste. Emilie, San Antonio, TX; Provincialate Community, San Antonio, TX

Represented in the Archdioceses of Galveston-Houston and San Antonio and in the Diocese of Brownsville. Also in Mexico City.

[3680] (S.H.J.M.)—SISTERS OF THE SACRED HEARTS OF JESUS AND MARY (P)

Founded in France in 1866. First foundation in United States in 1953.

Motherhouse: Essex, England

Regional House: 2150 Lake Shore Ave., Oakland, CA 94606. Tel: 510-839-5213; Fax: 510-839-5256. Sr. Lorna K. Walsh, S.H.J.M., Team Member.

Universal total in Congregation: 160; U.S. Community: 9.

Ministry in Pastoral Care; Adult Education; Counseling; Children's Faith Formation; Nursing.

Represented in the Dioceses of Oakland and Stockton.

[3690] (SS.CC.)—CONGREGATION OF THE SACRED HEARTS AND OF PERPETUAL ADORATION (P)

Founded in France in 1800 as a Congregation of men and

women. Members are consecrated to the Hearts of Jesus and Mary. Special Ministries are Perpetual Adoration, the education of youth, especially the poor, parish work and foreign missions. First Catholic missionaries to Hawaii in 1827: Sisters started Catholic Schools for girls in Hawaii 1859. First foundation in the continental United States in 1908.

Generalate: Via Aurelia 145, Scala C-Int 10-14, Rome, Italy, 00165. Sr. Rosa Maria Ferreiro, SS.CC., Supr. Gen.

Pacific Province: *Sisters of the Sacred Hearts*, 1120 Fifth Ave, Honolulu, HI 96816. Tel: 808-737-5822. Sr. Helene Wood, SS.CC., Prov.
Total in Community: 40.
Legal Holdings and Titles: Sisters of the Sacred Hearts Corporation; Regina Pacis Convent; Sacred Hearts Academy Corporation; Saint Anthony Retreat Center Corporation; Malia O Ka Malu Community, Honolulu, HI; Na Leo Ho'onani Community, Honolulu, HI; Paewalani Community, Honolulu, HI; Our Lady of Grace Community, Artesia, NM.

East Coast Region: *Sisters of the Sacred Hearts of Jesus and Mary and of Perpetual Adoration*, 35 Huttleston Ave., Fairhaven, MA 02719-3154. Tel: 508-994-9341; Fax: 508-990-1967. Sr. Muriel Ann Lebeau, SS.CC., Supr.
Total in Community: 3.
Represented in the Diocese of Fall River.

[3710] (C.S.A.)—CONGREGATION OF SISTERS OF SAINT AGNES (P)

Founded in the United States in 1858.

General Motherhouse: *St. Agnes Convent*, 320 County Rd. K, Fond Du Lac, WI 54937-8158. Tel: 920-907-2300; Fax: 920-923-3194. Sr. Joann Sambs, C.S.A., Gen. Supr.; Sr. Diane Bauknecht, C.S.A., Gen. Vicar. Councilors: Sr. Sharon Pollnow, C.S.A.; Sr. Doris Klein, C.S.A.
Total in Congregation : 272.
Ministry in the field of Academic and Religious Education; Hospitals; Homes for Aged; Parish Ministry; Foreign Missions; Social Services; Healthcare.
Properties owned or sponsored: Hazotte Ministries, Inc.; Marian University, Fond du Lac, WI; Agnesian HealthCare of Fond du Lac, WI, Inc.; St. Francis Home, Fond du Lac, WI; Waupun Memorial Hospital, Waupun, WI; The Monroe Clinic, Monroe, WI.
Represented in the Archdioceses of Chicago, Milwaukee, Mobile, New York, and St. Paul-Minneapolis and in the Dioceses of Allentown, Altoona-Johnstown, Columbus, Fort Wayne-South Bend, Gallup, Gary, Green Bay, Jackson, Joliet, Madison, Marquette, Memphis, Palm Beach, Phoenix, Providence, Raleigh, Salina, Toledo, Tucson and Venice. Also in Honduras and Nicaragua.

[3718] (S.S.A.)—SISTERS OF ST. ANN

Founded in Italy in 1834.

General Motherhouse: V.d. Aldobrandeschi, Rome, Italy, 100-00163. Sr. Ernestine Fernandes, S.S.A., Supr. Gen.
Universal total in Congregation: 1500.

U.S. Delegation (1952): *Mount St. Ann*, P.O. Box 328, Ebensburg, PA 15931. Tel: 814-472-9354; Fax: 814-472-9354. Sr. Anna Maria Lorenzon, S.S.A., Delegate; Sr. Melany Pereira, S.S.A., Community Archivist.
Total in Community: 9.
Ministry in the field of Education; Retreat Ministry; Foreign Mission; Pastoral Ministry.
Represented in the Dioceses of Altoona-Johnstown and Corpus Christi.

[3720] (S.S.A.)—SISTERS OF SAINT ANNE (P)

Founded in Vaudreuil, Province of Quebec, Canada, 1850. First foundation in the United States in 1866.
Legal Title: *The Community of the Sisters of St. Anne.*

General Motherhouse: 1950 Provost St., H85 1P7, Lachine, Canada Sr. Rita Larivee, Congregational Leader.

Saint Marie Province (1887): 720 Boston Post Rd. E., Marlborough, MA 01752. Tel: 508-481-4934; Tel: 508-481-4939. Provincial Leaders: Sr. Marguerite St. Amand, S.S.A.; Sr. Yvette E. Bellerose, S.S.A.
Total number in Province: 115; Total in Community: 580.
Properties owned and/or sponsored: Saint Anne Convent; Mary Martha House, Marlborough, MA; Esther House, Worcester, MA; Marie Esther Health Center, Inc., Marlborough, MA; St. Anne Regional, Worcester, MA.
Ministry in the field of Academic and Religious Education at all levels; Center for Spiritual Renewal; Campus Ministry; Various Apostolates; Retreat Work; Pastoral Ministry; Ministry to the Aged, Shut-ins and the Poor; Assisted Living Nursing; Foreign Ministries.
Represented in the Archdiocese of Boston and in the Dioceses of Fall River, Providence, Springfield in Massachusetts and Worcester.

[3730] (O.S.B.M.)—SISTERS OF THE ORDER OF ST. BASIL THE GREAT (P)
(International Byzantine Rite)

Founded in Cappadocia in the 4th Century by St. Basil the Great and his sister St. Macrina. First foundation in the United States in 1911.

Basilian Generalate: Via San Alessio 26, Rome, Italy, 00153. Sr. Miriam Claire Kowal, O.S.B.M., Gen. Supr.

Philadelphia-Ukrainian Byzantine Rite: *Provincial and Motherhouse*, 710 Fox Chase Rd., Jenkintown, PA 19046. Tel: 215-663-9153; Fax: 215-379-4843.
Solemnly Professed Sisters: 41.
Ministry in Education at all levels; Pastoral Ministry.
Represented in the Ukrainian Archdiocese of Philadelphia and in the Ukrainian Dioceses of Chicago, Parma and Stamford.

Pittsburgh Ruthenian Byzantine Rite-Motherhouse and Novitiate: *Mount St. Macrina*, 500 W. Main St., P.O. Box 878, Uniontown, PA 15401. Tel: 724-438-8644. Sr. Seraphim Olsafsky, O.S.B.M., Prov.
Professed Sisters: 71.
Legal Titles: Declaration of the Sisters of the Order of St. Basil the Great Endowment Trust; Declaration of Trust of the Sisters of the Order of St. Basil the Great Community Support Program; Mount St. Macrina Cemetery, Inc., Uniontown, PA.
Sister's serve in Diocesan, Parish and Religious Education Ministry; Health Care; Pastoral Ministry.
Represented in the Byzantine Archdiocese of Pittsburgh and in the Dioceses of Parma, Passaic and Van Nuys.

[3735] (C.S.B.)—CONGREGATION OF ST. BRIGID (P)

Founded in Ireland in 1807.

U.S. Foundation (1953): *St. Brigid's Convent*, 5118 Loma Linda Dr., San Antonio, TX 78201. Tel: 210-733-0701. Sr. Anne Drea, C.S.B., Reg. Coord.
Total in Community: 15.
Properties owned and/or sponsored: Regional House.
Pastoral Ministry in Parishes, Detention Center and Hospitals; Academic Education at all levels; Music Ministry.
Represented in the Archdioceses of Boston and San Antonio and in the Diocese of Wilmington.

[3740] (S.S.C.)—SISTERS OF ST. CASIMIR (P)

Founded by Servant of God, Mother Maria Kaupas in the United States in 1907.

General Motherhouse: 2601 W. Marquette Rd., Chicago, IL 60629. Tel: 773-776-1324; Fax: 773-776-8755. Sr. M. Immacula Wendt, S.S.C., Gen. Supr.; Sr. Margaret Zalot, S.S.C., Gen. Sec.; Sr. M. Christella, S.S.C., Archivist.
Total in Community: 90.
Properties owned and/or sponsored: Maria High School; Holy Cross Hospital, Chicago, IL; Villa Joseph Marie High School, Holland, PA.
Ministry in the field of Academic Education; Foreign Missions; Hospitals; Pastoral Ministry.
Represented in the Archdioceses of Chicago and Philadelphia and in the Diocese of Kalamazoo. Also in Argentina.

[3750] (S.S.CH.)—SISTERS OF ST. CHRETIENNE (P)

Founded in France in 1807. First foundation in the United States in 1903.

General Motherhouse: Metz (Moselle), France, 57000.

Provincial House: 297 Arnold St., Wrentham, MA 02093-1798. Tel: 508-384-8066; Fax: 508-384-3170. Sr. Lisette Michaud, S.S.Ch., Prov. Supr.
Total number in Province: 49.
Properties owned and/or sponsored: Our Lady Preschool Learning Center, Marlborough, MA; St. Chretienne Retirement Residence, Marlborough, MA.
Legal Titles: St. Chretienne Educational Institute, Inc., Marlborough, MA; St. Chretienne Educational Institute Trust Wrentham, MA.
Represented in the Archdiocese of Boston and in the Dioceses of Norwich, Providence, Portland in Maine and St. Petersburg.

[3760] (O.S.C.)—ORDER OF ST. CLARE
Poor Clares-Poor Clares of the Primitive Observance

Founded in Assisi, Italy in 1212. First permanent foundation in the United States in 1878.
3626 N. 65th Ave., Omaha, NE 68104-3299.

Monastery of St. Clare: 70 Nelson Ave., Wappingers Falls, NY 12590-1121. Tel: 845-297-1685; Fax: 845-297-7657; Web: www.poorclaresny.com.
Solemnly Professed Sisters: 10; Simply Professed: 1; Novices: 1.
Assisi, Italy, is called the Motherhouse of the Order, but the Abbess of said Monastery has no jurisdiction over other Communities of Poor Clares. Some Monasteries, such as those at Omaha, Evansville, New Orleans, Memphis, Jamaica Plain, Greenville, Lowell and Spokane, are subject to a Father General and to the Provincial of the Franciscan Province in which the Monastery is located. Monasteries at Aptos, Cleveland, Kokomo, Los Altos Hills, Newport News, Rockford, Roswell and Santa Barbara are Colettines.

St. Clare's Monastery of the Blessed Sacrament O.S.C: 720 Henry Clay Ave., New Orleans, LA 70118. Tel: 504-895-2019. Sr. Elizabeth Mortell, O.S.C., Abbess.
Total in Community: 9.
Cloistered.

Franciscan Monastery of St. Clare O.S.C: 6825 Nurrenbern Rd., Evansville, IN 47712-8518. Tel: 812-425-4396; Web: poorclare.org/evansville. Sr. Jeanne Maffet, O.S.C., Abbess; Sr. Catherine K. Janeway, O.S.C., Vicaress.
Total in Community: 9.

Monastery of St. Clare (1932): 1310 Dellwood Ave., Memphis, TN 38127. Tel: 901-357-6662. Sr. Mary Marguerite, O.S.C., Abbess.
Total in Community: 5.
Solemnly Professed Cloistered.

The Franciscan Monastery of St. Clare: 920 Centre St., Jamaica Plain, MA 02130. Tel: 617-524-1760; Fax: 617-983-5205. Sr. Clare Frances McAvoy, O.S.C., Abbess.
Total in Community: 22.

Monastery of St. Clare O.S.C: 150 White Pine Rd., Chesterfield, NJ 08515. Tel: 609-324-2638; Fax: 609-324-2938. Sr. Miriam Varley, O.S.C., Abbess.
Total in Community: 14.

Franciscan Monastery of Saint Clare: 1271 Langhorne-Newtown Rd., Langhorne, PA 19047-1297. Tel: 215-968-5775; Fax: 215-968-6254. Sr. Evelyn L. Eynon, O.S.C., Abbess.
Total in Community: 13.

Franciscan Monastery of St. Clare, Spokane, Washington: *Poor Clare Nuns*, 4419 N. Hawthorne St., Spokane, WA 99205. Tel: 509-327-4479. Sr. Rita Louise McLean, O.S.C., Abbess; Sr. Colleen Byrne, O.S.C., Vocation Directress.
Professed Nuns: 5.
Solemn Vows, Papal Enclosure Franciscan Province of Santa Barbara. Mother Bentivoglio Federation of Poor Clares.

St. Clare's Monastery: 421 S. Fourth St., Sauk Rapids, MN 56379. Tel: 320-251-3556; Fax: 320-203-7052. Mother Mary Matthew, O.S.C., Abbess.
Total in Community: 20.

St. Clare's Monastery of the Infant Jesus (1953): *Franciscan Poor Clare Nuns*, 8650 Russell Ave. S., Minneapolis, MN 55431-1998. Tel: 952-881-4766. Sr. Frances Getchell, O.S.C., Abbess.
Total in Community: 13; Novices: 1; Postulants: 1.
Legal Title: *Franciscan Poor Clare Nuns.*

Monastery of Poor Clares (1877): *Order of St. Clare-Poor Clare Colettine Nuns P.C.C.*, 3501 Rocky River Dr., Cleveland, OH 44111-2998. Tel: 216-941-2820. Mother Mary Dolores, P.C.C., Abbess.
Total in Community: 18.
Poor Clare Nuns (Colettines), observing the Primitive Rule of St. Clare. Strictly cloistered, Solemn Vows, Perpetual Exposition of the Most Blessed Sacrament.

Franciscan Monastery of St. Clare: *Order of St. Clare*, 1505 Miles Rd., Cincinnati, OH 45231-2427. Tel: 513-825-7177; Fax: 513-825-4071; Email: contactsisters@fuse.net; Web: www.poorclarescincinnati.org. Sr. Ann Bartko, O.S.C., Abbess.
Total in Community: 8.
Solemn vows; papal enclosure.

Corpus Christi Monastery (Solemn Vows, Papal Enclosure): *Poor Clare Colettines P.C.C.*, 2111 S. Main St., Rockford, IL 61102. Tel: 815-963-7343. Mother Mary Regina, P.C.C., Abbess.
Total in Community: 20.
Cloistered.

Annunciation Monastery: *Poor Clare Colettines P.C.C.*, 6200 E. Minooka Rd., Minooka, IL 60447-9458.

Monastery of Poor Clares-P.C.C. (1928): 215 E. Los Olivos St., Santa Barbara, CA 93105. Tel: 805-682-7670. Mother M. Clare of Jesus, Abbess.
Total in Community: 13.

Monastery of St. Clare: 445 River Rd., Andover, MA 01810-4213. Tel: 978-683-7599; Fax: 978-683-6085. Sr. Therese Marie Lacroix, O.S.C., Abbess.
Total in Community: 14.
Cloistered.

Poor Clare Monastery of Our Lady of Guadalupe: 809 E. 19th St., Roswell, NM 88201. Tel: 575-622-0868. Mother M. Angela, Abbess.
Total in Community: 22.
Legal Title: *The Community of Poor Clares of New Mexico, Inc.*
Cloistered.

Poor Clares Immaculate Heart Monastery: 28210 Natoma Rd., Los Altos Hills, CA 94022-3220. Tel: 650-948-2947. Mother Maura, P.C.C., Abbess.
Total in Community: 16.

Monastery of St. Clare: 37 McCauley Rd., Travelers Rest, SC 29690. Tel: 864-834-8015; Fax: 864-834-5402. Sr. Mary Connor, O.S.C., Abbess.
Total in Community: 18.
Cloistered.

Monastery of Poor Clares Colettine P.C.C: 5500 Holly Fork Rd., Barhamsville, VA 23011. Tel: 757-566-1684. Mother Mary Clare, P.C.C., Abbess; Sr. Mary Agnes, P.C.C., Archivist.
Total in Community: 13.
Solemn Vows. Cloistered.

Maria Regina Mater Monastery P.C.C: *Poor Clare Nuns*, 1175 N., 300 W., Kokomo, IN 46901. Tel: 765-457-5743. Mother Miriam, Abbess.
Total in Community: 10; Novices: 1.
Cloistered.

Christ the King Monastery of St. Clare O.S.C: 3900 Sherwood Blvd., Delray Beach, FL 33445. Tel: 561-498-3294. Sr. Leanna Chrostowski, O.S.C., Abbess.

Total in Community: 9.

Monastery of St. Clare of the Immaculate Conception O.S.C: *Poor Clares*, 200 Marycrest Dr., Saint Louis, MO 63129. Tel: 314-846-2618. Mother Mary Leo Hoffmann, O.S.C., Abbess.
Total in Community: 12.
Legal Title: *Nuns of the Order of St. Clare of St. Louis.*

San Damiano Monastery of St. Clare (Solemn Vows, Papal Enclosure): 6029 Estero Blvd., Fort Myers Beach, FL 33931-4325. Tel: 239-463-5599; Fax: 239-463-4993. Sr. Mary Frances Fortin, O.S.C., Abbess.
Cloistered Sisters: 8.

Monastery of St. Clare: 9300 Hwy. 105, Brenham, TX 77833. Tel: 979-836-2444. Sr. Angela Chandler, O.S.C., Abbess.
Sisters in Community: 4.

Poor Clares of Montana: 3020 18th Ave., S., Great Falls, MT 59405-5167. Tel: 406-453-7891; Fax: 406-453-8689. Sr. Catherine Cook, O.S.C., Abbess.

St. Joseph Monastery of the Poor Clares Colettine, P.C.C: P.O. Box 160, 1671 Pleasant Valley Rd., Aptos, CA 95001-0160. Tel: 831-761-9659. Mother Francis Maria, P.C.C., Abbess.
Total in Community: 12.
(Reform of St. Colette) Daily Exposition of the Most Blessed Sacrament.

Monastery of St. Clare: 4875 Shattuck Rd., Saginaw, MI 48603. Tel: 989-797-0593; Email: sisters@srsclare.com. Sr. Dianne Doughty, O.S.C., Abbess.
Solemnly Professed: 4.

[3765] (O.S.C.CAP.)—CAPUCHIN POOR CLARES (P)

Federation of Our Lady of the Angels in North America (1991): *Monastery of the Blessed Sacrament*, 4201 N.E. 18th St., Amarillo, TX 79107. Tel: 806-383-6771; Fax: 806-383-9877. Mother Theresa Cortes, O.S.C., Pres.

[3770] (O.S.C.)—SISTERS OF ST. CLARE (P)

"Bethlehem" the Generalate: 101 Harold's Cross Rd., Dublin 6W, Ireland Sr. Patricia Rogers, O.S.C., Abbess Gen.

Santa Clara: 1171 Via Santa Paulo, Vista, CA 92081. Tel: 760-295-0611. Sr. Madeline Fitzgerald, O.S.C., Contact Person; Sr. Patricia Rogers, O.S.C., Reg. Supr.-California Tel: 011-353-1-496-6791; Sr. Phyllis Shaughnessy, O.S.C., Reg. Supr.-Florida Tel: 727-643-2121.
Total in Congregation : 152; Total in Guatemala & El Salvador: 25; Total in U.S: 15.
Ministry in the field of Academic and Religious Education at all Levels; Pastoral & Social Ministry; Retreats; Ministry to the sick, poor and imprisoned.
Represented in the Dioceses of Orange, St. Petersburg, San Bernardino, San Diego and Wilmington. Also in Australia, El Salvador, England, Guatemala, Ireland and Wales.

[3780] (SS.C.M.)—SISTERS OF SAINTS CYRIL AND METHODIUS (P)

Founded in the United States in 1909.

General Motherhouse: Villa Sacred Heart, Danville, PA 17821-1698. Tel: 570-275-3581; Fax: 570-275-5997. Sr. Linda Marie Bolinski, SS.C.M., Gen. Supr.
Total in Community: 99.
Ministry in the field of Education; Parish Ministry and Religious Education; Retreat/Spiritual Direction; Hospital Chaplaincy; Deaf Apostolate; Homes for the Aged; Music Conservatory; Continuing Care Retirement Community.
Properties owned or sponsored: St. Cyril Preschool and Kindergarten; St. Cyril Academy Spiritual Center; Villa Sacred Heart; Maria Hall, Inc.; Maria Joseph Manor, Inc.; The Meadows at Maria Joseph Manor, Inc., Danville, PA; Villa St. Cyril, Highland Park, IL.
Represented in the Archdioceses of Chicago, New York and San Antonio and in the Dioceses of Bridgeport, Charleston, Gary, Harrisburg, Scranton and Syracuse.

[3790] (S.S.D.)—INSTITUTE OF THE SISTERS OF ST. DOROTHY (P)

Founded in Italy in 1834. First foundation in the United States in 1911.

General Motherhouse: Via del Gianicolo 4-a, Rome, Italy, 00165. Sr. Jaci Dutra-Pessoa, S.S.D., Gen. Coord.

Province of United States of America (1920): *St. Dorothy Provincialate*, 13 Monkeywrench Ln., Bristol, RI 02809-2916. Tel: 401-253-5434 Ext. 211. Sr. Dorothy Schwarz, S.S.D., Prov. Coord.
Universal total in Congregation: 1071; Total number in the U.S: 37.
Ministry in the field of Education; Spiritual Life Centers; Hospital Chaplaincies; Social work with immigrants.
Properties owned or sponsored: Villa Fatima, Taunton, MA; Mt. St. Joseph, Bristol, RI; Our Lady of Fatima High School, Warren, RI; St. Dorothy Academy, Staten Island, NY.

[3810] (X.S.)—SOCIETY OF CATHOLIC MISSION SISTERS OF ST. FRANCIS XAVIER, INC. (D)

(Xavier Sisters)

Founded in the United States in 1946.

Convent: 37179 Moravian Dr., Clinton Township, MI 48036. Tel: 586-465-5082; Fax: 586-465-1990. Sr. Mary Agnes Malburg.
Total in Community: 1.
Represented in the Archdiocese of Detroit.

[3820] (C.S.J.B.)—SISTERS OF ST. JOHN THE BAPTIST (P)

Founded in Italy in 1878. First foundation in the United States in 1906.

General Motherhouse: Rome, Italy Sr. Rosaria DiIorio, Supr. Gen.

U.S. Provincial House: 3308 Campbell Dr., Bronx, NY 10465-1358. Tel: 718-518-7820. Sr. Mary Cecile Swanton, C.S.J.B., Prov. Supr.
Total in Community: 99.
Legal Titles and Holdings: Mt. St. John Convent, Purchase, NY; St. John Villa Academy, Staten Island, NY; Providence Rest Nursing Home, Bronx, NY; Mt. St. John Convent, Gladstone, NJ.
Ministry in the field of Education; Health Care for Aged Women & Men; Child Day Care; Pastoral Ministry.

[3830] (C.S.J. OR S.S.J.)—SISTERS OF ST. JOSEPH

The Independent Motherhouses of the Sisters of St. Joseph are represented in the United States in the following Archdioceses and Dioceses:

[3830-01] BOSTON (D)

Motherhouse of the Congregation of the Sisters of St. Joseph of Boston-CSJ (1873): 637 Cambridge St., Brighton, MA 02135. Tel: 617-783-9090; Fax: 617-783-8246. Sr. Mary L. Murphy, C.S.J., Pres.; Sr. Mary Rita Grady, C.S.J., Community Archivist.
Total in Community: 435.
Legal Holdings or Titles: Motherhouse of the Sisters of Saint Joseph of Boston, Brighton, MA; Bethany Health Care Center, Inc., Framingham, MA; Bethany Hill School, Inc., Framingham, MA; St. Joseph Hall, Framingham, MA; Retreat Center, Cohasset, MA; The Merrimack Montessori School, Haverhill, MA; Walnut Park Montessori School, Newton, MA; Jackson School, Newton, MA; Fontbonne Academy, Milton, MA; Mount Saint Joseph Academy, Brighton, MA; Regis College, Weston, MA; Corporation for the Sponsored Ministries of the Sisters of St. Joseph of Boston, Brighton, MA; CSJ Ministries Connection, Inc., Brighton, MA; The Literacy Connection, Brighton, MA.; Casserly House, Roslindale, MA.

[3830-03] ORANGE (P)

Sisters of St. Joseph of Orange - Motherhouse: 480 S. Batavia St., Orange, CA 92868. Tel: 714-744-8121; Fax: 717-744-3165. Sr. Katherine Gray, C.S.J., Gen. Supr.; Sr. Adele Marie Kohummel, C.S.J., Community Archivist.
Total in Community: 157.
Legal Holdings and Titles: Sisters of St. Joseph of Orange; Sisters of St. Joseph Healthcare Foundation, Orange, CA; St. Joseph College, Orange, CA; St. Joseph Health System; St. Joseph Health System Foundation, Orange, CA; St. Jude Hospital, Inc. (dba St. Jude Medical Center); St. Jude Memorial Foundation, Fullerton, CA; St. Joseph Hospital Orange; St. Jude Hospital Yorba Linda, (dba St. Joseph Heritage Healthcare); Yorba Linda, CA; Mission Hospital Regional Medical Center, Mission Viejo, CA; Santa Rosa Memorial Hospital, Santa Rosa, CA; St. Joseph Hospital of Eureka, Eureka, CA; Redwood Memorial Hospital, Fortuna, CA; Redwood Memorial Foundation, Fortuna, CA; Queen of the Valley Hospital of Napa, Napa, CA; St. Mary of the Plains Hospital, Lubbock, TX; St. Mary Medical Center, Apple Valley, CA; St. Joseph Health Ministry.
Ministry in the field of Education; Health & Hospital Services; Pastoral and Social Services.
Represented in the Archdioceses of Los Angeles and San Francisco and in the Dioceses of Orange, San Bernardino, San Diego and Santa Rosa.

[3830-05] ROCKVILLE CENTRE (D)

St. Joseph's Convent - Congregation of the Sisters of Saint Joseph of Brentwood, NY CSJ: Brentwood, NY 11717. Tel: 516-273-4531. Sr. Jean Amore, C.S.J., Pres.; Sr. Virginia Dowd, C.S.J., Community Archivist.
Total in Community: 658.
Ministry in the field of Education; Health & Hospital Services; Social Services.
Represented in the Dioceses of Brooklyn and Rockville Centre. Also in Puerto Rico, Dominican Republic and Brazil.

[3830-06] BUFFALO (P)

Generalate - Congregation of the Sisters of St. Joseph SSJ: 10324 Main St., Clarence, NY 14031. Tel: 716-759-6454; Fax: 716-759-6415; Email: BUFFSSJ@aol.com. Sr. Loretta Young, S.S.J., Pres.; Sr. Suzanne Rodriguez, S.S.J., Community Archivist.
Total in Community: 127.
Ministry in the field of Education at all levels; School for Deaf; Youth Ministry; Justice Ministry; Pastoral Ministry; Hospital Chaplaincy; Prison Ministry; Spirituality Center.
Properties owned or sponsored: Administrative Office; Sisters of St. Joseph Residence.

[3830-09] ERIE (D)

Sisters of St. Joseph SSJ: 5031 W. Ridge Rd., Erie, PA 16506-1249. Tel: 814-836-4100; Fax: 814-836-4278. Sr. Mary Ellen Dwyer, S.S.J., Pres.
Total in Community: 120.
Legal Title: *Sisters of St. Joseph of Northwestern PA Inc.*
Ministry in the field of Education at all levels; Social Ministries; Nursing Home; Health Care; Pastoral Work and other Diocesan Ministries.
Institutions sponsored: Saint Vincent Health Center; St. Mary's Home of Erie; Villa Maria Elementary; Villa Maria Academy; Sisters of St. Joseph Neighborhood Network, Inc.; St. Patrick's Haven; Erie DAWN; Bethany House.
Represented in the Archdioceses of Chicago and Washington and in the Diocese of Cleveland and Louisville.

[3830-12] OGDENSBURG (D)

Motherhouse of the Society of the Sisters of St. Joseph SSJ: 1425 Washington St., Watertown, NY 13601-4533. Tel: 315-782-3460; Web: www.ssjwatertown.org. Sr. Bernadette Marie Collins, S.S.J., Major Supr.; Sr. Norma Bryant, S.S.J., Community Archivist.
Total in Community: 51.
Ministry in the field of Education at all levels; Parish and Diocesan Administration.
Represented in the Dioceses of Ogdensburg and Syracuse.

[3830-13] PITTSBURGH (P)

Sisters of St. Joseph CSJ - Motherhouse: Sisters of St. Joseph: 1020 State St., Baden, PA 15005. Tel: 724-869-2151; Fax: 724-869-3336. Leadership Team: Sr. Mary Pellegrino, Congregational Moderator; Sr. Carolyn Bodenschatz; Sr. Marguerite Coyne; Sr. Rosanne Oberleitner; Sr. Sally Witt, Community Archivist.
Total in Community: 214.
Properties owned and/or sponsored: Motherhouse and 18 residences.
Ministry in the field of Education; Health Care; Social Services; Spiritual Development; Congregational Services.
Represented in the Archdioceses of Boston, Detroit, Dubuque, Hartford, Miami, New York and Washington and in the Dioceses of Altoona-Johnstown, Arlington, Buffalo, Cheyenne, Erie, Fresno, Greensburg, Jackson, Pittsburgh, Richmond, Tucson and Wheeling-Charleston.

[3830-14] ROCHESTER (P)

Sisters of St. Joseph SSJ - Motherhouse: 150 French Rd., Rochester, NY 14618-3822. Tel: 585-641-8100; Fax: 585-641-8524. Sr. Mary Louise Mitchell, Congregational Pres.; Kathleen Urbanic, Archivist.
Total in Community: 280.
Ministry in the field of Education at all levels; Health Care; Pastoral Ministry; Home for Emotionally Disturbed Children; Parish and Diocesan Evangelization; College Campus Ministry; Social Service; Justice and Peace Office; Drug Dependency Programs; Retreats & Spiritual Direction; Prison and Jail Ministry.
Properties owned and sponsored: Nazareth Schools; Nazareth Convent; St. Joseph's Neighborhood Center; Day Star; Morning Star.
Sisters sponsor: Home Health Care; Food Kitchen; Health Care Center; Spirituality Center; Domestic and Foreign Missions.
Represented in the Archdioceses of Mobile and St. Louis and in the Diocese of Rochester. Also in Brazil.

[3830-15] SALINA (P)

General Administration Office (1884): *Nazareth Motherhouse - Sisters of St. Joseph of Concordia CSJ*, 215 Court St., P.O. Box 279, Concordia, KS 66901. Tel: 785-243-2149. Sr. Marcia Allen, C.S.J., Pres.

Motherhouse: *Sisters of St. Joseph*, 1300 Washington St., Concordia, KS 66901. Tel: 785-243-2113.
Total Sisters in Community: 152.
Properties owned and/or sponsored: Manna House of Prayer, Concordia, KS; St. Mary's, Silver City, NM.
Ministry in Care for Elderly; Homeless; Education; Parish and Diocesan Evangelization; Social Services; Justice and Peace Offices; Marriage and Family Counseling; Youth Formation; Healthcare; College Campus Ministry; Drug Dependency Programs; Prisons; Consultants; Refugees; Continuous Prayer.
Represented in the Archdioceses of Atlanta, Kansas City in Kansas and St. Paul-Minneapolis and in the Dioceses of El Paso, Kansas City, Las Cruces, Orange, Phoenix, Pueblo, St. Cloud, Salina and Wichita.

[3830-16] SPRINGFIELD (MA) (D)

Motherhouse: *The Congregation of the Sisters of St. Joseph of Springfield (SSJ)-Mont Marie*, 34 Lower Westfield Rd, Holyoke, MA 01040. Tel: 413-536-0853; Fax: 413-533-3275. Sr. Mary Quinn, S.S.J., Pres.; Sherry Enserro, Archivist.

Total in Community: 287.
Legal Holdings and Titles: Mont Marie Child Care Center, Inc.; Mont Marie Health Care Center, Inc.; Mont Marie Senior Residence, Inc., Holyoke, MA; St. Joseph Residence at Mont Marie.
Ministry in the field of Religious & Academic Education; Parish Ministry; Cross-Cultural; Diocesan Administration; Chaplaincy; Health Care, Social Services; Research and Study; Restorative Justice; AIDS Ministry; Creative Arts.
Represented in the Archdiocese of Washington and in the Dioceses of Bridgeport, Burlington, Fall River, Lake Charles, Norwich, Providence, Springfield (MA) and Worcester.

[3832] C.S.J.—CONGREGATION OF THE SISTERS OF ST. JOSEPH (P)

Legal Title: *Congregation of the Sisters of St. Joseph, Inc. d/b/a Congregation of St. Joseph.* 3430 Rocky River Dr., Cleveland, OH 44111-2297. Tel: 216-252-0440; Fax: 216-941-3430; Web: www.csjoseph.org.
Total in Community: 768.

Cleveland Center: 3430 Rocky River Dr., Cleveland, OH 44111-2997. Tel: 216-252-0440; Fax: 216-941-3430.
Legal Titles: The Sisters of St. Joseph; Legal Holdings: Saint Joseph Academy; Sisters of Saint Joseph Community Support Charitable Trust.
Ministry in the field of Academic and Religious Education at all levels; Parish and Pastoral Ministry; Deaf Apostolate; Parish Team Member; Justice Work; Health Care; Social Services; Radio; Social Concerns; Retreat Work.
Represented in the Archdioceses of Chicago and Washington and in the Dioceses of Cleveland, Youngstown and Venice.

LaGrange Center: 1515 W. Ogden Ave., La Grange Park, IL 60526. Tel: 708-354-9200; Fax: 708-354-9573.
Legal Titles: Sisters of St. Joseph of LaGrange; Legal Holdings: Nazareth Academy (LaGrange Park, IL); Sisters of St. Joseph of LaGrange Charitable Trust; Christ in the Wilderness.
Ministry in the field of Education; School Administration; Nursing; Pastoral Care in Hospitals; Nursing Homes; Work with the Elderly; Parish Ministry; Archdiocesan Administration; Spiritual Direction and Retreats; Administrative Services; Immigration Services.
Represented in the Archdiocese of Chicago and the Dioceses of Joliet, Jackson and Superior.

Medaille Center: 4010 Executive Park Dr., #320, Cincinnati, OH 45241. Tel: 513-761-2888; Fax: 513-761-0088.
Legal Titles: Sisters of St. Joseph of Medaille; Legal Holdings: St. Joseph's Academy (Baton Rouge, LA); People Program (New Orleans, LA); Ministry Against the Death Penalty; St. Joseph Spirituality Center (Baton Rouge, LA).
Ministry in the field of Academic Education at all levels; Health Care; Pastoral Ministry; Religious Education; Foreign Missions; Social Service; Centers for Christian Renewal; Services to the Poor and Minorities; Community Service; Diocesan Offices; Prison Ministry; Ministry Against the Death Penalty; Ministry for Retired-Elderly; Chemical Dependency; Adult Mentally Retarded; Care for Retired Sisters.
Represented in the Archdioceses of Chicago, Cincinnati, New Orleans and St. Paul-Minneapolis and in the Dioceses of Baton Rouge, Crookston, El Paso, Houma-Thibodaux, Rapid City, Superior and Wichita.

Nazareth Center: 3427 Gull Rd., Nazareth, MI 49074. Tel: 269-381-6290; Fax: 269-381-4909.
Legal Titles: The Sisters of St. Joseph of Nazareth; Legal holdings: Dillon Hall for Independent Living, Inc.; Ascension Health, Inc. (co-sponsor).
Ministry in the field of Education; Social Services; Parish and Church-related Ministries; Healthcare; Spirituality.
Represented in the Archdioceses of Detroit, Los Angeles, New Orleans and Santa Fe and in the Dioceses of Brooklyn, Fort Wayne-South Bend, Gaylord, Grand Rapids, Kalamazoo, Lafayette (LA), Lafayette in Indiana, Lansing, Lexington, Orange and Saginaw.

Tipton Center: 1440 W. Division Rd., Tipton, IN 46072. Tel: 765-675-4146; Fax: 765-675-7471.
Legal Title: *The Sisters of St. Joseph of Tipton, Indiana, Inc.*
Ministry in the fields of Education, Health Care, Pastoral Ministry, Social Service, Evangelization.
Represented in the Archdioceses of Indianapolis and Louisville and in the Dioceses of Lafayette in Indiana and Lansing.

Wheeling Center: 137 Mount St. Joseph Rd., Wheeling, WV 26003. Tel: 304-232-8160; Fax: 304-232-1404.
Legal Titles: The Sisters of St. Joseph of Wheeling, Inc.; Legal Holdings: Sisters of St. Joseph of Wheeling Foundation, Inc.; A.B.L.E. Families, Inc.; Holy Family Child Care & Development Center, Inc.; St. Joseph Health Initiative, Inc.; Sisters of St. Joseph Charitable Fund, Inc.; Sisters of St. Joseph Health and Wellness Foundation.
Ministry in the following areas: Parish Ministry; Pastoral Services; Elementary, Secondary, College Education; Health Care; Social Services; Spiritual Formation; Direction and Retreat Ministries; Diocesan, Administration and Service.
Represented in the Diocese of Wheeling-Charleston.

Wichita Center: 3700 E. Lincoln, Wichita, KS 67218. Tel: 316-686-7171; Fax: 316-689-4056.
Legal Titles: Sisters of St. Joseph of Wichita, Kansas; Legal holdings: Sisters of St. Joseph "Dear Neighbor" Ministries, Inc.; St. Joseph Adoption Referral Services, Inc.; Sheridan Village, Inc. (co-sponsor).
Ministry in the fields of Religious and Academic Education; Adult Religious Correspondence Courses; Diocesan Program for the Handicapped; Pro-Life Ministry to Women; Home Hospice; Hospital and Clinical Care; Pastoral Ministry; Campus Ministry; Senior Care; Social Services; Transitional Housing; Low Income Senior Housing; Retreat Ministry.
Represented in the Archdiocese of Kansas City in Kansas and in the Dioceses of Dodge City, Grand Island, Kansas City-St. Joseph, Salina and Wichita. Also in Japan.

[3840] (C.S.J.)—SISTERS OF ST. JOSEPH OF CARONDELET (P)

Founded in France in 1650. First foundation in the United States in 1836.

Congregational Offices: 2311 S. Lindbergh Blvd., St. Louis, MO 63131. Tel: 314-966-4048; Fax: 314-966-5041. Congregational Leadership Team for Provinces & Vice Province: Sr. Laura Bufano, C.S.J.; Sr. Francine Costello, C.S.J.; Sr. Susan Hames, C.S.J.; Sr. Catharine McNamee, C.S.J.; Sr. Elizabeth Ney, C.S.J.

Province of St. Louis (1836): *St. Joseph's Provincial House*, 6400 Minnesota Ave., St. Louis, MO 63111. Tel: 314-481-8800; Fax: 314-351-3111. Province Leadership Team: Sr. Patricia Clune, C.S.J.; Sr. Pat Giljum, C.S.J.; Sr. Helen Flemington, C.S.J.; Sr. Elizabeth Brown, C.S.J.; Sr. Suzanne Wesley, C.S.J.; Sr. Nancy Corcoran, C.S.J.; Sr. Jean Meier, C.S.J.
Total in Community: 387.
Legal Title: *Sisters of St. Joseph of Carondelet, St. Louis Province.*
Sponsored Institutions: Colleges 2; Academies 2; Institute for the Deaf 1.
Ministries in the field of Academic Education; Pastoral Ministries; Diocesan Offices; Health Care; Child Care; Geriatric Care; Foreign Missions; Social Services; Community Services; Special Services; Fine Arts.
Represented in the Archdioceses of Anchorage, Atlanta, Boston, Chicago, Denver, Indianapolis, Kansas City in Kansas, Los Angeles, Mobile, Omaha, St. Louis, St. Paul-Minneapolis and Seattle and in the Dioceses of Belleville, Brownsville, Charleston, Colorado Springs, El Paso, Green Bay, Honolulu, Jackson, Kansas City-St. Joseph, Marquette, Palm Beach, Peoria, San Diego, San Jose, Savannah and Venice.

Province of St. Paul (1851): *St. Joseph's Administration Center*, 1884 Randolph Ave., Saint Paul, MN 55105. Tel: 651-690-7000; Fax: 651-690-7039. Province Leadership Team: Sr. Margaret Gillespie, C.S.J.; Sr. Katherine Rossini, C.S.J.; Sr. Jean Wincek, C.S.J.; Sr. Mary Kraft, C.S.J., Archivist.
Total in Community: 286.
Legal Holdings or Titles: Sisters of St. Joseph of Carondelet.
Ministry in the fields of Education; Health; Social Services; Spirituality.
Represented in the Archdioceses of Baltimore, St. Louis and St. Paul-Minneapolis and in the Dioceses of Brownsville, Charlotte, El Paso, Jackson, Jefferson City, New Ulm, St. Cloud and Superior.

Province of Albany (1858): *St. Joseph's Provincial House*, 385 Watervliet-Shaker Rd., Latham, NY 12110-4799. Tel: 518-783-3500; Fax: 518-783-3672; Web: www.csjalbany.org. Province Leadership Team: Sr. Mary Anne Rodgers, C.S.J., Dir.; Sr. Nancy Gregg, C.S.J., First Counselor; Sr. Ann Christi Brink, C.S.J., Exec. Committee; Sr. Charla Commins, C.S.J.; Sr. Mary Jo Tallman, C.S.J.; Sr. Eileen McCann, C.S.J.; Sr. Anne L. Clark, C.S.J., Prov. Archivist; Rev. Geoffrey D. Burke, Chap.
Total in Community: 400.

Novitiate: 369 Watervliet-Shaker Rd., Latham, NY 12110. Tel: 518-783-3536.
Ministry in the fields of Academic and Special Education at all levels; Hospital and Infirmary Services; Hospital Pastoral Ministries; Parish Ministry and Religious Education; Diocesan Offices; Youth Ministry; Counseling; Retreat and Spiritual Direction; Social and Community Services; Fine Arts.
Represented in the Archdioceses of Anchorage, Boston, Cincinnati, Detroit, Indianapolis, Los Angeles, New York, St. Louis, Seattle, San Francisco and Washington and in the Dioceses of Albany, Birmingham, Brooklyn, Buffalo, Charleston, Erie, Harrisburg, Honolulu, Kansas City-St. Joseph, Ogdensburg, Palm Beach, Pensacola-Tallahassee, Pittsburgh, Rochester, Rockville Centre, Scranton, Shreveport, Spokane, Syracuse, Trenton, and Worcester. Also in Chile and Peru.

Province of Los Angeles (1878): *St. Mary's Provincialate and Carondelet Center*, 11999 Chalon Rd., Los Angeles, CA 90049-1524. Tel: 310-889-2100; Fax: 310-476-8735. Sr. Mary McKay, C.S.J., Prov. Supr.; Sr. Patricia Rose Shanahan, C.S.J., Archivist.
Professed Sisters: 357.
Legal Titles or Holdings: Sisters of St. Joseph in California; Sisters of St. Joseph in Arizona; Sisters of St. Joseph Ministerial Services.
Sisters serve in the fields of Education; Health Services; Social Services; Pastoral Ministry.
Represented in the Archdioceses of Boston, Los Angeles, St. Louis, San Francisco and Seattle and in the Dioceses of Boise, Fresno, Honolulu, Little Rock, Monterey, Oakland, Orange, Phoenix, Sacramento, San Bernardino, San Diego, San Jose, Spokane, Stockton, Tucson and Yakima.

Hawaii Vice-Province (1956): *Sisters of St. Joseph of Carondelet, Carondelet Center*, 5311 Apo Dr., Honolulu, HI 96821-1829. Tel: 808-373-3850. Sr. Margaret L. Perreira, C.S.J., Dir.
Professed Sisters: 30.
Legal Title: *Sisters of St. Joseph of Carondelet-Hawaii Vice-Province.*
Ministries include: Elementary and Secondary Schools; Services to the Elderly; Prayer & Spirituality; Administering Diocesan Offices; Religious Education Directors; Social Ministry.
Represented in the Diocese of Honolulu. Also in Chile.

[3850] (C.S.J.)—SISTERS OF ST. JOSEPH OF CHAMBERY (P)

Founded in France in 1650. First foundation in United States in 1885.

Generalate: Via Calandrelli 7, Rome, Italy, 00153. Sr. Sally Hodgdon, C.S.J., Supr. Gen.

Provincial House: *Convent of Mary Immaculate*, 27 Park Rd., West Hartford, CT 06119. Tel: 860-233-5126; Tel: 860-232-8252; Fax: 860-232-4649. Sr. Dolores Lahr, C.S.J., Prov. Supr.
Total in Community: 119.
Legal Title: *The Sisters of St. Joseph Corporation.*
Ministry in the field of Academic and Religious Education at all levels; Social Services; Pastoral and Parish Ministries; Law; Foreign Missions; Hospitals, Health Care and Prisons; Retreat work and Spiritual Direction.
Represented in the Archdioceses of Hartford and in the Dioceses of Bridgeport, Fairbanks, Lexington, Monterey, Oakland, San Antonio and Springfield in Massachusetts.

[3860] (S.J.C.)—SISTERS OF ST. JOSEPH OF CLUNY (P)

Founded in France in 1807.

Generalate: Paris, France Sr. Morag Collins, Supr. Gen.

American Novitiate: *Mary Immaculate Queen Novitiate*, 853 W 7th St., San Pedro, CA 90731. Tel: 310-834-5431. Sr. Genevieve Marie Vigil, S.J.C., Local Coord.

Provincialate: 7 Restmere Ter., Middletown, RI 02842. Tel: 401-846-4757. Sr. Joan Vander Zyden, S.J.C., Prov. of U.S. & Canada.
Professed Sisters in U.S. & Canada: 26.
Legal Title: *Sisters of St. Joseph of Cluny, Inc.*
Ministry in outreach ministry; pastoral work; retreats; healthcare; education.
Represented in the Archdiocese of Los Angeles and in the Dioceses of Newark and Providence. Also in Canada.

[3870] (C.S.J.)—SISTERS OF ST. JOSEPH OF LYONS, FRANCE (P)

Founded in France October 15, 1650. First foundation in United States in 1906 in Jackman, Maine.

General Motherhouse: Lyons, France Sr. Janet Gagnon, Supr. Gen.

Maine Province: *Sisters of St. Joseph*, 93 Halifax St., Winslow, ME 04901. Tel: 207-873-4512; Fax: 207-873-1976. Sr. Gilla Dube, C.S.J., Prov.
Total in Community: 33.
Ministry in Catechesis; Holistic Care; Spirituality and Ecology; Pastoral Ministry; Education; Pastoral Care; Mental Health; Social Work and Canon Law.
Properties owned and sponsored: Mount St. Joseph Holistic Care Community, Waterville, ME.
Represented in the Archdiocese of Los Angeles and in the Dioceses of Manchester and Portland (In Maine).

[3890] (C.S.J.P.)—SISTERS OF ST. JOSEPH OF PEACE (P)

Founded in England 1884. First United States foundation 1885.

Generalate: *Sisters of St. Joseph of Peace Generalate, Inc.*, 125 Michigan Ave., N.E., Washington, DC 20017. Tel: 202-884-9768; Fax: 202-884-9771. Sr. Margaret Byrne, C.S.J.P., Congregation Leader; Sr. Terry Donohue, C.S.J.P., Asst. Congregation Leader; Sr. Kristin Funari, C.S.J.P.; Sr. Anne Hayes, C.S.J.P.; Sr. Coralie Muzzy, C.S.J.P.
Total in Community: 230.
Ministry in the field of Education; Health & Social Services; Religious Education; Parish Ministry, Retreat Ministry, Social & Minority Ministry.
Represented in the Archdioceses of Anchorage, Los Angeles, Newark, New York, Portland in Oregon, San Francisco, Seattle and Washington and in the Dioceses of Camden, Juneau, Metuchen, Paterson, San Diego, Spokane and Yakima. Also in Canada and El Salvador.

Congregation Novitiate, Englewood Cliffs, NJ: *Mater Dei Convent*, 399 Hudson Dr., Englewood Cliffs, NJ 07632.
Total in Community: 4.
Sr. Margaret Byrne, C.S.J.P., Congregation Leader; Sr. Theresa Donahue, C.S.J.P., Asst.Congregation Leader.
Total number in the Eastern U.S: 101.
Properties owned or sponsored: St. Joseph's Home for the Blind; St. Ann's Home for The Aged; St. Mary's

Residence; St. Joseph's Home; The Nurturing Place (York Street Child Development Center); St. Joseph's School for the Blind; Stella Maris Retreat Center-Water Spirit; The York St. Project; St. Joseph Messenger Office; St. Michael Villa; The Kenmare School.

Wesstern U.S. (1909): *St. Mary's Provincialate*, 1663 Killarney Way, Box 248, Bellevue, WA 98009-0248. Tel: 425-451-1770; Fax: 425-462-9760. Sr. Margaret Byrne, C.S.J.P., Congregation Leader.
Total Number in Western U.S: 79.
Corporate Titles: Sisters of St. Joseph of Peace; Sisters of St. Joseph of Peace Charitable Trust, Bellevue, WA.
Properties owned: St. Mary's Residence, Bellevue, WA; Prospect House, Seattle, WA; St. Therese Residence, Seattle, WA; Grace House, Seattle, WA; Alicia Park House, Seattle, WA; Eugene Residence, Eugene, OR; Our Lady of Perpetual Help House, San Diego, CA; Casa Navidad, San Diego, CA.

[3893] (S.S.J.)—SISTERS OF SAINT JOSEPH OF CHESTNUT HILL, PHILADELPHIA (P)

Founded in France in 1650. First foundation in Philadelphia in 1847.

Motherhouse (1847): *Mount St. Joseph Convent*, 9701 Germantown Ave., Philadelphia, PA 19118-2694. Tel: 215-248-7200; Fax: 215-248-7277; Email: msjc@ssjphila.org; Web: www.ssjphila.org. Sr. Anne Patricia Myers, S.S.J., Congregational Pres.; Sr. Patricia Annas, S.S.J., Archivist.
Total in Congregation : 952.
Legal Holdings or Titles: Saint Joseph Villa; Saint Joseph Guild; Bethlehem Retirement Village, Flourtown, PA; Academy Village, McSherrystown, PA; Saint Joseph Housing Corporation; Saint Mary by-the-Sea Convent, Cape May Point, NJ; Cecilian, Philadelphia, PA; Mount Saint Joseph Academy, Flourtown, PA; Norwood-Fontbonne Academy, Philadelphia, PA; Holy Family, Bayonne, NJ; Chestnut Hill College, Philadelphia, PA; Cecilian Village, McSherrystown, PA; SSJ Center for Spirituality, Philadelphia, PA; Saint Joseph Academy, McSherrystown, PA; The Convent of the Sisters of St. Joseph, Chestnut Hill, PA; Elizabeth House, Philadelphia, PA; Saint Joseph Village, McSherrystown, PA; Sisters of Saint Joseph Welcome Center, Philadelphia, PA.
Ministry in the field of Academic and Religious Education at all levels; Institutes for Dependent Children; Pastoral Ministry; Campus Ministry; Care of the Aged; Social Services; Prison Ministry; Health Care; Psychologists; Hospice Ministry; Hospital Chaplaincy; Spiritual Directors; Drug and Alcohol Counselors.
Represented in the Archdioceses of Baltimore, Chicago, Miami, Newark, New York, Philadelphia, San Antonio and Washington and in the Dioceses of Allentown, Altoona-Johnstown, Arlington, Brooklyn, Camden, Charlotte, Fairbanks, Fort Wayne-South Bend, Harrisburg, Jackson, Metuchen, Paterson, Raleigh, St. Petersburg, Savannah, Trenton, Venice, Wheeling-Charleston and Wilmington. Also in Canada, France and Peru.

[3900] (S.S.J.)—SISTERS OF ST. JOSEPH OF ST. AUGUSTINE, FLORIDA (D)

Founded in France in 1650. First foundation in the United States in 1866. Classified as an American Congregation in 1899.

Motherhouse (1847): *St. Joseph Convent*, 241 St. George St., P.O. Box 3506, St. Augustine, FL 32085. Tel: 904-824-1752; Email: ssjfl@bellsouth.net. Sr. Ann Kuhn, S.S.J., Gen. Supr.; Sr. Thomas Joseph McGoldrick, S.S.J., Community Archivist.
Total in Community: 82.
Ministry in Hospital-Health Care Services; Social Services; Hospital Pastoral Care; Care of Aged; Academic and Religious Education at all levels; Parish Ministry; Diocesan Office Administration; Architectural Liturgical Design; Retreat Ministry; Ministry to the Handicapped.
Represented in the Archdiocese of Miami and in the Dioceses of Orlando, Palm Beach, Pensacola-Tallahassee, St. Augustine and St. Petersburg.

[3910] (S.J.S.M.)—SISTERS OF ST. JOSEPH OF ST. MARK (D)

Founded in France in 1845. First foundation in the United States in October, 1937.

Generalate: Colmar, France Sr. Sophie Moog, Gen. Supr.
Universal total in Congregation: 249.

General Motherhouse (Cleveland) (1939): 21800 Charden Rd., Euclid, OH 44117-2199. Mother Mary Therese Trunk, Supr. Gen.

Youngstown Diocese: *Sisters of St. Joseph of St. Mark, Community Center*, 2300 Reno Dr., Ste. 319, Louisville, OH 44641. Tel: 330-875-7967. Sr. Edwardine Baznik, S.J.S.M., Supr.
Total number in U.S: 12.
Represented in the Dioceses of Cleveland and Youngstown.

[3920] (S.J.W.)—SISTERS OF ST. JOSEPH THE WORKER (D)

General Motherhouse: *St. William Convent*, 1 St. Joseph Ln., Walton, KY 41094. Mother Celeste Marie Downes, S.J.W., Supr. Gen.
Total in Community: 16.
Properties owned and operated: Taylor Manor Nursing Home, Versailles, KY; 16-acre property in Walton, KY: Motherhouse Formation House.
Represented in the Dioceses of Covington and Lexington.

[3930] (SSJ-TOSF)—SISTERS OF ST. JOSEPH OF THE THIRD ORDER OF ST. FRANCIS (P)

Founded in the United States in 1901.

Corporate Office: 1300 Maria Dr., P.O. Box 305, Stevens Point, WI 54481-0305. Tel: 715-341-8457; Fax: 715-341-8830. Sr. Jane Blabolil, S.S.J.-T.O.S.F., Pres.; Sr. Michelle Wronkowski, S.S.J.-T.O.S.F., Vice Pres.; Sr. Dorothy Pagosa, S.S.J.-T.O.S.F., Vice Pres.; Sr. Linda Szocik, S.S.J.-T.O.S.F., Vice Pres.
Total number in the Congregation: 314.
Sponsors: Learning Center; 2 High Schools; Health Care Systems; Continuing Care Retirement Community.
Ministries in the following areas: Academic Education at all levels; Pastoral Ministry; Health Care Services; Ministry abroad in South America and Puerto Rico; 8th Day Center for Justice; Social Services.
Represented in the Archdioceses of Chicago, Detroit, Hartford, Los Angeles, Milwaukee, St. Paul-Minneapolis, and Washington DC and in the Dioceses of Arecibo (PR), Cleveland, Fort Wayne-South Bend, Gary, Grand Island, Hartford, Green Bay, Harrisburg, Joliet, Kalamazoo, Knoxville, La Crosse, Lansing, Madison, Norwich, Oakland, Phoenix, Rockford, St. Petersburg, Superior, Toledo and Youngstown. Also in Peru and Brazil.

[3935] (S.S.L.)—THE CONGREGATION OF THE SISTERS OF ST. LOUIS, JUILLY - MONAGHAN (P)

Founded in France in 1842. First foundation in the United States in 1949.

General Motherhouse: Louisville Monaghan, Ireland Sr. Donna Hansen, S.S.L.

Regional House: *Louisville Convent*, 22300 Mulholland Dr., Woodland Hills, CA 91364. Tel: 818-883-1678. Sr. Brid Long, S.S.L.
Finally Professed Sisters: 56.
Legal Title: *Sisters of St. Louis, Juilly-Monaghan, Inc.*
Ministry in the field of Education; Pastoral and Social Ministries.
Represented in the Archdioceses of Chicago and Los Angeles and in the Dioceses of Oakland, Orange, Raleigh and San Diego.

[3950] (S.S.M.N.)—SISTERS OF SAINT MARY OF NAMUR (P)

Founded in Namur, Belgium, in 1819. First foundation in the United States in 1863.

General Motherhouse: Namur, Belgium Sr. Rejeanne Roussel, Gen. Supr.
Universal total in Congregation: 420.

Eastern Province: *Provincial House*, 241 Lafayette Ave., Buffalo, NY 14213-1453. Tel: 716-884-8221; Fax: 716-884-6598. Sr. Caroline Smith, S.S.M.N., Prov. Supr.
Total in Community: 87.
Legal Holdings or Titles: 9 Residences.
Ministry in the field of Religious and Academic Education; Pastoral Ministry; Community Organization; Social Services; Diocesan and Health related services; Refugee Assistance.
Represented in the Dioceses of Bridgeport, Buffalo, Charleston and Savannah. Also in Canada.

Western Province: *Provincial House - Our Lady of Victory Center*, 909 W. Shaw St., Fort Worth, TX 76110. Tel: 817-923-8393. Sr. Patricia St. Marie, Prov.
Total in Community: 42.
Ministry in the field of Religious and Academic Education; Diocesan Offices; Pastoral Ministry; Social Services; Health Care and Missions.
Properties owned or sponsored: Our Lady of Victory Center, Fort Worth, TX; Our Lady of Victory Catholic School, Fort Worth, TX; Sisters of St. Mary of Namur, Fort Worth, TX; Notre Dame Convent; Mercy Convent, Wichita Falls, TX.
Represented in the Dioceses of Dallas and Fort Worth.

[3960] (S.S.M.O.)—SISTERS OF ST. MARY OF OREGON

Founded in Oregon in 1886.

General Motherhouse: *Sisters of St. Mary of Oregon*, 4440 S.W. 148th Ave., Beaverton, OR 97007. Tel: 503-644-9181. Sr. Barbara Jean Laughlin, Supr. Gen.
Total in Congregation : 69.
Ministry in the field of Education; Nursing Homes; and Parish Services.
Properties owned or sponsored: Maryville Nursing Home; Little Flower Development Center; SSMO Campus Schools.
Represented in the Archdioceses of Los Angeles and Portland in Oregon and in the Diocese of Helena.

[3980] (S.P.C)—SISTERS OF SAINT PAUL DE CHARTRES (P)

Founded in France in 1696.

General House: 193 Via della Vignaccia, Rome, Italy, 1-00163. Sr. Myriam Kitcharoent, S.P.C., Supr. Gen.
Universal total in Congregation: 4000.

U.S. Province: 1300 County Rd. 492, Marquette, MI 49855-9632. Tel: 906-226-3932. Sr. Gloria J. Schultz, S.P.C., Prov.
Total in Community: 15.
Legal Holding: Bishop Noa Home for Senior Citizens, Escanaba, MI.
Ministry in the field of Academic and Religious Education; Hospital Chaplaincy; Pastoral Ministry.
Represented in the Archdiocese of Washington and in the Diocese of Marquette.

[3990] (S.S.P.C.)—MISSIONARY SISTERS OF ST. PETER CLAVER (P)

Founded in 1894. First Foundation in the United States, 1914.

General House: 16 via dell' Olmata, Rome, Italy, 00184. Sr. Maria Moryl, S.S.P.C., Supr. Gen.
Legal Title: *The Sodality of St. Peter Claver for the African Missions-Missionary Sisters of St. Peter Claver.*

American Headquarters: 225 Century Ave., S., Saint Paul, MN 55125-1155. Tel: 651-738-9704.
Total in Community: 17.
Represented in the Archdioceses of Chicago, St. Louis and St. Paul-Minneapolis.

[4010] (O.S.A.)—SISTERS OF ST. RITA (D)

General Motherhouse: Friedrich-Spee-Str. 32, 97072 Wurzburg, Germany Sr. Rita Maria Kaes, O.S.A., Gen.
Universal total in Congregation: 130.

U.S. Address: *St. Rita's Convent*, 4014 Green Bay Rd., Racine, WI 53404. Tel: 262-639-1766. Sr. Irene Hanika, O.S.A., Supr.
Represented in the Archdiocese of Milwaukee.

[4020] (S.T.J.)—SOCIETY OF ST. TERESA OF JESUS (P)

(Teresian Sisters)

Founded in Spain in 1876. First foundation in the United States in 1910. Total Membership 1,499.

Generalate: Via Valcannuta, 134, Rome, Italy, 00166.

Provincial House: *St. Francis de Sales Province*, 18080 St. Joseph's Way, Covington, LA 70435-5623. Tel: 985-893-1470; Fax: 985-893-2476.

Formation House: 18158 St. Joseph's Way, Covington, LA 70435-5624. Tel: 985-893-1557. Sr. Martha L. Gonzalez, Community Archivist.
Total in Community: 33.
Properties owned and/or sponsored: St. Teresa's Convent, San Antonio, TX; Henry de Osso Convent, San Antonio, TX; Provincialate, Covington, LA; Blessed Mercedes Prat Convent, New Orleans, LA.
Ministry in the field of Academic Education at all levels; Education in underdeveloped areas; Youth Ministry; Pastoral Ministry.
Represented in the Archdioceses of Miami, New Orleans and San Antonio.

[4030] (S.S.T.V.)—CONGREGATION OF SISTERS OF ST. THOMAS OF VILLANOVA (P)

Founded in France in 1661. First foundation in the United States in 1948.

General Motherhouse: 52 Blvd. d'Argeson, Neuilly-sur-Seine, France, 92200. Tel: 01 47 47 42 20; Fax: 01 47 47 38 00; Email: neuillystv@wanado.com; Web: www.congregation-stv.org.
Universal total in Congregation: 250.

Sisters of St. Thomas of Villanova Convent: 76 W. Rocks Rd., Norwalk, CT 06851. Tel: 203-847-2885; Fax: 203-847-3740; Email: sstv_usa@sbcglobal.net; Web: www.saintthomasofvillanova.com. Mother Jean Marie Raymond, S.S.T.V., Supr.
Total in Community: 4.
Properties owned and/or sponsored: Notre Dame Convalescent Home.
Represented in the Diocese of Bridgeport.

[4040] (S.U.)—SOCIETY OF ST. URSULA (P)

Founded in Dole, France, in 1606. First foundation in the United States in 1901.

General Motherhouse: St. Cyr-Loire, France Sr. Mary Alice Mooney, S.U., Supr. Gen.

Provincialate: *American Regional Ctr.*, 50 Linwood Rd., Rhinebeck, NY 12572. Tel: 845-876-2341. Sr. Mary Dolan, S.U., Reg. Supr.
Total in Community: 28.
Ministry in the field of Education; Parish Ministry; Spiritual Direction and Retreats.
Represented in the Archdiocese of New York and in the Dioceses of Providence and Raleigh.

[4048] F.C.J.—SOCIETY OF THE SISTERS FAITHFUL COMPANIONS OF JESUS (P)

Founded in France in 1820. First founded in the United States in 1895.

General Motherhouse: *Stella Maris Convent*, North Foreland, Braodstairs, Kent, England, CT10 3NR.

Provincial Office: 300 Palmerston Ave., Toronto, Canada, M6J 2J4. Tel: 416-588-1791.

U.S. Provincial Business Office: 324 Cory's Ln.,

Portsmouth, RI 02871. Tel: 401-683-2222. Sr. Katherine Mary O'Flynn, F.C.J., Supr. Gen.; Sr. Patricia Binchy, F.C.J., Prov.; Sr. Marguerite Goddard, F.C.J., Novice Dir.
Sisters: 16.

[4050] (S.D.S.H.)—SISTERS OF THE SOCIETY DEVOTED TO THE SACRED HEART (D)

Founded in Hungary in 1940.

Motherhouse (1956): 9814 Sylvia Ave., Northridge, CA 91324. Tel: 818-772-9961; Fax: 818-772-2742; Web: www.sacredheartsisters.com. Sr. Jane Stafford, Supr. Gen.; Sr. Ida Peterfy, Foundress.

Novitiate House: 10480 Winnetka Ave., Chatsworth, CA 91311. Tel: 818-831-9710; Fax: 818-831-0790; Web: www.sdsh.org; Web: www.sacredheartsisters.com.
Total in Community: 50.
Properties owned and/or sponsored: Sacred Heart Motherhouse, Northridge CA; Heart of Jesus Retreat Center, Santa Ana, CA; Sacred Heart Novitiate, Chatsworth, CA; Sacred Heart Retreat Camp, Big Bear, CA; Sacred Heart Convent, Los Angeles, CA.
Ministry in Parish Religious Education Centers; Catechist Formation Centers; Camp for year-round Retreats and summer Family Retreats Camps; Catechesis; Youth Leadership Programs; Day Retreat Center for Children and Adults; Catechesis in Parochial Schools and Catholic High Schools; "Sacred Heart Kids' Club" Video/DVD Catechesis; Hispanic and Chinese Catechetical Center; Catechetical Programs on Military Bases; Catechetical Missions to Dioceses; Far East Mission in Taiwan; Mission in Hungary.
Represented in the Archdioceses of Los Angeles and St. Louis and the Dioceses of Orange and San Bernardino. Also in Taiwan and Hungary.

[4060] (S.H.C.J.)—SOCIETY OF THE HOLY CHILD JESUS (P)

Founded in England in 1846. First foundation in the United States in 1862.

Motherhouse: Via della Maglianella 379, Rome, Italy, 00166. Sr. Geraldine MacCarthy, S.H.C.J., Society Leader.

American Province: *Provincial Offices*, 460 Shadeland Ave., Drexel Hill, PA 19026-2312. Tel: 610-626-1400. Sr. Helen T. McDonald, S.H.C.J., Prov. Leader; Sr. Helena Mayer, S.H.C.J., Archivist.
Total number in Province: 178.
Ministry in a variety of Educational and Pastoral Work.
Properties owned or sponsored: Connelly School of the Holy Child, Potomac, MD; Cornelia Connelly School, Anaheim, CA; Mayfield Junior School of the Holy Child Jesus; Mayfield Senior School of the Holy Child Jesus, Pasadena, CA; Oak Knoll School of the Holy Child, Summit, NJ; Old Westbury School of the Holy Child, Old Westbury, NY; Rosemont School of the Holy Child, Rosemont, PA; School of the Holy Child, Drexel Hill, PA; School of the Holy Child, Rye, NY; Providence Center, Philadelphia, PA; Cornelia Connelly Center for Education; Holy Child Middle School, New York, NY.
Represented in the Archdioceses of Boston, Chicago, Hartford, Los Angeles, Milwaukee, Newark, New Orleans, New York, Philadelphia, Portland in Oregon and Washington and in the Dioceses of Camden, Charlotte, Orange, Paterson, Rockville Centre, San Diego, Trenton and Venice.

[4070] (R.S.C.J.)—SOCIETY OF THE SACRED HEART (P)

Founded in France in 1800. First foundation in the United States in 1818.

Generalate: Via Tarquinio Viper, 16, Rome, Italy, 00152. Sr. Kathleen Conan, Supr. Gen.

United States Provincial House: 4120 Forest Park Ave., St. Louis, MO 63108. Tel: 314-652-1500; Fax: 314-534-6800; Email: provincialhouse@rscj.org. Sr. Paula Toner, R.S.C.J., Prov.; Sr. Frances Gimber, Prov. Archivist.
Total number in the Province: 357.
Ministry in the field of Religious and Academic Education at all levels; Adult Education; Parish, Pastoral, Social and Health Care Ministries.
Province Corporations: Society of the Sacred Heart, United States Province, Inc.; California Province of the Society of the Sacred Heart, Inc.; Society of the Sacred Heart, Chicago Province, Inc.; Religious of the Sacred Heart, Washington Province, Inc.; Religious of the Sacred Heart, New York Province, Inc.; Ladies of the Sacred Heart, MO; Religious of the Sacred Heart in Massachusetts, Inc.; Network of the Sacred Heart Schools, Inc., 700 N. Third St., St. Charles, MO 63301, Phone: 636-724-7003.
Represented in the Archdioceses of Boston, Chicago, Cincinnati, Detroit, Galveston-Houston, Louisville, Miami, Milwaukee, New Orleans, New York, Omaha, St. Louis, San Francisco, Seattle and Washington and in the Dioceses of Albany, Baton Rouge, Fall River, Fort Wayne-South Bend, Lafayette (LA), Oakland, Portland, San Bernardino, San Diego, San Jose, and Trenton.

[4080] (S.S.S.)—SISTERS OF SOCIAL SERVICE OF LOS ANGELES, INC. (P)

Founded in Hungary. Established in the United States at Los Angeles, California in 1926.

General Motherhouse: 4316 Lanai Rd., Encino, CA 91436. Tel: 818-285-3355; Fax: 818-285-3366. Sr. Claire Graham, Gen. Dir.
Total in Community: 100.
Legal Titles: Sisters of Social Service of Los Angeles; Sisters of Social Service Support Trust Fund.
Social Service Work in Parishes and in Diocesan Agencies; Leadership Training of Youth and Adults; Summer Camps for Children and Families; Programs for the Elderly; Peace and Justice Work; Religious Education; Settlement Houses; Health Programs; Family Counseling Services; International houses in Mexico, Philippines and Taiwan.
Represented in the Archdioceses of Los Angeles, Portland in Oregon, San Francisco and Seattle and in the Dioceses of Oakland, Sacramento and San Diego.

[4090] (S.S.S.)—SISTERS OF SOCIAL SERVICE OF THE DIOCESE OF BUFFALO, INC. (P)

Founded in Budapest, Hungary in 1923; Sr. Margaret Slachta, Foundress.

H-1029, Bathori Laszlo u. 10, Budapest, Hungary

U.S. District Residence: 296 Summit Ave., Buffalo, NY 14214-1936. Tel: 716-834-0197; Fax: 716-834-6168. Sr. Teresina Joo, S.S.S., District Moderator; Sr. Agnes Pataki, S.S.S., Gen. Moderator.
Total number in the United States: 14.
Social Work; Parish Ministry; Health Care; Ministry for Justice and Human Rights.
Represented in the Archdiocese of Miami and in the Diocese of Buffalo.

[4100] (S.S.M.)—SISTERS OF THE SORROWFUL MOTHER (THIRD ORDER OF ST. FRANCIS) (P)

Founded in Italy in 1883. First foundation in the United States in 1889.

General Motherhouse: *Casa Generalizia della Suore dell'Addolorata*, Via Paolo III, Rome, Italy, I-00165. Sr. Teresina Mara, S.S.M., Gen. Supr.

U.S./Caribbean Province: 2935 Universal Ct., Ste. 100, Oshkosh, WI 54904. Tel: 920-230-2040; Fax: 920-230-2041. Sr. M. Sylvia Egan, S.S.M., Prov. Supr.
Total number in the U.S. Community: 139.
Legal Holding: Sisters of the Sorrowful Mother - Marian Health System, Inc.; Sisters of the Sorrowful Mother - US/Caribbean Province, Inc.
Ministry in the fields of Religious and Academic Education; Nursing Homes; Social Work; Hospitals and Hospital Administration.
Represented in the Archdiocese of Milwaukee and in the Dioceses of Camden, Green Bay, Las Cruces, La Crosse, Paterson, Superior, Tulsa, Wichita and Winona. Also in Dominican Republic, Trinidad, Grenada and Castries.

[4105] —THIRD ORDER REGULAR FRANCISCAN COMMON NOVITIATE

1550 Plainfield Rd., #3N, Joliet, IL 60435-3752. Tel: 815-730-8502; Email: novitiate1550@yahoo.com; Web: www.newfranciscans.org. Sr. Sharon Fitzpatrick, O.S.F., Assoc. Novice Mistress.

120 N. Elizabeth Ave., Saint Louis, MO 63135-2456. Web: www.newfranciscans.org. Sr. Rosalie Wisniewski, O.S.F.
Total participating congregations: 31.
Ministry in the develpment in each novice of Franciscan spirituality, charism, and prayer.
Represented in the Archdiocese of St. Louis.

[4110] (O.S.U.)—URSULINE NUNS (P)
(Roman Union)

Founded in Italy in 1535. First foundation in the United States New Orleans, Louisiana in 1727.

Generalate: Via Nomentana 236, Rome, Italy, 00162. Mother Cecilia Wang, O.S.U., Prioress Gen.

Eastern Province of the U.S. (1900): *Ursuline Provincialate*, 1338 North Ave., New Rochelle, NY 10804. Tel: 914-712-0060; Fax: 914-712-3134.
Total number in the Province: 131.
Legal Titles: Ursuline Provincialate, Eastern Province of the United States, Inc.; Marian Residence Fund, New Rochelle, NY; OSU Charitable Trust, New Rochelle, NY.
Ministry in the field of Academic Education at all levels; varied Pastoral and Social Services.
Represented in the Archdioceses of New Orleans, New York and Washington and in the Dioceses of Bridgeport, Ogdensburg, Orlando and Wilmington.

Central Province of the U.S: *Ursuline Provincialate*, 353 S. Sappington Rd., Saint Louis, MO 63122. Tel: 314-821-6884; Fax: 314-821-6888. Sr. Diane Fulgenzi, O.S.U., Prov. Prioress.
Total in Community: 127.
Ministry in the field of Religious and Academic Education.
Represented in the Archdioceses of Chicago, Galveston-Houston, New Orleans, St. Louis, St. Paul-Minneapolis and San Antonio and in the Dioceses of Dallas, Laredo, Peoria, Springfield-Cape Girardeau and Springfield (IL).

Western Province U.S. (1932): *Ursuline Provincialate*, 639 Angela Dr., Santa Rosa, CA 95403-1793. Tel: 707-545-6811; Fax: 707-579-8571. Sr. Margaret Johnson, O.S.U., Co-Prov.; Sr. Shirley Ann Garibaldi, O.S.U., Co-Prov.
Total number in the Province: 27.
Ministry in the field of Elementary and Secondary Education; Work with the Eskimos, American Indians, & Hispanics; Parish Ministry; Catechetical Coordinators; Spiritual Direction; Spiritual Growth Center; Counseling Services; Detention Ministry.
Represented in the Archdioceses of Anchorage, Los Angeles and San Francisco and in the Dioceses of Boise, Fairbanks, Great Falls-Billings, Juneau, and Santa Rosa.

Northeastern Province: *Ursuline Provincialate*, 45 Lowder St., Dedham, MA 02026-4200. Tel: 781-326-6219; Fax: 781-326-7296. Sr. Angela Krippendorf, O.S.U., Prov.
Total in Community: 30.
Ministry in the field of Education.
Represented in the Archdiocese of Boston and in the Diocese of Portland (In Maine).

[4120] (O.S.U.)—URSULINE NUNS, OF THE CONGREGATION OF PARIS (P)

Founded in Italy in 1535. First foundation in the United States in New Orleans, Louisiana in 1727.

Motherhouse (1845): *Ursulines of Brown County*, 20860 St. Rte. 251, Fayetteville, OH 45118-9705. Tel: 513-875-2020 Ext. 27; Fax: 513-875-2311; Web: www.ursulinesofbc.org. Sr. Patricia Homan, O.S.U., Supr.
Total in Community: 31.
Legal Title: *St. Ursula Literary Institute; Ursulines of Brown County; Ursuline Academy of Cincinnati, Chatfield College.*
Ministry in the field of Academic Education at all levels; Special Education; Adult Education; Catechetical Instruction; Administration; Retreats; Counseling; Organization Consultation; Social-Inner City & Rural; Senior Services; Campus and Parish Ministry.
Represented in the Archdiocese of Cincinnati and in the Diocese of Toledo.

[4120-01] CINCINNATI (P)

Motherhouse: *Ursulines of Cincinnati, St. Ursula Convent*, 1339 E. McMillan St. (Walnut Hills), Cincinnati, OH 45206. Tel: 513-961-3410. Sr. Mary Jerome Buchert, O.S.U.
Total in Community: 13.
Legal Title: *Ursuline Sisters, Inc.; Ursuline Sisters Charitable Trust.*
Ministry in the field of Academic Education at all levels; Parish and Diocesan Services; Social Services; Communications.
Represented in the Archdiocese of Cincinnati.

[4120-02] KANSAS CITY IN KANSAS (D)

Ursuline Convent of Our Lady of Lourdes: 901 E. Miami St., Paola, KS 66071. Tel: 913-557-2349. Sr. Kathleen Condry, O.S.U., Supr.
Total in Community: 26.
Legal Title: *Ursuline Sisters, Inc.; Ursuline Sisters Charitable Trust.*
Ministry in the field of Academic Education at all levels; Parish and Diocesan Services.
Represented in the Archdiocese of Kansas City in Kansas and in the Diocese of Kansas City-St. Joseph.

[4120-03] LOUISVILLE (P)

Ursuline Motherhouse of the Immaculate Conception: 3115 Lexington Rd., Louisville, KY 40206. Tel: 502-893-0125; Fax: 502-896-3913. Sr. Lynn Jarrell, O.S.U., Pres.
Total in Community: 125.
Legal Title: *Ursuline Society and Academy of Education aka Ursuline Sisters.*
Ministry in the field of Academic Education; Child Care; Pastoral Ministry; Social Services; Health Care.
Properties owned and sponsored: Sacred Heart Academy; Sacred Heart Model School; Marian Home, Louisville, KY.
Represented in the Archdioceses of Baltimore, Cincinnati, Indianapolis, Louisville and Philadelphia and in the Dioceses of Charleston, Covington, Davenport, Grand Island, Lexington and Wheeling-Charleston.

[4120-04] CLEVELAND (P)

Ursuline Motherhouse and Educational Center: 2600 Lander Rd., Cleveland, OH 44124. Fax: 440-449-3588. Sr. Angelita Zawada, O.S.U., Supr. Gen.; Sr. Colette Livingston, O.S.U., Community Archivist.
Total in Community: 192.
Legal Titles: The Ursuline Academy of Cleveland; The Ursuline Sisters of Cleveland.
Ministry in the field of Academic Education at all levels; Parish Ministry; Diocesan Offices; Seminary; Social Service Agency; Hospital and Health Care Ministry; Spiritual Direction and Retreat Ministry; Foreign Mission.
Properties sponsored: Ursuline College; Beaumont High School; Urban Community School; Villa Angela/St. Joseph High School.
Represented in the Archdioceses of San Antonio and in the Dioceses of Brownsville, Cleveland, Springfield-Cape Girardeau, Cincinnati, and Youngstown. Also in El Salvador.

[4120-05] OWENSBORO (P)

Mt. St. Joseph Ursuline Motherhouse: 8001 Cummings Rd., Maple Mount, KY 42356. Tel: 270-229-4103; Fax: 270-229-4127.
Total in Community: 176.
Legal Holdings and Titles: St. Joseph's Female Ursuline Academy; Brescia University, Owensboro, KY; Mount Saint Joseph Conference and Retreat Center, Maple Mount, KY.
Ministry in Colleges; High Schools; Elementary Schools; Parishes; Retreats and Spiritual Direction; Pastoral Care; Health Care; Social Services; Hispanic Outreach; Diocesan Offices.
Represented in the Archdioceses of Louisville, Santa Fe, St. Paul Minneapolis and Washington and in the Dioceses of Belleville, Gallup, Kansas City in Kansas, Kansas City-St. Joseph, Memphis, Owensboro, Shreveport, Springfield-Cape Girardeau and Springfield in Illinois. Also in Chile.

[4120-06] TOLEDO (P)

Ursuline Convent of the Sacred Heart: 4045 Indian Rd., Toledo, OH 43606. Tel: 419-536-9587. Sr. Donna Frey, O.S.U., Gen. Supr.
Total in Community: 53; Associates: 150.
Legal Title: *Ursuline Convent of the Sacred Heart.*
Ministry in the field of Administration; Religious and Academic Education; Health Care; Counseling Services; Pastoral Ministry; Pastoral Care; Retreat Work; Spiritual Direction; Education in Music; Home Health Care.
Properties owned or sponsored: St. Ursula Academy, Toledo, OH.
Represented in the Archdiocese of Washington and in the Dioceses of Fresno and Toledo. Also in Lima, Peru.

[4120-07] YOUNGSTOWN (P)

Motherhouse: *Ursuline Motherhouse and Educational Center*, 4250 Shields Rd., Canfield, OH 44406. Tel: 330-792-7636. Sr. Nancy Dawson, O.S.U., Gen. Supr.
Total in Community: 54.
Properties owned and/or sponsored: Ursuline Motherhouse; Ursuline Center; Ursuline Preschool & Kindergarten; Beatitude House.
Ministry in the field of Religious and Academic Education at all levels; Parish Ministry; Social Services; Hospital Services; Single Parenting; AIDS Ministry; Preschool; Kindergarten; Nursing Home Service.
Represented in the Dioceses of Cleveland and Youngstown.

[4130] (O.S.U.)—URSULINE SISTERS OF THE CONGREGATION OF TILDONK, BELGIUM (P)
International Congregation

Founded in Italy in 1535 by St. Angela Merici (Ursulines). Congregation of Tildonk founded in Belgium in 1832. First foundation in the United States in Ozone Park, New York, in 1924.

Generalate: Brussels, Belgium Sr. Judith O'Connor, O.S.U., Gen. Supr.

Ursuline Provincialate: 81-15 Utopia Pkwy., Jamaica, NY 11432. Tel: 718-591-0681. Sr. Mairead M. Barrett, Prov. Supr.
Total in Community: 59.
Properties owned and/or sponsored: St. Ursula Center, Blue Point, NY; Ursuline Provincialate, Jamaica NY.
Ministry in the field of Education in all its aspects; Retreat Work; Chaplaincies.
Represented in the Archdioceses of Hartford and New York and in the Dioceses of Bridgeport, Brooklyn, Burlington and Rockville Centre.

[4155] (M.T.G.)—SISTERS ADORERS OF THE HOLY CROSS (P)

Founded in 1670 in Vietnam by Bishop Pierre Lambert de la Motte. First foundation in the U.S. 1979.

General Motherhouse: *Holy Cross Convent*, 7408 S.E. Alder, Portland, OR 97215. Tel: 503-254-3284. Sr. Mary Trinh Nguyen, M.T.G., Supr.
Sisters: 29.
Represented in the Archdiocese of Portland in Oregon and in the Dioceses of Arlington and Sacramento.

[4160] (V.S.C.)—VINCENTIAN SISTERS OF CHARITY (P)

First foundation in the United States in 1902.

General Motherhouse and Novitiate: *St. Vincent Hill*, 8200 McKnight Rd., Pittsburgh, PA 15237. Tel: 412-364-3000; Fax: 412-364-9055. Sr. Charlene Reebel, V.S.C., Major Supr.
Professed Sisters: 111.
Ministry in the field of Education at all levels; Health Care in Nursing Homes; Child Care Center; Catechetical Centers; Social Apostolates; Pastoral Ministries.
Properties owned or sponsored: Vincentian Child Care Center; Vincentian Academy-Duquesne University Vincentian de Marillac; Vincentian Regency; Vincentian Home, Inc.; Marian Manor, Inc.
Represented in the Archdiocese of Mobile and in Dioceses of Greensburg, Madison, Pittsburgh, Steubenville and Venice. Also in Canada.

[4170] (V.S.C.)—VINCENTIAN SISTERS OF CHARITY (D)

Founded in Bedford in 1928.

Congregational Home: *Villa San Bernardo*, 1160 Broadway, Bedford, OH 44146-4523. Tel: 440-232-4755; Fax: 440-232-7832.

[4180] (M.P.V.)—RELIGIOUS VENERINI SISTERS (P)

Founded in Italy in 1685. First foundation in the United States in 1909.

General Motherhouse: via Gioachino Belli 31, Rome, Italy Mother Mariateresa Crescini, Supr. Gen.
Universal total in Congregation: 447.

Provincialhouse for the U.S: 23 Edward St., Worcester, MA 01605. Sr. Hilda Ponte, M.P.V., Prov.
Total in Community: 23.
Legal Holdings: Venerini Academy, Worcester, MA.
Ministry in the field of Education; Health Care; Social Services; Parish and Diocesan Ministry; Foreign Missions.
Represented in the Dioceses of Albany and Worcester.

[4190] (V.H.M.)—VISITATION NUNS (P)

Founded in France in 1610. First foundation in the United States in Georgetown, Washington, DC in 1799.

First Federation of North America
Mother Rose Marie Kinsella, V.H.M., Federation Pres.
Listed in the Order of Foundation established.

Monastery of the Visitation (1833): 2300 Springhill Ave., Mobile, AL 36607-3202. Tel: 251-473-2321; Fax: 251-476-9761; Web: www.VisitationMonasteryMobile-.org. Mother Rose Marie Kinsella, Supr.
Total in Community: 7.

Monastery of the Visitation: 14 Beach Rd., P.O. Box 432, Tyringham, MA 01264. Tel: 413-243-3995; Fax: 413-243-3543; Email: vistyr@aol.com; Web: www.vistyr.org. Mother Mary Ruth Dolch, Supr.
Total in Community: 18.
Legal Title: *Visitation of Holy Mary.*

Monastery of the Visitation: 12221 Bienvenue Rd., Rockville, VA 23146. Tel: 804-749-4885. Mother Mary Emmanuel Stahl, V.H.M., Supr.
Professed Sisters: 13.
Legal Title: *Visitation of Holy Mary.*

Monastery of the Visitation: 5820 City Ave., Philadelphia, PA 19131-1295. Tel: 215-473-5888. Mother Antoinette Marie Walker, V.H.M., Supr.
Professed Sisters Cloistered: 6.
Legal Title: *Sisters of the Visitation of Philadelphia.*

Monastery of the Visitation (Contemplative): 1745 Parkside Blvd., Toledo, OH 43607-1599. Tel: 419-536-1343; Fax: 419-536-0658; Email: vhm-toledo@toast.net; Web: www.toledovisitation.org. Mother Mary Bernard Grote, V.H.M., Supr.
Professed Sisters: 17; In Formation: 6.
Legal Title: *The Contemplative Order of the Visitation of Toledo, Ohio.*

Monastery of the Visitation (Strictly Cloistered): 2055 Ridgedale Dr., Snellville, GA 30078. Tel: 770-972-1060. Mother Mary Jozefa Kowalewski, V.H.M., Supr.
Professed Sisters: 12; Novices: 2.
Legal Title: *Order of the Visitation.*

Second Federation of North America

Monastery of the Visitation of Georgetown: 1500 35th St., N.W., Washington, DC 20007. Tel: 202-337-0305; Fax: 202-965-3845. Mother Mary Berchmans Hannan, Supr.; Sr. Mada-anne Gell, Community Archivist.
Total number in the school community: 480; Total in Community: 16.
Legal Holdings and Titles: Sisters of the Visitation of Georgetown; Georgetown Visitation Preparatory School.

Monastery of the Visitation (1833): 3020 N. Ballas Rd., St. Louis, MO 63131. Tel: 314-625-9260. Sr. Mary Veronica Haronik, V.H.M., Supr.
Total in Community: 14.
Legal Holdings: Visitation Academy of St. Louis County; Monastery of the Visitation, St. Louis, MO.
Ministry in Education.

Sisters of the Visitation of Holy Mary of Mount de Chantal, Inc. (1848): Wheeling, WV 26003. Tel: 304-232-1283. Sr. Joanne Gonter, V.H.M., Supr.
Total in Community: 10.
Legal Holdings or Titles: Sisters of the Visitation of Holy Mary of Mount de Chantal, Inc.; Mount de Chantal Visitation Academy, Inc.
Ministry in the field of Education.

Monastery of the Visitation (1855): 8902 Ridge Blvd., Brooklyn, NY 11209-5716. Tel: 718-745-5151; Fax: 718-745-3680. Mother Mary Pauline Baulis, V.H.M., Supr.
Professed Sisters: 19.
Legal Title: *Sisters of the Visitation of Brooklyn, NY.*

Monastery of the Visitation: 2455 Visitation Dr., St. Paul, MN 55120. Tel: 651-683-1700. Sr. Marie Therese Conaty, V.H.M., Supr.
Total in Community: 15.
Monastery located at 2000 16th Ave., Rock Island, IL 61201. Phone: 314-432-5353.
Ministry in Prayer and Education.

[4200] (S.V.M.)—SISTERS OF THE VISITATION OF THE CONGREGATION OF THE IMMACULATE HEART OF MARY (D)

Founded in France in 1610. First foundation in the United States in 1799.

Visitation Convent: 2950 Kaufmann Ave., Dubuque, IA 52001-1631. Tel: 563-556-2440. Sr. Patricia Clark, S.V.M., Pres.
Total in Community: 5.
Ministry in Higher Education; Adult Education; Parish Ministry.
Represented in the Archdiocese of Dubuque.

[4210] (S.D.V.)—VOCATIONIST SISTERS (P)
(Sisters of the Divine Vocations)

Founded in Italy in 1921. First established in the United States in 1967.

General Motherhouse: *Corso Duca D'Aosta*, 22 Pianura, Naples, Italy, 80126. Sr. Antonietta Colafemina, S.D.V., Supr. Gen.

U.S. Foundation: *Perpetual Help Day Nursery*, 170 Broad St., Newark, NJ 07104. Tel: 973-484-3535. Sr. Perpetua Da Conceicao, S.D.V., Supr.
Total in Community: 6.
Ministry in Nursery Schools & Kindergartens; CCD Program and Parish Services.
Represented in the Archdiocese of Newark.

Sister Joanna Formation House: 88 Brooklake Rd., Florham Park, NJ 07932. Tel: 973-966-9762. Sr. Gelsomina Mosca, Supr.; Sr. Luisa Gargione, Delegate.
Total in Community: 15.
Ministry in Nursery School; Formation House; Religious Education.
Represented in the Archdiocese of Newark and in the Dioceses of Paterson and Metuchen.

[4230] (X.M.M.)—XAVERIAN MISSIONARY SOCIETY OF MARY, INC. (P)

Founded in Italy in 1945. First established in the United States in 1954.

General Motherhouse: *Missionarie Saveriane Di Maria*, Via Omero 4, Parma, Italy Sr. Ines Frizza, X.M.M., Supr. Gen.
Total Membership: 265.

U.S. Headquarters: *Xaverian Missionary Society of Mary*, 242 Salisbury St., Worcester, MA 01609. Tel: 508-757-0514; Email: xavsistersusa@msn.com.
Ministry to Hispanics; Elderly; Families; CCD Programs and Mission Education.
Represented in the Diocese of Worcester.
Sr. Rosa Maria G. Serra, X.M.M., Supr.

SPECIAL CARE FACILITIES

(For a complete listing refer to the corresponding (Arch)Diocese.)

ALABAMA

Daphne
Archdiocese of Mobile

John McClure Snook Regional Center, 27296 County Rd. 13, Daphne, 36526. Tel: 251-625-2555; Fax: 251-625-2556. (Assisted living Alzheimer community.)

Mobile
Archdiocese of Mobile

Rendu Terrace West, Inc., c/o 6801 Airport Blvd., P.O. Box 850429, Mobile, 36685.

Pelham
Diocese of Birmingham

Contemplative Outreach Birmingham, 106 Red Stick Rd., Pelham, 35124. Tel: 205-991-6964. Email: tschached@bellsouth.net. Web: www.bham.net/cobweb.

ALASKA

Anchorage
Archdiocese of Anchorage

Brother Francis Shelter, 1021 E. Third Ave., Anchorage, 99501. Tel: 907-277-1731. Overnight shelter for homeless men and women.

Covenant House Alaska, 609 F St., Anchorage, 99501. Tel: 907-272-1255; Fax: 907-272-1466. Program for homeless and runaway youth.

AMERICAN SAMOA

Pago Pago
Diocese of Samoa-Pago Pago

Hope House, P.O. Box 596, Pago Pago, AS 96799. Tel: 684-699-2101; Fax: 684-699-6051.

ARIZONA

Phoenix
Diocese of Phoenix

Affordable Services for Seniors, Inc., 1201 E. Thomas Rd., Phoenix, 85014. Tel: 602-285-1800. Email: shastings@fsl.org.

Payson Senior Living, Inc., 1201 E. Thomas Rd., Phoenix, 85014. Tel: 602-285-1800; Fax: 602-285-1838. Email: jgreene@fsl.org. (Pineview Manor Apartments, Payson)

Diocese of Tucson

Valley Center for the Deaf, 3130 E. Roosevelt, Phoenix, 85008. Tel: 602-267-1921; Fax: 602-273-1872.

Tucson
Diocese of Tucson

Community Outreach Program for the Deaf, 268 W. Adams, Tucson, 85705. Tel: 520-792-1906; Fax: 520-770-8544.

Immigration Counseling Service, 140 W. Speedway, Ste. 130, Tucson, 85705. Tel: 520-623-0344; Fax: 520-770-8578.

St. Elizabeth's Health Center, 140 W. Speedway, Ste. 100, Tucson, 85705. Tel: 520-628-7871; Fax: 520-770-8528.

ARKANSAS

Little Rock
Diocese of Little Rock

ABBA House, Missionaries of Charity, 1014 S. Oak St., Little Rock, 72204. Tel: 501-666-9718 (Abba House); 501-663-3596 (convent). Home for expectant mothers, homeless women & children.

CALIFORNIA

Chatsworth
Archdiocese of Los Angeles

Rancho San Antonio, 21000 Plummer St., Chatsworth, 91311. Tel: 818-882-6400; Fax: 818-882-6404. Sponsored by Catholic Archdiocese of Los Angeles.

Culver City
Archdiocese of Los Angeles

Marycrest Manor (1956) 10664 St. James Dr., Culver City, 90230-5498. Tel: 310-838-2778; 310-838-0016 (Carmelite Sisters); Fax: 310-838-9647; 310-838-0024 (Carmelite Sisters). Email: marycrestocd@yahoo.com. Skilled Nursing Facility attended by priests from Loyola Marymount University.

El Cajon
Diocese of San Diego

St. Madeleine Sophie's Center for Adults with Developmental Disorders, 2119 E. Madison Ave., El Cajon, 92019-1111. Tel: 619-442-5129; Fax: 619-442-2590. Email: dturner@stmsc.org. Web: www.stmsc.org.

Hayward
Diocese of Oakland

St. Joseph's Center for Deaf and Hard of Hearing, 25580 Campus Drive, Hayward, 94542-1137. Tel: 510-881-2245 (Voice); 866-720-9221 (Video Phone); 510-881-2247 (TDD); Fax: 510-881-2248. Email: sjcd@sjcd.org. Web: www.sjcd.org.

Lancaster
Archdiocese of Los Angeles

Lancaster Community Shelter, 44611 Yucca Ave., Lancaster, 93534. Tel: 661-945-7524.

Los Angeles
Archdiocese of Los Angeles

Angel Guardian Home for Homeless Disabled Mothers with Minor Children (2000) 1660 Rockwood St., Los Angeles, 90026. Tel: 213-483-6654; Fax: 213-482-0522.

Bethany House, 850 N. Hobart Blvd., Los Angeles, 90029. Tel: 323-665-6937; Fax: 323-664-0754. Email: imas.bethania@hotmail.com.

Convent of the Good Shepherd-Good Shepherd Shelter (1904) Mailing Address: P.O. Box 19487, Los Angeles, 90019. Tel: 323-737-6111; Fax: 323-737-6113. Email: rgsla1@aol.com. Web: www.goodsheperdshelter.org. Shelter for Battered Women and Their Children.

Good Shepherd Center for Homeless Women and Children (1984) Languille Emergency Shelter, 267 N. Belmont Ave., Los Angeles, 90026. Tel: 213-250-5241; Fax: 213-250-5073. Email: srjuliamary@sbcglobal.net. Web: www.thegoodshepherdcenter.com. (A Program of Catholic Charities.)

Hawkes Transitional Residence/Women's Village (1998) 1640 Rockwood St., Los Angeles, 90026. Tel: 213-482-0281; Fax: 213-482-0299.

Little Flower Missionary House (1943) 2434 Gates St., Los Angeles, 90031-2824. Tel: 323-221-9248; Fax: 323-221-9831. Email: lflower@catholic.org. Web: www.rc.net/losangeles/littleflower. Attended by Salesian priests. Child and Kindergarten Care Center.

Mother-Child Transitional Residence Administrative Site (1992) 267 N. Belmont Ave., Los Angeles, 90026. Tel: 213-469-6540; Fax: 213-469-0370.

Order of Malta Los Angeles Clinic, Inc., 2222 W. Ocean View, #112, Los Angeles, 90057. Tel: 213-384-4323; Fax: 213-384-4097. Email: freemed112@sbcglobal.net. Primary Health Care for the frail elderly, the working poor and medically underserved children.

St. Anne's, 155 N. Occidental Blvd., Los Angeles, 90026. Tel: 213-381-2931; Fax: 213-381-7804. Email: stannes@stannes.org. Web: www.stannes.org. Residential treatment program, Transitional Housing, Mental Health, Family Based Services; Early Learning Center Services for pregnant and at risk children and families.

St. Anne's, 155 N. Occidental Blvd., Los Angeles, 90026. Tel: 213-381-2931, Ext. 218; Fax: 213-381-7804. Email: stannes@stannes.org. Web: www.stannes.org. Group Home for pregnant, parenting teens and their babies.

St. Joseph's Residence (1957) 1124 W. Adams Blvd., Los Angeles, 90007. Tel: 213-749-9577; Fax: 213-747-6468. Email: divine_providence@sbcglobal.net. Web: www.companyofmary.com.

St. Vincent Senior Citizen Nutrition Program, Inc. aka St. Vincent Meals on Wheels (1977) 2131 W. Third St., Los Angeles, 90057. Tel: 213-484-7778; Fax: 213-484-7276.

Napa
Diocese of Santa Rosa in California

Rainbow House, c/o 1219 Jefferson St., Ste. 2, Napa, 94559. Tel: 707-224-4403; Fax: 707-224-2889.

Placerville
Diocese of Sacramento

Mother Teresa Maternity Home, 3109 Sacramento St., Placerville, 95667. Tel: 530-295-8006.

Sacramento
Diocese of Sacramento

Lemon Hill, 5036 Lemon Hill Ave., Sacramento, 95824. Tel: 916-421-1620, Ext. 214; Fax: 916-421-3729.

McMahon, 8529 Florin Rd., Sacramento, 95828. Tel: 916-421-1620, Ext. 214; Fax: 916-421-3729.

San Diego
Diocese of San Diego

Bishop Maher Men's Center (1989) 1501 Imperial Ave., San Diego, 92101. Tel: 619-446-2100; Fax: 619-446-2129. Web: www.neighbor.org. Single men's center - 150 residents.

Joan Kroc Homeless Center (1987) 1501 Imperial Ave., San Diego, 92101. Tel: 619-446-2100; Fax: 619-446-2129. Web: www.neighbor.org. Housing for families & single women (326).

National Aids Foundation dba Josue Homes 3350 E St., San Diego, 92102. Tel: 619-466-4827; Fax: 619-446-2129. Web: www.neighbor.org. Housing for persons with AIDS (38).

Padre Luis Jayme International Outreach, 3350 E St., San Diego, 92101. Tel: 619-446-2100; Fax: 619-446-2129. Providing assistance to colonias, prison ministries and orphanages; earthquakes and flood relief in Mexico.

Paul Mirabile Center--Mirabile Housing Inc. (1994) 1501 Imperial Ave., San Diego, 92101. Tel: 619-446-2100; Fax: 619-446-2129. Emergency housing for 270 men & 80 women; free dining room (4000 meals daily).

Rachel's Women's Center--San Diego, San Diego, 92101. Tel: 619-236-9074.

Toussaint Academy of Arts & Sciences, 1404-5th St., San Diego, 92101. Tel: 619-687-1080, Ext. 3399; Fax: 619-446-2129. Web: www.neighbor.org. Residential for 35 homeless teens.

Villa Harvey Mandel, 72-17th St., San Diego, 92101. Tel: 619-446-2100; Fax: 619-446-2129. 95 units - Low to moderate income apts.

San Francisco
Archdiocese of San Francisco

Mount St. Joseph-St. Elizabeth (1976) 100 Masonic Ave., San Francisco, 94118. Tel: 415-567-8370; Fax: 415-351-5531. Email: slowery@msjse.org. Web: www.msjse.org. Successor Corporation to Mount St. Joseph Home for Girls and St. Elizabeth Infant Hospital. Organization name: Epiphany Center for Families in (a program of Mt. St. Joseph-St. Elizabeth) Recovery.

Peter Claver Community, 1340 Golden Gate, San Francisco, 94115. Tel: 415-749-3800; Fax: 415-569-3153. Email: scerreta@cccyo.org. Web: www.cccyo.org/programs/hiv.php.

Rita da Cascia, 1652 Eddy St., #8, San Francisco, 94115. Tel: 415-202-0941; Fax: 415-202-0937. Email: ehammerle@cccyo.org. Web: www.cccyo.org.

The Good Shepherd Gracenter (1986) 1310 Bacon St., San Francisco, 94134. Tel: 415-586-2845; Fax: 415-586-0355. Email: info@gsgracenter.org. Web: www.gsgracenter.org. Residential.

San Jose
Diocese of San Jose in California

The Roman Catholic Welfare Corporation of San Jose, 1150 N. First St., Ste. 100, San Jose, 95112. Tel: 408-983-0168; Fax: 408-983-0296. Email: serventi@dsj.org.

Santa Ana
Diocese of Orange in California

St. Francis Home for the Aged (1944) 1718 W. 6th St., Santa Ana, 92703. Tel: 714-542-0381; Fax: 714-542-4654. Email: stfrancishome@sbcglobal.net. Web: www.st-francis-home.org.

Santa Barbara
Archdiocese of Los Angeles

St. Vincent's (1858) 4200 Calle Real, Santa Barbara, 93110-1454. Tel: 805-683-6381; Fax: 805-967-7508. Email: info@sv-sb.org. Web: www.stvincents-sb.org. For single moms on welfare and/or very low income.

Santa Monica

Archdiocese of Los Angeles

Saint John's Child Study Center, Saint John's Hospital & Health Center, 1339 20th St., Santa Monica, 90404. Tel: 310-829-8921; Fax: 310-829-8455. Affiliated with Saint John's Hospital.

Santa Rosa
Diocese of Santa Rosa in California

Alzheimer's Respite/Resource Center, 987 Airway Ct., Santa Rosa, 95403. Tel: 707-528-8712; Fax: 707-575-4910. P.O. Box 4900, Santa Rosa, 95402.

Saratoga
Diocese of San Jose in California

Our Lady of Fatima Villa, 20400 Saratoga-Los Gatos Rd., Saratoga, 95070. Tel: 408-741-2950; Fax: 408-741-4930. Web: www.fatimavilla.org. Provides skilled nursing care and assisted living facility for aged women and men.

Sonora
Diocese of Stockton

Mother Lode Ombudsman Program Ombudsman Program, Legal Advocacy & Elder Abuse Prevention, Social Security Representative Payee Program., 14855 Mono Way, Ste. 105, Sonora, 95370. Tel: 209-532-7632; Fax: 209-532-8448. Email: ktoepel@ccstockton.org.

Spring Valley
Diocese of San Diego

Noah Homes (1983) 12526 Campo Rd., Spring Valley, 91978. Tel: 619-660-6200; Fax: 619-660-1481. Email: m.nocon@noahhomes.org. Web: www.noahhomes.org.

COLORADO

Aurora
Archdiocese of Denver

St. Anna's Home (Congregation of Sisters of Charity of St. Vincent de Paul, Colorado Chapter Inc.), 3147 S. Pagosa St., Aurora, 80013. Tel: 303-627-2986; Fax: 303-627-2986. Email: st.annashome@hotmail.com.

Canon City
Diocese of Pueblo

Centura Health-Progressive Care Center, 1338 Phay Ave., Canon City, 81212. Tel: 719-285-2540; Fax: 719-285-2256. An operating unit of Catholic Health Initiatives Colorado (an affiliate of Catholic Health Initiatives).

Colorado Springs
Diocese of Colorado Springs

Franciscan Community Counseling, 7665 Assisi Heights, Colorado Springs, 80919. Tel: 719-955-7008; Fax: 719-598-0346. Email: sharon@stfrancis.org. Web: www.franciscancommunitycounseling.org.

Medalion Retirement Community, 1719 E. Bijou St., Colorado Springs, 80909. Tel: 719-381-1000; Fax: 719-381-4978. An operating unit of Catholic Health Initiatives Colorado. An affiliate of Catholic Health Initiatives.

Namaste Alzheimer Center, 2 Penrose Blvd., Colorado Springs, 80906. Tel: 719-776-6300; Fax: 719-520-9709. An operating unit of Catholic Health Initiatives Colorado. An affiliate of Catholic Health Initiatives; Adult Day Programs for seniors with Alzheimer's or dementia.

Denver
Archdiocese of Denver

Archdiocesan Family Housing, Inc. (1968) 4045 Pecos St., Ste. A, Denver, 80211. Tel: 303-830-0215; Fax: 303-830-2885. Housing for Low-Income Families.

Archdiocesan Housing, Inc. (1968) 4045 Pecos St., Ste. A, Denver, 80211. Tel: 303-830-0215; Fax: 303-830-2885. Email: jrussell@archdiocesanhousing.org. Web: www.archdiocesanhousing.com.

Clare Gardens, Inc. (1972) 2626 Osceola St., Denver, 80212. Tel: 303-433-6268; Fax: 303-455-5359. Web: www.nfhealthcare.org. Housing Ministry, low-income family units.

Colorado Affordable Catholic Housing Corp. (1991) 4045 Pecos St., Ste. A, Denver, 80211. Tel: 303-830-0215; Fax: 303-830-2885. Web: www.archdiocesanhousing.org.

Decatur Place, Mailing Address: 1999 Broadway, #1000, Denver, 80202. 1155 Decatur St., Denver, 80204. Tel: 303-830-3300; Fax: 303-830-3301. Web: www.mercyhousing.org. Two year single parent transitional housing program.

Housing Management Services, Inc. (1986) 4045 Pecos St., Ste. A, Denver, 80211. Tel: 303-830-0215; Fax: 303-830-2885. Web: www.archdiocesanhousing.org.

Machebeuf Apartments, Inc., 4045 Pecos St., Ste. A, Denver, 80211. Tel: 303-830-0215. Email: jrussell@archdiocesanhousing.org. Web: www.archdiocesanhousing.org. Low income housing for families located in Glenwood Springs, CO.

Marycrest Assisted Living, 2850 Columbine Rd., Denver, 80221. Tel: 303-433-0906; Fax: 303-433-1254. Email: ppmarycrest@comcast.net. Web: www.marycrest.org.

Mercy Holly Park East (1996) 1999 Broadway, Ste. 1000, Denver, 80202. Tel: 303-830-3300; Fax: 303-830-3301. Affordable housing for singles and families.

Mercy Holly Park West (1996) 1999 Broadway, Ste. 1000, Denver, 80202. Tel: 303-830-3300; Fax: 303-830-3301. Affordable housing for singles and families.

Prairie Rose Plaza, 4045 Pecos St., Ste. A, Denver, 80211.

Special Religious Education-Pastoral Care of Developmentally Disabled Persons (1976) (An office of the Archdiocese of Denver), 3101 W. Hillside Pl., Denver, 80219. Tel: 303-934-1999; Fax: 303-935-7795. Religious education of mentally retarded children and adults.

Willow Street Apartments (1996) 1999 Broadway, Ste. 1000, Denver, 80202. Tel: 303-830-3300; Fax: 303-830-3301. Affordable housing for persons with chronic mental illness.

Grand Junction
Diocese of Pueblo

Grand Valley Catholic Outreach, 245 S. 1st St., Grand Junction, 81501. Tel: 970-241-3658; Fax: 970-254-1262. Email: gvcoaid@yahoo.com. Web: www.catholicoutreach.org.

Pueblo
Diocese of Pueblo

Centura Health-Villa Pueblo, 1111 Bonforte Blvd., Pueblo, 81001. Tel: 719-545-5911; 303-964-2355 (Chap. Svcs.); Fax: 719-544-1354. An operating unit of Catholic Health Initiatives Colorado (an affiliate of Catholic Health Initiatives).

Westminster
Archdiocese of Denver

Clare of Assisi Homes - Westminster, Inc. (1995) 2451 W. 82 Pl., Westminster, 80003. Tel: 303-427-4406; 303-462-9271 (Corporate). Housing and services for elderly and disabled.

CONNECTICUT

Danbury
Diocese of Bridgeport

The Pope John Paul II Center for Health Care, Inc., 33 Lincoln Ave., Danbury, 06810. Tel: 203-416-1355. Email: onedee98@aol.com.

Deep River
Diocese of Norwich

Mount St. John, 135 Kirtland St., Deep River, 06417-1816. Tel: 860-343-1340; Fax: 860-343-1394. Email: decerbod@mtstjohn.org; mckenneyv@mtstjohn.org. Web: www.mtstjohn.org.

Hamden
Archdiocese of Hartford

Clelian Adult Day Center (1988) 261 Benham St., Hamden, 06514-2898. Tel: 203-288-4151; Fax: 203-288-0551. Email: cleliancenter@juno.com. Web: www.clelianadultdaycenter.com. A day health care facility for elderly and disabled adults (interdenominational).

Hartford
Archdiocese of Hartford

**Malta House of Care, Inc.*, One State St., Ste. 2400, Hartford, 06103. Tel: 860-808-0195. Web: www.maltahouseofcare.org. To deliver charitable primary and/or preventative medical health care to the needy uninsured of the Greater Hartford region.

Meriden
Archdiocese of Hartford

Franciscan Family Care Center (1979) 267 Finch Ave., Meriden, 06451. Tel: 203-238-1441; Fax: 203-686-0807. Email: ssuzanne@franciscanhc.org.

West Hartford
Archdiocese of Hartford

Saint Agnes Home, Inc. (1914) 104 Mayflower St., West Hartford, 06110. Tel: 860-521-7516; Fax: 860-521-6160. Email: info@stagneshome.org. Web: www.stagneshome.org. For adolescent single mothers and their infants.

Willimantic
Diocese of Norwich

Holy Family Home and Shelter, Inc., 88 Jackson St., P.O. Box 884, Willimantic, 06226-0884. Tel: 860-423-7719; Fax: 860-423-3770. Email: sisterpeter@holyfamilywillimantic.org. Web: www.holyfamilywillimantic.org.

DELAWARE

New Castle
Diocese of Wilmington

Emmanuel Dining Room, South, 500 Rogers Rd., New Castle, 19720. Tel: 302-577-2951; Fax: 302-652-2576.

Wilmington
Diocese of Wilmington

Andrisani Building (1996) 1801 W. 6th St., Wilmington, 19805. Tel: 302-428-3702; Fax: 302-428-3705.

Angela Merici House (1993) 1105 W. 8th St., Wilmington, 19806-4605. Tel: 302-655-4817. Residence for Religious Sisters.

Benedictine Park, 731 W. 9th St., Wilmington, 19801. Tel: 302-652-5523; Fax: 302-652-1919.

Bethany House (1999) 601 N. Jackson St., Wilmington, 19805-3241. Tel: 302-656-8391. Email: mmatarese@ministryofcaring.org. Permanent housing for women with special needs.

CACFP (Child & Adult Care Food Program), 2604 W. 4th St., Wilmington, 19805. Tel: 302-655-9624; Fax: 302-654-9753.

Emmanuel Dining Room, East, 226 N. Walnut St., Wilmington, 19801-3934. Tel: 302-652-2577; Fax: 302-652-2576.

Emmanuel Dining Room, West (1979) 121 N. Jackson St., Wilmington, 19805-3670. Tel: 302-652-3228; Fax: 302-652-2576.

Francis X. Norton Center (2002) 917 N. Madison St., Wilmington, 19801. Tel: 302-594-9455; Fax: 302-428-3655. Multigenerational community center.

HIV/AIDS Services, 2601 W. 4th St., Wilmington, 19805. Tel: 302-655-9624; Fax: 302-654-6432.

House of Joseph I (1985) 1328 W. Third St., Wilmington, 19805-3662. Tel: 302-652-0904; Fax: 302-594-9472. Email: wnewson@ministryofcaring.org. Shelter for homeless employable men who are seeking employment.

House of Joseph II, 9 W. 18th St., Wilmington, 19802-4833. Tel: 302-594-9473; Fax: 302-594-9494. Email: srjean@ministryofcaring.org. Hospice for people with AIDS.

House of Joseph Transitional Residence (1998) 704 West St., Wilmington, 19801-1523. Tel: 302-652-7968; Fax: 302-594-9472. Email: wnewson@ministryofcaring.org. Transitional residence for employable, formerly homeless persons.

Il Bambino (2002) 903 N. Madison St., Wilmington, 19801. Tel: 302-594-9449; Fax: 302-594-9450. Infant day care program.

Job Placement Center (1985) 1100 Lancaster Ave., Wilmington, 19805-4009. Tel: 302-652-5522; Fax: 302-652-0917. Email: mking@ministryofcaring.org. Employment agency to assist the poor.

Maria Lorenza Longo House (2003) 822 Jefferson St., Wilmington, 19801. Transitional Residence for Families.

Mary Mother of Hope House I (1977) Temporary Address: 917 N. Madison St., Wilmington, 19801. Tel: 302-652-8532; Fax: 302-594-9434. Email: mmatarese@ministryofcaring.org. Emergency shelter for homeless women.

Mary Mother of Hope House II (1983) 121 N. Jackson St., Wilmington, 19805-3670. Tel: 302-652-1935; Fax: 302-594-9475. Emergency shelter for women with children.

Mary Mother of Hope House III (1988) 515 N. Broom St., Wilmington, 19805-3114. Tel: 302-652-0970; Fax: 302-594-9496. Emergency shelter for women with children.

Mary Mother of Hope House Transitional Residence, 818-820 Jefferson St., Wilmington, 19801-1432. Tel: 302-594-9448; Fax: 302-594-9434. Email: mmatarese@ministryofcaring.org. Transitional residence for single women.

Ministry of Caring Distribution Center, 1410 N. Claymont St., Wilmington, 19802-5227. Tel: 302-652-0969; Fax: 302-594-9478.

Ministry of Caring Guild (1990) 506 N. Church St., Wilmington, 19801. Tel: 302-427-9447; Fax: 302-778-5286.

Ministry of Caring, Inc. (1977) 506 N. Church St., Wilmington, 19801-4812. Tel: 302-652-5523; Fax: 302-652-1919. Email: mail@ministryofcaring.org.

Nazareth House I (1998) 106 N. Broom St., Wilmington, 19805. Tel: 302-652-0790; Fax: 302-594-9496.

Nazareth House II (1998) 898 Linden St., Wilmington, 19805-4423. Tel: 302-428-3635; Fax: 302-428-3636. Transitional residence for families.

Nazareth Long Term Housing (1998) 203 N. Jackson St., Wilmington, 19805-3649. Tel: 302-652-5523; Fax: 302-652-1919. Long term housing

Nazareth Long Term Housing, 207 S. Van Buren St., Wilmington, 19805. Tel: 302-652-5523; Fax: 302-652-1919. Transitional residence for families.

Nazareth Long Term Housing, 109-1/2 & 111 N. Jackson St., Wilmington, 19805. Tel: 302-652-5523; Fax: 302-652-1919. Transitional residence for families.

Nazareth Long Term Housing (1998) 807 W. 6th St., Wilmington, 19805. Tel: 302-652-5523; Fax: 302-652-1919. Long term housing

Office for Parish Social Ministry, 2601 W. 4th St., Wilmington, 19805. Tel: 302-655-9624; Fax: 302-655-9753.

Padre Pio House, 213 N. Jackson St., Wilmington, 19805. Email: wnewson@ministryofcaring.org. Permanent housing for men with special needs.

Pierre Toussaint Dental Office (1995) 830 Spruce St., Wilmington, 19801-4205. Tel: 302-652-8947; Fax: 302-652-8994. Dental office for the homeless.

Sacred Heart Administration, 903 N. Madison St., Wilmington, 19801. Tel: 302-888-1420; Fax: 302-594-9450.

Sacred Heart Convent, 700 W. 9th St., Wilmington, 19801. Tel: 302-692-8532.

Sacred Heart House (1997) 917 N. Madison St., Wilmington, 19801. Tel: 302-428-3652; Fax: 302-428-3655.

Sacred Heart Housing, Inc. (1998) 506 N. Church St., Wilmington, 19801. Tel: 302-652-5523; Fax: 302-652-1919.

Samaritan Outreach (1995) 1410 N. Claymont St., Wilmington, 19802-5227. Tel: 302-594-9476; Fax: 303-594-9478. Social outreach for the homeless.

St. Clare Medical Outreach (1992) 7th & Clayton Sts., Wilmington, 19805-3156. Tel: 302-575-8218. Mobile medical van which provides health services for the poor.

St. Francis Transitional Residence (1995) 103-107 & 111 N. Jackson St., Wilmington, 19805-3648. Transitional living for women and children.

DISTRICT OF COLUMBIA

Washington
Archdiocese of Washington

Lt. Joseph P. Kennedy, Jr., Institute, 801 Buchanan St., N.E., Washington, 20017. Tel: 202-529-7600; Fax: 202-529-2028. Email: gadair@kennedyinstitute.org. Web: www.kennedyinstitute.org. The Lt. Joseph P. Kennedy, Jr., Institute of the Archdiocese of Washington is a private, nonprofit organization providing education, training and employment, therapeutic and residential services to children and adults with developmental disabilities.

FLORIDA

Boca Raton
Diocese of Palm Beach

Cross International Catholic Outreach, Inc., 370 W. Camino Gardens Blvd., Boca Raton, 33432. Tel: 561-392-9212, Ext. 104; Fax: 561-367-0564. Email: info@crossinternational.org. Web: www.crosscatholic.org.

Jacksonville
Diocese of St. Augustine

L'Arche Harbor House (1985) 700 Arlington Rd. N., Jacksonville, 32211. Tel: 904-721-5992; Fax: 904-721-7143. Email: communityleader@bellsouth.net. Web: larchejacksonville.org. A residential community for adults with developmental disabilities and those who choose to share life with them (assistants). We also have an adult day program called the Rainbow Workshop.

Largo
Diocese of St. Petersburg

Bethlehem Centre, Inc., 10895 Hamlin Blvd., Largo, 34644. Tel: 727-596-9394; Fax: 727-596-6792. Senior Center offering programs in Fitness, Exercise, Social, Educational, Music, Art, Computers, and Religious Nature on Tuesday, Wednesday, and Friday. Hot luncheon is available on Tuesday and Friday (Oct.-April).

Miami
Archdiocese of Miami

Camillus Health Concern, Inc. (1984) P.O. Box 012408, Miami, 33101-2408. Tel: 305-374-1065; Fax: 305-373-7431. Web: www.camillus.org. Provides medical, dental, mental health and social services to the homeless and indigent.

Camillus House, Inc. (1960) 336 N.W. 5th St., Miami, 33128. Tel: 305-374-1065, Ext. 308; Fax: 305-372-1402. Email: dr.paul@camillus.org. Web: www.camillus.org. Provides services to the homeless: emergency services, substance abuse rehabilitation, transitional and permanent housing.

Gift of Hope, Missionaries of Charity (1981) 724 N.W. 17th St., Miami, 33136. Tel: 305-326-0032.

Soup Kitchen (1981) Miami. Tel: 305-326-0032.

Women's and Children's Shelter, Miami. Tel: 305-326-0032.

Panama City
Diocese of Pensacola-Tallahassee

Naomi House, 2941 E. 11th St., Panama City, 32401. Tel: 850-763-0475; Fax: 850-763-2969. Email: catholicchari@comcast.net. c/o Catholic Charities, 3128 E. 11th St., Panama City, 32401.

St. Barnabas House, 2943 E. 11th St., Panama City, 32401. Tel: 850-763-0475; Fax: 850-763-2969. Email: catholicchari@comcast.net. c/o Catholic Charities, 3128 E. 11th St., Panama City, 32401.

St. Augustine
Diocese of St. Augustine

Religious Education for Catholic Deaf and Blind, 30 Ocean Ave., St. Augustine, 32084-2813. Tel: 904-825-4272 (Voice/TDD); Fax: 904-825-4348. Email: religiouseduc90@bellsouth.net. Web: www.catholicdeaf.org. Florida School for the Deaf and Blind.

GEORGIA

Atlanta
Archdiocese of Atlanta

Good Shepherd Outreach Center, 2426 Shallowford Ter., Atlanta, 30341. Tel: 770-455-9379; Fax: 770-451-0156.

Our Lady of Perpetual Help Home, 760 Pollard Blvd., S.W., Atlanta, 30315. Tel: 404-688-9515; Fax: 404-588-9568. Web: olphhome.org. Nursing Home for Free Care of Cancer Patients.

Saint Joseph's Mercy Care Services (1985) 424 Decatur St., Atlanta, 30312-1848. Tel: 678-843-8500; Fax: 678-843-8501. Email: aebberwein@sjha.org. Division of Saint Joseph's Health System. Operates Saint Joseph's Mercy Care Services (Atlanta, Georgia). Operates Mercy Senior Care (Rome, Georgia).

Macon
Diocese of Savannah

Nazareth Life Ministries, 538 Orange St., Macon, 31201. Tel: 478-746-9803; Fax: 478-745-0847. Email: famsre@bellsouth.net. Pregnancy Services for birth parents/families/newborn, education & direct services.

Savannah
Diocese of Savannah

St. Mary's Home, 2170 E. Victory Dr., P.O. Box 3627-B, Savannah, 31414. Tel: 912-236-7164; Fax: 912-236-9699. Email: STMARYHOME@aol.com.

HAWAII

Hilo
Diocese of Honolulu

Mobile Care Health Project, 140-B Holomua St., Hilo, 96720. Tel: 808-935-3050; Fax: 808-935-3794.

Honolulu
Diocese of Honolulu

St. Francis Home Care Services, 2228 Liliha St., Ste. 106, Honolulu, 96817. Tel: 808-534-0777; Fax: 808-676-1300.

Kalaupapa
Diocese of Honolulu

Kalaupapa Nursing Facility (Molokai), P.O. Box 3333, Kalaupapa, 96742. Tel: 808-567-6911; Fax: 808-567-6916. Email: knfcef@aloha.net. Operated by the State Dept. of Health for Hansen's Disease Branch.

Lihue
Diocese of Honolulu

St. Francis Home Care Services-Kauai, 4472 Pahee St., Ste. N, Lihue, 96766. Tel: 808-245-6430; Fax: 808-246-8620.

ILLINOIS

Arlington Heights
Archdiocese of Chicago

Northwest Suburban Senior Services, 1801 W. Central, Arlington Heights, 60005. Tel: 847-797-5321; Fax: 847-253-9597.

Carpentersville
Diocese of Rockford

Provena Family Care, Carpentersville, 2201 Randall Rd., Carpentersville, 60110. Tel: 847-844-7800; Fax: 847-783-0628.

Chicago
Archdiocese of Chicago

Ada S. Niles Adult Day Care, 6717 S. Elizabeth, Chicago, 60639. Tel: 773-488-5400; Fax: 773-488-5878.

Ada S. Niles Senior Center and Adult Day Care Services, 653 W. 63rd St., Chicago, 60621. Tel: 312-745-3307; Fax: 312-745-3330.

Addiction Consultation and Educational Services, 651 W. Lake St., Chicago, 60661. Tel: 312-655-7453.

Archdiocesan AIDS Ministry Office, 651 W. Lake St., Chicago, 60661. Tel: 312-948-6500; Fax: 312-879-0208.

Bishop Edwin M. Conway Residence, 1900 N. Karlov Ave., Chicago, 60639. Tel: 773-252-8578; Fax: 773-525-9946.

Catholic Home Care, Inc., 721 N. La Salle St., Chicago, 60654. Tel: 312-655-7415; Fax: 312-337-2705.

Catholic Office of the Deaf, 3525 S. Lake Park Ave., Chicago, 60616. Tel: 312-534-7899 (Voice); 312-751-8368 (TDD); Fax: 312-534-0394. Email: cathdeafch@archchicago.org. Web: www.deafchurchchicago.parishesonline.com.

Central States Institute of Addiction, 651 W. Lake St., Chicago, 60661. Tel: 312-655-7530; Fax: 312-266-9027.

Child Welfare Counseling and Therapeutic Services, 651 W. Lake, Chicago, 60661. Tel: 312-655-7191; Fax: 312-236-5384.

Children & Adolescent Parent Program, 651 W. Lake St., Chicago, 60661. Tel: 312-655-7222; Fax: 312-236-5384.

Children's HealthCare Center, 4015 N. Oak Park Ave., Chicago, 60634. Tel: 773-205-3600; Fax: 773-205-3630.

**Claver House of Renewal, Inc.*, 8514 S. Avalon St., Chicago, 60619. Tel: 773-731-3294. Food pantry, soup kitchen, home-bound senior citizen care, after-school youth recreational programs; mentoring; tutoring and scholarship assistance to elementary and high school graduates continuing studies at Catholic educational institutions. Outreach to the homeless: clothing, toys and basic toiletries for local shelters.

Community Family Service Center, 1100 S. May, Chicago, 60607. Tel: 312-733-5661, Ext. 1467; Fax: 312-733-5211.

Forever Free, 6212 S. Sangamon, Chicago, 60621. Tel: 773-374-8165; Fax: 773-548-4522.

Franciscan Outreach Association, 1645 W. LeMoyne St., Chicago, 60622. Tel: 773-278-6724; Fax: 773-278-7120. Web: www.franoutreach.org. Owns & operates: Marquard Center (dining room for the homeless), Franciscan House of Mary & Joseph (shelter) and a Case Management Program for the homeless in Chicago.

Holbrook Center for Counseling and Psychotherapy, 641 W. Lake St., Chicago, 60661. Tel: 312-655-7719; Fax: 312-655-0678.

Homelessness Prevention Call Center, 721 N. LaSalle St., Chicago, 60610. Tel: 312-698-5070; Fax: 312-655-0678.

House of the Good Shepherd, 1114 W. Grace St., Chicago, 60613. Tel: 773-935-3434; Fax: 773-935-3523. Shelter for abused women with children.

Intact Family Services, 651 W. Lake St., Chicago, 60661. Tel: 312-655-7601; Fax: 773-292-5713.

Jadonal E. Ford Center for Adolescent Parenting, 11255 S. Michigan Ave., Chicago, 60628. Tel: 773-995-1737; Fax: 773-995-0125.

Joseph Cardinal Bernardin Family Shelter Program, 651 W. Lake St., Chicago, 60661. Tel: 312-655-7700; Fax: 773-483-5301.

**L'Arche Chicago*, 1049 S. Austin Blvd., Chicago, 60644. Tel: 773-287-8249; Fax: 708-863-1273 (Call first). Email: larchechicago@sbcglobal.net. Web: www.larchechicago.org. A Christian Community concerned with life sharing between persons with a developmental disability and persons who assist them.

LOSS (Loving Outreach to Survivors of Suicide), 651 W. Lake St., Chicago, 60661. Tel: 312-655-7283; Fax: 312-559-1530.

Maternity/Adoption Services, 651 W. Lake St., Chicago, 60661. Tel: 312-655-7071; Fax: 312-236-5384.

Misericordia/Heart of Mercy Center, 6300 N. Ridge, Chicago, 60660-1017. Tel: 773-973-6300; Fax: 773-973-5214. Web: www.misericordia.com. Children and adults with developmental disabilities.

Mother and Child Food and Nutrition (MAC) Warehouse, 1965 W. Pershing Rd., Chicago, 60608. Tel: 773-523-0299.

Mother and Child Food and Nutrition Program (MAC), 4940 W. Flournoy, Chicago, 60644. Tel: 773-378-3127; Fax: 773-261-0536.

Options for Housing, Inc. f/k/a Shelter for the Homeless, Inc., 721 N. LaSalle St., Chicago, 60610. Tel: 312-655-7305.

**Port Ministries*, 5013 S. Hermitage Ave., Chicago, 60609. Tel: 773-778-5955; Fax: 773-778-2451. Email: port532857@aol.com. Web: www.portministries.org. A Franciscan outreach to the poor and homeless; mobile soup kitchen, family transitional shelter, GED, ESL, family svcs., neighborhood gym and free clinic.

St. Ailbe Adult Day Care, 9249 S. Avalon, Chicago, 60619. Tel: 773-721-0177; Fax: 773-721-1228.

St. Mary of Providence, 4200 N. Austin Ave., Chicago, 60634. Tel: 773-545-8300; Fax: 773-545-8035. Email: SrRitaB@sbcglobal.net. Developmental training and residential care of developmentally disabled adults.

St. Rose Center, 4911 S. Hoyne Ave., Chicago, 60609. Tel: 773-436-1433; Fax: 773-436-2280. Email: strosecenter@aol.com. Web: www.strosecenter.org. Day Training Program for Developmentally Impaired young adults.

Villa Guadalupe Senior Services Corporation, 3201 E. 91st St., Chicago, 60617. Tel: 773-933-0344; Fax: 773-933-0827. Organization to provide affordable housing and related services for Senior Citizens in South Chicago.

Women Infant Children Food Centers Program, 4624 W. Diversey, Chicago, 60639. Tel: 312-951-7672; Fax: 773-205-1271. WIC Food Centers: 416 E. 43rd St., Chicago, IL 60653; 6202 S. Halsted St., Chicago, IL 60621; 2310 W. Roosevelt Rd., Chicago, IL 60608; 5332 S. Western, Chicago, IL 60609; 3110 W. Armitage, Chicago, IL 60647; 4500 W. Chicago Ave., Chicago, IL 60651 WIC Warehouse; 1643 W. Cermak Rd., Chicago, IL 60608; 1734 W. Chicago Ave., Chicago, IL 60622; 3932 W. Madison St., Chicago, IL 60624; 5125 W. Chicago, Chicago, IL 60651; 1802 E. 71st St., Chicago IL 60649; 11255 S. Michigan Ave., Chicago, IL 60628; 4622 W. Diversey Ave., Chicago, IL 60639; 8959 S. Commercial Ave., Chicago, IL 60617; 2400 S. Kedzie Ave., Chicago, IL 60623 and 1106 W. 79th St., Chicago, IL 60620.

Des Plaines
Archdiocese of Chicago

Child and Family Behavioral Health Center, 555 Wilson Ln., Des Plaines, 60016. Tel: 847-390-3000; Fax: 847-294-2788.

Maryville Academy, 1150 N. River Rd., Des Plaines, 60016. Tel: 847-294-1999; Fax: 847-824-7277. Web: www.maryvilleacademy.org.

North/Northwest Suburban Family Shelter Program, 1717 N. Rand Rd., Des Plaines, 60016. Tel: 847-376-2100; Fax: 847-390-8214.

Scott Nolan Residential Treatment Center, 555 Wilson Ln., Des Plaines, 60016. Tel: 847-768-5430; Fax: 847-768-5478.

Freeport
Diocese of Rockford

Provena St. Vincent's Community Living Facility and Supported Living Arrangement, 659 E. Jefferson St., Freeport, 61032. Tel: 815-232-6181; Fax: 815-232-6143.

Hampshire
Diocese of Rockford

Provena Family Care, Hampshire, 895 S. State St., Ste. 201, Hampshire, 60140. Tel: 847-683-7099; Fax: 847-683-7104.

Harvey
Archdiocese of Chicago

South Suburban Senior Services and Senior Activity Center, 15300 S. Lexington, Harvey, 60426. Tel: 708-596-2222; Fax: 708-596-6329.

St. Susanna Shelter Apartments, 14926 S. Honore, Harvey, 60426. Tel: 708-331-8211; Fax: 708-339-4398.

Hines
Archdiocese of Chicago

Cooke's Manor Transitional Housing For Men, Bldg. 14 Hines VA Campus, 5th Ave. & Roosevelt Rd., Hines, 60141. Tel: 708-273-6627; Fax: 708-343-4469.

Huntley
Diocese of Rockford

Provena Family Care, Huntley, 12155 Regency Sq. Pkwy., Huntley, 60142. Tel: 847-515-2100; Fax: 847-515-2328.

Joliet
Diocese of Joliet in Illinois

Guardian Angel Community Services, 1550 Plainfield Rd., Joliet, 60435. Tel: 815-729-0930; Fax: 815-744-6087. Email: Sheila@guardianangelhome.org. Web: www.guardianangelhome.org. Sponsored by the Sisters of St. Francis of Mary Immaculate; Child and family welfare agency: therapeutic school, foster care, domestic violence shelter, child abuse prevention center, counseling, transitional living program, and Rape Crisis Program.

Kankakee
Diocese of Joliet in Illinois

Lisieux Pastoral Outreach Center, 371 N. St. Joseph Ave., Kankakee, 60901-2741. Tel: 815-939-2913.

Provena St. Mary's Adult Day Center, 1025 E. Washington, Kankakee, 60901. Tel: 815-937-2447; Fax: 815-936-3245. Email: rebecca.barney@provena.org. Web: www.provena.org. 19065 Hickory Creek Dr., #300, Mokena, 60448.

Lake Zurich
Archdiocese of Chicago

Mt. St. Joseph Home, 24955 North Hwy. 12, Lake Zurich, 60047. Tel: 847-438-5050; Fax: 847-438-6313. Email: msjlz@aol.com. Intermediate care for developmentally disabled women.

Mokena
Diocese of Joliet in Illinois

Provena Senior Services, 19065 Hickory Creek Dr., Ste. 310, Mokena, 60448-8507. Tel: 708-478-7900; Fax: 708-478-5143. Email: connie.march@provena.org. Web: www.provena.org.

Provena St. Mary's Adult Day Center, 1025 E. Washington, Kankakee, 60901. Tel: 815-937-2447; Fax: 815-936-3245. Email: rebecca.barney@provena.org. Web: www.provena.org. 19065 Hickory Creek Dr., #300, Mokena, 60448.

Momence
Diocese of Joliet in Illinois

Good Shepherd Manor (1971) P.O. Box 260, Momence, 60954. Tel: 815-472-6492; 815-472-3700; Fax: 815-472-2160. Email: gsmanor@mchsi.com. Web: www.goodshepherdmanor.org. Adult Male DD-MR.

Normal
Diocese of Peoria

Homes of Hope, Inc., 401 Pine St., Ste. 1, Normal, 61761. Tel: 309-862-0607; Fax: 309-452-7131. Email: homesofhope1@verizon.net.

Oak Park
Archdiocese of Chicago

Accolade Adult Day Care, 112 S. Humphrey, Oak Park, 60302-2704. Tel: 708-445-1300; Fax: 708-445-9595.

Daughters of the Heart of Mary, 140 N. Euclid Ave., #401, Oak Park, 60302-1684. Tel: 708-386-0190; Fax: 708-383-1327. Email: ephpheta@sbcglobal.net. Web: www.dhmna.org.

Peoria
Diocese of Peoria

Saint Clare Home, 5533 N. Galena Rd., Peoria, 61614. Tel: 309-682-5428; Fax: 309-682-8478. Web: osfhealthcare.org. Skilled nursing facility.

River Forest
Archdiocese of Chicago

Big Sisters, P.O. Box 5728, River Forest, 60305. Tel: 708-488-8893. Web: bigsistersofchicago.org.

Round Lake
Archdiocese of Chicago

Lake County Senior Case Management Services, 116 N. Lincoln, Round Lake, 60073. Tel: 847-546-5733; Fax: 847-546-7114.

Savanna
Diocese of Rockford

Mercy Homecare/Hospice, 1121 N. 5th St., Savanna, 61074. Tel: 815-273-2628; Fax: 815-273-7025. Email: nocj@mercyhealth.com. Web: www.mercyclinton.com.

Springfield
Diocese of Springfield in Illinois

Brother James Court (1975) 2508 St. James Rd., Springfield, 62707. Tel: 217-544-4876; Fax: 217-747-5971. Email: administrator@brotherjamescourt.com. Web: www.brotherjamescourt.com. Residence for Mentally Retarded Male Adults.

St. Clare's Health Clinic, 700 N. 7th St., Ste. A, Springfield, 62702. Tel: 217-523-1474; Fax: 217-523-0194. Web: www.cc.dio.org.

St. John's Breadline, 430 N. Fifth St., Springfield, 62702. Tel: 217-528-6098; Fax: 217-528-3605. Email: stjohnsbreadline@sbcglobal.net. Web: www.cc.dio.org.

Tinley Park
Archdiocese of Chicago

St. Coletta's of Illinois, Inc., 18350 Crossing Dr., Tinley Park, 60487. Tel: 708-342-5200; Fax: 708-342-2579. Web: www.stcolettas.com. Sponsored by the Sisters of St. Francis of Assisi. Residential care, education, job training & job placement for developmentally disabled children and adults.

Waukegan
Archdiocese of Chicago

Lake County HIV/AIDS Case Management, 671 S. Lewis, Waukegan, 60085. Tel: 847-782-4144; Fax: 847-782-4133.

Lake County Senior Community Services & Nutrition Program Sites, 671 S. Lewis Ave., Waukegan, 60085. Tel: 847-782-4267; Fax: 847-782-4296.

West Peoria
Diocese of Peoria

Guardian Angel Home, 2900 W. Heading Ave., West Peoria, 61604. Tel: 309-636-7500; Fax: 309-673-3405. Web: www.ccdop.org. Treatment for Abused and Neglected Youth.

INDIANA

Crown Point
Diocese of Gary

Franciscan Home Care Services, Inc., 203 Franciscan Dr., Crown Point, 46307. Tel: 219-661-5321; Fax: 219-661-5305. Email: cgrantner@franciscancommunities.com.

East Chicago
Diocese of Gary

Office of Hispanic Ministry (1983) 1709 E. 138th St., P.O. Box 3027, East Chicago, 46312. Tel: 219-397-2125; Fax: 219-397-2168. Email: atorres@dcgary.org. Web: www.dcgary.org.

Hammond
Diocese of Gary

Heartland Center, 6819 Indianapolis Blvd., Hammond, 46324. Tel: 219-844-7515; Fax: 219-844-7566. Email: mail@heartlandctr.org. Web: www.heartlandctr.org. Office of Peace and Social Justice of the Diocese of Gary.

Senior Companion Program, 6919 Indianapolis Blvd., Hammond, 46324. Tel: 219-844-4883; Fax: 219-844-4885.

Spiritual Life/Seimetz Center, 1441 Hoffman St., Hammond, 46327. Tel: 219-932-8321; Fax: 219-932-8321. Email: xctb29c@prodigy.com.

Indianapolis
Archdiocese of Indianapolis

A Caring Place - Adult Day Services, c/o Fairview Presbyterian Church, 4609 N. Capitol Ave., Indianapolis, 46208. Tel: 317-466-0015; Fax: 317-475-3093.

Terre Haute
Archdiocese of Indianapolis

Gibault Children's Services, 6301 S. U.S. Hwy. 41, P.O. Box 2316, Terre Haute, 47802-0316. Tel: 812-299-1156; Fax: 812-298-3044. Email: gibault@gibault.org. Web: www.gibault.org. Residential treatment facility for males and females between the ages of 8 and 18, sponsored by the Knights of Columbus of Indiana.

St. Ann Community Outreach Services of Terre Haute, 1440 Locust St., Terre Haute, 47807. Tel: 812-232-6832; Fax: 812-232-2442. Email: stannchurch@gmail.com. Mailing Address: 1440 Locust St., Terre Haute, 47807.

IOWA

Clinton
Diocese of Davenport

Arch I, 402 S. Fourth St., Clinton, 52732. Tel: 563-243-3980.

Arch II, 734 Fifth Ave. S., Clinton, 52732. Tel: 563-242-5082.

Arch III, 505 7th Ave. S., Clinton, 52732. Tel: 563-242-8740; Fax: 563-242-8740.

Arch, Inc., Box 0278, Clinton, 52733-0278. Tel: 563-243-9035; Fax: 563-243-7796. Email: larchia@qwest.net.

Mercy Home Care and Hospice, 638 S. Bluff, Clinton, 52732. Tel: 563-244-3766; Fax: 563-244-3719. Email: meistesk@mercyhealth.com. Web: www.mercyclinton.com.

Des Moines
Diocese of Des Moines

House of Mercy, 1409 Clark St., Des Moines, 50314-1964. Tel: 515-643-6500; Fax: 515-643-6598. Email: tbeveridge@mercydesmoines.org. Web: houseofmercydesmoines.org.

Dubuque
Archdiocese of Dubuque

Caritas Center, 1130 Carmel Dr., Dubuque, 52003-7911. Tel: 563-556-3240. Email: bvmcenter@bvmcong.org. Web: www.bvmcong.org.

Holy Family Hall Infirmary, 3340 Windsor Ave., Dubuque, 52001-1300. Tel: 563-583-9786; Fax: 563-583-6080. Email: info@osfdbq.org. Web: www.osfdbq.org.

Marian Hall Infirmary, 1050 Carmel Dr., Dubuque, 52003. Tel: 563-556-5474; Fax: 563-588-1975. Email: bvmcenter@bvmcong.org. Web: www.bvmcong.org.

Iowa City
Diocese of Davenport

Mercy Outreach Iowa City, Inc., 500 E. Market St., Iowa City, 52245. Tel: 319-339-3540.

KANSAS

Great Bend
Diocese of Dodge City

Heartland Center for Wholistic Health (1988) 1005 Williams, Great Bend, 67530. Tel: 620-793-9067; Fax: 620-793-5817. Email: anita@hcwh.net. Web: www.hcwh.net. Body massage, herbals, chiropractic, natural remedies.

Kansas City
Archdiocese of Kansas City in Kansas

St. Joseph Adoption Referral Service, Inc. (2001) 8160 Parallel Pkwy., Ste. 103, Kansas City, 66112. Tel: 913-299-5222; 800-752-1737; Fax: 913-299-5111. Email: apeacefulblessing@yahoo.com. Web: www.catholicadoption.info.

Wichita
Diocese of Wichita

Guadalupe Clinic, Inc. (1985) 940 S. St. Francis, Wichita, 67211. Tel: 316-264-8974; Fax: 316-262-4938. Email: guadalupe@guadalupeclinic.kscoxmail.com. Web: www.guadalupeclinic.com.

Via Christi Healthcare Outreach Program for Elders, Inc. (HOPE) (2002) 2622 W. Central, Ste. 101, Wichita, 67203. Tel: 316-858-1111; Fax: 316-858-1166. Email: justin_loewen@via-christi.org. Web: viachristihope.org.

Via Christi Senior Services, Inc. (1985) 2622 W. Central, Ste. 100, Wichita, 67203. Tel: 316-946-5200; Fax: 316-946-5299. Email: jerry_carley@via-christi.org. Web: www.via-christi.org.

KENTUCKY

Louisville
Archdiocese of Louisville

**Nativity Academy*, 529 E. Liberty St., Louisville, 40202. Tel: 502-855-3300; Fax: 502-562-2192. Email: scarson@nativityacademy.org. (Grades 6-8)

Open Hand Kitchen and Community Center, 1026 S. Jackson St., Louisville, 40203. Tel: 502-584-2480; Fax: 502-587-1977.

Our Lady of Peace, 2020 Newburg Rd., Louisville, 40205. Tel: 502-451-3330; Fax: 502-479-4140. Email: michaelahrens@jhsmh.org. Web: www.jhsmh.org. Hospital for Psychiatric Illness.

Ozanam Inn, 1034 S. Jackson St., Louisville, 40203. Tel: 502-584-2480; Fax: 502-587-1977. (Men's Emergency & Transitional Shelter)

Pitt Academy, 6010 Preston Hwy., Louisville, 40219. Tel: 502-966-6979; Fax: 502-962-8878. Email: sdowney@pitt.com. Web: www.pitt.com.

Roberts Hall, 1032 E. Burnett Ave., Louisville, 40217. Tel: 502-636-3549; Fax: 502-587-1977. (Women's Housing)

Sacred Heart School for the Arts, 3105 Lexington Rd., Louisville, 40206. Tel: 502-897-1816; Fax: 502-896-3927. Email: lslaughter@sacredheartschools.org. Web: www.sacredheartschools.org.

Sacred Heart Village I, Inc. (Senior Housing Apartments), 2110 Payne St., Louisville, 40206. Tel: 502-895-6409; Fax: 502-895-8166.

Sacred Heart Village II, Inc. (Senior Housing Apartments), 2108 Payne St., Louisville, 40206. Tel: 502-895-8085; Fax: 502-895-8039.

Sacred Heart Village III, Inc. (Senior Housing Apartments), 3101 Wayside Dr., Louisville, 40216. Tel: 502-776-5004; Fax: 502-772-7695.

Sacred Heart Village, Inc. dba Sacred Heart Village 2120 Payne St., Louisville, 40206. Tel: 502-895-9425; Fax: 502-357-5549. Mercy Franciscan Health and Housing Services.

Simon Hall, 1022 S. Jackson St., Louisville, 40203. Tel: 502-584-2480; Fax: 502-587-1977. (Men's Recovery)

St. Jude Women's Recovery Center, 431 E. St. Catherine St., Louisville, 40203. Tel: 502-589-6024; Fax: 502-587-1977. (Women's Recovery)

Tranquil House (Housing For Mentally Ill), 1035 S. Preston St., Louisville, 40203. Tel: 502-584-2480; Fax: 502-587-1977.

LOUISIANA

Alexandria
Diocese of Alexandria

Our Lady of Sorrows Community Homes, 347 Browns Bend Rd., Alexandria, 71303. Tel: 318-487-8897; Fax: 318-487-9987. Email: carlabols@aol.com.

St. Mary's Residential Training School, Inc., P.O. Drawer 7768, Alexandria, 71306. Tel: 318-445-6443; Fax: 318-449-8520. Email: sistercarla@stmarys-rts.org. Web: www.stmarys-rts.org.

Arabi
Archdiocese of New Orleans

St. Bernard Health Center, Inc., 7718 W. Judge Perez, Arabi, 70032. Tel: 504-271-8952; Fax: 504-278-4692.

Baton Rouge
Diocese of Baton Rouge

Chateau Louise, 7565 Bishop Ott Dr., Baton Rouge, 70806. Tel: 225-926-5918. Housing for elderly and handicapped persons.

Maternity & Adoption, 1900 S. Acadian Thruway, Baton Rouge, 70808. Tel: 225-336-8708; Fax: 225-336-8703. Email: adopt@ccdiobr.org. Web: www.adoptbatonrouge.com. Mailing Address: P.O. Box 4785, Baton Rouge, 70821-4785.

Ollie Steele Burden Manor, 4250 Essen Ln., Baton Rouge, 70809-2196. Tel: 225-926-0091; Fax: 225-926-4937. Our Lady of the Lake Regional Medical Center, Our Lady of the Lake Pastoral Care.

Lafayette
Diocese of Lafayette

St. Bernadette Clinic, Lafayette. Tel: 337-264-6292.

St. Joseph Shelter for Men, 425 St. John St., Lafayette, 70501. Tel: 337-233-6816; Fax: 337-233-6829. Web: www.catholicservice.org.

Lake Charles
Diocese of Lake Charles

Our Lady Queen of Heaven Manor, Villa Maria, 3905 Kingston St., Lake Charles, 70605. Tel: 337-478-4780; Fax: 337-474-8822. Email: villamaria@suddenlink.net.

Metairie
Archdiocese of New Orleans

Sisters of Mercy Ministries dba Mercy Family Center Psychological and psychiatric evaluation, counseling and tutorial services., 110 Veterans Memorial Blvd., Ste. 425, Metairie, 70005. Tel: 504-838-8283; Fax: 504-838-9799. Email: sengro@mercyfamilycenter.com. Web: www.mercyfamilycenter.com.

New Orleans
Archdiocese of New Orleans

Baronne Street Transitional Housing, 2407 Baronne St., New Orleans, 70113-1621. Tel: 504-269-9311. Crisis & Residential Emergency Center.

Boys Hope Girls Hope (1980) Group Homes for Boys and Girls., P.O. Box 19307, New Orleans, 70179-0307. Tel: 504-484-7744; Fax: 504-484-6120. Web: www.bhghnola.org.

Ciara House, c/o 1000 Howard Ave., Ste. 1000, New Orleans, 70113. Housing for Chronically Mentally Ill Adults.

Daughters of Charity Services of New Orleans, 4164 Canal St., New Orleans, 70119. Tel: 504-482-2080; Fax: 504-483-6016. Email: jfirstley@dcsno.org.

Jefferson CARE Center, c/o 1000 Howard Ave., Ste. 1000, New Orleans, 70113. Temporary Residence for Homeless Families.

Ocean Avenue, c/o 1000 Howard Ave., Ste. 1000, New Orleans, 70113. Community Home for Developmentally Disabled Adults.

Ozanam Inn Shelter for Homeless Men, 843 Camp St., New Orleans, 70130-3751. Tel: 504-523-1184; Fax: 504-523-1187. Web: www.ozanaminn.org.

Project Lazarus (1986) Residential Program for Persons with AIDS, P.O. Box 3906, New Orleans, 70177-3906. Tel: 504-949-3609; Fax: 504-944-7944. Email: info@projectlazarus.net. Web: www.projectlazarus.net.

Ss. Mary & Elizabeth, c/o 1000 Howard Ave., Ste. 1000, New Orleans, 70113. Community Home for Developmentally Disabled Adults.

St. Jude the Apostle, c/o 1000 Howard Ave., Ste. 1000, New Orleans, 70113. Community Home for Developmentally Disabled Adults.

St. Peter the Fisherman, c/o 1000 Howard Ave., Ste. 1000, New Orleans, 70113. Community Home for Developmentally Disabled Adults.

St. Rosalie, c/o 1000 Howard Ave., Ste. 1000, New Orleans, 70113. Community Home for Developmentally Disabled Adults.

The Apartments at Mater Dolorosa, 1226 S. Carrollton Ave., New Orleans, 70118. Tel: 504-865-7222; Fax: 504-861-9225.

Villa St. Maurice II (Villa Additions) Not currently open due to Hurricane Katrina, 6101 Douglas St., New Orleans, 70117-2100. Residence for Senior Citizens & Handicapped

Shreveport
Diocese of Shreveport

St. Catherine Community Center, 331 E. 71st St., Shreveport, 71106-4305. Tel: 318-865-9817; Fax: 318-869-2549. Email: sccc@sport.rr.com. Web: www.rc.net/shreveport/stcatherine. Afterschool Enrichment, Summer Day Camp, Parenting, Arts, Anger Management, Computers, Health Services Program, Teen Mom Mentoring.

MAINE

Biddeford
Diocese of Portland (In Maine)

St. Andre Home, Inc., Admin. Office, 283 Elm St., Biddeford, 04005-3093. Tel: 207-282-3351; Fax: 207-282-8733. Web: www.SaintAndreHome.org. Pregnant and Parenting Young Women, Adoption Services, Infant Foster Care Homes, Emergency Placement; Public Information-Education; Community Outreach Services; Residences in Biddeford, Lewiston, Bangor.

Lewiston
Diocese of Portland (In Maine)

Neighborhood Housing Initiative, Inc., P.O. Box 7291, Lewiston, 04243-7291. Tel: 207-777-8802; Fax: 207-777-8800. Web: www.stmarysmaine.com.

**St. Martin de Porres Residence, Inc.*, Mailing Address: P.O. Box 7227, Lewiston, 04243-7227. 23 Bartlett St., Lewiston, 04243-7227. Tel: 207-786-4690; Fax: 207-786-8866. Email: smdporres02@aol.com.

MARYLAND

Baltimore
Archdiocese of Baltimore

Answers for the Aging, 3320 Benson Ave., Baltimore, 21227-1035. Tel: 410-646-0100; 888-502-7587; Fax: 410-646-0500.

Bon Secours Family Support Center, 26 N. Fulton Ave., Baltimore, 21223. Tel: 410-362-3629; Fax: 410-362-3649. Web: www.bonsecours.org/bshsi.

Cherry Hill SeniorLife Center, 606 Cherry Hill Rd., Ste. 201, Baltimore, 21225-1229. Tel: 410-354-5101; Fax: 410-354-5103.

Pastoral Care at the Jenkins Senior Living Community, 3320 Benson Ave., Baltimore, 21227. Tel: 410-646-6513; Fax: 410-646-0500.
Project FRESH Start (Family Relocation, Empowerment, and Self-Help), 228 W. Lexington St., Ste. 220, Baltimore, 21201-3432. Tel: 410-261-6777; Fax: 410-889-0203.
Project SERVE (Service and Education through Residential Volunteer Experience), 725 Fallsway, Baltimore, 21202. Tel: 413-986-9029; Fax: 410-962-8931.
St. Elizabeth Rehabilitation and Nursing Center (Jenkins Memorial Nursing Home, Inc.), 3320 Benson Ave., Baltimore, 21227-1035. Tel: 410-644-7100; Fax: 410-646-6589.
Trinitarian Counseling Services, Inc., 8400 Park Heights Ave., P.O. Box 5719, Baltimore, 21282. Tel: 410-486-5764; Fax: 410-486-0614. Email: treasurer@trinitarians.org.
Villa Maria Baltimore Child and Adolescent Response System (B-CARS), 1118 S. Light St., Baltimore, 21230. Tel: 410-727-4800; Fax: 410-727-5853.

Fort Washington
Archdiocese of Washington

**Prison Outreach Ministry* (1982) P.O. Box 44325, Fort Washington, MD 20749. Tel: 301-448-7026. Email: mbryantabc@msn.com.

Princess Anne
Diocese of Wilmington

Seton Center, 30632 Hampden Ave., P.O. Box 401, Princess Anne, MD 21853. Tel: 410-651-9608; Fax: 410-651-1437.

Rockville
Archdiocese of Washington

The Frost Center, Society of the Divine Savior (1976) 4915 Aspen Hill Rd., Rockville, MD 20853. Tel: 301-933-3451; Fax: 301-933-0330. Email: seanmcl@frostcenter.com. Web: www.frostcenter.com. A School and Therapy Program for Emotionally Disturbed and Autistic Students. Grades 1-12.

Silver Spring
Archdiocese of Washington

Saint Luke Institute, Inc., 8901 New Hampshire Ave., Silver Spring, MD 20903. Tel: 301-445-7970; Fax: 301-422-5400. Email: getinfo@sli.org. Web: www.sli.org. The Institute is a licensed and accredited treatment center for priests and religious, and a center for education and research.

Timonium
Archdiocese of Baltimore

St. Vincent's Center, 2600 Pot Spring Rd., Timonium, 21093. For additional information please see the Associated Catholic Charities section.
St. Vincent's Child Abuse Prevention Programs, 2600 Pot Spring Rd., Timonium, 21093. Tel: 410-666-7113; Fax: 410-561-8109.
Villa Maria Behavioral Health Clinics, 2300 Dulaney Valley Rd., Timonium, 21093. Tel: 410-252-7664; Fax: 410-561-9073.

MASSACHUSETTS

Boston
Archdiocese of Boston

Our Lady's Guild House - Residence for Women, 20 Charlesgate W., Boston, 02215. Tel: 617-536-3000; Fax: 617-536-8508.
St. Helena House, 89 Union Park St., Boston, 02118. Tel: 617-426-2922; Fax: 617-542-3460. Seniors, low income & disabled persons.
St. Mary's Women and Infants Center, 90 Cushing Ave., Boston, 02125. Center for pregnant women.; (See Guidance Centers for more information.)

Braintree
Archdiocese of Boston

Life Resources, Inc., 100 River Rd., Braintree, 02184. Tel: 781-849-7751; Fax: 781-849-7754. Web: www.liferesourcesinc.org.
Life Resources/Alpha-Omega, 140 Adams St., Braintree, 02184. Tel: 781-848-5510; Fax: 781-380-7565. Web: www.liferesourcesinc.org. A long term residence for 20 adolescent boys.

Brockton
Archdiocese of Boston

Catholic Charities South A Division of Catholic Charities, 686 N. Main St., Brockton, 02301. Tel: 508-587-0815; Fax: 508-580-0837. Email: lisa_lodge@ccab.org. Web: ccab.org.

Cambridge
Archdiocese of Boston

**Youville House, Inc.*, 1573 Cambridge St., Cambridge, 02138-4398. Tel: 617-491-1234; Fax: 617-491-8838. Email: joannecparsons@youvillehouse.org. Web: www.youvillehouse.com. Youville House is an assisted living facility housing retired priests from the Archdiocese of Boston and elders from the community.

Charlton
Diocese of Worcester

Ministry to Retired Priests, 188 Old Worcester Rd., Charlton, 01507. Tel: 508-868-9239; Fax: 508-248-3814.

Holyoke
Diocese of Springfield in Massachusetts

Broderick House, 56 Cabot St., P.O. Box 6269, Holyoke, 01041. Tel: 413-534-7610; Fax: 413-536-8536. SRO (single room occupency), permanent housing for low income sober men/women.
Kate's Kitchen, 51 Hamilton St., Holyoke, 01040. Tel: 413-532-0233; Fax: 413-536-1137. A community kitchen which provides one meal daily to anyone in need - no questions asked.
Loreto House, 51 Hamilton St., Holyoke, 01041. Tel: 413-533-5909; Fax: 413-536-1137. An around-the-clock shelter for homeless men.
Mary's Meadow, 12 Gamelin St., Holyoke, 01040. Tel: 413-420-2500; Fax: 413-322-7096.
Providence Ministries for the Needy, Inc., P.O. Box 6269, Holyoke, 01041-6269. Tel: 413-536-9109; Fax: 413-536-1137.

Lakeville
Archdiocese of Boston

Bishop Joseph John Ruocco House, 22 Highland Rd., Lakeville, 02347. Tel: 508-947-2823; Fax: 508-947-0305. Web: liferesourcesinc.org. Short term residence for 16 female adolescents. To provide comprehensive life skill services to residents and their families.

Lawrence
Archdiocese of Boston

**Greater Lawrence Mental Health Center, Inc.*, 30 General St., Lawrence, 01841. Tel: 978-683-3128; Fax: 978-686-7856.

Methuen
Archdiocese of Boston

St. Ann's Home Special Needs School, 100 A. Haverhill St., Methuen, 01844. Tel: 978-682-5276; Fax: 978-688-4932. Email: dgrandbois@st.annshome.org. Web: www.st.annshome.org. Ungraded special needs school for emotionally disturbed and behaviorally disordered children.
St. Ann's Home, Inc., 100A Haverhill St., Methuen, 01844. Tel: 978-682-5276; Fax: 978-688-4932. Email: dgrandbois@st.annshome.org. Web: www.st.annshome.org.

Roxbury
Archdiocese of Boston

Nazareth Residence for Mothers and Children, 91 Regent St., Roxbury, 02119. Tel: 617-541-0100; Fax: 617-541-8781. Email: nazareth_residence@ccab.org. Home for homeless mothers and children who are HIV positive.

Springfield
Diocese of Springfield in Massachusetts

Diocesan Office for Counseling, Prevention and Victim Services, 65 Elliot St., P.O. Box 1730, Springfield, 01102-1730. Tel: 413-732-3175; 413-452-0621; 413-452-0624; Fax: 413-452-0618. Web: www.diospringfield.org/MC.html.

Westfield
Diocese of Springfield in Massachusetts

Genesis Spiritual Life Center, 53 Mill St., Westfield, 01085-4253. Tel: 413-562-3627; Fax: 413-572-1060.

Whitinsville
Diocese of Worcester

St. Camillus Institute, 497 Hill St., Whitinsville, 01588.

Worcester
Diocese of Worcester

Mercy Centre (Developmental Disabilities), 25 W. Chester St., Worcester, 01605-1136. Tel: 508-852-7165; Fax: 508-856-9755. Special Education Day Program and Sheltered Workshop for Developmentally Disabled Youngsters and Adults.
Youville House Shelter for Homeless Families, 133 Granite St., Worcester, 01604-4500. Tel: 508-753-3084; Fax: 508-754-0139.

MICHIGAN

Detroit
Archdiocese of Detroit

Holy Cross Family & Community Support Program, 5690 Cecil Ave., Detroit, 48210. Tel: 313-895-2200; Fax: 313-895-4010. Email: fboylan@hccsnet.org. Web: www.hccsnet.org. Includes specialized foster care, supervised independent living, in-home family treatment.
St. Patrick Senior Center, Inc., 58 Parsons, Detroit, 48201. Tel: 313-833-7080; Fax: 313-833-0128. Web: www.stpatseniorcenter.com.
St. Thomas Center, 8333 Townsend, Detroit, 48213. Tel: 313-924-9515; Fax: 313-924-9547. Email: fboylan@hccsnet.org. Web: www.hccsnet.org.

Fraser
Archdiocese of Detroit

Sanctuary at Fraser Villa (a unit of Trinity Senior Living Communities), 33300 Utica Rd., Fraser, 48026. Tel: 586-293-3300. Email: sliwinsg@trinity-health.org. Web: www.trinityseniorsanctuary.org.

Lake Orion
Archdiocese of Detroit

Guest House Recovery Residence, 444 Nakomis Rd., Lake Orion, 48362. Tel: 248-693-8973.
Guest House for Women Religious, 1720 W. Scripps Rd., Box 68, Lake Orion, 48360. Tel: 248-391-3100; Fax: 248-393-0186. Web: www.guesthouse.org. A state-licensed and CARF accredited endorsed residential treatment center for Catholic sisters and women in formation.; Central Admissions Office, from U.S. & Canada call: 800-626-6910.

Livonia
Archdiocese of Detroit

**Angela Hospice Home Care, Inc.*, 14100 Newburgh Rd., Livonia, 48154-5010. Tel: 734-464-7810; Fax: 734-779-4601. Email: ahospice@aol.com. Web: www.angelahospice.org.
Marycrest Manor, 15475 Middlebelt Rd., Livonia, 48154. Tel: 734-427-9175; Fax: 734-427-5044. Ownership: Franciscan Sisters of St. Joseph.

Memphis
Archdiocese of Detroit

Sacred Heart Rehabilitation Center, Inc., 400 Stoddard Rd., Box 41038, Memphis, 48041-1038. Tel: 810-392-2167; Fax: 810-392-3385. Treatment for alcoholism and drug dependency to adult men and women. Detox and residential services.

Pontiac
Archdiocese of Detroit

Hispanic Outreach, Pontiac. Tel: 248-338-4250; Fax: 248-335-8130.

Port Huron
Archdiocese of Detroit

Port Huron Mercy Family Care, 2601 Electric Ave., P.O. Box 610669, Port Huron, 48061-0669. Tel: 810-985-1868. (A unit of Trinity Health).

Rochester Hills
Archdiocese of Detroit

Sanctuary at Bellbrook (A unit of Trinity Senior Living Communities), 873 W. Avon Rd., Rochester Hills, 48307. Tel: 248-656-3239. Email: moulism@trinity-health.org. Web: www.trinityseniorsanctuary.org.

Royal Oak
Archdiocese of Detroit

Sanctuary at Alexander (A unit of Trinity Senior Living Communities), 718 W. Fourth St., Royal Oak, 48067. Tel: 248-545-0571. Email: larsonjo@trinity-health.org. Web: www.trinityseniorsanctuary.org.

Saginaw
Diocese of Saginaw

Queen of Angels Center, 3400 S. Washington, Saginaw, 48601. Tel: 989-755-1971; Fax: 989-755-2780.

Warren

Archdiocese of Detroit

Sanctuary at the Abbey (a unit of Trinity Senior Living Communities), 12250 E. Twelve Mile Rd., Warren, 48093. Tel: 586-751-6200. Email: loriusl@trinity-health.org. Web: www.trinityseniorsanctuary.org.

St. John's Deaf Center, 14057 E. Nine Mile Rd., Warren, 48089. Tel: 586-758-0710 (TDD); 866-281-7108 (VP); 586-774-8476 (Voice); Fax: 586-774-8476.

Waterford
Archdiocese of Detroit

Lourdes Alzheimers Special Care Center, 2400 Watkins Lake Rd., Waterford, 48328. Tel: 248-674-4732; Fax: 248-618-6376. Web: www.lourdescampus.com.

MINNESOTA

Cold Spring
Diocese of St. Cloud

Bethany Home Contact John Krueger at Catholic Charities, 13 Eighth Ave. S., Cold Spring, 56320. Tel: 320-685-7899; Fax: 320-685-9808. Email: jkrueger@gw.stcdio.org. Supervised Living Situation for Persons with Developmental Disabilities.

Mother Teresa Home Contact Catholic Charities, 101 Tenth Ave., Cold Spring, 56320. Tel: 320-685-8626; Fax: 320-685-8626. Supervised Living Situation for Persons with Developmental Disabilities.

St. Anne's Home Contact Catholic Charities, 103 10th Ave. N., Cold Spring, 56320. Tel: 320-685-7898; Fax: 320-685-9819. Supervised Living Situation for Persons with Developmental Disabilities.

St. Luke's Home Contact Catholic Charities, 411 Eighth Ave. N., Cold Spring, 56320. Tel: 320-685-7750. Adults with mild to moderate developmental disabilities.

Fergus Falls
Diocese of St. Cloud

Catholic Charities Intensive Treatment Unit, 1010 Maryland Ln., Fergus Falls, 56537. Tel: 218-739-9325; Fax: 218-739-2242.

Little Falls
Diocese of St. Cloud

St. Camillus Place, 1100 S.E. Fourth St., Little Falls, 56345. Tel: 320-632-1212; Fax: 320-632-1383.

Paynesville
Diocese of St. Cloud

Adult Foster Care for Handicapped Individuals, 1790 W. Mill St., Paynesville, 56362. Tel: 320-243-3750; Fax: 320-243-3718.

Saint Paul
Archdiocese of St. Paul and Minneapolis

Guild Incorporated (1990) 130 S. Wabasha St., Ste. 90, Saint Paul, 55107. Tel: 651-450-2220; Fax: 651-450-2221. Email: info@guildincorporated.org. Web: www.guildincorporated.org. Formed by the Guild of Catholic Women. Guild Incorporated provides an array of recovery oriented behavioral health & human services for individuals with serious and persistent mental illness.

St. Cloud
Diocese of St. Cloud

LaPaz Community Inc., Catholic Charities Housing Services, 530 S. 16th St., St. Cloud, 56301. Mailing Address: 157 Roosevelt Rd., Ste. 200, St. Cloud, 56301.

St. Cloud Children's Home of the Diocese of St. Cloud, 1726 Seventh Ave. S., St. Cloud, 56301. Tel: 320-650-1500; Fax: 320-650-1508.

St. Elizabeth Home Contact John Krueger at Catholic Charities, 306 15th Ave. N., St. Cloud, 56303. Tel: 320-240-3350. Email: jkrueger@gw.stcdio.org. Board and Lodging Home for Functionally Impaired Adults.

St. Paul
Archdiocese of St. Paul and Minneapolis

Our House of Minnesota, Inc. I (1975) 1846 Dayton Ave., St. Paul, 55104. Tel: 651-644-6650; Fax: 651-646-1104.

Our House of Minnesota, Inc. II (1975) 1846 Portland, St. Paul, 55104. Tel: 651-644-2411; Fax: 651-646-1104.

Our Lady of Good Counsel Home (1941) 2076 St. Anthony Ave., St. Paul, 55104-5096. Tel: 651-646-2797; Fax: 651-646-7884. Web: www.ourladyhome.org; www.franciscancare.org.

WomanWell, 1784 La Crosse Ave., St. Paul, 55119-4808. Tel: 651-739-7953; Fax: 651-739-7475. Email: seeking@WomanWell.org. Web: www.womanwell.org.

Waite Park
Diocese of St. Cloud

St. Francis Home, P.O. Box 326, Waite Park, 56387. Tel: 320-251-7630; Fax: 320-240-8097. Supervised Living Situation for Persons with Developmental Disabilities.

West St. Paul
Archdiocese of St. Paul and Minneapolis

Saint Paul's Outreach, Inc., 110 Crusader Ave., W., West St. Paul, 55118. Tel: 651-451-6114; Fax: 651-453-0810. Email: info@spoweb.org. Web: www.spoweb.org.

MISSOURI

Blue Springs
Diocese of Kansas City-St. Joseph

St. Mary's Manor (1987) 111 Mock Ave., Blue Springs, 64014. Tel: 816-228-5655; Fax: 816-228-8480. Email: pkelley@carondelet.com. Long term care facility with skilled nursing care and residential care. Sponsored by Benedictine Health System and Sisters of St. Joseph of Carondelet.

Chesterfield
Archdiocese of St. Louis

St. Joseph Institute for the Deaf, 1809 Clarkson Rd., Chesterfield, 63017-5065. Tel: 636-532-3211 (Voice/TTY); Fax: 636-532-4560. Web: www.sjid.org. School for the Deaf; Auditory-oral day school for hearing-impaired children from birth-8th grade. Early intervention therapy for children 0-5; pre- & elementary school offering intense speech & academic prog.

Creve Coeur
Archdiocese of St. Louis

SSM Rehab, 10101 Woodfield Ln., Ste. 100, Exec. Offices, Creve Coeur, 63132. Tel: 314-768-5300; Fax: 314-768-5355. Web: www.ssmrehab.com. Member of SSM Health Care; For rehabilitation of pediatrics, adolescents and adults.

Florissant
Archdiocese of St. Louis

Child Center - Marygrove (1849) 2705 Mullanphy Ln., Florissant, 63031. Tel: 314-837-1702; Fax: 314-830-6263. Email: hnegri@ccstl.org. Web: www.marygroveonline.org. Owned and operated under the auspices of Catholic Charities; Residential treatment for emotionally disturbed males and females (ages 6-21). Special education, therapy and medical services. Overnight emergency care: and crisis nursery males and females (Birth-21). Transitional Services, Apartments, Sequoia House and Drury House. Male and Female (ages 17-21).

St. Elizabeth Adult Day Care Center of Florissant (1994) 1831 N. New Florissant Rd., Florissant, 63033. Tel: 314-838-5005; Fax: 314-838-5005.

Kansas City
Diocese of Kansas City-St. Joseph

Carondelet Manor, 621 Carondelet Dr., Kansas City, 64114. Tel: 816-943-4777. Owned and operated by Carondelet Long Term Care Facilities, Inc. Sponsored by Sisters of St. Joseph of Carondelet and Benedictine Health System.

Liberty
Diocese of Kansas City-St. Joseph

Immacolata Manor (1981) 2135 Manor Way, Liberty, 64068-9397. Tel: 816-781-4332; Fax: 816-781-8820. Email: info@imanor.org. Residential and day habilitation services for people with developmental disabilities; Operated by the Immacolata Board of Directors.

Normandy
Archdiocese of St. Louis

Maria Droste Residence (1979) 7660 Natural Bridge Rd., Normandy, 63121. Tel: 314-383-5553; Fax: 314-382-1325. Web: goodshepherdsisters.org. For Women in Need.

Springfield
Diocese of Springfield-Cape Girardeau

**McAuley Counseling Services, Inc.*, 2200 E. Sunshine, Ste. 201, Springfield, 65804. Tel: 417-823-0498.

St. John's Mercy Villa, 1100 E. Montclair, Springfield, 65807. Tel: 417-820-8500; Fax: 417-820-8547. Skilled Care of Long Term Nursing Home, for the Aged and Chronically Ill.

St. Louis
Archdiocese of St. Louis

Ascension Health, 4600 Edmundson Rd., St. Louis, 63134. Tel: 314-733-8000; Fax: 314-733-8013. Email: atersigni@ascensionhealth.org. Web: www.ascensionhealth.org. Co-sponsored by four of the United States Provinces of the Daughters of Charity: Northeast Prov., Albany, NY; Southeast Prov., Emmitsburg, MD; East Central Prov., Evansville, IN; West Central Prov., St. Louis, MO and by the Congregation of St. Joseph and the Congregation of the Sisters of St. Joseph of Carondelet.

Ascension Health-IS, Inc., 4600 Edmundson Rd., St. Louis, 63134. Tel: 314-733-8000; Fax: 314-733-8013. Email: atersigni@ascensionhealth.org. Web: www.ascensionhealth.org.

Boys Hope/Girls Hope of St. Louis, Inc., 755 S. New Ballas Rd., Ste. 120, St. Louis, 63141. Tel: 314-692-7477; Fax: 314-692-7810. Email: hopestlouis@bhgh.org. Web: www.hopestlouis.org. Residential Care for Adolescent Boys and Girls, Troubled by Family Disruptions, who are Capable of College Preparatory High School Work. Ages 10-18.

Cardinal Ritter Senior Services, 7601 Watson Rd., St. Louis, 63119. Tel: 314-961-8000; Fax: 314-961-1934. Email: swesley@ccstl.org. Web: www.cardinalritterseniorservices.org. Catholic Charities network of agencies provides social services, in home services, residences, adult day care, employment and volunteer services for the elderly.

Carondelet Health System, Inc., 4600 Edmundson Rd., St. Louis, 63134. Tel: 314-733-8000; Fax: 314-733-8013. Email: atersigni@ascensionhealth.org.

Cathedral Tower, 325 N. Newstead Ave., St. Louis, 63108. Tel: 314-367-5500, Ext. 121; Fax: 314-361-5099. Email: tgorski@ccstl.org. Web: www.ccstl.org. Building which houses several agencies of Catholic Charities: Queen of Peace Center; St. Elizabeth Hall; and Peace for Kids, Inc.

Catholic Deaf Ministry, 7530 Natural Bridge Rd., St. Louis, 63121. Tel: 314-727-2747 (TTY). Email: vbarnhart@archstl.org. Provides Services for Deaf and Hearing Impaired Persons.

Catholic Family Services (1992) 9200 Watson Rd., G101, St. Louis, 63126. Tel: 314-544-3800; 800-652-8055; Fax: 314-843-0552. Provides residential and social services, professional counseling and health care access to families and communities.

Department of Special Education (1950) 20 Archbishop May Dr., St. Louis, 63119. Tel: 314-792-7320; Fax: 314-792-7325. Email: ktichy@archstl.org. Special Education Ungraded classrooms at Ascension, Chesterfield; St. John the Baptist and Seven Holy Founders. Special Education Schools at Annunziata and the Academy at St. Rose Philippine Duchesne. Special Education Day Care, Preschool and Early Intervention Services at St. Mary's-North-South. Special Education Program for children with autism and developmental delays at St. Gemma Center. Special Education services for high school students with disabilities at partner Catholic high schools through St. Joseph's special services. Special religious education classes for children and adults with developmental disabilities or major learning disabilities. Psycho-Educational Testing Service. Administrative office for above programs and services.

Father Dempsey's Hotel, Inc., 3427 Washington Ave., St. Louis, 63103. Tel: 314-535-7221; Fax: 314-535-7289. Email: maboussie@archstl.org.

Father Jim's Home, 3427 Washington Ave., St. Louis, 63103. Tel: 314-535-7221; Fax: 314-535-7289. Email: maboussie@archstl.org.

Food and Fuel for Life, 100 N. Jefferson Ave., St. Louis, 63103. Tel: 877-238-3228; 314-881-6000; Fax: 314-531-6712. Email: info@svdpstl.org. Web: www.servingthepoor.org.

Guardian Angel Settlement Association, P.O. Box 2055, St. Louis, 63158-0055. Tel: 314-231-3188; Fax: 314-231-8126. Email: efmurphy@guardianangelsettlement.org. Web: www.guardianangelsettlement.org. Child Care Services and Social Services.

Guardian Angel at Hosea House, 2635 Gravois Ave., St. Louis, 63118. Tel: 314-773-9027; Fax: 314-773-6140.

Queen of Peace Center (1985) 325 N. Newstead Ave.,

St. Louis, 63108. Tel: 314-531-0511; Fax: 314-531-1458. Email: cneumann@ccstl.org. Comprehensive residential and outpatient behavioral healthcare for addicted women and their children. Specialty in pregnant women, trauma and dually diagnosed. Permanent and transitional housing programs. Licensed by the Department of Mental Health Division of Alcohol and Drug Abuse. Accredited by COA Council on Accreditation.

Rosati Center, 4220-24 N. Grand Ave., St. Louis, 63107. Tel: 314-534-6624; Fax: 314-535-4394. Permanent supportive housing for former homeless single adults. Managed by St. Patrick Center.

Rosati Group Home, Inc., 4218 N. Grand Blvd., St. Louis, 63107. Tel: 314-534-6624; Fax: 314-535-4394. Email: nboland@stpatrickcenter.org. Web: stpatrickcenter.org. Group Home for homeless mentally ill adults. Managed by St. Patrick Center.

Seton Institute, Ascension Health, 4600 Edmundson Rd., P.O. Box 45998, St. Louis, 63164. Tel: 314-733-8286; Fax: 314-733-8013. Email: jimpicciche@ascensionhealth.org. Web: www.setoninstitute.org.

St. Elizabeth Adult Day Care Center (1981) 3401 Arsenal St., St. Louis, 63118. Tel: 314-772-5107; Fax: 314-772-3674. Email: sjamiller@juno.com. Web: www.seadcc.org. Conducted by the Sisters of the Most Precious Blood to Provide Day Care for the Elderly and Handicapped.

St. Martha's Hall, P.O. Box 4950, St. Louis, 63108. Tel: 314-533-1313; Fax: 314-533-2035. Email: stmarthashall@sbcglobal.net. Web: www.saintmarthas.org; www.ccstl.org. Provides Shelter, Advocacy and Support to Abused Women & their Children.

St. Mary's Special Services (1952) 1724 Redman Ave., St. Louis, 63138. Tel: 314-653-2591; Fax: 314-653-6811. Web: www.special-education.org. Early Intervention therapies and child care for preschool children (ages 6 weeks-5 years) developmentally disabled in a normalized mainstream setting (capacity 100); Inclusionary early childhood education for children ages 3-6 years (capacity 20).

St. Philippine Home (1996) 1015 Goodfellow Blvd., St. Louis, 63112. Tel: 314-454-1012; Fax: 314-367-7455. Email: cneumann@ccstl.org. Transitional housing for drug affected homeless city women and their children.

MONTANA

Great Falls
Diocese of Great Falls - Billings

St. Thomas Child and Family Center, 1710 Benefis Ct., Great Falls, 59405. Tel: 406-761-6538; Fax: 406-727-0670. Email: carrie@stthomaskids.org. Web: stthomaskids.org.

NEBRASKA

Lincoln
Diocese of Lincoln

Villa Marie School and Home for the Educable Mentally Handicapped (1964) P.O. Box 80328, Lincoln, 68501. Tel: 402-786-3625; Fax: 402-488-6525.

NEW HAMPSHIRE

Laconia
Diocese of Manchester

Bishop Bradley Senior Living Community, 406 Court St., Laconia, 03246. Tel: 603-524-0466; Fax: 603-527-0884. Email: stt.administrator@nh-cc.org.

Manchester
Diocese of Manchester

St. Joseph Residence (1980) 495 Mammoth Rd., Manchester, 03104. Tel: 603-668-6011; Fax: 603-647-6648. Email: MJMakowski@presmarynh.org. New Hampshire Catholic Charities.

Nashua
Diocese of Manchester

Marguerite's Place, 87 Palm St., Nashua, 03060. Tel: 603-598-1582; Fax: 603-598-7574. Email: balves@margueritesplace.org. Web: www.margueritesplace.org.

NEW JERSEY

Hoboken
Archdiocese of Newark

Good Counsel, Inc. (St. Francis Home), 411 Clinton St., Hoboken, 07030. Tel: 201-798-9059; 201-795-0637; 800-723-8331 (Hotline); Fax: 201-795-0809. Email: cbell@goodcounselhomes.org. Web: www.goodcounselhomes.org; www.postabortionhelp.org. Housing, counseling and referrals for single women who are pregnant or single mothers with children. Counseling for men and women experiencing post abortion stress.

Jersey City
Archdiocese of Newark

Margaret Anna Cusack Care Center, Inc., 537 Pavonia Ave., Jersey City, 07306. Tel: 201-653-8300, Ext. 2152; Fax: 201-653-7705. Email: info@cusackcarecenter.org. Web: www.cusackcarecenter.org. Skilled Nursing Facility for Men & Women.

St. Joseph's Home, 81 York St., Jersey City, 07302. Tel: 201-413-9280; Fax: 201-451-0952. Transitional housing for homeless women and children.

St. Joseph's Home for the Blind (1886) (Skilled nursing facility for men and women), 537 Pavonia Ave., Jersey City, 07306. Tel: 201-653-8300; Fax: 201-653-7705. Email: info@cusackcarecenter.org. Web: www.cusackcarecenter.org.

St. Mary's Residence, 240 Washington St., Jersey City, 07302-3806. Tel: 201-432-6289; Fax: 201-451-0952. (Single working women of low income assisted; no children).

Keyport
Diocese of Trenton

Collier House, 386 Maple Pl., Keyport, 07735. Tel: 732-264-3222; Fax: 732-264-3277. Email: pauldes21@comcast.net. Web: www.collieryouthservices.org. Transitional Aging-Out Program for Women 18-21 years old.

Lawrenceville
Diocese of Trenton

Morris Hall / Saint Lawrence, Inc., 2381 Lawrenceville Rd., Lawrenceville, 08648. Tel: 609-896-9500; Fax: 609-895-0242. Email: cbrennan@slrc.org. Web: www.slrc.org. St. Lawrence Rehabilitation Center.

Morris Hall / Saint Lawrence, Inc. Morris Hall - St. Joseph's Nursing Center, 1 Bishops' Dr., Lawrenceville, 08648-2050. Tel: 609-896-0006; Fax: 609-896-8037; 609-895-0466. Email: epetroski@morrishall.org. Web: www.morrishall.org. Skilled Nursing Care Facility for the Chronically Ill.

Lodi
Archdiocese of Newark

**The Promise Outreach, Inc.* (1982) Volunteers visit, correspond with, and provide opportunity for spirituality and other basic needs to teens in programs, correctional institutions and centers of rehabilitation., 260 S. Main St., Lodi, 07644. Tel: 973-460-3229; Fax: 973-473-7126. Email: vimsters@aol.com. Web: home.catholicweb.com/thepromiseoutreachinc.

Pompton Lakes
Diocese of Paterson

Pathways Counseling Center, Inc., 16 Pompton Ave., Pompton Lakes, 07442. Tel: 973-835-6337; Fax: 973-616-4688. Email: pegb@pathwayscounseling.org. Web: www.pathwayscounseling.org.

Red Bank
Diocese of Trenton

Collier Group Home, 180 Spring St., Red Bank, 07701. Tel: 732-842-8337; Fax: 732-530-7096. Email: pauldes21@comcast.net. Web: www.collieryouthservices.org. 24 Hour Program-Therapy and Educational Services. Provided Under the Supervision of the Sisters of the Good Shepherd.

Wayne
Diocese of Paterson

Bethany Residence, 738 Rte. 23, Wayne, 07470. Tel: 973-628-8109.

Wickatunk
Diocese of Trenton

Collier Services, Collier High School, 160 Conover Rd., Wickatunk, 07765. Tel: 732-946-4771; Fax: 732-946-3519. Email: info@collieryouthservices.org. Web: www.collieryouthservices.org. Adolescent Boys and Girls.

NEW MEXICO

Albuquerque
Archdiocese of Santa Fe

Casa Angelica (1967) 5629 Isleta Blvd., S.W., Albuquerque, 87105. Tel: 505-877-5763; Fax: 505-873-2786. Email: lturner@casaangelica.org. Web: www.casaangelica.org. Home for developmentally disabled children and young adults.

Good Shepherd Center, Inc., 218 Iron St., S.W., P.O. Box 749, Albuquerque, 87103. Tel: 505-243-2527; Fax: 505-247-2207. Direct Service Agency for the Homeless.

Marie Amadea Shelter for Unwed Mothers (Alternative to Abortion), P.O. Box 708, Albuquerque, 87103. Tel: 505-242-1516; Fax: 505-243-0402. Home for unwed expectant women.

Santa Fe
Archdiocese of Santa Fe

Villa Therese Catholic Clinic, 219 Cathedral Pl., Santa Fe, 87501. Tel: 505-983-8561; Fax: 505-982-7863. Email: vtcc@cnsp.com.

NEW YORK

Albany
Diocese of Albany

Diocesan AIDS Services, 100 Slingerlands St., Albany, 12202. Tel: 518-449-3581; Fax: 518-426-3662.

Emmaus House, 45 Trinity Pl., Albany, 12202. Tel: 518-482-4966. Albany Catholic Worker Community.

Hospitality House Therapeutic Community Inc., 271 Central Ave., Albany, 12206. Tel: 518-434-6468; Fax: 518-434-6302. Email: lbecker@hospitalityhouse.info. A private, not-for-profit, intensive residential treatment program for males, 18 years or older, with a history of drug and/or substance abuse.

Saint Anne Institute, 160 N. Main Ave., Albany, 12206. Tel: 518-437-6500; Fax: 518-437-6555. Email: rriccio@s-a-i.org. Web: www.stanneinstitute.org. Residential and Community-based Preventive Service Center. Regents accredited and certified junior and senior H.S. for the emotionally handicapped and Preschool program for 3-4 year olds who are speech-impaired and emotionally disturbed. Residential care, critical care, and Day Treatment for young women ages 12-18. Family Services, Vocational Training, Sex Abuse Prevention and Juvenile Sex Offender Programs for male and female adolescents in crisis and their families.

St. Peter's Licensed Home Care Agency, 159 Wolf Rd., Albany, 12205. Tel: 518-525-6099; Fax: 518-525-6002. Email: bsmith@stpetershealthcareservices.org.

Allegany
Diocese of Buffalo

St. Elizabeth Motherhouse (1859) 115 E. Main St., Allegany, 14706. Tel: 716-373-0200; Fax: 716-372-5774. Email: fsa@fsallegany.org. Web: www.alleganyfranciscans.org.

Astoria
Diocese of Brooklyn

Peter J. Della Monica Center for Seniors, 23-56 Broadway, Astoria, 11106. Tel: 718-626-1500; Fax: 718-278-4432.

Provincial Office, 25-30 21st Ave., Astoria, 11105. Tel: 718-278-1155.

Steinway Senior Center, 20-43 Steinway St., Astoria, 11105. Tel: 718-728-8472; Fax: 718-278-5301.

Barryville
Archdiocese of New York

New Hope Manor, 35 Hillside Rd., Barryville, 12719. Tel: 845-557-8353; Fax: 845-557-6603. Email: newhopemnr@aol.com. Web: www.newhopemanor.org. See listing in the Miscellaneous section for further details.

Bay Shore
Diocese of Rockville Centre

Nursing Sisters Home Care, Inc. dba Catholic Home Care 15 Park Ave., Ste. 200, Bay Shore, 11706. Tel: 631-969-8200; Fax: 631-224-8678.

Bayside
Diocese of Brooklyn

Bayside Senior Center and Bayside Senior Center Transportation Program, 221-15 Horace Harding Expwy., Bayside, 11364. Tel: 718-225-1144; Fax: 718-229-7320.

Queens Day Habilitation Program, 61-58 Springfield Blvd., Bayside, 11364. Tel: 718-281-0480; Fax: 718-281-0478.

Beacon
Archdiocese of New York

Metropolitan Association of Contemplative Communities, Inc., 89 Hiddenbrooke Dr., Beacon, 12508. Tel: 845-831-5572; Fax: 845-831-5579. Web: macc.catholic.org.

Metropolitan Association of Contemplative Communities, Inc. (1967) 89 Hiddenbrooke Dr., Beacon, 12508. Tel: 845-831-5572; Fax: 845-831-5579. Web: macc.catholic.org.

Blauvelt
Archdiocese of New York

Friends of St. Dominic's Inc., 500 Western Hwy., Blauvelt, 10913. Tel: 845-359-3400; Fax: 845-398-0466. Email: sjm@stdominicshome.org. Web: www.stdominicshome.org/friends.

Saint Dominic's Home (1878) 500 Western Hwy., Blauvelt, 10913. Tel: 845-359-3400; Fax: 845-359-4253. Email: judyk@stdominicshome.org. Web: www.stdominicshome.org.

Bohemia
Diocese of Rockville Centre

Talbot House Alcohol Crisis Center, 30-C Carlough Rd., Bohemia, 11716. Tel: 631-589-4144; Fax: 631-589-3281.

Bronx
Archdiocese of New York

Beacon of Hope House Bronx Congregate Services, 1400 Waters Pl., Bronx, 10461. Tel: 718-892-3494; Fax: 718-892-5507.

East Bronx Supported Housing, 690 Mace Ave., Bronx, 10467. Tel: 718-654-2731; Fax: 718-655-2101.

Good Counsel, Inc., 1157 Fulton Ave., Bronx, 10456. Tel: 718-312-3980, Ext. 10; 800-723-8331 (For Info & Referrals); Fax: 718-312-3991. Email: delores_morgan@goodcounselhomes.org. Web: www.goodcounselhomes.org.

Highbridge Neighborhood Supported Housing Program, 1484 Nelson Ave., Suite A, Bronx, 10452. Tel: 718-503-8106; Fax: 718-293-0939.

Kolping-on-Concourse, 2916 Grand Concourse, Bronx, 10458. Tel: 718-733-6119. Web: www.kolpingresidence.com. (Catholic Kolping Society New York, Inc.)

Mount St. Ursula Speech Center, 2885 Marion Ave., Bronx, 10458. Tel: 718-584-7679; Fax: 718-584-7954. Email: msuspeech@aol.com.

New York Offices, 853 Longwood Ave., Ste. 202, Bronx, 10459. Tel: 917-645-9100; Fax: 917-645-9095. Web: www.stdominicshome.org.

Saint Dominic's Home - Prevention Program (ASTAAN) Parent Aide Counseling Advocacy Information and Referral., 2345 University Ave., Bronx, 10468. Tel: 718-584-4407; Fax: 718-584-4540. Email: annettet@stdominicshome.org. Web: www.stdominicshome.org.

St. Eleanora's Home for Convalescents (1901) Sisters of Charity Center, 6301 Riverdale Ave., Bronx, 10471. Tel: 718-549-9200, Ext. 261; Fax: 718-884-3013. Email: ghanley@scny.org. Web: scny.org.

St. Elizabeth House, 427 E. 155th St., Bronx, 10455. Tel: 212-234-9089. Web: www.franciscanfriars.com.

St. Joseph's School for the Deaf, 1000 Hutchinson River Pkwy., Bronx, 10465. Tel: 718-828-9000; 718-828-1671 (TDD); Fax: 718-792-6631. Email: darles@SJSDNY.org.

TORCH (To Reach Children), 2340 Andrews Ave., Bronx, 10468. Tel: 718-365-7238; Fax: 718-584-3057. Web: www.stdominicshome.org.

Terence Cardinal Cooke Residence, 2467 Bathgate Ave., Bronx, 10458. Tel: 718-367-6990; 718-367-5405 (TTY); Fax: 718-365-2544.

The Clubhouse, 512 Southern Blvd., Bronx, 10455. Tel: 718-993-1078; Fax: 718-993-0216.

Brooklyn
Diocese of Brooklyn

Advocate for Persons with Disabilities Services, 191 Joralemon St., 7th Fl., Brooklyn, 11201. Tel: 718-722-6232.

Bay Ridge Day Habilitation Program, 347 74th St., 2nd Fl., Brooklyn, 11209. Tel: 718-745-7117; Fax: 718-745-3741.

Bellerose Senior HDFC, Inc., 191 Joralemon St., Brooklyn, 11201. Tel: 718-479-4739; Fax: 718-479-6612.

Benson Ridge Senior Services Assistance Center, 6825 5th Ave., Brooklyn, 11220. Tel: 718-236-3205; Fax: 718-837-1957.

Bereavement Services, 191 Joralemon St., 7th Fl., Brooklyn, 11201. Tel: 718-722-6214.

Bethlehem Community HDFC Inc., 191 Joralemon St., Brooklyn, 11201. Tel: 718-722-6000; Fax: 718-722-6045.

Brooklyn Day Habilitation Program, 177 Livingston Ave., 2nd Fl., Brooklyn, 11201. Tel: 718-237-4063; Fax: 718-797-2059.

Casa Betsaida-Home for people with AIDS, 267 Hewes St., Brooklyn, 11211. Tel: 718-218-7890; Fax: 718-218-8264. Email: cbetsaidainc@aol.com.

Circle of Hope Brooklyn and Queens, 2520 Flatbush Ave., Ste. 10, Brooklyn, 11234. Tel: 718-338-4716; Fax: 718-338-5383.

Deafness Services, 191 Joralemon St., 7th Fl., Brooklyn, 11201. Tel: 718-722-6216; Teletype: 718-722-6226.

Glenwood Senior Center, 5701 Avenue H, Brooklyn, 11234. Tel: 718-241-7711; Fax: 718-241-1936.

Mercy Home for Children (1865) 243 Prospect Park W., Brooklyn, 11215. Tel: 718-832-1075; Fax: 718-832-7612. Email: info@mercyhomeny.org. Web: www.mercyhomeny.org. Under the sponsorship of the Sisters of Mercy.; Six Intermediate Care Facilities (Residences & 5 Individual Residential Alternatives) for adolescents & adults who are developmentally disabled: Visitation Residence; Harold Warren Residence; de Porres Residence; Littlejohn Residence; Santulli Residence; Kevin Keating Residence; Chrys Residence; Gail Addeo Residence; Rev. Michael J. McGivney Residence; Augusta Residence & Frank's Residence. Three all day Saturday Recreation Programs, for adolescents and adults with developmental disabilities and autistic children, we offer MSC Services for families and the individuals. Four all day recreational respite programs need of supportive services. In Home Respite Services; James P. Slattery, CPA, Creative Arts Program, Mercy-Mitsui USA & Co. Creative Arts Program.

MercyFirst, 6301 12th Ave., Brooklyn, 11219. Tel: 718-232-1500; Fax: 718-232-0331. Web: www.mercyfirst.org. Residential services provided in campus and group home settings, including diagnostic/group emergency foster care, non-secure detention, hard to place (JD and clinically intensive), abuse treatment and prevention, mother/child, and OMH programs.; Foster Boarding Home/Adoption, Aftercare and Preventive Services programs provide services in Nassau, Queens and Brooklyn.

Mount Carmel Senior HDFC, 191 Joralemon St., Brooklyn, 11201. Tel: 718-722-6000; Fax: 718-722-6045.

Narrows Senior Center, 1230 63rd St, Brooklyn, 11219. Tel: 718-232-3211; Fax: 718-232-0512.

Narrows at the Lodge, 7711 18th Ave., Brooklyn, 11214. Tel: 718-621-1081; Fax: 718-621-1407.

Northside Senior Center, 179 N. 6th St., Brooklyn, 11211. Tel: 718-387-2316; Fax: 718-387-3235.

Partnering with Autistic Citizens (PACT) Day Habilitation Program, 177 Livingston Ave., 2nd Fl., Brooklyn, 11201. Tel: 718-237-4063; Fax: 718-797-2059.

Pete McGuinness Senior Center, 715 Leonard St., Brooklyn, 11222. Tel: 718-383-1940; Fax: 718-383-1960.

Restorative Justice, 191 Joralemon St., 7th Fl., Brooklyn, 11201. Tel: 718-722-6113.

Services for Pregnant Women, 191 Joralemon St., 7th Fl., Brooklyn, 11201. Tel: 718-722-6121; 718-725-7800 24-Hour Emergency Helpline.

Sheepshead Bay Supportive Services (NORC), 3677 Nostrand Ave. #3-A, Brooklyn, 11229. Tel: 718-769-3579; Fax: 718-769-4155.

South Brooklyn Alzheimer's Adult Care Program, 5201 Avenue H., Brooklyn, 11234. Tel: 718-241-7711; 718-241-1936.

St. Catherine Laboure Special Education Program, Dept. of Educ., 21 Bay 11th St., Brooklyn, 11228. Tel: 718-256-2605; Fax: 718-449-1607. Web: www.dioceseofbrooklyn.org. Program for mentally challenged students ages 5-21 and learning disabled students grades 6-8.

St. Francis de Sales School for the Deaf (1960) 260 Eastern Pkwy., Brooklyn, 11225. Tel: 718-636-4573; Fax: 718-636-4577. Email: school@sfdesales.org. Web: www.sfdesales.org. Infant through Elementary Grades (8th Grade).

St. Jerome's Health Services Corp. dba Holy Family Home 1740 84th St., Brooklyn, 11214. Tel: 718-232-3666; Fax: 718-259-9180. Affiliated with Saint Vincent Catholic Medical Centers of New York.

St. Paul the Apostle Senior HDFC, 191 Joralemon St., Brooklyn, 11201. Tel: 718-722-6000; Fax: 718-722-6045.

St. Teresa of Avila Senior HDFC, 191 Joralemon St., Brooklyn, 11201. Tel: 718-722-6000.

The Bay Senior Center, 3643 Nostrand Ave., Brooklyn, 11230. Tel: 718-648-2053; Fax: 718-648-7213.

Archdiocese of New York

Kingsborough Intensive Supported Apartment Program, 647 Vanderbilt Ave., Brooklyn, 11238. Tel: 718-398-4556; Fax: 718-398-4807.

Buffalo
Diocese of Buffalo

Catholic Health System Program of All-Inclusive Care for the Elderly, Inc. (CHS PACE), Seton Professional Building, 2121 Main St., Ste. 300, Buffalo, 14214.

St. Francis of Buffalo, Inc. Formerly known as St. Francis Hospital., 34 Benwood Ave., Buffalo, 14214. Tel: 716-862-2500; Fax: 716-862-2505. Email: dcrispel@chsbuffalo.org. c/o Catholic Health Systems, 2121 Main St., Ste. 300, Buffalo, 14214.

The Franciscan Center, Inc., 1910 Seneca St., Buffalo, 14210-1842. Tel: 716-822-8017; Fax: 716-822-8537. Web: www.franciscancenterinc.org. Transitional Shelters for Adolescent Males 16-20: Transitional Indep. Living Program, Supported Residence.

Clifton Park
Diocese of Albany

Seton Health at Schuyler Ridge aka Leonard Nursing Home One Abele Dr., Clifton Park, 12065. Tel: 518-371-1400. Email: ssmith@setonhealth.org. Web: schuylerridge.org.

Seton Health at Schuyler Ridge aka Leonard Nursing Home One Abele Dr., Clifton Park, 12065. Tel: 518-371-1400; Fax: 518-371-1240. Email: ssmith@setonhealth.org. Web: schuylerridge.org.

Cornwall
Archdiocese of New York

Contemplative Outreach, Ltd., 10 Landmark Dr., Ste. 117, P.O. Box 208, Cornwall, 12518. Tel: 845-534-5180. Email: office@coutreach.org. Web: www.contemplativeoutreach.org.

East Islip
Diocese of Rockville Centre

Suffolk Hearing & Speech Center, Inc., 369 E. Main St., East Islip, 11730. Tel: 631-376-4001; Fax: 631-376-4208. A diagnostic and treatment center.

Flushing
Diocese of Brooklyn

Alzheimers Adult Day Care, 157-16 65th Ave., Flushing, 11357. Tel: 718-358-3541; Fax: 718-961-4712.

Garrison
Archdiocese of New York

St. Christopher's Inn (1908) Temporary shelter for homeless men. Outpatient chemical dependency services & primary healthcare., 21 Franciscan Way, P.O. Box 150, Garrison, 10524-0150. Tel: 845-335-1000; Fax: 845-335-1017. Email: bpalka@atonementfriars.org. Web: www.stchristophersinn-graymoor.org.

Germantown
Diocese of Albany

The Carmelite System, Inc., 646 Woods Rd., Germantown, 12526-5617. Tel: 518-537-7500; Fax: 518-537-7501. Email: xsusansan@carmelitesystem.org. Web: Carmelitesystem.org.

Harrison
Archdiocese of New York

Good Counsel/Daystar Program, 275 North St., Harrison, 10528. Tel: 914-925-9834; 800-723-8331 (Info. & Referrals); Fax: 914-925-9101. Web: www.goodcounselhomes.org; www.postabortionhelp.org.

Hawthorne
Archdiocese of New York

Rosary Hill Home (1901) Free home for incurable cancer patients., Hawthorne, 10532. Tel: 914-769-0114; Fax: 914-769-3916. Web: www.hawthorne.dominicans.org.

Hollis
Diocese of Brooklyn

Project Independence, 183-16 Jamaica Ave., Hollis, 11423. Tel: 718-217-0126; Fax: 718-217-0495.

Southwest Queens Senior Services, 186-16 Jamaica Ave., 2nd Fl., Hollis, 11423. Tel: 718-217-0126; Fax: 718-217-0495.

Jackson Heights
Diocese of Brooklyn

Catherine Sheridan Senior Center, 35-24 83rd St.,

Jackson Heights, 11372. Tel: 718-458-4600; Fax: 718-458-5665.

Jamaica
Diocese of Brooklyn

Hillcrest Senior Center, 168-01B Hillside Ave., Jamaica, 11432. Tel: 718-297-7171; Fax: 718-657-2247.

Lackawanna
Diocese of Buffalo

Baker Victory Services (1851) (formerly known as Baker Hall, Our Lady of Victory Infant Home, St. Joseph Orphanage and St. John's Protectory), 780 Ridge Rd., Lackawanna, 14218. Tel: 716-828-9500; 888-287-1160; Fax: 716-828-9526. Email: baker@buffnet.net. Web: www.bakervictoryservices.org. Bakery Victory Services assists children, adults and families in need through preventative, outpatient, educational, and residential programs, including international and domestic adoptions, foster care, early childhood education, and a dental clinic, as well as programs for individuals with developmental disabilities and young people who are emotionally, behaviorally, or mentally challenged.

Long Island City
Diocese of Brooklyn

Hour Children (1995) 36-11A 12th St., Long Island City, 11106. Tel: 718-443-4724; Fax: 718-433-4728. Email: hourchildren@verizon.net. Web: www.hourchildren.org.

Montrose
Archdiocese of New York

Kolping-on-Hudson (Catholic Kolping Society New York, Inc.), 95 Montrose Point Rd., Montrose, 10548. Tel: 914-736-0117.

Mount Vernon
Archdiocese of New York

St. Theresa's Residence, 30 S. 10th Ave., Mount Vernon, 10550. Tel: 914-664-5900; Fax: 914-664-6733.

Nesconset
Diocese of Rockville Centre

Cleary Deaf Child Center, Inc. (1925) 301 Smithtown Blvd., Nesconset, 11767. Tel: 631-588-0530 (Voice and TTY); Fax: 631-588-0016. Email: kenm@clearyschool.org. Web: www.clearyschool.org. Day School (Infants thru 21 years).

New Rochelle
Archdiocese of New York

Ursuline Social Outreach, Inc. (1996) 138 Centre Ave., New Rochelle, 10801. Tel: 914-633-7298; Fax: 914-633-7393. Email: usoalc@aol.com. Ursuline Outreach sponsors The Adult Learning Center, 572B Main St., New Rochelle, NY 10801.

New York
Archdiocese of New York

Catholic Charities Community Services Beacon of Hope House Division, Catholic Charities, 1011 First Ave., New York, 10022. Tel: 212-371-1000; Fax: 212-421-0021. Email: anne.tommaso@archny.org. Web: www.archny.org.

Catholic Charities Department of Housing, Housing Development Institute, Inc., 1011 First Ave., New York, 10022. Tel: 212-371-1000.

Catholic Near East Welfare Association (CNEWA) (1926) 1011 First Ave., New York, 10022. Tel: 212-826-1480; Fax: 212-826-8979. Email: cnewa@cnewa.org. Web: www.cnewa.org.

Centro Maria, Inc. For young students and working women., 539 W. 54th St., New York, 10019. Tel: 212-757-6989; Fax: 212-307-5687. Email: cenmariany@mindspring.com. Web: www.religiosasdemariainmaculada.

Cor Mariae, c/o 1011 First Ave., Rm. 1130, New York, 10022. Tel: 212-371-1000, Ext. 2435. Residence for formerly homeless senior women.

Covenant House Under 21 (Runaway and Homeless Youth.), 460 W. 41st St., New York, 10036. Tel: 212-727-4000; Fax: 212-727-4992.

Developmental Disabilities Clinic, 1249 Fifth Ave., New York, 10029. Tel: 212-360-3703; Fax: 212-360-3842. Comprehensive Outpatient medical, therapeutic and educational services. On site and off site OMRDD Article 16 services.

El Carmelo Residence, 249 W. 14th St., New York, 10011. Tel: 212-242-8224; Fax: 212-242-7233.

Emergency Food Services, 1011 First Ave., New York, 10022. Tel: 212-371-1000, Ext. 2481; Fax: 212-317-8719.

Grace Institute, 1233 Second Ave., New York, 10021. Tel: 212-832-7605; Fax: 212-486-2869. Email: info@graceinstitute.org. Web: www.graceinstitute.org.

John A. Coleman School, 590 Avenue of the Americas, New York, 10011. Tel: 646-459-3401; Fax: 646-459-3689. Email: sharon.herl@setonpediatric.org. Web: www.setonpediatric.org.

Kolping Society of New York Men's Residence (Catholic Kolping Society New York, Inc.) (1888) For young Catholic men., 165 E. 88th St., New York, 10128. Tel: 212-369-6647; Fax: 212-987-5652. Email: residence@kolpingny.org.

Lavelle School for the Blind, E. 221st St. and Paulding Ave., New York, 10469. Tel: 718-882-1212; Fax: 718-882-0005. Web: www.lavelleschool.org.

Little Sisters of the Assumption Family Health Service, Inc. (1958) 333 E. 115th St., New York, 10029. Tel: 646-672-5200; Fax: 212-348-8284. Email: gcarter@lsafhs.org.

New York Catholic Deaf Center, St. Elizabeth of Hungry Church, 211 E. 83rd St., New York, 10028. Tel: 212-988-8563 (Voice); 212-988-1903 (TTY); 866-810-3394 (Video Phone); Fax: 212-988-1903. Web: www.deafcathnyc.org.

New York Foundling Charitable Corp., 590 Avenue of the Americas, New York, 10011. Tel: 212-633-9300. Web: www.nyfoundling.org.

SVCMC Health Services Inc., 130 W. 12th St., Ste. 6-E, New York, 10011. Tel: 212-604-7536. Email: estclair@svcmcny.org.

Sacred Heart Residence Working or studying young ladies ages 19-29., 432 W. 20th St., New York, 10011. Tel: 212-929-5790; Fax: 212-924-0891. Email: sacredheartresidence@hotmail.com. Web: www.sacredheartresidence.com.

Sr. Una McCormack Maternity Services, Inc. (1997) 1011 First Ave., New York, 10022. Tel: 212-371-1000, Ext. 2100; Fax: 212-755-4110. Email: pgeorgini@cgshb.org.

St. Agnes' Residence For students and working women., 237 W. 74th St., New York, 10023. Tel: 212-874-1361.

St. Francis Counseling Center, Inc., 135 W. 31st St., New York, 10001. Tel: 212-736-8500; Fax: 212-736-8545. Web: www.stfrancisnyc.org.

St. Mary's Residence (1913) For students and young working women., 225 E. 72nd St., New York, 10021. Tel: 212-249-6850; Fax: 212-249-4336. Email: St.MarysRes72@aol.com.

The Dwelling Place (1977) For homeless women., 409 W. 40th St., New York, 10018. Tel: 212-564-7887; Fax: 212-695-3642.

The Jeanne d'Arc Residence (1896) 253 W. 24th St., New York, 10011. Tel: 212-989-5952; Fax: 212-691-0257. Email: jdresidence@gmail.com. Women.

The Leo House (1889) Clergy, Sisters & Other Travelers., 332 W. 23rd St., New York, 10011. Tel: 212-929-1010; Fax: 212-366-6801.

Thorpe Family Residence, Inc. (1988) 2252 Crotona Ave., New York, 10457. Tel: 718-933-7312; Fax: 718-933-7311. Email: SrBarbTFR@aol.com. Web: www.bronxmall.com/com/thorpe.

Ogdensburg
Diocese of Ogdensburg

St. Joseph's Home (1960) 950 Linden St., Ogdensburg, 13669. Tel: 315-393-3780; Fax: 315-393-3847. Email: administrator@stjh.org. Web: www.stjh.org.

Ossining
Archdiocese of New York

Cardinal McCloskey Emergency Residential School (1980) 155 N. Highland Ave., Ossining, 10562. Tel: 914-762-5302; Fax: 914-762-7844.

Dominican Sisters Family Health Service, Inc. (Central Services/Administration) (1974) Community-based, certified, voluntary Home Health Agency and Long Term Home Health Care and AIDS Programs serving all of Westchester, Suffolk and the South Bronx. Unique community outreach programs., 299 N. Highland Ave., Ossining, 10562. Tel: 914-941-1710; Fax: 914-941-0518. Email: VHanrahan@dsfhs.org. Web: www.dsfhs.org.

Ozone Park
Diocese of Brooklyn

Ferrini Welfare League, 98-21 101 Ave., Ozone Park, 11416. Tel: 718-845-0539.

Ozone Park Senior Center, 103-02 101st Ave., Ozone Park, 11416. Tel: 718-847-2100; Fax: 718-847-2166.

Poughkeepsie
Archdiocese of New York

Good Counsel, Inc., 38 N. Clinton St., Poughkeepsie, 12601. Tel: 845-452-2944; 800-723-8331 (Info. & Referrals); Fax: 845-452-6390. Web: www.goodcounselhomes.org; www.postabortionhelp.org.

Richmond Hill
Diocese of Brooklyn

Richmond Hill Senior Center, 87-25 118th St., Richmond Hill, 11418. Tel: 718-846-2877; Fax: 718-847-9089.

Rochester
Diocese of Rochester

Mercy Outreach Center, Inc. (1977) 142 Webster Ave., Rochester, 14609. Tel: 585-288-2634; Fax: 585-288-0252. Web: www.mercyoutreachcenter.org. Health and dental services for the uninsured and advocacy.

Rockaway Beach
Diocese of Brooklyn

Seaside Senior Center, 90-01 Rockaway Beach Blvd., Rockaway Beach, 11693. Tel: 718-634-4047; Fax: 718-634-6853.

Roosevelt
Diocese of Rockville Centre

Friends of Mother of Good Counsel Home, Inc., 290 Babylon Tpke., Roosevelt, 11575. Tel: 516-223-1013; Fax: 516-223-4254. Email: ossr290@earthlink.net.

Sloatsburg
Ukrainian Catholic Diocese of Stamford

St. Mary's Villa Spiritual, Cultural & Educational Center, 150 Sisters Servants Ln., P.O. Box 9, Sloatsburg, NY 10974-0009. Tel: 845-753-5100; Fax: 845-753-1956.

Spring Valley
Archdiocese of New York

Good Counsel, Inc., 22 Linden Ave., Spring Valley, 10977. Tel: 845-356-0517; 800-723-8331 (Info & Referrals); Fax: 845-356-0406. Web: www.goodcounselhomes.org; www.postabortionhelp.org.

Springfield Gardens
Diocese of Brooklyn

Martin De Porres Group Homes (1974) 136-25 218th St., Springfield Gardens, 11413. Tel: 718-527-0606; Fax: 718-723-1528. Email: phiro@nyc.rr.com. Web: mdp.org.

Staten Island
Archdiocese of New York

Beacon of Hope House Staten Island Supervised Programs, 777 Seaview Ave., Bldg. D, 2nd Fl., Staten Island, 10305. Tel: 718-980-1072; Fax: 718-980-1077.

Good Counsel, Inc., 38 Wiman Pl., Staten Island, 10305. Tel: 718-727-8266; 800-723-8331 (Info. & Referrals); Fax: 718-447-6625. Web: www.goodcounselhomes.org; www.postabortionhelp.org.

Pax Christi Hospice Hospice Care Services for the terminally ill., 1200 South Ave., Ste. 306, Staten Island, 10314. Tel: 718-876-1022; Fax: 718-876-1803.

Syosset
Diocese of Rockville Centre

MercyFirst (1894) 525 Convent Rd., Syosset, 11791-3864. Tel: 516-921-0808; Fax: 516-921-4542. Email: gmccaffery@mercyfirst.org. Web: www.mercyfirst.org. Residential services provided in campus and group home settings, including diagnostic/group emergency foster care, non secure detention, hard to place (JD and clinically intensive), abuse treatment and prevention, mother/child, and OMH programs.; Foster Boarding Home/Adoption, Aftercare and Prevention Services programs provide services in Nassau, Queens and Brooklyn.

Syracuse
Diocese of Syracuse

L'Arche of Syracuse, Inc., 1232 Teall Ave., Syracuse, 13206. Tel: 315-479-8088; Fax: 315-479-8118. Email: larchesyracuse@cnymail.com. Web: www.larchesyracuse.com. A Christian Community concerned with life sharing between persons with a developmental disability and persons who assist them; Homes at 310 Galster Ave, 4550 Cleveland Rd., 211 Croyden Ln., 140 Highland Ave., Syracuse.

Tarrytown
Archdiocese of New York

**Family Home Health Care, Inc.* (Licensed Home Health Care Affiliate), 65 S. Broadway, Tarrytown, 10591. Tel: 914-631-7200; Fax: 914-631-2382. Email: dozure@dsfhs.org.

Utica
Diocese of Syracuse

St. John and St. Joseph Home, Inc., 1408 Genesee St., Utica, 13502. Tel: 315-724-2158; Fax: 315-724-5318.

Wading River
Diocese of Rockville Centre

Little Flower Children & Family Services of New York (1929) 2450 N. Wading River Rd., Wading River, 11792-1402. Tel: 631-929-6200; Fax: 631-929-6121. Web: www.LittleFlowerNY.org. Affiliated with the Diocese of Brooklyn. Foster care, adoption & post-adoption svcs., intermediate care facilities, residential treatment center, Special Act school district, family day care, family care for MR/DD clients, foster homes for teen mothers & their babies. Therapeutic foster boarding homes. Eldercare Solutions: Counseling for employees of client organizations.

Watervliet
Diocese of Albany

St. Colman's Home, Watervliet, 12189. Tel: 518-273-4911; Fax: 518-273-3312.

West Park
Archdiocese of New York

St. Cabrini Home (1890)West Park, 12493. Tel: 845-384-6500; Fax: 845-384-6001. Email: info@cabrinihome.com. Web: cabrinihome.com.

White Plains
Archdiocese of New York

Cardinal McCloskey Services (1946) Two Holland Ave., White Plains, 10603. Tel: 914-997-8000; Fax: 914-997-2166. Email: bfinnerty@cardinalmccloskey.org. Web: www.cardinalmccloskeyservices.org. Statistical Information: Sisters 2; Hayden House Capacity: 20, Total Assisted: 39, Total Staff: 20; Foster Boarding Home Program Capacity: 350 Beds, Total Assisted: 437; Group Home Capacity: 8, Total Assisted: 8; Therapeutic Foster Boarding Home Program Capacity: 60 Beds, Total Assisted: 69; General Preventative Services Capacity: 225, Total Assisted: 934 children/319 families; Family Rehabilitation Services: 120, Total Assisted: 443 children/319 families; In Day Care: Site I Capacity: 850 (Family), Total Assisted: 1,451, Site II Capacity: 80 (Group), Total Assisted: 121 children/118 families; Site III CMS, University Heights DC: 77 (Group) - 102 (Family), Total Assisted: 263 children/240 families, MRDD Residences Capacity: 80, Total Staff: 487

RDC Center for Counseling and Human Development, Inc. (1991) 52 N. Broadway, White Plains, 10603. Tel: 914-949-0504; Fax: 914-997-1979. To provide counseling services for laity, religious and clergy. Individual and group counseling are offered as well as marital and family therapy.

Wyandanch
Diocese of Rockville Centre

Gerald J. Ryan Outreach Center, Inc., 1434 Straight Path, Wyandanch, 11798. Tel: 631-643-7591; Fax: 631-643-1871. Email: ryanouthreach@optonline.net.

NORTH CAROLINA

Belmont
Diocese of Charlotte

**Holy Angels Services, Inc.*, 6600 Wilkinson Blvd., Belmont, 28012. Tel: 704-825-4161; Fax: 704-825-0553. Email: info@holyangelsnc.org. Web: www.holyangelsnc.org. Mailing Address: P.O. Box 710, Belmont, 28012. Residential and developmental programs and svcs. for children and adults with mental retardation and physical disabilities.

McAuley Residence ICF/MR Group Homes, Belmont.

Morrow Center, Belmont. (Children 0-20)

Raleigh
Diocese of Raleigh

Catholic Parish Outreach, 2013 N. Raleigh Blvd., Raleigh, 27604. Tel: 919-873-0245; Fax: 919-873-0260. Web: www.cporaleigh.org.

Rosman
Diocese of Charlotte

**Frances Warde Health Service*, 9526 Rosman Hwy., Rosman, 28772. Tel: 828-884-7990; Fax: 828-966-9609. Email: jdewarrsm@juno.com.

NORTH DAKOTA

Dickinson
Diocese of Bismarck

Benedictine Living Communities, Inc. dba Benedict Court (2003) 830 2nd Ave. E., Dickinson, 58601. Tel: 701-456-7242; Fax: 701-456-7250. Email: Jon.frantsvog@bhshealth.org. Web: www.benedict-court.org.

Fargo
Diocese of Fargo

Villa Nazareth dba Friendship, Inc. 801 Page Dr., Fargo, 58103. Tel: 701-235-8217; Fax: 701-235-7538. Email: jeffpederson@catholichealth.net. A community-based facility providing an array of residential, vocational, educational, social and clinical services for children and adults with mental retardation and other developmental disabilities.

Sentinel Butte
Diocese of Bismarck

Home On The Range (1950) 16351 I-94, Sentinel Butte, 58654-9500. Tel: 701-872-3745; Fax: 701-872-3748. Email: jorluck@gohotr.org. Web: www.gohotr.org.

OHIO

Akron
Diocese of Cleveland

Interval Brotherhood Home Alcohol-Drug Rehabilitation Center (1970) 3445 S. Main St., Akron, 44319. Tel: 330-644-4095; Fax: 330-645-2031. Email: sam@ibh.org. Web: www.ibh.org.

**St. Patrick Manor, Inc. c/o Humility of Mary Housing, Inc.*, 3250 W. Market St., Ste. 204, Akron, 44333. Tel: 330-384-1555; Fax: 330-384-2144. Email: kradigan@hmhousing.org. Web: www.hmhousing.org.

Cincinnati
Archdiocese of Cincinnati

Friars Club, 1615 Vine St., Cincinnati, 45202. Tel: 513-381-5432; Fax: 513-381-7909. Email: atimmons@friarsclubinc.org. Web: www.friarsclubinc.org.

Cleveland
Diocese of Cleveland

Chemical Dependency Services - Midtown Professional Center, 3135 Euclid Ave., Room 202, Cleveland, 44115-2507. Tel: 216-391-2030; Fax: 216-391-8946.

Employment & Training Services - Midtown Professional Center, 3135 Euclid Ave., Room 101, Cleveland, 44115-2507. Tel: 216-426-9870; Fax: 216-426-9932.

Hispanic Senior Center, 7800 Detroit Ave., Cleveland, 44102. Tel: 216-939-3714; Fax: 216-631-3654.

St. Phillip Neri Family Center, 799 E. 82nd St., Cleveland, 44103. Tel: 216-391-4415.

Euclid
Diocese of Cleveland

Rose Mary, The Johanna Grasselli Rehabilitation and Education Center, 19350 Euclid Ave., Euclid, 44117. Tel: 216-481-4823; Fax: 216-481-4154. Web: rose-marycenter.com.

Garfield Heights
Diocese of Cleveland

Brendan Manor, Inc., 13401 Cranwood Dr., Garfield Heights, 44105. Tel: 216-475-5230; Fax: 216-475-5852. Email: dlkalchert@hotmail.com. Licensed nonprofit, nondenominational adult group home for chronically ill adults.

North Lima
Diocese of Youngstown

The Assumption Village, Marian Living Center (Assisted Living Facility), 9800 Market St., North Lima, 44452. Tel: 330-549-0740; Fax: 330-549-0701. Member: Catholic Healthcare Partners and Humility of Mary Health Partners.; Special Care Unit for residents with Alzheimer's or Dementia; Skilled Nursing Unit with Subacute Care Program; Intermediate Care.

Northfield
Diocese of Cleveland

St. Barnabas Villa, Inc. (1985) 9234 Olde Eight Rd., Northfield, 44067. Tel: 330-467-3758; Fax: 330-908-1186. A shared living facility for 11 people over 60 years of age.

Parma
Diocese of Cleveland

CCSC/Parmadale (1925) 6753 State Rd., Parma, 44134. Tel: 440-845-7700; Fax: 440-845-5910. Email: pdale@clevelandcatholiccharities.org. Web: www.clevelandcatholiccharities.org. Specialized Residential Services; Intensive Treatment Services; Chemical Dependency Treatment; Community Flexible Clinical Response; Specialized Foster Care; Whole Family Treatment; In-Home Services; Outpatient Services; Training and Consultation Services; and Volunteer Program; Adoption Services; Head Start.

Holy Family Home and Hospice (1956) 6707 State Rd., Parma, 44134. Tel: 440-888-7722; Fax: 440-866-6040. Email: info@holyfamilyhome.com. Web: www.holyfamilyhome.com. Inpatient and community-based end of life care.

Poland
Diocese of Youngstown

Hospice of the Valley, Hospice House, 9803 Sharrott Rd, Poland, 44514. Tel: 330-549-5850; Fax: 330-549-5859.

Sandusky
Diocese of Toledo

**Providence Residential Community Corp Apartment and Villa Home Independent Living*, 5000 Providence Dr., Sandusky, 44870. Tel: 419-624-1171; Fax: 419-624-1175. Email: jwindisch@providencecenters.org. Web: www.providencecenters.org.

Tiffin
Diocese of Toledo

St. Francis Home Inc., 182 St. Francis Ave., Tiffin, 44883. Tel: 419-447-2723; Fax: 419-448-1337. Email: ceo@stfrancishome.org. Web: www.stfrancishome.org.

Youngstown
Diocese of Youngstown

Beatitude House (1991) 238 Tod Ln., Youngstown, 44504. Tel: 330-744-3147; Fax: 330-744-3991. Email: info@beatitudehouse.com. Web: www.beatitudehouse.com. Permanent supportive housing, transitional housing, job preparation, job training, counseling, education and case management for economically disadvantaged women and children.

OKLAHOMA

Oklahoma City
Archdiocese of Oklahoma City

St. Ann's Home, Inc. (1950) 9400 St. Ann's Dr., Oklahoma City, 73162. Tel: 405-728-7888; Fax: 405-728-1302.

PENNSYLVANIA

Ambler
Archdiocese of Philadelphia

St. Mary's Villa for Children and Families, 701 Bethlehem Pike, P.O. Box 388, Ambler, 19002-0388. Tel: 215-643-7676; Fax: 215-542-9219. Email: fryer.diana@hfi-pgh.org. Web: www.hfi.org. Family centered organization providing residential care and treatment to youth ages 7-18. St. Mary's is committed to helping children, preserving families and strengthening communities by providing residential treatment and outpatient mental health counseling. It strives to empower children and families to lead responsible lives and develop healthy relationships built on faith, hope and love.

Aston
Archdiocese of Philadelphia

Assisi House, 600 Red Hill Rd., Aston, 19014. Tel: 610-459-8990; Fax: 610-558-5344. Email: JLAMANNA@osfPHILA.org. Web: www.osfphila.org. Home for retired Sisters of St. Francis of Philadelphia.

Audubon
Archdiocese of Philadelphia

St. Gabriel's Hall, Box 7280, Audubon, 19407-7280. Tel: 215-247-2776 (Philadelphia); 610-666-7970 (Audubon); Fax: 610-666-1479. Email: jlavoritano@chs_adphila.org. Offers residential treatment for court-committed delinquent boys, ages 10-18.

Bensalem
Archdiocese of Philadelphia

De La Salle Vocational Day Treatment Center, Box 344, Bensalem, 19020. Tel: 215-464-0344; Fax: 215-638-3767. Email: jlogan@chs-adphila.org. A community based day treatment program for court-committed delinquent boys, ages 15-18.

Bethlehem
Diocese of Allentown

Grace Mansion Assisted Living Residence of Catholic Senior Housing and Health Care Services, Inc., 1200 Spring St., Bethlehem, 18018. Tel: 610-865-6748; Fax: 610-997-8444. Email: kabruzzese@HFManor.org. Web: www.hfmanor.org. Personal care/assisted living facility for 25 elderly.

Holy Family Apartments of Catholic Housing Corporation of Bethlehem, 330-338 13th Ave., Bethlehem, 18018. Tel: 610-866-4603; Fax: 610-866-1622. Email: hfabeth@epix.net. Catholic housing for the elderly.

Holy Family Manor of Catholic Senior Housing and Health Care Services, Inc. (1963) Holy Family Manor: a division of Catholic Senior Housing and Health Care Services, Inc., 1200 Spring St., Bethlehem, 18018. Tel: 610-865-5595; Fax: 610-997-8454. Email: hkessler@hfmanor.org. Web: www.hfmanor.org. Skilled and intermediate nursing care facility for the aged, chronically ill, or invalid.

Trexler Pavilion, Assisted Living Residence of Catholic Senior Housing and Health Care Services, Inc., 1220 Prospect Ave., Bethlehem, 18018. Tel: 610-868-7776; Fax: 610-865-7775. Email: kabruzzese@HFManor.org. Web: www.hfmpc.org. Personal care/assisted living facility for 23 elderly.

Chambersburg
Diocese of Harrisburg

Chambersburg Family Outreach, 336 Philadelphia Ave., Chambersburg, 17201. Tel: 717-264-2332; Fax: 717-264-0654.

Chester
Archdiocese of Philadelphia

Bernardine Center, 2625 W. Ninth St., Chester, 19013. Tel: 610-497-3225; Fax: 610-497-3659. Email: director@bernardinecenter.org. Web: www.bernardinecenter.org. West Side Brunch, Emergency Food Cupboard, Supercupboard Program, Advocacy, Computer Lab, English as a Second Language (ESL), Citizenship Classes.

Clarion
Diocese of Pittsburgh

Amelia House (1995) Clarion. Tel: 814-226-6682. Web: www.providenceconnections.org. Purpose: To engage in educational activities and operation of day care centers and other related services to families in need.

Clarks Green
Diocese of Scranton

Lourdesmont (1889) 537 Venard Rd., Clarks Green, 18411. Tel: 570-587-4741; Fax: 570-586-0030. Email: msherman@lourdesmont.com. Web: www.lourdesmont.com.

Darby
Archdiocese of Philadelphia

Villa Saint Joseph, 1436 Lansdowne Ave., Darby, 19023-1298. Tel: 610-586-8535; Fax: 610-586-2810. Home for aged, infirm and convalescent priests of the Archdiocese of Philadelphia.

Downingtown
Archdiocese of Philadelphia

St. John Vianney Center, 151 Woodbine Rd., Downingtown, 19335. Tel: 610-269-2600; Fax: 610-873-8028. Web: www.sjvcenter.org. Center for Behavioral Healthcare for Priests, Brothers, and Sisters.

Erie
Diocese of Erie

Gannondale, Inc., 4635 E. Lake Rd., Erie, 16511. Tel: 814-899-7659; Fax: 814-898-4266. Email: gdale@gannondale.org. Web: www.gannondale.org.

St. Patrick Haven, Inc., 147 E. 12th St., Erie, 16501. Tel: 814-454-7219; 814-836-5301; Fax: 814-454-7219.

Harborcreek
Diocese of Erie

Harborcreek Youth Services, 5712 Iroquois Ave., Harborcreek, 16421. Tel: 814-899-7664; Fax: 814-899-3075. Email: jpetulla@hys-erie.org.

Harrisburg
Diocese of Harrisburg

Adoption Services, 806-C S. 29th St., Harrisburg, 17111. Tel: 717-564-7115; Fax: 717-238-6050.

Hollidaysburg
Diocese of Altoona-Johnstown

Dmitri Manor Priests' Residence, St. Mary's Ln., Hollidaysburg, 16648. Tel: 814-696-4698.

Lancaster
Diocese of Harrisburg

Intensive Day Treatment, 47 S. Mulberry St., Lancaster, 17603. Tel: 717-295-9630; Fax: 717-295-9525.

New Brighton
Diocese of Pittsburgh

McGuire Memorial (1963) 2119 Mercer Rd., New Brighton, 15066-3437. Tel: 724-843-3400; Fax: 724-847-2004. Email: mcgm@mcguirememorial.org. Web: www.mcguirememorial.org. Residential Facility-Intermediate Care for Developmentally Challenged; Private School, Licensed Adult Training, Community Homes.

Philadelphia
Archdiocese of Philadelphia

Casa del Carmen, 4400 N. Reese St., Philadelphia, 19140. Tel: 215-329-5660; Fax: 215-329-6722. Offers emergency crisis social services to the Spanish speaking community in Philadelphia and surrounding areas.

De La Salle-In-Towne Day Treatment Center, 25 S. Van Pelt St., Philadelphia, 19103. Tel: 215-567-5500; Fax: 215-567-6922. Email: cgaus@chs-adphila.org. A community-based day treatment program for court-committed delinquent boys, ages 14-17.

Drueding Center/Project Rainbow, 413 W. Master St., Philadelphia, 19122. Tel: 215-769-1830; Fax: 215-787-0999. Email: acollins@holyredeemer.com. Web: www.holyredeemer.com. Subsidiary of Holy Redeemer Health System; Provides transitional housing and support services for homeless women with children; daycare is provided for the children.

**Holy Redeemer Home Care and Hospice* Holy Redeemer Support Services, 12265 Townsend Rd., Ste. 400, Philadelphia, 19154. Tel: 215-671-9200; Fax: 215-671-1950. Web: www.holyredeemer.com. Affiliate of Holy Redeemer Health System. Sponsor: Sisters of the Holy Redeemer; Medicare certified home health agency serving patients in their own homes; Medicare certified hospice program serving terminally ill patients and their families.

Mercy Hospice, 334 S. 13th St., Philadelphia, 19107. Tel: 215-545-5153; Fax: 215-545-1872. Provides residential case management and referral services to homeless women, women in recovery who are single or are with their children. Mercy Hospice also provides lunch Monday thru Friday from 12:00 - 12:45 p.m. to homeless women and children. Showers, clothing and the use of a telephone are available on a limited basis.

Mount Nazareth, 2755 Holme Ave., Philadelphia, 19152. Tel: 215-338-8992; Fax: 215-338-8752. Home for retired and infirm sisters.

Norris Square Senior Community Center, 2121 N. Howard St., Philadelphia, 19133. Tel: 215-423-7241; Fax: 215-634-7751.

Saint Katharine Drexel Residence, 7919 Forrest Ave., Philadelphia, 19150. Tel: 215-549-5765; Fax: 215-549-2375.

St. Anne's Senior Community Center, 2607 E. Cumberland St., Philadelphia, 19125. Tel: 215-423-2772; Fax: 215-423-2423.

St. Charles Senior Community Center, 1941 Christian St., Philadelphia, 19146. Tel: 215-790-9530; Fax: 215-790-9765.

St. Francis Inn, 2441 Kensington Ave., Philadelphia, 19125. Tel: 215-423-5845; Fax: 215-423-2289. Email: stfrancisinn@aol.com. Web: www.stfrancisinn.org. Hot meals for the poor.

St. Gabriel's System, Administrative Offices, 227 N. 18th St., Philadelphia, 19103. Tel: 215-665-8777; Fax: 215-665-8821. Email: jlavoritano@chs-adphila.org. Web: www.saintgabrielssystem.org. Administrative and Intake services for residential treatment; Day Treatment for Court-committed delinquent boys, ages 12-17. (See St. Gabriel's Hall, De LaSalle in Towne, De LaSalle Vocational and St. Gabriel's System Reintegration Services and Brother Rousseau Academy).

St. Joachim's Hall Group Home (16 females ages 12-21), 1509 Church St., Philadelphia, 19124. Tel: 215-992-5402; Cell: 267-574-1100; Fax: 215-992-5189.

St. Joan of Arc Hall (16 females ages 12-21), 7201 Milnor St., Philadelphia, 19135. Tel: 215-992-5070; Cell: 215-275-4560; Fax: 215-624-8355.

St. John's Hospice for Men, 1221 Race St., Philadelphia, 19107. Tel: 215-563-7763; Fax: 215-563-0108. Web: www.saintjohnshospice.org. Staffed by Catholic Social Services Archdiocese of Philadelphia.

St. Joseph's Hall Group Home (12 females ages 12-21), 477 E. Locust Ave., Philadelphia, 19144. Tel: 215-849-1316; Cell: 215-300-2315; Fax: 215-842-0387.

St. Lucy Day School for Children with Visual Impairments and Archbishop Ryan Academy for the Deaf, 4251 L St., Philadelphia, 19124. Tel: 215-289-4220; Fax: 215-289-4229. Email: APLucy01@nni.com. Web: www.slds.org.

St. Mary's Residence, 247 S. 5th St., Philadelphia, 19106. Tel: 215-922-4228; Fax: 215-922-0192.

St. Vincent Homes, Administrative Office Building, 1509 Church St., Philadelphia, 19124. Tel: 215-992-5402; Fax: 215-992-5198. Operates the following programs for court adjudicated dependent females ages 12-21 who suffer from abuse and neglect. All facilities are staffed 24/7.

Star Harbor Senior Community Center, 4700 Springfield Ave., Philadelphia, 19143. Tel: 215-724-4414; Fax: 215-726-7496. Email: bjhartze@chs-adphila.org.

Thea Bowman's Women's Center, 2858 Kensington Ave., Philadelphia, 19134. Tel: 215-739-1137. Women's day activity center.

Visitation Homes, 2638 Kensington Ave., Philadelphia, 19125. Tel: 215-425-2080; Fax: 215-425-1412. Residential service program for families making the transition from homelessness to permanent housing. The program offers 18 furnished one to three bedroom apartments and on site case management and life skill services. Referrals come through the City's Office of Emergency Shelter and Services. For a period of up to 2 years, residents are helped to achieve economic self sufficiency and address the other issues which led to their homelessness.

Women of Hope, 251 N. Lawrence St., Philadelphia, 19106. Tel: 215-592-9116; Fax: 215-592-0650. Residential facility for chronically mentally ill homeless women.

Women of Hope Lombard, 1210 Lombard St., Philadelphia, 19147. Tel: 215-732-1341; Fax: 215-732-0659. Residential Facility for chronically mentally ill homeless women.

Phoenixville
Archdiocese of Philadelphia

St. Mary's Franciscan Shelter, 209 Emmett St., Phoenixville, 19460. Tel: 610-933-3097; Fax: 610-917-9845. Email: stmarysfs@verizon.net. Web: stmarysfs.org.

Pine Grove
Diocese of Scranton

St. Michael's Group Home, 25 Oak Grove Rd., Pine Grove, 17963. Tel: 570-345-1160; Fax: 570-345-6307. Email: pggirls1995@yahoo.com. Web: www.dioceseofscranton.org.

Pittsburgh
Diocese of Pittsburgh

DePaul School for Hearing and Speech (1908) 6202 Alder St., Pittsburgh, 15206. Tel: 412-924-1012; Fax: 412-924-1036. Email: mjmac@depaulinst.com. Web: www.speakmiracles.org. Auditory-Oral day school for children with hearing, speech and language impairments.

Marian Hall Home, Inc. (1970) 934 Forest Ave., Pittsburgh, 15202-1118. Tel: 412-761-1999; Fax: 412-761-2556. Email: marian27@verizon.net. Purpose: to provide programs, facilities, and services, including, but not limited to, residential personal care, and long-term care homes for the elderly, ill, or disabled, including supportive services.

Mercy Outreach Ministries, Inc., 3333 Fifth Ave., Pittsburgh, 15213. Tel: 412-578-6202; Fax: 412-578-6180. Email: mcdonoughfx@carlow.edu.

Providence Family Support Center (1994) 3113 Brighton Rd., Pittsburgh, 15212-2456. Tel: 412-766-6730; Fax: 412-766-6775. Web: www.providencecon-nections.org.

The Community at Holy Family Manor, Inc., 301 Bellevue Rd., Pittsburgh, 15229-2194. Tel: 412-931-6996; Fax: 412-931-7255.

Vincentian Home Inc. (1924) 111 Perrymont Rd., Pittsburgh, 15237. Tel: 412-366-5600; Fax: 412-366-1408. Web: www.vcs.org.

Vincentian de Marillac (1943) 5300 Stanton Ave., Pittsburgh, 15206. Tel: 412-361-2833; Fax: 412-361-1237. Email: mcoyne@vcs.org. Catholic, skilled nursing home.

Reading
Diocese of Allentown

Mary's Shelter, 325 S. 12th St., Reading, 19602-2021. Tel: 610-376-1973; Fax: 610-376-5391. Email: brenda@maryshelter.org. Web: www.marysshelter.org. A residence for pregnant, homeless young women and teens.

Sacred Heart Villa - Assisted Living Community of the Missionary Sisters of the Most Sacred Heart of Jesus (2003) 51 Seminary Ave., Reading, 19605. Tel: 610-929-5751; Fax: 610-929-0762. Email: sacredheart-villa@comcast.com. Web: sacredheartvilla-readingpa.org.

Scranton
Diocese of Scranton

St. Joseph's Center (1888) 2010 Adams Ave., Scranton, 18509. Tel: 570-342-8379; Fax: 570-342-6080. Email: torourke@stjosephscenter.org. Web: www.stjosephscenter.org.

Springfield
Archdiocese of Philadelphia

Cardinal Krol Center, 1799 S. Sproul Rd., Springfield, 19064. Tel: 484-475-2467; Fax: 610-544-1207. Web: catholicsocialservicesphilly.org; www.cssmrserv.org. A residential facility for 131 male adults with developmental/intellectual disabilities which provides an environment, both day and residential, that contributes to the individuals own growth and development by fulfilling their potential in the physical, mental, emotional, social, psychological, and spiritual areas of their lives.

Divine Providence Village, 686 Old Marple Rd., Springfield, 19064. Tel: 610-328-7730; Fax: 610-544-1710. Care & specialized training for developmentally disabled females.

Don Guanella School, 1797 S. Sproul Rd., Springfield, 19064-1195. Tel: 484-475-2474; Fax: 610-328-2136. Email: fr.dweber@chs-adphila.org. Web: www.catholicsocialservicesphilly.org. Provides specialized care and residential treatment program for boys with developmental/ intellectual disabilities ages 6-21.

Tunkhannock
Diocese of Scranton

St. Michael's Group Home-Tunkhannock, 28 Putnam St., Tunkhannock, 18657. Tel: 570-836-6932; Fax: 570-836-6979. Email: stmikes@epix.net. Web: www.dioceseofscranton.org.

St. Michael's School, Box 370, Tunkhannock, 18657. Tel: 570-388-6155; Fax: 570-388-6979. Email: stmikes@epix.net. Web: www.dioceseofscranton.org.

Upper Darby
Archdiocese of Philadelphia

Dominican Pastoral Counseling, 131 Copley Rd., Upper Darby, 19082. Tel: 215-635-6027; Fax: 215-635-2017. Email: cgaekeop@verizon.net. Web: www.elkinsparkop.org.

Ventnor
Archdiocese of Philadelphia

Villa St. Joseph by the Sea Summer residence for aged, infirm, and convalescent priests of the Archdiocese of Philadelphia., 114 S. Princeton Ave., Ventnor, 08406. Tel: 609-823-9383. Email: hmcconnell@chs.adphila.org.

Warminster
Archdiocese of Philadelphia

Regina Coeli Residence for Priests, 685 York Rd., Warminster, 18974. Tel: 215-441-4642. Home for retired priests of the Archdiocese of Philadelphia.

West Pittston
Diocese of Scranton

St. Michael's Group Home-West Pittston, 225-227 Damon St., West Pittston, 18643. Tel: 570-602-6579; Fax: 570-602-6979.

Wexford
Diocese of Pittsburgh

St. Anthony School Programs, 2000 Corporate Dr., Ste. 580, Wexford, 15090. Tel: 724-940-9020. Email: lgeorge@stanthonyschoolprograms.com. Resource rooms for students with special needs in 7 elementary schools, 2 high schools and 1 Post-Secondary Program.

Willow Grove
Archdiocese of Philadelphia

Our Lady of Confidence Day School, Willow Grove. Tel: 215-657-9311; Fax: 215-657-9312. Email: apConf01@nni.com. Web: www.ourladyofconfidence.com. Mentally Challenged.

PUERTO RICO

Bayamon
Archdiocese of San Juan, Puerto Rico

Hogar Del Nino "El Ave Maria" (For Abused Children), Carretera 861, km 2.0, Bo. Pajaros Americanos, Bayamon, 00957. Tel: 787-797-2382; 787-279-3003; Fax: 787-797-2382. Mailing Address: PMS 239, P.O. Box 607061, Bayamon, 00960-7061.

Hogar Escuela Sor Maria Rafaela (Girls with Problems), Carretera 871, km 1.0, Bo. El Volcan, Hato Tejas, Bayamon, 00961. Tel: 787-785-9517; 787-785-1125; Fax: 787-787-5324; 787-779-0449. Email: hogar.sormaria@gmail.com. P.O. Box 3024, Bayamon, PR 00960.

Hogar Fatima (Girls), Ave. Santa Juanita Final, Camino Esteban Cruz, Bayamon, 00961. Fax: 787-780-9763. Email: fatima001@prttc.net. Web: www.osrhogarfatimainc.com. P.O. Box 4228, Bayamon Garden Sta., Bayamon, 00958-4228. Tel: 787-787-2580.

Hogar Santisima Trinidad (Drug Addiction Rehabilitation Home), Lote A y Lote B, km 7.0, Bo Mucarabones, Carr. 861, Toa Alta, 00954. Tel: 787-799-6208; Fax: 787-799-1977. Email: trinita@prtc.net. PMB 326, P.O. Box 607061, Bayamon, 00960-7061.

Bayamon Garden Sta., Bayamon
Archdiocese of San Juan, Puerto Rico

Hogar Fatima (Girls), Ave. Santa Juanita Final, Camino Esteban Cruz, Bayamon, 00961. Fax: 787-780-9763. Email: fatima001@prttc.net. Web: www.osrhogarfatimainc.com. P.O. Box 4228, Bayamon Garden Sta., Bayamon, 00958-4228. Tel: 787-787-2580.

Canovanas
Diocese of Fajardo-Humacao, Puerto Rico

Hogar Teresa Toda (1993) (For Girls), P.O. Box 868, Canovanas, 00729. Tel: 787-886-2060; Fax: 787-886-2075. Email: hteresatoda@aol.com; teresatoda@prtc.net. Web: www.teresatodapr.org. Calle 5-A, R-14, Villa De Loiza, Loiza, 00729. Tel: 787-886-2060; Fax: 787-886-2075.

Dorado
Archdiocese of San Juan, Puerto Rico

Santuario del Espiritu Santo, Box 187, Dorado, 00646-0187. Tel: 787-796-2798; Fax: 787-796-1359. Email: espiritanospr@gmail.com. Web: www.espiritanos.com.

Loiza
Diocese of Fajardo-Humacao, Puerto Rico

Hogar Teresa Toda (1993) (For Girls), P.O. Box 868, Canovanas, 00729. Tel: 787-886-2060; Fax: 787-886-2075. Email: hteresatoda@aol.com; teresatoda@prtc.net. Web: www.teresatodapr.org. Calle 5-A, R-14, Villa De Loiza, Loiza, 00729. Tel: 787-886-2060; Fax: 787-886-2075.

Mayaguez
Diocese of Mayaguez, Puerto Rico

Asylum for the Poor and Aged, Calle Ramon E. Betances 162 Sur., Mayaguez, 00680.

Ponce
Diocese of Ponce, Puerto Rico

Missionaries of Charity (1989)Mailing Address: P.O. Box 32177, Ponce, 00732-2177. Tel: 787-841-5443.

Hna. Selma M.C. (D) Home for the Aged, 683 Ramos Antonini, El Tuque, Ponce, 00728.

Puerta De Tierra
Archdiocese of San Juan, Puerto Rico

Asylum For The Aged and Infirm (Hogar de la Providencia), Stop 5, Edif. 205, Puerta De Tierra, 00906-6571. Tel: 787-722-1331; 787-723-2419; 787-724-3574; Fax: 787-725-4308. P.O. Box 9066571, San Juan, 00906-6571.

Rio Piedras
Archdiocese of San Juan, Puerto Rico

Centro N. Sra. de la Providencia Sisters of Notre Dame., R.F.D. #2, Box 16T, Rio Piedras, 00928. Tel: 787-761-0273.

Centro Santa Luisa (1972) (Services for the Elderly), Carretera 842, Camino Los Romeros km 1.5, Bo. Caimito, Rio Piedras, 00926. Tel: 787-720-2764; Fax: 787-731-7795. Email: centrosantaluisa@yahoo.com. Web: www.geocities.com/centrosantaluisa. Mailing Address: R.R. 6 Box 9492, San Juan, 00926-9492.

San Juan
Archdiocese of San Juan, Puerto Rico

Asylum For The Aged and Infirm (Hogar de la Providencia), Stop 5, Edif. 205, Puerta De Tierra, 00906-6571. Tel: 787-722-1331; 787-723-2419; 787-724-3574; Fax: 787-725-4308. P.O. Box 9066571, San Juan, 00906-6571.

Casa La Providencia (Drug Addicted Women), Calle Norzagaray #200, San Juan, 00901. Tel: 787-725-5358; Fax: 787-725-0058. Email: casalaprovidencia@hotmail.com. P.O. Box 9020614, San Juan, 00902-0614.

Casa La Providencia, Inc. Drug Rehabilitation Center, P.O. Box 9020614, San Juan, 00902-0614. Tel: 787-725-5358; Fax: 787-725-0058. Email: casalaprovidencia@hotmail.com. Web: casalaprovidencia.org.

Casa de Ninos Manuel Fernandez Juncos (Orphans and Abused Boys) , Calle Villa Verde Esq. Refugio, Pda 11, Miramar, Santurce, 00940. Tel: 787-724-2904; 787-725-6328; Fax: 787-724-0980. P.O. Box 9020163, San Juan, 00902-0163.

Centro De Orientacion Vocacional Nuestra Senora del Consuelo (Teenagers/Single Mothers), Floral Park, 20 C. Matienzo Citron, San Juan, 00919. Tel: 787-250-6323; Fax: 787-250-6323. Email: oblahchr@prte.net.

Centro Medico de P.R., Calle 10 #1030, Puerto Nuevo, 00920. Apdo. 347, San Juan, 00936. Tel: 787-763-7272.

Centro Santa Luisa (1972) (Services for the Elderly), Carretera 842, Camino Los Romeros km 1.5, Bo. Caimito, Rio Piedras, 00926. Tel: 787-720-2764; Fax: 787-731-7795. Email: centrosantaluisa@yahoo.com. Web: www.geocities.com/centrosantaluisa. Mailing Address: R.R. 6 Box 9492, San Juan, 00926-9492.

Hogar Carmelitano Julian Bengochea Final (Elderly Retirement Hospice), Calle Julian Bengoechea Final, San Juan, 00924. Tel: 787-769-6510; 787-769-3110; Fax: 787-768-1240.

Hogares Rafaela Ibarra (Orphan or Abused Girls), Calle Torrelaguna 432, San Juan, 00923. Tel: 787-763-1204; Fax: 787-763-6266. Web: www.hogaresrafaelaybarra.com. 432 Calle Torrelaguna, San Juan, 00923-1773.

Politecnico Amigo (For School Dropout Boys), Calle Refugio #960, Pda II, Santurce, 00940. Tel: 787-725-2059; Fax: 787-722-3436. Email: polam@prtc.net. P.O. Box 13204, San Juan, 00908.

Santurce
Archdiocese of San Juan, Puerto Rico

Casa de Ninos Manuel Fernandez Juncos (Orphans and Abused Boys) , Calle Villa Verde Esq. Refugio, Pda 11, Miramar, Santurce, 00940. Tel: 787-724-2904; 787-725-6328; Fax: 787-724-0980. P.O. Box 9020163, San Juan, 00902-0163.

Politecnico Amigo (For School Dropout Boys), Calle Refugio #960, Pda II, Santurce, 00940. Tel: 787-725-2059; Fax: 787-722-3436. Email: polam@prtc.net. P.O. Box 13204, San Juan, 00908.

Toa Alta
Archdiocese of San Juan, Puerto Rico

Hogar Santisima Trinidad (Drug Addiction Rehabilitation Home), Lote A y Lote B, km 7.0, Bo Mucarabones, Carr. 861, Toa Alta, 00954. Tel: 787-799-6208; Fax: 787-799-1977. Email: trinita@prtc.net. PMB 326, P.O. Box 607061, Bayamon, 00960-7061.

Toa Baja
Archdiocese of San Juan, Puerto Rico

Hogar Divino Nino Jesus (Drug Addict Rehabilitation), Carretera 854, Km. 3.5, Toa Baja, 00949. Tel: 787-794-0020; Fax: 787-794-0020. Email: divinoninojesus@yahoo.es. P.O. Box 2464, Toa Baja, 00951.

RHODE ISLAND

Pawtucket
Diocese of Providence

Outreach and Tracking Program, 242 Dexter St., Pawtucket, 02860. Tel: 401-724-8380; Fax: 401-724-8899.

Tides' Hispanic Outreach Project, 242 Dexter St., Pawtucket, 02860. Tel: 401-724-8201; Fax: 401-724-8899.

Providence
Diocese of Providence

Holy Spirit Convent, 43 Westerly Ave., Providence, 02909. Tel: 401-946-5639.

Southern New England Rehabilitation Center, Providence. Tel: 401-456-4500; Fax: 401-456-4501. Web: www.snerc.com. A joint venture of St. Joseph Hospital and Rhode Island Hospital.

Woonsocket
Diocese of Providence

Woonsocket Outreach Project, 55 Main St., Ste. 1, Woonsocket, 02895. Tel: 401-766-9320; Fax: 401-766-9324.

SOUTH CAROLINA

Johns Island
Diocese of Charleston

Our Lady of Mercy Community Outreach Services, Inc. (1989) 1684 Brownswood Rd., Johns Island, 29455. Tel: 843-559-4109; Fax: 843-559-8819. Email: olmoutreach@aol.com. Web: olmoutreach.org. P.O. Box 607, Johns Island, 29457. Tel: 843-559-4109; Fax: 843-558-8819. Sponsored by Sisters of Charity of Our Lady of Mercy.

SOUTH DAKOTA

Manderson
Diocese of Rapid City

St. Francis Home, P.O. Box 122, Manderson, 57756-0122. Tel: 605-455-2077; Fax: 605-455-1680. Email: geraldineosf@aol.com. Home for abandoned and abused children (Licensed) 2-18 years of age. 6 children at a time.

Sioux Falls
Diocese of Sioux Falls

Community Outreach, 231 N. Weber Ave., Sioux Falls, 57103. Tel: 605-331-3935; Fax: 605-336-8924. Email: info@thecommunityoutreach.org.

TENNESSEE

Knoxville
Diocese of Knoxville

Columbus Home, Inc., 3227 Division St., Knoxville, 37919. Tel: 865-971-3560; Fax: 865-546-0433.

Memphis
Diocese of Memphis

Shelter, Memphis. Tel: 901-526-5456.

Nashville
Diocese of Nashville

Ladies of Charity Welfare Agency, Inc. (1617) 2212 State St., Nashville, 37203. Tel: 615-327-3430; Fax: 615-321-3312. Email: locwelfare@bellsouth.net.

Mid-Tennessee Rural Outreach Association, 30 White Bridge Rd., Nashville, 37205. Tel: 615-352-3087.

TEXAS

Amarillo
Diocese of Amarillo

Downtown Women's Center, Inc., 409 S. Monroe, Amarillo, 79101. Tel: 806-372-3625; Fax: 806-372-9026. Email: diann@dwcenter.org.

Beaumont
Diocese of Beaumont

Counseling Services, P.O. Box 829, Beaumont, 77704-0829. Tel: 409-924-4418; Fax: 409-832-0145. 2780 Eastex Fwy., Beaumont, 77703-4617.

Elijah's Place (2003) P.O. Box 829, Beaumont, 77704. Tel: 409-924-4419; Fax: 409-832-0145.

Hospitality Center, 3959 Gulfway Dr., Port Arthur, 77642. Tel: 409-982-4842; Fax: 409-983-7145. P.O. Box 829, Beaumont, 77704-0829.

El Paso
Diocese of El Paso

Catholic Counseling Services, Inc., 499 St. Matthews St., El Paso, 79907. Tel: 915-872-8424; Fax: 915-872-8425. Email: jcastrellon@elpasodiocese.org.

Fort Worth
Diocese of Fort Worth

Assessment Center of Tarrant, 2701 Burchill Rd. N., Fort Worth, 76105. Tel: 817-534-0814; Fax: 817-531-2996. (Children's Shelter)

Clinical Counseling Department, 2701 Burchill Rd., Fort Worth, 76104. Tel: 817-534-0814; Fax: 817-536-1556.

Houston
Archdiocese of Galveston-Houston

Casa Juan Diego (1980) P.O. Box 70113, Houston, 77270. Tel: 713-869-7376; Fax: 713-864-7295. Email: info@cjd.org. Web: www.cjd.org. 4818 Rose, Houston, 77007.

Casa de Esperanza De Los Ninos, Inc. (1982) P.O. Box 66581, Houston, 77266-6581. Tel: 713-529-0639; Fax: 713-529-9179. Email: casa@casahope.org. Web: www.casahope.org. Homes for children in crisis situations, foster care, adoption.

Covenant House Texas, 1111 Lovett Blvd., Houston, 77006. Tel: 713-523-2231; Fax: 713-523-6904. Email: Rgrobinson@covenanthouse.org. Web: www.covenanthousetx.org.

Magnificat Houses Inc. (1968) P.O. Box 25415, Houston, 77265. Tel: 713-520-0461; Fax: 713-520-0461. Email: magnificathousesion@sbcglobal.net. Web: www.mhihouston.org.

San Jose Clinic (1922) 2615 Fannin, Houston, 77002. Tel: 713-228-9411; Fax: 713-228-6371. Email: staciecokinos@sanjoseclinic.org. Web: www.sanjoseclinic.org.

Santa Maria Hostel, 2605 Parker Rd., Houston, 77093. Tel: 713-691-0900; 713-957-2413; Fax: 713-691-0910; 713-400-1119. Email: kaustin@santamariahostel.org. Web: www.santamariahostel.org. 807 Paschall, Houston, 77009. Tel: 713-222-0699; Fax: 713-222-6245. Intensive and supportive residential treatment; housing, shelter and outpatient services (substance abuse) for women ages 18 and above and women with their children. Treatment for co-occurring disorders is also provided.

Port Arthur
Diocese of Beaumont

Hospitality Center, 3959 Gulfway Dr., Port Arthur, 77642. Tel: 409-982-4842; Fax: 409-983-7145. P.O. Box 829, Beaumont, 77704-0829.

San Angelo
Diocese of San Angelo

Catholic Outreach Services, 410 N. Chadbourne, San Angelo, 76903. Tel: 915-658-4124; Fax: 915-481-0315. Email: cos.margie@verizon.net. Thrift Store Social Services.

San Antonio
Archdiocese of San Antonio

Bro. Charles Andersen Residence, 320 Brahan Blvd., San Antonio, 78215. Tel: 210-223-9117; Fax: 210-223-2081.

Catholic Counseling and Consultation Center, 7711 Madonna, San Antonio, 78216. Tel: 210-377-1133; Fax: 210-377-1230. See Curia Section - Department of Social & Community Services.

Christus Continuing Care dba Christus Homecare 4241 Woodcock Dr., Ste. A-100, San Antonio, 78228. Email: patrick.carrier@ChristusHealth.org. Web: www.christushomecare.org.

Guadalupe Home for Homeless Pregnant Women, 1223 S. Trinity St., San Antonio, 78207. Tel: 210-476-0707; Fax: 210-224-7388.

Project Rachel of San Antonio, 9862 Lorene Ln., Ste. 108, San Antonio, 78216. Tel: 210-342-4673; 210-722-4213 (Spanish); (800) 651-HOPE; Fax: 210-341-1572. Email: rachel@anewchoice.org. Web: www.anewchoice.org; www.projectrachelsanantonio.org.

Seton Home, 1115 Mission Rd., San Antonio, 78210. Tel: 210-533-3504; Fax: 210-533-3467. Email: margretstarkey@setonhomesa.org. Web: www.setonhomesa.org.

Visitation House Ministries, 945 W. Huisache, San Antonio, 78201. Tel: 210-735-6910; Fax: 210-738-8794. Web: www.vhmin.org. A nonprofit corporation chartered under the laws of the State of Texas; Provides a two year transitional housing program for homeless women and children, and training for women.

Splendora
Archdiocese of Galveston-Houston

Shalom Center, Inc. (1980) 13516 Morgan Dr., Splendora, 77372-3121. Tel: 281-399-0520; Fax: 281-399-3366. Email: info@shalomcenterinc.org. Web: www.shalomcenterinc.org. A residential treatment center for priests, brothers and sisters.

UTAH

Ogden
Diocese of Salt Lake City

Catholic Community Services Joyce Hansen Hall Food Bank & Social Services, 2504 F. Ave., Ogden, 84401. Tel: 801-394-5944; Fax: 801-621-8468. Mailing Address: P.O. Box 869, Ogden, 84402.

Salt Lake City
Diocese of Salt Lake City

Bishop Weigand Resource Center, 745 E. 300 S., Salt Lake City, 84102. Tel: 801-363-7710; Fax: 801-595-8532.

CCS-St. Mary's Treatment Program for Men, 745 E. 300 S., Salt Lake City, 84102. Tel: 801-328-1894; Fax: 801-328-1895. Residential Substance Abuse Treatment for Adult Males.

CCS-St. Vincent de Paul Resource Center, 745 E. 300 S., Salt Lake City, 84102. Tel: 801-363-7710; Fax: 801-595-8532.

CCS-Treatment Program for Women, 745 E. 300 S., Salt Lake City, 84102. Tel: 801-977-9119; Fax: 801-977-8227.

VIRGINIA

Lynchburg
Diocese of Richmond

Nott Homes, Inc., 3009-3011 Roundelay Rd., Lynchburg, 24502. Tel: 434-239-0722; Fax: 434-239-1042.

Virginia Beach
Diocese of Richmond

Assisi House, 3700 Big Ben Rd., Virginia Beach, 23452. Tel: 757-431-8522; Fax: 757-431-9776. Email: fpatroll@verizon.net.

WASHINGTON

Bellevue
Archdiocese of Seattle

Champion House, 1800 145th Pl., S.E., Bellevue, 98007-6209. Tel: 425-644-4477; Fax: 425-746-0438.

Elbert House, 16000 N.E. 8th St., Bellevue, 98008. Tel: 206-747-5111; Fax: 425-641-3141. Email: walterg@ccsww.org.

Chehalis
Archdiocese of Seattle

Providence Place, 350 S.E. Washington Ave., Chehalis, 98532. Tel: 360-740-8389; Fax: 360-740-6504. Sponsored by The Sisters of Providence.

Chewelah
Diocese of Spokane

DominiCare, 110 S. Third St. E., P.O. Box 1070, Chewelah, 99109. Tel: 509-935-4925; Fax: 509-935-4082. Email: joan.sisco@providence.org. Web: www.providence.org. A home care/chore service in Stevens & Spokane Counties.

Everett
Archdiocese of Seattle

Providence Hospice and Home Care of Snohomish County, 2731 Wetmore Ave., #500, Everett, 98201. Tel: 425-261-4800; Fax: 425-261-4850. Web: www.providence.org/phhc.

Olympia
Archdiocese of Seattle

Providence Mother Joseph Care Center, 3333 Ensign Rd., N.E., Olympia, 98506. Tel: 360-493-4900; Fax: 360-493-4000.

Providence Sound HomeCare and Hospice, 3432 South Bay Rd., Olympia, 98506. Tel: 800-869-7062; 360-459-8311; Fax: 360-493-4657. Web: www.providence.org.

Seattle

Archdiocese of Seattle

Chancery Place, 910 Marion St., # 1307, Seattle, 98104. Tel: 206-343-9415; Fax: 206-343-0680.
Heritage House at The Market, 1533 Western Ave., Seattle, 98101. Tel: 206-382-4119; Fax: 206-382-0201. Email: heritagehouse@providence.org.
Martin Luther King. Jr., Day Home Center, 1855 S. Ln., Seattle, 98144. Tel: 206-328-5670; Fax: 206-325-5922. Email: debb@ccsww.org.
Providence Mount St. Vincent, 4831 35th Ave. S., Seattle, 98126. Tel: 206-937-3700; Fax: 206-938-8999. Email: charlene.boyd@providence.org. Web: www.providence.org/themount.
Providence Peter Claver House, 7101 38th Ave. S., Seattle, 98118. Tel: 206-721-6265; Fax: 206-721-1327. Email: duong.nguyen@providence.org.
Providence Vincent House, 1423 First Ave., Seattle, 98101. Tel: 206-682-9307; Fax: 206-682-0548. Sponsored by Providence Health and Services.
Spruce Park Apartments, 155 21st Ave., Seattle, 98122. Tel: 206-322-0450; Fax: 206-328-6637.
St. Martin's on Westlake, 2008 Westlake Ave., Seattle, 98121. Tel: 206-340-0410; Fax: 206-682-8843. Email: marians@ccsww.org.
The Franciscan, 15237 21st Ave., S.W., Seattle, 98166. Tel: 206-431-8001; Fax: 206-431-1254.

Spokane
Diocese of Spokane

Bernadette Place, Mailing Address: P.O. Box 2253, Spokane, 99210-2253. Tel: 509-326-2023. 925 N. A St., #2, Spokane, 99210-2253. This complex houses twelve developmentally delayed women; 6 units of affordable housing for persons with disabilities and special needs.
Emilie Court Assisted Living, 34 E. 8th Ave., Spokane, 99202-1202. Tel: 509-474-2550; Fax: 509-474-2618. Email: charlene.longworth@providence.org.
St. Joseph's Counseling Center dba St. Joseph Family Center N. 1016 Superior St., Spokane, 99202-2059. Tel: 509-483-6495; Fax: 509-483-1541. Email: sjfc@stjosephfamilycenter.org. Web: www.stjosephfamilycenter.org.
St. Margaret's Shelter, P.O. Box 2253, Spokane, 99210-2253. Tel: 509-624-9788; Fax: 509-624-1461. Emergency and transitional shelter for women & children.
Transitional Living Center, 3128 N. Hemlock, Spokane, 99205. Tel: 509-325-2959; 509-328-6702; Fax: 509-325-8319. Email: ktalbott@help4women.org. Web: www.help4women.org. Housing for homeless women & children.
Transitional Programs for Women, 1002 N. Superior St., Spokane, 99202. Tel: 509-328-6702; Fax: 509-325-9877. Email: dmaurer@help4women.org. Web: www.help4women.org.
Women's Hearth, 920 W. Second Ave., Spokane, 99201. Tel: 509-456-3531; Fax: 509-456-3531. Web: www.help4women.org. A safe place for women at risk.

Tumwater
Archdiocese of Seattle

Tumwater Apartments, 5701 6th Ave., S.W., Tumwater, 98501-8517. Tel: 360-352-4321; Fax: 360-352-3557.

WEST VIRGINIA

Pineville
Diocese of Wheeling-Charleston

Children's Health Care, Inc., Box 430, Pineville, 24874. Tel: 304-732-7069; Fax: 304-732-7098. Email: ecatters@marshall.edu.

Rhodell
Diocese of Wheeling-Charleston

Rhodell Health Clinic (1975) P.O. Box 158, Rhodell, 25915. Tel: 304-683-4318; Fax: 304-683-4791.

WISCONSIN

Appleton
Diocese of Green Bay

Global Outreach, Inc. (1994) 4815 Whitetail Way, Appleton, 54914. Tel: 920-734-5967. Email: boryczkabb@sbcglobal.net. Web: www.globaloutreachprogram.com.

Brookfield
Archdiocese of Milwaukee

Wheaton Franciscan Home Health and Hospice, Inc. (1986) 13950 W. Capitol Dr., Brookfield, 53005. Tel: 414-874-6161. Web: www.mywheaton.org.

Chippewa Falls
Diocese of La Crosse

L.E. Phillips Libertas Treatment Center (1977) 2661 County Hwy. I, Chippewa Falls, 54729. Tel: 715-723-5585; 800-680-4578; Fax: 715-726-3504. Email: ddachel@sjcf.hshs.org. Web: www.stjoeschipfalls.com.

Green Bay
Diocese of Green Bay

McClosky Program, Inc., 2560 Shawano Ave., P.O. Box 10357, Green Bay, 54313. Tel: 920-434-8208; Fax: 920-662-0047. A Community based residential facility for women 18 years old and over who are pregnant or in a crisis situation and in need of transitional supervision and guidance. Needs addressed are personal and family problems. Also, shelter offered during crisis or unemployment.
Our Lady of Charity Center, Inc., 2560 Shawano Ave., P.O. Box 10357, Green Bay, 54313. Tel: 920-434-8208; Fax: 920-662-0047.

Kenosha
Archdiocese of Milwaukee

Assisi Homes - Kenosha, Inc. (1994) Independent Housing for Low Income Elderly, 1860 27th Ave., Kenosha, 53140. Tel: 262-551-9821; Fax: 262-551-9843. Web: www.wfhealthcare.org.
Assisi Homes - Saxony, Inc. (1994) Independent Housing for Low Income Elderly, 1876 22nd Ave., Kenosha, 53140. Tel: 262-551-9005; Fax: 262-551-7586. Web: www.wfhealthcare.org.
Franciscan Seniors, Kenosha, Inc. (1994) 1920 27th Ave., Kenosha, 53140. Tel: 630-462-9271; 262-551-0989; Fax: 262-551-8683. Web: www.wfhealthcare.org.

La Crosse
Diocese of La Crosse

Gerard Hall, La Crosse. Tel: 608-791-3985; Fax: 608-791-7802. 8 bed home for women with AODA, MH, or Pregnancy and Parenting Issues.

Madison
Diocese of Madison

Central City Counseling Services, 30 S. Franklin St., Madison, 53703. Tel: 608-256-2358; Fax: 608-256-2350.

Marshfield
Archdiocese of Milwaukee

Ministry Home Care, Inc. (1998) Marshfield. Tel: 715-389-3802; Fax: 715-387-9950.

Milwaukee
Archdiocese of Milwaukee

Adult Day Services & Resource Center, 1919 N. 60th St., Milwaukee, 53208. Tel: 414-771-2881; Fax: 414-771-9115.
Assisi Homes - Jefferson Court, Inc. (1993) 415 E. Knapp St., Milwaukee, 53202. Tel: 414-271-5370; Fax: 414-271-5988. Web: www.wfhealthcare.org.
Daystar, Inc., P.O. Box 2130, Milwaukee, 53201-2130. Tel: 414-385-0334; Fax: 414-385-0336. Email: daystar@daystarinc.org. Web: www.daystarinc.org. Transitional living program for formerly battered women without children, for up to two years.
Eastside Senior Services (1974) 2618 N. Hackett Ave., Milwaukee, 53211. Tel: 414-961-0661; Fax: 414-961-0661. Email: eastside@interfaithmilw.org. Corporate Title: Eastside Senior Services, Inc. - an Interfaith Outreach Program; Sponsored by SS. Peter and Paul, Lake Park Lutheran Church, ELCA, St. Mark's Episcopal Church, Plymouth Church, United Church of Christ, Our Lady of Divine Providence, Three Holy Women, Epikos Church, Immanuel Presbyterian, Cathedral of St. John the Evangelist, Old St. Mary's and Summerfield United Methodist, Milwaukee.
Rosalie Manor Community & Family Services, Inc., 4803 W. Burleigh St., Milwaukee, 53210. Tel: 414-449-2868; Fax: 414-449-2870. Email: d.groshek@rmcfs.org. Web: www.rosaliemanor.org. Community Programs that strengthen Milwaukee families by empowering parents to be nurturing & by guiding youth toward positive futures.
Sacred Heart Rehabilitation Institute, Inc. (1955) 2025 E. Newport Ave., Milwaukee, 53211. Tel: 414-326-1740; Fax: 414-326-1739. Ascension Health System.
St. Charles Youth and Family Services, Inc. (1920) 151 S. 84th St., Milwaukee, 53214. Tel: 414-476-3710; Fax: 414-778-5985. Email: scarpenter@stcharlesinc.org. Web: www.stcharlesinc.org.

Mount Calvary
Archdiocese of Milwaukee

Cristo Rey Ranch, Inc., N8102 Calvary St., Mount Calvary, 53057. Tel: 920-753-2026; 920-753-3211; Fax: 920-753-3100. Email: wbodden@villalorettonh.org; nunbetterfarm@hotmail.com. Provides weekend respite services to families caring for emotionally/behaviorally challenged children and adolescents. Program emphasis on pet therapy. Some day and evening programs thru County Social Services Department.

New Berlin
Archdiocese of Milwaukee

Adult Day Services & Resource Center, 13700 W. National Ave., New Berlin, 53151. Tel: 262-782-0740; Fax: 262-782-0024. Other Offices: Beaver Dam, Brookfield, Burlington, Fond du Lac, Fontana, Kenosha, Menomonee Falls, Port Washington, West Bend.

Oshkosh
Diocese of Green Bay

The Convent Project, Inc., 449 High Ave., Oshkosh, 54901. Tel: 920-233-1894. Email: baker8983@sbcglobal.net. For victims of domestic abuse.

Prairie du Chien
Diocese of La Crosse

Villa Succes, Prairie du Chien, 53821. Tel: 608-326-8424; Fax: 608-326-8638. 12 bed halfway house for AODA and AODA outpatient and Detox programs.

Rhinelander
Diocese of Superior

Retired Senior Volunteer Program, 1835 N. Stevens St., Ste. 22, Rhinelander, 54501. Tel: 715-362-1919.

Superior
Diocese of Superior

Retired Senior Volunteer Program, 1416 Cumming Ave., Superior, 54880. Tel: 715-394-4425; Fax: 715-394-5951.

Two Rivers
Diocese of Green Bay

Sisters Treatment Home, 3904 Martin Ln., Two Rivers, 54241. Tel: 920-553-1524; Fax: 920-553-2442. For physically and mentally handicapped children.

Woodruff
Archdiocese of Milwaukee

Dr. Kate Newcomb Convalescent Center, Inc. (1980) Woodruff. Tel: 715-356-8888; Fax: 715-356-8861.

WYOMING

Casper
Diocese of Cheyenne

Shelter, 324 E. H St., P.O. Box 1557, Casper, 82602. Tel: 307-577-8026; Fax: 307-577-0125.

An Alphabetical List of Diocesan and Religious Priests of the United States

REPORTED TO THE PUBLISHERS FOR THIS ISSUE
(Cardinals, Archbishops, Bishops, Archabbots and Abbots are listed in previous section)
ABBREVIATIONS

A.A.	Assumptionists
B.C.S.	Brothers of Christian Service
B.G.S.	Little Brothers of the Good Shepherd
B.S.O.	Basilian Salvatorian Fathers
C.F.A.	Alexian Brothers
C.F.C.	Congregation of Christian Brothers
C.F.M.M.	Brothers of Our Lady, Mother of Mercy
C.F.P.	Brothers of the Poor of St. Francis
C.F.R.	Franciscan Friars of the Renewal
C.F.X.	Brothers of St. Francis Xavier
C.I.C.M.	Missionhurst Congregation of the Immaculate Heart of Mary
C.J.	Josephite Fathers
C.J.M.	Congregation of Jesus and Mary
C.M.	Congregation of the Mission
C.M.C.	Congregation of Mother Coredemptrix
C.M.F.	Claretian Missionaries
C.M.I.	Carmelites of Mary Immaculate
C.M.L.M.	The Congregation of Maronite Lebanese Missionaries
C.M.M.	Congregation of Mananhill Missionar- ies, Marianhill Fathers & Brothers
C. M.Vd.	Mekhitarist Fathers
C.O.	Oratorians
C.P.	Congregation of the Passion
C.P.M.	Congregation of the Fathers of Mercy
C.PP.S.	Society of the Precious Blood
C.R.	Congregation of the Resurrection
C.R.	Theatine Fathers
C.R.I.C.	Canons Regular of the Immaculate Conception
C.R.L.	Canons Regular of the Lateran
C.R.M.	Adorno Fathers
C.R.S.	Somascan Fathers
C.R.S.P.	Clerics Regular of St. Paul
C.S.	Missionaries of St. Charles Scalabrin- ians
C.S.B.	Basilian Fathers
C.S.C.	Brothers of the Congregation of Holy Cross
C.S.C.	Priests of the Congregation of Holy Cross
C.S.J.	Congregation of St. Joseph
C.S.J.B.	Congregation of St. John the Baptist
C.S.P.	Paulist Fathers
C.S.P.X.	Brothers of Saint Pius X
C.S.S.	Stigmatine Fathers and Brothers.
C.S.Sp.	Congregation of the Holy Spirit
C.SS.R.	Redemptorist Fathers
C.S.V.	Clerics of St. Viator
D.L.P.	Diocesan Labor Priests
Er.Cam.	Camaldolese Hermits of the Congregation of Monte Corona
F.C.	Brothers of Charity
F.D.P.	Sons of Divine Providence
F.F.I.	Franciscan Friars of the Immaculate
F.F.S C.	Franciscan Brothers of the Holy Cross
F.I.C.	Brothers of Christian Instruction
F.J.	Congregation of St. John
F.M.M.	Brothers of Mercy
F.M.M.	Missionary Fraternity of Mary
F.M.S.	The Marist Brothers
F.M.S.I.	Sons of Mary Missionary Society
F.P.M.	Presentation Brothers
F.S.C.	Brothers of the Christian Schools
F.S.E.	Brothers of the Holy Eucharist
F.S.P.	Brothers of St. Patrick
F.S.R.	Brothers of the Congregation of Our Lady of the Holy Rosary
F.S.S.P.	Priestly Fraternity of St. Peter
G.H.M.	The Glenmary Home Missioners
H.J.D.	Los Hermanos de Juan Diego
H.M.C.	Hermits of Mount Carmel
I.C.	Institute of Charity
I.C.	Incarnational Consecration
I.H.M.	Brothers of the Immaculate Heart of Mary
I.M.C.	Consolata Missionaries
I.S.S.S.	Schoenstatt Institute of Secular Priests
L.B.S.F.	Little Brothers of Saint Francis
L.C.	Legionaries of Christ
M.Afr.	Missionaries of Africa
M.C.B.S.	Missionary Congregation of the Blessed Sacrament
M.C.C.J.	Comboni Missionaries of the Heart of Jesus (Verona)
M.Des.	Mercedarios Descalzos
M.E.P.	Paris Foreign Mission Society
M.G.	Guadalupe Missioners
M.H.M.	Mill Hill Missionaries
M.I.C.	Congregation of Marians of the Immaculate Conception
M.J.	Missionaries of St. Joseph (Mexico)
M.M.	Maryknoll
M.S.	The Missionaries of Our Lady of La Salette
M.S.A.	Missionaries of the Holy Apostles
M.S.C.	Missionaries of the Sacred Heart
M.S.F.	Congregation of the Missionaries of the Holy Family
M.S.P.	Missionaries of St. Paul
M.Sp.S.	Missionaries of the Holy Spirit
M.SS.CC.	Missionaries of the Sacred Hearts of Jesus and Mary
O.A.R.	Order of the Augustinian Recollects
O.Carm.	Carmelite Fathers and Brothers
O.Cart.	Order of Carthusians
O.C.D.	Discalced Carmelite Fathers
O.Cist.	Cistercian Fathers
O.C.S.O.	The Cistercian Order of the Strict Observance (Trappists)
O.de.M.	Order of Our Lady of Mercy
O.F.M.	Franciscan Friars
O.F.M-.Cap.	The Capuchin Friars
O.F.M-.Conv.	Conventual Franciscans
O.H.	Hospitaller Brothers of St. John of God
O.I.C.	Order of the Imitation of Christ
O.L P.	Brothers of Our Lady of Providence
O.M.	Minim Fathers
O.Mar.	Congregation of Maronite Monks
O.M.I.	Oblates of Mary Immaculate
O.M.V.	Oblates of the Virgin Mary
O.P.	Order of Preachers (Dominicans)
O.Praem.	Canons Regular of Premontre
O.R.C.	Operarios del Reina de Cristo
O.S.A.	The Augustinians
O.S.B.	Benedictine Monks
O.S.B-.Cam.	Camaldolese Hermits
O S.B.M.	Order of St. Basil the Great
O.S.C.	Canons Regular of the Order of the Holy Cross
O.S.Cam.	Camillian Fathers and Brothers
O.S.F.	Congregation of the Religious Brothers of the Third Order Regular of St. Francis
O.S.F.	Franciscan Brothers of Christ the King
O.S.F.	Franciscan Brothers of the Third Or- der Regular
O.S.F.	Franciscan Missionary Brothers of the Sacred Heart of Jesus
O.S.F.S.	Oblates of St. Francis de Sales
O.S.J.	Oblates of St. Joseph
O.S.M.	Servites
O.S-.P.P.E.	Pauline Fathers
O.Ss.S.	Brigittine Monks
O.SS.T.	Order of the Holy Trinity
P.I.M.E.	Pontifical Institute for Foreign Missions
R.C.J.	Rogationist Fathers
S.A.	Franciscan Friars of the Atonement
S.A.C.	Society of the Catholic Apostolate
S.C.	Brothers of the Sacred Heart
S.C.	Servants of Charity
S.Ch.	Society of Christ
Sch.P.	Piarist Fathers.
S.C.J.	Congregation of the Priests of the Sacred Heart
S.D.B.	Salesians of Don Bosco
S.D.S.	Society of the Divine Savior
S.D.V.	Vocationist Fathers
S.F.	Sons of the Holy Family
S.F.M.	Scarboro Foreign Missions
S.J.	Jesuit Fathers and Brothers
S.M.	Society of Mary (Marianists)
S.M.	Marist Fathers
S.M.A.	Society of African Missions
S.M.M.	Montfort Missionaries
S.M.P.	Society of Our Mother of Peace
S.O.Cist.	Cistercian Monks of the Strict Obser- vance
S.O.L.T.	Society of Our Lady of the Most Holy Trinity
s.P.	Servants of the Paraclete
S.P.S.	St. Patrick Missionary Society
S.S.	Society of the Priests of Saint Sulpice
S.S.C.	Society of St. Columban
SS.CC.	Congregation of the Sacred Hearts of Jesus and Mary
S.S.E.	Society of Saint Edmund
S.S.J.	St. Joseph's Society of the Sacred Heart
S.S.P.	Pauline Fathers and Brothers
S.S.S.	Congregation of the Blessed Sacrament
S.S.T.	Missionary Society of St. Thomas the Apostle
S.T.	Missionary Servants of the Most Holy Trinity
S.X.	Xaverian Missionary Fathers
S.V.D.	Society of the Divine Word
T.O.R.	Third Order Regular of Saint Francis
V.C.	Vincentian Congregation (India)
V.D.C.	Verbum Dei Community

The letters in parentheses designate the diocese. See the "Diocesan Abbreviations". Letters in brackets designate categories in the Institution Section.

A

Aapengnuo, Clement '88 (ARL) Arlington, VA St. Charles Borromeo.

Aaron, Andrew '96 (BAL) Walkersville, MD St. Timothy; Priest Personnel Board.

Aaron, Shawn *l.c.* '02 (ATL)[B] Dawsonville, GA Southern Catholic College.

Abad, Jose Antonio P. '82 (AGN) Tumon, GU Blessed Diego Luis de San Vitores Church; Archdiocesan Presbyteral Council.

Abalahin, Emiel *o.carm.* '06 (PMB) Boca Raton, FL St. Jude.

Abalon, Danilo *s.o.l.t.* '89 (SEA) Seattle, WA St. Alphonsus.

Abalon, Jose Amante M. '01 (NEW) On Duty Outside the Archdiocese.

Abalon, Jose M. (BO) Brockton, MA St. Patrick.

Abalon, Jose Manuel M. '00 (NEW) On Duty Outside the Archdiocese.

Aban, Adolfo Aristotle '83 (MO) DEPARTMENT OF VETERANS AFFAIRS HOSPITALS AND CHAPLAINS.

Abanulo, Athanasius '90 (NSH) Nashville, TN Assumption.

Abara, Lawrence N. '78 (LAF) Chataignier, LA Our Lady of Mount Carmel; Breaux Bridge, LA Our Lady of Mercy.

Abarrategui, Leandro *o.f.m.* '54 (SJN) Carolina, PR Santa Clara de Asis.

Abarratelegui, Leanadro *o.f.m.* '68 (SJN).

Abas, Peter '86 (ROC) Rochester, NY St. Thomas the Apostle; [K] Rochester, NY Sisters of Mercy of the Americas – New York, Pennsylvania, Pacific West Community; Rochester, NY St. Cecilia; Rochester, NY Christ the King.

Abata, Russell J. *c.ss.r.* '57 (NY)[EE] New York, NY Redemptorist Priests and Brothers, C.Ss.R.

Abaya, Pascual '96 (HON) Pearl City, HI Our Lady of Good Counsel.

Abba, Matthew '94 (NY) Mount Sinai Medical Center.

Abbatiello, Robert *o.f.m.cap.* (NY) New York, NY Good Shepherd.

Abbot, Kerry M. *o.f.m.conv.* '90 (MO) Air Force Chaplains.
Abbott, Donald S. '73 (CHR) Walterboro, SC St. Anthony.
Abbott, Eugene J. '57 (STP) Retired.
Abbott, Gregory E. '07 (STP) St. Michael, MN St. Michael.
Abbott, Kerry *o.f.m.conv.* '90 (MRY)[F] Arroyo Grande St. Joseph Cupertino Province, Provincial Center.
Abbott, William M. *s.j.* '72 (FgM) New York, NY Society of Jesus.
Abdallah, Geoffrey (SAM) Brooklyn, NY Cathedral of Our Lady of Lebanon.
Abdella, Peter *c.s.p.* '85 (LA)[AA] Los Angeles, CA University of California, Los Angeles, University Catholic Center; Los Angeles, CA St. Paul the Apostle.
Abdelsamad, Bashir Eldaw '86 (NSH)[F] Nashville, TN St. Thomas Hospital; Nashville, TN Christ the King.
Abdoo, Louis *i.m.c.* '73 (SB) Riverside, CA St. Francis de Sales.
Abe, John Adam '84 (RIC) Williamsburg, VA St. Bede.
Abegg, Victor P. *o.f.m.conv.* '74 (MRY) Pismo Beach, CA St. Paul the Apostle.
Abel, Robert M. '73 (L) Payneville, KY St. Mary Magdalen of Pazzi; Payneville, KY St. Theresa.
Abele, Alan Carl '73 (ANC) Retired.
Abell, Edward '67 (GAL) Houston, TX Retired.
Abella, Ray *o.s.f.s.* '93 (STO) Jamestown, CA Sierra Conservation Center.
Abellan, Jose Antonio Murcia '01 (CHI) Chicago, IL St. James.
Abels, Kevin P. '03 (BRK)[B] Elmhurst, NY Cathedral Preparatory Seminary of the Immaculate Conception; Vocations, Office of.
Abercrombie, Jamie M. *c.s.b.* '73 (GAL) Angleton, TX Most Holy Trinity; [B] Sugar Land, TX Basilian Fathers of Sugarland.
Abernethy, David S. *c.o.* '94 (PIT)[M] Pittsburgh, PA Congregation of the Oratory of St. Philip Neri; [P] Pittsburgh, PA Carnegie–Mellon University; [P] Pittsburgh, PA Chatham College; [P] Pittsburgh, PA University of Pittsburgh; Pittsburgh, PA.
Abert, Richard *s.j.* '76 (RC) Pine Ridge, SD Saint Ignatius Loyola; Pine Ridge, SD Holy Rosary; [C] Pine Ridge, SD Jesuit Community of Holy Rosary Mission; Pine Ridge, SD Our Lady of Sorrows.
Abi–chedid, Elie '85 (SAM) Jacksonville, FL St. Maron Maronite.
Abi–Sarkis, Elias '75 (OLL) Tulsa, OK St. Therese of the Child Jesus Maronite Catholic Church.
Abi–Sarkis, Elias '75 (TLS)[E] Tulsa, OK Saint Francis Hospital.
Abiamiri, Anthony (BAL) Baltimore, MD St. Anthony of Padua.
Abler, Lawrence E. *o.f.m.cap.* '64 (GB) Appleton, WI St. Joseph; [J] Appleton, WI St. Joseph Friary.
Abmayr, George J. *s.m.* '56 (CLV)[N] Cleveland, OH Marianist Community.
Aboagye–Tawiah, Joseph '86 (BRK) Bayside, NY Sacred Heart of Jesus.
Abog, Nestor *c.m.r.* '01 (CHR) Goose Creek, SC Immaculate Conception.
Aboh, Bede C. '88 (KNX) Alcoa, TN Our Lady of Fatima; Townsend, TN St. Francis of Assisi; Presbyteral Council.
Abomo, Paul Tango *s.j.* '07 (CHI)[C] Chicago, IL Jesuit Community at Loyola University Chicago.
Aboody, Rt. Rev. Charles '62 (NTN) Presbyteral Council Retired.
Aboyi, James *v.c.* '04 (TUC) Kearny, AZ Infant Jesus of Prague Roman Catholic Parish – Kearny.
Abraham, Anthony '08 (STV)[B] Catholic Charismatic Renewal; Charismatic Movement; St. Thomas, VI Holy Family Parish.
Abraham, Johnson C. '88 (OAK) Washington Hospital; Fremont, CA Holy Spirit.
Abraham, Joseph '90 (RNO) Judicial Vicar/Officialis; Curia; Priest Personnel Board; Diocesan Board of Consultors; Presbyteral Council; Reno, NV St. Rose of Lima.
Abraham, Mathew K. *a.l.c.p.* '99 (SP) Zephyrhills, FL St. Joseph Catholic Church.
Abraham, Thaddeus J. '91 (BRK) Flushing Hospital and Medical Center; Flushing, NY Mary's Nativity.
Abrahamczyk, Kazimierz *s.v.d.* '85 (MEM) Polish Catholic Ministry; Memphis, TN St. John's; Korean Catholic Ministry; [F] Memphis, TN Society of the Divine Word (Chicago Province).
Abrahams, John J. '79 (BAL) Retired.
Abrahim, Jirjis '67 (EST) Eparchial College of Consultors; West Bloomfield, MI St. Thomas Chaldean Catholic Parish.
Abramovic, Joseph M. *o.f.m.* '60 (STL) St. Louis, MO St. Joseph.
Abrego, Martin '92 (SJ) San Jose, CA St. Patrick.
Abreu, John E. '74 (PRO) Warren, RI St. Thomas the Apostle.
Abruzzese, Rev. Msgr. John A. '74 (BO) On Duty Outside the Archdiocese.
Abruzzese, Joseph A. '90 (PRO) Absent on Leave.
Absalon, Burt H. '01 (RCK) Loves Park, IL St. Bridget.
Abts, John J. *o.f.m.* '90 (FWT)[H] Crowley, TX St. Maximilian Kolbe Friary.
Abts, John *o.f.m.* '84 (FWT)[G] Crowley, TX St. Francis Village, Inc.
Abu–Lail, Samir '94 (NTN) Presbyteral Council; Seattle, WA St. Joseph Mission.
Abuah–Quansah, Francis '76 (LC) La Crosse, WI St. Joseph; Defensor Vinculi; Rockland, WI St. Peter.
Abuan, Antonio G. *m.s.* '84 (SB) Apple Valley, CA Our Lady of the Desert; Lucerne Valley, CA St. Paul.
Abuan–Gaona, Antonio G. '84 (SB) Council for Consecrated Life; [I] Apple Valley, CA Missionaries of Our Lady of La Salette. MS.
Abucewicz, Rev. Msgr. John A. '44 (BO) Senior Priests. Retired.
Abugel, Alexander G. '80 (BRK) Long Island City, NY St. Patrick.
Aburto, Elias Juan Tello *o.s.b.* '01 (SFS)[F] Marvin, SD Blue Cloud Abbey.
Abwanda, Joseph Okanda *o.c.d.* '05 (MIL)[P] Milwaukee Provincial Offices – Discalced Carmelites.
Acaba, Jose A. '82 (ARE) Quebradillas, PR San Raphael; Director of Youth.
Accardi, Joseph N. '90 (PH) Philadelphia, PA St. Bernard.
Accinni Reinhardt, Michael D. '01 (PHX) Glendale, AZ Our Lady of Perpetual Help Roman Catholic Parish.
Acebias, Anacleto '80 (BRK) Flushing, NY Mary's Nativity.
Acerbi, Luigi *p.i.m.e.* '50 (PAT)[N] Wayne, NJ P.I.M.E. Missionaries Residence.
Acero, Roman A. '08 (R) Chapel Hill, NC St. Thomas More.
Acervo, Lee E. '08 (DET) Plymouth, MI Our Lady of Good Counsel.
Acevedo, Antonio '73 (MIA) Retired.
Acevedo, Bertulfo '56 (ARE) Retired.
Acevedo, Edward '97 (MGZ) Las Marias, PR Immaculate Heart of Mary.
Acevedo, Jaime H. '99 (MIA) Miami, FL Mother of Our Redeemer.
Acevedo, Juan Burgos *o.p.* '89 (PCE) Yauco, PR Holy Rosary.
Acevedo, Luis H. '51 (ELP) Retired.
Acevedo, Milton '09 (ARL) Woodbridge, VA Our Lady of Angels.
Achadinha, James M. (BO) Cambridge, MA St. Anthony of Padua.
Achbach, Kevin Lee '03 (RC) Timber Lake, SD Holy Cross; [E] Philip, SD Priest Retirement and Aid Association/Pension Plan Board.
Acho, Jorge '95 (ARL) Falls Church, VA St. Anthony's.
Ackah, Jerome Francis '92 (RVC) Oceanside, NY South Nassau Communities Hospital.
Acker, Karl H. '63 (MIL) Retired.
Acker, Thomas S. *s.j.* '63 (DET)[K] Detroit Jesuit Provincial Office–Detroit Province of the Society of Jesus.
Ackeret, Dennis '68 (MIL) Eagle, WI St. Theresa; Archdiocesan Consultors.
Ackerman, Donald K. '61 (EVN) Clergy Personnel Board Retired.
Ackerman, J. Thomas '97 (BIR) Guntersville, AL St. William; Diocesan College of Consultors; Priests'/Presbyteral Council.
Ackerman, Phillip '78 (FAR) Grand Forks, ND Holy Family Church of Grand Forks; Deanery 3.
Ackerman, Raymond K. '91 (OKL) Norman, OK St. Thomas More University Parish; [K] Norman, OK Campus Ministry for the Archdiocese of Oklahoma City; Council of Priests Archdiocesan; Personnel Committee; Campus Ministry, Department of; Council of Priests Archdiocesan.
Acklin, Thomas *o.s.b.* '80 (GBG) President's Council:; [G] Latrobe, PA Saint Vincent Archabbey.
Aclan, Alejandro '93 (LA) Pomona, CA St. Madeleine.
Aclan, Alex '93 (LA) San Gabriel Region; Secretary & Treasurer.
Acob, Augusto '80 (OAK) Livermore, CA St. Charles Borromeo.
Acosta, Dempsey '99 (NY) New York, NY St. Agnes.
Acosta, Francisco '70 (BWN) Brownsville, TX Our Lady of Guadalupe.
Acosta, Jorge E. '02 (NEW) Hackensack, NJ Holy Trinity.
Acosta, Oscar M. Aguilera *o.s.m.* '05 (CHI)[N] Chicago Order of Friar Servants of Mary (Servites) United States of America Province, Inc.
Acosta, Raul *s.d.b.* (NY) Port Chester, NY Our Lady of the Rosary.
Acosta, Yovanny '96 (BRK) Jackson Heights, NY Our Lady of Fatima.
Acosta–Escobar, Bill John '02 (R) Pinehurst, NC Sacred Heart; Robbins, NC Saint Juan Diego.
Acquaro, Philip Anthony *c.s.b.* '70 (GAL)[O] Houston, TX Dillon House Retired.
Acrea, John '62 (DM) Retired.
Acrea, John '62 (STP)[A] St. Paul, MN St. John Vianney Seminary; [C] St. Paul, MN University of St. Thomas.
Acri, John A. '65 (HBG) Lancaster, PA St. Anthony of Padua Retired.
Acton, Rev. Msgr. John A. '48 (LA) Retired.
Acton, Thomas M. '57 (LA) Gardena, CA Maria Regina Retired.
Acuna–Delgado, Jesus '06 (TUC) Somerton, AZ Immaculate Heart of Mary Roman Catholic Parish – Somerton.
Adackapara, Matthew '60 (TR) Retired.
Adain, Dieuseul '98 (NEW) Elizabeth, NJ Our Lady of Most Holy Rosary/St. Michael.
Adajar, Winnie "Wayne" '98 (ORG) Fountain Valley, CA Holy Spirit.
Adam, Charles A. '86 (DAV)[A] Davenport, IA St. Ambrose University; [A] St. Ambrose University.
Adam, Nicholas J. '76 (DAV) Grinnell, IA St. Mary's; Diocesan Consultors.
Adam, Richard A. '88 (DAV) Kalona, IA Holy Trinity; Riverside, IA St. Mary of the Assumption; Riverside, IA St. Joseph.
Adamcik, Bryan F.J. '96 (NEW) Harrington Park, NJ Our Lady of Victories.
Adamczak, David *s.d.s.* '00 (MET) Great Meadows, NJ SS. Peter and Paul.
Adamczyk, Pawel *s.j.* '07 (WDC)[N] Washington, DC The Jesuit Community at Georgetown University.
Adame, Alejandro *c.s.v.* '00 (CHI)[N] Arlington Heights Viatorian Province Center–Clerics of St. Viator.
Adamiak, Rev. Msgr. Mitred Leo '46 (SJP) Presbyters Retired.
Adamian, Antoine '70 (OLN) Farmington, MI St. Vartan's.
Adamich, Albert R. '48 (CHI) Evergreen Park, IL Most Holy Redeemer Retired.
Adamko, Rev. Msgr. Cyril A. '53 (Y) Retired.
Adamo, Robert B. '98 (BRK) Brooklyn, NY Immaculate Heart of Mary; Art and Architecture Commission.
Adams, Alvin J. '67 (PIT)[C] Pittsburgh, PA Bishop Canevin High School, Inc.; Pittsburgh, PA Ascension.
Adams, Augustine C. (BRK) Flushing, NY Holy Family.
Adams, Daniel '80 (P) Absent on Leave.
Adams, David (KAL) Diocesan Consultors; Presbyteral Council Members; Presbyteral Council Members Retired.
Adams, Dudley R. C. *s.j.* '92 (BO)[U] Weston, MA Campion Health Center, Inc.
Adams, Edmond F. '52 (SC) Retired.
Adams, Rev. Msgr. George J. '50 (STU) Retired.
Adams, Rev. Msgr. George '50 (E) Retired.
Adams, Harry J. '68 (NO) Metairie, LA St. Philip Neri.
Adams, James F. '04 (STP) New Market, MN St. Nicholas.
Adams, James P. '82 (ATL)[C] Fayetteville, GA Our Lady of Mercy Catholic High School; Special or Other (Arch)Diocesan Assignment.
Adams, James '09 (KAL) Graduate Studies.
Adams, Joel K. *s.j.* '95 (P)[D] Portland, OR Jesuit High School.
Adams, John E. '69 (WDC) Special Ministries; [V] Washington, DC Community of Christ.
Adams, John Michael '85 (BIR) Birmingham, AL St. Peter the Apostle.
Adams, Joseph M. *o.s.b.* '09 (GBG)[G] Latrobe, PA Saint Vincent Archabbey.
Adams, Michael J. '59 (CHI) Chicago, IL Christ the King Retired.
Adams, Michael J. '06 (TYL) Presbyteral Council; Carthage, TX St. William of Vercelli.
Adams, Michael T. '68 (MRY) Retired.
Adams, Richard '65 (NY) New York, NY St. Agnes.
Adams, Rev. Msgr. Robert '45 (OAK) Retired.
Adams, Rodney T. '91 (OM) Omaha, NE St. Patrick (Elkhorn).
Adams, Sandy (LEX)[D] Ashland, KY Our Lady of Bellefonte Hospital, Inc.
Adams, Stephen E. '81 (DEN) Aurora, CO St. Pius X; Deaneries; Elected Representatives from Deanery to Presbyteral Council; College of Consultors.
Adams, T. Edmund *o.s.b.* '89 (PRO)[P] Portsmouth, RI Abbey of St. Gregory the Great.
Adams, Terrance *t.o.r.* '67 (WH) Moundsville, WV St. Francis Xavier's.
Adams, Thomas J. '64 (OM) Retired.
Adams, Walter C. '84 (NY) Absent on Sick Leave Retired.
Adams, William *c.ss.r.* '63 (LA) Whittier, CA St. Mary of the Assumption; [P] Whittier, CA Redemptorists of Whittier Retired.
Adams, William '78 (VEN) Fort Myers Beach, FL Ascension.
Adamski, Donald *o.f.m.conv.* '75 (LSC)[D] Mesilla Park, NM Holy Cross Retreat and Friary.
Adamski, John S. '71 (ATL) Atlanta, GA Our Lady of Lourdes.
Adamson, Fredrick J. '95 (PHX)[G] Phoenix, AZ Mount Claret Roman Catholic Retreat Center; Moderator of the Curia; Vicar General; College of Consultors; Finance and Administration; Presbyteral Council.
Adamson, Joseph J. '90 (CAM) Representatives by Deaneries; Gloucester County Deanery; Clergy Health Panel; Pitman, NJ Our Lady Queen of Peace R.C.

Church, Pitman N.J.
Adamson, Milton N. *c.s.c.* '66 (PHX) Phoenix, AZ St. Joseph's Hospital; [F] Phoenix, AZ Holy Cross Congregation/Casa Santa Cruz.
Adamson, Milton *c.s.c.* (FTW)[H] Notre Dame Congregation of Holy Cross, Indiana Province, Provincial House.
Adan, Aurelio '69 (CGS)[B] Aibonito, PR Casa Manresa; Diocesan Consultors; Priests Senate.
Adathiparampil, Thomas '87 (SYM) Loganville, GA Holy Family Knanaya Catholic Church.
Addai, Augustine '98 (NY) Yorktown Heights, NY St. Patrick.
Addari, Enzo '76 (LAN)[E] Chelsea, MI St. Louis Center for Exceptional Children & Adults.
Adebowale, Raymond (CHI) Chicago, IL St. Clotilde.
Adegboyega, John–Rita '00 (WOR) Worcester, MA St. Peter.
Adejoh, Patrick O. '92 (MO) DEPARTMENT OF VETERANS AFFAIRS HOSPITALS AND CHAPLAINS.
Adejoh, Patrick '92 (JC) Columbia, MO Veterans' Administration Medical Center.
Adekola, Patrick (NY) Spring Valley, NY St. Joseph.
Adeleke, Albert (WDC)[B] Washington, DC St. Joseph's Seminary.
Adeletta, David *o.p.* '98 (FgM) New York, NY Province of St. Joseph (Eastern).
Adelman, Norbert *c.pp.s* '56 (CIN)[N] Carthagena, OH St. Charles Retired.
Adelmann, Edward *o.carm.* '75 (JOL)[L] Darien Carmelite Provincial Office; Darien, IL Provincial Headquarters, Carmelite Provincial Office.
Adeniji, Michael (CHY) Cheyenne, WY St. Mary's Cathedral.
Adessa, Rev. Msgr. Dominick J. '47 (BRK) Retired.
Adewole, Olusola *o.p.* (HBG)[I] Carlisle, PA Dickinson School of Law; Carlisle, PA Saint Patrick.
Adhana, Gabre–Tinsaye '47 (GAL)[L] Houston, TX Pope John Paul XXIII Priests' Residence Retired.
Adhav, Satish Baburao '06 (BLX) Biloxi, MS Our Lady of Fatima.
Adibe, Anthony *c.s.sp.* '91 (DM)[D] Des Moines, IA Mercy Medical Center.
Adimakkeel, Joy Joseph '80 (MAR) Bessemer, MI St. Sebastian; Wakefield, MI Immaculate Conception of the Blessed Virgin Mary; [B] Bessemer, MI St. Sebastian School Endowment Fund; Vicars Forane.
Adione, Joachim '96 (NY) Bronxville, NY St. Joseph; Lawrence Hospital.
Adiukwu, Richard U. '96 (LKC) Cameron, LA Our Lady Star of the Sea; Cameron, LA Sacred Heart of Jesus; Grand Chenier, LA St. Eugene.
Adkins, Howard R. '07 (BR) Independence, LA Mater Dolorosa.
Adolf, Gregory P. '91 (TUC) Sierra Vista, AZ Saint Andrew the Apostle Roman Catholic Parish – Sierra Vista.
Adolfo, Geoffrey '00 (FgM) Boston, MA St. James the Apostle, Inc.
Adongo, Nicholas Olonde *o.c.d.* '07 (MIL)[P] Milwaukee Provincial Offices – Discalced Carmelites.
Adonizio, Joseph J. '56 (SCR) Retired.
Adorno, Anibal '92 (DAL) Dallas, TX St. Augustine Catholic Church.
Adrian, Stephen J. '39 (NU) Retired.
Adrian, Stephen J. '68 (STP) St. Paul, MN St. Matthew.
Adrian, Stephen '39 (PHX) Gilbert, AZ St. Anne Roman Catholic Parish Retired.
Adrians, Rev. Msgr. Thomas M. '67 (PBL) Pueblo, CO Christ the King; Vicar General; Presbyteral Council–College of Consultors; Presbyteral Council; Clergy Assemblies; Clergy Conference of the Diocese of Pueblo.
Adrians, Rev. Msgr. Thomas '67 (PBL) Personnel.
Adu, Martin K. '75 (MIA) Miami, FL St. James; Special Assignment.
Adu–Kwaning, Stephen '84 (NY) Bronx, NY St. Raymond.
Aduaka, Anthony '04 (LEX) Special Assignment.
Aduri, Chinnappa Reddy (NY) Ellenville, NY St. Mary and St. Andrew.
Aduri, Tom '03 (KCK) Meriden, KS St. Aloysius; Perry, KS St. Theresa's.
Adversario, Efran F. '89 (MO) Air Force Chaplains.
Adversario, Efren '89 (AGN) On Duty Outside the Archdiocese.
Aelavanthara, Anthony '68 (ALX) Powhatan, LA St. Francis of Assisi.
Aelavanthara, Antony '68 (ALX) College of Consultors; Appointed Members; Deans.
Aerts, John F. '02 (FAR) Lakota, ND St. Mary's Church of Lakota; Lakota, ND St. Lawrence O'Toole's Church of Michigan; Lakota, ND St. Joseph.
Afagbegee, Edmund Kofi *s.v.d.* '86 (OAK) Oakland, CA St. Bernard.
Affelt, Francis *o.f.m.* '52 (FTW)[I] Mishawaka, IN St. Francis Provincialate.
Affelt, Francis '52 (GRY)[H] Cedar Lake, IN Our Lady of Lourdes Friary.
Affonso, Alexander '68 (SJ) Absent on Sick Leave.
Affrim, Rev. Msgr. Richard '73 (LA) Sherman Oaks, CA St. Francis de Sales.
Afful, Samuel Ebulley '83 (BRK) Flushing, NY St. Ann.
Afoakwah, John Yaw '92 (ROC) Owego, NY Blessed Trinity; Owego, NY St. Patrick.
Afunugo, Emmanuel *d.d.* '83 (AMA) On Duty Outside the Diocese.
Agaloos, Reinerio '89 (NEW) Rahway, NJ St. Mary's.
Agamba, Clement (TUC) Tucson, AZ Roman Catholic Church of Saint Elizabeth Ann Seton – Tucson.
Agan, Rev. Msgr. Jose '70 (NEW) Retired.
Aganbi, Isaac '79 (NY) Mount Vernon, NY Mount Vernon Hospital.
Agapito, John *c.p.m.* '89 (LEX) Berea, KY St. Clare.
Agar, Bartholomew A. *o.praem.* '58 (GB)[J] De Pere, WI St. Norbert Abbey.
Agbagwa, Godswill (BAL)[N] Baltimore, MD St. Elizabeth Rehabilitation and Nursing Center.
Agbakwuo, John O. '91 (LR) Searcy, AR St. James; Searcy, AR St. Richard Church; Heber Springs, AR St. Albert Church.
Agbasiere, John *s.m.m.m.* '96 (BEL) Mound City, IL St. Patrick; Mound City, IL St. Catherine; Mound City, IL Church of the Immaculate Conception–St. Mary.
Agbenu, Rev. Msgr. Peter '72 (VIC) Victoria, TX Holy Family of Joseph, Mary & Jesus.
Agber, Philip *c.s.sp.* '01 (PH)[F] Bensalem, PA Holy Ghost Preparatory School; [Y] Bensalem, PA Congregation of the Holy Spirit.
Agbulu, Abel (BAL) Baltimore, MD St. Cecilia; Baltimore, MD Immaculate Conception.
Ageas, Cesar R. '83 (SAC) Special Assignment; Sacramento International Airport; Sacramento, CA Divine Mercy.
Agele, Comfort *c.s.c.* '04 (FTW)[H] Notre Dame Congregation of Holy Cross, Indiana Province, Provincial House.
Aggeler, Vincent *c.ss.r* '58 (KC)[J] Kansas City, MO Redemptorists Fathers of Kansas City, Missouri; Kansas City, MO Our Lady of Perpetual Help.
Agi, Lawrence '99 (SD) Scripps Mercy Hospital; San Diego, CA Holy Spirit; [H] San Diego, CA Scripps Mercy Hospital.
Agila, Vincente '91 (GAL) Houston, TX St. Cecilia.
Agliardo, Michael J. *s.j.* '94 (BUF)[O] Buffalo, NY Canisius Jesuit Community Inc.
Agnese, Sergio Dall *c.s.* '79 (WDC) Riverdale, MD Our Lady of Fatima Parish.
Agnew, Francis H. *c.m.* '60 (STL)[O] St. Louis, MO Lazarist Residence.
Agnew, Francis H. *c.m.* '60 (FgM) Earth City, MO Western Province.
Agnew, John C. '90 (POD)[JJ] New York, NY Prelature of the Holy Cross and Opus Dei; New York.
Agoha, Christopher *s.m.m.m.* '96 (BAK) La Grande, OR Our Lady of the Valley; Board of Education; Defenders of the Bond and Promoters of Justice; Council of Priests and Diocesan Consultors.
Agostinelli, Gianni *c.s.* '86 (ORL) Mount Dora, FL St. Patrick's; Leesburg, FL St. Paul's.
Agostino, Emil *o.carm.* (JOL)[L] Darien Carmelite Provincial Office Retired.
Agostino, Joseph V. *c.m.* '83 (PH)[B] Philadelphia, PA DePaul Novitiate.
Agostino, Steven J. *s.j.* '93 (Y) Girard, OH St. Rose.
Agresti, Albert A. *s.j.* '94 (BO)[U] Boston The Society of Jesus of New England–Provincial Offices.
Agresti, Albert A. *s.j.* '80 (MAN) Dartmouth–Hitchcock Medical Center.
Agresti, Frank P. '03 (PAT) Mendham, NJ St. Joseph's; Girl Scouting; Presbyteral Council.
Agu, Paschalis (CHI)[J] Chicago, IL St. Anthony Hospital.
Agudelo, Alvaro Mejia *o.s.m.* '04 (ORG) Fullerton, CA St. Philip Benizi.
Agudelo, German Correa '00 (FR) Fall River.
Agudelo, German Correa (FR) Fall River, MA Cathedral of St. Mary of the Assumption.
Agudo, Moises '97 (SFR) San Francisco, CA St. Charles Borromeo.
Agudo, Teodoro *o.f.m.cap.* '54 (NO) New Orleans, LA St. Theresa of Avila.
Aguera, Jorge *d.c.j.m.* (DEN) Littleton, CO St. Mary.
Aguggia, Rev. Msgr. Steven J. '93 (BRK) Middle Village, NY St. Margaret; [X] Brooklyn, NY Pro Sanctity Movement; Officialis–Judicial Vicar; Diocesan Judges; Committee for Eastern Orthodox–Catholic Relations; [X] Middle Village, NY National Italian Apostolate Conference.
Agughara, Fidelis '88 (BUR)[D] Burlington, VT St. Joseph/Kervick Home; Burlington, VT Fletcher Allen Health Care.
Aguilar, Arturo *s.s.c.* '84 (OM)[K] St. Columbans, NE Missionary Society of St. Columban.
Aguilar, Benjamin *o.carm.* '94 (CHI)[D] Chicago, IL; [N] Chicago Carmelite Priory of St. Cyril.
Aguilar, Benjamin *o.carm.* '94 (JOL)[L] Darien Carmelite Provincial Office.
Aguilar, Francis V. '09 (LA) Santa Fe Springs, CA St. Pius X.
Aguilar, Francisco Javier Aceves *o.f.m.* (LAR) Hebbronville, TX Our Lady of Guadalupe.
Aguilar, Genaro P. *c.s.c.* '83 (SCR)[C] Holy Cross Community.
Aguilar, Javier '98 (OAK) Walnut Creek, CA St. Mary.
Aguilar, Luis Roberto *o.p.* '92 (SAT) San Antonio, TX St. Ann; [L] San Antonio, TX Dominican Priory of San Juan Macias.
Aguilar, Ricardo '95 (AUS) Bastrop, TX Ascension Catholic Church.
Aguilar, Rogelio Mur *o.carm.* '56 (MGZ) Anasco, PR St. Anthony Abbot.
Aguilera, Salvador '84 (ELP) On Duty Outside of Diocese; Navy Chaplains.
Aguirre, Eduardo '08 (SB) San Bernardino, CA Our Lady of Hope Catholic Community, Inc.
Aguirre, Ignacio *o.s.b.* '53 (FAJ)[B] Humacao, PR San Antonio Abad Abbey of the Order of St. Benedict.
Aguirre, Jesus (BAL) Lansdowne, MD St. Clement.
Aguirre, Juan Carlos '99 (TUC) Eloy, AZ Saint Helen of the Cross Roman Catholic Church – Eloy.
Aguirre, Nery *o.f.m.* '74 (FgM) New York, NY Franciscan Province of the Immaculate Conception.
Aguirre, Osmar R. '93 (YAK) Prosser, WA Sacred Heart; Diocesan Consultors.
Aguirre, Rosalino *o.r.c.* (PCE) Adjuntas, PR St. Joachim.
Aguirre–Garza, Jesus *o.f.m.* '96 (STL)[O] St. Louis Franciscan Friary of St. Anthony of Padua; U.S. Religious Serving Elsewhere.
Aguste, Jean–Miguel '93 (BRK) Brooklyn, NY St. Jerome.
Agustin, Honesto '82 (RNO) Reno, NV St. Therese Church of the Little Flower.
Agustin, Richard *m.m.* '85 (FgM) Maryknoll, NY MARYKNOLL.
Aguwa, Henry *s.m.m.m.* '04 (PBL) Delta, CO St. Michael.
Aguwa, Jude '78 (NY) Croton Falls, NY St. Joseph.
Aguzey, William K. '93 (BRK) Jackson Heights, NY St. Joan of Arc.
Agwu, John Okeke *s.m.m.m.* '04 (FRS) Planada, CA Sacred Heart; Merced, CA Our Lady of Mercy/St. Patrick's.
Agwuoke, Emmanuel S. *c.s.sp.* (DM) Des Moines, IA St. Augustin's.
Agyemano, Rev. Msgr. Seth (NY) Nyack, NY St. Ann.
Agyepong, Alexander '00 (NY) Nyack, NY St. Ann.
Ahabyona, Titus '97 (OWN) Judges; Owensboro, KY St. Pius Tenth.
Ahanotu, Leonard '94 (TLS) Bixby, OK St. Clement of Rome; Diocesan Senators.
Ahearn, Donald J. '51 (CHI) Chicago, IL St. Juliana Retired.
Ahearn, John F. *m.m.* '73 (FgM) Maryknoll, NY MARYKNOLL.
Ahearn, John F. *m.m.* '73 (NY)[EE] Maryknoll Maryknoll Fathers and Brothers.
Ahearn, Richard F. '60 (BO) Senior Priests. Retired.
Ahearn, Thomas A. *m.m.* '68 (NY)[EE] Maryknoll, NY Maryknoll Fathers and Brothers Charitable Trust; [EE] Maryknoll Maryknoll Fathers and Brothers Retired.
Ahern, Bernard '54 (ALB) Retired.
Ahern, Bernie '54 (STA) Jacksonville, FL St. Joseph's.
Ahern, Dennis P. *s.j.* '70 (CIN)[F] Cincinnati, OH St. Xavier High School; [N] Cincinnati, OH Jesuit Community at St. Xavier High School.
Ahern, Rev. Msgr. John B. '54 (NY) New York, NY Our Lady of Loreto; [I] New York, NY Holy Name Centre for Homeless Men, Inc. Retired.
Ahern, John S. '54 (HRT) Retired.
Ahern, John V. '67 (SY) DeWitt, NY Holy Cross.
Ahern, Thomas W. '94 (BRK) Brooklyn, NY St. Augustine; Presbyteral Council.
Ahern, Thomas W. '48 (NOR) Old Lyme, CT Christ the King Retired.
Aherne, James *m.s.* '73 (SPR) Holyoke, MA Immaculate Conception.
Aherne, P. Vincent *c.m.* '52 (STL)[O] St. Louis Vincentian Residence.
Ahlbach, William J. '62 (SFR) San Mateo, CA St. Matthew.
Ahlemeyer, Richard J. '77 (BRK) Rockaway Beach, NY Saint Camillus–Saint Virgilius; Presbyteral Council.
Ahler, Richard H. *s.j.* '61 (MIL)[P] Wauwatosa, WI Jesuit Community at St. Camillus.
Ahles, Donald M. '71 (RCK) Sterling, IL St. Mary; Diocesan Consultors.
Ahlin, Robert J. '71 (PIT) Pittsburgh, PA Holy Angels; Judges.
Ahlstrom, Michael P. '69 (CHI) Brookfield, IL St. Barbara; Vicar for the Diaconate Community.
Ahn, Chol–Min (SD) San Diego, CA St. Columba.
Ahn, Peter *o.s.b.* '02 (PAT)[N] Newton, NJ St. Paul's Abbey.
Ahn, Simon Hyo–Sung '91 (RIC) Hampton, VA St. Rose of Lima; Hampton, VA Catholic Community of the Korean Martyrs.
Aho, Charles A. '70 (SY) Liverpool, NY Developmental Center; Special Assignment.
Ahrens, William B. '51 (STL) Retired.
Ahrensfield, Michael E. '80 (ALN) Lehighton, PA SS. Peter and Paul.

Ahumanda, Jose E. *c.s.c.* '83 (FTW)[H] Notre Dame Congregation of Holy Cross, Indiana Province, Provincial House.
Aiardi, Reno *i.m.c.* '65 (SB) San Bernardino, CA Mission Office of the Diocese of San Bernardino; Riverside, CA St. Francis de Sales.
Aichele, Raymond P. '58 (CIN) Retired.
Aidoo, Thomas '85 (RVC) Stony Brook, NY Stony Brook University Hospital.
Aiello, Anthony '69 (DM) Retired.
Aiello, John D. '69 (MIL) Racine, WI St. Joseph; Defenders of the Bond.
Aigner, Edward M. '72 (WIL) Salisbury, MD St. Francis De Sales; Eastern Correctional Institution.
Aiken, Rev. Msgr. Lloyd E. '70 (BAL) Glyndon, MD Sacred Heart.
Aiken, Rev. Msgr. Lloyd (BAL) Priest Personnel Board.
Aiken, Richard J. '70 (MIL) Milwaukee, WI St. Sebastian.
Ailer, Gellert Jozsef '06 (WDC) Gaithersburg, MD St. John Neumann.
Aime, Moise '80 (RVC) Lindenhurst, NY Our Lady of Perpetual Help.
Aineto, Louis *s.d.b.* (CHI) Chicago, IL St. John Bosco.
Ainikkal, Jose *c.m.i.* '85 (CAM) Marmora, NJ Church of the Resurrection, Marmora, N.J.; Woodbine, NJ St. Casimir's R.C. Church, Woodbine, N.J.
Airdi, Reno *i.m.c.* '65 (SB) Special or Other Diocesan Assignment.
Aisa, Francisco *sch.p.* (PCE) Ponce, PR Our Lady of Mt. Carmel.
Aita, Mark C. *s.j.* '83 (PH)[C] Jesuit Fathers; [Y] Loyola Center and Manresa Hall.
Aitcheson, William M. '88 (ARL) Chantilly, VA St. Timothy.
Ajamie, Albert '50 (IND) Retired.
Ajanma, Emmanuel '03 (BUR) Barre, VT St. Monica.
Ajemian, David J. '01 (BO) Health Leave.
Ajewole, Michael *m.s.p.* '96 (AUS) Austin, TX Holy Cross; [G] Austin, TX Missionary of St. Paul, MSP.
Ajibola, Peter '77 (WDC) Suitland, MD St. Bernardine.
Ajiboye, Michael (CHI) Chicago, IL St. Clotilde.
Ajiki, Pius T. '84 (WDC) Riverdale Park, MD St. Bernard.
Ajoko, Donatus O. '95 (BR)[F] Baton Rouge, LA Our Lady of the Lake Regional Medical Center.
Akajiufor, Pius '96 (LC)[D] Spiritual Services Dept.
Akalawa, Ambrose (LAF) On Special Assignment.
Akalue, Emmanuel '94 (ORL) Dunnellon, FL St. John the Baptist; African Ministry.
Akamike, Romanus Arinze '89 (SAN) Coleman, TX Sacred Heart; Winters, TX Our Lady of Mt. Carmel.
Akange, Stephen '86 (IND) Batesville, IN St. Louis.
Akano, Francis '99 (BAK) Council of Priests and Diocesan Consultors; Merrill, OR St. Augustine.
Akao, Michio *s.v.d.* '03 (WDC)[N] Washington, DC Divine Word House.
Akara, Boniface *c.m.f.* (PHX) Grand Canyon, AZ El Cristo Rey Roman Catholic Parish.
Akata, Anietie '94 (KNX) Johnson City, TN St. Mary.
Akeriwe, Raymond A. '03 (LFT) Zionsville, IN St. Alphonsus.
Akers, Bert *s.j.* '61 (BAL) Towson, MD Church of the Immaculate Conception; [S] Baltimore, MD Colombiere Jesuit Community.
Akho, Daniel '90 (HRT) Hartford, CT Cathedral of St. Joseph.
Akiki, Joseph G. '87 (SAM) Olean, NY St. Joseph.
Akin–Otiko, Peter '96 (STA) Jacksonville, FL St. Matthew's; Defenders of the Bond.
Akinlolu, Anthony *o.p.* '04 (WDC) Washington, DC Children's Medical Center; [W] Mount Rainier, MD Dominican Fathers & Brothers Inc. Province of Nigeria; Washington, DC National Rehabilitation Hospital; Washington, DC Washington Hospital Center.
Akiona, Lane *ss.cc.* '81 (HON) Honolulu, HI St. Augustine by the Sea; Office of Clergy Priest Retirement Committee; Presbyteral Council; Members; Members.
Akkalayil, Binoy *o.ss.t.* '05 (BAL)[S] The Trinitarians in India (Bangalore & Trichur).
Akoury, Tony (SAM) Uniontown, PA St. George.
Akpa, Onwuham *o.praem.* '04 (JKS)[E] Raymond, MS Priory of St. Moses the Black; Canton, MS Holy Child Jesus; Canton, MS Sacred Heart.
Akpabio, Felix '78 (BRK) Cambria Heights, NY Sacred Heart.
Akpan, Tersur Melchizedek *v.c.* '06 (TUC) Maricopa, AZ Our Lady of Grace Roman Catholic Parish – Maricopa.
Akpoghiran, Peter O. '92 (RIC) Tribunal Staff; Richmond, VA St. Patrick.
Akpunonu, Peter Damian *s.s.l.* '66 (CHI)[A] Mundelein, IL University of St. Mary of the Lake/Mundelein Seminary.
Akpunonu, Raymond (RVC) Dix Hills, NY St. Matthew.
Aksamit, Stanley J. '77 (SPR) Turners Falls, MA Our Lady of Peace; Presbyteral Council.
Akwue, Francis *c.s.sp.* '71 (MIA) Pompano Beach, FL St. Henry.
Al–Shaikh, Emad Hanna '00 (OLD) Saint Joseph's Mission; La Mesa, CA Our Mother of Perpetual Help Parish.
Alabart, Francis X. '40 (FRS) Retired.
Alagia, Vincent de P. *s.j.* '58 (CHL) Charlotte, NC St. Peter; [J] Mooresville, NC Jesuit Community.
Alaharasan, V. Antony '65 (NOR) North Stonington, CT St. Thomas More; Members.
Alam, Alam '81 (NTN) Retired.
Alamo, Emiliano '64 (PCE) Coamo, PR San Antonio de Padua.
Alamo, Jose *c.s.sp.* '85 (ARE) Orocovis, PR Our Lady of Fatima.
Alanis, Francisco Martin *c.o.r.c.* '03 (SB) San Bernardino, CA Our Lady of Guadalupe.
Alappat, Antoo '94 (BIR) Lanett, AL Holy Family.
Alappat, Joy '81 (NEW) Garfield, NJ Church of Our Lady of Sorrows; Garfield, NJ Syro–Malabar Catholic Mission of New Jersey; Chaplain to the India Catholic Association (Syro–Malabar Rite).
Alappat, Joy '81 (SYM) Garfield, NJ Blessed Kunjachan Syro–Malabar Catholic Mission, Staten Island, NY.
Alarcon, Felix '63 (RVC) Retired.
Alarcon, Rev. Msgr. Juan '64 (SFR) San Francisco, CA St. Anne Retired.
Alaribe, Ogechukww Kieran *o.s.b.* '91 (PBL) Trinidad, CO Most Holy Trinity, Trinidad Area Catholic Community (Trinidad Cluster).
Alava, Andres *o.a.r.* '63 (LSC) Anthony, NM St. Anthony's; Vicars; Presbyteral Council.
Alava, Basilio S. *o.s.a.* (NY) New York, NY Holy Rosary.
Alayón, Hermenegildo '79 (CGS) Caguas, PR Divino Nino.
Albacete, Rev. Msgr. Lorenzo '73 (WDC) On Duty Outside the Archdiocese.
Alba Infante, Saul '02 (BAK) Boardman, OR Our Lady of Guadalupe.
Albaladejo, Juan A. '85 (MET) On Duty Outside the Diocese.
Alban, Arthur P. '87 (GAL) Houston, TX Christ the Redeemer.
Albanese, Charles *o.c.s.o.* '05 (DEN)[N] Snowmass, CO St. Benedict's Monastery.
Albano, Alwyn M. '90 (MO) Army Chaplains.
Albano, Arturo L. '74 (SFR) San Francisco, CA Mission Dolores Basilica.
Albano, George M. '44 (TR)[N] Trenton, NJ St. Lawrence Rehabilitation Center Retired.
Albano, Peter J. *c.m.* '68 (MET)[I] Princeton, NJ Vincentian Residence.
Albano, Vincent *s.o.l.t.* '72 (CC)[G] Robstown, TX Society of Our Lady of the Most Holy Trinity.
Albarano, Richard '68 (LA) Burbank, CA St. Francis Xavier.
Albarracin, Luis '67 (VEN) LaBelle, FL Our Lady Queen of Heaven.
Albee, Rev. Msgr. Paul A. '84 (LA) Deanery 4.
Albee, Rev. Msgr. Paul M. '84 (LA) Moorpark, CA Holy Cross; Members.
Albenesius, Paul M. '97 (OM) Jackson, NE St. Patrick.
Alber, Michael '02 (GR) Grand Rapids, MI St. John Vianney.
Alber, Thomas L. '85 (JC) Marshall, MO St. Peter.
Alberg, Leo W. '91 (LA) Gardena, CA Maria Regina.
Albero, Steven J. *o.praem.* '92 (PH)[Y] Paoli, PA Daylesford Abbey.
Albers, Austin *o.f.m.* '64 (SFD) Montrose, IL St. Rose of Lima; Teutopolis, IL St. Francis of Assisi; [L] Teutopolis, IL St. Francis Assisi Friary.
Albers, Edwin *o.f.m.* '61 (STL)[O] St. Louis, MO Franciscan Friary of St. Anthony of Padua.
Albers, George *c.pp.s.* '62 (CIN)[N] Carthagena, OH St. Charles Retired.
Albers, James R. *o.s.b.* '00 (KCK)[I] Atchison, KS St. Benedict's Abbey; Atchison, KS.
Albers, Thomas *c.pp.s.* '67 (KC) Liberty, MO St. James.
Albert, Andrew *s.m.* (BO) Pastoral Care; Boston, MA.
Albert, Claude J. '64 (PRT) Diocesan Priests' Benefit Plan – Trustees Retired.
Albert, James R. '86 (PRT) Madawaska, ME Notre Dame du Mont Carmel Parish; Van Buren, ME Saint Peter Chanel Parish.
Albert, Patrick L. '92 (SCR) Forest City, PA Sacred Heart of Jesus; Pleasant Mount, PA St. James.
Alberth, Regis R. '80 (PIT) Allegheny County, PA Marian Manor, Inc.; [J] Pittsburgh, PA Marian Manor Corp.
Albertine, Richard P. *m.m.* '66 (FgM) Maryknoll, NY MARYKNOLL.
Alberts, Edward T. '75 (NSH) Brentwood, TN Holy Family; Deans.
Albertson, Eric J. '86 (ARL) On Duty Outside the Diocese; Military Chaplains; Army Chaplains.
Albertson, Lawrence '65 (KCK) Bucyrus, KS Queen of the Holy Rosary.
Albietz, Henry F. '74 (CIN) Fayetteville, OH St. Angela Merici; Fayetteville, OH St. Michael.
Albino, Brian E. '79 (FR) Fall River, MA St. Anthony of Padua.
Albino, Ramon E. '84 (MGZ) Aguadilla, PR La Milagrosa; [A] Aquadilla, PR Corpus Christi College.
Albosta, John T. '64 (SCR) Waymart, PA St. Mary.
Albrecht, Craig L. '95 (SAG) Bay City, MI St. Mary of the Assumption; Diocesan Council of Catholic Women.
Albrecht, James W. '58 (NY)[JJ] New York, NY Prelature of the Holy Cross and Opus Dei; New York.
Albrecht, Louis Henry '86 (BAK) La Grande, OR Our Lady of the Valley Retired.
Albrecht, Tomasz (NOR) Niantic, CT St. Agnes.
Albright, Matthew '07 (Y) Canton, OH St. Michael the Archangel.
Albright, R. Gerard *s.j.* '58 (DET)[K] Detroit, MI Jesuit Community at the University of Detroit Mercy.
Albright, Robert E. '72 (BAL) Retired.
Alburquerque, Messias '03 (FR) Falmouth, MA St. Patrick's; Vineyard Haven, MA Good Shepherd.
Alcantara, Miguel B. '65 (CHI) Other Assignments.
Alcarria, Antonio Munoz '64 (CGS) Caguas, PR San Pedro Apostol.
Alcazar, Emanuel '89 (ELP) El Paso, TX St. Paul the Apostle; Presbyteral Council.
Alcazar, Victor H. '01 (RCK) DeKalb, IL St. Mary.
Alchouefati, Kamil (SAM) Cary, NC Saint Sharbel Mission.
Alciati, Paul J. '77 (SY) Utica, NY Our Lady of Lourdes.
Alco, James J. '90 (SCR) Wilkes–Barre, PA St. Therese; Unassigned or Leave of Absence Retired.
Alcocer, Jose '60 (ELP) El Paso, TX San Jose.
Alcott, Stephen *o.p.* '01 (WIL)[O] Newark, DE Catholic Campus Ministry, Univ. of Delaware; Newark, DE University of Delaware; Newark, DE St. Thomas More Oratory; Catholic Campus Ministry.
Alcuin, William *o.f.m.cap.* '52 (GB)[J] Appleton, WI St. Fidelis Friary Retired.
Alcuino, Miguel '79 (ELP) Fort Davis, TX St. Joseph; Alpine, TX Our Lady of Peace.
Aldaz, Antonio M. '74 (LA) Baldwin Park, CA St. John the Baptist.
Alder, Ronald J. '69 (DET) Retired.
Alderson, John *o.f.m.* (PAT) Butler, NJ St. Anthony.
Aldrich, Louis G. *s.j.* '86 (FgM) Los Gatos, CA Society of Jesus.
Alecio–Rodriguez, Freddy '91 (SJN) On Duty Outside the Archdiocese.
Alejos, Raul *o.f.m.* '08 (SD) Oceanside, CA Mission San Luis Rey; [J] Oceanside, CA Mission San Luis Rey.
Alejunas, Richard P. '89 (NY)[DD] Port Chester, NY Don Bosco Community Center of Port Chester, Inc.
Alejunas, Richard *s.d.b.* '89 (NY) Port Chester, NY Our Lady of the Rosary.
Aleksa, Thomas M. '75 (E) Erie, PA St. Luke.
Alello, Michael J. '07 (BR) Labadieville, LA St. Philomena.
Alenchery, Joseph '87 (RVC) St. Margaret of Scotland.
Alengadan, George *s.d.b.* '82 (OAK) Orinda, CA Santa Maria; Deacon Council; Office of Priest and Deacon Formation.
Alers, Juan '69 (LKC) Retired.
Alesandro, Rt. Rev. Msgr. John A. '67 (RVC) Vicar General; Censors of Books; Senate of Priests (Presbyteral Council/College of Consultors); Chaplains of the Nassau County Police Department.
Alesandro, Rev. Msgr. John A. '66 (RVC) Nassau County Police Department.
Alessandrini, Raniero *c.s.* '57 (LA) Los Angeles, CA St. Peter.
Alex, Boby '94 (BR) St. Amant, LA Holy Rosary.
Alexander, Andrew *s.j.* '79 (OM)[K] Omaha, NE Jesuit Community at Creighton University.
Alexander, Fred *s.o.l.t.* '98 (CC)[G] Robstown, TX Society of Our Lady of the Most Holy Trinity.
Alexander, Fred *o.c.d.* '82 (MIL) Hubertus, WI St. Mary of the Hill; [P] Hubertus, WI Discalced Carmelite Monastery – Holy Hill Basilica of the National Shrine of Mary, Help of Christians, Holy Hill.
Alexander, John D. *s.j.* '54 (NY)[EE] Loyola Hall, Jesuit Community.
Alexander, Jon *o.p.* '86 (PRO)[P] Providence St. Thomas Aquinas Priory at Providence College.
Alexander, Jose Kadukunnel *c.m.i.* '86 (CAM) Lakeland, NJ Camden County Hospital at Lakeland.
Alexander, Joseph '73 (LAF) On Leave.
Alexander, Leon '66 (WH) Morgantown, WV St. Francis De Sales Catholic Church.
Alexander, Marc R. '85 (HON)[I] Kaneohe, HI Augustine Educational Foundation; Office of Clergy: Diocesan Screening Committee; Diocesan Board of Education; Vicar General, Moderator of the Curia, Diocesan Theologian, and Censor Liborum; Bishops Administrative Advisory Council; College of Consultors; Diocesan Finance Council; [F] Members of the Corporation:; Members; Clergy Personnel Board; Office of Clergy Priest Retirement Committee; Presbyteral Council; Diocesan Development Committee; [F] Board of Directors:; Diocesan Theological Commission; Diocesan Planning and Building Commission; Implementation Commission of Diocesan Road Map for Pastoral Program and Facility Needs.
Alexander, Marc '85 (HON) Hawaii Catholic Community Foundation.
Alexandrunas, Albert *o.f.m.cap.* '65 (WH) Belle, WV St.

John; [L] Charleston, WV Capuchins–St. Anthony Friary.
Alexius, Vincent *s.v.d.* '03 (BR) Baton Rouge, LA St. Paul the Apostle.
Alfaro, Gustavo A. '02 (NEW) On Duty Outside the Archdiocese.
Alfaro, Jose N. '03 (PMB)[A] Boynton Beach, FL St. Vincent de Paul Regional Seminary.
Alfaro, Rev. Msgr. Juan '62 (SAT) San Antonio, TX St. Rose of Lima.
Alfonso, Jairo Ariel *c.s.* (BRK) Brooklyn, NY St. Joseph Patron of the Universal Church.
Alfonso, San Juan *c.p.* '60 (SAC)[I] Citrus Heights, CA Christ the King Retreat.
Alforque, Benjamin E. *m.s.c.* '79 (SB) Riverside, CA St. Catherine of Alexandria; Riverside; Appointed Members; College of Consultors.
Algarin–Rosado, Rodney '01 (SJN) Carolina, PR San Felipe Apostol.
Ali, Peter Yakubu '82 (STP) Coon Rapids, MN Church of the Epiphany.
Alicea Rivera, Luis A. '96 (FAJ) Fajardo, PR Cathedral Santiago Apostol; [A] Fajardo, PR Colegio Santiago Apostol.
Alilonu, Augustine Chibuzo '00 (SPC) Fredericktown, MO St. Michael; [D] Cape Girardeau, MO Saint Francis Medical Center.
Alilonu, Augustine '00 (FAR) On Duty Outside the Diocese.
Alimaji, Christian A. *m.s.p.* '88 (SAV) Savannah, GA St. Benedict the Moor.
Alindogan, Peter J. '90 (TR) Defenders of the Bond; Promoter of Justice.
Alindogan, Peter James (TR) Cinnaminson, NJ St. Charles Borromeo.
Alisauskas, Peter J. '43 (SCR) Retired.
Aliunzi, Robert *a.j.* '91 (PHX) Glendale, AZ St. James Roman Catholic Parish; College of Consultors; Presbyteral Council; Deans.
Alkire, Thomas John *o.carm.* '63 (LA) Los Angeles, CA St. Raphael.
Alkire, Timothy M. '85 (LFT) Lafayette, IN St. Boniface; Vice Officialis; Greater Lafayette Catholic School Board; Presiding Judges.
Alla, Stanislaus *s.j.* '99 (BO)[U] Newton, MA The Jesuit Community at Boston College.
Allaire, Barry J. '72 (BUF) Olean, NY St. Mary of the Angels.
Allam, Show Reddy '94 (JOL) Elmhurst, IL Immaculate Conception.
Allard, George L. '60 (PRO)[P] Providence St. John Vianney Residence Retired.
Allard, Rev. Msgr. John C. '75 (PRO) Woonsocket, RI St. Agatha; Woonsocket, RI Precious Blood; [N] Woonsocket, RI Fr. Marot CYO Center.
Allard, John E. *o.p.* '86 (PRO)[P] Providence St. Thomas Aquinas Priory at Providence College.
Allard, Marcel M. '65 (MAN) Manchester, NH Ste. Marie Retired.
Allbright, Brian V. '83 (P) Newport, OR Sacred Heart Parish.
Allega, Ernest '76 (WOR) South Barre, MA St. Thomas–A–Becket.
Allegra, John Christopher '70 (L) Springfield, KY Holy Trinity; [M] St. Catharine, KY Sansbury Care Center, Inc.
Allegretto, William M. *c.m.* '85 (PH)[B] Philadelphia, PA DePaul Novitiate.
Allen, Charles H. *s.j.* '73 (BGP)[B] Fairfield, CT Fairfield University; [O] Fairfield, CT The Fairfield Jesuit Community–Fairfield University.
Allen, David E. '78 (BR) Port Allen, LA Holy Family.
Allen, David G. *s.j.* '79 (BAL)[S] Baltimore, MD Jesuit Community of Loyola University, Inc.
Allen, David '95 (DEN) Frisco, CO St. Mary; Deaneries; Elected Representatives from Deanery to Presbyteral Council.
Allen, Donald *m.m.* '67 (SJ)[M] Los Altos, CA Maryknoll.
Allen, Francis R. *s.j.* '56 (BO)[U] Weston, MA Campion Health Center, Inc.
Allen, Frederick J. *m.m.* '65 (NY)[EE] Retired.
Allen, Jeff *s.j.* (LA)[D] Los Angeles, CA Verbum Dei High School.
Allen, John A. '90 (CHL) Greensboro, NC St. Paul the Apostle.
Allen, Joseph P. *o.p.* '67 (FgM) New York, NY Province of St. Joseph (Eastern); New York, NY; New York, NY Dominican Mission Secretariate; Staff.
Allen, Joseph P. *o.p.* '67 (HRT) New Haven, CT St. Mary's Priory.
Allen, Kenneth '04 (NO) On Special Assignment.
Allen, Loren '94 (SR) Eureka, CA St. Bernard; Clergy Personnel Committee.
Allen, Nicholas '08 (NSH) Catholic Youth Office and Search Program; Franklin, TN St. Matthew; [B] Nashville, TN Father Ryan High School.
Allen, Peter A. '71 (RVC)[M] Amityville, NY St. Pius X Residence.
Allen, Peter J. *o.p.* '67 (WDC) Washington, DC St. Dominic Church & Priory.
Allen, Peter (RVC) Unassigned.
Allen, Philip T. '59 (OG) Adjutant Judicial Vicars.
Allen, Richard J. '97 (MO) Army National Guard Chaplains; On Duty Outside Diocese.
Allen, Richard L. '61 (GB) Neenah, WI St. Gabriel the Archangel.
Allen, Scott W. *f.s.s.p.* '90 (TYL) Tyler, TX St. Joseph the Worker Mission.
Allen, Shawn W. '99 (BO) Townsend, MA St. John the Evangelist.
Allen, Terry '61 (ALX) Retired.
Allende, Santiago Rivera '83 (MGZ) Mayaguez, PR Ascension.
Allender, Raymond '75 (SFR) San Francisco, CA St. Agnes.
Allender, Thomas *s.j.* '71 (SFR)[E] San Francisco, CA St. Ignatius College Preparatory (Coed); [N] San Francisco, CA Jesuit Community at St. Ignatius College Preparatory.
Aller, Domingo *o.s.a.* '61 (SJN) Bayamon, PR Santa Rita de Casia.
Allers, Rodney M. '08 (DUB) Marion, IA St. Joseph.
Alleyne, Rev. Msgr. Edward D. '60 (CAM) Judges Retired.
Allgaier, Sebastian *o.s.b.* '99 (KC) Stanberry, MO St. Peter's; [J] Conception, MO Conception Abbey.
Alliata, Peter R. '61 (WDC) Mechanicsville, MD Immaculate Conception.
Allie, Robert *o.m.i.* '51 (STP)[K] St. Paul, MN Oblate Residence.
Allie, Stanley J. '58 (ALB) Retired.
Allin, R. Benedict *o.s.b.* '67 (STL) St. Louis, MO St. Anselm; [O] St. Louis, MO The Abbey of St. Mary and St. Louis.
Alling, James '92 (PHX) Sun Lakes, AZ St. Steven Roman Catholic Parish.
Allison, Rev. Msgr. Bruce R. '61 (E) Erie, PA St. Julia; [C] Erie, PA Cathedral Preparatory School.
Allison, Jeffrey L. *c.s.c.* '96 (FTW) Members; [H] Notre Dame, IN Congregation of Holy Cross, Indiana Province, Provincial House.
Allison, Jeffrey *c.s.c.* '96 (P)[B] University of Portland; [L] Portland, OR Holy Cross Fathers & Brothers, C.S.C. – University of Portland.
Allison, Joseph C. '56 (CIN) Retired.
Allison, Michael P. '91 (E) Erie, PA St. Mark the Evangelist.
Allman, Matthew T. *c.ss.r.* '00 (WDC)[N] Washington, DC Holy Redeemer College.
Alloggia, Benoit *o.s.b.* '09 (GBG)[G] Latrobe, PA Saint Vincent Archabbey.
Allt, John F. '73 (TUC) Vail, AZ Saint Rita in the Desert Roman Catholic Parish – Vail; Directors.
Almade, Frank D. '78 (PIT) Sharpsburg, PA Saint Juan Diego Parish; Clergy Personnel Board.
Almagno, Romano S. *o.f.m.* '65 (NY)[EE] New York Franciscan Province of the Immaculate Conception.
Almagno, Romano *o.f.m.* '65 (PRO) Providence, RI Cathedral of SS. Peter and Paul.
Almarza, Juan *o.a.r.* (LSC) Anthony, NM St. Anthony's.
Almazan, Humberto *m.s.a.* '66 (NOR)[G] Cromwell Society of the Missionaries of the Holy Apostles.
Almazan, Jose A. '63 (CC) Corpus Christi, TX St. Theresa.
Almazan, Jose '63 (CC) Presbyteral Council.
Almazan, Leobardo *o.p.* '05 (NO)[P] New Orleans Dominican Friars, Southern Dominican Province of St. Martin de Porres.
Almeida, George F. '65 (FR) Retired.
Almendra, Leoncio T. '60 (NOR) Retired.
Almendras, Joel J. '75 (MRY) Salinas Valley State Prison.
Alminde, Joseph M. *s.j.* '62 (PH)[Y] Loyola Center and Manresa Hall.
Almonte, Alfred P. *c.s.* '61 (PRO) Providence, RI St. Bartholomew.
Almonte, Antonio '97 (NY) New York, NY Our Lady Queen of Martyrs.
Almonte, Yunior '05 (NEW) Ridgefield Park, NJ St. Francis of Assisi; Part–time Staff.
Almy, Rev. Msgr. Augustin '74 (MIA) Miami, FL St. James.
Alobaidi, Joseph *o.p.* '80 (WDC)[B] Washington, DC Dominican House of Studies.
Alonso, Armando '90 (MIA) Fort Lauderdale, FL St. Clement.
Alonso, Ignacio '60 (ARE) Manati, PR La Candelaria.
Alonso, Oscar *sch.p.* '68 (MIA)[C] Fort Lauderdale, FL Cardinal Gibbons High School.
Alookaran, Charles '91 (BIR) Athens, AL St. Paul's.
Alookaran, Joy '80 (BRK) Woodside, NY St. Sebastian.
Alparce, Emmanuel '99 (CHK) Kristo Rai Parish; Presbyteral Council; Diocesan Publications Office.
Alphonse, Anthony '92 (AUS) Bertram, TX Holy Cross; Burnet, TX Our Mother of Sorrows.
Alphonse, Justin Nelson *c.p.* '00 (L) Louisville, KY St. Agnes; [L] Louisville, KY Sacred Heart Retreat.
Alphonse, Satheesh C. '02 (LAN)[E] Chelsea, MI St. Louis Center for Exceptional Children & Adults.
Alphonso, John '68 (DAL) Dallas, TX St. Jude Chapel.
Alsola, Felix S. '86 (DET)[H] Southfield, MI Providence Hospital.
Alt, Kenneth G. *c.pp.s.* '78 (CIN)[N] Dayton, OH Provincial Office of the Cincinnati Province of the Society of the Precious Blood.
Altavilla, Philip A. '92 (SCR) Episcopal Vicars; Procurator/Advocates; Diocesan Commission on Ecumenism and Inter–Faith Matters; Diocesan Office of Ecumenism; Clarks Summit, PA The Slovak Catholic Federation (1911); Clarks Summit, PA Our Lady of the Snows; Diocesan Consultors.
Altavista, Salvatore D. *m.s.* '64 (HRT)[L] Hartford, CT Missionaries of LaSalette.
Altenbaugh, Richard L. '60 (PT) Retired.
Altermatt, Charles K. '08 (DET) Detroit, MI Holy Redeemer.
Altermatt, Gregory M. '76 (HRT) Special and other Archdiocesan Assignment; West Haven, CT Our Lady of Victory; [H] New Haven, CT Hospital of St. Raphael; West Haven, CT St. John Vianney.
Althoff, Arthur J. '55 (STL) Retired.
Altier, Robert J. '89 (STP)[H] Hastings, MN Regina Medical Center; [J] Hastings, MN Regina Retirement Center; Regina Medical Center.
Altine, Richard L. '95 (KAL) Scouting Apostolate; Sturgis, MI Holy Angels.
Altman, David *o.c.s.o.* '79 (SLC)[F] Huntsville, UT Abbey of Our Lady of the Holy Trinity of the Order of Cistercians; Huntsville, UT.
Altman, James T. '08 (LC) Boy Scouts; [C] Wisconsin Rapids, WI Assumption High School; [C] Wisconsin Rapids, WI Assumption Middle School.
Altman, Joseph W. '76 (CHI) Harvey, IL Ascension–St. Susanna; Markham, IL St. Gerard Majella.
Altmann, Robert T. '62 (LC) Archivist; [H] La Crosse, WI Holy Cross (Seminary) Diocesan Center Retired.
Altrui, Ronald P. '81 (NY) On Duty Outside the Archdiocese; On Leave of Absence.
Altstock, Edward '59 (P) Retired.
Altuna, Javier *s.j.* '66 (LA) Inglewood, CA St. John Chrysostom.
Alvarado, John Paul '88 (MET) South Plainfield, NJ Sacred Heart.
Alvarado, Roberto '89 (ELP) El Paso, TX El Buen Pastor Mission.
Alvarado de Jesus, Jose R. '94 (PCE) Ponce, PR San Conrado.
Alvardo de Jesus, Jose '94 (MO) Army National Guard Chaplains.
Alvares, Augustine '50 (P) Retired.
Alvares, Jacob *s.a.c.* '97 (FWT) Grapevine, TX St. Francis of Assisi.
Alvarez, Abel *o.s.a.* '58 (NY) New York, NY Holy Rosary.
Alvarez, Antonio M. '93 (MET) Bernardsville, NJ Our Lady of Perpetual Help.
Alvarez, Carlos A. '01 (PBL) Pagosa Springs, CO Immaculate Heart of Mary; Presbyteral Council–College of Consultors; Presbyteral Council; Personnel.
Alvarez, Eduardo *s.j.* '74 (MIA) Miami Dade College–Wolfson Campus; Miami, FL Gesu.
Alvarez, Enrique '03 (SAC) North Highlands, CA St. Lawrence the Martyr.
Alvarez, Fabio A. '04 (ATL) Cumming, GA St. Brendan the Navigator.
Alvarez, Fred *s.a.* '61 (NY)[EE] Garrison, NY Franciscan Friars of the Atonement.
Alvarez, Javier *o.f.m.* '89 (FRS) Delano, CA Our Lady of Guadalupe.
Alvarez, John J. '81 (POD)[P] Kirkwood, MO Prelature of the Holy Cross and Opus Dei; Kirkwood.
Alvarez, Jonathan (AGN) Defender of the Bond; Yigo, GU Our Lady of Lourdes.
Alvarez, Jose '03 (MIA)[A] Miami, FL St. John Vianney College Seminary; [C] Miami, FL St. Brendan High School.
Alvarez, Juan '88 (ARL) Alexandria, VA Good Shepherd.
Alvarez, Manuel Francisco '02 (MIA) Chaplain—Dade County – Serra Club; Parkland, FL Mary Help of Christians Church.
Alvarez, Miguel *sch.p.* '61 (PCE) Ponce, PR Our Lady of Mt. Carmel.
Alvarez, Milton *c.m.f.* '97 (SPC)[F] Springfield, MO Claretians Missionaries' Residence–Villa Claret; Aurora, MO Holy Trinity; Aurora, MO Sacred Heart.
Alvarez, Nolasco Tamayo '98 (PRO) Providence, RI St. Edward.
Alvarez, Pablo D. *f.s.s.p.* '86 (PCE) On Duty Outside the Diocese.
Alvarez, Perfecto *o.s.a.* '52 (PCE)[B] The Pontifical Catholic University of Puerto Rico.
Alvarez, Perfecto *o.s.a.* '53 (SJN) Bayamon, PR Ntra. Sra. de la Monserrate.
Alvarez, Pompilio '60 (NY) Bronx, NY St. Athanasius.
Alvarez, Porfirio '69 (LA) Oxnard, CA St. Anthony.
Alvarez, Ramon '81 (PCE)[G] Ponce, PR Prelature of the Holy Cross and Opus Dei; Ponce.
Alvarez, Ramon '82 (DAL) On Leave of Absence.
Alvarez, Xavier '73 (LA) Valinda, CA St. Martha.

Alvarez, Yuvan Arbey '04 (NEW) Kearny, NJ St. Cecilia's.
Alvarez–Garcia, Julio '75 (WDC) Retired.
Alvernaz, Dennis '71 (FRS) Retired.
Alvero, Joshua *d.s.* '99 (PHX) Mesa, AZ Holy Cross Roman Catholic Parish.
Alvero, Sammy '93 (MIA) Miami, FL Good Shepherd.
Alves, Francis '95 (WDC) Bethesda, MD St. Jane Frances de Chantal.
Alves, Rev. Msgr. Joseph T. '53 (BO) Senior Priests. Retired.
Alvey, Leonard J. '58 (OWN) Non–Parochial Assignments; [A] Owensboro, KY Brescia University; Judges.
Alvizures, Miguel A. '08 (GAL) Sugar Land, TX St. Theresa.
Alzate, Alberto '77 (LAV) North Las Vegas, NV St. Christopher.
Alzugaray, Rev. Msgr. Joseph '67 (SR) Napa, CA St. Apollinaris; Deans; Board of Consultors; Priests' Council.
Amabile, Patsy L. '73 (CAM) On Duty Outside the Diocese.
Amadeo, Michael '92 (DM) Des Moines, IA Holy Trinity; Defenders of the Bond.
Amador, Alfonso *c.ss.r.* '58 (SJN) San Juan, PR San Agustin Retired.
Amaechi, Jerome '94 (SY) North Syracuse, NY St. Rose of Lima.
Amagba, Paschal *c.m.f.* '97 (LA) Los Angeles, CA Our Lady Queen of the Angels.
Amah, Peter O. '05 (SPK) Colville, WA Immaculate Conception; Colville, WA Sacred Heart of Jesus; Colville, WA Pure Heart of Mary; Members.
Amalanathan, Chinnappan *h.g.n.* '01 (LEX)[M] Middlesboro, KY Herald of Good News Missionary Society, Inc.
Amalanathan, Chinnappan *h.g.n.* '02 (LEX) Middlesboro, KY St. Julian.
Amalanathan, Irudayaraj '91 (P) Sublimity, OR St. Boniface; Aumsville, OR St. Mary – Shaw.
Amaldoss, G. '78 (NO) Marrero, LA St. Joachim.
Amalfitano, Joseph A. '63 (PH) Marcus Hook, PA Immaculate Conception.
Amaliri, Paul Obi '00 (TLS) Air Force Reserve Chaplains; On Duty Outside the Diocese.
Amaliri, Paul (LAV) Military Chaplains.
Amalraj, Loyola '81 (NY) Croton–on–Hudson, NY Holy Name of Mary.
Aman, Gerald W. *s.j.* '73 (FgM) New York, NY Society of Jesus.
Amande, Lito D. '03 (RVC) Wantagh, NY St. Frances de Chantal.
Amandolare, Rev. Msgr. Ronald J. (PAT) Retired.
Amani, Bernard (FTW)[H] Notre Dame Congregation of Holy Cross, Indiana Province, Provincial House.
Amankwah–Danquah, Philip (NY) New York, NY St. Charles Borromeo.
Amann, John J. '66 (BRK) Brooklyn, NY Holy Family.
Amann, Steven J. '74 (MIL) Burlington, WI St. Charles.
Amann, William '54 (ROC) Penfield, NY St. Joseph Retired.
Amantia, Damian Vincent *t.o.r.* '90 (VEN) Bradenton, FL Our Lady of the Angels.
Amar, Joseph P. '74 (SAM)[B] University of Notre Dame Du Lac; On Duty Outside the Diocese.
Amar, Zab '74 (E) Coalport, PA St. Basil the Great; Ramey, PA Holy Trinity.
Amaral, Angelo '86 (TR) Riverside, NJ The Church of Jesus, the Good Shepherd, Riverside, N.J.
Amaral, Mark '04 (OAK) Pinole, CA St. Joseph.
Amaral, Stephen P. '78 (PRO) Coventry, RI Our Lady of Czenstochowa; Council Members.
Amaro, Arlindo A. *c.s.sp.* '56 (PRO) Central Falls, RI Immaculate Heart of Mary.
Amaro, Jorge '85 (NEW) Newark, NJ Our Lady of Fatima.
Amasa, Sheldon '90 (TR) Toms River, NJ St. Maximilian Kolbe.
Amato, Antonio '61 (PRT) Retired.
Amato, Frank *s.a.c.* '88 (BRK) Brooklyn, NY Our Lady of the Rosary of Pompeii; Consultors:.
Amato, Joseph '59 (ALB) Retired.
Amato, Rev. Msgr. Nicholas P. '70 (BAL) Monkton, MD Our Lady of Grace.
Amato, Salvatore '69 (BRK) Rego Park, NY Resurrection–Ascension.
Amaya, Alex Diaz '06 (ARL) Falls Church, VA St. Philip.
Amaya, Hernando Gomez '02 (SAC) Orland, CA St. Dominic.
Amayun, Alejandro A. '92 (LA) Rowland Heights, CA St. Elizabeth Ann Seton.
Ambalathingal, Robert *o.c.d.* '96 (BRK) Brooklyn, NY Holy Name; [S] Indian Latin Rite Apostolate.
Amberger, Frank G. '96 (CIN) Russia, OH St. Remy.
Ambert, Jorge *s.j.* '66 (SJN) San Juan, PR Nuestra Senora del Carmen.
Ambert–Rivera, Jorge (SJN) Judges.
Ambooken, Jose '75 (NY) Bronx, NY St. Margaret Mary.
Ambosta, Dawson '75 (NY) Bronxville, NY St. Joseph.
Ambrogi, James J. '64 (PH) Malvern, PA St. Patrick.
Ambrose, John Peter *m.s.f.s.* '98 (KAL) Bangor, MI Sacred Heart of Jesus; Permanent Diaconate.
Ambrose, John Peter *m.s.f.s.* '98 (TYL)[B] Whitehouse, TX The Missionaries of St. Francis de Sales.
Ambrose, Joseph *o.c.d.* '98 (LA) Downey, CA St. Raymond.
Ambrose, Malcolm '72 (LA) Santa Clarita, CA St. Clare.
Ambrosio, Rev. Msgr. Joseph F. '74 (NEW) Newark, NJ Our Lady of Mt. Carmel; Ironbound Deanery 21; Members; Italian Apostolate.
Ambrosy, David J. '85 (DUB)[H] Cedar Rapids, IA Mercy Medical Center–Cedar Rapids; Cedar Rapids, IA St. Matthew; Deanery Representatives.
Ameche, William *s.j.* '81 (SD) San Diego, CA Our Lady of Guadalupe.
Amedee, Rev. Msgr. Francis '48 (HT) Retired.
Amen, Maurice E. *c.s.c.* '61 (FTW)[H] Notre Dame Congregation of Holy Cross, Indiana Province, Provincial House.
Ament, Richard J. '66 (DUB) Cresco, IA Notre Dame.
Ament, Robert J. '52 (DUB) Retired.
Amepparambil, John Xaviour '98 (CC) Port Aransas, TX St. Joseph.
Amerando, Jerry '84 (FRS) Easton, CA St. Jude.
Amershek, Charles M. '75 (ALT) On Sabbatical.
Ames, Gregory '86 (DEN) Northglenn, CO Immaculate Heart of Mary; Deaneries; Elected Representatives from Deanery to Presbyteral Council.
Ames, John J. '82 (PH) On Special or Other Archdiocesan Assignment; Conshohocken, PA St. Matthew; [BB] Philadelphia, PA Newman Apostolate for Archdiocese of Philadelphia; Office for Catechetical Formation.
Amesse, Michael *o.m.i.* '84 (BWN) Brownsville, TX Immaculate Conception Cathedral.
Amey, Rev. Msgr. Robert G. '69 (WDC) Rockville, MD St. Mary; Advocates; [W] Rockville, MD Archdiocesan Council of Catholic Women.
Amezaga, Louis (LSC) Absent On Leave.
Amezcua, Alfonso '87 (LA) Los Angeles, CA Immaculate Conception.
Amezcua, Pedro Enrique (SB)[I] Corona, CA Confraternity of Operarios Del Reino De Cristo, C.O.R.C.
Amian, Arthur '89 (HON) Kula, HI Our Lady Queen of the Angels.
Amico, Alexander D. '73 (E) Erie, PA St. Paul.
Amico, Charles R. '52 (BUF)[A] East Aurora, NY Christ the King Seminary Retired.
Amico, Francis A. *c.s.b.* '75 (GAL)[O] Sugar Land Basilian Mission Center.
Amidar, Venancio '78 (ORG) Cypress, CA St. Irenaeus.
Amidon, Philip R. *s.j.* '74 (OM) Omaha, NE St. John; [K] Omaha, NE Jesuit Community at Creighton University.
Amiot, Ronald J. *s.j.* '78 (BAL) Towson, MD; [S] Baltimore, MD Jesuit Community of Loyola University, Inc.; [B] Jesuit Community of Loyola University, Inc.; [S] Towson, MD Maryland Province of the Society of Jesus.
Amiot, Ronald J. *s.j.* '78 (BO)[U] Boston The Society of Jesus of New England–Provincial Offices.
Amir, Andrews '90 (SFR)[A] Menlo Park, CA St. Patrick Seminary and University.
Amiro, Raymond M. '43 (SFE) Retired.
Amissah, Kofi Ntsiful '79 (ALB) Albany, NY Sacred Heart of Jesus; Menands, NY St. Joan of Arc.
Ammering, Bruce F. '54 (ROC)[K] Rochester, NY Sisters St. Joseph of Rochester Retired.
Amo, Steven '92 (SPR) Feeding Hills, MA Sacred Heart.
Amora, Eduardo '90 (NY) Staten Island, NY Holy Rosary; Staten Island University Hospital North.
Amora, Silvano B. '77 (TR) Keansburg, NJ St. Ann.
Amos, Rev. Msgr. John R. '73 (MOB) On Leave from the Archdiocese.
Ampong, Bernard Osei '96 (SY) Rome, NY St. Peter.
Amrhein, Quentin *c.p.* '53 (HRT)[L] West Hartford Holy Family Monastery/Retreat.
Amrhein, Quentin *c.p.* '53 (BRK)[T] Jamaica, NY Immaculate Conception Monastery Retired.
Amrhein, Robert *o.f.m.conv.* '62 (SY) Binghamton, NY SS. Cyril and Method; Binghamton, NY Holy Trinity.
Amritharaj, Andrews *s.d.b.* '90 (OAK) San Leandro, CA Our Lady of Good Counsel.
Amsberry, John '97 (P) Portland, OR Church of St. Joseph the Worker.
Amundsen, Rev. Msgr. Robert L. '69 (DEN) Lafayette, CO Immaculate Conception.
Amy, Rev. Msgr. Peter L. '64 (LA) Sylmar, CA St. Didacus.
Amyot, Andrew J. '64 (OG) Norfolk, NY Visitation of the B.V.M.; Norfolk, NY St. Raymond.
Anaeche, Collins I. '08 (HRT) Hartford, CT Cathedral of St. Joseph.
Anaele, Ignatius I. '98 (CHI) South Holland, IL St. Jude the Apostle.
Anala, Anthony A. *s.v.d.* '07 (LAF) Opelousas, LA Holy Ghost.
Anandan, Rajendran '91 (LC) Custer, WI Immaculate Conception.
Anane, Francis '98 (NY) Mount Kisco, NY Northern Westchester Hospital; Mt. Kisco, NY St. Francis of Assisi.
Anania, Alexis *o.f.m.* '58 (PIT) Pittsburgh, PA St. Pamphilus.
Anarado, Ethel '01 (RVC) Mineola, NY Corpus Christi; Mineola, NY Winthrop Hospital.
Anarcon, Angelito '82 (TR) Middletown, NJ St. Mary.
Anare, Lawrence '98 (BRK) Brooklyn, NY St. Therese of Lisieux.
Anastasia, Thomas '91 (SP) Plant City, FL St. Clement; [L] St. Petersburg, FL St. Clement Housing, Inc.
Anastasio, Thomas '58 (BRK) Brooklyn, NY St. Patrick Retired.
Anatuanya, Gregory '01 (ATL) Atlanta, GA Holy Cross.
Anawonah, Frederick '95 (BRK) South Ozone Park, NY St. Clement Pope.
Anaya–Estrada, Jose–Angel '09 (MIL) Lake Geneva, WI St. Francis de Sales.
Anaya–Maida, Fernando '94 (GAL) Humble, TX St. Mary Magdalene.
Ancharski, John J. '83 (TUC) Leave of Absence; Solomon, AZ Our Lady of Guadalupe Roman Catholic Parish – Solomon.
Ancona, Rev. Msgr. Gaspar F. '63 (GR) Retired.
Anctil, Peter Claude *o.s.b.* '67 (BUR)[E] Weston, VT Priory of Benedictine Monks.
Andalas, Patricius Mutiara *s.j.* '04 (OAK)[M] Berkeley, CA Jesuit Fathers and Brothers.
Andary, John S. '51 (SAM) Retired.
Andebo, Hillary '99 (JC) Jefferson City, MO Capital Region Medical Center; Jefferson City, MO Immaculate Conception.
Andel, David '95 (SB) Special or Other Diocesan Assignment; Judicial Vicar; Judges; Yucaipa, CA St. Frances Xavier Cabrini; College of Consultors.
Anderl, Peter J. '01 (FAR) Mantador, ND Sts. Peter & Paul Church of Mantador; Mooreton, ND St. Anthony's.
Anderlonis, Rev. Msgr. Joseph J. '69 (PH) Philadelphia, PA St. George; Vicar for Consecrated Life; On Special or Other Archdiocesan Assignment.
Anders, Rev. Msgr. Arnold '50 (VIC) On Duty Outside the Diocese.
Anders, Rev. Msgr. Arnold (CC)[E] Corpus Christi, TX Mount Carmel Home.
Andersen, Emil (E) Retired.
Andersen, Eric Michael '09 (P) Beaverton, OR St. Cecilia.
Anderson, Alexander R. '75 (STL) De Soto, MO St. Rose of Lima.
Anderson, Rev. Msgr. Andrew L. '74 (MIA) Judicial Vicar; Archdiocesan Council of Catholic Women; Catholic Funeral Directors' Guild; Catholic Lawyers' Guild; Special Assignment.
Anderson, Rev. Msgr. Andrew L. '74 (SAM) Judges.
Anderson, Anthony *s.o.l.t.* '91 (CC)[G] Robstown, TX Society of Our Lady of the Most Holy Trinity.
Anderson, Arthur C. '62 (RVC) Retired.
Anderson, Arthur T. '58 (CAM) Retired.
Anderson, Arthur (CHI)[N] Chicago, IL St. Peter's Friary.
Anderson, Barg G. '05 (SUP) Somerset, WI St. Anne.
Anderson, Bertil J. '74 (PRO) Warwick, RI St. Rita.
Anderson, Daniel J. *o.f.m.* '76 (CIN)[N] Cincinnati, OH Pleasant Street Friary; Councillors:.
Anderson, David *s.j.* '97 (SEA)[L] Seattle, WA Arrupe Jesuit Community at Seattle University; [A] Seattle, WA Seattle University.
Anderson, David '83 (STN) Ukiah, CA St. Peter Eastern Catholic Mission.
Anderson, Derek *so.l.t.* '03 (CC)[G] Robstown, TX Society of Our Lady of the Most Holy Trinity.
Anderson, Edward C. *c.s.v* '50 (LAV)[C] Las Vegas, NV Clerics of St. Viator Retirement Home.
Anderson, Edward *c.s.v.* '50 (CHI)[N] Arlington Heights Viatorian Province Center–Clerics of St. Viator.
Anderson, Edward '08 (SFS) Sioux Falls, SD St. Lambert.
Anderson, Edwin C. '08 (SUP) Spooner, WI St. Catherine; Spooner, WI St. Joseph; Spooner, WI St. Francis De Sales; Presbyteral Council & Diocesan Consultors; Catholic Boy and Girl Scout Chaplain.
Anderson, Gabriel C. '89 (DUB) Dubuque, IA St. Columbkille; Due Process Board.
Anderson, George M. *s.j.* '73 (NY)[EE] New York, NY Jesuit Community of the Immaculate Conception.
Anderson, Rev. Msgr. James B. '78 (GAL)[A] Houston, TX St. Mary's Seminary.
Anderson, James *m.s.a.* '77 (NOR)[G] Cromwell Society of the Missionaries of the Holy Apostles.
Anderson, John C. '93 (SUP) Tomahawk, WI St. Francis of Assisi; Tomahawk, WI St. Mary; East Deanery; Board of Directors; Personnel Placement Board.
Anderson, Rev. Msgr. John D. '62 (FAR) Retired.
Anderson, Rev. Msgr. John E. '66 (LSC) Las Cruces, NM Holy Cross; Bishops Administrative Council; Vicar General; Director of Clergy Personnel; Defenders of the Bond; Diocesan Consultors; Presbyteral Council; Clergy Personnel Board; Finance Council; Holy Childhood Association; Propagation of the

Faith; Priests Retirement Fund Committee.
Anderson, John '96 (ATL) Without Archdiocesan Assignment or Faculties.
Anderson, Jordan S. *o.praem.* '97 (ORG)[I] Silverado, CA Norbertine Fathers of Orange Inc.
Anderson, Joseph G. '63 (MIL) New Berlin, WI Holy Apostles Retired.
Anderson, Joseph W. '62 (PEO) Retired.
Anderson, Kenneth J. '87 (CHI) DeKalb, IL St. Mary; Winnetka, IL SS. Faith, Hope and Charity.
Anderson, Kevin '83 (SCL) Braham, MN St. Peter & Paul; Zimmerman, MN St. Edward's; Zimmerman, MN St. Pius X; Presbyteral Council; Diocesan Consultors.
Anderson, Knute *o.s.b.* '56 (SCL)[I] Collegeville, MN St. John's Abbey, of the Order of St. Benedict.
Anderson, Kurt J. *m.m.* '72 (FgM) Maryknoll, NY MARYKNOLL.
Anderson, Lawrence (PAT) Pompton Lakes, NJ Our Lady of the Assumption.
Anderson, Louis '63 (GR) Retired.
Anderson, Louis '07 (NY) Peekskill, NY Assumption.
Anderson, Luke *s.o.cist.* '54 (ALN)[K] New Ringgold, PA Cistercian Monastery; New Ringgold, PA.
Anderson, Michael F. '83 (STP) St. Paul, MN Church of St. Bernard; Deanery 3; Secretary.
Anderson, Philip *o.s.b.* '84 (TLS)[G] Hulbert, OK Our Lady of the Annunciation of Clear Creek Monastery; Hulbert, OK.
Anderson, R. Bentley *s.j.* '96 (STL)[C] Saint Louis University; [O] St. Louis, MO Jesuit Community Corporation at Saint Louis University – Jesuit Hall.
Anderson, R. Bentley *s.j.* '96 (NY)[EE] Cardinal Spellman Hall, Jesuit Community.
Anderson, Richard W. *s.j.* '66 (CHI)[D] Chicago, IL St. Ignatius College Prep.
Anderson, Robert Kevin *o.c.s.o.* '55 (WOR)[O] Spencer, MA St. Joseph's Abbey.
Anderson, Robert M. *o.s.m.* '65 (CHI)[N] Chicago Order of Friar Servants of Mary (Servites) United States of America Province, Inc.
Anderson, Robert S. *o.s.m.* '65 (P)[L] Portland, OR The Grotto, The National Sanctuary of Our Sorrowful Mother.
Anderson, Ronald '72 (DET) Milford, MI St. Mary, Our Lady of the Snows.
Anderson, Shawn Matthew *o.s.b.* '07 (GBG)[G] Latrobe Saint Vincent Archabbey.
Anderson, Stephen A. '86 (E) Western Vicariate.
Anderson, Stephen A. '79 (E) Conneaut Lake, PA Our Lady Queen of the Americas.
Anderson, Steven D. '03 (LAN) Montrose, MI Good Shepherd.
Anderson, Steven '95 (LAN)[B] Flint, MI Luke M. Powers Catholic High School.
Anderson, Terence '84 (SFS) Huron, SD Holy Trinity.
Anderson, Thomas S. *s.j.* '98 (MIL)[P] Milwaukee, WI Jesuit Community at Marquette University.
Anderson, Thomas '07 (SFS) Sioux Falls, SD St. Joseph Cathedral.
Anderson, William A. '63 (WH) Retired.
Anderson, William C. '52 (TR) Retired.
Anderson, William R. '42 (BO) Senior Priests. Retired.
Andert, Thomas *o.s.b.* '75 (SCL)[I] Collegeville, MN St. John's Abbey, of the Order of St. Benedict; Collegeville, MN.
Andinam, Emmanuel '77 (CHR) Clemson, SC St. Andrew; [H] Clemson, SC Clemson University, Southern Wesleyan University & TriCounty Technical College.
Andoh, Godfrey Nana (DET) Taylor, MI St. Alfred.
Andonian, Raphael *o.mech.* '65 (OLN) Belmont, MA Holy Cross; Business Chancellor.
Andrade, Antonio L. '63 (BO) Senior Priests. Retired.
Andrade, Bernardino '65 (OAK) Retired.
Andrade, David M. '86 (FR) Fall River, MA Holy Trinity.
Andrade, J. Anthony (STP) St. Paul, MN St. Pascal Baylon.
Andrae, Henry C. '78 (E) Sharon, PA Sacred Heart.
Andraschko, Rev. Msgr. James '59 (SFS) Retired.
Andre, Leonard J. '61 (MIL) Retired.
Andre, Rev. Msgr. Ludwig '57 (SJ) Retired.
Andreano, Rev. Msgr. Michael A. '00 (NEW) Newark, NJ Cathedral Basilica of the Sacred Heart; Members; Vice Chancellor and Secretary to the Archbishop; Vice Chancellor and Secretary to the Archbishop.
Andreassi, Anthony *c.o.* '07 (BRK) Brooklyn, NY St. Boniface; [T] Brooklyn, NY Oratory of Saint Philip Neri, Congregation Pontifical Rite.
Andreassi, Anthony *c.o.* '07 (NY)[F] New York, NY Regis High School.
Andreatta, Rev. Msgr. Tullio '38 (SB) Retired.
Andree, John Paul *c.ss.r.* '68 (CHI) Chicago, IL St. Michael in Old Town; [N] Chicago, IL The Redemptorist Fathers of Chicago.
Andrejek, Michael J. '98 (PEO) Oglesby, IL Holy Family.
Andres, Edmundo *c.m.f.* '56 (MET) Perth Amboy, NJ Our Lady of Fatima.
Andres, James *o.f.m.cap.* '63 (DET) Clinton Twp., MI St. Ronald.
Andres, Napoleon *m.s.* '85 (HON) Honolulu, HI St. Anthony.
Andres, Tim *o.carm.* '86 (JOL)[L] Darien Carmelite Provincial Office.
Andrews, Alexander *o.s.b.* '69 (SCL)[I] Collegeville, MN St. John's Abbey, of the Order of St. Benedict.
Andrews, Christopher *o.s.b.* '06 (TLS)[G] Hulbert, OK Our Lady of the Annunciation of Clear Creek Monastery.
Andrews, Daniel R. '01 (OM) Elgin, NE St. Boniface; Elgin, NE St. Bonaventure; [B] Elgin, NE Pope John XXIII Central Catholic High School at Elgin.
Andrews, Dave *s.j.* '79 (CI)[C] Kolonia, Pohnpei, FM Jesuit House.
Andrews, Edward *o.s.a.* '59 (CHI)[N] Olympia Fields, IL Tolentine Monastery at Tolentine Center.
Andrews, Eric *c.s.p.* '95 (LA)[BB] Pacific Palisades, CA Paulist Productions; Los Angeles, CA St. Paul the Apostle.
Andrews, John F. '62 (FR) Wellfleet, MA Our Lady of Lourdes.
Andrews, John S. '96 (OM) Osmond, NE St. Mary of the Seven Dolors; Randolph, NE St. Frances de Chantal; Deans; Deans.
Andrews, Mark W. *s.j.* '92 (CHI)[S] The Jesuit Retreat League of Chicago.
Andrews, Peter J. '88 (PRO) Tiverton, RI St. Christopher; Tiverton, RI St. Theresa.
Andrews, Robert F. *o.s.a.* '55 (PH)[Y] Villanova, PA St. Thomas Monastery.
Andrey, Roberto A. '83 (SFR) San Bruno, CA St. Robert.
Andrie, Donald A. *c.s.p.* '94 (GR) Campus Ministry; Allendale, MI St. Luke University Parish; [K] Allendale, MI St. Luke University Parish and Catholic Campus Ministry.
Andrino, Guilherme A. *s.v.d.* '07 (TR) Techny, IL; Trenton, NJ Blessed Sacrament–Our Lady of the Divine Shepherd Parish.
Andrus, Albin A. '73 (PRT) Portland, ME St. Patrick's Retired.
Andrus, Charles *s.s.j.* '76 (NO) New Orleans, LA Blessed Sacrament–St. Joan of Arc.
Andrus, David L. *s.j.* '79 (NO)[P] Pohnpei, FM Jesuits of Pohnpei.
Andrus, David *s.j.* (CI) Diocesan Consultors; Pohnpei–Kosrae.
Andrus, Richard *s.v.d.* '83 (CHI) Chicago, IL St. Elizabeth.
Andujar, J. Iriarte *o.p.* '86 (PRO)[P] Providence St. Thomas Aquinas Priory at Providence College.
Anello, Robert *m.s.a.* '07 (NOR)[G] Cromwell Society of the Missionaries of the Holy Apostles.
Anemelu, Charles I. '97 (NEW) Englewood, NJ Englewood Hospital & Medical Center.
Angadiath, Joseph *c.m.i.* '69 (LKC) Lake Charles Memorial Hospital; Lake Charles, LA Sacred Heart of Jesus.
Angel, A. Oliver '01 (BWN) Associate Judges; Canonical Assistance.
Angel, Ariel O. '01 (BWN) Mission, TX Our Lady of the Holy Rosary.
Angel, Fredy A. '05 (SAV) Adel, GA Queen of Peace.
Angel, Jose Rene '93 (BWN) Edinburg, TX Immaculate Conception; San Isidro, TX St. Isidore; Defenders of the Bond; Canonical Assistance.
Angel, Oliver '01 (LAR) Tribunal.
Angel, Rene '93 (SAT) Defenders of the Bond.
Angel–Neri, Gilberto '07 (NY) Bronx, NY Blessed Sacrament.
Angeles, Joey F. '00 (BR) Plaquemine, LA St. Joan of Arc; White Castle, LA Our Lady of Prompt Succor.
Angeles, Rodel '92 (CLV) Philippine–American Ministry; Cleveland, OH Cathedral of St. John the Evangelist; [X] Cleveland, OH St. John Cathedral Endowment Trust.
Angelicchio, Paul F. '77 (SY) Syracuse, NY Our Lady of Pompei/St. Peter; Presbyteral Council.
Angelini, Joseph *o.f.m.conv.* '65 (ALB) Albany, NY Holy Family Parish.
Angelini, Joseph '67 (MIA) Retired.
Angell, Charles *s.a.* '60 (NY)[EE] Garrison, NY St. Christopher's Inn; [EE] Garrison, NY St. Christopher's Friary.
Angell, Stephen J. '04 (SAV) Vidalia, GA Sacred Heart; Presbyteral Council.
Angelle, Rev. Msgr. Robert G. '56 (LAF) Retired.
Angelo, Thomas M. '85 (NOR) On Duty Outside the Diocese; Military Chaplains; Air Force Chaplains.
Angeloni, Michael A. '75 (WIL) Wilmington, DE Church of the Holy Child.
Angelov, Kiril '90 (STF) Diocesan Consultors; Syracuse; Administrative Council; Rochester, NY St. Josaphat.
Angelovic, Michael '65 (SEA) Seahurst, WA St. Francis of Assisi Retired.
Angelucci, Patrick *s.d.b.* (NY)[F] New Rochelle, NY Salesian High School.
Angert, James *t.o.r.* '71 (ARL) Herndon, VA St. Joseph.
Angi, Steven J. '85 (CIN) Adjutant Judicial Vicars.
Angilella, Joseph T. *s.j.* '65 (SFR)[N] San Francisco, CA Loyola House Jesuit Community.
Anginoli, Rev. Msgr. Joseph T. '75 (PAT) Mendham, NJ St. Joseph's; Adjutant Judicial Vicar.
Angkel, Julio '83 (CI)[C] Tunnuk, Chuuk, FM Vicariate Residence; Vocations.
Angken, Julio '83 (CI) Chuuk, FM St. Anthony's.
Anglaaere, Peter '86 (ROC) Hornell, NY Our Lady of the Valley.
Angle, Camillus *t.o.r.* '54 (ALT)[G] Newry, PA St. Bernardine Monastery Retired.
Angles, Rev. Msgr. Sebastian '44 (BRK) Retired.
Anglim, Ronald H. '65 (CHI) Retired.
Anglim, Thomas G. '54 (VEN) Retired.
Anglin, John *o.f.m.* '68 (SP)[N] St. Petersburg St. Anthony Friary.
Angostura, Marino '94 (HON) Honolulu, HI St. Philomena.
Angotti, Joseph A. '91 (GRY) La Porte, IN St. Peter.
Anguay, James *ss.cc.* '72 (HON)[D] Kaneohe, HI Sacred Hearts Center.
Angueira, Jose Francisco Quintero '89 (SJN) Bayamon, PR Nuestra Sra. de los Dolores.
Anguiano, James M. '82 (LA) Members; Vocations.
Anguiano, Jesus Gerardo '09 (SAT) Pleasanton, TX St. Andrew.
Angula, Michael '94 (SR) St. Helena, CA St. Helena.
Angulo, Raul '85 (MIA) Miami, FL Mother of Christ.
Anholzer, Daniel *o.f.m.cap.* '80 (SAG) Saginaw, MI St. Joseph.
Ani, Godwin *s.s.j.* (MOB) Mobile, AL Most Pure Heart of Mary; Prichard, AL St. James Major.
Anich, Kenneth *s.v.d.* '73 (DUB)[B] Epworth, IA Divine Word College.
Anichini, Albert *m.c.c.j.* '62 (FgM) Cincinnati, OH COMBONI MISSIONARIES (VERONA FATHERS).
Aniello, Frederick M. '79 (HRT) Waterbury, CT Our Lady of Mt. Carmel.
Anifer, Jeffrey J. '67 (DET) Melvindale, MI St. Mary Magdalen.
Anike, Anthony O. *m.s.p.* '95 (GAL) Houston, TX St. Peter the Apostle.
Aniszczyk, Leon S. '73 (MET) Bound Brook, NJ St. Mary of Czestochowa.
Ankenbrandt, Thomas F. *s.j.* '60 (DET)[K] Clarkston, MI Colombiere Center.
Anklan, Carlos *c.s.* '97 (PMB) Delray Beach, FL Our Lady Queen of Peace.
Ankley, Christopher '09 (KAL) Portage, MI St. Catherine of Siena.
Annese, Joseph P. '62 (LAV) Retired.
Annese, Lucius *o.f.m.* '58 (NY)[EE] New York Franciscan Province of the Immaculate Conception.
Annie, Rev. Msgr. Frederick P. '78 (WH) Diocesan (Home) Missions; Propagation of the Faith, Pontifical Society for; Vicar General and Moderator of the Curia; Diocesan Consultors; Catholic University, Friends of; Holy Childhood Association; Diocesan and Foreign Missions, Office of; Contacts to Report.
An Ninh, Vincent Nguyen '71 (DET) Detroit, MI Our Lady of Grace Vietnamese Parish.
Annino, Sebastian V. '61 (CAM) Rosenhayn, NJ St. Mary's Church, Rosenhayn, N.J.; [I] Newfield, NJ The Mater Dei Nursing Home, Newfield, New Jersey.
Annunziato, Michael *ss.cc.* '53 (FR)[G] Fairhaven, MA Damien Residence Retired.
Anonuevo, Salvador '86 (RIC) Bedford, VA Holy Name of Mary; Moneta, VA Resurrection.
Ansaldi, Rev. Msgr. Joseph C. '62 (NY)[F] Staten Island, NY St. Joseph by the Sea, High School; [T] Staten Island, NY Mission of the Immaculate Virgin.
Ansaloni, Edmund *o.f.m.* '49 (SP)[N] Clearwater Beach, FL St. Paul Friary.
Ansbro, Rev. Msgr. Francis J. '51 (NY) Peekskill, NY Assumption Retired.
Anschutz, Larry '82 (SFD) Mount Olive, IL Ascension; Mount Olive, IL Holy Trinity.
Anselment, Joseph '61 (ALB) Priests Retirement Board/ Priests Retirement Plan Board Retired.
Anselmi, Albert J. '71 (ALT) Retired.
Ansems, Bruce '05 (KCK) Further Studies.
Anslow, Thomas C. *c.m.* '72 (LA)[P] Los Angeles, CA Amat Residence II; Canonical Services, Vicar for; Canonical Services, Vicar for.
Anson, Cesar R. '77 (TR) Burlington, NJ The Church of St. Katharine Drexel, Burlington, N.J.
Antal, Andras '68 (CLV) Cleveland, OH St. Elizabeth of Hungary.
Antall, Rev. Msgr. Richard C. '80 (CLV) Casa Parroquial Inmaculada Concepcion.
Antao, Rev. Msgr. John S. '60 (NEW) Elizabeth, NJ Our Lady of Fatima; Portugese Apostolate.
Antczak, John '63 (JOL) Bradley, IL St. Joseph; Kankakee, IL Riverside Medical Center.
Antczak, Robert A. '64 (NEW) Jersey City, NJ St. Paul's; Members.
Antekeier, Charles R. '62 (GR) Retired.
Antes, Esteban Eugenio '93 (RIC) Petersburg, VA St. Joseph.
Anthony, Alphonse (TYL) On Duty Outside the Diocese.
Anthony, Angelo *c.pp.s.* '89 (CIN)[N] Dayton, OH

Provincial Office of the Cincinnati Province of the Society of the Precious Blood.
Anthony, Benedict '86 (LA) Woodland Hills, CA St. Mel.
Anthony, Dharmaraj *m.s.f.s.* '92 (TYL)[B] Whitehouse, TX The Missionaries of St. Francis de Sales.
Anthony, Eddy *s.j.* (CI) St. Joseph.
Anthony, Fred Jeffrey '09 (P) Sweet Home, OR St. Helen Catholic Church.
Anthony, Jerold G. '96 (CAM) Vineland, NJ St. Padre Pio Parish, Vineland, N.J.
Anthony, Joseph '80 (MO) DEPARTMENT OF VETERANS AFFAIRS HOSPITALS AND CHAPLAINS.
Anthony, Joseph (LAV) On Duty Outside the Diocese.
Anthony, Julian '66 (PBR) Latrobe, PA St. Mary's.
Anthony, Rev. Msgr. Paul G. '61 (STL) Retired.
Anthony, Raju '98 (NY) Bronx, NY St. Gabriel.
Anthonysamy, Richard S. *s.j.* '08 (DEN)[N] Denver, CO Xavier Jesuit Center.
Antillon, Omar '98 (MIL) Burlington, WI St. Charles.
Antillon, William R. '79 (RCK) Morrison, IL St. Mary.
Antinarelli, Ronald A. '74 (ROC) Rochester, NY Our Lady of Victory–St. Joseph.
Antiporek, James '81 (JOL) Warrenville, IL St. Irene.
Antl, Louis '48 (SFD)[L] Springfield, IL Our Lady of Angels Friary.
Antle, Nicholas C. (GAL) Retired.
Antle, Nicholas Neal (GAL)[L] Houston, TX Pope John Paul XXIII Priests' Residence Retired.
Antoine, James *o.f.m.cap.* '67 (GF) Lodge Grass, MT Our Lady of Loretto.
Antolini, Vincenzo *o.m.v.* '58 (LA) Hawaiian Gardens, CA St. Peter Chanel.
Anton, Ronald J. *s.j.* '83 (GAL) Retired.
Anton, Ronald J. *s.j.* '83 (BAL)[S] Baltimore, MD Jesuit Community of Loyola University, Inc. Retired.
Antoñanzas, Rev. Msgr. Jesùs R. Diez '57 (PCE) Diocesan Consultors; Coto Laurel, PR Our Lady of Mt. Carmel.
Antone, William *o.m.i.* '80 (WDC) Councilors:; [N] Washington, DC Provincial Offices of the United States Province of the Missionary Oblates of Mary Immaculate.
Antonelle, John N. '06 (NOR) Chaplains; Storrs, CT St. Thomas Aquinas.
Antonelli, Rev. Msgr. Louis '49 (CHK) Rota, MP San Isidro Parish; Presbyteral Council.
Antonelli, Robert *c.s.c.* '65 (P)[B] University of Portland; [L] Portland, OR Holy Cross Fathers & Brothers, C.S.C. – University of Portland.
Antonelli, Robert *c.s.c.* (FTW)[H] Notre Dame Congregation of Holy Cross, Indiana Province, Provincial House.
Antonellis, Joseph A. '72 (BO) Members; Absent on Leave.
Antonicelli, Rev. Msgr. Charles V. '93 (WDC) Washington, DC St. Joseph on Capitol Hill; Deans; Judges; Pastoral Center Special Ministries; Episcopal Vicar for Canonical Services.
Antonik, Jan '03 (VEN) Sarasota, FL St. Thomas More.
Antonucci, Richard J. *o.praem.* '72 (PH)[Y] Paoli, PA Daylesford Abbey; [B] Paoli, PA Daylesford Abbey; Paoli, PA.
Antony, Abraham '95 (SJ) Los Altos, CA St. Simon.
Antony, Albin Roby '86 (NY) Staten Island, NY St. Charles.
Antony, John Francis '91 (NY) Bronx, NY St. Barnabas.
Antony, John K. '96 (LR) Fayetteville, AR St. Joseph; Vice Chancellors; Adjutant Judicial Vicars; Judges.
Antony, Kye Mansoo '01 (CHK) Presbyteral Council.
Antony, Peter '89 (CC) Riviera, TX Our Lady of Consolation.
Antony, Varghese '91 (CC) Corpus Christi, TX Our Lady of the Rosary.
Antonydass, Pichaimuthu (PRT) Lewiston, ME Prince of Peace Parish.
Antonyian, Soosai (PRT) Lewiston, ME Prince of Peace Parish.
AntonySamy, S. R. '71 (CR) Crookston, MN Cathedral of the Immaculate Conception.
Antos, Paul J. '54 (ALB) Retired.
Antoun, Ziad *o.m.m.* '98 (OLL)[A] Ann Arbor, MI Maronite Order of the Blessed Virgin Mary; Ann Arbor, MI.
Antram, Cormac *o.f.m.* '54 (GLP) Radio; St. Michaels, AZ St. Michael.
Antry, Theodore J. *o.praem.* '66 (PH)[Y] Paoli, PA Daylesford Abbey.
Antunes, Enzio *s.d.v.* (NEW) Archdiocese of Newark Commitium.
Antunes, Ezio *s.d.v.* (PAT) Paterson, NJ St. Gerard Majella; Paterson, NJ St. Michael the Archangel.
Antunez, Roy L. *s.j.* '71 (P) Springfield, OR St. Alice; [L] Portland, OR Colombiere Community.
Antunez–Olea, Bardo Fabian '03 (TUC) Clifton, AZ Sacred Heart Roman Catholic Church and St. Mary's Mission – Clifton; Morenci, AZ Holy Cross Roman Catholic Church – Morenci.
Antus, Roland '62 (DUL) Retired.
Antweiler, Donald J. '73 (JC) Monroe City, MO St. Stephen; Monroe City, MO Holy Rosary.
Antwi, Eric B. '01 (WH) Chester, WV Sacred Heart; New Cumberland, WV Immaculate Conception.
Antwi–Boasiako, Dominic *a.b.* '81 (VIC) Wharton, TX Holy Family; Wharton, TX Our Lady of Mt. Carmel; Presbyteral Council.
Anumata, Christopher (CHI)[J] Oak Park, IL West Suburban Medical Center.
Anung, Ronelo '92 (NY) Staten Island, NY St. Patrick.
Anuszewski, Albeet M. *o.ss.t.* '91 (BAL)[S] The Trinitarians in Italy (Rome).
Anuta, Hyginus Chucks '97 (SFE) Tucumcari, NM St. Anne.
Anuzewski, Damian *o.ss.t.* '79 (BAL)[S] The Trinitarian Community in Adelphi, Maryland.
Anyaeche, Jude (PIT) Allegheny County, PA UPMC University of Pittsburgh Medical Center.
Anyagwa, Donald (HRT) New Britain, CT St. Ann; New Britain, CT St. Mary's.
Anyama, Vincent C. '09 (DAL) Frisco, TX St. Francis of Assisi.
Anyamele, Faustinus '06 (DEN) Aurora, CO Queen of Peace.
Anyanike, Vitalis E. '02 (OM) Hooper, NE St. Rose of Lima.
Anyanwu, Celestine '83 (BRK) East Elmhurst, NY St. Gabriel.
Anyanwu, Christopher (PAT) Paterson, NJ St. Joseph Hospital.
Anyanwu, Christopher (PAT)[K] Paterson, NJ St. Joseph's Hospital and Medical Center.
Anyanwu, Cornelius Kelechi '08 (HRT) Waterbury, CT St. Leo the Great; Waterbury, CT SS. Peter and Paul.
Anyanwu, Innocent '80 (LAV) Las Vegas, NV Holy Family.
Anyikwa, Felix '87 (LKC) Oberlin, LA St. Joan of Arc.
Anziano, James J. '81 (PH) Retired.
Anzoategui, Francisco J. '88 (BO) Framingham, MA St. Stephen.
Anzora, Juan '08 (ATL) Atlanta, GA Immaculate Heart of Mary.
Aolhunga, Joseph Okech '91 (NY) New Rochelle, NY Holy Family.
Apassa, Cyril '71 (RNO) Reno, NV St. Rose of Lima.
Apel, John *s.j.* '69 (DEN)[N] Centennial, CO Regis High Jesuit Community.
Apel, John *s.j.* '71 (BAK) Pendleton, OR St. Andrew's Indian Mission.
Apfelbeck, Keith B. '99 (LC) Special Assignment; Thorp, WI St. Bernard–St. Hedwig Parish.
Apfelbeck, Kurt J. '99 (LC) Leave of Absence.
Apfelbeck, Kurt (SAM)[F] Shelburne, VT Saint Rafka Retreat Center.
Apoldite, Dennis A. '78 (TR) Trenton, NJ Sacred Heart.
Apolinar, Moises R. '81 (LA) South El Monte, CA Epiphany.
Aponte, Jose *s.j.* '00 (MGZ) Mayaguez, PR Church De El Buen Pastor.
Aponte, Melvin Diaz '02 (PCE) Yauco, PR Santo Domingo de Guzman.
Aponte–Merced, Luis *o.f.m.* '03 (PEO) Peoria, IL St. Joseph; Peoria, IL Sacred Heart.
Apostol, Moises '78 (RCK) Saint Charles, IL St. Patrick.
Apostoli, Andrew D. *c.f.r.* '67 (NY)[A] Yonkers, NY St. Joseph's Seminary.
Apostoli, Andrew (NY)[EE] Yonkers, NY St. Leopold's Friary.
Apparcel, Gregory *c.s.p.* (NY)[EE] Jamaica Estates Paulist Fathers Generalate.
Appel, Paul J. '03 (DAV) Washington, IA St. James.
Appelby, Gerald J. '59 (ROC) Retired.
Appiah, Kwaku John '98 (KNX) Greeneville, TN Notre Dame; Presbyteral Council.
Appiasi, Samuel '83 (VIC) Blessing, TX St. Peter's; Procurator Advocate; Presbyteral Council.
Apple, Jason (STL) St. Louis, MO Oratory of St. Francis de Sales.
Appleby, Gerald '59 (ROC) Rochester, NY Guardian Angels.
Applegate, Rev. Msgr. Gary '81 (KCK) Judicial Vicar; Judges; Archdiocesan Consultors.
Applewhite, Mark (RVC) Smithtown, NY St. Catherine of Siena Hospital.
Appleyard, Rev. Msgr. George '68 (SJP) Carnegie, PA Holy Trinity; Consultors; Eparchial Corporation; Central Protopresbytery; Vicar for Religious; Liturgical Commission; Examiners of Clergy; Permanent Deacon Program; Presbyteral Council; Carbondale, IL Catholic Association of Diocesan Ecumenical and Interreligious Officers (CADEIO); Vicar General; Eparchial Convention; Arbitration Board; Presbyters.
Appleyard, Joseph A. *s.j.* '66 (BO)[U] Newton, MA The Jesuit Community at Boston College.
Apura, Nilo '75 (TR) Trenton, NJ St. Mary Cathedral.
Apuzzo, Pasquale '76 (RIC) Chesterfield, VA St. Gabriel.
Aquilera, George '83 (LA) Gardena, CA St. Anthony of Padua.
Aquino, Alexander '74 (SD) Chula Vista, CA St. Rose of Lima.
Aquino, Arnel *s.j.* '04 (BO)[U] Cambridge, MA Faber House.
Aquino, Francisco '90 (ORL) Orlando, FL Holy Family.
Aquino, Joseph G. *m.s.* '69 (ATL) Marietta, GA St. Ann.
Aquino, Rev. Msgr. Oscar A. '62 (NY) Judges; New York, NY St. Lucy.
Aquino, Peter M. '69 (NEW) Livingston, NJ St. Raphael.
Arachi, Grace G. '91 (NEW) Mountainside, NJ Church of Our Lady of Lourdes.
Aracich, Anthony *s.j.* '67 (NEW)[B] Jersey City, NJ Jesuit Center; [M] Jersey City, NJ Jesuits of Saint Peter's College, Inc.
Aracil, Javier '63 (NEW) Elizabeth, NJ St. Anthony's.
Arackal, Bony '93 (SAC) Elk Grove, CA St. Joseph.
Arackal, Joseph J. *v.c.* '67 (SYM) St. Cloud, MN St. Alphonsa Syro–Malabar Catholic Church Minnesota; Saint Cloud, MN.
Aragon, Ramon '50 (SFE) Retired.
Aragon, Salvador *o.f.m.* '55 (SFE)[H] Albuquerque, NM The Province of Our Lady of Guadalupe.
Arambasick, Dennis *o.f.m.* '85 (HRT) Winsted, CT St. Joseph.
Aramburo, Eugenio '88 (MRY) Los Gatos, CA Christ Child; Administrative Committee Priests' Pension Plan; Clergy Personnel Board; Vicar for Hispanic Clergy.
Aramburu, Jose A. *m.m.* '84 (FgM) Maryknoll, NY; Maryknoll, NY; [EE] Maryknoll Maryknoll Fathers and Brothers.
Aramendi, Juan '91 (POD) Guaynabo.
Aramendi, Juan '91 (SJN)[G] Guaynabo, PR Opus Dei.
Arana, Francisco '64 (SJN) Bayamon, PR Nuestra Senora de Covadonga; [E] San Juan, PR Centro Medico de P.R.
Arango, Andres *c.j.m.* '95 (PHX) Phoenix, AZ St. Jerome Roman Catholic Parish.
Arango, Fabio '66 (MIA)[J] Miami, FL Mercy Hospital.
Arango, Gilberto '75 (STO) Stockton, CA Cathedral of the Annunciation (Pastor of); School of Ministry.
Arango, John Jaime Tobon '96 (BRK) Brooklyn, NY St. Martin of Tours–Our Lady of Lourdes.
Arango–Medina, Miguel '65 (SAT) Von Ormy, TX St. Peter the Fisherman.
Aranha, George '75 (SJ) Palo Alto, CA St. Thomas Aquinas; [D] San Jose, CA Presentation High School.
Arano–Ponce, Gerardo '03 (KCK) Roeland Park, KS St. Agnes.
Aransi, John '97 (SP)[J] Tampa, FL St. Joseph's Hospital, Inc.
Araque, Alvaro U. '72 (STO) Stockton, CA St. Gertrude Church (Pastor of).
Arata, Miguel A. '95 (NEW) On Duty Outside the Archdiocese.
Araujo, Arturo *s.j.* '99 (SFE) Albuquerque, NM Immaculate Conception.
Araujo, Manuel *c.p.* (SJN) San Juan, PR Jesus Maestro.
Araujo, Robert J. *s.j.* '93 (BO)[U] Boston The Society of Jesus of New England–Provincial Offices.
Araujo, Robert J. *s.j.* '93 (CHI)[C] Chicago, IL Jesuit Community at Loyola University Chicago.
Arauz, Erick E. '85 (SFR) Half Moon Bay, CA Our Lady of the Pillar.
Arbanas, Harold P. '48 (GF) Retired.
Arbelaez, Ernesto *s.j.* (LA) Hospital Chaplains.
Arboleda, Dario H. *o.ss.t.* '03 (PCE) Ponce, PR La Santisima Trinidad; Episcopal Vicar for Sick.
Arboleda, Jorge W. '93 (STO) Modesto, CA St. Stanislaus Church (Pastor of); College of Consultors/ Presbyteral Council.
Arboleda, Vidal '55 (ORL) Retired.
Arcamo, Rev. Msgr. Floro B. '65 (SFR) San Francisco, CA Star of the Sea; Filipino Ministry; On Special Assignment; Episcopal Vicar for Filipinos.
Arce, Aaron *o.p.* '80 (STL)[O] St. Louis, MO St. Dominic Priory.
Arce, Neil A. '05 (BEA) Anahuac, TX Our Lady of Light.
Arce, Robert P. '64 (NY) Bronx, NY St. Margaret Mary.
Arce–Flores, Carlos '91 (R) Ex Officio; Vicar for Hispanics; Office of Hispanic Ministry; Cary, NC St. Michael the Archangel.
Arcega, Ruel '95 (FgM) Boston, MA St. James the Apostle, Inc.
Arceneaux, Chester '92 (LAF) Lafayette, LA Our Lady of Wisdom, University of Louisiana; [L] Lafayette, LA Our Lady of Wisdom Catholic Student Center; College Ministry.
Arceneaux, Jules '90 (LAF) On Leave.
Arceneaux, Louis *c.m.* '66 (NO)[P] New Orleans, LA Congregation of the Mission Western Province (Vincentians).
Arceo, Ernesto '83 (LA) Ventura, CA Sacred Heart.
Arceo, Ruben *s.j.* '02 (SFR)[N] San Francisco, CA Loyola House Jesuit Community.
Archambault, Donald '70 (DET) Detroit, MI Corpus Christi; Archdiocesan Vicars; Presbyteral Council.
Archambault, Rev. Msgr. Henry N. '59 (NOR) Taftville, CT Sacred Heart; College of Consultors; Members; Deans; Diocesan Pastoral Council; Lawyers, Guild of Catholic; Judges.

Archambault, Rev. Msgr. Henry '59 (NOR) Board of Education.
Archambault, James H. '67 (HRT) Retired.
Archambault, Richard L. '55 (NOR)[H] Putnam, CT Holy Spirit Provincial House; Project Northeast.
Archambault, Richard *m.afr.* '73 (SP)[N] St. Petersburg, FL Missionaries of Africa.
Archer, Arthur (NOR) Retired.
Archer, Richard R. *o.p.* '58 (R)[F] Raleigh, NC Dominican Priory.
Archer, Scott '90 (PEO) Fairbury, IL St. John the Baptist.
Archibong, Cosmas (HRT) West Haven, CT V.A. CT Health Care System.
Archibong, Cosmos (HRT) Waterbury, CT Waterbury Hospital.
Arcila, David *o.c.d.* '95 (CHI) Mundelein, IL Santa Maria Del Popolo.
Arciniegas, Hector Eduardo Mejia *m.s.c.* '06 (FgM) Aurora, IL MISSIONARIES OF THE SACRED HEART.
Arciszewski, Gilbert '59 (MIL) Retired.
Arcoleo, Douglas R. '98 (RVC) Freeport, NY Our Holy Redeemer.
Arcosa, Carl Tacuyan '07 (OAK) Brentwood, CA Immaculate Heart of Mary.
Arcuri, Carmen J. '61 (COL) Worthington, OH St. Michael Retired.
Ardagh, Brian '95 (CHI) Lemont, IL St. Alphonsus.
Ardinger, Scott R. '01 (ALN) Orefield, PA St. Joseph The Worker; Office of Worship; Appointed Members; Secretariat for Catholic Life and Evangelization.
Ardis, John B. *c.s.p.* '90 (LA) Los Angeles, CA St. Paul the Apostle.
Ardolf, Edward J. '64 (NU) Nicollet, MN St. Paul; New Ulm, MN St. Mary.
Ardouin, Rev. Msgr. Beaubrun '93 (NEW) Irvington, NJ St. Leo's; Haitian Apostolate; Members.
Arechiga, Dennis '00 (SAT) Converse, TX St. Monica.
Arechua, Ramon J. *m.j.* '96 (GAL) Houston, TX St. Stephen.
Areiza, Juan '08 (ATL) Roswell, GA St. Andrew.
Arejola, Rodolfo G. '68 (AGN) Tamuning, GU St. Anthony and St. Victor.
Arel, Don *o.m.i.* (OAK)[M] Oakland, CA Missionary Oblates of Mary Immaculate United States Province.
Arella, Rev. Msgr. Gerard J. '28 (BRK) Retired.
Arella, Rev. Msgr. Gerard '54 (BRK)[T] Douglaston, NY Bishop Mugavero Residence Retired.
Arellano, Edgardo M. '74 (WIL)[L] Dover, DE Secular Institute of the Two Hearts; [J] Dover, DE Oblate Apostles of the Two Hearts; [K] Dover, DE Leaven of the Immaculate Heart of Mary (LIHM).
Arellano, Jesus *c.m.* '73 (NY) New York, NY; New York, NY Holy Agony; [EE] New York, NY Vincentian Fathers.
Arellano, Josue *c.o.r.c.* '01 (SB)[I] Corona, CA Confraternity of Operarios Del Reino De Cristo, C.O.R.C.
Arellano–Reynoso, Josué *c.o.r.c.* '05 (SB) Corona, CA St. Edward.
Arends, Todd '02 (CR) Deans; Diocesan Consultors; Greenbush, MN Blessed Sacrament; Priests' Council.
Arens, John F. '74 (BO)[D] Needham, MA St. Sebastian's School, Inc.
Arens, Patrick O. '00 (WIN) Slayton, MN St. Ann's; Slayton, MN St. Columba's; Slayton, MN St. Mary; Appointed Members.
Arenz, James *s.j.* '65 (LA)[C] Los Angeles, CA Jesuit Community Retired.
Ares, Francisco J. '83 (BRK) Wyckoff Heights Hospital.
Arevalo, Jorge '94 (ATL) Atlanta, GA Cathedral of Christ the King.
Arevalo, Joseph V. '65 (RVC) Babylon, NY St. Joseph.
Arevalos Lupercia, Benjamin '09 (CHI) Chicago, IL Good Shepherd.
Arflack, Gregory A. '98 (OWN) Absent on Leave.
Argano, Christopher '09 (NY) Monroe, NY Sacred Heart Church.
Argent, Robert W. '55 (STL) Retired.
Argentieri, Nicholas J. '08 (PIT) Butler, PA St. Paul; Butler, PA St. Wendelin.
Argentino, Ralph J. '68 (SP) Permanent Diaconate Office; Tampa, FL Christ the King.
Argue, Patrick *ss.cc.* '62 (LA)[P] La Verne, CA Congregation of the Sacred Hearts of Jesus and Mary Retired.
Arguelles, I. Anthony '74 (BLX) Pascagoula, MS Our Lady of Victories; College of Consultors.
Arias, Alfredo '04 (FRS) Corcoran, CA Our Lady of Lourdes.
Arias, Ariel '85 (RNO) Reno, NV St. Therese Church of the Little Flower.
Arias, Gonzalo '00 (NY) Monticello, NY St. Peter.
Arias, Guillermo *s.j.* '72 (MIA)[K] Miami, FL Villa Javier.
Arias, Guillermo *s.j.* '72 (PMB)[A] Boynton Beach, FL St. Vincent de Paul Regional Seminary.
Arias, Guillermo '73 (RNO) Sun Valley, NV St. Peter Canisius.
Arias, Hernan '85 (PAT) Morristown, NJ St. Margaret of Scotland; Priestly Life Committee.
Arias, Jesus J. '92 (MIA) Miami, FL St. Joachim.
Aribe, Stephen '55 (NEW) Newark, NJ St. Lucy's.
Arico, Carl J. '60 (NEW) Bayonne, NJ St. Vincent de Paul Retired.
Aridas, Christopher J. '73 (RVC) St. Margaret of Scotland.
Arimond, Vincent '55 (DUL) Retired.
Arinze, Paul U. '99 (MAD) Appointed.
Arinze, Paul Ugo '99 (MAD) Dodgeville, WI St. Joseph.
Aririatu, Samuel '79 (RVC) Port Jefferson, NY Infant Jesus.
Aririatu, Samuel '79 (RVC) Port Jefferson, NY St. Charles Hospital, Port Jefferson, New York.
Aristil, Edmond *c.s.sp.* '03 (CHI) Chicago, IL St. Mary Magdalene; Chicago, IL St. Tarcissus; Chicago, IL St. Ambrose.
Ariza, Campo E. '75 (CGS) Diocesan Consultors; Priests Senate; Caguas, PR Cathedral Dulce Nombre de Jesus.
Ariza, Rev. Msgr. Vicente '75 (SJN)[G] Guaynabo, PR Opus Dei; Regional Vicar for Puerto Rico; Guaynabo.
Arizpe, Samuel '87 (BWN) San Benito, TX St. Theresa.
Arkins, Michael *s.s.s.* '73 (SP) Holiday, FL St. Vincent De Paul.
Arle, David '84 (VEN) Fort Myers, FL St. Vincent de Paul.
Arledge, Joseph H. '97 (OKL) Oklahoma City, OK Sacred Heart.
Arledge, Thaddaeus R. *o.s.b.* '56 (SEA)[L] Lacey, WA St. Martin's Abbey.
Arlia, William *o.f.m.* '06 (WIL)[J] Wilmington, DE Capuchin Franciscan Friars, St. Francis Renewal Center; [L] Wilmington, DE Secular Franciscan Order; [M] Wilmington, DE St. Francis Renewal Center.
Arlotta, Jack '92 (NY) Highland Falls, NY Sacred Heart of Jesus.
Armano, Patrick S. '03 (BO) Methuen, MA St. Monica.
Armato, Robert J. '95 (BRK) Art and Architecture Commission; Astoria, NY St. Joseph.
Armbruster, Timothy *c.pp.s.* '01 (KC) Liberty, MO St. James.
Armengol, Jose *c.m.f.* '67 (SJN) Bayamon, PR San Jose.
Armenio, Peter V. '80 (POD)[V] Chicago, IL Prelature of the Holy Cross and Opus Dei; Vicar for the Midwest; Chicago.
Armenta, Benito '87 (LA) Los Angeles, CA St. Alphonsus.
Armey, Charles R. '80 (WOR) Worcester, MA Our Lady of Loreto.
Arminio, Thomas G. '81 (NEW) Woodcliff Lake, NJ Our Lady Mother of the Church; Ministry to the Bereaved, Separated, Divorced, Retrouvaille Retired.
Armistead, Rev. Msgr. John M. '71 (STO) Stockton, CA Cathedral of the Annunciation (Pastor of); College of Consultors/Presbyteral Council.
Armshaw, Joseph R. *c.ss.r.* '52 (STL)[O] Liguori, MO St. Clement Health Care Center Retired.
Armshaw, Rev. Msgr. Patrick J. '62 (RVC)[K] Bethpage, NY Society of St. Vincent de Paul–Central Council.
Armstrong, Christopher R. '80 (CIN) Cincinnati, OH St. Antoninus; Imprimatur Censors; Judges.
Armstrong, John F. *s.j.* '78 (NO) Saint Louis, MO; [P] New Orleans, LA Jesuit Provincial Office; [C] New Orleans, LA Loyola University New Orleans.
Armstrong, John F. *s.j.* '78 (STL)[O] St. Louis, MO Sacred Heart Jesuit Community; [O] St. Louis, MO The Jesuits of the Missouri Province.
Armstrong, Regis *o.f.m.cap.* '67 (WDC)[C] Catholic University of America, The.
Armstrong, Richard G. (KNX) Christian Formation.
Armstrong, Richard (SJP) Presbyters.
Armstrong, Rev. Msgr. Robert A. '62 (BAL) Baltimore, MD Cathedral of Mary Our Queen; Consultors; Defenders of the Bond; Consultors.
Armstrong, Rev. Msgr. Robert '62 (BAL) Retired.
Armstrong, Rodney J. *s.s.j.* '91 (GAL) Baytown, TX Holy Family.
Arnao, Thomas V. '82 (RVC) Adjutant Judicial Vicar; Hewlett, NY St. Joseph's.
Arnaud, Allan '08 (RVC) Seaford, NY Maria Regina.
Arnaud, Michael '75 (LAF) New Iberia, LA Nativity of Our Lady.
Arnberg, Todd '76 (SAG) St. Charles, MI St. Mary; St. Charles, MI Immaculate Conception.
Arneson, James E. '67 (IND) Retired.
Arnhols, Rev. Msgr. Richard J. '73 (NEW) Bergenfield, NJ St. John the Evangelist; Vicar for Pastoral Life; Members; Members; Vicar for Pastoral Life.
Arnholt, Joseph M. '73 (PH) Philadelphia, PA St. Anne.
Arnister, Rev. Msgr. Edward J. '79 (TR) Vice Chancellors; Tribunal Judges; Trenton, NJ Divine Mercy Parish.
Arnold, Erik A. (BAL) Presbyteral Council.
Arnold, Erik J. '99 (BAL) Ellicott City, MD Our Lady of Perpetual Help.
Arnold, John D. *s.j.* '73 (STL)[O] St. Louis, MO Ignatius House.
Arnold, John P. '98 (TUC) Tucson, AZ Saint Ambrose Roman Catholic Parish – Tucson; Adjutant Judicial Vicar; Diocesan Consultors; Council of Priests; Vicars Forane; All Vicars Forane.
Arnold, Rex '04 (OKL) Clinton, OK St. Mary's.
Arnold, Wayne H. '00 (MEM) Bolivar, TN St. Mary Church; Selmer, TN St. Jude the Apostle Catholic Church; Scouting.
Arnold, William L. '80 (COL) Columbus, OH Holy Spirit.
Arnold, William '80 (COL) Diocesan Judges.
Arnoldt, David L. '68 (WIN) Retired.
Arnone, Allan '80 (SJ) On Leave of Absence.
Arnone, John C. '99 (NO) Saint Bernard, LA St. Bernard; Saint Bernard, LA Our Lady of Lourdes.
Arnone, Leo '93 (ALT) Johnstown, PA St. Clare of Assisi; Navy Reserve Chaplains.
Arnoult, Paul '02 (SFR) Larkspur, CA St. Patrick.
Arnout, Eric R. '96 (ALN) Allentown, PA Cathedral of St. Catharine of Siena; Appointed Members.
Arnsparger, Roger K. '77 (CHL) Gastonia, NC St. Michael; Education; Diocesan Consultors; Office of Faith Formation.
Arnzen, Mark '05 (SJ) Morgan Hill, CA St. Catherine of Alexandria; Council of Priests; College of Consultors; Ongoing Formation of Clergy.
Arocho, Jose A. '91 (FAJ) Luquillo, PR Madre del Redentor; Master of Ceremonies.
Arockiam, Amalraj (LC) Dodge, WI Most Sacred Heart.
Arockiam, Arockiam *s.v.d.* '02 (LAF) Maurice, LA St. Joseph.
Arockiaraj, Christy (BAL)[M] Baltimore, MD St. Agnes HealthCare, Inc.
Arockiasamy, Justin *s.v.d.* '00 (LAF) St. Martinville, LA Notre Dame de Perpetuel Secours.
Arockiassamy, Joseph '85 (ALB) Stamford, NY Sacred Heart/St. Philip Neri.
Arockiyasamy, Santhiyagu *m.s.f.s.* '96 (LAN) Flint, MI St. Mary.
Arogundade, Jude (NY) Elmsford, NY Our Lady of Mt. Carmel.
Arogyasami, Joseph *i.m.s.* '89 (BR) Albany, LA St. Margaret Queen of Scotland.
Arokiadass, Soosai Arpudam *h.g.n.* '00 (WH) Madison, WV St. Mary, Queen of Heaven.
Arokiam, Santhiyagu *m.s.f.s.* '96 (TYL)[B] Whitehouse, TX The Missionaries of St. Francis de Sales.
Arokiasamy, Kulan–Daisamy '71 (DET) Eastpointe, MI St. Veronica.
Arokiaselvam, Nithiyaselvam *m.s.f.s.* '00 (TYL)[B] Whitehouse, TX The Missionaries of St. Francis de Sales.
Arokiaselvam, Nithyaselvam '01 (LAN) Ann Arbor, MI St. Thomas the Apostle.
Arold, Richard J. '67 (NY) Retired.
Arong, Jose *o.m.i.* '66 (OAK) Oakland, CA Sacred Heart; Diocesan Planning Board.
Aronyu, Cuthbert '72 (OAK) Oakland, CA St. Benedict.
Arouje, Lonachan W. '70 (STO) College of Consultors/Presbyteral Council; Angels Camp, CA St. Patrick Church of Angels Camp (Pastor of).
Arps, Joseph W. '02 (PRT) Retired.
Arputham, Dominic '98 (LA) Pacific Palisades, CA Corpus Christi.
Arputham, Michael '78 (NY) Staten Island, NY St. Mary.
Arrambide, Jaime C. *c.ss.r.* '73 (GAL) Houston, TX St. Raphael the Archangel.
Arrando, Angelo S. '71 (BGP) Danbury, CT St. Gregory the Great.
Arrazola, Rodrigo A. '01 (HBG) Cornwall, PA Sacred Heart of Jesus.
Arrellano, Adondee '03 (HON) Kahului, HI Christ the King.
Arreola, Alberto *o.m.i.* '02 (LA) Pomona, CA Sacred Heart.
Arriaga, Joaquin S. '97 (FRS) Fresno, CA Our Lady of Mt. Carmel.
Arriaga, Jose Jesus '69 (WDC) Hyattsville, MD St. Mark.
Arribas, Santiago *c.m.* '66 (SJN)[I] San Juan, PR Servicios Pastorales Paules; Servicios Pastorales Paules; San Juan, PR Jesus Maestro.
Arrieta, David '62 (SJN) San Juan, PR Nuestra Senora de Lourdes.
Arrieta Correa, Juan Carlos '09 (CHI) Chicago, IL St. Bede the Venerable.
Arriola, Augustin *sch.p.* '60 (LA) Los Angeles, CA Santa Teresita.
Arrizurieta, Candido *c.m.* '54 (NY) New York, NY Holy Agony; [EE] New York, NY Vincentian Fathers; New York, NY.
Arroyave, Jesus Rodrigo '96 (TYL) Marshall, TX St. Joseph; Co Directors.
Arroyave, Jesus '96 (ORL) Apopka, FL St. Francis of Assisi.
Arroyave, Luis F. '88 (TYL) Nacogdoches, TX Sacred Heart; Nacogdoches, TX Our Lady of Guadalupe.
Arroyave, Pastor A. '90 (CGS) Las Piedras, PR San Juan Bautista.
Arroyo, Rev. Msgr. Brigido '61 (AGN) Tamuning, GU St. Anthony and St. Victor; Archdiocesan Presbyteral Council; Catholic Daughters of the Americas; Saint Anthony Parish.

Arroyo, Edward B. *s.j.* '75 (NO)[C] New Orleans, LA Loyola University New Orleans.
Arroyo, Edward B. *s.j.* '75 (MOB)[A] Mobile, AL Spring Hill College.
Arroyo, Edward B. *s.j.* '75 (MOB)[I] Mobile, AL Spring Hill College Campus Ministry.
Arroyo, Eric '92 (SR) Windsor, CA Our Lady of Guadalupe.
Arroyo, Mario J. '77 (GAL) Houston, TX St. Cyril of Alexandria.
Arroyo, Miguel *o.c.d.* '99 (CGS) Caguas, PR San Jose.
Arruda, Henry S. '67 (FR) Taunton, MA St. Anthony's; Diocesan Liaison with Portuguese Charismatic Groups.
Arsenault, Edward J. '91 (WDC)[W] Silver Spring, MD Saint Luke Institute, Inc.; On Duty Outside the Diocese.
Arsenault, Joseph B. *m.m.* '59 (NY)[EE] Maryknoll Maryknoll Fathers and Brothers Retired.
Arsenault, Joseph G. (BO) Abington, MA St. Bridget.
Arseneau, Vernon '72 (JOL) Chebanse, IL SS. Mary and Joseph; Clifton, IL St. Peter's.
Arseneault, David J. '81 (ALT)[I] Huntington, PA Juniata College; Huntingdon, PA Most Holy Trinity; State Correctional Institution.
Arsenius, '06 (BAK)[B] La Pine, OR Monastery of Annunciation Hermitage.
Arteaga, Peter *m.sp.s.* '97 (P) Area Vicars; Hillsboro, OR St. Matthew.
Arter, Ronald L. '61 (COL) Retired.
Arthasseril, Jerome S. '66 (NEW) Verona, NJ Our Lady of the Lake.
Arthur, David J. *c.s.c.* '54 (FR)[A] North Easton, MA Holy Cross Fathers Religious.
Arthur, E. Eugene *s.j.* '66 (COS)[F] Sedalia, CO Sacred Heart Jesuit Community; [H] Sedalia, CO Sacred Heart Jesuit Retreat House.
Arthur, James K. '83 (LC) Bloomer, WI St. Paul; Bloomer, WI St. John the Baptist.
Artis, George *s.v.d.* '62 (CHI)[N] Techny, IL Divine Word Residence.
Artmann, Robert J. '64 (MIL) Retired.
Arts, Paul–Louis '64 (SC) Retired.
Artunduaga, Henry '92 (CC) Corpus Christi, TX St. Joseph; Corpus Christi, TX The Shrine of Nuestra de San Juan de Los Lagos.
Arturi, Bradley K. '62 (POD)[JJ] Overlook Study Center; New Rochelle.
Artuso, Grazioso '64 (BGP) Bridgeport, CT St. Raphael.
Artysiewicz, Chet *g.h.m.* '73 (TLS) Idabel, OK St. Francis De Sales.
Artzer, James *s.v.d.* '50 (CHI)[N] Techny, IL Divine Word Residence.
Arul, John '70 (MRY) Retired.
Arulanandam, John Peter *m.s.f.s.* '01 (DET) White Lake, MI St. Patrick.
Arulanandam, John Peter *m.s.f.s.* '01 (TYL)[B] Whitehouse, TX The Missionaries of St. Francis de Sales.
Arulandu, Thaines '82 (FAR) Edgeley, ND Transfiguration Church of Edgeley; Edgeley, ND Holy Spirit Church of Nortonville.
Arulappa, Devaraj '86 (TYL) Fairfield, TX St. Bernard of Clairvaux.
Arulappa, Luckas *m.s.f.s.* '96 (NSH) Hendersonville, TN Our Lady of the Lake.
Arulappa, Luckas *m.s.f.s.* '96 (TYL)[B] Whitehouse, TX The Missionaries of St. Francis de Sales.
Arulsamy, Arputham '90 (BRK) Brooklyn, NY Our Lady of Angels.
Arumainathan, Antonyra *o.m.i.* '02 (MIA) Miami, FL Christ the King.
Arvay, Alfred S. '58 (NEW) Retired.
Arwady, Raymond '09 (DET) Livonia, MI St. Michael.
Arwo–Dogu, Seth N. (RVC) Babylon, NY St. Joseph.
Arzate, Roman '86 (LA) Canoga Park, CA Our Lady of the Valley.
Arzola, Roberto *o.p.* '74 (SJN) Catano, PR Nuestra Senora del Carmen.
Asagba, Francis '91 (BRK) Brooklyn, NY St. Catharine of Alexandria.
Asalemo, Asalemo '08 (SPP) Pago Pago, AS Cathedral of the Holy Family.
Asante, Augustine Nsiah '98 (VIC) El Campo, TX St. Philip the Apostle.
Asantemungu, Juvenalis '99 (MIL) Wauwatosa, WI St. Jude the Apostle.
Asare–Dankwah, John '94 (NO) New Orleans, LA Blessed Trinity.
Ascencio, Enrique '88 (MGZ) Moca, PR Our Lady of Monserrate.
Ascencio, Joseph A. '82 (COL) On Duty Outside the Diocese.
Ascheman, Thomas *s.v.d.* (FTW) Fort Wayne.
Ascheman, Thomas *s.v.d.* '82 (CHI)[N] Techny, IL Society of the Divine Word, Provincial Headquarters–Chicago Prov.
Ascheman, Thomas *s.v.d.* '82 (FTW) Fort Wayne, IN St. Patrick.
Aschenbrennen, George A. *s.j.* '65 (WDC)[N] Washington, DC The Jesuit Community of St. Aloysius Gonzaga.
Aschenbrenner, Ralph '61 (SAL) Retired.
Aschmann, Karl *c.ss.r.* '50 (ORL)[F] New Smyrna Beach, FL St. Alphonsus Villa–Redemptorist Fathers and Brothers Retired.
Asenjo, Jose Maria '65 (GAL) Retired.
Asghedom, Tesfaldet '85 (LA) Los Angeles, CA Sacred Heart.
Ashbaugh, William A. '93 (LAN) Father McGiveny House; Ann Arbor, MI St. Thomas the Apostle; St. Catherine House.
Ashbeck, David K. '68 (GB) On Duty Outside the Diocese.
Ashe, John F. '63 (NOR) Portland, CT St. Mary.
Ashe, Joseph C. '76 (NOR) Old Saybrook, CT St. John.
Ashe, Kevin P. '63 (NEW) Retired.
Ashe, Michael B. '59 (CC) Retired.
Ashenbrenner, Robert D. *o.s.f.s.* '54 (PH)[Y] Philadelphia, PA Father Louis Brisson Residence Retired.
Ashenbrenner, Robert D. *o.s.f.s.* '54 (WIL)[J] Childs, MD Retirement and Assisted Care Facility Retired.
Ashibuogwu, Michael '00 (PHX) Lake Havasu City, AZ Our Lady of the Lake Roman Catholic Parish.
Ashkar, Chorbishop Dominic F. '62 (SAM) Washington, DC Our Lady of Lebanon Church.
Ashley, Benedict M. *o.p.* '48 (STL)[O] St. Louis, MO St. Dominic Priory.
Ashman, Robert '86 (NY) Yonkers, NY St. Anthony.
Ashmore, Ronald M. '76 (IND) Unassigned.
Ashton, Rev. Msgr. John P. '55 (Y) College of Consultors; Priests Council Retired.
Asia, Thomas P. *m.m.h.c.* '98 (LA) Carson, CA St. Philomena.
Asih, Paul *m.s.p.* (BIR) Bessemer, AL St. Francis of Assisi.
Asir, Antony '82 (RVC) East Meadow, NY St. Raphael.
Askar, George F. '67 (LFT) Retired.
Asma, Lawrence F. *c.m.* '83 (STL) DePaul Health Center; [O] St. Louis Vincentian Residence; [O] St. Louis, MO Lazarist Residence.
Asma, Lawrence F. *c.m.* '83 (FgM) Earth City, MO Western Province.
Asmar, Rev. Msgr. Maroun '93 (SAM) Somerset, NJ St. Sharbel.
Aspinall, Campion W. *c.j.* '61 (LA) Santa Maria, CA St. Louis de Montfort Retired.
Assalone, John T. '09 (LAV) Henderson, NV St. Francis of Assisi.
Asselin, Jason '06 (FAR) Fargo, ND Holy Spirit Church of Fargo.
Assenmacher, Hugh *o.s.b.* '58 (LR)[A] Subiaco, AR Subiaco Abbey.
Assi, Nicholas '72 (LA) Manhattan Beach, CA American Martyrs.
Ast, Nicholas K. *o.s.b.* '01 (OKL)[I] Shawnee, OK St. Gregory's Abbey.
Astarita, Joseph J. '03 (NEW) Jersey City, NJ St. Aedan's.
Astorino, Robert F. *m.m.* '70 (FgM) Maryknoll, NY MARYKNOLL.
Astudillo, Roland '89 (LA) Montebello, CA Our Lady of the Miraculous Medal.
Astudillo, Tony P. '73 (LA) Walnut, CA St. Lorenzo Ruiz.
Astuto, Lucian S. '57 (OM) Retired.
Asucan, Julian '00 (BUR) Fairfax, VT St. Luke.
Asue, Daniel '97 (MIA) North Miami, FL Holy Family.
Asuming, Frederick '89 (NO) New Orleans, LA Blessed Trinity.
Asuncion, Leo Alban '79 (OAK) Deanery #5.
Asuncion, Leonardo '79 (OAK) Martinez, CA St. Catherine of Siena.
Asuquo, Godwin '03 (RCK)[L] DeKalb, IL Newman Foundation for Catholic Students of Northern Illinois University; DeKalb, IL Christ the Teacher, University Parish of Northern Illinois University.
Atadana, Joseph Ayeridaga '88 (STP) Minneapolis, MN St. Leonard of Port Maurice.
Atangana, Edouard '02 (BWN) Hidalgo, TX St. Frances Xavier Cabrini; Coordinator; Presbyteral Council; [E] San Juan, TX San Juan Nursing Home, Inc.
Atcher, Joseph *o.carm.* '76 (L) Ex Officio; Office of Lifelong Formation and Education; Louisville, KY Holy Spirit.
Atcher, Joseph *o.carm.* '76 (JOL)[L] Darien Carmelite Provincial Office.
Atehortua, Jairo L. *c.m.* '95 (SP) New Port Richey, FL Our Lady Queen of Peace.
Atem, Henry '08 (ATL) Roswell, GA St. Peter Chanel.
Aten, Robert L. '79 (STL) Special Assignment; [O] Rocky Mount, MO Contemplative Heart of Mary Hermitage.
Athappilly, Andrews *c.m.i.* '64 (COV) Burlington, KY Immaculate Heart of Mary.
Atienza, Abdon *o.s.a.* '61 (MGZ) San German, PR St. Rose of Lima.
Atienza, Brian '02 (SAC) Auburn, CA St. Joseph.
Atkin, Timothy *c.i.c.m.* '74 (FgM) Arlington, VA MISSIONHURST.
Atkins, Daniel '87 (IND) Corydon, IN Most Precious Blood; Corydon, IN St. Peter; Council of Priests.
Atkins, J. Daniel '87 (IND) Corydon, IN St. Joseph.
Atkins, James '75 (PRM) On Duty Outside the Diocese.
Atkins, James '72 (RVC) Serving Outside the Diocese.
Atkins, James '72 (NY)[EE] Yonkers, NY St. Felix Friary.
Atkins, James '75 (PBR) Toronto, OH St. Joseph.
Atkinson, Anselm *o.s.b.* '82 (WOR)[O] Petersham, MA St. Mary's Monastery.
Atkinson, John V. '61 (MEM) College of Consultors; Presbyteral Council Retired.
Atkinson, Sean '69 (JKS) Cleveland, MS Our Lady of Victories; Rosedale, MS Sacred Heart; [H] Cleveland, MS Delta State University Newman Center.
Ato, Lorenzo '88 (NY) New York, NY St. Brigid; New York, NY St. Emeric; Communications Office (Bureau of Information for the Media); New York, NY Immaculate Conception.
Atok, George *s.d.b.* '82 (NY)[GG] Stony Point, NY Don Bosco Retreat Center and Marian Shrine; [GG] Stony Point, NY Marian Shrine.
Atonio, Andrew *m.f.* '91 (SPP) Diocesan Consultors; Pago Pago, AS Church of the Immaculate Conception.
Atonio, Falaniko '92 (SPP) Faculty Members; Pago Pago, AS Church of Sacred Heart.
Atoyebi, John B. '94 (CHI) Chicago, IL St. Clotilde; Chicago, IL Holy Angels.
Atraga, Tamiru F. (BO) Malden, MA Immaculate Conception.
Attah, Magnus '80 (SEA) Lacey, WA Sacred Heart of Jesus.
Attak, Cyril '64 (PRM) Allen Park, MI St. Stephen.
Attakruh, John '89 (RVC) Patchogue, NY Brookhaven Memorial Hospital.
Attanasio, Raymond V. '58 (MET) Retired.
Attanasio, Scott '95 (NEW) North Arlington, NJ Queen of Peace.
Attansey, Matthew '79 (FAR) Mayville, ND St. Agnes; Mayville, ND Our Lady of Peace Church of Mayville.
Attard, Joseph '69 (BRK) Brooklyn, NY Most Precious Blood.
Atto, Dennis D. '02 (RCK) Savanna, IL St. John the Baptist; Mount Carroll, IL SS. John and Catherine.
Atuah, Charles *m.s.p.* '90 (BEA) Diocesan College of Consultors; Memorial Hermann Baptist Hospital; Port Arthur, TX Sacred Heart–St. Mary Parish; Presbyteral Council.
Atunzu, Kevin O. '79 (LR) Nashville, AR St. Martin Church; Hope, AR Our Lady of Good Hope.
Atusameso, Jean–Claude '00 (ARL) Alexandria, VA St. Mary's.
Atwell, Basil *o.s.b.* '02 (BIS) Fort Yates, ND St. Peter – Catholic Indian Mission; Fort Yates, ND St. Philomena; [A] Richardton, ND Assumption Abbey; Fort Yates, ND St. James; Fort Yates, ND St. Elizabeth; Fort Yates, ND Sacred Heart.
Atwine, Lucius *c.s.c.* '97 (FTW)[H] Notre Dame Congregation of Holy Cross, Indiana Province, Provincial House.
Atwood, Ray E. '94 (DUB) Elma, IA St. Peter; Elma, IA Immaculate Conception; Elma, IA Immaculate Conception; Elma, IA Our Lady of Lourdes; Elma, IA St. Bernard.
Atwood, Ronald E. '84 (OAK) Retired.
Atwood, Ronald J. '69 (COL) Columbus, OH St. Francis of Assisi.
Atwood, Wilbur J. *s.s.j.* '58 (NO)[P] New Orleans, LA The Josephite Faculty House of St. Augustine High School; [E] New Orleans, LA St. Augustine High School; [H] New Orleans, LA St. Augustine High School.
Atzeni, Roberto '88 (ARE) Sabana Hoyos, PR Nuestra Senora de Fatima.
Atzeni Marini, Roberto *c.m.v.* '88 (ARE) Priest's Senate (Consejo Presbiteral).
Au, Thomas Y. '79 (LIN) Roseland, NE Sacred Heart; Advocates; Deaneries and Deans; Diocesan Area CCD Directors.
Au, Vincent *c.m.c.* '00 (SB) Corona, CA St. Mary Magdalene; [I] Corona, CA Congregation of the Mother Co–Redemptrix, C.M.C.
Au, William A. '75 (BAL) Baltimore, MD SS. Philip and James.
Aubespin, Francis Borgia *s.v.d.* '65 (GAL) Houston, TX St. Mary of the Purification.
Aubin, Jean P. '01 (BO) Maynard, MA St. Bridget.
Aubin, Rev. Msgr. Joseph G. '55 (OG) Plattsburgh, NY St. Peter Retired.
Aubin, Joseph '61 (LAN) Retired.
Aubin, Pierre *m.s.c.* '58 (OG) Cape Vincent, NY The Catholic Community of Cape Vincent, Rosiere and Chaumont; [F] Watertown, NY Missionaries of the Sacred Heart; [J] Cape Vincent, NY Mission Project Service; Diocesan Consultors; Consultors:.
Aubin, Ronald '81 (SP) Land O'Lakes, FL Our Lady of the Rosary; Judicial Vicar; Judges; College of Consultors; [F] Land O Lakes, FL Our Lady of the Rosary Early Childhood Center – Mary's House – ECC.
Auble, Theodore J. '75 (ROC) Churchville, NY St. Vincent De Paul.
Aubrey, Robert J. '71 (DM) Dexter, IA Des Moines City

Chaplaincy Program; [J] Des Moines, IA City Hospital Chaplaincy Service.
Aubry, Ronald J. '81 (COL) Millersburg, OH St. Peter.
Auby, John R. '94 (MAD) Janesville, WI St. William; Personnel Board.
Auchter, Rev. Msgr. John A. '54 (ALN) Lake Harmony, PA St. Peter the Fisherman; Coplay, PA St. Peter.
Aucoin, Rev. Msgr. Robert H. '70 (OG)[A] Plattsburgh, NY Seton Catholic Central; Episcopal Vicar for Catholic Education; Diocesan Consultors; Director of Deacon Formation; Plattsburgh, NY St. Peter.
Auda, Rev. Msgr. Lawrence '60 (SFD) Gillespie, IL St. Joseph; Gillespie, IL SS. Simon and Jude; Litchfield Deanery.
Audet, Arthur J. '85 (HRT) Marlborough, CT St. John Fisher.
Audet, Dennis J. '78 (MAN) Meredith, NH St. Charles Borromeo; Long Range Planning Committee; Cabinet Secretary for Ministry Formation; Vicars Forane; Secretariat for Ministry Formation; Priest Personnel Board.
Audette, Albert '93 (BGP) Stamford, CT The Basilica of Saint John the Evangelist Retired.
Audu, John (NY) Kingston, NY St. Mary.
Auer, Benedict L. *o.s.b.* '80 (SEA)[L] Lacey, WA St. Martin's Abbey; [A] Lacey, WA Saint Martin's University.
Auer, Rev. Msgr. John J. '57 (BAL) Severna Park, MD St. John the Evangelist; Jessup, MD Clifton T. Perkins Hospital Retired.
Auer, John '79 (COS) Highlands Ranch, CO St. Mark Catholic Church.
Auer, Joseph E. '56 (CHI) Palos Park, IL Retired.
Auer, Peter *s.o.l.t.* '93 (MAD) Ridgeway, WI Immaculate Conception; Ridgeway, WI St. Bridget.
Auer, Robert F. '51 (DUB) Retired.
Auerbach, Shay W. *s.j.* '99 (RIC) Richmond, VA Sacred Heart.
Aufdermauer, Joseph A. '68 (MIL) New Berlin, WI St. Elizabeth Ann Seton.
Aufieri, Robert J. '74 (NY) Staten Island, NY Holy Rosary; Italian Apostolate, Office of the.
Aufiero, Louis D. '65 (BRK) Flushing, NY Holy Family Retired.
Augenstein, Eric '04 (IND) New Albany, IN Our Lady of Perpetual Help.
Auger, George J. *c.s.v.* '61 (CHI)[N] Arlington Heights, IL Viatorian Province Center–Clerics of St. Viator.
Auger, Gerald E. '55 (MAN) Retired.
Auger, Raymond D. '56 (PRT) Retired.
Augustine, Kenneth J. '77 (MIL) Brookfield, WI St. Luke.
Augustine, L. '92 (SCR) East Stroudsburg, PA St. Matthew's.
Augustine, Liju *c.m.i.* '03 (BRK) Astoria, NY Immaculate Conception.
Augustine, Rev. Msgr. Roger J. '59 (SC) Sioux City, IA Blessed Sacrament; Priests' Pension Plan – Board of Trustees Retired.
Augustine, Russell '89 (BGP) Redding Ridge, CT St. Patrick; Presbyteral Council.
Augustinowitz, Michael E. '75 (BUR) Priests' Benefit Fund; [G] Montpelier, VT Goddard College (Plainfield); Montpelier, VT St. Augustine.
Augustyn, Andrew M. '47 (GI) Retired.
Augustyn, Boguslaw Adam *c.ss.r.* '93 (MO) Army Reserve Chaplains.
Augustyn, James M. '63 (BUF) Judges Retired.
Augustyn, Kevin R. '04 (DEN) Boulder, CO St. Thomas Aquinas; Deaneries; Elected Representatives from Deanery to Presbyteral Council.
Augustyn, Richard H. '76 (BUF) Hospital Chaplains; Buffalo General Hospital; Buffalo, NY Immaculate Heart of Mary.
Aumaitre, Louis (NEW) Irvington, NJ St. Leo's.
Auman, Robert '47 (SFE) Retired.
Aumen, Paul *c.pp.s.* '49 (CIN)[N] Dayton Provincial Office of the Cincinnati Province of the Society of the Precious Blood.
Aureus, Antonio '77 (DAL) Sherman, TX St. Mary.
Aurilia, John C. *o.f.m.cap.* (SP) Tampa, FL Most Holy Redeemer.
Ausenbaugh, J. Andrew '95 (OWN) Absent on Leave.
Ausperk, Michael D. '89 (CLV) Cleveland, OH St. Vincent de Paul.
Austgen, Robert J. *c.s.c.* '58 (FTW)[B] University of Notre Dame Du Lac; [E] Notre Dame, IN University Health Services; [H] Notre Dame, IN Holy Cross Community, Corby Hall, University of Notre Dame.
Austin, Brian *f.s.s.p.* (VEN) Sarasota, FL Christ the King.
Austin, C. Gerard *o.p.* '59 (VEN)[D] Arcadia, FL Blessed Edmund Rice School for Pastoral Ministry.
Austin, David M. '03 (RCK) Fulton, IL Immaculate Conception; Albany, IL St. Patrick.
Austin, John J. '97 (PRT) Retired.
Austin, Jonathan '97 (DAL) On Leave of Absence.
Austin, Michael P. '00 (BLX) Moss Point, MS St. Joseph; Deans; Mission Office; Liturgy, Office of; Diocesan Liturgical Commission; Building and Real Estate Committee; Mission Board; Pontifical Association of the Holy Childhood; Propagation of the Faith; Presbyteral Council.
Austin, Nicholas *s.j.* '06 (BO)[U] Newton, MA The Jesuit Community at Boston College.
Austin, Stephen E. '84 (TLS) Tulsa, OK Resurrection.
Austin, Walter J. '81 (NO) La Place, LA Ascension of Our Lord; Army National Guard Chaplains.
Austriaco, Nicanor P.G. *o.p.* '04 (PRO)[P] Providence St. Thomas Aquinas Priory at Providence College.
Auth, Clifford H. '99 (SY)[F] Syracuse, NY Bishop Joseph T. O'Keefe, Inc.; [U] Syracuse, NY David W. Barry Foundation; Chancellor; Board of Diocesan Consultors; Management Team; Presbyteral Council; Defender of the Bond; Vicar for Administration; Administration; Building Commission; Clerical Fund Society of the Roman Catholic Diocese of Syracuse; Priests' Personnel Committee; [U] Syracuse, NY Grimes Foundation; Finance Committee; Special Assignment; Baldwinsville, NY St. Augustine.
Auth, James E. '61 (TOL) Advocate; Toledo, OH Regina Coeli; Judges.
Auth, William G. *o.s.f.s.* '69 (TOL)[I] Toledo Oblates of St. Francis de Sales.
Auther, John *s.j.* '90 (PHX) Phoenix, AZ St. Francis Xavier Roman Catholic Parish; [F] Phoenix, AZ Society of Jesus.
Auva'a, Eneliko (SPP) Pago Pago, AS Co–Cathedral of St. Joseph the Worker.
Auve, Perron J. '62 (YAK) Kennewick, WA Holy Spirit.
Avau, Felix A. *c.i.c.m.* '54 (SAT) Retired.
Avella, Alberto '80 (GLP) Grants, NM St. Teresa of Avila; Milan, NM St. Vivian; Milan, NM San Mateo; Milan, NM San Rafael; Vicars Forane; Presbyteral Council; Seboyeta, NM Our Lady of Sorrows.
Avella, Robert E. '75 (ARL) Arlington, VA Our Lady of Lourdes; Defenders of the Bond.
Avella, Steven M. '79 (MIL)[B] Hales Corners, WI Sacred Heart School of Theology; Special Assignment.
Avella, William '50 (RNO) Retired.
Avello, Vicente Salas *o.de.m.* '66 (PCE) Ponce, PR Santuario San Judas Tadeo.
Avendano, Alvaro '92 (ATL) Cumming, GA Good Shepherd; Dahlonega, GA St. Luke.
Aveni, Paul J. '98 (BO) Revere, MA St. Mary of the Assumption.
Avenido, Albert H. '95 (LA) Lakewood, CA St. Pancratius; Spiritual Moderator.
Avenido, Serafin P. '77 (SAN) Brownwood, TX St. Mary's.
Avicolli, Maurice C. *o.praem.* '68 (PH) Philadelphia, PA St. Gabriel; [Y] Paoli, PA Daylesford Abbey.
Avila, Carlos Antonio Massieu '89 (MIA)[Q] Coral Gables, FL House of the Divine Will, Inc.
Avila, Daniel C. '87 (FRS) Visalia, CA St. Thomas the Apostle; Visalia, CA Holy Family; Visalia, CA St. Mary.
Avila, Israel '91 (FRS) Cutler, CA St. Mary.
Avila, Jose Rodolfo Lache '81 (CHR) Camden, SC Our Lady of Perpetual Help.
Avila, Misael '99 (STO) Oakdale, CA St. Mary of the Annunciation Church (Pastor of).
Avila, Rev. Msgr. Stephen J. '81 (FR) Mansfield, MA St. Mary's; Attleboro Deanery; Office for Divine Worship; Television Apostolate.
Avila–Ibarra, Juan Pablo '08 (CHI) Chicago Heights, IL St. Paul; Chicago Heights, IL St. Agnes.
Aviles, Mario Alberto *c.o.* '98 (BWN) Hidalgo, TX Sacred Heart; [C] Pharr, TX Oratory Academy School of St. Philip Neri; [F] Pharr, TX Pharr Oratory of St. Philip Neri of Pontifical Right; Pharr, TX Oratory Academy School of St. Philip Neri; Pharr, TX Oratory School – Athenaeum for University Preparation; [B] Pharr, TX Oratory Athenaeum for University Preparation; Pharr, TX.
Aviles, Victor Perez *o.p.* '67 (PCE) Yauco, PR Holy Rosary.
Avis, William E. *i.c.r.s.s.* '07 (KC) Kansas City, MO Oratory of Old St. Patrick.
Avittappally, Baiju Augustine *m.s.* '01 (ORL) Orlando, FL Good Shepherd.
Avula, Maria Susai J. '80 (TYL) Sulphur Springs, TX St. James.
Avula, Susai '80 (TYL) Deans; Priests' Personnel Board.
Awada, Bechara '03 (OLL) Peoria, IL St. Sharbel Maronite Catholic Church.
Awalt, Rev. Msgr. William J. '47 (WDC) Potomac, MD Our Lady of Mercy Retired.
Award, Richard *c.p.* '81 (FgM) South River, NJ St. Paul of the Cross Province.
Award, *c.p.* '81 (MET)[I] South River Passionist Provincial Office.
Awuafor, Gabriel '91 (NY) Cold Spring, NY Our Lady of Loretto.
Axe, Thomas R. '60 (CIN) Retired.
Axe, William J. *o.ss.t.* '74 (BAL)[S] The Trinitarians in California.
Axe, William *o.ss.t.* '74 (LA) Los Angeles, CA St. Agatha.
Axtmann, David '06 (SFS) Webster, SD Christ the King.
Axtmann, Mark A. '01 (MO) DEPARTMENT OF VETERANS AFFAIRS HOSPITALS AND CHAPLAINS.
Axtmann, Mark '01 (SFS) Beresford, SD St. Teresa of Avila; Veteran's Hospital.
Ayala, Agustin Mateo '90 (WDC) Washington, DC St. Gabriel; Advocates.
Ayala, Daniel '86 (BRK) Rego Park, NY Our Lady of the Angelus.
Ayala, H. Alejandro '06 (CHL) Winston–Salem, NC St. Leo the Great.
Ayala, Juan *o.m.i.* '07 (LA) San Fernando, CA Santa Rosa.
Ayala, Osvaldo *c.m.* '01 (FgM) Philadelphia, PA Eastern Province.
Ayala, Robert M. '06 (MIA) Miami, FL St. John Bosco.
Ayamanthil, Mathew '59 (NEW)[M] Caldwell, NJ The Rev. Msgr. James F. Kelley Residence for Retired Priests Retired.
Ayang, John M. *s.o.l.t.* '98 (CC)[G] Robstown, TX Society of Our Lady of the Most Holy Trinity.
Ayangl, John M. *s.o.l.t.* (GAL) Houston, TX St. Monica.
Ayathupadam, Joseph '61 (CHL) Retired.
Ayaton, Achilles '79 (ALN) Bethlehem, PA Notre Dame of Bethlehem.
Aydt, Raymond A. '46 (BIS) Grenora, ND St. Boniface.
Ayem, Alfred A. *s.v.d.* (NO) New Orleans, LA St. Paul the Apostle.
Ayers, Dan '99 (COS)[C] Colorado Springs, CO Penrose Hospital.
Ayissi Nkoumu, Joseph '05 (BWN) McAllen, TX McAllen Medical Hospital.
Ayisu, Stephen *s.v.d.* '02 (SB) San Bernardino, CA St. Anthony.
Aylward, Gerald J. *c.s.p.* '53 (NY)[EE] New York, NY Paulist Fathers' Motherhouse Retired.
Aylward, James W. '64 (SFR) Retired.
Aylward, Richard *m.m.* '53 (NY)[EE] Maryknoll Maryknoll Fathers and Brothers Retired.
Ayo, Nicholas *c.s.c.* '59 (FTW)[B] University of Notre Dame Du Lac; [H] Notre Dame, IN Holy Cross Community, Corby Hall, University of Notre Dame.
Ayoob, John '65 (PIT) Moon Township, PA St. Margaret Mary.
Ayotte, David J. *s.j.* '92 (OAK)[M] Berkeley, CA Jesuit Fathers and Brothers.
Ayoub, Rev. Msgr. S. Paul '53 (BUF)[O] Lackawanna, NY Bishop Head Residence Retired.
Ayres, William G. '99 (PH) Philadelphia, PA Immaculate Conception; Philadelphia, PA St. Michael; Laotian Apostolate.
Ayuni Toh, Marcel *sch.p.* '06 (NY) New York, NY Annunciation; [EE] New York, NY Calasanzian Fathers (Piarists).
Ayuyu, Isaac M. '86 (CHK) Saipan, MP Cathedral of Our Lady of Mt. Carmel; Director of Worship; Presbyteral Council; Hospital Chaplaincy (Saipan); Main Contact.
Azar, Rt. Rev. John '88 (NTN) Atlanta, GA St. John Chrysostom; Presbyteral Council.
Azar, Nicholas G. '09 (ATL) Graduate Studies.
Azar, Rev. Msgr. Peter F. '80 (SAM) Lawrence, MA St. Anthony; Presbyteral Council; Protopresbyters (Deans); College of Consultors; Board of Pastors.
Azcoiti, Vicente '56 (BWN) Retired.
Azcoitia, Florentino *s.j.* '55 (MIA)[K] Miami, FL Villa Javier; Encuentros Familiares y Casa Manresa (Spanish).
Azcona, Jose Luis '85 (AUS) Luling, TX St. John the Evangelist.
Azevedo, Ferdinand T. *s.j.* '70 (FgM) Los Gatos, CA Society of Jesus.
Azhakath, Matthew '89 (NY) Phoenicia, NY St. Francis de Sales.
Azike, Emmanuel '01 (SEA) Burlington, WA St. Charles; La Conner, WA Sacred Heart; Mount Vernon, WA Immaculate Conception.
Azike, Emmanuel *o.p.* (SEA) Sedro Woolley, WA Immaculate Heart of Mary.
Azoon, Philip '94 (NTN) Retired.
Azpericueta, Lucas '69 (FRS) Retired.
Azrak, Albert *c.s.s.* '60 (NY) White Plains, NY Our Lady of Mt. Carmel.
Azu, Edmund (LA) Hospital Chaplains.
Azu, John '75 (LR) Little Rock, AR Our Lady of the Holy Souls.
Azuwike, Anthony '01 (MEM) Savannah, TN St. Mary Church.
Azzarto, Anthony J. *s.j.* '69 (NEW)[C] Jersey City, NJ Jesuit Community; [M] Jersey City, NJ Jesuit Community of St. Peter's Prep, Inc.

B

Baabuge, Martin Atanga '91 (TUC) Pearce, AZ Saint Jude Thaddeus Roman Catholic Parish – Pearce Sunsites.
Babcock, David J. *o.f.m.* '53 (FgM) New York, NY Holy Name Province.

Babcock, Rt. Rev. James K. '81 (NTN) Placentia, CA Holy Cross.
Babcock, Timothy F. '68 (DET) Special Assignment; Judges.
Babeu, Gill C. '87 (BGP) Stamford, CT St. Bridget of Ireland.
Babich, Ronald J. '77 (DET) Fraser, MI Our Lady Queen of All Saints.
Babick, Bryan P. '07 (CHR) Diocesan Master of Ceremonies; Mount Pleasant, SC Christ Our King.
Babicz, Edmund A. '84 (MAN) Center Ossipee, NH St. Joseph; Sanbornville, NH St. Anthony; Carroll County House of Correction.
Babiczuk, Fred '86 (FR) Fall River, MA Parish of the Good Shepherd.
Babin, Albert C. *c.ss.r.* '52 (STL)[O] Liguori, MO St. Clement Health Care Center.
Babin, Victor '75 (MIA) Hollywood, FL Nativity.
Babineau, Alexis A. *a.a.* '45 (WOR)[O] Worcester, MA Assumptionists (Augustinians of the Assumption).
Babineau, William E. '68 (MAN) Auburn, NH St. Peter Retired.
Babinski, Donald E. '81 (RVC) East Islip, NY St. Mary's.
Babiuch, Thomas '02 (ALB) Fort Edward, NY St. Joseph; Glens Falls, NY St. Alphonsus.
Babonas, Alphonse '62 (DET) Retired.
Babowitch, John F. '96 (PH) Philadelphia, PA St. Barnabas.
Bac, Isidore M. Dinh Thanh *c.m.c.* '83 (SPC)[F] Springfield, MO Congregation of Mother Coredemptrix, Our Lady of the Rosary House.
Baca, Al '89 (ORG) Ecumenical and Interreligious Affairs.
Baca, Alfred '89 (ORG) Tustin, CA St. Cecilia.
Baca, Jamie *c.s.p.* '06 (AUS)[L] Austin, TX University Catholic Center.
Baca, Joseph '01 (FRS) Absent on Sick Leave.
Bacatan, Francisco '94 (NY) Scarsdale, NY St. Pius X.
Baccaro, Gaetano T. '85 (SY) Oswego, NY St. Paul; Northern Area Vicar; Presbyteral Council.
Baccellieri, Joseph '66 (P) Retired.
Bacchi, Lee F. '77 (JOL) Joliet, IL St. Mary Nativity.
Bacchi, Robert A. '77 (CHI) La Grange, IL St. Francis Xavier.
Bacevice, Joseph A. '77 (CLV) Defenders of the Bond; Cleveland, OH St. Casimir.
Bacevicius, John J. *o.f.m.* '62 (PRT)[I] Kennebunkport, ME St. Anthony's Friary; Kennebunkport, ME.
Bach, Rev. Msgr. Frank J. '56 (SPK) Retired.
Bach, Gregory J. '99 (COV)[R] Highland Heights, KY Catholic Newman Club – Northern Kentucky University; Diocesan Consultors; Campus Ministry–Newman Center; Serra Club of Diocese of Covington; Vocations Office.
Bach, James Nguyen '94 (NO) Luling, LA St. Anthony of Padua; Ama, LA St. Mark.
Bach, John A. '71 (LFT)[D] Lafayette, IN St. Anthony Health Care Retired.
Bach, Lester *o.f.m.cap.* '57 (MAD)[I] Madison, WI San Damiano Friary Retired.
Bachand, Joseph G. *m.s.* '76 (FR)[G] Attleboro, MA La Salette Missionary Association.
Bachand, Joseph G. *m.s.* '76 (HRT) Hartford, CT Missionaries of Our Lady of La Salette; Hartford, CT; [L] Hartford, CT Missionaries of LaSalette Province of Mary, Mother of the Americas.
Bacher, Arthur A. '54 (CLV) Richfield, OH St. Victor; Brunswick, OH St. Colette Retired.
Bachkay, John M. '83 (PIT) Pittsburgh, PA St. Sylvester.
Bachman, Martin E. '09 (CIN) Cincinnati, OH St. James the Greater.
Bachman, Michael J. '84 (BGP) Norwalk, CT St. Ladislaus.
Bachmann, Kevin J. *o.s.b.* '01 (PBL) Pueblo, CO St. Joseph.
Bachmann, Mark *o.s.b.* '91 (TLS)[G] Hulbert, OK Our Lady of the Annunciation of Clear Creek Monastery.
Bachmeier, A. Bernard '68 (FAR) Retired.
Bachmeier, Brian '97 (FAR) Absent on Leave.
Bachmeier, Mark V. '89 (P) Eugene, OR St. Mary; Personnel Board.
Bachner, Daniel '05 (JOL) Plainfield, IL St. Mary Immaculate.
Bachner, James M. '96 (PIT) Pittsburgh, PA St. Catherine of Siena.
Bacik, James J. '62 (TOL) Toledo, OH Corpus Christi (University of Toledo); [L] Toledo, OH University of Toledo Campus Ministry; [M] Toledo, OH U.T. Newman Foundation for Student Education and Development.
Bacik, James J. (FTW)[B] University of Notre Dame Du Lac.
Bacik, Leonard M. '72 (CLV) Middleburg Heights, OH St. Bartholomew.
Bacino, Ben '75 (PBL) Personnel; Pueblo, CO St. Mary Help of Christians.
Backer, Dennis J. '07 (STP) Coon Rapids, MN Church of the Epiphany.
Backes, John J. '73 (NY) Dover Plains, NY St. Charles Borromeo.
Backherns, Robert *s.m.* '56 (CIN)[N] Dayton, OH Mercy Siena Gardens.
Backiel, Bernard *m.i.c.* '60 (SPR)[H] Stockbridge, MA Congregation of Marian Fathers of The Immaculate Conception of the Most Blessed Virgin Mary.
Backmann, Albert P. '00 (STP)[C] St. Paul, MN University of St. Thomas; [A] St. Paul, MN St. John Vianney Seminary.
Backous, Timothy *o.s.b.* '86 (SCL)[B] Saint John's University; [D] Collegeville, MN St. John's Preparatory School; [I] Collegeville, MN St. John's Abbey, of the Order of St. Benedict.
Bacleon, Misael '84 (NY) Bronx, NY Montefiore Medical Center.
Bacleon, Misael '83 (NY) Bronx, NY St. Ann.
Bacon, Jeffery W. '05 (CIN) Hamilton, OH Queen of Peace.
Bacovin, Rev. Msgr. Ronald J. '66 (TR) Pennington, NJ St. James; Office of Priest Personnel.
Badawi, Rev. Msgr. Alfred '91 (OLL) Lombard, IL Our Lady of Lebanon Maronite Catholic Church; Presbyteral Council.
Baddick, Rev. Msgr. Thomas D. '81 (ALN) College of Consultors; Bethlehem, PA Notre Dame of Bethlehem.
Badding, Joseph P. '69 (BUF) Ransomville, NY Immaculate Conception.
Badeaux, James '99 (PSC) Mont Clare, PA St. Michael.
Badeaux, Kevin *j.c.l.* '84 (BEA) On Leave.
Baden, Robert D. '77 (RC) Retired.
Badenes, Jose Ignacio *s.j.* '93 (LA)[C] Los Angeles, CA Jesuit Community.
Bader, Edward '82 (NY) Marlboro, NY St. Mary.
Bader, Paul A. '61 (CIN) Cincinnati, OH St. Matthias Retired.
Badger, Arthur A. '53 (TOL) Retired.
Badgerow, Rock J. '79 (GR) Personal Leave.
Badia, Leonard F. '60 (BRK) Retired.
Badilles, Roy Jose '82 (LUB) Snyder, TX St. Elizabeth's; Snyder, TX Our Lady of Guadalupe.
Badillo, Robert P. *m.id.* '95 (NY) Bronx, NY St. Dominic; Bronx, NY Our Lady of Solace; [EE] Bronx, NY Idente Missionaries – Santa Maria Residence.
Badiola, Jose Alexander *s.j.* '98 (BO)[U] Cambridge, MA Hopkins House.
Badnerosky, Myron M. '56 (PSC) Levittown, PA Our Lady of Perpetual Help.
Bado, Arsene Brice *s.j.* '09 (BO)[U] Cambridge, MA Hopkins House.
Badurina, Gabriel *t.o.r.* '62 (PIT) Washington County, PA West Penn Allegheny Health System–Canonsburg Hospital; Canonsburg, PA St. Patrick.
Badway, Gavin '00 (PMB) West Palm Beach, FL Holy Name of Jesus.
Bae, Constantine Kihyen '85 (LA)[BB] Los Angeles, CA Korean Catholic Renewal Movement of Southern California.
Bae, Stephen '02 (WDC) Potomac, MD Our Lady of Mercy.
Baehr, David J. '64 (VEN) Legion of Mary; Bradenton, FL Sacred Heart.
Baehr, David '64 (SY) Retired.
Baek, Augustine *s.d.b.* '95 (NY)[GG] Stony Point, NY Don Bosco Retreat Center and Marian Shrine; [GG] Stony Point, NY Marian Shrine.
Baenziger, Edward J. *c.s.b.* '76 (GAL)[O] Houston, TX Residence of the Basilian Fathers of the University of St. Thomas.
Baer, Campion *o.f.m.cap.* '56 (MIL)[B] Mount Calvary, WI St. Lawrence Seminary; [P] Mount Calvary, WI St. Lawrence Friary.
Baer, Chrysostum Anthony *o.praem* '04 (ORG)[D] Silverado, CA St. Michael's Preparatory School; [I] Silverado, CA Norbertine Fathers of Orange Inc.
Baer, Robert W. *c.s.p.* '54 (NY)[EE] Jamaica Estates Paulist Fathers Generalate.
Baer, Robert W. *c.s.p.* '54 (BO)[U] Boston, MA Paulist Fathers Residence.
Baer, Timothy K. '96 (WDC) Chaptico, MD Our Lady of the Wayside.
Baer, William J. '96 (STP)[A] St. Paul, MN St. John Vianney Seminary; [C] St. Paul, MN University of St. Thomas; Saint John Vianney Seminary.
Baerwald, Jeffrey C. *s.j.* '93 (SJ)[B] Santa Clara, CA Jesuit Community.
Baeten, David '62 (GB) Retired.
Baetzold, Anthony Marie *c.f.r.* '05 (NY) Bronx, NY; [EE] Bronx, NY Saint Lawrence Friary.
Baez, Ramon A. '05 (ARL) Notaries; Fairfax, VA St. Leo's.
Bafaro, Michael P. '53 (WOR) Worcester, MA Our Lady of Mt. Carmel and St. Ann.
Bagadiong, Francisco '65 (SFR) San Francisco, CA St. Anne Retired.
Bagan, T. Francis *o.m.i.* '52 (BO)[X] Tewksbury, MA Immaculate Heart of Mary Residence.
Bagatin, Tarcisio *c.s.* '54 (PRO) Providence, RI Holy Ghost.
Bagdonis, Raymond *o.carm.* '94 (NY) Middletown, NY Our Lady of Mt. Carmel.
Baggetta, Joseph J. '74 (BO) Boston, MA St. James the Greater; Metro Youth Service Center.
Bagh, Yusuf *o.f.m.* '85 (NY)[EE] New York Franciscan Province of the Immaculate Conception.
Bagienski, Ronald A. '69 (BUF) Absent on Leave.
Bagnarol, Marco S. *i.m.c.* (MET)[I] Somerset, NJ Consolata Society for Foreign Missions.
Bagnato, James D. *o.praem.* '79 (WIL)[J] Middletown, DE Immaculate Conception Priory of the Canons Regular of Premontre; [J] Middletown, DE Norbertine Fathers of Delaware, Inc.
Baguio, Daniel S. '91 (GAL) Humble, TX St. Mary Magdalene.
Bagyinski, Agoston *o.f.m.* '98 (WDC)[B] Silver Spring, MD Holy Name College.
Bahash, James '99 (SD) San Diego, CA St. Jerome; Presbyteral Council.
Bahena, Rosalino Aguirre *o.r.c.* '03 (PCE) Castaner, PR Our Lady of the Miraculous Medal.
Bahhuth, Albert '96 (LA) Burbank, CA St. Finbar; San Fernando Region.
Bahl, Greg E. '06 (DUB) Worship Commission; Manchester, IA St. Mary; Manchester, IA Immaculate Conception; Ryan, IA St. Patrick; Adult Members.
Bahlinger, Donald *s.j.* (TUC)[H] Nogales, AZ Kino Border Initiative.
Bai, Bonaventure *o.f.m.* '99 (CIN)[C] Cincinnati, OH St. Anthony Shrine, Franciscan Postulancy.
Baiardi, Sereno *o.f.m.* '66 (MIL)[Y] Waterford, WI General Secretariat of the Franciscan Missions, Inc.; Waterford, WI General Secretariat of the Franciscan Missions, Inc.
Baidoo, Joseph '85 (RVC) Roosevelt, NY Queen of the Most Holy Rosary.
Baidoo, Raphael *o.ss.t.* '77 (VIC) Goliad, TX Immaculate Conception.
Baidoo, Raphael *o.ss.t.* (BAL)[S] The Trinitarians in Texas (Victoria & vicinity).
Baier, Donald M. '70 (RVC) Coram, NY St. Frances Cabrini.
Baier, William J. '82 (STL) Florissant, MO St. Ferdinand.
Baikauskas, Patrick *o.p.* '08 (LFT)[H] West Lafayette, IN St. Thomas Aquinas Parish and Foundation for Catholic Students Attending Purdue University; West Lafayette, IN St. Thomas Aquinas.
Bailey, Casey *o.c.s.o.* '83 (P)[L] Lafayette, OR The Cistercian (Trappist) Abbey of Our Lady of Guadalupe.
Bailey, Douglas S. *s.d.s.* '77 (ORL)[G] Melbourne, FL Florida Institute of Technology Campus Ministry.
Bailey, Fred K. '83 (ORG) Aliso Viejo, CA Corpus Christi.
Bailey, J. Lawrence '86 (SEA) Military Chaplains; Air Force Chaplains.
Bailey, Paul F. '58 (BO) Plymouth, MA St. Mary; Senior Priests. Retired.
Bailey, Ricardo '03 (ATL) College of Consultors; [C] Roswell, GA Blessed Trinity Catholic High School; Special or Other (Arch)Diocesan Assignment.
Bailey, Robert L. '93 (PRO) Pawtucket, RI St. Maria Goretti.
Bailey, Thomas *o.s.b.* '04 (RCK)[G] Aurora, IL Marmion Abbey.
Bailey, Thomas *o.s.b.* '04 (KC)[A] Conception, MO Conception Seminary College.
Baillargeon, Daniel '07 (PRT)[M] Waterville, ME Colby College; [M] Waterville, ME Thomas College; Waterville, ME Corpus Christi Parish.
Bailleres, Anthony *l.c.* '81 (MAD)[F] Edgerton, WI Koshkonong Pastoral Center; [I] Edgerton, WI Oaklawn Incorporated.
Bailon, Abelardo B.M. '58 (LA) Retired.
Baima, Thomas A. '80 (CHI) Skokie, IL St. Peter; [A] Mundelein, IL University of St. Mary of the Lake/Mundelein Seminary; Mundelein Seminary/University of St. Mary of the Lake; Administrative Council; [A] Mundelein, IL University of St. Mary of the Lake/Mundelein Seminary; [A] Mundelein, IL Ministerial and Continuing Education; [A] Mundelein, IL Conference Center.
Bain, Andre '04 (BRK) Brooklyn, NY St. Patrick.
Bain, Daniel '64 (RIC) Retired.
Bain, John '70 (RNO) Retired.
Bain, Kenneth '90 (SFS) Garretson, SD St. Rose of Lima; Garretson, SD St. Joseph the Workman; [I] Yankton, SD The House of Mary Shrine, Inc.
Bain, Richard C. '80 (SFR) DEPARTMENT OF VETERANS AFFAIRS HOSPITALS AND CHAPLAINS Retired.
Bain, Thomas J. *s.j.* '56 (DET)[K] Clarkston, MI Colombiere Center.
Baird, James '93 (DEN) Conifer, CO Our Lady of The Pines.
Baird, Rev. Msgr. Lawrence J. '69 (ORG) Newport Beach, CA Our Lady of Mount Carmel; Diocesan Finance Council.
Baistra, Jorge '74 (SAT) Retired.
Bajek, Gerald A. '69 (NEW)[M] Rutherford, NJ St. John Vianney Residence for Priests.
Bajkowski, Dennis W. '71 (CAM) Pennsville, NJ Church of the Queen of the Apostles, Pennsville, N.J.

Bajorek, James R. '80 (PH) Wallingford, PA St. John Chrysostom.
Bajorek, Joseph *s.d.b.* '45 (NEW)[M] Ramsey, NJ Don Bosco Prep Salesian Residence; [C] Ramsey, NJ Don Bosco Preparatory High School Retired.
Bak, Charles *m.s.a.* '09 (NOR)[G] Cromwell Society of the Missionaries of the Holy Apostles.
Bak, Charles *m.s.a.* '09 (HRT) Waterbury, CT Basilica of the Immaculate Conception.
Baka, James '91 (TUC) Pirtleville, AZ Saint Bernard Roman Catholic Church – Pirtleville; Douglas, AZ Saint Luke Roman Catholic Church – Douglas; Douglas, AZ Immaculate Conception Roman Catholic Parish – Douglas.
Bakajika, Andre K. *c.i.c.m.* (SAT) San Antonio, TX St. Patrick.
Bakatu, Sebastien '83 (STP) Inver Grove Heights, MN Church of St. Patrick.
Baker, Rev. Msgr. Andrew R. '91 (ALN) Allentown, PA Cathedral of St. Catharine of Siena.
Baker, Bartley '93 (NEW) Elmwood Park, NJ St. Leo's.
Baker, Brad '00 (JOL) Joliet, IL The Cathedral of St. Raymond.
Baker, David D '07 (BUF) West Seneca, NY Queen of Heaven.
Baker, Donald C. '95 (NY) New York, NY Nativity; New York, NY St. Teresa.
Baker, Donald P. '80 (CHL) Absent On Leave.
Baker, Dwight '09 (BUR) Saint Johnsbury, VT St. Elizabeth; St. Johnsbury, VT St. John the Evangelist.
Baker, Gerald H. '83 (OWN) Morganfield, KY St. Ann.
Baker, Jack H. '93 (DET) Waterford, MI St. Perpetua.
Baker, James E. '63 (DOD) Judge Retired.
Baker, James E. '63 (MO) Judges.
Baker, James H. *s.j.* '69 (STL)[C] Saint Louis University; [O] St. Louis, MO Jesuit Community Corporation at Saint Louis University – Jesuit Hall.
Baker, Jay '92 (HT) Thibodaux, LA St. Joseph Co–Cathedral; Vicar General; Judges; Priests Council; Legal Services; Coordinator; Clergy Personnel; College of Consultors; Diocesan Finance Council.
Baker, John C. '82 (MIA) Key West, FL St. Mary, Star of the Sea; Local Chaplain.
Baker, John Sims '94 (NSH) Defenders of the Bond; Vanderbilt; Priest Benefit Foundation; Presbyteral Council.
Baker, Rev. Msgr. Joseph W. '51 (STL) Retired.
Baker, Justin J. '99 (BUR) Elected Members; Rutland, VT Christ the King; Wallingford, VT St. Patrick; Diocesan Consultors; Deans.
Baker, Kenneth J. '84 (CHI) Western Springs, IL St. John of the Cross.
Baker, Kenneth R. '62 (CIN) Englewood, OH St. Paul.
Baker, Kenneth *s.j.* '62 (PAT) Pequannock, NJ Our Lady of Fatima Chapel (Tridentine).
Baker, Nicholas J. '63 (LIN) Minden, NE St. John the Baptist; Deaneries and Deans; Diocesan Area CCD Directors.
Baker, Richard D. (NY) New York, NY St. Malachy's.
Baker, Richard M. *m.m.* '71 (FgM) Maryknoll, NY MARYKNOLL.
Baker, Robert R. *c.s.c.* '70 (FgM) New Rochelle, NY Eastern Brothers Province.
Baker, Stephen J. *o.s.a.* '90 (PH)[Y] Malvern, PA Augustinian Friars (O.S.A.); [F] Malvern, PA Malvern Preparatory School for Boys.
Baker, Thomas E. '89 (LA) Lancaster, CA Sacred Heart; Deanery 8; San Fernando Region.
Baker, W. Pierre '78 (MAN) Nashua, NH Blessed John XXIII Parish.
Baker, William S. '55 (SY) Retired.
Baker, William T. '82 (ALN) Appointed Members; Bethlehem, PA Incarnation of Our Lord Parish.
Bakewell, Donald V. '66 (DUB) Dubuque, IA St. Joseph.
Bakey, Christopher T. '98 (CAM) Woodbine, NJ St. Casimir's R.C. Church, Woodbine, N.J.
Bakey, Christopher T. '98 (CAM) Vocation Advisory Board.
Bakh, Antoine '88 (OLL) Fullerton, CA St. John Maron Maronite Catholic Church.
Bakka, Suresh '03 (OWN) Reed, KY St. Augustine; Owensboro, KY St. Peter of Alcantara.
Bakkar, Gabriel Mary *c.f.r.* '07 (NY)[EE] New York, NY St. Joseph's Friary.
Bakke, Lawrence M. '75 (MAD) Baraboo, WI St. Joseph; Elected; Personnel Board.
Bakker, Richard T. *s.m.a.* '59 (BO) Malden, MA Immaculate Conception.
Bakle, John L. *s.m.* '67 (COL) Cardington, OH Sacred Hearts.
Bakle, John L. *s.m.* '67 (STL)[O] St. Louis Marianists, Province of the United States (Society of Mary).
Bakwaph, Peter '03 (NY) Spring Valley, NY St. Joseph.
Baky, Isidore '72 (MIA) Fort Lauderdale, FL St. Helen; Vietnamese.
Bakyil, Alphonsus *s.o.l.t.* '85 (CC)[G] Robstown, TX Society of Our Lady of the Most Holy Trinity.
Bakyil, Alphonsus *s.o.l.t.* '85 (PHX) Phoenix, AZ Most Holy Trinity Roman Catholic Parish.
Bala, Paul '69 (SAG) Port Sanilac, MI St. Mary.
Balaban, Oryst '57 (SJP) Presbyters Retired.
Balado, Rev. Msgr. Armando '49 (MIA) Retired.
Balagapo, Victorio '66 (SFR) San Francisco, CA St. Anthony of Padua.
Balagtas, Rodel G. '91 (LA) Los Angeles, CA Immaculate Heart of Mary.
Balarote, Venancio R. '01 (RIC) Norfolk, VA St. Pius X.
Balas, David *o.cist.* '54 (DAL)[B] University of Dallas; [J] Irving, TX Cistercian Abbey of Our Lady of Dallas.
Balash, Michael D. '87 (Y) Warren, OH St. William.
Balashowreddy, Salibindla '80 (AMA) Canadian, TX Sacred Heart.
Balasko, George J. '67 (Y) East Liverpool, OH St. Ann.
Balazs, Richard *c.r.* '65 (CHI) Chicago, IL St. Stanislaus, Bishop and Martyr.
Balazy, Edwin W. '62 (DET) Dearborn Heights, MI St. John the Baptist.
Balbi, Abel E. '82 (SB) Colton, CA Immaculate Conception; Colton, CA San Salvador.
Balcerski, Duane *c.s.c.* (FTW)[H] Notre Dame Congregation of Holy Cross, Indiana Province, Provincial House.
Balcerski, Duane *c.s.c.* '71 (PHX)[F] Phoenix, AZ Holy Cross Congregation/Casa Santa Cruz.
Balchunas, Henry A. '65 (HRT) Wolcott, CT St. Pius X.
Balczeniuk, Mark G. '83 (SCR) Episcopal Vicars.
Baldacchino, Rev. Msgr. Peter '96 (NEW) On Duty Outside the Archdiocese.
Balderas, Jose Luis '68 (LAR) Laredo, TX Christ the King.
Balderas, Sergio A. '06 (BLX) Vocations; Biloxi, MS Our Lady of Fatima; Presbyteral Council.
Balderrama, Sergio '06 (MIL) Sheboygan, WI St. Clement.
Baldo, Jing '99 (CHY) Rock Springs, WY Holy Spirit Catholic Community.
Baldonado, Rev. Msgr. Bonifacio '85 (STO) Modesto, CA Our Lady of Fatima Church (Pastor of).
Baldonado, Luis *o.f.m.* '52 (PHX) Phoenix, AZ St. Mary's Roman Catholic Basilica Retired.
Baldonieri, Thomas F. '90 (CHI) Highwood, IL St. James.
Baldovin, John *s.j.* '75 (BO)[U] Cambridge, MA St. Edmund's House.
Balducelli, Roberto *o.s.f.s.* '36 (WIL) Wilmington, DE St. Anthony of Padua.
Balduck, Walter *o.f.m.cap.* '73 (TUC) Mammoth, AZ Blessed Sacrament Roman Catholic Parish – Mammoth.
Baldwin, Bradley *t.o.r.* '94 (ALT) Councilors:; Altoona, PA Bon Secours–Holy Family Campus; Catholic Chaplaincy Ministry; [G] Hollidaysburg, PA St. Joseph Friary.
Baldwin, Rev. Msgr. Edward J. '55 (DET) Retired.
Baldwin, John F. '59 (CHI) Retired.
Baldwin, Kevin '98 (ATL)[G] Alpharetta, GA Norcross Pastoral Center, Inc.
Baldwin, Michael E. '83 (WCH) Andover, KS St. Vincent de Paul.
Baldwin, Paul C. '97 (DUB) Eldora, IA St. Mary; Iowa Falls, IA St. Mark.
Baldyga, William L. '69 (HRT) Suffield, CT St. Joseph.
Balen, Adilso Luiz *c.s.* '91 (CHI)[N] Oak Park, IL Missionaries of Saint Charles.
Balen, Moacir *c.s.* '77 (BO) Somerville, MA St. Anthony of Padua.
Bales, Francis *o.s.b.* '87 (TLS)[G] Hulbert, OK Our Lady of the Annunciation of Clear Creek Monastery.
Bales, Robert '57 (MIL) Retired.
Bales, Rev. Msgr. Thomas E. '74 (RCK) Rockford, IL Holy Family.
Balestino, Francis P. '60 (ALT) Retired.
Balestrieri, Edward '59 (BEL) Retired.
Balili, Peter D. *s.t.d.* '89 (SFR) San Mateo, CA St. Timothy.
Balinda, Thadeus '92 (FTW) Culver, IN St. Mary of the Lake.
Balinong, Alfredo *s.j.* '64 (NY) New York, NY Blessed Sacrament.
Balint, Rev. Msgr. R. James '61 (DAL) Plano, TX Prince of Peace.
Balint, Stephen J. '65 (BGP) Norwalk, CT St. Ladislaus.
Balistreri, Anthony '93 (SJP) Eastern Protopresbytery; Vicar for Clergy; Presbyteral Council; Personnel Board; Presbyters.
Balizan, Daniel M. '89 (SFE) Raton, NM St. Patrick/St. Joseph.
Balkan, Paschal *o.c.s.o.* '55 (ARL)[H] Berryville, VA Cistercian Abbey of Our Lady of the Holy Cross.
Ball, Raymond A. '87 (MAN) Lancaster, NH Gate of Heaven; Catholic Scouting.
Ball, Richard D. '77 (SC) Granville, IA St. Joseph; [B] Granville, IA Spalding Catholic Schools, Inc.; Presbyteral Council; Diocesan Consultors; Deans.
Ball, Rev. Msgr. Thomas J. '66 (BUR) Canon 1742 Panel of Pastors; Burlington, VT Cathedral of the Immaculate Conception.
Ball, Wayne L (RIC) Richmond, VA St. Patrick.
Ball, Wayne '89 (RIC) Highland Springs, VA St. John the Evangelist; Judges; International Airport.
Ballance, Harvey '57 (NEW) Retired.
Ballard, Kevin *s.j.* '85 (SJ)[L] Los Altos, CA Jesuit Retreat Center of Los Altos.
Ballard, Mark E. '02 (BO) Green Harbor, MA Our Lady of the Assumption.
Ballecer, Robert *s.j.* '07 (WDC)[N] Washington, DC Leonard Neale House.
Ballesteros, Enrique '89 (OAK) Concord, CA Queen of All Saints.
Ballester Torres, Rev. Msgr. Pedro (PCE) Retired.
Balleza, John A. '85 (SFR) Redwood City, CA Our Lady of Mount Carmel.
Ballien, Paul K. '99 (DET) On Duty Outside the Archdiocese.
Balliett, Timothy R. '08 (E) Erie, PA St. George.
Ballman, Luke R. '01 (ATL) Vocations; Special or Other (Arch)Diocesan Assignment.
Ballou, Jeffrey A. '01 (SPR) Ware, MA St. Mary's; Presbyteral Council; Air Force Reserve Chaplains.
Balluff, John '88 (JOL) Gilman, IL Immaculate Conception; West Chicago, IL St. Mary; Continuing Formation for Priests.
Balluff, Thomas J. '06 (STP) St. Bonifacius, MN St. Boniface; Delano, MN St. Mary of Czestochowa.
Ballweg, John M. '56 (NEW) Retired.
Ballweg, Rev. Msgr. Lawrence F. '40 (RVC) Retired.
Balmeo, Simeon '65 (AGN) Agana, GU Our Lady of the Purification.
Balog, Robert A. '72 (RCK) McHenry, IL St. Mary.
Balser, Edward '56 (JKS) Retired.
Balser, Robert *c.ss.r.* '49 (GR) Grand Rapids, MI St. Alphonsus; [L] Grand Rapids, MI The Society of the Redemptorists of the City of Grand Rapids.
Balskus, Charles '65 (CHI) Chicago, IL St. Mary, Star of the Sea Retired.
Balta, Rev. Msgr. Raymond A. '69 (PBR) Johnstown, PA St. Mary's; Protopresbyters.
Baltes, Gabriel *o.s.b.* '91 (JOL) Lisle, IL St. Joan of Arc.
Baltes, Timothy '76 (SCL) Presbyteral Council; Chokio, MN St. Charles; Chokio, MN St. Mary's; Morris, MN Assumption of the Blessed Virgin Mary; Diocesan Consultors.
Balthazar, Ayala '43 (SJ) Retired.
Balthazar, Rev. Msgr. Norman '63 (SP) Clearwater, FL Miserere Guild, Inc.; Calvary Catholic Cemetery and Miserere Guild.
Baltrus, Michael '07 (NSH) McEwen, TN St. Patrick's.
Baltrusaitis, Gabriel *o.f.m.* '54 (PRT)[I] Kennebunkport, ME St. Anthony's Friary; Kennebunkport, ME.
Baltz, Albert G. '70 (BUR) Brandon, VT St. Mary's.
Baltz, David *m.c.c.j.* '67 (FgM) Cincinnati, OH COMBONI MISSIONARIES (VERONA FATHERS).
Baluyot, Michael '97 (BEA) On Leave.
Balwinski, Gerald E. '69 (SAG) Retired.
Balzer, Raymond '49 (FTW) Retired.
Bambenek, Oliver *o.f.m.cap.* '65 (MIL)[B] Mount Calvary, WI St. Lawrence Seminary; [P] Mount Calvary, WI St. Felix Friary.
Bamber, William J. *c.m.* '55 (PH)[Y] Philadelphia Congregation of the Mission[Y].
Bamberg, Callistus *o.f.m.* '61 (BO)[X] Boston, MA Saint Anthony Residence Retired.
Bambir, Vjekoslav *o.f.m.* '40 (CHI)[N] Chicago, IL St. Anthony's Friary.
Bambrick, John P. '91 (TR) Toms River, NJ St. Joseph.
Bambrick, John W. '70 (ALN) Ashland, PA St. Joseph; Ashland, PA St. Mauritius; Gordon, PA Our Lady of Good Counsel; Ashland – Court St. Joan of Arc #225.
Bammon, John *o.f.m.* '09 (IND) Terre Haute, IN St. Joseph University Parish.
Banach, Henry S. '48 (WOR) Retired.
Banach, Rev. Msgr. Michael '88 (WOR) On Special or Other Diocesan Assignment; On Duty Outside the Diocese.
Banal, Jose Vaughn '96 (LA) Culver City, CA St. Augustine.
Banas, James T. *c.s.c.* '57 (FTW)[H] Notre Dame Congregation of Holy Cross, Indiana Province, Provincial House; New Rochelle, NY Eastern Brothers Province.
Banas, Leonard N. *c.s.c.* '52 (FTW)[B] University of Notre Dame Du Lac; [H] Notre Dame, IN Holy Cross Community, Corby Hall, University of Notre Dame.
Banazak, Gregory '85 (DET) Special Assignment.
Banchs, Luis R. *s.e.m.v.* '02 (ARE) Arecibo, PR Our Lady of Guadalupe.
Bancroft, Martin '01 (RVC) Port Jefferson, NY Mather Memorial Hospital; Port Jefferson, NY Infant Jesus.
Banda, Brian *s.j.* '08 (BO)[U] Cambridge, MA St. Edmund's House.
Bandanadam, Jojappa (Joseph) '97 (FRS) Lemoore, CA St. Peter Prince of Apostles.
Banden, Joseph W. '69 (STL) Florissant, MO St. Sabina.
Bandico, Marcelino '85 (SD) Encinitas, CA St. John the Evangelist.
Bandiera, Colombo F. '52 (WH) Retired.
Bandres, Antonio *o.f.m.cap.* '75 (FWT) Fort Worth, TX Immaculate Heart of Mary.
Bandsuch, Mark *s.j.* '00 (LA)[C] Los Angeles, CA Jesuit Community.

Banduku, Charles Mbuyi '98 (MIL) Fox Point, WI St. Eugene.
Banet, Paul *s.s.j.* '55 (BAL)[S] Baltimore, MD St. Joseph's Manor.
Banet, Stephen '77 (IND) Indianapolis, IN St. Jude.
Bang–Doan, Joseph '74 (GAL)[S] Houston, TX The Catholic Chaplain Corps.
Bani, J. Cary '07 (BR) St. Francisville, LA Our Lady of Mount Carmel; Angola, LA Louisiana State Penitentiary.
Baniak, Walter '41 (ALB) Retired.
Banick, Rev. Msgr. Thomas V. '63 (SCR) Wilkes–Barre, PA St. Mary of the Immaculate Conception.
Banico, Wharren '00 (LA) Canonical Staff.
Banigan, Herbert '46 (DEN) Retired.
Bankemper, Stef M. '03 (COV) Fort Thomas, KY St. Catherine of Siena.
Bankemper, Stephen M. '03 (COV)[B] Newport, KY Newport Central Catholic High School.
Banken, Robert L. '68 (STL) Portage Des Sioux, MO St. Francis of Assisi.
Banker, Rick '88 (DUL)[G] Cloquet, MN Educational Endowment Trust, Queen of Peace Church; Cloquet, MN Holy Family; Cloquet, MN Queen of Peace.
Banks, Charles *o.m.i.* '66 (SAT)[K] San Antonio, TX Oblate Madonna Residence; [L] San Antonio, TX Oblate Vocation Office.
Banks, Gary *s.t.* (PAT)[N] Stirling, NJ Holy Spirit Missionary Cenacle.
Banks, Peter *o.f.m.cap.* '73 (LA) Solvang, CA Old Mission Santa Ines; Los Angeles, CA St. Lawrence of Brindisi; Definitors:.
Bankston, James '04 (STN) La Mesa, CA Our Lady of Perpetual Help.
Bankston, James (SD) La Mesa, CA Our Lady of Perpetual Help.
Bannan, Peter F. '67 (NY) Pelham, NY St. Catharine.
Bannantine, Thomas E. *s.j.* '65 (OM)[K] Omaha, NE Jesuit Community at Creighton University.
Banner, Russell '67 (CLV) Administrative Leave.
Bannes, Timothy L. '07 (STL) Ballwin, MO Holy Infant.
Bannon, Anthony *l.c.* '75 (NY)[II] Rye, NY Catholic WomenWork Inc.
Banos, Felix '58 (ORL) Lakeland, FL St. Joseph's Retired.
Bantz, William '60 (Y) Retired.
Banuelas, Rev. Msgr. Arturo '76 (ELP) El Paso, TX St. Pius X.
Banye, Anthony '94 (BRK) Brooklyn, NY St. Patrick.
Banzin, Robert S. '64 (CHI) Retired.
Banzon, Oscar (SD) San Diego, CA St. Michael.
Bao, Anthony '48 (OKL) Retired.
Baok, Dominikus *s.v.d.* (WH) Gassaway, WV St. Thomas.
Baptista, Diego '69 (SR) On Duty Outside the Diocese.
Baptista, Diogo '69 (SAC) Ione, CA Mule Creek State Prison; Ione, CA.
Baptiste, Eden Jean '83 (RVC) Brentwood, NY St. Anne's.
Baraan, Geoffrey '97 (OAK) Union City, CA St. Anne; Deanery #15.
Barachini, Nello '86 (BGP) Shelton, CT St. Margaret Mary Retired.
Barajas, Abel '96 (MIA) Pompano Beach, FL San Isidro; [Q] Pompano Beach, FL Word & Life Catholic Ministry, Inc.; [Q] Pompano Beach, FL Ministerio Catolico Verbo y Vida, Inc.
Barak, Christopher L. '87 (LIN) Palmyra, NE St. Leo's; Notaries; Commission for Sacred Liturgy and Sacred Music; Office of Religious Education (CCD); Evangelization Committee; Priests' Continuing Education Committee.
Barakeh, Imad *b.s.o.* (NTN) Lawrence, MA St. Joseph.
Baraki, Tesfamariam '75 (WDC) Washington, DC St. Gabriel; Washington, DC Kidane–Mehret Ge'ez Rite Catholic Church; Hospital & Nursing Home Ministries.
Baran, Blaise R. '82 (MET) Washington, NJ St. Joseph.
Baran, Jody '89 (PSC) Passaic, NJ St. Michael Cathedral.
Baran, John P. '84 (BGP) Fairfield, CT St. Anthony of Padua.
Baran, Joseph L. '47 (MIL) Retired.
Baran, Volodymyr '85 (PAT) Morristown, NJ Morristown Memorial Hospital; Dover, NJ Dover General Hospital; Rockaway, NJ Sacred Heart.
Baranek, Raymond '76 (CLV) Absent on Leave.
Baraniak, James T. *o.praem.* '93 (GB) De Pere, WI St. Norbert College; [B] De Pere, WI St. Norbert College; [J] De Pere, WI St. Joseph Priory.
Baraniewicz, Joseph *o.s.f.s.* '57 (TOL)[I] Childs, MD Annecy Hall Retired.
Baraniewicz, Joseph *o.s.f.s.* '57 (WIL)[J] Childs, MD Retirement and Assisted Care Facility Retired.
Baranowski, Arthur R. '68 (DET) Marysville, MI St. Christopher; [T] Marysville, MI National Alliance of Parishes Restructuring into Communities (NAPRC).
Baranowski, David J. '73 (HRT) Rocky Hill, CT St. James; Office for Divine Worship; Special and other Archdiocesan Assignment.
Baranowski, Stanley A. '55 (MIL) Retired.
Baranski, Andrew E. '92 (SY) Oswego, NY St. Joseph; Oswego, NY St. Stephen the King; Priests' Personnel Committee.
Baranski, Richard *o.f.m.* '06 (FWT)[H] Crowley, TX St. Maximilian Kolbe Friary.
Baransky, Francis J. '79 (ALN) Jim Thorpe, PA St. Joseph.
Baranyuk, Adrian F. '05 (WIL) Wilmington, DE St. John the Beloved.
Barasinski, John B. '81 (GRY) Beverly Shores, IN St. Ann.
Baratelli, David J. '82 (MO) Air Force Reserve Chaplains; Apostleship of the Air.
Barattini, John H. '44 (NO) Retired.
Baraza, Patrick '82 (SPK) Spokane, WA Cathedral of Our Lady of Lourdes.
Barba, Alfredo '09 (FWT) Denton, TX Immaculate Conception.
Barbato, Robert A. *o.f.m.cap.* '87 (LA)[B] Santa Ynez, CA San Lorenzo Seminary – Retreat Center; Definitors:.
Barbato, Robert A. *o.f.m.cap.* '87 (WDC)[B] Washington, DC St. Francis Friary–Capuchin College.
Barbella, John J. '87 (MET) Phillipsburg, NJ St. Philip & St. James.
Barber, Bradley A. '94 (MO) DEPARTMENT OF VETERANS AFFAIRS HOSPITALS AND CHAPLAINS.
Barber, Eugene J. *s.j.* '63 (BAL)[S] Towson Maryland Province of the Society of Jesus; Towson, MD Society of Jesus.
Barber, Hal '67 (SFS) Sioux Falls, SD St. Therese.
Barber, Michael C. *s.j.* '85 (SFR)[A] Menlo Park, CA St. Patrick Seminary and University; [E] San Francisco, CA St. Ignatius College Preparatory (Coed); [N] San Francisco, CA Jesuit Community at St. Ignatius College Preparatory.
Barber, Michael C. *s.j.* '85 (MO) Navy Reserve Chaplains.
Barber, Michael D. *s.j.* '79 (STL)[C] Philosophy and Letters, College of; [C] Saint Louis University; [O] St. Louis, MO Leo Brown Jesuit Community.
Barber, Michael L. *s.j.* '75 (BAL)[S] Baltimore, MD Colombiere Jesuit Community.
Barber, Michael *s.m.* '90 (SAT)[K] San Antonio, TX Marianist Residence: Skilled Nursing.
Barber, Stephen A. *s.j.* '98 (SFR) California State Prison; [N] San Francisco, CA Loyola House Jesuit Community.
Barbian, Leonard M. '65 (MIL) Retired.
Barbieto, Paciano A. (NEW) Kearny, NJ St. Stephen.
Barbone, Joseph F. '72 (NEW) Bayonne, NJ Our Lady of the Assumption.
Barbosa, Cristiano G. Borro '07 (MAN) Nashua, NH Blessed John XXIII Parish; Cambridge, MA St. Anthony of Padua.
Barbosa, Paulo (FR) Fall River, MA Cathedral of St. Mary of the Assumption.
Barbour, Claude–Marie (CHI)[B] Chicago, IL The Catholic Theological Union at Chicago.
Barbour, Hugh C. *o.praem.* '90 (ORG)[A] Silverado, CA St. Michael's Norbertine Postulancy, Novitiate and Juniorate; [I] Silverado, CA Norbertine Fathers of Orange Inc.; Ecumenical and Interreligious Affairs; Silverado, CA.
Barboutz, Paul '09 (PAT) Ringwood, NJ St. Catherine of Bologna.
Barcellona, Thomas J. '95 (CAM) Vocation Advisory Board.
Barcelona, Rogelio *s.o.l.t.* '95 (SEA) Seattle, WA St. Matthew.
Barcelos, Robert *o.c.d.* '08 (LA) Alhambra, CA St. Therese.
Barch, Howard C. '93 (MO) Navy Reserve Chaplains.
Barch, Howard C. '93 (RCK) Freeport, IL St. Mary; Freeport, IL St. Joseph.
Barcio, Rev. Msgr. Robert G. '47 (E) Erie, PA St. Peter Cathedral Retired.
Barclay, Robert F. '75 (BRK) Ozone Park, NY St. Elizabeth.
Barclift, Richard L. '66 (PEO) Retired.
Barczak, Rene *o.f.m.* '64 (PH)[D] Philadelphia, PA Archbishop Ryan High School; [Y] Philadelphia, PA St. Pius X Residence.
Bardes, Rev. Msgr. George F. '44 (NY)[EE] Bronx, NY John Cardinal O'Connor Residence Retired.
Barfknecht, David *o.s.b.* '89 (HON)[D] Waialua, HI Benedictine Monastery of Hawaii/Retreat Center; Waialua, HI.
Bargola, Cerino O. '84 (MO) Navy Chaplains.
Baribeau, Donald G. *m.s.* '75 (R) Swansboro, NC St. Mildred.
Barica, Daniel *o.f.m.* '99 (LA) Santa Barbara, CA Old Mission Santa Barbara; [P] Santa Barbara, CA Franciscan Friary, Order of Friars Minor (Old Mission).
Barile, Ralph '82 (BRK) Long Island City, NY St. Mary.
Barille, Nicholas J. *s.t.* '95 (SB) Riverside, CA Our Lady of Perpetual Help.
Baris, Bernard *m.s.* '69 (FR) Brewster, MA Our Lady of the Cape; [G] Attleboro, MA La Salette Missionary Association.
Barita, Joseph *a.l.c.p./o.s.s.* '87 (P) Portland, OR St. Birgitta.
Barius, Placid *o.f.m.* '43 (PRT)[I] Kennebunkport, ME St. Anthony's Friary; Kennebunkport, ME.
Barius, Placidas *o.f.m.* '43 (LIT) Lithuanian Franciscan Province of St. Casimir.
Barkemeyer, John F. '90 (CHI) Military Chaplains; Army Chaplains.
Barkenquest, Lehr *o.s.f.s.* '64 (LAN) Clarklake, MI St. Rita.
Barker, Brian '94 (BEL) Pinckneyville, IL St. Bruno.
Barker, Jack D. '92 (SB) Murrieta, CA St. Martha.
Barker, Jack '92 (SB) College of Consultors.
Barker, Rev. Msgr. James '80 (BAL) Forest Hill, MD St. Ignatius; Presbyteral Council.
Barker, Joseph A. '53 (ALB) Priests Retirement Board/ Priests Retirement Plan Board; Troy, NY Our Lady of Victory Retired.
Barker, Richard E. '92 (GAL) Huffman, TX St. Philip the Apostle.
Barker, Ronald A. '75 (BO) Wakefield, MA St. Joseph.
Barkett, James S. '91 (ARL) Fairfax, VA St. Mary of Sorrows.
Barkey, Patrick '90 (PIT) Wildwood, PA St. Catherine of Sweden.
Barkin, Martin F. '77 (PIT) Verona, PA St. Gerard Majella; Penn Hills, PA St. Susanna.
Barlaan, Dwight Dennis G. '97 (SFR) Daly City, CA Our Lady of Perpetual Help.
Barley, Tom '91 (SAN) Priests' Personnel Board; Judicial Vicar; Diocesan Consultors; Presbyteral Council; Deans; San Angelo, TX Cathedral of the Sacred Heart.
Barlow, James P. '73 (SAT) San Antonio, TX St. Luke.
Barman, Karl *o.s.b.* '65 (JC) Fulton, MO St. Peter.
Barman, William '81 (ORG) Lake Forest, CA Santiago de Compostela.
Barmann, Karl *o.s.b.* '65 (JC) Mokane, MO St. Jude Thaddeus.
Barmasse, Gerald R. *c.s.c.* '76 (FTW)[H] Notre Dame Congregation of Holy Cross, Indiana Province, Provincial House; New Rochelle, NY Eastern Brothers Province.
Barna, Darek '00 (RCK) Algonquin, IL St. Margaret Mary.
Barna, Dariusz *o.f.m.conv.* (BRK) Brooklyn, NY Most Holy Trinity – Saint Mary.
Barnard, Matthew D. '08 (STL) Maryland Heights, MO Holy Spirit.
Barnd, Donald *s.c.j.* '78 (MIL)[P] Franklin, WI Villa Maria.
Barnes, Charles *s.j.* '08 (SPK) Spokane, WA St. Aloysius; [J] Spokane, WA Regis Community.
Barnes, David J. '97 (BO) Beverly, MA St. Mary Star of the Sea.
Barnes, Gavin *o.s.b.* '52 (IND)[K] St. Meinrad, IN St. Meinrad Archabbey.
Barnes, James H. '69 (LA) Los Angeles, CA St. Joan of Arc.
Barnes, John G. '52 (DUB) Retired.
Barnes, Rev. Msgr. Joseph C. '58 (FRS) Retired.
Barnes, Thomas C. '87 (COV) Covington, KY Holy Cross.
Barnett, Daniel '00 (SPK) Pasco, WA St. Patrick; Members.
Barnett, Fred J. '52 (JC) Retired.
Barnett, Rev. Msgr. Stephen '70 (SFS) Plankinton, SD St. John.
Barnhardt, Bruno *o.s.b.cam.* '66 (MRY)[F] Big Sur, CA New Camaldoli Hermitage.
Barnhart, Victor A. '90 (STL) St. Louis, MO St. Andrew; Archdiocesan Deaf Ministry.
Barnhill, Robert K. '85 (MO) Cambridge, NE St. John's; [L] Mc Cool Junction, NE Camp Kateri; Commission for Sacred Liturgy and Sacred Music; Deaf Ministry; Scouting; Air National Guard Chaplains.
Barno, John R. '06 (NEW) Bayonne, NJ St. Andrew's.
Barnufsky, Stephen *o.f.m.* '76 (TUC) Tucson, AZ San Xavier Mission Roman Catholic Parish – Tucson; Council of Priests; Vicar for Native Americans; Vicars Forane; All Vicars Forane.
Barnum, James (RVC) Valley Stream, NY Franklin Medical Center Hospital.
Barnum, Martin '74 (CHI)[A] Mundelein, IL University of St. Mary of the Lake/Mundelein Seminary.
Barnum, Matthew J. '07 (GR) Muskegon, MI St. Mary's; Muskegon, MI St. Jean Baptiste.
Barnwell, Gerald P. '77 (FR) Retired.
Baroma, Roman '72 (SEA) Seattle, WA St. George; Seattle, WA St. Paul.
Baroma, Roy (SEA) Seattle, WA St. Edward.
Baron, Mark *m.i.c.* '04 (WDC)[B] Washington, DC Marian Fathers Scholasticate.
Barona, German *m.s.c.* '86 (RCK)[G].
Barona, Jaime '98 (ATL) Winder, GA St. Matthew.
Barone, Michael C. '08 (NEW) Rahway, NJ St. Mark's.
Barone, Michael J. '75 (TYL) Madisonville, TX St. Elizabeth Ann Seton.

Baroni, Barry J. '79 (ALT) Johnstown, PA Visitation of the B.V.M.
Baronti, David '76 (SPK) On Duty Outside the Diocese.
Baroody, Rt. Rev. Economos Sami W. '94 (NTN) Diocese of Newton for the Melkites in the USA, Inc., a Massachusetts Corporation.
Barota, Michael '04 (SPA) Ceres, CA St. Matthew's Assyrian–Chaldean Catholic Church.
Barousse, Raphael *o.s.b.* '55 (NO) Mandeville, LA St. Dymphna Catholic Center and Chapel; Mandeville, LA Southeast Louisiana Hospital; [P] St. Benedict, LA St. Joseph Abbey.
Barozzi, Italo '65 (BRK) Flushing, NY St. Mel.
Barr, Brian P. '93 (RVC) Rockville Centre, NY Campus Parish of Long Island; Vocations.
Barr, Brian '93 (RVC)[C] Hicksville, NY Holy Trinity Diocesan High School.
Barr, Rev. Msgr. Eric R. '84 (RCK) Durand, IL St. Mary; Special Assignment; Vicar for Clergy and Religious; Ministry to Priests Program; Priest Personnel; Diocesan Consultors.
Barr, Joseph F. '78 (BAL) Davidsonville, MD Holy Family; Presbyteral Council.
Barr, Rev. Msgr. Liam M. '74 (LIN) Lincoln, NE St. Joseph; Deaneries and Deans; Office of Stewardship & Development.
Barr, Mark D. (BO) Quincy, MA St. John the Baptist.
Barr, Philip R. '48 (PH) Retired.
Barr, Timothy J. '06 (RCK) Crystal Lake, IL St. Thomas the Apostle.
Barragan, Juan Carlos '97 (AMA) Dumas, TX SS. Peter and Paul.
Barragan, Victor D. Marino (BO) Lynn, MA St. Joseph.
Barrameda, Arnel B. '86 (GAL) Crosby, TX Sacred Heart.
Barrand, James '89 (VNN) Anchorage, AK Saint Nicholas of Myra.
Barras, Gregory '84 (BLX) Biloxi, MS Cathedral of the Nativity of the Blessed Virgin Mary; Biloxi, MS St. Michael.
Barras, Michael J. '73 (LKC) West Calcasieu Cameron Hospital; Westlake, LA St. John Bosco.
Barras, Robert '80 (GAL) Houston, TX St. Bernadette Soubirous.
Barratt, Anthony M. '85 (ALB) Frankfort, NY Our Lady Queen of Apostles; Ilion, NY Annunciation; Deans; Judges.
Barre, Michael L. *s.s.* '70 (BAL)[A] Baltimore, MD St. Mary's Seminary and University; Baltimore, MD; [S] Baltimore, MD St. Mary's Seminary & University.
Barre, Michael L. *s.s.* '70 (MEM) On Duty Outside the Diocese.
Barreda, Giles *o.f.m.* '61 (FR) Buzzards Bay, MA St. Margaret.
Barrera, Albino F. *o.p.* '93 (PRO)[P] Providence St. Thomas Aquinas Priory at Providence College.
Barrera, Constantino '06 (BEA)[A] Beaumont, TX Monsignor Kelly Catholic High School; Beaumont, TX St. Jude Thaddeus.
Barrera, Fernando '05 (STO) Absent on Leave.
Barrera, Filiberto '98 (OAK) Richmond, CA St. Cornelius.
Barrera, Rev. Msgr. Gustavo '79 (BWN) St. Philip; Promoter of Justice; Defenders of the Bond; Presbyteral Council; College of Consultors; Diocesan Finance Council; Parish Priests Consultors and Priests' Personnel Board; McAllen, TX Our Lady of Sorrows.
Barrera, Jose Alberto (SLC) West Valley City, UT Saints Peter and Paul LLC 243.
Barrera, Luis '95 (ORL) Casselberry, FL St. Augustine.
Barreto, Angel L. Soto '92 (MGZ) San German, PR San German de Auxerre.
Barrett, David S. '64 (GB) Menominee Pastoral Program; Gillett, WI St. John; Suring, WI St. Michael Retired.
Barrett, David '04 (STP) Kilkenny, MN St. Canice.
Barrett, Edward F. '61 (SCR) Scranton, PA Immaculate Conception.
Barrett, Edward J. '75 (CHI) Alsip, IL St. Terrence.
Barrett, Rev. Msgr. Francis X. '55 (ALN) Reading, PA Holy Guardian Angels Retired.
Barrett, Gerard *o.m.i.* '64 (BWN) Port Isabel, TX Our Lady Star of the Sea.
Barrett, James L. '82 (CHI) Chicago, IL St. Margaret Mary; Deans.
Barrett, James L. '56 (KAL) Marshall, MI; Diocesan Consultors; Presbyteral Council Members; Presbyteral Council Members Retired.
Barrett, John J. '78 (RVC) Wading River, NY St. John Baptist.
Barrett, John '59 (JOL) Retired.
Barrett, Joseph '05 (FAR) Jamestown, ND St. James Basilica of Jamestown.
Barrett, Kevin S. '92 (PCE) On Duty Outside the Diocese.
Barrett, Michael J. *s.t.d.* '85 (GAL) Houston, TX Holy Cross Chapel.
Barrett, Michael J. '85 (POD) Houston.
Barrett, Michael '85 (GAL)[N] Houston, TX Opus Dei.
Barrett, Michael '76 (MIL) Milwaukee, WI Congregation of the Blessed Trinity.
Barrett, Miles J. '82 (SC) On Duty Outside the Diocese; Navy Chaplains.
Barrett, Miles J. '82 (CAM) Cape May, NJ United States Coast Guard, Command Chaplain's Office.
Barrett, Thomas E. '93 (PMB) Palm Beach Gardens, FL Cathedral of St. Ignatius Loyola; [B] Fort Pierce, FL John Carroll High School, Inc.; Elected Members.
Barrett, Thomas G. '88 (ORL) Longwood, FL Church of the Nativity.
Barrett, Thomas M. '71 (BEL) Vienna, IL St. Francis de Sales.
Barrett, Thomas M. '71 (BEL) Vienna, IL St. Paul.
Barrett, Thomas *c.ss.r.* '67 (ROC)[L] Canandaigua, NY Notre Dame Retreat House.
Barrett, Rev. Msgr. Walter C. '75 (RIC) Richmond, VA Holy Rosary; Ladysmith, VA St. Mary of the Annunciation; Regional Vicars; Richmond, VA St. Elizabeth.
Barrett, William '59 (ROC) Retired.
Barrette, Eugene *m.s.* '67 (ATL) Smyrna, GA St. Thomas the Apostle.
Barricks, Robert L. '94 (P) Portland, OR Holy Family.
Barringer, Robert J. *c.s.b.* '74 (GAL)[O] Houston, TX Residence of the Basilian Fathers of the University of St. Thomas.
Barrios, Diego *c.m.f.* '42 (LA)[V] Rancho Dominguez, CA Dominguez Seminary Inc.
Barrios, Eduardo *s.j.* '72 (MIA)[K] Miami, FL Villa Javier; [D] Miami, FL Belen Jesuit Preparatory School.
Barron, Clemente *c.p.* '70 (SAT)[L] San Antonio, TX Casa Pasionista Guadalupe.
Barron, Dale F. *m.m.* '65 (FgM) Maryknoll, NY MARYKNOLL.
Barron, Daniel *o.m.v.* '92 (BO) Lowell, MA St. Patrick; [B] Boston, MA Our Lady of Grace Seminary.
Barron, Gerald *o.f.m.cap.* '66 (LA) Solvang, CA Old Mission Santa Ines.
Barron, John P. *s.j.* '82 (ALN)[A] Wernersville, PA Jesuit Center–Jesuit Community; [N] Wernersville, PA Jesuit Center.
Barron, Robert E. '86 (CHI)[A] Mundelein, IL University of St. Mary of the Lake/Mundelein Seminary.
Barron, Stanley C. '74 (PAT) Priestly Life Committee; Flanders, NJ St. Elizabeth Ann Seton; Vocations Board; Paterson, NJ Mission Office.
Barron, Wayne *c.m.f.* '58 (CHI)[N] Oak Park, IL Claretian Missionaries USA Eastern Province.
Barron, William R. '07 (E) Erie, PA Our Lady of Peace.
Barrons, Brian *m.m.* '84 (FgM) Maryknoll, NY MARYKNOLL.
Barrosa, Julian Michael A. *d.s.* '91 (GAL) Pasadena, TX St. Pius the Fifth.
Barrow, John A. '80 (PMB) Stuart, FL St. Andrew.
Barrow, Joseph A. '96 (NEW) On Duty Outside the Archdiocese.
Barruetabena, Felix *c.p.* '52 (SJN) Carolina, PR Santa Gema Galgani.
Barry, Bernard J. *s.j.* '00 (NY)[EE] Cardinal Spellman Hall, Jesuit Community.
Barry, David E. *s.j.* '61 (BAL)[S] Towson Maryland Province of the Society of Jesus.
Barry, David E. *s.j.* '78 (DEN)[N] Denver, CO Xavier Jesuit Center.
Barry, Rev. Msgr. Edward M. '73 (NY) Bronx (Northeast); Bronx, NY St. Barnabas.
Barry, Garrett J. '66 (BO) Randolph, MA St. Mary.
Barry, Gerard B. '50 (BO) Senior Priests. Retired.
Barry, James D. '61 (NU) Retired.
Barry, James F. '67 (CAM) Salem, NJ St. Mary's Catholic Church, Salem.
Barry, James J. '69 (BO) Chelsea, MA Our Lady of Grace; Vicariate IV; Vicariate IV.
Barry, James *c.p.* '69 (MET)[I] South River Passionist Provincial Office.
Barry, Rev. Msgr. John F. '61 (LA) Manhattan Beach, CA American Martyrs.
Barry, John G. *c.ss.r.* '48 (ORL) New Smyrna Beach, FL Sacred Heart.
Barry, John M. '88 (WDC) Bowie, MD St. Edward; [W] Bowie, MD Washington Catholic Charismatic Service Committee; Charismatic Renewal Regional Service Committee.
Barry, Rev. Msgr. John '61 (LA) Deanery 19; Members.
Barry, Maurice J. '67 (HRT) Windsor, CT St. Gertrude.
Barry, Michael W. *ss.cc.* '64 (LA)[P] La Verne, CA Congregation of the Sacred Hearts of Jesus and Mary.
Barry, Michael *ss.cc.* '64 (SB) Special or Other Diocesan Assignment; [I] Chino Hills, CA Congregation of the Sacred Hearts of Jesus & Mary, SS.CC.
Barry, Rev. Msgr. Patrick (NY) Chappaqua, NY St. John and St. Mary.
Barry, Paul '48 (WDC) Retired.
Barry, Peter J. *m.m.* '65 (FgM) Maryknoll, NY MARYKNOLL.
Barry, Raymond J. '65 (HRT) Retired.
Barry, Robert L. *o.p.* '73 (CHI)[N] St. Pius V Priory.
Barry, Robert L. *o.p.* '73 (MO) Air National Guard Chaplains.
Barry, Thomas J. '67 (HRT) Middlebury, CT St. John of the Cross.
Barry, William A. *s.j.* '62 (BO)[U] Weston, MA Campion Jesuit Community.
Barszczewski, Rev. Msgr. Francis A. '68 (PH) Retired.
Barta, Ardel H. '63 (DUB) Vinton, IA St. Mary; Walker, IA St. Mary; Vinton, IA Sacred Heart; Dubuque, IA St. Raphael Cathedral Retired.
Barta, Rev. Msgr. James O. '55 (DUB) College of Consultors; Continuing Formation of Priests; Finance Council; Lay Formation Advisory Board; Investment Committee; Directors Retired.
Bartchak, Rev. Msgr. Mark L. '81 (E) Erie, PA St. Stanislaus; Pennsylvania Catholic Conference; Judicial Vicar; Matrimonial Judges; Office of Conciliation & Arbitration; Pennsylvania Conference on Inter–Church Cooperation; Consultants.
Bartczyszyn, Steven *c.r.* '86 (CHI)[N] Chicago Provincial Office of the Congregation of the Resurrection.
Bartek, Valerian '82 (LIN) Trenton, NE St. James; Deaneries and Deans.
Bartek, William C. '61 (OM) Retired.
Bartel, Franklin '70 (PHX) Sun City, AZ St. Elizabeth Seton Roman Catholic Parish.
Bartel, Martin R. *o.s.b.* '85 (GBG) Greensburg, PA St. Benedict; Greensburg, PA St. Bruno.
Bartell, Ernest J. *c.s.c.* '61 (FTW)[B] University of Notre Dame Du Lac; [H] Notre Dame, IN Holy Cross Community, Corby Hall, University of Notre Dame.
Bartelme, James P. '82 (SUP) Ladysmith, WI St. Mary of Czestochowa; Ladysmith, WI Our Lady of Sorrows; Ladysmith, WI St. Anthony de Padua.
Barter, Robert '61 (PRM) Clinton Township, MI St. Nicholas; Sacred Liturgy Retired.
Barth, Rev. Msgr. Charles P. '56 (CAM) Hammonton, NJ St. Anthony of Padua Roman Catholic Church, Hammonton, N.J.; Friends of the Sacred Heart Retired.
Barth, John C. *m.m.* '91 (FgM) Maryknoll, NY MARYKNOLL.
Barth, Michael D. '94 (COV) Adjutant Judicial Vicars; Melbourne, KY St. Philip.
Barth, Michael *s.t.* '79 (JKS) Camden, MS Sacred Heart; Silver Spring, MD.
Barth, Raymond J. '85 (KAL) Retired.
Barthel, Charles '82 (STL) Manchester, MO Christ, Prince of Peace.
Bartholomew, Michael J. '09 (RVC) Huntington Station, NY St. Hugh of Lincoln.
Bartko, Gerald L. *o.s.f.s.* '66 (BUF)[D] Niagara Falls, NY Niagara Catholic High School; Lockport, NY All Saints.
Bartko, Louis *o.f.m.* '90 (CIN) Cincinnati, OH St. Clement; [N] Cincinnati, OH St. Clement Friary.
Bartkus, Rev. Msgr. Algimantas A. '65 (ALN) On Duty Outside the Diocese.
Bartkus, Rev. Msgr. Algimantas '65 (LIT) Lithuanian R. Catholic Religious Aid, Inc.
Bartlett, James *s.m.* '69 (HON)[D] Honolulu, HI Marianist Hall Community.
Bartlett, Richard *c.m.f.* '50 (CHI)[N] Oak Park Claretian Missionaries USA Eastern Province.
Bartley, David J. '70 (BO) Senior Priests. Retired.
Bartley, Denis *s.s.c.* '51 (OM)[K] St. Columbans Missionary Society of St. Columban.
Bartley, Denis *s.s.c.* '51 (PRO)[P] Bristol, RI St. Columban's Retirement House Retired.
Bartnik, James T. '75 (BUF) Buffalo, NY St. John the Evangelist Retired.
Bartniski, William D. '67 (GAL) Rosenberg, TX Holy Rosary; [S] Galveston, TX The Bishop's Palace.
Bartolay, Rolando '08 (OAK) El Cerrito, CA St. John the Baptist.
Bartollotta, Victor W. '90 (ROC) On Duty Outside the Diocese.
Bartolo, Salvador *o.carm.* '52 (JOL)[L] Darien Carmelite Provincial Office.
Bartoloma, James L. '03 (CAM) On Duty Outside the Diocese.
Bartolome, Cyrus '07 (BGP) Presbyteral Council; Bethel, CT St. Mary.
Bartolomeo, Thomas '06 (SPC) New Madrid, MO Immaculate Conception.
Bartolomeo, Thomas '06 (SPC) Caruthersville, MO Sacred Heart.
Bartolotta, Victor '90 (DAL)[C] Dallas, TX Bishop Lynch High School, Inc.; Dallas, TX St. Thomas Aquinas.
Barton, Michael *m.c.c.j.* '75 (FgM) Cincinnati, OH COMBONI MISSIONARIES (VERONA FATHERS).
Barton, Rev. Msgr. Raymond A. '66 (RIC) Virginia Beach, VA St. Nicholas; Vicar for Ecumenism & Ecumenical Affairs; Commission for Ecumenical & Interreligious Affairs.
Bartos, Andrzej '83 (CHI) Chicago, IL St. Christina.
Bartos, Francis J. '54 (PH) Retired.
Bartos, Kris '85 (MIA) Pembroke Pines, FL St. Boniface.
Bartosic, Mark A. '94 (CHI) Cicero, IL St. Frances of Rome; Cicero, IL Our Lady of Charity; Deans.
Bartosz, Andrzej '91 (CHI) Oak Lawn, IL St. Germaine.
Bartoszek, Richard '89 (DET) Grosse Pointe, MI Beaumont Hospital; Presbyteral Council.

Bartoul, William '77 (SAM) On Duty Outside the Diocese; Air Force Chaplains.
Bartsch, Edward C. '49 (VIC) Flatonia, TX St. Mary's.
Bartsch, Kenneth W. *o.f.m.conv.* '75 (MO) DEPARTMENT OF VETERANS AFFAIRS HOSPITALS AND CHAPLAINS.
Bartulica, Angelo '08 (KC) Blue Springs, MO St. John La Lande.
Bartylla, Rev. Msgr. James R. '01 (MAD) Vocations; Diocesan Consultors; Madison; Appointed; [F] Madison, WI Bishop O'Connor Catholic Pastoral Center.
Baru, Joseph Uri *o.c.d.* '05 (MIL)[P] Milwaukee Provincial Offices – Discalced Carmelites.
Barusefski, Ronald '89 (PSC) Minersville, PA SS. Peter and Paul; Syncellus; Eparchial College of Consultors; Presbyteral Council.
Barut, Joel '67 (HON) Pahala, HI Sacred Heart; Pahala, HI Holy Rosary.
Barwig, Regis N. '59 (GB)[J] Oshkosh, WI Community of Our Lady; Community of Our Lady.
Barwin, John G. '80 (E) Johnsonburg, PA St. Anne Retired.
Baryski, Wojciech *s.ch.* '65 (CHI) Chicago, IL Five Holy Martyrs.
Basarab, John G. '79 (PSC) Annandale, VA Epiphany of Our Lord; Syncellus; Eparchial College of Consultors; Presbyteral Council.
Basarte, Aldrin '96 (SAC) Legion of Mary; Yreka, CA St. Joseph; McCloud, CA St. Joseph; Fort Jones, CA Sacred Heart.
Baseford, Paul '57 (SB) Retired.
Basekela, Cletus '71 (STP) Maplewood, MN St. Jerome.
Bash, Cletus '56 (OKL) Retired.
Bashista, Brian G. '99 (ARL) Arlington, VA Our Lady of Lourdes; Vocations, Office of; Advocates.
Basil, John E. '62 (NEW) Retired.
Basile, Gioacchino '95 (NEW) On Duty Outside the Archdiocese.
Basile, Gioacchino '95 (BRK) East Elmhurst, NY St. Gabriel.
Basilio, Allan '94 (BRK) Astoria, NY Immaculate Conception.
Basilious, Reynolds *o.c.d.* '97 (BRK) Brooklyn, NY St. Mary Mother of Jesus.
Basinow, Leonard '53 (SAM) Retired.
Basler, Rev. Msgr. Howard B. '58 (BRK) Retired.
Basquel, Thomas *c.s.sp.* '76 (BRK)[T] Long Island City, NY Holy Ghost Fathers of Ireland; [X] Long Island City, NY World Compassion Link; Long Island City, NY; Councilors:.
Basquerizo, Christian Jaramillo '09 (NEW) Union City, NJ Sts. Joseph and Michael.
Bass, Frank B. '03 (BR) Baton Rouge, LA St. George.
Bass, Michael E. '87 (LR) Little Rock, AR Christ the King.
Bass, Rev. Msgr. Ricardo E. '74 (DET) West Bloomfield, MI Prince of Peace; College of Consultors; Defenders of Bond.
Bassano, Michael *m.m.* '75 (FgM) On Duty Outside the Diocese; Maryknoll, NY MARYKNOLL.
Bassett, Frank W. '00 (NY) Nanuet, NY St. Anthony.
Bassey, Anthony *m.s.p.* '91 (NY) Yonkers, NY St. Bartholomew.
Bassil, Pierre '98 (OLL) Dayton, OH Our Lady of Lebanon Maronite Catholic Mission; Dayton, OH Saint Ignatius of Antioch Maronite Catholic Church.
Basso, Anthony *s.d.v.* '93 (LSC) Truth or Consequences, NM Our Lady of Perpetual Help.
Basso, Richard '62 (SEA) Retired.
Bastan, Jose M. Garcia *o.s.a.* '62 (SJN) Bayamon, PR San Juan Bautista de la Salle.
Bastia, Rev. Msgr. Raymond B. '75 (PRO) Providence, RI St. Joseph; Secretary for Planning & Financial Services; Finance Council; Secretariat for Planning and Financial Services; Insurance Commission; Council Members; College of Consultors.
Bastian, James R. '95 (BUF) Air Force Reserve Chaplains; [D] Buffalo, NY St. Joseph's Collegiate Institute; Cheektowaga, NY St. Aloysius Gonzaga.
Bastianelli, Daniel P. *s.s.j.* '64 (LAF) Rayne, LA Our Mother of Mercy.
Bastidas, Alexis '82 (NY) New York, NY Blessed Sacrament.
Bastien, Emmanuel '09 (MIA) Miami, FL Good Shepherd.
Bastress, Rev. Msgr. Arthur '51 (BAL) Baltimore, MD St. Alphonsus, Shrine of.
Basulto–Pitol, Marco A. '00 (TUC) Coolidge, AZ Saint James Roman Catholic Parish – Coolidge.
Basznianin, Richard '84 (TR) Forked River, NJ St. Pius X.
Batausa, Nilo '97 (HT) Houma, LA Maria Immacolata.
Batch, Thomas A. '76 (SAC) Retired.
Batcha, James J. '85 (PRM) Burton, OH Church of Mariapoch; Eparchial Shrine of the Weeping Madonna of Mariapoch; Sexual Allegation Review Board; Parma, OH Holy Spirit; Presbyteral Council; Eparchial Finance Council; Cantors' Institute Faculty; Office of Evangelization and Missionary Activity; Priest's Pension Board; Stewardship Office.
Batchelder, George '05 (MRY) Atascadero, CA St. William's.
Batcheldor, C. Joseph '57 (L) Bardstown, KY Basilica of St. Joseph Proto–Cathedral Retired.
Batcho, Robert '88 (STF) Syracuse, NY St. John the Baptist; Holy Name Societies.
Bateman, John B. '96 (HBG) Appointed; Waynesboro, PA St. Andrew.
Bateman, John '96 (HBG)[I] Waynesboro, PA Penn State University, Mont Alto Campus, South Mountain.
Bates, David (SEA)[H] Olympia, WA Providence Mother Joseph Care Center.
Bates, Donald J. *o.s.a.* '60 (JOL) New Lenox, IL St. Jude.
Bates, James R. '63 (LFT) Retired.
Bath, Winston L. '72 (ALB) Hudson, NY Parish of the Holy Trinity; Priests Retirement Board/Priests Retirement Plan Board.
Bathineni, Mohana R. '01 (GLP) Farmington, NM St. Mary's.
Batikha, George '97 (NTN) West Paterson, NJ St. Ann.
Batista, Jiobani '93 (VEN) Sarasota, FL St. Jude.
Batmomolin, Lukas *s.v.d.* '91 (CHI)[N] Techny, IL Divine Word Residence.
Batsis, Thomas *o.carm.* '70 (LA) North Hollywood, CA St. Jane Frances de Chantal.
Batt, Anthony R. '04 (STU) St. Clairsville, OH St. Mary's.
Battafarano, Gregory A. *o.carm.* (PAT) Consulting Psychologist.
Battafarano, Gregory *o.carm.* '67 (NEW) Bogota, NJ St. Joseph's.
Battaglia, Pio *c.s.* '71 (VEN) Immokalee, FL Our Lady of Guadalupe.
Batterberry, Michael J. '70 (SEA)[B] Burien, WA John F. Kennedy Catholic High School.
Battersby, Gerard '98 (DET) Graduate Studies.
Battiato, Patrick (COS) Retired.
Battiato, Ronald A. '61 (OM) Fremont, NE St. Patrick.
Battisti, Lewis A. '62 (CAM) Retired.
Battle, Rev. Msgr. Lawrence '49 (SB) Retired.
Battolini, Ottaviano *o.f.m.* '43 (FgM) New York, NY Franciscan Province of the Immaculate Conception.
Batts, Peter *o.p.* '81 (PRO)[P] Providence St. Thomas Aquinas Priory at Providence College.
Batule, Rev. Msgr. Robert J. '85 (RVC) Academic Leave; Greenlawn, NY St. Francis of Assisi.
Batung, Anthony '76 (CHR) Aiken, SC St. Gerard.
Bature, Anthony '96 (BRK) Brooklyn, NY St. Teresa of Avila.
Batykefer, John J. '90 (PIT) Canonsburg, PA St. Patrick.
Bau, Chau Xuan *c.ss.r.* '62 (LA)[P] Baldwin Park Vietnamese Redemptorist Mission.
Baudry, Jean–Marie *i.v.e.* '05 (SJ) San Jose, CA St. Leo the Great.
Bauer, Carl E. '63 (WH) Retired.
Bauer, Carl (CHR) Hampton, SC St. Mary.
Bauer, Charles A. '78 (MEM) Memphis, TN Holy Rosary.
Bauer, Daniel *s.v.d.* '74 (FgM) Techny, IL.
Bauer, Donald J. '01 (LC) Cadott, WI St. Rose of Lima; Cadott, WI St. Anthony; Deans.
Bauer, Donald J. '48 (SY) Retired.
Bauer, Elmer *c.m.* '93 (PH)[B] Philadelphia, PA St. Vincent's Seminary; Philadelphia, PA; [B] Philadelphia, PA DePaul Novitiate.
Bauer, Elmer *c.m.* '88 (PH)[Y] Philadelphia Congregation of the Mission.
Bauer, Erwin J. '47 (DET) Memphis, MI Holy Family Retired.
Bauer, Rev. Msgr. Henry '48 (KC) Retired.
Bauer, Jacob F. '48 (GI) Retired.
Bauer, John F. '65 (E) Retired.
Bauer, John J. '08 (STP) St. Paul, MN The Nativity of Our Lord.
Bauer, John M. '73 (PIT) Carmichaels, PA St. Hugh; Carmichael, PA Our Lady of Consolation.
Bauer, John M. '79 (STP) Minneapolis, MN The Basilica of St. Mary Co–Cathedral.
Bauer, John *c.ss.r.* (BAL) Baltimore, MD Sacred Heart of Jesus.
Bauer, Karl A. '67 (NY) Yonkers, NY St. Anthony.
Bauer, Mark '86 (GR) Caledonia, MI Holy Family.
Bauer, Richard W. *m.m.* '85 (FgM) Maryknoll, NY MARYKNOLL.
Bauer, Robert A. '87 (DET) Maybee, MI St. Joseph; Carleton, MI St. Patrick.
Bauer, Roy R. '59 (SFD) Retired.
Bauer, Scott A. '98 (LC) Leave of Absence.
Bauer, Stephen F. '77 (STL) St. Charles, MO St. Peter.
Bauer, Stephen *o.s.c.* '92 (PHX)[F] Phoenix, AZ Crosier Community of Phoenix (Canons Regular of the Order of the Holy Cross).
Bauer, Steven '04 (CHI)[U] Chicago, IL University of Illinois at Chicago – John Paul II Newman Center.
Bauer, Sylvester W. '42 (JC) Rural Life Movement Retired.
Bauer, Sylvester '42 (SPC) Diocesan Peace and Justice Commission Retired.
Bauerle, Bernhard *o.carm.* '64 (JOL)[L] Darien, IL St. Simon Stock Priory; [L] Darien, IL Carmelite Provincial Office; Darien, IL; Councilors:.
Baugh, David G. '57 (CLV) Wickliffe, OH Our Lady of Mount Carmel Retired.
Bauhoff, Rev. Msgr. Richard C. '73 (RVC) Carle Place, NY Church of Our Lady of Hope; Judges for Interdiocesan Tribunal; Priests' Retirement Board.
Bauler, Rev. Msgr. Gary P. '67 (LA) Simi Valley, CA St. Peter Claver.
Baum, Matthew '09 (ALT) State College, PA Our Lady of Victory.
Baum, Terrence A. *s.j.* '81 (KC)[D] Kansas City, MO Rockhurst High School; [J] Kansas City, MO Rockhurst Jesuit Community.
Bauman, Dale A. '82 (FTW) Pierceton, IN St. Francis Xavier; Advisory Board; Fort Wayne, IN Cathedral of the Immaculate Conception.
Bauman, John '78 (NY) White Plains, NY Burke Rehabilitation Center.
Bauman, Kevin M. '08 (FTW) Elkhart, IN St. Vincent de Paul; Elkhart.
Bauman, Rodger '82 (STP) White Bear Lake, MN St. Mary of the Lake.
Bauman, William A. '60 (KC) Administrative Committee Retired.
Baumann, Charles R. *s.j.* '80 (OM)[K] Omaha, NE Jesuit Community at Creighton University.
Baumann, John A. *s.j.* '69 (OAK)[M] Oakland, CA Jesuit Fathers and Brothers; [R] Oakland, CA PICO National Network.
Baumann, Lawrence L. '64 (PHX) Retired.
Baumann, Richard J. *s.j.* '75 (CHI)[N] Chicago Chicago Province of the Society of Jesus–Provincial Office; Chicago, IL Society of Jesus.
Baumann, Silas *o.f.m.cap.* '51 (GB)[J] Appleton, WI St. Fidelis Friary Retired.
Baumann, Stephen A. '92 (ORL) Longwood, FL Annunciation.
Baumberger, Richard '89 (SFS) Dante, SD Assumption B.V.M.; Wagner, SD St. John the Baptist.
Baumert, Frank J. '78 (OM) Omaha, NE Holy Name; Deans; Age Groups; Deans.
Baumgaertner, Rev. Msgr. William L. '46 (STP)[C] St. Paul, MN University of St. Thomas Retired.
Baumgartner, Rev. Msgr. A. Thomas '58 (BAL) Baltimore, MD St. Ursula; Baltimore, MD St. Joseph.
Baumgartner, Rev. Msgr. A. Thomas '58 (BAL) Priest Personnel Board Retired.
Baumgartner, Andrew *o.s.b.* '60 (B)[C] Jerome, ID Monastery of the Ascension.
Baumgartner, Rev. Msgr. David '90 (CR) Adoption Referral/Post Adoption Search; Catholic Campaign for Human Development; Catholic Relief Services; Vicar General & Moderator of the Curia; Information Officer; Promoter of Justice; Diocesan Consultors; Finance Council; Holy Childhood Association; Natural Family Planning; Priests' Council; Priests' Personnel Board; Propagation of the Faith; Diocesan Board of Review for the Protection of Children and Young People; Catholic Charities; Defenders of the Bond.
Baumgartner, John H. '63 (MIL) Lyons, WI St. Joseph.
Baumhart, Raymond C. *s.j.* '57 (CHI)[C] Chicago, IL Jesuit Community at Loyola University Chicago; Office of the Archbishop; Personal Consultant to the Cardinal.
Baur, Joseph A. *o.f.m.* '52 (PHX) Guadalupe, AZ Our Lady of Guadalupe Roman Catholic Parish.
Bausch, Michael '79 (ROC) Pittsford, NY Church of the Transfiguration.
Bausch, William J. '55 (TR) Retired.
Bauschka, Joseph '55 (GB) Retired.
Bautista, Antonio (MO) Navy Chaplains.
Bautista, Gaspar '75 (FRS) Mendota, CA Our Lady of Guadalupe.
Bautista, Jose A. '99 (LA) Military Chaplains.
Bautista, Jose '91 (ORL) Judges; Kissimmee, FL St. Catherine of Siena; Appointed Members; Defenders of the Bond.
Bautista, Renato J. '07 (NEW) Franklin Lakes, NJ Most Blessed Sacrament.
Bautista, Tony '05 (NY)[B] Staten Island, NY Society of St. Paul.
Bautista–Peráza, Pedro '04 (SPK) Connell, WA St. Vincent; Eltopia, WA St. Paul; Ritzville, WA St. Ambrose; Ritzville, WA St. Agnes; Ritzville, WA Holy Trinity.
Bauwens, Thomas E. '87 (OM) Humphrey, NE St. Francis; Consultors; Ex Officio (Consultors).
Bauza, Ricardo '05 (LSC) Las Cruces, NM St. Genevieve; Finance Council.
Bava, David '73 (WDC) Washington, DC Holy Redeemer.
Bavaro, John *o.f.m.* '63 (MAN) Manchester, NH Blessed Sacrament.
Baver, John J. '91 (PIT) Bethel Park, PA St. Germaine.
Baver, Rev. Msgr. William F. '81 (ALN) Bethlehem, PA SS. Simon and Jude; Cemeteries.
Bavinger, Bruce *s.j.* '78 (R)[F] Raleigh Jesuit Community; Wilson, NC Church of St. Therese.
Bawyn, Anthony '82 (SEA) Seattle, WA St. Catherine of

Siena; Special Assignment; Judicial Vicar; Judges; Due Process; Presbyteral Council; Seattle, WA Our Lady of the Lake.
Baxa, Henry '90 (SAL) Abilene, KS St. Andrew Parish; Chapman, KS St. Michael Parish; Moderator.
Baxter, Gregory P. '88 (OM) Deans; Omaha, NE St. Margaret Mary; Moderator of the Curia; Deans; Finance Council; Propagation of the Faith; Archbishop's Appointees.
Baxter, M. Shane '03 (BEA) Beaumont, TX Our Lady of the Assumption; Vocations; [D] Beaumont, TX Lamar University–Catholic Student Center; Vocation Board; Presbyteral Council.
Baxter, Nicholas *o.f.m.* '62 (SAT) San Antonio, TX San Jose y San Miguel.
Baxter, Stephen R. '81 (WCH) Halstead, KS Sacred Heart Parish; Judges; Cursillo (English language); Kansas State Industrial Reformatory.
Baxter, Rev. Msgr. Thomas F. '76 (MAD) Madison, WI St. James; Madison, WI Saint Joseph.
Baxter, Thomas–Benedict *o.s.b.* '79 (CHI)[N] Chicago, IL Monastery of the Holy Cross.
Bay, Joseph N. '94 (COL) Columbus, OH Sts. Augustine and Gabriel; Columbus, OH Columbus Vietnamese Catholic Community; Presiding Judges of First Instance.
Bay, Richard '04 (PAT) Unassigned; [A] Boonton, NJ Domus Bartimaeus.
Bayard, Michael S. *s.j.* '98 (SEA)[A] Seattle, WA Seattle University; [L] Seattle, WA Arrupe Jesuit Community at Seattle University.
Baybay, Felicito S. '74 (ORL) Candler, FL Immaculate Heart of Mary.
Bayer, Edward J. '56 (BAL) Retired.
Bayer, Ernest '01 (DEN) Steamboat Springs, CO Holy Name.
Bayer, Lawrence J. '58 (CLV) Parma, OH St. Bridget Retired.
Bayer, Peter T. '71 (ROC) Rochester, NY St. Margaret Mary; St. Ann's Home/Heritage; [E] Rochester, NY St. Ann's Home for the Aged; [E] Rochester, NY St. Ann's Nursing Home Co., Inc.; [E] Rochester, NY Chapel Oaks:.
Bayhi, M. Jeffery '79 (BR) Zachary, LA St. John the Baptist.
Bayhi, M. Jeffery '79 (NO) Closer Walk Ministries.
Bayhi, Peter W. *s.j.* '66 (STL)[O] St. Louis, MO Jesuit Community Corporation at Saint Louis University – Jesuit Hall.
Bayim, Cyril Obi '81 (RVC) Bay Shore, NY St. Patrick's.
Bayle, Stephen (BO)[C] Boston, MA Emmanuel College.
Bayler, Frederick C. '09 (FBK) Fairbanks, AK Sacred Heart Cathedral Catholic Church Fairbanks; [C] Fairbanks, AK Kobuk Center.
Baylis, Thomas J. '59 (HRT) Retired.
Bayne, Joseph *o.f.m.conv.* '85 (BUF)[J] Buffalo, NY The Franciscan Center, Inc.; Buffalo Fire Department and Erie County Emergency Services; [D] Athol Springs, NY St. Francis High School; [O] Athol Springs, NY St. Francis of Assisi Friary.
Baysinger, Leo *s.d.b.* '67 (LA)[F] Bellflower, CA St. John Bosco High School.
Bayuk, Richard *c.pp.s.* '75 (KC)[J] Liberty, MO Precious Blood Society Provincial Office; [A] Kansas City, MO Gaspar Mission House; Liberty, MO; [A] Liberty, MO Society of the Precious Blood Provincial Offices.
Baz, Rev. Msgr. Louis '81 (OLL) Detroit, MI St. Maron Maronite Catholic Church.
Bazan, Rev. Msgr. Joaquin '62 (WDC)[M] Washington, DC Little Sisters of the Poor of Washington, D.C., Inc. Retired.
Bazan, Michael J. '84 (ARL) Manassas, VA Sacred Heart.
Bazar, Christopher G. '04 (TOL) Mansfield, OH St. Peter; Youth, Young Adult and Campus Ministry.
Bazar, Ty J. '02 (VIC) Bloomington, TX St. Patrick's.
Bazikila, Ghislain C. (SFR) San Francisco, CA St. Benedict Parish at St. Francis Xavier Church.
Bazyouros, Christopher '03 (LA) Rancho Dominguez, CA St. Albert the Great; Liturgical Commision.
Bazzel, Kevin M. '01 (BIR) Tribunal; Chancellor; Diocesan College of Consultors; [H] Birmingham, AL The Chapel of St. Stephen the Martyr Campus Center; Birmingham, AL St. Paul's Cathedral; Priests'/ Presbyteral Council; Diocesan College of Vicars.
Bazzi, Michael J. '64 (SD) El Cajon, CA St. Peter Cathedral.
Bazzi, Michael J. '64 (SPA) El Cajon, CA St. Peter Chaldean Cathedral.
Bazzoli, Robert L. *o.s.f.s.* '88 (PH) Philadelphia, PA Our Mother of Consolation; Provincial Councilors:.
Beach, Rev. Msgr. Francis W. '76 (PH) West Chester, PA SS. Simon and Jude.
Beach, R. Paul '01 (L) Defenders of the Bond; Graduate Studies.
Beacom, John F. '37 (OM) Retired.
Beacom, Vincent L. '44 (SC) Retired.
Beal, John P. '74 (E) On Duty Outside Diocese; Matrimonial Judges.
Beal, John P. '74 (WDC)[C] Catholic University of America, The.
Beale, Kenneth R. '92 (NEW) Military Chaplains; Air Force Chaplains.
Bean, Charles S. '62 (CAM) Retired.
Bean, E. Gray '03 (BIR) Gadsden, AL St. James; Fort Payne, AL Our Lady of the Valley.
Beard, Mark B. '09 (BR) Paulina, LA St. Michael the Archangel; Paulina, LA Most Sacred Heart of Jesus; Paulina, LA St. Joseph.
Bearis, Marvin *o.f.m.cap.* '09 (HON) Waimanalo, HI St. George.
Bearss, James M. '97 (GAY) Gaylord, MI St. Mary Cathedral; Elmira, MI St. Thomas Aquinas; Grayling, MI St. Mary; Gaylord, MI Holy Redeemer.
Beaskoa, Ruben '66 (MGZ) San Sebastian, PR San Sebastian Martir.
Beat, Jerome A. '63 (WCH) Presbyteral Council/College of Consultors; Cursillo (Spanish language).
Beat, Jerry '63 (WCH)[C] Wichita, KS St. Joseph Campus.
Beath, James D. '79 (CHI) Chicago, IL St. Mary, Star of the Sea.
Beaton, Kevin J. *s.f.o.* '87 (SAM) New Castle, PA St. John the Baptist.
Beaton, Kevin (SAM) Pro–Life Director.
Beattie, Rev. Msgr. James T. '61 (WDC) Bethesda, MD St. Bartholomew; Priest Council.
Beattie, Joseph A. *o.s.f.s.* '65 (VEN)[G] Fort Myers, FL Oblates of St. Francis de Sales.
Beatty, James H. '74 (CLV) Avon Lake, OH Holy Spirit.
Beatty, Michael D. '64 (CIN) Cincinnati, OH St. Simon the Apostle; Judges.
Beatty, Steven L. '07 (BEL) Belleville, IL Cathedral of St. Peter.
Beaubien, David W. '93 (WDC) Derwood, MD St. Francis of Assisi.
Beauchamp, E. William *c.s.c.* '82 (FTW)[H] Notre Dame, IN Congregation of Holy Cross, Indiana Province, Provincial House.
Beauchamp, Henry *c.ss.r.* '78 (PCE) Guayama, PR St. Anthony of Padua.
Beauchamp, William *c.s.c.* '82 (P)[B] University of Portland; [B] University of Portland; [L] Portland, OR Holy Cross Fathers & Brothers, C.S.C. – University of Portland; Provincial Councilors:.
Beauchemin, Ronald A. *m.s.* '68 (FR)[G] Attleboro, MA La Salette Shrine.
Beauclair, Stephen *o.s.b.* '67 (SCL) Richmond, MN SS. Peter and Paul; [I] Collegeville, MN St. John's Abbey, of the Order of St. Benedict; Deans.
Beaudet, Christopher J. '00 (STP) Judicial Vicar; [A] Saint Paul, MN The Saint Paul Seminary; [C] St. Paul, MN University of St. Thomas.
Beaudin, William R. '82 (BUR)[G] Middlebury, VT Middlebury College; Middlebury, VT Assumption of the Blessed Virgin Mary; Elected Members.
Beaudoin, Andrew *s.s.s.* '54 (CLV)[N] Cleveland Congregation of the Blessed Sacrament Provincial House.
Beaudoin, Andrew *s.s.s.* '54 (SP) Spring Hill, FL St. Frances Xavier Cabrini.
Beaudry, David B. '82 (GB) Kimberly, WI Holy Spirit.
Beaulaurier, Brooks F. '08 (YAK) Director of Planned Giving; Development Office/Stewardship.
Beaulieu, Kerry '74 (ORG) Newport Beach, CA Our Lady Queen of Angels.
Beaulieu, Peter R. '83 (WOR)[K] Worcester, MA Saint Vincent Hospital, Inc.
Beaulieu, Raymond A. '42 (PRO) Retired.
Beaulieu, Richard C. '76 (BO) Winchester, MA St. Mary.
Beaumier, Casey C. *s.j.* '05 (BO)[U] Newton, MA The Jesuit Community at Boston College.
Beaumont, Gregory J. '96 (FRS) Kingsburg, CA Holy Family; Ecumenical Affairs.
Beaumont, Richard '58 (FWT) Retired.
Beaupre, R. Bradley *c.s.c.* '68 (ORL) Viera, FL St. John the Evangelist.
Beauregard, Andrew F. *f.p.o.* '08 (BO)[U] Lawrence, MA Franciscans of Primitive Observance.
Beauregard, David N. *o.m.v.* '80 (BO)[B] Boston, MA Our Lady of Grace Seminary; [Z] Boston, MA St. Clement Archdiocesan Eucharistic Shrine.
Beauregard, James E. '70 (BUR) Retired.
Beausoleil, Charles *o.m.i.* '56 (BO)[Z] Lowell, MA St. Joseph the Worker Residence; [X] Tewksbury, MA Immaculate Heart of Mary Residence.
Beausoleil, Kent A. *s.j.* '07 (CIN) Cincinnati, OH St. Robert Bellarmine; [R] Cincinnati, OH Xavier University Campus Ministry; [N] Cincinnati, OH Jesuit Community at Xavier University.
Beauvais, David E. '62 (RCK) Retired.
Beaven, Robert W. '68 (CHI) Chicago, IL St. Benedict.
Beaver, Carlton '74 (IND) Council of Priests.
Beaver, Nelson G. '76 (TOL) Lexington, OH Resurrection; St. Juan Diego Deanery.
Beaver, William A. *o.s.b.* '85 (PIT) Pittsburgh, PA St. Peter.
Beavers, Carl '68 (CHY) Rock Springs, WY Holy Spirit Catholic Community; [G] Rock Springs, WY Rock Springs Catholic School Foundation; St. Joseph's Society for Priests (Clergy Mutual Benefit Society); Diocesan Schools Advisory Group.
Bebak, Brian D. '86 (WCH) El Dorado Correctional Facility; El Dorado, KS St. John the Evangelist.
Bebek, Dominic L. '53 (LA) Retired.
Bebek, Dominic (ORG) Retired.
Bebel, Alfred J. '58 (SY) Binghamton, NY; Presbyteral Council Retired.
Becerra, Rafael *c.s.* (GAL) Houston, TX St. Leo the Great.
Becerra, Robert L. '89 (LSC) Hurley, NM Infant Jesus; Vicars; Santa Clara, NM Santa Clara; Presbyteral Council.
Becerra, Robert L. '89 (NEW) On Duty Outside the Archdiocese.
Becerril, Julian *o.de.m.* '75 (BWN) Alton, TX San Martin de Porres.
Bechamps, Vincent *o.ss.t.* (BAL)[S] The Trinitarians in Bristol, Pennsylvania.
Bechamps, Vincent *o.ss.t.* '66 (PH) Bristol, PA St. Ann.
Bechard, Bernard J. *s.s.e.* '49 (BUR) Sheldon Springs, VT St. Anthony.
Bechard, Gerard V. '80 (DET) Westland, MI SS. Simon and Jude.
Becher, Albert B. '84 (DAL) Lancaster, TX St. Francis of Assisi.
Becherer, David A. '48 (MOB)[E] Mobile, AL Little Sisters of the Poor, Home For the Aged, Inc. Retired.
Becherer, James R. '54 (CLV) Retired.
Bechtel, David W. '08 (SCR) Williamsport, PA St. Joseph the Worker, Williamsport; [D] Williamsport, PA Saint John Neumann Regional Academy High School Campus.
Bechtel, James C. '71 (ALN) Tamaqua, PA St. Jerome; Carbon/Schuylkill Serra Club.
Beck, Rev. Msgr. Albert J. '49 (GAL) Retired.
Beck, David J. '67 (TOL) Retired.
Beck, Edward L. *c.p.* '85 (NY)[II] Pelham, NY Passionist Communications, Inc.; [II] Pelham, NY Passionist Communications Center; [EE] Pelham Manor, NY St. Vincent's Residence.
Beck, Erwin G. *s.j.* '60 (NY)[EE] New York, NY Murray–Weigel Hall.
Beck, Henry *o.f.m.* '80 (ELP) Catholic Campus Ministry; [I] El Paso, TX Catholic Campus Ministry at University of Texas at El Paso.
Beck, Joseph C. '84 (PIT) Pittsburgh, PA St. Rosalia; Allegheny County, PA Forbes Road Nursing Center; Allegheny County, PA Kane Regional Center – Glen Hazel; Allegheny County, PA Woodhaven Convalescent Center; Allegheny County, PA Health South Hospital of Pittsburgh; Allegheny County, PA Independent Court of Monroeville; Allegheny County, PA Manorcare Health Services North Hills.
Beck, Lawrence J. '88 (LA) On Duty Outside the Archdiocese.
Beck, Lawrence J. '88 (SAC) Westwood, CA Our Lady of the Snows; Vicars Forane; Quincy, CA St. John.
Beck, R. Patrick '76 (BEA) Military Chaplains; Air Force Chaplains.
Beck, Richard P. '55 (MIL) Retired.
Beck, Richard W. '74 (SCR) Hawley, PA Blessed Virgin Mary, Queen of Peace.
Beck, Richard *o.m.i.* '67 (SAT)[K] San Antonio, TX Oblate Madonna Residence.
Beck, Robert R. '66 (DUB)[L] Dubuque, IA Mt. St. Francis; [C] Loras College.
Becka, Robert R. *s.j.* '60 (FgM) Los Gatos, CA Society of Jesus.
Becker, Anthony J. '47 (RCK) Retired.
Becker, Arthur '73 (ALB) Cohoes, NY Holy Trinity; Advocates; Ministers to Active Priests and Priests in Special Circumstances.
Becker, Bruno *o.s.b.* '51 (P)[L] St. Benedict, OR Mt. Angel Abbey.
Becker, Charles P. '86 (CHI) Other Assignments.
Becker, Daniel J. '96 (WOR) Warren, MA St. Paul; West Warren, MA St. Stanislaus.
Becker, David R. '66 (ALT) Retired.
Becker, Dennis E. '62 (NU) Retired.
Becker, Donald '67 (BUF) Retired.
Becker, Edward '05 (ORG) Education Leave.
Becker, Rev. Msgr. Frederick J. '59 (NY) Bronx, NY St. Lucy; Montefiore Medical Center – North Division.
Becker, John J. '72 (GB) Green Bay, WI Nativity of Our Lord; Priests' Personnel Board; College of Consultors; Appointed Members; Gillett, WI St. John; Suring, WI St. Michael.
Becker, Joseph P. *o.s.f.s.* '69 (ALN) Lehigh Valley Hospital at Cedar Crest; [B] Center Valley, PA DeSales University; [K] Center Valley, PA Oblates of St. Francis de Sales.
Becker, Rev. Msgr. Michael A. '75 (ALT) Campus Ministry; [I] Johnstown, PA University of Pittsburgh at Johnstown; St. Michael, PA St. Michael's; [I] Saint Michael, PA Office of Youth and Campus Ministry.
Becker, Rev. Msgr. Michael '99 (STP)[C] St. Paul, MN University of St. Thomas; [A] St. Paul, MN St. John Vianney Seminary.
Becker, Nickolas L. '02 (SC) On Duty Outside the Diocese.
Becker, Nickolas *o.s.b.* '02 (SCL)[I] Collegeville, MN St.

John's Abbey, of the Order of St. Benedict.
Becker, Paul D. '73 (BIS) Bismarck, ND Corpus Christi.
Becker, Richard F. '72 (PBL) Trinidad, CO Most Holy Trinity, Trinidad Area Catholic Community (Trinidad Cluster); [E] Trinidad, CO Trinidad Area Catholic Community; Diocesan Council of Catholic Women.
Becker, Robert T. '64 (SFD) Retired.
Becker, Robert '79 (AUS) Lockhart, TX St. Mary.
Becker, Russell C. *o.f.m.* '72 (FgM)[II] New York, NY Franciscan Missionary Union, Province of the Most Holy Name; New York, NY Holy Name Province; Provincial Councilors:.
Becker, Russell *o.f.m.* (NEW)[M] East Rutherford, NJ Sacred Heart Friary.
Becker, Thomas '80 (SCL) Greenwald, MN St. Andrew's; Greenwald, MN St. John's; Greenwald, MN St. Michael's; Diocesan Consultors; Deans.
Becker, Rev. Msgr. Vincent J. '62 (BUF) Vicars; Judges; Wellsville, NY Immaculate Conception; Bolivar, NY St. Mary.
Becker, William M. '88 (WIN) Winona, MN St. Mary's; Censors of Books and Periodicals.
Beckermann, Julius *o.s.b.* '03 (SCL) Cold Spring, MN St. James; [H] Cold Spring, MN Assumption Home; [H] Cold Spring, MN John Paul Apartments; [H] Cold Spring, MN Assumption Court; [I] Collegeville, MN St. John's Abbey, of the Order of St. Benedict.
Beckfelt, John W. '74 (LC) Retired.
Beckley, Clarence *s.s.c.* '66 (OM)[K] St. Columbans Missionary Society of St. Columban Retired.
Beckley, John *s.m.* (WH)[G] Wheeling, WV Good Shepherd Nursing Home.
Beckman, David M. '92 (DUB) Protivin, IA Holy Trinity; Protivin, IA St. John Nepomucene; Protivin, IA Assumption of the B.V.M.; Deanery Representatives; Priests' Council; [F] Protivin, IA Trinity Catholic School; Lawler, IA Our Lady of Mt. Carmel; St. Lucas, IA St. Luke; Waucoma, IA St. Mary.
Beckman, Gary L. '95 (DAV) Houghton, IA St. John's; Houghton, IA St. James.
Beckman, John *s.j.* '54 (CIN)[N] Cincinnati, OH Faber Jesuit Community.
Beckman, Joseph F. '54 (CIN)[B] Cincinnati, OH Mt. St. Mary's Seminary of the West Retired.
Beckman, Mark '90 (NSH) Franklin, TN St. Matthew; Presbyteral Council; Clergy Personnel Board.
Beckman, Martin A. '58 (STP) Retired.
Beckman, Richard J. '56 (OKL) Retired.
Beckman, Robert E. *s.j.* '56 (DET)[K] Clarkston, MI Colombiere Center.
Beckman, Robert E. *s.j.* '56 (CHI)[N] Chicago Chicago Province of the Society of Jesus–Provincial Office.
Beckmann, Rev. Msgr. Donald M. '70 (RVC) Long Beach, NY St. Ignatius Martyr; Ecumenical & Interreligious Affairs.
Becnel, Rev. Msgr. Terry B. '64 (NO) Norco, LA Sacred Heart of Jesus.
Bedard, Andre L. '57 (MAN) Nashua, NH Blessed John XXIII Parish Retired.
Bedard, Paul *s.d.b.* '65 (NY)[GG] Stony Point, NY Don Bosco Retreat Center and Marian Shrine; [GG] Stony Point, NY Marian Shrine.
Bedel, Jason Edward '08 (CIN) Sidney, OH Holy Angels.
Bedenikovic, Stephen *o.f.m.* '85 (CHI) Chicago, IL Sacred Heart.
Bedillion, James R. '75 (PIT) Boyers, PA St. Alphonsus; Judges.
Bednar, Gerald J. '83 (CLV)[A] Wickliffe, OH St. Mary Seminary and Graduate School of Theology.
Bednar, Martin *o.f.m.* '64 (SP)[N] St. Petersburg St. Anthony Friary.
Bednarik, John F. *o.f.m.cap.* '68 (HBG) Secretary for Catholic Life and Evangelization; Prison Ministry; [I] Harrisburg, PA Catholic Campus Ministry; Harrisburg, PA St. Francis of Assisi.
Bednark, Walter '47 (SCL) Paynesville, MN St. Margaret's Retired.
Bednarowicz, Andrzej '01 (BUR) Graniteville, VT St. Sylvester.
Bednartz, Rev. Msgr. August C. '52 (BRK) Retired.
Bednarz, Jan '72 (SLC) Taylorsville, UT Saint Martin de Porres LLC 236.
Bedoya, Carlos '90 (ORL) Deltona, FL St. Clare.
Bedoya, Dario '91 (TYL) On Duty Outside the Diocese.
Bedoya, Hector '91 (ORG) Santa Ana, CA Immaculate Heart of Mary.
Bedoya, Hugo '56 (BRK) Flushing, NY St. John Vianney Retired.
Bedoya, Martin E. '03 (CHI) Des Plaines, IL St. Mary.
Bedoya, Omar A. '94 (ARE) Bajadero, PR La Milagrosa; Cursillos de Cristiandad.
Bedoya Sanchez, Ruben D. '91 (LAV) Las Vegas, NV Prince of Peace.
Bedrossian, Armenag '99 (OLN) Wynnewood, PA St. Mark's Armenian Catholic.
Bedzinski, Robert *s.ch.* '02 (DET) Sterling Heights, MI Our Lady of Czestochowa.
Beebe, Rev. Msgr. Charles J. '70 (PEO) Roanoke, IL St. John; Roanoke, IL St. Joseph; Permanent Diaconate, Office of.
Beebe, David E. '61 (CAM) Retired.
Beeching, Roy T. '74 (GRY) Merrillville, IN St. Joan of Arc; Merrillville, IN Ss. Peter and Paul; Hammond, IN Saint John–Saint Joseph; Cemeteries; Council of Catholic Women.
Beeda, Rev. Msgr. Francis J. '61 (SCR) Wilkes Barre, PA Retired.
Beegan, James *m.s.f.* '00 (STL)[N] St. Louis, MO Little Sisters of the Poor, Home for the Aged.
Beek, Alois Van '73 (MIL) Neosho, WI St. Matthew.
Beek, John van der *o.s.a.* '53 (CHI)[N] Olympia Fields, IL Tolentine Monastery at Tolentine Center.
Beekman, Carl E. '00 (RCK) Amboy, IL St. Patrick; Amboy, IL St. Flannen; Amboy, IL St. Mary; Amboy, IL St. Patrick.
Beeman, William Daniel '07 (RIC) Norfolk, VA Holy Trinity.
Beerman, Andrew J. '96 (WIN)[A] Winona, MN Immaculate Heart of Mary Seminary; Censors of Books and Periodicals; Additional Diocesan Assignments.
Beerntsen, Harold '61 (GB) Green Bay, WI Retired.
Beers, Ervan *o.f.m.* '55 (FRS) Delano, CA Our Lady of Guadalupe.
Beers, J. Michael '79 (ALN) Frackville, PA St. Joseph; Frackville – Court St. James #1029.
Beers, John Michael '79 (MO) Air Force Reserve Chaplains.
Beeson, Rev. Msgr. Lawrence A. '60 (DM) Judges; Priests' Pension Fund Society Retired.
Beeson, Terry P. '05 (STP) South St. Paul, MN St. John Vianney.
Beever, Carlton J. '74 (IND) Indianapolis, IN St. Philip Neri.
Beezer, Arnold R. *s.j.* '64 (SPK)[J] Spokane, WA Regis Community Retired.
Befort, Daryl '95 (WCH) Wichita, KS St. Francis of Assisi.
Befort, Earl *o.f.m.cap.* '69 (SAL) Hays, KS Our Lady Help of Christians Parish; Catharine, KS St. Catherine Parish; Hays, KS St. Anthony Parish; [A] Hays, KS Thomas More Prep–Marian Alumni Assoc.; [D] Hays, KS St. Joseph's Friary.
Begay, Joseph N. *s.s.j.* '59 (WDC) Washington, DC St. Luke.
Begg, Christopher T. '77 (WDC) Washington, DC St. Joseph on Capitol Hill; Special Ministries; [C] Catholic University of America, The.
Beggane, Thomas (LSC) Absent On Leave.
Beggiani, Chorbishop Seely '61 (SAM)[A] Washington, DC Our Lady of Lebanon Maronite Seminary; Presbyteral Council; Lebanon Commission; Finance Council.
Beggin, Thomas M. '79 (GF) Retired.
Begin, Daniel L. '75 (CLV) Cleveland, OH St. Cecilia.
Begin, Rev. Msgr. Raymond F. '52 (PRT) Retired.
Begin, Robert T. '64 (CLV) Cleveland, OH St. Colman; Avon, OH Our Lady of the Wayside.
Begley, James J. '82 (RIC) Mechanicsville, VA Church of the Redeemer.
Begley, John J. *s.j.* '62 (BO)[U] Boston The Society of Jesus of New England–Provincial Offices.
Begley, John J. *s.j.* '62 (SCR)[C] Scranton, PA The University of Scranton.
Begley, Thomas B. '60 (SPR) Retired.
Begley, Thomas M. '89 (STL) Retired.
Begly, Mark S. '84 (ALT) Altoona Deanery; Lakemont, Altoona, PA St. John the Evangelist; Inter–Faith Minister.
Begnaud, Adam *o.s.b.* '96 (NO)[P] St. Benedict, LA St. Joseph Abbey.
Begolly, Rev. Msgr. Michael J. '81 (GBG) New Kensington, PA Mt. St. Peter.
Begue, Joseph E. *c.m.* '55 (STL)[O] St. Louis, MO Lazarist Residence; [V] St. Louis, MO The Vincentian Press Religious Supply.
Behan, George P. '56 (PRO) Retired.
Behan, Hugh F. '64 (JC) Absent on Leave.
Behan, Rev. Msgr. Philip A. '70 (SB) Palm Springs, CA St. Theresa; Judges.
Behan, Thomas W. *o.s.a.* '58 (LA) Los Angeles, CA Our Mother of Good Counsel.
Behen, John *c.pp.s.* '46 (CIN)[N] Carthagena, OH St. Charles Retired.
Behl, Rev. Msgr. Richard A. '66 (MET) Old Bridge, NJ St. Thomas the Apostle; Office of Pontifical Mission Societies; Commission for Pro–Life Action.
Behnen, Robert *o.f.m.* '60 (SFD)[L] Springfield, IL Our Lady of Angels Friary.
Behnke, John *c.s.p.* '76 (WDC)[B] Washington, DC St. Paul's College.
Behnke, Robert C. '73 (CHI) Other Assignments.
Behrend, Thomas J. '00 (CLV) Presbyteral Conveners; Presbyteral Council; Wickliffe, OH Our Lady of Mount Carmel.
Behrens, James Stephen *o.c.s.o.* '74 (ATL)[G] Conyers The Monastery of the Holy Spirit.
Behringer, William *s.m.* '60 (CLV) Cleveland, OH St. Aloysius – St. Agatha.
Beierwaltes, Charles *c.ss.r.* '67 (MIL)[S] Oconomowoc, WI The Redemptorist Retreat Center.
Beighlie, James T. *c.m.* '79 (STL) House Springs, MO Our Lady, Queen of Peace.
Beighlie, James '79 (STL)[O] St. Louis Vincentian Residence.
Beirne, Charles J. *s.j.* '69 (NY)[EE] Cardinal Spellman Hall, Jesuit Community.
Beirne, Gerald E. '62 (PRO) Retired.
Beirne, M. Christen '69 (NEW) Short Hills, NJ St. Rose of Lima.
Beirne, Robert M. '63 (PRO) Providence, RI Assumption of the Blessed Virgin Mary Retired.
Beischel, Thomas *c.pp.s.* '58 (CIN)[N] Carthagena, OH St. Charles Retired.
Beisel, Rev. Msgr. James D. '80 (PH) Warrington, PA St. Robert Bellarmine.
Beitans, John '73 (IND) Indianapolis, IN St. Lawrence.
Beiter, Eugene J. '64 (LAN) Retired.
Beiter, Robert G. '64 (BUF) Depew, NY St. Barnabas Retired.
Beiting, Rev. Msgr. Ralph '49 (LEX) Louisa, KY St. Jude; Father Beiting Appalachian Mission Center.
Bejan, Ciprian '00 (BGP) Greenwich, CT St. Michael the Archangel.
Bejarano, Cesar Rafael *o.f.m.* (NY) Bronx, NY St. Luke.
Bejarano, Ramon '98 (STO) Personnel Board; Modesto, CA St. Stanislaus Church (Pastor of).
Bejgrowicz, Joseph S. '70 (NEW) Kenilworth, NJ St. Theresa's; Union North Deanery 23; Members; Members.
Bejo, Lauro *s.o.l.t.* (KC) Kansas City, MO Our Lady of Peace.
Bejo, Stephen *o.f.m.conv.* (OAK)[M] Castro Valley, CA Conventual Franciscans (Province of St. Joseph of Cupertino).
Bekkedahl, Mark '85 (B)[B] Nampa, ID Mercy Medical Center.
Beksha, Francis W. '46 (BO) Senior Priests. Retired.
Belanger, C. Francis *o.p.* '05 (MAN)[K] Hanover, NH Order of Preachers; [O] Hanover, NH The Catholic Student Center at Dartmouth, Aquinas House, Aquinas at Dartmouth, Inc.
Belanger, Daniel R. *c.s.v.* '07 (CHI)[N] Arlington Heights Viatorian Province Center–Clerics of St. Viator.
Belanger, Daniel R. *c.s.v.* '07 (JOL) Bourbonnais, IL St. George.
Belanger, Francis C. *o.p.* '05 (MAN) Hanover, NH St. Denis.
Belanger, Gerald R. '75 (MAN) Peterborough, NH Divine Mercy Parish; Presbyteral Council; College of Consultors; Priest Personnel Board.
Belanger, Thomas G. '06 (CHI) Chicago, IL St. Philip Neri.
Belanggoy, Plutarco *c.i.c.m.* '96 (SAT) San Antonio, TX St. James the Apostle.
Belanich, Giordano '75 (NEW) Fairview, NJ St. John the Baptist; Secaucus, NJ Hudson County Juvenile Correctional Center.
Belardi, Todd *l.c.* '04 (ATL)[L] Norcross, GA Home and Family, Inc.; [D] Cumming, GA Pinecrest Academy, Inc.; [G] Alpharetta, GA Norcross Pastoral Center, Inc.
Belauskas, August J. '68 (CHI)[A] Mundelein, IL University of St. Mary of the Lake/Mundelein Seminary; [A] Mundelein, IL University of St. Mary of the Lake/Mundelein Seminary.
Belchez, Caesar '95 (HBG)[I] Gettysburg, PA Gettysburg College; Gettysburg, PA St. Joseph the Worker.
Belczak, Edward A. '72 (DET) Troy, MI St. Thomas More.
Belczak, Thomas A. '80 (DET) Plymouth, MI St. Kenneth.
Belden, Cory '02 (STP) White Bear Lake, MN St. Pius X; Rush City, MN Sacred Heart.
Belfield, John '58 (STU) Retired.
Belford, Rev. Msgr. William J. '74 (NY) New York, NY.
Belgarde, George H. *s.j.* '88 (NY)[EE] New York Jesuit Provincial's Office.
Belgarde, George H. *s.j.* '88 (OG)[J] Hogansburg, NY St. Regis Mission.
Belger, Jeffry W. '03 (DAV)[E] Iowa City, IA Newman Catholic Student Center; Scouting; Iowa City, IA St. Mary.
Belgica, Erwin '94 (SP) Temple Terrace, FL Corpus Christi.
Belhumer, Roger E. '61 (PRO)[P] Providence St. John Vianney Residence Retired.
Belhumeur, Paul *m.s.* '61 (BUR) Windsor, VT St. Francis of Assisi.
Belhumeur, Roger E. '61 (PRO) Retired.
Beligotti, Richard J. '68 (ROC) Rochester, NY St. Salome.
Beligotti, Robert L. '68 (ROC) Fairport, NY Assumption of the Blessed Virgin Mary.
Belinda, Augustine *t.o.r.* '93 (ALT)[G] Loretto, PA St. Francis Friary at Mount Assisi.
Belinsky, Michael T. *c.s.c.* '89 (FTW)[H] Notre Dame Congregation of Holy Cross, Indiana Province, Provincial House.
Belinsky, Michael T. *c.s.c.* '89 (P)[P] Portland, OR University of Portland; [B] University of Portland;

[L] Portland, OR Holy Cross Fathers & Brothers, C.S.C. – University of Portland.
Belisch, Carl L. *c.s.b.* '65 (GAL)[O] Houston, TX Dillon House Retired.
Belisle, Ronald '62 (SEA) Shelton, WA St. Edward.
Belitz, Justin *o.f.m.* '61 (IND) Indianapolis, IN Sacred Heart of Jesus.
Belitz, Ronald C. '79 (GB) Green Bay, WI Prince of Peace; Wausaukee, WI St. Agnes; Wausaukee, WI St. Augustine; Vicariate.
Belizaire, Hilaire '00 (BRK) Brooklyn, NY St. Therese of Lisieux; Art and Architecture Commission.
Belizario, Nelson *o.carm.* '68 (JOL)[L] Darien Carmelite Provincial Office.
Belizario, Nelson *o.carm.* '68 (NY) Bronx, NY St. Simon Stock.
Bell, Brian '70 (PHX) Scottsdale, AZ St. Bernard of Clairvaux Roman Catholic Parish.
Bell, Rev. Msgr. Carl F. '66 (LA) Encino, CA St. Cyril.
Bell, Edward H. '77 (PH) Media, PA Nativity of the Blessed Virgin Mary; Diocesan Priests' Compensation and Benefits Committee.
Bell, Edward M. '64 (WH) Retired.
Bell, Gerald L. '73 (L) Lebanon, KY Holy Name of Mary; Lebanon, KY St. Augustine; Deans.
Bell, Gerald P. *s.j.* '57 (WDC)[E] North Bethesda, MD Georgetown Preparatory School.
Bell, Gerard P. *s.j.* '57 (WDC)[W] Silver Spring, MD Apostleship of Prayer.
Bell, Gerard P. *s.j.* '57 (NY)[EE] New York Jesuit Provincial's Office.
Bell, Rev. Msgr. John P. '75 (DAL) Allen, TX Our Lady of Angels; Judicial Vicar; Judicial Vicar.
Bell, Joseph '74 (SPK) Spokane Valley, WA St. John Vianney.
Bell, Richard A. *m.m.* '57 (NY)[EE] Maryknoll Maryknoll St. Teresa's Residence Retired.
Bell, Steven *c.s.p.* '08 (AUS) Austin, TX St. Austin.
Bellafiore, I. Michael *s.j.* '03 (BO)[U] Boston The Society of Jesus of New England–Provincial Offices.
Bellafiore, I. Michael *s.j.* '03 (SCR)[C] Scranton, PA The University of Scranton.
Bellamah, Timothy F. *o.p.* '98 (PRO)[P] Providence St. Thomas Aquinas Priory at Providence College.
Bellamah, Timothy *o.p.* '98 (WDC)[B] Washington, DC Dominican House of Studies.
Belland, David '87 (SCL) Special Assignment.
Bellantonio, Albert '69 (SCR) Tobyhanna, PA St. Ann; Hispanic Ministry Outreach.
Bellantonio, Albert '69 (BRK) Released from Diocesan Assignment.
Bellefeuille, Albert A. '54 (MAN) Retired.
Bellenoit, George C. '72 (FR) South Yarmouth, MA St. Pius Tenth; Cape Cod Deanery.
Belleque, Thomas '85 (SEA) Bellevue, WA St. Louise.
Bellerive, Joseph V. '86 (ORL) Judges.
Bellerive, Vigny Joseph '86 (ORL) Orlando, FL St. Andrew.
Bellesorte, Anthony R. *o.c.s.o.* '69 (SAC)[A] Vina, CA Abbey of New Clairvaux, Trappist Seminary; [I] Vina, CA Abbey of New Clairvaux, Trappist.
Belletty, Emile Ignatius '78 (LA) Retired.
Bellew, Rev. Msgr. Francis P. '66 (NY) Wappingers Falls, NY St. Mary; Dutchess.
Bellew, Lawrence *c.p.* '53 (BRK)[T] Jamaica, NY Immaculate Conception Monastery.
Belli, Brian W. '02 (ARL) Alexandria, VA St. Mary's.
Bellinghausen, David *o.s.b.* '86 (LR)[A] Subiaco, AR Subiaco Abbey; Subiaco, AR.
Bellino, Samuel P. *s.j.* '88 (YAK)[H] Yakima, WA Central Washington Catholic Foundation; Diocesan Catholic Committee on Scouting.
Bellisario, Andrew E. *c.m.* '84 (LA)[P] Montebello, CA DePaul Evangelization Center; [V] Montebello, CA DePaul Evangelization Center.
Bellisario, Andrew E. *c.m.* '84 (SJ)[N] Los Altos Hills, CA Daughters of Charity of St. Vincent de Paul, Seton Provincialate.
Bellittiere, David A. '89 (BUF) Dunkirk, NY Holy Trinity.
Belliveau, Gary J. '85 (MAN) Hudson, NH St. Kathryn.
Belliveau, Paul D. *m.m.* '69 (NY)[EE] Maryknoll Maryknoll Fathers and Brothers Retired.
Bello, Carlos '09 (DEN) Westminster, CO Holy Trinity.
Bello, David *o.p.* '81 (FgM)[M] Oakland Order of Preachers (Province of the Most Holy Name of Jesus – Western Dominican Province); Oakland, CA Province of the Holy Name (Western Dominican Province).
Bello, Giles *o.f.m.* '55 (PAT)[N] Ringwood, NJ Holy Name Friary, Inc.
Bello, Jorge Luis '03 (MIA) Miami, FL St. Kevin.
Bello, Juan Carlos *t.o.r.* '08 (SAT) San Antonio, TX St. Leonard's.
Bello, Manuel Aznar *c.m.* '66 (MGZ) Mayaguez, PR San Vicente.
Bello, Wilson '98 (NEW) Elizabeth, NJ Immaculate Conception.
Bellonce, Fritzner '06 (MIA) Pompano Beach, FL St. Elizabeth of Hungary Catholic Church.
Bellopede, Louis P. '91 (PH) Ridley Park, PA St. Madeline.
Bellow, Rev. Msgr. Richard '70 (CHL) Diocesan Consultors; Huntersville, NC St. Mark.
Belluomini, Rev. Msgr. Ralph '60 (FRS) Bakersfield Memorial Hospital & San Joaquin Community Hospital.
Belmonte, John M. *s.j.* '96 (MIL)[P] Milwaukee, WI Jesuit Community at Marquette University; [E] Milwaukee, WI Marquette University High School.
Belmonte, Luis Gerardo *o.c.d.* '07 (SAT) San Antonio, TX Basilica of the National Shrine of the Little Flower, Our Lady of Mt. Carmel and St. Therese Parish.
Belmontes, Jesus '04 (DAL) Dallas, TX San Juan Diego (Quasi Parish).
Belogi, James '81 (ALB) Schenectady, NY St. Madeleine Sophie; Schenectady, NY St. Gabriel the Archangel.
Beloin, Robert L. '73 (HRT)[Q] New Haven, CT Yale University–St. Thomas More Catholic Center and Chapel; Special and other Archdiocesan Assignment.
Belongea, David *o.f.m.cap.* '59 (GB)[J] Appleton, WI St. Fidelis Friary.
Belongia, Brian S. '05 (GB) Priests' Personnel Board; Waupaca, WI St. Mary Magdalene.
Belschner, Wayne L. '95 (BO) East Boston, MA Sacred Heart.
Belsole, Kurt J. *o.s.b.* '78 (GBG)[G] Latrobe Saint Vincent Archabbey.
Belsome, Garland T. '90 (BR) Defenders of the Bond; Board Members; Presbyteral Council.
Belsome, Gary T. '90 (BR) Gonzales, LA St. Theresa of Avila.
Belt, David D. '90 (OM) Norfolk, NE Sacred Heart.
Beltowski, Andrew '90 (CHI) Palatine, IL St. Theresa.
Beltrami, Robert *o.f.m.* '63 (P) Portland, OR Ascension.
Beltran, Jacinto '02 (HT) Thibodaux, LA St. Joseph Co–Cathedral.
Beltran, Jacque B. '87 (CHI)[A] Mundelein, IL University of St. Mary of the Lake/Mundelein Seminary.
Beltran, JoAndre '01 (CHI) Chicago, IL Notre Dame de Chicago.
Beltran, Justo '69 (BRK) Woodhull Medical & Mental Health Center.
Beltzner, Lucian W. *o.carm.* '63 (NY) Tarrytown, NY Transfiguration.
Belzer, Rev. Msgr. Paul J. '54 (BUF) Retired.
Benacchio, Onorio *c.s.* '50 (VEN) Immokalee, FL Our Lady of Guadalupe.
Benack, Henry I. '51 (RVC) Retired.
Benak, Wes E. *o.s.a.* '91 (CHI)[N] Chicago, IL St. Rita Monastery.
Benavente, Rev. Msgr. James L.G. '94 (AGN) Agana, GU Dulce Nombre de Maria Cathedral – Basilica; Archdiocesan College of Consultors; Archdiocesan Finance Council; Archdiocesan Presbyteral Council; Catholic Cemetery Office.
Benda, Eugene M. '60 (DAV) Retired.
Benda, Frederick J. *s.j.* '72 (DET)[K] Detroit, MI Jesuit Community at the University of Detroit Mercy.
Bendel, Eugene F. '57 (STL) O'Fallon, MO Assumption Retired.
Benden, Stephen *c.ss.r.* '89 (KC) Kansas City, MO Our Lady of Sorrows; [N] Kansas City, MO Our Lady of Perpetual Help Charitable Trust; Kansas City, MO Our Lady of Perpetual Help; [J] Kansas City, MO Redemptorists Fathers of Kansas City, Missouri.
Bender, Arthur C. *s.j.* '78 (NY)[F] New York, NY Regis High School; [EE] New York, NY St. Ignatius Loyola Residence.
Bender, James W. *c.pp.s.* '52 (CIN)[N] Dayton Provincial Office of the Cincinnati Province of the Society of the Precious Blood.
Bender, Philip M. '64 (ALT) State College, PA Good Shepherd.
Bender, Rev. Msgr. Thomas G. '56 (COL) Retired.
Bendernagel, Cajetan *c.p.* '52 (HRT)[L] West Hartford Holy Family Monastery/Retreat.
Bendik, Rev. Msgr. John J. '67 (SCR) Pittston, PA St. John the Evangelist; Deans.
Bendorf, Richard *o.f.m.* '87 (STL)[O] St. Louis Franciscan Friary of St. Anthony of Padua.
Bendorf, Richard *o.f.m.* '87 (MO) Army Chaplains.
Bendzella, Sylvester J. '59 (ALT) Retired.
Bene, Philip J. '94 (STL) Special Assignment.
Benecki, Stanley '84 (COL) Columbus, OH St. Mary Magdalene; Deaf Apostolate.
Benedetto, James F. '70 (NEW)[M] Caldwell, NJ The Rev. Msgr. James F. Kelley Residence for Retired Priests Retired.
Benedetto, William F. '07 (NEW) Glen Rock, NJ St. Catharine.
Benedict, Joseph '97 (SJ) Special Assignment; Los Altos, CA St. William; Deacon Formation.
Benedicto, Benjamin '62 (ORG) Retired.
Benefiel, Rev. Msgr. Harry E. '60 (LAF) Diocesan Consultors Retired.
Beneleit, Edward L. '74 (Y) Navarre, OH St. Clement.
Benestad, Rev. Msgr. Thomas J. '70 (ALN) Retired.
Bengert, Tony '65 (ELP) Absent on Leave.
Bengford, Ronald J. '94 (PRO) Woonsocket, RI Sacred Heart.
Bengochea, Gerardo *s.j.* (RVC) Hempstead, NY Our Lady of Loretto.
Bengurria, Juan B. *c.p.* '57 (ARE) Lares, PR St. Joseph.
Benicewicz, Joseph *o.f.m.conv.* '88 (BAL)[W] Ellicott City, MD AnthonyCorps, Inc.; [S] Baltimore, MD Immaculate Heart of Mary Friary; [W] Ellicott City, MD Fr. Justin Ministry Fund, Inc.
Beninati, Francis H. *m.m.* '55 (FgM) Maryknoll, NY MARYKNOLL.
Benintende, Joseph '70 (ALB) Oneonta, NY St. Mary; [R] Albany, NY Noonan Community Service Corporation; Presbyteral Council; Diocesan Board of Consultors.
Benioff, Edward C. '07 (LA) San Pedro, CA Holy Trinity.
Beniot, Vincent *o.p.* '84 (P)[L] Portland, OR Holy Rosary Priory.
Benischeck, Bernard J. '53 (PH) Retired.
Benish, William '72 (AUS) Retired.
Benitez, Carlos A. '04 (WDC) Rockville, MD St. Raphael.
Benitez, Eduardo '66 (ORL) Retired.
Benitez, Gustavo '96 (TUC) Nogales, AZ Sacred Heart of Jesus Roman Catholic Parish – Nogales.
Benjamin, John J. '93 (SB) Retired.
Benjamin, Mariasoosai '84 (NY) Larchmont, NY SS. John and Paul.
Benjamin, Robert L. '00 (SR) Ferndale, CA Church of the Assumption.
Benjamine, Anthony '94 (CHR) Yonges Island, SC St. Mary.
Benko, Robert *o.f.m.conv.* '00 (R) Burlington, NC Blessed Sacrament; [F] Elon, NC Conventual Franciscans; Deans; Council of Priests.
Benkovic, Theodore *o.f.m.* '41 (CHI)[N] Chicago, IL St. Anthony's Friary.
Benkowski, Gregory '84 (OM) Omaha, NE Holy Ghost.
Benliro, Fernando C. '58 (OM) Retired.
Benn, Walter J. '77 (PH) Pottstown, PA St. Aloysius.
Bennerfield, Herbert '99 (LAF) Delcambre, LA Our Lady of the Lake; Delcambre, LA Saint Martin de Porres; Diocesan Co Chaplains.
Bennett, Ambrose *o.s.b.* '04 (STL)[F] Creve Coeur, MO St. Louis Priory School; [O] St. Louis, MO The Abbey of St. Mary and St. Louis.
Bennett, Rev. Msgr. Austin P. '49 (BRK)[T] Brooklyn, NY Curial Residence; [U] Brooklyn, NY Monastery of the Sisters Adorers of the Precious Blood; Confraternity of the Precious Blood Retired.
Bennett, Christopher '90 (SJ) San Jose, CA Santa Teresa; Deans.
Bennett, Rev. Msgr. Donald T. '67 (RVC) Hicksville, NY St. Ignatius Loyola.
Bennett, Rev. Msgr. John F. '71 (RVC) Huntington, NY St. Patrick's.
Bennett, Joseph R. '66 (CHI) Other Assignments.
Bennett, Joseph T. *s.j.* '57 (BO)[D] Dorchester, MA Boston College High School.
Bennett, Melvin J. '69 (LFT) Associate Judges; Carmel, IN St. Elizabeth Ann Seton.
Bennett, Michael X. '71 (HBG) On Duty Outside the Diocese.
Bennett, Noel I. '59 (MIA) Retired.
Bennett, Norman S. *c.ss.r.* '71 (BRK) Brooklyn, NY Our Lady of Perpetual Help Basilica.
Bennett, Richard '72 (JOL) Absent on Leave.
Bennett, Rolland *o.m.i.* '61 (SAT)[K] San Antonio, TX Oblate Madonna Residence.
Bennett, Thomas F. '68 (HRT) Washington Depot, CT Our Lady of Perpetual Help; Medical Leave.
Bennett, Thomas *l.c.* '91 (PHX) Queen Creek, AZ Our Lady of Guadalupe Roman Catholic Parish.
Bennis, Terrence W. '04 (GRY) North Judson, IN Ss. Cyril and Methodius.
Beno, Joseph '57 (P) Retired.
Beno, Patrick C. '04 (GB) Oconto Falls, WI St. Anthony; Oconto Falls, WI St. Patrick; Oconto, WI Holy Trinity.
Benoit, Adrian J. '65 (SPR) Retired.
Benoit, Bryan *s.c.j.* '93 (MIL)[P] Hales Corners Priests of the Sacred Heart.
Benoit, Charles J. *o.s.b.* '01 (NO)[P] St. Benedict, LA St. Joseph Abbey; [A] St. Benedict, LA St. Joseph Seminary College.
Benoit, Lloyd F. '90 (LAF) Franklin, LA Assumption B.V.M.
Benoit, Louis '79 (RIC) Clifton Forge, VA St. Joseph; Covington, VA Sacred Heart.
Benoit, Raymond P. '89 (BO) Lowell, MA St. Margaret.
Benoit, Vincent *o.p.* '84 (P) Portland, OR Holy Rosary Parish & Dominican Priory.
Benonis, Richard R. '58 (PH) On Duty Outside the Archdiocese.
Benonis, Richard '52 (SAT) Retired.
Benonis, William J. '52 (PH) Retired.
Bensman, Gerald E. *s.t.l.* '64 (CIN) Retired.
Bensman, John L. '56 (CIN)[N] Carthagena, OH St. Charles Retired.
Benson, Joseph A. '84 (NO) New Orleans, LA Blessed Francis Xavier Seelos.

Benson, Richard B. *c.m.* '78 (LA)[A] Camarillo, CA St. John's Seminary; Members.
Bentil, Augustine Kofi (LC) Milladore, WI St. Kilian; Junction City, WI St. Michael; Milladore, WI St. Wenceslaus.
Bentil, Gabriel (VIC) Inez, TX St. Joseph's; School Board.
Bentivegna, Salvatore *o.s.j.* '63 (SCR)[B] Pittston, PA St. Joseph's Oblate Seminary.
Benton, James '73 (LIN) Harvard, NE St. Joseph's; Apostolate to the Spanish Speaking.
Bentz, John B. '66 (COL) Retired.
Bentz, John C. *s.j.* '04 (SEA)[L] Seattle, WA Jesuit House, Seattle; Presbyteral Council.
Bentz, John C. *s.j.* '04 (P) Portland, OR; [L] Portland, OR Jesuit Provincial Office (Society of Jesus, Oregon Prov.); Portland, OR Society of Jesus.
Benusa, Jeffrey M. '03 (HEL) Harlowton, MT St. Joseph; White Sulphur Springs, MT St. Bartholomew.
Benwell, Rev. Msgr. William '80 (MET) Vicars General; Moderator; Canonical Staff; College of Consultors.
Benya, Edward G. *s.j.* '84 (NO)[P] New Orleans Jesuit Provincial Office.
Benz, Rev. Msgr. David H. '75 (PH) Morrisville, PA St. John the Evangelist.
Benz, Gary '99 (BIS) Hazelton, ND St. Paul; Linton, ND St. Anthony; Linton, ND St. Katherine.
Benz, James J. '74 (STL) St. Charles, MO St. Cletus; [V] St. Louis, MO Archdiocesan Stewardship Education Committee.
Benz, Thomas G. *s.j.* '00 (SY)[A] Syracuse, NY Saint Andrew Hall.
Benzmiller, James T. '99 (LC) Leave of Absence.
Beof, Marlon *o.a.r.* '97 (NY)[B] Suffern, NY Tagaste Monastery.
Beof, Marlon *o.a.r.* '97 (LA)[P] Oxnard, CA St. Augustine Priory O.A.R.; Oxnard, CA Mary Star of the Sea.
Beran, Mark T. '02 (OM) Wayne, NE St. Mary; Age Groups.
Berardi, Rev. Msgr. Ferdinando D. '77 (NY) New Rochelle, NY Holy Family.
Berardi, James J. '59 (CLV) Retired.
Berardi, Thomas F. '76 (ALB) Lake George, NY Sacred Heart; [Q] Cobleskill, NY State University of New York College of Agricultural & Technology at Cobleskill; Bolton Landing, NY Blessed Sacrament.
Berardi, Thomas '76 (ALB) Presbyteral Council; Diocesan Board of Consultors; Ministers to Active Priests and Priests in Special Circumstances.
Berbary, Richard J. '04 (NEW) Bayonne, NJ St. Henry's.
Berbena, Christopher '80 (OAK) San Leandro, CA Assumption of the Blessed Virgin Mary.
Berberian, David V. '74 (ALB) Delmar, NY St. Thomas the Apostle; Judges; Administrative Review Board (Due Process); Priests Placement Committee.
Berberich, Thomas E. '59 (HRT) Kent, CT Sacred Heart; Appointed.
Bercasio, Rafael '93 (PHX) Phoenix, AZ Corpus Christi Roman Catholic Parish.
Berchmans, Britto '81 (CHI) Park Ridge, IL St. Paul of the Cross; [A] Chicago, IL St. Joseph College Seminary.
Berchmanz, Anthony '67 (MO) Military Chaplains; Navy Chaplains.
Bercier, Barry *a.a.* '85 (WOR)[O] Worcester, MA Assumptionists of Assumption College.
Bercik, Michael *o.f.m.* '79 (BO)[U] Boston, MA St. Christopher Friary.
Berdis, Donald E. '63 (E) Farrell, PA Our Lady of Fatima–St. Ann.
Berdugo, Hernan '83 (SJN) Carolina, PR Inmaculada Concepcion.
Berean, Christopher H. '87 (NY) Saugerties, NY St. Mary of the Snow.
Bereda, Stanislaw J. '65 (GAY) Retired.
Berendt, George *p.i.m.e.* '74 (DET)[K] Detroit, MI P.I.M.E. Missionaries.
Berendt, Peter *c.p.* '57 (GAL)[O] Houston, TX Congregation of the Passion, Holy Name Passionist Community and Retreat Center; [Q] Houston, TX Holy Name Retreat Center.
Berens, Cyprian *o.f.m.* '51 (CIN)[M] Cincinnati, OH Archbishop Leibold Home for the Aged; [N] Cincinnati St. Francis Seraph Friary Retired.
Beres, Kevin J. '00 (ARL) Annandale, VA St. Michael.
Beretta, J. Christian *o.s.f.s* '97 (VEN)[B] Fort Myers, FL Bishop Verot High School; [G] Fort Myers, FL Oblates of St. Francis de Sales; [K] Fort Myers, FL The Bishop Verot High School Foundation.
Bereza, Stepan '93 (STF) New Britain, CT St. Josaphat.
Berg, Blaise R. '98 (SAC)[L] Chico, CA St. Thomas Aquinas Newman Center Chico; Chico, CA St. John the Baptist; Vicars Forane; Theological Commission.
Berg, Daniel J. '00 (BIS) Diocesan Corporate Board; Diocesan Finance Council.
Berg, Daniel J. '00 (BIS) Priests' Benefit Association; Flasher, ND St. Theresa the Child Jesus; Flasher, ND St. Lawrence; Flasher, ND St. Gertrude.
Berg, Donald M. '47 (LC) Retired.
Berg, Peter M. '71 (OG) Newcomb, NY St. Henry; Newcomb, NY St. Therese.
Berg, Ralph *c.m.f.* '64 (FRS) Fresno, CA St. Anthony Claret.
Berg, Richard V. '52 (STP) Retired.
Berg, Richard *c.s.c.* '63 (P)[B][L] Portland, OR Holy Cross Fathers & Brothers, C.S.C. – University of Portland Retired.
Berg, Richard *c.s.c.* (FTW)[H] Notre Dame Congregation of Holy Cross, Indiana Province, Provincial House.
Berg, Stephen '99 (FWT) Fort Worth, TX St. Peter The Apostle; Vicar General; Diocesan Pastoral Council; Presbyteral Council and Consultors; Diocesan Finance Council; Catholic Foundation of North Texas; Clergy and Religious Personnel Services; Priests' Care Fund.
Berg, Thomas V. '00 (NY) Hopewell Junction, NY St. Columba.
Bergamo, Rev. Msgr. John A. '65 (SCR)[D] East Stroudsburg, PA Notre Dame High School; East Stroudsburg, PA St. Matthew's.
Bergbower, Daniel J. '88 (MO) Air National Guard Chaplains; Military Services.
Bergen, William J. *s.j.* '55 (NY) New York, NY St. Ignatius Loyola; [EE] New York, NY St. Ignatius Loyola Residence.
Berger, Bernard M. '64 (GI) Crawford, NE St. John the Baptist.
Berger, David '06 (VIC) Victoria, TX Our Lady of Victory Cathedral.
Berger, John G. '67 (NU) Lafayette, MN St. Gregory the Great; Lafayette, MN St. George; St. Peter Regional Treatment Center; [F] St. Peter, MN St. Peter Regional Treatment Center; Vice–Chancellor; Judicial Vicar (Officialis); On Special or Other Diocesan Assignment.
Berger, John W. '98 (HON) Honolulu, HI Cathedral of Our Lady of Peace.
Berger, Lawrence B. '66 (LC) La Crosse, WI Holy Trinity; Appointed Members.
Berger, Peter '05 (MIL) Mequon, WI Lumen Christi.
Berger, Robert F. '62 (HBG) Myerstown, PA Mary, Gate of Heaven.
Bergeron, Rev. Msgr. Albert G. '62 (HT) Retired.
Bergeron, C. Paul '81 (LAF) Retired.
Bergeron, Marc H. '70 (FR) Fall River, MA St. Anne's; Procurator–Advocates; Ecumenical Officer.
Bergeron, Michael A. '96 (HT) Houma, LA Annunziata.
Bergeron, Michael '96 (HT)[E] Thibodaux, LA Marian Servants of the Word.
Bergeron, Robert E. '52 (BO) Senior Priests. Retired.
Berggreen, Rev. Msgr. Robert H. '64 (BR) Baton Rouge, LA St. Agnes.
Berghammer, Robert J. '49 (MIL) Retired.
Berghout, Paul A. '96 (ARL) Defenders of the Bond; Arlington, VA Cathedral of St. Thomas More.
Bergin, James *s.v.d.* '69 (DUB)[B] Epworth, IA Divine Word College.
Bergin, John J. *s.v.d.* '67 (BO)[U] Duxbury, MA Society of the Divine Word.
Bergin, John J. *s.j.* '67 (STL)[O] St. Louis, MO De Smet Jesuit High School Community.
Bergin, Karl '04 (ORL) 25–45; Merritt Island, FL Divine Mercy Catholic Community.
Bergin, Paschal '57 (CC) Retired.
Bergin, Patrick A. *m.m.* '59 (NY)[EE] Retired.
Bergin, Rev. Msgr. Thomas J. '61 (NY) Archdiocesan Consultors; Staten Island, NY St. Charles.
Bergkamp, Roger *o.m.i.* '64 (ANC) Pastoral Team:; Pastoral Team:; Pastoral Team:.
Bergman, Charles B. '58 (PIT)[M] Pittsburgh, PA St. John Vianney Manor Retired.
Bergman, Eric L. '07 (SCR) On Special or Other Diocesan Assignment; Scranton, PA St. Clare.
Bergman, Richard '55 (DM) Retired.
Bergman, Rev. Msgr. Robert '71 (KCK) Louisburg, KS Immaculate Conception.
Bergner, David J. *s.d.s.* '76 (MO) Navy Reserve Chaplains.
Bergner, David *s.d.s.* '76 (MIL)[P] Milwaukee Salvatorian Provincial Offices; Milwaukee, WI.
Bergner, David *s.d.s.* '76 (FgM) Milwaukee, WI SALVATORIAN MISSIONS.
Bergquist, Patrick D. '90 (FBK) Fairbanks, AK St. Raphael Catholic Church Fairbanks; Vicar General; Presbyteral Council; Finance Advisory Board.
Bergs, David '76 (LSC) Retired.
Bergsbaken, Dennis L. '78 (GB) Greenleaf, WI St. Clare Corp.
Bergschneider, Matthew '05 (RCK) Secretary to the Bishop & Diocesan Master of Ceremonies; Special Assignment.
Bergstadt, John P. '68 (GB) Green Bay, WI St. John the Baptist.
Berinti, Benjamin A. *c.pp.s.* '85 (ORL) Vice Chairman; Appointed Members; [E] Winter Park, FL San Pedro Spiritual Development Center; [F] Winter Park, FL Franciscan Friars, T.O.R., San Pedro Friary.
Berinti, Benjamin *c.pp.s.* '85 (CIN)[N] Dayton, OH Provincial Office of the Cincinnati Province of the Society of the Precious Blood.
Beristain, Juan M. '71 (SJN) Levittown, PR Santisima Trinidad.
Berkery, Patrick J. '56 (HRT) Retired.
Berkey, William G. '02 (GBG) Greensburg, PA Blessed Sacrament Cathedral.
Berkhout, Frans J. '87 (ALN)[O] Kutztown, PA Albright College (Reading); [O] Kutztown, PA Kutztown University (Kutztown).
Berko–Attah, Abraham (NY) Bronx, NY Christ the King.
Berland, Mark '74 (SAL) Oberlin, KS Sacred Heart Parish; Selden, KS Sacred Heart Parish; Oberlin, KS Immaculate Conception of the Blessed Virgin Mary Parish.
Bermejo, Donardo S. '91 (JC) Shelbina, MO St. Patrick; Shelbina, MO St. Mary.
Bermudez, Alberto '86 (NO) Kenner, LA St. Jerome.
Bermudez, Duvan '96 (PMB) Lake Worth, FL Sacred Heart.
Bermudez, Jaime E. (POD) Ponce.
Bermudez, Jose '80 (SPR) Holyoke, MA Our Lady of Guadalupe.
Bermudez–Hernandez, Mauricio '09 (DEN) Fort Morgan, CO St. Helena.
Bermudez Onopa, Jaime (PCE)[G] Ponce, PR Prelature of the Holy Cross and Opus Dei.
Berna, Francis *o.f.m.* '80 (PH)[Y] Philadelphia, PA St. Pius X Residence; Provincial Councilors:.
Bernabe, Humberto '75 (LA) Los Angeles, CA Ascension.
Bernacki, William J. *o.p.* '56 (CHI)[D] Oak Park, IL Fenwick High School; [N] St. Pius V Priory.
Bernadicou, Paul J. *s.j.* '65 (LA)[P] Los Angeles, CA Colombiere House.
Bernal, Edward '87 (SAT) San Antonio, TX St. Benedict.
Bernal, Luis Rodolfo *o.f.m.* '89 (ELP) El Paso, TX Our Lady of Guadalupe.
Bernaola, Javier '85 (POD) Guaynabo.
Bernaola, Javier '85 (SJN)[G] Guaynabo, PR Opus Dei.
Bernard, Andre '73 (SR) Retired.
Bernard, George C. *c.s.c.* '49 (P)[B][L] Portland, OR Holy Cross Fathers & Brothers, C.S.C. – University of Portland Retired.
Bernard, George *c.s.c.* (FTW)[H] Notre Dame Congregation of Holy Cross, Indiana Province, Provincial House.
Bernard, Larry *o.f.m.* '66 (GLP) Pueblo of Acoma, NM San Esteban, Acoma Catholic Indian Mission; Laguna, NM St. Joseph.
Bernardi, Peter J. *s.j.* '87 (NO)[C] New Orleans, LA Loyola University New Orleans.
Bernardi, Peter J. *s.j.* '87 (CHI)[C] Chicago, IL Jesuit Community at Loyola University Chicago.
Bernardino, Eduardo '91 (SD) Escondido, CA Church of the Resurrection.
Bernardo, Joseph C. '03 (LIN) Advocates; Lincoln, NE St. Michael.
Bernardy, Patrick '60 (GB) Retired.
Bernas, Anthony (PEO) Monmouth, IL Immaculate Conception.
Bernas, Eugene '66 (NEW) Retired.
Bernas, Thomas A. '94 (CHI) Chicago, IL St. Richard.
Bernauer, Edmund G. '61 (NEW) Retired.
Bernauer, James W. *s.j.* '75 (BO)[U] Newton, MA The Jesuit Community at Boston College.
Bernauer, James '52 (CR) Retired.
Bernbrock, John *s.j.* '56 (PHX) Scottsdale, AZ Our Lady of Perpetual Help Roman Catholic Parish.
Berndt, Wayne *o.f.m.cap.* '83 (FgM) White Plains, NY Province of St. Mary.
Bernelli, Rev. Msgr. Matthew '64 (BGP) Bridgeport, CT St. Mary.
Berner, Albert J. '68 (NEW) Verona, NJ Our Lady of the Lake.
Berner, Francis '70 (NO) On Medical Leave of Absence.
Berner, Michael '86 (DM) Logan, IA St. Anne; Missouri Valley, IA St. Patrick.
Bernhardt, Gary *o.f.m.* '99 (SFD)[L] Quincy, IL Holy Cross Friary.
Bernier, Michael F. '03 (SPR) Springfield, MA St. Mary's.
Bernier, Paul '00 (FR) Fall River, MA Cathedral of St. Mary of the Assumption.
Bernier, Paul *s.s.s.* '64 (CLV) Highland Heights, OH St. Paschal Baylon; [N] Cleveland, OH Congregation of the Blessed Sacrament.
Bernier, Philip J. *o.f.m.cap.* '01 (CLV)[N] Cleveland, OH St. Paul Friary; Garfield Heights, OH Holy Spirit Parish.
Berning, James C. '91 (WIN) Albert Lea, MN St. Theodore; Albert Lea, MN St. James; [J] Albert Lea, MN St. Theodore Catholic School Endowment; [C] Albert Lea, MN St. Theodore School.
Berning, James *s.d.b.* '93 (NY)[GG] Stony Point, NY Marian Shrine; [GG] Stony Point, NY Don Bosco Retreat Center and Marian Shrine.
Bernotas, Robert J. '83 (LFT) Kentland, IN St. Joseph; Members; Kentland, IN St. John the Baptist; Kentland, IN SS. Peter and Paul.

Bernott, Ernest J. '48 (GR) Retired.
Berns, Eric R. '96 (LC) Mauston, WI St. Patrick.
Berny, Paul W. '72 (ATL) Flowery Branch, GA Prince of Peace; College of Consultors.
Berran, Donald M. '60 (BRK) Brooklyn, NY St. Ephrem; South Ozone Park, NY; South Ozone Park, NY Our Lady of Perpetual Help Retired.
Berret, Anthony J. *s.j.* '71 (PH)[C] Jesuit Fathers; [Y] Philadelphia, PA St. Alphonsus House.
Berrette, Hugues '91 (BRK) Brooklyn, NY St. Jerome.
Berrigan, Daniel J. *s.j.* '52 (NY)[EE] New York, NY Jesuit Community of the Immaculate Conception.
Berrio, Augusto *s.j.* '63 (LA) Santa Barbara, CA Our Lady of Sorrows.
Berrio, Diego '08 (CHI) Arlington Heights, IL St. Edna.
Berrio, Ignacio D. '66 (BO) Marlborough, MA Immaculate Conception; Presbyteral Council.
Berrios, Angel '65 (PCE) Santa Isabel, PR St. James.
Berrios, Israel '96 (CGS) Aibonito, PR Church of St. Joseph; Diocesan Consultors; Priests Senate; Vocations.
Berrios, Israel (CGS)[F] Casa del Apostol San Andres.
Berry, Dennis M. *s.t.* '74 (MOB)[J] Hurtsboro, AL Blessed John XXIII Center; Silver Spring, MD.
Berry, Dennis M. *s.t.* '74 (PT)[E] Tallahassee, FL Missionary Servants of the Most Holy Trinity.
Berry, Michael *o.c.d.* '06 (MIL) Milwaukee, WI St. Florian.
Berry, William F. '66 (WDC) Retired.
Berryman, Harold L. '58 (GB) New Holstein, WI Holy Rosary; New Holstein, WI St. Ann; [E] New Holstein, WI Divine Savior Catholic Elementary School, Inc.
Bersabal, Rey '91 (SAC) Presbyteral Council; Folsom, CA St. John the Baptist.
Berschied, Paul L. '86 (COV) Southgate, KY St. Therese of the Infant Jesus.
Bersman, Eric L. '07 (SCR)[I] Scranton, PA Mercy Hospital of Scranton.
Bertelli, Ameilio James '59 (BO) Senior Priests. Retired.
Bertelli, Mark '06 (SB) On Sabbatical; Montclair, CA Our Lady of Lourdes.
Bertels, George '55 (KCK) Judges Retired.
Bertels, Henry J. *s.j.* '62 (NY)[EE] Cardinal Spellman Hall, Jesuit Community.
Bertha, Joseph '80 (PSC) Pittston, PA St. Michael; Evangelization; Retirement Plan Board.
Berthelette, Ernest H. '74 (PRO) Providence, RI Cathedral of SS. Peter and Paul.
Bertin, Gerard L. '89 (MAN) Goffstown, NH St. Lawrence.
Bertino, Dominic V. '75 (GRY) Hobart, IN St. Bridget.
Bertocchi, Luigi *o.s.b.* '70 (SCL)[I] Collegeville, MN St. John's Abbey, of the Order of St. Benedict.
Bertogli, John '77 (DM) Des Moines, IA St. Ambrose Cathedral.
Bertolacci, Caesar *m.c.* '96 (DET)[K] Plymouth, MI Miles Christi.
Bertolotti, David P. '91 (BRK) Woodhull Medical & Mental Health Center; Brooklyn, NY All Saints.
Bertone, Thomas C. *c.s.c.* '81 (SCR)[C] King's College.
Bertoni, Albert *s.m.* '79 (RVC)[D] Uniondale, NY Kellenberg Memorial High School.
Bertoniere, Gabriel *o.c.s.o.* '58 (WOR)[O] Spencer, MA St. Joseph's Abbey.
Bertram, Keith '04 (DUL) Aurora, MN Holy Rosary; Biwabik, MN St. John; Hoyt Lakes, MN Queen of Peace.
Bertrand, Armand J. '89 (SC) Cherokee, IA Immaculate Conception; Marcus, IA Holy Name; Presbyteral Council; Deans.
Bertrand, Conley '59 (LAF)[M] Lafayette, LA Come Lord Jesus! Inc.
Bertrand, Conley (NO) Come, Lord Jesus Program of Prayer and Scripture.
Bertrand, Emmanuel *o.p.* '58 (COL)[I] Columbus, OH Mohun Health Care Center.
Bertrand, Richard D. *s.j.* '79 (BO)[U] Boston The Society of Jesus of New England–Provincial Offices.
Bertrand, Richard D. *s.j.* '79 (PRT) Portland, ME Sacred Heart/St. Dominic; Portland, ME Cathedral of the Immaculate Conception; Portland, ME St. Christopher's; Portland, ME St. Louis; Portland, ME St. Peter's.
Bertrand, Victor E. *c.s.v.* '62 (CHI)[N] Arlington Heights Viatorian Province Center–Clerics of St. Viator.
Bertrand, Vincent E. '87 (SPC) Adjutant Judicial Vicars; Judges.
Berube, Paul W. '60 (BO) Newburyport, MA Immaculate Conception; Senior Priests. Retired.
Berube, Richard N. *s.s.e.* '70 (BUR)[E] Colchester, VT Society of St. Edmund; [A] Colchester, VT St. Michael's College.
Beseau, Steven '95 (KCK)[L] Lawrence, KS St. Lawrence Catholic Campus Center at the University of Kansas and Residence.
Besel, Patrick '06 (BAL) Grantsville, MD St. Ann; Special Assignment.
Besendorfer, Ralph L. '59 (STA) Callahan, FL Our Lady of Consolation; Promoter of Justice.
Beshara, Rev. Msgr. Ronald '71 (SAM) Greenacres, FL Mary Mother of Light Maronite Mission; Office of Outreach.
Beshara, Rev. Msgr. Ronald '71 (PMB) Defenders of the Bond.
Beshoner, Sebastian *o.s.b.* '55 (LR)[A] Subiaco, AR Subiaco Abbey.
Beshoner, Seraphim *t.o.r.* '05 (STU)[H] Steubenville, OH Holy Spirit Friary; [A] Steubenville, OH Franciscan University of Steubenville.
Besinga, Dino J. '82 (MO) Army Chaplains.
Besse, Joseph A. '45 (PRO) Retired.
Bessellieu, Mel '97 (FWT) Presbyteral Council and Consultors; Burleson, TX St. Ann.
Best, Richard '61 (JOL) Retired.
Best, Russell W. '86 (BO) Roxbury, MA St. Patrick; Permanent Disability.
Besterwitch, Ralph *s.a.c.* '83 (DET) Redford, MI Our Lady of Loretto; Presbyteral Council; [K] Redford, MI Society of the Catholic Apostolate–Indian Province of the State of Michigan.
Bestler, Joseph '57 (GB) Retired.
Betances–Torres, Martin '87 (NY) On Leave of Absence.
Betancourt, Cesar '09 (SAT) Helotes, TX Our Lady of Guadalupe.
Betancourt, Jorge R. *o.carm.* '03 (ARE) Ciales, PR Holy Rosary.
Betancourt, Juan Carlos '96 (ATL) Athens, GA St. Joseph.
Betancourt, Juan Miguel *s.e.m.v.* '01 (STP)[A] Saint Paul, MN The Saint Paul Seminary; St. Paul, MN St. Francis De Sales; St. Paul, MN St. James.
Betancourt Ramirez, Jorge '03 (SJN) Awaiting Assignment.
Betancur, Nelson '75 (PAT) Paterson, NJ St. George.
Betancurt, Rigoberto '83 (SHP) Bossier City, LA Christ the King.
Bethel, Francis *o.s.b.* '83 (TLS)[G] Hulbert, OK Our Lady of the Annunciation of Clear Creek Monastery.
Betley, Michael E. '80 (GB) Antigo, WI SS. Mary & Hyacinth; Niagara, WI St. Anthony; Vicariate.
Betoni, John P. *o.s.a.* '62 (PH)[C] Villanova University; [Y] Villanova, PA St. Thomas Monastery.
Betrand, Conley '59 (LAF) Retired.
Betrozoff, Larry '73 (MRY) Tres Pinos, CA Retired.
Betschart, Joseph '99 (P) Special Assignment.
Bettaso, Emmanuel *o.c.d.* '05 (MIL)[P] Hubertus, WI Discalced Carmelite Monastery – Holy Hill Basilica of the National Shrine of Mary, Help of Christians, Holy Hill.
Bettendorf, James B. '59 (LAN) Retired.
Betters, John D. '03 (CLV) Hudson, OH St. Mary; Euclid, OH SS. Robert & William.
Betti, Frederick G. *s.j.* '90 (BUF)[O] Buffalo, NY Canisius Jesuit Community Inc.; [D] Buffalo, NY Canisius High School.
Betti, Mark J. '96 (R) Fuquay–Varina, NC St. Bernadette.
Bettinger, Eugene Joseph *o.carm.* '76 (NEW) Paramus, NJ Carmelite Chapel of St. Therese; Teaneck, NJ St. Anastasia's.
Bettinger, Mark T. '93 (PBL) Montrose, CO St. Mary; Personnel.
Bettley, Emil '83 (NY) Nyack, NY St. Ann.
Betts, David R. '98 (SCR) Veteran's Administration Hospital; Tunkhannock, PA Nativity of Blessed Virgin Mary; Tunkhannock, PA St. Mary of the Lake.
Betts, John C. '68 (P) Albany, OR Our Lady of Perpetual Help (St. Mary).
Betz, James F. '71 (MO) Diocesan Historian; Army Chaplains; On Duty Outside the Diocese.
Betz, James S. '89 (WDC) Laurel, MD St. Nicholas.
Betz, Kenneth '65 (EVN) Haubstadt, IN St. James.
Betz, Robert '73 (MIL) South Milwaukee, WI Divine Mercy.
Betz, Thomas *o.f.m.cap.* '91 (PH) Chinese Apostolate; Definitors:; Vocations Co–Directors:; Philadelphia, PA St. John the Evangelist.
Betzen, James G. *c.pp.s.* '81 (JC) Sedalia, MO St. Patrick; Sedalia, MO Sacred Heart.
Beugos, Felipe Santiago *c.ss.r.* (SJN) San Juan, PR San Agustin.
Beuth, William J. *c.pp.s.* '59 (CIN)[N] Dayton Provincial Office of the Cincinnati Province of the Society of the Precious Blood.
Beuther, Richard J. '96 (BRK) Brooklyn, NY SS. Peter and Paul; Diocesan Consultors; Presbyteral Council.
Beuzer, Vincent J. *s.j.* '58 (FBK)[E] St. Marys, AK Brother Joe Prince Jesuit Community.
Beuzer, Vincent *s.j.* '58 (ANC)[F] Anchorage, AK Anchorage Jesuit Community.
Bevacqua, James M. '03 (LA) Glendale, CA Holy Family.
Bevan, James J. '75 (LAV) Retired.
Bevans, Stephen B. *s.v.d.* '71 (CHI)[B] Chicago, IL The Catholic Theological Union at Chicago; [N] Chicago, IL Edward McGuinn, S.V.D. Residence.
Bevenour, Richard F. '57 (DAV) Retired.
Beveridge, John P. '72 (SFD) Collinsville, IL SS. Peter and Paul.
Bevilacqua, Jerome F. *o.s.a.* '65 (SD)[J] San Diego, CA Augustinian Community.
Bevilacqua, Jerry *o.s.a.* '65 (SD)[O] San Diego, CA Spirit Ministries.
Bevington, William S. '51 (NSH)[L] Hendersonville, TN Legion of Mary; [L] Hendersonville, TN Priests Eucharistic League; Judges Retired.
Bevins, John J. '58 (HRT) Waterbury, CT Basilica of the Immaculate Conception.
Beyer, Gregory *o.f.m.cap.* '62 (SAL)[D] Victoria, KS St. Fidelis Friary.
Beyer, Lawrence A. '96 (DAL) Plano, TX Prince of Peace Retired.
Beyer, Leroy O. '66 (WH) Retired.
Beyer, Richard J. '81 (MO) On Duty Outside the Diocese; DEPARTMENT OF VETERANS AFFAIRS HOSPITALS AND CHAPLAINS.
Beyer, Richard '81 (AUS) Temple, TX V.A. Hospital; Waco, TX V.A. Hospital.
Beyette, Paul V. '50 (OG) Retired.
Bezunartea, Rev. Msgr. Herman O. '58 (FRS) Retired.
Biagi, Vincent L. *s.j.* '78 (NY)[EE] New York, NY St. Ignatius Loyola Residence; [EE] New York, NY Society of Jesus, New York Province; New York, NY.
Biain, Jose *o.f.m.* '48 (MIA) Judges.
Bialek, Mark '06 (BAL) Forest Hill, MD St. Ignatius.
Bialkowski, David W. '88 (BUF) Legion of Mary; Cheektowaga, NY St. John Gualbert.
Bialkowski, Jacek J. '96 (SCR) Mansfield, PA Holy Child; Mansfield, PA St. John Neumann.
Bialkowski, Peter '00 (RIC) Smithfield, VA Good Shepherd; Suffolk, VA St. Mary of the Presentation.
Bialoncik, Emmanuel *o.f.m.* '73 (BWN) Alamo, TX Resurrection.
Biancalana, Angelo G. *m.c.c.j.* '58 (LA)[BB] Covina, CA Comboni Mission Center.
Bianchi, Raymond S. '52 (TR) Retired.
Bianco, Anthony M. *c.r.s.p.* '51 (ALN)[K] Bethlehem, PA The Barnabite Fathers Barnabite Spiritual Center.
Bianco, Louis A. '05 (BAL) Priests Sick or Absent.
Biase, Justin A. *o.f.m.conv.* '70 (FgM) AMERICAN CONVENTUAL FRANCISCAN MISSIONS; Rensselaer, NY.
Biase, Justin *o.f.m.conv.* '70 (ALB)[A] Rensselaer, NY Conventual Franciscan Friars; [L] Rensselaer, NY Provincialate, Immaculate Conception Friary – Order of Friars Minor Conventual; [R] Rensselaer, NY Franciscans in Collaborative Ministry, Inc.
Biasiotto, Richard *o.f.m.* '64 (ALB)[B] Siena College; [R] Albany, NY St. Francis Chapel.
Biber, Joseph Morton '85 (RIC) Richmond, VA St. Mary.
Bichl, William M. *s.j.* '67 (CLV)[B] University Heights, OH John Carroll Jesuit Community.
Bichsel, William *s.j.* (SEA)[C] Tacoma, WA Bellarmine Preparatory School.
Bickel, Timothy C. '92 (MIL) Butler, WI St. Agnes.
Bickett, Anthony '83 (OWN) Hardinsburg, KY St. Romuald; Consultors; Diocesan Liturgical Committee; Clergy Personnel Director.
Bico, Anthony '93 (NEW)[B] School of Diplomacy and Intl. Rels.
Bico, Antonio I. '93 (NEW) Members; [A] South Orange, NJ Immaculate Conception Seminary.
Bicomong, Sergio '79 (CAM) Fairton, NJ Federal Correctional Institution; Millville, NJ The Church of St. John Bosco, Millville, N.J.
Bicomong, Sergio '79 (TR) On Duty Outside the Diocese.
Bicsko, Stephen C. *c.m.* '70 (BRK)[T] Queens Village, NY DePaul Residence.
Bicz, Marian '88 (RVC) Cutchogue, NY Our Lady of Ostrabrama.
Biczak, Arkad '63 (SFE) Albuquerque, NM St. John the Apostle; Mission Office.
Bida, John A. '73 (NY) Bangall, NY Immaculate Conception; Pine Plains, NY St. Anthony.
Bidawid, Kamal Warda '68 (SPA) Turlock, CA St. Thomas Assyrian–Chaldean Parish; El Dorado Hills, CA Our Lady of Perpetual Help Chaldean/Assyrian Catholic Church.
Bidinger, Bruce M. *s.j.* '86 (PH)[Y] Loyola Center and Manresa Hall; [C] Jesuit Fathers.
Bido, Miguel S. (ARE) Quebradillas, PR San Raphael.
Bidwell, Michael L. '89 (CIN) New Carlisle, OH Sacred Heart.
Bidwill, Joseph E. *o.p.* '55 (STP) Minneapolis, MN St. Albert the Great.
Bie, Paul R. '83 (RVC) Medical Leave.
Biebel, Rev. Msgr. William E. '62 (E) Erie, PA St. Peter Cathedral; Northern Vicariate.
Bieberle, Victor '51 (WCH) Retired.
Bieganowski, Ronald *s.j.* '72 (MIL)[P] Milwaukee, WI Jesuit Community at Marquette University.
Biegler, Patrick *m.s.a.* '05 (NOR)[G] Cromwell Society of the Missionaries of the Holy Apostles.
Biegler, Patrick *m.s.a.* '05 (WIL) New Castle, DE Our Lady of Fatima.
Biegler, Steven '93 (RC) Rapid City, SD Cathedral of Our Lady of Perpetual Help; Diocesan Consultors.
Biegun, Marek (PAT)[Q] Chester, NJ Nazareth Village; Unassigned; Totowa, NJ St. James of the Marches.
Biehl, August *s.m.* '58 (SAT)[K] San Antonio, TX Marianist Residence: Skilled Nursing.

Bielak, Andrew '95 (NY) Manhattan, NY Bird S. Coler Memorial Hospital and Home; Manhattan, NY Goldwater Memorial Hospital; New York, NY Our Lady of Peace; New Rochelle, NY Sound Shore Medical Center.
Bielasiewicz, Slawomir (STA) Jacksonville, FL Sacred Heart.
Bielawa, Thomas *s.d.s.* '72 (NSH) Retired.
Bielecki, Michael *o.s.a.* '83 (PH)[C] Radnor, PA Cabrini College.
Bielewicz, Harry R. '86 (PIT) Clergy Personnel Board; Secretary for Clergy; Chaplain Services, Office for; Pittsburgh, PA Our Lady of Loreto; Vicar for Clergy; Priest Council.
Bien, Dan '85 (AGN) Dededo, GU Santa Barbara.
Bienvenu, Kenneth A. '60 (LAF) St. Martinville, LA St. Martin of Tours Retired.
Bienvenu, Paul G. '92 (LAF) Opelousas, LA Our Lady of Mercy.
Bier, Louis C. '76 (PH) Philadelphia, PA St. Francis de Sales.
Biermann, John G. *s.a.c.* '69 (BAL) Baltimore, MD St. Jude Shrine.
Biernacki, Jacob S. '67 (SPC) Retired.
Biernat, Leon J. '92 (BUF) Lancaster, NY Our Lady of Pompeii.
Biernat, Ryszard S. '09 (BUF) Orchard Park, NY Nativity of Our Lord.
Biernat, Wayne C. '04 (SPR) Williamstown, MA SS. Patrick and Raphael.
Biersack, Thomas E. '81 (MIL) Lomira, WI St. Andrew; Mayville, WI St. Mary.
Bierschenk, Stephen W. '76 (DAL) Dallas, TX St. Monica; Personnel Board.
Bierster, Rev. Msgr. Leo N. '52 (HBG) Retired.
Bies, Michael '04 (PEO) Rantoul, IL St. Malachy.
Biesinger, Robert J. '56 (BUF)[O] Buffalo, NY Sheehan Residence for Priests Retired.
Biewend, Michael *c.j.* '80 (P) Portland, OR St. Mary Magdalene.
Biffar, William *c.ss.r.* '47 (ALB)[L] Saratoga Springs, NY St. John Neumann Residence.
Bigelow, William R. '67 (BUF) Hamburg, NY St. Mary of the Lake.
Biggane, Edward J. *s.m.a.* '58 (NEW)[M] Tenafly, NJ Society of African Missions, Provincialate, S.M.A. Fathers.
Bigirimana, Pascal (CHI) Chicago, IL SS. Peter and Paul.
Bigley, Michael *s.d.s.* '87 (GB) St. Nazianz, WI St. Gregory; Kiel, WI Holy Trinity.
Biglin, Martin J. '67 (NY) New Rochelle, NY Holy Name of Jesus.
Bignall, Douglas '93 (DET)[A] The School of Theology.
Bihr, Rev. Msgr. Louis J. '68 (PAT) Presbyteral Council; College of Consultors; Straight and Narrow, Inc.; Special Assignment.
Bik, Michael *o.s.b.* '93 (SCL)[I] Collegeville, MN St. John's Abbey, of the Order of St. Benedict.
Bikoma, Rev. Msgr. Edward J. '51 (EST) Chicago, IL St. Ephrem's Church.
Bilinsky, Rev. Msgr. Canon William M. '65 (STN) Retired.
Bilinsky, Rev. Msgr. William '65 (NO) Retired.
Bill, J. Armand '56 (PRT) Retired.
Bill, Rev. Msgr. Ronald C. '57 (SY) Ecumenical Commission; Fayetteville, NY Immaculate Conception Retired.
Bill, Thomas *c.s.c.* (FTW)[H] Notre Dame Congregation of Holy Cross, Indiana Province, Provincial House.
Billac, Christopher A. *s.j.* '65 (GAL)[E] Houston, TX Strake Jesuit College Preparatory Inc.
Biller, Andrew *s.v.d.* '61 (MIL)[P] East Troy, WI Divine Word Missionaries Retired.
Biller, Rev. Msgr. Bernard N. '70 (ALT) Retired.
Billett, Robert *c.m.f.* '57 (LA)[V] Rancho Dominguez, CA Dominguez Seminary Inc.
Billian, Michael R. '84 (TOL) Delegate of the Bishop; Ex Officio Members; Episcopal Vicar, Moderator of the Curia and Chancellor; Mareda, Inc.; Members; Members; Toledo, OH Queen of the Most Holy Rosary Cathedral.
Billiard, Don *o.f.m.* '83 (SFE)[H] Albuquerque, NM The Province of Our Lady of Guadalupe; [L] Albuquerque, NM Anselm Weber Fund; [L] Albuquerque, NM Roger Huser Fund.
Billiard, Don *o.f.m.* '83 (GLP) Pueblo of Acoma, NM San Esteban, Acoma Catholic Indian Mission; Laguna, NM St. Joseph.
Billicky, Louis S. '49 (BO) Senior Priests. Retired.
Billing, Rev. Msgr. Jerome D. '71 (STL) Chancellor for Canonical Affairs; Promoter of Justice; Archdiocesan Archives; Priests' Purgatorial Society; St. Louis Roman Catholic Theological Seminaries, Inc.; [V] St. Louis, MO St. Louis City Catholic Church Real Estate Corporation; [V] St. Louis, MO St. Louis County Catholic Church Real Estate Corporation; [V] St. Louis, MO Franklin County Catholic Church Real Estate Corporation; [V] St. Louis, MO Jefferson County Catholic Church Real Estate Corporation; [V] St. Louis, MO Lincoln County Church Real Estate Corporation; [V] St. Louis, MO Perry County Catholic Church Real Estate Corporation; [V] St. Louis, MO St. Charles County Catholic Church Real Estate Corporation; [V] St. Louis, MO St. Francois County Catholic Church Real Estate Corporation; [V] St. Louis, MO Ste. Genevieve County Catholic Church Real Estate Corporation; [V] St. Louis, MO Warren County Catholic Church Real Estate Corporation; [V] St. Louis, MO Washington County Catholic Church Real Estate Corporation; St. Louis, MO Basilica of St. Louis, King of France; Defender of the Bond.
Billinger, James J. '83 (WCH) Wichita, KS Holy Savior; Presbyteral Council/College of Consultors; Building Commission.
Billings, Kit '95 (OM)[G] Omaha, NE Archbishop Bergan Mercy Medical Center.
Billman, George '72 (FAR) Retired.
Billote, Dindo '09 (JOL) Naperville, IL St. Raphael.
Billotte, Philip J. '66 (ROC) Retired.
Billotti, Joseph E. *s.j.* '63 (BUF)[O] Buffalo, NY Canisius Jesuit Community Inc.
Billy, Dennis J. *c.ss.r.* '80 (PH) Philadelphia, PA St. Peter the Apostle; [A] Wynnewood, PA Theological Seminary of St. Charles Borromeo, Overbrook.
Billy, Dennis *c.ss.r.* '80 (NY)[EE] Esopus, NY Redemptorist Priests and Brothers C.Ss.R. (Province of Baltimore).
Bilodeau, Florent '57 (MAN) Manchester, NH St. Anthony of Padua Retired.
Bilodeau, Leopold J. '73 (BUR) Barre, VT St. Monica; Graniteville, VT St. Sylvester; Elected Members.
Bilodeau, Roger P. '65 (MAN) Nashua, NH St. Joseph Retired.
Bilot, James D. '92 (DET) Dearborn, MI Divine Child.
Bily, John C. '58 (VIC) Weimar, TX St. Michael; Judges.
Bily, Rev. Msgr. Lambert S. '63 (SAT) San Antonio, TX St. Clare.
Bilyk, Ivan (STF) Willimantic, CT Protection of B.V.M.
Bilyk, Stepan '01 (PHU) Shamokin, PA Assumption of B.V.M.; Shamokin, PA Transfiguration of Our Lord.
Binaghi, Maurizio *m.c.c.j.* '99 (CHI) Chicago, IL St. Martin De Porres.
Binder, Mark J. '71 (SPC) Piedmont, MO St. Catherine of Siena.
Bindner, Charles J. '58 (L) Retired.
Binet, Scott *m.i.* '03 (MIL)[P] Milwaukee, WI St. Camillus Provincialate; [Y] Milwaukee, WI Servants of Saint Camillus Disaster Relief Services, Inc.
Binh Dinh Do, Luke M. *c.m.c.* '77 (SB)[I] Corona, CA Congregation of the Mother Co–Redemptrix, C.M.C.
Biniek, Joseph P. '78 (ARL) Retired.
Biniszkiewicz, Rev. Msgr. Leonard E. '63 (BUF) Retired.
Binlayo, Hermes *s.j.* '94 (RNO) Carlin, NV Sacred Heart.
Binlayo, Hermes *s.j.* '02 (RNO) Elko, NV St. Joseph's; Eureka, NV St. Brendan's; Wells, NV St. Thomas Aquinas.
Binsfeld, Douglas '98 (SFS) Florence, SD Blessed Sacrament; Henry, SD St. Henry.
Binsfeld, Steven '79 (SCL) Alexandria, MN St. Mary's; Deans.
Binta, Robert '91 (PHX) Phoenix, AZ St. Paul Roman Catholic Parish.
Binzer, Joseph R. '94 (CIN) Cincinnati, OH St. Louis; Vicar General; Archdiocesan Department Directors; Ex Officio Members; Consultors; Director; Chancellor; Judges.
Biondi, Lawrence H. *s.j.* '70 (STL)[C] St. Louis, MO Saint Louis University; [O] St. Louis, MO Jesuit Community Corporation at Saint Louis University – Jesuit Hall; [C] Saint Louis University.
Birarelli, Carl A. '58 (CIN) Retired.
Birch, Donald G. '67 (PH) Fallsington, PA St. Joseph the Worker.
Birch, Keith L. '71 (DUB) Monticello, IA Sacred Heart.
Birch, Rev. Msgr. Thomas J. '59 (ALN) Shillington, PA St. John Baptist de la Salle; Douglassville, PA Immaculate Conception Retired.
Bircumshaw, Rev. Msgr. Colin F. '75 (SLC) Salt Lake City, UT Saint Ann LLC 215; College of Consultors; Deans; Finance Council; Liturgical Commission; Priests' Personnel Board; Promoter of Justice; Vocation Office.
Bird, Stephen J. '76 (OKL) Oklahoma City, OK Church of the Epiphany of the Lord; Special Assignment; Worship and Spiritual Life, Office of.
Bird, Steven '00 (PEO) On Leave of Absence.
Birdsall, Anthony J. '60 (GB) Retired.
Birdsall, Anthony J. (GB) Regional Vicars.
Birdsall, Hugh G. *s.d.s.* '62 (MIL)[P] Greendale, WI; [B] Hales Corners, WI Sacred Heart School of Theology.
Bireley, Robert L. *s.j.* '64 (CHI)[C] Chicago, IL Jesuit Community at Loyola University Chicago.
Biren, Timothy E. '99 (WIN)[I] Mankato, MN St. Thomas More Newman Center, Minnesota State University; Emmaus House of Formation.
Birge, Rev. Msgr. George D. '58 (BGP) Retired.
Biriruka, Ernest '81 (MIA) Miramar, FL Blessed John XXIII Church.
Birk, John G. '63 (MO) Pasco, WA St. Patrick; CIVIL AIR PATROL Retired.
Birk, John W. '70 (L) Byzantine Rite Faithful Retired.
Birk, John '63 (SPK) Special Ministry; [F] Pasco, WA Lourdes Medical Center Retired.
Birkel, John B. '96 (LIN) Fairbury, NE St. Michael's.
Birket, Dwight J. '72 (DOD) Hoisington, KS St. John the Evangelist Catholic Church of Hoisington, Kansas; Hoisington, KS Holy Family Catholic Church of Odin, Kansas; On Duty Outside the Diocese.
Birkle, Rev. Msgr. Walter A. '58 (NY) Retired.
Birkmaier, James E. '68 (GF) Retired.
Birkmaier, James '68 (GF) Clerical Benefit Association.
Birmingham, Kevin M. '97 (CHI) Hazel Crest, IL St. Anne.
Birmingham, Robert F. '93 (HRT) Retired.
Birney, Timothy P. '98 (DET) Office of Priestly Vocations.
Biron, Gerald *m.s.* '60 (HRT)[L] Hartford, CT Missionaries of LaSalette.
Biron, Robert G. '74 (MAN) New London, NH Our Lady of Fatima; Priest Personnel Board; Ecumenical and Interreligious Affairs; Presbyteral Council; College of Consultors.
Biroschak, Robert V. '93 (LA) Retired.
Biroschak, Robert V. '93 (BGP) Judges.
Birungyi, George '75 (RCK) Special Assignment; [D] Elgin, IL Provena Saint Joseph Hospital.
Bisaillon, Rene *m.s.* '59 (HON) Koloa, HI St. Raphael Retired.
Bisbee, Burnell B. *s.j.* '75 (OM)[K] Omaha, NE Jesuit Community at Creighton University.
Bischof, Donald R. '83 (PIT) Fenelton, PA St. John.
Bischoff, Albert J. *s.j.* '56 (CIN)[N] Cincinnati, OH Jesuit Community at Xavier University; [R] Cincinnati, OH Xavier University Campus Ministry.
Bisgrove, Charles *s.c.j.* '90 (MIL)[P] Hales Corners, WI Priests of the Sacred Heart.
Bisharat, Rt. Rev. George Said '93 (NTN) North Hollywood, CA St. Anne.
Bishop, Clifton E. '98 (ALN)[H] Bethlehem, PA Holy Family Manor of Catholic Senior Housing and Health Care Services, Inc.; Allentown, PA Our Lady Help of Christians; Assistants.
Bishop, E. Louis *s.j.* '64 (PHX)[B] Phoenix, AZ Brophy College Preparatory; [F] Phoenix, AZ Society of Jesus.
Bishop, Marc J. '01 (BO) Navy Reserve Chaplains; Methuen, MA Our Lady of Good Counsel; Methuen, MA St. Monica.
Bishop, Rev. Msgr. Patrick A. '74 (ATL) Marietta, GA Church of the Transfiguration.
Bishop, Robert *c.m.f.* '71 (LA)[V] Rancho Dominguez, CA Dominguez Seminary Inc.
Bishop, Robert (OLL) Defender of the Bond; Promoter of Justice.
Bishop, Thomas G. '70 (Y) Canton, OH All Saints; Canton, OH St. Anthony; Priests Council.
Bishop, Thomas '75 (CHI) Barrington, IL St. Anne.
Bisig, Josef *f.s.s.p.* '77 (LIN) Denton, NE; [A] Denton, NE Our Lady of Guadalupe Seminary.
Bisignano, Joseph '81 (NY) Yorktown Heights, NY St. Patrick.
Bisoffi, Joseph L. *m.i.* '72 (MIL)[P] Milwaukee, WI St. Camillus Provincialate; Milwaukee, WI.
Bissinger, Karl C. '05 (FR) Secretary to the Bishop; Vocations.
Bisson, Andrew R. *o.f.m.* '93 (PRT)[I] Kennebunkport, ME St. Anthony's Friary; Kennebunkport, ME.
Bisson, Eddy N. '68 (MAN) Pelham, NH St. Patrick.
Bisson, Joseph *s.v.d.* '63 (FgM) Techny, IL.
Bisson, Roger *m.afr.* '55 (SP)[N] St. Petersburg, FL Missionaries of Africa.
Bissonette, James B. '88 (DUL) Duluth, MN St. James; Chancellor; Judicial Vicar; Vicar for Canonical Affairs; Diocesan Corporate Board; Cemeteries.
Bissot, Robert H. '57 (GAY) Ossineke, MI St. Gabriel; Ossineke, MI St. Catherine; Holy Childhood Pontifical Association; Propagation of the Faith.
Biswas, Tony *ss.cc.* (FR)[G] Fairhaven National Center of the Enthronement.
Biszek, Rev. Msgr. Robert J. '65 (ALN) Bethlehem, PA Holy Infancy.
Bitanga, Rev. Msgr. Fred A. '64 (SFR) San Francisco, CA St. Monica Retired.
Bitangjol, Albert P. '56 (SFR) Retired.
Bitchapogu, Anthony (KAL) Kalamazoo, MI St. Joseph.
Bitsko, Daniel J. '65 (PSC) Retired.
Bittel, Patrick M. '82 (OWN) Philpot, KY St. William; Knottsville, KY St. Lawrence; Deans/Coordinators.
Bitterman, John L. *s.s.* '69 (STO) On Duty Outside the Diocese.
Bitterman, John L. *s.s.* '69 (BAL)[S] Baltimore Society of St. Sulpice, Province of the United States; [O] Baltimore, MD St. Charles Villa.
Bittmenn, David J. '94 (SLC) Orem, UT St. Francis of Assisi LLC 221.
Bittner, Gregory T. '85 (BIR) Members; Tribunal; Birmingham, AL St. Francis Xavier; Priests'/Presbyteral Council; Diocesan College of Vicars.
Bittner, Wayne W. '64 (MIL) Retired.
Bitz, Al M. '69 (FAR) Jamestown, ND St. Margaret

Alacoque; Jamestown, ND St. James Basilica of Jamestown; Jamestown, ND St. Michael; Jamestown, ND St. Mathias Church of Windsor; [J] Jamestown, ND Jamestown College; Deanery 7.
Biven, L. Russell '57 (MOB)[E] Mobile, AL Little Sisters of the Poor, Home For the Aged, Inc. Retired.
Biven, Louis Russell '57 (MOB)[J] Mobile, AL Catholic University, Friends of Retired.
Bixenman, Joseph E. '72 (AMA)[I] Amarillo, TX Roman Catholic Diocese of Amarillo Deposit and Loan Fund.
Bixenman, Rev. Msgr. Joseph '72 (AMA) Perryton, TX Immaculate Conception; College of Consultors; Presbyteral Council.
Bizaca, Mate '73 (LA) Los Angeles, CA St. Anthony.
Bizzotto, Giovanni *c.s.* '72 (LA)[B] Sun Valley, CA Scalabrini House of Discernment (Seminary).
Bjorum, James L. '76 (DET) St. Clair Shores, MI Our Lady of Hope; Judges.
Blacet, Rev. Msgr. William J. '46 (KC) Kansas City, MO Our Lady of Good Counsel; Censor Librorum.
Blach, Leo M. '53 (DEN) Retired.
Black, Frank A. '80 (BRK) Brooklyn, NY St. Laurence.
Black, James P. '88 (COL) Delaware, OH St. Mary.
Black, Michael G. '00 (RCK) Rockford, IL St. Edward.
Blackall, John C. '51 (HRT) Appointed Retired.
Blackall, Randall L. '54 (HRT) Retired.
Blackburn, Michael *o.f.m.* (SPK) Spokane, WA St. Francis of Assisi; Members.
Blackwell, Edward A. '76 (HBG) On Duty Outside the Diocese.
Blackwell, Edward A. '76 (MIA)[B] St. Thomas University.
Blackwell, Michael J. '73 (WDC) Landover Hills, MD St. Mary's Catholic Church Retired.
Bladt, Joel S. *s.t.* '61 (SAV) Blakely, GA Holy Family.
Blaes, Donald A. '56 (BEL) Retired.
Blaes, James F. *c.s.c.* '55 (FTW) South Bend, IN Faith & Hope & Charity Chapel; [H] Holy Cross House Retired.
Blaes, Paul '51 (KC) Retired.
Blaeser, Donald *o.f.m.* '70 (SFD)[L] Quincy, IL St. Francis Solanus Friary.
Blaettler, James R. *s.j.* '80 (SFR) San Francisco, CA St. Ignatius; [N] San Francisco, CA Loyola House Jesuit Community.
Blahnik, Jason J. '09 (GB) Oshkosh, WI St. Raphael the Archangel; Omro, WI St. Mary; Winneconne, WI St. Mary.
Blain, Lionel A. '54 (PRO) Woonsocket, RI St. Anthony Retired.
Blaine, James E. '77 (SLC) American Fork, UT Saint Peter LLC 242; American Fork, UT Utah State Prison; Correctional Institution Ministry.
Blaine, Philip *o.f.m.conv.* '63 (NY)[EE] Staten Island, NY St. Francis Friary.
Blair, Guy *s.c.j.* '82 (GB) Green Bay, WI St. John.
Blair, Rev. Msgr. Raymond O. '60 (MAN) Retired.
Blair, Rev. Msgr. Raymond '60 (PMB) Defenders of the Bond.
Blais, George '90 (ORG) Irvine, CA St. Thomas More.
Blais, Melvin J. '42 (STP) Retired.
Blais, Robert L. '63 (PRO) Retired.
Blais, Roland O. '44 (MAN) Retired.
Blake, Andrew P. '63 (RVC) Sag Harbor, NY St. Andrew's Retired.
Blake, Carlyle R. *c.ss.r.* '62 (NY)[EE] New York, NY Redemptorist Priests and Brothers, C.Ss.R.
Blake, David D. *o.f.m.* '95 (BUF)[O] St. Bonaventure, NY St. Bonaventure Friary; [C] St. Bonaventure, NY Friar Community.
Blake, Gary W. '08 (PEO) Mendota, IL SS. Peter and Paul; Mendota, IL Holy Cross.
Blake, Jerry W. '00 (DUB) Traer, IA St. Paul; Waterloo, IA St. Mary of Mt. Carmel; La Porte City, IA Sacred Heart.
Blake, John Vincent *o.p.* '51 (CHI)[N] St. Pius V Priory.
Blake, Lawrence R. '99 (STP) Air Force Reserve Chaplains; Waconia, MN St. Joseph.
Blake, Peter M. '84 (STL) St. Louis, MO Our Lady of Sorrows.
Blake, Philip C. *s.j.* '61 (SJ)[M] Los Gatos, CA Sacred Heart Jesuit Center.
Blake, Richard *s.j.* '69 (BO)[U] Newton, MA The Jesuit Community at Boston College.
Blake, Robert '77 (SR) Santa Rosa, CA Holy Spirit.
Blake, William B. '63 (SCR) Jessup, PA St. James; Jessup, PA St. Mary's Assumption.
Blakely, Leonard J. '80 (WIL) Galena, MD St. Dennis.
Blakely, Paige (ORL) Judges.
Blaker, John R. '96 (OAK) Richmond, CA St. David of Wales; Deanery #22.
Blanch, Jose Maria *s.f.* '51 (SFE) Santa Cruz, NM Holy Cross.
Blanchard, David *o.carm.* '87 (JOL)[L] Darien Carmelite Provincial Office.
Blanchard, David *o.carm.* '87 (WDC)[B] Washington, DC Whitefriars Hall.
Blanchard, Donald V. '69 (BR) Retired.
Blanchard, Peter R. *s.m.* '67 (NO)[P] New Orleans, LA Marist Fathers.
Blanchet, Leo '86 (MOB) Whistler, AL St. Bridget; Holy Childhood Association; Pontifical Mission Societies of the United States.
Blanchett, Edward H. (TR) Lakewood, NJ St. Mary of the Lake; Riverside, NJ The Church of Jesus, the Good Shepherd, Riverside, N.J.
Blanchette, Brian D. '85 (PRT) Bridgton, ME St. Joseph; Windham, ME Our Lady of Perpetual Help.
Blanchette, Melvin C. *s.s.* '73 (WDC)[A] Washington, DC Theological College of the Catholic University of America; [C] Catholic University of America, The.
Blanchette, Melvin C. *s.s.* '67 (BAL)[S] Baltimore Society of St. Sulpice, Province of the United States.
Blanchette, Melvin *s.s.* (WDC)[C] Washington, DC Catholic University of America, The.
Blanchette, Melvin *s.s.* (DET) On Duty Outside the Archdiocese.
Blanchette, Oliver (Robert) *a.a.* '44 (WOR)[O] Worcester, MA Assumptionists (Augustinians of the Assumption).
Blanchfield, David W. '82 (BGP) Norwalk, CT St. Jerome; Members of the Clergy Personnel Committee.
Blanco, Adalberto (LA) Carpinteria, CA St. Joseph.
Blanco, Gonzalo *o.s.b.* '92 (BIS)[A] Richardton, ND Assumption Abbey; Richardton, ND Assumption Abbey.
Blanco, Ignacio A. *c.m.f.* '51 (SAT) San Antonio, TX Immaculate Heart of Mary.
Blanco, Ildefonso *o.s.a.* '64 (MGZ) Aguada, PR St. Francis of Assisi.
Blanco, Joseph '84 (DEN) Akron, CO St. Joseph.
Blanco, Miguel A. (ARE) Arecibo, PR Church of San Martin de Porres.
Blanco, Telesforo R. *o.s.a.* '60 (BEA) Port Arthur, TX Our Lady of Guadalupe.
Blanco, Vincent '90 (ANC) Anchorage, AK Our Lady of Guadalupe; Notaries.
Bland, Thomas A. '74 (SAC) Carmichael, CA St. John the Evangelist; Presbyteral Council; Priests' Personnel Board, Diocesan.
Blanda, William C. '91 (LAF) Abbeville, LA St. Mary Magdalen.
Blandon, Francisco '96 (SR) Napa, CA St. John the Baptist.
Blaney, Dennis J. '58 (GRY) Sharing Meadows Retired.
Blaney, James *o.m.i.* '65 (JUN) Haines, AK Sacred Heart.
Blaney, Robert J. '07 (BO) West Roxbury, MA St. Theresa of Avila.
Blaney, Robert M. '92 (BO) Weymouth, MA St. Jerome; Presbyteral Council.
Blangiardi, B. Jeffrey *s.j.* '86 (BO)[U] Boston The Society of Jesus of New England–Provincial Offices.
Blangiardi, B. Jeffrey *s.j.* '86 (SD) La Jolla, CA Veterans Administration Hospital.
Blank, Matthew '07 (SAC) Truckee, CA Assumption of the Blessed Virgin Mary.
Blank, Severius '58 (FWT) Retired.
Blank, William H. '87 (NO) Garyville, LA St. Hubert.
Blankenhorn, Bernard *o.p.* '06 (OAK)[M] Oakland Order of Preachers (Province of the Most Holy Name of Jesus – Western Dominican Province).
Blankinship, Calvin '96 (B) Fruitland, ID Corpus Christi Catholic Church.
Blantz, James R. *c.s.c.* '59 (FTW)[H] Holy Cross House.
Blantz, James R. *c.s.c.* '59 (PHX)[F] Phoenix, AZ Holy Cross Congregation/Casa Santa Cruz.
Blantz, Thomas E. *c.s.c.* '60 (FTW)[B] University of Notre Dame Du Lac; [H] Notre Dame, IN Holy Cross Community, Corby Hall, University of Notre Dame; [H] Notre Dame, IN Congregation of Holy Cross, Indiana Province, Provincial House.
Blas, Mario W. '83 (MO) DEPARTMENT OF VETERANS AFFAIRS HOSPITALS AND CHAPLAINS.
Blas, Wilson '83 (DAL) Bonham, TX St. Elizabeth; Bonham, TX Sam Rayburn Memorial Veterans Center.
Blasco, Ignacio '62 (MIA) Retired.
Blaser, John R. '64 (TOL) Retired.
Blasich, Bernard '67 (MIL)[P] Milwaukee, WI St. Camillus Provincialate.
Blasick, George *c.ss.r.* (BAL) Annapolis, MD St. Mary.
Blaska, John A. '53 (DET) Retired.
Blasko, Joseph A. '99 (GAY) Roscommon, MI St. Michael; Prudenville, MI Our Lady of the Lake; Higgins Lake, MI St. Hubert; Higgins Lake, MI St. James.
Blasko, Zvonko '82 (CLV) Cleveland, OH St. Paul.
Blastic, Michael *o.f.m.* '75 (BUF)[O] St. Bonaventure, NY St. Bonaventure Friary; [C] St. Bonaventure, NY Friar Community.
Blaszczak, Gerald R. *s.j.* '79 (BGP)[O] Fairfield, CT The Fairfield Jesuit Community–Fairfield University; [B] Fairfield, CT Fairfield University; [V] Fairfield, CT Fairfield University.
Blaszkowski, Andy '08 (STA) St. Augustine, FL Cathedral – Basilica of St. Augustine.
Blaszkowski, Remigiusz '05 (STA) Seminarians; Ponte Vedra Beach, FL Our Lady Star of the Sea; Vocations.
Blattner, Joseph H. '58 (STL) On Duty Outside the Archdiocese.
Blau, Thomas J. *o.p.* '99 (PRO)[P] Providence St. Thomas Aquinas Priory at Providence College.
Blau, Thomas *o.p.* '99 (COL) Columbus, OH St. Patrick.
Blaufuss, Tony '58 (KCK) Retired.
Blauvelt, Robert '59 (BRK)[T] Douglaston, NY Bishop Mugavero Residence Retired.
Blay, Rev. Msgr. Roberto Garcia '86 (PCE) Mercedita, PR Church of the Resurrection; Vicar General; Diocesan Consultors; Diocesan Board of Administration; Administrator; Committee for Community Planning; Episcopal Vicar for Diocesan Administration.
Blazak, Camillus '51 (BIR) Signal Mountain, TN Retired.
Blazejewski, Richard W. '74 (BUF) Perry, NY St. Isidore.
Blazek, Camilius '51 (KNX)[D] Signal Mountain, TN Alexian Village of Tennessee.
Blazek, David J. '97 (DET) Holly, MI St. Rita; Presbyteral Council; Archdiocesan Vicars.
Blazek, Eugene '76 (HON) On Duty Outside the Diocese.
Blazek, James F. '79 (CHI) Schiller Park, IL St. Maria Goretti.
Blazek, John J. *c.s.c.* '67 (FTW)[H] Holy Cross House.
Blazek, John *c.s.c.* '67 (CLV)[D] Gates Mills, OH Gilmour Academy.
Blazewicz, William J. '59 (LC)[H] La Crosse, WI Holy Cross (Seminary) Diocesan Center Retired.
Blazine, Rev. Msgr. James A. '62 (BEL) Retired.
Blazovich, Victor M. '00 (SPK) Spokane, WA St. Francis Xavier; Spokane, WA St. Patrick.
Bleboo, Lawrence T. '79 (MO) Army Reserve Chaplains.
Blecha, Rev. Msgr. Charles A. '40 (LC) Retired.
Blee, Edward C. *s.m.* '55 (SFR)[N] San Francisco, CA Marist Center of the West Retired.
Bleem, Gerald *o.f.m.* '82 (CHI)[N] Cicero, IL San Damiano Friary Order of Friars Minor.
Bleeser, Peter '67 (NY) Hartsdale, NY Sacred Heart; [II] White Plains, NY Deutschsprachige Katholische Gemeinde New York–German Speaking Catholic Congregation New York.
Bleich, Rev. Msgr. Russell M. '60 (DUB) On Special or Other Archdiocesan Assignment; Episcopal Vicar for Cedar Rapids Region; College of Consultors; Building Commission; Pastoral Council; Ex Officio Members; Archbishop's Cabinet; Vinton, IA St. Mary; Walker, IA St. Mary; Vinton, IA Sacred Heart; Archdiocesan Pastoral Center.
Bleichner, Howard P. '67 (PIT) On Duty Outside the Diocese.
Bleichner, Howard P. *s.s.* '67 (BAL)[S] Baltimore Society of St. Sulpice, Province of the United States Retired.
Bleichner, Howard P. '67 (SFR)[A] Menlo Park, CA St. Patrick Seminary and University.
Bleiler, William James '66 (CAM) Leesburg, NJ New Jersey State Medium Security Prison Retired.
Blenker, Ambrose J. '62 (LC) Plum City, WI St. John the Baptist.
Blenkle, Joseph A. '90 (NY) Valhalla, NY Holy Name of Jesus.
Blesnuk, Donald J. '85 (BUF) Absent on Leave.
Blessing, Gerald '05 (STL) Wildwood, MO St. Alban Roe.
Blessing, Howard '76 (LAF) Lafayette, LA Holy Cross.
Blessing, Loren '81 (FRS) Fresno, CA St. Anthony of Padua.
Blessinger, James '64 (EVN) Evansville, IN Corpus Christi; Clergy Personnel Board.
Blewett, John Patrick '09 (MAD) Sauk City, WI St. Aloysius.
Blicharski, Michael *o.cist.* '95 (CHI)[N] Willow Springs, IL Cistercian Fathers, Our Lady Mother of the Church Polish Mission; Argo, IL Our Lady, Mother of the Church Polish Mission.
Blicharz, Dariusz Piotr '91 (BRK) Brooklyn, NY St. Catharine of Alexandria.
Blick, Ned J. '92 (WCH) On Duty Outside the Diocese.
Blick, Ned '02 (MO) Army Chaplains.
Blick, Ned (OG) U.S. Army Headquarters.
Blickhan, Donald '74 (SFD) Quincy, IL Illinois Veterans' Home.
Blind, Thomas F. '82 (NEW) Bloomfield, NJ Church of St. Thomas the Apostle; [P] Union, NJ Kean University.
Bline, David '98 (CLV) Presbyteral Council.
Bline, G. David '98 (CLV) Akron, OH St. Francis de Sales.
Blinn, Richard J. *s.j.* '69 (SJ)[M] Los Gatos, CA Sacred Heart Jesuit Center.
Bliss, Rev. Msgr. Michael C. '91 (PEO)[H] East Peoria, IL Saint Francis Medical Center; Vicariates and Vicars; [I] Peoria, IL Saint Clare Home.
Blissert, Richard *c.ss.r.* '56 (FgM) Baltimore Province.
Bliszcz, Michael '87 (SJP) Grand Rapids, MI St. Michael's; On Assignment Outside the Diocese; Presbyters.
Bliven, Edmond '50 (P) Retired.
Blocher, James F. *c.s.b.* '75 (GAL)[E] Houston, TX St. Thomas High School.
Block, John G. '63 (PMB) Retired.

Block, John '63 (ORG) Retired.
Blocklinger, James L. '66 (DUB) Retired.
Blomberg, John F. '59 (STL) Retired.
Blondell, Robert H. '66 (DET) Harrison Township, MI St. Hubert.
Blonski, Joachim '92 (GLP) Show Low, AZ St. Rita; St. Johns, AZ St. John the Baptist; Presbyteral Council; Diocesan Consultors.
Blonski, Joachim '92 (GLP) Priests' Retirement Board.
Blood, Francis J. *o.s.f.s.* (CAM) Camden, NJ The Church of the Immaculate Conception, Camden, N.J.
Blood, Rev. Msgr. Francis X. '79 (STL) St. Louis, MO Our Lady of Providence; Holy Childhood, Pontifical Association; Latin American Apostolate, Archdiocese of St. Louis; Pan y Amor; Society for the Propagation of the Faith; New York, NY A. The Pontifical Society for the Propagation of the Faith.
Bloom, Phillip A. '71 (SEA) Monroe, WA St. Mary of the Valley.
Bloomer, Matthew A. '99 (SFR)[R] San Francisco, CA Prelature of the Holy Cross and Opus Dei; San Francisco.
Bloomfield, Andrew '05 (DET) Absent on Leave.
Bloshchynskyy, Ihor '03 (PHU) Philadelphia, PA St. Josaphat's.
Blostic, Leonard *t.o.r.* '63 (ALT)[G] Newry, PA St. Bernardine Monastery Retired.
Blotsky, Hugo L. *o.s.b.* '88 (BIS)[A] Richardton, ND Assumption Abbey.
Blotsky, Hugo L. *o.s.b.* '88 (CHY) Thermopolis, WY St. Francis.
Blottman, William P. '65 (FR) Retired.
Blount, Anthony *s.o.l.t.* '96 (CC)[G] Robstown, TX Society of Our Lady of the Most Holy Trinity.
Blount, Anthony *s.o.l.t.* '96 (PBL) Capulin, CO St. Joseph.
Blount, James *s.o.l.t.* '99 (CC)[G] Robstown, TX Society of Our Lady of the Most Holy Trinity.
Blout, Daniel L. '86 (GBG) Kittanning, PA St. Mary, Our Lady of Guadalupe; Yatesboro, PA St. Mary.
Blowers, Leslie F. *m.m.* '63 (CIN)[N] Cincinnati, OH The Catholic Foreign Mission Society of America, Inc.
Blowey, David *o.f.m.conv.* '87 (BAL)[S] Ellicott City Order of Friars Minor Conventual.
Blubaugh, Homer D. '69 (COL) London Correctional Institution; Columbus, OH St. Agnes; Columbus, OH St. Aloysius.
Blue, Peter W. *o.s.b.* '70 (PAT)[N] Newton St. Paul's Abbey; Newton, NJ St. Paul's Abbey.
Bluejacket, David '88 (DEN) Arvada, CO Spirit of Christ Catholic Community.
Bluett, Anthony '69 (ORL) Lake Wales, FL Holy Spirit.
Bluett, James K. '67 (PT) On Leave of Absence.
Bluett, John J. '63 (ORL) Winter Springs, FL St. Stephen.
Blum, Charlie E. (STO) Judges.
Blum, John '96 (SP) St. Pete Beach, FL St. John Vianney.
Blum, Stephen J. '76 (TOL) Lima, OH St. Charles Borromeo; Blessed Junipero Serra Deanery.
Blum, William G. *c.s.c.* '65 (FTW)[H] Notre Dame, IN Columba Hall; [H] Notre Dame Congregation of Holy Cross, Indiana Province, Provincial House; [H] Holy Cross House.
Blume, David '04 (STP) Oak Grove, MN St. Patrick.
Blumenfeld, Donald E. '79 (NEW)[A] South Orange, NJ Immaculate Conception Seminary; [B] School of Diplomacy and Intl. Rels.; Censores Librorum.
Blumeyer, A. James *s.j.* '63 (KC) Kansas City, MO St. Francis Xavier; [J] Kansas City, MO Rockhurst Jesuit Community.
Blums, Burton *o.s.b.* '45 (SCL)[I] Collegeville, MN St. John's Abbey, of the Order of St. Benedict.
Blute, Robert H. '56 (BO) Senior Priests. Retired.
Bly, Walter J. '64 (FTW)[C] South Bend, IN Saint Joseph's High School Retired.
Blyman, Robert Y. '70 (RVC) Hicksville, NY Our Lady of Mercy.
Blyskosz, Joseph J. '95 (FR) Awaiting Assignment; [G] Fall River, MA Priests' Hostel.
Boachie–Yiadom, Godfred '95 (CIN) Cincinnati, OH Our Lord, Christ the King.
Boackle, Paul H. '89 (SAM) Retired.
Boadt, Lawrence *c.s.p.* '69 (NEW)[M] Mahwah, NJ Paulist Fathers – Paulist Press; [R] Mahwah, NJ Paulist Press.
Boateng–Mensah, Anthony (VIC) Victoria, TX St. Mary's.
Boateng–Mensah, Samanhyia '73 (MO) DEPARTMENT OF VETERANS AFFAIRS HOSPITALS AND CHAPLAINS.
Boateng–Mensah, Semanhyia '73 (PH) Coatesville, PA St. Cecilia.
Bobadilla, Tomas '81 (NY) Newburgh, NY St. Patrick.
Bobal, Rev. Msgr. Joseph K. '63 (E) Retired.
Bober, Charles S. '72 (PIT) Cranberry Township, PA St. Kilian; [Q] Pittsburgh, PA Priests' Benefit Plan of the Diocese of Pittsburgh; College of Consultors; Priest Council.
Bober, Marjan L. '63 (CAM) Retired.
Boberek, Aurelius *o.s.b.* '57 (IND)[K] St. Meinrad, IN St. Meinrad Archabbey.
Bobola, Adam *s.ch.* '92 (JOL) Lombard, IL Divine Mercy Polish Mission.
Bobrek, Edwin *o.f.m.* '51 (NY)[EE] New York Franciscan Province of the Immaculate Conception.
Boccabella, James D. '09 (WDC) Washington, DC Blessed Sacrament, Shrine of the Most.
Boccaccio, Michael A. '71 (BGP) Norwalk, CT St. Philip; Judges.
Boccafola, Rev. Msgr. Kenneth '63 (RVC) Serving Outside the Diocese.
Boccali, Ronald *p.i.m.e.* '60 (COL) Heath, OH St. Leonard Retired.
Boccardi, Raymond C. '52 (PIT) Retired.
Boccio, Rev. Msgr. Charles P. '61 (BRK) Astoria, NY Immaculate Conception Retired.
Bochanski, Philip G. *c.o.* '99 (PH) Philadelphia, PA St. Francis Xavier; [Z] Philadelphia, PA Sister Servants of the Holy Spirit of Perpetual Adoration (S.Sp-.S.A.P.); [Y] Philadelphia, PA The Philadelphia Congregation of The Oratory of St. Philip Neri.
Bochenek, Joseph G. '71 (BAL) Baltimore, MD St. Brigid.
Bochicchio, Rev. Msgr. Paul L. '71 (NEW) Nutley, NJ Holy Family; Archdiocesan Stewardship Advisory Committee; [Q] Totowa, NJ The Association of the Marian Apostolate of Mercy, Inc.; Members.
Bochinski, Mark J. '58 (SCR)[N] Dunmore, PA Villa St. Joseph Retired.
Bochnak, Zenon A. '85 (MET) On Duty Outside the Diocese.
Bocian, Rev. Msgr. Ronald C. '72 (ALN) Shenandoah, PA St. Casimir; Shenandoah, PA St. Stanislaus; Father Walter Ciszek Prayer League, Inc. (The); Shenandoah, PA St. Stephen.
Bocianowski, Thaddeus Nicholas '71 (BUF) Buffalo, NY St. Adalbert; Buffalo, NY St. John Kanty; Buffalo, NY St. Stanislaus.
Bock, Lawrence R. '62 (HRT) Consultors – Canon 1742; Newington, CT Church of the Holy Spirit; College of Consultors; Episcopal Vicars; Ex Officio Members.
Bockenfeld, Elgar *o.f.m.* '44 (STP) New Prague, MN St. Benedict; New Prague, MN St. John the Evangelist.
Bocklage, Richard F. *s.j.* '55 (STL)[O] St. Louis, MO Jesuit Community Corporation at Saint Louis University – Jesuit Hall.
Bockskopf, Richard J. '70 (STL) Maryland Heights, MO Holy Spirit.
Boczek, Zenon *s.d.s.* '96 (MET) Port Murray, NJ St. Theodore.
Boczek, Zenon *s.d.s.* '96 (NEW)[M] Verona, NJ The Salvatorian Fathers.
Bodah, Henry J. '78 (PRO) Providence, RI St. Joseph; [S] Providence, RI Brown University.
Bodde, Frederick A. '53 (DET) Retired.
Bodden, Charles J. *o.s.a.* '78 (FgM) Olympia Fields, IL Province of Our Mother of Good Counsel (Midwestern).
Boddie, James R. '78 (STA) Orange Park, FL St. Catherine's; Scouts; Multicultural Ministry.
Bodensteiner, Peter C. '45 (DUB) Retired.
Bodin, Daniel J. '05 (STP) Taylors Falls, MN St. Joseph's.
Bodnar, Edward W. *s.j.* '52 (WDC)[N] Washington, DC The Jesuit Community at Georgetown University Retired.
Bodo, Murray L. *o.f.m.* '64 (CIN)[N] Cincinnati, OH Pleasant Street Friary; [U] Cincinnati, OH Franciscans Network.
Bodziak, Charles F. '67 (ALT) Cassandra, PA St. Agnes; Wilmore, PA St. Bartholomew's.
Bodziony, Ralph A. '58 (CLV) Cleveland, OH St. John Cantius Retired.
Boeckman, Scott A. '03 (OKL) Woodward, OK St. Peter's; Council of Priests Archdiocesan.
Boedy, Thomas *s.j.* '70 (STP) Shakopee, MN St. Mark.
Boeff, Dismas *o.s.b.* '76 (CLV) Brook Park, OH St. Peter the Apostle; SouthWest General Hospital; [N] Cleveland Benedictine Order of Cleveland.
Boeglin, John '78 (EVN) Jasper, IN Holy Family; Rural Life Conference.
Boehling, Michael G. '06 (RIC) Chesapeake, VA St. Mary; Portsmouth, VA Church of the Holy Angels; Portsmouth, VA Church of the Resurrection; Portsmouth, VA St. Paul.
Boehm, Rev. Msgr. James A. '58 (STU) Retired.
Boehm, Michael J. '75 (CHI) Chicago, IL Blessed Sacrament.
Boehm, Michael P. '94 (STL) Washington, MO Our Lady of Lourdes.
Boehman, John *o.f.m.* '59 (CIN)[N] Cincinnati St. Francis Seraph Friary Retired.
Boehme, Arnold *o.c.d.* '68 (MIL)[P] Milwaukee Provincial Offices – Discalced Carmelites.
Boehme, Ferdinand '97 (LIN) Curtis, NE St. James.
Boehme, Walter E. *s.j.* '70 (MIL)[P] Milwaukee, WI Arrupe House Jesuit Community.
Boehning, Rev. Msgr. John A. '62 (NY) New York, NY St. Thomas More.
Boeke, Anselm F. '43 (CIN)[N] Carthagena, OH St. Charles Retired.
Boekelman, Timothy J. '77 (SC) Madrid, IA St. Malachy's; Ogden, IA St. John's; Madrid, IA St. John of God; Woodward State Hospital and School.
Boel, Joseph H. *s.j.* '59 (DET)[K] Clarkston, MI Colombiere Center.
Boenzi, Joseph *s.d.b.* '79 (OAK)[M] Berkeley Salesians of Don Bosco; [A] Berkeley, CA Dominican School of Philosophy and Theology.
Boes, Clair L. '65 (SC) Retired.
Boes, Edward *s.a.* '98 (NY)[EE] Garrison Franciscan Friars of the Atonement, Minister General Office.
Boes, Marvin '62 (SC) Retired.
Boes, Steven '85 (OM) Boys Town, NE Immaculate Conception B.V.M.; [I] Boys Town, NE Father Flanagan's Boys' Home.
Boesel, Rev. Msgr. James E. '54 (RVC) Hicksville, NY Our Lady of Mercy Retired.
Boeshans, Rev. Msgr. Francis G. '48 (NO)[S] New Orleans, LA Stella Roman Foundation, Inc. Retired.
Boettcher, John '91 (SR) On Duty Outside the Diocese.
Boettner, David '94 (KNX) Gatlinburg, TN St. Mary; Moderator of the Curia; Moderator of the Curia; Presbyteral Council; Knoxville, TN Cathedral of the Sacred Heart of Jesus; Episcopal Vicar; Diocesan Finance Council.
Boever, Richard *c.ss.r.* '73 (MIL)[S] Oconomowoc, WI The Redemptorist Retreat Center.
Boff, Bernard J. '61 (TOL) Mission of Accompaniment Retired.
Bogacki, Phillip A. '08 (MIL) Brookfield, WI St. John Vianney.
Bogacz, John A. '09 (TR) Toms River, NJ St. Justin.
Bogan, Robert F. '58 (SY) Clinton, NY Church of the Annunciation.
Bogda, Rev. Archpriest Dennis M. '67 (PBR) Munhall, PA St. John the Baptist Cathedral; Consultors; Vocations; Revitalization and Renewal Commission; Presbyteral Council.
Bogdan, Rev. Msgr. Henry S. '48 (TR)[N] Trenton, NJ Villa Vianney Retired.
Bogdan, Rev. Msgr. Leonard A. '60 (KAL) Sun City West, AZ Retired.
Bogdan, Palka *s.d.s.* '92 (NEW)[M] Verona, NJ The Salvatorian Fathers.
Bogert, James '67 (RVC) Retired.
Boghossian, G. Scott '02 (PSC) Linden, NJ St. George's; Eparchial Newspaper.
Bognanno, Rev. Msgr. Frank E. (DM) Des Moines, IA Christ the King.
Bogniak, Rev. Msgr. Casimir '57 (E) Retired.
Boguslawski, Steven C. *o.p.* '87 (DET)[T] Washington, DC Operations Office.
Boguslawski, Steven C. *o.p.* '87 (WDC)[B] Washington, DC Dominican House of Studies; New York, NY; Consultants.
Bogusz, Dennis A. '79 (GBG) Mount Pleasant, PA Frick Community Health Center; Connellsville, PA Highlands Hospital & Health Center; Connellsville, PA St. John the Evangelist.
Bohan, Philip *o.f.m.cap.* (NY) New York, NY Good Shepherd.
Bohlin, Rev. Msgr. Thomas G. '97 (POD)[JJ] New York, NY Prelature of the Holy Cross and Opus Dei; Regional Vicar for the United States; New York.
Bohn, John '97 (JKS) Starkville, MS St. Joseph; [H] Starkville, MS Mississippi State University Catholic Student Association; Approved Advocate and Auditors.
Bohner, Allan G. '98 (SR) Retired.
Bohnert, Edward A. '85 (SFR) Belmont, CA St. Mark.
Bohnsack, David *m.c.c.j.* '94 (CHI)[N] Chicago, IL Comboni Missionaries Theologate (M.C.C.J.), Verona Fathers.
Bohnsak, Christopher G. '09 (TOL) Findlay, OH St. Michael the Archangel.
Bohorquez, Carlos M. '99 (SFD) Pierron, IL St. Gertrude; Pierron, IL Immaculate Conception; Pierron, IL St. Nicholas; Comite Diocesano de Ministerio Hispano – Diocesan Committee for Hispanic Ministry; Air National Guard Chaplains.
Bohorquez, Hernan D. '02 (BGP) Darien, CT St. John; Leave of Absence.
Bohorquez, Jesus Alberto '01 (MIA) Miami Beach, FL St. Patrick.
Bohr, Rev. Msgr. David A. '71 (SCR) Scranton, PA St. Peter's Cathedral; Scranton, PA Holy Family; Permanent Diaconate Office.
Boileau, David A. '56 (NO) Retired.
Boisaubin, Robert D. '69 (STL) Retired.
Boissey, M. David (CHL) Greensboro, NC St. Benedict.
Boisvert, Gilbert O. '71 (OG) Altona, NY Holy Angels; Altona, NY St. Louis.
Boisvert, Keith W. '79 (BAL) Frederick, MD St. Katharine Drexel Roman Catholic Congregation, Inc.
Boisvert, Marc *o.m.i.* '84 (FgM) Washington, DC AMERICAN OBLATE MISSIONS.
Boisvert, Ralph J. '99 (PRT) Augusta, ME St. Michael Parish.
Boisvert, Robert G. '58 (MAN) Retired.
Boivin, Henry P. '57 (BO) Senior Priests. Retired.
Boivin, John '76 (CHI) Chicago, IL Holy Name Cathedral.

Boivin, Louis R. '48 (FR) Retired.
Bojczuk, Thaddeus J. '73 (CHI) Chicago, IL St. Symphorosa and Seven Sons; Deans.
Boji, Manuel Y. '68 (EST) Southfield, MI Our Lady of Chaldeans Cathedral, Mother of God Chaldean Parish; Vicar General; Eparchial College of Consultors; Diocesan Corporation–The Chaldean Catholic Church of U.S.A.
Bok, James M. *o.f.m.* '74 (CIN)[N] Cincinnati St. Francis Seraph Friary.
Bok, John P. *o.f.m.* '62 (GAL) Galveston, TX Holy Family.
Bokenkotter, Thomas '50 (CIN) Cincinnati, OH Assumption of the Blessed Virgin Mary.
Bokinskie, Richard '79 (SAG) Chicago, IL National Organization for Continuing Education of Roman Catholic Clergy, Inc. (NOCERCC); Chesaning, MI Our Lady of Perpetual Help; Oakley, MI St. Michael; Territorial Vicars.
Bokota, Marek '81 (NEW) Mahwah, NJ Immaculate Heart of Mary.
Boks, Lawrence E. '66 (GAY) Retired.
Bolan, John *c.pp.s.* '53 (CIN)[N] Dayton Provincial Office of the Cincinnati Province of the Society of the Precious Blood.
Boland, Eamonn '69 (DUL) Moose Lake, MN Holy Angels; Moose Lake State Hospital.
Boland, Edward F. '44 (PRO)[M] Pawtucket, RI Jeanne Jugan Residence Retired.
Boland, Rev. Msgr. Eugene (PAT) Little Falls, NJ Retired.
Boland, Jeremiah M. '81 (CHI) Chicago, IL Holy Family; College of Consultors; Archbishop's Delegate for Extern and International Priests.
Boland, Rev. Msgr. John P. '55 (PH) Defenders of the Bond; Diocesan Priests' Compensation and Benefits Committee; Philadelphia, PA St. Christopher Retired.
Boland, Rev. Msgr. John V. '65 (PAT) McAfee, NJ St. Francis de Sales.
Boland, John '75 (GLP) On Leave of Absence.
Boland, Michael M. '86 (CHI) Chicago, IL Holy Name Cathedral; [G] Chicago, IL Catholic Charities of the Archdiocese of Chicago–Archdiocesan Offices; [G] Chicago, IL Mission of the Holy Cross; Health/Hospital Affairs; Administrative Council; Department Directors; Director; Catholic Charities of Chicago.
Boland, Thomas L. '65 (L) Louisville, KY St. Patrick; Archdiocesan Examiners.
Bolatete, Ramon '85 (ORL)[G] Lakeland, FL Florida Southern College Newman Center; Lakeland, FL St. Joseph's.
Bolcar, Andrew J. '65 (CAM) Retired.
Bolda, Eugeniusz *s.ch.* '89 (PHX) Phoenix, AZ Our Lady of Czestochowa Roman Catholic Parish.
Bolderson, John J. '81 (KC) Butler, MO St. Patrick's; Montrose, MO Immaculate Conception.
Bolding, Robert '09 (PHX) Phoenix, AZ SS. Simon and Jude Roman Catholic Cathedral; [A] Phoenix, AZ St. Mary's Roman Catholic High School.
Bolduc, John *s.m.* '70 (FgM) THE SOCIETY OF MARY.
Bolduc, Marcel *o.m.i.* '39 (BO)[X] Tewksbury, MA Immaculate Heart of Mary Residence.
Bolduc, Richard *o.m.i.* '64 (BO)[X] Tewksbury, MA Immaculate Heart of Mary Residence.
Boles, Joseph M. '65 (SCR)[N] Dunmore, PA Villa St. Joseph Retired.
Boley, Robert *o.carm.* '75 (JOL)[L] Joliet, IL St. Elias Carmelites.
Bolez, Edward C. '74 (ALN) Retired.
Bolger, Anthony '69 (HON) Retired.
Bolger, Jesse '07 (BAL) Bel Air, MD St. Margaret.
Bolger, John A. *c.c.* (GAL) Houston, TX Queen of Peace.
Bolger, Michael J. '92 (RCK) Shannon, IL St. Wendelin; [B] Freeport, IL Aquin Central Catholic High School.
Bolger, Rev. Msgr. Richard T. '66 (PH) Willow Grove, PA St. David.
Bolger, Rev. Msgr. William '53 (SD) Retired.
Bolha, Jeremy J. *o.s.b.* '59 (GBG)[G] Latrobe, PA Saint Vincent Archabbey.
Bolha, Jeremy *o.s.b.* '59 (E) St. Marys, PA Sacred Heart of Jesus.
Bolieau, Henry G. '72 (NOR) Absent on Leave.
Bolivar, Carlos Alberto '01 (CC) Alice, TX St. Joseph.
Boll, John E. '70 (SAC) Sacramento, CA St. Anthony.
Boll, John *o.p.* '82 (COL) Columbus, OH St. Patrick.
Bollea, Richard C. '62 (HRT) Waterbury, CT Waterbury Hospital; Beacon Falls, CT St. Michael; Special and other Archdiocesan Assignment; Coordinator of the Hospital Apostolate.
Boller, Kenneth J. *s.j.* '75 (NY)[F] Bronx, NY Fordham Preparatory School; [EE] Jesuit Community, Kohlmann Hall.
Bolling, Francis Joseph '04 (MOB)[E] Mobile, AL Little Sisters of the Poor, Home For the Aged, Inc. Retired.
Bolling, Joseph M. '91 (MOB) Mobile, AL St. Matthew.
Bollman, Richard W. *s.j.* '69 (CIN) Cincinnati, OH St. Robert Bellarmine; [D] Cincinnati, OH Xavier University; [N] Cincinnati, OH Jesuit Community at Xavier University.
Bolman, Anthony P. '60 (SFE) Retired.
Bolser, Charles G. *c.s.v.* '73 (CHI) Chicago, IL St. Viator; [N] Arlington Heights Viatorian Province Center–Clerics of St. Viator.
Bolser, Robert T. *c.s.v.* '95 (CHI)[N] Arlington Heights Viatorian Province Center–Clerics of St. Viator.
Bolser, Robert T. *c.s.v.* '95 (LAV) Henderson, NV St. Thomas More.
Bolster, M. Thomas '82 (GR) Hart, MI St. Gregory's.
Bolte, Richard G. '83 (COV) Union, KY St. Timothy.
Bolte, Thomas L. '80 (CIN) Cincinnati, OH St. Teresa of Avila.
Bolton, Bill *s.d.b.* '86 (LA)[V] Rosemead, CA St. Joseph's Salesian Youth Renewal Center.
Bolton, Donald *c.ss.r.* '52 (ALB)[L] Saratoga Springs, NY St. John Neumann Residence.
Bolton, Norman B. '83 (SPR)[N] Chicopee, MA Bay Path College; Chicopee, MA Nativity of the Blessed Virgin Mary; Chicopee, MA St. Mary's; [N] Chicopee, MA American International College; Ludlow, MA St. John the Baptist; [N] Springfield, MA Newman Apostolates and Campus Ministries.
Bolton, Paul J. '62 (PRO) Retired.
Boly, Craig *s.j.* '74 (P) Portland, OR St. Pius X[D].
Bomar, Rev. Msgr. Fred '60 (AUS) Austin, TX St. Peter the Apostle; Consultors.
Bomba, Paul M. '77 (WOR) Deans; Presbyteral Council; Blackstone, MA St. Theresa.
Bombardier, Dennis P. '68 (SPR) Retired.
Bombardier, Paul A. '82 (SPR) Shelburne Falls, MA St. Joseph's.
Bombera, Alex *t.o.r.* '46 (ALT)[G] Loretto, PA St. Francis Friary at Mount Assisi.
Bomberger, Ray P. *s.s.j.* (BAL) Baltimore, MD St. Peter Claver; Baltimore, MD St. Pius V.
Bommarito, Rev. Msgr. Vincent R. '77 (STL) St. Louis, MO St. Ambrose.
Bona, Joseph F. *s.j.* '72 (DEN)[N] Denver, CO Xavier Jesuit Center.
Bona, Richard '03 (CLV) Translators; North Royalton, OH St. Albert the Great.
Bonacci, Louis A. *s.j.* '73 (SCR)[C] Scranton, PA The University of Scranton.
Bonacci, Paul '91 (ROC) Watkins Glen, NY St. Benedict; Watkins Glen, NY St. Mary of the Lake.
Bonacci, Thomas *c.p.* '72 (OAK) Antioch, CA St. Ignatius of Antioch.
Bonacci, Thomas *c.p.* '72 (MET)[I] South River Passionist Provincial Office Retired.
Bonadies, Kenneth P. '65 (HRT) Retired.
Bonadio, Joseph J. *s.s.* '64 (BAL)[O] Baltimore, MD St. Charles Villa; [S] Baltimore Society of St. Sulpice, Province of the United States Retired.
Bonafed, Joseph E. '92 (GBG) Connellsville, PA Immaculate Conception; Connellsville, PA St. John the Evangelist; Connellsville, PA St. Rita.
Bonanno, Raphael *o.f.m.* '62 (BO)[Z] Boston, MA St. Anthony Shrine.
Bonano, Salvatore *c.m.f.* '43 (LA)[V] Rancho Dominguez, CA Dominguez Seminary Inc. Retired.
Bonar, Clyde A. '84 (ORL) Retired.
Bonarrigo, David *t.o.r.* '78 (ALT)[G] Loretto, PA St. Francis Friary at Mount Assisi.
Bonavitacola, John M. '88 (PH) On Duty Outside the Archdiocese.
Bonavitacola, John '88 (PHX) Tempe, AZ Our Lady of Mt. Carmel Roman Catholic Parish.
Bonczewski, Rev. Msgr. William D. '83 (OLL) Murray, UT Saint Jude Maronite Catholic Church.
Bonczewski, Rev. Msgr. William '76 (SLC) Murray, UT Saint Jude.
Bond, B. Daniel (RIC) Retired.
Bond, Ernest W. '88 (COS) Burlington, CO St. Catherine of Siena; Stratton, CO St. Charles Borromeo.
Bond, William D. '99 (OM) Omaha, NE St. Joseph.
Bonderenko, Thomas '80 (BAL) Priests Sick or Absent.
Bondi, Richard A. '74 (SPR) South Hadley, MA St. Theresa of Lisieux.
Bondi, Steven '86 (JOL) Wilmington, IL St. Rose.
Bondy, Alberto P. '86 (DET) Warren, MI St. Anne.
Boned, Enrique '57 (MIA) Retired.
Bonela, Anthony *m.s.f.s.* '97 (STA) Jacksonville, FL St. Joseph's.
Bonela, Anthony *m.s.f.s.* '97 (TYL)[B] Whitehouse, TX The Missionaries of St. Francis de Sales.
Bonelli, Charles *i.m.c.* '69 (MET)[I] Somerset, NJ Consolata Society for Foreign Missions; Somerset, NJ; Somerset, NJ Consolata Missionaries.
Bonello, Joseph *o.f.m.* '85 (FgM) New York, NY Franciscan Province of the Immaculate Conception.
Bonello, Pablo *i.v.e.* '84 (WDC) Mount Rainier, MD St. James.
Bonenge, Jean R. *c.m.* '96 (MET)[I] Princeton, NJ Vincentian Residence.
Bonetti, Henry *s.d.b.* '73 (FgM) New Rochelle, NY SALESIANS OF DON BOSCO.
Boney, Vincent *c.p.* '57 (SCR)[M] Scranton, PA Saint Ann's Passionist Monastery.
Bonfadini, Leo '74 (PBL) Absent on Leave.
Bonfiglio, Gregory R. *s.j.* '94 (SAC)[D] Sacramento, CA Jesuit High School; [I] Carmichael, CA Sacramento Jesuit Community.
Bongard, Joseph W. '86 (PH) Lafayette Hill, PA St. Philip Neri; [D] Philadelphia, PA Roman Catholic High School for Boys; Approved Advocates.
Bongila, Jean Pierre '91 (STP)[C] St. Paul, MN University of St. Thomas.
Bonifas, Roger D. '45 (TOL) Cloverdale, OH St. Barbara Retired.
Bonifazi, Remo J. *c.s.sp.* '45 (FgM) Bethel Park, PA CONGREGATION OF THE HOLY SPIRIT.
Bonikowski, Leon V. *o.s.f.s.* '65 (FgM)[Y] Philadelphia, PA Father Louis Brisson Residence; Wilmington, DE OBLATES OF ST. FRANCIS DE SALES MISSIONS.
Bonin, Harold A. '65 (CHI) Retired.
Bonjean, Jerry *s.d.b.* '67 (OAK)[E] Richmond, CA Salesian High School.
Bonk, Karl *s.j.* '82 (CLV)[D] Cleveland, OH St. Ignatius High School.
Bonk, Matthew S. *c.ss.r.* '04 (STL) St. Louis, MO St. Alphonsus Liguori; [O] St. Louis, MO Redemptorist Fathers.
Bonke, James R. '70 (IND) Indianapolis, IN SS. Peter and Paul Cathedral; Indianapolis, IN Christ The King; Defenders of the Bond; Promoter of Justice.
Bonnar, David J. '88 (PIT) Pittsburgh, PA St. Bernard.
Bonneau, Normand *o.m.i.* '76 (WDC)[N] Washington, DC Provincial Offices of the United States Province of the Missionary Oblates of Mary Immaculate; Washington, DC AMERICAN OBLATE MISSIONS.
Bonneau, Roger *o.carm.* '60 (JOL)[L] Darien Carmelite Provincial Office.
Bonnell, Rev. Msgr. Victor G. '60 (SLC) Layton, UT Saint Rose of Lima LLC 245; Ecumenical Commission.
Bonner, Charles E. '65 (PH) Philadelphia, PA St. Cecilia.
Bonner, Dismas *o.f.m.* '58 (STL)[S] Dittmer, MO Il Ritiro–The Little Retreat.
Bonner, Michael J. *s.v.d.* '66 (CHI) Wheeling, IL St. Joseph the Worker.
Bonner, Patrick J. *o.s.b.* '59 (PAT)[N] Newton St. Paul's Abbey.
Bonner, William J. '67 (LA) Los Angeles, CA St. Stephen of Hungary.
Bonneville, Lionel E. '63 (SPR) Northampton, MA Veterans Administration Hospital; DEPARTMENT OF VETERANS AFFAIRS HOSPITALS AND CHAPLAINS Retired.
Bonnici, John S. '91 (NY) Chester, NY St. Columba.
Bonnici, William C. '67 (DET) Retired.
Bonnot, Bernard R. '67 (Y) College of Consultors; Struthers, OH St. Nicholas; Priests Council.
Bono, James P. '03 (PAT) On Duty Outside the Diocese.
Bono, Jamie (NY)[X] Suffern, NY Good Samaritan Hospital of Suffern.
Bonoan, Tito '80 (OAK)[E] Hayward, CA Moreau Catholic High School.
Bonsignore, Dennis '81 (ROC) Monroe Community Hospital; Strong Health System; Rochester, NY St. Anne; Highland Hospital.
Bonsignore, Mark '95 (HRT)[H] Hartford, CT Saint Francis Hospital and Medical Center.
Bonsor, Jack '74 (SJ) Absent on Sick Leave.
Bonvouloir, Philip '54 (WOR) Fiskdale, MA St. Anne's and St. Patrick's.
Bonzagni, Rev. Msgr. John J. '80 (SPR) Presbyteral Council; Lenox Dale, MA St. Vincent de Paul's; Judicial Vicar; Diocesan Diaconate Council; Bishop's Commission for Clergy; Diocesan Consultors.
Book, Theodore '02 (ATL) Liturgical Commission; [B] Dawsonville, GA Southern Catholic College.
Booms, Andrew D. '07 (SAG) Port Austin, MI St. Michael.
Boone, Scott F. '01 (DUB)[O] Webster City, IA St. Thomas Aquinas Foundation; Webster City, IA St. Thomas Aquinas; Williams, IA St. Mary; Deanery Representatives.
Boor, Colin J. '50 (WCH) Retired.
Boosel, Brian D. *o.s.b.* '03 (GBG)[G] Latrobe, PA Saint Vincent Archabbey; [G] Latrobe Saint Vincent Archabbey.
Booth, Edward '74 (STA) St. Augustine, FL Cathedral – Basilica of St. Augustine.
Booth, Jim W. '07 (BIR) Birmingham, AL Our Lady of Sorrows.
Booth, John A. '82 (SY) Binghamton, NY St. Patrick.
Booth, John J. '82 (SY) Deposit, NY St. Joseph; Windsor, NY Our Lady of Lourdes; Binghamton Psychiatric Hospital; Binghamton, NY Binghamton Psychiatric Hospital; Binghamton, NY St. Thomas Aquinas.
Booth, Raymond '57 (ROC) Pittsford, NY St. Louis Retired.
Boquet, Gregory M. *o.s.b.* '88 (NO)[A] St. Benedict, LA St. Joseph Seminary College; [P] St. Benedict, LA St. Joseph Abbey.
Boquet, Shenan J. '93 (HT) Houma, LA St. Gregory Barbarigo; College of Consultors; Priests Council.
Boras, Kurt D. '86 (CHI) Chicago, IL St. Mary of the Woods.
Borawski, Gerald J. '72 (LFT) Monticello, IN Our Lady

of the Lakes; Associate Judges.
Borba, Joseph '97 (SB) On Sabbatical.
Borbon, Samuel '07 (FRS) Porterville, CA St. Anne.
Borbridge, David *s.j.* '63 (MOB)[A] Mobile, AL Spring Hill College.
Borca, Dennis L. '81 (MAR) Retired.
Borchardt, Edgar '96 (SPK) Colbert, WA St. Joseph.
Borcherding, Martin '73 (LAF) Lafayette, LA St. Elizabeth Seton.
Borcic, Rev. Msgr. John J. '76 (STL) St. Louis, MO St. Mary Magdalen; Council of Catholic Youth; Archdiocesan Office of the Permanent Diaconate; Office of Youth Ministry.
Borcz, Casimir Adalbert *o.c.d.* '45 (GRY)[H] Munster, IN Discalced Carmelite Fathers Monastery.
Bordeaux, Henry *o.c.d.* '62 (SAT)[L] San Antonio, TX Discalced Carmelite Fathers of San Antonio; San Antonio, TX Basilica of the National Shrine of the Little Flower, Our Lady of Mt. Carmel and St. Therese Parish.
Bordeleau, Beau–Pierre G. '85 (BRK) Released from Diocesan Assignment.
Bordelon, Kevin '05 (LAF) Rayne, LA St. Leo IV; Diocesan Consultors; Continuing Education of Priests.
Bordelon, Rev. Msgr. Roland '50 (ALX) Retired.
Bordenave, Ian G. *o.p.* (GAL) Houston, TX Holy Rosary.
Bordonaro, Joseph C. '89 (PH) Holland, PA St. Bede the Venerable.
Bordonaro, Richard D. '76 (BUF) Millard Fillmore Suburban Hospital.
Borek, Derek J. '99 (BO) Priests Pursuing Higher Studies.; [A] Brighton, MA St. John Seminary.
Borel, Albert '81 (LKC) Westlake, LA St. John Bosco; Judges.
Boren, Edward *o.f.m.* '64 (SAT) San Antonio, TX St. Timothy's; San Antonio, TX San Jose y San Miguel.
Borer, Robert D. '76 (STU) Cambridge, OH Christ Our Light Parish.
Boretto, Krzysztof '87 (SY) Binghamton, NY Saints John & Andrew; Binghamton, NY Our Lady of Lourdes Memorial Hospital.
Borg, Marcellinus *o.f.m.* '59 (ALB)[A] Catskill, NY St. Anthony Friary.
Borg, Ronald *c.s.b.* '79 (DET) Detroit, MI St. Bartholomew/St. Rita.
Borgelt, Daniel E. '93 (TOL) Napoleon, OH St. Augustine; Our Lady, Queen of Peace Deanery.
Borgen, Alfonso '98 (LA) Gardena, CA St. Anthony of Padua.
Borger, Marvin G. '91 (TOL) Ecclesiastical Notary; Perrysburg, OH St. Rose; Judges.
Borger, Theodore R. '83 (DAV) Retired.
Borgerding, Terry J. '77 (STL) St. Charles, MO St. Cletus.
Borgers, Charles *o.m.i.* '41 (SAT)[K] San Antonio, TX Oblate Madonna Residence.
Borges, Charles *s.j.* '81 (BAL)[B] Timonium, MD Loyola Graduate Center–Timonium Campus; [S] Baltimore, MD Jesuit Community of Loyola University, Inc.; [B] Jesuit Community of Loyola University, Inc.
Borges, Jose A. *s.j.* '69 (SJN)[H] San Juan, PR Comunidad Jesuita.
Borges, Laurence J. '59 (BO) Dorchester, MA St. Gregory.
Borges, Marcos Vinicius T. *c.ss.r.* '95 (NEW) Newark, NJ St. James.
Borges, Mario L. '82 (OAK) Castro Valley, CA Transfiguration.
Borges, Robert '04 (FRS) Clovis, CA Our Lady of Perpetual Help.
Borgesen, Ken *o.ss.t.* (BAL)[S] The Trinitarians in New Jersey.
Borgesen, Kenneth G. *o.ss.t.* '87 (TR) Trenton, NJ The Church of the Incarnation–St. James.
Borgia, Anthony A. '84 (TOL) Mansfield, OH St. Peter.
Borgmeyer, Dean '81 (WH) Weirton, WV St. Joseph the Worker.
Borho, Charles D. '57 (P) Retired.
Borino, David J. '86 (HRT) Retired.
Borja, Charlito A. '03 (CHK) Saipan, MP San Jude Parish; Presbyteral Council.
Bork, Vincent P. '95 (ARL) On Leave of Absence.
Borkenhagen, Jason W. '01 (WCH) Parsons, KS St. Patrick.
Borkowski, Francis '77 (NY) On Leave of Absence.
Borkowski, Mark '96 (DET) Detroit, MI St. Josaphat; Detroit, MI St. Joseph; Detroit, MI Sweetest Heart of Mary.
Borkowski, Raymond *o.f.m.conv.* '61 (FgM) Cromwell, CT St. John; Ellicott City, MD Franciscan Mission Association.
Borkowski, Thomas '81 (KC) On Duty Outside the Diocese; [O] Wheaton, IL Wheaton Franciscan Services, Inc.
Borkowski, Tomasz J. '01 (WOR) Clinton, MA Our Lady of the Rosary; Clinton, MA Our Lady of Jasna Gora.
Borkowski, Walter '85 (SAC) Sacramento, CA St. Peter; Sacramento, CA All Hallows.
Borlang, Stephen M. '86 (SAC) Vallejo, CA St. Vincent Ferrer; Presbyteral Council.
Borlik, Dan Paul *c.m.* '76 (DAL)[J] Dallas, TX Congregation of the Mission, Western Province.
Bormann, Charles P. '58 (PHX) Retired.
Bormann, Paul D. '85 (SC) Bancroft, IA St. John the Baptist's; Ledyard, IA Sacred Heart.
Bornhauser, Emmanuel '98 (NEW) On Duty Outside the Archdiocese.
Borno, Saint Charles '04 (BRK) Brooklyn, NY St. Teresa of Avila.
Borntrager, Conrad M. *o.s.m.* '60 (CHI) Chicago, IL Annunciata; [N] Chicago, IL Order of Friar Servants of Mary (Servites) United States of America Province, Inc.; [N] Chicago, IL Annunciata Priory; Chicago, IL.
Boroch, Andrzej '95 (SAG) Marlette, MI St. Elizabeth.
Borodach, Joseph '60 (PBR) Bradenville, PA St. Mary's; Protopresbyters.
Boroughs, Philip L. *s.j.* '78 (WDC)[C] Washington, DC Georgetown University; [N] Washington, DC The Jesuit Community at Georgetown University.
Borowczyk, Martin R. '42 (CHI) Retired.
Borowiak, David J. '71 (BUF) Cheektowaga, NY St. Philip the Apostle.
Borowiak, Kenneth A. '87 (LIN) Lincoln, NE St. Michael; Bishop Bruskewitz Charity and Stewardship Appeal (DDP); Office of Information and Media; Newspaper.
Borowski, Charles E.J. '66 (WOR) Southbridge, MA St. Hedwig.
Borowski, Paul *c.ss.r.* '87 (ALB) Saratoga Springs, NY St. Clement.
Borre, Robert J. '60 (MAD) Retired.
Borrelli, Rev. Msgr. Anthony A. '54 (COL) Retired.
Borrelli, Rev. Msgr. Anthony '54 (COL) Diocesan Judges.
Borrero, Victor R. *s.e.m.v.* '89 (ARE) Arecibo, PR Our Lady of Guadalupe.
Borro Barbosa, Cristiano G. '07 (MAN) Brazilian Apostolate.
Borruel, Alberto J. '06 (AUS) Round Rock, TX St. William; Associate Directors.
Borski, Charles J. *o.m.i.* '70 (GAL) Alvin, TX St. John the Baptist.
Borski, Rev. Msgr. Chester L. '67 (GAL) Kingwood, TX St. Martha; [S] Houston, TX Martha's Kitchen Food Services; Appointees; College of Consultors; Priests Personnel Committee.
Borski, Jerome *o.s.b.* '92 (PAT)[N] Morristown, NJ St. Mary's Abbey; [O] Convent Station, NJ St. Anne Villa.
Borstelmann, James E. '67 (NY) Kingston, NY St. Colman.
Borsuk, Ronald W. '58 (PBR) Retired.
Bortz, Thomas P. '04 (ALN) Allentown, PA Cathedral of St. Catharine of Siena; Bethlehem, PA St. Anne; Elected Members.
Boruszewski, Rev. Msgr. Joseph A. '53 (BUF) Retired.
Borzaga, Rinaldo '47 (BRK) Retired.
Borzaga, Rinaldo *a.f.s.c.* '47 (NY)[EE] Bronx, NY Brothers of the Christian Schools of Manhattan College, Inc.
Borzuchowski, John W. '68 (NY) Kingston, NY Immaculate Conception.
Borzych, Alexander J. '80 (MO) Military Chaplains; Navy Chaplains.
Bosack, Albert J. '43 (BUF)[O] Lackawanna, NY Bishop Head Residence Retired.
Bosch, Joseph J. '63 (P) Brookings, OR Star of the Sea.
Bosch, Stan *s.t.* '86 (LA) Los Angeles, CA St. Michael.
Bosch, William J. *s.j.* '60 (SY)[Q] Syracuse, NY Jesuits at LeMoyne, Inc.
Boschert, Bert *s.j.* (OM) Omaha, NE Christ the King.
Boschert, Hubert G. *s.j.* '68 (OM)[K] Omaha, NE Jesuit Community at Creighton University.
Boschert, Joseph N. '60 (COV) Retired.
Boschetto, Dan *s.x.* '70 (PAT)[N] Wayne Xaverian Missionary Fathers; Wayne, NJ XAVERIAN MISSIONARY FATHERS.
Boschi, Marcelo *f.d.p.* '95 (BO)[S] East Boston, MA Don Orione Nursing Home; [Z] Boston, MA Madonna Queen Shrine.
Bosco, John M. '71 (LAN) Morrice, MI St. Mary.
Bosco, Mark G. *s.j.* '99 (CHI)[C] Chicago, IL Jesuit Community at Loyola University Chicago.
Boscoe, John L. *c.s.b.* '72 (GAL)[O] Sugar Land, TX Basilian Mission Center.
Boscutti, Darrio L. '86 (CHI) Hickory Hills, IL St. Patricia; Western Springs, IL St. John of the Cross.
Bosken, Robert E. *s.j.* '56 (STL)[O] St. Louis, MO De Smet Jesuit High School Community.
Boslett, Donald E. '59 (ALT) Retired.
Bosnich, David A. '95 (PBR) Elected Deanery Representatives; Duquesne, PA SS. Peter and Paul.
Bosque, Peter J. '83 (SAC) Absent on Leave.
Bosque, Peter '83 (SB) Chino, CA St. Margaret Mary.
Bosse, Dennis *o.f.m.* '90 (CIN)[N] Cincinnati St. Francis Seraph Friary.
Bosse, Dennis *o.f.m.* '90 (IND)[B] Indianapolis, IN Marian University; Indianapolis, IN Sacred Heart of Jesus.
Bossi, Paul R. '69 (BUF) Buffalo, NY Blessed Sacrament.
Bossi, Stephen E. *c.s.p* '86 (WDC)[B] Washington, DC St. Paul's College.
Bossie, Robert W. *s.c.j.* '75 (CHI)[N] SCJ Novitiate.
Bossman, David M. *o.f.m.* '65 (NY)[EE] New York Franciscan Friars, Holy Name Province.
Bosso, Rev. Msgr. Stephen C. '78 (PT) On Duty Outside the Diocese.
Bosso, Rev. Msgr. Stephen '78 (PMB)[A] Boynton Beach, FL St. Vincent de Paul Regional Seminary.
Bostwick, John *o.praem.* '76 (GB)[B] St. Norbert College; [J] De Pere, WI St. Joseph Priory.
Bostwick, John '69 (RIC) Unassigned.
Boteju, Bernard '85 (TYL) Waskom, TX St. Lawrence Brindisi; Priests' Pension Board.
Boteler, William M. *m.m.* '68 (WDC)[B] Washington, DC Maryknoll Fathers and Brothers.
Boteler, William M. *m.m.* '68 (SJ)[M] Los Altos, CA Maryknoll.
Botello, Camillo *m.s.f.* '03 (BWN) Donna, TX St. Joseph.
Botenhagen, Paul *o.f.m.* '82 (LSC) Mescalero, NM St. Joseph; Presbyteral Council; Priestly Life and Ministry Committee.
Botheroyd, Thomas '00 (JOL) Lombard, IL Sacred Heart.
Botsko, Jerome G. '82 (PBR) Brownsville, PA St. Nicholas; Elected Deanery Representatives.
Botte, Gregory *o.f.m.* '68 (NY)[EE] New York Franciscan Province of the Immaculate Conception.
Botthof, Robert J. *o.p.* '87 (CHI)[N] Chicago Dominicans (Provincial Office); Chicago, IL; Hillside, IL St. Domitilla; [N] St. Pius V Priory.
Bottino, Rev. Msgr. Dominic J. '78 (CAM) Adjutant Judicial Vicars; Judges; Vineland, NJ Divine Mercy, Vineland, N.J.
Bottino, Rev. Msgr. Edward J. '52 (BRK) Flushing, NY Mary's Nativity Retired.
Botz, Roger *o.s.b.* '60 (SCL)[G] St. Cloud, MN St. Cloud Hospital; [I] Collegeville, MN St. John's Abbey, of the Order of St. Benedict.
Bou, Pedro L. *s.v.d.* '74 (TR) Red Bank, NJ St. Anthony.
Bouchaaya, Georges *m.l.m.* (SAM) Glen Allen, VA St. Anthony.
Bouchard, Charles E. *o.p.* '79 (STL)[O] St. Louis, MO Dominican Community of St. Louis; [O] St. Louis, MO Dominican Community of St. Louis.
Bouchard, Denis *f.s.s.p.* '00 (Y) Vienna, OH Queen of the Holy Rosary.
Bouchard, Lucien *o.m.i.* '55 (MIA) Miami, FL Christ the King.
Bouchard, Marcel H. '72 (FR) East Sandwich, MA Corpus Christi.
Bouchard, Norman '88 (PBL) Absent on Leave.
Bouchard, Rev. Msgr. Paul L. '72 (MAN) Merrimack, NH Our Lady of Mercy; Promoter of Justice; Defender of the Bond; Presbyteral Council.
Bouchard, Robert P. '84 (PRT) Special or Other Diocesan Assignment.
Bouchard, Thomas '53 (DUL) Retired.
Boucher, Edward F. '60 (SAG) Retired.
Boucher, Gerard A. '53 (MAN) Retired.
Boucher, Gilmond '58 (PMB) Riviera Beach, FL St. Francis of Assisi.
Boucher, Kevin '91 (FAR) Fargo, ND Nativity Church of Fargo.
Boucher, Peter P. '04 (MAN) Concord, NH Immaculate Heart of Mary.
Boucher, Richard R. *m.s.* '60 (HRT)[H] Hartford, CT Missionaries of LaSalette.
Boucher, Roger R. '73 (WOR) On Duty Outside the Diocese.
Boucree, Thaddeus *s.v.d.* '52 (BLX)[D] Bay St. Louis, MS St. Augustine's Residence.
Boudoin, Burt '82 (SD) Escondido, CA St. Mary.
Boudreau, C. Paul '83 (NOR) On Duty Outside the Diocese.
Boudreau, George R. *o.p.* '83 (STL)[B] St. Louis, MO Aquinas Institute of Theology.
Boudreau, George '83 (NO)[P] New Orleans Dominican Friars, Southern Dominican Province of St. Martin de Porres.
Boudreau, Paul B. '07 (MAN) Keene, NH St. Bernard; Presbyteral Council; Keene, NH Mary, Queen of Peace Parish; Keene, NH St. Margaret Mary; Keene, NH Immaculate Conception; College of Consultors.
Boudreau, Thomas C. '95 (BO) Quincy, MA St. Ann.
Boudreau, Thomas Francis '56 (LA) Retired.
Boudreaux, Claude P. *s.j.* '55 (NO)[P] New Orleans, LA Ignatius Residence Retired.
Boudreaux, John S. '73 (MOB) Mobile, AL Corpus Christi.
Boudreaux, Ronald J. *s.j.* '06 (FWT)[J] Lake Dallas, TX Montserrat Jesuit Retreat House.
Bouffard, Rev. Msgr. James F. '70 (NEW) Westfield, NJ St. Helen.
Bouffard, Lionel A. *m.m.* '63 (NY)[EE] Maryknoll Maryknoll Fathers and Brothers Retired.
Bouffier, Robert *s.m.* '74 (HON)[D] Honolulu, HI Chaminade Pohaku Marianist Community.
Boufford, Thomas F. '81 (GR) Ionia, MI SS. Peter and Paul.

Boughton, Michael *s.j.* '79 (BO)[U] Newton, MA The Jesuit Community at Boston College.
Bouhall, William G. '94 (CLV) Brooklyn, OH St. Thomas More; Presbyteral Conveners; Presbyteral Council.
Boulanger, Andre '65 (PHX) Retired.
Boulanger, Gerard J. *m.s.* '73 (LKC) Sulphur, LA Our Lady of Prompt Succor.
Boulet, Marshall '71 (LKC) Elton, LA St. Paul.
Boulette, Rev. Msgr. Michael '76 (SAT) College of Consultors; In Rural Area; Archdiocesan Presbyteral Council; Priests Personnel Board; [S] Ingram, TX St. Peter Upon the Water, A Center For Spiritual Direction and Formation.
Bouley, Allan *o.s.b.* '62 (SCL)[I] Collegeville, MN St. John's Abbey, of the Order of St. Benedict.
Boulin, Jean Wesner '04 (PMB) Vero Beach, FL St. Helen.
Boulos, Peter '93 (SAM) Protopresbyters (Deans); Tampa, FL Mission of Sts. Peter & Paul; Presbyteral Council; College of Consultors.
BouMerhi, Jibran '88 (OLL) St. Louis, MO St. Raymond Maronite Catholic Cathedral.
Bourcy, Robert Scott '82 (ROC) Mendon, NY St. Catherine of Siena.
Bourdon, Norman W. '73 (PRO) Cumberland, RI St. Joan of Arc; Deans.
Bourek, David F. '79 (LIN) Friend, NE St. Joseph's; Advocates; Rural Life Conference.
Bouressa, Donald J. '61 (PRO) Retired.
Bourg, Rodney P. '78 (NO) Covington, LA Most Holy Trinity.
Bourgault, Ronald L. '63 (BO) Senior Priests. Retired.
Bourgea, Roger *s.m.* '59 (BO)[U] Boston, MA Marist Fathers of Our Lady of Victories (Boston Prov.); Pastoral Care.
Bourgeois, Bernard W. '95 (BUR)[B] South Burlington, VT Rice Memorial High School; Winooski, VT St. Francis Xavier.
Bourgeois, Donald E. '85 (SY) "The Catholic Sun".
Bourgeois, Donald '85 (SY) Endicott, NY St. Ambrose.
Bourgeois, Francis L. '61 (LAF) Retired.
Bourgeois, Rev. Msgr. Lloyd '57 (SD) San Diego, CA San Rafael Retired.
Bourgeois, Louis D. '59 (BO) Hamilton, MA St. Paul.
Bourgeois, Roger *s.s.s.* '57 (CLV) Highland Heights, OH St. Paschal Baylon; [N] Cleveland, OH Congregation of the Blessed Sacrament.
Bourgeois, Roy L. *m.m.* '72 (NY)[EE].
Bourget, Laurence *o.c.s.o.* '42 (WOR)[O] Spencer, MA St. Joseph's Abbey.
Bourgoin, Raymond *o.m.i.* '66 (FgM) Washington, DC AMERICAN OBLATE MISSIONS.
Bourke, Charles E. '70 (BO) Winthrop, MA St. John the Evangelist.
Bourke, John F. '60 (CAM) Retired.
Bourke, Martin '74 (SEA) Burlington, WA St. Charles; La Conner, WA Sacred Heart; La Conner, WA St. Paul; Mount Vernon, WA Immaculate Conception; Sedro Woolley, WA Immaculate Heart of Mary; Mount Vernon, WA Skagit Valley Catholic Churches.
Bourke, Nathaniel J. '59 (GF) Retired.
Bourke, Ulick *s.m.a.* '68 (BO)[U] Dedham, MA African Mission House.
Bourque, Rev. Msgr. Charles J. '62 (BO) Canton, MA St. John the Evangelist; Senior Priests. Retired.
Bourque, Rev. Msgr. Joseph A. '55 (LKC) Retired.
Bourque, Thomas *t.o.r.* '82 (PIT)[M] Pittsburgh, PA Franciscan Friars, T.O.R.
Boursiquot, Gaetan (ORL) Orlando, FL St. Andrew.
Boursiquot, Jean Gaetan '81 (ORL) Haitian Ministry.
Bouska, Jerome Anthony '56 (LA) Los Angeles, CA St. Basil's Retired.
Bousquet, Roland '54 (FR) Retired.
Bouterie, Thomas '80 (HT) On Duty Outside the Diocese.
Boutin, Emile R. '91 (BO) Walpole, MA Blessed Sacrament.
Bouton, Thomas F. '83 (BO) Dorchester, MA St. Ambrose; Emergency Response Group.
Boutros, Peter '00 (NTN) Phoenix, AZ St. John of the Desert; Presbyteral Council; Ambassadors.
Bouzi, Quilin *o.m.i.* '07 (MIA) Miramar, FL St. Stephen.
Bouzigard, Michael A. *s.j.* '01 (NO)[C] New Orleans, LA Loyola University New Orleans.
Bova, Eugene R. '57 (BIS) Retired.
Bova Conti, Michael J. '71 (BO) Sudbury, MA Our Lady of Fatima.
Bovard, William R. '64 (PIT)[M] Pittsburgh, PA St. John Vianney Manor Retired.
Bove, Ralph A. '78 (SY) Norwich, NY Roman Catholic Community of Norwich, St. Paul & St. Bartholomew.
Bovee, Brian '81 (RCK) Rockford, IL St. Mary Oratory.
Bovenzi, Robert *c.p.* '85 (CHI)[M] Chicago, IL Resurrection Life Center.
Bovenzi, Robert *c.p.* '85 (GAL)[O] Houston, TX Congregation of the Passion, Holy Name Passionist Community and Retreat Center.
Bowden, John V. '62 (TR) Cursillo; [N] Trenton, NJ Villa Vianney Retired.
Bowden, Lloyd '49 (JOL) Retired.
Bowe, John F. '73 (PH) Warrington, PA St. Joseph.
Bowen, Gerard J. '77 (BAL) Elkridge, MD St. Augustine.
Bowen, John W. *s.s.* '49 (BAL)[O] Baltimore, MD St. Charles Villa; [S] Baltimore Society of St. Sulpice, Province of the United States Retired.
Bowen, Joseph D. '57 (PH) Retired.
Bowens, Lorin M. '74 (MAD) La Valle, WI Holy Family; Lime Ridge, WI St. Boniface; Lime Ridge, WI St. Patrick; Council of Catholic Women.
Bower, Alan '89 (STA) Gainesville, FL St. Patrick Church.
Bower, Lawrence C. '88 (BAK) Navy Reserve Chaplains Retired.
Bowering, Gerhard H. *s.j.* '70 (BGP)[O] Fairfield, CT The Fairfield Jesuit Community–Fairfield University.
Bowers, Mark R. '98 (TOL) Health Leave.
Bowers, Phillip T. '64 (LFT) Fishers, IN Holy Spirit Church.
Bowers, Ronald J. '64 (SFE) Associate Judges.
Bowers, Ronald J. '64 (SFE) Retired.
Bowker, Jeffrey *l.c.* '94 (SAC) Sacramento, CA Our Lady of Guadalupe Shrine.
Bowlds, Kent '93 (JKS) Office of Vocations; Madison, MS St. Francis of Assisi.
Bowler, James M. *s.j.* '74 (BGP)[B] Fairfield, CT Fairfield University; [O] Fairfield, CT The Fairfield Jesuit Community–Fairfield University.
Bowler, Joseph D. *o.s.f.s.* '49 (WIL)[J] Childs, MD Retirement and Assisted Care Facility Retired.
Bowler, Michael J. '57 (CHI) Retired.
Bowles, Rev. Msgr. Richard J. '61 (PT) Retired.
Bowles, William H. '91 (MIA) Fort Lauderdale, FL St. John the Baptist.
Bowling, Theodore B. *s.j.* '53 (FgM) Chicago, IL Society of Jesus.
Bowling, William M. '97 (L) Shelbyville, KY Annunciation of the Blessed Virgin Mary; Vocations.
Bowman, Eric A. '04 (CIN) Cincinnati, OH St. Jude the Apostle.
Bowman, John '65 (SEA) Seattle, WA St. Anne.
Bowman, R. Peter '55 (CHI) Retired.
Bowman, Ronald P. '82 (ALN) Reading, PA St. Catharine of Siena; Serra Club of Reading; Elected Members.
Bowski, Eugene '77 (GLP) Vanderwagen, NM St. Patrick.
Boxleitner, Rev. Msgr. J. Jerome '56 (STP) Retired.
Boyack, Kenneth G. *c.s.p.* '79 (WDC)[B] Washington, DC St. Paul's College; [W] Washington, DC Paulist National Catholic Evangelization Assoc.
Boyalla, Balaji *s.a.c.* '99 (FWT) Fort Worth, TX Holy Family.
Boyce, James *o.carm.* '77 (NEW) Commissary Provincials:; Tenafly, NJ Our Lady of Mount Carmel.
Boyd, C. Morris '78 (CHL) Asheville, NC Basilica of St. Lawrence.
Boyd, Douglas A. '79 (PIT) Braddock, PA Good Shepherd.
Boyd, Ian '63 (NEW)[B] School of Diplomacy and Intl. Rels.
Boyd, James A. '63 (BRK) On Leave/Unassigned.
Boyd, James '63 (SD) San Diego, CA Port of San Diego; Apostleship of the Sea.
Boyd, Norman *s.a.* '65 (NY)[EE] Garrison, NY Franciscan Friars of the Atonement.
Boyd, Norman *s.a.* '65 (BO)[N] Brockton, MA Chapel of Our Savior–Catholic Pastoral and Information Center; [U] Brockton, MA Chapel of Our Savior; [Z] Brockton, MA Chapel of Our Saviour.
Boyer, Mark G. '76 (SPC) Nixa, MO St. Francis of Assisi.
Boyer, Millard G. '75 (LAF) On Special Assignment.
Boyer, Thomas J. '68 (OKL) Norman, OK Church of St. Mark the Evangelist; Personnel Committee.
Boyer, Wayne M. '87 (JC) Jefferson City, MO St. Francis Xavier; Priestly and Religious Vocations Committee.
Boyhan, J. Patrick *m.s.a.* '77 (NOR)[G] Cromwell Society of the Missionaries of the Holy Apostles.
Boyhan, J. Patrick *m.s.a.* '77 (VEN) Fort Myers, FL Blessed Pope John XXIII.
Boykins, Charles *s.v.d.* '65 (CHI)[N] Techny, IL Divine Word Residence.
Boylan, Martin M. '80 (SCR) Canton, PA St. Michael; Towanda, PA SS. Peter and Paul.
Boyle, Daniel J. '78 (SPR) Adams, MA Pope John Paul the Great Parish.
Boyle, David (STL)[J] Bridgeton, MO SSM De Paul Health Center Foundation.
Boyle, Dennis P. '73 (PH) Philadelphia, PA St. Jerome.
Boyle, Rev. Msgr. Eugene '46 (SJ) Retired.
Boyle, Rev. Msgr. Francis V. '55 (NY) Staten Island, NY Blessed Sacrament; [EE] Bronx, NY John Cardinal O'Connor Residence Retired.
Boyle, George J. '52 (PH) Retired.
Boyle, Gregory *s.j.* '84 (LA) Los Angeles, CA Dolores Mission.
Boyle, James E. '66 (ROC) Penfield, NY St. Joseph Retired.
Boyle, James F. *c.s.c.* '57 (FR)[G] North Dartmouth, MA Holy Cross Residence Retired.
Boyle, James '61 (SEA) Retired.
Boyle, John B. '76 (SCR) Pocono Pines, PA St. Maximilian Kolbe, Pocono Pines.
Boyle, John T. '69 (CHI) Other Assignments.
Boyle, Michael J. *c.m.* '59 (PHX) Gilbert, AZ St. Anne Roman Catholic Parish.
Boyle, Michael '95 (RVC) Ronkonkoma, NY St. Joseph's.
Boyle, Neil *s.s.c.* '43 (FgM) St Columbans, NE House of Post–Graduate Studies.
Boyle, Rev. Msgr. Patrick J. '65 (NY) Rye, NY Resurrection; Central Westchester; Retirement Plan for Priests.
Boyle, Patrick J. *s.j.* '63 (CHI)[A] Mundelein, IL University of St. Mary of the Lake/Mundelein Seminary.
Boyle, Patrick M. *o.s.m.* '56 (CHI)[N] Chicago Order of Friar Servants of Mary (Servites) United States of America Province, Inc.
Boyle, Patrick *o.f.m.* '80 (NY)[EE] New York, NY Franciscan Province of the Immaculate Conception; New York, NY.
Boyle, Patrick *o.c.s.o.* '67 (SLC)[F] Huntsville, UT Abbey of Our Lady of the Holy Trinity of the Order of Cistercians.
Boyle, Rev. Msgr. Raymond J. '56 (PEO) Seneca, IL St. Patrick's; Vicariates and Vicars.
Boyle, Richard P. *s.j.* '75 (BO)[U] Boston The Society of Jesus of New England–Provincial Offices.
Boyle, Richard P. *s.j.* '75 (TUC)[D] Tucson, AZ Jesuit Community of the Vatican Observatory.
Boyle, Richard R. *o.s.m.* '84 (CHI)[N] Chicago Order of Friar Servants of Mary (Servites) United States of America Province, Inc.
Boyle, Richard *o.s.m.* '84 (OAK) Union City, CA St. Anne.
Boyle, Rev. Msgr. Robert J. '51 (BO) Senior Priests. Retired.
Boyle, Robert J. '63 (PIT) Finleyville, PA St. Isaac Jogues; Finleyville, PA St. Francis of Assisi.
Boyle, Robert (PIT) Allegheny County, PA Jefferson Regional Medical Center.
Boyle, Silvan *o.carm.* '48 (PHX)[F] Phoenix, AZ Carmelite Community Retired.
Boyle, Stephen M. '95 (BO) Newton, MA Corpus Christi – St. Bernard; Emmanuel College.
Boyle, Thomas '56 (PHX) Retired.
Boyle, Valentine *o.carm.* '46 (PHX) Phoenix, AZ; Diocesan Judges; [F] Phoenix, AZ St. Therese Priory.
Boyle, Victor J. '60 (BRK) Retired.
Boymer, Lloyd J. '43 (CLV) Macedonia, OH Our Lady of Guadalupe; Cleveland, OH Retired.
Bozada, Mark S. '81 (STL) Catawissa, MO St. James; Villa Ridge, MO St. Mary of Perpetual Help.
Bozek, Miroslaw *s.j.* '04 (CHI)[N] Chicago, IL Sacred Heart Mission House.
Bozek, Robert '78 (WDC) Absent On Leave; Bethesda, MD Our Lady of Lourdes.
Bozel, Rev. Msgr. Robert A. '48 (BAL) Retired.
Bozeman, Anthony M. '00 (PH) On Duty Outside the Archdiocese.
Bozeman, Anthony *s.s.j.* '00 (NO) Board of Directors:; New Orleans, LA St. Raymond–St. Leo the Great.
Boznar, Joseph P. '70 (CLV)[Y] Cleveland, OH St. Vitus Development Corporation; Cleveland, OH St. Vitus.
Bozung, James M. '61 (GR) Retired.
Bozza, Nicholas (PAT) Netcong, NJ St. Michael's; Charismatic Renewal.
Bozzelli, Joseph V. '67 (WIL) Chester, MD St. Christopher.
Bozzelli, Rev. Msgr. Richard J. '94 (BAL) Baltimore, MD Corpus Christi.
Bozzo, Kenneth '80 (FRS) Lindsay, CA Sacred Heart.
Braak, Thomas E. '59 (DUB) Retired.
Braaten, James B. '89 (BIS) Dickinson, ND St. Wenceslaus; Diocesan Corporate Board; Diocesan Finance Council.
Braathan, Scott *s.o.l.t.* '03 (CC)[G] Robstown, TX Society of Our Lady of the Most Holy Trinity.
Braband, James *s.v.d.* '80 (CHI)[N] Techny, IL Divine Word Residence; [W] Techny, IL Divine Word Techny Community Corporation; [N] Techny, IL Society of the Divine Word, Provincial Headquarters–Chicago Prov.
Brabandt, James Paul *o.f.m.* '95 (WDC)[N] Washington, DC Franciscan Monastery USA Inc.; Washington, DC COMMISSARIAT OF THE HOLY LAND; Washington, DC.
Bracamonte, Jose '93 (SCL) Multicultural Ministry; Pastoral Council.
Bracco, Theodore *o.f.m.* '66 (SFD)[L] Teutopolis, IL St. Francis Assisi Friary; Teutopolis, IL St. Francis of Assisi.
Bracke, James *c.s.c.* '80 (FTW)[B] University of Notre Dame Du Lac; [H] Notre Dame, IN Holy Cross Community, Corby Hall, University of Notre Dame.
Bracken, Jerome *c.p.* '68 (BRK)[T] Jamaica, NY Immaculate Conception Monastery.
Bracken, Joseph A. *s.j.* '62 (CIN)[N] Cincinnati, OH Jesuit Community at Xavier University.

Bracken, W. Jerome *c.p.* '68 (NEW)[A] South Orange, NJ Immaculate Conception Seminary; [B] School of Diplomacy and Intl. Rels.
Bracken, Walter *s.v.d.* '71 (BLX)[D] Bay St. Louis, MS St. Augustine's Residence.
Bracket, Louis P. '47 (MAR) Retired.
Brackett, Christopher *l.c.* '93 (HRT)[B] Cheshire, CT Novitiate of the Legion of Christ; Thornwood, NY.
Brackin, James D. *s.c.j.* '75 (MIL)[P] Franklin, WI Villa Maria; [P] Hales Corners, WI Priests of the Sacred Heart.
Brackley, J. Dean *s.j.* '76 (FgM) New York, NY Society of Jesus.
Bradbury, Henry M. *c.m.* '59 (BRK)[T] Jamaica, NY Vincentian Residence.
Braddock, Stephen '98 (MIL)[P] Milwaukee, WI St. Camillus Provincialate.
Braden, Michael *s.j.* '79 (NEW)[B] Jersey City, NJ Jesuit Center; [M] Jersey City, NJ Jesuits of Saint Peter's College, Inc.
Braden, Patrick O. *c.s.b.* '52 (GAL)[O] Houston, TX Residence of the Basilian Fathers of the University of St. Thomas.
Bradford, Richard S. '98 (BO) Boston, MA Congregation of Saint Athanasius.
Bradler, Robert C. '62 (ROC)[N] Rochester, NY Holy Childhood Association; The Society for the Propagation of the Faith Retired.
Bradley, Alfred *c.ss.r.* '88 (NY)[EE] New York, NY Redemptorist Priests and Brothers, C.Ss.R.
Bradley, Bruce '78 (DAL) At Large Members; Van Alstyne, TX Holy Family; McKinney, TX St. Michael; Accreditation Board.
Bradley, Dennis J. '77 (PIT)[M] Pittsburgh, PA St. John Vianney Manor.
Bradley, Ed '75 (OWN) Board Members.
Bradley, Edward C. *s.j.* '79 (PH)[Y] Loyola Center and Manresa Hall.
Bradley, Rev. Msgr. Edward G. '66 (NEW)[C] West Orange, NJ Seton Hall Preparatory School; Ex Officio Members; Ministry to Retired Priests; Members.
Bradley, Hugh J. '89 (CAM) Blue Anchor, NJ Parish of Blessed John the Twenty–Third, Blue Anchor, N.J.
Bradley, J. Edward '75 (OWN) Henderson, KY Holy Name of Jesus.
Bradley, J. Richard '81 (TLS) Owasso, OK St. Henry; Diocesan Senators.
Bradley, James F. *o.s.f.s.* '61 (TOL)[I] Toledo, OH Retired.
Bradley, James P. '73 (BRK)[M] Brooklyn, NY Advocate for Persons with Disabilities Services.
Bradley, James P. *s.j.* '58 (NO)[P] New Orleans, LA Ignatius Residence; [P] New Orleans, LA Loyola Jesuit Community.
Bradley, James P. *s.j.* '58 (WDC)[E] North Bethesda, MD Georgetown Preparatory School.
Bradley, James *s.d.s.* '61 (LA) Whittier, CA St. Bruno.
Bradley, John A. '65 (ORG) Retired.
Bradley, John J. '67 (ALB) Albany, NY Blessed Sacrament.
Bradley, John J. '63 (PH) Philadelphia, PA Sacred Heart of Jesus Retired.
Bradley, John '67 (ALB) Deans.
Bradley, Joseph A. '91 (SFR) San Mateo, CA St. Gregory Retired.
Bradley, Matthew '72 (BO)[W] Scituate, MA Foyer of Charity; Foyer of Charity.
Bradley, Michael J. '78 (CHI) Chicago, IL St. Gertrude.
Bradley, Michael '91 (TUC) Leave of Absence.
Bradley, Michael '78 (CHI) Judges.
Bradley, Michael *o.m.i.* '66 (FgM) Washington, DC AMERICAN OBLATE MISSIONS.
Bradley, Michael (SAG) Promoter of Justice.
Bradley, Robert M. '57 (LA) Retired.
Bradley, Robert '73 (CC)[K] San Antonio, TX Padua Place Retired.
Bradley, Valentine J. '06 (ALT) Bellefonte, PA St. John the Evangelist's; Spring Mills, PA Blessed Kateri Tekakwitha; Bellefonte, PA State Correctional Institution – Rockview Our Lady of the Mount.
Bradley, Rev. Msgr. William J. '57 (NY) New Rochelle, NY Blessed Sacrament.
Bradlo, Antoni *c.ss.r.* (CHI) Chicago, IL St. Adalbert.
Bradshaw, Alexander H. '85 (ROC) Rochester, NY Our Mother of Sorrows.
Bradshaw, Benjamin P. '06 (MEM) Memphis, TN St. Paul The Apostle.
Bradshaw, Jordan *o.p.* '92 (SEA)[O] Seattle, WA University of Washington, Catholic Newman Center; Seattle, WA Blessed Sacrament.
Bradshaw, Paul F. '70 (FTW)[B] University of Notre Dame Du Lac.
Bradshaw, Terry L. '80 (L) Louisville, KY St. Athanasius; College of Consultors; Ex Officio.
Bradtke, Thomas '62 (DEN) Retired.
Brady, Charles '55 (SAC) Sacramento, CA Holy Spirit Retired.
Brady, Daniel J. '61 (CHI) Arlington Heights, IL Our Lady of the Wayside Retired.
Brady, Daniel O. '84 (RIC) Glen Allen, VA St. Michael.
Brady, Edmund P. '59 (BRK) Long Island City, NY Our Lady of Mount Carmel Retired.
Brady, Edward E. '90 (PH) Quakertown, PA St. Isidore.
Brady, Gerald '83 (SPR) Diocesan Charismatic Renewal; The Catholic Charismatic Renewal of Springfield, Inc. Retired.
Brady, Rev. Msgr. Gerard J. '59 (SR) Napa, CA St. Thomas Aquinas; Parish Priest Consultors.
Brady, James J. '57 (ALN)[J] Bethlehem, PA Holy Family Villa Retired.
Brady, James J. '72 (TR) Brick Town, NJ St. Dominic.
Brady, James J. '53 (MIL) Retired.
Brady, James *s.o.l.t.* '89 (CC)[G] Robstown, TX Society of Our Lady of the Most Holy Trinity.
Brady, James '06 (LAF) Diocesan Consultors.
Brady, James *s.m.m.* '92 (HRT)[L] Litchfield, CT Montfort Missionaries; [U] Litchfield, CT Lourdes Shrine Guild, Inc.
Brady, Jeremiah A. *s.s.j.* '51 (MOB) Mobile, AL St. Joseph.
Brady, John A. *s.j.* '49 (LA)[F] Los Angeles, CA Loyola High School of Los Angeles.
Brady, Rev. Msgr. John B. '55 (WDC) Archdiocesan Chaplain Coordinator/Catholic Committee on Boy Scouts, Girl Scouts & Camp fire Retired.
Brady, John '55 (SFS) Retired.
Brady, Jude W. *o.s.b.* '80 (ALT) Carrolltown, PA St. Benedict's.
Brady, Justin '05 (B) Knights of Columbus; Burley, ID St. Theresa; Rupert, ID St. Nicholas; Priest Personnel Commission.
Brady, Michael '01 (STO) Manteca, CA St. Anthony Church of Manteca (Pastor of).
Brady, Rev. Msgr. Patrick A. '61 (WIL) Retired.
Brady, Patrick J. '64 (CAM) Pleasantville, NJ St. Peter's Catholic Church, Pleasantville, N.J.; Northfield, NJ The Church of St. Bernadette, Northfield, N.J.
Brady, Patrick J. '93 (PH)[A] Wynnewood, PA Theological Seminary of St. Charles Borromeo, Overbrook.
Brady, Philip W. '43 (BGP) Retired.
Brady, Reginald '93 (DET) Absent on Leave.
Brady, Richard J. '59 (BO) Senior Priests. Retired.
Brady, Rev. Msgr. Roger J. '58 (BO) Senior Priests. Retired.
Brady, Theodore E.A. *s.j.* '61 (BAL)[M] Baltimore, MD Mercy Health Services Inc.; [S] Baltimore, MD Ferdinand Wheeler Jesuit Community.
Brady, Rev. Msgr. Thomas C. '54 (RCK) Vicars General; Diocesan Consultors; Cemeteries Retired.
Brady, Rev. Msgr. Thomas F. '59 (BRK) Brooklyn, NY Good Shepherd Retired.
Brady, Timothy *o.de.m* '03 (BUF)[O] LeRoy, NY Order of the BVM of Mercy/Mercedarian Friars; LeRoy, NY Our Lady of Mercy; [O] LeRoy, NY St. Raymond Nonnatus Novitiate.
Brady, Vincent M. '95 (PSC) Orlando, FL Holy Dormition.
Brady, William J. '80 (SFR) San Francisco, CA St. Emydius.
Braeser, Donald *o.f.m.* '70 (SFD) Quincy, IL St. Francis Solanus.
Braganca, Socorro *o.c.d.* '03 (NY) New York, NY Our Lady of Victory.
Braganza, Joseph '83 (NY) New York, NY St. Agnes.
Brahill, John *o.s.b.* '82 (RCK)[G] Aurora, IL Marmion Abbey.
Brahm, Harvey '51 (MIL) Retired.
Braida, Ernest E. '64 (DAV) Retired.
Brailsford, William M. '04 (WDC) Hospital & Nursing Home Ministries; Washington, DC St. Ann.
Brainard, Ernest B. '45 (OAK) Retired.
Brainerd, Winthrop J. '87 (WDC)[M] Washington, DC Cardinal O'Boyle Residence for Priests Retired.
Brajkovich, Thomas R. '61 (PEO) Retired.
Braley, James E. '75 (BO) Plymouth, MA Blessed Kateri Tekakwitha.
Brambilla, Charles A. '71 (STP) Blaine, MN St. Timothy's.
Brambilla, Sigmund *o.f.m.* '55 (NY)[EE] New York Franciscan Province of the Immaculate Conception.
Bramble, Donald *o.p.* '76 (LAV)[C] Las Vegas, NV Dominican Rectory, Fra Angelico House.
Bramlage, Gregory D. '96 (IND) Sunman, IN St. Charles Borromeo; Sunman, IN St. Nicholas; Sunman, IN St. Pius.
Bramlage, James A. '64 (CIN) Cincinnati, OH St. Peter in Chains Cathedral; Judges.
Bramwell, Bevil *o.m.i.* '85 (WDC)[N] Washington, DC Oblate Community.
Bramwell, Bevil *o.m.i.* (ARL)[C] Hamilton, VA The Catholic Distance University.
Bran–Flores, Marco *s.j.* '04 (CHI)[C] Chicago, IL Jesuit Community at Loyola University Chicago.
Branch, Edward B. '74 (ATL)[J] Atlanta, GA Atlanta University Complex–The Catholic Center; Special or Other (Arch)Diocesan Assignment; Council of Priests.
Branch, Edward B. '74 (L) On Duty Outside the Archdiocese; Consultants.
Brancich, John A. *f.s.s.p.* '04 (OM) Omaha, NE Immaculate Conception, B.V.M.
Brand, Fred '67 (SFE) Retired.
Brand, William *o.f.m.* '74 (OAK)[M] Oakland, CA Franciscan Friars (Province of Santa Barbara).
Brandenberger, Robert J. *c.m.* '52 (PH)[Y].
Brandenhoff, Peter B. '70 (WIN) On Duty Outside the Diocese.
Brandes, John F. '51 (STP) Minneapolis, MN St. Boniface Retired.
Brandl, Mark J. '09 (MIL) Greendale, WI St. Alphonsus.
Brando, Joseph J. '72 (KNX) Retired.
Brandow, Stephen J. '96 (MO) Diocesan, Region 5 & Louisiana Purchase Council Chaplain; Pineville, LA Central Louisiana State Hospital; Pineville, LA Veterans Administration Medical Center; DEPARTMENT OF VETERANS AFFAIRS HOSPITALS AND CHAPLAINS.
Brandstrup, Christian '79 (STA) Absent or Sick Leave.
Brandt, Daniel J. '99 (CHI) Chicago, IL Nativity of Our Lord.
Brandt, Joseph D. '83 (PH) Philadelphia, PA St. Anne.
Brandt, Paul C. '84 (PH) Limerick, PA Blessed Teresa of Calcutta.
Brandt, Timothy '09 (GB) Green Bay, WI Annunciation of the Blessed Virgin Mary; Green Bay, WI St. Joseph; Green Bay, WI St. Jude; Green Bay, WI St. Patrick.
Brankatelli, Joseph R. '08 (CLV) Parma, OH Holy Family.
Brankin, Anthony J. '75 (CHI) Berwyn, IL St. Odilo.
Brankin, Patrick M. '79 (CHI) On Duty Outside the Archdiocese.
Brankin, Rev. Msgr. Patrick M. '79 (TLS) Special Assignment; Office of Divine Worship; Office of Permanent Diaconate.
Brannan, Patrick P. *s.j.* '63 (PH)[Y] Loyola Center and Manresa Hall.
Brannen, Brett A. '91 (SAV) On Duty Outside the Diocese.
Brannen, Brett A. '91 (BAL)[A] Emmitsburg, MD Mount St. Mary's Seminary; [A] Emmitsburg, MD Mount St. Mary's Seminary.
Brannigan, John *s.s.c.* '67 (LA) Los Angeles, CA St. Columban.
Brannigan, John *s.s.c.* '67 (OM)[K] St. Columbans Missionary Society of St. Columban.
Branon, Philip J. '51 (BUR) Retired.
Bransfield, Christopher '98 (SJ) San Jose, CA St. Martin of Tours; Building Committee.
Bransfield, J. Brian '94 (PH) Censores Librorum; Assistant General Secretary; Staff; Staff; On Duty Outside the Archdiocese; Staff; Staff Coordinator; Staff Coordinator; Staff Coordinator.
Bransfield, Sean P. '02 (PH)[A] Wynnewood, PA Theological Seminary of St. Charles Borromeo, Overbrook; On Special or Other Archdiocesan Assignment; Assistant Judicial Vicars.
Branson, Bernard E. '59 (KC) Independence, MO St. Ann's.
Branson, Dale A. '97 (TUC) Hayden, AZ Saint Joseph Roman Catholic Parish – Hayden; Diocesan Consultors; Council of Priests; Vicars Forane; All Vicars Forane.
Branson, Keith *c.pp.s.* '00 (JC) Warsaw, MO St. Ann.
Brant, David A. '65 (SEA) Seattle, WA St. James Cathedral Retired.
Brant, Paul W. *s.j.* '77 (R)[F] Raleigh Jesuit Community; Windsor, NC Catholic Community of Bertie & Washington Counties; Goldsboro, NC St. Mary.
Brantman, Thomas E. '75 (RCK) Somonauk, IL St. John the Baptist.
Braquet, David J. '94 (ALX) On Duty Outside the Diocese.
Brasher, C. John '75 (SFE) Las Vegas, NM Our Lady of Sorrows Church.
Brassard, Leo *a.a.* '69 (BO)[U] Boston Assumptionist Center.
Brassard, Ronald E. '74 (PRO) Cranston, RI Immaculate Conception.
Brassil, Rev. Msgr. James A. '62 (RVC) North Merrick, NY Sacred Heart Retired.
Brassil, Kevin J. '58 (PRO) Retired.
Bratek, Martin *c.r.* '72 (CHI)[D] Chicago, IL Gordon Tech High School.
Brath, John A. '68 (SPC) Retired.
Bratkowski, Allen J. '89 (MIL) Racine, WI St. Edward.
Bratus, Walter N. '56 (GBG) Retired.
Braudis, Joseph M. '77 (ALN)[J] Bethlehem, PA Holy Family Villa Retired.
Brauer, Frank J. '86 (BAL) Hunt Valley, MD Catholic Community of St. Francis Xavier.
Brauer, Mark S. '92 (DET) Farmington, MI Our Lady of Sorrows.
Braukman, Donald '86 (CR) Warroad, MN St. Mary's.
Brault, Bernard *s.m.m.* '68 (HRT)[L] Litchfield, CT Montfort Missionaries.
Brault, Gilles '76 (STA) Absent or Sick Leave.
Brault, Laurence V. '77 (WOR) Upton, MA Holy Angels.
Brault, Y. David '77 (WDC) Clinton, MD St. Mary.
Braun, Brian *o.f.m.cap.* '60 (MIL)[P] Milwaukee, WI St. Conrad Friary.

Braun, Rev. Msgr. Francis '54 (BUF) Buffalo, NY St. Mark.
Braun, Gary G. '77 (STL)[T] St. Louis, MO Washington University Newman Centers.
Braun, Gerald E. *s.j.* '46 (NY)[EE] New York, NY Murray–Weigel Hall.
Braun, H. Gerard '85 (FAR) Grand Forks, ND St. Michael's Church of Grand Forks.
Braun, John J. *m.afr.* '57 (SP)[N] St. Petersburg, FL Missionaries of Africa.
Braun, John S. '87 (SPC) Webb City, MO Sacred Heart.
Braun, Rev. Msgr. Michael '67 (FRS) Bakersfield, CA Our Lady of Perpetual Help; Defenders of the Bond; Finance Committee; Deposit and Loan Fund; [A] Bakersfield, CA Garces Memorial High School.
Braun, Virgil R. '60 (SCL) Eden Valley, MN The Church of the Assumption; Directors.
Braunreuther, Robert J. *s.j.* '65 (BO)[U] Boston The Society of Jesus of New England–Provincial Offices.
Braunreuther, Robert J. *s.j.* '65 (CHI)[C] Chicago, IL Jesuit Community at Loyola University Chicago.
Brausch, Anthony M. '02 (CIN)[B] Cincinnati, OH Mt. St. Mary's Seminary of the West.
Bravata, Kevin W. '00 (MEM) Memphis, TN Blessed Sacrament.
Bravo, Flavio *s.j.* '05 (GAL)[E] Houston, TX Strake Jesuit College Preparatory Inc.
Bravo, Jorge *c.s.* '04 (DAL) Irving, TX St. Luke.
Bravo, Joseph '77 (SFR) Retired.
Brawner, Frank '05 (LEX) Berea, KY St. Clare; [L] Berea, KY St. Clare Church–Berea College.
Bray, Kevin '67 (FRS) Absent on Sick Leave.
Brazaskas, Robert '66 (TUC) Council of Priests; Vicars Forane; All Vicars Forane; Sierra Vista, AZ Our Lady of the Mountains Roman Catholic Parish – Sierra Vista.
Breaker, Donald J. '64 (CIN) On Special and Archdiocesan Assignment.
Breaker, Donald J. '64 (JC) Retired.
Bream, James I. '64 (SFS) Retired.
Breault, Charles *o.m.i.* '59 (BO)[U] Lowell, MA St. Eugene House (Residence).
Breault, William F. *s.j.* '62 (SAC)[I] Carmichael, CA Sacramento Jesuit Community; Archives.
Breaux, John G. '04 (LAF) Loreauville, LA St. Joseph; Diocesan Consultors.
Breaux, Louis Allen '81 (LAF) Scott, LA Sts. Peter and Paul.
Breaux, O. Joseph '68 (LAF) Maurice, LA St. Alphonsus.
Breaux, Overton Joseph '68 (LAF) Defenders of the Bond.
Brecht, David L. *o.s.a.* '65 (DET)[E] Macomb, MI Austin Catholic Academy.
Breck, Steven H. '00 (CLV) Bay Village, OH St. Raphael.
Breckensiek, Marne *o.f.m.* '65 (CIN)[N] Cincinnati St. Francis Seraph Friary Retired.
Breczinski, Paul '98 (BAL) Bradshaw, MD St. Stephen.
Bredeck, Martin J. *s.j.* '64 (KC)[J] Kansas City, MO Rockhurst Jesuit Community.
Bredemeyer, Ryan '07 (PEO)[B] Peoria, IL Peoria Notre Dame High School; Peoria, IL St. Jude's.
Breen, Bernard J. '72 (L) Louisville, KY St. Frances of Rome; Louisville, KY St. Leonard.
Breen, Brendan *c.p.* '50 (MET)[I] South River Passionist Provincial Office Retired.
Breen, Brendan *c.p.* '50 (SCR)[M] Scranton, PA Saint Ann's Passionist Monastery.
Breen, Damian B. *o.s.b.* '98 (PAT)[N] Morristown St. Mary's Abbey.
Breen, Damian '98 (MET) East Brunswick, NJ St. Bartholomew.
Breen, Rev. Msgr. Edward J. '58 (BRK) Jackson Heights, NY Our Lady of Fatima Retired.
Breen, Francis J. *m.m.* '70 (NY)[EE] Maryknoll Maryknoll Fathers and Brothers.
Breen, Gregory '04 (RVC) Garden City, NY St. Joseph's.
Breen, James E. '80 (BGP)[O] Stamford, CT The Catherine Dennis Keefe Queen of the Clergy Retired Priests' Residence Retired.
Breen, James J. '80 (BGP) Retired.
Breen, Joseph P. '61 (NSH) Nashville, TN St. Edward.
Breen, Philip M. '65 (NSH) Nashville, TN St. Ann; [L] Nashville, TN Ladies of Charity Welfare Agency, Inc.; Vicar for Catholic Charities; Clergy Personnel Board.
Breen, Phillip '65 (NSH) Deans; Presbyteral Council; Priest Benefit Foundation.
Breen, Robert H. '57 (PH) Retired.
Breidenbach, John '87 (EVN) Absent on Medical Leave.
Breier, Donald P. '69 (PIT) Pittsburgh, PA St. Paul Cathedral; St. Paul Cathedral.
Breier, Rev. Msgr. Henry J. '94 (STL) St. Louis, MO St. Raphael The Archangel.
Breig, Gary R. '78 (STL) Military Chaplains; Air Force Chaplains.
Breighner, Joseph F. '71 (BAL) Baltimore, MD Cathedral of Mary Our Queen; Special Assignment.
Breindel, Charles L. (RIC) Danville, VA Sacred Heart; Diocesan Pastoral Planning Commission.
Breit, Melvin P. '62 (MIL) Retired.
Breitbach, Richard C. '61 (MIL) Retired.
Brelsford, William J. '70 (LA) Los Angeles, CA Visitation.
Brembah, Philip (FWT) Fort Worth, TX St. Mary of the Assumption.
Brembor, Janusz '90 (PH) Philadelphia, PA St. John Cantius.
Brembos, Rev. Msgr. George M. '56 (MET) Woodbridge, NJ St. James Retired.
Bremer, Al '02 (OWN) Sebree, KY St. Michael.
Brenberger, Thomas *c.pp.s.* '66 (CIN) Celina, OH Immaculate Conception of the Blessed Virgin Mary; Rockford, OH St. Teresa; [T] Dayton, OH Community Support Charitable Trust.
Brenes–Chaves, Fabio De Jesus '85 (NEW) Elizabeth, NJ Immaculate Heart of Mary and Saint Patrick.
Breneville, Garcia (BO) Cambridge, MA St. John the Evangelist; Brockton, MA Christ the King.
Brenk, Frederick E. *s.j.* '63 (MIL)[P] Milwaukee Jesuit Provincial Office, Wisconsin Province.
Brenkle, Rev. Msgr. John J. '58 (SR) St. Helena, CA St. Helena; Promoter of Justice; Diocesan Judges; Finance Committee; Review Board.
Brenkus, Pavol '01 (ATL) Duluth, GA St. Monica.
Brenna, William D. '09 (SUP) Hudson, WI St. Patrick.
Brennan, Anthony V. *m.m.* '61 (FgM) Maryknoll, NY MARYKNOLL.
Brennan, Bernard F. '62 (SFR) Retired.
Brennan, Brian C. '79 (NY) Mahopac, NY St. John the Evangelist.
Brennan, Cathal '52 (P) Retired.
Brennan, Rev. Msgr. Dermot R. '56 (NY)[EE] Bronx, NY John Cardinal O'Connor Residence; Yorktown Heights, NY St. Patrick Retired.
Brennan, Donald *o.s.a.* '53 (TLS)[B] Tulsa, OK Cascia Hall Preparatory School.
Brennan, Edmund J. '82 (ALN) Unassigned.
Brennan, Eugene P. '70 (STL) Lambert – St. Louis International Airport; Florissant, MO St. Sabina Retired.
Brennan, Francis C. *s.j.* '58 (STL)[O] St. Louis, MO Jesuit Community Corporation at Saint Louis University – Jesuit Hall.
Brennan, George P. '68 (MO) DEPARTMENT OF VETERANS AFFAIRS HOSPITALS AND CHAPLAINS Retired.
Brennan, George '87 (VEN) Retired.
Brennan, George '75 (ALB) Special Assignment; Catholic Charities Agencies and Commissions; Ecumenical and Interreligious Affairs of the Roman Catholic Diocese of Albany, Commission for; Watervliet, NY Immaculate Heart of Mary.
Brennan, Gerard M. '50 (BO) Senior Priests. Retired.
Brennan, James F. '55 (BO) Senior Priests. Retired.
Brennan, Rev. Msgr. John A. '56 (TYL) Gun Barrel City, TX St. Jude.
Brennan, John D. '70 (PIT) East McKeesport, PA St. Robert Bellarmine.
Brennan, John J. '78 (SPR) Agawam, MA St. John the Evangelist.
Brennan, John P. *s.m.a.* '64 (LA)[A] Camarillo, CA St. John's Seminary.
Brennan, John W. *o.s.f.s.* '65 (WIL)[J] Childs, MD Retirement and Assisted Care Facility Retired.
Brennan, Joseph (Dennis) *o.s.b.* '74 (LA)[P] Valyermo, CA St. Andrew's Abbey.
Brennan, Joseph F. *s.j.* '56 (BO)[U] Weston, MA Campion Health Center, Inc.
Brennan, Joseph F. '59 (LAF) Retired.
Brennan, Joseph T. *s.j.* '69 (CHI)[D] Chicago, IL St. Ignatius College Prep; [D] Chicago, IL St. Ignatius Jesuit Community.
Brennan, Joseph T. *o.s.f.s.* '98 (R) Durham, NC Holy Infant.
Brennan, Joseph *o.s.c.* '45 (SCL)[I] Onamia, MN Crosier Priory.
Brennan, Rev. Msgr. Joseph '80 (LA) San Pedro, CA Holy Trinity; San Pedro Region.
Brennan, Rev. Msgr. Keith R. '84 (PMB)[A] Boynton Beach, FL St. Vincent de Paul Regional Seminary; Special Assignment.
Brennan, Keith *s.d.s.* '70 (MIL)[P] Milwaukee Salvatorian Provincial Offices Retired.
Brennan, Lawrence C. '76 (STL)[A] St. Louis, MO Kenrick School of Theology.
Brennan, Rev. Msgr. Mark E. '76 (WDC) Gaithersburg, MD St. Martin of Tours; Advocates; Priest Council.
Brennan, Matthew '62 (BIR) Retired.
Brennan, Rev. Msgr. Michael J. '71 (BRK) Jackson Heights, NY Our Lady of Fatima.
Brennan, Michael *c.p.* '53 (BRK)[T] Jamaica, NY Immaculate Conception Monastery.
Brennan, P. Paul '59 (ROC) Willard, NY Drug Treatment Center; Romulus, NY Five Points Correctional Facility.
Brennan, Patrick A. *o.s.a.* '63 (SB) Upland, CA St. Anthony; Fontana, CA Blessed John XXIII Catholic Community, Inc.
Brennan, Patrick *c.p.* '73 (LA)[P] Sierra Madre, CA Passionist Residence; [V] Sierra Madre, CA Mater Dolorosa Passionist Retreat Center, Inc.
Brennan, Patrick '77 (P) Portland, OR St. Rita; Vicar for Clergy; Clergy; College of Consultors; Ex Officio; Judicial Vicar; Judges; Clergy Personnel; Board Members.
Brennan, Paul P. '59 (ROC) Retired.
Brennan, Pierce A. *s.j.* '76 (NY)[F] New York, NY Xavier High School; [EE] New York, NY Xavier Jesuit Community; [EE] Loyola Hall, Jesuit Community.
Brennan, Pierce A. *s.j.* '76 (RVC) Oceanside, NY St. Anthony.
Brennan, Rev. Msgr. Ralph '57 (AUS) Retired.
Brennan, Rev. Msgr. Robert J. '89 (RVC) Rockville Centre, NY St. Agnes Cathedral; Vicar General and Moderator of the Curia; Senate of Priests (Presbyteral Council/College of Consultors); Priests' Personnel Assignment Board; Vicar General.
Brennan, Robert M. '65 (NEW)[M] Rutherford, NJ St. John Vianney Residence for Priests Retired.
Brennan, Robert '49 (NY)[B] Beacon, NY St. Lawrence of Brindisi Friary Retired.
Brennan, Robert *c.s.c.* '68 (ORL) Cocoa Beach, FL Church of Our Saviour; [F] Cocoa Beach, FL Congregation of Holy Cross, Eastern Province.
Brennan, Ronan P. '50 (SAC) Sutter Creek, CA Immaculate Conception; Coordinator for Retired Priests Retired.
Brennan, Rev. Msgr. Seamus F. '72 (MET) Somerville, NJ Immaculate Conception; College of Consultors; Deans.
Brennan, Terrence M. *s.j.* '76 (MIL)[P] Milwaukee, WI Pere Marquette Jesuit Community; [E] Milwaukee, WI Marquette University High School.
Brennan, Terrence P. '99 (SFE) Ohkay Owingeh, NM St. John the Baptist; Ohkay Owingeh, NM Tewa Missions.
Brennan, Thomas J. '74 (PH) Coatesville, PA Our Lady of the Rosary.
Brennan, Thomas J. *s.j.* '96 (PH)[C] Jesuit Fathers; [Y] Loyola Center and Manresa Hall.
Brennan, Thomas '89 (LAN) Retired.
Brennan, Thomas '66 (TR) Retired.
Brennan, Thomas *s.d.b.* '82 (NY)[EE] New Rochelle, NY Salesian Provincial House.
Brennan, Thomas *s.d.b.* '82 (NEW)[M] Ramsey, NJ Don Bosco Prep Salesian Residence; [C] Ramsey, NJ Don Bosco Preparatory High School.
Brennan, Timothy J. *o.s.b.* '78 (PAT)[N] Morristown St. Mary's Abbey.
Brennan, Walter G. *s.j.* '60 (FgM) Los Gatos, CA Society of Jesus.
Brennan, William J. '49 (L) Retired.
Brennan, William J. *s.j.* '51 (MIL)[P] Wauwatosa, WI Jesuit Community at St. Camillus.
Brennan, Rev. Msgr. William P. '63 (CAM) Haddonfield, NJ Church of Christ the King, Haddonfield, N.J.; Camden Central Deanery; College of Consultors.
Brennell, John J. '78 (STL) Imperial, MO St. Joseph.
Brennell, Rev. Msgr. John J. (STL) Archdiocesan Consultors.
Brennen, Christopher J. '83 (PH)[Y] Rosemont, PA Saxony Hall.
Brennen, John E. '00 (TOL) Galion, OH St. Joseph.
Brenner, Raymond '69 (EVN) Jasper, IN St. Joseph; Deans.
Brenner, Rev. Msgr. Thomas R. '61 (HBG) Retired.
Brenny, Kenneth '63 (SCL) Deans Retired.
Brenon, Terence V. '91 (SAN) Abilene, TX St. Vincent Pallotti.
Brensinger, Richard C. '92 (ALN) Bethlehem, PA Our Lady of Perpetual Help.
Brentrup, Bruce *s.d.s.* '59 (MIL)[P] Milwaukee Salvatorian Provincial Offices.
Brentshelton, James '01 (KNX) Townsend, TN St. Francis of Assisi.
Brenyah, Stephen (NY) Katonah, NY St. Mary of the Assumption.
Brenza, William J. '70 (HRT) Plantsville, CT Mary Our Queen; Consultors – Canon 1742.
Breski, Martin *o.f.m. conv.* '69 (ATL) Lithia Springs, GA St. John Vianney.
Breslawski, William G. '79 (RVC) Lynbrook, NY Our Lady of Peace; Procurator & Advocates; Senate of Priests (Presbyteral Council/College of Consultors); Priests' Personnel Assignment Board.
Breslin, Cornelius J. '00 (WIL) Regina Coeli Society; Wilmington, DE St. Mary of the Immaculate Conception; Wilmington, DE St. Patrick; Wilmington, DE Wilmington Hospital.
Breslin, J. Michael '65 (RIC) Cape Charles, VA St. Charles Borromeo.
Breslin, John B. *s.j.* '73 (NY)[EE] New York, NY Murray–Weigel Hall.
Breslin, Rev. Msgr. John E. '61 (PH) Philadelphia, PA Holy Family Retired.
Breslin, John S. '85 (CHI) Chicago, IL St. Michael the Archangel.
Breslin, John *s.m.m.* '56 (BRK)[T] Ozone Park Montfort Missionaries Provincialate (Missionaries of the Company of Mary).
Breslin, Paul *o.f.m.* '88 (FgM) New York, NY Holy

Name Province.
Breslin, William E. '74 (DEN) Boulder, CO Sacred Heart of Jesus.
Bresnahan, James F. *s.j.* '59 (BO)[U] Newton, MA The Jesuit Community at Boston College.
Bresnahan, John E. *o.s.a.* '36 (PH)[Y] Villanova, PA St. Thomas Monastery.
Bresnahan, John J. '60 (CHI) Schiller Park, IL St. Beatrice Retired.
Bresnahan, Richard F. '58 (PEO) Retired.
Bresnahan, Thomas J. '60 (MAN) Pelham, NH St. Patrick Retired.
Brethour, Gary G. '89 (LIN) McCook, NE St. Patrick.
Bretl, James J. *s.d.s.* '65 (NSH) McMinnville, TN St. Catherine Retired.
Bretl, James *s.d.s.* (MIL)[P] Milwaukee Salvatorian Provincial Offices Retired.
Breton, Albert '54 (SPR) Retired.
Breton, Raymond G. '68 (OAK) Judicial Vicar; Presbyteral Council; Judicial Vicar & Director; Judges; Vicars for Religious; Pastoral Leadership Placement Board (PLPB).
Breton, Richard D. '08 (NOR) North Grosvenordale, CT St. Joseph.
Bretone, Richard J. '89 (BRK) Ridgewood, NY St. Matthias; [X] Jackson Heights, NY Eternal Flame of Hope Ministries, Inc.; Long Island City, NY Our Lady of Mount Carmel.
Brett, Frank X. '59 (KNX) Retired.
Brett, Stephen F. *s.s.j.* '76 (BAL)[S] Baltimore, MD St. Joseph's Manor.
Bretzke, James T. *s.j.* '81 (BO)[U] Newton, MA The Jesuit Community at Boston College.
Breu, David L. '73 (NU) Graceville, MN Holy Rosary.
Breunig, Rudy V. *s.t.* '65 (SAV) Bainbridge, GA St. Joseph's.
Brewczynski, Jacek M. '96 (DET) Absent on Leave.
Brewer, Dexter S. '89 (NSH) Nashville, TN Christ the King; Judicial Vicar; Judges; Presbyteral Council; Priest Benefit Foundation.
Brewer, Dexter (KNX) Marriage Tribunal.
Brewer, James P. '77 (PRT) Lyman, ME St. Philip.
Brewer, Mark Alan '03 (ROC) Rochester, NY St. Charles Borromeo.
Brewer, Timothy M. '79 (WOR) Leominster, MA Our Lady of the Lake.
Brey, Christopher J. '97 (SFD) Beardstown, IL St. Fidelis; Beardstown, IL St. Alexius; Comite Diocesano de Ministerio Hispano – Diocesan Committee for Hispanic Ministry; Coordinator of Hispanic Ministry; Ashland, IL St. Augustine.
Brey, Christopher J. '97 (SFD) Virginia, IL St. Luke.
Breza, Paul J. '63 (WIN) Retired.
Brezovec, John F. '66 (ALT) Johnstown, PA St. John Gualbert Cathedral; Johnstown, PA Memorial Medical Center.
Brice, Donald '58 (WDC) Advocates; Washington, DC Annunciation.
Brice, Rev. Msgr. Frederick J. '69 (MIA) Lighthouse Point, FL St. Paul the Apostle.
Brice, Steven J. '82 (LC) Wausau, WI St. Anne.
Briceland, Alan *s.j.* '63 (BRK) Elmhurst General Hospital.
Briceland, W. Alan *s.j.* '65 (NY)[EE] New York, NY Jesuit Community of the Immaculate Conception.
Briceno, Joseph C. '81 (PHX) On Leave.
Brick, Donald *o.c.d.* '00 (MIL)[P] Hubertus, WI Discalced Carmelite Monastery – Holy Hill Basilica of the National Shrine of Mary, Help of Christians, Holy Hill.
Brick, Paul T. *s.d.s.* '63 (SAV) Retired.
Brick, Paul *s.d.s.* '63 (MIL)[P] Milwaukee Salvatorian Provincial Offices Retired.
Brickler, R. Richard '61 (ROC) Rochester, NY St. Boniface; Judges.
Brickner, Charles W. '75 (RIC) Woodlawn, VA St. Joseph's.
Brickner, Joseph *l.c.* '04 (HRT)[B] Cheshire, CT Novitiate of the Legion of Christ.
Brickner, Ronald J. '92 (TOL)[B] Fremont, OH St. Joseph Central Catholic High School; Kelley's Island, OH St. Michael; Put–In–Bay, OH Mother of Sorrows; St. Vincent dePaul Society.
Bride, Harold L. *c.s.c.* '49 (FTW)[H] Notre Dame Congregation of Holy Cross, Indiana Province, Provincial House.
Bride, Rev. Msgr. Thomas R. '67 (NOR) Old Lyme, CT Christ the King; Vicar General; College of Consultors; Members; Diocesan Pastoral Council; Notaries; Diocesan Finance Council; Board of Education; Advisory Ministry Evaluation Committee.
Bridge, George H. *c.ss.r.* '48 (ALB)[L] Saratoga Springs, NY St. John Neumann Residence.
Bridges, Clarence S. '88 (ALT) Johnstown, PA St. John Gualbert Cathedral.
Bridges, Rev. Msgr. James P. '62 (SAN) Midland, TX St. Stephen's.
Bridgman, Mark M. '96 (OM) Bellevue, NE St. Mary.
Bried, William *o.f.m.* '58 (SP)[N] St. Petersburg St. Anthony Friary.
Brieffies, John *m.s.f.* '56 (RIC) West Point, VA Our Lady of the Blessed Sacrament; West Point, VA; [K] West Point, VA Missionaries of the Holy Family, General Mission Office–M.S.F., Inc.
Brien, Paul J. *m.m.* '60 (FgM) Maryknoll, NY MARYKNOLL.
Brien, Peter C. *m.m.* '60 (FgM) Maryknoll, NY MARYKNOLL.
Brienz, Edward R. '96 (Y) Youngstown, OH Cathedral of St. Columba.
Brierley, Andrew '08 (PMB) Palm Beach Gardens, FL Cathedral of St. Ignatius Loyola.
Briers, Fred *c.r.* '04 (MOB) Montgomery, AL Resurrection Catholic Church.
Bries, Marvin J. '73 (DUB)[F] Guttenberg, IA St. Mary and Immaculate Conception School System; Guttenberg, IA Immaculate Conception; Guttenberg, IA St. Joseph; Guttenberg, IA St. Mary.
Briese, Dominic *o.p.* '96 (OAK)[M] Oakland, CA Order of Preachers (Province of the Most Holy Name of Jesus – Western Dominican Province).
Briese, Michael W. '09 (WDC) Silver Spring, MD St. John the Evangelist.
Brietske, Rev. Msgr. Richard C. '62 (TR) Building Commission Retired.
Briffa, Salvino '71 (DET) Westland, MI St. Bernardine.
Brigandi, Rev. Msgr. Paul A. '54 (SY)[Q] Syracuse, NY Tommy Coyne Residence Dillon Hall Retired.
Brigandi, Stephen J. '97 (RVC) Bayville, NY St. Gertrude's.
Briganti, Philip J. '73 (PAT) On Duty Outside the Diocese.
Briggman, Michael J. '68 (ALN) Bally, PA Most Blessed Sacrament; [J] Bethlehem, PA Holy Family Villa; Elected Members Retired.
Briggs, Michael J. *m.m.* '76 (FgM) Maryknoll, NY MARYKNOLL.
Brighenti, Kenneth D. '88 (MET) On Duty Outside the Diocese; Navy Reserve Chaplains.
Brighenti, Kenneth D. (BAL)[A] Emmitsburg, MD Mount St. Mary's Seminary.
Brignac, H. L. '83 (NO) Retired.
Brillantes, Edgar B. '80 (HON) Wahiawa, HI Our Lady of Sorrows.
Brillantes, Michael '83 (SFR) San Bruno, CA St. Bruno.
Brimley, Wilfred A. *c.s.p.* '62 (NY)[EE] Jamaica Estates Paulist Fathers Generalate.
Brimley, Wilfred A. *c.s.p.* '62 (BO)[U] Boston, MA Paulist Fathers Residence.
Brincat, George '57 (LA) Retired.
Brindamour, Maurice L. '74 (PRO) Woonsocket, RI Our Lady, Queen of Martyrs; Deans.
Bringas, Daniel '76 (FRS) Wasco, CA State Prison.
Bringas, Salvador '87 (HON) Mountain View, HI St. Theresa.
Brink, Joseph C. '63 (COV) Edgewood, KY St. Pius X; [I] Edgewood, KY St. Elizabeth Medical Center, Inc. Retired.
Brinker, Brian J. '88 (RVC)[M] Amityville, NY St. Pius X Residence.
Brinker, William *c.s.c.* (FTW)[H] Notre Dame Congregation of Holy Cross, Indiana Province, Provincial House.
Brinkman, Barry '91 (SAL) Concordia, KS Our Lady of Perpetual Help Parish; Chancellor; Associate Judges; Personnel Board; Lay Review Board–Diocesan Committee Regarding Alleged Cases of Child Sexual Abuse; Ex Officio; Office of Communications; Belleville, KS St. Isidore Parish; Belleville, KS St. George Parish; Belleville, KS St. Edward Parish.
Brinkman, Gerard *c.ss.r.* '61 (PH) Philadelphia, PA St. Peter the Apostle.
Brinkman, James J. '81 (SUP) New Richmond, WI St. Patrick; New Richmond, WI Immaculate Conception; Board of Directors.
Brinkman, John T. *m.m.* '71 (FgM) Maryknoll, NY MARYKNOLL.
Brinkman, Terence P. '73 (GAL) Baytown, TX St. John the Evangelist.
Brinkman, Terence '73 (GAL) Censor Librorum.
Brinkmoeller, David E. '71 (CIN) Dayton, OH St. Helen; Dayton, OH Our Lady of the Immaculate Conception; Vicarri Foranei (Deans).
Brinn, Adrian J. '68 (SB) Retired.
Brinn, Rev. Msgr. John J. '62 (NY) Poughkeepsie, NY St. Mary.
Brinsmade, John F. '81 (HRT) Plainville, CT Our Lady of Mercy.
Briody, Hugh J. '63 (SUP) Retired.
Briones, Jesus *s.v.d.* '76 (TR) Lakewood, NJ St. Anthony Claret.
Briones Cesped, Osvaldo Enrique '09 (MAD) Sauk City, WI St. Aloysius.
Brioni, Luigi *s.x.* '61 (PAT)[N] Wayne Xaverian Missionary Fathers; Wayne, NJ XAVERIAN MISSIONARY FATHERS.
Brioso–Texidor, Luis '93 (MO) DEPARTMENT OF VETERANS AFFAIRS HOSPITALS AND CHAPLAINS.
Briseno, Miguel *o.f.m.conv.* '90 (LSC) Presbyteral Council; [D] Mesilla Park, NM Holy Cross Retreat and Friary.
Briseno, Rev. Msgr. Pedro '81 (BWN) Harlingen, TX Immaculate Heart of Mary; [K] Harlingen, TX RGV Educational Broadcasting, Inc.
Brislin, Thomas *c.p.* '68 (FgM) South River, NJ St. Paul of the Cross Province.
Brislin, Thomas *c.p.* '68 (MET)[I] South River Passionist Provincial Office.
Brisotti, William F. '68 (RVC) Wyandanch, NY Our Lady of the Miraculous Medal.
Brissette, Reginald R. '63 (PRT) Westbrook, ME St. Anthony of Padua Parish.
Brisson, Robert A. '85 (NY)[JJ] New York, NY Prelature of the Holy Cross and Opus Dei; New York.
Bristow, David '98 (FWT) Fort Worth, TX St. Mary of the Assumption; Deans.
Brito, Cristiano Aparecido *o.s.b.* '91 (RIC) Virginia Beach, VA St. Gregory the Great.
Brito, Lawrence R. '00 (SFE) Taos, NM Nuestra Senora De Guadalupe.
Britt, William J. '53 (STL) Retired.
Brittain, Gerald W. '62 (MIL) West Bend, WI Holy Angels.
Britto, Antony *s.a.c.* '88 (GR) Edmore, MI St. Bernadette of Lourdes; Edmore, MI St. Margaret Mary.
Britto, Rev. Msgr. Federico A. '82 (PH) Philadelphia, PA Saint Cyprian.
Britto, Sean *c.s.j.* '01 (NEW) Orange, NJ Mt. Carmel.
Brixius, Hilary R. '68 (WIN) Worthington, MN St. Mary's; Elected At–Large Representatives.
Brizio, Michael *i.m.c.* (TR) Freehold, NJ St. Rose of Lima.
Broadhurst, T. Paul *c.s.b.* '60 (ROC)[J] Rochester, NY Basilian Residence.
Brobst, James *o.m.i.* '90 (BEL)[H] Belleville, IL King's House Retreat and Renewal Center.
Brobst, Richard A. '65 (Y) Retired.
Brocato, John K. '03 (ALX) Military Chaplains; Army Chaplains.
Brocato, Robert S. '95 (SJ) On Duty Outside the Diocese.
Broccolo, Gerard T. '65 (CHI) Retired.
Brock, David F. '56 (DET) Retired.
Brock, John '62 (JKS) Retired.
Brockett, Norman L. '87 (HRT)[J] West Hartford, CT Saint Mary Home; Special and other Archdiocesan Assignment.
Brockhaus, Rev. Msgr. Edward '64 (SD) Lemon Grove, CA St. John of the Cross; Vicars Forane.
Brockland, John A. '91 (STL) St. Charles, MO Sts. Joachim and Ann.
Brockland, Robert J. *c.m.* '74 (STL)[O] St. Louis, MO Lazarist Residence.
Brockman, Blaise N. '77 (LA) Santa Clarita, CA Blessed Kateri Tekakwitha.
Brockman, Rev. Msgr. David D. '90 (R) Diocesan Judges; Vicar General; Diocesan Consultors; Ex Officio.
Brockman, Leon *o.c.s.o.* '55 (SPC)[F] Ava, MO Assumption Abbey (Trappist).
Brockman, Norbert C. *s.m.* '73 (SAT)[C] San Antonio, TX St. Mary's University of San Antonio, Texas; [L] San Antonio, TX Woodlawn Marianist Community.
Brockmyre, Philip C. '02 (SY) Phoenix, NY St. Stephen.
Brockson, Scott D. '96 (PH) Philadelphia, PA St. William.
Broderick, C. Michael '87 (WOR) Whitinsville, MA St. Patrick.
Broderick, James M. '60 (BO) Senior Priests.; Newburyport, MA Immaculate Conception Retired.
Broderick, John W. '89 (SY) Absent on Leave.
Broderick, Leo P. '56 (DET) Retired.
Broderick, Richard '70 (ALB) Special Assignment.
Broderick, Sean A. *c.s.sp.* '65 (MET) Hillsborough, NJ Mary, Mother of God.
Brodersen, Rev. Msgr. Charles F. '48 (OM) Retired.
Brodersen, Steven W. '85 (SC) Boone, IA Sacred Heart; Presbyteral Council.
Brodeski, Rev. Msgr. Aaron R. '98 (RCK) Woodstock, IL St. Patrick; Woodstock, IL St. Mary; [B] Woodstock, IL Marian Central Catholic High School.
Brodeur, Henry C. *m.s.* '66 (FR)[G] Attleboro, MA La Salette Shrine.
Brodeur, Scott N. *s.j.* '90 (BO)[U] Boston The Society of Jesus of New England–Provincial Offices.
Brodeur, Theodore J. '66 (MAR) Brimley, MI St. Francis Xavier; Brimley, MI Blessed Kateri Tekakwitha; Vicars Forane.
Brodniak, Anthony B. *m.m.* '54 (NY)[EE].
Brodnick, Edward J. '76 (COV) Crescent Springs, KY St. Joseph.
Brodnick, Joseph '69 (CLV) Administrative Leave.
Brody, Donald *o.f.m.cap.* '47 (GB)[J] Appleton, WI St. Fidelis Friary Retired.
Brodzeller, Robert E. *s.j.* '63 (MIL)[P] Wauwatosa, WI Jesuit Community at St. Camillus.
Broering, Raymond L. '53 (COV) Administrative Leave Retired.
Brogan, Leo '67 (PHX) Retired.
Brogan, William (NY) Bronx, NY St. Raymond.
Brogus, Albert G. '45 (SCR) Retired.
Brohammer, Ronald '60 (MIA) Retired.

Broheimer, John P. '03 (OM)[B] Elgin, NE Pope John XXIII Central Catholic High School at Elgin; Neligh, NE St. Francis; Tilden, NE Our Lady of Mt. Carmel; Age Groups; [O] Neligh, NE Legion of Mary.
Broker, William H. *c.ss.r.* '49 (STL)[O] Liguori, MO Liguori Mission House/Redemptorists.
Brokman, James P. '97 (DUB) Sumner, IA Immaculate Conception; Fayette, IA St. Francis of Assisi.
Bromenshenkel, Fintan *o.s.b.* '45 (SCL) Collegeville, MN St. John's Abbey; [I] Collegeville, MN St. John's Abbey, of the Order of St. Benedict.
Bromley, Vincent M. '65 (SUP) Winter, WI Sacred Heart; Winter, WI St. Peter Retired.
Brommer, Joshua R. '06 (HBG) Mechanicsburg, PA St. Joseph.
Bromwich, James S. '03 (L) Campbellsville, KY Our Lady of Perpetual Help; Campbellsville, KY Our Lady of the Hills.
Broniak, Leonard *c.ss.r.* '79 (GAL) Houston, TX Holy Ghost; Deaf Apostolate.
Bronk, Philip *s.t.* '51 (SD) La Mesa, CA Little Flower Haven; [I] La Mesa, CA Little Flower Haven.
Bronkiewicz, Rev. Msgr. Laurence R. '73 (BGP) Diocesan Censors; Ridgefield, CT St. Mary.
Brookbank, Scott F. *o.f.m.* '08 (PRO)[N] Providence, RI St. Francis Chapel & City Ministry Center; [P] Providence, RI St. Francis Friary; Providence, RI St. Mary.
Brooker, Richard L. *m.m.* '55 (NY)[EE] Retired.
Brooks, Armand L. '97 (FAR) Special Assignment.
Brooks, Bryan V. '93 (TLS) Muskogee, OK Saint Joseph Church; Priests' Personnel Committee.
Brooks, Charles R. '65 (GB) Retired.
Brooks, David R. *s.j.* '78 (WDC)[N] Washington, DC The Jesuit Community of St. Aloysius Gonzaga.
Brooks, Jason *l.c.* '04 (CHI)[N] Hillside, IL Legion of Christ.
Brooks, Jeddie P. '77 (SPR) Monson, MA St. Patrick's; Procurators–Advocate; Brimfield, MA St. Christopher's.
Brooks, John E. *s.j.* '59 (WOR)[O] Worcester, MA Jesuits of the Holy Cross, Inc.
Brooks, Michael J. *ss.cc.* '61 (LA)[P] La Verne, CA Congregation of the Sacred Hearts of Jesus and Mary.
Brooks, Robert C. '61 (ARL) Retired.
Brooks, Robert E. '95 (SAC) Tahoe City, CA Corpus Christi.
Brooks, Thomas M. '78 (E) Erie, PA St. Jude the Apostle.
Brooks, Rev. Msgr. William C. '76 (AUS) Austin, TX St. Theresa.
Broom, Edward *o.m.v.* '86 (LA) Hawaiian Gardens, CA St. Peter Chanel.
Broome, William *m.s.a.* '05 (NOR)[G] Cromwell Society of the Missionaries of the Holy Apostles.
Brophy, Edward G. '93 (BRK) Brooklyn, NY St. Edmund.
Brophy, John L. '69 (SFS) On Duty Outside the Archdiocese; Britton, SD St. John de Britto.
Brophy, Michael *s.j.* '69 (CHI)[N] Chicago Chicago Province of the Society of Jesus–Provincial Office.
Brophy, R. Michael *s.j.* '69 (DET)[K] Clarkston, MI Colombiere Center.
Brosk, Steven J. '90 (MO) Military Chaplains; Air Force Reserve Chaplains.
Broski, Mark *o.s.b.* '91 (KCK) Catholic Scouts.
Brosmer, John '05 (EVN) Diocesan Council of Priests; Dale, IN St. Joseph; Santa Claus, IN St. Nicholas.
Brosmer, Thomas J. '69 (COL) Columbus, OH St. Cecilia.
Brosnahan, Bruce C. '01 (TLS) Fairfax, OK Sacred Heart.
Brosnan, Rev. Msgr. Dermot '57 (SAT) Retired.
Brosnan, Rev. Msgr. Liam P. '59 (SAT) Retired.
Brosnan, Thomas F. '81 (BRK) Bayside, NY Sacred Heart of Jesus.
Brossart, Scott *s.o.l.t.* '00 (CC)[G] Robstown, TX Society of Our Lady of the Most Holy Trinity.
Brossart, Scott *s.o.l.t.* '00 (FAR) Belcourt, ND St. Ann; Belcourt, ND St. Ann.
Brost, Corey D. *c.s.v.* '06 (CHI) Arlington Heights, IL; [N] Arlington Heights Viatorian Province Center–Clerics of St. Viator; [D] Arlington Heights, IL St. Viator High School.
Brost, Frederick '56 (SUP) Stetsonville, WI Sacred Heart of Jesus.
Brothersen, Maynard J. '48 (DAV)[J] Davenport, IA St. Vincent Center Retired.
Broudou, Joseph G. '96 (OM)[N] Crofton, NE St. Joseph Church of Constance Endowment Trust Fund; [N] Crofton, NE St. Rose Church Cemetery Endowment Trust Fund; Omaha, NE St. Vincent de Paul.
Brougher, Douglas C. '62 (NO) New Orleans, LA Touro Infirmary; Ministry to Sick Priests; New Orleans, LA Good Shepherd.
Brouillard, John '56 (P) Retired.
Brouillard, Louis A. (AGN) Retired.
Brouillette, Daniel E. '09 (NO) Destrehan, LA St. Charles Borromeo.
Brouillette, Thomas S. '96 (LIN) Diocesan Consultors.
Brouillette, Thomas '96 (LIN) Weston, NE St. John Nepomucene; Presbyteral Council.
Broussard, A. Rex '66 (LAF) Duson, LA St. Basil.
Broussard, Dennis A. '91 (MAN) Absent on Leave.
Broussard, F. David '93 (LAF) Kaplan, LA Our Lady of the Holy Rosary.
Broussard, Henry J. '72 (LAF) Cankton, LA St. John Berchmans.
Broussard, Hubert C. '52 (HT) Retired.
Broussard, John S. *c.s.b.* '48 (GAL) Manvel, TX Sacred Heart of Jesus.
Broussard, Ken *o.s.b.* '03 (LAF) Assessors; On Special Assignment.
Broussard, Paul '98 (LAF) Erath, LA Our Lady of Lourdes.
Broussard, Richard Dale '00 (LAF) Pine Prairie, LA St. Peter.
Broussard, Rev. Msgr. Ronald '88 (LAF) New Iberia, LA St. Edward.
Broussard, Theodore '98 (LAF) Evangeline, LA St. Joseph; [K] Opelousas, LA Cursillo Center; Cursillo.
Broussard, Warren J. *s.j.* '88 (LAF) Retreats; New Orleans, LA.
Broussard, Warren J. *s.j.* '88 (NO)[P] New Orleans, LA Jesuit Provincial Office.
Brouwers, Hans A.L. '78 (PH) On Duty Outside the Archdiocese.
Brovey, Rev. Msgr. Steven L. '91 (CHR) Taylors, SC Prince of Peace; College of Consultors; Deans; Building & Renovation Commission; Divine Worship & Sacraments, Administrator for; Office of Prayer & Worship; Personnel Committee.
Brown, Rev. Msgr. Anthony M. '49 (HEL) Retired.
Brown, Arthur A. '57 (BO) Senior Priests. Retired.
Brown, Avram E. '04 (SAC) On Duty Outside the Diocese.
Brown, Benedict J. '74 (L) Unassigned.
Brown, Bruce '63 (P) Portland, OR Sacred Heart Retired.
Brown, Charles D. '93 (GR) Holland, MI St. Francis de Sales.
Brown, Charles E. '71 (WDC) Burtonsville, MD Resurrection Parish Retired.
Brown, Charles L. '73 (BRK) On Leave/Unassigned.
Brown, Charles L. '67 (WIL) Wilmington, DE St. John the Beloved; Deans.
Brown, Rev. Msgr. Charles '89 (NY) On Duty Outside the Archdiocese.
Brown, Charles '87 (PSC) Retired.
Brown, Charles '58 (SFE) Retired.
Brown, Charles *s.c.j.* '84 (MIL)[P] Milwaukee, WI SCJ Community; [B] Hales Corners, WI Sacred Heart School of Theology.
Brown, David A. *s.j.* '02 (NO)[P] New Orleans Jesuit Provincial Office.
Brown, David G. *o.s.b.* '75 (CHL)[A] Belmont, NC Belmont Abbey College; [J] Belmont, NC Belmont Abbey; Belmont, NC.
Brown, David M. *o.s.m.* '48 (CHI) Chicago, IL Assumption of the Blessed Virgin Mary; [N] Chicago, IL Assumption Priory.
Brown, David '07 (P) Florence, OR St. Mary, Our Lady of the Dunes; Reedsport, OR St. John the Apostle.
Brown, Dennis *o.m.v.* '89 (BO)[Z] Boston, MA St. Francis Chapel; [U] Milton, MA Oblate Residence (St. Joseph House).
Brown, Dom Lawrence *o.s.b.* '84 (BUR)[F] Westfield, VT Monastery of the Immaculate Heart of Mary.
Brown, Douglas T. '06 (CLV) Brecksville, OH St. Basil the Great.
Brown, Erin '07 (TR) West Long Branch, NJ St. Jerome.
Brown, Eugene M. '60 (NU) St. Mary's Care Center; [C] Winsted, MN St. Mary's Care Center Retired.
Brown, Everett *s.m.m.* '61 (RVC)[M] Bay Shore, NY Montfort Missionaries.
Brown, Francis Xavier *o.s.b.* '84 (TLS)[G] Hulbert, OK Our Lady of the Annunciation of Clear Creek Monastery.
Brown, George *o.m.i.* '64 (BO)[U] Lowell, MA Missionary Oblates of Mary Immaculate.
Brown, Gerald L. *s.s.* '64 (SFR)[A] Menlo Park, CA St. Patrick Seminary and University.
Brown, Gerald L. *s.s.* '64 (BAL)[S] Baltimore Society of St. Sulpice, Province of the United States.
Brown, Gerald '81 (MET) Retired.
Brown, Gregory J. *o.f.m.cap.* '04 (PIT) Rochester, PA St. Cecilia; [M] Beaver, PA St. Fidelis Friary.
Brown, Harold C. *c.pp.s.* '59 (TOL) Liaison Team Priest.
Brown, James E. '72 (TOL) Spiritual Directors; Toledo, OH Our Lady of Lourdes.
Brown, James T. '97 (NEW) Bloomfield, NJ Sacred Heart.
Brown, James V. *o.a.r.* '46 (LA)[P] Oxnard, CA St. Augustine Priory O.A.R.
Brown, Jerry W. '01 (OAK) Brentwood, CA Immaculate Heart of Mary.
Brown, Rev. Msgr. John J. '83 (BRK) Belle Harbor, NY St. Francis de Sales; Defenders of the Marriage Bond.
Brown, John T. *g.h.m.* '84 (SAV) Swainsboro, GA Holy Trinity.
Brown, Joseph A. *s.j.* '72 (MIL)[P] Milwaukee Jesuit Provincial Office, Wisconsin Province.
Brown, Joseph E. *s.j.* '56 (STL)[O] St. Louis, MO Jesuit Community Corporation at Saint Louis University – Jesuit Hall.
Brown, Joseph Mary *c.s.j.* '97 (PEO)[K] Princeville, IL Congregation of St. John.
Brown, Joseph *c.pp.s.* '61 (CIN)[N] Carthagena, OH St. Charles Retired.
Brown, Keenan Wynn '02 (LAF) Arnaudville, LA St. John Francis Regis; Arnaudville, LA St. Catherine.
Brown, Kenneth A. '77 (STL) University City, MO All Saints.
Brown, Kenneth J. '06 (MRY) Arroyo Grande, CA St. Patrick; Diocesan Consultors; Presbyteral Council; Vicars Forane; Diocesan Consultors.
Brown, Konstantin K. '88 (ROM) Unassigned.
Brown, Lawrence *o.s.b.* '84 (TLS)[G] Hulbert, OK Our Lady of the Annunciation of Clear Creek Monastery.
Brown, Len *c.m.f.* '82 (ATL) Stone Mountain, GA Corpus Christi.
Brown, Leonard *c.m.f.* '82 (ATL)[J] Atlanta, GA Dekalb Community College; Special or Other (Arch)Diocesan Assignment.
Brown, Lewis E. '67 (ROC) Corning, NY All Saints Retired.
Brown, Matthew F. '63 (SY) Vestal, NY Our Lady of Sorrows; Vestal, NY Binghamton Nursing Homes Retired.
Brown, Matthew J. *o.s.b.* '49 (OKL)[I] Shawnee, OK St. Gregory's Abbey.
Brown, Michael O. '74 (TOL) Toledo, OH St. Clement; [C] Toledo, OH St. Francis de Sales High School; College of Consultors; St. Agnes Deanery; Members.
Brown, Michael R. '89 (ROC) Sonyea, NY Livingston Correctional Facility and Seneca Correctional Facility; Sonyea, NY Groveland Correctional Facility; Auburn, NY St. Hyacinth; Auburn, NY Auburn Correctional Facility.
Brown, Michael '89 (ROC) Auburn, NY St. Francis of Assisi; Auburn, NY Sacred Heart; Auburn, NY St. Hyacinth.
Brown, Ned *l.c.* '98 (WDC)[N] Potomac, MD Legionaries of Christ.
Brown, Nicholas *s.c.j.* '76 (SAT) San Antonio, TX St. Luke's Baptist Hospital; University Hospital; [L] San Antonio, TX Hospital Ministry House.
Brown, Rev. Msgr. Patrick E. '78 (PAT) Stirling, NJ St. Vincent de Paul; Morris County Jail.
Brown, Patrick *o.c.s.o.* '74 (WOR)[O] Spencer, MA St. Joseph's Abbey.
Brown, Phillip J. '89 (BAL)[S] Baltimore Society of St. Sulpice, Province of the United States.
Brown, Phillip '89 (BIS) On Duty Outside the Diocese.
Brown, Richard '58 (SD) Lemon Grove, CA St. John of the Cross.
Brown, Rev. Msgr. Robert L. '69 (NOR) Uncasville, CT St. John the Evangelist; Chancellor; College of Consultors; Members; Diocesan Pastoral Council; Notaries; Catholic Relief Services; Advisory Ministry Evaluation Committee.
Brown, Robert P. '63 (SC) Royal, IA St. Louis; Defenders of the Bond.
Brown, Robert W. '66 (ORL) Orlando, FL St. Joseph.
Brown, Rev. Msgr. Robert '69 (NOR) Board of Education.
Brown, Robert *o.s.f.s.* '67 (R) Buxton, NC Our Lady of the Seas.
Brown, Roderick M. *o.p.* '79 (CHI)[N] St. Pius V Priory.
Brown, Russell D. '04 (MRY) San Luis Obispo, CA San Luis Obispo.
Brown, Shaun S. '94 (NTN) Military Chaplain; Navy Chaplains.
Brown, Stephan *s.v.d.* '93 (SP)[A] St. Leo, FL Saint Leo University, Office of Assessment and Institutional Research.
Brown, Steven P. '77 (SJ) San Jose, CA St. Maria Goretti; Priests' Retirement Board.
Brown, Sylvester F. '56 (WIN) Retired.
Brown, Theophile W. *o.s.b.* '56 (RIC)[K] Richmond, VA Mary Mother of the Church Abbey; [K] Richmond, VA Mary Mother of the Church Abbey.
Brown, Thomas E. '78 (E) Corry, PA St. Thomas The Apostle; Corry, PA St. Elizabeth.
Brown, Thomas J. '99 (GR) Muskegon, MI St. Michael's; Muskegon Heights, MI Sacred Heart; Deans.
Brown, Thomas *o.m.i.* '55 (FgM) Washington, DC AMERICAN OBLATE MISSIONS.
Brown, Timothy B. *s.j.* '86 (BAL)[S] Baltimore, MD Jesuit Community of Loyola University, Inc.; [B] Jesuit Community of Loyola University, Inc.
Brown, Timothy '88 (ROC) Rochester, NY St. Pius Tenth; Rochester, NY Holy Ghost.
Brown, W. P. '80 (PT) Panama City, FL Our Lady of the Rosary.
Brown, Walter '94 (JKS) Belzoni, MS All Saints; Yazoo City, MS St. Mary; Yazoo City, MS St. Francis.
Brown, Warren A. *o.m.i.* '82 (SAT)[C] Oblate School of Theology; [L] San Antonio, TX De Mazenod House;

[L] San Antonio, TX Missionary Oblates of Mary Immaculate; Judicial Vicar.
Brown, Warren *o.m.i.* '82 (WDC)[N] Washington, DC Provincial Offices of the United States Province of the Missionary Oblates of Mary Immaculate.
Brown, Wilbur J. '04 (LAF) Retired.
Brown, Wilbur Joseph '04 (LAF) Church Point, LA Our Lady of the Sacred Heart.
Brown, William E. '88 (SFR) Daly City, CA Our Lady of Mercy.
Brown, William M. *o.m.v.* '94 (BO)[B] Boston, MA Oblate Provincialate; Boston, MA.
Brown, William P. '80 (PT) Panama City, FL Our Lady Queen of Peace Mission.
Browne, Denis P. *m.m.* '47 (FgM) Maryknoll, NY MARYKNOLL.
Browne, Dennis '79 (SJ) On Leave of Absence.
Browne, Rev. Msgr. George T. '55 (DET) Pastoral Care for Senior Priests Retired.
Browne, Gerald '81 (MET)[I] Somerset, NJ Maria Regina Residence Retired.
Browne, Rev. Msgr. J. Patrick '67 (SJ) San Jose, CA Cathedral Basilica of St. Joseph; College of Consultors; Priests' Retirement Board; [O] San Jose, CA San Jose Cathedral Foundation.
Browne, Joseph P. *c.s.c.* '55 (FTW)[H] Holy Cross House; South Bend, IN Faith & Hope & Charity Chapel Retired.
Browne, Robert M. '61 (BO) Senior Priests. Retired.
Browne, Ronald T. '91 (DET) On Duty Outside the Archdiocese.
Browne, Ronald T. '91 (MAR) Consultors; Ministry Personnel Services, Dept. of; Vicars General.
Browne, Stanley '81 (GB) Retired.
Browne, William E. '04 (CLV) Parma, OH St. Columbkille.
Brownell, Patrick P. '94 (KNX) Signal Mountain, TN St. Augustine; Presbyteral Council; Diocesan Consultors; Army National Guard Chaplains.
Brownell, Robert A. '69 (RIC) Richmond, VA St. Peter.
Brownfield, David L. '90 (DAV) Grand Mound, IA Church of St. Philip and James; Delmar, IA St. Patrick's; Delmar, IA St. Anne.
Brownholtz, Andrew C. '01 (PH) Hatfield, PA St. Maria Goretti.
Brownsey, Brian K. '96 (PEO) Vocations Office.
Brownstein, Donald P. '81 (COS) Parker, CO Ave Maria; Northern Deanery; Vicars Forane.
Brozat, Charles *s.a.* '57 (NY)[EE] Garrison Franciscan Friars of the Atonement, Minister General Office.
Brozena, Joseph M. '58 (SCR) Retired.
Brozonowicz, Gregory (NOR) Advisory Board.
Brozonowicz, Grzegorz P. '96 (NOR) Groton, CT St. Mary Mother of the Redeemer; Members; Continuing Education and Formation Commission for the Clergy.
Brozovic, Matthew R. *o.f.m.* '56 (GBG)[G] Uniontown, PA St. Anthony Friary.
Brozyniak, Pawel W. *s.j.* '06 (CHI)[C] Chicago, IL Jesuit Community at Loyola University Chicago.
Brubaker, Claude '55 (VEN) Retired.
Brubaker, George J. '80 (WIL) Milford, DE St. John the Apostle; Judicial Vicar; Court of First Instance Judges; College of Consultors; Contact; Catholic Relief Services, Inc.
Brubaker, W. Scott '82 (PHX) Mesa, AZ St. Bridget Roman Catholic Parish.
Bruce, Joseph J. *s.j.* '81 (BO)[U] Boston The Society of Jesus of New England–Provincial Offices.
Bruce, Joseph J. *s.j.* '81 (PRO) Woonsocket, RI St. Charles; Deaf and Hard of Hearing Apostolate.
Bruce, Terry '67 (KC) Kansas City, MO St. Elizabeth's; Deans.
Bruch, James A. '65 (SC) Sioux City, IA St. Boniface.
Bruch, Lynn '86 (SC) Auburn, IA St. Mary's; Lake City, IA St. Mary's; Lake City, IA St. Joseph's.
Bruck, Donald '68 (DM) Glenwood, IA Our Lady of the Holy Rosary.
Bruck, Raymond E. '58 (GR) Retired.
Brucker, G. Fredrick '76 (GR) Belding, MI St. Joseph's; Belding, MI St. Mary's; On Special Assignment.
Brucker, George W. '56 (ALB) Retired.
Brucksch, James L. '69 (GAY) Retired.
Brucz, James *c.s.p.* '74 (STP)[K] Minneapolis, MN Paulist Fathers; [R] Minneapolis, MN Newman Center at St. Lawrence; Minneapolis, MN St. Lawrence–Newman Center.
Brudzynski, Peter F. '50 (BO) Senior Priests. Retired.
Bruecken, Albert *o.s.b.* '77 (KC)[A] Conception, MO Conception Seminary College; [J] Conception, MO Conception Abbey.
Bruemmer, Joseph A. '48 (CIN) Retired.
Bruemmer, Joseph *o.s.c.* '45 (SCL)[I] Onamia Crosier Priory.
Bruening, Allen '51 (CLV) Life of Prayer and Penance.
Bruening, Bernard H. '59 (CIN) Retired.
Bruening, Joseph B. '53 (CIN) Retired.
Bruetsch, Joseph J. '70 (LFT) Retired.
Bruggeman, Donald R. '62 (DUB) Retired.
Bruggeman, Gerald H. '49 (COS)[C] Colorado Springs, CO Penrose Hospital Retired.
Bruggeman, Sidney B. '09 (GI) St. Libory, NE St. Libory's.
Brugger, Rev. Msgr. Robert L. '68 (E) Erie, PA St. George; Finance Council.
Brum, Rev. Msgr. Louis L. '74 (BWN) McAllen, TX Holy Spirit; Vicar for Religious.
Brumleve, Matthew '88 (KC) Kansas City, MO Holy Family.
Brummel, Mark J. *c.m.f.* '60 (CHI)[N] Chicago, IL Claretian Missionaries, St. Jude League, Inc.; [N] Oak Park, IL Claretian Missionaries Community Support Trust; [W] Chicago, IL Villa Guadalupe Senior Services Corporation; Chicago, IL Holy Cross/ Immaculate Heart of Mary; Oak Park, IL; [N] Oak Park Claretian Missionaries USA Eastern Province.
Brummel, Thomas *c.m.f.* '59 (CHI)[N] Oak Park, IL Claretian Missionaries USA Eastern Province.
Brummer, Lawrence *o.f.m.* '58 (SAT) San Antonio, TX San Francisco de la Espada.
Brundage, John L. '70 (MET) South River, NJ Corpus Christi.
Brundage, Thomas T. '88 (MIL) On Duty Outside the Archdiocese.
Brundage, Thomas T. '88 (ANC) Glennallen, AK Holy Family; Palmer, AK St. Michael; Judicial Vicar; Diocesan Consultors; Moderator of the Curia.
Brundage, Tom '88 (FBK) Defenders of the Bond.
Brune, Meinrad *o.s.b.* '61 (IND)[K] St. Meinrad, IN St. Meinrad Archabbey.
Brunelle, J. Ernest *m.m.* '59 (NY)[EE] Maryknoll Maryknoll Fathers and Brothers Retired.
Brunelle, Richard *a.a.* '63 (BO)[U] Boston Assumptionist Center.
Brunet, Rev. Msgr. Frederic J. '60 (HT) Chauvin, LA St. Joseph; Finance Officer; Diocesan Finance Council.
Brunet, Jules A. '55 (BR) Retired.
Brunetta, M. Juan–Diego *o.p.* '01 (HRT) New Haven, CT St. Mary's Priory; Defender of the Bond; Judges; Appointed Members.
Brunette, Larry H. '99 (SFD) Granite City, IL Holy Family.
Bruney, James L. '84 (PIT) Pittsburgh, PA St. Cyril of Alexandria; Defender of the Bond.
Brungardt, Aloysius '71 (SAL) Junction City, KS St. Francis Xavier Parish.
Brungardt, John B. '98 (WCH) Presbyteral Council/ College of Consultors; Ongoing Formation of the Clergy Committee; Chancellor; Finance Committee; Wichita, KS Christ the King.
Bruni, John E. '76 (CAM) Landisville, NJ Queen of Angels Parish, Buena Borough, N.J.; Continuing Education & Spiritual Formation of Priests (CESF).
Brunick, Charles *c.s.p.* '70 (P)[Q] Portland, OR Paulist Fathers Catholic Center for Evangelization.
Bruning, David R. '78 (TOL) Fremont, OH St. Joseph.
Bruning, William '93 (KCK) Topeka, KS Mother Teresa of Calcutta; Holton, KS St. Dominic; Holton, KS St. Francis Xavier.
Brunkan, Rev. Msgr. Walter L. '56 (DUB) Greene, IA St. Mary; Greene, IA St. Mary; Deanery Representatives; Directors.
Brunner, Rev. Msgr. James C. '54 (VIC) Victoria, TX St. Mary's; Vicars General; Diocesan Consultors; Presbyteral Council; Priests' Personnel Board; Diocesan Finance Board; Respect Life–Pro Life.
Brunner, John H. '62 (NU) Watkins, MN Church of St. Anthony; Property Committee.
Brunner, Michael *o.s.b.* '05 (STL)[F] Creve Coeur, MO St. Louis Priory School; [O] St. Louis, MO The Abbey of St. Mary and St. Louis.
Brunner, William *s.s.c.* '62 (OM)[K] St. Columbans Missionary Society of St. Columban.
Brunnert, Edward J. *m.s.* '63 (LKC) Dequincy, LA Our Lady of La Salette.
Brunnert, Jude *m.s.* '64 (LKC) De Ridder, LA St. Joseph's.
Brunnert, Theodore J. '54 (STL) St. Louis, MO St. Joan of Arc Retired.
Bruno, Anthony J. '68 (HRT) Enfield, CT St. Adalbert's; Wethersfield, CT Connecticut Department of Correction; Special and other Archdiocesan Assignment.
Bruno, John *r.c.j.* '74 (LA) Van Nuys, CA St. Elisabeth; [P] Van Nuys, CA Rogationist Fathers.
Bruno, Robert A. *o.f.m.* '77 (MO) Air Force Chaplains; Presbyteral Council.
Bruno, Robert *o.f.m.* (CIN)[N] Cincinnati St. Francis Seraph Friary.
Bruno, Steven V. '05 (NO) Vocation Office; Marrero, LA The Visitation of Our Lady.
Brunovsky, Michael *o.s.b.* '93 (CLV)[D] Cleveland, OH Benedictine High School; [N] Cleveland Benedictine Order of Cleveland.
Brunovsky, Steven K. '92 (CLV) Fairlawn, OH St. Hilary.
Brunskill, Richard W. '83 (PEO) Havana, IL St. Patrick's.
Brunsman, Barry *o.f.m.* '56 (MRY)[H] San Juan Bautista, CA St. Francis Retreat Center; [F] San Juan Bautista, CA Franciscan Friars.
Brunton, Daniel B. '60 (SPR) Procurators–Advocate Retired.
Brusato, Martin '89 (SAC) Absent on Leave.
Brusatti, Louis *c.m.* '75 (AUS)[A] St. Edward's University.
Bruse, James C. '84 (ARL) Kilmarnock, VA St. Francis de Sales.
Brusky, David *s.d.s.* '52 (MIL)[P] Milwaukee, WI Salvatorians – Jordan Hall Retired.
Bruso, Robert D. '93 (WOR) Fitchburg, MA St. Anthony of Padua; Fitchburg, MA St. Joseph's; Deans; Hmong Ministry; Presbyteral Council.
Brutus, Ferry '80 (MIA) Homestead, FL Sacred Heart.
Bryan, Francis E. '62 (IND) Archdiocesan Judges Retired.
Bryan, Kevin J. '76 (L) Jamestown, KY Holy Redeemer; Jamestown, KY Holy Spirit; Ex Officio.
Bryan, Paul *c.ss.r.* '59 (HBG)[G] Ephrata St. Clement's Mission House.
Bryant, F. Michael '69 (WDC) Washington, DC Holy Comforter—St. Cyprian; Special Ministries; [W] Washington, DC District of Columbia Detention Facility; [W] Fort Washington, MD Prison Outreach Ministry.
Bryant, Michael '78 (SCR) Scranton, PA Saint John Neumann, Scranton.
Bryce, Edward M. '60 (PIT) Pittsburgh, PA St. Bede.
Bryce, Vincent W. *o.p.* '57 (STL)[O] St. Louis, MO St. Dominic Priory.
Bryda, Ronald J. '66 (CLV) Litchfield, OH Our Lady Help of Christians Parish.
Bryerton, Robert R. '74 (TUC) Hereford, AZ Retired.
Bryk, John J. '53 (CLV) Retired.
Bryl, Thaddeus J. '66 (MIL) Retired.
Brylka, Vincent R. '65 (OAK)[L] Oakland, CA Bishop Begin Villa Retired.
Brynda, Rev. Msgr. Gerald J. '57 (TUC) Retired.
Brynes, John *o.s.a.* '55 (PH) Philadelphia, PA St. Nicholas of Tolentine; [Y] Philadelphia, PA Augustinian Community (O.S.A.).
Bryon, Paul J. '46 (R) Retired.
Bryon, Thomas C. '63 (STL) Kirkwood, MO St. Gerard Majella.
Bryson, John H. '50 (MAN) Retired.
Brzek, Jon J. '81 (PIT) Military Chaplains; Navy Chaplains.
Brzezicki, Zbigniew Canon '88 (STF) Fresh Meadows, NY Annunciation of the B.V.M.
Brzezinski, Hilary *o.f.m.* '76 (MIL) Milwaukee, WI St. Anthony of Padua.
Brzezinski, Jerome A. '69 (DET) Auburn Hills, MI St. John Fisher Chapel University Parish.
Brzezniak, Aurelian W. *o.f.m.conv.* '45 (BUF)[D] Athol Springs, NY St. Francis High School; [O] Athol Springs, NY St. Francis of Assisi Friary Retired.
Brzoska, David '00 (GBG)[A] Latrobe, PA St. Vincent Seminary; On Duty Outside the Diocese.
Brzostowski, Hilary *o.f.m.conv.* '66 (TR) Delran, NJ The Church of the Resurrection, Delran Township, N.J.
Brzozowski, Simon *m.s.f.* '64 (L)[K] Louisville, KY St. Joseph Home for the Aged.
Bubel, Robert '08 (NY) Warwick, NY St. Stephen.
Buby, Bertrand A. *s.m.* '64 (CIN)[D] Dayton, OH The University of Dayton; [N] Dayton, OH Marianist Community.
Bucaria, James A. '72 (SP) Masaryktown, FL St. Mary, Our Lady of Sorrows.
Bucaro, Michael '80 (SB) Chino, CA California Institute for Men.
Buccafurni, Ferdinand '58 (PH) Philadelphia, PA St. Donato.
Buccellato, Sebastian *o.f.m.* '51 (NY)[EE] New York, NY Padua Friary; [GG] Wappingers Falls, NY Mt. Alvernia Retreat House.
Bucchino, John *o.f.m.* '73 (MAN) Manchester, NH Blessed Sacrament.
Bucci, Michael J. '62 (GBG) Retired.
Bucci, Richard A. '73 (PRO) West Warwick, RI Sacred Heart Church.
Bucciantini, Charles '72 (JKS) Leland, MS St. James; Approved Advocate and Auditors; Trustees.
Bucciantini, Charles '72 (BLX) Trustees.
Bucciarelli, Michael '75 (TUC) Benson, AZ The Roman Catholic Parish of Our Lady of Lourdes – Benson; Defenders of the Bond; Council of Priests; Vocations.
Buccicone, Ananias *o.s.b.* '93 (ALT) Patton, PA Queen of Peace.
Bucciferro, William *s.d.b.* '83 (NY)[GG] Stony Point, NY Don Bosco Retreat Center and Marian Shrine; [GG] Stony Point, NY Marian Shrine.
Bucek, Timothy P. '76 (GAL) Bellville, TX Sts. Peter & Paul.
Buchanan, Caleb A. '97 (BRK)[S] West Indian Apostolate; Brooklyn, NY St. Gregory the Great.
Buchanan, David '93 (BIR) Jasper, AL St. Cecilia.
Buchanan, Donald E. '65 (IND) Retired.
Buchanan, Robert E. '68 (SB) Retired.
Bucher, Mel *o.f.m.* '61 (SD)[J] Oceanside, CA Mission San Luis Rey Retired.
Bucher, Otto N. *o.f.m.cap.* '59 (MIL)[B] Hales Corners, WI Sacred Heart School of Theology.
Bucher, Otto N. *o.f.m.cap.* '59 (SUP) Rib Lake, WI Good Shepherd.
Bucher, Rev. Msgr. Philip A. '61 (SPC) Retired.

Bucher, Raymond J. *o.f.m.* '64 (OAK)[O] Danville, CA San Damiano Retreat.
Buchheit, Edward *c.p.* '63 (SCR)[M] Scranton, PA Saint Ann's Passionist Monastery.
Buchheit, Rev. Msgr. Jerome J. '51 (STL) Retired.
Buchheit, Rev. Msgr. Richard A. '51 (STL) Florissant, MO St. Norbert Retired.
Buchholz, Athanasius *o.s.b.* '54 (P)[L] St. Benedict, OR Mt. Angel Abbey.
Buchholz, Samuel James '01 (R) Elizabeth City, NC Holy Family; Deans; Council of Priests.
Buchignani, Rev. Msgr. Peter P. '65 (MEM) Cordova, TN St. Francis of Assisi; Vicar General; Clergy Personnel Board; College of Consultors; Adjutant Judicial Vicar; Presbyteral Council.
Buchignani, Richard G. '62 (NSH) Judges Retired.
Buchlein, Neil R. '98 (WH) Hurricane, WV Catholic Church of the Ascension.
Buchleitner, Donald N. '70 (PIT) Pittsburgh, PA Guardian Angels; Pittsburgh, PA Holy Innocents.
Buchman, Joel R. '91 (LA)[J] San Pedro, CA Providence Little Company of Mary San Pedro Peninsula Hospital Pavillion; [J] Torrance, CA Providence Little Company of Mary Sub–Acute Center–South Bay.
Buchmeier, Francis X. *s.j.* '73 (FgM) Milwaukee, WI Society of Jesus.
Buchmeier, Robert P. '91 (WDC) Oxon Hill, MD St. Columba.
Buchmelter, Brendan '80 (STA) Absent or Sick Leave.
Buchmiller, Ronald J. '69 (SD) Lakeside, CA Our Lady of Perpetual Help; Presbyteral Council; Clergy Personnel Board.
Buck, Daniel P. '71 (CHI) Other Assignments.
Buck, Frank '85 (ORL) Lakeland, FL St. John Neumann.
Buckalew, Jack '74 (SEA) Tracyton, WA Holy Trinity.
Buckel, John '80 (IND) On Disability Leave.
Bucki, John P. *s.j.* '79 (BUF)[O] Buffalo, NY Canisius Jesuit Community Inc.; [R] Buffalo, NY Canisius College, Campus Ministry Office; [C] Buffalo, NY Canisius College.
Buckius, Walter A. *s.j.* '52 (WH)[A] Wheeling, WV Wheeling Jesuit University.
Buckles, David J. '88 (LFT) West Lafayette, IN Blessed Sacrament; Special Assignment; Presiding Judge; Defenders of the Bond.
Buckles, Luke D. *o.p.* '78 (OAK)[M] Oakland Order of Preachers (Province of the Most Holy Name of Jesus – Western Dominican Province).
Buckley, Brendan P. *o.f.m.cap.* '81 (BO)[U] Jamaica Plain, MA St. Francis of Assisi Friary; Jamaica Plain, MA Our Lady of Lourdes.
Buckley, Charles J. *o.s.b.* '70 (OKL)[I] Shawnee, OK St. Gregory's Abbey.
Buckley, Cornelius M. *s.j.* '62 (LA)[C] Santa Paula, CA Thomas Aquinas College.
Buckley, Francis J. *s.j.* '58 (SJ)[M] Los Gatos, CA Sacred Heart Jesuit Center.
Buckley, Frank C. *s.j.* '08 (SFR) San Francisco, CA St. Agnes.
Buckley, Gerald J. '57 (SY) Binghamton Psychiatric Hospital; Binghamton, NY Binghamton Psychiatric Hospital; [Q] Binghamton, NY McDevitt Residence for Retired Priests; Presbyteral Council Retired.
Buckley, Gerald *o.p.* '57 (OAK)[M] Oakland, CA Order of Preachers (Province of the Most Holy Name of Jesus – Western Dominican Province).
Buckley, Harold P. '53 (RVC) Retired.
Buckley, James B. *f.s.s.p.* '65 (LIN)[A] Denton, NE Our Lady of Guadalupe Seminary; Denton, NE.
Buckley, James F. '59 (FR) Retired.
Buckley, James M. '90 (OM) Omaha, NE St. Patrick; Deans; Deans.
Buckley, John J. *c.m.* '57 (PH)[Y].
Buckley, John M. *s.j.* '56 (NEW)[B] Jersey City, NJ Jesuit Center; [M] Jersey City, NJ Jesuits of Saint Peter's College, Inc.
Buckley, John *s.s.c.* '68 (OM)[K] St. Columbans Missionary Society of St. Columban.
Buckley, John *s.s.c.* '68 (PRO)[P] Bristol, RI St. Columban's Retirement House.
Buckley, Michael J. *s.j.* '62 (SJ)[B] Santa Clara, CA Jesuit Community.
Buckley, Michael *o.c.d.* '47 (SR)[L] Oakville, CA Carmelite House of Prayer.
Buckley, Patrick (NY) Staten Island, NY St. Teresa.
Buckley, Thomas E. *s.j.* '70 (OAK)[A] Berkeley, CA Jesuit School of Theology at Santa Clara University; [M] Berkeley, CA Jesuit Fathers and Brothers.
Buckley, Thomas J. *s.j.* '74 (WDC)[N] Washington, DC The Jesuit Community at Georgetown University.
Buckley, Thomas R. '76 (ALN) Coopersburg, PA St. Joseph.
Buckley, Thomas W. '55 (BO) Senior Priests. Retired.
Buckley, Timothy J. '92 (PH) Warminster, PA Nativity of Our Lord.
Buckman, Frank (ORG) Retired.
Buckman, Tom '00 (OWN) Paducah, KY St. John the Evangelist.
Buckner, Christopher M. '80 (ARL) On Leave of Absence.
Buckner, Mark A. '02 (OWN) Owensboro, KY St. Mary Magdalene.
Bucko, Raymond A. *s.j.* '83 (OM)[K] Omaha, NE Jesuit Community at Creighton University.
Buckon, Neal J. '95 (CLV) Military Chaplains; Army Chaplains.
Bucon, Raymond H. '79 (MO) Army Reserve Chaplains; Dearborn Heights, MI St. Sabina.
Bucsek, Basil '68 (STN) Retired.
Buczyna, Andrew L. '87 (JOL) Absent on Leave.
Buda, Jacek *o.p.* '95 (NY)[II] New York, NY Polish Dominicans, Inc.
Budde, Rev. Msgr. John G. '77 (DET) Davisburg, MI Divine Mercy.
Budde, Todd '01 (MIL) Germantown, WI St. Boniface.
Budden, William A. '68 (RCK) Retired.
Buddendorff, Kenneth A. *s.j.* '61 (NO)[P] New Orleans, LA Ignatius Residence.
Budenholzer, Francis *s.v.d.* '72 (FgM) Techny, IL.
Budez, Jorge H. '02 (BUF) Absent on Leave.
Budhi, Adrianus *m.s.c.* '89 (SB) Riverside, CA St. Catherine of Alexandria; Riverside, CA Riverside Community Hospital.
Budka, Dennis G. '84 (MIL) Lomira, WI St. Mary; St. Theresa, WI St. Theresa.
Budke, Jon *l.c.* '01 (DEN)[S] Centennial, CO LC Pastoral Services Inc.
Budnar, Randy J. '88 (MAD) Darlington, WI Holy Rosary; Deaneries.
Budney, Rev. Msgr. David F. '57 (CAM) Retired.
Budovic, Francis X. *s.j.* '49 (DET)[K] Clarkston, MI Colombiere Center.
Budwick, Rev. Msgr. John J. '64 (NY) Middletown, NY St. Joseph.
Budzikowski, Kenneth A. '80 (CHI) Chicago, IL St. Thecla; Deans.
Buebendorf, Victor J. '64 (NY) Staten Island, NY St. Mary.
Bueche, Charles C. *c.ss.r.* '53 (STL)[O] Liguori, MO St. Clement Health Care Center Retired.
Bueche, William *c.ss.r.* '78 (STP) Brooklyn Center, MN St. Alphonsus; [K] Brooklyn Center, MN Redemptorist Fathers of Hennepin County.
Buechele, Andrew C. *sch.p.* '69 (WDC)[B] Washington, DC Queen of Pious Schools House of Studies–Piarist Fathers.
Buehler, John A. '74 (SY) Utica, NY St. John.
Buelt, Rev. Msgr. Edward '82 (DEN) Foxfield, CO Our Lady of Loreto; Members At Large; College of Consultors; Promoter of Justice.
Buena, Joey R. *c.s.s.* '06 (MRY) Pacific Grove, CA St. Angela Merici Church.
Buenaflor, Evelio '85 (HT) Amelia, LA St. Andrew.
Buendia, Francisco Jimenez '05 (BO)[U] Cambridge, MA Rahner House.
Buening, Matthew T. '03 (BAL)[V] Ellicott City, MD The St. Paul's Parish Endowment Trust; Ellicott City, MD St. Paul.
Buening, Robert B. '58 (CIN) Cincinnati, OH Corpus Christi Retired.
Bueno, Alberto *t.o.r.* '86 (WDC)[N] Washington, DC St. Louis Friary.
Bueno, Jaime '88 (CHY) Evanston, WY St. Mary Magdalen.
Buentello, Michael A. *c.s.b.* '95 (GAL)[R] Houston, TX University of St. Thomas Campus Ministry; [O] Houston, TX Residence of the Basilian Fathers of the University of St. Thomas.
Buentello, Michael *c.s.b.* '95 (GAL)[C] Houston, TX University of St. Thomas.
Buermann, Eric *o.s.b.* '45 (FAJ)[B] Humacao, PR San Antonio Abad Abbey of the Order of St. Benedict.
Buersmeyer, David A. '80 (DET) Washington, MI SS. John and Paul; Archdiocesan Vicars; Presbyteral Council.
Buerster, Rev. Msgr. James A. '79 (BEL) Germantown, IL St. Boniface; Sandoval, IL St. Lawrence; Diocesan Deans.
Buescher, David G. '71 (JC) Retired.
Bueter, Paul '59 (FTW) Cursillo.
Bueter, Robert *s.j.* '73 (CIN)[N] Cincinnati, OH Jesuit Community at Xavier University.
Buettner, George J. '52 (BAL) Retired.
Buettner, Matthew R. '03 (CHL) Lincolnton, NC St. Dorothy.
Bueya, Emmanuel *s.j.* '05 (BO)[U] Newton, MA The Jesuit Community at Boston College.
Bueza, Ritche '03 (SJ) Santa Clara, CA St. Justin; Deans; Diocesan Clergy Personnel Board; Council of Priests.
Buffardi, Joseph G. '76 (PAT) Parsippany, NJ St. Christopher.
Buffer, Thomas J. '91 (COL) Columbus, OH Saint Stephen the Martyr; Censor of Books.
Buffington, Jon '81 (P)[J] Portland, OR Providence Portland Medical Center.
Bufogle, Arthur '04 (WH) Hinton, WV Sacred Heart; Hinton, WV St. Patrick.
Buga, John '99 (ROM) Retired.
Bugarin, Fred '72 (ANC) Anchorage, AK St. Anthony; Diocesan Consultors.
Bugarin, Rev. Msgr. G. Michael '91 (DET) St. Clair Shores, MI St. Joan of Arc; Archdiocesan Vicars; Presbyteral Council; Special Assignment.
Bugas, Joel O. '09 (SFE) Albuquerque, NM Annunciation.
Bugay, Stephen R. '84 (GBG) Republic, PA Madonna of Czestochowa; Republic, PA Holy Rosary.
Bugayong, Demetrio L. '70 (LA) Carson, CA St. Philomena.
Buggert, Donald W. *o.carm.* '66 (WDC)[B] Washington, DC Whitefriars Hall.
Buggert, William *o.carm.* (FTW)[B] University of Notre Dame Du Lac.
Bughagar, Desmond *s.j.* '05 (BAL)[S] Baltimore, MD Ferdinand Wheeler Jesuit Community.
Bugler, Rev. Msgr. Henry J. '75 (NO) Destrehan, LA St. Charles Borromeo.
Bugman, Rev. Msgr. John H. '52 (BUF) Lackawanna, NY Our Lady of Victory National Shrine Retired.
Bugner, Joseph *s.v.d.* '63 (CHI)[N] Techny, IL Divine Word Residence.
Bugno, Krzystof *s.d.s.* '85 (SAT)[L] Falls City, TX Salvatorian Fathers Community of Texas.
Bugno, Krzysztof *s.d.s.* (ORL) Titusville, FL St. Teresa.
Buhake, Longin '96 (ORL) Kissimmee, FL Holy Redeemer.
Buhl, Wilbert L. '60 (GB) Maplewood, WI Retired.
Buhler, Richard O. *s.j.* '70 (STL) St. Louis, MO St. Francis Xavier; [O] St. Louis, MO The Jesuits of the Missouri Province; Saint Louis, MO; [O] St. Louis, MO Jesuit Community Corporation at Saint Louis University – Jesuit Hall.
Buhman, Jay M. '05 (LIN) Advocates; Lincoln, NE Cathedral of the Risen Christ.
Buhman, Leo T. '48 (JC) Retired.
Buholzer, Robert E. '56 (MAD) Retired.
Buhr, Donald L. '66 (STL) St. Louis, MO Our Lady of the Holy Cross.
Buhr, Eugene S. '54 (LA) Hawthorne, CA St. Joseph Retired.
Buhrman, Donald A. '86 (GI) St. Libory, NE St. Libory's; Spalding, NE St. Michael's; Diocesan Consultors.
Bui, Dong '92 (JOL) Naperville, IL Sts. Peter and Paul.
Bui, Dung Quang '02 (STA) Gainesville, FL St. Patrick Church.
Bui, Francis Quyet '90 (HT) Larose, LA Our Lady of the Rosary.
Bui, Francis Ty '75 (LA) Winnetka, CA St. Joseph the Worker.
Bui, Joseph Hoang Huy '04 (GAL) Spring, TX Christ the Good Shepherd.
Bui, Joseph T.P. '97 (GAL) Houston, TX Christ, The Incarnate Word.
Bui, Joseph '91 (ORL) Indialantic, FL Holy Name of Jesus.
Bui, Joseph *p.i.m.e.* '00 (PHX) Glendale, AZ St. Louis The King Roman Catholic Parish.
Bui, Khue Si '01 (BEA) Beaumont, TX St. Joseph.
Bui, Marion Joseph *o.c.d.* '95 (LR)[A] Little Rock, AR Marylake – Carmelite Novitiate.
Bui, Minh Cong '01 (ORG) Adjutant Judicial Vicars; Judges; Special Assignment.
Bui, Minh '00 (ORG) Santa Ana, CA Christ Our Savior Cathedral.
Bui, Peter Dai '03 (PHX) Mesa, AZ Christ the King Roman Catholic Parish.
Bui, Peter Tam '01 (WOR) Worcester, MA Our Lady of Vilna.
Bui, Peter *s.d.b.* '90 (LA)[D] Rosemead, CA Don Bosco Technical Institute.
Bui, Phong (ORL) Special Assignment.
Bui, Phong (TUC) Tucson, AZ Arizona State Prison.
Bui, Tam M. '01 (WOR) Vietnamese Apostolate; Vietnamese Ministry.
Bui, Thaddeus *o.h.* (LA)[K] Ojai, CA St. Joseph's Health and Retirement Center.
Bui, Tho *s.d.b.* '07 (MRY)[F] Watsonville, CA Saint Francis Salesian Community; [B] Watsonville, CA St. Francis Central Coast Catholic High School; Watsonville, CA Our Lady Help of Christians.
Bui, Tin Mahn '75 (SFE) Albuquerque, NM Our Lady of Lavang.
Bui, Tuan *c.ss.r.* '97 (DAL) Garland, TX Mother of Perpetual Help.
Bui, Vincent D. *s.s.* '95 (BAL)[S] Baltimore Society of St. Sulpice, Province of the United States.
Bui, Vincent *s.s.* '95 (LAN) On Duty Outside the Diocese.
Buitrago, Alex '67 (DAL) Dallas, TX St. Elizabeth.
Buitrago, Luis '67 (DAL) Dallas, TX Parkland Health & Hospital System.
Buitrago, Tarsicio '64 (ARL) Basye, VA Our Lady of the Shenandoah.
Buitron, Luis Segundo '00 (CR) Kelliher, MN St. Patrick.
Bujnak, George A. '65 (PSC) McAdoo, PA St. Michael.
Bukala, Casimir R. *s.j.* '66 (CLV)[B] University Heights, OH John Carroll Jesuit Community.
Bukauskas, Raimundas *o.f.m.* '04 (PRT)[I] Kennebunkport, ME St. Anthony's Friary.

Bukofsky, James W. '71 (BRK) On Leave/Unassigned.
Bukowski, Jan *cor* (CHI) Bridgeview, IL St. Fabian; Chicago, IL St. Helen.
Bula, Sebastine *v.c.* '04 (TUC) San Manuel, AZ Saint Bartholomew Roman Catholic Parish – San Manuel.
Bulala, Matthew (CHR) Myrtle Beach, SC St. Andrew.
Bulfer, Stephen C. '73 (FRS) Mariposa, CA St. Joseph.
Bulger, John '64 (SEA) Retired.
Bulinda, Ernest Livasia '88 (RIC) Norfolk, VA Basilica of St. Mary of the Immaculate Conception.
Bulinski, Marcin J. '07 (CHI) Oak Lawn, IL St. Linus.
Bullene, Richard S. *c.s.c.* '83 (FTW)[B] University of Notre Dame Du Lac; [H] Notre Dame, IN Holy Cross Community, Corby Hall, University of Notre Dame.
Buller, Ruben J. '08 (LKC) Lake Charles, LA St. Henry; Vocation Recruiters.
Bullman, Rudolph '00 (HEL) Kalispell, MT Risen Christ; Presbyteral Council; Deaneries; Montana Association of Churches; Diocesan Ecumenical Officer.
Bullock, Gabriel G. *o.s.b.* '61 (PEO)[A] Peru, IL St. Bede Abbey.
Bullock, John *l.c.* '02 (LA)[P] Arcadia, CA Legionaries of Christ.
Bullock, Scott E. '91 (DUB)[A] Dubuque, IA Seminary of St. Pius X; Dubuque, IA St. Catherine; Bellevue, IA St. Donatus; Bellevue, IA St. Joseph; Judges; Newly Ordained Program; Seminarians; Seminary Admissions and Advisory Board; Worship Commission; On Special or Other Archdiocesan Assignment; Priestly Life and Ministry Committee.
Bullock, Stewart '06 (BAL) Severna Park, MD St. John the Evangelist.
Bulwith, Richard E. '67 (CHI)[G] Chicago, IL Catholic Charities of the Archdiocese of Chicago–Archdiocesan Offices; [G] Hines, IL Cooke's Manor Transitional Housing For Men; Associate Administrators; Chicago, IL Our Lady of Lourdes.
Bumbar, Rev. Canon Philip '68 (SJP) Carnegie, PA Holy Trinity.
Bumbar, Rev. Archpriest Philip (SJP) Arbitration Board; Presbyters.
Bumbarger, Bruce *m.ss.cc.* '92 (BIR) Clanton, AL Church of the Resurrection.
Bumpus, Rev. Msgr. Harold '63 (SP) Retired.
Bunch, Randall (JC)[B] Jefferson City, MO St. Mary Health Center.
Bunch, Timothy S. '79 (CIN) Hamilton, OH St. Peter in Chains; Vicarri Foranei (Deans).
Bunda, Roland *s.m.* '67 (HON) Wailuku, HI St. Anthony of Padua.
Bunda, Roland *s.m.* '78 (HON)[D] Wailuku, HI Wailuku Marianist Community.
Bundac, Nito (NY) Ossining, NY St. Ann.
Bundz, Michael '81 (STF) Utica, NY St. Michael; Utica, NY St. Volodymyr the Great.
Bunger, Kevin J. '83 (SY) Port Crane, NY St. Joseph.
Bungo, Samuel '77 (E) New Bethlehem, PA St. Charles.
Buni, Leon Salvador A. '75 (TR) Toms River, NJ St. Joseph.
Bunik, Wasyl '93 (PHU) Warrington, PA Presentation of Our Lord; Warrington, PA St. Anne's.
Bunnell, Adam *o.f.m.conv.* '73 (L) Louisville, KY St. Paul; [A] Bellarmine University.
Bunnell, Thomas J. *s.j.* '74 (YAK) Sunnyside, WA St. Joseph's.
Bunny, Rev. Msgr. Michael '65 (LA) Newbury Park, CA St. Julie Billiart.
Bunofsky, Walter *s.v.d.* '60 (DUB)[B] Epworth, IA Divine Word College.
Bunse, Gerald L. '83 (SFD) Farmersville, IL St. Mary; Morrisonville, IL St. Maurice; Raymond, IL St. Raymond.
Bunse, Gerald '51 (SFD) Graham Correctional Center.
Bunsic, Albert *o.c.d.* '67 (TUC)[D] Tucson, AZ Discalced Carmelite Friars of St. Margaret Mary's; Tucson, AZ Saint Margaret Mary Alacoque Roman Catholic Parish – Tucson.
Buntel, Richard A. '71 (BO) Permanent Disability.
Bunyan, Gregory '96 (AMA) Memphis, TX Sacred Heart; Spearman, TX Sacred Heart; Gruver, TX Cristo Redentor.
Buonanno, Vito A. '81 (BRK) Art and Architecture Commission; Liturgical Commission.
Buonanno, Vito A. '81 (BRK)[R] Washington, DC Basilica of the National Shrine of the Immaculate Conception; Released from Diocesan Assignment.
Buongirno, Robert F. (NOR) Lebanon, CT St. Francis of Assisi.
Buono, Carmen '07 (PAT)[C] Denville, NJ Morris Catholic High School; Dover, NJ Sacred Heart.
Buono, Joseph *c.ss.r.* '43 (ALB)[L] Saratoga Springs, NY St. John Neumann Residence.
Buonopane, Gerald '06 (NEW) Livingston, NJ St. Philomena.
Buontempo, Giovanni '98 (WDC)[A] Hyattsville, MD Redemptoris Mater Archdiocesan Missionary Seminary.
Buote, Martin L. '60 (FR) Retired.
Bur, George W. *s.j.* '72 (PH)[F] Philadelphia, PA St. Joseph's Preparatory School; [Y] Philadelphia, PA Jesuit Community, Arrupe House.
Burak, Paul '72 (CHI) Orland Park, IL St. Michael.
Burakowski, Wieslaw '92 (NSH) Retired.
Buranosky, Dennis M. '72 (PIT) Bellevue, PA Assumption of the Blessed Virgin Mary on the Beautiful River.
Burasa, James *c.s.c.* '95 (FTW)[H] Notre Dame Congregation of Holy Cross, Indiana Province, Provincial House.
Burba, Edward A. '75 (CLV) Akron, OH St. Mary.
Burbach, Jude *o.s.b.* '53 (KCK)[I] Atchison, KS St. Benedict's Abbey Retired.
Burbank, Robert J. '64 (HRT) Branford, CT St. Mary Retired.
Burch, Edward '03 (R) Kinston, NC Holy Spirit Catholic Church.
Burch, Francis F. *s.j.* '63 (PH)[Y] Loyola Center and Manresa Hall.
Burch, Thaddeus J. *s.j.* '61 (MIL)[P] Milwaukee, WI Jesuit Community at Marquette University.
Burchell, Richard '75 (CLV) Solon, OH St. Rita.
Burchfield, Michael A. '93 (FRS) On Special Assignment; Judicial Vicar; Tribunal Judges.
Burchfield, Michael '93 (FRS) Fresno, CA Shrine of St. Therese.
Burchill, John P. *o.p.* '65 (PRO) Providence, RI St. Pius V; [P] Providence, RI St. Pius Priory.
Burckhart, William C. '53 (BO) Senior Priests.; Westwood, MA St. Denis Retired.
Burda, Andriy (STN) Dearborn Heights, MI Our Lady of Perpetual Help.
Burden, George W. *s.s.j.* '91 (MOB) Mobile, AL Prince of Peace.
Burdess, James J. '88 (ALN) Summit Hill, PA St. Joseph.
Burdick, Thomas J. '84 (SB) Hemet; Appointed Members; Winchester, CA Blessed Teresa of Calcutta Catholic Community, Inc.
Burdzy, Krystian '03 (MET) East Brunswick, NJ St. Bartholomew.
Burek, Frank J. '71 (CHI) Chicago, IL St. Robert Bellarmine.
Bures, Francis *s.v.d.* '53 (FgM) Techny, IL.
Burgaleta, Claudio M. *s.j.* '92 (NY)[EE] Cardinal Spellman Hall, Jesuit Community.
Burgard, David G. '94 (DET) Wayne, MI St. Mary; Inkster, MI Holy Family Parish.
Burge, Robert '71 (CLV) Retired.
Burger, Edward K. *s.j.* '70 (STL)[O] St. Louis, MO Ignatius House.
Burger, Francis '69 (KCK) Archdiocesan Consultors.
Burger, Frank '69 (KCK) Olathe, KS Prince of Peace; Priests' Council.
Burger, John *s.s.c.* '73 (FgM) St Columbans, NE U.S. Foundation & Administration.
Burger, Joseph '54 (OKL) Retired.
Burger, Mark J. '80 (CIN) West Chester, OH St. John; Vicarri Foranei (Deans); Consultors; Ex Officio Members.
Burger, Philip G. '83 (HBG) Hershey, PA St. Joan of Arc; [I] Harrisburg, PA Hershey Medical Center; Deans; Pastoral Council, Diocesan.
Burger, Rev. Msgr. Raymond '60 (KCK) Vice–Chancellor; Defenders of the Bond Retired.
Burger, Robert '48 (KCK) Retired.
Burget, Joel *o.f.m.conv.* '66 (IND) Terre Haute, IN St. Benedict.
Burghoff, Theodore H. '55 (STL) Retired.
Burgoon, Charles E. '64 (STL) St. Louis, MO St. Richard; Deaneries/Deans.
Burgos, Adnel T. '89 (BRK) Richmond Hill, NY Our Lady of the Cenacle.
Burgos, Jose Ramon (BRK) Brooklyn, NY St. Lucy–St. Patrick.
Burgos, Roman *t.o.r.* '02 (AUS) Waco, TX St. Francis on the Brazos; Waco, TX.
Burgoyne, Sidney C. '54 (PH) Retired.
Burgues, Jose P. *sch.p.* '81 (MIA)[Q] Miami, FL SEPI Evangelization and Education Foundation, Inc.; [O] Miami, FL Southeast Regional Office for Hispanic Ministry, Inc.; [O] Miami, FL Southeast Pastoral Institute.
Burian, Rev. Msgr. Ed '65 (SFS) Woonsocket, SD St. Joseph Retired.
Burk, Robert J. *m.s.a.* '03 (WIL) Georgetown, DE St. Michael the Archangel.
Burk, Robert *m.s.a.* '03 (NOR)[G] Cromwell Society of the Missionaries of the Holy Apostles.
Burkard, Rev. Msgr. Paul J.E. '69 (BUF)[J] Lackawanna, NY Baker Victory Services; Finance Council; Vicars; Lackawanna, NY Our Lady of Victory National Shrine.
Burkardt, Donald (GB) Retired.
Burkart, James M. '93 (GAL) Liturgical Commission.
Burkart, James M. '93 (GAL) Houston, TX St. Luke the Evangelist.
Burkauskas, Peter M. '79 (PH) Philadelphia, PA St. Andrew; Philadelphia, PA St. Casimir.
Burke, Adrian *o.s.b.* '97 (IND)[K] St. Meinrad, IN St. Meinrad Archabbey.
Burke, Alfred M. *o.s.a.* '57 (FgM)[N] Olympia Fields, IL Tolentine Monastery at Tolentine Center; Olympia Fields, IL Province of Our Mother of Good Counsel (Midwestern).
Burke, Alfred '69 (NEW) Union, NJ Holy Spirit.
Burke, Christopher R. '86 (PBR) Boardman, OH Infant Jesus of Prague.
Burke, Clement J. '61 (DUB) Retired.
Burke, Donal *o.f.m.cap.* '75 (SFR)[N] Burlingame, CA Capuchin Provincial House.
Burke, Edmund M. '77 (NY) Kingston, NY St. Mary; Kingston, NY St. Peter.
Burke, Edmund '77 (NY) Kingston, NY Kingston City Hospital.
Burke, Edward P. '73 (PH) Philadelphia, PA Cathedral Basilica of SS. Peter and Paul.
Burke, Eugene A. *c.s.c.* '53 (FTW)[H] Holy Cross House.
Burke, Geoffrey D. '79 (ALB) Latham, NY Our Lady of the Assumption; [M] Latham, NY Provincial House of the Sisters of St. Joseph of Carondelet (Albany Province); Province Leadership Team:; Deans.
Burke, Gilbert J. *o.s.b.* '62 (GBG)[G] Latrobe, PA Saint Vincent Archabbey.
Burke, Gregory '51 (HEL)[E] Butte, MT St. James Health Care, Sisters of Charity of Leavenworth Health System Retired.
Burke, Harry '63 (NY)[E] Bronx, NY Cardinal Hayes High School.
Burke, Herbert '92 (CHL) Forest City, NC Immaculate Conception.
Burke, Rev. Msgr. James A. '56 (NEW) Midland Park, NJ Nativity Retired.
Burke, James C. '64 (ROC) Retired.
Burke, James G. '77 (BO) Westwood, MA St. Denis; Defenders of the Bond; Canonical Affairs Committee.
Burke, Rev. Msgr. James M. '64 (PMB) Assessors; Port St. Lucie, FL St. Lucie; Advocates Retired.
Burke, James *c.ss.r.* '56 (CHR) Sumter, SC St. Anne; Sumter, SC St. Jude.
Burke, James *o.p.* (GAL) Houston, TX Holy Rosary.
Burke, John F. '55 (WOR) Retired.
Burke, John R. '54 (E) Retired.
Burke, John R. '72 (L) Louisville, KY St. William; Louisville, KY Good Shepherd.
Burke, Joseph F. *s.j.* '78 (BUF)[A] East Aurora, NY Christ the King Seminary; [O] Buffalo, NY Canisius Jesuit Community Inc.
Burke, Kevin F. *s.j.* '86 (OAK)[A] Berkeley, CA Jesuit School of Theology at Santa Clara University; [A] Berkeley, CA Jesuit School of Theology at Santa Clara University; [M] Berkeley, CA Jesuit Fathers and Brothers.
Burke, Kevin F. *s.j.* '86 (SJ)[B] Santa Clara University.
Burke, Lawrence A. *o.f.m.* (NY)[EE] New York Franciscan Friars, Holy Name Province.
Burke, Mark J. *s.j.* '93 (BO)[U] Boston The Society of Jesus of New England–Provincial Offices.
Burke, Michael A. '76 (PAT) Prospect Park, NJ St. Paul's.
Burke, Rev. Msgr. Michael J. '62 (PH) Primos, PA St. Eugene Retired.
Burke, Michael J. (PAT) Pro–Synodal Judges; Catholic Family and Community Services.
Burke, Rev. Msgr. Michael L. '74 (MAD) Madison, WI St. Maria Goretti; Diocesan Consultors; Appointed.
Burke, Michael M. *o.p.* '68 (NO) New Orleans, LA St. Anthony of Padua.
Burke, Michael '50 (CC) Retired.
Burke, Michael *s.c.j.* '63 (MIL)[P] Franklin, WI Villa Maria.
Burke, Paul A. '96 (ATL)[B] Dawsonville, GA Southern Catholic College; Atlanta, GA Holy Spirit.
Burke, Richard *c.p.* '76 (SCR)[R] Scranton, PA St. Ann's Foundation; [M] Scranton, PA Saint Ann's Passionist Monastery.
Burke, Robert M. *o.s.a.* '55 (PH)[Y] Villanova, PA St. Thomas Monastery.
Burke, Robert *s.s.c.* '49 (OM)[K] St. Columbans Missionary Society of St. Columban Retired.
Burke, Ronald A. '54 (SFR) Retired.
Burke, Ronald '72 (HON) Retired.
Burke, Ronald '72 (LSC) Retired.
Burke, Thomas J. *o.ss.t.* '78 (BAL) Councilors:; [S] Baltimore, MD.
Burke, Thomas J. '01 (PIT) Braddock, PA Good Shepherd; Priest Council; College of Consultors.
Burke, Thomas J. *o.ss.t.* '78 (WDC)[E] Hyattsville, MD De Matha Catholic High School.
Burke, Thomas *c.ss.r.* '81 (CHR) Sumter, SC St. Anne.
Burke, Vincent *s.v.d.* '61 (FgM) Techny, IL.
Burke, William A. '65 (CHI) Retired.
Burke, Rev. Msgr. William F. '59 (BAL) Baltimore, MD St. Francis of Assisi; Catholic Campaign For Human Development, Archdiocese of Baltimore, Inc.
Burke, William F. '75 (MEM) Millington, TN St. William.
Burke, William *s.j.* (GF)[G] Billings, MT St. Vincent Healthcare.
Burke, William *o.p.* '60 (WDC) Washington, DC St. Dominic Church & Priory.
Burkemper, Robert W. '81 (STL) Overland, MO All Souls.

Burkert, Gerald F. '61 (IND)[I] Beech Grove, IN St. Paul Hermitage Retired.
Burkert, William C. '71 (MIL) Milwaukee, WI Our Lady of Lourdes.
Burkey, Blaine *o.f.m.cap.* '61 (DEN)[N] Denver, CO St. Francis of Assisi Friary; [N] Denver, CO Capuchin Province of Mid–America, Inc.
Burkhalter, Ross C. '94 (OM) Graduate Studies.
Burkhard, John *o.f.m.conv.* '67 (WDC)[N] Silver Spring, MD Gemelli House; Rensselaer, NY.
Burkhardt, Alan T. '86 (LC) Stevens Point, WI St. Joseph; [L] Stevens Point, WI St. Joseph's Congregation, Stevens Point Endowment Trust.
Burkhardt, Odilo *o.s.b.* '50 (SFS)[F] Marvin, SD Blue Cloud Abbey.
Burkle, Raymond A. '90 (DUB) Holy Cross, IA Holy Trinity; Holy Cross, IA St. Joseph; Holy Cross, IA SS. Peter and Paul; Holy Cross, IA Holy Cross; Holy Cross, IA St. Francis of Assisi; [F] Holy Cross, IA LaSalle Elementary Schools.
Burkley, John T. '70 (CLV) Middlefield, OH St. Lucy; Parkman, OH St. Edward.
Burks, William P. '86 (L) Louisville, KY St. Pius X.
Burkus, John '40 (ELP) Retired.
Burla, Frank J. '63 (NEW) Montclair, NJ Immaculate Conception.
Burnell, Robert J. '70 (CHI) Lyons, IL St. Hugh.
Burnett, Eugene David *o.f.m.* '54 (LA)[P] Los Angeles, CA St. Joseph Friary.
Burnett, George P. '61 (HRT) Ansonia, CT Assumption Retired.
Burnett, James E. '74 (DAV) On Duty Outside the Diocese; DEPARTMENT OF VETERANS AFFAIRS HOSPITALS AND CHAPLAINS.
Burnett, James E. '74 (MO) Presbyteral Council.
Burnett, James '68 (JOL) Absent on Leave.
Burnett, James '74 (CHI) Hines V.A. Hospital.
Burnett, Timothy J. *o.s.b.* '80 (NO) Folsom, LA St. John the Baptist.
Burnette, John '85 (SFD) Quincy, IL St. Peter.
Burnette, Kurt '89 (VNN) Albuquerque, NM Our Lady of Perpetual Help; Commission for the Implementation of the Particular Law; College of Consultors; Adjutant Judicial Vicar; Pension Committee.
Burnette, Kurt '89 (LAV) Defender of the Bond; Diocesan Judges.
Burnham, Martin J. '02 (BAL) Annapolis, MD St. Andrew by the Bay; [V] Annapolis, MD St. Andrew by the Bay Endowment Trust.
Burnia, Scott A. '88 (SD) Jamul, CA St. Pius X.
Burnie, James *c.s.sp.* '84 (LR) Hattieville, AR St. Mary.
Burns, Basil David *o.s.b.* '01 (NO)[P] St. Benedict, LA St. Joseph Abbey.
Burns, Basil (NO)[A] St. Benedict, LA St. Joseph Seminary College.
Burns, Charles F. *s.j.* '72 (MIL)[P] Milwaukee Jesuit Provincial Office, Wisconsin Province.
Burns, Claude Thomas '02 (EVN) Evansville, IN Holy Spirit.
Burns, Douglas C. *o.s.f.s.* '99 (ALN)[B] Center Valley, PA DeSales University; [K] Center Valley, PA Oblates of St. Francis de Sales.
Burns, Edward J. '54 (FR) Retired.
Burns, Edward M. '04 (CIN)[R] Fairborn, OH Catholic Campus Ministry.
Burns, Rev. Msgr. G. Thomas '57 (NEW) Retired.
Burns, Gerald H. '69 (BR) Baton Rouge, LA St. Aloysius.
Burns, Gerald '09 (SEA) Aberdeen, WA Our Lady of Good Help; Aberdeen, WA St. Mary; Aberdeen, WA SS. Peter and Paul; Aberdeen, WA St. Jerome.
Burns, Hugh *o.p.* '82 (NY) Pleasantville, NY Holy Innocents.
Burns, James P. '93 (STP)[C] St. Paul, MN University of St. Thomas; Graduate Studies.
Burns, Rev. Msgr. John A. '48 (BRK) Brooklyn, NY Mary Queen of Heaven Retired.
Burns, John F. '48 (BO) Senior Priests. Retired.
Burns, John M. *o.carm.* '82 (STP)[L] Lake Elmo, MN Carmel of Our Lady of Divine Providence; [K] Lake Elmo, MN Carmelite Hermitage of the Blessed Virgin Mary; Lake Elmo, MN.
Burns, John P. '03 (FRS) Retired.
Burns, John R. '90 (PEO) Galva, IL St. John's; Woodhull, IL St. John's; [O] Moline, IL The Order of the Legion of Little Souls of the Merciful Heart of Jesus.
Burns, John '65 (ALB) Deans.
Burns, John '65 (ALB) Morris, NY Holy Cross.
Burns, Joseph Clement *o.p.* '54 (CIN)[N] Cincinnati, OH St. Gertrude Priory; Cincinnati, OH St. Gertrude.
Burns, Joseph '60 (CAM) Retired.
Burns, Rev. Msgr. Lawrence E. '56 (MAN) Retired.
Burns, Lawrence E. '62 (BUF) Blasdell, NY Our Mother of Good Counsel.
Burns, Malcolm J. '85 (RVC) Farmingville, NY Church of the Resurrection.
Burns, Michael J. '58 (SJ) Los Altos, CA St. Simon Retired.
Burns, Michael J. '73 (TR) Bordentown, NJ St. Mary; Legion of Mary.
Burns, Michael *s.d.s.* '05 (MIL)[N] Milwaukee, WI St. Anne's Salvatorian Campus.
Burns, Norbert C. *s.m.* '53 (CIN)[D] Dayton, OH The University of Dayton; [N] Dayton, OH Marianist Community.
Burns, Patrick G. '92 (BRK) Jackson Heights, NY Blessed Sacrament.
Burns, Patrick J. *s.j.* '63 (MIL)[P] Milwaukee, WI Arrupe House Jesuit Community; [P] Milwaukee, WI Jesuit Provincial Office, Wisconsin Province.
Burns, Paul D. *c.s.s.* '61 (SPR) Springfield, MA Our Lady of Mt. Carmel.
Burns, Peter *s.j.* '53 (SJ)[M] Los Gatos, CA Sacred Heart Jesuit Center.
Burns, Robert A. *o.p.* '61 (TUC) Tucson, AZ Saint Thomas More Roman Catholic Newman Parish – Tucson; [G] Tucson, AZ University of Arizona.
Burns, Robert O. *s.j.* '57 (OM)[K] Omaha, NE Jesuit Community at Creighton University.
Burns, Thomas J. '54 (SFR) Retired.
Burns, Thomas J. *m.m.* '69 (FgM) Maryknoll, NY MARYKNOLL.
Burns, Thomas *s.c.j.* '65 (SP)[N] Pinellas Park, FL Priests of the Sacred Heart.
Burns, Tom *m.s.c.* '64 (SB) Crestline, CA St. Frances Xavier Cabrini.
Burns, Vincent M. *s.j.* '57 (BGP)[O] Fairfield, CT The Fairfield Jesuit Community–Fairfield University.
Burns, Rev. Msgr. Vincent P. '67 (PH) On Duty Outside the Archdiocese.
Burns, Vincent '67 (JKS) Aberdeen, MS St. Francis of Assisi.
Burns, William L. '85 (HRT) Hartford, CT St. Lawrence O'Toole Retired.
Burr, Jeremiah R. *m.m.* '67 (FgM) Maryknoll, NY MARYKNOLL.
Burr, Stephen '02 (DET)[A] The College of Liberal Arts.
Burr, Thomas E. '73 (RCK) Retired.
Burrascano, Anthony P. *o.s.a.* '79 (PH) Bryn Mawr, PA Our Mother of Good Counsel; [Y] Villanova, PA Provincial Offices of the Order of St. Augustine, Province of St. Thomas of Villanova; [Y] Bryn Mawr, PA Augustinians Friars (O.S.A.); Counselors:; Villanova, PA Province of St. Thomas of Villanova (Eastern).
Burrell, David B. *c.s.c.* '59 (FgM) New Rochelle, NY Eastern Brothers Province.
Burrows, Michael *o.s.b.* '80 (RCK)[G] Aurora, IL Marmion Abbey.
Burshek, James J. *s.j.* '75 (STL)[O] St. Louis, MO; [S] St. Louis, MO Retreat House.
Burshnick, Frank *s.c.j.* '70 (SP)[N] Pinellas Park, FL Priests of the Sacred Heart.
Burson, James *c.j.m.* '63 (SD) San Diego, CA Blessed Sacrament.
Burt, Donald X. *o.s.a.* '55 (PH)[Y] Villanova, PA St. Thomas Monastery.
Burt, Michael E. '09 (GR) Remus, MI St. Michael's.
Burtchaell, James *c.s.c.* (FTW)[H] Notre Dame Congregation of Holy Cross, Indiana Province, Provincial House.
Burtka, Joseph *l.c.* (HRT)[B] Cheshire, CT Novitiate of the Legion of Christ.
Burton, C. Jefferies *s.j.* '67 (BAL)[S] Baltimore, MD Colombiere Jesuit Community.
Burton, Charles '80 (KNX) Chattanooga, TN St. Jude.
Burton, Rev. Msgr. John H. '72 (CAM) Vineland, NJ The Catholic Church of the Sacred Heart, Vineland, N.J.; Vineland, NJ The Church of Saint Isidore the Farmer, Vineland, N.J.; Liturgical Art and Architectural Commission; College of Consultors; Vicars General; Cumberland Deanery; Liturgical Commission; Ex Officio Members; Ex Officio Members; Ex Officio Members.
Burton, Richard T. '03 (BO) Peabody, MA St. Thomas the Apostle; Peabody, MA Our Lady of Fatima.
Burton, Rev. Msgr. Richard W. '63 (WDC)[M] Washington, DC Cardinal O'Boyle Residence for Priests Retired.
Burton, William *o.f.m.* '89 (CHI)[N] Chicago, IL St. Peter's Friary.
Burtschi, J. Richard *s.j.* '71 (STL)[O] St. Louis, MO Jesuit Community Corporation at Saint Louis University – Jesuit Hall.
Burusu, Valery '92 (SPC)[D] Joplin, MO St. John's Regional Medical Center; Mercy Lifecare Systems; Joplin, MO Joplin Hospital Ministry.
Burwinkel, Elmer J. '84 (IND)[P] Madison, IN Mary's King's Village Schoenstatt Center, Inc. Retired.
Bury, Anthony '91 (CHI) Chicago, IL St. Bruno.
Bury, Antoni *s.ch.* '56 (LA) Los Angeles, CA Our Lady of the Bright Mount.
Bury, Harold J. '55 (STP) Retired.
Buryadnyk, Mykola '02 (STN) Chicago, IL St. Joseph.
Buryadnyk, Mykola '02 (CHI)[J] Chicago, IL Resurrection Medical Center.
Buryska, James F. '65 (WIN) On Special or Other Diocesan Assignment; [D] Rochester, MN Saint Mary Hospital; Coordinator of Diocesan Health Ministry; Hospitals.
Burzawa, Janusz '86 (SP) St. Petersburg, FL The Mercy of God Polish Mission.
Burzynski, Michael H. '89 (BUF) Council of Priests; Niagara Falls, NY St. Mary of the Cataract.
Bus, Anthony *c.r.* '84 (CHI) Chicago, IL St. Stanislaus Kostka.
Busch, Arthur '58 (WCH) Retired.
Busch, August '56 (EVN) Retired.
Busch, Joseph '80 (ALB) Queensbury, NY Our Lady of the Annunciation.
Busch, Robert A. '93 (OKL)[A] Shawnee, OK St. Gregory's University.
Busch, Robert '93 (AMA) On Duty Outside the Diocese.
Busch, Vernon *o.f.m.cap.* '60 (PIT)[M] Pittsburgh, PA St. Augustine Friary.
Busch, Vincent J. *s.s.c.* '74 (FgM) St Columbans, NE House of Post–Graduate Studies.
Busco, Rev. Msgr. John J. '40 (PH) Retired.
Buse, Harold J. '77 (OM) Omaha, NE St. Leo; [O] Omaha, NE St. Vincent de Paul Society.
Busemeyer, Louis E. *s.j.* '70 (CHI)[D] Chicago, IL St. Ignatius Jesuit Community.
Busemeyer, Louis *s.j.* '70 (RCK) Aurora, IL St. Rita of Cascia.
Bush, Bernard J. *s.j.* '65 (SJ)[L] Los Altos, CA Jesuit Retreat Center of Los Altos.
Bush, Carson '03 (CHR) Absent On Leave.
Bush, Frederick '51 (ROC) Rochester, NY St. Mark Retired.
Bush, Robert '69 (SAN) Abilene, TX Sacred Heart.
Bush, Scott '92 (HON) Vicars Forane; College of Consultors; Ewa Beach, HI Our Lady of Perpetual Help; Presbyteral Council.
Bush, Thomas M. '99 (LIN) Nebraska City, NE St. Joseph's; Advocates.
Bush, William C. '62 (LEX) Nicholasville, KY St. Luke.
Busher, Robert J. '76 (DAV) Davenport, IA Sacred Heart Cathedral; Judges.
Bushmaker, Godfrey E. *o.praem.* '00 (ORG)[I] Silverado, CA Norbertine Fathers of Orange Inc.
Bushmaker, Godfrey *o.praem* '00 (LA) Wilmington, CA SS. Peter and Paul.
Bushy, Tim '83 (PHX) Chandler, AZ Chandler Regional Hospital; Gilbert, AZ Mercy Gilbert Medical Center.
Bushy, Timothy F. '83 (CR) On Duty Outside the Diocese.
Busichio, Salvatore A. '60 (R) Raleigh, NC Cathedral of the Sacred Heart.
Busichio, Salvatore '60 (NEW) On Duty Outside the Archdiocese.
Busieka, George S. *c.m.* '05 (STL)[O] St. Louis, MO Lazarist Residence.
Buslon, Arlou '85 (NEW) Leonia, NJ St. John the Evangelist's.
Bussen, Rev. Msgr. Robert J. '71 (SLC) College of Consultors; Priests' Personnel Board; Park City, UT Saint Mary of the Assumption LLC 238; Board of Directors.
Bussmann, Frank A. '06 (JC) Ministry to Priests; Jonesburg, MO St. Patrick; Montgomery City, MO Immaculate Conception.
Bustamante, David '05 (FRS) Visalia, CA Holy Family; Visalia, CA St. Mary; Visalia, CA St. Thomas the Apostle.
Bustamante, John Christopher '03 (DET) Detroit, MI Assumption Grotto.
Bustamante–Agudelo, Carlos–Mario '99 (ATL) Johns Creek, GA St. Benedict.
Busto, George *c.o.* '05 (HON) Honolulu, HI Holy Trinity; [C] Honolulu, HI St. Francis Healthcare System of Hawaii.
Busto, George *c.o.* (STN) Honolulu, HI St. Sophia Byzantine Missions.
Bustonera, Ian '03 (ORG) Yorba Linda, CA St. Martin de Porres.
Bustos, Javier '01 (MIL) Special Assignment; [B] Hales Corners, WI Sacred Heart School of Theology.
Butawan, Roberto '82 (DAL) Plano, TX Prince of Peace.
Butcavage, Leonard M. '72 (SCR) Wyoming, PA St. Joseph's; Wyoming, PA Our Lady of Sorrows.
Butch, Brian T. '93 (TR) Neptune, NJ Holy Innocents; Leave of Absence.
Butera, Christopher S. '07 (ALN) Allentown, PA St. Thomas More.
Butera, George J. '68 (BO) Revere, MA St. Anthony of Padua; Health Leave.
Butler, Allan L. W. '67 (BO) Senior Priests. Retired.
Butler, David A. *o.p.* '57 (WDC) Washington, DC St. Dominic Church & Priory.
Butler, David Aloysius *o.p.* '57 (NY)[EE] New York NY St. Catherine of Siena Priory.
Butler, Francis *s.s.j.* '85 (LAF) Church Point, LA Our Mother of Mercy.
Butler, James P. '86 (BO) Senior Priests. Retired.
Butler, James '69 (R) Retired.
Butler, John J. '54 (L)[M] Louisville, KY Ursuline Motherhouse of the Immaculate Conception Retired.
Butler, John J. '60 (MO) DEPARTMENT OF VETERANS AFFAIRS HOSPITALS AND CHAPLAINS.
Butler, John M. '72 (GBG) Leckrone, PA Our Lady of

Perpetual Help (St. Mary); Masontown, PA All Saints.
Butler, John T. *s.j.* '00 (BO) Watertown, MA; [U] Watertown, MA The Society of Jesus of New England–Provincial Offices.
Butler, John *s.j.* '00 (BO)[U] Newton, MA The Jesuit Community at Boston College.
Butler, John '60 (HON) On Duty Outside the Diocese.
Butler, Kevin M. '07 (RCK) Rockford, IL St. Peter Cathedral.
Butler, Leo J. '98 (NEW) Norwood, NJ Immaculate Conception.
Butler, Michael A. '85 (R) Greenville, NC St. Gabriel.
Butler, Rev. Msgr. Michael T. '89 (STL) Air Force Chaplains; Military Chaplains.
Butler, Michael '84 (COS) Colorado Springs, CO Our Lady of the Pines–Black Forest.
Butler, Norman H. *m.s.* '75 (HRT)[L] Hartford, CT Missionaries of LaSalette.
Butler, Patrick J. '82 (ALB) Clifton Park, NY St. Edward the Confessor; Spiritual Director.
Butler, Paul F. '87 (RVC) Seaford, NY St. William the Abbot.
Butler, Paul '04 (ALB) Albany, NY All Saints Catholic Church; [Q] Albany, NY New York State University at Albany; Special Assignment; Presbyteral Council; Diocesan Board of Consultors; Members.
Butler, Rene *m.s.* (BUR) Windsor, VT St. Francis of Assisi.
Butler, Richard J. '62 (BO) Brookline, MA St. Mary of the Assumption; Senior Priests. Retired.
Butler, Robert J. '62 (BO) Milton, MA St. Agatha; Senior Priests. Retired.
Butler, Robert R. *m.s.* '69 (HRT)[L] Hartford, CT Missionaries of LaSalette.
Butler, Thomas W. '82 (LAN) Hillsdale, MI St. Anthony.
Butler, Thomas *o.carm.* '50 (TUC)[A] Tucson, AZ Salpointe Catholic High School; [D] Tucson, AZ Carmelite Priory Retired.
Butler, Thomas '82 (LAN) Priests' Assignment Commission.
Butler, Timothy A. '88 (MO) Military & VA Chaplains.; Air Force Chaplains.
Butler, Timothy (TUC) Tucson, AZ Christ the King Chapel.
Butler, Victor *s.v.d.* '64 (TR)[N] Bordentown, NJ Society of the Divine Word.
Butler, Vincent E. *s.j.* (NY)[EE] Loyola Hall, Jesuit Community.
Butor, Walter *o.m.i.* '03 (CR) Ogema, MN Most Holy Redeemer.
Butta, C. Gregory '91 (WDC) Washington, DC St. Francis Xavier.
Butters, Craig M. '83 (ORG) Rancho Santa Margarita, CA San Francisco Solano Church; Liturgical Commission.
Butters, Joseph '65 (JOL) On Duty Outside the Diocese.
Buttini, Mario *o.s.j.* '39 (SCR)[B] Pittston, PA St. Joseph's Oblate Seminary.
Buttner, Michael J. '78 (CHL) Clemmons, NC Holy Family.
Buttner, Michael T. '75 (BAL) Retired.
Butts, James *s.d.v.* '01 (NEW) Palisades Park, NJ St. Nicholas.
Butz, Crispin C. *o.f.m.* '50 (SFE)[I] Santa Fe, NM Discalced Carmelite Monastery; [H] Albuquerque, NM The Province of Our Lady of Guadalupe.
Butz, Joseph *c.ss.r.* '70 (STL)[O] Liguori, MO Liguori Mission House/Redemptorists.
Butz, Robert J. '00 (MAD) Muscoda, WI St. Joseph; Boscobel, WI Immaculate Conception; Muscoda, WI St. Malachy; Muscoda, WI St. John the Baptist.
Buu, Francis X. '74 (NY) New York, NY Immaculate Conception.
Buvala, Andrew G. *o.f.m.* '47 (GAY) Suttons Bay, MI St. Wenceslaus; Suttons Bay, MI Blessed Kateri Tekakwitha; Native American Apostolate.
Buvens, Edward P. *s.j.* '69 (ATL)[I] Atlanta, GA Ignatius House.
Buxkemper, Rev. Msgr. Roland '65 (LUB) Retired.
Buxman, Donald R. '70 (P) Milwaukie, OR Christ the King; Personnel Board.
Buyansky, Timothy *o.s.b.* '69 (CLV)[D] Cleveland, OH Benedictine High School; [N] Cleveland, OH.
Buzga, John P. '59 (E)[K] San Antonio, TX Padua Place Retired.
Buzzelli, Aaron N. *o.s.b.* '77 (GBG)[G] Latrobe, PA Saint Vincent Archabbey.
Buzzerio, Joseph E. '77 (NEW) Retired.
Bwayo, Peter K. *a.j.* '89 (SP) Tampa, FL St. Lawrence.
Bwezani Phiri, Wilfred (CHI) Cicero, IL St. Frances of Rome.
Byabato, Deus–Dedit B. '93 (PEO)[H] Galesburg, IL St. Mary Medical Center.
Byarugaba, George '92 (OAK) Oakland, CA St. Lawrence O'Toole–St. Cyril of Jerusalem.
Byaruhanga, Frederick '89 (LA) Los Angeles, CA St. Joan of Arc.
Byeck, Mitch *o.m.i.* '81 (DUL) International Falls, MN St. Thomas Aquinas; International Falls, MN St. Columban.
Byekwaso, Celestine '82 (GB) Regional Vicars; Coleman, WI St. Anne Parish Corp.
Byer, James M. '81 (CHL) Taylorsville, NC Holy Trinity.
Byerley, E. Joseph '93 (CAM) Haddon Heights, NJ Church of St. Rose, Haddon Heights, N.J.
Byerley, Timothy E. '85 (CAM)[P] Deptford, NJ Collegium Center for Faith and Culture.
Byers, Dohrman W. '74 (CIN) Georgetown, OH St. Mary; Ripley, OH St. George; Ripley, OH St. Michael the Archangel.
Byers, George D. *c.p.m.* '92 (COL)[A] Columbus, OH Pontifical College Josephinum.
Byers, John '95 (LAN) Lansing, MI Immaculate Heart of Mary.
Byington, Edward J. '70 (FR) Providence, RI St. Augustine Retired.
Bynon, Rev. Msgr. Joseph P. '56 (BRK) Rego Park, NY Resurrection–Ascension; [T] Douglaston, NY Bishop Mugavero Residence Retired.
Byomuhangi, Deusdedit (CHI) Western Springs, IL St. John of the Cross.
Byrd, Charles A. '01 (ATL) Jasper, GA Our Lady of the Mountains.
Byrd, Freddie '88 (OWN) Waverly, KY Sacred Heart; Waverly, KY St. Peter.
Byrd, Howard W. *s.s.j.* '75 (NO) New Orleans, LA St. Raymond–St. Leo the Great.
Byrne, Rev. Msgr. Albert J. '79 (ALN) Allentown, PA Immaculate Conception.
Byrne, Basil *o.c.s.o.* '76 (WOR)[O] Spencer, MA St. Joseph's Abbey.
Byrne, Bernard M. '06 (SUP) Boulder Junction, WI St. Anne; Boulder Junction, WI St. Rita; Boulder Junction, WI St. Mary.
Byrne, Bernard P. *m.m.* '56 (SJ)[M] Los Altos, CA Maryknoll.
Byrne, David '88 (WIN) On Special or Other Diocesan Assignment.
Byrne, Edward G. '64 (NY) Ossining, NY St. Ann.
Byrne, Frederick *o.s.b.* '82 (GBG)[G] Latrobe, PA Saint Vincent Archabbey.
Byrne, George '69 (SD) Retired.
Byrne, Glenn F. '75 (BAL) Graduate Studies.
Byrne, Rev. Msgr. Harry J. '46 (NY) New York, NY Epiphany; [EE] Bronx, NY John Cardinal O'Connor Residence Retired.
Byrne, Harry M. *o.p.* '78 (STL)[B] St. Louis, MO Aquinas Institute of Theology.
Byrne, Hugh A. '62 (BRK)[T] Douglaston, NY Bishop Mugavero Residence Retired.
Byrne, James F. *o.s.f.s.* '60 (CHL) High Point, NC Immaculate Heart of Mary.
Byrne, James O. '37 (CIN)[N] Carthagena, OH St. Charles Retired.
Byrne, Joel *o.f.m.* '51 (CIN)[N] Cincinnati, OH St. Clement Friary Retired.
Byrne, John F. *s.s.j.* '66 (BAL)[S] Baltimore, MD St. Joseph Society of the Sacred Heart House of Central Administration Retired.
Byrne, Joseph F. '69 (BO) Senior Priests. Retired.
Byrne, Joseph L. '54 (HEL) Townsend, MT Holy Cross; Holy Childhood Association; Propagation of the Faith.
Byrne, Keith '04 (LA) Rancho Palos Verdes, CA St. John Fisher.
Byrne, Rev. Msgr. Laserian '48 (FRS) Fresno, CA St. Anthony of Padua Retired.
Byrne, Laurence *s.d.b.* '52 (SFR)[N] San Francisco, CA Salesian Provincial Residence Retired.
Byrne, Luke J. *s.j.* '65 (KC)[J] Kansas City, MO Rockhurst Jesuit Community.
Byrne, Mark *s.o.l.t.* '98 (CC)[G] Robstown, TX Society of Our Lady of the Most Holy Trinity.
Byrne, Patrick J. '55 (COL) Retired.
Byrne, Peter D. *s.j.* '75 (P)[L] Portland, OR Jesuit Provincial Office (Society of Jesus, Oregon Prov.); [L] Portland, OR Colombiere Community.
Byrne, Peter J. '84 (NY) Staten Island, NY Immaculate Conception.
Byrne, Peter *f.s.s.p.* '03 (TLS) Tulsa, OK Parish of Saint Peter.
Byrne, Rev. Msgr. Raymond J. '57 (NY) Irvington–on–the–Hudson, NY Immaculate Conception.
Byrne, Robert H. '75 (SAG) Frankenmuth, MI Blessed Trinity.
Byrne, Robert Paul '50 (LA) Retired.
Byrne, Thomas J. *c.s.sp.* '64 (GAL)[O] Houston, TX Congregation of the Holy Spirit, Province of the United States.
Byrne, Thomas R. '58 (DET) Retired.
Byrne, William D. '94 (WDC) Washington, DC St. Peter; [T] College Park, MD University of Maryland Catholic Student Center; Secretariats; Secretary for Pastoral Ministry and Social Concerns; Pastoral Center Special Ministries.
Byrne, William D. '88 (WIN)[D] Rochester, MN Saint Mary Hospital.
Byrnes, Rev. Msgr. Donald M. '55 (NO) Retired.
Byrnes, Francis J. '51 (BRK) Retired.
Byrnes, James J. '80 (STL) St. Louis, MO Mary, Mother of the Church.
Byrnes, Rev. Msgr. James T. '86 (NY)[E] Goshen, NY John S. Burke Catholic High School.
Byrnes, John D. '94 (ALT) Judicial Vicar; Cresson, PA St. Aloysius; Tribunal.
Byrnes, John P. '45 (TR) Retired.
Byrnes, John W. '47 (BRK)[Q] Queens Village, NY Queen of Peace Residence Retired.
Byrnes, Michael J. '96 (DET)[A] Detroit, MI Sacred Heart Major Seminary, Inc.; Detroit, MI Presentation/Our Lady of Victory.
Byrnes, Rev. Msgr. Paul A. '62 (BAL) Retired.
Byrnes, Robert R. '67 (GBG) Greensburg, PA Excela Health – Westmoreland Hospital; [J] Greensburg, PA The Bishop William G. Connare Center.
Byrnes, Thomas J. '99 (NY) Monroe, NY Sacred Heart Church.
Byrolly, Bruce '58 (WIL) Retired.
Byron, J. Michael '89 (STP) St. Paul, MN St. Cecilia; [A] Saint Paul, MN The Saint Paul Seminary; [C] St. Paul, MN University of St. Thomas; Censores Librorum.
Byron, William J. *s.j.* '61 (PH)[Y] Loyola Center and Manresa Hall; [C] Jesuit Fathers.
Byron, William '62 (YAK) Goldendale, WA Holy Trinity.
Byrth, Peter *o.carm.* '59 (NEW) Tenafly, NJ Our Lady of Mount Carmel.
Byrth, Peter *o.carm.* '59 (JOL)[L] Darien Carmelite Provincial Office.
Bzdyra, Stephen H. '79 (HRT) Seymour, CT St. Augustine; Special and other Archdiocesan Assignment; Ansonia–Derby Deanery.

C

Cabala, Thomas S. '79 (CHI) Hometown, IL Our Lady of Loretto.
Caballejo, Romeo J. '97 (MO) Army Reserve Chaplains.
Caballejo, Yuen '06 (MO) Army Reserve Chaplains; Marietta, GA Cobb County Jail; Special or Other (Arch)Diocesan Assignment.
Caballero, Francisco '53 (TOL) Retired.
Caballero, Gilberto *c.m.* '03 (FgM) Philadelphia, PA Eastern Province.
Caban, Carmen '06 (SP)[J] Tampa, FL St. Joseph's Hospital, Inc.
Cabanas, Jaime '55 (BWN) Retired.
Cabarcas–Rua, Fabian '89 (ATL) Lilburn, GA Our Lady of the Americas.
Cabardo, Donato '99 (NEW) Demarest, NJ Parish of St. Joseph.
Cabasagan, Arbel '07 (SAC) Folsom, CA St. John the Baptist.
Cabasino, Philip A. *c.ss.r.* '47 (BO) Boston, MA Our Lady of Perpetual Help.
Cabatuan, Julito A. '83 (NY) New York, NY Holy Family.
Cabazi, Ruta A. '65 (IND)[G] Beech Grove, IN St. Francis Hospital and Health Centers.
Cabell, Barry E. *c.s.c.* '89 (AUS) Austin, TX St. Paul.
Cabello, Tomas *c.m.f.* (CGS) Caguas, PR Inmaculado Corazon de Maria.
Cabezas, Francisco Javier '79 (NEW) Newark, NJ Northern State Prison.
Cabezas, Richard E. '99 (NEW) Kearny, NJ St. Stephen.
Cabico, Jon '09 (HON) Aiea, HI St. Elizabeth.
Caboboy, Juan '76 (ORG) Garden Grove, CA St. Columban.
Cabra, M. Arturo '98 (R) Washington, NC Mother of Mercy.
Cabral, Clifford J. '79 (PRO) Pascoag, RI St. Joseph.
Cabral, Fernando A. '86 (PRO) West Warwick, RI St. Anthony.
Cabral, Jeffrey '02 (FR) Graduate Studies.
Cabrera, Alberto '99 (MRY) Santa Cruz, CA Star of the Sea.
Cabrera, Alberto *c.p.* '65 (BRK)[T] Jamaica, NY Immaculate Conception Monastery.
Cabrera, Encarnacion J. '08 (CC) Rockport, TX Sacred Heart.
Cabrera, Jose '07 (SAG) Outside the Diocese.
Cabrera, Juan Evangelista *o.c.d.* '09 (OKL) Oklahoma City, OK Our Lady of Mount Carmel and St. Therese Little Flower.
Cabrera, Mario F. '81 (LA) Lynwood, CA St. Emydius.
Cabrera, Rodolfo R. (ARE) Camuy, PR St. Joseph.
Cabrera, Rolando '93 (MIA) Miami, FL Epiphany.
Cabrera, Sergio '73 (MIA) Miami, FL St. Brendan Retired.
Cabrerizo, Juan L. *sch.p.* '77 (SJN) San Juan, PR Santisimo Salvador; [B] San Juan, PR Colegio Calasanz.
Cabrisos, Cromwell '78 (ORL) Clermont, FL Blessed Sacrament; Judges.
Cabrita, Paul M. *s.m.* '86 (STP) St. Paul, MN St. Louis King of France.
Caccavale, Charles '81 (BRK) Released from Diocesan Assignment.

Caccavale, Charles '91 (RVC)[A] Huntington, NY Diocesan Seminary of the Immaculate Conception; Censors of Books.
Caccavelle, Pius *o.f.m.cap.* (NEW) Part–time Staff.
Cacciapuoti, Antonio '90 (LA) Los Angeles, CA Christ the King; Board of Directors.
Caceres, Rev. Msgr. Alonso '59 (ORG) Retired.
Caceres, Angel Diaz '76 (SJN)[A] Bayamon Central University.
Caceres, Angel Diaz '76 (ARE) Vega–Alta, PR Santa Ana.
Caceres, Blas *c.ss.r.* '87 (NY) New York, NY Most Holy Redeemer.
Caceres, Jacob Antonio '08 (SAC) Vacaville, CA St. Joseph.
Caceres, Leonardo M. '03 (NEW) On Duty Outside the Archdiocese.
Caceres, Luis Albert '08 (AUS) Giddings, TX St. Margaret.
Caceres, Marco A. '67 (MET) New Brunswick, NJ St. John the Baptist.
Cachat, Leo P. *s.j.* '66 (DET)[P] Bloomfield Hills, MI Manresa Jesuit Retreat House.
Cadavid, Diego F. '02 (CHI) Chicago, IL Our Lady of Lourdes.
Cadavid, Jose Augusto '97 (HON) Kihei, HI St. Theresa.
Cadavid–Rivera, Gonzalo '09 (BAL) Cockeysville, MD St. Joseph; [V] Cockeysville, MD St. Joseph, Texas Endowment Trust.
Cadden, Donald R. *s.j.* '58 (SPK)[B] Spokane, WA Gonzaga University.
Caddy, James L. '64 (CLV) Gates Mills, OH St. Francis of Assisi.
Cadigan, Timothy J. *s.j.* '91 (SCR)[C] Scranton, PA The University of Scranton.
Cadorette, Curtis R. *m.m.* '77 (NY)[EE].
Cadran, Raymond G. *m.s.* '78 (ATL) Marietta, GA St. Ann.
Cadrecha, Robert '04 (SP) Temple Terrace, FL Corpus Christi; Elected Pastors.
Cadusale, Jose '60 (BRK) Rego Park, NY Our Lady of the Angelus; Queens Hospital Center—Pastoral Care Office.
Cadwallader, George B. '92 (PH) Richboro, PA St. Vincent de Paul.
Cadwallader, Simon '97 (FgM) Boston, MA St. James the Apostle, Inc.
Cady, Frank G. '81 (TUC) Tucson, AZ Saint Odilia Roman Catholic Community – Tucson.
Caesar, Floyd '75 (ALN) Weatherly, PA Our Lady of Lourdes Parish; Catholic Daughters of the Americas; Father Henry Baker Council #12105, Weatherly.
Caesar, Roger J. *s.s.j.* '77 (BAL)[S] Baltimore, MD St. Joseph Society of the Sacred Heart House of Central Administration.
Cafarelli, Francis (FTW)[B] University of Notre Dame Du Lac.
Cafarelli, Frank *c.s.c.* (FTW)[A] Notre Dame, IN Moreau Seminary; [A] Notre Dame, IN Moreau Seminary.
Caffe, John I. '62 (STL) Dardenne Prairie, MO Immaculate Conception.
Caffery, James D. *m.s.* '60 (HRT)[L] Hartford, CT Missionaries of LaSalette.
Caffrey, Benet W. *o.s.b.* '58 (PAT)[N] Morristown, NJ St. Mary's Abbey.
Caffrey, Edward '57 (SPK) Retired.
Caffrey, Gerald *c.m.f.* '80 (PHX) Prescott, AZ United States Veterans Hospital (Prescott); Prescott, AZ Sacred Heart Roman Catholic Parish.
Caffrey, Gerald *c.m.f.* '80 (MO) DEPARTMENT OF VETERANS AFFAIRS HOSPITALS AND CHAPLAINS.
Caffrey, William J. *s.v.d.* '59 (SB)[I] Riverside, CA Divine Word Seminary.
Caffrey, William *s.v.d.* '58 (ORG)[G] Fullerton, CA St. Jude Medical Center.
Cafone, Rev. Msgr. James M. '65 (NEW)[B] Seton Hall University; Censores Librorum; [B] School of Diplomacy and Intl. Rels.
Cagantas, Dennis '95 (NY) Bronx, NY St. Clare of Assisi.
Caggianelli, Gregg '02 (VEN) Sarasota, FL Incarnation; Vocations/Seminarian Formation; Air Force Reserve Chaplains.
Caggiano, Kyrin *o.carm.* (JOL)[L] Darien Carmelite Provincial Office Retired.
Cahalan, Patrick J. *s.j.* '65 (LA)[C] Los Angeles, CA Loyola Marymount University; [C] Los Angeles, CA Jesuit Community.
Cahalane, Rev. Msgr. Thomas '63 (TUC) Tucson, AZ Our Mother of Sorrows Roman Catholic Parish – Tucson; Diocesan Consultors; Council of Priests; Vicars Forane; Ecumenical Commission; All Vicars Forane.
Cahill, Brendan J. '90 (GAL)[A] Houston, TX St. Mary's Seminary.
Cahill, Clemente *c.ss.r.* '51 (CGS) Aguas Buenas, PR Church of Tres Santos Reyes.
Cahill, Daniel '73 (TR) Keansburg, NJ St. Ann.
Cahill, Dennis H. '77 (DUB) Cedar Rapids, IA St. Pius X; Hiawatha, IA St. Elizabeth Ann Seton Parish.
Cahill, Edward B. '60 (PH) Retired.
Cahill, Frank '68 (MIA) Retired.
Cahill, J. Donald *s.m.* '61 (STL)[O] St. Louis, MO Cure of Ars Marianist Community Retired.
Cahill, J. Patrick '07 (CHL) Charlotte, NC St. Gabriel.
Cahill, James '61 (CHL) Retired.
Cahill, John W. '73 (COV) Hispanic Ministry; Erlanger, KY Cristo Rey.
Cahill, John W. '63 (RCK) Retired.
Cahill, Joseph W. '76 (PRT) Berwick, ME Our Lady of the Angels; York, ME St. Christopher–by–the–Sea; Kittery, ME St. Raphael's.
Cahill, Rev. Msgr. Richard M. '58 (BUF) Retired.
Cahill, Rev. Msgr. Richard '39 (NY) New York, NY National Catholic Community Service.
Cahill, William C. '61 (SY) Rome, NY Transfiguration; Mohawk, NY Oneida Correctional Facility I.; Special Assignment.
Cahn, Cao Xuan '87 (ROC) Rochester, NY St. Helen.
Cahoon, John E. '89 (GAL) Houston, TX St. Cecilia; Promoter of Justice; Western Vicariate.
Cahouet, Eugene *o.p.* '62 (WDC) Washington, DC St. Dominic Church & Priory.
Caiazzo, Gregory G. '76 (RIC) Military Chaplains; Navy Chaplains.
Caiazzo, Gregory G. '76 (MO) Presbyteral Council.
Caiazzo, Nicholas '92 (NOR) On Duty Outside the Diocese.
Caime, James M. *s.j.* '02 (NO)[C] New Orleans, LA Loyola University New Orleans.
Caimi, Luke A. '58 (WDC) Retired.
Cain, Dennis R. '79 (DUB) Epworth, IA St. John; Epworth, IA St. Patrick; Epworth, IA St. Joseph; Epworth, IA St. Clement.
Cain, Frederick L. '70 (PIT) Priest Council; Vicariate 2; College of Consultors; Clergy Personnel Board.
Cain, Gervase *t.o.r.* '57 (ALT)[G] Loretto, PA St. Francis Friary at Mount Assisi.
Cain, Harry J. *s.j.* '63 (BO)[U] Weston, MA Campion Jesuit Community.
Cain, J. C. *o.m.i.* '89 (BEL)[F] Belleville, IL Shrine of Our Lady of the Snows.
Cain, Rev. Msgr. James E. '50 (STO) Diamond Springs, CA Retired.
Cain, Rev. Msgr. James R. '56 (OM) Omaha Priests Retirement Plan and Trust, The Retired.
Cain, John F. '56 (SC) Spencer, IA Retired.
Cain, Joseph *o.s.c.* '44 (SCL)[I] Onamia Crosier Priory.
Cain, Randy N. '88 (CC) Taft, TX Holy Family.
Cain, Robert K.C. '95 (TLS) On Duty Outside the Diocese; Navy Reserve Chaplains.
Cain, William F. *s.j.* '69 (SJ)[M] Los Gatos, CA Sacred Heart Jesuit Center.
Caindec, Ferdinando '79 (NY) Nanuet, NY St. Anthony.
Cairns, John L. '63 (ALB) Retired.
Cairns, Stephen P. '68 (TOL) North Baltimore, OH Holy Family.
Cairone, A. Robert '64 (CAM) Retired.
Cal–Ortiz, Rodolfo L. '93 (GAL) Pearland, TX St. Helen.
Calabrese, Charles L. '72 (FWT)[L] Fort Worth, TX Texas Christian University Catholic Community; On Duty Outside the Diocese.
Calabrese, Charles '72 (FWT) Youth & Young Adult Ministry and Campus Ministry.
Calabrese, Peter M. *c.r.s.p.* '00 (BUF)[B] Youngstown, NY St. Anthony M. Zaccaria Seminary; [T] Youngstown, NY Basilica of the National Shrine of Our Lady of Fatima, Inc.; Youngstown, NY Holy Family.
Calabria, Michael D. *o.f.m.* '03 (BUF)[O] St. Bonaventure, NY St. Bonaventure Friary; [C] St. Bonaventure, NY Friar Community.
Calabro, John E. '73 (PH) Philadelphia, PA Holy Spirit.
Calabro, Nicholas J. '66 (BGP)[O] Stamford, CT The Catherine Dennis Keefe Queen of the Clergy Retired Priests' Residence Retired.
Calais, Floyd J. '50 (LAF) Retired.
Calamari, Joseph M. *s.s.j.* '45 (BAL)[S] Baltimore, MD St. Joseph's Manor.
Calasara, Mansuelo '61 (JC) Retired.
Caldarella, James J. '71 (WOR) Princeton, MA Prince of Peace.
Caldas, Rev. Msgr. Constantino R. '51 (BGP) Retired.
Calder, Kenneth J. '60 (BRK) Brooklyn, NY Our Lady of Angels Retired.
Calderon, Cruz '08 (DAL) McKinney, TX St. Michael.
Calderon, Francisco *o.p.* '50 (MIA) Miami, FL St. Brendan.
Calderon, Jaime '05 (RVC) Westbury, NY St. Brigid.
Calderon, Juan Luis *o.a.r.* '94 (NEW) Centro Guadalupe.
Calderon, Vicente '63 (ELP) El Paso, TX St. Raphael.
Calderon, Wilfredo *s.d.b.* (ARE) Orocovis, PR San Juan Bautista.
Calderon Calderon, Wilfredo *s.d.b.* (ARE) Priest's Senate (Consejo Presbiteral).
Calderone, Joseph D. *o.s.a.* '73 (PH)[C] Villanova University; [Y] Villanova, PA St. Thomas of Villanova Friary.
Calderone, Joseph D. *o.s.a.* '73 (MO) Navy Reserve Chaplains.
Caldognetto, Dominic *s.x.* '66 (MIL)[B] Franklin, WI Xaverian Missionary Fathers College Seminary.
Caldwell, Rev. Msgr. Frank J. *c.s.w.* '81 (RVC) Uniondale, NY St. Martha; Rockville Centre Deanery.
Caldwell, Fred '95 (DAL) Retired.
Caldwell, J. Ripley '54 (SJ)[M] Los Gatos, CA Sacred Heart Jesuit Center.
Caldwell, James A. '03 (TLS) Krebs, OK St. Joseph's.
Caldwell, James V. '60 (SD) Retired.
Caldwell, John A. '70 (L) Pewee Valley, KY St. Aloysius.
Caldwell, Thomas A. *s.j.* '56 (MIL)[P] Milwaukee, WI Jesuit Community at Marquette University.
Caldwell, Rev. Msgr. William '68 (KC) Excelsior Springs, MO St. Ann.
Calegari, Leonard J. '63 (SFR) San Francisco, CA St. Stephen Retired.
Calero, Luis F. *s.j.* '83 (SJ)[B] Santa Clara, CA Jesuit Community.
Calero Gómez, Nomar Jose '91 (MGZ) Mayaguez, PR Cathedral of Our Lady of Purification.
Calgaro, John *o.f.m.conv.* '74 (FgM)[N] Chicago Conventual Franciscans of St. Bonaventure Province; Chicago, IL Province of Saint Bonaventure.
Calhoun, Gerald '61 (OWN) Madisonville, KY Christ the King; Consultors; Committee for Administration; Committee for Education; Priest Personnel Committee.
Calhoun, Lawrence E. *c.s.c.* '63 (FTW)[H] Notre Dame Congregation of Holy Cross, Indiana Province, Provincial House.
Calhoun, Michael '02 (PEO)[A] Peru, IL St. Bede Abbey.
Calhoun, Ronald G. '72 (BO) Hudson, MA St. Michael.
Caliba, Jude '94 (NEW) East Orange, NJ Holy Name of Jesus.
Calicchio, Isaac J. *o.f.m.* '56 (HRT) Meriden, CT St. Rose of Lima.
Caligiuri, Rev. Msgr. Angelo M. '58 (BUF)[O] Tonawanda, NY O'Hara Residence; Finance Council Retired.
Caligiuri, Rev. Msgr. Anthony J. '49 (BUF)[O] Tonawanda, NY O'Hara Residence Retired.
Calimeri, Anthony F. '47 (ROC) Retired.
Calis, Joseph A. '99 (WDC) Bowie, MD Ascension.
Calise, Rev. Msgr. Joseph P. '80 (BRK) Brooklyn, NY Annunciation of the Blessed Virgin Mary; Brooklyn, NY Our Lady of Mount Carmel Shrine Church.
Calkins, Rev. Msgr. Arthur B. '70 (NO) On Duty Outside the Archdiocese.
Calkins, Rev. Msgr. Howard W. '67 (NY) Mt. Vernon, NY Sacred Heart; Westchester (South Shore).
Calkins, Ronald L. '78 (NO) Mandeville, LA Mary Queen of Peace; Deans.
Callaghan, Rev. Msgr. Aloysius R. '71 (ALN) On Duty Outside the Diocese.
Callaghan, Rev. Msgr. Aloysius R. '71 (STP)[C] St. Paul, MN University of St. Thomas; [A] Saint Paul, MN The Saint Paul Seminary; The Saint Paul Seminary School of Divinity.
Callaghan, Michael J. *c.m.* '76 (BRK)[T] Jamaica, NY Vincentian Residence.
Callaghan, Michael J. *c.o.* '90 (BRK) Brooklyn, NY St. Boniface; [T] Brooklyn, NY Oratory of Saint Philip Neri, Congregation Pontifical Rite.
Callaghan, Nicholas E. '04 (NY) Blauvelt, NY St. Catharine.
Callahan, Daniel *s.a.* '87 (NY)[EE] Garrison Franciscan Friars of the Atonement, Minister General Office.
Callahan, David P. '87 (BO) Quincy, MA St. Mary.
Callahan, Rev. Msgr. Francis J. '72 (SCR) Wilkes–Barre, PA St. Therese; Deans.
Callahan, Francis X. '63 (BAL) Bel Air, MD St. Margaret Retired.
Callahan, Francis X. '49 (HRT) Milford, CT St. Agnes.
Callahan, James A. '73 (PH) Philadelphia, PA Christ the King.
Callahan, James B. '98 (WOR) Leominster, MA St. Anna.
Callahan, James F. '75 (WIN) St. Charles, MN Holy Redeemer; St. Charles, MN St. Charles Borromeo; St. Charles, MN St. Aloysius.
Callahan, Rev. Msgr. James P. '74 (STL) St. Charles, MO St. Joseph.
Callahan, John J. *s.j.* '70 (STL)[O] St. Louis, MO Jesuit Community Corporation at Saint Louis University – Jesuit Hall.
Callahan, John J. *s.j.* '70 (BR)[J] Convent, LA Manresa House of Retreats.
Callahan, Joseph F. *c.s.c.* '70 (FR)[A] North Easton, MA Holy Cross Fathers Religious; [I] North Easton, MA Holy Cross Retreat House.
Callahan, Joseph H. '86 (CLV) Cleveland, OH Our Lady of Lourdes; Presbyteral Council.
Callahan, Joseph W. '66 (PH) Retired.
Callahan, Joseph (CLV)[V] Cleveland, OH Our Lady of Lourdes.
Callahan, Rev. Msgr. Kevin G. '84 (MO) Ellisville, MO St. Clare of Assisi; DEPARTMENT OF VETERANS AFFAIRS HOSPITALS AND CHAPLAINS.
Callahan, Nelson J. '53 (CLV) Bay Village, OH St.

Raphael Retired.
Callahan, Richard B. *m.m.* '64 (NY)[EE] Maryknoll Maryknoll Fathers and Brothers; [EE] Maryknoll, NY M.M.A.F. Charitable Trust; [EE] Maryknoll, NY Maryknoll Fathers and Brothers Charitable Trust; [FF] Maryknoll, NY Maryknoll Sisters Charitable Trust; [II] Maryknoll, NY The Asian Catholic News Fund.
Callahan, Ronan P. *c.p.* '51 (NOR)[A] Cromwell, CT Holy Apostles College and Seminary.
Callahan, Ronan *c.p.* '51 (HRT)[L] West Hartford, CT Holy Family Monastery/Retreat.
Callahan, Rev. Msgr. Steven F. '87 (SD) San Diego, CA St. Brigid; Vicar General; Adjutant Judicial Vicar; Clergy Personnel Board; College of Consultors; Finance Council; Presbyteral Council; Victim Assistance Coordinator.
Callahan, Vincent '75 (SFD)[M] Springfield, IL St. Francis Convent; [L] Springfield, IL Our Lady of Angels Friary.
Callahan, Zachary '58 (RVC) Merrick, NY Curé of Ars Retired.
Callan, Dennis *s.v.d.* '87 (FgM) Techny, IL.
Callan, John *sch.p.* '82 (MIA)[C] Fort Lauderdale, FL Cardinal Gibbons High School.
Callan, Patrick J. '61 (RVC) Point Lookout, NY Our Lady of the Miraculous Medal.
Callanan, Michael G. *m.m.* '60 (LA) Monrovia, CA Annunciation; [P] Monrovia, CA Retired.
Callaway, Donald *m.i.c.* '03 (SPR)[H] Provincial Office.
Calle, Diomedes '94 (SPR) Springfield, MA Blessed Sacrament; Springfield, MA All Souls.
Calle, Juan de la '54 (PMB) Retired.
Calle–Perez, Sergio '98 (ATL) Without Archdiocesan Assignment or Faculties.
Callea, Michael *m.i.c.* '02 (SPR)[H] Stockbridge, MA Association of Marian Helpers, Marian Helpers Center; [H] Stockbridge, MA Congregation of Marian Fathers of The Immaculate Conception of the Most Blessed Virgin Mary.
Calledo, James '94 (RVC) East Northport, NY St. Anthony of Padua.
Calleja, Rev. Msgr. Guido '53 (MOB) Magnolia Springs, AL St. John the Baptist.
Callery, Peter J. *s.j.* '72 (BR)[J] Convent, LA Manresa House of Retreats.
Callery, William '01 (FAR) Lamoure, ND Assumption of Mary; La Moure, ND Holy Rosary Church of La Moure; Lamoure, ND St. Raphael's Church of Verona.
Calles, Rev. Msgr. Robert S. '63 (ELP) El Paso, TX Most Holy Trinity.
Callipare, Joseph P. '85 (PT) Vicar for Permanent Deacons and Chairman; Permanent Deacon Formation Team; Permanent Deacon Formation Board; Office of the Permanent Diaconate and Permanent Deacon Formation.
Callipare, Joseph P. '85 (PT) Pensacola, FL St. John the Evangelist; Executive Committee of Permanent Deacons.
Callis, Elbert '76 (MEM) Bartlett, TN St. Ann.
Caloca–Rivas, Rigoberto *o.f.m.* '82 (OAK)[M] Oakland, CA Franciscan Friars (Province of Santa Barbara); [R] Berkeley, CA Multicultural Institute.
Calovini, Rev. Msgr. Gerald E. '73 (STU) Steubenville, OH Holy Family; Defenders of the Bond; Presbyteral Council; College of Consultors; Priests Personnel Board.
Calter, Arthur M. '56 (BO) Senior Priests. Retired.
Caluda, Charles J. '62 (NO) Retired.
Calumba, Faron '79 (HRT) Hamden, CT Our Lady of Mt. Carmel.
Calvo, Gabriel '52 (WDC)[B] Washington, DC Diocesan Laborer Priests, House of Studies.
Caly, Roman (FBK) Emmonak, AK Sacred Heart Catholic Church Emmonak.
Calzada, Teodoro *c.m.* '55 (SJN) San Juan, PR Nuestra Senora del Pilar.
Camacho, Henry A. *o.p.* '60 (HRT) New Haven, CT St. Mary's Priory.
Camacho, Jesus '75 (B) Prison Ministry; Boise, ID St. Mary's.
Camacho, Jesus '06 (SAT) Del Rio, TX St. Joseph's.
Camacho, Orlando *c.s.sp.* (ARE) Propagation of Faith; Holy Childhood.
Camacho, Robert '79 (RCK) Special Assignment.
Camacho–Monserrate, Enrique Manuel '07 (SJN) Catholic Charities; Caritas of Puerto Rico.
Camacho–Monserrate, Enrique Manuel '07 (SJN)[I] San Juan, PR Caritas de Puerto Rico, Inc.; Carolina, PR Ntra. Sra. Reina de Los Angeles.
Camacho–Torres, Jose Orlando *c.s.sp.* '92 (SJN)[F] Dorado, PR Santuario del Espiritu Santo; Propagation of the Faith; Holy Childhood Association.
Camadella, Christian F. *o.f.m.* '56 (PAT) Paterson, NJ St. Bonaventure.
Camaioni, Matthew J. '07 (RCK) Rockford, IL St. Rita.
Camara, Michael M. '89 (FR) New Bedford, MA Our Lady of Mt. Carmel.
Camarda, Ronald A. '90 (STA) Unassigned.
Camargo, Carlos '06 (B) Aberdeen, ID Presentation of the Lord.
Camarillo, Joel Arciga '98 (CAM) Camden, NJ St. Joseph Catholic Church, East Camden, N.J. (Pro–Cathedral).
Cambi, Michael '07 (ALB) Saratoga Springs, NY St. Peter.
Cambra, Daniel '87 (LIT) Marian Province of Mary Mother of Mercy.
Cambra, Daniel *m.i.c.* '86 (JOL) Plano, IL St. Mary.
Cambra, Daniel *m.i.c.* '86 (SPR)[H] Provincial Office.
Cambra, Raymond '77 (FR) Fall River, MA Sacred Heart.
Cameli, Louis J. '69 (CHI) Chicago, IL Holy Name Cathedral.
Camera, Bede G. *o.s.b.* '88 (MAN)[K] Manchester, NH St. Anselm Abbey.
Cameron, Ben *c.p.m.* '97 (OWN)[F] Auburn, KY Fathers of Mercy; Auburn, KY.
Cameron, Hilary J. '64 (PRT) Retired.
Cameron, Lachlan T. '08 (RVC) New Hyde Park, NY Holy Spirit; Massapequa, NY St. Rose of Lima.
Cameron, Peter John *o.p.* (HRT) New Haven, CT St. Mary's Priory.
Cameron, Robert M. '59 (KC) Special Assignment; Holy Childhood Association; Priests' Purgatorial Society; Propagation of the Faith.
Camet, Ronald '01 (BUR) Burlington, VT Christ the King–St. Anthony.
Camilleri, Anthony E. '07 (DET) Lake Orion, MI St. Joseph.
Camilleri, Joseph M. '74 (BR) Amite, LA St. Helena.
Camilli, E. Michael *m.s.c.* '60 (ALN)[A] Center Valley, PA Sacred Heart Villa, Missionaries of the Sacred Heart; Ex Officio Members; Secretariat for Catholic Life and Evangelization.
Camilo, Gabriel *m.j.* '87 (GAL) Houston, TX St. Stephen.
Caminiti, Antonino '08 (AGN) Asan, GU Nino Perdido Y Sagrada Familia; Nino Perdido Parish (Asan).
Camire, Bernard J. *s.s.s.* '66 (NY) New York, NY St. Jean Baptiste.
Cammayo, Ruben '80 (NY) Bronx, NY Our Lady of Solace.
Cammisa, James N. '49 (TR)[N] Trenton, NJ St. Lawrence Rehabilitation Center Retired.
Camora, Anthony '70 (BRK) Brooklyn, NY Sacred Hearts of Jesus and Mary and St. Stephen.
Camora, Antonio (BRK) Special Assignment; [S] Apostleship of the Sea.
Camorlinga, Angel *m.c.c.j.* '96 (CHI)[N] La Grange Park, IL Comboni Missionaries.
Camp, Alfred L. '57 (JKS) Madison, MS St. Francis of Assisi Retired.
Camp, Steven '87 (RVC) Baldwin, NY St. Christopher; Senate of Priests (Presbyteral Council/College of Consultors).
Campagna, Robert M. *o.f.m.* '77 (NY)[EE] New York, NY Franciscan Province of the Immaculate Conception; [II] Mount Vernon, NY Franciscan Mission Associates; [II] Mount Vernon, NY St. Dymphna Devotion; New York, NY; Definitors:.
Campagnone, Nicholas '65 (ALB) Retired.
Campana, Thomas J. '80 (CHI) Chicago, IL Our Lady of Mount Carmel.
Campbell, Andrew S. *o.s.b.* '81 (GBG)[G] Latrobe, PA Saint Vincent Archabbey.
Campbell, Bernard J. *o.f.m.cap* '68 (MAN) Manchester, NH St. Anne–St. Augustin; N.H. State Prison.
Campbell, Bernie *c.s.p.* '68 (OAK) Berkeley, CA Holy Spirit Parish/Newman Hall.
Campbell, Brian '09 (PMB) Palm Beach Gardens, FL St. Patrick.
Campbell, Donald *c.s.p.* '62 (NY)[EE] New York, NY Paulist Fathers' Motherhouse.
Campbell, Douglas '76 (WCH) Judges; Temporary Leave of Absence.
Campbell, Dwight '91 (PEO) On Duty Outside the Diocese; Northlake, IL St. John Vianney, Cure of Ars.
Campbell, Rev. Msgr. Francis '73 (P) Retired.
Campbell, Gerard J. *s.j.* '51 (WDC)[N] Washington, DC The Jesuit Community at Georgetown University Retired.
Campbell, Howard W. '88 (PIT) Aliquippa, PA Our Lady of Fatima.
Campbell, Rev. Msgr. Hugh P. '61 (PH) Retired.
Campbell, Rev. Msgr. J. Michael '71 (STU) Presbyteral Council; College of Consultors; Vicar for Religious.
Campbell, James C. '06 (E) Port Allegany, PA St. Gabriel the Archangel; Coudersport, PA St. Eulalia.
Campbell, Rev. Msgr. James F. '64 (BUF) Finance Council; Buffalo, NY St. Joseph's Cathedral.
Campbell, Joe '99 (KNX) LaFollette, TN Our Lady of Perpetual Help.
Campbell, Rev. Msgr. John G. '55 (ORG) Judges.
Campbell, Rev. Msgr. John Michael '71 (STU) Marietta, OH St. Mary's; [L] Marietta, OH Marietta College.
Campbell, Rev. Msgr. John S. '66 (ALN) Northampton, PA Queenship of Mary Parish.
Campbell, Rev. Msgr. John '55 (ORG) Retired.
Campbell, Joseph C. '06 (E) Ridgway, PA St. Leo the Great.
Campbell, Joseph '99 (KNX) La Follette, TN Christ the King.
Campbell, Joseph '60 (FAR) Retired.
Campbell, Rev. Msgr. Mark A. '71 (SD) Diocesan Judges; San Diego, CA Immaculate Conception; Presbyteral Council.
Campbell, Norbert J. '60 (PIT) Wilmerding, PA St. Jude the Apostle.
Campbell, Paul F. '65 (WOR) Dudley, MA St. Anthony.
Campbell, Paul J. '82 (WIL) Chestertown, MD Sacred Heart; Chestertown, MD Washington College; [O] Newark, DE Washington College.
Campbell, Paul *s.j.* '88 (CHI)[N] Chicago, IL Clark Street Jesuit Residence.
Campbell, Peter E. *m.s.c.* '60 (RCK)[G] Aurora, IL Missionaries of the Sacred Heart Community.
Campbell, Robert E. *o.praem.* '08 (SFE)[H] Albuquerque, NM Santa Maria de la Vid Priory.
Campbell, Robert J. *m.s.* '58 (FR) Brewster, MA Our Lady of the Cape.
Campbell, Robert *o.praem* '08 (SFE) Presbyterian Hospital.
Campbell, Roy Edward '07 (WDC) Washington, DC St. Augustine.
Campbell, Shane A. '08 (STP) Coon Rapids, MN Church of the Epiphany.
Campbell, Stephen *s.j.* '85 (MOB)[A] Mobile, AL Spring Hill College.
Campbell, Theodore C. '72 (STP) Golden Valley, MN Good Shepherd; Deanery 9.
Campbell, Thomas L. '48 (FR)[A] North Easton, MA Holy Cross Fathers Religious.
Campbell, Wayne '86 (OAK) Moraga, CA St. Monica.
Campbell, William D. '58 (SCR) Carbondale, PA St. Rose of Lima.
Campbell, William F. *s.j.* '98 (BO)[G] Roxbury, MA Nativity Preparatory School.
Campbell, William G. '63 (FR) Retired.
Campbell, William R. *s.j.* '64 (PRT)[C] Portland, ME Cheverus High School.
Campbell, William W. '52 (BO) Senior Priests. Retired.
Campechano, Javier '95 (STO) Stockton, CA St. George Church (Pastor of).
Campellone, Joseph G. *o.s.f.s.* '96 (PH)[D] Philadelphia, PA Father Judge High School for Boys; [Y] Philadelphia, PA Father Louis Brisson Residence.
Campi, Vincent L. '45 (WH) Retired.
Campion, John R. '48 (HBG) Doylesburg, PA Our Lady of Refuge; Doylesburg, PA Our Lady of Refuge Mission Retired.
Campion, Joseph J. '73 (ALN) Whitehall, PA St. John the Baptist.
Campion, Joseph J. *s.s.j.* '91 (NO) New Orleans, LA St. David.
Campion, Owen F. '66 (NSH) On Duty Outside the Diocese.
Campion, Thomas B. '52 (HRT) Wethersfield, CT Corpus Christi; Wethersfield, CT Sacred Heart.
Campion, Rev. Msgr. Thomas F. '57 (MAD)[D] Monroe, WI The Monroe Clinic, Inc.; Apostolate to the Handicapped.
Campion, William T. '77 (ALN) Palmerton, PA Sacred Heart; Palmerton Hospital.
Campo, Frank D. '09 (BO) Franklin, MA St. Mary.
Campo, Gustavo *i.v.e.* (BGP) Bridgeport, CT St. George; [O] Bridgeport, CT Instituto Verbo Encarnado.
Campo, Lance J. '93 (NO) Center of Jesus the Lord; Hispanic Apostolate Pastoral Services.
Campoli, Timothy J. '74 (SPR) Greenfield, MA Blessed Sacrament; Deans.
Campos, Daniel '04 (TLS) Hispanic Ministry; Muskogee, OK Saint Joseph Church.
Campos, Miguel *sch.p.* '96 (LA)[P] Los Angeles, CA Piarist Fathers.
Campos, Miguel '98 (FRS) Tipton, CA St. John The Evangelist.
Campos, Pedro '02 (CHI) Chicago, IL St. Kevin.
Campos, Randy Raul '08 (LA) El Monte, CA Nativity.
Camps, Enrique M. *o.s.m.* '04 (ELP) El Paso, TX Our Lady of Sorrows.
Campuzano, Guillermo *c.m.* '90 (CHI)[N] Chicago, IL Vincentian Community, Congregation of the Mission, Western Province.
Camuso, Robert '92 (SEA) Shoreline, WA St. Luke.
Can–Vasquez, Gregorio Filipe '88 (GAL) Houston, TX St. John Vianney.
Canaan, Timothy G. '93 (OG) Plattsburgh, NY Newman Parish, John XXIII College Community; Campus Ministry; Plattsburgh, NY St. John the Baptist.
Canal, Manuel '58 (MRY) Retired.
Canales, Rene L. '06 (CAM) Carney's Point, NJ St. James' Church, Pennsgrove, N.J.
Canales, William '00 (ATL) Gainesville, GA St. Michael.
Canarro, John '01 (SY) Presbyteral Council.
Canary, John F. '69 (CHI) Vicar General; Administrative Council; Vicar General; Chaplaincies/Chaplain Affairs; Chicago, IL Cardinal's Residence; Vice Chairmen.

Canas, Eugene *o.m.i.* '64 (GAL) Cursillos in Christianity; Houston, TX Immaculate Heart of Mary.
Canavan, Edward P. *o.s.f.s.* '64 (TOL)[I] Childs, MD Annecy Hall Retired.
Canavan, Gerald D. '69 (PH) Eddystone, PA St. Rose of Lima.
Canavan, John D. '55 (DET) Retired.
Canavan, Mark P. '71 (CHI) Oak Lawn, IL St. Louis De Montfort.
Canavan, Rev. Msgr. Mitred Martin A. '68 (SJP) Presbyters.
Canavera, Lawrence J. '67 (GB) Menasha, WI St. John; Menasha, WI St. Mary; Menasha, WI St. Patrick.
Canceran, Danilo A. '89 (MET) Old Bridge, NJ St. Thomas the Apostle.
Cancro, Francis T. '81 (CHL) Belmont, NC Queen of the Apostles.
Candalisa, Frank '02 (NO) Metairie, LA St. Christopher the Martyr.
Candanedo, Wilmo *o.p.* '99 (DAL)[J] Irving, TX Dominican Priory of St. Albert the Great and Novitiate; Seagoville, TX Federal Correctional Institution.
Candela, Rafael '59 (SJN) Retired.
Candelaria, Dino '04 (SFE) Questa, NM St. Anthony.
Candelaria, Ernest *c.s.j.* '58 (LA) Lancaster, CA Blessed Junipero Serra.
Candelas, Ignacio *o.f.m.* (GLP) Fort Defiance, AZ Our Lady of Blessed Sacrament; St. Michaels, AZ St. Michael.
Candreva, Arthur A. *i.v.dei* (BRK) Middle Village, NY Our Lady of Hope.
Candreva, Rev. Msgr. Thomas D. '63 (RVC) Judges for Interdiocesan Tribunal Retired.
Cane–Gombau, Pere '93 (MIL)[V] Racine, WI Community of St. Paul, Inc.; Special Assignment.
Canela, Jorge '09 (GI) Lexington, NE St. Ann's.
Canepa, Jorge A. *c.s.c.* '56 (FTW)[H] Notre Dame Congregation of Holy Cross, Indiana Province, Provincial House.
Canete, Hernan '96 (LA) Reseda, CA St. Catherine of Siena.
Canez, Jorge '79 (PHX) Avondale, AZ St. Thomas Aquinas Roman Catholic Parish.
Canfield, Francis E. *s.j.* '67 (CLV)[D] Cleveland, OH St. Ignatius High School.
Canino, Louis *o.f.m.* '69 (CHL)[J] Stoneville, NC Franciscan Friary; [Q] Greensboro, NC Franciscan Center; [M] Stoneville, NC St. Francis Springs Prayer Center.
Canizares, David (GAL) Area Representatives.
Canizares, Dwight M. '81 (GAL) Baytown, TX St. Joseph.
Canjar, John A. '49 (DEN) Retired.
Cann, Hilarion V. '53 (WH) Retired.
Canna, Joseph '70 (LA) Irwindale, CA Our Lady of Guadalupe.
Cannariato, Paul A. '83 (NEW) Closter, NJ St. Mary; Part–time Staff; Magnificat, A Ministry to Catholic Women.
Canniff, James B. '60 (BO) Malden, MA Immaculate Conception; Senior Priests. Retired.
Canning, Wilfred S. *c.s.b.* '55 (GAL)[O] Houston, TX Dillon House Retired.
Cannoles, Antonio *c.ss.r.* '69 (FgM) Brooklyn, NY AMERICAN REDEMPTORIST FATHERS.
Cannon, Col. Robert R. '78 (VEN) Military Chaplains; Air Force Chaplains.
Cannon, Hugh D. '66 (RVC) East Islip, NY St. Mary's.
Cannon, John '04 (SFE) Cimarron, NM Immaculate Conception Church; Springer, NM St. Joseph; College of Consultors; Presbyteral Council of the Archdiocese of Santa Fe; Vicars Forane (Deans).
Cannon, Kenneth V. '97 (BO) Scituate, MA St. Mary of the Nativity.
Cannon, Maro *c.f.a.* '85 (KNX)[D] Signal Mountain, TN Alexian Village of Tennessee; [F] Signal Mountain, TN Alexian Brothers.
Cannon, Michael J. '81 (VEN) Lake Placid, FL St. James.
Cannon, Richard E. '86 (MO) Quincy, MA St. John the Baptist; Navy Reserve Chaplains.
Cannuli, Richard G. *o.s.a.* '99 (PH)[C] Villanova University; [Y] Villanova, PA St. Thomas of Villanova Friary.
Canny, Michael '77 (SAC) Mount Shasta, CA St. Anthony; Dunsmuir, CA St. John the Evangelist.
Canny, Stephen '61 (SR) Retired.
Cano, Nicolas *o.s.b.* '97 (BIS)[A] Richardton, ND Assumption Abbey; Richardton, ND Assumption Abbey.
Cano, Roberto *f.s.s.p.* '07 (LIN)[L] Lincoln, NE St. Francis of Assisi Church; 1962 Mass Apostolate.
Canoll, Anthony *s.j.* '99 (CHI)[N] Chicago, IL Woodlawn Jesuit Community.
Canon, Hector U. (AGN) Malojlo, GU San Isidro.
Cano Ramirez, Jorge Andres '09 (KNX) Oak Ridge, TN St. Mary.
Canorro, John '01 (SY) Mexico, NY St. Anne, Mother of Mary.
Canoy, Charles '05 (LAN) Saline, MI St. Andrew; Priests' Assignment Commission.
Canterbury, Keith E. '94 (SAC) Retired.
Canterna, Charles J. '76 (BAL) Baltimore, MD Maryland Correctional Adjustment Center; Special Assignment.
Canterna, Chuck (BAL) Baltimore, MD Maryland Penitentiary Complex.
Cantley, Rev. Msgr. Michael J. '55 (BRK)[T] Douglaston, NY Bishop Mugavero Residence Retired.
Cantones, Joel P. '81 (NO) Edgard, LA St. John the Baptist.
Cantore, John A. *c.m.* '63 (STL)[O] Perryville, MO Congregation of the Mission.
Cantu, Jose Helio *l.c.* '06 (SAC) Sacramento, CA Our Lady of Guadalupe Shrine.
Cantwell, Edward F. '58 (ALB) Hudson, NY Parish of the Holy Trinity Retired.
Cantwell, Edward F. '54 (ALB) Retired.
Cantwell, John '69 (SAC) Placerville, CA St. Patrick's.
Cantwell, William J. *c.s.p.* '56 (NY)[EE] Jamaica Estates Paulist Fathers Generalate.
Cantwell, William J. *c.s.p.* '56 (PMB)[H] Vero Beach, FL Paulist Fathers Residence.
Canu, John '63 (ELP) El Paso, TX Our Lady of Assumption.
Canuel, Paul E. '66 (FR) Nantucket, MA St. Mary's, Our Lady of the Isle; Nantucket.
Canzio, Celestino *o.f.m.* '73 (NY)[EE] New York Franciscan Province of the Immaculate Conception.
Cao, Bill T. '01 (ORG) Santa Ana, CA Our Lady of La Vang.
Cao, Duy '01 (CHI)[A] Chicago, IL St. Joseph College Seminary.
Cao, John Vu *c.m.c.* '01 (SB)[I] Corona, CA Congregation of the Mother Co–Redemptrix, C.M.C.
Cao, Joseph T. '00 (DEN) Arvada, CO St. Joan of Arc.
Cao, Nghia *c.ss.r.* '05 (SAT)[L] San Antonio, TX Redemptorists of Texas–San Antonio #1.
Cao, Paul Binh The *s.d.d.* '01 (P) Portland, OR Our Lady of Lavang.
Cao, Paul '01 (CHI)[R] Chicago, IL Kolping Center.
Cao, Peter *c.ss.r.* '04 (BRK) Brooklyn, NY Our Lady of Perpetual Help Basilica.
Cao, Victor *c.s.j.b.* '06 (BRK)[T] Elmhurst, NY Congregation of St. John the Baptist of China; Flushing, NY St. John Vianney.
Cao Phuong Ky, Joseph *s.s.* '59 (SPC)[F] Carthage, MO Congregation of the Mother Coredemptrix, United States Assumption Province.
Capacillo, Euben *o.a.r.* '75 (LA) Los Angeles, CA Cristo Rey.
Capacillo, Euben '75 (ORG) Santa Ana, CA Our Lady of the Pillar.
Capalbo, Kenneth *o.f.m.* '74 (FgM) U.S. Religious Serving Elsewhere; [O] St. Louis Franciscan Friary of St. Anthony of Padua.
Capalbo, Kenneth *o.f.m.* '74 (SFD)[L] Quincy, IL Holy Cross Friary.
Caparas, Allain B. '06 (CAM) Merchantville, NJ St. Peter's Catholic Church, Merchantville, N.J.; [P] Landisville, NJ Padre Pio Shrine, Buena Borough, N.J., Inc.
Capato, Justin *o.s.b.* '80 (PAT) Cedar Knolls, NJ Notre Dame of Mt. Carmel; [N] Morristown St. Mary's Abbey.
Capdepon, Federico '83 (MIA) Miami Shores, FL St. Martha.
Capdeville, Henri *o.s.b.* '93 (TUC)[D] St. David, AZ Holy Trinity Monastery; Saint David, AZ.
Capeding, Lito J. (MOB) Daphne, AL Shrine of the Holy Cross; Apostleship of the Sea.
Capella, Joseph A. '90 (CAM) Lindenwold, NJ Our Lady of Guadalupe Parish, Lindenwold, N.J.
Capella, Joseph P. '90 (CAM) Representatives by Ordination Seniority; Consultants.
Capellan, Carlos Manuel Grullon '08 (PCE) Awaiting Assignment.
Capen, George *o.m.i.* '59 (BEL)[E] Belleville, IL Our Lady of the Snows Apartment Community Retirement Home; [F] Belleville, IL Missionary Oblates of Mary Immaculate – St. Henry's Oblate Residence.
Capetola, Nicholas *c.r.m.* '62 (CHR) Goose Creek, SC Immaculate Conception; Ramsey, NJ.
Capewell, Timothy J. '83 (TR) Princeton Jct., NJ Church of St. David the King.
Capik, Rev. Msgr. William J. '54 (MET) Retired.
Capilla, Oscar *l.c.* '07 (HRT)[B] Cheshire, CT Novitiate of the Legion of Christ.
Capitani, Sylvan P. '64 (HBG) New Freedom, PA St. John the Baptist.
Capitolo, Mario L. *s.j.* '59 (SJ)[M] Los Gatos, CA Sacred Heart Jesuit Center.
Capitolo, Paul F. *s.j.* '69 (SFR)[E] San Francisco, CA St. Ignatius College Preparatory (Coed); [N] San Francisco, CA Jesuit Community at St. Ignatius College Preparatory.
Capizzi, Marc F. '06 (PH) Bryn Mawr, PA St. John Neumann.
Caplis, Roger J. '58 (CHI) Retired.
Capo, Rafael *sch.p.* '96 (SJN) San Juan, PR Santisimo Salvador; [B] San Juan, PR Colegio Calasanz.
Capolarello, Salvatore '78 (BRK) On Leave/Unassigned.
Capone, Albert L. '80 (BO) Lowell, MA St. Michael.
Capone, Robert '00 (ORG) Placentia, CA St. Joseph.
Caponi, Francis J. *o.s.a.* '89 (PH)[C] Villanova University; [F] Malvern, PA Malvern Preparatory School for Boys; [Y] Malvern, PA Augustinian Friars (O.S.A.).
Caporali, Paul M. *s.d.b.* '54 (LA)[V] Rosemead, CA St. Joseph's Salesian Youth Renewal Center.
Caporiccio, Louis *c.p.m.* '97 (OWN) Auburn, KY; [F] Auburn, KY Fathers of Mercy.
Capoverdi, Giacomo '97 (PRO) Pawtucket, RI St. Leo the Great.
Capozzelli, Rev. Msgr. Emmanuel M. '49 (NEW)[M] Caldwell, NJ The Rev. Msgr. James F. Kelley Residence for Retired Priests Retired.
Cappel, Charles H. *m.m.* '44 (NY)[EE] Maryknoll Maryknoll Fathers and Brothers Retired.
Cappelletti, Edward *s.d.b.* '50 (NY)[EE] New Rochelle, NY Salesian Provincial House.
Cappelletti, Joseph '82 (CLV) Retired.
Cappelloni, David P. '86 (SCR) Dunmore, PA St. Rocco's; Dunmore, PA St. Anthony of Padua.
Cappelloni, Thomas A. '76 (SCR) Harleigh, PA Sacred Heart of Jesus; Hazleton, PA Queen of Heaven, Hazleton; Hazleton, PA St. Nazarius; [R] Harleigh, PA National Shrine of the Sacred Heart.
Capperella, Thomas S. '01 (CAM) Woodbury, NJ St. Patrick's Church, Woodbury.
Cappleman, Garry J. *o.p.* '03 (SFR)[N] San Francisco, CA St. Dominic Priory; San Francisco, CA St. Dominic.
Cappucci, Chester J. *o.m.i.* '63 (BO)[X] Tewksbury, MA Immaculate Heart of Mary Residence.
Cappuccino, Gregory J. '73 (RVC) Wantagh, NY St. Frances de Chantal.
Caprio, Albert A. *o.p.* '66 (HRT) New Haven, CT St. Mary's Priory Retired.
Caprio, Robert J. *o.f.m.* '63 (BO)[U] Andover St. Francis Friary; [W] Andover, MA Franciscan Center – Retreat House; [O] Brighton, MA Caritas St. Elizabeth's Medical Center of Boston, Inc.
Capriola, David (STV).
Capriolo, Victor R. '71 (MIL) Fond du Lac, WI Holy Family.
Capuano, Vincent J. *s.j.* '98 (FgM)[S] Towson Maryland Province of the Society of Jesus; Towson, MD Society of Jesus.
Capucci, Giovanni '06 (DEN) Graduate Studies.
Capuci, John M. '90 (BO) Burlington, MA St. Malachy.
Caputo, Ralph J. '75 (BRK) Brooklyn, NY St. Bernard of Clairvaux.
Caputo, Salvatore *s.s.c.* '76 (OM)[K] St. Columbans, NE Missionary Society of St. Columban.
Caraballo, Antonio '81 (ARE) Retired.
Caraballo Galindo, Gerardo E. '09 (MGZ) Lajas, PR Our Lady of the Purification.
Carabello, Francis J. '68 (NO) Retired.
Carasala, Arul '94 (KCK) Onaga, KS St. Columbkille; Corning, KS St. Patrick's; Kelly, KS St. Bede; Onaga, KS St. Vincent de Paul.
Caravia, Santiago Flor '00 (AGN) Hagatna, GU Nuestra Senora de la Paz y Buen Viaje.
Carazo, Jacob *o.f.m.conv.* '04 (OAK) San Pablo, CA St. Paul.
Carbajales, Ignacio '60 (MIA) Retired.
Carballo, Rafael '06 (ATL) Carrollton, GA Church of Our Lady of Perpetual Help.
Carberry, John '81 (SFD) Quincy, IL St. Anthony of Padua Retired.
Carbine, Rev. Msgr. Francis A. '62 (PH) Philadelphia, PA St. Katherine of Siena Retired.
Carbonaro, Dennis J. '81 (PH) Philadelphia, PA Our Lady of Consolation.
Carbone, Anthony J. '93 (GBG) Latrobe, PA St. John the Evangelist; Judges.
Carbone, Joseph M. *o.s.m.* '59 (CHI)[N] Chicago Order of Friar Servants of Mary (Servites) United States of America Province, Inc.
Carbone, Joseph M. *o.s.m.* '59 (DEN) Denver, CO Our Lady of Mount Carmel.
Carboneau, Dominic '99 (FTW) Presbyteral Council.
Carboneau, Dominique A. '99 (FTW) Yoder, IN St. Aloysius; Advisory Board.
Carbonneau, Robert *c.p.* '78 (NEW)[M] Passionist Archives.
Carbonneau, Robert *c.p.* '78 (BAL)[S] Baltimore, MD St. Joseph's Passionist Community; Baltimore, MD St. Joseph Passionist Monastery Parish.
Carboy, Daniel *c.ss.r.* (RIC) Hampton, VA St. Joseph; Fort Monroe, VA St. Mary Star of the Sea.
Carcerano, Michael J. '76 (LA) Ventura, CA San Buenaventura Mission.
Carchidi, Rudolph V. *c.s.c.* '55 (FR)[A] North Easton, MA Stonehill College; [A] North Easton, MA Holy Cross Fathers Religious.
Cardelli, Rev. Msgr. Daniel E. '57 (OAK)[R] Oakland, CA Italian Catholic Federation; Danville, CA St. Isidore Retired.
Cardenas, Eugenio *m.sp.s.* '82 (LA)[A] Camarillo, CA St. John's Seminary.
Cardenas, Gonzalo Arias '00 (NY) New York, NY Our Lady of Lourdes.

Cardenas, Hugo G. *i.v.e.* '04 (FR)[M] New Bedford, MA The Institute of the Incarnate Word, Inc.; New Bedford; New Bedford, MA St. Kilian.
Cardenas, Juan Raul '00 (PMB) Stuart, FL St. Joseph.
Cardenas, Marco *c.m.f.* '91 (CHI) Chicago, IL St. Basil/Visitation; [N] Oak Park Claretian Missionaries USA Eastern Province.
Cardenas, Prisciliano '50 (SJN) San Juan, PR Francisca Javiera Cabrini.
Cardenas–Martinez, Arcangel *s.s.p.* '90 (ATL) Marietta, GA Church of the Transfiguration.
Cardenas–Robles, Sergio *c.r.* '99 (PBL) Antonito, CO Our Lady of Guadalupe.
Cardenas Bonilla, Jose C. *c.s.* '99 (PRO) Providence, RI Blessed Sacrament.
Cardente, Edward S. '74 (PRO) Providence, RI St. Edward; North Providence, RI St. Anthony.
Cardiel, Gabriel *o.f.m.* '99 (AMA) Amarillo, TX St. Laurence Cathedral; Bishop's Appointee.
Cardillo, Clement *s.d.b.* (PAT) Clifton, NJ St. Paul.
Cardinal, Maurice *m.s.* '50 (HON) Hawi, HI Sacred Heart.
Cardinale, Kenneth R. '98 (WOR) West Boylston, MA Our Lady of Good Counsel.
Cardona, Carlos Garcia '92 (LKC) Kinder, LA St. Philip Neri.
Cardona, George '53 (MIA) Hialeah, FL St. John the Apostle Retired.
Cardona, Jorge D. '93 (CGS) Maunabo, PR San Isidro Labrador; Priests Senate.
Cardona, Orlando D. *c.m.* '97 (BRK) Brooklyn, NY St. John the Baptist; [T] Brooklyn, NY St. John the Baptist Rectory.
Cardona, Orlando *c.m.* '97 (RVC)[M] Oyster Bay, NY Vincentian Community.
Cardona Matta, Jose Miguel '98 (SJN) Puerto Nuevo, PR San Pablo.
Cardone, Joseph P. '87 (TOL) Special Assignment; Sylvania, OH St. Joseph.
Cardone, Thomas A. *s.m.* '85 (RVC)[D] Uniondale, NY Kellenberg Memorial High School; [M] Mineola, NY Provincial Residence and Novitiate; Councilors:.
Cardoni, Albert A. *s.j.* '60 (BO)[U] Weston, MA Campion Health Center, Inc.
Cardoso, Carlos *s.a.c.* '05 (NY) New York, NY Our Lady of Mt. Carmel; [EE] New York, NY Pallottine Fathers.
Cardoso, Luis A. '58 (FR) Retired.
Cardoso, Reinaldo M. '60 (PRO)[M] Pawtucket, RI Jeanne Jugan Residence Retired.
Cardoso, Roney M. *o.s.a.* '01 (SAT) San Antonio, TX St. Jude.
Cardoza, Edward '57 (SB) Retired.
Cardoza, Manuel '09 (SB) Temecula, CA St. Catherine of Alexandria.
Cardoza, Timothy N. '83 (FRS) Fresno, CA St. Mary Queen of Apostles Catholic Church.
Cardozo, Orlando *o.p.* '06 (NO) New Orleans, LA St. Anthony of Padua.
Cardy, William *o.f.m.* '72 (STL)[J] St. Louis, MO St. Anthony's Medical Center; [O] St. Louis, MO Franciscan Friary of St. Anthony of Padua.
Carek, Peter P. '60 (MIL) Retired.
Carew, Lawrence F. '66 (BGP) Trumbull, CT Christ the King.
Carey, David C. '04 (HRT) Meriden, CT St. Laurent; Meriden, CT Our Lady of Mount Carmel; Appointed Members.
Carey, David M. '62 (BAL) Retired.
Carey, Dennis G. '98 (NOR) Waterford, CT St. Paul; Part Time; Priests' Retirement Plan Board.
Carey, Gerald P. '98 (PH) Philadelphia, PA St. Paul.
Carey, J. Peter *s.j.* '64 (CIN)[N] Cincinnati, OH Faber Jesuit Community.
Carey, James H. '66 (SY) Pompey, NY Immaculate Conception; Tully, NY St. Leo; Health Care; Lafayette, NY St. Joseph.
Carey, John *o.f.m.cap.* '53 (PIT)[M] Butler, PA St. Mary's Friary.
Carey, Joseph H. *c.s.c.* '69 (FTW)[B] University of Notre Dame Du Lac; [H] Notre Dame, IN Holy Cross Community, Corby Hall, University of Notre Dame; [H] Notre Dame Congregation of Holy Cross, Indiana Province, Provincial House.
Carey, Rev. Msgr. Leo P. '51 (PAT)[Q] Chester, NJ Nazareth Village Retired.
Carey, Michael R. *o.p.* '77 (STL)[O] St. Louis, MO Dominican Community of St. Louis; [B] St. Louis, MO Aquinas Institute of Theology.
Carey, Michael *o.p.* '77 (OAK)[M] Oakland, CA Order of Preachers (Province of the Most Holy Name of Jesus – Western Dominican Province).
Carey, Paul V. '71 (SY) Lee Center, NY St. Joseph; Presbyteral Council.
Carey, Richard T. '65 (WOR) Presbyteral Council; North Brookfield, MA St. Joseph; Deans.
Carey, Richard W. '55 (LA) Retired.
Carey, Shawn P. '09 (BO) Assistant Director of the Office of the Deaf Apostolate; Hopkinton, MA St. John the Evangelist.
Carey, Stephen A. '98 (NEW) Fort Lee, NJ Madonna.
Carey, Stephen '62 (CAM) Retired.
Carey, William F. '67 (BGP) Greenwich, CT St. Agnes.
Carey, William G. '81 (BGP) New Canaan, CT St. Aloysius.
Carey, William H. '53 (SHP) Retired.
Carfagna, Rev. Msgr. Frank A. '67 (Y) Finance Council; Canton, OH St. Joseph; [Q] Youngstown, OH Catholic Cemeteries of the Diocese of Youngstown, Inc.; Judges.
Cargill, Rev. Msgr. Eugene '59 (GAL) League City, TX St. Mary.
Cargo, Jason '07 (DAL) Plano, TX St. Elizabeth Ann Seton.
Cargo, Thomas '78 (JOL) Kankakee, IL St. Teresa.
Caridi, Michael A. '94 (PIT) Pittsburgh, PA St. Louise de Marillac.
Carie, Giles *o.f.m.conv.* '61 (ELP) Judges.
Carie, Giles *o.f.m.conv.* '61 (LSC) Judges; [D] Mesilla Park, NM Holy Cross Retreat and Friary.
Cariglio, Rev. Msgr. Michael J. '70 (Y) Youngstown, OH Our Lady of Mt. Carmel; College of Consultors; Department of Canonical Services; Judicial Vicar; Priests Council.
Carignan, Armand *o.m.i.* '53 (FgM) Washington, DC AMERICAN OBLATE MISSIONS.
Carignan, Raymond P. *s.s.j.* '61 (BLX) Gulfport, MS St. Therese.
Carignan, Ronald *o.m.i.* '59 (SAT)[K] San Antonio, TX Oblate Madonna Residence.
Carillo, Victor '87 (SAT)[A] San Antonio, TX Assumption Seminary.
Carina, Chester H. '85 (MET) Matawan, NJ Most Holy Redeemer; Holy Name Society.
Carini, James P. '65 (NOR) Tolland, CT St. Matthew; Members; Deans; District Moderators; Liturgical Commission; Advisory Board.
Carkenord, David '62 (FTW) Waterloo, IN St. Michael the Archangel.
Carkhuff, Thomas R. *o.s.c.* '76 (PHX)[F] Phoenix, AZ Crosier Community of Phoenix (Canons Regular of the Order of the Holy Cross); [F] Phoenix, AZ Crosier Provincial House Province of St. Odilia.
Carkhuff, Thomas *o.s.c.* '76 (FgM) Phoenix, AZ CROSIER FATHERS MISSIONS.
Carl, Scott M. '00 (STP)[C] St. Paul, MN University of St. Thomas; Graduate Studies; [A] Saint Paul, MN The Saint Paul Seminary.
Carles, Alexander J. '88 (MET) Somerville, NJ Immaculate Conception.
Carleton, Robert J. *m.m.* '64 (SJ)[M] Los Altos, CA Maryknoll.
Carley, Patrick F. '69 (SLC) West Jordan, UT Saint Joseph the Worker LLC 232.
Carlin, Bernard *c.ss.r.* '78 (GR) Grand Rapids, MI St. Alphonsus; [L] Grand Rapids, MI The Society of the Redemptorists of the City of Grand Rapids.
Carlin, George *s.o.l.t.* '84 (CC)[G] Robstown, TX Society of Our Lady of the Most Holy Trinity.
Carlin, John T. '76 (CLV) Parma, OH St. Charles Borromeo; Retirement Board.
Carlin, Warren *o.carm.* '58 (JOL)[L] Darien Carmelite Provincial Office Retired.
Carlino, Richard A. '79 (ALB) Schenectady, NY St. Anthony; Schenectady, NY St. John the Evangelist.
Carlo, Cyprian '73 (LA) Ventura, CA Sacred Heart.
Carlo, Edgar '97 (MGZ) Vocations.
Carlo, Joseph C. '63 (BUF) Retired.
Carlo, Raymond J. '87 (CHR) Garden City, SC St. Michael.
Carlone, Carmen A. '69 (CAM) Hammonton, NJ St. Joseph's Church, Hammonton, N.J.
Carlos, Joseph P. *o.f.m.* '75 (SFD) Dieterich, IL St. Isidore the Farmer Church; [L] Teutopolis, IL St. Francis Assisi Friary.
Carlos, Miguel '95 (LAN) On Leave of Absence.
Carlsen, James F. '00 (MOB) Mobile, AL St. Pius X.
Carlson, Curtis *o.f.m.cap.* '95 (SAL) Ellis, KS St. Mary Parish; [D] Hays, KS St. Joseph's Friary.
Carlson, Edward A. '83 (CHI) Chicago, IL St. Edward.
Carlson, Rev. Msgr. George F. '66 (BO) West Roxbury, MA Holy Name; Elected.
Carlson, Gerald J. '63 (GI) Retired.
Carlson, Gregory I. *s.j.* '74 (OM)[K] Omaha, NE Jesuit Community at Creighton University.
Carlson, James R. '73 (SAG) Saginaw, MI St. John Vianney; Ecumenism Ministry.
Carlson, Kenneth F. '98 (CHI) Army Chaplains; Military Chaplains.
Carlson, Michael A. '07 (HRT)[D] Bristol, CT St. Paul Catholic High School; Newington, CT Church of the Holy Spirit.
Carlson, Richard D. '69 (NEW) Montclair, NJ St. Peter Claver.
Carlson, Robert D. '63 (GAL) Retired.
Carlson, Steven V. '96 (R) Wilmington, NC Christ the King; Wilmington, NC St. Mark.
Carlton, Maurice T. '68 (MET) High Bridge, NJ St. Joseph.
Carman, Bernard '80 (BRK) Brooklyn, NY Our Lady of the Rosary of Pompeii.
Carman, Paul '00 (SY) Absent on Leave.
Carmichael, Eugene *s.j.* '73 (CIN)[N] Cincinnati, OH Jesuit Community at Xavier University.
Carmichael, John F. '97 (BO) Marshfield, MA St. Ann by the Sea.
Carmody, Emeric *o.carm.* '54 (JOL)[L] Darien Carmelite Provincial Office Retired.
Carmody, James F. '70 (WOR) Northbridge, MA St. Peter.
Carmody, James P. '63 (RVC) Retired.
Carmody, Lawrence W. '90 (COS) Security, CO St. Dominic.
Carmody, Michael J. '83 (GAL) Houston, TX St. Catherine of Siena.
Carmody, Stephen F. *o.p.* '81 (COL) Somerset, OH St. Joseph's; Somerset, OH Holy Trinity.
Carmody, Stephen Francis *o.p.* '81 (NY) New York, NY St. Catherine of Siena.
Carmola, Michael J. '64 (SY) Special Assignment; [S] Syracuse, NY Christ the King Retreat House; Laymen & Laywomen Retreat Movements.
Carmona, Henry '78 (B) Boise, ID Cathedral of St. John the Evangelist; Mountain Home, ID Our Lady of Good Counsel; Judicial Vicar; Judges; College of Consultors.
Carmona, Hugo '85 (PRO) Woonsocket, RI All Saints Parish; Woonsocket, RI St. Charles.
Carmone, Anthony F. '47 (PRO) Retired.
Carneiro, Denis '68 (CHI) Buffalo Grove, IL St. Mary.
Carnes, Matthew E. *s.j.* '03 (WDC)[N] Washington, DC The Jesuit Community at Georgetown University.
Carnes, Valerie (KNX)[D] Signal Mountain, TN Alexian Village of Tennessee.
Carnevale, Michael *o.f.m.* '61 (NY) New York, NY St. Francis of Assisi.
Carney, Angus N. *o.s.a.* '43 (PH)[Y] Villanova, PA St. Thomas Monastery.
Carney, Bryan J. '07 (BRK) Belle Harbor, NY St. Francis de Sales.
Carney, Edward '63 (PEO) Retired.
Carney, James R. *s.j.* '56 (NY)[EE] New York, NY Murray–Weigel Hall.
Carney, John F. '91 (SFE) Los Alamos, NM Immaculate Heart of Mary.
Carney, John J. '63 (BAL) Retired.
Carney, John J. *c.m.* '82 (FgM) Philadelphia, PA Eastern Province.
Carney, Joseph T. '68 (MIA) Miami Springs, FL Blessed Trinity.
Carney, Lawrence D. '07 (WCH) Arma, KS St. Joseph; Girard, KS St. Michael.
Carney, Rev. Msgr. Patrick J. '55 (NY) Hartsdale, NY Sacred Heart.
Carney, Robert E. '91 (TUC) Tucson, AZ Saint Francis de Sales Roman Catholic Parish – Tucson.
Carney, Thomas *m.s.c.* '54 (ALN)[A] Center Valley, PA Sacred Heart Villa, Missionaries of the Sacred Heart.
Caro, Eddie *o.f.m.* (SJN)[C] Sabana Seca, PR Post–Noviciado San Jose Obrero.
Caro, Luis A. *c.ss.r.* '75 (BRK) Brooklyn, NY Our Lady of Perpetual Help Basilica.
Caro, Robert V. *s.j.* '70 (LA)[C] Los Angeles, CA Loyola Marymount University; [C] Los Angeles, CA Jesuit Community.
Carola, Joseph A. *s.j.* '93 (NO)[P] New Orleans Jesuit Provincial Office.
Carolan, Craig G. '91 (BWN) St. Andrew; Presbyteral Council; College of Consultors; Mission, TX San Cristobal Magallanes & Companions.
Carolan, Emmet '62 (SAT) San Antonio, TX Holy Family; Judges.
Carolan, John J. '51 (CHI) Oak Park, IL St. Catherine of Siena–St. Lucy Retired.
Carolan, Thomas '58 (SFD)[L] Springfield, IL Our Lady of Angels Friary.
Carolin, Joseph C. '66 (HBG) South Mountain, PA Restoration Center.
Caroluzza, Rev. Msgr. Thomas '58 (RIC) Virginia Beach, VA Retired.
Caro Morales, Jorge L. '89 (MGZ) Sabana Grande, PR Church of San Isidro.
Caron, Antonin R. '69 (PRT) Retired.
Caron, David G. *o.p.* '89 (NO) New Orleans, LA St. Dominic; New Orleans, LA St. Anthony of Padua.
Caron, Eduardo *c.s.sp.* '57 (SJN)[F] Dorado, PR Santuario del Espiritu Santo.
Caron, Gerard J. '94 (PRO) Harrisville, RI St. Theresa of the Child Jesus.
Caron, Gerard *s.m.* '54 (BO)[U] Boston, MA Marist Fathers Lourdes Residence; [Z] Boston, MA Marist Fathers Residence.
Caron, Rev. Msgr. Marc B. '89 (PRT) Diocesan Consultors; Diocesan Office for Worship; Lewiston, ME Prince of Peace Parish.
Caron, Paul A. '83 (FR) Mattapoisett, MA St. Anthony's; Marion, MA St. Rita's.
Caronan, John E. *o.praem.* '94 (ORG)[I] Silverado, CA Norbertine Fathers of Orange Inc.
Caronan, John *o.praem.* '94 (ORG) Judges.
Carongay, Jovito B. '92 (BRK) Elmhurst, NY Ascension.
Carosella, Jerome A. '63 (VEN) Boca Grande, FL Our

Lady of Mercy; Pension Plan Board of Trustees (Archdiocese of Miami/Diocese of Venice).
Carota, Peter '97 (STO) Ripon, CA St. Patrick Church of Ripon (Pastor of).
Carotenuto, Anthony M. '68 (TR) Red Bank, NJ St. Anthony.
Carpender, John W. '53 (DUB) Retired.
Carpender, Thomas J. '48 (DUB) Retired.
Carpenter, Brian Kumar '09 (ROC) Rochester, NY Peace of Christ Roman Catholic Parish of Rochester, NY.
Carpenter, Christopher '95 (PHX) On Leave.
Carpenter, Edward C. '95 (ELP) Clint, TX San Lorenzo; San Elizario, TX San Elceario; Advocates; Presbyteral Council.
Carpenter, Sean G. '09 (SCR) Brodheadsville, PA Our Lady Queen of Peace.
Carpenter, Todd *o.f.m.* '99 (NY) Bronx, NY Holy Cross.
Carpenter, Todd *o.f.m.* '99 (WIL) Wilmington, DE St. Paul's.
Carpenter, William *c.s.v.* '77 (CHI)[N] Arlington Heights Viatorian Province Center–Clerics of St. Viator.
Carpentier, Normand E. '71 (PRT) Diocesan Review Board; Diocesan Priests' Benefit Plan – Trustees; Personnel Board; Bath, ME All Saints Parish.
Carpentier, Robert A. '67 (PRO) Absent on Leave.
Carpine, Eric *o.f.m.* '75 (NY) New York, NY St. Stephen of Hungary.
Carpinelli, Vincent G. '71 (CAM) Glassboro, NJ The Church of Our Lady of Lourdes, Glassboro, N.J.
Carr, Alton *c.ss.r.* '60 (SAT)[L] San Antonio, TX Redemptorists of Texas–San Antonio #1; San Antonio, TX St. Gerard Majella.
Carr, Andrew *c.ss.r.* '55 (BAL) Baltimore, MD St. Michael; Baltimore, MD St. Patrick.
Carr, Brendan '72 (BAL) Retired.
Carr, David W. '80 (PMB)[B] West Palm Beach, FL Cardinal Newman High School, Inc.
Carr, Ephrem *o.s.b.* '67 (IND)[K] St. Meinrad St. Meinrad Archabbey.
Carr, Eugene R. '63 (SCR) Retired.
Carr, Gary M. '82 (SPC) Leave of Absence.
Carr, Rev. Msgr. James A. '55 (CAM) Retired.
Carr, James P. *s.j.* '92 (BO)[W] Gloucester, MA Eastern Point Retreat House.
Carr, James V. '69 (RIC) Retired.
Carr, Joseph A. '06 (PIT) Cranberry Township, PA St. Kilian.
Carr, Mark A. *s.j.* '05 (MIL)[P] Milwaukee, WI Pere Marquette Jesuit Community; [E] Milwaukee, WI Marquette University High School.
Carr, Michael '68 (CHY) Torrington, WY St. Rose; College of Consultors; Lusk, WY St. Leo's; Judges.
Carr, Neil J. *s.j.* '51 (NY)[EE] New York, NY Murray–Weigel Hall.
Carr, Raymond J. *s.m.* '63 (WDC)[N] Washington, DC Marist Center.
Carr, Raymond *s.m.* '63 (WH)[G] Wheeling, WV Good Shepherd Nursing Home.
Carr, Richard T. '01 (ARL) Front Royal, VA St. John the Baptist.
Carr, Robert J. (BO) Somerville, MA St. Benedict.
Carr, Walter '92 (AUS) Retired.
Carr, Rev. Msgr. William H. '69 (RIC) Richmond, VA St. Bridget.
Carr, Rev. Msgr. William '59 (WCH) Retired.
Carrano, Michael A. '70 (BRK) Middle Village, NY Our Lady of Hope; Assignment Board.
Carranza, Claudio Cabrera '02 (MRY) King City, CA St. John the Baptist.
Carranza, Fernando '95 (NEW) On Duty Outside the Archdiocese.
Carranza, Fernando '95 (DAL)[A] Dallas, TX The Redemptoris Mater House of Formation.
Carranza, Manuel Fragoso '05 (TUC) Parker, AZ Sacred Heart Roman Catholic Parish – Parker.
Carranza, Riz '80 (LA) Santa Maria, CA St. Mary of the Assumption.
Carrara, Christopher C. '94 (OG) Committee on Assignments; Lowville, NY St. Hedwig; Lowville, NY St. Mary; Lowville, NY St. Peter.
Carraro, Francesco '95 (NEW) Bergenfield, NJ St. John the Evangelist.
Carre, Joseph P. Edwidge '83 (NSH) Nashville, TN Church of the Most Holy Name.
Carreiro, Walter A. '95 (BO) Cambridge, MA St. Anthony of Padua; Vicariate IV; Portuguese.
Carrella, Eugene J. '84 (NY) Staten Island, NY St. Adalbert.
Carreon, Noe '92 (DEN) Denver, CO Our Lady of Grace; Ex Officio Members.
Carreon, Regidor '75 (PHX) Sun City, AZ St. Elizabeth Seton Roman Catholic Parish Retired.
Carrero, Angel Dario *o.f.m.* '95 (SJN) Sabana Seca, PR San Jose Obrero; [A] Bayamon Central University.
Carri, Sebastian J. *s.j.* '67 (FgM) Chicago, IL Society of Jesus.
Carrier, J. Victor '69 (SPR) Springfield, MA Holy Cross.
Carrier, Mark F. '99 (ARL) Alexandria, VA St. Louis.
Carrier, Michael J. '95 (WIL) Wilmington, DE Church of the Holy Child; Office of Worship; Catholic Scouting Program.
Carrier, Paul E. *s.j.* '78 (BGP)[O] Fairfield, CT The Fairfield Jesuit Community–Fairfield University.
Carrier, Paul E. *s.j.* '77 (BO)[U] Boston The Society of Jesus of New England–Provincial Offices.
Carriero, John P. *s.j.* '63 (ROC)[B] Rochester, NY McQuaid Jesuit High School.
Carrigan, Thomas C. '60 (SAC) Retired.
Carrigg, George A. '57 (BO) Dorchester, MA St. Christopher.
Carrigg, William J. '56 (BO) Senior Priests. Retired.
Carrillo, Rev. Msgr. Arsenio S. '56 (TUC) Retired.
Carrillo, Arthur *c.p.* '70 (CHI)[N] Chicago, IL Passionist Missions of India; [N] Chicago, IL Passionist Missions, Inc.; Chicago, IL Holy Cross Province (Western).
Carrillo, Arthur *c.p.* '70 (GAL)[O] Houston, TX Congregation of the Passion, Holy Name Passionist Community and Retreat Center.
Carrillo, Ron *s.f.* '74 (SFE) Chimayo, NM Holy Family.
Carrillo, Sergio '82 (MIA) Retired.
Carrington, Richard J. '76 (NEW) Union City, NJ Sts. Joseph and Michael; Holy Name Federation.
Carrion, Michael J. '77 (BAL) Judge.
Carrion, Michael W. '77 (BAL) Baltimore, MD Immaculate Heart of Mary; [V] Baltimore, MD The Immaculate Heart of Mary School Endowment Trust; [W] Millersville, MD Holy Name Society (Union).
Carrion, Patrick '82 (BAL) Baltimore, MD Holy Cross; Baltimore, MD St. Mary, Star of the Sea; Baltimore, MD Our Lady of Good Counsel.
Carrion Leyva, José Antonio (SJN) Carolina, PR Ntra. Sra. de Fatima.
Carrol, Michael '67 (LA) Newbury Park, CA St. Julie Billiart.
Carrola, Rudy T. '88 (SAT) San Antonio, TX St. John Berchmans.
Carroll, Rev. Msgr. Aidan M. '63 (LA) Valinda, CA St. Martha; [D] La Puente, CA Bishop Amat Memorial High School.
Carroll, Alban *s.a.* '55 (NY)[EE] Garrison, NY Franciscan Friars of the Atonement.
Carroll, Brian '62 (JKS) Flowood, MS St. Paul.
Carroll, Daniel *o.carm.* '60 (CHI)[D] Chicago, IL; [N] Chicago, IL Carmelite Priory of St. Cyril Retired.
Carroll, Edward E. '50 (MIL) Retired.
Carroll, Edward G. '67 (BO) Permanent Disability.
Carroll, Emmett H. *s.j.* '62 (SEA) Bainbridge Island, WA St. Cecilia; [L] Seattle, WA Arrupe Jesuit Community at Seattle University.
Carroll, Emmett *o.f.m.conv.* '54 (TR) Seaside Park, NJ St. Catharine of Siena; Tribunal Judges.
Carroll, Francis P. *s.s.c.* '62 (PRO) St Columbans, NE House of Post–Graduate Studies; [P] Bristol, RI St. Columban's Retirement House.
Carroll, Francis *s.s.c.* '62 (OM)[K] St. Columbans Missionary Society of St. Columban.
Carroll, Gilbert A. '41 (CHI) Palm Harbor, FL Retired.
Carroll, J. Alfred *s.j.* '59 (SPK)[B] Spokane, WA Gonzaga University.
Carroll, Rev. Msgr. James J. '45 (COL) Retired.
Carroll, James J. '56 (NEW) Retired.
Carroll, James M. '68 (BO) Vicariate IV; Georgetown, MA St. Mary.
Carroll, James *o.f.m.* '79 (PSC) Mahanoy City, PA St. Mary's; [A] Sybertsville, PA Holy Dormition Friary.
Carroll, John A. *s.s.j.* '66 (WDC) Washington, DC Incarnation.
Carroll, Rev. Msgr. John J. '66 (PAT) Kinnelon, NJ Our Lady of the Magnificat; Presbyteral Council; Pro–Synodal Judges.
Carroll, John J. *s.j.* '55 (FgM) New York, NY Society of Jesus.
Carroll, John P. '53 (BO) Senior Priests. Retired.
Carroll, John R. (BO) Woburn, MA St. Anthony of Padua.
Carroll, Rev. Msgr. Joseph A. '74 (SD)[L] San Diego, CA St. Vincent de Paul Village; [L] Campo, CA Rancho San Vincente; [L] San Diego, CA S.V.D.P. Management Inc.; [O] San Diego, CA Catholic Committee on Scouting.
Carroll, Joseph '55 (HON) Retired.
Carroll, Keith M. '09 (HBG) Chambersburg, PA Corpus Christi.
Carroll, Rev. Msgr. Lawrence J. '81 (BGP) Fairfield, CT St. Pius X; Diocesan Consultors; Vicariate III (Fairfield, Easton, West Bridgeport); Members of the Clergy Personnel Committee; Pastors' Vocation Advisory Board; Presbyteral Council; Parochial Examiners.
Carroll, Michael A. '72 (SAC) Auburn, CA St. Teresa of Avila Parish.
Carroll, Rev. Msgr. Michael J. *c.m.* '77 (PH)[B] Philadelphia, PA St. Vincent's Seminary; [Y] Philadelphia Congregation of the Mission.
Carroll, Michael J. *c.m.* '77 (FgM) Philadelphia, PA Eastern Province; Philadelphia, PA.
Carroll, Rev. Msgr. Michael J. '61 (PH) Wayne, PA St. Katharine of Siena; Office for Ecumenical and Interreligious Affairs Retired.
Carroll, Michael J. *c.m.* '77 (PH) Philadelphia, PA Immaculate Conception.
Carroll, Michael '70 (GB) Absent on Leave, Sick or Disabled.
Carroll, Michael '67 (LA) Westlake Village, CA St. Maximilian Kolbe.
Carroll, Norman P. '93 (WIL) Wilmington, DE St. Elizabeth.
Carroll, Patrick '53 (NY) Retired.
Carroll, Rev. Msgr. Ralph E. '58 (NO) Retired.
Carroll, Rev. Msgr. Robert B. '63 (PAT) Highland Lakes, NJ Our Lady of Fatima.
Carroll, Rev. Msgr. Robert J. '75 (PH) West Chester, PA St. Maximilian Kolbe.
Carroll, Roger '63 (STP) Retired.
Carroll, Sean *s.j.* (TUC)[H] Nogales, AZ Kino Border Initiative.
Carroll, Thomas J. *s.j.* '84 (SJ)[L] Los Altos, CA Jesuit Retreat Center of Los Altos.
Carroll, Thomas R. *sch.p.* '70 (LEX)[B] Martin, KY The Piarist School; [G] Martin, KY Piarist Fathers.
Carroll, William R. '70 (BO) Marian Devotions; Melrose, MA St. Mary of the Annunciation.
Carroll, William *s.j.* '69 (SJ)[M] Los Gatos, CA Sacred Heart Jesuit Center.
Carrozza, Andrew P. '90 (NY) Yonkers, NY St. Ann.
Carrozzo, Anthony M. *o.f.m.* '66 (NY) New York, NY St. Francis of Assisi.
Carruthers, Rev. Msgr. Michael '91 (MIA)[A] Miami, FL St. John Vianney College Seminary.
Carscallen, Rev. Msgr. Edward C. '47 (TUC) Retired.
Carson, John '64 (NY) Yonkers, NY St. Ann.
Carson, Michael '98 (SJ) San Jose, CA Queen of Apostles; Priests' Retirement Board; Council of Priests.
Carson, Robert E. *o.praem.* '46 (GB)[J] De Pere, WI St. Norbert Abbey.
Carson, Rev. Msgr. Stanley B. '79 (ALT) Altoona, PA Sacred Heart.
Cartagena, Antonio '85 (CGS) Caguas, PR San Juan Apostol y Evangelista; Vicar General; Diocesan Consultors; Priests Senate.
Cartaya, Pedro *s.j.* '67 (MIA)[D] Miami, FL Belen Jesuit Preparatory School; [K] Miami, FL Villa Javier.
Carten, Thomas F. *c.s.c.* '79 (SCR)[C] Holy Cross Community.
Carter, Augustine W. *o.carm.* '51 (LA)[P] Encino, CA Our Lady of Mount Carmel Priory.
Carter, Daniel E. '79 (SFR) San Francisco, CA Our Lady of Lourdes.
Carter, David '05 (KNX) Presbyteral Council.
Carter, Francis T. '86 (HRT) New Haven, CT St. Bernadette.
Carter, Rev. Msgr. James A. '66 (CHR) Mount Pleasant, SC Christ Our King.
Carter, James C. *s.j.* '58 (NO)[C] New Orleans, LA Loyola University New Orleans.
Carter, John T. '70 (BAL) Williamsport, MD St. Augustine Retired.
Carter, Rev. Msgr. John T. '49 (E) Retired.
Carter, Kevin E. '86 (NEW) Jersey City, NJ St. Nicholas; Our Lady of Fatima First Saturday Family; Members.
Carter, Mark *o.f.m.cap.* (BAL) Baltimore, MD St. Ambrose.
Carter, Mark *o.f.m. cap.* '92 (PIT)[M] Butler, PA St. Mary's Friary; Cabot, PA St. Joseph; Butler, PA St. Mary of the Assumption.
Carter, Martin *s.a.* '75 (NY)[EE] Garrison, NY Franciscan Friars of the Atonement.
Carter, Raymond J. '49 (COL) Retired.
Carter, Robert E. *s.j.* '63 (NY)[EE] New York, NY Murray–Weigel Hall.
Carter, Stephen *o.f.m.cap.* '82 (WDC) Washington, DC Shrine of the Sacred Heart.
Carton, A. Richard '93 (PAT) Boonton, NJ Our Lady of Mount Carmel.
Carton, Rev. Msgr. William J. '59 (TR)[N] Trenton, NJ Villa Vianney Retired.
Cartwright, Christopher M. *s.j.* '80 (SJ)[B] Santa Clara, CA Jesuit Community.
Carty, John A. *s.j.* '59 (FgM) Watertown, MA Society of Jesus.
Carty, John T. '50 (PRO) Retired.
Carucci, David P. '95 (MOB) Montgomery, AL St. Bede the Venerable Catholic Church.
Carusi, Angelo N. '98 (PRO) Providence, RI Blessed Sacrament; Catholic Scouting–Boy Scouts, Girl Scouts, Camp Fire.
Caruso, Daniel M. (SY) Binghamton, NY St. Paul.
Caruso, Daniel '94 (SY) Binghamton, NY St. Mary of the Assumption.
Caruso, Michael *s.j.* '82 (LA)[C] Los Angeles, CA Jesuit Community.
Caruso, Philip J. '78 (NY) New Rochelle, NY St. Joseph.
Caruso, Robert J. '80 (PHX) Mesa, AZ All Saints Roman Catholic Parish; Defenders of the Bond.
Carvajal, Damian '53 (SJN) San Juan, PR Cristo Redentor.
Carvajal, Rev. Msgr. Felipe N. '68 (PAT) Passaic, NJ St. Nicholas.
Carvajal, Raul H. '65 (MRY) Retired.

Carvajal–Bastro, Tomas '08 (PBL) Office of Hispanic Ministry.
Carvalho, Antonio '93 (COL) Columbus, OH Holy Name of Jesus.
Carvalho, Gordian '85 (HON) Honolulu, HI St. Pius X; Clergy Personnel Board; Honolulu, HI Sacred Heart.
Carvalho, Joaquim *o.s.b.* '82 (KCK)[I] Atchison, KS St. Benedict's Abbey.
Carven, John W. *c.m.* '60 (PH)[B] Philadelphia, PA St. Vincent's Seminary[Y].
Carver, Dennis J. '94 (BLX) Pass Christian, MS Holy Family Parish; Deans; Personnel Board; Vocations; Presbyteral Council; College of Consultors; CDB Seminarian Education, Inc.
Carver, Joseph P. *s.j.* (SEA)[L] Seattle, WA Jesuit House, Seattle.
Carvill, Michael *f.s.c.b.* '90 (DEN) Broomfield, CO Nativity of Our Lord.
Carville, John '63 (BR) Retired.
Cary, Liam '92 (P) Medford, OR Sacred Heart of Jesus.
Cary, Robert M. *c.s.p.* '84 (CHI) Chicago, IL Old St. Mary.
Cary, William J. '58 (SUP) Retired.
Carzon, Thomas *o.m.v.* '96 (DEN) Denver, CO Holy Ghost.
Casabon, Luis '61 (MIA) Retired.
Casadia, James A. '01 (CAM) Atco, NJ The Church of the Assumption, Atco, N.J.; Representatives by Ordination Seniority.
Casadillo, Guillermo (BIR)[I] Birmingham, AL Congregation of the Passion: Holy Family Community, Inc.
Casagram, Michael *o.c.s.o.* '82 (L)[L] Trappist, KY Abbey of Our Lady of Gethsemani, of the Order of Cistercians of the Strict Observance.
Casale, Charles B. '69 (FRS) Retired.
Casale, Rev. Msgr. Franklyn M. '67 (MIA)[B] St. Thomas University.
Casale, Rev. Msgr. Franklyn M. '67 (NEW) On Duty Outside the Archdiocese.
Casaleggio, David E. '81 (LAV) Las Vegas, NV St. Anne; Presbyteral Council for the Diocese of Las Vegas.
Casari, Michael T. '95 (WIL) Ocean City, MD St. Luke and St. Andrew.
Casarotto, Secondo *c.s.* '66 (BUF) Buffalo, NY St. Anthony of Padua.
Casaus, Vicente *sch.p.* '52 (LA) Los Angeles, CA St. Lucy.
Casavantes, Carlos S. *f.s.s.p.* '86 (CC) Corpus Christi, TX St. Michael the Archangel Latin Mass Community.
Casavates, Carlos '86 (CC) Corpus Christi, TX Our Lady of Perpetual Help.
Casazza, Rev. Msgr. David J. '43 (NEW) River Edge, NJ St. Peter the Apostle Retired.
Cascino, Marion *o.f.m.* '49 (NY)[EE] New York Franciscan Province of the Immaculate Conception.
Cascione, James *c.ss.r.* '83 (PH) Philadelphia, PA Visitation B.V.M.
Casciotti, James A. *s.j.* '78 (BAL) Towson, MD; Presbyteral Council; [S] Towson, MD Maryland Province of the Society of Jesus; [S] Baltimore, MD Colombiere Jesuit Community.
Casciotti, James A. *s.j.* (BAL)[W] Baltimore, MD Radio Mass of Baltimore, Inc.
Case, Frank *s.j.* '69 (SEA)[A] Seattle, WA Seattle University; [L] Seattle, WA Arrupe Jesuit Community at Seattle University.
Case, Lowell D. *s.s.j.* '80 (WDC) Washington, DC St. Augustine.
Case, Lowell D. *s.s.j.* '80 (GAL) Houston, TX Our Mother of Mercy; Houston, TX Our Lady Star of the Sea.
Case, Richard D. *s.j.* '75 (SPK) Spokane, WA St. Aloysius.
Case, Richard *s.j.* '75 (SPK) Members; [B] Spokane, WA Gonzaga University.
Caserta, Angelo C. '45 (CIN) Piqua, OH St. Boniface Retired.
Caserta, Charles W. '54 (CIN) Retired.
Caserta, Rev. Msgr. Thomas G. '79 (BRK) Brooklyn, NY St. Bernadette.
Casey, Anthony C. '58 (BRK)[Q] Queens Village, NY Queen of Peace Residence Retired.
Casey, Christopher J. '07 (BO) Dracut, MA St. Francis of Assisi; Dracut, MA Ste. Marguerite d'Youville.
Casey, Daniel '58 (SAC) Retired.
Casey, David J. *s.j.* '69 (SY)[Q] Syracuse, NY Jesuits at LeMoyne, Inc.
Casey, Denis '57 (TLS)[E] Tulsa, OK Saint Francis Hospital Retired.
Casey, Diarmid *c.s.sp.* '69 (SFR) Millbrae, CA St. Dunstan.
Casey, Donald A. '43 (SB) Retired.
Casey, Donald A. '43 (LAV) Henderson, NV St. Peter the Apostle Retired.
Casey, Edward J. '79 (PH) Broomall, PA St. Pius X; [D] Radnor, PA Archbishop John Carroll High School.
Casey, James R. '00 (PH) Philadelphia, PA Annunciation B.V.M.; [D] Philadelphia, PA Roman Catholic High School for Boys.
Casey, John D. '55 (HRT) North Haven, CT St. Therese Retired.
Casey, Rev. Msgr. John F. '54 (BRK) Queens Village, NY Our Lady of Lourdes; Presbyteral Council Retired.
Casey, Rev. Msgr. John H. '57 (CAM) Retired.
Casey, John J. *m.m.* '56 (NY)[EE] Maryknoll Maryknoll Fathers and Brothers.
Casey, John P. *m.m.* '56 (NY)[EE] Retired.
Casey, John W. '45 (SCR) Retired.
Casey, John *s.a.c.* '67 (FWT) Weatherford, TX St. Stephen.
Casey, Joseph H. *s.j.* '49 (BO)[U] Weston, MA Campion Health Center, Inc.
Casey, Joseph M. '66 (PAT) Retired.
Casey, Kevin P. *s.j.* '72 (SD) Santee, CA Guardian Angels.
Casey, Kevin *c.p.* '67 (MET)[I] South River Passionist Provincial Office.
Casey, M. Joseph *s.j.* '67 (CIN) Cincinnati, OH St. Francis Xavier.
Casey, Noah J. '76 (IND) Indianapolis, IN St. Luke; Priests' Personnel Board.
Casey, Patrick L. '65 (NU) Darwin, MN St. John.
Casey, Patrick M. *s.j.* '72 (FgM) Chicago, IL Society of Jesus; Chicago, IL Society of Jesus.
Casey, Patrick T. *o.m.i.* '80 (JUN) Petersburg, AK St. Catherine of Siena; Wrangell, AK St. Rose of Lima.
Casey, Patrick '97 (DET) Canton, MI St. Thomas a Becket; Presbyteral Council; Archdiocesan Vicars.
Casey, Peter J. '68 (BO) Milton, MA St. Agatha.
Casey, Richard L. '65 (BO) Littleton, MA St. Anne; Emergency Response Group.
Casey, Robert E. '87 (BO) South Boston, MA St. Brigid; South Boston, MA Gate of Heaven; Vicariate II.
Casey, Robert G. '94 (CHI) Brookfield, IL St. Barbara.
Casey, Thomas J. *o.s.a.* '69 (PH)[Y] Villanova, PA St. Thomas Monastery.
Casey, Thomas Joseph *s.j.* '57 (STL)[O] St. Louis, MO Jesuit Community Corporation at Saint Louis University – Jesuit Hall.
Casey, William '69 (KNX) Retired.
Casey, William *c.p.m.* '91 (OWN)[F] Auburn, KY Fathers of Mercy; Auburn, KY.
Cash, Richard '89 (OWN) Morganfield, KY St. Ann.
Cashen, Michael E. '91 (TLS) Tulsa, OK St. Catherine.
Cashin, James '65 (SAT) Comfort, TX Sacred Heart.
Cashman, Christopher T. '89 (BRK) Brooklyn, NY St. Mary Star of the Sea.
Cashman, James *o.s.c.* '48 (SCL)[I] Onamia Crosier Priory.
Cashman, Jeremiah '55 (LC) Cornell, WI Holy Cross.
Cashman, John *c.p.* '67 (MET)[I] South River Passionist Provincial Office.
Cashman, Joseph C. '60 (WIN) Absent on Leave.
Casillas, Rafael '72 (LA) Los Angeles, CA St. Joseph.
Casillas, Richard *s.v.d.* '97 (LA) Los Angeles, CA Our Lady of Loretto.
Casimir, Benjamin *c.s.* '03 (VEN) Immokalee, FL Our Lady of Guadalupe.
Casipong, Guillermo *c.i.c.m.* '07 (SAT)[H] San Antonio, TX Christus Santa Rosa Health Care Corporation; San Antonio, TX Santa Rosa Hospital System.
Caskey, John '82 (SCL) Special Assignment.
Caskey, Virgil '44 (HBG)[G] Ephrata, PA St. Clement's Mission House.
Casper, Paul *s.c.j.* '57 (MIL)[P] Franklin, WI Villa Maria.
Cassabon, Michael P. (R) Fayetteville, NC St. Patrick.
Cassar, Edward A. '69 (BRK) Brooklyn, NY Our Lady of Grace.
Cassar, Julian '77 (BAK) Health and Retirement Board; Baker, OR Cathedral of St. Francis De Sales.
Cassato, Rev. Msgr. David L. '72 (BRK) Brooklyn, NY St. Athanasius; Parish Services Corp.; Police Department; Peter Turner Insurance Co.; Diocesan Insurance Committee.
Cassel, Harry A. *o.s.a.* '50 (PH)[Y] Villanova, PA St. Thomas Monastery Retired.
Cassem, Ned H. *s.j.* '70 (BO)[U] Weston, MA Campion Jesuit Community.
Casserly, Eugene D. '69 (PT) Vicars Forane; Defender of the Bond; Priests' Pension Plan, Board for; Pensacola, FL Little Flower.
Cassese, Anthony '77 (CLV) Cleveland, OH St. Jerome.
Cassese, John *o.f.m.* '50 (BRK) Brooklyn, NY Our Lady of Peace.
Cassese, John–Marie *o.f.m.* '50 (NY)[EE] New York, NY Padua Friary; [EE] New York Franciscan Province of the Immaculate Conception.
Cassidy, Bernard F. *s.j.* '63 (SJ)[M] Los Gatos, CA Sacred Heart Jesuit Center.
Cassidy, Rev. Msgr. Charles C. (PAT) Retired.
Cassidy, Daniel J. '78 (CHI) Chicago, IL Saint Ita.
Cassidy, Daniel J. *o.p.* '57 (PRO)[P] Providence St. Thomas Aquinas Priory at Providence College.
Cassidy, Felix F. *o.p.* '54 (SFR) San Francisco, CA St. Dominic; [N] San Francisco, CA St. Dominic Priory.
Cassidy, Francis J. '59 (LA) Monrovia, CA Immaculate Conception Retired.
Cassidy, Francis P. '57 (CHI) Chicago, IL; Chicago, IL St. Daniel the Prophet Retired.
Cassidy, James M. '61 (CLV) Ashland, OH St. Edward.
Cassidy, Rev. Msgr. James P. '51 (NY) New York, NY Cathedral of St. Patrick Retired.
Cassidy, James '78 (STP) Minneapolis, MN St. Joan of Arc.
Cassidy, John M. '58 (CHI) Chicago, IL St. Daniel the Prophet Retired.
Cassidy, Rev. Msgr. John T. '79 (PT) Pensacola, FL St. Thomas More; Vicar for Priests; Finance, Diocesan Commission for; Priests' Pension Plan, Board for; Priest Personnel Board.
Cassidy, John V. '69 (LC) Retired.
Cassidy, Kevin W. '60 (MAD) Sun City, AZ Retired.
Cassidy, Rev. Msgr. Martin J. '57 (MIA) Lauderdale–by–the–Sea, FL Assumption.
Cassidy, Matthew J. *s.j.* '99 (FgM) New York, NY Society of Jesus.
Cassidy, Richard '67 (DET) Special Assignment.
Cassidy, Terry A. '84 (PEO) Peoria, IL St. Ann; Cursillo Program.
Cassidy, Theodore *s.m.* '68 (CAM)[O] Cape May Point, NJ Marianist Family Retreat Center.
Cassidy, Rev. Msgr. Thomas J. '57 (ARL) Vienna, VA St. Mark Retired.
Cassidy, Thomas *s.c.j.* '71 (MIL)[P] Milwaukee, WI SCJ Community; [P] Hales Corners, WI Priests of the Sacred Heart.
Cassin, Rev. Msgr. Andrew J. '54 (WDC) Waldorf, MD St. Peter Retired.
Cassista, Fernand *m.s.* '65 (FR)[G] Attleboro, MA La Salette Shrine; [I] Attleboro, MA La Salette Retreat Center.
Casstevens, Jennifer (BO)[CC] Cambridge, MA The Youville House, Inc.
Castaldi, Joseph '63 (NOR) New London, CT St. Joseph; Defenders of the Bond; Priests' Retirement Plan Board.
Castanada, Heibar '94 (MRY) Hollister, CA Sacred Heart/St. Benedict Catholic Community.
Castaneda, Brian '99 (LA) Los Angeles, CA Holy Spirit; Los Angeles, CA St. Mary Magdalen; Our Lady of the Angels Region.
Castañeda, Luis *o.c.d.* '03 (OKL) Oklahoma City, OK Our Lady of Mount Carmel and St. Therese Little Flower.
Castaneda, Mario '95 (PMB) West Palm Beach, FL St. John Fisher; Spanish.
Castaneda, Rev. Msgr. Oscar F. '87 (MIA)[O] Miami, FL National Shrine of Our Lady of Charity; Archicofradia Nuestra Senora de la Caridad (Spanish); [Q] Miami, FL Opus Caritatis Corp.
Castaneda, Severiano '71 (LA) Los Angeles, CA San Francisco Church.
Castano, Jairo (LAF) On Special Assignment.
Casteel, Michael J. '84 (SPC) Benton, MO St. Denis; Benton, MO St. Lawrence.
Castejon, Antonio Garcia '81 (SJN) Police Chaplains.
Castellani, Paul J. '96 (PH) Lansdowne, PA St. Philomena.
Castellano, Rev. Msgr. Francis J. '60 (SCR) Retired.
Castellanos, Ricardo C. '70 (MIA) Lauderhill, FL Retired.
Castellanos Ruiz, Yesid Ricardo '82 (SJN) San Juan, PR Santa Luisa de Marillac.
Castellino, Albert J. *c.ss.r.* '62 (STL)[O] Liguori, MO Liguori Mission House/Redemptorists.
Castelow, Ralph T. '89 (WIL) Newark, DE St. John the Baptist–Holy Angels.
Caster, Gary C. '92 (PEO) On Duty Outside the Diocese.
Caster, Gary C. (SPR)[N] Williamstown, MA.
Castillo, Alex '81 (SB) Ontario, CA Our Lady of Guadalupe.
Castillo, Carlos C. *c.m.f.* '73 (LA)[V] Rancho Dominguez, CA Dominguez Seminary Inc.
Castillo, Eduardo (POD) San Antonio.
Castillo, Francisco '67 (BWN) Mission, TX Our Lady of St. John of the Fields.
Castillo, Gustavo '01 (LA) Azusa, CA St. Frances of Rome; San Gabriel Region.
Castillo, Javier del '05 (POD) Chicago.
Castillo, Jose '80 (SD) San Ysidro, CA Our Lady of Mt. Carmel.
Castillo, Miguel Gonzalez '06 (YAK) Sunnyside, WA St. Joseph's; Youth/Young Adult Hispanic Ministry.
Castillo, Miguel '58 (NY) Haverstraw, NY St. Peter.
Castillo, Paulino Matus *o.f.m.conv.* '88 (ATL) Lithia Springs, GA St. John Vianney.
Castillo, Pedro '85 (AUS) Lampasas, TX St. Mary of the Immaculate Conception; Lampasas, TX Good Shepherd.
Castillo, Rene '89 (RIC) Rocky Mount, VA Francis of Assisi; Salem, VA Salem VA Medical Center; Roanoke, VA St. Gerard.
Castillo, Ricardo '03 (CHI) Chicago, IL St. Bronislava; Chicago, IL Immaculate Conception of the Blessed Virgin Mary.
Castillo, Richard '83 (PT) On Leave of Absence.
Castillo, Rolando '94 (MIA) Absent on Leave.

Castillo, Rolo B. '92 (RIC) Waynesboro, VA St. John the Evangelist.
Castillo, Ruben Dario (PAT) Paterson, NJ Cathedral of St. John the Baptist.
Castillo, Santos '04 (JOL) Wheaton, IL St. Michael.
Castillo, Ysidro Valero '73 (SJN) San Juan, PR San Miguel Arcangel.
Castillo DelGadillo, Guillermo '74 (BIR) Birmingham, AL St. Joseph's.
Castle, Nathan *o.p.* '85 (SJ) Stanford, CA Catholic Community at Stanford.
Castles, Patrick J. '69 (TR) Allentown, NJ St. John.
Castoldi, Heitor *c.s.* (BO) Framingham, MA St. Tarcisius.
Castor, Timothy William '01 (RC) Belle Fourche, SD St. Paul; Spearfish, SD St. Joseph.
Castori, Michael T. T. *s.j.* '90 (SJ)[B] Santa Clara, CA Jesuit Community.
Castrillo, Jesus Saez *o.de.m.* '69 (PCE) Ponce, PR La Merced.
Castrillo, Jesus *c.m.f.* '49 (LA) El Monte, CA Our Lady of Guadalupe.
Castro, Alberto '79 (MGZ) Diocesan Board of Administration.
Castro, Angel '08 (LA) Los Angeles, CA St. Columbkille.
Castro, Antonio '84 (GAL) Deer Park, TX St. Hyacinth.
Castro, Dominic Joseph '98 (MRY) Seaside, CA St. Francis Xavier.
Castro, Geronimo *m.s.* '99 (HON) Makawao, HI St. Joseph; Diocesan Pastoral Council.
Castro, John G. *o.m.i.* '62 (SAT)[D] San Antonio, TX Antonian College Preparatory High School; [L] San Antonio, TX.
Castro, Mario A. '00 (BWN) Brownsville, TX Church of the Good Shepherd.
Castro, Oscar M. '93 (GAL) Pasadena, TX St. Pius the Fifth; Central Vicariate.
Castro, Patrick *o.f.m.cap.* '88 (AGN) Agana Heights, GU Our Lady of the Blessed Sacrament; [F] Agana Heights, GU St. Fidelis Friary; Archdiocesan Presbyteral Council.
Castro, Robert '85 (SR) Imola, CA Napa State Hospital.
Castronovo, Edmund A. '76 (SY) Georgetown, NY Camp Georgetown; Camp Pharsalia.
Castronovo, Edmund A. '76 (SCR) Scranton, PA St. Michael's; [M] Elmhurst, PA Priestly Fraternity of St. Peter (F.S.S.P.), North American District Headquarters.
Caswell, Thomas C. '66 (SPK) Archivist; Ecumenical Relations Retired.
Catagnus, James N. '70 (PH) Philadelphia, PA St. Ambrose.
Catalana, Mark '91 (SJ) Special Assignment.
Catalano, James A. *s.j.* '95 (BUF) Buffalo, NY St. Michael.
Catalano, James *o.s.j.* '63 (MRY) Davenport, CA St. Vincent De Paul; [F] Shrine of St. Joseph.
Catallo, Sylvester *o.f.m.cap.* '54 (NY)[B] Beacon, NY St. Lawrence of Brindisi Friary.
Catanach, Richard '88 (LSC) Priests Retirement Fund Committee; Defenders of the Bond; Vicars; Presbyteral Council; Clergy Personnel Board; Priestly Life and Ministry Committee; Mesilla, NM Basilica of San Albino.
Catania, Thomas M. '74 (BRK) Richmond Hill, NY Holy Child Jesus.
Catanise, Joseph R. '82 (ROC) Hilton, NY St. Leo.
Cataudo, Anthony I. *o.p.* '60 (CAM)[M] Camden, NJ Dominican Sisters of the Perpetual Rosary Chaplain's Residence; [N] Camden, NJ Monastery of the Dominican Nuns of the Perpetual Rosary.
Catena, Paul G. '07 (ALB) Margaretville, NY Sacred Heart; Albany, NY Christ the King.
Catoir, John T. '60 (PAT)[Q] Chester, NJ Nazareth Village; [Q] Passaic, NJ St. Jude Media Ministries; Pro-Synodal Judges Retired.
Catucci, Thomas F. '82 (SY) Kirkwood, NY St. Mary.
Catungal, Mario T. *o.c.d.* '04 (MO) Air Force Chaplains.
Caufield, Kenneth J. *s.j.* '67 (NY)[EE] New York, NY St. Ignatius Loyola Residence.
Caul, Robert F. '61 (PRO) North Providence, RI Mary, Mother of Mankind Retired.
Cauley, Thomas F. '81 (PMB) Port St. Lucie, FL Holy Family.
Caulfield, John P. '03 (WDC) Priest Council.
Caulfield, John '59 (ORL) Lakeland, FL St. Joseph's.
Caulfield, Sean '49 (B) Judges Retired.
Cauterucci, Francis J. '90 (PH) Philadelphia, PA Our Lady of Mt. Carmel.
Cavagnaro, John A. '75 (CAM) Collings Lakes, NJ Church of Our Lady of the Lakes, Collings Lakes, N.J.
Cavagnaro, Mark R. '70 (CAM) Blackwood, NJ St. Agnes' Church, Blackwood Terrace, N.J.; Elected Members.
Cavagnuolo, Salvatore F. '67 (HRT) Yalesville, CT Our Lady of Fatima.
Cavalier, Robert C. '72 (NO) Abita Springs, LA St. Jane de Chantal.
Cavalier, Wayne A. *o.p.* '93 (SAT) San Antonio, TX St. Ann.
Cavalier, Wayne *o.p.* '93 (SAT)[L] San Antonio, TX Dominican Priory of San Juan Macias.
Cavallaro, Rev. Msgr. Galliano J. '42 (PRO) Retired.
Cavalli, Victor *o.p.* '48 (SAC) Benicia, CA St. Dominic Retired.
Cavalluzzi, Kevin P. '93 (BRK) Brooklyn, NY The Cathedral-Basilica of St. James; [E] Brooklyn, NY Campus Ministers and Ministry Centers; Brooklyn, NY St. Brendan.
Cavanagh, Brian M. '58 (LA) Covina, CA Sacred Heart Retired.
Cavanagh, David J. '85 (BO)[T] Cambridge, MA Opus Dei, Prelature of the Holy Cross and Opus Dei; Cambridge.
Cavanagh, Gerald F. *s.j.* '64 (DET)[K] Detroit, MI Jesuit Community at the University of Detroit Mercy.
Cavanagh, James '80 (LA) On Sick Leave.
Cavanagh, Joseph A. *s.j.* '62 (CI)[C] Kolonia, Pohnpei, FM Jesuit House; New York, NY Society of Jesus.
Cavanagh, Michael J. '59 (PBL) Retired.
Cavanaugh, Brian *t.o.r.* '82 (STU)[A] Steubenville, OH Franciscan University of Steubenville; [H] Steubenville, OH Holy Spirit Friary.
Cavanaugh, Daniel J. '66 (PH) Media, PA Nativity of the Blessed Virgin Mary.
Cavanaugh, Harry M. *c.pp.s.* '54 (CIN)[N] Carthagena, OH St. Charles Retired.
Cavanaugh, James K. '51 (Y) Retired.
Cavanaugh, John '90 (FAR) Reynolds, ND Our Lady of Perpetual Help Church of Reynolds; Thompson, ND St. Jude's Church of Thompson.
Cavanaugh, Kevin P. '86 (HRT) Manchester, CT St. James; Hartford Vicariate; Army National Guard Chaplains; Manchester Deanery; Manchester, CT Assumption.
Cavanaugh, Michael *o.s.f.s.* '76 (WH) Martinsburg, WV St. Joseph's.
Cavanaugh, Thomas J. '03 (PH) Philadelphia, PA St. Matthew.
Cavazos-Gonzales, Gilberto *o.f.m.* '85 (CHI)[B] Chicago, IL The Catholic Theological Union at Chicago; [N] Chicago, IL Holy Spirit Friary, Order of Friars Minor.
Caveglia, Patrick *o.s.b.* '94 (KC)[A] Conception, MO Conception Seminary College; [J] Conception, MO Conception Abbey; [N] Conception, MO The St. Benedict Education Foundation.
Cavell, Lawrence Arthur '89 (HT) Administrative Leave.
Cavellier, Richard '79 (DET) Auburn Hills, MI Sacred Heart; Defenders of Bond.
Caverly, Rev. Msgr. J. Bernard '65 (SP) St. Petersburg, FL St. Raphael; Ecumenical and Inter-Religious Affairs.
Caverly, Rev. Msgr. Patrick J. '61 (ORL) Longwood, FL Annunciation; Vicar General; Ex Officio Members.
Caverte, Rolando A. '62 (SFR) San Francisco, CA Church of the Epiphany Retired.
Cavey, Donald J. '76 (RIC) Hampton, VA VA Medical Center; DEPARTMENT OF VETERANS AFFAIRS HOSPITALS AND CHAPLAINS.
Caviedes, Victor '99 (VEN) Hispanic, Migrant and Spanish Speaking Apostolates; Lake Placid, FL Communidad Catolica Hispana Santiago Apostol (Santiago Mission); Sebring, FL St. Catherine.
Caviglia, Caesar J. '55 (LAV) Retired.
Cavitt, Arthur J. *o.p.* '02 (STL) St. Louis, MO St. Elizabeth, Mother of John the Baptist.
Cavoto, Joseph F. *s.a.* '80 (NY) New York, NY St. Francis of Assisi; [EE] Garrison, NY Franciscan Friars of the Atonement.
Cawley, John *c.m.* '65 (LA)[A] Camarillo, CA St. John's Seminary.
Cawley, Martin *o.c.s.o.* '61 (P)[L] Lafayette, OR The Cistercian (Trappist) Abbey of Our Lady of Guadalupe.
Cawley, Patrick T. '70 (GAY) Beaver Island, MI Holy Cross.
Cawley, Patrick '70 (GR) Retired.
Cawley, Thomas *c.m.* '57 (KC)[J] Independence, MO Vincentian Parish Mission Center.
Cawley, William M. '73 (HBG) On Duty Outside of the Diocese; York, PA St. Patrick; [A] York, PA York Catholic High School.
Cayer, John B. '96 (PT) Crestview, FL Our Lady of Victory.
Cayetano, Alvin *s.o.l.t.* '95 (PHX) Camp Verde, AZ St. Frances Cabrini Roman Catholic Parish.
Caylor, Dennis J. '75 (CIN) Springfield, OH St. Joseph; Springfield, OH St. Raphael; Vicarri Foranei (Deans); Defenders of the Bond.
Cazares, Felix A. '03 (BWN) Rio Hondo, TX St. Helen.
Cazares Haro, Salvador A. '00 (TUC) Leave of Absence.
Cazayoux, Clair M. *s.j.* '62 (LAF) Grand Coteau, LA St. Charles Borromeo.
Cazenavette, Joseph E. '05 (NO) Mandeville, LA Our Lady of the Lake Roman Catholic Church; Legion of Mary.
Cebula, Joseph '75 (ALB) Schenectady, NY Our Lady of the Assumption.
Cebula, Thomas W. '68 (Y) Massillon, OH St. Barbara.
Cebulka, Peter R. *c.o.* '93 (MET)[I] New Brunswick, NJ The New Brunswick Congregation of the Oratory of St. Philip Neri; New Brunswick, NJ St. Peter the Apostle; New Brunswick, NJ.
Cebulka, Peter *c.o.* '93 (MET)[N] New Brunswick, NJ Catholic Center at Rutgers University; Office of Vocations.
Cecero, John J. *s.j.* '89 (NY)[EE] New York, NY Jesuit Community at Fordham University; [EE] Cardinal Spellman Hall, Jesuit Community.
Cecil, Bruce K. *c.s.c.* '92 (SB) Coachella, CA Our Lady of Soledad; [I] Coachella, CA Congregation of Holy Cross.
Cecil, Bruce *c.s.c.* (FTW)[H] Notre Dame Congregation of Holy Cross, Indiana Province, Provincial House.
Cecil, Ivo E. '54 (L) Shepherdsville, KY St. Benedict; Shepherdsville, KY St. Aloysius Retired.
Cecil, Patrick G. '78 (CHI) Wadsworth, IL St. Patrick; Deans.
Cedolia, Robert J. '78 (PIT) Pittsburgh, PA St. Anne.
Cedro, Michael '04 (NY) New City, NY St. Augustine.
Ceja, Miguel R. '90 (SB) Moreno Valley, CA St. Christopher.
Cejudo, Serafin '56 (GAL) Retired.
Celano, Freddy '87 (TYL) Jacksonville, TX Our Lady of Sorrows.
Celano, Joseph G. '87 (MET) Bridgewater, NJ St. Bernard of Clairvaux.
Celano, Leo J. *o.praem.* '72 (ORG)[I] Silverado, CA Norbertine Fathers of Orange Inc.
Celentano, Christopher '08 (SY) Binghamton, NY Saints John & Andrew; Presbyteral Council.
Celeste, Charles R. '80 (ALB) Leave of Absence; Albany Medical Center Hospital.
Celiano, Alfred V. '53 (NEW)[B] School of Diplomacy and Intl. Rels. Retired.
Celichowski, John *o.f.m.cap.* '93 (FgM) Detroit, MI Province of St. Joseph; Detroit, MI.
Celichowski, John *o.f.m.cap.* '93 (DET)[K] Detroit, MI Provincialate; [K] Detroit St. Bonaventure Friary.
Celino, Anthony C. '98 (ELP) Judges; El Paso, TX Santa Lucia; Diocesan Tribunal; Presbyteral Council; Priests' Personnel Advisory Committee.
Celis Quintero, Marco A. '09 (NEW) Summit, NJ St. Teresa's.
Cella, John *o.f.m.* '78 (MIL)[Y] Franklin, WI Franciscan Pilgrimage Programs, Inc.; [P] Provincial Offices of the Franciscan Friars, Assumption BVM Province, Inc.; Judges for Second Instance; [B] Hales Corners, WI Sacred Heart School of Theology.
Cellini, Ronald R. '79 (CHR) Bluffton, SC St. Gregory the Great.
Cellucci, Carl D. '53 (PH) Retired.
Celso, B. Thomas '79 (ROC) Unassigned.
Celuch, Martin '03 (Y) Advocates; Graduate Studies.
Cely, Alfonso '01 (ORL) Ocala, FL Blessed Trinity.
Cely, Manuel '05 (BIS)[A] Richardton, ND Assumption Abbey.
Cembor, Thomas M. '79 (NEW) Montclair, NJ Mountainside Hospital; Montclair, NJ Our Lady of Mt. Carmel.
Cencula, Leonard T. '63 (STU) Retired.
Cendrowicz, Jaroslaw *o.s.p.p.e.* (CHI) Harwood Heights-Norridge, IL St. Rosalie.
Cenefeldt, Harry E. '54 (TR)[N] Trenton, NJ Villa Vianney Retired.
Centeno, Yader F. *sch.p.* '96 (MIA) Miami, FL St. Timothy.
Centina, Gilbert Luis R. *o.s.a.* (NY) New York, NY Holy Rosary.
Centner, David *o.c.d.* '71 (WDC)[W] Washington, DC Spiritual Life; [B] Washington, DC Discalced Carmelite Friars.
Cepeda, Arturo '96 (SAT) Vice Rector; [A] San Antonio, TX Assumption Seminary; Vocation Office; Pre-Seminary Program; [Q] San Antonio, TX National Foundation for Mexican-American Vocations.
Ceperley, Eugene F. '55 (SC) Retired.
Cera, James B. '64 (MIL) Retired.
Cerank, Gerald A. '72 (OG) Mooers Forks, NY St. Joseph; Mooers Forks, NY St. Ann.
Ceranowski, Albert B. '64 (TOL) Retired.
Ceranowski, Gerald L. '67 (TOL) Retired.
Cerbin, Walter *s.s.j.* '55 (LAF) Lebeau, LA Immaculate Conception.
Cerbone, James L. *s.d.b.* '80 (NY)[EE] New Rochelle, NY Salesian Provincial House.
Cerbone, James *s.d.b.* '80 (NEW)[M] Ramsey, NJ Don Bosco Prep Salesian Residence; [C] Ramsey, NJ Don Bosco Preparatory High School.
Cereceda, Jaime *o.m.i.* (SJN) San Juan, PR Nuestra Sra. de Guadalupe.
Cerezo, Alberto F. '60 (YAK) Retired.
Ceriello, Joseph A. '78 (BRK) Brooklyn, NY Queen of All Saints.
Cerio, Frank '86 (ORL) Deltona, FL Our Lady of the Lakes.
Cerkas, John W. '70 (GB) Laona, WI St. Leonard; Laona, WI St. Norbert; Laona, WI St. Hubert Mission.

Cermak, Michael Gilmary *o.mar.* '95 (SAM)[B] Petersham, MA Maronite Monks of Adoration Most Holy Trinity Monastery.
Cerniglia, George *s.m.* '69 (STL)[O] St. Louis, MO Marianists, Province of the United States (Society of Mary); Councilors:; [O] St. Louis, MO Marianist Community.
Cernoch, Gerard '64 (VIC) Bay City, TX Our Lady of Guadalupe.
Cerny, George F. '64 (CHI) Retired.
Cerpich, Richard J. '61 (MIL) Sheboygan, WI St. Peter Claver Retired.
Cerratos, Ramon *s.x.* '99 (PAT)[N] Wayne Xaverian Missionary Fathers; Wayne, NJ XAVERIAN MISSIONARY FATHERS.
Cerretto, Michael P. *c.s.b.* '69 (LSC) Director of Deacon Formation; Las Cruces, NM Cathedral of the Immaculate Heart of Mary; [B] Las Cruces, NM Basilian Fathers; Agua Viva Editorial Advisory Board.
Cerrone, Michael J. '81 (SAV) Retired.
Cerulo, Thomas *o.ss.t.* (BAL)[S] Leadership; [S] Baltimore, MD.
Cervantes, Fidel '55 (ELP) Retired.
Cervantes, Leo (RIC) Retired.
Cervantes, Luis Cananza *m.c.c.j.* '75 (LA) Los Angeles, CA Holy Cross.
Cervantes, Timothy '00 (GLP) Cuba, NM Immaculate Conception.
Cervenak, Andrew '78 (TR) Retired.
Cervero, Joseph '89 (BGP) New Fairfield, CT St. Edward the Confessor.
Cervine, Keith '09 (MET) Clinton, NJ Immaculate Conception; Office of Vocations.
Cervini, Rev. Msgr. John '68 (RVC) Serving Outside the Diocese.
Cervinski, Paul '61 (BIS) Retired.
Cerwonka, Clarence J. '61 (PBL) Retired.
Cerwonka, Clarence '61 (SY) Maine, NY Most Holy Rosary.
Cesa, Dean '98 (CHL) Cashiers, NC St. Jude; Highlands, NC Our Lady of the Mountains.
Cesanek, Damian *o.f.m.* '69 (CIN)[N] Cincinnati, OH St. Francis Seraph Friary.
Cesaro, Nicholas J. '54 (HRT) Newington, CT St. Mary Retired.
Cesarone, Jeffrey T. *o.praem* '94 (CAM) Lindenwold, NJ Our Lady of Guadalupe Parish, Lindenwold, N.J.
Cespedes, Carlos J. '75 (MIA)[O] Miami, FL National Shrine of Our Lady of Charity.
Cessario, Romanus *o.p.* '71 (BO)[A] Brighton, MA St. John Seminary.
Cesta, James M. '74 (SY) Utica, NY St. Mary of Mt. Carmel/Blessed Sacrament; Oswego, NY Oswego County Jail.
Cestaro, Joseph A. '62 (BRK) Retired.
Ch'e, James '54 (AGN) Tamuning, GU St. Anthony and St. Victor.
Cha, Simeon Ho Chan (CHI) Des Plaines, IL St. Paul Chong Hasang.
Chaanine, George '96 (LAV) Administrative Leave.
Chaback, Rev. Msgr. Michael J. '70 (ALT)[K] Hollidaysburg, PA Conference of Slovak Clergy.
Chaback, Rev. Msgr. Michael J. '70 (ALN) Permanent Diaconate Office; Northampton, PA Queenship of Mary Parish.
Chabak, Rev. Msgr. Robert M. '72 (NEW) Retired.
Chabala, Brian J. '77 (DET) Farmington Hills, MI St. Fabian.
Chabot, Peter L. *m.m.* '65 (CIN)[N] Cincinnati, OH The Catholic Foreign Mission Society of America, Inc.
Chabot, Robert A. *s.s.s.* '66 (GAL) Houston, TX Corpus Christi.
Chabot, Roger P. '65 (PRT) Retired.
Chachlowski, Marek '82 (NEW) Berkeley Heights, NJ Church of the Little Flower.
Chackaleckel, Davis *m.s.f.s.* '80 (NSH) Columbia, TN St. Catherine.
Chackaleckel, Davis *m.s.f.s.* '80 (TYL)[B] Whitehouse, TX The Missionaries of St. Francis de Sales.
Chacko, Jose Brahmakulam '87 (BIR) Birmingham, AL Our Lady Queen of the Universe.
Chacko, Joseph Ampatt '77 (SHP) Bossier City, LA Mary, Queen of Peace.
Chacko, Joseph C. '68 (MET) U.S. Veterans Medical Center.
Chacko, Rev. Msgr. Joseph C. '68 (MO) DEPARTMENT OF VETERANS AFFAIRS HOSPITALS AND CHAPLAINS.
Chacko, Joseph P. '94 (WIN) On Special or Other Diocesan Assignment; [D] Rochester, MN Saint Mary Hospital.
Chacko, Joseph '84 (NOR) Preston, CT St. Catherine of Siena.
Chacko, Joy T. '92 (TR) Howell, NJ St. Veronica.
Chacko, Philip '85 (FAR) Bisbee, ND Holy Rosary; Rolette, ND Sacred Heart; Willow City, ND Notre Dame de la Victoire Church of Willow City.
Chacko, Tom '95 (WH) Spencer, WV Holy Redeemer.
Chacko, Vincent *i.m.s.* '80 (AUS) Chappell Hill, TX St. Stanislaus.
Chacon, Frank '89 (GLP) Winslow, AZ St. Joseph's; Winslow, AZ Madre de Dios; Presbyteral Council; Diocesan Consultors.
Chacon, Gilbert *s.j.* '73 (FRS) Buttonwillow, CA St. Mary.
Chacon, Humberto *c.s.* '07 (SJ) San Jose, CA Holy Cross.
Chacon, J. Humberto *c.s.* '07 (GAL) Houston, TX St. Leo the Great.
Chacon, Jaime H. '04 (YAK) Mabton, WA Immaculate Conception; Diocesan Consultors; Hispanic Ministries/Hispanic Ministry Formation; Grandview, WA Blessed Sacrament; Benton City, WA St. Frances Xavier Cabrini.
Chacon, Jorge '74 (NEW) Elizabeth, NJ Immaculate Conception.
Chacon, William '91 (BRK) Brooklyn, NY All Saints.
Chadwick, Brian D. '01 (GRY) Judicial Vicar; Judges; Charismatic Apostolate; Priests' Personnel Board; Merrillville, IN St. Andrew.
Chadwick, Lawrence A. '75 (RVC) Dix Hills, NY St. Matthew.
Chadwick, Matthew C. *o.f.m.conv.* '88 (PH) Philadelphia, PA St. Matthew.
Chae, Dong–Ho '89 (COS) Colorado Springs, CO St. Andrew Kim Quasi Parish.
Chaffman, Rev. Msgr. Charles J. '84 (LA) Los Angeles, CA Christ the King; Judicial Vicar; Judges.
Chaisson, John C. '66 (BO) Senior Priests. Retired.
Chaker, Victor '03 (NOR) Coventry, CT St. Mary.
Chakian, Joy '78 (DET) Troy, MI Beaumont Hospital; Rochester, MI Crittendon Hospital.
Chakkiath, Janil Joseph *o.ss.t.* '08 (BAL)[S] The Trinitarians in India (Bangalore & Trichur).
Chakkittamuriyil, Sajy '95 (SYM) Carrollton, TX St. Alphons Syro Malabar Catholic Church.
Chalackal, A. David '88 (MET) Old Bridge, NJ St. Thomas the Apostle; Raritan Bay Medical Center–Old Bridge.
Chalackal, Poulose *o.ss.t.* '05 (BAL)[S] The Trinitarians in India (Bangalore & Trichur).
Chalany, Robert '52 (WH) Retired.
Chalbhagam, George *c.m.i.* '86 (SAL) Mankato, KS Sacred Heart Parish; Mankato, KS St. Theresa Parish; Smith Center, KS St. Mary Parish.
Chalissery, Joy '90 (BIR) Huntsville, AL Our Lady Queen of the Universe.
Chalkey, Andrew G. *o.m.i.* '56 (BEL)[F] Belleville, IL Missionary Oblates of Mary Immaculate – St. Henry's Oblate Residence.
Challancin, James '68 (MAR) Ishpeming, MI St. Joseph; Republic, MI St. Augustine.
Challinor, Michael F. '91 (NY) Bronx, NY St. Mary Star of the Sea.
Challman, Stephen G. '96 (NY) Staten Island, NY Holy Rosary.
Chalmers, H. Edward '79 (WOR) Fitchburg, MA St. Bernard; Diocesan College of Consultors.
Chalupa, Fred '73 (AUS) Retired.
Chalupka, Anselm *o.s.p.p.e.* '95 (BUF) Buffalo, NY Corpus Christi.
Chamberlain, Francis P. *s.j.* '68 (FgM) Chicago, IL Society of Jesus.
Chamberlain, Henry T. *s.j.* '61 (CHI)[N] Chicago Chicago Province of the Society of Jesus–Provincial Office.
Chamberlain, Henry *s.j.* '61 (CIN)[Q] Milford, OH Jesuit Spiritual Center at Milford.
Chamberlain, Rev. Msgr. Michael J. '66 (DEN) Byers, CO Our Lady of the Plains; Defenders of the Bond.
Chamberlain, Robert F. '57 (GI) Retired.
Chamberlain, Rev. Msgr. Robert J. '64 (DM) Des Moines, IA St. Joseph's.
Chamberlain, Tom '70 (AUS) Temple, TX St. Matthew; Temple, TX Our Lady of Guadalupe Catholic Church – Temple, Texas.
Chamberland, Gary S. *c.s.c.* '98 (FTW)[H] Notre Dame Congregation of Holy Cross, Indiana Province, Provincial House.
Chamberland, Gary *c.s.c.* '98 (P)[P] Portland, OR University of Portland; [B] University of Portland.
Chamberlin, Gregory D. *o.s.b.* '65 (IND)[K] St. Meinrad St. Meinrad Archabbey.
Chamberlin, Gregory D. *o.s.b.* '65 (EVN) Evansville, IN St. Benedict Cathedral; Evansville, IN Holy Trinity.
Chamberlin, Gregory *o.s.b.* '65 (EVN) Diocesan Council of Priests.
Chamberlin, Rev. Msgr. Mark '68 (CC) Deans; College of Consultors; Personnel Board – Priests; Presbyteral Council; Judges; Portland, TX Our Lady of Mount Carmel.
Chambers, Francis E. '78 (PH)[Y] Villanova, PA St. Thomas Monastery.
Chambers, Henry G. '65 (BO) Millis, MA St. Thomas the Apostle.
Chambers, James *s.j.* '55 (CHI) Chicago, IL John H. Stroger, Jr. Hospital of Cook County; [D] Chicago, IL St. Ignatius Jesuit Community.
Chambers, James *o.m.i.* '06 (FgM) Washington, DC AMERICAN OBLATE MISSIONS.
Chambers, Thomas E. *c.s.c.* '61 (FTW)[H] Notre Dame, IN Congregation of Holy Cross, Indiana Province, Provincial House; [H] Notre Dame Congregation of Holy Cross, Indiana Province, Provincial House; Members.
Chambers, Thomas E. *c.s.c.* '61 (NO)[S] Metairie, LA Willwoods Community.
Chamblain, Joseph M. *o.s.m.* '84 (CHI)[N] Chicago, IL Assumption Priory.
Chamblain, Joseph *o.s.m.* '84 (CHI) Chicago, IL Assumption of the Blessed Virgin Mary.
Champagne, Michael '94 (LAF)[M] Lafayette, LA Community of Jesus Crucified; Diocesan Consultors.
Champagne, Rene *c.p.* '49 (DET)[K] Detroit, MI St. Paul of the Cross Community, Congregation of the Passion.
Champagne, Rene *c.p.* '49 (L)[L] Louisville, KY Sacred Heart Retreat.
Champagne, Robert E. *s.m.* '51 (BO)[W] Framingham, MA The Marist House.
Champigny, Richard *o.carm.* '65 (PMB) Boca Raton, FL St. Jude.
Champigny, Roger G. '60 (PRO) Retired.
Champigny, Thomas R. '81 (SPR) Easthampton, MA Our Lady of Good Counsel.
Champlin, Michael A. *o.p.* '66 (SUP)[H] Webster, WI Thomas More Center for Preaching and Prayer, Inc.
Champlin, William E. '93 (WOR) Worcester, MA Immaculate Conception; Deans; Presbyteral Council; St. Vincent dePaul Society—.
Champoli, Daniel '09 (BRK) Graduate Studies.
Champoux, Thomas C. '67 (YAK) Clergy Personnel Board; Richland, WA Christ the King; Defenders of the Bond; Diocesan Coordinator for Health Affairs; St. Vincent de Paul Society.
Chan, Lucas *s.j.* '06 (BO)[U] Newton, MA The Jesuit Community at Boston College.
Chan, Paul '50 (NY)[II] New York, NY Chinese Catholic Information Center.
Chan–A–Sue, Andrew '00 (MIA) Coral Springs, FL St. Andrew.
Chan–Yong, Peter Lim '97 (BRK) Bayside, NY Sacred Heart of Jesus.
Chanama, Oliver '80 (NY) East Elmhurst, NY Otis Bantum Correctional Center; New York, NY Holy Innocents.
Chanas, Stefan '96 (NY) New York, NY St. John Nepomucene.
Chanassery, Johnson *o.c.d.* (BRK) Brooklyn, NY St. John the Evangelist.
Chancler, Joseph *t.o.r.* '83 (ALT)[A] Loretto, PA St. Francis University.
Chandler, Anthony L. '89 (L) Brandenburg, KY St. John the Apostle; Vine Grove, KY St. Martin of Tours; Defenders of the Bond.
Chandler, John *s.j.* '64 (HON)[D] Honolulu, HI Jesuit Fathers House; Honolulu, HI Newman Center–Holy Spirit Parish.
Chandy, James '90 (SYM) Houston, TX St. Mary's Knanaya Catholic Mission of Houston.
Chaney, Robert E. '88 (SAV) Savannah, GA Resurrection of Our Lord; Director of African American Ministry.
Chang, Benedict '63 (SFR) San Francisco, CA Star of the Sea Retired.
Chang, Cornelius P. *o.s.b.* '62 (GBG)[G] Latrobe Saint Vincent Archabbey.
Chang, Jeffrey G.L. *s.j.* '99 (FgM)[S] Towson Maryland Province of the Society of Jesus; Towson, MD Society of Jesus.
Chang, John O. (TR) Lakewood, NJ St. Mary of the Lake.
Chang, Joseph *o.s.b.* '57 (JOL)[L] Lisle, IL St. Procopius Abbey.
Chant, William S. '88 (BUR) Retired.
Chap, Robert W. *c.m.* '66 (FgM) Earth City, MO Western Province.
Chapa, Emilio Landeros '08 (TUC) Yuma, AZ Saint Francis of Assisi Roman Catholic Parish – Yuma.
Chapa, Robert *s.o.l.t.* '07 (CC)[G] Robstown, TX Society of Our Lady of the Most Holy Trinity.
Chapdelaine, Gerard E. *s.j.* '66 (SEA)[C] Tacoma, WA Bellarmine Preparatory School; [C] Tacoma, WA Bellarmine Preparatory School.
Chapel, Rev. Msgr. Joseph R. '92 (NEW)[A] South Orange, NJ Immaculate Conception Seminary; [A] South Orange, NJ Immaculate Conception Seminary[B].
Chapin, Daniel L. '72 (OG) Croghan, NY St. Stephen; Ecumenical Commission.
Chapin, Jacinto Mary *f.i.* (IND)[K] Bloomington, IN Marian Friary of Our Lady Coredemptrix, Franciscan of the Immaculate.
Chaplin, John G. '68 (E) Clearfield, PA St. Francis.
Chapman, Lawrence J. '77 (MIL) East Troy, WI St. Peter.
Chapman, Michael A. '82 (PH) Philadelphia, PA Ascension of Our Lord.
Chapman, Michael L. '69 (OKL) Oklahoma City, OK Holy Angels; Region I–A; Priests' Retirement Board.
Chapman, Robert J. '67 (PH) Narberth, PA St. Margaret.
Chappell, Arthur B. *o.s.a.* '69 (PH)[Y] Villanova, PA St.

John Stone Friary.
Chappell, James T. '67 (DUB) Maquoketa, IA Sacred Heart; Maquoketa, IA St. John; Maquoketa, IA St. Lawrence.
Chappetto, Rev. Msgr. Raymond F. '71 (BRK) Floral Park, NY Our Lady of the Snows; Diocesan Consultors; Vicar for Clergy, Consecrated Life and Apostolic Organizations; Presbyteral Council.
Charboneau, Marion *o.s.b.* '06 (KCK)[I] Atchison, KS St. Benedict's Abbey; [A] Atchison, KS Benedictine College.
Charbonneau, Damian M. *o.s.m.* '50 (CHI) Chicago, IL Assumption of the Blessed Virgin Mary; [N] Chicago, IL Assumption Priory.
Charbonneau, Roger L. '71 (BUR) Propagation of the Faith; Defenders of the Bond; National Shrine of the Immaculate Conception, Washington; Colchester, VT Holy Cross; Notaries.
Charbonneau, Rev. Msgr. William R. '73 (HRT) Military Chaplains; Air Force Chaplains.
Charbonnet, Clayton "Beau" '03 (NO) Harahan, LA St. Rita.
Charelus, Ronel *s.m.m.* '95 (RVC) Westbury, NY St. Brigid.
Charest, Glenn S. '77 (STA) Ponte Vedra Beach, FL Our Lady Star of the Sea.
Charest, Roger M. *s.m.m.* '42 (RVC)[M] Bay Shore, NY Montfort Missionaries Retired.
Charipar, Henry W. '68 (DUB) Retired.
Charland, George A. '60 (WOR) East Brookfield, MA St. John the Baptist.
Charland, Paul A. '71 (PRO) Providence, RI St. Joseph.
Charlebois, Rev. Msgr. Robert L. '57 (GRY) Retired.
Charles, Jean Gabriel (BO) Dorchester, MA St. Matthew.
Charles, Lewis *s.j.* (FgM) Chicago, IL Society of Jesus.
Charles, Patrick '06 (MIA) Miramar, FL St. Bartholomew.
Charles, Robes C. '99 (MIA) Fort Lauderdale, FL St. Clement.
Charlot, Lucien '61 (BRK) Brooklyn, NY St. Augustine Retired.
Charlton, Robert *ss.cc.* '88 (BWN) Presbyteral Council; Edinburg, TX Sacred Heart.
Charlton, Terrence P. *s.j.* '76 (FgM) Chicago, IL Society of Jesus.
Charm, Robert '77 (OAK) Retired.
Charman, Eugene J. '71 (HRT) Cheshire, CT St. Thomas Becket; Waterbury Vicariate.
Charnley, George '76 (DET) Novi, MI St. James.
Charnoki, Rev. Msgr. William G. '65 (GBG) Ligonier, PA Holy Trinity; Judges.
Charpentier, Alfred *o.m.i.* '71 (FgM) Washington, DC AMERICAN OBLATE MISSIONS.
Charron, Jason '08 (SJP) Garner, NC SS. Volodymyr and Olha Mission; Presbyters.
Charters, Thomas S. *g.h.m.* '75 (WH) Logan, WV St. Francis of Assisi; Man, WV St. Edmund.
Chase, Charles E. '79 (OG) Retired.
Chase, Francis G. '57 (BO) Senior Priests. Retired.
Chase, Kenneth M. '84 (DET) South Lyon, MI St. Joseph.
Chase, Lee P. '93 (ROC) Absent on Leave.
Chase, Martin *s.j.* '91 (NY)[EE] Cardinal Spellman Hall, Jesuit Community.
Chase, Maurice '53 (SD) Retired.
Chase, P. Geoffrey *o.s.b.* '59 (PRO)[P] Portsmouth, RI Abbey of St. Gregory the Great.
Chase, Raymond '78 (BAL) Baltimore, MD St. Charles Borromeo; [L] Timonium, MD Villa Maria Continuum; Special Assignment.
Chase, Terrence R. '84 (GRY) Michigan City, IN Queen of All Saints; Bishop's Council of Priests.
Chassaniol, Warren F. '65 (HT) Retired.
Chasse, Joseph S. *s.m.* '52 (BO)[W] Framingham, MA The Marist House Retired.
Chasse, Lucien *s.m.* '43 (BO)[U] Boston, MA Marist Fathers of Our Lady of Victories (Boston Prov.).
Chateau, Ixon '06 (BO) Medford, MA St. Clement.
Chateau, Paul F. '66 (DET) Oak Park, MI Our Lady of Fatima.
Chau, Pedro Bismarck '08 (NEW) Garfield, NJ Our Lady of Mt. Virgin.
Chaupetta, Victor *m.s.* '70 (FR)[G] Attleboro, MA La Salette Shrine.
Chauvin, Gregory S. '07 (LAF) Church Point, LA Our Lady of the Sacred Heart.
Chavannes, Jacques Eddy '85 (PRO) Providence, RI St. Michael the Archangel; Providence, RI Rhode Island Hospital.
Chavarria, Horacio '66 (BWN) Harlingen, TX Our Lady of the Assumption.
Chavarria, Jerome L. *c.ss.r.* '84 (ORL)[F] New Smyrna Beach, FL St. Alphonsus Villa–Redemptorist Fathers and Brothers; [F] New Smyrna Beach, FL Redemptorist Fathers of the Vice Province of Richmond; New Smyrna Beach, FL.
Chavarria, Juan *c.m.* '95 (PH)[Y].
Chavez, Arturo '91 (SB) Retired.
Chavez, Carlos '84 (SFE) Clovis, NM Sacred Heart.
Chavez, Frank '76 (SAN) Midland, TX Our Lady of San Juan de Los Lagos.
Chavez, Gerald F. '73 (FRS) Absent on Sick Leave.
Chavez, Johnny Lee '76 (SFE) Albuquerque, NM Queen of Heaven.
Chavez, Jose Luis *c.ss.r.* '84 (LA) Whittier, CA St. Mary of the Assumption; [P] Whittier, CA Redemptorists of Whittier.
Chavez, Jose M. '98 (GI) Elm Creek, NE Immaculate Conception.
Chavez, Jose '96 (MRY) On Leave.
Chavez, Luis N. '91 (TUC) Retired.
Chavez, Manual '96 (SR) Calistoga, CA Our Lady of Perpetual Help.
Chavez, Manuel '96 (SR) Clergy Personnel Committee; Vocations.
Chavez, Patrick J. '68 (SFE) El Rito, NM San Juan Nepomuceno.
Chavez, Phillip *s.o.l.t.* '93 (CC)[G] Robstown, TX Society of Our Lady of the Most Holy Trinity.
Chavez, Ricardo A. '63 (OAK) Pittsburg, CA St. Peter, Martyr of Verona.
Chavez, Rigoberto *s.t.* '08 (LA) Compton, CA Our Lady of Victory.
Chavez, Vincent P. '91 (SFE) Albuquerque, NM St. Therese of the Infant Jesus of the Little Flower.
Chcvenia, Jose C. '89 (SEA) Enumclaw, WA Sacred Heart of Jesus.
Cheah, Joseph M. *o.s.m.* '92 (CHI)[N] Chicago Order of Friar Servants of Mary (Servites) United States of America Province, Inc.
Cheah, Joseph *o.s.m.* '92 (HRT) Avon, CT St. Ann's.
Cheatham, Louis W. '45 (GBG)[F] Greensburg, PA Neumann House Retired.
Cheble, Michel '02 (NTN) Warren, MI Our Lady of Redemption.
Checchia, Jose *c.ss.r.* '63 (CGS) Aguas Buenas, PR Church of Tres Santos Reyes.
Checchio, Rev. Msgr. James F. '92 (CAM) On Duty Outside the Diocese.
Check, Paul N. '97 (BGP) Norwalk, CT St. Mary.
Check, Ronald '07 (PH) Philadelphia, PA St. Monica.
Checon, Amaricho *s.j.* '57 (BRK) Queens Village, NY Our Lady of Lourdes.
Chelakat, Anthony *s.j.* '67 (FgM) Chicago, IL Society of Jesus.
Chelena, Thomas '68 (PRM) Absent on Leave.
Chelich, James A. '76 (GR) Grand Rapids, MI St. Thomas the Apostle.
Cheline, Paschal *o.s.b.* '64 (P)[A] St. Benedict, OR Mount Angel Seminary; [L] St. Benedict, OR Mt. Angel Abbey.
Chellan, Steephan '94 (CAM) International Priests Representatives; Gloucester, NJ St. Mary's Church, Gloucester.
Chemazar, Blase *o.f.m.* '53 (CHI)[N] Lemont, IL The Slovene Franciscan Fathers, Order of Friars Minor, Commissariat of the Holy Cross; [S] Lemont, IL St. Mary's Retreat House; Lemont, IL.
Chemino, S. Scott '93 (ALX) Cheneyville, LA St. Joseph; Echo, LA St. Francis de Sales.
Chemino, Stephen Scott '93 (ALX) Vicar General; Administrator and Assessor, Code of Pastoral Conduct; Director of Pastoral Planning and Lay Ecclesial Ministry; Judges; Ex Officio; Louisiana Interchurch Council.
Chen, Anthony K. '52 (CHI) Retired.
Chen, Paul Feng '07 (OAK) Chinese Pastoral Center.
Chen, Peter Tianzhi (BAL) Catonsville, MD St. Mark.
Chen, Peter '96 (DAL) Retired.
Chen, Rafael (ORG) Retired.
Chen, Raphael '45 (AMA) Retired.
Chen, Tommy '08 (VIC) Shiner, TX SS. Cyril and Methodius.
Chen, Vincent P. '57 (MET) Phillipsburg, NJ St. Philip & St. James; Chinese Apostolate.
Chenault, Richard A. '08 (BIR)[A] Birmingham, AL John Carroll Catholic High School; Birmingham, AL Our Lady of the Valley.
Chenevy, Anthony *s.s.p.* '58 (Y)[A] Canfield, OH Society of St. Paul.
Cheney, Craig I. '03 (MAN) Coos County House of Corrections; Colebrook, NH North American Martyrs Parish.
Cheney, James '95 (FAR) Fargo, ND St. Paul's Newman Church of Fargo; [I] Fargo, ND St. Paul's Newman Church of Fargo; Navy Reserve Chaplains.
Cheney, Jesse C. '43 (LR)[G] Little Rock, AR St. John Manor Retired.
Cheng, Joseph '03 (NEW) Hackensack, NJ Holy Trinity; Chinese Apostolate.
Cheng, Thomas '60 (BRK) Retired.
Chenier, Michael D. '09 (MAR) Menominee, MI Resurrection.
Chennapallil, George '87 (NSH) Springfield, TN Our Lady of Lourdes.
Chenot, Paul *c.p.* '51 (BRK) Creedmoor Psychiatric Center; [T] Jamaica, NY Immaculate Conception Monastery.
Cheon, Joachim '01 (FRS) Bakersfield, CA San Clemente Mission Parish.
Chepaitis, Peter *o.f.m.* '72 (ALB) Special Assignment; [N] Middleburgh, NY Bethany Ministries.
Cheplic, Rev. Msgr. Peter A. '72 (NEW)[M] Rutherford, NJ St. John Vianney Residence for Priests Retired.
Chepponis, James J. '85 (PIT) Pittsburgh, PA St. John Capistran; Music, Office for.
Cheramie, Lonnie '00 (HT) Administrative Leave.
Cherayath, Davis '72 (SYM) Oklahoma City, OK Holy Family Syro–Malabar Catholic Church Oklahoma.
Cheri, Fernand *o.f.m.* '78 (BEL)[F] East St. Louis, IL St. Benedict the Black Friary.
Chermeil, Tony '91 (VEN) Naples, FL St. Peter the Apostle; West Collier County.
Chern, James N. '99 (NEW)[P] Upper Montclair, NJ Newman Catholic Center at Montclair State University.
Cherolikal, John '74 (LUB) Lubbock, TX St. Patrick; Vicars Forane.
Cherrez, Ornoldo '97 (LA) Huntington Park, CA St. Matthias.
Cherry, Athanasius C. *o.s.b.* '68 (GBG)[G] Latrobe, PA Saint Vincent Archabbey.
Cherry, Richard W. *s.j.* '69 (FgM) Detroit, MI Detroit Province.
Cherubini, Perry A. '85 (CAM) Representatives by Deaneries; Absecon, NJ Church of Saint Elizabeth Ann Seton, Absecon, N.J.; Elected Members; Consultants.
Cherukarakunnel, Alexander J. '63 (HRT) Waterbury, CT Basilica of the Immaculate Conception.
Cherunilath, Skariajohnus *v.c.* '94 (SCL) Little Falls, MN Our Lady of Lourdes.
Cherup, Rev. Msgr. Michael A. '81 (PT) Fort Walton Beach, FL St. Mary Church; Vicars Forane.
Cherup, Rev. Msgr. Michael '81 (PT) Priest Personnel Board.
Cheruparambil, Francis *v.c.* '82 (TR) Keyport, NJ Holy Family.
Cheruvil, James A.C. '90 (GAL) Sugar Land, TX St. Thomas Aquinas.
Chervenak, Gregory *o.f.m.cap.* '79 (HBG) Community General Osteopathic Hospital; Harrisburg, PA Pinnacle Health System; Harrisburg, PA St. Francis of Assisi.
Chervenak, Stephen M. '60 (PIT) White Oak, PA St. Angela.
Chesney, Michael *s.j.* '91 (MIA)[K] Miami, FL Villa Javier.
Chethipuzha, Varghese I. '69 (NY) New City, NY St. Augustine.
Chetty, Melchoir '83 (CAM) Woodbury, NJ St. Patrick's Church, Woodbury.
Chevalier, Martin '83 (DM) On Duty Outside the Diocese.
Chevalier, Thomas H. '80 (ALB) Voorheesville, NY St. Matthew.
Chew, Randolph G. '71 (PRO) Portsmouth, RI St. Barnabas; Deans; Council Members.
Chewning, Seraphim John '93 (PBR) Retired.
Chia, Luis P. '59 (GAL) Retired.
Chiaka, Raphael '76 (CHY) Lusk, WY St. Leo's; Wyoming Women's Center (Correctional Facility).
Chiang, John B. '53 (NY) Retired.
Chiang, Rev. Msgr. Joseph '59 (NEW)[M] Rutherford, NJ St. John Vianney Residence for Priests Retired.
Chiapa–Villarreal, Hector '06 (DEN) Roggen, CO Sacred Heart.
Chiara, Rev. Msgr. Peter A. '48 (RVC) East Islip, NY St. Mary's Retired.
Chiaramonte, Anthony J. '65 (ALB) Special Assignment; Office; Members.
Chiaravalle, Dominic M. '65 (PH) Chadds Ford, PA St. Cornelius.
Chiarello, Leonir Mario '95 (NY)[II] New York, NY Scalabrini International Migration Network.
Chiarilli, Rev. Msgr. Patrick S. '61 (CAM) Clayton, NJ Retired.
Chiarinoti, Juan Carlos (YAK) Chelan, WA St. Anne's; Chelan, WA St. Francis de Sales.
Chica, Esterminio '06 (NEW) Elizabeth, NJ St. Mary of the Assumption; Part–time Staff.
Chichetto, James W. *c.s.c.* '68 (FR)[A] North Easton, MA Stonehill College; [A] North Easton, MA Holy Cross Fathers Religious.
Chidiac, Bakhos '91 (OLL) Wheeling, WV Our Lady of Lebanon Maronite Catholic Church.
Chidozie, Marcus '93 (DAL) Garland, TX St. Michael the Archangel.
Chieffo, Rev. Msgr. Ralph J. '75 (PH) Media, PA St. Mary Magdalen.
Chiesa, Robert E. *s.j.* '68 (FgM) Los Gatos, CA Society of Jesus.
Chiffriller, Edward J. *s.s.j.* '74 (BAL)[S] Baltimore, MD St. Joseph Society of the Sacred Heart House of Central Administration; [V] Baltimore, MD St. Joseph Manor Foundation, Inc.; [V] Baltimore, MD The Josephite Seminarian Education Trust; [V] Baltimore, MD The Josephite Retirement and Disability Benefits Trusts; Baltimore, MD.
Chigbo, Kenneth '96 (NY) Valhalla, NY Westchester Medical Center; Sleepy Hollow, NY The Magdalene; Valhalla, NY Westchester Medical Center.

Chikawe, Hugh '71 (SP) Tampa, FL St. Peter Claver.
Chikezie, Emmanuel '89 (BEA)[B] Beaumont, TX CHRISTUS Health Southeast Texas – CHRISTUS Hospital – St. Elizabeth.
Chikweto, Timothy C. '03 (BAL)[S] Baltimore Society of St. Sulpice, Province of the United States.
Chilagorom, Desmond '79 (BAK) Pendleton, OR St. Mary.
Chilagorom, Desmond '79 (RVC) Smithtown, NY St. Patrick.
Child, John F. '59 (DET) Dearborn, MI Sacred Heart Retired.
Childs, G. Anthony '00 (ALB) Priestly Life and Ministry Council.
Childs, Guy A. '00 (ALB) South Glens Falls, NY St. Michael the Archangel.
Chilen, Rev. Msgr. Michael D. '69 (CC) Retired.
Chiles, Richard P. *o.praem.* '87 (JKS) Raymond, MS Immaculate Conception; [E] Raymond, MS Priory of St. Moses the Black.
Chillog, Thomas A. '84 (STU) St. Clairsville, OH St. Mary's; [L] St. Clairsville, OH Ohio University – Eastern; Episcopal Vicar for Pastoral Planning & Personnel; Auditors; Defenders of the Bond; Pastoral Staff; Presbyteral Council; College of Consultors; Priests Personnel Board; Continuing Education of Priests; Health Panel of the Clergy; Vicar for Priests.
Chilson, Elbert '78 (DEN) Aurora, CO St. Therese.
Chilson, Richard *c.s.p.* '72 (STP) Minneapolis, MN St. Lawrence–Newman Center; [K] Minneapolis, MN Paulist Fathers; Fairview University Medical Center.
Chilufya, Lewis B. '00 (BAL)[S] Baltimore Society of St. Sulpice, Province of the United States.
Chimera, Angelo M. '69 (BUF) Awaiting Assignment.
Chimiak, Rev. Msgr. Karl A. '80 (WDC) Deans; Valley Lee, MD St. George.
Chin, Donald J. *o.f.m.* '67 (FgM) New York, NY Holy Name Province.
Chinchar, Gerald T. *s.m.* '82 (CIN)[D] Dayton, OH The University of Dayton; [N] Dayton, OH Marianist Community; [R] Dayton, OH University of Dayton Campus Ministry.
Chinchilla, Ricardo *c.j.m.* '93 (SD) Carlsbad, CA St. Patrick.
Ching, Herbert '47 (HON) Retired.
Ching, Philip '09 (DET) Utica, MI St. Lawrence.
Chingandu, Pedro *m.s.* '96 (FR)[G] Attleboro, MA La Salette Shrine.
Chinh, Michael M. Do Quang *c.m.c.* (SPC)[F] Carthage, MO Congregation of the Mother Coredemptrix, United States Assumption Province.
Chinnacode, Peter Piamote *c.s.s.* '94 (BO)[U] Waltham, MA Stigmatine Fathers & Brothers Provincial House.
Chinnapa, John Britto *m.s.f.s.* (DET) Macomb, MI St. Isidore.
Chinnappa, Ambrose (TYL) Mount Vernon, TX Sacred Heart.
Chinnappa, Johnbritto *m.s.f.s.* '97 (TYL)[B] Whitehouse, TX The Missionaries of St. Francis de Sales.
Chinnappan, Benjamin '88 (MO) Maywood, IL St. Eulalia; Hines V.A. Hospital; DEPARTMENT OF VETERANS AFFAIRS HOSPITALS AND CHAPLAINS.
Chinnici, Joseph P. *o.f.m.* '72 (OAK)[A] Berkeley, CA Franciscan School of Theology; [M] Berkeley, CA Franciscan Friars (Province of Santa Barbara).
Chinyanwa, Smart H. *s.s.* '01 (BAL)[S] Baltimore Society of St. Sulpice, Province of the United States.
Chiodo, Rev. Msgr. Frank '76 (DM) Des Moines, IA St. Anthony's.
Chiola, Richard L. '72 (SFD) Springfield, IL St. Frances Cabrini; Ongoing Formation of Clergy.
Chipson, Joseph (BIS) Hettinger, ND Sacred Heart; Hettinger, ND Sacred Heart; Hettinger, ND Holy Trinity.
Chirackal, Francis *c.m.i.* '92 (SAC) Sacramento, CA St. Mary.
Chirakkarottu, Koshy '99 (DET) Warren, MI St. Anne.
Chiraphurathel, Felix *o.praem.* '72 (TYL) Atlanta, TX St. Catherine of Siena Church.
Chirayath, Chummar *o.s.j.* '78 (FRS) Bakersfield, CA Our Lady of Guadalupe.
Chirayath, Jacob George '97 (WDC) Landover Hills, MD St. Mary's Catholic Church.
Chirayath, Joseph Vadake '75 (TLS) Hugo, OK St. Agnes; Hugo, OK Immaculate Conception.
Chircop, Manuel J. *c.s.b.* '77 (DET) Garden City, MI St. Dunstan; Detroit, MI Ste. Anne de Detroit.
Chiriaco, William J. '86 (PH) Media, PA St. Mary Magdalen; [D] Springfield, PA Cardinal O'Hara High School.
Chirichella, Vincent G. '07 (BRK) Whitestone, NY St. Luke.
Chirichiello, Richard *o.s.b.* '95 (GBG)[G] Latrobe, PA Saint Vincent Archabbey.
Chirico, Peter F. *s.s.* '56 (BAL)[S] Baltimore Society of St. Sulpice, Province of the United States Retired.
Chirico, Peter *s.s.* '56 (SEA) Retired.
Chirovsky, Rt. Rev. Andriy '80 (STN) Tucson, AZ St. Michael.
Chirovsky, Ivan (SJP) Pittsburgh, PA St. John the Baptist; Liturgical Commission; St. Josaphat Sacerdotal Society; Arbitration Board; Presbyters.
Chisanga, Tresphord *s.d.b.* '00 (OAK)[M] Berkeley Salesians of Don Bosco.
Chisholm, Gregory C. *s.j.* '93 (BO)[U] Boston The Society of Jesus of New England–Provincial Offices.
Chisholm, Gregory *s.j.* '93 (OAK)[M] Oakland, CA Jesuit Fathers and Brothers; Oakland, CA St. Patrick; [A] Berkeley, CA Jesuit School of Theology at Santa Clara University.
Chisholm, Thomas *o.s.b.* '89 (JOL)[L] Lisle, IL St. Procopius Abbey.
Chitteth, Biju (BIS) Crosby, ND St. Patrick; Crosby, ND St. Luke; Crosby, ND St. John the Baptist.
Chiusano, Louis *o.f.m.cap.* '57 (FgM) White Plains, NY Province of St. Mary.
Chizmar, Rev. Msgr. John G. '75 (ALN) Lake Harmony, PA St. Peter the Fisherman; Vicars Forane; Strengthening Our Future in Faith (SOFF).
Chladek, Melchior *o.cist.* '55 (DAL)[J] Irving, TX Cistercian Abbey of Our Lady of Dallas.
Chlebo, John C. '80 (CLV) Rocky River, OH St. Christopher.
Chleborad, Gerald '60 (CHY) Retired.
Chlopecki, Robert J. '74 (BEL) Retired.
Chmiel, Bronislaus '69 (CHI) Chicago, IL St. Pancratius.
Chmiel, Gerald J. '70 (TOL) Toledo, OH St. John the Baptist; Toledo, OH St. Michael the Archangel; Members.
Chmielecki, Janusz *o.f.m.conv.* (BO) South Boston, MA Our Lady of Czestochowa.
Chmielewski, Francis J. '73 (BUF) Buffalo, NY St. Bernard; Buffalo, NY St. Casimir.
Chmielewski, Philip J. *s.j.* '81 (LA)[C] Los Angeles, CA Jesuit Community.
Chmielewski, Philip J. *s.j.* '81 (CHI)[N] Chicago Chicago Province of the Society of Jesus–Provincial Office.
Chmil, John J. '95 (SCR) Wellsboro, PA St. Peter's.
Chmura, Gary '78 (CLV) Cleveland, OH Our Lady of Peace; Northcoast Behavioral Healthcare System North Campus; Northfield, OH Northcoast Behavioral Healthcare System South.
Chmura, Julian '64 (DET) Retired.
Chmurski, Marek '95 (FR) New Bedford, MA St. Lawrence Martyr.
Cho, Alexander '75 (SAL) Osborne, KS St. Aloysius Gonzaga Parish; Osborne, KS St. Mary Parish.
Cho, Hooyeon '05 (NEW) Maplewood, NJ St. Andrew Kim.
Cho, Jae Jin '93 (MIA) Korean.
Cho, Minhyun '99 (NEW) Maplewood, NJ St. Andrew Kim; Korean Apostolate.
Choate, Lawrence M. *o.s.m.* '78 (CHI) Chicago, IL St. Francis of Assisi/Our Lady of the Angels; [N] Berwyn, IL Servants of Mary (Servite) Development Office; Chicago, IL; [N] Chicago, IL Order of Friar Servants of Mary (Servites) United States of America Province, Inc.
Choc, Pedro *o.s.b.* '90 (SFS)[F] Marvin, SD Blue Cloud Abbey.
Chocarro, Antonio (CGS) Retired.
Chochol, Ronald C. '64 (STL) Special Assignment.
Chodakowski, Iraneusz *m.i.c.* '78 (MIL) Kenosha, WI St. Peter.
Chodakowski, Ireneusz *m.i.c.* '78 (SPR)[H] On Duty Outside of House:.
Chodzynski, Jacek *o.c.d.* '88 (GRY)[H] Munster, IN Discalced Carmelite Fathers Monastery.
Choe, James Bong–Won '77 (LA) Los Angeles, CA Holy Trinity.
Choi, Gi Weon (STA) Jacksonville, FL St. Francis Choe Chapel.
Choi, Jae Peter (IND) Indianapolis, IN St. Lawrence.
Choi, Jang Won '03 (PIT) Chaplain to Korean Catholic Community.
Choi, Mark '94 (LA) Norwalk, CA St. Linus.
Choi, Yong Hoon *s.s.c.* '01 (OM)[K] St. Columbans Missionary Society of St. Columban.
Choiniere, John Marie *o.mar.* '95 (SAM)[B] Petersham, MA Maronite Monks of Adoration Most Holy Trinity Monastery.
Chojda, Arthur *o.c.d.* '03 (STA)[H] Bunnell, FL Discalced Carmelite Fathers of Florida.
Chojnacki, Anthony *o.f.m.* '68 (GB)[J] Pulaski, WI Friary.
Chojnacki, Bernard '09 (VEN) Port Charlotte, FL St. Charles Borromeo.
Cholewa, Gregory T. *o.m.i.* '76 (CHI)[N] Chicago, IL The Oblate House of Theology.
Choma, Rev. Msgr. James S. '86 (NEW)[B] Seton Hall University; [B] School of Diplomacy and Intl. Rels.
Chompoochan, Weerasak '06 (OAK) Rodeo, CA St. Patrick.
Chong, Peter L. '92 (OAK) Fijian Pastoral Center; Oakland, CA St. Theresa of the Infant Jesus (The Little Flower).
Chong, Sammy *s.j.* '07 (BO)[U] Newton, MA The Jesuit Community at Boston College.
Chong, Vicente *s.j.* '09 (BO)[U] Cambridge, MA Zipoli House.
Chontos, Joseph '82 (KCK) Special Assignment.
Choo, Thomas *ss.cc.* '69 (HON) Honolulu, HI St. Patrick; [D] Honolulu, HI St. Patrick's Monastery.
Choong, Norbert '84 (AMA) Retired.
Choorackunnel, John V. *c.m.i.* '64 (TLS)[E] Tulsa, OK Saint Francis Hospital; Special Assignment.
Choorapanthiyil, Mathew *o.c.d.* '89 (IND)[C] Clarksville, IN Our Lady of Providence Junior – Senior High School; New Albany, IN Our Lady of Perpetual Help.
Choorathottiyil, Paul *v.c.* (FTW) South Bend, IN St. Catherine of Siena Parish at St. Jude; South Bend, IN St. Catherine of Siena Parish at Sacred Heart of Jesus.
Chooshukunnel, Kurian Stephen *o.s.h.* '94 (GAL) Missouri City, TX Holy Family.
Choozhukunnel, Kurian Steephen *o.s.h.* '94 (GAL)[O] Missouri City, TX The Society of the Oblates of Sacred Heart.
Choquet, Alexei H. '83 (CHL) On Duty Outside the Diocese.
Choquette, David P. '98 (NOR) Somersville, CT All Saints.
Chorey, Robert '02 (RNO) Fernley, NV St. Robert Bellarmine; Diocesan Board of Consultors; Presbyteral Council; Lists of Deans; Liturgy Commission.
Chornyak, Joseph I. '53 (PBR) Retired.
Chorpenning, Joseph F. *o.s.f.s.* '79 (PH)[C] Jesuit Fathers; [Y] Wyndmoor, PA Villa de Sales Oblate Residence; [Y] Wyndmoor, PA Oblates of St. Francis de Sales (O.S.F.S.).
Chortos, Donald '66 (PIT) Washington, PA Immaculate Conception; Absent on Sick Leave.
Chortos, George F. '64 (PIT) Monongahela, PA Transfiguration.
Chouinard, Lionel G. '65 (PRT) Lisbon Falls, ME Holy Trinity; Sabattus, ME Our Lady of the Rosary.
Chouinard, Marcel G. '56 (PRT)[G] Waterville, ME Mt. St. Joseph Holistic Care Community Retired.
Choutapalli, Joseph '90 (SAN) San Angelo, TX St. Margaret; Carlsbad, TX St. Therese of the Child Jesus.
Chovanec, Paul R. '72 (GAL) Houston, TX St. Justin Martyr.
Chow, Louis Y. '89 (HRT) Retired.
Chow, Luke L. '54 (PH) Retired.
Chowning, Daniel '88 (WH)[L] Hinton, WV Monastery of Christ on the Mountain.
Chowning, Michael *o.f.m.* '68 (LEX) Hazard, KY Mother of Good Counsel; [K] Hazard, KY Father Farrell Spiritual Life Center; College of Consultors; Mountain East.
Chretien, Richard L. '67 (FR) Fall River, MA Notre Dame de Lourdes; Fall River, MA Our Lady of the Immaculate Conception.
Chripko, Vladimir *c.o.* '95 (NY) Tappan, NY Our Lady of the Sacred Heart.
Chrismer, Mark A. '09 (STL) Valley Park, MO Sacred Heart.
Christ, John P. *o.s.c.* '65 (DET) Royal Oak, MI St. Dennis.
Christ, John *o.s.c.* '65 (PHX)[F] Phoenix, AZ Crosier Community of Phoenix (Canons Regular of the Order of the Holy Cross).
Christal, Jonas (BO) Roxbury, MA St. Patrick.
Christensen, Brian Patrick '99 (RC) Fort Pierre, SD St. John; Vocation Program.
Christensen, Brian '99 (RC) Deaneries.
Christensen, Christian *i.s.p.* '71 (AUS)[G] Austin, TX Schoenstatt Fathers.
Christensen, Christian *i.s.s.s.* '71 (MIL)[T] Waukesha, WI Secular Institute of Schoenstatt Fathers.
Christensen, Joseph '97 (FAR) Fargo, ND St. Mary's Cathedral of Fargo; [F] Minto, ND Saint Gianna's Home Inc.
Christensen, Michael R. '79 (LIN) Lincoln, NE St. Peter.
Christensen, William *s.m.* '73 (STL)[O] St. Louis Marianists, Province of the United States (Society of Mary).
Christenson, Lawrence *c.m.* '84 (DEN) Denver, CO Church of the Risen Christ.
Christian, George G. *o.p.* '55 (L) Louisville, KY St. Louis Bertrand; [L] Louisville, KY St. Louis Bertrand Priory.
Christian, Lawrence J. '83 (SAT)[A] San Antonio, TX Assumption Seminary; Department of Assumption–St. John's Seminary.
Christian, Robert *o.p.* '76 (OAK)[M] Oakland Order of Preachers (Province of the Most Holy Name of Jesus – Western Dominican Province).
Christiansen, Andrew J. *s.j.* '72 (NY)[EE] New York, NY "America;" Residence and publication office of the America Press; [II] New York, NY America Press, Inc.
Christiansen, Cal '08 (SEA) Tacoma, WA Sacred Heart; Tacoma, WA Holy Rosary; Tacoma, WA St. Joseph; Tacoma, WA St. Ann; Tacoma, WA St. John of the Woods; Tacoma, WA Visitation.
Christie, Frank M. *o.s.m.* '56 (CHI)[N] Chicago Order of

Friar Servants of Mary (Servites) United States of America Province, Inc.
Christman, Rev. Msgr. Bernard E. '59 (OG) Judges Retired.
Christman, Ralph F. *m.m.* '56 (NY)[EE].
Christman, Robert '79 (MIA) Absent on Leave.
Christofferson, Kevin '97 (HEL) Frenchtown, MT St. John the Baptist.
Christopher, Brian J. *s.j.* (FgM) St. Louis, MO Society of Jesus.
Christopher, Mark '62 (ORL) Sanford, FL All Souls Retired.
Christopher, Mark '57 (PMB) Retired.
Christopher, Patrick J. '91 (MO) House Springs, MO Our Lady, Queen of Peace; Deaneries/Deans; DEPARTMENT OF VETERANS AFFAIRS HOSPITALS AND CHAPLAINS.
Christudasl, Velanmarukudiyil *o.s.b.* '86 (TR) Brick, NJ Visitation.
Christy, Timothy '92 (MET) Flemington, NJ St. Magdalen de Pazzi.
Christy, William H. *c.s.sp.* '92 (FgM) Bethel Park, PA CONGREGATION OF THE HOLY SPIRIT.
Chriszt, Dennis *c.pp.s.* '82 (CIN)[N] Dayton Provincial Office of the Cincinnati Province of the Society of the Precious Blood.
Chrobot, Leonard F. '64 (FTW) South Bend, IN St. Hedwig; South Bend, IN St. Patrick; South Bend, IN Faith & Hope & Charity Chapel.
Chrusciel, Bogumil '68 (NEW) Newark, NJ St. Stanislaus.
Chrysostom, Francis X. '60 (LA)[J] Inglewood, CA Daniel Freeman Memorial Hospital.
Chryst, Robert D. '68 (SY) Syracuse, NY St. Anthony of Padua; Special Assignment; Spanish Apostolate.
Chrzan, John P. '03 (CHI) Park Ridge, IL St. Paul of the Cross.
Chrzanowski, Jaroslaw *s.j.* '00 (WDC)[N] Washington, DC The Jesuit Community at Georgetown University.
Chrzastek, Brian *o.p.* '92 (WDC)[B] Washington, DC Dominican House of Studies.
Chu, Peter M.Q. *s.j.* '68 (SJ)[D] San Jose, CA Bellarmine College Preparatory.
Chu, Peter Ngoc Thanh '55 (GAL)[L] Houston, TX Pope John Paul XXIII Priests' Residence Retired.
Chu, Quang Vinh '91 (ORG) Stanton, CA St. Polycarp.
Chua, Freddie T. '98 (LA) Tujunga, CA Our Lady of Lourdes.
Chubirko, Michael *s.d.b.* '60 (SP)[P] Tampa, FL Salesian Society of Florida, Inc.
Chudy, Carl S. *s.x.* '86 (FgM)[N] Wayne, NJ Xaverian Missionary Fathers; Wayne, NJ XAVERIAN MISSIONARY FATHERS.
Chukwu, Christopher '80 (MAN) Dartmouth–Hitchcock Medical Center.
Chukwu, Donatus '93 (CHI) Chicago, IL St. Margaret Mary; [J] Chicago, IL Saint Joseph Hospital.
Chukwu, Kenneth (LA)[J] Tarzana, CA Providence Tarzana Medical Center.
Chukwu, Peter M. '93 (GR) Fremont, MI All Saints; White Cloud, MI St. Joseph's.
Chukwube, Stanislaus '88 (RVC) West Islip, NY Our Lady of Lourdes.
Chukwuleta, Daniel '91 (FTW) Fort Wayne, IN St. Joseph Medical Center.
Chukwuma, Francis '96 (FTW) Bluffton, IN St. Joseph; Judicial Vicar.
Chumo, Augustine '98 (ROC) Henrietta, NY Church of the Good Shepherd.
Chun, Francis '63 (P) Retired.
Chun, Glen *s.j.* '08 (CIN)[N] Cincinnati, OH Jesuit Community at St. Xavier High School.
Chung, Alex '88 (LA) Los Angeles, CA St. Gregory Nazianzen.
Chung, Anthony '71 (SFR) Retired.
Chung, Brian '00 (LA) Cursillo Movement.
Chung, Eugene *o.c.s.o.* '06 (ROC)[J] Piffard, NY Abbey of the Genesee.
Chung, Francis '93 (AUS) Austin, TX St. Andrew Kim Taegon Korean Catholic Church.
Chung, Hee Ook '76 (LAV) Las Vegas, NV St. Paul Jung–Ha–Sang.
Chuong, Joseph Doan Huy '64 (GAL)[O] New Caney, TX Congregation of the Mother Coredemptrix Retired.
Church, Rev. Msgr. James F. '58 (SAC) College of Consultors; Propagation of the Faith; Sacramento, CA St. Rose.
Church, Timothy A. '95 (DAL) Allen, TX St. Jude.
Church, Wenceslaus '59 (CHI)[N] Chicago, IL St. Peter's Friary.
Churchwell, Rev. Msgr. Stephen T. '76 (ATL) Dawsonville, GA Christ Redeemer Catholic Church; College of Consultors; Adjutant Judicial Vicars.
Chuwa, Leonard *a.j.* '99 (PIT) Pittsburgh, PA St. Bede.
Chwalek, John '48 (SPR) Retired.
Chwalek, Kazimierz *m.i.c.* '87 (SPR)[H] Stockbridge, MA Association of Marian Helpers, Marian Helpers Center; [H] Stockbridge, MA Congregation of Marian Fathers of The Immaculate Conception of the Most Blessed Virgin Mary; Provincial Councilors:; [H] Provincial Office.
Chwaliszewski, Roman *o.f.m.conv.* '60 (FR) New Bedford, MA Our Lady of Perpetual Help.
Chwieroth, Edward J. '50 (PH) Bensalem, PA Retired.
Chycinski, Gregory A. '71 (MIL) Milwaukee, WI Blessed Savior Parish.
Chylewski, Rev. Msgr. Anthony '52 (SD) Retired.
Chylinski, Keith J. '07 (PH) Philadelphia, PA St. Anselm.
Chylko, Gerard *c.ss.r.* '79 (WDC)[N] Washington, DC Holy Redeemer College.
Ciaccio, Accursio *f.s.c.b.* '09 (DEN) Broomfield, CO Nativity of Our Lord.
Cialone, Donald F. '75 (NEW) Westfield, NJ Holy Trinity.
Ciampaglio, Rev. Msgr. Joseph A. (PAT) Diocesan Council of Catholic Women.
Ciampaglio, Rev. Msgr. Joseph M. (PAT) Retired.
Ciancimino, David S. *s.j.* '88 (FgM) New York, NY; [EE] New York, NY Society of Jesus, New York Province; New York, NY Society of Jesus; [EE] New York, NY Xavier Jesuit Community.
Ciandella, Roch *o.f.m.* '72 (NY)[GG] Wappingers Falls, NY Mt. Alvernia Retreat House.
Ciano, Kenneth J. '95 (IND) Retired.
Ciappi–Azcorra, Angel L. '98 (SJN) Diocesan Consultors; Legion of Mary; Vicar of Development; Vicar of Economic Affairs.
Ciaramitaro, James M. *o.f.m.conv.* '88 (MIL) Milwaukee, WI Basilica of St. Josaphat.
Ciaramitaro, Rev. Msgr. Victor P. '72 (MEM) Memphis, TN St. Michael's; College of Consultors; Judges; Presbyteral Council.
Ciaramitaro, Rev. Msgr. Victor '72 (MEM) Clergy Personnel Board.
Ciaravolo, Ronald '54 (NY) Retired.
Ciardiello, Bruno *o.f.m.* '45 (BRK) Brooklyn, NY Our Lady of Peace Retired.
Ciaston, Krzysztof D. '07 (CHI) Chicago, IL St. Tarcissus.
Ciavaglia, Julio M. *c.r.s.p.* '66 (BUF)[B] Youngstown, NY St. Anthony M. Zaccaria Seminary; [T] Youngstown, NY Basilica of the National Shrine of Our Lady of Fatima, Inc.
Ciba, Thomas J. '74 (NEW) Jersey City, NJ Our Lady of Czestochowa.
Cibangu, Sylvain '95 (SEA) Everett, WA Immaculate Conception; Everett, WA Our Lady of Perpetual Help.
Cibelli, Ernest W. '09 (BAL) Graduate Studies.
Ciccarino, Christopher M. '96 (NEW)[B] School of Diplomacy and Intl. Rels.; [A] South Orange, NJ Immaculate Conception Seminary.
Ciccolini, Samuel R. '69 (CLV) Akron, OH Immaculate Conception; [T] Akron, OH Interval Brotherhood Home Alcohol–Drug Rehabilitation Center.
Ciccone, Joseph A. *c.s.p.* '89 (KNX) Knoxville, TN Immaculate Conception; Knoxville, TN Calvary Cemetery; Presbyteral Council.
Ciccone, Joseph J. *c.s.p.* '89 (KNX) Cemeteries.
Ciccone, Mark *s.j.* '85 (LA)[P] Los Angeles, CA Colombiere House; [J] Burbank, CA Providence Saint Joseph Medical Center; [J] Burbank, CA Providence Saint Joseph Medical Center.
Ciccone, Michael *o.p.* '75 (COL)[A] Columbus, OH Pontifical College Josephinum.
Cicerale, Charles W. '75 (MET) Woodbridge, NJ St. James; College of Consultors; Deans.
Cichon, Michael W. '85 (NY) Staten Island, NY Assumption/St. Paul; Staten Island, NY St. Paul.
Cicinato, Michael '76 (MRY) San Luis Obispo, CA Nativity of Our Lady.
Cid, Roberto '07 (MIA) Plantation, FL St. Gregory.
Cidlevich, Brian J. *s.m.* '08 (DET)[D] Pontiac, MI Notre Dame Preparatory School and Marist Academy.
Ciemiega, Wieslaw *o.f.m.conv.* '93 (BO) South Boston, MA Our Lady of Czestochowa.
Cieniewicz, Donald W. '83 (ALN) Hamburg, PA St. Mary.
Cienik, Kenneth *s.a.* '77 (MO) Navy Reserve Chaplains.
Cienik, Kenneth *s.a.* '77 (STU)[A] Steubenville, OH Franciscan University of Steubenville; [H] Steubenville, OH Holy Spirit Friary.
Cienik, Kenneth *s.a.* '77 (NY)[EE] Garrison, NY Franciscan Friars of the Atonement.
Ciesielski, Marek *s.ch.* '96 (LA) Los Angeles, CA Our Lady of the Bright Mount.
Ciesla, Marek *s.chr.* '82 (ATL) Lawrenceville, GA St. Marguerite D'Youville.
Ciesla, Walter M. '81 (GRY) Michigan City, IN St. Stanislaus Kostka; Blue Army.
Cieslak, William M. *o.f.m.cap.* '73 (OAK)[R] Board of Directors:.
Cieslak, William *o.f.m.cap.* '73 (DET)[K] Detroit, MI Provincialate; Detroit, MI.
Cieslak, William *o.f.m.cap.* '73 (CHI)[N] Chicago, IL St. Clare Friary.
Cieslewicz, Vincent P. '94 (E) Mount Jewett, PA St. Joseph; Smethport, PA St. Elizabeth; Bradford, PA Federal Correction Institution.
Cieslik, R. Dale '82 (L) Louisville, KY St. Elizabeth Ann Seton; Archivist; Clergy Personnel Commission.
Cieslikowski, Thomas J. '88 (HRT) New Britain, CT St. Jerome; New Britain, CT St. Maurice.
Cieslinski, Robert '43 (P) Retired.
Cieutat, John Gregory '06 (DEN) Denver, CO St. Catherine of Siena.
Ciferni, Andrew D. *o.praem.* '68 (PH)[B] Paoli, PA Daylesford Abbey; [Y] Paoli, PA Daylesford Abbey; Paoli, PA.
Cifuentes, Patricio Gallego '79 (PCE) Patillas, PR Inmaculado Corazon de Maria.
Cigan, John J. *j.c.b.* '74 (PSC) Binghamton, NY Holy Spirit; Presbyteral Council; Retirement Plan Board.
Ciganek, William *c.f.x.* (BAL) Baltimore, MD Sacred Heart of Mary.
Cihak, John '98 (P) On Duty Outside the Archdiocese.
Cilano, Richard J. '05 (BUF) United Memorial Medical Center; East Bethany, NY Immaculate Conception; Pavilion, NY St. Mary.
Cilia, Rev. Msgr. Francis V. '79 (SJ) Special Assignment; [O] San Jose, CA Roman Catholic Seminary Corporation of San Jose; Roman Catholic Seminary Corporation; Vicar General and Moderator of the Curia; College of Consultors; Roman Catholic Welfare Corporation; Priests' Retirement Board; Council of Priests; Building Committee; Lay Retirement Board; Diocesan Leadership Team.
Cilia, Jose *o.carm.* '68 (JOL) Joliet, IL Mount Carmel.
Ciliberti, Francis J. *o.praem.* '44 (WIL)[J] Middletown, DE Immaculate Conception Priory of the Canons Regular of Premontre.
Cilibraise, Michael '08 (GR) Presbyteral Council; Scottville, MI St. Jerome; Custer, MI St. Mary's.
Cilinski, Robert C. '79 (ARL) Manassas, VA All Saints; Deans; Diocesan Consultors.
Cilwick, Theodore T. '43 (CHR) Retired.
Cima, Jose '58 (SB) Retired.
Cima, Thomas E. '67 (CHI) Deans; Chicago, IL St. Michael the Archangel.
Cimarrusti, Francis A. '64 (CHI) Chicago, IL St. Matthias; [G] Chicago, IL Catholic Charities of the Archdiocese of Chicago–Archdiocesan Offices Retired.
Cimbala, Edward G. '88 (PSC) Hillsborough Township, NJ St. Mary's; Priesthood & Diaconate Formation Programs.
Cimerman, Krizolog *o.f.m.* '73 (NY) New York, NY St. Cyril; Councilors:.
Cimino, Michael '86 (SFE) Albuquerque, NM Our Lady of the Assumption.
Cimperman, Victor J. '43 (CLV) Cleveland, OH St. Vitus Retired.
Cimpl, Charles L. '78 (SFS) Sioux Falls, SD St. Michael; Vicar General; Tribunal Judges; Diocesan Consultors; Presbyteral Council; Personnel Board.
Cincinnati, Anthony '87 (WH) Priests' Health and Retirement Association; Diocesan Consultors; Episcopal Vicar for Clergy; Permanent Diaconate Formation; Contacts to Report; [H] Wheeling, WV Welty Trust, Inc.; Wheeling, WV St. Joseph's Cathedral.
Cincotta, Anthony '74 (SY) On Duty Outside the Diocese.
Cindric, John R. '74 (GBG)[J] Greensburg, PA The Bishop William G. Connare Center.
Cingle, Martin A. '73 (ALT) Nanty–Glo, PA St. Mary's.
Cini, Rev. Msgr. J. Thomas '68 (WIL) Vicar General for Administration and Moderator of the Curia; Diocesan Planning; Diocesan Real Estate Committee; Catholic Ministry to the Elderly; College of Consultors; Diocesan Building Committee; Public Affairs Advisory Committee; Catholic Diocese of Wilmington, Inc.; Catholic Ministry to the Elderly, Inc.; Catholic Press of Wilmington, Inc.; Catholic Charities, Inc.; Catholic Youth Organization, Inc.; Children's Home, Inc.; Seton Villa, Inc.; Siena Hall, Inc.; Delawareans United for Education; Wilmington, DE St. Ann.
Cink, James J. '85 (MOB) Victim Assistance Coordinator.
Cink, James J. '85 (MOB) Mobile, AL St. Dominic; Officers; Archdiocesan Consultors.
Cinnante, Justin S. '07 (NY) Hopewell Junction, NY St. Columba.
Cinque, Stephen J. '81 (NEW) Washington Township, NJ Our Lady of Good Counsel.
Cinquegrani, David *c.p.* '96 (HRT)[L] West Hartford Holy Family Monastery/Retreat; [P] West Hartford, CT Holy Family Passionist Retreat Center; Commission for Priests' Retreats.
Cinquegrani, R. Bruce '79 (MEM) Memphis, TN St. Brigid.
Cinson, Victor '74 (STU) Minerva, OH St. Francis Xavier; Minerva, OH St. Gabriel the Archangel.
Cintron, Angel Luis '91 (FAJ) Catechetical Vicar.
Cintron, Freddy '87 (BRK) Brooklyn, NY St. Catharine of Alexandria.
Cintron, Segismundo '89 (PCE) Yauco, PR St. Martin de Porres.
Cintron, Segismundo (PCE)[B] The Pontifical Catholic University of Puerto Rico.

Cintron Ortiz, Angel L. '91 (FAJ) Fajardo, PR Cathedral Santiago Apostol.
Cintula, Francis M. '65 (CHL) Eden, NC St. Joseph of the Hills Retired.
Cio, Robert J. '74 (NEW) Harrison, NJ Holy Cross.
Cioch, Gregory '00 (DEN) Fort Collins, CO St. Elizabeth Ann Seton; Deaneries; Elected Representatives from Deanery to Presbyteral Council.
Cioffi, Alfred '85 (MIA) Hialeah, FL Immaculate Conception.
Cioffi, Phillip F. '81 (CHI) Highland Park, IL Immaculate Conception; Highwood, IL St. James.
Cioffi, Ronald J. '69 (TR) Keyport, NJ St. Joseph; Social Concerns.
Ciolak, Jakub '04 (NY) New York, NY Our Lady of Good Counsel.
Ciolek, Dominik *s.j.* '07 (OAK)[M] Berkeley, CA Jesuit Fathers and Brothers; Polish Center.
Ciomek, Christopher '98 (CHI)[A] Mundelein, IL University of St. Mary of the Lake/Mundelein Seminary.
Cioppa, John A. *m.m.* '59 (FgM) Maryknoll, NY MARYKNOLL.
Cioppi, Martin T. '81 (PH) Hatboro, PA St. John Bosco.
Ciordia, Jose Antonio '61 (NEW) Union City, NJ St. Augustine's.
Ciordia, Pedro M. '61 (LA) Retired.
Ciorra, Anthony J. '73 (NY)[C] Bronx, NY Fordham University.
Ciotola, Rev. Msgr. Romano '65 (COL) Columbus, OH Our Lady of Victory.
Ciotoli, Vincent '76 (ALB) Hoosick Falls, NY Immaculate Conception.
Cipagauta, Uriel Salamanca '87 (BEL) Cobden, IL St. Joseph.
Cipar, Daniel '61 (Y) East Palestine, OH Our Lady of Lourdes Retired.
Cipolla, Richard G. '84 (BGP) Norwalk, CT St. Mary.
Cipot, Edwin H. '00 (NY) Staten Island, NY Holy Child.
Cippel, Rev. Msgr. John A. '60 (SP) Brandon, FL Church of the Nativity Retired.
Ciprian, Carl A. '76 (CLV)[E] Parma Heights, OH Incarnate Word Academy; [O] Parma Heights, OH Sisters of the Incarnate Word and Blessed Sacrament Retired.
Cipriani, Peter A. '04 (BGP) Trumbull, CT St. Theresa; [C] Fairfield, CT Notre Dame Catholic High School.
Cipriano, Joseph F. '59 (SCR)[N] Dunmore, PA Villa St. Joseph Retired.
Cipriano, Robert P. '87 (SFR) East Palo Alto, CA St. Francis of Assisi Retired.
Ciranni, Salvatore *r.c.j.* '55 (FRS) Sanger, CA St. Mary; Sanger, CA Retired.
Cirata, David J. '06 (TOL) Walbridge, OH St. Jerome.
Cirba, Richard J. '89 (SCR) Hazleton, PA SS. Cyril & Methodius, Hazleton; Hazleton, PA St. Stanislaus; Deans.
Circe, Scott M. '05 (ORL) Orlando, FL St. James Cathedral.
Cirera, Arsenio G. '89 (SFR) Belmont, CA Immaculate Heart of Mary.
Ciriaco, Dominic G. *o.s.f.s.* '99 (WIL)[B] Wilmington, DE Salesianum School.
Ciriaco, Dominic G. '99 (NEW)[D] Paramus, NJ Paramus Catholic High School; Hohokus, NJ St. Luke's.
Cirignani, Anthony *o.f.m.* '83 (GB) Green Bay, WI St. Philip the Apostle; Green Bay, WI St. Bernard.
Cirilli, Matthew R. '64 (PIT) Retired.
Cirillo, Nicholas A. '95 (BGP)[A] Stamford, CT St. John Fisher Seminary Residence; [C] Stamford, CT Trinity Catholic High School; Pastors' Vocation Advisory Board.
Cirino, Andre *o.f.m.* '67 (NY)[EE] Mount Vernon, NY St. Bernardine of Siena Friary.
Ciriza, Jesus M. *m.ss.cc.* '59 (SJN) Bayamon, PR Santiago Apostol.
Cirone, Theodore *c.m.f.* '55 (CHI)[N] Chicago, IL Claret House.
Ciryak, Michael A. '98 (FR) Swansea, MA Saint Francis of Assisi; Bristol Community College; [L] Fall River, MA Bristol Community College Newman Center; Director.
Cisco, Bede *o.s.b.* '78 (IND)[K] St. Meinrad, IN St. Meinrad Archabbey; Deacon Formation; [A] St. Meinrad, IN Saint Meinrad School of Theology.
Cisco, Mariano '82 (BRK) Brooklyn, NY St. Joseph Patron of the Universal Church.
Cisek, Herman W. *m.m.* '65 (CHI) Chicago, IL; [N] Chicago, IL Maryknoll Fathers & Brothers.
Cisetti, Joseph I. '91 (KC) Kansas City, MO Holy Cross; Permanent Diaconate.
Cisetti, Joseph '91 (KC) Kansas City, MO St. Anthony; Deans.
Cisewski, John '71 (NO) New Orleans, LA St. Katharine Drexel.
Ciski, Michael *t.o.r.* '00 (FWT) Arlington, TX St. Maria Goretti.
Cisneros, Daniel '03 (SAT) San Antonio, TX Our Lady of Perpetual Help.
Cisneros, Ramon '99 (ORG) Santa Ana, CA St. Anne's.
Cisneros, Richard Mederich Marcelino '98 (NY) Bronx, NY St. Peter and St. Paul.
Cisneros, Salvador *c.r.* '05 (DEN) Denver, CO Our Lady of Guadalupe.
Ciszkowski, Slawomir '00 (NY) Ossining, NY St. Augustine.
Citero, Sam *o.carm.* '84 (WDC)[B] Washington, DC Whitefriars Hall.
Citino, Angelo R. '77 (PH) Warminster, PA Nativity of Our Lord.
Citro, Anthony M. '94 (GAY) Traverse City, MI Immaculate Conception.
Ciuba, Rev. Msgr. Edward J. '59 (NEW) Upper Saddle River, NJ Church of the Presentation Retired.
Ciuciulla, Peter *m.c.c.j.* '92 (CHI) Cincinnati, OH U.S. Headquarters, Comboni Mission Center; Cincinnati, OH; [W] Chicago, IL The Peace Corner, Incorporated.
Ciuciulla, Peter *m.c.c.j.* '92 (CIN)[N] Cincinnati, OH Comboni Missionaries (Verona Fathers)–Comboni Mission Center; [N] Cincinnati, OH Comboni Missionaries (Verona Fathers)–Comboni Mission Center.
Ciupek, James D. '97 (BUF) Alden, NY St. John the Baptist.
Ciurej, Richard S. '54 (OM) Retired.
Ciurpita, John '89 (PHU) Presbyteral Council; Chester, PA Holy Ghost; Clifton Heights, PA SS. Peter and Paul.
Civille, John R. '66 (CIN) Middletown, OH Holy Family.
Cizik, Ladis '87 (PIT) Allegheny County, PA Beverly Manor of Monroeville; Allegheny County, PA Seneca Place; Hamilton Hills Personal Care; Allegheny County, PA Ladies of the Grand Army Republic (LGAR); Allegheny County, PA Manorcare Health Services Monroeville; Allegheny County, PA Presbyterian Seniorcare Westminister Place; Seneca Hills Retirement Village; Seneca Manor Assisted Living; Sunrise Assisted Living; Seneca Place; Pittsburgh, PA Our Lady of Joy.
Clagett, Rev. Msgr. Carl P. '55 (COL) Retired.
Clair, John J. '82 (CHI)[L] Chicago, IL Misericordia/ Heart of Mercy Center.
Clancy, "Ray" '74 (AUS) Retired.
Clancy, Rev. Msgr. Douglas P. '71 (HRT) West Hartford, CT St. Brigid; West Hartford, CT St. Helena.
Clancy, Frank *s.c.j.* '74 (BWN) Retired.
Clancy, Richard F. '91 (BO)[AA] Cambridge, MA Massachusetts Institute of Technology Catholic Community; Campus Ministry; Massachusetts Institute of Technology.
Clancy, Richard F. (BO) Dorchester, MA St. Gregory.
Clancy, Robert E. '74 (CLV) Akron, OH Sacred Heart of Jesus; Akron General Hospital.
Clancy, Timothy R. *s.j.* '89 (SPK)[B] Spokane, WA Gonzaga University; Nine Mile Falls, WA Our Lady of the Lake.
Clanton, Bruce *s.d.s.* '78 (MIL)[P] Milwaukee Salvatorian Provincial Offices.
Clapham, Bruce '95 (MO) DEPARTMENT OF VETERANS' AFFAIRS HOSPITALS AND CHAPLAINS.
Clapsaddle, Harlan (RCK) Retired.
Clarin, Rolando *o.s.c.* '93 (LA) Valinda, CA St. Martha.
Clark, Anthony '79 (LSC) Retired.
Clark, Anthony *s.v.d.* '85 (MEM)[F] Memphis, TN Society of the Divine Word (Chicago Province); African American Catholics; Memphis, TN St. Joseph's; Secretary for Multicultural Ministries.
Clark, Augustine '97 (ORL) Orlando, FL St. Charles Borromeo.
Clark, Dana '01 (SAL) Colby, KS Sacred Heart Parish; Catholic Charities Board.
Clark, David '84 (P) On Duty Outside the Archdiocese.
Clark, Rev. Msgr. Dennis R. '66 (SD) San Diego, CA St. Vincent de Paul.
Clark, Douglas K. '76 (SAV) Censor Librorum; College of Consultors; Newspaper; Diocesan Worship Commission; Savannah, GA Cathedral of St. John the Baptist.
Clark, Rev. Msgr. Eugene V. '51 (NY)[II] New York, NY Friends of American Art in Religion, Inc.
Clark, Howard T. '57 (WIL) Retired.
Clark, J. Michael '95 (OWN) Utica, KY St. Anthony; Judicial Vicar; Director of Ecumenism.
Clark, James B. '95 (BO) Unassigned.
Clark, James E. '96 (ALB) Catholic Deaf Ministry; Fort Plain, NY Parish of Our Lady of Hope.
Clark, James P. '52 (NY) Bronx, NY St. Frances of Rome Retired.
Clark, James W. '84 (GBG) Uniontown, PA Uniontown Hospital; Republic, PA Madonna of Czestochowa.
Clark, Jason *l.c.* '04 (SAC) Sacramento, CA Our Lady of Guadalupe Shrine.
Clark, John F. *c.m.* '70 (STL)[O] St. Louis, MO Lazarist Residence; [Q] St. Louis, MO Marillac Provincial Offices.
Clark, John R. '96 (WDC) Rockville, MD Shrine of St. Jude.
Clark, John W. *s.j.* '59 (LA)[P] Culver City, CA Ignatius House, The Novitiate of the California Province, Society of Jesus.
Clark, John W. *s.j.* '59 (SJ)[M] Los Gatos, CA Sacred Heart Jesuit Center.
Clark, Joseph J. '96 (ARL) Annandale, VA St. Michael.
Clark, Joseph L. '76 (RIC) Retired.
Clark, Keith *o.f.m.cap.* '65 (GB)[M] Appleton, WI Monte Alverno Retreat & Spirituality Center.
Clark, Luke *o.p.* '04 (RIC) Charlottesville, VA St. Thomas Aquinas; Lay Fraternity of St. Dominic.
Clark, Matthew R. *o.s.b.* '87 (NO)[P] St. Benedict, LA St. Joseph Abbey; [A] St. Benedict, LA St. Joseph Seminary College; [A] St. Benedict, LA St. Joseph Seminary College.
Clark, Patrick S. '61 (SEA) Seattle, WA St. Patrick.
Clark, Paul M. '03 (HBG) Harrisburg, PA Cathedral Parish of St. Patrick; Auditor; Advocates.
Clark, Peter A. *s.j.* '92 (PH)[C] Jesuit Fathers; [Y] Loyola Center and Manresa Hall.
Clark, Peter J. '02 (LAN) Williamston, MI St. Mary; [P] Lansing, MI Diocesan Service Committee; Vicar for Charismatic Communities.
Clark, Ray '91 (OWN) Non–Parochial Assignments; Society for the Propagation of the Faith; Holy Childhood Association.
Clark, Richard '93 (MRY) Retired.
Clark, Robert J. '99 (CHI) La Grange, IL St. Cletus; Deans.
Clark, Robert J. *o.s.b.* '87 (MO) Navy Reserve Chaplains.
Clark, Robert *s.s.c.* '65 (OM)[K] St. Columbans Missionary Society of St. Columban.
Clark, Steven E. '90 (NY) Mt. Kisco, NY St. Francis of Assisi.
Clark, Thomas F. *s.j.* '81 (BO)[U] Boston The Society of Jesus of New England–Provincial Offices.
Clark, Thomas F. *s.j.* '81 (BR) Baton Rouge, LA Immaculate Conception.
Clark, Thomas R. '62 (L) New Haven, KY Immaculate Conception Retired.
Clark, Timothy *o.c.s.o.* '80 (P)[L] Lafayette, OR The Cistercian (Trappist) Abbey of Our Lady of Guadalupe.
Clark, Timothy '80 (SEA) Seattle, WA Our Lady of the Lake.
Clark, Vernon F. '80 (CHY) Cody, WY St. Anthony; Vicars Forane.
Clark, William A. *s.j.* '93 (WOR)[O] Worcester, MA Jesuits of the Holy Cross, Inc.
Clark, William *o.m.i.* '55 (BEL)[F] Belleville, IL Missionary Oblates of Mary Immaculate – St. Henry's Oblate Residence.
Clarke, Brian J.T. '07 (SCR) On Duty Outside the Diocese; Judges.
Clarke, Brian J.W. '02 (SCR) Vice Chancellor; Scranton, PA St. Peter's Cathedral.
Clarke, David M. *s.j.* '64 (DEN)[B] Denver, CO Regis University; [N] Denver, CO Regis Jesuit Community (The Jesuits at Regis University).
Clarke, Fergus *o.f.m.* '73 (FgM) Washington, DC COMMISSARIAT OF THE HOLY LAND.
Clarke, Rev. Msgr. James A. '70 (Y) North Canton, OH St. Paul.
Clarke, Rev. Msgr. James T. '38 (SCR)[N] Dunmore, PA Villa St. Joseph Retired.
Clarke, James '81 (LA)[A] Camarillo, CA St. John's Seminary; Chair.
Clarke, Jeremy *s.j.* '02 (BO)[U] Newton, MA The Jesuit Community at Boston College.
Clarke, Rev. Msgr. John A. '59 (CAM) Retired.
Clarke, Kevin T. *s.j.* '73 (P)[J] Portland, OR Providence Portland Medical Center.
Clarke, Peter J. '04 (PAT) Boy Scouting; [C] Wayne, NJ De Paul High School.
Clarke, Peter '63 (CHR) Gloverville, SC Our Lady of the Valley Retired.
Claro, Carlos Luis *c.s.v.* '98 (CHI)[N] Arlington Heights Viatorian Province Center–Clerics of St. Viator.
Claro, Mario R. '67 (WH) Franklin, WV St. Elizabeth Ann Seton.
Clary, Brian M. '97 (BO) Brookline, MA St. Mary of the Assumption; Priests' Recovery Program.
Clary, Michael '77 (KC) Lee's Summit, MO Our Lady of the Presentation.
Class, Michael D. *s.j.* '90 (MIL)[P] Milwaukee, WI Jesuit Community at Marquette University.
Classen, Rev. Msgr. Joseph F. '03 (STL) St. Louis, MO St. Margaret Mary Alacoque.
Classick, Bede *o.s.b.* '67 (SEA)[L] Lacey, WA St. Martin's Abbey; [A] Lacey, WA Saint Martin's University.
Clauder, J. Gibbs '73 (MAD) Leave of Absence.
Claudio, Antonio '75 (SJ) Santa Clara County Jail; Detention Ministry for Juveniles; Special Assignment; Milpitas, CA St. Elizabeth.
Claudio, Miguel '06 (CGS) Catholic Youth; Caguas, PR Maria Madre de la Iglesia.
Clausen, Rev. Msgr. William J. '62 (RCK) Retired.
Claver, Peter '93 (NY) Cornwall, NY The Cornwall Hospital; Newburgh, NY St. Luke Hospital.
Clavero, Jose M. *sch.p.* '64 (NY) New York, NY Annunciation; [EE] New York, NY Calasanzian Fathers (Piarists).
Clavey, William J. '98 (CHI) Berwyn, IL St. Mary of Celle.
Clavijo, Manuel A. '05 (WOR) Milford, MA St. Mary of the Assumption; St. Mary.

Clavin, M. Oliver '70 (SPC) Kelso, MO St. Augustine; Scott City, MO St. Joseph.
Clavin, Nicholas P. '73 (SD) San Diego, CA St. Gregory The Great.
Clay, Catesby '07 (LEX) Lawrenceburg, KY St. Lawrence.
Clay, Chris '07 (LEX) Priests' Retirement Board.
Clay, Christopher R. '98 (SCR) Unassigned or Leave of Absence.
Clay, David J. *s.s.c.* (FgM) St Columbans, NE House of Post–Graduate Studies.
Clay, John C. '51 (STP) St. Paul, MN St. Stanislaus.
Clay, Rev. Msgr. Michael G. '80 (R) Council of Priests; Clayton, NC St. Ann.
Clayton, Daniel '68 (DAL) Dallas, TX Methodist Dallas Medical Center; Dallas, TX Methodist Charlton Medical Center.
Clayton, Rev. Msgr. Murray '56 (SHP) Retired.
Cleary, Christopher *c.p.* '86 (BRK)[T] Jamaica, NY Immaculate Conception Monastery; [V] Jamaica, NY Bishop Molloy Retreat House.
Cleary, Dennis W. *m.m.* '77 (NY)[EE] Maryknoll Maryknoll Fathers and Brothers.
Cleary, Donald M. '71 (OM) North Bend, NE St. Charles Borromeo; Snyder, NE St. Leo.
Cleary, Donald R. '68 (KC) Retired.
Cleary, Edward L. *o.p.* '57 (PRO)[P] Providence St. Thomas Aquinas Priory at Providence College.
Cleary, Francis X. *s.j.* '63 (STL)[O] St. Louis, MO Jesuit Community Corporation at Saint Louis University – Jesuit Hall.
Cleary, Gerard M. '61 (BLX) Gulfport, MS St. John the Evangelist.
Cleary, Herbert J. *s.j.* '68 (BO)[S] South Boston, MA Marian Manor; [D] Dorchester, MA Boston College High School.
Cleary, James L. *o.f.m.cap.* '70 (LA) Los Angeles, CA St. Lawrence of Brindisi.
Cleary, Rev. Msgr. Kevin '48 (FRS) Retired.
Cleary, Paul '74 (SAT) LaCoste, TX Our Lady of Grace; Defenders of the Bond.
Cleary, Philip C. '79 (CHI) Missionary Work.
Cleary, Richard T. *s.j.* '66 (BO)[U] Weston, MA Campion Health Center, Inc.
Cleary, Richard *o.s.b.* '55 (LR)[H] Jonesboro, AR Holy Angels Convent–Motherhouse.
Cleary, William M. *o.s.a.* '61 (PH)[Y] Villanova, PA St. Thomas Monastery.
Cleary, William '61 (WDC) Washington, DC St. Mary, Mother of God.
Cleary, William '04 (NY) Graduate Studies.
Cleary, William *c.ss.r.* '62 (SEA)[L] Seattle, WA The Redemptionist Society of Washington; Seattle, WA Sacred Heart of Jesus.
Cleaton, C. Thomas '75 (CLV) Avon, OH St. Mary of the Immaculate Conception.
Cleator, Gerard B. *o.p.* '65 (CHI)[N] St. Pius V Priory.
Cleaveland, Raymond '06 (SEA) Seattle, WA Christ the King.
Clegg, Thomas E. '90 (IND) Jeffersonville, IN Sacred Heart; Jeffersonville, IN St. Augustine.
Clegg, Timothy '71 (LFT) On Duty Outside the Diocese.
Clemens, Bailey '98 (BAK) Pendleton, OR St. Mary; Council of Priests and Diocesan Consultors.
Clemens, John W. '72 (CHI)[W] Chicago, IL The Aquin Guild; College of Consultors; Rosemont, IL Our Lady of Hope.
Clemens, Neal C. '01 (MO) Air Force Chaplains.
Clemens, Neal '01 (OAK) Military Chaplains.
Clement, D. Blaine '08 (LAF) New Iberia, LA Our Lady of Perpetual Help.
Clement, Frederick *m.ss.cc.* '94 (CAM)[M] Linwood, NJ Villa Pieta. Missionaries of the Sacred Hearts of Jesus & Mary.
Clement, Philip Dac '08 (SP) Brandon, FL Church of the Nativity.
Clement, Richard H. '85 (ALN) Shillington, PA St. John Baptist de la Salle; Elected Members.
Clement, Thomas '95 (SFS) Alexandria, SD St. Mary of Mercy; Emery, SD St. Martin; Presbyteral Council.
Clement, Youssef *b.s.o.* (NTN) Methuen, MA Basilian Salvatorian Order.
Clemente, Joseph J. '81 (SY) East Syracuse, NY St. Matthew.
Clemente, Michael '55 (ALB) Retired.
Clemente, Santiago Rubio (NY) Bronx, NY St. Brendan.
Clemente, Vincent L. '76 (VEN) Wauchula, FL St. Michael.
Clementich, LeRoy E. *c.s.c.* '57 (FTW)[H] Notre Dame Congregation of Holy Cross, Indiana Province, Provincial House.
Clements, Charles '62 (MIA) Miami, FL St. Richard Retired.
Clements, Daniel A. '54 (NSH) Retired.
Clements, George H. '57 (CHI) Retired.
Clements, Robert '90 (PHX) Phoenix, AZ SS. Simon and Jude Roman Catholic Cathedral.
Clements, Thomas P. '55 (CHL) Retired.
Clements, Thomas P. '55 (MO) DEPARTMENT OF VETERANS AFFAIRS HOSPITALS AND CHAPLAINS.
Clemo, Ronald M. *s.j.* '67 (SJ)[D] San Jose, CA Bellarmine College Preparatory.
Clemons, Delma '66 (OWN) Retired.
Clennon, Raymond *o.carm.* '67 (CHI) Gurnee, IL St. Paul the Apostle.
Clerkin, Robert J. '80 (RVC) Glen Head, NY St. Paul the Apostle; Senate of Priests (Presbyteral Council/ College of Consultors); Priests' Retirement Board.
Clerkin, Thomas J. *c.s.p.* '85 (LA) Los Angeles, CA St. Paul the Apostle.
Clermont, John *o.f.m.cap.* '53 (NY) White Plains, NY Province of St. Mary; New York, NY St. John the Baptist.
Cleto, Jorge Luis *o.s.a.* '08 (NY) Staten Island, NY Our Lady of Good Counsel.
Cletus, Sales T. (Ranjan) '84 (AUS) Temple, TX St. Mary.
Cleu, Paul '74 (OAK) Retired.
Cleves, Simeon *o.f.m.* '55 (CIN)[N] Cincinnati, OH St. Francis Seraph Friary.
Cleves, Rev. Msgr. William '78 (COL)[A] Columbus, OH Pontifical College Josephinum; [A] Columbus, OH Pontifical College Josephinum.
Click, Patrick R. '71 (LFT) Fishers, IN St. Louis de Montfort.
Clifford, Donald P. '61 (BO) Senior Priests. Retired.
Clifford, James *o.s.a.* '72 (P)[L] Myrtle Creek, OR Augustinian Community; [J] Medford, OR Providence Medford Medical Center.
Clifford, Jerome *s.c.j.* '61 (MIL)[P] Hales Corners Priests of the Sacred Heart.
Clifford, Joseph G. '89 (VEN) Fort Myers, FL St. Columbkille.
Clifford, Leo *o.f.m.* '46 (BO)[X] Boston, MA Saint Anthony Residence Retired.
Clifford, Michael J. '60 (GB) Peshtigo, WI St. Mary Retired.
Clifford, Paul T. (BO) Hopkinton, MA St. John the Evangelist.
Clifford, Peter C. '76 (ROC) Fairport, NY St. John of Rochester; Newly Ordained Priests.
Clifford, Richard J. *s.j.* '66 (BO)[B] Chestnut Hill, MA The Ecclesiastical Faculty at Boston College; [C] The School of Theology and Ministry; [U] Cambridge, MA Claver House.
Clifford, Richard L. *m.m.* '53 (FgM) Maryknoll, NY MARYKNOLL.
Clifford, Richard (FTW)[B] University of Notre Dame Du Lac.
Clifford, Thomas F. *s.j.* '81 (WDC)[E] Washington, DC Gonzaga College High School; [N] Washington, DC The Jesuit Community of St. Aloysius Gonzaga; Washington, DC St. Aloysius.
Clifton, James F. *s.j.* '88 (OM) Omaha, NE St. Frances Cabrini; [K] Omaha, NE Jesuit Community at Creighton University.
Clinch, Kevin D. '83 (TUC) Casa Grande, AZ Saint Anthony of Padua Roman Catholic Parish – Casa Grande; [G] Casa Grande, AZ Central Arizona College, Holy Family Newman Center; Members.
Cline, Martin E. '05 (OG) Fort Covington, NY St. Mary; Fort Covington, NY St. Patrick; Fort Covington, NY St. Joseph.
Clinton, Donald E. '90 (MAN) Manchester, NH Sacred Heart of Jesus; Manchester, NH Ste. Marie; Elliott Hospital.
Clinton, Kevin I. '74 (STP) New Prague, MN St. Scholastica; New Prague, MN St. Joseph; New Prague, MN St. Wenceslaus; New Prague, MN St. Thomas.
Clisch, Norman A. '65 (MAR) Caspian, MI St. Cecilia; Iron River, MI St. Agnes.
Clody, Rev. Msgr. Albert W. '65 (BUF) Buffalo, NY All Saints.
Clogan, Paul M. '99 (PRT) Retired.
Cloherty, Francis J. '62 (BO) Brockton, MA Our Lady of Lourdes.
Cloherty, John J. '60 (SFR) San Francisco, CA St. Anne Retired.
Cloherty, Thomas '74 (DAL) Dallas, TX All Saints; Personnel Board.
Cloney, Michael W. '68 (SR) McKinleyville, CA Christ the King; Priests' Council.
Cloonan, Dennis '03 (CHY) Retired.
Clooney, Rev. Archpriest David '64 (PHU) Northampton, PA St. John the Baptist.
Clooney, Francis X. *s.j.* '78 (BO)[U] Cambridge, MA La Farge House.
Cloquet, Victor '50 (SEA) Retired.
Clore, Victor '65 (DET) Detroit, MI Christ the King; [T] Detroit, MI Dominican Center for Religious Development.
Close, Frederick J. '01 (WDC) Washington, DC St. Anthony; Priest Council.
Close, James J. '63 (CHI)[H] Chicago, IL Mission of Our Lady of Mercy–Mercy Home for Boys and Girls; Mercy Home for Boys and Girls Retired.
Close, Rev. Msgr. John A. '69 (PH) Wayne, PA St. Katharine of Siena.
Close, John L. '82 (MO) Navy Reserve Chaplains.
Close, John '82 (ALB) New Lebanon, NY Immaculate Conception.
Closner–Benavidez, Jonathan *o.m.i.* '03 (MIA) Miramar, FL St. Stephen.
Cloud, Charles W. '89 (TUC) Florence, AZ Assumption of the Blessed Virgin Mary Roman Catholic Parish – Florence.
Clough, Wulfstan F. *o.s.b.* '96 (GBG)[G] Latrobe, PA Saint Vincent Archabbey.
Clougherty, Paul L. '60 (BO) Senior Priests. Retired.
Cloutier, Roland C. '66 (NOR) Putnam, CT St. Mary Church of the Visitation; [J] Portland, CT Affirmation Counseling Center; Members; Continuing Education and Formation Commission for the Clergy.
Cloutier, Ronald F. '72 (GAL) Harris County Jail; Correctional Ministries (Jail Chaplains); Elected Members; Houston, TX All Saints.
Cloutier, Timothy D. '83 (STP) Waverly, MN St. Mary.
Clovis, Stephen M. '89 (MO) Eugene, OR St. Paul; Navy Reserve Chaplains.
Clubb, Ronald E. *s.t.p.* '86 (STP) Retired.
Clune, Malachy *o.p.* '60 (SJN)[C] San Juan, PR Fraternidad San Antonio.
Clutario, Reynaldo *s.o.l.t.* '93 (PHX) Camp Verde, AZ St. Frances Cabrini Roman Catholic Parish; Mayer, AZ St. Joseph Roman Catholic Mission Mayer, A Quasi–Parish.
Clyne, Rev. Msgr. Vincent F. '45 (NY) Retired.
Co, Anthony '05 (PEO) Champaign, IL St. John's Catholic Chapel; [M] Champaign, IL St. John's Catholic Newman Center at the University of Illinois, Urbana–Champaign.
Coady, Frank '76 (SAL) Salina, KS St. Elizabeth Ann Seton Parish; Art and Architecture Commission; Priests' Continuing Formation Committee; Director Adult Faith Formation; Office of Liturgy; Office of Deacons.
Coady, John '59 (GF) Retired.
Coakley, John P. *s.j.* '70 (CHI)[D] Chicago, IL St. Ignatius Jesuit Community; [J] Maywood, IL Loyola University Medical Center.
Coakley, Patrick *m.s.c.* '86 (AUS) Austin, TX St. Catherine of Siena.
Coan, Gregory S. '03 (WDC) Newburg, MD Holy Ghost.
Coates, John T. '45 (PH) Retired.
Cobb, Clement '03 (KCK) Olathe, KS St. Paul.
Cobb, Gerald T. *s.j.* '81 (SEA)[A] Seattle, WA Seattle University; [L] Seattle, WA Arrupe Jesuit Community at Seattle University.
Cobb, Richard E. *s.j.* '62 (SJ)[D] San Jose, CA Bellarmine College Preparatory.
Cobel, Lawrence F. '73 (BUF) Springville, NY St. Aloysius; West Valley, NY St. John the Baptist.
Cobenas, Pedro A. '92 (LA) Los Angeles, CA Our Lady of Guadalupe.
Cobona, Kusitino '84 (LAN) Grand Blanc, MI Holy Family.
Cobos, Jose A. (GAL) Houston, TX Resurrection.
Coby, Thomas W. '73 (RVC) Riverhead, NY St. John the Evangelist.
Cocca, Stephen M. '96 (WDC) Absent On Leave.
Cocco, William T. '04 (WIL)[A] Wilmington, DE St. Mark's High School; Hockessin, DE St. Mary of the Assumption.
Cochran, George L. *o.p.* '62 (PRO)[P] Providence St. Thomas Aquinas Priory at Providence College.
Cochran, Paul M. *s.j.* '94 (SPK)[J] Spokane, WA Regis Community.
Cochran, Paul W. '88 (LFT) Alexandria, IN St. Mary; Elwood, IN St. Joseph; Diocesan Consultors; Associate Judges; Presbyteral Council; Members.
Cochran, Ronald '01 (SD) El Cajon, CA St. Luke.
Cocio, Carlos '83 (TUC) Administrative Leave of Absence.
Cockayne, John E. '85 (HRT) Retired.
Cocucci, Joseph M.P.R. '96 (WIL) Wilmington, DE Cathedral of St. Peter; Office of Priestly and Religious Vocations and Seminarians and Newly Ordained; Diocese of Wilmington – Serra Club Information.
Coda, Joseph F. '63 (NEW)[M] Rutherford, NJ St. John Vianney Residence for Priests Retired.
Codd, Rev. Msgr. Kevin A. '79 (SPK) Othello, WA Sacred Heart.
Codd, Kevin '79 (SPK) Members.
Coddaire, Louis '78 (SR) Fortuna, CA St. Joseph; Garberville, CA Our Lady of the Redwoods; Scotia, CA St. Patrick.
Code, Sean K. '93 (ALT) Fallentimber, PA St. Thomas Aquinas; Fallentimber, PA St. Joan of Arc.
Codega, John C. '99 (PRO) West Warwick, RI Christ the King.
Codori, Joseph B. '00 (PIT) Canonsburg, PA St. Patrick.
Cody, Aelred *o.s.b.* '57 (IND)[K] St. Meinrad, IN St. Meinrad Archabbey.
Cody, Daniel '62 (STA) Jacksonville, FL St. Joseph's; Diocesan Consultors; Family Life, Diocesan Center for; Presbyteral Council.
Cody, Henry P. '58 (HRT) West Hartford, CT The Church of St. Timothy.

Cody, Rev. Msgr. John K. '73 (COL) Columbus, OH St. Christopher; Adjutant Judicial Vicar; Presiding Judges of First Instance.
Cody, John R. *c.ss.r.* '81 (TR)[R] Long Branch, NJ San Alfonso Retreat House.
Cody, Kevin W. '93 (MO) Military Chaplains; Air Force Chaplains.
Cody, Thomas '68 (STA) Absent or Sick Leave.
Coe, Austin J. '85 (MO) Army Reserve Chaplains.
Coelho, Adilso *c.o.* '01 (CHR) Rock Hill, SC St. Anne; [E] Rock Hill, SC Oratory of St. Philip Neri, Congregation of the Oratory of Pontifical Rite.
Coelho, Blaise (CHI) Tinley Park, IL St. George.
Coelho, Brian Alick '07 (WDC) Rockville, MD St. Elizabeth.
Coelho, Gabriel P. '78 (CC) Tivoli, TX Our Lady of Guadalupe.
Coelho, Oscar '08 (SFE) Santa Fe, NM The Cathedral Basilica of St. Francis of Assisi.
Coelho, Paul *s.j.* '88 (OM)[K] Omaha, NE Jesuit Community at Creighton University.
Coelho–Harguindeguy, Rev. Msgr. John '67 (FRS) Lemoore, CA St. Peter Prince of Apostles.
Coello, Demetrio *s.d.b.* '60 (ARE) Orocovis, PR San Juan Bautista.
Coen, Rev. Msgr. Charles P. '68 (NY) Red Hook, NY St. Christopher.
Coenen, Thomas '77 (DM) On Sabbatical.
Coens, Frank *o.f.m.* '73 (SHP) West Monroe, LA St. Paschal.
Coerber, Joseph H. '66 (MIL) New Holstein, WI St. Mary; Fond Du Lac, WI St. John the Baptist.
Coerver, Richard V. '76 (STL) Washington, MO St. Ann; Washington, MO St. Gertrude.
Coerver, Rev. Msgr. Robert M. '80 (DAL) Deans; Rockwall, TX Our Lady of the Lake; Consultors of Pastors; Censor Librorum.
Coffaro, Nicholas F. '08 (SAG) Midland, MI St. Brigid.
Coffas, William '04 (ROC) Geneva, NY Our Lady of Peace Roman Catholic Church of Geneva, NY.
Coffey, Rev. Msgr. Andrew V. '47 (SAC) Davis, CA St. James; Charismatic Renewal Retired.
Coffey, Brian *m.h.m.* '72 (NY) Suffern, NY Good Samaritan Hospital; Suffern, NY Sacred Heart.
Coffey, James Brian *m.h.m.* '72 (NY)[EE] Hartsdale, NY Mill Hill Fathers Residence.
Coffey, Joseph L. '96 (MO) Military Chaplains; Navy Chaplains.
Coffey, Michael J. '91 (CAM) Cherry Hill, NJ Holy Eucharist Parish, Cherry Hill, N.J.
Coffey, Peter *s.d.s.* (MIL)[P] Milwaukee Salvatorian Provincial Offices Retired.
Coffey, Stephen M. *o.s.b.* '07 (SFE)[H] Pecos, NM Our Lady of Guadalupe Abbey.
Cogan, James J. '04 (VEN) Bradenton, FL SS. Peter and Paul the Apostles.
Cogan, Patrick *s.a.* '77 (NY)[EE] Garrison Franciscan Friars of the Atonement, Minister General Office.
Cogan, William B. *s.j.* '55 (NY)[EE] New York, NY Murray–Weigel Hall.
Coghlan, Rev. Msgr. Brian '63 (ORG) Seal Beach, CA Holy Family Retired.
Coghlan, John '74 (MOB) Citronelle, AL St. Thomas; Mount Vernon, AL St. Cecilia.
Cohan, Dennis J. '74 (NEW) Clark, NJ St. Agnes.
Cohea, Victor H. '80 (NO)[Q] New Orleans, LA Sisters of the Holy Family Motherhouse, S.S.F.; [S] New Orleans, LA Pan African Roman Catholic Clergy Conference; Members At Large:; New Orleans, LA St. Maria Goretti.
Coine, Robert E. '76 (WIL) Easton, MD SS. Peter and Paul.
Coiro, Gregory *o.f.m.cap.* '82 (SFR)[B] San Francisco, CA Capuchin Franciscan Order San Buenaventura Friary.
Coiro, Mark J. '94 (BO) Holliston, MA St. Mary; Presbyteral Council.
Cokonougher, Brian K. '99 (DET) Port Huron, MI Holy Trinity.
Cokus, Rev. Msgr. Joseph J. '58 (LA) Retired.
Colacicco, Rev. Msgr. Gerardo J. '82 (NY) Hopewell Junction, NY St. Columba.
Colacino, John A. *c.pp.s.* '80 (ROC)[J] Rochester, NY Missionaries of the Precious Blood.
Colagreco, Michael A. '77 (PH) Lenni, PA St. Francis de Sales.
Colaj, Rene Otzoy *o.s.b.* '82 (RCK)[G] Aurora, IL Marmion Abbey.
Colamaria, Francis A. '01 (BRK) Richmond Hill, NY Holy Child Jesus.
Colamarino, Dennis J. '73 (PIT) Duquesne, PA St. Joseph; Duquesne, PA Christ the Light of the World.
Colankin, Dimitrij '76 (AUS) Caldwell, TX St. Mary; Caldwell, TX Holy Rosary.
Colapietro, Peter M. '76 (NY) New York, NY Holy Cross; New York Sanitation Department.
Colaresi, Robert E. *o.carm.* '67 (JOL)[L] Darien, IL St. Simon Stock Priory; [N] Darien, IL Carmelite Spiritual Center; [O] Darien, IL Society of the Little Flower; [O] Darien, IL National Shrine of St. Therese; Councilors:.
Colarusso, Darin V. '06 (BO) Braintree, MA St. Francis of Assisi.
Colasito, Basil C. '59 (RVC) Great Neck, NY St. Aloysius Retired.
Colasurdo, Peter '77 (STA) Retired.
Colautti, Federico '92 (DEN)[A] Denver, CO Redemptoris Mater House of Formation.
Colavechio, Xavier G. *o.praem.* '55 (GB)[J] De Pere, WI St. Norbert Abbey.
Colavechio, Xavier *o.praem.* '55 (JKS) Diocesan Judges.
Colberg, Rev. Msgr. James Philip '55 (LA) Santa Maria, CA St. Mary of the Assumption Retired.
Colbert, Richard K. *s.m.* '64 (WDC)[N] Washington, DC Marist Center Retired.
Colbert, Richard *c.pp.s.* '69 (KC)[J] Liberty, MO Precious Blood Center.
Colborn, Francis R. '63 (LA) Retired.
Colchin, Stephen E. '84 (FTW) New Haven, IN St. Louis; Monroeville, IN St. Rose of Lima.
Cole, Barry '82 (PEO)[N] Urbana, IL Opus Dei.
Cole, Basil Burr *o.p.* '66 (WDC)[B] Washington, DC Dominican House of Studies.
Cole, Edwin J. '64 (JC) Laurie, MO Shrine of St. Patrick; VII. Sedalia/Lake Ozark; Appointed Members.
Cole, G. Barry '82 (POD) Urbana.
Cole, James J. '71 (BGP)[P] Monroe, CT Sisters of the Holy Family of Nazareth, C.S.F.N.
Cole, Rev. Msgr. Raymond L. '72 (MET) Hillsborough, NJ St. Joseph.
Cole, Robert F. '72 (MAN) Priest Personnel Board.
Cole, Robert F. '71 (MAN) Wolfeboro, NH St. Katharine Drexel; Presbyteral Council.
Cole, Robert J. '72 (CLV) Oberlin, OH Sacred Heart.
Cole, Robert J. '06 (RIC) Virginia Beach, VA St. John the Apostle Church.
Cole, Vincent P. *m.m.* '71 (FgM) Maryknoll, NY MARYKNOLL.
Colella, David *o.ss.t* '57 (BAL)[S] Baltimore, MD.
Colello, Michael A. '01 (PRO) Providence, RI Cathedral of SS. Peter and Paul; Bishop's Office & Chancery Office.
Coleman, Rev. Msgr. Brian P. '63 (GB) Vice–Chancellor; Adjutant Judicial Vicars; College of Consultors; Judges Retired.
Coleman, C. Michael '67 (KC) Special Assignment; Judge; Archivist.
Coleman, Christopher C. '06 (CIN) Dayton, OH St. Anthony of Padua.
Coleman, Christopher L. '94 (BRK) Members At Large:; Brooklyn, NY Queen of All Saints; Brooklyn, NY Saint Martin de Porres.
Coleman, Christopher (NO)[S] New Orleans, LA Pan African Roman Catholic Clergy Conference.
Coleman, Donald E. '74 (SD) Carlsbad, CA St. Elizabeth Seton.
Coleman, Gerald D. *s.s.* '68 (SFR) Redwood City, CA St. Pius.
Coleman, Gerald D. *s.s.* '68 (BAL)[S] Baltimore Society of St. Sulpice, Province of the United States.
Coleman, Gerald J. '78 (TLS)[E] Tulsa, OK St. John Medical Center, Inc.; Special Assignment.
Coleman, Rev. Msgr. James G. '62 (HRT) Consultors – Canon 1742; Waterbury, CT SS. Peter and Paul; Episcopal Vicars; College of Consultors; Waterbury, CT St. Leo the Great; Ex Officio Members; Archbishop's Annual Appeal Retired.
Coleman, James Montini '99 (MOB) Belle Fontaine, AL St. Philip Neri.
Coleman, James '76 (COL) Columbus, OH Our Lady of the Miraculous Medal.
Coleman, James '73 (P) On Duty Outside the Archdiocese.
Coleman, John A. '67 (SFR)[N] San Francisco, CA Loyola House Jesuit Community; San Francisco, CA St. Ignatius.
Coleman, John J. '54 (NY) Retired.
Coleman, John K. '71 (SFR) Veterans' Hospital.
Coleman, John Kenneth '71 (MO) DEPARTMENT OF VETERANS AFFAIRS HOSPITALS AND CHAPLAINS.
Coleman, John R. '88 (PHX) Chandler, AZ St. Andrew the Apostle Roman Catholic Parish.
Coleman, John R. '50 (SFR) East Palo Alto, CA St. Francis of Assisi Retired.
Coleman, John *o.carm.* '78 (LA)[P] Encino, CA Our Lady of Mount Carmel Priory.
Coleman, John '71 (SFR) On Duty Outside the Archdiocese.
Coleman, Rev. Msgr. John '50 (SJ) Retired.
Coleman, Michael A. '81 (JC) Moberly, MO St. Pius X; Moberly, MO Moberly Correctional Center; Teens Encounter Christ (TEC).
Coleman, Paul '03 (OAK) Danville, CA St. Isidore.
Coleman, R. Ed '86 (P) Molalla, OR St. James.
Coleman, Rev. Msgr. Robert F. '78 (NEW)[A] South Orange, NJ Immaculate Conception Seminary; [B] School of Theology; [B] School of Diplomacy and Intl. Rels.
Coleman, Robert J. '87 (JOL) Beaverville, IL St. Mary; Beaverville, IL St. Martin; Deans.
Coleman, Robert P. '78 (CHI) Other Assignments.
Coless, Gabriel M. *o.s.b.* '57 (PAT)[N] Morristown, NJ St. Mary's Abbey.
Coletta, Rev. Msgr. Thomas J. '63 (PAT) Clergy Personnel Office; Paterson, NJ Our Lady of Victories.
Coletti, Arnold F. '62 (BO) Lexington, MA Sacred Heart; Presbyteral Council.
Coley, James E. '47 (TR) Retired.
Coley, James '47 (TR)[N] Trenton, NJ St. Lawrence Rehabilitation Center Retired.
Colgan, John '48 (SP) Retired.
Colgan, John (LSC) Retired.
Colgan, Thomas A. *s.j.* '75 (BUF)[O] Buffalo, NY Canisius Jesuit Community Inc.; [R] Buffalo, NY Canisius College, Campus Ministry Office.
Colgan, Rev. Msgr. Thomas J. '49 (RVC) Northport, NY St. Philip Neri Retired.
Colgan, Tobias *o.s.b.* '82 (EVN)[F] Ferdinand, IN Sisters of St. Benedict of Ferdinand, IN, Inc., Monastery Immaculate Conception; Saint Meinrad, IN.
Colgan, Tobias *o.s.b.* '82 (IND)[K] St. Meinrad, IN St. Meinrad Archabbey.
Colhour, David *c.p.* '94 (SAC)[I] Citrus Heights, CA Christ the King Retreat; [K] Citrus Heights, CA Christ the King Passionist Retreat Center.
Colibraro, Daniel '56 (CHY) Retired.
Colibraro, Philip '57 (CHY) Retired.
Colicchio, Damian '62 (NEW)[B] Lodi, NJ Lodi Campus; [N] Lodi, NJ Immaculate Conception Convent.
Colicchio, Ralph M. '67 (HRT) New Haven, CT St. Anthony; New Haven, CT St. Michael.
Colin, Alberto '09 (SAT) Kerrville, TX Notre Dame.
Colina, Jose '89 (SP) Tampa, FL St. Paul.
Coll, Eduardo *i.v.e.* '88 (PH) Philadelphia, PA St. Veronica.
Coll, Jerome B. *s.j.* '59 (PH)[Y] Loyola Center and Manresa Hall.
Coll, John J. *s.j.* '56 (WH)[A] Wheeling, WV Wheeling Jesuit University.
Coll, Rev. Msgr. Robert J. '59 (ALN) Bethlehem, PA Assumption B.V.M. Retired.
Collado, Domingo '93 (BRK) Jamaica, NY Presentation of the Blessed Virgin Mary.
Collard, Bruce W. '80 (MAN) Nashua, NH St. Christopher; [L] Manchester, NH St. George Manor.
Colleary, Patrick '74 (PHX) On Leave.
Colleoni, Xavier *m.c.c.j.* '52 (LA) Los Angeles, CA St. Cecilia.
Coller, Jerome *o.s.b.* '59 (SCL)[I] Collegeville, MN St. John's Abbey, of the Order of St. Benedict.
Colleran, James A. '63 (CHI) Retired.
Collet, John *o.m.i.* '67 (SAT)[A] San Antonio, TX Assumption Seminary.
Colletta, Ralph V. '61 (CLV) Retired.
Collette, Rev. Msgr. Richard '52 (WOR) Retired.
Colletti, Arnold F. (BO) Lexington, MA St. Brigid.
Colletti, Peter '84 (CLV) Independence, OH St. Michael.
Colletti, Richard M. '78 (WIN) Winona, MN Cathedral of the Sacred Heart; Winona, MN St. Casimir's; Diocesan Consultors.
Collier, Joseph '58 (SD) Retired.
Colligan, James P. *m.m.* '55 (LA)[P] Los Angeles, CA Retired.
Colling, Paul J. '87 (GI) Lexington, NE St. Ann's; Hispanic Ministry; Priests' Advisory Board (Presbyteral Council); CEC (Catholics Encounter Christ); Diocesan Consultors.
Collini, Rev. Msgr. Celsus O. '47 (BRK) Retired.
Collins, Austin I. *c.s.c.* '82 (FTW)[B] University of Notre Dame Du Lac; [H] Notre Dame, IN Holy Cross Community, Corby Hall, University of Notre Dame.
Collins, Carl '91 (HT) Houma, LA Our Lady of the Most Holy Rosary; Priests Council; Terrebonne Deanery; College of Consultors.
Collins, Charles E. '72 (BO) Cambridge, MA St. John the Evangelist.
Collins, Charles Reid '05 (PT) Panama City, FL St. Dominic.
Collins, Charlie I. '82 (WIN) Rochester, MN St. Pius X; Propagation of the Faith.
Collins, Christopher S. *s.j.* '06 (BO)[U] Newton, MA The Jesuit Community at Boston College.
Collins, Corwin *o.s.b.* '57 (SCL) Richmond, MN St. Catherine's; St. Martin, MN St. Martin; [I] Collegeville, MN St. John's Abbey, of the Order of St. Benedict.
Collins, Daniel J. '58 (CHI) Chicago, IL St. Mary of the Lake Retired.
Collins, David J. *s.j.* '98 (WDC)[N] Washington, DC The Jesuit Community at Georgetown University.
Collins, Denis E. *s.j.* '69 (LA) Santa Barbara, CA Our Lady of Sorrows.
Collins, Edward A. '68 (PAT)[K] Paterson, NJ St. Joseph's Hospital and Medical Center; Paterson, NJ St. Joseph Hospital.
Collins, Edwin J. '54 (RVC) Retired.
Collins, James B. '04 (NY) Bronx, NY St. Benedict.
Collins, James J. '64 (PH) Philadelphia, PA Saint Martha; [C] Philadelphia, PA Holy Family University; On Special or Other Archdiocesan Assignment.

Collins, James M. *s.j.* '58 (BO)[U] Weston, MA Campion Health Center, Inc.
Collins, James M. '95 (CHL) Newton, NC St. Joseph.
Collins, James R. '68 (CIN) Retired.
Collins, James R. '81 (PRO) Cranston, RI St. Matthew.
Collins, James *s.j.* '05 (CHI) Chicago, IL St. Procopius.
Collins, John E. *c.s.p.* '70 (NY)[EE] New York, NY Paulist Fathers' Motherhouse.
Collins, John Michal '69 (LA) On Active Leave.
Collins, John P. '72 (PH) Yeadon, PA St. Louis.
Collins, John *c.ss.r.* '87 (PH)[C] Gwynedd Valley, PA Gwynedd–Mercy College.
Collins, John (CHI) College of Consultors; Vicar for Priests.
Collins, John '98 (LA) Burbank, CA St. Robert Bellarmine.
Collins, Kevin A. *o.m.i.* '82 (GAL) Houston, TX Immaculate Conception.
Collins, Kevin S. *c.m.* '85 (CHI)[N] Chicago DePaul Vincentian Residence.
Collins, Lawrence E. '77 (CHI) Cicero, IL Our Lady of the Mount.
Collins, Leonard J. *c.s.c.* '69 (FTW) South Bend, IN St. Adalbert; South Bend, IN St. Augustine.
Collins, Michael J. '67 (BR) Baton Rouge, LA Most Blessed Sacrament.
Collins, Michael T. *o.praem.* '78 (PH)[Y] Paoli, PA Daylesford Abbey.
Collins, Michael T. *o.praem.* '78 (WIL)[B] Claymont, DE Archmere Academy.
Collins, Rev. Msgr. Michael '43 (ORG) Seal Beach, CA St. Anne's Retired.
Collins, Neil J. '58 (NEW) Retired.
Collins, Patrick '64 (PEO) Retired.
Collins, Raymond F. '59 (PRO) Retired.
Collins, Raymond *c.ss.r.* (BO) Boston, MA Our Lady of Perpetual Help.
Collins, Richard '04 (FWT) Henrietta, TX St. Jerome; Henrietta, TX St. Mary; Henrietta, TX St. William; Henrietta, TX St. Joseph.
Collins, Robert C. *s.j.* '67 (NY)[EE] New York, NY "America;" Residence and publication office of the America Press.
Collins, Robert '88 (BRK) On Leave/Unassigned.
Collins, Seamus *o.p.* '58 (SP) Hudson, FL St. Michael the Archangel.
Collins, Shannon *c.p.m.* '00 (L) Glasgow, KY St. Helen.
Collins, Stephen L. '83 (E) Retired.
Collins, Terrence '71 (R) Hampstead, NC St. Jude the Apostle.
Collins, Thomas E. '92 (NY)[E] White Plains, NY Archbishop Stepinac High School.
Collins, Thomas S. '92 (PT) Santa Rosa Beach, FL Christ the King Mission; Santa Rosa Beach, FL St. Rita.
Collins, Rev. Msgr. Timothy '58 (NY) New York, NY Our Lady of the Rosary; [EE] Bronx, NY John Cardinal O'Connor Residence Retired.
Collins, Vincent *o.c.s.o.* '72 (ARL)[H] Berryville, VA Cistercian Abbey of Our Lady of the Holy Cross.
Collins, Rev. Msgr. William A. '95 (BAL) Randallstown, MD Holy Family.
Collins, William A. '61 (BAL) Retired.
Collins, William B. '74 (PAT) Hamburg, NJ St. Jude the Apostle; Vocations Board.
Collins, William Emmett *c.ss.r.* '52 (STL)[O] Liguori, MO St. Clement Health Care Center Retired.
Collins, William F. '65 (CAM) Retired.
Collins, Rev. Msgr. William J. '60 (NY) Livingston Manor, NY St. Aloysius.
Collins, William P. '56 (RCK) Retired.
Collins, William *m.s.c.* '67 (SAT) San Antonio, TX Immaculate Conception; [L] San Antonio, TX Missionaries of the Sacred Heart; Sectional Leadership Team.
Colliou, Alain M. '09 (WDC) Waldorf, MD St. Peter.
Collison, Craig A. '78 (SC) Sioux City, IA Sacred Heart; Presbyteral Council.
Collogan, Robert '82 (JOL) Absent on Leave.
Collopy, Rev. Msgr. John C. '56 (BAL) Hydes, MD St. John the Evangelist; Lutherville Timonium, MD Retired.
Collucci, Bennett *o.f.m.cap.* '57 (SAL)[D] Victoria, KS St. Fidelis Friary.
Collum, Patrick '92 (NO) Bogalusa, LA Annunciation Catholic Church.
Colnaghi, Andrew *o.s.b.cam.* '79 (MRY)[F] Big Sur New Camaldoli Hermitage.
Colnaghi, Andrew '79 (OAK)[M] Berkeley, CA Incarnation Monastery, Camaldolese Benedictines.
Colohan, Edward A. '61 (BGP)[O] Stamford, CT The Catherine Dennis Keefe Queen of the Clergy Retired Priests' Residence Retired.
Colom, Marti '00 (MIL)[V] Racine, WI Community of St. Paul, Inc.; On Duty Outside the Archdiocese.
Coloma, Alberto Vasquez '93 (PHX) Phoenix, AZ St. Vincent de Paul Roman Catholic Parish.
Colombo, Ronald A. '72 (GB) Denmark, WI St. James; Denmark, WI All Saints; De Pere, WI St. Mary; Kellnersville, WI St. Joseph; Denmark, WI Holy Trinity Mission.
Colominas, Octavio '02 (MIA) Absent on Leave.
Colon, Alberto Diaz '85 (ARE) Priest's Senate (Consejo Presbiteral); Defenders of the Bond.
Colon, Angel '95 (CGS) Gurabo, PR San Jose.
Colon, Hector *c.ss.r.* '76 (CGS) Aguas Buenas, PR Church of Tres Santos Reyes.
Colon, Jackson '90 (CHI) Chicago, IL St. Ignatius.
Colon, Jorge *c.ss.r.* (SJN) San Juan, PR San Agustin.
Colon, Jose E. '63 (PCE) On Duty Outside the Diocese.
Colon, Jose '01 (ARE) Vega Baja, PR Parroquia de San Martin de Porres.
Colon, Rev. Msgr. Jose '61 (PCE) Retired.
Colon, Rene A. (ARE) Arecibo, PR Our Lady of Guadalupe.
Colon, Vincent A. '50 (STP) Retired.
Colopelnic, Vasile '04 (STF) Spring Valley, NY SS. Peter and Paul; Catechetics (Heritage Schools).
Colopy, James L. '86 (COL) Columbus, OH St. Dominic; OSU Hospital East.
Colosimo, Felix R. '65 (SY) New Hartford, NY Our Lady of the Rosary.
Colozzi, Charles J. '02 (CAM) Barrington, NJ Church of St. Francis de Sales, Barrington, N.J.
Colpitts, Albert B. '73 (PRT) Limerick, ME St. Matthew.
Colter, Dennis J. '66 (DUB) Gilbertville, IA Immaculate Conception; Gilbertville, IA St. Joseph; [G] Gilbertville, IA Don Bosco High School.
Colton, Bernard '50 (PHX) Retired.
Colton, Gary P. '68 (HON) Lahaina, HI Maria Lanakila; Presbyteral Council.
Colucci, Bennett '57 (SAL) Retired.
Colvin, Andrew '02 (MO) Navy Chaplains; Military Services.
Colwell, Michael P. '94 (SAT) Defenders of the Bond.
Colwell, Rev. Msgr. Michael P. '94 (AMA) Marriage Encounter; Promoter of Justice; [I] Amarillo, TX Project Solidarity; [I] Amarillo, TX Marriage Encounter; College of Consultors; [I] Amarillo, TX Pope John Paul II House of Discernment; Borger, TX St. John the Evangelist.
Coman, Christopher M. '08 (SAG) Lexington, MI St. Patrick; Lexington, MI St. Denis.
Comandini, Glenn J. '86 (MET) Theological Commission.
Comandini, Glenn J. *s.t.d.* '86 (MET) Basking Ridge, NJ St. James.
Comboy, Richard *s.j.* '69 (STL)[O] St. Louis, MO Jesuit Community Corporation at Saint Louis University – Jesuit Hall.
Combs, Gordon *o.f.m.cap.* '64 (HON) Office of Clergy Priest Retirement Committee; Honolulu, HI Cathedral of Our Lady of Peace Retired.
Combs, J. Derran *o.f.m.* '94 (JOL) Joliet, IL St. John the Baptist; [A] Joliet, IL University of St. Francis; [L] Joliet, IL St. John the Baptist Friary.
Combs, Ronald P. '03 (CIN) Dayton, OH St. Henry.
Combs, Will '04 (SAT) San Antonio, TX St. Mary Magdalen.
Combs, William H. '04 (SAT)[S] San Antonio, TX Brothers of the Beloved Disciple.
Comeau, Ronald R. '71 (LFT) On Duty Outside the Diocese.
Comer, John P. '64 (STL) Crestwood, MO St. Elizabeth of Hungary Retired.
Comer, Michael E. '80 (COV) Burlington, KY Immaculate Heart of Mary; Diocesan Consultors.
Comerford, Christopher J. '96 (SFD) Granite City, IL St. Elizabeth.
Comerford, John J. *o.carm.* '77 (JOL)[L] Joliet, IL St. Elias Carmelites.
Comerford, Patrick '69 (LA)[J] Santa Monica, CA Saint John's Health Center; [L] Santa Monica, CA Saint John's Child Study Center, Saint John's Hospital & Health Center; Hospital Chaplains.
Comesanas, Raul E.L. '77 (NEW) Newark, NJ St. Thomas Aquinas.
Comeskey, John H. '56 (SY) Utica, NY St. Elizabeth Hospital; [M] Utica, NY St. Elizabeth Medical Center Retired.
Comesky, Clement *o.f.m.* '55 (FgM) New York, NY Holy Name Province.
Comiskey, Rev. Msgr. James '50 (LUB) Kansas City, MO Retired.
Comiskey, John P. '60 (NY)[E] Staten Island, NY Monsignor Farrell High School.
Comisky, John *c.s.c.* '68 (FgM) St Columbans, NE House of Post–Graduate Studies.
Commons, Patrick M. '51 (IND)[I] Beech Grove, IN St. Paul Hermitage Retired.
Commyn, James E. '86 (DET) St. Clair Shores, MI St. Lucy.
Comparan, Jose Luis '03 (DUB) Waterloo, IA Queen of Peace.
Compbell, Gerardo *c.ss.r.* (SJN) San Juan, PR San Agustin.
Compentente, Virgilio '67 (NY) Yonkers, NY Immaculate Conception.
Complo, Daniel C. '54 (DET) Retired.
Compton, Matthew Ross '04 (CHI) Chicago, IL Holy Name Cathedral.
Comstock, Douglas G. '67 (OG) Diocesan Consultors; Alexandria Bay, NY St. Cyril of Alexandria (Catholic Community of Alexandria).
Comtois, Norman *o.m.i.* '73 (BO)[U] Lowell, MA Missionary Oblates of Mary Immaculate.
Conahan, Rev. Msgr. John J. '62 (PH) Jenkintown, PA Immaculate Conception.
Conan, Constantine J. *c.s.sp.* '48 (PIT)[O] Bethel Park, PA The Spiritan Center.
Conard, James A. *m.m.* '56 (FgM) Maryknoll, NY MARYKNOLL.
Conard, Ray J. '55 (GB) Retired.
Conaty, Charles '88 (CAM) Hammonton, NJ St. Martin de Porres Roman Catholic Church, Hammonton, N.J.
Conboy, Michael F. '62 (ROC)[J] Rochester, NY Becket Hall; Priests' Personnel Board; Pension Committee (Lay and Priests).
Conboy, Michael '62 (ROC) Rochester, NY St. Thomas More; Department of Priest Personnel; Office of Vocations; Priest Consultors.
Conboy, Richard L. *s.t.l.* '60 (PIT) Allegheny County, PA Kane Regional Center – Scott.
Conboy, Richard '60 (PIT)[N] Coraopolis, PA Our Lady of the Sacred Heart Convent.
Concannon, Stephen F. '64 (PRT) Retired.
Concannon, Stephen F. '64 (MAN) Hampton, NH Our Lady of the Miraculous Medal.
Concepcion, Mervin P. '03 (SAC) Tulelake, CA Holy Cross; Weed, CA Holy Family; Vicars Forane.
Concepcion, Pablo J. '93 (POD)[G] Guaynabo, PR Opus Dei; San Juan.
Concepcion, Pablo '93 (PCE)[G] Ponce, PR Prelature of the Holy Cross and Opus Dei.
Concha, Alfonso J. '76 (MO) Military Chaplains; Navy Chaplains.
Concha, Antonio *s.j.* '63 (ELP) El Paso, TX Sacred Heart.
Concha, Augusto M. '72 (PH) Lansdale, PA St. Stanislaus.
Concik, Michael (NY) East Elmhurst, NY Correctional Institution for Men.
Concordia, George Lawrence *o.p.* '58 (NY)[EE] New York, NY St. Catherine of Siena Priory; [II] New York, NY Dominican Shrine of St. Jude, Inc.
Conde, Francis Enrico '74 (PAT) Paterson, NJ St. Joseph Hospital.
Conde, Norberto '89 (GAL) Houston, TX Our Lady of Sorrows.
Conde, Ramon (PCE) San Judas Tadeo.
Conde, Thomas P. '87 (CHI) Chicago, IL Christ the King; Deans.
Condon, Daniel J. '81 (ROC) Chancellor; Chancellor and Director of the Department of Legal Services; College of Consultors; Board of Directors; Vicar for Religious; Pension Committee (Lay and Priests); Priest Consultors.
Condon, Denis '78 (CHI) Schaumburg, IL St. Marcelline.
Condon, Edwin D. '61 (BO) Senior Priests.; Presbyteral Council; Pastoral Care of Clergy Retired.
Condon, Gerald A. '56 (DUB) Retired.
Condon, Gerald W. '55 (BAK) Northern; Heppner, OR St. Patrick's; Heppner, OR St. William.
Condon, Liam '63 (ALB) Cambridge, NY St. Patrick; Salem, NY Holy Cross.
Condon, Robert M. '56 (SC) Retired.
Condon, Sean '57 (ORG) Newport Beach, CA Our Lady of Mount Carmel Retired.
Condon, Rev. Msgr. T. Mark '89 (PAT) Little Falls, NJ Our Lady of the Holy Angels; Theological Commission; Deans; Defenders of the Bond; Office of Worship and Spirituality; Liturgical Commission.
Condon, Thomas M. *o.p.* '88 (MEM) Memphis, TN St. Peter Church; [F] Memphis, TN The Dominican Friars of Memphis, Inc.
Condon, William F. '54 (RIC) Retired.
Condon, William G. *c.s.c.* '61 (MO) Navy Reserve Chaplains.
Condon, William G. *c.s.c.* '61 (FR)[G] North Dartmouth, MA Holy Cross Residence; [G] North Dartmouth, MA St. Joseph's Hall Retired.
Condron, Robert F. '69 (HRT) Ansonia, CT Assumption.
Conelly, Marcos A. '03 (ARE) Arecibo, PR Our Lady of Guadalupe.
Conen, Paul F. *s.j.* '57 (DET)[K] Clarkston, MI Colombiere Center.
Conesa, Rev. Msgr. Diego '57 (STA) Retired.
Confer, Bernard T. *o.p.* '73 (HRT) New Haven, CT St. Mary's Priory.
Confer, Thomas B. *o.p.* '73 (HRT)[M] North Guilford, CT Monastery of Our Lady of Grace; [M] North Guilford, CT Monastery of Our Lady of Grace.
Congdon, John '00 (MO) Army Chaplains; On Duty Outside the Diocese.
Congdon, Robert J. '87 (BO) Brookline, MA St. Mary of the Assumption.
Congro, Basil P. '78 (CHR) Absent On Leave.
Conheeney, Thomas P. '55 (NEW) Bayonne, NJ St. Mary Star of the Sea.
Coning, Jeffrey '97 (COL) Office of Vocations; Dublin, OH St. Brigid of Kildare.

Conka, Francis *c.o.* '98 (NY) Tappan, NY Our Lady of the Sacred Heart.
Conkle–Ryan, Francisco *s.t.* '78 (FAJ) Loiza, PR Santiago Apostol, El Mayor.
Conlan, Rev. Msgr. F. Allan '54 (SCR) Retired.
Conlan, Timothy *o.p.* '67 (FgM)[M] Oakland Order of Preachers (Province of the Most Holy Name of Jesus – Western Dominican Province); Oakland, CA Province of the Holy Name (Western Dominican Province).
Conlan, Walter J. *s.j.* '76 (BGP)[B] Fairfield, CT Fairfield University; [O] Fairfield, CT The Fairfield Jesuit Community–Fairfield University.
Conley, Brian J. *s.j.* '01 (WDC)[L] Washington, DC Georgetown University Hospital; [N] Washington, DC The Jesuit Community at Georgetown University.
Conley, Brian J. *s.j.* '01 (BO)[U] Boston The Society of Jesus of New England–Provincial Offices.
Conley, Charles '74 (MIL) Wauwatosa, WI St. Jude the Apostle.
Conley, John E. *c.s.c.* '79 (FTW)[B] University of Notre Dame Du Lac; [H] Notre Dame, IN Holy Cross Community, Corby Hall, University of Notre Dame.
Conley, John *c.p.* '76 (L) Louisville, KY St. Agnes; [L] Louisville, KY Sacred Heart Retreat.
Conley, John *s.j.* '83 (BAL)[S] Baltimore, MD Jesuit Community of Loyola University, Inc.; [B] Jesuit Community of Loyola University, Inc.
Conley, Lawrence '67 (PRT) Gorham, ME St. Anne; [M] Gorham Campus; Pastoral Associates.
Conley, Martin P. '57 (OM) Retired.
Conley, Michael T. *s.j.* '07 (CHI)[N] Chicago, IL Miguel Pro Jesuit Community; Chicago, IL St. Procopius.
Conley, Rev. Msgr. Peter V. '64 (BO) Norfolk, MA St. Jude; Elected.
Conley, Rory T. '89 (WDC) Gaithersburg, MD St. John Neumann; Special Ministries.
Conley, Roy H. '61 (PIT)[M] Pittsburgh, PA St. John Vianney Manor Retired.
Conley, Seraphin J. *t.o.r.* '61 (ORL)[F] New Smyrna Beach, FL Villa Madonna Retired.
Conlin, Matthew T. *o.f.m.* '45 (ALB) Mount McGregor Correctional Facility; [B] Siena College.
Conlon, Anthony J. '62 (WH) Retired.
Conlon, Arthur F. '54 (TR) Retired.
Conlon, Christopher W. *s.m.* '66 (CIN)[D] Dayton, OH The University of Dayton; [N] Dayton, OH Marianist Community.
Conlon, Colmbanus '59 (ORG) Retired.
Conlon, James P. '02 (LAN) Westphalia, MI St. Mary.
Conlon, James '64 (OAK)[B] Holy Names University.
Conlon, Philip J. '55 (MAD) Forsyth, MO Our Lady of the Ozarks Retired.
Conlon, Richard '90 (BRK) Jackson Heights, NY Blessed Sacrament.
Conlon, Timothy *o.s.c.* '79 (PHX)[F] Phoenix, AZ; Phoenix, AZ Sacred Heart Roman Catholic Parish.
Conn, James J. *s.j.* '74 (BO)[U] Newton, MA The Jesuit Community at Boston College.
Conn, James J. *s.j.* '74 (BAL)[S] Towson Maryland Province of the Society of Jesus; Canonical & Theological Consultants to the Archbishop.
Connaghan, Daniel H. '90 (HRT) Retired.
Connall, Darrin '92 (SPK)[A] Spokane, WA Bishop White Seminary; Vocation Director; Bishop White Seminary.
Connaughton, James '50 (MIA) Deerfield Beach, FL St. Ambrose Retired.
Connaughton, Rev. Msgr. Lawrence M. '70 (NY) New York, NY Our Lady of the Scapular and St. Stephen; New York, NY Sacred Hearts of Jesus and Mary.
Connealy, Gerald A. '87 (OM) Stanton, NE St. Peter.
Connell, Rev. Msgr. Andrew F. '51 (BO) Senior Priests. Retired.
Connell, James E. '87 (MIL) Sheboygan, WI St. Clement; Sheboygan, WI Holy Name; Judges for Second Instance; Special Assignment.
Connell, James E. (MIL) Vice Chancellor.
Connell, John Andrew '81 (PAT) Randolph, NJ Resurrection.
Connell, John F. '62 (WOR) Retired.
Connell, John M. '85 (LR) Springdale, AR St. Raphael; Presbyteral Council.
Connell, Kevin *s.j.* (SPK)[D] Spokane, WA Gonzaga Preparatory School.
Connell, Loren *o.f.m.* '76 (CIN)[M] Centerville, OH St. Leonard; [U] Centerville, OH St. Leonard Faith Community; [N] Cincinnati St. Francis Seraph Friary.
Connell, Mark J. '86 (NY)[II] Chappaqua, NY Newburgh San Miguel Program; [H] Newburgh, NY San Miguel Academy of Newburgh.
Connell, Mark '86 (NY) Newburgh, NY Sacred Heart.
Connell, Martin T. *s.j.* '94 (FgM) Detroit, MI Detroit Province; [K] Detroit Jesuit Provincial Office–Detroit Province of the Society of Jesus.
Connell, Patrick J. '92 (DET) Berkley, MI Our Lady of La Salette.
Connell, Stephen J. '62 (WIL) Braintree, MA Retired.
Connell, Rev. Msgr. William J. '76 (Y) Poland, OH Holy Family; Judges.
Connell, William R. '75 (MAD) Oregon, WI Holy Mother of Consolation.
Connelly, Brennan *o.f.m.* '56 (BO)[Z] Boston, MA St. Anthony Shrine.
Connelly, Rev. Msgr. Christopher D. '93 (SPR) Springfield, MA St. Michael's Cathedral; Springfield, MA Holy Family; Vicars General; Bishop's Commission for Clergy; Bishop's Cabinet; Diocesan Consultors; Massachusetts Catholic Conference; Judges; Defenders of the Bond; Presbyteral Council.
Connelly, Donald F. '58 (WIN) Retired.
Connelly, Edward C. '65 (BAL) Crofton, MD St. Elizabeth Ann Seton.
Connelly, Fidelis *c.p.* '50 (PMB)[H] North Palm Beach, FL Our Lady of Florida Spiritual Center.
Connelly, Rev. Msgr. James E. '55 (PH) Philadelphia, PA St. Monica Retired.
Connelly, Rev. Msgr. James N. '49 (BUF)[O] Tonawanda, NY O'Hara Residence Retired.
Connelly, James *c.s.c.* (FTW)[H] Notre Dame Congregation of Holy Cross, Indiana Province, Provincial House.
Connelly, John J. '50 (BO) Newton, MA Sacred Heart; Dorchester, MA St. Ann.
Connelly, Laurence D. (GAL) Retired.
Connelly, Mark J. '87 (WIL) Lewes, DE St. Jude The Apostle.
Connelly, Peter *o.s.b.* '87 (WOR)[O] Still River, MA Benedictine Monks, St. Benedict Abbey.
Connelly, Xavier *o.s.b.* '89 (WOR)[O] Still River, MA Benedictine Monks, St. Benedict Abbey; Still River, MA.
Conner, James *o.c.s.o.* '57 (L)[L] Trappist, KY Abbey of Our Lady of Gethsemani, of the Order of Cistercians of the Strict Observance.
Conner, Michael P. '85 (GAY) Kingsley, MI St. Mary.
Conner, Paul M. *o.p.* '67 (PRO)[P] Providence St. Thomas Aquinas Priory at Providence College.
Conner, Steven '94 (NEW) Fort Lee, NJ Holy Trinity; Southeast Bergen Region Deanery 6.
Conners, John P. '99 (CAM) On Leave of Absence.
Conners, Quinn *o.carm.* '71 (WDC)[B] Washington, DC Whitefriars Hall; Councilors:.
Connerton, Rev. Msgr. Barry R.L. '70 (PRO) Providence, RI St. Augustine; Deans.
Connery, J. Thomas '63 (ALB) Priests Retirement Board/Priests Retirement Plan Board Retired.
Connery, Sean P. *o.s.f.s.* '71 (WIL) Elsmere, DE Veteran's Hospital; [B] Wilmington, DE Salesianum School.
Connery, Sean P. *o.s.f.s.* '71 (MO) DEPARTMENT OF VETERANS AFFAIRS HOSPITALS AND CHAPLAINS.
Connery, Thomas '83 (ORL) DeLand, FL St. Peter's Church; [G] Deland, FL Stetson University Catholic Campus Ministry; Eastern.
Connery, Thomas '63 (ALB) Glenville, NY Immaculate Conception.
Connole, Marlin J. '68 (SEA) Retired.
Connolly, Andrew P. '56 (RVC) Patchogue, NY; Port Washington, NY Our Lady of Fatima Retired.
Connolly, Brian W. '55 (PIT) Retired.
Connolly, Charles B. *s.j.* '74 (BO)[U] Boston, MA Loyola House.
Connolly, Rev. Msgr. Clement J. '64 (LA) South Pasadena, CA Holy Family.
Connolly, Edward B. '66 (ALN) Girardville, PA St. Joseph; Holy Name Societies; Girardville, PA St. Vincent de Paul; Girardville – Court St. Cecilia #1529.
Connolly, Fidelis *c.p.* '50 (MET)[I] South River Passionist Provincial Office Retired.
Connolly, Gerard M. *t.o.r.* '69 (ALT)[G] Newry, PA St. Bernardine Monastery; [G] Hollidaysburg, PA Province Econome's Office.
Connolly, James M.T. '78 (ALN) Military Chaplains; Navy Reserve Chaplains.
Connolly, James P. '54 (NY) New York, NY St. John the Evangelist; Holy Name Society Archdiocesan Union of New York.
Connolly, Jerry '67 (GF) Retired.
Connolly, John G. '63 (BO) Senior Priests. Retired.
Connolly, John J. '94 (BO) Dorchester, MA St. Brendan; Boston, MA Holy Trinity; Professional Standards and Oversight.
Connolly, John T. '78 (PAT) Clifton, NJ Sacred Heart; Deans; Advocates.
Connolly, Joseph F. *t.o.r.* '68 (VEN) Sarasota, FL Our Lady Queen of Martyrs.
Connolly, Joseph M. *c.s.s.* '57 (BO)[X] Waltham, MA Stigmatine Fathers and Brothers Retired.
Connolly, Joseph *s.v.d.* '60 (BO)[U] Duxbury, MA Society of the Divine Word.
Connolly, Joseph *t.o.r.* '68 (VEN) College of Consultors; Venice Diocesan Council of Catholic Women.
Connolly, K. Scott '95 (SEA) Bellingham, WA Assumption; Presbyteral Council; Deans.
Connolly, Kevin '85 (WIN) Fairmont, MN Holy Family; Fairmont, MN St. John Vianney; Elected At–Large Representatives; Priest Assignments Committee.
Connolly, Leo L. '81 (COL) Columbus, OH St. Cecilia; Diocesan Judges; Priests Personnel Board.
Connolly, Rev. Msgr. Leon L. '58 (DUB) On Special or Other Archdiocesan Assignment; Vicar for Hispanic Ministry; Vicar for Hispanic Ministry Retired.
Connolly, Mark '57 (BGP)[W] Greenwich, CT Clemons Productions, Inc.; Communications Retired.
Connolly, Michael C. *o.s.f.s.* '74 (WIL)[B] Wilmington, DE Salesianum School.
Connolly, Michael J. *s.j.* '68 (SPK)[B] Spokane, WA Gonzaga University.
Connolly, Michael J. *s.j.* '68 (BO)[U] Boston The Society of Jesus of New England–Provincial Offices.
Connolly, Michael '78 (NY)[EE] Yonkers, NY St. Clare Friary.
Connolly, Rev. Msgr. Neil A. '58 (NY) New York, NY St. Mary.
Connolly, Patrick *s.j.* '66 (LA)[C] Los Angeles, CA Jesuit Community.
Connolly, Paul E. '83 (DAV) DeWitt, IA St. Joseph's.
Connolly, Paul '83 (DAV) Diocesan Consultors.
Connolly, Peter *c.ss.r.* '77 (TUC) Tucson, AZ Santa Catalina Roman Catholic Parish – Tucson; [F] Tucson, AZ Redemptorist Society of Arizona Redemptorist Renewal Center.
Connolly, Robert P. '79 (PIT) Burgettstown, PA Our Lady of Lourdes.
Connolly, Thomas *s.j.* '63 (B) DeSmet, ID Sacred Heart.
Connolly, Thomas '52 (SFS) Retired.
Connolly, Thomas '00 (SPK) Clarkston, WA Holy Family.
Connolly, William J. *s.j.* '56 (BO)[U] Weston, MA Campion Health Center, Inc.
Connor, Brian P. '89 (LIN) Lincoln, NE North American Martyrs.
Connor, Charles P. '90 (SCR) On Duty Outside the Diocese; Censor Librorum; Diocesan Historian.
Connor, Gerald T. '54 (ROC) Retired.
Connor, J. Patrick '61 (NSH) Presbyteral Council; Priest Benefit Foundation.
Connor, J. Patrick '61 (NSH) Retired.
Connor, James E. '60 (PRT) Retired.
Connor, James L. *s.j.* '59 (BAL)[S] Baltimore, MD Jesuit Community of Loyola University, Inc.
Connor, James '78 (HEL) Polson, MT Immaculate Conception; Ronan, MT Sacred Heart; [E] Polson, MT St. Joseph Hospital Corporation.
Connor, John F. '64 (NEW) Newark, NJ Immaculate Conception; Newark, NJ Our Lady of Good Counsel Retired.
Connor, John M. *c.ss.r.* '65 (TR)[R] Long Branch, NJ San Alfonso Retreat House.
Connor, John S. *c.s.c.* '70 (SB) Coachella, CA Our Lady of Soledad; [I] Coachella, CA Congregation of Holy Cross.
Connor, John *c.s.c.* (FTW)[H] Notre Dame Congregation of Holy Cross, Indiana Province, Provincial House.
Connor, John *c.p.* '84 (SCR)[M] Scranton, PA Saint Ann's Passionist Monastery.
Connor, Kevin T. '87 (MAN) Absent on Leave.
Connor, Martin P. '64 (BO)[CC] Hanover, MA League of Catholic Women of the Archdiocese of Boston; Hanover, MA St. Mary of the Sacred Heart; Senior Priests. Retired.
Connor, Patrick L. '83 (ROC) Addison, NY St. Stanislaus; Bradford, NY St. Catherine of Siena.
Connor, Patrick *s.v.d.* '57 (TR)[N] Bordentown, NJ Society of the Divine Word.
Connor, Robert A. (POD) South Orange.
Connor, Sean M. '01 (BO) Dorchester, MA St. Ann.
Connor, Vincent '71 (SB) Corona, CA Retired.
Connor, William J. '46 (COL) Retired.
Connors, Albert *c.m.f.* '73 (LA)[V] Rancho Dominguez, CA Dominguez Seminary Inc. Retired.
Connors, Cletus *o.s.b.* '72 (SCL) Cold Spring, MN St. Boniface; [I] Collegeville, MN St. John's Abbey, of the Order of St. Benedict.
Connors, Edmund P. '66 (NY) Katonah, NY St. Mary of the Assumption; [E] Staten Island, NY Moore Catholic High School.
Connors, Francis E. '73 (BUR) Island Pond, VT St. James the Greater.
Connors, John E. '01 (SPR) Northampton, MA Sacred Heart; Ludlow, MA St. Mary.
Connors, Martin *o.p.* '51 (NY)[FF] Hawthorne, NY Motherhouse & Novitiate of the Sisters of St. Dominic, Congregation of St. Rose of Lima; Pleasantville, NY Holy Innocents; Hawthorne, NY Rosary Hill Home.
Connors, Michael E. *c.s.c.* '84 (FTW)[H] Notre Dame, IN Holy Cross Community, Corby Hall, University of Notre Dame.
Connors, Michael *c.s.c.* '84 (FTW)[B] University of Notre Dame Du Lac.
Connors, Quinn *o.carm.* '71 (NY)[EE] Middletown, NY Brandsma Priory.
Connors, Richard P. '79 (PH) Philadelphia, PA Nativity of the Blessed Virgin Mary.
Connors, Robert L. '71 (BO) Dracut, MA St. Francis of

Assisi; Dracut, MA Ste. Marguerite d'Youville; Presbyteral Council.
Connors, Rev. Msgr. Terrence L. '75 (MAD) Sun Prairie, WI St. Albert the Great.
Conoboy, Shawn '06 (Y) Boardman, OH St. Charles Borromeo.
Conole, Robert W. '91 (BO) Haverhill, MA Sacred Hearts.
Conoscenti, Frederick M. '65 (BUF) Retired.
Conover, James A. '78 (TR) Keyport, NJ St. Joseph.
Conrad, Brian P. '76 (HBG) On Medical Leave.
Conrad, John F. '63 (GB) Retired.
Conrad, Sebastian *m.s.f.s.* '90 (TYL)[B] Whitehouse, TX The Missionaries of St. Francis de Sales.
Conrad, Simon *o.f.m.cap.* (SAL)[D] Victoria, KS St. Fidelis Friary.
Conroy, Donald B. '64 (WDC)[W] Washington, DC National Institute for the Family.
Conroy, Francis M. '64 (BO) Newton, MA Corpus Christi – St. Bernard; Senior Priests. Retired.
Conroy, J. Peter *s.j.* '71 (NY)[EE] Cornwall, NY Jogues Retreat Center.
Conroy, James R. *s.j.* '78 (BAL)[W] Baltimore, MD Ignatian Volunteer Corps.
Conroy, James *s.j.* '78 (BO)[U] Newton, MA The Jesuit Community at Boston College.
Conroy, John Jerome *o.p.* '49 (NY)[EE] New York, NY St. Catherine of Siena Priory.
Conroy, Kevin M. '82 (CLV) Released from Diocesan Assignment.
Conroy, Kevin M. '68 (FgM) Maryknoll, NY MARYKNOLL.
Conroy, Michael '65 (CHI)[N] Chicago, IL St. Patrick's Missionary Society.
Conroy, Patrick J. *s.j.* '83 (P)[D] Portland, OR; [L] Portland, OR Jesuit Provincial Office (Society of Jesus, Oregon Prov.).
Conroy, Philip M. '64 (BO) Nahant, MA St. Thomas Aquinas; Senior Priests. Retired.
Conroy, Robert *m.c.* (KCK) Topeka, KS Our Lady of Guadalupe.
Conry, Austin '65 (MOB) Fairhope, AL St. Lawrence.
Conry, Roy *o.carm.* '56 (TUC)[A] Tucson, AZ Salpointe Catholic High School; [D] Tucson, AZ Carmelite Priory Retired.
Consani, Robert E. '59 (KAL) Kalamazoo, MI St. Monica.
Consani, Robert E. '63 (KAL) Retired.
Consemino, Angelo R. (LUB) Floydada, TX St. Mary Magdalen.
Conserva, Stephen *o.m.i.* '74 (LA) San Fernando, CA St. Ferdinand.
Considine, James F. '02 (MET) Piscataway, NJ St. Frances Cabrini.
Considine, Matthew J. *s.m.m.* '77 (BRK)[T] Ozone Park, NY Montfort Missionaries Provincialate (Missionaries of the Company of Mary); Ozone Park, NY; Ozone Park, NY St. Mary Gate of Heaven.
Considine, William *s.m.m.* '73 (HRT)[U] Litchfield, CT Lourdes Shrine Guild, Inc.; [L] Litchfield, CT Montfort Missionaries; Counselors:.
Consiglio, Cyprian *o.s.b.cam.* '98 (MRY)[F] Big Sur, CA New Camaldoli Hermitage.
Constant, Van '93 (HT) Army National Guard Chaplains; Gibson, LA Most Blessed Sacrament Faith Community.
Constantin, Rodrigue '03 (OLL) St. Paul, MN Holy Family Maronite Catholic Church.
Constantine, Bennett P. '58 (LAN) Eaton Rapids, MI St. Peter; Defenders of the Bond.
Constantine, Cyprian G. *o.s.b.* '77 (GBG)[A] Latrobe, PA St. Vincent Seminary; [G] Latrobe, PA Saint Vincent Archabbey.
Contadino, Eugene *s.m.* '70 (CIN)[D] Dayton, OH The University of Dayton; [N] Dayton, OH Marianist Community.
Contardi, Michael *o.de.m.* '60 (CLV) Cleveland, OH St. Rocco.
Conte, James W. '48 (NY) Retired.
Conte, John P. '58 (ALN)[J] Bethlehem, PA Holy Family Villa Retired.
Conte, Rev. Msgr. John P. '64 (HRT) Consultors – Canon 1742; Madison, CT St. Margaret; Episcopal Vicars; College of Consultors; Ex Officio Members.
Contell, Andres Codoner '08 (NEW) Newark, NJ St. Columba's.
Conterno, Austin *s.d.b.* '48 (SFR) San Francisco, CA SS. Peter and Paul.
Conti, Cornelius *o.f.m.* '62 (SP)[N] St. Petersburg, FL St. Anthony Friary.
Conti, John P. '46 (NY) Retired.
Conti, Vincent G. *s.j.* '01 (WDC)[E] Washington, DC Gonzaga College High School; [N] Washington, DC The Jesuit Community of St. Aloysius Gonzaga.
Contons, Rev. Msgr. Albert J. '48 (BO) Senior Priests. Retired.
Contons, Rev. Msgr. Albert '48 (LIT) Lithuanian R. Catholic Priests' League of America.
Contran, Sergio *m.c.c.j.* '50 (LA)[BB] Covina, CA Comboni Mission Center.
Contreras, Arnulfo '05 (KC) Kansas City, MO Holy Cross.
Contreras, David '93 (AMA) Advocates; Hereford, TX San Jose; Priests' Pension Plan Retirement Committee.
Contreras, Humberto E. (RVC) Central Islip, NY St. John of God.
Contreras, Marcos A. Cepeda *m.n.m.* (ARE) Camuy, PR Our Lady of Asumption.
Contreras, Rodolfo (MRY) Campus Ministry Department.
Contreras, Wilfredo '03 (MIA) Fort Lauderdale, FL St. Clement.
Contreras Tribaldo, Carlos Alberto (SJN) Trujillo Alto, PR Exaltacion de la Santa Cruz; [B] Trujillo Alto, PR Santa Cruz.
Conva, Mathias T. '62 (NEW) Paramus, NJ Our Lady of the Visitation Retired.
Conva, Matthias T. '62 (NEW) Retired.
Converse, Brian J. '91 (MO) Army National Guard Chaplains.
Converset, John *m.c.c.j.* '71 (FgM) Cincinnati, OH COMBONI MISSIONARIES (VERONA FATHERS).
Convertino, David *o.f.m.* '77 (BO)[Z] Boston, MA St. Anthony Shrine.
Convery, Paul C. *c.o.* '84 (PH)[Y] Philadelphia, PA The Philadelphia Congregation of The Oratory of St. Philip Neri; Philadelphia, PA St. Francis Xavier.
Convey, Edwin H. *s.j.* '53 (BAL)[S] Baltimore, MD Jesuit Community of Loyola University, Inc.
Conway, David '52 (WDC) Retired.
Conway, Dennis *m.c.c.j.* '68 (CHI)[W] Chicago, IL The Peace Corner, Incorporated; [N] La Grange Park, IL Comboni Missionaries.
Conway, Edward *o.f.m.cap.* '98 (NY) New York, NY St. John the Baptist.
Conway, Gerald W. '56 (WIN) Retired.
Conway, James '65 (SAT) Castroville, TX St. Louis.
Conway, Rev. Msgr. Jeffrey '73 (NY) Staten Island, NY Our Lady Star of the Sea.
Conway, John E. *m.m.* '73 (FgM) Maryknoll, NY MARYKNOLL.
Conway, Rev. Msgr. John L. '56 (GBG) Retired.
Conway, John R. '69 (SFE) Associate Judges.
Conway, John T. '00 (ATL) Blue Ridge, GA St. Anthony.
Conway, Rev. Msgr. John T. '77 (PH) King of Prussia, PA Mother of Divine Providence.
Conway, John '69 (SFE) Retired.
Conway, Laurence '59 (MIA) Retired.
Conway, Michael J. *o.ss.t.* (DAL) Dallas, TX Santa Clara.
Conway, Rev. Msgr. Michael '60 (PAT) Retired.
Conway, Michael *o.ss.t.* (BAL)[S] (Dallas, Texas).
Conway, Michael *s.d.b.* '92 (SP)[B] St. Petersburg, FL St. Petersburg Catholic High School, Inc.
Conway, Neil '63 (CLV) Absent on Leave Retired.
Conway, Richard C. '63 (BO) Dorchester, MA St. Peter; Dorchester, MA Blessed Mother Teresa of Calcutta; Emergency Response Group.; Dorchester, MA St. Ambrose; Dorchester, MA Holy Family.
Conway, Richard T. '83 (BO) Andover, MA St. Robert Bellarmine.
Conway, Robert *c.pp.s.* '53 (CIN)[N] Carthagena, OH St. Charles Retired.
Conway, Thomas A. *c.pp.s.* '57 (KC)[J] Liberty, MO Precious Blood Center; [A] Liberty, MO Society of the Precious Blood Provincial Offices Retired.
Conway, Thomas E. *o.f.m.* (TR) Brant Beach, NJ St. Francis of Assisi.
Conway, Thomas S. '86 (BLX) Defenders of the Bond; Deans; Campus Ministry; Trustees; Presbyteral Council.
Conway, Thomas '86 (BLX) Hattiesburg, MS St. Thomas Aquinas; University of Southern Mississippi..
Conway, Thomas '86 (JKS) Trustees.
Conway, Tommy '72 (BLX)[F] Hattiesburg, MS University of Southern Mississippi.
Conway, William '77 (JOL) Downers Grove, IL Divine Savior.
Conwell, Joseph *s.j.* '50 (SPK)[B] Spokane, WA Gonzaga University.
Conyard, James R. *s.j.* '62 (P)[L] Portland, OR Colombiere Community.
Conyers, Richard *c.s.c.* '69 (CHI) Chicago, IL Queen of All Saints Basilica; [D] Niles, IL Notre Dame College Prep.
Conyers, Richard *c.s.c.* (FTW)[H] Notre Dame Congregation of Holy Cross, Indiana Province, Provincial House.
Coogan, Roch A. *o.f.m.* '54 (SP)[N] St. Petersburg St. Anthony Friary Retired.
Coogan, Roch A. *o.f.m.* '54 (MO) Air Force Reserve Chaplains.
Coogan, Thomas M. '97 (RVC) Bay Shore, NY St. Patrick's.
Coogan, Thomas '97 (RVC) Islip Deanery; Senate of Priests (Presbyteral Council/College of Consultors).
Cook, Adrian L. '72 (MOB) Brewton, AL St. Maurice.
Cook, Brian J. '85 (CHL) Winston–Salem, NC St. Leo the Great.
Cook, Damien '99 (OM) Omaha, NE St. Peter.
Cook, Daniel '90 (GR) Faculties Suspended.
Cook, Rev. Msgr. Douglas '94 (ORG) Orange, CA Cathedral of the Holy Family; Judicial Vicar; Judges; Council of Priests; Consultors; Special Assignment; Office of Canonical Services.
Cook, Edward J. '67 (MIL) Milwaukee, WI Congregation of the Great Spirit.
Cook, John B. '49 (TR) Retired.
Cook, John Joseph Mary *f.i.* '02 (SY)[U] Maine, NY Mount St. Francis Hermitage, Inc.
Cook, Joseph T. '86 (CHI) Chicago Heights, IL St. Kieran.
Cook, Kevin A. '01 (FR) Vocations; [B] Taunton, MA Coyle and Cassidy High School; Taunton, MA Annunciation of the Lord; Morton Hospital.
Cook, Michael J. '73 (WIL) Newark, DE St. John the Baptist–Holy Angels.
Cook, Michael L. *s.j.* '66 (SPK)[B] Spokane, WA Gonzaga University.
Cook, Rev. Msgr. Paul G. '59 (BAL) Cockeysville, MD St. Joseph; Consultors; Consultors; [V] Cockeysville, MD St. Joseph, Texas Endowment Trust.
Cook, Philip C. *o.s.a.* '97 (CHI)[N] Chicago, IL St. Augustine Friary.
Cook, Rob '03 (B) College of Consultors; Vocations.
Cook, Robert J. '65 (LC) Deans; Viroqua, WI Annunciation of the Blessed Virgin Mary.
Cook, Robert W. '00 (CHY)[B] Lander, WY Wyoming Catholic College.
Cook, Stephen M. '97 (KC) Kansas City, MO St. Peter's.
Cook, Thomas E. '97 (WIN) Madelia, MN St. Mary; St. James, MN St. James; Madelia, MN St. Katherine.
Cook, Thomas R. *o.s.a.* '57 (PH)[Y] Villanova, PA St. Augustine Friary.
Cook, Thomas S. '88 (LA) Lompoc, CA La Purisima Concepcion.
Cook, Timon *o.f.m.* '50 (SFE)[H] Albuquerque, NM The Province of Our Lady of Guadalupe Retired.
Cook, Timothy R. '83 (STL) Ferguson, MO Blessed Teresa of Calcutta.
Cook, William G. '88 (NEW) East Orange, NJ Holy Name of Jesus.
Cooke, Christopher R. '06 (PH) Philadelphia, PA St. Martin of Tours.
Cooke, Rev. Msgr. Colman M. '65 (SP) College of Consultors.
Cooke, Rev. Msgr. Colman '65 (SP) Retired.
Cooke, Philip *s.j.* '08 (RC) Manderson, SD St. Agnes; Porcupine, SD Church of Christ the King.
Cooke, Phillip *s.j.* '08 (RC)[C] Pine Ridge, SD Jesuit Community of Holy Rosary Mission; Pine Ridge, SD Holy Rosary.
Cooke, Vincent M. *s.j.* '67 (BUF)[O] Buffalo, NY Canisius Jesuit Community Inc.; [C] Buffalo, NY Canisius College.
Cookson, Edmund L. *m.m.* '65 (FgM) Maryknoll, NY MARYKNOLL.
Cool, Brian '93 (ROC)[M] Rochester, NY Catholic Newman Community at the University of Rochester; [M] Eastman School of Music Catholic Students Organization; Rochester, NY St. Stanislaus.
Cooley, John Edward '48 (LA) Retired.
Cooley, Stephen *o.carm.* '67 (LA)[P] Encino, CA Our Lady of Mount Carmel Priory.
Coolong, Raymond E. *s.m.* '71 (BO)[U] Boston, MA Marist Fathers and Brothers Provincial House; [W] Framingham, MA The Marist House; Boston, MA.
Coon, David N. '93 (SPC) Poplar Bluff Hospital Ministry; Doniphan, MO St. Benedict; Poplar Bluff, MO Sacred Heart.
Coon, John Clancy '01 (BEA) Diocesan College of Consultors; Port Arthur, TX St. James.
Coonan, Robert J. '65 (SPR) Hatfield, MA St. Joseph's; Hatfield, MA Holy Trinity; Deans.
Cooney, Arthur *o.f.m.cap.* '76 (GB)[O] Green Bay, WI The Diocesan Charismatic Renewal Center.
Cooney, Camillus *o.s.b.* '56 (LR)[A] Subiaco, AR Subiaco Abbey.
Cooney, David *s.d.s.* '67 (NSH) McMinnville, TN St. Catherine; Smithville, TN St. Gregory.
Cooney, Dennis J. '74 (VEN) Lehigh Acres, FL St. Raphael; Respect Life Department.
Cooney, Francis C. *m.s.* '69 (HRT) Hartford, CT Our Lady of Sorrows; [L] Hartford, CT Our Lady of Sorrows Rectory.
Cooney, Gerald '50 (FWT) Retired.
Cooney, Rev. Msgr. James J. '64 (BRK)[B] Elmhurst, NY Cathedral Preparatory Seminary of the Immaculate Conception Retired.
Cooney, John M. '62 (HRT) Watertown, CT St. John the Evangelist; Cursillo Movement, Archdiocesan Director of.
Cooney, Michael N. '75 (DET) Mount Clemens, MI St. Peter; Archdiocesan Vicars; Presbyteral Council.
Cooney, Patrick *o.s.b.* '91 (MO) Air National Guard Chaplains.
Cooney, Patrick *o.s.b.* '91 (IND)[A] St. Meinrad, IN Saint Meinrad School of Theology; [K] St. Meinrad, IN St. Meinrad Archabbey; Defenders of the Bond.
Cooney, Robert R. *c.s.v.* '57 (CHI)[N] Arlington Heights, IL Viatorian Province Center–Clerics of St. Viator.

Cooney, Rev. Msgr. Roger P. '70 (COV) Fort Thomas, KY St. Thomas.
Cooney, Romaeus *o.carm.* '58 (ALB) Troy, NY Holy Trinity; Troy, NY St. Joseph.
Cooney, Sean K. '59 (ORL) Representative for Retired Priests Retired.
Cooney, Stephen A. '76 (LIN) Health Care Facilities.
Cooney, Theophane *c.p.* '52 (BRK) Jamaica, NY Immaculate Conception; [T] Jamaica, NY Immaculate Conception Monastery.
Cooney, Xavier *s.v.d.* '83 (WH) Summersville, WV St. John The Evangelist.
Cooper, Angus *o.f.m.* '61 (LA)[P] Los Angeles, CA St. Joseph Friary; [F] Los Angeles, CA Loyola High School of Los Angeles.
Cooper, Brian G. *c.s.v.* '00 (CHI)[N] Arlington Heights Viatorian Province Center–Clerics of St. Viator.
Cooper, David E. '70 (MIL) Milwaukee, WI St. Matthias.
Cooper, Donald A. '53 (NEW) Retired.
Cooper, Donald J. '63 (E) Retired.
Cooper, James W. '80 (LIN) Osceola, NE St. Vincent Ferrer; Advocates; Presbyteral Council.
Cooper, Jeffrey A. *c.s.c.* '94 (OAK)[M] Berkeley, CA Priests of the Congregation of Holy Cross.
Cooper, Jeffrey *c.s.c.* (FTW)[H] Notre Dame Congregation of Holy Cross, Indiana Province, Provincial House.
Cooper, John A. '80 (LIN) Lincoln, NE Sacred Heart.
Cooper, Joseph M. '95 (MAN) Manchester, NH St. Joseph Cathedral.
Cooper, Leo '43 (KCK) Retired.
Cooper, Mark A. *o.s.b.* '76 (MAN)[K] Manchester, NH St. Anselm Abbey.
Cooper, Michael W. *s.j.* '73 (CHI)[N] Chicago Chicago Province of the Society of Jesus–Provincial Office.
Cooper, Michael *s.j.* '73 (SP)[A] St. Leo, FL Saint Leo University, Office of Assessment and Institutional Research.
Cooper, Patrick E. '91 (CHR) Simpsonville, SC St. Elizabeth Ann Seton.
Cooper, Robert T. '07 (NO) Covington, LA St. Peter.
Cooper, Ronald C. '83 (CIN) Priests On Administrative Leave.
Cooper, Warren L. '71 (NO) Marrero, LA Immaculate Conception; Deans; Blue Army of Our Lady of Fatima.
Coopmans, Joseph R. *o.praem.* '81 (GB)[J] De Pere, WI St. Norbert Abbey.
Copeland, Leonard R. *o.c.d.* '67 (MIL) Milwaukee, WI St. Florian; [H] West Allis, WI Mary Queen of Saints Catholic Academy; West Allis, WI Holy Assumption.
Copeland, Robert F. '99 (LAN) Flint, MI St. Pius X.
Copelin, Boniface T. *o.s.b.* '08 (OKL)[I] Shawnee, OK St. Gregory's Abbey.
Copenhaver, John L. '88 (LIN) Wahoo, NE St. Wenceslaus.
Copon, Ricardo (LA) Oxnard, CA Mary Star of the Sea.
Copp, Rodney J. '73 (BO) Waltham, MA St. Charles Borromeo; Trustees; Promoter of Justice; Defenders of the Bond; Canonical Affairs Committee.
Coppenrath, Rev. Msgr. Leonard A. '53 (BO) Senior Priests. Retired.
Coppinger, Edmund '59 (OAK) Richmond, CA St. Cornelius Retired.
Coppinger, John W. *s.a.* '72 (NY)[EE] Garrison, NY Franciscan Friars of the Atonement.
Coppola, Anthony '02 (SP) Pinellas Park, FL Sacred Heart.
Coppola, Vincent J. *c.s.c.* '01 (BUR) Bennington, VT Sacred Heart St. Francis de Sales; Readsboro, VT St. Joachim.
Cops, Augustin *o.f.m.cap.* '86 (MAD)[I] Madison, WI San Damiano Friary Retired.
Cops, Peter (LC)[H] La Crosse, WI Holy Cross (Seminary) Diocesan Center.
Copsey, Robert A. '78 (SAC) Galt, CA St. Christopher.
Corali, Serafino A. '47 (RVC)[M] Amityville, NY St. Pius X Residence Retired.
Corapi, John *s.o.l.t.* '91 (CC)[G] Robstown, TX Society of Our Lady of the Most Holy Trinity.
Corbally, Christopher *s.j.* '76 (TUC)[D] Tucson, AZ Jesuit Community of the Vatican Observatory.
Corbaton, P. Jose Alcocer *m.ss.cc.* '64 (SJN) Trujillo Alto, PR San Bartolome.
Corbelli, Vincent F. *m.m.* '60 (FgM) Maryknoll, NY MARYKNOLL.
Corbett, Eugene J. *s.j.* '62 (SJ)[D] San Jose, CA Bellarmine College Preparatory.
Corbett, Eugene *s.j.* '62 (SJ) Santa Clara Valley Medical Center.
Corbett, John B. '56 (PIT) Pittsburgh, PA Retired.
Corbett, John Dominic *o.p.* '80 (WDC)[B] Washington, DC Dominican House of Studies.
Corbett, John F. '95 (NEW) Apostleship of the Sea; Elizabeth, NJ Our Lady of Fatima.
Corbett, Michael E. '54 (PBL) Retired.
Corbett, Robert L. '51 (STL) Manchester, MO Christ, Prince of Peace Retired.
Corbett, Rev. Msgr. W. Joseph '95 (ATL) Special or Other (Arch)Diocesan Assignment; College of Consultors; Vicars General; Board of Directors.
Corbin, Don '70 (TOL)[G] Oregon, OH St. Charles Mercy Hospital.
Corbin, Raymond G. '04 (BUF) Cheektowaga, NY Infant of Prague; Roswell Park Memorial Institute.
Corbino, Thomas A. '72 (JOL) Lombard, IL St. Pius X.
Corbo, Alfred P. '56 (CHI) Retired.
Corces, Pedro M. '88 (MIA) Weston, FL St. Katharine Drexel.
Corcione, Michael *o.f.m.* '01 (NY)[EE] St. Peter Friary.
Corciulo, Rev. Msgr. Cosimo '56 (SB) Retired.
Corcoran, Anthony J. *s.j.* (NO)[P] New Orleans Jesuit Provincial Office.
Corcoran, Brian '72 (SD) Encinitas, CA St. John the Evangelist.
Corcoran, Rev. Msgr. Clifton J. '54 (AMA)[C] Panhandle, TX St. Ann's Nursing Home Retired.
Corcoran, Edward G. '56 (CHI) Retired.
Corcoran, Frank '54 (JKS) Greenville, MS St. Joseph Retired.
Corcoran, John J. '55 (RVC) Center Moriches, NY St. John the Evangelist Retired.
Corcoran, John J. *m.m.* '63 (FgM) Maryknoll, NY MARYKNOLL.
Corcoran, Kevin '88 (SY) Canastota, NY St. Agatha; Presbyteral Council.
Corcoran, Lawrence E. *s.j.* '63 (BO)[U] Weston, MA Campion Health Center, Inc.
Corcoran, Shawn D. '00 (COL) Chancellor; Presbyteral Council; Columbus, OH St. Joseph Cathedral; College of Consultors; Bishop's Council; Diocesan Finance Council.
Corcoran, Stanley D. '90 (DAL) Retired.
Corcoran, T. Kevin '99 (PAT) Priest Secretary to the Bishop; Vocations Office; Special Assignment; Vice Chancellors.
Corcoran, Thomas B. '98 (BO) Somerville, MA St. Ann; Somerville, MA St. Catherine of Genoa.
Corcoran, William T. '81 (CHI) Oak Lawn, IL St. Linus; Deans.
Corcuera, Manuel R. '70 (CHK) Saipan, MP Santa Soledad Mission Parish; Vicar General; Presbyteral Council; College of Consultors; Diocesan Pastoral Council; Commission on Family Life; Legion of Mary.
Cordeiro, Anthony *o.p.* '67 (SAC) Benicia, CA St. Dominic Retired.
Cordeno, Peter (ORL) Orlando, FL Holy Cross.
Corder, Stephen *s.j.* '01 (ORG)[H] Orange, CA Loyola Institute for Spirituality; [I] Anaheim, CA Manresa Jesuit Residence.
Cordero, Carlos *o.s.a.* '99 (SJN)[E] San Juan, PR Centro Medico de P.R.; [C] Bayamon, PR Seminario Agustiniano Sto. Tomas De Villanueva; Bayamon, PR Ntra. Sra. de la Monserrate.
Cordero, Rev. Msgr. Faustino '71 (BRK) Brooklyn, NY St. Rocco.
Cordero, Martin G. '99 (LSC) La Mesa, NM San Jose; Charismatic Renewal Liaisons.
Cordero, Mert '74 (NEW) Ridgewood, NJ Our Lady of Mount Carmel; Ridgewood, NJ Valley Hospital.
Cordery, Robert J. '80 (MO) Air Force Reserve Chaplains.
Cordery, Robert J. '80 (BO) Unassigned.
Cordes, Christopher L. '95 (JC) Kirksville, MO Mary Immaculate; Board of Trustees; Priestly and Religious Vocations Committee.
Cordes, John '03 (KCK) Topeka, KS Our Lady of Guadalupe.
Cordier, Michael L. '02 (CIN) Milford, OH St. Elizabeth Ann Seton.
Cordisco, Philip *o.ss.t.* (BAL)[S] The Trinitarians in New Jersey.
Coreas, Edwin A. '92 (GAL) Houston, TX Our Lady of St. John; Defenders of the Bond.
Corel, Joseph S. '00 (JC) Cursillo Movement; Ministry Formation; Ministry to Priests; Priestly and Religious Vocations Committee; Youth Ministry.
Coric, Christopher *o.f.m.conv.* '71 (BUF) Veterans Hospital; Lackawanna, NY Our Lady of Bistrica.
Coriden, James A. '57 (GRY) On Duty Outside the Diocese.
Corigliano, Anthony M. *c.s.s.* '55 (SPR) Springfield, MA Our Lady of Mt. Carmel.
Corkery, Daniel '55 (ALX) Hessmer, LA St. Martin of Tours Retired.
Corkery, Raymond *o.carm.* '59 (JOL) Retired.
Corkery, Raymond *o.carm.* '59 (TUC) Tucson, AZ Sacred Heart Roman Catholic Parish – Tucson.
Corl, Ronald *o.p.* '66 (DET)[P] Detroit, MI St. Paul of the Cross Passionist Retreat and Conference Center, Inc.
Corl, Ronald *c.p.* '66 (DET)[K] Detroit, MI St. Paul of the Cross Community, Congregation of the Passion.
Corley, Joseph '75 (PH) Darby, PA Blessed Virgin Mary.
Corley, Malachy *o.c.s.o.* '55 (ATL)[G] Conyers, GA The Monastery of the Holy Spirit.
Corley, Theodosius *o.f.m.cap.* '74 (BUR) Proctor, VT St. Dominic; Rutland, VT St. Peter.
Corley, Thomas '85 (JOL) Retired.
Cormack, James B. *c.m.* '76 (STL) St. Louis, MO St. Catherine Laboure.
Cormack, James *c.m.* '76 (STL) Society of St. Vincent de Paul, Council of St. Louis.
Cormack, Michael J. '54 (SAC) Roseville, CA St. Rose of Lima Retired.
Cormier, Gregory P. '83 (LAF) Baldwin, LA Sacred Heart; Baldwin, LA St. Peter the Apostle.
Cormier, Leo G. '57 (BO) Senior Priests. Retired.
Cormier, Michael Robert '00 (SP) Port Richey, FL St. James the Apostle.
Cormier, Robert J. '82 (NEW) Newark, NJ St. Rose of Lima.
Cormier, Robert '82 (NEW) Newark, NJ Northern State Prison.
Cormier, Roger C. '61 (BO) Senior Priests. Retired.
Cormier, William N. '71 (WOR) Douglas, MA St. Denis; Diocesan Building Commission Members.
Cornea, Sergiu '96 (ROM) Aurora, IL Ss. Peter and Paul Church.
Corneille, Cecil C. '95 (MO) Army National Guard Chaplains.
Corneille, Cecil '95 (STV) On Duty Outside the Diocese.
Cornejo, Quirino '91 (SAN) Midland, TX St. Stephen's.
Cornejo, Vincent C. '56 (MET) Retired.
Cornejo–Castillero, Justino '05 (NEW) Elizabeth, NJ Immaculate Heart of Mary and Saint Patrick.
Corneli, Luis R. *s.s.* '91 (BAL)[S] Baltimore, MD St. Mary's Seminary & University; [A] Baltimore, MD St. Mary's Seminary and University.
Cornelia, Jose D. *d.s.* '99 (PHX) Scottsdale, AZ St. Bernadette Roman Catholic Parish; Phoenix, AZ John C. Lincoln Hospital – N. Mountain.
Cornelio, Noel *p.i.m.e.* '03 (DET)[K] Detroit, MI P.I.M.E. Missionaries; Detroit, MI St. Hedwig.
Cornelius, Rev. Msgr. William R. '58 (STU) Retired.
Cornell, Richard P. (BO) Ashland, MA St. Cecilia.
Cornely, Francis J. '48 (PH) Retired.
Cornely, Joseph *s.t.* '60 (SB) Riverside, CA Our Lady of Perpetual Help.
Cornett, David '85 (STU) Nelsonville, OH Holy Cross; Nelsonville, OH St. Mary of the Hills; [L] Nelsonville, OH Hocking Technical College; Presbyteral Council; College of Consultors.
Corniel, Rafael G. '75 (NY) Advocates; New York, NY Our Lady of the Scapular and St. Stephen.
Cornish, Ron '68 (KCK) Retired.
Cornwell, Malcolm *c.p.* '69 (SCR)[M] Scranton, PA Saint Ann's Passionist Monastery.
Corominas, John *c.m.f.* '49 (LA)[V] Rancho Dominguez, CA Dominguez Seminary Inc.
Corona, Andrew J. '93 (GRY) Portage, IN Nativity of Our Savior.
Corona, Enrique '07 (PAT) Office of Multicultural Ministries; Dover, NJ Sacred Heart; Dover, NJ Our Lady Queen of the Most Holy Rosary.
Corona, John '71 (RNO) Retired.
Corona, Rev. Msgr. Michael J. '68 (MET) Raritan, NJ The Catholic Church of St. Ann; Department of Education; Catholic Scouting Apostolate; College of Consultors.
Corona, Miguel *m.sp.s.* '05 (SB) Indio, CA Our Lady of Perpetual Help.
Coronado, Genero '51 (LA) Retired.
Coronado, Victorino B. *c.i.c.m.* '95 (CAM) Williamstown, NJ Our Lady of Peace Parish, Monroe Township, N.J.
Coronado–Arrascue, Rev. Msgr. Ricardo '90 (COS) Judicial Vicar and Chancellor; Judicial Vicar; Vicar for Religious; Presbyteral Council; Judicial Vicar and Chancellor; Chancellor and Judicial Vicar.
Coroztieta, Jose Madoz '53 (SJN) Retired.
Corpora, Joseph *c.s.c.* '84 (FTW)[H] Notre Dame Congregation of Holy Cross, Indiana Province, Provincial House; [B] University of Notre Dame Du Lac; [H] Notre Dame, IN Holy Cross Community, Corby Hall, University of Notre Dame.
Corr, Rev. Msgr. John F. '51 (PAT) Retired.
Corradi, Frank '85 (LC)[D] Chippewa Falls, WI St. Joseph's Hospital.
Corrado, Dennis M. *c.o.* '70 (BRK) Brooklyn, NY St. Boniface; [T] Brooklyn, NY Oratory of Saint Philip Neri, Congregation Pontifical Rite; Brooklyn, NY.
Corral, Jose M. '79 (SFR) San Francisco, CA St. Finn Barr; [S] Tiburon, CA Charismatic Movement.
Corral, Roberto *o.p.* '88 (OAK) Antioch, CA Most Holy Rosary.
Corrales, Alirio '78 (LAR) Laredo, TX Santa Margarita de Escocia; Presbyteral Council.
Corrales, Dominador '85 (SFR) Daly City, CA St. Andrew.
Correa, Gino *o.f.m.* '76 (SFE)[H] Albuquerque, NM The Province of Our Lady of Guadalupe; Albuquerque, NM.
Correa–Garcia, Luis Norberto '04 (SJN) San Juan, PR Santa Maria de Los Angeles; Adjunct Vicar; Judges.
Correia, Edward E. '68 (FR) Fall River, MA St. Michael.
Correio, Bruce '85 (LA) Santa Barbara, CA St. Raphael.
Correz, Steven '00 (ORG) Garden Grove, CA St. Columban; Council of Priests; Council of Priests.
Corriere, Basil *e.c.* '87 (STU)[H] Bloomingdale, OH Holy Family Hermitage.
Corrigan, Allen F. '82 (CLV) Richfield, OH St. Victor.

Corrigan, Rev. Msgr. Bernard J. '47 (NY) Warwick, NY St. Stephen Retired.
Corrigan, George C. *o.f.m.* '07 (SP) Tampa, FL Sacred Heart.
Corrigan, Gregory M. '86 (WIL) Wilmington, DE Corpus Christi; KAIROS Ministries, Inc.
Corrigan, Rev. Msgr. Hugh J. '63 (NY) Yonkers, NY Immaculate Conception; Westchester (Yonkers).
Corrigan, J. David *s.j.* '65 (STL)[O] St. Louis, MO Jesuit Community Corporation at Saint Louis University – Jesuit Hall.
Corrigan, Michael T. (GAL) Retired.
Corriveau, Ernest *m.s.* '64 (LKC) Sulphur, LA Our Lady of Prompt Succor.
Corriveau, Michel G. *c.p.m.* '05 (FR) Sturdy Memorial Hospital.
Corriveau, Michel G. *c.p.m.* '05 (FR) Seekonk, MA St. Mary's.
Corriveau, Raymond *c.ss.r.* '62 (CHI)[N] Glenview, IL The Redemptorists of Glenview, Illinois.
Corriveau, Real *o.m.i.* '61 (FgM) Washington, DC AMERICAN OBLATE MISSIONS.
Corriveau, Roger R. *a.a.* '74 (WOR)[O] Worcester, MA Assumptionists of Assumption College.
Corry, Francis J. '74 (NY) Bronx, NY St. Frances of Rome.
Corso, Charles W. *c.s.c.* '75 (FTW)[H] Notre Dame Congregation of Holy Cross, Indiana Province, Provincial House.
Cortes, Antonio '96 (MRY) On Leave.
Cortes, Ariel '96 (TYL) Diocesan Christian Initiation Team; Presbyteral Council.
Cortes, Hernando *s.f.* '91 (WDC)[B] Silver Spring, MD Holy Family Seminary.
Cortes, Jesse '63 (LAV) Las Vegas, NV St. Bridget Catholic Church.
Cortes, Oscar '94 (RCK) McHenry, IL Church of Holy Apostles.
Cortes, Raul '62 (LA) Reseda, CA St. Catherine of Siena.
Cortes, Victor '96 (POD) Miami.
Cortes, Victor '96 (MIA)[P] Miami, FL Prelature of the Holy Cross and Opus Dei.
Cortes, Victor '96 (PMB)[G] Delray Beach, FL Prelature of the Holy Cross and Opus Dei.
Cortes–Campos, Roberto J. '02 (WDC) Washington, DC Our Lady Queen of the Americas; Lexington Park, MD Immaculate Heart of Mary.
Cortese, Francis X. *o.praem.* '62 (PH)[Y] Paoli, PA Daylesford Abbey.
Cortese, Patrick S. '48 (SCR) Retired.
Cortez, Fernando '77 (OAK) San Leandro, CA St. Leander.
Cortez, Jose '73 (TYL) Jacksonville, TX Our Lady of Guadalupe; Rusk, TX Jerry H. Hodge Unit and Sky View Unit, Texas Department of Corrections; Auditor.
Cortez, Ramiro *o.m.i.* '70 (GAL) Houston, TX Immaculate Heart of Mary.
Cortinovis, Charles '09 (WDC) Graduate Studies.
Cortney, Edward P. '63 (GI) Retired.
Coruna, Roberto '77 (MET) Bloomsbury, NJ Church of the Annunciation.
Corvera, Jose Maria A. '97 (TUC) Patagonia, AZ Saint Therese of Lisieux Roman Catholic Parish – Patagonia.
Coryer, Francis J. '82 (OG) Charismatic Renewal.
Corzo, Wilson O. '98 (FTW) Ligonier; Ligonier, IN St. Patrick.
Cos, Rafael '82 (MIA) Tamarac, FL St. Malachy.
Cosby, Rev. Msgr. R. Roy '54 (ARL) Retired.
Coschignano, Joseph C. '69 (RVC) Center Moriches, NY St. John the Evangelist.
Cosentino, Jack '70 (FAR) Venice, FL Epiphany Cathedral Retired.
Cosgrove, Edward *c.ss.r.* '55 (STL)[O] Liguori, MO St. Clement Health Care Center.
Cosgrove, Francis J. '65 (JKS) Meridian, MS St. Patrick; Meridian, MS St. Joseph; East Mississippi State Hospital; Priests' Council; Diocesan Consultors; Approved Advocate and Auditors.
Cosgrove, Jerome P. '63 (SC) Retired.
Cosgrove, John *s.d.b.* '02 (NY)[GG] Stony Point, NY Don Bosco Retreat Center and Marian Shrine; [GG] Stony Point, NY Marian Shrine.
Cosgrove, Joseph J. '92 (BAL) Edgewater, MD Our Lady of Perpetual Help.
Cosgrove, Rev. Msgr. Joseph '60 (LA) Retired.
Cosgrove, William B. '74 (NY)[II] Scarsdale, NY Catholic Charismatic Renewal Office; Canon 1742 Panel of Pastors; Charismatic Renewal Office; New City, NY St. Augustine.
Cosgrove, William P. '99 (BIS) Retired.
Cosgrove, William '55 (ROC) Canandaigua, NY Veteran's Hospital Retired.
Cosmic, John J. '90 (OG) Carthage, NY St. James Minor Retired.
Coss, John *f.m.s.i.* '56 (BO)[B] Framingham, MA Sylva Maria; Framingham, MA.
Cossavella, Anthony J. '81 (PH) West Chester, PA St. Agnes.
Cossette, Raymond '55 (DUL) Retired.
Costa, Anthony J. '90 (PH)[A] Wynnewood, PA Theological Seminary of St. Charles Borromeo, Overbrook.
Costa, Caetano F. '64 (RVC) Deer Park, NY SS. Cyril and Methodius.
Costa, Carl A. *m.m.* '71 (FgM) Maryknoll, NY MARYKNOLL.
Costa, David A. '85 (FR) North Attleboro, MA St. Mary's; North Attleboro, MA Sacred Heart.
Costa, Eugene *o.de.m.* '74 (BUF)[O] LeRoy, NY Order of the BVM of Mercy/Mercedarian Friars; [O] LeRoy, NY St. Raymond Nonnatus Novitiate.
Costa, Gabriel B. '79 (NEW)[B] School of Diplomacy and Intl. Rels.
Costa, Lucas Torrell deAlmeida *o.s.b.* '67 (GBG)[G] Latrobe Saint Vincent Archabbey.
Costa, Thomas C. '78 (RVC) Glen Cove, NY St. Patrick's; Procurator & Advocates; Oyster Bay Deanery.
Costa, Thomas E. '05 (FR)[B] Attleboro, MA Bishop Feehan High School; Seekonk, MA Our Lady of Mt. Carmel.
Costales, Frederick A. *m.s.* '02 (SB) Moreno Valley, CA St. Christopher; [I] Moreno Valley, CA Missionaries of Our Lady of La Salette, MS.
Costantino, Joseph S. *s.j.* '87 (NY) New York, NY St. Francis Xavier; [EE] New York, NY Xavier Jesuit Community.
Costanza, Jared J. '99 (PRO) Bristol, RI St. Elizabeth.
Costanzo, John J. '64 (PBL) Retired.
Costello, Andrew *c.ss.r.* '65 (BAL) Annapolis, MD St. Mary.
Costello, Bernard B. '63 (PIT)[Q] Pittsburgh, PA Cardinal Dearden Center Retired.
Costello, Brian L. '00 (SFR) South San Francisco, CA Mater Dolorosa.
Costello, Coleman J. '67 (BRK)[T] Douglaston, NY Bishop Mugavero Residence Retired.
Costello, Daniel F. '98 (CHI) Chicago, IL St. Thomas of Canterbury.
Costello, David '95 (FgM) Boston, MA St. James the Apostle, Inc.
Costello, David *o.c.d.* '62 (SR)[L] Oakville, CA Carmelite House of Prayer.
Costello, Edward *o.f.m.conv.* '61 (NY) Staten Island, NY Seaview Hospital Rehabilitation Center and Home; [EE] Staten Island, NY St. Francis Friary.
Costello, Frank B. *s.j.* '52 (SPK)[B] Spokane, WA Gonzaga University Retired.
Costello, James J. *s.j.* '66 (STL) St. Louis, MO St. Francis Xavier.
Costello, James. J. *s.j.* '66 (STL)[O] St. Louis, MO Jesuit Community Corporation at Saint Louis University – Jesuit Hall.
Costello, John F. *s.j.* '83 (CHI)[N] Chicago, IL Clark Street Jesuit Residence.
Costello, John F. '96 (VEN) Venice, FL Epiphany Cathedral.
Costello, John J. '89 (BRK) Released from Diocesan Assignment.
Costello, Rev. Msgr. John M. '72 (STL) Kirkwood, MO St. Peter.
Costello, John M. *s.j.* '84 (NY)[EE] New York, NY Murray–Weigel Hall; [F] Bronx, NY Fordham Preparatory School.
Costello, Mark Joseph *o.f.m.cap.* '91 (CHI)[N] Chicago, IL St. Clare Friary; Councilors:.
Costello, Raymond *m.s.c.* '45 (ALN)[A] Center Valley, PA Sacred Heart Villa, Missionaries of the Sacred Heart.
Costello, Robert B. '53 (BO) Senior Priests. Retired.
Costello, Robert T. *s.j.* '63 (STL)[O] St. Louis, MO Jesuit Community Corporation at Saint Louis University – Jesuit Hall.
Costello, Ted '85 (SP) Clearwater, FL St. Michael The Archangel.
Costello, Vincent F. '76 (CHI) Vicar for Priests; Commission on the Mission and Life of Diocesan Priests; Chicago, IL St. Clement.
Costello, William J. '64 (CHI) Retired.
Costello, William M. '74 (FR) East Falmouth, MA St. Anthony's.
Coster, Henry G. *s.j.* '59 (ALN)[A] Wernersville, PA Jesuit Center–Jesuit Community.
Costigan, Christopher M. '08 (RVC) Levittown, NY St. Bernard.
Costigan, George (PAT) Retired.
Costigan, James P. *c.p.m.* '02 (OWN)[F] Auburn, KY Fathers of Mercy.
Costigan, Rev. Msgr. P. James '68 (SAV) Savannah, GA St. Peter the Apostle Church; Savannah Deanery.
Costigan, Richard F. *s.j.* '64 (STL)[O] St. Louis, MO Jesuit Community Corporation at Saint Louis University – Jesuit Hall.
Cotant, Charles *c.ss.r.* '41 (FgM) Denver, CO Denver Province.
Cote, David P. '68 (PRT) Madawaska, ME Notre Dame du Mont Carmel Parish; Van Buren, ME Saint Peter Chanel Parish.
Cote, Duaine '62 (FAR)[J] Fargo, ND Cursillo Movement; Fargo, ND Sts. Anne & Joachim Church of Fargo Retired.
Cote, E. Joseph '69 (BAL)[T] Baltimore, MD The School Sisters of Notre Dame Atlantic–Midwest Province.
Cote, Gerald M. '56 (TUC) Retired.
Cote, Joseph E. (BAL) Advocates.
Cote, Joseph J. '69 (BAL) Special Assignment.
Cote, Mark '04 (JOL) Bloomingdale, IL St. Isidore.
Cote, Norman J. '58 (OG) Retired.
Cote, Normand C. '58 (OG) Rouses Point, NY St. Joseph; Plattsburgh, NY St. John the Baptist Retired.
Cote, Paul E. '71 (PRT) Special or Other Diocesan Assignment.
Cote, Roland P. '71 (MAN) Manchester, NH Parish of the Transfiguration.
Cotone, Michael *o.s.c.* '74 (PHX)[F] Phoenix, AZ Crosier Provincial House Province of St. Odilia.
Cotta, Rev. Msgr. Myron J. '87 (FRS) On Special Assignment; Vicar General and Moderator of the Curia; Diocesan Consultors; Finance Committee; Holy Childhood Association; Personnel Board; Priests' Council; The Society for the Propagation of the Faith/The Society of St. Peter Apostle; Vicar for Priests; Continuing Formation of Priests.
Cotter, George C. *m.m.* '60 (NY)[EE] Maryknoll Maryknoll Fathers and Brothers.
Cotter, John F. '80 (SAG) Territorial Vicars; Gladwin, MI Sacred Heart.
Cotter, Lawrence E. '52 (OG) Colton, NY St. Patrick; Defenders of the Bond; Censor Librorum Retired.
Cotter, Pius *o.f.m.cap.* '88 (GB) Brussels, WI St. Francis–St. Mary Parish.
Cotter, Raymond C. '86 (GAY) Hillman, MI Jesus the Good Shepherd; Hillman, MI St. Augustine; Mio, MI St. Mary; Lewiston, MI St. Francis of Assisi.
Cotter, Robert L. '47 (OG) Judges Retired.
Cotter, Vincent '83 (OAK) Concord, CA St. Agnes.
Cotton, Charles E. '73 (COL) Columbus, OH St. Elizabeth; Parochial Examiners; Deanery 4: Northland; Presbyteral Council.
Cottrell, James '68 (SP) Retired.
Coucelo, Andres '68 (MIA) Retired.
Coughlan, Rev. Msgr. Michael J. '52 (SD) Retired.
Coughlan, Robert '90 (SFE) Retired.
Coughlin, Bernard J. *s.j.* '55 (SPK)[B] Spokane, WA Gonzaga University.
Coughlin, Daniel P. '60 (CHI) On Duty Outside the Archdiocese.
Coughlin, Edward J. *s.j.* '74 (NY)[EE] Cornwall, NY Jogues Retreat Center.
Coughlin, James K. *s.j.* '83 (ROC)[B] Rochester, NY McQuaid Jesuit High School.
Coughlin, John C. *o.f.m.* '02 (CAM) Camden, NJ St. Anthony of Padua Roman Catholic Church, Camden, N.J.; Continuing Education & Spiritual Formation of Priests (CESF).
Coughlin, John J. *o.f.m.* (FTW)[B] University of Notre Dame Du Lac.
Coughlin, Kenneth F. '90 (LAN) Grand Blanc, MI Holy Family.
Coughlin, Paul E. '66 (PRT) Retired.
Coughlin, Paul F. '91 (BO) Peabody, MA St. John the Baptist.
Coughlin, Roger J. '51 (CHI)[G] Chicago, IL Catholic Charities of the Archdiocese of Chicago–Archdiocesan Offices; Associate Administrators; Maternity Fund Retired.
Coughlin, Thomas '77 (HON) On Duty Outside the Diocese.
Coughlin, Thomas *o.p.miss.* '77 (SAT) Deaf and Hard of Hearing Ministry; [B] San Antonio, TX Dominican Missionaries for the Deaf Apostolate House of Studies; [S] San Antonio, TX Deaf Ministry of San Antonio.
Coughlin, William D. '66 (BO) Wakefield, MA Most Blessed Sacrament; Members.
Couhig, Michael D. *c.s.c.* '80 (FTW)[H] Notre Dame Congregation of Holy Cross, Indiana Province, Provincial House.
Couhig, Michael *c.s.c.* '80 (AUS) Austin, TX St. Ignatius Martyr.
Coulter, Gary '99 (LIN) Ashland, NE St. Mary's; Promoters Justitiae; Defensores Vinculi.
Coulter, Lawrence W. '86 (GI) Priests' Pension and Welfare Board Retired.
Coulthard, Gregory *s.d.s.* '67 (GB)[J] New Holstein, WI Salvatorian Public Relations.
Counce, Paul D. '79 (BR) Baton Rouge, LA St. Joseph Cathedral; Judicial Vicar; College of Consultors; Presbyteral Council.
Counce, Paul '79 (NO)[A] St. Benedict, LA St. Joseph Seminary College.
Courier, Rick L. '85 (MAR) Escanaba, MI St. Thomas the Apostle; Escanaba, MI St. Anthony.
Cournoyer, Alfred C. '85 (SPR) On Duty Outside the Diocese.
Cournoyer, Michael R. '98 (ALB) Leave of Absence.
Courteau, Allen *o.m.i.* '76 (FgM) Washington, DC AMERICAN OBLATE MISSIONS.
Courtemanche, Normand L. '65 (PRO) Retired.
Courtney, Edward '55 (HEL) Retired.

Courtney, Patrick E. '87 (LFT) Unassigned.
Courtney, Scott M. '00 (LIN) Bellwood, NE St. Peter's; Advocates.
Courtney, William "Liam" '99 (PBL) Pueblo, CO Shrine of St. Therese.
Courtright, Lawrence P. '61 (TLS) Retired.
Courtright, Raymond P. '92 (FAR) Fargo, ND St. Anthony of Padua's Church of Fargo.
Courville, Rev. Msgr. J. Douglas '76 (LAF) St. Martinville, LA St. Martin of Tours.
Courville, Robert '63 (LAF) Retired.
Coury, Charles *c.ss.r.* '76 (FgM) Baltimore Province.
Coury, Paul *c.ss.r.* '72 (TUC)[F] Tucson, AZ Redemptorist Society of Arizona Redemptorist Renewal Center.
Coury, Phillip *c.m.* '71 (PBL) Aguilar, CO St. Anthony; Deans.
Cousens, Dennis L. '77 (L) Radcliff, KY St. Christopher.
Cousineau, Robert H. *s.j.* '60 (NY)[EE] Loyola Hall, Jesuit Community.
Cousins, John P. *o.f.m.cap.* '76 (COS) Colorado Springs, CO St. Francis of Assisi; [F] Colorado Springs, CO Solanus Casey Friary.
Couterier, David *o.f.m.cap.* (BO) Pastoral Planning.
Coutinha, Paul *s.a.c.* '82 (DET) Redford, MI St. Valentine.
Coutinho, Absalom (PAT) Retired.
Coutinho, Paul J. *s.j.* '81 (STL)[C] Saint Louis University; [O] St. Louis, MO Jesuit Community Corporation at Saint Louis University – Jesuit Hall.
Couto, Nelson '79 (NY) Bronx, NY St. Philip Neri.
Couto, Robert '96 (MAN) Londonderry, NH St. Jude.
Couture, Paul E. *s.s.e.* '56 (BUR)[E] Colchester, VT Society of St. Edmund.
Couture, Roger *o.m.i.* '55 (NOR)[G] Willimantic, CT Missionary Oblates of Mary Immaculate; [I] Willimantic, CT Immaculata Retreat House.
Couture, Roland '53 (BO)[U] Lowell, MA Andre Garin Retirement Residence.
Couturier, David *o.f.m.cap.* (BO)[U] Jamaica Plain, MA St. Francis of Assisi Friary.
Couturier, George M. '81 (HRT) On Duty Outside the Archdiocese; Glastonbury, CT St. Dunstan.
Covarrubias, Raul R. '83 (B) Idaho Falls, ID Christ the King; Idaho Falls, ID Holy Rosary; Priest Retirement Committee; Priest Personnel Commission.
Covarrubias–Pina, Salomon '91 (YAK) Wapato, WA St. Peter Claver; Defenders of the Bond; Jail Ministry; Presbyteral Council Executive Committee.
Coveney, James B. '64 (ALT) Altoona, PA St. Mark's.
Coveny, Richard C. '56 (BUF)[O] Lackawanna, NY Bishop Head Residence Retired.
Cover, Phillip B. '70 (LFT) On Duty Outside the Diocese.
Covington, Charles L. '85 (AUS) Ecumenism.
Covington, Larry '85 (AUS) Austin, TX St. Louis.
Covos, Ruben '06 (SAN) Military Chaplains.
Covos, Ruben '06 (BLX) Keesler Airforce Base.
Cowan, George R. '65 (BRK)[T] Douglaston, NY Bishop Mugavero Residence Retired.
Cowan, Steven '99 (RIC) Unassigned.
Coward, Robert *c.p.* '68 (FgM)[N] Chicago Passionist Provincial Office.
Cowart, Conrad '96 (STA) Starke, FL St. Edward.
Cowell, Raymond '57 (CHI) Retired.
Cower, D. Craig '54 (RC) Retired.
Cowhig, Edward D. '45 (BO) Senior Priests. Retired.
Cowie, Donald *s.m.* '61 (SAT)[F] San Antonio, TX Central Catholic High School; [L] San Antonio, TX Central Catholic Marianist Community.
Cowles, James '86 (RIC) Gloucester, VA St. Therese, the Little Flower.
Cox, Alan B. '76 (LFT) Retired.
Cox, Bernard '91 (IND) Danville, IN Mary Queen of Peace.
Cox, Christopher *c.s.c.* '99 (FTW) South Bend; South Bend, IN St. Casimir; South Bend, IN St. Adalbert; [H] Notre Dame Congregation of Holy Cross, Indiana Province, Provincial House.
Cox, Rev. Msgr. Craig A. '78 (LA) Members; [A] Camarillo, CA St. John's Seminary.
Cox, Rev. Msgr. David D. '81 (JC) Rolla, MO St. Patrick; Diocesan Consultors; VI. Rolla; Senators; Ministry to Priests; [D] Rolla, MO Catholic Newman Center, Missouri University of Science and Technology; Priestly and Religious Vocations Committee.
Cox, Francis '50 (WCH) Retired.
Cox, Rev. Msgr. Gregory A. '76 (LA) Los Angeles, CA St. Anastasia; [X] Los Angeles, CA Catholic Charities of Los Angeles, Inc.; [X] Los Angeles, CA Central Administrative Offices; Executive Director; Members; Board of Directors.
Cox, James M. '98 (PH) Philadelphia, PA St. Cecilia.
Cox, Rev. Msgr. James '51 (NY) Retired.
Cox, John T. *o.m.i.* '87 (MIA) Miami, FL Holy Redeemer.
Cox, John *o.m.i.* '87 (BO)[Z] Lowell, MA St. Joseph the Worker Residence.
Cox, Joseph C. '46 (MAD) Retired.
Cox, Joseph *o.s.b.* '91 (IND)[K] St. Meinrad, IN St. Meinrad Archabbey.
Cox, Paul '54 (ALB) Warrensburg, NY St. Cecilia; Ministers to Retired Priests Retired.
Coy, Richard D. '00 (MEM) Bartlett, TN St. Ann; College of Consultors; Presbyteral Council.
Coy, William J. *m.m.* '55 (NY)[EE] Maryknoll Maryknoll Fathers and Brothers Retired.
Coyle, Arthur M. (BO) Ex Officio; Merrimack Region; Lowell, MA St. Rita; College of Consultors; Presbyteral Council.
Coyle, Dan '89 (FRS) Bakersfield, CA Sacred Heart.
Coyle, Rev. Msgr. Edward J. '80 (ALN) Bally, PA Most Blessed Sacrament; Army National Guard Chaplains.
Coyle, Eugene P. '54 (BRK)[T] Douglaston, NY Bishop Mugavero Residence Retired.
Coyle, Patrick J. *s.m.* '45 (SFR)[N] San Francisco, CA Marist Center of the West Retired.
Coyle, Patrick P. *ss.cc.* '61 (LA)[P] La Verne, CA Congregation of the Sacred Hearts of Jesus and Mary Retired.
Coyle, Robert '91 (RVC) Mineola, NY Corpus Christi; Navy Reserve Chaplains; Serving Outside the Diocese.
Coyle, Thomas J. '70 (MAD) Jefferson, WI St. John the Baptist; Sullivan, WI St. Mary Help of Christians; Jefferson, WI St. Lawrence.
Coyne, Christopher J. (BO) Westwood, MA St. Margaret Mary.
Coyne, Edwin J. '62 (BGP) Retired.
Coyne, Emmett A. '66 (MAN) Retired.
Coyne, Rev. Msgr. George R. '59 (STU) Retired.
Coyne, George V. *s.j.* '65 (TUC)[D] Tucson, AZ Jesuit Community of the Vatican Observatory.
Coyne, Gregory '89 (POD)[U] Washington, DC Tenley Study Center; Washington.
Coyne, James P. '75 (SEA) Covington, WA St. John the Baptist; Deans; Presbyteral Council.
Coyne, Liam '98 (ATL) Fort Oglethorpe, GA St. Gerard Majella.
Coyne, Martin P. *s.j.* '66 (FgM) Chicago, IL Society of Jesus.
Coyne, Rev. Msgr. Michael J. '55 (CAM) Retired.
Coyne, Robert F. *m.m.* '83 (FgM) Maryknoll, NY MARYKNOLL.
Coyne, Robert R. '76 (PIT) Bairdford, PA St. Victor.
Coyne, Ronald D. '73 (BO) Randolph, MA St. Mary.
Coyte, Thomas '74 (DEN) Denver, CO Holy Cross.
Coz, Richard T. *s.j.* '58 (SJ)[M] Los Gatos, CA Sacred Heart Jesuit Center.
Cozzens, Andrew H. '97 (STP)[A] Saint Paul, MN The Saint Paul Seminary; [C] St. Paul, MN University of St. Thomas; Worship.
Cozzens, Donald '65 (CLV) Retired.
Cozzi, Phillip M. '06 (ARL) Notaries; Presbyteral Council; Warrenton, VA St. John the Evangelist.
Cozzini, Robert P. '60 (NEW)[M] Caldwell, NJ The Rev. Msgr. James F. Kelley Residence for Retired Priests Retired.
Cozzubbo, Gregory P. *c.m.* '84 (PH) Philadelphia, PA Immaculate Conception; Philadelphia, PA Philadelphia Prison System; Prison Ministry Program.
Crabb, John T. *s.j.* '79 (BO)[U] Boston The Society of Jesus of New England–Provincial Offices; [U] Weston, MA Campion Jesuit Community.
Crable, John M. '53 (OG) Retired.
Craddock, Joseph F. '04 (PRO) Providence, RI Rhode Island Hospital; Cranston, RI St. Mark.
Crafts, George A. (POD) Providence.
Crafts, George '65 (PRO)[O] Providence, RI Prelature of the Holy Cross and Opus Dei.
Crager, Richard '85 (NEW) Elizabeth, NJ St. Anthony's.
Craig, Bruce *s.d.b.* '74 (SP) Tampa, FL Mary Help of Christians; [P] Tampa, FL Salesian Society of Florida, Inc.
Craig, Christopher A. '93 (IND) Shelbyville, IN St. Joseph.
Craig, Dale *s.o.l.t.* '97 (CC)[G] Robstown, TX Society of Our Lady of the Most Holy Trinity.
Craig, Donald R. '74 (CHI) Chicago, IL St. Mary of Perpetual Help.
Craig, John V. *s.j.* '77 (STL)[O] St. Louis, MO De Smet Jesuit High School Community.
Craig, Patrick H. '05 (KAL) Decatur, MI Holy Family.
Craig, Paul *o.f.m.cap.* '66 (FgM) Detroit, MI Province of St. Joseph; [K] Detroit St. Bonaventure Friary.
Craig, Richard J. '61 (BO) Senior Priests. Retired.
Craig, Robert G. '64 (MO) DEPARTMENT OF VETERANS AFFAIRS HOSPITALS AND CHAPLAINS.
Craig, Robert N. *o.f.m.cap.* '67 (MO) DEPARTMENT OF VETERANS AFFAIRS HOSPITALS AND CHAPLAINS.
Craig, Robert *o.f.m.cap.* '67 (PIT)[M] Pittsburgh, PA St. Augustine Friary; University Drive; H.J. Heinz III (Aspinwall).
Craig, Rod L. '77 (FRS) Visalia, CA St. Mary; Visalia, CA Holy Family; Visalia, CA St. Thomas the Apostle.
Craig, Samuel L. '76 (WDC) Laurel, MD St. Nicholas Retired.
Craig, Thomas '82 (FWT) Arlington, TX St. Vincent de Paul; Mission Council; Society for the Propagation of the Faith; Priests' Pension Plan Trustees; Presbyteral Council and Consultors.
Craig, William R. *o.praem.* '55 (PH)[Y] Paoli, PA Daylesford Abbey.
Cramblitt, Rev. Msgr. Richard E. '72 (BAL) Baltimore, MD Shrine of the Sacred Heart; Consultors; Consultors.
Cramer, David W. '91 (SCR) Great Bend, PA St. Lawrence; Jackson, PA St. Martin of Tours; Legion of Mary; Susquehanna, PA St. John the Evangelist.
Cramer, Donald W. '01 (HBG)[I] Bloomsburg, PA Bloomsburg University of Pennsylvania.
Cramer, Harry N. '84 (WH) Bridgeport, WV All Saints.
Cramer, Joseph '77 (KCK) Gardner, KS Sacred Heart; Archdiocesan Council of Catholic Women (ACCW).
Cramer, Terry A. '99 (ARL) Alexandria, VA Blessed Sacrament.
Cramer, William N. '77 (PAT) Absent on Leave.
Crane, Mark W. '05 (TR) Manalapan, NJ St. Thomas More.
Crane, Rev. Msgr. Thomas E. '57 (BUF) Censors—Board of Diocesan Censors of Books and Vigilance for the Faith; [O] Tonawanda, NY O'Hara Residence Retired.
Cranor, Bernard *o.s.b.* '62 (SFE)[H] Abiquiu, NM Monastery of Christ in the Desert.
Crasta, Rudolf '89 (LUB) Vicars Forane.
Crasta, Rudy '89 (LUB) Presbyteral Council.
Crawford, Rev. Msgr. C. Slade '65 (PT) Seminarian Candidate Review Board; Seminarians, Office of.
Crawford, Cyril K. *o.s.b.* '07 (NO)[P] St. Benedict, LA St. Joseph Abbey.
Crawford, Douglas Y. '07 (NY) Poughkeepsie, NY St. Martin de Porres.
Crawford, John G. '63 (CLV) Brook Park, OH Assumption of Mary; Parma, OH St. Francis de Sales Retired.
Crawford, Larry P. '66 (IND) Indianapolis, IN St. Gabriel the Archangel.
Crawford, Richard E. '75 (PEO) Retired.
Crawford, Robert F. *m.m.* '61 (FgM) Maryknoll, NY MARYKNOLL.
Crawford, Rev. Msgr. Slade '65 (PT) Orders & Ministries, Commission for; Miramar Beach, FL Church of the Resurrection.
Crawley, Richard *o.f.m.cap.* '09 (BUR) Rutland, VT St. Peter.
Cray, David G. *s.s.e.* '72 (BUR) Charlotte, VT Our Lady of Mount Carmel; Hinesburg, VT St. Jude the Apostle.
Craycroft, Bernard L. '57 (L) Retired.
Creagan, Michael '97 (STP) West St. Paul, MN St. Joseph.
Creagan, Robert F. '88 (KAL) Battle Creek, MI St. Joseph; Knights of Columbus.
Creagh, Kevin G. *c.m.* '96 (BRK)[T] Jamaica, NY St. Vincent's House.
Creagh, Richard C. '76 (CHI) Chicago, IL St. Gabriel.
Crean, Hugh F. '62 (SPR)[G] Holyoke, MA Providence Place, Inc. Retired.
Creane, Anthony '56 (SPR) Retired.
Creary, Rev. Msgr. J. Edwin '73 (MEM) Germantown, TN Our Lady Of Perpetual Help; Defenders of the Bond.
Creason, Richard H. '67 (STL) St. Louis, MO Most Holy Trinity.
Credo, Alejandro P. *o.s.a.* '86 (RIC) Elkton, VA Holy Infant; Quinque, VA Shepherd of the Hills.
Creed, Peter M. '67 (RIC) Norge, VA St. Olaf, Patron of Norway.
Creed, Peter '67 (SY) On Duty Outside the Diocese.
Creed, William E. *s.j.* '71 (CHI)[C] Chicago, IL Jesuit Community at Loyola University Chicago.
Creeden, Brendan D. *o.s.b.* '78 (CHI)[N] Chicago, IL Monastery of the Holy Cross.
Creedon, Gerard '68 (ARL) Arlington, VA St. Charles Borromeo.
Creedon, Joseph D. '68 (PRO) Kingston, RI Christ the King; [S] Kingston, RI University of Rhode Island Catholic Center; Council Members.
Creegan, Kevin G. '01 (PEO) DePue, IL St. Mary's.
Creel, Jesse '57 (R) Retired.
Cregan, David A. *o.s.a.* '99 (PH)[Y] Villanova, PA Fray de Leon Community; [C] Villanova University.
Cregan, Francis A. *o.a.r.* '95 (NY) Bronx, NY St. John's.
Cregan, James F. '63 (PT) Retired.
Cregan, John C. '87 (ARL) Alexandria, VA Blessed Sacrament; Bishop's Delegate for Clergy; Deans; Permanent Diaconate; Clergy Personnel Board.
Cregan, John J. '61 (CLV) Cleveland, OH Our Lady of Angels.
Cregan, Mark T. *c.s.c.* '83 (FR)[A] North Easton, MA Stonehill College; [A] North Easton, MA Holy Cross Fathers Religious; Prov. Councilors:.
Cregan, Mark T. *c.s.c.* (NY)[II] New Rochelle, NY Holy Cross International, Inc.
Crehan, Lawrence F. '74 (PH) Ardsley, PA Queen of Peace.
Crehan, Matthias J. *o.f.m.* '75 (MO) DEPARTMENT OF VETERANS AFFAIRS HOSPITALS AND CHAPLAINS.

Crehan, Matthias *o.f.m.* '75 (CIN)[N] Cincinnati St. Francis Seraph Friary.
Crehan, Matthias *o.f.m.* '75 (PHX) Phoenix, AZ United States Veterans Affairs Medical Center.
Creider, Philip B. '77 (OKL) Military Chaplains; Navy Chaplains.
Creighton, Bernard R. *o.f.m.* '67 (PAT)[N] Butler, NJ St. Anthony Friary.
Creighton, Rev. Msgr. Edward '47 (SD) Retired.
Creighton, James J. *s.j.* '60 (CHI)[D] Chicago, IL St. Ignatius Jesuit Community; [J] Maywood, IL Loyola University Medical Center.
Creighton, Matthew E. *s.j.* '57 (DET)[K] Clarkston, MI Colombiere Center.
Cremaldi, Angelo '60 (LAF) Opelousas, LA Our Lady Queen of Angels.
Cremin, Michael *s.a.c.* '83 (DET) Wyandotte, MI St. Joseph.
Cremins, John J. '69 (BRK) Forest Hills, NY Our Lady of Mercy.
Cremis, Luis '00 (BAL) Baltimore, MD Our Lady of Pompei.
Cremonie, Louis D. '72 (HRT) Manchester, CT Manchester Memorial Hospital; East Hartford, CT St. Mary; Special and other Archdiocesan Assignment.
Crescenzi, Rocco *f.d.p.* '43 (BO)[S] East Boston, MA Don Orione Nursing Home.
Creson, Michael '87 (KNX) Soddy Daisy, TN Holy Spirit Catholic Church.
Crespin, George E. '62 (OAK) Berkeley, CA St. Joseph The Worker Retired.
Crespo, Charles '01 (STV) Hispanic Ministry; Diocesan Newspaper; Charlotte Amalie, VI Cathedral of Sts. Peter and Paul; [B] St. Thomas, VI Hispanic Ministry.
Crespo, Hipolito (ARE) Arecibo, PR Church of San Martin de Porres.
Cressman, Richard *s.d.b.* '80 (BO)[M] Salesian Staff:.
Crevcoure, Stuart '01 (TLS) Stillwater, OK St. John the Evangelist Parish and Newman Center; [I] Stillwater, OK St. John's University Parish and Catholic Student Center; Campus Ministry.
Crewe, Ronald O. '63 (MIL) Racine, WI Sacred Heart Congregation.
Crews, Clyde F. '73 (L)[A] Bellarmine University.
Crews, John S. '71 (SR)[G] Sonoma, CA Hanna Boys Center; Diocesan Judges.
Cribben, Andrew G. *o.praem.* '94 (GB)[J] De Pere, WI St. Norbert Abbey.
Cribben, Rev. Msgr. Philip J. '62 (PH) Newtown Square, PA St. Anastasia.
Cribbin, Austin J. '56 (BAK) Retired.
Cricchio, Santo *o.f.m.conv.* '91 (MO) Navy Reserve Chaplains.
Cricchio, Santo *o.f.m.conv.* (BRK) Brooklyn, NY Most Holy Trinity – Saint Mary.
Crilly, James F. *c.s.v.* '56 (CHI)[N] Arlington Heights, IL Viatorian Province Center–Clerics of St. Viator.
Crilly, Marc *o.s.b.* '93 (WOR)[O] Still River, MA Benedictine Monks, St. Benedict Abbey.
Crimmins, Rev. Msgr. Michael (NY) New York, NY St. Gregory.
Crino, Patrick '88 (TUC) Tucson, AZ Saint Augustine Cathedral Roman Catholic Parish – Tucson.
Criqui, J. Kenneth '63 (KC) Carrollton, MO St. Mary's; Consultors; Deans.
Criscitelli, Anthony M. *t.o.r.* '80 (STP) Minneapolis, MN St. Bridget; Minneapolis, MN.
Criscuolo, Rev. Msgr. Salvatore A. '78 (WDC) Washington, DC St. Patrick; Special Ministries.
Crisman, James H. '01 (DEN) Director; Denver, CO Mother of God; Lakewood, CO Our Lady of Fatima.
Crisostomo, Abraham *o.f.m.conv.* '96 (FgM)[N] Chicago Conventual Franciscans of St. Bonaventure Province; Chicago, IL Province of Saint Bonaventure.
Crisostomo, Armando '93 (NEW) West New York, NJ St. Joseph of the Palisades.
Crisostomo, Michael '96 (AGN) Hagatna, GU Immaculate Heart of Mary; Catholic Campus Ministry, Newman Center, University of Guam; [H] Hagatna, GU Office of Youth, Young Adult & Campus Ministry; Archdiocesan Presbyteral Council; Youth and Young Adults Ministry.
Crisp, Michael L. '97 (SUP) Iron River, WI St. Peter; Iron River, WI St. Florian; Iron River, WI St. Michael; Iron River, WI SS. Peter and Paul.
Crisp, Robert R. '75 (DAL) Deans; Rowlett, TX Sacred Heart.
Crispo, Roderick A. *o.f.m.* '55 (BO)[B] Chestnut Hill, MA Redemptoris Mater Archdiocesan Missionary House of Formation.
Crispo, Roderick *o.f.m.* '55 (NY)[EE] Mount Vernon, NY St. Bernardine of Siena Friary; [EE] New York Franciscan Province of the Immaculate Conception.
Cristancho, Lisandro '91 (RCK) Elgin, IL St. Mary.
Criste, Ambrose *o.praem.* '08 (ORG)[A] Silverado, CA St. Michael's Norbertine Postulancy, Novitiate and Juniorate; [I] Silverado, CA Norbertine Fathers of Orange Inc.
Cristina, Mark Mary *m.v.f.a.* '03 (BIR)[E] Birmingham, AL Franciscan Missionaries of the Eternal Word, A Public Association of the Christian Faithful.
Cristler, Richard F. '00 (TLS) Collinsville, OK St. Therese Church and Diocesan Eucharistic Shrine of Saint Therese.
Cristobal, Daniel *o.f.m.cap.* '59 (AGN) Talofofo, GU San Miguel; [F] Agana Heights, GU St. Fidelis Friary; [H] Agana, GU Secular Franciscans; Secular Franciscans (Third Order).
Critch, Gerard F. '89 (VEN) Naples, FL St. Peter the Apostle.
Crivello, Peter A. '93 (MRY) Monterey, CA Cathedral of San Carlos Borromeo; Special Assignment; Vicar General; Diocesan Consultors; Diocesan Consultors; Finance Council; Presbyteral Council; Clergy Personnel Board.
Crkva, Odilo *o.s.b.* '53 (JOL)[L] Lisle, IL St. Procopius Abbey.
Croak, David P. '66 (DEN) Arvada, CO Shrine of St. Anne.
Croak, Thomas *c.m.* '65 (CHI)[N] Chicago, IL Vincentian Community, Congregation of the Mission, Western Province.
Croal, Thomas '58 (ORG) Retired.
Croce, Albert A. *c.s.c.* '50 (FR)[G] North Dartmouth, MA Holy Cross Residence Retired.
Crochet, Barry F. '93 (LAF) New Iberia, LA Our Lady of Prompt Succor.
Crocker, John R. *s.j.* '61 (CHI)[D] Chicago, IL St. Ignatius Jesuit Community.
Croell, John B. *o.p.* '98 (FgM) New York, NY Province of St. Joseph (Eastern).
Croft, J. George *o.m.i.* '44 (BO) Tewksbury, MA St. William.
Crofut, Robert J. '72 (BGP) Norwalk, CT St. Thomas the Apostle; Parochial Examiners; Presbyteral Council.
Croghan, James P. *s.j.* '85 (FgM) New York, NY Society of Jesus.
Croghan, John P. '75 (SY) Clinton, NY St. Mary; [T] Clinton, NY Hamilton College Newman Center.
Croglio, James C. '80 (BUF)[D] Buffalo, NY St. Joseph's Collegiate Institute.
Crohan, Robert F. *m.m.* '62 (NY) Maryknoll, NY MARYKNOLL[EE] Retired.
Croisetiere, David N. '77 (SD) San Diego, CA Our Lady of Refuge; Promoter of Justice.
Croke, Alfred M. '63 (NY) Livingston Manor, NY St. Aloysius; [EE] Bronx, NY John Cardinal O'Connor Residence Retired.
Crombie, Francis H. '68 (SPR) Springfield, MA St. Patrick's.
Cromley, Nathan *c.s.j.* '07 (PEO)[K] Princeville, IL Congregation of St. John.
Cron, Steven D. '78 (GR) Wyoming, MI St. Joseph The Worker.
Cron, Walter D. '60 (NEW) Retired.
Cronauer, Patrick T. *o.s.b.* '84 (GBG)[G] Latrobe, PA Saint Vincent Archabbey; [A] Latrobe, PA St. Vincent Seminary.
Crone, Patrick H. '71 (CIN) Cincinnati, OH St. Saviour.
Crone, Terence '02 (ATL) Toccoa, GA St. Mary.
Cronin, Brian '74 (ALB) Schenectady, NY St. Joseph Retired.
Cronin, Daniel C. '55 (NOR) Columbia, CT St. Columba.
Cronin, Edward J. '80 (CHI) Palos Heights, IL St. Alexander.
Cronin, Harry C. *c.s.c.* '62 (FTW)[H] Notre Dame Congregation of Holy Cross, Indiana Province, Provincial House.
Cronin, Harry *c.s.c.* '62 (OAK)[M] Berkeley, CA Priests of the Congregation of Holy Cross.
Cronin, James J. '62 (HRT) Milford, CT St. Mary; Pro–Life Activities; Special and other Archdiocesan Assignment.
Cronin, James *o.s.b.* '54 (ROC)[J] Pine City, NY Mount Saviour Monastery; Pine City, NY.
Cronin, Joseph R. '98 (HRT) West Haven, CT Our Lady of Victory; West Haven, CT St. John Vianney.
Cronin, Kevin M. *o.f.m.* '74 (PAT)[N] Butler, NJ St. Anthony Friary; [N] Franciscan Ministry of the Word.
Cronin, Michael J. '73 (CHI) Lemont, IL St. Patrick.
Cronin, Michael J. '95 (WIN) Absent on Leave.
Cronin, Rev. Msgr. Patrick '67 (SAT) San Antonio, TX Prince of Peace.
Cronin, Peadar *ss.cc.* '72 (LA) San Dimas, CA Holy Name of Mary; [P] La Verne, CA Congregation of the Sacred Hearts of Jesus and Mary.
Cronin, Peter J. *s.s.c.* '54 (BUF)[M] Silver Creek, NY St. Columbans on the Lake, Home for the Aged.
Cronin, Peter *s.s.c.* '54 (OM)[K] St. Columbans Missionary Society of St. Columban.
Cronin, Richard F. *o.s.b.* '66 (PAT)[N] Morristown, NJ St. Mary's Abbey.
Cronin, Richard '60 (JC) Retired.
Cronin, Robert J. *s.o.l.t.* '83 (FAR) Belcourt, ND St. Ann; Belcourt, ND St. Ann.
Cronin, Robert J. *s.o.l.t.* '83 (CC)[G] Robstown, TX Society of Our Lady of the Most Holy Trinity.
Cronin, Robert W. '52 (NOR) Members; Censor of Books Retired.
Cronin, Sean '73 (LA) On Administrative Leave.
Cronin, Sylvester J. '88 (MET) Department of Stewardship and Development; College of Consultors; Metuchen, NJ Cathedral of St. Francis of Assisi.
Cronin, Thomas '69 (KC) Retired.
Cronin, Rev. Msgr. Timothy P. '85 (STL)[A] St. Louis, MO Cardinal Glennon College; Cardinal Glennon College.
Cronin, Tom '69 (RNO) Virginia City, NV St. Mary in the Mountains Retired.
Cronin, William F. *o.s.cam.* (WOR)[S] Whitinsville, MA St. Camillus Institute, Inc.
Cronin, William *m.i.* '76 (MIL)[P] Milwaukee, WI St. Camillus Provincialate.
Cronk, James F. '69 (DET) Bloomfield Hills, MI St. Owen.
Cronkleton, Thomas E. '86 (CHY) Judicial Vicar; Cheyenne, WY Holy Trinity; College of Consultors; Ex Officios, Non–Voting; Judicial Vicar; Judges; St. Joseph's Society for Priests (Clergy Mutual Benefit Society).
Cronogue, Michael P. *s.s.e.* '77 (FgM)[E] Colchester, VT Society of St. Edmund; Colchester, VT SOCIETY OF ST. EDMUND; Colchester, VT; Colchester, VT Society of St. Edmund.
Cronouge, Michael *s.s.e.* '77 (NOR)[M] Mystic, CT St. Edmund's of Connecticut, Inc.
Crook, David G. '81 (BEL) Retired.
Crooker, Robert W. *c.s.b.* '53 (GAL)[O] Houston, TX Residence of the Basilian Fathers of the University of St. Thomas.
Crookston, James F. '71 (ALT) Johnstown, PA St. John Gualbert Cathedral.
Crookston, Michael J. '80 (GBG) Uniontown, PA St. John The Evangelist; Bishop's Priests Council.
Crosara, Lawrence *s.x.* '58 (MIL)[B] Franklin, WI Xaverian Missionary Fathers College Seminary.
Crosby, Rev. Msgr. Charles E. '56 (MAN) Retired.
Crosby, Dan *o.f.m.cap.* '64 (LC)[G] Marathon City, WI St. Anthony Spirituality Center.
Crosby, Michael *o.f.m.* '64 (STL)[S] Dittmer, MO Il Ritiro–The Little Retreat.
Crosby, Michael *o.f.m.cap.* '66 (MIL) Milwaukee, WI St. Benedict the Moor.
Crosby, Neil A. '81 (CLV) Cuyahoga Falls, OH St. Eugene.
Crosby, Theodore A. '00 (OG) Lyon Mountain, NY St. Bernard.
Crosby, Vincent R. *o.s.b.* '72 (GBG)[G] Latrobe, PA Saint Vincent Archabbey.
Crosier, Rev. Msgr. Raymond '75 (AMA) Amarillo, TX St. Hyacinth's; Priests' Pension Plan Retirement Committee.
Cross, Michael L. '62 (MRY) Felton, CA St. John's.
Cross, Robert A. '52 (CHI) Retired.
Cross, William D. '85 (STU) Judicial Vicar; Pastoral Staff; Wintersville, OH Blessed Sacrament; Wintersville, OH Our Lady of Lourdes.
Cross, William H. '74 (CIN) Cincinnati, OH St. Andrew; Cincinnati, OH St. Margaret – St. John Parish.
Crosse, Charles G. '53 (SEA) Lakewood, WA St. John Bosco Retired.
Crossen, Jason '00 (DAV) Muscatine, IA SS. Mary and Mathias of Muscatine; Columbus Junction, IA St. Joseph.
Crosser, Raymond G. '56 (ALT) Retired.
Crossin, John W. *o.s.f.s.* '76 (WDC)[B] Washington, DC Deshairs Community–Oblates of St. Francis de Sales Residence.
Crossman, James '46 (DUL) Retired.
Crossmyer, Robert *c.p.* '88 (BIR) Birmingham, AL Holy Family; [I] Birmingham, AL Congregation of the Passion: Holy Family Community, Inc.
Crossthwait, Joseph (GAL)[L] Houston, TX Pope John Paul XXIII Priests' Residence Retired.
Crosthwait, Rev. Msgr. Joseph H. '41 (GAL) Retired.
Crosthwaite, Alejandro *o.p.* '98 (OAK)[M] Oakland Order of Preachers (Province of the Most Holy Name of Jesus – Western Dominican Province).
Croteau, Roger H. '67 (MAN) Derry, NH Holy Cross; Advocates.
Crotty, Christopher *c.p.m.* '01 (OWN)[F] Auburn, KY Fathers of Mercy.
Crotty, Columban *ss.cc.* '58 (WDC) Seat Pleasant, MD St. Margaret.
Crotty, John M. '47 (NY) Retired.
Crotty, John '47 (NY)[EE] Bronx, NY John Cardinal O'Connor Residence.
Crotty, Thomas M. *o.s.m.* '60 (CHI)[N] Chicago Order of Friar Servants of Mary (Servites) United States of America Province, Inc.
Crotty, Thomas M. *o.s.m.* '60 (ORG)[I] Anaheim, CA Servite Fathers and Brothers.
Crowe, Francis R. *o.p.* '47 (CHI)[N] St. Pius V Priory.
Crowe, George W. '65 (PH) Retired.
Crowe, Hugh '58 (LA) Los Angeles, CA St. Ann Retired.
Crowe, Raymond *o.m.i.* '54 (BO)[X] Tewksbury, MA Immaculate Heart of Mary Residence.
Crowe, William R. '08 (LA) Simi Valley, CA St. Peter Claver.
Crowley, Cale J. *s.s.* '69 (BAL)[S] Baltimore Society of

St. Sulpice, Province of the United States.
Crowley, Charles G. *s.j.* '51 (BO)[U] Weston, MA Campion Health Center, Inc.
Crowley, Daniel J. '68 (BO) Senior Priests.; Middleborough, MA Sacred Heart Retired.
Crowley, Dennis J. '89 (PAT) Morristown, NJ Assumption of the Blessed Virgin Mary.
Crowley, Edmund G. '70 (MAN) Hooksett, NH Holy Rosary; Suncook, NH St. John the Baptist; Air National Guard Chaplains.
Crowley, James M. '87 (CHR) Greenwood, SC Our Lady of Lourdes.
Crowley, John A. '61 (PMB) Delray Beach, FL; Vero Beach, FL St. John of the Cross; Elected Members Retired.
Crowley, John C. '03 (PH) Graduate Studies.
Crowley, Joseph P. '06 (HRT)[D] West Hartford, CT Northwest Catholic High School; New Britain, CT St. Joseph's; New Britain, CT St. Peter.
Crowley, Pat *ss.cc.* '63 (SB)[I] Chino Hills, CA Congregation of the Sacred Hearts of Jesus & Mary, SS.CC.
Crowley, Patrick J. *ss.cc.* '72 (LA)[P] La Verne, CA Congregation of the Sacred Hearts of Jesus and Mary.
Crowley, Paul G. *s.j.* '92 (SJ)[B] Santa Clara, CA Jesuit Community.
Crowley, R. Kevin '68 (MET) Retired.
Crowley, Richard P. '64 (BO) Middleborough, MA Sacred Heart.
Crowley, Thomas F. '76 (WDC) Waldorf, MD Our Lady Help of Christians.
Crowley, William F. *c.s.sp.* '49 (PIT)[B] Pittsburgh, PA Duquesne University of the Holy Spirit; [O] Bethel Park, PA The Spiritan Center Retired.
Crowley, William '74 (B) Coeur d'Alene, ID St. Thomas; Adjutant Judicial Vicars; Judges.
Crozzoletto, Provvido *m.c.c.j.* '70 (NEW)[M] Montclair, NJ Comboni Missionaries of the Heart of Jesus (Verona Fathers).
Crucet, Jose '88 (PMB) West Palm Beach, FL St. Juliana.
Cruez, Luis (SJN) San Juan, PR Jesus Mediador.
Crumbley, Charles W. '67 (Y) Warren, OH St. James.
Crumley, William *c.s.c.* '64 (LAF) Charenton, LA Immaculate Conception.
Crump, Michael Edward *s.o.l.t.* '09 (CC) Robstown, TX St. Anthony; [G] Robstown, TX Society of Our Lady of the Most Holy Trinity.
Cruz, Alberto Dela '94 (CHK) Saipan, MP Santa Remedios Parish; Presbyteral Council.
Cruz, Alexander '91 (NEW) Linden, NJ St. Elizabeth of Hungary.
Cruz, Carlos de la *s.j.* '75 (LAF)[J] Grand Coteau, LA Jesuit Spirituality Center (St. Charles College).
Cruz, Cecilio de la (SJN)[F] Rio Piedras, PR Hogar Santa Teresa Jornet for the Aged.
Cruz, David R. '86 (LUB)[A] Lubbock, TX Office for Cursillo Movement.
Cruz, David '86 (LUB) Lubbock, TX Our Lady of Grace; Cursillo Movement.
Cruz, Dennys W. *c.p.* (ARE) Lares, PR St. Joseph.
Cruz, Domingo '73 (HT) Schriever, LA St. Bridget; Priests Council.
Cruz, Eric '02 (NY) Bronx, NY Christ the King.
Cruz, Faustino M. *s.m.* '88 (OAK)[A] Berkeley, CA Franciscan School of Theology; [A] Berkeley, CA Franciscan School of Theology.
Cruz, Fidel '05 (NY) Bronx, NY Blessed Sacrament.
Cruz, Francisco '69 (CHR) Joanna, SC St. Boniface; Newberry, SC St. Mark; [H] Gaffney, SC Limestone College.
Cruz, Gilbert J. '81 (SJN) Retired.
Cruz, Gilbert '81 (LA) Altadena, CA Sacred Heart.
Cruz, Gustavo '74 (LAV) Las Vegas, NV Prince of Peace; Priests' Pension Board; Presbyteral Council for the Diocese of Las Vegas.
Cruz, Hector *sch.p.* '04 (PCE)[C] Coto Laurel, PR Colegio Ponceno.
Cruz, Hector *s.m.* '77 (BWN) Brownsville, TX San Felipe de Jesus; Olmito, TX Our Heavenly Father; San Pedro, TX San Pedro.
Cruz, James A. '05 (NY) New York, NY; Secretary to the Archbishop.
Cruz, Jose Gabrie Rodriguez '98 (CHR) Johns Island, SC Church of the Holy Spirit.
Cruz, Jose '07 (LA) Los Angeles, CA Immaculate Conception.
Cruz, Luciano '86 (PAT) Paterson, NJ St. Therese.
Cruz, Luis Antonio Rivera '83 (CGS) San Lorenzo, PR Sagrado Corazon de Jesus y 12 Apostoles.
Cruz, Rev. Msgr. Remberto '49 (SJN) Retired.
Cruz, Robert Joel '96 (HT) Thibodaux, LA Our Lady of Prompt Succor; Pontifical Societies for the Propagation of the Faith.
Cruz, Saul E. '92 (RCK) DeKalb, IL St. Mary; Special Assignment.
Cruz–Davila, Carlos D. '80 (SJN) San Juan, PR Nuestra Senora de la Esperanza; Santurce, PR Doctors Community Hospital; [E] San Juan, PR Doctor's Community Hospital; [E] San Juan, PR Centro Medico de P.R.
Cruz Velazquez, Johnny *o.ss.t.* '91 (SJN) Santurce, PR Ashford Presbyterian Community Hospital.
Cryan, James F. *o.s.f.s.* '65 (TOL) Toledo, OH Gesu; [I] Toledo, OH Provincial Residence.
Cryan, John J. '81 (NEW) Jersey City, NJ Our Lady of Mercy; Jersey City, NJ Church of Our Lady of Sorrows; Jersey City South Deanery 12; Archdiocesan Judges.
Cryans, Andrew W. '75 (MAN) Durham, NH St. Thomas More; [O] Durham, NH St. Thomas More Catholic Student Center at the University of New Hampshire.
Crynes, Rev. Msgr. J. Peter '67 (SCR) Unassigned or Leave of Absence; [N] Dunmore, PA Villa St. Joseph.
Csaszar, James C. '99 (COL) Corning, OH St. Bernard; New Lexington, OH Church of the Atonement; New Lexington, OH St. Patrick; New Lexington, OH St. Rose of Lima; Deanery 8: Muskingum–Perry; Parochial Examiners; Presbyteral Council.
Cserhati, Rev. Msgr. Ferenc '71 (ATH) "Eletunk" (Our Life).
Csete, Ivan L. '81 (NY) Forestburgh, NY St. Thomas Aquinas.
Csizmar, Richard A. '68 (BUF) Vicars; Clergy Personnel Board; Albion, NY Holy Family.
Cuadrado, Angel *o.de.m.* '86 (PCE) Ponce, PR Santuario San Judas Tadeo.
Cuadrado, Hector F. *c.m.f.* '91 (SJN) Bayamon, PR San Jose.
Cuadros, Jesus '66 (BRK) Brooklyn, NY Holy Family–Saint Thomas Aquinas.
Cuario, Bruno *d.s.* '91 (PHX) Williams, AZ St. Joseph's Roman Catholic Parish; Seligman, AZ St. Francis Roman Catholic Parish; Ashfork, AZ St. Anne Roman Catholic Mission Ashfork, A Quasi–Parish.
Cuario, Dindo Bruno *d.s.* '91 (PHX) Grand Canyon, AZ El Cristo Rey Roman Catholic Parish.
Cuarto, Jonathan '05 (SJ) Campbell, CA St. Lucy.
Cuba, I. Enrique Castro '94 (LC) Abbotsford, WI St. Bernard.
Cubas–Ramirez, Franklin *s.m.* '89 (SB) Indio, CA Our Lady of Perpetual Help.
Cucarella, Diego Ramon Sario *m.afr.* '01 (WDC) Washington, DC; Washington, DC MISSIONARIES OF AFRICA; [N] Washington, DC Missionaries of Africa.
Cuccaro, John J. '79 (PBR) Pittsburgh, PA St. John Chrysostom.
Cuccia, Salvatore H. *o.praem.* '66 (GB) De Pere, WI St. Norbert College; [J] De Pere, WI St. Norbert Abbey; [B] De Pere, WI St. Norbert College.
Cudak, Emil (CHI) Chicago, IL St. Bruno.
Cudden, Jerome *o.p.* '07 (OAK) Oakland, CA; [M] Oakland, CA Order of Preachers (Province of Holy Name of Jesus – Western Dominican Province).
Cuddigan, John D. *s.j.* '62 (OM)[K] Omaha, NE Jesuit Community at Creighton University.
Cuddihy, Rev. Msgr. William '56 (SD) Retired.
Cuddy, Rev. Msgr. John J. '53 (SAV) Retired.
Cuddy, Michael J. *o.p.* '07 (PRO)[B] Providence, RI Providence College; [P] Providence St. Thomas Aquinas Priory at Providence College.
Cuddy, William F. '79 (BO) Military & VA Chaplains.; Navy Chaplains.
Cuddy, William F. '79 (MO) Presbyteral Council.
Cudnik, Chester C. '48 (CLV) Cleveland, OH St. Barbara Retired.
Cuenca, Fernando *o.m.v.* '84 (LA) Hawaiian Gardens, CA St. Peter Chanel.
Cuenca–Wilson, Mauricio '01 (PBL) San Luis, CO Sangre de Cristo.
Cuenin, Walter H. '70 (BO)[AA] Waltham, MA Brandeis University Catholic Chaplaincy; Brandeis University; Allston, MA St. Anthony of Padua.
Cuevas, Alberto R. '98 (SFR) Menlo Park, CA St. Anthony.
Cuevas, Diego O. '03 (MAD) University Hospitals.
Cuevas, Geronimo '86 (MRY) On Leave.
Cuevas, Jose Luis '74 (LA) Long Beach, CA St. Athanasius.
Cuevas, Randy M. '82 (MO)[K] Hammond, LA St. Albert the Great Catholic Student Center; Air Force Reserve Chaplains.
Cuevas, Wilson '81 (ELP) El Paso, TX Corpus Christi.
Cuff, John P. *m.m.* '69 (FgM) Maryknoll, NY MARYKNOLL.
Cuic, Jozo *o.f.m.* '74 (DET) Troy, MI St. Lucy.
Culhane, Alberic *o.s.b.* '57 (SCL)[I] Collegeville, MN St. John's Abbey, of the Order of St. Benedict.
Culkin, Rev. Msgr. Francis J. '44 (SY) Rome, NY St. Mary of the Assumption Retired.
Culkin, Michael J. (HBG) Lancaster, PA St. John Neumann.
Culkin, Michael '78 (WDC) On Duty Outside the Archdiocese.
Cull, Rev. Msgr. Lawrence W. '69 (NEW) Ramsey, NJ St. Paul.
Cullen, Anthony F. '75 (SPR) Holyoke, MA St. Jerome.
Cullen, Bernard J. *o.c.s.o.* '48 (DUB)[K] Peosta, IA New Melleray Abbey, Order of Cistercians of the Strict Observance.
Cullen, Christopher M. *s.j.* '94 (NY)[EE] Cardinal Spellman Hall, Jesuit Community.
Cullen, Daniel *s.m.a.* '47 (NEW)[M] Tenafly, NJ Society of African Missions, Provincialate, S.M.A. Fathers.
Cullen, Donald '71 (KCK) Overland Park, KS Queen of the Holy Rosary.
Cullen, Harold '68 (TR) West Long Branch, NJ St. Jerome.
Cullen, Hugh G. '75 (GAL) Houston, TX St. Thomas More.
Cullen, Rev. Msgr. J. Peter '67 (BGP) Greenwich, CT St. Michael the Archangel; Vicars General; Presbyteral Council; Finance Council; Pastors' Vocation Advisory Board; Diocesan Consultors.
Cullen, John J. '99 (BUF) Canaseraga, NY St. Mary.
Cullen, Kevin L. *s.j.* '86 (KC)[J] Kansas City, MO Rockhurst Jesuit Community; [B] Kansas City, MO Rockhurst University.
Cullen, Patrick P. '68 (BIR) Bessemer, AL St. Aloysius Church; [I] Bessemer, AL St. Aloysius Educational Foundation; Diocesan College of Consultors; Apostolate with Mentally Retarded Persons; Priests'/Presbyteral Council; Diocesan College of Vicars.
Cullen, Patrick *s.p.s.* '52 (NEW)[M] Cliffside Park, NJ St. Patrick's Missionary Society Retired.
Cullen, Paul M. *o.s.m.* '65 (CHI) Chicago, IL Annunciata; [N] Chicago, IL Annunciata Priory.
Cullen, Robert J. '05 (BO) Medford, MA St. Raphael.
Cullen, William J. *s.j.* '65 (BO)[U] Weston, MA Campion Health Center, Inc.
Cullen, William '48 (JOL) Retired.
Cullen, William '83 (JKS) Retired.
Culler, Eric J. '08 (TOL)[B] Tiffin, OH Calvert High School; Sycamore, OH St. Pius X; Tiffin, OH St. Mary.
Culleton, Thomas '91 (SLC) Retired.
Culley, Brian *c.m.f.* '84 (CHI)[N] Chicago, IL Barbastro House (Claretian Candidate House).
Culligan, Kevin *o.c.d.* '63 (BO)[U] Boston, MA Carmelite Monastery.
Culligan, Martin J. *c.m.* '57 (STL)[O] St. Louis, MO Lazarist Residence Retired.
Culligan, Michael A. '59 (SR) Petaluma, CA St. James.
Cullinan, John F. '46 (PHX) Retired.
Cullinane, Brian *o.f.m.* '71 (NEW) Wood Ridge, NJ Our Lady of the Assumption.
Cullinane, Briant *o.f.m.conv.* '57 (ALB) Special Assignment; [L] Rensselaer, NY Provincialate, Immaculate Conception Friary – Order of Friars Minor Conventual.
Cullinane, Jeremiah J. '59 (WH) Retired.
Cullinane, John F. *p.e.* '56 (BRK) Rockaway Point, NY Blessed Trinity Roman Catholic Church Retired.
Cullings, David Ronald '67 (P) Retired.
Cullings, David '67 (P)[C] Eugene, OR Marist Catholic High School.
Culloty, John P. '72 (BO) Norwood, MA St. Timothy.
Culnane, William R. '60 (SCR)[N] Dunmore, PA Villa St. Joseph Retired.
Culotta, Joachim *o.p.* '64 (SFE)[K] Albuquerque, NM St. Thomas Aquinas (Newman Center) University Parish; Albuquerque, NM St. Thomas Aquinas University Parish.
Culotta, Joseph G. '83 (BIR) Birmingham, AL St. Mark the Evangelist; Diocesan College of Consultors; Priests'/Presbyteral Council; Diocesan College of Vicars.
Culotta, Rev. Msgr. Salvador J. '53 (BEA) Retired.
Culver, Garry '64 (DM) Retired.
Culver, James A. '55 (SY) Rome, NY St. Peter Retired.
Culver, Richard J. '85 (OAK) Bay Point, CA Our Lady, Queen of the World; Deanery #7.
Cumberland, Matthew T. '92 (LA) La Puente, CA St. Joseph.
Cummings, Brian J. *s.s.e.* '96 (BUR)[A] Colchester, VT St. Michael's College; [E] Colchester, VT Society of St. Edmund; [H] Isle La Motte, VT St. Anne's Shrine; Councilors:; Board Members.
Cummings, Rev. Msgr. Carl F. '75 (BAL) Pasadena, MD St. Jane Frances de Chantal; [W] Woodstock, MD Catholic War Veterans, Inc.
Cummings, Charles J. '68 (SCR) Diocesan Consultors; Deans Retired.
Cummings, Charles J. *o.c.s.o.* '71 (SLC)[A] Huntsville, UT Abbey of Our Lady of the Holy Trinity; [F] Huntsville, UT Abbey of Our Lady of the Holy Trinity of the Order of Cistercians.
Cummings, Gabriel '84 (SAV) St. Marys, GA Our Lady Star of the Sea.
Cummings, Rev. Msgr. George '43 (SP) Citrus Springs, FL St. Elizabeth Ann Seton Retired.
Cummings, John J. '88 (LFT) Reynolds, IN St. Joseph.
Cummings, Jose Emilio '72 (SJN) San Juan, PR Catedral de San Juan Bautista; [D] San Juan, PR Santa Ana Chapel.
Cummings, Juniper *o.f.m.conv.* '50 (FgM) Mount Saint Francis, IN Province of Our Lady of Consolation.
Cummings, Leo P. '64 (SCR)[N] Dunmore, PA Villa St. Joseph.
Cummings, Marilyn '97 (SP)[J] Tampa, FL St. Joseph's Hospital, Inc.
Cummings, Maurice H. *o.carm.* '71 (DOD) Ashland, KS St. Joseph Catholic Church of Ashland, Kansas.

Cummings, McLean (BAL) Ellicott City, MD Our Lady of Perpetual Help; [A] Emmitsburg, MD Mount St. Mary's Seminary.
Cummings, Patrick J. '78 (GAL)[S] Houston, TX The Catholic Chaplain Corps.
Cummings, Paul J. '55 (LAN) Retired.
Cummings, Thomas W. *s.j.* '69 (STL)[F] St. Louis, MO St. Louis University High School, George H. Backer Memorial; [O] Saint Louis, MO St. Louis University High School Jesuit Community.
Cummings, Timothy '08 (SP) Scouting Office, Boys; Elected Parochial Vicars; Dunedin, FL Our Lady of Lourdes.
Cummings–Espada, Rev. Msgr. Jose E. '72 (SJN) Diocesan Consultors; Subcommission for Sacred Art.
Cummins, Anthony O. '65 (SAT) Boerne, TX St. Peter the Apostle.
Cummins, Charles T. '68 (SLC) Ogden, UT Saint Florence Catholic Community LLC 254; Ogden, UT Saint Joseph LLC 230; [H] Ogden, UT Weber State University, Newman Center.
Cummins, Joseph V. *c.m.* '72 (PH) Philadelphia, PA St. Francis of Assisi.
Cummins, Michael E. '95 (KNX) East Tennessee State University; Deaf Ministry; Vocation Discernment Office.
Cummins, Michael J. *c.m.* '77 (BRK)[T] Queens Village, NY DePaul Residence.
Cummins, Michael '95 (KNX) Johnson City, TN St. Mary; [H] Johnson City, TN ETSU–Catholic Center.
Cummins, Robert L. '86 (RIC) Mathews, VA Church of Francis de Sales; Topping, VA Church of the Visitation.
Cuneo, Rev. Msgr. J. James '67 (BGP) Stratford, CT Holy Name of Jesus; Catholic Lawyers; Adjutant Judicial Vicar.
Cuneo, James J. '63 (DEN) Retired.
Cunha, Egionor '92 (MO) Navy Reserve Chaplains.
Cunnane, Rev. Msgr. Jarlath '77 (LA) Los Angeles, CA St. Thomas the Apostle; Deanery 15; Members.
Cunnane, Michael A. '61 (SD) Santee, CA Guardian Angels; Clergy Personnel Board.
Cunneen, Rev. Msgr. Sean R. '67 (NEW) Scotch Plains, NJ Immaculate Heart of Mary.
Cunney, Henry M. '59 (BO) Senior Priests. Retired.
Cunniff, Charles *c.s.p.* '83 (COL)[J] Columbus, OH Campus Ministry.
Cunniff, Vincent '53 (P) Retired.
Cunnigham, James K. '95 (BRK) Far Rockaway, NY St. Mary Star of the Sea and St. Gertrude.
Cunningham, Donald M. *s.j.* '64 (STL)[O] St. Louis, MO Jesuit Community Corporation at Saint Louis University – Jesuit Hall.
Cunningham, Douglas D. '87 (SY) Air National Guard Chaplains; Endicott, NY St. Anthony of Padua.
Cunningham, Edward *o.m.i.* '58 (SAT)[K] San Antonio, TX Oblate Madonna Residence.
Cunningham, Gerard M. '93 (ORL) Lady Lake, FL St. Timothy.
Cunningham, James B. '87 (BUF) Buffalo, NY St. Teresa.
Cunningham, James K. '95 (BRK) Presbyteral Council.
Cunningham, James *c.s.s.* '50 (BO)[X] Waltham, MA Stigmatine Fathers and Brothers Retired.
Cunningham, John D. *s.j.* '05 (CHI)[C] Chicago, IL Jesuit Community at Loyola University Chicago.
Cunningham, John E. '51 (DM) Retired.
Cunningham, John F. '74 (PHX) Retired.
Cunningham, John H. '65 (ALX) Retired.
Cunningham, John Vianney *t.o.r.* '70 (ORL)[E] Winter Park, FL San Pedro Spiritual Development Center.
Cunningham, John (BAL) Bel Air, MD St. Margaret.
Cunningham, Rev. Msgr. Joseph C. '71 (PH) Retired.
Cunningham, Joseph L. '63 (BRK) Bellerose, NY St. Gregory the Great.
Cunningham, Joseph L. '56 (MIL) Retired.
Cunningham, Leonard A. *o.c.s.o.* '50 (CHR)[E] Moncks Corner, SC Mepkin Abbey.
Cunningham, Lloyd *s.v.d.* '81 (CHI)[N] Techny, IL Divine Word Residence.
Cunningham, Mark '99 (ALB) Herkimer, NY St. Francis de Sales; Members; Mohawk, NY Blessed Sacrament.
Cunningham, Michael '86 (OAK) Concord, CA Queen of All Saints.
Cunningham, Nicholas J. '79 (TOL) Shelby, OH Most Pure Heart of Mary.
Cunningham, Rev. Msgr. Peter J. '56 (MOB) Mobile, AL St. Mary; Archdiocesan Consultors.
Cunningham, Robert W. *s.j.* '55 (FgM) Los Gatos, CA Society of Jesus.
Cunningham, Vianney *t.o.r.* '70 (ORL)[F] Winter Park, FL Franciscan Friars, T.O.R., San Pedro Friary.
Cuny, W. Timothy *o.s.a.* '70 (KAL)[E] Douglas, MI Order of St. Augustine; Douglas, MI St. Peter.
Cuomo, Rocco A. '64 (TR) Retired.
Cupp, Edwin F. '69 (WH) Retired.
Cupple, Gerard J. '85 (DET) Lincoln Park, MI St. Henry.
Cupps, David W. '09 (RIC) Portsmouth, VA St. Paul; Portsmouth, VA Church of the Resurrection; Chesapeake, VA St. Mary; Portsmouth, VA Church of the Holy Angels.
Curalli, Joseph M. *c.ss.r.* '78 (STL)[O] Liguori, MO Liguori Mission House/Redemptorists.
Curbelo, Luis *s.e.m.v.* '94 (STP) St. Paul, MN St. James; St. Paul, MN St. Francis De Sales.
Curci, Rev. Msgr. Richard G. '72 (GBG)[J] Greensburg, PA The Bishop William G. Connare Center.
Curesky, Mark *o.f.m.conv.* '75 (HRT) Kensington, CT St. Paul.
Cureton, Anthony J. '04 (GAY) Higgins Lake, MI St. James; Prudenville, MI Our Lady of the Lake.
Curiel, James A. *o.c.d.* '95 (SAT) San Antonio, TX Basilica of the National Shrine of the Little Flower, Our Lady of Mt. Carmel and St. Therese Parish; [L] San Antonio, TX Discalced Carmelite Fathers of San Antonio.
Curley, Augustine J. *o.s.b.* '88 (NEW)[M] Newark, NJ Newark Abbey.
Curley, Rev. Msgr. Joseph K. '62 (RVC) Centereach, NY Assumption of the Blessed Virgin Mary.
Curley, Patrick '70 (JKS) Vicksburg, MS St. Michael.
Curley, Patrick '08 (NY) New York, NY Epiphany.
Curley, Terence P. '72 (BO) Health Leave.
Curley, Thomas J. '70 (NY) Red Hook, NY St. Christopher; Tivoli, NY St. Sylvia.
Curnutte, William G. '82 (SLC) Retired.
Curran, Anthony T. '83 (ATL) Retired.
Curran, Anthony '72 (ALB) Schenectady, NY St. John the Evangelist; Schenectady, NY St. Paul the Apostle; Albany County Nursing Home; Special Assignment.
Curran, Brendan A. *o.p.* '01 (CHI) Chicago, IL St. Pius V; [N] Chicago, IL Dominican Community.
Curran, Charles E. '58 (ROC) On Duty Outside the Diocese.
Curran, Francis D. '50 (CLV) Willoughby, OH Immaculate Conception Retired.
Curran, Rev. Msgr. Francis L. '38 (MAN) Retired.
Curran, Francis T. '69 (GI) Retired.
Curran, Rev. Msgr. Hugh D. '54 (NY) Retired.
Curran, Rev. Msgr. James P. '63 (CAM) Gloucester, NJ St. Mary's Church, Gloucester.
Curran, Rev. Msgr. James P. '63 (CAM) Parent–Teachers Association.
Curran, James *s.d.b.* '51 (NO) Harvey, LA St. Rosalie.
Curran, John F. *s.j.* '59 (CI)[C] Kolonia, Pohnpei, FM Jesuit House; Vicar General; Finance Committee; Notaries; New York, NY Society of Jesus.
Curran, John M. *o.m.i.* '78 (FgM) Pacoima, CA Mary Immaculate; Washington, DC AMERICAN OBLATE MISSIONS.
Curran, John W. *o.f.m.conv.* '71 (IND) Sellersburg, IN St. Joseph.
Curran, John '71 (IND) Clarksville, IN St. Anthony of Padua.
Curran, Joseph L. '76 (BO) Watertown, MA Sacred Heart.
Curran, Rev. Msgr. Michael J. '81 (BRK) Rockaway Point, NY Blessed Trinity Roman Catholic Church.
Curran, Oliver '76 (RNO) Fallon, NV St. Patrick.
Curran, Oliver (GLP) On Duty Outside of Diocese.
Curran, Patrick '01 (STO) San Andreas, CA St. Andrew Church of San Andreas (Pastor of).
Curran, Paul E. '59 (BO) Senior Priests. Retired.
Curran, Rev. Msgr. Paul F. '57 (PH) Springfield, PA Holy Cross Retired.
Curran, Peter *o.m.i.* '71 (FgM) Washington, DC AMERICAN OBLATE MISSIONS.
Curran, Richard G. '76 (BO) Unassigned.; Watertown, MA Sacred Heart.
Curran, Thomas B. *o.s.f.s.* '84 (KC)[B] Kansas City, MO Rockhurst University; [J] Kansas City, MO Rockhurst Jesuit Community.
Curran, Thomas M. '70 (BO) Permanent Disability.
Curran, Vincent J. '98 (HRT) East Hartford, CT St. Christopher; Hamden–North Haven Deanery.
Curran, William J. '69 (CHI) Tinley Park, IL St. George.
Curran, William *m.afr.* '66 (FgM) Washington, DC MISSIONARIES OF AFRICA.
Currans, Clement W. '74 (SC) Emmetsburg, IA Holy Family.
Current, Maurice H. '80 (LIN) Beaver Crossing, NE Sacred Heart; Adjutant Judicial Vicars; Commission for Sacred Liturgy and Sacred Music; Ecumenical Affairs, Commission for; Priests' Continuing Education Committee.
Currie, Charles A. '59 (SY) Endicott, NY St. Ambrose.
Currie, Charles L. *s.j.* '63 (WDC)[N] Washington, DC Leonard Neale House; [W] Washington, DC Association of Jesuit Colleges and University.
Currie, John A. '97 (BO) Hingham, MA St. Paul.
Currie, Joseph A. *s.j.* '68 (NY)[EE] Cardinal Spellman Hall, Jesuit Community.
Currie, Joseph *s.j.* '68 (NY)[HH] Bronx, NY Fordham University at Rosehill.
Currin, John M. '98 (DET) Romulus, MI St. Aloysius.
Curry, Andrew '08 (FTW) Fort Wayne, IN St. Elizabeth Ann Seton.
Curry, Frederic F. '49 (TUC) Tucson, AZ Saint Joseph Roman Catholic Parish – Tucson Retired.
Curry, James J. *s.j.* '74 (NY)[F] New York, NY Loyola School; [EE] New York, NY St. Ignatius Loyola Residence.
Curry, Rev. Msgr. Joseph M. '86 (MET) Episcopal Vicars; Spotswood, NJ Immaculate Conception.
Curry, Richard J. *s.j.* '09 (WDC)[N] Washington, DC The Jesuit Community at Georgetown University.
Curry, Robert S. *s.j.* '64 (PH)[Y] Loyola Center and Manresa Hall.
Curry, Stephen M. *o.s.a.* '96 (CAM)[C] Richland, NJ St. Augustine Preparatory School.
Curry, Terrence M. *s.j.* '77 (WOR)[O] Worcester, MA Jesuits of the Holy Cross, Inc.; [K] Worcester, MA Saint Vincent Hospital, Inc.
Curry, Thomas P. *o.s.b.* '03 (GBG) Latrobe, PA St. Vincent Basilica; [G] Latrobe, PA Saint Vincent Archabbey.
Curso, Manuel '72 (SFR) Colma, CA Holy Angels.
Curtin, Cornelius L. *s.j.* '56 (DET)[K] Clarkston, MI Colombiere Center.
Curtin, Eugene P. '56 (BO) Senior Priests. Retired.
Curtin, James F. '51 (BO) Senior Priests. Retired.
Curtin, Jim '69 (JOL) Lockport, IL St. Dennis.
Curtin, Martin *o.f.m.cap.* '90 (BO)[U] Jamaica Plain, MA San Lorenzo Friary.
Curtin, Vincent C. *s.j.* '68 (CHL) Mooresville, NC St. Therese; [J] Mooresville, NC Jesuit Community.
Curtis, Howard *o.c.s.o.* '57 (P)[L] Lafayette, OR The Cistercian (Trappist) Abbey of Our Lady of Guadalupe.
Curtis, John C. '84 (LEX) Carlisle, KY Shrine of Our Lady of Guadalupe; Paris, KY Annunciation of the Blessed Virgin Mary; HIV/AIDS Ministry.
Curtis, Joseph C. '69 (CHI) Indian Creek, IL St. Mary of Vernon.
Curtiss, Donald J. '71 (ROC) Clifton Springs, NY St. Dominic; Clifton Springs, NY St. Felix/St. Francis Parish Cluster.
Curtsinger, George '52 (FWT) Retired.
Cusack, Rev. Msgr. Francis V. '54 (MOB) Mobile, AL Our Lady of Lourdes; Archdiocesan Consultors; Vicar General.
Cusack, Francis *c.p.* '58 (CHI)[N] Chicago, IL Passionist Community–Immaculate Conception Monastery.
Cusack, Rev. Msgr. John J. '71 (PAT) Military Chaplains.
Cusack, John J. *c.m.* '45 (PH)[Y].
Cusack, Rev. Msgr. John J. (TUC) Tucson, AZ Christ the King Chapel.
Cusack, Paul *c.p.* '59 (MET)[I] South River Passionist Provincial Office.
Cusack, Thomas *s.s.c.* '62 (LA)[P] Los Angeles, CA Columban Fathers, Procure House.
Cusack, Thomas *s.s.c.* '62 (OM)[K] St. Columbans Missionary Society of St. Columban.
Cusatis, Girard J. '63 (PH) Drexel Hill, PA St. Andrew Retired.
Cusato, Michael F. *o.f.m.* '81 (BUF)[O] St. Bonaventure, NY St. Bonaventure Friary; [C] St. Bonaventure University; [C] St. Bonaventure, NY Friar Community.
Cuschieri, Rev. Msgr. Albert '61 (DAL) Retired.
Cush, John P. '98 (BRK) Censors of Books; [B] Elmhurst, NY Cathedral Preparatory Seminary of the Immaculate Conception.
Cushing, Matthew A. '09 (COV)[B] Erlanger, KY St. Henry District High School; Erlanger, KY Mary, Queen of Heaven.
Cushing, Robert A. '78 (SAV) Cordele, GA St. Theresa.
Cushing, Vincent de Paul *o.f.m.* '63 (WDC)[N] Silver Spring, MD Gemelli House.
Cushing, Walter F. '56 (ROC) Rochester, NY St. Cecilia Retired.
Cusick, Eugene G. '64 (PH) Retired.
Cusick, John C. '70 (CHI) Chicago, IL Old St. Patrick; Young Adult Ministry/Singles; Archdiocesan Council of Catholic Men.
Cusick, Kevin M. '92 (MO) Upper Marlboro, MD Saint Mary of the Assumption; Navy Reserve Chaplains.
Cusick, Thomas H. '64 (DET) Belleville, MI St. Anthony.
Cusick, Timothy S. '00 (STA) Presbyteral Council.
Cusick, Timothy *s.s.* (STA) Palm Coast, FL St. Elizabeth Ann Seton.
Cusimano, Joseph Gabriel *o.s.b.* '76 (SFE)[H] Abiquiu, NM Monastery of Christ in the Desert.
Cusimano, Salvatore J. '49 (BUF)[O] Tonawanda, NY O'Hara Residence Retired.
Cusmano, John C. '64 (DET) Retired.
Custer, Edward O. *m.m.* '72 (FgM) Maryknoll, NY MARYKNOLL.
Custer, John S. '83 (PSC) Westbury, NY Resurrection; Westbury, NY St. Andrew the Apostle.
Cutcher, Anthony E. '99 (CIN) St. Marys, OH Holy Rosary; Priest Councilors; Consultors.
Cutler, Shawn W. '05 (BGP) Greenwich, CT St. Michael the Archangel.
Cutrara, Vincent *c.s.* '57 (CIN) Cincinnati, OH Sacred Heart.
Cutrone, Dominick F. '55 (BRK) Brooklyn, NY Our Lady of Grace Retired.

Cwiekowski, Bruce '79 (P)[J] Portland, OR Providence Portland Medical Center.
Cwiekowski, Frederick J. *s.s.* '62 (SFR)[A] Menlo Park, CA St. Patrick Seminary and University.
Cwiekowski, Frederick J. *s.s.* '62 (HRT) On Duty Outside the Archdiocese.
Cwiekowski, Frederick J. *s.s.* '62 (BAL)[S] Baltimore Society of St. Sulpice, Province of the United States Retired.
Cwik, Thomas G. *s.j.* '00 (KC)[J] Kansas City, MO Rockhurst Jesuit Community; Kansas City, MO St. Francis Xavier.
Cybulski, David '09 (DET) Farmington, MI Our Lady of Sorrows.
Cyktor, Ronald L. '00 (GBG) Brady's Bend, PA St. Patrick.
Cylwicki, Albert W. *c.s.b.* '60 (ROC)[J] Rochester, NY Basilian Residence.
Cymbor, Rev. Msgr. John A. '50 (STU) Retired.
Cymerman, Alexander B. *o.f.m.conv.* '65 (SPR) Holyoke, MA Mater Dolorosa.
Cyr, Joel R. '71 (PRT) Benedicta, ME St. Benedict's; East Millinocket, ME Christ the Divine Mercy Parish.
Cyr, John F. '02 (PEO) Bloomington, IL Holy Trinity.
Cyr, John '02 (PEO) Bloomington, IL St. Patrick Church of Merna.
Cyr, L. Chanel '53 (PRT) Retired.
Cyr, L. Philip '69 (PRT) St. Agatha, ME Our Lady of the Valley.
Cyr, Lawrence *c.pp.s.* '44 (CIN)[N] Carthagena, OH St. Charles Retired.
Cyr, Myles *o.m.i.* '54 (PRT) Lincoln, ME St. Mary.
Cyr, Richard E. '60 (DET) Retired.
Cyr, Roger *o.m.i.* '59 (PRT) Howland, ME St. Leo The Great; Lincoln, ME St. Mary.
Cyr, Terrence *o.carm.* '75 (JOL)[L] Darien Carmelite Provincial Office.
Cyr, William E. '71 (SPR) Office of Lay Ministry Formation.
Cyr, William F. '71 (SPR) North Adams, MA Our Lady of Mercy Shrine; North Adams, MA Saint Elizabeth of Hungary Parish; [N] North Adams, MA Massachusetts College of Liberal Arts.
Cyscon, Peter J. '73 (CHI) Bridgeview, IL St. Fabian.
Cyscon, Philip E. '84 (CHI) Chicago, IL Holy Innocents.
Cyvas, Matthew '41 (ALB) Retired.
Cyza, Mark L. '04 (LIN) Advocates; Nebraska City, NE St. Mary's; Apostolate to the Spanish Speaking; Diocesan Consultors; Legion of Mary; Presbyteral Council.
Czabala, Teodor (STF) Johnson City, NY Sacred Heart Ukrainian Catholic Church.
Czachor, Richard E. '77 (SCR) Tannersville, PA Our Lady of Victory.
Czahur, John P. '77 (TR) Mount Holly, NJ Sacred Heart.
Czaicki, Franciszek *o.c.d.* '97 (GRY)[H] Munster, IN Discalced Carmelite Fathers Monastery.
Czaja, Blaise *c.p.* '64 (DET)[K] Detroit, MI St. Paul of the Cross Community, Congregation of the Passion.
Czaja, Joseph S. '46 (Y) Retired.
Czajka, Norman M. '61 (CHI) Retired.
Czajkowski, Andrew A. '74 (LAN) Davison, MI St. John the Evangelist; Regional Vicars.
Czajkowski, Richard S. *m.m.* '61 (FgM) Maryknoll, NY MARYKNOLL.
Czapinski, Richard J. '58 (PIT) Retired.
Czapla, Bruce *o.f.m.* '03 (MAN) Derry, NH St. Thomas Aquinas.
Czapla, Donald J. '03 (DUB) Marshalltown, IA St. Henry.
Czarcinski, Edward A. '88 (MET) Milltown, NJ Our Lady of Lourdes.
Czarkowski, Joseph R. '74 (E) Erie, PA Holy Rosary.
Czarnecki, Andrew '98 (DET) Roseville, MI St. Angela.
Czarnecki, Rev. Msgr. Anthony S. '66 (WOR) Webster, MA St. Joseph Basilica; Defender of the Bond; Deans; Presbyteral Council; Polish Ministry.
Czarnecki, Edward R. '66 (BUF) Defenders of the Bond; Blasdell, NY Our Mother of Good Counsel.
Czarnecki, Mark '96 (GAL) Spring, TX St. Edward; Houston, TX Holy Name.
Czarnecki, Stanislaw *s.j.* '97 (CHI)[N] Chicago, IL Sacred Heart Mission House; [N] Chicago, IL Jan Beyzym Society, Inc.
Czarnicki, Eryk '01 (CHI) Franklin Park, IL St. Gertrude.
Czarnota, Paul '03 (DET) Yale, MI Sacred Heart; Emmett, MI Our Lady of Mount Carmel.
Czarnota, Stanislaus '56 (LAN) Retired.
Czartorynski, David F. '84 (ALN) On Duty Outside the Diocese; DEPARTMENT OF VETERANS AFFAIRS HOSPITALS AND CHAPLAINS.
Czaster, Herman *o.f.m.conv.* '65 (BRK) Elmhurst, NY St. Adalbert.
Czaus, Joseph C. '89 (ALN) Unassigned.
Czech, Edward M. '73 (CLV) Cleveland, OH Holy Name Retired.
Czeck, Thomas *o.f.m.conv.* '98 (RNO) Reno, NV St. Thomas Aquinas Cathedral.
Czelusniak, Donald '78 (ALB) Gloversville, NY Church of the Holy Spirit; Deans.
Czemerda, Edward M. '87 (PIT) Absent on Sick Leave; [M] Pittsburgh, PA St. John Vianney Manor.
Czerniak, Ryszard *s.ch.* '00 (CHI) Argo, IL St. Blasé.
Czerwonka, Paul G. '03 (LC) On Duty Outside the Diocese.
Czok, Robert W. '66 (BRK) Brooklyn, NY St. Anthony of Padua–St. Alphonsus.
Czudek, Jan '99 (BRK) Forest Hills, NY Our Lady, Queen of Martyrs; [S] Czech/Slovak Apostolate.
Czyzewski, Michael *o.s.p.p.e.* '04 (PH)[Y].
Czyzynski, John *s.c.j.* '63 (CHI)[N] SCJ Novitiate.

D

D'Abele, Peter *s.m.m.* '75 (BRK)[T] Ozone Park Montfort Missionaries Provincialate (Missionaries of the Company of Mary).
D'Achille, Arnold V. '59 (DET) Retired.
D'Aco, Joseph '99 (FAR) Cando, ND Sacred Heart Church of Cando; Cando, ND St. Vincent de Paul Church of Leeds.
D'Addezio, Rev. Msgr. Louis A. '61 (PH) On Special or Other Archdiocesan Assignment; Philadelphia, PA St. Patrick.
D'Agostino, Carl L. '59 (CLV) Independence, OH St. Michael; Cleveland, OH Holy Redeemer Retired.
D'Agostino, Joseph '41 (ALB) Retired.
D'Agostino, Rodolfo *r.c.j.* '64 (LA) Van Nuys, CA St. Elisabeth; [P] Van Nuys, CA Rogationist Fathers.
D'Albro, Thomas G. '71 (BRK) Bayside, NY Our Lady of the Blessed Sacrament.
D'Alliessi, Daniel '04 (NY) Washington, DC St. Mary, Mother of God; Graduate Studies.
D'Almeida, Edward P. '09 (LR) Fort Smith, AR Immaculate Conception; Fort Smith, AR St. Leo's.
D'Ambrosia, Peter J. *s.m.* '85 (PRO) Coventry, RI SS. John and Paul.
D'Amico, Carmen A. '82 (PIT) Pittsburgh, PA St. Benedict the Moor; Pittsburgh, PA Epiphany; Pittsburgh, PA St. Mary of Mercy.
D'Amico, Frank A. '87 (STL) Wentzville, MO St. Patrick.
D'Amico, Joseph A. '95 (NEW) Archdiocesan Judges.
D'Amico, Joseph A. '95 (NEW) Jersey City, NJ St. Aloysius.
D'Andrea, Edward R. '73 (RVC) Blue Point, NY Our Lady of the Snow; South Brookhaven Deanery.
D'Andrea, Steven D. '97 (NEW) Wallington, NJ Most Sacred Heart of Jesus.
D'Angelico, Rev. Msgr. Anthony J. '74 (PH) Southampton, PA Our Lady of Good Counsel.
D'Angelo, Anthony *s.d.b.* '67 (BIR) Birmingham, AL Holy Rosary.
D'Angelo, Donald S. '68 (SFR) Retired.
D'Angelo, Joseph '68 (RVC) Nassau County Police Department; North Merrick, NY Sacred Heart; Chaplains of the Nassau County Police Department.
D'Angelo, Paul R. '09 (VEN) Naples, FL St. William.
D'Angelo, Thomas P. '84 (NY)[E] Bronx, NY Cardinal Spellman High School; Pastoral Life Conference; Absent on Sick Leave.
d'Anjou, John R. *s.j.* '72 (PRT) Portland, ME St. Patrick's; Portland, ME St. Pius X.
d'Anjou, John R. *s.j.* '72 (BO)[U] Boston The Society of Jesus of New England–Provincial Offices.
D'Anjou, Lawrence C. (OAK) Confraternity of Eucharistic Devotion (CEDDO).
D'Anjou, Lawrence C. '00 (OAK) Deacon Council; Vocations.
D'Antonio, John A. '73 (SP)[F] Palm Harbor, FL St. Luke Early Childhood Center; Palm Harbor, FL St. Luke the Evangelist; Vicars Forane; Incardination Committee.
D'Antonio, Ronald M. '77 (BRK) Brooklyn, NY St. Athanasius.
D'Aquila, Ulysses L. '04 (SFR) San Francisco, CA St. Kevin.
d'Auby, Phillip *s.m.* '61 (SFR)[N] San Francisco, CA Marist Center of the West Retired.
D'Aurora, Joseph A. '73 (RIC) Lexington, VA St. Patrick; Navy Reserve Chaplains.
D'Aversa, Robert *t.o.r.* '76 (ORL) Mount Dora, FL St. Patrick's.
D'costa, Maxy *s.f.x.* '96 (P) Milwaukie, OR St. John the Baptist.
D'Cruz, Ferreolus '59 (ALX) Deans; Tallulah, LA St. Edward; College of Consultors; Appointed Members.
D'Cruz, Michael *o.f.m.* '57 (NY)[EE] New York Franciscan Province of the Immaculate Conception.
D'Cunha, Theodore *s.a.c.* '90 (DET) Canton, MI Saint John Neumann.
D'Emma, Gregory J. '70 (NEW) Military Chaplains; Army Chaplains.
D'Eon, Earl '89 (PHX) Retired.
d'Escoto, Miguel F. *m.m.* '61 (NY)[EE] Maryknoll Maryknoll Fathers and Brothers Retired.
D'heedene, Walter O. *c.i.c.m.* '67 (SAT) San Antonio, TX Sacred Heart.
D'Imperio, Robert J. '07 (CAM) Glassboro, NJ The Church of Our Lady of Lourdes, Glassboro, N.J.
D'Incecco, Alfred '75 (NY) Absent on Sick Leave.
D'Mello, John '73 (PMB) West Palm Beach, FL St. Ann.
D'Mello, Norbert *c.s.c.* '90 (SUP) Presbyteral Council & Diocesan Consultors; Barron, WI St. Boniface.
D'Mello, Norbert *c.s.c.* '90 (SUP) Barron, WI St. Joseph; Barron, WI St. Peter.
D'Onofrio, Joseph J. '05 (BO) Arlington, MA Saint Agnes.
D'Silva, Joseph R. '67 (MO) DEPARTMENT OF VETERANS AFFAIRS HOSPITALS AND CHAPLAINS.
D'Silva, Valerian *o.f.m.cap.* '82 (NY) New York, NY St. John the Baptist.
D'Sousa, Maurice *c.s.c.* '77 (MO) DEPARTMENT OF VETERANS AFFAIRS HOSPITALS AND CHAPLAINS.
D'Souza, Claude J. '65 (RVC) Retired.
D'Souza, Gerard *o.c.s.o.* '01 (ROC)[J] Piffard, NY Abbey of the Genesee.
D'Souza, Gilbert P. '73 (BGP) Norwalk, CT St. Joseph.
D'Souza, Maurice *c.s.c.* '77 (CLV) Cleveland, OH Veterans Administration Hospitals, Brecksville V.A.
D'Souza, Michael '77 (NSH) Nashville, TN Assumption; Nashville, TN St. Pius X.
D'Souza, Robert '73 (FTW) Fort Wayne, IN St. Jude; Fort Wayne, IN Parkview Memorial Hospital.
D'Souza, Sudhir (BGP) Norwalk, CT St. Thomas the Apostle.
D'Souza, William '76 (GF) Forsyth, MT Immaculate Conception; Diocesan Consultors; Colstrip, MT St. Margaret Mary; Priests' Council.
Dabash, G. Adrian *o.p.* '71 (PRO)[P] Providence St. Thomas Aquinas Priory at Providence College.
Dabbene, Bernard *s.d.b.* '66 (SFR)[N] San Francisco, CA Salesian Provincial Residence Retired.
Dabhi, James *s.j.* '88 (OAK)[M] Berkeley, CA Jesuit Fathers and Brothers.
Dabney, Philip *c.ss.r.* '78 (BO) Boston, MA Our Lady of Perpetual Help.
Dabria, Jerry J. '55 (NO) Retired.
Dabrowski, George J. *c.m.* '58 (HRT)[L] Manchester DePaul Provincial Residence Retired.
Dabrowski, James O. '84 (CAM) Bellmawr, NJ The Church of the Annunciation BVM, Bellmawr, N.J.; Representatives by Deaneries.
Dabrowski, Klemens *s.ch.* '82 (WDC)[W] Silver Spring, MD Friends of John Paul II Foundation.
Dabrowski, Klemens *s.ch.* '87 (MIA) Pompano Beach, FL Our Lady of Czestochowa Mission; Polish – (Our Lady of Czestochowa Polish Mission).
Dabruzzi, James S. '53 (SUP) Retired.
Dacechen, Mario *o.s.b.m.* '88 (STN) Warren, MI St. Josaphat.
Dacey, Donald '53 (DET) Retired.
Dachauer, Andrew C. *s.j.* '64 (STO) Mammoth Lakes, CA St. Joseph Church of Mammoth Lakes.
Da Costa, Darrell '97 (BRK) Corona, NY St. Paul the Apostle.
DaCosta, Lee '73 (BWN) Weslaco, TX St. Joan of Arc.
da Cunha, Domingos M. '71 (PRO) Cumberland, RI Our Lady of Fatima.
Dada, Jacek '93 (CHI) Mt. Prospect, IL St. Emily.
DaDamio, Paul A. '00 (ALN) Unassigned.
Dadatt, Gelso '98 (PH) Portuguese and Brazilian Apostolates; Philadelphia, PA St. Martin of Tours.
Dadey, Neil R. '81 (ALT) Northern Deanery; Bellefonte, PA St. John the Evangelist's; Spring Mills, PA Blessed Kateri Tekakwitha.
Daffron, Justin *s.j.* '05 (CHI)[C] Chicago, IL Jesuit Community at Loyola University Chicago.
Daganta, Felizardo J. *o.a.r.* '88 (LA) Montebello, CA St. Benedict.
Dagelen, Anthony L. *s.j.* '65 (MIL)[P] Wauwatosa, WI Jesuit Community at St. Camillus.
Dagher, Rt. Rev. George *b.s.o.* '43 (NTN) Methuen, MA Basilian Salvatorian Order; Methuen, MA Retired.
Dagit, Rick D. '86 (DUB) Colo, IA St. Gabriel; Colo, IA St. Patrick; Colo, IA St. Joseph; Colo, IA St. Mary.
Dagle, Harold F. '59 (ALN) DEPARTMENT OF VETERANS AFFAIRS HOSPITALS AND CHAPLAINS; Lebanon, PA Assumption of the Blessed Virgin Mary Retired.
Dagle, Harold '58 (HBG) Lebanon, PA Veterans Administration Hospital.
Dagle, Thomas W. '02 (WH) White Sulphur Springs, WV St. Catherine of Siena; White Sulphur Springs, WV St. Charles Borromeo.
Dagnoli, Albert *ss.cc.* '68 (FR)[G] Fairhaven, MA Damien Residence.
Daguplo, Genaro '84 (TR) Hamilton, NJ St. Raphael–Holy Angels Parish.
Daher, Richard '95 (OLD) Notre Dame de L'Assomption.
Dahl, Henry J. '96 (FR) Provincetown, MA St. Peter the Apostle; Auditors; Diocesan Consultors.
Dahl, Philip *o.cart.* '65 (BUR)[E] Arlington, VT Carthusian Foundation in America, Inc., Charterhouse of the Transfiguration.
Dahlberg, Daniel J. '67 (SUP) Hudson, WI St. Patrick; Vicar General; Ex Officio Members; Presbyteral Council & Diocesan Consultors.
Dahlby, Charles '77 (SFD) Retired.
Dahlheimer, Ronald W. '59 (STP) Retired.

Dahlinger, James H. *s.j.* '91 (SY)[Q] Syracuse, NY Jesuits at LeMoyne, Inc.
Dahlinger, James H. *s.j.* '91 (NY)[EE] Loyola Hall, Jesuit Community.
Dahlke, Robert W. *s.j.* '65 (NY)[EE] New York, NY Murray–Weigel Hall.
Dahm, Charles W. *o.p.* '64 (CHI)[N] Chicago, IL Dominican Community.
Dahm, Paul J. '62 (RVC) Retired.
Dahms, Paul G. '58 (MO) DEPARTMENT OF VETERANS AFFAIRS HOSPITALS AND CHAPLAINS.
Dahms, Paul '58 (RC) Retired.
Dai, Ba Thai *s.v.d.* '05 (FgM) Techny, IL.
Daiber, Rev. Msgr. Sean J. '67 (CAM) On Duty Outside the Diocese.
Daigle, Christopher '78 (TLS) Pawhuska, OK Immaculate Conception.
Daigle, David A. '03 (MO) Navy Chaplains.
Daigle, David (BGP) On Duty Outside the Diocese.
Daigle, Eugene *c.ss.r.* '72 (ORL)[F] New Smyrna Beach, FL St. Alphonsus Villa–Redemptorist Fathers and Brothers Retired.
Daigle, Gregory J. '93 (BR) Lakeland, LA Immaculate Conception.
Daigle, Karl J. '97 (SHP) Shreveport, LA St. Joseph; Advocates; Church Vocations Board & Vocations Office.
Daigle, Robert E. '63 (VNN) On Special Assignment.
Daigle, Roland *o.f.m.cap.* '84 (FgM) White Plains, NY Province of St. Mary.
Daigle, Steven '89 (DUL) Willow River, MN St. Isidore; Willow River, MN St. Mary.
Dailey, Gary M. '85 (SPR) Springfield, MA St. Michael's Cathedral; Vocations; Presbyteral Council.
Dailey, Joseph E. '77 (DET) Lake Orion, MI Christ the Redeemer.
Dailey, Stanley L. (Stash) '08 (COL) Deanery 3: North High; Worthington, OH St. Michael; Presbyteral Council.
Dailey, Thomas F. *o.s.f.s.* '87 (ALN)[B] Center Valley, PA DeSales University; [K] Center Valley, PA Oblates of St. Francis de Sales.
Dailey, William R. *c.s.c.* '01 (FTW)[H] Notre Dame Congregation of Holy Cross, Indiana Province, Provincial House.
Dailey, William R. *c.s.c.* '01 (NY) New York, NY Holy Trinity.
Dailey, William '59 (RVC)[M] Amityville, NY St. Pius X Residence Retired.
Daily, Vincent E. '58 (BO) Dorchester, MA St. Gregory; Senior Priests. Retired.
Dair, Richard J. '80 (ARL) Retired.
Daisy, George '97 (LAN) Lansing, MI Immaculate Heart of Mary.
Dakes, John T. '87 (WDC) Leonardtown, MD St. Aloysius; Advocates; Priest Council; Archdiocesan College of Consultors.
Dakin, Kenneth M. '88 (SAT) Hondo, TX St. John the Evangelist.
Dalbon, Luis '47 (CGS)[C] Aibonito, PR Casa Salesiana de Retiros.
Dale, Douglas '88 (ORG) Brea, CA St. Angela Merici.
Daleo, Joseph P. '71 (BEA) Eastern Vicariate; Orange, TX St. Mary.
Dalessandro, Dennis G. '83 (HBG) Berwick, PA St. Joseph's.
Daley, Brian E. *s.j.* '70 (CHI)[N] Chicago Chicago Province of the Society of Jesus–Provincial Office.
Daley, Brian *s.j.* '70 (FTW)[B] University of Notre Dame Du Lac; [K] South Bend, IN Jesuit Community.
Daley, Daniel P. '70 (GLP) Quemado, NM Sacred Heart; Pinetop, AZ St. Mary of the Angels; Springerville, AZ St. Peter.
Daley, E. Raymond *o.p.* '52 (NY)[EE] New York, NY St. Vincent Ferrer Priory.
Daley, Rev. Msgr. Ernest J. '55 (E) Erie, PA St. Jude the Apostle; Episcopal Delegate for Retired Priests; Members Retired.
Daley, Francis E. '66 (BO) Lakeville, MA Saints Martha and Mary.
Daley, Frederick D. '74 (SY) Syracuse, NY All Saints; Utica, NY Mohawk Valley Psychiatric Center.
Daley, Jacques de Paul *o.s.b.* '71 (GBG) Greensburg, PA Excela Health – Westmoreland Hospital; [G] Latrobe, PA Saint Vincent Archabbey.
Daley, James D. '54 (ALB) Delmar, NY St. Thomas the Apostle Retired.
Daley, Joseph A. '68 (CHY) Retired.
Dalimpuo, Felix '93 (ROC) Newark, NY St. Michael.
Dalin, Jonathan J. '09 (PH) Collegeville, PA St. Eleanor.
Dall, Lincoln '08 (JKS) Jackson, MS Holy Family; Priests' Council; Jackson, MS St. Richard of Chichester; Co Chairmen.
Dallas, Benjamin '02 (SAV) Savannah, GA Most Blessed Sacrament.
Dallen, James '69 (SAL) Retired.
Dalpiaz, Alex *c.s.* (ORL) Winter Garden, FL Resurrection.
Dalpiaz, Gino *c.s.* (CHI)[N] Chicago, IL Scalabrini House of Theology.
Dalseth, Gerald '64 (SCL) Pierz, MN St. Michael's; Pierz, MN St. Joseph's; Diocesan Commission on Ecumenical and Interreligious Affairs.
Dalton, Brendan '69 (MIA) Hollywood, FL St. Bernadette; [C] Fort Lauderdale, FL Archbishop Edward A. McCarthy High School.
Dalton, Rev. Msgr. Desmond '70 (FgM) Boston, MA St. James the Apostle, Inc.
Dalton, Donald T. '60 (STL) Retired.
Dalton, George R. '84 (PIT) Cranberry Township, PA St. Ferdinand.
Dalton, James '68 (SEA) Arlington, WA Immaculate Conception.
Dalton, James *o.s.f.s.* '72 (WIL)[B] Wilmington, DE Salesianum School; Provincial Councilors:.
Dalton, John Bryan '70 (MIA) Deerfield Beach, FL St. Ambrose.
Dalton, Rev. Msgr. John W. '58 (DUB) Retired.
Dalton, Michel *o.f.m.cap.* '78 (HON) Ewa, HI Immaculate Conception Church; Bishops Administrative Advisory Council; Implementation Commission of Diocesan Road Map for Pastoral Program and Facility Needs; Presbyteral Council.
Dalton, Peadar '70 (MOB) On Leave from the Archdiocese.
Dalton, Robert *g.h.m.* '62 (CIN)[N] Cincinnati Headquarters of Glenmary Home Missioners Retired.
Dalupang, Arturo O. '95 (CHR) Florence, SC St. Anthony's All Souls Memorial.
Daly, Anthony C. *s.j.* '72 (STL)[C] Saint Louis University; [O] St. Louis, MO Jesuit Community Corporation at Saint Louis University – Jesuit Hall.
Daly, Bartholomew *m.h.m.* '62 (NY) New York, NY Our Lady of Peace; [EE] Hartsdale, NY Mill Hill Fathers Residence; Hartsdale, NY.
Daly, Rev. Msgr. Charles W. '51 (HRT)[A] In Res. at the Archbishop Daniel A. Cronin Retirement Residence at St. Thomas Seminary Retired.
Daly, Christopher H. '60 (NY)[EE] Bronx, NY John Cardinal O'Connor Residence Retired.
Daly, David *l.c.* '01 (ATL)[G] Alpharetta, GA Norcross Pastoral Center, Inc.
Daly, Denis E. *s.j.* '64 (STL)[C] Saint Louis University; [O] St. Louis, MO Jesuit Community Corporation at Saint Louis University – Jesuit Hall.
Daly, Rev. Msgr. Desmond '66 (SP) Tampa, FL Christ the King.
Daly, Edwin J. *s.j.* '59 (FgM) Chicago, IL Society of Jesus.
Daly, Francis J. *s.j.* '72 (CIN)[F] Cincinnati, OH St. Xavier High School; [N] Cincinnati, OH Jesuit Community at St. Xavier High School.
Daly, J. Daniel *s.j.* '92 (DEN)[N] Denver, CO Regis Jesuit Community (The Jesuits at Regis University).
Daly, Jerome R. '87 (ARL) Retired.
Daly, John J. '58 (HRT) North Haven, CT St. Barnabas Retired.
Daly, John J. '59 (LA) Los Angeles, CA Holy Trinity Retired.
Daly, John P. *s.j.* '56 (LA)[C] Los Angeles, CA Jesuit Community.
Daly, John R. *s.j.* '63 (DEN)[N] Denver, CO Xavier Jesuit Center.
Daly, John V. *s.j.* '66 (FgM) Milwaukee, WI Society of Jesus.
Daly, Joseph V. *c.m.* '60 (BRK)[T] Jamaica, NY St. Vincent's House.
Daly, Kevin *o.f.m.* '80 (NEW) East Rutherford, NJ St. Joseph's; [M] East Rutherford, NJ Sacred Heart Friary.
Daly, Manus P. '65 (JC) Retired.
Daly, Peter J. '86 (WDC) Prince Frederick, MD St. John Vianney.
Daly, Raymond (NY) Judges.
Daly, Richard L. '58 (BEL) Retired.
Daly, Robert J. *s.j.* '63 (BO)[U] Newton, MA The Jesuit Community at Boston College; Watertown, MA; [U] Watertown, MA The Society of Jesus of New England–Provincial Offices.
Daly, Robert L. '41 (MET) Spotswood, NJ Immaculate Conception Retired.
Daly, Shawn T. '95 (HRT) Meriden, CT St. Joseph; Meriden, CT St. Mary; New Haven Vicariate; Meriden Deanery.
Daly, Simeon *o.s.b.* '48 (IND)[K] St. Meinrad, IN St. Meinrad Archabbey.
Daly, Thomas A. '87 (SFR) Serra Club of San Francisco (Downtown); On Special Assignment; [D] Kentfield, CA Marin Catholic College Preparatory (Coed); [P] San Francisco, CA Catholic Charities CYO of the Archdiocese of San Francisco; College of Consultors; Deans; Office of Vocations.
Daly, Rev. Msgr. Thomas J. '52 (BO) Senior Priests. Retired.
Daly, Timothy P. '96 (ORL) Daytona Beach, FL Basilica of Saint Paul; [G] Daytona Beach, FL.
Daly, Vincent M. '71 (BRK) South Ozone Park, NY Our Lady of Perpetual Help.
Dam, LoXuan *m.m.* '00 (FgM) Maryknoll, NY MARYKNOLL.
Dama, Martin L. '82 (SY) Syracuse, NY St. John the Baptist.
Damboise, Aaron L. '08 (PRT) Caribou, ME Parish of the Precious Blood.
Damhorst, Joseph *s.j.* '68 (FgM) St. Louis, MO Society of Jesus.
Damian, Lawrence P. '71 (BUF) Depew, NY St. James.
Damian, Rinaldo '88 (MO) DEPARTMENT OF VETERANS AFFAIRS HOSPITALS AND CHAPLAINS.
Damian, Ronald '88 (WOR) On Duty Outside the Diocese.
Damico, Rodney M. '92 (COL) Westerville, OH St. Paul the Apostle.
Damien, Paul (SAM) Easton, PA Our Lady of Lebanon.
Damis, Frank J. '84 (NY) Kingston, NY St. Joseph.
Dammay, Dante U. '77 (STO) Manteca, CA St. Anthony Church of Manteca (Pastor of).
Dammeir, James L. '79 (MIL) Retired.
Da Mota, Idomor '08 (ARL) Alexandria, VA St. Louis.
Damron, Robert '83 (LEX) Prestonsburg, KY St. Martha; Salyersville, KY St. Luke.
Damroth, William J. '93 (NY) Staten Island, NY Our Lady, Queen of Peace.
Dan, Bernard '04 (ROC) Rochester, NY Our Lady Queen of Peace; Rochester, NY St. Thomas More.
Danaher, Rev. Msgr. Mortimer '53 (STA) Jacksonville, FL Holy Family Retired.
Danaher, Philip '83 (JOL) Woodridge, IL Christ The Servant Parish.
Danaher, Thomas E. *m.m.* '62 (FgM) Maryknoll, NY MARYKNOLL.
Danber, Bernard R. *o.s.a.* '86 (CHI)[J] Chicago, IL Holy Cross Hospital; [N] Chicago, IL St. Rita Monastery.
Danber, Bernard *o.s.a.* '86 (CHI) Chicago, IL St. Rita of Cascia.
Dance, Kevin *c.p.* '65 (BRK) Brooklyn, NY All Saints.
Danczyk, Mark J. '92 (MIL) Caledonia, WI St. Louis.
Danda, Sean '09 (IND) Graduate Studies.
Dande, Benjamin *m.s.f.s.* '01 (DOD) Jetmore, KS St. Lawrence Catholic Church of Jetmore, Kansas; Jetmore, KS St. Anthony Catholic Church of Hanston, Kansas.
Dande, Benjamin *m.s.f.s.* '01 (TYL)[B] Whitehouse, TX The Missionaries of St. Francis de Sales.
Dandelet, James D. '54 (WIN) Retired.
Dandry, Anthony M. '89 (MET) Retired.
Dandurand, Douglas E. '82 (STP) Deephaven, MN St. Therese.
Dandurand, Michael G. '97 (TOL)[L] Bowling Green, OH Bowling Green State University Campus Ministry; Bowling Green, OH St. Thomas More University Parish; Youth, Young Adult and Campus Ministry.
Dane, James E. '83 (MOB) Orange Beach, AL St. Thomas by the Sea.
Dane, John '91 (LEX) Retired.
Danek, Michael *c.r.* '86 (CHI)[N] Chicago, IL Provincial Office of the Congregation of the Resurrection; Chicago, IL.
Danek, Michael *c.r.* (STL)[O] St. Louis, MO Congregation of the Resurrection.
Danel, Joseph B. *s.j.* '52 (FgM)[L] Portland Jesuit Provincial Office (Society of Jesus, Oregon Prov.); Portland, OR Society of Jesus.
Danella, Francis W. *o.s.f.s.* '73 (CAM) St. Pius X Spiritual Life Center; [M] Blackwood, NJ Bishop's Residence.
Dang, Bernadine Tan Minh (GAL) Houston, TX St. Elizabeth Ann Seton.
Dang, Chin Van '83 (MO) Military Chaplains; Navy Chaplains.
Dang, Ha '05 (BGP) Bridgeport, CT St. Augustine Cathedral.
Dang, Hai Duc '99 (GAL) New Caney, TX St. John of the Cross.
Dang, Joseph *s.v.d.* '93 (BEA) Beaumont, TX St. Pius X.
Dang, Quy Ngoc *s.v.d.* '09 (DUB)[B] Epworth, IA Divine Word College.
Dang, Thomas Thien *o.s.b.* '93 (P)[L] St. Benedict, OR Mt. Angel Abbey.
Dang, Vincent H. '95 (SCR) Wyoming, PA St. Frances Cabrini.
Dang, Vincent Tinh '08 (SJ) Los Altos, CA St. Nicholas.
Dang Ha, Dominic Thuy '84 (SLC) Salt Lake City, UT Our Lady of Perpetual Help LLC 261.
Daniel, John C. '92 (SFE) College of Consultors; Albuquerque, NM St. Jude Thaddeus.
Daniele, Anthony J. '56 (BO) Senior Priests. Retired.
Daniels, Jerrell Michael '01 (JKS) On Leave.
Daniels, Joel *o.f.m.cap.* '67 (NY)[EE] Yonkers, NY St. Clare Friary.
Daniels, John W. '36 (GRY) Retired.
Daniels, Joseph E. '90 (PRT) Lewiston, ME Prince of Peace Parish.
Daniels, Lawrence *o.c.d.* '65 (MIL)[P] Milwaukee Provincial Offices – Discalced Carmelites.
Daniels, Leo Francis *c.o.* '65 (BWN) Pharr, TX St. Jude Thaddeus; [F] Pharr, TX Pharr Oratory of St. Philip Neri of Pontifical Right; Pharr, TX; [C] Pharr, TX Oratory Academy School of St. Philip Neri; [B] Pharr, TX Oratory Athenaeum for University Preparation.
Daniels, Paul A. '57 (MIL) Retired.

Daniels, William S. *o.p.* '05 (MEM)[F] Memphis, TN The Dominican Friars of Memphis, Inc.; Memphis, TN St. Peter Church.
Danielsen, Thomas *c.ss.r.* '64 (STL)[O] Liguori, MO Liguori Mission House/Redemptorists.
Danielson, Charles R. '92 (BUR) Cambridge, VT St. Mary; Underhill Center, VT St. Thomas.
Danielson, Daniel E. '63 (OAK) Piedmont, CA Corpus Christi Retired.
Danielson, Harold *s.d.b.* '66 (SFR) San Francisco, CA SS. Peter and Paul.
Danik, Daniel A. '48 (NEW) Bloomfield, NJ Sacred Heart; Serra Club of West Essex Retired.
Daniszewski, Rev. Msgr. Alfred '45 (MAN) Manchester, NH St. Hedwig.
Daniszewski, Rev. Msgr. John D. '43 (E) Retired.
Danko, Michael S. '52 (LIN) Aurora, MO Retired.
Dankoski, Francis '09 (STU)[J] Hopedale, OH The Order of the Sacred and Immaculate Hearts of Jesus and Mary.
Danna, Rev. Msgr. Anthony '67 (BRK) Ridgewood, NY Our Lady of the Miraculous Medal.
Danneker, David L. '82 (HBG) Elizabethtown, PA St. Peter; [I] Elizabethtown, PA Elizabethtown College; Appointed; Consultors, College; Catholic Physicians League.
Danneker, Edward A.J. '64 (ATL) Atlanta, GA Holy Cross Retired.
Danner, Brian '95 (SC) Milford, IA St. Joseph's.
Danner, James L. '74 (MO) Military Chaplains; Navy Chaplains.
Danner, Michael A. '65 (GR) Retired.
Danos, Dean F. '80 (HT) Thibodaux, LA St. Genevieve.
Danowski, Alexander J. '59 (PBL) Retired.
Dansak, Thomas J. '73 (PIT) SCI Pittsburgh.
Danso, Thomas '83 (BR)[F] Baton Rouge, LA Our Lady of the Lake Regional Medical Center.
Dant, J. Nicholas '77 (IND) Indianapolis, IN Our Lady of Lourdes; Indianapolis, IN St. Bernadette.
Dant, John W. '06 (L) Bardstown, KY St. Monica; Bardstown, KY St. Thomas.
Dant, Nicholas J. '77 (IND) Archdiocesan Judges.
Dante, Neal F. '64 (CAM) Retired.
Danter, Albert F. '43 (STL) Retired.
Dantinne, Gary J. '68 (GB) Suamico, WI St. Pius; Suamico, WI St. Benedict.
Danylo, Bohdan '96 (STF)[A] Stamford, CT Ukrainian Catholic Seminary Inc. St. Basil College; Presbyteral Council; Vocations; Liturgical Commission.
Danyluk, Richard J. *ss.cc.* '75 (LA)[P] La Verne, CA Congregation of the Sacred Hearts of Jesus and Mary.
Danzi, Rocco C. *s.j.* '89 (NY)[EE] New York, NY Xavier Jesuit Community; [EE] New York, NY Society of Jesus, New York Province.
Dao, Anthony C. *o.p.* '82 (SB) Montclair, CA Our Lady of Lourdes; Elected Members.
Dao, Joseph Nam H. '00 (CHI) Winnetka, IL SS. Faith, Hope and Charity.
Dao, Ngo Van *c.ss.r.* '86 (LA)[P] Baldwin Park Vietnamese Redemptorist Mission.
Dao, Thanh X. '03 (SEA) Des Moines, WA St. Philomena.
Dao, Vincent Van '05 (SPK) Valley, WA St. Mary of the Rosary; Valley, WA Sacred Heart; Valley, WA Holy Ghost.
Daoust, Joseph P. *s.j.* '69 (DET)[K] Detroit Jesuit Provincial Office–Detroit Province of the Society of Jesus.
Dao Vu, Joseph *s.v.d.* '88 (MEM) Memphis, TN Sacred Heart Church.
Daprai, Damien *o.s.b.* '08 (RCK)[G] Aurora, IL Marmion Abbey.
Daprile, James M. '76 (Y) Youngstown, OH St. Brendan.
Darbouze, Joseph '55 (NY) Bronx, NY St. Raymond.
Darby, Thomas J. '47 (NY)[EE] Bronx, NY Retired.
Darcy, Brendan *s.m.a.* '67 (NEW)[M] Tenafly, NJ Society of African Missions, Provincialate, S.M.A. Fathers; Tenafly, NJ.
Darcy, David M. '94 (SPR) Chicopee, MA Assumption; Chicopee, MA Holy Name of Jesus; Bishop's Commission for Clergy; Deans; Presbyteral Council.
Darcy, James F. '66 (BO) Senior Priests. Retired.
Darcy, Rev. Msgr. John J. '79 (PRO) Providence, RI St. Maron; [U] Providence, RI Miscellaneous Listings for the Diocese of Providence; Secretary for Ministerial Services; Chancellor; Secretariat for Ministerial Services; Priests' Personnel; Clergy Benefit Fund; Vicars General; Judges; Vicars General; College of Consultors; Officers; East Providence, RI St. Francis Xavier.
Darcy, Michael J. *c.o.* '02 (PIT)[M] Pittsburgh, PA Congregation of the Oratory of St. Philip Neri.
Darcy, Michael P. '00 (WIL) Catholic Scouting Program; Bethany Beach, DE St. Ann.
Dargan, Peter S. '61 (HRT) Orange, CT Holy Infant.
Dargis, Andre E. '67 (WOR) Gardner, MA Our Lady of the Holy Rosary.
Daries, Joseph *c.m.f.* '56 (LA)[V] Rancho Dominguez, CA Dominguez Seminary Inc.
Darilek, Rev. Msgr. Dennis '73 (SAT) Seguin, TX St. James.
Darin, David M. '91 (BEL) Belleville, IL St. Luke; Diocesan Liturgical Commission; Belleville, IL St. Teresa of the Child Jesus.
Darling, Franklin '58 (SPR) Retired.
Darling, George E. '84 (GR) Grand Rapids, MI Blessed Sacrament; Clergy Fund.
Darling, William G. '73 (ROC) Canadaigua, NY St. Mary; East Bloomfield, NY St. Bridget.
Darnell, Lawrence T. *o.m.v.* '82 (LA) Hawaiian Gardens, CA St. Peter Chanel.
Darow, Robert G. '63 (CHI) Retired.
DaRoza, George *s.s.c.* '85 (OM)[K] St. Columbans Missionary Society of St. Columban.
Darragh, John J. '69 (HEL) Hamilton, MT St. Francis; Personnel Board.
Dasari, Joseph '97 (BGP) Danbury, CT St. Joseph.
Dascenzo, Joseph J. '58 (PIT) Ellwood City, PA Holy Redeemer Parish Retired.
Daschbach, Richard *s.v.d.* '64 (FgM) Techny, IL.
Dash, Alan J. '67 (R) Retired.
Dash, George J. *o.f.m.cap.* '92 (NY) Beacon, NY Fishkill Correctional Facility; East Elmhurst, NY Anna M. Kross Center.
Da Silva, A. Paul '98 (MET) Legion of Mary.
DaSilva, Aex Assuncao *o.f.m.* '04 (CHI)[N] Chicago, IL St. Peter's Friary.
DaSilva, Antonio F. '88 (NEW) Newark, NJ Our Lady of Fatima.
da Silva, Antonio L. *s.d.v.* '83 (NEW) Newark, NJ St. Michael's.
DaSilva, Arlindo Paul '98 (MET) Office for Multicultural Ministries; Piscataway, NJ Our Lady of Fatima.
DaSilva, Colbert *s.d.b.* '84 (BRK) Brooklyn, NY Our Lady of Guadalupe.
da Silva, Darci Donizetti (BO) Rockland, MA Holy Family.
da Silva, Jorge *s.m.* '71 (SJ)[M] Living In Other Residences:.
Da Silva, Jose Carlos '92 (BRK)[S] Brazilian Apostolate; Long Island City, NY St. Rita.
da Silva, Rev. Msgr. Joseph '72 (B) Boise, ID Risen Christ Catholic Community; Vicars General; Ex Officio; Priest Personnel Commission; Ecumenical Commission; Ex Officio; Finance Council.
Das Neves, Antonio '61 (SB) Sun City, CA St. Vincent Ferrer.
Dass, Ajith Kumar *ss.cc.* '06 (FR)[G] Fairhaven National Center of the Enthronement.
Dass, Joseph '89 (LA) Van Nuys, CA St. Bridget of Sweden; Alhambra, CA All Souls.
Dassanayake, Vincent Paul (NY) Pawling, NY St. John the Evangelist; Pawling, NY St. John the Evangelist.
Datko, James *o.m.i.* (DUL) Duluth, MN Holy Family.
Dattilo, Anthony A. '90 (STL) Apple Creek, MO St. Joseph; Perryville, MO St. Maurus; Deaneries/Deans.
Dattilo, Anthony M. '84 (CIN) Cincinnati, OH St. Catharine of Siena.
Datzman, Harold L. *o.s.b.* '65 (PEO) Peru, IL St. Joseph's; [A] Peru, IL St. Bede Abbey.
Dau, Luyen *c.ss.r.* '08 (PH) Philadelphia, PA Visitation B.V.M.
Daugherty, Daniel L. '94 (TYL) Whitehouse, TX Prince of Peace.
Daugherty, Patrick *c.p.* '02 (PMB)[H] North Palm Beach, FL Our Lady of Florida Spiritual Center.
Daugherty, Scott '83 (FRS) Porterville, CA St. Anne.
Dauphinais, Louis Marie *m.m.a.* '70 (SAM)[B] Petersham, MA Maronite Monks of Adoration Most Holy Trinity Monastery; Petersham, MA.
Dauphine, Marc Rene '09 (MRY) Watsonville, CA St. Patrick.
Dauses, Jeffrey S. '90 (BAL) Baltimore, MD Basilica of the National Shrine of the Assumption of the Blessed Virgin Mary.
Dauss, Francis '48 (SP) Retired.
Dautremont, Charles R. '60 (GR) Grand Rapids, MI St. Dominic.
Davadilla, Joel '88 (FRS) Tehachapi, CA St. Malachy.
Davalos, Rev. Msgr. Carlos '78 (SAT) Helotes, TX Our Lady of Guadalupe; College of Consultors; Archdiocesan Presbyteral Council.
Davalos, Juan Pablo '07 (BWN)[K] La Joya, TX Boy Scouts; La Joya, TX Our Lady, Queen of Angels.
Davantes, Carlo B. '79 (MO) Navy Reserve Chaplains.
Davanzo, Joseph V. '97 (RVC) Commack, NY Christ the King.
Dave, Kyle V. '01 (NO) Lacombe, LA Sacred Heart.
Davenport, Christopher M. '61 (PRO) West Warwick, RI SS. Peter and Paul.
Davenport, Clement A. '48 (SFR) Menlo Park, CA The Church of the Nativity Retired.
Davern, Rev. Msgr. Robert B. '51 (SY)[Q] Syracuse, NY Tommy Coyne Residence Dillon Hall.
Davern, Rev. Msgr. Robert '51 (SY) Retired.
Davern, Timothy R. '78 (PHX) Censor Librorum; Presbyteral Council; Diocesan Judges; Gilbert, AZ St. Anne Roman Catholic Parish.
Davey, Edward M. '53 (PAT)[Q] Chester, NJ Nazareth Village Retired.
Davey, Philip D. *o.s.b.* '75 (PEO)[A] Peru, IL St. Bede Abbey.
Davich, Rev. Msgr. George '62 (SLC) Retired.
David, Craig '96 (MO) Military Chaplains; DEPARTMENT OF VETERANS AFFAIRS HOSPITALS AND CHAPLAINS.
David, George '71 (ROM) Roebling, NJ St. Mary; Trenton, NJ St. Basil; Finance Council; College of Consultors; Protosyncellus; Director of Vocations; Trenton Deanery.
David, Jamin S. '08 (WDC) Washington, DC St. Stephen Martyr.
David, John M. (RIC) Richmond, VA Church of the Vietnamese Martyrs.
Davidson, John '64 (EVN) Evansville, IN St. Anthony.
Davies, Daniel *o.p.* '58 (NY) Pleasantville, NY Holy Innocents.
Davies, Julian A. *o.f.m.* '60 (ALB)[B] Siena College.
Davies, Maximos '06 (ROM)[A] Pearblossom, CA Holy Resurrection Monastery.
Davignon, Charles P. '56 (BUR) Retired.
Davignon, Philip A. '62 (FR) Osterville, MA Our Lady of the Assumption.
Davila, Andres (ARE) On Duty Outside the Diocese.
Davila, Jose Alexis (SLC) Layton, UT Saint Rose of Lima LLC 245.
Davila, Rafael R. *m.m.* '58 (GAL)[A] Houston, TX St. Mary's Seminary; [O] Houston Maryknoll Fathers and Brothers.
Davila, Rito '05 (AUS) Bastrop, TX Ascension Catholic Church.
Davin, Neil W. *c.p.* '52 (MET)[I] Somerset, NJ Maria Regina Residence; [I] South River Passionist Provincial Office; Canonical Staff.
Davin, Neil *c.p.* '52 (BRK)[T] Jamaica, NY Immaculate Conception Monastery.
Davin, William *c.p.* '56 (PIT)[M] Pittsburgh, PA St. Paul of the Cross Monastery.
Davino, Michael J. '86 (CHR) Absent On Leave.
Davis, Anthony '85 (SEA) Mercer Island, WA St. Monica.
Davis, Augustine *o.s.b.* '59 (IND)[K] St. Meinrad, IN St. Meinrad Archabbey.
Davis, Christopher J. '98 (CHL) Asheboro, NC St. Joseph.
Davis, Christopher *o.s.b.* '58 (PRO)[P] Portsmouth, RI Abbey of St. Gregory the Great.
Davis, Clement T. '70 (IND) Columbus, IN St. Bartholomew; Archdiocesan Judges.
Davis, Clyde F. *m.m.* '63 (SJ)[M] Los Altos, CA Maryknoll.
Davis, Cyprian *o.s.b.* '56 (IND)[A] St. Meinrad, IN Saint Meinrad School of Theology; [K] St. Meinrad, IN St. Meinrad Archabbey.
Davis, D.G. "Skip" '98 (E) Titusville, PA St. Titus; Titusville, PA St. Walburga.
Davis, Daniel C. *o.p.* '94 (LFT) West Lafayette, IN St. Thomas Aquinas; [H] West Lafayette, IN St. Thomas Aquinas Parish and Foundation for Catholic Students Attending Purdue University; Members; Aquinas Educational Foundation, Inc.; Newman Apostolate, Purdue University.
Davis, Edward J. '49 (NOR) Retired.
Davis, Edward V. *m.m.* '61 (FgM) Maryknoll, NY MARYKNOLL.
Davis, Ernest P. '02 (KC) Priestly Life and Ministry; Kansas City, MO St. Therese Little Flower; Administrative Committee.
Davis, F. Hampton (LAF) Lafayette, LA Our Lady Queen of Peace.
Davis, Gary G. '75 (L) Louisville, KY St. Peter the Apostle Parish.
Davis, Henry *s.s.j.* '93 (BEA) Beaumont, TX Blessed Sacrament; Beaumont, TX Our Mother of Mercy.
Davis, James J. *o.p.* '53 (PRO)[P] Providence St. Thomas Aquinas Priory at Providence College Retired.
Davis, John E. '69 (FAR) Retired.
Davis, John P. '63 (PRT) Retired.
Davis, John *o.p.* '66 (NY)[HH] New York, NY New York University; New York, NY St. Joseph.
Davis, Joseph P. '72 (PAT) Succasunna, NJ St. Therese.
Davis, Karl *o.m.i.* '05 (OAK) Oakland, CA Sacred Heart.
Davis, Leo D. '64 (SPK)[J] Spokane, WA Regis Community.
Davis, Mark E. '96 (TOL) Bowling Green, OH St. Aloysius.
Davis, Michael J. '87 (PH) Croydon, PA St. Thomas Aquinas; Council of Priests.
Davis, Michael W. '90 (CIN) Fort Lauderdale, FL St. Jerome; [B] Cincinnati, OH Mt. St. Mary's Seminary of the West; [B] Cincinnati, OH Mt. St. Mary's Seminary of the West.
Davis, Noel '62 (LAR) Encinal, TX Immaculate Heart of Mary.
Davis, Raphael *o.praem.* '99 (LA) Long Beach, CA Holy Innocents.
Davis, Richard P. '63 (LR) Bigelow, AR St. Elizabeth; Bigelow, AR St. Boniface; Bigelow, AR St. Francis of

Assisi Church; Presbyteral Council.
Davis, Richard *t.o.r.* '80 (STU)[A] Steubenville, OH Franciscan University of Steubenville; [H] Steubenville, OH Holy Spirit Friary.
Davis, Terrence '69 (SJ) Retired.
Davis, Thomas R. '83 (R) Absent on Leave.
Davis, Rev. Msgr. Wilbur '64 (ORG) Newport Beach, CA Our Lady Queen of Angels Retired.
Davis, William E. *o.s.f.s.* '82 (WIL)[J] Childs, MD Retirement and Assisted Care Facility; Provincial Staff:.
Davis, Rev. Msgr. William F. '56 (MEM) Retired.
Davis, William F. *o.s.f.s.* '61 (WDC)[B] Washington, DC Oblates of St. Francis de Sales.
Davis, William *o.m.i.* (LAR) Laredo, TX San Francisco Javier.
Davison, Andreas R. '07 (BO) West Roxbury, MA St. Theresa of Avila.
Davison, Ben '92 (SD) El Cajon, CA St. Kieran.
Davison, Don *c.p.p.s.* '80 (IND) Bloomington, IN St. Charles Borromeo.
Davison, Donald *c.pp.s.* '80 (CIN)[N] Dayton Provincial Office of the Cincinnati Province of the Society of the Precious Blood.
Davison, Timothy L. '85 (TLS) Tulsa, OK SS. Peter and Paul; Diocesan Senators.
Davitti, Michael *s.x.* '70 (CHI) Chicago, IL St. Therese Catholic Chinese Church.
DaVola, Rev. Msgr. F. Robert '67 (BWN) Retired.
Davoren, Steve V. '96 (LA) Ventura, CA Our Lady of the Assumption; Santa Barbara Region.
Davy, Andy *m.i.c.* '09 (JOL) Yorkville, IL St. Patrick.
Davy, Kavungal Lonappan *c.m.i.* '96 (COV) Carrollton, KY St. John the Evangelist.
Daw, Timothy M. '91 (CLV) Cleveland, OH Annunciation; Rocky River, OH St. Christopher.
Dawber, Stephen F. *s.j.* '69 (BO)[U] Weston, MA Campion Health Center, Inc.
Dawis, Ralph '54 (NY) Staten Island, NY Richmond University Medical Center.
Dawley, Robert (RVC) Melville, NY Good Shepherd Hospice (Nassau).
Daws, Dominic '55 (B) Retired.
Dawson, Rev. Msgr. James D. '54 (LIN)[E] Lincoln, NE Bonacum House; Evangelization Committee Retired.
Dawson, Richard '81 (PT) Bonifay, FL Blessed Trinity; De Funiak Springs, FL St. Margaret.
Dawson, Wayne (MRY) Paso Robles, CA St. Rose.
Dawson, William A. *s.j.* '58 (BAL)[S] Baltimore, MD Colombiere Jesuit Community.
Dawson, William F. '54 (DAV)[A] St. Ambrose University Retired.
Day, Charles J. '81 (CHR) Retired.
Day, Dennis C. '76 (B) Sandpoint, ID St. Joseph's; College of Consultors; Deans.
Day, James R. *o.ss.t.* '72 (PH) Bristol, PA St. Ann; Councilors:.
Day, James R. *o.ss.t.* '72 (BAL)[S] The Trinitarians in Bristol, Pennsylvania.
Day, James Richard '96 (NO) Gretna, LA St. Joseph.
Day, Jeffrey '99 (DET) Dearborn Heights, MI St. Sebastian; Archdiocesan Vicars; Presbyteral Council.
Day, Jerome J. *o.s.b.* '95 (MAN) Manchester, NH St. Raphael; [K] Manchester, NH St. Anselm Abbey.
Day, John P. *c.p.* '72 (CHI)[N] Chicago Passionist Provincial Office.
Day, John Patrick *c.p.* '72 (STL) Sullivan, MO Church of the Holy Martyrs of Japan.
Day, L. Dudley *o.s.a.* '53 (CHI)[N] Chicago, IL St. Monica Monastery.
Day, Martin *o.f.m.conv.* '91 (WDC)[B] Forestville, MD St. Bonaventure Friary.
Day, Michael '71 (SJ) On Leave of Absence.
Day, Wilfred E. '67 (IND) New Albany, IN Holy Family; Deaneries and Deans.
Day, William F. '86 (GLP) Priests' Retirement Board Retired.
Daya, John *o.f.m.cap.* '78 (PIT) Pittsburgh, PA Our Lady of the Angels; Priest Council.
Dayanan, Renerio '01 (HT) Thibodaux, LA St. Joseph Co–Cathedral.
Daz, Rev. Msgr. Rudolph A. '54 (SLC) Bountiful, UT Saint Olaf LLC 239.
Daza, Wilmer de Jesus '99 (DAL)[M] Dallas, TX Nuestra Senora del Pilar Land & Development Trust; Dallas, TX Nuestra Senora del Pilar.
Deaconson, James '85 (AUS) Temple, TX St. Mary.
DeAdder, James W. '55 (BO) Senior Priests. Retired.
De Agostini, Claudio *c.s.j.* '58 (LA) San Pedro, CA St. Peter.
DeAguiar, Luiz Antonio '85 (BRK) Jamaica, NY St. Pius V.
DeAguilar, Arturo '97 (CHL) Absent On Leave.
DeAmato, Norbert *o.f.m.* '48 (BO) Cambridge, MA St. Francis of Assisi.
Dean, Frederic D. '65 (PRO)[P] Providence St. John Vianney Residence Retired.
Dean, Gregory '54 (CC) Retired.
Dean, Harry '96 (AUS) Priestly Life and Formation Committee; Vicar for Clergy.
Dean, John T. '72 (SPR)[N] Westfield, MA Westfield State College Retired.
Dean, Joseph R. *s.c.j.* '84 (RC)[C] Lower Brule, SD SCJ Community House; Lower Brule, SD St. Mary's.
Dean, Joseph *s.c.j.* '84 (MIL)[P] Hales Corners, WI Priests of the Sacred Heart.
Dean, Joseph *s.c.j.* '84 (SFS) Fort Thompson, SD St. Joseph; Lower Brule, SD Immaculate Conception.
Dean, Mark *o.m.i.* '83 (SFD)[A] Godfrey, IL Immaculate Heart of Mary Novitiate.
Dean, William E. '76 (PH) Philadelphia, PA Sacred Heart of Jesus.
de Anda, James R. '05 (OM) Fremont, NE St. Patrick.
Deane, Declan '72 (OAK) Pleasant Hill, CA Christ the King.
Deane, J. Peter *s.j.* '66 (DET)[K] Clarkston, MI Colombiere Center.
Deane, Joseph Mary *c.f.r.* (NY)[EE] Yonkers, NY St. Leopold's Friary.
Deane, Joseph Mary *c.f.r.* (FWT)[H] Fort Worth, TX Sacred Heart Friars of the Renewal.
Deane, Rev. Msgr. Joseph '59 (AUS) Retired.
de Angel, Miguel A. '05 (CGS) Yabucoa, PR Santos Angeles Cutodios; Priests Senate.
De Angelis, Mark J. '88 (BO) Society of St. James the Apostle.
De Angelis, Sante *o.f.m.* '62 (MIL)[Y] Waterford, WI General Secretariat of the Franciscan Missions, Inc.
DeAngelo, Jude T. *o.f.m.conv.* '84 (CHL) Winston–Salem, NC Our Lady of Mercy; [L] Winston–Salem, NC Wake Forest University and Winston–Salem University.
DeAntoniis, Paul J. *o.praem* '63 (PH)[Y] Paoli, PA Daylesford Abbey; [S] Darby, PA Mercy Fitzgerald Hospital.
Deardorff, Joseph F. *c.pp.s.* '82 (CIN)[N] Dayton Provincial Office of the Cincinnati Province of the Society of the Precious Blood.
Dearhammer, John W. '91 (CHI) Schaumburg, IL Church of the Holy Spirit.
de Armas, Alexio Jose *o.c.d.* '58 (PCE) Ponce, PR San Jose.
Deary, John F. *o.s.a.* '66 (VEN) Cape Coral, FL Saint Katharine Drexel.
Deas, Rev. Msgr. George T. '51 (BRK)[T] Douglaston, NY Bishop Mugavero Residence Retired.
DeAscanis, Michael '04 (BAL) Priest Personnel Board; Glen Burnie, MD Church of the Good Shepherd; Glen Burnie, MD Crucifixion, Church of the; Glen Burnie, MD Holy Trinity; [V] Glen Burnie, MD The Church of the Good Shepherd Parish Endowment Trust.
Dease, Dennis J. '69 (STP)[C] St. Paul, MN University of St. Thomas.
Deasey, Ken '87 (LA) Holy Childhood Association.
Deasio, August J. '75 (ROM) Formation Council Retired.
Deasy, Jeremiah '67 (BIR) Tuscaloosa, AL Holy Spirit; [I] Tuscaloosa, AL The Harrison Family Endowment Trust for the Benefit of Holy Spirit School; Diocesan College of Consultors; Priests'/Presbyteral Council; Diocesan College of Vicars.
Deasy, Kenneth '87 (LA) Los Angeles, CA St. Brendan.
Deasy, Rev. Msgr. Timothy J. '58 (MOB) Daphne, AL Christ the King Retired.
Deasy, Wayman P. *m.m.* '59 (NY)[EE] Maryknoll Maryknoll Fathers and Brothers; [EE] Maryknoll, NY Maryknoll Fathers and Brothers Charitable Trust.
Deatrick, John D. '66 (L) Retired.
Deaver, Stephen F. '59 (GI) Council of Catholic Women, Diocesan Retired.
de Avila y Romero, Rafael Antonio '74 (SFR) San Francisco, CA Visitacion, Church of the.
de Azevedo, Antonio Carvalho '62 (BGP) Danbury, CT Immaculate Heart of Mary.
Debany, Edgar J. *s.j.* '84 (BAL)[S] Towson Maryland Province of the Society of Jesus; Towson, MD Society of Jesus.
DeBellis, John A. '85 (NY) Carmel, NY St. James the Apostle.
DeBellis, Peter '97 (ROC) Absent on Leave.
Debes, Donald *o.f.m.cap.* '70 (FgM) Denver, CO Province of Mid–America.
DeBiase, William *o.f.m.* '66 (PH)[Y] Philadelphia, PA Order of Friars Minor of the Province of the Most Holy Name.
Debicki, John P. '64 (POD) Washington.
Debicki, John '64 (WDC)[U] Washington, DC Prelature of the Holy Cross and Opus Dei; [G] Potomac, MD The Heights School.
DeBisschop, James P. '88 (PEO) Coal Valley, IL St. Maria Goretti; Orion, IL Mary, Our Lady of Peace.
Debitetto, Ronald E. '63 (WOR) Retired.
DeBlanc, Rev. Msgr. Jefferson J. '77 (LAF) Church Point, LA Our Lady of the Sacred Heart.
De Blas, Alonso *o.f.m.* '64 (PHX)[G] Scottsdale, AZ Franciscan Renewal Center, Inc. (Casa de Paz Y Bien).
de Blas, Mariano *l.c.* '72 (LA)[P] Arcadia, CA Legionaries of Christ.
DeBlase, Dominic *s.d.b.* '61 (WDC) Washington, DC Nativity.
DeBlasio, Dominck A. '40 (PIT) Retired.
DeBlasio, Ernie '88 (MEM) Memphis, TN Church of the Resurrection; College of Consultors; Presbyteral Council.
DeBlock, Matthew '08 (RCK) Elgin, IL St. Mary.
Debo, William D. '95 (JC) Hermann, MO St. George; Rhineland, MO Church of the Risen Savior.
DeBock, Rev. Msgr. William A. '49 (MAD)[F] Madison, WI Bishop O'Connor Catholic Pastoral Center Retired.
DeBoe, Stanley W. *o.ss.t.* '83 (BAL)[S] The Trinitarians in Texas (Victoria & vicinity).
De Boe, Stanley *o.ss.t.* (VIC) Victoria, TX Our Lady of Sorrows.
DeBona, Guerric *o.s.b.* '86 (IND)[A] St. Meinrad, IN Saint Meinrad School of Theology; [K] St. Meinrad, IN St. Meinrad Archabbey; Officers.
De Brito Alves, Joseph '67 (BGP) Bridgeport, CT Our Lady of Fatima.
de Bruijn, Johan *o.cart.* '91 (BUR)[E] Arlington, VT Carthusian Foundation in America, Inc., Charterhouse of the Transfiguration.
DeBruycker, James R. '82 (STP) Minneapolis, MN St. Joan of Arc.
Debski, Joseph E. '64 (MIL) Retired.
Dec, Ignatius (Allen) *o.mar.* '84 (SAM)[B] Petersham, MA Maronite Monks of Adoration Most Holy Trinity Monastery.
Decaen, Ramon E. '00 (LIN) Dawson, NE St. Mary's; Apostolate to the Spanish Speaking; Advocates; Diocesan Area CCD Directors.
Decal, Wilfredo '77 (HT) Cut–Off, LA Sacred Heart.
De Candia, Anthony '07 (R) Jacksonville, NC Shrine of the Infant of Prague, Church of the Holy Spirit.
de Cardenas, Rev. Msgr. Javier Garcia '85 (NY)[JJ] New York, NY Prelature of the Holy Cross and Opus Dei; New York.
DeCarlo, Philip J. '55 (PIT) Retired.
DeCarlo, Thomas M. '69 (DM)[E] Johnston, IA Bishop Drumm Retirement Center.
De Carlo Mena, Francisco '50 (SJN) Retired.
DeCarolis, Joseph R. '59 (HRT) Retired.
DeCarolis, Vito C. '54 (HRT) Retired.
Decasa, George '78 (SD) San Diego, CA St. Charles.
De Celles, John C. '96 (ARL) Alexandria, VA St. Mary's.
Decewicz, Michael W. '78 (PIT) Beaver, PA SS. Peter and Paul; [P] Monroeville, PA Community College of Allegheny County – Boyce Campus.
Dechant, Leo *c.s.j.* '80 (LA) Lancaster, CA Blessed Junipero Serra.
Dechant, Paul *o.s.f.s.* '90 (CHL) Kernersville, NC Holy Cross.
Dechering, Rev. Msgr. Anton '62 (SP) St. Petersburg, FL Blessed Trinity; Scouting Office, Girls; College of Consultors.
Decipeda, Raymond *m.m.h.c.* '91 (LA) Lomita, CA St. Margaret Mary Alacoque.
Deck, Allan F. *s.j.* '76 (WDC)[N] Washington, DC Leonard Neale House.
Deck, Marion *t.o.r.* '69 (ALT)[G] Loretto, PA St. Francis Friary at Mount Assisi.
Decker, Chris (NO)[A] St. Benedict, LA St. Joseph Seminary College.
Decker, Christopher J. '07 (BR) Baton Rouge, LA St. Thomas More; Presbyteral Council.
Decker, Douglas A. '78 (OG) Adams, NY St. Cecilia; Advocates; Air National Guard Chaplains.
Decker, Jonathan *s.j. m.j.* '76 (OLL) Portland, OR Saint Sharbel Maronite Catholic Church.
Decker, Lawrence J. '84 (ALB) Amsterdam, NY St. Joseph–St. Michael–Our Lady of Mount Carmel.
Decker, Neil F. *s.j.* '58 (BO)[U] Weston, MA Campion Health Center, Inc.
Decker, Raymond G. '58 (SFR) Retired.
Decker, Robert L. '83 (OG) Harrisville, NY St. Francis Solanus; Star Lake, NY St. Hubert; Campus Ministry.
Decker, W. Johnathan *s.j.m.j.* (OLL)[D] Philippi, WV Our Lady of Solitude Maronite Hermitage, Inc.
Deckman, Peter '64 (ROC) Retired.
DeClippel, Ludo *c.j.* '68 (LA) Santa Barbara, CA Holy Cross.
DeClue, Richard '07 (CHL) Charlotte, NC St. Vincent de Paul; Graduate Studies.
DeCneudt, Rev. Msgr. Ferdinand '39 (DET) Retired.
DeCola, Vincent P. *s.j.* '88 (NY)[EE] New York, NY St. Ignatius Loyola Residence.
DeConciliis, Anthony J. *c.s.c.* '78 (NO)[C] New Orleans, LA Our Lady of Holy Cross College.
DeCondorpusa, Alfonso R. '95 (MET) Iselin, NJ St. Cecelia.
De Condorpusa, Alfonso R. '95 (NEW) On Duty Outside the Archdiocese.
DeCorte, Allan *o.f.m.* '77 (JOL) Joliet, IL St. John the Baptist.
DeCosta, George '64 (HON) Retired.
DeCosta, Joseph F. '90 (NOR) Gales Ferry, CT Our Lady of Lourdes; District Moderators.
DeCoste, Wade '03 (ALX) On Duty Outside the Diocese.
Decoteau, Vernon P. '75 (SPR) Belchertown, MA St.

Francis of Assisi; Diocesan Commission for the Liturgy.
DeCrans, Joseph '84 (CR) Deans; Ada, MN St. Joseph's; Priests Retirement Board of Trustees.
DeCrans, William '08 (CR) East Grand Forks, MN Sacred Heart.
de Cristobal, Fernando '65 (GRY) East Chicago, IN St. Patrick Retired.
Dede, Paul M. '64 (IND) Retired.
de Dios, Alfredo *o.a.r.* '60 (ORG)[I] Santa Ana, CA Augustinian Recollects; Santa Ana, CA Our Lady of Guadalupe.
de Dios, Francisco Mendez '60 (ARL) Manassas, VA All Saints.
de Dios Oliveros, Juan '99 (ATL) Dalton, GA St. Joseph's.
DeDomenico, Dominic *o.p.* '66 (OAK)[M] Oakland, CA Order of Preachers (Province of the Most Holy Name of Jesus – Western Dominican Province); [R] Oakland, CA Dominican Community Support Charitable Trust; [M] Oakland, CA Order of Preachers (Province of the Most Holy Name of Jesus – Western Dominican Province); Oakland, CA.
De Dominici, Lorenzo '46 (LA) San Pedro, CA Mary, Star of the Sea Retired.
Dee, Rev. Msgr. Dacian '56 (SP) Promoter of Justice; Defender of the Bond Retired.
Deegan, James *o.m.i.* '70 (STP)[N] Buffalo, MN Christ the King Retreat Center.
Deegan, John E. *o.s.a.* '61 (PH)[Y] Villanova, PA St. John Stone Friary; Counselors:.
Deegan, Ronan *t.o.r.* '58 (ALT)[G] Loretto, PA St. Francis Friary at Mount Assisi.
Deehan, Robert J. '83 (BO) Milton, MA St. Agatha; Clergy Personnel; Ex Officio.
Deehr, Anselm *s.t.* '90 (LA) Veterans Affairs Medical Center.
Deehr, Anselm *s.t.* '90 (WDC)[N] Adelphi, MD Father Judge Missionary Cenacle.
Deeke, Von C. '03 (BEL) O'Fallon, IL St. Clare; Diocesan Pastoral Council.
Deeker, Geoffrey J. *c.s.s.* '60 (SPR) Diocesan Commission for the Liturgy; Pittsfield, MA St. Joseph's.
Deeley, Kevin J. '74 (BO) Military & VA Chaplains.; Navy Chaplains.
Deeley, Rev. Msgr. Robert P. '73 (BO) On Duty Outside the Archdiocese.
Deely, John *o.m.i.* '70 (FgM) Washington, DC AMERICAN OBLATE MISSIONS.
Deeney, Charles J. *o.m.i.* '71 (ORL) Longwood, FL Annunciation.
Deering, Rev. Msgr. Mark '53 (AUS) Retired.
Deering, Michael J. '02 (BIR) Gardendale, AL St. Elizabeth Ann Seton; Diocesan College of Consultors; Priests'/Presbyteral Council; Diocesan College of Vicars.
Deery, Lawrence *o.m.i.* '41 (BO)[X] Tewksbury, MA Immaculate Heart of Mary Residence.
Deeves, John F. *s.j.* '58 (DAL)[D] Dallas, TX Jesuit College Preparatory School; Procurator–Advocates.
Deevy, Edward '62 (ALX) Absent on Leave.
Defayette, Jeffrey M. '88 (WDC) Lanham, MD St. Matthias Apostle; Advocates.
DeFazio, Vincent G. '92 (SFE) Retired.
DeFelice, Jonathan P. *o.s.b.* '74 (MAN)[B] Manchester, NH Saint Anselm College; [K] Manchester, NH St. Anselm Abbey.
De Feydeau, Francois *o.s.b.* '83 (TLS)[G] Hulbert, OK Our Lady of the Annunciation of Clear Creek Monastery.
Deffenbaugh, J. (PT) Saufley Field Federal Prison Camp.
Deffenbaugh, Joseph T. '79 (Y) On Duty Outside the Diocese.
Deffenbaugh, Terry A. *o.s.a.* '75 (CHI)[N] Matteson, IL Austin Friary.
DeFolco, Joseph '85 (SEA) Snohomish, WA St. Michael; Lake Stevens, WA Holy Cross Parish.
DeForest, Matthew J. '09 (ARL) Manassas, VA All Saints.
DeForge, Michael W. '79 (BUR) Diocesan Consultors; Canon 1742 Panel of Pastors; Shelburne, VT St. Catherine of Siena; Deans; [G] Northfield, VT Norwich Newman Apostolate.
De Francisco, Joseph '75 (DAV)[A] St. Ambrose University.
DeFrancisco, Joseph '75 (BEA) On Duty Outside the Diocese.
De Franco, Anthony '38 (ALB) Schenectady, NY St. Anthony; Schenectady, NY St. John the Evangelist Retired.
DeFrange, Jonathan M. *o.s.b.* '78 (NO)[P] St. Benedict, LA St. Joseph Abbey; Covington, LA St. Benedict.
DeFronzo, Anthony P. '81 (PSC) Special or Other Diocesan Assignment.
de Gaal, Emery '00 (CHI)[A] Mundelein, IL University of St. Mary of the Lake/Mundelein Seminary.
DeGaetano, Louis J. '79 (BRK) Flushing, NY St. Kevin.
Degagne, Richard E. '82 (FR) East Freetown, MA St. John Neumann.
Degaris, Herbert P. '91 (NY) Yorktown Heights, NY St. Patrick.
Degen, Jerome A. '59 (SC) Retired.
Degenhardt, Gervase *o.f.m.cap.* '58 (PIT)[M] Pittsburgh, PA St. Augustine Friary; [N] Pittsburgh, PA Sisters of St. Francis of the Neumann Communities, Western Pennsylvania Region.
DeGeorge, Salvatore *o.m.i.* (GAL) Houston, TX St. Patrick; Central Vicariate.
DeGerolami, Michael '74 (SAT) San Antonio, TX St. Philip of Jesus.
Degeyter, Edward '70 (LAF) Retired.
DeGiacomo, Albert J. '08 (LEX) Lexington, KY The Newman Center, Holy Spirit; [L] Lexington, KY The Newman Center Holy Spirit Parish University of Kentucky.
DeGiovine, Christopher '77 (ALB) Special Assignment; [B] Albany, NY The College of Saint Rose; Priestly Life and Ministry Council.
Deglaire, Pierre L. *c.s.sp.* '70 (SB) Highland, CA St. Adelaide.
Degnan, Charles *s.s.c.* '43 (OM)[K] St. Columbans Missionary Society of St. Columban.
Degnan, Charles *s.s.c.* '43 (PRO)[P] Bristol, RI St. Columban's Retirement House Retired.
Degnan, Rev. Msgr. Henry B. '48 (PH) Norristown, PA St. Paul Retired.
Degnan, James F. '55 (BO) Senior Priests. Retired.
Degnan, John F. '51 (JC) Retired.
DeGrand, Robert L. '80 (SFD) Effingham, IL St. Mary Help of Christians; Sigel, IL Sacred Heart; Sigel, IL St. Mary of the Assumption; Sigel, IL St. Michael the Archangel.
DeGrandis, Robert *s.s.j.* '59 (WDC)[B] Washington, DC St. Joseph's Seminary.
DeGrocco, Rev. Msgr. Joseph '88 (RVC) Senate of Priests (Presbyteral Council/College of Consultors).
DeGrood, Donald E. '97 (STP) Forest Lake, MN St. Peter.
DeGroot, Francis J. '93 (MAR) Escanaba, MI St. Anne; Advocates; Vicars Forane.
DeGroot, Ignatius *o.f.m.* '64 (TUC) Topawa, AZ San Solano Missions Roman Catholic Parish – Topawa.
De Groot, Kenneth J. *o.praem.* '61 (GB) Green Bay, WI St. Willebrord.
DeGuzman, Dennis U. '91 (OM) Military Chaplains.
De Guzman, Dennis '91 (MO) Air Force Chaplains.
De Heredia, Agnel '80 (SFR) South San Francisco, CA All Souls.
De Herrera, Christopher *o.s.* '97 (PCE) Penuelas, PR Sacred Heart; [H] Penuelas, PR Oblates of Wisdom.
Dehetre, Mark '93 (LAN) On Leave of Absence.
Dehne, Carl A. *s.j.* '70 (STL)[O] St. Louis, MO Jesuit Community Corporation at Saint Louis University – Jesuit Hall.
DeHondt, Ronald '73 (DET) St. Clair Shores, MI St. Margaret of Scotland.
Deibel, David L. '83 (SR)[L] Napa, CA Provincialate Community.
Deibel, David L. '83 (SAC) Judges.
Deibel, David L. (CHY) Defenders of the Bond.
Deichert, Joseph '84 (BIS) On Duty Outside the Diocese; Air Force Chaplains.
Deig, Robert A. '50 (EVN) Retired.
Deikel, Jeffrey '76 (LA) Covina, CA Sacred Heart.
Deimeke, L. Edward '75 (ALB) Priests Placement Committee; Leadership Team:.
Deimel, George *c.ss.r.* '37 (ALB)[L] Saratoga Springs, NY St. John Neumann Residence.
Deis, Dennis *o.m.i.* '65 (SFS) Rosholt, SD St. John the Baptist.
Deisch, Raymond J. '62 (RC) Retired.
Deister, Charles C. '63 (STL)[Q] Saint Louis, MO School Sisters of Notre Dame.
Deitch, Richard S. '86 (SFR) Retired.
Deitelhoff, Bernard H. '57 (MAD) Retired.
Deiters, James E. '91 (BEL) O'Fallon, IL St. Clare; Chicago, IL National Organization for Continuing Education of Roman Catholic Clergy, Inc. (NOCERCC); Diocesan Consultors.
Deiters, James R. '91 (BEL) Formation of Priests.
Deiters, Robert M. *s.j.* '58 (FgM) Chicago, IL Society of Jesus.
Deitz, Christopher L. '85 (MRY)[F] Arroyo Grande, CA St. Joseph Cupertino Province, Provincial Center.
Deitz, Christopher *o.f.m.conv.* '85 (MRY) Arroyo Grande, CA; [F] Arroyo Grande, CA St. Joseph Cupertino Friary.
Deitzer, Gerald E. *c.m.* '55 (PH)[Y].
DeJardin, Joseph R. *s. j.* '61 (SPK)[J] Spokane, WA Regis Community.
de Jesumaria, Marcelo *c.r.* '04 (SB)[I] Fontana, CA Congregation of the Resurrection, CR; Fontana, CA Blessed John XXIII Catholic Community, Inc.
De Jesus, Dwight '85 (ALX) Winnsboro, LA St. Mary; Elected Members.
de Jesus, Hector Bruno '85 (TYL) Gilmer, TX St. Francis of Assisi.
De Jesus, Rev. Msgr. Herminio '69 (PCE)[B] The Pontifical Catholic University of Puerto Rico; Chancellor; Diocesan Consultors.
de Jesus, Orlando (CGS) Diocesan Tribunal of Caguas.
de Jesus Gomez, Orlando '86 (CGS) Cidra, PR Nuestra Senora del Carmen.
de Jesus Puertas, Cristobal (NEW) Orange, NJ St. John's.
de Jesus Reynaga, Jose '04 (FRS) Merced, CA Sacred Heart.
de Jong, Jan *s.c.j.* '64 (MIL)[B] Hales Corners, WI Sacred Heart School of Theology; [P] Hales Corners, WI Priests of the Sacred Heart.
DeJulio, David '90 (SP) Tampa, FL St. Mark the Evangelist.
DeJulio, Robert J. '72 (NY) Pelham Manor, NY Our Lady of Perpetual Help.
Deka, Robbie '07 (GAY) Pellston, MI St. Clement; Pellston, MI Sacred Heart.
Dekaa, Thomas T. '82 (TUC) Safford, AZ Saint Rose of Lima Roman Catholic Parish – Safford.
Dekat, Carl '53 (KCK) Wamego, KS St. Joseph Retired.
Dekat, Earl '66 (KCK) Horton, KS St. Leo's; Horton, KS St. Mary's.
Deken, John C. '72 (STL) New Haven, MO St. Paul; New Haven, MO Assumption.
Dekrem, Bruno '92 (RVC) Floral Park, NY Our Lady of Victory.
de la Calle, Juan '54 (PMB) Indiantown, FL Holy Cross.
De La Cruz, Damian *c.r.* '05 (DEN) Fort Collins, CO Holy Family.
De la Cruz, Jenaro *o.c.d.* '66 (SAT)[L] San Antonio, TX Discalced Carmelite Fathers of San Antonio; San Antonio, TX Basilica of the National Shrine of the Little Flower, Our Lady of Mt. Carmel and St. Therese Parish.
de la Cruz, Juan '57 (ATL) Snellville, GA St. Oliver Plunkett.
Delacruz, Leandro '83 (TR) Hamilton, NJ St. Raphael–Holy Angels Parish.
Dela Cruz, Manuel C. *m.s.* '90 (HON) Honolulu, HI St. Anthony.
de la Cruz, Martin '01 (BWN)[A] Mission, TX The Saint Joseph and Saint Peter Seminary; Pharr, TX St. Margaret Mary.
De la Cruz, Nicolas *c.r.l.* (ARE) Corozal, PR La Milagrosa.
De la Cruz, Perlito '03 (SAC) Weaverville, CA St. Patrick.
DeLa Cruz, Vicente '90 (HT) Judicial Vicar; Judges; Houma, LA Cathedral of St. Francis De Sales.
de la Cruz Fernandez, Pedro '95 (DOD) Great Bend, KS Prince of Peace Catholic Church of Great Bend, Kansas.
DeLacy, Stephen P. '04 (PH)[D] Radnor, PA Archbishop John Carroll High School; Newtown Square, PA St. Anastasia.
deLadurantaye, Paul F. '88 (ARL) Arlington, VA Cathedral of St. Thomas More; Diocesan Judges; Catholic Education, Office of Catechetics; Liturgy, Office of Sacred.
Delaere, Paul *c.i.c.m.* '43 (FgM) Arlington, VA MISSIONHURST.
De La Garza, Joseph '51 (SAT) Retired.
Delahanty, Patrick D. '69 (L) Louisville, KY St. Martin de Porres; Louisville, KY St. Augustine.
Delahunty, Richard A. '65 (ORG) Laguna Woods, CA St. Nicholas; Council of Priests.
Delahunty, Thomas P. '55 (SAC) Retired.
de Laire, Georges F. '97 (MAN) On Duty Outside the Diocese.
del Almeida, Felipe R.J. *o.s.b.* '07 (GBG)[G] Latrobe Saint Vincent Archabbey.
de la Madrid, James Gil *m.ss.cc.* '97 (SJN) Bayamon, PR San Juan Bautista de la Salle.
DeLand, Robert J. '73 (SAG) Bay City, MI St. James; Judicial Vicar; Judges.
Delaney, Brian '75 (LA) Montebello, CA Our Lady of the Miraculous Medal; North Hills, CA Our Lady of Peace.
Delaney, Charles A. *c.s.c.* '49 (FgM)[H] Notre Dame Congregation of Holy Cross, Indiana Province, Provincial House; New Rochelle, NY Eastern Brothers Province.
Delaney, Rev. Msgr. Dennis M. '76 (STL) St. Louis, MO St. John the Apostle and Evangelist; Catholic Cemeteries of St. Louis.
Delaney, Donald *s.d.b.* '76 (NY) Port Chester, NY Corpus Christi.
Delaney, Rev. Msgr. Howard L. '40 (PBL) Retired.
Delaney, James *c.s.sp.* '54 (BRK)[T] Long Island City, NY Holy Ghost Fathers of Ireland; [X] Long Island City, NY World Compassion Link Retired.
Delaney, James *c.s.sp.* '54 (NEW) Jersey City, NJ St. Aloysius.
Delaney, John C. '06 (CAM) On Leave of Absence.
Delaney, John J. '62 (NY) Retired.
Delaney, John W. (BO) North Andover, MA St. Michael; Vicariate III.
Delaney, Rev. Msgr. John W. '64 (MIA) Fort Lauderdale, FL St. Helen Retired.
Delaney, John '81 (FTW) South Bend, IN St. Catherine of Siena Parish at St. Jude; Advisory Board; South Bend, IN St. Catherine of Siena Parish at Sacred

Heart of Jesus.
Delaney, Larry '90 (CR) Deans; East Grand Forks, MN Sacred Heart.
Delaney, Lawrence '67 (LAN)[M] De Witt, MI St. Francis Retreat Center.
Delaney, Matthew S. '51 (LA) Retired.
Delaney, Rev. Msgr. Michael J. '85 (SCR) Scranton, PA St. Paul's.
DeLaney, Michael M. *c.s.c.* '87 (FgM) New Rochelle, NY Eastern Brothers Province.
Delaney, Michael V. *s.j.* '85 (STL)[O] St. Louis, MO Jesuit Community Corporation at Saint Louis University – Jesuit Hall.
DeLaney, Michael *c.s.c.* (FTW)[H] Notre Dame Congregation of Holy Cross, Indiana Province, Provincial House.
Delaney, Thomas '57 (JKS) Crystal Springs, MS St. John the Evangelist.
Delaney, Thomas *o.m.i.* '60 (FgM) Washington, DC AMERICAN OBLATE MISSIONS.
Delaney, William I. '61 (RVC) Retired.
Delaney, William J. *c.pp.s.* '63 (LA) Los Angeles, CA St. Agnes.
Delaney, William J. '54 (NY) New York, NY Holy Innocents.
Delaney, William K. *s.j.* '85 (LA)[P] Los Angeles, CA Colombiere House.
Delaney, Rev. Msgr. William '44 (CHY) Cheyenne, WY Holy Trinity Retired.
Delaney, William *s.j.* '85 (LA)[BB] Burbank, CA SCRC (Southern California Renewal Communities).
Delange, Maurice '71 (COV) Retired.
del Angel, Jesus '00 (FRS) Sabbatical.
Delano, Kenneth J. '60 (FR) Retired.
de la Pena, Cosme R. '92 (CAM) International Priests Representatives; Absecon, NJ Church of Saint Elizabeth Ann Seton, Absecon, N.J.
De la Pena, Jose Manuel '00 (NEW) Bayonne, NJ St. Mary Star of the Sea.
De La Pena, Ordanico '98 (NEW) Hoboken, NJ Our Lady of Grace and Saint Joseph Parish.
DeLaPena, Richard '82 (NY) Castle Point, NY V.A. Hudson Valley Healthcare.
De la Pena, Uldarico '82 (MO) Kingston, NY St. Joseph; DEPARTMENT OF VETERANS AFFAIRS HOSPITALS AND CHAPLAINS.
De La Pinera, Fernando '51 (NO) Retired.
de la Puebla, Tomàs *c.m.* '49 (MGZ) Mayaguez, PR San Vicente Retired.
Delargy, Torlach C. '66 (POD)[R] San Francisco, CA Prelature of the Holy Cross and Opus Dei; Menlo Park.
De La Riva, John *o.f.m.cap.* '99 (MO) DEPARTMENT OF VETERANS AFFAIRS HOSPITALS AND CHAPLAINS.
de la Rosa, Frank '78 (SJN)[E] Carolina, PR Hospital Universitario de Carolina.
De La Rosa, Jose Luis '84 (SAT) Selma, TX Our Lady of Perpetual Help.
de la Rosa, Roger *s.j.* '03 (STL)[O] St. Louis, MO Leo Brown Jesuit Community.
de la Rosa, Roger *s.j.* '03 (SFR)[N] San Francisco, CA Loyola House Jesuit Community.
de la Rosa Peguero, Frank '78 (SJN) Carolina, PR San Francisco de Asis.
Delarue, Louis '75 (BEA) Retired.
de la Torre, Bartholomew *o.p.* '67 (FgM) Oakland, CA Province of the Holy Name (Western Dominican Province).
dela Torre, Bartholomew *o.p.* '67 (OAK)[M] Oakland Order of Preachers (Province of the Most Holy Name of Jesus – Western Dominican Province).
de la Torre, Jorge '97 (FRS) Arvin, CA St. Thomas the Apostle.
Delauney, Herbert C. '75 (LAF) Absent on Sick Leave.
De Laura, Felice J. '63 (BRK) Retired.
DeLay, Dominic *o.p.* '93 (LA) Los Angeles, CA St. Dominic.
Delay, Donald R. '83 (BO) Walpole, MA St. Mary; Presbyteral Council.
DeLazzer, Dorino '59 (DEN) Retired.
Delbel, James A. '81 (OG) Champlain, NY St. Mary; Mineville, NY Moriah Shock Incarceration Correctional Facility.
Del Bosque, Alejandro *l.c.* '87 (SAT) Devine, TX St. Joseph's.
Delcambre, Michael L. '05 (LAF) Cecilia, LA St. Joseph; Cecilia, LA St. Rose of Lima.
Del Campo, Cristian *s.j.* '05 (BO)[U] Cambridge, MA Faber House.
Del Carmen, Leo '91 (LA) Canoga Park, CA Our Lady of the Valley.
del Castillo, F. Javier '05 (CHI)[V] Chicago, IL Prelature of the Holy Cross and Opus Dei.
DelConte, Eugene *o.s.a.* '55 (PH) Philadelphia, PA St. Rita of Cascia.
DelDuca, John A. '68 (CAM) Elected Members; Blackwood, NJ St. Agnes' Church, Blackwood Terrace, N.J.
DeLeers, Stephen V. '84 (MIL) Retired.
DeLeers, Vincent J. *o.praem.* '46 (SFE)[H] Albuquerque, NM Santa Maria de la Vid Priory.
DeLeeuw, John '44 (LAF) Retired.
de Leis, Sean *c.s.sp.* '81 (PMB) Fort Pierce, FL St. Mark the Evangelist.
DeLellis, Francis V. '49 (PRO) Retired.
Delendick, Rev. Msgr. John '77 (BRK) Brooklyn, NY St. Jude Shrine Church; Fire Department; Diocesan Real Estate Board.
DeLeo, Roy James '69 (NEW) Elizabeth, NJ St. Genevieve's.
DeLeon, Angeles '04 (RNO) Winnemucca, NV St. Paul; Liturgy Commission.
DeLeon, Benedict '80 (SAC) Priests' Personnel Board, Diocesan; Redding, CA St. Joseph.
De Leon, Eddie *c.m.f.* '91 (CHI)[N] Oak Park, IL Claretian Missionaries USA Eastern Province; [N] Oak Park, IL Claretian Missionaries Community Support Trust.
de Leon, Edward T. *o.m.i.* '80 (SAN) Midland, TX Our Lady of Guadalupe; Diocesan Liturgical Commission.
DeLeon, Esteban *s.v.d.* (RIC) Virginia Beach, VA Star of the Sea.
de Leon, Jose A. '81 (CGS) Barranquitas, PR San Andres Apostol; Vocations.
DeLeon, Jose Raul '08 (WDC) Takoma Park, MD Our Lady of Sorrows.
DeLeon, Juancho G. '94 (NEW) Bloomfield, NJ St. Valentine.
DeLeon, Marco Tulio '01 (PMB) Jensen Beach, FL St. Martin de Porres.
De Leon, Michael '95 (LAR) Laredo, TX Divine Mercy.
DeLeon, Robert E. *c.s.c.* '85 (ALB) Albany Medical Center Hospital; [L] Valatie, NY St. Joseph Center; Special Assignment.
De Leonardis, Gerard *o.f.m.cap.* '49 (NY)[B] Beacon, NY St. Lawrence of Brindisi Friary Retired.
DeLerno, Kevin T. (NO) Metairie, LA St. Christopher the Martyr.
Delfra, Louis A. *c.s.c.* '04 (FTW)[B] University of Notre Dame Du Lac; [H] Notre Dame, IN Holy Cross Community, Corby Hall, University of Notre Dame.
Delgado, Alfonso *ss.cc.* '95 (GAL) Houston, TX Prince of Peace.
Delgado, Alvaro H. '02 (STO) Stockton, CA St. Edward Church (Pastor of).
Delgado, Enrique '96 (MIA) Key Largo, FL St. Justin Martyr.
Delgado, Jose A. '04 (CHI) Other Assignments.
Delgado, Jose D. *c.s.b.* '01 (GAL)[O] Sugar Land Basilian Mission Center.
Delgado, Jose Manuel *c.m.* '04 (FgM) Philadelphia, PA Eastern Province.
Delgado, Joseph '95 (SJ) On Leave of Absence.
Delgado, Juan R. Mora '92 (ARE) Adjutant Judges.
Delgado, Lenin *c.ss.r.* '91 (NY) New York, NY Most Holy Redeemer.
Delgado, Leslie N. '55 (LA) Los Angeles, CA Our Lady of Guadalupe Sanctuary.
Delgado, Rafael Diaz *o.p.* (SJN) Carolina, PR Cristo Rey.
Delgado, Ruben '90 (BWN) Elsa, TX Sacred Heart; Presbyteral Council; College of Consultors.
Del Giudice, Carl '81 (CHL) Brevard, NC Sacred Heart.
Delich, David L. *o.p.* '63 (STL)[O] St. Louis, MO St. Dominic Priory.
De Lillio, Richard R. *o.s.f.s.* '66 (WIL)[B] Wilmington, DE Salesianum School.
de Lima, Roberto Aparacido *c.ss.r.* '96 (WOR) Brazilian Ministry.
Deliman, Rev. Msgr. Edward M. '73 (PH) Philadelphia, PA St. Martin of Tours.
de Lira, Noel R. '99 (BAL)[S] Baltimore, MD St. Mary's Seminary & University.
de Lira, Noel '00 (SFR)[A] Menlo Park, CA St. Patrick Seminary and University.
Delis, Robert *s.d.b.* '79 (MO) Navy Chaplains.
Delis, Robert *s.d.b.* '79 (SFR)[N] San Francisco Salesian Provincial Residence.
Delisi, Anthony *o.c.s.o.* '54 (ATL)[G] Conyers, GA The Monastery of the Holy Spirit.
Delisle, Eric T. '03 (MAN) Southern N.H. Regional Medical Center and Nursing Homes; St. Joseph Hospital; Nashua, NH Blessed John XXIII Parish.
DeLisle, Henri A. *o.m.i.* '58 (MAN)[K] Colebrook, NH Shrine of Our Lady of Grace.
Delisle, Richard *m.s.* '59 (MAN) Lebanon, NH Sacred Heart.
Dell, Robert S. *c.o.* '90 (CHR)[E] Rock Hill, SC Oratory of St. Philip Neri, Congregation of the Oratory of Pontifical Rite.
Dell, Robert *c.o.* '90 (SEA)[L] Seattle, WA Seattle Oratory.
Dell'Anno, Anthony V. '69 (BRK) Brooklyn, NY St. Edmund Retired.
Dellaert, Brian M. '05 (DUB) Garner, IA St. Wenceslaus; Forest City, IA St. James; Garner, IA St. Boniface; Forest City, IA St. Patrick; Britt, IA St. Patrick; Forest City, IA St. Patrick.
Dellagiovanna, Mariano N. '07 (NEW) West New York, NJ Holy Redeemer.
Della Neve, Louis '52 (BUF) Retired.
De Llano, Domingo '68 (CC) Retired.
della Picca, Paul B. '59 (ALN) Retired.
Della Pietra, Douglas '96 (ROC) Absent on Leave.
Dellaporte, Dominick M. '85 (NEW) Hoboken, NJ St. Francis.
Dellinger, Jonathan '05 (DEN) Wray, CO St. Andrew; Yuma, CO St. John the Evangelist.
Dello Russo, John F. *o.s.a.* '87 (NY) Staten Island, NY Our Lady of Good Counsel.
Dellos, Richard E. '68 (SY) Utica, NY St. Joseph and St. Patrick.
Dell'Oro, Italo *c.r.s.* '82 (GAL) Houston, TX Christ the King; Priests Personnel Committee; Director of Ministry to Priests.
Delmonte, Albert L. '69 (ROC) Pittsford, NY St. Louis Retired.
Delmore, Eugene *s.j.* '69 (YAK) Yakima, WA St. Joseph Parish.
Del Olmo, Jose '92 (VEN) Hispanic, Migrant and Spanish Speaking Apostolates.
Delonnay, Lawrence '75 (DET) Waterford, MI Our Lady of the Lakes.
DeLora, John '94 (NY) Staten Island University Hospital North; Staten Island, NY Staten Island University Hospital South.
DeLorenzo, John R. '76 (SY) Jordan, NY St. Patrick.
DeLoreto, Anthony '54 (B) Pocatello, ID Holy Spirit Catholic Community Retired.
DeLorme, R. Daniel '57 (SY) Homer, NY St. Margaret.
de los Reyes, Joel '75 (AGN) Cursillo in Christianity; Dededo, GU Santa Barbara.
De Los Rios, Enrique '00 (LA) Los Angeles, CA St. Alphonsus.
De Los Santos, Rev. Msgr. Jorge '91 (DEN) Vicar for Hispanic Ministry; Ex Officio Members; Vicar for Hispanic Ministry.
DeLoza, Jose '87 (YAK) On Duty Outside the Diocese.
Del Prado, Jerry (NY) Staten Island, NY Our Lady Help of Christians.
Del Prete, Rev. Msgr. Frank G. '77 (NEW) Hoboken, NJ SS. Peter and Paul's; Archdiocesan Judges.
Del Priore, John *s.j.s.* '08 (MAD) Mazomanie, WI St. Barnabas; Sauk City, WI St. Norbert; Sauk City, WI St. Aloysius; Mazomanie, WI St. John the Baptist.
Del Priore, Kenneth '83 (SD) Escondido, CA Church of the Resurrection.
del Rosario, Mark *s.s.s.* '80 (HON) Honolulu, HI Star of the Sea; Office of Clergy: Diocesan Screening Committee.
del Toro, Alejandro '07 (RCK) DeKalb, IL Christ the Teacher, University Parish of Northern Illinois University; [L] DeKalb, IL Newman Foundation for Catholic Students of Northern Illinois University.
Del Toro, Jose L. *t.o.r.* '95 (MO) Air Force Chaplains.
Del Toro, Jose (RC) Ellsworth AFB.
DelToro, José Jaime *c.s.b.* '08 (DET) Detroit, MI Ste. Anne de Detroit.
DeLuca, Anthony '53 (PIT) Retired.
DeLuca, David *m.s.c.* '66 (OG)[F] Watertown, NY Missionaries of the Sacred Heart.
DeLuca, Paul F. '81 (CIN) Cincinnati, OH Nativity of Our Lord.
DeLuca, Stephen J. '65 (BGP) Greenwich, CT Greenwich Hospital.
DeLucia, Gerald M. '78 (Y) Campbell, OH St. Lucy; Campbell, OH St. Rose of Lima.
DeLucia, Pierluigi *s.j.* '09 (BO)[U] Cambridge, MA St. Edmund's House.
DeLucia, Vincent G. *o.p.* '94 (NY) New York, NY St. Joseph; [HH] New York, NY New York University.
De Luney, Gerald C. '69 (SB) Corona, CA Corpus Christi.
Delva, Jean M. '07 (BRK) Queens Village, NY SS. Joachim and Anne.
Del Valle, Thomas '79 (NY) New York, NY Holy Cross.
Del Valle, Tomas '79 (SJN) On Duty Outside the Archdiocese.
Delvard, Quesnel *s.d.b.* '03 (PMB) Belle Glade, FL St. Philip Benizi.
Del Vecchio, Joseph F. *s.s.j.* '36 (WDC) Washington, DC St. Luke.
DelVecchio, Rev. Msgr. Michael E. '54 (BUF) Retired.
Delzell, David G. '50 (TR) Retired.
Delzingaro, Richard M. *c.r.s.p.* '96 (BUF)[T] Youngstown, NY Basilica of the National Shrine of Our Lady of Fatima, Inc.; [B] Youngstown, NY St. Anthony M. Zaccaria Seminary.
de M. Pereira, Luciano J. '54 (FR) Somerset, MA St. John of God Retired.
DeMaio, Dominic *o.p.* '08 (ANC) Hispanic Ministry; Anchorage, AK Holy Family Cathedral.
DeMaio, Joseph *o.carm.* '65 (ROC)[B] Rochester, NY McQuaid Jesuit High School; [J] Rochester, NY Whitefriars Priory.
DeMan, Thomas *o.p.* '62 (P)[N] McKenzie Bridge, OR St. Benedict Lodge Dominican Retreat & Conference Center.
Demarais, Garvin J. '81 (OG) Malone, NY Franklin Correctional Facility; Malone, NY Upstate Correctional Facility; Advocates.
DeMarco, David G. *s.j.* '05 (CHI)[N] Chicago Chicago Province of the Society of Jesus–Provincial Office.

DeMarco, David G. *s.j.* '05 (DET)[B] Berkley, MI Loyola House.
DeMarco, Peter A. '60 (BGP) Deaf, Apostolate for; [O] Stamford, CT The Catherine Dennis Keefe Queen of the Clergy Retired Priests' Residence Retired.
DeMarinis, Rev. Msgr. John H. '62 (Y) Finance Council; Youngstown, OH St. Anthony.
DeMartinis, Michael G. '97 (E) Erie, PA St. Andrew; [C] Erie, PA Cathedral Preparatory School.
De Martinis, O. Robert '86 (ALB) Schenectady, NY Immaculate Conception.
DeMartino, Robert J. '92 (ARL) Stafford, VA St. William of York.
DeMattia, John '68 (PAT) Dover, NJ St. Mary's.
deMayo, Martin P. '03 (BGP) Stratford, CT St. Mark.
Demecias, Genaro C. '82 (FRS) Taft, CA St. Mary.
DeMeersman, Clement *c.i.c.m.* '52 (FgM) Arlington, VA MISSIONHURST.
Demek, Martin H. '75 (BAL) Baltimore, MD St. William of York.
Demers, Bertrand '48 (KNX) Retired.
Demers, Francis L. *o.m.i.* '55 (MAN) Diocesan Judges.
Demers, Francis *o.m.i.* '55 (BO)[X] Tewksbury, MA Immaculate Heart of Mary Residence.
Demers, Gerard A. *s.m.* (BO) Boston, MA Our Lady of Victories.
Demers, Gerard *s.m.* '59 (BO)[U] Boston, MA Marist Fathers of Our Lady of Victories (Boston Prov.).
Demers, Normand J. '58 (PRO) Retired.
Demers, Paul R. *s.c.* '81 (MAN)[B] Nashua, NH Rivier College.
Demers, Richard D. '83 (OG) Absent on Sick Leave, Disabled.
Demers, Wilfred G. '59 (MAN) Retired.
Demers, Wilfred '55 (MAN) Manchester, NH Ste. Marie.
Demets, Laurent *f.s.s.p.* '00 (LR)[K] North Little Rock, AR Priestly Fraternity of St. Peter.
DeMeulemeester, Patrick '95 (PEO) Granville, IL Sacred Heart Of Jesus; Granville, IL St. Patrick's.
DeMeulenaere, Martin *o.s.b.* '73 (KC) Maryville, MO St. Gregory Barbarigo; [J] Maryville, MO; Deans; Presbyteral Council.
Deming, Robert N. '58 (KC) Retired.
Demkiv, Ivan '92 (PHU) Philadelphia, PA Immaculate Conception of Blessed Virgin Mary, Cathedral; College of Archeparchial Consultors; Presbyteral Council; Protopresbyters (Deans).
Demko, James J. '82 (PSC) Beaver Meadows, PA SS. Peter and Paul.
Demkovich, Rev. Msgr. John J. '65 (PAT) Passaic, NJ Assumption of the Blessed Virgin Mary; Pro–Synodal Judges; Paterson, NJ Mission Office; Legion of Mary.
Deml, Francis S. '57 (DEN) Retired.
Demmer, Donald L. '75 (DET) Troy, MI St. Alan; Birmingham, MI St. Columban.
DeMolen, Richard '98 (RNO) Retired.
Dempsey, Dennis '80 (STP) Northfield, MN St. Dominic.
Dempsey, Edward M. '67 (NOR) Absent on Leave.
Dempsey, Rev. Msgr. James '56 (BEA) Retired.
Dempsey, John G. '64 (STL) Arnold, MO Immaculate Conception.
Dempsey, Rev. Msgr. Michael J. '58 (BRK) Forest Hills, NY Our Lady, Queen of Martyrs Retired.
Dempsey, Nicholas '71 (SD) San Diego, CA St. Therese of Carmel.
Dempsey, Richard J. '58 (CHI) Retired.
Dempsey, Rev. Msgr. Robert J. '80 (CHI) Northfield, IL St. Philip the Apostle; College of Consultors.
Dempsey, Sean T. '08 (PH)[Y] Loyola Center and Manresa Hall.
Dempsey, Terrence E. *s.j.* '85 (STL)[C] Saint Louis University; [O] St. Louis, MO Jesuit Community Corporation at Saint Louis University – Jesuit Hall.
Dempsey, Rev. Msgr. Thomas J. '61 (RCK) Retired.
Dempsey, Rev. Msgr. Thomas J. '62 (STL) Ballwin, MO Holy Infant.
Demse, Thomas P. '76 (MIL) Milwaukee, WI St. Gregory The Great.
Demski, Ronald G. '69 (TYL) New Boston, TX St. Mary of the Cenacle; New Boston, TX Telford Unit, Texas Department of Corrections.
Demuth, Rev. Msgr. George R. '46 (SCR) Retired.
Demuth, Paul E. '68 (GB) Green Bay, WI Resurrection; Vicar for Ministers; Priests' Personnel Board; Special Assignment; Ex Officio.
De Nard, Silvio *s.c* '79 (PH)[B] Springfield, PA Servants of Charity; [M] Rosemont, PA St. Edmond's Home for Children.
DeNardi, Charles A. '36 (OWN) Retired.
Dendinger, Robert L. '75 (TOL) Upper Sandusky, OH Transfiguration of the Lord.
Dene, Charles J. '58 (ALN) Shenandoah, PA Annunciation.
Dene, Joseph '62 (WH) Retired.
Denemark, Emil J. *s.j.* '81 (FgM) Milwaukee, WI Society of Jesus; Army Reserve Chaplains.
De Nguyen–Dang, Thomas '82 (ORG) Tustin, CA St. Cecilia.
Denha, Suleiman '59 (EST) Oak Park, MI Mar Addai Chaldean Parish; Eparchial College of Consultors.
Denig, Philip P. '85 (DEN) On Duty Outside the Archdiocese.
Denig, Stephen J. *c.m.* '75 (BUF)[O] Niagara University, NY Vincentian Community at Niagara University; [C] Niagara University, NY Niagara University; [G] Niagara Falls, NY Catholic Academy of Niagara Falls.
Deniger, Joseph L. *c.s.sp.* '58 (SB) Hemet, CA Our Lady of the Valley.
DeNigris, Emanuele '05 (WDC) Germantown, MD Mother Seton Parish.
DeNinno, Dale E. '78 (PIT) Pittsburgh, PA Saint Elizabeth of Hungary.
DeNinno, Louis L. '76 (PIT) Pittsburgh, PA Holy Wisdom; Matrimonial Concerns, Office for; Matrimonial Concerns, Office for; Judges.
Denison, Frederick J. '73 (IND) Floyds Knobs, IN St. John the Baptist.
Denk, Kurt M. *s.j.* '07 (OAK)[M] Berkeley, CA Jesuit Fathers and Brothers.
Denk, Michael J. '07 (CLV) Northfield, OH St. Barnabas.
Denn, James J. *c.s.c.* '61 (FTW)[H] Notre Dame Congregation of Holy Cross, Indiana Province, Provincial House.
Dennehy, John D. '81 (NEW)[B] School of Diplomacy and Intl. Rels.
Dennehy, Martin J. '51 (BGP) Retired.
Dennemann, Thomas J. '73 (CIN) Cincinnati, OH St. Ann.
Dennerlein, Arno A. '69 (JOL) Absent on Leave.
Dennerlein, John L. '74 (JOL) Shorewood, IL Holy Family Retired.
Denning, John F. *c.s.c.* '87 (FR)[A] North Easton, MA Stonehill College; [A] North Easton, MA Holy Cross Fathers Religious.
Dennis, George T. *s.j.* '54 (SJ)[M] Los Gatos, CA Sacred Heart Jesuit Center.
Dennis, John J. *o.s.f.s.* '45 (PH)[Y] Philadelphia, PA Father Louis Brisson Residence Retired.
Dennis, John J. *o.s.f.s.* '45 (WIL)[J] Childs, MD Retirement and Assisted Care Facility Retired.
Dennis, John M. *s.j.* '86 (BAL)[S] Baltimore, MD Jesuit Community of Loyola University, Inc.; [B] Jesuit Community of Loyola University, Inc.
Dennis, Patrick '78 (B) Retired.
Dennis, Peter K. *ss.cc.* '62 (LA)[P] La Verne, CA Congregation of the Sacred Hearts of Jesus and Mary.
Dennis, Peter K. *ss.cc.* '62 (SB)[I] Chino Hills, CA Congregation of the Sacred Hearts of Jesus & Mary, SS.CC.
Dennis, Sam *o.s.b.* '57 (SFE)[H] Pecos, NM Our Lady of Guadalupe Abbey.
Dennis, Thomas J. '92 (SFD) Absent on Leave.
Dennis, Tyler '09 (RC) Rapid City, SD Cathedral of Our Lady of Perpetual Help.
Dennison, Arthur '73 (MIA) Coral Gables, FL Little Flower.
Denniston, John '79 (RVC) Serving Outside the Diocese; New Hyde Park, NY Notre Dame.
Denny, Charles J. '69 (TOL) Oregon, OH St. Charles Mercy Hospital; [G] Oregon, OH St. Charles Mercy Hospital.
Denny, Charles J. '69 (TOL) Toledo, OH St. Anne Mercy Hospital; [G] Toledo, OH St. Anne Mercy Hospital.
Denny, John T. *o.s.a.* '90 (CHL) Maggie Valley, NC St. Margaret of Scotland.
Denny, Thomas F. *s.j.* '68 (NY)[EE] New York, NY St. Ignatius Loyola Residence.
Deno, Rev. Msgr. Lawrence M. '59 (OG) Cadyville, NY St. James Church.
DeNoble, Augustine *o.s.b.* '55 (P)[L] St. Benedict, OR Mt. Angel Abbey.
Denron, Christopher J. *s.j.* '01 (CHI)[N] Chicago, IL Miguel Pro Jesuit Community.
Densmore, Anthony M. '04 (MO) Air Force Reserve Chaplains.
Dente, Thomas A. '93 (NEW) Jersey City, NJ Our Lady of Czestochowa; Members; Office of Divine Worship.
Dentici, Rev. Msgr. Thomas '53 (DEN) Steamboat Springs, CO Holy Name Retired.
Dentinger, Roy E. '50 (L) Ex Officio Retired.
Denys, Charles *c.i.c.m.* '44 (ARL)[H] Arlington, VA Missionhurst, C.I.C.M.–Central House and Provincialate.
Denzer, Joseph W. '68 (BRK)[T] Douglaston, NY Bishop Mugavero Residence Retired.
Denzer, Thomas F. *s.j.* '61 (STL)[O] St. Louis, MO Jesuit Community Corporation at Saint Louis University – Jesuit Hall.
De Oca, Jose Monte '96 (NEW) Jersey City, NJ St. Aloysius.
de Oliveira, Pedro *o.f.m.conv.* '00 (R)[F] Pittsboro, NC Our Lady of Guadalupe Friary; Siler City, NC St. Julia.
DePalma, Michael '03 (SFE) Presbyteral Council of the Archdiocese of Santa Fe; Vocations; Presbyteral Council of the Archdiocese of Santa Fe; Rio Rancho, NM St. Thomas Aquinas.
De Pascale, Daniel '61 (ALB) Retired.
DePasquale, Leonard *i.m.c.* '71 (SB) San Bernardino, CA St. Bernardine.
Depatie, Donald L. '78 (PRO) Cumberland, RI St. Aidan.
De Paula, Cristobal '02 (MIA) Miami Springs, FL Blessed Trinity.
de Paulo, Craig (SJP) On Leave; Presbyters.
Depeaux, Bernard F. '50 (BUR) Retired.
De Peaux, Rowland C. *o.praem.* '51 (GB)[J] De Pere, WI St. Joseph Priory.
DePew, Daniel R. '85 (GR) Spring Lake, MI St. Mary's.
DePeyster, Aaron J. '05 (DET) Lapeer, MI Immaculate Conception of the Blessed Virgin Mary.
DePietro, Arthur J. '63 (BO) Senior Priests. Retired.
Depinet, Robert L. *m.m.* '61 (NY)[EE] Maryknoll Maryknoll Fathers and Brothers Retired.
DePinto, Basil '58 (OAK) Piedmont, CA Corpus Christi Retired.
Depman, Rev. Msgr. Francis J. '81 (PH) West Grove, PA Assumption B.V.M.
Deponai, Joseph J. '83 (NY) Nanuet, NY St. Anthony.
De Porter, Arnold W. '63 (WDC) Retired.
DePra, Italo '51 (P) Retired.
DePrinzio, Kevin M. *o.s.a.* '04 (PH)[Y] Villanova, PA Provincial Offices of the Order of St. Augustine, Province of St. Thomas of Villanova.
DePrinzio, Kevin *o.s.a.* '04 (PH)[C] Villanova University; [Y] Drexel Hill, PA Bellesini Friary.
DeProfio, Rev. Msgr. Louis A. '56 (BGP) Diocesan Consultors; Retired Priests; Presbyteral Council; [O] Stamford, CT The Catherine Dennis Keefe Queen of the Clergy Retired Priests' Residence Retired.
DeProspero, Nicholas '70 (PSC) Pottstown, PA St. John the Baptist.
Deptula, Michael '84 (PHX) On Leave.
Deptula, Rev. Msgr. Stanley L. '96 (PEO)[O] Peoria, IL Archbishop Fulton J. Sheen Foundation; Vice Chancellors; Liturgy, Churches and Chapels; Divine Worship, Office of; Assistant Directors.
DeRammelaere, Bruce A. '06 (DAV) Burlington, IA SS. John & Paul.
DeRamos, Fidel '64 (WDC) Retired.
de Ranitz, Richard *o.p.* '70 (CHI)[N] Chicago Dominicans (Provincial Office).
Derasmo, John '81 (RVC) Westbury, NY St. Brigid.
Derbes, Louis J. *c.m.* '51 (STL)[O] Perryville, MO Congregation of the Mission.
Derbish, Michael *o.f.m.* '62 (SJP) Presbyters Retired.
Derda, Christopher '06 (KAL) Augusta, MI St. Ann; Vocations; Presbyteral Council Members; Presbyteral Council Members.
DeRea, Philip *m.s.c.* '68 (RCK) Washington, DC MIVA–America Missionary Vehicle Association Inc.; [G] Aurora, IL Missionaries of the Sacred Heart Community.
Derenne, Karin (GB)[G] Appleton, WI St. Elizabeth Hospital, Inc.; [G] Oshkosh, WI Mercy Medical Center of Oshkosh, Inc.
Deresienski, Stanley *s.s.e.* '78 (BUR) Councilors:; [E] South Burlington, VT Edmundnite House of Formation.
deRezende, Roberto F. (BO) Stoughton, MA Immaculate Conception.
Derfus, Kenneth J. '56 (MIL) Retired.
Dericks, Rev. Msgr. John H. '41 (PAT) Morristown, NJ Retired.
Derise, Mark '97 (LAF) New Iberia, LA Our Lady of Perpetual Help; Knights of Columbus.
DeRiso, John M. *c.s.c.* '02 (FTW) South Bend, IN St. Joseph; [H] Notre Dame Congregation of Holy Cross, Indiana Province, Provincial House.
De Ritis, Gilbert J. *m.m.* '54 (NY)[EE] Retired.
Derivan, Rev. Msgr. Thomas B. '72 (NY) Bronx, NY St. Helena.
Derivaux, Donald F. '55 (JKS) Retired.
Dermody, Thomas '62 (SAC) Retired.
Dermond, Rev. Msgr. John K. '68 (TR) Trenton, NJ St. Mary Cathedral; Assistant Chancellors; Judicial Vicar; Mercer County.
Dermott, William R. '82 (MO) Military Chaplains; Navy Chaplains.
Dernbach, Rev. Msgr. Arthur '53 (P) Retired.
Dernek, Richard J. '70 (WIN) Lake City, MN St. Mary's of the Lake; Lake City, MN St. Patrick of West Albany.
DeRoche, Wilfred L. '65 (OG) Retired.
de Rosa, Francis M. '01 (ARL) Colonial Beach, VA St. Elizabeth of Hungary.
Derosa, Vincent '08 (WDC) Silver Spring, MD St. Bernadette.
DeRose, Martin '88 (ALB) Hagaman, NY St. Stephen.
DeRosia, Volney J. '03 (MAN) Epping, NH St. Joseph.
Derosier, Edmond M. '73 (BO) Ayer, MA St. Mary; Shirley, MA St. Anthony of Padua.
DeRouen, Rev. Msgr. Keith J. '83 (LAF) Lafayette, LA Cathedral of St. John the Evangelist; Office of Worship.
DeRouen, Robert R. *s.j.* '54 (DEN)[N] Denver, CO Xavier Jesuit Center.
Derrane, Mark G. '95 (BO) Lynn, MA Sacred Heart.

Derrenbacher, James W. '45 (NY)[EE] Bronx, NY John Cardinal O'Connor Residence Retired.
Derrera, Ferdinand *s.j.* '61 (LAF) Grand Coteau, LA St. Charles Borromeo.
Derry, Daniel '63 (SJ) Gilroy, CA St. Mary.
Dery, Henry R. '48 (HRT)[A] In Res. at the Archbishop Daniel A. Cronin Retirement Residence at St. Thomas Seminary Retired.
Dery, Peter (BRK) Brooklyn, NY St. Columba.
Derzack, Rev. Msgr. Thomas A. '76 (ALN) College of Consultors; Bangor, PA Our Lady of Good Counsel; Clarks Summit, PA The Slovak Catholic Federation (1911).
DeSa, Walter *o.s.f.s.* '65 (FgM) Wilmington, DE OBLATES OF ST. FRANCIS DE SALES MISSIONS.
DeSalvo, Donald D. '69 (RCK) Retired.
DeSalvo, William '88 (JOL) Westmont, IL Holy Trinity; Deans.
Desam, Balaraju '03 (SCR) Honesdale, PA St. John the Evangelist.
DeSanctis, Peter A. '79 (BRK) Released from Diocesan Assignment.
DeSanctis, Peter (RVC) Shelter Island Heights, NY Our Lady of the Isle.
DeSandre, John G. '64 (TR) Deal, NJ St. Mary of the Assumption.
De Santi, Bruno *c.s.j.* '51 (LA) San Pedro, CA St. Peter.
DeSantis, Rev. Msgr. Joseph A. '75 (ALN) Reading, PA Sacred Heart; Appointed Members.
DeSantis, Linus *o.f.m.conv.* '71 (SY)[T] Syracuse, NY Syracuse University, St. Thomas More Foundation, Inc.; Syracuse, NY Assumption B.V.M.
DeSanto, Joseph A. '54 (NY) Nanuet, NY St. Anthony Retired.
Desaulniers, Richard P. '70 (PRO) Manville, RI St. James.
Desautels, Alfred R. *s.j.* '50 (BO)[U] Weston, MA Campion Health Center, Inc.
Desch, Paul *o.f.m.* '56 (CIN)[N] Cincinnati, OH St. John the Baptist Friary.
Deschamps, Wilfred H. '90 (MAN) Jaffrey, NH St. Patrick.
DeSciose, Michael C. '75 (PBL) Parkview Hospital.
Descoteaux, Lee R. '07 (RVC) Deer Park, NY SS. Cyril and Methodius.
Des Forges, Edmond *o.f.m.conv.* '77 (CHI)[N] Libertyville, IL Marytown, Our Lady of Fatima Friary.
Deshaies, Richard A. *s.j.* '92 (BO)[U] Newton, MA The Jesuit Community at Boston College.
Desharnais, Gary L. '00 (YAK) Yakima, WA Holy Family.
Deshautelle, Blake Paul '07 (ALX) Vocations and Seminarians; Cottonport, LA St. Mary Assumption.
Deshotels, James M. *s.j.* '93 (NO) Gray, LA Byzantine Catholic Mission.
Deshotels, James M. *s.j.* '93 (PBR) New Orleans, LA St. Nicholas of Myra Mission.
Desiano, Francis P. *c.s.p.* '72 (NY)[EE] Jamaica Estates, NY Paulist Fathers Generalate.
DeSiano, Francis P. *c.s.p.* (BRK)[T] Jamaica Estates, NY Paulist Fathers – Generalate.
DeSiano, Francis P. *c.s.p.* '72 (WDC)[B] Washington, DC St. Paul's College; [W] Washington, DC Paulist National Catholic Evangelization Assoc.
Desiderio, Frank *c.s.p.* '82 (LA) Los Angeles, CA St. Paul the Apostle.
DeSilva, L. Praxid '69 (NY) Briarcliff Manor, NY St. Theresa.
DeSilva, Lionel A. *c.s.p.* '59 (NY) Roosevelt Site; [EE] New York, NY Paulist Fathers' Motherhouse.
DeSimone, David A. '87 (NY) Poughkeepsie, NY St. Peter; Poughkeepsie, NY Vassar Brothers Hospital; New York, NY Sacred Heart of Jesus.
DeSimone, Russell J. *o.s.a.* '51 (PH)[Y] Villanova, PA St. Thomas Monastery.
DeSimone, Thomas '06 (NY) White Plains, NY Our Lady of Sorrows.
Desir, Jean Hugues '04 (ORL) Clermont, FL St. Faustina Catholic Church.
Desjardins, George A. '59 (MAN) Retired.
Desjardins, James M. *s.j.* '77 (FgM)[S] Towson Maryland Province of the Society of Jesus; Towson, MD Society of Jesus.
Desjardins, Raymond S. '42 (MAN) Retired.
Deskevich, Andrew J. '97 (PBR) Erie, PA SS. Peter and Paul; Revitalization and Renewal Commission; Communications; Presbyteral Council.
DeSloover, A. Robert '74 (TOL) Miller City, OH St. Nicholas; Miller City, OH Holy Family.
Desmarais, Paul E. '79 (PRO) Carolina, RI St. Mary.
Desmond, David A. '02 (SFS) Hartford, SD St. George; [C] Sioux Falls, SD O'Gorman High School; Diocesan Consultors; Presbyteral Council.
Desmond, Hubert E. '58 (BO) Senior Priests. Retired.
Desmond, Rev. Msgr. Joseph E. '47 (MAN) Retired.
Desmond, Joseph L. '74 (MET) Robert Wood Johnson University Hospital; Edison, NJ St. Matthew the Apostle.
Desmond, Rev. Msgr. Michael J. '71 (NEW) Caldwell, NJ St. Aloysius; Elected Members.
Desmond, Nicholas R. '84 (CHI) Chicago, IL St. Aloysius; Chicago, IL St. Stephen, King of Hungary; Deans.
DeSocio, John A. '78 (MO) Navy Reserve Chaplains; Elmira, NY St. Mary.
Desormeaux, Roland *c.s.* '82 (PMB) Delray Beach, FL Our Lady of Perpetual Help Mission.
DeSouza, Carl '66 (RIC) Retired.
de Souza, Owen '70 (LA) Hospital Chaplains; On Sick Leave.
DesRochers, Emery N. *m.s.* '48 (HRT)[L] Hartford, CT Missionaries of LaSalette.
Desrochers, Rev. Msgr. Timothy H. '64 (MAR) Retired.
Des Rosiers, Denis A. '69 (OAK) Walnut Creek, CA St. Stephen.
DesRosiers, N. Wilfrid *s.s.j.* '55 (BAL)[S] Baltimore, MD St. Joseph Society of the Sacred Heart House of Central Administration Retired.
Desrosiers, Paul H. '75 (NO) New Orleans, LA University of New Orleans; New Orleans, LA Transfiguration of the Lord.
Desrosiers, Philip J. '66 (BO) Senior Priests. Retired.
DesRosiers, Ronald G. *s.m.* '63 (DET)[K] Livonia, MI Marist Fathers & Brothers Community.
DesRuisseaux, Charles E. '60 (MAN) Presbyteral Council; College of Consultors Retired.
Desruisseaux, G. Frantz '78 (BGP) Norwalk, CT St. Joseph; Episcopal Vicar for Haitians; Promoter of Justice.
Desso, Leo C. '79 (ANC) Retired.
DeStefano, Rev. Msgr. Richard A. '62 (BEA) Diocesan Building Commission; [G] Beaumont, TX The Catholic Foundation of the Diocese of Beaumont, Inc. Retired.
DeStefano, Salvatore '08 (NY) Larchmont, NY SS. John and Paul.
DeStephano, Mark T. *s.j.* '88 (NEW)[B] Jersey City, NJ Jesuit Center; [M] Jersey City, NJ Jesuits of Saint Peter's College, Inc.
Deston, David C. '09 (FR) South Yarmouth, MA St. Pius Tenth.
DeSutter, Mark A. '82 (PEO) Clergymen's Aid, Inc.; Morton, IL Blessed Sacrament.
DeTemple, Michael *o.p.* '81 (WIL) Newark, DE University of Delaware; Catholic Campus Ministry.
DeTemple, Michael *o.p.* '01 (WIL) Newark, DE St. Thomas More Oratory.
Determan, Joseph *o.p.* '51 (SAT) San Antonio, TX Methodist Hospital; [L] San Antonio, TX Dominican Priory of San Juan Macias.
Deters, Frederick J. *s.j.* '67 (IND)[D] Indianapolis, IN Brebeuf Jesuit Preparatory School, Inc.; [G] Beech Grove, IN St. Francis Hospital and Health Centers.
Deters, Gregory J. '87 (DET) St. Clair, MI St. Mary.
Detig, Joseph *s.v.d.* (TR)[N] Bordentown, NJ Society of the Divine Word.
Detisch, John J. '88 (E) Erie, PA Sacred Heart; Deans.
Detisch, Scott P. '87 (E) Fairview, PA Holy Cross; The Bishop's Theological Advisory Committee.
DeTomasi, Gerardo *m.c.c.j.* '63 (CHI) Blue Island, IL St. Donatus.
De Tommaso, Louis D. *o.f.m.* '54 (NY)[EE] New York, NY Padua Friary; [EE] New York Franciscan Province of the Immaculate Conception.
DeTore, Richard *c.m.f.* '64 (LA)[V] San Gabriel, CA Claretian Missionaries – Western Province, Inc.
Detscher, Rev. Msgr. Alan F. '71 (BGP) Riverside, CT St. Catherine of Siena.
Dettenwanger, Dennis '64 (CIN) Retired.
Dettling, William *o.p.* '59 (COL)[A].
Dettmer, Alfred J. '56 (GRY) Retired.
Dettmer, David J. '80 (BRK) Whitestone, NY St. Luke.
Deutsch, Rev. Msgr. Daniel J. '94 (RCK) Batavia, IL Holy Cross; Bishop's Secretary for Retired Priests; Diocesan Consultors; Deans; Clergy Relief Society, Priests' Retirement Committee.
Deutsch, George E. '57 (TR) Retired.
Deutsch, Marvin *m.m.* '57 (SJ)[M] Los Altos, CA Maryknoll.
Deutsch, Paul *s.j.* '90 (NO)[P] New Orleans, LA Jesuit Provincial Office.
Deutsch, Paul (JC)[B] Jefferson City, MO St. Mary Health Center.
Deutsch, Timothy '94 (DUL) Crosby, MN St. Joseph; Crosby, MN St. Joseph; Youth Conservation Camp.
Devadhason, Masilamony '94 (SD) Sharp Grossmont Hospital; Kaiser Permanente Medical Center; Alvarado Hospital; Spring Valley, CA Santa Sophia.
Devamapalle, George (NY) Kingston, NY St. Joseph.
Devane, John F. *s.j.* '52 (BO)[U] Weston, MA Campion Health Center, Inc.
Devaney, Michael J. *o.m.i.* '57 (BO)[X] Tewksbury, MA Immaculate Heart of Mary Residence.
Devany, John *c.p.* '45 (DET)[K] Detroit, MI St. Paul of the Cross Community, Congregation of the Passion.
Devaraj, Chinnappan M. *o.f.m.* '94 (PMB)[F] West Palm Beach, FL Lourdes–Noreen McKeen Residence for Geriatric Care.
Devaraj, Peter *s.a.c.* '81 (RVC) Bridgehampton, NY Queen of the Most Holy Rosary; Senate of Priests (Presbyteral Council/College of Consultors); Sag Harbor, NY St. Andrew's.
Devassy, Joy Mankulam '82 (NY) Pearl River, NY St. Margaret of Antioch.
Deveau, Adhemar *o.m.i.* '52 (BO)[U] Lowell, MA Andre Garin Retirement Residence.
Deveau, Daniel R. '75 (MAN) Groveton, NH St. Marguerite d'Youville Parish.
DeVeer, Richard S. (BO) Weymouth, MA St. Francis Xavier.
DeVelis, Mark *o.c.d.* (MAN) Dover, NH Parish of the Assumption.
Dever, Rev. Msgr. Daniel J. '52 (HON) Retired.
Dever, Dennis A. '60 (BO) Medford, MA St. Clement.
Dever, James T. *o.s.f.s.* '73 (TR) Riverton, NJ Sacred Heart.
Dever, Rev. Msgr. William '65 (MIA) Fort Lauderdale, FL St. Helen.
Devera, Percival P. '91 (ORL) Apopka, FL St. Francis of Assisi.
Devereaux, Martin C. '54 (PMB) Retired.
Devereaux, Thomas W. '68 (SR) Cloverdale, CA St. Peter's; Ecumenical and Interreligious Affairs.
Devereux, James A. *s.j.* '58 (PH)[Y] Loyola Center and Manresa Hall.
Devereux, Peter *l.c.* '99 (ATL)[L] Norcross, GA Home and Family, Inc.; [G] Norcross, GA Legionaries of Christ, Incorporated.
Devereux, Raymond P. '68 (CHI) Schiller Park, IL St. Beatrice Retired.
de Verteuil, Jack '89 (FBK) Healy, AK Holy Mary of Guadalupe Catholic Church Healy; Presbyteral Council; Consultors.
Devery, Thomas P. '77 (NY) Priest Personnel, Office of; Pastoral Life Conference; Priest Personnel Board.
Devett, Aaron *o.s.b.* '75 (RCK)[G] Aurora, IL Marmion Abbey.
DeViese, James R. '09 (WH) Graduate Studies.
DeVille, George T. '57 (PIT) Muse, PA Holy Rosary.
DeVille, William H. '62 (COL) Retired.
Devin, John C. *c.ss.r.* '49 (BO) Boston, MA Our Lady of Perpetual Help.
Devine, Charles F. '65 (SB) Idyllwild, CA Retired.
Devine, Daniel P. '65 (PH) Drexel Hill, PA St. Charles Borromeo.
Devine, Donald G. *s.j.* '65 (NY)[F] Bronx, NY Fordham Preparatory School; [EE] Jesuit Community, Kohlmann Hall.
Devine, James T. '60 (BRK)[T] Douglaston, NY Bishop Mugavero Residence Retired.
Devine, Joseph T. '80 (HRT) Hartford, CT St. Lawrence O'Toole; Hartford Vicariate.
Devine, Kevin A. *c.s.p.* '56 (NY)[EE] New York, NY Paulist Fathers' Motherhouse.
Devine, Rev. Msgr. Michael F. '57 (SP) Clearwater, FL St. Brendan Retired.
Devine, Patrick A. '69 (HBG) Danville, PA State Hospital Retired.
Devine, Paul '63 (OAK) Retired.
Devine, Richard J. *c.m.* '55 (BRK)[T] Queens Village, NY DePaul Residence.
Devine, Stephen M. '64 (FRS) Hanford, CA Immaculate Heart of Mary.
Devine, Terry '85 (OWN) Uniontown, KY St. Agnes.
Devine, Thomas J. *o.a.r.* '68 (NEW) Union City, NJ St. Augustine's.
Devine, William B. '58 (SC) Retired.
Devine, William D. '73 (BO) Military & VA Chaplains.; Navy Chaplains.
Devine, William G. *s.j.* '57 (BO)[U] Weston, MA Campion Health Center, Inc.
Devine, William J. (CHI) Retired.
Devine, William P. '52 (DUB) Retired.
Deviney, Raymond L. '59 (SCR) Nanticoke, PA St. Mary of Czestochowa Retired.
Devino, Terrence P. *s.j.* '87 (BO)[U] Boston The Society of Jesus of New England–Provincial Offices.
Devino, Terrence P. *s.j.* '87 (SCR)[C] Scranton, PA The University of Scranton.
Deviny, Edward *c.p.* '66 (MET)[I] South River Passionist Provincial Office.
Deviny, Edward *c.p.* '66 (SCR)[M] Scranton, PA Saint Ann's Passionist Monastery.
Devis, Sanjai *v.c.* '97 (CAM) Sewell, NJ Church of the Holy Family, Washington Township; International Priests Representatives.
De Vita, James C. '57 (RVC) Retired.
Devito, Darius *o.f.m.cap.* '57 (NY)[EE] Yonkers, NY St. Clare Friary.
DeVito, Michael C. '76 (HRT) Suffield, CT Sacred Heart; Enfield Deanery.
Devlin, Rev. Msgr. Charles V. '55 (PH) Media, PA Nativity of the Blessed Virgin Mary Retired.
Devlin, David J. *o.s.f.s.* '77 (PH) Philadelphia, PA Our Mother of Consolation.
Devlin, Francis X. *o.s.a.* '73 (CAM)[C] Richland, NJ St. Augustine Preparatory School.
Devlin, James E. '72 (BRK) Brooklyn, NY Good Shepherd; Presbyteral Council; Diocesan Consultors.
Devlin, Joseph D. *s.j.* '66 (BO)[U] Weston, MA Campion Health Center, Inc.
Devlin, Joseph P. '91 (PH) Philadelphia, PA St. Bridget.
Devlin, Kevin '54 (OKL) Retired.

Devlin, Mark '79 (TR) Hopewell, NJ St. Alphonsus; Keyport, NJ Holy Family.
Devlin, Philip T. *c.s.c.* '56 (FTW)[H] Instituto de Estudios Aymaras; New Rochelle, NY Eastern Brothers Province.
Devlin, Raymond A. *s.j.* '55 (SJ)[M] Los Gatos, CA Sacred Heart Jesuit Center.
Devlin, Vianney *o.f.m.* '55 (BO)[X] Boston, MA Saint Anthony Residence Retired.
DeVolder, Philip '80 (FTW) Warsaw, IN Our Lady of Guadalupe.
DeVolder, Philip '80 (FTW) Pro–Synodal Judges.
Devorak, James W. '72 (NU) Granite Falls, MN St. Andrew; Montevideo, MN St. Joseph; Priests' Council.
Devore, Daniel B. '79 (BGP) On Duty Outside the Diocese.
Devore, Gerald T. '62 (BGP) Retired.
DeVore, John C. *m.s.f.s.* '86 (ATL)[G] Snellville, GA The Missionaries of St. Francis De Sales.
Devore, John *m.s.f.s.* '86 (TYL)[B] Whitehouse, TX The Missionaries of St. Francis de Sales.
Devot, Paul *s.j.* '72 (LA) Santa Barbara, CA Our Lady of Sorrows.
DeVous, Phillip W. '04 (COV)[B] Newport, KY Newport Central Catholic High School; Bellevue, KY Divine Mercy; Dayton, KY St. Bernard.
DeVries, Thomas D. '89 (MIL) Wauwatosa, WI Christ King.
Devron, Christopher *s.j.* (CHI)[D] Chicago, IL Christ the King Jesuit College Preparatory School.
Dewaele, Joseph *c.i.c.m.* '49 (ARL)[H] Arlington, VA Missionhurst, C.I.C.M.–Central House and Provincialate.
DeWalt, Rev. Msgr. Homer C. '50 (E)[I] Canton, OH House of Loreto Retired.
Dewan, Wilfred *c.s.p.* '53 (NY)[EE] Jamaica Estates Paulist Fathers Generalate.
Dewan, William G. '86 (JOL) Shorewood, IL Holy Family; Vicar for Priests.
Dewane, Daniel '71 (GB) Retired.
DeWane, E. Thomas *o.praem.* '58 (MO) DEPARTMENT OF VETERANS AFFAIRS HOSPITALS AND CHAPLAINS.
Dewane, Rev. Msgr. John B. '62 (GB) Retired.
deWasseige, Eric *o.p.* '65 (CHI)[N] Chicago Dominicans (Provincial Office).
deWater, Joseph M. '67 (NO) On Duty Outside the Archdiocese.
Dewes, John W. '65 (CHI) Retired.
DeWitt, David D. '84 (PIT) Pittsburgh, PA Incarnation of the Lord; Pittsburgh, PA Risen Lord.
Dewitt, Phil (GB)[G] Oshkosh, WI Mercy Medical Center of Oshkosh, Inc.
Deye, Walter C. *s.j.* '75 (FgM) Chicago, IL Society of Jesus.
Deye, Walter C. *s.j.* '75 (DET)[K] Chicago, IL Jesuit Provincial Office–Detroit Province of the Society of Jesus.
DeYoung, Thomas J. '83 (GR) Retired.
Deziel, William *o.s.c.* '97 (STP) Cottage Grove, MN Church of St. Rita.
Deziel, William *o.s.c.* '97 (PHX)[F] Phoenix, AZ Crosier Provincial House Province of St. Odilia.
Dhabliwala, Neil '08 (ATL) Atlanta, GA Cathedral of Christ the King.
Dhairiam, Arul *s.s.s.* '90 (GAL)[S] Houston, TX The Catholic Chaplain Corps.
Dhanwar, Walter *i.m.s.* '91 (AUS) Lott, TX Church of the Visitation.
Dharmaraj, Anthony *m.s.f.s.* '92 (ALX) Cottonport, LA St. Mary Assumption.
Dhein, William A. '02 (LC) Eau Claire, WI Sacred Heart of Jesus–St. Patrick; [C] Eau Claire, WI Regis Middle School; [C] Eau Claire, WI Regis High School; Navy Reserve Chaplains.
Dhondt, Edward F. '69 (LFT) Anderson, IN St. Ambrose; Associate Judges Retired.
Diachak, Rev. Msgr. Robert (PAT) Chester, NJ Retired.
Diaghek, Rev. Msgr. Robert M. '71 (PAT)[Q] Chester, NJ Nazareth Village.
Diala, Innocent Onwukwe '91 (BAK) Chiloquin, OR Our Lady of Mt. Carmel.
Diamond, David E. '83 (PH)[A] Wynnewood, PA Theological Seminary of St. Charles Borromeo, Overbrook.
Diamond, Matthew J. '71 (BRK) Flushing, NY St. Andrew Avellino Retired.
Dianda, Carl F. '59 (WDC) Washington, DC St. Francis de Sales; Ladies of Charity.
Dias, D. Francis '71 (NY) Sloatsburg, NY St. Joan of Arc.
Dias, John F. *c.s.c.* '63 (FR)[G] North Dartmouth, MA St. Joseph's Hall; [G] North Dartmouth, MA Holy Cross Residence Retired.
Dias da Costa, Josias *o.s.b.* '86 (KCK)[I] Atchison, KS St. Benedict's Abbey.
Diaz, Alberto '85 (ARE) Corozal, PR Holy Family.
Diaz, Alberto (SJN) Clergy Social Security (Prevision Social del Clero).
Diaz, Alvaro '73 (CAM) Ocean City, NJ St. Augustine's Catholic Church, Ocean City, N.J.
Diaz, Alvaro '45 (SJN) Retired.
Díaz, Angel R. '85 (ARE) Caonillas–Utuado, PR Nuestra Senora del Monte Carmelo.
Diaz, Cesar Jaime Guzman '96 (AUS) Austin, TX San Francisco; Austin, TX San Juan Diego Mission of Dolores – Stoney Point.
Diaz, Claudio '00 (CHI) Chicago, IL Providence of God; Consejo Pastoral Arquidiocesano Hispano – Americano; Ethnic Offices.
Diaz, Claudio '00 (BWN)[K] Brownsville, TX Asociacion Nacional de Sacerdotes Hispanos.
Diaz, Dairo E. '01 (HRT) Appointed Members; Hartford, CT St. Peter.
Diaz, Dario E. '01 (HRT)[A] Bloomfield, CT St. Thomas Seminary.
Díaz, David '79 (CGS) Cidra, PR Nuestra Senora del Carmen.
Diaz, Edwin '98 (NY) New York, NY St. Thomas More.
Diaz, Erno (NY)[II] New York, NY Chapel San Lorenzo Ruiz (Philippine Pastoral Center).
Diaz, Francisco G. '77 (MIA) Miami, FL Prince of Peace.
Diaz, Francisco '87 (FRS) Delano, CA Kern Valley State Prison.
Diaz, Gilbert M. '94 (KNX) Chattanooga, TN St. Stephen; Presbyteral Council.
Diaz, Gonzalo '63 (MGZ) On Special Assignment.
Diaz, Gonzalo '52 (POD)[G] Guaynabo, PR Opus Dei; Guaynabo.
Diaz, Rev. Msgr. Gonzalo '63 (MGZ) Vicar General; Diocesan Consultors.
Diaz, Rev. Msgr. Gonzalo '63 (PCE) Mayaguez.
Diaz, Rev. Msgr. Heberto M. '89 (BWN) Brownsville, TX St. Luke; Catholic Foundation of the Rio Grande Valley Board; [K] Brownsville, TX Asociacion Nacional de Sacerdotes Hispanos; St. John; Office of the Chancellor; Moderator of the Curia/Brownsville/San Juan; Presbyteral Council; College of Consultors; Campaign for Human Development; [K] Brownsville, TX Catholic Foundation of the Rio Grande Valley; [D] Executive Board:.
Diaz, Hector '82 (MO)[E] San Juan, PR Centro Medico de P.R.; DEPARTMENT OF VETERANS AFFAIRS HOSPITALS AND CHAPLAINS.
Diaz, Hernando '71 (SLC) Tooele, UT St. Marguerite LLC 235; College of Consultors.
Diaz, J. Glenn '87 (SP) Safety Harbor, FL Espiritu Santo.
Diaz, Jaime A. *o.p.* '00 (SAT) In Metropolitan Area; Archdiocesan Presbyteral Council; Priests Personnel Board.
Diaz, Jose Juan Cardona '01 (MGZ) Communications Media; Mayaguez, PR Santa Teresita.
Diaz, Joseph A. '94 (HON) Kapolei, HI St. Jude.
Díaz, José Matías '89 (WDC)[A] Hyattsville, MD Redemptoris Mater Archdiocesan Missionary Seminary.
Diaz, Libardo Ladino (CHI) Chicago, IL St. Turibius.
Diaz, Martin '78 (SLC) Midvale, UT Saint Therese of the Child Jesus LLC 246; Deans; Team.
Diaz, Michael '73 (SD) Oceanside, CA St. Mary, Star of the Sea.
Diaz, Nelson '01 (LUB) Lubbock, TX San Ramon; St. Francis of Assisi Mission.
Diaz, Oscar '94 (SR) Priests' Council; Hispanic Ministry; Parish Priest Consultors; Cotati, CA St. Joseph.
Diaz, Raul '97 (FRS) Dinuba, CA St. Catherine of Siena.
Diaz, Segundo Enrique '91 (AUS) San Marcos, TX St. John the Evangelist.
Diaz, Thomas '81 (SR) Yountville, CA St. Joan of Arc; Vocations.
Diaz, Tony *c.m.f.* '95 (LA) Los Angeles, CA St. Camillus De Lellis; San Gabriel, CA San Gabriel Mission.
Diaz–Munoz, Javier A. '98 (TR) Trenton, NJ St. Joseph; The Hispanic and Portuguese Apostolate.
Diaz–Torre, Emilio *l.c.* '93 (ATL)[G] Norcross, GA Legionaries of Christ, Incorporated.
Diaz De Leon, Juan Ramon '72 (SR) Special Assignment.
Díaz Delgado, Rafael (SJN) Catano, PR Nuestra Senora del Carmen.
Diaz Vilar, J. Juan *s.j.* '69 (NEW)[M] Jersey City, NJ Jesuits of Saint Peter's College, Inc.
DiBacco, John V. '67 (WH) Star City, WV St. Mary's.
DiBardino, Anthony R. '76 (CAM) Mullica Hill, NJ Church of the Holy Name of Jesus, Mullica Hill, N.J.; Continuing Education & Spiritual Formation of Priests (CESF); Woodstown, NJ St. Joseph's Catholic Church, Woodstown, N.J.
Dibble, Michael '60 (NY) Retired.
Dibble, Michael (OAK) Pleasant Hill, CA Christ the King.
Dibeashi, Ignatius '89 (SD) Campo, CA St. Adelaide of Burgundy Parish.
DiBiccaro, Dominic M. '04 (HBG) Columbia, PA St. Peter.
DiBuo, Roger F. '89 (WIL) Bear, DE St. Elizabeth Ann Seton.
DiCicco, Mario *o.f.m.* '59 (OAK)[A] Berkeley, CA Franciscan School of Theology.
DiCicco, Mario *o.f.m.* (CHI)[N] Chicago, IL St. Peter's Friary.
Dick, Firmus '54 (EVN) Retired.
Dick, Gregory M. *o.praem.* '96 (ORG)[A] Silverado, CA St. Michael's Norbertine Postulancy, Novitiate and Juniorate; [I] Silverado, CA Norbertine Fathers of Orange Inc.
Dick, John '96 (DAL) Ennis, TX Epiphany (Quasi Parish); Ennis, TX St. John Nepomucene.
Dickenson, William R. '89 (CLV) Released from Diocesan Assignment.
Dickerson, Anthony E. '06 (KNX) Knoxville, TN All Saints Catholic Church; [A] Knoxville, TN Knoxville Catholic High School.
Dickey, Bryon A. '09 (SEA) Tacoma, WA St. Charles Borromeo.
Dickie, Rev. Msgr. John A. '56 (SD) San Diego, CA St. Mary Magdalene Retired.
Dickinson, Andrew '06 (SFS) Brookings, SD St. Paul; [H] Brookings, SD Pius XII Student Center.
Dickinson, William '89 (PH)[CC] Exton, PA Catholic Leadership Institute; West Chester, PA SS. Simon and Jude.
Dickman, John W. '48 (L) Retired.
Dickman, Richard C. '93 (LC) Kendall, WI St. Patrick; Kendall, WI St. Joseph; Kendall, WI St. John the Baptist.
Dickmann, Louis H. '59 (COV) Retired.
Dickrell, Cyril *s.d.s.* '53 (MIL)[P] New Holstein, WI Retired.
Dicks, Thomas '87 (NY) Goshen, NY St. John the Evangelist.
Dicks, Tom (NY)[R] Bronx, NY District Council of the Bronx.
Dickson, Norman *s.j.* '54 (GAY) Kalkaska, MI St. Aloysius; Kalkaska, MI St. Mary of the Woods.
Dicristina, Frank T. '86 (SB) Phelan, CA Blessed Junipero Serra Church; Phelan, CA Our Lady of the Snows.
Didier, Jacques R. *m.e.p.* '53 (SFR)[N] San Francisco, CA Paris Foreign Mission Society Residence; San Francisco, CA.
Didone, Matthew *c.s.* '67 (BRK)[T] Jamaica, NY Saint Charles House of Studies.
Diebel, Thomas '79 (LUB) Retired.
Dieckhaus, Anthony W. '62 (PH) On Special or Other Archdiocesan Assignment; Philadelphia, PA St. Jerome.
Dieckhaus, Joseph C. '74 (PH) Exton, PA SS. Philip and James; Archdiocesan Judges.
Dieckmann, Rev. Msgr. Michael '74 (STL) Fenton, MO St. Paul; Archdiocesan Consultors.
Diederich, Donald F. '58 (RVC) Priests' Retirement Board Retired.
Diederich, Everett A. *s.j.* '52 (STL)[C] Saint Louis University; [O] St. Louis, MO Jesuit Community Corporation at Saint Louis University – Jesuit Hall.
Diederichs, Carl E. '02 (MIL) Milwaukee, WI All Saints.
Diedrick, Charles T. '78 (CLV) Elyria, OH St. Mary; Associate Judges.
Diegel, Rev. Msgr. Ron L. '75 (TYL) Deans; Presbyteral Council.
Diegel, Rev. Msgr. Ronald L. '75 (TYL) College of Consultors; Priests' Pension Board; Priests' Personnel Board; Holly Lake Rach, TX Holy Spirit Church.
Diegelman, Robert W. '93 (R) Durham, NC St. Matthew.
Diehl, Dennis P. '74 (BAL) Fulton, MD St. Francis of Assisi.
Dieker, James P. '93 (DOD) Liberal, KS St. Anthony of Padua Catholic Church of Liberal, Kansas; Satanta, KS St. Alphonsus Catholic Church of Satanta, Kansas; Deans.
Diekhans, Joseph '65 (GF) Chester, MT St. Mary; Chester, MT Our Lady of Ransom.
Diekhoff, Bernard *c.pp.s.* '47 (CIN)[N] Carthagena, OH St. Charles Retired.
Diem, Joseph '85 (BO) Medford, MA St. Joseph.
Diem, Simon Le Phuc *c.m.c.* '03 (SPC) Springfield, MO Immaculate Conception.
Diemand, James E. '68 (SPR) Retired.
Dien, Tran Gia '08 (LA)[P] Baldwin Park, CA Vietnamese Redemptorist Mission.
Dienert, Robert T. '62 (LR) North Little Rock, AR Immaculate Heart of Mary.
Dieringer, James J. '58 (P) Retired.
Diermeier, Joseph '78 (LC) Marathon City, WI Nativity of the Blessed Virgin Mary.
Diesbourg, Raymond *m.s.c.* '74 (RCK)[G].
Diesbourg, Raymond *m.s.c.* '74 (PH) Ottsville, PA St. John the Baptist.
Diesbourg, Raymond *m.s.c.* '74 (FgM) Aurora, IL; Aurora, IL MISSIONARIES OF THE SACRED HEART.
Diesen, Edwin Bryan '07 (GLP) Milan, NM St. Vivian; Milan, NM San Mateo; Milan, NM San Rafael; Grants, NM St. Teresa of Avila.
Dieter, Thomas M. '83 (JOL) On Duty Outside the Diocese; DEPARTMENT OF VETERANS AFFAIRS

HOSPITALS AND CHAPLAINS.
Dieter, Xavier L. *o.c.s.o.* '58 (DUB)[K] Peosta, IA New Melleray Abbey, Order of Cistercians of the Strict Observance; [L] Dubuque, IA Our Lady of the Mississippi Abbey.
Dietlein, Damian *o.s.b.* '57 (IND)[A] St. Meinrad, IN Saint Meinrad School of Theology.
Dietlein, Damian *o.s.b.* '57 (BIS)[A] Richardton, ND Assumption Abbey.
Dietlein, Raymond *o.s.b.* '54 (BIS)[A] Richardton, ND Assumption Abbey Retired.
Dietrich, Christopher *o.f.m.cap.* '59 (NY) Yonkers, NY Sacred Heart.
Dietrich, Douglas D. '96 (LIN) Lincoln, NE St. Mary; Permanent Deacon Continuing Education Committee.
Dietrich, John J. '93 (BAL)[A] Emmitsburg, MD Mount St. Mary's Seminary; [A] Emmitsburg, MD Mount St. Mary's Seminary.
Dietrich, John J. '93 (HRT) On Duty Outside the Archdiocese.
Dietrich, Severin *o.f.m.conv.* '53 (TR)[M] Yardville, NJ Villa Maria Sanitarium.
Dietsch, William '71 (EVN) Retired.
Dietz, Rev. Msgr. Conrad R. '57 (BRK)[B] Douglaston, NY Cathedral Seminary Residence of the Immaculate Conception; Oceanside, NY St. Anthony; [T] Douglaston, NY Bishop Mugavero Residence Retired.
Dietz, Elias *o.c.s.o.* '03 (L)[L] Trappist, KY Abbey of Our Lady of Gethsemani, of the Order of Cistercians of the Strict Observance; Trappist, KY.
Dietz, Joseph '87 (NY) Sleepy Hollow, NY The Magdalene; Valhalla, NY Westchester Medical Center.
Dietz, Rev. Msgr. Norbert J. '49 (STL) University City, MO Our Lady of Lourdes Retired.
Dietzen, John J. '54 (PEO) Retired.
Dietzenbach, Rev. Msgr. John A. '80 (BAL) Ellicott City, MD Resurrection.
Dietzenbach, John '80 (BAL) Consultors.
Dietzler, William J. '69 (MIL) Racine, WI St. Paul the Apostle.
Diez, Rev. Msgr. Antonio '59 (SP) Riverview, FL Resurrection; Spanish Speaking Spiritual Moderator.
Diez, Jose L. *o.s.a.* '72 (MGZ) Diocesan Consultors.
Diez, Oscar '68 (DAL) Retired.
Di Fede, Thomas V. *o.p.* '59 (L) Louisville, KY St. Louis Bertrand; [L] Louisville, KY St. Louis Bertrand Priory.
Diffley, Patrick J. '63 (BRK) Retired.
DiFilippo, John V. *o.s.f.s.* '45 (PH)[Y] Philadelphia, PA Father Louis Brisson Residence Retired.
DiFiore, John *s.d.b.* '97 (NO)[D] Marrero, LA Archbishop Shaw High School.
DiFolco, Thomas P. '83 (CIN) Cincinnati, OH St. Agnes; Cincinnati, OH St. Martin De Porres; Priestly Formation.
Digal, Danilo C. '78 (NO) Chalmette, LA Our Lady of Prompt Succor; Deans.
DiGeronimo, Michael A. '76 (WOR) Advocates; Sutton, MA St. Mark.
DiGiacomo, James J. *s.j.* '56 (NY)[EE] New York, NY "America;" Residence and publication office of the America Press.
DiGiovanni, Alfonso '96 (NEW) On Duty Outside the Archdiocese.
Di Giovanni, Rev. Msgr. Stephen M. '77 (BGP) Stamford, CT The Basilica of Saint John the Evangelist.
DiGiralamo, Gerald *s.a.* '81 (BO)[N] Brockton, MA Chapel of Our Savior–Catholic Pastoral and Information Center; [U] Brockton, MA Chapel of Our Savior; [Z] Brockton, MA Chapel of Our Saviour.
DiGiralamo, Gerald *s.a.* '81 (NY)[EE] Garrison, NY Franciscan Friars of the Atonement.
DiGirolamo, Dante '48 (NEW) Retired.
DiGirolamo, Rev. Msgr. Paul A. '83 (PH) Philadelphia, PA Old St. Mary's; Assistant Judicial Vicars; Diocesan Priests' Compensation and Benefits Committee.
DiGiulio, Richard S. '69 (BUF) Orchard Park, NY St. Bernadette; Charismatic Renewal Program; Advocates.
Dignan, Eamon '59 (WDC) Hollywood, MD St. John Francis Regis Retired.
Dignan, Thomas L. '57 (BIS) Retired.
DiGregorio, Joseph L. '66 (PH) Philadelphia, PA St. Martin of Tours.
DiGuglielmo, Anthony J. '03 (PH) Graduate Studies; Lafayette Hill, PA St. Philip Neri.
DiIorio, Michael C. '77 (PH) Levittown, PA St. Michael the Archangel.
Dike, Anthony O. (GLP) Holbrook, AZ Our Lady of Guadalupe.
Dikete, Fidele C. '02 (SAT) San Antonio, TX Our Lady of Good Counsel; In Metropolitan Area; Archdiocesan Presbyteral Council; Priests Personnel Board.
Di Lella, Alexander A. *o.f.m.* '55 (WDC)[C] Catholic University of America, The Retired.
DiLella, Rev. Msgr. Christopher C. '79 (PAT) Medical Leave.
DiLella, Rev. Msgr. Christopher C. (PAT) Apostleship of Prayer; Priests Eucharistic League.
Di Lella, Mario *o.f.m.* '53 (SP)[N] St. Petersburg, FL St. Anthony Friary.
DiLeo, Anthony '64 (SB) Retired.
Dileo, Richard *s.c.j.* '81 (GAL) Houston, TX Our Lady of Guadalupe.
Dilg, Donald W. *c.s.c.* '75 (COS) Woodland Park, CO Our Lady of the Woods; [F] Cascade, CO Holy Cross Novitiate.
Dilg, Donald W. *c.s.c.* '75 (FTW)[H] Notre Dame Congregation of Holy Cross, Indiana Province, Provincial House.
Dilgen, William M. *s.m.m.* '47 (RVC)[M] Bay Shore, NY Montfort Missionaries Retired.
Dilger, Basil *o.s.b.* '61 (SFS)[F] Marvin, SD Blue Cloud Abbey; Marvin, SD Blue Cloud Abbey.
Dilger, Donald '59 (EVN) Retired.
Diliberto, Peter J. '43 (LA)[P] Montebello, CA DePaul Evangelization Center; [V] Montebello, CA DePaul Evangelization Center Retired.
Dilion, Joseph A. '46 (HRT) Retired.
Dilipy, Basilio '94 (CI) Chuuk, FM Holy Family Church; [C] Tunnuk, Chuuk, FM Vicariate Residence.
Dill, Edwin *s.t.* '59 (WDC)[N] Riverdale, MD Holy Spirit Missionary Cenacle; [N] Adelphi, MD Father Judge Missionary Cenacle.
Dillabough, Rev. Msgr. Daniel J. '74 (SD)[B] San Diego, CA University of San Diego; Defenders of the Bond; College of Consultors; Presbyteral Council.
Dillane, Maurice '63 (SAT) Retired.
Dillard, Daniel C. '09 (OWN) Paducah, KY St. Thomas More.
Dillard, Steven C. *s.j.* '86 (WDC)[N] Washington, DC Leonard Neale House.
Dillard, William '98 (SD) San Diego, CA St. John the Evangelist; Spiritual Direction for Candidates and Priests; Spiritual Direction for Candidates and Priests; [A] San Diego, CA St. Francis De Sales Center.
Dillenburg, Rev. Msgr. James E. '65 (GB) Green Bay, WI St. Elizabeth Ann Seton; Regional Vicars.
Dillinger, Joseph A. '96 (SC) Arcadia, IA St. John the Baptist; Breda, IA Our Lady of Mt. Carmel; Breda, IA St. Bernard's.
Dillingham, Charles C. '73 (WIL) Hockessin, DE St. Mary of the Assumption.
Dillman, Alan M. '59 (ATL) Retired.
Dillon, Ciarian *o.m.i.* '54 (OAK) Crockett, CA St. Rose of Lima.
Dillon, David *o.carm.* '65 (JOL) Retired.
Dillon, Dennis T. *s.j.* '69 (LAN) Ann Arbor, MI St. Mary Student Parish; [J] Ann Arbor, MI Detroit Province of the Society of Jesus – Jesuit Residence.
Dillon, Rev. Msgr. Desmond P. '41 (YAK) Kennewick, WA St. Joseph's Retired.
Dillon, Rev. Msgr. Edward J. '67 (ATL) Atlanta, GA Holy Spirit; Advisory Board on Sexual Abuse of Minors; Archdiocesan Judges; [L] Atlanta, GA The Solidarity Association.
Dillon, Edward J. *o.f.m.* '55 (SP)[N] St. Petersburg St. Anthony Friary Retired.
Dillon, Edward J. (PAT) Retired.
Dillon, Edward J. '60 (ROC) Geneseo, NY St. Luke the Evangelist Roman Catholic Church Society of Livingston County; [M] Geneseo, NY State University College at Geneseo (Geneseo), Newman Catholic Community at the Interfaith Center Retired.
Dillon, Geoffrey R. *s.j.* '83 (SFR)[N] San Francisco, CA Loyola House Jesuit Community.
Dillon, Gerald F. *c.s.b.* '62 (GAL)[O] Houston, TX Dillon House Retired.
Dillon, Jeffry T. '81 (BRK) Springfield Gardens, NY Christ the King; South Ozone Park, NY St. Clement Pope; Springfield Gardens, NY St. Mary Magdalene.
Dillon, Jerome V. '77 (OM) Military Chaplains; Navy Chaplains.
Dillon, John D. '59 (ROC) Retired.
Dillon, John J. '98 (WDC) Hyattsville, MD St. Mark; Priest Council; Archdiocesan College of Consultors.
Dillon, John T. *s.j.* '63 (CHI)[C] Chicago, IL Jesuit Community at Loyola University Chicago; [A] Mundelein, IL University of St. Mary of the Lake/ Mundelein Seminary.
Dillon, Kevin J. '03 (RVC) Williston Park, NY St. Aidan's Church.
Dillon, Kevin M. '00 (HRT) Plantsville, CT St. Aloysius.
Dillon, Richard J. '61 (NY) On Duty Outside the Archdiocese.
Dillon, Robert W. '97 (NY) Staten Island, NY St. John Neumann.
Dillon, Thomas J. '59 (GI) Retired.
DiLorenzo, Thomas A. '79 (BO) Winthrop, MA Holy Rosary.
DiLoreto, Anthony '54 (B) Retired.
DiLuzio, James M. *c.s.p.* '93 (NY)[EE] New York, NY Paulist Fathers' Motherhouse.
Dilworth, Kevin L. *s.j.* '84 (SJ)[D] San Jose, CA Bellarmine College Preparatory; Council of Religious.
Dimaranan, Vitaliano *s.d.b.* (AGN)[B] Hagatna, GU The Father Duenas Memorial School.
DiMarco, Rev. Msgr. Abel A. '56 (PCE)[B] The Pontifical Catholic University of Puerto Rico; Sacred Music Commission.
DiMarco, Anthony J. '06 (NOR) Chaplains; Middlefield, CT St. Colman.
DiMaria, Peter J. '93 (PH) Philadelphia, PA Stella Maris.
DiMaria, Sean E. '05 (BUF) Alfred, NY SS. Brendan and Jude; Almond, NY Blessed Sacrament.
Di Marzio, Vito '75 (LA)[P] Van Nuys, CA Rogationist Fathers.
Di Marzio, Vito *r.c.j.* '75 (LA) Van Nuys, CA St. Elisabeth.
DiMascola, Charles J. '81 (SPR) Turners Falls, MA Our Lady of Czestochowa.
DiMattei, Robert A. '91 (BAL) Curtis Bay, MD St. Athanasius.
DiMauro, John C. *o.f.m.* '56 (BO)[U] Andover St. Francis Friary; [W] Andover, MA Franciscan Center – Retreat House.
Di Mauro, Joseph A. *o.s.f.s.* '73 (WIL)[D] Wilmington, DE Nativity Preparatory School.
DiMauro, Rev. Msgr. Joseph V. '67 (CAM) Woodbury, NJ St. Patrick's Church, Woodbury; Appointed Members; College of Consultors.
Di Mauro, Joseph *s.a.* '78 (NY)[EE] Garrison, NY Franciscan Friars of the Atonement.
Dimengo, Michael '77 (CLV) Absent on Leave.
Dimic, Milan '85 (BGP) Newtown, CT St. Rose of Lima.
Dimler, G. Richard *s.j.* '63 (BAL)[S] Towson Maryland Province of the Society of Jesus.
Dimler, Richard *s.j.* '63 (LA) Venice, CA St. Mark.
Dimock, R. Giles *o.p.* '66 (WDC)[B] Washington, DC Dominican House of Studies.
Dinan, John '58 (WCH) Retired.
DiNardo, Daniel A. '66 (CAM) Bridgeton, NJ The Church of the Immaculate Conception, Bridgeton, N.J.
DiNardo, Lawrence A. '74 (PIT) Pittsburgh, PA Holy Wisdom; Director, Department for Canon and Civil Law Services; Judges; Canon and Civil Law Services, Dept. for; Canonical Services, Office for; Health Care Liaison, Office of the; Diocesan Review Board; Vicar for Canonical Services; Promoter of Justice; Priest Council; Vicar for Canonical Services.
DiNardo, Mark A. '58 (CLV) Cleveland, OH St. Patrick; Presbyteral Conveners; Presbyteral Council.
Dinda, John J. '62 (PH) Retired.
Dindorf, Meinrad *o.s.b.* '58 (SCL)[H] St. Cloud, MN St. Benedict's Senior Community; [I] Collegeville, MN St. John's Abbey, of the Order of St. Benedict; Diocesan Planning Council.
Dineen, Michael P. '49 (MIL) Retired.
Dinelli, William J. '61 (SAC) Retired.
Dinello, John E. '85 (PIT) Pittsburgh, PA Immaculate Conception–St. Joseph; Army Reserve Chaplains.
Dineros, Santiago A. '55 (RVC) Retired.
Dinga, William '75 (RIC) Retired.
Dinges, Anthony '57 (RIC) Retired.
Dinguis, Jorge L (BRK) Flushing, NY St. Michael.
Dinh, Hai D. (DAV) Vicar for Vietnamese.
Dinh, Hai Duc '08 (DAV) Davenport, IA St. Paul the Apostle; [M] Davenport, IA Vietnamese Catholic Community of the Quad Cities; Davenport, IA Sacred Heart Cathedral.
Dinh, Hao '93 (SJ) San Jose, CA St. Thomas of Canterbury; Deans.
Dinh, Hoan '07 (ROC) Webster, NY St. Rita.
Dinh, Hoan *o.f.m.* '06 (WDC)[B] Silver Spring, MD Holy Name College.
Dinh, J.M. Huy Quang *c.s.sp.* '00 (GAL)[B] Houston, TX Holy Ghost Fathers and Brothers.
Dinh, Joseph Long '00 (CHL) Jefferson, NC St. Francis of Assisi.
Dinh, Ky Ngoc *s.v.d.* '08 (SB) Corona, CA St. Matthew.
Dinh, Peter '00 (DEN) Denver, CO Assumption of the Blessed Virgin Mary.
Dinh, Quang Duc *s.v.d.* '92 (CHI)[N] Chicago, IL Divine Word Theologate.
Dinh, Thomas Tranh *i.c.m.* '65 (BR)[H] Baton Rouge, LA Incarnatio Consecratio Missio.
Dinh, Tran Thuc '61 (OAK) San Leandro, CA St. Felicitas Retired.
Dinh, Tri M. *s.j.* '00 (OAK)[M] Oakland, CA Jesuit Fathers and Brothers.
Dinh, Trung Hoa *s.j.* '06 (BO)[U] Newton, MA The Jesuit Community at Boston College.
Dinh, Van '02 (OAK) Air Force Reserve Chaplains; Military Chaplains.
Dinh, Victor T. '03 (FRS) Fresno, CA St. Genevieve; Fresno, CA Veterans Administration Medical Center.
Dinh–Van–Thiep, Philip '83 (GB) Stockbridge, WI St. Mary; Sherwood, WI St. John–Sacred Heart; Hilbert, WI St. Mary.
Dinh Hau, Vincent Nguyen '09 (SAC)[I] Walnut Grove, CA Monastery of Chau Son Sacramento.
Dinh Van, Anton Quang '04 (SAT) San Antonio, TX San Francesco di Paola (Italian).
Dinh Viet Luan, Felix M. *c.m.c.* '89 (SPC)[F] Carthage, MO Congregation of the Mother Coredemptrix, United States Assumption Province.
Dinh Vuong Can, Anselm M. *c.m.c.* '77 (SPC)[F]

Carthage, MO Congregation of the Mother Coredemptrix, United States Assumption Province.
Dini, Tekle '73 (SR) Willits, CA St. Anthony of Padua.
Dininni, Nicholas J. '93 (PH) Coatesville, PA St. Cecilia.
Diniz, Rev. Msgr. Pedro D. '71 (BGP) Danbury, CT St. Peter.
Dinkel, Harvey *o.f.m.cap.* '61 (SAL)[C] Hays, KS St. John's Hays; [C] Victoria, KS St. John's Victoria; [D] Victoria, KS St. Fidelis Friary.
Dinkha, Samuel '80 (SPA) Campbell, CA St. Mary Assyrian–Chaldean Parish.
Dinkins, Rev. Msgr. Jack M. '63 (GAL) Katy, TX Epiphany of the Lord.
Dinneen, James J. *s.j.* '60 (NEW)[C] Jersey City, NJ Jesuit Community; [M] Jersey City, NJ Jesuit Community of St. Peter's Prep, Inc.
DiNoia, Joseph Augustine *o.p.* '70 (WDC) On Duty Outside the Archdiocese.
DiNola, Leonard J. '58 (NY) Retired.
Dinovo, Anthony A. '01 (COL) Kenton, OH Immaculate Conception.
Dinsdale, Samuel '03 (SLC) Presbyteral Council; Team; Salt Lake City, UT Saint Patrick LLC 257.
Dio, Jacob *m.s.f.s.* '04 (NSH) Murfreesboro, TN St. Rose of Lima.
Diochi, Michael '80 (KC) Chillicothe, MO St. Columban.
Diogo, Louis M. '46 (PRO) Retired.
Dioka, Jude T. '80 (LC) Alma Center, WI Immaculate Conception; Fairchild, WI St. John Cantius; Fairchild, WI St. Joseph.
Diokno, Rev. Msgr. Rolando V. '70 (GAL) Houston, TX Notre Dame.
Diomartich, Rev. Msgr. Felix S. '37 (LA) Retired.
Dion, Richard H. '99 (MAN) Manchester, NH St. Anthony of Padua; Nashua Hispanic Parish Ministry.
Dionisio, Romeo '84 (PHX) Tempe, AZ Church of the Resurrection Roman Catholic Parish; Mesa, AZ Banner Desert Medical Center.
Dionne, Adrian L. *o.p.* '49 (WDC) Washington, DC St. Dominic Church & Priory.
Dionne, Francis '81 (SP) Retired.
Dionne, J. Joseph *c.ss.r.* (CHL) Concord, NC St. James.
Dionne, Rene *m.afr.* '61 (FgM) Washington, DC MISSIONARIES OF AFRICA.
DiOrio, John R. '99 (PH) Secane, PA Our Lady of Fatima; Council of Priests.
Diorio, Ralph A. '57 (WOR) On Special or Other Diocesan Assignment; Apostolate of Divine Mercy.
DiPasquale, Donald '62 (NEW) Cliffside Park, NJ Epiphany.
DiPerri, James M. '88 (BO) Waltham, MA Our Lady, Comforter of the Afflicted; [A] Weston, MA Blessed John XXIII National Seminary.
Diphe, Juan M. '76 (HEL) Military Chaplains.
DiPietro, Leroy A. '70 (PIT) Retired Priests, Office for; Pittsburgh, PA St. Athanasius.
DiPietro, Rodric J. '76 (COL) Hilliard, OH St. Brendan.
Dipre, Gilio L. '55 (E)[B] Erie, PA Gannon University Retired.
Direen, John '01 (OAK) Berkeley, CA St. Joseph The Worker; Chaplains.
DiRenzo, Michael J. '70 (STU) Fort MacArthur Annex; On Duty Outside the Diocese.
Di Renzo, Michael '70 (ORL)[A] Melbourne, FL Central Catholic High School, Inc.
Dirkx, Dennis A. '72 (MIL) Whitefish Bay, WI Holy Family; Shorewood, WI St. Robert.
Dirscherl, Denis A. *s.j.* '67 (CHI)[N] Chicago Chicago Province of the Society of Jesus–Provincial Office.
Di Russo, Anthony '63 (MAN) Lunenburg, MA Retired.
DiSalvatore, Remo *o.f.m.cap.* '97 (CHL) Charlotte, NC St. Thomas Aquinas.
Dischler, Raymond J. '73 (MAD) Poynette, WI St. Thomas; Poynette, WI St. Joseph; Deaneries.
DiSciacca, Joseph V. '73 (HRT) Bristol, CT St. Joseph; Special and other Archdiocesan Assignment; Office of Ministry for Priests; Ex Officio.
Disco, Bernard *o.s.b.* '06 (MAN)[K] Manchester, NH St. Anselm Abbey.
DiSenso, Gerard '53 (NY)[EE] Bronx, NY John Cardinal O'Connor Residence Retired.
Diskin, Francis X. *c.s.p.* '46 (NY)[EE] Jamaica Estates Paulist Fathers Generalate; [EE] New York, NY Paulist Fathers' Motherhouse Retired.
Diskin, Michael L. '77 (PHX) Glendale, AZ St. Louis The King Roman Catholic Parish; Assistant Chancellor; College of Consultors; Catholic Cemeteries; Ecumenical and Interreligious Affairs; Presbyteral Council.
Di Spigno, Francis J. *o.f.m.* '96 (WDC)[B] Silver Spring, MD Holy Name College.
DiSpigno, Gennaro J. '81 (RVC) Bellport, NY Mary Immaculate.
Dissanayake, Texie '87 (NOR) New London, CT St. Joseph.
Dissek, Jerome M. '69 (BUF) Cuba, NY Our Lady of the Angels; Belmont, NY Holy Family of Jesus, Mary & Joseph.
Dissi, Elias M. *a.j.* '91 (BAK) Hermiston, OR Our Lady of Angels.
DiStefano, Rev. Msgr. John '52 (BEA) Retired.
DiStefano, Joseph '84 (ORG) Absent on Sick Leave.
DiStefano, Salvatore '03 (NEW) West Orange, NJ St. Joseph's; Kearny, NJ Our Lady of Sorrows.
Distefano, Simeon C. *o.f.m.* '63 (NY)[EE] New York Franciscan Province of the Immaculate Conception.
Dister, John E. *s.j.* '62 (CLV)[B] University Heights, OH John Carroll Jesuit Community.
Distor, Leo *s.s.c.* '96 (OM)[K] St. Columbans Missionary Society of St. Columban.
Distor, Leo *s.s.c.* '96 (CHI)[N] Chicago, IL Columban Fathers Theologate.
Ditenhafer, John A. '61 (STL) Ladue, MO Church of the Annunziata Retired.
Ditillo, James J. *s.j.* '74 (ALN)[A] Wernersville, PA Jesuit Center–Jesuit Community.
DiTomasso, Peter *m.ss.cc.* '06 (CAM)[M] Linwood, NJ Villa Pieta. Missionaries of the Sacred Hearts of Jesus & Mary; Linwood, NJ.
Ditta, Angelo J. '86 (RVC)[M] Amityville, NY St. Pius X Residence; Unassigned.
Dittberner, Jerome M. *s.t.d.* '64 (STP)[A] Saint Paul, MN The Saint Paul Seminary; [C] St. Paul, MN University of St. Thomas.
Dittmeier, Charles R. '70 (FgM) On Duty Outside the Archdiocese; Maryknoll, NY MARYKNOLL.
Dittmer, Antonio (WIN)[A] Winona, MN Immaculate Heart of Mary Seminary; Additional Diocesan Assignments.
Ditto, Anthony W. '90 (GBG) Donegal, PA St. Raymond of the Mountains; Donegal, PA St. Boniface.
Ditullio, Brian '06 (PAT) Morristown, NJ St. Margaret of Scotland.
DiTullio, Peter S. *s.c.* '68 (PRO) East Providence, RI Sacred Heart.
Diulio, Albert J. *s.j.* '74 (WDC)[N] Washington, DC Leonard Neale House.
Diurczak, Eugene '68 (NEW) Linden, NJ Holy Family.
Diver, Patrick *s.d.b.* (NEW) Elizabeth, NJ St. Anthony's.
Divine, Finbarr '70 (LA) Whittier, CA St. Gregory the Great.
Divis, Daniel O. '79 (CLV) Lorain, OH Mary Mother of God.
Divis, M. James '76 (LIN)[A] Seward, NE St. Gregory the Great Seminary; Deaneries and Deans; Censores Librorum; Ecumenical Affairs, Commission for; Commission on Alcohol and Drug Abuse.
Dixey, Edward *o.s.a.* '57 (PH)[Y] Villanova, PA St. Augustine Friary.
Dixon, David C. '57 (PIT)[M] Pittsburgh, PA St. John Vianney Manor Retired.
Dixon, Francis F. *o.carm.* '76 (NY) Middletown, NY Our Lady of Mt. Carmel; [HH] New Rochelle, NY Iona College.
Dixon, Isadore (WDC) Hyattsville, MD St. Jerome.
Dixon, J. Isidore '64 (WDC) Retired.
Dixon, James M. *s.j.* '73 (GRY)[H] East Chicago, IN Roque Gonzalez Residence–Jesuit Fathers; [M] Hammond, IN Heartland Center; Catholic Campaign for Human Development; Global Solidarity Partnership Program; Peace and Social Justice, Office of; Rural Life Conference.
Dixon, James R. '70 (NO) Retired.
Dixon, James *s.j.* '73 (GRY) Heartland Center; Indiana Catholic Conference.
Dixon, Jerome A. '57 (PIT) Pittsburgh, PA; Allegheny County, PA Little Sisters of the Poor (James P. Wall Home for the Aged); [J] Pittsburgh, PA Little Sisters of the Poor Home for the Aged Retired.
Diyaolu, Francis (CHI) Chicago, IL St. Helena.
Dlabal, Norbert '72 (SAL) Goodland, KS Our Lady of Perpetual Help Parish; Goodland, KS Holy Ghost Parish; Personnel Board; Board of Trustees; College of Consultors.
Dlabal, Norbert '72 (SAL) Vicariate Representatives; Council of Priests.
Dlugos, Raymond F. *o.s.a.* '83 (BO)[C] Our Mother of Good Counsel Monastery.
Dlugos, Raymond F. *o.s.a.* '83 (PH)[C] Villanova, PA Villanova University.
Dmoch, Paul '76 (NY) Washingtonville, NY St. Mary.
Do, Rev. Msgr. Dominic Dinh '80 (SJ) San Jose, CA St. Maria Goretti.
Do, Joseph Chung Van *o.p.* '95 (GAL) Houston, TX Our Lady of Lavang Church.
Do, Peter Quan '02 (L) Louisville, KY St. Bartholomew; Ex Officio.
Do, Peter *o.p.* '09 (SLC) Salt Lake City, UT Saint Catherine of Siena LLC 218; [H] Salt Lake City, UT University of Utah, Newman Center.
Do, Tuan Anh '00 (CIN) Priests On Personal Leave.
Do, Tung Minh '04 (L) Graduate Studies.
Do, Vien Van '90 (PEO) Wyoming, IL St. John the Baptist; Wyoming, IL St. Patrick; Wyoming, IL St. Dominic's.
Do, Vincentius Toan '07 (BRK)[S] Chinese Apostolate–Brooklyn; Brooklyn, NY St. Rosalia–Regina Pacis.
Doai, Dang Kim '08 (BRK)[T] Jamaica, NY Vincentian Residence.
Doan, John Baptist Minh *o.p.* (GAL) Houston, TX Our Lady of Lavang Church.
Doan, Peter Khoi Anh Hoang *s.d.d.* '09 (P) Portland, OR Our Lady of Lavang.
Doan Nguyen, Joseph Tan *o.f.m.* '86 (STL)[O] St. Louis Franciscan Friary of St. Anthony of Padua.
Doan Quang Bau, Mark M. *c.m.c.* '77 (SPC)[F] Carthage, MO Congregation of the Mother Coredemptrix, United States Assumption Province.
Doan Toan, Basil M. *c.m.c.* '99 (SPC) El Dorado Springs, MO St. Elizabeth of Hungary.
Do Ba Ai, Joseph '51 (SPC)[F] Carthage, MO Congregation of the Mother Coredemptrix, United States Assumption Province.
Do Ba Cong, James '61 (SPC)[F] Carthage, MO Congregation of the Mother Coredemptrix, United States Assumption Province.
Dobbin, Edmund J. *o.s.a.* '62 (PH)[C] Villanova University; [Y] Villanova, PA St. Thomas Monastery.
Dobbin, J. D. '64 (GF) Fort Shaw, MT St. Ann Retired.
Dobbins, Michael J. '99 (ARL) Winchester, VA Sacred Heart of Jesus.
Dobbins, Robert R. *s.j.* '67 (NY)[EE] Loyola Hall, Jesuit Community.
Dobbs, Jeffrey L. '08 (WIN) Fulda, MN St. Gabriel's; Fulda, MN Immaculate Heart of Mary; Fulda, MN St. Anthony's.
Dober, Edward J. '76 (LA) Norwalk, CA St. John of God.
Dobes, Rev. Msgr. George E. '68 (CHI) Judges; On Duty Outside the Archdiocese.
Dobihal, Robert F. '50 (STP) Retired.
Dobkowski, Rev. Msgr. Paulin J. '54 (BEL) Retired.
Dobosiewcz, Leon W. '46 (Y) Retired.
Dobosiewicz, Rev. Msgr. Leo '46 (ORL) Lake Wales, FL Holy Spirit Retired.
Dobosz, Jerzy George '95 (TYL) On Duty Outside the Diocese.
Dobosz, Jerzy '95 (SAG) Linwood, MI St. Anne; Kawkawlin, MI St. Valentine; Kawkawlin, MI Sacred Heart.
Dobrosky, John M. '83 (TR) Leave of Absence.
Dobrowolski, Thomas R. '68 (FTW) Mishawaka, IN St. Michael Ukrainian Catholic Church.
Dobrowolski, Rev. Archpriest Thomas '88 (STN) Retired.
Dobrowski, Peter P. '71 (PHX) Bullhead City, AZ St. Margaret Mary Roman Catholic Parish; Defenders of the Bond.
Dobrzenski, Francis G. '77 (MAR) Lake Linden, MI St. Joseph; Consultors.
Dobrzynski, Martin J. '84 (GRY) Schererville, IN St. Michael; Worship and Spirituality, Office of.
Dobson, Christopher *t.o.r.* '78 (ALT)[A] Loretto, PA St. Francis University; [I] Loretto, PA St. Francis University (Loretto).
Dobson, Gregory J. '83 (BUF)[G] Olean, NY Southern Tier Catholic School; Vicars; Olean, NY St. Mary of the Angels.
Do Carmo Araujo, Rosenilton '02 (ATL) Atlanta, GA St. Jude.
Dockendorf, Ronald '82 (SCL) Grey Eagle, MN St. Joseph's; Grey Eagle, MN St. John the Baptist.
Dockerill, Walter '60 (PMB) Retired.
Doctor, Daniel E. '06 (KAL) Coldwater, MI St. Charles Borromeo.
Doctor, John *o.f.m.* '76 (SFD)[B] Quincy, IL Quincy University; [L] Quincy, IL Holy Cross Friary.
Doda, Eugene J. '77 (MIL) Waterford, WI St. Thomas Aquinas.
Dodd, Michael A. '00 (TLS) Broken Arrow, OK St. Anne.
Dodd, Michael *s.s.c.* '61 (OM)[K] St. Columbans, NE Missionary Society of St. Columban; Religious Orders.
Dodd, Michael *o.c.d.* '79 (MIL)[P] Milwaukee Provincial Offices – Discalced Carmelites.
Dodd, Ronald E. '05 (PEO) Streator, IL St. Stephen's; Streator, IL St. Anthony of Padua; Streator, IL Immaculate Conception.
Dodds, Michael J. *o.p.* '77 (OAK) Berkeley, CA St. Mary Magdalen.
Dodds, Michael *o.p.* '77 (OAK)[A] Berkeley, CA Dominican School of Philosophy and Theology.
Dodge, Erwin J. *o.s.a.* '57 (CHI)[N] Chicago, IL St. Monica Monastery.
Dodge, Terry '05 (FAR) Wahpeton, ND St. John's Church of Wahpeton.
Dodo, Wilfred Y. (NY) Staten Island, NY Holy Child.
Dodrai, Alexius '97 (FTW) Fort Wayne, IN St. Patrick.
Doefler, John F. (GB)[O] Green Bay, WI Sacred Heart Seminary Corporation.
Doerfler, John F. '91 (GB) Chancellor; Conciliation and Arbitration Board; Priests' Personnel Board; Cecil, WI St. Martin; Special Assignment; College of Consultors; Vicars General; Ex Officio; The Shrine of Our Lady of Good Help, Inc.
Doerfler, John F. '91 (GB)[O] New Franken, WI The Chapel of Our Lady of Good Help, Inc.; [L] New Franken, WI The Chapel of Our Lady of Good Help (Diocesan Shrine)–Robinsonville.
Doerfler, Rev. Msgr. Marvin G. '59 (SAT) Canyon Lake, TX St. Thomas the Apostle.
Doerhoff, Rev. Msgr. Dennis E. '76 (STL) Creve Coeur,

MO St. Monica.
Doering, Christopher E. '98 (CHI) Chicago, IL Our Lady of Victory.
Doerner, David L. *s.a.* '60 (NY)[EE] Garrison, NY Franciscan Friars of the Atonement Retired.
Doerr, Brian M. '98 (LFT) Special Assignment; Vocation Director; Carmel, IN St. Elizabeth Ann Seton.
Doerr, Richard J. '93 (LFT) Carmel, IN Our Lady of Mount Carmel; [I] Carmel, IN Our Lady of Mount Carmel Parochial School.
Doerre, Edmund J. '63 (LC) Trempealeau, WI St. Mary; Trempealeau, WI St. Bartholomew.
Doersching, Lawrence *s.m.* '73 (MIA)[D] Hollywood, FL Chaminade–Madonna College Preparatory.
Doffing, Gordon M. '60 (STP) Retired.
Dogali, Michael F. '92 (BGP) Danbury, CT St. Joseph.
Dogaru, Alin Nadir '00 (ROM) East Chicago, IN St. Nicholas; Communications Director.
Doheny, Thomas R. '58 (MAD) Retired.
Doherty, Charles '58 (CC) Retired.
Doherty, D. G. *o.p.* '57 (FgM) New York, NY Province of St. Joseph (Eastern).
Doherty, Daniel J. *s.s.* '94 (SCR) On Duty Outside the Diocese.
Doherty, Daniel J. *s.s.* '94 (BAL)[A] Baltimore, MD St. Mary's Seminary and University; [S] Baltimore Society of St. Sulpice, Province of the United States.
Doherty, Declan M. *o.s.m.* '60 (CHI)[N] Chicago Order of Friar Servants of Mary (Servites) United States of America Province, Inc.
Doherty, Donald J. *m.m.* '62 (NY)[EE] Retired.
Doherty, Edward C. *m.s.a.* '69 (NOR)[G] Cromwell, CT Society of the Missionaries of the Holy Apostles.
Doherty, Edward C. *o.s.a.* '57 (PH)[Y] Villanova, PA St. Thomas Monastery.
Doherty, Glennon C. '78 (STL) On Leave of Absence.
Doherty, Henry F. '56 (BO) Senior Priests. Retired.
Doherty, James '72 (GAY) Suttons Bay, MI St. Gertrude; Suttons Bay, MI St. Michael the Archangel.
Doherty, James *c.s.c* '78 (FR) Falmouth, MA St. Patrick's.
Doherty, John R. '64 (NEW) Bayonne, NJ St. Andrew's Retired.
Doherty, Rev. Msgr. John T. '45 (NY)[EE] Bronx, NY John Cardinal O'Connor Residence Retired.
Doherty, Louis *c.p.* '57 (CHI)[N] Chicago Passionist Provincial Office; [N] Chicago, IL Passionist Community–Immaculate Conception Monastery.
Doherty, Michael *o.f.m.* '76 (LA)[V] Malibu, CA Serra Retreat; Definitors:.
Doherty, Neil '69 (MIA) Retired.
Doherty, Rev. Msgr. Patrick J. '55 (BWN) Retired.
Doherty, Patrick J. '59 (MAD) Retired.
Doherty, Paul J. '95 (WOR) On Administrative Leave of Absence.
Doherty, Raymond J. *s.s.e.* '58 (BUR)[E] Colchester, VT Society of St. Edmund; [A] Colchester, VT St. Michael's College.
Doherty, Robert G. *s.j.* '60 (BO)[U] Weston, MA Campion Jesuit Community.
Doherty, Robert J. '70 (BO) Senior Priests. Retired.
Doherty, Terrance *s.m.a.* '70 (NEW)[M] Tenafly, NJ Society of African Missions, Provincialate, S.M.A. Fathers Retired.
Doherty, Rev. Msgr. Timothy L. '76 (RCK) Special Assignment; Dundee, IL St. Catherine of Siena; Ethicist for Health Care Issues, Diocesan; Dundee, IL St. Mary's Mission of Gilberts.
Dohman, William '73 (B) Retired.
Dohner, Stephen J. '76 (CLV) Medina, OH Holy Martyrs.
Dohogne, David J. '92 (SPC) Dexter, MO Sacred Heart; Campbell, MO St. Teresa; Campbell, MO St. Ann; Region IX; Diocesan Pastoral Council.
Doiron, David E. '69 (WOR) Paxton, MA St. Columba.
Doktoczyk, Stephen '05 (ORG) Staff.
Doktorczyk, Stephen '05 (ORG) Promoter of Justice; Costa Mesa, CA St. Joachim; Adjutant Judicial Vicars.
Doktorczyk, Steve '05 (ORG) Judges; Special Assignment.
Dolan, Bernard M. '66 (BGP) Trumbull, CT Christ the King.
Dolan, Charles *c.s.s.* '58 (BO)[U] Waltham, MA Stigmatine Fathers & Brothers Provincial House.
Dolan, Daniel D. *m.m.* '54 (NY)[EE] Retired.
Dolan, Edward *s.s.c.* '58 (OM)[K] St. Columbans, NE Missionary Society of St. Columban.
Dolan, Gerald M. *o.f.m.* '56 (SP)[N] St. Petersburg, FL St. Anthony Friary.
Dolan, Hugh '57 (PT) Retired.
Dolan, James L. *o.p.* '60 (FgM) Metairie, LA St. Martin de Porres Province (Southern Dominican Province).
Dolan, James Linus *o.p.* '60 (NO)[P] New Orleans Dominican Friars, Southern Dominican Province of St. Martin de Porres.
Dolan, James W. '75 (PIT) Butler, PA St. Michael the Archangel; Butler, PA St. Peter.
Dolan, Jarlath '74 (LA) Camarillo, CA Blessed Junipero Serra.
Dolan, John P. '89 (SD) Chula Vista, CA St. Rose of Lima; Vicars Forane.
Dolan, John R. *m.s.* '79 (FR) Brewster, MA Our Lady of the Cape.
Dolan, Joseph M. '92 (WOR) Fitchburg, MA St. Camillus de Lellis; [R] Fitchburg, MA Fitchburg State College (Fitchburg).
Dolan, Joseph V. *s.j.* '52 (NY)[EE] Loyola Hall, Jesuit Community.
Dolan, Joseph '60 (BRK) Retired.
Dolan, Laurence *o.f.m.* '65 (SD)[J] Oceanside, CA Mission San Luis Rey.
Dolan, Leo A. '52 (STP) Retired.
Dolan, Rev. Msgr. Leo M. '60 (SAT) San Antonio, TX St. Helena.
Dolan, Mark A. '76 (STL) Webster Groves, MO Annunciation.
Dolan, Michael F. '97 (WDC) Retired.
Dolan, Michael J. '96 (HRT)[Q] Hartford, CT University of Hartford Newman Center; Special and other Archdiocesan Assignment; [A] Bloomfield, CT St. Thomas Seminary; Vocations.
Dolan, Rev. Msgr. Neal T. '64 (SD) Poway, CA St. Michael.
Dolan, Patrick G. '71 (JC) Ministry to Priests; Jefferson City, MO Immaculate Conception.
Dolan, Patrick J. '78 (L) Liberty, KY St. Bernard; Army National Guard Chaplains; Defenders of the Bond.
Dolan, Patrick '95 (DEN) Denver, CO Most Precious Blood; [S] Denver, CO Archbishops Guild.
Dolan, Paul '84 (RVC) Port Jefferson, NY Infant Jesus.
Dolan, Peter C. '54 (PMB) Port St. Lucie, FL St. Lucie Retired.
Dolan, Raymond '56 (B) On Duty Outside the Diocese.
Dolan, Robert L. *s.j.* '73 (FgM) Chicago, IL Society of Jesus.
Dolan, Robert *s.j.* '76 (LA) Los Angeles, CA Dolores Mission.
Dolan, Thomas D. '51 (BRK) Ozone Park, NY St. Elizabeth Retired.
Dolan, Timothy E. '83 (STP) Pine Island, MN St. Michael; Zumbrota, MN St. Paul.
Dolan, Walter *o.f.m.* '61 (CLV)[N] Brooklyn, OH St. Anthony of Padua Friary; Cleveland, OH St. Rose of Lima.
Dolan, William S. *s.j.* '82 (SY)[Q] Syracuse, NY Jesuits at LeMoyne, Inc.; [T] Syracuse, NY LeMoyne College Campus Ministry.
Dolbec, Jacques *s.o.l.t.* '95 (CC)[G] Robstown, TX Society of Our Lady of the Most Holy Trinity.
Dolciamore, John V. '52 (CHI)[A] Mundelein, IL University of St. Mary of the Lake/Mundelein Seminary Retired.
Dolciamore, John V. '52 (VEN) Judicial Vicar; Judges.
Dolcic, Maurus *t.o.r.* '99 (WDC)[N] Washington, DC St. Louis Friary.
Dolehide, John R. *o.p.* '47 (CHI)[N] St. Pius V Priory.
Dolejsi, Bryan '05 (SEA) Issaquah, WA St. Joseph.
Dolezal, Richard R. '76 (MIL) Retired.
Dolezal, Thomas '70 (KCK) Lenexa, KS Holy Trinity.
Dolinic, Louis S. '66 (BUF)[G] North Tonawanda, NY North Tonawanda Catholic School; North Tonawanda, NY Our Lady of Czestochowa.
Dolinksi, Pawel *s.d.s.* '97 (MET) Great Meadows, NJ SS. Peter and Paul.
Dolinski, Pawel *s.d.s.* '97 (NEW)[M] Verona, NJ The Salvatorian Fathers.
Doll, Donald A. *s.j.* '68 (OM)[K] Omaha, NE Jesuit Community at Creighton University.
Dollard, Mark E. '91 (MAN) Henniker, NH St. Theresa; Vicars Forane; Hillsborough, NH St. Mary.
Dollen, Bernard '53 (ROC) Retired.
Dollinger, Rev. Msgr. John M. '57 (E) Retired.
Dollins, Randy '07 (DEN) Craig, CO Saint Michael.
Dolski, V. Anthony '59 (GB) Retired.
Dolter, Dennis *s.o.l.t.* '02 (CC)[G] Robstown, TX Society of Our Lady of the Most Holy Trinity.
Domagas, Reynaldo '87 (NY) Manhattan, NY New York Downtown Hospital – New York Infirmary; New York, NY Our Lady of Victory.
Domandich, Anthony '58 (SEA) Retired.
Domas, John R. '50 (SB) Retired.
Domaszewicz, Chester '78 (VEN) LaBelle, FL Our Lady Queen of Heaven.
Dombroski, Dean W. '64 (GB) Luxemburg, WI St. Thomas the Apostle; New Franken, WI St. Kilian; New Franken, WI St. Joseph; Peshtigo, WI St. Mary; Porterfield, WI SS. Joseph & Edward.
Dombrow, Rev. Msgr. William A. '70 (PH)[T] Darby, PA Villa Saint Joseph; [T] Ventnor, PA Villa St. Joseph by the Sea; Department Retired Clergy; On Special or Other Archdiocesan Assignment.
Dombrowski, Francis *o.f.m.cap.* '59 (MIL)[S] South Milwaukee, WI The Dwelling Place.
Dombrowski, John *o.f.m.* '84 (JOL) Joliet, IL St. John the Baptist; [L] Joliet, IL St. John the Baptist Friary; Councilors:.
Dombrowski, Ronald J. '72 (SAG) Saginaw, MI St. John the Baptist; Saginaw, MI St. Josaphat; Saginaw, MI St. Matthew.
Dombrowski, Stanley J. *o.s.f.s.* '83 (VEN) Fort Myers, FL St. Cecilia.
Dombrowski, Steven G. '89 (CHI) Mt. Prospect, IL St. Raymond de Penafort.
Dombrowski, Timothy '73 (LAN)[G] Ann Arbor, MI St. Joseph Mercy Hospital.
Dome, Thomas J. *c.r.i.c.* '98 (LA) Santa Paula, CA St. Sebastian; [B] Santa Paula, CA Dom Grea House (House of Formation) Canons Regular of the Immaculate Conception, (C.R.I.C.); [P] Santa Paula, CA Canons Regular of the Immaculate Conception.
Domec, Rev. Msgr. Charles C. '56 (GAL) The Woodlands, TX Sts. Simon and Jude.
Domek, Kazimierz '73 (SP) Tampa, FL Blessed Sacrament.
Domfang, Martin–Claude *s.j.* '06 (MIL)[P] Milwaukee, WI Jesuit Community at Marquette University.
Domfeh–Boateng, Joseph '95 (NY) Bedford, NY St. Patrick.
Domhoff, Ronald J. '72 (L) Louisville, KY St. Peter the Apostle Parish.
Domin, Rev. Msgr. Edward R. '88 (ALN) Reading, PA St. Catharine of Siena.
Domin, John M. '50 (P)[K] Beaverton, OR Maryville Nursing Home Retired.
Domingo, Alberto *c.m.f.* '79 (LA)[V] Rancho Dominguez, CA Dominguez Seminary Inc. Retired.
Domingo, Santiago '65 (LAR) Laredo, TX Santo Nino.
Domingue, Kenneth J. '91 (LAF) Leonville, LA St. Leo the Great; Leonville, LA St. Catherine.
Dominguez, Jesus '02 (RCK) Sterling, IL St. Mary.
Dominguez, Julio '03 (CHL) Lenoir, NC St. Francis of Assisi.
Dominguez, Ramon '00 (FR) On Duty Outside the Diocese.
Dominguez, Ramon *y.a.* '00 (ARL)[L] McLean, VA Youth Apostles Institute, An Association of Christian Faithful.
Dominguez, Vincent '02 (SFE) Albuquerque, NM Queen of Heaven.
Do Minh Van, Luke M. *c.m.c.* '77 (SPC)[F] Carthage, MO Congregation of the Mother Coredemptrix, United States Assumption Province.
Dominiak, Thomas M. '61 (GAY) Retired.
Dominic, Francis J. '52 (MAD) Retired.
Dominic, Joseph *s.a.c.* '80 (MIL)[P] Milwaukee, WI Pallotti House; Hartford, WI St. Lawrence; Allenton, WI Resurrection.
Dominic, Michael M. '88 (MO) Army Reserve Chaplains.
Dominik, Kevin J. '88 (PIT) Pittsburgh, PA St. Winifred.
Dominik, Stanley J. '58 (GRY) Whiting, IN Immaculate Conception; Whiting, IN St. Adalbert; Whiting, IN St. John the Baptist Retired.
Dominik, Stanley '58 (GRY) Whiting, IN Sacred Heart.
Dominique, Todd M. '94 (TOL) Defiance, OH St. John the Evangelist; [D] Defiance, OH Holy Cross Catholic School of Defiance.
Domme, Edward C. '79 (SFE) Albuquerque, NM Our Lady of the Assumption; Finance Council.
Domme, Edward '79 (SFE) Presbyteral Council of the Archdiocese of Santa Fe; Presbyteral Council of the Archdiocese of Santa Fe.
Dommer, Ian *o.s.b.* '79 (SCL)[I] Collegeville, MN St. John's Abbey, of the Order of St. Benedict.
Domond, Osner *c.m.* (PCE) Ponce, PR San Vicente–Cantera.
Dompke, Ramon *c.ss.r.* '64 (CHI)[N] Glenview, IL The Redemptorists of Glenview, Illinois.
Domurat, Thomas S. '79 (BO) East Boston, MA Most Holy Redeemer.
Don, Sextus '79 (FTW) Wabash, IN St. Bernard.
Donadio, Vincent J. '73 (TR) Leave of Absence.
Donaghey, John *s.v.d.* '54 (CHI)[N] Techny, IL Divine Word Residence.
Donaghey, Patrick H.M. '85 (ATL) Lilburn, GA St. Stephen the Martyr.
Donaghue, Denis *s.j.* '05 (SEA)[L] Seattle, WA Arrupe Jesuit Community at Seattle University.
Donaghy, Thomas J. '79 (BAL) Ellicott City, MD St. Paul Retired.
Donaghy, Thomas J. '79 (PH) Norwood, PA St. Gabriel Retired.
Donahoe, Patrick *t.o.r.* '74 (ARL) Herndon, VA St. Joseph.
Donahoe, Rev. Msgr. Thomas '54 (SC) Presbyteral Council Retired.
Donahue, Aidan N. '86 (HRT) Bloomfield, CT Sacred Heart; Ecumenical Affairs, Commission for; Farmington Valley Deanery; Special and other Archdiocesan Assignment.
Donahue, Rev. Msgr. Brian G. '83 (FAR) Military Chaplains.
Donahue, Brian G. '83 (MO) Army Reserve Chaplains.
Donahue, Cecil J. *o.s.b.* '54 (MAN)[K] Manchester, NH St. Anselm Abbey.
Donahue, Charles *c.s.p.* '05 (KNX) Knoxville, TN John XXIII University Parish/Catholic Center; [H] Knoxville, TN UT–Knoxville, Newman Foundation, Inc.
Donahue, Denis M. '90 (ARL) Alexandria, VA St. Rita.
Donahue, Edward J. '80 (ALN) Unassigned.
Donahue, Eugene *s.j.* '70 (GB)[M] Oshkosh, WI Jesuit

Retreat House.
Donahue, John A. *s.j.* '79 (FgM) Los Gatos, CA Society of Jesus.
Donahue, John G. '60 (STP) Stillwater, MN St. Michael Retired.
Donahue, John J. *s.j.* '64 (BAL)[A] Baltimore, MD St. Mary's Seminary and University.
Donahue, John R. *s.j.* '64 (BAL)[S] Baltimore, MD Jesuit Community of Loyola University, Inc.
Donahue, L. Scott '82 (CHI) Chicago, IL St. Robert Bellarmine; [H] Chicago, IL Mission of Our Lady of Mercy–Mercy Home for Boys and Girls.
Donahue, Martin P. '61 (WOR) Deans; Presbyteral Council Retired.
Donahue, Richard T. '68 (BO) On Duty Outside the Archdiocese.
Donahue, Scott (CHI) Mercy Home for Boys and Girls; [G] Chicago, IL Mercy Home for Boys & Girls.
Donahue, Stephen D. '86 (IND) Aurora, IN St. Mary of the Immaculate Conception.
Donahue, William H. *c.s.c.* '49 (FTW) South Bend, IN Faith & Hope & Charity Chapel Retired.
Donahue, William P. '70 (GBG) Latrobe, PA St. Rose.
Donahue, William P. '86 (SR) Sonoma, CA St. Leo; Advocates; Priests' Council.
Donahue, William P. '86 (SR) Clergy Personnel Committee.
Donahugh, Donald E. '62 (RCK) Active Outside the Diocese; [B] Port Arthur, TX CHRISTUS Health Southeast Texas – CHRISTUS Hospital – St. Mary.
Donajkowski, Charles G. '91 (GAY) East Tawas, MI Holy Family; Oscoda, MI Sacred Heart; Elected Members; Members of the College of Consultors.
Donald, John R. *s.j.* '72 (FgM) Los Gatos, CA Society of Jesus.
Donald, Michael L. '72 (STL) Creve Coeur, MO St. Monica.
Donaldson, Raymond J. *s.j.* '05 (R) Durham, NC Holy Cross; [F] Raleigh Jesuit Community.
Donaldson, Thomas J. '68 (LC) Personnel Council Retired.
Donaldson, Thomas *c.ss.r.* '77 (CHI)[N] Chicago, IL The Redemptorist Fathers of Chicago; Chicago, IL St. Michael in Old Town.
Donarski, Richard *o.c.s.o.* '86 (ATL)[G] Conyers, GA The Monastery of the Holy Spirit.
Donat, Robert J. '66 (SB) Retired.
Donatelli, Gino *s.j.* '81 (LEX) Lexington, KY Cathedral of Christ the King.
Donato, John P. *c.s.c.* '91 (FTW)[H] Notre Dame Congregation of Holy Cross, Indiana Province, Provincial House.
Donato, John *c.s.c.* '91 (P)[L] Portland, OR Holy Cross Fathers & Brothers, C.S.C. – University of Portland[B].
Dondanville, Joseph '95 (PEO) Kickapoo (Edwards), IL St. Mary of Kickapoo; [B] Champaign, IL High School of St. Thomas More.
Donders, Sjef *m.afr.* '57 (WDC)[N] Washington, DC Missionaries of Africa; Washington, DC MISSIONARIES OF AFRICA; Washington, DC.
Donehue, Ambrose *o.f.m.* '51 (ALB)[B] Siena College; [R] Albany, NY St. Francis Chapel.
Donellen, Rev. Msgr. Thomas J. '56 (BAL) Retired.
Doner, Roy '81 (SAC) Colusa, CA Our Lady of Lourdes; College of Consultors.
Dong, Quang Minh '91 (OAK) Deanery #13.
Dong, Quang Minh '91 (OAK) Oakland, CA Cathedral Parish of Christ the Light.
Dongkore, Greg '86 (LA) La Canada Flintridge, CA St. Bede the Venerable.
Dongmo, Saturnin Tsayem *s.j.* '07 (OAK)[M] Berkeley, CA Jesuit Fathers and Brothers.
Dongo, Bruno *a.j.* '01 (CAM) Westmont, NJ The Church of the Holy Saviour, Westmont, N.J.
Donia, John E. '07 (PH) Philadelphia, PA St. Timothy.
Donini, Leone '95 (NEW) On Duty Outside the Archdiocese.
Donio, Frank S. *s.a.c.* '94 (BAL) South Orange, NJ; [W] Baltimore, MD Union of Catholic Apostolate USA, Inc.
Donio, Frank S. *s.a.c.* '94 (WDC)[B] West Hyattsville, MD Pallottine Seminary at Green Hill.
Donio, Thomas S. '95 (CAM) Hammonton, NJ St. Martin de Porres Roman Catholic Church, Hammonton, N.J.; Continuing Education & Spiritual Formation of Priests (CESF); Central Deanery.
Donish, Peter M. '70 (PSC) Retirement Plan Board; Hazleton, PA St. Mary's; Presbyteral Council.
Donlan, Paul A. '62 (POD) Los Angeles.
Donlan, Paul A. '62 (LA)[W] Los Angeles, CA Prelature of the Holy Cross and Opus Dei.
Donlan, Robert '67 (SP) Retired.
Donlon, James I. '75 (ALB) Special Assignment; Vicar Judicial; Judges; Bishop's Delegate for Marriage Dispensations; Presbyteral Council; Diocesan Board of Consultors.
Donlon, James W. '65 (PH) Conshohocken, PA St. Matthew.
Donnarumma, Francesco '05 (PCE) Penuelas, PR St. Joseph.
Donnay, Raymond '50 (SCL) Retired.
Donnelly, Eamonn *s.v.d.* '70 (LA) Los Angeles, CA Our Lady of Lourdes.
Donnelly, Rev. Msgr. Edward J. '54 (RVC) Valley Stream, NY Holy Name of Mary Retired.
Donnelly, Eugene F. '48 (BRK) Jackson Heights, NY Our Lady of Fatima Retired.
Donnelly, Francis '79 (GAL)[O] Houston, TX Companions of the Cross (Texas).
Donnelly, J. Patrick *s.j.* '65 (MIL)[P] Milwaukee, WI Jesuit Community at Marquette University.
Donnelly, Joseph T. '71 (HRT) Southbury, CT Sacred Heart; Suburban Waterbury Deanery.
Donnelly, Joseph–Benedict *o.c.s.o.* '43 (P)[L] Lafayette, OR The Cistercian (Trappist) Abbey of Our Lady of Guadalupe.
Donnelly, Rev. Msgr. Lawrence Edward '49 (LA) Retired.
Donnelly, Michael *s.s.c.* '63 (OM)[K] St. Columbans Missionary Society of St. Columban.
Donnelly, P. Martin '64 (TOL) Toledo, OH Blessed Sacrament.
Donnelly, Robert W. *m.m.* '59 (NY)[EE] Maryknoll Maryknoll Fathers and Brothers Retired.
Donnelly, Robert '91 (ALB) Retired.
Donnelly, Sean J. '82 (CLV) Madison, OH Immaculate Conception.
Donnelly, Stephen H. '97 (RVC) Leave of Absence.
Donnelly, Thomas F. *m.m.* '57 (SJ)[M] Los Altos, CA Maryknoll.
Donnelly, Thomas '61 (RNO) Zephyr Cove, NV Our Lady of Tahoe Retired.
Donnelly, Timothy *o.s.b.* '65 (LR) Winslow, AR Our Lady of the Ozarks Shrine; Van Buren, AR St. Michael.
Donnelly, William F. *s.j.* '63 (SJ)[B] Santa Clara, CA Jesuit Community.
Donnelly, William J. *o.s.a.* '67 (PH) Counselors:; Rosemont, PA St. Thomas of Villanova Parish.
Donnelly, William J. *m.m.* '65 (CHI)[N] Chicago, IL Maryknoll Fathers & Brothers.
Donnelly, William P. '64 (PH) Retired.
Donnelly, William '71 (JOL) Hinsdale, IL St. Isaac Jogues.
Donnelly, William '64 (ROC) Rochester, NY St. Mary.
Donney, David N *o.s.c.* '01 (PHX)[F] Phoenix, AZ Crosier Community of Phoenix (Canons Regular of the Order of the Holy Cross).
Dono, Abram E. *s.t.* '64 (TUC) Tucson, AZ Blessed Kateri Tekakwitha Roman Catholic Missions Parish – Tucson; [H] South Tucson, AZ Blessed Kateri Tekakwitha Parish Center.
Donoghue, Henry A. '64 (WOR) Worcester, MA Blessed Sacrament.
Donoghue, Henry Thomas *o.p.* '57 (WDC)[B] Washington, DC Dominican House of Studies.
Donoghue, Patrick '82 (P) Portland, OR St. Anthony.
Donoghue, Paul *s.m.* '68 (STL)[O] St. Louis Marianists, Province of the United States (Society of Mary).
Donoher, Edward (TOL)[H] Oregon, OH Sacred Heart Home.
Donohoe, Rev. Msgr. Edward '50 (STO) Diamond Springs, CA Retired.
Donohoe, Patrick K. '82 (CC) Beeville, TX St. Joseph.
Donohoe, Peter '50 (SFD) Retired.
Donohoe, Philip M. '53 (OKL) Retired.
Donohoe, Richard E. '84 (BIR) Diocesan Finance Council; Annual Catholic Charities Appeal; Diocesan College of Vicars.
Donohoe, Stephen S. '92 (MO) Chelmsford, MA St. Mary; Navy Reserve Chaplains; Presbyteral Council.
Donohoe, Thomas E. '61 (RVC) Long Beach, NY St. Mary of the Isle; Point Lookout, NY Our Lady of the Miraculous Medal Retired.
Donohoe, Thomas P. '52 (BO) Carlisle, MA St. Irene.
Donohoo, Daniel B. '86 (IND) Indianapolis, IN SS. Peter and Paul Cathedral; Archdiocesan Cathedral.
Donohoo, Lawrence J. *o.p.* '85 (BAL)[A] Emmitsburg, MD Mount St. Mary's Seminary.
Donohue, Charles *c.s.p.* '05 (KNX) University of Tennessee–Knoxville.
Donohue, Edward *o.f.m.* '56 (PAT)[N] Butler, NJ St. Anthony Friary.
Donohue, James *c.r.* '83 (BAL)[B] Emmitsburg, MD Mount Saint Mary's University.
Donohue, John J. '48 (CHI) Retired.
Donohue, John J. '73 (NEW) Bloomfield, NJ St. Valentine.
Donohue, John J. *s.j.* '59 (FgM) Watertown, MA Society of Jesus.
Donohue, John W. *s.j.* '50 (NY)[EE] Loyola Hall, Jesuit Community.
Donohue, John '73 (NEW) Belleville, NJ Clara Maass Medical Center.
Donohue, Michael F. '75 (NOR) Building Commission.
Donohue, Michael T. '75 (NOR) East Lyme, CT St. Matthias; Deans; Campaign for Human Development; Navy Reserve Chaplains; Members; College of Consultors.
Donohue, Patrick W. '75 (NEW) Hackensack, NJ Holy Trinity.
Donohue, Paul *m.c.c.j.* '75 (CIN)[N] Cincinnati, OH Comboni Missionaries (Verona Fathers)–Comboni Mission Center; [U] Cincinnati, OH The Comboni Missionaries Auxiliary, Inc.; Cincinnati, OH Comboni Missionaries of the Heart of Jesus, Inc. (Verona Fathers).
Donohue, Peter M. *o.s.a.* '79 (PH)[C] Villanova, PA Villanova University; [Y] Villanova, PA Fray de Leon Community.
Donohue, Raymond A.J. '85 (BUF) Retired.
Donohue, Steve *s.p.s.* '59 (SJ)[M] Saratoga, CA St. Patrick's Missionary Society Retired.
Donoso, Fermin J. *c.s.c.* '67 (FTW)[H] Notre Dame Congregation of Holy Cross, Indiana Province, Provincial House.
Donovan, Bernard Thomas '05 (MO) Carlinville, IL SS. Mary & Joseph; Air National Guard Chaplains.
Donovan, Charles *c.ss.r.* '72 (CHR) Sumter, SC St. Jude.
Donovan, Daniel E. *c.m.* '42 (PH)[Y].
Donovan, Dennis *s.d.b.* '83 (SP)[T] St. Petersburg, FL The Salesian Society of St. Petersburg, Inc.; [P] Tampa, FL Salesian Society of Florida, Inc.
Donovan, Edward M. '04 (NEW) Members.
Donovan, Edward R. *c.s.p.* '59 (NY)[EE] Jamaica Estates Paulist Fathers Generalate.
Donovan, Edward *c.s.p.* '59 (LA) Los Angeles, CA St. Paul the Apostle Retired.
Donovan, J. Michael '65 (SY) Marcellus, NY St. Francis Xavier.
Donovan, J. Paul '58 (TLS) Owasso, OK St. Henry Retired.
Donovan, James J. '87 (CHI) Diocesan Priests' Placement Board; Chicago, IL St. Barnabas.
Donovan, James W. *c.s.p.* '68 (SFR) San Francisco, CA Old St. Mary's Cathedral.
Donovan, John L. '54 (BO) Senior Priests. Retired.
Donovan, John P. '86 (SY) Johnson City, NY St. James; Adjutant Judicial Vicar; Priests' Personnel Committee.
Donovan, Rev. Msgr. John T. '44 (MIL) Retired.
Donovan, Joseph J. *m.m.* '79 (LA)[P] Los Angeles, CA.
Donovan, Kevin G. '88 (HRT) East Haven, CT St. Clare; Branford, CT St. Elizabeth.
Donovan, Michael A. '62 (DET) Roseville, MI St. Donald.
Donovan, Michael '04 (NEW) Franklin Lakes, NJ Most Blessed Sacrament.
Donovan, Michael *o.de.m.* (CLV)[N] Cleveland, OH Mercedarians; Cleveland, OH Our Lady of Mount Carmel.
Donovan, Michael (PAT)[C] Wayne, NJ De Paul High School.
Donovan, Patrick J. *m.m.* '57 (NY)[EE] Retired.
Donovan, Patrick M. *o.s.m.* '55 (CHI)[N] Chicago Order of Friar Servants of Mary (Servites) United States of America Province, Inc.
Donovan, Patrick *o.s.m.* '55 (ORG) Fullerton, CA St. Juliana Falconieri; [M] Fullerton, CA California State University Fullerton, Newman Center.
Donovan, Patrick *c.s.sp.* '57 (SFR) Millbrae, CA St. Dunstan.
Donovan, Paul A. *s.j.* '56 (PH)[Y] Loyola Center and Manresa Hall.
Donovan, Richard R. '58 (RVC) Malverne, NY Our Lady of Lourdes Retired.
Donovan, Richard *o.f.m.* '85 (BO)[W] Andover, MA Franciscan Center – Retreat House; [U] Andover St. Francis Friary.
Donovan, Robert C. '70 (FR) Pocasset, MA St. John the Evangelist.
Donovan, Robert '53 (ROC) Retired.
Donovan, Rev. Msgr. Thomas F. '57 (BRK) Lawyers; Diocesan Judges; [T] Douglaston, NY Bishop Mugavero Residence Retired.
Donovan, Rev. Msgr. Thomas F. '57 (LAV) Diocesan Judges.
Donovan, Rev. Msgr. Walter J. '44 (ATL) Retired.
Donovan, William G. '94 (PH) Diocesan Priests' Compensation and Benefits Committee; [A] Wynnewood, PA Theological Seminary of St. Charles Borromeo, Overbrook.
Donovan, Rev. Msgr. William L. '43 (SCR)[N] Dunmore, PA Villa St. Joseph Retired.
Donovan, Rev. Msgr. William '50 (SY) Retired.
Donton, Joseph P. '91 (PEO) Washington, IL St. Patrick's.
Doody, Cyril F. '57 (BRK) Brooklyn, NY St. Mark Retired.
Doody, Michael J. *s.j.* '78 (BGP)[O] Fairfield, CT The Fairfield Jesuit Community–Fairfield University; [B] Fairfield, CT Fairfield University; [V] Fairfield, CT Fairfield University.
Doody, Rev. Msgr. Peter J. '71 (PAT) Wayne, NJ Annunciation; Minister to Priests.
Doogan, James A. *s.j.* '98 (LA) Los Angeles, CA Blessed Sacrament.
Doolan, Ailbe *o.c.d.* '53 (SJ)[M] San Jose, CA Carmelite Monastery, Novitiate.
Doolan, John M. *s.j.* '63 (NY)[EE] New York, NY Murray–Weigel Hall.

Doolan, Vincent P. '80 (BO) Quincy, MA St. Joseph.
Dooley, Harry J. *c.s.p.* '58 (NY)[EE] Jamaica Estates Paulist Fathers Generalate.
Dooley, Rev. Msgr. Joseph P. '56 (ALN) Retired.
Dooley, Kevin F. '84 (MAD) Evansville, WI St. Paul; Footville, WI St. Augustine.
Dooley, Matthew R. '09 (NEW) River Edge, NJ St. Peter the Apostle.
Dooley, Michael D. *s.j.* '85 (NO)[P] New Orleans, LA Jesuit Provincial Office; New Orleans, LA Immaculate Conception.
Dooley, Peter C. '76 (RVC) Bellmore, NY St. Barnabas the Apostle; Priests' Retirement Board.
Dooley, Thomas V. '91 (DM) Des Moines, IA St. Anthony's.
Dooling, Patrick '82 (MRY) Monterey, CA Cathedral of San Carlos Borromeo; Clergy Life and Ministry Board.
Dooner, William B. '70 (PH) Penndel, PA Our Lady of Grace; Diocesan Priests' Compensation and Benefits Committee.
Do Quang Chau, Peter '73 (NSH) Vietnamese Ministry.
Dora, Rev. Msgr. Peter A. '72 (ATL) Defenders of the Bond.
Dora, Rev. Msgr. Peter P. '67 (BGP) Stamford, CT Stamford Hospital.
Dorado, Jaime '93 (PMB) West Palm Beach, FL Holy Name of Jesus; Elected Members.
Dorais, Gerald A. '55 (WOR) Gardner, MA Sacred Heart of Jesus.
Doran, Austin C. '78 (LA) Encino, CA Our Lady of Grace.
Doran, Brian D. '71 (LA) West Hollywood, CA St. Ambrose; Vernon, CA Holy Angels Parish of the Deaf Retired.
Doran, Edward E. *o.s.a.* '61 (PH)[Y] Villanova, PA St. Thomas Monastery.
Doran, Edward P. '84 (BRK) Brooklyn, NY St. Charles Borromeo.
Doran, James *o.s.b.* '00 (WOR)[O] Still River, MA Benedictine Monks, St. Benedict Abbey.
Doran, Rev. Msgr. John E. '72 (NEW) Members; Members; Members; Vicar General, Moderator of the Curia and Acting Chancellor; [R] Newark, NJ Catholi-Care, Inc.; [R] Newark, NJ New Jersey Caritas Corporation, Inc.; Newark, NJ Cathedral Basilica of the Sacred Heart; Archdiocesan Implementation Team.
Doran, Rev. Msgr. John E. '66 (WOR) Leominster, MA St. Leo; Members.
Doran, Joseph *s.d.b.* '66 (NY)[GG] Stony Point, NY Marian Shrine; [GG] Stony Point, NY Don Bosco Retreat Center and Marian Shrine.
Doran, Robert M. *s.j.* '69 (MIL)[P] Milwaukee, WI Jesuit Community at Marquette University.
Doran, William J. *s.j.* '55 (OM)[C] Omaha, NE Creighton Preparatory School.
Dore, M.J. Bernard '82 (PRO) Foster, RI St. Paul the Apostle.
Dore, Robert '89 (JKS) Columbus, MS Annunciation; West Point, MS Immaculate Conception; [H] Columbus, MS Mississippi University for Women Student Center.
Dore, Thomas M. '61 (CHI) Oak Park, IL St. Giles; Chicago, IL St. Pascal Retired.
Dore, Timothy *o.f.m.conv.* (BRK) Brooklyn, NY Most Holy Trinity – Saint Mary.
Dorff, Francis W. *o.praem.* '60 (SFE)[H] Albuquerque, NM Santa Maria de la Vid Priory.
Dorgan, Gerard L. '58 (BO) Danvers, MA St. Mary of the Annunciation.
Dorgan, John J. '65 (RIC) Retired.
Dorhauer, Robert '63 (STL) Florissant, MO Sacred Heart.
Dorin, Robert R. *s.j.* '67 (BO)[D] Dorchester, MA Boston College High School.
Doriot, Thomas E. '49 (FTW) Retired.
Doris, John A. '75 (SCR) Dunmore, PA Our Lady of Mount Carmel Parish.
Dorley, Paul D. '49 (TOL) Retired.
Dormer, David J. '77 (SCR) Military Chaplains; Army Chaplains.
Dormido, Arecio '83 (NY) Fishkill, NY Downstate Correctional Facility.
Dorn, John *o.ss.t.* '81 (BAL) Hanover, MD St. Lawrence Martyr; [S] Baltimore, MD.
Dorn, Louis E. '72 (JC) Louisiana, MO St. Joseph; Bowling Green, MO Northeast Correctional Center; Senators; Mediation and Arbitration Board; Prison Ministry; Residents Encounter Christ.
Dorn, Rupert *o.f.m.cap* '51 (MAD)[I] Madison, WI San Damiano Friary Retired.
Dorn, Thomas E. '03 (CIN) Fort Recovery, OH Mary Help of Christians; Fort Recovery, OH St. Peter; Fort Recovery, OH St. Joseph; Fort Recovery, OH St. Paul.
Dornak, Melvin '92 (AUS) Franklin, TX St. Francis of Assisi.
Dornbos, William '68 (HEL) Special Assignments; Butte, MT Holy Spirit.
Dorner, Joseph E. '95 (GB) Marinette, WI Holy Family; Regional Vicars.
Dorner, William E. '07 (PIT) Conway, PA Our Lady of Peace.
Dorney, Rev. Msgr. Dennis C. '67 (TLS) Priests' Personnel Committee; Tulsa, OK Church of St. Mary; Diocesan Senators; Diocesan Consultors; Seminary Board; Clergy Education.
Dorney, Rev. Msgr. James J. '58 (NY) Staten Island, NY St. Peter; Staten Island.
Dorney, Rev. Msgr. James (NY)[G] Staten Island, NY Seton Foundation for Learning, Inc.
Dorniak, Joseph *o.f.m.conv.* '79 (BAL)[S] Ellicott City, MD Friary of St. Joseph Cupertino; [O] Baltimore, MD St. Joseph's Nursing Home.
Doroin, Elias E. '64 (GAL) Retired.
Dorpe, Ray Van *c.m.* '82 (STL)[O] St. Louis, MO Lazarist Residence.
Dorr, James F. *c.m.* '58 (BRK)[T] Jamaica, NY Vincentian Residence.
Dorrill, James F. '60 (MOB) Retired.
Dorrler, Michael E. *s.j.* '83 (CHI)[N] Chicago, IL Clark Street Jesuit Residence.
Dorrmann, William J. '55 (CIN) Harrison, OH St. John the Baptist Retired.
Dorsch, Henry L. '68 (SPR) Southwick, MA Our Lady of the Lake.
Dorsch, Larry W. '75 (WH) Weirton, WV St. Paul's.
Dorsel, John F. '61 (R) Retired.
Dorsey, Dan *g.h.m.* '78 (CIN)[N] Fairfield, OH; Cincinnati, OH.
Dorsey, Garrett D. '59 (PIT) Allison Park, PA St. Ursula.
Dorsey, Joseph A. *c.s.c.* '57 (FTW)[H] Notre Dame Congregation of Holy Cross, Indiana Province, Provincial House; New Rochelle, NY Eastern Brothers Province.
Dorsey, Patrick *s.j.* '96 (CHI)[C] Chicago, IL Jesuit Community at Loyola University Chicago.
Dorson, James E. '77 (RIC) Retired.
Dorsonville, Mario E. '85 (WDC)[I] Washington, DC Spanish Catholic Center, Inc./Division of Immigrant and Refuge Services; Priest Council.
Dorta, Juan Manuel *s.j.* '55 (MIA)[D] Miami, FL Belen Jesuit Preparatory School; [K] Miami, FL Villa Javier; [K] Belen Jesuit Alumni Association.
Dorton, John '70 (DM) Panama, IA St. Mary of the Assumption; Westphalia, IA St. Boniface; Advocates; Portsmouth, IA St. Mary.
Dorula, Douglas E. '02 (GBG) Harrison City, PA St. Barbara.
Dorvil, Pierre A *s.m.m.* '84 (SP) Tampa, FL Epiphany of Our Lord.
Dorwart, William D. *c.s.c.* '80 (FTW)[H] Notre Dame Congregation of Holy Cross, Indiana Province, Provincial House.
Dorwart, William D. *c.s.c.* '80 (MO) Navy Chaplains.
Dory, Michael '76 (MO) Military Chaplains; Navy Chaplains.
Dosch, Leander *o.c.s.o.* '50 (SLC)[F] Huntsville, UT Abbey of Our Lady of the Holy Trinity of the Order of Cistercians.
Dosch, Michael Mary *o.p.* '05 (CIN) Cincinnati, OH St. Gertrude; [N] Cincinnati, OH St. Gertrude Priory.
Doscher, Joseph *s.c.j.* '73 (SP)[N] Pinellas Park, FL Priests of the Sacred Heart Retired.
Dosh, Mark B. '58 (STP) Excelsior, MN St. John the Baptist; Censores Librorum.
Doskey, Rev. Msgr. Clinton J. '54 (NO) New Orleans, LA St. Pius X; Adjutant Judicial Vicar; Archdiocesan Consultors Retired.
dos Reis, Antonio Jose '82 (SJ) San Jose, CA Five Wounds Portuguese National Church.
dos Reis, Jose Q. '64 (PRO) Providence, RI Rhode Island Hospital; [C] Warwick, RI Bishop Hendricken High School.
dos Remedios, Francis *o.s.b.* '82 (BIS)[A] Richardton, ND Assumption Abbey Retired.
dos Santos, Antonio *c.s.s.* '00 (SAC) Special Assignment; West Sacramento, CA Holy Cross; Sacramento, CA St. Elizabeth.
dos Santos, Egidio Alves (BO) Cape Verdean.
Dos Santos, Jose A.F. '53 (FR) Retired.
Dos Santos, Stephen *c.pp.s.* '06 (CIN)[N] Dayton Provincial Office of the Cincinnati Province of the Society of the Precious Blood.
dos Santos, Stephen *c.pp.s.* '06 (LA) Los Angeles, CA St. Agnes.
Dosyak, Mykhaylo (STF) Staten Island, NY Holy Trinity.
Do Thai Iloa, Bartholomew M. *c.m.c.* '77 (SPC)[F] Carthage, MO Congregation of the Mother Coredemptrix, United States Assumption Province.
Do Thanh Cao, Philip M. *c.m.c.* (SPC)[F] Carthage, MO Congregation of the Mother Coredemptrix, United States Assumption Province.
Dotson, Rev. Msgr. Paul J. '68 (LA) Redondo Beach, CA St. Lawrence Martyr.
Doty, Craig A. '97 (LIN) Wilber, NE St. Wenceslaus; Adjutant Judicial Vicars.
Dou, Paul Dao (KCK) Easton, KS St. Joseph–St. Lawrence.
Doucet, David A. '69 (BO) Stow, MA St. Isidore.
Doudican, James '48 (CHY) Cheyenne, WY Holy Trinity Retired.
Dougher, James P. '03 (SCR) Pittston, PA St. John the Evangelist.
Dougherty, Bill '63 (TUC) Tucson, AZ Saint Pius X Roman Catholic Parish – Tucson Retired.
Dougherty, C. Peter '61 (LAN) Retired.
Dougherty, Charles *c.p.* '68 (MET)[I] South River Passionist Provincial Office Retired.
Dougherty, Damien *o.f.m.* '75 (STL)[O] St. Louis, MO Franciscan Friary of St. Anthony of Padua.
Dougherty, Daniel J. '70 (PH) Retired.
Dougherty, Denis *o.s.b.* '56 (SPC) Springfield, MO St. Joseph's.
Dougherty, Edward C. *s.j.* '72 (WDC) Port Tobacco, MD St. Ignatius.
Dougherty, Edward J. '53 (TR) Retired.
Dougherty, Edward M. *m.m.* '79 (FgM) Maryknoll, NY; Maryknoll, NY; [EE] Maryknoll Maryknoll Fathers and Brothers.
Dougherty, Edward '53 (TR)[N] Trenton, NJ Villa Vianney Retired.
Dougherty, Eugene J. '53 (PIT)[M] Pittsburgh, PA St. John Vianney Manor Retired.
Dougherty, Hugh J. '69 (PH) Pottstown, PA St. Thomas More.
Dougherty, James J. *s.j.* '59 (STL)[O] St. Louis, MO Jesuit Community Corporation at Saint Louis University – Jesuit Hall.
Dougherty, James R. '68 (BEL) Retired.
Dougherty, James '67 (JOL) Glen Ellyn, IL St. Petronille.
Dougherty, John J. *c.s.c.* '94 (P) Portland, OR Holy Redeemer.
Dougherty, John *c.s.c.* (FTW)[H] Notre Dame Congregation of Holy Cross, Indiana Province, Provincial House.
Dougherty, Joseph V. '05 (E) Galeton, PA St. Bibiana.
Dougherty, Rev. Msgr. Paul V. '80 (PH) Huntingdon Valley, PA St. Albert the Great.
Dougherty, Stephen J. '73 (PH) Narberth, PA St. Margaret; [A] Wynnewood, PA Theological Seminary of St. Charles Borromeo, Overbrook.
Dougherty, Stephen '03 (CC)[G] Robstown, TX Society of Our Lady of the Most Holy Trinity; Corpus Christi, TX Our Lady of Perpetual Help.
Dougherty, Terrence *o.c.d.* '63 (BO)[U] Boston, MA Carmelite Monastery.
Dougherty, Terrence *o.c.d.* (WOR) Worcester, MA Our Lady of the Angels.
Dougherty, William J. *o.s.f.s.* '59 (WIL) Elsmere, DE Veteran's Hospital; [J] Wilmington, DE DeSales House.
Dougherty, William N. *o.s.f.s.* '65 (ARL) Reston, VA St. John Neumann.
Doughterty, Charles T. *c.p.* '68 (SFE) Albuquerque, NM St. John the Apostle.
Doughtery, Edward M. '79 (STP)[K] Bloomington, MN Maryknoll Fathers and Brothers, Catholic Foreign Mission Society of America.
Doughty, Edward F. '95 (BO) South Boston, MA Gate of Heaven; South Boston, MA St. Brigid.
Doughty, Rees W. '94 (NY) Nyack, NY St. Ann.
Douglas, David M. '65 (LFT) Retired.
Douglas, Gordon W. '68 (SEA)[B] Seattle, WA Bishop Blanchet High School Retired.
Douglas, John '81 (MET)[I] South River, NJ Passionist Provincial Office.
Douglas, John '81 (FgM) South River, NJ St. Paul of the Cross Province.
Douglas, Louis '58 (ALB) Retired.
Douglas, Norman K. '74 (CLV) Akron, OH St. Bernard; Ministers.
Douglass, Vincent *c.ss.r.* '66 (ORL)[F] New Smyrna Beach, FL St. Alphonsus Villa–Redemptorist Fathers and Brothers Retired.
Doussan, Rev. Msgr. Douglas A. '60 (NO) New Orleans, LA St. Gabriel the Archangel; Continuing Formation for Priests; Priest Personnel Office.
Do Van Quang, Michael M. *c.m.c.* '93 (SPC) Seneca, MO St. Mary.
Dove, Thomas J. '61 (NY)[EE] Jamaica Estates Paulist Fathers Generalate.
Dove, Thomas J. *c.s.p.* '61 (SFR) San Francisco, CA Old St. Mary's Cathedral Retired.
Dover, Edward '85 (LA) La Crescenta, CA St. James the Less; Montrose, CA Holy Redeemer; Vice Chairman; San Fernando Region.
Dovick, Robert E. '53 (CHI) Retired.
Dovzhuk, Mykola '91 (STN) Houston, TX Protection of the Mother of God.
Dow, Emanuel (LA) Hospital Chaplains.
Dowalgo, Mitchell G. *c.s.b.* '82 (LSC) Las Cruces, NM St. Albert the Great Newman Parish; [B] Las Cruces, NM Basilian Fathers.
Dowalgo, Mitchell *c.s.b.* '82 (LSC) Campus Ministry.
Dowd, Barry G. '82 (BUR) On Duty Outside the Diocese.
Dowd, Barry '82 (ORL) Orlando, FL Basilica of the National Shrine of Mary Queen of the Universe.

Dowd, Brian P. '91 (BRK) Long Island City, NY Queen of Angels.
Dowd, James '56 (P) Oakridge, OR St. Michael Retired.
Dowd, John *c.ss.r.* '61 (CHI) Chicago, IL St. Michael in Old Town; [N] Chicago, IL The Redemptorist Fathers of Chicago Retired.
Dowd, Robert A. *c.s.c.* '94 (FTW)[B] University of Notre Dame Du Lac; [H] Notre Dame, IN Holy Cross Community, Corby Hall, University of Notre Dame; Members; [H] Notre Dame, IN Congregation of Holy Cross, Indiana Province, Provincial House.
Dowd, Thomas M. '54 (GI) Retired.
Dowd, William J. '67 (NEW) Special Assignment in the Archdiocese.
Dowdel, Lawrence '91 (LA) Covina, CA St. Louise de Marillac.
Dowdell, Aaron M. *o.ss.t.* '74 (BAL) Hanover, MD St. Lawrence Martyr; [S] Baltimore, MD.
Dowdell, Rev. Msgr. Joseph M. '63 (BUF) Lakewood, NY Sacred Heart.
Dowdell, Thomas '71 (OKL) Perry, OK St. Rose of Lima.
Dowdle, David P. '79 (CHI) Western Springs, IL St. John of the Cross.
Dowling, Edward T. *s.j.* '69 (NY)[EE] Loyola Hall, Jesuit Community.
Dowling, Finbarr *o.s.b.* '68 (STL) Marthasville, MO St. Ignatius Loyola.
Dowling, John C. '51 (NEW) Retired.
Dowling, John J. *o.s.a.* '68 (FgM) Olympia Fields, IL Province of Our Mother of Good Counsel (Midwestern).
Dowling, John R. '83 (KNX) Knoxville, TN St. John Neumann.
Dowling, Joseph K. '80 (NSH) Centerville, TN Christ the Redeemer; Hohenwald, TN Holy Trinity; Hohenwald, TN St. Cecilia; Air Force Reserve Chaplains.
Dowling, Joseph *o.m.i.* '07 (ANC) Pastoral Team:; Pastoral Team:; Pastoral Team:.
Dowling, Kevin '80 (NSH)[L] Nashville, TN Diocesan Council of Catholic Women.
Dowling, Lawrence R. '91 (CHI) Chicago, IL St. Agatha; Deans; College of Consultors.
Dowling, P. Finbarr *o.s.b.* '68 (STL)[O] St. Louis, MO The Abbey of St. Mary and St. Louis.
Dowling, Patrick '82 (JC) Eldon, MO Sacred Heart; Jefferson City, MO Algoa Correctional Center; Fulton, MO Diagnostic and Reception Center; Tipton, MO Tipton Treatment Center; Fulton, MO Fulton State Hospital.
Dowling, Raymond '61 (GB) Retired.
Dowling, Sean P. '09 (BUR) Catholic Golden Age; Burlington, VT Christ the King–St. Anthony.
Dowling, Timothy '93 (PAT) Parsippany, NJ St. Ann.
Downey, Alvin T. *o.s.b.* '70 (GBG)[G] Latrobe, PA Saint Vincent Archabbey.
Downey, Christopher J. '09 (AUS) College Station, TX St. Mary; [L] College Station, TX St. Mary's Catholic Center.
Downey, David C. '03 (PMB) Boca Raton, FL St. Joan of Arc.
Downey, Donald '81 (CC) On Special Assignment; [D] Corpus Christi, TX CHRISTUS Spohn Hospital Corpus Christi – Shoreline.
Downey, Joseph F. *s.j.* '48 (DET)[K] Clarkston, MI Colombiere Center.
Downey, Kevin *o.f.m.* (PAT) Pompton Lakes, NJ Our Lady of the Assumption.
Downey, Michael '72 (SAC) Fairfield, CA Holy Spirit.
Downie, Arley T. '88 (GLP) Retired.
Downing, Andrew N. *s.j.* '07 (FTW)[K] South Bend, IN Jesuit Community.
Downing, Andrew N. *s.j.* '07 (BO)[U] Boston The Society of Jesus of New England–Provincial Offices.
Downing, Andrew N. *s.j.* '07 (CHI)[N] Chicago Chicago Province of the Society of Jesus–Provincial Office.
Downing, Charles H. '65 (PRO) West Warwick, RI St. Joseph.
Downs, Gregory Todd '91 (LAF) Absent on Sick Leave.
Downs, James A. '70 (PIT) Hillsville, PA Christ the King; Lawrence County, PA Lawrence County Jail.
Downs, James E. '02 (WIL) Rehoboth Beach, DE St. Edmond.
Downs, James *m.s.a.* '02 (NOR)[G] Cromwell Society of the Missionaries of the Holy Apostles.
Downs, John L. '55 (OG) Retired.
Downs, R. Bruce '94 (PHX) Glendale, AZ St. Helen Roman Catholic Parish.
Downs, Walter *m.s.c.* '43 (ALN)[A] Center Valley, PA Sacred Heart Villa, Missionaries of the Sacred Heart.
Dowsey, Gary '98 (SP) Dunedin, FL Our Lady of Lourdes.
Doyen, Mitchell S. '91 (STL) St. Louis, MO St. Simon the Apostle; [E] St. Louis, MO Saint Mary's High School.
Doyle, Alan T. *m.m.* '64 (FgM) Maryknoll, NY MARYKNOLL.
Doyle, Brendan '63 (JC) Jefferson City, MO Immaculate Conception; [A] Jefferson City, MO Helias High School; Vice–Chancellors; Judicial Vicar.
Doyle, Charles E. '53 (GRY) Retired.
Doyle, Daniel E. *o.s.a.* '86 (PH)[C] Villanova University; [Y] Rosemont, PA Saxony Hall.
Doyle, Daniel *s.m.* '67 (MIA) Catholic Charismatic Services—Archdiocese of Miami; Catholic Law Enforcement Ministry.
Doyle, Dennis J. '65 (STL) Shrewsbury, MO St. Michael.
Doyle, Dennis M. '92 (STL) Judges; [A] St. Louis, MO Kenrick School of Theology; [A] St. Louis, MO Cardinal Glennon College.
Doyle, Donald '53 (ALB) Retired.
Doyle, Edward F. '64 (JC) Retired.
Doyle, Eugene '76 (SCL) Becker, MN Immaculate Conception; Big Lake, MN Our Lady of the Lake; Mora, MN St. Mary's; Mora, MN St. Kathryn's; Diocesan Planning Council.
Doyle, Francis J. *o.s.a.* '70 (FgM) Villanova, PA Province of St. Thomas of Villanova (Eastern).
Doyle, Rev. Msgr. James F. '59 (NY) Bronxville, NY St. Joseph.
Doyle, Rev. Msgr. James Michael '57 (SFS) Retired.
Doyle, James '61 (LKC) Lake Charles, LA St. Theodore; Defenders of the Bond.
Doyle, James '49 (ROC) Retired.
Doyle, Rev. Msgr. Jerald A. '69 (BGP) Stratford, CT Our Lady of Grace; Episcopal Vicar for Administration; Judicial Vicar; Diocesan Consultors; Presbyteral Council.
Doyle, John J. '70 (CHI) Flossmoor, IL Infant Jesus of Prague.
Doyle, John J. '58 (JOL) Crest Hill, IL St. Ambrose; Crest Hill, IL St. Anne.
Doyle, John L. '52 (BO) Senior Priests. Retired.
Doyle, John T. *o.s.f.s.* '52 (WIL)[J] Childs, MD Retirement and Assisted Care Facility Retired.
Doyle, John '52 (DUL) Virginia, MN Sacred Heart; Virginia, MN Holy Spirit; Virginia, MN Sacred Heart Retired.
Doyle, Joseph C. '72 (NEW) Fair Lawn, NJ St. Anne's.
Doyle, Joseph M. *s.s.j.* '68 (NO)[E] New Orleans, LA St. Augustine High School; [H] New Orleans, LA St. Augustine High School; [P] New Orleans, LA The Josephite Faculty House of St. Augustine High School; [S] New Orleans, LA Pierre Toussaint Foundation of New Orleans, Inc.
Doyle, Kenneth '66 (ALB) Albany, NY Parish of Mater Christi; Chancellors; Presbyteral Council; Public Information.
Doyle, Kevin '08 (SFS) Pierre, SD SS. Peter and Paul.
Doyle, Lawrence Michael *o.s.m.* '65 (CHI)[N] Chicago, IL Assumption Priory.
Doyle, Mathias *o.f.m.* '62 (BO) Presbyteral Council.
Doyle, Mattias *o.f.m.* '62 (ALB)[B] Siena College.
Doyle, Michael A. '94 (TYL) On Duty Outside the Diocese.
Doyle, Michael J. '85 (BO) Navy Reserve Chaplains; Military & VA Chaplains.
Doyle, Rev. Msgr. Michael J. '59 (CAM) Camden, NJ The Church of Sacred Heart; Representatives by Deaneries.
Doyle, Michael M. '89 (NU) Redwood Falls, MN St. Catherine; Building Committee.
Doyle, Michael *o.s.m.* '65 (CHI) Chicago, IL Assumption of the Blessed Virgin Mary.
Doyle, N. Brendan '89 (ATL) On Leave of Absence; Without Archdiocesan Assignment or Faculties.
Doyle, Oliver '78 (GF) Great Falls, MT St. Ann's Cathedral; Special Assignment.
Doyle, Patrick '75 (IND) Indianapolis, IN Nativity of Our Lord Jesus Christ.
Doyle, Paul F. *c.s.c.* '77 (FTW)[B] University of Notre Dame Du Lac; [H] Notre Dame, IN Holy Cross Community, Corby Hall, University of Notre Dame.
Doyle, Philip R. '48 (NY) Retired.
Doyle, Rev. Msgr. Seamus '56 (MIA) Miami Shores, FL St. Rose of Lima; Deans and Deaneries.
Doyle, Stephen *o.f.m.* '62 (BO)[X] Boston, MA Saint Anthony Residence Retired.
Doyle, Thomas D. '82 (BUF) Clarence, NY Our Lady of Peace; Wende Correctional Facility.
Doyle, Thomas F. '66 (PH) Wayne, PA St. Katharine of Siena.
Doyle, Thomas J. '08 (RCK)[B] Woodstock, IL Marian Central Catholic High School; Special Assignment.
Doyle, Thomas P. *o.p.* '71 (CHI)[N] Chicago Dominicans (Provincial Office).
Doyle, Thomas P. *c.s.c.* '98 (FTW)[H] Notre Dame, IN Congregation of Holy Cross, Indiana Province, Provincial House.
Doyle, Thomas R. '62 (DAV) Retired.
Doyle, Thomas V. '84 (BRK) Brooklyn, NY St. Thomas Aquinas.
Doyle, Rev. Msgr. Thomas '54 (LA) Retired.
Doyle, Thomas *c.s.c.* '98 (P) Finance Council; [B] University of Portland; [L] Portland, OR Holy Cross Fathers & Brothers, C.S.C. – University of Portland; [B] University of Portland.
Doyle, Rev. Msgr. Vincent J. '65 (NEW) Defenders of the Bond Retired.
Doyne, David A. '56 (PH) Retired.
Drab, John P. '46 (RVC) Retired.
Drabek, Howard E. '91 (GAL) Richmond, TX Sacred Heart; Air Force Reserve Chaplains.
Drabik, Richard *m.i.c.* '60 (SPR)[H] Stockbridge, MA Congregation of Marian Fathers of The Immaculate Conception of the Most Blessed Virgin Mary.
Drabiska, Frank J. '76 (PIT) Pittsburgh, PA Word of God.
Dragga, Thomas M. '83 (CLV)[A] Wickliffe, OH Borromeo Seminary; [A] Wickliffe, OH St. Mary Seminary and Graduate School of Theology; [Y] Wickliffe, OH Center for Pastoral Leadership Services, Inc.
Dragon, Joseph W. '78 (PH) Absent on Sick Leave.
Drake, Sebastian *o.f.m.* '45 (OAK)[M] Oakland, CA Franciscan Friars (Province of Santa Barbara).
Drake, Timothy A. '71 (RIC) Clintwood, VA St. Joseph; Norton, VA St. Anthony; Big Stone Gap, VA Sacred Heart; Jonesville, VA Church of the Holy Spirit.
Dralega, Caesar '93 (WIN) Additional Diocesan Assignments; Rochester, MN Pax Christi.
Drammer, Noel *o.f.m.conv.* (TOL) Carey, OH Our Lady of Consolation, Basilica–National Shrine.
Drapeau, Benoit *c.j.m.* '59 (PHX) Phoenix, AZ St. Jerome Roman Catholic Parish; Presbyteral Council.
Draper, Andrew *t.o.r.* '88 (CHL) Mocksville, NC St. Francis of Assisi.
Draugialis, Josef '63 (LA) Los Nietos, CA Our Lady of Perpetual Help.
Draves–Arpaia, Cornelius '79 (PHX) On Leave.
Drea, Michael E. '04 (BO) Cambridge, MA St. Paul; [AA] Cambridge, MA Harvard Catholic Student Center; Pilgrimages; Harvard University.
Dreasen, Rev. Msgr. John R. '79 (RVC) East Northport, NY St. Anthony of Padua; East Northport, NY St. Anthony of Padua.
Dreese, Rev. Msgr. John J. '59 (COL) Diocesan Judges Retired.
Dreffein, Larry *o.f.m.* '76 (JOL)[K] Plainfield, IL Mayslake Village– Plainfield Campus, Inc.; [K] Oak Brook, IL Mayslake Annex II, NFP.
Dreger, Rev. Msgr. Francis X. '51 (PH) Retired.
Dreher, Daniel A. '08 (AMA) Catholic Student Center at West Texas A & M University; [H] Canyon, TX Catholic Student Center at West Texas A & M University; Canyon, TX St. Ann's.
Dreher, John D. '64 (PRO) Woonsocket, RI St. Agatha Retired.
Dreiling, Gerald G. *c.pp.s.* '58 (CIN)[N] Dayton Provincial Office of the Cincinnati Province of the Society of the Precious Blood.
Dreiling, Rev. Msgr. Raymond C. '75 (FRS) Visalia, CA St. Thomas the Apostle; Visalia, CA Holy Family; Diocesan Consultors; Vicars Forane; Personnel Board; Priests' Council; Visalia, CA St. Mary.
Dreisbach, Charles V. '59 (BAK) Retired.
Drendel, Ralph J. *s.j.* '53 (SJ)[M] Los Gatos, CA Sacred Heart Jesuit Center.
Drennan, Jimmy David '96 (SAT) Spring Branch, TX St. Joseph.
Drennan, Lawrence J. '61 (BO) Senior Priests. Retired.
Drennan, Rev. Msgr. William A. '55 (STL) Wildwood, MO St. Alban Roe Retired.
Drennen, Christopher J. *o.s.a.* '83 (PH)[C] Villanova University.
Drenzek, Peter C. '69 (MIL) Wauwatosa, WI St. Bernard.
Dressler, Philip J. '61 (CHI) Chicago, IL St. Juliana Retired.
Dressman, James J. *s.j.* '61 (BO)[U] Weston, MA Campion Health Center, Inc.
Dressman, Richard E. '72 (CIN) Cincinnati, OH St. Aloysius–on–the–Ohio.
Dressman, Robert C. *s.j.* '55 (DET)[K] Clarkston, MI Colombiere Center.
Dreves, Mark '95 (LEX) Lexington, KY Cathedral of Christ the King; Vicar General; Secretariat of the Vicar General.
Drew, Andrew *o.f.m.cap.* '61 (NY)[EE] Yonkers, NY St. Clare Friary Retired.
Drew, Geoffrey D. '04 (CIN) Consultors; Ex Officio Members; Liberty Township, OH St. Maximilian Kolbe.
Drew, George *c.ss.r.* '50 (ALB)[L] Saratoga Springs, NY St. John Neumann Residence.
Drew, James F. '74 (RVC) Elmont, NY St. Vincent de Paul.
Drewniak, Stanley '78 (JOL) Lockport, IL St. John Vianney.
Drexel, John *o.m.i.* '62 (FgM) Washington, DC AMERICAN OBLATE MISSIONS.
Drexler, Harold J. '55 (DUB) Dubuque, IA Sacred Heart Retired.
Driesch, Albert *t.o.r.* '46 (STU)[H] Steubenville, OH Holy Spirit Friary.
Driesch, David A. '82 (PIT) Pittsburgh, PA Our Lady of Joy.
Drilling, Peter J. '67 (BUF)[A] East Aurora, NY Christ the King Seminary; [A] East Aurora, NY Christ the King Seminary; Council of Priests; Consultors, College of.
Drinane, Gerald A. *s.j.* '62 (FgM) Detroit, MI Detroit Province.
Driscoll, Arthur J. '52 (BO) Senior Priests. Retired.

Driscoll, Daniel '76 (HEL) Whitehall, MT St. Teresa of Avila.
Driscoll, Donald '64 (NY) Retired.
Driscoll, Rev. Msgr. Eugene J. '70 (LUB) Lubbock, TX Holy Spirit; Priests Personnel Board; Defender of the Bond; Defender of the Bond–Appeal; Presbyteral Council; Diocesan Building Commission.
Driscoll, James A. *o.p.* '54 (PRO)[P] Providence St. Thomas Aquinas Priory at Providence College.
Driscoll, James E. '55 (OAK) Danville, CA St. Isidore Retired.
Driscoll, Jeremy *o.s.b.* '81 (P)[L] St. Benedict, OR Mt. Angel Abbey.
Driscoll, John M. *o.s.a.* '51 (PH)[Y] Villanova, PA St. Thomas Monastery.
Driscoll, John P. '47 (FR) Retired.
Driscoll, John '54 (JOL) Romeoville, IL St. Andrew the Apostle Retired.
Driscoll, Joseph J. '79 (BO) On Duty Outside the Archdiocese.
Driscoll, Michael A. '68 (MET) Retired.
Driscoll, Michael '76 (FTW)[B] University of Notre Dame Du Lac; Liturgical Commission.
Driscoll, Michael '77 (HEL) On Duty Outside the Diocese; Consultant.
Driscoll, Michael *o.carm.* '67 (PMB) Boca Raton, FL St. Jude; Liturgy.
Driscoll, Nicholas J. '69 (BO) Permanent Disability.
Driscoll, Patrick J. '08 (STL) Ellisville, MO St. Clare of Assisi.
Driscoll, Patrick Remmers '04 (MOB) Montgomery, AL St. Peter; Montgomery, AL St. John the Baptist.
Driscoll, Paul G. '64 (RVC) Retired.
Driscoll, Richard A. '55 (BO) Senior Priests. Retired.
Driscoll, Richard *s.d.s.* '65 (NSH) Shelbyville, TN St. William.
Driscoll, Samuel *o.f.m.cap.* '59 (FgM) Pittsburgh, PA Province of St. Augustine.
Driscoll, Rev. Msgr. Thomas J. '61 (BGP) Easton, CT Notre Dame (of Easton); Vicars General; Judges; Diocesan Censors; Diocesan Consultors; Presbyteral Council; Finance Council; Pastors' Vocation Advisory Board.
Driscoll, Timothy Paul '99 (FR) Taunton, MA Annunciation of the Lord.
Driscoll, William D. '55 (NEW) Retired.
Drobach, William *s.a.* '88 (NY)[EE] Garrison, NY St. Christopher's Inn; [EE] Garrison, NY St. Christopher's Friary.
Drobin, Paul J. '66 (SY)[T] Utica, NY Newman Center at SUNY Institute of Technology; [T] Utica, NY Utica College Newman Center.
Drobinski, Joseph J. '75 (WIL) Wilmington, DE St. Matthew.
Droessler, Jeffrey A. '09 (ORG) Education Leave.
Droessler, Joseph '95 (ORG) Westminster, CA Blessed Sacrament.
Droessler, Wayne J. '69 (DUB) Coggon, IA St. Joseph; Central City, IA St. Stephen; Coggon, IA St. John the Evangelist; Anamosa, IA St. Patrick.
Drofych, Mykola '08 (STF) Yonkers, NY St. Michael.
Drogon, Greg (PAT) Medical Leave.
Droll, Rev. Msgr. Larry J. '73 (SAN) Priests' Personnel Board; Presbyteral Council; Vicar General; Defensores Vinculi; Diocesan Consultors; Board of Directors; Midland, TX St. Ann's; Priests' Pension Plan.
Drolshagen, Jerome '04 (CC)[G] Robstown, TX Society of Our Lady of the Most Holy Trinity.
Drongowski, Stanley *o.p.* '79 (IND) Bloomington, IN St. Paul Catholic Center.
Droski, Norman P. '64 (GR) Coopersville, MI St. Michael's Retired.
Drouin, Marc B. '90 (MAN) Laconia, NH St. Joseph; Lakeport, NH Our Lady of the Lakes; Laconia, NH Sacred Heart.
Drouncheck, Anthony M. '89 (ALN) Nesquehoning, PA St. Francis of Assisi Parish.
Drozak, Lukasz *c.ss.r.* '06 (MET) Manville, NJ Sacred Heart of Jesus.
Drozd, Henry J. '62 (DAL) Retired.
Drozd, Henry J. '62 (SAV) Retired.
Drozd, Marian '91 (MET) South Amboy, NJ Sacred Heart.
Drozdovsky, Michael '92 (SJP) Parma, OH Pokrova Ukrainian Catholic Parish; Presbyters.
Droze, D. Anthony '85 (CHR) Columbia, SC Our Lady of the Hills.
Drucker, James N. '78 (PSC) Retired.
Druding, John C. '76 (ATL) Judges Retired.
Druding, Vincent '09 (NY) Bronx, NY Our Lady of Angels.
Druggan, Dennis *o.f.m.cap.* '84 (MIL)[P] Mount Calvary, WI St. Lawrence Friary; [B] Mount Calvary, WI St. Lawrence Seminary.
Drum, John *c.ss.r.* '54 (ALB)[L] Saratoga Springs, NY St. John Neumann Residence.
Drummond, Alexander R. '94 (ARL) Great Falls, VA St. Catherine of Siena.
Drummond, Elsyn J. '54 (NOR) Retired.
Drummy, John A. '71 (SUP) Amery, WI St. Joseph; Balsam Lake, WI Our Lady of the Lakes; Clear Lake, WI St. John; Southwest Deanery; Personnel Placement Board.
Drupieski, Stanley R. *o.s.f.s.* '64 (WIL) Wilmington, DE St. Anthony of Padua; Court of First Instance Judges.
Drury, Dennis G. '82 (GB) Denmark, WI St. Therese de Lisieux; Denmark, WI St. Isidore the Farmer.
Drury, George *s.j.* '52 (BO)[U] Newton, MA The Jesuit Community at Boston College.
Drury, Michael J. '74 (PAT) Long Valley, NJ St. Luke.
Drury, Michael '84 (HEL) Cut Bank, MT St. Margaret; Shelby, MT St. William; Valier, MT St. Francis.
Drury, Robert '79 (OWN) Franklin, KY St. Mary.
Drutowski, Robert J. '79 (MIL) Pewaukee, WI Queen of Apostles.
Drybka, Krzysztof *o.s.p.p.e.* (NY) Yonkers, NY St. Casimir.
Drywal, Justin *o.s.b.* '98 (CLV) Broadview Heights, OH Assumption.
Drzaic, Frank '62 (LA) Los Angeles, CA Our Lady of Loretto.
Drzal, Stanislaw *s.ch.* '69 (DET) Sterling Heights, MI Our Lady of Czestochowa.
Duaime, Jeffrey T. *c.s.sp.* '86 (FgM) Bethel Park, PA; Eastern Province; Bethel Park, PA CONGREGATION OF THE HOLY SPIRIT.
Duaime, Jeffrey T. *c.s.sp.* '86 (PH)[F] Bensalem, PA Holy Ghost Preparatory School; [Y] Bensalem, PA Congregation of the Holy Spirit.
Duane, Robert J. '53 (NY) Ardsley, NY Our Lady of Perpetual Help; [EE] Bronx, NY John Cardinal O'Connor Residence Retired.
Duane, Rev. Msgr. Thomas J. '71 (PH) Lansdale, PA St. Stanislaus.
Duarte, Danilo Martinez '03 (SJN)[F] Rio Piedras, PR Hogar Santa Teresa Jornet for the Aged.
Duarte, J. Scott '78 (RIC) Quinton, VA St. Elizabeth Ann Seton.
Duarte, Scott '78 (RIC) Vicar for the Causes of Saints.
Duases, Jeffrey (BAL) Priest Personnel Board.
Dubay, Thomas E. *s.m.* '50 (WDC)[N] Washington, DC Marist Center.
Dube, Gregory P. '07 (PRT) Saco, ME Good Shepherd Parish.
Dube, Marcel *o.carm.* '54 (VEN) Englewood, FL St. Francis of Assisi.
Dubell, Rev. Msgr. James H. '65 (TR) Cemeteries; Medford, NJ St. Mary of the Lakes.
Dubert, James W. '98 (DUB) Rockwell, IA St. Patrick; Rockford, IA Holy Name; Rockwell, IA Sacred Heart.
Dubi, Leonard A. '68 (CHI) Calumet City, IL St. Victor.
Dubitsky, Roman '65 (PHU) Perth Amboy, NJ Assumption of B.V.M.
Dublinski, Steve '85 (SPK) Vicars General; Moderator of the Curia; Members; Diocesan Pastoral Council; Diocesan Liturgical Commission.
Dublinski, Steven L. '85 (SPK) Spokane, WA Cathedral of Our Lady of Lourdes; Washington, DC Federation of Diocesan Liturgical Commissions.
Dubois, Rev. Msgr. Andrew '95 (PRT) Guardian; Diocesan Consultors; Staff; Diocesan Priests' Benefit Plan – Trustees; Diocesan Finance Council; Personnel Board; Special or Other Diocesan Assignment; Ex Officio; Vicars General; Moderator of the Curia; Auburn, ME Immaculate Heart of Mary Parish; Department of Administrative & Ministerial Services; Ministerial Services; Rumford, ME Parish of the Holy Savior.
Dubois, Rev. Msgr. Charles J. '64 (LKC) Lake Charles, LA St. Theodore.
DuBois, David J. '80 (GAL) Pattison, TX Sacred Heart.
DuBois, Francis J. '70 (ALB) Latham, NY St. Ambrose.
Dubois, Patrick '04 (VEN) Defenders of the Bond; Venice, FL Our Lady of Lourdes.
Dubois, Raymond *s.s.s.* '49 (CLV)[N] Cleveland Congregation of the Blessed Sacrament Provincial House; [N] Richfield, OH Regina Health Center.
DuBois, Rev. Msgr. William '48 (SP) Retired.
Dubovici, Rev. Archpriest Mihai '94 (STF) Bridgeport, CT Protection of B.V.M.; [A] Stamford, CT Ukrainian Catholic Seminary Inc. St. Basil College; Vice Econome; Notary Publics; Presbyteral Council; Administrative Council; Development Office; Ecumenical Commission.
Dubriske, Edward J. *s.s.e.* '64 (BUR)[E] Colchester, VT Society of St. Edmund; Colchester, VT SOCIETY OF ST. EDMUND.
Dubrouillet, James N. '97 (CHR) Simpsonville, SC St. Mary Magdalene.
Dubuisson, William *o.m.i.* '55 (SAT)[K] San Antonio, TX Oblate Madonna Residence.
Duc, Dominic Tran Minh '90 (PH) East Lansdowne, PA St. Cyril of Alexandria.
Ducaji, John '54 (JOL) Wheaton, IL St. Mark.
Ducci, Alex '61 (STA) Retired.
Ducette, Rev. Msgr. John I. '62 (BUF) Apostleship of the Sea; [O] Buffalo, NY Sheehan Residence for Priests Retired.
Duch, Robert G. '64 (PIT) Retired.
Duchaine, Rev. Msgr. R. Mark '78 (SC) Mapleton, IA St. Mary's; Episcopal Vicar for Canonical Affairs; Judicial Vicar; Judges; Diocesan Finance Council; Presbyteral Council; Diocesan Consultors; Priests' Pension Plan – Board of Trustees; Vicar General; Catholic School Foundation of the Diocese of Sioux City; Priests' Personnel Board.
DuCharme, Paul '55 (GB) Retired.
DuChez, Daniel B. *o.s.* (LC)[D] Chippewa Falls, WI St. Joseph's Hospital; Chippewa Falls, WI Notre Dame.
Duchnowicz, Arthur F. '01 (GAY) Rogers City, MI St. Monica; Onaway, MI St. Paul; Posen, MI St. Casimir; Rogers City, MI St. Ignatius.
Duchschere, Paul C. '90 (FAR) Special Assignment; Permanent Diaconate; Vocation Director.
Ducle, Rico (CAM) Camden, NJ The Church of St. Joan of Arc, West Collingswood, N.J.
Duc Minh, Joseph N. '61 (LA) Retired.
Ducre, Kennon Y. '83 (ELP) El Paso, TX All Saints.
Duda, Robert '84 (JOL) Villa Park, IL St. John the Apostle.
Dudak, Rev. Msgr. George A. '56 (PAT)[Q] Chester, NJ Nazareth Village Retired.
Dudash, Derrick F. '74 (GRY) Hebron, IN St. Helen; Bishop's Council of Priests.
Dudek, Bernard *o.f.m. conv.* '54 (BAL) Baltimore, MD St. Clement Mary Hofbauer.
Dudek, Stanislaus '87 (HRT) New Britain, CT Sacred Heart of Jesus.
Dudek, Stanislaw '62 (BUF) Retired.
Dudek, Stephen S. '84 (GR) Grand Rapids, MI Holy Name of Jesus; On Special Assignment; [L] Grand Rapids, MI The Society For The Propagation Of The Faith; [L] Grand Rapids, MI The Society For The Propagation Of The Faith.
Dudkevych, Andriy '95 (PHU) Passaic, NJ St. Nicholas.
Dudkiewicz, Stanley '52 (SY) Syracuse, NY Sacred Heart Basilica.
Dudley, James *m.s.c.* '56 (SAT)[L] San Antonio, TX Missionaries of the Sacred Heart; Sectional Leadership Team.
Dudo, Nicholas '08 (CAM) Blackwood, NJ St. Agnes' Church, Blackwood Terrace, N.J.
Dudziak, Rev. Msgr. Paul M. '69 (WDC) Gaithersburg, MD St. Rose of Lima.
Dudzik, Dariusz '95 (NOR) Groton, CT Sacred Heart.
Dudzik, Jozef '00 (BUF) Clymer, NY Christ Our Hope.
Dudzinski, Andrew J. '96 (LFT) Muncie, IN St. Mary.
Dudzinski, Brian A. '97 (LFT) Fishers, IN St. John Vianney Parish; Members.
Dudzinski, Paul L. '86 (ARL) Washington, VA St. Peter.
Dudzinski, Theodore C. '97 (LFT) Kokomo, IN St. Joan of Arc; Kokomo, IN St. Patrick; Office of the Permanent Diaconate.
Due, Rev. Msgr. J. Michael '00 (COV) Diocesan Consultors; Religious; Vicars General.
Duell, James S. '82 (CIN) Troy, OH St. Patrick.
Duenas, Jaime H. '50 (NY) Bronx, NY Nativity of Our Blessed Lady Retired.
Duenas, Jose Luis *o.a.r.* '59 (ELP) El Paso, TX Guardian Angel.
Dueñas, Manuel '07 (NEW) Bergenfield, NJ St. John the Evangelist.
Dueppen, David '99 (MIA) Absent on Leave.
Duerr, Rt. Rev. Gregory *o.s.b.* '64 (P)[L] St. Benedict, OR Mt. Angel Abbey; Saint Benedict, OR.
Duesdieker, Robert W. '80 (JC) Boonville, MO SS. Peter and Paul; Fayette, MO St. Joseph; Defenders of the Bond; I. Columbia; Personnel Board.
Duesman, Rev. Msgr. Jerome P. '68 (DAL) Irving, TX Holy Family of Nazareth; Building Commission.
Duesman, Rev. Msgr. Leon '65 (DAL) Coppell, TX St. Ann; Defensor Vinculi.
Duesterhaus, Michael R. '91 (MO) Navy Reserve Chaplains; Military Chaplains; On Duty Outside the Diocese; Spotsylvania, VA St. Matthew.
Duet, Jerod '08 (HT) Houma, LA St. Bernadette; Catholic Daughters of the Americas; Priests Council.
Dueweke, Robert *o.s.a.* '79 (ELP) Permanent Diaconate Office; Tepeyac Institute.
Duff, Daniel Joseph '07 (LFT) Kokomo, IN St. Patrick; Kokomo, IN St. Joan of Arc.
Duff, John J. '77 (NY) Pawling, NY St. John the Evangelist.
Duffe, Stephen J. '96 (NEW) Washington Township, NJ Our Lady of Good Counsel.
Duffeck, David A. '06 (GB) De Pere, WI Immaculate Conception; Oneida, WI St. Joseph.
Duffell, John P. '69 (NY) New York, NY Ascension.
Duffey, Joseph A. '52 (PH)[Y] Villanova, PA St. Thomas Monastery Retired.
Dufficy, Edward C. '50 (CHI) Retired.
Duffner, Paul A. *o.p.* '40 (P) Portland, OR Holy Rosary Parish & Dominican Priory; [L] Portland, OR Holy Rosary Priory Retired.
Duffner, Ralph J. '56 (SPC) Chaffee, MO St. Ambrose; Priests' Mutual Benefit Society Retired.
Duffy, Darrell G. '05 (BUF) Jamestown, NY St. James.
Duffy, Donald J. '43 (CHI) Retired.
Duffy, Donald '59 (NO) Lafitte, LA St. Anthony Retired.
Duffy, Rev. Msgr. Francis J. '70 (PAT) Morris Plains, NJ St. Virgilius; Deacon Internship Program.
Duffy, Rev. Msgr. Francis X. '49 (NY) Cornwall–on–

Hudson, NY St. Thomas of Canterbury; [EE] Bronx, NY John Cardinal O'Connor Residence Retired.
Duffy, G. Ralph '65 (WDC) Rockville, MD Shrine of St. Jude Retired.
Duffy, George A. *s.j.* '55 (BO)[U] Weston, MA Campion Health Center, Inc.
Duffy, George '63 (MIA) Retired.
Duffy, Hugh E. *o.s.f.s.* '60 (WIL)[J] Childs, MD Retirement and Assisted Care Facility Retired.
Duffy, Hugh P. *s.j.* '68 (SEA)[A] Seattle, WA Seattle University; [L] Seattle, WA Arrupe Jesuit Community at Seattle University.
Duffy, Hugh '66 (PMB) Okeechobee, FL Sacred Heart.
Duffy, James D. *s.m.* '79 (ATL) Atlanta, GA Our Lady of the Assumption; Advocates.
Duffy, James F. *s.j.* '06 (WDC)[N] Washington, DC The Jesuit Community at Georgetown University.
Duffy, James H. '56 (MIL) Special Assignment.
Duffy, John F. *c.s.p.* '75 (NY)[EE] Jamaica Estates, NY Paulist Fathers Generalate; Jamaica, NY.
Duffy, John F. *c.s.p.* (BRK)[T] Jamaica Estates, NY Paulist Fathers – Generalate.
Duffy, Joseph P. *s.j.* '57 (BO)[U] Newton, MA The Jesuit Community at Boston College.
Duffy, Michael A. *o.f.m.* '71 (PH)[Q] Philadelphia, PA St. Francis Inn; [Y] Philadelphia, PA Order of Friars Minor of the Province of the Most Holy Name.
Duffy, Michael M. '76 (RIC) Bumpass, VA Immaculate Conception; Mineral, VA St. Jude; Judges; Adjutant Judicial Vicar.
Duffy, Patrick '81 (SFE) Retired.
Duffy, Paul J. *m.m.* '79 (FgM) Maryknoll, NY MARYKNOLL.
Duffy, Raymond '68 (FRS) Retired.
Duffy, Richard *o.f.m.* '58 (FgM) Saint Louis, MO Sacred Heart Province.
Duffy, Thomas J. '66 (PH) Retired.
Duffy, Rev. Msgr. Thomas M. '53 (WDC) Priest Council; Washington, DC Our Lady of Victory Retired.
Dufner, Daniel G. '96 (YAK) Cashmere, WA St. Francis Xavier; Leavenworth, WA Our Lady of the Snows; Diocesan Finance Council; Clergy Personnel Board.
Dufner, Thomas W. '83 (STP) St. Louis Park, MN Holy Family.
Dufour, David W. '94 (NO) Kenner, LA Divine Mercy.
Dufour, George J. '70 (BO) Salem, MA St. Anne.
DuFour, Louis C. '58 (BO) Senior Priests. Retired.
DuFour, Rene *o.m.i.* '54 (BEL)[F] Belleville, IL Missionary Oblates of Mary Immaculate – St. Henry's Oblate Residence.
Dufresne, Vincent J. '83 (BR) Paulina, LA St. Michael the Archangel; Paulina, LA Most Sacred Heart of Jesus; Paulina, LA St. Joseph; Promoter of Justice; Defenders of the Bond.
Dufresne, Vincent (NO)[A] St. Benedict, LA St. Joseph Seminary College.
Duga, Bernard '99 (NEW) Hackensack, NJ Hackensack University Medical Center.
Dugal, James H. *c.pp.s.* '56 (CIN) Montezuma, OH Our Lady of Guadalupe.
Dugan, Dennis *s.o.l.t.* '09 (CC)[G] Robstown, TX Society of Our Lady of the Most Holy Trinity.
Dugan, J. Thomas '70 (E) Sharon, PA St. Joseph.
Dugan, James L. *s.j.* '73 (NY)[EE] New York, NY St. Ignatius Loyola Residence; New York, NY St. Ignatius Loyola.
Dugan, James M. '89 (ALT) Southern Deanery; Meyersdale, PA SS. Philip and James; Somerset, PA State Correctional Institution.
Dugan, Paul J. *s.j.* '56 (BUF)[O] Buffalo, NY Canisius Jesuit Community Inc.
Dugan, T. Michael '88 (DAL) Deans; Dallas, TX St. Elizabeth; Consultors of Pastors; Liturgy Office.
Dugan, Thomas P. *c.s.b.* '60 (GAL)[O] Sugar Land Basilian Mission Center.
Dugan, William M. '49 (SPK) Retired.
Dugandzic, Peter '95 (RVC) Valley Stream, NY Blessed Sacrament; Academic Leave.
Dugandzic, Peter '95 (NY)[A] Yonkers, NY St. Joseph's Seminary.
Dugas, Jerome A. '62 (BR) Retired.
Dugas, Scott '77 (HT) Administrative Leave.
Dugas, Willard '77 (LAF) Retired.
Dugay, Anthony *s.v.d.* '62 (FgM) Techny, IL.
Duggan, Donald J. *s.j.* '55 (SJ)[M] Los Gatos, CA Sacred Heart Jesuit Center.
Duggan, Edmund Brendan *c.s.sp.* '75 (BRK)[S] Irish Apostolate; Woodside, NY Blessed Virgin Mary, Help of Christians.
Duggan, Eugene F. '46 (SFR) Sausalito, CA St. Mary Star of the Sea Retired.
Duggan, J. Edward '50 (CHI) Retired.
Duggan, John J. '56 (PRO) Coventry, RI SS. John and Paul Retired.
Duggan, Joseph P. '64 (VEN) Retired.
Duggan, Karl '98 (ATL) On Leave of Absence; Without Archdiocesan Assignment or Faculties.
Duggan, Kevin F.X. '98 (SEA) Sammamish, WA Mary, Queen of Peace.
Duggan, Kevin P. '87 (MET) Jamesburg, NJ St. James the Less.
Duggan, Kevin *s.m.* '86 (MRY) Campus Ministry Department; [I] San Luis Obispo, CA California State Polytechnic Institute/Cuesta College; [F] San Luis Obispo, CA Society of Mary (Marists)–S.M.
Duggan, Michael A. *m.m.* '59 (NY)[EE] Maryknoll Maryknoll Fathers and Brothers.
Duggan, Nicholas '62 (SAC) Retired.
Duggan, Oliver '71 (SEA) Seattle, WA St. Catherine of Siena; Seattle, WA Assumption.
Duggan, Paul O'Donnell '70 (PAT) Clifton, NJ SS. Cyril and Methodius.
Duggan, Peter '55 (SEA) Seattle, WA St. Peter Retired.
Duggan, Robert J. *c.s.b.* '64 (GAL) Angleton, TX Most Holy Trinity; Southern Vicariate.
Duggan, Sean B. *o.s.b.* '88 (NO)[P] St. Benedict, LA St. Joseph Abbey.
Duggimpudi, Jaya Prathap '99 (BIR) Birmingham, AL Our Lady of Sorrows.
Duggins, Dominic R. *g.h.m.* '74 (CIN)[N] Fairfield, OH; [T] Fairfield, OH Glenmary Home Missioners Charitable Trust; Cincinnati, OH.
Duhaime, James H. '61 (PRO) Retired.
Duhaime, John N. '71 (WH) Retired.
Duhe, Thomas P. '78 (BR) College of Consultors; Continuing Formation for the Clergy; Baton Rouge, LA St. Thomas More; Presbyteral Council.
Duhon, Edward J. '07 (LAF) Eunice, LA St. Anthony of Padua.
Dukart, George '59 (BIS)[G] Bismarck, ND Emmaus Place Retired.
Dukart, Norman J. '67 (BIS) Retired.
Duke, Rev. Msgr. Charles J. '47 (NO) Retired.
Duke, Jerome J. '68 (CLV) Lakewood, OH SS. Cyril and Methodius; Associate Judges.
Dukehart, C. Henry *s.s.* '43 (BAL)[S] Baltimore Society of St. Sulpice, Province of the United States Retired.
Dukehart, Claude H. *s.s.* '43 (BAL)[O] Baltimore, MD St. Charles Villa Retired.
Dukeley, Boris '98 (SJP) Presbyters Retired.
Duker, Rev. Msgr. Russell A. *s.e.o.d.* '70 (PBR) Pittsburgh, PA Holy Spirit; Protosyncellus; Consultors; Priests' Pension Board; Presbyteral Council; Pittsburgh, PA St. Pius X.
Dukowski, James G. *o.m.i.* '67 (FgM) Washington, DC AMERICAN OBLATE MISSIONS.
Dulaney, William R. '73 (BRK) Bellerose, NY St. Gregory the Great.
Dulce, Thomas Joseph T.J. '09 (GAL) Kingwood, TX St. Martha.
Dulek, Lawrence V. '73 (MIL) On Leave.
Dull, James C. (R) Wake Forest, NC St. Catherine of Siena.
Dullahan, Robert J. '57 (ALN)[A] Wernersville, PA Jesuit Center–Jesuit Community.
Dullea, Denis '61 (ATL) Retired.
Dulli, Brian '08 (MAD) Sun Prairie, WI Sacred Hearts of Jesus and Mary.
Dulock, Vincent *c.s.b.* '69 (GAL)[B] Sugar Land, TX Basilian Fathers of Sugarland.
Duma, Rt. Rev. Msgr. Gregory '64 (ROM) Canton, OH St. George Cathedral; College of Consultors; Canton Deanery.
Dumadag, Christopher (BAL)[S] Baltimore, MD Ferdinand Wheeler Jesuit Community.
Dumag, Peter '92 (HON) Vocations Director; Honolulu, HI Co–Cathedral of St. Theresa of the Child Jesus.
Dumais, George J. *s.j.* '71 (HEL) Missoula, MT St. Francis Xavier; Special Assignments.
Dumais, Marcel *o.m.i.* '63 (CHI)[W] Chicago, IL Oblates for International Pastoral.
Dumais, Paul H. '04 (PRT)[M] Standish, ME Saint Joseph's College; Pastoral Associates.
Duman, Charles J. '52 (SFS) Salem, SD St. Mary Retired.
Dumas, Emile E. *m.m.* '67 (FgM) Maryknoll, NY MARYKNOLL.
Dumas, Terrence J. '87 (LAN) Ann Arbor, MI St. Francis of Assisi Retired.
Dumenko, Oleksandr '01 (PHU) St. Clair, PA St. Nicholas; Shenandoah, PA St. Michael's.
Duminiak, John J. '60 (ALN)[J] Bethlehem, PA Holy Family Villa Retired.
Dumm, Demetrius R. *o.s.b.* '47 (GBG)[G] Latrobe, PA Saint Vincent Archabbey.
Dumm, Wilfred M. *o.s.b.* '45 (GBG)[G] Latrobe, PA Saint Vincent Archabbey.
Dummer, Anthony *o.m.i.* (OAK)[M] Oakland, CA Missionary Oblates of Mary Immaculate United States Province.
Dumont, C. Peter '71 (MAN) Auburn, NH St. Peter; Long Range Planning Committee; Presbyteral Council; College of Consultors; Candia, NH St. Paul.
Dumont, Gerald '80 (BRK) Brooklyn, NY Our Lady of Miracles.
Dumont, Jacob *l.c.* '08 (CHI)[N] Hillside, IL Legion of Christ.
Dumoulin, Marcel L. '61 (PRT) Retired.
Dumphrey, Joseph C. *o.s.f.s.* '64 (BUF) Lockport, NY St. John the Baptist.
Dumpson, Roland J. '83 (NY) Retired.
Dunavan, Thomas B. '98 (LIN) Tecumseh, NE St. Andrew's; Lincoln, NE Nebraska Penal Complex; Apostolate to the Spanish Speaking.
Dunbar, Francis '55 (ALB) Retired.
Duncan, Andrew D. '93 (CHY) Riverton, WY St. Margaret's; College of Consultors; Diocesan Schools Advisory Group.
Duncan, Rev. Msgr. Edward J. '41 (PEO)[M] Champaign, IL St. John's Catholic Newman Center at the University of Illinois, Urbana–Champaign; Champaign, IL St. John's Catholic Chapel Retired.
Duncan, Rev. Msgr. John C. '60 (LFT) Carmel, IN Our Lady of Mount Carmel; Associate Judges.
Duncan, Rev. Msgr. Joseph P. '89 (PH) Bensalem, PA St. Charles Borromeo; Regional Vicars; Priests' Personnel Board.
Duncan, Rev. Msgr. Joseph (IND)[I] Indianapolis, IN St. Augustine Home, Little Sisters of the Poor.
Duncan, Rev. Msgr. William H. '90 (GR) Byron Center, MI St. Sebastian's; On Special Assignment; Vicar General/Moderator of the Curia; College of Consultors; Moderator of the Curia; Diocesan Finance Council Membership.
Duncanson, Rev. Msgr. Richard F. '71 (SD) San Diego, CA Mission Basilica San Diego De Alcala.
Duncanson, Rev. Msgr. Richard '71 (SD) Vicars Forane; Censores Librorum.
Duncklee, Lawrence T. '80 (RVC) Inwood, NY Our Lady of Good Counsel; Procurator & Advocates.
Dundon, Robert W. *s.j.* '69 (FgM) Milwaukee, WI Society of Jesus.
Dunfee, Dirk J. *s.j.* '97 (KC)[J] Kansas City, MO Rockhurst Jesuit Community.
Dunfee, James M. '84 (STU) Mingo Junction, OH St. Agnes; Censores Librorum; Judges; Deans.
Dung, Nguyen Luke Hung (NO) New Orleans, LA Chapel of the Vietnamese Martyrs.
Dung, Nguyen Quoc *c.ss.r.* '05 (LA)[P] Baldwin Park Vietnamese Redemptorist Mission.
Dunghe, Adelino P. *s.j.* '95 (SY)[Q] Syracuse, NY Jesuits at LeMoyne, Inc.
Dunham, Larry C. *o.f.m.* '74 (SFE)[H] Albuquerque, NM The Province of Our Lady of Guadalupe.
Dunklee, Lawrence G. '78 (LC)[D] Eau Claire, WI Sacred Heart Hospital; Hospitals and Health Affairs.
Dunkley, George '70 (SD) San Marcos, CA St. Mark.
Dunkley, George '70 (WOR) On Duty Outside the Diocese.
Dunlap, Christopher J. '06 (STL) St. Louis, MO St. Francis of Assisi.
Dunlap, William M. '74 (TR) Brick, NJ Visitation.
Dunleavy, Thomas J. '75 (PH) Philadelphia, PA St. Anselm.
Dunleavy, Thomas J. *m.m.* '75 (FgM) Maryknoll, NY MARYKNOLL.
Dunmyer, Raymond A. '76 (BIR) Montevallo, AL St. Thomas the Apostle; [H] Montevallo, AL University of Montevallo.
Dunn, Bob '85 (CC) Corpus Christi, TX Most Precious Blood.
Dunn, Charles J. *s.j.* '55 (WOR)[O] Worcester, MA Jesuits of the Holy Cross, Inc.
Dunn, Christopher J. *o.f.m.* '82 (FgM) New York, NY Holy Name Province.
Dunn, Didacus *o.f.m.cap.* '56 (SAL)[D] Hays, KS St. Joseph's Friary.
Dunn, Rev. Msgr. Donald F. '61 (COS) Retired.
Dunn, Edmond J. '72 (DAV) Oxford, IA St. Peter's; Oxford, IA St. Mary's; [A] St. Ambrose University.
Dunn, Rev. Msgr. Edward C. '43 (TOL) Retired.
Dunn, Gerald R. '57 (MAN) Retired.
Dunn, Harold *m.s.a.* '78 (NOR)[G] Cromwell Society of the Missionaries of the Holy Apostles.
Dunn, Jerome *o.f.m.cap.* '68 (BAL)[S] Cumberland, MD SS. Peter and Paul Friary; Cumberland, MD SS. Peter and Paul.
Dunn, John F. '54 (DET) Retired.
Dunn, Laurence J. '68 (CHI) Lake Forest, IL St. Patrick.
Dunn, Lawrence *m.i.c.* '87 (WDC)[B] Washington, DC Marian Fathers Scholasticate.
Dunn, Michael G. '03 (TR) Burlington, NJ The Church of St. Katharine Drexel, Burlington, N.J.
Dunn, Michael L. '94 (BGP) Trumbull, CT St. Theresa; Presbyteral Council.
Dunn, Richard B. '80 (SY) Military Chaplains; Air Force Chaplains.
Dunn, Richard B. '80 (BLX) Keesler Airforce Base.
Dunn, Rev. Msgr. Richard F. '58 (BRK)[T] Douglaston, NY Bishop Mugavero Residence Retired.
Dunn, Robert M. '92 (NY)[AA] Bronx, NY Jeanne Jugan Residence.
Dunn, Stephen *c.p.* '64 (MET)[I] South River Passionist Provincial Office.
Dunn, Stephen '71 (SD) Unassigned.
Dunn, Rev. Msgr. William A. '65 (COL) Logan, OH St. John; College of Consultors.
Dunn, William S. '06 (BO) Chelmsford, MA St. Mary.
Dunne, Dermot J. '00 (OM) Madison, NE St. Leonard; Deans; Officers; Deans.
Dunne, Edward *c.ss.r* '49 (ALB)[L] Saratoga Springs, NY St. John Neumann Residence.

Dunne, George W. *s.s.s.* '82 (ORL) Winter Springs, FL St. Stephen.
Dunne, Gerald M. *o.s.f.s.* '77 (PH)[Y] Wyndmoor, PA Villa de Sales Oblate Residence.
Dunne, Gerard *s.s.c.* '67 (OM)[K] St. Columbans Missionary Society of St. Columban.
Dunne, James M. '61 (BRK) Rockaway Beach, NY Saint Camillus–Saint Virgilius Retired.
Dunne, John S. *c.s.c.* '54 (FTW)[B] University of Notre Dame Du Lac; [H] Notre Dame, IN Holy Cross Community, Corby Hall, University of Notre Dame.
Dunne, Rev. Msgr. Joseph A. '42 (NY)[EE] Bronx, NY Retired.
Dunne, Mark '02 (TYL) Lindale, TX Holy Family.
Dunne, Rev. Msgr. Peter F. '44 (OM) Boys Town, NE Immaculate Conception B.V.M. Retired.
Dunne, Raymond A. *s.j.* '50 (DET)[K] Clarkston, MI Colombiere Center.
Dunne, Thomas *s.d.b.* '72 (NY)[EE] New Rochelle, NY Salesian Cooperators of St. John Bosco; New Rochelle, NY; New Rochelle, NY SALESIANS OF DON BOSCO.
Dunning, James P. '63 (ORG) Mission Viejo, CA St. Kilian.
Dunnivan, John '53 (KCK) Retired.
Dunphy, James R. *m.s.* '57 (STL)[O] LaSalette Spirituality Center.
Dunphy, Larry *o.f.m.* '60 (SAC) Sacramento, CA St. Francis of Assisi.
Dunphy, Richard W. *s.j.* '73 (COS)[F] Sedalia, CO Sacred Heart Jesuit Community; [H] Sedalia, CO Sacred Heart Jesuit Retreat House.
Dunphy, Robert J. '65 (CAM) Audubon, NJ Church of the Holy Maternity, Audubon, NJ; Mount Ephraim, NJ Church of the Sacred Heart, Mt. Ephraim, N.J.
Dunphy, Thomas R. '58 (CLV) Valley City, OH St. Martin of Tours.
Dunson, Donald '82 (CLV)[A] Wickliffe, OH Borromeo Seminary; [A] Wickliffe, OH St. Mary Seminary and Graduate School of Theology.
Dunyo, Andrew (BRK) Brooklyn, NY St. Mark.
Duoba, Jonas *m.i.c.* '46 (CHI)[N] Chicago, IL Congregation of Marian Fathers of the Immaculate Conception Retired.
Duong, Cu Minh '87 (MOB) Mobile, AL St. Monica; Vicar for Vietnamese Affairs.
Duong, Duc '00 (BEA) Port Arthur, TX St. Catherine of Siena.
Duong, James Duc H. '01 (CHL) Greensboro, NC St. Benedict.
Duong, Paul '74 (SJ) San Jose, CA Christ the King.
Duong, Tien H. '01 (CHL) Franklin, NC St. Francis of Assisi.
Duong, Tri Minh *c.m.* '05 (BRK)[T] Jamaica, NY Vincentian Residence.
Duplessis, Donald *o.s.m.* '61 (CHI)[N] Chicago Order of Friar Servants of Mary (Servites) United States of America Province, Inc.
Duplissey, James Joshe '09 (LSC) Deming, NM Holy Family.
DuPont, Arthur J. '54 (HRT) Bristol, CT St. Gregory the Great; Appointed Retired.
Dupont, Bernard *o.p.* '68 (WDC)[B] Washington, DC Dominican House of Studies.
Dupre, Matthew C. '98 (BR) Brusly, LA St. John the Baptist; College of Consultors; Presbyteral Council.
Dupre, Stephane *f.s.s.p.* (COS) Security, CO Immaculate Conception Parish.
DuPreez, Frank V. '86 (LR) North Little Rock, AR St. Patrick; North Little Rock, AR St. Augustine.
Duprey, Rev. Msgr. Dennis J. '70 (OG) Malone, NY Notre Dame; Advocates; Deans.
Dupuis, George H. '50 (BUR) Retired.
Dupuis, Philip '51 (LAN) Retired.
DuQuesnay, Damian *o.s.b.* '46 (SP)[N] St. Leo, FL St. Leo Abbey.
Duquet, Heribert *m.e.p.* '39 (SFR)[K] San Francisco, CA Home for the Aged of the Little Sisters of the Poor; [N] San Francisco, CA Paris Foreign Mission Society Residence Retired.
Duquette, Don Bosco *o.f.m.cap.* '64 (PRT) Portland, ME St. Joseph's.
Duquette, Roy H. '58 (SPR) Retired.
Dura, Eduardo '77 (SFR) San Francisco, CA St. Patrick.
Durack, Jerome F. *s.j.* '60 (FgM) Chicago, IL Society of Jesus.
Duran, Ernesto '42 (BRK) Retired.
Duran, Jorge '75 (SAT) On Leave.
Duran, Said '95 (TYL) On Duty Outside the Diocese.
Duran–Ortega, Alfonso *o.de m.* '98 (SB) Riverside, CA Our Lady of Guadalupe Shrine.
Durand, Donald '58 (P) Retired.
Durant, Thomas M. '76 (SY) Whitesboro, NY St. Anne; Whitesboro, NY St. Paul.
Durante, Charles '94 (RNO) Carson City, NV St. Teresa of Avila; Vicar General; Diocesan Board of Consultors; Finance Council; Seminary Board; Presbyteral Council; Priest Personnel Board; Life, Peace & Justice Commission.
Durazo, Marco Antonio '07 (LA) Oxnard, CA Santa Clara.
Durbin, John G. '79 (R) Chapel Hill, NC St. Thomas More.
Durchholz, Jack J. '95 (EVN) Diocesan Council of Priests.
Durchholz, Jack '95 (EVN) Clergy Personnel Board.
Durchholz, Jack '95 (EVN) Ferdinand, IN St. Ferdinand.
Durette, Mathias D. *o.s.b.* '93 (MAN)[K] Manchester, NH St. Anselm Abbey.
Durette, Robert *o.m.i.* '60 (FgM) Washington, DC AMERICAN OBLATE MISSIONS.
Durham, DePorres C. *o.p.* '90 (CHI)[D] Oak Park, IL Fenwick High School; [N] River Forest, IL St. Thomas Aquinas Priory.
Durham, Neil *s.d.s.* '82 (MIL)[P] Milwaukee, WI Salvatorians – Jordan Hall Retired.
Durian, Ariel *c.s.* '05 (LA) Sun Valley, CA Our Lady of the Holy Rosary.
Durig, D. Kent '93 (WH) Weirton, WV Sacred Heart of Mary.
Duris, Lawrence M. '69 (CHI) Chicago, IL St. Ailbe.
Durkee, David R. '80 (CLV) Uniontown, OH Queen of Heaven.
Durken, Daniel *o.s.b.* '56 (SCL)[I] Collegeville, MN St. John's Abbey, of the Order of St. Benedict.
Durkin, Daniel '73 (FTW) Fort Wayne, IN St. Henry; Fort Wayne, IN Sacred Heart.
Durkin, Edward J. *s.j.* '75 (BUF)[O] Buffalo, NY Canisius Jesuit Community Inc.; [G] Cheektowaga, NY Catholic Central School.
Durkin, Eugene F. '49 (CHI) Chicago, IL Holy Name Cathedral Retired.
Durkin, James J. '68 (CAM) Vocation Advisory Board; [I] Cherry Hill, NJ St. Mary's Catholic Home, Cherry Hill, N.J.
Durkin, John F. '99 (ATL) Duluth, GA St. Monica.
Durkin, John L. '67 (NY) Amenia, NY Immaculate Conception.
Durkin, Patrick J. *c.s.v.* '52 (LAV)[C] Las Vegas, NV Clerics of St. Viator Retirement Home.
Durkin, Patrick J. *c.s.v.* '52 (CHI)[N] Arlington Heights Viatorian Province Center–Clerics of St. Viator.
Durney, Charles W. '63 (PH) Retired.
Durr, Edmund J. '65 (SY) Retired.
Durso, Michael H. *s.j.* '66 (STL)[O] St. Louis, MO De Smet Jesuit High School Community.
Duru, Hippolytus '97 (NEW) Livingston, NJ St. Barnabas Medical Center; West Orange, NJ Our Lady of Lourdes; Bronx, NY St. Francis Xavier; Bronx, NY North Central Bronx Hospital; Bronx Municipal Hospital Center, Abraham Jacobi Hospital, Nathan B. VanEtten Hospital.
Duschl, Frederick J. '65 (TOL) College of Consultors; Retrouvaille Retired.
Dusecina, Regis J. '73 (PBR) Greensburg, PA St. Nicholas of Myra.
Dushack, Rev. Msgr. Douglas L. '72 (MAD) Middleton, WI St. Bernard; Vicar for Priests.
Dusheck, Leo *s.v.d.* '61 (TR)[N] Bordentown, NJ Society of the Divine Word.
Dussan, Luis *c.m.f.* '49 (SAT) San Antonio, TX Immaculate Heart of Mary Retired.
Dusseault, Emile C. *m.s.* '54 (HRT)[L] Hartford, CT Missionaries of LaSalette.
Duster, Charles *s.s.c.* '61 (CHI) Council:; [N] Chicago, IL Columban Fathers Mission Center.
Duster, Charles *s.s.c.* '61 (OM)[K] St. Columbans Missionary Society of St. Columban.
Duston, Alan *o.p.* (SEA) Defenders of the Bond.
Duston, Thomas L. '92 (MAN) Londonderry, NH St. Mark the Evangelist; Deaf Ministry; Pastoral Council; Public Policy Commission.
Dusza, Donald W. '83 (ALT) Bedford, PA St. Thomas.
Dutel, Gilbert J. '70 (LAF) Eunice, LA Annunciation of the B.V.M.; Eunice, LA St. Anthony of Padua.
Dutkiewicz, Eugene M. *s.j.* '61 (MIL)[Y] Milwaukee, WI The Jesuit Partnership; [P] Milwaukee, WI Jesuit Provincial Office, Wisconsin Province; Milwaukee, WI; [P] Milwaukee, WI Jesuit Community at Marquette University.
Dutra, David '07 (STO)[G] Stockton, CA St. John Vianney House of Formation; Stockton, CA St. Mary of the Assumption Church (Pastor of); Modesto, CA St. Stanislaus Church (Pastor of); Vocations.
Dutra, Luis C. '55 (LAF)[H] Lafayette, LA De La Salle Christian Brothers Retired.
Dutram, Charles J. '58 (WOR) Retired.
DuVall, W. Scott '09 (RCK) Huntley, IL St. Mary.
Duvelius, Dennis M. '96 (IND) Tell City, IN St. Paul; Deaneries and Deans; Tell City, IN St. Mark.
DuWell, Ralph '00 (ORL) Northern; Lady Lake, FL St. Timothy.
Dux, Rev. Msgr. John H. '73 (STA) Retired.
Duyka, Stephen J. '97 (TYL) Advocates.
Duyka, Stephen '97 (TYL) Rusk, TX Sacred Heart; Rusk, TX Jerry H. Hodge Unit and Sky View Unit, Texas Department of Corrections.
Duyshart, Edwin C. '84 (LA) Altadena, CA St. Elizabeth of Hungary.
Dvorak, Donald *o.p.* '57 (DAL)[J] Irving, TX Dominican Priory of St. Albert the Great and Novitiate.
Dvorak, Franklin A. '70 (OM) Deans; Deans; Omaha, NE St. Elizabeth Ann.
Dvorak, Gerald '79 (STP) Hopkins, MN St. Joseph's.
Dvorscak, James '76 (JOL) Mokena, IL St. Mary Church.
Dwomoh, Charles '86 (VIC) Defenders of the Bond; Palacios, TX St. Anthony's; Diocesan Consultors; Edna Deanery; Presbyteral Council; Priests' Personnel Board.
Dworak, Joseph '65 (ALB) Priests Retirement Board/ Priests Retirement Plan Board; Hudson Falls, NY Church of St. Mary's/St. Paul's.
Dworak, Walter W. '72 (PIT) Pittsburgh, PA St. Philip.
Dwyer, Arthur J. *m.m.* '49 (SJ)[M] Los Altos, CA Maryknoll; [M] Los Altos, CA Maryknoll.
Dwyer, Daniel P. *o.f.m.* '88 (ALB)[B] Siena College; Provincial Councilors:.
Dwyer, David P. *c.s.p.* '00 (NY)[EE] New York, NY Paulist Fathers' Motherhouse.
Dwyer, Rev. Msgr. Donald M. '79 (NY) Bronx, NY Our Lady of the Assumption; Bronx (East).
Dwyer, Eugene F. *s.j.* '59 (DET)[K] Clarkston, MI Colombiere Center.
Dwyer, James *s.s.c.* '58 (PRO)[P] Bristol, RI St. Columban's Retirement House.
Dwyer, James *s.s.c.* '58 (OM)[K] St. Columbans Missionary Society of St. Columban.
Dwyer, John A. '74 (WOR) Lunenburg, MA St. Boniface.
Dwyer, John F. '56 (NY) Tappan, NY Our Lady of the Sacred Heart.
Dwyer, John '56 (NY) Retired.
Dwyer, Kevin F. *o.s.a.* '62 (BO)[C] North Andover, MA Merrimack College.
Dwyer, Robert D. '62 (SY) Bainbridge, NY St. John the Evangelist.
Dwyer, Thomas P. *o.s.a.* '53 (FgM) Villanova, PA Province of St. Thomas of Villanova (Eastern).
Dwyer, Timothy *s.m.* '68 (SAT)[L] San Antonio, TX Casa Maria Marianist Community.
Dy, Angel '69 (DOD) Fowler, KS St. Anthony Catholic Church of Fowler, Kansas; Meade, KS St. John the Baptist Catholic Church of Meade, Kansas; Plains, KS St. Patrick Catholic Church of Plains, Kansas.
Dyachok, Petro '89 (STN) San Francisco, CA Immaculate Conception Catholic Church; Santa Clara, CA St. Volodymyr.
Dybas, Richard W. '59 (ALB) Schenectady, NY St. John the Evangelist Retired.
Dye, David M. '92 (ATL) Norcross, GA Mary Our Queen Catholic Church.
Dye, Robert M. '91 (TLS) Hispanic Ministry; Tulsa, OK St. Francis Xavier Church and Diocesan Marian Shrine & Expiatory Temple of Our Lady of Guadalupe.
Dyer, Francis X. *o.p.* '69 (CHI)[N] Chicago Dominicans (Provincial Office).
Dyer, Gene J. '85 (CHI) Des Plaines, IL St. Mary.
Dyer, George J. '53 (CHI) Wadsworth, IL St. Patrick Retired.
Dyer, Hugh Vincent *o.p.* '08 (HRT) New Haven, CT St. Mary's Priory.
Dyer, James W. '97 (STL) Farmington, MO St. Joseph.
Dyer, Joseph '74 (JKS) Forest, MS St. Michael; Forest, MS St. Michael; [H] Forest, MS East Central Community College Newman Center; Priests' Council.
Dyer, Raymond E. '46 (PRO) Retired.
Dyer, Thomas P. '69 (Y)[C] Louisville, OH St. Thomas Aquinas High School; [P] Louisville, OH St. Thomas Aquinas High School Endowment Fund; Sebring, OH St. Ann.
Dyer, Rev. Msgr. Timothy J. '74 (LA) Los Angeles, CA Nativity; Los Angeles, CA St. Columbkille; Deanery 16; Our Lady of the Angels Region; Members.
Dygula, Rafal *s.ch.* (CHI) Chicago, IL Five Holy Martyrs.
Dygula, Rafal '96 (JOL) Lombard, IL Divine Mercy Polish Mission.
Dykas, Benjamin '71 (ALT) Retired.
Dyke, Neil Van '98 (CHI) Stickney, IL St. Pius X.
Dylag, Michael R. '65 (GBG) Retired.
Dymek, Mariusz Andrej *o.s.p.p.e.* (NY) Yonkers, NY St. Casimir.
Dymowski, Thomas H. *o.ss.t.* (SAT) Special Assignment.
Dymowski, Tom *o.ss.t.* '85 (BAL)[S] Individuals in Other Locations:.
Dymski, J. Daniel '60 (E) Retired.
Dynek, Wieslaw A. '74 (MO) Army Chaplains.
Dyrcz, Michael S. '73 (CLV) Retired.
Dyrwal, Justin *o.s.b.* '98 (CLV)[N] Cleveland, OH.
Dysinger, Luke *o.s.b.* '86 (LA)[P] Valyermo, CA St. Andrew's Abbey; Members; [A] Camarillo, CA St. John's Seminary.
Dytkowski, Louis M. '60 (BGP) Retired.
Dzengelski, Martin G. '07 (BO) West Roxbury, MA Holy Name.
Dzermejko, David F. '74 (PIT) Charleroi, PA Mary Mother of the Church.
Dziadek, Vladimir '82 (SP) Gulfport, FL Most Holy

Name of Jesus.
Dziak, Theodore A. *s.j.* '83 (NO)[C] New Orleans, LA Loyola University New Orleans.
Dziak, Theodore A. *s.j.* (BO)[U] Boston The Society of Jesus of New England–Provincial Offices.
Dziedziak, Robert T. '05 (VEN) Sarasota, FL St. Patrick.
Dziedzic, Gerald H. '74 (HRT) Terryville, CT Immaculate Conception; Terryville, CT St. Casimir; Appointed Members.
Dzieglewicz, John T. *s.j.* '83 (NY)[EE] Cardinal Spellman Hall, Jesuit Community.
Dziekan, Wayne H. '94 (GAY) Justice and Peace.
Dzielak, Rev. Msgr. Thomas L. '63 (RCK) Rock Falls, IL St. Andrew; Tampico, IL St. Mary; Deans; Council of Catholic Women, Diocesan; Ecumenism, Office of; Pro Synodal Judges.
Dzien, Joseph Duc '83 (NO) Des Allemands, LA St. Gertrude; Paradis, LA St. John the Baptist.
Dzien, Marek (STA) St. Augustine, FL San Sebastian.
Dzieszko, Thaddeus '88 (CHI) Chicago, IL St. Constance; [T] Chicago, IL Catholic League for Religious Assistance to Poland.
Dzikowski, Piotr *s.ch.* '87 (SEA) Tacoma, WA SS. Peter & Paul; Polish Speaking, Ministry to.
Dziob, Rev. Msgr. Michael W. '42 (PRO)[P] Providence St. John Vianney Residence Retired.
Dziordz, Walter *m.i.c.* '84 (JOL) Darien, IL Our Lady of Peace.
Dziorek, Anthony *c.r.* '75 (CHI) Chicago, IL St. Stanislaus, Bishop and Martyr; Councilors:.

E

Eagan, Joseph F. *s.j.* '53 (MIL)[P] Wauwatosa, WI Jesuit Community at St. Camillus.
Eagan, William J. *s.j.* '75 (BGP)[O] Fairfield, CT The Fairfield Jesuit Community–Fairfield University; [E] Fairfield, CT Fairfield College Preparatory School.
Eagle, Raphael *t.o.r.* '67 (FWT) Fort Worth, TX St. Bartholomew.
Eale, Francois–Xavier (HRT) Orange, CT Holy Infant.
Earl, John '94 (RCK) Elgin, IL St. Joseph.
Earl, Marcellus R. *o.c.s.o.* '63 (ROC)[J] Piffard, NY Abbey of the Genesee.
Earl, Patrick F. (CHL) Charlotte, NC St. Peter.
Earley, James Kiernan *c.p.* '57 (MET)[I] South River Passionist Provincial Office Retired.
Earley, Jerome *o.c.d.* '95 (DAL)[H] Dallas, TX Mount Carmel Center; [J] Dallas, TX Mt. Carmel Center.
Earley, Phillip B. '74 (BO) Wilmington, MA St. Thomas of Villanova; Catholic Charities Senior Management.
Earls, John Patrick *o.s.b.* '65 (SCL)[I] Collegeville, MN St. John's Abbey, of the Order of St. Benedict.
Early, Francis J. '85 (WDC) Bushwood, MD Sacred Heart.
Early, William F. '68 (BRK) Retired.
Earner, Rev. Msgr. Thomas '62 (SP) Retired.
Earthedath, Sebastian *m.s.t.* '86 (SP) New Port Richey, FL Our Lady Queen of Peace.
Earthman, Michael G. '07 (GAL) Houston, TX Holy Name; Houston, TX Our Lady of Walsingham.
East, Rev. Msgr. Raymond G. '81 (WDC) Washington, DC St. Teresa of Avila.
Easterling, William T. '82 (LA) Covina, CA Sacred Heart.
Eastman, Patrick W. '84 (TLS) Retired.
Easton, Rev. Msgr. Frederick '66 (IND) Indianapolis, IN St. Gabriel the Archangel; Vicariate Judicial Metropolitan Tribunal.
Easton, Rev. Msgr. William H. '70 (DET) Presbyteral Council; Royal Oak, MI National Shrine of the Little Flower; [D] Royal Oak, MI Shrine Catholic High School; Archdiocesan Vicars.
Eaton, John *o.f.m.* '78 (NSH) Nashville, TN St. Vincent de Paul; Presbyteral Council; [H] Nashville, TN Franciscan Friars.
Ebach, Aloys *c.pp.s.* '74 (KC)[A] Kansas City, MO Gaspar Mission House; [A] Liberty, MO Society of the Precious Blood Provincial Offices; [J] Liberty, MO Precious Blood Society Provincial Office; Liberty, MO; Kansas City, MO Sacred Heart–Guadalupe.
Ebarb, Walter E. '62 (SHP) Retired.
Ebarb, Walter '62 (SAT) San Antonio, TX Retired.
Ebben, Betrand E. *o.p.* '59 (R)[F] Raleigh, NC Dominican Priory.
Ebbesmier, John '78 (PHX) Youngtown, AZ Church of St. Joachim & St. Anne Roman Catholic Parish.
Ebejer, Lino P. '91 (WH) Retired.
Ebel, Stephen P. '70 (DAV) Knoxville, IA St. Anthony's; Melcher, IA Sacred Heart.
Eberhart, Lewis '04 (LAN) University of Michigan Hospitals/Pastoral Dept.
Eberle, Paul '05 (BIS) Hague, ND St. Mary; Strasburg, ND Sts. Peter and Paul; Strasburg, ND St. Michael.
Eberle, Richard *o.s.f.s.* '82 (LAN) Hudson, MI Sacred Heart; Manitou Beach, MI St. Mary on the Lake.
Ebert, Douglas '09 (STP) Lakeville, MN All Saints.
Ebert, James A. '09 (ALB) Ballston Spa, NY St. Mary.
Ebert, Mark S. '76 (STL) Ballwin, MO Holy Infant.
Ebey, Carl F. *c.s.c.* '72 (FTW)[B] University of Notre Dame Du Lac; [H] Notre Dame, IN Holy Cross Community, Corby Hall, University of Notre Dame.
Ebker, Daniel '06 (PEO) Canton, IL St. Mary's.
Eble, James E. *m.m.* '88 (FgM) Maryknoll, NY MARYKNOLL.
Eblen, James '64 (SEA) Special Assignment; Theological Resources; Judges Retired.
Ebner, Patrick '04 (AUS) Bryan, TX St. Anthony; Bryan, TX San Salvador.
Ebright, James A. '05 (CHL) Salisbury, NC Sacred Heart.
Ebrom, Robert L. '71 (CHI) Elk Grove Village, IL Queen of the Rosary.
Ebron, Jose Erlito '93 (NEW) Kenilworth, NJ St. Theresa's.
Ebulueme, Theophilus '95 (NSH) Clarksville, TN Immaculate Conception.
Eburn, Brian '68 (STA) Fernandina Beach, FL St. Michael's.
Ebuziem, Cajetan '96 (LFT)[E] Lafayette, IN Emmaus House; [C] Lafayette, IN St. Elizabeth Central.
Ecandon, Luis '06 (DEN) Denver, CO St. Mary Magdalene.
Eccleston, John '55 (SCL) Retired.
Echekwu, Kyrian C. '92 (BRK) Elmhurst, NY Ascension.
Echert, John P. '87 (MO) South St. Paul, MN Holy Trinity; South St. Paul, MN St. Augustine; Air National Guard Chaplains.
Echeverria, Miguel *o.a.r.* '61 (LSC) Chaparral, NM St. Thomas More Church.
Echeverria, Pedro Faustino '84 (PCE) Aguirre, PR Sacred Heart.
Echevia, Les Suberi '61 (RCK) Retired.
Eck, Ivan C. '51 (WCH) Mount Hope, KS St. Rose; Mount Hope, KS St. Joseph; Mt. Hope, KS St. Louis.
Eck, John E. *c.s.v.* '63 (CHI)[N] Arlington Heights Viatorian Province Center–Clerics of St. Viator; [N] Chicago, IL Viatorian Residence.
Eck, Reinhard C. '50 (WCH) Andale, KS St. Joseph.
Eckard, John '00 (BAL) Priests Sick or Absent.
Eckart, Frank K. '69 (TOL) Toledo, OH Sacred Heart of Jesus; Toledo, OH St. Stephen; Members.
Eckart, Placidus *o.s.b.* '49 (LR)[A] Subiaco, AR Subiaco Abbey.
Eckberg, Joseph A. '00 (WCH) Hutchinson, KS Church of the Holy Cross.
Ecker, Rev. Msgr. John A. '58 (YAK) Yakima, WA St. Paul Cathedral; Naches, WA St. John; Vicar General; Diocesan Consultors; Ecumenical Liaison; Diocesan Finance Council; Clergy Personnel Board; Presbyteral Council Executive Committee; Lay Advisory Board.
Ecker, Rev. Msgr. Robert J. '51 (BRK) Retired.
Eckerman, Felix *s.v.d.* '47 (CHI)[N] Techny, IL Divine Word Residence.
Eckermann, Rev. Msgr. Charles H. '56 (SY) Retired.
Eckert, John C. '72 (PH) Morrisville, PA Holy Trinity.
Eckert, Sidney J. '66 (DET) Warren, MI St. Cletus.
Eckert, Thomas J. *c.s.c.* '03 (FTW)[H] Notre Dame, IN Holy Cross Community, Corby Hall, University of Notre Dame.
Eckert, Tom *c.s.c.* '03 (FTW)[B] University of Notre Dame Du Lac.
Eckert, William F. '64 (CAM) Retired.
Eckhoff, Evan *o.f.m.* '57 (KNX)[B] Knoxville, TN St. Mary's Health System, Inc.
Eckinger, Ambrose *o.p.* '81 (WIL) Newark, DE St. Thomas More Oratory; Catholic Campus Ministry; Newark, DE University of Delaware; [O] Newark, DE Catholic Campus Ministry, Univ. of Delaware.
Eckley, Michael P. '91 (OM) Winnebago, NE St. Joseph; Winnebago, NE St. Augustine's; Macy, NE Our Lady of Fatima; Homer, NE St. Cornelius.
Eckman, Mark A. '85 (PIT) Pittsburgh, PA St. Thomas More; College of Consultors; Clergy Personnel Board; Priest Council.
Eckroth, Leonard A. '58 (BIS) Retired.
Eckroth, Richard *o.s.b.* '52 (SCL)[I] Collegeville, MN St. John's Abbey, of the Order of St. Benedict.
Eckstein, Francis J. '58 (IND) Retired.
Eco, Roy V. '80 (ORL) Ocala, FL Blessed Trinity.
Edakkulathoor, Joseph *c.m.i.* '89 (COV) Falmouth, KY St. Francis Xavier.
Edamattan, Thomas '66 (RVC) Huntington, NY St. Patrick's; Huntington, NY Huntington Hospital.
Edassery, Davis *s.a.c.* '88 (MIL)[P] Milwaukee, WI Pallotti House.
Edathumparambil, Binu *m.s.f.s.* '00 (TYL)[B] Whitehouse, TX The Missionaries of St. Francis de Sales.
Edayadiyil, Jose *v.c.* '73 (SCL) Isanti, MN St. Elizabeth Ann Seton.
Eddy, William A. '75 (CHI) Chicago, IL St. Hilary.
Edelen, Luke A. *o.s.b.* '80 (NEW)[M] Newark, NJ Newark Abbey; Archdiocesan Commission of Christain Unity; [P] Jersey City, NJ New Jersey City University, Gilligan Student Union.
Edelen, Mark D. '08 (LEX) West Liberty, KY Prince of Peace.
Edelen, Richard D. '75 (LEX) Lexington, KY Pax Christi Catholic Church.
Edelen, Thomas '01 (TYL) Trinity, TX Most Holy Trinity; Diocesan Catholic School Advisory Council.
Eden, Timothy E. *s.m.* '77 (HON)[A] Honolulu, HI Chaminade University of Honolulu; [A] Honolulu, HI Chaminade University of Honolulu.
Eden, Timothy *s.m.* '77 (HON)[D] Honolulu, HI Center Marianist Community; [G] Honolulu, HI Our Lady the Mystical Rose Chapel; Members.
Edens, William L. *c.s.p.* (OAK) Berkeley, CA Holy Spirit Parish/Newman Hall.
Eder, Donald '54 (LAN) Retired.
Eder, Donald '60 (LFT) Retired.
Ederer, John A. '77 (SAG) Retired.
Edgerly, Leo J. '84 (OAK) Piedmont, CA Corpus Christi; Cursillo Movement.
Ediza, Manuel '79 (SD) San Diego, CA St. Michael; Presbyteral Council.
Edlefsen, Frederick H. '01 (ARL)[K] Fredericksburg, VA University of Mary Washington; Fredericksburg, VA St. Mary of the Immaculate Conception.
Edmunds, Garret *o.f.m.* '82 (FgM) Oakland, CA St. Barbara Province.
Edmunds, Garrett *o.f.m.* '82 (OAK)[M] Oakland Franciscan Friars (Province of St. Barbara); Washington, DC.
Edmunds, Garrett *o.f.m.* '82 (FgM) Washington, DC COMMISSARIAT OF THE HOLY LAND; [N] Washington, DC Franciscan Monastery USA Inc.; [N] Washington, DC Commissariat of the Holy Land, Franciscan Monastery – Mount St. Sepulchre.
Edmunds, John S. *s.t.* '76 (FgM) Silver Spring, MD MISSIONARY SERVANTS OF THE MOST HOLY TRINITY; Silver Spring, MD; Silver Spring, MD Missionary Servants of the Most Holy Trinity (Trinity Missions).
Edmunds, John S. *s.t.* '76 (WDC)[N] Silver Spring, MD Missionary Servants of the Most Holy Trinity; [N] Riverdale, MD Holy Spirit Missionary Cenacle.
Edney, Mark *o.p.* (NO)[S] Metairie, LA International Dominican Foundation.
Edogwo, Linus V. '86 (NEW) Newark, NJ St. Mary's.
Edomobi, Eustace '75 (NEW) Newark, NJ St. Michael Medical Center; [G] Newark, NJ Saint Michael's Medical Center; Newark, NJ The Parish of the Transfiguration.
Eduarte, Edmund P. '93 (GAL) Freeport, TX St. Mary: Star of the Sea; Humble, TX St. Mary Magdalene; George Bush Intercontinental Airport.
Eduvala, Andre *o.f.m.cap.* '04 (AGN)[F] Agana Heights, GU St. Fidelis Friary.
Edwards, Brice *c.p.* '70 (MET)[I] South River Passionist Provincial Office Retired.
Edwards, Brice *c.p.* '70 (SCR)[M] Scranton, PA Saint Ann's Passionist Monastery.
Edwards, Byron H. '87 (SPC) Retired.
Edwards, Charles A. '86 (SFD) Highland, IL St. Paul.
Edwards, Cyril D. '84 (SCR) Scranton, PA Holy Rosary; Scranton, PA St. Anthony of Padua; Scranton, PA St. Joseph's.
Edwards, Dale '83 (FWT) Retired.
Edwards, David A. '02 (BEA) Diocesan College of Consultors; Mont Belvieu, TX Holy Trinity; Presbyteral Council.
Edwards, Guy F. '85 (OG) Dannemora, NY St. Joseph; Altona, NY Altona Correctional Facility; Dannemora, NY Clinton Correctional Facility.
Edwards, J. Daniel '94 (LAF) Lafayette, LA St. Jules.
Edwards, James T. '76 (STL) On Medical Leave Retired.
Edwards, Michael W. '79 (PMB) Propagation of the Faith & Missionary Cooperative Plan; Assessors; Consultors; Ex Officio.
Edwards, Michael W. '79 (PMB) Vero Beach, FL St. Helen; Vicars Forane.
Edwards, Philip *o.s.b.* '67 (LA)[P] Valyermo, CA St. Andrew's Abbey; [V] Valyermo, CA St. Andrew's Abbey Retreat Center (All Groups).
Edwards, Robert '81 (Y) Lisbon, OH St. George; Charismatic Prayer Group.
Edwards, Tom J. '90 (OAK)[L] Oakland, CA Bishop Begin Villa.
Edyk, Rev. Msgr. Eugene '61 (DET) Retired.
Effiong, Noel *m.s.p.* '89 (RVC) West Hempstead, NY St. Thomas, the Apostle.
Efiong, Emmanuel '89 (CHR) Pickens, SC Holy Cross.
Efodigbue, Ayo E. *m.s.p.* '94 (BR) Donaldsonville, LA St. Catherine of Siena; Presbyteral Council.
Eftink, Rev. Msgr. Edward M. '66 (SPC) Priests' Mutual Benefit Society Retired.
Eftink, Glenn A. '93 (SPC) Charleston, MO St. Henry; Sikeston, MO St. Francis Xavier's.
Egan, Arthur B. '57 (CLV) Avon, OH St. Mary of the Immaculate Conception Retired.
Egan, Brennan R. *o.f.m.* (BO)[U] Boston, MA St. Christopher Friary.
Egan, Brennan *o.f.m.* (FR)[G] Onset, MA St. Joseph Friary–Franciscan Friars.
Egan, Rev. Msgr. Brian '50 (BIR) Birmingham, AL Our Lady of Sorrows Retired.
Egan, Rev. Msgr. Eugene E. '54 (WIN) Retired.
Egan, Gerard P. '65 (CHI) Other Assignments.
Egan, Harvey D. *s.j.* '69 (BO)[U] Newton, MA The

Jesuit Community at Boston College.
Egan, John Martin *o.p.* '56 (WDC)[B] Washington, DC Dominican House of Studies.
Egan, Patrick '66 (LAN)[P] Ann Arbor, MI Catholic Men's Movement.
Egan, Patrick *o.s.b.* '08 (BIR) Cullman, AL Sacred Heart.
Egan, Philip '82 (KC) Clinton, MO Holy Rosary; Deans.
Egan, Robert J. *s.j.* '62 (SEA)[L] Seattle, WA Arrupe Jesuit Community at Seattle University.
Egan, Robert J. *s.j.* '73 (SPK)[B] Spokane, WA Gonzaga University.
Egan, Robert M. *c.s.v.* '78 (CHI)[D] Arlington Heights, IL St. Viator High School; [N] Arlington Heights Viatorian Province Center–Clerics of St. Viator.
Egan, Thomas F. '75 (WOR) Leominster, MA Holy Family of Nazareth.
Egan, Thomas R. *m.m.* '74 (FgM) Maryknoll, NY MARYKNOLL.
Egargo, Fernando '92 (RVC) West Hempstead, NY St. Thomas, the Apostle.
Egbe, Dozie '95 (PIT) Pittsburgh, PA Word of God.
Egbe, Paul '95 (MOB) Ozark, AL St. John.
Egbeji, Jude '89 (NY) Sleepy Hollow, NY St. Teresa of Avila.
Egbers, James B. '96 (COV) Deans; Alexandria, KY St. Mary of the Assumption.
Egedegbe, William *m.s.p.* '98 (BR) Prairieville, LA St. John the Evangelist.
Eggert, Rev. Msgr. Francis X. '58 (SFE) Albuquerque, NM Our Lady of Fatima.
Eggert, Rev. Msgr. Francis '58 (SFE) College of Consultors; Presbyteral Council of the Archdiocese of Santa Fe.
Egging, Martin L. '93 (GI) Loup City, NE St. Josaphat's; Ravenna, NE Our Lady of Lourdes; Diocesan Consultors.
Eggleston, Earl '96 (SD) San Diego, CA Our Lady of Angels; Liturgy and Spirituality.
Eggleton, Christopher T. *o.p.* '88 (FgM) Metairie, LA St. Martin de Porres Province (Southern Dominican Province).
Eggleton, Christopher *o.p.* '80 (NO)[P] New Orleans Dominican Friars, Southern Dominican Province of St. Martin de Porres.
Eghiabumhe, Fabian '04 (NY) Beacon, NY St. John the Evangelist.
Egierd, Henry A. '80 (MET) Retired.
Egitto, Philip J. '88 (ORL) Daytona Beach, FL Our Lady of Lourdes.
Egloff, Adolph '40 (EVN) Retired.
Eglsaer, Harry S. *s.j.* '51 (MIL)[P] Wauwatosa, WI Jesuit Community at St. Camillus.
Ego, Anthony M. '85 (PEO) Milan, IL St. Ambrose.
Eguaras, Jesus *c.m.* '70 (NY) New York, NY Holy Agony; [EE] New York, NY Vincentian Fathers; New York, NY.
Eguiguren, Jose Martin '61 (CGS) Caguas, PR Santisimo Sacramento.
Eguino, Desiderio *o.p.* '78 (MIA) Miami, FL St. Dominic; [K] Miami, FL Dominican Fathers of Miami, Inc.
Ehalt, William L. '99 (IND) Spencer, IN St. Jude the Apostle.
Ehiemere, Michael '81 (CHY) Greybull, WY Sacred Heart.
Ehli, Joshua J. '09 (BIS) Dickinson, ND Queen of Peace Church; [C] Dickinson, ND Trinity High School.
Ehmke, Lyle *o.s.c.* '70 (PHX)[F] Crosiers Serving Abroad.
Ehmke, Matthew (STP) Edina, MN Our Lady of Grace.
Ehr, Donald J. *s.v.d.* '55 (CHI) Chicago, IL St. Anselm.
Ehrhardt, Joseph B. *o.f.m.* '67 (FgM) New York, NY Holy Name Province.
Ehrich, John D. '00 (PHX) Phoenix, AZ St. Thomas the Apostle Roman Catholic Parish; Presbyteral Council.
Ehrman, Dale W. '90 (LFT)[I] Noblesville, IN Hamilton County Catholic High School Corporation, Blessed Theodore Guerin High School; [B] Noblesville, IN Saint Theodore Guerin High School; Westfield, IN St. Maria Goretti; Associate Directors.
Ehrman, Terrence P. *c.s.c.* '00 (FTW)[H] Notre Dame Congregation of Holy Cross, Indiana Province, Provincial House.
Ehwald, Joseph A. '62 (COL) Retired.
Eichenberger, Thomas P. '76 (MIL) Mequon, WI St. Francis Borgia.
Eichenseer, Rev. Msgr. Donald W. '61 (BEL) Defensores Vinculi; Diocesan Finance Council; Albers, IL St. Bernard; Damiansville, IL St. Damian.
Eichhoff, Paul '70 (TLS) Diocesan Senators; Claremore, OK St. Cecilia; Diocesan Consultors.
Eichhorst, Franklin *o.f.m.cap.* '57 (LSC) Carrizozo, NM St. Rita.
Eichner, Philip K. *s.m.* '66 (RVC)[D] Uniondale, NY Kellenberg Memorial High School.
Eichor, Rev. Msgr. Edward C. '59 (STL) Retired.
Eichorn, Harry B. *c.s.c.* '57 (FTW)[H] Notre Dame Congregation of Holy Cross, Indiana Province, Provincial House.
Eickhoff, Jeffrey R. '95 (LIN)[A] Seward, NE St. Gregory the Great Seminary; Pro Life.
Eickhoff, Matthew '89 (LIN) Brainard, NE Holy Trinity; Commission for Sacred Liturgy and Sacred Music; Engaged Encounter; Evangelization Office; Evangelization Committee; Family Life Office; Marriage Encounter; Natural Family Planning; PREP; Teens Encounter Christ (TEC); Ecumenical Affairs, Commission for.
Eid, Elie '07 (NTN) Plymouth, MI St. Michael.
Eid, Rev. Msgr. Frederick M. '47 (NEW) Retired.
Eifler, John G. '61 (L) Retired.
Eikens, Leroy F. '62 (WIN) Stewartville, MN Retired.
Eilen, Allan Paul '09 (STP) Hastings, MN St. Elizabeth Ann Seton.
Eilerman, Craig R. '87 (COL) Columbus, OH Christ the King.
Eilers, Brian Joseph '04 (AUS)[L] San Marcos, TX Texas State University, H.L. Grant Catholic Student Center.
Eilert, Rev. Msgr. Edward J. '64 (NEW)[M] Rutherford, NJ St. John Vianney Residence for Priests Retired.
Eimer, Frank J. '58 (L) Retired.
Eiroa, Andres '88 (MGZ)[D] Mayaguez, PR Opus Dei (Prelature of the Holy Cross and Opus Dei); Mayaguez.
Eis, Charles R. '66 (SPK) DEPARTMENT OF VETERANS AFFAIRS HOSPITALS AND CHAPLAINS Retired.
Eisel, Howard P. *s.s.c.* '54 (PRO)[P] Bristol, RI St. Columban's Retirement House Retired.
Eisel, Howard *s.s.c.* '54 (OM)[K] St. Columbans Missionary Society of St. Columban.
Eisele, Francis X. '54 (RVC) East Rockaway, NY St. Raymond's.
Eisele, James F. '88 (LAN) College of Consultors; Priests' Assignment Commission; Grand Ledge, MI St. Michael.
Eisele, Paul F. '68 (SC) Alton, IA St. Mary's; Hospers, IA St. Anthony's.
Eisemann, Frederick F. '53 (ROC) Rochester, NY Holy Cross Retired.
Eisweirth, Thomas '74 (Y) Leetonia, OH St. Patrick; Salem, OH St. Paul.
Eivers, Rev. Msgr. Michael J. '55 (MIA) Pembroke Pines, FL St. Edward.
Ejaidu, Cyril Ngbede '95 (AUS) Waco, TX St. John the Baptist.
Ejike, John '78 (FAR) Rugby, ND St. Theresa, Little Flower Church of Rugby.
Ejimabo, Nichodemus '96 (AUS) Blanco, TX St. Ferdinand.
Ejimadu, Festus N. '93 (DET) Farmington, MI St. Gerald.
Ejimofor, Francis *s.s.sp.* '90 (TOL)[G] Toledo, OH St. Vincent Mercy Medical Center; Toledo, OH St. Vincent Mercy Medical Center; Toledo, OH St. Hedwig.
Ejimofor, Joseph '77 (LR) Fordyce, AR Good Shepherd; Sheridan, AR Holy Cross; Benton, AR Our Lady of Fatima.
Ejiofo, Lawrence '99 (LIN) David City, NE St. Mary's.
Ekada, Santulino *o.c.d.* '03 (MIL)[P] Milwaukee Provincial Offices – Discalced Carmelites.
Ekaitis, Timothy M. '07 (MAR) Marquette, MI St. Peter Cathedral.
Ekdahl, Kenneth W. '91 (TR) Keyport, NJ Jesus the Lord.
Eke, Anselm *m.s.p.* '92 (BEA) Orange, TX St. Therese.
Eke, Casimir *c.s.sp.* '74 (CHI) Blue Island, IL St. Isidore.
Eke, Peter O. '97 (GAY) Judge; Gaylord, MI St. Mary Cathedral; Elmira, MI St. Thomas Aquinas; Grayling, MI St. Mary; Gaylord, MI Holy Redeemer.
Eke, Rafael E. '01 (SAT) Army Chaplains; Military Chaplains.
Ekechukwu, Alexander *c.s.sp.* '73 (MIA) Miami, FL St. Agatha; FIU–University Park; Nigerian Apostolate.
Ekekwe, Kenneth '00 (BUR) Bethel, VT St. Anthony.
Ekemgba, Fidelis '81 (SCR)[I] Williamsport, PA Divine Providence Hospital of the Sisters of Christian Charity.
Ekenachi, Donatus '83 (LA) Santa Clarita, CA Our Lady of Perpetual Help.
Ekeocha, James '07 (AUS) Austin, TX St. Thomas More; Associate Directors.
Ekeocha, James '07 (AUS) Serra Club – Austin.
Ekeocha, John Onyenanu '93 (CAM) Woodbury, NJ St. Patrick's Church, Woodbury.
Ekete, Damian (NY) Bronx, NY Our Lady of Mercy.
Ekiert, Ireneusz *o.ss.t.* '00 (BAL)[S] The Trinitarians in New Jersey.
Ekiert, Ireneusz *o.ss.t* '00 (TR) Asbury Park, NJ Our Lady of Mt. Carmel.
Ekka, Louis T. '89 (LAN) Flushing, MI St. Robert.
Ekpo, Joseph '86 (CHI) Bellwood, IL St. Simeon; [D] Oak Park, IL Fenwick High School.
Ekwoanya, John C. (NU) New Ulm, MN St. Mary.
Ekwueme, Clifford '83 (NY) Port Jervis, NY Immaculate Conception.
Ekwugh, Francis '82 (BAK) Council of Priests and Diocesan Consultors.
Ekwugha, Francis Xavier '82 (BAK) Burns, OR Holy Family.
El–Hayek, Nehmatallah '62 (SAM) Retired.
El–Khalli, Georges Y. '81 (SAM) Williamsville, NY St. John Maron; Religious Education; Presbyteral Council; Protopresbyters (Deans); College of Consultors.
Elam, Ray *o.s.a.* '70 (MIL) Racine, WI St. Rita.
Elambassery, Xavier '66 (SJP) Latrobe, PA Assumption of B.V.M.; Arbitration Board; Presbyters.
Elamparayil, Joseph *o.c.d.* '96 (ARL) Falls Church, VA St. James.
Elanjileth, J. Matthew '45 (PIT) Retired.
Elanjileth, John M. '50 (PIT) Allegheny County, PA McKeesport UPMC.
Elanjimattathil, Michael *c.m.i.* '96 (SAL) Oakley, KS St. Joseph Parish; Oakley, KS St. Paul Parish; Council of Priests.
Elayidathamadam, Mathew *m.s.f.s.* '96 (TYL)[B] Whitehouse, TX The Missionaries of St. Francis de Sales.
El Basha, Assaad *m.l.m.* '92 (OLL) Lewisville, TX Our Lady of Lebanon Maronite Catholic Church; [A] Houston, TX The Congregation of Maronite Lebanese Missionaries.
Elbert, William '73 (MIA) North Miami Beach, FL St. Lawrence; Spiritual Moderators.
Elder, Gregory '06 (SB) Ecumenical Office; Murrieta, CA St. Martha.
Elder, John W. *s.j.* '65 (BGP)[O] Fairfield, CT The Fairfield Jesuit Community–Fairfield University Retired.
Elder, Leonard F. *s.c.j.* '96 (JKS) Holly Springs, MS St. Joseph; [E] Nesbit, MS St. Michael Community House.
Elder, William S. '81 (NY) New York, NY Our Lady of Good Counsel; Judicial Vicar; Judges.
Eldred, Richard W. '99 (IND) Bedford, IN St. Vincent de Paul; Mitchell, IN St. Mary/Assumption.
Eldredge, Richard *t.o.r.* '78 (FWT) Diocesan Pastoral Council; Presbyteral Council and Consultors; Colleyville, TX Good Shepherd; Mission Council.
Eldridge, Darren J. '07 (LAF) Eunice, LA St. Mathilda.
Eldridge, Francis *s.a.* '77 (LA) Los Angeles, CA St. Odilia.
Eldridge, Francis *s.a.* '77 (NY)[EE] Garrison Graymoor Ecumenical and Interreligious Institute.
Eldringhoff, John P. '68 (KC) Retired.
Elejalde, Manuel *c.p.* '49 (SJN) Carolina, PR Nuestra Senora de la Piedad.
Eles, Joseph '65 (PSC) Retired.
Elewaut, Thomas J. *c.j.* '86 (LA)[F] Santa Barbara, CA Bishop Garcia Diego High School Inc.
Elford, Hugh Ricardo *c.ss.r.* (TUC)[F] Cortaro, AZ Redemptorist Society of Arizona Desert House of Prayer.
Elford, Ricardo *c.ss.r.* '64 (DEN)[N] Denver The Redemptorists/Denver Province.
Eli, Jude *o.p.* '76 (OAK)[M] Oakland, CA Order of Preachers (Province of the Most Holy Name of Jesus – Western Dominican Province); Oakland, CA.
Eli, Judi *o.p.* '76 (LA) Los Angeles, CA St. Dominic.
Elia, Chorbishop Faouzi '77 (OLL) Peoria, IL St. Sharbel Maronite Catholic Church; [F] St. Louis, MO Eparchial Endowments; Pastoral Center; College of Consultors; Office for Immigration; Presbyteral Council.
Elia, Victor *c.m.* '57 (NY) New York, NY Holy Agony; [EE] New York, NY Vincentian Fathers; New York, NY.
Elias, Benjamin (BRK) Brooklyn, NY St. Mary Mother of Jesus.
Elias, Mario '93 (SD) San Diego, CA St. Columba.
Elias–Haddix, Ralph *o.c.d.* '98 (MIL) Milwaukee, WI St. Florian.
Elie, Matthew '05 (BEL) Belleville, IL Our Lady Queen of Peace; Belleville, IL Blessed Sacrament.
Elis, Patrick H. '69 (BUF) Buffalo, NY St. Rose of Lima.
Elis, Tomas Alfonso '70 (LA) Goleta, CA St. Mark University Parish Retired.
Elizardo, Pedro T. '01 (CC) On Special Assignment; Presbyteral Council.
Elizardo, Pedro (Pete) T. '01 (CC) Corpus Christi, TX Corpus Christi Cathedral.
Elizardo, Pete '01 (CC) Office of Youth And Young Adult Ministry; Office of Worship; [I] Corpus Christi, TX Search Retreats; [I] Corpus Christi, TX FirePower Retreats; [I] Corpus Christi, TX Teens Encounter Christ and Church "TECC".
Elizondo, Ernesto '00 (AUS) Manor, TX St. Joseph.
Elizondo, Ruben *o.m.i.* '62 (FgM) Washington, DC AMERICAN OBLATE MISSIONS.
Elizondo, Virgil '63 (SAT) San Antonio, TX St. Rose of Lima.
Elizondo, Virgilio P. (FTW)[B] University of Notre Dame Du Lac.
Elkhoury, Armando '04 (OLL) Lakewood, CO St. Rafka Maronite Catholic Church.
El Khoury, Armando (OLL) Eparchial Webmaster; Presbyteral Council; Office of Priestly Vocations.
El Khoury, Pierre '98 (OLL)[A] Houston, TX The Congregation of Maronite Lebanese Missionaries; Houston, TX Our Lady of the Cedars Maronite

Catholic Church.
Elkin, Rev. Msgr. Frederic F. '77 (SY) Military Chaplains.
Elko, Joseph M. '70 (HRT) New Haven, CT Saint Martin de Porres.
Eller, Hugh *o.f.m.* '53 (PAT)[N] Butler, NJ St. Anthony Friary.
Ellerman, Thomas E. *s.m.* '67 (OAK)[M] Berkeley, CA Marist Fathers and Brothers.
Ellias, John J. '64 (ALT) Retired.
Ellickal, Saji *m.c.b.s.* '00 (MEM) Memphis, TN St. Louis.
Elliot, Thomas *c.s.c.* '67 (BGP)[P] Wilton, CT Lourdes Health Care Center, Inc.
Elliott, Gregg '00 (TLS)[E] Tulsa, OK Jane Phillips Health Corp.
Elliott, Joseph W. '71 (OG) Willsboro, NY Catholic Community of St. Philip of Jesus of Willsboro (1909) & St. Joseph of Essex (1872).
Elliott, Joseph *c.ss.r.* '49 (LA) Whittier, CA St. Mary of the Assumption; [P] Whittier, CA Redemptorists of Whittier Retired.
Elliott, Patrick H. '00 (SLC) Ogden, UT Holy Family LLC 205.
Elliott, Roger *c.p.* '58 (SCR)[M] Scranton, PA Saint Ann's Passionist Monastery.
Elliott, Ron '73 (OM)[G] Omaha, NE Archbishop Bergan Mercy Medical Center.
Elliott, Ronald J. '02 (KC) Blue Springs, MO St. John La Lande; Consultors; Permanent Diaconate.
Elliott, Thomas A. '99 (LR) Fort Smith, AR Christ the King; [B] Fort Smith, AR Trinity Junior High; Presbyteral Council.
Elliott, Thomas F. *c.s.c.* '67 (FTW)[H] Notre Dame Congregation of Holy Cross, Indiana Province, Provincial House.
Elliott, Thomas *c.s.c.* '67 (BGP)[P] Wilton, CT School Sisters of Notre Dame Motherhouse (Northeastern Province).
Elliott, Timothy P. '82 (STL) Lake Saint Louis, MO Saint Gianna.
Elliott, Trumie C. '88 (L) Springfield, KY St. Dominic.
Elliott, W. Gregg '00 (TLS) Special Assignment.
Elliott, William J. *s.j.* '61 (WDC)[E] North Bethesda, MD Georgetown Preparatory School.
Elliott, Rev. Msgr. William '60 (SD) Retired.
Elliott, Zachary *o.f.m.* '08 (NEW) East Rutherford, NJ St. Joseph's; [M] East Rutherford, NJ Sacred Heart Friary.
Ellis, Alfred J. *o.s.a.* '63 (ALB) Troy, NY St. Augustine.
Ellis, John H.R. '91 (VEN) Retired.
Ellis, Kail C. *o.s.a.* '67 (PH)[C] Villanova University; [Y] Villanova, PA St. John Stone Friary.
Ellis, Matthew '88 (DET) Marine City, MI Our Lady on the River.
Ellorin, Raymund '91 (HON) Honokaa, HI Our Lady of Lourdes.
Ellos, William J. *s.j.* '68 (MIL)[P] Milwaukee Jesuit Provincial Office, Wisconsin Province.
Elmer, Rev. Msgr. Charles '53 (AUS) On Duty Outside the Diocese; [A] Houston, TX St. Mary's Seminary.
Elmer, Gregory *o.s.b.* '76 (LA)[P] Valyermo, CA St. Andrew's Abbey.
Elmer, John *o.f.m.conv.* '73 (IND)[J] Mount St. Francis, IN Mount Saint Francis Friary and Retreat Center; Clarksville, IN St. Anthony of Padua.
Elmer, Richard J. *c.s.b.* '57 (DET)[E] Novi, MI Catholic Central High School.
Elmer, Timothy S. '73 (SY) Western Area Vicars; Management Team; Presbyteral Council; Judicial Vicar; Syracuse, NY St. Daniel; Board of Diocesan Consultors.
Elorriaga, Javier *o.ss.t.* '68 (PCE) Ponce, PR La Santisima Trinidad.
Elsasser, Thomas G. '88 (CLV) Mentor, OH St. Mary of the Assumption.
Elsbernd, James H. '90 (CIN) On Special and Archdiocesan Assignment; Hamilton, OH St. Joseph.
Elsen, Vincent *o.f.m.* '47 (FWT)[H] Crowley, TX St. Maximilian Kolbe Friary.
Elser, William '86 (LR) Benton, AR Our Lady of Fatima.
Elshoff, Matthew G. *o.f.m.cap.* '82 (SFR)[N] Burlingame, CA Capuchin Provincial House.
Elskamp, Frederick J. '62 (JC) Diaconate Office; California, MO Annunciation; Tipton, MO St. Andrew.
Elsner, Martin L. *s.j.* '62 (SAT) San Antonio, TX Our Lady of Guadalupe.
Elston, Joseph G. '85 (SCR) On Special or Other Diocesan Assignment; Ministry with Deaf and Hard of Hearing.
Elukunnel, Joseph Dominic *s.a.c.* '80 (MIL)[P] Milwaukee, WI Pallotti House.
Eluvathingal, Jose *s.a.c.* '85 (MIL)[P] Milwaukee, WI Pallotti House.
Ely, Peter B. *s.j.* '69 (SEA)[A] Seattle, WA Seattle University; [L] Seattle, WA Arrupe Jesuit Community at Seattle University.
Elyse, Esteker *s.m.m.* '64 (MIA) Miami, FL St. Mary's Cathedral.
Elzi, Joseph *c.m.* '52 (CHL) Charlotte, NC Our Lady of Guadalupe Church.
Emagalit, Zeverin '72 (NY)[X] Poughkeepsie, NY St. Francis Hospital; Poughkeepsie, NY St. Francis Hospital.
Emanuel, John '92 (TUC) Retired.
Emanuel, Steve (OM)[B] Omaha, NE Daniel J. Gross Catholic High School of Omaha.
Emechete, Innocent '72 (MO) Navy Reserve Chaplains.
Emeh, Augustine (BRK) Peninsula Hospital Center; St. John's Episcopal Hospital; Far Rockaway, NY St. Mary Star of the Sea and St. Gertrude.
Emeh, Martins '02 (RCK) Geneva, IL St. Peter; Vice Chancellor; Special Assignment.
Emeli, Edwin '88 (TUC)[C] Tucson, AZ Carondelet St. Mary's Hospital.
Emerick, Stephen J. '58 (CIN) Retired.
Emerson, George F. '56 (BO) Norwood, MA St. Timothy; Senior Priests.; Presbyteral Council; College of Consultors Retired.
Emery, Rev. Msgr. Robert E. '87 (NEW) South Orange, NJ Our Lady of Sorrows.
Emezie, Charles '83 (SFS)[D] Aberdeen, SD Avera St. Luke's; [D] Aberdeen, SD Avera St. Luke's.
Emille, Cyprien (NY) Bronx, NY Our Lady of Grace.
Emmanuel, Joseph '81 (NY) Tuckahoe, NY Immaculate Conception.
Emmons, Rayford E. '74 (PH) Philadelphia, PA Our Lady of Hope.
Empereur, James L. *s.j.* '65 (SAT) San Antonio, TX St. Matthew's.
Emrisek, Gene *o.f.m.cap.* '68 (DEN) Denver, CO Sacred Heart; [N] Denver, CO San Antonio Friary.
Emusa, Peter '97 (LAF) Carencro, LA Our Lady of the Assumption; Scott, LA Saint Martin de Porres.
Encinares, Rev. Msgr. Cesar E. '77 (SB) Loma Linda, CA Loma Linda Community Hospital; Loma Linda, CA Loma Linda U.M.C. East Campus.
Enciso, Dario Moreno *m.s.c.* '04 (FgM) Aurora, IL MISSIONARIES OF THE SACRED HEART.
Endebrock, Rev. Msgr. Donald M. '51 (MET) Carteret, NJ St. Joseph Retired.
Endejan, John '57 (MIL) Retired.
Enderle, Gilbert *c.ss.r.* (STL)[O] Liguori, MO Liguori Mission House/Redemptorists.
Enderlin, Joseph J. '46 (LR)[G] Little Rock, AR St. John Manor Retired.
Enderlin, R. E. '69 (PEO) Retired.
Enderlin, Ronald '69 (PEO) Lacon, IL Immaculate Conception.
Endiape, Dario '93 (MET) Basking Ridge, NJ St. James.
Endres, David J. '09 (CIN) Dayton, OH St. Albert the Great.
Endres, Gilbert J. '52 (STP) Retired.
Endres, James F. '82 (PH)[D] Warminster, PA Archbishop Wood Catholic High School; [T] Warminster, PA Regina Coeli Residence for Priests.
Endres, John C. *s.j.* '76 (OAK)[A] Berkeley, CA Jesuit School of Theology at Santa Clara University; [M] Berkeley, CA Jesuit Fathers and Brothers.
Endres, William '69 (ROC) Scottsville, NY St. Mary of the Assumption; Strong Health System; East Rochester, NY St. Jerome.
Endress, James '60 (EVN) Retired.
Ene, Herbert '97 (MEM) African Catholic Ministry; Memphis, TN Cathedral of the Immaculate Conception.
Enegbuma, Richard J. '80 (NY) Staten Island, NY St. Christopher.
Enelichi, Alphonsus *m.s.p.* '90 (GAL) Barrett Station, TX St. Martin de Porres; Houston, TX St. Peter the Apostle.
Enette, Rawlin B. *s.s.j.* '59 (GAL) Houston, TX St. Peter Claver; Houston, TX Our Lady Star of the Sea.
Engbarth, David R. '76 (RCK) Aurora, IL Our Lady of Good Counsel.
Engbers, Thomas '67 (MIA) Retired.
Engel, Paul *o.f.m.cap.* '64 (NY)[EE] White Plains, NY St. Conrad Friary.
Engel, Paul '55 (ALB) Delanson, NY Our Lady of Fatima Retired.
Engelbrecht, S. Stephen '00 (PEO) Andalusia, IL St. Patrick Church.
Engelhardt, Charles F. *o.s.f.s.* '77 (PH) Philadelphia, PA Resurrection of Our Lord; [Y] Wyndmoor, PA Villa de Sales Oblate Residence.
Engelhardt, Rev. Msgr. Herbert G. '40 (BUF) Retired.
Engelhart, Henry R. '63 (BEL) Retired.
Engels, Richard J. '60 (WIN) Retired.
Engen, Bruce '89 (DUL) Pine River, MN Our Lady of Lourdes Retired.
Engh, Michael E. *s.j.* '81 (SJ)[B] Santa Clara University.
England, Barry C. '68 (FTW) Mishawaka, IN St. Bavo.
Engle, Richard F. '56 (COL) Zaleski, OH St. Sylvester Retired.
Engler, Chapin '07 (WH) Inwood, WV St. Leo.
Engler, Clarence A. *m.m.* '59 (FgM) Maryknoll, NY MARYKNOLL.
Engler, Ernest J. '51 (DUB) Retired.
Engler, Simon Mary *t.o.r.* '49 (ALT)[G] Loretto, PA St. Francis Friary at Mount Assisi.
Englert, Michael *o.f.m.conv.* '89 (PMB) Port St. Lucie, FL St. Lucie.
English, James M. *s.j.* '66 (BAL)[S] Baltimore, MD Colombiere Jesuit Community.
English, Joseph *o.f.m.cap.* '90 (AGN)[F] Agana Heights, GU St. Fidelis Friary; Archdiocesan Presbyteral Council.
English, Paul F. *c.s.b.* '85 (GAL)[B] Sugar Land, TX Basilian Fathers of Sugarland.
English, Robert K. '88 (OM) Omaha, NE Mary Our Queen.
English, Rev. Msgr. Tobias P. '63 (LA) Pasadena, CA St. Andrew Retired.
English, William J. '60 (BO) Quincy, MA Holy Trinity.
English, Rev. Msgr. William J. '69 (WDC) Potomac, MD Our Lady of Mercy.
Engo, Michael '97 (FR) On Duty Outside the Diocese.
Enin, James *m.i.c.* '91 (JOL) Darien, IL Our Lady of Peace.
Enke, Rev. Msgr. Paul P. '72 (COL) Granville, OH St. Edward the Confessor.
Enlow, Rev. Msgr. Leo J. '75 (SFD)[E] Effingham, IL St. Anthony High School; Effingham, IL St. Anthony of Padua; Shumway, IL Annunciation; Effingham Deanery.
Enman, Frederick *s.j.* '88 (BO)[U] Newton, MA The Jesuit Community at Boston College.
Enneking, Marvin '91 (SCL) Vicar General; Judges; Diocesan Consultors; Diocesan Corporate Board; Diocesan Finance Council; Presbyteral Council; Diocesan Priests Pension Plan Trustees; Personnel Committee; St. Cloud, MN St. Wendelin's; Directors.
Enneking, Thomas A. *o.s.c.* '84 (PHX) Provincial Councilors:; [F] Phoenix, AZ Crosier Community of Phoenix (Canons Regular of the Order of the Holy Cross).
Enneking, Thomas *o.s.c.* '84 (CHI)[N] Chicago, IL Crosier Community of Chicago.
Ennis, Timothy *o.carm.* '02 (ALB) Troy, NY St. Joseph.
Ennis, William '64 (ORL) Orlando, FL Holy Family.
Enright, Edward J. *o.s.a.* '73 (BO)[C] Our Mother of Good Counsel Monastery.
Enright, Edward *o.s.a.* (PH)[C] Villanova University.
Enright, James C. '69 (BUF) Retired.
Enright, John P. '53 (CHI) Retired.
Enright, Michael P. '84 (CHI) Chicago, IL St. Paul.
Enright, Thomas M. '66 (CHI) Niles, IL Our Lady of Ransom.
Enriquez, Alex '85 (TR) Red Bank, NJ St. James.
Enriquez, David '06 (FRS) Orange Cove, CA St. Isidore the Farmer.
Enriquez, Juan '80 (LA) Lynwood, CA St. Philip Neri.
Enriquez, Miguel '08 (DEN) Aurora, CO St. Pius X.
Enriquez, Rean F. '93 (MO) Navy Chaplains.
Ensey, Eric S. '95 (SCR) Unassigned or Leave of Absence.
Enslow, Batholomew *s.s.j.* '49 (BLX) Pass Christian, MS Our Mother of Mercy.
Ensman, Raymond E. '66 (TOL) Retired.
Enverga, Edgardo *c.r.m.* '86 (CHR) Moncks Corner, SC St. Philip Benizi.
Enyan–Boadu, Peter '84 (ROC) Brockport, NY Nativity of the Blessed Virgin Mary.
Enzler, Rev. Msgr. John J. '73 (WDC) Washington, DC Blessed Sacrament, Shrine of the Most; Archdiocesan College of Consultors; Vicar of Development.
Enzler, Rev. Msgr. John '73 (WDC) Priest Council; Staff.
Enzweiler, Rev. Msgr. Donald A. '87 (COV) Kenton, KY St. Matthew; Diocesan Tribunal.
Enzweiler, Raymond N. '06 (COV)[B] Covington, KY Covington Latin School; Covington, KY Cathedral, Basilica of the Assumption.
Ephraim, John B. '99 (RVC) Roslyn, NY St. Francis Hospital.
Epie, Franklin N. '06 (BWN) McAllen, TX Rio Grande Regional Hospital.
Epima, Felix '00 (PIT) Pittsburgh, PA Word of God.
Eppenbrock, Donald J. '60 (SAG) Cass City, MI St. Pancratius; Gagetown, MI St. Agatha Retired.
Epperley, Wayne *c.s.sp.* '83 (SB) Hemet, CA Our Lady of the Valley.
Epperson, Frank '01 (SR) Crescent City, CA St. Joseph; Deans; Board of Consultors; Priests' Council.
Epping, Robert L. *c.s.c.* '70 (COS) Colorado Springs, CO Sacred Heart; Metro–South Deanery (Colorado Springs); Presbyteral Council; College of Consultors; Vicars Forane.
Eppler, Jeff *s.o.l.t.* '03 (CC)[G] Robstown, TX Society of Our Lady of the Most Holy Trinity.
Eppler, Jeff *s.o.l.t.* '03 (FAR) Dunseith, ND St. Michael the Archangel Dunseith.
Era, John *c.m.* (CHI)[N] Chicago DePaul Vincentian Residence.
Eraly, Mathew '75 (MO) DEPARTMENT OF VETERANS AFFAIRS HOSPITALS AND CHAPLAINS.
Eraly, Mathew '87 (NEW) East Orange, NJ Veterans Administration Hospital.
Eraly, Matthew '75 (NEW) Livingston, NJ St. Philomena.

Erb, Francis J. '54 (ROC) Addison, NY St. Stanislaus Retired.
Erbacher, Joseph '72 (EVN) Loogootee, IN St. John; Loogootee, IN St. Martin; Loogootee, IN St. Joseph; Loogootee, IN St. Mary's; Defender of the Bond.
Erbacher, William J. '87 (ARL) On Leave of Absence.
Erbland, Philip N. *m.m.* '66 (FgM) Maryknoll, NY MARYKNOLL.
Ercolano, Anthony S. '73 (BRK) On Leave/Unassigned.
Erdei, Joseph J. *o.s.b.m.* '58 (PSC)[A] Matawan, NJ Basilian Fathers of Mariapoch.
Erdeljac, Frank G. '83 (PIT) Retired.
Erden, Harry J. *o.s.a.* '57 (PH)[Y] Malvern, PA Augustinian Friars (O.S.A.).
Erdle, Thomas M. '55 (ROC) Rochester, NY St. Margaret Mary Retired.
Erdlen, Harry J. *o.s.a.* '57 (PH)[F] Malvern, PA Malvern Preparatory School for Boys.
Erestain, Alfonso E. '64 (MO) DEPARTMENT OF VETERANS AFFAIRS HOSPITALS AND CHAPLAINS.
Erhart, Henry J. *s.j.* '55 (PH)[Y] Loyola Center and Manresa Hall.
Erhimeyoma, Edwin (NY) Bronx, NY Holy Rosary.
Ericksen, Matthew '09 (SAV) Augusta, GA St. Joseph.
Erickson, David '97 (PEO) On Duty Outside the Diocese.
Erickson, David '98 (CHY) Lander, WY Holy Rosary.
Erickson, John Paul '06 (STP) St. Paul, MN St. Agnes; Worship.
Erickson, Matthew *o.p.* '90 (WDC)[B] Washington, DC Dominican House of Studies.
Erickson, Philip Lee '95 (L) Louisville, KY Our Lady of Mount Carmel; Louisville, KY St. Thomas More; Adjutant Judicial Vicar.
Erickson, Richard M. '85 (MO) Air Force Reserve Chaplains.
Erickson, Robert E. *c.s.v.* '67 (CHI)[N] Arlington Heights, IL Viatorian Province Center–Clerics of St. Viator.
Erickson, Robert J. '58 (SB) Retired.
Erickson, Robert L. *s.j.* '74 (GF) Hays, MT St. Paul's Indian Mission.
Erickson, Scott Matthew *o.p.* '90 (NY)[EE] New York, NY St. Catherine of Siena Priory; New York, NY.
Erikson, Richard M. '85 (BO) Vicar General and Moderator of the Curia; Presbyteral Council; Vicars General; Members; College of Consultors; Ex Officio; West Roxbury, MA Holy Name; [CC] Braintree, MA Caritas Christi Retirement Plan and Trust; Ex Officio; Health Benefit Trust, Insurance and Pension Trusts, Caritas Christi Retirement Plan; Chair; Trustees.
Erlander, Michael '68 (STP)[C] St. Paul, MN University of St. Thomas Retired.
Erlander, Michael (STP) Retired.
Erlenbush, Ryan '09 (GF) Special Assignment.
Ermatinger, Cliff *l.c.* '97 (CHI) Cicero, IL St. Frances of Rome.
Ermer, James '78 (FAR) Casselton, ND St. Thomas; Casselton, ND St. Leo's Church of Casselton.
Ermis, Norman '83 (SAT) San Antonio, TX St. Margaret Mary.
Ernest, Bryan D. '82 (GI) Ogallala, NE St. Luke's; Personnel Board; Priests' Advisory Board (Presbyteral Council).
Ernest, Matthew S. '04 (NY) Graduate Studies.
Ernest, Stephen *s.v.d.* '67 (OAK) Oakland, CA St. Bernard.
Ernst, Anthony '98 (EVN) Fort Branch, IN Holy Cross; Haubstadt, IN SS. Peter and Paul; Fort Branch, IN St. Bernard.
Ernst, Jeff *o.f.m.cap.* '96 (COS)[I] Colorado Springs, CO Catholic Center at the Citadel; [F] Colorado Springs, CO Our Lady of the Angels Friary.
Ernst, Rev. Msgr. Norbert A. '72 (STL) St. Louis, MO St. Margaret Mary Alacoque.
Ernst, Stephen T. *s.t.* '86 (WDC)[N] Adelphi, MD Father Judge Missionary Cenacle.
Ernst, William W. '64 (IND) Retired.
Ernster, James M. '55 (MIL) Retired.
Ernster, Milo L. '55 (WIN) Retired.
Ernstmann, Rev. Msgr. Mark C. '51 (SPC) Retired.
Erondu, Isaac Emeka '93 (BWN) St. James; San Benito, TX Our Lady, Queen of the Universe.
Erpelding, Edward '66 (FTW) Avilla, IN St. Mary of the Assumption.
Erpelding, Michael J. '89 (SC) Sioux City, IA St. Joseph; Presbyteral Council; Judges; Adjutant Judicial Vicar.
Erps, James *s.j.* '80 (LA)[C] Los Angeles, CA Jesuit Community.
Errecalde, Javier *o.de.m.* '54 (SJN) San Juan, PR Nuestra Senora de la Merced.
Erro, Sabino *o.f.m.cap.* '54 (FWT) Fort Worth, TX Our Lady of Guadalupe.
Errosti, Mariano *o.f.m.* '50 (SJN) San Juan, PR Resurreccion del Senor.
Ertle, Thomas J. *o.p.* '56 (PRO)[P] Providence St. Thomas Aquinas Priory at Providence College.
Ertzbischoff, Edmond L. '76 (LAN) Ypsilanti, MI St. Joseph.
Eruo, Basil '99 (JC) Jefferson City, MO St. Peter.
Eruppakkatt, Joseph *s.s.p.* '88 (NY)[B] Staten Island, NY Society of St. Paul; Staten Island, NY.
Ervin, Mark W. '90 (WDC) Germantown, MD Mother Seton Parish.
Ervin, Thomas '74 (SFR) On Duty Outside the Archdiocese.
Erving, James *o.m.i.* (LAR) Eagle Pass, TX Our Lady of Refuge.
Erwin, Michael J. '98 (MIL) New Munster, WI St. Alphonsus; Twin Lakes, WI St. John the Evangelist.
Erwin, Patrick O. '68 (PAT) Absent on Leave.
Ery, Marianna '87 (RCK) Aurora, IL Holy Angels.
Esarey, Brian '04 (IND) Guilford, IN St. Paul; Guilford, IN St. Martin.
Escalante, Agustin '88 (LAR) Zapata, TX Our Lady of Lourdes.
Escalante, Augustin '88 (SFR) On Duty Outside the Archdiocese.
Escalante, Peter '78 (SD) San Diego, CA St. Joseph Cathedral; Clergy Personnel Board; Presbyteral Council.
Escalante, Ronald S. '95 (ARL) Purcellville, VA St. Francis de Sales.
Escanilla, Elias '84 (HON) Paia, HI Holy Rosary.
Escano, Mariano Regalado '09 (P) Eugene, OR St. Mary.
Esch, Aaron J. '09 (MIL) Study Leave.
Esch, Eugene *o.s.b.* '54 (B) Glenns Ferry, ID Our Lady of Limerick Station; [C] Jerome, ID Monastery of the Ascension.
Eschbach, Victor J. '72 (PH) Parkesburg, PA Our Lady of Consolation; Diocesan Priests' Compensation and Benefits Committee.
Eschweiler, Edward R. '48 (MIL) Retired.
Esclanda, Derrick '99 (DAL)[I] Irving, TX Opus Dei; Irving.
Escobar, Agustin '87 (ORG) Orange, CA St. Norbert.
Escobar, Joseph A. '88 (PRO) Providence, RI Our Lady of the Rosary; College of Consultors.
Escobedo, Armando '64 (BWN) Retired.
Escobedo, Gilberto '00 (ORG) Costa Mesa, CA St. Joachim.
Escurel, Armando P. '79 (SD) San Diego, CA St. Rita.
Eseke, Anthony M. '96 (STA) Gainesville, FL St. Augustine.
Esenther, Keith J. *s.j.* '71 (CHI)[C] Chicago, IL Jesuit Community at Loyola University Chicago.
Esguerra, Bernadino '87 (TR) Brick Town, NJ Epiphany; Lakewood, NJ St. Mary of the Lake.
Esguerra, Martin *m.id.* (NY) Bronx, NY Santa Maria.
Esguerra–Lopez, Martin *id.m.* '08 (BRK)[E] Brooklyn, NY Campus Ministers and Ministry Centers.
Esker, Karl *c.ss.r.* '76 (FgM) Baltimore Province.
Eskind, Rev. Msgr. Jace F. '87 (LKC) Lake Charles, LA Immaculate Conception Cathedral; Diocesan Board of Administration; Vicar Judicial; Judges; Diocesan Consultors; Office For Worship; Presbyteral Council.
Esmilla, Efren V. '93 (PH) Philadelphia, PA Our Lady of Hope; Filipino Apostolate; College of Consultors.
Esmond, William '55 (ALB) Retired.
Espadas, Miguel Angel '09 (MEM) Memphis, TN Church of the Resurrection.
Espaillat, Joseph '03 (NY) Yonkers, NY St. Peter.
Esparza, Erik L. '08 (SB) Barstow, CA St. Joseph.
Espejel, Rene *c.s.b.* '87 (LSC)[B] Las Cruces, NM Basilian Fathers; Las Cruces, NM Cathedral of the Immaculate Heart of Mary.
Espelage, Arthur J. *o.f.m.* '71 (VEN) Venice, FL Our Lady of Lourdes; Judicial Vicar.
Espelage, Arthur *o.f.m.* '71 (CIN)[N] Cincinnati St. Francis Seraph Friary; Cincinnati, OH.
Espelage, Thomas '70 (CIN) Cincinnati, OH St. John the Evangelist.
Esper, Abraham L. '85 (SY) Baldwinsville, NY St. Augustine; Baldwinsville, NY St. Mary of the Assumption.
Esper, John C. '83 (DET)[T] Bloomfield Hills, MI Detroit Catholic Charismatic Renewal Center; Madison Heights, MI St. Vincent Ferrer.
Esper, Joseph M. '82 (DET) Lakeport, MI St. Edward's on the Lake.
Esper, Thomas '51 (DET) Retired.
Espina, Ernesto E. *c.m.* '71 (SFR) San Francisco, CA St. Finn Barr.
Espinal, David '02 (BRK) On Leave/Unassigned.
Espinel, Luis *o.p.* '59 (SJN)[A] Bayamon Central University.
Espino, Jose '83 (MIA) Hialeah, FL San Lazaro.
Espinosa, Anthony L. '96 (OM) Schuyler, NE Divine Mercy.
Espinosa, David F. '98 (BRK) On Leave/Unassigned.
Espinosa, Donald *a.a.* '71 (BO)[U] Boston, MA Assumptionist Center; [U] Boston Assumptionist Center.
Espinosa, Eduardo *o.f.m.* '04 (GLP) Presbyteral Council; Diocesan Consultors.
Espinosa, Gabriel D. '07 (VIC) Wharton, TX Holy Family; Wharton, TX Our Lady of Mt. Carmel.
Espinosa, Julio *o.a.r.* (NEW) Union City, NJ St. Augustine's.
Espinosa, Melesio Peter '95 (AUS) Austin, TX Santa Barbara Catholic Church –Austin, Texas.
Espinoza, Carlos *o.f.m.* '85 (LSC) Garfield, NM San Isidro.
Espinoza, Eduardo *o.f.m.* '04 (GLP) Gallup, NM St. Francis of Assisi.
Espinoza, Galo *o.a.r.* '92 (LA) Los Angeles, CA Cristo Rey.
Espinoza, Luis A. '87 (TUC) Pirtleville, AZ Saint Bernard Roman Catholic Church – Pirtleville; Douglas, AZ Saint Luke Roman Catholic Church – Douglas; Douglas, AZ Immaculate Conception Roman Catholic Parish – Douglas.
Espinoza–Espinoza, Pedro '02 (MRY) Educational Leave.
Espiritu, Bernard *s.v.d.* (CHI) Chicago, IL St. Anselm.
Espona Jimenez, Juan (PCE) On Duty Outside the Diocese.
Esposito, Alberto '01 (STA) Flagler Beach, FL Santa Maria Del Mar.
Esposito, Anthony '56 (Y) Retired.
Esposito, Augustine M. *o.s.a.* '79 (PH)[F] Malvern, PA Malvern Preparatory School for Boys; [A] Wynnewood, PA Theological Seminary of St. Charles Borromeo, Overbrook; [Y] Malvern, PA Augustinian Friars (O.S.A.).
Esposito, Charles P. '99 (GBG) Kent, PA Church of the Good Shepherd.
Esposito, Rev. Msgr. Ernest T. '67 (BGP)[L] Trumbull, CT St. Joseph's Manor; Episcopal Vicar for Religious; Office for Clergy Personnel; District Spiritual Directors; Family Life Ministry Diocesan Office; Presbyteral Council; Trumbull, CT St. Stephen.
Esposito, Lawrence J. '76 (WOR) Linwood, MA Good Shepherd.
Esposito, Luigi '64 (BAL) Baltimore, MD Our Lady of Pompei; Baltimore, MD.
Esposito, Mario *o.carm.* '77 (ALB)[M] Germantown, NY Postulation Office; Middletown, NY.
Esposito, Mario *o.carm.* '77 (NY)[EE] Middletown, NY Carmelite Friars (North American Province of St. Elias).
Esposito, Ralph J. '67 (LR) Retired.
Esposito, Samuel J. '78 (PIT) McMurray, PA St. Benedict the Abbot.
Esposito, Stanislao '03 (WIL) Elkton, MD Immaculate Conception.
Esposito, William C. '58 (SY) Retired.
Esposito–Garcia, Juan '08 (WDC) Rockville, MD Shrine of St. Jude.
Esquerra, Martin I. '08 (NY)[EE] Bronx, NY Idente Missionaries – Santa Maria Residence.
Esquerro, Angel Miguel '68 (SJN) San Juan, PR San Jose Obrero.
Esquerro–Preciado, Miguel (SJN)[B] San Juan, PR Colegio Angeles Custodios.
Esquivel, Carlos *o.s.j.* '83 (FRS) Madera, CA St. Joachim; Councilors:.
Esquivel, Giovanni Ruiz '00 (CGS)[B] San Lorenzo, PR Casa Charlie Rodriguez; [E] San Lorenzo, PR Diocesan Shrine Our Lady of Mount Carmel.
Esquivel, Rev. Msgr. John '68 (FRS) Reedley, CA St. Anthony of Padua; Advocates; Diocesan Consultors; Vicars Forane; Personnel Board; Priests' Council.
Ess, Thomas '66 (CHI)[N] Chicago, IL St. Peter's Friary.
Esseff, Rev. Msgr. John A. '53 (SCR)[N] Dunmore, PA Villa St. Joseph Retired.
Esselman, Thomas E. *c.m.* '80 (STL)[O] St. Louis, MO Vincentian Residence; [O] St. Louis, MO Vincentian Residence; Earth City, MO Western Province.
Essen, Peter Von *o.f.m.cap.* '56 (FgM) White Plains, NY Province of St. Mary.
Esser, James *o.f.m.* '67 (GB) Krakow, WI St. Casimir; [J] Wausaukee, WI Villa Alverna.
Esser, Paul M. '57 (MIL) Retired.
Essex, Rev. Msgr. Donald S. '73 (WDC) Bethesda, MD St. Jane Frances de Chantal.
Essig, Edward J. '94 (ALN) Frackville, PA St. Ann; Frackville, PA Annunciation B.V.M.
Essig, Herbert '74 (JOL) Bolingbrook, IL St. Francis of Assisi.
Essman, Ronald '80 (DET) Clinton Twp., MI St. Paul of Tarsus.
Essuon, James (NY) Staten Island, NY St. Clare.
Esswein, Michael J. '98 (STL) Kirkwood, MO St. Peter.
Estabrook, Kevin E. '09 (CLV) Parma, OH St. Columbkille.
Estada, Julio '59 (MIA)[J] Miami, FL Mercy Hospital.
Estadilla, Lino *o.m.v.* '06 (BO)[B] Boston, MA Oblate Provincialate.
Esteban, Antonio '85 (LA) South El Monte, CA Epiphany.
Esteban, Pedro Antonio '85 (LA) On Sick Leave.
Estensoro, Jose '60 (ARE) Retired.
Estepa, Isaias *o.a.r.* '94 (CC) Odem, TX Sacred Heart.
Estephan, Andre S. *m.l.m.* '90 (OLL) Houston, TX Our Lady of the Cedars Maronite Catholic Church; [A] Houston, TX The Congregation of Maronite Lebanese Missionaries.
Estephan, Andre *m.l.m.* (GAL)[M] Splendora, TX Shalom Center, Inc.
Estes, Dan *s.o.l.t.* '99 (CC)[G] Robstown, TX Society of Our Lady of the Most Holy Trinity; [I] Corpus Christi, TX.

Esteves, Jose *o.dem.* '58 (PCE)[D] Ponce, PR Residencia Santa Marta.
Estevez, Leobardo Almazan *o.p.* '05 (FgM) Metairie, LA St. Martin de Porres Province (Southern Dominican Province).
Estibalez, Inocencio '52 (SP) Retired.
Estilette, Grady J. '63 (LAF) Retired.
Estiverne, Saint–Martin (BRK) Brooklyn, NY St. Matthew.
Estok, Edward T. '85 (CLV) North Royalton, OH St. Albert the Great; Translators.
Estok, Edward T. '85 (CLV) Presbyteral Council.
Estorgue, Roger O. *o.p.* '85 (GAL) Houston, TX St. Dominic.
Estrada, Enrique J. '93 (MIA) Miami Beach, FL St. Joseph; Priests' Personnel Board.
Estrada, Enrique '79 (DOD) Liberal, KS St. Anthony of Padua Catholic Church of Liberal, Kansas.
Estrada, Hector Diaz '82 (SJN)[E] San Juan, PR VA Medical Center.
Estrada, Ignacio *s.v.d.* '03 (ORG)[G] Fullerton, CA St. Jude Medical Center.
Estrada, J. Manuel '86 (SFR) San Francisco, CA St. Peter.
Estrada, Jorge L. '07 (CHI) Argo, IL St. Blasé.
Estrada, Lawrence E. '80 (LA) Monterey Park, CA St. Stephen Martyr.
Estrada, Rafael A. '05 (SAV) Baxley, GA Good Shepherd.
Estrada, Richard *c.m.f.* '78 (LA) Los Angeles, CA Our Lady Queen of the Angels.
Estrada, Sabino '72 (BRK) Woodside, NY St. Sebastian Retired.
Estrada–Fernandez, Agustin '00 (SAT) San Antonio, TX St. Vincent de Paul.
Estrem, John '86 (STP) Special Assignment.
Esty, Gregory L. '75 (STP) St. Paul Park, MN St. Thomas Aquinas.
Esukpa, Emmanuel *m.s.p.* '92 (GAL) Houston, TX St. Peter the Apostle.
Etafo, Benedict (BRK) Brooklyn, NY St. Columba.
Ethen, Jeffrey D. '88 (SCL) Belgrade, MN St. Francis De Sales; Brooten, MN St. Donatus; Elrosa, MN SS. Peter and Paul; Navy Reserve Chaplains; Presbyteral Council.
Etheredge, F. William '83 (RCK) Special Assignment; [B] Aurora, IL Aurora Central Catholic High School.
Etienne, Bernard '93 (EVN) Diocesan Council of Priests; Special Assignment; Diocesan Consultors; Deans; Evansville, IN Holy Rosary; Vocation Office.
Etienne, Paul D. '92 (IND) Archdiocesan Review Board.
Etienne, Zachary J. '04 (EVN) Ireland, IN Annunciation of the Blessed Virgin Mary.
Etim, Idongesit A. '09 (WIL) New Castle, DE Our Lady of Fatima.
Etlinger, Peter J. *c.s.b.* '47 (ROC) Rochester, NY Christ the King.
Ettel, Dale *o.s.c.* '82 (PHX)[F] Phoenix, AZ Crosier Provincial House Province of St. Odilia.
Ettlinger, Gerard H. *s.j.* '66 (NY)[EE] New York Jesuit Provincial's Office.
Ettner, Wilhelm J. '93 (ARL) Woodstock, VA St. John Bosco.
Ettolil, Sebastian *m.c.b.s.* '68 (MAR) Ewen, MI Sacred Heart; Watersmeet, MI Immaculate Conception; Watersmeet, MI Lac Vieux Desert Reservation.
Etuale, Kolio '03 (SPP) Pago Pago, AS St. Paul; Director of Vocations; Faculty Members; Auditors; Diocesan Consultors; Pago Pago, AS St. Joseph the Worker Futiga.
Etuale, Viane '90 (SPP) Vicar General of Diocese; Pago Pago, AS Christ the King; Diocesan Consultors; Diocesan Pastoral Council; Faculty Members; Judges.
Eturi, Balaraju '95 (SCR) Jessup, PA St. James; Jessup, PA St. Mary's Assumption.
Etxeandia Ormaetzea, Jesús *c.p.* '59 (SJN) Carolina, PR Nuestra Senora de la Piedad.
Etzel, Peter J. *s.j.* '94 (MIL)[P] Milwaukee, WI Arrupe House Jesuit Community.
Etzel, Raymond A. '50 (TOL) Retired.
Euker, John T. '74 (GBG) Apollo, PA St. James the Greater; East Vandergrift, PA Our Lady, Queen of Peace.
Eurico, Francisco '94 (HRT) Waterbury, CT Our Lady of Fatima.
Eut, Vincent E. '86 (NY) White Plains, NY St. John the Evangelist.
Euteneuer, Thomas J. '88 (PMB) Released from Diocesan Assignment.
Euteneuer, Thomas J. '88 (ARL)[L] Front Royal, VA Human Life International.
Euteneuer, Thomas J. (MIA)[Q] Miami, FL Vida Humana Internacional.
Euvrard, Scott A. '94 (BO) Sharon, MA Our Lady of Sorrows.
Evancho, George '64 (PBR) Retired.
Evancho, Robert '79 (PSC) Saint Petersburg, FL St. Therese; Syncellus.
Evangelisto, Louis Anthony '54 (HRT) Retired.
Evanick, Michael '60 (PRM) Merrillville, IN St. Michael.
Evanish, Robin '83 (PIT) Carnegie, PA St. Elizabeth Ann Seton.
Evanko, Joseph J. '91 (SCR) Mountaintop, PA St. Jude.
Evanofski, Bernard P. '86 (VEN) Sarasota, FL Incarnation.
Evans, Edward '80 (WDC) Retired.
Evans, G. William '78 (TR) Eatontown, NJ St. Dorothea; [N] Trenton, NJ Villa Vianney.
Evans, George P. '77 (BO) Weston, MA St. Julia; Presbyteral Council.
Evans, George *s.s.s.* '57 (CLV)[N] Cleveland Congregation of the Blessed Sacrament Provincial House; [N] Richfield, OH Regina Health Center.
Evans, James L. '94 (AUS) Austin, TX St. John Neumann.
Evans, John R. '09 (RCK) Batavia, IL Holy Cross.
Evans, John '80 (FAR) On Duty Outside the Diocese.
Evans, John *o.p.* '04 (OAK)[M] Oakland, CA Order of Preachers (Province of the Most Holy Name of Jesus – Western Dominican Province).
Evans, John *o.p.* '04 (LA) Los Angeles, CA St. Dominic.
Evans, John '80 (WIN)[D] Rochester, MN Saint Mary Hospital.
Evans, Ken '86 (NEW) Roselle Park, NJ The Assumption.
Evans, Larry '01 (NEW)[D] Paramus, NJ Paramus Catholic High School; Archdiocesan Stewardship Advisory Committee.
Evans, Michael A. *s.j.* '83 (DET)[K] Detroit Jesuit Provincial Office–Detroit Province of the Society of Jesus; Detroit, MI Detroit Province.
Evans, Michael J. '92 (LA) Arcadia, CA Holy Angels.
Evans, Richard A. '82 (CLV) Parma, OH Holy Family.
Evans, Robert T. '03 (STL) Overland, MO Our Lady of the Presentation.
Evans, Timothy W. '94 (MOB) On Administrative Leave.
Evans, Wilfred F. '68 (SY) Syracuse, NY Veterans Administration Hospital Retired.
Evans, William Morris '81 (CHL) Retired.
Evard, Paul A. '61 (IND) Retired.
Evardoni, Luis '99 (GAL) Houston, TX St. Matthew the Evangelist.
Evardoni, Luis Paolo Agostino V. *d.s.* '99 (GAL)[O] Houston, TX St. Matthew the Evangelist.
Eve, Paul W. '82 (L) Louisville, KY Holy Spirit.
Evenson, Robert '91 (SEA) Snohomish County Jail; Seattle, WA Our Lady of Fatima; Special Assignment.
Everding, Richard F. '66 (STL) Retired.
Everett, Willis E. '90 (MO) On Duty Outside the Diocese; DEPARTMENT OF VETERANS AFFAIRS HOSPITALS AND CHAPLAINS.
Everitt, Edward E. *o.p.* '68 (BR) Hammond, LA Holy Ghost; Tickfaw, LA Our Lady of Pompeii; Presbyteral Council.
Evernden, Michael *c.s.p.* '74 (P) Portland, OR St. Philip Neri; [Q] Portland, OR Paulist Fathers Catholic Center for Evangelization; Area Vicars.
Evers, Gerard A. '40 (CIN) Retired.
Evers, Leonard M. '68 (GB) Cecil, WI St. Martin; Shawano, WI Sacred Heart; Gresham, WI St. Francis Solanus; Keshena, WI St. Michael.
Evers, Linus *c.pp.s.* '71 (JC) Senators; Sedalia, MO St. Patrick; Sedalia, MO Sacred Heart.
Evers, Rev. Msgr. Paul C. '54 (WIN) Retired.
Evers, Paul H. '80 (HON) On Duty Outside the Diocese.
Evers, Robert B. '60 (GRY) Retired.
Eversley, Garth *o.carm.* '03 (NY)[EE] Middletown, NY St. Albert's Priory.
Eversole, Paul M. '95 (ARL) Woodbridge, VA Our Lady of Angels.
Everts, Donald E. '95 (GB) Green Bay, WI Annunciation of the Blessed Virgin Mary; Green Bay, WI St. Joseph; Green Bay, WI St. Jude; Green Bay, WI St. Patrick.
Ewah, Boniface '98 (ROC) Corning, NY All Saints.
Ewald, Daniel P. '86 (JC) Milan, MO St. Mary; Marceline, MO St. Bonaventure.
Ewen, Sharbel *o.s.b.* '88 (SD)[J] Oceanside, CA Prince of Peace Abbey.
Ewenteang, Tatieru *m.s.c.* (CI) Chuuk, FM Mortlock.
Ewers, Paul J. *m.c.c.j.* '65 (CHI) Blue Island, IL St. Donatus.
Ewert, Michael *o.f.m.* '59 (SFD)[L] Springfield, IL Our Lady of Angels Friary.
Ewing, Matt J. *o.carm.* '54 (LA)[P] Encino, CA Our Lady of Mount Carmel Priory.
Extejt, John I. *o.s.f.s.* '85 (TOL)[C] Toledo, OH St. Francis de Sales High School; [I] Toledo, OH.
Extejt, Thomas J. '73 (TOL) Fremont, OH St. Ann.
Exume, Gilbert '08 (ATL) Johns Creek, GA St. Brigid.
Eybel, John W. *m.m.* '70 (CHI) Chicago, IL; [N] Chicago, IL Maryknoll Fathers & Brothers.
Eyerman, Matthew S. '95 (CHI) Chicago, IL St. Columbanus.
Eyman, Bryan R. '85 (PRM) Mentor–on–the–Lake, OH St. Michael; Mentor–on–the–Lake, OH St. Andrew the Apostle; Ohio; Building Commission.
Ezaki, Bernard J. '88 (ALN) Bethlehem, PA Notre Dame of Bethlehem; [C] Bethlehem, PA Bethlehem Catholic High School.
Ezaqnikatt, Francis *c.ss.r.* (CHL) Concord, NC St. James.
Eze, Cyprian '88 (LAF) On Special Assignment.
Ezeanokwasa, Jude '89 (MIA) Fort Lauderdale, FL Our Lady Queen of Martyrs.
Ezeatu, Mike Steve '94 (CAM) West Collingswood, NJ Church of the Transfiguration, West Collingswood, N.J.
Ezeh, Christian '95 (STO) Stockton, CA St. Mary of the Assumption Church (Pastor of).
Ezeh, Gabriel I. '94 (BWN) La Feria, TX St. Francis Xavier; St. Paul.
Ezeh, Gabriel U. *s.m.m.m.* '05 (BAK) Milton Freewater, OR St. Francis of Assisi.
Ezeh, Raphael *m.s.p.* (CHI) Chicago, IL Corpus Christi.
Ezeibekwe, Samuel '79 (FAR) Pisek, ND Sts. Peter & Paul Church of Bechyne; Pisek, ND St. Joseph's Church of Lankin; Deanery 4; Pisek, ND St. John Nepomucene's Church of Pisek.
Ezeigbo, Pius '99 (SAT) Brackettville, TX St. Mary Magdalen.
Ezeiruaku, Vitus '96 (SFE) Penasco, NM San Antonio de Padua; Dixon, NM St. Anthony.
Ezenwa, Hilary '96 (RVC) Bethpage, NY New Island Hospital.
Ezenwachi, Ferdinand (BAL) Columbia, MD St. John the Evangelist.
Ezeoke, Benedict (CHI) Melrose Park, IL Sacred Heart; [J] Chicago, IL St. Anthony Hospital.
Ezeoke, Christopher '91 (BRK) South Ozone Park, NY St. Anthony of Padua.
Ezeonyeka, Aloysius *o.s.b.* '02 (LA) Azusa, CA St. Frances of Rome.
Ezeonyido, John Paul '03 (ATL) Lilburn, GA St. Stephen the Martyr.
Ezeugwa, Romanus *m.s.p.* (MOB) Tuskegee Institute, AL St. Joseph; [I] Tuskegee Institute, AL Tuskegee University Newman Center.
Ezharath, Joseph '66 (TYL) Gladewater, TX St. Theresa of the Infant Jesus; Palestine, TX Beto I Unit and Louie C. Powledge Unit, Texas Department of Corrections.
Ezop, Dwight M. '97 (LAN) De Witt, MI St. Jude; [P] FAITH Magazine.
Ezurike, Paschal '95 (P) Grants Pass, OR St. Anne.

F

Faber, Emmet N. '55 (LC) Retired.
Fabian, Andrew C. *o.p.* '56 (WIN) Additional Diocesan Assignments.
Fabian, John C. *o.p.* '59 (CHI)[N] Chicago Dominicans (Provincial Office).
Fabian, John V. '68 (DET) Special Assignment.
Fabian, John '68 (MAR)[H] Paradise, MI Companions of Christ the Lamb.
Fabiano, Philip *o.f.m.cap.* '64 (NY) New York, NY St. John the Baptist.
Fabing, Robert J. *s.j.* '74 (SJ)[L] Los Altos, CA Jesuit Retreat Center of Los Altos; [O] Los Altos, CA Jesuit Institute for Family Life.
Fabish, Rapael A. *o.p.* '53 (CHI)[N] St. Pius V Priory.
Fabj, Frank T. '84 (GAL) Houston, TX St. Frances Cabrini.
Fabre, Jacques E. *c.s.* '86 (ATL) Forest Park, GA San Felipe de Jesus.
Fabre, Richard '73 (LAF) St. Martinville, LA St. Rita.
Facci, John *s.a.c.* '71 (ALB)[R] Cohoes, NY Apostolate for the Suffering Retired.
Fackler, Neil E. '98 (CHI) Chicago, IL St. Robert Bellarmine.
Facura, Joseph '68 (RIC) Virginia Beach, VA St. Matthew; Defenders of the Bond.
Fadallan, Elbert A. '80 (MO) Air Force Chaplains.
Fador, Francis R. '96 (HRT) Sharon, CT St. Bridget; Sharon, CT St. Bernard.
Fadrowski, Rev. Msgr. William J. '87 (NEW) North Arlington, NJ Queen of Peace; Priest Personnel Policy Board.
Faesser, Arthur A. '76 (GI) Sidney, NE St. Patrick's.
Fafinski, Donald S. '66 (BUF) Retired.
Fagan, Christopher '09 (LA) Palmdale, CA St. Mary.
Fagan, Edward J. *o.a.r.* '63 (NY) Bronx, NY St. John's.
Fagan, Rev. Msgr. Emmet '55 (BRK)[M] Brooklyn, NY Ecclesial Consultants, Inc.
Fagan, Rt. Rev. Msgr. Emmet '55 (RVC) Priests' Retirement Board.
Fagan, George V. '69 (COS) Limon, CO Our Lady of Victory; Defender of the Bond; Eastern Deanery; Presbyteral Council; Vicars Forane.
Fagan, George V. (PBL) Defensores Vinculi.
Fagan, John E. *s.j.* '83 (WOR)[O] Worcester, MA Jesuits of the Holy Cross, Inc.
Fagan, John E. *s.j.* '83 (NY)[EE] New York, NY Xavier Jesuit Community.
Fagan, Joseph K. '67 (BO)[A] Weston, MA Blessed John XXIII National Seminary; Senior Priests. Retired.
Fagan, Paul R. *c.p.* '86 (NY)[EE] Riverdale, NY Passionist Spiritual Center; [GG] Bronx, NY The Passionist Spiritual Center/Cardinal Spellman Retreat House.

Fagan, Rev. Msgr. Robert Emmet (RVC) Retired.
Fagan, Robert R. '58 (ALN) Easton, PA St. Jane Frances de Chantal Retired.
Fagin, Gerald M. *s.j.* '69 (NO)[C] New Orleans, LA Loyola University New Orleans.
Fagone, Benedict *o.f.m.conv.* '67 (SPR) Chicopee, MA St. Anthony of Padua.
Fagot, Hacker J. *s.j.* '57 (NO)[P] New Orleans, LA Ignatius Residence Retired.
Faherty, William B. *s.j.* '44 (STL) Saint Louis, MO; [O] St. Louis, MO Jesuit Community Corporation at Saint Louis University – Jesuit Hall; [O] St. Louis, MO The Jesuits of the Missouri Province.
Fahey, Rev. Msgr. Charles J. '58 (BRK)[M] Brooklyn, NY Ecclesial Consultants, Inc.; [EE] Loyola Hall, Jesuit Community; On Duty Outside the Diocese.
Fahey, Edward J. '89 (WIL) Claymont, DE Holy Rosary; Nursing Homes.
Fahey, Rev. Msgr. Gerard '51 (SR) Santa Rosa, CA Star of the Valley; Cemeteries.
Fahey, James L. '59 (BO) Senior Priests. Retired.
Fahey, James W. '70 (FR) North Easton, MA Immaculate Conception.
Fahey, John H. '61 (WH) Retired.
Fahey, John M. '54 (TUC) Retired.
Fahey, John Peter '84 (LA) Retired.
Fahey, Michael A. *s.j.* '64 (BO)[U] Newton, MA The Jesuit Community at Boston College.
Fahey, Robert E. *s.m.* '53 (SFR)[N] San Francisco, CA Marist Center of the West Retired.
Fahey, Thomas C. *o.f.m.* '47 (FTW)[I] Huntington, IN Victory Noll—Motherhouse of Our Lady of Victory Missionary Sisters Retired.
Fahey, Thomas C. '47 (CHY) Retired.
Fahey–Guerra, John P. *c.ss.r.* '96 (CHI)[N] Chicago, IL Redemptorist Theology Residence.
Fahnestock, John *m.s.c.* '71 (SB) Hesperia, CA Holy Family.
Fahrbach, Paul A. '84 (TOL) Bellevue, OH St. Gaspar del Bufalo; Attica, OH Our Lady of Hope.
Faiella, William W. *c.s.c.* '79 (FTW)[H] Notre Dame Congregation of Holy Cross, Indiana Province, Provincial House.
Faiella, William W. *c.s.c.* '79 (PHX)[F] Phoenix, AZ Holy Cross Congregation/Casa Santa Cruz; Scottsdale, AZ St. Bernard of Clairvaux Roman Catholic Parish.
Fain, John '03 (LAN) Owosso, MI St. Paul; Priests' Assignment Commission.
Faiola, Fabio '08 (AGN) Agana, GU Our Lady of Guadalupe.
Faiola, Rev. Msgr. Samuel J. '49 (BUF) Censors—Board of Diocesan Censors of Books and Vigilance for the Faith Retired.
Faiola, Thomas *o.f.m.cap.* '85 (NY) New York, NY Our Lady of Sorrows.
Fairbanks, Gregory J. '90 (PH) On Duty Outside the Archdiocese.
Fairbanks, Patrick A. *s.j.* '00 (CHI)[D] Chicago, IL St. Ignatius College Prep; [N] Chicago, IL Chicago Province of the Society of Jesus–Provincial Office; Chicago, IL; Detroit, MI; [D] Chicago, IL St. Ignatius Jesuit Community.
Fairchild, Rev. Msgr. Edward '59 (COL) Retired.
Fairman, Derek '06 (ALT) Johnstown, PA St. Benedict's.
Fairman, Timothy J. '88 (CHI) Ingleside, IL St. Bede.
Fait, Thomas G. '74 (MIL) Personal Leave.
Faix, William R. *o.s.a.* '63 (FgM) Villanova, PA Province of St. Thomas of Villanova (Eastern).
Fajardo, Ramil E. '04 (CHI) Chicago, IL St. Clement.
Fajardo, Ricardo (NY) New York, NY St. Catherine of Genoa.
Fajella, Francis *m.s.a.* '82 (NOR)[G] Cromwell Society of the Missionaries of the Holy Apostles.
Faker, Dennis '08 (LFT) Lafayette, IN St. Mary Cathedral; Lafayette, IN St. Lawrence.
Falabella, Robert '61 (CHR) Simpsonville, SC St. Mary Magdalene.
Falana, Arek '06 (CHI) Chicago, IL Queen of All Saints Basilica.
Falardeau, Ernest R. *s.s.s.* '56 (NY) New York, NY St. Jean Baptiste.
Falbo, Samuel J. '60 (LAV) Las Vegas, NV St. Anthony of Padua.
Falbo, Samuel '60 (SFE) Retired.
Falco, Frank M. *o.s.m.* '67 (CHI)[N] Chicago Order of Friar Servants of Mary (Servites) United States of America Province, Inc.; Chicago, IL; [N] Chicago, IL Order of Friar Servants of Mary (Servites) United States of America Province, Inc.
Falco, Frank *o.s.m.* '67 (ORG) Fullerton, CA St. Juliana Falconieri; [I] Fullerton, CA Servite Fathers and Brothers.
Falco, Ronald G. '81 (WOR) Office of Ongoing Priestly Formation; Worcester, MA St. George.
Falcone, Emilio '57 (RCK) Active Outside the Diocese Retired.
Falcone, Mark D. *o.praem* '66 (GB)[J] De Pere, WI St. Norbert Abbey.
Falcone, Sebastian '51 (ROC)[A] Rochester, NY St. Bernard's School of Theology & Ministry Retired.
Faletoi, Konelio '92 (HON) Kailua–Kona, HI St. Michael The Archangel; College of Consultors; Vicars Forane; Presbyteral Council.
Faliskie, Edmund *c.ss.r.* '91 (BRK)[T] Brooklyn, NY Redemptorist Fathers of New York, Inc.–Baltimore Province.
Falk, Gerald R. '59 (GB) Appleton, WI St. Thomas More.
Falk, Robert *s.d.b.* '63 (FgM) New Rochelle, NY SALESIANS OF DON BOSCO.
Falkenhan, Pierre M. '80 (PIT) Donora, PA Our Lady of the Valley.
Falkenthal, Thomas W. '75 (CHI) Military Chaplains.
Falkenthal, Thomas W. '75 (MIA) Apostleship of the Sea; [Q] Aventura, FL Apostleship of the Sea (Archdiocese of Miami); [Q] Miami Shores, FL Stella Maris Seamen Center, Inc.
Falla, Gustavo A. '96 (BGP) Stamford, CT Saint Benedict – Our Lady of Montserrat; Pastors' Vocation Advisory Board.
Faller, Rodel '08 (BEA) Beaumont, TX St. Anne.
Falletta, Frank J. '66 (ROC) Rochester, NY St. Lawrence.
Falletta, Joseph '72 (ALB) Copake Falls, NY Parish of Our Lady of Hope; Presbyteral Council; Diocesan Board of Consultors.
Fallgren, Matthew '01 (RC) Eagle Butte, SD All Saints.
Fallon, Daniel R. '76 (CHI) Chicago, IL St. Cornelius.
Fallon, James P. *s.s.j.* '68 (LAF) Breaux Bridge, LA St. Francis of Assisi; Crowley, LA St. Theresa.
Fallon, John C. '71 (ATL) Prison Apostolate.
Fallon, John C.K. '71 (ATL) Atlanta, GA Holy Spirit.
Fallon, John F. '58 (BO) Senior Priests. Retired.
Fallon, John J. '46 (BO) Senior Priests. Retired.
Fallon, John P. '95 (FAR) Absent on Leave.
Fallon, John P. *o.s.f.s.* '60 (STO)[A] Stockton, CA St. Mary's High School; Diocesan Finance Council.
Fallon, John '69 (BIR) Birmingham (Hoover), AL Prince of Peace.
Fallon, Joseph '96 (NY) Walden, NY Most Precious Blood.
Fallon, Marc F. *c.s.c.* '91 (FR) Taunton; [A] North Easton, MA Holy Cross Fathers Religious; New Bedford, MA St. Lawrence Martyr.
Fallon, Vince *ss.cc.* '91 (RNO) Diocesan School Board; [F] Reno, NV University of Nevada, Newman Community; Reno, NV Our Lady of Wisdom; Diocesan Board of Consultors; Presbyteral Council.
Fallon, Vincent *ss.cc.* '91 (LA)[P] La Verne, CA Congregation of the Sacred Hearts of Jesus and Mary.
Fallone, Thomas H. '02 (PAT) Vocations Office; Sussex County Jail; [A] Boonton, NJ Domus Bartimaeus.
Falotico, Ronald S. '69 (CAM) Egg Harbor City, NJ St. Nicholas' Church, Egg Harbor City; Hammonton, NJ St. Joseph's Church, Hammonton, N.J.
Falsey, James E. '72 (SAG) AuGres, MI St. Mark.
Falter, John F. *c.pp.s.* '61 (CIN)[N] Dayton Provincial Office of the Cincinnati Province of the Society of the Precious Blood.
Faluszczak, James G. '96 (E) Sheffield, PA St. Anthony; Warren State Hospital.
Falvey, Edmund F. '61 (WOR) Retired.
Falzon, Angelo *o.f.m.* '84 (FgM) New York, NY Franciscan Province of the Immaculate Conception.
Fama, Lawrence J. '92 (NEW) Maywood, NJ Our Lady Queen of Peace; Elected Members.
Famania, Edison *c.m.* '94 (FgM) Philadelphia, PA Eastern Province.
Fambrini, Robert *s.j.* '79 (SD) San Diego, CA Our Lady of Guadalupe.
Famiglietti, Rocco *o.f.m.* '47 (FgM) New York, NY Franciscan Province of the Immaculate Conception.
Familar, Rex '93 (ORL) Orlando, FL St. John Vianney.
Famiyeh, Emmanuel '90 (LC) Richland Center, WI St. Mary (Assumption of B.V.M.).
Fanale, James F. *c.s.v.* '69 (CHI)[N] Arlington Heights Viatorian Province Center–Clerics of St. Viator.
Fanale, James *c.s.v.* '69 (JOL) St. Anne, IL St. Anne.
Fane, Kevin R. *o.p.* '69 (CHI) River Forest, IL St. Vincent Ferrer; [J] Chicago, IL Resurrection Medical Center.
Fanelli, Charles V. '71 (CHI) Chicago, IL St. Thomas More; [W] Chicago, IL Italian Catholic Federation.
Fanelli, James G. '56 (HRT)[A] In Res. at the Archbishop Daniel A. Cronin Retirement Residence at St. Thomas Seminary Retired.
Fangman, James E. '63 (SC) Carroll, IA Retired.
Fangman, Paul J. '49 (OM) Retired.
Fangman, Robert M. '54 (SC) Retired.
Fangman, Thomas M. '92 (OM) Omaha, NE Sacred Heart; [O] Omaha, NE Christian Urban Education Service.
Fangmann, Frederick C. '63 (DUB) Retired.
Fanning, John E. '68 (NY) New York, NY Our Lady of Victory.
Fanning, Patrick F. *ss.cc.* '83 (FR)[G] Fairhaven National Center of the Enthronement.
Fannon, Noel '61 (BLX) Kiln, MS St. Matthew the Apostle.
Fanrak, James M. '71 (LR) Mountain Home, AR St. Peter the Fisherman; Mountain View, AR St. Mary Church.
Fanta, Thomas G. '88 (CLV) Shaker Heights, OH St. Dominic; [X] Shaker Heights, OH St. Dominic Endowment Fund.
Fanucci, Santino J. '58 (SCR)[N] Dunmore, PA Villa St. Joseph Retired.
Faour, George '91 (NEW) Orange, NJ St. John's; Central Essex Deanery 17.
Farace, Frederick A. '55 (HBG) Retired.
Faraci, Douglas F. '69 (BUF) Retired.
Faraci, Francis '59 (LAN) Otisville, MI St. Francis Xavier Retired.
Farana, Mario P. '71 (SFR) San Francisco, CA St. Paul; Deans; Council of Priests.
Farano, Michael A. '68 (ALB) Special Assignment; Vicar General and Moderator of the Curia; Propagation of the Faith–Pontifical Society; Presbyteral Council; Loudonville, NY St. Pius X.
Farao, John *o.f.m.conv.* '88 (MRY) California Men's Colony West; California Men's Colony East; Pismo Beach, CA St. Paul the Apostle.
Farbolin, Alberic R. *o.c.s.o.* '02 (DUB)[K] Peosta, IA New Melleray Abbey, Order of Cistercians of the Strict Observance.
Fardellone, Emil *s.d.b.* '44 (NO)[D] Marrero, LA Archbishop Shaw High School.
Fares, Lawrence T. '50 (DET) Retired.
Faretra, Albert M. '86 (BO) Belmont, MA St. Joseph.
Farfaglia, Salvatore James (CC) Corpus Christi, TX Saint Helena of the True Cross of Jesus.
Farfan, Carlos *p.e.s.* '04 (SAC) Dixon, CA St. Peter.
Farge, William J. *s.j.* '78 (NO)[C] New Orleans, LA Loyola University New Orleans.
Faria, Carl M.D. '88 (MRY) Archives.
Farias, Joseph A. *s.d.b.* '64 (LA) Los Angeles, CA St. Mary; [P] Los Angeles, CA Dominic Savio Salesian Residence.
Farias, Joseph G. '75 (PAT) Convent Station, NJ St. Thomas More; [P] Madison, NJ Drew University Catholic Campus Ministry; [P] Madison, NJ Catholic Campus Ministry.
Faricy, Robert L. *s.j.* '62 (MIL)[P] Milwaukee, WI Jesuit Community at Marquette University.
Farina, Carlo A. *s.j.* '64 (SJ)[M] Los Gatos, CA Sacred Heart Jesuit Center.
Farina, Rev. Msgr. Michael D. '54 (WDC)[M] Washington, DC Cardinal O'Boyle Residence for Priests.
Farina, Rev. Msgr. Michael F. '54 (WDC) Retired.
Faris, Chorbishop John D. '76 (SAM) Utica, NY St. Louis Gonzaga; On Duty Outside the Diocese.
Farke, Rodney '72 (SFS) Brookings, SD St. Thomas More; Tribunal Judges; Cursillo.
Farland, Rev. Msgr. George A. '68 (SPR) Springfield, MA Sacred Heart; Vicars for the Clergy; Bishop's Commission for Clergy; Deans; Co Vicars For Clergy; Clergy Counseling Service.
Farland, Norman '66 (ORL) Wahneta, FL Our Lady of Guadalupe.
Farleo, Brennan–Joseph *o.f.m.conv.* '86 (NY)[EE] Staten Island, NY St. Francis Friary.
Farley, Bernard C. '68 (PH)[V] Philadelphia, PA St. John Neumann Nursing Home; On Special or Other Archdiocesan Assignment.
Farley, Daniel H. '98 (LC) Almond, WI St. Maximilian Maria Kolbe; Army National Guard Chaplains.
Farley, James V. '65 (PRO) Ashaway, RI Our Lady of Victory; Bradford, RI St. Vincent de Paul.
Farley, John B. '93 (PBL) Grand Junction, CO Immaculate Heart of Mary; Deans.
Farley, Rev. Msgr. John J. '62 (NY) Poughkeepsie, NY St. Mary.
Farley, Rev. Msgr. John '62 (NY) Poughkeepsie, NY Vassar Brothers Hospital.
Farley, John *s.v.d.* '60 (BO)[U] Duxbury, MA Society of the Divine Word.
Farley, Leo O. '54 (NEW)[M] Caldwell, NJ The Rev. Msgr. James F. Kelley Residence for Retired Priests Retired.
Farley, Leslie A. '93 (LR) West Memphis, AR St. Michael; West Memphis, AR Sacred Heart Church.
Farley, Patrick '05 (PHX) Carefree, AZ Our Lady of Joy Roman Catholic Parish; Advocates.
Farley, Thomas B. '79 (P) Portland, OR St. Clare.
Farley, Thomas F. '02 (PRT) Old Town, ME Parish of the Resurrection of the Lord.
Farmer, J. Kevin '93 (BAL) Middletown, MD Holy Family Catholic Community.
Farmer, Rev. Msgr. James '79 (BAL) Baltimore, MD St. Ursula.
Farmer, Kevin (BAL) Presbyteral Council.
Farmer, Rev. Msgr. Michael L. '95 (MOB) Mobile AL Cathedral of the Immaculate Conception; Mobile, AL St. Joseph; Vicar General; Chancellor; Archdiocesan Consultors; Apostleship of Prayer; Catholic Housing of Mobile, Inc.; Censor Librorum; Liturgical Commission; Officers; [J] Mobile, AL Apostleship of Prayer.
Farmer, Regis M. '73 (PIT) Wildwood, PA St. Catherine of Sweden; College of Consultors; Priest Council.
Farmer, Terrence '03 (PRM) Columbus, OH St. John Chrysostom; Young Adults; Presbyteral Council.
Farnan, Donald P. '87 (KC) Kansas City, MO St.

Thomas More; Consultors; Administrative Committee.
Farnan, James B. '00 (PIT) Beaver Falls, PA St. Philomena; [P] New Brighton, PA Geneva College; Beaver Falls, PA Divine Mercy.
Farnik, John *c.ss.r.* '62 (SAT)[L] San Antonio, TX Redemptorists of Texas–San Antonio #1; San Antonio, TX St. Gerard Majella.
Farnum, David E. *c.s.p.* '00 (NY)[EE] New York, NY Paulist Fathers' Motherhouse.
Faroh, Paul *o.f.m.conv.* '85 (TOL) Carey, OH Our Lady of Consolation, Basilica–National Shrine.
Faron, Wieslaw *s.j.* '06 (CHI)[N] Chicago, IL Sacred Heart Mission House.
Farrar, Brandon '06 (KCK) Baldwin, KS Annunciation; Edgerton, KS Assumption.
Farre, Raymond *sch.p.* '53 (LA) Los Angeles, CA Santa Teresita.
Farrell, Bernard P. '65 (BLX) Ocean Springs, MS St. Elizabeth Ann Seton; Catholic Housing Board; Personnel Board.
Farrell, Charles A. *o.p.* '54 (CIN) Cincinnati, OH St. Gertrude; [N] Cincinnati, OH St. Gertrude Priory.
Farrell, David E. *c.s.c.* '68 (FgM) New Rochelle, NY Eastern Brothers Province.
Farrell, Dennis J. '73 (BRK) Holy Name Society; Brooklyn, NY Resurrection.
Farrell, Emmet L. '65 (SD) San Diego, CA St. Jude.
Farrell, Rev. Msgr. Francis '55 (BLX) Biloxi, MS Our Lady of Fatima Retired.
Farrell, George A. '96 (MET) North Plainfield, NJ St. Joseph.
Farrell, Gerald J. *m.m.* '57 (FgM) Maryknoll, NY MARYKNOLL.
Farrell, James M. '75 (IND) Retreat & Renewal Ministries and Fatima Retreat House; [J] Indianapolis, IN Our Lady of Fatima Retreat House, Inc.; Priests' Personnel Board.
Farrell, John E. '62 (BO) Lynnfield, MA Our Lady of the Assumption; Vicariate I; Vicariate I.
Farrell, John J. *o.s.a.* '59 (PH)[C] Villanova University; [Y] Villanova, PA St. Thomas Monastery Retired.
Farrell, Joseph J. '74 (TR) New Egypt, NJ The Church of the Assumption.
Farrell, Joseph L. '95 (PH) Council of Priests; Jamison, PA St. Cyril of Jerusalem.
Farrell, Joseph L. *o.s.a.* '91 (PH)[C] Villanova University; [Y] Drexel Hill, PA Bellesini Friary.
Farrell, Kevin R. '65 (JOL) Wood Dale, IL Holy Ghost.
Farrell, Kurt '98 (WIN) Dodge Center, MN St. John Baptist de La Salle; Dodge Center, MN St. Vincent de Paul; Dodge Center, MN St. Francis de Sales.
Farrell, Lawrence M. '01 (KAL) Kalamazoo, MI St. Monica; Advocates.
Farrell, Lawrence *o.p.* '71 (SB)[I] Riverside, CA St. Vincent Ferrer House.
Farrell, Lawrence '01 (KAL) Holy Childhood Association and Propagation of the Faith; Missions.
Farrell, Michael A. '70 (ORL) Merritt Island, FL Divine Mercy Catholic Community.
Farrell, Michael J. *s.s.j.* '60 (BAL)[S] Baltimore, MD St. Joseph's Manor.
Farrell, Patrick J. *o.c.d.* '62 (MIL)[P] Hubertus, WI Discalced Carmelite Monastery – Holy Hill Basilica of the National Shrine of Mary, Help of Christians, Holy Hill.
Farrell, Rev. Msgr. Patrick '60 (JKS) Vicksburg, MS St. Paul; Diocesan Consultors; Association of Priests; Personnel Board.
Farrell, Patrick (BLX) Association of Priests (Diocese of Biloxi and Jackson).
Farrell, Paul A. *c.ss.r.* '52 (STL)[O] Liguori, MO St. Clement Health Care Center.
Farrell, Philip N. '93 (PIT) Vicariate 4; Priest Council; College of Consultors; Clergy Personnel Board.
Farrell, Richard T. '84 (ROC) Elmira, NY Blessed Sacrament Roman Catholic Church of Elmira, NY; Elmira, NY Elmira Correctional Facility, Center and Camp Monterey; Pine City, NY Southport Correctional Facility.
Farrell, Richard *c.m.f.* '52 (CHI) Chicago, IL Our Lady of Guadalupe; [N] Oak Park, IL Claretian Missionaries USA Eastern Province.
Farrell, Robert J. '80 (CIN) Mason, OH St. Susanna.
Farrell, Robert *s.j.* '64 (BO)[U] Newton, MA The Jesuit Community at Boston College.
Farrell, Ronald J. '00 (CHR) Georgetown, SC St. Mary Our Lady of Ransom; Georgetown, SC St. Cyprian.
Farrell, Seamus J. '67 (OAK) Hayward, CA St. Bede; Consultors; Priest Representatives; Presbyteral Council.
Farrell, Thomas F. '43 (HRT)[A] In Res. at the Archbishop Daniel A. Cronin Retirement Residence at St. Thomas Seminary Retired.
Farrell, Thomas J. '92 (GB) Appleton, WI St. Pius X.
Farrell, Thomas P. '82 (LEX) Danville, KY SS. Peter & Paul; College of Consultors; Bluegrass West.
Farrell, Timothy W. '89 (GLP) Farmington, NM Sacred Heart; Priests' Retirement Board.
Farrell, Walter L. *s.j.* '47 (DET)[P] Bloomfield Hills, MI Manresa Jesuit Retreat House.
Farrelly, John *o.s.b.* '55 (WDC)[N] Washington, DC St. Anselm's Abbey.
Farrelly, Rev. Msgr. Terence J. '50 (ORL) Rockledge, FL St. Mary's Retired.
Farren, John A. *o.p.* '64 (WDC)[W] Washington, DC Rosary Shrine of St. Jude.
Farren, John *o.p.* '64 (NY)[II] New York, NY The Dominican Foundation of Dominican Friars, Province of St. Joseph, Inc.; [II] New York, NY St. Jude Dominican Missions; [EE] New York, NY St. Vincent Ferrer Priory.
Farris, William *o.f.m.* '77 (CIN)[E] Cincinnati, OH Roger Bacon High School; [T] Cincinnati, OH Roger Bacon High School Endowment; Councillors:; [N] Cincinnati, OH St. Clement Friary.
Farrugia, David J. *o.p.* '60 (OAK) Berkeley, CA St. Mary Magdalen; Deanery #20.
Farrugia, William C. '63 (BRK) Astoria, NY St. Joseph; Astoria, NY St. Joseph.
Farry, John A. '65 (CHI) Chicago, IL St. Andrew Retired.
Farry, John J. '67 (PH) Levittown, PA Queen of the Universe.
Farsaci, Francis A. *o.s.a.* '64 (PH)[Y] Villanova, PA St. Thomas Monastery.
Fasano, Eric R. '02 (RVC) Procurator & Advocates.
Fasano, Jerome W. '77 (ARL) Front Royal, VA St. John the Baptist.
Fasano, Paul J. '08 (RCK) Batavia, IL Holy Cross.
Fasching, Jeffery A. '97 (WCH) Ava, MO Immaculate Heart of Mary; Springfield, MO St. Elizabeth Ann Seton; On Duty Outside the Diocese; Mountain Grove, MO Sacred Heart.
Fasching, Jeffrey A. '97 (SPC) Diocesan Hospital Ministry.
Fasciglione, Massimo S. '74 (CAM) Ocean City, NJ The Church of Our Lady of Good Counsel, Ocean City, N.J.
Fasline, Anthony '62 (Y) Retired.
Fasnacht, Matthew J. '07 (WIN) Stewartville, MN St. Bridget's; Stewartville, MN St. Bernard's; Rochester, MN Resurrection; Appointed Members.
Faso, Charles '67 (CHI)[N] Chicago, IL St. Peter's Friary.
Fassero, Jonathan *o.s.b.* '78 (IND)[A] St. Meinrad, IN Saint Meinrad School of Theology; [K] St. Meinrad, IN St. Meinrad Archabbey.
Fassett, Edward S. *s.j.* '88 (WDC)[N] Washington, DC Leonard Neale House.
Fasuga, Eugeniusz *c.ss.r.* '97 (MET) Manville, NJ Sacred Heart of Jesus; Somerville, NJ Somerset Medical Center.
Fata, Joseph A. '68 (Y) Boardman, OH St. Luke.
Fater, Rev. Msgr. Douglas '70 (SAT) Retired.
Fath, Robert '07 (FBK) North Pole, AK St. Nicholas Catholic Church North Pole; Presbyteral Council.
Fatooh, Rev. Msgr. Charles G. '85 (MRY) Cayucos, CA St. Joseph.
Faucher, Eugene J. '51 (CHI) Arlington Heights, IL St. Edna Retired.
Faucher, W. Thomas '71 (B) Boise, ID St. Mary's; Judges.
Faugno, Valerian *o.f.m.* '58 (ALB)[A] Catskill, NY St. Anthony Friary.
Faul, Charles J. '80 (RIC) Wytheville, VA St. Mary the Mother of God.
Faulhaber, Gregory M. '79 (BUF) Defenders of the Bond; Council of Priests; [A] East Aurora, NY Christ the King Seminary; [A] East Aurora, NY Christ the King Seminary.
Faulk, Peter A. '06 (ALX) Alexandria, LA St. Francis Xavier Cathedral; Alexandria, LA Rapides Regional Medical Center.
Faulkner, Joseph J. '05 (LIN) Lincoln, NE St. Peter; Advocates.
Faulstich, Paul J. *s.j.* '68 (CHI)[D] Wilmette, IL Loyola Academy; [N] Chicago, IL Chicago Province of the Society of Jesus–Provincial Office; Chicago, IL.
Fauser, Steven W. '03 (HBG) Danville, PA St. Joseph.
Faust, Gary J. '78 (STL) Lemay, MO St. Bernadette.
Faust, Louis J. '74 (WDC) Brandywine, MD St. Michael; Germantown, MD Mother Seton Parish.
Faustner, William J. '76 (COL) Newcomerstown, OH St. Francis de Sales; Deanery 10: Tuscarawas–Holmes–Coshocton; Presbyteral Council; Parochial Examiners.
Fausz, Kevin *c.m.* '91 (SAT) In Metropolitan Area; Archdiocesan Presbyteral Council; San Antonio, TX Holy Redeemer.
Fauz, Kevin *c.m.* '91 (SAT) Priests Personnel Board; [D] San Antonio, TX St. Gerard Catholic High School.
Favara, Joseph F. '41 (SAG) Retired.
Favazza, Robert D. '09 (MEM) Brownsville, TN St. John Church; Jackson, TN St. Mary Church.
Fawcett, Brian '97 (RC) Lemmon, SD St. Mary's; Deaneries; Presbyteral Council.
Fawcett, Rev. Msgr. Henry F. '64 (SD) San Diego, CA Our Lady of Mt. Carmel; College of Consultors; Presbyteral Council Retired.
Fawls, Daniel J. '97 (BUF) Medina, NY Holy Trinity.
Fay, David E. '64 (CIN) Cincinnati, OH St. Gabriel; Cincinnati, OH St. Matthias; Judges.
Fay, Gregory J. '76 (STA) Jacksonville, FL Holy Family.
Fay, Rev. Msgr. William P. '74 (BO) Brighton, MA St. Columbkille.
Fayle, Vaughn *o.f.m.* (CHI)[N] Chicago, IL St. Peter's Friary.
Faylona, Joey '03 (SAN) Andrews, TX Our Lady of Lourdes.
Fayos, Javier *l.c.* '97 (SAT)[G] San Antonio, TX Rolling Hills Academy, Inc.
Fazio, Cosimo R. '48 (NY) New Rochelle, NY St. Joseph Retired.
Fazio, Paul *o.f.m.conv.* '74 (OAK)[M] Castro Valley, CA Conventual Franciscans (Province of St. Joseph of Cupertino).
Fecher, Rev. Msgr. Vincent '50 (SAT)[K] San Antonio, TX Casa De Padres Retired.
Fechner, Erich A. '92 (STL) St. Louis, MO St. Simon the Apostle.
Fecht, Geoffrey *o.s.b.* '88 (SCL)[I] Collegeville, MN St. John's Abbey, of the Order of St. Benedict.
Fecko, Leonard J. '89 (CIN) On Special and Archdiocesan Assignment.
Fecteau, Raymond L. '72 (WDC) Darnestown, MD Our Lady of the Visitation; Irving, TX National Catholic Committee on Scouting Executive Committee (1934).
Fedak, Dennis Z. '98 (PH) Philadelphia, PA Nativity of the Blessed Virgin Mary; Philadelphia, PA Our Lady Help of Christians.
Fedak, Paul C. '98 (FR) St. Anne's Hospital; Fall River, MA Holy Name.
Fedders, William '68 (LEX) Special Assignment.
Fedek, Robert '05 (CHI)[A] Mundelein, IL University of St. Mary of the Lake/Mundelein Seminary; Mundelein, IL St. Mary of the Annunciation.
Fedele, Giuseppe '05 (NEW) Newark, NJ Cathedral Basilica of the Sacred Heart.
Federico, Cesidio J. '62 (WH) Retired.
Federline, Thomas A. '85 (GBG) Greensburg, PA St. Paul; Diocesan Ecumenical Office.
Feders, Joseph *o.s.b.* '99 (SCL) St. Joseph, MN St. Joseph's; [I] Collegeville, MN St. John's Abbey, of the Order of St. Benedict; Presbyteral Council.
Federspiel, Nicholas T. '04 (RCK) Saint Charles, IL St. Patrick.
Fedewa, Matthew '58 (LAN) Retired.
Fedewa, Rev. Msgr. Sylvester L. '54 (LAN) Cursillo Retired.
Fedigan, James J. *s.j.* '65 (NY)[EE] Loyola Hall, Jesuit Community.
Fedigan, James (BRK) Jackson Heights, NY Our Lady of Fatima.
Fedor, Gregory F. '83 (Y) Austintown, OH St. Joseph; College of Consultors; Priests Council.
Fedor, Lawrence L. *o.s.b.* '65 (MIL)[P] Benet Lake, WI St. Benedict's Abbey.
Fedor, Mark Q. '72 (CLV) Cleveland, OH St. Mel; Promoters of Justice.
Fedor, Robert P. '61 (E) Retired.
Fedora, Joseph *m.m.* '84 (FgM) Maryknoll, NY MARYKNOLL.
Fedorowich, Rev. Msgr. Michael '55 (PHU) Retired.
Fee, James M. *o.m.i.* '71 (BUF) Buffalo, NY Holy Angels.
Fee, John M. *ss.cc.* '56 (DET) Harper Woods, MI Our Lady Queen of Peace.
Fee, John *ss.cc.* (FR)[G] Fairhaven, MA Damien Residence.
Fee, Pat '61 (ORG) Retired.
Feehan, Kenneth *s.v.d.* '59 (BO)[U] Brighton, MA Divine Word Missionaries.
Feehan, Stephen S. '62 (NEW) Retired.
Feehily, John W. '73 (OKL) Moore, OK St. Andrew's.
Feela, Paul F. '78 (STP) St. Paul, MN Church of Lumen Christi.
Feeley, Paul *o.carm.* '53 (NY) New York, NY St. John the Martyr Retired.
Feeley, Sylvester E. *c.ss.r.* '48 (BRK) Brooklyn, NY Our Lady of Perpetual Help Basilica.
Feely, Rev. Msgr. James B. '58 (GB) Hortonville, WI SS. Peter and Paul; Priests' Personnel Board Retired.
Feely, Thomas H. *s.j.* '75 (NY) New York, NY; Watertown, MA; [EE] New York, NY Society of Jesus, New York Province; [EE] New York, NY Xavier Jesuit Community; Towson, MD.
Feely, Thomas J. *s.j.* '75 (BO)[U] Watertown, MA The Society of Jesus of New England–Provincial Offices.
Feenan, Rev. Msgr. J. Francis '53 (PAT) Retired.
Feeney, John J. '54 (PRT) Retired.
Feeney, Joseph J. *s.j.* '65 (PH)[C] Jesuit Fathers; [Y] Philadelphia, PA St. Alphonsus House.
Feeney, Kevin J. '77 (CHI)[A] Mundelein, IL University of St. Mary of the Lake/Mundelein Seminary; Mundelein Seminary/University of St. Mary of the Lake; [A] Mundelein, IL University of St. Mary of the Lake/Mundelein Seminary.
Feeney, Robert T. '86 (PH) Philadelphia, PA St. Leo.
Feeney, Thomas M. '48 (PH) Retired.
Feeney, Rev. Msgr. Thomas P. '79 (CC) Office of the Bishop; Diaconal Screening Committee; Tribunal;

Judges; Canonical Affairs; Judicial Vicar; Presbyteral Council.
Feeney, William P. '72 (PIT) Judges; Washington, PA Immaculate Conception; Priest Council.
Feeser, William '77 (SAC) Sacramento, CA Immaculate Conception.
Fegan, Peter *o.p.* '01 (Y) Youngstown, OH St. Dominic.
Fehn, Jerome W. '78 (MO) Military Chaplains; Army National Guard Chaplains.
Fehn, Jerry (STP) Fairview–Southdale Hospital; Methodist Hospital.
Fehrenbacher, Henry '48 (SCL) Retired.
Fehring, Fabian *o.f.m.cap.* '53 (GF) Hardin, MT St. Joseph.
Feicht, Donald L. '70 (Y) Alliance, OH St. Joseph.
Feierfeil, Gerald F. '67 (SC) Sioux City, IA Nativity of Our Lord Jesus Christ; Board of Education; Episcopal Representative for Hospitals and Health Care.
Feigh, Conan E. *o.s.b.* '57 (GBG)[G] Latrobe, PA Saint Vincent Archabbey.
Feil, Carl M. *o.s.m.* '61 (CHI)[N] Chicago Order of Friar Servants of Mary (Servites) United States of America Province, Inc.
Feil, Carl *o.s.m.* '61 (ORL) Melbourne, FL Our Lady of Lourdes Retired.
Feild, Rev. Msgr. Martin Eugene '59 (BAL) Taneytown, MD St. Joseph; Presbyteral Council.
Feiss, Hugh *o.s.b.* '66 (B)[C] Jerome, ID Monastery of the Ascension.
Feit, Matthias '56 (PHX)[G] Phoenix, AZ Mount Claret Roman Catholic Retreat Center Retired.
Fekete, George J. '65 (GR) Retired.
Feketie, Michael J. '57 (NEW) Plainfield, NJ St. Mary Retired.
Felago, John F. *m.m.* '68 (SJ)[M] Los Altos, CA Maryknoll.
Felczak, Leonard J. '44 (CHI) Retired.
Feld, Norbert F. *s.s.c.* '49 (PRO)[P] Bristol, RI St. Columban's Retirement House Retired.
Feld, Norbert *s.s.c.* '49 (OM)[K] St. Columbans Missionary Society of St. Columban.
Feldcamp, Rev. Msgr. William J. '65 (SCR) Scranton, PA St. Clare; Deans; Scranton, PA St. Paul's.
Feldhaus, Rev. Msgr. Eugene A. '46 (BRK) Little Neck, NY; [T] Douglaston, NY Bishop Mugavero Residence Retired.
Feldhaus, Thomas F. '76 (CIN) Priests On Administrative Leave.
Feldmeier, Russell J. *m.m.* '80 (FgM) Maryknoll, NY MARYKNOLL.
Felice, John M. *o.f.m.* '68 (NY) New York, NY St. Francis of Assisi.
Felice–Pace, Albert *o.p.* '60 (LAV) Presbyteral Council for the Diocese of Las Vegas; St. Thomas Aquinas Catholic Newman Community at UNLV; [E] Las Vegas, NV St. Thomas Aquinas Catholic Newman Community at UNLV; [C] Las Vegas, NV Dominican Rectory, Fra Angelico House.
Felices–Sanchez, Rev. Msgr. Fernando B. '82 (SJN) Censor Librorum; Spiritual Directors.
Feliciano, Abraham *s.d.b.* '05 (WDC) Washington, DC Nativity.
Felicitas, Godofredo '82 (BRK) Bayside, NY St. Robert Bellarmine; [S] Filipino Apostolate.
Felion, Jerome '47 (BWN) Retired.
Felipe, Marvin P. *s.d.b.* '92 (SFR) San Francisco, CA St. Anne.
Felix, Bernard H. '92 (DOD) Belpre, KS St. Bernard Catholic Church of Belpre, Kansas; Larned, KS Sacred Heart of Jesus Catholic Church of Larned, Kansas; Presbyteral Council.
Felix, Paul G. '90 (GAL) Dickinson, TX Shrine of the True Cross; Southern Vicariate.
Felix, William P. '81 (LC) Chippewa Falls, WI St. Charles Borromeo; Chippewa Falls, WI St. Peter; [M] Chippewa Falls, WI Institute of St. Joseph.
Felker, Joseph F. '73 (SB) Riverside, CA St. Thomas the Apostle.
Fell, John N. *s.t.d.* '88 (MET) Bernardsville, NJ Our Lady of Perpetual Help; [L] Bernardsville, NJ Sacred Heart Chapel.
Fell, Timothy J. '99 (BAL) Baltimore, MD St. Agnes.
Fellenz, Ralph *o.f.m.cap.* '68 (GB)[J] Appleton, WI St. Fidelis Friary Retired.
Feller, Richard J. '53 (CHI) Retired.
Feller, Robert M. *o.praem.* '55 (GB)[J] De Pere, WI St. Norbert Abbey.
Fellrath, Frank W. '89 (MET) Edison, NJ Our Lady of Peace.
Felt, James W. *s.j.* '56 (SJ)[B] Santa Clara, CA Jesuit Community.
Felt, Richard R. '69 (PHX) Mesa, AZ Holy Cross Roman Catholic Parish; College of Consultors; Presbyteral Council; Deans.
Felter, Francis J. *m.m.* '69 (FgM) Maryknoll, NY MARYKNOLL.
Feltes, Victor C. '09 (LC)[C] Marshfield, WI Columbus High School; [C] Marshfield, WI Columbus Catholic Middle School; Marshfield, WI St. John the Baptist; Marshfield, WI Christ the King.
Feltman, Philip S. '66 (TOL) Retired.
Feltman, Thomas '01 (FAR) Wishek, ND St. David; Wishek, ND St. Patrick; Wishek, ND St. Andrew's Church of Zeeland.
Felton, Daniel J. '81 (GB) Newton, WI St. Thomas the Apostle; Manitowoc, WI St. Francis of Assisi.
Feltz, John G. '73 (BUR) Army National Guard Chaplains; Defenders of the Bond; Fairfax, VT St. Luke; Milton, VT St. Ann; Notaries.
Feltz, Joseph E. '79 (PIT) Monongahela, PA St. Anthony.
Feltz, Joseph M. '02 (IND) Council of Priests.
Feltz, Joseph M. '02 (IND) Brownsburg, IN St. Malachy.
Feltz, Thomas '85 (LA) Encino, CA Our Lady of Grace.
Felux, Jonathan W. '09 (SAT) Vocation Office; San Antonio, TX St. Brigid.
Feminelli, John '87 (CC) Retired.
Fenech, Francis X. '50 (PMB) Lake Worth, FL Sacred Heart Retired.
Fenelon, David '70 (DM) Retired.
Fenger, Guy '77 (MIA) Pembroke Pines, FL St. Boniface.
Fenili, J. Robert *c.ss.r.* '62 (CHI)[N] Chicago, IL Redemptorist Theology Residence.
Fenlon, Brian '75 (PHX) Special Assignment.
Fenlon, John P. '70 (SY) Syracuse, NY St. Patrick; Pastoral Examiners.
Fenlon, Thomas B. '61 (NY) Bronx, NY St. Augustine.
Fennell, Joseph G. *s.j.* '45 (BO)[U] Weston, MA Campion Health Center, Inc.
Fennell, Patrick A. *o.s.b.* '89 (PEO)[A] Peru, IL St. Bede Abbey.
Fenner, Eric *o.f.m.conv.* '46 (TR) Seaside Park, NJ St. Catharine of Siena.
Fennessy, Rev. Msgr. James J. '68 (ATL) Atlanta, GA St. Jude; College of Consultors.
Fennessy, James '02 (ROC) Waterloo, NY St. Patrick; Waterloo, NY St. Mary.
Fennessy, Joseph H. '56 (HBG) Retired.
Fennessy, Keith '84 (NY) Staten Island, NY St. Margaret Mary.
Fennessy, Peter J. *s.j.* '70 (DET)[P] Bloomfield Hills, MI Manresa Jesuit Retreat House.
Fenske, Donald J. '58 (CHI) Calumet City, IL Our Lady of Knock Retired.
Fenstermaker, James *c.s.c.* '84 (FR) South Easton, MA Holy Cross.
Fenton, Cornelius *c.pp.s.* '49 (CIN)[N] Carthagena, OH St. Charles Retired.
Fenton, Joe *s.m.* '94 (LA)[AA] Claremont, CA Claremont Colleges.
Fenton, Joseph *s.m.* '72 (WDC)[N] Washington, DC Marist Center.
Fenton, Lawrence E. '63 (GI) Retired.
Fenton, Patrick '08 (TYL) Kilgore, TX Christ the King.
Fenzl, Rod *o.praem.* '55 (SFE)[H] Albuquerque, NM Santa Maria de la Vid Priory.
Ferdinand, Cruz Cruz '05 (PCE) Villalba, PR Our Lady of Mt. Carmel.
Ference, Damian J. '03 (CLV)[A] Wickliffe, OH Borromeo Seminary.
Fereochia, Leonard *c.s.s.* '55 (BO)[X] Waltham, MA Stigmatine Fathers and Brothers Retired.
Feret, Rev. Msgr. Francis S. '62 (PH) Philadelphia, PA St. Adalbert; Polish Apostolate.
Ferguson, Gary M. '71 (TOL) Archbold, OH St. Peter; Fayette, OH Our Lady of Mercy.
Ferguson, James A. '85 (ALX) Defender of the Bond and Promoter of Justice; Alexandria, LA St. Francis Xavier Cathedral; College of Consultors; Elected Members; [A] Alexandria, LA Holy Savior Menard Central.
Ferguson, James J. *c.s.c.* '64 (PHX)[F] Phoenix, AZ Holy Cross Congregation/Casa Santa Cruz; Glendale, AZ St. Helen Roman Catholic Parish.
Ferguson, John G. *s.j.* '54 (SJ)[M] Los Gatos, CA Sacred Heart Jesuit Center.
Ferguson, Justin R. '06 (SAV) Macon, GA St. Joseph; Presbyteral Council.
Ferguson, Paul Anthony '02 (EVN) Evansville, IN Holy Redeemer.
Ferguson, Peter A. '90 (GAL) Retired.
Ferguson, Robert *f.s.s.p.* '02 (LIN)[A] Denton, NE Our Lady of Guadalupe Seminary.
Ferguson, Thomas P. '94 (ARL) Diocesan Judges; McLean, VA St. Luke; Episcopal Vicar for Faith Formation and Director of the Diaconate Formation Program; Diaconal Formation Program.
Ferguson, William J. '06 (COL) Buckeye Lake, OH Our Lady of Mt. Carmel.
Ferland, Martin *o.mar.* '95 (SAM)[B] Petersham, MA Maronite Monks of Adoration Most Holy Trinity Monastery.
Ferland, Thomas J. '87 (PRO) Providence, RI St. Michael the Archangel; Providence, RI Rhode Island Hospital.
Ferlita, Ernest *s.j.* '62 (NO)[C] New Orleans, LA Loyola University New Orleans.
Fermeglia, Charles '88 (BRK) Released from Diocesan Assignment.
Fernan, Matthew F. '89 (NY) Hastings–on–Hudson, NY St. Matthew.
Fernandes, Albano (CHI) Wilmette, IL St. Joseph.
Fernandes, Babasino '75 (FTW)[F] Avilla, IN Provena Sacred Heart Home.
Fernandes, Cosme S. '95 (NY) Bronx, NY St. Martin of Tours.
Fernandes, Cyril '88 (FTW) Fort Wayne, IN St. John the Baptist.
Fernandes, David A. '97 (PH) Norwood, PA St. Gabriel.
Fernandes, Earl K. '02 (CIN) Imprimatur Censors; [A] Cincinnati, OH The Athenaeum of Ohio; [B] Cincinnati, OH Mt. St. Mary's Seminary of the West; [B] Cincinnati, OH Mt. St. Mary's Seminary of the West.
Fernandes, John '77 (OAK) Retired.
Fernandes, Jose Manuel '59 (NEW) Elizabeth, NJ Our Lady of Fatima.
Fernandes, Lourdino '69 (FTW) Albion, IN Blessed Sacrament.
Fernandes, Mark E. '04 (PH) Sellersville, PA St. Agnes.
Fernandes, Mauro de Souza *o.s.b.* '84 (GBG)[G] Latrobe Saint Vincent Archabbey.
Fernandes, Patrick O. '83 (BUF) Buffalo General Hospital.
Fernandes, Peter *s.f.x.* '85 (P) Milwaukie, OR St. John the Baptist.
Fernandes, Peter *s.f.x.* '99 (CHI) Chicago, IL St. Timothy.
Fernandes, Roque A.D. '69 (LA) Azusa, CA St. Frances of Rome Retired.
Fernandes, Sydney '79 (HON) Kahuku, HI St. Roch.
Fernandez, Agostino *o.s.b.* '05 (CHL)[J] Belmont, NC Belmont Abbey.
Fernandez, Archelito '93 (TLS) Bartlesville, OK St. James.
Fernandez, Cesar A. '95 (LA) La Puente, CA St. Louis of France.
Fernandez, Eduardo C. *s.j.* '92 (OAK)[A] Berkeley, CA Jesuit School of Theology at Santa Clara University; [M] Berkeley, CA Jesuit Fathers and Brothers.
Fernandez, Edward P. '70 (DAL) Retired.
Fernandez, Elias *o.ss.t.* '69 (ARE) Isabela, PR St. Anthony.
Fernandez, Emmanuel '79 (LAF) Erath, LA St. John.
Fernandez, Fabio Jose '04 (CAM) Glassboro, NJ St. Bridget's Catholic Church, Glassboro, N.J.
Fernandez, Felipe *o.s.a.* '71 (SJN) Bayamon, PR San Agustin.
Fernandez, Francis X. *o.f.m.cap.* '58 (FWT) Fort Worth, TX Our Lady of Guadalupe; Cursillo Center.
Fernandez, Frank '79 (PHX) Phoenix, AZ St. Theresa Roman Catholic Parish.
Fernandez, Gerardo '91 (SD) Calexico, CA Our Lady of Guadalupe.
Fernandez, Gustavo D. *s.j.* '67 (FgM) Los Gatos, CA Society of Jesus.
Fernandez, Ismael *o.p.* '07 (PCE) Yauco, PR Holy Rosary.
Fernandez, Javier (SJN) San Juan, PR Nuestra Senora de la Merced.
Fernandez, Jose A. '60 (BGP) Retired.
Fernandez, Joseph *s.d.b.* '76 (OAK) Berkeley, CA St. Ambrose.
Fernandez, Julio '57 (MGZ) Censor Librorum; Religious Consultor; Religious Coordinator.
Fernandez, Luis J. '71 (NO) Retired.
Fernandez, Manuel A. '62 (ORL) Eustis, FL St. Mary of the Lakes.
Fernandez, Marcellus '68 (B) Retired.
Fernandez, Maxim '97 (SAN) Fort Stockton, TX St. Agnes; Fort Stockton, TX St. Joseph's.
Fernandez, Nelson '56 (MIA) Retired.
Fernandez, Rafael Castano '88 (ATL) Cedartown, GA St. Bernadette's.
Fernandez, Rafael *o.f.m.* '87 (FgM) New York, NY Franciscan Province of the Immaculate Conception.
Fernandez, Ricardo *c.m.* (SJN) San Juan, PR Nuestra Senora del Pilar.
Fernandez, Romualdo *c.m.f.* '53 (SJN) Bayamon, PR Santa Maria; Bayamon, PR San Jose; Bayamon, PR San Antonio Maria Claret.
Fernandez, Samuel *o.c.d.* '07 (CGS) Caguas, PR San Jose.
Fernandez, Simine G. *o.ss.t.* '04 (BAL)[S] The Trinitarians in India (Bangalore & Trichur).
Fernandez–Diaz, Mariano *s.t.* '05 (FAJ) Luquillo, PR San Jose.
Fernandez–Marino, Vicente '82 (SJN) Guaynabo, PR Maria Madre de la Misericordia; Cursillos De Cristiandad.
Fernandez Minguez, Serapio '50 (ARE) Retired.
Fernando, Antony '85 (CR) Bemidji, MN St. Philip's.
Fernando, Augustine '64 (RVC) Farmingdale, NY St. Kilian.
Fernando, Bernard '65 (NEW) Retired.
Fernando, Camillus '80 (BAK) Vale, OR St. Patrick.
Fernando, Cresus '82 (NY) Suffern, NY Sacred Heart.
Fernando, Gamini E. '71 (NY) Poughkeepsie, NY Holy Trinity; Stormville, NY Green Haven Correctional Facility.

Fernando, Joachim '62 (BRK) Rosedale, NY St. Pius X Retired.
Fernando, Joseph Paul '62 (RVC) Long Beach, NY St. Ignatius Martyr; Long Beach, NY Long Beach Memorial Medical Center.
Fernando, Lionel '87 (SAN) Sonora, TX St. Ann's.
Fernando, Peter Damian '70 (LA) Ventura, CA San Buenaventura Mission.
Fernando, Peter '64 (BAK) Enterprise, OR St. Katherine's.
Fernando, Polycarp '78 (FTW) Bremen, IN St. Dominic.
Fernando, Roger Marcus '75 (P) Portland, OR St. Therese of the Child Jesus.
Fernando, Sebastian M. '70 (NEW) Glen Rock, NJ St. Catharine; Paramus, NJ Bergen Regional Medical Center.
Fernando, Simon '60 (RVC) Retired.
Fernando, Stanislaus K. (CHI) Bellwood, IL St. Simeon.
Fernando, Susil '87 (LKC) Vinton, LA St. Joseph; Diocesan Consultors; Presbyteral Council; Vocation Recruiters.
Fernando, Rev. Msgr. Venantius M. '61 (NEW) Hillside, NJ Christ the King.
Ferone, John M. *s.j.* '83 (CIN)[N] Cincinnati, OH Faber Jesuit Community.
Ferraioli, Rev. Msgr. Frank B. '61 (PAT) Parsippany, NJ St. Christopher Retired.
Ferraioli, Joseph *o.m.i.* '77 (STP) St. Paul, MN St. Casimir.
Ferrante, Frank *c.m.f.* '70 (LA) Coordinators.
Ferrara, Alberto A. *c.s.b.* '00 (GAL)[O] Sugar Land Basilian Mission Center.
Ferrara, Angelus '90 (NTN) Warren Center, PA Our Lady of Solitude Cloister & Retreat.
Ferrara, Bede *o.f.m.* '50 (BO)[U] Lynn, MA Franciscan Community (Province of Immaculate Conception).
Ferrara, Charles F. '90 (STL) Lemay, MO St. Martin of Tours.
Ferrara, John *o.m.v.* '82 (BO)[U] Milton, MA Oblate Residence (St. Joseph House).
Ferrara, Joseph R. '77 (CAM) Berlin, NJ Saint Simon Stock Parish, Berlin, N.J.
Ferrarese, Rev. Msgr. Fernando '77 (BRK)[M] Brooklyn, NY Italian Board of Guardians; Liturgical Commission; Astoria, NY Immaculate Conception.
Ferrari, Rev. Msgr. Steven A. '80 (BRK) Brooklyn; Assignment Board; Presbyteral Council; Brooklyn, NY Immaculate Heart of Mary.
Ferraro, Joseph A. '90 (NEW) Newark, NJ St. Anthony's; Members; Members.
Ferraro, Rev. Msgr. Joseph '67 (OAK) Retired.
Ferraro, Michael M. '68 (BO) Lynn, MA St. Mary.
Ferraro, Pat '92 (Y) Streetsboro, OH St. Joan of Arc.
Ferraro, Ronald A. '60 (HRT) Waterbury, CT Our Lady of Lourdes; Waterbury, CT St. Lucy.
Ferraro, Vincent J. '70 (BUF)[K] Buffalo, NY Kenmore Mercy Hospital; Kenmore, NY St. Andrew.
Ferras, Jesus '04 (MIL)[T] Waukesha, WI Secular Institute of Schoenstatt Fathers.
Ferras, Jesus *i.s.p.* '04 (AUS) Office of Youth, Young Adult and Campus Ministry; [G] Austin, TX Schoenstatt Fathers.
Ferrazoli, Henry R. '61 (NEW) Retired.
Ferreira, Alphonse *o.f.m.* '72 (BO)[U] Lynn, MA Franciscan Community (Province of Immaculate Conception); [U] Lynn, MA "The Listening Place" (Counseling Center); The Listening Place; The Listening Place; The Listening Place.
Ferreira, Jose S. '56 (BO) Senior Priests. Retired.
Ferreira, Joseph A. '59 (OAK)[L] Oakland, CA Bishop Begin Villa Retired.
Ferreira, Manuel P. '60 (FR) Retired.
Ferrence, John J. *o.s.a.* '52 (PH)[Y] Villanova, PA St. Thomas Monastery.
Ferrer, Charles M. '64 (CHI) Chicago, IL St. Mary of the Angels; [V] Chicago, IL Midtown Residence; Chicago.
Ferrer, Chris '01 (AUS) Austin, TX St. Julia.
Ferrer, Christopher *m.f.* '01 (AUS) Judicial Vicar; Diocesan Tribunal Judges.
Ferrer, Jorge *s.j.* '77 (MGZ) Mayaguez, PR Church De El Buen Pastor.
Ferrer, Melchor *s.d.b.* '74 (NY) New York, NY St. Rose of Lima; Manhattan, NY New York Presbyterian Hospital.
Ferrer, Michael M. *s.d.b.* '74 (NY) Manhattan, NY Presbyterian Medical Center.
Ferrer, Peter C. '61 (LA) Retired.
Ferretti, Samuel J. '74 (SCR) Scranton, PA St. Lucy's; Scranton, PA SS. Peter and Paul; Deans.
Ferri, Greg (BAL) Baltimore, MD St. Rita.
Ferri, Gregory J. '98 (BAL) Special Assignment.
Ferrick, Michael P. '99 (E) St. Marys, PA Queen of the World.
Ferrick, Raymond J. '77 (PRO) Barrington, RI Holy Angels.
Ferrie, Francis '65 (NO) Retired.
Ferrier, Francis V. *s.j.* '61 (BR) Special Assignment.
Ferrier, Ronald J. '68 (PH) Philadelphia, PA St. Katherine of Siena.
Ferrigan, Robert E. '61 (CHI) Retired.
Ferris, Aaron R. '09 (GR) Muskegon, MI Our Lady of Grace; Muskegon, MI St. Thomas the Apostle.
Ferris, Carl A. '55 (GI) Retired.
Ferris, James *c.ss.r.* '35 (ALB)[L] Saratoga Springs, NY St. John Neumann Residence.
Ferris, Robert M. '01 (CHL) Hickory, NC St. Aloysius.
Ferris, Thomas B. '63 (PIT) Retired.
Ferris, Timothy F. '03 (TOL) Bluffton, OH St. Mary; Lima, OH St. Rose of Lima; [B] Lima, OH Central Catholic High School.
Ferrito, Rev. Msgr. Joseph L. (PAT) Retired.
Ferro, Ralph '71 (RVC) New Hyde Park, NY Holy Spirit; East Meadow, NY Nassau County Correctional Center; Chaplains.
Ferruzzi, William *s.d.b.* (BO)[M] Salesian Staff:.
Ferry, James P. '06 (NEW) West Orange, NJ Our Lady of Lourdes.
Ferry, James T. *m.m.* '56 (FgM) Maryknoll, NY MARYKNOLL.
Ferry, James '84 (FR) Fall River, MA Espirito Santo.
Ferry, Rev. Msgr. John T. '84 (NY) Scarsdale, NY Immaculate Heart of Mary.
Fesen, Thomas A. '99 (TR) Hamilton Square, NJ St. Gregory the Great.
Feser, Victor *o.s.b.* '64 (BIS)[A] Richardton, ND Assumption Abbey; [B] Bismarck, ND University of Mary.
Fesniak, Mark '03 (PHU) Minersville, PA Nativity of B.V.M.; Minersville, PA St. Nicholas.
Fesniak, Mark (PHU) Presbyteral Council.
Fessio, Joseph D. *s.j.* '72 (SJ)[M] Los Gatos Sacred Heart Jesuit Center.
Fesuh, Tesfay Woldemarian '88 (WDC) Washington, DC St. Anthony; [W] Washington, DC Ethiopian and Eritrean Catholic Mission, USA.
Fesuh, Tesfaye (WDC) Washington, DC Blessed Sacrament, Shrine of the Most.
Fetcho, John E. '64 (SY) Syracuse, NY Our Lady of Peace.
Fetscher, James F. '68 (MIA) Pinecrest, FL St. Louis.
Fetscher, James '68 (MIA) Deans and Deaneries; [M] Pinecrest, FL MorningStar Renewal Center, Inc.
Fetters, Donald G. *c.s.c.* '76 (FgM) New Rochelle, NY Eastern Brothers Province.
Fetzer, Jose *s.j.* '08 (FWT)[J] Lake Dallas, TX Montserrat Jesuit Retreat House.
Feucht, Urban C. '55 (SEA)[L] Lacey, WA St. Martin's Abbey.
Feudjio, Rev. Msgr. Jerome '90 (STV) Vicar for Clergy and Religious; Charlotte Amalie, VI Cathedral of Sts. Peter and Paul; Diocesan Consultors; Vocations; Catholic Television Network (CTN); Prison Ministry.
Feusahrens, Frederick J. '72 (RIC) Richmond, VA St. Paul Retired.
Fevlo, Anthony *s.m.a.* '98 (BO)[U] Dedham, MA African Mission House.
Fey, Albert *c.pp.s.* '46 (CIN)[N] Carthagena, OH St. Charles Retired.
Fey, George *c.pp.s.* '43 (CIN)[N] Carthagena, OH St. Charles Retired.
Fey, Joseph H. *c.s.c.* '51 (FTW)[H] Holy Cross House Retired.
Fey, Thomas J. '70 (ALX) Retired.
Fey, William *o.f.m.cap.* '68 (FgM) Pittsburgh, PA Province of St. Augustine.
Fiala, Timothy R. '96 (CHI) Hillside, IL St. Domitilla; [A] Chicago, IL St. Joseph College Seminary.
Fiala, Vit *o.f.m.* '98 (Y) Definitors:; Youngstown, OH; [J] Youngstown, OH Mt. Alverna Friary.
Fiala, Vit *o.f.m.* (NY)[EE] Mt. Vernon, NY Franciscan Mission Associates.
Fialkowski, Edward R. '78 (CHI) Arlington Heights, IL Our Lady of the Wayside; College of Consultors; Deans.
Fialkowski, Thomas M. '66 (E) Board of Members.
Fice, Joseph J. *s.j.* '72 (SJ)[L] Los Altos, CA Jesuit Retreat Center of Los Altos.
Ficek, Ryszard '98 (RVC) Glen Head, NY St. Hyacinth; Riverhead, NY St. Isidore's.
Fichteman, William L. '81 (L) Louisville, KY Cathedral of the Assumption; Archdiocesan Examiners.
Fichter, Stephen J. '00 (NEW) Haworth, NJ Sacred Heart.
Fichtner, Joseph *o.s.c.* '43 (SCL)[I] Onamia Crosier Priory.
Fichtner, Rev. Msgr. Robert C. '55 (BO) Senior Priests. Retired.
Fickel, William *s.s.s.* '81 (CLV)[N] Cleveland, OH Congregation of the Blessed Sacrament; Highland Heights, OH St. Paschal Baylon.
Fickes, Daniel R. '91 (CLV) Garfield Heights, OH St. Therese.
Ficorilli, Chad R. *o.s.b.* '79 (GBG)[G] Latrobe, PA Saint Vincent Archabbey.
Fictum, Robert A. '78 (MIL) Ripon, WI St. Catherine of Siena.
Fidalgo, Federico '63 (CC) Retired.
Fider, William '66 (DUL) Duluth, MN St. Joseph; Duluth, MN St. Lawrence.
Fiebelkorn, Daniel F. '97 (BUF) Silver Creek, NY Our Lady of Mt. Carmel.
Fiedler, Donald J. '59 (DOD) Retired.
Fiedler, Rev. Msgr. Kenneth J. '71 (MAD) Madison, WI Our Lady, Queen of Peace; Deaneries.
Fiedler, Lloyd *s.v.d.* '70 (FgM) Techny, IL.
Fiedorowicz, Joseph '75 (OAK) On Sabbatical.
Fiedurek, Jan *s.ch.* (WDC) Silver Spring, MD Our Lady Queen of Poland and Saint Maximilian Kolbe.
Field, Eugene J. '94 (NEW) Ridgefield Park, NJ St. Francis of Assisi; Boy Scouts of America/Catholic Committee on Scouting.
Field, James A. '90 (BO) Melrose, MA Incarnation of Our Lord and Savior Jesus Christ.
Fields, Rev. Archpriest John M. '86 (PHU)[D] Philadelphia, PA Ascension Manor, Inc.; College of Archeparchial Consultors; Presbyteral Council; Protopresbyters (Deans); Frackville, PA St. Michael's; Board Members; Frackville, PA St. John the Baptist.
Fields, Rev. Archpriest John M. (ALN) Rev. James A. Hogan Council #2580, Frackville.
Fields, Robert H. '82 (JC) Camdenton, MO St. Anthony; Hermitage, MO St. Bernadette.
Fields, Stephen M. *s.j.* '86 (WDC)[N] Washington, DC The Jesuit Community at Georgetown University.
Fields, William *o.p.* '91 (MOB) Daphne, AL Christ the King.
Fier, Brian J. '89 (STP) St. Louis Park, MN Most Holy Trinity.
Fierro, Rev. Msgr. David G. '76 (ELP) El Paso, TX St. Matthew; Vicar for Clergy; Diocesan Pastoral Staff; Defenders of the Bond; Vicar for Clergy; Finance Council; Ex Officio Members; Priests' Personnel Advisory Committee.
Fierros, Rick '78 (FRS) Delano, CA St. Mary of the Miraculous Medal.
Fifagrowicz, Joseph G. '62 (BUF) Eggertsville, NY St. Benedict Retired.
Figaredo, Tarsicio Gotay *o.carm.* '73 (SJN) San Juan, PR Santa Teresita Del Nino Jesus; San Juan–Santurce; Subcommission for Popular Piety.
Figel, Terence *o.m.i.* '64 (DUL) Duluth, MN Holy Family.
Figge, Urban *o.m.i.* '57 (BEL)[F] Belleville, IL Missionary Oblates of Mary Immaculate – St. Henry's Oblate Residence.
Figler, Michael B. '98 (TR) Atlantic Highlands, NJ St. Agnes.
Figlia, Sidney *s.d.b.* '68 (NO) Harvey, LA St. John Bosco.
Figliola, Nicholas J. '64 (RVC) Sayville, NY St. Lawrence the Martyr.
Figliozzi, Rev. Msgr. Richard M. '79 (RVC) Franklin Square, NY St. Catherine of Sienna.
Figueiredo, Rev. Msgr. Anthony J. '94 (NEW) On Duty Outside the Archdiocese.
Figueredo, Sergio *s.j.* '60 (MIA) Miami, FL Gesu.
Figueroa, Edward *o.m.i.* '60 (FgM) Washington, DC AMERICAN OBLATE MISSIONS.
Figueroa, Francisco (OAK) Chaplains.
Figueroa, Honecimo '99 (MO) Army National Guard Chaplains; On Assignment Outside the Diocese.
Figueroa, Jose I. '96 (DAL) Dallas, TX Blessed Sacrament.
Figueroa, Ruben C. *o.f.m.* (TYL) Hispanic Ministry Advisory Council.
Figueroa, Ruben '70 (TYL) Tyler, TX Our Lady of Guadalupe; Priests' Personnel Board.
Figueroa Esquer, Francisco J. '01 (OAK) Bishop's Representative for Catholic Charismatics (Spanish); Oakland, CA St. Jarlath.
Figurelli, Nicholas G. '82 (NEW)[B] School of Diplomacy and Intl. Rels.; Newark, NJ Our Lady of Mt. Carmel.
Filacchione, Rev. Msgr. Marc A. '80 (NY) New York, NY Our Lady of Victory; New York Fire Department.
Filardi, Rev. Msgr. Edward J. '94 (WDC) Bethesda, MD Our Lady of Lourdes.
Filary, Richard M. '82 (SAG) Midland, MI Assumption of the Blessed Virgin Mary; Judges.
Filho, Felix I. '99 (NEW) Harrison, NJ Holy Cross.
Filiatreau, Hilary *o.s.b.* '49 (LR) Altus, AR St. Mary.
Filice, Francis P. '79 (SFR) San Francisco, CA St. Thomas the Apostle Retired.
Filice, Peter F. *s.j.* '71 (LA)[F] Los Angeles, CA Loyola High School of Los Angeles.
Filipkowski, Peter '86 (PAT) Newton, NJ St. Joseph.
Filippelli, John L.M. *s.s.j.* '57 (WDC)[B] Washington, DC St. Joseph's Seminary.
Filippello, Michael A. '00 (PH) Philadelphia, PA Immaculate Heart of Mary.
Filippini, Renato *s.x.* '97 (PAT)[N] Wayne Xaverian Missionary Fathers; Wayne, NJ XAVERIAN MISSIONARY FATHERS.
Filipski, Raymond R. '75 (NEW) Bergenfield, NJ St. John the Evangelist.
Fillion, Stephen '79 (SAG) Bay City, MI Our Lady of the Visitation.
Fillman, G. Allan '77 (TOL) Paulding, OH Divine Mercy Parish; St. Maximilian Kolbe Deanery.
Filmanski, Francis E. '53 (RVC) Retired.
Filmer, Eric R. '04 (SAV) Moultrie, GA Immaculate Conception; Presbyteral Council.

Filmyer, Bernard G. *s.j.* '52 (BAL)[S] Towson Maryland Province of the Society of Jesus.
Filut, David C. '68 (MIL) New Berlin, WI Holy Apostles.
Fimbel, Duane G. '57 (BUF) North Tonawanda, NY DeGraff Memorial Hospital; North Tonawanda, NY St. Jude the Apostle.
Fimian, Kevin J. '06 (ARL) Notaries; Potomac Falls, VA Our Lady of Hope.
Fimiani, Rev. Msgr. Louis F. '60 (NEW) Cranford, NJ St. Michael's Retired.
Finamore, Robert A. '70 (WDC) Fort Washington, MD St. Ignatius.
Finan, James '59 (WDC)[M] Washington, DC Cardinal O'Boyle Residence for Priests Retired.
Finch, Joseph E. '58 (ALB)[M] Germantown, NY St. Teresa's Motherhouse.
Finch, Joseph E. '58 (OM) Retired.
Finch, Raymond J. *m.m.* '76 (FgM) Maryknoll, NY MARYKNOLL.
Fincutter, John F. *s.v.d.* '50 (MIL)[P] East Troy, WI Divine Word Missionaries Retired.
Fincutter, Patrick *s.v.d.* '55 (MIL)[P] East Troy, WI Divine Word Missionaries Retired.
Finder, James '91 (JC) Cuba, MO St. Francis; Cuba, MO Holy Cross; Cuba, MO St. Michael.
Findikyan, Michael D. (FTW)[B] University of Notre Dame Du Lac.
Findlan, Rev. Msgr. Joseph G. '38 (PIT)[M] Pittsburgh, PA St. John Vianney Manor Retired.
Finegan, Gerard '67 (VEN) Longboat Key, FL St. Mary Star of the Sea; Presbyteral Council.
Finegan, Lawrence J. '70 (SFR) San Francisco, CA Cathedral of St. Mary (Assumption).
Finelli, Jay A. '92 (PRO) Tiverton, RI Holy Ghost.
Finelli, Rev. Msgr. Victor F. '89 (ALN) Catasauqua, PA Annunciation B.V.M.–St. Mary's; Judges; Elected Members.
Finelli, Victor '89 (LEX) Associate Judges.
Fineo, Richard '02 (FAR) Cooperstown, ND Sacred Heart Church of Aneta; Cooperstown, ND St. George; Cooperstown, ND St. Olaf; Cooperstown, ND St. Lawrence; Diocesan College of Consultors.
Fineran, A. Gerard *s.j.* '50 (NO)[P] New Orleans Jesuit Provincial Office.
Finerty, Bernard *o.f.m.cap.* '61 (BAL) Cresaptown, MD St. Ambrose; Cumberland, MD SS. Peter and Paul; [S] Cumberland, MD SS. Peter and Paul Friary.
Finerty, D. Bryan '59 (PRO) Retired.
Finerty, Raymond J. *o.p.* '71 (LA)[AA] Los Angeles, CA Occidental College, Catholic Campus Ministry.
Finerty, Raymond *o.p.* '71 (LA) Los Angeles, CA St. Dominic.
Fink, Rev. Msgr. Charles R. '76 (RVC)[A] Huntington, NY Diocesan Seminary of the Immaculate Conception.
Fink, Daniel *o.f.m.conv.* '84 (HBG) Trevorton, PA St. Patrick.
Fink, David G. *o.f.m.conv.* '84 (HBG) Coal Township, PA Our Lady of Hope.
Fink, John L. '67 (IND) Bradford, IN St. Michael.
Fink, John L. '69 (IND) Depauw, IN St. Bernard; Depauw, IN St. Joseph.
Fink, John '71 (MIA) Special Assignment; Catholic Charismatic Services—Archdiocese of Miami.
Fink, Joseph '83 (STP) West St. Paul, MN St. Joseph.
Fink, Karel '91 (AUS) Killeen, TX St. Joseph.
Fink, Peter E. *s.j.* '69 (NY)[EE] New York, NY Xavier Jesuit Community; New York, NY St. Francis Xavier.
Fink, Philip *o.f.m.cap.* '77 (PIT) Beaver County, PA Villa St. Joseph; [M] Allison Park, PA St. Conrad Friary.
Finlan, Robert T. '94 (ALN) Bethlehem, PA Sacred Heart of Jesus; [C] Bethlehem, PA Bethlehem Catholic High School; Elected Members; College of Consultors.
Finlay, Joseph F. '57 (STA) Retired.
Finley, James F. '63 (MO) Navy Chaplains; Military Chaplains.
Finley, James F. '63 (TUC) Yuma, AZ MCAS Chapel.
Finley, Jeffrey *c.pp.s.* '90 (OAK) Washington Hospital.
Finley, John Thomas '75 (LAF) On Special Assignment.
Finley, Thomas M. *c.m.* '54 (PH)[Y].
Finley, Thomas M. *c.m.* '54 (GR)[J] Spring Lake, MI St. Lazare Retreat House.
Finley, William (ORL) Retired.
Finn, Daniel J. '72 (BO) Dorchester, MA St. Mark; Presbyteral Council.
Finn, David C. '03 (RCK) Special Assignment; Sterling, IL Sacred Heart; [B] Sterling, IL Newman Central Catholic High School.
Finn, Dominick F. *o.s.f.s.* '56 (PH) Norristown, PA Norristown State Hospital.
Finn, Edward S. '52 (SCR) On Special or Other Diocesan Assignment Retired.
Finn, Firmin *o.f.m.conv.* '55 (ALB)[J] Latham, NY Our Lady of Hope Residence; [L] Rensselaer, NY Provincialate, Immaculate Conception Friary – Order of Friars Minor Conventual; Special Assignment.
Finn, Gregory T. *o.s.j.* '89 (SCR) Hazleton, PA Annunciation, Hazelton; [B] Pittston, PA St. Joseph's Oblate Seminary; [M] Pittston, PA Our Lady of Sorrows Province of the Oblates of St. Joseph; Councilors:.
Finn, John A. *o.s.f.s.* '62 (WIL) Wilmington, DE St. Francis Hospital; [J] Wilmington, DE DeSales House.
Finn, John P. '81 (NO) Retired.
Finn, Joseph P. '98 (LIN) Lincoln, NE St. Mary; Health Care Facilities.
Finn, Michael E. '77 (SCR) Lake Ariel, PA St. Thomas More.
Finn, Rev. Msgr. Peter G. '65 (NY) Staten Island, NY Blessed Sacrament; [I] New York, NY The Ladies of Charity of the Catholic Charities of the Archdiocese of New York; Archdiocesan Consultors; Staten Island.
Finn, Rev. Msgr. Peter '65 (NY)[G] Staten Island, NY Seton Foundation for Learning, Inc.
Finn, Raymond C. *o.p.* '70 (NO) Metropolitan Tribunal; New Orleans, LA St. Dominic.
Finn, Robert E. *s.j.* '91 (CHI) Chicago, IL John H. Stroger, Jr. Hospital of Cook County; [N] Chicago, IL Woodlawn Jesuit Community.
Finn, Seamus P. *o.m.i.* '76 (WDC)[N] Washington, DC Provincial Offices of the United States Province of the Missionary Oblates of Mary Immaculate; [N] Washington, DC Oblate Community.
Finn, William P. *c.m.* '48 (PH)[Y].
Finnane, Daniel P. '63 (MAD) Waunakee, WI St. Mary of the Lake.
Finnegan, Charles *o.f.m.* '58 (BO)[Z] Boston, MA St. Anthony Shrine.
Finnegan, Gerald F. *s.j.* '67 (BO)[U] Boston The Society of Jesus of New England–Provincial Offices.
Finnegan, Gerald F. *s.j.* '67 (PRO) Woonsocket, RI St. Charles.
Finnegan, J. Kevin '96 (STP) Faribault, MN Divine Mercy Catholic Church.
Finnegan, John P. '54 (CHI) Retired.
Finnegan, John S. '56 (SY) Baldwinsville, NY St. Elizabeth Ann Seton.
Finnegan, Joseph '65 (HEL) Retired.
Finnegan, Kevin H. '90 (GLP) Crownpoint, NM St. Paul; Promoter of Justice; Defenders of the Bond; Vicars Forane; Presbyteral Council.
Finnegan, Kevin '96 (STP) Shieldsville, MN St. Patrick; Kenyon, MN St. Michael.
Finnegan, Robert K. *o.praem.* '52 (GB)[J] De Pere, WI St. Norbert Abbey; [O] De Pere, WI Canons Regular of Magnovarad, Ltd.; [O] De Pere, WI Norbertine Generalate, Inc.; Bishop's Finance Council.
Finnegan, Rev. Msgr. Thomas J. '51 (BO) Senior Priests. Retired.
Finnegan, William J. '57 (CHI) Orland Park, IL St. Michael Retired.
Finnell, John H. '78 (WH) South Charleston, WV Blessed Sacrament.
Finnell, Terrell '92 (KC) Kansas City, MO St. Monica; Deans.
Finnerty, Rev. Msgr. D. Joseph '63 (BRK) Flushing, NY St. Kevin.
Finnerty, Rev. Msgr. James J. '55 (NEW) Jersey City, NJ St. Paul's Retired.
Finnerty, Rev. Msgr. Joseph L. '57 (SD) Poway, CA St. Michael Retired.
Finnerty, Vincent H. *c.m.* '79 (CHL) Charlotte, NC Our Lady of Guadalupe Church.
Finnestad, Jerald L.C. '80 (FAR) Lisbon, ND St. Vincent's Church of Gwinner; Lisbon, ND St. Aloysius Church of Lisbon.
Finney, Donald T. '94 (PMB) Jupiter, FL St. Peter.
Finnigan, Francis *c.p.* '68 (MET)[I] South River Passionist Provincial Office.
Finnigan, Francis *c.p.* (FgM) South River, NJ St. Paul of the Cross Province.
Finnigan, John B. '61 (MAN) Suncook, NH St. John the Baptist Retired.
Finnigan, Rev. Msgr. John C. '59 (Y) Canton, OH St. Peter.
Finno, James '72 (CHI) Tinley Park, IL St. Stephen, Deacon and Martyr.
Finsterbach, Thomas P. *s.j.* '76 (SJ)[M] Los Gatos, CA Sacred Heart Jesuit Center.
Finucan, J. Thomas '55 (LC)[H] La Crosse, WI Holy Cross (Seminary) Diocesan Center Retired.
Finucane, Robert '54 (B) Genesee, ID St. Mary Station Retired.
Fiore, Arthur B. '75 (WIL) Newark, DE St. John the Baptist–Holy Angels.
Fiore, John J. *c.s.b.* '57 (GRY)[H] Merrillville, IN Basilian Fathers Residence Retired.
Fiore, Joseph A. '70 (BUF) Darien Center, NY Immaculate Heart of Mary.
Fiore, Peter A. *o.f.m.* '55 (ALB)[B] Siena College.
Fiorelli, Lewis S. *o.s.f.s.* '70 (ARL) Vienna, VA Our Lady of Good Counsel.
Fiorillo, Antimo '43 (NY) Bronx, NY Santa Maria Retired.
Fiorino, Alfred L. *s.j.* '60 (NY)[EE] Loyola Hall, Jesuit Community.
Fiorino, Dominic J. '61 (NEW)[M] Caldwell, NJ The Rev. Msgr. James F. Kelley Residence for Retired Priests Retired.
Firestone, Thomas '78 (LAN) Flint, MI St. John Vianney; [P] Fenton, MI Alma Redemptoris Mater.
Firko, Frank A. '77 (PBR) Hermitage, PA St. Michael; Elected Deanery Representatives; Presbyteral Council.
Firmin, Daniel F. '04 (SAV) Savannah, GA Cathedral of St. John the Baptist; Catholic Relief Services; Mission Cooperative Appeal; Presbyteral Council; Chancellor; Chancery; Tribunal Judges; Staff.
Firpo, John A. '77 (ROC) Rochester, NY St. Charles Borromeo.
Fisch, Gerald M. '57 (SC) Retired.
Fischer, Adrian *o.f.m.* '75 (SHP) Monroe, LA Little Flower of Jesus.
Fischer, Andrew C. (PIT) Pittsburgh, PA St. Paul Cathedral.
Fischer, Barry J. *c.pp.s.* '73 (CIN)[N] Dayton Provincial Office of the Cincinnati Province of the Society of the Precious Blood.
Fischer, Benedict *o.s.b.* '07 (BIS)[B] Bismarck, ND University of Mary; [A] Richardton, ND Assumption Abbey.
Fischer, Brian J. '79 (CHI) Chicago, IL St. Gregory, the Great.
Fischer, Brian R. '03 (STL) Master of Ceremonies; Office of Youth Ministry; Special Assignment.
Fischer, Charles H. '71 (KAL) Battle Creek, MI St. Philip; Advocates.
Fischer, Charles '90 (FAR) Fargo, ND St. Mary's Cathedral of Fargo.
Fischer, Clarence L. '61 (HON) Office of Clergy Priest Retirement Committee.
Fischer, Rev. Msgr. Don L. '67 (DAL) Richardson, TX St. Joseph.
Fischer, Eugene '65 (SD) Retired.
Fischer, G. William *o.s.f.s.* '69 (E)[K] Erie, PA Saint Mary's Home of Erie.
Fischer, Henry J. '71 (BEL) Bartelso, IL St. Cecilia.
Fischer, Hilary *m.s.c.* '57 (SB) Anza, CA Sacred Heart.
Fischer, James J. *s.j.* '55 (ROC)[B] Rochester, NY McQuaid Jesuit High School.
Fischer, John M. '63 (E) Girard, PA Retired.
Fischer, John P. '76 (CIN) Cincinnati, OH St. Michael; Judges.
Fischer, John '86 (SFS) Vermillion, SD St. Agnes.
Fischer, Jonathan *o.s.b.* '61 (STP)[H] St. Paul, MN HealthEast St. Joseph's Hospital; St. Joseph's Hospital.
Fischer, Jonathan *o.s.b.* '61 (SCL)[I] Collegeville, MN St. John's Abbey, of the Order of St. Benedict.
Fischer, Kenneth J. '71 (CHI) River Forest, IL St. Luke.
Fischer, Mark F. *f.s.s.p.* '95 (ATL) Mableton, GA St. Francis De Sales.
Fischer, Norman '00 (LEX) Lexington, KY St. Peter Claver.
Fischer, Philip C. *s.j.* '61 (STL)[O] St. Louis, MO Jesuit Community Corporation at Saint Louis University – Jesuit Hall.
Fischer, Richard O. '76 (MO) Air Force Reserve Chaplains; Southern; Klamath Falls, OR St. Pius X.
Fischler, James *c.i.c.m.* '76 (SAT) Priests Personnel Board; Del Rio, TX Sacred Heart; In Rural Area; Archdiocesan Presbyteral Council.
Fisette, Carl B. '06 (PRO) Providence, RI St. Augustine.
Fisette, Kevin R. '81 (PRO) Absent on Leave.
Fish, Alfred H. '77 (OG) St. Regis Falls, NY Church of the Holy Cross; St. Regis Falls, NY St. Ann.
Fish, Eugene J. '97 (FAR) Retired.
Fish, Justin '05 (DUL) Aitkin, MN St. James; Aitkin, MN Our Lady of Fatima; Aitkin, MN Holy Family.
Fish, Michael *o.s.b.cam.* '78 (MRY)[F] Big Sur, CA New Camaldoli Hermitage.
Fishel, Gregory *s.d.b.* '89 (CHI) Chicago, IL St. John Bosco.
Fisher, A. J. '56 (BAK) Retired.
Fisher, Albert '81 (BIR) On Duty Outside the Diocese.
Fisher, Albert '81 (SAV) Special Assignment.
Fisher, Andrew J. '98 (ARL) Annandale, VA St. Ambrose; Vocations, Office of.
Fisher, Bernard *s.v.d.* '45 (CHI)[N] Techny, IL Divine Word Residence.
Fisher, Clarence L. '61 (HON) Office of Clergy: Diocesan Screening Committee; Diocesan Ecumenical Commission Retired.
Fisher, David E. '86 (LAN) Owosso, MI St. Joseph.
Fisher, David T. *s.j.* '53 (SJ)[M] Los Gatos, CA Sacred Heart Jesuit Center.
Fisher, David '84 (OLL) Cincinnati, OH St. Anthony of Padua Maronite Catholic Church.
Fisher, Donald C. '61 (PIT) Retired.
Fisher, Edward K. '92 (MEM) Paris, TN Holy Cross.
Fisher, Rev. Msgr. Edward T. '49 (BUF) Retired.
Fisher, Harold *o.m.i.* '00 (LA) San Fernando, CA Santa Rosa.
Fisher, Kyle *c.ss.r.* '63 (STL) St. Louis, MO St. Alphonsus Liguori; [O] St. Louis, MO Redemptorist Fathers.
Fisher, Martin J. '86 (ALB) Greenwich, NY St. Joseph; Schuylerville, NY Notre Dame–Visitation.
Fisher, Martin '51 (GF) Retired.
Fisher, Rev. Msgr. Michael W. '90 (WDC) Secretariats;

Continuing Education for Clergy; Archdiocesan College of Consultors; Priest Council; Pastoral Center Special Ministries; Hyattsville, MD St. Mark.
Fisher, Rev. Msgr. Michael William (WDC) Secretariat for Ministerial Leadership and Vicar for Clergy.
Fisher, Paul '95 (HBG) Bloomsburg, PA St. Columba.
Fisher, Raymond A. '71 (TOL)[J] Fremont, OH St. Bernardine Home.
Fisher, Robert D. '80 (DEN) Englewood, CO All Souls; Deaneries; Elected Representatives from Deanery to Presbyteral Council.
Fisher, Robert J. '92 (DET) Utica, MI St. Lawrence.
Fisher, Robert *s.v.d.* '65 (BLX) Diocesan Liturgical Commission; [D] Bay St. Louis, MS St. Augustine's Residence.
Fisher, Roe '02 (STA) Absent or Sick Leave.
Fisher, Terry '85 (FTW) Mishawaka, IN St. Joseph; Presbyteral Council; School Board, Diocesan.
Fisher, William F. *o.s.f.s.* '61 (DET) Monroe, MI St. Anne; Monroe, MI St. Joseph.
Fisher, William '93 (KCK) Regional Pastoral Leaders; Ottawa, KS Sacred Heart.
Fishwick, Joseph '75 (MIA) Special Assignment; [J] Miami, FL Mercy Hospital Retired.
Fister, Daniel '09 (LEX) Lexington, KY Cathedral of Christ the King.
Fister, Stephen J. '82 (P)[N] Gold Hill, OR St. Rita's Retreat Center.
Fitch, John '02 (VEN) Venice, FL Epiphany Cathedral.
Fitterer, Paul *s.j.* '63 (P)[A] Portland, OR Jesuit Novitiate of Sheridan Orgeon.
Fittin, Edward Seton *o.s.b.* '93 (PAT)[N] Morristown, NJ St. Mary's Abbey.
Fitts, Robert L. *s.j.* '69 (SPK) Spokane, WA St. Ann.
Fitz, James *s.m.* '74 (STL)[O] St. Louis, MO Marianists, Province of the United States (Society of Mary); Saint Louis, MO; [O] St. Louis, MO Maryland Avenue Marianist Community.
Fitz–Henry, Edward '85 (MRY) San Juan Bautista, CA San Juan Bautista; Administrative Committee Priests' Pension Plan.
Fitz–Patrick, David M. '79 (MO) Military Chaplains; Air Force Chaplains.
Fitzgerald, Allan *o.s.a.* '67 (PH) Rosemont, PA St. Thomas of Villanova Parish; [C] Villanova University.
Fitzgerald, Christopher *i.c.* '58 (SP) Seffner, FL St. Francis of Assisi.
Fitzgerald, David E. *s.a.* '65 (R) Apex, NC St. Andrew the Apostle.
Fitzgerald, David T. *s.p.* '78 (SB) Commission for Ministry with Families of Gay and Lesbian Catholics; San Bernardino, CA Our Lady of the Assumption; Office of the Vicar for Clergy; Officers.
Fitzgerald, David *s.a.* '65 (NY)[EE] Garrison Graymoor Ecumenical and Interreligious Institute.
Fitzgerald, Edmund H. '57 (PRO) Retired.
Fitzgerald, Rev. Msgr. Edmund J. '68 (FR) Somerset, MA St. Thomas More; Diocesan Consultors; Fall River Deanery; Diocesan Health Facilities.
Fitzgerald, Edward T. '59 (SPR) Ware, MA All Saints.
Fitzgerald, Edward W. '95 (CHR) Hanahan, SC Divine Redeemer; Chancellor; College of Consultors.
Fitzgerald, Garrett J. *s.j.* '55 (NY)[EE] New York, NY Murray–Weigel Hall.
Fitzgerald, George R. *c.s.p.* '65 (NY)[EE] Jamaica Estates Paulist Fathers Generalate.
Fitzgerald, George R. *c.s.p.* '65 (SFR) San Francisco, CA Old St. Mary's Cathedral.
Fitzgerald, Howard E. '78 (DM) On Sabbatical; Advocates.
Fitzgerald, Rev. Msgr. J. Terrence '62 (SLC) Vicar General and Moderator of the Curia; College of Consultors; Board of Directors; Priests' Personnel Board; Defenders of the Bond; Board For Formation of Priests.
Fitzgerald, James E. *s.j.* '66 (MIL)[P] Wauwatosa, WI Jesuit Community at St. Camillus.
Fitzgerald, John B. '55 (LA) Retired.
Fitzgerald, John E. '57 (PH) Philadelphia, PA St. Anselm Retired.
Fitzgerald, John E. '63 (STO) Twain Harte, CA All Saints Church (Pastor of); College of Consultors/ Presbyteral Council; Deans.
Fitzgerald, Rev. Msgr. John G. '62 (LA) Lompoc, CA Our Lady Queen of Angels.
Fitzgerald, John J. *o.s.a.* '41 (PH)[Y] Villanova, PA St. Thomas Monastery.
Fitzgerald, John J. '58 (RVC) Setauket, NY St. James Retired.
FitzGerald, Rev. Msgr. John L. '67 (BAL) Special Assignment; [W] Baltimore, MD Stella Maris Maritime Center.
Fitzgerald, John P. '74 (PIT) Conway, PA Our Lady of Peace; Air National Guard Chaplains; Chicago, IL National Conference of Catholic Airport Chaplains (NCCAC).
Fitzgerald, Joseph *c.m.* '05 (FgM) Philadelphia, PA Eastern Province.
Fitzgerald, Joseph '07 (RVC)[C] Hicksville, NY Holy Trinity Diocesan High School.
FitzGerald, Kevin T. *s.j.* '88 (WDC)[N] Washington, DC The Jesuit Community at Georgetown University.
Fitzgerald, Rev. Msgr. Michael J. '80 (PH) On Special or Other Archdiocesan Assignment; Judicial Vicar; College of Consultors; Priests' Personnel Board; Philadelphia, PA St. Patrick; [A] Wynnewood, PA Theological Seminary of St. Charles Borromeo, Overbrook.
Fitzgerald, P. Timothy '75 (DM) On Special Assignment; Office of Lay Ministry.
Fitzgerald, Paul J. *s.j.* '92 (BGP)[B] Fairfield, CT Fairfield University; [O] Fairfield, CT The Fairfield Jesuit Community–Fairfield University.
Fitzgerald, R. Martin '89 (R) On Duty Outside the Diocese.
Fitzgerald, R. Martin '89 (MO) Air Force Chaplains.
Fitzgerald, R. Patrick *o.f.m.* '61 (NY) New York, NY St. Francis of Assisi.
Fitzgerald, Raymond R. *s.j.* '91 (NO)[E] New Orleans, LA Jesuit High School; [P] New Orleans, LA Jesuit Provincial Office.
Fitzgerald, Richard W. (BO) Wellesley, MA St. Paul; Vicariate II.
Fitzgerald, Robert H. *s.j.* '66 (MIL)[P] Wauwatosa, WI Jesuit Community at St. Camillus.
Fitzgerald, Thomas J. '75 (PAT) Clifton, NJ St. Clare's.
Fitzgerald, Thomas J. '68 (MAD) Retired.
Fitzgerald, Thomas P. '66 (STP) Centerville, MN St. Genevieve.
Fitzgerald, Thomas *s.s.s.* '64 (SP) Holiday, FL St. Vincent De Paul.
Fitzgerald, Timothy *c.p.* '56 (PIT)[M] Pittsburgh, PA St. Paul of the Cross Monastery; [O] Pittsburgh, PA St. Paul of the Cross Retreat Center.
Fitzgerald, Timothy (DM) Altoona, IA SS. John and Paul.
Fitzgerald, Rev. Msgr. William F. '50 (TR)[N] Trenton, NJ Villa Vianney; Diocesan Consultors Retired.
Fitzgerald, William J. '58 (PHX) Scottsdale, AZ Our Lady of Perpetual Help Roman Catholic Parish Retired.
Fitzgerald, William *c.ss.r.* '43 (DEN)[N] Denver The Redemptorists/Denver Province.
Fitzgerald, Rev. Msgr. William '57 (KAL) Retired.
Fitzgerald, William *c.ss.r.* '43 (FgM) Denver, CO Denver Province.
Fitzgibbon, Edmond J. '59 (STL) Retired.
Fitzgibbons, John A. '68 (PH) Retired.
Fitzgibbons, John P. *s.j.* '85 (MIL)[P] Milwaukee, WI Jesuit Community at Marquette University.
Fitzgibbons, Peter L. '84 (MO) Albemarle, NC Our Lady of the Annunciation; Military Chaplains; Army Reserve Chaplains.
Fitzmaurice, James '84 (ALB) Albany, NY Christ the King; Presbyteral Council; Diocesan Board of Consultors.
Fitzmaurice, Rev. Msgr. V. Paul '73 (GBG) North Huntingdon, PA St. Agnes.
Fitzmyer, Joseph A. *s.j.* '51 (WDC)[N] Washington, DC The Jesuit Community at Georgetown University Retired.
Fitzpatrick, Bede *o.f.m.* '55 (FgM) New York, NY Holy Name Province.
Fitzpatrick, Daniel J. *s.j.* '66 (NY)[EE] Loyola Hall, Jesuit Community; [II] New York, NY Brooklyn Prep Alumni Association; [II] Bronx, NY Metro New York Christian Life Communities, Inc.
Fitzpatrick, Rev. Msgr. Donnelly J. '63 (PEO) Retired.
Fitzpatrick, Edmund J. '47 (CHI) Retired.
Fitzpatrick, Edward J. '70 (DAV)[E] Iowa City, IA Newman Catholic Student Center; [J] Iowa City, IA O'Keefe Hall; Judges.
Fitzpatrick, Edward T. *o.s.f.s.* (R) Kitty Hawk, NC Holy Redeemer by the Sea.
Fitzpatrick, Gerald J. *s.j.* '71 (WDC)[Q] Faulkner, MD Loyola Retreat House.
Fitzpatrick, J. Vincent '92 (FAR) Absent on Leave.
Fitzpatrick, Rev. Msgr. James J. '84 (PH) Morrisville, PA St. John the Evangelist.
Fitzpatrick, James M. '84 (FR) Absent on Sick Leave.
Fitzpatrick, James M. '71 (SAG) Standish, MI Resurrection of the Lord; Territorial Vicars.
Fitzpatrick, Rev. Msgr. John E. '70 (PAT) Oak Ridge, NJ St. Thomas, the Apostle.
Fitzpatrick, John P. '60 (BO) Senior Priests. Retired.
Fitzpatrick, John P. '52 (STP) Retired.
Fitzpatrick, Joseph F. *s.j.* '65 (NY)[EE] New York, NY Murray–Weigel Hall.
Fitzpatrick, Mallick J. *s.j.* '60 (NY)[EE] Jesuit Community, Kohlmann Hall; [F] Bronx, NY Fordham Preparatory School.
Fitzpatrick, Michael J. '83 (PH) Honey Brook, PA St. Peter.
Fitzpatrick, Michael J. *s.j.* '77 (BAK) Pendleton, OR St. Andrew's Indian Mission.
Fitzpatrick, Michael Joseph '03 (FR) University of Massachusetts Dartmouth; [L] North Dartmouth, MA Catholic Campus Ministry University of Massachusetts Dartmouth; New Bedford, MA Our Lady of Guadalupe; St. Luke's Hospital.
Fitzpatrick, Michael *s.j.* '77 (SPK)[O] Spokane, WA Kateri Northwest Ministry Institute.
Fitzpatrick, Paul E. *s.m.* '77 (BO)[A] Weston, MA Blessed John XXIII National Seminary.
Fitzpatrick, Paul K. '98 (LA) San Marino, CA Saints Felicitas and Perpetua.
Fitzpatrick, R. Michael '71 (OM) Omaha, NE St. Stanislaus; Promoter of Justice; Defenders of the Bond; Consultors; Finance Council; Ex Officio (Consultors).
Fitzpatrick, Robert J. '54 (CHI) Ingleside, IL St. Bede Retired.
Fitzpatrick, Robert J. '73 (STP) Roseville, MN St. Rose of Lima.
Fitzpatrick, Robert *o.m.i.* '71 (FgM) Washington, DC AMERICAN OBLATE MISSIONS.
Fitzpatrick, Thomas J. *s.j.* '68 (MAN) Salem, NH Mary, Queen of Peace; Salem, NH St. Joseph.
Fitzpatrick, Thomas J. *s.j.* '68 (BO)[U] Boston The Society of Jesus of New England–Provincial Offices.
Fitzpatrick, Thomas P. '61 (SY) Syracuse, NY Our Lady of Lourdes.
Fitzpatrick, Thomas '04 (SFS) Sioux Falls, SD St. Joseph Cathedral; Sioux Falls, SD Our Lady of Guadalupe.
Fitzsimmons, Donald J. *c.s.v.* '60 (CHI)[N] Arlington Heights, IL Viatorian Province Center–Clerics of St. Viator.
Fitzsimmons, Rev. Msgr. Eugene J. '60 (CAM) Haddonfield, NJ The Church of St. Vincent Pallotti, Haddon Township, N.J. Retired.
Fitzsimmons, Gerald J. *s.m.m.* '75 (BRK) Ozone Park, NY St. Mary Gate of Heaven; Presbyteral Council.
Fitzsimmons, J. Thomas '62 (CIN) Eaton, OH Visitation of the Blessed Virgin Mary; Eaton, OH St. John the Evangelist.
Fitzsimmons, Rev. Msgr. Richard '56 (PEO) Retired.
Fitzsimmons, Robert Philip *o.p.* '55 (NY)[EE] New York, NY St. Catherine of Siena Priory.
Fitzsimmons, Rev. Msgr. Thomas B. '62 (CAM) Retired.
Fitzsimons, Patrick '01 (LEX) Special Assignment.
Fiuk, Stanislaw '90 (SAT) La Vernia, TX St. Ann.
Fix, Donald P. '80 (PIT) Military Chaplains; Navy Chaplains.
Fix, Joseph J. '68 (GR) Evart, MI Sacred Heart; Evart, MI St. Agnes; Deans.
Fix, Robert H. '53 (CHR) Retired.
Fixsen, Patrick '07 (PEO) Pekin, IL St. Joseph's.
Flach, Carl '58 (P) Retired.
Flach, James A. '86 (SFD) Wood River, IL Holy Angels.
Flach, Rev. Msgr. Thomas D. '71 (BEL) Marion, IL St. Joseph; Defensores Vinculi.
Flack, Robert S. *s.j.* '74 (CHI)[S] The Jesuit Retreat League of Chicago.
Fladung, Charles J. '92 (DAV) Keota, IA Holy Trinity; Sigourney, IA St. Mary's; Deans.
Flagg, Wayne N. '88 (VIC) New Ulm, TX SS. Peter and Paul; Alleyton, TX St. Roch.
Flaherty, Charles *s.s.c.* '50 (OM)[K] St. Columbans Missionary Society of St. Columban.
Flaherty, Daniel J. '54 (DEN) Louisville, CO St. Louis Retired.
Flaherty, Daniel L. *s.j.* '60 (CHI)[N] Evanston, IL Canisius House.
Flaherty, Edward F. *s.j.* '65 (DEN)[N] Denver, CO Xavier Jesuit Center.
Flaherty, Frederick R. *m.s.* '57 (HRT)[L] Hartford, CT Missionaries of LaSalette.
Flaherty, Rev. Msgr. J. Francis '55 (CAM) Retired.
Flaherty, Rev. Msgr. James J. '80 (PT) Pensacola, FL Holy Spirit; Judicial Vicar; Judges; College of Consultors; Administrative Council; Continuing Education & Formation; Members Elected by Deanery.
Flaherty, James P. *s.j.* '92 (MIL)[P] Milwaukee, WI Jesuit Community at Marquette University.
Flaherty, Jay M. '85 (KNX) Pigeon Forge, TN Holy Cross.
Flaherty, John J. *o.s.a.* '55 (CHI)[N] Olympia Fields, IL Tolentine Monastery at Tolentine Center.
Flaherty, John R. '90 (DUB) Manchester, IA St. Mary; [E] Manchester, IA St. Paul School of Religion; Manchester, IA Immaculate Conception; Ryan, IA St. Patrick.
Flaherty, Kevin H. *s.j.* '83 (CHI)[N] Chicago Chicago Province of the Society of Jesus–Provincial Office.
Flaherty, Kevin H. *s.j.* '83 (FgM) Chicago, IL Society of Jesus.
Flaherty, Leon *c.pp.s.* '61 (CIN)[N] Dayton Provincial Office of the Cincinnati Province of the Society of the Precious Blood.
Flaherty, Leon *c.pp.s.* (GRY) Whiting, IN St. John the Baptist.
Flaherty, Malachy *o.c.s.o.* '60 (SLC)[F] Huntsville, UT Abbey of Our Lady of the Holy Trinity of the Order of Cistercians.
Flaherty, Malachy *o.f.m.cap.* (RVC) Melville, NY Long Island Developmental Center.
Flaherty, Michael T. '73 (CIN) Cincinnati, OH St. Veronica.
Flaherty, Richard C. *o.f.m.* '82 (BO)[Z] Boston, MA St. Anthony Shrine.
Flaherty, William J. '52 (CHI) Winnetka, IL SS. Faith, Hope and Charity Retired.

Flajole, John Paul *o.f.m.* '64 (GAL) Galveston, TX Holy Family.
Flamm, Paul M. *c.s.sp.* '99 (FgM) Bethel Park, PA CONGREGATION OF THE HOLY SPIRIT.
Flammia, Paul G. '96 (BO) Wilmington, MA St. Thomas of Villanova.
Flanagan, Rev. Msgr. Bernard A. '82 (ALN) Shenandoah, PA St. Mary Magdalen; Shenandoah, PA Annunciation; Shenandoah, PA St. George; Shenandoah, PA Our Lady of Mt. Carmel; Shenandoah – Court Annunciation #175.
Flanagan, Brian '98 (PMB) Palm Beach Gardens, FL St. Patrick.
Flanagan, Damian '91 (MIA) Miami, FL St. Catherine of Siena.
Flanagan, David J. '87 (MAD) Benton, WI St. Patrick; Cuba City, WI St. Rose of Lima.
Flanagan, Edward R. '88 (MET) Monroe Township, NJ Nativity of Our Lord.
Flanagan, Edward *o.f.m.* '64 (WDC)[N] Washington, DC Franciscan Monastery USA Inc.
Flanagan, Hubert *s.c.a.* '67 (DET)[K] Wyandotte, MI Society of the Catholic Apostolate (Pallottine Fathers); [K] Wyandotte, MI Pallottine Missionary Center (Irish Province).
Flanagan, James D. '71 (NY) Bronx, NY Holy Family.
Flanagan, James E. *c.s.s.* '50 (BO)[X] Waltham, MA Stigmatine Fathers and Brothers Retired.
Flanagan, James W. '61 (DUB) Retired.
Flanagan, James *s.o.l.t.* '52 (CC)[G] Robstown, TX Society of Our Lady of the Most Holy Trinity.
Flanagan, James '08 (ATL) Atlanta, GA Holy Spirit.
Flanagan, John B. '97 (PH) Primos, PA St. Eugene; [D] Springfield, PA Cardinal O'Hara High School.
Flanagan, John J. '74 (SAT) San Antonio, TX St. Jerome; In Metropolitan Area; Archdiocesan Presbyteral Council; Priests Personnel Board.
Flanagan, John P. '59 (SY) Utica, NY St. John Retired.
Flanagan, Joseph F. X. *s.j.* '59 (BO)[U] Newton, MA The Jesuit Community at Boston College.
Flanagan, Michael J. *m.s.* '60 (HRT)[L] Hartford, CT Missionaries of LaSalette.
Flanagan, Rev. Msgr. Michael T. '65 (JC) Columbia, MO Our Lady of Lourdes; Episcopal Vicars; Diocesan Consultors; Personnel Board; Ex Officio Members; Finance Committee; Board of Trustees.
Flanagan, Rev. Msgr. P. Kevin '59 (PAT) Clifton, NJ; Clifton, NJ St. Philip the Apostle Retired.
Flanagan, Rev. Msgr. Patrick J. '56 (SAT) Retired.
Flanagan, Patrick S. *c.m.* (BRK)[T] Jamaica, NY Vincentian Residence.
Flanagan, Patrick Sean *c.m.* '92 (RVC)[M] Oyster Bay, NY Vincentian Community.
Flanagan, Rev. Msgr. Sean B. '59 (LA) Los Angeles, CA L.A. City Fire Dept. Retired.
Flanagan, Rev. Msgr. Thomas J. '49 (BRK) Retired.
Flanagan, William F. '64 (JC) Retired.
Flanigan, Rev. Msgr. Gerald A. '51 (DET) Retired.
Flanigan, James F. *c.s.c.* '62 (FTW)[B] University of Notre Dame Du Lac; [H] Notre Dame, IN Holy Cross Community, Corby Hall, University of Notre Dame.
Flanigan, Rev. Msgr. Thomas P. '69 (PH) Lansdale, PA Corpus Christi.
Flannagan, Bruce G. '78 (BO) Danvers, MA St. Richard of Chichester.
Flannagan, Thomas J. (SC) Spencer, IA Sacred Heart.
Flannery, John C. *o.p.* '60 (P)[L] Portland, OR Holy Rosary Priory; Portland, OR Holy Rosary Parish & Dominican Priory Retired.
Flannery, Kevin L. *s.j.* '87 (DET)[K] Detroit Jesuit Provincial Office–Detroit Province of the Society of Jesus.
Flannery, Michael '97 (ALB) Fort Ann, NY St. Ann; Whitehall, NY Our Lady of Hope.
Flannery, Rev. Msgr. Michael '64 (JKS) Madison, MS St. Francis of Assisi; Office of Vicar General; Promoter of Justice; Diocesan Consultors.
Flannery, Patrick R. '97 (NEW) Caldwell, NJ St. Aloysius.
Flannery, Robert B. '73 (BEL) Carbondale, IL St. Francis Xavier; Carterville, IL Church of the Holy Spirit; Diocesan Deans; Ecumenical and Interreligious Affairs; Carbondale, IL Catholic Association of Diocesan Ecumenical and Interreligious Officers (CADEIO).
Flaska, Michael J. '97 (DEN) Longmont, CO St. John the Baptist; Conifer, CO Our Lady of The Pines; Evergreen, CO Christ the King.
Flater, Gerald *o.m.i.* '57 (BO)[X] Tewksbury, MA Immaculate Heart of Mary Residence.
Flatley, Brian M. '66 (BO) Arlington, MA Saint Agnes.
Flattery, John J. '55 (PEO) Retired.
Flavin, James A. '87 (BO) Pastoral Care of Priests and Clergy Fund; Boston, MA St. Mary – St. Catherine of Siena.
Flavin, James *o.m.i.* '63 (BO)[X] Tewksbury, MA Immaculate Heart of Mary Residence.
Flavin, John E. '61 (CHI) Retired.
Flax, Myron *o.f.m.cap.* '64 (COS)[I] Colorado Springs, CO Catholic Center at the Citadel; [F] Colorado Springs, CO Solanus Casey Friary.
Fleck, David G. '75 (EVN) Vincennes, IN St. Vincent de Paul; Judges; Diocesan Consultors; Diocesan Council of Priests; Deans; Vincennes, IN St. John the Baptist.
Fleck, John W. '59 (TOL) Delphos, OH St. John the Baptist; Delphos, OH St. Patrick.
Fleck, Kenneth J. '76 (CHI) Tinley Park, IL St. George.
Fleckenstein, John D. '02 (KAL) Vocations; Portage, MI St. Catherine of Siena; Diocesan Finance Council.
Fleckenstein, John '02 (KAL) Cemeteries; Presbyteral Council Members; Presbyteral Council Members.
Flecky, Michael J. *s.j.* '77 (OM)[K] Omaha, NE Jesuit Community at Creighton University.
Fleischhacker, John J. *o.s.c.* '61 (SCL)[I] Onamia, MN Crosier Priory.
Fleischman, Richard J. '68 (MIL) Belgium, WI St. Mary; Fredonia, WI Holy Rosary; Random Lake, WI Our Lady of the Lakes.
Fleischmann, George R. '56 (MIL) Retired.
Fleiter, Robert V. '61 (STL) Herculaneum, MO Church of the Assumption of B.V.M.
Fleming, Alfred J. *m.m.* '60 (FgM) Maryknoll, NY MARYKNOLL.
Fleming, Austin H. '73 (BO) Concord, MA Holy Family.
Fleming, Brendan '52 (P) Retired.
Fleming, Daniel J. '96 (ATL) Newnan, GA St. Mary Magdalene.
Fleming, David L. *s.j.* '65 (STL) Saint Louis, MO; [O] St. Louis, MO Ignatius House; [V] St. Louis, MO Review for Religious.
Fleming, David '90 (DM) Council Bluffs, IA St. Patrick.
Fleming, George '94 (ALB) Troy, NY St. Bonaventure; Schaghticoke, NY Church of the Holy Trinity.
Fleming, James *s.j.* '95 (BO)[U] Newton, MA The Jesuit Community at Boston College.
Fleming, Jeffrey M. '92 (HEL) Missoula, MT Christ the King; [G] Missoula, MT University of Montana; Presbyteral Council; Diocesan Pastoral Council; Diocesan Consultors; Defenders of the Bond; Members.
Fleming, John M. '61 (CAM) Retired.
Fleming, John W. '96 (MAN) Auditors; Finance Council; Manchester, NH Parish of the Transfiguration.
Fleming, Joseph W. '74 (ALT) Chest Springs, PA St. Monica's; Dysart, PA St. Augustine.
Fleming, Martin M.P. '52 (STP) Retired.
Fleming, Rev. Msgr. Patrick V. '48 (ALT) Retired.
Fleming, Raymond H. '82 (ROC) Rochester, NY Emmanuel Church of the Deaf of the Diocese of Rochester; Rochester, NY St. Monica.
Fleming, Rodger P. '07 (STL) St. Charles, MO St. Joseph.
Fleming, T.J. '85 (SAG) New Lothrop, MI St. Michael.
Fleming, Terence K. '67 (ROC) On Duty Outside the Diocese.
Fleming, Rev. Msgr. Terrance L. '73 (LA) Los Angeles, CA St. Brendan; Propagation of the Faith; Judges; Mission Office.
Fleming, Thomas J. '59 (BO) Senior Priests. Retired.
Fleming, Thomas '55 (JOL) Retired.
Flemming, James K. '86 (VEN) Retired.
Flens, Daniel A. '89 (CHI) Chicago, IL Cardinal's Residence; Office of the Archbishop.
Fletcher, Luke Mary *c.f.r.* '03 (NY)[EE] New York, NY St. Joseph's Friary; [EE] Yonkers, NY St. Leopold's Friary.
Fletcher, Patrick '85 (MO) On Duty Outside the Diocese; Air Force Chaplains.
Fleury, Joseph M. *s.m.* '84 (WDC)[N] Washington, DC Marist Center.
Fleury, Joseph M. *s.m.* '84 (MO) Army Chaplains.
Fleury, Joseph M. *s.m.* '84 (HON) Military Chaplains.
Flickinger, Don D. '64 (FRS) Retired.
Flickinger, Don D. '64 (SFR) San Francisco, CA St. Paul.
Flickinger, Robert E. '75 (KAL) Advocates; Diocesan Consultors; Presbyteral Council Members; South Haven, MI St. Basil; Presbyteral Council Members.
Flint, Edward A. *s.j.* '69 (DET)[K] Clarkston, MI Colombiere Center.
Flint, James *o.s.b.* '83 (JOL) Lisle, IL; [A] Lisle, IL Benedictine University; [L] Lisle, IL St. Procopius Abbey.
Flint, Kenneth '42 (NOR) Retired.
Flisk, Louden–Hans W. '01 (FAR) Retired.
Fliss, James W. '75 (BUF) Farnham, NY St. Anthony's.
Fliss, Paul J. '92 (MIL) Fox Point, WI St. Eugene; Whitefish Bay, WI St. Monica.
Fliss, Richard L. '66 (LC) On Duty Outside the Diocese Retired.
Floch, W. Roy '77 (SPK) Spokane, WA St. Paschal.
Flock, Robert H. '82 (LC) Foreign Missions.
Floeder, John P. '07 (STP) Anoka, MN St. Stephen; Appointees.
Floersh, Philip M. *c.m.* '62 (STL)[O] St. Louis Vincentian Residence.
Flood, Augustine A. *o.s.b.* '64 (GBG)[G] Latrobe, PA Saint Vincent Archabbey.
Flood, Charles J. *o.ss.t.* '90 (BAL)[S] The Trinitarians in New Jersey.
Flood, Charles J. *o.ss.t.* '90 (TR) Asbury Park, NJ Our Lady of Mt. Carmel; Jersey Shore Medical Center.
Flood, Eric *f.s.s.p.* '00 (SCR)[M] Elmhurst, PA Priestly Fraternity of St. Peter (F.S.S.P.), North American District Headquarters; Elmhurst, PA.
Flood, Francis *o.s.b.* '93 (NEW)[M] Newark, NJ Newark Abbey.
Flood, Rev. Msgr. J. Michael '68 (PH) Glenside, PA St. Luke the Evangelist; [BB] Glenside, PA Arcadia University.
Flood, James F. '62 (CLV)[M] Fairlawn, OH St. Edward Home; [M] Fairlawn, OH St. Edward Home.
Flood, Rev. Msgr. James J. '58 (PH) Philadelphia, PA St. Timothy Retired.
Flood, Matthew C. *s.j.* '61 (NY)[F] Bronx, NY Fordham Preparatory School; [EE] Loyola Hall, Jesuit Community.
Flood, Maurice *o.c.s.o.* '91 (ARL)[H] Berryville, VA Cistercian Abbey of Our Lady of the Holy Cross.
Flood, Maurice *o.c.s.o.* '91 (SR)[M] Whitethorn, CA Our Lady of the Redwoods Abbey.
Flood, Paul '90 (ATL) Johns Creek, GA St. Benedict.
Flood, Rev. Msgr. Peter J. '69 (TR) Retired.
Flood, Rev. Msgr. William J. '57 (BRK) BMT Holy Name Society; Bayside, NY Our Lady of the Blessed Sacrament Retired.
Flor, Carlos F. '97 (BO) Revere, MA Immaculate Conception.
Flor, Carlos '97 (NEW) On Duty Outside the Archdiocese.
Flora, Carmel *o.f.m.cap.* '53 (FgM) Detroit, MI Province of St. Joseph; [K] Detroit St. Bonaventure Friary.
Flora, Giandomenico '06 (BGP) Bridgeport, CT St. Raphael.
Florczyk, Walter '62 (SY) Retired.
Florea, Eugene '07 (PHX) Phoenix, AZ St. Gregory Roman Catholic Parish; [A] Phoenix, AZ Bourgade Catholic High School.
Florek, Rev. Msgr. Frederick J. '64 (SD) San Diego, CA St. Therese.
Florek, Richard T. *o.f.m.conv.* '72 (PMB) Boynton Beach, FL St. Mark.
Florek, Thomas W. *s.j.* '86 (CHI)[N] Chicago Chicago Province of the Society of Jesus–Provincial Office.
Florek, Thomas *s.j.* '86 (FTW)[K] South Bend, IN Jesuit Community; [B] University of Notre Dame Du Lac.
Florenciani, Javier Aquino '06 (MGZ) San German, PR San German de Auxerre.
Flores, Alejandro Francisco '09 (BWN) Brownsville, TX San Felipe de Jesus.
Flores, Alejandro '99 (MIA) Miami, FL St. Joachim.
Flores, Alejandro '09 (JOL) Shorewood, IL Holy Family.
Flores, Antonio '05 (PBL) Durango, CO Sacred Heart.
Flores, Arthur *o.m.i.* '92 (SAT) San Antonio, TX San Juan De Los Lagos Shrine.
Flores, Benjamin '93 (ELP) El Paso, TX San Antonio.
Flores, Cirilo '91 (ORG)[K] Santa Ana, CA Catholic Charities of Orange County, Inc.; Diocesan Finance Council; Special Assignment; Council of Priests; Consultors.
Flores, Efrain '91 (ORG) Westminster, CA Blessed Sacrament; Clergy Personnel Board.
Flores, Francisco '00 (B) Caldwell, ID Our Lady of the Valley; [F] Caldwell, ID The College of Idaho; Priest Personnel Commission; Priest Retirement Committee.
Flores, Gabriel '85 (SFR) San Francisco, CA St. Anthony of Padua.
Flores, Guillermo Ulises Ortrz *o.f.m.* (LAR) Hebbronville, TX Our Lady of Guadalupe.
Flores, Guillermo *m.sp.s.* '03 (LA) Oxnard, CA Our Lady of Guadalupe Parish.
Flores, Javier *s.d.v.* '08 (NEW) Newark, NJ St. Michael's.
Flores, Jesus '85 (ROC) Office of Migrant Ministry.
Flores, Jose A. '73 (CGS) Yabucoa, PR Santos Angeles Cutodios.
Flores, Jose Alfredo Siesquen '88 (SPR) Westfield, MA St. Mary's.
Flores, Juan M. '98 (YAK) Zillah, WA Resurrection; Toppenish, WA St. Aloysius.
Flores, Juan Manuel '03 (YAK) Diocesan Commission on Public Worship.
Flores, Juan Manuel '03 (FRS) Exeter, CA Sacred Heart.
Flores, Lee A. '85 (GAL) Rosenberg, TX Our Lady of Guadalupe.
Flores, Louis Fernando Orozco '05 (MRY) Salinas, CA Sacred Heart.
Flores, Luzvimindo '79 (ANC) Big Lake, AK Corp. of Our Lady of the Lake Church.
Flores, Miguel '94 (FRS) Bakersfield, CA St. Joseph.
Flores, Ramiro '95 (OAK) Richmond, CA St. Mark.
Flores, Raymond J. '05 (LSC) Hatch, NM Our Lord of Mercy; Office of Vocations; Clergy Personnel Board; Presbyteral Council; Priestly Life and Ministry Committee.
Flores, Richard '84 (FWT) Fort Worth, TX St. Patrick Cathedral; Vocations and Seminarians.
Flores, Roberto *s.v.d.* '96 (OAK) Oakland, CA St. Bernard.
Flores–Alva, Luis M. '06 (BAK) Madras, OR St. Patrick.

Flores Alferez, Juan M. '98 (YAK) Diocesan Commission for the Catechumenate.
Florez, Andrew '93 (NY) Rosendale, NY St. Peter.
Florez, Hernan '05 (DEN) Frederick, CO St. Theresa.
Florez, Jhon J. (CGS) Priests Senate.
Florez, José Luis *o.s.a.* '81 (LA) Claremont, CA Our Lady of the Assumption.
Florez, Juan Pablo (BRK) Flushing, NY St. Michael.
Florez, Luis '59 (STA) Retired.
Florez–Ardilla, Carlos '03 (MIL) Milwaukee, WI Prince of Peace/Principe de Paz; Milwaukee, WI St. Vincent de Paul; Milwaukee, WI St. Hyacinth.
Florez–Coicedo, Horacio '89 (SAT) Charlotte, TX St. Rose of Lima.
Flori, David J. '86 (DAL) Richardson, TX St. Paul the Apostle; Deans.
Floridi, Nicholas A. '00 (PHX) Phoenix, AZ St. Joan of Arc Roman Catholic Parish; Advocates.
Florido, Robert A. '79 (CHI) Chicago, IL Transfiguration of Our Lord.
Florido, Robert '79 (MO) DEPARTMENT OF VETERANS AFFAIRS HOSPITALS AND CHAPLAINS.
Florio, Philip A. *s.j.* '01 (PH)[BB] Philadelphia, PA University of Pennsylvania; [Y] Loyola Center and Manresa Hall; Philadelphia, PA St. Agatha–St. James.
Florvil, Telamaque (NY) New York, NY St. Charles Borromeo.
Flott, Phil '02 (GI) Scottsbluff, NE Our Lady of Guadalupe.
Flower, Thomas A. '65 (HRT) Tariffville, CT St. Bernard.
Flowers, Thomas A. '77 (WIL) Smyrna, DE St. Polycarp; Delaware Home & Hospital for the Chronically Ill; Catholic Charismatic Renewal.
Floyd, Ronnie Paul '08 (FR) Wareham, MA St. Patrick's.
Fluet, Gregoire J. '82 (NOR) Moodus, CT St. Bridget of Kildare; Deans; Part Time; Archivist; [A] Cromwell, CT Holy Apostles College and Seminary; Members; Director and Chaplain.
Fluetsch, John P. '91 (FRS) Wasco, CA St. John the Evangelist.
Flum, Martin '01 (STU)[H] Bloomingdale, OH Holy Family Hermitage.
Flusche, Vincent '90 (LR) Texarkana, AR St. Edward; Ashdown, AR St. Elizabeth Ann Seton Church; Foreman, AR Sacred Heart Church; Deans; Vicars for Religious; Presbyteral Council.
Flusk, Rev. Msgr. Joseph F. '53 (NEW) Retired.
Flynn, Arthur C. '52 (BO) Senior Priests. Retired.
Flynn, Brian L. '03 (BO) Brockton, MA St. Edith Stein.
Flynn, Charles P. '69 (DUL) Eveleth, MN Resurrection; Gilbert, MN St. Joseph.
Flynn, D. Michael *s.j.* '73 (NY) Staten Island, NY St. Mary of the Assumption; Staten Island, NY Our Lady of Mt. Carmel–St. Benedicta.
Flynn, Edmund *o.c.s.o.* '70 (ARL)[H] Berryville, VA Cistercian Abbey of Our Lady of the Holy Cross.
Flynn, Edward R. '54 (SD) Retired.
Flynn, Francis J. '69 (OG) Constable, NY The Catholic Community of Constable, Westville and Trout River; Constable, NY St. Bridget's Oratory.
Flynn, George R. '56 (BO) Senior Priests. Retired.
Flynn, George '56 (FgM) Boston, MA St. James the Apostle, Inc.
Flynn, J. Joseph *o.f.m.cap.* (NY)[C] New Rochelle, NY The College of New Rochelle.
Flynn, James B. '64 (WOR) Southborough, MA St. Matthew; [B] Worcester, MA Holy Name Central Catholic Junior/Senior High School.
Flynn, James E. '55 (L) Retired.
Flynn, James E. '67 (CHI) Deans.
Flynn, James F. '67 (CHI) Chicago, IL Holy Name of Mary; Chicago, IL Sacred Heart Mission of Holy Name of Mary.
Flynn, James R. *o.s.a.* '72 (PH)[F] Malvern, PA Malvern Preparatory School for Boys; [Y] Malvern, PA Augustinian Friars (O.S.A.).
Flynn, James '06 (FWT) Fort Worth, TX St. John the Apostle.
Flynn, James '73 (SJ)[L] Los Altos, CA Jesuit Retreat Center of Los Altos.
Flynn, John C. '55 (NY) Bronx, NY St. Martin of Tours.
Flynn, John F. *o.s.a.* '53 (LAN) Flint, MI St. Matthew.
Flynn, John H. '55 (BO) Senior Priests. Retired.
Flynn, John J. *s.j.* '69 (SJ)[M] Los Gatos, CA Sacred Heart Jesuit Center.
Flynn, John Joseph *o.f.m.cap.* (NY)[HH] New Rochelle, NY College of New Rochelle.
Flynn, John L. *s.j.* '64 (SJ)[M] Los Gatos, CA Sacred Heart Jesuit Center.
Flynn, John R. *o.s.a.* '71 (PH) Philadelphia, PA St. Rita of Cascia; [Y] Villanova, PA Provincial Offices of the Order of St. Augustine, Province of St. Thomas of Villanova.
Flynn, Rev. Msgr. John '52 (TYL) Advocates Retired.
Flynn, Joseph *o.f.m.cap.* '66 (NY)[EE] White Plains, NY St. Conrad Friary.
Flynn, Lawrence W. *m.m.* '87 (NY)[EE] Maryknoll Maryknoll Fathers and Brothers Retired.
Flynn, Mark F. '72 (HRT) Farmington, CT St. Patrick.
Flynn, Matthew *o.c.s.o.* '58 (WOR)[O] Spencer, MA St. Joseph's Abbey.
Flynn, Michael E. '77 (CHI) Chicago, IL St. Thomas More.
Flynn, Michael F. '91 (BGP) Trumbull, CT St. Theresa.
Flynn, Michael J. '94 (PT) On Duty Outside the Diocese; [A] Boynton Beach, FL St. Vincent de Paul Regional Seminary.
Flynn, Rev. Msgr. Michael P. '71 (RVC) Farmingdale, NY St. Kilian.
Flynn, Michael *o.carm.* '60 (CHI) Chicago, IL Nativity of Our Lord.
Flynn, Michael *o.carm.* '61 (JOL)[L] Darien Carmelite Provincial Office.
Flynn, Patrick *c.ss.r.* '69 (BAL) Annapolis, MD St. Mary.
Flynn, Paul *o.s.a.* '82 (ORG) Santa Ana, CA St. Barbara Catholic Church.
Flynn, Rev. Msgr. Sean P. '75 (TR) Sea Girt, NJ St. Mark.
Flynn, Stephen A. '08 (CLV) Solon, OH St. Rita.
Flynn, Thomas A. '60 (CLV) North Olmsted, OH St. Clarence Retired.
Flynn, Thomas A. '49 (SCR) Retired.
Flynn, Rev. Msgr. Thomas M. '58 (CAM) Retired.
Flynn, Thomas P. '60 (DET) Retired.
Flynn, Thomas '61 (HEL) On Duty Outside the Diocese.
Flynn, William J. '64 (NOR) Taftville, CT Sacred Heart Retired.
Flynn, William J. *s.s.* '59 (SCR)[N] Dunmore, PA Villa St. Joseph Retired.
Flynn, William J. *s.s.* '59 (BAL)[S] Baltimore Society of St. Sulpice, Province of the United States Retired.
Fobare, Scott D. '87 (OG) Port Henry, NY The Church of All Saints; Port Henry, NY St. Patrick; Committee for the Continuing Education of Clergy.
Foeckler, Christopher *m.j.* (CHI)[W] Chicago, IL Men's Formation Center.
Foelker, James *o.m.i.* '55 (CC) Sarita, TX Our Lady of Guadalupe.
Foeller, Rev. Msgr. Charles J. '50 (COL) Legion of Mary Retired.
Fogal, Joseph B. '75 (WIN) Austin, MN St. Augustine's; Austin, MN St. Edward's; Priest Assignments Committee.
Fogarty, Declan *o.s.a.* '59 (SB) Norco, CA St. Mel.
Fogarty, Gerald P. *s.j.* '70 (WDC)[N] Washington, DC The Jesuit Community at Georgetown University; Towson, MD.
Fogarty, James '54 (SLC) Retired.
Fogarty, John (PIT)[B] Pittsburgh, PA Duquesne University of the Holy Spirit.
Fogarty, John *c.s.sp.* '81 (PIT)[M] Bethel Park, PA Congregation of the Holy Spirit Province of the United States; [M] Bethel Park, PA Holy Spirit Fathers and Brothers Provincialate; [Q] Bethel Park, PA Spiritan Support Trust; Councilors:; Priest Council.
Fogarty, Joseph A. *o.p.* (MAD) Madison, WI.
Fogarty, Rev. Msgr. Noel '57 (MIA) Plantation, FL St. Gregory; Members.
Fogarty, Rev. Msgr. Paul '67 (ATL) Decatur, GA St. Thomas More.
Fogarty, Thomas *s.s.p.* '57 (Y)[A] Canfield, OH Society of St. Paul.
Fogle, Bruce '83 (OWN) Earlington, KY Holy Cross; Dawson Springs, KY Resurrection; Earlington, KY Immaculate Conception.
Foglio, John '61 (LAN) Retired.
Fohlin, Paul *o.c.d.* '72 (BO)[U] Boston, MA Carmelite Monastery.
Fohn, Kurt M. '01 (CHL) Statesville, NC St. Philip the Apostle.
Foisy, Leonard R. '57 (MAN) Retired.
Foken, Herman J. '43 (TLS) Retired.
Folbrecht, Robert A. '75 (LA) L.A. County Fire Dept.; Covina, CA St. Louise de Marillac.
Folchetti, John T. '74 (TR) Lincroft, NJ St. Leo the Great.
Folda, Rev. Msgr. John T. '89 (LIN)[A] Seward, NE St. Gregory the Great Seminary; Notaries; Vicars For Religious; Censores Librorum; Catholic Physicians Guild; Members; Diocesan Health Ministries, Inc.; Diocesan Housing Ministries, Inc.; Priests' Continuing Education Committee.
Foley, Augustine E. *o.s.b.* '89 (NO)[A] St. Benedict, LA St. Joseph Seminary College; [P] St. Benedict, LA St. Joseph Abbey; [A] St. Benedict, LA St. Joseph Seminary College.
Foley, Brendan P. '55 (HT) Retired.
Foley, Daniel R. '60 (SPR)[G] Springfield, MA St. Michael's Residence; Judges; Promoter of Justice Retired.
Foley, David M. '72 (MEM) Retired.
Foley, Dennis *c.ss.r.* '61 (TR)[R] Long Branch, NJ San Alfonso Retreat House.
Foley, Edward *o.f.m.cap.* (CHI)[B] Chicago, IL The Catholic Theological Union at Chicago; Detroit, MI.
Foley, Edwin *c.ss.r.* '47 (BAL) Baltimore, MD Our Lady of Fatima.
Foley, Francis P. '84 (MO) Military Chaplains; Navy Chaplains.
Foley, George '58 (FWT) Mansfield, TX St. Jude.
Foley, Gerald J. '59 (GB) Appointed Members Retired.
Foley, J. Patrick '73 (RNO) Ongoing Formation for Permanent Deacons.
Foley, Rev. Msgr. James J. '66 (PH) Collegeville, PA St. Eleanor.
Foley, Jerome P. '84 (SFR) San Francisco, CA St. James.
Foley, John B. *s.j.* '72 (STL)[C] Saint Louis University; [O] St. Louis, MO Jesuit Community Corporation at Saint Louis University - Jesuit Hall.
Foley, John J. *c.s.p.* '67 (PAT)[A] Oak Ridge, NJ Paulist Novitiate; [J] Oak Ridge, NJ Mount Paul Retreat Center.
Foley, John J. '74 (WOR) Shrewsbury, MA St. Anne.
Foley, John J. *c.s.p.* '67 (NY) Jamaica, NY Catholic Missionary Union; [EE] New York, NY Paulist Fathers' Motherhouse.
Foley, Rev. Msgr. John Kieran '59 (LA) Montrose, CA Holy Redeemer Retired.
Foley, John P. *s.j.* '67 (CHI) Chicago, IL St. Procopius; [N] Chicago, IL Miguel Pro Jesuit Community.
Foley, John P. *s.j.* '59 (CHI)[W] Chicago, IL Cristo Rey Network.
Foley, John '74 (WOR) Diocesan Building Commission Members.
Foley, Joseph P. *c.m.* '68 (BRK)[T] Queens Village, NY DePaul Residence.
Foley, Joseph *s.m.a.* '67 (NEW)[M] Tenafly, NJ Society of African Missions, Provincialate, S.M.A. Fathers Retired.
Foley, Marc *o.c.d.* '81 (WDC)[B] Washington, DC Discalced Carmelite Friars.
Foley, Matthew E. '89 (CHI) Army Chaplains; Military Chaplains.
Foley, Rev. Msgr. Matthew F. '56 (BRK) Retired.
Foley, Matthew *o.f.m.conv.* '09 (BAL)[S] Baltimore, MD Immaculate Heart of Mary Friary; [C] Baltimore, MD Archbishop Curley High School.
Foley, Michael G. '86 (CHI) Orland Park, IL St. Michael.
Foley, Rev. Msgr. Michael G. '70 (WOR) Westborough, MA St. Luke the Evangelist.
Foley, Michael '70 (PT) Tallahassee, FL Good Shepherd.
Foley, Patrick '72 (PT) Pensacola, FL St. Joseph; Members At Large.
Foley, Patrick '73 (SD) Unassigned.
Foley, Patrick *t.o.r.* '06 (STP) Minneapolis, MN St. Bridget; [K] Minneapolis, MN St. Bridget Friary.
Foley, Peter J. '67 (PH) Retired.
Foley, Peter '67 (SP) St. Pete Beach, FL St. John Vianney.
Foley, Thomas C. '57 (BO) Senior Priests.; Quincy, MA St. Ann Retired.
Foley, Thomas F. '77 (SFR) San Francisco, CA Old St. Mary's Cathedral.
Foley, Thomas S. '86 (BO) Parish Life and Leadership; Ex Officio; Presbyteral Council; Quincy, MA St. John the Baptist.
Foley, Timothy M. '65 (STL) University City, MO Christ the King.
Foley, Walter W. '76 (ATL) Retired.
Foley, William B. *s.j.* '77 (BO)[U] Weston, MA Campion Jesuit Community.
Foley, William E. '79 (WDC) Upper Marlboro, MD Saint Mary of the Assumption; Deans.
Foley, Rev. Msgr. William J. '67 (NY) Stony Point, NY Immaculate Conception.
Folger, Benedict *ss.cc.* '57 (FR)[G] Fairhaven, MA Damien Residence.
Folino, Frank *o.f.m.* '05 (SHP)[F] Ruston, LA E. Donn Piatt Catholic Student Center at Louisiana Tech University; Ruston, LA St. Thomas Aquinas.
Follmann, Roland F. *o.s.a.* '60 (TLS)[B] Tulsa, OK Cascia Hall Preparatory School.
Follmar, A. Joseph '59 (LC) Greenwood, WI St. Mary Help of Christians; Greenwood, WI Holy Family.
Folorunso, Stephen (SAL) Atwood, KS Sacred Heart Parish; Atwood, KS St. John Nepomucene Parish; Atwood, KS Assumption of Mary Parish.
Folsey, William David *o.p.* '60 (PRO)[P] Providence St. Thomas Aquinas Priory at Providence College.
Folsom, Cassian *o.s.b.* '84 (IND)[K] St. Meinrad St. Meinrad Archabbey.
Folsom, Paul '65 (SCL) Retired.
Folsom, William P. '91 (MOB) Retired.
Foltyn, Rev. Msgr. Emilian '64 (AUS) Jarrell, TX Holy Trinity Catholic Church – Corn Hill, Texas; Rural Life.
Foltz, Rev. Msgr. Michael H. '89 (CR) Adjutant Judicial Vicar; Finance Council; Diocesan Consultors; Moorhead, MN St. Joseph's; Priests' Council; Priests' Personnel Board.
Folzenlogen, John N. *s.j.* '65 (GAL)[E] Houston, TX Strake Jesuit College Preparatory Inc.
Folzenlogen, Joseph D. *s.j.* '71 (CIN)[N] Cincinnati, OH Claver Jesuit Community.
Fonck, Benet *o.f.m.* '72 (JOL)[K] Joliet, IL Our Lady of Angels Retirement Home.
Fonck, Benet *o.f.m.* '72 (CHI)[N] Countryside, IL St.

Gratian Friary, Franciscan Friars.
Fones, Michael S. *o.p.* '92 (TUC) Tucson, AZ Saint Thomas More Roman Catholic Newman Parish – Tucson; [G] Tucson, AZ University of Arizona Retired.
Fones, Michael *o.p.* '92 (OAK)[A] Berkeley, CA Dominican School of Philosophy and Theology.
Fong, Franklin *o.f.m.* '06 (OAK)[M] Oakland, CA Franciscan Friars (Province of Santa Barbara); Definitors:.
Fonscea, Joaquin Mayorqa (SJN) San Juan, PR Santos Pedro y Pablo los Apostoles.
Fonseca, Erwin A. *c.s.c.* '91 (FTW)[H] Notre Dame Congregation of Holy Cross, Indiana Province, Provincial House.
Fonseca, Rev. Msgr. Harvey '92 (FRS) Livingston, CA St. Jude Thaddeus; Diocesan Consultors; Vicars Forane; Priests' Council.
Fonseca, Luis '09 (SAV) Valdosta, GA St. John the Evangelist.
Fonseca, Oscar D. '07 (NEW) South Kearny, NJ Hudson County Correctional Center; Air Force Reserve Chaplains.
Fonseca, Oscar D. '69 (NEW) West New York, NJ St. Joseph of the Palisades.
Fonseca, Rolando '94 (ELP) Advocates; Presbyteral Council; Marfa, TX St. Mary's.
Fonseka, Matthew '69 (NEW) Saddle Brook, NJ St. Philip the Apostle.
Fontaine, David A. *o.carm.* '79 (SAC) Fairfield, CA Our Lady of Mount Carmel,.
Fontana, Alphonso R. '97 (HRT) Bristol, CT St. Anthony.
Fontana, Charles S. '69 (DET) Dearborn, MI St. Clement.
Fontana, Glenn J. '92 (PEO) Cullom, IL St. John's.
Fontana, John M. *o.s.m.* '78 (CHI)[N] Chicago Order of Friar Servants of Mary (Servites) United States of America Province, Inc.; [N] Chicago, IL Order of Friar Servants of Mary (Servites) United States of America Province, Inc.; Chicago, IL.
Fontanella, Andrew J. '56 (HBG) Retired.
Fontanella, Paul C. '02 (SCR) Williamsport, PA St. Ann's.
Fontanini, Christopher '97 (DM) St. Mary's, IA Assumption; [C] West Des Moines, IA Dowling Catholic High School; St. Marys, IA St. Patrick; St. Marys, IA Immaculate Conception.
Fontenot, Anthony '01 (LKC) Jennings, LA Immaculate Conception; Vocation Recruiters; Diocesan Consultors; Presbyteral Council.
Fonti, Joseph G. '92 (BRK)[V] Brooklyn, NY Ss. Peter and Paul Spirituality Center Brooklyn Campus; Ministerial Development Program; [V] Douglaston, NY Ss. Peter and Paul Spirituality Center Queens Campus; [B] Douglaston, NY Cathedral Seminary Residence of the Immaculate Conception; Secretariat for Pastoral Support.
Foote, Job *o.s.b.* '89 (ALT) Nicktown, PA St. Nicholas.
Foote, Job *o.s.b.* '89 (MO) Navy Reserve Chaplains.
Foppiano, Michael '07 (BAL) Towson, MD Church of the Immaculate Conception.
Foppiano, Steven Eugene '02 (SAC) Paradise, CA St. Thomas More; Presbyteral Council.
Foradori, V. David '86 (E) Du Bois, PA St. Joseph; Du Bois, PA St. Michael.
Foran, Peter '74 (LA) Westlake Village, CA St. Jude.
Forbes, Eric *o.f.m.cap.* '90 (AGN)[F] Agana Heights, GU St. Fidelis Friary; Archdiocesan College of Consultors; Archdiocesan Presbyteral Council.
Forbes, John J. '91 (R) Council of Priests; Raleigh, NC Our Lady of Lourdes; Deans.
Forbes, Richard L. '67 (CAM) Retired.
Forbes, Wayne '61 (P) Portland, OR St. John Fisher; Area Vicars.
Forbidussi, John E. '94 (PIT) Richeyville, PA St. Agnes.
Forbus, John J. '06 (CC) Corpus Christi, TX Saint John the Baptist.
Forcelle, Joseph '80 (SFS) Watertown, SD Immaculate Conception.
Forcier, Richard–Jacob *o.f.m.conv.* '86 (NOR) Stafford Springs, CT St. Edward.
Forcier, Robert H. '03 (PRO) Cranston, RI Holy Apostles.
Ford, Christopher M. '87 (HRT) Branford, CT St. Mary; Judges.
Ford, Harold LeRoy '49 (LA) Long Beach, CA St. Joseph Retired.
Ford, Rev. Msgr. J. Joseph '67 (PRT) Falmouth, ME Holy Martyrs; Gray, ME St. Gregory; Diocesan Consultors; Diocesan Priests' Benefit Plan – Trustees; Personnel Board.
Ford, James Michael '66 (LA) Retired.
Ford, John T. *c.s.c.* '59 (FTW)[H] Notre Dame Congregation of Holy Cross, Indiana Province, Provincial House.
Ford, John T. Ford, C.S.C. T. '59 (WDC)[C] Catholic University of America, The.
Ford, Lawrence D. *o.f.m.* '96 (NY) New York, NY Holy Name of Jesus.
Ford, Michael F. *s.j.* '75 (BO)[U] Cohasset, MA Bellarmine House; [U] Newton, MA The Jesuit Community at Boston College.
Ford, Nevin *o.f.m.* '54 (LA)[P] Santa Barbara, CA Franciscan Friary, Order of Friars Minor (Old Mission).
Ford, Rev. Msgr. Robert A. '44 (NY)[EE] Bronx, NY John Cardinal O'Connor Residence Retired.
Ford, William A. '82 (STO) Diamond Springs, CA Retired.
Forester, Raymond L. '66 (WIL) Rehoboth Beach, DE St. Edmond; Deans.
Forgach, Carl J. '60 (Y) Retired.
Forgarty, Austin '81 (ATL) Newnan, GA St. George.
Forge, Michael D. '97 (DAL) Dallas, TX Mary Immaculate.
Forget, Timothy W. '02 (OM) Clarkson, NE SS. Cyril and Methodius; Leigh, NE St. Mary.
Forgit, Ambrose *ss.cc.* '55 (FR)[F] Fairhaven, MA Our Lady's Haven of Fairhaven Inc.; [G] Fairhaven, MA Damien Residence.
Forintos, Bradley '91 (DET) Trenton, MI St. Joseph.
Forish, Andrew J. '42 (DET) Retired.
Foriska, John M. '70 (GBG) Jeannette, PA Sacred Heart; Jeannette, PA Ascension; Bishop's Priests Council.
Forlani, Joseph *m.c.c.j.* '58 (LA) Los Angeles, CA St. Cecilia; [BB] Covina, CA Comboni Mission Center.
Forlano, Albert (STF) Catechetics (Heritage Schools); Family Life; Religious Education.
Forlano, Philip M. '03 (PH) Philadelphia, PA Cathedral Basilica of SS. Peter and Paul; On Special or Other Archdiocesan Assignment.
Forler, Christopher A. '08 (EVN) Evansville, IN Holy Redeemer.
Forliti, John E. '62 (STP) Retired.
Forman, Bruce H. '74 (STL) St. Louis, MO Sts. Peter and Paul.
Forman, Patrick J. '89 (BUR) Elected Members; Catholic Daughters of The Americas; Engaged Encounter; Saint Johnsbury, VT St. Elizabeth; St. Johnsbury, VT St. John the Evangelist; Deans.
Formolo, Frank *l.c.* '03 (DAL)[J] Irving, TX Legionaries of Christ; [D] Irving, TX The Highlands School; [E] Irving, TX The Highlands School.
Fornal, Andrzej J. *o.p.* '94 (NY) New York, NY Notre Dame; [HH] New York, NY Columbia University; [II] New York, NY Polish Dominicans, Inc.
Fornasari, Archimede *m.c.c.j.* '50 (CHI)[B] Chicago, IL The Catholic Theological Union at Chicago; [N] Chicago, IL Comboni Missionaries Theologate (M.C.C.J.), Verona Fathers.
Forner, Craig M. '75 (SFR) San Rafael, CA St. Isabella.
Forni, John V. '77 (ROC) Rochester, NY St. John the Evangelist.
Forno, R. Adam '87 (ALB) Rensselaer, NY Parish of St. John the Evangelist and St. Joseph's.
Foro, Emmanuel *s.j.* '04 (OAK)[M] Berkeley, CA Jesuit Fathers and Brothers.
Forrest, Stephen '04 (MIL)[Y] Kenosha, WI St. Mark Latin American Center; Kenosha, WI St. Mark; [V] Racine, WI Community of St. Paul, Inc.
Forrest, Thomas *c.ss.r.* '54 (WDC)[N] Washington, DC Holy Redeemer College.
Forrey, William C. '90 (HBG) Deans; Carlisle, PA Saint Patrick.
Forsen, James '79 (LA) Vocations; Los Angeles, CA St. Columbkille.
Forsman, David '01 (DUL) Pine City, MN Immaculate Conception; Pine City, MN St. Mary.
Forst, Aloysius A. '49 (STL) Retired.
Forst, Rev. Msgr. Charles J. '49 (STL) Retired.
Forst, Rev. Msgr. Charles '45 (STL) St. Louis, MO St. Mark Retired.
Forst, Rev. Msgr. Robert M. '51 (ALN) Allentown, PA Our Lady Help of Christians Retired.
Forster, Francis P. *o.s.b.* '64 (CHL)[J] Belmont, NC Belmont Abbey.
Forster, Rev. Msgr. William J. '54 (BO) Senior Priests. Retired.
Forsyth, Kevin J. '86 (HRT) Naugatuck, CT St. Vincent Ferrer.
Forsythe, Daniel A. '09 (PBR) Munhall, PA St. Elias.
Forsythe, Patrick Don Bosco '04 (BIR) Tuscumbia, AL Our Lady of the Shoals.
Forte, Anthony J. *s.j.* '83 (BO)[U] Boston The Society of Jesus of New England–Provincial Offices.
Forte, Anthony '91 (NEW) Newark, NJ Our Lady of Mt. Carmel.
Forte, John Paul *o.p.* '93 (SD)[N] San Diego, CA University of California at San Diego (Campus Ministry).
Fortenberry, Jerome *c.m.* '55 (STL)[O] Perryville, MO Congregation of the Mission.
Fortener, Kenneth R. '69 (L) Howardstown, KY St. Ann; Associate Judges; New Hope, KY St. Vincent de Paul.
Fortier, Joe *s.j.* '90 (SPK)[B] Spokane, WA Gonzaga University.
Fortier, Joel '69 (JOL) Naperville, IL St. Thomas the Apostle; [D] Naperville, IL All Saints Catholic Academy.
Fortier, Theodore L. *a.a.* '53 (WOR)[O] Worcester, MA Assumptionists (Augustinians of the Assumption).
Fortin, John R. *o.s.b.* '76 (MAN)[K] Manchester, NH St. Anselm Abbey.
Fortin, Philip '00 (PT) Port St. Joe, FL St. Joseph.
Fortin, Richard A. '62 (WOR) Millbury, MA Assumption.
Fortin, Robert *a.a.* '58 (WOR)[O] Worcester, MA Assumptionists (Augustinians of the Assumption).
Fortman, Anthony *c.pp.s.* (TOL) Glandorf, OH St. John the Baptist.
Fortner, Douglas F. '70 (COV) Administrative Leave.
Fortney, Kenneth E. '79 (HEL) Plains, MT St. James; Thompson Falls, MT St. William.
Fortuna, Joseph J. '80 (CLV) Cleveland, OH Ascension.
Fortuna, Stanley *c.f.r.* '90 (NY)[EE] Bronx, NY Our Lady of the Angels Friary; [II] Bronx, NY Francesco Productions Inc.
Fortunato, Anthony M. *o.de.m.* '67 (CLV) Cleveland, OH Our Lady of Mount Carmel; [N] Cleveland, OH Mercedarians.
Fortunato, Vincent *o.f.m.cap.* '80 (NEW) Hoboken, NJ St. Ann's.
Fortunio, Carlo *o.p.* '85 (NEW) West New York, NJ Holy Redeemer; North Hudson Deanery 8; Members.
Foschiatto, Edi *s.x.* '81 (PAT) Wayne, NJ XAVERIAN MISSIONARY FATHERS; [N] Wayne Xaverian Missionary Fathers.
Foshage, Nathanael *o.s.b.* '68 (OM)[K] Elkhorn, NE Mount Michael Benedictine Abbey.
Foshage, Nathanael *o.s.b.* '68 (PBL) Ouray, CO St. Daniel the Prophet; Ouray, CO St. Patrick; Telluride, CO St. Patrick; Presbyteral Council–College of Consultors; Presbyteral Council; Personnel.
Foshage, Ronald B. *m.s.* '75 (BEA) Northern Vicariate; Jasper, TX St. Michael; Jasper, TX Our Lady of La Salette Mission; Jasper, TX St. Raymond Mission.
Fosnot, James '94 (RIC) Retired.
Fossa, Leandro *c.s.* (CHI) Melrose Park, IL St. Charles Borromeo.
Fossati, Sergio *p.i.m.e.* '89 (DET)[T] Detroit, MI PIME Foster Parents; [K] Detroit, MI P.I.M.E. Missionaries.
Fosselman, Albert M. '60 (RNO) Judges Retired.
Fosselman, Rev. Msgr. John Anthony '42 (LA) Downey, CA Rancho Los Amigos Medical Center Retired.
Foster, Clyde K. '75 (CLV) Akron, OH St. Bernard; [V] Akron, OH Parishes with Ministry to Spanish Speaking: St. Bernard.
Foster, Dominic *t.o.r.* '05 (STU)[A] Steubenville, OH Franciscan University of Steubenville; [H] Steubenville, OH Holy Spirit Friary.
Foster, Edward '51 (DUL) Retired.
Foster, James A. '72 (ALX) Nachitoches, LA Immaculate Conception.
Foster, James J. '80 (STL) New Haven, MO Holy Family.
Foster, James K. *c.s.c.* '95 (FTW)[B] University of Notre Dame Du Lac; [H] Notre Dame, IN Holy Cross Community, Corby Hall, University of Notre Dame.
Foster, John F. *s.j.* '68 (SEA)[A] Seattle, WA Seattle University; [L] Seattle, WA Arrupe Jesuit Community at Seattle University.
Foster, John J. '51 (PH) Retired.
Foster, John J. M. '91 (WDC)[C] Catholic University of America, The.
Foster, John J.M. '91 (STO) Defenders of the Bond; On Duty Outside the Diocese.
Foster, John Mary *f.j.* '87 (SAT) Special Assignment.
Foster, Jonathan D. *o.f.m.* '60 (JOL)[N] Lombard, IL Mayslake Ministries, Inc.
Foster, Joseph R. '91 (BO) Medford, MA St. Francis of Assisi.
Foster, Rev. Msgr. Michael S. '80 (BO) Tribunal Court.
Foster, Raymond *o.carm.* '73 (JOL)[L] Joliet, IL St. Elias Carmelites.
Foster, Reginald *o.c.d.* '66 (MIL)[P] Milwaukee Provincial Offices – Discalced Carmelites.
Foster, Thomas J. '86 (DUL)[C] Duluth, MN St. Mary's Medical Center; [G] Duluth, MN St. Mary's Medical Center.
Foster, Thomas W. *s.j.* '72 (SJ)[M] Los Gatos, CA Sacred Heart Jesuit Center.
Fostner, Jay J. *o.praem.* '88 (GB)[B] De Pere, WI St. Norbert College; [B] St. Norbert College.
Foudy, Rev. Msgr. John T. '40 (SFR) Retired.
Foudy, Thomas F. '67 (MIA) Pompano Beach, FL St. Coleman.
Fountain, Michael *o.f.m.cap.* '73 (MIL)[Y] Milwaukee, WI House of Peace.
Fournier, Denis *o.s.b.* '60 (BIS)[A] Richardton, ND Assumption Abbey; New Town, ND St. Anthony.
Fournier, Peter J. '09 (FR) Hyannis, MA St. Francis Xavier's; Cape Cod Hospital.
Fournier, Raymond A. *s.m.* '49 (BO)[W] Framingham, MA The Marist House Retired.
Fournier, Raymond J. *o.c.s.o.* '81 (ROC)[J] Piffard, NY Abbey of the Genesee.
Fournier, William J. '73 (ANC) Wasilla, AK Sacred Heart; Big Lake, AK Corp. of Our Lady of the Lake Church; Moderator of the Curia; Talkeetna, AK St. Bernard.

Fournier, William '73 (DUL) On Duty Outside the Diocese.
Fouser, Otto *o.f.m.conv.* '55 (TR) Seaside Park, NJ St. Catharine of Siena.
Foutts, Patrick D. *o.praem.* '93 (ORG)[H] Silverado, CA St. Michael's Summer Camp.
Fowler, Rev. Msgr. Eugene A. '48 (NY) Lake Katrine, NY St. Catherine Laboure Retired.
Fowler, J. Richard '91 (HRT) Bristol, CT Bristol Hospital.
Fowler, John W. '53 (DAL) Retired.
Fowler, Joseph M. '61 (L) Retired.
Fowler, Joseph '02 (PT) Pensacola, FL St. Paul; Seminarian Candidate Review Board; Priest Personnel Board.
Fowler, Joseph '84 (PT) Orders & Ministries, Commission for.
Fowler, Michael *o.f.m.* '76 (GAY) Indian River, MI Cross in the Woods Catholic Shrine.
Fowler, T. Joseph '02 (PT) Judges.
Fowlkes, Eric L. '89 (NSH) Hendersonville, TN Our Lady of the Lake.
Fox, Anthony *o.f.m.conv.* '82 (CHI)[N] Libertyville, IL Marytown, Our Lady of Fatima Friary.
Fox, Brian *s.s.j.* '91 (WDC)[B] Washington, DC St. Joseph's Seminary.
Fox, Charles D. '06 (DET) Office of the Archbishop; Marriage Permissions/Dispensations.
Fox, Daniel A. '82 (LA) Woodland Hills, CA St. Bernardine of Siena.
Fox, Daniel J. *o.f.m.cap.* '75 (DET)[T] St. Clair Shores, MI Catholic Kolping Society of America, Detroit Branch, Inc.
Fox, Daniel *o.f.m.cap.* (SAG) Sanford, MI St. Agnes.
Fox, Donal R. *o.s.b.* '66 (PAT)[N] Morristown, NJ St. Mary's Abbey.
Fox, Gabriel '74 (GAY) Retired.
Fox, George W. '61 (MAD) Retired.
Fox, James E. '74 (DEN) Aurora, CO St. Michael the Archangel.
Fox, James R. '90 (DEN) Craig, CO Saint Michael; Meeker, CO Holy Family.
Fox, John J. '60 (BUF) Retired.
Fox, Joseph E. *o.p.* (TOL) Assessors.
Fox, Leonard '55 (SFS) Retired.
Fox, Martin E. '03 (CIN) Piqua, OH St. Boniface; Piqua, OH St. Mary.
Fox, Martin F. '65 (GB) Retired.
Fox, Melvin E. '63 (GR) Retired.
Fox, Rev. Msgr. Patrick '52 (SD) Retired.
Fox, Richard E. '92 (SCR) Elmhurst, PA St. Eulalia.
Fox, Richard '85 (SFS) Sioux Falls, SD Christ the King.
Fox, Robert J. '59 (GF) Retired.
Fox, Robert L. '01 (CHY) Casper, WY Our Lady of Fatima; [G] Torrington, WY Catholic Charities of Wyoming, Inc.
Fox, Sean P. '53 (SEA) Mountlake Terrace, WA St. Pius X; Catholic Archdiocese of Seattle Clergy Medical Plan Veba Trust; Priests' Pension Plan.
Fox, Thomas E. '60 (LFT) Remington, IN Sacred Heart.
Fox, Thomas *o.f.m.* '62 (IND) Indianapolis, IN Sacred Heart of Jesus.
Foxen, David K. *m.s.c.* '97 (SB) Palm Springs, CA Our Lady of Solitude.
Foxhoven, H. Christopher '04 (STU) Wintersville, OH Blessed Sacrament; Wintersville, OH Our Lady of Lourdes.
Foye, Thomas M. '55 (NEW) Bayonne, NJ St. Andrew's Retired.
Foynes, Rev. Msgr. Aiden '61 (SP) Clearwater, FL St. Cecelia Retired.
Foyo, Alexis *o.s.b.* '83 (SD)[J] Oceanside, CA Prince of Peace Abbey.
Fracaro, Mark A. '67 (JOL) Minooka, IL St. Mary.
Frade, Paulo '97 (NEW) Newark, NJ St. Aloysius.
Fraenzle, Wilfred '64 (LEX) Pikeville, KY St. Francis of Assisi.
Fragomeni, Richard '75 (ALB) On Duty Outside the Diocese; Special Assignment.
Fragomeni, Richard '75 (CHI)[B] Chicago, IL The Catholic Theological Union at Chicago.
Fraher, Joseph P. '50 (CHY) Retired.
Fraher, Kevin *c.ss.r.* '73 (CHI)[N] Glenview, IL The Redemptorists of Glenview, Illinois.
Fraher, Leonard W. '56 (SUP) Retired.
Fraile, Mariano *o.c.d.* '47 (PCE) Ponce, PR San Jose.
Fraile, Tomas *c.r.* '63 (DEN) Denver, CO St. Cajetan.
Frain, Brian *s.j.* '02 (ROC)[B] Rochester, NY McQuaid Jesuit High School.
Fraini, Frederick D. '08 (WOR) Athol, MA Our Lady Immaculate; Petersham, MA St. Peter; Athol, MA St. Francis.
Frambes, John *o.f.m.* '79 (WIL) Wilmington, DE St. Paul's; Wilmington, DE St. Joseph's R.C. Church of Wilmington, Inc.
Franca, Hugo '04 (OAK) San Lorenzo, CA St. John the Baptist.
Francavilla, Rt. Rev. Joseph F. '68 (NTN) McLean, VA Holy Transfiguration; Presbyteral Council.
Francavilla, Rt. Rev. Joseph (NTN) Protopresbyters; College of Eparchial Consultors.
Franceschini, Mark M. *o.s.m.* '59 (CHI)[N] Chicago Order of Friar Servants of Mary (Servites) United States of America Province, Inc.
Franceschini, Mark *o.s.m.* '59 (DEN) Denver, CO Our Lady of Mount Carmel.
Franceschini, Rev. Msgr. Philip J. '66 (NY) Staten Island, NY Our Lady of Pity.
Francesco, Richard G. '87 (NEW) West Orange, NJ St. Joseph's.
Francez, James *m.c.c.j.* '57 (FgM) Cincinnati, OH COMBONI MISSIONARIES (VERONA FATHERS).
Franchomme, Emilio '04 (DEN) Johnstown, CO St. John the Baptist.
Francik, Gerard C. '87 (BAL) Special Assignment; [W] Baltimore, MD Serra Club; Vocation Office.
Francik, Gerard C. '87 (BAL) Baltimore, MD Cathedral of Mary Our Queen.
Francis, Bernard C. '69 (NO) Hahnville, LA Our Lady of the Holy Rosary.
Francis, Daniel *c.ss.r.* '91 (NY)[II] Bronx, NY Perpetual Help Center.
Francis, Daniel *c.ss.r.* (BAL)[W] Baltimore, MD Redemptorist Office for Mission Advancement.
Francis, Rev. Msgr. Eugene (GAL) Retired.
Francis, George '85 (SP)[J] Tampa, FL St. Joseph's Hospital, Inc.
Francis, John '90 (BRK) Woodhaven, NY St. Thomas Apostle.
Francis, Joseph A. *o.p.* '78 (NY) New York, NY St. Monica.
Francis, Joseph '94 (LA) South El Monte, CA Epiphany.
Francis, Mark R. *c.s.v.* '82 (CHI)[N] Arlington Heights Viatorian Province Center–Clerics of St. Viator.
Francis, Mathew (KCK) Onaga, KS St. Vincent de Paul.
Francis, Paul R. '41 (BO) Senior Priests. Retired.
Francis, Peter *o.f.m.* '80 (RVC) Northport, NY St. Philip Neri.
Francis, R. Peter '80 (MO) DEPARTMENT OF VETERANS AFFAIRS HOSPITALS AND CHAPLAINS.
Francis, Sean M. '04 (PIT) Wexford, PA St. Alphonsus.
Francis, Sunny *s.v.d.* '88 (CHI)[N] Techny, IL Divine Word Residence.
Francisco, Joey '93 (NY) Bronx, NY St. Raymond.
Francisco, Ramon J. '96 (HON) Waihee, HI St. Ann.
Francisko, Gary '82 (PRM) Eparchial Shrine of the Weeping Madonna of Mariapoch; Burton, OH Church of Mariapoch.
Franck, James E. *c.pp.s.* '64 (CIN)[N] Dayton Provincial Office of the Cincinnati Province of the Society of the Precious Blood.
Franck, James *c.pp.s.* '64 (OAK) Newark, CA St. Edward.
Franck, John *c.pp.s.* '67 (LA) Los Angeles, CA St. Agnes.
Franck, John *c.pp.s* '67 (CIN)[N] Dayton Provincial Office of the Cincinnati Province of the Society of the Precious Blood.
Franck, John *a.a.* '77 (WOR)[O] Worcester, MA Assumptionists of Assumption College.
Franco, Rev. Msgr. Hilary '55 (NY) Ossining, NY St. Augustine.
Franco, Joseph E. '04 (MO) DEPARTMENT OF VETERANS AFFAIRS HOSPITALS AND CHAPLAINS; Bronx, NY Sacred Heart.
Franco, Juan Carlos '03 (DAL) Dallas, TX St. Philip.
Franco, Juan '08 (OAK) Fremont, CA Our Lady of Guadalupe.
Franco, Maurilio *m.g.* '66 (LA) Los Angeles, CA St. Paul.
Franco, Robert J. '82 (CLV) Catholic Renewal Ministries; North Ridgeville, OH St. Peter.
Franco, Robert M. '73 (PIT) Beaver Falls, PA Christ the Divine Teacher.
Franco, Rodolfo '99 (BWN) Brownsville, TX The Parish of the Lord of Divine Mercy.
Franco, Ronald A. *c.s.p.* '95 (NY) New York, NY St. Paul the Apostle; [EE] New York, NY Paulist Fathers' Motherhouse.
Franco, Victor *l.c.* '81 (MAN)[A] Center Harbor, NH Immaculate Conception Apostolic School.
Franco Henao, Luis Fernando (ARL) Springfield, VA St. Bernadette.
Francois, Ducasse *i.v. dei.* '98 (PMB) West Palm Beach, FL Holy Name of Jesus.
Francois, Jean Augustin '90 (BRK) Brooklyn, NY Holy Family.
Francois, Marc Arthur (NEW) Jersey City, NJ St. Patrick and Assumption/All Saints Church.
Francois, Yves '05 (PMB) Vocations; Vocations; Seminarians.
Franczek, J. August '48 (GAY) Hale, MI St. Pius X; Whittemore, MI St. James.
Franey, John A. '63 (PH) Retired.
Frank, Chrysostom '85 (DEN) Denver, CO St. Elizabeth of Hungary.
Frank, Edward R. '57 (SAV) Augusta, GA St. Mary on the Hill Retired.
Frank, Gerald W. '70 (BWN) Brownsville, TX St. Joseph.
Frank, Paul G. '04 (LIN) Red Cloud, NE Sacred Heart; Advocates.
Frank, Paul *o.m.i.* '50 (MIA) Fort Lauderdale, FL St. John the Baptist.
Frank, Richard C. *m.m.* '53 (FgM) Maryknoll, NY MARYKNOLL.
Frank, Richard W. '72 (JC) Canton, MO St. Joseph; Ewing, MO Queen of Peace.
Frank, Thomas *s.s.j.* (LA) Los Angeles, CA St. Brigid's.
Frank, Rev. Msgr. Tom '70 (AUS) Austin, TX San Jose.
Franken, William F. '88 (BAL) Hydes, MD St. John the Evangelist.
Frankenberger, William J. *c.s.b.* '62 (GAL) Houston, TX St. Anne.
Franklin, Claude W. '97 (SAM) Roanoke, VA St. Elias.
Franklin, David W. '85 (BGP) Danbury, CT St. Joseph.
Franklin, George '86 (STV) Diocesan Consultors.
Franklin, Mark '02 (SHP) Minden, LA St. Paul.
Franklin, Osvaldo (NY) Yonkers, NY Our Lady of Fatima; Yonkers, NY Immaculate Conception.
Frankman, Greg '81 (SFS)[D] Sioux Falls, SD Avera McKennan; Sioux Falls, SD.
Franko, George M. '50 (Y) Retired.
Franko, John *o.m.i.* '67 (GAL) Alvin, TX St. John the Baptist.
Frankovich, Francis A. *c.c.* '68 (GAL)[S] Houston, TX Catholic Charismatic Center.
Frankovich, Lawrence *o.f.m.* '66 (MIL) West Allis, WI St. Augustine.
Frankowski, Miroslaw *s.ch.* '98 (DET) Hamtramck, MI St. Florian.
Franks, Donald E. '79 (COL) Lancaster, OH St. Mary; [L] Lancaster, OH St. Mary of the Assumption Foundation.
Franks, Gabriel '57 (VIC) On Special or Other Diocesan Assignment.
Franks, T. Becket *o.s.b.* '86 (JOL)[L] Lisle, IL St. Procopius Abbey.
Franks, Thomas Becket *o.s.b.* '86 (JOL)[A] Lisle, IL Benedictine University.
Franks, Thomas *o.f.m.cap.* '08 (NY) New York, NY St. John the Baptist.
Fransco, Peter J. '58 (SC) Retired.
Fransiscus, Thomas J. *c.ss.r.* '65 (LAV) Promoters of Justice; Diocesan Advocates.
Fransiscus, Thomas *c.ss.r.* '65 (RNO) Adjutant Judicial Vicar; Diocesan Board of Consultors; Dayton, NV St. Ann; Presbyteral Council; Lists of Deans.
Frantz, Henry *c.pp.s.* '54 (CIN)[N] Carthagena, OH St. Charles Retired.
Franxman, Thomas W. *s.j.* '64 (COV) Fort Mitchell, KY Blessed Sacrament.
Franz, Lou *c.m.* (GLP) Retired.
Franz, Paul R. '66 (BO) Senior Priests. Retired.
Franz, S. Michael '69 (CLV) Cleveland, OH St. Stephen.
Franzinell, Benjamin '50 (LAV) Retired.
Franzman, Thomas R. '70 (CHI)[A] Mundelein, IL University of St. Mary of the Lake/Mundelein Seminary.
Frapaul, Sam *o.f.m.cap.* '78 (PAT) Passaic, NJ St. Mary Hospital.
Frapaul, Sam *o.f.m.cap.* (NEW) Hackensack, NJ Church of St. Francis of Assisi.
Fra Paul, Sam *o.f.m.cap.* (PAT)[K] Passaic, NJ St. Mary's Hospital.
Frappier, Rev. Msgr. George L. '56 (PRO) Council Members Retired.
Frascadore, Henry C. '59 (HRT) Retired.
Fraser, Bernard '00 (DET) Absent on Leave.
Fraser, Christopher J. '01 (PHX) College of Consultors; Judicial Vicar; Presbyteral Council.
Fraser, Daniel J. '99 (TOL) Retired.
Fraser, Donald D. '74 (B) McCall, ID Our Lady of the Lake.
Fraser, Gerald C. '72 (BO) Permanent Disability.
Fraser, James F. '65 (BRK) Whitestone, NY Holy Trinity.
Fraser, John '96 (NY) Hawthorne, NY Holy Rosary.
Fraser, Michael B. '75 (NO) On Administrative Leave.
Fraszczak, Zbigniew *s.v.d.* '93 (OAK) Hayward, CA St. Joachim.
Fratt, Gregory '98 (HT) Morgan City, LA Sacred Heart of Jesus.
Fratts, Ralph J. '60 (ROC) Retired.
Frawley, Gerard *s.a.c.* '68 (DET) Wyandotte, MI; Ortonville, MI St. Anne.
Frawley, John P. '44 (CHI) Chicago, IL St. Thomas More Retired.
Frawley, Patrick J. '78 (BRK) Jackson Heights, NY Our Lady of Fatima; Released from Diocesan Assignment.
Frayna, Ramon '86 (AUS) Dime Box, TX St. Joseph; Dime Box, TX Holy Family Catholic Church – Lexington, Texas.
Frazer, Christopher '07 (SAC) Chico, CA St. John the Baptist.
Frazer, Edward J. *s.s.* '61 (BAL)[O] Baltimore, MD St. Charles Villa; [S] Baltimore Society of St. Sulpice, Province of the United States Retired.
Frazer, J. Francis '75 (PIT) Clarksville, PA St. Thomas; Greene County, PA State Correctional Institute at Greene.

Frazer, Joseph '84 (AUS) Retired.
Frazier, Lawrence K. '71 (BAL) Buckeystown, MD St. Joseph–on–Carrollton Manor.
Frazier, Richard W. '96 (COV) Administrative Leave.
Frazier, William B. *m.m.* '56 (NY)[EE] Maryknoll Maryknoll Fathers and Brothers.
Frechette, Christopher *s.j.* '99 (BO)[U] Cambridge, MA Claver House.
Frechette, Leo L. '55 (MAN) Rochester, NH Retired.
Frechette, Rt. Rev. Paul G. '78 (NTN) Worcester, MA Our Lady of Perpetual Help; Continuing Education of Clergy Office.
Frechette, Paul *s.m.* '76 (FgM) THE SOCIETY OF MARY.
Frechette, Richard *c.p.* '79 (FgM) South River, NJ St. Paul of the Cross Province.
Frechette, Richard *c.p.* '79 (MET)[I] South River Passionist Provincial Office.
Frechette, Thomas A. '86 (FR) Attleboro Falls, MA St. Mark's.
Frecker, Rev. Msgr. A. Anthony '72 (COL) Canal Winchester, OH Pope John XXIII.
Frederici, David C. '01 (FR)[L] Hyannis, MA Cape Cod Campus Ministry; In Res; Cape Cod Campus Ministry; Cape Cod Hospital; Catholic Scouting Program.
Frederick, Curt J. '75 (MIL) Archdiocesan Consultors; Waukesha, WI St. William; Judges for Second Instance.
Frederick, Joseph B. '56 (MIL) Retired.
Frederick, Rev. Msgr. Lawrence A. '66 (LR)[B] Little Rock, AR Catholic High School.
Frederick, Robert A. '00 (ATL)[J] Atlanta, GA North Georgia College; Special or Other (Arch)Diocesan Assignment; Dahlonega, GA St. Luke; Boy Scouts.
Fredericks, James L. '77 (SFR) On Duty Outside the Archdiocese.
Fredericks, James '77 (LA)[C] Los Angeles, CA Jesuit Community.
Fredericks, Michael '87 (MO) Air Force Reserve Chaplains; Colton, CA Immaculate Conception.
Frederico, Charles A. *s.j.* '06 (NY)[EE] New York, NY "America;" Residence and publication office of the America Press; [EE] New York, NY Society of Jesus, New York Province.
Free, Daniel *c.p.* '52 (HRT)[L] West Hartford Holy Family Monastery/Retreat.
Free, Daniel *c.p.* '52 (BRK)[T] Jamaica, NY Immaculate Conception Monastery Retired.
Free, Henry *c.p.* '58 (HRT)[L] West Hartford Holy Family Monastery/Retreat.
Free, Henry *c.p.* '58 (BRK)[T] Jamaica, NY Immaculate Conception Monastery Retired.
Freed, Eric '90 (SR)[J] Arcata, CA Newman Community, Humboldt State University; Eureka, CA St. Bernard.
Freed, Eric '90 (SFR) Japanese Mission.
Freed, Robert '83 (ALN) Bally, PA Most Blessed Sacrament Retired.
Freed, Robert '83 (WCH) Retired.
Freedy, Joseph M. '08 (PIT) Ambridge, PA Good Samaritan; Baden, PA St. John the Baptist; Priest Council.
Freeh, Vincent T. *m.s.c.* '59 (OG)[F] Watertown, NY Missionaries of the Sacred Heart.
Freel, Francis *c.ss.r.* '46 (ALB)[L] Saratoga Springs, NY St. John Neumann Residence.
Freeman, Brendan *o.c.s.o.* (ROC)[N] Piffard, NY Cistercian Publications, Inc.
Freeman, James '65 (DM) Retired.
Freeman, John A. '73 (PH) Boothwyn, PA St. John Fisher.
Freeman, Joseph '05 (SD) San Diego, CA Good Shepherd.
Freeman, Roland P. '67 (DEN)[G] Denver, CO Special Religious Education–Pastoral Care of Developmentally Disabled Persons.
Freemesser, Paul J. '59 (ROC) Rochester, NY St. Theodore Retired.
Freer, Douglas '07 (TR) Belmar, NJ St. Rose.
Fregapane, Rev. Msgr. Mercurio A. '51 (HBG) Retired.
Frego, Max '63 (SAG) Retired.
Freiburger, Jason Eugene '07 (FTW) Fort Wayne, IN St. Vincent de Paul.
Freiburger, Jason (FTW) Presbyteral Council.
Freiermuth, Harry '59 (MRY) Retired.
Freihofer, Michael A. '87 (MO) Air Force Reserve Chaplains.
Freihofer, Michael '06 (DEN) Granby, CO St. Anne.
Freitag, Patrick '96 (SEA) Mercer Island, WA St. Monica.
Freitas, Daniel L. '49 (FR) Retired.
Freitas, Fernando P. '48 (PRO) Retired.
Freitas, Patrick '65 (HON) Haiku, HI St. Rita; Clergy Personnel Board.
Fremgen, Edward George '92 (LA) Retired.
French, D. James *s.j.* '75 (RVC) Oceanside, NY St. Anthony.
French, Donald J. '76 (HRT) Hamden, CT Blessed Sacrament.
French, James R. '78 (STL) Park Hills, MO Immaculate Conception.
French, John F. '54 (ALB) Retired.
French, Michael D. *s.j.* '46 (STL)[C] Saint Louis University.
French, Michael D. *s.j.* '75 (STL)[O] St. Louis, MO Jesuit Community Corporation at Saint Louis University – Jesuit Hall.
French, Raymond D. *c.s.sp.* '91 (PIT)[B] Pittsburgh, PA Duquesne University of the Holy Spirit.
French, Robert E. '63 (RIC) Retired.
French, Rev. Msgr. Thomas A. '49 (SAT)[K] San Antonio, TX Incarnate Word Retirement Community; [M] San Antonio, TX Incarnate Word Retirement Community Retired.
French, Thomas *s.m.* '97 (SFR)[N] San Francisco, CA Marianist Community; [D] San Francisco, CA Archbishop Riordan High School (Boys).
French, Walter V. '65 (NEW) Retired.
Frenier, Steven G. *o.f.m.conv.* '82 (BUF)[O] Athol Springs, NY St. Maximilian Kolbe Friary; Athol Springs, NY St. Francis of Assisi; Council of Priests.
Frenoy, Fortune C. *s.m.* '54 (SFR)[N] San Francisco, CA Marist Center of the West Retired.
Frerichs, Glenn K. '00 (WIN) Diocesan Consultors; Wabasha, MN St. Felix; Wabasha, MN St. Agnes; [A] Winona, MN Immaculate Heart of Mary Seminary; Appointed Members.
Frerker, Jack W. '63 (BEL) Retired.
Frerkes, James '62 (MRY) Retired.
Freson, Kenan *o.f.m.* '67 (CIN)[C] Cincinnati, OH St. Anthony Shrine, Franciscan Postulancy; [T] Cincinnati, OH Community Support Charitable Trust; Councillors:.
Freund, John B. *c.m.* '65 (BRK)[T] Jamaica, NY Vincentian Residence.
Freund, Joseph *c.ss.r.* '66 (NY)[GG] Esopus, NY Mount St. Alphonsus Redemptorist Retreat Center.
Frey, Rev. Msgr. Andrew F. '48 (BR) Retired.
Frey, Rev. Msgr. Francis '58 (SAN) Retired.
Frey, Jerome V. '50 (LAF)[M] Lafayette, LA Community of Jesus Crucified Retired.
Frey, Rev. Msgr. John T. '70 (CAM) Representatives by Deaneries; Avalon, NJ The Church of Maris Stella, Avalon, N.J.; Stone Harbor, NJ St. Paul's Church, Stone Harbor, N.J.; Amicus; English Cursillo.
Freyer, Timothy '89 (ORG) Anaheim, CA St. Boniface; [G] Fullerton, CA St. Jude Medical Center; Clergy Personnel Board.
Frias, Rev. Msgr. Carlos '60 (ELP) Retired.
Frias, Martin '03 (PBL) Walsenburg, CO Sacred Heart; Walsenburg, CO St. Mary.
Frias, Ramon *o.f.m.cap.* '72 (NY) New York, NY St. John the Baptist.
Frias, Rev. Msgr. Santiago C. '59 (RIC) Retired.
Friberg, Daniel '62 (STP) Retired.
Fricdel, John (J) F. '86 (SPC)[J] Joplin, MO Newman Club, Missouri Southern State University.
Fride, Edward O. '86 (LAN) Ann Arbor, MI Christ the King.
Fridrich, Sylvester W. '51 (CLV) Gates Mills, OH St. Francis of Assisi Retired.
Friebel, Richard *c.pp.s.* '78 (CIN) Dayton, OH Holy Trinity; Priest Councilors.
Fried, Francis L. '68 (STP) Roseville, MN Corpus Christi.
Friedel, James *o.s.a.* '65 (CHI)[N] Olympia Fields, IL Tolentine Monastery at Tolentine Center.
Friedel, John (J.) F. '86 (SPC) Joplin, MO St. Peter The Apostle; Vocations–Seminarians; Diocesan Consultors; Presbyteral Council; Campus Ministries.
Friedel, Robert E. '57 (CLV) Twinsburg, OH SS. Cosmas and Damian Retired.
Friedell, John C. '54 (DUB)[C] Retired.
Friedell, Ronald G. '66 (DUB)[I] Dubuque, IA Holy Family Hall Infirmary.
Friedl, Erwin J. '71 (CHI) Melrose Park, IL Sacred Heart.
Friedl, Rev. Msgr. Francis P. '43 (DUB) Retired.
Friedl, Thomas '92 (CR) Boy Scouts; Park Rapids, MN St. Peter the Apostle; Pastoral Leadership Program Board.
Friedley, Craig '07 (PHX) Phoenix, AZ St. Vincent de Paul Roman Catholic Parish.
Friedman, Cecil H. '50 (SC) Retired.
Friedman, Daniel L. '72 (BEL) Aviston, IL St. Francis of Assisi.
Friedman, Greg '76 (CIN) Cincinnati, OH St. Francis Seraph.
Friedman, Gregory *o.f.m.* '76 (CIN)[N] Cincinnati, OH Pleasant Street Friary; [N] Cincinnati, OH St. Francis Seraph Friary.
Friedrich, James '89 (SFS) Woonsocket, SD St. Joseph; Woonsocket, SD St. Wilfrid; Defenders of the Matrimonial Bond.
Friedrich, Lawrence '47 (SFS) Retired.
Friedrich, Ralph '43 (Y) Retired.
Friedrichs, Richard M. '70 (PRO) Warwick, RI St. Catherine.
Friedrichsen, Timothy A. '84 (SC) Presbyteral Council.
Friedricikson, Tim '84 (SC) Denison, IA St. Rose of Lima.
Friel, Edward M. '89 (CAM) Westmont, NJ The Church of the Holy Saviour, Westmont, N.J.; Elmer, NJ St. Ann's Catholic Church, Elmer, N.J.
Friel, John F. '70 (TUC) Yuma, AZ Saint John Neumann Roman Catholic Church – Yuma.
Friel, Mark M. '63 (BUF)[O] Buffalo, NY Sheehan Residence for Priests Retired.
Friend, Rev. Msgr. R. Scott '87 (LR) Vicar General; Diocesan Consultors; Monsignor James E. O'Connell Diocesan Seminarian Fund, Inc.; Vocations; Priests Personnel Board (Diocesan); Presbyteral Council.
Frient, Lawrence '84 (Y) Niles, OH Our Lady of Mt. Carmel.
Fries, Richard R. *m.m.* '76 (FgM) Maryknoll, NY MARYKNOLL.
Frigo, Martin A. *o.praem.* '49 (WIL)[J] Middletown, DE Immaculate Conception Priory of the Canons Regular of Premontre.
Frigo, William *o.f.m. cap.* '63 (MAD)[I] Madison, WI San Damiano Friary Retired.
Frilot, Rev. Msgr. Eugene P. '55 (LA) Glendale, CA Church of the Incarnation Retired.
Frink, John A. '87 (ALN)[C] Reading, PA Holy Name High School; Shillington, PA St. John Baptist de la Salle.
Frink, Thomas J. *s.j.* '05 (FgM) Watertown, MA Society of Jesus.
Frinsko, Donald S. *t.o.r.* '79 (STU)[H] Steubenville, OH Holy Spirit Friary; [A] Steubenville, OH Franciscan University of Steubenville.
Frisch, Carl M. *o.ss.t.* '06 (BAL)[S] Leadership; [S] Baltimore, MD.
Frisch, Kenneth J. '78 (MAD) Highland, WI SS. Anthony and Philip; Montfort, WI St. Thomas; Personnel Board.
Frisch, Michael F. *o.praem.* '97 (GB)[J] De Pere, WI St. Norbert Abbey.
Frisch, Ralph *s.t.* (PAT)[N] Stirling, NJ Holy Spirit Missionary Cenacle.
Frische, Emile *m.h.m.* '70 (NY) New York, NY Holy Family; Coordinator for Special & Pastoral Ministries; [EE] Hartsdale, NY Mill Hill Fathers Residence.
Friske, Joseph P. '62 (SAG) Outside the Diocese Retired.
Frison, Ted '72 (P) Salem, OR Hillcrest Youth Correctional Facility.
Frisoni, Matthew H. '05 (ALB) Delhi, NY St. Peter; Walton, NY St. John the Baptist; [Q] Delhi, NY State University of New York College of Agricultural & Technology at Delhi.
Frister, Jerome '57 (JUN) Retired.
Fritsch, Albert *s.j.* '67 (LEX) Ravenna, KY St. Elizabeth of Hungary; Stanton, KY Our Lady of the Mountains.
Fritsch, Michael C. '85 (IND) Bloomington, IN St. John the Apostle; Archdiocesan Judges.
Fritschen, Thomas M. *f.s.s.p.* '00 (ATL) Mableton, GA St. Francis De Sales.
Fritz, Henry H. *o.s.b.* '52 (PEO)[A] Peru, IL St. Bede Abbey Retired.
Fritz, John '00 (WDC)[B] Washington, DC St. Joseph's Seminary.
Fritz, Peter *o.f.m.* '50 (SFD)[L] Springfield, IL Our Lady of Angels Friary.
Fritz, Richard A. '75 (KAL) Bronson, MI St. Mary's.
Fritz, Robert J. '75 (CAM) Pitman, NJ Our Lady Queen of Peace R.C. Church, Pitman N.J.
Fritzen, James C. '69 (SY) Liverpool, NY Christ the King.
Frizzell, Lawrence E. '62 (NEW)[B] School of Diplomacy and Intl. Rels.
Froehle, Charles L. '63 (STP) Minneapolis, MN Our Lady of Lourdes.
Froehlich, James P. *o.f.m.cap.* '82 (WDC)[B] Washington, DC St. Francis Friary–Capuchin College; [A] Washington, DC Theological College of the Catholic University of America.
Froehlich, Rev. Msgr. Mark J. '69 (STU) Barnesville, OH Assumption; Barnesville, OH St. Mary's; Judges.
Froelich, Canice *o.f.m.cap.* '47 (SAL) Hays, KS St. Joseph Parish; [D] Hays, KS St. Joseph's Friary.
Frohlich, Attila '01 (EVN) Evansville, IN Good Shepherd.
Froidurot, Michael '78 (SD) Poway, CA St. Gabriel.
Fromageot, Robert *f.s.s.p.* '01 (LIN) Presbyteral Council; [A] Denton, NE Our Lady of Guadalupe Seminary; [L] Lincoln, NE St. Francis of Assisi Church.
Fromholzer, Francis J. '58 (ALN) Retired.
Fronckewicz, Stephen *o.s.b.* '57 (NOR)[F] Willimantic, CT Holy Family Home and Shelter, Inc.
Fronckowiak, Dennis F. '77 (BUF) Tonawanda, NY St. Timothy.
Fronczak, Dennis A. '75 (BUF) Defenders of the Bond; Council of Priests; Holland, NY St. Joseph.
Fronek, Randy '05 (RCK) Rockford, IL Holy Family.
Fronk, Christopher S. *s.j.* '97 (MO) Navy Reserve Chaplains.
Fronk, Christopher *s.j.* (PIT) Pittsburgh, PA St. Bernard.
Fronske, Edward *o.f.m.* '67 (GLP) Cibecue, AZ St. Catherine; Whiteriver, AZ St. Francis.

Frontiero, Anthony F. '91 (MAN) On Duty Outside the Diocese.
Frost, Arthur *c.ss.r.* '41 (LA) Whittier, CA St. Mary of the Assumption; [P] Whittier, CA Redemptorists of Whittier Retired.
Frost, John M. '87 (DM) Avoca, IA St. Mary, Mediatrix of All Graces; Avoca, IA St. Patrick; Diocesan Consultors.
Frost, Rev. Msgr. Stephen A. '77 (FRS) Bakersfield, CA Christ the King.
Frost, Rev. Msgr. Stephen '77 (RNO) Judges.
Frost, Thomas *o.f.m.* '60 (MRY)[F] San Miguel, CA Novitiate House for the Franciscan Friars, O.F.M.; [F] San Miguel, CA Franciscan Friars, O.F.M.; San Miguel, CA San Miguel.
Frozena, Kenneth R. '60 (GB) Retired.
Frueh, Robert '63 (BRK) Kingsboro Psychiatric Center; Brooklyn, NY St. Saviour.
Fruge, Rev. Msgr. Donald J. '72 (GAL) Retired.
Frugoli, Francis A. *s.j.* '45 (SJ)[M] Los Gatos, CA Sacred Heart Jesuit Center.
Frundt, Oscar H. '56 (WIL) Retired.
Frutades, Alfredo *i.v.e.* '01 (PHX) Phoenix, AZ Immaculate Heart of Mary Roman Catholic Parish; Phoenix, AZ St. Anthony Roman Catholic Parish.
Fruth, Paul '74 (DUL) McGregor, MN Our Lady of Fatima; McGregor, MN Holy Family; Council of Catholic Women.
Fry, James Q. '79 (ORG) Retired.
Fry, Wallace Blake '07 (ELP) El Paso, TX St. Raphael; Dell City, TX San Isidro.
Fryar, James A. *f.s.s.p.* '04 (VEN) Sarasota, FL Christ the King.
Fryar, Rev. Msgr. Thomas S. '78 (DEN) Denver, CO Cathedral Basilica of the Immaculate Conception; College of Consultors; Defenders of the Bond; Vicar General and Moderator of the Curia; Archdiocesan Finance Council; Ex Officio Members; Vicars General; Moderator of the Curia.
Fryda, William *m.m.* '88 (FgM) Maryknoll, NY MARYKNOLL.
Frydrych, Jerszy *s.ch.* '85 (SD) San Diego, CA St. Maximilian Kolbe Mission.
Fryer, Rev. Msgr. Patrick L. '73 (WH) Martinsburg, WV St. Joseph's.
Fu, Joseph '60 (NEW) Retired.
Fuccile, Dominic G. '66 (NEW) Retired.
Fucheck, Robert '66 (ORL) Retired.
Fuchs, Eric W. '04 (WDC)[N] Washington, DC Holy Redeemer College.
Fuchs, John *s.j.* '75 (SEA)[C] Tacoma, WA Bellarmine Preparatory School.
Fuchs, Moritz A. '55 (SY) Pastoral Examiners Retired.
Fuchs, Ronald G. '90 (ATL) Without Archdiocesan Assignment or Faculties.
Fucinaro, Rev. Msgr. Thomas J. '89 (LIN) On Duty Outside the Diocese.
Fuemmeler, James R. '58 (JC) Retired.
Fuenmayor, Jose Maria '84 (DEN)[A] Denver, CO Redemptoris Mater House of Formation.
Fuente, Alberto *o.a.r.* '94 (NEW) Union City, NJ Holy Family.
Fuentes, Pablo '95 (NO) Metairie, LA Our Lady of Divine Providence.
Fuentes, Ruben *o.f.m.* '64 (SD) Lemon Grove, CA St. John of the Cross.
Fuentes, Theo *c.m.f.* '51 (LA) San Gabriel, CA San Gabriel Mission.
Fuentes Rodriguez, Jose '45 (SJN) Retired.
Fuentez, Trinidad '78 (ELP) El Paso, TX Queen of Peace; Defenders of the Bond.
Fugee, Michael (NEW) Newark, NJ St. Antoninus.
Fugini, Francis *o.f.m.cap.* '54 (PIT)[M] Pittsburgh, PA St. Augustine Friary; Pittsburgh, PA Province of St. Augustine.
Fugle, James L. '08 (BUF) Niagara Falls, NY St. Vincent de Paul.
Fugolo, Joseph *c.s.* '67 (NY)[II] New York, NY American Committee on Italian Migration, Inc.
Fuhrman, Bruno *o.s.b.* '54 (LR)[A] Subiaco, AR Subiaco Abbey.
Fuhrman, Rev. Msgr. Robert J. '81 (NEW) Saddle River Borough, NJ St. Gabriel the Archangel; Propagation of the Faith; Society of St. Peter the Apostle; Holy Childhood Association; Missionary Union of Priests & Religious.
Fuhrmann, Nicholas *o.s.b.* '54 (LR)[A] Subiaco, AR Subiaco Abbey.
Fuino, Crispin *o.f.m.conv.* '48 (TR) Point Pleasant Beach, NJ St. Peter's Retired.
Fujihara, Fidelis *s.a.* '65 (NY)[EE] Garrison Franciscan Friars of the Atonement, Minister General Office.
Fukes, Gary M. '88 (MO) Military Chaplains; Army Chaplains.
Fukes, James *o.f.m.conv.* '98 (R) Siler City, NC St. Julia; [F] Pittsboro, NC Our Lady of Guadalupe Friary.
Fuks, Mariusz K. '08 (SAV) Savannah, GA St. Peter the Apostle Church.
Fulcher, Titus '96 (CHR) Hanahan, SC Our Lady Protectress of All Christians; Office of Child Protective Services.
Fulcher, Titus '95 (CHR) Office of Ongoing Formation for Recently Ordained Clergy.
Fulcher, Titus '96 (CHR) Bishop's Office.
Fulco, William J. *s.j.* '66 (LA)[C] Los Angeles, CA Jesuit Community.
Fuld, Charles L. '86 (SD) Retired.
Fuld, Charles '86 (SD) "Southern Cross"—(Diocesan Newspaper).
Fuld, Chuck '86 (LA) State Chaplain.
Fulgenzi, Mario '68 (RIC) Virginia Beach, VA St. Gregory the Great.
Fullam, T. Dominick '94 (BLX) Biloxi, MS St. Mary; Vicar General; Defenders of the Bond; Catholic Foundation–Diocese of Biloxi; Catholic Housing Board; Finance Council; Insurance Committee; Catholic University, Friends of; Moderator of Curia; College of Consultors; Personnel Board; Presbyteral Council.
Fullam, Rev. Msgr. Vincent F. '65 (BRK) Rego Park, NY Resurrection–Ascension; Legion of Mary; Presbyteral Council.
Fullen, John N. '95 (BAL) Retired.
Fuller, Jon D. *s.j.* '90 (BO)[D] Dorchester, MA Boston College High School.
Fuller, Leigh A. *s.j.* '66 (BAL)[S] Towson Maryland Province of the Society of Jesus.
Fuller, Michael J.K. '97 (CHI)[A] Mundelein, IL University of St. Mary of the Lake/Mundelein Seminary; Special Assignment.
Fuller, Neil *s.v.d.* '69 (SB) Corona, CA St. Matthew.
Fuller, Orlando R. '75 (MO) Army Chaplains.
Fuller, Orlando R. (SAL) Fort Riley Catholic Community.
Fuller, Rev. Msgr. Robert D. '56 (TUC) Tucson, AZ Saint Frances Cabrini Roman Catholic Parish – Tucson; Directors; [H] Tucson, AZ St. Frances Cabrini Foundation, Inc.
Fuller, Samuel *o.f.m.cap.* '08 (NOR) Middletown, CT St. Pius X.
Fuller, Timothy M. '93 (OKL) Midwest City, OK St. Philip Neri; Archdiocesan Finance Council; Master of Ceremonies; Air National Guard Chaplains.
Fullerton, Daniel J. '91 (MO) Navy Chaplains.
Fullerton, Daniel '91 (SCR) Military Chaplains.
Fullmer, Hugh '72 (JOL) Aurora, IL Our Lady of Mercy.
Fullum, John J. '67 (BRK) East Glendale, NY Sacred Heart.
Fullum, Rev. Msgr. Vincent (BRK) Diocesan Consultors.
Fulmer, Jeffrey M. '97 (CIN) Priests On Personal Leave.
Fulton, Rev. Msgr. David I. '67 (MET) Baptistown, NJ Our Lady of Victories.
Fulton, Rev. Msgr. David I. (BAL)[A] Baltimore, MD St. Mary's Seminary and University.
Fulton, David L. '02 (OM) Fordyce, NE St. Joseph; Fordyce, NE St. John the Baptist; Fordyce, NE St. Boniface; [N] Fordyce, NE Cemetery Endowment for St. Boniface Church.
Fulton, Eugene J. '67 (NY)[GG] Larchmont, NY Trinity Retreat; Spiritual Development, Office of.
Fulton, Eugene '67 (PSC) On Duty Outside Diocese.
Fulton, Kenneth S. '50 (TLS) Retired.
Fulton, Rev. Msgr. Robert W. '62 (MOB) Gulf Shores, AL Our Lady of the Gulf.
Fulton, Terry '94 (SAC) Woodland, CA Holy Rosary; Sacramento, CA St. Maria Goretti.
Funaro, Rev. Msgr. Joseph A. '65 (BRK) Forest Hills, NY Our Lady, Queen of Martyrs.
Funesti, Peter K. '88 (NEW) Midland Park, NJ Nativity.
Funk, David J. *o.f.m.cap.* '68 (GB) Little Chute, WI St. John Nepomucene; Omro, WI St. Mary.
Funk, Rev. Msgr. David R. '74 (COL) Reynoldsburg, OH St. Pius X.
Funk, Peter C. '64 (PH) On Duty Outside the Archdiocese.
Funk, Peter C. '64 (BEA) Commission for Continuing Education of Clergy & Religious; [E] Beaumont, TX Holy Family Retreat Center.
Funk, Peter *o.s.b.* '04 (CHI)[N] Chicago, IL Monastery of the Holy Cross.
Funk, Virgil C. '63 (RIC) Retired.
Funke, Gerald '80 (B) Nampa, ID St. Paul's; Adjutant Judicial Vicars; Judges; College of Consultors; Deans; St. Vincent de Paul Society.
Funke, Rev. Msgr. Richard P. '60 (DUB) Defenders of the Bond Retired.
Funke, Ronald R. *s.j.* '68 (SEA)[L] Seattle, WA Arrupe Jesuit Community at Seattle University.
Funtila, Aloysius '83 (CHI) Waukegan, IL St. Anastasia.
Furca, Marian *c.ss.r.* '87 (MET) Perth Amboy, NJ St. Stephen.
Furdzik, Pawel *o.c.d.* '95 (GRY)[H] Munster, IN Discalced Carmelite Fathers Monastery.
Furey, J. Barry '71 (BGP) Darien, CT St. Thomas More; Members of the Clergy Personnel Committee; Presbyteral Council.
Furey, John *c.ss.r.* '60 (BO) Boston, MA Our Lady of Perpetual Help.
Furey, Matthew J. '99 (NY) Bronx, NY St. Francis Xavier.
Furey, Thomas J. '73 (PH) Schwenksville, PA St. Mary.
Furfaro, Virgil '73 (SFE) Retired.
Furlan, Gerard *s.x.* '58 (BO)[U] Holliston, MA Xaverian Missionaries.
Furlan, Michael J. '75 (CHI) Oak Lawn, IL St. Germaine.
Furlong, Aidan M. *a.a.* '53 (WOR)[O] Worcester, MA Assumptionists (Augustinians of the Assumption).
Furlong, J. Daryl '66 (MAD) Retired.
Furlong, Richard V. '72 (BUF) On Duty Outside the Diocese.
Furlong, Rev. Msgr. Thomas D. '60 (OM) Bellevue, NE St. Matthew The Evangelist Church of Bellevue Retired.
Furman, Henry P. '02 (BUR)[G] Castleton, VT Castleton State College; Castleton, VT St. John the Baptist; Castleton, VT St. Paul.
Furnari, Casper J. '68 (BRK) Flushing, NY Holy Family.
Furnari, Salvatore C. *s.a.c.* '05 (BAL) Baltimore, MD St. Leo.
Furrell, Reynold '98 (ORG) Ladera Ranch, CA Holy Trinity.
Furrevig, Edward G. '67 (NEW) Retired.
Furtado, Al *c.s.sp.* '64 (SFR) Belmont, CA St. Mark.
Fusare, Francis *c.p.m.* '96 (OWN)[F] Auburn, KY Fathers of Mercy.
Fusco, Albin *o.f.m.* '61 (ALB)[A] Catskill, NY St. Anthony Friary.
Fusco, Frederick *o.f.m.* '42 (ALB)[A] Catskill, NY St. Anthony Friary.
Fusco, Frederick *o.f.m.* '42 (NY)[EE] New York Franciscan Province of the Immaculate Conception.
Fusco, Thomas M. '85 (RVC) Syosset, NY St. Edward Confessor.
Fuselier, Karl '94 (LKC) On Leave.
Fushek, Rev. Msgr. Dale J. '78 (PHX) On Leave.
Fuss, Edward *s.m.* '89 (NO)[P] New Orleans, LA Marist Fathers.
Fussner, Donald T. '60 (NY) New York, NY St. Peter Retired.
Futie, Richard F. '82 (BGP) Defenders of the Bond; Stamford, CT Sacred Heart.
Futo, Yoshio Ignatius *s.j.* '81 (FgM) St. Louis, MO Society of Jesus.
Futter, Volker *o.s.b.* '69 (OM)[K] Schuyler, NE Benedictine Mission House; Schuyler, NE.
Fynn, Isaac A. '79 (TUC) Tucson, AZ Saint Joseph Roman Catholic Parish – Tucson; Tucson, AZ St. Joseph's Hospital; [C] Tucson, AZ Carondelet St. Joseph's Hospital.

G

Gaa, David *o.f.m.* '98 (FgM) Oakland, CA St. Barbara Province.
Gaa, David *o.f.m.* '98 (OAK)[M] Oakland Franciscan Friars (Province of St. Barbara).
Gaalaas, Rev. Msgr. Patrick J. '72 (TLS)[J] Tulsa, OK Priest Retirement Trust of the Roman Catholic Diocese of Tulsa; Vicar General; Ex Officio; Diocesan Consultors; Priests' Personnel Committee; Seminary Board; Ecumenism; Tulsa, OK St. Bernard of Clairvaux.
Gabage, John B. '07 (WIL) Dover, DE Holy Cross.
Gabel, Emanuel '57 (DEN) Retired.
Gabel, Martin M. '68 (JOL) Homer Glen, IL St. Bernard.
Gabela, Jose Luis Diez *o.s.a.* '72 (MGZ) Aguada, PR St. Francis of Assisi.
Gaberle, Jiri '89 (MIL) Special Assignment.
Gabet, George *f.s.s.p.* (FTW) Fort Wayne, IN Sacred Heart.
Gabin, John D. '75 (PH) Springfield, PA Holy Cross.
Gabler, Michael J. *o.s.b.* '08 (GBG)[G] Latrobe, PA Saint Vincent Archabbey.
Gaborit, Mauricio *s.j.* '78 (FgM) St. Louis, MO Society of Jesus.
Gaboury, Victor *s.s.c.* '57 (OM)[K] St. Columbans Missionary Society of St. Columban Retired.
Gaboury, Victor *s.s.c.* '57 (PRO)[P] Bristol, RI St. Columban's Retirement House Retired.
Gabriel, Abelardo *s.v.d.* '06 (CHI) Chicago, IL St. Anselm.
Gabriel, Eduardo *o.p.* '92 (MIA)[K] Miami, FL Dominican Fathers of Miami, Inc.; Miami, FL St. Dominic.
Gabriel, John B. '98 (MO) Army Chaplains.
Gabriel, John D. '87 (NEW) Vocations Office; Members; Emmaus House of Discernment; Director of Vocations; Members.
Gabriel, John *m.s.* '91 (ATL) Marietta, GA St. Ann.
Gabriel, Michael A. '84 (CHI) Chicago, IL St. Josaphat.
Gabriel, Paul *o.f.m.conv.* '05 (R)[F] Elon, NC Conventual Franciscans; Burlington, NC Blessed Sacrament.
Gabrielli, Theodore E. *s.j.* '96 (FgM) Los Gatos, CA; Los Gatos, CA Society of Jesus.
Gabrielli, Theodore *s.j.* '96 (SJ) San Jose, CA Most Holy Trinity; [O] Los Gatos, CA California Jesuit Missions.
Gabrus, Alois '72 (STL)[O] St. Louis, MO Franciscan

Friary of St. Anthony of Padua.
Gabuzda, Richard J. '81 (OM)[P] Omaha, NE Institute for Priestly Formation; On Duty Outside the Diocese.
Gacad, Manuel *m.j.* '78 (LA)[P] Los Angeles, CA Missionaries of Jesus, Inc.; Los Angeles, CA St. Kevin; Los Angeles, CA Precious Blood.
Gaddy, Rev. Msgr. James '65 (LKC) Lake Charles, LA Our Lady Queen of Heaven.
Gaddy, Kenneth F. *c.ss.r.* '88 (FgM) Christiansted, VI Church of the Holy Cross; Christiansted, St. Croix, VI Blessed Peter Donder's Formation Residence; Baltimore Province.
Gadenz, Pablo T. '96 (TR) On Duty Outside the Diocese; Censores Librorum.
Gadenz, Pablo T. '96 (NEW)[B] School of Diplomacy and Intl. Rels.; [A] South Orange, NJ Immaculate Conception Seminary.
Gadient, Peter J. '45 (LIN) Legion of Mary; [E] Lincoln, NE Bonacum House Retired.
Gadziala, Timothy '94 (ATL) Atlanta, GA St. Anthony of Padua; AACCW.
Gaeke, Thomas M. '75 (CIN) Medical Leave of Absence.
Gaelens, Albert R. *c.s.b.* '60 (GAL)[E] Houston, TX St. Thomas High School.
Gaesser, Ronald E. '61 (ROC) Auburn, NY Holy Family Retired.
Gaeta, Bernard N. '73 (Y) Advocates; Priests Council; Judges.
Gaeta, David R. '80 (SLC) On Duty Outside the Diocese.
Gaeta, Rev. Msgr. Francis X. '63 (RVC) Deer Park, NY SS. Cyril and Methodius.
Gaetano, Francis M. *s.a.c.* '48 (NEW) Fairview, NJ Our Lady of Grace.
Gaetano, Rev. Msgr. Lewis F. '73 (Y) Canton, OH Our Lady of Peace; Canton, OH St. Paul; Priests Council.
Gaffey, Eugene F. '69 (PRT)[M] Portland, ME University of Maine at Machias; Calais, ME Blessed Kateri Tekakwitha Parish; Machias, ME Saint Peter the Fisherman Parish.
Gaffey, Rev. Msgr. James P. '60 (SR) Diocesan Judges Retired.
Gaffey, Kevin P. '57 (SFR) Retired.
Gaffigan, Charles A. '62 (ALB) Corinth, NY Holy Mother and Child Parish.
Gaffigan, William J. '64 (ALB) Retired.
Gaffney, Brian R. *c.o.* '05 (PH)[Y] Philadelphia, PA The Philadelphia Congregation of The Oratory of St. Philip Neri; Philadelphia, PA St. Francis Xavier.
Gaffney, David F. '00 (PRO)[C] Warwick, RI Bishop Hendricken High School; [A] Providence, RI Seminary of Our Lady of Providence; Seminary of Our Lady of Providence.
Gaffney, Edward M. *o.p.* '49 (HBG)[H] Lancaster, PA Dominican Nuns of the Perpetual Rosary, Incorporated.
Gaffney, Francis P. '64 (CAM) Adjutant Judicial Vicars; Judges; Gibbstown, NJ St. Michael's Church, Gibbstown, N.J.
Gaffney, J. Michael '73 (OG) Massena, NY The Catholic Community of St. Mary's & St. Joseph's.
Gaffney, J. Patrick *s.m.m.* '54 (RVC)[M] Bay Shore, NY Montfort Missionaries.
Gaffney, James F. '85 (ALN) Unassigned.
Gaffney, John H. *o.s.a.* '45 (TLS)[B] Tulsa, OK Cascia Hall Preparatory School.
Gaffney, John *s.o.l.t.* '09 (CC) Robstown, TX St. John Nepomucene; [G] Robstown, TX Society of Our Lady of the Most Holy Trinity.
Gaffney, Joseph P. '67 (LA) Retired.
Gaffney, Michael (OG) Committee on Assignments.
Gaffney, Patrick D. *c.s.c.* '74 (FTW)[B] University of Notre Dame Du Lac; [H] Notre Dame, IN Holy Cross Community, Corby Hall, University of Notre Dame.
Gaffney, William *c.ss.r.* '60 (TR)[R] Long Branch, NJ San Alfonso Retreat House.
Gaffny, David J. '57 (NSH) Dover, TN St. Francis of Assisi.
Gaffny, David J. '06 (NSH) Clarksville, TN Immaculate Conception.
Gaffny, David (NSH) Deans.
Gagala, John '58 (DET) Judges Retired.
Gagan, Charles R. *s.j.* '68 (SFR) San Francisco, CA St. Ignatius; [N] San Francisco, CA Loyola House Jesuit Community; [P] San Francisco, CA Catholic Charities CYO of the Archdiocese of San Francisco.
Gagan, Philip R. '79 (STA) Special Assignment.
Gage, George '79 (ROM) Boardman, OH St. Mary; College of Consultors; Diocesan Collections Coordinator.
Gage, Philip S. *s.m.* '69 (WDC)[N] Washington, DC Marist Center.
Gaggawala, Paul O. *a.j.* '80 (ALN)[P] Shenandoah, PA Apostles of Jesus; [P] Northampton, PA Apostles of Jesus.
Gaglia, Fred R. '63 (SB) Retired.
Gagliano, Philip J. '76 (NY) Ardsley, NY Our Lady of Perpetual Help.
Gagliardi, Richard '62 (OAK) Pinole, CA St. Joseph Retired.
Gagliardo, Anthony F. '61 (BUF) Retired.
Gagliardo, Anthony (COS) Retired.
Gaglione, John R. '76 (BUF) Air Force Reserve Chaplains; Snyder, NY Christ the King; Finance Council.
Gaglioni, Joseph B. *c.s.sp.* '64 (SB)[I] Hemet, CA Congregation of the Holy Spirit Retired.
Gagne, Donald *s.m.* '54 (PRT) Lewiston, ME Central Maine Medical Center.
Gagne, Marc R. '85 (MAN) Dover, NH Parish of the Assumption.
Gagne, Roger C. '75 (PRO) Warwick, RI St. Peter.
Gagne, Ronald G. *m.s.* '71 (FR)[G] Attleboro, MA La Salette Shrine.
Gagne, Ronald '66 (DUL) Retired.
Gagne, Walter *s.a.* '71 (NY)[EE] Garrison, NY Franciscan Friars of the Atonement.
Gagnepain, John F. *c.m.* '62 (SPC) Ecumenism; Diocesan Director of Continuing Formation of Clergy; Presbyteral Council.
Gagnepain, John F. *c.m.* '62 (STL)[O] Perryville, MO Congregation of the Mission.
Gagnier, John F. '78 (ROC) Rochester, NY Holy Name of Jesus; Rochester, NY Our Lady of Mercy.
Gagnon, Andre J. '57 (MAN)[J] Laconia, NH St. Francis Rehabilitation and Nursing Center Retired.
Gagnon, Daniel *o.m.i.* '87 (FgM) Washington, DC AMERICAN OBLATE MISSIONS.
Gagnon, Herve *o.m.i.* '45 (BO)[U] Lowell, MA St. Eugene House (Residence) Retired.
Gagnon, Joseph A. '61 (DET) Retired.
Gagnon, Leo G. '72 (MAN) Richmond, VA Retired.
Gagnon, Mariano *o.f.m.* '57 (FgM) New York, NY Holy Name Province.
Gagnon, Raymond E. '72 (MAN) Franklin, NH St. Paul.
Gagnon, Richard *s.d.s.* '65 (NSH) Smyrna, TN St. Luke; Hispanic Ministry.
Gagnon, Ronald P. '56 (TUC) Retired.
Gago, Jose *o.m.i.* '56 (SAT)[K] San Antonio, TX Oblate Madonna Residence.
Gahagan, William H. '70 (KNX) Helenwood, TN St. Jude Parish; Norris, TN St. Joseph; Clinton, TN St. Therese.
Gahan, James L. '68 (STL) St. Charles, MO Sts. Joachim and Ann; [E] St. Charles, MO Duchesne High School.
Gahan, Timothy '07 (CHR) Spartanburg, SC St. Paul the Apostle.
Gaiardo, Martin J. '70 (SCR) Retired.
Gaines, G. Timothy '87 (DEN) Louisville, CO St. Louis.
Gaitan, Ramon *o.a.r.* '60 (NY)[B] Suffern, NY Tagaste Monastery.
Gaiter, Chester E. *s.j.* '76 (STL)[O] St. Louis, MO Jesuit Community Corporation at Saint Louis University – Jesuit Hall.
Gajardo, Leonardo J. '06 (GRY) On Duty Outside the Diocese.
Gajda, Piotr J. '55 (CC) Military Chaplains; Air Force Chaplains.
Gajdos, Rev. Msgr. T. George '70 (MIL) Wauwatosa, WI Christ King; Archdiocesan Consultors.
Gajdzinski, Norman A. '63 (CLV) Garfield Heights, OH St. Therese Retired.
Gajewski, Rev. Msgr. Chester A. '50 (SCR)[N] Dunmore, PA Villa St. Joseph Retired.
Gajewski, Robert S. '07 (NEW) New Milford, NJ St. Joseph's.
Galambos, Stephen *o.f.m.* '96 (NY)[EE] New York Franciscan Province of the Immaculate Conception.
Galan, Jose M. '65 (PCE) Mercedita, PR Church of the Sacred Heart.
Galang, Danilo C. *m.s.* '96 (HON) Kekaha, HI St. Theresa.
Galang, Jose '78 (SJ) Saratoga, CA Church of the Ascension.
Galant, Andrzej *s.ch.* '81 (MIL) Milwaukee, WI SS. Cyril and Methodius; Milwaukee, WI St. Maximilian Kolbe.
Galarneault, Thomas '07 (DUL) Bigfork, MN Our Lady of the Snows; Bigfork, MN St. Catherine; Bigfork, MN St. Michael.
Galarza, Edison *o.c.c.s.s.* '99 (STP) Minneapolis, MN SS. Cyril & Methodius.
Galasso, Michael S. '71 (HRT) East Hartford, CT Blessed Sacrament.
Galaz, Jesse C. '81 (LA) Paramount, CA Our Lady of the Rosary.
Galdon, Joseph A. *s.j.* '59 (FgM) New York, NY Society of Jesus.
Galdon, Peter P. '68 (NEW) Retired.
Galea, Michael A. '80 (BR) Sorrento, LA St. Anthony of Padua; Sorrento, LA St. Anne.
Galeana, David (CHI) Round Lake, IL St. Joseph.
Galeano, John J. '02 (NEW) Lodi, NJ St. Francis de Sales.
Galek, Peter '83 (CHI) Hillside, IL St. Domitilla.
Galens, Jeffrey R. '90 (NY) Rhinebeck, NY The Good Shepherd.
Galetto, Paul W. *o.s.a.* '82 (CAM)[C] Richland, NJ St. Augustine Preparatory School.
Gali, Anthony J. '95 (SCR) Mountaintop, PA St. Jude.
Galic, Rev. Msgr. Bernard J. '70 (FTW) South Bend, IN Holy Family; Budget Committee; Vocations.
Galic, Josip N. *o.f.m.* '66 (CHI)[N] Chicago, IL St. Anthony's Friary.
Galido, Ariel *m.s.c.* '04 (MI) Cathedral of the Assumption; Prefecture Consultors.
Galier, Victor A. '98 (ATL) Tyrone, GA St. Matthew; Advocates; Vicars for Clergy.
Galinada, Michael–Dwight Colin '78 (ORG) Brea, CA St. Angela Merici.
Galindo, Igor *sch.p.* (NY)[EE] New York, NY Calasanzian Fathers (Piarists).
Galindo, Mario *m.s.f.* '07 (SAT) New Braunfels, TX Holy Family.
Galipeau, Roland J. '64 (SPR) Holyoke, MA Holy Cross.
Galivan, James F. '81 (CHI) Other Assignments.
Gall, Jacob M. '62 (FTW) Retired.
Gallagher, Adrian *o.f.m.conv.* '92 (HBG) Coal Township, PA Our Lady of Hope; Trevorton, PA St. Patrick.
Gallagher, Anthony (TOL) Retired.
Gallagher, Brian *s.s.c.* '52 (PRO)[P] Bristol, RI St. Columban's Retirement House Retired.
Gallagher, Brian *s.s.c.* '52 (OM)[K] St. Columbans Missionary Society of St. Columban.
Gallagher, Cathal *s.s.c.* '74 (SFS) Armour, SD St. Paul the Apostle.
Gallagher, Cathal *s.s.c.* '74 (OM)[K] St. Columbans Missionary Society of St. Columban.
Gallagher, Charles A. *s.j.* '58 (NEW)[B] Jersey City, NJ Jesuit Center; [M] Jersey City, NJ Jesuits of Saint Peter's College, Inc.
Gallagher, Charles G. '44 (CHI) La Grange, IL St. Cletus Retired.
Gallagher, Cyrus *o.f.m.cap.* '65 (COS)[D] Colorado Springs, CO St. Francis Nursing Center; [F] Colorado Springs, CO Solanus Casey Friary.
Gallagher, Daniel B. '99 (GAY) Special Assignment.
Gallagher, Daniel J. '51 (PH) Retired.
Gallagher, Daniel N. '65 (MO) DEPARTMENT OF VETERANS AFFAIRS HOSPITALS AND CHAPLAINS.
Gallagher, Daniel '65 (JKS) Defenders of the Bond; Cursillo Movement; [C] Jackson, MS St. Dominic–Jackson Memorial Hospital.
Gallagher, David F. *c.s.s.* '59 (BO)[X] Waltham, MA Stigmatine Fathers and Brothers Retired.
Gallagher, Dennis J. *o.s.a.* '65 (PH)[C] Villanova University; [Y] Villanova, PA St. Thomas Monastery.
Gallagher, Dennis *a.a.* '78 (WOR)[A] Worcester, MA Assumption College; [O] Worcester, MA Assumptionists of Assumption College; [R] Worcester, MA Assumption College; Councilors:.
Gallagher, Edward H. *o.p.* '36 (PRO)[P] Providence St. Thomas Aquinas Priory at Providence College Retired.
Gallagher, Edward L. '53 (BO) Senior Priests. Retired.
Gallagher, Edward M. '78 (AGN) Barrigada, GU San Vicente Ferrer.
Gallagher, Edward *s.a.* '71 (NY)[EE] Garrison Franciscan Friars of the Atonement, Minister General Office Retired.
Gallagher, Eugene P. '38 (NY) Retired.
Gallagher, Francis L. '48 (BO) Senior Priests. Retired.
Gallagher, Francis M. '64 (PH) Retired.
Gallagher, Francis (PEO) On Leave of Absence.
Gallagher, Gregory *o.m.i.* '72 (BEL)[F] Belleville, IL Shrine of Our Lady of the Snows.
Gallagher, J. Peter '92 (IND) Lawrenceburg, IN St. Lawrence.
Gallagher, Jack *o.s.cam.* '81 (WOR)[L] Whitinsville, MA St. Camillus.
Gallagher, James E. '87 (RIC) Appomattox, VA Our Lady of Peace; Hurt, VA St. Victoria.
Gallagher, James R. '65 (CHI)[J] Evergreen Park, IL Little Company of Mary Hospital and Health Care Centers Retired.
Gallagher, James T. *c.s.c.* '07 (FTW)[A] Notre Dame, IN; [H] Notre Dame Congregation of Holy Cross, Indiana Province, Provincial House; [B] University of Notre Dame Du Lac; [H] Notre Dame, IN Holy Cross Community, Corby Hall, University of Notre Dame.
Gallagher, Rev. Msgr. John A. '55 (NY) Yonkers, NY St. Paul the Apostle.
Gallagher, John C. *c.s.b.* '60 (GAL)[O] Houston, TX Residence of the Basilian Fathers of the University of St. Thomas.
Gallagher, John E. '59 (BO) Senior Priests. Retired.
Gallagher, Rev. Msgr. John Gerald '57 (CAM) Retired.
Gallagher, John J. *o.s.cam.* '81 (WOR)[L] Whitinsville, MA St. Camillus Hospice, Inc.
Gallagher, John J. '55 (BAL) Retired.
Gallagher, John M. '71 (GB) Retired.
Gallagher, John P. '80 (DAV) Davenport, IA St. Anthony's; Defenders of the Bond; Blue Grass, IA St. Andrew.
Gallagher, John P. '57 (PH) Retired.
Gallagher, John P. '68 (PIT) Cranberry Township, PA St. Ferdinand.
Gallagher, John R. '93 (WH) Glen Dale, WV St. Jude.
Gallagher, John '92 (PMB) English; Released from Diocesan Assignment.
Gallagher, John *m.i.* '81 (WOR)[O] Whitinsville, MA St. Camillus Community.

Gallagher, John *o.f.m.cap.* '78 (FgM)[EE] White Plains, NY St. Conrad Friary; White Plains, NY Province of St. Mary; White Plains, NY.
Gallagher, Joseph J. '63 (PH) Retired.
Gallagher, Kevin J. '02 (PH) Lansdale, PA Corpus Christi.
Gallagher, Kevin M. '98 (NY) Pine Bush, NY The Infant Saviour.
Gallagher, Kevin P. '83 (ALN) Mahanoy City, PA Blessed Teresa of Calcutta Parish.
Gallagher, Laurence *c.ss.r.* '02 (LA) Pacific Palisades, CA Corpus Christi.
Gallagher, Maurice O. '50 (PBL) Retired.
Gallagher, Michael J. '69 (WIL) On Duty Outside the Diocese.
Gallagher, Michael J. '66 (SD) El Cajon, CA Our Lady of Grace.
Gallagher, Michael S. *s.j.* '84 (NO)[P] New Orleans Jesuit Provincial Office.
Gallagher, Otmar *o.f.m.cap.* '48 (PIT)[M] Pittsburgh, PA St. Augustine Friary Retired.
Gallagher, Rev. Msgr. Patrick J. '70 (MOB) Dothan, AL St. Columba; [I] Dothan, AL George C. Wallace Jr. Community College Newman Center; Vicars Forane.
Gallagher, Patrick *o.f.m.conv.* '65 (ALB) Fonda, NY St. Cecilia; Tribes Hill, NY Sacred Heart.
Gallagher, Paul V. '63 (RIC) Retired.
Gallagher, Paul *o.f.m.* '82 (CHI)[N] Cicero, IL San Damiano Friary Order of Friars Minor.
Gallagher, Philip P. '78 (LAN) Retired.
Gallagher, Raymond '90 (SAN) Retired.
Gallagher, Richard '36 (SEA) Retired.
Gallagher, Richard '44 (TR) Leave of Absence.
Gallagher, Richard '60 (SEA) Federal Detention Center Retired.
Gallagher, Robert A. '77 (STU) Little Hocking, OH St. Ambrose.
Gallagher, Rev. Msgr. Robert J. '73 (LA) North Hollywood, CA St. Charles Borromeo; Deanery 7; Members; Members.
Gallagher, Roger P. '54 (WDC)[M] Washington, DC Cardinal O'Boyle Residence for Priests Retired.
Gallagher, Simeon *o.f.m.cap.* '71 (DEN)[N] Denver, CO St. Francis of Assisi Friary.
Gallagher, Simon P. *o.s.b.* '73 (PAT) Morris Plains, NJ Greystone Park Psychiatric Hospital; [N] Morristown, NJ St. Mary's Abbey.
Gallagher, Thomas G. '68 (RVC) North Merrick, NY Sacred Heart.
Gallagher, Thomas J. *s.j.* '70 (BO)[U] Weston, MA Campion Health Center, Inc.
Gallagher, Thomas J. '61 (CLV) Retired.
Gallagher, Thomas M. *o.f.m.* '82 (HRT) Hartford, CT St. Patrick–St. Anthony.
Gallagher, Thomas N. *s.j.* '61 (SEA)[C] Tacoma, WA Bellarmine Preparatory School.
Gallagher, Thomas P. *o.s.f.s.* '67 (PH)[Y] Wyndmoor, PA Villa de Sales Oblate Residence.
Gallagher, Timothy M. *o.m.v.* '79 (BO)[B] Boston, MA Our Lady of Grace Seminary.
Gallagher, Timothy '09 (ATL) Conyers, GA St. Pius X.
Gallagher, Tom *s.j.* '61 (SPK)[B] Spokane, WA Gonzaga University.
Gallagher, William E. '46 (SEA) Retired.
Gallagher, William G. '53 (RVC) Retired.
Gallagher, William J. '47 (WOR) Retired.
Gallagher, Rev. Msgr. William J. '69 (BUF) Orchard Park, NY St. John Vianney; Finance Council.
Gallant, Jon–Paul '78 (FR) South Attleboro, MA St. Theresa of the Child Jesus.
Gallant, Rodrigue J. '47 (MAN) Retired.
Gallardo, David '84 (LA) Pico Rivera, CA St. Mariana de Paredes.
Gallardo, Joseph *o.a.r.* '94 (NEW)[M] West Orange, NJ Augustinian Recollects.
Gallarelli, George A. *s.j.* '62 (BGP)[E] Fairfield, CT Fairfield College Preparatory School; [O] Fairfield, CT The Fairfield Jesuit Community–Fairfield University.
Gallaro, George D. '72 (NTN) Priests Serving Outside the Eparchy.
Gallaro, George D. '72 (PBR) Gibsonia, PA St. Andrew the Apostle; [A] Pittsburgh, PA Byzantine Catholic Seminary of SS. Cyril and Methodius.
Gallaro, George D. '72 (PBR) Presbyteral Council; Vicar for Canonical Services; Judicial Vicar.
Gallas, John '05 (STP) Loretto, MN SS. Peter and Paul.
Gallatin, Joseph G. '97 (STP)[G] Eagan, MN Faithful Shepherd Catholic School; Mendota, MN St. Peter.
Gallatin, Paul H. '58 (OKL) Oklahoma City, OK Retired.
Gallaugher, Daniel T. '09 (WDC) Clinton, MD St. Mary.
Galle, Maciej '08 (CHI) Chicago, IL St. Constance; Advocates.
Gallego, Jose M. *o.m.* '57 (SJN) San Juan, PR Ntra. Sra. de Fatima.
Gallegos, David M. *o.s.m.* '66 (CHI)[N] Chicago Order of Friar Servants of Mary (Servites) United States of America Province, Inc.
Gallegos, David *o.s.m.* '66 (ORG) Fullerton, CA St. Philip Benizi.
Gallegos, Joseph *c.r.* '69 (PBL) Cortez, CO St. Margaret Mary; Cortez, CO St. Rita.
Gallegos, Jospeph Larry *c.r.* (DEN)[N] Denver, CO The Theatine Fathers.
Gallegos, Stephen *c.m.* '88 (FgM) Earth City, MO Western Province.
Gallegos, Valentine '09 (SAT) San Antonio, TX St. Matthew's.
Gallen, Francis H. '47 (PH) Retired.
Gallen, John '69 (HT) Thibodaux, LA Christ The Redeemer.
Gallen, John *s.j.* '63 (NY)[EE] New York, NY Murray–Weigel Hall.
Gallenbach, Thomas E. '58 (LAV) Las Vegas, NV St. Joseph, Husband of Mary.
Gallenbach, Thomas '58 (SFD) On Duty Outside the Diocese.
Gallenstein, Joseph A. '90 (COV) Taylor Mill, KY St. Anthony; [B] Covington, KY Covington Catholic High School.
Gallerini, Philip G. '62 (SPR) Retired.
Galles, Rev. Msgr. Francis A. '52 (WIN) Retired.
Galli, Clarence F. '53 (SFE) Retired.
Gallia, Andrew R. '62 (SCR) Retired.
Galligan, Charles H. '87 (PRO) Pawtucket, RI St. Edward.
Galligan, James L. *o.s.a.* '50 (PH)[Y] Villanova, PA St. Thomas Monastery.
Gallina, Leo J. '65 (E) Bradford, PA St. Bernard.
Gallinger, Carl '89 (CHY) Laramie, WY St. Paul's Newman Center; [F] Laramie, WY St. Paul's Newman Center, University Catholic Community (University of Wyoming); College of Consultors; Vicars Forane; Defenders of the Bond.
Gallipeau, Mark T. '06 (WH) Marlinton, WV St. John Neumann.
Gallipoli, Mario *c.p.* '61 (BRK)[T] Jamaica, NY Immaculate Conception Monastery.
Gallivan, Rev. Msgr. David M. '66 (BUF) Buffalo, NY Holy Cross.
Gallo, Dennis '85 (MRY) San Luis Obispo, CA San Luis Obispo.
Gallo, Gerardo '85 (NEW) Fairview, NJ St. John the Baptist.
Gallo, Jhon Jaime Florez '96 (CGS) Caguas, PR San Pablo Apostol.
Gallo, Regis *o.f.m.* '62 (ALB)[A] Catskill, NY St. Anthony Friary.
Gallo, Vincent '60 (BRK) Glendale, NY St. Pancras Retired.
Gallogly, Francis X. '65 (PH)[Y] Villanova, PA St. Thomas Monastery.
Gallus, David *o.s.c.* '66 (SCL)[I] Onamia, MN Crosier Priory.
Galluzzo, James '90 (P) Absent on Leave.
Gally, Lourduraj Gregory (SLC) Salt Lake City, UT Saint Ambrose LLC 214; Salt Lake City, UT Veterans Administration Hospital.
Galonek, David B. '96 (WOR) West Brookfield, MA Sacred Heart of Jesus; West Brookfield, MA St. Mary's.
Galos, Artemio '85 (DET) Sterling Heights, MI St. Michael.
Galovich, George '71 (STL) Retired.
Galt, Ronald '92 (CHI)[J] Maywood, IL Loyola University Medical Center; Chicago, IL Immaculate Conception of the Blessed Virgin Mary; Chicago, IL St. Joseph.
Galuppi, Michael '07 (SY) Camillus, NY St. Joseph.
Galvan, Alfred '65 (LSC) Ruidoso, NM St. Eleanor; Vicars; Presbyteral Council.
Galvan, John *s.j.* '99 (LA)[C] Los Angeles, CA Jesuit Community.
Galvez, Elias *o.f.m.* '56 (FgM) Oakland, CA St. Barbara Province.
Galvez, Jesus Manuel *o.f.m. conv.* '91 (OAK) Hayward, CA St. Bede.
Galvez, Mariano Martínez *o.m.i.* '84 (SJN) San Juan, PR Nuestra Sra. de Guadalupe.
Galvez, Miguel *s.j.s.* '01 (MAD) Sauk City, WI St. Norbert; Sauk City, WI St. Aloysius.
Galvez–Pineda, Rafael I. '06 (NEW) Westwood, NJ St. Andrew's.
Galvin, Edward *s.m.a.* '62 (NEW)[M] Tenafly, NJ Society of African Missions, Provincialate, S.M.A. Fathers Retired.
Galvin, Gregory P. '94 (NOR) Storrs, CT St. Thomas Aquinas; Seminarian Advisory Board; Director of Vocations; Members.
Galvin, James Gerard '94 (SAT) San Antonio, TX San Juan Capistrano.
Galvin, James M. '51 (LA)[V] Santa Barbara, CA St. Mary's Seminary Center.
Galvin, John P. '68 (WDC)[C] Catholic University of America, The; On Duty Outside the Archdiocese.
Galvin, John *s.m.* '63 (FgM) THE SOCIETY OF MARY.
Galvin, Thomas J. '82 (PIT) Pittsburgh, PA St. John the Baptist.
Galvin, William J. *m.m.* '56 (FgM) Maryknoll, NY MARYKNOLL.
Galvis Rios, Hector F. '09 (NEW) Jersey City, NJ Our Lady of Mt. Carmel.
Galyo, Rev. Msgr. John M. '54 (PH) Retired.
Gamache, Barry J. '81 (PRO) Bristol, RI St. Mary.
Gamallo, Edito '75 (NEW) Newark, NJ St. Anthony's.
Gamas, Giovanni '07 (SAC) Vallejo, CA St. Basil.
Gamba, Jose I. '86 (NEW) Fairview, NJ St. John the Baptist; Hispanic Apostolate.
Gambaro, Giampiero *o.f.m.cap.* '90 (NY)[EE] White Plains, NY Capuchin Friars International, Inc.; [EE] White Plains, NY St. Francis of Assisi Foundation.
Gambatese, Angelus *o.f.m.* '59 (NY) New York, NY St. Stephen of Hungary; [II] New York, NY Shrine of St. Jude, Inc.
Gamber, Matthew T. *s.j.* '95 (CHI)[N] Chicago Chicago Province of the Society of Jesus–Provincial Office.
Gamber, William K. '64 (STP) Retired.
Gambet, Daniel G. *o.s.f.s.* '57 (ALN)[B] Center Valley, PA DeSales University; [K] Center Valley, PA Oblates of St. Francis de Sales.
Gamboriko, Elias Rinaldo *a.j.* '99 (SFS) Sioux Falls, SD St. Josephine Bakhita Catholic Church.
Gambro, John M. *o.p.* '57 (CHI)[N] St. Pius V Priory.
Gamel, Robert E. '90 (FRS) Los Banos, CA St. Joseph.
Gameros, Ignacio L. '81 (TUC) Retired.
Gamez, Francisco J. '03 (SFR) San Francisco, CA Cathedral of St. Mary (Assumption).
Gamez, Rigoberto (CHI) Defenders of the Bond.
Gamez, Steven '08 (SAT) San Antonio, TX Cathedral of San Fernando.
Gamez–Alfonso, Rigoberto '95 (CHI) Chicago, IL Our Lady of Tepeyac; Chicago, IL Providence of God.
Gamm, David B. '72 (COV) Florence, KY St. Paul.
Gamm, Joseph *c.m.f.* '45 (LA)[V] Rancho Dominguez, CA Dominguez Seminary Inc.
Gammad, Engelberto '84 (SJ) Judges; Special Assignment; Adjutant Judicial Vicar.
Gamrot, Jaroslaw '91 (WDC) La Plata, MD Sacred Heart.
Ganahl, James A. '56 (SB) Retired.
Gancarz, Eugeniusz '71 (SP) Tampa, FL Incarnation.
Gancayco, Richard K. '92 (WDC) Washington, DC St. Benedict the Moor.
Ganci, William Philip '09 (PT) Tallahassee, FL Good Shepherd.
Gancila, Joseph A. '01 (BRK) Brooklyn, NY St. Bernadette.
Gandara, Juan Luis '67 (LAF) New Iberia, LA Sacred Heart of Jesus; On Special Assignment.
Gang, Dennis *t.o.r.* '76 (STU)[A] Steubenville, OH Franciscan University of Steubenville; [H] Steubenville, OH Holy Spirit Friary.
Gangolu, Babu *s.a.c.* '92 (SP) St. Petersburg, FL St. Paul.
Ganiel, Joseph F. '83 (CAM) Longport, NJ Church of the Epiphany, Longport, N.J.; Ventnor, NJ St. James Catholic Church, Ventnor, N.J.
Ganley, Thomas P. '85 (MET)[H] Somerset, NJ McCarrick Care Center; [I] Somerset, NJ Maria Regina Residence; Robert Wood Johnson University Hospital.
Gann, Seán J. '94 (RVC) Kings Park, NY St. Joseph's.
Gannon, Bernard J. '71 (CAM) Retired.
Gannon, Brian P. '97 (BGP) Ridgefield, CT St. Mary.
Gannon, Daniel J. *s.j.* '68 (CHY) Saint Stephens, WY St. Stephen's; [D] Saint Stephens, WY St. Stephens Mission – Jesuit Community.
Gannon, Dismas *o.c.s.o.* '50 (P)[L] Lafayette, OR The Cistercian (Trappist) Abbey of Our Lady of Guadalupe.
Gannon, George J. '02 (BAL) Baltimore, MD Sacred Heart of Mary; [V] Baltimore, MD The Sacred Heart of Mary Cemetery Continuing Care Trust.
Gannon, James *o.f.m.* '87 (MIL)[C] Milwaukee, WI Cardinal Stritch University; Milwaukee, WI St. Anthony of Padua.
Gannon, Joseph T. '75 (STP) Retired.
Gannon, Josephjude C. '03 (BRK) Hollis, NY St. Gerard Majella.
Gannon, Patrick J. '60 (LA) Retired.
Gannon, Patrick '76 (NO) New Orleans, LA Holy Name of Mary (Algiers).
Gannon, Thomas M. *s.j.* '67 (DET)[K] Clarkston, MI Colombiere Center.
Gannon, William Robert *o.p.* '53 (NY)[EE] New York, NY St. Vincent Ferrer Priory.
Ganshert, Rev. Msgr. Daniel T. '74 (MAD) Vicars General; Diocesan Consultors; Presbyteral Council; Personnel Board; Building Commission; Saint Raphael Society Clergy Retirement Plan; [I] Madison, WI The Catholic Diocese of Madison Foundation, Inc.; [F] Madison, WI Bishop O'Connor Catholic Pastoral Center.
Ganss, Karl P. '68 (RCK) Elburn, IL St. Gall.
Gantley, Donald M. *o.s.m.* '79 (CHI)[N] Chicago Order of Friar Servants of Mary (Servites) United States of America Province, Inc.
Gantley, Mark J. '91 (LAV) Henderson, NV St. Francis of Assisi.
Gantley, Mark J. '91 (HON) Defender of the Bond and Promoter of Justice.
Gantley, Mark '91 (SY) On Duty Outside the Diocese.

Ganuza, Felix *sch.p.* '76 (NY) New York, NY Annunciation; [EE] New York, NY Calasanzian Fathers (Piarists).
Ganz, Richard H. *s.j.* '84 (P)[L] Portland, OR Colombiere Community.
Ganz, Richard H. *s.j.* '84 (SPK)[B] Spokane, WA Gonzaga University.
Ganza, Jean Baptiste *s.j.* '05 (SEA)[L] Seattle, WA Arrupe Jesuit Community at Seattle University.
Gappa, Herbert T. *m.m.* '68 (NY)[EE] Maryknoll Maryknoll Fathers and Brothers Retired.
Gaquit, Teodulo '70 (HON) Honolulu, HI St. Anthony; Honolulu, HI Diocesan Hospital Ministry.
Garamendi, Martin *o.m.* '52 (SJN) San Juan, PR Ntra. Sra. de Fatima.
Garand, J. Douglas '01 (TOL) Toledo, OH St. Catherine of Siena.
Garanzini, Michael J. *s.j.* '80 (CHI)[C] Chicago, IL President's Office; [C] Chicago, IL Jesuit Community at Loyola University Chicago.
Garavel, Andrew J. *s.j.* '92 (BO)[U] Boston The Society of Jesus of New England–Provincial Offices.
Garavel, Andrew J. *s.j.* '92 (SJ)[B] Santa Clara, CA Jesuit Community.
Garaventa, Louis *s.j.* '76 (NY)[F] New York, NY Xavier High School.
Garbaciak, Dariusz *s.v.d.* '96 (CHI)[N] Techny, IL Divine Word Residence; [N] Techny, IL Blessed Arnold Charitable Trust; [N] Techny, IL DWTCRE Charitable Trust; [N] Techny, IL S.V.D. Funds, Inc.; Techny, IL; [N] Techny, IL Society of the Divine Word, Provincial Headquarters–Chicago Prov.; [W] Techny, IL Divine Word Techny Community Corporation.
Garbacz, Casimir *s.v.d.* (CHI) Ethnic Offices.
Garbacz, Kazimierz *s.v.d.* '70 (CHI)[N] Techny, IL Divine Word Residence.
Garbacz, Marcin Stanislaw '04 (RC) Faith, SD St. Joseph; [E] Philip, SD Priest Retirement and Aid Association/Pension Plan Board.
Garbarino, Joseph J. '83 (PAT) Montville, NJ St. Pius X; Deans.
Garbin, Raymond '63 (JOL) Elmhurst, IL Immaculate Conception.
Garbo, Francis Mark P. '90 (SFR) San Mateo, CA St. Timothy.
Garceau, Hildebrand *o.praem.* '84 (ORG) Costa Mesa, CA St. John the Baptist.
Garced, Wilberto Reyes *l.d.* '93 (NY)[II] New York, NY Lumen Dei.
Garces, Francis *o.f.m.cap.* '66 (FWT) Fort Worth, TX Our Lady of Guadalupe.
Garces–Solis, Rafael '99 (SB) Chino, CA St. Margaret Mary.
Garcia, Abraham R. *m.g.* '82 (LA)[P] Los Angeles, CA Guadalupe Missioners Procure.
Garcia, Albert *ss.cc.* '69 (HON)[D] Kaneohe, HI Sacred Hearts Center.
Garcia, Alfredo '02 (COS) Colorado Springs, CO Our Lady of Guadalupe.
Garcia, Alfredo *ss.cc.* '63 (BWN) Edinburg, TX Sacred Heart.
Garcia, Alonzo M. '05 (TUC) Tucson, AZ Holy Family Roman Catholic Parish – Tucson.
Garcia, Andres '93 (PH) Kennett Square, PA St. Patrick.
Garcia, Antonio '81 (SJN) Carolina, PR Ntra. Sra. Del Carmen.
Garcia, Antonio *o.de.m.* '67 (PCE) Ponce, PR Santuario San Judas Tadeo.
Garcia, Antonio *o.m.* (CGS) Cayey, PR Nuestra Senora de la Asuncion.
Garcia, Armand D. '05 (PH) Philadelphia, PA St. Katherine of Siena.
Garcia, Rev. Msgr. Avelino R. '68 (SP) St. Petersburg, FL Transfiguration.
Garcia, Camilo '00 (STO) Modesto, CA St. Joseph Church of Modesto (Pastor of).
Garcia, Camilo '08 (B) Buhl, ID Immaculate Conception; Twin Falls, ID St. Edward The Confessor.
Garcia, Daniel E. '88 (AUS) Austin, TX St. Vincent de Paul; Consultors; Associate Directors.
Garcia, David '75 (SAT) College of Consultors; Archdiocesan Presbyteral Council; San Antonio, TX Old Spanish Missions; San Antonio, TX St. Margaret Mary.
Garcia, Dennis M. '00 (SFE) Defenders of the Bond; Albuquerque, NM San Felipe de Neri; Presbyteral Council of the Archdiocese of Santa Fe; Albuquerque, NM San Ignacio.
Garcia, Edgar *o.m.i.* '85 (LA) South Gate, CA St. Helen.
Garcia, Eduardo H. '90 (CC) Beeville, TX St. Joseph Retired.
Garcia, Emilio '57 (ORL) Retired.
Garcia, Esau '87 (ORL) Deans; Orlando, FL Holy Cross; Ex Officio Members.
Garcia, Fernando (NSH) Antioch, TN Our Lady of Guadalupe.
Garcia, Francisco Gius '95 (RVC) Wantagh, NY St. Frances de Chantal.
Garcia, Francisco *o.f.m.cap.* '78 (PCE)[E] Ponce, PR Fraternidad Santa Teresita, Frailes Capuchinos; [H] Ponce, PR Albergue La Providencia para El Bienestar Social, Inc.
Garcia, George A. '73 (MIA) Coconut Grove, FL St. Hugh.
Garcia, Gildardo '85 (MO) Air Force Chaplains.
Garcia, Guillermo C. '75 (LA) Bell Gardens, CA St. Gertrude; Members.
Garcia, Hector *o.carm.* (MGZ) Anasco, PR St. Anthony Abbot.
Garcia, Hector *c.ss.r.* (CGS)[B] Aguas Buenas, PR Casa Cristo Redentor.
Garcia, Hignio '99 (SD) San Diego, CA St. Jude.
Garcia, Isidor *c.m.f.* '54 (LA)[V] Rancho Dominguez, CA Dominguez Seminary Inc.
Garcia, J. Jesus '98 (LA) Maywood, CA St. Rose of Lima.
Garcia, Jacinto '97 (DAL) Dallas, TX St. Rita.
Garcia, Jaime A. '08 (PRO) Providence, RI Rhode Island Hospital; Providence, RI St. Michael the Archangel.
Garcia, Jeffrey T. '86 (RIC) Amelia, VA Good Samaritan; Powhatan, VA St. John Neumann.
Garcia, Jesus A. '94 (SJN) San Juan, PR San Jorge.
Garcia, Jorge E. (B) Hailey, ID St. Charles Borromeo; Sun Valley, ID Our Lady of the Snows.
Garcia, Jose Isidoro *o.m.i.* '64 (CC) Kingsville, TX St. Martin.
Garcia, Jose L. (ARE) Retired.
Garcia, Jose Luis '00 (BWN) Edinburg, TX St. Joseph the Worker.
Garcia, Jose Maria '08 (CHI) Chicago, IL St. Sylvester.
Garcia, Jose '52 (MIA) Retired.
Garcia, Jose '09 (DEN) Brighton, CO St. Augustine.
Garcia, Rev. Msgr. Juan F. '67 (SPR) Springfield, MA All Souls; Springfield, MA Blessed Sacrament; Presbyteral Council.
Garcia, Juan L. *d.l.p.* '70 (SB)[A] Grand Terrace, CA Blessed Junipero Serra House of Formation; Blessed Junipero Serra House of Formation; [I] Grand Terrace, CA Diocesan Laborer Priests, DLP; Special or Other Diocesan Assignment.
Garcia, Rev. Msgr. Juan *c.r.i.c.* '67 (SPR) Procurators–Advocate; Diocesan Consultors.
Garcia, Juan '95 (FRS) Porterville, CA St. Anne.
Garcia, Juan Bosco Jimenez *s.d.b.* (CHI) Arlington Heights, IL Mission San Juan Diego.
Garcia, Justiniano '98 (SJN)[G] Guaynabo, PR Opus Dei; Guaynabo.
Garcia, Lino Ayala *c.s.* (BO) Everett, MA St. Anthony of Padua.
Garcia, Louis '93 (STO) Stockton, CA St. Mary of the Assumption Church (Pastor of).
Garcia, Rev. Msgr. Luis Javier '76 (BWN)[A] Mission, TX The Saint Joseph and Saint Peter Seminary; Canonical Assistance; Judicial Department and Diocesan Tribunal; Presiding Judge; Office of Permanent Deacons; Office for Propagation of the Faith; Office for the Church in Latin America.
Garcia, Luis '97 (MIA) Pompano Beach, FL St. Coleman.
Garcia, Manuel '75 (SJN)[E] San Juan, PR Centro Medico de P.R.
Garcia, Marcelino *s.j.* '70 (MIA)[K] Miami, FL Villa Javier.
Garcia, Marcial I. '95 (VEN) College of Consultors; Clewiston, FL St. Margaret.
Garcia, Mario *o.f.m.cap.* '88 (DAL)[J] Dallas, TX Capuchin Franciscan Friars, Vice Province of Texas; Dallas, TX Our Lady of Lourdes; Dallas, TX.
Garcia, Martin '09 (SAT) San Antonio, TX St. Rose of Lima.
Garcia, Michael A. *o.p.* '81 (CHI) River Forest, IL St. Vincent Ferrer.
Garcia, Michel '04 (MIA) Absent on Leave.
Garcia, Miguel A. *c.ss.r.* (SJN) San Juan, PR San Agustin.
Garcia, Millan '62 (SFE) Retired.
Garcia, Nelson *s.j.* '67 (MIA)[D] Miami, FL Belen Jesuit Preparatory School; [K] Miami, FL Villa Javier.
Garcia, Rev. Msgr. Otto L. '73 (BRK) Jackson Heights, NY St. Joan of Arc; Diocesan Judges.
Garcia, Patrick Kenny Q. '89 (AGN) Yigo, GU Our Lady of Lourdes.
Garcia, Pedro '65 (GR) Retired.
Garcia, Rev. Msgr. Pedro '64 (MIA) Princeton, FL St. Ann Mission; Rural Life Ministry.
Garcia, Philip *o.f.m.* '82 (SD)[J] Oceanside, CA Mission San Luis Rey.
Garcia, Rafael *s.j.* '93 (SFE) Albuquerque, NM Immaculate Conception; Presbyteral Council of the Archdiocese of Santa Fe.
Garcia, Rev. Msgr. Ramon V. '55 (SAT)[K] San Antonio, TX Padua Place.
Garcia, Raul Valencia '03 (TUC) San Luis, AZ Saint Jude Thaddeus Roman Catholic Parish – San Luis.
Garcia, Rev. Msgr. Raymond '55 (SAT) Retired.
Garcia, Raymundo '74 (TYL) Malakoff, TX Mary, Queen of Heaven Church; Athens, TX St. Edward Church; Presbyteral Council.
Garcia, Reynaldo A. *s.j.* '76 (MAR) Mackinac Island, MI Ste. Anne de Michilimackinac.
Garcia, Ricardo '92 (BWN) Defenders of the Bond; Presbyteral Council; Brownsville, TX Mary, Mother of the Church.
Garcia, Rev. Msgr. Roberto '86 (PCE)[B] The Pontifical Catholic University of Puerto Rico.
García, Rodolfo '97 (DAL) Irving, TX Church of the Incarnation; Vocations; [L] Irving, TX University of Dallas.
Garcia, Rodrigo Dallos *o.ss.t.* '94 (SJN) Bayamon, PR Ascension Del Senor.
Garcia, Rolando G. '86 (MIA) Miami, FL St. Agatha; FIU–University Park.
Garcia, Ruben *o.c.d.* '97 (SAT) San Antonio, TX St. Cecilia.
Garcia, Salomon '09 (ATL) Peachtree City, GA Holy Trinity.
Garcia, Saul A. *m.s.p.* '02 (LA) Los Angeles, CA Our Lady of Solitude; Los Angeles, CA Santa Isabel.
Garcia, Sebastian J. '07 (NEW) Jersey City, NJ St. Aedan's.
Garcia, Severiano *c.m.f.* '50 (SJN) Bayamon, PR San Jose.
Garcia–Ferrer, Eduardo '93 (CHI) Chicago, IL St. Stanislaus Kostka.
Garcia–Gonzalez, Francisco Javier '80 (R) Fuquay–Varina, NC St. Bernadette.
Garcia–Icedo, Mario '78 (PHX) Cashion, AZ St. William Roman Catholic Parish.
Garcia–Martinez, Antonio *o.m.* '67 (SJN) San Juan, PR Ntra. Sra. de Fatima.
Garcia–Miro, Sergio '78 (MIA) Retired.
Garcia–Ramirez, Pedro '92 (AUS) Pflugerville, TX St. Elizabeth.
Garcia–Rodriguez, Porfirio *o.m.i.* '08 (BUF) Buffalo, NY Holy Angels.
Garcia–Sanchez, Pedro *o.f.m.* (SB) Ontario, CA Our Lady of Guadalupe.
Garcia–Tunon, Guillermo *s.j.* '00 (MIA)[D] Miami, FL Belen Jesuit Preparatory School; [K] Miami, FL Villa Javier.
Garcia–Valencia, Joaquin (CHI) Chicago, IL St. Genevieve.
Garcia Almodovar, Angel L. '03 (ALN) Allentown, PA Sacred Heart of Jesus.
Garcia Echevarria, Roberto (PCE) Coto Laurel, PR Retired.
Garcia Flores, Efren Fergus '02 (SAC) Burney, CA St. Francis of Assisi.
Garcia Granados, Enrique '09 (MEM) Memphis, TN St. Michael's.
Gardin, Rev. Msgr. Vernon E. '71 (STL) Richmond Heights, MO Immacolata; [H] St. Louis, MO Department of Special Education; [H] St. Louis, MO St. Mary's Special Services; Archdiocesan Consultors; Moderator of the Curia.
Gardiner, Christopher B. '68 (MAR) Munising, MI Sacred Heart of Jesus.
Gardiner, James K. '69 (GAY) Bellaire, MI St. Luke; East Jordan, MI St. Joseph.
Gardiner, James *s.a.* '69 (NY)[EE] Garrison, NY Franciscan Friars of the Atonement.
Gardiner, Richard E. '67 (WDC) Solomons, MD Our Lady Star of the Sea; Priest Council.
Gardner, Clement G. '67 (ALT) Juniata Deanery; Hollidaysburg, PA St. Michael's.
Gardner, Daniel '78 (KCK) Kansas City, KS All Saints; [J] Kansas City, KS; Regional Pastoral Leaders.
Gardner, Giles *c.ss.r.* '39 (FgM) Baltimore Province.
Gardner, Rev. Msgr. Glenn D. '70 (DAL) Forney, TX St. Martin of Tours; Terrell, TX State Hospital; Adjutant Judicial Vicars; College of Consultors; Censor Librorum; Appointed Members.
Gardner, Jerome J. '79 (CIN) Cincinnati, OH St. Margaret Mary.
Gardner, John Paul '05 (BIS) Priests' Benefit Association.
Gardner, Royal J. '51 (SPR) Retired.
Gardner, William M. '92 (PEO) Spring Valley, IL St. Mary; Peru, IL St. Valentine.
Gardner, William P. '62 (TR) Retired.
Gardocki, Patrick M. *o.f.m.* '81 (MO) DEPARTMENT OF VETERANS AFFAIRS HOSPITALS AND CHAPLAINS; Navy Reserve Chaplains.
Gardocki, Patrick *o.f.m.* '81 (BUF) Veterans Hospital; Cheektowaga, NY St. John Gualbert.
Gardocki, Thomas F. '65 (WIL) Retired.
Gardon, Emmanuel *c.p.* '50 (PMB)[H] North Palm Beach, FL Our Lady of Florida Spiritual Center.
Gareau, Timothy W. '88 (CLV) Bay Village, OH St. Raphael.
Gargantiel, Isidro T. '68 (GR) Retired.
Gargotta, Anthony '01 (PIT) Pittsburgh, PA St. Edward; Pittsburgh, PA St. Francis of Assisi; Priest Council.
Garibaldi, Anthony *o.f.m.* '76 (SAC) Sacramento, CA St. Francis of Assisi.
Gariboldi, Ronald J. '61 (BO) Gloucester, MA Holy Family.
Gariepy, Andre M. '58 (WOR) Retired.
Gariepy, Robert E. '63 (WOR) Retired.
Gariepy, Thomas P. *c.s.c.* '74 (FR)[A] North Easton, MA

Stonehill College; [A] North Easton, MA Holy Cross Fathers Religious.
Garinger, Grant *s.j.* '97 (LA)[C] Los Angeles, CA Jesuit Community.
Gariolo, Joseph M. *c.r.s.p.* '50 (BUF)[B] Youngstown, NY St. Anthony M. Zaccaria Seminary.
Garisto, James A. '77 (NY) Poughkeepsie, NY St. Peter.
Garkowski, John G. '66 (BRK) South Ozone Park, NY Our Lady of Perpetual Help.
Garland, Reynolds *o.f.m.* '60 (LEX) Jackson, KY Holy Cross.
Garland, William T. *o.s.a.* '62 (PH)[C] Villanova, PA Villanova University; Counselors:.
Garland, William T. *o.s.a.* '62 (BO)[C] Our Mother of Good Counsel Monastery.
Garlick, Thomas B. '84 (WOR) Southborough, MA St. Anne.
Garneau, James F. '84 (R) Council of Priests; Mount Olive, NC St. Mary; Diocesan Consultors; Home Mission Society of the Diocese of Raleigh; Deans; Office of Permanent Diaconate.
Garner, Andy '01 (OWN) Non–Parochial Assignments.
Garner, D. Andrew '01 (OWN) Consultors; Vocations Office; Priest Personnel Committee.
Garner, Dominic Mary *m.f.v.a.* '04 (BIR)[E] Birmingham, AL Franciscan Missionaries of the Eternal Word, A Public Association of the Christian Faithful.
Garner, Joel P. *o.praem.* '65 (SFE) Albuquerque, NM Our Lady of Most Holy Rosary; [H] Albuquerque, NM Santa Maria de la Vid Priory; [L] Albuquerque, NM Norbertine Community of New Mexico, Inc.
Garner, Kirby '77 (AUS) Defenders of the Bond; Buda, TX Santa Cruz.
Garner, Steven M. '09 (DUB) Dubuque, IA Church of the Resurrection.
Garnica, Antonio *m.s.c.* '79 (LA)[P] Cudahy, CA Misioneros del Sagrado Corazon y Santa Maria de Guadalupe; Deanery 17; San Pedro Region.
Garnier, David W. '09 (GAL) Houston, TX Co–Cathedral of the Sacred Heart.
Garoffolo, Vincent '41 (NEW) Retired.
Garon, Robert E. J. '05 (LA) North Hollywood, CA St. Charles Borromeo; Ventura, CA Our Lady of the Assumption.
Garone, Thomas *o.f.m.* '73 (NY)[GG] Wappingers Falls, NY Mt. Alvernia Retreat House.
Garr, T. Mattingly *s.j.* '75 (FgM) Chicago, IL Society of Jesus.
Garrahy, Michael '51 (WCH) Retired.
Garramone, Dominic M. *o.s.b.* '92 (PEO)[A] Peru, IL St. Bede Abbey; [C] Peru, IL St. Bede Academy; Peru, IL.
Garrett, Benton Lee '06 (WDC) Military Chaplains; Lexington Park, MD Immaculate Heart of Mary.
Garrett, John C. '04 (TR) Tuckerton, NJ St. Theresa.
Garrett, Patrick Stuart '09 (GAL) Spring, TX St. Edward.
Garrett, Scott '03 (ANC) Dillingham, AK Holy Rosary; Defenders of the Bond.
Garrett, Scott '03 (FBK) Defenders of the Bond.
Garrido, Alejandro '92 (CHI) Chicago, IL Seminary Formation House–Casa Jesus.
Garrigan, Gerard *o.s.b.* '89 (STL) St. Louis, MO St. Anselm; [O] St. Louis, MO The Abbey of St. Mary and St. Louis.
Garrione, Robert '89 (ALX) Campti, LA Nativity of The Blessed Virgin Mary.
Garrison, G. Matthew '04 (LR) Little Rock, AR Cathedral of St. Andrew.
Garrity, Charles *o.c.d.* '66 (SB)[L] Redlands, CA El Carmelo Retreat House; [I] Redlands, CA Discalced Carmelites, OCD.
Garrity, Francis D. '56 (BO) Senior Priests. Retired.
Garrity, G. Patrick '76 (KNX) Morristown, TN St. Patrick; Deans of the Diocese; Presbyteral Council; Diocesan Consultors; Ministries of the Five Rivers Deanery.
Garrity, Rev. Msgr. Paul V. '73 (BO) Lynn, MA St. Mary; Vicariate II; Vicariate II; Trustees.
Garrity, Robert M. '81 (RCK) Active Outside the Diocese.
Garrity, Sean M. *c.s.b.* '88 (LSC) Las Cruces, NM Cathedral of the Immaculate Heart of Mary; [B] Las Cruces, NM Basilian Fathers.
Garrity, Stephen M. *s.j.* '70 (ALN)[A] Wernersville, PA Jesuit Center–Jesuit Community.
Garrote, Sancho E. '76 (NY) Bronx, NY Bronx Psychiatric Center.
Garrote, Sancho G. '76 (NY) Bronx Municipal Hospital Center, Abraham Jacobi Hospital, Nathan B. VanEtten Hospital.
Garrote, Sancho (NY) Bronx, NY St. Brendan.
Garrott, William P. *o.p.* '94 (WDC) New York, NY; [B] Washington, DC Dominican House of Studies.
Garry, Peter J. '68 (RVC) Northport, NY St. Philip Neri.
Garry, Ron '83 (RC)[E] Philip, SD Priest Retirement and Aid Association/Pension Plan Board; Philip, SD Sacred Heart.
Gartland, Daniel B. '82 (LFT) Lafayette, IN St. Mary Cathedral; Lafayette, IN St. Lawrence; Deans; Diocesan Consultors; Members.
Gartland, James G. *s.j.* '93 (CHI)[D] Chicago, IL Cristo Rey Jesuit High School, Inc.; [N] Chicago, IL Miguel Pro Jesuit Community.
Gartland, R. Vincent '81 (TR) Lawrenceville, NJ St. Ann.
Gartner, Charles A. '58 (RVC) Homestead, FL; [M] Amityville, NY St. Pius X Residence Retired.
Garvey, Rev. Msgr. Francis J. '59 (NU) Grove City, MN Church of Our Lady; Vicar for Retired Priests.
Garvey, James W. '76 (PIT) Retired.
Garvey, John F. *s.j.* '74 (NY)[EE] New York, NY St. Ignatius Loyola Residence.
Garvey, John M. *m.s.* '53 (HRT)[L] Hartford, CT Missionaries of LaSalette.
Garvey, Michael '71 (Y) Mantua, OH St. Joseph.
Garvey, Roderick *c.ss.r.* '49 (STL)[O] Liguori, MO St. Clement Health Care Center Retired.
Garvin, Rev. Msgr. Joseph P. '73 (PH) Philadelphia, PA St. Christopher; Council of Priests.
Garvin, Thomas R. *s.j.* '58 (SPK)[J] Spokane, WA Regis Community Retired.
Gary, Paul Q. '84 (CHL) Charlotte, NC St. Luke.
Gary, Paul '84 (CHL) Diocesan Consultors.
Garza, Amador '85 (BWN) Rio Grande City, TX Immaculate Conception.
Garza, David '07 (SFS) Sioux Falls, SD Our Lady of Guadalupe.
Garza, Juan G. '02 (WCH) Newton, KS Our Lady of Guadalupe; Kansas State Industrial Reformatory.
Garza, Roberto '96 (MIA) Catholic Charities of the Archdiocese of Miami, Inc.; Vocations; Miami, FL St. Mary's Cathedral.
Garzarelli, Santo R. '61 (PH) Retired.
Garzon, Fabio H. *s.d.b.* '86 (KAL) Fennville, MI San Felipe de Jesus; Hartford, MI Immaculate Conception; Presbyteral Council Members; Presbyteral Council Members.
Gaskin, Grant '06 (WDC) Laurel, MD St. Mary.
Gaskin, Matthew L. *o.f.m.* '50 (PAT)[N] Ringwood, NJ Holy Name Friary, Inc.
Gasnick, Roy *o.f.m.* '60 (SP)[N] St. Petersburg, FL St. Anthony Friary.
Gaspar, Antony '98 (LA) Artesia, CA Holy Family.
Gaspar, Jonathan M. '04 (BO) Divine Worship and Spiritual Life.
Gaspar, Mark S. '98 (PH) Brookhaven, PA Our Lady of Charity.
Gaspar, Panimayakumar '84 (NY) Staten Island, NY Our Lady Star of the Sea.
Gasparik, Francis *o.f.m.cap.* '86 (NY) New York, NY St. John the Baptist; White Plains, NY Province of St. Mary; Definitors:.
Gasparin, Giampietro *c.s.j.* '79 (LA)[D] Lancaster, CA Paraclete High School; Lancaster, CA Blessed Junipero Serra.
Gasparini, Louis *m.c.c.j.* '66 (FgM) Cincinnati, OH U.S. Headquarters, Comboni Mission Center; Cincinnati, OH; Cincinnati, OH Comboni Missionaries of the Heart of Jesus, Inc. (Verona Fathers).
Gasparini, Louis *m.c.c.j.* '66 (CIN)[N] Cincinnati, OH Comboni Missionaries (Verona Fathers)–Comboni Mission Center.
Gaspeny, Peter J. '83 (SAG) Midland, MI Blessed Sacrament; Diocesan Presbyteral Council; Territorial Vicars.
Gass, Michael W. '77 (DEN) On Duty Outside the Archdiocese.
Gass, Rev. Msgr. Robert J. '53 (OM) Retired.
Gastalver, Alfredo '76 (SJN)[G] Guaynabo, PR Opus Dei; Guaynabo.
Gaston, Rev. Msgr. James T. '70 (GBG) Lower Burrell, PA St. Margaret Mary; Deaneries; Bishop's Priests Council; College of Deans.
Gately, R. Troy '89 (GAL) Houston, TX St. John Vianney.
Gately, Robert E. '52 (COL) Retired.
Gathenya, John '86 (ROC) Weedsport, NY Our Lady of the Snow.
Gatlin, Bernard '68 (LA) Piru, CA San Salvador.
Gatlin, Jeffrey D. '00 (L) Louisville, KY St. Albert the Great.
Gatman, Ronald P. *o.s.b.* '79 (SAV)[B] Savannah, GA Benedictine Military School; [E] Savannah, GA The Benedictine Priory.
Gatschet, Fred '93 (SAL)[G] Hays, KS Comeau Catholic Campus Center; [A] Hays, KS Thomas More Prep–Marian.
Gattari, Valentine A. '54 (DET) Retired.
Gatti, Daniel J. *s.j.* '72 (NY)[F] New York, NY Xavier High School; [EE] New York, NY "America;" Residence and publication office of the America Press.
Gatto, Joseph C. '83 (BUF)[A] East Aurora, NY Christ the King Seminary; Williamsville, NY St. Gregory the Great.
Gatto, Reynold J. *s.j.* '68 (SJ)[M] Los Gatos, CA Sacred Heart Jesuit Center.
Gatto, Rev. Msgr. Vincent S. '55 (WDC) Rockville, MD St. Raphael Retired.
Gatzak, John P. '75 (HRT) Special and other Archdiocesan Assignment; Office of Radio and Television; Waterbury, CT Blessed Sacrament; Office of WJMJ–FM.
Gau, David H. *s.j.* '62 (CHY) Riverton, WY St. Margaret's.
Gauchat, Eric *o.f.m.cap.* '92 (WH)[L] Wheeling, WV Capuchin Hermitage of St. Joseph.
Gauci, Albert *o.f.m.* '71 (FgM) New York, NY Franciscan Province of the Immaculate Conception.
Gauci, John *c.ss.r.* '59 (BRK) Brooklyn, NY Our Lady of Perpetual Help Basilica.
Gaudet, Joseph A. '57 (BO) Senior Priests. Retired.
Gaudio, Dean A. '03 (TR) Brick Town, NJ St. Dominic.
Gaudio, Robert '74 (ROC) North Chili, NY St. Christopher; [M] Rochester, NY Roberts Wesleyan College c/o St. Christopher Church.
Gaudreau, Bernard E. '75 (BUR) South Burlington, VT St. John Vianney; Elected Members.
Gaudreau, James E. '69 (BO) Lynn, MA St. Joseph.
Gaudreau, Walter *s.m.* '64 (BO)[W] Framingham, MA The Marist House.
Gaudreault, Lucien *s.v.d.* '88 (MIL)[P] East Troy, WI Divine Word Missionaries.
Gaughan, Joseph '94 (FTW) Fort Wayne, IN Most Precious Blood; Presbyteral Council.
Gaughan, Rev. Msgr. Patrick '68 (STU) Athens, OH St. Paul's; Deans; Priests Personnel Board.
Gaughan, Paul '52 (RIC) Virginia Beach, VA St. John the Apostle Church Retired.
Gaughan, Thomas E. *c.s.c.* '87 (FTW)[B] University of Notre Dame Du Lac; [H] Notre Dame, IN Holy Cross Community, Corby Hall, University of Notre Dame.
Gaugler, Robert *c.ss.r.* '39 (ALB)[L] Saratoga Springs, NY St. John Neumann Residence.
Gaul, Richard G. '68 (DUB) Monona, IA St. Mary; Monona, IA St. Patrick; Deans; Deanery Representatives; Monona, IA St. Bridget.
Gaul, Thomas J. '73 (R) Hope Mills, NC Good Shepherd Retired.
Gaulin, Frederick J. *c.m.* '50 (PH)[Y].
Gaumond, Paul J. '74 (NOR) Essex, CT Our Lady of Sorrows; District Moderators.
Gaunt, Thomas P. *s.j.* '81 (WDC)[N] Washington, DC Leonard Neale House; [W] Washington, DC Jesuit Conference, Inc.; Washington, DC; Washington, DC Jesuit Conference, Inc.
Gaus, Rev. Msgr. Arnold L. '59 (ALT) Ebensburg, PA Holy Name.
Gauthier, Donald F. '75 (MAN) Intervale, NH Our Lady of the Mountains.
Gauthier, Ernest '62 (KC) Retired.
Gauthier, John C. '65 (PHX) Retired.
Gauthier, Lawrence T. '55 (MAR) Catholic Relief Services; Holy Childhood Association; Propagation of the Faith Retired.
Gauthreaux, Rev. Msgr. L. Earl '56 (NO) New Orleans, LA St. Maria Goretti; Judges.
Gautreau, Henry W. '79 (BR) Catholic Charismatic Renewal Retired.
Gautreaux, Francis *c.ss.r.* '50 (FgM) Denver, CO Denver Province.
Gauvin, Leo *o.m.i.* '51 (SAT)[K] San Antonio, TX Oblate Madonna Residence.
Gauvin, Maurice O. '86 (FR) West Harwich, MA Holy Trinity.
Gavaler, Campion P. *o.s.b.* '59 (GBG)[G] Latrobe, PA Saint Vincent Archabbey.
Gavancho, Juan C. '07 (CHI) Berwyn, IL St. Odilo.
Gavin, Carney E. '65 (BO) Brighton, MA St. Columbkille.
Gavin, Emmett *o.carm.* '87 (NEW) Teaneck, NJ St. Anastasia's; Metropolitan Tribunal.
Gavin, James *o.f.m.cap.* '65 (BRK)[T] Brooklyn, NY St. Michael's Friary.
Gavin, John F. *s.j.* '02 (BO)[U] Boston The Society of Jesus of New England–Provincial Offices.
Gavin, John R. *o.s.a.* '48 (CHI)[N] Olympia Fields, IL Tolentine Monastery at Tolentine Center.
Gavin, Kenneth J. *s.j.* '75 (WDC)[W] Washington, DC Jesuit Refugee Service; [N] Washington, DC Leonard Neale House.
Gavin, Patrick *o.carm.* '97 (PHX) Phoenix, AZ St. Agnes Roman Catholic Parish.
Gavin, Robert A. *o.f.m.* '59 (NY) New York, NY St. Francis of Assisi.
Gavin, Thomas M. *s.j.* '75 (CAM) Camden, NJ The Church of the Holy Name, Camden, N.J.
Gaviola, Raul R. '95 (NEW) Dumont, NJ St. Mary's.
Gaviria, Antonio (PAT) Vocations Board.
Gaviria, Jesus A. '06 (PAT) Madison, NJ St. Vincent Martyr.
Gaviria, Omar Bedoya '94 (PCE)[A] Arecibo, PR Pontificia Universidad Catholica de Puerto Rico, Recinto de Arecibo; [B] The Pontifical Catholic University of Puerto Rico.
Gavit, James F. '54 (SAG) Retired.
Gavit, Steven M. '97 (SAG) Hemlock, MI St. Mary.
Gavitt, J. Duane '84 (SCR) Freeland, PA Our Lady of the Immaculate Conception.
Gavotto, Robert W. *o.s.a.* '64 (SD)[J] San Diego, CA Augustinian Community; [C] San Diego, CA St. Augustine High School.

Gawienowski, John '00 (SPR)[N] Amherst, MA University of Massachusetts; Florence, MA Annunciation.
Gawlik, Gilbert *s.v.d.* '54 (CHI)[N] Techny, IL Divine Word Residence.
Gawlik, Jerzy *s.v.d.* (CHI) Wheeling, IL St. Joseph the Worker.
Gawlowski, Michael R. '02 (DET) Centerline, MI St. Clement; Warren, MI St. Teresa of Avila.
Gawlowski, Paul *o.f.m.conv.* '99 (SFR) San Francisco, CA St. Paul of the Shipwreck; Arroyo Grande, CA.
Gawronski, Gerald '01 (LAN) Ann Arbor, MI St. Patrick.
Gawronski, Marc A. '91 (DET) Monroe, MI St. Mary; Archdiocesan Vicars.
Gawronski, Mark '91 (DET) Presbyteral Council.
Gawronski, Raymond T. *s.j.* '86 (BAL)[S] Towson Maryland Province of the Society of Jesus.
Gawrych, Andrew *c.s.c.* '08 (PHX) Goodyear, AZ Saint John Vianney Roman Catholic Parish.
Gawrylewski, Patrick M. *o.f.m.* '76 (GB) Seymour, WI St. Stanislaus; Pulaski, WI Assumption of the Blessed Virgin Mary; Hortonville, WI St. Denis; Hortonville, WI St. Patrick; [J] Wausaukee, WI Villa Alverna.
Gay, G. Gregory *c.m.* '80 (FgM) Philadelphia, PA Eastern Province.
Gay, G. Gregory *c.m.* '70 (PH)[Y].
Gayam, Francis '78 (NY) Bronx, NY St. Francis Xavier.
Gayarre, Eugenio '61 (ARE) Arecibo, PR Church of Christ the King.
Gaydos, Anthony M. *o.s.m.* '48 (SPC) Ironton, MO Ste. Marie Du Lac.
Gaydos, Anthony M. *o.s.m.* '48 (CHI)[N] Chicago Order of Friar Servants of Mary (Servites) United States of America Province, Inc.
Gaydosik, David L. '87 (STU) Pastoral Staff; Woodsfield, OH St. John the Baptist; Woodsfield, OH St. Sylvester; Woodsfield, OH St. John Bosco Mission; Catholic Rural Life.
Gaynor, James E. *c.pp.s.* '67 (CIN)[N] Dayton Provincial Office of the Cincinnati Province of the Society of the Precious Blood.
Gaytan, Alfredo *s.o.l.t.* '82 (CC)[G] Robstown, TX Society of Our Lady of the Most Holy Trinity.
Gaytan, Jose Alfredo *s.o.l.t.* '82 (LAR) Laredo, TX St. Frances Cabrini.
Gaytan Ramirez, Rodolfo '02 (CHI) Mt. Prospect, IL St. Raymond de Penafort.
Gayton, John J. '86 (WIL) Claymont, DE Holy Rosary.
Gayton, John J. *m.i.c.* '86 (MO) Navy Reserve Chaplains.
Gaza, J. Patrick '68 (GRY) Gary, IN SS. Monica–St. Luke; Gary, IN St. Mark.
Gazdowicz, Krzysztof '04 (SP) Spring Hill, FL St. Frances Xavier Cabrini.
Gazzingan, Mark '07 (SJ) San Jose, CA St. Christopher.
Gazzingan, Michael '03 (SJ) San Jose, CA St. Maria Goretti.
Geaney, James *o.carm.* '59 (FgM) Darien, IL Provincial Headquarters, Carmelite Provincial Office.
Geaney, James *o.carm.* '59 (TUC) Tucson, AZ Sacred Heart Roman Catholic Parish – Tucson.
Geaney, John J. *c.s.p.* '64 (MEM) Memphis, TN St. Augustine; Media Consultant; Diocesan Spokesperson.
Geany, Nash P. (NY) Stewart Field.
Gearhart, Edwin F. '73 (CIN) Springfield, OH St. Teresa of the Child Jesus; Adjutant Judicial Vicars.
Gearhart, James '77 (JC)[B] Jefferson City, MO St. Mary Health Center.
Gearhart, Lawrence M. '03 (CIN) Mechanicsburg, OH St. Michael's; Mechanicsburg, OH Immaculate Conception.
Gearheard, William J. '94 (LAF) Milton, LA St. Joseph.
Gearing, Barry T. '00 (CLV) Berea, OH St. Adalbert.
Geary, Brian A. '98 (RCK) Belvidere, IL St. James.
Geary, Edward P. '64 (BO) Senior Priests. Retired.
Geary, Patrick G. '56 (DUB) Retired.
Gebbia, Gregory V. *o.f.m.* '86 (NEW) Jersey City, NJ St. John the Baptist; [C] Newark, NJ Christ the King Preparatory School of Newark, N.J., Corp.
Gebelein, Gary M. '74 (STL) St. Louis, MO St. Francis of Assisi; Deaneries/Deans.
Gebhard, Robert L. '87 (BUF) Vicars.
Gebhard, Robert L. '87 (MO) DEPARTMENT OF VETERANS AFFAIRS HOSPITALS AND CHAPLAINS.
Gebhardt, Paul L. '91 (CIN) Cincinnati, OH St. Vivian.
Gebremichael, Abayneh (BO) Eritrean; Ethiopian.
Geders, Joseph *c.m.* '84 (CHY) Jackson, WY Our Lady of the Mountains.
Geditz, Roger '69 (SFS) Geddes, SD St. Ann Retired.
Gedvila, Izidorius '48 (GF) Retired.
Gee, Daniel N. '95 (ARL)[A] Front Royal, VA Christendom College.
Gee, John F. '53 (WOR) Auburn, MA North American Martyrs; [S] Auburn, MA Kateri Tekakwitha Development, Inc.
Geelan, Thomas E. '62 (SC) Retired.
Geer, Steve '06 (P) Stayton, OR Immaculate Conception; Area Vicars.
Geers, Frank *o.f.m.* '58 (CIN)[C] Cincinnati, OH St. Anthony Shrine, Franciscan Postulancy.
Geers, Harold *o.f.m.* '60 (CIN)[N] Cincinnati St. Francis Seraph Friary.
Geffrard, Yves '01 (PMB) Haitian Ministry; Fort Pierce, FL Notre Dame Mission.
Gegotek, Tadeusz '91 (MO) Military Chaplains; Navy Chaplains.
Gehl, Rev. Msgr. James C. '74 (LA) La Canada Flintridge, CA St. Bede the Venerable; Deanery 6.
Gehl, James E. '69 (SY) Cicero, NY Sacred Heart.
Gehlen, Elzear *s.v.d.* '44 (CHI)[N] Techny, IL Divine Word Residence.
Gehling, Kenneth B. '62 (DUB)[H] Mason City, IA Mercy Medical Center–North Iowa; Deans.
Gehring, Robert P. '66 (GRY) Retired.
Gehringer, Andrew N. '00 (ALN) Whitehall, PA Holy Trinity; Vocations Office; Elected Members.
Geib, David *o.p.* '67 (LA) Los Angeles, CA St. Dominic.
Geigel, Francis '38 (GB) Retired.
Geiger, Angelo Mary *f.i.* '91 (NOR)[G] Griswold, CT Marian Friary of Our Lady of Guadalupe; Griswold, CT.
Geiger, Bernard *o.f.m.conv.* '59 (CHI)[N] Chicago Conventual Franciscans of St. Bonaventure Province.
Geiger, Damon *o.ss.t.* '71 (BAL)[S] Individuals in Other Locations:.
Geiger, Damon *o.ss.t.* '71 (NTN) Liturgical Commission.
Geiger, Damon *o.ss.t.* '71 (GAL)[A] Houston, TX St. Mary's Seminary.
Geiger, Rev. Msgr. James A. '50 (COL) Retired.
Geiger, Rev. Msgr. James A. '50 (COL) Diocesan Judges; Logan, OH St. John Retired.
Geiger, James *c.ss.r.* '60 (RIC)[M] Hampton, VA Holy Family Retreat.
Geiger, Michael A. '02 (TOL) Shelby, OH Sacred Heart of Jesus; Crestline, OH St. Joseph.
Geinzer, Eugene M. *s.j.* '74 (FgM) Towson, MD Society of Jesus; [S] Towson Maryland Province of the Society of Jesus.
Geinzer, John A. '67 (PIT) Pittsburgh, PA St. John the Baptist.
Geinzer, Patrick *c.p.* '95 (PIT)[M] Pittsburgh, PA St. Paul of the Cross Monastery; [O] Pittsburgh, PA St. Paul of the Cross Retreat Center.
Geis, John F. '64 (IND) Floyds Knobs, IN St. Mary–of–the–Knobs.
Geiser, Allen A. '90 (GB) Absent on Leave, Sick or Disabled.
Geisinger, Robert J. *s.j.* '91 (CHI)[N] Chicago Chicago Province of the Society of Jesus–Provincial Office.
Geisser, Raymond E. '60 (PH)[Y] Villanova, PA St. Thomas Monastery.
Geissler, Robert '47 (NY) Montgomery, NY Holy Name of Mary Retired.
Geiszel, John I. *s.j.* '57 (SJ)[M] Los Gatos, CA Sacred Heart Jesuit Center.
Geitner, John E. *m.m.* '53 (FgM) Maryknoll, NY MARYKNOLL.
Gelati, Dario '53 (PIT) Retired.
Gelencser, Paul L. *o.praem.* '41 (ORG)[I] Silverado, CA Norbertine Fathers of Orange Inc. Retired.
Geleney, Joseph F. '01 (AUS) Washington, TX Blessed Virgin Mary; Somerville, TX St. Ann.
Gelfant, Michael L. '05 (BRK) Brooklyn, NY St. Anselm.
Gelfenbien, Gary Paul '71 (ALB) Chatham, NY St. James.
Gelfer, Peter (LA) Hospital Chaplains.
Gelido, Manuel T. '79 (WH) Nitro, WV Christ the King; Nitro, WV Holy Trinity; Wheeling, WV St. Patrick.
Gelinas, Rene *m.s.* '60 (HRT)[L] Hartford, CT Missionaries of LaSalette.
Gelinas, Robert James '05 (NEW) Bayonne, NJ St. Henry's.
Gelineau, Rev. Msgr. Edward J. '42 (BUR) Retired.
Gelineau, Raymond H. '69 (WOR) On Duty Outside the Diocese.
Gellel, Lawrence *s.j.* '54 (BRK) Astoria, NY St. Joseph.
Geller, Charles H. '73 (BEL) Special Assignment.
Gelpi, Donald L. *s.j.* '64 (OAK)[A] Berkeley, CA Jesuit School of Theology at Santa Clara University; [M] Berkeley, CA Jesuit Fathers and Brothers; [A] Berkeley, CA Jesuit School of Theology at Santa Clara University.
Gelsomino, Rev. Msgr. Peter (NY) Port Chester, NY Sacred Heart of Jesus.
Gelson, James N. *s.j.* '60 (BAL)[S] Towson Maryland Province of the Society of Jesus.
Gelthaus, Harry J. '85 (L) Louisville, KY SS. Simon and Jude; Louisville, KY Most Blessed Sacrament.
Gelthaus, Lawrence J. '88 (L) Edmonton, KY Christ the Healer.
Gembala, Joseph J. '87 (DET) Sterling Heights, MI St. Malachy.
Gemme, Stephen M. '02 (WOR) Northboro, MA St. Bernadette.
Gemperline, Joachim *c.p.* '53 (L)[L] Louisville, KY Sacred Heart Retreat.
Gemza, Richard J. '95 (BGP) Greenwich, CT St. Mary.
Genabia, Joel S. '03 (SAC) Chico, CA Our Divine Savior.
Gendreau, Claude R. '93 (PRT) Special or Other Diocesan Assignment.
Gendreau, Michael P. '90 (PRT) Special or Other Diocesan Assignment.
Gendreau, Richard R. '69 (FR) Swansea, MA St. Louis de France.
Gendron, Michael E. '95 (MAN) Advocates; Charlestown, NH All Saints Parish.
Genello, Patrick J. '83 (SCR) Hazleton, PA Holy Rosary.
Genereux, Wayne C. *o.de.m.* '97 (SP)[N] St. Petersburg, FL St. Peter Nolasco Residence; Saint Petersburg, FL Cathedral of St. Jude the Apostle.
Generose, Rev. Msgr. Anthony J. '99 (SCR) Wilkes–Barre, PA St. Aloysius; Judicial Vicar; Vicar for Consecrated Life; Retirement Fund for Religious; Consecrated Life Office.
Genest, Gilles M. *m.s.* '62 (FR)[G] Attleboro, MA La Salette Shrine Retired.
Geng, Dennis *o.c.d.* '89 (MIL)[P] Milwaukee Provincial Offices – Discalced Carmelites.
Gengaro, Nicholas S. '81 (NEW)[B] School of Diplomacy and Intl. Rels.
Genito, Joseph A. *o.s.a.* '75 (PH) Philadelphia, PA St. Rita of Cascia; [CC] Philadelphia, PA National Shrine of Saint Rita of Cascia.
Gennardo, Vincent *c.s.* '64 (CHI) Chicago, IL Santa Maria Addolorata.
Genovard, Juan J. *m.ss.cc.* '56 (SJN) Movimiento "Por Un Mundo Mejor".
Genovese, Anthony M. *o.s.a.* '73 (PH) Counselors:; [Y] Villanova, PA St. Thomas Monastery.
Genovese, Seamus D. '75 (OAK) Oakland, CA Our Lady of Lourdes.
Genovesi, Vincent J. *s.j.* '69 (PH)[C] Jesuit Fathers; [Y] Loyola Center and Manresa Hall.
Genska, Depaul *o.f.m.* (PAT)[N] Ringwood, NJ Holy Name Friary, Inc.
Gensler, Harry J. *s.j.* '74 (CLV)[B] University Heights, OH John Carroll Jesuit Community.
Gentile, Carl J. '60 (PIT) Pittsburgh, PA St. John Fisher.
Gentile, Emile A. *t.o.r.* '64 (ORL)[F] New Smyrna Beach, FL Villa Madonna Retired.
Gentile, Robert A. '03 (SPR) Holyoke, MA Blessed Sacrament; Deans; Presbyteral Council; Diocesan Consultors.
Gentile, Thomas E. '73 (L) Ex Officio; Louisville, KY Mary Queen of Peace Parish.
Gentili, Rev. Msgr. Joseph P. '87 (PH) Buckingham, PA Our Lady of Guadalupe.
Gentleman, Gerard J. '97 (RVC) Hicksville, NY Holy Family.
Gentleman, Gerard '97 (RVC) Senate of Priests (Presbyteral Council/College of Consultors).
Gentleman, John W. '87 (BO) Essex, MA St. John the Baptist; Manchester by the Sea, MA Sacred Heart.
Genua, Ronald L. '65 (HRT)[A] In Res. at the Archbishop Daniel A. Cronin Retirement Residence at St. Thomas Seminary Retired.
Genuardi, Gasper A. '68 (PH) Conshohocken, PA SS. Cosmas and Damian.
Genuario, Rev. Msgr. William A. '56 (BGP) Judges; [O] Stamford, CT The Catherine Dennis Keefe Queen of the Clergy Retired Priests' Residence Retired.
Geo, Patrick '93 (FRS) Rosamond, CA St. Mary of the Desert.
Geoghegan, James *o.c.d,* '60 (SJ)[M] San Jose, CA Carmelite Monastery, Novitiate.
Geoghegan, John F. '45 (STL) Retired.
George, Abraham K. '95 (NY) Staten Island, NY St. Ann.
George, Rev. Msgr. Alexander C. '65 (LA) Retired.
George, Augustin '93 (MAR) Hancock, MI Resurrection.
George, Benny *c.m.i.* '88 (LA) Burbank, CA St. Francis Xavier.
George, Rev. Msgr. David M. '76 (SAM) On Sabbatical.
George, Francis M. '87 (LAN) Howell, MI St. John The Baptist.
George, Gary *c.ss.r.* '92 (OLL) Youngstown, OH St. Maron Maronite Catholic Church; Office of Youth Ministries; Presbyteral Council; College of Consultors.
George, Gary (SAM) Youth Ministry Office.
George, George C. '86 (AUS) Chaplains of the Military; DEPARTMENT OF VETERANS AFFAIRS HOSPITALS AND CHAPLAINS.
George, J. Clark '56 (ALT) Retired.
George, Jacob C. '97 (WDC) Landover Hills, MD Syro–Malankara Mission.
George, James '70 (HRT) Watertown, CT St. John the Evangelist.
George, Jose '77 (TYL) Crockett, TX Crockett State School.
George, Jose '77 (SP) Tampa, FL Incarnation.
George, Rev. Msgr. Joseph '62 (LA) Retired.
George, Lloyd *s.j.* '73 (BAL)[D] Baltimore, MD Loyola Blakefield.
George, Madhu '98 (TUC) Tucson, AZ Our Mother of Sorrows Roman Catholic Parish – Tucson.

George, Mark *s.j.* '98 (DET)[E] Detroit, MI University of Detroit Jesuit High School and Academy; Detroit, MI SS. Peter and Paul Jesuit.
George, Mathew C. '97 (DET) Canton, MI St. Thomas a Becket.
George, Patrick *t.o.r.* '55 (ALT)[G] Loretto, PA St. Francis Friary at Mount Assisi.
George, Rejimon *c.m.i.* '03 (BEA) Port Arthur, TX St. Therese the Little Flower of Jesus.
George, Richard E. '95 (PMB) Fort Pierce, FL Notre Dame Mission; Fort Pierce, FL St. Anastasia; Elected Members.
George, Robert J. '95 (ALN)[C] Easton, PA Notre Dame High School; Bethlehem, PA Sacred Heart of Jesus.
George, Robert J. '76 (PIT)[N] Pittsburgh, PA Sisters of Mercy of the Americas – New York, Pennsylvania, Pacific West Community.
George, Sebastian K. *c.m.i.* '80 (STA) Branford, FL San Juan Mission; High Springs, FL St. Madeleine Sophie Parish.
George, Sojan *h.g.n.* '00 (FWT) Bridgeport, TX St. John the Baptizer; Decatur, TX Assumption of the Blessed Virgin Mary; Bridgeport, TX St. Mary.
George, William L. '73 (WDC)[E] North Bethesda, MD Georgetown Preparatory School.
George–Obilonu, Kingsley (GLP) Quemado, NM Sacred Heart; Springerville, AZ St. Peter.
Georgekutty, Ponnachan '83 (BRK) Brooklyn, NY St. Bernadette.
Georgekutty, Ponnachan '83 (NY) Patterson, NY Sacred Heart.
Georgia, John J. '75 (HRT) Consultors – Canon 1742; Bristol, CT St. Gregory the Great; Waterbury Vicariate; Bristol Deanery.
Georgis, Pieter '00 (SPA) Perris, CA St. Hormizdah Mission.
Gephart, John B. '46 (L)[L] Louisville, KY Bishop David Apartments Retired.
Gepiga, Rufino '99 (SP) Tampa, FL Christ the King.
Gera, Francis '64 (PSC) Retired.
Geraci, Anthony J. '75 (CIN) South Charleston, OH St. Charles Borromeo; Yellow Springs, OH St. Paul.
Geraghty, Rev. Msgr. Martin T. '64 (BRK) Bayside, NY St. Robert Bellarmine.
Gerald, John J. '82 (SC) Carroll, IA Holy Spirit; St. Anthony Regional Hospital; [C] Carroll, IA St. Anthony Regional Hospital.
Gerald, Selvam '93 (TR) Lincroft, NJ St. Leo the Great.
Gerathy, Rev. Msgr. Kenneth A. '54 (NY)[EE] Bronx, NY Retired.
Gerber, Brian C. '08 (MAR) Garden, MI St. Mary Magdalene; Garden, MI St. John the Baptist; Garden, MI St. Andrew.
Gerber, Martin '76 (ORL) Orlando, FL Basilica of the National Shrine of Mary Queen of the Universe.
Gerber, Nicholas J. '08 (AMA) Amarillo, TX St. Mary's.
Gerdes, Harry J. '62 (CIN) Retired.
Gerend, Lawrence '76 (GB) Retired.
Gerg, Joseph U. *o.s.b.* '65 (GBG)[G] Latrobe, PA Saint Vincent Archabbey.
Gergel, Stephen J. '62 (ALT) Retired.
Gergel, Stephen J. '62 (SAV) Retired.
Geris, Thierry '09 (SJ) Palo Alto, CA St. Thomas Aquinas.
Gerken, Theodore J. '57 (ALB) Columbia County Jail Retired.
Gerl, Robert '79 (LAN) On Duty Outside the Diocese.
Gerlach, Dominic *c.pp.s.* '50 (CIN)[N] Carthagena, OH St. Charles Retired.
Gerlach, John *o.p.* '63 (MAD)[G] Sinsinawa, WI Dominican Motherhouse.
Gerlach, Matthew J. '96 (TLS)[I] Tulsa, OK St. Philip Neri Newman Center at The University of Tulsa; Campus Ministry; Propagation of the Faith; Vocations; Diocesan Senators; Seminary Board.
Gerlach, Michael J. '82 (PH) Upper Darby, PA St. Laurence.
Gerlach, William Peter '04 (FAR) Grand Forks, ND St. Michael's Church of Grand Forks.
Gerlich, Robert S. *s.j.* '73 (NO)[C] New Orleans, LA Loyola University New Orleans.
Gerlock, Stanley J. '60 (SY) Broome County Jail; [Q] Binghamton, NY McDevitt Residence for Retired Priests Retired.
Germain, Levelt '02 (NY) Bronx, NY Our Lady of Grace.
Germaine, Kenneth *s.d.b.* '67 (BIR) Birmingham, AL Holy Rosary.
German, Michael J. '68 (NEW) River Edge, NJ St. Peter the Apostle.
Germann, Lauren '78 (SCL) Sartell, MN St. Francis Xavier; Diocesan Consultors; Diocesan Corporate Board; Presbyteral Council; Diocesan Education Council.
Gerosa, Julian *c.r.s.* '78 (GAL) Houston, TX Assumption.
Gerres, Daniel W. '66 (WIL) Wilmington, DE St. Thomas; Howard R. Young Correctional Institution; Deans.
Gerrety, James P. '57 (COV) Retired.
Gerrietts, Darrel (DUB) Review Board for Sexual Abuse of Minors by Clergy and Other Church Personnel.
Gerritts, John R. '91 (SUP) Rhinelander, WI St. John; Presbyteral Council & Diocesan Consultors; Rhinelander, WI Nativity of Our Lord.
Gerrity, Raymond J. '45 (CHI) Retired.
Gersbach, Karl A. *o.s.a.* '61 (PH)[Y] Villanova, PA St. Thomas Monastery.
Gerth, Kenneth *m.c.c.j.* '65 (CIN)[N] Cincinnati, OH Comboni Missionaries (Verona Fathers)–Comboni Mission Center.
Gerth, Kenneth *m.c.c.j.* '64 (SP)[J] Tampa, FL St. Joseph's Hospital, Inc.
Gerum, Jerome G. '50 (LC) Retired.
Gerut, William F. *s.j.* '67 (OM)[K] Omaha, NE Jesuit Community at Creighton University.
Gerut, William F. *s.j.* '67 (DM)[J] Griswold, IA Creighton University Retreat Center.
Gervacio, Adrian R. '67 (LA) Naval Air Station; Naval Construction Battalion Center.
Gervacio, Adrian R. '67 (HON) Honolulu, HI Our Lady of the Mount; Clergy Personnel Board.
Gervasio, Rev. Msgr. Thomas N. '82 (TR) Hamilton, NJ Our Lady of Sorrows–St. Anthony Parish.
Gese, David '78 (SEA) Elma, WA St. Joseph.
Gessner, Glenn *o.f.m.cap.* '60 (FgM) Detroit, MI Province of St. Joseph.
Gessner, Glenn *o.f.m.cap.* '60 (DET)[K] Detroit St. Bonaventure Friary.
Gesty, John *o.f.m.cap.* '66 (PIT)[M] Allison Park, PA St. Conrad Friary.
Gesy, Lawrence J. '75 (BAL) Retired.
Getchel, Richard '76 (GB) Green Bay, WI St. Agnes; Adjutant Judicial Vicars; Judges; Vicariate.
Getigan, Bernardito '85 (SAN) Odessa, TX Holy Redeemer.
Getsinger, Ronald A. '68 (WH) Retired.
Getsurin, Peter Tenchai *c.ss.r.* '96 (STL)[B] St. Louis, MO St. John Neumann House.
Gettinger, Rev. Msgr. Robert J. '64 (STL) St. Louis, MO St. Augustine.
Getz, Joseph *o.s.a.* '51 (ALB) Troy, NY St. Augustine.
Getz, Rev. Msgr. Robert L. '61 (LSC) Episcopal Vicar for Clergy and Personnel; Diocesan Consultors; Clergy Personnel Board; Priests Retirement Fund Committee.
Getz, Rev. Msgr. Robert '61 (LSC) Retired.
Geyer, Kenneth A. *o.s.b.* '53 (CHL)[J] Belmont, NC Belmont Abbey.
Geyman, Donald R. '96 (GAY) Vocations and Pastoral Care of Seminarians, Delegate for.
Ghaby, Jean '92 (NTN) Cliffside Park, NJ St. Demetrius; West Paterson, NJ St. Ann.
Ghanoum, Rt. Rev. Exarch Gabriel *b.s.o.* '93 (NTN) Delray Beach, FL St. Nicholas; Continuing Education of Clergy Office; Order of St. Nicholas; Victim Assistance Coordinator; College of Eparchial Consultors.
Gherardi, Marc *o.s.f.s.* '08 (ALN)[B] Center Valley, PA DeSales University; [K] Center Valley, PA Oblates of St. Francis de Sales.
Ghezzi, Giancarlo *p.i.m.e.* '84 (PAT)[N] Wayne, NJ P.I.M.E. Missionaries Residence.
Ghezzi, Richard G. '86 (SCR)[L] Wilkes–Barre, PA Little Flower Manor of the Diocese of Scranton; [L] Wilkes–Barre, PA St. Therese Residence.
Ghiloni, Mark V. '83 (COL) Westerville, OH St. Paul the Apostle.
Ghio, John J. '80 (STL) St. Louis, MO Assumption.
Ghiorso, David A. '81 (SFR) San Carlos, CA St. Charles.
Ghisalberti, Giacomo G. '70 (R) Retired.
Ghozairan, Poulos '75 (SPA) Scottsdale, AZ Mar Auraha Chaldean Catholic Parish.
Ghyselinck, Mark R. *c.s.c.* '88 (FTW)[H] Notre Dame Congregation of Holy Cross, Indiana Province, Provincial House.
Ghyselinck, Mark *c.s.c.* '88 (FgM) New Rochelle, NY Eastern Brothers Province.
Giachino, Valeriano *s.s.p.* '57 (LA)[P] Los Angeles, CA The Society of St. Paul; Los Angeles, CA.
Giacinti, Gaston *i.v.e.* '05 (BRK) Brooklyn, NY St. Michael – Saint Malachy.
Giacomini, Salvatore H. *s.d.b.* '51 (SFR) San Francisco, CA SS. Peter and Paul.
Gialogo, Rev. Msgr. Agustin '73 (STO) Stockton, CA St. Michael Church of Stockton (Pastor of).
Giamello, Anthony '05 (WIL) Wilmington, DE St. Elizabeth; Air National Guard Chaplains.
Giammona, Rev. Msgr. John J. '59 (GR) Retired.
Giampietro, Anthony E. *c.s.b.* '93 (GAL)[O] Houston, TX Residence of the Basilian Fathers of the University of St. Thomas.
Giandurco, Rev. Msgr. Joseph R. '87 (NY) Suffern, NY Sacred Heart; Canon 1742 Panel of Pastors; [II] Cause:.
Gianelli, Gene E. '70 (HRT) Consultors – Canon 1742; Woodbridge, CT Church of the Assumption; New Haven Vicariate; West Shore Line Deanery.
Gianfreda, Fausto *s.j.* '08 (OAK)[M] Berkeley, CA Jesuit Fathers and Brothers.
Giangiacomo, Tosello *c.s.sp.* '48 (ARE) Orocovis, PR Our Lady of Fatima.
Giannamore, Rev. Msgr. Anthony J. '56 (STU) Retired.
Giannamore, Pete A. '90 (WH) Follansbee, WV St. Anthony.
Gianni, Vincent J. '70 (BO) Wakefield, MA St. Florence; Emergency Response Group.
Giannini, Stephen W. '93 (IND) Indianapolis, IN St. John the Evangelist.
Giannini, Stephen '93 (IND) Assistant Chancellor; Priests' Personnel Board; Vicariate for Clergy and Parish Life Coordinators: Formation and Personnel; Personnel: Priests and Parish Life Coordinators; Archdiocesan Judges; Council of Priests; Board of Consultors.
Giannitelli, Michael C. '91 (NOR) Colchester, CT St. Andrew; Seminarian Advisory Board.
Giannone, Ronald *o.f.m.cap.* '90 (WIL) Wilmington, DE Sacred Heart; [G] Wilmington, DE Ministry of Caring, Inc.; [J] Wilmington, DE St. Felix Friary; [K] Wilmington, DE Monastery of St. Veronica Giuliani; Definitors:.
Giannone, Ronald *o.f.m.cap.* '90 (NEW)[M] Union City, NJ Capuchin Friars – Province of the Sacred Stigmata of St. Francis; [M] Union City, NJ Capuchin Friars – Province of the Sacred Stigmata of St. Francis.
Gianola, William '62 (CHY) Retired.
Giaquinto, Albert C. '48 (NOR) Retired.
Giaquinto, Albert C. *s.s.* '48 (BAL)[O] Baltimore, MD St. Charles Villa; [S] Baltimore Society of St. Sulpice, Province of the United States Retired.
Giardina, Robert J. '76 (PRO) Providence, RI St. Charles Borromeo; Deans.
Giardino, Andrew *o.f.m.* '62 (HRT) Hartford, CT St. Patrick–St. Anthony.
Giardino, Louis '75 (BIR) Judges; Huntsville, AL Good Shepherd.
Gibas, Robert G. '62 (Y) Judges Retired.
Gibbeaut, Wayne *o.f.m.* '83 (SFE) Pena Blanca, NM Nuestra Senora De Guadalupe; [H] Albuquerque, NM The Province of Our Lady of Guadalupe.
Gibbons, Donald Patrick '91 (SFD) Grafton, IL St. Patrick; Jerseyville, IL St. Francis Xavier.
Gibbons, Edward '97 (VEN) Sarasota, FL Incarnation.
Gibbons, Ian R. *s.j.* '06 (KC)[D] Kansas City, MO Rockhurst High School; [J] Kansas City, MO Rockhurst Jesuit Community.
Gibbons, James *o.m.i.* '69 (FgM) Washington, DC AMERICAN OBLATE MISSIONS.
Gibbons, John J. '58 (NEW) Bayonne, NJ Saint Michael and Saint Joseph Retired.
Gibbons, John M. '89 (ALN) Reading, PA St. Margaret.
Gibbons, John M. '56 (DEN) Retired.
Gibbons, Rev. Msgr. John '60 (TR) Retired.
Gibbons, John *o.f.m.* '01 (OAK)[M] Oakland Franciscan Friars (Province of St. Barbara); Oakland, CA St. Barbara Province.
Gibbons, Patrick '91 (SFD) Priests' Personnel Board.
Gibbons, Rev. Msgr. Robert C. '81 (SP) St. Petersburg, FL St. Paul; Judges; College of Consultors; [T] Saint Petersburg, FL Partners with Haiti, Inc.; Elected Pastors.
Gibbons, Thomas F. *m.m.* '48 (NY)[EE] Retired.
Gibbs, Donald J. *o.s.b.* '05 (MIL) Kenosha, WI Our Lady of Mount Carmel; [P] Benet Lake, WI St. Benedict's Abbey.
Gibbs, Phillip G. '94 (DUB) Decorah, IA St. Benedict.
Gibino, Joseph R. '81 (BRK) Whitestone, NY Holy Trinity; Liturgical Commission.
Giblin, William M. '59 (NEW)[M] Caldwell, NJ The Rev. Msgr. James F. Kelley Residence for Retired Priests Retired.
Gibney, Robert G. '54 (NEW)[M] Caldwell, NJ The Rev. Msgr. James F. Kelley Residence for Retired Priests Retired.
Gibowski, Boguslaw T. '69 (PRO) Retired.
Gibson, Beryl '96 (SAL) Retired.
Gibson, Brendan *s.j.c.* '05 (CHI) Chicago, IL St. John Cantius; [P] Chicago, IL Canons Regular of Saint John Cantius.
Gibson, Bruno *o.p.* '60 (OAK) Berkeley, CA St. Mary Magdalen.
Gibson, Christopher *c.p.* '75 (CHI)[N] Chicago, IL Passionist Community–Immaculate Conception Monastery.
Gibson, Jack *s.d.b.* '70 (LA) Bellflower, CA St. Dominic Savio.
Gibson, James M. *c.r.* '79 (SB)[I] Fontana, CA Congregation of the Resurrection, CR; Fontana, CA Blessed John XXIII Catholic Community, Inc.
Gibson, James *c.r.* '79 (CHI)[N].
Gibson, Rev. Msgr. Lawrence J. '55 (LA) Retired.
Gibson, Robert J. '58 (SCR) Unassigned or Leave of Absence.
Gibson, Stephen C. *c.s.c.* '70 (FTW)[H] Notre Dame Congregation of Holy Cross, Indiana Province, Provincial House.
Gibson, Stephen G. '81 (GRY) East Chicago, IN St. Mary.
Gick, Francois *s.j.* '80 (BO)[U] Boston The Society of Jesus of New England–Provincial Offices.

Gideon, Peter M. '76 (COL) Lancaster, OH St. Mark.
Gideon, Stephen G. '97 (NSH) Gallatin, TN St. John Vianney.
Gieb, Harry F. '92 (WH)[A] Wheeling, WV Wheeling Jesuit University.
Giedgaudas, Francis *o.f.m.* '47 (PRT)[I] Kennebunkport, ME St. Anthony's Friary; Kennebunkport, ME.
Giel, John C. '78 (ORL) Leesburg, FL St. Paul's; Ex Officio Members.
Giel, John '78 (ORL) Deans; Judges.
Gielow, Richard *c.m.* '70 (KC)[J] Independence, MO Vincentian Parish Mission Center; Saint Louis, MO Ladies of Charity of the United States of America (LCUSA).
Gier, Rev. Msgr. Gregory A. '67 (TLS) Tulsa, OK Holy Family Cathedral.
Giermek, Joachin *o.f.m.conv.* '69 (BAL)[S] Ellicott City, MD Order of Friars Minor Conventual.
Giese, Samuel C. '85 (WDC) Landover Hills, MD St. Mary's Catholic Church; Army National Guard Chaplains.
Giesen, Cal '47 (FWT)[H] Crowley, TX St. Maximilian Kolbe Friary.
Giesige, Randy P. '98 (TOL) New Riegel, OH All Saints.
Giesing, Rev. Msgr. Anthony '55 (SD) Retired.
Giesler, Michael E. '79 (STL)[P] Kirkwood, MO Prelature of the Holy Cross and Opus Dei; Kirkwood.
Gietl, Joseph A. '73 (GAL) Spring, TX St. Edward; Northern Vicariate; College of Consultors; Appointees.
Gietzen, Albin J. '56 (GAY) Retired.
Gigante, Louis R. '59 (NY) Retired.
Gigantiello, Rev. Msgr. Jamie J. '95 (BRK) Brooklyn, NY Mary Queen of Heaven; Secretariat for Development.
Giggi, Rev. Msgr. J. Robert '53 (BO) Natick, MA St. Linus.
Giglio, Michael E. '94 (ORL) Port Orange, FL Epiphany.
Gigliotti, James *t.o.r.* '80 (FWT) Arlington, TX St. Maria Goretti.
Gigliotti, Vincent J. '76 (GBG) Brownsville, PA St. Peter; Smock, PA St. Cecilia.
Gignac, Francis T. *s.j.* '67 (WDC)[C] Catholic University of America, The; [N] Washington, DC The Jesuit Community at Georgetown University.
Gikonyo, David Kamau *i.m.c.* '97 (MET)[I] Somerset, NJ Consolata Society for Foreign Missions.
Gil, Fernando '88 (ORL) Judicial Vicar; Director of Tribunal; 46–55; Judges.
Gil–Sang, Andrew Lee (CIN)[U] Cincinnati, OH St. Andrew Kim Korean Catholic Community.
Gilb, Rev. Msgr. Eugene A. '57 (LA) Rancho Palos Verdes, CA St. John Fisher Retired.
Gilbaugh, Eric C. '05 (HEL) Three Forks, MT Holy Family.
Gilbert, Dennis M. '71 (MRY) On Leave.
Gilbert, Dennis (SJ) Sunnyvale, CA Church of The Resurrection.
Gilbert, Rev. Msgr. Donald J. '68 (MAN) Diocesan Review Board; Judicial Vicar; Diocesan Judges.
Gilbert, John Mary '03 (LC)[M] Chippewa Falls, WI Institute of St. Joseph; Appointed Members.
Gilbert, Maurice L. '66 (WOR) Millville, MA St. Augustine.
Gilbert, Paul T. '01 (MAN)[L] Concord, NH Monastery of Discalced Carmelites; Concord Hospital.
Gilbert, Philip F. *c.pp.s.* '60 (LFT)[A] Rensselaer, IN Saint Joseph's College.
Gilbert, Robert J. '98 (CHI) Chicago, IL St. Joachim.
Gilbert, Thomas R. '05 (BRK) South Richmond Hill, NY St. Benedict Joseph Labre.
Gilbertson, Lee C. '63 (SPR) Retired.
Gilbo, Robert *c.s.c.* '67 (FgM) New Rochelle, NY Eastern Brothers Province.
Gilbo, Roberto M. *c.s.c.* '67 (FTW)[H] Notre Dame Congregation of Holy Cross, Indiana Province, Provincial House.
Gilborges, Anthony *o.s.f.s.* '89 (VEN) Fort Myers, FL Our Lady of Light.
Gilchrist, Rev. Msgr. John J. '57 (NEW) Harrison, NJ Holy Cross; Archdiocesan Commission for Interreligious Affairs Retired.
Gilday, Robert J. '75 (IND) Council of Priests; Adjunct Vicars Judicial; Indianapolis, IN St. Therese of the Infant Jesus (Little Flower).
Gilde, Lothar M. '06 (LIN) Wahoo, NE St. Wenceslaus; Advocates.
Gildea, Arthur *c.ss.r.* '67 (PH) Philadelphia, PA St. Peter the Apostle.
Gildea, Charles *c.ss.r.* '53 (ALB)[L] Saratoga Springs, NY St. John Neumann Residence.
Gildea, John J. '66 (BRK) Brooklyn, NY Our Lady of Mercy; Brooklyn, NY Holy Family.
Gildner, Leo H. '53 (PEO) Retired.
Gile, Honesto '87 (SFR) Redwood City, CA St. Pius.
Gile, Joseph M. '88 (WCH)[A] Wichita, KS Newman University; Ongoing Formation of the Clergy Committee; Wichita, KS Blessed Sacrament.
Gilg, Rev. Msgr. James E. '66 (OM) Omaha, NE St. Mary Magdalene; Catholic Schools Office; Age Groups.
Gilgun, Bernard E. '54 (WOR) Shrewsbury, MA St. Anne Retired.
Giljum, Stephen P. '03 (STL) Dardenne Prairie, MO Immaculate Conception.
Gill, David H. *s.j.* '67 (BO)[U] Boston The Society of Jesus of New England–Provincial Offices.
Gill, David H. *s.j.* '67 (OAK)[A] Berkeley, CA Jesuit School of Theology at Santa Clara University; [M] Berkeley, CA Jesuit Fathers and Brothers; Oakland, CA St. Patrick.
Gill, G. Dennis '83 (PH) Philadelphia, PA Cathedral Basilica of SS. Peter and Paul; Office for Worship; On Special or Other Archdiocesan Assignment.
Gill, Ilyas *o.f.m.* '93 (BRK)[S] Pakistani Apostolate; Brooklyn, NY Mary Queen of Heaven.
Gill, Joseph C. *s.j.* '59 (MIL)[P] Wauwatosa, WI Jesuit Community at St. Camillus.
Gill, Michael J. '66 (NOR) Norwichtown, CT Sacred Heart.
Gill, Rev. Msgr. Richard '56 (BUF) Retired.
Gill, Richard *l.c.* '91 (NY)[II] Thornwood, NY Alpha Omega Family Center, Inc.
Gill, Rev. Msgr. William J. '55 (RVC) Southold, NY Retired.
Gilleece, Rev. Msgr. Thomas E. '67 (NY) Archdiocesan Consultors; Chappaqua, NY St. John and St. Mary.
Gillelan, Robert M. '89 (HBG) York, PA Immaculate Conception of the Blessed Virgin Mary; Deans.
Gillen, Gabriel *o.p.* (NY) New York, NY St. Catherine of Siena.
Gillen, George D. '71 (NEW) Elizabeth, NJ St. Genevieve's; Members; Elected Members.
Gillen, Rev. Msgr. James G. '52 (WDC) Retired.
Gillen, Rev. Msgr. John J. '45 (NY) Retired.
Gillen, Kevin *o.p.* '00 (NY) Manhattan, NY Memorial Sloan Kettering Cancer Center; Manhattan, NY Hospital for Special Surgery; Manhattan, NY New York Presbyterian Hospital.
Gillen, Niles *o.carm.* '56 (VEN) Englewood, FL St. Raphael.
Gillen, Peter D. '78 (BRK) Woodside, NY Corpus Christi.
Gillen, Thomas M. '52 (NO) Retired.
Giller, Roderic *o.s.b.* '62 (KCK)[I] Atchison, KS St. Benedict's Abbey; Bendena, KS St. Benedict; Troy, KS St. Charles; Wathena, KS St. Joseph's.
Gilles, Brian *c.ss.r.* '03 (STP) Brooklyn Center, MN St. Alphonsus.
Gilles, Rev. Msgr. Richard W. '94 (LC) Special Assignment; [A] La Crosse, WI Holy Cross Seminary House of Formation; [J] La Crosse, WI Catholic Charities of the Diocese of La Crosse, Inc.; Diocesan Administrator and Moderator of the Curia; Ecclesiastical Notaries; Promoter of Justice; Diocesan Judges; Building Commission; Pastoral Council; Ex Officio; Consultors; Ex Officio; International Priests.
Gilles, Thomas C. '67 (CLV) Chardon, OH St. Mary.
Gillespie, Barnabas *o.s.b.* '80 (IND) Tell City, IN St. Michael; Tell City, IN St. Pius; [K] St. Meinrad St. Meinrad Archabbey; Tell City, IN St. Paul.
Gillespie, C. Kevin *s.j.* '86 (BAL)[B] Timonium, MD Loyola Graduate Center–Timonium Campus.
Gillespie, Edward F. '57 (RCK) Retired.
Gillespie, Francis J. '72 (CHR) Hardeeville, SC St. Anthony.
Gillespie, Francis T. '59 (ALN)[J] Bethlehem, PA Holy Family Villa Retired.
Gillespie, Hugh '06 (BRK) Ozone Park, NY St. Mary Gate of Heaven.
Gillespie, Jerome F. '82 (BO) Awaiting Assignment.
Gillespie, John D. '72 (STA) Gainesville, FL St. Augustine.
Gillespie, John '95 (R) Lumberton, NC St. Francis De Sales.
Gillespie, Joseph P. *o.p.* '70 (STP) Minneapolis, MN St. Albert the Great.
Gillespie, Joseph '50 (PHX) Retired.
Gillespie, Kevin *s.j.* (BAL)[S] Baltimore, MD Ferdinand Wheeler Jesuit Community.
Gillespie, Martin Joseph '00 (BLX) Columbia, MS Most Holy Trinity; Industrial and Training School.
Gillespie, Robert B. '43 (GR) Retired.
Gillespie, Thomas E. '72 (MAD) Marshall, WI St. Mary's of the Nativity; Waterloo, WI St. Joseph.
Gillespie, Thomas J. *o.s.f.s.* '60 (VEN) Naples, FL St. Ann.
Gillespie, Thomas M. '68 (BO) North Reading, MA St. Theresa of Lisieux.
Gillespie, Thomas '61 (SB) Retired.
Gillespie, Thomas *o.s.b.* '64 (SCL)[I] Collegeville, MN St. John's Abbey, of the Order of St. Benedict.
Gillespie, Victor *o.s.b.* '56 (LR)[A] Subiaco, AR Subiaco Abbey.
Gillette, James R. *c.p.* '71 (NY)[EE] Bronx, NY Passionist Residence.
Gillette, Peter '91 (SEA) Camas, WA St. Thomas Aquinas.
Gilley, Charles F. *i.v.dei.* '96 (BRK) Long Island City, NY St. Patrick.
Gillgannon, Michael '58 (KC) Mission Duty.
Gillick, Lawrence D. *s.j.* '72 (OM)[K] Omaha, NE Jesuit Community at Creighton University.
Gilligan, Adrian *o.s.a.* '68 (PH)[Y] Villanova, PA St. Thomas Monastery.
Gilligan, James M. *m.m.* '55 (NY)[EE] Maryknoll Maryknoll Fathers and Brothers Retired.
Gilligan, Michael J. '69 (CHI) Other Assignments; [W] South Holland, IL American Catholic Press.
Gillin, Thomas M. *s.j.* '52 (NO)[P] New Orleans, LA Ignatius Residence Retired.
Gillin, Thomas P. '74 (PH)[F] Bryn Mawr, PA Country Day School of the Sacred Heart; Springfield, PA St. Kevin.
Gillis, David C. '79 (ALN) On Duty Outside the Diocese.
Gillis, David C. '79 (ORL) DeBary, FL St. Ann's.
Gillis, Edward F. '46 (BO) Senior Priests. Retired.
Gillis, James B. *c.s.c.* '56 (FTW)[H] Holy Cross House Retired.
Gillis, Ralph J. '59 (GB) Crandon, WI St. Joseph.
Gillis, Roger S. *s.j.* '78 (SEA)[A] Seattle, WA Seattle University; [L] Seattle, WA Arrupe Jesuit Community at Seattle University.
Gillis, Ronald S. '67 (BAL)[A] Emmitsburg, MD Mount St. Mary's Seminary.
Gillis, Ronald S. (POD) Reston.
Gillmeyer, Patrick *o.s.b.* '03 (RCK)[G] Aurora, IL Marmion Abbey.
Gillon, James A. *s.j.* '74 (BO)[U] Cambridge, MA Zipoli House.
Gil Londono, William A. '00 (LA) Paramount, CA Our Lady of the Rosary.
Gillooly, Patrick J. '53 (WH) Berkeley Springs, WV St. Vincent de Paul Retired.
Gills, Thomas '78 (BAL) Military Chaplains; Air Force Chaplains.
Gillum, William *o.f.m.cap.* '76 (PIT) Rochester, PA St. Cecilia; [M] Beaver, PA St. Fidelis Friary.
Gillum, William *o.f.m.cap.* (PIT) Beaver County, PA McGuire Memorial Home.
Gilman, Leonard *o.carm.* '98 (NEW) Tenafly, NJ Our Lady of Mount Carmel.
Gilmartin, Rev. Msgr. John D. '72 (RVC) Garden City, NY St. Anne.
Gilmartin, Rev. Msgr. John E. '56 (BGP)[O] Stamford, CT The Catherine Dennis Keefe Queen of the Clergy Retired Priests' Residence Retired.
Gilmartin, Paul P. *s.j.* '62 (BO)[U] Weston, MA Campion Health Center, Inc.
Gilmore, Alan *o.c.s.o.* '70 (L)[L] Trappist, KY Abbey of Our Lady of Gethsemani, of the Order of Cistercians of the Strict Observance.
Gilmore, Lawrence *s.d.b.* '84 (FgM) New Rochelle, NY SALESIANS OF DON BOSCO.
Gilmore, Vincent M. *o.praem.* '90 (ORG)[I] Silverado, CA Norbertine Fathers of Orange Inc.
Gilmour, James *c.ss.r.* (MET) Co Directors.
Gilmour, Robert G. *c.s.c.* '68 (FgM) New Rochelle, NY Eastern Brothers Province.
Gilroy, Robert G. *s.j.* '97 (BO)[U] Weston, MA Campion Jesuit Community.
Gilsdorf, Daniel C. '60 (GB) Retired.
Gilsdorf, Gordon J. '49 (GB) Special Assignment; Censores Librorum.
Gilsenan, Rev. Msgr. John P. '56 (WCH) Colwich, KS St. Mark; Promoter of Justice; Defenders of the Bond.
Gilsenan, Michael J. *ss.cc.* '59 (SB)[I] Chino Hills, CA Congregation of the Sacred Hearts of Jesus & Mary, SS.CC.
Gilson, Michael C. *s.j.* '02 (SAC)[I] Carmichael, CA Sacramento Jesuit Community; [D] Sacramento, CA Jesuit High School.
Gimeno, Fabian G. '60 (ORL) St. Cloud, FL St. Thomas Aquinas.
Gimpl, Carl '55 (P) Judges; [P] Monmouth, OR Western Oregon University (Monmouth).
Gimpl, Rev. Msgr. Carl '55 (P) Independence, OR St. Patrick Church.
Ginel, Robert J. '78 (NY) Bronx, NY Holy Cross.
Ging, Regis B. *m.m.* '66 (FgM) Maryknoll, NY MARYKNOLL.
Gingras, Dennis C. '90 (HRT) Unassigned.
Gingras, Jerome R. '78 (ALB) Glenville, NY Immaculate Conception.
Gini, John E. *o.f.m.* '63 (MRY)[F] San Miguel, CA Franciscan Friars, O.F.M.; San Miguel, CA San Miguel.
Gins, Paul M. *o.s.m.* '75 (CHI)[N] Chicago Order of Friar Servants of Mary (Servites) United States of America Province, Inc.
Gins, Paul M. *o.s.m.* '75 (ORG)[I] Anaheim, CA Servite Fathers and Brothers; Fullerton, CA St. Juliana Falconieri.
Ginther, Lawrence P. '46 (WIN) Retired.
Ginther, Richard '83 (IND) Terre Haute, IN St. Patrick; Terre Haute, IN St. Margaret Mary.
Gintoli, Rev. Msgr. Blase M. '69 (BGP) Fairfield, CT Our Lady of the Assumption.
Ginty, Rev. Msgr. Thomas M. '85 (HRT) Waterbury, CT Our Lady of Loreto; Waterbury Deanery; Waterbury, CT St. Stanislaus Kostka.
Gioeli, Leonard '05 (VEN) Port Charlotte, FL San Antonio.

Gion, Chad '02 (BIS) Mandan, ND Spirit of Life; Mandan, ND St. Martin; Pro–Synodal Judges; Mandan, ND St. Anthony.
Gionet, Urbain J. '51 (WOR) Retired.
Gioppato, Alfonso *o.m.i.* '64 (SAT) Nixon, TX St. Joseph's; Smiley, TX St. Philip Benizi.
Giorda, Adolph *o.f.m.* '46 (NY)[EE] New York, NY Padua Friary.
Giordani, Rev. Msgr. Mark J. '69 (PAT) Paterson, NJ Cathedral of St. John the Baptist; Passaic County Jail; Deans.
Giordano, John C. '67 (MET) Retired.
Giordano, Joseph *c.i.c.m.* '72 (ARL)[H] Arlington, VA Missionhurst, C.I.C.M.–Central House and Provincialate.
Giordano, Pasquale T. *s.j.* '72 (FgM) New York, NY Society of Jesus.
Giorno, Stephen J. *s.t.* '86 (NEW) Jersey City, NJ Christ, the King.
Giovanoni, Peter M. '01 (WDC) Washington, DC Our Lady Queen of Peace.
Gipson, Rev. Msgr. Robert W. '62 (LA) Pasadena, CA Assumption of the Blessed Virgin Mary.
Gira, Steve *c.r.* (BEL) Columbia, IL Immaculate Conception of the B.V.M.
Giraldo, Alonso Escobar (PCE) Arroyo, PR Our Lady of Mt. Carmel.
Giraldo, Jesus Antonio '97 (KNX) Knoxville, TN All Saints Catholic Church.
Girard, Charles A. *s.m.* '66 (ATL)[D] Atlanta, GA Marist School.
Girardeau, Robert A. '93 (SAV) Americus, GA St. Mary; College of Consultors.
Girardin, Peter T. '60 (BO) Senior Priests. Retired.
Girnius, Charles F. *m.m.* '44 (NY)[EE] Retired.
Giroir, Rev. Msgr. Frank J. '81 (NO) Parish Sites & Boundaries Committee; Serra Club of West St. Tammany; Madisonville, LA St. Anselm.
Girone, Joseph F. *o.s.a.* '81 (NY) Bronx, NY St. Nicholas of Tolentine.
Girotti, John W. '02 (GB) College of Consultors.
Girotti, John W. '02 (GB) Bear Creek, WI St. Rose; Green Bay, WI St. Francis Xavier Cathedral; Bear Creek, WI St. Mary.
Girouard, Robert J. '59 (PRT) Retired.
Giroux, Garry B. '76 (OG) Potsdam, NY St. Mary; Advocates; Campus Ministry.
Giroux, Harry E. '76 (OG) Absent on Sick Leave, Disabled Retired.
Giroux, Joseph W. '00 (OG) Old Forge, NY St. Anthony of Padua; Old Forge, NY St. Bartholomew; Old Forge, NY St. William.
Giroux, Peter *f.p.o.* '98 (BO)[U] Lawrence, MA Franciscans of Primitive Observance.
Giroux, Regis J. '70 (SPR) Absent on Leave.
Giroux, Richard M. '69 (MAN) Tilton, NH St. Mary of the Assumption.
Giroux, William P. '80 (BUR) Burlington, VT St. Mark's.
Girres, Edward M. '79 (SC) Presbyteral Council; Algona, IA St. Cecelia.
Girzone, Joseph '55 (ALB) Retired.
Gismondi, Carl N. *f.s.s.p.* '02 (SCR)[M] Elmhurst, PA Priestly Fraternity of St. Peter (F.S.S.P.), North American District Headquarters; Elmhurst, PA.
Gismondi, Carl *f.s.s.p.* '02 (SD) San Diego, CA St. Anne.
Gitau, Paul '94 (ROC) Rochester, NY Immaculate Conception; Rochester, NY St. Bridget.
Gito, Nicholas B. *m.s.c.* '73 (SB) Riverside, CA St. Catherine of Alexandria.
Gitonga, Patrick '02 (PH) Philadelphia, PA St. Katherine of Siena.
Gits, Douglas J. '53 (WIN) Retired.
Gitter, Paul '93 (STP)[C] St. Paul, MN University of St. Thomas; [A] St. Paul, MN St. John Vianney Seminary.
Gittins, Anthony *c.s.sp.* '67 (CHI)[B] Chicago, IL The Catholic Theological Union at Chicago.
Gitzen, Patrick *o.m.i.* '75 (FgM) Washington, DC AMERICAN OBLATE MISSIONS.
Giudice, Anthony *o.f.m.cap.* '54 (NEW) Hackensack, NJ Church of St. Francis of Assisi.
Giudice, Francis J. '56 (PRO) Providence, RI St. Charles Borromeo Retired.
Giuffre, Carmelo '07 (MIL) Fond du Lac, WI Holy Family.
Giuffre, Frank A. '97 (PH)[A] Wynnewood, PA Theological Seminary of St. Charles Borromeo, Overbrook.
Giuliani, John B. '60 (BGP)[N] West Redding, CT The Benedictine Grange.
Giuliani, John P. *c.o.* '80 (CHR) Fort Mill, SC St. Philip Neri; [E] Rock Hill, SC Oratory of St. Philip Neri, Congregation of the Oratory of Pontifical Rite.
Giuliani, John '60 (BGP) Retired.
Giuliani, Scott *s.o.l.t.* '09 (CC)[G] Robstown, TX Society of Our Lady of the Most Holy Trinity.
Giuliani, Scott *s.o.l.t.* '09 (PBL) Capulin, CO St. Joseph.
Giuliano, Anthony J. '84 (NY) Yonkers, NY Christ the King.
Giuliano, Carmen *s.a.* '61 (NY)[EE] Garrison, NY Franciscan Friars of the Atonement.
Giuliano, Mario *o.f.m.conv.* (CHL) Winston–Salem, NC Our Lady of Mercy.
Giuliano, Steven B. '80 (WIL) Middletown, DE St. Joseph; Deans.
Giulietti, Julio *s.j.* '79 (BO)[U] Boston The Society of Jesus of New England–Provincial Offices.
Giunta, Jose *i.v.e.* '91 (NY) Bronx, NY St. Thomas Aquinas.
Giuntini, Robert J. '76 (RVC)[J] Huntington, NY St. Joseph's Guest Home for the Aged, Inc. Retired.
Giusta, Rev. Msgr. Frank J. '63 (ATL) Special or Other (Arch)Diocesan Assignment Retired.
Givey, David W. '71 (PH) Retired.
Gizler, John B. '02 (PIT) McKeesport, PA St. Martin de Porres.
Gjengdahl, Nels H. '07 (STP) Shoreview, MN St. Odilia.
Gjergji, Nue '73 (DET) Southfield, MI Our Lady of Albanians.
Gjonaj, Damien *o.s.b.* '00 (DET)[B] Oxford, MI St. Benedict Monastery.
Glab, Joseph *c.r.* '75 (CHI) Schaumburg, IL St. Matthew; Councilors:.
Glab, Stephen *c.r.* '82 (RCK) Woodstock, IL Resurrection.
Glabik, Peter S. '07 (PAT) Rockaway, NJ Sacred Heart; Rockaway, NJ St. Cecilia's.
Glabinski, Janusz '86 (LAR) Rio Bravo, TX Santa Rita de Casia Independent Mission.
Glabinski, Jozef '89 (LAR) Crystal City, TX Sacred Heart.
Glackin, Thomas J. '68 (VEN) Retired.
Gladstone, James J. *s.j.* '66 (MIL)[P] Wauwatosa, WI Jesuit Community at St. Camillus; Milwaukee, WI; [P] Milwaukee, WI Jesuit Provincial Office, Wisconsin Province.
Glahn, Carl '52 (OWN) Retired.
Glancy, Christopher J. *c.s.v.* '93 (CHI)[N] Arlington Heights Viatorian Province Center–Clerics of St. Viator.
Glandorf, Ken (DUB)[H] Cedar Rapids, IA Mercy Medical Center–Cedar Rapids.
Glanzmann, Edward J. *o.s.b.* '79 (CHI)[N] Chicago, IL Monastery of the Holy Cross.
Glapiak, Edward '61 (WIL) Retired.
Glaros, Matthew J. '99 (MO) Military Chaplains; Air Force Chaplains.
Glaser, Kenneth J. '00 (DUB) Associate Directors; [N] Cedar Falls, IA St. Stephen the Witness Catholic Student Center, University of Northern Iowa; On Special or Other Archdiocesan Assignment; Christian Initiation Advisory Committee.
Glaser, Lawrence A. *o.c.s.o.* '58 (SAC)[A] Vina, CA Abbey of New Clairvaux, Trappist Seminary; [I] Vina, CA Abbey of New Clairvaux, Trappist.
Glasgow, Dennis T. *s.j.* '84 (LAN) Ann Arbor, MI St. Mary Student Parish; [J] Ann Arbor, MI Detroit Province of the Society of Jesus – Jesuit Residence.
Glasgow, Mark W. '62 (PIT) Homestead, PA St. Maximilian Kolbe; Military Chaplains; Highland Drive.
Glasgow, Robert K. '85 (MAN) Military Chaplains.
Glasgow, Robert K. '85 (MO) Army Chaplains.
Glasgow, Rev. Msgr. T. Gaspard '69 (NO) Retired.
Glass, James M. *o.s.b.* '04 (RIC) Blackstone, VA Immaculate Heart of Mary; Farmville, VA St. Theresa; [K] Richmond, VA Mary Mother of the Church Abbey.
Glass, Robert H. *c.s.b.* '74 (GAL)[E] Houston, TX St. Thomas High School.
Glass, Senan *o.f.m.cap.* '57 (PH) Philadelphia, PA St. John the Evangelist.
Glassmire, David R. '94 (MO) Navy Reserve Chaplains; Military Chaplains.
Glastetter, Donald A. '65 (STL) Wentzville, MO St. Patrick.
Glastetter, Michael J. *o.f.m.conv.* '99 (PEO) Peoria, IL Holy Family.
Glatts, Joseph M. '66 (PH) West Chester, PA SS. Simon and Jude.
Glaves, John J. '56 (LIN) Retired.
Glavin, Leonard *o.f.m.cap.* '54 (NY) New York, NY St. John the Baptist Retired.
Glavin, Patrick *o.f.m.cap.* '08 (MAN) Manchester, NH St. Anne–St. Augustin.
Gleason, Carl *s.d.s.* '56 (FgM) Milwaukee, WI SALVATORIAN MISSIONS.
Gleason, Jack '95 (TLS) Tulsa, OK Church of the Madalene; Diocesan Senators; Diocesan Consultors; Seminary Board.
Gleason, James '50 (STL)[O] Liguori, MO Liguori Mission House/Redemptorists.
Gleason, Joseph F. '87 (PH)[A] Wynnewood, PA Theological Seminary of St. Charles Borromeo, Overbrook.
Gleason, Laurence J. '96 (PH) West Chester, PA St. Agnes.
Gleason, Rev. Msgr. Paul D. '47 (PRT) Retired.
Gleason, Richard J. '67 (LA) Culver City, CA St. Augustine.
Gleba, Rev. Msgr. Peter W. '53 (SY) Syracuse, NY Sacred Heart Basilica.
Gleba, William P. '58 (SY) Retired.
Gleeson, Edward D. '69 (CHI) Lemont, IL St. James at Sag Bridge.
Gleeson, Martin J. *o.p.* '98 (NO) New Orleans, LA St. Dominic; [P] Metairie, LA Dominican Friars, Southern Dominican Province of St. Martin de Porres; [P] Metairie, LA Southern Dominican Foundation; [S] Metairie, LA Southern Dominican Foundation; Metairie, LA St. Martin de Porres Province (Southern Dominican Province); Metairie, LA.
Gleeson, Michael '75 (LA) Long Beach, CA St. Cornelius.
Gleeson, Stephen J. '63 (BGP) Trumbull, CT St. Stephen; Nurses, Council of Catholic; Pastors' Vocation Advisory Board.
Gleeson, Thomas F. *s.j.* '68 (ALN)[N] Wernersville, PA Jesuit Center.
Gleeson, Thomas F. *s.j.* '68 (PH)[Y] Loyola Center and Manresa Hall.
Gleeson, William T. '66 (PBL) Pueblo, CO St. Joseph; Avondale, CO Sacred Heart; Pueblo, CO St. Therese.
Gleissner, Leopold *o.f.m.cap.* '52 (GB)[J] Appleton, WI St. Fidelis Friary Retired.
Gleixner, Joseph *m.s.c.* '65 (RCK)[G].
Glenn, Gregory A. (SLC) Salt Lake City, UT Cathedral of the Madeleine LLC 202.
Glenn, Rev. Msgr. Michael G. '90 (DEN)[A] Denver, CO Saint John Vianney Theological Seminary; College of Consultors; St. John Vianney Theological Seminary; Ex Officio Members.
Glenn, Nicholas '98 (STN)[A] Eagle Harbor, MI Holy Transfiguration Skete.
Glennon, Bertin *s.t.* '71 (KNX) Chattanooga, TN SS. Peter and Paul.
Glennon, James G. *o.s.a.* '52 (PH)[Y] Villanova, PA St. Thomas Monastery.
Glennon, Thomas G. *s.s.c.* '79 (CHI)[N] Chicago, IL Columban Fathers Mission Center.
Glennon, Thomas *s.s.c.* '79 (OM)[K] St. Columbans Missionary Society of St. Columban.
Glepko, Robert J. '76 (CLV) Lorain, OH Nativity of the Blessed Virgin Mary.
Gliatta, Ronald *o.f.m.* '77 (NY)[EE] New York Franciscan Province of the Immaculate Conception.
Glimm, Rev. Msgr. Francis X. '35 (RVC)[J] Huntington, NY St. Joseph's Guest Home for the Aged, Inc.; Censors of Books Retired.
Glinkowski, Raphael K. *o.s.p.p.e.* '62 (GBG) Kittanning, PA Armstrong County Hospital; [G] Kittanning, PA Pauline Fathers Monastery.
Glisson, Nicholas '79 (OAK) Oakland, CA St. Lawrence O'Toole–St. Cyril of Jerusalem.
Glockner, Michael W. *c.s.c.* '70 (FTW)[H] Notre Dame Congregation of Holy Cross, Indiana Province, Provincial House.
Glogowski, John F. '71 (SFR) Redwood City, CA St. Matthias.
Glogowski, John J. '62 (ROC) Retired.
Glorie, Rev. Msgr. John W. '60 (MIA) Retired.
Glorioso, Charles '95 (SHP) Bossier City, LA Christ the King; Church Vocations Board & Vocations Office.
Gloss, John C. '03 (MET) Colonia, NJ St. John Vianney.
Glosser, Rev. Msgr. William F. '84 (ALN) Saint Clair, PA St. Clare of Assisi Parish.
Gloudeman, Francis M. *o.praem.* '91 (ORG)[I] Silverado, CA Norbertine Fathers of Orange Inc.
Gloudeman, Robert J. '64 (MIL) Retired.
Glover, Donald F. *m.m.* '70 (NY)[EE] Maryknoll Maryknoll Fathers and Brothers Retired.
Glover, Francis N. *s.j.* '58 (FgM) New York, NY Society of Jesus.
Glover, George R. *o.s.b.* '88 (RCK) Aurora, IL Annunciation of the Blessed Virgin Mary; [G] Aurora, IL Marmion Abbey.
Glover, Jason A. *s.t.l.* '02 (E)[B] Erie, PA Gannon University.
Glover, Mark '08 (SPR) Wilbraham, MA St. Cecilia's.
Glover, S. Matthew '04 (PRO)[S] Kingston, RI University of Rhode Island Catholic Center.
Glovik, Rev. Msgr. Karl L. '61 (DUB) Retired.
Gluc, Vincent *o.f.m.conv.* '79 (BAL)[S] Baltimore, MD Immaculate Heart of Mary Friary; [C] Baltimore, MD Archbishop Curley High School.
Glueckert, Leopold *o.carm.* '68 (WDC)[B] Washington, DC Whitefriars Hall.
Glynn, Canon Thomas '64 (STN) Chicago, IL St. Joseph.
Glynn, Edward *s.j.* '67 (BAL)[S] Baltimore, MD Colombiere Jesuit Community.
Glynn, Francis M. '70 (BO) Allston, MA St. Anthony of Padua.
Glynn, Joseph *c.s.sp.* '76 (SFR) Millbrae, CA St. Dunstan; Long Island City, NY.
Glynn, Martin G. '78 (PAT) Denville, NJ St. Mary's.
Glynn, Robert *s.j.* '91 (FgM) Los Gatos, CA Society of Jesus.
Glynn, Seamus A. '58 (ORG) Anaheim, CA San Antonio de Padua Del Cañon Church Retired.
Glynn, Thomas Joseph '54 (LA) Long Beach, CA Our Lady of Refuge Retired.
Glynn, Rev. Msgr. William F. '47 (BO) Senior Priests. Retired.

Gmerek, Ronald E. '71 (E) Erie, PA Our Mother of Sorrows.
Gnall, Julian (VNN) On Special Assignment.
Gnanapragasm, M. Susai '94 (CC) Corpus Christi, TX Our Lady of Perpetual Help.
Gnanaraj, Michael '76 (BWN) Brownsville, TX Valley Baptist Health Systems–Brownsville.
Gnanasegaram, Frank '84 (RVC) Shoreham, NY St. Mark.
Gnarackatt, Joseph '67 (TR) Brick Town, NJ St. Dominic.
Gniewyk, Eugene '90 (NEW) Fairfield, NJ St. Thomas More.
Gnirk, Lloyd A. '78 (OM) Valley, NE St. John; [B] Omaha, NE Roncalli Catholic High School of Omaha.
Gnoinski, Piotr '05 (CHI) Chicago, IL St. Francis Borgia.
Gobbo, Paolo '94 (SJ) Santa Clara, CA St. Clare.
Gober, Christopher M. '00 (CHL) Spruce Pine, NC St. Lucien; Vocations; Linville, NC St. Bernadette.
Gobitas, Rev. Msgr. Gerald E. '75 (ALN) Chancellor; Secretary to the Bishop; Secretariat for Clergy; Priest Personnel Office; College of Consultors; Ex Officio Members.
Goblirsch, Robert P. '60 (NU) Ortonville, MN St. James; Ortonville, MN St. John; Ortonville, MN St. Joseph; Board of Trustees for Pension Plan for Priests.
Gockel, Guido *m.h.m.* '69 (NY)[II] New York, NY Catholic Near East Welfare Association (CNEWA).
Goda, Paul J. *s.j.* '66 (SJ)[B] Santa Clara, CA Jesuit Community.
Godecker, Jeff '69 (IND) Indianapolis, IN Christ The King.
Godecker, Jeffrey H. '69 (IND)[O] Indianapolis, IN Butler University; Council of Priests.
Godenciuc, Iura '94 (STF) New Haven, CT St. Michael.
Godenciuc, Vasile '81 (STF) Elmira Heights, NY St. Nicholas; Sayre, PA Ascension of Our Lord.
Godfrey, Donal *s.j.* '92 (SFR)[N] San Francisco, CA Loyola House Jesuit Community.
Godfrey, Joseph J. *s.j.* '69 (PH)[C] Jesuit Fathers; [Y] Philadelphia, PA St. Alphonsus House.
Godfrey, Timothy S. *s.j.* '85 (WDC)[N] Washington, DC The Jesuit Community at Georgetown University.
Godic, Frank G. '73 (CLV) Cleveland, OH Immaculate Conception.
Godin, Normand J. '73 (PRO) Providence, RI St. Agnes.
Godina, Juan Manuel '07 (YAK) Waterville, WA St. Joseph's; Natural Family Planning Advisory Committee; Natural Family Planning; Respect Life Committee; Social Justice and Human Life Commission; Kennewick, WA St. Joseph's; Benton City, WA St. Frances Xavier Cabrini.
Godinez, Rodolfo '91 (STA) Williston, FL Holy Family.
Godinez–Ramos, Eulices '08 (LEX) Lexington, KY Mary, Queen of the Holy Rosary.
Godleski, David A. *s.j.* '98 (CHI)[C] Chicago, IL Jesuit Community at Loyola University Chicago.
Godley, Patrick '53 (SEA) Retired.
Goebel, Joseph A. '50 (CLV) Euclid, OH St. Christine Retired.
Goebel, Robert A. *s.j.* '63 (SEA)[C] Tacoma, WA Bellarmine Preparatory School.
Goebel, Robert A. *s.j.* '63 (SPK)[J] Spokane, WA Regis Community Retired.
Goebel, Robert W. '74 (CIN) Cincinnati, OH St. Therese, The Little Flower.
Goeckner, Jeffrey '95 (SFD) Edwardsville, IL St. Boniface; Priests' Personnel Board.
Goedde, Bernard C. '72 (BEL) Nashville, IL Our Lady of Perpetual Help; Pinckneyville, IL St. Mary Magdalen; Office of Youth Ministry.
Goedert, Robert A. *o.p.* '51 (CHI)[N] St. Pius V Priory.
Goedert, William O. '55 (CHI) Oak Lawn, IL St. Germaine Retired.
Goeeselin, Fernand L. *m.m.* '70 (NY)[EE] Retired.
Goehring, Rev. Msgr. Raymond J. '64 (LAN) Lansing, MI Resurrection; Bellevue, MI St. Ann; Judicial Vicar; Tribunal Judges.
Goeke, James F. *s.j.* '88 (STL)[C] Saint Louis University; [O] St. Louis, MO Bellarmine House of Studies.
Goekler, Thomas F. *m.m.* '67 (FgM) Maryknoll, NY MARYKNOLL.
Goellen, Richard M. '63 (FAR) Retired.
Goergen, David *m.afr.* '69 (FgM) Washington, DC MISSIONARIES OF AFRICA.
Goergen, Donald J. *o.p.* '75 (CHI)[N] Chicago Dominicans (Provincial Office).
Goergen, Donald *o.p.* '75 (STL)[O] St. Louis, MO St. Dominic Priory.
Goergen, Michael A. '62 (CHI) Chicago, IL St. Bartholomew Retired.
Goering, Rev. Msgr. Joseph P. '00 (FAR) Moderator of the Curia; Vicar General; Vicar for Clergy; Corporate Board; Diocesan Finance Council; Arbitration & Conciliation Board.
Goerner, James E. '93 (PH) Philadelphia, PA St. Bartholomew.
Goertz, Rev. Msgr. Alois J. '48 (SAT)[K] San Antonio, TX Casa De Padres Retired.
Goertz, Bernard C. '52 (AUS) Retired.
Goertz, Howard '77 (AUS) Kyle, TX St. Anthony Marie De Claret.
Goertz, Rev. Msgr. Victor '52 (AUS) Retired.
Goethals, Gregory M. *s.j.* '88 (LA)[F] Los Angeles, CA Loyola High School of Los Angeles.
Goettemoeller, Leonard *c.pp.s* '49 (CIN)[N] Carthagena, OH St. Charles Retired.
Goetz, Donald R. '68 (L) Louisville, KY St. Brigid; Louisville, KY St. James; Defenders of the Bond.
Goetz, Gerald E. *s.j.* '73 (MIL)[P] Milwaukee, WI Jesuit Community at Marquette University.
Goetz, J. Raymond '81 (OWN) Bowling Green, KY Holy Spirit.
Goetz, Joseph W. '60 (CIN) Retired.
Goetz, Martin G. '92 (DAV) Director of Vocations; Vocations; [J] Davenport, IA St. Vincent Center.
Goff, William P. *c.m.* '66 (PH)[Y].
Gofigan, Paul M. '04 (AGN) Dededo, GU Santa Barbara; El Shaddai (PPFI), Prayer Partner International, Guam Chapter.
Goggin, Cornelius J. '56 (MAN) Retired.
Goggin, John T. '64 (NU) On Duty Outside the Diocese.
Goggins, James K. '94 (DEN) Lakewood, CO St. Bernadette; Deaneries; Elected Representatives from Deanery to Presbyteral Council.
Goguen, Rev. Msgr. Francis T. '66 (WOR) Leominster, MA St. Cecilia; Diocesan College of Consultors; Deans; Presbyteral Council.
Goh, Joseph *o.f.m.* (OAK)[M] Berkeley, CA Franciscan Friars (Province of Santa Barbara).
Gohlke, Nathan '08 (JOL) Joliet, IL The Cathedral of St. Raymond.
Gohm, Robert S. '75 (SAG) Bay City, MI Holy Trinity.
Gohring, William '84 (ORL) Special Assignment.
Goicoechea, Greg *o.f.m.cap.* '45 (FWT) Fort Worth, TX Immaculate Heart of Mary.
Goin, James A. '92 (OKL) Region IV; Chickasha, OK Holy Name; Council of Priests Archdiocesan.
Gojuk, Peter P. *o.m.v.* '81 (BO)[B] Boston, MA Our Lady of Grace Seminary; [A] Brighton, MA St. John Seminary.
Golas, Eugene S. '55 (GR) Retired.
Golas, John S. '81 (HRT) Consultors – Canon 1742; Unionville, CT St. Mary; Hartford Vicariate.
Golasinski, Rev. Msgr. Donald '62 (BEA) Southern Vicariate; Catholic Women, Council of; Groves, TX Immaculate Conception.
Golasinski, Rev. Msgr. James L. '58 (GAL) Houston, TX Annunciation.
Golba, Gregorz '97 (PAT) Passaic, NJ Holy Rosary.
Gold, William '65 (SD) Retired.
Goldasich, Mark '81 (KCK) Tonganoxie, KS Sacred Heart; Newspaper "The Leaven".
Goldbach, Edmund *o.f.m.conv.* '65 (CLV) Lorain, OH St. Anthony of Padua.
Goldbach, Peter D. *c.m.* '44 (BRK)[T] Jamaica, NY Vincentian Residence Retired.
Goldberg, James M. '76 (GBG) Slickville, PA St. Sylvester.
Golden, Edward '61 (ROC) Retired.
Golden, James '48 (DUL) Retired.
Golden, Patrick '96 (RIC) Richmond, VA Cathedral of the Sacred Heart.
Golden, Paul L. *c.m.* '65 (DEN)[N] Denver, CO Congregation of the Mission Western Province: De Paul House.
Golden, Thomas '63 (GB) Retired.
Goldian, Edward R. *s.j.* '69 (STL) St. Louis, MO St. Mary Magdalen.
Golding, Edward '88 (ALB) Round Lake, NY Corpus Christi; Worcester, NY St. Joseph.
Goldrick, Timothy J. '72 (FR) North Dighton, MA St. Nicholas of Myra Parish.
Gole, Joseph '43 (MIL)[B] Hales Corners, WI Sacred Heart School of Theology; [P] Franklin Villa Maria.
Golemba, Rev. Msgr. Roman '75 (STF) Fall River, MA St. John–the–Baptist; Woonsocket, RI St. Michael; Presbyteral Council.
Golias, Rev. Msgr. Andrew J. '70 (PH) Norristown, PA St. Teresa of Avila.
Golini, Ronald '68 (NTN) Leave of Absence.
Golino, Arthur A. '80 (NY) New York, NY St. Columba.
Golish, Robert *m.m.* '53 (NY)[EE] Retired.
Golka, James R. '94 (GI) Ongoing Formation for Clergy and Liturgy; Personnel Board.
Golka, James R. '94 (GI) North Platte, NE St. Patrick.
Gollatz, Ronald J. '72 (CHI) Wauconda, IL Transfiguration.
Gollob, Timothy A. '58 (DAL) Dallas, TX Holy Cross; DEPARTMENT OF VETERANS AFFAIRS HOSPITALS AND CHAPLAINS.
Gollob, Timothy A. '58 (SAT) Defenders of the Bond.
Gollob, Timothy '58 (DAL) Dallas, TX VA – North Texas Health Care System.
Golobich, John '48 (DUL) Duluth, MN Retired.
Golombek, Rev. Msgr. Robert K. '65 (BUF) Retired.
Goloran, Mauricio O. '84 (LA) Valinda, CA St. Martha.
Golueke, Thomas J. '77 (BAL) Priests Sick or Absent.
Golyzniak, Gregory '98 (COS) Colorado Springs, CO St. Joseph's.
Gomes, Angelo *s.f.x.* (BRK) Brooklyn, NY Holy Spirit.
Gomes, Antonio '62 (P) Salem, OR St. Joseph.
Gomes, Benedict '69 (KCK) Rossville, KS St. Stanislaus; St. Marys, KS Immaculate Conception.
Gomes, Christopher *o.f.m.conv.* (BO) Roxbury, MA St. Patrick.
Gomes, Herman *ss.cc.* '78 (HON) Kaneohe, HI St. Ann; Presbyteral Council.
Gomes, John A. '69 (FR) South Dartmouth, MA St. Mary's.
Gomes, Martin *ss.cc.* '69 (FR)[G] Fairhaven National Center of the Enthronement.
Gomes, Robert M. '66 (CAM) Retired.
Gomes, Ronald A. '87 (BO) Permanent Disability.
Gomes, Stanley '95 (NEW)[A] South Orange, NJ Seton Hall University College Seminary; [B] School of Diplomacy and Intl. Rels.; Adjunct Clergy Personnel; Ex Officio Members.
Gomes, William J. '69 (RVC) Elmont, NY St. Boniface.
Gomez, Anthony J. '98 (LA) Norwalk, CA St. Linus.
Gomez, Arturo S. *c.m.f.* '80 (SB) Rialto, CA St. Catherine of Siena.
Gomez, Aurelio Yanez '74 (NEW) Hillside, NJ St. Catherine of Siena.
Gomez, Carlos '03 (PHX) Phoenix, AZ St. Augustine Roman Catholic Parish.
Gomez, Cesar '98 (WIL) Georgetown, DE St. Michael the Archangel.
Gomez, Edmund '93 (SB) Elected Members; Perris, CA St. James; Elected Members.
Gomez, Edmundo '69 (NY) Bronx, NY St. Helena.
Gomez, Eduardo '07 (BWN) Harlingen, TX Immaculate Heart of Mary.
Gomez, Edwin A. '05 (WOR) St. Peter; St. Louis; Worcester, MA St. Peter; Webster, MA St. Louis.
Gómez, Enrique '77 (CGS) Las Piedras, PR Inmaculada Concepcion.
Gomez, F. Augustin Anda (BO) Brighton, MA St. Columbkille.
Gomez, Francisco *o.m.i.* '07 (FgM) Washington, DC AMERICAN OBLATE MISSIONS.
Gomez, Francisco '09 (BGP) Darien, CT St. John.
Gomez, Frank '61 (BWN) Retired.
Gomez, Gustavo '02 (YAK) Mattawa, WA Our Lady of the Desert; Charismatic Renewal, Spanish.
Gomez, Rev. Msgr. Henry '58 (LA) Retired.
Gomez, Humberto '88 (SAC) Vacaville, CA St. Mary.
Gomez, Jerry '93 (CAM) Mullica Hill, NJ Church of the Holy Name of Jesus, Mullica Hill, N.J.
Gomez, Jhon Jairo '09 (TYL) Graduate Studies.
Gomez, Jhon '07 (BGP) Bridgeport, CT St. Augustine Cathedral.
Gomez, Jorge A. '04 (BWN) Parish Priests Consultors and Priests' Personnel Board; [A] Mission, TX The Saint Joseph and Saint Peter Seminary.
Gomez, Jose '95 (AMA) Amarillo, TX Our Lady of Guadalupe; Advocates.
Gómez, José Luis *s.d.b.* '61 (SJN) San Juan, PR San Juan Bosco.
Gomez, Juan Fernando (CC) Mathis, TX Sacred Heart.
Gomez, Rev. Msgr. Leo '63 (GLP) Retired.
Gomez, Rev. Msgr. Leo '63 (SFE) Retired.
Gomez, Lorenzo *l.c.* '73 (DET)[T] Clarkston, MI Clarkston Pastoral Center, Inc.; [T] Bloomfield Hills, MI Logos, Inc. (Michigan); [P] Oxford, MI Queen of the Family Retreat Center.
Gomez, Lorenzo *s.d.v.* (PAT) Paterson, NJ St. Gerard Majella; Paterson, NJ St. Michael the Archangel.
Gomez, Marco Tulio *s.j.* '08 (DEN)[N] Denver, CO Regis Jesuit Community (The Jesuits at Regis University).
Gomez, Miguel '81 (MIA) Hialeah, FL Santa Barbara.
Gomez, Miguel '02 (MRY) On Leave.
Gomez, Orlando Perez *o.s.b.* '01 (RCK)[G] Aurora, IL Marmion Abbey.
Gomez, Orlando '97 (SAC) Fairfield, CA Holy Spirit.
Gomez, Otoniel J. '90 (PRO) Westerly, RI Immaculate Conception.
Gomez, Rafael '73 (BRK) Woodhaven, NY St. Thomas Apostle; Ozone Park, NY St. Elizabeth.
Gomez, Ramon '85 (OAK) Hayward, CA St. Clement; Deanery #17.
Gomez, Roberto '09 (SJ) San Jose, CA St. Maria Goretti.
Gomez, Silvestre *o.p.* '97 (SJN) Bayamon, PR Santo Domingo de Guzman; Bayamon, PR Nuestra Senora del Perpetuo Socorro.
Gomez, Walter '80 (MO) Air National Guard Chaplains.
Gomez–Baca, Walter '80 (SJN) Military Services; Guaynabo–Puerto Nuevo; Guaynabo, PR Maria Madre de la Misericordia.
Gomez–Medina, Oscar '02 (SAC) Sacramento, CA All Hallows; Sacramento, CA St. Peter.
Gomez del Valle, Jorge *m.sp.s.* '73 (SEA) Mill Creek, WA St. Elizabeth Ann Seton.
Gómez Urias, Ceferino '65 (SJN) Catano, PR Nuestra Senora del Carmen.
Gomide, Tomaz '71 (RVC) Mineola, NY Corpus Christi.
Gomolski, Joseph T. '81 (WIL) Absent on Sick Leave.
Gomori, Marcus '06 (LAV) Las Vegas, NV St. Elizabeth Ann Seton; Auditors; Pension Committee.
Gomori, Marcus '06 (LAV) Diocesan Advocates.
Gomori, Mark A. '06 (VNN) Las Vegas, NV St. Gabriel

the Archangel.
Gonchar, John Joseph *o.f.m.* '56 (GBG)[G] Uniontown, PA St. Anthony Friary.
Gonda, Gerard *o.s.b.* '80 (CLV)[N] Cleveland, OH; [D] Cleveland, OH Benedictine High School.
Gondek, Albert J. *o.s.f.s.* '66 (CHL) Lexington, NC Our Lady of the Rosary.
Gondek, Joseph A. '37 (MAR) Retired.
Gonderinger, Gerald E. '74 (OM) West Point, NE St. Aloysius; West Point, NE St. Boniface; West Point, NE St. Anthony; West Point, NE Assumption B.V.M.
Gonet, Charles F. '58 (SPR)[G] Springfield, MA St. Michael's Residence Retired.
Goni, Galadima G. '72 (SPR) Haydenville, MA Our Lady of the Hills.
Goni, Joachim *o.a.r.* '40 (ORG) Santa Ana, CA Our Lady of the Pillar Retired.
Gonsalves, Lino '86 (NY) New York, NY Our Lady of Guadalupe at St. Bernard's.
Gonsalves, Valerian *o.s.b.* '90 (TLS) Durant, OK St. William.
Gonser, Richard A. '62 (CLV) North Ridgeville, OH St. Julie Billiart.
Gonyo, Lance M. '93 (ROC) Spencerport, NY St. John the Evangelist; Conciliation Board.
Gonyo, Roland G. '73 (OG) Absent on Sick Leave, Disabled.
Gonzales, Adam *o.c.d.* '05 (SJ)[M] San Jose, CA Carmelite Monastery, Novitiate.
Gonzales, Rev. Msgr. Gabriel '84 (LA) North Hollywood, CA St. Charles Borromeo.
Gonzales, George '71 (SB) Judges Retired.
Gonzales, Jose de Jesus '08 (B) St. Anthony, ID Mary Immaculate.
Gonzales, Loren '89 (PHX) Peoria, AZ St. Charles Borromeo Roman Catholic Parish.
Gonzales, Rev. Msgr. Loreto '78 (LA) Long Beach, CA St. Barnabas.
Gonzales, Masseo *o.f.m.conv.* '96 (RNO) Reno, NV St. Thomas Aquinas Cathedral.
Gonzales, Ramon J. *o.p.* '09 (BR) Ponchatoula, LA St. Joseph.
Gonzales, Randy *c.i.c.m.* '04 (ARL)[H] Arlington, VA Missionhurst, C.I.C.M.–Central House and Provincialate.
Gonzales, Richard '98 (CC) Corpus Christi, TX St. Pius X.
Gonzales, Robert A. '78 (TUC) Tucson, AZ Saint John the Evangelist Roman Catholic Parish – Tucson.
Gonzales, Ronald *s.j.* '03 (SAT) San Antonio, TX Our Lady of Guadalupe.
Gonzales–Cabrera, Javier '08 (SB) Fontana, CA Kaiser Permanente Hospital.
Gonzalez, Alvaro Pio '03 (PT) Gulf Breeze, FL Saint Sylvester.
Gonzalez, Angel '52 (FRS) Retired.
Gonzalez, Anthony '92 (LA) Santa Monica, CA St. Clement.
Gonzalez, Anthony '93 (NY) Staten Island, NY St. Rita.
Gonzalez, Antonio '50 (FRS) Retired.
Gonzalez, Rev. Msgr. Antonio '62 (LUB) Retired.
Gonzalez, Aquilino D. *o.s.a.* '72 (FgM) Villanova, PA Province of St. Thomas of Villanova (Eastern).
Gonzalez, Arnold J. *c.m.f.* '58 (LA) San Gabriel, CA San Gabriel Mission.
Gonzalez, Avelino Armando '06 (WDC) Gaithersburg, MD St. Martin of Tours.
González, Carlos *s.f.m.* '04 (MGZ) Mayaguez, PR Our Lady of Mt. Carmel.
Gonzalez, Charles G. *s.j.* '67 (WDC)[C] Washington, DC Georgetown University; [N] Washington, DC The Jesuit Community at Georgetown University.
Gonzalez, Ciro '90 (KCK) Kansas City, KS All Saints.
Gonzalez, Cristobal Guardado '85 (LA) Rancho Dominguez, CA St. Albert the Great.
Gonzalez, Cruz Gil '48 (SJN) Retired.
Gonzalez, Daniel '92 (TYL) On Duty Outside the Diocese.
Gonzalez, Daniel '92 (SUP) Butternut, WI Immaculate Conception; Park Falls, WI St. Francis of Assisi; Park Falls, WI St. Anthony of Padua.
Gonzalez, Domingo N. (ORL) Lakeland, FL Church of the Resurrection Retired.
Gonzalez, Eliseo *o.a.r.* '03 (NEW)[M] West Orange, NJ Augustinian Recollects.
Gonzalez, Elkin '08 (TLS) Hispanic Ministry; Tulsa, OK SS. Peter and Paul.
Gonzalez, Emilio '88 (SEA) Lynden, WA St. Joseph.
Gonzalez, Fernando '95 (BWN) La Joya, TX Our Lady, Queen of Angels.
Gonzalez, Flavio V. '77 (CHI) Des Plaines, IL St. Stephen Protomartyr.
Gonzalez, Gabriel Jose T. *s.j.* '00 (NY)[EE] Loyola Hall, Jesuit Community.
Gonzalez, George G. '67 (MO) Military Chaplains; Army Chaplains.
Gonzalez, George '87 (BWN) Harlingen, TX Jail Ministry.
Gonzalez, Gonzalo *o.s.a.* '49 (SJN) Bayamon, PR San Agustin; Bayamon, PR Santa Rita de Casia; [E] Bayamon, PR Hospital Universitario.
Gonzalez, Hugo '89 (PHX) On Leave.
Gonzalez, Isaac *o.c.s.o.* '81 (ATL)[G] Conyers, GA The Monastery of the Holy Spirit.
Gonzalez, Rev. Msgr. Ivan '01 (RVC) Shoreham, NY St. Mark.
Gonzalez, J. Eduardo '81 (DAL) Appointed Members; [M] Dallas, TX Cathedral Restoration and Preservation Fund, Inc.; Dallas, TX Cathedral–Santuario de Guadalupe; College of Consultors.
Gonzalez, Jaime '90 (VEN) Fort Myers, FL Jesus the Worker Mission (Jesus Obrero); Fort Myers, FL San Jose Mission.
Gonzalez, Jamie '90 (TR) Mount Holly, NJ Christ the Redeemer.
Gonzalez, Jesus (SJN) Bayamon, PR Santa Elena.
Gonzalez, Joel (TYL) Longview, TX St. Matthew Catholic Church.
Gonzalez, John Alex '02 (R) Raleigh, NC Doggett Center at Aquinas House; [I] Raleigh, NC Doggett Center for Catholic Campus Ministry at Aquinas House.
Gonzalez, John–Paul '06 (LA) Norwalk, CA St. John of God.
Gonzalez, Jorge L. *s.d.b.* '89 (SJN) Catano, PR San Francisco de Sales.
Gonzalez, Jose Antonio '91 (VEN) Deans; Presbyteral Council.
Gonzalez, Jose G. '54 (SP) St. Petersburg, FL St. Raphael Retired.
Gonzalez, Jose Luis '98 (P) Gresham, OR St. Anne.
Gonzalez, Jose Marcos *o.f.m.* '05 (MIL) Beaver Dam, WI St. Katharine Drexel.
Gonzalez, Jose Navarro *m.g.* '75 (LA) Los Angeles, CA St. Paul.
Gonzalez, Jose R. *o.f.m.cap.* '04 (PCE)[E] Ponce, PR Fraternidad Santa Teresita, Frailes Capuchinos.
Gonzalez, Jose '69 (SR) Santa Rosa, CA Resurrection.
Gonzalez, Jose '91 (VEN) Lake Placid, FL Communidad Catolica Hispana Santiago Apostol (Santiago Mission); [I] Lake Placid, FL Campo San Jose; Hispanic, Migrant and Spanish Speaking Apostolates; Juventud Hispana (Hispanic Youth Ministry); Sebring, FL St. Catherine.
Gonzalez, Juan Francisco '94 (LA) Monrovia, CA Immaculate Conception.
Gonzalez, Juan J. *s.m.* '82 (BRK) Brooklyn, NY St. Francis of Assisi–St. Blaise.
Gonzalez, Juan Jose *m.sp.s.* '00 (P) Hillsboro, OR St. Matthew.
Gonzalez, Juan Jose Saliva '90 (PCE) Arroyo, PR Our Lady of Mt. Carmel.
Gonzalez, Juan *c.pp.s.* '76 (GRY) East Chicago, IN Our Lady of Guadalupe.
Gonzalez, Julio A. Vera '98 (MGZ) Moca, PR Our Lady of Monserrate.
Gonzalez, Julio Angel '98 (MO) Army National Guard Chaplains.
Gonzalez, Julio *s.f.* '00 (SFE) Chimayo, NM Holy Family.
Gonzalez, Julio '09 (LA) North Hollywood, CA St. Charles Borromeo.
Gonzalez, Lorenzo '03 (RCK) Woodstock, IL St. Mary.
Gonzalez, Lorenzo '01 (VEN) Moore Haven, FL St. Joseph the Worker.
Gonzalez, Luis O. '00 (NEW) Newark, NJ St. Columba's.
Gonzalez, Luis P. '94 (NEW) Newark, NJ Immaculate Conception; Newark, NJ Our Lady of Good Counsel.
Gonzalez, Marcos '94 (LA) Advisory Members to the Commission; Inglewood, CA St. John Chrysostom.
Gonzalez, Marcos '06 (MAN) Portsmouth, NH Corpus Christi Parish.
Gonzalez, Mario *o.s.a.* '58 (SJN) Bayamon, PR Ntra. Sra. de la Monserrate; [C] Bayamon, PR Seminario Agustiniano Sto. Tomas De Villanueva.
Gonzalez, Mario '55 (VEN) Retired.
Gonzalez, Miguel '98 (ORL) Vocations.
Gonzalez, Octavio '01 (PCE) Penuelas, PR St. Joseph.
Gonzalez, Octavio '01 (NEW) On Duty Outside the Archdiocese.
Gonzalez, Oreste '86 (NY)[JJ] Overlook Study Center.
Gonzalez, Orestes '86 (POD) New Rochelle.
Gonzalez, P. Carlos '04 (MGZ)[C] Mayaguez, PR Comunidad Belen.
Gonzalez, Primitivo '62 (LA) Maywood, CA St. Rose of Lima.
Gonzalez, Rafael J. *c.r.l.* '93 (ARE) Corozal, PR La Milagrosa.
Gonzalez, Rev. Msgr. Ricardo '57 (NEW) Orange, NJ St. John's Retired.
Gonzalez, Rudolph F. '87 (NY) Spring Valley, NY St. Joseph.
Gonzalez, Salvador '01 (FRS) Fresno, CA St. Helen; Priests' Council; Vocations.
Gonzalez, Salvador *o.m.i.* '03 (NOR)[G] Willimantic, CT Missionary Oblates of Mary Immaculate.
Gonzalez, Tomas '01 (SJN)[C] Rio Piedras, PR Seminario Mayor Regional San Juan Bautista.
Gonzalez, Victoriano *ss.cc.* (SJN) San Juan, PR San Juan M. Vianney.
Gonzalez, Vidal '09 (PAT) Passaic, NJ St. Anthony of Padua.
Gonzalez–Abreu, Hector '79 (MIA) Retired.
Gonzalez–Ballesteros, Rodolfo '88 (TR) Brick, NJ Visitation.
Gonzalez–Flores, Jose Duvan '96 (ATL) College of Consultors.
Gonzalez–Florez, Jose Duvan '96 (ATL) Alpharetta, GA St. Thomas Aquinas.
Gonzalez–Gaytan, Jose Enrique '03 (CHL) Boonville, NC Divine Redeemer (Divino Redentor).
Gonzalez–Gonzalez, Tomas '01 (SJN) Cursillos De Cristiandad.
Gonzalez–Hernandez, Marco Antonio '07 (R) Wilmington, NC St. Mark; Wilmington, NC Christ the King.
Gonzalez–Martinez, Eduardo '98 (DAL)[A] Dallas, TX The Redemptoris Mater House of Formation.
Gonzalez–Medina, Ruben *c.m.f.* (SJN) "El Visitante".
Gonzalez Chao, Luis '58 (SJN) Retired.
Gonzalez Pola, Antonio '63 (SJN)[A] Bayamon Central University.
Goode, Francis *o.p.* '80 (SFR) San Francisco, CA St. Dominic.
Goode, Francis *o.p.* '87 (SFR)[N] San Francisco, CA St. Dominic Priory.
Goode, James *o.f.m.* '72 (NY)[EE] New York, NY St. Clare Friary; Definitors:; [EE] New York, NY Franciscan Province of the Immaculate Conception; New York, NY Franciscan Province of the Immaculate Conception.
Goode, Rev. Msgr. Joseph J. '73 (PAT) Long Valley, NJ St. Mark the Evangelist; Canonical Advisor; Deans; Catholic Deaf Society.
Goode, Lawrence C. '64 (SFR) East Palo Alto, CA St. Francis of Assisi; [S] East Palo Alto, CA Legion of Mary.
Goode, Michael *c.pp.s.* '79 (KC)[N] Liberty, MO St. Gaspar Society; [A] Liberty, MO Precious Blood Center; [J] Liberty, MO Precious Blood Center; [N] Liberty, MO R.J. Stukenborg Corporation.
Goode, William F. '60 (WDC) Bowie, MD Ascension Retired.
Goodly, Timothy '93 (LKC) Lake Charles, LA Immaculate Conception Cathedral; Presbyteral Council; Diocesan Consultors.
Goodman, Julian '66 (RIC) Retired.
Goodman, Leo M. '91 (HBG) Lancaster, PA Assumption of the Blessed Virgin Mary; Presbyteral Council.
Goodrow, David C. (BO) Natick, MA St. Patrick.
Goodrum, James R. '57 (LFT) Associate Judges Retired.
Goodson, Todd Michael '02 (IND) Indianapolis, IN St. Monica; Council of Priests.
Goodwin, Calvin R. *f.s.s.p.* '79 (LIN)[A] Denton, NE Our Lady of Guadalupe Seminary; Denton, NE.
Goodwin, Christopher P. '04 (LIN) Advocates; Benkelman, NE St. Joseph's.
Goodwin, James '97 (FAR) Larimore, ND St. Stephen's Church of Larimore; Presbyteral Council; Judges.
Goodwin, Owen F. *ss.cc.* '54 (FR)[G] Fairhaven, MA Damien Residence Retired.
Goodwin, Patrick '69 (OAK) Oakland, CA St. Theresa of the Infant Jesus (The Little Flower).
Goodwin, Raymond M. '69 (WOR) North Grafton, MA St. Mary; Grafton, MA St. Philip's.
Goodwin, Robert T. '57 (MAN) Retired.
Goodwin, Thomas L. '85 (CC) Corpus Christi, TX St. Joseph.
Goodyear, Michael *l.c.* '94 (PHX)[H] Queen Creek, AZ John Paul II Catholic Newman Center; Queen Creek, AZ Our Lady of Guadalupe Roman Catholic Parish; [A] Scottsdale, AZ Notre Dame Preparatory Roman Catholic High School.
Goodyear, Robert *s.t.* '75 (JKS) Philadelphia, MS Holy Rosary; Approved Advocate and Auditors.
Gooley, Laurence L. *s.j.* '65 (SPK)[J] Spokane, WA Regis Community.
Gooley, Lawrence L. *s.j.* '65 (B) Priest River, ID St. Catherine's.
Goolsby, Gregory D. '93 (ATL) Alpharetta, GA St. Thomas Aquinas; Judges.
Goopio, Jose Rodriguez *s.v.d.* '73 (SB)[I] Riverside, CA Divine Word Seminary.
Gootee, Jason E. '99 (ALX)[I] Natchitoches, LA Northwestern State University; Nachitoches, LA Holy Cross.
Gootee, Paul *s.v.d.* '55 (FgM) Techny, IL.
Gopaul, Antonius P. '97 (BRK) Brooklyn, NY St. Thomas Aquinas.
Goraieb, Charles '91 (PHX) Mesa, AZ Queen of Peace Roman Catholic Parish; Tempe, AZ St. Margaret Roman Catholic Parish.
Gorantla, Charles *h.g.n.* '02 (FWT) Wichita Falls, TX Sacred Heart; Knox City, TX Santa Rosa; Megargel, TX St. Mary; Munday, TX St. Joseph; Seymour, TX Sacred Heart.
Gorap, George E. (BRK) Rosedale, NY St. Pius X.
Gorczyca, Andrzej *m.i.c.* (SPR)[H] Stockbridge, MA Congregation of Marian Fathers of The Immaculate Conception of the Most Blessed Virgin Mary.
Gorczyca, Grzegorz P. '05 (CHI) Palatine, IL St. Theresa.

Gordinier, William J. '58 (ROC) Retired.
Gordon, Charles *c.s.c.* '87 (FTW)[H] Notre Dame Congregation of Holy Cross, Indiana Province, Provincial House.
Gordon, Charles *s.t.* '67 (FgM) Silver Spring, MD MISSIONARY SERVANTS OF THE MOST HOLY TRINITY.
Gordon, Charles *c.s.c.* '87 (P)[B] University of Portland; [L] Portland, OR Holy Cross Fathers & Brothers, C.S.C. – University of Portland.
Gordon, Dennis *f.s.s.p.* '08 (SCR) Scranton, PA St. Michael's.
Gordon, Gerald R. *s.j.* '60 (SPK)[B] Spokane, WA Gonzaga University Retired.
Gordon, Gerald *t.o.r.* '69 (FWT) Fort Worth, TX St. Andrew; Fort Worth, TX St. Andrew.
Gordon, Rev. Msgr. Gregory W. '88 (LAV) On Duty Outside the Diocese.
Gordon, Jacob A. '06 (TOL) Delphos, OH St. John the Evangelist.
Gordon, James E. '81 (RIC) Chesapeake, VA St. Therese of Lisieux.
Gordon, James *i.c.* '69 (SP) Seminole, FL Blessed Sacrament.
Gordon, James *f.s.s.p.* '04 (KCK)[E] Maple Hill, KS St. John Vianney Preparatory School.
Gordon, John B. '85 (MET) Perth Amboy, NJ Our Lady of Hungary; Perth Amboy, NJ La Asuncion; [A] South Amboy, NJ Cardinal McCarrick High School.
Gordon, John F. '88 (NEW) Nutley, NJ Holy Family.
Gordon, John J. *o.m.i.* '01 (SAT) San Antonio, TX St. Mary.
Gordon, Joseph A. '71 (SFR) Retired.
Gordon, Kevin M. '83 (SUP) On Special or Other Diocesan Assignment; Presbyteral Council & Diocesan Consultors; Diocesan Coordinator of Health Affairs; Personnel Placement Board.
Gordon, Kevin M. '83 (SUP) Saxon, WI St. Ann.
Gordon, L. William '65 (OG) Chazy, NY Sacred Heart.
Gordon, Terrence *f.s.s.p.* (OM) Omaha, NE Immaculate Conception, B.V.M.
Gore, Robert D. '65 (BEL) Hecker, IL St. Augustine of Canterbury.
Gore, William R. *o.s.f.s.* '69 (FgM)[J] Wilmington, DE DeSales House; Wilmington, DE OBLATES OF ST. FRANCIS DE SALES MISSIONS.
Gorecho, Welthy '99 (WIL)[J] Dover, DE Oblate Apostles of the Two Hearts.
Gorena, Pedro *o.ss.t.* '66 (SJN) Bayamon, PR Ascension Del Senor; [F] Toa Alta, PR Hogar Santisima Trinidad.
Gorges, Bernard X. '95 (WCH) Chanute, KS St. Patrick; Humboldt, KS St. Joseph.
Gorges, Peter '68 (JUN) Diocesan Consultors Retired.
Gorgis, Noel '89 (LA) North Hollywood, CA St. Paul Assyrian–Chaldean.
Gorgis, Noel '89 (SPA) North Hollywood, CA St. Paul Assyrian–Chaldean Catholic Parish.
Gorham, Francis X. *o.m.i.* '58 (BO)[X] Tewksbury, MA Immaculate Heart of Mary Residence.
Gori, Peter G. *o.s.a.* (BO) Andover, MA St. Augustine; Court Advocate/Respondent; Canonical Affairs Committee; Presbyteral Council.
Gorka, Thaddeus '88 (PH) Philadelphia, PA St. Adalbert.
Gorman, Charles '54 (GF) Retired.
Gorman, Cyril *o.s.b.* '90 (SCL)[I] Collegeville St. John's Abbey, of the Order of St. Benedict.
Gorman, Edward M. *o.p.* '92 (NY) New York, NY St. Catherine of Siena; [II] New York, NY Dominican Shrine of St. Jude, Inc.
Gorman, Edward M. *o.p.* '92 (PRO)[P] Providence, RI St. Pius Priory; Providence, RI St. Pius V.
Gorman, Edward M. *o.p.* '92 (MO) Navy Reserve Chaplains.
Gorman, Rev. Msgr. Francis P. '59 (NY) Sleepy Hollow, NY St. Teresa of Avila.
Gorman, James P. '73 (PH) Philadelphia, PA Nativity of the Blessed Virgin Mary.
Gorman, James '81 (STP) Burnsville, MN Church of the Risen Savior.
Gorman, John E. *s.d.s.* '69 (MIL)[P] Milwaukee Salvatorian Provincial Offices.
Gorman, John '58 (SB) Retired.
Gorman, Joseph F. '55 (HRT) Waterbury, CT St. Leo the Great; Waterbury, CT St. Joseph; Waterbury, CT St. Patrick Retired.
Gorman, Kevin D. *o.s.b.* '51 (PEO)[A] Peru, IL St. Bede Abbey Retired.
Gorman, Michael J. '80 (LC) Diocesan Judges; Deans; St. Joseph's Priest Fund, Inc., (Benevolent Society); La Crosse, WI St. Joseph the Workman Cathedral; [C] La Crosse, WI Aquinas Catholic Schools.
Gorman, Richard F. '82 (NY)[E] Bronx, NY Cardinal Spellman High School.
Gorman, Robert G. '80 (MET) Old Bridge, NJ St. Ambrose.
Gorman, Rody Ignatius '55 (LA) Huntington Park, CA St. Matthias Retired.
Gorman, Thomas J. '59 (TOL) Retired.
Gorman, William A. '73 (ALB) Dolgeville, NY St. Joseph; Newport, NY St. John the Baptist.
Gorman, William N. '76 (MOB) Dauphin Island, AL St. Edmund–by–the–Sea.
Gormley, Brendan '07 (NY) Congers, NY St. Paul.
Gormley, Charles E. '51 (PH) Bala Cynwyd, PA St. Matthias Retired.
Gormley, Eugene *l.c.* '83 (MAD)[F] Edgerton, WI Koshkonong Pastoral Center; [I] Edgerton, WI Oaklawn Incorporated.
Gormley, George *s.v.d.* '07 (BLX)[D] Bay St. Louis, MS Southern Province of St. Augustine – Provincial Offices; Bay Saint Louis, MS; [D] Bay St. Louis, MS St. Augustine's Residence.
Gormley, Gerard '85 (SR) Arcata, CA St. Mary's.
Gormley, James W. '54 (PH) Retired.
Gormley, Kevin '64 (JC) Marshall, MO St. Peter; Marshall, MO Marshall State School–Hospital.
Gormley, Raymond P. '92 (CAM) Runnemede, NJ Church of St. Teresa of the Infant Jesus, Runnemede, N.J.; Representatives by Deaneries; Camden South Deanery.
Gormley, William J. *c.m.* '49 (PH)[Y].
Gorney, Joseph *c.ss.r.* '51 (ORL)[F] New Smyrna Beach, FL St. Alphonsus Villa–Redemptorist Fathers and Brothers Retired.
Gorny, Ed *g.h.m.* '68 (CIN)[N] Cincinnati Headquarters of Glenmary Home Missioners Retired.
Gorny, Edward V. *g.h.m.* '68 (SAV) Retired.
Gorospe, Paterno '66 (NEW) Teaneck, NJ Holy Name Hospital; [G] School of Nursing.
Gorowski, Roman *c.m.* '72 (HRT) Derby, CT St. Michael the Archangel.
Gorsic, Gregor '97 (JOL) Romeoville, IL St. Andrew the Apostle.
Gorski, Eugene F. *c.s.c.* '60 (FTW)[B] University of Notre Dame Du Lac; [H] Notre Dame, IN Holy Cross Community, Corby Hall, University of Notre Dame.
Gorski, Rev. Msgr. J. Donald '59 (CHR) Retired.
Gorski, John F. *m.m.* '63 (FgM) Maryknoll, NY MARYKNOLL.
Gorski, John J. '64 (CLV) Avon, OH Holy Trinity Retired.
Gorski, Lawrence E. '75 (CHI) Chicago, IL Our Lady of Grace.
Gorski, Robert E. '80 (MAN) Manchester, NH St. Pius X; Long Range Planning Committee; College of Consultors; Priest Personnel Board; Propagation of the Faith; Moderator of the Curia; Presbyteral Council; Real Estate Board.
Gorski, Terrence *o.f.m.* '75 (BWN) Grulla, TX Holy Family.
Gorton, Timothy J. '82 (PRO) Woonsocket, RI St. Agatha; Woonsocket, RI Precious Blood.
Gosciniak, Dariusz '92 (HRT) Cheshire, CT Manson Youth Institution; New Britain, CT Holy Cross.
Gosma, Robert D. '59 (MIL) Burlington, WI Immaculate Conception Retired.
Gosnell, David H. '65 (GRY) Retired.
Gosnell, Stephen D. '78 (BAL) Special Assignment.
Goss, Francis G. '47 (BO) Senior Priests. Retired.
Gosselin, Rev. Msgr. Homer P. '69 (SPR) Vicars for the Clergy; Ludlow, MA St. John the Baptist.
Gosselin, Joseph *m.s.* '65 (LKC) Sulphur, LA Our Lady of Prompt Succor.
Gosselin, Larry *o.f.m.* '81 (MRY)[F] San Miguel, CA Novitiate House for the Franciscan Friars, O.F.M.; [H] San Miguel, CA San Miguel Retreat House; [F] San Miguel, CA Franciscan Friars, O.F.M.; San Miguel, CA San Miguel.
Gosselin, Rt. Rev. Lawrence '76 (NTN) Lansing, MI St. Joseph; Presbyteral Council.
Gosselin, Richard R. '59 (BO) Senior Priests. Retired.
Gossman, John A. '71 (DUB) Marion, IA St. Joseph; Mount Vernon, IA St. John the Baptist; Springville, IA St. Isidore; Anamosa, IA St. Patrick; Deans; Vocation Awareness Advisory Committee.
Goth, Dennis J. '84 (LFT) Muncie, IN St. Lawrence.
Gothe, Marcus '59 (P) Retired.
Gothie, George J. '67 (PAT) Hopatcong, NJ St. Jude's.
Gothman, Augie '93 (CR) Pastoral Office of Worship/RCIA; Vocations; Catechumenal Commission; Commission on Building and Planning; Commission on Liturgy, Sacred Music and Art.
Gothman, August '93 (CR) Priests' Personnel Board.
Gotimer, Rev. Msgr. James E. '53 (BRK) Retired.
Gott, Camillus *o.f.m.conv.* '60 (SAT)[B] San Antonio, TX San Damiano Friary, Prenovitiate House of Formation; [L] San Antonio, TX San Damiano Friary.
Gotta, Paul A. '06 (HRT) Hamden, CT St. Rita; [Q] New Haven, CT Southern Connecticut State University Catholic Center.
Gottemoeller, Mark '76 (IND) Mooresville, IN St. Thomas More.
Gottschalk, David *o.f.m.cap.* '69 (DEN)[N] Denver, CO St. Francis of Assisi Friary.
Gottschalk, Matthew *o.f.m.cap.* '53 (MIL)[Y] Milwaukee, WI House of Peace.
Gotwalt, Joseph F. '65 (HBG) Hanover, PA St. Joseph; Deans.
Goudreau, George W. '48 (PRT) Retired.
Goudreau, Rev. Msgr. Joseph L. '63 (PRT) Retired.
Goudreau, Paul '60 (SP) Retired.
Goudreau, William G. *s.j.* '52 (FgM) Detroit, MI Detroit Province.
Gouger, John *c.ss.r.* '65 (FgM) Denver, CO Denver Province.
Gouin, Joseph O. '65 (MAR) Kingsford, MI American Martyrs.
Gould, Clayton '81 (LR) Dardanelle, AR St. Augustine.
Gould, Rev. Msgr. James C. *s.j.* '74 (MI) Former Prelate.
Gould, James C. *s.j.* '74 (FgM) New York, NY Society of Jesus.
Gould, James R. '81 (ARL) Springfield, VA St. Raymond of Penafort.
Gould, Lawrence *s.a.c.* '76 (MO) DEPARTMENT OF VETERANS AFFAIRS HOSPITALS AND CHAPLAINS.
Gould, Lawrence *s.a.c.* '76 (SFR) San Francisco, CA St. Monica; Veterans' Hospital.
Gould, Louis J. '62 (WOR) Retired.
Gould, Michael A. *m.m.* '54 (FgM) Maryknoll, NY MARYKNOLL.
Gould, William R. '65 (B) Post Falls, ID St. George's.
Goulding, Laurence B. *g.h.m.* '62 (LEX) Grayson, KY Ss. John & Elizabeth.
Goulding, Laurence *g.h.m.* '62 (COV) Vanceburg, KY Holy Redeemer.
Goulding, Laurence *g.h.m.* '62 (CIN)[N] Cincinnati Headquarters of Glenmary Home Missioners Retired.
Gouldrick, John W. *c.m.* '69 (PH)[Y].
Gouldrick, John W. *c.m.* '69 (FgM) Philadelphia, PA Eastern Province.
Goulet, Daniel '07 (BAL) Frederick, MD St. John the Evangelist.
Goulet, Raymond O. '57 (BO) Senior Priests. Retired.
Goulet, Wayne F. '74 (PHX) On Leave.
Goulet, Xavier *o.f.m.conv.* (TOL) Carey, OH Our Lady of Consolation, Basilica–National Shrine.
Gousse, Paul M. '99 (MAN) Gonic, NH St. Leo; Rochester, NH Our Lady of the Holy Rosary.
Gouthro, Arthur *s.a.* '69 (NY)[EE] Garrison Franciscan Friars of the Atonement, Minister General Office.
Governale, Russell *o.f.m.conv.* '88 (BRK) Brooklyn, NY Immaculate Heart of Mary.
Governale, Russell *o.f.m.conv.* '88 (WDC)[B] Forestville, MD St. Bonaventure Friary.
Govin, Lazarus J. '08 (MIA) Coral Springs, FL St. Andrew.
Govindu, Balaswamy '77 (SFR) South San Francisco, CA St. Augustine.
Govorchin, Vincent '55 (SLC) Retired.
Gow, John '08 (RCK) Cary, IL SS. Peter & Paul.
Gowen, Daniel F. '89 (TR) Highlands, NJ Our Lady of Perpetual Help.
Gower, James M. '53 (PRT) Retired.
Gower, Peter J. '84 (PRO) Warren, RI St. Jean Baptiste; Warren, RI St. Mary of the Bay.
Goyette, Giles R. *o.mar.* '82 (SAM)[B] Petersham, MA Maronite Monks of Adoration Most Holy Trinity Monastery.
Goyette, Michael J. '04 (CAM) Continuing Education & Spiritual Formation of Priests (CESF); On Leave of Absence.
Goyo, Jimwell '89 (DAL) Dallas, TX St. James.
Gozaloff, Rev. Msgr. Paul J. '56 (WDC) Retired.
Graap, Augustin (NY) Poughkeepsie, NY Our Lady Health of the Sick.
Graap, Augustine *o.carm.* '66 (NY) Warwick, NY Mid–Orange Correctional Facility; Otisville, NY Otisville Correctional Facility; Poughkeepsie, NY Hudson River Psychiatric Center.
Grab, Michael J. '77 (HBG) Enola, PA Our Lady of Lourdes.
Grabara, Tomasz *m.s.f.* '95 (SAT) Seguin, TX Our Lady of Guadalupe.
Grabert, Colman *o.s.b.* '65 (IND)[K] St. Meinrad, IN St. Meinrad Archabbey.
Grabish, Rev. Msgr. John J. '72 (ALN) Allentown, PA Sacred Heart of Jesus.
Grabner, Donald *o.s.b.* '54 (KC)[A] Conception, MO Conception Seminary College; [J] Maryville, MO.
Grabner, Eugene W. '59 (WCH) Retired.
Grabner, Kenneth E. *c.s.c.* '60 (FTW)[H] Notre Dame, IN Holy Cross Village; [H] Notre Dame Congregation of Holy Cross, Indiana Province, Provincial House.
Grabner, Robert J. '00 (STP) South St. Paul, MN St. Augustine.
Grabowski, Dennis '76 (Y) Retired.
Grabowski, Eugene M. '89 (R) Retired.
Grabowski, Walter P. '81 (BUF) Eden, NY Immaculate Conception.
Grabowsky, Rev. Msgr. Myron '67 (PHU) Special Assignment.
Grabrian, Dennis '70 (COS) On Duty Outside Diocese.
Grabrian, John '70 (DEN) Lakewood, CO Christ on the Mountain Parish.
Grace, Edward D. '67 (CHI) Chicago, IL Queen of All Saints Basilica.
Grace, Gerald '65 (PMB) Advocates; Highland Beach, FL St. Lucy; Consultors; Elected Members.
Grace, Hugh R. '64 (NY) Wesley Hills, NY St. Boniface.

Grace, James N. '59 (CHI) Retired.
Grace, John A. '79 (RIC) Blacksburg, VA St. Mary.
Grace, John J. '48 (SAC) South Lake Tahoe, CA St. Theresa Retired.
Grace, John J. (CHI) Retired.
Grace, John M. '88 (MAN) Nashua, NH Parish of the Resurrection.
Grace, John *o.s.a.* '62 (ORG) Special Assignment.
Grace, Joseph W. '53 (LFT) U.S. Veteran's Hospital; DEPARTMENT OF VETERANS AFFAIRS HOSPITALS AND CHAPLAINS Retired.
Grace, Patrick J.T. '79 (BRK) Brooklyn, NY Good Shepherd.
Grace, Patrick '79 (RVC) Serving Outside the Diocese.
Grace, Peter *c.p.* '72 (BRK)[T] Jamaica, NY Immaculate Conception Monastery.
Grace, Thomas A. *c.m.* '64 (STL)[O] Perryville, MO Congregation of the Mission.
Gracey, John '93 (FRS) Bishop, CA Our Lady of Perpetual Help.
Gracz, Rev. Msgr. Henry C. '65 (ATL) Atlanta, GA Shrine of the Immaculate Conception; Advocates; Vicars for Clergy.
Graczyk, Carl *o.f.m.* '73 (PH) Philadelphia, PA St. Jerome; [Y] Philadelphia, PA St. Pius X Residence.
Graczyk, Randolph *o.f.m.cap.* '68 (GF) Pryor, MT St. Charles Borromeo Church.
Graden, John *o.s.f.s.* '76 (BUF)[T] Stella Niagara, NY DeSales Resources and Ministries, Inc.
Gradilone, Rev. Msgr. Thomas J. '50 (BRK)[T] Douglaston, NY Bishop Mugavero Residence Retired.
Grady, Bernard C. '68 (DUB) Hampton, IA St. Patrick; Hampton, IA St. Mary; Deans; Personnel Advisory Board; Stewardship Committee.
Grady, Brian D. '00 (RCK) Crystal Lake, IL St. Elizabeth Ann Seton.
Grady, Francis J. *s.s.c.* '63 (CHI) Forest Park, IL St. Bernardine.
Grady, Francis *s.s.c.* '63 (OM)[K] St. Columbans Missionary Society of St. Columban.
Grady, John P. *m.m.* '55 (NY)[EE] Retired.
Grady, Michael '94 (MIA) Hollywood, FL Nativity.
Grady, Peter W. '53 (FAR) Retired.
Graef, Rev. Msgr. Franz '57 (SHP) Judges; Censor of Books; Hodge, LA St. Lucy Retired.
Graehler, Kenneth '63 (EVN) Retired.
Graf, Gary M. '84 (CHI) Chicago, IL St. Gall; Waukegan, IL Most Blessed Trinity.
Graf, Harold P. '68 (PHX) Retired.
Graf, Henry C. '49 (PH) Retired.
Graf, James W. '72 (L) Springfield, KY Holy Rosary; Ex Officio; Raywick, KY St. Francis Xavier Church.
Graf, Rev. Msgr. John W. '74 (PH) West Grove, PA Assumption B.V.M.
Graf, Paul '82 (LFT)[C] Lafayette, IN St. Elizabeth Central.
Graf, William E. '60 (ROC) Censores Librorum; Staff; Ministry to Priests Retired.
Graf, William '60 (ROC) Retired.
Graff, Francis C. '65 (PIT) Retired.
Graff, Joseph P. '76 (GAY) Harbor Springs, MI Holy Cross; Harbor Springs, MI St. Ignatius; Harbor Springs, MI Holy Childhood of Jesus; Cross Village, MI St. Nicholas; Ecumenical and Interreligious Affairs, Delegate for.
Graff, Timothy G. '85 (FgM) Maryknoll, NY MARYKNOLL.
Graffis, Joseph T. '71 (L) Louisville, KY St. Edward.
Grafsky, George J. '71 (STP) Le Sueur, MN St. Anne.
Graham, Bill *o.f.m.cap.* (BAL) Baltimore, MD St. Ambrose.
Graham, Edgar *s.j.* '54 (PH)[Y] Loyola Center and Manresa Hall.
Graham, George Nelson (LC) New Lisbon, WI Our Lady of the Lake; New Lisbon, WI St. Paul.
Graham, Rev. Msgr. George P. '52 (RVC) Levittown, NY St. Bernard; Censors of Books; Judges for Interdiocesan Tribunal; Priests' Retirement Board; Catholic Lawyer's Guild Retired.
Graham, Rev. Msgr. George P. '52 (ALB) Interdiocesan Tribunal for the Province of NY Archdiocese.
Graham, J. David '91 (MEM) Memphis, TN St. Anne's.
Graham, James G. '66 (PIT) Pittsburgh, PA St. Lawrence O'Toole.
Graham, Rev. Msgr. James J. '73 (PH) Havertown, PA St. Denis; Archdiocesan Judges.
Graham, James K. '93 (SJ) San Jose, CA St. Elias; San Jose, CA St. John Vianney.
Graham, Jerry *sj* '00 (SEA) La Conner, WA St. Paul.
Graham, John J. '90 (BO) Arlington, MA Saint Agnes.
Graham, Rev. Msgr. John K. '74 (NY) Bronx, NY St. Raymond; Canon 1742 Panel of Pastors.
Graham, John *c.ss.r.* '53 (ALB)[L] Saratoga Springs, NY St. John Neumann Residence.
Graham, Joseph B. '63 (PH) Philadelphia, PA St. Jerome.
Graham, Michael J. *s.j.* '88 (CIN)[D] Cincinnati, OH Xavier University; [N] Cincinnati, OH Jesuit Community at Xavier University.
Graham, Rev. Msgr. Neil '59 (NY) White Plains, NY St. John the Evangelist.
Graham, Robert *s.m.* '50 (BO)[W] Framingham, MA The Marist House.
Graham, Rev. Msgr. Thomas A. '62 (BRK) Rosedale, NY St. Pius X.
Graham, Thomas D. '48 (PH) Retired.
Graham, Walter F. *c.m.* '49 (BRK)[T] Jamaica, NY Vincentian Residence Retired.
Graham, Rev. Msgr. William P. '65 (CAM) Retired.
Graham, William *o.f.m.cap.* '72 (WDC)[B] Washington, DC St. Francis Friary–Capuchin College.
Graham, William *o.f.m.cap.* (BAL) Judicial Vicar; [S] Baltimore, MD St. Ambrose Friary.
Grajeda, Miguel Angel '97 (MRY) Watsonville, CA St. Patrick; Clergy Personnel Board.
Grajek, Lawrence '57 (SB) Retired.
Grala, Paul E. *s.o.l.t.* '95 (SAT) Harper, TX St. Anthony's.
Grala, Paul *s.o.l.t.* '95 (CC)[G] Robstown, TX Society of Our Lady of the Most Holy Trinity.
Gralapp, Robert W. '64 (SC) Manilla, IA Sacred Heart; Manning, IA Sacred Heart.
Gramaje, Arhtur *c.m.f.* '94 (PHX) Prescott, AZ Sacred Heart Roman Catholic Parish.
Gramata, Raymond '70 (E) Meadville, PA St. Agatha.
Grambow, Arnold J. '69 (MAR) Gladstone, MI All Saints; Executive Board.
Gramigna, Francis J. '64 (CAM) Retired.
Gramlich, Anthony *m.i.c.* '02 (SPR)[H] The National Shrine of The Divine Mercy; [H] Stockbridge, MA Congregation of Marian Fathers of The Immaculate Conception of the Most Blessed Virgin Mary.
Grams, Rev. Msgr. Douglas L. '87 (NU) New Ulm, MN St. Mary; Vicar General; Associate Judges; College of Consultors; Committee on Parishes; Corporate Board; Priest Personnel; Priest Personnel Board; Bishop's Delegate in Matters Pertaining to Sexual Misconduct; Board of Trustees for Pension Plan for Priests; On Special or Other Diocesan Assignment; Priests' Council.
Gramza, Ronald J. '73 (MIL) Racine, WI St. Richard of Chichester.
Granadino, David F. '81 (LA) On Administrative Leave.
Granado, Jason '08 (AGN) Agat, GU Our Lady of Mount Carmel.
Granados, Carlos E. '88 (ARE) Vega Baja, PR N.S. de la Providencia.
Granados, John J. '98 (BRK) Brooklyn, NY Our Lady of Guadalupe.
Granata, Rev. Msgr. Joseph P. '75 (RVC) Huntington Station, NY St. Hugh of Lincoln.
Granato, John *s.m.* '06 (BO) Boston, MA Our Lady of Victories; [U] Boston, MA Marist Fathers of Our Lady of Victories (Boston Prov.).
Granato, Rev. Msgr. Joseph J. '55 (NEW) Newark, NJ St. Lucy's.
Granato, Rev. Msgr. Joseph J. '66 (NEW) Retired.
Grancini, Steven M. *c.r.s.p.* '57 (SD) San Diego, CA Our Lady of the Rosary.
Grande, Kenneth J. '78 (BRK) Brooklyn, NY St. Nicholas.
Grandon, Douglas A. '08 (PEO) Moline, IL Sacred Heart.
Grandpre, Louis '61 (DET) Retired.
Grandstrand, Charles P. '66 (NEW) Bergen Pascack Valley Deanery 2P.
Graner, Thomas '94 (FAR) Rugby, ND St. Mary's Church of Knox; Rugby, ND St. Theresa, Little Flower Church of Rugby; Rural Life.
Graney, William F. '71 (WIL) Wilmington, DE Parish of the Resurrection.
Granfield, David *o.s.b.* '52 (WDC)[N] Washington, DC St. Anselm's Abbey.
Granfield, Patrick *o.s.b.* '57 (WDC)[C] Catholic University of America, The; [N] Washington, DC St. Anselm's Abbey Retired.
Grange, John O. '66 (NY) Bronx, NY St. Athanasius.
Granich, Rev. Msgr. Bernard E. '53 (STL) Retired.
Granillo, Paul C. '97 (SB) On Leave of Absence.
Granito, Mark E. '98 (SFE) Tijeras, NM Holy Child.
Grankauskas, Paul M. '00 (ARL) Arlington, VA St. Ann; Notaries.
Grankowski, Zbigniew '83 (DET) Detroit, MI St. Cunegunda; Dearborn, MI St. Barbara.
Granstrand, Charles P. '66 (NEW) Park Ridge, NJ Our Lady of Mercy; Bergen Pascack Valley Deanery 2P.
Grant, Benedict *f.p.o.* '08 (BO)[U] Lawrence, MA Franciscans of Primitive Observance.
Grant, Frederick A. '62 (BO) Senior Priests. Retired.
Grant, James A. '66 (PH) Warrington, PA St. Joseph.
Grant, Jeffery A. '82 (SFD) Decatur, IL Saints James and Patrick Parish; Board of Catholic Education.
Grant, Paul '84 (CHI) Chicago; [V] Chicago, IL Northview University Center.
Grant, Robert J. '93 (HRT) Hartford, CT St. Augustine.
Grant, Robert L. '80 (DAV)[A] St. Ambrose University; Blue Grass, IA St. Andrew.
Grant, Robert '84 (DM) On Duty Outside the Diocese.
Grant, W. Douglas '80 (PRO) North Providence, RI Mary, Mother of Mankind.
Grant, William D. '86 (LIN) Evangelization Committee; Apostolate to the Spanish Speaking.
Grant, William David '86 (LIN) Lincoln, NE Cristo Rey; Lincoln, NE St. Joseph.
Grantz, Leon *c.p.* '46 (L)[L] Louisville, KY Sacred Heart Retreat.
Granzotto, Peter *s.d.b.* '57 (NY) Port Chester, NY Corpus Christi.
Grappoli, Frank B. *s.x.* '63 (FgM)[N] Wayne, NJ Xaverian Missionary Fathers; Wayne, NJ XAVERIAN MISSIONARY FATHERS.
Grasher, Al '86 (SPK) Deer Park, WA St. Mary Presentation.
Grasing, John '88 (WIL) Middletown, DE St. Joseph.
Grass, Aloysius P. *c.m.* '51 (PH)[Y].
Grassel, Martin *o.s.b.* '04 (P)[L] St. Benedict, OR Mt. Angel Abbey; [Q] St. Benedict, OR The Abbey Foundation of Oregon.
Grasselli, Rev. Msgr. Renato '94 (NEW)[A] Kearny, NJ Redemptoris Mater Archdiocesan Missionary Seminary; Members; [Q] Kearny, NJ Eucharistic Shrine of the Adorable Face of Jesus.
Grassi, Dominic J. '73 (CHI) Chicago, IL St. Gertrude.
Grassi, Timothy J. '00 (WH) Thomas, WV St. Thomas Aquinas.
Grassl, Joseph A. '50 (LC) Mosinee, WI St. Francis Xavier; Mosinee, WI St. John the Baptist.
Grasso, Aldo *o.s.j.* '44 (MRY)[F] Shrine of St. Joseph.
Grasso, Anthony R. *c.s.c.* '78 (SCR)[C] Holy Cross Community.
Grasso, Joseph A. *c.pp.s.* '91 (MO) DEPARTMENT OF VETERANS AFFAIRS HOSPITALS AND CHAPLAINS.
Grasso, Philip A. '43 (MAD) Retired.
Grasso, Richard '63 (PAT) On Duty Outside the Diocese.
Grathwohl, John M. '55 (KAL) Kalamazoo, MI Retired.
Gratkowski, Eugene W. '67 (CHI) River Grove, IL St. Cyprian.
Grattaroti, Robert A. '62 (WOR) Charlton City, MA St. Joseph's; Cursillo.
Gratto, Stephen H. '73 (OG) Port Leyden, NY St. Martin.
Grauls, Paul *s.d.b.* '62 (WDC) Washington, DC Nativity.
Grave de Peralta, Miguel '96 (NTN) Augusta, GA St. Ignatios of Antioch.
Graven, Thomas J. '68 (STU) Maynard, OH St. Joseph; Maynard, OH St. Stanislaus.
Graves, Clarence Edwin '92 (LR) Wynne, AR St. Peter.
Graves, Edwin '92 (LR) Wynne, AR St. Mary Church.
Grawe, Michael *o.f.m.* '70 (STL)[O] St. Louis, MO Franciscan Friary of St. Anthony of Padua.
Gray, Brian M. '86 (BGP) Leave of Absence.
Gray, Daniel J. '76 (PRO) Portsmouth, RI St. Anthony.
Gray, Edward J. *c.ss.r.* '58 (ORL) New Smyrna Beach, FL Sacred Heart.
Gray, Howard J. *s.j.* '55 (WDC)[N] Washington, DC The Jesuit Community at Georgetown University.
Gray, James C. '88 (STL) Maplewood, MO Immaculate Conception; Barnes – Jewish Hospital.
Gray, Rev. Msgr. Jason A. '97 (PEO) Judges; Peoria, IL St. Vincent De Paul.
Gray, Rev. Msgr. Jason '97 (PEO) Judicial Vicar.
Gray, John W. '58 (PRO) Retired.
Gray, John '86 (PT) Ecumenical & Interreligious Affairs, Office of Retired.
Gray, Jude J. *o.s.b.* '68 (MAN)[K] Manchester, NH St. Anselm Abbey.
Gray, Kevin J. '84 (HRT) Waterbury, CT Sacred Heart–Sagrado Corazon; [S] Waterbury, CT Spanish–Speaking Center.
Gray, Michael '08 (LFT) Lafayette, IN St. Lawrence.
Gray, Peter W. *s.s.* '79 (BAL)[S] Baltimore Society of St. Sulpice, Province of the United States.
Gray, Rev. Msgr. Philip A. '60 (SCR) Diocesan Building Commission; [N] Dunmore, PA Villa St. Joseph Retired.
Gray, Richard *m.s.a.* '03 (NOR)[G] Cromwell Society of the Missionaries of the Holy Apostles.
Gray, Richard *m.s.a.* (BAL) Frederick, MD St. John the Evangelist; Baltimore, MD St. Rita.
Gray, Robert B. '57 (L) Louisville, KY St. Elizabeth of Hungary; Louisville, KY St. Therese Retired.
Gray, Robert '88 (SJ) On Leave of Absence.
Gray, Sherman '70 (BGP) Leave of Absence.
Gray, Timothy *s.c.j.* '78 (JKS) Southaven, MS Christ the King; Hernando, MS Holy Spirit; Senatobia, MS St. Gregory the Great; [E] Nesbit, MS St. Michael Community House; Robinsonville, MS Good Shepherd Catholic Church.
Graziadio, Rev. Msgr. Domenick T. '66 (RVC) Plainview, NY St. Pius X; Judges for Interdiocesan Tribunal.
Graziano, Damien '67 (JOL) Propagation of the Faith.
Graziano, George R. *s.j.* '59 (FgM) New York, NY Society of Jesus.
Graziano, Gerard J. '61 (NEW) Hackensack, NJ Immaculate Conception.
Graziano, J. Damien '67 (JOL) Oakbrook Terrace, IL Ascension of Our Lord.
Graziano, Peter N. '63 (FR) Retired.
Grazulis, Antanas *s.j.* '78 (LIT) Lithuanian Jesuit Province.
Grazulis, Antanas *s.j.* '78 (CHI)[N] Lemont, IL Baltic

Jesuits Advancement Office.
Grbavac, Charbel *o.praem.* '06 (ORG) Council of Priests; [I] Silverado, CA Norbertine Fathers of Orange Inc.
Grbes, Jozo *o.f.m.* '93 (CHI) Chicago, IL St. Jerome; Councilors:.
Greaney, Thomas M. *o.s.m.* '70 (CHI)[N] Chicago Order of Friar Servants of Mary (Servites) United States of America Province, Inc.
Greatorex, Robert W. '57 (LC)[I] Stevens Point, WI St. Joseph Motherhouse Retired.
Greaves, Gerald F. '74 (NEW) Livingston, NJ St. Raphael.
Greaves, John G. '58 (PRO) Retired.
Greb, John '06 (PHX) Phoenix, AZ St. Joseph Roman Catholic Parish.
Greb, Michael P. *o.f.m.cap.* '89 (PIT) Freedom, PA St. Felix; Rochester, PA St. Cecilia; [M] Beaver, PA St. Fidelis Friary.
Grecco, Robert J. '93 (PIT) Pittsburgh, PA Sacred Heart.
Greco, Anthony F. '79 (WIL) Ocean City, MD St. Mary, Star of the Sea.
Greco, Evan *o.f.m.* (PAT)[L] Totowa, NJ St. Joseph's Home for the Elderly.
Greco, Michael *o.f.m.cap.* '06 (BRK)[T] Brooklyn, NY St. Michael's Friary.
Greco, Raymond *o.s.b.* '63 (MRY)[F] San Luis Obispo, CA Men's Residence Retired.
Greco, Robert *o.carm.* '55 (NY) Middletown, NY Our Lady of Mt. Carmel.
Greeley, Andrew M. '54 (CHI) Retired.
Greeley, Rev. Msgr. Joseph F. '74 (LA) Lakewood, CA St. Pancratius.
Green, Bernard *s.d.s.* '73 (PHX) Tempe, AZ Our Lady of Mt. Carmel Roman Catholic Parish.
Green, Charles C. '95 (WDC) Washington, DC St. Augustine Retired.
Green, David E. '88 (PRO) Warwick, RI St. Kevin.
Green, Fred J. *s.j.* '58 (FgM) Los Gatos, CA Society of Jesus.
Green, Rev. Msgr. Gerard L. '56 (BUF) Council of Priests Retired.
Green, Gregory A. *c.s.c.* '62 (FTW)[B] University of Notre Dame Du Lac; [H] Notre Dame, IN Holy Cross Community, Corby Hall, University of Notre Dame.
Green, Michael R. *o.s.b.* '70 (DET)[K] Detroit, MI St. Sylvester Monastery; [B] Oxford, MI St. Benedict Monastery; Detroit, MI St. Scholastica.
Green, Romuald *o.f.m.* '55 (WDC) Washington, DC; [N] Washington, DC Franciscan Monastery USA Inc.
Green, Ronald L. '96 (MRY) Nipomo, CA St. Joseph.
Green, Ronald L. *m.m.* '85 (NY)[EE] Maryknoll Maryknoll Fathers and Brothers.
Green, Rev. Msgr. Thomas J. '63 (BGP) On Duty Outside the Diocese; [C] Catholic University of America, The.
Green, Thomas P. *s.j.* '61 (NY) New York, NY St. Aloysius.
Green, William H. '63 (SUP) Retired.
Greene, Daniel '58 (YAK) Retired.
Greene, Gordon L. '94 (KAL) Watervliet, MI St. Joseph.
Greene, John C. '85 (GAY) Special Assignment.
Greene, John L. '76 (SFR) San Francisco, CA St. Monica; San Francisco Fire Department.
Greene, Michael M. '79 (BRK) On Leave/Unassigned.
Greene, Michael *c.p.* '82 (NY)[EE] Riverdale, NY Passionist Spiritual Center; [GG] Bronx, NY The Passionist Spiritual Center/Cardinal Spellman Retreat House.
Greene, Padraig '76 (OAK) Pleasanton, CA The Catholic Community of Pleasanton.
Greene, Rev. Msgr. Richard '65 (LAF) New Iberia, LA Sacred Heart of Jesus.
Greene, Thomas P. *s.j.* '07 (FgM)[W] Washington, DC Jesuit Missions, Inc.; [W] Washington, DC Jesuit Social and International Ministries–National Office; Washington, DC National Headquarters; Washington, DC.
Greene, Thomas P. *s.j.* '07 (NO)[C] New Orleans, LA Loyola University New Orleans.
Greene, Rev. Msgr. William L. '50 (BR) Judges Retired.
Greenfield, David '08 (MAD) Madison, WI St. Maria Goretti.
Greenfield, James J. *o.s.f.s.* '90 (WDC)[T] Washington, DC George Washington Univ. Newman Center; Wilmington, DE.
Greenfield, James J. *o.s.f.s.* '90 (WIL) Wilmington, DE Oblates of St. Francis de Sales (O.S.F.S.); [P] Wilmington, DE Brisson Fund; [J] Wilmington, DE Wilmington–Philadelphia Province of the Oblates of St. Francis de Sales.
Greenhalgh, Donald C. '84 (ARL) Arlington, VA St. Ann.
Greenlaw, Martin F. '68 (SFR) Retired.
Greenleaf, Daniel P. '95 (PRT) Special or Other Diocesan Assignment.
Greenleaf, Daniel (WDC)[A] Washington, DC Theological College of the Catholic University of America.
Greenough, Patrick *o.f.m.conv.* '87 (CHI)[N] Chicago, IL Conventual Franciscans of St. Bonaventure Province; [P] Libertyville, IL Marytown, U.S. National Center of the Militia of the Immaculata Movement; Chicago, IL Province of Saint Bonaventure; Chicago, IL.
Greenough, Patrick *o.f.m.conv.* '87 (DET)[K] Dearborn Heights, MI All Saints Friary.
Greenway, George G. '87 (SPR) Retired.
Greenway, George G. '87 (SAV) Retired.
Greenwell, Charles C. '82 (SAN) San Angelo, TX Holy Angels; Defensores Vinculi.
Greenwell, Joseph M. *c.ss.r* '48 (STL)[O] Liguori, MO St. Clement Health Care Center Retired.
Greenwell, Michael *o.carm.* '79 (JOL)[L] Darien Carmelite Provincial Office.
Greenwell, Michael *o.carm.* '79 (SFR) Kaiser Hospital San Francisco; St. Mary's Medical Center; [J] San Francisco, CA St. Mary's Medical Center.
Greer, Austin *o.p.* (GAL) Houston, TX Holy Rosary.
Greer, Bradley '09 (STU) St. Clairsville, OH St. Mary's.
Greer, G. Michael '81 (COV) Covington, KY St. John.
Greer, Michael '75 (MIA) Miami, FL Good Shepherd; Spiritual Moderators; Worship & Spiritual Life Commission.
Grega, Bernard F. '62 (ALT) Colver, PA Holy Family.
Gregoire, Paul L. '55 (MAN) Retired.
Gregoire, Wilfrid G. '56 (PRO) Westerly, RI Immaculate Conception.
Gregor, Robert M. *c.p.m.* '00 (L)[D] Louisville, KY Holy Angels Academy, Inc.
Gregorek, Joseph C. '65 (E)[B] Erie, PA Gannon University; Deans.
Gregorek, Stan M. '66 (PIT) Cecil, PA St. Mary; [Q] Wildwood, PA Cursillo Movement–Diocese of Pittsburgh.
Gregori, Anthony F. '53 (GF) Retired.
Gregori, Emidio O. '58 (BGP) Retired.
Gregorie, Jocelyn *c.s.sp.* '86 (PIT)[B] Pittsburgh, PA Duquesne University of the Holy Spirit.
Gregorio, Juan J. *s.d.b.* '56 (MGZ) San Antonio, PR San Jose Obrero.
Gregorio, Robert J. '68 (CAM) Serra Clubs International; Marmora, NJ Church of the Resurrection, Marmora, N.J.
Gregoris, Nicholas L. '97 (SCR) On Duty Outside the Diocese.
Gregory, James T. '99 (HRT) Oakville, CT St. Mary Magdalen; [D] Waterbury, CT Sacred Heart High School.
Gregory, Kenneth '73 (ALB) Grafton, NY Parish of Our Lady of the Snow; Albany Medical Center Hospital; Special Assignment; [G] Watervliet, NY St. Colman's Home.
Gregory, Peter A. '73 (SPR) Pittsfield, MA St. Charles.
Gregory, Rev. Msgr. Robert S. '69 (KC) Consultors; Presbyteral Council; Deans; Finance Council; Kansas City, MO Cathedral of Immaculate Conception.
Grehl, Paul F. *o.s.f.s.* '60 (LAN) Manitou Beach, MI St. Mary on the Lake; [B] Jackson, MI Lumen Christi Catholic High School.
Greig, Rev. Msgr. Harry D. '76 (LKC) Big Lake, LA St. Mary of the Lake; Defenders of the Bond.
Greig, Rev. Msgr. Kenneth R. '67 (BEA) Diocesan College of Consultors; Diocesan Judges; Groves, TX St. Peter the Apostle; Presbyteral Council.
Grein, Blane *o.f.m.* '62 (GLP) Chinle, AZ Our Lady of Fatima; Lukachukai, AZ St. Isabel; Ministry Formation Program.
Greiner, James A. '63 (OKL) Mustang, OK Church of the Holy Spirit.
Greiner, Robert '93 (BAK) Prineville, OR St. Joseph; Health and Retirement Board.
Greisen, Thomas A. '82 (OM) Omaha, NE St. Rose; Servant Minister.
Greiten, Gregory J. '92 (MIL) Menomonee Falls, WI St. Mary.
Greiwe, Edward *o.s.c.* '64 (SCL)[I] Onamia, MN Crosier Priory.
Grek, Richard *c.r.* '67 (CHI)[N].
Greka, Rev. Msgr. David '62 (AMA) Retired.
Grelak, Andrew T. '71 (BO) Chelsea, MA St. Stanislaus.
Grell, Loras K. '96 (LIN) Lawrence, NE Sacred Heart; Diocesan Area CCD Directors.
Grellinger, R. Michael '62 (MIL) Retired.
Grembocki, Joseph L. '71 (ALN) Slatington, PA Assumption B.V.M.
Gremillion, Rickey J. '98 (ALX) Catholic Relief Services; [H] Alexandria, LA Catholic Charities and Special Ministries; Director of Catholic Charities and Special Ministries.
Gremmels, John '91 (FWT) On Leave of Absence.
Grenache, Claude *a.a.* '66 (BO)[U] Boston, MA Assumptionist Center; [AA] Waltham, MA Bentley University Spiritual Life Center; Bentley College.
Grendler, Albert O. '59 (SC) Retired.
Grenham, John P. '80 (NO) Metairie, LA St. Benilde; Metairie, LA St. Benilde.
Grenier, Louis L. *s.j.* '49 (FgM) Watertown, MA Society of Jesus.
Grennan, James '44 (SAL) Retired.
Grennan, Larry '66 (SAL) Personnel Board; Council of Priests.
Grennan, Lawrence E. '66 (SAL) Clay Center, KS Saints Peter and Paul Parish; Clay Center, KS St. Anthony Parish.
Grennon, John *o.c.d.* '97 (MIL)[P] Hubertus, WI Retreat Center.
Grenon, Paul R. '78 (PRO) Coventry, RI SS. John and Paul.
Gres–Gayer, Jacques '69 (WDC)[C] Catholic University of America, The.
Greschel, Mark '01 (CHI) Military Chaplains; Army Chaplains.
Greskiewicz, Joseph A. '69 (SCR) Plains, PA SS. Peter and Paul; Diocesan Building Commission.
Gresko, Gregory *o.s.b.* '04 (RIC)[K] Richmond, VA Mary Mother of the Church Abbey; [B] Richmond, VA Benedictine High School.
Greskoviak, Neri *o.f.m.* '63 (PEO) Metamora, IL St. Mary of Lourdes.
Greskowiak, David '09 (FRS) Merced, CA Our Lady of Mercy/St. Patrick's; Planada, CA Sacred Heart.
Greskowiak, Stephen '89 (VNN) On Leave.
Gresock, Thomas G. '85 (BUF) Retired.
Gretchko, A. Edward '72 (PBR) Massillon, OH St. Nicholas.
Gretchko, A. Edward '72 (Y) Massillon, OH Saint Mary; [P] Massillon, OH National Shrine of St. Dymphna.
Gretz, James R. '94 (PIT) Worship Commission; Worship, Dept. for; New Castle, PA St. Vitus.
Grevatch, William N. '64 (LC) Wausau, WI St. Michael; Consultors; Wausau, WI Church of the Resurrection; Ex Officio.
Greving, Daniel M. '97 (SC) Merrill, IA Assumption Church; Merrill, IA St. Joseph; Merrill, IA St. Joseph's; Priests' Personnel Board.
Grewe, Michael W. '79 (OM) Gretna, NE St. Patrick; Vicar General; Consultors; Finance Council; Omaha Priests Retirement Plan and Trust, The; Ex Officio (Consultors).
Grey, Joseph B. '09 (KAL) Battle Creek, MI St. Joseph.
Grey, Michael T. *c.s.sp* '79 (GAL) Houston, TX St. Michael.
Greytak, William '56 (HEL) Boulder, MT St. Catherine; Boulder River School and Hospital.
Grib, Philip J. *s.j.* '72 (CHI) Chicago, IL St. Eugene; [D] Chicago, IL St. Ignatius Jesuit Community.
Grib, Robert I. *s.j.* '72 (CHI)[D] Chicago, IL St. Ignatius Jesuit Community.
Gribbin, Rev. Msgr. Robert C. '47 (HBG) Abbottstown, PA Immaculate Heart of Mary Retired.
Gribble, G. Michael '81 (COL) Columbus, OH St. Joseph Cathedral; Deanery 1: Center–South Columbus; Presbyteral Council; Diocesan Judges; Priests Continuing Education; Parochial Examiners.
Gribble, Richard E. *c.s.c.* '89 (FR)[A] North Easton, MA Stonehill College; [A] North Easton, MA Holy Cross Fathers Religious.
Gribble, Richard E. *c.s.c.* '89 (FTW)[H] Notre Dame Congregation of Holy Cross, Indiana Province, Provincial House.
Gribbon, Michael C. '81 (BRK) Rockaway Point, NY Blessed Trinity Roman Catholic Church.
Gribik, John '89 (SJP) Jeannette, PA St. Demetrius; Presbyters.
Grice, Edward M. '80 (MO) Army Reserve Chaplains; Westwego, LA Our Lady of Prompt Succor.
Gricius, Aurelijus *o.f.m.* '96 (PRT)[I] Kennebunkport, ME St. Anthony's Friary.
Grieco, Frank M. '01 (RVC) East Northport, NY St. Anthony of Padua.
Grieco, Michael S. '83 (LA) Oxnard, CA Santa Clara.
Grieco, Rev. Msgr. Nicholas V. '59 (BGP) Weston, CT St. Francis of Assisi.
Grieman, Gerald G. '79 (STP) Retired.
Griener, George E. *s.j.* '73 (OAK)[A] Berkeley, CA Jesuit School of Theology at Santa Clara University; [M] Berkeley, CA Jesuit Fathers and Brothers.
Grier, Matthew *m.h.m.* '69 (NY)[EE] Hartsdale, NY Mill Hill Fathers Residence; Hartsdale, NY Mill Hill Missionaries.
Gries, Andrew *o.c.s.o.* '59 (ARL)[H] Berryville, VA Cistercian Abbey of Our Lady of the Holy Cross.
Gries, Eugene *o.praem.* '68 (SFE) Albuquerque, NM Our Lady of Most Holy Rosary; [H] Albuquerque, NM Santa Maria de la Vid Priory.
Gries, Jason '04 (EVN) Vincennes, IN Sacred Heart; Special Assignment; Associate Directors; Bicknell, IN St. Philip Neri.
Gries, Jeremy M. '09 (IND) Indianapolis, IN St. Monica.
Griesbach, Rev. Msgr. John '76 (FRS) Advocates; On Special Assignment; [F] Three Rivers, CA St. Anthony's Retreat Center; Co Directors.
Griesbach, Seamus P. '07 (PRT) Bangor, ME Saint Paul the Apostle Parish.
Griesedieck, Rev. Msgr. Edmund O. '65 (STL)[A] St. Louis, MO Kenrick School of Theology; [V] St. Ann, MO St. Louis Catholic Charismatic Renewal; Charismatic Renewal Retired.
Griesemer, Edward *s.c.j.* '57 (MIL)[W] Wauwatosa, WI Milwaukee Archdiocesan Holy Name Union; [P] Franklin, WI Villa Maria.
Griesgraber, Paul Gerard '06 (LA) Reseda, CA St.

Catherine of Siena; Pasadena, CA St. Andrew.
Griffey, M. Brendan '74 (JC) Boonville, MO SS. Peter and Paul; Columbia Catholic Hospital Ministry.
Griffin, Carter '04 (WDC) Graduate Studies.
Griffin, Charles R. '56 (COL) Chillicothe, OH St. Peter; Chillicothe, OH Ross Correctional Institution Retired.
Griffin, Rev. Msgr. Charles T. '58 (BUF)[O] Tonawanda, NY O'Hara Residence Retired.
Griffin, David G. '66 (BUF) Retired.
Griffin, David R. *o.s.b.* '76 (ALT)[I] University Park, PA Penn State University, University Park; [J] University Park, PA Penn State Catholic Community.
Griffin, Edward V. *o.s.a.* '49 (PH)[Y] Villanova, PA St. Thomas Monastery.
Griffin, James C. '82 (RIC) Virginia Beach, VA St. Mark.
Griffin, John C. '77 (MRY) Carmel, CA San Carlos Borromeo Basilica; Advocates; Contact Persons.
Griffin, John '72 (SR) Rohnert Park, CA St. Elizabeth Seton.
Griffin, Joseph J. *o.s.f.s.* '56 (WIL)[J] Childs, MD Retirement and Assisted Care Facility Retired.
Griffin, Joseph M. '82 (SAG) Argyle, MI St. Joseph; Ubly, MI St. Columbkille; Ubly, MI St. John the Evangelist.
Griffin, Michael J. '49 (MAN) Retired.
Griffin, Michael '90 (SFS) Pierre, SD SS. Peter and Paul; Bishop's Bulletin; Personnel Board.
Griffin, Michael *o.c.d.* '50 (MIL)[P] Hubertus, WI Discalced Carmelite Monastery – Holy Hill Basilica of the National Shrine of Mary, Help of Christians, Holy Hill.
Griffin, Noel '64 (LA) On Sick Leave.
Griffin, Patrick J. *c.m.* '79 (RVC)[A] Huntington, NY Diocesan Seminary of the Immaculate Conception.
Griffin, Patrick J. *c.m.* '79 (NY)[C] Staten Island, NY St. John's University Staten Island Campus.
Griffin, Patrick J. *c.m.* '79 (BRK)[D] St. John's University; [T] Jamaica, NY St. Vincent's House.
Griffin, Robert E. *s.j.* '61 (SJ)[M] Los Gatos, CA Sacred Heart Jesuit Center.
Griffin, Thomas A. *s.j.* '58 (MIA) Miami, FL Gesu.
Griffin, Thomas *o.s.a.* '83 (CHI)[J] Chicago, IL Holy Cross Hospital.
Griffin, Thomas *o.s.a.* '83 (MO) Navy Reserve Chaplains.
Griffin–Smolenski, Thomas J. *s.j.* '00 (LA)[P] Los Angeles, CA Colombiere House.
Griffith, Daniel F. '02 (STP) North Saint Paul, MN St. Peter; College of Consultors.
Griffith, Darragh '97 (ATL) Marietta, GA Holy Family.
Griffith, Sidney H. *s.t.d.* '65 (WDC)[C] Catholic University of America, The; [N] Riverdale, MD Holy Spirit Missionary Cenacle.
Griffith, Thomas *s.v.d.* '69 (BO)[U] Duxbury, MA Society of the Divine Word.
Griffiths, Charles L. '05 (TR) Howell, NJ St. Veronica.
Griffiths, John M. '76 (CHI) Chicago, IL Queen of Angels; Judges.
Griffiths, John (WIN) Defenders of the Bond.
Griffiths, Thomas *c.p.* '57 (BRK)[T] Jamaica, NY Immaculate Conception Monastery.
Griffiths, Thomas *s.v.d.* (BO) Presbyteral Council.
Grifone, Fabian *o.f.m.* '54 (NY) New York, NY Most Precious Blood.
Grigassy, Daniel P. *o.f.m.* '77 (PAT) Paterson, NJ St. Bonaventure.
Grigus, John *o.f.m.conv.* '89 (RCK) Rockford, IL St. Anthony of Padua.
Grile, Harry *c.ss.r.* '68 (SEA) Seattle, WA Sacred Heart of Jesus; [L] Seattle, WA The Redemptionist Society of Washington.
Grile, Patrick *c.ss.r.* '71 (STP) Brooklyn Center, MN St. Alphonsus.
Grilliot, Thomas J. '76 (CIN) Piqua, OH St. Mary.
Grillo, Simon '03 (SEA) Des Moines, WA St. Philomena.
Grimaldi, Joseph A. '90 (MRY) On Duty Outside the Diocese; Corralitos, CA Holy Eucharist.
Grimaldi, Joseph A. '90 (MO) Defenders of the Bond.
Grimaldi, Joseph R. '83 (BRK) Brooklyn, NY St. Mark; Diocesan Consultors; Brooklyn, NY St. Margaret Mary; Presbyteral Council; Diocesan Real Estate Board; Diocesan Judges.
Grimaldi, Robert B. *s.j.* '68 (FgM) Los Gatos, CA Society of Jesus.
Grimalia, Rev. Msgr. Vincent J. '68 (SCR) Scranton, PA St. Peter's Cathedral; Office of Pastoral Planning; Diocesan Office for Clergy Formation; Diocesan Consultors; Diocesan Finance Council.
Grimard, Rocky *o.m.i.* '91 (SAT)[C] Oblate School of Theology; Retreats, Men.
Grimard, Rocky *o.m.i.* '91 (SAT)[N] San Antonio, TX Oblate Renewal Center.
Grimes, John C. '00 (MET) Sayreville, NJ Our Lady of Victories.
Grimes, John J. (BO) Dover, MA Most Precious Blood; Vicariate III.
Grimes, Rev. Msgr. Kenneth F. '57 (COL) Columbus, OH St. Andrew Retired.
Grimes, Rev. Msgr. Kevin '57 (COL) Retired.
Grimes, Price D. '88 (OKL) Absent on Sick Leave.
Grimes, Raymond P. '55 (PBL) Las Animas, CO St. Mary Retired.
Grimes, Robert R. *s.j.* '84 (NY)[C] Bronx, NY Fordham University; [EE] Cardinal Spellman Hall, Jesuit Community.
Grimm, John S. '02 (WIL) Special or Other Diocesan Assignment.
Grimm, John S. '02 (NEW)[B] School of Diplomacy and Intl. Rels.; [A] South Orange, NJ Immaculate Conception Seminary.
Grimm, Robert B. *s.j.* '76 (P)[L] Portland Jesuit Provincial Office (Society of Jesus, Oregon Prov.).
Grimm, William J. *m.m.* '77 (FgM) Maryknoll, NY MARYKNOLL.
Grimme, D. Timothy '77 (ALT) Altoona, PA St. Therese of the Child Jesus.
Grimmer, James A. '54 (BUF) Retired.
Griner, William S. '61 (L) Clergy Personnel Commission Retired.
Grinko, Frank X. *o.f.m. cap.* '81 (COS)[I] Colorado Springs, CO Catholic Center at the Citadel; [F] Colorado Springs, CO Our Lady of the Angels Friary.
Grinnell, Horace H. '74 (ARL) Falls Church, VA St. Anthony's.
Grinnen, Jack *t.o.r.* '72 (ALT)[G] Loretto, PA St. Francis Friary at Mount Assisi.
Grinsell, John *s.d.b.* '71 (NEW) Orange, NJ Our Lady of the Valley.
Grippe, Louis A. '69 (SCR) Hazleton, PA Church of the Most Precious Blood.
Grippo, Robert F. '72 (NY) Bronx, NY St. Theresa of the Infant Jesus; Canon 1742 Panel of Pastors.
Gripshover, Ronald J. '96 (ARL) Fredericksburg, VA St. Patrick; Advocates.
Grise, Clifford J. '45 (BGP)[O] Stamford, CT The Catherine Dennis Keefe Queen of the Clergy Retired Priests' Residence Retired.
Grispino, Frank *s.m.* '56 (DET)[K] Livonia, MI Marist Fathers & Brothers Community.
Grissom, Joel *s.m.* '03 (BWN) Brownsville, TX San Felipe de Jesus.
Griswold, Edward J. '73 (TR) On Duty Outside the Diocese.
Griswold, Edward '73 (BAL)[A] Baltimore, MD St. Mary's Seminary and University.
Grix, Robert *o.f.m.cap.* '78 (NY)[B] Beacon, NY St. Lawrence of Brindisi Friary.
Grix, Robert *o.f.m.cap.* (PAT)[N] Ringwood, NJ Holy Name Friary, Inc.
Grizzelle–Reid, Paul *s.c.j.* '72 (MIL)[P] Hales Corners, WI Priests of the Sacred Heart.
Groarke, Francis P. '73 (PH) Philadelphia, PA Holy Name of Jesus.
Grob, Jeffrey S. '92 (CHI) Elmwood Park, IL St. Celestine.
Grochowski, Bernard J. '63 (WOR) Retired.
Grodecki, Henry *c.m.* '75 (SPC) Neosho, MO St. Canera.
Groden, Rev. Msgr. Michael F. '65 (BO) On Duty Outside the Archdiocese.
Grodnicki, Robert S. '88 (TR) Toms River, NJ St. Luke.
Groeschel, Benedict J. *c.f.r.* '59 (BRK)[O] Brooklyn, NY St. Francis Home for Boys; Counselors:.
Groeschel, Benedict J. *c.f.r.* '59 (NEW)[K] Hoboken, NJ Good Counsel, Inc. (St. Francis Home); [K] Hoboken, NJ Good Counsel, Inc.
Groeschel, Benedict Joseph *c.f.r.* '59 (NY)[A] Yonkers, NY St. Joseph's Seminary; [EE] Bronx, NY Franciscan Friars of the Renewal; [GG] Larchmont, NY Trinity Retreat; [GG] Larchmont, NY St. Francis Retreat, Inc.; [S] Spring Valley, NY Good Counsel, Inc.; [II] Cause:; [II] Larchmont, NY The Oratory of Divine Love, Inc.
Grogan, Brendan '61 (MIA) Absent on Leave.
Grogan, Gerald P. '60 (VEN) Retired.
Grogan, J. Clyde '68 (BEL) Red Bud, IL St. Patrick.
Grogan, Richard P. *s.j.* '73 (NY)[EE] New York, NY Murray–Weigel Hall.
Grogan, Todd '90 (CIN) Cincinnati, OH Annunciation of the Blessed Virgin Mary.
Grogan, Vincent B. *o.f.m.* '63 (PAT)[N] Butler, NJ St. Anthony Friary; Advocates; Provincial Councilors:.
Grogan, William E. '83 (PH) Philadelphia, PA All Saints.
Grogan, William P. '76 (CHI) Chicago, IL St. Ignatius; Health/Hospital Affairs; Bio Ethics Commission.
Groh, Christopher '79 (JOL) Joliet, IL Holy Cross; Joliet, IL St. Mary Nativity.
Grohe, Eugene J. *c.ss.r.* '50 (NY) Esopus, NY Sacred Heart; [EE] Esopus, NY Redemptorist Priests and Brothers C.Ss.R. (Province of Baltimore).
Groher, Robert C. '66 (GB) Special Assignment.
Grollmes, Eugene E. *s.j.* '64 (STL)[O] St. Louis, MO Jesuit Community Corporation at Saint Louis University – Jesuit Hall.
Gromadzki, Michael '01 (MET) Port Reading, NJ St. Anthony of Padua; Woodbridge, NJ Our Lady of Mount Carmel.
Gromadzki, Stanley G. '89 (MET) South River, NJ St. Mary of Ostrabrama.
Gron, Ryszard '88 (CHI) Palatine, IL St. Thomas of Villanova.
Groncki, Rev. Msgr. Richard F. '66 (NEW) Newark, NJ Cathedral Basilica of the Sacred Heart; Office of Divine Worship; Members.
Grondin, Charles R. '03 (PRO) East Greenwich, RI Our Lady of Mercy.
Grondz, David '06 (KAL)[E] Kalamazoo, MI St. Philip Neri House; Kalamazoo, MI St. Mary.
Groner, Eric *s.v.d.* '96 (BEA) Cleveland, TX St. Mary.
Groner, John W. '71 (JC) St. Robert, MO St. Jude; St. Robert, MO St. Robert Bellarmine.
Gronert, Stephen F. '86 (WCH) Eureka, KS Sacred Heart; Eureka, KS St. John; Eureka, KS St. Teresa of Avila.
Gronski, Peter '71 (STF)[F] Stamford, CT Missionary Sisters of Mother of God.
Groody, Daniel G. *c.s.c.* '93 (FTW)[B] University of Notre Dame Du Lac; [H] Notre Dame, IN Holy Cross Community, Corby Hall, University of Notre Dame.
Groover, Henry B. *o.p.* '82 (BR) Hammond, LA Holy Ghost; Tickfaw, LA Our Lady of Pompeii.
Gros, Edwin L. *s.j.* '80 (ELP) El Paso, TX Sacred Heart.
Gros, Paul A. '09 (BR) Denham Springs, LA Immaculate Conception.
Grosch, Robert D. '74 (GF) Judicial Vicar; Clerical Benefit Association.
Grosch, Robert '74 (GF) Billings, MT St. Patrick Co–Cathedral; Holy Cross Cemetery (Billings).
Grosch, Robert (HEL) Promoter of Justice.
Groshek, Rev. Msgr. Richard '62 (LAN) Vicar General Retired.
Grosko, Joseph R. '59 (PIT) West Mifflin, PA St. Agnes; West Mifflin, PA Holy Trinity.
Gross, Barry R. '75 (WDC)[E] Olney, MD Our Lady of Good Counsel High School.
Gross, Barry '75 (LFT) On Duty Outside the Diocese.
Gross, Donald L. '59 (LFT) Ambia, IN St. Mary; Fowler, IN Sacred Heart of Jesus; Deans; Defenders of the Bond; Members; Ministry to Priests' Program; Diocesan Consultors.
Gross, G. Robert '07 (DUB) Deanery Representatives; Dyersville, IA Basilica of St. Francis Xavier; Worthington, IA St. Paul.
Gross, Gary L. '83 (MO) Army Chaplains.
Gross, Gary '83 (LIN) On Duty Outside the Diocese.
Gross, Gerard *o.c.s.o.* '78 (ATL)[G] Conyers, GA The Monastery of the Holy Spirit.
Gross, James '99 (FAR) Velva, ND Sts. Peter & Paul Church of Karlsruhe; Velva, ND St. Cecilia's Church of Velva; Deanery 6.
Gross, Joseph J. *o.ss.t* '70 (BAL)[S] Baltimore, MD.
Gross, Kenneth '71 (DM) Imogene, IA St. Patrick; Red Oak, IA St. Mary.
Gross, Lawrence A. '66 (ROC) Honeoye Falls, NY St. Paul of the Cross.
Gross, Lawrence F. '66 (ROC) Lima, NY St. Rose.
Gross, Lee W. '87 (ARL) On Duty Outside the Diocese.
Gross, Lee W. '87 (BAL)[A] Emmitsburg, MD Mount St. Mary's Seminary; [A] Emmitsburg, MD Mount St. Mary's Seminary.
Gross, Matthew *o.f.m.cap.* '61 (DEN)[N] Denver, CO St. Francis of Assisi Friary.
Gross, Nile C. '09 (NO) Metairie, LA St. Clement of Rome.
Gross, Ralph C. '70 (MIL) Dousman, WI St. Bruno; Archdiocesan Consultors.
Gross, Richard C. '62 (NU) Retired.
Gross, Richard J. '63 (FAR) Retired.
Gross, Richard K. *s.j.* '76 (BO)[U] Boston The Society of Jesus of New England–Provincial Offices.
Gross, Stephen *o.f.m.conv.* '69 (MRY)[F] Arroyo Grande, CA St. Joseph Cupertino Province, Provincial Center.
Gross, Steve *o.f.m.conv.* (LA) Hermosa Beach, CA Our Lady of Guadalupe.
Gross, Thomas L. '75 (HON) Kailua, HI St. John Vianney; Clergy Personnel Board.
Gross, Rev. Msgr. Val '63 (FAR) Fargo, ND Holy Spirit Church of Fargo Retired.
Grossenburg, Tony '99 (RC) McLaughlin, SD St. Bonaventure's; McLaughlin, SD St. Bernard; McLaughlin, SD Standing Rock Reservation.
Grossi, Anthony J. *o.s.b.* '99 (GBG)[G] Latrobe, PA Saint Vincent Archabbey.
Grosskopf, Albert A. *s.j.* '83 (SFR) San Francisco, CA St. Ignatius; [N] San Francisco, CA Loyola House Jesuit Community.
Grosso, James D. '79 (BGP) Stamford, CT St. Leo.
Grote, Alan W. '82 (GBG) Legion of Mary; New Kensington, PA St. Joseph; New Kensington, PA St. Mary of Czestochowa.
Groth, Rev. Msgr. Ronald '69 (LKC) Jennings, LA St. Lawrence; Presbyteral Council; Diocesan Consultors.
Grous, Rev. Msgr. Albin J. '87 (PH) Drexel Hill, PA St. Andrew.
Grove, Kevin *c.s.c.* '10 (FTW) South Bend, IN St. Joseph.
Grove, Stanley *m.s.a.* '00 (HRT) Waterbury, CT Basilica of the Immaculate Conception.
Grove, Stanley *m.s.a.* '00 (NOR)[G] Cromwell Society of the Missionaries of the Holy Apostles.

Grovenburg, Gregg H. *s.j.* '88 (KC)[J] Kansas City, MO Rockhurst Jesuit Community.
Grover, David A. '83 (CAM) Gibbstown, NJ St. Michael's Church, Gibbstown, N.J.; Paulsboro, NJ St. John's Church, Paulsboro, N.J.; Representatives by Deaneries.
Grover, Peter *o.m.v.* '90 (BO)[B] Boston, MA Our Lady of Grace Seminary; [Z] Boston, MA St. Clement Archdiocesan Eucharistic Shrine.
Groves, Edmund '49 (PHX) Retired.
Grozio, Stephen M. *c.m.* (RVC) Hispanic Apostolate of the South Fork.
Grubb, Paul *s.j.* '08 (P)[D].
Grubba, Dale W. '66 (MAD) Princeton, WI St. James; Princeton, WI St. John the Baptist; Deaneries.
Gruben, John *o.a.r.* '74 (NY)[B] Suffern, NY Tagaste Monastery.
Gruber, Rev. Msgr. Aloys Conrad '67 (STO) Oakdale, CA St. Mary of the Annunciation Church (Pastor of); Deans.
Gruber, Anthony P. '70 (NOR) Retired.
Gruber, Eric J. '91 (ALN) Catasauqua, PA St. Andrew; Catasauqua, PA St. Lawrence the Martyr.
Gruber, Kevin W. '80 (RVC) Bohemia, NY St. John Nepomucene.
Gruber, Mark F.X. *o.s.b.* '83 (GBG)[G] Latrobe, PA Saint Vincent Archabbey.
Grubisch, Rev. Msgr. Donald W. '53 (WIN) Diocese of Winona Incardination Board Retired.
Gruden, William J. '79 (SAG) Munger, MI St. Norbert; Reese, MI St. Elizabeth; Territorial Vicars.
Grudowski, Rev. Msgr. Robert J. '61 (PH) Holland, PA St. Bede the Venerable Retired.
Gruenes, Bernard '98 (SCL) St. Cloud, MN St. Michael; Waite Park, MN St. Joseph's; Office of Diaconate.
Grullon, Carlos Manuel '07 (PCE) Guayanilla, PR Immaculate Conception.
Grummer, James E. *s.j.* '82 (MIL)[P] Milwaukee Jesuit Provincial Office, Wisconsin Province.
Grumsey, Dennis *o.f.m.conv.* '86 (HBG) Shamokin, PA Mother Cabrini; Pastoral Council, Diocesan.
Grundhaus, Rev. Msgr. Roger L. '66 (CR) Judicial Vicar; Fertile, MN St. Joseph; Mentor, MN St. Lawrence.
Grundowski, Francis M. '71 (ALN) Retired.
Grunewald, Bernard *er.o.l.s* '77 (OLL)[D] Philippi, WV Our Lady of Solitude Maronite Hermitage, Inc. Retired.
Grunow, Stephen E. '97 (CHI) Lake Forest, IL St. Mary.
Grupczynski, Gerald *s.ch.* '88 (LAV) Las Vegas, NV St. Anthony of Padua.
Gruss, Rev. Msgr. Robert D. '94 (DAV) On Duty Outside the Diocese.
Gruver, David '85 (ORG) Lake Forest, CA Santiago de Compostela.
Gryga, Theodore '64 (SY) Military Chaplains.
Gryszko, Alojzy *s.d.b.* '72 (LA) Paramount, CA Our Lady of the Rosary.
Grytner, Eugeniusz '79 (ORL) Titusville, FL St. Teresa.
Grytner, Eugeniusz *s.d.s.* '79 (SAT)[L] Falls City, TX Salvatorian Fathers Community of Texas.
Grytsyuk, Volodymyr '06 (SJP) Solon, OH Protection B.V.M.; Presbyters.
Grzela, Marek B. '92 (CHI) Other Assignments.
Grzelak, Thaddeus A. '65 (BRK) Retired.
Grzymski, Donald *o.f.m.conv.* '80 (BAL) Baltimore, MD St. Clement Mary Hofbauer; [W] Owings Mills, MD Knights of Columbus; Consultors; Consultors; Presbyteral Council.
Gschwend, James P. *s.j.* '65 (CHI)[S] The Jesuit Retreat League of Chicago.
Guadagnoli, Michael '97 (DAL) Dallas, TX St. Pius X; Personnel Board.
Guadarrama, Jesus *c.m.* '04 (PH) Philadelphia, PA St. Francis of Assisi.
Guagliardo, Salvatore J. '59 (RCK) Retired.
Guaipo, Jose Gregorio '88 (SJN) Guaynabo, PR Santa Rosa de Lima.
Guajardo, Hilario '89 (AUS) China Spring, TX St. Philip Catholic Church – China Spring, Texas; McGregor, TX St. Eugene Catholic Church – McGregor, Texas; McGregor, TX Our Lady of San Juan Catholic Mission Church – Moody, Texas.
Gualano, Kevin M. '04 (ALN) Orefield, PA St. Joseph The Worker.
Gualtieri, Raymond A. '64 (PIT) Retired.
Guanchez, Omar '09 (SCL) Elk River, MN The Church of St. Andrew.
Guardiola, Louis *c.p.m.* '01 (OWN)[F] Auburn, KY Fathers of Mercy.
Guarino, Rt. Rev. Msgr. Charles A. '67 (RVC) Promoter of Justice; Defenders of the Bond.
Guarino, Rev. Msgr. Charles A. '67 (RVC) Garden City, NY St. Joseph's.
Guarino, Mario *f.d.p.* '81 (BO)[S] East Boston, MA Don Orione Nursing Home.
Guarino, Mario *f.d.p.* '81 (NY) New York, NY St. Ann.
Guarino, R. Michael '68 (BO) Revere, MA St. Anthony of Padua.
Guarino, Thomas G. '77 (NEW)[A] South Orange, NJ Immaculate Conception Seminary; [B] School of Diplomacy and Intl. Rels.; Censores Librorum.
Guarnica, Luis Felipe Rodriguez '97 (SJN) Guaynabo, PR Cristo Salvador.
Guarnieri, Lee (RIC)[E] Newport News, VA Bernardine Franciscan Sisters Foundation, Inc.
Guarnieri, Leo J. '77 (RIC) West Point, VA Our Lady of the Blessed Sacrament.
Guarnieri, Richard '71 (NY) Bronx, NY St. Clare of Assisi.
Guarnizo, Jhon '03 (STA) Crescent City, FL St. John the Baptist; Presbyteral Council; Multicultural Ministry.
Guarnizo, Jhon '03 (BWN)[K] Brownsville, TX Asociacion Nacional de Sacerdotes Hispanos.
Guarracino, Ralph '54 (BRK) Retired.
Guasp Santos, Walter '01 (CAM) On Duty Outside the Diocese.
Guastella, Luke *o.f.m.cap.* '55 (NY)[B] Beacon, NY St. Lawrence of Brindisi Friary.
Guastella, Rev. Msgr. Richard J. '72 (NY) Staten Island, NY St. Clare.
Guay, Robert F. '73 (PIT) Judges; Priest Council; Vicars General; Vicariate 1; College of Consultors; Diocesan Development Board; Clergy Personnel Board.
Guay, Robert '73 (PIT)[N] Pittsburgh, PA Motherhouse, Sisters of the Holy Spirit (S.H.S.).
Guba, Michael '65 (NEW) Garfield, NJ Church of Our Lady of Sorrows.
Gubbels, Wayne '71 (DM) Audubon, IA St. Patrick; Audubon, IA Holy Trinity.
Gubbins, John '70 (MIA) Military Chaplains.
Gubbins, William B. '55 (CHI) Orland Hills, IL St. Elizabeth Seton Retired.
Gubbiotti, Jeffrey '04 (HRT) West Haven, CT St. Louis.
Gubernat, Michael E. '77 (NEW) Paramus, NJ Our Lady of the Visitation.
Guberovic, Zeljko J. '06 (NEW) Union City, NJ St. Anthony of Padua.
Guckin, Matthew W. '99 (PH)[D] Downingtown, PA Bishop Shanahan High School; Downingtown, PA St. Joseph; Council of Priests.
Gudalefsky, Adam B. *m.m.* '59 (FgM) Maryknoll, NY MARYKNOLL.
Gudewicz, John L. '70 (PIT) Pittsburgh, PA All Saints.
Guenter, Frank '66 (GAL) Houston, TX St. Gregory the Great.
Guenter, Frank '70 (GAL) Houston, TX Federal Correctional Center.
Guenter, Frank (GAL) Retired.
Guenther, Daniel C. '82 (SC) Sioux City, IA Immaculate Conception; Continuing Education for Priests.
Guenther, Rev. Msgr. Donald E. '62 (NEW) Summit, NJ St. Teresa's; Elected Members Retired.
Guentner, Francis J. *s.j.* '47 (STL)[O] St. Louis, MO Jesuit Community Corporation at Saint Louis University – Jesuit Hall.
Guentner, Hugh M. *o.s.m.* '91 (DEN) Minturn, CO St. Patrick.
Guentner, Hugh *o.s.m.* '91 (CHI)[N] Chicago Order of Friar Servants of Mary (Servites) United States of America Province, Inc.
Guererro, Larry '83 (STO) Modesto, CA St. Joseph Church of Modesto (Pastor of).
Guerin, Louis T. '87 (PMB)[K] Diocese of Palm Beach Health Plan Trust; [A] Boynton Beach, FL St. Vincent de Paul Regional Seminary; Released from Diocesan Assignment.
Guerin, Louis '87 (PMB) Elected Members.
Guerin, Peter J. *o.s.b.* '63 (MAN)[K] Manchester, NH St. Anselm Abbey; Presbyteral Council; Manchester, NH.
Guerin, William A. *o.s.f.s.* '57 (PH)[Y] Wyndmoor, PA Villa de Sales Oblate Residence.
Guerini, Ademir *c.s.* '87 (ORL) Portuguese/Brazilian Ministry; Winter Garden, FL Resurrection.
Guerra, Alcibiades *c.m.* '90 (FgM) Philadelphia, PA Eastern Province.
Guerra, Aroldo '54 (NY) New York, NY Incarnation.
Guerra, Heriberto '76 (PAT) Paterson, NJ Blessed Sacrament.
Guerra, Juan Gabriel *l.c.* '91 (ATL)[G] Alpharetta, GA Norcross Pastoral Center, Inc.
Guerra, Robert F. '00 (VIC) Eagle Lake, TX Parish of the Nativity; Presbyteral Council.
Guerra–Mayaudon, Gerardo *o.p.* '69 (AUS)[G] Austin, TX Dominican Friars of Austin.
Guerreiro, Clarence L. *ss.cc.* '70 (HON) Honolulu, HI St. Patrick.
Guerreiro, Clarence *ss.cc.* '76 (HON)[D] Honolulu, HI St. Patrick's Monastery.
Guerreiro, Clyde L. *ss.cc.* '76 (HON) Kaunakakai, HI Saint Damien Catholic Parish; Members.
Guerrera, Richard P. *s.j.* '73 (FgM) Watertown, MA Society of Jesus.
Guerrera, Rev. Msgr. Vittorio '91 (HRT) On Duty Outside the Archdiocese.
Guerrero, Abraham '97 (TUC) Nogales, AZ San Felipe de Jesus Roman Catholic Parish – Nogales.
Guerrero, Rev. Msgr. Andres '57 (PCE) Juana Diaz, PR St. Raymond Nonato.
Guerrero, Eugenio Villafranca *c.m.* '53 (SJN) San Juan, PR Sagrado Corazon de Jesus.
Guerrero, Felix Leon *o.f.m.cap.* '86 (AGN)[F] Agana Heights, GU St. Fidelis Friary; Notary; Confraternity of Christian Mothers.
Guerrero, J. Jesus *o.s.a.* '98 (GAL) Baytown, TX Our Lady of Guadalupe.
Guerrero, Jose Ma. (ARE) On Duty Outside the Diocese.
Guerrero, Robert '92 (SB) Chino, CA Our Lady of Guadalupe.
Guerrero, Toribio C. '96 (LAR) Laredo, TX St. Peter The Apostle; Cursillo Movement.
Guerrette, William J. '55 (BO) Senior Priests. Retired.
Guerrini, Brian *ss.cc.* '08 (LA)[P] La Verne, CA Congregation of the Sacred Hearts of Jesus and Mary.
Guerrini, Brian '08 (LSC) Artesia, NM Our Lady of Grace; Members.
Guerrini, Roderic M. '63 (LA) Retired.
Guertin, Donald F. *c.s.c.* '64 (FTW)[H] Notre Dame Congregation of Holy Cross, Indiana Province, Provincial House.
Guesnier, Rene *o.s.b.* '61 (DOD) Seward, KS St. Francis Xavier Catholic Church of Seward, Kansas.
Guest, Richard M. '94 (ARL) Ashburn, VA St. Theresa.
Guevara, Alfonso M. '77 (BWN) McAllen, TX St. Joseph the Worker; [A] Mission, TX The Saint Joseph and Saint Peter Seminary.
Guevara, Jose Maria '68 (LAR) Laredo, TX St. Jude; College of Consultors.
Guevara, Miguel H. '67 (GI) Retired.
Guevin, Benedict M. *o.s.b.* '85 (MAN)[K] Manchester, NH St. Anselm Abbey; Lay Ministry Formation Commission.
Guffey, David L. *c.s.c.* (FTW)[H] Notre Dame Congregation of Holy Cross, Indiana Province, Provincial House.
Guffey, David *c.s.c.* '91 (LA) Santa Monica, CA St. Monica.
Guglielmelli, Michael V. '70 (NEW) Hoboken, NJ St. Francis.
Guglielmi, Donald A. '84 (BGP) Stratford, CT St. Mark; Office for the Continuing Education of Clergy.
Guglielmo, Alan F. '68 (NEW) Coordinator for Health Care Apostolate Continuing Education; Newark, NJ Office of Health Care Personnel; Secaucus, NJ Immaculate Conception Retired.
Gugliotta, Francis *s.x.* '52 (FgM)[N] Wayne Xaverian Missionary Fathers; Wayne, NJ XAVERIAN MISSIONARY FATHERS.
Gugliotta, Kevin A. '96 (NEW) Scotch Plains, NJ St. Bartholomew.
Guianan, Francisco *s.o.l.t.* (KC) Kansas City, MO Our Lady of Peace.
Guiao, Raymond P. *s.j.* '90 (CHI)[N] Chicago, IL Clark Street Jesuit Residence; [N] Chicago, IL Chicago Province of the Society of Jesus–Provincial Office.
Guiao, Raymond P. *s.j.* '99 (DET)[K] Chicago, IL Jesuit Provincial Office–Detroit Province of the Society of Jesus.
Guichard, Alvaro '69 (MIA) Absent on Leave.
Guichard, Benoit *f.s.s.p.* '04 (PAT) Pequannock, NJ Our Lady of Fatima Chapel (Tridentine).
Guida, Amedeo G. '85 (SY) Johnson City, NY St. James.
Guido, Joseph J. *o.p.* '81 (PRO)[P] Providence St. Thomas Aquinas Priory at Providence College; [B] Providence, RI Providence College.
Guido, Luis '08 (SB) San Bernardino, CA Our Lady of the Assumption.
Guido, Paul R. *o.f.m.* '66 (HRT) New Britain, CT St. Francis of Assisi.
Guido, Thomas J. '87 (PT) Miramar Beach, FL Church of the Resurrection; Orders & Ministries, Commission for.
Guido, Thomas '87 (PT) Members At Large.
Guidon, Patrick *o.m.i.* '50 (SAT)[G] San Antonio, TX St. Anthony's School.
Guidry, Joseph *s.v.d.* '57 (CHI)[N] Techny, IL Divine Word Residence.
Guidry, Michael '91 (LAF) Minister to Priests.
Guidry, Michael '71 (LAF) Morrow, LA St. Peter.
Guidry, Mitchell '97 (LAF) Absent on Sick Leave.
Guidry, Raymond *s.v.d.* '57 (CHI)[N] Techny, IL Divine Word Residence.
Guijarro, Rev. Msgr. Mario (SJN) Hermandad N. Sra. De La Caridad; [B] Guaynabo, PR Colegio San Pedro Martir.
Guijarro de Corzo, Rev. Msgr. Mario A. '78 (SJN) Guaynabo, PR San Pedro Martir de Verona.
Guilbeau, Aubrey V. '82 (LKC) Sulphur, LA Immaculate Conception of the B.V.M.; Deans; Diocesan Consultors; Deaf Apostolate; Presbyteral Council.
Guilbeau, Jeremy Aquinas *o.p.* '02 (NY) New York, NY St. Vincent Ferrer; [EE] New York, NY St. Vincent Ferrer Priory.
Guilbert, Norman J. '97 (BGP) Bridgeport, CT St. Patrick Church.
Guillaume, Lemier '92 (ORL) Ocala, FL St. Jude's Catholic Community.
Guillemette, Robert C. '90 (MAN) Nashua, NH Immaculate Conception.

Guillen, Fernando E. '90 (NEW) Elizabeth, NJ Blessed Sacrament.
Guillen, Juan '74 (TUC) Administrative Leave of Absence.
Guillen, Oswaldo *s.d.b.* '02 (CHI) Chicago, IL St. John Bosco.
Guillen, Randy '96 (NEW) Santa Ana, CA St. Anne's; On Duty Outside the Archdiocese.
Guillen, Robert '70 (WDC) Washington, DC Holy Name.
Guillen–Santoyo, Patricio '57 (SB) Retired.
Guillermo–Cordoba, Luis '00 (ATL) Lilburn, GA Our Lady of the Americas.
Guillory, Brad D. '09 (LAF) Abbeville, LA St. Mary Magdalen.
Guillory, Joshua P. '07 (LAF) Ville Platte, LA St. Joseph; Graduate Studies.
Guillot, Rev. Msgr. Leo '56 (BR) Baton Rouge, LA St. Louis, King of France Retired.
Guillot, Raymond Joseph (NO) Abita Springs, LA St. Jane de Chantal.
Guilmain, Roland *a.a.* '53 (BO)[U] Boston, MA Assumptionist Center.
Guilmette, Leo *o.m.i.* '63 (FgM) Washington, DC AMERICAN OBLATE MISSIONS.
Guimon, Michael M. *o.s.m.* '70 (CHI)[N] Chicago Order of Friar Servants of Mary (Servites) United States of America Province, Inc.
Guimon, Michael *o.s.m.* '70 (OAK) Alta Bates Campus of the Alta Bates Summit Medical Center; Herrick Campus of the Alpha Bates Summit Medical Center; [M] Berkeley, CA Servites.
Guimond, John *o.f.m. cap.* '83 (DET)[P] Washington, MI Capuchin Retreat.
Guinan, Frank '66 (PMB) Retired.
Guinan, Michael D. *o.f.m.* '63 (OAK)[A] Berkeley, CA Franciscan School of Theology.
Guinan, Michael '53 (GF) Retired.
Guiney, John *s.m.a.* '61 (JOL) Retired.
Guiney, John *s.m.a.* '61 (NEW)[M] Tenafly, NJ Society of African Missions, Provincialate, S.M.A. Fathers Retired.
Guiry, Robert W. '60 (BRK) On Leave/Unassigned.
Guise, Cyril *o.c.d.* '59 (MIL)[P] Hubertus, WI Discalced Carmelite Monastery – Holy Hill Basilica of the National Shrine of Mary, Help of Christians, Holy Hill.
Guitron, Steven '94 (LA) Pacoima, CA Guardian Angel.
Gula, Richard M. *s.s.* '73 (BAL)[S] Baltimore Society of St. Sulpice, Province of the United States.
Gula, Richard *s.s.* '73 (OAK)[A] Berkeley, CA Franciscan School of Theology.
Gula, Richard *s.s.* (E) On Duty Outside Diocese.
Gulash, George M. '92 (ALT) Cresson, PA St. Francis Xavier.
Guldon, Pat *o.m.i.* '50 (SAT)[L] San Antonio, TX Oblate Benson Residence (Southwest Area).
Gulino, Stephen S. '97 (NOR) Uncasville, CT St. John the Evangelist.
Guljas, Andrew *c.s.c.* '68 (FTW)[H] Notre Dame Congregation of Holy Cross, Indiana Province, Provincial House.
Gullan–Steele, Stuart '80 (ALB) Ravena, NY St. Patrick.
Gulley, Anthony D. '56 (ALB) Retired.
Gulley, James '81 (ALB) Retired.
Gullo, Joseph A. '86 (BUF) Arcade, NY St. Mary.
Gully, Anthony '56 (ALB) Albany, NY Blessed Sacrament.
Gully, Bernard L. '62 (SAN) Priests' Personnel Board; Presbyteral Council; Cursillos de Cristiandad; Deans; Big Spring, TX Holy Trinity Parish.
Gumapo, Polycarpo (Pol) R. '70 (SAC) Citrus Heights, CA Holy Family; Vicars Forane.
Gumataotao, Agustin *o.f.m.cap.* '82 (AGN) Sinajana, GU Saint Jude Thaddeus; [F] Agana Heights, GU St. Fidelis Friary; Archdiocesan Presbyteral Council.
Gumbert, Kenneth R. *o.p.* '85 (FR) Fall River, MA Notre Dame de Lourdes.
Gummersheimer, Gary P. '79 (BEL) Murphysboro, IL St. Andrew.
Gumprecht, Thomas *s.a.* '68 (NY)[EE] Garrison Graymoor Ecumenical and Interreligious Institute.
Gumprecht, Thomas *s.a.* '68 (R) Apex, NC St. Andrew the Apostle.
Gunderson, Gerald T. '76 (CHI) Park Ridge, IL Mary, Seat of Wisdom.
Gunn, Francis *o.f.m.* (PAT) Pompton Lakes, NJ Our Lady of the Assumption.
Gunn, Rev. Msgr. James L. '77 (MAD) Waunakee, WI St. John the Baptist.
Gunn, Terence (NY)[II] Hyde Park, NY Focolare Movement National Center (Men's Branch).
Gunning, Eugene L. '55 (SCR) Retired.
Gunningham, John '07 (SB) Fontana, CA St. Joseph.
Gunnoud, James B. '59 (HRT) Retired.
Gunter, David W. '09 (BO) Methuen, MA St. Monica.
Gunti, Charles *o.f.m.* '68 (SAT) San Antonio, TX San Jose y San Miguel.
Guntzelman, Louis J. '57 (CIN) Retired.
Gunwall, Kurtis '08 (FAR) Fargo, ND Sts. Anne & Joachim Church of Fargo.
Gunzel, Raymond *s.p.* '69 (STL)[O] Saint Louis, MO Servants of the Paraclete.
Guppenberger, August '61 (CIN)[N] Cincinnati Headquarters of Glenmary Home Missioners Retired.
Gural, Marion A. '56 (BRK) Retired.
Gurath, Guy '64 (MIL) Random Lake, WI Our Lady of the Lakes; Belgium, WI St. Mary; Fredonia, WI Holy Rosary.
Gurdak, Joseph *o.f.m.cap.* '70 (MAN) Manchester, NH St. Anne–St. Augustin; Manchester Hispanic Parish Ministry.
Gurgul, Walter *m.i.c.* '60 (SPR)[H] Stockbridge, MA Congregation of Marian Fathers of The Immaculate Conception of the Most Blessed Virgin Mary.
Gurka, Gerald J. '80 (SCR) St. John the Baptist.
Gurnee, William H. '00 (WDC) Avenue, MD Holy Angels; Advocates.
Gurnick, Michael K. '98 (CLV)[A] Wickliffe, OH Borromeo Seminary; Vocations Office.
Gurovich, Rev. Archpriest Daniel '74 (PHU) Presbyteral Council; Bethlehem, PA St. Josaphat's; Adjunct Judicial Vicars; Priests Beneficial Fund.
Gurrieri, John A. '67 (BRK) Flushing, NY St. Andrew Avellino.
Gurtler, Gary *s.j.* '79 (BO)[U] Newton, MA The Jesuit Community at Boston College.
Gurtner, Mark '96 (FTW) South Bend, IN St. Anthony de Padua; Pro–Synodal Judges; Consultors; Presbyteral Council; Environment and Art; Liturgical Commission.
Gurtubay, Ramon *c.p.* '80 (SJN)[C] Dorado, PR Estudiantado Pasionista.
Gurzynski, Rev. Msgr. James C. '63 (AMA) Defenders of the Bond Retired.
Gusiora, Alphonsus '83 (PCE) On Duty Outside the Diocese.
Gusmer, Rev. Msgr. Charles W. '66 (NEW) Cedar Grove, NJ St. Catherine of Siena; Elected Members; Office of Divine Worship; Members; Censores Librorum.
Gusmer, Charles '66 (NEW) Retired.
Gussoni, Lino '44 (NY) Retired.
Gustafson, Christopher M. '95 (CHI) Niles, IL Our Lady of Ransom.
Guste, Placid *s.m.p.* '61 (SPC)[F] Marionville, MO The Society of Our Mother of Peace, Sons of Our Mother of Peace.
Guste, Placid *s.m.p.* '61 (STL)[O] High Ridge, MO Society of Our Mother of Peace; [S] High Ridge, MO Society of Our Mother of Peace at Mary the Font Solitude.
Guste, Rev. Msgr. Robert I. '50 (NO) Kenner, LA Our Lady of Perpetual Help; Ministry of Evangelization & Spiritual Renewal; Jesus Caritas Fraternity of Priests; Living Waters Program (Radio Ministry).
Gustin, Clement N. *o.s.c.* '55 (SCL)[I] Onamia, MN Crosier Priory.
Gutgsell, Michael F. '74 (OM) Defenders of the Bond; Officers; Omaha, NE St. Cecilia Cathedral; Consultors; Ex Officio (Consultors).
Gutgsell, Stephen J. '84 (OM) On Leave of Absence.
Guthneck, Peter E. '71 (GF) Box Elder, MT St. Margaret Mary; Vicars Forane; Personnel Board.
Guthrie, Alfred '30 (BRK) Retired.
Guthrie, Alfred '55 (BRK) College Point, NY St. Fidelis Retired.
Guthrie, John G. '90 (BIS) Bismarck, ND Cathedral of the Holy Spirit; Vicar General; Diocesan Corporate Board; Diocesan Finance Council; Presbyteral Council.
Guthrie, Paul *o.f.m.* '53 (PSC)[A] Sybertsville, PA Holy Dormition Friary; Sybertsville, PA Assumption B.V.M. Province.
Guthrie, Raymond P. '84 (PEO) Ottawa, IL St. Columba; Silvis, IL Our Lady of Guadalupe.
Gutierrez, Alfonso '85 (SAV) Tifton, GA Our Divine Saviour.
Gutierrez, Alvin P. '61 (PIT) Retired.
Gutierrez, Celestino '64 (VEN) Hispanic, Migrant and Spanish Speaking Apostolates; Sarasota, FL St. Jude.
Gutierrez, David *t.o.r.* '92 (SAT) San Antonio, TX St. Leonard's.
Gutierrez, Francisco '01 (YAK) Yakima, WA Holy Redeemer.
Gutierrez, Franco '65 (SJN) Trujillo Alto, PR Maria Llena de Gracia.
Gutierrez, Fulgencio '00 (BRK) Brooklyn, NY St. Barbara.
Gutierrez, Gilberto '73 (PAT) Passaic, NJ Our Lady of Fatima.
Gutierrez, Guido '08 (CHI) Chicago, IL St. Michael the Archangel.
Gutierrez, Ismael '04 (OAK) Pastoral Leadership Placement Board (PLPB); Oakland, CA Cathedral Parish of Christ the Light.
Gutierrez, Javier *s.f.* '91 (SFE) Santa Cruz, NM Holy Cross.
Gutierrez, Jeronimo '81 (SJ) San Jose, CA Christ the King.
Gutierrez, Jose Gregorio '97 (NY) Bronx, NY St. Rita of Cascia Shrine Church.
Gutierrez, Jose Luis '08 (STO) Stockton, CA Presentation Church (Pastor of).
Gutierrez, Jose '73 (STP) Retired.
Gutierrez, Juan Antonio *o.f.m.* '97 (LSC) Roswell, NM St. John the Baptist.
Gutierrez, Juan Rogelio '07 (BWN) McAllen, TX Our Lady of Sorrows.
Gutierrez, Luis '98 (JOL) Addison, IL St. Joseph.
Gutierrez, Michael D. '93 (LA) Santa Monica, CA St. Anne.
Gutierrez, Oscar '96 (PHX) Glendale, AZ Our Lady of Perpetual Help Roman Catholic Parish.
Gutierrez, Rogelio '09 (YAK) Wenatchee, WA St. Joseph's.
Gutirerrez, Jose '76 (CC) On Special Assignment.
Gutmann, David '83 (P) Beaverton, OR Holy Trinity.
Gutmann, Donald '91 (P) Newberg, OR St. Peter; Area Vicars.
Gutowski, Edmund *c.m.* '60 (HRT)[L] Manchester, CT DePaul Provincial Residence.
Gutowski, Matthew J. '88 (OM) Omaha, NE St. Bernard; Catholic Faith Formation Office.
Gutting, James G. '75 (E) Erie, PA St. Mary of the Immaculate Conception; Inner–City Outreach.
Gutting, John C. '54 (LA) Retired.
Guyer, James B. *s.j.* '72 (DEN)[N] Denver, CO Regis Jesuit Community (The Jesuits at Regis University).
Guz, Edmund F. '55 (CHI) Burnham, IL Mother of God Retired.
Guz, Leonard J. '55 (JOL) Retired.
Guz, Witalij *s.ch.* '03 (DET) Sterling Heights, MI Our Lady of Czestochowa.
Guzik, Michael A. *s.j.* '03 (BUF)[D] Buffalo, NY Canisius High School; [O] Buffalo, NY Canisius Jesuit Community Inc.
Guzinski, Joseph D. *c.p.* '51 (BRK)[T] Jamaica, NY Immaculate Conception Monastery.
Guzman, Alfonso *o.f.m.* '71 (SJN) Sabana Seca, PR San Jose Obrero.
Guzman, Armando '86 (SEA) Snohomish, WA St. Michael.
Guzman, Bandilio *s.j.* (SJN) Rio Piedras, PR Academia San Ignacio de Loyola; [B] San Juan, PR Academia San Ignacio de Loyola; Maranatha House of Prayer.
Guzmán, Baudilio *s.j.* '91 (SJN) San Juan, PR San Ignacio de Loyola; [D] San Juan, PR Renovacion Conyugal; [H] San Juan, PR Comunidad Jesuita; Renovacion Conyugal (Fundacion Fernando Martinez Calle, Inc.).
Guzman, David *m.x.y.* '88 (NY)[EE] Bronx, NY Yarumal Mission Society, Inc.
Guzman, Javier Uribe *m.n.m.* '58 (SAT) Del Rio, TX Our Lady of Guadalupe.
Guzman, Jesus Aguirre '89 (BAL) Glen Burnie, MD Holy Trinity.
Guzman, Johnny R. *s.d.b.* (CGS)[C] Aibonito, PR Casa Salesiana de Retiros.
Guzman, Juan Jose *o.a.r.* '08 (ORG) Santa Ana, CA Our Lady of Guadalupe.
Guzman, Juan Santa '85 (SJN) Carolina, PR Santo Cristo de la Agonia.
Guzman, Julian *s.d.s.* '68 (WDC)[B] Silver Spring, MD Salvatorian Community.
Guzman, Julian *s.d.s.* (MIL)[P] Milwaukee Salvatorian Provincial Offices.
Guzman, Mark A. '08 (SEA) Marysville, WA St. Mary.
Guzman, Miguel *c.r.* '06 (DEN) Denver, CO Our Lady of Guadalupe.
Guzman, Ronaldo *m.s.* '95 (HON) Waipahu, HI St. Joseph.
Gúzman, Salvador '00 (DAL) Dallas, TX Our Lady of Perpetual Help.
Guzman, Walter F. '02 (HBG) Hershey, PA St. Joan of Arc.
Guzman Alfaro, Alfonso *o.f.m.* '71 (FgM)[EE] New York Franciscan Friars, Holy Name Province; New York, NY Holy Name Province.
Guzman Alfaro, Alfonso *o.f.m.* '71 (SJN) Secretary to the Archbishop; Vicar of Religious.
Gwiazda, Francis A. '69 (PH) Philadelphia, PA St. Laurentius.
Gwinner, David E. '84 (COL) Westerville, OH St. Paul the Apostle.
Gwozdz, John P. '86 (HRT) Glastonbury, CT St. Paul; South Glastonbury, CT St. Augustine.
Gwozdz, Thomas L. *s.b.d.* '75 (NO)[A] St. Benedict, LA St. Joseph Seminary College; [A] St. Benedict, LA St. Joseph Seminary College.
Gwudz, John S. '72 (NOR) On Duty Outside the Diocese.
Gyabbah, Andrew (NY) Brewster, NY St. Lawrence O'Toole.
Gyamfi, Paul M. '88 (BRK) Ozone Park, NY Nativity of the Blessed Virgin Mary.
Gyan, Eric V. '86 (BR) Prairieville, LA St. John the Evangelist.
Gye–Chun, John (B) Lee '97 (WIL) Korean Catholics; Korean Catholic Community, Inc.
Gyhra, Richard A. '99 (LIN) Graduate Studies.
Gyure, William Louis '91 (TUC) Payson, AZ Saint Philip the Apostle Roman Catholic Church – Payson.

H

Ha, Abraham '02 (ALN) Schuylkill Haven, PA St. Ambrose.
Ha, Dominic Vinh Van '93 (CHI) Chicago, IL St. Henry.
Ha, Hieu Minh '00 (ATL) Army Chaplains; Military Chaplains.
Ha, Louis Pham *c.m.c.* '94 (FWT) Fort Worth, TX Christ the King; Wichita Falls, TX Immaculate Conception of Mary.
Ha, Peter '74 (LA) North Hills, CA Our Lady of Peace.
Ha, Simon Hyung–Min '92 (PH) Springfield, PA Holy Cross; Korean Apostolate.
Ha, Thomas Do Thanh '63 (ORG) Retired.
Haag, Michael B. '05 (SFD) Commission for the Care of Infirm and Retired Priests; Casey, IL St. Charles Borromeo; Greenup, IL Christ the King; Marshall, IL St. Mary.
Haag, Ralph L. *c.s.c.* '04 (FTW)[A] Notre Dame, IN; [B] University of Notre Dame Du Lac; [H] Notre Dame, IN Holy Cross Community, Corby Hall, University of Notre Dame.
Haag, Theodore *o.f.m.* '79 (CLV)[D] Parma, OH Padua Franciscan High School; [N] Brooklyn, OH St. Anthony of Padua Friary.
Haake, Chris G. '97 (PEO) Earlville, IL St. Teresa of Avila; [B] Ottawa, IL Marquette High School.
Haake, Gregory P. *c.s.c.* '07 (FTW)[H] Notre Dame Congregation of Holy Cross, Indiana Province, Provincial House.
Haake, Thomas *o.m.v.* '81 (KC) Bishop's Representative for Health Care Issues; Deans; Gladstone, MO St. Andrew the Apostle.
Haaland, Byron *s.c.j.* '77 (MIL)[P] Franklin, WI St. Francis Residence.
Haas, Dietrich A. '67 (MIL)[T] Waukesha, WI Schoenstatt Fathers.
Haas, Joseph H. '59 (MIL) Retired.
Haas, Lawrence W. '63 (FAR) Retired.
Haas, Robert L. '62 (TOL) Retired.
Haas, Roger *o.f.m.conv.* '69 (PAT) Clifton, NJ St. John Kanty.
Haase, Albert *o.f.m.* '83 (CHI)[N] Chicago, IL Holy Spirit Friary, Order of Friars Minor; [N] Countryside, IL St. Gratian Friary, Franciscan Friars.
Haase, Howard G. '83 (MIL) Union Grove, WI St. Robert Bellarmine; Kansasville, WI St. Mary–Dover.
Hababag, Jimmy '82 (PMB) Boca Raton, FL St. Joan of Arc.
Habash, Yousif A. '75 (OLD) North Hollywood, CA Sacred Heart Parish.
Habash, Chorbishop Yousif '75 (LA) North Hollywood, CA Sacred Heart Syriac Catholic Parish.
Habchi, Nabil *o.m.m.* '02 (OLL)[A] Ann Arbor, MI Maronite Order of the Blessed Virgin Mary; Ann Arbor, MI.
Habe, Robert W. '62 (PIT) Retired.
Haber, Thomas N. '01 (BGP) Leave of Absence.
Haberkorn, Timothy A. '92 (KCK) Topeka, KS Sacred Heart–St. Joseph.
Haberman, C. Robert '75 (PBL) On Duty Outside the Diocese.
Haberman, Clayton J. '50 (WIN) Retired.
Haberman, Robert '75 (SFR)[C] San Rafael, CA Dominican University of California.
Habetz, Thomas E. '01 (LAF) Centerville, LA St. Joseph.
Habib, Fadi '04 (EST) Oak Park, MI Mar Addai Chaldean Parish.
Habiger, Rev. Msgr. James D. '51 (WIN) Retired.
Habiger, Rev. Msgr. James D. '51 (STP)[C] St. Paul, MN University of St. Thomas.
Habiger, Matthew *o.s.b.* '68 (KCK)[I] Atchison, KS St. Benedict's Abbey.
Habing, Paul '80 (SFD) On Sabbatical.
Habison, Gerhart '76 (LA) Torrance, CA Nativity.
Hablewitz, James A. '67 (GB) Little Chute, WI St. John Nepomucene; Vicariate.
Haby, Gerald *s.m.* '69 (SAT)[L] San Antonio, TX Central Catholic Marianist Community Retired.
Haby, Marie–Elie '96 (DET) Archdiocesan Vicars; Detroit, MI St. Stephen–Mary Mother of the Church.
Hachey, Paul J. *s.m.* '84 (ATL) Special or Other (Arch)Diocesan Assignment; [D] Atlanta, GA Marist School; Judicial Vicar.
Hachi, Yuon '88 (ORL) Barefoot Bay, FL St. Luke.
Hack, Michael A. '70 (CHI) Judicial Vicar; Judges; Chicago, IL Notre Dame de Chicago.
Hack, Michael A. '70 (KAL) Defender of the Bond.
Hack, Rev. Msgr. Michael A. (RCK) Defenders of the Bond.
Hack, Thomas '55 (GR) Retired.
Hackel, Daniel H. '02 (LC) Colby, WI St. Mary Help of Christians; Appointed Members.
Hackenmueller, Jerome B. '69 (STP) St. Paul, MN St. Patrick.
Hackert, Eugene C. '51 (NU) Retired.
Hackett, Denis *o.f.m.conv.* '74 (TR) Seaside Park, NJ St. Catharine of Siena.
Hackett, James F. '68 (L) Louisville, KY St. Raphael the Archangel.
Hackman, Marvin R. '71 (CIN) Retired.
Hadberg, Dennis C. '72 (E) On Leave of Absence.
Haddad, Wayne M. '97 (MO) On Duty Outside the Diocese; Navy Chaplains.
Hadden, Robert F. '09 (CIN) Cincinnati, OH Immaculate Heart of Mary.
Hadden, Rev. Msgr. Thomas P. '58 (R) Diocesan Judges; Ex Officio; Office of African Ancestry Ministry and Evangelization; Vicar for African American Ancestry Ministry Retired.
Hadel, Richard E. *s.j.* '65 (STL)[O] St. Louis, MO; [S] St. Louis, MO Retreat House.
Hadgkiss, Joseph *s.o.l.t.* '93 (CC)[G] Robstown, TX Society of Our Lady of the Most Holy Trinity.
Hadley, Christopher *s.j.* '09 (BO)[U] Cambridge, MA St. Edmund's House.
Hadnagy, John R. *o.f.m.conv.* '90 (TOL) Carey, OH Our Lady of Consolation, Basilica–National Shrine.
Hadusek, Paul J. '69 (NU) Retired.
Haefeli, Joaquin C. '51 (LA) Retired.
Haefling, Maurice C. *o.s.b.* '94 (KCK)[I] Atchison, KS St. Benedict's Abbey; Canon City, CO.
Haefling, Maurice C. *o.s.b.* '94 (PBL)[H] Florence, CO Trinity Ranch Conference & Renewal Center, Inc.
Haefner, Douglas J. '83 (MET) Somerset, NJ St. Matthias.
Haemmerle, Gerald R. '67 (CIN) Dayton, OH St. Charles Borromeo; Judges.
Haesaert, William F. *c.s.v.* '80 (LAV) Las Vegas, NV St. Viator; [C] Las Vegas, NV Clerics of St. Viator Retirement Home.
Haesaert, William F. *c.s.v.* '80 (CHI)[N] Arlington Heights Viatorian Province Center–Clerics of St. Viator.
Hafeman, Harry G. '76 (GB) Green Bay, WI SS. Peter and Paul.
Hafemann, George '99 (NY) Port Jervis, NY Immaculate Conception.
Haffey, Thomas P. '69 (HEL) Butte, MT Holy Spirit; Butte, MT St. Ann; Director for Ministry to Priests; Associate Judges; Deaneries; Continuing Formation of the Clergy; Butte, MT St. John the Evangelist.
Haffey, Thomas '69 (HEL) Personnel Board.
Hafner, Gerard '62 (ROC) Retired.
Haft, Ronald C. '07 (CIN) Dayton, OH St. Charles Borromeo.
Hagan, Aelred *o.c.s.o.* '89 (CHR)[E] Moncks Corner, SC Mepkin Abbey.
Hagan, Rev. Msgr. Charles H. '70 (PH) Doylestown, PA Our Lady of Mount Carmel.
Hagan, Harry *o.s.b.* '86 (IND)[A] St. Meinrad, IN Saint Meinrad School of Theology; [K] St. Meinrad, IN St. Meinrad Archabbey.
Hagan, James '69 (SFR) On Duty Outside the Archdiocese.
Hagan, Paul '82 (LFT) Unassigned.
Hagan, Robert A. *s.j.* '72 (NO) New Orleans, LA Holy Name of Jesus.
Hagan, Robert *o.s.a.* '03 (PH)[Y] Villanova, PA Fray de Leon Community; [C] Villanova University.
Hagan, Thomas *o.s.f.s.* '69 (FgM) Wilmington, DE OBLATES OF ST. FRANCIS DE SALES MISSIONS.
Hagan, Vincent J. '66 (RVC) Retired.
Hagarman, Vincent A. *s.j.* '54 (DET)[K] Clarkston, MI Colombiere Center.
Hagearty, Charles B. '59 (HRT) Retired.
Hagedorn, Thomas J. '71 (CLV) Cleveland, OH St. Patrick.
Hagee, Robert J. *s.j.* '61 (CIN)[N] Cincinnati, OH Faber Jesuit Community.
Hagemann, John *o.s.b.* '75 (OM)[C] Elkhorn, NE Mount Michael Benedictine School; [K] Elkhorn, NE Mount Michael Benedictine Abbey.
Hagen, Gerald A. '91 (SUP) Phillips, WI St. Paul the Apostle; Phillips, WI St. Therese of Lisieux; Phillips, WI St. John the Baptist; Presbyteral Council & Diocesan Consultors.
Hagen, John J. *o.s.a.* '57 (PH)[C] Villanova University; [Y] Villanova, PA St. Thomas Monastery.
Hagen, Joseph B. *o.f.m.* '46 (STL)[O] St. Louis, MO Franciscan Friary of St. Anthony of Padua.
Hagen, William *o.m.i.* '61 (BEL)[F] Belleville, IL Shrine of Our Lady of the Snows.
Hagenbach, George G. '54 (PH) Retired.
Hagendorf, Thomas A. *o.praem.* '63 (GB) Green Bay, WI Holy Cross.
Hager, Raymond D. '97 (STL) Elsberry, MO Sacred Heart.
Hager, Van Allen *i.m.c.* '73 (MET)[I] Somerset, NJ Consolata Society for Foreign Missions.
Hagerman, James W. '86 (MET) Parlin, NJ St. Bernadette.
Hagerty, Rev. Msgr. John B. '55 (E) Episcopal Delegate for Retired Priests; Erie, PA Blessed Sacrament; Members Retired.
Haggar, Rt. Rev. Exarch Joseph S. '66 (NTN) Lincoln, RI St. Basil the Great; Woonsocket, RI St. Elias; Defender of the Bond and Promoter of Justice; Protopresbyters; College of Eparchial Consultors; Presbyteral Council; Diocese of Newton for the Melkites in the USA, Inc., a Massachusetts Corporation; Finance Council.
Haggar, Rt. Rev. Exarch Joseph '66 (NTN) Protosyncellus.
Haggerty, Donald F. '89 (NY)[A] Yonkers, NY St. Joseph's Seminary; Censors Librorum.
Haggerty, Shaun Thomas '09 (SFS) Sioux Falls, SD Holy Spirit.
Haggerty, Rev. Msgr. Thomas M. '64 (BRK) Brooklyn, NY St. John the Evangelist; Alcoholism Committee; Lake Orion, MI National Catholic Council on Alcoholism and Related Drug Problems, Inc.
Haggerty, Thomas '79 (RVC) East Meadow, NY St. Raphael; Procurator & Advocates.
Haggins, Martin *o.f.m.cap* '64 (SFR)[B] San Francisco, CA Capuchin Franciscan Order San Buenaventura Friary.
Hagileiram, John S. *s.j.* '85 (CI) Yap, FM St. Ignatius; Diocesan Consultors; Yap; New York, NY Society of Jesus.
Haglof, Anthony '71 (WH)[L] Hinton, WV Monastery of Christ on the Mountain.
Hagstrom, Thomas '93 (SFD) Quincy, IL St. Anthony of Padua; Priests' Personnel Board.
Hahn, Bernardine '43 (STL)[O] St. Louis, MO Franciscan Friary of St. Anthony of Padua.
Hahn, Dominic D. '80 (SEA) Vancouver, WA St. James.
Hahn, Francis *o.m.i.* '72 (FgM) Washington, DC AMERICAN OBLATE MISSIONS.
Hahn, Gerald T. '79 (NEW) Northvale, NJ St. Anthony's; Northern Valley Bergen Deanery 2N.
Hahn, James David '61 (SCL) Cambridge, MN Christ the King; Diocesan Priests Pension Plan Trustees.
Hahn, Peter I. '02 (HBG) Lancaster, PA St. Leo the Great.
Hahn, Raymond W. '74 (E) Erie, PA Our Lady of Mt. Carmel.
Hahn, Scott R. '03 (WDC) Camp Springs, MD St. Philip the Apostle.
Hahn, William P. '04 (COL) Chillicothe, OH St. Peter; Waverly, OH St. Mary, Queen of the Missions.
Hahr, Karl A. '04 (BUR) Knights of Columbus; Richford, VT All Saints.
Hai, Dinh Minh *c.ss.r.* '95 (LA)[P] Baldwin Park Vietnamese Redemptorist Mission.
Hai, Nguyen Tat *c.ss.r.* '95 (LA)[P] Baldwin Park Vietnamese Redemptorist Mission.
Haig, Frank R. *s.j.* '60 (BAL)[S] Baltimore, MD Jesuit Community of Loyola University, Inc.; [B] Jesuit Community of Loyola University, Inc.
Haight, Roger D. *s.j.* '67 (NY)[EE] New York, NY "America;" Residence and publication office of the America Press.
Hain, Rev. Msgr. Raymond B. '48 (LIN)[E] Lincoln, NE Bonacum House Retired.
Haines, Jeffrey R. '85 (MIL) West Bend, WI St. Frances Cabrini; Archdiocesan Consultors.
Haines, Kevin J. '87 (LFT) Westfield, IN St. Maria Goretti.
Haiss, Maurice *s.t.* '56 (WDC)[N] Adelphi, MD Father Judge Missionary Cenacle.
Hajduk, Rev. Msgr. Edward J. '53 (NEW)[M] Rutherford, NJ St. John Vianney Residence for Priests Retired.
Hakala, Thomas *o.carm.* '78 (JOL)[L] Darien Carmelite Provincial Office.
Hake, Rev. Msgr. James E. '60 (SAL) Lincoln, KS St. Joseph Parish; Lincoln, KS St. Patrick Parish; Defender of the Bond; College of Consultors; Council of Priests; Personnel Board; Art and Architecture Commission; Ex Officio; Consultors; Vicars General.
Halabura, Stephen J. '61 (ALN) Retired.
Haladej, Peter '02 (Y) Wellsville, OH Immaculate Conception; East Liverpool, OH St. Aloysius.
Haladus, Victorian *o.f.m.* '61 (SFD)[L] Springfield, IL Our Lady of Angels Friary.
Halaiko, David J. '67 (CLV) Akron, OH Nativity Of the Lord Jesus.
Halbing, William J. '82 (NEW) Newark, NJ St. Antoninus.
Halborg, John T. '80 (NY)[II] New York, NY St. Ansgar Scandinavian Catholic League Retired.
Halbur, Kenneth '09 (DM) West Des Moines, IA St. Francis of Assisi.
Haldane, Richard S. '92 (B) Cottonwood, ID Assumption; Cottonwood, ID St. Anthony's; Cottonwood, ID St. Mary's.
Haldas, Piotr *s.d.s.* (NEW) Garfield, NJ St. Stanislaus Kostka.
Hale, Robert *o.s.b.cam.* '66 (MRY)[F] Big Sur, CA New Camaldoli Hermitage.
Haley, James A. *c.s.p.* '68 (NY)[EE] New York, NY Paulist Fathers' Motherhouse; [EE] Jamaica Estates, NY Paulist Fathers Generalate.
Haley, Thomas '78 (STL) Saint Louis, MO Our Lady of the Rosary.
Haley, William J. '52 (BO) Senior Priests. Retired.
Halfacre, Philip '91 (PEO) Ottawa (Naplate), IL St. Mary's; Ottawa, IL St. Patrick's; Censor Librorum.
Halfmann, Rev. Msgr. Curtis T. '59 (LUB) Retired.
Halfpenny, Rev. Msgr. Patrick F. '75 (DET) Contact; Grosse Pointe Farms, MI St. Paul Catholic Church; Carbondale, IL Catholic Association of Diocesan

Ecumenical and Interreligious Officers (CADEIO); Office for Clergy and Consecrated Life; Ecumenical/Interfaith Relations.
Halka, Frantisek A. '98 (ALT) Army Chaplains; Military Chaplains.
Halkovic, Thomas M. *c.s.c.* '71 (FR)[A] North Easton, MA Stonehill College; [A] North Easton, MA Holy Cross Fathers Religious.
Hall, Adrian B. '64 (NO) Retired.
Hall, Charles D. '79 (GR) Holland, MI Our Lady of the Lake.
Hall, Conan *s.a.* '74 (NY)[EE] Garrison, NY St. Francis of Assisi Novitiate.
Hall, Daleasha (P)[J] Eugene, OR Sacred Heart Medical Center.
Hall, Daniel B. *c.s.v.* '88 (CHI)[N] Arlington Heights Viatorian Province Center–Clerics of St. Viator.
Hall, Daniel R. *c.s.v.* '88 (CHI)[D] Arlington Heights, IL St. Viator High School.
Hall, Douglas C. '79 (OM) Military Chaplains; Air Force Chaplains.
Hall, Howard B. '62 (BR) Retired.
Hall, Howard *o.f.m.* '53 (LA)[P] Santa Barbara, CA Franciscan Friary, Order of Friars Minor (Old Mission).
Hall, James W. '70 (ELP) El Paso, TX St. Thomas Aquinas; Judges.
Hall, John F. '55 (DET) Retired.
Hall, John M. '80 (IND) Martinsville, IN St. Martin of Tours; French Lick, IN Our Lady of the Springs; Council of Priests; French Lick, IN Our Lord Jesus Christ the King.
Hall, John '82 (PHX) On Leave.
Hall, Joseph S. '85 (L) Retired.
Hall, Martin J. '52 (RVC)[M] Amityville, NY St. Pius X Residence Retired.
Hall, Michael *o.s.b.* '65 (WDC)[N] Washington, DC St. Anselm's Abbey.
Hall, R. Eric (WH) Parkersburg, WV St. Francis Xavier's.
Hall, Ralph T. *o.p.* '55 (PRO)[P] Providence St. Thomas Aquinas Priory at Providence College Retired.
Hall, Richard *o.m.i.* '93 (LAR) College of Consultors; Laredo, TX Our Lady of Guadalupe; Priests Personnel Board; Ex Officio Members.
Hall, Robert C. '79 (ALT) Conemaugh, PA Church of the Transfiguration.
Hall, Robert Eric '01 (WH) Parkersburg, WV St. Monica's.
Hall, Robert '85 (HEL) Butte, MT Butte Catholic Community North; Butte, MT Immaculate Conception; Butte, MT St. Joseph; Butte, MT St. Patrick; [G] Butte, MT Montana College of Mineral Science and Technology; Presbyteral Council.
Hall, Rodney '91 (SAC) Retired.
Hall, Roger L. *o.f.m.* '03 (HRT)[L] Waterbury, CT St. Michael Rectory; Waterbury, CT St. Michael.
Hall, Sidney '57 (SAC) Retired.
Hall, Thomas P. *c.s.p.* '77 (NY)[EE] Jamaica Estates Paulist Fathers Generalate.
Hall, Thomas P. *c.s.p.* '77 (MO) Navy Chaplains.
Hall, Timothy J. '06 (WIN) Adrian, MN St. Adrian; Lismore, MN St. Anthony's; Adrian, MN Our Lady of Good Counsel; Lismore, MN St. Kilian.
Hall, Warren R. '89 (NEW)[D] Jersey City, NJ Hudson Catholic Regional High School; Jersey City, NJ St. Aloysius.
Halladay, Paul A. '00 (MOB) On Leave for Military; Army Chaplains.
Hallahan, Kenneth P. '75 (CAM) Blackwood, NJ St. Agnes' Church, Blackwood Terrace, N.J.; Campaign for Human Development.
Hallahan, Timothy J. '57 (SPR) Retired.
Hallahan, William *o.m.i.* '59 (OAK)[M] Oakland, CA Missionary Oblates of Mary Immaculate United States Province.
Hallee, Roger *o.m.i.* '63 (FgM) Washington, DC AMERICAN OBLATE MISSIONS.
Hallegado, Salvador Den '03 (CHI) Chicago, IL St. Genevieve.
Halleman, John L. '55 (STL) Retired.
Halleron, James E. '97 (TOL) Montpelier, OH Sacred Heart; Bryan, OH St. Patrick.
Hallett, Garth L. *s.j.* '59 (STL)[O] St. Louis, MO Jesuit Community Corporation at Saint Louis University – Jesuit Hall.
Halley, James L. '04 (LA) Hospital Chaplains; Long Beach, CA St. Anthony.
Halligan, Damian O. *s.j.* '67 (RVC)[O] Manhasset, NY St. Ignatius Retreat House, Inisfada.
Halligan, John J. *s.j.* '61 (FgM) New York, NY Society of Jesus.
Halligan, Raymond Ferrer *o.p.* '60 (NY)[EE] New York, NY St. Vincent Ferrer Priory.
Hallin, Rev. Msgr. Albert W. '61 (PEO) Ivesdale, IL St. Joseph's; Seymour, IL St. Boniface; Vicariates and Vicars; Commission for Ecumenism; Thomasboro, IL St. Elizabeth of Hungary.
Hallinan, Edward J. '83 (PH) Philadelphia, PA St. Martin De Porres.
Hallinan, Mark C. *s.j.* '95 (NY)[EE] New York, NY Society of Jesus, New York Province; [EE] New York, NY St. Ignatius Loyola Residence; New York, NY; [II] New York, NY Centro Altagracia de Fe y Justicia, Inc. (Altagracia Center of Faith and Justice, Inc.).
Hallissey, Rev. Msgr. James T. '40 (B) Retired.
Hallissey, La Salle *o.p.* '79 (LA) Los Angeles, CA St. Dominic.
Hallock, Addison *m.s.a.* '74 (NOR)[A] Cromwell, CT Holy Apostles College and Seminary; [G] Cromwell, CT Society of the Missionaries of the Holy Apostles; Cromwell, CT Missionaries of the Holy Apostles, Society of the; Cromwell, CT.
Halloran, James F. '43 (COS) Retired.
Halloran, Rev. Msgr. John C. '62 (PRO) Retired.
Halloran, Joseph H. '47 (COS) Retired.
Halloran, Joseph '53 (ALB) Retired.
Halloran, Paul F. '53 (WIN) Retired.
Hallsten, Thomas J. '90 (PHX) Tempe, AZ Holy Spirit Roman Catholic Parish; Dolan Springs, AZ Our Lady of the Desert.
Halovatch, Paul J. '70 (HRT) Special and other Archdiocesan Assignment.
Halphen, Jude '94 (LAF) New Iberia, LA St. Peter; Family Life Ministry.
Halpin, Joseph A. '79 (TR) Retired.
Halpin, Joseph W. *m.m.* '52 (FgM) Maryknoll, NY MARYKNOLL.
Halpine, Rev. Msgr. James F. '52 (TLS) Tulsa, OK Holy Family Cathedral Retired.
Halsema, Douglas G. '00 (PT) Pensacola, FL St. Paul; Independent Review Board; Permanent Deacon Formation Board; Pensacola; Permanent Deacon Formation Team.
Halstead, James R. *o.s.a.* '76 (CHI)[N] Chicago, IL St. John Stone Friary.
Halstead, John (TOL)[G] Tiffin, OH Mercy Hospital.
Halter, Robert *c.ss.r.* '70 (DEN)[N] Denver, CO The Redemptorists/Denver Province; Denver, CO.
Halus, Robert E. '82 (PBR) Perryopolis, PA St. Nicholas.
Halvey, William *s.v.d.* '76 (CHI)[N] Techny, IL Divine Word Residence.
Halvorson, Richard '04 (KCK) Archdiocesan Council on Finances; Paola, KS Holy Trinity.
Ham, Rev. Msgr. Jerome '68 (PEO) Ottawa, IL St. Francis of Assisi; Diocesan College of Consultors.
Hamaday, Ronald A. *o.s.a.* '78 (CAM)[C] Richland, NJ St. Augustine Preparatory School; Richland, NJ.
Hamaday, Ronald A. *o.s.a.* '78 (MO) Navy Reserve Chaplains.
Hamak, William '92 (SFS) Clark, SD St. Michael.
Hamanna, Thomas J. *s.j.* '97 (P)[N] Portland, OR Nestucca Sanctuary.
Hambach, Lawrence *s.v.d.* '61 (FgM) Techny, IL.
Hambrough, Rev. Msgr. Patrick K. '85 (STL) St. Louis, MO St. Mark.
Hamel, J. Thomas *s.j.* '58 (WOR)[O] Worcester, MA Jesuits of the Holy Cross, Inc.
Hamel, James A. '92 (NEW) Military Chaplains; Air Force Chaplains.
Hamel, Joseph L. *m.m.* '85 (FgM) Maryknoll, NY MARYKNOLL.
Hamel, Philip N. '85 (FR) New Bedford, MA St. Joseph–St. Therese.
Hamel, Robert F. '83 (STP) Retired.
Hamernick, Joseph M. *s.j.* '62 (BAL)[S] Baltimore, MD Colombiere Jesuit Community.
Hamernik, Peter P. '56 (WOR) Retired.
Hamill, Gregory J. '94 (PH) Oxford, PA Sacred Heart.
Hamill, William A. *o.s.a.* '68 (TLS)[B] Tulsa, OK Cascia Hall Preparatory School.
Hamilton, Daniel E. '72 (ARL) On Leave of Absence.
Hamilton, Rev. Msgr. Daniel S. '58 (RVC) Lindenhurst, NY Our Lady of Perpetual Help Retired.
Hamilton, Donald Joseph *o.c.s.o.* '46 (SPC)[F] Ava, MO Assumption Abbey (Trappist).
Hamilton, Edward A. '59 (ORL) Retired.
Hamilton, James J. '53 (PRO) Retired.
Hamilton, James '58 (CC) Judges Retired.
Hamilton, John W. '70 (BUR)[D] Rutland, VT St. Joseph/Kervick Residence Retired.
Hamilton, Ken *s.v.d.* '82 (OAK) Oakland, CA St. Lawrence O'Toole–St. Cyril of Jerusalem.
Hamilton, Mark M. '94 (L) New Haven, KY Immaculate Conception; New Haven, KY St. Catherine.
Hamilton, Stephen V. '99 (OKL) Kingfisher, OK SS. Peter and Paul; Region IX; Council of Priests Archdiocesan; Defenders of the Bond.
Hamilton, Terence J. '73 (CIN) Cincinnati, OH St. Martin of Tours; Priest Councilors.
Hamilton, Thomas M. '88 (SFR) San Francisco, CA St. Gabriel; Young Ladies' Institute.
Hamilton, Thomas *o.f.m.conv.* (OAK)[M] Castro Valley, CA Conventual Franciscans (Province of St. Joseph of Cupertino).
Hamilton, William J. *s.j.* '63 (BO)[D] Dorchester, MA Boston College High School; [U] Boston The Society of Jesus of New England–Provincial Offices.
Hamilton, William J. *s.j.* '63 (MO) DEPARTMENT OF VETERANS AFFAIRS HOSPITALS AND CHAPLAINS.
Hamilton, William J. '80 (SPR) Northampton, MA St. Mary of the Assumption.
Hamlet, Ralph '62 (RIC) Retired.
Hamlett, Christopher M. '82 (E) Erie, PA Mount Calvary.
Hamm, David A. *s.t.* '75 (BLX) Pass Christian, MS St. Stephen.
Hamm, M. Dennis *s.j.* '70 (OM)[K] Omaha, NE Jesuit Community at Creighton University.
Hamm, Robert E. *s.j.* '68 (FgM)[S] Towson Maryland Province of the Society of Jesus; Towson, MD Society of Jesus.
Hamm, Thomas F. '00 (STU) Caldwell, OH St. Michael; Caldwell, OH Immaculate Conception; [M] Caldwell, OH RCIA; Diocesan Director of Ecumenism; RCIA.
Hammel, Gerald R. *s.m.* '78 (STL) St. Louis, MO Our Lady of the Pillar.
Hammel, Gerald *s.m.* '06 (STL)[O] St. Louis, MO Marianist Community, Our Lady of the Pillar Parish.
Hammelman, William *o.s.b.* '71 (P) Silverton, OR St. Paul; [L] St. Benedict, OR Mt. Angel Abbey; Area Vicars.
Hammer, James *o.f.m.cap.* '65 (PRT) Portland, ME St. Joseph's; [M] Portland, ME.
Hammer, Jefferson J. '60 (NY) Retired.
Hammer, Michael J. '69 (MIL) Special Assignment; Coordinator of Catholic AIDS Ministry.
Hammer, William D. '80 (L) Bardstown, KY Basilica of St. Joseph Proto–Cathedral; Deans; Ex Officio; Fairfield, KY St. Michael.
Hammerl, Rev. Msgr. Leo E. '44 (BUF)[O] Tonawanda, NY O'Hara Residence Retired.
Hammerschmitt, Clemens '73 (PMB) Lake Worth, FL St. Matthew; [K] Palm Beach Gardens, FL Diocesan Council of Catholic Women; Council of Catholic Women.
Hammerstein, Harold *o.s.b.* '48 (IND)[K] St. Meinrad St. Meinrad Archabbey.
Hammes, Greg '07 (KCK)[B] Shawnee Mission, KS Bishop Miege High School.
Hammes, Gregory '07 (KCK) Leawood, KS Curé of Ars.
Hammett, Peter E. *o.s.b.* '72 (NO)[P] St. Benedict, LA St. Joseph Abbey; Franklinton, LA Holy Family.
Hammond, Charles '76 (SAG) Sandusky, MI St. Joseph.
Hammond, Gerard E. *m.m.* '60 (FgM) Maryknoll, NY MARYKNOLL.
Hammond, H. Martin '73 (BAL) Baltimore, MD St. Isaac Jogues.
Hammond, John *o.s.b.* '50 (BUR)[E] Weston, VT Priory of Benedictine Monks.
Hammond, Joseph '89 (KNX) Morristown, TN St. Patrick.
Hammond, Mark J. '89 (COL) Mt. Vernon, OH St. Vincent de Paul; Defenders of the Bond; Health Affairs Department (Hospitals).
Hammond, Robert '52 (FTW) Retired.
Hamon, Victor '93 (TYL) Diboll, TX Our Lady of Guadalupe.
Hampe, Rev. Msgr. Raymond A. '54 (STL) St. Charles, MO St. Peter; St. Charles, MO St. Joseph Health Center; [J] St. Charles, MO SSM St. Joseph Health Center.
Hamperzonian, Jerry '70 (MO) On Duty Outside Diocese; DEPARTMENT OF VETERANS AFFAIRS HOSPITALS AND CHAPLAINS.
Hamperzonian, Jerry '70 (SD) San Diego, CA Blessed Sacrament; La Jolla, CA Veterans Administration Hospital.
Hampsch, John *c.m.f.* '52 (LA)[V] Rancho Dominguez, CA Dominguez Seminary Inc.
Hamrogue, John *c.ss.r.* '63 (BRK) Brooklyn, NY Our Lady of Perpetual Help Basilica.
Han, Kwang Seog (HON) Honolulu, HI Korean Catholic Community.
Han, Thomas '83 (LA) West Covina, CA St. Christopher.
Han, Young Seung J. '98 (SB) Norco, CA St. Andrew Kim Korean Community.
Hanbury, Rev. Msgr. Kevin M. '72 (NEW) Livingston, NJ St. Philomena; [B] School of Diplomacy and Intl. Rels.; Office of the Superintendent of Schools/Vicariate for Education; Members; Vicar for Education and Superintendent of Schools.
Hanchon, Rev. Msgr. Donald F. '74 (DET) Presbyteral Council; Detroit, MI Holy Redeemer.
Hancock, Rev. Msgr. George H. '47 (OWN) Age Group Six Representative.
Hancock, Rev. Msgr. George '47 (OWN) Retired.
Hand, Dennis M. '75 (GRY) On Duty Outside the Diocese.
Hand, John D. '98 (PH) Philadelphia, PA Saint Cyprian.
Hand, Kenneth J. '72 (BRK) On Leave/Unassigned.
Hand, Raymond *o.f.m.cap.* '62 (NY)[EE] Yonkers, NY St. Clare Friary.
Hand, Robert T. '97 (SAV) Columbus, GA Our Lady of Lourdes Retired.
Handal, Ephrem '03 (NTN) McLean, VA Holy Transfiguration.
Handges, Rev. Msgr. William E. '64 (ALN) Coplay, PA St. Peter.

Handrahan, John B. *s.j.* '58 (BO)[U] Weston, MA Campion Health Center, Inc.
Handwerker, Rev. Msgr. Valentine N. '74 (MEM) Memphis, TN Cathedral of the Immaculate Conception; [C] Memphis, TN Immaculate Conception Cathedral School.
Hanefeldt, Joseph G. '84 (OM) On Duty Outside the Archdiocese.
Hanel, Charles T. '83 (MIL) Hubertus, WI St. Gabriel.
Haney, John R. '61 (PIT) Pittsburgh, PA St. Gabriel of the Sorrowful Virgin; Clergy Personnel Board; Priest Council.
Haney, Michael *o.f.m.* '74 (SUP) Bayfield, WI Holy Family; Washburn, WI St. Ann; Bayfield, WI St. Joseph; Bayfield, WI St. Francis; Washburn, WI St. Louis.
Haney, T. Ronald '58 (HBG) New Cumberland, PA St. Theresa of the Infant Jesus Retired.
Haney, William *o.f.m.* '84 (MRY)[F] San Juan Bautista, CA Franciscan Friars; [H] San Juan Bautista, CA St. Francis Retreat Center.
Haney, William *o.f.m.* '84 (SJ) San Jose, CA Our Lady of Guadalupe.
Hanh, Joseph Phan Trong '70 (KC) Kansas City, MO Church of the Holy Martyrs.
Hanhauser, Martin *o.f.m.* (PAT)[N] Ringwood, NJ Holy Name Friary, Inc.
Hanic, John D. '83 (CHL) North Wilkesboro, NC St. John Baptist de LaSalle.
Hanic, Jonathan '67 (CHL) Absent On Leave.
Hanifan, Mark '07 (RNO) Respect Life Commission; Reno, NV St. Albert the Great.
Hanifin, Michael P. '87 (ORG) Yorba Linda, CA Santa Clara de Asis; Boy Scouts/Girl Scouts; Council of Priests.
Hanincik, Frank A. '08 (PSC) New Britain, CT Holy Trinity; Trumbull, CT St. John the Baptist.
Hankee, Robert Jason '02 (IND) Greensburg, IN Immaculate Conception; Napoleon, IN St. Maurice; Greensburg, IN St. Denis; Council of Priests.
Hankiewicz, Edward A. '79 (GR) On Special Assignment; Grand Rapids, MI Sacred Heart of Jesus; Tribunal Office.
Hankiewicz, Edward A. '79 (KAL) Judges.
Hankiewicz, Edward J. (GR) Deans.
Hankomoone, Cornelius *s.s.* '96 (BAL)[S] Baltimore Society of St. Sulpice, Province of the United States.
Hanks, Gregory '89 (AUS) Rockdale, TX St. Joseph.
Hanks, Sebastian '81 (PH)[Y].
Hankus, David J. '84 (JOL) Oswego, IL St. Anne.
Hanley, Rev. Msgr. Andrew W. '40 (SD) Retired.
Hanley, Daniel F. '05 (ARL) Falls Church, VA St. James; Advocates.
Hanley, Dennis P. '81 (HRT) Military Chaplains.
Hanley, Foster *o.carm.* '63 (TUC)[A] Tucson, AZ Salpointe Catholic High School; [D] Tucson, AZ Carmelite Priory.
Hanley, Gerald T. '73 (RNO) Retired.
Hanley, James R. *s.j.* '58 (SJ)[M] Los Gatos, CA Sacred Heart Jesuit Center.
Hanley, John A. *o.s.f.s.* '86 (ALN)[B] Center Valley, PA DeSales University; [K] Center Valley, PA Oblates of St. Francis de Sales; [O] Center Valley, PA DeSales University (Center Valley).
Hanley, John P. '94 (PAT) Paterson, NJ St. Casimir's; Auditors Retired.
Hanley, John W. *o.m.i.* (BO) Tewksbury, MA St. William; Presbyteral Council.
Hanley, John '56 (PHX)[G] Phoenix, AZ Mount Claret Roman Catholic Retreat Center Retired.
Hanley, Rev. Msgr. Joseph F. '68 (CHR) Deans; Personnel Committee.
Hanley, Rev. Msgr. Joseph F. '68 (CHR) North Charleston, SC St. John; Charleston, SC Blessed Sacrament; College of Consultors.
Hanley, Lawrence F. '52 (CHI) Retired.
Hanley, Thomas E. '65 (WIL) Absent on Sick Leave.
Hanley, William '69 (ORL) Melbourne, FL Our Lady of Lourdes.
Hanlon, Rev. Msgr. Andrew J. '68 (PH) Brookhaven, PA Our Lady of Charity.
Hanlon, Berard J. *o.f.m.* '63 (FgM) New York, NY Holy Name Province.
Hanlon, Capistran *o.f.m.* '60 (ALB)[B] Siena College.
Hanlon, Edward J. '86 (WOR) South Grafton, MA St. James.
Hanlon, Francis *o.s.f.s.* '76 (VEN) Fort Myers, FL St. Cecilia.
Hanlon, Kevin J. *m.m.* '89 (NY)[EE] Maryknoll Maryknoll Fathers and Brothers.
Hanlon, Robert M. *s.j.* '64 (BO)[U] Boston The Society of Jesus of New England–Provincial Offices.
Hanly, Denis J. *m.m.* '59 (FgM) Maryknoll, NY MARYKNOLL.
Hanly, Michael A. '67 (NEW) Verona, NJ Our Lady of the Lake.
Hann, Michael *c.i.c.m.* '73 (ARL)[H] Arlington, VA Missionhurst, C.I.C.M.–Central House and Provincialate.
Hanna, Ayad '99 (EST) Troy, MI St. Joseph Chaldean Parish.
Hanna, Dominique '07 (SAM) Atlanta, GA St. Joseph's Maronite Church.
Hanna, George *s.d.b.* '66 (WDC) Washington, DC Nativity.
Hanna, Jack H. *c.s.b.* '74 (GAL)[E] Houston, TX St. Thomas High School.
Hannafey, Francis T. *s.j.* '93 (BGP)[B] Fairfield, CT Fairfield University; [O] Fairfield, CT The Fairfield Jesuit Community–Fairfield University.
Hannafin, Steven J. '01 (RVC) Leave of Absence.
Hannah, Raymond *s.v.d.* '60 (TR)[N] Bordentown, NJ Society of the Divine Word.
Hannan, Gabriel *s.t.* '55 (WDC)[N] Adelphi, MD Father Judge Missionary Cenacle.
Hannan, James E. *o.s.a.* '44 (SD)[J] San Diego, CA Augustinian Community.
Hannan, James G. '81 (BRK) On Leave/Unassigned.
Hannan, John K. '55 (SAC) Priests' Personnel Board, Diocesan; Sacramento, CA St. Philomene Retired.
Hannan, John *s.m.* '68 (FgM) THE SOCIETY OF MARY.
Hannappel, Joseph A. '84 (GI) Kearney, NE St. James; Diocesan Consultors; Personnel Board.
Hanneke, Rev. Msgr. Richard E. '76 (STL) Office of Priests' Personnel and Continuing Formation of Priests; St. Louis, MO St. Stephen, Protomartyr.
Hanneman, Dennis A. '72 (OM) Deans; Bellevue, NE St. Mary; Deans.
Hannes, David A. '83 (PRM) Flushing, MI St. Michael; Presbyteral Council; Judge.
Hannick, Anthony S. '58 (YAK) Retired.
Hannigan, John T. '76 (MO) Navy Chaplains; Military Chaplains.
Hannigan, Raymond (HEL) Retired.
Hannigan, Rev. Msgr. Thomas J. '49 (MAN) Manchester, NH St. Catherine; Presbyteral Council Retired.
Hannon, James J. '57 (RVC) Retired.
Hannon, Rev. Msgr. James W. '88 (BAL) Frostburg, MD St. Michael; Grantsville, MD St. Ann; Midland, MD St. Joseph; Westernport, MD St. Peter; [V] Frostburg, MD St. Michael School Endowment Trust; Lonaconing, MD St. Mary of the Annunciation; Consultors; Advocates; Consultors.
Hannon, Jim (RVC) Westbury, NY St. Brigid.
Hannon, John M. '60 (BO) Hanson, MA St. Joseph the Worker.
Hannon, Joseph F. *s.d.b.* '73 (MO) Army Chaplains.
Hannon, Joseph (KCK) Fort Leavenworth, KS St. Ignatius Chapel.
Hannon, Ken *o.m.i.* '72 (SAT)[C] Oblate School of Theology; [L] San Antonio, TX De Mazenod House.
Hannon, Kevin '75 (SY) Manlius, NY St. Ann.
Hannon, Michael '47 (ORL) Retired.
Hannon, Patrick *c.s.c.* '89 (P)[B] University of Portland; [L] Portland, OR Holy Cross Fathers & Brothers, C.S.C. – University of Portland.
Hannon, Richard T. '93 (GAY) Retired.
Hannon, Robert J. '79 (Y) Canton, OH St. Therese Little Flower Retired.
Hannon, W. *c.s.c.* (FTW)[H] Notre Dame Congregation of Holy Cross, Indiana Province, Provincial House.
Hanouille, Roger M. *o.s.a.* '59 (PH)[Y] Villanova, PA St. Thomas Monastery.
Hanowsky, Rev. Canon Andrew '88 (SJP) Cleveland, OH Ss. Peter and Paul; Administrative Council; Consultors; St. Josaphat Sacerdotal Society; Presbyters.
Hanrahan, Denis G. '59 (OKL) Guthrie, OK St. Mary's.
Hanrahan, Edward J. *s.j.* '61 (BO)[U] Weston, MA Campion Health Center, Inc.
Hanrahan, John A. '66 (RCK) Retired.
Hanrahan, John W. '55 (L) Retired.
Hanrahan, William P. '69 (NEW) Military Chaplains.
Hanrahan, William '69 (ANC) Diocesan Consultors; Notaries.
Hansen, Howard *o.f.m.conv.* '57 (STP)[N] Prior Lake, MN Franciscan Retreats.
Hansen, Lawrence H. '68 (NU) Retired.
Hansen, Michael H. '66 (NEW) Retired.
Hansen, Michael '67 (NEW)[M] Rutherford, NJ St. John Vianney Residence for Priests.
Hansen, Stephen '06 (KC) Lexington, MO Immaculate Conception.
Hanser, F. Patrick *c.m.* '70 (DAL)[J] Dallas, TX Congregation of the Mission, Western Province.
Hanson, Rev. Msgr. Donald M. '71 (RVC) East Hampton, NY Most Holy Trinity.
Hanson, Rev. Msgr. James E. '61 (STL) Ste. Genevieve, MO St. Joseph.
Hanson, John Henry *o.praem.* '06 (ORG)[I] Silverado, CA Norbertine Fathers of Orange Inc.; [D] Silverado, CA St. Michael's Preparatory School.
Hanson, Kirby C. '70 (SFR) Retired.
Hanson, Richard N. '75 (CHL) Unassigned.
Hanson, Rev. Msgr. William A. '72 (RVC) Port Jefferson Station, NY St. Gerard Majella; North Brookhaven Deanery.
Hanudel, Francis A. *o.f.m.* (NY) New York, NY St. Anthony of Padua.
Hanus, Thomas J. '66 (AUS) Retired.
Hanwell, John J. *s.j.* '91 (BGP)[E] Fairfield, CT Fairfield College Preparatory School; [O] Fairfield, CT The Fairfield Jesuit Community–Fairfield University.
Hao, William T. '09 (ATL) Douglasville, GA St. Theresa.
Hapanowicz, Arthur R. '56 (SY) Utica, NY Holy Trinity.
Hapka, Jerome A. *s.a.c.* '55 (MIL)[P] Milwaukee, WI Pallotti House.
Harahan, Rev. Msgr. Robert E. '74 (NEW) Wyckoff, NJ St. Elizabeth.
Harak, G. Simon *s.j.* '79 (MIL)[P] Milwaukee, WI Jesuit Community at Marquette University.
Harak, G. Simon *s.j.* '79 (BO)[U] Boston The Society of Jesus of New England–Provincial Offices.
Haran, F. Ignatius '59 (SAC) Folsom, CA St. John the Baptist; [O] Sacramento, CA The Parochial Fund, Inc.; Members Retired.
Haran, James E. '44 (BUF) Retired.
Harbaugh, Paul E. '74 (BEL) Leave of Absence.
Harbaugh, Russell D. '04 (MEM) Dyersburg, TN Holy Angels Church.
Harbour, Gerald G. '73 (PRO) Pawtucket, RI St. John the Baptist.
Harbour, Linn S. '86 (MOB) On Leave for Military; Air Force Chaplains.
Harcarik, Bernard M. '63 (PIT) Pittsburgh, PA Prince of Peace.
Harder, Kenneth J. '96 (TLS) Stillwater, OK St. Francis Xavier; Judges; Adjutant Judicial Vicar.
Hardesty, Ernest L. '75 (LR)[I] Russellville, AR St. Leo the Great University Parish; Russellville, AR St. Leo the Great University Parish; Atkins, AR Assumption B.V.M.
Hardiman, Rev. Msgr. Michael J. '78 (BRK) Woodside, NY St. Sebastian.
Hardin, Boniface *o.s.b.* '59 (IND)[K] St. Meinrad St. Meinrad Archabbey.
Hardin, John S. *o.f.m.* '86 (SFR) San Francisco, CA St. Boniface.
Hardin, John *o.f.m.* '82 (OAK)[M] Oakland, CA Franciscan Friars (Province of St. Barbara); [R] Oakland, CA Province of Saint Barbara Fraternal Care Trust.
Harding, Ignatius *o.f.m.* '72 (FgM) New York, NY Holy Name Province.
Harding, Pius X *o.s.b.* '93 (P)[L] St. Benedict, OR Mt. Angel Abbey.
Hardon, John *s.j.* '47 (WDC)[W] Kensington, MD Inter Mirifica.
Hardy, J. Patrick '06 (SUP) Lac du Flambeau, WI St. Anthony of Padua; Manitowish Waters, WI Our Lady Queen of Peace.
Hardy, L. Richard '06 (PAT) Parsippany, NJ St. Peter the Apostle.
Haren, Thomas A. '73 (CLV) Garfield Heights, OH St. Monica; Holy Name Societies, Cleveland Diocesan Union.
Harfmann, John G. *s.s.j.* '62 (BAL)[S] Baltimore, MD St. Joseph Society of the Sacred Heart House of Central Administration.
Harfmann, John G. *s.s.j.* '62 (NO) New Orleans, LA Corpus Christi–Epiphany.
Hargaden, Kevin J. '99 (ATL) LaGrange, GA St. Peter; [J] LaGrange, GA LaGrange Jr. College; Special or Other (Arch)Diocesan Assignment.
Harger, Bruce E. '01 (NEW) Hillsdale, NJ St. John the Baptist.
Hargesheimer, Thomas J. '68 (WIN) Diocesan Consultors; Winona, MN St. Stanislaus; Deans; Council of Catholic Women; Winona, MN St. John Nepomucene.
Hargreaves, Henry G. *s.j.* '47 (SPK)[J] Spokane, WA Regis Community.
Harhager, John H. *s.m.* '79 (ATL)[D] Atlanta, GA Marist School.
Harhager, John *s.m.* '79 (FgM) Boston, MA U.S. Mission Promoter.
Harkins, Conrad *o.f.m.* '61 (STU)[A] Steubenville, OH Franciscan University of Steubenville; [H] Steubenville, OH Holy Spirit Friary.
Harkins, John M. '65 (PH) Philadelphia, PA St. Ambrose.
Harkins, Kenneth *o.p.* '67 (WDC)[B] Washington, DC Dominican House of Studies.
Harkins, Michael J. '79 (BO) Jamaica Plain, MA St. Thomas Aquinas.
Harkins, Rev. Msgr. Thaddeus '55 (JKS) Retired.
Harkrader, Edward O. '69 (PEO) Retired.
Harlow, Denis '58 (BLX) Retired.
Harlow, Lance W. '93 (BUR) Elected Members; Deans; Charismatic Renewal; Bellows Falls, VT St. Charles.
Harlow, Sean R. *o.carm.* '69 (NY) New York, NY St. John the Martyr.
Harman, Paul F. *s.j.* '68 (WOR)[O] Worcester, MA Jesuits of the Holy Cross, Inc.
Harman, Peter C. '99 (SFD) Springfield, IL St. Katharine Drexel; Springfield, IL Cathedral of the Immaculate Conception.
Harmening, Adrian W. *o.s.b.* '55 (RIC) Richmond, VA St. Joseph; [K] Richmond, VA Mary Mother of the Church Abbey.
Harmless, William J. *s.j.* '87 (OM)[K] Omaha, NE Jesuit Community at Creighton University.
Harmon, Alban *c.p.* '58 (BAL)[S] Baltimore, MD St.

Joseph's Passionist Community; Defenders of the Bond; Baltimore, MD St. Joseph Passionist Monastery Parish.
Harmon, Barry J. '90 (SFD) Arcola, IL St. John the Baptist; Tuscola, IL Forty Martyrs; Comite Diocesano de Ministerio Hispano – Diocesan Committee for Hispanic Ministry.
Harmon, John '93 (DM) Urbandale, IA St. Pius X.
Harms, Rev. Msgr. William C. '65 (NEW) Westfield, NJ St. Helen; Archdiocesan Implementation Team.
Harnan, James A. *m.s.c.* '64 (SAT) Stonewall, TX St. Francis Xavier; [L] San Antonio, TX Missionaries of the Sacred Heart.
Harness, H. Robert '82 (DAV) Davenport, IA Holy Family.
Harnett, Brendan G. '73 (PRT) Auburn, ME Immaculate Heart of Mary Parish; Norway, ME Blessed Teresa of Calcutta Parish.
Harnett, Edward F. '58 (CHI) Wilmette, IL St. Francis Xavier Retired.
Harnett, Rev. Msgr. Timothy '56 (SD) Retired.
Harney, Thomas C. '62 (GF) Laurel, MT St. Anthony.
Harnischfeger, William '93 (PHX) Retired.
Haro–Palos, Arturo '99 (ATL) Cleveland, GA St. Paul the Apostle; Blairsville, GA St. Francis of Assisi.
Harold, Rev. Msgr. Thomas J. '91 (RVC) Valley Stream, NY Holy Name of Mary; Belmont Deanery; Priests' Personnel Assignment Board.
Harpe, David L. '94 (GR) Faculties Suspended.
Harpel, John *s.v.d.* '44 (DUB)[H] New Hampton, IA Mercy Medical Center–New Hampton.
Harper, Henry *s.s.j.* '50 (BAL) Baltimore, MD St. Peter Claver.
Harper, John H. '87 (GB) De Pere, WI St. Francis Xavier; De Pere, WI St. Mary.
Harr, Gerald J. '62 (GI) Gering, NE Christ the King.
Harr, Richard *o.m.i.* '52 (BO)[X] Tewksbury, MA Immaculate Heart of Mary Residence.
Harren, Robert C. '66 (SCL) St. Stephen, MN St. Stephen's; Adjutant Judicial Vicar; Judges; Censores Librorum.
Harren, Robert '66 (SCL) Promoter Justitiae.
Harrer, Ronald *o.m.i.* '70 (STP)[K] St. Paul, MN Oblate Residence; Regions Medical Center.
Harrigan, Maurice D. '96 (LA) Los Angeles, CA Holy Trinity.
Harrigan, Philip K. *s.j.* '56 (BO)[U] Weston, MA Campion Health Center, Inc.
Harriman, Rev. Msgr. Michael D. '68 (SFR) San Francisco, CA St. Cecilia; College of Consultors; Apostleship of the Sea.
Harrington, Ashley J. *o.carm.* '67 (NEW) Englewood, NJ St. Cecilia's.
Harrington, Ashley *o.carm.* '67 (JOL)[L] Darien Carmelite Provincial Office.
Harrington, Brian J. '67 (FR) Seekonk, MA Our Lady of Mt. Carmel.
Harrington, Daniel J. *s.j.* '71 (BO)[U] Cambridge, MA Jogues House.
Harrington, Donald J. *c.m.* '73 (BRK)[D] Queens, NY St. John's University; [T] Jamaica, NY St. Vincent's House.
Harrington, Donald J. *c.m.* '73 (NY)[C] Staten Island, NY St. John's University Staten Island Campus.
Harrington, Ignatius '82 (NTN) Westerville, OH Holy Resurrection; Zanesville, OH Holy Trinity; Continuing Education of Clergy Office.
Harrington, James J. '53 (BO) Senior Priests. Retired.
Harrington, Jay M. *o.p.* '85 (STL)[O] St. Louis, MO St. Dominic Priory.
Harrington, Jay *o.p.* '85 (CHI)[N] Chicago Dominicans (Provincial Office).
Harrington, Jeremy *o.f.m.* '59 (CIN)[T] Cincinnati, OH Community Support Charitable Trust; Washington, DC Commissariat of the Holy Land; Washington, DC; [N] Cincinnati St. Francis Seraph Friary.
Harrington, Jeremy *o.f.m.* '59 (FgM)[N] Washington, DC Franciscan Monastery USA Inc.; Washington, DC COMMISSARIAT OF THE HOLY LAND; [N] Washington, DC Commissariat of the Holy Land, Franciscan Monastery – Mount St. Sepulchre.
Harrington, John P. '66 (BRK) Astoria, NY St. Joseph.
Harrington, John P. '04 (FR) Awaiting Assignment.
Harrington, Rev. Msgr. Joseph D. '56 (HEL)[B] Helena, MT Carroll College; Diocesan Consultors; Episcopal Vicar for Senior Status Priests Retired.
Harrington, Rev. Msgr. Joseph '56 (HEL) Friends of The Catholic University; Diocesan Finance Council.
Harrington, Kevin '75 (FR) New Bedford, MA St. Francis of Assisi.
Harrington, Rev. Msgr. Kieran E. '01 (BRK) Brooklyn, NY St. Joseph; Public Information Office; Office of Legislative Affairs; Secretariat for Communications.
Harrington, Mark '79 (PHX) Anthem, AZ St. Rose Philippine Duchesne Roman Catholic Parish.
Harrington, Michael C. (BO) Dorchester, MA St. Ann; Vocations.
Harrington, Richard L. '66 (BO) Senior Priests. Retired.
Harrington, Rev. Msgr. Robert J. '71 (NEW) Elizabeth, NJ St. Mary of the Assumption; Archdiocesan Judges.
Harrington, Rev. Msgr. Russell J. '79 (LAF) Church Point, LA Assumption of the Blessed Virgin Mary; Chancellor & Vicar for Priests; Vicar for Priests; Diocesan Consultors; Secretariat of Religious Personnel.
Harrington, Rev. Msgr. Thomas J. '64 (FR) Defenders of the Bond Retired.
Harris, Alfred J. '94 (WDC) Washington, DC St. Mary, Mother of God.
Harris, Anton T. *s.j.* '75 (NY)[EE] Cardinal Spellman Hall, Jesuit Community.
Harris, Arlen *o.f.m.cap.* (NY) New York, NY Good Shepherd.
Harris, Daniel E. *c.m.* '74 (STL)[B] St. Louis, MO St. John Neumann House; [O] St. Louis, MO Lazarist Residence.
Harris, Daniel (STL)[B] St. Louis, MO Aquinas Institute of Theology.
Harris, David G. '06 (GAL) Danbury, TX St. Anthony de Padua.
Harris, David W. '08 (L) Pewee Valley, KY St. Aloysius.
Harris, Edwin B. *s.j.* '75 (SJ)[D] San Jose, CA Bellarmine College Preparatory; Los Gatos, CA.
Harris, Gerald P. '79 (SUP) River Falls, WI St. Bridget.
Harris, Glenn H. '92 (PEO) Chillicothe, IL St. Edward's.
Harris, Rev. Msgr. Jack D. '74 (LR) Stuttgart, AR Holy Rosary; Presbyteral Council; Priests Personnel Board (Diocesan); Stuttgart, AR SS. Cyril and Methodius; [K] Stuttgart, AR Holy Rosary Catholic School "Vision 2000" Educational Trust Fund.
Harris, Rev. Msgr. James E. '85 (LAR) Presbyteral Council; Laredo, TX St. John Neumann.
Harris, Julian P. '91 (PMB) Boynton Beach, FL St. Thomas More.
Harris, Rev. Msgr. Martin P. '55 (WDC) Hollywood, MD St. John Francis Regis Retired.
Harris, Michael B. '89 (SCR) Unassigned or Leave of Absence.
Harris, Raymond L. '94 (BAL) Graduate Studies.
Harris, Richard D. '93 (CHR) Columbia, SC St. Joseph; Building & Renovation Commission; Vocations.
Harris, Richard '93 (CHR) Vocations Board; College of Consultors; Personnel Committee.
Harris, Rev. Msgr. Robert M. '59 (BRK)[O] Brooklyn, NY St. Vincent's Services, Inc.; [M] Brooklyn, NY St. Vincent's Services, Inc.; Released from Diocesan Assignment.
Harris, Robert '96 (DM) Des Moines, IA All Saints.
Harris, Scott T. *m.m.* '78 (FgM) Maryknoll, NY MARYKNOLL.
Harris, Steven J. '80 (PH) Wayne, PA St. Isaac Jogues; Archdiocesan Judges.
Harris, Timothy *t.o.r.* '06 (ARL) Herndon, VA St. Joseph.
Harris, Rev. Msgr. Wallace A. '72 (NY) Archdiocesan Consultors.
Harris, Whitney G. '80 (LKC) On Duty Outside the Diocese.
Harris, William R. '78 (SEA) Shoreline, WA St. Mark.
Harrison, Brian W. *o.s.* '85 (PCE) On Duty Outside the Diocese.
Harrison, Rev. Msgr. Craig F. '87 (FRS) Bakersfield, CA St. Francis of Assisi; Diocesan Consultors; Vicars Forane; Personnel Board; Priests' Council.
Harrison, Eugene *c.ss.r* '01 (NO) New Orleans, LA St. Alphonsus; New Orleans, LA St. Mary's Assumption; New Orleans, LA St. Mary's Chapel.
Harrison, George E. '68 (FR) Fall River, MA Holy Name.
Harrison, James '55 (ATL) Lawrenceville, GA St. Marguerite D'Youville.
Harrison, Jeffrey D. *s.j.* '87 (FgM) St. Louis, MO Society of Jesus.
Harrison, Jeffrey D. *s.j.* (STL) St. Louis, MO St. Matthew, Apostle.
Harrison, John *c.ss.r.* '67 (BAL) Annapolis, MD St. Mary.
Harrison, Michael *s.s.c.* '48 (PRO)[P] Bristol, RI St. Columban's Retirement House Retired.
Harrison, Michael *s.s.c.* '48 (OM)[K] St. Columbans Missionary Society of St. Columban.
Harrison, Patrick C. '91 (OM) Omaha, NE St. Joan of Arc; Judicial Vicar; Archbishop's Appointees.
Harrison, Robert '64 (NY)[E] Bronx, NY Cardinal Hayes High School.
Harrison, Robert *c.ss.r.* '05 (PH) Philadelphia, PA St. Peter the Apostle.
Harrison, Timothy A. '91 (BO) Gloucester, MA Holy Family.
Harrison, William S. '72 (PH) Cheltenham, PA St. Joseph; Cheltenham, PA Presentation of Blessed Virgin Mary.
Harrity, Rev. Msgr. Dennis '60 (DET) Retired.
Harrity, Patrick V. *c.m.* '68 (CHI)[N] Chicago, IL Vincentian Community, Congregation of the Mission, Western Province.
Harrold, John J. '92 (GBG) Herminie, PA St. Edward.
Harrold, Rev. Msgr. Michael '50 (VIC) Victoria, TX Our Lady of Victory Cathedral; Diocesan Consultors; Victoria Deanery; Presbyteral Council; Judges; Priests' Personnel Board.
Harry, William *o.carm.* '83 (TUC)[A] Tucson, AZ Salpointe Catholic High School; [D] Tucson, AZ Carmelite Priory.
Harshaw, Albert E. '73 (CAM) Camden, NJ St. Joseph Catholic Church, East Camden, N.J. (Pro–Cathedral).
Hart, Brian '63 (SEA) Retired.
Hart, Charles *o.f.m.* '79 (SFD)[L] Springfield, IL Our Lady of Angels Friary.
Hart, E. James '96 (FWT) Chancellor and Moderator of the Curia; Diocesan Pastoral Council; Presbyteral Council and Consultors; Diocesan Finance Council; Catholic Foundation of North Texas; St. Joseph's Health Care Trust; Building Commission; Diocesan Pastoral Finance Committee; Conduct Review Board.
Hart, Edward J. '55 (BUR) Shelburne, VT Retired.
Hart, Gregory G. '84 (LR) Harrison, AR Mary, Mother of God; Deans; Yellville, AR St. Andrew Church; Vicars for Religious; Presbyteral Council.
Hart, James '65 (KC) Retired.
Hart, Jean F. *s.o.l.t.* '90 (CC) Corpus Christi, TX St. Anselm Anglican Use Community; [G] Robstown, TX Society of Our Lady of the Most Holy Trinity; [F] Corpus Christi, TX Queen of Peace Retreat Center.
Hart, Jean '92 (CC)[I] Corpus Christi, TX.
Hart, John B. '60 (SLC) Retired.
Hart, Rev. Msgr. John E. '81 (PAT) Morristown, NJ Assumption of the Blessed Virgin Mary; Pro–Synodal Judges; Presbyteral Council; College of Consultors; Theological Commission.
Hart, Jonathan '96 (FgM) Boston, MA St. James the Apostle, Inc.
Hart, Joseph A. '73 (ROC) Rochester, NY Our Lady Queen of Peace; Rochester, NY St. Thomas More; Vicars General; Moderator of the Pastoral Center; Censores Librorum; Board of Directors; Pension Committee (Lay and Priests); Priest Consultors.
Hart, Rev. Msgr. Kevin T. '74 (WDC) Rockville, MD St. Patrick; Promoter of Justice; Priests Retirement Board.
Hart, Paul S. '89 (NO) New Orleans, LA St. Andrew the Apostle; Deans.
Hart, Richard J. '01 (SAV) Dublin, GA Immaculate Conception.
Hart, Richard *o.f.m.cap.* (MIL)[P] Milwaukee, WI St. Conrad Friary.
Hart, Robert H. '00 (STP) Oakdale, MN Transfiguration; Deanery 4; College of Consultors.
Hart, Rolland A. '64 (OG) Retired.
Hart, Ronald '71 (JOL)[K] Naperville, IL St. John Vianney Villa.
Hart, Thomas J. '74 (SC) Mallard, IA St. Mary's; West Bend, IA SS. Peter and Paul.
Hart, Thomas Joseph '07 (LR) Camden, AR St. Louis; Magnolia, AR Immaculate Heart of Mary.
Hart, Thomas M. *o.s.b.* '88 (GBG)[G] Latrobe, PA Saint Vincent Archabbey.
Hart, William H. '58 (CAM) Retired.
Harte, Rev. Msgr. F. Joseph '61 (ORL) Retired.
Harte, Paul D. '76 (CAM) Carneys Point, NJ The Church of Corpus Christi, Carneys Point, N.J.; Carney's Point, NJ St. James' Church, Pennsgrove, N.J.; Representatives by Ordination Seniority; Consultants.
Harte, Paul D. '76 (CAM) Southwest Deanery.
Harten, Dennis *o.s.a.* '75 (VEN) Naples, FL St. Elizabeth Seton.
Hartenbach, William *c.m.* '64 (STL)[O] St. Louis, MO Vincentian Residence.
Hartenbach, William *c.m.* '68 (EVN)[F] Evansville, IN Daughters of Charity of St. Vincent de Paul of Indiana, Inc.
Harter, Michael G. *s.j.* '74 (STL)[O] St. Louis, MO The Jesuits of the Missouri Province; Saint Louis, MO; [O] St. Louis, MO Sacred Heart Jesuit Community.
Hartford, Kevin F. '04 (WOR) Leominster, MA St. Leo; Chaplains.
Hartgen, Rev. Msgr. Dennis T. '73 (ALN) Reading, PA Holy Guardian Angels; Vicars Forane.
Hartgen, William E. *s.s.* '76 (BAL)[S] Baltimore Society of St. Sulpice, Province of the United States Retired.
Harth, Charles F. '36 (BRK)[Q] Queens Village, NY Queen of Peace Residence Retired.
Harth, John M. '87 (SPC) Region VII; Priests' Mutual Benefit Society; Diocesan Development Fund; The Mirror Advisory Board; Jackson, MO Immaculate Conception; Leopold, MO St. John.
Hartigan, Daniel J. *o.s.a.* '45 (CHI)[N] Chicago, IL St. Monica Monastery.
Hartigan, Dennis P. '80 (TOL) Toledo, OH Historic Church of Saint Patrick; [B] Toledo, OH Central Catholic High School; Blessed Teresa of Calcutta Deanery.
Hartlage, Albert J. '56 (L) Fairfield, KY St. Michael Retired.
Hartlage, William C. '41 (L) Retired.
Hartle, Thomas R. *o.f.m.* '71 (BO)[X] Boston, MA Saint Anthony Residence.
Hartlein, Rev. Msgr. Jerome D. '58 (BEL) Mascoutah, IL Holy Childhood of Jesus; Diocesan Consultors;

Building Commission, Chancery Office.
Hartley, Matthew '06 (DEN) Northglenn, CO Immaculate Heart of Mary.
Hartley, Paul M. '81 (JC) Kahoka, MO St. Michael the Archangel; Kahoka, MO The Shrine of St. Patrick; Il. Hannibal.
Hartling, Charles W. '79 (NEW) Rutherford, NJ Church of St. Mary.
Hartman, Augustine *o.p.* '66 (SEA) Seattle, WA Blessed Sacrament.
Hartman, Glenn '76 (CAM) Bellmawr, NJ The Church of Mary, Mother of the Church, Bellmawr, N.J.
Hartman, Raymond S. '68 (COV) Covington, KY Mother of God.
Hartman, Rev. Msgr. Thomas J. '71 (RVC) Chaplains of the Nassau County Police Department; Nassau County Police Department; [M] Amityville, NY St. Pius X Residence.
Hartmann, Edward J. '76 (NY) On Duty Outside the Archdiocese.
Hartmann, Rev. Msgr. John F. '53 (BRK) Madison, CT Retired.
Hartmann, Joseph A. '78 (DEN) Estes Park, CO Our Lady of the Mountains; Loveland, CO St. John the Evangelist; [S] Loveland, CO St. John the Evangelist Education Foundation.
Hartmann, Paul B.R. '94 (MIL)[Y] Waukesha, WI St. Thomas More Lawyers Society; Special Assignment; Judicial Vicar; Judges for First Instance; Judges for Second Instance; Office for Marital Reconciliation–Separation; Archdiocesan Court of Equity; [D] Waukesha, WI Catholic Memorial High School.
Hartmann, Richard A. '73 (DET) Flat Rock, MI St. Roch.
Hartmayer, Gregory J. *o.f.m.conv.* '79 (ATL) Jonesboro, GA St. Philip Benizi; College of Consultors.
Hartnett, Daniel F. *s.j.* '74 (CHI)[C] Chicago, IL Jesuit Community at Loyola University Chicago.
Hartnett, George F. '74 (SY) Solvay, NY St. Cecilia.
Hartnett, James L. *s.m.* '55 (WDC)[N] Washington, DC Marist Center Retired.
Hartnett, James '72 (ORG) Judges; Seal Beach, CA Holy Family.
Hartnett, Rev. Msgr. Robert L. '79 (BAL) Baltimore, MD Our Lady of Mount Carmel; Presbyteral Council.
Hartnett, Rev. Msgr. Robert (BAL) Advocates.
Hartrich, Kurt *o.f.m.* '66 (CHI) Chicago, IL St. Peter's; [W] Chicago, IL S.F.V., Inc.; [N] Chicago, IL St. Peter's Friary.
Hartsfield, John H. '01 (BIR) Oneonta, AL Corpus Christi; Priests'/Presbyteral Council.
Hartshorn, Christopher '94 (DM) Winterset, IA St. Joseph; [J] Des Moines, IA Roman Catholic Pastoral Center Foundation; Vicar General; Diocesan Consultors; Diocesan Corporation Board; Priests' Pension Fund Society; [J] Des Moines, IA Endowment for Educational Excellence.
Hartwell, James W. '02 (BUF) Warsaw, NY St. Michael.
Hartz, Gerald A. '59 (SC) Retired.
Hartzer, John '54 (IND) Retired.
Hartzler, Joseph *s.m.* '87 (OAK)[A] Berkeley, CA Franciscan School of Theology.
Hartzler, Joseph *s.m.* '87 (SJ)[M] Cupertino, CA The Alcalde House.
Harvey, Charles K. '52 (WCH) Retired.
Harvey, David W. '68 (LAN) Fenton, MI St. John.
Harvey, David '68 (LAN) Gaines, MI St. Joseph.
Harvey, Fred R. '00 (BIS) Priests' Personnel Board.
Harvey, Frederick R. '00 (BIS) Minot, ND St. Therese the Little Flower.
Harvey, James P. '96 (KNX) Crossville, TN St. Alphonsus.
Harvey, Jeffrey H. *c.m.* '93 (STL)[O] St. Louis, MO Lazarist Residence.
Harvey, John A. '66 (PIT) Retired.
Harvey, John D. *o.f.m.cap.* '72 (PH) Philadelphia, PA St. Callistus.
Harvey, John F. *o.s.f.s.* '44 (NY)[II] New York, NY Courage International, Incorporated.
Harvey, John F. *o.s.f.s.* '44 (ALN)[B] Center Valley, PA DeSales University; [K] Center Valley, PA Oblates of St. Francis de Sales.
Harvey, John L. '86 (CHI) Chicago, IL St. Mary of the Assumption; Riverdale, IL Queen of Apostles.
Harvey, L. Warren '88 (LR) Pine Bluff, AR St. Joseph.
Harvey, Michael K. '99 (BO) Haverhill, MA All Saints.
Harvey, Michael L. *o.f.m.* '89 (ORG) Huntington Beach, CA SS. Simon and Jude; Consultors; Council of Priests.
Harvey, Peter J. *o.s.f.s.* '60 (WIL)[J] Childs, MD Retirement and Assisted Care Facility Retired.
Harvey, Warren '88 (LR) Deans; Diocesan Council for Black Catholics; [B] Pine Bluff, AR St. Joseph Catholic Jr./Sr. High School; Vicars for Religious; Presbyteral Council; Priests Personnel Board (Diocesan).
Harvey, Wilfred *o.m.i.* '63 (BO)[U] Lowell, MA Missionary Oblates of Mary Immaculate.
Haryasz, Francis S. '58 (STA) Retired.
Hascall, John S. *o.f.m.cap.* '67 (MAR) Sault Sainte Marie, MI Holy Family Mission; Sault Sainte Marie, MI St. Isaac Jogues Mission; Sault Sainte Marie, MI St. Isaac Jogues.
Haschka, David *s.j.* '75 (STP)[E] Minneapolis, MN Cristo Rey Jesuit High School – Twin Cities; [S] Minneapolis, MN Cristo Rey Corporate Internship Program – Twin Cities.
Haschka, Jonathan *s.j.* '75 (FgM)[P] Milwaukee Jesuit Provincial Office, Wisconsin Province; Milwaukee, WI Society of Jesus.
Haschke, Jonathan J. '09 (LIN) Lincoln, NE St. Teresa's; Advocates.
Hascinger, Philip S. '72 (LFT) Grissom, IN Grissom Air Force Base, St. Michael's Chapel.
Haselhorst, Rev. Msgr. Vincent '57 (BEL) Retired.
Hasenberg, Aloysius J. '49 (MAR) Retired.
Hasenkamp, Robert '63 (KCK) Retired.
Hasey, Adam '50 (FAR) Retired.
Hasieber, Joseph S. '73 (ALX) Coatesville, PA St. Joseph Retired.
Haskamp, Gregory '93 (KC) Smithville, MO Church of the Good Shepherd.
Haske, Henry B. *s.j.* '57 (SCR)[E] Scranton, PA Scranton Preparatory School; [C] Scranton, PA The University of Scranton.
Haskin, Jay C. '67 (BUR) Canon 1742 Panel of Pastors; Colchester, VT Our Lady of Grace; Lisle, IL The National Catholic Risk Retention Group, Inc.; Elected Members.
Haslach, Stephen *c.p.* '54 (HRT)[L] West Hartford Holy Family Monastery/Retreat.
Haslach, Stephen *c.p.* '54 (BRK)[T] Jamaica, NY Immaculate Conception Monastery.
Hasler, Clifford P. '71 (WDC)[N] Washington, DC La Salette Formation Community.
Haspedis, George '56 (SPK) Spokane, WA St. Peter Retired.
Hasse, Benjamin J. '09 (MAR) Marquette, MI St. Michael; [G] Marquette, MI Catholic Campus Ministry–Northern Michigan University.
Hasse, James A. *s.j.* '69 (CIN)[N] Cincinnati, OH Claver Jesuit Community.
Hasser, David Joseph '07 (LFT) Kokomo, IN St. Joan of Arc; Kokomo, IN St. Patrick.
Hassett, James F. '75 (BUF) Barker, NY Our Lady of the Lake.
Hasso, Bede J. *o.s.b.* '57 (GBG)[G] Latrobe, PA Saint Vincent Archabbey.
Hasso, Daniel *c.m.* '97 (CHI)[N] Chicago DePaul Vincentian Residence.
Hast, James C. *o.f.m.cap.* '77 (DET)[K] Detroit, MI St. Mary's Friary; [T] Detroit, MI Solanus Casey Center.
Hastings, Eric F. '05 (DUL) Censor of Books; Vice Chancellor; Adjutant Judicial Vicar; Duluth, MN St. Benedict.
Hastings, Joel '99 (DUL) Proctor, MN St. Rose; Proctor, MN St. Philip Neri; Department of Liturgy.
Hastings, Scott A. '08 (OM) Norfolk, NE Sacred Heart.
Hastings, William J. '73 (CHI) Chicago, IL St. William.
Hastrich, Rev. Msgr. George M. '50 (MAD)[H] Madison, WI Saint Martin House Retired.
Hastrich, George M. '50 (RCK)[M] St. Charles, IL Queen of Americas Guild.
Hatcher, John *s.j.* '74 (RC) St. Francis, SD St. Charles Borromeo; St. Francis, SD St. Francis Mission/ Rosebud Educational Society; [C] Howes, SD Kino Jesuit Community.
Hatcher, Rev. Msgr. William C. '71 (NEW) Springfield, NJ St. James the Apostle; Commission for the Men's Apostolate.
Hater, Robert J. '59 (CIN) Cincinnati, OH St. Clare Retired.
Hathaway, Christopher *f.s.s.p.* '01 (RC) Rapid City, SD Cathedral of Our Lady of Perpetual Help.
Hathaway, Edward C. '91 (ARL) Chantilly, VA St. Veronica.
Hatrick, Brian M. '79 (BUF) Retired.
Hattie, Eugene F. *s.j.* '53 (FgM) Detroit, MI Detroit Province.
Hatton, Ronald '95 (PSC) Lansford, PA St. John the Baptist.
Hattrup, Theobald *o.f.m.* '56 (CIN)[N] Cincinnati St. Francis Seraph Friary Retired.
Hauber, Douglas L. '89 (JOL) Herscher, IL St. Margaret Mary; Kankakee, IL St. James The Apostle; Bonfield, IL Sacred Heart.
Hauck, Herbert C. '64 (STL) On Duty Outside the Archdiocese.
Hauck, Herbert '64 (PHX) Carefree, AZ Our Lady of Joy Roman Catholic Parish.
Hauer, Joseph L. '81 (DUB) Dubuque, IA Church of the Resurrection; Judges; Finance Council.
Hauer, Maurus *o.f.m.conv.* '45 (LSC) Carlsbad, NM St. Edward.
Hauf, Edward *o.m.i.* '66 (BEL) Fayetteville, IL St. Pancratius; [F] Belleville, IL Shrine of Our Lady of the Snows.
Haugan, Daniel C. '03 (STP) Saint Paul, MN Holy Spirit.
Haugen, John S. '84 (DUB) On Special or Other Archdiocesan Assignment; [C] Dubuque, IA Loras College; Campus Ministry; Vocation Awareness Advisory Committee.
Haugh, John '61 (DAL) Retired.
Haughey, John C. *s.j.* '61 (WDC)[N] Washington, DC Woodstock Jesuit Community; [W] Washington, DC Woodstock Theological Center.
Haughney, Rev. Msgr. William J. '47 (MET)[I] Somerset, NJ Maria Regina Residence Retired.
Haupt, Lloyd '54 (SCL) Retired.
Haus, Robert A. *s.j.* '55 (BUF)[O] Buffalo, NY Canisius Jesuit Community Inc. Retired.
Hauser, Albert J. '81 (OG) Plattsburgh, NY Our Lady of Victory; Advocates; Apostleship of Prayer; Priests' Eucharistic League; Plattsburgh, NY St. Mary of the Lake.
Hauser, Albert *o.s.b.* '60 (KCK) Axtell, KS St. Michael's; Summerfield, KS Holy Family; [I] Atchison, KS St. Benedict's Abbey.
Hauser, Gerald B. '45 (MIL) Retired.
Hauser, John G. '71 (BRK) On Leave/Unassigned.
Hauser, Nathanael *o.s.b.* '83 (SCL)[I] Collegeville, MN St. John's Abbey, of the Order of St. Benedict.
Hauser, Richard J. *s.j.* '68 (OM)[K] Omaha, NE Jesuit Community at Creighton University.
Hausfeld, Bruce *o.f.m.* '61 (LSC) Alamogordo, NM Immaculate Conception.
Hausfeld, Bryant *o.f.m.* '65 (LSC) Alamogordo, NM Immaculate Conception; Presbyteral Council.
Hausladen, Robert T. '01 (IND) Indianapolis, IN St. Pius X; [C] Indianapolis, IN Bishop Chatard High School.
Hausman, Jacob *c.f.r.* '09 (NY)[EE] Yonkers, NY St. Leopold's Friary.
Hausmann, Leo '92 (RC) Wall, SD St. Patrick's; Officialis.
Hausmann, William C. *s.j.* '66 (SPK)[B] Spokane, WA Gonzaga University.
Haut, Rev. Msgr. Vincent J. '68 (STA) Jacksonville, FL Blessed Trinity; Diocesan Consultors; Cursillos de Cristiandad.
Haut, Rev. Msgr. Vincent '68 (STA) Presbyteral Council.
Hautz, Roland *g.h.m.* '53 (RIC) Gate City, VA St. Bernard.
Hauver, James H. '97 (NY) Stony Point, NY Immaculate Conception.
Hauver, James '97 (DUL) On Duty Outside the Diocese.
Havel, Elias *o.mar.* '95 (SAM)[B] Petersham, MA Maronite Monks of Adoration Most Holy Trinity Monastery.
Havel, Gregory G. '90 (WIN) La Crescent, MN Holy Cross; La Crescent, MN The Church of the Crucifixion.
Havener, John R. '55 (PH)[Y] Villanova, PA St. Thomas Monastery.
Havens, James A. (MOB) Mobile, AL St. Dominic.
Havey, Lee *c.p.* '04 (BRK) Jamaica, NY Immaculate Conception.
Havey, Lee *c.p.* '06 (SCR)[M] Scranton, PA Saint Ann's Passionist Monastery.
Haviland, William T. '62 (HBG) Sunbury, PA St. Monica.
Havrilka, Joseph '05 (SFD) Ramsey, IL St. Joseph; Vandalia, IL Mother of Dolors; Commission for the Care of Infirm and Retired Priests.
Havron, Daniel *o.f.m.* '77 (ALN)[M] Easton, PA St. Francis Retreat House; [K] Easton, PA St. Francis Friary.
Hawes, Rev. Msgr. Cletus J. '52 (DUB)[E] Calmar, IA Christian Family School of Religion; Ossian, IA St. Francis de Sales; Ossian, IA Our Lady of Seven Dolors.
Hawes, Donald J. '53 (DUB)[F] Calmar, IA Calmar–Festina–Spillville Catholic School; Spillville, IA St. Wenceslaus; Calmar, IA St. Aloysius.
Hawes, Roger '01 (VIC) Presbyteral Council; Yorktown, TX Holy Cross.
Hawk, Patrick *c.ss.r.* '69 (TUC)[F] Tucson, AZ Redemptorist Society of Arizona Redemptorist Renewal Center.
Hawk, Vincent J. '02 (CLV) Ministers; Loudonville, OH St. Peter; Presbyteral Council; Presbyteral Conveners; [W] Loudonville, OH University of Ashland.
Hawken, Michael '94 (KCK) Shawnee, KS St. Joseph; Regional Pastoral Leaders.
Hawker, James '63 (CHL) Retired.
Hawkes–Teeples, Steven B. *s.j.* '93 (FgM) St. Louis, MO Society of Jesus.
Hawkins, Allan R.G. '94 (FWT) Arlington, TX Church of St. Mary the Virgin.
Hawkins, Charles '78 (PMB) Boca Raton, FL Ascension.
Hawkins, Donald A. *s.j.* '76 (NO) New Orleans, LA Holy Name of Jesus.
Hawkins, Douglas W. *c.s.c.* '57 (FR)[G] North Dartmouth, MA Holy Cross Residence Retired.
Hawkins, John *o.s.c.* '66 (SCL)[I] Onamia, MN Crosier Priory.
Hawkins, Robert F. '75 (PRO) Barrington, RI St. Luke; College of Consultors.
Hawkins, Thomas J. D. '70 (KC) Higginsville, MO St. Mary's.

Hawley, Gerard L. '92 (SCR) Unassigned or Leave of Absence.
Hawthorne, Patrick J. '82 (WOR) Auburn, MA St. Joseph's.
Hawver, Carl *o.f.m.* '74 (IND) Oldenburg, IN Holy Family; [L] Oldenburg, IN Motherhouse of the Congregation of the Sisters of the Third Order of St. Francis.
Hay, John N. '07 (WCH) Pittsburg, KS Our Lady of Lourdes.
Hay, Theodore H. *s.t.l.* '55 (MOB) Retired.
Hay, W. Michael '92 (CIN) Cincinnati, OH St. Aloysius Gonzaga.
Hayatsu, Richard K. '65 (SEA) Seahurst, WA St. Francis of Assisi; Federal Way, WA St. Theresa.
Haycock, Anthony J. '72 (SEA) Seattle, WA St. Mary; [E] Seattle, WA Catholic Seamen's Club.
Haycock, Donald J. *c.s.c.* '58 (ROC) Rochester, NY St. Lawrence.
Hayde, Rev. Msgr. Ronald '81 (RVC) Medical Leave.
Hayden, Rev. Msgr. Carl T. '45 (GI) Retired.
Hayden, Hilary *o.s.b.* '56 (WDC)[N] Washington, DC St. Anselm's Abbey.
Hayden, James P. '91 (GAY) Elected Members Retired.
Hayden, Johnrose '95 (LUB) Retired.
Hayden, Joseph F. '63 (L) Retired.
Hayden, Joseph J. *s.j.* '70 (WH)[A] Wheeling, WV Wheeling Jesuit University.
Hayden, Joseph M. '48 (CAM) Retired.
Hayden, Joseph *s.j.* '70 (WH) Benwood, WV St. John's; McMechen, WV St. James; Diocesan Consultors.
Hayden, Kyle *o.f.m.* '97 (NY) New York, NY St. Stephen of Hungary.
Hayden, Michael M. *o.c.s.o.* '54 (ROC)[J] Piffard Abbey of the Genesee.
Hayden, Michael T. '85 (SUP) Hurley, WI St. Mary of the Seven Dolors; Mercer, WI St. Isaac Jogues and Companions; Presbyteral Council & Diocesan Consultors.
Hayden, Patrick T. '90 (STL) On Duty Outside the Archdiocese.
Hayden, Robert L. '70 (RVC) Seaford, NY St. William the Abbot.
Hayden, Ted *s.m.a.* '58 (FgM) Tenafly, NJ SOCIETY OF AFRICAN MISSIONS.
Hayden, Terence '77 (NO) Gretna, LA Ochsner Medical Center, West Bank; Belle Chasse, LA Our Lady of Perpetual Help.
Hayden, Thomas E. *s.m.a.* '58 (NEW)[M] Tenafly, NJ Society of African Missions, Provincialate, S.M.A. Fathers.
Haydinger, Christian J. '76 (RIC) Ashland, VA St. Ann.
Haydock, Kenneth '80 (SEA) Edmonds, WA Holy Rosary.
Hayduk, Rev. Archpriest Michael '77 (PRM) Parma, OH Saint John the Baptist, Cathedral; Syncellus for Doctrine and Worship; Presbyteral Council; Eparchial Pastoral Council; Eparchial Consultors; Sacred Liturgy; Cantors' Institute Faculty; Seminary Education Formation Board.
Hayek, Herbert C. *o.p.* '71 (CHI) River Forest, IL St. Vincent Ferrer.
Hayek, Rev. Msgr. Sami '59 (SAM) Retired.
Hayek, Rev. Msgr. Stanley J. '59 (DUB) Building Commission; Directors Retired.
Hayer, James '89 (PSC) Wilkes–Barre, PA St. Mary's; Wyoming Valley Protopresbyterate; Communications and Telecommunications; Eparchial Newspaper.
Hayes, Bonaventure *o.f.m.* '67 (PAT)[N] Ringwood, NJ Holy Name Friary, Inc.
Hayes, Brian '92 (SD) El Cajon, CA Holy Trinity.
Hayes, Dennis J. '86 (NO) New Orleans, LA St. Rita.
Hayes, Dennis J. '76 (SY) Marietta, NY Corpus Christi.
Hayes, Edward A. *m.m.* '59 (FgM) Maryknoll, NY MARYKNOLL.
Hayes, Edward '58 (KCK) Retired.
Hayes, Finbarr *o.p.* '57 (OAK)[M] Oakland, CA Order of Preachers (Province of the Most Holy Name of Jesus – Western Dominican Province).
Hayes, Gary '90 (OWN) Absent on Leave.
Hayes, Gerard C. '60 (HT) Retired.
Hayes, James A. *s.s.j.* '55 (BAL)[S] Baltimore, MD St. Joseph Society of the Sacred Heart House of Central Administration Retired.
Hayes, James L. '38 (DET) Retired.
Hayes, James M. *s.j.* '85 (WOR)[R] Holy Cross College; [O] Worcester, MA Jesuits of the Holy Cross, Inc.
Hayes, James *s.s.s.* '77 (NY) New York, NY St. Andrew.
Hayes, Jerry *s.j.* '07 (LA)[F] Los Angeles, CA Loyola High School of Los Angeles.
Hayes, John H. '87 (ROC) Honeoye, NY St. Mary, Our Lady of the Hills; Livonia, NY St. Matthew Catholic Church Society.
Hayes, John J. '60 (CLV) Cleveland, OH Immaculate Conception Retired.
Hayes, Lawrence J. *o.f.m.* '89 (WDC) Silver Spring, MD St. Camillus.
Hayes, Leo J. '61 (BEL) Ava, IL St. Elizabeth; Ava, IL St. Ann; Ava, IL St. Joseph.
Hayes, Martin E. '84 (OWN) Leitchfield, KY St. Elizabeth of Hungary; Leitchfield, KY St. Paul; Committee for Administration.
Hayes, Maurice C. *o.f.m.conv.* '69 (ELP) El Paso, TX Our Lady of Mt. Carmel; El Paso, TX Our Lady of the Valley.
Hayes, Rev. Msgr. Paul J. '48 (NEW) New Providence, NJ Our Lady of Peace Retired.
Hayes, Robert E. '71 (SJ) Defender of the Bond; Ongoing Formation of Clergy; Special Assignment.
Hayes, Robert '71 (MRY) Defenders of the Bond.
Hayes, Samuel '83 (CHY) Rawlins, WY St. Joseph's; Vicars Forane; Defenders of the Bond.
Hayes, Stephen Dominic *o.p.* '88 (L) Springfield, KY St. Rose.
Hayes, Terrence M. '72 (STP) Minneapolis, MN Our Lady of Victory.
Hayes, Thomas J. '73 (ALB) Waterford, NY St. Mary's Church; Deans; Members.
Hayes, Thomas J. *o.m.i.* '64 (BEL)[F] Belleville, IL Missionary Oblates of Mary Immaculate – St. Henry's Oblate Residence.
Hayes, Thomas *o.p.* '59 (OAK)[M] Oakland, CA Order of Preachers (Province of the Most Holy Name of Jesus – Western Dominican Province).
Hayes, Thomas *o.p.* '59 (SFR)[K] San Francisco, CA Home for the Aged of the Little Sisters of the Poor; [N] San Francisco, CA St. Dominic Priory Retired.
Hayes, Timothy M. '85 (COL) Columbus, OH St. Timothy; Diocesan Judges.
Hayes, William E. *s.j.* '58 (P)[D].
Hayes, Xavier *c.p.* '59 (NY)[EE] Bronx, NY Passionist Residence.
Hayes, Zachary *o.f.m.* '59 (SFD)[L] Springfield, IL Our Lady of Angels Friary.
Hayman, Robert W. '66 (PRO) Providence, RI St. Sebastian.
Hayn, Carl H. *s.j.* '47 (SJ)[B] Santa Clara, CA Jesuit Community.
Haynes, Mark J. '85 (PH) Havertown, PA Annunciation B.V.M.
Haynes, Scott *s.j.c.* '07 (CHI) Chicago, IL St. John Cantius; [P] Chicago, IL Canons Regular of Saint John Cantius.
Hays, Henry Bryan *o.s.b.* '62 (SCL)[I] Collegeville, MN St. John's Abbey, of the Order of St. Benedict.
Hays, John S. '93 (SP) Ridge Manor, FL St. Anne.
Hays, Kevin W. '77 (CHI) Missionary Work.
Hays, Kevin '77 (FgM)[U] Boston, MA The Society of St. James the Apostle, Inc.; Boston, MA St. James the Apostle, Inc.
Hays, Richard Rex *c.m.* '93 (DAL) Dallas, TX Holy Trinity; [J] Dallas, TX Congregation of the Mission, Western Province.
Hays, Timothy '96 (SPK) Walla Walla, WA Assumption of the Blessed Virgin Mary.
Hayward, William *m.i.c.* '89 (MIL) Kenosha, WI St. Peter.
Hazard, Rev. Msgr. Michael D. '72 (KAL) Kalamazoo, MI St. Joseph; Vicar General; Diocesan Consultors; Presbyteral Council Members; Presbyteral Council Members.
Hazebrouck, Maurice L. '45 (PRO) Retired.
Hazel, Terrence J. '75 (Y) Canfield, OH St. Michael; Defenders of the Bond; Physically and Developmentally; Deaf and Hearing Impaired.
Hazel, Terrence '75 (Y) Scouting, Diocesan Office.
Hazelton, James '61 (HEL) Helena, MT Santo Tomas; On Duty Outside the Diocese.
Hazewski, Eugene J. '59 (NEW)[M] Rutherford, NJ St. John Vianney Residence for Priests Retired.
Hazler, George F. '67 (DET) Bloomfield Hills, MI Voluntas Dei Institute (1958); [T] Bloomfield Hills, MI Voluntas Dei Institute.
Hazuka, Jeremy L. '97 (LIN) Nebraska City, NE St. Benedict's; Legion of Mary; [C] Nebraska City, NE Lourdes Central Catholic Schools.
Hazzard, William M. '63 (WIL) Wilmington, DE St. Matthew Retired.
Hazzouri, Alex J. '57 (SCR)[N] Dunmore, PA Villa St. Joseph Retired.
Head, Bernard '53 (IND) St. Mary–of–the–Woods, IN St. Mary–of–the–Woods; West Terre Haute, IN St. Leonard of Port Maurice Retired.
Headley, Donald J. '58 (CHI) Chicago, IL St. Mary of the Woods Retired.
Headley, William '64 (SD)[B] University of San Diego.
Heagerty, John J. '54 (SY) Retired.
Heagerty, Kevin *o.f.m.cap.* '61 (FgM) Detroit, MI Province of St. Joseph.
Heagerty, Kevin *o.f.m.cap.* '61 (DET)[K] Detroit St. Bonaventure Friary.
Heagle, John L. '65 (LC) On Duty Outside the Diocese.
Healey, Bernard A. '95 (PRO) Albion, RI St. Ambrose; Government Liaison; Newspaper.
Healey, Charles J. *s.j.* '65 (BO)[U] Boston The Society of Jesus of New England–Provincial Offices.
Healey, Charles *s.j.* '65 (SY)[A] Syracuse, NY Saint Andrew Hall.
Healey, Edward J. '87 (FR) West Harwich, MA Holy Trinity.
Healey, Fergus *o.f.m.* '54 (BO)[Z] Boston, MA St. Anthony Shrine.
Healey, John E. '70 (MAN) St. Joseph Hospital; Nashua, NH St. Patrick; Southern N.H. Regional Medical Center and Nursing Homes.
Healey, Joseph G. *m.m.* '66 (FgM) Maryknoll, NY MARYKNOLL.
Healey, Kenneth *s.m.* '70 (BO)[D] Reading, MA Austin Preparatory School.
Healey, William B. '55 (SCR)[N] Dunmore, PA Villa St. Joseph Retired.
Healy, Cornelius J. '66 (SFR) Ross, CA St. Anselm.
Healy, Daniel H. '01 (MET)[M] Oxford, NJ The Anawim Community.
Healy, Daniel (ROC)[N] Corning, NY Anawim Community Center.
Healy, Gabriel *ss.cc.* '57 (FR)[G] Fairhaven, MA Damien Residence Retired.
Healy, George *c.s.sp.* '53 (SB)[I] Hemet, CA Congregation of the Holy Spirit Retired.
Healy, George '02 (MIA) Absent on Leave.
Healy, Rev. Msgr. Gerard M. '61 (MAD) Stoughton, WI St. Ann.
Healy, J. Cletus *s.j.* '51 (MIL)[P] Wauwatosa, WI Jesuit Community at St. Camillus.
Healy, Jack *o.carm.* '70 (ROC)[B] Rochester, NY McQuaid Jesuit High School; [J] Rochester, NY Whitefriars Priory.
Healy, James E. '72 (KC) Blue Springs, MO St. Robert Bellarmine.
Healy, James F. '66 (NY) Mamaroneck, NY St. Vito.
Healy, John J. '66 (SAC) Hospitals, Diocesan Liaison for Catholic.
Healy, John '41 (SR) Retired.
Healy, John '66 (SAC) College of Consultors; AIDS, Ministry to.
Healy, Kieran J. *o.p.* '61 (OAK)[M] Oakland, CA Order of Preachers (Province of the Most Holy Name of Jesus – Western Dominican Province); [M] Oakland, CA Order of Preachers (Province of the Most Holy Name of Jesus – Western Dominican Province).
Healy, Michael J. '70 (SFR) San Francisco Police Department; San Mateo, CA St. Bartholomew.
Healy, Patrick F. *o.m.i.* '47 (BO)[X] Tewksbury, MA Immaculate Heart of Mary Residence; Pastoral Care.
Healy, Patrick *s.s.j.* (MOB) Mobile, AL Most Pure Heart of Mary; Prichard, AL St. James Major.
Healy, Rev. Msgr. Peter C. '53 (LA) Burbank, CA St. Robert Bellarmine Retired.
Healy, Stephen M. '85 (BO) Monponsett, MA Our Lady of the Lake.
Healy, Terence P. '62 (ALB) Richfield Springs, NY St. Joseph the Worker.
Healy, Thomas F. *s.j.* '65 (HEL) Missoula, MT St. Francis Xavier.
Healy, Thomas F. *s.j.* '65 (SPK)[J] Spokane, WA Regis Community.
Healy, Thomas I. '52 (CHI)[W] Chicago, IL St. Bonaventure Oratory Retired.
Healy, Thomas J. '66 (BRK) Corona, NY Our Lady of Sorrows.
Healy, Thomas '67 (SAV) Augusta, GA St. Joseph.
Healy, William P. '66 (PHX) Retired.
Healy, William *o.c.d.* '46 (MIL) Milwaukee, WI St. Florian.
Heames, Denis M. (SAG) Outside the Diocese.
Heaney, John F. '57 (PRO) Retired.
Heaney, John J. *s.j.* '52 (DAL) Dallas, TX St. Rita.
Heaney, Joseph P. '53 (PRO) Retired.
Hearn, Philip A. '66 (SY) Rome, NY St. Mary of the Assumption; Rome, NY St. Peter; Eastern Area Vicars; Board of Diocesan Consultors; Presbyteral Council.
Hearne, James P. '05 (CHI) Oak Park, IL St. Giles.
Hearty, Joseph *f.s.s.p.* (DEN) Littleton, CO Our Lady of Mount Carmel (Latin Mass Community).
Heaslip, Andrew J. '09 (LIN) Hastings, NE St. Cecilia's; Advocates.
Heath, Christopher '88 (ORG) Dana Point, CA St. Edward the Confessor.
Heath, Thomas R. *o.p.* '50 (FgM) New York, NY Province of St. Joseph (Eastern).
Hebda, Martin J. '67 (CHI)[J] Chicago, IL Mercy Hospital and Medical Center.
Hebda, Michael J. '96 (SAC) Vicar Episcopal for Clergy; Ongoing Education of Clergy; Sacramento, CA St. Anthony.
Hebda, Michael '96 (SAC) Presbyteral Council.
Hebden, W. Scott '99 (CHI)[A] Mundelein, IL University of St. Mary of the Lake/Mundelein Seminary.
Heberlein, Kenneth '71 (GAL) Retired.
Heberlein, Rev. Msgr. Louis J. '51 (E) Retired.
Hebert, Adrien T. *c.s.sp.* '58 (FgM) Bethel Park, PA CONGREGATION OF THE HOLY SPIRIT.
Hebert, Daniel J. '79 (ANC) Anchorage, AK Holy Cross.
Hebert, Earl '52 (SPR) Retired.
Hebert, Gerard A. '81 (FR) Westport, MA St. George's; Defenders of the Bond.
Hebert, Rev. Msgr. J. Gaston '60 (LR) Presbyteral Council; Priests Personnel Board (Diocesan).
Hebert, John M. '51 (LIN) Retired.
Hebert, Joseph E. *m.afr.* '63 (SP)[N] St. Petersburg, FL Missionaries of Africa.

Hebert, Oliver J. *t.o.r.* '71 (PBR) Northern Cambria, PA St. John the Baptist; Patton, PA SS. Peter and Paul.
Hebert, Rev. Msgr. Ray P. '52 (NO) Retired.
Hebert, Roland G. '47 (WOR) Retired.
Hebert, Ronald '65 (SD) San Diego, CA Sacred Heart.
Hebert, T. J. '49 (LAF) Retired.
Hebl, Rev. Msgr. John H. '61 (MAD) Retired.
Hechenberger, Gerald R. '96 (BEL) Smithton, IL St. John the Baptist.
Heck, Quintin T. '00 (MIL) On Duty Outside the Archdiocese.
Heck, Thomas A. '76 (VEN) Port Charlotte, FL St. Charles Borromeo.
Heckathorne, Brad *o.f.m.conv.* '81 (FgM) Ellicott City, MD Province of Saint Anthony of Padua.
Heckel, Guerric Frederick A. '66 (CHR)[E] Moncks Corner, SC Mepkin Abbey.
Hecker, Rev. Msgr. Lawrence A. '58 (NO) Retired.
Hecktor, Brian E. '08 (STL) Chesterfield, MO Ascension.
Hedderman, James A. '95 (BIR) Russellville, AL Good Shepherd Church.
Hederman, James J. *s.j.* '99 (BO)[D] Dorchester, MA Boston College High School.
Hederman, Kevin F. '75 (STL) On Leave of Absence.
Hedges, John P. '87 (DET) New Boston, MI St. Stephen.
Hedrick, John H. '70 (MAD) Pardeeville, WI St. Andrew; Markesan, WI St. Mary; Markesan, WI St. Joseph; Pardeeville, WI St. Mary of the Most Holy Rosary; Elected.
Hedrick, Rev. Msgr. Kenneth J. '73 (NO) Metairie, LA St. Angela Merici.
Heeg, Lawrence M. '57 (GRY) Bishop's Council of Priests Retired.
Heekin, John M. '63 (PAT) Retired.
Heelan, Patrick A. *s.j.* '58 (WDC)[N] Washington, DC The Jesuit Community at Georgetown University.
Heemrood, Jan *o.m.i.* '45 (SAT)[K] San Antonio, TX Oblate Madonna Residence.
Heenan, Michael F. '55 (RVC) Retired.
Heerdink, Eugene '51 (EVN) Spanish Speaking Ministry Retired.
Heese, Henry '61 (CC) Retired.
Heet, Donald J. *o.s.f.s.* '76 (WDC)[B] Washington, DC Deshairs Community–Oblates of St. Francis de Sales Residence; [C] Catholic University of America, The; Officers; Provincial Councilors:.
Hefferan, John E. '56 (CHI) Retired.
Heffern, Colman *o.s.b.* '76 (SFE)[H] Pecos, NM Our Lady of Guadalupe Abbey.
Heffernan, Henry G. *s.j.* '62 (WDC)[N] Washington, DC The Jesuit Community of St. Aloysius Gonzaga.
Heffernan, James F. '50 (BRK) Retired.
Heffernan, John J. *o.f.m.* '89 (ARL) Triangle, VA St. Francis of Assisi.
Heffernan, Joseph A. '65 (FRS) Retired.
Heffernan, Raymond '57 (SEA) Friday Harbor, WA St. Francis.
Heffernan, Robert G. '63 (HRT) Hamden, CT St. Stephen.
Heffner, Carroll '61 (NO) Retired.
Heffron, William *ss.cc.* '68 (FR)[G] Fairhaven, MA Damien Residence.
Hefner, Rev. Msgr. Helmut A. '69 (LA) Liturgical Commision.
Hefner, Rev. Msgr. Helmut A. '69 (LA) Woodland Hills, CA St. Mel.
Heft, James L. *s.m.* '73 (LA)[BB] Los Angeles, CA The Institute for Advanced Catholic Studies.
Hegarty, Daniel P. '63 (BO) Senior Priests. Retired.
Hegarty, Frederick J. *m.m.* '53 (NY)[EE].
Hegarty, Michael P. '95 (CAM) Audubon, NJ Church of the Holy Maternity, Audubon, NJ.
Hegedus, Gaspar '65 (SAV) Grovetown, GA St. Teresa of Avila.
Hegedusich, William '06 (WDC) Washington, DC St. Peter.
Hegenbarth, Robert S. '56 (LC) Bangor, WI St. Mary; West Salem, WI St. Leo the Great.
Hegnauer, Edward Anthony '09 (WDC) Laurel, MD St. Mary.
Hegyi, Martin A. *s.j.* '63 (NY)[II] Bronx, NY Saint Jutta Foundation, Inc.; [EE] New York, NY Murray–Weigel Hall.
Heher, Rev. Msgr. Michael '78 (ORG) Staff; Vicar General; Moderator of the Curia; Clergy Personnel Board; Council of Priests; Consultors; Land Advisory Board; Garden Grove, CA St. Columban; Diocesan Finance Council; Special Assignment.
Hehir, J. Bryan '66 (BO) Catholic Charitable Bureau of the Archdiocese of Boston, Inc.; Catholic Relief Services; Wellesley, MA St. John the Evangelist.
Hehman, Lawrence W. '65 (LEX) Priests' Retirement Board Retired.
Hehn, Robert E. '63 (DEN) Rifle, CO St. Mary.
Heiar, Rev. Msgr. Donald J. '00 (MAD) Madison, WI St. Thomas Aquinas.
Heiar, James *s.v.d.* '70 (BO)[U] Duxbury, MA Society of the Divine Word.
Heidecke, Albert J. '93 (JOL) Manteno, IL St. Joseph.
Heidenblut, Gregory *o.s.a.* '04 (LA)[F] Ojai, CA Villanova Preparatory School.
Heidenreich, Robert J. '69 (CHI) Winnetka, IL Sacred Heart.
Heidenrich, Peter J. '77 (CHI) Chicago, IL St. Walter.
Heidgen, Warren *o.s.b.* '60 (BIS)[A] Richardton, ND Assumption Abbey.
Heidt, Charles A. '59 (BIS) Priests' Benefit Association Retired.
Heier, Thomas *c.m.m.* '58 (DET)[K] Vocation Office; Dearborn Heights, MI.
Heier, Vergil *c.m.m.* '63 (DET)[K] Vocation Office.
Heier, Vincent A. '77 (STL) On Medical Leave.
Heikkala, Gregory R. '91 (MAR) Special Assignment; Champion, MI Sacred Heart; Ishpeming, MI St. John the Evangelist; Republic, MI St. Augustine; Vocation Office.
Heil, John P. *s.s.d.* '74 (STL) Special Assignment.
Heil, John P. *s.s.d.* '74 (WDC)[C] Catholic University of America, The.
Heille, Gregory J. *o.p.* '75 (STL)[B] St. Louis, MO Aquinas Institute of Theology; [O] St. Louis, MO Dominican Community of St. Louis.
Heilman, Richard M. '88 (MAD) Mount Horeb, WI St. Ignatius; Cross Plains, WI St. Mary of Pine Bluff; Appointed.
Heim, Edward L. '71 (STL) Augusta, MO Immaculate Conception.
Heim, John P. *s.j.* '65 (CIN)[N] Cincinnati, OH Jesuit Community at St. Xavier High School; Reading, OH Sts. Peter and Paul.
Heim, Joseph A. *m.m.* '61 (NY)[EE] Maryknoll Maryknoll Fathers and Brothers Retired.
Heim, Michael J. '82 (PH) Philadelphia, PA St. Dominic.
Heiman, Andrew '05 (WCH) Wellington, KS St. Anthony/St. Rose.
Heiman, Lawrence *c.pp.s.* '43 (CIN)[N] Carthagena, OH St. Charles Retired.
Heimer, Michael G. '71 (GRY) Walkerton, IN St. Anthony of Padua; Walkerton, IN St. John Kanty.
Heimerman, Francis D. '44 (DUB) Retired.
Heimos, Robert L. '67 (STL) Retired.
Heimsoth, Larry '99 (AUS) On Duty Outside the Diocese.
Hein, Gary (MAD)[D] Madison, WI St. Mary's Hospital.
Hein, John '63 (RVC) Hewlett, NY St. Joseph's Retired.
Heina, Steve '82 (SAL) Ellsworth, KS St. Bernard Parish; Ellsworth, KS St. Ignatius Loyola Parish; Propagation of the Faith.
Heina, Steven '82 (SAL) Holy Childhood, Pontifical Association.
Heine, Michael *o.f.m.conv.* '90 (FgM) Ellicott City, MD Province of Saint Anthony of Padua; [S] Ellicott City Order of Friars Minor Conventual.
Heineman, Rev. Msgr. Donald P. '47 (DUB) Retired.
Heinen, Francis A. '59 (NEW)[M] Caldwell, NJ The Rev. Msgr. James F. Kelley Residence for Retired Priests Retired.
Heinen, Miles J. *c.m.* '82 (PH)[B] Philadelphia, PA DePaul Novitiate.
Heinen, Virgil O. '60 (SUP) Retired.
Heines, Timothy '94 (DAL) On Leave of Absence.
Heiney, Lawrence W. '75 (CHL) Winston–Salem, NC St. Benedict the Moor.
Heinlein, Gregory (RVC) Massapequa Park, NY Our Lady of Lourdes.
Heinlein, Rev. Msgr. John T. '61 (RVC) Sayville, NY St. Lawrence the Martyr; Mastic Beach, NY St. Jude.
Heinrich, Harold D. '56 (HRT) Retired.
Heinsz, Vernon R. *s.j.* '73 (KC)[J] Kansas City, MO Rockhurst Jesuit Community.
Heintz, Andrew J. '05 (ARL) Notaries; Alexandria, VA Queen of Apostles.
Heintz, Daniel '54 (SY) North Syracuse, NY St. Rose of Lima Retired.
Heintz, Rev. Msgr. Michael W. '93 (FTW) South Bend, IN St. Matthew Cathedral; [B] University of Notre Dame Du Lac; Presbyteral Council; Consultors; Censor Librorum; Liturgical Commission; Inter City Catholic League.
Heintz, Robert L. '49 (SFD) Retired.
Heintzelman, Edward F. '84 (CAM) Mays Landing, NJ Church of St. Vincent de Paul, Mays Landing, N.J.
Heintzelman, Gerard T. '59 (HBG) Retired.
Heinz, David C. '77 (PEO) Bartonville, IL St. Anthony.
Heinz, Rev. Msgr. Martin G. '94 (RCK) Aurora, IL Holy Angels.
Heinz, Robert P. '80 (CHI) Northbrook, IL St. Norbert.
Heinz, Walter E. '62 (STU) Pomeroy, OH Sacred Heart.
Heinze, Arthur G. '69 (MIL) Menomonee Falls, WI St. James.
Heis, Clarence G. '82 (CIN) On Special and Archdiocesan Assignment.
Heise, Bert *o.f.m.* '57 (PEO) Peoria, IL Sacred Heart; Peoria, IL St. Joseph Retired.
Heiser, James '05 (CHY) Worland, WY St. Mary Magdalen; Advocates; College of Consultors.
Heiser, W. Charles *s.j.* '53 (STL)[C] Saint Louis University; [O] St. Louis, MO Jesuit Community Corporation at Saint Louis University – Jesuit Hall.
Heisig, James *s.v.d.* '69 (FgM) Techny, IL.
Heisig, Kazimierz '78 (HRT) Hartford, CT SS. Cyril and Methodius.
Heisler, John F. '99 (ARL) On Duty Outside the Diocese; [A] Columbus, OH Pontifical College Josephinum.
Heisler, John '99 (COL)[A] Columbus, OH Pontifical College Josephinum.
Heithoff, James E. '77 (GI) Personnel Board.
Heithoff, James H. '77 (GI) Alliance, NE Holy Rosary.
Heiting, R. Paul '87 (WIN)[A] Winona, MN Immaculate Heart of Mary Seminary; Judicial Officers; Misconduct Issues.
Heitkamp, Samuel '67 (SAT) Retired.
Heitz, Louis S. '57 (LFT) Retired.
Heitz, Warren *o.s.b.* '66 (IND)[K] St. Meinrad, IN St. Meinrad Archabbey.
Heitzman, Clarence J. '56 (COV) Southgate, KY St. Therese of the Infant Jesus.
Hejdak, Andrew '84 (CC) Woodsboro, TX St. Therese, The Little Flower.
Hejna, Lewis E. '81 (SPC) Springfield, MO Immaculate Conception.
Helbing, Brendan *o.s.b.* '65 (OKL)[I] Shawnee, OK St. Gregory's Abbey.
Helfrich, P. Frederick '71 (ROC) Webster, NY Holy Spirit.
Helfrich, Paul D. *b.h.* (BO)[AA] Boston, MA The Catholic Center at Boston University; Boston University.
Helfrich, Peter G. '76 (OG) Absent on Sick Leave, Disabled.
Helfrich, Thomas J. *o.s.f.s.* '78 (LAN)[N] Adrian, MI Siena Heights University; Parr Hwy. Correctional Facility.
Heller, Rev. Msgr. Christopher J. '79 (RVC) Babylon, NY St. Joseph; Babylon Deanery.
Heller, James '68 (SAG) Saginaw, MI St. Stephen.
Hellmann, Andreas '00 (GB)[O] Green Bay, WI Oratory of St. Joseph.
Hellmann, David E. '73 (LFT) Crawfordsville, IN St. Bernard.
Hellmann, Rev. Msgr. Donald F. '53 (COV) Florence, KY St. Paul; Diocesan Consultors; Priest Personnel; Defenders of the Bond Retired.
Hellmann, Wayne *o.f.m.conv.* '67 (IND)[J] Mount St. Francis, IN Mount Saint Francis Friary and Retreat Center.
Hellwig, Carl '06 (PMB) Port St. Lucie, FL St. Elizabeth Ann Seton.
Hellwig, Lee W. '86 (HRT) Military Chaplains; Navy Chaplains.
Helly, Victor J. *s.j.* '54 (FgM) New York, NY Society of Jesus.
Helman, Bradford N. '68 (Y) Canton, OH St. Michael the Archangel.
Helmick, Raymond G. *s.j.* '63 (BO) West Roxbury, MA St. Theresa of Avila; [U] Newton, MA The Jesuit Community at Boston College.
Helmick, Rev. Msgr. William M. '62 (BO) West Roxbury, MA St. Theresa of Avila; Trustees.
Helmin, Virgil A. '75 (SCL) Clear Lake, MN St. Marcus; Judicial Vicar; Notaries; Diocesan Priests Pension Plan Trustees.
Helmin, Virgil '75 (CR) Defenders of the Bond.
Helmlinger, Peter '04 (CIN) Cincinnati, OH Our Lady of the Rosary.
Helms, Michael L. '90 (DOD) Deerfield, KS Christ the King Catholic Church of Deerfield, Kansas; Lakin, KS St. Anthony of Padua Catholic Church of Lakin, Kansas; Syracuse, KS St. Raphael Catholic Church of Syracuse, Kansas.
Helms, Walter '69 (DAV) Coralville, IA St. Thomas More; [M] Coralville, IA St. Thomas More New Season Charitable Trust.
Helmueller, John '01 (SFS) Flandreau, SD SS. Simon and Jude; Spanish–Speaking Apostolate.
Helou, Nadim *m.l.m.* (SAM) Fall River, MA St. Anthony of the Desert.
Helwig, Paul C. '74 (HBG) Camp Hill, PA Good Shepherd; Consultors, College; Appointed.
Heman, Richard J. '67 (STL) Retired.
Hemann, David '85 (SC) Holstein, IA Our Lady of Good Counsel; Ida Grove, IA Sacred Heart; Odebolt, IA St. Martin's.
Hemann, Everett '71 (DUB) Cedar Falls, IA St. Patrick.
Hemann, Rev. Msgr. John W. '60 (DUB) Retired.
Hemann, Maurice *o.m.i.* '50 (FgM) Washington, DC AMERICAN OBLATE MISSIONS.
Hemann, Melvin D. '59 (DUB) Marriage Retorno Retired.
Hemauer, Gilbert *o.f.m.cap.* (GB)[J] Appleton, WI St. Fidelis Friary Retired.
Hemberger, Kent A. '88 (WCH)[G] Wichita, KS Spiritual Life Center; Building Commission; Retreats; Ongoing Formation of the Clergy Committee.
Hemberger, Rev. Msgr. Robert E. '70 (WCH) Victim Assistance Coordinator; [F] Wichita, KS Wichita Center, Congregation of the Sisters of St. Joseph; Vicar General; Moderator of the Diocesan Curia; Director of Diocesan Planning; Presbyteral Council/College of Consultors; Judges; Ongoing Formation of

the Clergy Committee; Building Commission; Finance Committee; Health Affairs – Diocesan Liaison.
Hembrow, William '60 (SFD) Jerseyville, IL St. Mary; Jerseyville, IL Holy Ghost.
Hemler, Edward B. '64 (BAL) Fallston, MD St. Mark.
Hemm, Thomas *c.pp.s.* '78 (CIN) Saint Henry, OH St. Bernard; St. Henry, OH St. Aloysius; St. Henry, OH St. Francis; St. Henry, OH St. Henry; Saint Henry, OH St. Wendelin; [N] Dayton Provincial Office of the Cincinnati Province of the Society of the Precious Blood; Provincial Council:.
Hemmelgarn, Larry J. *c.pp.s.* '84 (CIN)[N] Dayton, OH Provincial Office of the Cincinnati Province of the Society of the Precious Blood; [N] Dayton Provincial Office of the Cincinnati Province of the Society of the Precious Blood.
Hemmer, Joseph *o.f.m.* '54 (FBK) Kaltag, AK St. Teresa Catholic Church; Saint Louis, MO Sacred Heart Province; Presbyteral Council; Consultors.
Hemmerle, R. Joseph '67 (L) Loretto, KY Holy Cross; St. Francis, KY St. Francis of Assisi.
Hemmerling, Henry L. '66 (MET) Retired.
Hemming, Philip M. '67 (P) Banks, OR St. Francis of Assisi.
Hemp, Lawrence '67 (LUB) Retired.
Hemphill, Anthony *s.v.d.* '58 (CHI)[N] Techny, IL Divine Word Residence.
Hemrick, Eugene F. '63 (JOL) On Duty Outside the Diocese.
Hemrick, Eugene '63 (WDC) Washington, DC St. Joseph on Capitol Hill.
Hemsing, John D. '88 (MIL) Archdiocesan Consultors; Mequon, WI Lumen Christi.
Henao, Luis '74 (NO) Slidell, LA Trinity Neurologic Rehabilitation Center at Slidell; Slidell, LA Greenbriar Nursing & Convalescent Home; Slidell, LA Guest House of Slidell Nursing Home; Slidell, LA St. Margaret Mary.
Henault, James A. *m.s.* '80 (ATL) Snellville, GA St. Oliver Plunkett.
Henault, John *o.m.i.* '63 (FgM) Washington, DC AMERICAN OBLATE MISSIONS.
Henchal, Rev. Msgr. Michael J. '73 (PRT) Scarborough, ME St. Maximilian Kolbe; Cape Elizabeth, ME St. Bartholomew; Vicars General; Promoter of Justice; Associate Judges; Diocesan Consultors; Ex Officio Members; Diocesan Finance Council; Staff.
Henchal, Rev. Msgr. Michael J. '73 (PRT) South Portland, ME St. John the Evangelist; South Portland, ME Church of the Holy Cross; [M] Portland, ME Southern Maine Community College.
Henchey, Joseph *c.s.s.* '56 (BO)[U] Waltham, MA Bertoni Hall – Formation House.
Henchey, Joseph *c.s.s.* '56 (NY)[A] Yonkers, NY St. Joseph's Seminary.
Hendel, Lawrence '77 (SJ) San Jose, CA St. Anthony.
Henden, Brian *o.carm.* '93 (LA) North Hollywood, CA St. Jane Frances de Chantal.
Henderson, Christopher '94 (SAM) Retired.
Henderson, Donald '70 (PEO) Clergymen's Aid, Inc.; Peoria, IL St. Philomena.
Henderson, James B. *o.c.s.o.* '60 (DUB)[K] Peosta, IA New Melleray Abbey, Order of Cistercians of the Strict Observance.
Henderson, John A. '87 (JC) Perry, MO St. William.
Henderson, John *o.f.m.conv.* '84 (P) Corvallis, OR St. Mary; [P] Corvallis, OR Trinity Court (Student Housing); Area Vicars.
Henderson, Robert J. '65 (COV)[I] Edgewood, KY St. Elizabeth Medical Center, Inc. Retired.
Henderson, Roy '90 (BGP) Bridgeport, CT St. Andrew.
Henderson, Timothy J. '04 (STL) Ellisville, MO St. Clare of Assisi.
Hendren, Lucian '63 (SFE) Retired.
Hendrick, Rev. Msgr. Frank J. '54 (ARL) Retired.
Hendrick, Rev. Msgr. Matthew D. '85 (R) Wrightsville Beach, NC St. Therese.
Hendricks, Clare '63 (GRY) On Duty Outside the Diocese.
Hendricks, Rev. Msgr. Donald W. '55 (NY) Buchanan, NY St. Christopher.
Hendricks, Edward S. '77 (BAL) Special Assignment; [U] Frostburg, MD Frostburg State University.
Hendricks, Rev. Msgr. Joseph M. '72 (COL) Dublin, OH St. Brigid of Kildare; [L] Columbus, OH Diocesan Retirement Community Corp.; [G] Columbus, OH The Villas at St. Therese Independent Living, Inc.; [G] Columbus, OH The Villas at St. Therese Assisted Living, Inc.
Hendricks, Theodore J. '65 (GB) Black Creek, WI St. Mary; Bonduel, WI St. Lawrence.
Hendrickson, Daniel *s.j.* '94 (NY)[EE] New York, NY Xavier Jesuit Community.
Hendrickson, Michael D. '01 (MO) San Jose, CA St. Victor; Navy Reserve Chaplains.
Hendry, Rev. Msgr. Owen J. '60 (NEW) Retired.
Hendry, Simon J. *s.j.* '77 (DET)[K] Detroit, MI Jesuit Community at the University of Detroit Mercy.
Heneghan, James A. '83 (CHI) Chicago, IL Immaculate Heart of Mary.
Heneghan, Jarlath '55 (SEA) Retired.
Heneghan, John F. '55 (YAK) Judges Retired.
Henehan, Patrick '98 (PEO) Wapella, IL St. Patrick Church; [B] Bloomington, IL Central Catholic High School.
Henehan, Thomas P. *m.m.* '65 (FgM) Maryknoll, NY MARYKNOLL.
Henery, Ronald *o.p* '78 (NY)[EE] New York St. Vincent Ferrer Priory.
Heney, David '78 (LA) Thousand Oaks, CA St. Paschal Baylon.
Hengle, John R. '68 (CLV) Tallmadge, OH Our Lady of Victory; Associate Judges.
Heninger, Michael B. '00 (ATL) On Leave of Absence.
Henke, Donald E. '93 (STL)[A] St. Louis, MO Kenrick School of Theology; [D] St. Louis, MO Paul VI Institute of Catechetical and Pastoral Studies.
Henke, Rev. Msgr. James '66 (SAT) San Antonio, TX St. Francis of Assisi; Judges.
Henkels, Edmund *o.s.b.* '59 (WDC)[N] Washington, DC St. Anselm's Abbey.
Henkes, Donald E. '66 (SAG) Rosebush, MI St. Henry/ St. Charles.
Henkle, Charles *o.f.m.conv.* '97 (CLV) Lorain, OH St. Anthony of Padua; Lorain, OH St. Peter.
Henley, Earl *m.s.c.* '69 (SB) Native American Ministry; Special or Other Diocesan Assignment; San Jacinto, CA St. Joseph Mission.
Henn, William *o.f.m.cap.* '78 (PIT)[M] Pittsburgh, PA St. Augustine Friary.
Hennecke, William '07 (SPC) Jackson, MO Immaculate Conception; Leopold, MO St. John.
Hennelly, Michael F. '91 (PH) Levittown, PA Queen of the Universe.
Hennen, David R. '05 (STP) Buffalo, MN St. Francis Xavier.
Hennen, Joseph *o.s.c.* '67 (PHX)[F] Phoenix, AZ Crosier Provincial House Province of St. Odilia.
Hennen, Joseph '67 (HON) Hilo, HI Malia Puka O' Kalani (Mary Gate of Heaven); Hilo, HI St. Joseph.
Hennen, Thomas Joseph '04 (DAV) Clinton, IA Jesus Christ, Prince of Peace.
Hennessey, Daniel F. '02 (BO) Vocations; Waltham, MA St. Mary.
Hennessey, John E. '67 (CHI) Libertyville, IL St. Joseph.
Hennessey, John J. *c.ss.r.* (BO) Boston, MA Our Lady of Perpetual Help.
Hennessey, Joseph M. '88 (BO) Associates; Weston, MA St. Julia.
Hennessey, Lawrence R. '71 (CHI)[A] Mundelein, IL University of St. Mary of the Lake/Mundelein Seminary; [W] Mundelein, IL Civitas Dei Foundation.
Hennessey, Rev. Msgr. William J. '61 (MIA) Special Assignment; [B] St. Thomas University; [Q] Miami Shores, FL Archdiocese of Miami Millennium Appeal, Inc.; [Q] Miami Shores, FL Archdiocese of Miami, Inc.; Vicars General; Moderator of the Curia; Consultors; Incardination Committee; Priests' Personnel Board; Executive Director; Catholic Charities of the Archdiocese of Miami, Inc.; Members.
Hennessy, Brian P. '99 (PH) Office of the Vicar for Clergy; Philadelphia, PA St. Madeleine Sophie; On Special or Other Archdiocesan Assignment.
Hennessy, Rev. Msgr. Douglas J. '63 (PEO) Bloomington, IL Holy Trinity.
Hennessy, Rev. Msgr. Douglas '63 (PEO) Clergymen's Aid, Inc.
Hennessy, James W. '61 (WIN) Retired.
Hennessy, John A. *s.j.* '69 (MIL)[P] Wauwatosa, WI Jesuit Community at St. Camillus.
Hennessy, John '78 (FWT) On Leave of Absence.
Hennessy, Joseph I. '63 (PHX) Retired.
Hennessy, Thomas C. *s.j.* '47 (NY)[EE] New York, NY Murray–Weigel Hall.
Hennessy, Thomas J. '96 (ATL) Norcross, GA Saint Patrick.
Henning, Edward *o.f.m.cap.* (SP) Tampa, FL Most Holy Redeemer.
Henning, James P. *o.f.m.conv.* '82 (PEO) Clinton, IL St. John the Baptist Catholic Church; Farmer City, IL Sacred Heart.
Henning, Michael L. '74 (STL) Saint Louis, MO Holy Name of Jesus.
Henning, Phillip D. '93 (SAT) Floresville, TX Sacred Heart.
Henning, Richard G. '92 (RVC)[A] Huntington, NY Diocesan Seminary of the Immaculate Conception.
Henninger, George '85 (VIC) On Duty Outside the Diocese.
Henninger, Mark *s.j.* '78 (WDC)[N] Washington, DC The Jesuit Community at Georgetown University.
Hennington, Bruce M. '68 (MAD) Columbus, WI St. Jerome; Doylestown, WI St. Patrick.
Henrich, Steven *o.s.c.* '74 (PHX)[F] Phoenix, AZ; Provincial Councilors:.
Henrick, John C. '62 (NSH) Antioch, TN St. Ignatius of Antioch; Defenders of the Bond; Presbyteral Council.
Henricksen, Rev. Msgr. Francis C. '55 (DAV) Promoters of Justice; Vicar for Religious; Vicar for Clergy Retired.
Henriot, Peter J. *s.j.* '70 (FgM) Portland, OR Society of Jesus.
Henriques, Eduardo T. *s.j.* '03 (WOR)[O] Worcester, MA Jesuits of the Holy Cross, Inc.
Henriquez, Carlos S. '95 (ARE) Vega–Alta, PR Immaculate Conception of Blessed Virgin Mary.
Henriquez, Genaro '99 (BWN) Pharr, TX St. Anne, Mother of Mary.
Henriquez, Juan Carlos *s.j.* '99 (BO)[U] Newton, MA The Jesuit Community at Boston College.
Henritzy, Elias *o.p.* '92 (WDC)[B] Washington, DC Dominican House of Studies.
Henry, Charles W. *o.s.b.* '53 (NEW)[M] Newark, NJ Newark Abbey.
Henry, David *s.j.* (SEA)[A] Seattle, WA Seattle University; [L] Seattle, WA Arrupe Jesuit Community at Seattle University.
Henry, Donald H. '71 (VEN) Sarasota, FL St. Thomas More; Presbyteral Council.
Henry, Earl J. *o.s.b.* '64 (GBG)[G] Latrobe, PA Saint Vincent Archabbey.
Henry, James R. '71 (MRY) Salinas, CA Madonna Del Sasso; Diocesan Consultors; Diocesan Consultors; Presbyteral Council.
Henry, James *s.v.d.* '59 (LA)[D] Lakewood, CA Saint Joseph High School.
Henry, James '71 (MRY) Vicars Forane.
Henry, John F. *s.j.* '55 (BAL)[S] Towson Maryland Province of the Society of Jesus.
Henry, John P. '52 (RVC) Tarpon Springs, FL St. Ignatius of Antioch Retired.
Henry, Joseph P. '58 (PRO) Retired.
Henry, Joseph *s.j.* '47 (SCR)[C] Scranton, PA The University of Scranton.
Henry, Lawrence J. *c.s.c.* '61 (FTW)[H] Notre Dame Congregation of Holy Cross, Indiana Province, Provincial House.
Henry, Lawrence *c.s.c.* '61 (GRY)[D] Michigan City, IN Saint Anthony Memorial Health Centers.
Henry, Leo G. '55 (PIT) Retired.
Henry, Patrick J. '92 (SAC) Susanville, CA Sacred Heart.
Henry, Patrick J. (CHI) Oak Lawn, IL St. Catherine of Alexandria.
Henry, Paul J. '70 (BAL) Special Assignment.
Henry, Paul J. '68 (ORL) Orlando, FL St. John Vianney.
Henry, Paul J. '70 (MO) DEPARTMENT OF VETERANS AFFAIRS HOSPITALS AND CHAPLAINS.
Henry, Paul '68 (ORL) Vicar for Clergy; Ex Officio Members.
Henry, Perry *c.m.* '83 (STL)[O] Earth City, MO Congregation of the Mission Western Province (Vincentians).
Henry, Perry *c.m.* '83 (FgM) Earth City, MO Western Province; Earth City, MO.
Henry, Peter J. '68 (ORL) DeBary, FL St. Ann's; Representative for Incardinated Priests.
Henry, Robert P. '79 (NY) Scarsdale, NY Immaculate Heart of Mary.
Henry, Ronald H. *o.p.* '58 (GAL) Houston, TX Holy Rosary.
Henry, Terence *t.o.r.* '76 (STU)[A] Steubenville, OH Franciscan University of Steubenville; [H] Steubenville, OH Holy Spirit Friary.
Henry, William F. '84 (JKS) Charismatic Renewal.
Henry, William '84 (JKS) Jackson, MS St. Therese; Personnel Board.
Henseler, J. Thomas '63 (PEO) On Duty Outside the Diocese.
Henseler, J. Thomas '63 (SFD) Mount Sterling, IL Holy Family; Mount Sterling, IL St. Thomas; Mount Sterling, IL Western Illinois Correctional Center.
Henseler, Michael *s.d.s.* '77 (MIL)[P] Milwaukee Salvatorian Provincial Offices.
Henseler, Philip E. '00 (CHI) Other Assignments.
Hensell, Eugene *o.s.b.* '69 (IND)[A] St. Meinrad, IN Saint Meinrad School of Theology; [K] St. Meinrad, IN St. Meinrad Archabbey.
Henson, Darren '01 (KCK) On Leave of Absence.
Henson, Jerome '77 (ORG) Administrative Leave.
Henson, Joel '93 (LA)[A] Camarillo, CA St. John's Seminary; Liturgical Commision.
Henson, Paul *o.carm.* '02 (LA)[F] Encino, CA Crespi Carmelite High School; [P] Encino, CA Our Lady of Mount Carmel Priory.
Hensy, Patrick E. *c.s.p.* '78 (LA) Los Angeles, CA St. Paul the Apostle Retired.
Hentges, James *o.s.c.* '76 (PHX)[F] Crosiers Serving Abroad.
Hentz, Otto H. *s.j.* '68 (WDC)[N] Washington, DC The Jesuit Community at Georgetown University.
Hentzner, John T. '45 (MIL) Retired.
Henyk, Christopher '08 (Y) North Canton, OH St. Paul.
Henz, Kenneth W. '51 (CIN) Retired.
Heon, Charles *o.m.i.* '64 (FgM) Washington, DC AMERICAN OBLATE MISSIONS.
Hepburn, Timothy M. '93 (ATL)[J] Atlanta, GA Georgia Institute of Technology; Permanent Diaconate; Office of Evangelization; Special or Other (Arch)Diocesan Assignment.
Hephner, John J. '59 (GB) Wausaukee, WI St. Agnes;

Wausaukee, WI St. Augustine Retired.
Hepnar, Bede '57 (GB)[J] Green Bay, WI St. Mary of the Angels Friary.
Hepner, Ernest C. '61 (CLV) Retired.
Heppe, Patrick E. '77 (MIL) Special Assignment; Archbishop's Executive Council; Vicars General; Vicar for Ordained and Lay Ecclesial Ministry.
Heppen, Michael J. *c.s.c.* '63 (FTW)[H] Holy Cross House.
Her, Chundo '94 (SAC) Sacramento, CA St. Jeong–Hae Elizabeth.
Hera, Marianus Pale *s.v.d.* '04 (WDC)[N] Washington, DC Divine Word House.
Herald, Robert '89 (AUS) Hearne, TX St. Mary.
Heramb, James '68 (JOL) Absent on Leave.
Heras, Rev. Msgr. Michael '84 (CC) Corpus Christi, TX Our Lady of Perpetual Help; Presbyteral Council.
Heraty, John T. '67 (RCK) Retired.
Herba, Stanislaw '64 (SLC) West Valley City, UT Saints Peter and Paul LLC 243.
Herbein, Rev. Msgr. John J. '74 (E) Franklin, PA St. Patrick; Deans.
Herbek, Rev. Msgr. Adrian F. '59 (LIN) Building Commission; Members Retired.
Herbek, Rev. Msgr. Adrian F. '59 (LIN)[E] Lincoln, NE Bonacum House.
Herber, Alvin *c.pp.s.* '50 (CIN)[N] Carthagena, OH St. Charles Retired.
Herber, John *c.pp.s.* '68 (CIN)[N] Carthagena, OH St. Charles.
Herber, Stanley J. '64 (IND) Connersville, IN St. Gabriel; Knightstown, IN St. Rose; Liberty, IN St. Bridget; New Castle, IN St. Anne; Deaneries and Deans.
Herberger, Edward *s.v.d.* '60 (CHI)[N] Techny, IL Divine Word Residence.
Herberger, Roy T. '68 (BUF) Sheehan Memorial Emergency Hospital; Buffalo, NY SS. Columba–Brigid.
Herbers, Simon *c.p.* '50 (GAL)[O] Houston, TX Congregation of the Passion, Holy Name Passionist Community and Retreat Center.
Herbert, Eugene '81 (LA) Monrovia, CA Annunciation.
Herbert, G. Paul '86 (WDC) Poolesville, MD Our Lady of the Presentation; Pastoral Center Special Ministries; Judges; Defenders of the Bond; Air Force Reserve Chaplains.
Herbert, G. Paul '86 (MO) Judges.
Herbert, John J. '83 (BUR)[D] Rutland, VT Loretto/Kervick Home Retired.
Herbert, Rev. Msgr. Leo P. '67 (ATL) Lookout Mountain, GA Our Lady of the Mount.
Herbert, Michael J. '05 (RIC) Lebanon, VA Good Shepherd; St. Paul, VA St. Therese.
Herbst, Robert M. *o.f.m.conv.* '91 (OAK) Adjutant Judicial Vicars; Judges; Vicars for Religious; Consultors; Court of Second Instance; Presbyteral Council.
Herbst, Robert *o.f.m.conv.* '91 (OAK) Alameda, CA St. Barnabas.
Herbst, Thomas *o.f.m.* '92 (SD)[J] Oceanside, CA Mission San Luis Rey.
Herbster, Rev. Msgr. Kenneth J. '63 (NEW) North Caldwell, NJ Notre Dame; Minister for Priests.
Hercek, Joseph R. '72 (MRY) Retired.
Hercik, Terry A. '80 (GBG) Coral, PA Our Lady of the Assumption.
Herda, Jerome '90 (MIL) Whitefish Bay, WI St. Monica; Fox Point, WI St. Eugene.
Heredia, Juan Victor '91 (BWN) Raymondville, TX St. Anthony.
Hereford, Thomas D. '85 (JC) Absent on Leave.
Hereley, Peter J. *o.p.* '63 (CHI) River Forest, IL St. Vincent Ferrer; [T] River Forest, IL American Friends of the Ecole Biblique.
Hereshko, David M. '00 (HBG) Abbottstown, PA Immaculate Heart of Mary; Appointed.
Herff, Jerome R. *c.m.* '67 (GLP) Kayenta, AZ Our Lady of Guadalupe; Defenders of the Bond; Diocesan Review Board for Sexual Abuse & Misconduct by Clergy, Religious and Other Church Personnel.
Hergenrother, John C. '66 (CHI) Judges; Other Assignments.
Herhenrerder, Peter V. '59 (SCR) Retired.
Heria, Fernando '96 (MIA) Judges; Miami, FL St. Brendan.
Herian, Kenneth J. *s.j.* '55 (MIL) Milwaukee, WI Gesu Parish.
Heric, William '81 (SEA) Redmond, WA St. Jude; Duvall, WA Holy Innocents.
Herle, Clifford *o.f.m.* '55 (LSC) Tularosa, NM St. Francis de Paula.
Herlihy, Rev. Msgr. Daniel J. '67 (MET) South Bound Brook, NJ Our Lady of Mercy; Episcopal Vicars.
Herlihy, Neil '05 (ATL) The Rock, GA St. Peter the Rock.
Herlong, Theophilus L. '58 (LKC) Advocates Retired.
Herman, Charles A. '97 (FTW) South Bend, IN St. John the Baptist.
Herman, Gerald *o.f.m.conv.* '57 (SAT)[L] San Antonio, TX San Damiano Friary.
Herman, Gerard *o.f.m.conv.* '57 (SAT)[B] San Antonio, TX San Damiano Friary, Prenovitiate House of Formation.
Herman, John A. *c.s.c.* '95 (PHX)[J] Goodyear, AZ St. John Vianney School Development Fund.
Herman, John A. *c.s.c.* '94 (PHX) Goodyear, AZ Saint John Vianney Roman Catholic Parish; College of Consultors; Presbyteral Council.
Herman, John *c.s.c.* (FTW)[H] Notre Dame Congregation of Holy Cross, Indiana Province, Provincial House.
Herman, Norbert H. '88 (SAT) Runge, TX St. Anthony's; Kenedy, TX Our Lady Queen of Peace.
Herman, Robert D. '60 (WIN) Medford, MN Christ the King Retired.
Herman, William J. '00 (DET) Harper Woods, MI Our Lady Queen of Peace.
Hermann, Rev. Msgr. Carlton P. '52 (SFS) Retired.
Hermanns, Mel *o.f.m.cap.* '64 (CHI) Chicago, IL Our Lady Gate of Heaven.
Hermes, Alphonsus B. *o.praem.* '01 (ORG)[D] Silverado, CA St. Michael's Preparatory School; [I] Silverado, CA Norbertine Fathers of Orange Inc.
Hermes, Rev. Msgr. Daniel J. '69 (RCK) Crystal Lake, IL St. Thomas the Apostle; Diocesan Consultors.
Hermes, Rev. Msgr. Eustace '41 (VIC) Retired.
Hermes, Joseph H. *m.m.* '62 (FgM) Maryknoll, NY MARYKNOLL.
Hermes, Michael '91 (KCK)[B] Kansas City, KS Bishop Ward High School; Leawood, KS Church of the Nativity.
Hermes, Richard C. '98 (SP)[C] Tampa, FL Jesuit High School.
Hermes, Thomas W. '82 (KC) Chillicothe, MO St. Columban; Consultors; Deans.
Hermoso, Joseph '57 (ELP) El Paso, TX St. Joseph's.
Hermoso, Rev. Msgr. Seth F. '67 (GAL) Houston, TX St. John Neumann; Ethnic Vicars.
Hernanco, Henry L. '67 (LA) Federal Correctional Institution.
Hernandez, Alfred Ricardo '66 (SAT) Military Chaplains.
Hernandez, Alfred '82 (LA) Torrance, CA Nativity.
Hernandez, Rev. Msgr. Alfred '55 (LA) Retired.
Hernandez, Alfredo '92 (PMB) West Palm Beach, FL St. Juliana; Ex Officio; Vicars Forane.
Hernandez, Angelo '93 (PH) Pottstown, PA St. Aloysius.
Hernandez, Anselmo *l.c.* '01 (MO) Army Chaplains.
Hernandez, Rev. Msgr. Anthony '95 (BRK)[X] Brooklyn, NY Casa Betsaida–Home for people with AIDS; Chancellor; Diocesan Consultors; Presbyteral Council; Brooklyn, NY Transfiguration; Vicar for Canonical Affairs.
Hernandez, Anthony '00 (VNN) Los Gatos, CA St. Basil the Great; Director of Religious Education.
Hernandez, Antonio X. '92 (SAT) On Leave; Sabinal, TX St. Patrick's.
Hernandez, Antonio *c.ss.r.* '67 (CGS) Aguas Buenas, PR Church of Tres Santos Reyes.
Hernandez, Apolinar '90 (SR) On Leave.
Hernandez, Ariel '02 (CAM) Continuing Education & Spiritual Formation of Priests (CESF).
Hernandez, Ariel '03 (CAM) Bridgeton, NJ The Church of the Immaculate Conception, Bridgeton, N.J.; Cedarville, NJ St. Michael's Roman Catholic Church; Bridgeton, NJ The Church of St. Teresa Avila, Bridgeton, N.J.
Hernandez, Benito A. *c.r.* '03 (DEN) Denver, CO Our Lady of Guadalupe.
Hernandez, Bernardo *c.m.* '63 (ARE) Manati, PR Sagrada Familia.
Hernandez, Bradford '08 (AUS) Brenham, TX St. Mary of the Immaculate Conception.
Hernández, Edwin R. '83 (CGS) Barranquitas, PR Church of St. Anthony of Padua.
Hernandez, Eliseo *c.o.r.c.* '82 (SB) San Bernardino, CA Our Lady of Guadalupe; [I] Corona, CA Confraternity of Operarios Del Reino De Cristo, C.O.R.C.
Hernandez, Enrico '96 (SJ) On Leave of Absence.
Hernandez, Esteban '87 (BWN) Los Fresnos, TX St. Cecilia; Presbyteral Council.
Hernandez, Fernando A. '90 (NY) Newburgh, NY St. Patrick.
Hernandez, Fidel *o.a.r.* '97 (LA) Oxnard, CA Mary Star of the Sea; [P] Oxnard, CA St. Augustine Priory O.A.R.
Hernandez, Francis G. *s.j.* '63 (SAC)[D] Sacramento, CA Jesuit High School; [I] Carmichael, CA Sacramento Jesuit Community.
Hernandez, Francisco J. '90 (LAR) Laredo, TX San Agustin Cathedral.
Hernandez, Francisco J. '94 (MIA) Hialeah, FL Immaculate Conception.
Hernandez, Francisco J. '90 (YAK) On Duty Outside the Diocese Retired.
Hernandez, Francisco '95 (CGS) Formacion Diac. Permanentes; Caguas, PR Nuestra Senora del Perpetuo Socorro.
Hernandez, Rev. Msgr. Gonzalo Diaz '63 (MGZ) Hormigueros, PR Shrine of Our Lady of Monserrate; Diocesan Board of Administration; Parish Priests Consultors.
Hernandez, Hugo *m.g.* '95 (OAK) Concord, CA St. Francis of Assisi.
Hernandez, Ivan '09 (FRS) Bakersfield, CA St. Philip the Apostle.
Hernandez, Jimmy '83 (ARE) Retired.
Hernandez, Jorge *o.f.m.* '98 (SFR) San Francisco, CA St. Boniface.
Hernandez, Jose A. '60 (SFE) Tome, NM Immaculate Conception.
Hernandez, Jose Luis '99 (SPK) Cheney, WA St. Rose of Lima.
Hernandez, Rev. Msgr. Joseph F. '81 (LA) Vice Chancellor; Continuing Formation for Clergy; Continuing Formation.
Hernandez, Rev. Msgr. Joseph '81 (LA) Los Angeles, CA St. Teresa of Avila; ACC Liaison to Brothers' Council; Executive Director.
Hernandez, Juan Pedro '89 (PT) Quincy, FL St. Thomas the Apostle.
Hernandez, Juan Ramon *c.ss.r.* '80 (CGS) San Lorenzo, PR Nuestra Senora de la Mercedes.
Hernandez, Lawrence C. *o.ss.t.* '78 (BAL)[S] The Trinitarian Community in Adelphi, Maryland.
Hernandez, Manuel Santiago '85 (PCE) Catholic Youth Organization.
Hernandez, Manuel '96 (CC) Retired.
Hernandez, Martin '97 (DEN) Edwards, CO St. Clare of Assisi.
Hernandez, Miguel A. '02 (ORG) Stanton, CA St. Polycarp.
Hernandez, Nils '04 (DUB) Clarion, IA St. John; Eagle Grove, IA Sacred Heart; Belmond, IA St. Francis Xavier.
Hernandez, Pablo A. '06 (L) Lebanon, KY St. Augustine; Lebanon, KY Holy Name of Mary.
Hernandez, Pedro '89 (ARE) Vega Alta, PR Our Lady of Mt. Carmel.
Hernandez, Rafael Mendez '94 (SJN) Bayamon, PR Santo Domingo De Guzman.
Hernandez, Ramon '73 (SP) Tampa, FL St. Mary.
Hernandez, Reynaldo '99 (FRS) Tulare, CA St. Rita.
Hernandez, Ricardo '00 (RCK) Rockford, IL St. Patrick.
Hernandez, Ricardo '98 (SJN) Clergy Social Security (Prevision Social del Clero).
Hernandez, Victor '06 (TYL) Grand Saline, TX St. Celestine; Emory, TX St. John the Evangelist Church.
Hernandez–Ayala, Jose Luis '06 (ATL) Special or Other (Arch)Diocesan Assignment; [C] Atlanta, GA St. Pius X Catholic High School.
Hernandez–Gomez, Francisco J. '01 (SAC) Yuba City, CA St. Isidore; Presbyteral Council.
Hernandez Morales, Ricardo '98 (SJN) Spiritual Director.
Hernandez Ralat, Edwin '01 (SJN) Graduate Studies.
Hernandez Velez, Daniel Enrique '03 (MGZ) Mayaguez, PR Church of the Resurrection.
Hernando, Henry L. '67 (LA)[BB] San Pedro, CA Apostleship of the Sea, Catholic Maritime Ministry; Apostleship of the Sea.
Hernando, Jose L. '62 (MIA) Key Biscayne, FL St. Agnes; Deans and Deaneries.
Herne, Robert G. '47 (CHI) Palos Hills, IL Sacred Heart Retired.
Herold, Anthony J. '79 (DAV) Clinton, IA Jesus Christ, Prince of Peace; Deans.
Heron, J. Thomas '78 (PH) Elkins Park, PA St. James.
Herondi, Fernandes de Araujo *s.x.* '76 (PAT) Wayne, NJ XAVERIAN MISSIONARY FATHERS; [N] Wayne Xaverian Missionary Fathers.
Herpin, Rev. Msgr. Michael '66 (LAF) On Leave.
Herpin, Wayne D. *s.j.* '74 (LSC) Alamogordo, NM St. Jude.
Herr, Kenneth H. '68 (EVN) Evansville, IN St. Boniface; Clergy Personnel Board.
Herrador, Blas P. '52 (GAL) Houston, TX Resurrection.
Herrea, Henry Erazo '98 (DAL) Dallas, TX Cathedral–Santuario de Guadalupe.
Herrejon–Lopez, Armando '07 (ATL) Lilburn, GA St. John Neumann.
Herrera, Anthony W. '91 (OAK) Hayward, CA All Saints.
Herrera, David '89 (SAN) San Angelo, TX St. Mary's.
Herrera, Edward '91 (LSC) Sunland Park, NM St. Martin de Porres; Presbyteral Council; Clergy Personnel Board.
Herrera, Rev. Msgr. Emigdio '77 (LA) Lynwood, CA St. Emydius.
Herrera, Enrique '96 (MRY) Greenfield, CA Holy Trinity.
Herrera, Francisco '67 (ELP) Presbyteral Council Retired.
Herrera, Jorge '03 (RNO) Diocesan Board of Consultors; Yerington, NV Holy Family; Hawthorne, NV Our Lady of Perpetual Help; Presbyteral Council.
Herrera, Jose F. '88 (BRK) Woodside, NY Corpus Christi.
Herrera, Jose G. '89 (MO) Army Chaplains.
Herrera, Jose M. '09 (YAK) Grandview, WA Blessed Sacrament; Mabton, WA Immaculate Conception.
Herrera, Jose '89 (STV) On Duty Outside the Diocese.

Herrera, Manuel Victor (NY) Bronx, NY Our Lady of Grace.
Herrera, Pedro E. *c.s.v.* '80 (CHI)[N] Arlington Heights Viatorian Province Center–Clerics of St. Viator.
Herrera, Ruben '06 (RCK) Elgin, IL St. Joseph.
Herrera–Castaneda, Roberto '08 (ATL) Lawrenceville, GA St. Lawrence.
Herrera–Ciro, Albeiro '08 (PBL) Holly, CO St. Frances of Rome; Lamar, CO St. Francis De Sales–Our Lady of Guadalupe; Springfield, CO Annunciation.
Herrera–Diaz, Nixon Andres '99 (NY) Bronx, NY St. Margaret Mary.
Herrero, Rev. Msgr. Nicolas '59 (FRS) Retired.
Herring, James B. *o.praem.* '02 (GB)[A] De Pere, WI St. Norbert Abbey; [J] De Pere, WI St. Norbert Abbey; [O] De Pere, WI NORBERT & CO.; De Pere, WI.
Herrmann, Francis R. *s.j.* '74 (BO)[U] Newton, MA The Jesuit Community at Boston College.
Herrmann, Gilbert P. '49 (DOD) Retired.
Herrmann, James *o.s.c.* '70 (STP) Crystal, MN St. Raphael.
Herrmann, James *o.s.c.* '70 (PHX)[F] Crosiers Serving Abroad.
Herrmann, Richard J. '44 (LC) Retired.
Herrmann, Robert W. '58 (PIT) Retired.
Herron, Rev. Msgr. Denis M. '73 (BRK) Woodside, NY St. Teresa.
Herron, Francis X. '55 (PH) Retired.
Herron, Jack B. '74 (FAR) Military Chaplains.
Herron, John B. '74 (MO) Army Chaplains.
Herron, Rev. Msgr. Joseph P. '62 (CAM) Retired.
Hersey, Bryan L. '98 (SEA) Presbyteral Council; Deans.
Hersey, Bryan L. '98 (SEA) Everett, WA Immaculate Conception; Everett, WA Our Lady of Perpetual Help.
Hertel, James R. (PAT) Retired.
Hertel, John *o.carm.* '53 (JOL)[K] Darien, IL Carmelite Carefree Retirement Village.
Hertel, Joseph M. *o.f.m.* '66 (PAT)[Q] Paterson, NJ St. Anthony's Guild.
Hertel, Joseph M. *o.f.m.* '66 (NEW)[M] East Rutherford, NJ Sacred Heart Friary; [M] East Rutherford, NJ Sacred Heart Friary.
Hertges, Donald A. '07 (DUB) Cedar Rapids, IA St. Jude.
Hertweck, Robert *s.m.* '64 (SJ)[M] Cupertino, CA The Marianist Center.
Hertzfeld, Adam L. '02 (TOL) Office of Vocations: Priesthood and Consecrated Life; Perrysburg, OH St. Rose; Northwest Ohio Guild of the Catholic Medical Association.
Hervey, Paul '95 (SP) Knights of Columbus Retired.
Herzing, Joseph '99 (SCL) Menahga, MN Holy Cross; Perham, MN St. Henry's; Personnel Committee; Presbyteral Council.
Herzog, John M. '56 (DUB) Retired.
Herzog, Lawrence A. '80 (STL) Richmond Heights, MO Little Flower.
Herzog, Mark J. '79 (TOL) Oregon, OH St. Ignatius; Blessed Kateri Tekakwitha Deanery; Members; Diocesan Council of Catholic Women (DCCW).
Herzstein, Joseph M. *c.s.sp.* '63 (FgM) Bethel Park, PA CONGREGATION OF THE HOLY SPIRIT.
Hesburgh, Theodore M. *c.s.c.* '43 (FTW)[H] Holy Cross House.
Heskamp, Charles *s.v.d.* '58 (MIL)[P] East Troy, WI Divine Word Missionaries Retired.
Hesketh, John E. *o.s.b.* '94 (PAT)[N] Morristown, NJ St. Mary's Abbey.
Heskin, Thomas M. *o.s.m.* '55 (CHI)[N] Chicago Order of Friar Servants of Mary (Servites) United States of America Province, Inc.
Hesko, Daniel C. '84 (TR) Middletown, NJ St. Catherine.
Heslin, Rev. Msgr. James J. '54 (STA) Retired.
Heslin, Philip J. '57 (SUP) On Special or Other Diocesan Assignment; Moderator of the Curia; Ex Officio Members.
Heslin, Sean '67 (ORL) Cocoa Beach, FL Church of Our Saviour; Deans; Ex Officio Members; 64+.
Hess, James D. *o.carm.* '76 (PBR) North Huntingdon, PA St. Stephen's.
Hess, Larry J. '79 (ALN) Reading, PA St. Anthony of Padua; Charismatic Renewal; Catholic Men of Good News (CMOGN).
Hess, Michael N. '71 (DM) West Des Moines, IA Sacred Heart.
Hess, Stephen M. *s.j.* '50 (SPK)[B] Spokane, WA Gonzaga University.
Hesse, Anthony R. '01 (NU) Winsted, MN Holy Trinity; College of Consultors; Worship Committee; Priests' Council.
Hesse, Paul A. '91 (CC)[I] Corpus Christi, TX Fire-Power Retreats; Corpus Christi, TX Saint John the Baptist.
Hesse, Thomas '63 (KCK) Retired.
Hessel, Gerald (MIL) Milwaukee, WI Our Lady of Divine Providence.
Hesseling, Jason E. '00 (MAD) Military Chaplains.
Hesseling, Jason E. '73 (MO) Army Chaplains.
Hession, Anthony '99 (FAR) Munich, ND St. Mary; Munich, ND Assumption Church of Starkweather.
Hession, Mark R. '84 (FR) Centerville, MA Our Lady of Victory; Auditors; Continuing Education of the Clergy; Diocesan Council of Catholic Nurses.
Hessling, Ambrose B. *o.s.b.* '57 (PEO)[A] Peru, IL St. Bede Abbey.
Hessling, Daniel '04 (JOL) Hopkins Park, IL Sacred Heart; Momence, IL St. Patrick.
Hester, John '59 (SJ) Stanford Medical Center.
Heston, Charles '02 (NY) Amenia, NY Immaculate Conception.
Heter, Bernard P. '74 (NY) Cornwall–on–Hudson, NY St. Thomas of Canterbury.
Hetzler, Leo A. *c.s.b.* '55 (ROC)[J] Rochester, NY Basilian Residence.
Heuberger, Joseph '70 (P) Salem, OR St. Vincent de Paul; Building Commission.
Heuberger, Mark L. '80 (VEN) Cape Coral, FL St. Andrew; Presbyteral Council.
Heumann, Carl J. *s.j.* '92 (STL)[F] St. Louis, MO St. Louis University High School, George H. Backer Memorial; [O] Saint Louis, MO St. Louis University High School Jesuit Community.
Heuring, Rev. Msgr. Alvan P. '44 (DUB) Retired.
Heuschkel, Regis *o.p.* '50 (Y) Youngstown, OH St. Dominic.
Heusel, Daniel '00 (STU) Tiltonsville, OH St. Joseph; Tiltonsville, OH St. Lucy's; Auditors; Notaries; Assistant Directors; Defenders of the Bond.
Heuser, James *s.d.b.* '84 (NY)[EE] New Rochelle, NY Salesian Provincial House.
Heuser, James *s.d.b.* (OAK)[M] Berkeley Salesians of Don Bosco.
Heusser, John F. (PAT) Retired.
Hever, Rev. Msgr. Thomas '62 (PHX) Scottsdale, AZ Our Lady of Perpetual Help Roman Catholic Parish.
Hevern, Vincent W. *s.j.* '76 (SY)[Q] Syracuse, NY Jesuits at LeMoyne, Inc.
Hevia, Todd O. '67 (PT) Retired.
Hewe, Manuel A. '97 (HON) Mililani Town, HI St. John Apostle and Evangelist; College of Consultors; Vicars Forane; Presbyteral Council.
Hewes, James E. '74 (ROC) Rush, NY St. Joseph.
Hewes, Robert S. '78 (RVC) Seaford, NY St. James; Air Force Reserve Chaplains.
Hewes, Russell L. '01 (OKL) Ada, OK St. Joseph; [K] Ada, OK East Central State University.
Hewett, Alfred J. '56 (CAM) Haddon Heights, NJ Church of St. Rose, Haddon Heights, N.J. Retired.
Hewitt, Anthony '99 (VEN) Defenders of the Bond; Auditors; Sarasota, FL St. Jude.
Hewitt, Kenneth R. (PAT) Retired.
Hewitt, Matthew A. '04 (SC) Le Mars, IA St. James; Presbyteral Council.
Heyd, James F. '89 (CHI) Other Assignments.
Heyd, Joseph J. *o.s.b.* '56 (PEO)[A] Peru, IL St. Bede Abbey Retired.
Heyer, Bryan O. '04 (VIC) Presbyteral Council; Port Lavaca, TX Our Lady of the Gulf.
Heying, John '00 (RC) Buffalo, SD St. Anthony.
Heyman, George P. '81 (ROC) Priests' Sabbatical Committee; Fairport, NY Church of the Resurrection.
Heyman, George '81 (ROC)[A] Rochester, NY St. Bernard's School of Theology & Ministry.
Heymen, Richard '56 (GB) Retired.
Heyrosa, Alfred '83 (SD) San Marcos, CA St. Mark.
Hezel, Francis X. *s.j.* '69 (FgM)[A] Pohnpei, FM Micronesian Seminar; [C] Kolonia, Pohnpei, FM Jesuit House; New York, NY Society of Jesus.
Hezel, Kenneth J. *s.j.* '66 (AGN) New York, NY Society of Jesus; [F] Tamuning, GU Society of Jesus Micronesia.
Hezel, Kenneth J. *s.j.* '66 (CI)[C] Manresa Jesuit House.
Hezel, Kenneth *s.j.* '66 (AGN) Archdiocesan College of Consultors; Archdiocesan Presbyteral Council.
Hgi, Francis (WDC) Washington, DC Shrine of the Sacred Heart.
Hibner, Cyprian *o.carm.* '67 (TUC)[A] Tucson, AZ Salpointe Catholic High School; [D] Tucson, AZ Carmelite Priory Retired.
Hibner, Jerome H. '64 (BEL) Retired.
Hicarte, Mateo H. '53 (LA) Los Angeles, CA Immaculate Heart of Mary Retired.
Hickel, Rev. Msgr. John J. '55 (STL) St. Paul, MO St. Paul.
Hickey, Christopher J. '94 (BO) Hanover, MA St. Mary of the Sacred Heart.
Hickey, Daniel J. '59 (BO) Malden, MA Sacred Hearts.
Hickey, Dennis W. *c.s.p.* '76 (NY)[EE] New York, NY Paulist Fathers' Motherhouse.
Hickey, Fred *o.c.d.* '07 (MIL)[P] Milwaukee Provincial Offices – Discalced Carmelites.
Hickey, George W. '73 (PRT) Hallowell, ME Sacred Heart.
Hickey, Gerald J. '63 (BO) Senior Priests. Retired.
Hickey, Gregory J. '79 (PH)[AA] Malvern, PA St. Joseph's–in–the–Hills; On Special or Other Archdiocesan Assignment.
Hickey, James C. *s.m.a.* '46 (NEW)[M] Tenafly, NJ Society of African Missions, Provincialate, S.M.A. Fathers Retired.
Hickey, James F. '68 (BO) Rockland, MA Holy Family.
Hickey, Jerome J. *o.c.s.o.* '59 (ATL)[G] Conyers, GA The Monastery of the Holy Spirit Retired.
Hickey, Rev. Msgr. John '81 (AMA) Retired.
Hickey, Joseph W. '56 (NY) DEPARTMENT OF VETERANS AFFAIRS HOSPITALS AND CHAPLAINS; Castle Point, NY V.A. Hudson Valley Healthcare Retired.
Hickey, Kieran *o.f.m.* '49 (GB)[J] Appleton, WI St. Fidelis Friary Retired.
Hickey, Michael '62 (VEN) Retired.
Hickey, Thomas E. '70 (CHI) Glenview, IL Our Lady of Perpetual Help.
Hickey, Thomas F. *c.ss.r.* '54 (BRK) Brooklyn, NY Our Lady of Perpetual Help Basilica.
Hickey, Timothy J. *c.s.sp.* '67 (ARL) Arlington, VA Our Lady, Queen of Peace.
Hickey, Timothy *c.s.sp.* (PIT)[P] Pittsburgh, PA Duquesne University; Councilors:.
Hickie, J. Noel '67 (P)[J] Eugene, OR Sacred Heart Medical Center; On Duty Outside the Diocese.
Hickin, Michael '97 (FAR) On Duty Outside the Diocese.
Hickl, Robert *o.m.i.* '79 (FgM) Washington, DC AMERICAN OBLATE MISSIONS.
Hickman, J. Stephen '82 (RIC) Retired.
Hickman, J. Stephen '82 (SFE) Retired.
Hicks, Alfred J. *s.j.* '66 (BO)[G] Roxbury, MA Nativity Preparatory School; Watertown, MA Society of Jesus.
Hicks, Boniface *o.s.b.* '04 (GBG)[G] Latrobe, PA Saint Vincent Archabbey.
Hicks, Francis J. '00 (LA) Los Angeles, CA St. Basil's; Cardinal McIntyre Fund for Charity.
Hicks, Frank '00 (LA) Director.
Hicks, Ronald A. '94 (CHI) Missionary Work.
Hicks, Steven '82 (SAN) Military Chaplains; Navy Chaplains.
Hidaka, Ronald E. *s.j.* '74 (FgM) Portland, OR Society of Jesus.
Hiebl, Charles J. '62 (LC) Athens, WI St. Anthony de Padua; Athens, WI Holy Family; Deans; Athens, WI St. Thomas.
Hien, Joachim L. '74 (SPK) Spokane, WA St. Anthony; Vietnamese Apostolate; Spokane, WA St. Joseph.
Higdon, C. Paul '46 (DET)[H] Port Huron, MI St. Joseph Mercy Port Huron Retired.
Higdon, Francis B. *m.m.* '67 (FgM) Maryknoll, NY MARYKNOLL.
Higginbotham, Matthew P. '94 (LAF) Crowley, LA Immaculate Heart of Mary.
Higginbotham, Robert P. '75 (BLX) Diberville, MS Sacred Heart; Personnel Board.
Higgins, Brian J. '99 (ATL) Dunwoody, GA All Saints.
Higgins, Charles J. '75 (BO) Kingston, MA St. Joseph; Newton, MA Mary Immaculate of Lourdes; [BB] Braintree, MA Massachusetts Catholic Self–Insurance Group, Inc.; Clerk.
Higgins, Rev. Msgr. E. Edward '57 (PEO) Retired.
Higgins, Edward F. '54 (GBG)[F] Greensburg, PA Neumann House Retired.
Higgins, Edward J. '76 (PSC) Philadelphia, PA Holy Ghost; Commission for Ecumenism; Presbyteral Council.
Higgins, Francis C. '68 (SAV) Retired.
Higgins, Rev. Msgr. Grant J. '56 (BUF) Retired.
Higgins, Jerome *o.f.m.cap.* '54 (MIL)[B] Mount Calvary, WI St. Lawrence Seminary; [P] Mount Calvary, WI St. Lawrence Friary Retired.
Higgins, John F. *m.s.* '72 (HRT)[L] Hartford, CT Missionaries of LaSalette.
Higgins, John J. '96 (NY) Peekskill, NY Assumption.
Higgins, John '01 (BEL) Leave of Absence.
Higgins, John '81 (LA) Downey, CA St. Raymond.
Higgins, John *s.j.* '66 (BO)[U] Newton, MA The Jesuit Community at Boston College; [U] Watertown, MA The Society of Jesus of New England–Provincial Offices.
Higgins, Rev. Msgr. Joseph P. '58 (MAD) Retired.
Higgins, Rev. Msgr. Laurence E. '53 (SP) Tampa, FL St. Lawrence Retired.
Higgins, Leonard H. '82 (TLS) McAlester, OK St. John.
Higgins, Michael *c.p.* '70 (CHI)[N] Chicago, IL Passionist Community–Immaculate Conception Monastery.
Higgins, Michael *o.carm.* '68 (TUC)[D] Tucson, AZ Carmelite Priory Retired.
Higgins, Peter '56 (VIC) Retired.
Higgins, Raymond (DM) Stuart, IA All Saints; Stuart, IA St. John.
Higgins, Robert F. '05 (CHR) North Myrtle Beach, SC Our Lady Star of the Sea; Building & Renovation Commission.
Higgins, Thomas M. '85 (PH) Philadelphia, PA Holy Innocents; Pastors Review Board; Council of Priests.
Higgs, Donald X. '88 (WH) Wheeling–Charleston Diocesan Council of Catholic Women; Elkins, WV St. Brendan; Vicars Forane; Coalton, WV St. Patrick Church.
Highberger, Donald E. *s.j.* '81 (DEN)[N] Denver, CO

Regis Jesuit Community (The Jesuits at Regis University).
Highberger, Rev. Msgr. George '61 (PHX) Wickenburg, AZ St. Anthony of Padua Roman Catholic Parish.
Highfill, Brian H. '74 (NO) Retired.
Hight, Michael '82 (RC) Retired.
Hightower, Craig *s.j.* '04 (SPK)[B] Spokane, WA Gonzaga University.
Hightower, Craig *s.j.* '04 (SEA)[C] Tacoma, WA Bellarmine Preparatory School.
Hightower, Oliver Lee '61 (SEA) Lakewood, WA St. John Bosco; Lacey, WA Sacred Heart of Jesus.
Higley, Rev. Msgr. Gregory L. '81 (JC) Holts Summit, MO St. Andrew; Vicar General; Moderator of the Curia; Adjutant Judicial Vicar; Diocesan Consultors; Personnel Board; Ex Officio Members; Finance Committee; Board of Trustees; Priestly and Religious Vocations Committee.
Higuera, Federico '82 (BEL) Anna, IL St. Mary.
Higuera, Francisco '01 (YAK) On Duty Outside the Diocese.
Higuera, Francisco '01 (MAD) Dane, WI St. Michael; Lodi, WI St. Patrick.
Hiland, Gerard P. '85 (CIN) Owensville, OH St. Louis; Owensville, OH St. Philomena.
Hilander, Augustine *o.p.* '08 (P) Eugene, OR St. Thomas More Church.
Hilbert, J. Robert *s.j.* '56 (CHY) Saint Stephens, WY St. Stephen's; [D] Saint Stephens, WY St. Stephens Mission – Jesuit Community.
Hilbert, Joseph C. '52 (HBG) Lancaster, PA St. Joseph Retired.
Hilbert, Michael P. *s.j.* '83 (NY)[EE] New York Jesuit Provincial's Office.
Hildebrandt, Henry F. '87 (DOD) Ness City, KS Sacred Heart Catholic Church of Ness City, Kansas; Ness City, KS St. Aloysius Catholic Church of Ransom, Kansas; Presbyteral Council.
Hilden, Michael J. *o.s.a.* '73 (FgM) Villanova, PA Province of St. Thomas of Villanova (Eastern).
Hilderbrand, H. Michael '76 (IND) Lanesville, IN St. Mary; Priests' Personnel Board.
Hilderbrand, Ryan Paul '09 (EVN) Montgomery, IN St. Peter; All Saints; Petersburg, IN SS. Peter and Paul.
Hilferty, John G. '78 (ALN)[G] Allentown, PA Sacred Heart Hospital.
Hilfiker, Robert G. '87 (NY) New Windsor, NY St. Joseph.
Hilgartner, Richard B. '95 (BAL) On Duty Outside the Archdiocese.
Hilgartner, Richard '95 (BAL) Presbyteral Council; Staff.
Hilgeman, Edward J. '52 (STL) Spiritual Directors Retired.
Hilgeman, James L. *m.m.* '65 (NY)[EE] Maryknoll Maryknoll Fathers and Brothers Retired.
Hilgendorf, Patrick '97 (DAV) Burlington, IA SS. John & Paul.
Hilgert, E. John *c.p.* '75 (CHI)[N] Chicago, IL Passionist Community–Immaculate Conception Monastery.
Hilinski, Joseph T. '76 (CLV) Cleveland, OH Our Lady of Mercy.
Hilinski, Joseph T. '74 (CLV) Diocesan Interfaith Commission; Continuing Education for Formation of Ministers.
Hill, Allan J. '83 (HRT) Harwinton, CT Immaculate Heart of Mary.
Hill, Rev. Msgr. Charles E. '64 (LA) Hospital Chaplains Retired.
Hill, Clifton *c.s.sp.* '65 (BR) Baton Rouge, LA St. Agnes.
Hill, Donald M. '94 (L) Louisville, KY St. Albert the Great.
Hill, Edward T. '60 (BAL) Retired.
Hill, Eric J. '00 (ATL) Decatur, GA Sts. Peter and Paul.
Hill, Frederick '67 (RVC) Smithtown, NY St. Patrick; Smithtown, NY St. Catherine of Siena Hospital.
Hill, George H. '68 (NY)[HH] Bronx, NY Manhattan College; Bronx, NY St. Gabriel.
Hill, George H. '68 (WOR) On Duty Outside the Diocese.
Hill, Kyle J. '06 (SPC) Leave of Absence.
Hill, Michael *o.f.m.* '77 (OAK)[R] Oakland, CA Province of Saint Barbara Fraternal Care Trust.
Hill, Patrick J. '68 (LA) Canonical Services Coordinator.
Hill, Rev. Msgr. Philip W. '70 (NY) Military Chaplains; Army Chaplains.
Hill, Rev. Msgr. Robert Cary '66 (WDC) Garrett Park, MD Holy Cross.
Hill, Scott *o.m.i.* (OAK) Oakland, CA Sacred Heart.
Hill, Thomas F. *o.f.m.cap.* '66 (STP) Rosemount, MN St. Joseph.
Hill, W. Paul '64 (WDC) Retired.
Hill, William '06 (CHY) St. Joseph's Society for Priests (Clergy Mutual Benefit Society); Gillette, WY St. Matthew's.
Hiller, Everett J. '54 (RCK) Retired.
Hilley, Stephen J. '79 (MIA) Miami, FL St. Richard.
Hilliard, Richard '79 (SJ) Ongoing Formation of Clergy; Special Assignment.
Hillier, David A. '76 (TR) On Duty Outside the Diocese.
Hillier, David A. (HBG)[I] Shippensburg, PA Shippensburg University; Shippensburg, PA Our Lady of the Visitation; Presbyteral Council.
Hillier, John '88 (NOR)[A] Cromwell, CT Holy Apostles College and Seminary.
Hillyard, Matthew J. *o.s.f.s.* '91 (CAM) Camden, NJ The Church of the Immaculate Conception, Camden, N.J.; Camden, NJ The Church of the Holy Name, Camden, N.J.; Camden, NJ Our Lady of Mount Carmel, Camden, N.J./Church of Our Lady of Fatima, Camden, N.J.; Ex Officio Members.
Hilton, Francis G. *s.j.* '92 (BAL)[S] Baltimore, MD Jesuit Community of Loyola University, Inc.; [B] Jesuit Community of Loyola University, Inc.
Hilton, Hank *s.j.* '92 (BAL)[B] Timonium, MD Loyola Graduate Center–Timonium Campus.
Hilton, John L. '82 (DEN) Westminster, CO Holy Trinity.
Hilz, Robert *t.o.r.* '70 (FWT) Fort Worth, TX St. Andrew.
Himawan, Ignatius *m.s.f.* '92 (SAT) New Braunfels, TX Holy Family.
Himes, Kenneth R. *o.f.m.* '76 (NY)[EE] New York Franciscan Friars, Holy Name Province.
Himes, Kenneth *o.f.m.* '76 (BO)[U] Newton, MA The Jesuit Community at Boston College.
Himes, Michael J. '72 (BRK) Released from Diocesan Assignment.
Himes, Robert P. '58 (YAK) Grand Coulee, WA St. Henry's; Coulee City, WA St. Patrick's.
Himmelsbach, James R. '77 (STP) Minneapolis, MN Annunciation.
Himsworth, Raymond J. '62 (PH)[BB] Elkins Park, PA Moss Rehab Einstein at Elkins Park.
Hincapie, Lisimaco (ARE) Sabana Hoyos, PR Inmaculado Corazon de Maria.
Hinch, Rev. Msgr. Lawrence E. '59 (BRK)[T] Douglaston, NY Bishop Mugavero Residence Retired.
Hincks, Michael *o.r.c.* '98 (DET)[K] Grosse Pointe, MI Order of Canons Regular of the Holy Cross.
Hinde, Peter *o.carm.* '52 (JOL)[L] Darien Carmelite Provincial Office; Darien, IL Provincial Headquarters, Carmelite Provincial Office.
Hindel, Richard *o.s.b.* '47 (IND)[K] St. Meinrad, IN St. Meinrad Archabbey.
Hindelang, Joseph C. *s.m.* '78 (DET)[D] Pontiac, MI Notre Dame Preparatory School and Marist Academy.
Hindley, Robert J. *o.s.f.s.* '58 (FgM) Wilmington, DE OBLATES OF ST. FRANCIS DE SALES MISSIONS.
Hindman, John '75 (SB) On Leave of Absence.
Hinds, William H. '87 (COV) Williamstown, KY St. William; [S] Fort Mitchell, KY Mission Share.
Hindsley, Leonard P. '84 (FR) Westport, MA St. John the Baptist.
Hines, Bede *t.o.r.* '47 (ALT)[G] Loretto, PA St. Francis Friary at Mount Assisi.
Hines, George C. '04 (BO) Wrentham, MA St. Mary; Elected.
Hines, Hugh *o.f.m.* '60 (NY) New York, NY St. Francis of Assisi.
Hines, J. William '72 (WDC) Rockville, MD Shrine of St. Jude; Priest Council.
Hinfey, Donald J. *s.j.* '63 (FgM) New York, NY Society of Jesus.
Hinken, Michael *s.o.l.t.* '96 (CC)[G] Robstown, TX Society of Our Lady of the Most Holy Trinity.
Hinkley, Michael F.X. *s.t.d.* '91 (HRT) Waterbury, CT Blessed Sacrament; Waterbury, CT Shrine of Saint Anne for Mothers.
Hinnebusch, John Frederick *o.p.* '50 (WDC)[B] Washington, DC Dominican House of Studies.
Hinnen, James W. '71 (MAD) Mineral Point, WI Congregation of St. Mary–St. Paul; Judges.
Hinni, Thomas R. *c.m.* '63 (STL)[O] St. Louis, MO Lazarist Residence.
Hinojal, Ricardo *o.a.r.* '62 (LSC) Las Cruces, NM Our Lady of Health; [B] Mesilla, NM Augustinian Recollect Fathers.
Hinojos, Jaime '02 (DET) Detroit, MI St. Gabriel; Presbyteral Council.
Hinojosa, Jose Alfredo '04 (ELP) Presidio, TX Santa Teresa de Jesus.
Hinojosa, P. Nolasco '96 (LAR) Laredo, TX Holy Family.
Hinojosa, Rafael '09 (YAK) Yakima, WA St. Paul Cathedral.
Hinrichsen, Rev. Msgr. Carl D. '55 (NEW) Park Ridge, NJ Our Lady of Mercy Retired.
Hinsvark, John '66 (FBK) Retired Retired.
Hinton, Frederick M. '70 (BUF) Park Creek Senior Living Community.
Hinton, John T. '73 (NO) New Orleans, LA Mater Dolorosa.
Hintz, Rev. Msgr. David R. '86 (LIN) Lincoln, NE St. Patrick's; [L] Lincoln, NE Calvary Cemetery and Mausoleum; Cemeteries.
Hippee, Rev. Msgr. Michael E. '73 (MAD) Madison, WI St. Bernard; Judicial Vicar; Judges; Appointed; Building Commission.
Hipskind, J. Timothy *s.j.* '00 (CIN)[N] Cincinnati, OH Claver Jesuit Community.
Hipskind, J. Timothy *s.j.* '00 (CHI)[N] Chicago Chicago Province of the Society of Jesus–Provincial Office.
Hipsley, Milton A. '70 (BAL) Retired.
Hipwell, Patrick J. '77 (STP) St. Paul, MN The Nativity of Our Lord; Deanery 2; College of Consultors.
Hiramatsu, Joseph *s.a.* '82 (NY)[EE] Garrison Franciscan Friars of the Atonement, Minister General Office.
Hire, Richard '70 (FTW) Syracuse, IN St. Martin de Porres; Diocesan Council of Catholic Women.
Hirniak, Mark '98 (STF) Notary; Communications; Yonkers, NY St. Michael.
Hirsch, Rev. Msgr. Clinton F. '45 (EVN) Judges Retired.
Hirsch, Joseph W. '86 (LC) Special Assignment; [H] La Crosse, WI Holy Cross (Seminary) Diocesan Center; Ex Officio; Consultors; Ex Officio.
Hirt, Alan *o.f.m.* '77 (CIN) Cincinnati, OH Holy Name; Cincinnati, OH St. Monica–St. George Parish Newman Center; [R] Cincinnati, OH University of Cincinnati Newman Center.
Hirten, Timothy J. '93 (BRK) Air Force Chaplains; Military Chaplains.
Hirtz, Daniel J. '73 (SPC) Salem, MO Sacred Heart; Region V.
Hislop, Edward '73 (HEL) Missoula, MT Blessed Trinity Parish; Diocesan Consultors; Deaneries; Liturgical Commission.
Hissey, L. Pierre '66 (PHX) Sun Lakes, AZ St. Steven Roman Catholic Parish.
Hissrich, John E. '86 (PIT) Pittsburgh, PA Nativity.
Hitch, David '68 (DAV) Tipton, IA St. Mary's.
Hitchcock, Martin B. '51 (BGP) Retired.
Hitchens, Robert '94 (PHU) Washington, DC Ukrainian Catholic National Shrine of the Holy Family; College of Archeparchial Consultors; Archeparchial Seminary Advisory and Admissions Board; Presbyteral Council; [A] Washington, DC St. Josaphat Seminary.
Hitchko, Daniel D. '64 (SCR) Exeter, PA St. Cecilia.
Hite, Gregory R. '81 (TOL) Toledo, OH St. Joan of Arc; St. Katherine Drexel Deanery; Judges.
Hite, Jordan F. *t.o.r.* '70 (MO) Defenders of the Bond.
Hite, Jordan *t.o.r.* '70 (BAL) Baltimore, MD St. Wenceslaus.
Hite, Jordan *t.o.r.* '70 (HBG) Diocesan Judges.
Hite, Richard B. *m.s.a.* '70 (WH)[E] Old Fields, WV Holy Spirit Hermitage.
Hite, Richard *m.s.a.* '70 (NOR)[G] Cromwell Society of the Missionaries of the Holy Apostles.
Hitosis, Lito *s.s.s.* '97 (CLV)[N] Cleveland, OH Congregation of the Blessed Sacrament.
Hitpas, Joseph H. *o.m.i.* '65 (WDC)[N] Washington, DC Provincial Offices of the United States Province of the Missionary Oblates of Mary Immaculate; [N] Washington, DC Oblate Community; [W] Washington, DC Archdiocese of Cotabato; Councilors:.
Hitpas, Joseph *o.m.i.* '65 (CHI)[W] Chicago, IL Oblates for International Pastoral.
Hitpas, Rev. Msgr. William J. '67 (BEL) O'Fallon, IL St. Nicholas.
Hjelstrom, Timothy '07 (DEN) Lakewood, CO Our Lady of Fatima.
Hladik, Dusan '83 (CHI) Brookfield, IL Czech Mission of Saints Cyril and Methodius.
Hladni, Mirko '71 (CLV) Cleveland, OH St. Paul; Judges in Second Instance.
Hlavaty, Kirby '99 (VIC) Priests' Personnel Board; Diocesan Consultors; Cuero Deanery; Presbyteral Council; Cuero, TX Our Lady of Guadalupe; Cuero, TX St. Michael.
Hlond, Waclaw *c.m.* '55 (HRT) Ansonia, CT St. Joseph Retired.
Hlubik, Joseph G. '93 (TR) Trenton Psychiatric Hospital; [T] Trenton, NJ Bede House, College of New Jersey; Jobstown, NJ St. Andrew's Church, Jobstown.
Hmircik, Donald A. '56 (MIL) Retired.
Hnatkivskyy, Vasyl (STN) Denver, CO Transfiguration of Our Lord.
Hnatyshyn, Rev. Canon Robert '64 (SJP) Presbyters Retired.
Ho, Antonio *c.s.j.b.* '95 (LA)[BB] Monterey Park, CA Congregation of St. John the Baptist.
Ho, Antonius *c.s.j.b.* '95 (BRK)[S] Chinese Apostolate–Queens; [T] Elmhurst, NY Congregation of St. John the Baptist of China; [T] Elmhurst, NY Our Lady of China Chapel; Flushing, NY St. John Vianney.
Ho, David *o.s.b.* (BAL) Baltimore, MD St. Benedict.
Ho, Joseph Khanh '90 (BEA) Western Vicariate; Diocesan College of Consultors; Diocesan Judges; Winnie, TX St. Louis; Presbyteral Council.
Ho, Liang D. *o.s.b.* (GBG)[G] Latrobe Saint Vincent Archabbey.
Ho, M. Justin Cong Huu *o.cist.* '06 (SB)[I] Lucerne Valley, CA The Cistercian Congregation of the Holy Family, St. Joseph Monastery.
Ho, Matthias '55 (ORG) Retired.
Ho, Mau *s.d.d.* (PT) Pensacola, FL Our Lady Queen of Martyrs, Mission.
Ho, Nicholas '79 (SAC) West Sacramento, CA Our Lady of Grace.
Ho, Thuc Si '04 (SJ) Santa Clara, CA St. Lawrence, the Martyr; College of Consultors.

Ho, Viet Peter '00 (ORG) Anaheim, CA San Antonio de Padua Del Cañon Church; Adjutant Judicial Vicars; Defenders of the Bond.
Ho, Xuan *s.v.d.* '03 (FgM) Techny, IL.
Hoag, Timothy S. '95 (RC) Belle Fourche, SD St. Paul; Spearfish, SD St. Joseph; Deaneries.
Hoagland, Victor *c.p.* '59 (NEW)[M] "Compassion" Magazine; [M] Union City, NJ Congregation of the Passion (Passionists)–St. Michael's Residence; [M] Passionist Press, Inc.
Hoak, Jack W. *o.f.m.* '75 (MO) Navy Reserve Chaplains.
Hoak, Jack *o.f.m.* '75 (NY)[EE] New York Franciscan Province of the Immaculate Conception.
Hoak, Jack *o.f.m.* '75 (HRT) Meriden, CT St. Rose of Lima; Appointed Members.
Hoan, Basil P. '77 (TYL) Retired.
Hoan, Michael Mai Khai '72 (ORG) Santa Ana, CA St. Barbara Catholic Church.
Hoang, Dat '03 (GAL) Seminarian Support; Vocations Office.
Hoang, Doan T. *s.j.* '97 (LA) Apostleship of Prayer; Los Gatos, CA; [P] Culver City, CA Ignatius House, The Novitiate of the California Province, Society of Jesus.
Hoang, Dominic Hung '90 (OKL) Oklahoma City, OK St. Andrew Dung–Lac.
Hoang, Francis Dang *s.j.* '95 (LA) West Covina, CA St. Christopher.
Hoang, John Minh Toan '68 (GAL) Retired.
Hoang, John Nghia *c.m.c.* (FWT) Arlington, TX Church of the Vietnamese Martyrs.
Hoang, Joseph Vien *s.d.b.* '83 (NO) Harvey, LA St. John Bosco.
Hoang, Joseph Viet '94 (SD) San Diego, CA St. Rita.
Hoang, Joseph '99 (P) Absent on Leave.
Hoang, Joseph '04 (ORG) Huntington Beach, CA St. Bonaventure.
Hoang, Khanh '94 (HON) Honolulu, HI Cathedral of Our Lady of Peace; Members; Clergy Personnel Board; Members; Episcopal Vicar for Clergy; Office of Clergy: Diocesan Screening Committee; Presbyteral Council; Implementation Commission of Diocesan Road Map for Pastoral Program and Facility Needs; Bishops Administrative Advisory Council; Office of Clergy Priest Retirement Committee.
Hoang, Linh *o.f.m.* '09 (ALB)[B] Siena College.
Hoang, Louis '95 (HON) Lahaina, HI Maria Lanakila.
Hoang, Luat V. *s.j.* '98 (LA)[D] Los Angeles, CA Verbum Dei High School; [F] In Res.
Hoang, Peter Thien Van *o.p.* '72 (GAL) Houston, TX Our Lady of Lourdes.
Hoang, Petrus B. '96 (P) Portland, OR St. Stephen.
Hoang, Phuong '89 (SEA) Seattle, WA Immaculate Conception; Vietnamese, Ministry to.
Hoang, Simon Thoi *s.v.d.* '07 (MEM)[F] Memphis, TN Society of the Divine Word (Chicago Province); Memphis, TN Church of the Ascension.
Hoang, Son Linh '03 (PMB) Port St. Lucie, FL St. Bernadette.
Hoang, Tat *c.ss.r.* '06 (BRK)[C] Bronx, NY St. Alphonsus Formation Residence.
Hoang, Tat–Thang *c.ss.r.* '06 (NY) Bronx, NY Immaculate Conception.
Hoang, Thang *s.v.d.* '04 (DUB)[B] Epworth, IA Divine Word College.
Hoang, Thuan V. '97 (SFR) San Francisco, CA Visitacion, Church of the; Promoter of Justice; On Special Assignment; Defenders of the Bond.
Hoar, Richard J. *s.j.* '56 (BUF) Buffalo, NY St. Michael.
Hoar, Thomas F.X. *s.s.e.* '78 (NOR)[I] Mystic, CT St. Edmund's Retreat; [M] Mystic, CT St. Edmund's of Connecticut, Inc.
Hoare, Liam *s.p.* '68 (STL)[O] Saint Louis, MO Servants of the Paraclete; [S] Dittmer, MO Vianney Renewal Center; Cedar Hill, MO; [V] Dittmer, MO Servants of the Paraclete Missouri Generalate Corporation.
Hoare, Patrick T. '07 (CHL) Charlotte, NC St. John Neumann.
Hoare, Richard '69 (BRK) South Ozone Park, NY St. Teresa of Avila.
Hoarer, Eric '01 (PBL)[H] Crestone, CO Spiritual Life Institute of America, Inc.
Hoat, Rochus Vu Dinh '60 (BAL) Baltimore, MD St. Mary of the Assumption Retired.
Hoban, Michael *s.s.c.* '70 (FgM) St Columbans, NE House of Post–Graduate Studies.
Hoban, Rev. Msgr. Thomas E. '60 (ALN) Retired.
Hobbes, Thomas F. '56 (SY) Endwell, NY Christ the King.
Hobbs, Rev. Msgr. James V. '57 (BAL) Retired.
Hober, Raymond *s.v.d.* '60 (PIT)[M] Pittsburgh, PA Society of The Divine Word.
Hobert, James M. '85 (TUC) Tucson, AZ Saint Monica Roman Catholic Parish – Tucson; Ministry to Priests Program; Defenders of the Bond.
Hobson, J. Mark '86 (CLV) Solon, OH Resurrection of Our Lord.
Hobson, Michael A. (BO) Middleton, MA St. Agnes; Presbyteral Council.
Hochheim, William A. '60 (STA) Retired.
Hochreiter, Robert S. '68 (SCR) Military Chaplains.
Hochstatter, Theodore '80 (PEO) On Duty Outside the Diocese.
Hock, Andreas '92 (DEN) Denver, CO Cathedral Basilica of the Immaculate Conception.
Hock, G. Harry *s.j.* '64 (RIC) Richmond, VA Sacred Heart.
Hockman, Richard C. *c.s.c.* '80 (SCR)[C] King's College; [C] Holy Cross Community.
Hoctor, Thomas D. '57 (ROC) Retired.
Hodapp, Timothy L. '85 (WIN) Absent on Leave.
Hoderny, Thomas S. '79 (E) Du Bois, PA St. Catherine.
Hodge, Rev. Msgr. William A. '74 (CAM) Representatives by Deaneries; Atlantic City, NJ Church of St. Nicholas, Atlantic City, N.J.; Delegate for Inter–Parochial Affairs; Diocesan Finance Council.
Hodges, Gabriel *o.s.b.* '06 (IND)[K] St. Meinrad, IN St. Meinrad Archabbey; St. Meinrad, IN.
Hodges, Leo '86 (ORL) Palm Bay, FL Our Lady of Grace; Southern.
Hodges, Robert *o.praem.* '74 (ORG) Costa Mesa, CA St. John the Baptist.
Hodgson, William M. '79 (SPC) Carthage, MO St. Ann; Secretariat for Cursillo; Charismatic Prayer Groups.
Hodnett, John J. *c.m.* '59 (PH)[Y].
Hoeberechts, Dwight *o.m.i.* '97 (BO)[U] Lowell, MA Oblate Vocation Office, Northeast / Southeast; [U] Lowell, MA St. Eugene House (Residence).
Hoebing, Philibert *o.f.m.* '50 (SFD)[B] Quincy, IL Quincy University; [L] Quincy, IL Holy Cross Friary Retired.
Hoeffner, Robert J. '73 (ORL) Palm Bay, FL St. Joseph; 56–63.
Hoefgen, Francis *o.s.b.* '79 (SCL)[I] Collegeville, MN St. John's Abbey, of the Order of St. Benedict.
Hoefler, David J. '02 (SFD) Springfield, IL Blessed Sacrament; Priests' Personnel Board.
Hoefler, Robert A. '85 (DM) Harlan, IA St. Michael.
Hoegerl, Carl W. *c.ss.r.* '50 (BRK)[T] Brooklyn, NY Redemptorist Fathers of New York, Inc.–Baltimore Province; Brooklyn, NY.
Hoehn, Daniel '04 (JOL) Peotone, IL St. Paul the Apostle; Manhattan, IL St. Patrick.
Hoelscher, James '58 (SAT)[K] San Antonio, TX Padua Place Retired.
Hoelsken, Mark *s.j.* (SPK) Wellpinit, WA St. Philip Benizi; Wellpinit, WA Sacred Heart; Wellpinit, WA Our Lady of Lourdes.
Hoene, Robert E. *s.j.* '53 (MIL)[P] Wauwatosa, WI Jesuit Community at St. Camillus.
Hoening, Gerald '52 (DAV) Retired.
Hoerburger, Henry R. '43 (LC) Elk Mound, WI St. Joseph Retired.
Hoernig, Alphonse X. *c.m.* '56 (STL)[O] Perryville, MO Congregation of the Mission.
Hoerning, Richard P. '73 (RVC) Rocky Point, NY St. Anthony of Padua.
Hoerter, James '06 (RC) McLaughlin, SD St. Bonaventure's; McLaughlin, SD St. Bernard; McLaughlin, SD Standing Rock Reservation.
Hoeser, Jerome G. '63 (LC) Eau Galle, WI St. Henry; Eau Galle, WI St. Joseph.
Hoesing, Kenneth F. '97 (LIN) David City, NE St. Francis; [C] David City, NE Aquinas/St. Mary's Schools; [L] David City, NE Aquinas High School Endowment Fund.
Hoesing, Paul C. '02 (OM) Vocations Office; Omaha, NE St. Margaret Mary.
Hoesli, Frederick Damien *o.p.* '64 (NY)[EE] New York St. Vincent Ferrer Priory.
Hoewischer, Harry E. *s.j.* '57 (DEN)[N] Denver, CO Xavier Jesuit Center.
Hoey, James F. '65 (WOR) Spencer, MA Mary, Queen of the Rosary.
Hofer, Andrew *o.p.* (FTW)[A] Notre Dame, IN Moreau Seminary.
Hofer, Kenneth Andrew *o.p.* '02 (FgM) New York, NY Province of St. Joseph (Eastern).
Hofer, Kenneth Andrew *o.p.* '02 (CIN)[N] Cincinnati, OH St. Gertrude Priory; Cincinnati, OH St. Gertrude.
Hoff, Wilfred G. *o.p.* '47 (CHI)[N] St. Pius V Priory.
Hoffa, Allen J. '09 (ALN) Allentown, PA Cathedral of St. Catharine of Siena.
Hoffenkamp, Robert A. '89 (JOL) Carol Stream, IL Corpus Christi.
Hoffer, Steven R. '05 (LAV) Las Vegas, NV St. Elizabeth Ann Seton; Building Committee.
Hoffman, Andrew W. '74 (SC) Pocahontas, IA Church of the Resurrection; Pocahontas, IA St. Margaret's.
Hoffman, Daniel R. '09 (E) Greenville, PA St. Michael.
Hoffman, David J. '96 (GB) Freedom, WI St. Nicholas.
Hoffman, Dennis H. '70 (DUL) Nashwauk, MN St. Mary; Nashwauk, MN St. Cecilia's; Nashwauk, MN St. Kevin.
Hoffman, Dennis L. '90 (DAV) Pella, IA St. Mary's; Colfax, IA Immaculate Conception.
Hoffman, Emmett G. '53 (GF) Retired.
Hoffman, Frank J. '92 (POD)[V] Chicago, IL Prelature of the Holy Cross and Opus Dei; Chicago.
Hoffman, James A. *o.f.m.* '67 (CHI)[N] Chicago, IL St. Peter's Friary.
Hoffman, James A. '67 (SUP) Woodruff, WI Holy Family.
Hoffman, John R. '75 (CHI) La Grange, IL St. Francis Xavier.
Hoffman, Joseph M. '79 (BRK) Elmhurst, NY St. Bartholomew; Fire Department.
Hoffman, Mark A. '90 (E) Grove City, PA Beloved Disciple.
Hoffman, Michael J. '05 (GRY) Valparaiso, IN St. Paul.
Hoffman, Michael *s.d.s.* '82 (MIL)[P] Milwaukee Salvatorian Provincial Offices.
Hoffman, Pio Maria *c.f.r.* '07 (NY)[EE] Bronx, NY Our Lady of the Angels Friary.
Hoffman, Raniero *o.s.b.cam.* '75 (MRY)[F] Big Sur, CA New Camaldoli Hermitage; Big Sur, CA.
Hoffman, Rev. Msgr. Robert B. '62 (RCK) Retired.
Hoffman, Robert E. *m.m.* '60 (FgM) Maryknoll, NY MARYKNOLL.
Hoffman, Robert M. *c.s.c.* '47 (FTW)[H] Holy Cross House Retired.
Hoffman, Robert '56 (PEO) Retired.
Hoffman, Steven B. (STP) Eagan, MN St. John Neumann.
Hoffman, Thomas W. *s.j.* '76 (LSC) Alamogordo, NM St. Jude.
Hoffman, Thomas '80 (CHI) Zion–Beach Park, IL Our Lady of Humility.
Hoffman, William A. '80 (GB) Appleton, WI St. Therese.
Hoffman, Rev. Msgr. William G. '61 (ATL) Boy Scouts Retired.
Hoffmann, Charles G. '63 (GB) Antigo, WI St. John.
Hoffmann, Christopher '87 (MO) Kissimmee, FL Holy Redeemer; Air Force Reserve Chaplains.
Hoffmann, Christopher '87 (ORL) Appointed Members; Chairman.
Hoffmann, Edward '61 (PIT) Retired.
Hoffmann, Francis T. '90 (BGP) Riverside, CT St. Catherine of Siena; Presbyteral Council.
Hoffmann, Frank T. '90 (BGP) Vicariate I (Stamford, Darien, Glenbrook, Greenwich, Byram, Riverside).
Hoffmann, Frank '71 (RNO) Retired.
Hoffmann, Henry '03 (BGP) Brookfield, CT St. Joseph.
Hoffmann, Lawrence R. '71 (DM) Des Moines, IA St. Theresa of the Child Jesus; Defenders of the Bond; Diocesan Consultors.
Hoffmann, Philip '64 (GB) Absent on Leave, Sick or Disabled.
Hoffmann, Pio Maria *c.f.r.* '07 (NY)[II] Bronx, NY The Saint Padre Pio Shelter Corporation.
Hoffmaster, Harry E. '70 (DET) Retired.
Hofmann, Charles A. *s.j.* '66 (CIN)[N] Cincinnati, OH Faber Jesuit Community.
Hofmann, Raymond *c.r.* '56 (L)[L] Louisville, KY Villa Pacis, Resurrectionist Retirement Home; Louisville, KY.
Hofmann, Rev. Msgr. Thomas X. '77 (CHR) Canonical Consultant; Office of Tribunal.
Hofschulte, Charles *c.j.* '71 (LA) Santa Maria, CA St. Louis de Montfort; Deanery 1; [P] Santa Maria, CA American Region of the Josephite Fathers Charitable Trust.
Hofstede, John '75 (STP) Minneapolis, MN Abbot–Northwestern Hospital; Minneapolis, MN Minneapolis Children's Hospital.
Hofstetter, Robert J. '54 (KNX) Newport, TN Good Shepherd; Diocesan Consultors; Censor Librorum; Presbyteral Council.
Hogan, Colm '98 (FgM) Boston, MA St. James the Apostle, Inc.
Hogan, Rev. Msgr. Daniel M. '53 (STL) O'Fallon, MO St. Barnabas.
Hogan, Francis T. '46 (BUF) Retired.
Hogan, George G. (BO) North Andover, MA St. Michael.
Hogan, James J. '61 (HEL) Retired.
Hogan, John A. '57 (GRY) Retired.
Hogan, John F. '88 (SY) Rome, NY St. John the Baptist.
Hogan, John J. *o.m.i.* '65 (BO) Tewksbury, MA St. William.
Hogan, John P. '73 (LC) Fall Creek, WI St. Raymond of Penafort; [I] Eau Claire, WI St. Bede Monastery.
Hogan, John P. *o.f.m.* '75 (BO)[Z] Boston, MA St. Anthony Shrine.
Hogan, John *s.s.c.* '62 (ORG)[H] Westminster, CA Korean Catholic Ministry; [I] Westminster, CA Columban Fathers.
Hogan, John *s.s.c.* '62 (PRO)[P] Bristol, RI St. Columban's Retirement House.
Hogan, John *s.s.c.* '62 (OM)[K] St. Columbans Missionary Society of St. Columban.
Hogan, Joseph F. '88 (MET) Retired.
Hogan, Joseph T. '88 (PEO) Urbana, IL St. Patrick's.
Hogan, Michael C. '51 (ROC) Fairport, NY St. John of Rochester Retired.
Hogan, Michael '65 (ALB) Rotterdam Junction, NY St. Margaret of Cortona; Schenectady, NY St. Joseph.
Hogan, Rev. Msgr. Michael '66 (ATL) Retired.
Hogan, Phil D. *o.f.m.* '62 (CHI)[D] Chicago, IL Hales Franciscan High School, Inc.; [N] Chicago, IL Holy Spirit Friary, Order of Friars Minor.
Hogan, Ralph R. '52 (PRO)[P] Providence St. John Vianney Residence Retired.

Hogan, Richard '81 (STP) Crystal, MN St. Raphael.
Hogan, Richard '86 (DET) Absent on Leave.
Hogan, Robert C. *s.j.* '64 (FgM) New York, NY Society of Jesus.
Hogan, Robert E. '83 (SAT)[S] San Antonio, TX Brothers of the Beloved Disciple; San Antonio, TX St. Mary Magdalen.
Hogan, Sean M. *c.s.sp.* '67 (PIT)[B] Pittsburgh, PA Duquesne University of the Holy Spirit; [B] School of Health Sciences.
Hogan, Rev. Msgr. Terence '80 (MIA) Miami, FL St. Mary's Cathedral; Presbyteral Council; Executive Director; Celebration and Rite Committee.
Hogan, Thomas J. *s.j.* '65 (STL)[O] St. Louis, MO Jesuit Community Corporation at Saint Louis University – Jesuit Hall.
Hogan, Thomas *s.m.* '46 (SJ)[M] Cupertino, CA The Marianist Center.
Hogan, Timothy A. '66 (L) Louisville, KY St. Boniface.
Hogan, Timothy D. '82 (DET) Novi, MI Holy Family; Presbyteral Council.
Hogan, Timothy J. '82 (SC) Sanborn, IA St. Cecilia's; Sanborn, IA Sacred Heart.
Hogan, Verne F. '57 (COV) Flemingsburg, KY St. Charles; May's Lick, KY St. Rose of Lima.
Hogan, William A. '66 (GF) Retired.
Hogan, William F. *c.ss.r.* '49 (STL)[O] Liguori, MO St. Clement Health Care Center.
Hogarty, Paul '48 (PT) Retired.
Hoge, James *o.s.b.* '43 (SP)[N] St. Leo, FL St. Leo Abbey.
Hohenbrink, Michael G. '74 (TOL) Findlay, OH St. Michael the Archangel; St. Francis of Assisi Deanery.
Hohenstein, Robert J. '68 (ALB) Schenectady, NY Our Lady of Mt. Carmel; Catholic Women's Service League; Priests Placement Committee.
Hohenwarter, Norman C. '96 (HBG) Lancaster, PA St. Anne.
Hohl, Alan *o.c.s.o.* '63 (SLC)[F] Huntsville, UT Abbey of Our Lady of the Holy Trinity of the Order of Cistercians.
Hohlmayer, Louis R. '53 (CIN) Retired.
Hohman, Andrew *o.f.m.cap.* '54 (CLV) Cleveland, OH Conversion of St. Paul; [N] Cleveland, OH St. Paul Friary.
Hohman, George R. *s.j.* '58 (WH)[A] Wheeling, WV Wheeling Jesuit University.
Hohosha, Ihor '07 (SJP) Aliquippa, PA Ss. Peter and Paul; McKees Rocks, PA St. John the Baptist; Alternates.
Hohosho, Ihor (SJP) Presbyteral Council; Presbyters.
Hoi, Joseph '84 (JC) Edina, MO St. Joseph; Memphis, MO St. John; Edina, MO St. Aloysius.
Hoisington, Thomas M. '95 (WCH) Wichita, KS St. Francis of Assisi; Administrative Assistant to the Bishop; Wichita, KS St. Jude; Presbyteral Council/ College of Consultors; Respect Life and Social Justice Office; [K] Wichita, KS Father Kapaun Guild.
Hokanson, Richard P. '74 (CHL) Absent on Medical Leave.
Hoke, John R. '76 (HBG) On Duty Outside the Diocese; Navy Chaplains.
Hoke, Thomas R. (HBG) York, PA St. Rose of Lima.
Holahan, Thomas J. *c.s.p.* '77 (NY)[EE] Jamaica Estates Paulist Fathers Generalate.
Holbrook, William M. '70 (CHI) Chicago, IL St. Monica Retired.
Holbrook, William M. '70 (LFT) On Duty Outside the Diocese Retired.
Holbus, Brian T. '81 (MIL) Milwaukee, WI St. Roman.
Holcomb, Joseph T. '80 (BRK) Flushing, NY St. Andrew Avellino.
Hold, William '77 (SAC) Retired.
Holden, Robert A. '62 (TOL) Retired.
Holder, Thomas '95 (KC) Kansas City, MO St. John Francis Regis.
Holdren, Benjamin P. '07 (LIN) Lincoln, NE St. Thomas Aquinas; [I] Lincoln, NE University of Nebraska, Newman Club; Vocations; Advocates.
Holian, John P. '63 (NEW) Retired.
Holicky, Gregory '72 (GRY)[D] Hammond, IN St. Margaret Mercy Healthcare Centers – North Campus.
Holihan, John W. '49 (NY)[EE] Bronx, NY Retired.
Holinga, Rev. Msgr. Thomas P. '74 (SFD) Springfield, IL St. Joseph; Springfield Deanery; Commission for the Care of Infirm and Retired Priests.
Holl, James E. '48 (STP) Retired.
Holl, Kermit *o.s.c.* '90 (SCL)[I] Onamia, MN Crosier Priory.
Holland, Daniel F. '65 (ROC) Spencerport, NY St. John the Evangelist Retired.
Holland, Edward T. '97 (CLV) South Euclid, OH St. Gregory the Great.
Holland, Francis M. '52 (BUR) Retired.
Holland, Rev. Msgr. George T. '48 (PBL) Retired.
Holland, James P. '98 (PIT) Moon Township, PA St. Margaret Mary.
Holland, Jeremiah *ss.cc.* '67 (SB)[I] Chino Hills, CA Congregation of the Sacred Hearts of Jesus & Mary, SS.CC.; Hemet, CA Holy Spirit.
Holland, Jeremiah *ss.cc.* '67 (LA)[P] La Verne, CA Congregation of the Sacred Hearts of Jesus and Mary.
Holland, Kilian '56 (SD) Retired.
Holland, Paul D. *s.j.* '80 (BO)[U] Weston, MA Campion Jesuit Community; [U] Weston, MA Campion Health Center, Inc.
Holland, Stanley *t.o.r.* '96 (SP) Tampa, FL St. Patrick.
Hollas, Eric *o.s.b.* '75 (SCL)[I] Collegeville, MN St. John's Abbey, of the Order of St. Benedict.
Holleman, John L. '81 (MOB) Semmes, AL Holy Name of Jesus.
Hollenbach, David *s.j.* '71 (BO)[U] Newton, MA The Jesuit Community at Boston College.
Holler, Martin J. '66 (STU) Athens, OH Christ the King University Parish; [L] Athens, OH Christ the King University Parish – Ohio University; Campus Ministry.
Holleran, Rev. Msgr. J. Warren '52 (SFR)[A] Menlo Park, CA St. Patrick Seminary and University Retired.
Holleran, Michael K. '79 (NY) Bronx, NY St. Frances de Chantal; New York, NY Sacred Hearts of Jesus and Mary; New York, NY Sacred Hearts of Jesus and Mary.
Holleran, Rev. Msgr. Warren '52 (SFR) Censor Librorum.
Hollfelder, Eugene F. '68 (MAD) Middleton, WI St. Peter's; Cross Plains, WI St. Martin of Tours.
Holliday, John J. *c.m.* '05 (PH) Philadelphia, PA Immaculate Conception.
Hollis, Kevin J. *o.s.a.* '02 (CAM)[C] Richland, NJ St. Augustine Preparatory School.
Hollis, Mark L. '72 (CLV)[A] Wickliffe, OH St. Mary Seminary and Graduate School of Theology.
Holloran, Michael J. '82 (CIN) Dayton, OH St. Adalbert; Dayton, OH Holy Cross; Dayton, OH Our Lady of the Rosary; Dayton, OH St. Stephen.
Holloway, David L. '82 (KC) Kansas City, MO St. Bernadette's.
Holloway, Gerald '98 (BIR) Tuscaloosa, AL St. Francis of Assisi University Parish; [H] Tuscaloosa, AL Diocesan Campus Ministry Office; [H] Tuscaloosa, AL University of Alabama in Tuscaloosa.
Holloway, James P. '70 (WDC) Retired.
Holloway, James '70 (SAV) Retired.
Holloway, Thomas B. '99 (PEO) Bushnell, IL St. Bernard; Bushnell, IL St. Augustine.
Hollowell, John J. '09 (IND) Brownsburg, IN St. Malachy; [C] Indianapolis, IN Cardinal Ritter High School.
Holly, Dennis *g.h.m.* '64 (NSH) Lafayette, TN Holy Family.
Holly, Dennis *g.h.m.* '64 (OWN) Scottsville, KY Christ the King.
Holly, John *o.f.m.cap.* '80 (CHI)[N] Chicago, IL St. Clare Friary.
Holmberg, J. Michael '73 (FWT) The Colony, TX Holy Cross.
Holmer, James J. '76 (TOL) Vermilion, OH St. Mary.
Holmes, Albert '93 (SCL) Special Assignment.
Holmes, Del *g.h.m.* '63 (CIN)[N] Cincinnati Headquarters of Glenmary Home Missioners Retired.
Holmes, Emmett P. *s.j.* '59 (CLV)[D] Cuyahoga Falls, OH Walsh Jesuit High School.
Holmes, Rev. Msgr. Kevin D. '84 (MAD) Madison, WI Cathedral Parish of St. Raphael; Diocesan Consultors; Appointed.
Holmes, Paul A. '81 (NEW)[B] School of Diplomacy and Intl. Rels.
Holmes, Paul (NEW)[B] Seton Hall University.
Holmes, Raymond M. '65 (NEW) Hasbrouck Heights, NJ Corpus Christi.
Holmes, Stephen '00 (ARL) Chantilly, VA St. Veronica.
Holmes, Thomas '91 (ALB) Middleburgh, NY Parish of Our Lady of the Valley; Deans; Cobleskill, NY St. Vincent de Paul.
Holoman, Rev. Msgr. Thomas L. '55 (LIN) Retired.
Holoubek, K. William '97 (LIN) Sutton, NE St. Mary's; Holy Childhood, Pontifical Association; Missionary Union of the Clergy; Propagation of the Faith.
Holoubek, Roger '69 (MIA) Dania Beach, FL St. Maurice.
Holpp, Lawrence V. '62 (PIT) Bobtown, PA St. Ignatius of Antioch.
Holquin, Rev. Msgr. Arthur A. '74 (ORG) San Juan Capistrano, CA Mission Basilica – San Juan Capistrano; Council of Priests; Judges; Consultors; Liturgical Commission; Building and Renovation Committee of the Liturgical Commission.
Holroyd, Patrick '74 (ARL) Vienna, VA St. Mark.
Holscher, Raymond T. *s.j.* '72 (FgM) New York, NY Society of Jesus.
Holt, Paul Stephen '72 (MO) DEPARTMENT OF VETERANS AFFAIRS HOSPITALS AND CHAPLAINS; Presbyteral Council.
Holt, Paul–Stephen '72 (WDC) Military Chaplains.
Holterhoff, Edward G. '70 (PAT) On Duty Outside the Diocese.
Holterhoff, Edward J. '70 (MRY) Cayucos, CA St. Joseph; Morro Bay, CA St. Timothy.
Holthaus, Paul G. '70 (BAL) Retired.
Holtman, Rev. Msgr. Elmer '64 (AUS) Consultors Retired.
Holtman, Jeffrey *o.f.m.* '85 (SFD)[L] Teutopolis, IL St. Francis Assisi Friary.
Holtman, Jeffry *o.f.m.* '85 (SFD) Teutopolis, IL St. Francis of Assisi.
Holtmann, Christopher F. '00 (STL) Hillsboro, MO Church of the Good Shepherd.
Holtschneider, Dennis H. *c.m.* '89 (CHI)[C] Chicago, IL De Paul University; [N] Chicago DePaul Vincentian Residence.
Holtschneider, Dennis H. *c.m.* '89 (PH)[Y].
Holtz, Albert T. *o.s.b.* '69 (NEW)[M] Newark, NJ Newark Abbey.
Holtz, Dominic *o.p.* '06 (STL)[B] St. Louis, MO Aquinas Institute of Theology; [O] St. Louis, MO St. Dominic Priory.
Holtz, Robert '03 (TR) Maple Shade, NJ Our Lady of Perpetual Help.
Holtz, Vernon A. *o.s.b.* '62 (GBG)[G] Latrobe, PA Saint Vincent Archabbey.
Holtzinger, William '00 (P) Grants Pass, OR St. Anne.
Holtzman, Jerome '57 (SFS) Retired.
Holup, James '59 (JOL) Ashkum, IL Assumption of the Blessed Virgin Mary.
Holy, Richard C. '08 (GRY) Munster, IN St. Thomas More; Adjutant Defenders of the Bond.
Holz, Robert A. '08 (RVC) Baldwin, NY St. Christopher.
Holzer, Claudio *c.s.* (CHI) Melrose Park, IL St. Charles Borromeo; Deans; Melrose Park, IL Our Lady of Mount Carmel.
Holzhauser, J. Joseph '82 (SFS) Aberdeen, SD St. Mary; Personnel Board.
Holzhauser, John J. '82 (MO) Army National Guard Chaplains.
Holzmann, Michael '88 (RVC) Bay Shore, NY St. Patrick's; [C] West Islip, NY St. John the Baptist.
Homa, Richard M. '73 (CHI) Orland Hills, IL St. Elizabeth Seton.
Homan, Daniel J. *o.s.b.* '69 (DET)[B] Oxford, MI St. Benedict Monastery.
Homann, Frederick A. *s.j.* '62 (PH)[Y] Loyola Center and Manresa Hall.
Hombach, Leo J. *s.j.* '61 (SJ)[M] Los Gatos, CA Sacred Heart Jesuit Center.
Homes, Dennis '72 (BAK) Retired.
Homes, Ronald G. '93 (LIN) Bruno, NE St. Anthony.
Homick, Cajetan P. *o.s.b.* '03 (GBG)[G] Latrobe Saint Vincent Archabbey.
Hommel, George W. '66 (NY) Phoenicia, NY St. Francis de Sales; Woodstock, NY St. John; Canon 1742 Panel of Pastors.
Hommrich, Thomas A. '63 (L) Associate Judges Retired.
Homrich, Eugene *c.s.c.* '55 (FgM) New Rochelle, NY Eastern Brothers Province.
Honan, Eugene D. '67 (SPR) Easthampton, MA Immaculate Conception.
Honhart, Mark A. '80 (SCR) Wapwallopen, PA Our Lady Help of Christians.
Honkomp, Clinton P. *o.p.* '88 (DEN) Denver, CO St. Dominic; [N] Denver, CO Dominican Friars.
Honold, Thomas G. '87 (MIA) Sunny Isles Beach, FL St. Mary Magdalen.
Honor, Michael P. '69 (MO) Army Chaplains.
Honorio, Gregorio S. *m.s.* '95 (HON) Waipahu, HI St. Joseph; Presbyteral Council.
Hont, Leon *o.s.b.* '80 (GBG) Crabtree, PA St. Bartholomew.
Hontiveros, Romeo (NY) New York, NY Our Lady of Victory.
Hood, Carl J. '86 (MEM) Memphis, TN St. Therese the Little Flower; Continuing Education for Clergy.
Hood, Jared M. *s.j.s.* '06 (MAD) Merrimac, WI St. Mary, Health of the Sick; Mazomanie, WI St. John the Baptist; Sauk City, WI St. Norbert; Sauk City, WI St. Aloysius; Appointed.
Hood, Rev. Msgr. Mervin J. '54 (SC) Retired.
Hoog, Eric *c.ss.r.* (BAL) Annapolis, MD St. Mary.
Hook, Stephen '03 (BAL) Williamsport, MD St. Augustine.
Hoolahan, Michael *c.p.* '61 (CHI)[N] Chicago, IL Province Finance Office.
Hoolahan, Michael *c.p.* '61 (LA)[P] Sierra Madre, CA Passionist Residence; [V] Sierra Madre, CA Mater Dolorosa Passionist Retreat Center, Inc.
Hoon Gyeom Kim, John '92 (HRT) Wethersfield, CT Sacred Heart.
Hooper, J. Leon *s.j.* '75 (WDC)[N] Washington, DC Woodstock Jesuit Community; [W] Washington, DC Woodstock Theological Center.
Hooper, J. Leon *s.j.* '75 (MIL)[Y] Milwaukee, WI Theological Studies, Inc.
Hooper, Robert K. '70 (PAT) Succasunna, NJ St. Therese.
Hoorman, Albert F.H. '67 (PHX) Phoenix, AZ Corpus Christi Roman Catholic Parish.
Hoover, Brett C. *c.s.p.* '97 (OAK)[A] Berkeley, CA Dominican School of Philosophy and Theology; Berkeley, CA Holy Spirit Parish/Newman Hall.
Hoover, Conrad '89 (CHL) Retired.

Hoover, Gary *o.s.b.* '83 (CLV)[D] Cleveland, OH Benedictine High School; [N] Cleveland, OH; Cleveland, OH.
Hoover, James '60 (SAL) Wilson, KS St. Joseph Parish; Wilson, KS St. Mary Parish; Washington, KS St. Augustine Parish; Wilson, KS St. Wenceslaus Parish.
Hoover, John P. '76 (CHL) Special Assignment.
Hoover, Matthew N. '95 (COL) Dover, OH St. Joseph; College of Consultors.
Hopcus, Daniel R. '64 (IND)[L] Saint Mary Of The Woods, IN Sisters of Providence General Administration.
Hopcus, Daniel '64 (ORG) On Duty Outside the Diocese.
Hope, Abbott J. '54 (CAM) Retired.
Hope, Donald E. '76 (SLC) East Carbon, UT Good Shepherd LLC 204; Price, UT Notre Dame de Lourdes LLC 207; Deans; Presbyteral Council.
Hopefl, Gregory J. '76 (SUP) Stone Lake, WI St. Ignatius; Stone Lake, WI St. Francis of Solanus; Stone Lake, WI St. Philip; Holy Childhood Association; Propagation of the Faith.
Hopka, John '79 (DAL) Dallas, TX St. Monica.
Hopkins, John P. '78 (WIL) Newark, DE St. Margaret of Scotland; College of Consultors; Priests' Council; Priests' Continuing Formation Committee.
Hopkins, John *l.c.* (WDC)[W] Bethesda, MD Alpha Omega, Inc.
Hopkins, John '91 (WDC)[N] Potomac, MD Legionaries of Christ.
Hopkins, John *l.c.* '01 (BAL)[W] Crownsville, MD Springhill Center for Family Development.
Hopkins, Michael *c.ss.r.* '63 (NY)[EE] New York, NY Redemptorist Priests and Brothers, C.Ss.R.
Hopkins, Peter *l.c.* '91 (NY)[II] Thornwood, NY Legion of Christ, Incorporated.
Hopkins, Richard J. '44 (GF) Retired.
Hopmeir, Ronald J. '91 (STL) Saint Louis, MO Sts. Mary and Joseph Chapel; St. Louis, MO St. Stephen, Protomartyr.
Hopp, Raymond '65 (BAK) Retired.
Hopp, Thomas R. (CIN) Priests Commended to a Life of Prayer and Penance.
Hoppe, Arthur '47 (SCL) Freeport, MN St. Rose of Lima Retired.
Hoppe, Lawrence '60 (GBG)[F] Greensburg, PA Neumann House.
Hoppe, Leslie *o.f.m.* '71 (MIL)[P] Provincial Offices of the Franciscan Friars, Assumption BVM Province, Inc.
Hoppe, Rev. Msgr. Ronald C. '58 (ALX) College of Consultors Retired.
Hoppe, Sean *o.s.b.* '82 (IND)[K] St. Meinrad, IN St. Meinrad Archabbey.
Hoppe, William M. '78 (BRK) Corona, NY St. Leo.
Hoppe, William '78 (BRK) Promoter of Justice.
Hoppenjans, Terence E. '55 (LEX) Paintsville, KY St. Michael Catholic Church; College of Consultors; Big Sandy/Licking.
Hopper, Jeffrey G. '06 (L) Elizabethtown, KY St. James; White Mills, KY St. Ignatius; Ex Officio.
Hopper, Thomas W. '04 (GAL) Conroe, TX Sacred Heart.
Hopping, John Paul '85 (ORG) On Duty Outside the Diocese.
Hopping, John Paul '85 (STL) Saint Louis, MO Our Lady of Guadalupe.
Hoppough, Gregory J. *c.s.s.* '74 (BO)[A] Weston, MA Blessed John XXIII National Seminary; [U] Waltham, MA Stigmatine Fathers & Brothers Provincial House; [X] Waltham, MA Stigmatine Fathers and Brothers.
Hora, Robert J. '83 (BUF) Boston, NY St. John the Baptist.
Horak, Rev. Msgr. Donald E. '63 (STU) Retired.
Horak, Mark F. *s.j.* '94 (WDC) Washington, DC Holy Trinity.
Horan, Brendan *s.j.* '93 (CHI)[C] Chicago, IL Jesuit Community at Loyola University Chicago.
Horan, George E. '72 (LA) Los Angeles, CA Sacred Heart; Los Angeles, CA Office of Restorative Justice; Los Angeles, CA L.A. Men's Central Jail; Co Directors.
Horan, Gerald M. *o.s.m.* '82 (ORG) Fullerton, CA St. Philip Benizi; Membership; Vicar for Faith Formation; Catholic Schools and Parish Faith Formation; Staff; Special Assignment.
Horan, Gerald M. *o.s.m.* '82 (CHI)[N] Chicago Order of Friar Servants of Mary (Servites) United States of America Province, Inc.; Chicago, IL; [N] Chicago, IL Order of Friar Servants of Mary (Servites) United States of America Province, Inc.
Horan, Gerald *o.s.m.* '82 (ORG) Office for Faith Formation.
Horan, James *s.d.b.* '82 (NEW)[C] Ramsey, NJ Don Bosco Preparatory High School; [M] Ramsey, NJ Don Bosco Prep Salesian Residence.
Horan, John F. *o.carm.* '84 (WDC)[W] Washington, DC Carmelite Institute; [B] Washington, DC Whitefriars Hall.
Horan, John '46 (SEA) Retired.
Horan, Mike '80 (SAT) On Sabbatical.
Horan, Ray '68 (ATL) Retired.
Horan, Terence J. '68 (SFR) Retired.
Horan, Thomas A. '62 (ALN) Gordon, PA Our Lady of Good Counsel Retired.
Horan, Thomas C. *o.m.i.* '94 (SFD)[A] Godfrey, IL Immaculate Heart of Mary Novitiate.
Horan, Thomas '73 (ALN)[J] Bethlehem, PA Holy Family Villa Retired.
Horan, Timothy E. '79 (ROC) Rochester, NY St. Margaret Mary; Office of Vocations.
Horanzy, Joseph M. '59 (SCR)[N] Dunmore, PA Villa St. Joseph Retired.
Horath, George B. '63 (MAD) Fennimore, WI St. John Nepomucene; Fennimore, WI St. Mary; Fennimore, WI St. Lawrence O'Toole.
Horath, James R. '73 (SUP) Merrill, WI St. Francis Xavier.
Horath, William G. '75 (SUP) Three Lakes, WI St. Kunegunda; Three Lakes, WI St. Theresa; Defender of the Bond.
Horejsi, Jeffrey P. '91 (NU) Regional Treatment Center; [F] Willmar, MN Willmar Regional Treatment Center; Finance Council; Social Concerns Committee; Spicer, MN Our Lady of the Lakes.
Horgan, Daniel B. '98 (MO) Released from Diocesan Assignment; Air Force Chaplains.
Horgan, John E. '72 (WOR) Ashburnham, MA St. Denis; Ashburnham, MA St. Anne.
Horgan, Joseph E. '53 (PRO) Retired.
Horgan, Paul L. *s.j.* '68 (FgM) New York, NY Society of Jesus.
Horgan, Timothy J. '55 (NEW) Retired.
Horgas, Robert '91 (E) Morrisdale, PA St. Agnes.
Horihan, Robert S. '02 (WIN) Censors of Books and Periodicals.
Horkan, Edward R. '03 (ARL) Alexandria, VA St. Rita; Notaries; Catholic Scouting Information.
Horley, Ray J. '58 (CLV)[M] Cleveland, OH Little Sisters of the Poor Retired.
Horn, Francis J. *o.s.a.* '75 (CAM)[C] Richland, NJ St. Augustine Preparatory School.
Horn, John P. *s.j.* '85 (OM)[K] Omaha, NE Jesuit Community at Creighton University.
Horn, Joseph K. *o.praem.* '81 (ORG)[I] Silverado, CA Norbertine Fathers of Orange Inc.
Horn, Joseph R. '97 (DET) Archdiocesan Vicars; Memphis, MI Holy Family; Presbyteral Council.
Hornacek, Joseph F. '66 (MIL) Archdiocesan Consultors; Pewaukee, WI St. Anthony on the Lake.
Hornat, Stephen *s.s.e.* '76 (MOB)[G] Selma, AL Edmundite Fathers.
Horner, Timothy *o.s.b.* '53 (STL)[O] St. Louis, MO The Abbey of St. Mary and St. Louis.
Hornicak, John Joseph '03 (JOL) South Wilmington, IL Sacred Heart; South Wilmington, IL St. Lawrence.
Hornick, J. Michael '69 (ANC) Retired.
Hornick, Joseph R. '05 (SCR) Dushore, PA St. Basil's.
Horning, Edward '04 (SD) El Centro, CA St. Mary.
Horning, Roy Theodore '01 (LAN) Flushing, MI St. Robert.
Hornung, Eugene H. '03 (SUP) Retired.
Horowski, Janusz '95 (CHI)[N] Techny, IL Divine Word Residence.
Horrigan, Kevin P. '70 (BO) Wilmington, MA St. Dorothy.
Horrigan, Rev. Msgr. Leo R. '59 (DEN) Denver, CO Notre Dame.
Horrigan, Sean P. '98 (GAL) Houston, TX Christ the Redeemer.
Horrigan, Sean '98 (GAL) Area Representatives.
Horton, Geoffrey '08 (PEO) Peoria, IL St. Bernard's; Peoria, IL St. Peter's; Peoria, IL St. Mark's.
Horton, John C. '66 (PEO) Mahomet, IL Our Lady of the Lake.
Horton, W. Peter '79 (PIT)[B] Pittsburgh, PA La Roche College; [P] Pittsburgh, PA Office for Campus Ministry; Campus Ministry, Office for; [P] Pittsburgh, PA La Roche College.
Horvat, Francis '58 (KCK) Kansas City, KS St. John the Baptist.
Horvat, Matthew '65 (KCK) Retired.
Horvath, Arpad *s.j.* '07 (ATH) "A Sziv".
Horvath, Gerlac A. *o.praem.* '46 (ORG)[I] Silverado, CA Norbertine Fathers of Orange Inc. Retired.
Horvath, Joseph K. *o.de.m.* '02 (PH) Philadelphia, PA Our Lady of Lourdes; [Y] Philadelphia, PA Monastery of Our Lady of Mercy.
Horvath, Pius L. *o.s.b.* '53 (SFR)[N] Portola Valley, CA Woodside Priory.
Horvath, Stephen G. '40 (TR)[N] Trenton, NJ St. Lawrence Rehabilitation Center Retired.
Horvath, Stephen '50 (Y) Retired.
Horzen, Bernard A. *o.s.b.* '53 (PEO)[A] Peru, IL St. Bede Abbey Retired.
Hosak, Peter J. '83 (PSC) Bethlehem, PA SS. Peter and Paul; South Pennsylvania Protopresbyterate.
Hosak, Peter J. *m.s.* (ALN)[C] Bethlehem, PA Bethlehem Catholic High School.
Hose, Samuel '91 (AUS) Lakeway, TX Church of the Resurrection, Emmaus.
Hosey, P. Keith '56 (LFT) Retired.
Hosie, James J. *s.j.* '65 (BO)[D] Dorchester, MA Boston College High School.
Hosie, Stanley W. *s.m.* '46 (WDC)[N] Washington, DC Marist Center Retired.
Hosinski, Thomas *c.s.c.* '73 (P)[B] University of Portland; [L] Portland, OR Holy Cross Fathers & Brothers, C.S.C. – University of Portland.
Hosinski, Thomas *c.s.c.* (FTW)[H] Notre Dame Congregation of Holy Cross, Indiana Province, Provincial House.
Hosko, George H. *c.s.b.* '68 (GAL)[O] Houston, TX Residence of the Basilian Fathers of the University of St. Thomas.
Hosler, Gregory '01 (PSC) East Brunswick, NJ Nativity of Our Lord.
Hospodar, Robert J. '78 (PSC) New York, NY St. Mary's; Syncellus; Chancellor; Eparchial College of Consultors; Promoter of Justice; Respect Life; Eparchial Historian; Retirement Plan Board; White Plains, NY St. Nicholas of Myra; Presbyteral Council.
Hospodar, Robert (NY) Promoter of Justice; Defenders of the Bond.
Hossan, Rev. Msgr. John B. '53 (BGP) Retired.
Host, Dick '74 (GR) Grand Rapids, MI St. Mary's.
Hostetter, Larry '87 (OWN) Non–Parochial Assignments; [A] Owensboro, KY Brescia University; Committee for Education; Priest Personnel Committee.
Hostettler, Paul A. '50 (KNX) Retired.
Hostios, Jaime E. '07 (CAM) Atlantic City, NJ Our Lady, Star of the Sea, Atlantic City, N.J.
Hotard, Rev. Msgr. Howard H. '55 (NO) Retired.
Hotovy, Dennis W. '57 (LIN) Wymore, NE St. Mary's.
Hottinger, Paul '75 (JOL) Naperville, IL St. Margaret Mary; [D] Naperville, IL All Saints Catholic Academy.
Hottinger, Theodore J. *s.j.* '63 (WIN) Retrouvaille.
Hottle, Maximilian J. *o.f.m.* '61 (LSC) Tularosa, NM St. Francis de Paula.
Hottovy, Jamie S. '99 (LIN) Prague, NE St. John's; Advocates; Building Commission; Diocesan Area CCD Directors.
Hotze, John V. '93 (WCH) Presbyteral Council/College of Consultors; Judicial Vicar; Judges; [K] Wichita, KS Father Kapaun Guild.
Hotze, John V. '93 (DOD) Judicial Vicar.
Houck, Gregory *o.carm.* '92 (JOL) Councilors:; [L] Darien Carmelite Provincial Office.
Houck, Peter '46 (ANC) Retired.
Houde, Daniel *o.ss.t.* (BAL)[S] The Trinitarians in New Jersey.
Houde, Daniel *o.ss.t.* '87 (TR) Trenton, NJ The Church of the Incarnation–St. James.
Hougan, Andrew C. '01 (RCK) Sandwich, IL St. Paul.
Hough, Marianus *c.s.j.* '99 (NEW) Orange, NJ Mt. Carmel.
Hough, Roger '64 (SAL) Retired.
Houghton, Rev. Msgr. Francis J. '51 (NEW) Newark Ecclesial Team Retired.
Houlahan, Richard A. *o.m.i.* '58 (SAT)[K] San Antonio, TX Oblate Madonna Residence.
Houle, Andre *o.m.i.* '52 (BO)[X] Tewksbury, MA Immaculate Heart of Mary Residence.
Houle, Michael R. '79 (STA)[A] Jacksonville, FL Bishop Kenny High School, Inc.; Special Assignment; Jacksonville, FL St. Pius the Fifth; Jacksonville, FL Holy Rosary; Jacksonville, FL Church of the Crucifixion.
Houle, Michael '79 (STA)[A] St. Augustine, FL St. Joseph's Academy, Inc.
Houle, Roger A. '77 (PRO) North Scituate, RI St. Joseph; Senior Priest Advisor.
Houle, Thomas R. *o.f.m.cap.* '78 (NY) New York, NY St. John the Baptist.
Houle, Wilfred Andre '74 (BUR) St. Albans, VT Immaculate Conception.
Houlihan, John J. '64 (GF) Retired.
Houlihan, Michael K. '79 (LIN) Hastings, NE St. Michael's; Advocates.
Houlihan, Ralph D. *s.j.* '65 (STL)[F] St. Louis, MO St. Louis University High School, George H. Backer Memorial; [O] Saint Louis, MO St. Louis University High School Jesuit Community.
Houndje, Cyprien Ephrem *o.p.* '01 (ARL) Fairfax, VA St. Mary of Sorrows.
Hourican, John J. '05 (MEM) Covington, TN St. Alphonsus Church.
Hourigan, Michael '66 (MIA) Sunrise, FL St. Bernard.
Hourihan, Raymond B. '87 (CHL) Retired.
House, Christopher A. '02 (SFD) Springfield, IL Cathedral of the Immaculate Conception; Liturgical Ministry: Liturgical Leadership; Parish Life Ministry; Office for Vocations; Springfield, IL St. Katharine Drexel; Advisory Board.
House, Richard M. '92 (YAK) Military Chaplains; Navy Chaplains.
Householder, Paul C. '73 (PIT) Aliquippa, PA St. Titus.
Houseknecht, Eric '95 (PHX) Mesa, AZ St. Timothy Roman Catholic Parish.
Houser, Michael J. '08 (STL) St. Ann, MO Holy Trinity.
Houser, Samuel E. '76 (HBG) York, PA St. Patrick.
Housey, Walter L. *c.m.* '56 (LA)[P] Santa Barbara, CA

St. Mary's Evangelization Center; [V] Santa Barbara, CA St. Mary's Seminary Center Retired.
Houston, James A. '68 (WOR) Northboro, MA St. Rose of Lima.
Houston, Michael *c.ss.r.* '98 (FgM) Brooklyn, NY AMERICAN REDEMPTORIST FATHERS.
Hovanec, Craig M. '03 (CLV) Lorain, OH St. Peter.
Hovley, Vincent E. *s.j.* '69 (COS)[F] Sedalia, CO Sacred Heart Jesuit Community; [H] Sedalia, CO Sacred Heart Jesuit Retreat House.
Howard, Arthur '06 (KAL) Kalamazoo, MI St. Monica.
Howard, C. Donald *s.a.* '72 (ARL) Sterling, VA Christ the Redeemer.
Howard, Clarence J. '61 (L) Retired.
Howard, David G. '06 (CIN) Reading, OH Sts. Peter and Paul.
Howard, Dennis J. '90 (LAN) Fowler, MI Most Holy Trinity; Regional Vicars.
Howard, Edward F. *s.j.* '66 (BO)[U] Weston, MA Campion Jesuit Community.
Howard, Evan Arthur *o.f.m.* '55 (OAK)[O] Danville, CA San Damiano Retreat Retired.
Howard, Rev. Msgr. James J. '52 (PH) Retired.
Howard, John W. *s.j.* '68 (BO)[U] Weston, MA Campion Jesuit Community.
Howard, John *c.j.m.* '67 (SD) Solana Beach, CA St. James.
Howard, Joseph '89 (SHP) Bossier City, LA St. Jude.
Howard, Joseph *f.s.s.p.* '02 (PAT) Pequannock, NJ Our Lady of Fatima Chapel (Tridentine).
Howard, Kenneth J. *s.s.j.* '87 (GAL) Houston, TX St. Francis Xavier.
Howard, Phillip R. *c.s.sp.* '79 (SB) Hemet, CA Our Lady of the Valley; Prov. Councilors:.
Howard, Randy '01 (OWN) Leitchfield, KY St. Joseph's; Sunfish, KY St. John the Evangelist.
Howard, Rev. Msgr. Robert E. '62 (LA) Retired.
Howard, Theodore J. '65 (RVC) Shoreham, NY St. Mark.
Howard, Rev. Msgr. Vincent '47 (LAN) Retired.
Howarth, Joseph E. '80 (PH) Philadelphia, PA Resurrection of Our Lord; Approved Advocates.
Howe, Christopher K. *o.s.a.* '89 (CHI)[N] Olympia Fields, IL Tolentine Monastery at Tolentine Center.
Howe, J. Norbert '56 (TOL) Retired.
Howe, Robert J. '94 (SAG) Bad Axe, MI Sacred Heart; Rapson, MI St. Joseph.
Howe, Timothy A. *s.j.* '98 (CHI) Chicago, IL St. Procopius; [N] Chicago, IL Miguel Pro Jesuit Community.
Howe, Timothy A. *s.j.* '98 (CIN)[F] Cincinnati, OH St. Xavier High School; [N] Cincinnati, OH Jesuit Community at St. Xavier High School.
Howell, Charles W. '98 (LEX) Frankfort, KY Good Shepherd.
Howell, David W. '65 (BGP) Retired.
Howell, David '78 (LAN) Brighton, MI St. Mary Magdalen Church; Regional Vicars; College of Consultors.
Howell, Rev. Msgr. Michael '74 (CC) Robstown, TX St. Thomas the Apostle; Presbyteral Council; Judges.
Howell, Patrick J. *s.j.* '72 (SEA)[A] Seattle, WA Seattle University; [L] Seattle, WA Arrupe Jesuit Community at Seattle University.
Howell, Stephen H. '74 (SFR) Belmont, CA Immaculate Heart of Mary; [E] Belmont, CA Notre Dame High School (Girls).
Hower, William J. '64 (MAD) Retired.
Howes, Marc C. '04 (LAV) Board of Trustees; Las Vegas, NV St. Joseph, Husband of Mary; Presbyteral Council for the Diocese of Las Vegas.
Howley, Rev. Msgr. Edward J. '47 (BGP) New Milford, CT Retired.
Howley, Vincent DePaul (NY) Carmel, NY St. James the Apostle.
Howren, John T. '95 (ATL) Cumming, GA St. Brendan the Navigator.
Hoy, Daniel J. '48 (PH) Strafford, PA Our Lady of the Assumption Retired.
Hoye, Rev. Msgr. Daniel F. '72 (FR) Mashpee, MA Christ The King; Promotor Justitiae; Defenders of the Bond.
Hoye, Justin E. '06 (KC) Nevada, MO St. Mary; Presbyteral Council.
Hoye, Ronald J. *c.m.* '91 (CHI)[N] Chicago DePaul Vincentian Residence.
Hoyer, Michael '80 (MIA) Fort Lauderdale, FL Our Lady Queen of Martyrs; Presbyteral Council.
Hoying, David A. *c.pp.s.* '83 (LFT) Bryant, IN Holy Trinity; Members.
Hoying, John *c.pp.s.* '62 (CIN)[N] Carthagena, OH St. Charles Retired.
Hoying, Leo A. '56 (CIN)[N] Carthagena, OH St. Charles Retired.
Hoying, Mark *c.pp.s.* (TOL) Kalida, OH St. Michael.
Hoying, Vincent *c.pp.s.* '58 (CIN)[N] Carthagena, OH St. Charles Retired.
Hoying, William *c.pp.s.* '61 (CIN)[N] Carthagena, OH St. Charles Retired.
Hoyles, Monte J. '06 (TOL) Graduate Studies.
Hoynes, Richard '88 (LA) Los Angeles, CA St. Francis Xavier Chapel.
Hoyos, Jose Eugenio '84 (ARL) Spanish Apostolate; Falls Church, VA St. Philip.
Hoyt, Stephen *o.f.m.cap.* (PAT)[K] Passaic, NJ St. Mary's Hospital.
Hoyumpa, Santiago '09 (GAY) Cadillac, MI St. Ann; Lake City, MI St. Theresa; Lake City, MI St. Stephen.
Hrebenko, Pawel '04 (BGP) Brookfield, CT St. Marguerite Bourgeoys; Presbyteral Council.
Hreha, James D. '87 (WIL) Lewes, DE St. Jude The Apostle.
Hreno, Frank *s.d.v.* '05 (PAT) Wayne, NJ Our Lady of the Valley.
Hrezo, Paul '03 (STU) On Duty Outside the Diocese.
Hrezo, Paul '00 (COL)[A] Columbus, OH Pontifical College Josephinum; [A] Columbus, OH Pontifical College Josephinum.
Hribsek, Aloysius J. '49 (BGP) Retired.
Hricko, Michael A. *s.j.* '73 (PH) Philadelphia, PA Old St. Joseph's.
Hrisko, Zachary *o.s.b.* '57 (JOL)[L] Lisle, IL St. Procopius Abbey.
Hritsko, William A. '98 (COL) Coshocton, OH Sacred Heart.
Hritz, Paul J. '53 (CLV) Cleveland, OH St. Malachi Retired.
Hrubiak, Rev. Archpriest Dennis M. '70 (PRM) Fairview Park, OH St. Mary Magdalene; Chancellor; Eparchial Consultors; Cantors' Institute Faculty; Office of Vocations; Seminary Education Formation Board; Priest's Pension Board.
Hruby, Paul '82 (LA) Glendale, CA Church of the Incarnation.
Hruska, Eugene P. '58 (GF) Retired.
Hruska, Timothy W. '96 (MAR) Grand Marais, MI Holy Rosary Church.
Hrydziuszko, Michael '95 (DET) Macomb, MI St. Isidore.
Hrynkiw, Wasyl '91 (STF) Hempstead, NY St. Vladimir.
Hrynuck, Rev. Msgr. Stephen '38 (PHU) Retired.
Hsu, Peter '57 (BEL) Retired.
Hu, Paul *s.o.l.t.* '94 (CC)[G] Robstown, TX Society of Our Lady of the Most Holy Trinity.
Huan, Joseph Van Tran '73 (RIC) Military Chaplains.
Huar, Ralph '81 (STP) Long Lake, MN St. George.
Huard, Jeff '94 (STP)[C] St. Paul, MN University of St. Thomas.
Huard, Jeffrey H. '94 (STP)[A] Saint Paul, MN The Saint Paul Seminary.
Huard, Leo *o.carm.* '65 (JOL)[L] Darien Carmelite Provincial Office.
Huba, Rev. Msgr. David C. '74 (NEW) North Essex Deanery 16.
Hubba, Rev. Msgr. David C. '74 (NEW) Nutley, NJ St. Mary's.
Hubbard, J. Randall '90 (L) Louisville, KY St. Stephen, Martyr.
Hubbard, Jeffrey A. '05 (OG) On Duty Outside the Diocese.
Hubbard, Jeffrey A. '05 (BAL)[S] Baltimore, MD St. Mary's Seminary & University.
Hubbard, Jeffrey '05 (SFR)[A] Menlo Park, CA St. Patrick Seminary and University.
Hubbard, Lawrence E. '68 (STP) Special Assignment; [S] Minneapolis, MN Sagrado Corazon de Jesus.
Hubbard, William '08 (ORG) La Habra, CA Our Lady of Guadalupe.
Hubbert, Joseph G. *c.m.* '77 (BUF)[O] Niagara University, NY Vincentian Community at Niagara University; [C] Niagara University, NY Niagara University.
Hubbs, Timothy L. '84 (CAM) On Duty Outside the Diocese; Army Chaplains.
Huber, Rev. Msgr. Daniel R. '50 (PBL) Retired.
Huber, Henry P. '02 (DUB) Garner, IA St. Boniface; Deanery Representatives; Britt, IA St. Patrick; Forest City, IA St. Patrick; Garner, IA St. Wenceslaus; Forest City, IA St. James; Forest City, IA St. Patrick.
Huber, J. William '59 (PBL) Pueblo, CO St. Pius X.
Huber, John *c.s.b.* '92 (GAL)[E] Houston, TX St. Thomas High School.
Huber, Kevin R. '91 (GRY) Bishop's Council of Priests; Priestly Life; Vocations; Hammond, IN St. Casimir.
Huber, Larry T. '95 (STL) Wentzville, MO St. Joseph.
Huber, Rev. Msgr. Mark D. '94 (LIN) Denton, NE St. Mary's; Diocesan Consultors; Officialis; Presbyteral Council; Building Commission; Priests' Continuing Education Committee.
Huber, Matthew P. '87 (HEL) Associate Judges; Stevensville, MT St. Mary.
Huber, Richard *m.s.c.* '59 (OG) Cape Vincent, NY Cape Vincent Correctional Facility; [F] Watertown, NY Missionaries of the Sacred Heart.
Huber, Vincent J. '64 (STU) Judges; Priests' Retirement Board; Vicar for Retired Priests; Wintersville, OH Blessed Sacrament Retired.
Hubert, Raymond P. '58 (PMB) Delray Beach, FL Emmanuel Retired.
Hubertus, Rev. Msgr. Albert '50 (SAT)[K] San Antonio, TX Casa De Padres; Judges Retired.
Huberty, Mark A. '96 (STP) Maplewood, MN Presentation of the Blessed Virgin Mary; Archdiocesan Finance Council (AFC).
Huberty, Ronald V. '90 (NU) Fairfax, MN St. Andrew; Franklin, MN Sacred Heart; Gibbon, MN St. Willibrord; Winthrop, MN St. Francis de Sales; Committee on Parishes; Priest Personnel Board.
Hubmann, William G. *c.pp.s.* '79 (CHI)[J] Chicago, IL Saints Mary and Elizabeth Medical Center.
Huck, Chuck '06 (CR) Red Lake Falls, MN St. Joseph's.
Huck, Joseph '69 (MIA) Retired.
Hudak, Mark J. *o.f.m.* '93 (CIN)[E] Cincinnati, OH Roger Bacon High School; [N] Cincinnati, OH Pleasant Street Friary.
Hudak, Ralph '77 (CLV) Cleveland, OH Immaculate Heart of Mary; Cleveland Diocesan Council, NCCW.
Hudak, Richard E. '68 (CLV) South Euclid, OH St. Margaret Mary.
Hudak, Thomas R. '73 (SCR) Unassigned or Leave of Absence.
Hudepohl, Howard *o.f.m.* '54 (CIN)[N] Cincinnati, OH St. Clement Friary.
Hudert, John P. *m.m.* '62 (NY)[EE] Maryknoll Maryknoll St. Teresa's Residence[EE] Retired.
Hudgin, Christopher J. *o.s.f.s.* '81 (ALN)[B] Center Valley, PA DeSales University; [K] Center Valley, PA Oblates of St. Francis de Sales.
Hudgins, David William '01 (LAN) Adrian, MI St. Joseph.
Hudgins, James C. '98 (ARL)[D] Arlington, VA Bishop Denis J. O'Connell High School; Falls Church, VA St. James.
Hudock, Paul A. '98 (WH) Vocations, Office of; Priest–Secretary for Bishop.
Hudson, Gerald F. *s.j.* '94 (SJ)[L] Los Altos, CA Jesuit Retreat Center of Los Altos.
Hudson, Richard '96 (AUS) Belton, TX Christ the King.
Hudzan, Volodymyr '93 (STN) Chicago, IL St. Nicholas Ukrainian Catholic Cathedral.
Hudziak, Jerome M. '64 (MIL)[B] Hales Corners, WI Sacred Heart School of Theology; Archdiocesan Consultors Retired.
Huebner, Terrance J. '74 (MIL) Lake Geneva, WI St. Francis de Sales.
Huebsch, Rev. Msgr. Joseph R. '50 (FAR) Retired.
Huegelmeyer, Charles T. *m.m.* '51 (NY)[EE] Retired.
Huehlefeld, Matthew H. '96 (VIC) Judges; Yoakum, TX St. Joseph.
Huelsing, Justin H. *o.m.i.* '54 (BEL)[F] Belleville, IL Missionary Oblates of Mary Immaculate – St. Henry's Oblate Residence.
Huerta, Enrique '86 (LA) Pico Rivera, CA St. Francis Xavier.
Huerta, Roque '08 (WIN) Winona, MN St. Casimir's.
Huertas, Alvaro '81 (MIA) Miami, FL St. Thomas the Apostle.
Huertas–Colon, Rev. Msgr. Ivan L. '93 (SJN)[C] Rio Piedras, PR Seminario Mayor Regional San Juan Bautista; San Juan Bautista Regional Seminary.
Huesca, Omar A. '81 (MIA) Miami, FL St. Raymond Retired.
Huesing, Paul D. *c.s.p.* '82 (BO)[N] Boston, MA Paulist Center; [U] Boston, MA Paulist Fathers Residence; [Z] Boston, MA Chapel of the Holy Spirit.
Huesman, Edward G. '41 (BAL) Retired.
Huff, Thomas M. (LC) Eastman, WI St. Wenceslaus.
Huffman, David L. '72 (STU) Ironton, OH St. Joseph; Ironton, OH St. Lawrence; Ironton, OH St. Mary; [K] Franklin Furnace, OH Our Lady of Fatima Shrine; [M] Ironton, OH Boy Scouts.
Huffman, Timothy J. '93 (STU) Lowell, OH St. Henry; Lowell, OH Our Lady of Mercy; Priests Personnel Board; Presbyteral Council.
Huffstetter, Stephen *s.c.j.* '89 (SFS)[B] Chamberlain, SD St. Joseph Indian School.
Hug, James E. *s.j.* '72 (WDC)[N] Washington, DC Leonard Neale House; [W] Washington, DC Center of Concern.
Huggins, Michael '89 (L)[A] Bellarmine University.
Huggins, Scott '01 (JOL) Paxton, IL St. Mary.
Huggins, William A. '67 (SPC) Retired.
Hughes, Albert C. '57 (BO) Senior Priests. Retired.
Hughes, Anthony '93 (LAV) Pahrump, NV Our Lady of the Valley.
Hughes, Barnabas B. *o.f.m.* '53 (LA)[P] Encino, CA Our Lady of Mount Carmel Priory.
Hughes, Brian C. '81 (SC) Estherville, IA St. Patrick's; Building Commission; Presbyteral Council.
Hughes, Brian '81 (SC) Armstrong, IA St. Mary's; Diocesan Consultors.
Hughes, Charles J. '74 (BO) Lowell, MA St. Anthony of Padua.
Hughes, Charles *g.h.m.* '54 (CIN)[N] Cincinnati Headquarters of Glenmary Home Missioners Retired.
Hughes, Charles *g.h.m.* '54 (SAV) Augusta, GA St. Mary on the Hill Retired.
Hughes, Christopher '98 (SFS) Mellette, SD All Saints.
Hughes, Dennis E. '75 (SP) Vicars Forane; Incardination Committee; Trinity, FL St. Peter the Apostle Catholic Church in Trinity, Inc.
Hughes, Derek '86 (MRY) Carmel Valley, CA Our Lady of Mt. Carmel.
Hughes, Edward R. '58 (RCK) Retired.

Hughes, Eugene E. *s.m.* '57 (ATL) Atlanta, GA Our Lady of the Assumption Retired.
Hughes, Francis J. '80 (BRK) Brooklyn, NY St. Columba; Brooklyn, NY Our Lady of Miracles.
Hughes, James A. '80 (BRK) Long Island City, NY Most Precious Blood.
Hughes, James F. '52 (PH) Retired.
Hughes, James L. '81 (BRK) Brooklyn, NY St. Sylvester.
Hughes, Rev. Msgr. John Charles '49 (LA) Camarillo, CA St. Mary Magdalen Retired.
Hughes, John Jay '54 (STL) University City, MO Christ the King Retired.
Hughes, John *m.s.* '53 (WOR) Fitchburg, MA St. Joseph's.
Hughes, John '94 (BEA) Beaumont, TX St. Jude Thaddeus.
Hughes, Joseph B. '67 (BAL) Retired.
Hughes, Joseph W. '70 (TR) Leave of Absence.
Hughes, Kenneth J. *s.j.* '66 (BO)[U] Cambridge, MA Faber House.
Hughes, Mark '82 (WDC) Kensington, MD Holy Redeemer.
Hughes, Michael J. *o.s.a.* '75 (VEN) Bokeelia, FL Our Lady of the Miraculous Medal.
Hughes, Peter *c.s.sp.* '61 (FAR) Special Assignment.
Hughes, Peter '81 (OWN) Owensboro, KY St. Martin.
Hughes, Raymond E. '02 (TR) Toms River, NJ St. Maximilian Kolbe.
Hughes, Raymond *c.r.* '75 (VEN) Naples, FL St. William.
Hughes, Rev. Msgr. Richard A. '52 (WDC) Forestville, MD Mt. Calvary Retired.
Hughes, Robert E. '90 (CAM)[A] Haddonfield, NJ Paul VI High School, Haddon Township, N.J.; Continuing Education & Spiritual Formation of Priests (CESF); Liturgical Art and Architectural Commission; Sewell, NJ Church of the Holy Family, Washington Township; Consultants.
Hughes, Robert E. *s.m.* '59 (CIN)[N] Dayton, OH Marianist Community.
Hughes, Robert W. '68 (MAD) Johnson Creek, WI St. Mary Magdalene; Lake Mills, WI St. Francis Xavier.
Hughes, Ronald J. '82 (SCR) Old Forge, PA St. Mary; Old Forge, PA Prince of Peace, Old Forge.
Hughson, D. Thomas *s.j.* '71 (MIL)[P] Milwaukee, WI Arrupe House Jesuit Community.
Hughson, Robert S. '79 (BUF) Niagara Falls, NY St. Vincent de Paul; Vicars.
Hugli, Richard H. '95 (MO) Defenders of the Bond.
Hugo, Joseph Gaspar D. '94 (BRK) Astoria, NY Immaculate Conception.
Hugo, William *o.f.m.cap.* '80 (MIL)[P] Milwaukee, WI St. Conrad Friary.
Huguley, Vernon '93 (BIR) Adamsville, AL St. Patrick's; Diocesan College of Vicars; Birmingham, AL St. Stanislaus.
Huhn, Thomas J. *m.s.* '69 (HRT)[L] Hartford, CT Our Lady of Sorrows Rectory; Hartford, CT Our Lady of Sorrows.
Hulko, Joseph D. '67 (ALN)[J] Bethlehem, PA Holy Family Villa Retired.
Hull, Francis M. *s.s.j.* '57 (ARL) Alexandria, VA St. Joseph's.
Hull, Rev. Msgr. Michael F. '93 (NY) New York, NY Guardian Angel; Censors Librorum; [A] Yonkers, NY St. Joseph's Seminary.
Hullinger, Jon '99 (KCK) Topeka, KS Mater Dei.
Hullinger, Ty S. '04 (BAL) Mount Savage, MD St. Patrick; Cumberland, MD Federal & State Correctional Facilities; Cumberland, MD St. Mary.
Hullings, Clifford '61 (SPK) Retired.
Hulot, Vincent *o.s.b.* '97 (TLS)[G] Hulbert, OK Our Lady of the Annunciation of Clear Creek Monastery.
Hulscher, Alfred J. *o.s.b.* '60 (SEA)[L] Lacey, WA St. Martin's Abbey; Lacey, WA.
Hulshof, David F. '82 (SPC) Cape Girardeau, MO St. Vincent de Paul; Advocates for the Respondent; Presbyteral Council; Diocesan Lay Endowment Board; Diocesan Council of Catholic Women (DCCW); Diocesan Consultors.
Hultberg, William J. *o.s.f.s.* '62 (WIL)[J] Wilmington Wilmington–Philadelphia Province of the Oblates of St. Francis de Sales.
Hultquist, Thomas H. '76 (WOR) Barre, MA St. Joseph's.
Humbrecht, Rev. Msgr. T. Allen '72 (KNX) Knoxville, TN Cathedral of the Sacred Heart of Jesus; Deans of the Diocese; Presbyteral Council; Diocesan Consultors; Ecumenism; Ministries of the Smoky Mtn. Deanery.
Hume, Kenneth '63 (P) Retired.
Humenay, Robert L. '69 (MO) Air National Guard Chaplains.
Huminski, Gregory J. '80 (BGP) Leave of Absence.
Humitz, Rev. Msgr. Robert S. '60 (DET) Retired.
Hummel, Donald K. '78 (NEW) Clark, NJ St. Agnes; Continuing Education and Formation of Priests; Boy Scouts of America/Catholic Committee on Scouting; Archdiocesan Girl Scouts; Office of the Permanent Diaconate.
Hummel, Kenneth J. '98 (PEO) Raritan, IL Church of St. Patrick; [M] Macomb, IL St. Francis of Assisi Newman Center.
Hummell, John F. '65 (PH)[BB] Oxford, PA Lincoln University.
Hummer, Lawrence L. '73 (COL) Chillicothe, OH St. Mary; Chillicothe, OH Chillicothe Correctional Institution.
Humphrey, Arthur F. (NEW) South Central Bergen Deanery 5.
Humphrey, Arthur Frank '75 (NEW) Little Ferry, NJ St. Margaret of Cortona.
Humphrey, Delos A. *m.m.* '54 (FgM) Maryknoll, NY MARYKNOLL.
Humphrey, Steven (BEL) Retired.
Humphries, Ryan P. '05 (ALX) Nachitoches, LA Immaculate Conception; Elected Members.
Humphrys, Richard A. '57 (SB) Bloomington, CA St. Charles Borromeo.
Hund, Francis '82 (KCK) Leawood, KS Church of the Nativity.
Hund, Joseph *o.f.m.* '89 (CIN)[N] Cincinnati St. Francis Seraph Friary.
Hund, William *c.s.c.* '60 (P)[B] University of Portland; [L] Portland, OR Holy Cross Fathers & Brothers, C.S.C. – University of Portland Retired.
Hund, William *c.s.c.* (FTW)[H] Notre Dame Congregation of Holy Cross, Indiana Province, Provincial House.
Hundt, Rev. Msgr. George F. '81 (PAT) Madison, NJ St. Vincent Martyr; Presbyteral Council; Defenders of the Bond; College of Consultors.
Hundt, Rev. Msgr. Robert P. '61 (LC) Judicial Vicar; Diocesan Judges; [H] La Crosse, WI Holy Cross (Seminary) Diocesan Center.
Hundt, Robert P. (DEN) Metropolitan Judges.
Huneger, Richard '73 (P) Oregon City, OR St. John the Apostle; Board Members; Diaconate Office.
Hung, Bernard Nguyen '97 (AUS) Kingsland, TX St. Charles Borromeo Catholic Church – Kingsland, Texas; Horseshoe Bay, TX Our Lady of the Lake.
Hung, Le Trong *c.s.s.r.* '08 (LA)[P] Baldwin Park Vietnamese Redemptorist Mission.
Hung, Peter '67 (CHI) Indochinese Catholic Center Retired.
Hung, Pham Quoc *c.ss.r.* '94 (LA)[P] Baldwin Park, CA Vietnamese Redemptorist Mission; [BB] Baldwin Park, CA The Redemptorist Vietnamese Mission Corporation.
Hung, Tran Duy '05 (ATL) Holy Vietnamese Martyr's Mission.
Hung, Trinh Peter '65 (CHI) Chicago, IL St. Thomas of Canterbury.
Hunke, Norman F. '73 (OM) Gretna, NE St. Charles Borromeo; Consultors; Ex Officio (Consultors).
Hunkeler, Edward J. '44 (OM) Retired.
Hunkler, Jerome '83 (FAR) Steele, ND St. Francis de Sales; Steele, ND St. Paul; Steele, ND St. Mary's Church of Medina.
Hunko, Gerard A. '91 (GAY) Charlevoix, MI St. Mary; Beaver Island, MI Holy Cross.
Hunt, Dennis M. (LIN) Aurora, NE St. Mary's.
Hunt, Doug '92 (PBL) Ignacio, CO St. Ignatius Parish.
Hunt, George *s.j.* '67 (NY)[EE] Cardinal Spellman Hall, Jesuit Community.
Hunt, Henry Clay '09 (SAT) Helotes, TX Our Lady of Guadalupe.
Hunt, Rev. Msgr. James A. '55 (BRK) Retired.
Hunt, James M. '83 (GI) Broken Bow, NE St. Joseph's; Procurator; Advocates.
Hunt, John W. '68 (PRO) Cumberland, RI St. Joseph.
Hunt, Kevin *o.c.s.o.* '79 (WOR)[O] Spencer, MA St. Joseph's Abbey.
Hunt, Rev. Msgr. Luke '67 (PT) Gulf Breeze, FL St. Ann; Vicar General; Building & Renovation, Diocesan Commission for; Finance, Diocesan Commission for; Knights of Columbus; Priests' Pension Plan, Board for; Members Ex Officio; College of Consultors.
Hunt, Mark J. '85 (PH) On Special or Other Archdiocesan Assignment; Fallsington, PA St. Joseph the Worker; [C] Philadelphia, PA Holy Family University; [A] Wynnewood, PA Theological Seminary of St. Charles Borromeo, Overbrook.
Hunt, Mark '01 (NSH) Nashville, TN Holy Rosary.
Hunt, Richard D. *s.j.* '71 (ROC)[M] Rochester, NY Newman (Catholic Campus) Parish, RIT/NTID; [B] Rochester, NY McQuaid Jesuit High School.
Hunt, Robert *c.pp.s.* '54 (CIN)[N] Dayton Provincial Office of the Cincinnati Province of the Society of the Precious Blood.
Hunter, Alan M. '77 (SFD) Kincaid, IL St. Rita; Stonington, IL Holy Trinity; Taylorville, IL St. Mary.
Hunter, Eric '72 (SP) Clearwater, FL St. Brendan; Personnel Board.
Hunthausen, John F. '52 (HEL)[B] Helena, MT Carroll College Retired.
Hunthausen, John M. *s.j.* '70 (STL)[O] St. Louis, MO Jesuit Community Corporation at Saint Louis University – Jesuit Hall; [A] St. Louis, MO Kenrick School of Theology.
Huntimer, Donald W. *c.s.v.* '59 (CHI)[N] Arlington Heights Viatorian Province Center–Clerics of St. Viator.
Huntstiger, Thomas '65 (STP) Retired.
Huntzinger, Rev. Msgr. Ralph J. '50 (COL) Retired.
Huon, Phan Phat *c.ss.r.* '53 (LA)[P] Baldwin Park Vietnamese Redemptorist Mission.
Huong, Joseph '85 (SAC) Marysville, CA St. Joseph.
Huppenbauer, Walter E. '57 (CHI) Retired.
Hurbanczuk, Adam '91 (HRT) Union City, CT St. Hedwig; Union City, CT St. Mary.
Hurd, R. Scott '00 (WDC) Special Ministries; Pastoral Center Special Ministries.
Hurd, Robert E. *s.j.* '91 (CIN)[N] Cincinnati, OH Jesuit Community at Xavier University.
Hurd, Scott '00 (WDC) Executive Director, Permanent Diaconate; Secretariat for Ministerial Leadership and Vicar for Clergy.
Hurd, Steven F. *s.j.* '80 (CHI)[C] Chicago, IL Jesuit Community at Loyola University Chicago.
Hurd, Timothy C. '92 (SHP) Zwolle, LA St. Joseph; Vicars Forane; Advocates; Deans; Diocesan Liturgy Commission; College of Consultors; Ex Officio Members.
Hurkes, Charles *o.m.i.* '58 (WDC)[N] Washington, DC Oblate Community.
Hurlbert, James F. '90 (CHI) Chicago, IL St. Alphonsus.
Hurley, Brendan *s.j.* '93 (BAL)[S] Towson Maryland Province of the Society of Jesus.
Hurley, Brian K. '02 (DET) Temperance, MI St. Anthony.
Hurley, Daniel A. *o.f.m.* '45 (BUF)[Q] West Clarksville, NY Mount Irenaeus, Franciscan Mountain Retreat & Holy Peace Friary; [R] St. Bonaventure, NY St. Bonaventure University; [C] West Clarksville, NY Holy Peace Friary.
Hurley, Rev. Msgr. Daniel J. '59 (RVC) Massapequa, NY St. Rose of Lima.
Hurley, Rev. Msgr. Edward '70 (DM) Vicar for Finance; Priests' Pension Fund Society; [J] West Des Moines, IA St. Francis of Assisi Roman Catholic School Foundation; West Des Moines, IA St. Francis of Assisi.
Hurley, Francis J. *c.s.c.* '53 (FR)[A] North Easton, MA Stonehill College; [A] North Easton, MA Holy Cross Fathers Religious.
Hurley, George '55 (JOL) Retired.
Hurley, Gerard '76 (JKS) Pearl, MS St. Jude; Rankin County Prison; Mississippi State Hospital; Co Chairmen.
Hurley, John E. *c.s.p.* (AUS) Austin, TX St. Austin.
Hurley, John J. *o.s.f.s.* '68 (FgM)[J] Wilmington, DE DeSales House; Wilmington, DE OBLATES OF ST. FRANCIS DE SALES MISSIONS.
Hurley, John J. '56 (CHI) Arlington Heights, IL St. Edna Retired.
Hurley, John W. '74 (CHI) Prospect Heights, IL St. Alphonsus Liguori.
Hurley, John '82 (WDC) Washington, DC St. Matthew Cathedral Retired.
Hurley, Rev. Msgr. Leonard F. '58 (WDC) Special Ministries; Hospital & Nursing Home Ministries; [M] Washington, DC Cardinal O'Boyle Residence for Priests; [W] Washington, DC Carroll Manor Nursing & Rehabilitation Center; Cardinal O'Boyle Residence for Priests.
Hurley, Michael *o.p.* '07 (SAC) Benicia, CA St. Dominic.
Hurley, Patrick M. *o.s.b.* '76 (PAT)[J] Morristown, NJ St. Mary's Abbey Retreat Center; [N] Morristown, NJ St. Mary's Abbey.
Hurley, Paul K. '95 (MO) Military & VA Chaplains.; Army Chaplains.
Hurley, Phillip R. *s.j.* '08 (MIL)[P] Milwaukee, WI Jesuit Community at Marquette University; [Y] Milwaukee, WI Apostleship of Prayer.
Hurley, Steven P. '03 (WIL) Wilmington, DE St. Ann.
Hurley, Thomas J. '93 (CHI) Chicago, IL Old St. Patrick.
Hurrell, Johnathan *ss.cc.* '05 (HON) Waialua, HI St. Michael.
Hurst, Paul F. '77 (CIN) Springfield, OH St. Bernard.
Hurst, Thomas R. *s.s.* '73 (ALB) On Duty Outside the Diocese.
Hurst, Thomas R. *s.s.* '73 (BAL)[A] Baltimore, MD St. Mary's Seminary and University; [S] Baltimore Society of St. Sulpice, Province of the United States; [A] Baltimore, MD St. Mary's Seminary and University.
Hurtado, Tomas '04 (ORL) Orlando, FL St. John Vianney.
Hurtado–Badillo, Domingo '93 (CHI)[J] Hoffman Estates, IL St. Alexius Medical Center.
Hurtuk, Joseph *s.m.* '74 (STP) St. Paul, MN St. Louis King of France.
Husain, Nicolas F. '86 (CHI)[M] Wheeling, IL Addolorata Villa.
Huse, Charles F. *o.a.r.* '61 (NEW)[M] West Orange, NJ Augustinian Recollects.
Huse, Ralph G. *s.j.* '75 (STL)[O] St. Louis, MO Jesuit Community Corporation at Saint Louis University – Jesuit Hall; [O] St. Louis, MO Jesuit Community Corporation at Saint Louis University – Jesuit Hall.

Huse, Robert *o.a.r.* '58 (LA)[P] Oxnard, CA St. Augustine Priory O.A.R.
Hushen, Mark A. *o.s.f.s.* '91 (WIL)[J] Wilmington Wilmington–Philadelphia Province of the Oblates of St. Francis de Sales.
Huske, Leonard G. '56 (CHI) Retired.
Hussey, Daniel C. '85 (GLP) On Duty Outside of Diocese.
Hussey, Daniel '85 (RNO) Elko, NV St. Joseph's; Lists of Deans.
Hussey, Edmund M. '58 (CIN) Retired.
Hussey, Gerald W. '78 (PRO) Little Compton, RI St. Catherine of Siena; Tiverton, RI St. Madeleine Sophie.
Hussey, Michael *o.m.i.* '60 (BEL)[F] Belleville, IL Missionary Oblates of Mary Immaculate – St. Henry's Oblate Residence.
Hussey, Robert M. *s.j.* '00 (R) Raleigh, NC St. Raphael the Archangel; [F] Raleigh Jesuit Community.
Hussli, Edward J. '67 (MIL) Retired.
Hussmann, John R. '54 (DUB) Retired.
Husted, Richard *o.f.m.* '65 (BUF) Allegany, NY St. Bonaventure.
Huston, Richard '95 (SD) San Diego, CA Good Shepherd Retired.
Huszti, Michael J. '75 (PRM) On Duty Outside the Diocese; Vicar Adjutant; Cantors' Institute Faculty.
Huszti, Michael '76 (PBR)[D] Uniontown, PA Monastery and Novitiate of the Sisters of St. Basil the Great; Pro–Synodal Judges.
Hut, Clemens '36 (EVN) Retired.
Hutcherson, Bartholomew J. *o.p.* '97 (TUC) Tucson, AZ Saint Thomas More Roman Catholic Newman Parish – Tucson; [G] Tucson, AZ University of Arizona.
Hutchins, James '67 (PH) Broomall, PA St. Pius X.
Hutchins, Michael *s.v.d.* '75 (DUB)[B] Epworth, IA Divine Word College.
Hutchinson, Ronald D. '94 (GR) Jenison, MI Holy Redeemer; On Special Assignment; Vocations Office.
Hutchison, William J. *s.j.* '66 (STL) St. Louis, MO St. Matthew, Apostle; [O] St. Louis, MO St. Matthew Jesuit Community.
Hutmacher, Robert '79 (CHI)[N] Chicago, IL St. Peter's Friary.
Hutsko, Basil '79 (PRM) Marblehead, OH St. Mary; Presbyteral Council; Priest's Pension Board.
Hutsko, Joseph '79 (VNN) Fontana, CA St. Nicholas; College of Consultors; Youth.
Hutsko, Rev. Archpriest Michael '84 (PHU) Absent on Leave; Board Members.
Hutter, John P. '92 (PH) Philadelphia, PA Maternity B.V.M.
Hutton, Leon '80 (LA)[A] Camarillo, CA St. John's Seminary.
Hutzler, James '80 (AMA)[C] Panhandle, TX St. Joseph's Home for Retired Priests Retired.
Huvane, James H. *m.m.* '70 (CLV)[N] Cleveland, OH Maryknoll Fathers & Brothers; Cleveland, OH.
Huyett, Gerald T. *s.j.* '73 (NY)[EE] New York, NY Jesuit Community of the Immaculate Conception.
Huynh, Andrew (ORG) Retired.
Huynh, Joseph Dinh C. '67 (PH) Philadelphia, PA St. Thomas Aquinas; Vietnamese Apostolate.
Huynh, Peter Loi '02 (SJ) San Jose, CA St. Francis of Assisi; Ongoing Formation of Clergy.
Huynh, Viet Tan '93 (PT) Madison, FL St. Vincent de Paul; Madison, FL St. Margaret.
Huytran, Stephen *o.carm.* '07 (NY) Middletown, NY Our Lady of Mt. Carmel.
Hvozdovic, Andrew S. '87 (SCR) Deans.
Hvozdovic, Andrew S. '87 (SCR) Sayre, PA Church of the Epiphany; Sayre, PA St. John the Evangelist.
Hwang, Bernard *o.s.b.* '49 (P) Retired.
Hwang, Matthias Seon Ki '88 (SJ) Sunnyvale, CA Holy Korean Martyrs.
Hwang, Xavier Jeong–yeon *s.j.* '06 (OAK)[M] Berkeley, CA Jesuit Fathers and Brothers.
Hy, Hilary Tran–Khac '57 (WDC) Silver Spring, MD Our Lady of Vietnam Retired.
Hyatt, Donald *c.s.b.* '68 (LSC) Truth or Consequences, NM Our Lady of Perpetual Help.
Hyatt, John R. *s.j.* '77 (NY) Staten Island, NY St. Mary of the Assumption.
Hyatt, Martin A. *b.s.o.* '84 (NTN) Methuen, MA Basilian Salvatorian Order; Methuen, MA.
Hyatt, Robert A. '63 (RVC) Amityville, NY South Oaks Psychiatric Hospital Retired.
Hybner, Joseph '63 (VIC) Flatonia, TX SS. Cyril and Methodius; Flatonia, TX Sacred Heart.
Hyclak, Walter J. '69 (CLV) Olmsted Falls, OH St. Mary of the Falls; Presbyteral Council.
Hyde, Gregory J. *s.j.* '98 (DET)[P] Bloomfield Hills, MI Manresa Jesuit Retreat House.
Hyde, Mark *s.d.b.* '81 (FgM) New Rochelle, NY SALESIANS OF DON BOSCO.
Hyde, Robert P. '88 (MO) DEPARTMENT OF VETERANS AFFAIRS HOSPITALS AND CHAPLAINS.
Hyde, Robert P. '88 (SY) Promoters of Justice; Syracuse, NY Crouse Irving Memorial Hospital; Syracuse, NY St. Margaret.
Hying, Donald J. '89 (MIL)[A] St. Francis, WI Saint Francis de Sales Seminary; Special Assignment.
Hykavy, Roman *o.s.b.m.* '94 (STN) Hamtramck, MI Immaculate Conception of B.V.M.
Hyl, Robert J. '63 (BGP) Stamford, CT Holy Spirit.
Hyland, James M. '81 (CHI) Evergreen Park, IL Most Holy Redeemer.
Hyland, Rev. Msgr. John M. '68 (DAV)[J] Davenport, IA St. Vincent Center; Finance Council; Vicar General and Moderator of the Curia; Diocesan Consultors; Diocesan Corporate Board; Pastoral Services; Notaries.
Hyland, Sean '84 (MIA) Absent on Leave.
Hyman, David L. *o.f.m.* '60 (ATL) Special or Other (Arch)Diocesan Assignment; [J] Athens, GA University of Georgia – Catholic Student Center; Athens, GA Catholic Student Center at The University of Georgia.
Hyman, David *o.f.m.* '60 (NY)[II] New York, NY Franciscans of Holy Name Province Benevolence Trust, Inc.
Hyman, Robert A. '61 (TUC) Retired.
Hyman, Robert (GLP) McNary, AZ St. Anthony.
Hymel, Ray A. '87 (NO) New Orleans, LA St. Rita.
Hyndman, Ernest R. '96 (MOB) Bay Minette, AL St. Agatha Church.
Hynes, Aidan '81 (PMB) Hobe Sound, FL St. Christopher; Ex Officio; Vicars Forane.
Hynes, Rev. Msgr. Christopher J. '92 (NEW)[B] School of Diplomacy and Intl. Rels.; Assistant to the Archbishop for Public Affairs.
Hynes, Gerald *c.p.* '51 (BAL) Baltimore, MD St. Ursula Retired.
Hynes, Gerald *c.p.* '51 (MET)[I] South River Passionist Provincial Office.
Hynes, James B. '94 (NY) Staten Island, NY St. Charles.
Hynes, James P. '49 (PRO)[P] Providence St. John Vianney Residence Retired.
Hynes, James '73 (SAT) San Antonio, TX Our Lady of the Angels.
Hynes, John F. '55 (DAV) Retired.
Hynes, John M. '65 (WIL) Wilmington, DE St. Catherine of Siena.
Hynes, Joseph P. '55 (PRO) Retired.
Hynes, Richard P. '72 (CHI) Chicago, IL Nativity of Our Lord; Department Directors; Department of Evangelization, Catechesis and Worship; Administrative Council.
Hynes, Thomas J. *c.m.* '59 (PH)[Y].
Hynes, Rev. Msgr. William '49 (SR) Sebastopol, CA St. Sebastian.
Hynous, David M. *o.p.* '59 (CHI) Judges; [N] St. Pius V Priory.
Hypolite, Douglas *s.j.* '80 (SP)[C] Tampa, FL Jesuit High School.

I

Iacona, Francesco *c.m.f.* '02 (CHI)[N] Oak Park Claretian Missionaries USA Eastern Province.
Iaconis, Anthony '97 (RVC) Islip Terrace, NY St. Peter the Apostle.
Iacovacci, Rev. Msgr. Nicholas J. '51 (PRO) Warwick, RI St. Peter; Council Members Retired.
Iacovone, Angelo *c.p.* '46 (BRK)[T] Jamaica, NY Immaculate Conception Monastery Retired.
Iannizzotto, Christopher J. *o.carm.* '08 (NY) Bronx, NY St. Simon Stock.
Iannone, Raphael *o.f.m.cap.* '64 (NY)[EE] New Paltz, NY St. Joseph Friary; New Paltz, NY St. Joseph.
Ianotti, Pascal '61 (ALB) Retired.
Iantosca, August J. '77 (BRK) Forest Hills, NY Our Lady of Mercy; Creedmoor Psychiatric Center.
Ianucci, Thomas '94 (MO) Navy Chaplains.
Iaquinta, Patsy J. '70 (WH) Retired.
Iaquinto, Richard *o.s.b.* '68 (BUR)[E] Weston, VT Priory of Benedictine Monks; Weston, VT.
Iaquinto, Robert '81 (NEW) Retired.
Iasiello, Louis V. *o.f.m.* '78 (SP)[N] St. Petersburg, FL St. Anthony Friary.
Iaucci, Thomas '94 (RIC) Military Chaplains.
Ibach, Michael J. '73 (YAK) Judicial Vicar; Judges; Diocesan Consultors.
Ibach, William D. *s.j.* '59 (BO)[U] Weston, MA Campion Jesuit Community.
Ibanez, Armando *o.p.* '93 (NO)[P] New Orleans Dominican Friars, Southern Dominican Province of St. Martin de Porres.
Ibarguen–Gomez, Gilber '94 (AUS) Goldthwaite, TX St. Peter; San Saba, TX St. Mary.
Ibarra, Arnold '00 (SAT)[A] San Antonio, TX Assumption Seminary.
Ibarra, Brando '99 (PAT) Passaic, NJ St. Anthony of Padua; Spanish Cursillos.
Ibarra, Dairo Hernando Arboleda *o.ss.t.* (PCE)[H] Ponce, PR Pastoral Care of the Sick.
Ibarra, Manuel '98 (LSC) Lovington, NM St. Thomas Aquinas; Clergy Personnel Board.
Ibarra, Martin D. '07 (CHI) Chicago, IL St. Agnes of Bohemia.
Ibarra, Martin *o.f.m.* '08 (OAK) Oakland, CA St. Elizabeth; [M] Oakland, CA Franciscan Friars (Province of Santa Barbara).
Ibay, Eulalio (Yul) P. '98 (CC) Corpus Christi, TX Our Lady Star of the Sea.
Ibe, Anselm '01 (LC)[D] Spiritual Services Dept.
Ibe, Bartholomew '98 (ALX) Evergreen, LA Little Flower.
Ibe, Ignatius A. *s.m.m.m.* '03 (ALX) Marksville, LA Holy Ghost.
Ibe, Sanctus K. '00 (MAD) Clinton, WI St. Stephen.
Ibe, Titus (HRT) West Haven, CT St. Paul's.
Ibebuike, Chuma P. '79 (LR) McGehee, AR St. Mary; Crossett, AR Holy Cross.
Ibeh, Eliseus *m.s.p.* '89 (AUS) Florence, TX Santa Rosa.
Ibekwe, James O. '85 (HRT) Hartford, CT Hartford Hospital; Hartford, CT St. Augustine.
Ibemere, Julian '98 (OWN) LaCenter, KY St. Mary; Paducah, KY Rosary Chapel.
Ibok, Augustine *s.m.p.* '07 (SPC)[F] Marionville, MO The Society of Our Mother of Peace, Sons of Our Mother of Peace.
Ibok, Matthew '96 (MIA) Miami, FL Our Lady of Lourdes.
Idagbo, Osang *c.m.* '05 (BEL) Waterloo, IL SS. Peter and Paul.
Idler, Peter M. '97 (CAM) On Leave of Absence.
Idra, Augustine *a.j.* '97 (KNX) Chattanooga, TN Our Lady of Perpetual Help; [A] Chattanooga, TN Notre Dame High School.
Idranyi, Edmund M. '54 (VNN) San Luis Obispo, CA Saint Anne Retired.
Idzik, George '73 (NEW) Retired.
Ifeanyi, Ethel Iwu '90 (PAT) Denville, NJ St. Clare Hospital.
Iffert, John C. '97 (BEL) Salem, IL St. Theresa of Avila; Mount Vernon, IL St. Mary.
Iffert, Wilbert J. '52 (BEL) Retired.
Ifionu, Bartholomew *s.m.m.m.* '04 (BAK) John Day, OR St. Elizabeth.
Ifkovits, Edward M. *s.j.* (BAL) Baltimore, MD St. Ignatius Church.
Igboanusi, Gerald "Chi" '08 (OM) Omaha, NE St. Stephen the Martyr.
Iglesias, Clement '58 (BEA) Retired.
Iglesias, Fernando Gonzalez '56 (LA) Retired.
Ignaci, Antony Roja (NY) Bronx, NY St. Theresa of the Infant Jesus.
Ignaci, Antonyraja '98 (NY) Bronx, NY Calvary Hospital.
Ignacio, Alejandro '74 (FRS) Fresno, CA Sacred Heart.
Ignacio, Pilar Bernal (SD).
Ignacio, Roberto '00 (TR) Riverton, NJ Sacred Heart.
Ignasik, Slawomir (JOL) Itasca, IL St. Peter the Apostle.
Ignaszak, Michael A. '84 (MIL)[H] Milwaukee, WI Holy Wisdom Academy; Milwaukee, WI St. Helen; Milwaukee, WI St. John Kanty; Milwaukee, WI St. Alexander.
Ignatius, Lourduraj *s.a.c.* '88 (PEO) Ottawa, IL St. Patrick's; Ottawa (Naplate), IL St. Mary's.
Igoe, Martin S. '62 (BGP) District Spiritual Directors Retired.
Igrobay, Manuel D. '89 (SFR) San Francisco, CA St. Charles Borromeo.
Igwe, Evaristus A. *c.m.* '07 (BRK)[T] Jamaica, NY Vincentian Residence.
Igwe, Paschal '96 (DET) Farmington Hills, MI Botsford Hospital.
Igwenwanne, Fidelis '90 (PHX) Phoenix, AZ Maricopa Medical Center.
Igweonu, Romanus '92 (BUR) Ludlow, VT Annunciation of the Blessed Virgin Mary.
Iheaka, Emmanuel K. '90 (MO) DEPARTMENT OF VETERANS AFFAIRS HOSPITALS AND CHAPLAINS.
Iheaka, Emmanuel K. '90 (PH) Coatesville, PA Veterans Administration Medical Center; Honey Brook, PA St. Peter.
Iheanaho, Kenneth '90 (TLS) Tulsa, OK St. Augustine's; Tulsa, OK St. Monica's.
Ihedioha, Hilary A. '85 (SAN) Brady, TX St. Patrick's.
Ihedoro, Christian *c.m.f.* '66 (LA)[V] Rancho Dominguez, CA Dominguez Seminary Inc.
Iheke, Uche G. *s.m.m.m.* '98 (MO) Army Chaplains.
Ihemedu, Emmanuel I. '06 (HRT) Hartford, CT St. Justin; Hartford, CT St. Michael.
Ihewulezi, Cajetan *c.ss.p.* (STL) Saint Louis, MO Sts. Teresa and Bridget.
Ihnatowicz, Janusz '62 (GAL)[O] Houston, TX Residence of the Basilian Fathers of the University of St. Thomas.
Ihrie, Bernard R. '55 (WDC) Retired.
Ihuoma, Alphonsus (PBL) La Junta, CO Our Lady of Guadalupe/St. Patrick.
Ijeoma, John Vianney '88 (MO) Army Chaplains.
Ijere, Ignatius (GRY)[D] Dyer, IN St. Margaret Mercy Healthcare Centers, South Campus.
Ikalowych, Jerry '08 (SJP) Conyers, GA Mother of God; Presbyters.
Ikataere, John *m.s.c.* '72 (CI) Chuuk, FM Mortlock.
Ike, Anthony '94 (STA) Switzerland, FL San Juan Del Rio.

Ike, Roberto '94 (JC) Jefferson City, MO St. Francis Xavier.
Ikemelu, Hyacinth I. '99 (BRK) Floral Park, NY Our Lady of the Snows; Long Island Jewish Hospital.
Ikeocha, Ikechukwu '00 (LA) Canoga Park, CA Our Lady of the Valley.
Ikhane, Irenaeus '01 (NY) Beacon, NY St. John the Evangelist.
Ikwuegbu, Charles (HRT) Forestville, CT St. Matthew.
Ilango, Xavier '88 (CR) Callaway, MN Assumption; Frazee, MN Sacred Heart; Priests' Council.
Ilano, Francis '06 (LA) Hacienda Heights, CA St. John Vianney.
Ilano, Jovencio '96 (RIC) Retired.
Ileka, Sylvester C. '00 (BRK) The Mount Sinai Hospital of Queens; Long Island City, NY St. Rita.
Ilgen, Timothy W. '03 (SEA) Longview, WA St. Rose de Viterbo.
Ililau, John Paul '90 (CI) Palau, PW St. John Baptist; [C] Manresa Jesuit House.
Illechukwu, Pius N. '80 (FTW) Walkerton, IN St. Patrick.
Illig, A. Mark '85 (BUF) Bowmansville, NY Sacred Heart.
Illikattil, Mathew (KAL) Mattawan, MI St. John Bosco.
Illo, Joseph P. '91 (STO) Modesto, CA St. Joseph Church of Modesto (Pastor of); Deans.
Illuri, Irudaya Raj '89 (SCR) Swoyersville, PA Holy Name/St. Mary's.
Ilnicki, Theodosius (Roman) *o.s.b.m.* '88 (RVC)[M] Glen Cove, NY St. Josaphat's Monastery, Novitiate and Retreat House.
Ilnicki, Theodosius *o.s.b.m.* '88 (STF) Judge; Ecumenical Commission; [B] Glen Cove, NY Basilian Fathers Novitiate of the Order of St. Basil the Great.
Ilnitskyi, Marko '05 (BUF) Lackawanna, NY Our Lady of Victory National Shrine.
Ilogon–Llabore, Denish *o.s.m.* '96 (P)[L] Portland, OR The Grotto, The National Sanctuary of Our Sorrowful Mother.
Ilokaba, Damian O. '86 (MO) Army Chaplains.
Imamshah, Harold '90 (ALX) Cloutierville, LA St. John the Baptist; Elected Members.
Imbarrato, Stephen '05 (SFE) Bernalillo, NM Our Lady of Sorrows.
Imbelli, Robert P. '66 (BO) On Duty Outside the Archdiocese; Newton, MA Sacred Heart.
Imberi, Anthony '62 (SFS) Retired.
Imbroll, Gregory E. *o.f.m.* '57 (NY)[EE] New York Franciscan Province of the Immaculate Conception.
Imfeld, Thomas J. '59 (LEX) Retired.
Imgrund, Norman P. '64 (ALT) Everett, PA St. John the Evangelist; Clearville, PA Seven Dolors B.V.M.
Imhangbe, Samson '02 (NY) Yonkers, NY St. Eugene.
Imhof, James *s.m.* '51 (SJ)[M] Cupertino, CA The Marianist Center.
Imholte, Otto *s.s.c.* '63 (FgM) St Columbans, NE House of Post–Graduate Studies.
Imming, Donald '60 (SFS) Retired.
Imo, Cletus '91 (SB) Alta Loma, CA St. Peter & St. Paul.
Imokhai, Charles '68 (NY) New Rochelle, NY Blessed Sacrament.
Imoru, Godwin '03 (BEA) Beaumont, TX Blessed Sacrament; Beaumont, TX Our Mother of Mercy.
Inbaraj, Victor '95 (LC) Boyceville, WI St. Luke; Mondovi, WI St. Joseph; Elk Mound, WI St. Joseph.
Incardona, Victor *m.i.c.* (SPR)[H] Stockbridge, MA Congregation of Marian Fathers of The Immaculate Conception of the Most Blessed Virgin Mary.
Ince, Michael W. '64 (STP) Elysian, MN St. Andrew; Waterville, MN Holy Trinity.
Ince, Owen F. '00 (NEW) On Duty Outside the Archdiocese; Newark, NJ Immaculate Conception.
India, Stephen J. *c.m.* '49 (PH)[Y].
Infante, Angel *t.o.r.* '08 (FWT) Fort Worth, TX All Saints.
Infante, Joseph '94 (RNO) Reno, NV St. Albert the Great.
Infante, Richard A. '92 (PIT) Pittsburgh, PA Our Lady of Grace.
Ingalls, Fred D. '74 (BUF) Retired.
Ingelmo–Benavente, Manuel '99 (DAL) Grand Prairie, TX Immaculate Conception.
Ingels, Gregory G. '74 (SFR) Absent on Leave.
Ingels, Kyle Thomas '05 (WDC) Special Ministries.
Ingemie, Dominic '67 (ALB) Saratoga Springs, NY St. Peter; Presbyteral Council; Diocesan Board of Consultors.
Ingham, G. Nicholas *o.p.* '81 (PRO)[P] Providence St. Thomas Aquinas Priory at Providence College.
Ingham, Rev. Msgr. Jeffrey A. '75 (R) Southern Pines, NC St. Anthony of Padua; Deans; Diocesan Consultors; Council of Priests.
Inghilterra, Vincent J. '72 (MO) Military Chaplains; Army Chaplains.
Ingiyimbere, Fidele *s.j.* '09 (BO)[U] Cambridge, MA Rahner House.
Inglot, Mark '81 (LAN) East Lansing, MI St. John the Evangelist Church and Student Center; East Lansing, MI St. Thomas Aquinas; [N] East Lansing, MI St. John the Evangelist Church and Student Center; Priests' Assignment Commission.
Ingold, Michael L. '91 (GB) Neenah, WI St. Margaret Mary.
Ingram, Brian '90 (RVC) Priests' Personnel Policy Board.
Ingram, Walter (Mike) '02 (SAV) Macon, GA Holy Spirit; Macon Deanery.
Inmaculada, Juan Evangelista de Maria *o.c.d.* '09 (SAT)[L] San Antonio, TX Discalced Carmelite Fathers of San Antonio.
Inman, Robert D. '03 (YAK) On Duty Outside the Diocese.
Innes, Ben R. *o.f.m.* '84 (P) Portland, OR Ascension; Aumsville, OR St. Mary – Shaw.
Innocenti, Mark '99 (SCL) Little Falls, MN Holy Family; Little Falls, MN Our Lady of Lourdes; Presbyteral Council; Advocates.
Innocenzi, Rev. Msgr. James G. '76 (TR) Titusville, NJ St. George; Assistant Chancellors; Associate Judicial Vicars.
Intal, Arlan G. *m.s.* '05 (SB) Lucerne Valley, CA St. Paul; [I] Apple Valley, CA Missionaries of Our Lady of La Salette. MS; Apple Valley, CA Our Lady of the Desert.
Intovigne, Raymond D. '64 (NOR) Co–Directors; Coventry, CT St. Mary.
Intranuovo, Ralph *s.c.j.* '83 (SP)[N] Pinellas Park, FL Priests of the Sacred Heart.
Introini, Rev. Msgr. Elso C. (PAT) Retired.
Inverso, Leon J. '85 (TR) Leave of Absence.
Inwang, Augustine Etemma *m.s.p.* '90 (BAL) Baltimore, MD St. Veronica.
Inwang, Augustine *m.s.p.* (BAL)[M] Baltimore, MD Mercy Health Services Inc.
Inyanwachi, Edward S. '94 (SFR) Burlingame, CA St. Catherine of Siena.
Inzina, Joseph Robert '60 (SHP) Priests' Retirement Board Retired.
Iodice, Ciro *o.f.m.* '72 (NY)[EE] New York Franciscan Province of the Immaculate Conception.
Iorio, Peter J. '93 (KNX)[K] Knoxville, TN Diocesan Council of Catholic Women; Priestly Life and Ministry; Vocations; Cleveland, TN St. Therese of Lisieux.
Iovino, Paul '61 (PAT) Auditors Retired.
Ipasu, Gabriel '03 (ORL) Lakeland, FL Church of the Resurrection.
Ipolito, Pascal D. '70 (BUF) West Falls, NY St. George.
Ippolito, Robert F. *m.s.* '73 (R) Shallotte, NC St. Brendan the Navigator.
Irace, Dominic P. '75 (ARL) Retired.
Ireland, David R. '83 (CLV) South Euclid, OH St. Gregory the Great.
Irish, Robert '92 (LAN) On Duty Outside the Diocese.
Irizarry, Alan M. '83 (MO) On Duty Outside the Diocese; Army Chaplains.
Irizarry, Elvin A. '97 (ARE) Utuado, PR Our Lady of Sorrows.
Irizarry, Kenneth D. Moore *s.e.m.v.* '09 (ARE) Arecibo, PR Our Lady of Guadalupe.
Irizarry Roman, Elvin A. '97 (ARE) Priest's Senate (Consejo Presbiteral); Prison Services.
Irizzary, Jose Fernando *o.f.m.cap.* '01 (SJN)[C] Rio Piedras, PR Fraternidad Santa Maria de Los Angeles.
Iroh, Anthony '94 (BRK) Brooklyn, NY St. Catherine of Genoa; Rosedale, NY St. Clare.
Iromenu, Anthony '95 (FRS) Bakersfield, CA St. Joseph.
Ironuma, Donatus (SPR)[E] Springfield, MA CHE – The Mercy Hospital, Inc.; Springfield, MA Our Lady of Hope.
Irrgang, Kenneth E. '68 (NU) Retired.
Irudamoney, Arul Joseph '91 (BIS) Glen Ullin, ND Sacred Heart of Jesus; Glen Ullin, ND St. Joseph; Hebron, ND St. Clement.
Irudaya, Jerard Raj Irudayanathan *c.pp.s* '97 (CIN)[N] Dayton Provincial Office of the Cincinnati Province of the Society of the Precious Blood.
Irudayanathan, Arokiasamy '83 (NEW) Montclair, NJ Immaculate Conception.
Irudayaraj, Arul Pragasam *s.v.d.* '06 (SB) San Bernardino, CA San Bernardino Community Hospital.
Irudayaraj, Nalazala '93 (SCR) Hazleton, PA SS. Cyril & Methodius, Hazleton; Hazleton, PA St. Stanislaus.
Irudeya, Jerard Raj Irudayanathan *c.pp.s.* '96 (OAK) Newark, CA St. Edward.
Irvin, Charles '67 (LAN) College of Consultors; Promoter of Justice Retired.
Irving, Alfred E. '71 (PRT) Portland, ME St. Louis; Portland, ME Maine Medical Center.
Irving, G. Peter '83 (LA) Long Beach, CA Holy Innocents.
Irwin, Jaime *c.s.c.* '65 (SB)[I] Coachella, CA Congregation of Holy Cross; Coachella, CA Our Lady of Soledad.
Irwin, James W. *c.s.c.* '65 (FTW)[H] Notre Dame Congregation of Holy Cross, Indiana Province, Provincial House.
Irwin, Joseph F. '62 (NY) Mamaroneck, NY Most Holy Trinity.
Irwin, Joseph M. '05 (OKL) Duncan, OK Assumption.
Irwin, Rev. Msgr. Kevin W. '71 (NY) On Duty Outside the Archdiocese; [C] Catholic University of America, The.
Irwin, Michael Den '01 (MOB) Mobile, AL St. Vincent de Paul; Priests' Eucharistic League.
Irwin, Patrick F. '59 (MAN) Retired.
Irwin, Rev. Msgr. Patrick '69 (SP)[F] Clearwater, FL Little Nazareth Early Childhood Center; Clearwater, FL St. Cecelia; Incardination Committee.
Irwin, Robert C. '95 (BAK) Council of Priests and Diocesan Consultors; Eastern; Board of Education; Campus Ministry Apostolate; Ontario, OR Blessed Sacrament.
Irwin, Robert '78 (FAR) On Duty Outside the Diocese.
Isaac, Dominic *j.c.d.* '87 (PH) Apostleship of the Sea; Philadelphia, PA St. William; Pakistani Apostolate.
Isaacson, James *s.j.c.* '04 (CHI) Chicago, IL St. John Cantius; [P] Chicago, IL Canons Regular of Saint John Cantius.
Isacc, Jose '75 (RNO) Priest Personnel Board.
Isacsson, Alfred *o.carm.* '58 (NY) Middletown, NY Our Lady of Mt. Carmel.
Isaza, Pedro Alejandro Moscoso '03 (PCE) Ponce, PR Cathedral of Our Lady of Guadalupe.
Ischay, Matthew A. '75 (CLV) Cleveland, OH Blessed Sacrament.
Ishida, Michael L. '06 (SPK) Wilbur, WA St. Joseph; Wilbur, WA Sacred Heart; Members.
Ishmael, Keith E. '03 (ALX) Jena, LA St. Mary; Elected Members.
Isi, Emmanuel (BIR) Bessemer, AL St. Francis of Assisi.
Isidor, Rahab '06 (SPC) Billings, MO St. Joseph.
Isinta, Christopher D. '04 (NEW) Roseland, NJ Our Lady of the Blessed Sacrament.
Isla, Elias (NY) New York, NY St. Jude.
Isla Chavez, Mario Genaro '04 (PCE) Salinas, PR Our Lady of Monserrat.
Isopo, Dominic '80 (ALB) Schenectady, NY St. Luke.
Issac, Jose '75 (RNO) Sparks, NV Holy Cross Catholic Community; Diocesan Board of Consultors; Presbyteral Council.
Issing, Daniel J. *c.s.c.* '90 (SCR)[C] Holy Cross Community.
Ittiyappara, Mathew '67 (SR) Retired.
Itube, Rene J. '64 (SFR) Deans.
Itukulapati, Joji '88 (SFS) Faulkton, SD St. Thomas the Apostle.
Iturbe, Rene *s.m.* '74 (SFR) San Francisco, CA Notre Dame des Victoires.
Iturreta, Pablo Daniel Munoz *i.v.e.* '06 (WDC) Mount Rainier, MD St. James.
Iturrizaga, Johnny C. *c.m.v.* '97 (ARE) Sabana Hoyos, PR Nuestra Senora de Fatima.
Itzaina, John *s.d.b.* '74 (SFR) San Francisco, CA SS. Peter and Paul.
Iulio, Vaiula '06 (SPP) Pago Pago, AS Church of St. Peter and Paul; Pago Pago, AS St. Peter Chanel–Sa'ilele.
Ivan, Nicholas '56 (PRM) Retired.
Ivanov, Mykola '05 (PHU) Pottstown, PA SS. Peter and Paul; Pottstown, PA St. Michael's; Defender of the Bond.
Ivanovich, Martin J. '08 (PH) West Chester, PA St. Maximilian Kolbe.
Ivans, Joseph *o.c.d.* '53 (GRY)[H] Munster, IN Discalced Carmelite Fathers Monastery.
Ivany, Mark '08 (WDC) Bethesda, MD Little Flower.
Ivers, Rev. Msgr. Leslie J. '79 (NY) Bronx, NY St. Frances de Chantal; Archdiocesan Consultors; Prison Apostolate.
Ivers, Victor J. '45 (CHI) Retired.
Ivey, David J. '86 (AUS) Brenham, TX St. Mary of the Immaculate Conception; Vandenberg Air Force Base.
Ivory, Rev. Msgr. Thomas P. '64 (NEW) West Orange, NJ St. Joseph's Retired.
Iwan, Janusz '76 (DET) Detroit, MI St. Hyacinth.
Iwaniec, Wieslaw '86 (SAT) Uvalde, TX Sacred Heart.
Iwanowski, Thomas B. '75 (NEW) Office of Divine Worship.
Iwasiw, Nestor '93 (PHU) Presbyteral Council; Archeparchial Seminary Advisory and Admissions Board; Olyphant, PA SS. Cyril and Methodius; Simpson, PA SS. Peter and Paul; Procurator/Advocate.
Iwele, Gooe *o.m.i.* (NY) New York, NY St. Andrew.
Iwen, Emmanuel E. '84 (SEA) Vancouver, WA St. Joseph.
Iwu, Ifeanyi '90 (PAT) Dover, NJ St. Mary's.
Iwu, Pius A. '77 (LR) On Special or Other Diocesan Assignment; Presbyteral Council.
Iwuala, Ishamel '87 (NY) Bronx, NY Bronx–Lebanon Hospital Center.
Iwuala, Peter O. '09 (NEW) New Providence, NJ Our Lady of Peace.
Iwuc, Anthony D. '53 (PRO)[P] Providence St. John Vianney Residence Retired.
Iwuchukwu, Azuka (WDC)[L] Washington, DC Georgetown University Hospital.
Iwuji, Luke Okecukwu '97 (DET)[H] Livonia, MI St. Mary Mercy Hospital.

Iwuji, Luke '97 (DET) Dearborn, MI Oakwood Hospital.
Iwuji, Matthew C. '74 (AUS) Austin, TX Sacred Heart.
Iwuji, Matthew C. '74 (SAT) Defenders of the Bond.
Iwuji, Paulinus *s.m.m.m.* '01 (AUS) Austin, TX Seton/Brackenridge Hospital.
Iwuoha, Anastasius (SLC) Sandy, UT Saint Thomas More Catholic Church LLC 248; [E] Salt Lake City, UT Christus Health Utah.
Iwuoha, Kevin '97 (SFE) Moriarty, NM Estancia Valley Catholic Parish.
Izac, Andre C. '64 (WDC) On Duty Outside the Archdiocese.
Izczuk, Cyril *o.s.b.m.* '89 (STF) New York, NY St. George.
Izen, Michael J. '05 (STP) Maple Lake, MN St. Timothy.
Izer, Rt. Rev. Wesley W. '77 (VNN) Gilbert, AZ St. Thomas the Apostle; Finance Officer; Building Commission; Eparchial Finance Commission; Chancellor; College of Consultors; Finance Officer; Finance Council; Building and Sacred Arts; Pension Committee.
Izer, Rt. Rev. Wesley '77 (VNN) Personnel Board.
Izral, John '56 (BLX) Retired.
Izral, John '56 (SJP) Ford City, PA St. Mary; Arnold, PA St. Vladimir; Presbyters.
Izuka, Emmanuel '97 (SFE) Albuquerque, NM St. Jude Thaddeus.
Izyk, Andrew (CHI) Chicago, IL St. Monica.
Izzo, Brian A. '98 (PH) Priests' Personnel Board; Springfield, PA Holy Cross.
Izzo, D. Dominic *o.p.* '94 (FgM) New York, NY Province of St. Joseph (Eastern).
Izzo, David Dominic *o.p.* '94 (NY)[EE] New York, NY St. Vincent Ferrer Priory; [II] New York, NY St. Thomas Aquinas Foundation; New York, NY.
Izzo, Januarius *o.f.m.* '62 (NY)[EE] New York Franciscan Province of the Immaculate Conception.

J

Jablonske, William (LC)[D] Chippewa Falls, WI St. Joseph's Hospital.
Jablonski, Edward J. '96 (PH) Downingtown, PA St. Joseph; [W] Downingtown, PA Catholic Health Care Services–Villa Saint Martha; [V] Downingtown, PA St. Martha Manor.
Jablonski, Joseph *m.s.c.* '76 (RCK)[G].
Jablonski, Rev. Msgr. William W. '63 (RVC) East Rockaway, NY St. Raymond's.
Jabo, Scott W. '90 (E)[C] Erie, PA Cathedral Preparatory School; [D] Erie, PA Villa Maria Academy; Erie, PA St. James.
Jabusch, Willard F. '56 (CHI)[W] Wilmette, IL Musica Pacis Retired.
Jach, Edward M. *s.m.* '64 (CIN) Cincinnati, OH St. Francis de Sales; [N] Cincinnati, OH De Sales Crossings Marianist Community; Priest Councilors.
Jacinto, Martin Borbon '01 (NEW) Jersey City, NJ Our Lady of Mercy.
Jack, Cuthbert A. *o.s.b.* '90 (GBG)[G] Latrobe, PA Saint Vincent Archabbey.
Jack, Cuthbert A. *o.s.b.* '90 (PBR) Homer City, PA St. Mary's Holy Protection.
Jack, Duane C. '67 (PEO) Colona, IL St. Patrick's.
Jack, J. Robert '92 (CIN)[B] Cincinnati, OH Mt. St. Mary's Seminary of the West.
Jackiewicz, Frederick W. '71 (TR) Leave of Absence.
Jacklin, Richard '84 (JOL) Kankakee, IL Shapiro Development Center; Bonfield, IL Sacred Heart.
Jackovic, George V. '46 (PIT) Retired.
Jackson, James M. '75 (WIL) Delaware State Correctional Center.
Jackson, James R. *m.m.* '58 (FgM) Maryknoll, NY MARYKNOLL.
Jackson, James *f.s.s.p.* '85 (DEN) Littleton, CO Our Lady of Mount Carmel (Latin Mass Community).
Jackson, Joseph M. '74 (CHI) Chicago, IL St. Ignatius.
Jackson, Lawrence J. '60 (DET) Retired.
Jackson, Robert H. '84 (CLV) Barberton, OH Prince of Peace; Presbyteral Council; Presbyteral Conveners.
Jackson, Robert '54 (RCK) Retired.
Jackson, Thomas Martin *o.p.* '92 (SFE) Albuquerque, NM St. Thomas Aquinas University Parish; [K] Albuquerque, NM St. Thomas Aquinas (Newman Center) University Parish; ALBQ: Aquinas Newman Center.
Jacob, Abraham M. '80 (CHI) Chicago, IL Our Lady of Victory; [J] Chicago, IL Our Lady of the Resurrection Medical Center.
Jacob, Abraham Mutholath '80 (SYM) Vicar General (Syncellus).
Jacob, Anthony J. *o.s.b.* '65 (JOL)[L] Lisle, IL St. Procopius Abbey; Lisle, IL.
Jacob, Jerome J. '92 (CHI) Arlington Heights, IL St. Edna.
Jacob, Jose K. *s.m.m.* (BEL) Waterloo, IL St. Patrick; Waterloo, IL Immaculate Conception.
Jacob, Joseph E. (LFT) Retired.
Jacob, Leonardo M. '88 (RCK) Elizabeth, IL St. Mary; Hanover, IL St. John the Evangelist.
Jacob, Lijoy *o.carm* '04 (WDC)[B] Washington, DC Whitefriars Hall.
Jacobi, Arthur '81 (DET) Retired.
Jacobi, Joseph A. '91 (OKL) Oklahoma City, OK St. Eugene's; Consultors Archdiocesan; Council of Priests Archdiocesan.
Jacobs, Charles E. '86 (HRT) Hartford, CT Holy Trinity.
Jacobs, Gilbert H. *o.praem.* '55 (GB)[J] De Pere, WI St. Norbert Abbey.
Jacobs, James T. '43 (GB) Retired.
Jacobs, Richard A. (PAT) Retired.
Jacobs, Richard M. *o.s.a.* '83 (JOL)[L] New Lenox, IL Augustinian Friary.
Jacobs, Richard *o.s.a.* '76 (PH)[C] Villanova University.
Jacobs, William '03 (KAL) Benton Harbor, MI Ss. John & Bernard; Diocesan Finance Council.
Jacobson, Clifford '96 (CHY) Clergy Continuing Education Grants; Gillette, WY St. Matthew's; Vicars Forane.
Jacobson, Gary '65 (P) Retired.
Jacobson, James *s.j.* (SPK)[J] Spokane, WA Regis Community.
Jacobus, Michael J. '08 (MAR) Ontonagon, MI Holy Family; Ontonagon, MI St. Mary; White Pine, MI St. Jude.
Jacquel, John B. '83 (E) Co Directors; Erie, PA St. John the Baptist.
Jacquemin, George '72 (CIN) Cincinnati, OH St. Clare; Vicarri Foranei (Deans).
Jacques, Alfred '60 (PRT) Rumford, ME Parish of the Holy Savior Retired.
Jacques, Donald W. '53 (PRT) Retired.
Jacques, Ernest J. *s.j.* '66 (NO)[P] New Orleans, LA Ignatius Residence.
Jacques, Eugene F. '80 (NO) Gretna, LA St. Cletus.
Jacques, Michael P. *s.s.e.* '82 (NO) New Orleans, LA St. Peter Claver; Deans; Archdiocesan Consultors.
Jacques, Roger N. '78 (BO) Awaiting Assignment.; Health Leave.
Jacunski, Robert D. '56 (NEW)[M] Caldwell, NJ The Rev. Msgr. James F. Kelley Residence for Retired Priests Retired.
Jadin, Samuel D. *o.praem.* '55 (GB)[K] Manitowoc, WI Holy Family Convent of Franciscan Sisters of Christian Charity.
Jadotte, Jean '06 (MIA) Miami, FL Notre Dame d'Haiti; Haitians.
Jadwisiak, Edmund '79 (PRM) Retired.
Jaeb, Maurus P. *o.s.b.* '95 (OKL)[I] Shawnee, OK St. Gregory's Abbey.
Jaeger, David *o.f.m.* '86 (FgM) Washington, DC COMMISSARIAT OF THE HOLY LAND.
Jaeger, David Maria A. *o.f.m.* '86 (SAT) Judges.
Jaeger, James A. '06 (MIL) Elkhorn, WI St. Patrick.
Jaeger, James P. '86 (ROC) Hammondsport, NY St. Gabriel; Bath, NY St. Mary; Air National Guard Chaplains.
Jaeger, Louis M. '73 (DUB) Lay Formation Advisory Board; American Martyrs Retreat House Advisory Board; [G] Waterloo, IA Columbus High School; Waterloo, IA Sacred Heart; [G] Waterloo, IA Cedar Valley Catholic Schools; Priestly Life and Ministry Committee.
Jaeger, Rev. Msgr. Robert E. '90 (COS) Colorado Springs, CO Saint Paul; Vicar General; Vicar for Clergy; Presbyteral Council; College of Consultors; Vicar General; Vicar General.
Jaenicke, Alfred J. '54 (HRT) Retired.
Jaffe, J.D. '03 (ARL) Fairfax, VA St. Leo's.
Jaffe, Joel D. '03 (ARL)[D] Fairfax, VA Paul VI Catholic High School.
Jagdfeld, Lawrence *o.f.m.* '75 (CHI)[N] Cicero, IL San Damiano Friary Order of Friars Minor.
Jagela, Walter M. '94 (WH) New Martinsville, WV St. Vincent de Paul; [O] Bethany, WV St. John Fisher Catholic Chapel; [O] West Liberty, WV West Liberty State College, St. Thomas Aquinas Campus Ministry.
Jagielski, James J. '77 (DET) Retired.
Jagodensky, Joe *s.d.s.* '80 (MIL)[N] Milwaukee, WI Alexian Village of Milwaukee, Inc.
Jagodzinski, Charles *o.f.m.conv.* '68 (BUF)[O] Athol Springs, NY St. Francis of Assisi Friary.
Jagodzinski, Rev. Msgr. John J. '62 (PH) Broomall, PA St. Pius X.
Jagoe, Bede R. *o.p.* '60 (CHI)[N] River Forest, IL St. Thomas Aquinas Priory.
Jagudilla, Julian *o.f.m.* '08 (R) Raleigh, NC St. Francis of Assisi.
Jakel, Pat G. '85 (SFD) Troy, IL St. Jerome.
Jakobiak, Arthur '56 (SFE) Retired.
Jakopac, George I. '00 (BAL) Special Assignment.
Jakows, Ronald M. '90 (PH) Doylestown, PA Our Lady of Mount Carmel.
Jaksina, Edward S. '55 (HRT) Seymour, CT Good Shepherd.
Jakub, Joseph A. '06 (TR)[B] Lawrenceville, NJ Notre Dame High School; Campaign for Human Development.
Jakubauskas, Richard A. '99 (WOR) Petersham, MA St. Peter; Athol, MA St. Francis; Athol, MA Our Lady Immaculate; Members.
Jakubco, Bernard *m.s.c.* '64 (PT) Perry, FL Immaculate Conception.
Jakubek, Eugene J. *s.j.* '54 (OM)[K] Omaha, NE Jesuit Community at Creighton University.
Jakubik, Richard '93 (CHI) Wilmette, IL St. Francis Xavier; Associate Administrators.
Jakubowicz, Greg *o.f.m.* '04 (ALB)[B] Loudonville, NY Siena College; [B] Siena College; [Q] Loudonville, NY Siena College.
Jakubowicz, Gregory P. *o.f.m.* '04 (ALB)[B] Siena College.
Jakubowski, Allen F. '75 (LC) Durand, WI St. Mary's Assumption; Durand, WI Holy Rosary; Durand, WI Sacred Heart of Jesus; Personnel Council.
Jalbert, Edward *c.j.* '87 (LA)[B] Santa Maria, CA St. Joseph Seminary (Josephite Fathers' Novitiate); [D] Santa Maria, CA St. Joseph High School.
Jalbert, Jason Y. '03 (MAN) Masters of Ceremonies; Vocations Office; Office for Worship.
Jalbert, Robert A. *m.m.* '79 (NY)[EE] Maryknoll Maryknoll Fathers and Brothers.
Jallas, Robert J. '84 (SFD) Springfield, IL St. Agnes.
Jamail, Rev. Msgr. Michael A. '60 (BEA) Vicar General and Moderator of the Curia; Diocesan College of Consultors; Promoter of Justice; Defender of Bond; Psychologists for the Tribunal; Diaconate Formation; Beaumont, TX St. Anne; Presbyteral Council.
James, David J. '91 (SY) Syracuse, NY Veterans Administration Hospital.
James, David John '91 (MO) DEPARTMENT OF VETERANS AFFAIRS HOSPITALS AND CHAPLAINS.
James, Rev. Msgr. David L. '96 (ALN) Allentown, PA St. Francis of Assisi; Promoter of Justice; Advocates; College of Consultors; Appointed Members; Defenders of the Bond.
James, Rev. Msgr. Joseph W. '57 (LUB)[B] Slaton, TX Our Lady of Mercy Retreat Center Retired.
James, Peter Paul *o.f.m.* '51 (CIN)[N] Cincinnati, OH St. Francis Seraph Friary Retired.
James, Thomas *s.v.d.* '69 (LAF) Lafayette, LA Immaculate Heart of Mary.
James, V. Warwick '80 (SJ) Los Altos, CA St. Simon.
James, Rev. Msgr. William R. '54 (MOB) Robertsdale, AL St. Patrick.
Jameson, Rev. Msgr. W. Ronald '68 (WDC) Washington, DC St. Matthew Cathedral; Deans; Archdiocesan Sacred Arts Committee; Commission on Sacred Art and Architecture.
Jamieson, Andrew '88 (TR) Tabernacle, NJ Holy Eucharist.
Jamin, David S. '08 (BR) Special Assignment.
Jamin, David (NO)[A] St. Benedict, LA St. Joseph Seminary College.
Jamison, Dale *o.f.m.* '74 (PHX) Sacaton, AZ St. Peter's; Native American Ministry Office; Native American Ministry – Field Office.
Jamison, Dale '74 (PHX) Laveen, AZ St. John The Baptist.
Jamnicky, John A. '72 (CHI) Antioch, IL St. Raphael the Archangel.
Jamros, Daniel P. *s.j.* '76 (BO)[U] Boston The Society of Jesus of New England–Provincial Offices.
Jamros, Daniel P. *s.j.* '76 (BUF)[O] Buffalo, NY Canisius Jesuit Community Inc.
Jamroz, Sigmund S. *m.m.* '66 (FgM) Maryknoll, NY MARYKNOLL.
Janaczek, Joseph J. '71 (BUF) Falconer, NY St. Patrick; Falconer, NY Our Lady of Loreto.
Janak, Gary W. '88 (VIC) Vice–Chancellor; Diocesan Consultors; El Campo Deanery; Judges; Priests' Personnel Board; Victim Assistance Coordinator; Presbyteral Council; El Campo, TX St. Philip the Apostle.
Janas, Camillus *o.f.m.* '60 (CHI)[N] Chicago, IL Holy Name Friary.
Janasik, Daniel R. '09 (MIL) Mequon, WI St. Francis Borgia.
Jancarz, Janusz Jay '83 (VEN) Parrish, FL Saint Frances Xavier Cabrini.
Janczak, Krzysztof '05 (CHI) Niles, IL St. John Brebeuf.
Janda, James A. '72 (SLC) Retired.
Jandernoa, Ronald L. '94 (MET) Blairstown, NJ St. Jude; College of Consultors; Deans.
Janeczek, Vladimir '59 (GRY) Hammond, IN St. Casimir Retired.
Janelli, Rev. Msgr. Anthony '64 (FRS) Yosemite National Park, CA Our Lady of the Snows Retired.
Janes, David A. '83 (SFS) Retired.
Janes, David '75 (P) Yamhill, OR St. John.
Janette, Paul '63 (MIL) Retired.
Janezic, Lawrence *o.f.m.* '78 (CHI)[N] Chicago, IL St. Peter's Friary.
Jang, Min–ho '99 (PHX) Tempe, AZ St. Columba Kim Roman Catholic Mission.
Janicki, Carl F. '94 (PH) Flourtown, PA St. Genevieve; [D] Philadelphia, PA Cardinal Dougherty High School.
Janicki, Laurian *o.f.m.* '64 (PSC) Provincial Councilors:; [A] Sybertsville, PA Holy Dormition Friary; Sybertsville, PA Assumption B.V.M. Province.
Janiezic, Lawrence *o.f.m.* '78 (WDC)[B] Silver Spring, MD Holy Name College.

Janiga, Bruce G. '83 (NEW)[C] West Orange, NJ Seton Hall Preparatory School.
Janiga, Joseph '45 (DET) Retired.
Janik, Anthony F. *o.f.m.* '70 (GRY)[D] Crown Point, IN Saint Anthony Medical Center; [H] Cedar Lake, IN Our Lady of Lourdes Friary.
Janik, Bruno '66 (CHI) Chicago, IL St. Bruno Retired.
Janik, Leszek T. '92 (NOR) Willimantic, CT St. Joseph; Members; Judicial Vicar; Advisory Board; Seminarian Advisory Board.
Janish, Rev. Msgr. James '69 (SAT) Judges; Macdona, TX Our Lady Queen of Heaven; Von Ormy, TX Sacred Heart; College of Consultors; Archdiocesan Presbyteral Council.
Janiszeski, Joseph J. *t.o.r.* '78 (PIT) Pittsburgh, PA St. Matthew.
Janiunas, Albin F. '48 (BO) Senior Priests. Retired.
Jank, Tadeusz '96 (NEW) Linden, NJ St. Theresa of the Child Jesus.
Jankaitis, Ronald V. '79 (ALN)[I] St. Clair, PA Neumann Apartments of Catholic Housing Corporation of St. Clair.
Janko, John *s.d.b.* '78 (NEW)[C] Ramsey, NJ Don Bosco Preparatory High School.
Janko, John *s.d.b.* (NEW)[M] Ramsey, NJ Don Bosco Prep Salesian Residence.
Janko, Joshua Moran '06 (LFT) Zionsville, IN St. Alphonsus.
Jankowiak, Patrick M. '92 (SAG) Clare, MI St. Cecilia.
Jankowski, James M. *o.f.m.conv.* '99 (MIL) Milwaukee, WI Basilica of St. Josaphat.
Jankowski, Lawrence *o.f.m.* '73 (CHI)[O] Chicago, IL Mother of Good Counsel Provincialate.
Jankowski, Peter G. '96 (JOL) Joliet, IL St. Patrick.
Jankowski, Richard '92 (SP) Spring Hill, FL St. Frances Xavier Cabrini; Vicars Forane; College of Consultors; Diocesan Finance Council.
Jankowski, Stanislaw *c.r.* '94 (CHI) Chicago, IL St. Hedwig.
Jankowski, Valentine M. *o.f.m.conv.* '61 (LSC) Carlsbad, NM San Jose; Loving, NM Our Lady of Grace; Vicars; Diocesan Consultors; Presbyteral Council.
Jann, Francis J. '47 (BUF) Rushford, NY St. Mark Retired.
Janoch, Edward J. '00 (CLV) Cleveland, OH St. Patrick.
Janocha, Carl William '91 (OKL) Elk City, OK St. Matthew's; Region V.
Janoski, Steven A. '88 (SFD) Special or Other Diocesan Assignment.
Janovec, James J. '64 (GI) Wood River, NE St. Mary's.
Janowiak, Paul A. *s.j.* '84 (SEA)[A] Seattle, WA Seattle University; [L] Seattle, WA Arrupe Jesuit Community at Seattle University.
Janowicz, Barney J. '57 (SAG) Retired.
Janowicz, Richard '80 (STN) Springfield, OR Nativity of the Mother of God; Diocesan Consultors; Personnel Board; South–West; Presbyteral Council.
Janowski, Lawrence *o.f.m.* '73 (CHI)[N] Chicago, IL Holy Name Friary.
Janowski, Michael S. '03 (GAY) Empire, MI St. Philip Neri; Lake Leelanau, MI St. Mary; Members of the College of Consultors.
Janowski, Rock J. '64 (LA) Retired.
Janowski, Wesley '93 (LC) Stevens Point, WI St. Casimir.
Janowski, Wesley *c.r.* '93 (LC) Stevens Point, WI St. Mary.
Jansch, Ronald *o.f.m.cap.* '50 (MIL)[P] Mount Calvary, WI St. Lawrence Friary Retired.
Jansen, Anthony G. *s.m.* '43 (STL)[O] St. Louis Marianists, Province of the United States (Society of Mary).
Jansen, Raymond L. '99 (LIN) Ulysses, NE Immaculate Conception; Presbyteral Council.
Jansen, William J. *m.c.c.j.* '66 (CIN)[N] Cincinnati, OH Comboni Missionaries (Verona Fathers)–Comboni Mission Center; [U] Cincinnati, OH Hispanic Ministry Office at St. Charles Borromeo, Archdiocese of Cincinnati; Archdiocesan Office of Hispanic Ministry.
Janski, Jerome J. '50 (STP) Retired.
Janson, Christian A. *s.m.* '73 (SAT)[L] San Antonio, TX Holy Rosary Marianist Community; San Antonio, TX Holy Rosary.
Janssen, Henri *o.m.i.* '43 (SAT)[K] San Antonio, TX Oblate Madonna Residence.
Janton, Anthony W. '77 (PH) Abington, PA Our Lady Help of Christians.
Janus, Mark–David *c.s.p.* '79 (GR) Ecumenical Affairs; Evangelization; On Special Assignment; Grand Rapids, MI Cathedral of St. Andrew; [L] Grand Rapids, MI Catholic Information Center.
Janvier, Paul '00 (TR) Asbury Park, NJ Holy Spirit.
Janya, Mateusz *s.j.* (NY)[EE] New York, NY Xavier Jesuit Community.
Janze, John E. '75 (ORG) Irvine, CA St. Thomas More; Council of Priests; Consultors.
Jaques, Domingos '47 (OAK) Retired.
Jara, Arnulfo *c.m.* (RVC) Hispanic Apostolate of the South Fork.
Jaramillo, Jose G. *m.g.* '80 (SB) Highland, CA St. Adelaide; Special or Other Diocesan Assignment; Grand Terrace, CA Christ the Redeemer.
Jaramillo, Leonardo '92 (PAT) Stirling, NJ St. Vincent de Paul.
Jaramillo, Luis '60 (SFE) Retired.
Jaramillo, Misael '01 (PAT) Paterson, NJ Cathedral of St. John the Baptist.
Jaramillo, Oscar '90 (B) Emmett, ID Sacred Heart.
Jaramillo, Pablo *o.f.m.cap.* '08 (DAL)[J] Dallas, TX Capuchin Franciscan Friars, Vice Province of Texas; Dallas, TX Our Lady of Lourdes.
Jaramillo, Peter '81 (KCK)[K] Kansas City, KS Society of St. Augustine – Public Association of the Faithful; Kansas City, KS Holy Family; Kansas City, KS St. Mary–St. Anthony.
Jaramillo, Peter '81 (MO) Army National Guard Chaplains.
Jaramillo, Roberto L. '93 (ATL) Lilburn, GA Our Lady of the Americas.
Jaranilla, Roberto '96 (LA) Pomona, CA St. Joseph.
Jarboe, Rev. Msgr. J. Bruce '86 (BAL) Glen Burnie, MD Holy Trinity; [V] Glen Burnie, MD The Church of the Good Shepherd Parish Endowment Trust; Glen Burnie, MD Church of the Good Shepherd; Presbyteral Council; Glen Burnie, MD Crucifixion, Church of the; Baltimore, MD Cathedral of Mary Our Queen.
Jarboe, Raymond '89 (BAK) Retired.
Jardiniano, Rolly P. '84 (LA) Granada Hills, CA St. Euphrasia.
Jarecki, Michael S. '44 (OG) Retired.
Jarmoluk, Rev. Msgr. Joseph F. '84 (RCK) Spring Grove, IL St. Peter.
Jaron, Glenn Giovanni '91 (SAC) Rocklin, CA SS. Peter and Paul.
Jaros, Joseph P. '56 (TOL) Judges Retired.
Jarosch, Eugene H. *s.a.c.* '51 (MIL)[P] Milwaukee, WI St. Vincent Community.
Jarosewic, Daniel '71 (CHI) Homewood, IL St. Joseph.
Jarosz, Peter '89 (JOL) Lombard, IL Christ the King.
Jarosz, Stanley '65 (MET) Helmetta, NJ Holy Trinity.
Jaroszeski, Paul A. '76 (STP) Ramsey, MN St. Katharine Drexel.
Jarreau, Niel *s.j.* '56 (ATL)[I] Atlanta, GA Ignatius House.
Jarrell, Stephen '73 (IND) Greencastle, IN St. Paul the Apostle; Council of Priests; Indiana State Farm; [O] Greencastle, IN DePauw University.
Jarret, Peter A. *c.s.c.* '92 (FTW)[B] University of Notre Dame Du Lac; [B] University of Notre Dame Du Lac; [H] Notre Dame, IN Congregation of Holy Cross, Indiana Province, Provincial House; [H] Notre Dame, IN Holy Cross Community, Corby Hall, University of Notre Dame; Provincial Councilors:; Members.
Jarvis, Edward A. *s.j.* '54 (PH)[Y] Loyola Center and Manresa Hall.
Jarvis, Paul '05 (STP) Chaska, MN Guardian Angels.
Jarzabek, Mariusz *m.i.c.* (SPR)[H] Stockbridge, MA Congregation of Marian Fathers of The Immaculate Conception of the Most Blessed Virgin Mary.
Jarzombek, Casimir '60 (VIC) Bay City, TX Holy Cross.
Jarzombek, Dennis '79 (SAT) Stockdale, TX St. Mary.
Jasany, Robert J. '79 (CLV) Cleveland, OH St. John Nepomucene; Presbyteral Conveners.
Jasinski, Andrew '98 (FAR)[A] Fargo, ND Cardinal Muench Seminary; Diocesan College of Consultors; Continuing Education of Priests; Special Assignment.
Jasinski, Rev. Msgr. Anthony J. '49 (BUF)[O] Lackawanna, NY Bishop Head Residence Retired.
Jasinski, Raymond J. '54 (CHI)[M] Justice, IL Rosary Hill Home Retired.
Jaskot, Rev. Msgr. Robert '98 (BAL) Baltimore, MD Cathedral of Mary Our Queen; [A] Baltimore, MD St. Mary's Seminary and University; Special Assignment.
Jaskowiak, Wojciech B. '03 (NEW) On Duty Outside the Archdiocese.
Jaskowiak, Wojciech B. '03 (AGN) Merizo, GU San Dimas and Our Lady of the Rosary; Merizo, GU San Dionisio; [A] Yona, GU Redemptoris Mater Archdiocesan Missionary Seminary.
Jaskula, Edward *c.r.* '55 (CHI)[D] Chicago, IL Gordon Tech High School.
Jaskulski, Bronislaus *o.f.m.* '46 (GRY)[H] Cedar Lake, IN Our Lady of Lourdes Friary.
Jaskulski, George *o.f.m.* '55 (CLV)[N] Garfield Heights, OH Marymount Convent; [O] Garfield Heights, OH Marymount Congregational Home; [M] Garfield Heights, OH Village at Marymount.
Jaskulski, Nathan *o.f.m.* '61 (CHI)[O] Chicago, IL Mother of Good Counsel Provincialate; [N] Chicago, IL Holy Name Friary.
Jasney, Robert J. '79 (CLV) Presbyteral Council.
Jasper, Frank *o.f.m.* '73 (CIN)[C] Cincinnati, OH St. Anthony Shrine, Franciscan Postulancy; [N] Cincinnati, OH St. Francis Seraph Friary.
Jasper, John '00 (BAK) Retired.
Jasper, Louis H. '51 (COV) Retired.
Jaspers, David Leo '09 (P) Salem, OR St. Joseph.
Jaspers, J. Dennis '66 (CIN) Cincinnati, OH All Saints; Priest Councilors.
Jasso, Jaroslav *c.m.* '93 (CHI)[N] Chicago DePaul Vincentian Residence.
Jasso, Stephen *t.o.r.* '65 (FWT) Fort Worth, TX All Saints; Diocesan School Advisory Council.
Jastrab, David J. '75 (PIT) Sewickley, PA St. Mary.
Jastrzebski, Edmund *c.r.* '74 (CHI) Chicago, IL St. Stanislaus Kostka.
Jaszczuk, Radoslaw *c.ss.r.* '91 (CHI) Cicero, IL St. Mary of Czestochowa.
Jaszek, Stanislaw '88 (FBK) Presbyteral Council; Pilot Station, AK St. Charles Spinola Catholic Church Pilot Station; Consultors.
Jaume, John *c.r.* '66 (NY) Plattekill, NY Our Lady of Fatima.
Jauregui, Luke '05 (SD) Chula Vista, CA St. Pius X.
Java, Miguel B. '73 (LA) La Puente, CA St. Louis of France.
Javier, Nazareno '98 (BRK) On Leave/Unassigned.
Javillo, Joseph *s.s.p.* '84 (NY)[B] Staten Island, NY Society of St. Paul; Staten Island, NY.
Jawa, Stanley *s.v.d.* (LAF) Opelousas, LA Holy Ghost.
Jawidzik, Edward M. '81 (TR) Freehold, NJ St. Robert Bellarmine.
Jaworowski, Rev. Msgr. Anthony E. '44 (PH) Swedesburg, PA Sacred Heart Retired.
Jaworowski, Grzegorz '94 (HRT) Manchester, CT Assumption; Manchester, CT St. James.
Jayachandra, Hermanagild '68 (DEN) Boulder, CO St. Martin de Porres.
Jayaraj, M. Jones '83 (TYL) Frankston, TX St. Charles Borromeo.
Jayasuriya, Jerome '61 (DAL) Retired.
Jayasuriya, Jerome (FWT) Albany, TX Jesus of Nazareth; Breckenridge, TX Sacred Heart.
Jazdzewski, Brian J. '99 (LC) Chippewa Falls, WI Notre Dame; Jim Falls, WI Sacred Heart of Jesus.
Jazmin, Romeo D. '85 (RIC) Chesapeake, VA Prince of Peace.
Jazmines, Vicente F. '79 (OG) Ogdensburg, NY St. Lawrence Psychiatric Center; Ogdensburg, NY St. Mary's Cathedral.
Jazon, Yvans '07 (CAM) Galloway, NJ The Church of the Assumption.
Jazowski, Rev. Msgr. John F. '48 (BGP) Retired.
Jean, Agapit H. '95 (MAN) Merrimack, NH St. John Neumann; Vicars Forane.
Jean, Aland *c.i.c.m.* '02 (CAM) Pleasantville, NJ St. Peter's Catholic Church, Pleasantville, N.J.
Jean, Antonio '99 (VEN) North Port, FL San Pedro.
Jean, Franky '93 (MIA) North Miami, FL Holy Family.
Jean, Lesly '83 (MIA) Key West, FL St. Mary, Star of the Sea.
Jean, Thony R. '00 (ATL) On Leave of Absence.
Jean–Louis, Isaie '88 (BRK) Brooklyn, NY St. Teresa of Avila.
Jean–Mary, Reginald '01 (MIA) Miami, FL Notre Dame d'Haiti; Haitians.
Jeanfreau, James J. '92 (NO) Kenner, LA St. Jerome; Pontifical Mission Societies/Holy Childhood Association/Propagation of the Faith; Missionaries of St. Therese.
Jean Paul, Souvenir *s.m.* '97 (BRK) Kings County Hospital Center.
Jeanty, Charnel '04 (MIA) Miami Shores, FL St. Rose of Lima.
Jeanty, Charnel '04 (MIA) Judges.
Jeanty, Succes (BO) Chelsea, MA St. Rose of Lima.
Jecewicz, Jerome (BRK) Long Island City, NY St. Raphael.
Jednaki, P. Gregorz '08 (NOR) Norwich, CT St. Patrick Cathedral.
Jedrejko, Romuald *o.p.* '05 (NY) New York, NY Notre Dame; [II] New York, NY Polish Dominicans, Inc.
Jedrychowski, Janusz '95 (STF) Pittsfield, MA St. John the Baptist; Hudson, NY St. Nicholas.
Jedrzejewski, Richard '74 (BUF) Buffalo, NY Assumption.
Jeffers, Robert A. '54 (NY) New York, NY Our Lady of the Rosary Retired.
Jeffrey, C. James '59 (FAR) Retired.
Jeffrey, Donald P. '64 (LKC) Sulphur, LA St. Theresa.
Jeffrey, George A. '65 (SCR)[N] Dunmore, PA Villa St. Joseph; Clarks Summit, PA Clarks Summit State Hospital Retired.
Jeffries, Brian E. '73 (HRT) Canaan, CT St. Joseph; Canaan, CT Immaculate Conception.
Jelinek, Anthony (MIL)[N] Kenosha, WI St. Joseph's Home for the Aged.
Jendrek, Michael J. '87 (BAL) Ijamsville, MD St. Ignatius of Loyola.
Jendrysik, Mark '85 (JOL) Addison, IL St. Philip The Apostle; Cursillo Movement.
Jenemann, Albert H. *s.j.* '60 (PH)[Y] Loyola Center and Manresa Hall.
Jenga, Fred *c.s.c.* (FTW)[H] Notre Dame Congregation of Holy Cross, Indiana Province, Provincial House.
Jenik, Rev. Msgr. John J. '70 (NY) Bronx, NY Our Lady of Refuge; Bronx (Northwest); Priests Council of the Archdiocese of New York.
Jenkins, Aaron M. '08 (IND)[C] Indianapolis, IN Father Thomas Scecina Memorial High School; Priestly and Religious Vocations.

Jenkins, Alan *s.v.d.* '73 (SB) San Bernardino, CA Our Lady of the Rosary Cathedral; Elected Members.
Jenkins, J. Michael '79 (SFD) Absent on Leave.
Jenkins, J. Wayne '72 (L) Louisville, KY St. Barnabas; Clergy Personnel Commission.
Jenkins, John I. *c.s.c.* '83 (FTW)[B] University of Notre Dame Du Lac; [B] University of Notre Dame Du Lac; [H] Notre Dame, IN Holy Cross Community, Corby Hall, University of Notre Dame.
Jenkins, John M. '60 (CLV) Akron, OH St. Paul; Euclid, OH Holy Cross; Cleveland, OH Euclid Hospital Retired.
Jenkins, Joseph A. '86 (WDC) Mitchellville, MD Holy Family.
Jenkins, Kenneth F. '80 (SB) On Leave of Absence.
Jenkins, Rev. Msgr. Ron '89 (AUS) On Duty Outside the Diocese.
Jenkins, Rev. Msgr. Ronny E. '89 (DAL) Defensor Vinculi.
Jenkins, Rev. Msgr. Ronny (BAL) Canonical & Theological Consultants to the Archbishop.
Jenkins, Walter E. *c.s.c.* '04 (FR)[A] North Easton, MA Stonehill College.
Jenkins, Walter E. '04 (SFR) San Francisco, CA St. James.
Jenkins, Wayne *s.c.j.* '77 (MIL)[P] Hales Corners, WI Priests of the Sacred Heart.
Jenne, Walter H. '70 (CLV) Brecksville, OH St. Basil the Great; Presbyteral Conveners; Presbyteral Council.
Jennett, Rev. Msgr. Michael J. '74 (LA) Santa Barbara, CA San Roque; Santa Barbara Region.
Jenniges, Leonard J. '48 (NU) Retired.
Jennings, Henry J. '62 (BO) Somerville, MA St. Joseph.
Jennings, John A. '50 (SEA) Retired.
Jennings, Rev. Msgr. Joseph '43 (MOB) Retired.
Jennings, Michael T. '69 (KNX) Rogersville, TN St. Henry; Sneedville, TN St. James the Apostle.
Jennings, Paul F. '74 (WIL) Chester, MD St. Christopher; Deans.
Jennings, Thomas J. '69 (WIN) Luverne, MN St. Catherine's; Elected Deanery Representatives; Luverne, MN St. Mary's.
Jennings, Tommie '88 (SD) San Diego, CA Christ the King; San Diego, CA St. John the Evangelist.
Jennings, William E. '40 (WIL) Retired.
Jenniskens, Thomas J. *s.j.* '56 (NO)[P] New Orleans, LA Ignatius Residence Retired.
Jennrich, Michael *o.f.m.* '87 (FgM) Saint Louis, MO Sacred Heart Province.
Jensen, Daniel P. *m.m.* '62 (NY)[EE] Retired.
Jensen, Jens–Peter (Jay) '01 (TUC) Tucson, AZ Saint Augustine Cathedral Roman Catholic Parish – Tucson.
Jensen, Joseph *o.s.b.* '54 (WDC)[C] Catholic University of America, The; [N] Washington, DC St. Anselm's Abbey; [W] Washington, DC Catholic Biblical Association.
Jensen, Larry '88 (SAM) Waterville, ME St. Joseph.
Jenson, Glen T. '95 (STP) Minneapolis, MN Holy Cross; Minneapolis, MN St. Anthony of Padua; Minneapolis, MN St. Hedwig.
Jenson, Jens–Peter '01 (COS) On Duty Outside Diocese.
Jenuwine, David John '09 (SAG) Mount Pleasant, MI Sacred Heart.
Jeon, Andrew Soo Hong '91 (JOL) Itasca, IL St. Andrew Kim.
Jeon, Dong Hyuk '01 (DET) Northville, MI St. Andrew Kim Korean Catholic Church.
Jeong–Ho An, Isidore *s.j.* '02 (ATL) Doraville, GA Korean Martyrs Catholic Church.
Jerabek, Bryan W. '08 (BIR) Huntsville, AL Holy Spirit; [A] Huntsville, AL Pope John Paul II Catholic High School.
Jerek, John M. '88 (Y) Campbell, OH St. John the Baptist.
Jerek, John '88 (Y) College of Consultors; Office of Vocations; Office of Clergy Services; Department of Clergy and Religious Services; Priests Council.
Jeremiah, Ian '08 (BGP) Presbyteral Council; New Canaan, CT St. Aloysius.
Jerge, Lawrence A. *c.s.c.* '68 (FR) South Easton, MA Holy Cross.
Jerome, Rev. Msgr. Harry J. '61 (BEL) Diocesan Consultors.
Jerome, Louis '88 (NY) Staten Island, NY Sacred Heart.
Jeronimo–Garcia, Adalberto *c.o.r.c.* '90 (SB) Redlands, CA The Holy Name of Jesus Catholic Community, Inc.
Jerse, William M. '80 (CLV) Adjunct Judicial Vicars; Middleburg Heights, OH St. Bartholomew.
Jervis, Rev. Msgr. Paul W. '83 (BRK) Brooklyn, NY Saint Martin de Porres.
Jeselnick, Stephen E. '77 (E) On Duty Outside Diocese; Air National Guard Chaplains.
Jesionowski, Richard A. '68 (BUF) Cheektowaga, NY Our Lady Help of Christians.
Jeske, Richard *o.f.m.* '59 (STL) St. Louis, MO St. Anthony of Padua; [O] St. Louis, MO Franciscan Friary of St. Anthony of Padua.
Jessing, Joseph *s.v.d.* '68 (BEA) Liberty, TX Immaculate Conception.
Jette, Mark R. '72 (HRT) West Haven, CT St. Lawrence; West Haven, CT St. Paul's.
Jewison, Harry P. '54 (WIN) Retired.
Jezierski, John '08 (LFT) Lafayette, IN St. Lawrence.
Jicha, John J. '95 (BAL) Pasadena, MD St. Jane Frances de Chantal.
Jimenez, Adrian N. '87 (ARE) Vega–Alta, PR Immaculate Conception of Blessed Virgin Mary.
Jimenez, Alvaro (ORL) Deltona, FL Our Lady of the Lakes.
Jimenez, Amiro '90 (ALN) Reading, PA St. Paul.
Jimenez, Ben *s.j.* '01 (DET) Detroit, MI SS. Peter and Paul Jesuit; [E] Detroit, MI University of Detroit Jesuit High School and Academy.
Jimenez, David J. '95 (YAK) Judges; Selah, WA Our Lady of Lourdes; Adjutant Judicial Vicar.
Jimenez, Eduardo '82 (MIA)[O] Miami Shores, FL Family Life Ministry; Family Life Ministry; Special Assignment.
Jimenez, Eloy (FTW) Plymouth, IN St. Michael; Plymouth.
Jimenez, Emilio '99 (CC) Corpus Christi, TX Our Lady of Guadalupe.
Jimenez, Fernando '09 (FTW) Fort Wayne, IN Cathedral of the Immaculate Conception.
Jimenez, Francisco '88 (ARE) Retired.
Jimenez, John T. '98 (SFR) San Francisco, CA St. Peter.
Jimenez, John '00 (SFR) San Francisco General Hospital.
Jimenez, Jose Carmelo '99 (OWN) Hopkinsville, KY SS. Peter and Paul.
Jimenez, Jose Luis *o.a.r.* '59 (ORG) Santa Ana, CA St. Barbara Catholic Church Retired.
Jimenez, Jose Orlando Cheverria '97 (CHR) Batesburg–Leesville, SC St. John of the Cross.
Jimenez, Jose Pio *c.m.* '68 (FgM) Philadelphia, PA Eastern Province.
Jimenez, Ryan '03 (CHK) Saipan, MP Cathedral of Our Lady of Mt. Carmel; Chancellor; Diocesan Curia Staff; Presbyteral Council; Diocesan Publications Office; Electronic Media; Cursillo Movement; Superintendent of Catholic Schools; Commission on Heritage Cultural of the Church.
Jimenez, Victorino (ARE) Retired.
Jimenez–Londono, Fredy A. '93 (PRO) Absent on Leave.
Jimenez Ortiz, Adrian N. '87 (ARE) Vicar of Diocesan Pastoral Affairs; Priest's Senate (Consejo Presbiteral).
Jimenez Vargas, Luis A. '04 (HBG) Lancaster, PA Iglesia Catolica San Juan Bautista.
Jindra, Frank E. '84 (OM) Genoa, NE St. Rose of Lima; Genoa, NE SS. Peter and Paul; Silver Creek, NE St. Lawrence; [M] Elkhorn, NE Apostolic Sodales.
Jirak, John F. '02 (WCH) On Duty Outside the Diocese; Totus Tuus of Wichita.
Jirovsky, Lee T. '06 (LIN) Lincoln, NE St. John the Apostle; Advocates.
Joaquin, Joseph M. '81 (BGP) Retired.
Joaquin, M. Joseph '81 (BGP) Danbury, CT St. Peter.
Jocco, Joseph P. *o.s.f.s.* '84 (ALN) Robesonia, PA St. Francis de Sales.
Jocelyn, Yves '62 (MIA) Fort Lauderdale, FL St. Helen.
Jocson, Edgardo P. '01 (NEW) Cranford, NJ St. Michael's.
Jocson, Salvador '57 (SFR) Retired.
Joda, Robert J. *s.j.* '58 (MIL)[P] Milwaukee, WI Jesuit Community at Marquette University.
Joensen, William M. '89 (DUB)[A] Dubuque, IA Seminary of St. Pius X; [C] Loras College; Medical–Moral Commission.
Joerger, Robert *c.p.* '77 (NY)[EE] Pelham Manor, NY St. Vincent's Residence.
John, Arun *i.m.s.* '92 (BR) Grosse Tete, LA St. Joseph; Livonia, LA St. Frances Xavier Cabrini; Grosse Tete, LA Immaculate Heart of Mary.
John, Jacob '02 (PH) Horsham, PA St. Catherine of Siena.
John, Richard *o.s.c.* '46 (SCL)[I] Onamia, MN Crosier Priory.
John, Sunny *o.carm.* '97 (NY) New York, NY St. John the Martyr.
Johns, Thomas W. '78 (CLV) Mentor, OH St. John Vianney.
Johnson, Andrew R. '04 (SFR) On Special Assignment; San Francisco, CA St. Thomas More.
Johnson, Andrew *o.c.s.o.* '91 (WOR)[O] Spencer, MA St. Joseph's Abbey.
Johnson, Andrew *o.s.c.o.* '91 (FR) Fall River, MA St. Michael; Charlton Memorial Hospital.
Johnson, Arthur M. *s.a.* '77 (ARL) Sterling, VA Christ the Redeemer.
Johnson, Arthur *o.s.a.* '63 (MIA)[K] Miami Gardens, FL Casa San Lorenzo.
Johnson, Bernard M. *o.praem.* '81 (ORG)[I] Silverado, CA Norbertine Fathers of Orange Inc.
Johnson, Brian A. '97 (OWN) Clarkson, KY St. Augustine; Clarkson, KY St. Anthony; Clarkson, KY St. Benedict.
Johnson, Brian '97 (OWN) Deans/Coordinators.
Johnson, Brian *c.ss.r.* '86 (STP) Brooklyn Center, MN St. Alphonsus.
Johnson, Carl D. '78 (NY) Port Ewen, NY Presentation of the Blessed Virgin Mary.
Johnson, Carl '77 (LEX) Special Assignment.
Johnson, Carl (HBG) Lewisburg, PA U.S. Penitentiary.
Johnson, Rev. Msgr. Charles B. '60 (HRT)[A] In Res. at the Archbishop Daniel A. Cronin Retirement Residence at St. Thomas Seminary Retired.
Johnson, Charles K. *o.p.* '06 (NO)[P] New Orleans Dominican Friars, Southern Dominican Province of St. Martin de Porres.
Johnson, Charles W. '94 (MO) Navy Chaplains; Chaplains of the Military.
Johnson, Charles *o.p.* '06 (FgM) Metairie, LA St. Martin de Porres Province (Southern Dominican Province).
Johnson, Christopher *o.p.* '60 (NY)[EE] New York, NY St. Catherine of Siena Priory.
Johnson, Christopher *o.c.d.* '93 (NY) Port Chester, NY Our Lady of Mercy.
Johnson, Dan '54 (ORG) Retired.
Johnson, Daniel E. '51 (HRT) Diocesan Labor Institute Retired.
Johnson, David P. '89 (OWN) Whitesville, KY St. Mary of the Woods.
Johnson, David W. *s.j.* '69 (OAK)[A] Berkeley, CA Jesuit School of Theology at Santa Clara University; [M] Berkeley, CA Jesuit Fathers and Brothers.
Johnson, Doug '83 (SFS) Retired.
Johnson, Edward D. '55 (PRO) Retired.
Johnson, Rev. Msgr. Edward Joseph '58 (LA) Retired.
Johnson, Eric Matthew '02 (IND) Priestly and Religious Vocations.
Johnson, Eric '02 (IND) Nashville, IN St. Agnes.
Johnson, Francis P. '60 (HRT) West Hartford, CT St. Helena Retired.
Johnson, Gary W. *o.f.m.conv.* '00 (SAT)[B] San Antonio, TX San Damiano Friary, Prenovitiate House of Formation; [L] San Antonio, TX San Damiano Friary.
Johnson, George '98 (CC) George West, TX St. George.
Johnson, Gerald T. '04 (SFE) Presbyteral Council of the Archdiocese of Santa Fe.
Johnson, Gerald '04 (SFE) Pecos, NM St. Anthony of Padua.
Johnson, H. Thomas '78 (DET) Shelby Twp., MI St. Kieran.
Johnson, Henry Joseph '57 (LA) Retired.
Johnson, Henry '76 (STO) Diamond Springs, CA Retired.
Johnson, Howard J. '54 (MIL) Retired.
Johnson, Howard '60 (WDC)[B] Washington, DC St. Joseph's Seminary Retired.
Johnson, James B. '80 (SP) Inverness, FL Our Lady of Fatima; [R] Floral City, FL Our Lady of Good Counsel Camp; Air Force Reserve Chaplains.
Johnson, James B. '80 (SP) Our Lady of Good Counsel Camp; Vicars Forane; Personnel Board; [R] Inverness, FL.
Johnson, James '60 (Y) Retired.
Johnson, James '00 (SEA) Seattle, WA Our Lady of Fatima; Presbyteral Council; Deans.
Johnson, James *o.f.m. cap.* '68 (LA)[B] Santa Ynez, CA San Lorenzo Seminary – Retreat Center.
Johnson, James '00 (SEA) Special Assignment.
Johnson, Jeff G. '92 (MAR) Marquette, MI Marquette General Hospital; Marquette, MI St. Christopher.
Johnson, Jerome A. '86 (MET) Iselin, NJ St. Cecelia.
Johnson, Joachim *o.c.s.o.* '02 (L)[L] Trappist, KY Abbey of Our Lady of Gethsemani, of the Order of Cistercians of the Strict Observance.
Johnson, Rev. Msgr. John G. '74 (COL) Hilliard, OH St. Brendan; Presiding Judges of First Instance.
Johnson, John J. '66 (STL) St. Louis, MO St. James the Greater.
Johnson, John R. '72 (SAG) Saginaw, MI SS. Peter and Paul.
Johnson, John R. '07 (SAV) On Duty Outside the Diocese.
Johnson, Joseph R. '98 (STP) St. Paul, MN Cathedral of Saint Paul; St. Paul, MN St. Vincent de Paul; Censores Librorum.
Johnson, Kevin '87 (PT) Tallahassee, FL St. Louis; Vicars Forane.
Johnson, Lawrence M. '83 (BAL) Special Assignment; [O] Timonium, MD Stella Maris.
Johnson, Lawrence P. '76 (MO) On Duty Outside the Diocese; Navy Chaplains.
Johnson, Lyle '76 (LIN) Lincoln, NE St. John the Apostle.
Johnson, Marcus '02 (LKC) Lake Charles, LA Immaculate Heart of Mary; [A] Lake Charles, LA St. Louis High School; Deans; Diocesan Consultors; Vocation Recruiters; Presbyteral Council.
Johnson, Maxwell E. '78 (FTW)[B] University of Notre Dame Du Lac.
Johnson, Michael *o.f.m.* '02 (WDC) Silver Spring, MD St. Camillus.
Johnson, Michael '09 (STP) New Brighton, MN St. John the Baptist.

Johnson, Rev. Msgr. Oliver F. '62 (AUS) Retired.
Johnson, Patrick D. *c.s.p.* '74 (MO) Navy Reserve Chaplains.
Johnson, Patrick *c.s.p.* '74 (STP)[K] Minneapolis, MN Paulist Fathers; [R] Minneapolis, MN Newman Center at St. Lawrence; Deanery 13; Minneapolis, MN St. Lawrence–Newman Center.
Johnson, Patrick *c.s.p.* '74 (STP) Minneapolis, MN All Saints.
Johnson, Paul *s.o.l.t.* (PAT)[J] Branchville, NJ Sanctuary of Mary–Our Lady of the Holy Spirit.
Johnson, Paul *o.p.* '59 (STP) Minneapolis, MN St. Albert the Great.
Johnson, Peter '91 (CHY) Buffalo, WY St. John the Baptist; Ecumenism Commission; Rural Life Ministry.
Johnson, Rev. Msgr. Philip L. '64 (FWT) Diocesan Finance Council; Catholic Foundation of North Texas.
Johnson, Rev. Msgr. Philip '64 (FWT) Bedford, TX St. Michael.
Johnson, Richard *c.p.* '51 (CHI)[N] Chicago Passionist Provincial Office.
Johnson, Rijo *s.d.v.* '08 (NEW) Newark, NJ St. Michael's.
Johnson, Robert Jules '09 (PT) Pensacola, FL St. Mary.
Johnson, Rev. Msgr. Robert K. '90 (WOR) Office for Divine Worship; Worcester, MA St. Paul Cathedral; Diocesan Building Commission Members.
Johnson, Rev. Msgr. Robert '51 (DAL) Retired.
Johnson, Robert *s.v.d.* '92 (FgM) Techny, IL.
Johnson, Stephen D. '72 (WOR) Leicester, MA St. Joseph; Leicester, MA St. Pius X.
Johnson, Terrence M. '94 (CHI)[B] Chicago, IL The Catholic Theological Union at Chicago.
Johnson, Thomas '78 (DET) College of Consultors.
Johnson, Timothy A. '93 (SC) Carroll, IA St. Mary's; St. Anthony Regional Hospital; [C] Carroll, IA St. Anthony Regional Hospital; Priests' Personnel Board; Carroll, IA Holy Spirit.
Johnson, Timothy K. '71 (OAK) Oakland, CA St. Leo the Great; Deanery #10.
Johnson, Timothy '01 (FAR) Oriska, ND St. Agatha's Church of Hope; Oriska, ND St. Bernard's Church of Oriska; Oriska, ND Sacred Heart Church of Sanborn.
Johnson, Rev. Msgr. W. Robert '51 (FWT)[G] Crowley, TX St. Francis Village, Inc. Retired.
Johnson, Walter W. *m.m.* '53 (NY)[EE] Retired.
Johnson, William T. *s.j.* '91 (OM)[K] Omaha, NE Jesuit Community at Creighton University.
Johnson, William '83 (OAK) Pittsburg, CA St. Peter, Martyr of Verona; Mount Diablo Hospital Medical Center; Contra Costa Regional Medical Center and VA Administrative Skilled Nursing Center.
Johnston, Christian R. '05 (KAL) Wayland, MI SS. Cyril and Methodius; Wayland, MI St. Therese of Lisieux.
Johnston, German Bartolome Vasquez '93 (TUC) Sierra Vista, AZ Saint Andrew the Apostle Roman Catholic Parish – Sierra Vista.
Johnston, Jeffrey (RVC) Medical Leave.
Johnston, Kenneth J. '68 (CAM) Mantua, NJ R.C. Church of the Incarnation, Township of Mantua, New Jersey.
Johnston, Michael O. '70 (NSH) Nashville, TN St. Henry.
Johnston, Michael '96 (P) Dallas, OR St. Philip; Judges.
Johnston, Paul *s.o.l.t.* '03 (CC)[G] Robstown, TX Society of Our Lady of the Most Holy Trinity.
Johnston, Paul (ATL)[L] Covington, GA Society of Our Lady of the Most Holy Trinity.
Johnston, Robert F. '71 (SAT) Retired.
Johnstone, Brian *c.s.s.r.* '58 (WDC)[C] Catholic University of America, The.
Johnstone, Brian *c.ss.r.* '64 (WDC)[N] Washington, DC Holy Redeemer College.
Johri, Mauro *o.f.m.cap.* (FgM) AMERICAN CAPUCHIN MISSIONS.
Joly, Henry L. '58 (ALT) Retired.
Joly, Michael D. '94 (PAT) On Duty Outside the Diocese.
Joly, Michael '94 (RIC) Yorktown, VA St. Joan of Arc.
Joly, Philip '01 (VEN) Cape Coral, FL St. Andrew.
Jonas, Lawrence A. *s.j.* '59 (MIL) Milwaukee, WI Gesu Parish.
Joncas, Jan Michael '69 (STP)[C] St. Paul, MN University of St. Thomas.
Jonczyk, Dariusz J. '97 (PRO) Central Falls, RI St. Joseph; Woonsocket, RI St. Stanislaus.
Jones, Anthony '89 (OWN) Owensboro, KY The Immaculate.
Jones, Brandon H. '08 (CHL) Huntersville, NC St. Mark.
Jones, C. Gregory *c.s.v.* '96 (CHI)[N] Chicago, IL Viatorian Residence; [N] Arlington Heights Viatorian Province Center–Clerics of St. Viator.
Jones, Carleton Parker *o.p.* '87 (NY)[EE] New York, NY St. Vincent Ferrer Priory.
Jones, Carlton P. *o.p.* (NY) New York, NY St. Vincent Ferrer.
Jones, Charles F. '63 (KC) Retired.
Jones, Clarence Edward *c.o.* '94 (CHR)[E] Rock Hill, SC Oratory of St. Philip Neri, Congregation of the Oratory of Pontifical Rite.
Jones, Clarence Edward *c.o.* '94 (SEA)[L] Seattle, WA Seattle Oratory; Seattle, WA Our Lady of Mount Virgin.
Jones, Daniel J. '97 (DET) Special Assignment; Presbyteral Council.
Jones, David A. '89 (CHI) Chicago, IL St. Benedict the African (East); Deans; College of Consultors.
Jones, David J. *m.m.* '62 (NY)[EE] Maryknoll Maryknoll Fathers and Brothers Retired.
Jones, David J. *m.m.* '62 (ALB) Troy, NY St. Patrick.
Jones, Donald R. '86 (PIT) Retired.
Jones, Edward T. '03 (PT) Florida State University; Members Elected by Deanery; Tallahassee, FL Co–Cathedral of St. Thomas More.
Jones, Frank W. '67 (GAL) Retired.
Jones, Frank '86 (FgM) Boston, MA St. James the Apostle, Inc.
Jones, Glenn '08 (SFE) Clayton, NM St. Francis Xavier.
Jones, Herbert J. *o.carm.* '60 (BO)[Z] Peabody, MA St. Theresa Carmelite Chapel; Presbyteral Council; [U] Peabody, MA Our Lady of the Scapular Priory.
Jones, Herbert *o.f.m.* '77 (SAT) San Antonio, TX San Francisco de la Espada.
Jones, J. Overton '64 (CAM) Retired.
Jones, James W. *o.f.m.cap.* '77 (NY)[B] Beacon, NY St. Lawrence of Brindisi Friary Retired.
Jones, James *o.f.m.* '76 (SP)[N] St. Petersburg St. Anthony Friary Retired.
Jones, John E. '59 (L) Retired.
Jones, Joseph F. *c.ss.r.* '73 (BRK)[T] Brooklyn, NY Redemptorist Fathers of New York, Inc.–Baltimore Province.
Jones, Joseph R. *c.p.* '65 (MET)[I] South River Passionist Provincial Office; South River, NJ.
Jones, Joseph R. *c.p.* '65 (FgM) South River, NJ St. Paul of the Cross Province.
Jones, Kenneth '69 (NEW) Plainfield, NJ St. Mary.
Jones, Levester '04 (WDC) Largo, MD St. Joseph; Priest Council.
Jones, Mark R. '92 (MIL) Racine, WI St. Lucy.
Jones, Martin J. '94 (NOR) Colchester, CT St. Andrew.
Jones, Michael K. '92 (BGP) Shelton, CT St. Lawrence; Office for the Continuing Education of Clergy; Pastors' Vocation Advisory Board.
Jones, Michael P. *o.f.m.* '01 (HRT) Hartford, CT St. Patrick–St. Anthony.
Jones, Michael T. '85 (MO) Bowie, MD St. Pius X; Air Force Reserve Chaplains.
Jones, Michael *o.f.m.* (NOR) Haitian Ministries Board.
Jones, Neil G. *m.s.* '72 (ATL) Snellville, GA St. Oliver Plunkett.
Jones, Paul W. '96 (JC) Retired.
Jones, Ralph O. *s.o.l.t.* '03 (CC)[G] Robstown, TX Society of Our Lady of the Most Holy Trinity; Fulton, TX Stella Maris Chapel.
Jones, Rev. Msgr. Raymond N. '59 (DEN) Retired.
Jones, Richard S. '88 (PIT) Coraopolis, PA St. Joseph.
Jones, Rick L. '90 (SPC) Branson, MO Our Lady of the Lake; Forsyth, MO Our Lady of the Ozarks; Diocesan Development Fund; Presbyteral Council; DEPARTMENT OF VETERANS AFFAIRS HOSPITALS AND CHAPLAINS.
Jones, Robert J. *c.m.* '69 (LA) Los Angeles, CA St. Camillus De Lellis; Los Angeles, CA Norris Cancer and USC University Hospital; [P] Montebello, CA DePaul Evangelization Center; [V] Montebello, CA DePaul Evangelization Center.
Jones, Robert J. *s.j.* '70 (SPK) Keller, WA St. Rose of Lima; Omak, WA St. Joseph; Inchelium, WA St. Michael's Mission; Nespelem, WA Sacred Heart Mission; [J] Spokane, WA Regis Community.
Jones, Robert M. *s.v.d.* '68 (BO)[U] Duxbury, MA Society of the Divine Word; Norfolk County Correctional Facility.
Jones, Robert S. '60 (SY) Special Assignment.
Jones, Robert W. '92 (RCK) Sugar Grove, IL St. Katharine Drexel Parish.
Jones, Ronald A. '73 (RCK) Retired.
Jones, Scott *s.d.s.* '04 (MIL) Consultors:; [P] Greendale, WI.
Jones, Thomas J. *c.s.c.* '72 (FTW) Notre Dame, IN Sacred Heart; [H] Notre Dame Congregation of Holy Cross, Indiana Province, Provincial House; [B] University of Notre Dame Du Lac; [H] Notre Dame, IN Holy Cross Community, Corby Hall, University of Notre Dame.
Jones, Thomas P. *o.f.m.* '59 (FgM) New York, NY Holy Name Province.
Jones, W. Thomas *s.m.* '47 (SFR)[N] San Francisco, CA Marist Center of the West Retired.
Jones, Rev. Msgr. William H. '47 (DEN) Retired.
Jones, William P. '69 (ALN) Retired.
Jones, William R. '67 (SY) On Sabbatical.
Jong, Lyndon A. '91 (MO) Army Chaplains.
Jonientz, Bernard '63 (SEA) Retired.
Jonikas, Gintaras '89 (DET) Detroit, MI St. Anthony; Southfield, MI Divine Providence.
Joo, Andrew '05 (BRK) Woodside, NY Blessed Virgin Mary, Help of Christians.
Joppa, Mark J. '07 (STP) Forest Lake, MN St. Peter.
Jorda, Mario Busquets '58 (MIA)[Q] Miami, FL Peruvian Mission, Inc.
Jordain, Floyd McCoy '84 (MGZ) Hormigueros, PR Shrine of Our Lady of Monserrate.
Jordan, Brian *o.f.m.* '83 (NY) New York, NY Holy Name of Jesus.
Jordan, Daniel J. '99 (BUR) Elected Members; Judicial Vicar; Enosburg Falls, VT St. John the Baptist; Judges.
Jordan, Francis G. '60 (DOD) Ingalls, KS St. Stanislaus Catholic Church of Ingalls, Kansas Retired.
Jordan, Rev. Msgr. Harry J. '61 (CAM)[M] Cherry Hill, NJ Sacred Heart Residence for Priests, Inc.; Representative for Retired Priests; [M] Cherry Hill, NJ Sacred Heart North; [M] Cherry Hill, NJ Sacred Heart South Retired.
Jordan, Rev. Msgr. John J. '69 (SCR) On Duty Outside the Diocese.
Jordan, John M. '83 (PIT) Absent on Sick Leave; [Q] Pittsburgh, PA Cardinal Dearden Center.
Jordan, Rev. Msgr. John W. (WDC)[W] Washington, DC Foundation for the Nativity & Miguel Schools.
Jordan, Joseph A. *o.s.a.* '58 (PH)[Y] Villanova, PA St. Thomas Monastery.
Jordan, Maryon *o.s.b.* '83 (BLX) V.A. Center.
Jordan, Michael *s.o.l.t.* '83 (CC)[G] Robstown, TX Society of Our Lady of the Most Holy Trinity.
Jordan, Phelim *s.v.d.* '81 (WDC) Washington, DC Providence Hospital; [L] Washington, DC Providence Hospital; [N] Washington, DC Divine Word House; [N] Washington, DC Divine Word House.
Jordan, Regis *o.c.d.* '64 (WDC)[B] Washington, DC Discalced Carmelite Friars; [W] Washington, DC Spiritual Life.
Jordan, Thomas *o.carm.* '70 (FgM)[L] Darien Carmelite Provincial Office; Darien, IL Provincial Headquarters, Carmelite Provincial Office.
Jorden, James A. '83 (PT) Retired.
Jorgensen, Alan P. '05 (KAL) Allegan, MI Blessed Sacrament.
Jose, Henrick '71 (MIA) Miami, FL St. Richard.
Jose, L.F. (BRK)[T] Brooklyn, NY Carmelites of Mary Immaculate, Inc.
Joseph, Alex '94 (NY) New York, NY St. Peter.
Joseph, Antony A. '75 (CHI) Evanston, IL St. Mary.
Joseph, Augustine '90 (OAK) San Leandro, CA St. Felicitas.
Joseph, Augustine *m.s.f.s.* '04 (KNX)[C] Signal Mountain, TN Alexian Village Health Care Center; [D] Signal Mountain, TN Alexian Village of Tennessee.
Joseph, Eappen '77 (BLX) Bassfield, MS St. Peter.
Joseph, Eugene Newman (NEW) New Providence, NJ Our Lady of Peace.
Joseph, Francis A. *o.c.d.* '79 (STO) Tracy, CA St. Bernard Church (Pastor of).
Joseph, George '99 (AUS) Elgin, TX Sacred Heart.
Joseph, George '94 (NEW) Jersey City, NJ Jersey City Medical Center; Jersey City, NJ St. Aloysius.
Joseph, Irudamoney Arul *m.s.f.x.* '91 (BIS) Hebron, ND St. Ann.
Joseph, Jacob *c.m.i.* '83 (CHR) North Myrtle Beach, SC Our Lady Star of the Sea.
Joseph, James *s.d.b.* (GI) Gordon, NE St. Leo's.
Joseph, Jean–Ronald '93 (VEN) On Administrative Leave.
Joseph, Jiang *s.j.* '08 (BO)[U] Newton, MA The Jesuit Community at Boston College.
Joseph, Jimmy *v.c.* '97 (SCL) St. Cloud, MN St. Anthony of Padua; St. Cloud, MN Holy Spirit; St. Cloud, MN St. John Cantius.
Joseph, Joy *t.o.r.* '95 (FWT) Fort Worth, TX St. Patrick Cathedral.
Joseph, Lawrence '84 (LA) Glendora, CA St. Dorothy.
Joseph, Rev. Msgr. Milam J. '64 (DAL) College of Consultors; Appointed Members; Episcopal Vicar; Diocesan Judges; Episcopal Vicar.
Joseph, Paul Chemplamparampil *c.m.i.* '83 (NY) White Plains, NY St. John the Evangelist.
Joseph, Peter *h.g.n.* '01 (LEX) Barbourville, KY St. Gregory; Williamsburg, KY Our Lady of Perpetual Help; [L] Barbourville, KY St. Gregory Church–Union College.
Joseph, Reji *c.m.i.* '05 (NY) Stony Point, NY Immaculate Conception.
Joseph, Sajeev *o.ss.t.* '08 (BAL)[S] The Trinitarians in India (Bangalore & Trichur).
Joseph, Sajo Puthenpurackal *h.g.n.* '99 (WH) Vienna, WV St. Michael's.
Joseph, Saju '94 (SJ) San Jose, CA St. Christopher; Council of Priests.
Joseph, Satish Antony '94 (CIN) Dayton, OH Our Lady of the Immaculate Conception; Dayton, OH St. Helen.
Joseph, Theopilos '74 (BRK) Brooklyn, NY St. Ephrem.
Joseph, Thomas '05 (STP) Carver, MN St. Nicholas.
Joseph, Tomy P. *m.s.f.s.* '94 (NSH) Loretto, TN Sacred Heart; Loretto, TN St. Joseph.
Joseph, V. Arul '78 (LC) Chippewa Falls, WI Holy Ghost; Chippewa Falls, WI St. Bridget.
Joseph, Valentine (LC) Lyndon Station, WI St. Mary.

Joseph, Varkey V. '79 (LC) Elmwood, WI Sacred Heart; Spring Valley, WI Sacred Heart of Jesus.
Joseph, Vincent Ezhanikatt '84 (WH) Wellsburg, WV St. John The Evangelist.
Joseph, Vio O. *s.a.c.* '79 (COL) Chillicothe, OH Veteran's Affairs Medical Center.
Joseph, Vio O. *s.a.c.* '79 (MO) DEPARTMENT OF VETERANS AFFAIRS HOSPITALS AND CHAPLAINS.
Joseph, William '62 (PT) Retired.
Joseph, William (ORL) Retired.
Joslyn, James W. '73 (MO) Military Chaplains; Navy Chaplains.
Josoma, Stephen S. (BO) Dedham, MA St. Susanna.
Jost, Aloys *o.f.m.* '80 (SHP) Hispanic Ministry and Immigration Services.
Jost, C. Thomas *s.j.* '68 (DEN)[N] Denver, CO Society of Jesus – St. Ignatius Loyola Jesuit Community.
Jost, Edward F. '96 (BUF) North Tonawanda, NY St. Jude the Apostle.
Josten, Paul '87 (SFS) Yankton, SD St. Benedict.
Joung, Matthew Un Kwang (RIC) Richmond, VA St. Kim Taegon.
Jovanovic, Rev. Msgr. Robert P. '61 (STL) St. Charles, MO St. Elizabeth Ann Seton.
Jowdy, Albert W. '84 (ATL) Lawrenceville, GA St. Lawrence; Judges; Deans; College of Consultors.
Joy, Laurence '60 (LA) Foreign Mission Retired.
Joy, William P. (BO) Mattapan, MA St. Angela Merici; Dorchester, MA St. Matthew.
Joyce, Brian '63 (OAK) Pleasant Hill, CA Christ the King.
Joyce, Daniel R.J. *s.j.* '01 (PH)[C] Jesuit Fathers; [Y] Loyola Center and Manresa Hall.
Joyce, Rev. Msgr. David J. '68 (SPR) Springfield, MA Our Lady of Hope; Vicars for the Clergy; Bishop's Commission for Clergy; Diocesan Consultors; Presbyteral Council; Co Vicars For Clergy; Springfield, MA Holy Name.
Joyce, Donald J. *o.m.i.* '58 (SAT)[K] San Antonio, TX Oblate Madonna Residence.
Joyce, Edward *c.pp.s.* '56 (CIN)[N] Dayton Provincial Office of the Cincinnati Province of the Society of the Precious Blood.
Joyce, George V. '43 (WDC) Retired.
Joyce, Gerald P. '61 (CHI) Westchester, IL Divine Infant Retired.
Joyce, James F. *s.j.* '75 (BUF)[G] Cheektowaga, NY Catholic Central School.
Joyce, James K. '72 (SPR) Pittsfield, MA Sacred Heart.
Joyce, James M. '48 (SFS) Worldwide Marriage Encounter.
Joyce, James '48 (SFS) Retired.
Joyce, John J. '89 (BEL) Okawville, IL St. Barbara.
Joyce, John M. '54 (ORG) Irvine, CA St. John Neumann Retired.
Joyce, Kevin P. '80 (SJ) Campbell, CA St. Lucy.
Joyce, Michael P. *c.m.* '76 (STL)[O] St. Louis, MO Lazarist Residence.
Joyce, Michael P. *c.m.* '76 (MEM) Chancellor; Presbyteral Council; Judicial Vicar; Secretary for Administration; Secretary for Ministry Services; Clergy Personnel Board.
Joyce, Michael S. *o.f.m.* '67 (PRO)[N] Providence, RI St. Francis Chapel & City Ministry Center; [P] Providence, RI St. Francis Friary.
Joyce, Michael *o.f.m.cap.* '85 (CLV)[A] Wickliffe, OH Borromeo Seminary.
Joyce, Michael '63 (OAK) Retired.
Joyce, Rev. Msgr. Peter M. '92 (CAM) Judges.
Joyce, Rev. Msgr. Peter M. '92 (CAM)[C] Richland, NJ St. Augustine Preparatory School.
Joyce, Peter '83 (WOR) Southbridge, MA St. Mary; St. Mary.
Joyce, Randal *c.p.* '50 (DET)[K] Detroit, MI St. Paul of the Cross Community, Congregation of the Passion.
Joyce, Raymond '62 (WCH)[C] Wichita, KS Via Christi Regional Medical Center, Inc. Retired.
Joyce, Thomas *c.p.* '69 (BRK)[T] Jamaica, NY Immaculate Conception Monastery.
Joyce, Thomas *c.m.f.* '59 (CHI)[N] Chicago, IL Barbastro House (Claretian Candidate House).
Joyce, Timothy J. '59 (BO)[U] Hingham, MA Glastonbury Abbey.
Joyce, William F. '60 (BO) Readville, MA St. Anne.
Joynes, Rev. Msgr. Joseph P. '64 (CAM) Retired.
Jozefiak, Gregory '92 (PEO) Rock Island, IL St. Mary; Rock Island, IL Sacred Heart; Rock Island, IL St. Joseph's; [B] Rock Island, IL Alleman High School.
Jozefiak, Matthew *c.pp.s.* (TOL) Cloverdale, OH St. John the Baptist; Ottawa, OH SS. Peter and Paul.
Jozwaik, Lawrence W. (GAL) Houston, TX Co-Cathedral of the Sacred Heart.
Jozwiak, Lawrence W. '87 (GAL) Metropolitan Tribunal.
Jozwiak, Richard '59 (SAG) Retired.
Jozwiak, Ronald J. '79 (DET) Troy, MI St. Elizabeth Ann Seton; Judges.
Ju, Minkee '98 (JOL) Darien, IL Our Lady of Korean Martyrs Mission.
Ju, Yong Don '94 (RVC) Woodbury, NY Holy Name of Jesus.
Juan, Dennis R. '98 (ATL) Griffin, GA Sacred Heart.
Juan, Francisco '63 (ARE) Orocovis, PR San Juan Bautista.
Juan, Marcial '66 (LA) Glendale, CA Holy Family.
Juan, Vincent R. '03 (SAC) On Duty Outside the Diocese.
Juantorena, Raphael '98 (BR) Hispanic Apostolate.
Juarez, Federico (Rene) *o.f.m.* '69 (LA) Los Angeles, CA Divine Saviour.
Juarez, J. Alejandro *o.f.m.* '88 (ELP)[B] El Paso, TX St. Anthony's School of Theology; El Paso, TX St. Francis of Assisi Mission.
Juarez, Lawrence '75 (CIN) Cincinnati, OH Old St. Mary.
Juarez, Lucio '91 (LA) Santa Maria, CA St. John Neumann.
Juarez, Mario '09 (ORG) Dana Point, CA St. Edward the Confessor.
Juarez, Miguel Angel Gusatvo Ruiz '06 (SPK) Brewster, WA Sacred Heart; Twisp, WA St. Genevieve.
Juarez, Robert Jesus '80 (LA) On Administrative Leave.
Juarez, Rudolph T. '80 (DAV) Vicar for Hispanics; Iowa City, IA St. Patrick's; Judges; Diocesan Consultors; Vicar for Hispanics.
Juarez, Thomas *s.d.b.* '66 (LAR) Laredo, TX San Luis Rey.
Juchniewicz, Leon '80 (SAC) Vallejo, CA St. Basil; College of Consultors; Priests' Personnel Board, Diocesan.
Judd, Stephen P. *m.m.* '78 (FgM) Maryknoll, NY MARYKNOLL.
Judd, Timothy '56 (LUB) Retired.
Jude, Robert J. '49 (STP) Retired.
Judge, Anthony *c.ss.r.* '79 (CHI) Chicago, IL St. Michael in Old Town; [N] Chicago, IL The Redemptorist Fathers of Chicago.
Judge, James G. '72 (BUF) Council of Priests; Buffalo, NY St. Martin; Buffalo, NY St. Thomas Aquinas.
Judge, Rev. Msgr. John G. '69 (NEW) Upper Montclair, NJ St. Cassian.
Judge, Philip G. *s.j.* '93 (NY)[F] New York, NY Regis High School; [EE] New York, NY St. Ignatius Loyola Residence.
Judge, Robert K. *s.j.* '65 (BAL)[S] Baltimore, MD Colombiere Jesuit Community.
Judge, Russell R. '78 (JC) Vandalia, MO Sacred Heart; Vandalia, MO Women's Eastern Missouri Reception, Diagnostic and Correctional Center.
Judge, Timothy M. '79 (PH) Royersford, PA Sacred Heart; Diocesan Priests' Compensation and Benefits Committee; Navy Reserve Chaplains.
Judie, John T. '87 (L) Louisville, KY Christ the King; Louisville, KY Immaculate Heart of Mary; Ex Officio.
Judy, Albert G. *o.p.* '62 (CHI) River Forest, IL St. Vincent Ferrer.
Judy, Myron *o.carm.* '63 (JOL)[L] Darien Carmelite Provincial Office.
Juelfs, Daniel '73 (RC) Rapid City, SD Blessed Sacrament; Rapid City, SD St. Rose of Lima; Vicar General; Diocesan Consultors.
Juenker, Rev. Msgr. Paul R. '45 (BUF)[O] Tonawanda, NY O'Hara Residence Retired.
Juettner, Mark R. '79 (STP) St. Paul, MN St. Andrew.
Jugan, Joseph J. '58 (PBR) Canonsburg, PA St. Michael; Protopresbyters.
Jugenheimer, James R. '87 (GB) Vicariate.
Jugenheimer, James R. '87 (GB) Oshkosh, WI Most Blessed Sacrament.
Juhas, John J. '75 (CLV) Kirtland, OH Divine Word Retired.
Juhl, Dennis D. '73 (DUB) Waterloo, IA Blessed Sacrament; Church Design/Renovation Commission.
Juknialis, Joseph J. '69 (MIL) Eden, WI Shepherd of the Hills (Good Shepherd).
Juleen, Stuart '77 (SAT) San Antonio, TX St. John The Evangelist.
Julian, Mario F. *o.f.m.* '81 (ALB) Troy, NY St. Anthony of Padua (Shrine Church).
Julien, Eddy '67 (RVC) Haitian–American Apostolate; Elmont, NY St. Boniface.
Julien, Roland M. '65 (STA) Gainesville, FL St. Patrick Church; [L] Gainesville, FL Spirit Radio of North Florida, Inc.; Deans.
Julius, James A. '65 (STL) Retired.
Jun–Seok, Abel Han '03 (PH) Philadelphia, PA Holy Angels.
Junak, Jacek *c.r.* '95 (RCK) Johnsburg, IL St. John the Baptist.
Juncer, Bartholomew *s.j.c.* '08 (CHI) Chicago, IL St. John Cantius; [P] Chicago, IL Canons Regular of Saint John Cantius.
Jung, Benedict *s.j.* '04 (WDC)[N] Washington, DC The Jesuit Community at Georgetown University.
Jung, Cheol Hyun (SAV) Augusta, GA St. Joseph.
Jung, Dennet *o.f.m.* '63 (GRY)[H] Cedar Lake, IN San Damiano Friary; Councillors:.
Jung, Dennet *o.f.m.* '63 (PEO) Bloomington, IL St. Mary's.
Jung, Dominic *c.pp.s.* (BO) Korean.
Jung, Jerome L. '93 (POD) Berkeley.
Jung, Jerome L. '93 (OAK)[Q] Berkeley, CA Opus Dei.
Jung, Joseph B. '56 (PH) Retired.
Jung, Michael *o.s.b.* '63 (BR) Baton Rouge, LA St. Agnes; Baton Rouge, LA Baton Rouge General Medical Center.
Jung, Michael *o.s.b.* '63 (NO)[P] St. Benedict, LA St. Joseph Abbey.
Junge, Heiko '96 (P) Absent on Leave.
Jungmann, William '03 (DEN) Holyoke, CO St. Patrick.
Jungwirth, Alphonse *c.pp.s.* '43 (CIN)[N] Carthagena, OH St. Charles Retired.
Juniet, Paul *o.f.m.* '66 (SFE) Jemez Pueblo, NM San Diego Indian Missions.
Junio, Joven T. *m.s.* '86 (SB)[I] Moreno Valley, CA Missionaries of Our Lady of La Salette, MS; Moreno Valley, CA St. Christopher.
Junius, Richard *o.m.i.* '56 (FgM) Washington, DC AMERICAN OBLATE MISSIONS.
Junker, Nicholas G. '08 (BEL) Belleville, IL St. Luke; Belleville, IL St. Teresa of the Child Jesus.
Jupin, Alan D. '62 (ALB) Retired.
Jura, Jacek A. '04 (CHI) Glenview, IL Our Lady of Perpetual Help; Niles, IL St. John Brebeuf.
Juracek, Joseph *o.f.m.* '83 (NY) Obernburg, NY St. Mary.
Juran, Michael P. '76 (BUF) On Duty Outside the Diocese.
Juran, Michael '76 (SP) Valrico, FL St. Stephen.
Juras, Callistus *o.f.m.conv.* '54 (BAL)[S] Ellicott City Order of Friars Minor Conventual Retired.
Jurcak, Lawrence '81 (CLV) Cleveland, OH Cathedral of St. John the Evangelist; Adjunct Judicial Vicars; Secretary; Senior Priests; Washington, DC Canon Law Society of America.
Jurek, Daniel J. '73 (BEL) Prairie du Rocher, IL St. Joseph; Diocesan Consultors; Diocesan Deans; Modoc, IL St. Leo; Big Muddy River Correctional Center.
Jurewicz, Francis Z. '59 (PIT) Retired.
Jurgelonis, Joseph J. '73 (WOR) East Templeton, MA Holy Cross; Templeton Developmental Center; Otter River, MA St. Martin Mission.
Jurgensmeier, Charles *s.j.* '88 (CHI)[C] Chicago, IL Jesuit Community at Loyola University Chicago.
Juric, Ante *o.f.m.* '72 (SJ) San Jose, CA St. Mary of the Assumption.
Juric, Jakov (GLP) On Duty Outside of Diocese.
Jurisich, Melvin A. *o.f.m.* '70 (OAK)[R] Oakland, CA Province of Saint Barbara Fraternal Care Trust.
Jurisich, Melvin A. *o.f.m.* '70 (LA)[V] Malibu, CA Serra Retreat.
Jurjewicz, Hubert '09 (PAT) East Hanover, NJ St. Rose of Lima.
Jurkiewicz, Andrezej '83 (ORL) Representative for Unincardinated Priests; Polish Ministry.
Jurkiewicz, Andrzej '83 (ORL) Orlando, FL St. Joseph.
Jurkovich, Robb M. '04 (MAR) Vicars Forane; Menominee, MI Resurrection.
Jurkowski, Joseph V. '58 (CAM) Atlantic City, NJ Church of St. Nicholas, Atlantic City, N.J.
Jurkus, Alan F. '70 (MIL) Greendale, WI St. Alphonsus.
Juroszek, Robert S. '05 (MO) CIVIL AIR PATROL.
Juroszek, Robert *t.o.r.* '05 (ALT) Altoona, PA Our Lady of Mt. Carmel.
Jurzyk, Marek '91 (JOL) Bolingbrook, IL St. Dominic.
Jussa, Inacio *s.j.* '07 (NY)[B] Bronx, NY Ciszek Hall.
Just, Felix N.W. *s.j.* '91 (ORG)[I] Anaheim, CA Manresa Jesuit Residence; [H] Orange, CA Loyola Institute for Spirituality.
Justavino, Teodoro *c.m.* '90 (FgM) Philadelphia, PA Eastern Province.
Justice, Joseph Charles '75 (ORG) Absent on Sick Leave.
Juszczak, John W. *c.ss.r.* '88 (MO) Air Force Chaplains.
Jutt, Anthony J. '51 (SPR) Retired.
Jutte, Edgar *c.pp.s.* '62 (CIN)[N] Dayton Provincial Office of the Cincinnati Province of the Society of the Precious Blood.
Jutton, David J. '66 (SY) Retired.
Juya, Filemon '81 (CHR) Batesburg–Leesville, SC St. John of the Cross; Vicar for Hispanic Ministry; Personnel Committee; Office of Hispanic Ministries.
Juza, Philip J. '95 (SUP) Hayward, WI St. Joseph; South Central Deanery; Pastoral Consultors; Personnel Placement Board.
Juzix, Richard *o.f.m.* '75 (LA) Los Angeles, CA St. Francis of Assisi.
Juzix, Richard *o.f.m.* '75 (ORG) Huntington Beach, CA SS. Simon and Jude.

K

Kabali, Joseph '96 (MET) Flemington, NJ St. Magdalen de Pazzi; Hunterdon Medical Center.
Kabango, Jean–Marie *o.f.m.* '99 (WDC) Silver Spring, MD St. Camillus.
Kabat, Daniel *o.f.m.cap.* '60 (LA) Solvang, CA Old Mission Santa Ines.
Kabat, Robert J. '79 (GB) Seymour, WI St. John; Judicial Vicar; Conciliation and Arbitration Board;

Bonduel, WI St. Lawrence; Judges; Seymour, WI St. Sebastian.
Kaberia, Silvio '83 (RIC) Virginia Beach, VA St. Luke.
Kabiru, Francis '07 (DUL) Grand Rapids, MN St. Joseph.
Kabongo–Mukuna, Jean Pierre '82 (MIL) Milwaukee, WI Froedtert Memorial Lutheran Hospital; Wauwatosa, WI St. Jude the Apostle.
Kabot, Damian *s.v.d.* '02 (LA) Los Angeles, CA St. John, The Evangelist.
Kacalo, Robert C. '06 (MIL) Whitefish Bay, WI Holy Family.
Kacerguis, Edward '82 (ALB)[Q] Troy, NY The Rensselaer Newman Foundation; [Q] Troy, NY University Parish of Christ Sun of Justice; Campus Ministry.
Kachappilly, Xavier *o.ss.t.* '08 (BAL)[S] The Trinitarians in India (Bangalore & Trichur).
Kachel, Czeslaw L. '57 (PRO)[P] Providence St. John Vianney Residence Retired.
Kachel, Steven J. '95 (LC) Tomah, WI St. Mary (Immaculate Conception); Warrens, WI St. Andrew; Deans; St. Joseph's Priest Fund, Inc., (Benevolent Society); DEPARTMENT OF VETERANS AFFAIRS HOSPITALS AND CHAPLAINS.
Kachuba, Rt. Rev. Mitred Archpriest John S. '74 (PRM) Euclid, OH St. Stephen; Ex Officio; Protosyncellus; Presbyteral Council; Eparchial Pastoral Council; Eparchial Finance Officer; Eparchial Consultors; Office of Religious Education; Seminary Education Formation Board; Priest's Pension Board.
Kachuba, Samuel S. '08 (BGP) Fairfield, CT St. Pius X.
Kachur, Oleh '03 (SJP) On Assignment Outside the Diocese; Presbyters.
Kachurka, Edward M. '89 (BRK) Flushing, NY St. Ann.
Kacinko, Elmer A. '61 (GBG) Retired.
Kacirk, Raymond J. *s.m.* '59 (STL)[O] St. Louis Marianists, Province of the United States (Society of Mary).
Kacprzak, Stanley '85 (ROC) Webster, NY St. Paul.
Kaczkowski, Conrad J. *s.m.* '68 (SAT)[C] San Antonio, TX St. Mary's University of San Antonio, Texas Retired.
Kaczmarczyk, Pawel '03 (DET) Royal Oak, MI National Shrine of the Little Flower.
Kaczmarek, David *t.o.r.* '06 (ORL) Cursillos de Cristiandad; [F] Winter Park, FL Franciscan Friars, T.O.R., San Pedro Friary; [E] Winter Park, FL San Pedro Spiritual Development Center.
Kaczmarek, Rev. Msgr. James A. '69 (MAR) Iron Mountain, MI Immaculate Conception of the Blessed Virgin Mary; Veterans Administration Center.
Kaczmarek, Peter '69 (RVC) Greenlawn, NY St. Francis of Assisi.
Kaczmarek, Thaddeus J. '71 (GBG) Murrysville, PA Mother of Sorrows; Finance Council.
Kaczorowski, Edward J. '58 (WIL) Bear, DE Retired.
Kaczorowski, James T. '73 (CHI) Chicago, IL Queen of Angels; Deans.
Kaczowka, Julian *s.ch.* '88 (JOL) Joliet, IL St. Mary Nativity; Joliet, IL Holy Cross.
Kaczynski, Krzysztof '93 (MET) Milford, NJ St. Edward the Confessor.
Kadambukatt, Ambrose Joseph *o.c.d.* '98 (LA)[J] Lynwood, CA St. Francis Medical Center.
Kadavil, Antony '67 (MOB) Mobile, AL St. Mary.
Kaddo, Chorbishop Joseph F. '72 (SAM) Fall River, MA St. Anthony of the Desert; Presbyteral Council.
Kaddo, Chorbishop Joseph (OLL) Order of St. Sharbel.
Kadera, Thomas R. '87 (CHY) Cheyenne, WY U.S. Veterans Administration Hospital 1; Defenders of the Bond; St. Joseph's Society for Priests (Clergy Mutual Benefit Society); Air Force Reserve Chaplains; Adjutant Judicial Vicar; Adjutant Judicial Vicar.
Kaderabek, Matthew *l.c.* (CHI)[N] Hillside, IL Legion of Christ.
Kadlec, Jared '97 (FAR) Kindred, ND St. Maurice; Horace, ND St. Benedict's Church of Wild Rice; Judges.
Kado, Paul '06 (FRS) Ridgecrest, CA St. Ann.
Kadrmas, Christopher J. '00 (BIS) Menoken, ND St. Hildegard; Judicial Vicar; Presbyteral Council.
Kadukappillil, Thomas '91 (SYM) Somerset, NJ St. Thomas Syro–Malabar Catholic Church.
Kadungamparambil, Josep Augustine '87 (RVC) Merrick, NY Curé of Ars.
Kaduppil, Roy Joseph '91 (SYM) Chancellor & Secretary to Bishop; Eparchial Consultors.
Kaduthodil, Abraham (CHI) Forest Park, IL St. Bernardine; [M] Northlake, IL Villa Scalabrini Nursing and Rehabilitation Center.
Kaech, Paul A. '06 (SEA) Raymond, WA St. Lawrence; Seaview, WA St. Mary.
Kaeding, Robert F. '73 (TR) On Duty Outside the Diocese.
Kaelin, Dennis J. '76 (NEW) Rahway, NJ St. Mark's; Elizabeth, NJ; Rahway, NJ St. Mary's.
Kafara, Andrew '85 (SAT) Pearsall, TX Immaculate Heart of Mary.
Kagan, Rev. Msgr. David D. '75 (RCK) Special Assignment; Vicars General; Moderator of the Curia; Diocesan Consultors; Newspaper; Pro Synodal Judges.
Kaggwa, Denis '04 (SFE) Ohkay Owingeh, NM St. John the Baptist.
Kagoma, Clement (NEW) Newark, NJ St. Michael Medical Center.
Kagoo, Edwin '80 (AUS) St. John Vianney.
Kahan, Paul *s.v.d.* '99 (BLX)[D] Bay St. Louis, MS Southern Province of St. Augustine – Provincial Offices.
Kahan, Paul *s.v.d.* '99 (FWT) Fort Worth, TX St. Rita.
Kahle, George G. *c.s.c.* '53 (FTW)[H] Holy Cross House.
Kahle, Jason J. '09 (TOL) Sandusky, OH St. Mary; [D] Sandusky, OH Sandusky Central Catholic School.
Kahlhamer, Bernard '59 (SCL) Foley, MN St. Lawrence's; Sauk Rapids, MN St. Patrick.
Kahlich, Daniel P. '66 (VIC) Columbus, TX St. Anthony's; Defenders of the Bond.
Kahn, Eric *o.f.m.* '55 (STL)[O] St. Louis Franciscan Friary of St. Anthony of Padua Retired.
Kahrs, Lee J. '65 (GB) Defenders of the Bond Retired.
Kahumburu, Joseph '83 (NY) Mamaroneck, NY Most Holy Trinity.
Kaicher, Edward '80 (SD) Vista, CA St. Francis of Assisi.
Kaichiramattathil, Stephen *s.a.c.* '96 (MIL)[P] Milwaukee, WI Pallotti House.
Kail, Chorbishop Michael J. '74 (OLL) Livonia, MI St. Rafka Maronite Catholic Mission; Warren, MI St. Sharbel Maronite Catholic Church; College of Consultors; Office of Liturgy; Presbyteral Council; Protopresbyters.
Kaim, Phillip '03 (MO) Active Outside the Diocese; Air Force Chaplains.
Kaimann, Gerald J. '70 (JC) Brookfield, MO Immaculate Conception; Marceline, MO St. Bonaventure; Ministry to Priests; Milan, MO St. Mary.
Kain, Rev. Msgr. Peter V. '65 (BRK) Brooklyn, NY St. Ephrem; Presbyteral Council; Peter Turner Insurance Co.; Diocesan Insurance Committee; Diocesan Consultors.
Kaipayil, Joseph *m.c.b.s.* '86 (NOR) Old Saybrook, CT St. John.
Kairouz, Elie G. '01 (SAM) Troy, NY St. Ann.
Kairu, James Kimani '94 (OAK) Richmond, CA St. David of Wales.
Kais, Paul D. '02 (POD)[N] Houston, TX Opus Dei; Vicar for Texas; Houston.
Kaiser, Gary Edward '06 (EVN) Diocesan Council of Priests; Jasper, IN Precious Blood; Diocesan Consultors.
Kaiser, Joseph W. '55 (RCK) Retired.
Kaiser, Lawrence B. '73 (DEN) Denver, CO Guardian Angels.
Kaiser, Lawrence H. '64 (DET) Retired.
Kaiser, Rev. Msgr. Ralph L. '54 (KC) Buckner, MO Church of the Santa Fe.
Kaithackal, Sebastian D. *c.m.i.* '81 (MET) Woodbridge, NJ St. James; Perth Amboy, NJ Raritan Bay Medical Center.
Kajoh, Robert T. *m.s.p.* (GAL) Houston, TX St. Philip Neri.
Kakareka, Joseph R. '72 (SCR) Sugar Notch, PA Holy Family Parish.
Kakascik, Rev. Msgr. Edward '55 (STU) Marietta, OH St. Mary's Retired.
Kakaty, Rt. Rev. Edward G. '72 (NTN) Waterford, CT St. Ann.
Kakaty, Rt. Rev. Edward '72 (NTN) National Association of Melkite Women.
Kakkuzhiyil, John *s.d.b.* '86 (MO) DEPARTMENT OF VETERANS AFFAIRS HOSPITALS AND CHAPLAINS.
Kakkuzhiyil, John *s.d.b.* '86 (GI) Valentine, NE St. Nicholas.
Kakwezi, Benedict (FTW) Decatur, IN St. Mary of the Assumption.
Kalabat, Frank '95 (EST) West Bloomfield, MI St. Thomas Chaldean Catholic Parish; Eparchial College of Consultors; Diocesan Corporation–The Chaldean Catholic Church of U.S.A.
Kalachalil, Roy Kurian *o.ss.t.* '08 (BAL)[S] The Trinitarians in India (Bangalore & Trichur).
Kalaj, Frederik '01 (DET) Erie, MI St. Joseph.
Kalam, Thomas *c.m.i.* '69 (NSH)[K] Liberty, TN Carmel Center of Spirituality; [A] Nashville, TN Aquinas College; [L] Nashville, TN Dominican Campus.
Kalamaja, Theodore M. *s.j.* '67 (NO) New Orleans, LA Orleans Parish Criminal Sheriff's Office Community Correctional Center; [P] New Orleans, LA Ignatius Residence.
Kalampatt, George '81 (AMA) Umbarger, TX St. Mary's; Happy, TX Holy Name of Jesus.
Kalamuzi, Ivan '05 (COV)[B] Maysville, KY St. Patrick High School; Maysville, KY St. Patrick.
Kalappura, George *c.m.i.* '60 (BEA) Beaumont, TX St. Anthony Cathedral Basilica; Convalescent Home Ministry.
Kalarickal, Joseph *m.s.t.* '90 (SP) New Port Richey, FL Our Lady Queen of Peace.
Kalarickal, Luka U. *m.s.f.s.* '88 (TYL)[B] Whitehouse, TX The Missionaries of St. Francis de Sales.
Kalas, Ronald N. '59 (CHI) Park Ridge, IL Mary, Seat of Wisdom; Deans Retired.
Kalata, Dominic P. '65 (ALN) Tremont, PA Most Blessed Trinity Parish.
Kalathil, Francis Osana *o.c.d.* '79 (LA) Downey, CA St. Raymond.
Kalaw, Teodoro *c.r.m.* (CHR)[H] Spartanburg, SC Converse College; Spartanburg, SC Jesus Our Risen Savior.
Kalayil, Roy Jacob (CC) Aransas Pass, TX St. Mary, Star of the Sea.
Kalb, Howard E. *s.j.* '54 (OM)[K] Omaha, NE Jesuit Community at Creighton University.
Kalchik, Paul J. '99 (CHI) Chicago, IL Resurrection.
Kalck, Michael V. '74 (CHI) Chicago, IL Holy Rosary.
Kalema, Josephat Kato *o.c.s.o.* '85 (NEW) Newark, NJ The Parish of the Transfiguration.
Kalema, Mark '88 (CHI) Chicago, IL Our Lady of Peace.
Kalemeera, Augustine (MIL) Shorewood, WI St. Robert.
Kaler, Adolph *o.m.i.* '57 (SAT)[K] San Antonio, TX Oblate Madonna Residence.
Kalert, David *o.m.i.* '64 (SAT)[L] San Antonio, TX De Mazenod House; [C] Oblate School of Theology.
Kaley, Richard *o.f.m.conv.* '75 (IND) Terre Haute, IN St. Joseph University Parish.
Kalich, Patrick J. '94 (GRY) Crown Point, IN St. Mary.
Kalicky, John E. *c.pp.s.* '61 (GRY) Whiting, IN St. John the Baptist; Whiting, IN St. Adalbert; Whiting, IN Immaculate Conception; Whiting, IN Sacred Heart.
Kalil, Gordon '94 (SR) Napa, CA St. John the Baptist; Priests' Council.
Kalin, William A. '59 (LIN)[E] Lincoln, NE Bonacum House Retired.
Kalina, Isaac *o.s.b.* '89 (LA)[P] Valyermo, CA St. Andrew's Abbey.
Kalinowski, Dariusz '99 (FR) Graduate Studies.
Kalinowski, Joseph J. '79 (MO) On Duty Outside Diocese; Army Chaplains.
Kalinowski, Loren M. '75 (SAG) Mount Pleasant, MI Sacred Heart.
Kalinowski, Ryszard *s.v.d.* '74 (LAF) Jeanerette, LA Our Lady of the Rosary.
Kalinski, Eugene E. '60 (GB)[J] Oshkosh, WI Community of Our Lady.
Kalisch, Jonathan *o.p.* '03 (HRT)[Q] Hamden, CT Catholic Community at Quinnipiac University.
Kalisch, Jonathan *o.p.* '03 (MAN)[K] Hanover, NH Order of Preachers; [O] Hanover, NH The Catholic Student Center at Dartmouth, Aquinas House, Aquinas at Dartmouth, Inc.
Kalist, Pancrose '88 (NY) Staten Island, NY Our Lady, Queen of Peace.
Kalista, Timothy D. '03 (CLV) Chardon, OH St. Mary.
Kalita, Thomas M. '74 (WDC) Olney, MD St. Peter.
Kalivela, Prabhakar '97 (OKL) Okeene, OK St. Anthony's.
Kaliyadan, William V. *m.s.* '94 (MAN) Lebanon, NH Sacred Heart; Vicars Forane.
Kalkman, Richard '56 (SCL) Retired.
Kall, Anthony *o.f.m.conv.* '71 (ALB)[R] Rensselaer, NY Assisi in Albany, Inc.; Albany, NY Holy Family Parish; Presbyteral Council; Diocesan Board of Consultors.
Kallabat, Stephen H. '66 (EST) Oak Park, MI Mar Addai Chaldean Parish; Eparchial College of Consultors; Eparchial Tribunal.
Kalladan, Joseph K. '69 (GAL) Sugar Land, TX St. Thomas Aquinas.
Kallaher, Timothy S. '72 (CIN) Cincinnati, OH St. John the Baptist; Judges; Priest Councilors.
Kallarackal, Lijo *o.s.b.silv.* (STL) Eureka, MO Sacred Heart.
Kallarackal, Sebastian *c.m.i.* '77 (SHP) Monroe, LA Our Lady of Fatima; [F] Monroe, LA Catholic Campus Ministry at the University of Louisiana at Monroe.
Kallock, Michael J. *c.s.p.* '73 (NY)[EE] Jamaica Estates, NY Paulist Fathers Generalate.
Kallock, Michael J. *c.s.p.* '73 (CHI) Chicago, IL Old St. Mary.
Kallookalam, Joseph *c.m.i.* '71 (SHP) Shreveport, LA St. Pius X.
Kallukalam, Jose '72 (STA) Jacksonville Beach, FL St. Paul's.
Kallumady, Thomas '73 (NY) New York, NY Holy Innocents.
Kallumkalkudy, George *c.m.i.* '76 (STP) Minneapolis, MN St. Austin.
Kalluvilayil, Job (GAL) Houston, TX St. Thomas More.
Kalombo, Jean Rene '95 (OWN) Owensboro, KY SS. Joseph and Paul.
Kalonga, Simon '84 (DEN) Denver, CO Cure D'Ars.
Kalousieh, George '81 (OLN) Little Falls, NJ Sacred Heart.
Kalscheuer, Henry N. '59 (MAD) Retired.
Kalscheuer, Roger '80 (OM) Omaha, NE St. James.
Kalscheuer, Gregory *s.j.* '01 (BO)[U] Newton, MA The Jesuit Community at Boston College.
Kaltenbach, Victor J. '62 (SFD) Greenville, IL St. Lawrence.

Kaltreider, Carl E. '79 (CHL) Andrews, NC Holy Redeemer.
Kalu, Clement '84 (NY) Staten Island, NY Richmond University Medical Center.
Kalu, Hyacinth '95 (LA) Walnut, CA St. Lorenzo Ruiz.
Kalu, Samuel '95 (LFT) Associate Judges.
Kalungi, John *a.j.* '89 (NY) Bronx, NY St. Angela Merici.
Kaluza, Michael C. '07 (STP) St. Paul, MN St. Vincent de Paul; St. Paul, MN Cathedral of Saint Paul.
Kamas, John A. *s.s.s.* '75 (NY) New York, NY St. Francis de Sales.
Kamas, John *s.s.s.* '75 (CLV)[N] Cleveland Congregation of the Blessed Sacrament Provincial House.
Kamau, Thomas (NY) Hawthorne, NY Holy Rosary.
Kamber, Kenneth L. '53 (L) Retired.
Kambitsch, Larry '69 (MRY) Tres Pinos, CA Immaculate Conception.
Kamenski, Thomas *o.f.m.* '82 (MIL)[P] Burlington, WI Queen of Peace Friary.
Kamide, Rev. Msgr. Paul T. '63 (ORL) Retired.
Kamienski, Gabriel *s.d.s.* '82 (SAT) Hobson, TX St. Boniface; [L] Falls City, TX Salvatorian Fathers Community of Texas.
Kamienski, Joseph J. *s.j.* '77 (NY)[F] Bronx, NY Fordham Preparatory School.
Kamiensky, Joseph J. *s.j.* '76 (NY)[EE] Jesuit Community, Kohlmann Hall.
Kaminski, Dariusz K. '91 (PAT) Paterson, NJ St. Stephen's.
Kaminski, Edward J. *c.s.c.* '75 (PHX) Phoenix, AZ Our Lady of the Valley Roman Catholic Parish; Glendale, AZ St. Raphael Roman Catholic Parish.
Kaminski, Edward J. *c.s.c.* '75 (FTW)[H] Notre Dame Congregation of Holy Cross, Indiana Province, Provincial House.
Kaminski, Frank T. *s.j.* '76 (WDC)[Q] Faulkner, MD Loyola Retreat House.
Kaminski, Louis T. '77 (MO) Army National Guard Chaplains; Old Forge, PA St. Mary; Old Forge, PA Prince of Peace, Old Forge.
Kaminski, Mark P. '01 (SY) Cortland, NY St. Anthony of Padua; Cortland, NY St. Mary.
Kaminski, Stephen J. '91 (CLV) Wickliffe, OH Our Lady of Mount Carmel; Concord, OH Tri Point Medical Center; Willoughby, OH Lake Health Hospital, Willoughby Campus.
Kaminski, Thomas J. '66 (CHI) Chicago, IL St. Helena.
Kaminsky, Joseph T. '61 (HRT) Wallingford, CT Resurrection.
Kammen, Paul A. '07 (STP) Chanhassen, MN St. Hubert.
Kammer, Alfred C. *s.j.* '76 (NO)[C] New Orleans, LA Loyola University New Orleans.
Kammer, Matt (SPK)[F] Chewelah, WA St. Joseph's Hospital (of Chewelah).
Kammerer, James '97 (SAT) On Leave.
Kammerer, Joseph '98 (LA) Redondo Beach, CA St. James.
Kammerer, Raymond '64 (CIN) Waynesville, OH St. Augustine.
Kammerer, Richard F. '80 (RVC) Deer Park, NY SS. Cyril and Methodius; Hicksville, NY Our Lady of Mercy.
Kamp, Francis J. *s.v.d.* '47 (CHI)[N] Techny, IL Divine Word Residence.
Kampschneider, Daniel J. '79 (OM) Omaha, NE St. Vincent de Paul.
Kamundo, Leopold '87 (ALB) Schenectady, NY St. John the Evangelist.
Kanagarajan, Lourdusamy '93 (DUL) Sandstone, MN Sacred Heart; Sandstone, MN St. Joseph; Sandstone, MN St. Luke.
Kanai, Charles '95 (MO) Army Reserve Chaplains.
Kanat, Joseph Kurian '58 (LAF) Lafayette, LA Cathedral of St. John the Evangelist.
Kanat, Kurian (LAF) On Special Assignment.
Kanavalil, Joseph Thomas *c.m.i.* '99 (SFE) Santa Rosa, NM St. Rose of Lima.
Kandathikudy, Jos '71 (SYM) Bronx, NY St. Thomas Syro–Malabar Catholic Church; Eparchial Consultors.
Kandathiparambil, Joseph John '94 (BIS) Garrison, ND St. Nicholas; Garrison, ND Immaculate Conception; Garrison, ND Sacred Heart.
Kandathiparampil, Joseph '63 (WIL) Retired.
Kandra, Antone *o.f.m.conv.* '57 (ALB) Nassau, NY St. Mary; [L] Rensselaer, NY Franciscan Mission House.
Kandrac, Antone *o.f.m.conv.* '57 (ALB)[L] Rensselaer, NY Provincialate, Immaculate Conception Friary – Order of Friars Minor Conventual.
Kandt, Gregory '90 (RIC) Charlottesville, VA Church of the Incarnation.
Kandyuk, Valeriy '90 (STN) Detroit, MI St. John the Baptist.
Kane, Brian P. '00 (MO) Morse Bluff, NE St. George; [C] Wahoo, NE Bishop Neumann Jr.–Sr. High School; Army National Guard Chaplains; [L] Wahoo, NE Bishop Neumann High School Endowment Fund; Presbyteral Council.
Kane, Edward R. '78 (BRK) Brooklyn, NY Holy Family.
Kane, Farrell J. *o.carm.* '65 (CHI) Gurnee, IL St. Paul the Apostle.
Kane, George J. '51 (CHI) Retired.
Kane, Rev. Msgr. James D. '58 (SY)[Q] Binghamton, NY McDevitt Residence for Retired Priests Retired.
Kane, James E. '51 (DEN) Retired.
Kane, James J. '71 (ALB) Mechanicville, NY Assumption–St. Paul.
Kane, James '71 (ALB) Stillwater, NY St. Peter the Apostle; Presbyteral Council; Diocesan Board of Consultors; Ecumenical and Interreligious Affairs of the Roman Catholic Diocese of Albany, Commission for.
Kane, John E. *c.m.* '70 (MOB) Opelika, AL St. Mary of the Mission; Hispanic Apostolate.
Kane, John '69 (SP) Retired.
Kane, Joseph F. '46 (SY)[Q] Syracuse, NY Tommy Coyne Residence Dillon Hall Retired.
Kane, Joseph M. '70 (BO) Senior Priests. Retired.
Kane, Joseph P. *s.j.* '68 (NY)[EE] New York, NY Murray–Weigel Hall.
Kane, Rev. Msgr. Joseph T. '62 (PH) Retired.
Kane, Joseph '67 (EVN) Retired.
Kane, Michael '80 (PSC) Coconut Creek, FL Our Lady of the Sign.
Kane, Paul '96 (MIA) Pompano Beach, FL St. Elizabeth of Hungary Catholic Church.
Kane, Philip M. '88 (JC) Pilot Grove, MO St. Joseph.
Kane, Terence '68 (ATL) Hartwell, GA Sacred Heart of Jesus.
Kane, Thomas A. *c.s.p.* '75 (NY)[EE] Jamaica Estates Paulist Fathers Generalate.
Kane, Rev. Msgr. Thomas A. '52 (WDC) Retired.
Kane, Rev. Msgr. Thomas S. '67 (RVC) Retired.
Kane, Timothy J. '82 (DET) Detroit, MI St. Gregory the Great; Detroit, MI Madonna; Highland Park, MI St. Benedict.
Kane, Rev. Msgr. William J. '60 (WDC) Retired.
Kanfush, Philip M. *o.s.b.* '00 (GBG)[G] Latrobe, PA Saint Vincent Archabbey.
Kang Gun–Lee, Vincent '94 (SFR) San Francisco, CA St. Michael Korean Catholic Church; Korean Catholic Ministry.
Kania, Donald A. '09 (SUP) Superior, WI St. Anthony; Superior, WI St. William; Superior, WI St. Anthony.
Kaniampadickal, Sebastian '00 (SYM) Garland, TX St. Thomas the Apostle Catholic Church (Syro–Malabar).
Kanicki, Philip A. '85 (RIC) Navy Chaplains; Unassigned.
Kanka, Robert '56 (ROC) Hornell, NY Our Lady of the Valley Retired.
Kannai, Niby *c.m.i.* '05 (COV) Elsmere, KY St. Henry.
Kannampuzha, Jose J. '92 (TYL) Lufkin, TX St. Andrew.
Kannee, Arturo '91 (DAL) Dallas, TX St. Pius X.
Kanonik, Stephen F. '82 (CHI) Chicago, IL St. Juliana.
Kantner, William R. '75 (MEM) Memphis, TN St. James.
Kantor, Rev. Msgr. Adolph A. '43 (SY) Retired.
Kantor, Robert Joseph '98 (MO) Navy Reserve Chaplains.
Kantor, Robert Joseph '98 (VEN) Naples, FL St. Agnes.
Kantor, Robert '98 (VEN) Presbyteral Council; Deans.
Kantz, Robert J. '01 (CAM) Westville Grove, NJ Church of the Most Holy Redeemer, Westville Grove, N.J.; Defenders of the Bond.
Kanu, Charles U. '92 (LR) Helena, AR St. Mary; Marianna, AR St. Andrew.
Kanu, Clement N. *m.s.p.* '03 (GAL) Houston, TX St. Philip Neri.
Kanzic, Gerald (PAT) On Duty Outside the Diocese.
Kao, Paulus '59 (LSC) Bayard, NM Our Lady of Fatima; Hurley, NM Infant Jesus.
Kapa, Benedict E. '00 (WH) Salem, WV Sacred Heart; Clarksburg, WV St. James the Apostle.
Kapfer, Leon *s.j.* '53 (SPK)[J] Spokane, WA Regis Community.
Kapitan, John *o.f.m.* '95 (PRM)[C] Dayton, OH St. Barbara Prayer Community.
Kapitz, Donald '73 (SFE) Retired.
Kaplan, Jan F. '67 (CHI) Chicago, IL St. Ladislaus.
Kappalumakkel, Mathew T. '89 (HRT) Washington Depot, CT Our Lady of Perpetual Help.
Kappe, John H. '71 (GAL) Hitchcock, TX Our Lady of Lourdes.
Kappes, Christiaan W. '02 (IND) Graduate Studies.
Kappes, Joseph B. *s.j.* '77 (CHL) Mooresville, NC St. Therese; [J] Mooresville, NC Jesuit Community.
Kappler, Stephan '94 (OAK) Study Leave.
Kapral, Richard J. '70 (SY) Oneida, NY St. Joseph; Oneida, NY St. Patrick.
Kapron, Alan '94 (PSC) Leave of Absence.
Kapushion, Rev. Msgr. Marvin J. '56 (PBL) Rye, CO St. Aloysius; Judicial Expert; Presbyteral Council–College of Consultors; Presbyteral Council Retired.
Kapusnak, Joseph '66 (PBR) Leisenring, PA St. Stephen; Revitalization and Renewal Commission.
Kapustka, Gerald *o.m.i.* '65 (FgM) Washington, DC AMERICAN OBLATE MISSIONS.
Karalus, Peter J. '97 (BUF) Vicars; North Collins, NY Epiphany of Our Lord; Council of Priests; Consultors, College of.
Karam, Hanna '01 (SAM) Wilkes–Barre, PA St. Anthony + St. George.
Karam, Peter '88 (OLL) Cleveland, OH St. Maron Maronite Catholic Church; Presbyteral Council; Victim Assistance Coordinator; Office of Protection of Minors.
Karamitis, Dennis R. *s.j.* '75 (CHI) Chicago, IL Notre Dame de Chicago.
Karanauskas, Tomas '98 (LA) Los Angeles, CA St. Casimir.
Karani, Stephen '93 (ROC) Wayland, NY Holy Family Catholic Community.
Karas, Stephen '65 (Y) Retired.
Karasek, Edward '87 (AUS) West, TX St. Mary, Church of the Assumption; Clerical Endowment Fund.
Karava, Norbert *o.f.m.cap.* '80 (MO) Navy Chaplains.
Karban, Roger R. '64 (BEL) Renault, IL Our Lady of Good Counsel.
Karcher, Jerome T. '83 (ORG) Huntington Beach, CA St. Vincent de Paul.
Karcsinski, Joseph J. '79 (BGP) Monroe, CT St. Jude.
Karczewski, Julian A. '74 (CAM) Swainton, NJ Retired.
Kardian, Richard S. *m.m.* '56 (NY)[EE] Retired.
Kardong, Terrence *o.s.b.* '63 (BIS)[A] Richardton, ND Assumption Abbey.
Kardzis, Christopher '84 (TOL) Sandusky, OH Holy Angels.
Karels, Ambrose G. '59 (KC) Retired.
Karempelis, Daniel *m.s.a.* '94 (NOR)[G] Cromwell, CT Society of the Missionaries of the Holy Apostles.
Karenbauer, Richard P. '70 (GBG) New Kensington, PA St. Mary of Czestochowa; New Kensington, PA St. Joseph; Holy Name Society.
Karepin, James M. *o.p.* '90 (CHI)[N] St. Pius V Priory.
Karepin, James M. *o.p.* '90 (STN) Chancellor; Presbyteral Council; Personnel Board; Diocesan Consultors; Eparchial Ecumenical Officer.
Karepin, James *o.p.* '90 (STN) Mishawaka, IN St. Michael.
Karg, Rev. Msgr. Andrew H. '64 (E) Greenville, PA St. Michael.
Karg, Rev. Msgr. William C. '57 (E) Oil City, PA St. Stephen; Priest Personnel Board.
Karg, William D. '64 (CLV) Akron, OH St. Sebastian Retired.
Kargul, A. Waine '67 (HRT) Hartford, CT St. Luke.
Kari, Arnold '77 (RC) Sturgis, SD St. Francis of Assisi.
Kariamadam, Jose *c.m.i.* '74 (NSH) Fayetteville, TN St. Anthony; [K] Liberty, TN Carmel Center of Spirituality; Deans.
Karieakatt, Paul *o.s.b.* '77 (LUB) Post, TX Holy Cross; Spur, TX St. Mary; Presbyteral Council.
Karikunnel, Joseph (NY) Staten Island, NY St. Clare.
Karimadam, Jose *c.m.i.* '74 (NSH) Pulaski, TN Immaculate Conception.
Karimatton, Joseph (NY) Larchmont, NY St. Augustine.
Kariu, James K. '94 (OAK) Kenyan Pastoral Center.
Kariuki, Alphonsus Mwariri *i.m.c.* '86 (MET) Phillipsburg, NJ St. Philip & St. James; Phillipsburg, NJ Warren Hospital.
Kariukikamau, Joseph (VIC) La Grange, TX SS. Peter and Paul.
Karkees, Rev. Msgr. Polis '61 (SPA) El Cajon, CA St. Peter Chaldean Cathedral.
Karl, Kevin '69 (OWN) Absent on Leave.
Karl, Robert J. '57 (PBR) Warren, OH SS. Peter and Paul's; [B] Warren, OH Infant of Prague Manor; Revitalization and Renewal Commission; Presbyteral Council.
Karle, William J. '72 (SCR) Swoyersville, PA Holy Name/St. Mary's; Swoyersville, PA Holy Trinity.
Karlen, Donald H. '64 (SY) Forestport, NY St. Patrick.
Karls, Victor *c.ss.r.* '70 (STL)[O] Liguori, MO Liguori Mission House/Redemptorists.
Karmanocky, Bernard *o.f.m.* '73 (ALT) Johnstown, PA St. Therese of the Child Jesus; Councilors:.
Karnik, George W. '58 (DUB) CEW Advisory Board Retired.
Karnish, Robert '66 (GI) Kimball, NE St. Joseph's.
Karns, David W. '74 (ALN) Port Carbon, PA St. Stephen.
Karoor, Isaac M. '69 (BAL) Retired.
Karott, Abraham *m.c.b.s.* '95 (MIL)[P] Kenosha, WI Missionary Congregation of the Blessed Sacrament, Inc., Zion Province.
Karpiey, Daniel J. '59 (HRT)[A] In Res. at the Archbishop Daniel A. Cronin Retirement Residence at St. Thomas Seminary Retired.
Karpyn, Gregory R. '87 (ALN) Allentown, PA St. Paul; Good Shepherd Home and Rehabilitation Hospital; Allentown, PA Manor Care Nursing Home; Macungie, PA Lehigh Center Nursing Home; Macungie, PA Lehigh Commons Personal Care Home.
Karris, Robert *o.f.m.* '65 (CHI)[N] Chicago, IL St. Peter's Friary.
Karris, Robert *o.f.m.* '65 (BUF)[O] St. Bonaventure, NY St. Bonaventure Friary; [C] St. Bonaventure, NY Friar Community.

Kartje, John F. '02 (CHI)[U] Evanston, IL Northwestern University, Sheil Center.
Karuhn, Robert J. '65 (GB) Appleton, WI Sacred Heart; College of Consultors.
Karuvelil, George *s.j.* '89 (WDC)[N] Washington, DC Woodstock Jesuit Community.
Karuvelil, John *s.j.* '98 (BO)[U] Cambridge, MA Claver House.
Karvelis, Francis V. '49 (HRT) Retired.
Karwacki, Bart *o.f.m.conv.* '75 (BAL)[S] Ellicott City, MD Friary of St. Joseph Cupertino.
Karwacki, Francis J. '83 (HBG) Mount Carmel, PA Our Lady of Mount Carmel; Charismatic Renewal; Deans; Presbyteral Council.
Karwin, John J. *s.j.* '67 (BO)[U] Weston, MA Campion Health Center, Inc.
Karwowski, Edmund K. '87 (HRT) Windsor, CT St. Gabriel.
Karwowski, Ephrem *o.f.m.cap.* '88 (NOR) Middletown, CT St. Pius X.
Kasanziki, Pascal *s.x.* '94 (CHI)[N] Chicago, IL Xaverian Missionaries (S.X.).
Kaschenbach, Rev. Msgr. Arthur J. '51 (SCR) Scranton, PA St. Patrick's Retired.
Kasel, Randal J. '05 (STP) Bayport, MN St. Charles.
Kasela, Adam J. '01 (SAV) Macon, GA St. Peter Claver.
Kaserow, John M. *m.m.* '69 (NY)[EE] Maryknoll Maryknoll Fathers and Brothers.
Kaseta, Peter *o.f.m.cap.* '67 (PRT) Portland, ME St. Joseph's; [M] Portland, ME.
Kash, Robert J. '52 (CHI) Retired.
Kashangaki, David *c.s.c.* '99 (FTW)[H] Notre Dame Congregation of Holy Cross, Indiana Province, Provincial House.
Kashen, David *o.f.m.conv.* (NOR) Stafford Springs, CT St. Edward.
Kashmer, George B. '58 (GRY) Retired.
Kasinskas, Clement *c.p.* '57 (HRT)[L] West Hartford Holy Family Monastery/Retreat.
Kasinski, James J. '66 (BUF) Niagara Falls, NY St. Mary of the Cataract; Niagara Falls Memorial Medical Centers.
Kasiyan, Andriv '02 (STF) Lackawanna, NY Our Lady of Perpetual Help.
Kasiyan, Ihor '92 (SJP) Parma, OH St. Andrew; Administrative Council; Alternates; Presbyters.
Kaska, E. William '69 (DAV)[J] Iowa City, IA O'Keefe Hall; State University of Iowa Hospital.
Kaskie, Brian '92 (JKS) McComb, MS St. Alphonsus; Approved Advocate and Auditors; Chatawa, MS St. Teresa.
Kaslyn, Robert J. *s.j.* '85 (WDC)[N] Washington, DC The Jesuit Community of St. Aloysius Gonzaga.
Kaslyn, Robert J. *s.j.* '85 (WDC)[C] Washington, DC Catholic University of America, The.
Kasparek, John A. '69 (PMB) Palm City, FL Holy Redeemer.
Kasper, John *o.s.f.s.* '79 (OAK) Lafayette, CA St. Perpetua; Deanery #4.
Kasperczuk, Marek '99 (CHI) Chicago, IL Holy Innocents; Bishop Abramowicz Seminary; Seminary Formation House–Bishop Abramowicz Seminary.
Kasperek, David D. '63 (GB) Green Bay, WI SS. Edward and Isidore.
Kasprick, Roger *o.s.b.* '59 (SCL)[I] Collegeville, MN St. John's Abbey, of the Order of St. Benedict.
Kasprzak, John F. '75 (BUF) Lackawanna, NY Queen of Angels.
Kasprzyk, James H. '65 (BUF) Retired.
Kasprzyk, Rev. Msgr. Leon J. '61 (MET)[I] Somerset, NJ Maria Regina Residence Retired.
Kasputis, Thomas R. '76 (CHI) Chicago, IL St. Rene Goupil.
Kass, Thomas G. *c.s.v.* '77 (CHI)[N] Chicago, IL Viatorian Residence; [N] Arlington Heights Viatorian Province Center–Clerics of St. Viator.
Kassian, Jeffery '96 (KAL) On Leave of Absence.
Kassis, Daniel F. '81 (GLP) Shiprock, NM Christ the King; Waterflow, NM Sacred Heart; Presbyteral Council; Vicars Forane.
Kassis, Paskal '02 (OLD) Paroisse Saint Ephrem.
Kasteel, Rev. Msgr. Ben '64 (LUB) Lubbock, TX Cathedral Christ the King; [D] Lubbock, TX Christ the King Cathedral School Foundation.
Kasten, Edward F. '54 (MIL) Retired.
Kastenholz, John P. *o.praem.* '65 (GB)[J] De Pere, WI St. Norbert Abbey; [O] De Pere, WI NORBERT & CO.; De Pere, WI; Hortonville, WI St. Denis; Hortonville, WI St. Patrick.
Kastenholz, Nicholas E. '02 (STL) University City, MO Our Lady of Lourdes; Judges.
Kaster, Alfred D. '60 (DUL) On Duty Outside the Diocese.
Kastigar, James J. '82 (CHI) Chicago, IL St. Mary of the Lake.
Kastigar, John J. '52 (CHI) Retired.
Kastl, Gary '07 (TLS) Tulsa, OK Church of St. Mary.
Kastner, Edwin H. '51 (BEL) Retired.
Kasu, Show Reddy '92 (BIR) Birmingham, AL St. Paul's Cathedral; [H] Birmingham, AL The Chapel of St. Stephen the Martyr Campus Center.
Kasuboski, Walter *o.f.m.cap.* '74 (FgM) Detroit, MI Province of St. Joseph; [K] Detroit St. Bonaventure Friary.
Kasule, Gerald *c.s.sp.* (BAL)[S] Baltimore, MD Congregation of the Holy Spirit.
Kasun, Paul L. *o.s.b.* '94 (OM) On Duty Outside the Archdiocese; [K] Schuyler, NE Benedictine Mission House.
Kasza, Rev. Msgr. John C. '93 (DET)[A] Orchard Lake, MI SS. Cyril and Methodius Seminary.
Kaszczak, Rev. Archpriest Ivan '85 (STF) Presbyteral Council; Air Force Reserve Chaplains; [A] Stamford, CT Ukrainian Catholic Seminary Inc. St. Basil College.
Kaszczak, Rev. Archpriest Ivan (STF) Stamford, CT Holy Protection of the Mother of God.
Kasznel, Richard C. '65 (STL) St. Mary, MO Immaculate Conception.
Katanga, Wenceslaus '03 (FAR) Towner, ND St. Cecilia's Church of Towner.
Katcher, Eugene '92 (DET) Roseville, MI Sacred Heart.
Katende, Fulgentius *c.s.c.* '91 (FTW)[H] Notre Dame Congregation of Holy Cross, Indiana Province, Provincial House.
Kathenge, Jonathan K. '03 (GAL) Houston, TX St. Vincent de Paul.
Katoa, Sione Laina '98 (SFR) Tongan Ministry; San Mateo, CA St. Timothy.
Katompa, Zephyrin K. '98 (NEW) Elizabeth, NJ Our Lady of Most Holy Rosary/St. Michael.
Katorski, Robert '63 (MIL) Retired.
Katricak, Kenneth J. *o.s.b.* '83 (CLV) Broadview Heights, OH Assumption; [N] Cleveland Benedictine Order of Cleveland.
Katsouros, Stephen N. *s.j.* '98 (NY)[F] New York, NY Loyola School; [EE] New York, NY St. Ignatius Loyola Residence.
Kattackal, Jacob '58 (SYM) Santa Ana, CA St. Thomas Apostle Syro–Malabar Catholic Church.
Kattakkara, Joseph *c.m.i.* '89 (BEA) Beaumont, TX St. Martin de Porres Mission; Beaumont, TX St. Mary.
Kattan, Charles '05 (NTN) West Roxbury, MA Annunciation Cathedral.
Katz, Jerome A. '71 (SY) Marathon, NY St. Stephen; Whitney Point, NY The Catholic Community of St. Stephen–St. Patrick.
Katz, Roger L. '89 (DUB) Retired.
Katzenberger, Scott *c.ss.r.* '97 (GAL) Houston, TX Holy Ghost.
Katziner, Stephen F. '74 (PH) Bensalem, PA Saint Ephrem.
Kaucheck, Kenneth R. '76 (DET) Absent on Leave; Judges.
Kauffman, Dennis *c.s.b.* '79 (DET)[E] Novi, MI Catholic Central High School.
Kauffman, Niles J. *o.f.m.cap.* '58 (MIL)[P] Milwaukee, WI St. Conrad Friary.
Kauffman, William B. '90 (WIL) On Duty Outside the Diocese; DEPARTMENT OF VETERANS AFFAIRS HOSPITALS AND CHAPLAINS.
Kauffmann, James '76 (RIC) Richmond, VA Saint Benedict; Nocturnal Adoration Society.
Kaufman, Harry J. '02 (BO) German; Burlington, MA St. Margaret.
Kaufman, Kent R. '93 (TOL) Rossford, OH All Saints; Members.
Kaufman, William C. '74 (PH) Philadelphia, PA St. Richard; Council of Priests; Pastors Review Board.
Kaukus, Edwin J. '57 (BUF) Retired.
Kaul, John L. '75 (DET) Military Chaplains.
Kaump, Joey '05 (MEM) Quest; Leadership Camp; Voyage.
Kaump, Richard J. '04 (MEM) Camden, TN St. Mary Church.
Kautzman, Jerome G. '59 (BIS)[G] Bismarck, ND Emmaus Place Retired.
Kauvaetupu, Lomano *m.s.c.* (CI) Chuuk, FM Holy Cross.
Kauzlarich, John J. '55 (CHI) Retired.
Kavanagh, Aelred *o.s.b.* '94 (NO)[P] St. Benedict, LA St. Joseph Abbey.
Kavanagh, Rev. Msgr. Edward J. '48 (SAC) Sacramento, CA St. Rose; Diocesan Council of Catholic Women Retired.
Kavanagh, James F. '64 (LA) Redondo Beach, CA St. James.
Kavanagh, Kevin J. '83 (COL) Columbus, OH Our Lady of Peace; College of Consultors; Diocesan Judges.
Kavanagh, Rev. Msgr. Richard T. '36 (IND) Retired.
Kavanaugh, John F. *s.j.* '71 (STL)[O] St. Louis, MO Jesuit Community Corporation at Saint Louis University – Jesuit Hall.
Kavanaugh, John J. *s.j.* '71 (STL)[C] Saint Louis University.
Kavanaugh, John J. '57 (WIL) Wilmington, DE Christ Our King Retired.
Kavanaugh, John P. '48 (SFR) Knights of Malta Retired.
Kavanaugh, Kieran *o.c.d.* '55 (WDC)[B] Washington, DC Discalced Carmelite Friars; [W] Washington, DC Institute of Carmelite Studies and ICS Publications.
Kavanaugh, Michael J. '85 (SAV) Port Wentworth, GA Our Lady of Lourdes; Finance Council; Ecumenism and Interreligious Affairs; Presbyteral Council.
Kavanaugh, Rev. Msgr. Richard '36 (IND)[I] Beech Grove, IN St. Paul Hermitage Retired.
Kavcak, John P. *m.s.c.* '73 (SB) Palm Springs, CA Our Lady of Solitude; Palm Springs, CA Our Lady of Guadalupe.
Kaveney, Thomas J. '47 (CHI) Berwyn, IL St. Odilo Retired.
Kaverenge, Fausto K. '92 (MO) Army Chaplains.
Kavipurayidam, Mathew *t.o.r.* '75 (FWT) Carrollton, TX St. Catherine of Siena.
Kavishe, Apolinary *a.j.* '98 (PRT) Bangor, ME Eastern Maine Medical Center; Bangor, ME Saint Paul the Apostle Parish.
Kavookjian, Rev. Msgr. Perry '87 (FRS) Personnel Board; Ecclesiastical Notaries; Bakersfield, CA St. Elizabeth Ann Seton.
Kavumkal, Sebastian *m.s.t.* '79 (MAR) Sault Sainte Marie, MI Holy Name of Mary; Sault Sainte Marie, MI Sacred Heart.
Kawa, Edward *s.d.s.* '64 (GRY)[H] Merrillville, IN Salvatorian Fathers (Society of the Divine Savior).
Kawa, Rev. Msgr. Robert J. '69 (STU) Beverly, OH St. Bernard; [M] Beverly, OH Marriage Encounter; Deans.
Kawai, Thomas '91 (PHX) Phoenix, AZ St. Edward Confessor Roman Catholic Parish; Phoenix, AZ St. Martin de Porres Roman Catholic Parish.
Kawalec, Pawel '95 (VEN) Venice, FL Our Lady of Lourdes.
Kawalec, Zachary M. '02 (CLV) Medina, OH St. Francis Xavier.
Kawamura, Peter *o.s.b.* '88 (SCL)[I] Collegeville St. John's Abbey, of the Order of St. Benedict.
Kawcznski, Ronald L. '90 (MO) Navy Chaplains.
Kawczynski, Ronald '90 (FAR) Military Chaplains.
Kawecki, Andrew M. '80 (GBG) Fairchance, PA SS. Cyril and Methodius; Fairchance, PA St. Hubert.
Kawiak, Matthew (ROC)[M] Brockport, NY State University College at Brockport, the Newman Oratory of Brockport.
Kawka, Frederick J. '64 (SAG) Shepherd, MI St. Vincent De Paul Retired.
Kay, Colin Adrian '05 (NEW) Fair Lawn, NJ St. Anne's.
Kay, Joseph *m.afr.* '48 (SP)[N] St. Petersburg, FL Missionaries of Africa.
Kay, Kieran R. *o.f.m.conv.* '55 (TOL) Carey, OH Our Lady of Consolation, Basilica–National Shrine.
Kayajan, Daniel R. *c.s.c.* '97 (SP) Dade City, FL St. Rita.
Kayammakal, Thomas '80 (SFE) Ribera, NM San Miguel Del Vado; Villanueva, NM Our Lady of Guadalupe.
Kayatta, Francis P. '80 (PRO) Narragansett, RI St. Mary, Star of the Sea; Deans; Air Force Reserve Chaplains.
Kayiwa, Julius '62 (PHX) Bullhead City, AZ St. Margaret Mary Roman Catholic Parish.
Kaylor, Lee '81 (SFR) Retired.
Kaylor, Robert W. '70 (Y) Brewster, OH St. Therese; [C] Canton, OH Central Catholic High School.
Kayondo, Leonard (BO) Dorchester, MA St. Mark.
Kayrouz, Rev. Msgr. Victor '64 (OLL) El Paso, TX St. Anthony of the Desert Maronite Catholic Mission/ Holy Family Church.
Kayrouz, Rev. Msgr. Victor '64 (ELP) El Paso, TX Holy Family.
Kayser, DeWayne '98 (SFS) Bowdle, SD St. Augustine; Presbyteral Council.
Kayser, Leonard '59 (SFS) Retired.
Kayser, Robert '52 (RVC) Dix Hills, NY St. Matthew; [M] Amityville, NY St. Pius X Residence Retired.
Kaywell, Jerome P. '91 (VEN) Punta Gorda, FL Sacred Heart.
Kaza, Rev. Msgr. Charles A. '72 (E) Brockway, PA Holy Cross; Brockway, PA St. Tobias; Eastern Vicariate; Administrative Cabinet; College of Consultors; Finance Council.
Kazarnowicz, Anthony S. '75 (MO) Army Chaplains; Military Chaplains.
Kazer, Michael '80 (DET) Livonia, MI St. Edith.
Kazibwe, John C. '03 (RIC) Clarksville, VA St. Catherine of Siena; South Boston, VA St. Paschal Baylon; South Hill, VA Good Shepherd.
Kazista, Rev. Msgr. Francis G. '66 (WDC) Silver Spring, MD St. John the Baptist.
Kazmierczak, Carl M. '55 (MIL) Retired.
Kcira, Anton '67 (DET) Rochester Hills, MI St. Paul Albanian Catholic Community.
Keahi, Christopher *ss.cc.* '65 (HON) Kaneohe, Oahu, HI; [D] Kaneohe, HI Congregation of the Sacred Hearts of Jesus and Mary (Hawaii Province SS.CC.); [D] Kaneohe, HI Sacred Hearts Center; Members.
Kealey, Edward J. '89 (RVC) Medford, NY St. Sylvester.
Kealy, Hubert J. '64 (GAL) Conroe, TX Sacred Heart; Northern Vicariate; Priests Personnel Committee.
Kealy, Sean *c.s.sp.* '65 (PIT)[B] Pittsburgh, PA Duquesne University of the Holy Spirit.
Kean, Brian M. '08 (PH) Downingtown, PA St. Joseph.

Kean, James F. '97 (DET)[T] Pontiac, MI Mt. Hope Catholic Cemetery Association; Pontiac, MI St. Damien of Molokai Parish.
Keane, Aquinas *o.c.s.o.* '73 (WOR)[O] Spencer, MA St. Joseph's Abbey; [Q] Spencer, MA St. Joseph Abbey.
Keane, Denis J. '63 (GF) Red Lodge, MT St. Agnes.
Keane, Rev. Msgr. Dennis P. '71 (NY) Crestwood, NY Church of the Annunciation.
Keane, Edward M. '39 (BRK) Flushing, NY Holy Family Retired.
Keane, Rev. Msgr. James P. '45 (SFR) Retired.
Keane, James T. '55 (LFT) Muncie, IN St. Mary.
Keane, John F. '65 (BO) Senior Priests. Retired.
Keane, John J. '62 (HRT) Hamden, CT St. Ann; New Haven, CT St. John the Baptist.
Keane, John J. *s.a.* '62 (WDC)[B] Washington, DC Atonement Seminary–Franciscan Friars of the Atonement.
Keane, John J. '62 (PIT) Retired.
Keane, Michael F. '90 (NY) Croton–on–Hudson, NY Holy Name of Mary; Canon 1742 Panel of Pastors.
Keane, Patrick A. '03 (R) Newton Grove, NC Our Lady of Guadalupe.
Keane, Patrick J. *o.s.a.* '52 (LA) Ojai, CA St. Thomas Aquinas Retired.
Keane, Patrick J. *o.s.a.* '52 (SD)[J] San Diego, CA Augustinian Community.
Keane, Philip S. *s.s.* '67 (BAL)[S] Baltimore Society of St. Sulpice, Province of the United States.
Keane, Philip S. *s.s.* '67 (SY) Syracuse, NY St. Charles Borromeo; On Duty Outside the Diocese.
Keane, Robert E. '78 (STP) Retired.
Keane, Robert L. *s.j.* '78 (MO) Navy Chaplains.
Keane, Robert L. *s.j.* '78 (BO)[U] Boston The Society of Jesus of New England–Provincial Offices.
Keane, Thomas F. '56 (BO) Senior Priests. Retired.
Keane, Rev. Msgr. Vincent A. '58 (BRK) Apostleship of Prayer; [T] Douglaston, NY Bishop Mugavero Residence Retired.
Keane, William F. *s.d.b.* '74 (NY) New Rochelle, NY; Port Chester, NY Our Lady of the Rosary.
Keaney, Francis *s.s.c.* '65 (PRO)[P] Bristol, RI St. Columban's Retirement House Retired.
Keaney, Francis *s.s.c.* '65 (OM)[K] St. Columbans Missionary Society of St. Columban.
Keaney, Rev. Msgr. James P. '54 (R) Retired.
Keaney, John B. *m.m.* '55 (NY)[EE] Retired.
Kearney, A. Damian *o.s.b.* '56 (PRO)[P] Portsmouth, RI Abbey of St. Gregory the Great.
Kearney, Brendan *s.j.* '68 (LA) Redondo Beach, CA St. James.
Kearney, Christopher *o.f.m.cap.* '68 (OAK)[M] Saint Conrad Friary.
Kearney, Daniel S. '87 (NY) New York, NY St. Elizabeth.
Kearney, John T. '83 (NY) Lake Katrine, NY St. Catherine Laboure.
Kearney, Joseph A. '67 (SCR) Wilkes Barre, PA Blessed Sacrament; Wilkes–Barre, PA St. Dominic; Wilkes–Barre, PA Geisinger Wyoming Valley Hospital.
Kearney, Lawrence T. *o.p.* '50 (CHI)[N] St. Pius V Priory.
Kearney, Michael J. '82 (BO) Bellingham, MA St. Blaise.
Kearney, Timothy E. '96 (BO) Hull, MA St. Mary of the Assumption.
Kearney, William '83 (SP) Retired.
Kearns, Adam '54 (TR)[N] Trenton, NJ Villa Vianney Retired.
Kearns, Edward A. '63 (MET) Retired.
Kearns, Edward T. '77 (PH) Philadelphia, PA St. Dominic.
Kearns, Harold M. '61 (HRT) Retired.
Kearns, John P. '88 (BO) Plymouth, MA St. Mary.
Kearns, Lawrence *c.ss.r.* '65 (FgM) Baltimore Province.
Kearns, Owen *l.c.* '83 (HRT)[B] Cheshire, CT Novitiate of the Legion of Christ.
Kearns, Thomas '60 (KCK) Overland Park, KS Holy Cross Retired.
Keating, Carroll J. *s.j.* '61 (SJ)[M] Los Gatos, CA Sacred Heart Jesuit Center.
Keating, Earl *c.p.* '58 (SCR)[M] Scranton, PA Saint Ann's Passionist Monastery.
Keating, Edward C. *o.f.m.* '58 (SP) Tampa, FL St. Lawrence Retired.
Keating, Edward J. '94 (HBG) Selinsgrove, PA St. Pius X; Selinsgrove, PA Selinsgrove Center; [I] Selinsgrove, PA Susquehanna University Catholic Campus Ministry.
Keating, George M. '54 (NEW) Kenilworth, NJ St. Theresa's; [R] Union, NJ Association of St. Philomena's Helpers and Servants to the Suffering & the Poor Retired.
Keating, James R. *o.s.a.* '84 (PH) Philadelphia, PA St. Nicholas of Tolentine; [Y] Philadelphia, PA Augustinian Community (O.S.A.).
Keating, John R. *s.j.* '61 (NY)[EE] Loyola Hall, Jesuit Community.
Keating, Joseph R. '57 (LC) Retired.
Keating, Michael J. '02 (STP)[C] St. Paul, MN University of St. Thomas.
Keating, Michael P. '97 (OM) Columbus, NE St. Bonaventure.
Keating, Patrick '05 (BRK) Assignment Board; Elmhurst, NY St. Bartholomew.
Keating, Thomas *o.c.s.o.* '49 (DEN)[N] Snowmass, CO St. Benedict's Monastery.
Keating, Timothy G. *s.m.* '85 (WDC)[B] Washington, DC Marist College, The Scholasticate.
Keating, Timothy G. *s.m.* '85 (ATL)[G] Atlanta, GA; Atlanta, GA.
Keck, Barnabas *o.f.m.cap.* '51 (NY) New Paltz, NY St. Joseph; [EE] New Paltz, NY St. Joseph Friary.
Keck, Edward '73 (COL) Bolivar, OH Church of the Holy Trinity.
Keck, Robert J. *s.j.* '60 (NY)[EE] New York, NY Jesuit Community of the Immaculate Conception.
Kedati, Andreas A. *s.v.d.* (LKC) Iowa, LA St. Raphael.
Kedjierski, Walter F. '02 (RVC) Floral Park, NY Our Lady of Victory; Procurator & Advocates.
Kedzierski, Casimir '60 (PIT) Glassport, PA Queen of the Rosary.
Kee, Rev. Msgr. James S. '95 (MOB) Judicial Vicar; Archdiocesan Consultors; Mobile, AL St. Catherine of Siena.
Keebler, Paul J. '66 (SY) Windsor, NY Our Lady of Lourdes Retired.
Keebler, William '91 (PEO) Tolono, IL St. Patrick's.
Keech, William J. *o.s.f.s.* '57 (WIL)[J] Wilmington, DE DeSales House.
Keefe, Bernard A. '63 (BGP) New Canaan, CT St. Aloysius Retired.
Keefe, Charles R. '76 (MIL)[N] Milwaukee, WI Milwaukee Catholic Home; Special Assignment.
Keefe, Daniel G. '83 (HRT) Hamden, CT St. Joan of Arc; New Haven Vicariate.
Keefe, Daniel T. '54 (OG) Judges Retired.
Keefe, Donald J. *s.j.* '62 (NY)[EE] Loyola Hall, Jesuit Community.
Keefe, Francis J. '58 (PRO)[P] Providence St. John Vianney Residence Retired.
Keefe, Gerald E. '47 (STP) Retired.
Keefe, Jeffrey *o.f.m.conv.* '52 (SY) Syracuse, NY Assumption B.V.M.
Keefe, John J. '68 (LIN) Lincoln, NE Cristo Rey; Apostolate to the Spanish Speaking.
Keefe, John P. *c.s.c.* '59 (PHX)[F] Phoenix, AZ Holy Cross Congregation/Casa Santa Cruz.
Keefe, John *c.s.c.* (FTW)[H] Notre Dame Congregation of Holy Cross, Indiana Province, Provincial House.
Keefe, Joseph L. '71 (WIN) Rochester, MN SS. Peter and Paul; Rochester, MN Pax Christi.
Keefe, Thomas H. *m.m.* '55 (NY)[EE] Maryknoll Maryknoll Fathers and Brothers Retired.
Keefer, Hugh *o.s.b.* '67 (KCK)[I] Atchison, KS St. Benedict's Abbey.
Keeffe, Anthony J. '63 (SY) Retired.
Keegan, James M. *s.j.* '71 (BO)[U] Boston, MA Loyola House.
Keegan, John E. *m.m.* '60 (NY)[EE] Maryknoll Maryknoll Fathers and Brothers Retired.
Keegan, John W. *s.j.* '69 (BO)[U] Boston The Society of Jesus of New England–Provincial Offices.
Keegan, John W. *s.j.* '69 (MAN) Milford, NH St. Patrick.
Keegan, Martin P. *m.m.* '65 (NY)[EE] Maryknoll Maryknoll Fathers and Brothers Retired.
Keegan, Terence *o.p.* '68 (PRO)[P] Providence St. Thomas Aquinas Priory at Providence College.
Keegstra, Garret *o.f.m.cap.* '86 (MIL)[P] Mount Calvary, WI St. Felix Friary.
Keehan, John J. '67 (CHI) Other Assignments.
Keehan, Terence M. '86 (CHI) Chicago, IL Transfiguration of Our Lord; Inverness, IL Holy Family.
Keehner, John E. '93 (Y) Judges.
Keehner, John '93 (Y) Youngstown, OH Cathedral of St. Columba; Youngstown, OH St. Casimir; Priests Council.
Keel, Edwin *s.m.* '70 (WH) Wheeling, WV St. Vincent de Paul.
Keelen, Kevin J. '91 (TR) Bayville, NJ St. Barnabas; Secretary.
Keeley, Isaac *o.c.s.o.* '92 (WOR)[O] Spencer, MA St. Joseph's Abbey.
Keeley, Patrick J. *c.m.* '58 (STL)[O] Perryville, MO Congregation of the Mission.
Keeling, Paul M. *c.r.s.p.* '75 (BUF)[B] Youngstown, NY St. Anthony M. Zaccaria Seminary; [T] Youngstown, NY Basilica of the National Shrine of Our Lady of Fatima, Inc.
Keenan, Alexander J. '76 (BO) East Boston, MA Most Holy Redeemer; Health Leave.
Keenan, Basil *o.s.b.* '67 (OKL) Seminole, OK Immaculate Conception; [I] Shawnee, OK St. Gregory's Abbey.
Keenan, Rev. Msgr. Charles J. '42 (LIN) Retired.
Keenan, Christopher B. *o.f.m.* '71 (NY) New York, NY St. Stephen of Hungary; Manhattan, NY St. Vincent Hospital & Medical Center.
Keenan, Desmond R. '49 (R) Retired.
Keenan, Eugene '71 (TR) Retired.
Keenan, Francis X. *c.p.* '61 (CHI)[N] Chicago, IL Passionit Community–Immaculate Conception Monastery.
Keenan, James F. *s.j.* '69 (NY)[H] New York, NY Nativity Mission Center, Inc.; New York, NY; [EE] New York, NY Society of Jesus, New York Province; [EE] New York, NY Xavier Jesuit Community.
Keenan, James R. '99 (RCK) Dixon, IL St. Patrick.
Keenan, James *s.j.* '82 (BO)[U] Newton, MA The Jesuit Community at Boston College.
Keenan, Rev. Msgr. John C. '51 (ORG) Retired.
Keenan, John J. *s.j.* '55 (ALN)[A] Wernersville, PA Jesuit Center–Jesuit Community.
Keenan, Joseph F. '84 (PIT)[M] Pittsburgh, PA St. John Vianney Manor.
Keenan, Joseph P. *s.t.* '79 (JKS) Boswell Retardation Center.
Keenan, Joseph *s.t.* '79 (BLX) Pass Christian, MS St. Stephen.
Keenan, Rev. Msgr. Patrick J. '69 (NY) Cortlandt Manor, NY St. Columbanus.
Keenan, Terence '65 (FR) Retired.
Keenan, Thomas E. '55 (MAN) Retired.
Keenan, Thomas L. '63 (PRO) Retired.
Keenan, Vincent P. *s.s.j.* '52 (BAL)[S] Baltimore, MD St. Joseph's Manor.
Keenan, William R. *o.f.m.* '56 (FgM) New York, NY Holy Name Province.
Keene, James H. *s.j.* '73 (LA)[C] Los Angeles, CA Jesuit Community.
Keene, Kenneth R. '95 (PIT) McKees Rocks, PA Holy Trinity.
Keene, Mark A. '84 (COV) Fort Wright, KY St. Agnes; Priests' Retirement Committee.
Keene, Warren '81 (STA) Jacksonville, FL Immaculate Conception.
Keener, Michael '92 (MIA) Absent on Leave.
Keener, Robert J. '95 (CHI) Navy Chaplains; Military Chaplains.
Keeney, Charles P. '78 (BRK)[E] Brooklyn, NY Campus Ministers and Ministry Centers; Brooklyn, NY St. Augustine.
Keeney, Timothy E. '96 (RIC) Bristol, VA St. Anne.
Keenoy, John A. '87 (STL) Pacific, MO St. Bridget Church.
Keese, John H. '74 (LA) Rowland Heights, CA St. Elizabeth Ann Seton.
Keferl, Francis J. '73 (CIN) Vandalia, OH St. Christopher.
Keffer, Robert F. '68 (WDC) Burtonsville, MD Resurrection Parish.
Keffer, Robert *o.cist.* '97 (LC)[H] Sparta, WI Our Lady of Spring Bank, Cistercian Abbey.
Keffler, Leopold *o.f.m.conv.* '63 (IND)[B] Indianapolis, IN Marian University; [P] Indianapolis, IN Mount Saint Francis Sanctuary, Inc.
Kegel, William M. *s.j.* '42 (MIL)[P] Wauwatosa, WI Jesuit Community at St. Camillus.
Kegler, Maynard *o.m.i.* (OAK)[M] Oakland, CA Missionary Oblates of Mary Immaculate United States Province.
Kegley, Jeffrey '96 (TR) Hamilton, NJ St. Raphael–Holy Angels Parish.
Kehew, Donal R. '63 (PRO) Retired.
Kehoe, Charles B. '73 (BRK) Retired.
Kehoe, Rev. Msgr. Daniel J. '39 (PH) Sharon Hill, PA Holy Spirit Retired.
Kehoe, James P. '70 (CHI) Evanston, IL St. Joan of Arc; Navy Reserve Chaplains.
Kehoe, Joseph F. '66 (SY) Durhamville, NY St. Francis; Munnsville, NY St. Therese of the Infant Jesus.
Kehoe, Mark '99 (MET) Piscataway, NJ Our Lady of Fatima.
Kehoe, Richard J. *c.m.* '57 (MET)[I] Princeton, NJ Vincentian Residence.
Kehres, Frank '68 (TOL) Members.
Kehres, Franklin P. '68 (TOL) Norwalk, OH St. Paul; Members.
Kehres, Paul S. *s.j.* '51 (FgM) Detroit, MI Detroit Province.
Keifer, John J. '70 (LFT) Newman Foundation, Ball State, Inc.
Keigher, Bernard '74 (TR) Lakehurst, NJ St. John.
Keighron, Robert E. '06 (BRK) Howard Beach, NY St. Helen.
Keiser, Jerome F. '71 (STP) Lake St. Croix Beach, MN St. Francis Of Assisi.
Keiser, Raymond W. '70 (BIR) Retired.
Keiter, Adam '08 (WCH) Wichita, KS Cathedral of the Immaculate Conception.
Keiter, James E. '01 (OM) Omaha, NE Assumption, B.V.M.; [D] Omaha, NE Assumption–Guadalupe Grade School; [O] Omaha, NE Cristo Rey Work/Study Program of Omaha; [B] Omaha, NE St. Peter Claver Cristo Rey Catholic High School of Omaha.
Keitz, Bernard Lawrence *o.p.* '54 (NY)[EE] New York, NY St. Vincent Ferrer Priory; New York, NY St. Vincent Ferrer; [EE] New York, NY St. Vincent Ferrer Priory.
Kejicki, Timothy P. *s.j.* '94 (CHI)[N] Evanston, IL Canisius House.
Kelash, David '94 (PHX) Cottonwood, AZ Immaculate

Conception Roman Catholic Parish; Presbyteral Council.
Kelber, Vincent M. *o.p.* '07 (ANC) Anchorage, AK Holy Family Cathedral.
Kelchak, Joseph M. '50 (SUP) Retired.
Keleher, Rev. Msgr. J. Patrick '68 (BUF)[R] Amherst, NY State University of New York at Buffalo (North Campus) Newman Center.
Keleta, Negusse Fesseha '84 (SEA) Mercer Island, WA St. Monica.
Keliher, Michael P. *c.s.v.* '76 (LAV) Henderson, NV St. Thomas More.
Keliher, Michael P. *c.s.v.* '76 (CHI)[N] Arlington Heights Viatorian Province Center–Clerics of St. Viator.
Kelleher, Cornelius '56 (DUL) Hinckley, MN St. Joseph; Hinckley, MN St. Patrick.
Kelleher, James R. *s.o.l.t.* '96 (CC)[I] Corpus Christi, TX; [G] Robstown, TX Society of Our Lady of the Most Holy Trinity.
Kelleher, John P. *o.s.b.* '89 (BO)[U] Hingham, MA Glastonbury Abbey.
Kelleher, John P. *o.s.b.* '89 (FR) Centerville, MA Our Lady of Victory.
Kelleher, Joseph '53 (CHL) Retired.
Kelleher, Lawrence A. '93 (GAY) Retired.
Kelleher, Mark A. '96 (WIL) Centreville, MD Our Mother of Sorrows; Air Force Reserve Chaplains.
Kelleher, Michael '65 (BLX) Pascagoula, MS Sacred Heart.
Kelleher, Robert J. '06 (SCR) Plymouth, PA All Saints.
Kelleher, Robert N. '59 (BO) Senior Priests. Retired.
Kelleher, Timothy J. '71 (BO) Walpole, MA Blessed Sacrament.
Kelleher, Walter T. *m.m.* '56 (NY)[EE] Retired.
Kellen, Elmer W. '50 (WIN)[D] Wabasha, MN Saint Elizabeth's Medical Center Retired.
Keller, Brendan '60 (MOB) Retired.
Keller, Daniel E. '82 (OM) On Medical Leave.
Keller, Gerald J. '65 (CLV) Berea, OH St. Adalbert Retired.
Keller, Herbert B. *s.j.* '81 (SCR)[C] Scranton, PA The University of Scranton; [E] Scranton, PA Scranton Preparatory School.
Keller, J. Rod '54 (ORG) Retired.
Keller, John D. *o.s.a.* '64 (SD)[J] San Diego, CA Augustinian Community; Counselors:.
Keller, John R. '54 (ORG) Huntington Beach, CA St. Bonaventure Retired.
Keller, John T. '74 (GAL) Houston, TX Prince of Peace.
Keller, Ken '69 (AMA) Dimmitt, TX Immaculate Conception; Nazareth, TX Holy Family; [I] Amarillo, TX Holy Family Parish of Nazareth, Texas Endowment Foundation.
Keller, Lawrence E. '47 (STP) Retired.
Keller, Matthew A. '02 (GLP) Gallup. Cure of Ars House of Discernment; Chancellor; Vocations; Priests' Retirement Board.
Keller, Neil J. '55 (CIN) Retired.
Keller, Paul J. *c.m.f.* '96 (LA)[V] San Gabriel, CA Claretian Missionaries – Western Province, Inc.; San Gabriel, CA; [V] Los Angeles, CA Tepeyac House (Novitiate).
Keller, Paul J. *o.p.* '93 (Y) Youngstown, OH St. Dominic.
Keller, Robert J. '74 (MO) Harper Woods, MI St. Peter the Apostle; Air Force Reserve Chaplains.
Keller, Robert L. '67 (CIN) Cincinnati, OH Resurrection of Our Lord.
Keller, Robert *o.p.* '83 (IND) Bloomington, IN St. Paul Catholic Center; [O] Bloomington, IN Indiana University, Bloomington.
Keller, Theodore A. '46 (LEX) Lexington, KY St. Peter Retired.
Keller, Thomas G. '97 (STL) Florissant, MO St. Angela Merici.
Keller, Thomas W. '58 (LR) Carlisle, AR St. Rose of Lima Church; England, AR Holy Trinity Church.
Keller, Thomas *m.s.c.* '55 (ORG) Placentia, CA St. Joseph; Defenders of the Bond; Adjutant Judicial Vicars; Special Assignment.
Keller, Thomas '84 (B) Weiser, ID St. Agnes.
Kellerman, Raymond C. '73 (CIN) Cincinnati, OH Holy Trinity Church; Judges.
Kellermann, Leonard P. *s.m.* '46 (WDC)[N] Washington, DC Marist Center Retired.
Kellermann, Leonard P. *s.m.* '46 (CLV)[M] Cleveland, OH Little Sisters of the Poor.
Kelley, Aloysius P. *s.j.* '62 (NY)[EE] Cardinal Spellman Hall, Jesuit Community.
Kelley, Arnold E. '56 (BO) Senior Priests.; Haverhill, MA All Saints Retired.
Kelley, Charles F. *s.j.* '84 (BO)[U] Boston The Society of Jesus of New England–Provincial Offices.
Kelley, Charles F. *s.j.* '84 (WDC)[N] Washington, DC Leonard Neale House; Washington, DC.
Kelley, Clark T. *o.s.f.s.* '64 (STO)[A] Stockton, CA St. Mary's High School.
Kelley, Daniel '95 (FWT) Presbyteral Council and Consultors; Arlington, TX St. Joseph's.
Kelley, David F. '88 (WIL) Bethany Beach, DE St. Ann; College of Consultors.
Kelley, David *o.s.a.* '73 (ALB) Waterford, NY St. Mary of the Assumption.
Kelley, Donald *s.s.c.* '62 (OM)[K] St. Columbans Missionary Society of St. Columban Retired.
Kelley, Edward J. '66 (MAN) Presbyteral Council Retired.
Kelley, Edward J. '68 (PRO) On Duty Outside the Diocese; Army Chaplains.
Kelley, Rev. Msgr. Francis H. '68 (BO) Roslindale, MA Sacred Heart; Vicariate I; Presbyteral Council.
Kelley, John '91 (AUS) Marlin, TX Sacred Heart; Marlin, TX St. Joseph.
Kelley, Joseph J. '87 (PH) Philadelphia, PA St. Monica; Diocesan Priests' Compensation and Benefits Committee.
Kelley, Laurence E. '60 (BO) Senior Priests. Retired.
Kelley, Michael A. '00 (PRO) Westerly, RI Immaculate Conception; Coventry, RI St. Vincent de Paul.
Kelley, Michael J. '75 (WDC) Washington, DC St. Martin of Tours.
Kelley, Omer C. '49 (GB)[G] Antigo, WI Langlade Hospital – Hotel Dieu of St. Joseph of Antigo Wisconsin Retired.
Kelley, Raymond H. *m.m.* '58 (FgM) Maryknoll, NY MARYKNOLL.
Kelley, Richard J. '72 (MAN) Presbyteral Council; Nashua, NH St. Christopher.
Kelley, Robert E. '79 (WOR) Oxford, MA St. Roch.
Kelley, Rev. Msgr. Thomas J. '51 (PH) Philadelphia, PA St. Matthew Retired.
Kelley, Thomas L. '88 (MAD) Cross Plains, WI St. Francis Xavier; Deaneries.
Kelley, William H. *c.s.c.* '70 (FR) Taunton, MA St. Mary's; Taunton.
Kelley, William *s.j.* '85 (SJ)[D] San Jose, CA Bellarmine College Preparatory.
Kellick, John W. '52 (GAL) Retired.
Kelliher, Michael M. *s.j.* '67 (SEA)[A] Seattle, WA Seattle University; [L] Seattle, WA Arrupe Jesuit Community at Seattle University.
Kellner, Winfried '63 (ROC) Rochester, NY Our Mother of Sorrows Retired.
Kellogg, Michael '02 (SCL) Bowlus, MN St. Stanislaus Kostka; Bowlus, MN St. Edward's; Freeport, MN St. Francis of Assisi; Bowlus, MN St. Mary; Diocesan Planning Council.
Kelly, Albert P. '72 (MOB) Elmore, AL Our Lady of Guadalupe.
Kelly, Andrew E. '70 (DAV) Mechanicsville, IA St. Mary's.
Kelly, Anthony *s.a.c.* '59 (NY) New York, NY Our Lady of Mt. Carmel.
Kelly, Augustine G. *o.s.b.* '88 (MAN)[K] Manchester, NH St. Anselm Abbey.
Kelly, Bernard A. *c.s.sp.* '62 (CHI) Chicago, IL St. Mary Magdalene.
Kelly, Brendan R.J. '05 (LIN) Advocates; Lincoln, NE Blessed Sacrament.
Kelly, Brian F. '77 (SCR) Military Chaplains.
Kelly, Charles F. '48 (CHI) Retired.
Kelly, Charles F. '64 (MET)[I] Somerset, NJ Maria Regina Residence Retired.
Kelly, Charles M. '07 (NEW) North Arlington, NJ Queen of Peace.
Kelly, Charles '99 (SAC) Priests' Personnel Board, Diocesan; Vocations.
Kelly, Columba *o.s.b.* '58 (IND)[A] St. Meinrad, IN Saint Meinrad School of Theology; [K] St. Meinrad, IN St. Meinrad Archabbey.
Kelly, Daniel A. '87 (PAT) Wayne, NJ Immaculate Heart of Mary.
Kelly, Daniel J. '56 (LC) Retired.
Kelly, Daniel L. '72 (RIC) Amherst, VA St. Francis of Assisi; Lovingston, VA St. Mary.
Kelly, Darrell C. *s.v.d.* '05 (JKS) Jackson, MS Holy Ghost; [H] Jackson, MS Tougaloo College Newman Center; Priests' Council.
Kelly, David A. *c.pp.s.* '82 (CIN)[N] Dayton Provincial Office of the Cincinnati Province of the Society of the Precious Blood.
Kelly, David A. *c.pp.s.* '82 (CHI)[W] Chicago, IL Kolbe House; [W] Chicago, IL Precious Blood Ministry of Reconciliation.
Kelly, David C. *m.m.* '57 (NY)[EE] Maryknoll Maryknoll Fathers and Brothers.
Kelly, David (NO)[A] New Orleans, LA Notre Dame Seminary Graduate School of Theology.
Kelly, Donald F. '63 (ALB) Retired.
Kelly, E. Francis '67 (SCR)[L] Scranton, PA Home for Aged of the Little Sisters of the Poor, Holy Family Residence.
Kelly, Edward C. '90 (PH) Jenkintown, PA Immaculate Conception; [D] Wyncote, PA Bishop McDevitt High School.
Kelly, Edward E. '65 (MEM) Retired.
Kelly, Edward J. '68 (PH) Norristown, PA Visitation B.V.M.
Kelly, Edward M. '68 (MIA) Coral Springs, FL St. Elizabeth Ann Seton.
Kelly, Eugene L. *o.s.f.s.* '65 (PH)[Y] Philadelphia, PA Father Louis Brisson Residence Retired.
Kelly, Eugene L. *o.s.f.s.* '65 (WIL)[J] Childs, MD Retirement and Assisted Care Facility Retired.
Kelly, Evangelist *o.f.m.cap.* '49 (LA)[B] Santa Ynez, CA San Lorenzo Seminary – Retreat Center.
Kelly, Rev. Msgr. Francis D. '63 (WOR) On Duty Outside the Diocese.
Kelly, Francis E. '55 (PH) Retired.
Kelly, Francis '57 (LA) Veterans Administration Wadsworth Hospital Center Retired.
Kelly, Frank F. '77 (GF) Retired.
Kelly, George F. *c.ss.r.* '59 (ORL)[F] New Smyrna Beach, FL St. Alphonsus Villa–Redemptorist Fathers and Brothers Retired.
Kelly, Gerald E. *m.m.* '67 (GAL)[O] Houston, TX Maryknoll Fathers and Brothers.
Kelly, Gerard P. *c.m.* '82 (CHI)[G] Chicago, IL Catholic Charities of the Archdiocese of Chicago–Archdiocesan Offices; [N] Chicago, IL Vincentian Community, Congregation of the Mission, Western Province.
Kelly, Gerard (CHI) Associate Administrators.
Kelly, Gregory '82 (DAL) Ex Officio Members; Vicar for Clergy; Procurator–Advocates; Consultors of Pastors; College of Consultors; Personnel Board; Priest Personnel; Accreditation Board; I. Vicar for Clergy.
Kelly, J. Patrick *o.f.m.* '71 (NY)[EE] New York Franciscan Friars, Holy Name Province.
Kelly, Rev. Msgr. James A. '82 (POD)[R] San Francisco, CA Prelature of the Holy Cross and Opus Dei; Los Angeles.
Kelly, James E. *c.s.c.* '58 (FTW)[H] Notre Dame, IN Congregation of Holy Cross, Indiana Province, Provincial House.
Kelly, Rev. Msgr. James G. '62 (BUF) Buffalo, NY St. Margaret; Clergy Personnel Board.
Kelly, Rev. Msgr. James J. '60 (BRK) Brooklyn, NY St. Brigid.
Kelly, James J. '83 (LA) Covina, CA Sacred Heart.
Kelly, James J. '50 (PH) Plymouth Meeting, PA Epiphany of Our Lord Retired.
Kelly, James Joseph '50 (PH) Retired.
Kelly, James M. *c.m.* '53 (BRK)[Q] Bayside, NY Ozanam Hall of Queens Nursing Home, Inc.; [T] Jamaica, NY Vincentian Residence.
Kelly, Rt. Rev. Msgr. James P. '62 (RVC) Rockville Centre, NY St. Agnes Cathedral Retired.
Kelly, James T. '92 (BO) Newburyport, MA Immaculate Conception.
Kelly, James *g.h.m.* '48 (CIN)[N] Cincinnati Headquarters of Glenmary Home Missioners; [T] Fairfield, OH Glenmary Home Missioners Charitable Trust Retired.
Kelly, James '44 (DOD) Retired.
Kelly, James *o.f.m.* '78 (CLV)[N] Brooklyn, OH St. Anthony of Padua Friary.
Kelly, James *c.s.c.* '58 (P)[B][L] Portland, OR Holy Cross Fathers & Brothers, C.S.C. – University of Portland Retired.
Kelly, James *s.j.* '03 (BAL)[S] Baltimore, MD Jesuit Community of Loyola University, Inc.; [B] Jesuit Community of Loyola University, Inc.
Kelly, Joel *o.s.b.* '66 (SCL)[I] Collegeville St. John's Abbey, of the Order of St. Benedict.
Kelly, John D. '86 (ARL) Clifton, VA St. Andrew the Apostle; Deans.
Kelly, John E. '73 (BO) Stoughton, MA St. James.
Kelly, John E. '87 (BUF) Military Chaplains; Navy Chaplains.
Kelly, John F. '84 (PT) Gulf Breeze, FL Saint Sylvester; Priests' Pension Plan, Board for.
Kelly, John J. '64 (BLX) Retired.
Kelly, John J. '87 (PH) Drexel Hill, PA St. Bernadette.
Kelly, John J. *s.j.* '74 (PH)[Y] Loyola Center and Manresa Hall.
Kelly, John L. '54 (BAL) Glen Burnie, MD Church of the Good Shepherd Retired.
Kelly, John P. '45 (BO) Senior Priests. Retired.
Kelly, John R. '68 (R) Retired.
Kelly, John T. '61 (ALB) Memorial Hospital; Special Assignment.
Kelly, John Thomas *s.j.* '74 (WDC)[Q] Faulkner, MD Loyola Retreat House.
Kelly, John W. *c.ss.r.* '51 (HBG)[G] Ephrata St. Clement's Mission House.
Kelly, John *o.s.f.s.* '71 (CHL) High Point, NC Immaculate Heart of Mary.
Kelly, John *s.c.a.* '72 (DET)[K] Wyandotte, MI Pallottine Missionary Center (Irish Province).
Kelly, Joseph J. '78 (NY) Bronx, NY St. Anthony.
Kelly, Joseph L. *c.s.sp.* '50 (PIT)[O] Bethel Park, PA The Spiritan Center.
Kelly, Rev. Msgr. Joseph P. '66 (SCR) Wilkes–Barre, PA Holy Rosary; [Q] Tunkhannock, PA Camp St. Andrew; [R] Scranton, PA St. Francis of Assisi Kitchen; Catholic Social Services; Hispanic Ministry Outreach.
Kelly, Justin J. *s.j.* '66 (DET)[E] Detroit, MI Loyola High School.
Kelly, Kenneth W. '79 (KCK) Mission, KS St. Pius X.
Kelly, Kevin J. '02 (PH) North Wales, PA St. Rose of Lima.
Kelly, Kevin *c.o.* '06 (MET) New Brunswick, NJ St. Peter the Apostle; [I] New Brunswick, NJ The New

Brunswick Congregation of the Oratory of St. Philip Neri.
Kelly, Martin T. '89 (MAN) Nashua, NH St. Patrick.
Kelly, Rev. Msgr. Martin '47 (NEW) Retired.
Kelly, Martin '65 (FgM) Boston, MA St. James the Apostle, Inc.
Kelly, Maurus *o.f.m.* '56 (LA)[P] Santa Barbara, CA Franciscan Friary, Order of Friars Minor (Old Mission).
Kelly, Michael D. '76 (SFS) Groton, SD St. Elizabeth Ann Seton.
Kelly, Rev. Msgr. Michael E. '66 (NEW)[C] West Orange, NJ Seton Hall Preparatory School; Liaison to the Irish Community.
Kelly, Michael J. '82 (PH) Hilltown, PA Our Lady of the Sacred Heart.
Kelly, Michael M. '81 (SR) Sonoma, CA St. Francis Solano; Parish Priest Consultors.
Kelly, Michael *ss.cc.* '63 (FR)[G] Fairhaven National Center of the Enthronement.
Kelly, Michael '73 (STO) Personnel Board; Lockeford, CA St. Joachim Church of Lockeford (Pastor of); Deans.
Kelly, Neil '91 (NY) Bronx, NY St. Lucy.
Kelly, Patrick J. '48 (BO) Woburn, MA St. Charles Borromeo; Senior Priests. Retired.
Kelly, Patrick *s.j.* '99 (SEA)[A] Seattle, WA Seattle University; [L] Seattle, WA Arrupe Jesuit Community at Seattle University.
Kelly, Paul J. '74 (OG) Saranac Lake, NY St. Bernard; Bloomingdale, NY St. Paul; Lake Clear, NY St. John in the Wilderness.
Kelly, Paul Maurice '47 (LA) Retired.
Kelly, Paul '83 (SC) Denison, IA St. Rose of Lima; Vail, IA St. Ann's.
Kelly, Paul *s.c.j.* '77 (MIL)[P] Milwaukee, WI SCJ Community.
Kelly, Philip J. '93 (NY) New York, NY St. Joseph of the Holy Family.
Kelly, Randy J. '94 (SAG) Saginaw, MI St. Thomas Aquinas; Territorial Vicars.
Kelly, Rev. Msgr. Raymond J. '61 (BRK)[M] Brooklyn, NY District Council of Kings; [T] Douglaston, NY Bishop Mugavero Residence Retired.
Kelly, Raymond M. '49 (PRO) Retired.
Kelly, Richard J. '88 (NEW) Woodcliff Lake, NJ Our Lady Mother of the Church; Members.
Kelly, Robert D. '00 (PRM) Cleveland, OH St. Nicholas; Lakewood, OH St. Gregory the Theologian.
Kelly, Robert G. *s.j.* '57 (NY)[EE] New York, NY Murray–Weigel Hall.
Kelly, Robert J. '74 (ALT) Holy Childhood; Propagation of the Faith; Philipsburg, PA SS. Peter and Paul; Catholic Relief Services & Foreign Mission Outreach.
Kelly, Robert L. '77 (SY) Rome, NY St. Paul; Presbyteral Council.
Kelly, Robert *s.v.d.* '86 (CHI)[N] Techny, IL Divine Word Residence.
Kelly, Robert *o.p.* '89 (LAN)[K] Adrian, MI Motherhouse of the Sisters of St. Dominic, Congregation of the Most Holy Rosary.
Kelly, Stephen M. *s.j.* '90 (OAK)[M] Oakland, CA Jesuit Fathers and Brothers.
Kelly, Thomas D. '77 (MO) On Duty Outside the Archdiocese; Air Force Reserve Chaplains.
Kelly, Thomas E. J. *s.j.* '79 (STL)[C] Saint Louis University; [O] St. Louis, MO Jesuit Community Corporation at Saint Louis University – Jesuit Hall.
Kelly, Thomas F. '41 (BRK) Retired.
Kelly, Thomas F. '56 (PEO) Retired.
Kelly, Rev. Msgr. Thomas F. '47 (Y) Retired.
Kelly, Thomas J. '68 (ALB) Ballston Spa, NY St. Mary.
Kelly, Thomas J. '86 (HRT) East Haven, CT St. Vincent de Paul.
Kelly, Thomas M. '90 (BIR) Birmingham, AL St. Peter the Apostle; [I] Birmingham, AL St. Peter's Endowment Foundation.
Kelly, Thomas P. '70 (BO) Emergency Response Group.
Kelly, Rev. Msgr. Thomas R. '67 (NY) Larchmont, NY St. Augustine.
Kelly, Thomas *o.f.m.* '62 (NEW) Wood Ridge, NJ Our Lady of the Assumption.
Kelly, Timothy J. '99 (TYL) Flint, TX St. Mary Magdalene Church; Presbyteral Council.
Kelly, Timothy *o.s.b.* '61 (SCL)[I] Collegeville, MN St. John's Abbey, of the Order of St. Benedict.
Kelly, Tony *s.a.c.* '55 (NY)[EE] New York, NY Pallottine Fathers.
Kelly, Vincent J. *c.ss.r.* '39 (ALB)[L] Saratoga Springs, NY St. John Neumann Residence.
Kelly, Vincent J. '57 (SY) Oriskany Falls, NY St. Joseph.
Kelly, Rev. Msgr. Vincent T. '56 (MIA) Fort Lauderdale, FL St. John the Baptist; [C] Fort Lauderdale, FL St. Thomas Aquinas High School; Consultors; Incardination Committee; Vicar for Christian Formation; Archbishop Hurley Scholarship Fund.
Kelly, William A. '59 (STA) Jacksonville Beach, FL St. Paul's; Vicar General; Diocesan Consultors; Presbyteral Council; Deans; Finance Committee; Diocesan Investment Committee; Building Commission.
Kelly, William J. '48 (CHI) Retired.
Kelly, William J. *s.j.* '54 (MIL)[P] Milwaukee, WI Jesuit Community at Marquette University.
Kelly, William J. *o.praem.* '05 (PH)[B] Paoli, PA Daylesford Abbey; [Y] Paoli, PA Daylesford Abbey.
Kelly, Rev. Msgr. William M. '47 (SY) Rome, NY St. Paul Retired.
Kelly, William T. '78 (GAL) Plantersville, TX St. Mary Retired.
Kelly, William T. (BO) Support and Ongoing Formation; Quincy, MA Sacred Heart.
Kelly, William *s.d.s.* '79 (NSH) Lewisburg, TN St. John the Evangelist.
Kelly, William *o.praem.* '05 (CAM) Bridgeton, NJ The Church of the Immaculate Conception, Bridgeton, N.J.
Kelpsas, A. *m.i.c.* '53 (JOL) Retired.
Kelpsas, Jaunius '94 (CHI) Chicago, IL Immaculate Conception.
Kelso, Francis E. '61 (MAN) Retired.
Kelso, Ronald *s.s.c.* '73 (FgM) St Columbans, NE House of Post–Graduate Studies.
Keltos, Adam *o.f.m.conv.* '62 (SY) Syracuse, NY Assumption B.V.M.
Kelty, Edward J. *o.s.* '89 (PCE) On Duty Outside the Diocese.
Kelty, Rev. Msgr. Leo A. '60 (TR) Retired.
Kelty, Matthew *o.c.s.o.* '46 (L)[L] Trappist, KY Abbey of Our Lady of Gethsemani, of the Order of Cistercians of the Strict Observance.
Kemayou, Louis '92 (STV) Kingshill, VI Church of St. Joseph; [B] St. Croix, VI Hispanic Ministry; Hispanic Ministry.
Kemberling, Andrew '88 (DEN) Centennial, CO St. Thomas More; Deaneries; Elected Representatives from Deanery to Presbyteral Council.
Kemeter, Robert '72 (PSC) Somerset, NJ SS. Peter and Paul.
Kemetse, Anthony '96 (NY) Poughkeepsie, NY St. Martin de Porres; Millbrook, NY St. Joseph.
Kemme, Allen M. '91 (SFD) Newton, IL St. Thomas the Apostle; Ste. Marie, IL St. Mary.
Kemme, Rev. Msgr. Carl A. '86 (SFD) Sherman, IL St. John Vianney; [O] Springfield, IL Catholic Care Center, Inc.; Diocesan Administrator; Corporate Board Members; Board of Catholic Education; Lay Employees' Pension Plan Administrative Committee; Commission for Buildings and Property; Moderator of the Curia; Priests' Personnel Board; Consultants; Diocesan Health Insurance Program Committee; [O] Springfield, IL Diocesan Care Management, Inc.; Comite Diocesano de Ministerio Hispano – Diocesan Committee for Hispanic Ministry.
Kemme, Joseph A. '64 (ALN)[A] Wernersville, PA Jesuit Center–Jesuit Community.
Kemmery, Robert J. '54 (MAN) Retired.
Kemner, Kieran *o.f.m.* '53 (CHI)[N] Countryside, IL St. Gratian Friary, Franciscan Friars.
Kemo, Rev. Msgr. Kurt H. '83 (STU) Wintersville, OH Blessed Sacrament; Wintersville, OH Our Lady of Lourdes; Censores Librorum; Stewardship and Development; Vicar General; Moderator of the Curia; Diocesan Finance Office; Diocesan/Parish Share Campaign; Child Protection Review Board; Pastoral Staff; Presbyteral Council; Priests Personnel Board; Diocesan Finance Council; College of Consultors; Victim Assistance Coordinator.
Kemp, Raymond B. '67 (WDC) Special Ministries; [W] Washington, DC Woodstock Theological Center.
Kemp, Thomas L. '52 (BUF) Retired.
Kempa, Rev. Msgr. Stanislaw (BO) Lowell, MA Holy Trinity.
Kempen, Gerald B. *o.praem.* '51 (GB)[J] De Pere, WI St. Norbert Abbey.
Kemper, Jeffrey M. '79 (CIN) Imprimatur Censors; Harrison, OH St. John the Baptist.
Kemper, John C. *s.s.* '83 (HBG) On Duty Outside the Diocese.
Kemper, John C. *s.s.* '83 (BAL)[R] Baltimore, MD St. Mary's Spiritual Center; [S] Baltimore Society of St. Sulpice, Province of the United States; [W] Baltimore, MD Mother Seton House on Paca Street, Inc.
Kempf, Joseph G. '80 (STL) O'Fallon, MO Assumption.
Kempf, William G. '84 (STL) Normandy, MO St. Ann; [T] St. Louis, MO University of Missouri, St. Louis, Catholic Newman Center; Archdiocesan Council of Priests.
Kempfirl, Fred '65 (NY) Milton, NY St. James.
Kempinger, Stephen *c.s.c.* '01 (FTW)[A] Notre Dame, IN Moreau Seminary; [A] Notre Dame, IN Moreau Seminary.
Kempski, Leonard J. '66 (WIL) Liaison for Non–Christian Religions; Wilmington, DE St. Thomas Retired.
Kenaston, Perry '99 (JUN) Craig, AK St. John by the Sea; Diocesan Consultors.
Kendall, Jeffrey A. '97 (CHR) Kingstree, SC St. Ann; Lake City, SC St. Philip the Apostle.
Kendall, Philip E. *c.s.v.* '62 (CHI)[N] Arlington Heights Viatorian Province Center–Clerics of St. Viator.
Kendall, Philip *c.s.v.* '62 (KCK) Defenders of the Bond.
Kendall, R. Daniel *s.j.* '70 (SFR)[N] San Francisco, CA Loyola House Jesuit Community.
Kendzierski, James '81 (GRY)[H] Cedar Lake, IN Our Lady of Lourdes Friary.
Kendzierski, James *o.f.m.* '82 (FTW)[I] Mishawaka, IN Our Lady of the Angels Convent.
Kendzierski, Norbert V. '64 (DET) Farmington Hills, MI St. Colman.
Kenealy, John J. *s.j.* '58 (FgM) Chicago, IL Society of Jesus.
Kenefick, Paul F. '56 (HRT)[A] In Res. at the Archbishop Daniel A. Cronin Retirement Residence at St. Thomas Seminary Retired.
Kenehan, David A. *o.s.f.s.* '74 (MO) Army Chaplains.
Kenkel, Benedict J. '53 (DM) Retired.
Kenkel, Leonard A. '60 (DM) Retired.
Kenlon, Knute *o.f.m.cap.* '58 (NY)[FF] Hastings–on–Hudson, NY Sisters of St. Francis of the Neumann Communities; [EE] Yonkers, NY St. Clare Friary.
Kenna, Daniel T. *o.f.m.* '73 (NY) New York, NY Holy Name of Jesus.
Kenna, Joseph J. '67 (YAK) On Duty Outside the Diocese Retired.
Kenna, Joseph R. '99 (ARL) Annandale, VA Holy Spirit.
Kennard, George V. *s.j.* '50 (SJ)[M] Los Gatos, CA Sacred Heart Jesuit Center.
Kenneally, Rev. Msgr. John A. '69 (SAV) Vicar General; Finance Council; Clergy Personnel; Valdosta–Brunswick Deanery; College of Consultors; St. Simons Island, GA St. William.
Kenneally, William F. '53 (BO) Senior Priests. Retired.
Kenneally, William G. '61 (CHI) Retired.
Kennealy, Thomas P. *s.j.* '62 (CIN)[N] Cincinnati, OH Jesuit Community at Xavier University.
Kennedy, Alex '90 (TLS) Grove, OK St. Elizabeth; Vinita, OK Holy Ghost.
Kennedy, Andrew '63 (BIR) Birmingham, AL Our Lady of Lourdes.
Kennedy, Arthur L. '67 (BO)[A] Brighton, MA St. John Seminary.
Kennedy, Bernard *o.f.m.* '88 (CHI) Provincial Councilors:; [N] Chicago, IL St. Joseph Interprovincial Post–Novitiate Formation House.
Kennedy, Charles J. '66 (PH) Philadelphia, PA Incarnation of Our Lord.
Kennedy, Rev. Msgr. David W. '53 (GAL) Retired.
Kennedy, David W. '97 (OWN) Oak Grove, KY St. Michael the Archangel.
Kennedy, Rev. Msgr. David '53 (GAL) Defenders of the Bond.
Kennedy, Rev. Msgr. Edward J. '59 (CAM) Retired.
Kennedy, Edward J. '68 (PH) On Special or Other Archdiocesan Assignment; Darby, PA Blessed Virgin Mary; [V] Darby, PA St. Francis Country House.
Kennedy, Ernest E. '56 (CHR) Retired.
Kennedy, Francis M. '64 (SPR) Retired.
Kennedy, Gary L. '68 (PBL) Pueblo, CO St. Mary Corwin Medical Center; [C] Pueblo, CO Centura Health–St. Mary–Corwin Medical Center.
Kennedy, Glenn (RVC) Leave of Absence.
Kennedy, Rev. Msgr. J. Nevin '58 (MET)[I] Somerset, NJ Maria Regina Residence Retired.
Kennedy, Rev. Msgr. James M. '54 (SY) North Syracuse, NY St. Rose of Lima.
Kennedy, James '54 (SY) Pastoral Examiners.
Kennedy, Jerrold F. '66 (OAK) Pleasanton, CA The Catholic Community of Pleasanton.
Kennedy, John D. '93 (SHP) Retired.
Kennedy, John F. '63 (NEW) Retired.
Kennedy, John F. *m.m.* '55 (FgM) Maryknoll, NY MARYKNOLL.
Kennedy, Rev. Msgr. John J. '49 (STL) Retired.
Kennedy, John V. *c.m.* '49 (PH)[Y].
Kennedy, John '56 (SFD) Retired.
Kennedy, Joseph P. '73 (WDC) Retired.
Kennedy, Joseph *s.j.* '55 (BAL)[S] Baltimore, MD St. Joseph's Manor; [S] Baltimore, MD Colombiere Jesuit Community.
Kennedy, Kevin '99 (SFR) Redwood City, CA St. Pius.
Kennedy, Kevin '00 (SFR) Sequoia Hospital.
Kennedy, Laurence W. '57 (SY) Syracuse, NY St. Brigid and St. Joseph.
Kennedy, Leo R. *m.m* '59 (NY)[EE] Maryknoll Maryknoll Fathers and Brothers; [EE] Maryknoll Maryknoll Fathers and Brothers Retired.
Kennedy, Leo *o.f.m.conv.* '90 (SAV) Brunswick, GA St. Francis Xavier.
Kennedy, Louis J. '57 (BRK)[T] Douglaston, NY Bishop Mugavero Residence Retired.
Kennedy, Malcolm M. '61 (POD)[JJ] New Rochelle, NY; New York.
Kennedy, Michael J. *c.m.* '51 (BAL) Emmitsburg, MD St. Joseph; [S] Emmitsburg, MD Vincentian House.
Kennedy, Michael J. '67 (STP) Retired.
Kennedy, Oliver *s.s.c.* '47 (OM)[K] St. Columbans Missionary Society of St. Columban.
Kennedy, Paddy '59 (SP)[F] Lutz, FL St. Timothy Catholic Early Childhood Learning Center.
Kennedy, Patrick A. '77 (STP) Eden Prairie, MN Pax Christi.
Kennedy, Patrick J. '53 (DEN) Retired.

Kennedy, Patrick J. R. '70 (NO) Retired.
Kennedy, Patrick '59 (SP) Lutz, FL St. Timothy.
Kennedy, Paul M. '77 (PH) Philadelphia, PA St. Katherine of Siena; Interparochial Cooperation, Commission for; Priests' Personnel Board.
Kennedy, Richard C. '73 (ORG) Santa Ana, CA St. Barbara Catholic Church.
Kennedy, Richard *m.s.c.* '67 (OG) Watertown, NY Our Lady of the Sacred Heart; [F] Watertown, NY Missionaries of the Sacred Heart.
Kennedy, Robert E. *s.j.* '65 (NEW)[B] Jersey City, NJ Jesuit Center; [M] Jersey City, NJ Jesuits of Saint Peter's College, Inc.
Kennedy, Robert J. '74 (ROC) Rochester, NY Blessed Sacrament; Priest Consultors.
Kennedy, Robert R. '66 (BO) South Boston, MA St. Monica–St. Augustine.
Kennedy, Robert T. '59 (NY) Retired.
Kennedy, Russell F. '75 (NOR) St. Mary Church – Spanish Apostolate; Part Time; Willington, CT St. Jude; Ashford, CT St. Philip the Apostle.
Kennedy, Stanley T. *m.s.* '70 (HRT)[L] Hartford, CT Missionaries of LaSalette.
Kennedy, Stanley (NOR)[J] Portland, CT Affirmation Counseling Center.
Kennedy, T. Frank *s.j.* '76 (BO)[U] Newton, MA The Jesuit Community at Boston College.
Kennedy, Thaddeus J. *o.c.s.o.* '58 (DUB)[K] Peosta, IA New Melleray Abbey, Order of Cistercians of the Strict Observance.
Kennedy, Thomas R. *c.m.* '64 (PH)[Y].
Kennedy, Thomas '07 (FWT) Bedford, TX St. Michael.
Kennedy, Victor P. '77 (NEW) Jersey City, NJ Parish of the Resurrection; Jersey City Downtown Deanery 11; Boy Scouts of America/Catholic Committee on Scouting.
Kennedy, William M. '87 (MO) Military & VA Chaplains.; Navy Chaplains.
Kennedy, William M. '71 (CIN) Cincinnati, OH Church of the Assumption.
Kennedy–Warley, David G. '57 (BUR) Retired.
Kennehan, John P. '62 (OG) On Duty Outside the Diocese.
Kennehan, John P. (STL) St. Louis, MO St. Richard; St. Louis, MO St. John's Mercy Medical Center; [J] Creve Coeur, MO St. John's Mercy Medical Center.
Kennelley, James J. '70 (E) Mercer, PA Immaculate Heart.
Kennelly, Daniel '77 (BGP)[J] Bridgeport, CT St. Vincent's Medical Center.
Kennelly, Michael F. *s.j.* '46 (NO)[P] New Orleans, LA Ignatius Residence Retired.
Kennelly, Stephen '69 (SAN) Retired.
Kenney, Albert A. '94 (PRO)[A] Providence, RI Seminary of Our Lady of Providence; [E] Providence, RI La Salle Academy; College of Consultors; Council Members; Seminary of Our Lady of Providence.
Kenney, Brian A. '02 (L) Clergy Personnel Commission; Lebanon, KY St. Charles; Defenders of the Bond.
Kenney, C. Douglas '99 (BAL) Hagerstown, MD St. Ann.
Kenney, Daniel J. *s.j.* '63 (MIL)[P] Wauwatosa, WI Jesuit Community at St. Camillus.
Kenney, Francis J. *s.m.* '49 (CIN)[N] Dayton, OH Mercy Siena Gardens.
Kenney, Gerard J. '97 (LUB) Lubbock, TX St. John Neumann; Diocesan Council of Catholic Women.
Kenney, Gerard '97 (LUB) Priests' Retirement Board.
Kenney, Henry *s.j.* '52 (LEX) Special Assignment; Lexington, KY St. Peter Retired.
Kenney, Rev. Msgr. Jeremiah F. '72 (BAL) Retired.
Kenney, Kevin T. '94 (STP) St. Paul, MN Our Lady of Guadalupe.
Kenney, Paul C. *s.j.* '72 (BO)[U] Weston, MA Campion Jesuit Community.
Kenney, Peter J. *s.s.j.* '44 (BAL)[S] Baltimore, MD St. Joseph's Manor.
Kenney, Sean W. '91 (MET) Warren, NJ Our Lady of the Mount.
Kenney, Timothy *s.m.* '82 (STL)[O] St. Louis, MO Cure of Ars Marianist Community.
Kenney, W. Henry *s.j.* '52 (LEX) Lexington, KY Veterans' Administration Hospital.
Kenney, William J. *c.s.p.* '51 (NY)[EE] Jamaica Estates Paulist Fathers Generalate.
Kenney, William J. '56 (STP) Retired.
Kenny, Donald '66 (JOL) Retired.
Kenny, Edward '74 (BAL) Priest Personnel Board.
Kenny, Eugene '53 (DOD) Retired.
Kenny, Gregory D. *c.m.f.* '59 (ATL) Stone Mountain, GA Corpus Christi.
Kenny, James E. '49 (OM) Retired.
Kenny, John F. *o.s.f.s.* '69 (WIL)[J] Childs, MD Retirement and Assisted Care Facility Retired.
Kenny, John J. *c.s.p.* '58 (GR) Evangelization.
Kenny, Joseph H. *o.p.* '50 (FgM) Chicago, IL Province of St. Albert the Great (Central).
Kenny, Joseph P. *o.p.* '63 (CHI)[N] Chicago Dominicans (Provincial Office).
Kenny, P. Edward '74 (BAL) Baltimore, MD Blessed Sacrament Church; Priests Sick or Absent.
Kenny, Peter *s.s.c.* '58 (LA)[P] Los Angeles, CA Columban Fathers, Procure House.
Kenny, Peter *s.s.c.* '58 (OM)[K] St. Columbans Missionary Society of St. Columban.
Kenny, Pierce *c.ss.r.* '69 (BRK) Brooklyn, NY Our Lady of Perpetual Help Basilica.
Kenny, Robert J. '03 (SEA) Seattle, WA St. Paul; Seattle, WA St. Edward; Seattle, WA St. George.
Kenny, Stephen K. '91 (MEM) Somerville, TN St. Philip the Apostle.
Kenny, Thomas A. '46 (NEW) Retired.
Kenny, Thomas J. *s.j.* '09 (BO)[U] Newton, MA The Jesuit Community at Boston College.
Kenny, Rev. Msgr. Walter F. '54 (NY) Larchmont, NY St. Augustine Retired.
Kenny, William J.M. '71 (LAV) Las Vegas, NV Christ the King; Las Vegas, NV Holy Spirit Catholic Church.
Kenny, William '71 (LAV) Presbyteral Council for the Diocese of Las Vegas.
Kenshol, Joseph W. '73 (GR) Sand Lake, MI Mary Queen of Apostles; Deans.
Kenshol, Joseph '73 (GR) Presbyteral Council.
Kent, Daniel '63 (MIA) Retired.
Kent, James *o.f.m.conv.* '91 (IND)[J] Mount St. Francis, IN Province of Our Lady of Consolation, Inc.; [K] Mount St. Francis, IN Provincial Headquarters for the Conventual Franciscan Province; Mount Saint Francis, IN Province of Our Lady of Consolation.
Keogh, James J. *s.j.* '52 (ALN)[A] Wernersville, PA Jesuit Center–Jesuit Community.
Keogh, Thomas '45 (SR) Retired.
Keohan, Edward M. '59 (BO) Beverly, MA St. Margaret; Senior Priests.; Salem, MA Immaculate Conception Retired.
Keohane, Daniel G. '78 (BRK) Rego Park, NY Our Lady of the Angelus; [T] Douglaston, NY Bishop Mugavero Residence Retired.
Keohane, Daniel T. '78 (SFR) San Francisco, CA St. Cecilia.
Keohane, Donal '68 (LA) Los Angeles, CA St. Martin of Tours.
Keohane, Donal '68 (SAV) Retired.
Keolker, Richard F. '63 (YAK) On Duty Outside the Diocese.
Keon, James J. *c.s.b.* '52 (GAL)[O] Houston, TX Residence of the Basilian Fathers of the University of St. Thomas.
Keough, Joseph F. '96 (HRT) Newington, CT St. Mary.
Keppel, Tim *c.r.* (SB) Diocesan Building Committee.
Keppel, Timothy F. *c.r.* '77 (SB)[I] Fontana, CA Congregation of the Resurrection, CR.
Keppeler, Richard J. '54 (BUF) Retired.
Keppens, Gustaaf M. *s.j.* '61 (WDC)[L] Washington, DC Georgetown University Hospital; [N] Washington, DC The Jesuit Community at Georgetown University.
Keppler, Daniel J. '58 (DUB) Retired.
Keppler, Rev. Msgr. John F. '60 (BRK)[T] Douglaston, NY Bishop Mugavero Residence Retired.
Kerbawy, Kevin '76 (SAG) Bay City, MI Holy Trinity; Bay City, MI St. Hedwig.
Kerber, John V. '58 (STL) Festus, MO Our Lady.
Kerber, Joseph P. '88 (SFD) Glen Carbon, IL St. Cecilia.
Kerber, Justin *c.p.* '72 (R) Greenville, NC St. Peter's; Deans; Council of Priests.
Kerby, Robert '70 (NTN) Retired.
Kerdiejus, John B. *s.j.* '58 (BO)[U] Weston, MA Campion Health Center, Inc.
Kerestes, Michael '89 (PSC) Beltsville, MD St. Gregory of Nyssa; Retirement Plan Board.
Kerestus, Thomas J. '69 (ALN) Retired.
Kereszty, Rochus *o.cist.* '60 (DAL)[J] Irving, TX Cistercian Abbey of Our Lady of Dallas.
Kerin, Rev. Msgr. Joseph A. '57 (CHL) Charlotte, NC Retired.
Kerin, Mike *g.h.m.* '88 (CIN)[N] Fairfield, OH.
Kerkemeyer, Carl '02 (TLS) Miami, OK Sacred Heart.
Kerketta, George '81 (BWN) Brownsville, TX Christ the King.
Kerketta, Pankratius '85 (LAN) Lansing, MI Resurrection.
Kern, Rev. Msgr. Crosby W. '65 (NO) New Orleans, LA St. Louis Cathedral; New Orleans, LA Shrine of St. Lazarus of Jerusalem; Newspaper; Old Ursuline Convent.
Kern, John R. '68 (MIL) Milwaukee, WI St. Catherine.
Kern, Joseph R. '57 (IND) Indianapolis, IN Retired.
Kern, Joseph '57 (IND) Deaneries and Deans.
Kern, Martin F. '94 (ALN) Boyertown, PA St. Columbkill; Cursillo Movement.
Kernan, Rev. Msgr. Eugene J. '49 (CAM) Retired.
Kernan, William A. '93 (SD) San Diego, CA St. Charles Borromeo; San Diego, CA San Diego Airport.
Kerner, Terrence D. '72 (DET) Dearborn, MI St. Martha; Dearborn, MI St. Joseph.
Kerns, John '85 (P) Portland, OR St. Juan Diego Catholic Church.
Kerper, Michael '85 (MAN) Rockingham County House of Corrections; Vicars Forane; Advocates; Portsmouth, NH Corpus Christi Parish; Public Policy Commission.
Kerr, Cherubin F. *o.s.a.* '44 (PH)[Y] Villanova, PA St. Thomas Monastery.
Kerr, John W. '98 (LR) Leave of Absence.
Kerr, Robert '95 (KC) Kansas City, MO St. Catherine of Siena; Gallatin, MO Mary Immaculate.
Kerr, Robert '84 (STA) Absent or Sick Leave.
Kerr, Seamus '60 (YAK) Retired.
Kerrigan, Bernard A. '48 (WIN)[F] Wabasha, MN St. Elizabeth's Health Care Center Retired.
Kerrigan, James P. '70 (WOR) Rutland, MA St. Patrick; Advocates.
Kerrigan, Joseph J. '90 (MET) New Brunswick, NJ Sacred Heart; Catholic Relief Services.
Kerrigan, Michael F. '64 (DEN) Idaho Springs, CO St. Paul.
Kerrigan, Michael *c.s.p.* '87 (NEW)[M] Mahwah, NJ Paulist Fathers – Paulist Press; [R] Mahwah, NJ Paulist Press.
Kerschen, Leon J. '62 (WCH) Retired.
Kerscher, Francis '55 (GB) Retired.
Kersgieter, Paul J. '45 (STL) Retired.
Kerst, Patrick '90 (SPK) Walla Walla, WA St. Francis of Assisi; Walla Walla, WA St. Patrick; Priests' Personnel Board.
Kersten, Edward J. *o.s.a.* '56 (MIL)[P] Racine, WI Augustinian Novitiate; Racine, WI St. Rita.
Kersten, Jay J. '98 (MO) On Duty Outside the Diocese; Navy Chaplains.
Kersten, John *s.v.d.* '40 (CHI)[N] Techny, IL Divine Word Residence.
Kersten, Kevin *s.j.* '72 (BO)[U] Newton, MA The Jesuit Community at Boston College.
Kertys, Martin *c.o.* '95 (NY) Tappan, NY Our Lady of the Sacred Heart.
Kertz, Leo *o.m.i.* '63 (FgM) Washington, DC AMERICAN OBLATE MISSIONS.
Kertz, Rev. Msgr. Raymond N. '67 (MAD) Cottage Grove, WI St. Patrick; Personnel Board.
Kerul'–Kmec, Miron '90 (PRM) Barberton, OH St. Nicholas.
Kerwan, Francis T. '43 (HRT) Enfield, CT Holy Family.
Kerwin, Art *o.p.* (GAL) Houston, TX Holy Rosary.
Kerze, William F. '69 (LA) Malibu, CA Our Lady of Malibu.
Kesicki, Michael T. '88 (E)[A] Erie, PA St. Mark's Seminary; [B] Erie, PA Gannon University; [M] Erie, PA Holy Family Monastery; The Bishop's Theological Advisory Committee; St. Mark Seminary.
Kesicki, Timothy P. *s.j.* '94 (FgM) Detroit, MI; Chicago, IL Society of Jesus; Detroit, MI Detroit Province.
Kesicki, Timothy P. *s.j.* '94 (DET)[K] Chicago, IL Jesuit Provincial Office–Detroit Province of the Society of Jesus; Chicago, IL.
Kesicki, Timothy P. *s.j.* '73 (CIN)[U] Cincinnati, OH St. Xavier Church Property Corporation.
Kessel, Gerald *o.f.m.cap.* '82 (DET)[P] Washington, MI Capuchin Retreat.
Kessing, Bernardine *o.f.m.* '60 (BO)[X] Boston, MA Saint Anthony Residence Retired.
Kessinger, David R. *o.s.b.* '58 (CHL)[J] Belmont, NC Belmont Abbey.
Kessler, Mathew *c.ss.r.* '91 (STL)[V] Liguori, MO Redemptorist Fathers.
Kessler, Thomas '84 (CHL) Monroe, NC Our Lady of Lourdes.
Kessler, Thomas '75 (EVN) Mt. Vernon, IN St. Philip.
Kessler, William Thomas '74 (COL) Lancaster, OH St. Bernadette; Censor of Books; Bremen, OH St. Mary.
Kessler, William '99 (SFD) Oconee, IL Sacred Heart; Pana, IL St. Patrick.
Kester, Kevin A. '81 (LA) La Canada Flintridge, CA St. Bede the Venerable.
Kester, William J. '70 (STL) St. Louis, MO St. Ambrose.
Kestermeier, Charles T. *s.j.* '75 (OM)[K] Omaha, NE Jesuit Community at Creighton University.
Kestler, Theodore E. *s.j.* '75 (FBK) St. Marys, AK Church of the Nativity Catholic Church St. Marys; [E] St. Marys, AK Brother Joe Prince Jesuit Community; Office of Native Permanent Diaconate; [E] St. Marys, AK Native Ministry Training Program.
Ketcham, Rev. Msgr. Gregory K. '94 (PEO) Champaign, IL St. John's Catholic Chapel; [M] Champaign, IL St. John's Catholic Newman Center at the University of Illinois, Urbana–Champaign.
Ketcham, Robert W. '08 (RVC) Valley Stream, NY Holy Name of Mary.
Ketteler, Ronald M. '61 (COV) Crescent Springs, KY St. Joseph; Ecumenism.
Kettenring, Michael J. '01 (NO) Marrero, LA The Visitation of Our Lady.
Ketter, Daniel '08 (ATL) Atlanta, GA St. Jude.
Kettleberger, John A. *c.m.* '78 (BRK)[T] Jamaica, NY St. Vincent's House.
Kettron, W. Michael '57 (LFT) Cicero, IN Sacred Heart.
Keulman, Kenneth P. '69 (NO)[C] New Orleans, LA Loyola University New Orleans.
Keulman, Kenneth P. '69 (SJ) On Leave of Absence.
Keusenkothen, Stephen *c.m.f.* '03 (CHI)[N] Oak Park Claretian Missionaries USA Eastern Province.

Keveny, M. Valentine (WDC) Rockville, MD St. Mary.
Keville, Joseph F. '96 (BO) Health Leave.; Brighton, MA St. Columbkille.
Kew, Larry J. '66 (GRY) Hammond, IN St. Catherine of Siena.
Key, Oren W. *s.j.* '53 (SFE) Albuquerque, NM Immaculate Conception.
Key, Paul '07 (TYL)[A] Tyler, TX Trinity Mother Frances Health System; West Central Deanery; Tyler, TX St. Peter Claver.
Key, William W. '75 (MIL)[W] Whitewater, WI Cursillos in Christianity; Waukesha, WI St. Joseph.
Keyes, Jeffrey R. *c.pp.s.* '91 (OAK) Newark, CA St. Edward.
Keyes, Jeffrey R. *c.pp.s.* '91 (CIN)[N] Dayton Provincial Office of the Cincinnati Province of the Society of the Precious Blood.
Keyes, Patrick A. *c.ss.r.* '89 (STL)[B] St. Louis, MO St. John Neumann House.
Keyes, Patrick A. *c.ss.r.* '89 (BRK)[C] Bronx, NY St. Alphonsus Formation Residence.
Keyes, Patrick *c.ss.r.* '89 (NY) Bronx, NY Immaculate Conception.
Keyes, Paul T. '63 (BO) North Andover, MA St. Michael.
Keyes, Rev. Msgr. Raphael P. '64 (JC) Camdenton, MO St. Anthony; Appointed Members; Board of Trustees; Hermitage, MO St. Bernadette.
Keyes, Thomas E. '73 (BO) Methuen, MA St. Lucy.
Keymont, Walter F. '80 (BO) East Bridgewater, MA St. John the Evangelist.
Keys, Rev. Msgr. Thomas J. '70 (SR) Santa Rosa, CA Star of the Valley; National Council of Catholic Women.
Kezmarsky, Kenneth E. '86 (PIT) Pittsburgh, PA St. Athanasius.
Khachan, Chorbishop Bernard C. '60 (OLL) Retired.
Khachan, Charles H. *m.l.m.* '99 (OLL) San Antonio, TX St. George Maronite Catholic Church; [A] Houston, TX The Congregation of Maronite Lebanese Missionaries.
Khai Vu, Joseph '96 (NEW) Elizabeth, NJ St. Genevieve's.
Khalil, Joseph *o.m.m.* '01 (OLL) Ann Arbor, MI; [A] Ann Arbor, MI Maronite Order of the Blessed Virgin Mary.
Khalil, Naim *b.s.o.* '90 (NTN) Brooklyn, OH St. Elias; Presbyteral Council.
Khammi, Rev. Msgr. Polis (SD) El Cajon, CA St. Peter Cathedral.
Khan, Joseph Nguyen '63 (DAV) Retired.
Khanh, Hilary *c.m.c.* '94 (STP) Minneapolis, MN Church of St. Anne – St. Joseph Hien.
Kharuk, Wasyl '92 (PHU) Presbyteral Council; Board Members; Washington, DC Ukrainian Catholic National Shrine of the Holy Family; [A] Washington, DC St. Josaphat Seminary.
Khin, Theodore '99 (WCH) Erie, KS St. Ambrose; St. Paul, KS St. Francis.
Khoa, Joseph M. Vu Toan *c.m.c.* '06 (SPC)[F] Carthage, MO Congregation of the Mother Coredemptrix, United States Assumption Province.
Khoi, Jim Ngo–Hoang *c.m.c.* '91 (LIN) Lincoln, NE Immaculate Heart of Mary.
Khong, Ambrose *c.s.j.b.* '08 (BRK)[T] Elmhurst, NY Congregation of St. John the Baptist of China.
Khoueiry, Joseph '00 (SAM) Dover, NH St. George.
Khoury, Ghattas '90 (OLL) Phoenix, AZ St. Joseph Maronite Catholic Church.
Khoury, Rev. Msgr. James T. '75 (SAM) Retired.
Khue, Thomas '91 (OAK) Fremont, CA Holy Spirit.
Kibby, Patrick J. '84 (NSH) Old Hickory, TN St. Stephen.
Kibirige, Charles '98 (LAN)[D] Ann Arbor, MI Spiritus Sanctus Academy.
Kibler, Gary R. '71 (BUF) Lockport, NY St. Mary.
Kibler, Joshua *c.o.* '09 (PIT)[P] Pittsburgh, PA University of Pittsburgh; [M] Pittsburgh, PA Congregation of the Oratory of St. Philip Neri; [P] Pittsburgh, PA Chatham College.
Kibler, Joshua *c.o.* '09 (PIT)[P] Pittsburgh, PA Carnegie–Mellon University; Pittsburgh, PA.
Kichak, Francis *c.s.sp.* '54 (SB)[I] Hemet, CA Congregation of the Holy Spirit Retired.
Kidaagen, Baiju *v.c.* '01 (COV)[C] Villa Hills, KY Villa Madonna Academy High School; Edgewood, KY St. Pius X.
Kidd, Wayne R. '73 (LC) Coon Valley, WI St. Mary.
Kidd, William J. *s.j.* '63 (MIL)[P] Milwaukee, WI Jesuit Community at Marquette University.
Kidder, Rev. Msgr. James C. '67 (SAC) El Dorado Hills, CA Holy Trinity; Priests' Personnel Board, Diocesan; Vicars Forane.
Kiddy, Curtis A. '92 (MIA) Miami Gardens, FL Visitation.
Kidner, M. Paul *o.s.b.* '58 (STL)[F] Creve Coeur, MO St. Louis Priory School; [O] St. Louis, MO The Abbey of St. Mary and St. Louis.
Kidney, Rev. Msgr. Liam J. '68 (LA) Pacific Palisades, CA Corpus Christi.
Kidney, Timothy '71 (SJ) Mountain View, CA St. Joseph.
Kiedinger, Daniel J. '91 (LC) Leave of Absence.
Kiefer, Joel E. '04 (ALN) Bethlehem, PA Notre Dame of Bethlehem.
Kiefer, John D. '70 (LFT) Muncie, IN St. Francis of Assisi; [H] Muncie, IN Newman Foundation–Ball State University.
Kiefer, R. David '62 (GB) Neopit, WI St. Anthony; Phlox, WI St. Joseph–Holy Family Parish; White Lake, WI SS. James–Stanislaus.
Kiefer, Robert '91 (SJ) San Jose, CA St. Frances Cabrini.
Kiefer, Thomas P. '81 (SPC) Cape Girardeau, MO Cathedral of St. Mary of the Annunciation; Vice Chancellor; Adjutant Judicial Vicars; Priests' Mutual Benefit Society; Diocesan Consultors; Judges.
Kiefer, William J. '58 (SB) Retired.
Kieffer, Charles G. '80 (PHX) Phoenix, AZ St. Theresa Roman Catholic Parish; Diocesan Judges; Deans.
Kieffer, Charles '80 (PHX) Phoenix, AZ St. Mark Roman Catholic Parish; Phoenix, AZ St. Philip the Deacon Roman Catholic Mission, A Quasi–Parish.
Kieffer, John L. *s.j.* '68 (LEX) Monticello, KY St. Peter; [J] Mount Vernon, KY Appalachia Science in the Public Interest.
Kieffer, Joseph '04 (SAL) Beloit, KS St. John the Baptist Parish; College of Consultors; Council of Priests.
Kieffer, Lawrence J. '50 (MAD) Retired.
Kieffer, Merlin '60 (SAL) Retired.
Kieffer, Robert '69 (SCL) Foley, MN St. John's.
Kieffer, Thomas A. *orat.* '65 (MRY)[F] Monterey, CA Oratorian Community–Congregation of the Oratory of Pontifical Right; [K] Monterey, CA Newman Institute for Historical and Religious Studies.
Kiel, William J. '93 (GBG) Indiana, PA St. Bernard.
Kielb, John T. '75 (TR) Monmouth Beach, NJ Church of the Precious Blood.
Kielbasa, Richard '59 (SC) Retired.
Kieliszewski, Jan M. '73 (MIL) Milwaukee, WI St. Augustine of Hippo.
Kielkowski, Andrzej *s.d.s.* '81 (NEW)[M] Verona, NJ The Salvatorian Fathers.
Kielkowski, Andzej C. *s.d.s.* '81 (CAM) Oaklyn, NJ St. Aloysius Catholic Church, Oaklyn, N.J.
Kieltyka, Robert '58 (MOB) Retired.
Kiely, Benedict C. '94 (BUR) Diocesan Consultors; Office of Continuing Education for Clergy; Stowe, VT Blessed Sacrament.
Kiely, Brian R. '78 (BO) Natick, MA St. Patrick.
Kiely, Cornelius '67 (BAK) On Duty Outside the Diocese; Boston, MA St. James the Apostle, Inc.
Kiely, Thomas P. '88 (NY) Cortlandt Manor, NY Holy Spirit.
Kiely, Thomas R. '03 (CAM) Office of Vocations; Pennsauken, NJ St. Stephen's R.C. Church, Pennsauken Township, N.J.; Elected Members.
Kiem, Anthony '46 (PT) Retired.
Kiene, Joachim *o.f.m.conv.* '64 (IND) Veterans' Administration Hospital.
Kiene, Joseph *o.f.m.conv.* '64 (MO) DEPARTMENT OF VETERANS AFFAIRS HOSPITALS AND CHAPLAINS.
Kienzle, Jerome C. '72 (MIL) Sick Leave.
Kiepura, Kenneth '69 (CHI) Libertyville, IL St. Joseph.
Kieran, John C. '67 (ATL) Conyers, GA St. Pius X.
Kieran, Richard A. '65 (ATL) On Leave of Absence.
Kiernan, Edward J. '54 (BRK) Retired.
Kiernan, James W. '62 (DM) Retired.
Kiernan, John G. '55 (PBL) Retired.
Kiernan, Joseph *o.f.m.* '69 (PAT)[N] Ringwood, NJ Holy Name Friary, Inc.
Kiernan, Michael F. '73 (SAC)[F] Sacramento, CA St. Patrick Children's Home, Inc.; [M] Sacramento, CA Catholic Charities of Sacramento, Inc.; [M] Sacramento, CA Catholic Social Service of Sacramento; [M] Auburn, CA Grand Council, Catholic Ladies Relief Society of the Diocese of Sacramento; Director of Social Services; Vicars Forane; College of Consultors; Catholic Charities of Sacramento, Inc.; Presbyteral Council; Ecumenical & Interreligious Affairs; Department of Social Services.
Kiernan, Michael F. '73 (SAC) Sacramento, CA Cathedral of the Blessed Sacrament.
Kiernan, Rev. Msgr. R. Donald '49 (ATL) Dunwoody, GA All Saints; Judges.
Kiernan, Robert J. *o.s.b.* '60 (BUR)[E] Weston, VT Priory of Benedictine Monks.
Kiernan, Thomas '48 (SY) Retired.
Kierney, Bede *o.s.b.* '83 (WOR)[O] Petersham, MA St. Mary's Monastery.
Kiesel, James P. '95 (BAL) Baltimore, MD St. Dominic; Presbyteral Council.
Kiesel, Leo C. '63 (EVN)[H] Loogootee, IN American–Innsbruck Alumni Association Retired.
Kieselbach, Joseph '61 (CR) Retired.
Kiesling, John *s.a.* '68 (NY)[EE] Garrison, NY St. Christopher's Inn.
Kieton, Dennis J. '85 (PRO) Cumberland, RI Our Lady of Fatima.
Kiff, Herbert J. '95 (NO) Harahan, LA St. Rita.
Kiffmeyer, James G. '85 (CIN) Cincinnati, OH Holy Family.
Kifolo, Patrick J. *o.s.f.s.* '07 (WIL)[B] Wilmington, DE Salesianum School.
Kiggins, Roy '64 (ROC) Retired.
Kightlinger, Jon T. '03 (BAL) Priests Sick or Absent.
Kigozi, Denis S. '91 (COL) Columbus, OH St. Thomas the Apostle.
Kihm, Frederick C. '93 (STU) Flushing, OH St. Paul's; Lafferty, OH St. Mary.
Kihm, Peter J. '81 (NY) Poughkeepsie, NY Our Lady of Mt. Carmel.
Kihneman, Rev. Msgr. Louis F. '77 (CC) Finance Council; Rockport, TX Sacred Heart.
Kijauskas, Gediminas *s.j.* '63 (CHI)[N] Lemont, IL Baltic Jesuits Advancement Office.
Kilasara, Thomas '85 (NO) Slidell, LA St. Margaret Mary; Slidell, LA Greenbriar Nursing & Convalescent Home; Slidell, LA Guest House of Slidell Nursing Home; Slidell, LA Trinity Neurologic Rehabilitation Center at Slidell.
Kilbride, Eugene M. '59 (HRT) West Hartford, CT St. Helena Retired.
Kilbridge, Robert *o.p.* '47 (CHI)[N] St. Pius V Priory.
Kilburg, Jack *m.s.f.* '79 (SAT) Seguin, TX Our Lady of Guadalupe.
Kilburn, Clay *c.m.* (GLP) Keams Canyon, AZ St. Joseph's Indian Mission; Vicars Forane; Presbyteral Council.
Kilcarr, Stephen M. '56 (NEW)[C] West Orange, NJ Seton Hall Preparatory School Retired.
Kilcawley, Sean P. '05 (LIN) Advocates; Graduate Studies.
Kilcline, Francis I. '81 (LFT) Peru, IN St. Charles Borromeo; Deans; Diocesan Consultors.
Kilcomons, Richard '06 (PAT) Morris Plains, NJ St. Virgilius.
Kilcourse, George A. '76 (L)[A] Bellarmine University.
Kilcoyne, Patrick '75 (SJ) Retired.
Kilcoyne, Terence T. '76 (WOR) Westminster, MA St. Edward the Confessor; Advocates; Deans; Presbyteral Council.
Kilcrann, John *c.s.sp.* (PIT)[B] Pittsburgh, PA Duquesne University of the Holy Spirit.
Kileo, Albert *a.l.c.p.* '92 (SLC) Roosevelt, UT Saint Helen LLC 224; Vernal, UT Saint James the Greater LLC 227.
Kileu, Barnabas S. *c.s.sp.* '05 (SB) Hemet, CA Our Lady of the Valley.
Kiley, Francis *o.f.m.conv.* '54 (CHI)[N] Chicago Conventual Franciscans of St. Bonaventure Province.
Kiley, J. Cletus '74 (CHI) On Duty Outside the Archdiocese.
Kiley, John A. '66 (PRO) Warwick, RI St. Francis of Assisi; Ecumenical Officer.
Kiley, John G. '70 (BO) Ipswich, MA Our Lady of Hope.
Kiley, Philip *s.j.* '71 (BO)[U] Newton, MA The Jesuit Community at Boston College.
Kiley, Phillip C. '78 (CHI) Chicago, IL St. George.
Kiley, Raymond P. '96 (BO) Watertown, MA St. Patrick; Emergency Response Group.
Kilgallen, John J. *s.j.* '65 (CHI)[C] Chicago, IL Jesuit Community at Loyola University Chicago.
Kilgallon, John J. '69 (PH) Southampton, PA Our Lady of Good Counsel.
Kilian, Waldemar Aleksander '87 (MO) Navy Reserve Chaplains.
Kilianski, Edward *s.c.j.* '83 (GAL) Houston, TX Our Lady of Guadalupe.
Kilidjian, Vincent *m.s.a.* '68 (NOR)[G] Cromwell Society of the Missionaries of the Holy Apostles.
Kilkelly, Timothy *m.m.* '90 (FgM) Maryknoll, NY MARYKNOLL.
Kill, Donald *s.s.c.* '72 (FgM) St Columbans, NE House of Post–Graduate Studies.
Kill, Robert J. '71 (TOL) Defiance, OH St. Michael; Defiance, OH St. Isidore.
Killackey, Cyprian *o.c.d.* '52 (TUC) Tucson, AZ Saint Margaret Mary Alacoque Roman Catholic Parish – Tucson; [D] Tucson, AZ Discalced Carmelite Friars of St. Margaret Mary's.
Killackey, Edward R. *m.m.* '57 (NY)[EE] Retired.
Killeen, Bernard D. '49 (HRT) Retired.
Killeen, John C. '59 (CAM) Cherry Hill, NJ St. Mary's R.C. Church, Delaware Township, N.J.
Killeen, John P. '57 (CC) Retired.
Killeen, Rev. Msgr. Michael F. '59 (LA) Rowland Heights, CA St. Elizabeth Ann Seton Retired.
Killeen, Thomas *o.m.i.* '58 (ANC) Cordova, AK St. Joseph.
Killeen, William E. '75 (CHI) Other Assignments.
Killeen, William J. '59 (HRT) Retired.
Killian, Anthony J. '08 (ARL) Alexandria, VA Blessed Sacrament; Notaries.
Killian, Wayne E. '84 (ALN) Bethlehem, PA Holy Ghost; [O] Bethlehem, PA Lehigh University (Bethlehem); [O] Bethlehem, PA Moravian College (Bethlehem); Campus Ministry Office.
Killilea, Patrick *ss.cc.* '69 (FR) Fairhaven, MA St. Mary's.
Kilmartin, John *f.d.p.* '86 (BO) East Boston, MA St.

Joseph–St. Lazarus; East Boston, MA.
Kilmurray, Fintan J. '77 (BLX) Wiggins, MS St. Francis Xavier; Army National Guard Chaplains.
Kilpatrick, Andrew W. '96 (SCR) Unassigned or Leave of Absence.
Kilpatrick, John J. '61 (SCR) Retired.
Kilroy, Brendan K. *s.p.s.* '62 (NEW)[C] Ramsey, NJ Don Bosco Preparatory High School; [M] Cliffside Park, NJ St. Patrick's Missionary Society.
Kilroy, C.A. *o.p.* '61 (STP) Minneapolis, MN St. Albert the Great.
Kilroy, Paul E. '70 (BO)[AA] Weston, MA Regis College Office of Campus Ministry; Allston, MA St. Anthony of Padua.
Kilty, Cornelius F. *o.s.f.s.* '69 (PH) Philadelphia, PA Mater Dolorosa.
Kilumanga, Raphael '71 (SP) St. Petersburg, FL Holy Cross.
Kilumbu, Claudes '94 (MO) Army Chaplains.
Kilzer, James *o.s.b.* '98 (BIS)[A] Richardton, ND Assumption Abbey.
Kim, Adrian *c.p.* '02 (FRS) Clovis, CA Our Lady of Perpetual Help; Community Medical Center, Clovis.
Kim, Alapaki '82 (HON) Nanakuli, HI St. Rita; Diocesan Pastoral Council; Presbyteral Council.
Kim, Alex K. '91 (ORG)[H] Anaheim, CA St. Thomas Korean Catholic Center.
Kim, Alfonso *m.m.* '97 (FgM) Maryknoll, NY MARYKNOLL.
Kim, Andrew M. '98 (BRK) Bayside, NY St. Robert Bellarmine.
Kim, Bede '07 (MET) Metuchen, NJ Cathedral of St. Francis of Assisi.
Kim, Carlos C. '93 (BO) Bridgewater, MA St. Thomas Aquinas.
Kim, Choong Seob '94 (R) New Hill, NC St. Ha–Sang Paul Jung.
Kim, Chrysostom *o.s.b.* '60 (SCL)[I] Collegeville, MN St. John's Abbey, of the Order of St. Benedict.
Kim, Dominic '90 (OAK) Korean Pastoral Center.
Kim, Dong Kyum '07 (NEW) Demarest, NJ Parish of St. Joseph.
Kim, Francis K. *o.f.m.* '96 (NY)[EE] New York, NY All Saints Friary; [II] New York, NY Franciscan Missionary Charities, Inc.; New York, NY All Saints.
Kim, Gabriel '04 (IND)[A] St. Meinrad, IN Saint Meinrad School of Theology.
Kim, Hong–Tae '95 (MET) Woodbridge, NJ Our Lady of Korea.
Kim, James Jong–Seong '00 (STP) Belle Plaine, MN Our Lady of the Prairie.
Kim, Jinsu Lawrence '00 (OKL) Oklahoma City, OK Korean Martyrs.
Kim, Jiwan A. *o.f.m.conv.* '93 (LA) Ventura, CA San Buenaventura Mission.
Kim, John Bosco *o.s.b.* (FgM) Newton, NJ St. Paul's Abbey.
Kim, John Dea Ha (BRK) Flushing, NY St. Paul Chong Ha–Sang Roman Catholic Chapel.
Kim, Joseph Sy '90 (LAN) Burton, MI Blessed Sacrament; [O] Blessed Sacrament Educational Trust Fund.
Kim, Joseph Y. '74 (BAL) Baltimore, MD Holy Korean Martyrs.
Kim, Joseph (NY) New York, NY St. Francis of Assisi.
Kim, Jungsoo '03 (NEW) Demarest, NJ Parish of St. Joseph.
Kim, Mary Joseph *o.cart.* '92 (BUR)[E] Arlington, VT Carthusian Foundation in America, Inc., Charterhouse of the Transfiguration.
Kim, Nam J. *s.s.* '90 (SFR)[A] Menlo Park, CA St. Patrick Seminary and University.
Kim, Nam J. *s.s.* '90 (BAL)[S] Baltimore Society of St. Sulpice, Province of the United States.
Kim, Nam Joseph '90 (ELP) On Duty Outside of Diocese.
Kim, Peter Sang Yun *s.d.b.* '02 (NY)[GG] Stony Point, NY Marian Shrine; [GG] Stony Point, NY Don Bosco Retreat Center and Marian Shrine.
Kim, Peter '00 (COL) Columbus, OH Korean Catholic Community.
Kim, Peter *l.c.* '00 (MAN)[A] Center Harbor, NH Immaculate Conception Apostolic School.
Kim, Peter '68 (HON) Honolulu, HI Korean Catholic Community.
Kim, Philip Sanghyo (R) Fayetteville, NC St. Andrew Kim.
Kim, Pio *o.f.m.* '01 (NY) New York, NY St. Francis of Assisi.
Kim, Rosario (TR) Eatontown, NJ Immaculate Conception.
Kim, Roy '94 (ORG) Inactive Leave.
Kim, Sae–Eul '84 (AUS) On Duty Outside the Diocese.
Kim, Samuel *o.s.b.* '95 (PAT)[N] Newton, NJ St. Paul's Abbey; Newton, NJ.
Kim, Silvester T. '06 (BAL) Baltimore, MD Cathedral of Mary Our Queen.
Kim, Sung Heum (John) '91 (CAM) Cherry Hill, NJ St. Yi Yun Il John Korean Catholic Mission; Absecon, NJ St. Andrew Kim Korean Catholic Mission, Inc.
Kim, Tae Sun '88 (DAL) Farmers Branch, TX St. Andrew Kim.
Kim, Tu–Din Paul '00 (LA)[P] Sierra Madre, CA Passionist Residence.
Kimani, Muthumbi wa *s.j.* '07 (STL)[O] St. Louis, MO Jesuit Community Corporation at Saint Louis University – Jesuit Hall.
Kimaryo, Simon (CLV)[K] Parma, OH Holy Family Home and Hospice.
Kimbrough, Conrad '78 (CHL) Retired.
Kime, David W. '97 (GRY) La Porte, IN St. Joseph; Deans; Bishop's Council of Priests; Consultors; Priests' Personnel Board.
Kimecz, Aloysius *o.cist.* '53 (DAL)[J] Irving, TX Cistercian Abbey of Our Lady of Dallas.
Kimes, John Paul '00 (OLL) Special Assignment.
Kimes, John Paul '00 (SAM) Judges.
Kimla, James '76 (MIL) Wauwatosa, WI St. Joseph Congregation.
Kimm, Gregory C. '87 (SJ) Cupertino, CA St. Joseph of Cupertino.
Kimminau, Bernard '94 (LIN) David City, NE St. Mary's.
Kimminau, Irenaeus *o.f.m.* '49 (SFD)[L] Quincy, IL Holy Cross Friary Retired.
Kimmons, Steven E. *s.j.* '94 (CHI)[C] Chicago, IL Jesuit Community at Loyola University Chicago.
Kinane, Gerard P. '73 (NO) On Administrative Leave.
Kinane, William P. '57 (SAC) Colfax, CA St. Dominic Retired.
Kinast, Robert L. '68 (ATL) On Duty Outside the Archdiocese.
Kincl, Robert L. '67 (AUS) Diocesan Tribunal Judges.
Kindall, John J. *s.j.* '57 (SPK)[J] Spokane, WA Regis Community.
Kindangen, George *c.m.i.* '92 (BEA) Orange, TX St. Helen.
Kindel, Joseph C. '04 (CIN) On Special and Archdiocesan Assignment.
Kinderman, Dennis *c.pp.s.* '67 (CIN)[N] Dayton Provincial Office of the Cincinnati Province of the Society of the Precious Blood.
Kinderman, Dennis *c.pp.s.* '67 (CHI)[W] Chicago, IL Precious Blood Ministry of Reconciliation.
Kindon, W. Frederick '74 (PH) New Hope, PA St. Martin of Tours.
Kinerk, Edward *s.j.* '72 (COS)[F] Sedalia, CO Sacred Heart Jesuit Community; [H] Sedalia, CO Sacred Heart Jesuit Retreat House.
King, Andrew '96 (NY)[A] Yonkers, NY Cathedral Prep Program; [A] Yonkers, NY St. Joseph's Seminary.
King, Arthur *o.m.i.* '59 (BUF) Buffalo, NY Holy Angels.
King, Brian Madison '97 (LKC)[B] Lake Charles, LA CHRISTUS Health Southwestern Louisiana.
King, Brian '00 (PMB) Episcopal Secretary.
King, Bruce *i.c.* '85 (PEO) Farmington, IL St. Matthew's.
King, Rev. Msgr. Charles '56 (FWT) Denton, TX Immaculate Conception; Deans; Ecumenism, Office of.
King, Donald E. '74 (Y) Warren, OH Blessed Sacrament; Priests Council.
King, Edward L. '55 (BO) Senior Priests. Retired.
King, Francis *o.c.s.o.* '58 (P)[L] Lafayette, OR The Cistercian (Trappist) Abbey of Our Lady of Guadalupe.
King, Rev. Msgr. George L. '53 (B) Kamiah, ID St. Catherine's of Siena; Orofino, ID St. Theresa's; Judges Retired.
King, Gerald J. *t.o.r.* '71 (FgM) Loretto, PA THIRD ORDER REGULAR MISSIONS.
King, Gregory C. '76 (LA) North Hollywood, CA St. Patrick.
King, James B. *c.s.c.* '88 (FTW)[H] Notre Dame, IN Holy Cross Community, Corby Hall, University of Notre Dame.
King, James E. '71 (NTN) Retired.
King, James E. '71 (PBL) Canon City, CO St. Michael; Finance Advisory Council; Clergy Benefit Society of the Diocese of Pueblo, Inc.
King, James J. *s.j.* '63 (CLV)[D] Cuyahoga Falls, OH Walsh Jesuit High School.
King, Rev. Msgr. James P. '46 (BRK)[T] Douglaston, NY Bishop Mugavero Residence Retired.
King, James W. '91 (BRK) Brooklyn, NY Assumption of the Blessed Virgin Mary.
King, James *c.s.c.* '88 (FTW)[B] University of Notre Dame Du Lac.
King, Jeffrey '87 (GLP) Reserve, NM Santo Nino; Catholic Committee on Scouting.
King, Jeremy *o.s.b.* '76 (IND)[K] St. Meinrad, IN St. Meinrad Archabbey.
King, John R. *m.m.* '53 (NY)[EE] Maryknoll Maryknoll Fathers and Brothers Retired.
King, John *o.m.i.* '54 (BO)[U] Lowell, MA Missionary Oblates of Mary Immaculate.
King, John '48 (PEO) Retired.
King, Larry '89 (GR) Portland, MI St. Patrick's; Deans; College of Consultors.
King, Leo *ss.cc.* '45 (FR)[G] Fairhaven, MA Damien Residence Retired.
King, Martin '96 (P) On Duty Outside the Archdiocese; Air Force Chaplains.
King, Michael J. '77 (WDC) Owings, MD Jesus the Good Shepherd; Deans.
King, Nicholas '66 (ORL) Rockledge, FL St. Mary's.
King, Norman A. '88 (RNO) Sparks, NV Immaculate Conception.
King, Philip J. '49 (BO) Senior Priests. Retired.
King, Stephen *o.f.m.conv.* (OAK)[M] Castro Valley, CA Conventual Franciscans (Province of St. Joseph of Cupertino).
King, Thomas F. '64 (LA) Los Angeles, CA St. Anastasia.
King, Thomas M. '73 (CIN) Cincinnati, OH Guardian Angels.
King, Thomas *c.s.c.* '69 (FTW)[H] Notre Dame Congregation of Holy Cross, Indiana Province, Provincial House.
King, Thomas *o.f.m.* '93 (FgM) Oakland, CA St. Barbara Province.
King, Thomas *c.s.c.* '69 (KAL) Niles, MI St. Mark.
King, Tommy *o.f.m.* '93 (OAK)[M] Oakland Franciscan Friars (Province of St. Barbara).
King, Rev. Msgr. William J. '83 (HBG) Consultors, College; Mechanicsburg, PA St. Elizabeth Ann Seton; Vicar General; Moderator of the Curia; Youth Protection Program; Diocesan Staff.
King, William J. (SAM) Promoter of Justice.
King, William M. *s.j.* '64 (WDC)[C] Washington, DC Georgetown University.
Kingbury, John *c.ss.r.* '80 (BAL) Annapolis, MD St. Mary.
Kingery, Michael G. '99 (ATL) Peachtree City, GA Holy Trinity.
Kingery, Michael '99 (ATL) Deans.
Kingery, Patrick J. '93 (ATL) Rome, GA St. Mary's.
Kingery, Victor *o.f.m.* '49 (SFD)[L] Springfield, IL Our Lady of Angels Friary.
Kingori, James *i.m.c.* '87 (BUF)[O] Williamsville, NY Consolata Fathers.
Kingsbury, John G. *c.ss.r.* '80 (NY)[GG] Esopus, NY Mount St. Alphonsus Redemptorist Retreat Center.
Kingsley, Richard M. '83 (TUC) Tucson, AZ Corpus Christi Roman Catholic Parish – Tucson; [H] Tucson, AZ Parish Pooled Investment Trust.
Kingsley, S. Thomas '03 (CHR) Charleston, SC Church of the Nativity.
Kiniry, Rev. Msgr. Lawrence R. '65 (GBG)[F] Greensburg, PA Neumann House.
Kinkel, Rev. Msgr. Robert J. '70 (DEN) College of Consultors; Edwards, CO St. Clare of Assisi.
Kinkel, Rev. Msgr. Robert '70 (DEN) Members At Large.
Kinkopf, John J. '57 (CLV) Chagrin Falls, OH St. Joan of Arc Retired.
Kinn, James W. '57 (CHI) Retired.
Kinnally, Robert M. '05 (BGP)[A] Stamford, CT St. John Fisher Seminary Residence; Office of Vocations; Westport, CT Church of the Assumption.
Kinnaman, Leroy G. '73 (LFT) Tipton, IN St. John the Baptist.
Kinnane, James F. '63 (HRT) Special and other Archdiocesan Assignment; Judges; Office for Religious; Adjutant Judicial Vicar; Newington, CT Church of the Holy Spirit.
Kinney, Donald *o.c.d.* '88 (SJ)[M] San Jose, CA Carmelite Monastery, Novitiate.
Kinney, James J. '98 (SUP) Solon Springs, WI St. Anthony of Padua; Solon Springs, WI St. Mary; Solon Springs, WI St. Pius X; Pastoral Consultors.
Kinney, John M. '76 (LFT) Military Chaplains; Air Force Chaplains.
Kinney, Leo '92 (FAR) Harwood, ND St. William; Hillsboro, ND St. Rose of Lima's Church of Hillsboro.
Kinney, M. Eugene '84 (MIL) On Duty Outside the Archdiocese.
Kinney, M. Eugene '84 (LAV) Las Vegas, NV Holy Family.
Kinoti, Elias (CHI) Chicago, IL St. Ignatius.
Kinsella, Charles R. '65 (BO) Senior Priests. Retired.
Kinsella, Rev. Msgr. John '64 (BAL) Priests Sick or Absent.
Kintanar, Chris '05 (SD) Alpine, CA Queen of Angels.
Kinter, John P. '67 (WDC) Washington, DC St. Thomas More; Hospital & Nursing Home Ministries.
Kintiba, Georges *s.v.d.* '96 (WDC)[N] Washington, DC Divine Word House.
Kinzer, Gary '70 (ORG) Absent on Sick Leave.
Kinzler, Dale H. '74 (FAR) Devils Lake, ND St. Joseph's Church of Devils Lake; [J] Devils Lake, ND Marriage Encounter; Deanery 5; Healthcare Director.
Kinzler, Herman *o.carm.* (NEW) Englewood, NJ St. Cecilia's.
Kiocha, Process Milton *a.j.* '01 (Y)[K] Canton, OH Sancta Clara Monastery.
Kipfer, David M. '88 (PEO) Ottawa, IL St. Columba.
Kipper, Nicholas A. '06 (LIN) Newspaper; Lincoln, NE St. Patrick's; Advocates.
Kiran, Ravi '04 (GLP) Gallup, NM Cathedral of the Sacred Heart.
Kirby, Daniel J. '94 (DM) Carter Lake, IA Our Lady of Carter Lake; Council Bluffs, IA Holy Family; Council

Bluffs, IA Our Lady, Queen of Apostles.
Kirby, Daniel '94 (DM) On Special Assignment; Seminarians.
Kirby, Donald J. *s.j.* '72 (SY)[Q] Syracuse, NY Jesuits at LeMoyne, Inc.
Kirby, Edward A. '61 (PT) Retired.
Kirby, Gerald S. '84 (NOR) Norwich, CT St. Mary.
Kirby, Jeffrey '07 (CHR) Graduate Studies; Vocations Board.
Kirby, Jim '96 (DM) Carlisle, IA St. Elizabeth Seton.
Kirby, Louis *o.s.b.* '48 (KCK)[I] Atchison, KS St. Benedict's Abbey.
Kirby, Mark *o.s.b.* '86 (TLS) Special Assignment.
Kirby, Martin F. '67 (BRK)[T] Douglaston, NY Bishop Mugavero Residence Retired.
Kirby, Robert F. '59 (FR) Retired.
Kirby, Shane L. '04 (SCR) Williamsport, PA St. Joseph the Worker, Williamsport.
Kirby, Thomas M. '57 (PIT)[N] Elizabeth, PA Divine Redeemer Motherhouse Retired.
Kirch, Jeffrey S. *c.pp.s.* '04 (LFT)[A] Rensselaer, IN Saint Joseph's College.
Kirch, Jeffrey *c.pp.s.* '04 (CIN)[N] Dayton Provincial Office of the Cincinnati Province of the Society of the Precious Blood.
Kirchen, Jude Geilen '73 (DEN) Rifle, CO St. Mary.
Kirchgessner, Christopher A. *o.s.b.* '80 (CHL)[J] Belmont, NC Belmont Abbey.
Kirchhoefer, Thomas A. '98 (MO) Military Chaplains; Army Chaplains.
Kirchner, Donnell *c.ss.r.* '66 (STL) Denver, CO Denver Province; [O] Liguori, MO Liguori Mission House/ Redemptorists.
Kirchner, James A. '63 (NEW) Retired.
Kirchner, Peter K. '93 (SCL) Glenwood, MN Sacred Heart; Glenwood, MN St. Bartholomew's; Directors.
Kirigia, Lazarus '07 (DM) West Des Moines, IA Sacred Heart.
Kirila, Michael '87 (ROM) Retired.
Kirk, Rev. Msgr. Albert E. '68 (MEM) Memphis, TN Church of the Holy Spirit.
Kirk, David R. '83 (TOL) Military Chaplains; Army Chaplains.
Kirk, James T. '86 (WIL) Wilmington, DE St. Mary Magdalen.
Kirk, John L. '70 (NSH) Catholic Charismatic Renewal; Spring Hill, TN Church of the Nativity.
Kirk, Rev. Msgr. Raymond '59 (SD) Retired.
Kirk, Rev. Msgr. Thomas D. '69 (MEM) Brownsville, TN St. John Church; Jackson, TN St. Mary Church; Dean of the Jackson Deanery.
Kirk, William S. '72 (PH) Philadelphia, PA Our Lady of Calvary.
Kirke, Eugene K. '62 (BO) Senior Priests. Retired.
Kirkhoff, Gerald J. '69 (IND) Indianapolis, IN St. Andrew the Apostle; Indianapolis, IN St. Pius X; Deaneries and Deans; Priests' Personnel Board; Vicariate for Advocacy to Priests.
Kirkhoff, Gerald '69 (IND) Council of Priests; Board of Consultors.
Kirkness, Michael D. '77 (GF) On Duty Outside of the Diocese.
Kirkness, Michael D. '77 (LA) Lompoc, CA Lompoc Federal Correctional Institution; Lompoc, CA US Penitentiary.
Kirkpatrick, James W. '08 (BUF) Hamburg, NY SS. Peter and Paul.
Kirlin, Bernard G. '71 (MIA) Coral Gables, FL St. Augustine; Deans and Deaneries; University of Miami.
Kirrane, James A. '46 (BRK) Retired.
Kirsch, Gerard D. *o.s.b.* '70 (SEA)[L] Lacey, WA St. Martin's Abbey; [A] Lacey, WA Saint Martin's University.
Kirsch, Gregory A. '81 (E) Houtzdale, PA Christ the King; Deans; Presbyteral Council; Defender of the Bond; College of Consultors.
Kirsch, Myron M. *o.s.b.* '73 (GBG)[G] Latrobe, PA Saint Vincent Archabbey.
Kirsch, Patrick V. '81 (SB) Alta Loma, CA St. Peter & St. Paul; Elected Members.
Kirtz, Raymond R. *o.m.i.* '58 (STP)[N] Buffalo, MN Christ the King Retreat Center.
Kirwan, Thomas P. '69 (DET) Retired.
Kirwen, Michael C. *m.m.* '63 (FgM) Maryknoll, NY MARYKNOLL.
Kirwin, George *o.m.i.* '58 (BUF) Buffalo, NY Our Lady of Hope.
Kirwin, Jerry *c.s.sp.* '83 (BRK) Councilors:; [T] Long Island City, NY Holy Ghost Fathers of Ireland.
Kirwin, John D. '66 (ALB) Ministers to Retired Priests.
Kirwin, John '66 (ALB) Retired.
Kirwin, Michael J. '76 (SCR) Laflin, PA St. Maria Goretti.
Kirwin, Peter *o.f.m.* (PHX)[G] Scottsdale, AZ Franciscan Renewal Center, Inc. (Casa de Paz Y Bien).
Kirwin, Rev. Msgr. Robert J. '45 (RVC) Williston Park, NY St. Aidan's Church Retired.
Kis–Horvath, Pascal *o.cist.* '57 (DAL)[J] Irving, TX Cistercian Abbey of Our Lady of Dallas.
Kisala, Robert *s.v.d.* '85 (FgM) Techny, IL.
Kiselica, John J. '84 (DET) Special Assignment.
Kiser, Karl *s.j.* '97 (DET)[E] Detroit, MI University of Detroit Jesuit High School and Academy.
Kish, Carl '62 (Y) Cortland, OH St. Robert Bellarmine Parish.
Kish, Jerome '98 (JOL) Downers Grove, IL St. Joseph.
Kish, Leslie P. '97 (B) Lewiston, ID Our Lady of Lourdes; [F] Lewiston, ID Lewis Clark State College; Lewiston, ID St. Stanislaus; Lewiston, ID St. James.
Kish, Matthew J. '43 (GRY) Retired.
Kish, Michael A. '65 (MIA) Pinecrest, FL St. Louis; Miami Dade College–Kendall Campus; Police Chaplains.
Kishore, Vimal *s.j.* '02 (OAK)[M] Berkeley, CA Jesuit Fathers and Brothers.
Kiss, Barnabas G. *o.f.m.* '78 (ATH) Delegate in North America; American Hungarian Catholic Priests' Association (USA).
Kiss, Barnabas G. *o.f.m.* '78 (DET) Detroit, MI Holy Cross.
Kissane, Rev. Msgr. James M. '92 (RVC) Central Islip, NY St. John of God; Chaplains of the Suffolk County Police Department.
Kissane, Maurice J. '64 (CHI) Retired.
Kissel, Anthony '73 (EVN) On Duty Outside the Diocese.
Kissel, Anthony '73 (SP)[A] St. Leo, FL Saint Leo University, Office of Assessment and Institutional Research.
Kissel, Francis J. *s.m.* '71 (ATL)[D] Atlanta, GA Marist School.
Kissel, Ignatius M. *o.s.m.* '65 (CHI)[N] Chicago Order of Friar Servants of Mary (Servites) United States of America Province, Inc.
Kissel, Ignatius M. *o.s.m.* '65 (P)[L] Portland, OR The Grotto, The National Sanctuary of Our Sorrowful Mother.
Kissell, Terrence '78 (DEN) Commerce City, CO Our Lady Mother of the Church.
Kissell, Wilbur T. '51 (MOB) Montgomery, AL St. Andrew; [I] Montgomery, AL Alabama State University Newman Center.
Kissinger, Rodney T. *s.j.* '53 (NO)[P] New Orleans, LA Ignatius Residence Retired.
Kissling, John M. '53 (DUB) Retired.
Kist, Harold W. '74 (CIN) Russells Point, OH St. Mary of the Woods; Priest Councilors; Consultors.
Kistler, Leonard A. *c.pp.s.* '61 (CIN)[N] Carthagena, OH St. Charles Retired.
Kistner, Hilarion *o.f.m.* '55 (CIN)[N] Cincinnati, OH St. Francis Seraph Friary.
Kita, John M. '98 (SCR) Elkland, PA St. Thomas the Apostle; Mansfield, PA Holy Child.
Kitchin, George R. '70 (BLX) Gulfport, MS St. James; Charismatic Renewal.
Kitenge, Denis '87 (SP)[J] Tampa, FL St. Joseph's Hospital, Inc.
Kitsmiller, Robert J. '04 (COL) West Jefferson, OH SS. Simon and Jude.
Kitt, William J. '43 (CLV) Elyria Township, OH St. Vincent de Paul Retired.
Kitten, Marvin C. *s.j.* '65 (NO)[C] New Orleans, LA Loyola University New Orleans.
Kitten, Marvin *s.j.* '65 (MOB)[A] Mobile, AL Spring Hill College; Jesuit.
Kittock, Francis R. '55 (STP) Deanery 18; College of Consultors Retired.
Kitz, Raphael *o.c.d.* '59 (LR)[A] Little Rock, AR Marylake – Carmelite Novitiate.
Kitzhaber, Keith '08 (LC) Cashton, WI St. Augustine of Hippo; Cashton, WI Nativity of the Blessed Virgin Mary; Cashton, WI St. John the Baptist.
Kitzke, Timothy L. '89 (MIL) Milwaukee, WI Old St. Mary; Milwaukee, WI Three Holy Women Catholic Parish.
Kivel, Joseph G. '61 (STP) Retired.
Kiwale, Methodius S. *a.l.c.p.* '96 (SFR) San Francisco, CA St. John of God.
Kiwan, Naji (SAM) Waterbury, CT Our Lady of Lebanon.
Kiwanuka, Deogratias '91 (PEO)[H] Bloomington, IL OSF St. Joseph Medical Center.
Kiwera, Thaddeus Simon *s.o.l.t.* '96 (CC)[G] Robstown, TX Society of Our Lady of the Most Holy Trinity.
Kiwus, John *c.ss.r.* (NY)[EE] Esopus, NY Redemptorist Priests and Brothers C.Ss.R. (Province of Baltimore).
Kizewski, Justin '08 (LC)[C] Chippewa Falls, WI McDonell Central Catholic High School; Chippewa Falls, WI Holy Ghost; Chippewa Falls, WI St. Bridget.
Kizhakkedam, Augustine '84 (SYM) Morrisville, NC Lourdes Matha Syro–Malabar Catholic Church.
Kizhakkethazhe, Francis Z. *m.s.f.s.* '87 (GAL) Houston, TX Notre Dame.
Kizhakkethazhe, Francis *m.s.f.s.* '87 (TYL)[B] Whitehouse, TX The Missionaries of St. Francis de Sales.
Kizhakumpurath, Philip Thomas *m.s.f.s.* '87 (TYL)[B] Whitehouse, TX The Missionaries of St. Francis de Sales.
Kizis, Kenneth G. '59 (SCR)[N] Dunmore, PA Villa St. Joseph Retired.
Kizito, John Fisher '02 (FAR) Ellendale, ND St. Helena's Church of Ellendale; Ellendale, ND St. Patrick.
Klaas, Gregory '67 (SR)[G] Sonoma, CA Hanna Boys Center.
Klaers, Marvin J. '50 (STP) Retired.
Klag, Michael A. '03 (WCH) Winfield, KS St. Mary; Winfield, KS Holy Name.
Klaiber, Jeffrey L. *s.j.* '74 (FgM)[N] Chicago Chicago Province of the Society of Jesus–Provincial Office; Chicago, IL Society of Jesus.
Klajbor, Richard J. '79 (CHI) Chicago, IL Our Lady, Mother of the Church.
Klak, Jan Piotr '79 (SAT)[C] Oblate School of Theology.
Klak, Jan '79 (SAT) San Antonio, TX St. Anthony Mary Claret.
Klamut, Charles '99 (PEO) Peoria, IL St. Mark's.
Klanichka, Volodymyr '01 (PHU) Wilmington, DE St. Nicholas.
Klapperich, Giles R. *o.p.* '53 (CHI)[N] St. Pius V Priory.
Klapps, William J. '58 (WIL) Wilmington, DE St. Matthew Retired.
Klarer, Michael E. '79 (MAD) Monroe, WI St. Victor; Navy Reserve Chaplains.
Klasek, Stephen A. '83 (NSH) Manchester, TN St. Mark; Tullahoma, TN St. Paul the Apostle; Diocesan Finance Board; Priest Benefit Foundation; Clergy Personnel Board; Diocesan Planning.
Klasinski, George '51 (KCK) Retired.
Klasinski, Stanley J. '77 (CLV) Lyndhurst, OH St. Clare.
Klassen, Roger *o.s.b.* '66 (SCL) Freeport, MN Sacred Heart; New Munich, MN Immaculate Conception; Freeport, MN St. Rose of Lima; [I] Collegeville, MN St. John's Abbey, of the Order of St. Benedict; Personnel Committee; Defensor Vinculi.
Klatka, Joseph S. '67 (MAN) Retired.
Klauck, Michael '94 (BIR) Absent on Leave.
Klauck, Rev. Msgr. Peter N. '55 (GB) Retired.
Klauck, Stanley B. '46 (MIL) Retired.
Klauer, Gary *o.f.m.conv.* '75 (MRY)[F] Arroyo Grande, CA St. Joseph Cupertino Province, Provincial Center.
Klauer, Gary *o.f.m.conv.* '75 (OAK) San Pablo, CA St. Paul; Deanery #21.
Klaus, John Mark *t.o.r.* '99 (VEN) Liturgical Commission; Sarasota, FL Our Lady Queen of Martyrs; Department of Worship and Ministries.
Kleas, Rev. Msgr. Milam '51 (GAL) Houston, TX St. Maximilian Kolbe Retired.
Kleba, Gerald J. '67 (STL) St. Louis, MO St. Cronan.
Kleber, Cecil *o.f.m.* '50 (SFE)[H] Albuquerque, NM The Province of Our Lady of Guadalupe.
Klecha, Joseph A. *m.m.* '69 (SJ)[M] Los Altos, CA Maryknoll.
Kleczewski, Kieran '78 (PHX) Avondale, AZ St. Thomas Aquinas Roman Catholic Parish; Worship and Liturgy, Office of; Avondale, AZ St. Michael Roman Catholic Parish; Deans.
Klee, Joseph C. '01 (COL)[I] Portsmouth, OH St. Joseph Adoration Monastery, Poor Clares of Perpetual Adoration; Lucasville, OH Southern Ohio Correctional Facility; New Boston, OH St. Monica.
Klees, Raymond F. '73 (CHI)[D] Niles, IL Notre Dame College Prep.
Kleffman, James '60 (DM) Council Bluffs, IA Retired.
Kleiber, Kenneth R. '68 (MO) Other Assignments; DEPARTMENT OF VETERANS AFFAIRS HOSPITALS AND CHAPLAINS.
Kleiber, Kenneth '68 (PHX) Phoenix, AZ United States Veterans Affairs Medical Center.
Klein, Bernard C. '49 (STP) Retired.
Klein, Charles R. '59 (BAL)[V] Glen Burnie, MD The Church of the Good Shepherd Parish Endowment Trust Retired.
Klein, David F. *s.j.* '71 (SAC)[D] Sacramento, CA Jesuit High School; [I] Carmichael, CA Sacramento Jesuit Community.
Klein, David J. '90 (CAM) Officers; Chancellor; Judicial Vicar; Judicial Vicar; Ex Officio Members; Vocation Advisory Board; College of Consultors; Ex Officio Members; Judges; Ex Officio Members; The Church of the Holy Spirit, Atlantic City, N.J.; [M] Blackwood, NJ Bishop's Residence.
Klein, David O. *c.s.b.* '70 (MO) DEPARTMENT OF VETERANS AFFAIRS HOSPITALS AND CHAPLAINS.
Klein, David *c.s.b.* '70 (SFE) Veterans Administration Medical Center; Albuquerque, NM Sacred Heart.
Klein, Dennis D. '66 (BRK) On Leave/Unassigned Retired.
Klein, Donald L. '65 (DUB)[F] Cedar Rapids, IA Regis Middle School; Cedar Rapids, IA St. Pius X; Personnel Advisory Board; Finance Council.
Klein, Douglas M. '96 (SC) Rock Valley, IA St. Mary's.
Klein, Eugene M. '74 (WIN) On Duty Outside the Diocese; Springfield, MO St. Joseph's.
Klein, Eugene M. '74 (SPC) Springfield, MO U.S. Medical Center; Fordland, MO Ozark Correctional Center.
Klein, George W. '59 (CHI) Northfield, IL St. Philip the Apostle Retired.

Klein, George W. '54 (CIN) Trenton, OH Holy Name.
Klein, Gregory L. *o.carm.* '75 (VEN) Osprey, FL Our Lady of Mount Carmel.
Klein, J. Leo *s.j.* '64 (CIN)[N] Cincinnati, OH Jesuit Community at Xavier University.
Klein, James J. '02 (COS) Colorado Springs, CO Divine Redeemer.
Klein, James T. '78 (CLV) Lakewood, OH St. James.
Klein, John J. '70 (PAT) Paterson, NJ St. George.
Klein, John P. '78 (LAN) Lansing, MI St. Gerard; Regional Vicars.
Klein, John '02 (JOL) Bensenville, IL St. Charles Borromeo.
Klein, Lawrence J. '84 (BWN) Brownsville, TX Our Lady of Good Counsel.
Klein, Leonard R. '06 (WIL) Wilmington, DE Wilmington Hospital; Censor of Books; St. Thomas More Society; Wilmington, DE Immaculate Heart of Mary.
Klein, Louis S. '81 (BUF) Cheektowaga, NY Queen of Martyrs.
Klein, Martin L. '91 (RVC) Glen Cove, NY St. Patrick's.
Klein, Pascal L. '87 (DOD) Elkhart, KS St. Joan of Arc Catholic Church of Elkhart, Kansas; Hugoton, KS St. Helen Catholic Church of Hugoton, Kansas.
Klein, Peter J. '74 (WIN) Janesville, MN St. Ann's; Janesville, MN St. Joseph's; Priest Assignments Committee.
Klein, Pius *o.s.b.* '74 (IND)[K] St. Meinrad, IN St. Meinrad Archabbey.
Klein, Terrance W. '84 (COL) On Duty Outside the Diocese.
Klein, Theodore J. '69 (NOR) Retired.
Kleiner, James '67 (DEN) Retired.
Kleiner, Robert *m.c.c.j.* '71 (LA) Los Angeles, CA Holy Cross.
Kleinfehn, Walter J. '60 (DUB) College of Consultors Retired.
Kleinheinz, Joseph L. '54 (SUP) Retired.
Kleinhenz, John H. *s.j.* '52 (DET)[K] Clarkston, MI Colombiere Center.
Kleinmann, Dennis W. '93 (ARL) Alexandria, VA St. Mary's.
Kleinschmidt, John '02 (FAR) Minto, ND Sacred Heart Church of Minto; Minto, ND St. Stanislaus Church of Warsaw.
Kleinschmidt, Sylvester '50 (SCL) Retired.
Kleinschmidt, Thomas *o.m.v.* '84 (BO)[B] Boston, MA Oblate Provincialate.
Kleinstuber, Joseph J. '64 (WDC) Retired.
Kleinwachter, John '77 (CR) Oklee, MN St. Francis Xavier's; Priests' Personnel Board.
Kleissler, Rev. Msgr. Thomas A. '57 (NEW) Special Assignment in the Archdiocese; [R] Plainfield, NJ RENEW International; Renew International.
Klem, Daniel N. '83 (RIC) Norfolk, VA Sacred Heart.
Klem, Robert J. *c.s.b.* '56 (GAL)[O] Sugar Land, TX Basilian Mission Center.
Klemash, Dennis J. *o.f.m.cap.* '90 (WH) Charleston, WV St. Anthony; Elkview, WV Our Lady of the Hills; [L] Charleston, WV Capuchins–St. Anthony Friary.
Klemme, Dennis C. '57 (VEN) Judges.
Klemme, Dennis C. '57 (MIL)[Q] Pewaukee, WI Carmel of the Mother of God; Judges for Second Instance Retired.
Klemme, Robert '91 (LFT) Oxford, IN St. Patrick; Oxford, IN St. Charles.
Klemmer, Marvin J. '66 (BIS) Bismarck, ND Ascension; Pro–Synodal Judges; Vicar for Presbyters; Priests' Personnel Board; Ecumenism.
Klepac, Rev. Msgr. Kenneth J. '58 (MOB) Mobile, AL St. Joan of Arc; Associate Judges.
Klepac, Richard *s.o.l.t.* '06 (CC)[G] Robstown, TX Society of Our Lady of the Most Holy Trinity.
Klepac, Richard *s.o.l.t.* '06 (PHX) Phoenix, AZ Most Holy Trinity Roman Catholic Parish.
Klepacki, Michael S. '78 (CHL) Military Chaplains; Navy Chaplains.
Klepec, George '71 (JOL) Joliet, IL St. Paul the Apostle.
Kleppner, Joseph J. '71 (PIT) Aliquippa, PA St. Frances Cabrini; Theological Commission.
Klettner, Frederick J. '65 (DET) Retired.
Kletzel, Thomas P. '83 (PH) East Norriton, PA St. Titus.
Klevence, John P. '85 (WIL) New Castle, DE St. Peter the Apostle.
Klikunas, Bruce J. *o.s.m.* '72 (OAK)[M] Berkeley, CA Servites.
Klikunas, Bruce M. *o.s.m.* '72 (CHI)[N] Chicago Order of Friar Servants of Mary (Servites) United States of America Province, Inc.
Klim, Vincent '89 (PAT)[Q] Chester, NJ Nazareth Village Retired.
Klima, James A. '76 (COL) Pickerington, OH Seton Parish; Deanery 6: East; Parochial Examiners; Presbyteral Council.
Klimas, George H. '51 (SAG) Retired.
Klimczyk, John '81 (FTW) South Bend, IN St. Hedwig; South Bend, IN Faith & Hope & Charity Chapel; South Bend, IN St. Patrick.
Klimek, Rev. Msgr. Edmund J. '53 (LC) Eau Claire, WI Newman Community; [D] Eau Claire, WI Sacred Heart Hospital; [K] Eau Claire, WI Newman Parish; Hospitals and Health Affairs.
Klimek, Jan '71 (CR) Park Rapids, MN St. Mary's.
Klimowicz, Sigmund *o.f.m.cap.* '45 (NY)[B] Beacon, NY St. Lawrence of Brindisi Friary.
Kline, Donald J. '95 (PHX) Phoenix, AZ St. Joan of Arc Roman Catholic Parish.
Kline, Donald '95 (PHX)[J] Phoenix, AZ Cursillo Movement.
Kline, Edmond G. '04 (WCH) Council Grove, KS St. Rose; Council Grove, KS St. Anthony of Padua.
Kline, Edwin J. *c.s.b.* '56 (DET)[E] Novi, MI Catholic Central High School.
Kline, John J. '47 (CLV) Retired.
Kline, Omer U. *o.s.b.* '49 (GBG)[G] Latrobe, PA Saint Vincent Archabbey.
Kline, Robert J. '04 (RVC) Center Moriches, NY St. John the Evangelist; Lindenhurst, NY Our Lady of Perpetual Help.
Kline, Robert W. '48 (CLV) Mentor, OH St. John Vianney Retired.
Kline, Rev. Msgr. Roy F. '51 (ALT) Altoona, PA Cathedral of the Blessed Sacrament Retired.
Kline, Rev. Msgr. Roy '50 (ALT) Retired.
Klingeisen, Richard H. '72 (GB) Regional Vicars.
Klingeisen, Richard H. '72 (GB) Diocesan Health Services; Special Assignment; Manitowoc, WI St. Francis of Assisi.
Klingele, Brian '02 (KCK) Garnett, KS Holy Angels; Greeley, KS St. John the Baptist's; Legion of Mary.
Klinger, Charles F. '83 (COL) Westerville, OH St. Paul the Apostle; Diocesan Judges.
Klinger, Rev. Msgr. Nevin J. '82 (ALN) On Duty Outside the Diocese.
Klinger, Rev. Msgr. Nevin J. (SAM) Advocates.
Klinger, Rev. Msgr. Nevin '82 (COL)[A] Columbus, OH Pontifical College Josephinum.
Klingler, Donald P. '61 (KAL) Otsego, MI St. Margaret; Diocesan Council of Catholic Women (D.C.C.W.).
Klingler, John *s.c.j.* '67 (MIL)[P] Milwaukee, WI SCJ Community.
Klingler, Ronald M. '65 (Y) Canton, OH St. John the Baptist.
Klink, Anthony G. '58 (MIL) Retired.
Klink, Delbert D. '60 (MAD) Retired.
Klink, Eugene A. '63 (LC) Eau Claire, WI Immaculate Conception; Deans; Consultors; Ex Officio.
Klink, Kenneth J. '66 (MAD) Belleville, WI St. Mary of Lourdes; Belleville, WI St. James; Elected.
Klink, Peter J. *s.j.* '81 (RC) Pine Ridge, SD Holy Rosary; [C] Pine Ridge, SD Jesuit Community of Holy Rosary Mission.
Klintworth, William P. *s.j.* '61 (FgM) New York, NY Society of Jesus.
Klinzing, Rev. Msgr. Thomas J. '71 (PMB) Judicial Vicar; Judges; Consultors; Ex Officio.
Klismet, Kurt J. *o.ss.t.* '02 (BAL)[S] Leadership; Councilors:; Councilors:; [S] Baltimore, MD.
Klizek, Duane R. '82 (BUF) Niagara Falls, NY Holy Family of Jesus, Mary and Joseph.
Kloak, David G. '78 (MO) Military Chaplains; Navy Chaplains.
Kloak, David '78 (HON) Military Chaplains.
Klobuka, John *s.m.* '78 (HON)[D] Honolulu, HI Marianist Hall Community.
Klocek, Andrew '89 (BRK) Music Commission.
Klocek, Andrzej (BRK) Astoria, NY St. Joseph.
Klockeman, John A. '00 (STP)[A] Saint Paul, MN The Saint Paul Seminary.
Klockeman, John '00 (STP)[C] St. Paul, MN University of St. Thomas.
Kloda, Marshall J. '89 (PH) On Special or Other Archdiocesan Assignment.
Kloepfer, John S. '53 (JOL) Retired.
Kloepfer, John S. '53 (RIC) Blackstone, VA Immaculate Heart of Mary Retired.
Klores, Stanley P. '82 (NO) New Orleans, LA St. Patrick; Ecumenical Officer.
Klos, Joseph '80 (BUF) Judges.
Klos, Michael E. '00 (LC) Waumandee, WI St. Boniface; Deans; Arcadia, WI Holy Family.
Kloskowski, Rev. Msgr. Stanley E. '58 (CAM) Retired.
Kloss, Anthony *o.s.b.* '91 (WOR)[O] Still River, MA Benedictine Monks, St. Benedict Abbey.
Kloster, Donald '95 (SAT) San Antonio, TX Audie Murphy VA Hospital.
Kloster, George M. '68 (CHL) Murphy, NC St. William.
Klosterman, Timothy Clement '08 (LA) Santa Monica, CA St. Monica.
Kloton, Michael J. '87 (SCR) Plains, PA SS. Peter and Paul.
Klotter, Frederick W. '96 (L) Louisville, KY St. Martin of Tours; Associate Judges; Ex Officio.
Klotz, David *o.s.a.* (GAL) Pasadena, TX St. Juan Diego.
Kluba, Zbigniew '73 (PAT) Morristown, NJ Morristown Memorial Hospital.
Klucinec, Benedict *m.s.a.* '87 (NOR)[G] Cromwell Society of the Missionaries of the Holy Apostles.
Klucinec, Benedict *m.s.a.* '87 (PT) Panama City, FL St. Dominic.
Klug, Richard L. '51 (CIN) Imprimatur Censors; Judges Retired.
Kluge, Stephen *o.f.m.* '01 (TR) Brant Beach, NJ St. Francis of Assisi.
Klump, Gregory S. '98 (STL) Ste. Genevieve, MO Ste. Genevieve.
Klunk, David '09 (ORG) Newport Beach, CA Our Lady Queen of Angels.
Klunk, Timothy '79 (BAL) Baltimore, MD Our Lady of Victory.
Klybus, Edward George '01 (NEW) On Duty Outside the Archdiocese.
Kmiec, Roman *c.m.* '86 (HRT) New Haven, CT St. Stanislaus.
Kmiotek, Michael *c.f.r* '06 (FWT)[H] Fort Worth, TX Sacred Heart Friars of the Renewal.
Knab, George *o.m.i.* '67 (CHI) Chicago, IL St. Malachy.
Knapek, John A. *s.j.* '57 (DET)[K] Clarkston, MI Colombiere Center.
Knapik, Andrew G. '57 (ALT) Retired.
Knapik, Andrew '78 (CLV) Cleveland, OH Immaculate Heart of Mary.
Knapp, Charles '63 (TUC) Defenders of the Bond Retired.
Knapp, Eric J. *s.j.* '04 (CIN) Cincinnati, OH St. Francis Xavier; [U] Cincinnati, OH St. Xavier Church Property Corporation; Priest Councilors.
Knapp, Eric *s.j.* '04 (CHI) Chicago, IL St. Procopius.
Knapp, Gerard J. *c.ss.r.* '75 (BAL) Baltimore, MD Sacred Heart of Jesus.
Knapp, James G. *s.j.* '81 (STL)[F] St. Louis, MO St. Louis University High School, George H. Backer Memorial; [O] Saint Louis, MO St. Louis University High School Jesuit Community.
Knapp, John M. (NY) Bronx, NY St. Gabriel.
Knapp, Rev. Msgr. Kenneth R. *a.c.s.w.* '63 (EVN) Evansville, IN Christ the King; Evansville, IN St. Theresa; Special Assignment; Vicar General; Diocesan Consultors; Diocesan Council of Priests; Ex Officio.
Knapp, Rev. Msgr. Richard L. '55 (SFR) Retired.
Knapp, Rev. Msgr. Richard S. '55 (SFR)[K] San Rafael, CA Nazareth House of San Rafael, Inc.
Knapp, Roger A. '85 (DET) Absent on Leave; Gibraltar, MI St. Victor.
Knapp, William L. '48 (SFR)[K] San Rafael, CA Nazareth House of San Rafael, Inc. Retired.
Knappik, Richard *c.ss.r.* '58 (ALB)[L] Saratoga Springs, NY St. John Neumann Residence.
Knappik, Richard '58 (HBG)[G] Ephrata, PA St. Clement's Mission House.
Knauer, Rev. Msgr. Paul F. '64 (PAT) Chester, NJ St. Lawrence the Martyr.
Knauf, Randall *o.f.m.cap* '91 (MIL)[P] Milwaukee, WI St. Conrad Friary.
Kneafsey, Rev. Msgr. Cornelius T. '58 (BRK) South Richmond Hill, NY St. Benedict Joseph Labre Retired.
Kneal, Rev. Msgr. Ellsworth '44 (STP) Retired.
Kneeland, David L. '06 (MAN) Bedford, NH St. Elizabeth Seton; Presbyteral Council.
Kneemiller, William C. '99 (DAV) Army Reserve Chaplains; Military Chaplains.
Kneifl, Rodney V. '85 (OM) Platte Center, NE St. Joseph; Platte Center, NE St. Michael; [O] Platte Center, NE Servants of the Heart of the Father; Platte Center, NE St. Stanislaus.
Kneip, Paschal N. *o.s.b.* '51 (RIC) Chincoteague Island, VA St. Andrew the Apostle.
Knepper, Daniel J. '70 (DUB) Dubuque, IA St. Anthony; College of Consultors; Deanery Representatives; Worship Commission.
Knepper, Timothy *c.pp.s.* '03 (LFT) Rensselaer, IN St. Augustine.
Knerr, Joseph '80 (ORG) Yorba Linda, CA St. Martin de Porres; Council of Priests.
Knestout, Rev. Msgr. Barry C. '89 (WDC) Washington, DC Annunciation.
Knestout, Mark D. '98 (WDC) Washington, DC St. Matthew Cathedral; Pastoral Center Special Ministries; Office of Worship.
Knickerbocker, Knick '09 (SAN) Junction, TX St. Theresa of the Child Jesus; Menard, TX Sacred Heart.
Knies, G. Jerome *o.s.a.* '62 (CHI)[N] Olympia Fields, IL The Augustinians–Provincialate; [N] Matteson, IL Austin Friary; Olympia Fields, IL.
Knight, David B. '61 (MEM) Retired.
Knight, Dennis '77 (LEX) Priests' Retirement Board.
Knight, Rev. Msgr. Jeffrey N. '88 (STL) Villa Ridge, MO St. John the Baptist.
Knight, Robert '83 (STL) St. Clair, MO St. Clare.
Knipe, Michael J. '88 (TLS) Judicial Vicar; Judges; Tulsa, OK St. Pius X.
Knippel, Kenneth P. '76 (MIL) Brookfield, WI St. John Vianney.
Knippenberg, Robert E. '00 (VIC) Shiner, TX SS. Cyril and Methodius; School Board.
Knipper, Daniel J. '67 (DUB) Lansing, IA St. Joseph; Lansing, IA Immaculate Conception.
Knittel, Kilian J. '60 (CHI) Retired.
Knoblach, Thomas '87 (SCL) St. Cloud, MN Holy Spirit; St. Cloud, MN St. Anthony of Padua; St. Cloud, MN

St. John Cantius; Directors; Health Ministry.
Knoebel, Thomas L. '69 (MIL)[B] Hales Corners, WI Sacred Heart School of Theology; Special Assignment.
Knoernschild, John *o.carm.* '70 (JOL)[L] Darien, IL St. Simon Stock Priory.
Knoll, Charles *o.f.m.cap.* '54 (PIT)[M] Pittsburgh St. Augustine Friary.
Knoll, Charles *o.f.m.cap* (WDC)[B] Washington, DC St. Francis Friary–Capuchin College.
Knoll, Jerome E. *c.s.c.* '60 (FTW)[A] Notre Dame, IN Moreau Seminary; [H] Notre Dame Congregation of Holy Cross, Indiana Province, Provincial House.
Knoll, Lester *o.f.m.cap.* '64 (PIT) Clairton, PA St. Clare of Assisi.
Knoll, Lester *o.f.m.cap* '64 (GBG)[A] Latrobe, PA St. Vincent Seminary.
Knoll, Urban H. '69 (STL) Retired.
Knop, Andrew *o.m.i.* '89 (SFS) Sisseton, SD St. Catherine; Sisseton, SD St. Peter.
Knopik, Andrew J. '83 (BEL) Nashville, IL St. Ann.
Knopp, Benjamin *o.f.m.conv.* '55 (L) Louisville, KY St. Paul.
Knopp, John '78 (ELP) Absent on Leave.
Knotek, Michael P. '96 (CHI) Chicago, IL St. John de la Salle; Presbyteral Council.
Knott, J. Ronald '70 (L) On Duty Outside the Archdiocese; [A] St. Meinrad, IN Saint Meinrad School of Theology.
Knott, William P. '59 (RCK) Retired.
Knox, James '51 (PRT) Retired.
Knox, Sean Vincent '01 (PT) Chipley, FL St. Joseph the Worker; Marianna, FL St. Anne; Cursillo Movement.
Knox, Stephen J. '89 (RCK) Huntley, IL St. Mary; Diocesan Consultors.
Knudsen, Ronald '72 (SEA) Mountlake Terrace, WA St. Pius X.
Knueven, Gerald E. '68 (TOL) Retired.
Knueven, Rev. Msgr. Harold L. '58 (IND) Greensburg, IN St. Mary Retired.
Knuffman, Donald E. '65 (SFD) Retired.
Knurek, Dennis A. '77 (BGP) Retired.
Knusel, Frank '89 (P) Retired.
Knusel, Frank '73 (VNN) Scappoose, OR St. Irene Byzantine Catholic Church.
Ko, Benedict *m.s.c.* '05 (MIL)[Y] Milwaukee, WI The Korean Catholic Community of Milwaukee.
Ko, Moo–Chan Benedict *m.s.c.* '04 (RCK)[G].
Kobak, David *o.f.m.* '03 (IND) Oldenburg, IN Holy Family.
Kobasiuk, Maxim *o.s.b.m.* '77 (STF)[A] Stamford, CT Ukrainian Catholic Seminary Inc. St. Basil College; Diocesan Consultors.
Kobbeman, Rev. Msgr. Gerald P. '66 (RCK) Rockford, IL St. Rita; Pro Synodal Judges; Deans.
Kobe, Robert S. '79 (ELP) El Paso, TX Christ The Savior; Adjutant Vicars; Judges.
Kobel, Stanley *o.f.m.cap.* '96 (CHL) Charlotte, NC St. Thomas Aquinas.
Kobida, Vincent F. '80 (MIL) Milwaukee, WI St. Margaret Mary.
Kobos, Martin *o.f.m.conv.* '76 (HRT) Kensington, CT St. Paul.
Kobti, Rev. Msgr. Labib '75 (SFR) Brazilian Ministry; San Francisco, CA St. Thomas More; St. Thomas More Society; [Q] San Francisco, CA Newman Center, San Francisco State University; Arab–American Catholic Ministry; San Francisco State Univ., Newman Center.
Kobus, Boguslaw '92 (PAT) Franklin, NJ Immaculate Conception.
Kobus, Damian M. *o.s.m.* '49 (CHI)[N] Chicago Order of Friar Servants of Mary (Servites) United States of America Province, Inc.
Kobus, Damian M. *o.s.m.* '49 (P)[L] Portland, OR The Grotto, The National Sanctuary of Our Sorrowful Mother.
Kobus, John J. '77 (CHI) Other Assignments.
Kobuszewski, Thomas P. '64 (SY) Syracuse, NY Transfiguration.
Koch, Rev. Msgr. Charles J. '63 (EVN) Retired.
Koch, David J. '69 (GB) Denmark, WI All Saints; Denmark, WI Holy Trinity Mission; [G] Green Bay, WI St. Mary's Hospital–Medical Center; Special Assignment; Denmark, WI St. James; Kellnersville, WI St. Joseph.
Koch, Donald J. '60 (STL) On Duty Outside the Archdiocese Retired.
Koch, Edward H. '01 (RVC) St. James, NY SS. Philip and James.
Koch, Eugene R. '59 (DM) Advocates Retired.
Koch, George J. *s.j.* '59 (SJ)[M] Los Gatos, CA Sacred Heart Jesuit Center.
Koch, Ivor '84 (FWT) Catholic Women, Council of.
Koch, Joseph A. *c.v.* '82 (MO) Navy Chaplains.
Koch, Joseph (NOR) Groton, CT U.S. Submarine Base–New London.
Koch, Kevin A. '85 (CHY) Casper, WY St. Anthony of Padua; [C] Casper, WY St. Anthony Manor; Vicars Forane; [G] Casper, WY St. Anthony Tri–Parish School Foundation.
Koch, Mariusz *c.f.r.* (NEW) Members; [M] Newark, NJ Franciscan Friars of the Renewal.
Koch, Michael R. '53 (GB)[I] Green Bay, WI The McCormick Memorial Home for the Aged; McCormick Memorial Home for the Aged Retired.
Koch, Paul M. '61 (DM) Retired.
Kochan, Frederick A. '55 (WIL) Retired.
Kochanowicz, Piotr *s.j.* '98 (CHI)[N] Chicago, IL Sacred Heart Mission House.
Kocher, Donald '63 (JOL) Lisle, IL St. Joan of Arc Retired.
Kocherry, Varghese *c.ss.r.* '62 (PH) Philadelphia, PA St. Peter the Apostle.
Kochery, Peter '70 (TR) Manalapan, NJ St. Thomas More.
Kochu, Paul '74 (SP) St. Petersburg, FL Holy Cross; Propagation of the Faith.
Kochuparambil, Johnson *o.s.j.* '91 (SCR) Hazleton, PA Annunciation, Hazelton.
Kochuparambil, Jose Matthew *o.s.b.* '97 (LUB) Officialis.
Kochuparambil, Jose '97 (LUB) Idalou, TX St. Philip Benizi.
Kochuparampil, Jose *c.m.f.* '87 (ATL) McDonough, GA St. James the Apostle.
Kochupurackal, Santy *m.s.f.s.* '95 (TYL)[B] Whitehouse, TX The Missionaries of St. Francis de Sales.
Kochupurackal, Sebastian *c.m.i.* '76 (HRT) Plainville, CT Our Lady of Mercy.
Kochupurackel, Abraham George *c.m.i.* '91 (STP) Hastings, MN St. Elizabeth Ann Seton; Mound, MN Our Lady of the Lake.
Kocik, Francis W. '76 (SY) On Duty Outside the Diocese; Binghamton, NY St. Mary of the Assumption; Binghamton, NY St. Paul.
Kocik, Thomas M. '97 (FR) Fall River, MA Santo Christo.
Kociolek, Charles J. *c.s.c.* '79 (SCR)[C] Holy Cross Community.
Kodakarakaran, Paul '75 (TLS) Special Assignment; [E] Tulsa, OK Saint Francis Hospital.
Kodakassery, Thomas *o.s.b.* '76 (FTW) North Manchester, IN St. Robert Bellarmine.
Koday, Mishael J. '08 (BWN) Elsa, TX Sacred Heart.
Koehl, Keith '97 (AUS) Associate Directors; Hutto, TX St. Patrick.
Koehler, John '65 (SEA) Retired.
Koehler, Jon C. '74 (BR) St. Amant, LA Holy Rosary.
Koehler, Kenneth '72 (DEN) Westminster, CO St. Mark.
Koehler, Steven C. '82 (DET) Sterling Heights, MI St. Rene Goupil.
Koehr, Louis '87 (BEL) Albers, IL Retired.
Koelker, Harry H. '68 (DUB) Oelwein, IA Sacred Heart; Fairbank, IA Immaculate Conception.
Koelsch, John '56 (B) Gooding, ID St. Elizabeth's; Shoshone, ID St. Peter's Retired.
Koen, Stephen A. '58 (BO) Senior Priests. Retired.
Koenig, Paul *o.f.m.cap.* '93 (FgM) Detroit, MI Province of St. Joseph; [K] Detroit St. Bonaventure Friary.
Koenig, Rev. Msgr. William E. '83 (RVC) Rockville Centre, NY St. Agnes Cathedral.
Koenigsfeld, James F. '68 (PBL) Durango, CO St. Columba; Deans; Personnel.
Koenigsknecht, William J. '68 (LAN) Lansing, MI Resurrection.
Koeninger, Francis F. '79 (STL) Hawk Point, MO St. Mary.
Koeplin, John P. *s.j.* '91 (SFR)[N] San Francisco, CA Loyola House Jesuit Community.
Koesel, Douglas '78 (CLV) North Ridgeville, OH St. Peter.
Koester, Timothy J. '83 (MO) Navy Chaplains; Military Chaplains.
Koester, Timothy '83 (HON) Military Chaplains.
Koesterer, David L. *s.j.* '64 (STL)[O] St. Louis, MO Jesuit Community Corporation at Saint Louis University – Jesuit Hall.
Koeth, Stephen M. *c.s.c.* '07 (FTW)[A] Notre Dame, IN Moreau Seminary; [H] Notre Dame Congregation of Holy Cross, Indiana Province, Provincial House.
Koetter, David A. '07 (SAV) Savannah, GA St. James.
Koetter, Paul D. '77 (IND) Indianapolis, IN Holy Spirit.
Koetter, Rev. Msgr. Paul '77 (IND) Board of Consultors; Deaneries and Deans; Priests' Personnel Board.
Koeune, August '84 (CHY) Casper, WY Saint Patrick's.
Koeune, George '95 (CHI) Chicago, IL St. Eugene.
Kofchock, Joseph T. (HBG) Retired.
Kofitse, Ted K. '84 (BO) Hanover, MA St. Mary of the Sacred Heart.
Kofski, James W. *m.m.* '91 (FgM)[B] Washington, DC Office of Justice and Peace; Maryknoll, NY MARYKNOLL.
Koharchik, Edward *c.s.p.* '05 (AUS) Dripping Springs, TX St. Martin de Porres.
Koharchik, George D. '74 (ALT) Mount Union, PA St. Catherine of Siena.
Kohler, Edward '77 (HEL) Browning, MT Church of the Little Flower; Deaneries.
Kohler, Girard J. *c.s.sp.* '63 (PIT)[M] Bethel Park, PA Holy Spirit Fathers and Brothers Provincialate; [O] Bethel Park, PA The Spiritan Center.
Kohler, Lawrence A. *m.s.* '61 (LKC) Sulphur, LA Our Lady of LaSalette.
Kohler, Peter D. '68 (WDC)[N] Washington, DC La Salette Formation Community.
Kohler, Russell E. '73 (DET)[Q] Detroit, MI Pope John XXIII Hospitality House; [Q] Onsted, MI St. Patrick's Retreat; Detroit, MI Most Holy Trinity; [Q] Harrisville, MI The Oratory.
Kohler, William (Guillo) *c.ss.r.* '83 (TUC) Tucson, AZ Saint Joseph Roman Catholic Parish – Tucson; Tucson, AZ Tucson Medical Center.
Kohler, William E. '67 (MIL) Muskego, WI St. Leonard Congregation.
Kohler, William F. '55 (PIT) Retired.
Kohlerman, Charles W. *c.s.c.* '63 (FTW)[H] Holy Cross House; [H] Notre Dame, IN Congregation of Holy Cross, Indiana Province, Provincial House.
Kohlerman, Charles *c.s.c.* '63 (FTW)[A] Notre Dame, IN Moreau Seminary; [A] Notre Dame, IN Moreau Seminary.
Kohli, Charles F. '61 (RVC) Retired.
Kohlmann, Vernon *s.d.v.* '98 (PAT) Florham Park, NJ; [N] Florham Park, NJ Father Justin Vocationary; Florham Park, NJ.
Kohls, Rev. Msgr. Eugene C. '57 (STA) Vicar for Senior Priests Retired.
Kohner, David W. '90 (STP) Archdiocesan Council on Catholic Women; Little Canada, MN St. John of Little Canada.
Kohrman, Glenn '92 (FTW) Elkhart, IN St. Vincent de Paul; Elkhart; Fort Wayne.
Kohut, David *o.f.m.* '79 (CIN)[N] Cincinnati, OH St. Clare Friary.
Kohut, Rev. Msgr. Joseph J. '62 (BGP)[O] Stamford, CT The Catherine Dennis Keefe Queen of the Clergy Retired Priests' Residence Retired.
Koilparampil, Augustine '64 (OAK) Livermore, CA St. Michael; VA Palo Alto Health Care System Home; DEPARTMENT OF VETERANS AFFAIRS HOSPITALS AND CHAPLAINS.
Kojo, Francis Kule (P)[L] Portland Holy Cross Fathers & Brothers, C.S.C. – University of Portland.
Kokeram, Sudash J. '99 (MO) Military Chaplains; Army Chaplains.
Kokose, Pius E. *c.s.sp.* (CHI) Calumet Park, IL Seven Holy Founders.
Kolakowski, Marcel *o.f.m.* '49 (PH) Philadelphia, PA St. John Cantius Retired.
Kolakowski, Robert B. '02 (MET) Lambertville, NJ St. John the Evangelist; Canonical Staff.
Kolarec, William T. *s.j.* '69 (MIL)[P] Wauwatosa, WI Jesuit Community at St. Camillus.
Kolasa, Stanley *ss.cc.* '70 (FR)[I] Wareham, MA Sacred Hearts Retreat Center.
Kolb, James *c.s.p.* '76 (NY)[EE] Jamaica Estates Paulist Fathers Generalate.
Kolb, James '76 (P) Portland, OR St. Elizabeth of Hungary.
Kolb, Jim *c.s.p.* '76 (P) Portland, OR Oregon Health Sciences University.
Kolb, Joseph C. '53 (OKL) Retired.
Kolb, Joseph E. *s.j.* '63 (WH)[A] Wheeling, WV Wheeling Jesuit University.
Kolb, Michael R. *s.j.* '82 (MIL)[P] Milwaukee, WI Arrupe House Jesuit Community.
Kolberg, Lawrence R. '68 (ORG) Absent on Sick Leave.
Kolcun, Stephen J. '46 (PBR) Retired.
Kolczaski, Richard '55 (PEO) Retired.
Kolde, Steven J. '00 (CIN) Cincinnati, OH St. John Neumann.
Kolencheril, Varghese '86 (CC) Edroy, TX Our Lady of Guadalupe Mission.
Kolenkiewicz, Louis J. '93 (PH) Milmont Park, PA Our Lady of Peace.
Kolenski, Robert D. '62 (LAN) Retired.
Kolesar, Rev. Msgr. John C. '64 (STU) Adena, OH St. Casimir's; Adena, OH St. Adalbert; Diocesan Director of Cemeteries; Council Members.
Kolf, Gerald S. '95 (POD) Washington.
Kolf, Gerald S. '95 (WDC)[U] Washington, DC Tenley Study Center.
Kolf, Gerard '95 (WDC)[G] Potomac, MD The Heights School.
Kolibas, Kenneth R. '94 (MET) Raritan, NJ St. Joseph.
Kolinovsky, Sebastian *c.p.* '51 (SCR)[M] Scranton, PA Saint Ann's Passionist Monastery.
Kolinovsky, Sebastian *c.p.* '51 (MET)[I] South River Passionist Provincial Office Retired.
Kolinski, Dennis *s.j.c.* '04 (CHI) Volo, IL St. Peter; [P] Chicago, IL Canons Regular of Saint John Cantius.
Kolinsky, Arthur J. *c.m.* '71 (PH)[Y].
Kolitsos, Andrew '94 (ROM) Director of Religious Education; Unassigned.
Kolla, Edward R. '01 (CAM) Ocean City, NJ The Church of St. Frances Cabrini, Ocean City, N.J.
Kollapallil, Kurian *m.s.f.s.* '97 (LAN) Howell, MI St. Joseph.
Kollapallil, Kurian *m.s.f.s.* '97 (TYL)[B] Whitehouse, TX The Missionaries of St. Francis de Sales.
Kollar, Anton *o.carm.* '51 (JOL)[L] Darien Carmelite

Provincial Office.
Kollar, Anton *o.carm.* '51 (SD)[O] San Diego, CA Christ Child Society.
Kollar, Rene M. *o.s.b.* '74 (GBG)[G] Latrobe, PA Saint Vincent Archabbey.
Kollath, Robert '97 (GB)[L] Chilton, WI St. Peregrine Shrine; Chilton, WI Good Shepherd; Kiel, WI SS. Peter and Paul.
Koller, Gerold *c.pp.s.* '49 (CIN)[N] Carthagena, OH St. Charles Retired.
Koller, Michael '04 (KCK) Seneca, KS SS. Peter and Paul's; Archdiocesan Consultors.
Koller, Thomas *o.c.d.* '90 (SB)[I] Redlands, CA Discalced Carmelites, OCD; [L] Redlands, CA El Carmelo Retreat House.
Kolling, James L. '65 (LA) Los Angeles, CA Visitation Retired.
Kolling, James L. '65 (LA) Retired.
Kollithanath, Philip '84 (CHL) High Point, NC Christ the King.
Kollman, Paul V. *c.s.c.* '91 (FTW)[B] University of Notre Dame Du Lac; [H] Notre Dame, IN Holy Cross Community, Corby Hall, University of Notre Dame.
Kollross, Dennis D. '81 (SFD) Mattoon, IL Immaculate Conception.
Kolmaga, Jan *o.s.p.p.e.* '82 (PH)[Y] Doylestown, PA.
Kolo, Vincent F. '95 (PIT) Allegheny County, PA West Penn Allegheny Health System–Allegheny General; Pittsburgh, PA Holy Wisdom.
Kolodziej, Jack *o.s.f.s.* '99 (PH)[D] Philadelphia, PA Father Judge High School for Boys; [Y] Philadelphia, PA Father Louis Brisson Residence.
Kolodziej, Ludwik (BRK) Brooklyn, NY Our Lady of Consolation.
Kolodziej, Ludwik *s.d.s.* (NEW)[M] Verona, NJ The Salvatorian Fathers.
Kolodziej, Michael *o.f.m.conv.* '70 (FgM)[S] Ellicott City, MD Order of Friars Minor Conventual; Ellicott City, MD Province of Saint Anthony of Padua; Ellicott City, MD.
Kolodziej, Ryszard '96 (R) Castle Hayne, NC St. Stanislaus.
Kolodziejczyk, Sebastian J. '99 (LC) Foreign Missions.
Kolodziejski, Karl *o.f.m.conv.* '78 (ALT) Davidsville, PA St. Anne; Hooversville, PA Holy Family.
Kolp, Rev. Msgr. James '50 (Y) Alliance, OH St. Joseph Retired.
Kolson, Lawrence F. '74 (BAL) Bradshaw, MD St. Stephen.
Kolton, Stanislaus J. '46 (CAM) Retired.
Kolumber, Denis A. *m.s.* (HRT)[L] Hartford, CT Missionaries of LaSalette Province of Mary, Mother of the Americas.
Kolzow, Andrew K. *o.p.* '58 (SAT)[L] San Antonio, TX Dominican Priory of San Juan Macias; San Antonio, TX St. Ann.
Koma, Joseph W. *c.s.c.* '61 (FTW)[H] Holy Cross House.
Komar, John E. '64 (NEW)[M] Rutherford, NJ St. John Vianney Residence for Priests Retired.
Komatz, David *o.praem* '75 (CHI)[N] Chicago, IL Premonstratensian Fathers and Brothers (Norbertines).
Kombo, Honore M. '90 (HRT) Manchester, CT Assumption; Manchester, CT St. James.
Kommer, Venard *o.f.m.* '46 (JOL) Clarendon Hills, IL Notre Dame.
Kommers, Thomas M. '80 (STP) Red Wing, MN Church of St. Joseph.
Komo, George '09 (DM) Council Bluffs, IA Our Lady, Queen of Apostles; Council Bluffs, IA Holy Family; Carter Lake, IA Our Lady of Carter Lake.
Komonchak, Joseph A. '64 (WDC)[C] Catholic University of America, The Retired.
Komorowski, Louis A. *o.s.f.s.* '56 (LAN) Adrian, MI St. Mary of Good Counsel.
Komperda, Pawel '06 (CHI) Chicago, IL St. Thecla.
Komu, Michael Ngei (BO) Lowell, MA St. Michael.
Kon, Placyd *o.f.m.* '96 (CLV) Cleveland, OH St. Stanislaus; [N] Cleveland, OH St. Stanislaus Friary.
Koncik, Michael *c.ss.r.* '82 (NY) Cincinnati, OH American Catholic Correctional Chaplains Association; [EE] New York, NY Redemptorist Priests and Brothers, C.Ss.R.
Konda, Bernard '67 (JUN) Retired.
Kondeja, Stanley '62 (RVC) Southampton, NY Our Lady of Poland.
Konderla, David '95 (AUS)[L] College Station, TX St. Mary's Catholic Center; College Station, TX St. Mary; Associate Directors.
Kondik, Curtis L. '00 (CLV) Absent on Leave.
Kondzielski, Thaddeus T. '67 (E) Edinboro, PA St. Philip.
Kondziolka, Ronald L. '76 (CHI)[J] Chicago Heights, IL St. James Hospital and Health Centers; Chicago, IL St. Anthony of Padua.
Konen, Lyle *c.ss.r.* '61 (SEA)[L] Seattle, WA The Redemptionist Society of Washington; Seattle, WA Sacred Heart of Jesus.
Konerman, Gregory J. '93 (CIN) Urbana, OH Sacred Heart (St. Paris); Urbana, OH St. Mary.
Konicki, William C. '78 (WOR) Hopedale, MA Sacred Heart of Jesus.
Konieczka, Edward J. '63 (SAG) Bay City, MI St. Hyacinth.
Konieczny, Stan J. '06 (BEL) Waterloo, IL SS. Peter and Paul.
Konka, Balaswamy '95 (OKL) Guymon, OK St. Peter's.
Konka, Rayappa '89 (LIN) Nebraska City, NE St. Mary's.
Konkala, Chinnapa Reddy '04 (OKL) Shawnee, OK St. Benedict.
Konkel, Eugene J. *s.s.* '57 (SFR)[A] Menlo Park, CA St. Patrick Seminary and University.
Konkel, Eugene J. *s.s.* '57 (MIL) On Duty Outside the Archdiocese.
Konkel, Eugene J. *s.s.* '57 (BAL)[S] Baltimore Society of St. Sulpice, Province of the United States Retired.
Konkel, Joseph D. *o.p.* '70 (GAL) Houston, TX Holy Rosary.
Konkler, Paul Jerome *o.c.s.o.* '68 (SAC)[A] Vina, CA Abbey of New Clairvaux, Trappist Seminary; [I] Vina, CA Abbey of New Clairvaux, Trappist.
Konkol, Robert *o.f.m.* '94 (GB) Maplewood, WI St. Mary; Casco, WI St. Peter–St. Hubert.
Kono, Mario '91 (VEN) North Fort Myers, FL St. Therese.
Konold, Lon *o.m.i.* '77 (STP)[N] Buffalo, MN Christ the King Retreat Center.
Konopa, Brian D. '98 (LC) Eau Claire, WI St. Olaf; Appointed Members.
Konopa, Robert *o.f.m.* '91 (JKS) Greenwood, MS St. Francis of Assisi.
Konopacky, Joseph R. '82 (LC) Leave of Absence.
Konopelski, Louis *s.d.b.* (NO)[D] Marrero, LA Archbishop Shaw High School; [G] Marrero, LA Archbishop Shaw Junior High School.
Konopik, Michael J. '07 (SFR) San Francisco, CA St. Gabriel.
Konopka, Edward F. '45 (DET) Retired.
Konopka, Edward M. '60 (NOR) Retired.
Konopka, Thomas E. '90 (ALB) Colonie, NY St. Clare; Special Assignment; Office.
Konowalek, Zenon '89 (CC) Refugio, TX St. James the Apostle.
Konrad, Erwin '89 (JC) Retired.
Konrade, Jarett '05 (SAL) Council of Priests; Boy Scouts; Priests' Continuing Formation Committee; Office of Priestly Vocations; Office of Priestly Vocations; College of Consultors; Salina, KS Sacred Heart Cathedral Parish.
Konzen, Joel M. *s.m.* '79 (ATL)[D] Atlanta, GA Marist School.
Koo, Matthew '88 (SJ) San Jose, CA St. Leo the Great; Santa Clara, CA Chinese Catholic Community Retired.
Kookoothe, Neil P. '95 (CLV) North Olmsted, OH St. Clarence.
Koons, Rev. Msgr. Thomas P. '97 (ALN) Allentown, PA St. Francis of Assisi; [L] Coopersburg, PA Carmelite Monastery; Judges; Vicar for Religious.
Koons, Thomas P. '97 (LEX) Associate Judges.
Koopman, Dennis *o.f.m.* '70 (CHI)[N] Countryside, IL St. Gratian Friary, Franciscan Friars.
Koopman, Joseph M. '01 (CLV)[A] Wickliffe, OH St. Mary Seminary and Graduate School of Theology.
Koopmann, Robert *o.s.b.* '81 (SCL)[B] Saint John's University; [I] Collegeville, MN St. John's Abbey, of the Order of St. Benedict.
Koos, Rev. Msgr. Gerald J. '66 (E) Erie, PA Hamot Medical Center; Erie, PA Our Mother of Sorrows.
Kopacek, Jerry F. '88 (DUB) Courage; Waterloo, IA St. Edward; Review Board for Sexual Abuse of Minors by Clergy and Other Church Personnel; Priestly Life and Ministry Committee.
Kopacek, Jerry F. '88 (DUB) Deans.
Kopacz, Joseph R. '77 (SCR) Mount Pocono, PA St. Mary of the Mount; Tobyhanna, PA St. Ann; Diocesan Consultors; Diocesan Finance Council; Hispanic Ministry Outreach.
Kopacz, K. S. '95 (FAR) Judicial Vicar; Presiding Judge; Special Assignment.
Kopacz, Rev. Msgr. Matthew S. '63 (BUF) Retired.
Kopacz, Stephen A. '72 (NEW) North Arlington, NJ Queen of Peace.
Kopaczynski, Germain *o.f.m.conv.* '74 (PMB) Boynton Beach, FL St. Mark.
Kopchik, Martin *m.s.f.s.* '86 (ATL) Snellville, GA St. Oliver Plunkett; [G] Snellville, GA The Missionaries of St. Francis De Sales; Special or Other (Arch)Diocesan Assignment.
Kopchik, Martin *m.s.f.s.* '86 (TYL)[B] Whitehouse, TX The Missionaries of St. Francis de Sales.
Kopczewski, Linus E. *o.f.m.* '65 (MIL)[N] Milwaukee, WI St. Ann Rest Home.
Kopczynski, Sean P. '00 (MAR)[E] Iron Mountain, MI Monastery of the Holy Cross.
Kopec, Chester C. *o.p.* '63 (SB) Retired.
Kopec, Christopher A. '93 (WIL) Military Chaplains.
Kopec, Edward S. '92 (PEO) Toluca, IL St. Ann's.
Kopec, Jerome E. '79 (BUF) Williamsville, NY SS. Peter and Paul.
Kopec, Krzysztof A. '93 (MO) Army Chaplains.
Kopec, Krzysztof (TUC) Fort Huchuca, AZ Fort Huchuca Army Post.
Kopec, Rajmund '92 (MO) Military Chaplains; Army Chaplains.
Kopel, Jerome '77 (SFS) Gettysburg, SD Sacred Heart.
Koper, Rev. Msgr. Francis B. '71 (WIL) On Duty Outside the Diocese.
Koper, Rev. Msgr. Francis '71 (DET)[A] Orchard Lake, MI SS. Cyril and Methodius Seminary.
Koper, Ryszard '78 (BRK) Maspeth, NY Holy Cross.
Kopera, Jacek *o.p.* '06 (NY) New York, NY Notre Dame; [II] New York, NY Polish Dominicans, Inc.; [HH] New York, NY Columbia University.
Koperski, Matthew J. '04 (GI) Personnel Board; Vocations; Kearney, NE St. James; [D] Kearney, NE University of Nebraska at Kearney Newman Apostolate.
Kopfensteiner, Thomas R. '81 (STL) On Duty Outside the Archdiocese.
Kopil, Michael J. '08 (GRY) Adjutant Defenders of the Bond; Schererville, IN St. Michael.
Kopinski, Rev. Msgr. Richard P. '64 (RVC) Glen Head, NY St. Hyacinth; Judges for Interdiocesan Tribunal.
Koplik, Rev. Msgr. William J. '62 (NEW) Ridgefield, NJ St. Matthew's Retired.
Koplinka, Steven '79 (PRM) Cleveland, OH St. Mary; Syncellus for Clergy and Religious; Presbyteral Council; Eparchial Pastoral Council; Sacred Liturgy; Seminary Education Formation Board.
Kopp, Rev. Msgr. Richard M. '69 (SY) Western Area Vicars; Board of Diocesan Consultors; Presbyteral Council; Vicar for Priests; Building Commission; Finance Committee; Priest Personnel; Priests' Personnel Committee.
Kopp, Thomas A. (BO)[CC] Boston, MA Pontifical Association of the Holy Childhood, Pontifical Society for the Propagation of the Faith & Pontifical Society of St. Peter the Apostle; Pontifical Society of Saint Peter the Apostle; Presbyteral Council.
Koppala, Leo Charles '94 (WIN) Blue Earth, MN SS. Peter and Paul's; Blue Earth, MN St. Mary's.
Koppes, Albert P. *o.carm.* '59 (JOL)[L] Darien Carmelite Provincial Office.
Koppes, Albert P. *o.carm.* '59 (LA)[C] Los Angeles, CA Jesuit Community; [C] Los Angeles, CA Loyola Marymount University.
Koprowski, Mitchell J. '41 (GI) Retired.
Kopystynski, A. Rafal *c.m.* (HRT)[L] Manchester, CT DePaul Provincial Residence.
Korabik, Joseph *c.r.* '38 (CHI)[D] Chicago, IL Gordon Tech High School.
Korba, Rev. Msgr. Frank '66 (PRM) Munster, IN Saint Nicholas; Presbyteral Council; Eparchial Consultors; Midwest; Associates; Catechetical Board.
Korban, Janusz '97 (RC) Rapid City, SD Blessed Sacrament.
Korbelak, John J. '74 (NEW) Hillsdale, NJ St. John the Baptist.
Korcz, Krzysztof '94 (WOR) Southborough, MA St. Anne.
Korda, J. James '79 (Y) Girard, OH St. Rose.
Kordas, Edward J. '68 (CLV) Hudson, OH St. Mary; Associate Judges.
Kordek, Frank *o.f.m.* '72 (IND) Indianapolis, IN Sacred Heart of Jesus.
Kordsmeier, Rev. Msgr. John '49 (LR)[G] Little Rock, AR St. John Manor; Defenders of the Bond Retired.
Korenek, Gregory E. '93 (VIC) Victoria, TX Holy Family of Joseph, Mary & Jesus; Judges.
Koressel, James '69 (EVN) All Saints; Montgomery, IN St. Peter; Diocesan Council of Priests; Deans; Petersburg, IN SS. Peter and Paul; Diocesan Consultors.
Korf, Joseph '74 (SCL) Elk River, MN The Church of St. Andrew; Advocates; Deans; Diocesan Corporate Board.
Korie, Ikechi *o.p.* '96 (ELP) El Paso, TX Santo Nino De Atocha; [J] El Paso, TX Blue Army.
Kormeyer, Thomas E. '90 (OG) Lake Clear, NY St. John in the Wilderness.
Kornacki, Thomas J. *o.f.m.* '77 (FgM) New York, NY Holy Name Province.
Kornath, Edwin M. '84 (MIL) Kewaskum, WI St. Michael; Kewaskum, WI Holy Trinity.
Kornitsky, Vasyl '05 (STF) Riverhead, NY St. John the Baptist.
Kornmeyer, Thomas E. '90 (OG) Bloomingdale, NY St. Paul; Saranac Lake, NY St. Bernard; Deans; Campus Ministry.
Korogi, Dale J. '83 (STP) Minneapolis, MN Christ the King.
Korpi, Wilson I. '08 (ARL) Fredericksburg, VA St. Mary of the Immaculate Conception; Notaries.
Korte, Owen W. '81 (OM) Fremont, NE St. Patrick.
Korte, William L. '83 (JC) New Cambria, MO St. Mary of the Angels; Salisbury, MO St. Joseph; Legion of Mary.
Kortendick, Steven J. '85 (MAD) Beloit, WI St. Jude; Beloit, WI St. Thomas the Apostle.
Korth, David M. '92 (OM) Homer, NE St. Cornelius; Winnebago, NE St. Joseph; Macy, NE Our Lady of Fatima; Winnebago, NE St. Augustine's; [N] Winnebago, NE FEATHERS.

Kos, Donald *o.f.m.conv.* '61 (BAL)[S] Ellicott City Order of Friars Minor Conventual.
Kos, Stanislaw '96 (RCK) Scales Mound, IL Holy Trinity; Galena, IL St. Mary.
Kosak, Rev. Msgr. Michael F. '70 (STV) Kingshill, VI Church St. Ann; [B] Lumen 2000/Caribbean Region; Diocesan Consultors; Caribbean Catholic Network (CCN); Communications Coordinator.
Kosaka, Paulo R. *o.f.m.cap.* '84 (HON) Kaneohe, HI Our Lady of Mt. Carmel.
Kosanke, Rev. Msgr. Charles G. '85 (DET)[T] Orchard Lake, MI American Friends of the Vatican Library.
Kosanke, Rev. Msgr. Charles '85 (DET)[A] Orchard Lake, MI SS. Cyril and Methodius Seminary.
Kosasih, Benny *ss.cc.* '02 (HON) Kaneohe, HI St. Ann.
Kosatka, Leonard *c.p.* '59 (FgM).
Kosch, Leo D. '93 (LIN) Davey, NE St. Mary's; Commission for Sacred Liturgy and Sacred Music.
Kosciesza, Bogumil '94 (WDC) Silver Spring, MD St. Catherine Laboure.
Kosciesza, Bogumil (DUL) Retired.
Kosco, William J. '00 (PHX) Buckeye, AZ Saint Henry Roman Catholic Parish; Presbyteral Council.
Kosek, Robert B. *c.r.s.p.* '89 (ALN)[K] Bethlehem, PA The Barnabite Fathers Barnabite Spiritual Center.
Kosem, Frank P. '70 (CLV) Elyria, OH St. Jude.
Koser, Albert C. '59 (PIT)[M] Pittsburgh, PA St. John Vianney Manor Retired.
Koser, Rudolph J. '74 (GBG) Clymer, PA Church of the Resurrection.
Koshko, Dennis '75 (HON) Vicars Forane; Kailua, HI St. Anthony of Padua; College of Consultors; Clergy Personnel Board; Presbyteral Council; Office of Clergy Priest Retirement Committee.
Koshyk, Ihor '05 (STN) Chicago, IL SS. Volodymyr and Olha.
Koshyk, Ihor (CHI)[J] Chicago, IL Saints Mary and Elizabeth Medical Center.
Kosicki, Bohdan W. '50 (DET) Retired.
Kosicki, George *c.s.b.* '54 (ROC)[J] Rochester Basilian Residence.
Kosinski, Stephen D. '81 (GRY) Hammond, IN All Saints.
Kosisko, Richard J. '85 (GBG) Mount Pleasant, PA St. Pius X; Mount Pleasant, PA Visitation of the Blessed Virgin Mary; Judges; Bishop's Priests Council.
Kosler, Timothy '71 (VIC) Schulenburg, TX St. John The Baptist; Schulenburg, TX Nativity of the Blessed Virgin Mary; Schulenburg, TX St. Rose of Lima; Diocesan Consultors; Schulenburg Deanery; Presbyteral Council; Defenders of the Bond; Priests' Personnel Board.
Kosmicki, Raymond '68 (GI) St. Paul, NE SS. Peter and Paul.
Kosmoski, David B. '83 (MET) Avenel, NJ St. Andrew.
Kosmowski, Gary J. '90 (MAN) Hampton, NH Our Lady of the Miraculous Medal; Belknap County House of Corrections.
Kosnac, Benjamin '93 (DET) Sterling Heights, MI SS. Cyril and Methodius.
Kosnik, Eugene '60 (NY) Absent on Sick Leave.
Kosowicz, Wojciech '65 (LAR) Laredo, TX St. Patrick; Finance Council.
Kosse, Gerald C. '76 (WIN) Pipestone, MN St. Leo's; Pipestone, MN St. Martin's; Deans; Advocates; Pipestone, MN St. Joseph's.
Kosse, Theodore C. '71 (CIN) Peebles, OH St. Mary Queen of Heaven; West Union, OH Holy Trinity.
Kostek, John S. '72 (NY) Staten Island, NY St. Ann.
Kostelnik, Rev. Msgr. Kevin J. '82 (LA) Los Angeles, CA Cathedral of Our Lady of the Angels; Master of Ceremonies for Stational Liturgies.
Kostelz, Richard F. '52 (JOL) Cabery, IL St. Joseph Retired.
Koster, Dale F. '54 (SC) Retired.
Koster, Kenneth J. '76 (SFS) Kranzburg, SD Holy Rosary; Tribunal Judges.
Kosterman, Richard A. '93 (GAY) Retired.
Kostiuk, Stepan '06 (STN)[M] Niles, IL Saint Andrew Life Center; [M] Park Ridge, IL Resurrection Nursing and Rehabilitation Center; [J] Des Plaines, IL Holy Family Medical Center; Chicago, IL SS. Volodymyr and Olha.
Kostka, Leonard J. *c.pp.s.* '40 (LFT)[A] Rensselaer, IN Saint Joseph's College Retired.
Kostrzomb, Stanley '77 (NEW) Lyndhurst, NJ St. Michael's.
Kosty, Robert J. '74 (WDC) Port Tobacco, MD St. Ignatius Loyola; Port Tobacco, MD St. Catherine of Alexandria.
Kostyk, Jaroslaw (STF) Directors.
Kostyk, Marian '90 (STF) Amsterdam, NY St. Nicholas; Amsterdam, NY St. Nicholas.
Kostyk, Yaroslaw (STF) Campbell Hall, NY St. Volodymyr; Campbell Hall, NY St. Andrew's; Administrative Council.
Kostyuk, Volodymyr '98 (PHU) Jenkintown, PA St. Michael the Archangel.
Koszarek, Rev. Msgr. Paul P. '54 (GB) Armstrong Creek, WI St. Stanislaus Kostka; Goodman, WI St. Joan of Arc Retired.
Koszarek, Robert J. '74 (SUP) Eagle River, WI St. Peter the Fisherman; Presbyteral Council & Diocesan Consultors.
Koszyk, Dariusz '04 (RVC) Oyster Bay, NY St. Dominic's.
Koszyk, Severyn J. *s.a.c.* '59 (BUF)[O] North Tonawanda, NY Society of the Catholic Apostolate.
Kot, Luke C. *o.c.s.o.* '48 (ATL)[G] Conyers, GA The Monastery of the Holy Spirit Retired.
Kotara, James A. '76 (SAT) Defenders of the Bond; San Antonio, TX St. Thomas More.
Kotecki, Ronald E. '72 (MIL) Milwaukee, WI Immaculate Conception.
Koterski, Joseph W. *s.j.* '92 (NY)[EE] Cardinal Spellman Hall, Jesuit Community.
Kotlanger, Michael J. *s.j.* '78 (SFR)[E] San Francisco, CA St. Ignatius College Preparatory (Coed); [N] San Francisco, CA Jesuit Community at St. Ignatius College Preparatory.
Kotlarczyk, Mark E. '88 (SB) Wildomar, CA St. Frances of Rome; Officers.
Kotlarz, Robert J. '69 (DET) Detroit, MI Our Lady of Good Counsel; Detroit, MI St. Raymond.
Kotlinski, Bede *o.s.b.* '84 (CLV)[D] Cleveland, OH Benedictine High School; [N] Cleveland, OH; Translators.
Kotlinsky, Eugene *c.m.* (BGP) Stamford, CT Holy Name of Jesus.
Kotnis, Gregory M. '56 (PHX) Retired.
Kottacka, Paul (LA)[J] Tarzana, CA Providence Tarzana Medical Center.
Kottackal, Paul '73 (SYM) San Fernando, CA St. Alphonsa Syro–Malabar Catholic Church of Los Angeles; Henderson, NV Bl. Mother Theresa Syro–Malabar Catholic Church.
Kottana, Kishore '09 (TOL) Maumee, OH St. Joseph.
Kottar, Michael T. '94 (CHL) Shelby, NC St. Mary's.
Kottaram, Mathew '63 (RVC) Retired.
Kottarathil, Benny '01 (STO) Modesto, CA St. Joseph Church of Modesto (Pastor of).
Kottas, Charles '70 (DM) Council Bluffs, IA St. Peter.
Kottayarikil, Cyriac *m.c.b.s.* '67 (MAR) Rudyard, MI St. Joseph.
Kottayil, Joseph '79 (MIA)[A] Miami, FL St. John Vianney College Seminary.
Kottenstette, William P. '73 (JC)[D] Kirksville, MO Catholic Newman Center, Truman State University.
Kouba, Charles J. '51 (CHI) Retired.
Koury, James '92 (NTN) Leave of Absence.
Koury, Rev. Msgr. Joseph A. '50 (JKS) Retired.
Koury, Joseph J. '77 (PRT) Bridgton, ME St. Joseph; Windham, ME Our Lady of Perpetual Help; Associate Judges.
Koury, Joseph N. '07 (LEX) Corbin, KY Sacred Heart; Williamsburg, KY St. Boniface.
Koury, Joseph (NTN) Judges.
Koutnik, Jerome P. '99 (RCK) South Beloit, IL St. Peter.
Kouts, Michael '91 (SJP) Brooksville, FL St. Andrew; Presbyters.
Kovach, John '65 (PRM) Whiting, IN Assumption of the Blessed Virgin.
Kovacic, Rev. Msgr. Anthony '47 (CHL) Retired.
Kovacik, Jozef '98 (ALT) Lock Haven, PA St. Agnes.
Kovacik, Mark '07 (DEN) Denver, CO Church of the Ascension.
Kovacs, Matthew *o.cist.* '57 (DAL)[J] Irving, TX Cistercian Abbey of Our Lady of Dallas.
Kovalcin, John A. '81 (STL) On Duty Outside the Archdiocese.
Kovalik, George J. '47 (STP) Retired.
Kovalyshin, Severyn '00 (SJP) North Port, FL Entrance of B.V.M. into the Temple (St. Mary's); Presbyters.
Kovanis, Joel '94 (SP) Sun City Center, FL Prince of Peace.
Kovarik, Peter '91 (RC) Custer, SD St. John the Baptist; Hot Springs, SD St. Anthony of Padua.
Kovash, Russell P. '09 (BIS) Bismarck, ND Cathedral of the Holy Spirit.
Kovatch, Thomas G. '07 (IND) Lawrenceburg, IN St. Teresa Benedicta of the Cross.
Kowal, Jacek L. '09 (MEM) Bartlett, TN St. Ann.
Kowalczyk, Adolph M. '88 (BUF) Orchard Park, NY Our Lady of the Sacred Heart.
Kowalczyk, Henry '94 (SPR) Sheffield, MA Our Lady of the Valley.
Kowalczyk, Joseph W. *m.m.* '61 (SJ)[M] Los Altos, CA Maryknoll.
Kowalczyk, Miroslaw *f.d.p.* (BO) East Boston, MA St. Joseph–St. Lazarus.
Kowalczyk, Sigismund C. '56 (DET) Retired.
Kowalczyk, Thomas M. '67 (SAG) Retired.
Kowalewski, John A. *o.s.f.s.* '77 (WIL)[J] Childs, MD Retirement and Assisted Care Facility; Wilmington, DE OBLATES OF ST. FRANCIS DE SALES MISSIONS.
Kowalik, Jacek '79 (VEN) Military Chaplains; Air Force Reserve Chaplains.
Kowalske, Kevin J. '95 (MIL) Newburg, WI Holy Trinity.
Kowalski, Al '51 (NEW) Kenilworth, NJ St. Theresa's Retired.
Kowalski, Aleksy (PAT) Theological Commission.
Kowalski, Alfred J. '51 (NEW) Retired.
Kowalski, Eric '93 (CHL) Mt. Airy, NC Holy Angels.
Kowalski, George '56 (DET) Retired.
Kowalski, Janusz '89 (LC) Rothschild, WI St. Therese of the Child Jesus.
Kowalski, Kazimierz A. (NY) New York, NY Our Lady of Good Counsel.
Kowalski, Lawrence T. '69 (OKL) Enid, OK St. Gregory the Great.
Kowalski, Matthew *o.s.b.* '87 (SFS)[F] Marvin, SD Blue Cloud Abbey.
Kowalski, Wladyslaw J. '51 (SUP) Mosinee, WI St. John the Baptist Retired.
Kowatch, Thomas P. '85 (CLV) Uniontown, OH Queen of Heaven.
Kownacki, Raymond F. '60 (BEL) Retired.
Koyickal, Joseph Chandy *s.a.c.* '80 (SFD) Effingham, IL St. Anthony of Padua.
Koyickal, Joseph *s.a.c.* '80 (MIL) Milwaukee, WI; [P] Milwaukee, WI Pallotti House.
Koyickal, Thomas '70 (PT) Cantonment, FL St. Jude Thaddeus.
Koys, Thomas R. '85 (CHI) Chicago, IL Immaculate Conception.
Kozacheson, Roman *o.f.m.cap* '61 (BAL)[S] Baltimore, MD St. Ambrose Friary; Baltimore, MD St. Ambrose.
Kozak, David J. '83 (ALN) Defenders of the Bond; Reading, PA St. Peter the Apostle.
Kozak, Lawrence F. '04 (PH) Graduate Studies.
Kozak, Remigius A. '54 (BLX) Retired.
Kozak, Richard J. '67 (CHI) Homewood, IL St. Joseph.
Kozak, Timothy J. '04 (STU) Ironton, OH St. Joseph; Ironton, OH St. Lawrence; Propagation of the Faith.
Kozanko, Andrzej J. '00 (FR) Awaiting Assignment; [G] Fall River, MA Priests' Hostel.
Kozar, Rev. Msgr. John E. '71 (NY) Propagation of the Faith, National Office; New York, NY A. The Pontifical Society for the Propagation of the Faith; New York, NY B. The Society of St. Peter Apostle; New York, NY C. The Pontifical Missionary Union; New York, NY D. Holy Childhood Association; New York, NY St. Teresa.
Kozar, Rev. Msgr. John E. '71 (PIT) On Duty Outside the Diocese.
Kozar, Joseph F. *s.m.* '77 (CIN) Troy, OH St. Patrick; [D] Dayton, OH The University of Dayton; [N] Dayton, OH Marianist Community.
Kozar, Petro (STN) Sacramento, CA St. Andrew the Apostle.
Kozel, Rev. Msgr. Robert F. '61 (ALN) Allentown, PA St. John the Baptist.
Kozen, Bert S. '63 (MO) Army National Guard Chaplains.
Kozen, Bert S. '82 (SCR) Military Chaplains.
Kozhaya Akoury, Tanios '82 (SAM) Advocates.
Kozhippandan, Santhosh George *o.ss.t.* '07 (BAL)[S] The Trinitarians in India (Bangalore & Trichur).
Koziczuk, Andrew A. '79 (SAC) Isleton, CA St. Therese's; Walnut Grove, CA St. Anthony.
Koziel, Piotr A. '97 (CC) Deans; College of Consultors; Personnel Board – Priests; Kingsville, TX St. Thomas Aquinas, University Catholic Center; Kingsville, TX St. Gertrude; Presbyteral Council.
Kozikowski, Thad '75 (GF) Retired.
Kozina, Vladimir '45 (OAK) Retired.
Koziol, John *o.f.m.conv.* '88 (ATL) Jonesboro, GA St. Philip Benizi.
Koziol, Ryszard Andrzej '97 (CC) Bishop, TX St. James.
Koziol, Stanley N. '58 (BGP) Retired.
Koziola, Marcin '05 (VEN) Naples, FL St. John the Evangelist.
Koziolkiewicz, Piotr '07 (NEW) Cedar Grove, NJ St. Catherine of Siena.
Kozlowski, Joseph F. '73 (BUF) Holley, NY St. Mary; Holley, NY St. Mark; Council of Priests.
Kozlowski, Joseph P. '49 (RVC) Glen Head, NY St. Hyacinth Retired.
Kozlowski, Lukasz '09 (SY) Cortland, NY St. Mary.
Kozlowski, Theodore '58 (GR) Grand Rapids, MI Our Lady of Sorrows; Deans; College of Consultors.
Kozminski, Andrew *s.a.c.* '88 (VEN) Sarasota, FL St. Martha.
Kozminski, Rev. Msgr. Max M. '60 (BUF) Retired.
Kozoil, Micah E. '76 (GBG) Uniontown, PA Nativity of the Blessed Virgin Mary.
Kozub, Tomasz '93 (CC) Corpus Christi, TX St. Thomas More Parish.
Kozyra, Oscar *o.de.m.* '73 (SP)[N] St. Petersburg, FL St. Peter Nolasco Residence; [S] St. Petersburg, FL Eckerd College – Catholic Campus Ministry.
Kraeger, David *t.o.r.* '68 (FWT) St. Boniface; Windthorst, TX St. Mary.
Kraemer, Edwin '55 (SCL) Retired.
Kraemer, John A. '57 (RCK) Retired.
Kraeszig, Charles J. '52 (IND) Retired.
Krafchak, John S. '56 (SCR) Retired.
Krafft, Joseph M. '02 (NO)[A] New Orleans, LA Notre Dame Seminary Graduate School of Theology.
Krafinski, Thomas S. *c.m.* '68 (MET)[I] Princeton, NJ Vincentian Residence.

Kraft, Philip G. '62 (SFD) Retired.
Kraft, Thomas *o.p.* '84 (FgM) New York, NY Province of St. Joseph (Eastern).
Kraft, William '86 (STO) Sonora, CA St. Patrick Church of Sonora (Pastor of).
Krah, James B. '71 (PIT) Darlington, PA St. Rose of Lima.
Krahenbuhl, Gary L. '84 (MAD) Beloit, WI Our Lady of the Assumption.
Krahman, Philip G. '72 (STL) St. Peters, MO All Saints.
Kraig, Robert J. '72 (CLV) Strongsville, OH St. John Neumann.
Kraizyi, Melecio (STF) Long Island City, NY Holy Cross.
Krajcovic, Bernard '56 (STU) Retired.
Krajewski, Joseph A. '73 (MET) New Brunswick, NJ St. Joseph.
Krajewski, Paul A. (PAT) Retired.
Krajnak, Jozef *s.d.b.* (NEW) West New York, NJ St. Joseph of the Palisades.
Krajnik, Paul A. '50 (CLV) Retired.
Kraker, Joseph H. '64 (CLV) Akron, OH St. Vincent.
Kraker, Lames J. '65 (SUP) Retired.
Kraljic, John R. '69 (NY)[E] Bronx, NY Cardinal Spellman High School.
Krall, Jack '63 (P) Retired.
Krall, Kenneth R. *s.j.* '71 (SPK)[B] Spokane, WA Gonzaga University.
Kralovich, Louis W. '60 (TR) Toms River, NJ St. Luke; Tribunal Judges Retired.
Kramarz, Andreas *l.c.* '03 (HRT)[B] Cheshire, CT Novitiate of the Legion of Christ.
Kramberg, Donald F. '74 (OG) Dannemora, NY St. Joseph; Redford, NY Church of the Assumption.
Kramer, Carl '52 (SAL) Hays, KS Retired.
Kramer, Daniel J. *c.m.* '47 (PH)[Y].
Kramer, Gary J. '93 (PH) Phoenixville, PA St. Mary of the Assumption.
Kramer, George '62 (JC) Retired.
Kramer, James F. '68 (CLV) Copley, OH Guardian Angels.
Kramer, Lawrence A. '60 (FTW) Columbia City, IN St. Paul of the Cross; Pro–Synodal Judges.
Kramer, Richard R. '66 (RCK) Oregon, IL St. Mary.
Kramer, Scott T. *c.pp.s.* '90 (CIN)[T] Dayton, OH Community Support Charitable Trust.
Kramer, Scott *c.pp.s.* '90 (COL) Columbus, OH St. James–the–Less.
Kramer, Thomas E. '58 (BIS) Presbyteral Council; [G] Bismarck, ND Emmaus Place Retired.
Kramer, Thomas J. '77 (DET) Dearborn Heights, MI St. Mel.
Kramer, William J. '73 (CIN) Cincinnati, OH Our Lady of the Visitation.
Kramer, William *c.pp.s.* '44 (CIN)[N] Carthagena, OH St. Charles Retired.
Kramis, Joseph '57 (SEA) Retired.
Kramlich, Lloyd *s.d.s.* (MIL)[P] Milwaukee Salvatorian Provincial Offices.
Kramper, James V. '73 (OM) Ewing, NE St. John The Baptist; Ewing, NE St. Peter de Alcantara; Deans; Council of Catholic Women, Archdiocesan; Deans.
Krank, Michael T. '52 (BIS) Retired.
Krantz, Ernest *c.pp.s.* '76 (CIN)[N] Dayton Provincial Office of the Cincinnati Province of the Society of the Precious Blood.
Krantz, Robert V. '78 (SFS) Humboldt, SD St. Ann; Montrose, SD St. Patrick; Personnel Board.
Kranyc, Andrew G. '87 (WH)[O] Philippi, WV Alderson–Broaddus College Newman Center; Absent on Leave.
Kranz, Stephen *o.s.b.* '55 (BIS) Mandaree, ND St. Anthony; New Town, ND St. Anthony; [A] Richardton, ND Assumption Abbey; Mandaree, ND St. Joseph.
Krapfl, Daniel A. '58 (DUB) College of Consultors; Directors; Retired Priests' Representatives; Board of Directors/Priest Pension Plan Board of Trustees Retired.
Krapfl, Gary F. '72 (DUB) On Special or Other Archdiocesan Assignment.
Krasevac, Edward *o.p.* '77 (OAK) Antioch, CA Most Holy Rosary; [A] Berkeley, CA Dominican School of Philosophy and Theology.
Krasic, Ljubo *o.f.m.* (CHI)[N] Chicago, IL St. Anthony's Friary.
Krastel, Francis W. '54 (WDC)[T] St. Mary's City, MD St. Mary's College Campus Ministry.
Krastel, Joseph F. *c.ss.r.* '64 (FgM) Baltimore Province.
Krasulski, Andrew '98 (SJP) Presbyters; Johnstown, PA St. John the Baptist.
Kraszewski, Thomas P. '97 (Y) Niles, OH St. Stephen.
Kratz, Alexander *o.f.m.* '99 (DET) Detroit, MI St. Aloysius; Presbyteral Council.
Kratz, Conrad J. *o.praem.* '73 (GB)[A] De Pere, WI St. Norbert Abbey; [J] De Pere, WI St. Joseph Priory; [M] De Pere, WI Norbertine Center for Spirituality; De Pere, WI.
Kraus, David E. *o.m.i.* '57 (BEL)[H] Belleville, IL King's House Retreat and Renewal Center.
Kraus, David H. '67 (DOD) Promoter of Justice; Defender of the Bond; Presbyteral Council Retired.
Kraus, Leonard E. *s.j.* '72 (STL)[O] St. Louis, MO Jesuit Community Corporation at Saint Louis University – Jesuit Hall; [O] St. Louis, MO; [S] St. Louis, MO Retreat House.
Kraus, Philip D. *s.j.* '75 (STL)[O] St. Louis, MO Jesuit Community Corporation at Saint Louis University – Jesuit Hall.
Kraus, Stephen '75 (ROC) Rochester, NY St. Theodore.
Kraus, Rev. Msgr. Theodore W. '63 (OAK) Orinda, CA Santa Maria.
Kraus, William *o.f.m.cap.* '73 (FgM) Denver, CO Province of Mid–America; [N] Denver, CO San Antonio Friary.
Krause, Bruce J. *c.m.* '82 (BUF)[C] Niagara University, NY Niagara University; [O] Niagara University, NY Vincentian Community at Niagara University; [R] Niagara University, NY Niagara University.
Krause, Edward C. *c.s.c.* '66 (FTW)[H] Notre Dame Congregation of Holy Cross, Indiana Province, Provincial House.
Krause, Edward *c.s.c.* '66 (E)[B] Erie, PA Gannon University; The Bishop's Theological Advisory Committee; [M] Erie, PA Congregation of the Divine Spirit.
Krause, Edward *c.s.c.* '40 (STL)[V] St. Louis, MO Central Bureau of the C.C.V.A.
Krause, Joseph A. '68 (TUC) Judge Retired.
Krauth, Lothar '73 (GF) Great Falls, MT Our Lady of Lourdes.
Krautsack, Blaise R. *o.praem.* '74 (PH)[Y] Paoli, PA Daylesford Abbey.
Krautsack, Blaise R. *o. praem* '74 (WIL)[B] Claymont, DE Archmere Academy.
Krawchuk, Thaddeus *c.ss.r.* '60 (PHU) Mount Carmel, PA SS. Peter and Paul.
Krawczenko, Arthur '07 (SY) Clayville, NY St. Patrick–St. Anthony.
Krawontka, Stephen A. '77 (SCR) Mocanaqua, PA St. Mary, Our Lady of Perpetual Help; Mocanaqua, PA St. Martha.
Kraynak, Nicholas '59 (PSC) Retired.
Kraynak, William B. '81 (Y) Canton, OH St. Joan of Arc.
Krebill, Dan (GF) Montana Association of Churches.
Krebs, Bruce D. '78 (BIS) Minot, ND Our Lady of Grace; Pro–Synodal Judges; Presbyteral Council.
Krebs, Rev. Msgr. Donald H. '55 (CR) Retired.
Krebs, Rev. Msgr. Henry L. '60 (E) Clearfield, PA St. Francis.
Krebs, John F. '57 (CHI) Retired.
Krebs, Paul F. '57 (COV) Wilder, KY St. John the Baptist Retired.
Krebs, Peter *s.t.* '69 (PAT)[N] Stirling, NJ Holy Spirit Missionary Cenacle; [N] Stirling, NJ Shrine of St. Joseph.
Kreckel, Robert G. '54 (ROC) Penfield, NY St. Joseph Retired.
Kredel, Thomas E. '72 (PIT) New Brighton, PA Holy Family.
Kredensor, Daniel M. '08 (PH) Newtown, PA St. Andrew.
Kreder, Mark '03 (TR) Toms River, NJ St. Justin.
Kreder, Michael J. '85 (NEW) Rutherford, NJ Church of St. Mary; Archdiocesan Stewardship Advisory Committee.
Kreher, Eugene A. (BEL) Trenton, IL St. Mary.
Kreidler, Rodney A. '05 (CLV) Parma, OH St. Anthony of Padua.
Kreidler, Thomas W. '77 (CIN) Cincinnati, OH Immaculate Heart of Mary.
Kreilein, Philip '74 (EVN) Evansville, IN Resurrection.
Kreilein, Ronald '07 (EVN) Celestine, IN St. Peter Celestine; Dubois, IN St. Raphael.
Kreimer, Richard *g.h.m.* '79 (CIN)[N] Cincinnati Headquarters of Glenmary Home Missioners Retired.
Kreinheder, Gregory J. '07 (SY) Syracuse, NY Holy Family.
Kreiser, Thomas L. '94 (NY) Garnerville, NY St. Gregory Barbarigo.
Kreitinger, Todd '00 (MOB) On Leave from the Archdiocese.
Kreitinger, Todd '00 (BIS) Dickinson, ND St. Patrick; Priests' Personnel Board.
Krejci, Rev. Msgr. Albert L. '41 (OM) Retired.
Krekelberg, Richard G. '73 (LA) Sierra Madre, CA St. Rita; Deanery 10.
Krekelberg, William '70 (ORG) Irvine, CA St. Thomas More; Archivist; Special Assignment.
Krelovich, Michael '95 (SB) Big Bear Lake, CA St. Joseph.
Kremen, Timothy M. *o.s.m.* '61 (CHI)[N] Chicago Order of Friar Servants of Mary (Servites) United States of America Province, Inc.
Kremen, Timothy M. *o.s.m.* '61 (DEN) Denver, CO Our Lady of Mount Carmel.
Kremer, John R. '59 (DUB) Delhi, IA St. John; Hopkinton, IA St. Luke; Deans.
Kremer, Philip *o.s.b.* '57 (RCK)[G] Aurora, IL Marmion Abbey.
Kreml, Curt *o.f.m.conv.* (TR) Point Pleasant Beach, NJ St. Peter's.
Kremmell, William T. '66 (BO) Reading, MA St. Athanasius; Pax Christi USA.
Kremp, Bruno *o.f.m.* '65 (CIN)[N] Cincinnati, OH St. John the Baptist Friary.
Krempa, Adam J. '90 (BUR)[G] Poultney, VT Green Mountain College; Middletown Springs, VT St. Anne; Poultney, VT St. Raphael.
Krempa, Stanley J. '70 (ARL) Winchester, VA Sacred Heart of Jesus.
Krempel, Matthew *o.f.m.* '74 (PHX) Kingman, AZ St. Mary Roman Catholic Parish.
Krenik, Michael J. '84 (STP) Chanhassen, MN St. Hubert.
Krenik, Robert L. '84 (RIC) Retired.
Krenik, Thomas '77 (STP) Richfield, MN St. Richard.
Krenzke, John W. '57 (COS) Retired.
Kresak, Stephen A. '05 (PIT) McKeesport, PA St. Pius V.
Kresinski, Daniel J. '70 (E) Farrell, PA St. Adalbert; Sharon, PA St. Anthony.
Kress, Dennis '99 (KNX) Elizabethton, TN St. Elizabeth; Mountain City, TN St. Anthony of Padua Catholic Church.
Kret, John A. *o.s.a.* '61 (JOL)[L] New Lenox, IL Augustinian Friary; [C] New Lenox, IL Providence Catholic High School.
Kretowicz, Antoni '87 (RCK) Aurora, IL St. Peter.
Krettek, Daniel F. '78 (DM) Elkhart, IA St. Mary/Holy Cross; [H] Des Moines, IA Emmaus House; Judges; Charismatic Renewal Liaison.
Krettek, G. Thomas *s.j.* '82 (MIL)[Y] Milwaukee, WI The Jesuit Partnership; [P] Milwaukee, WI Jesuit Provincial Office, Wisconsin Province; Milwaukee, WI Society of Jesus; Milwaukee, WI; [P] Milwaukee, WI Arrupe House Jesuit Community.
Kretz, James C. '91 (PEO) Retired.
Kreul, Ronald G. *o.p.* '78 (MAD) Elected; Madison, WI Blessed Sacrament.
Kreutz, William H. *s.j.* '69 (FgM) New York, NY Society of Jesus.
Kreutzer, Dan '98 (OWN) Hardinsburg, KY St. Romuald.
Kribs, Charles R. '51 (BEL) Retired.
Kribs, Don Richard '61 (LA) Los Angeles, CA Martin Luther King, Jr., Drew Medical Center Retired.
Kricek, Henry C. '80 (CHI) Wilmette, IL St. Joseph; [A] Chicago, IL St. Joseph College Seminary.
Krick, Howard K. '58 (PH) Retired.
Krieg, Charles F. *c.m.* '63 (MET)[I] Princeton, NJ Vincentian Residence.
Krieg, Rev. Msgr. Gerard C. '53 (ROC) Pittsford, NY St. Louis Retired.
Krieg, Rev. Msgr. Gerard '53 (ROC) Defender of the Bond Retired.
Krieg, Peter *o.f.m.* '43 (OAK)[M] Oakland, CA Franciscan Friars (Province of Santa Barbara).
Krieg, Thomas J. '92 (LC)[K] Menomonie, WI The Ministry to the University of Wisconsin–Stout; Deans; Menomonie, WI St. Joseph.
Kriegel, Rev. Msgr. Henry A. '70 (E) Erie, PA St. Hedwig; Erie, PA St. Patrick.
Kriegshauser, J. Laurence *o.s.b.* '69 (STL)[O] St. Louis, MO The Abbey of St. Mary and St. Louis.
Krier, John P. '69 (GF) On Duty Outside of the Diocese; Medical Lake, WA St. Anne.
Krier, John (SPK) Medical Lake, WA Mary Queen of Heaven.
Krile, Stephen L. '83 (COL) Circleville, OH St. Joseph.
Kriley, Victor *o.f.m.cap.* '64 (PIT)[M] Pittsburgh St. Augustine Friary.
Krill, Jude Michael *o.f.m.conv.* '83 (PH)[C] Aston, PA Neumann College.
Kringe, Charles J. '64 (SCR) Unassigned or Leave of Absence.
Krisak, Anthony F. '75 (WDC)[W] Washington, DC Paulist National Catholic Evangelization Assoc.
Krisak, Anthony F. *s.s.* '75 (TR) On Duty Outside the Diocese.
Krisanda, Stephen J. *m.s.* '60 (ORL) Orlando, FL Good Shepherd.
Krische, Francis '57 (KCK) Retired.
Krische, James J. '91 (BRK) Brooklyn, NY St. Cecilia; Army Reserve Chaplains.
Krische, Rev. Msgr. Vincent E. '64 (KCK) Retired.
Kriski, Frank *c.ss.r.* '63 (KC) Kansas City, MO Our Lady of Perpetual Help; [J] Kansas City, MO Redemptorists Fathers of Kansas City, Missouri.
Krisman, Ronald (ORL) Judges.
Kriss, Aaron J. '91 (PIT) Tarentum, PA Holy Martyrs.
Kriss, Zigford J. '58 (HRT) West Hartford, CT St. Helena Retired.
Kristancic, Dennis J. '83 (CLV) Garfield Heights, OH St. Monica.
Kristofak, Terence J. *c.p.* '69 (HRT)[P] West Hartford, CT Holy Family Passionist Retreat Center; [L] West Hartford, CT Holy Family Monastery/Retreat.
Kristy, Mark *o.c.d.* '85 (SR)[L] Oakville, CA Carmelite House of Prayer.
Krivak, John A. '82 (ALN)[O] Allentown, PA The

Newman Center; [O] Allentown, PA Cedar Crest College (Allentown); [O] Allentown, PA Muhlenberg College (Allentown); Legatus.
Kriz, Dennis *o.s.m.* '99 (CHI) Chicago, IL Annunciata; [N] Chicago, IL Annunciata Priory.
Krizner, William R. '79 (CLV) Brunswick, OH St. Colette.
Krlis, William F. '68 (BRK) Diocesan Real Estate Board; Long Island City, NY Most Precious Blood.
Krlis, William '68 (BRK) Presbyteral Council; Diocesan Consultors.
Kroeger, James H. *m.m.* '75 (FgM) Maryknoll, NY MARYKNOLL.
Kroeger, John '72 (CIN) On Special and Archdiocesan Assignment.
Kroeger, Timothy '90 (LFT) Lebanon, IN St. Joseph.
Kroes, Ralph S. *m.m.* '58 (FgM) Maryknoll, NY MARYKNOLL.
Kroger, Daniel *o.f.m.* '73 (CIN)[U] Cincinnati, OH St. Anthony Messenger; [U] Cincinnati, OH St. Anthony Messenger Press and Franciscan Communications; [C] Cincinnati, OH St. Anthony Shrine, Franciscan Postulancy.
Kroger, John H. '55 (COV) Bellevue, KY Divine Mercy; [I] Edgewood, KY St. Elizabeth Medical Center, Inc.; Vicar for Retired Priests; Bellevue, KY Retired.
Krogman, David '81 (SFS) Sioux Falls, SD St. Mary; Diocesan Consultors; Presbyteral Council.
Krogman, Philip J. '60 (MAD) Green Lake, WI Our Lady of the Lake.
Krol, Boleslaus '61 (DET) Detroit, MI St. Louis the King.
Krol, Miroslaw K. '99 (NEW) On Duty Outside the Archdiocese.
Krol, Miroslaw '99 (DET)[A] Orchard Lake, MI SS. Cyril and Methodius Seminary.
Krolczyk, David B. '72 (CHI) Sauk Village, IL St. James.
Kroll, Anthony '61 (SCL) Pastoral Council Retired.
Kromenaker, Joseph '47 (SFD) Retired.
Kromholtz, Bryan *o.p.* '00 (OAK)[A] Berkeley, CA Dominican School of Philosophy and Theology; [M] Oakland, CA Order of Preachers (Province of the Most Holy Name of Jesus – Western Dominican Province).
Kronkowski, Leonard J. '55 (GRY) Retired.
Kropac, Robert J. '82 (CLV) Concord Twp., OH St. Gabriel.
Kropf, Richard '58 (GAY)[H] Johannesburg, MI Stella Maris Hermitage.
Kropf, Richard '58 (LAN) On Duty Outside the Diocese.
Kropiwnicki, Henry '58 (FR) Retired.
Kropp, Steven *o.f.m.cap.* '04 (MIL) Mount Calvary, WI Holy Cross; St. Cloud, WI St. Cloud; St. Cloud, WI St. Joseph.
Kros, Donald M. '59 (OM) Retired.
Krosfield, George '70 (ALX) Tioga, LA Immaculate Heart of Mary.
Krosnicki, Thomas *s.v.d.* '66 (FgM) Techny, IL.
Krotec, Rt. Rev. Mitred Archpriest Ivan (STN) Chicago, IL SS. Volodymyr and Olha.
Krotkiewicz, Luke '83 (DET) Warren, MI Henry Ford Macomb Hospital.
Krouse, Dennis '68 (SD)[B] University of San Diego.
Krozser, John J. '56 (NEW) Retired.
Kruc, James '89 (RIC) Philadelphia, PA Retired.
Krudwig, William C. '61 (SPC) Retired.
Krueger, Robert '56 (P) Portland, OR St. Francis of Assisi Retired.
Kruesuwan, John Bosco Prasit '99 (FRS) Visalia, CA Holy Family; Visalia, CA St. Mary; Visalia, CA St. Thomas the Apostle.
Krug, Clement M. *c.ss.r.* '65 (NEW) Newark, NJ St. James; Brazilian Apostolate.
Krug, Clement *c.ss.r.* '65 (FgM) Baltimore Province.
Krugel, Stephen A. '88 (HRT) Enfield, CT Willard–Cybulski Correction Institute; Cheshire, CT Cheshire Correctional Institution; Suffield, CT Macdougall – Walker Correctional Institute; Special and other Archdiocesan Assignment; Cheshire, CT Webster Correctional Institute.
Kruger, Brent A. *c.s.c.* '97 (FTW)[H] Notre Dame Congregation of Holy Cross, Indiana Province, Provincial House.
Kruger, Brent A. *c.s.c.* (OAK)[M] Berkeley, CA Priests of the Congregation of Holy Cross.
Kruis, Ron '52 (PBL)[D] Pueblo, CO Centura Health–Villa Pueblo.
Krul, Valentine C. '77 (SY) New York Mills, NY Church of Sacred Heart and St. Mary; Presbyteral Council.
Krulak, Michael '84 (PSC) New Port Richey, FL St. Anne's.
Krull, Michael G. '86 (MET) Hopelawn, NJ Our Lady of the Most Holy Rosary; Perth Amboy, NJ Holy Spirit.
Krumm, John E. '76 (CIN) Jamestown, OH St. Augustine; Xenia, OH St. Brigid.
Krummert, Gary W. '02 (PIT) Bentleyville, PA Ave Maria.
Krupa, Stephen T. *s.j.* '88 (CHI)[C] Chicago, IL Jesuit Community at Loyola University Chicago.
Krupa, Thomas '71 (ALB) Castleton On Hudson, NY Sacred Heart; Advocates; Deans; Priestly Life and Ministry Council.
Krupich, Thomas '88 (FAR) Walhalla, ND Sts. Nereus & Achilleus Church of Neche; Walhalla, ND St. Boniface Church of Walhalla.
Krupka, Michael '77 (SJP) Consultors; Presbyters; Personnel Board.
Krupka, Rev. Canon Michael '77 (SJP) Wheeling, WV Our Lady of Perpetual Help.
Krupnik, Marion I. '54 (HRT) Retired.
Krupp, Albert A. '65 (CLV) Elyria, OH St. Agnes; Presbyteral Council; Presbyteral Conveners.
Krupp, Joseph J. '98 (LAN) East Lansing, MI St. Thomas Aquinas; East Lansing, MI St. John the Evangelist Church and Student Center.
Kruse, David B. '94 (BAL) Military Chaplains; Air Force Chaplains.
Kruse, James E. '96 (PEO) Assistant Directors.
Kruse, James E. '96 (ARL) McLean, VA St. John the Beloved.
Kruse, Phillip F. '81 (DUB)[D] Dyersville, IA Beckman High School; Worthington, IA St. Paul; Dyersville, IA Basilica of St. Francis Xavier; Deans; Vocation Awareness Advisory Committee.
Kruse, Robert J. *c.s.c.* '58 (FR)[A] North Easton, MA Stonehill College; [A] North Easton, MA Holy Cross Fathers Religious.
Kruszynski, Marek *s.j.* '09 (OAK)[M] Berkeley, CA Jesuit Fathers and Brothers; Polish Center.
Krutcik, Stanley F. '80 (WOR) Manchaug, MA St. Anne.
Krutewicz, Jan (CHI) Zion–Beach Park, IL Our Lady of Humility.
Krutewicz, Jan '00 (JOL) Westmont, IL Holy Trinity.
Kruthaupt, Timothy J. '07 (GBG) Clymer, PA Church of the Resurrection; Office for Clergy Vocations; Indiana, PA Indiana Hospital; St. Thomas More Society for Lawyers.
Krutzik, Norman '57 (GB) Retired.
Krylowicz, Mark J. '91 (CHI) Chicago, IL St. Anthony of Padua.
Krylowicz, Mark J. '91 (CHI)[W] Chicago, IL Holy Rosary.
Krymski, Christopher M. *o.s.m.* '83 (CHI) Chicago, IL Our Lady of Sorrows, Basilica of; Chicago, IL; [N] Chicago, IL National Shrine of St. Peregrine, O.S.M.; [N] Chicago, IL Order of Friar Servants of Mary (Servites) United States of America Province, Inc.
Krynen, Joseph G. '46 (PHX) Tempe, AZ Church of the Resurrection Roman Catholic Parish Retired.
Krysa, Czeslaw M. *s.l.d.* '80 (BUF)[A] East Aurora, NY Christ the King Seminary.
Krysa, Czeslaw M. '80 (BUF) Worship, Office Of; Finance Council.
Krystosek, Glenn A. '07 (SCL) Paynesville, MN St. Margaret's; Paynesville, MN St. Louis; Paynesville, MN St. Agnes.
Krystosek, Robert H. '56 (GI) Retired.
Kryszkiewicz, Pawel '93 (CAM) Camden, NJ St. Joseph's Catholic Church, Camden, N.J.
Kryvokulsky, Oleh '98 (STN) Eparchial Office of Religious Education & Catechesis; Chicago, IL SS. Volodymyr and Olha.
Kryzwda, Leonard *c.r.* '65 (SB) Lake Arrowhead, CA Our Lady of the Lake; Running Springs, CA St. Anne in the Mountains; Fontana, CA Blessed John XXIII Catholic Community, Inc.
Krzanowski, Lukasz *m.s.* '91 (SPR) Westfield, MA Holy Trinity.
Krzemien, Filip *o.cist.* '04 (CHI)[N] Willow Springs, IL Cistercian Fathers, Our Lady Mother of the Church Polish Mission.
Krzemien, Filip *o.cist.* '04 (CHI) Argo, IL Our Lady, Mother of the Church Polish Mission.
Krzewinski, Charles *o.m.i.* '52 (FgM) Washington, DC AMERICAN OBLATE MISSIONS.
Krzewinski, Charles *o.m.i.* '52 (SAT)[K] San Antonio, TX Oblate Madonna Residence.
Krzysiak, Rev. Msgr. Casimir J. '50 (SY) Utica, NY St. Stanislaus.
Krzyston, Stanley '85 (TR) Yardville, NJ St. Vincent de Paul.
Krzywda, Jerzy '89 (LAR) Carrizo Springs, TX Our Lady of Guadalupe; Presbyteral Council.
Krzywda, Leonard *c.r.* '65 (SB)[I] Lake Arrowhead, CA; Chicago, IL.
Krzywicki, Lance P. '83 (PT) Military Chaplains.
Krzyzaniak, Timothy D. '91 (LAN) Manchester, MI St. Mary.
Krzyzanowski, Casimir *m.i.c.* '56 (WDC)[B] Washington, DC Marian Fathers Scholasticate.
Krzyzopolski, Al '50 (SFS) Tribunal Judges Retired.
Kselman, John J. *s.s.* '67 (TR) On Duty Outside the Diocese.
Kselman, John S. *s.s.* '67 (BAL)[S] Baltimore Society of St. Sulpice, Province of the United States.
Kselman, John S. *s.s.* '67 (SFR)[A] Menlo Park, CA St. Patrick Seminary and University.
Ku, Theodore John Baptist *o.p.* '99 (WDC)[B] Washington, DC Dominican House of Studies.
Kub, Francis Q. '65 (CHI) Chicago, IL St. Simon the Apostle.
Kuba, William M. '62 (E) East Brady, PA St. Eusebius.
Kubacki, William J. '78 (TOL) Vicar for Priests; Continuing Formation for Priests; Deacon Formation; Toledo, OH Queen of the Most Holy Rosary Cathedral.
Kubajak, James '77 (PRM) Northwood, OH St. Michael the Archangel; Ex Officio; Great Lakes; Defender of the Bond; Promoter of Justice; Presbyteral Council.
Kubala, Daniel I. '76 (MIA) Miami, FL St. Thomas the Apostle.
Kubart, Rev. Msgr. Francis E. '41 (OM) Retired.
Kubat, Christopher K. '99 (LIN)[L] Lincoln, NE Catholic Social Services; Apostolate of Suffering; Catholic Social Services; Diocesan Housing Ministries, Inc.; [K] Lincoln, NE Catholic Social Services.
Kubat, Christopher (GI) Charities.
Kubeck, John C. '65 (MIL)[O] Brookfield, WI Prelature of the Holy Cross and Opus Dei Layton Study Center; Brookfield.
Kubiak, Joseph *o.f.m.cap.* '74 (MET) Colonia, NJ St. John Vianney.
Kubicki, James M. *s.j.* '83 (MIL)[Y] Milwaukee, WI Apostleship of Prayer; [P] Milwaukee, WI Jesuit Community at Marquette University.
Kubina, Eugene *t.o.r.* '53 (ALT)[G] Newry, PA St. Bernardine Monastery Retired.
Kubinski, Scott '84 (ROC) Lansing, NY All Saints; Freeville, NY Holy Cross; Groton, NY St. Anthony.
Kubisa, Jan '82 (GAL) Houston, TX St. Joseph; Houston, TX Holy Name.
Kubishyn, Ivan '79 (SJP) Presbyters; Apopka, FL St. Mary's.
Kubrak, Wladyslaw Z. '06 (BRK) Ridgewood, NY St. Matthias.
Kuca, Stanislaw '91 (CHI) La Grange, IL St. Francis Xavier.
Kucan, Jerome *o.f.m.* '51 (CHI)[N] Chicago, IL St. Anthony's Friary Retired.
Kucer, Peter *m.s.a.* '03 (NOR)[G] Cromwell Society of the Missionaries of the Holy Apostles.
Kucera, David G. '98 (DUB) Church Design/Renovation Commission; Manly, IA Sacred Heart.
Kucera, Edward C. '73 (GAL) Plantersville, TX St. Mary.
Kucera, Edward J. *o.s.b.* '53 (JOL)[L] Lisle, IL St. Procopius Abbey.
Kucera, Jeremy G. '04 (NU) Minneota, MN St. Edward.
Kuchar, Joseph *s.a.c.* '05 (BAL) Baltimore, MD St. Jude Shrine.
Kuchar, Michael W. '80 (LAN) Goodrich, MI St. Mark the Evangelist.
Kucharczyk, Dennis H. '85 (SAG) Caro, MI Sacred Heart; Navy Reserve Chaplains.
Kucharczyk, John J. '99 (BAL) Priests Sick or Absent.
Kucharski, Steven M. '77 (MAN) Keene, NH St. Bernard; Keene, NH Mary, Queen of Peace Parish; Keene, NH St. Margaret Mary; Keene, NH Immaculate Conception.
Kuchera, Michael J. *s.j.* '87 (BAL)[S] Towson Maryland Province of the Society of Jesus.
Kuchinsky, William J. '97 (WH) Fort Ashby, WV Annunciation of Our Lord; Ridgeley, WV St. Anthony; Romney, WV Our Lady of Grace.
Kuczmanski, Gregory M. '75 (BWN) Mission, TX St. Paul.
Kuczynski, Edward P. '77 (PH) On Special or Other Archdiocesan Assignment; Philadelphia, PA St. Charles Borromeo.
Kuczynski, Edwin *o.s.a.* '47 (CHI)[N] Olympia Fields, IL Tolentine Monastery at Tolentine Center.
Kuczynski, James H. *m.s.* '73 (HRT) Hartford, CT; [L] Hartford, CT Missionaries of LaSalette Province of Mary, Mother of the Americas.
Kuczynski, James H. *m.s.* '73 (ATL) Smyrna, GA St. Thomas the Apostle.
Kuczynski, Kazimierz '76 (NEW) Jersey City, NJ St. Ann's.
Kuder, Donald E. *c.s.b.* '63 (GAL)[O] Houston, TX Dillon House Retired.
Kuder, Stephen R. *s.j.* '73 (SPK)[B] Spokane, WA Gonzaga University.
Kudilil, James '63 (FRS) Retired.
Kudilil, Joseph (JOL) Rockdale, IL St. Joseph.
Kudleychuk, Bohdan (STN) St. Joseph, MO St. Joseph's; Omaha, NE St. George's; Omaha, NE Assumption of B.V.M.
Kudlo, Frank '88 (MIA) Absent on Leave.
Kudukkamthadam, Anthony K. Joseph '87 (SYM) Marlboro, NY Syro–Malabar Catholic Mission, Rockland.
Kueber, Michael I. '00 (P) Special Assignment.
Kuebler, A.M. Seamus '75 (WDC) On Duty Outside the Archdiocese.
Kuehler, Rev. Msgr. Norbert '55 (AMA) Retired.
Kuehnemund, H. Thomas '93 (DET) Waterford, MI St. Benedict.
Kuehner, John *c.ss.r.* '03 (CHI) Chicago, IL St. Michael in Old Town; [N] Chicago, IL The Redemptorist Fathers of Chicago.
Kuehner, Rev. Msgr. Ralph J. '50 (WDC) Derwood, MD St. Francis of Assisi Retired.

Kuenzig, Peter A. '46 (PIT) Retired.
Kuffel, Thomas '89 (LIN) Exeter, NE St. Stephen's; Presbyteral Council; Diocesan Area CCD Directors.
Kuffner, Patrick J. '02 (MET) Middlesex, NJ Our Lady of Mount Virgin; Deans.
Kugler, Michael '89 (GLP) On Duty Outside of Diocese.
Kuhlmann, John L. '68 (BUF) Retired.
Kuhlmann, Steven *o.p.* '92 (JC) Columbia, MO Sacred Heart; Columbia Catholic Hospital Ministry.
Kuhn, Aaron J. '07 (SCL) St. Cloud, MN St. Mary's Cathedral of St. Cloud; St. Cloud, MN St. Augustine; St. Cloud, MN Christ Church.
Kuhn, Christopher J. '97 (RCK) Galena, IL St. Mary; Galena, IL St. Michael; Scales Mound, IL Holy Trinity.
Kuhn, Christopher *c.s.c.* (FTW)[H] Notre Dame Congregation of Holy Cross, Indiana Province, Provincial House.
Kuhn, Dennis R. '82 (CHL) Absent On Leave.
Kuhn, George J. '64 (NY) Yonkers, NY St. Joseph Parish.
Kuhn, James G. '71 (MAD) Janesville, WI St. Patrick.
Kuhn, Michael F. *y.a.* '97 (ARL)[L] McLean, VA Youth Apostles Institute, An Association of Christian Faithful.
Kuhn, Michael F. '97 (FR) On Duty Outside the Diocese.
Kuhn, Richard W. '53 (DUB)[F] Farley, IA Seton Catholic Schools; Peosta, IA Holy Family; Peosta, IA St. John the Baptist Church of Peosta, Iowa.
Kuhn, Richard *s.m.* (BAL)[S] Baltimore, MD Society of Mary (Marianists).
Kuhn, Thomas A. '67 (CIN) Priests On Administrative Leave.
Kuhneman, Timothy '06 (RIC) Virginia Beach, VA Holy Spirit.
Kuhns, Howard *c.s.c.* '46 (PHX)[F] Phoenix, AZ Holy Cross Congregation/Casa Santa Cruz Retired.
Kuhns, Howard *c.s.c.* (FTW)[H] Notre Dame Congregation of Holy Cross, Indiana Province, Provincial House.
Kuhns, James '61 (SPK) Priests' Personnel Board Retired.
Kuhr, William '67 (GB)[K] Oshkosh, WI SSM Franciscan Courts; Omro, WI St. Mary.
Kuizon, Antonio '77 (NEW) Scotch Plains, NJ Immaculate Heart of Mary.
Kujawinski, Matthew J. '03 (E) Sharpsville, PA St. Bartholomew.
Kujovsky, Rev. Msgr. Thomas J. '57 (HBG) Retired.
Kujovsky, Rev. Msgr. Thomas J. '57 (HBG) Catholic History and Archives, Office of.
Kukatla, Jones '83 (CAM)[I] Vineland, NJ Bishop McCarthy Residence; Vineland, NJ Divine Mercy, Vineland, N.J.
Kuklich, Stepan '95 (BUF) Kenmore, NY St. John the Baptist; Millard Fillmore Suburban Hospital; Lakeview Shock Incarceration Correctional Facility.
Kukulka, Janusz *s.t.l.* '85 (HRT) Derby, CT St. Mary the Immaculate Conception.
Kukulka, Tadeusz *s.j.* '97 (CHI)[N] Chicago, IL Sacred Heart Mission House.
Kukura, Joseph W. '67 (NEW) On Duty Outside the Archdiocese.
Kula, Francis J. *m.s.* '54 (HRT)[L] Hartford, CT Missionaries of LaSalette.
Kulacz, Sean R. '09 (BGP) Trumbull, CT St. Stephen.
Kulah, Henry N. '84 (CHR) Charleston, SC St. Patrick; Charleston, SC Our Lady of Mercy.
Kulak, Joseph F. '66 (RCK) Elgin, IL St. Laurence.
Kulandairajan, S. '78 (NY) Shrub Oak, NY Saint Elizabeth Ann Seton.
Kulandaisamy, Amaldas *o.s.b.cam.* (LC) Prairie du Chien, WI St. John Nepomucene.
Kulas, Francis J. *m.s.* '54 (HRT) Rocky Hill, CT Veterans' Home and Hospital.
Kulas, John *o.s.b.* '57 (SCL)[I] Collegeville, MN St. John's Abbey, of the Order of St. Benedict.
Kulas, Robert A. '54 (WIN) Retired.
Kulas, William J. '74 (WIN) Blooming Prairie, MN St. Columbanus; Blooming Prairie, MN Sacred Heart; Associate Judges; Priests' Pension Board.
Kulathinal, Jose J. *c.m.i.* '92 (STA) Jacksonville, FL St. Patrick; Diocesan Consultors; Presbyteral Council; Deans.
Kulathingal, Francis *o.ss.t.* '09 (BAL)[S] The Trinitarians in India (Bangalore & Trichur).
Kulathumkal, Babu '96 (OWN) Hardin, KY St. Henry; Cadiz, KY St. Stephen.
Kulavich, John J. '83 (SCR)[L] Dallas, PA Mercy Center Nursing Unit, Inc.
Kulbicki, Timothy *o.f.m.conv.* '86 (BAL) Baltimore, MD St. Casimir; [A] Baltimore, MD St. Mary's Seminary and University.
Kulczynski, Jason '89 (PH) Lansdowne, PA St. Philomena; [D] Philadelphia, PA SS. John Neumann and Maria Goretti Catholic High School.
Kulesa, Daniel J. '62 (Y) Judges Retired.
Kulhawik, Frank '40 (CR) Retired.
Kulick, Larry J. '92 (GBG) Greensburg, PA Our Lady of Grace; Catholic Business and Professional Women's Association; Office for Clergy Vocations.
Kulick, Michael '09 (SJP) Parma, OH St. Josaphat Cathedral; Presbyters.
Kulig, Rev. Msgr. Anthony J. '61 (NEW)[B] School of Diplomacy and Intl. Rels.; Members; [A] South Orange, NJ Immaculate Conception Seminary.
Kulig, Christopher *o.carm* '00 (KCK) Leavenworth, KS Immaculate Conception–St. Joseph.
Kulig, Krzysztof A. '07 (CHI) Arlington Heights, IL St. James.
Kuligowski, Peter J. '97 (ALT) Absent on Leave.
Kuligowski, Peter '97 (ALX) Deville, LA St. John the Baptist.
Kulik, Rev. Msgr. Alexander T. '54 (SCR)[N] Dunmore, PA Villa St. Joseph Retired.
Kulik, Francis J. '69 (SCR) Unassigned or Leave of Absence.
Kull, John J. *o.f.m.* '66 (PAT)[N] Butler, NJ St. Anthony Friary.
Kull, Martin R. '76 (BRK) Brooklyn, NY St. Anselm.
Kulleck, Rev. Msgr. Donald R. '54 (SD) Chula Vista, CA St. Pius X Retired.
Kulleck, Thomas G. '74 (BWN) Associate Judges; Office of the Chancellor; Harlingen, TX St. Anthony.
Kullmann, Charles R. *c.s.p.* '78 (SFR) San Francisco, CA Old St. Mary's Cathedral.
Kulma, Ryszard '02 (GAL) Katy, TX St. Edith Stein.
Kulwiec, Richard *o.m.i.* '81 (LAR) Eagle Pass, TX St. Joseph.
Kumai, Felix K. '86 (MO) Army Chaplains.
Kumar, Joseph Nirmal '87 (CC) Corpus Christi, TX Holy Family.
Kumarthusseril, Joy *m.f.* '88 (OAK) Alameda, CA St. Albert; Alameda, CA St. Philip Neri.
Kumbakeel, Boby Kurian *o.ss.t.* '08 (BAL)[S] The Trinitarians in New Jersey.
Kumbakeel, Boby Kurian *o.ss.t.* '08 (TR) Asbury Park, NJ Our Lady of Mt. Carmel.
Kumbakkeel, James *o.s.b.* '86 (FTW) Fort Wayne, IN St. Charles Borromeo.
Kumbalaprampil, Xavier '66 (SAV) Retired.
Kumblumkal, Jose *c.m.i.* '90 (TYL) Winnsboro, TX Clyde Johnston Unit, Texas Department of Corrections.
Kummer, John R. '72 (CIN) Retired.
Kummer, William '75 (FTW) Plymouth, IN St. Michael; Retired Clergy Committee; Presbyteral Council.
Kummerer, Timothy M. '83 (TOL) Defiance, OH St. Mary.
Kumo, Michael (BO) Kenyan.
Kumplam, Chacko K. '80 (HRT) Milford, CT St. Mary.
Kumse, John M. '79 (CLV) Cleveland, OH St. Mary; [Y] Cleveland, OH Cleveland Slovenian Community Center; College of Consultors.
Kuna, Lech '74 (HRT)[J] Enfield, CT The Home for the Aged of the Little Sisters of the Poor.
Kuna, Vincent A. *c.s.c.* '09 (COS) Colorado Springs, CO Sacred Heart.
Kuna, Vincent A. *c.s.c.* '09 (FTW)[H] Notre Dame Congregation of Holy Cross, Indiana Province, Provincial House.
Kunath, Thomas '85 (TR) Barnegat, NJ St. Mary.
Kunco, Edward J. '69 (PIT) Cranberry Township, PA St. Ferdinand.
Kunderevych, Orest '98 (PHU) Edwardsville, PA St. Vladimir's; Mount Carmel, PA SS. Peter and Paul.
Kunes, James F. *s.m.* '60 (STL)[O] St. Louis Marianists, Province of the United States (Society of Mary).
Kunigonis, Mark S. '00 (PH) Springfield, PA St. Francis of Assisi.
Kunisch, Robert *c.pp.s.* '56 (TOL)[I] Bellevue Mary Lay Center; [K] Bellevue, OH Sorrowful Mother Shrine.
Kunisch, William J. '02 (HON) Vicars Forane; Honolulu, HI Co–Cathedral of St. Theresa of the Child Jesus; Diocesan Ecumenical Commission; Diocesan Ecumenical Interfaith Officer; Presbyteral Council; College of Consultors.
Kunkel, A. Henry '70 (BAL) Pylesville, MD St. Mary.
Kunkel, Albert A. '57 (CLV)[M] Akron, OH Francesca Residence; [O] Akron, OH Provincial Motherhouse and Novitiate of the Daughters of Divine Charity; Barberton, OH Prince of Peace.
Kunkel, Charles *o.s.c.* '67 (SCL)[I] Onamia, MN Crosier Priory.
Kunkel, George C. '77 (CIN) Cincinnati, OH St. Vincent Ferrer.
Kunkel, James E. '73 (PIT) Turtle Creek, PA St. Colman; Judges.
Kunkel, Ronald T. '00 (CHI)[A] Mundelein, IL University of St. Mary of the Lake/Mundelein Seminary.
Kunkel, Steve '01 (PHX) Mesa, AZ Christ the King Roman Catholic Parish.
Kunkle, Albert A. '57 (CLV) Retired.
Kunnakkattuthara, Rev. Msgr. Zacharias S. '75 (TYL) Palestine, TX Sacred Heart; Palestine, TX Beto I Unit and Louie C. Powledge Unit, Texas Department of Corrections; Tennessee Colony, TX Coffield Unit, Texas Department of Corrections; Tennessee Colony, TX Gurney Unit; Tennessee Colony, TX Michael Unit; College of Consultors; Deans; Priests' Pension Board; Priests' Personnel Board.
Kunnalakatt, Peter '85 (CHI)[J] Melrose Park, IL Westlake Community Hospital.
Kunnaseril, John Joseph *i.m.s.* '80 (BR) Livonia, LA St. Frances Xavier Cabrini; Grosse Tete, LA St. Joseph; Grosse Tete, LA Immaculate Heart of Mary.
Kunnath, Matthew '60 (NEW) Nutley, NJ St. Mary's.
Kunnath, Sebastian '73 (NEW) Paramus, NJ Our Lady of the Visitation.
Kunnathu, Varghese *m.c.b.s.* '74 (VIC) Wharton, TX Holy Family.
Kunnathukizhakethil, K. Joseph *s.d.b.* '83 (CHI) Chicago, IL St. Symphorosa and Seven Sons.
Kunnel, Lawrence K. '60 (TR) Neptune, NJ Holy Innocents Retired.
Kunnel, Thomas *t.o.r.* '88 (STP) Columbia Heights, MN Immaculate Conception; College of Consultors.
Kunnumpuram, Paul *m.s.f.s.* '76 (ALX) Marksville, LA Our Lady of Lourdes.
Kunnumpuram, Paul *m.s.f.s.* '76 (TYL)[B] Whitehouse, TX The Missionaries of St. Francis de Sales.
Kunst, Richard '98 (DUL) Auditor; Department of Vocations and Priestly Formation; Duluth, MN St. John; Duluth, MN St. Joseph.
Kuntz, Donald B. '41 (DET) Retired.
Kuntz, Kenneth E. '77 (DAV) Iowa City, IA St. Mary; Diocesan Consultors.
Kunz, David C. '80 (LC) Independence, WI SS. Peter and Paul; Personnel Council; Whitehall, WI St. John the Apostle.
Kunz, Eric J. '08 (STL) Oakville, MO Queen of All Saints.
Kunz, Francis P. '49 (WIN) Retired.
Kunz, James H. '73 (WIN) On Special or Other Diocesan Assignment; [D] Rochester, MN Saint Mary Hospital.
Kunz, John M. '76 (WIN) Deans; Mankato, MN St. John the Baptist.
Kunz, Thomas W. '04 (PIT) Graduate Studies.
Kunze, Robert W. '74 (NEW) Retired.
Kunzman, Richard T. '63 (CAM) Retired.
Kuolt, Benedict J. '47 (NY)[EE] Bronx, NY John Cardinal O'Connor Residence Retired.
Kuper, Raymond L. '64 (EVN) Judges Retired.
Kupisz, Julian '74 (FAR) Esmond, ND St. Boniface; Esmond, ND St. William; Esmond, ND Our Lady of Mt. Carmel Church of Balta.
Kupka, Marek S. '01 (PRO) Providence, RI St. Adalbert.
Kupke, Rev. Msgr. Raymond J. '73 (PAT) Florham Park, NJ Holy Family; Archivist; Theological Commission; Deans.
Kuppe, Paul *o.f.m.cap.* '70 (PH) Philadelphia, PA Our Lady of the Blessed Sacrament.
Kuras, Alexander A. '69 (DET) Westland, MI Church of the Divine Savior.
Kurash, Stanley J. '71 (SCR) Unassigned or Leave of Absence.
Kurber, Robert '60 (ORL) Retired.
Kurc, Slawomir '95 (CHI) Chicago, IL St. Daniel the Prophet.
Kurdziel, Dennis M. '75 (ALT) Loretto, PA Basilica of St. Michael the Archangel.
Kurgan, Charles *o.carm.* '65 (PHX)[F] Phoenix, AZ St. Therese Priory; Phoenix, AZ.
Kurgan, John '04 (SY) Tully, NY St. Leo; Lafayette, NY St. Joseph; Priests' Personnel Committee.
Kuriachen, Binu E. *m.s.f.s.* '00 (STL) Manchester, MO St. Joseph.
Kuriachen, Binu (CHI)[J] Elk Grove Village, IL Alexian Brothers Medical Center.
Kuriakose, Thomas '83 (HT) Montegut, LA St. Charles Borromeo.
Kurian, Santy M. *m.s.f.s.* '95 (GAL) Sugar Land, TX St. Laurence.
Kuriappilly, Johnson '90 (BIS) Beulah, ND St. Joseph; Hazen, ND St. Martin.
Kurilec, Robert E. '68 (SB) Retired.
Kurimay, Michael D. *s.j.* '73 (MIL)[P] Wauwatosa, WI Jesuit Community at St. Camillus.
Kurimsky, Frank M. '86 (PIT) Oakmont, PA St. Irenaeus.
Kurkowski, Innocent *o.f.m.conv.* '56 (BUF)[D] Athol Springs, NY St. Francis High School; [O] Athol Springs, NY St. Francis of Assisi Friary Retired.
Kurnath, Joseph G.M. '91 (HRT) Lakeville, CT St. Mary.
Kuroly, James A. '07 (BRK) Corona, NY Our Lady of Sorrows.
Kurovsky, Andrew '85 (SCR) Gouldsboro, PA St. Rita.
Kurowski, Canon Andrzej *s.a.c.* '76 (BRK) Brooklyn, NY St. Frances de Chantal.
Kurowski, Clement *o.f.m.* '53 (PH) Philadelphia, PA St. Monica Retired.
Kurpel, Yaroslav '93 (PHU) Philadelphia, PA Christ the King.
Kurpios, Szymon *sch.p.* (HRT) New Britain, CT Holy Cross.
Kurps, Jack *s.c.j.* '77 (JKS)[I] Walls, MS Sacred Heart League; [I] Walls, MS Sacred Heart Southern Missions Housing Corporation; [I] Walls, MS Sacred Heart Southern Missions, Inc.; [E] Nesbit, MS St.

Michael Community House.
Kurt, Allan J. '55 (DUB) Retired.
Kurtenbach, Harold R. '60 (GI) Charismatic Renewal Retired.
Kurtenbach, Harold '60 (GI) U.S. Veterans' Hospital Retired.
Kurtyka, Rev. Msgr. Edward J. '71 (PAT) Prospect Park, NJ St. Paul's; Judicial Vicar.
Kurtz, James *o.f.m.cap.* '87 (BAL) Cumberland, MD SS. Peter and Paul; [S] Cumberland, MD SS. Peter and Paul Friary; Cresaptown, MD St. Ambrose.
Kurtz, Jeffrey A. '90 (MAR) Crystal Falls, MI Guardian Angels; Channing, MI St. Rose.
Kurtz, R. James *s.j.* '77 (DET)[K] Clarkston, MI Colombiere Center.
Kurtzke, John *c.s.c.* (FTW)[H] Notre Dame Congregation of Holy Cross, Indiana Province, Provincial House.
Kurucz, Frank A. '98 (CHI) Chicago, IL St. Cajetan.
Kurumbel, Joseph *o.s.b.* '76 (LUB) Lamesa, TX St. Margaret Mary; Lamesa, TX St. Margaret Mary.
Kurutz, Joseph V. '59 (PIT) Bethel Park, PA Retired.
Kuruvila, Prince '92 (CC) Sandia, TX St. Francis of Assisi Mission; Orange Grove, TX St. John of the Cross.
Kuruvilla, Baby V. '90 (HT) Thibodaux, LA St. Lawrence the Martyr.
Kuruvilla, Prince (SYM) San Antonio, TX St. Thomas Syro–Malabar Catholic Mission of San Antonio; Orange Grove, TX St. Alphonsa Syro–Malabar Catholic Church Austin, TX.
Kurwicki, Rev. Msgr. Robert A. '85 (JC) Jefferson City, MO St. Joseph Cathedral; Personnel Board; Senators; Vice–Chancellors.
Kury, Ignatius '06 (SJP) Akron, OH Holy Ghost; Akron, OH St. Nicholas; Consultors; St. Josaphat Sacerdotal Society; Presbyters.
Kurylowicz, Martin '79 (GR) Faculties Suspended.
Kuryvial, George *o.m.i.* '58 (BEL)[F] Belleville, IL Missionary Oblates of Mary Immaculate – St. Henry's Oblate Residence.
Kurz, Andrew J. '02 (LIN) Advocates.
Kurz, Andrew '02 (LIN) Doniphan, NE St. Ann's; Doniphan, NE Sacred Heart.
Kurz, Rev. Msgr. Michael A. '75 (RCK) Rockford, IL St. Rita; Special Assignment; Judicial Vicar.
Kurz, William S. *s.j.* '70 (MIL)[P] Milwaukee, WI Jesuit Community at Marquette University.
Kurzaj, Rev. Msgr. Franciszek '76 (SAT) San Antonio, TX St. Paul; College of Consultors; Archdiocesan Presbyteral Council.
Kurzak, John F. '75 (SC) On Duty Outside the Diocese.
Kurzawa, Ronald '64 (DET) Presbyteral Council Retired.
Kurzyna, Andrew E. '74 (NY) Verplanck, NY St. Patrick.
Kurzynski, James R. '03 (LC) Eau Claire, WI Sacred Heart of Jesus–St. Patrick.
Kus, Robert J. '98 (R) Wilmington, NC St. Mary; Holy Childhood Pontifical Association; Pontifical Mission Societies in the United States.
Kus, Sebastian *o.f.m.* '57 (GB)[J] Pulaski, WI Friary.
Kuse, Rev. Msgr. Michael '67 (SFD) Quincy Deanery; Quincy, IL Blessed Sacrament.
Kusek, Wojciech *c.ss.r.* '04 (MET) Perth Amboy, NJ St. Stephen.
Kushnir, Volodymyr '09 (STN) Chicago, IL St. Joseph.
Kusi, Gordon P. '95 (BRK) Jamaica, NY St. Bonaventure–St. Benedict the Moor RC Church; Presbyteral Council.
Kusibab, Justin *o.f.m.conv.* '87 (DET)[K] Dearborn Heights, MI All Saints Friary.
Kusibab, Miroslaw *c.s.m.a.* '91 (NEW) Cliffside Park, NJ Epiphany.
Kusmirek, Mark '77 (TYL) Rusk, TX Jerry H. Hodge Unit and Sky View Unit, Texas Department of Corrections; Presbyteral Council; Jacksonville, TX Our Lady of Sorrows.
Kuss, Allen R. '84 (MO) On Duty Outside the Diocese; Navy Chaplains.
Kusugh, Richard '04 (TUC) Yuma, AZ Immaculate Conception Roman Catholic Parish & Guadalupe Mission – Yuma.
Kusy, Jerzy '86 (CLV) Perry, OH St. Cyprian.
Kutch, Joseph P. '88 (SCR) Glen Lyon, PA Corpus Christi.
Kutch, Peter *o.f.m.cap.* '66 (CHI)[N] Chicago, IL St. Clare Friary.
Kutiuk, Casimir '57 (GB) Retired.
Kutner, Rev. Msgr. Raymond W. '64 (BRK) Diocesan Real Estate Board; Diocesan Judges.
Kutsch, Eugene C. '51 (DUB) Retired.
Kuttiyanickal, Thomas *s.a.c.* '77 (MIL)[P] Milwaukee, WI Pallotti House.
Kuttiyanickal, Thomas *s.a.c.* '77 (CHI)[J] Evanston, IL Saint Francis Hospital; Evanston, IL Divine Liturgy–Ascension Church.
Kuttner, David '09 (SPK) Spokane, WA St. Thomas More.
Kuttukaran, Rafi '92 (BEL) Evansville, IL St. Boniface.
Kutubebi, Frederick '96 (RVC) Glen Cove, NY North Shore University Hospital at Glen Cove; Sea Cliff, NY St. Boniface Martyr.
Kutys, Rev. Msgr. Daniel J. '80 (PH) West Chester, PA SS. Peter and Paul.
Kutz, Lawrence A. (POD) Reston.
Kutzner, Roger '90 (JOL) Joliet, IL St. Joseph.
Kuusangnayir, Martin '01 (ROC) Ithaca, NY St. Catherine of Siena.
Kuusegmeh, Konaku *c.s.sp.* '95 (NY)[AA] New York, NY Cabrini Center for Nursing & Rehabilitation.
Kuykendall, Andrew '78 (WCH) Wichita, KS St. Peter the Apostle.
Kuykendall, Henry '86 (EVN) Evansville, IN Nativity; Deaf Ministry.
Kuykendall, Thomas S. '94 (YAK) Wenatchee, WA St. Joseph's; Diocesan Commission on Public Worship; Ministry & Education Center; Presbyteral Council Executive Committee.
Kuzara, George (Yuri) J. *c.pp.s.* '78 (TOL)[I] Bellevue Mary Lay Center; [K] Bellevue, OH Sorrowful Mother Shrine.
Kuzdal, Anthony P. '56 (NOR) Retired.
Kuzhichalil, Joseph (NY) Pearl River, NY St. Margaret of Antioch.
Kuzhikottayil, John *s.d.b.* '82 (HRT) Branford, CT St. Mary.
Kuzhippallil, George (PAT) Retired.
Kuzhupil, Joseph *m.s.f.s.* '85 (KNX)[D] Signal Mountain, TN Alexian Village of Tennessee; [C] Signal Mountain, TN Alexian Village Health Care Center.
Kuzhupil, Joseph *m.s.f.s.* '85 (TYL)[B] Whitehouse, TX The Missionaries of St. Francis de Sales.
Kuzia, Anthony *c.m.* '76 (MAN) Concord, NH St. Peter; Concord, NH Sacred Heart; N.H. State Prison.
Kuzilla, John A. '55 (E) Kersey, PA St. Boniface.
Kuzinskas, John A. '52 (CHI) Vicar for Senior Priests Retired.
Kuzma, Rev. Archpriest Mykhailo '81 (STN) Palatine, IL Immaculate Conception; Diocesan Consultors; Personnel Board; Chicago; Presbyteral Council.
Kuzmann, Robert J. '85 (ALN) Unassigned.
Kuzmeski, Charles H. '75 (SPR) Granby, MA Immaculate Heart of Mary.
Kuzmich, Rev. Msgr. John M. '65 (FTW) Fort Wayne, IN St. Vincent de Paul; Presbyteral Council.
Kuzniewski, Anthony J. *s.j.* '79 (WOR)[O] Worcester, MA Jesuits of the Holy Cross, Inc.
Kuznik, Robert '98 (RVC) Riverhead, NY St. Isidore's; Senate of Priests (Presbyteral Council/College of Consultors).
Kvedas, Leonard J. '61 (HRT) Beacon Falls, CT St. Michael; Waterbury Vicariate.
Kwak, Peter Hoin '81 (ARL) Fairfax, VA St. Paul Chung.
Kwang–Sung, An '89 (ANC) Korean Ministry; Anchorage, A Corp. of St. Andrew Kim Parish of the Korean Community.
Kwapisz, Gregory *o.f.m.conv.* '60 (BAL)[S] Ellicott City Order of Friars Minor Conventual.
Kwatera, Michael *o.s.b.* '77 (SCL)[I] Collegeville, MN St. John's Abbey, of the Order of St. Benedict.
Kweder, Joseph J. '85 (ALN) New Philadelphia, PA Holy Cross Parish.
Kwiatek, Piotr *o.f.m.cap* '00 (PH) Philadelphia, PA St. John the Evangelist.
Kwiatkowski, Joseph '06 (NEW) Paramus, NJ Church of the Annunciation.
Kwiatkowski, Mike '78 (SPK) Otis Orchards, WA St. Joseph.
Kwiatkowski, Paul M. '64 (TOL) Retired.
Kwiatkowski, Richard P. '72 (NEW) Leonia, NJ St. John the Evangelist's.
Kwiatkowski, Robert M. '83 (HRT) Woodbury, CT St. Teresa; Waterbury Vicariate.
Kwiatkowski, Sylvester '89 (SAC) Downieville, CA Immaculate Conception; Grass Valley, CA St. Patrick; Nevada City, CA St. Canice.
Kwiecien, John S. '76 (BUF) Collins Correctional Facility; North Collins, NY Holy Spirit.
Kwiecien, Mark *o.carm.* '80 (CHI)[D] Chicago, IL.
Kwiecien, Michael *o.carm.* '80 (CHI)[N] Chicago Carmelite Priory of St. Cyril.
Kwiecien, Wojciech '79 (CHI) Chicago, IL St. James.
Kwofie, Emmanuel '97 (BWN) Harlingen, TX Harlingen Medical Center.
Kwoka, Edward '78 (TR) Marlboro, NJ St. Gabriel.
Ky, Joseph T. *s.s.* '59 (BAL)[S] Baltimore Society of St. Sulpice, Province of the United States Retired.
Ky, Joseph T. *s.s.* '59 (HON) Retired.
Kyabuta, Jean Baptiste '88 (NSH) Decherd, TN Good Shepherd; Univ. of South–Sewanee.
Kyazze, Richard *c.s.c.* '03 (FTW)[H] Notre Dame Congregation of Holy Cross, Indiana Province, Provincial House.
Kye, Antony '01 (CHK) Saipan, MP Korean Catholic Community.
Kyeah, Barnabas (LC) Marathon, WI Sacred Heart; Mosinee, WI St. Patrick.
Kyebasuuta, John '98 (LA) Panorama City, CA St. Genevieve.
Kyeremeh, George (NY) Highland, NY St. Augustine.
Kyeremeh, John (NY) Millbrook, NY St. Joseph.
Kyfes, Robert J. '77 (CHI) Chicago, IL St. John Fisher.
Kyle, Eric F. *o.f.m.* '52 (PAT)[N] Ringwood, NJ Holy Name Friary, Inc.
Kynam, Victor '07 (GR) Lake Odessa, MI St. Edward's; Saranac, MI St. Anthony.
Kyom, Daniel J. '97 (NY) New York, NY St. John the Evangelist.
Kyrpczak, James A. '96 (MET) Phillipsburg, NJ St. Philip & St. James.
Kysely, Andrew T. '07 (GB) Appleton, WI St. Pius X.
Kyte, Michael G. *o.p.* '87 (CHI) River Forest, IL St. Vincent Ferrer.
Kythe, Jay K. '02 (STP) Cannon Falls, MN St. Pius V; Deanery 6; Miesville, MN St. Joseph.

L

L'Arche, Jeffrey '75 (ALB)[J] Albany, NY Teresian House; [P] Altamont, NY La Salette Shrine; Special Assignment.
L'Estrange, Peter *s.j.* '79 (WDC)[N] Washington, DC The Jesuit Community at Georgetown University.
L'Heureux, Ernest L. '62 (PRT) Retired.
L'Heureux, William D. '91 (OM) Omaha, NE St. Adalbert; Omaha, NE Our Lady of Lourdes.
Laba, Gerald *c.p.* '73 (PIT)[M] Pittsburgh, PA St. Paul of the Cross Monastery; [O] Pittsburgh, PA St. Paul of the Cross Retreat Center.
Labacevich, Ihar '06 (PRM) Minneapolis, MN St. John the Baptist.
LaBaff, Arthur J. '66 (OG) Clayton, NY St. Mary's of Clayton; Clayton, NY St. John the Evangelist; Deans; Diocesan Consultors; Committee on Assignments.
LaBaire, Steven M. '87 (WOR) Uxbridge, MA St. Mary's.
Labak, Joseph L. '77 (CLV) Wadsworth, OH Sacred Heart of Jesus.
Labaka, Francisco *o.f.m.* (SJN) Carolina, PR Santa Clara de Asis.
Labaky, Mansour (OLL)[F] St. Louis, MO Our Lady of Smiles Orphanage.
Labarda, Nathaniel C. '93 (HRT) Milford, CT St. Mary.
LaBarge, Christopher W. '85 (WIL) Salisbury, MD St. Francis De Sales.
Labarre, Renald D. '60 (PRT) Retired.
Labasano, Paterno B. *s.s.s.* '02 (HON) Honolulu, HI Star of the Sea.
Labat, Dennis C. '74 (NU) Springfield, MN St. Raphael; On Special or Other Diocesan Assignment; Riverbend TEC (Together Encounter Christ); Priest Personnel Board; Pastoral Administrators.
LaBat, Sean J. '99 (SJP) Raleigh, NC St. Basil The Great Mission; Presbyters.
LaBau, Anthony F. *s.j.* '46 (NY)[EE] New York, NY Murray–Weigel Hall.
LaBauve, J. Joel '70 (BR) Napoleonville, LA St. Anne; Napoleonville, LA Assumption of the Blessed Virgin Mary.
LaBauve, Joel (NO)[A] St. Benedict, LA St. Joseph Seminary College.
Labbe, Clifton *s.v.d.* '69 (BEA) Diocesan College of Consultors; Livingston, TX St. Martin de Porres Mission; Livingston, TX St. Joseph; Presbyteral Council.
Labbe, Donavan J. '97 (LAF) Lydia, LA St. Nicholas; New Iberia, LA St. Marcellus.
Labbe, Jason M. '01 (BR) Belle Rose, LA St. Jules; Paincourtville, LA St. Elizabeth.
Labbe, Joseph P. '75 (CLV) Administrative Leave.
Labbe, Wilfred P. '99 (PRT)[M] Orono, ME University of Maine; Newman Apostolate; Diocesan Consultors; Old Town, ME Parish of the Resurrection of the Lord.
Labbe, Wilfred '99 (PRT) Campus Ministry.
Labedis, Anthony *o.f.m.conv.* (RCK) Rockford, IL St. Anthony of Padua.
Labella, Robert '54 (CLV) Retired.
LaBelle, Jeffrey T. *s.j.* '88 (MIL)[P] Milwaukee, WI Jesuit Community at Marquette University.
LaBelle, Joseph *o.m.i.* '92 (SAT)[C] Oblate School of Theology; [L] San Antonio, TX De Mazenod House.
LaBelle, Patrick *o.p.* '65 (SFR)[M] Menlo Park, CA Vallombrosa Center.
Labinski, Jacek '83 (TR) Trenton, NJ St. Hedwig.
Labinsky, Paul '81 (PHU) Cherry Hill, NJ SS. Peter and Paul.
Labita, Francis J. '49 (BRK) Brooklyn, NY St. Ephrem Retired.
Labo, Timothy P. '86 (ORL) Apopka, FL St. Francis of Assisi.
Laboe, Timothy A. '99 (DET) Graduate Studies.
Labonte, Richard H. '70 (WOR) Retired.
LaBonte, Roger A. *m.afr.* '62 (FgM) Washington, DC MISSIONARIES OF AFRICA.
Labonte, Roger '94 (LA) On Administrative Leave.
Labonte, Youville *m.afr.* '52 (SP)[N] St. Petersburg, FL Missionaries of Africa.
Laboon, Joseph D. '57 (PIT) Retired.
Laborde, Lucas '05 (P)[P] Corvallis, OR Newman Center at Oregon State University (Corvallis).

Labosky, James M. '79 (R) Special Assignment; Pinehurst, NC Sacred Heart.
LaBove, M. Keith '81 (LAF) Lafayette, LA St. Patrick; Diocesan Consultors; Hospitals.
Labrador, Rene '91 (DOD) LaCrosse, KS Holy Trinity Catholic Church of Timken, Kansas; LaCrosse, KS St. Michael Catholic Church of LaCrosse, Kansas; Liebenthal, KS St. Joseph Catholic Church of Liebenthal, Kansas.
LaBranch, Derek R. P. '07 (SAC) Williams, CA Sacred Heart; Air Force Reserve Chaplains.
LaBrecque, Frederick '67 (CHR) Conway, SC St. James.
LaBree, Paul '03 (PRT) Special or Other Diocesan Assignment.
Labrie, Jean–Paul '82 (PRT) Caribou, ME Parish of the Precious Blood; Deans.
LaBrie, Joseph *s.j.* '97 (LA)[C] Los Angeles, CA Jesuit Community.
Labrie, Ray J. '03 (MAN) Litchfield, NH St. Francis of Assisi; Manchester, NH St. Catherine.
Labrie, Robert G. '64 (BO) Pastoral Care; Salem, MA St. James.
LaBuda, David E. *m.m.* '71 (NY)[EE] Maryknoll Maryknoll Fathers and Brothers.
LaBurt, Brian '86 (SAV) Columbus, GA Our Lady of Lourdes; [H] Columbus, GA Our Lady of Lourdes; Presbyteral Council.
Labus, Gregory T. '06 (BWN) Mercedes, TX Our Lady of Mercy; San Juan Diego Lay Ministry Institute; Presbyteral Council.
LaCanne, Stephen J. '76 (STP) St. Joseph's Hospital; [H] St. Paul, MN HealthEast St. Joseph's Hospital; HealthEast, Inc. & HealthEast Hospice; Deanery 17.
La Casa, Vicente Paz en '66 (PBL) Westcliffe, CO Our Lady of the Assumption.
LaCasse, Andre–Joseph *o.p.* '92 (COL) Columbus, OH St. Patrick; Presbyteral Council; New York, NY.
Lacasse, Eugene *o.c.s.o.* '54 (WOR)[O] Spencer, MA St. Joseph's Abbey.
Lacasse, J.A. Roger '53 (PRO) Woonsocket, RI All Saints Parish.
LaCasse, James *s.j.* '74 (FRS)[A] Bakersfield, CA Garces Memorial High School.
LaCasse, John P. '74 (DET) Retired.
Lacasse, Roger '53 (PRO) Retired.
LaCaze, Rev. Msgr. J. Carson '57 (SHP) Ecumenism and Interreligious Affairs; Shreveport, LA St. John Berchmans Cathedral.
Lacerna, Rodolfo '68 (ELP) Van Horn, TX Our Lady of Fatima.
Lacey, Joseph P. *s.j.* '71 (BAL) Woodstock, MD St. Alphonsus Rodriguez.
Lacey, Mark W. '95 (ATL) Without Archdiocesan Assignment or Faculties.
Lacey, Michael '78 (OAK) Deanery #18; San Lorenzo, CA St. John the Baptist.
Lacey, Robert Edward '05 (SFS) Yankton, SD Sacred Heart.
Lacey, Thomas *c.ss.r.* '55 (TOL) Lima, OH St. Gerard.
LaChance, Charles P. '84 (CHI) Other Assignments.
LaChance, Matthew G. '03 (TLS) Cushing, OK SS. Peter and Paul; Cushing, OK St. John.
LaChance, Paul '68 (CHI)[N] Chicago, IL St. Peter's Friary.
LaChance, Roger '67 (B) Coeur d'Alene, ID St. Pius X; Catholic Scouts.
LaChance, Roger (B)[F] Coeur d'Alene, ID North Idaho College.
LaChapelle, Hector *m.s.* '68 (R) Shallotte, NC St. Brendan the Navigator.
LaCharite, Roger J. *s.s.e.* '55 (MOB)[G] Selma, AL Edmundite Fathers.
Lache Avila, Jose Rodolfo '81 (CHR) Columbia, SC Our Lady of the Hills.
Lachendro, Vincent *o.f.m.conv.* '63 (FgM)[S] Ellicott City Order of Friars Minor Conventual; Ellicott City, MD Province of Saint Anthony of Padua.
Lachica, Jose Nestor Pocong '02 (CC) Corpus Christi, TX St. Paul the Apostle.
Lachowicz, Francis B. '60 (PIT) Retired.
Lachowitzer, Charles V. '90 (STP) Eagan, MN St. John Neumann; [G] Eagan, MN Faithful Shepherd Catholic School.
Lack, Chris '90 (CIN) Cincinnati, OH St. Dominic.
Lackenmier, James R. *c.s.c.* '64 (FR)[L] North Easton, MA Wheaton College Newman Center; Wheaton College; [A] North Easton, MA Holy Cross Fathers Religious.
Lacki, Marek *o.s.p.p.e.* '06 (PH)[Y].
Lackie, Dan *o.f.m.* '96 (ORG)[I] Huntington Beach, CA Franciscan Friars.
Lackland, Anthony F. '06 (DAL) Vocations; Dallas, TX Christ the King.
Lackner, Bede *o.cist.* '52 (DAL)[J] Irving, TX Cistercian Abbey of Our Lady of Dallas.
Lackner, Joseph *s.m.* '72 (STL)[O] St. Louis, MO Marianists, Province of the United States (Society of Mary); [O] St. Louis, MO Marianist Community; Councilors:.
Lacomara, Aelred *c.p.* '57 (FgM) South River, NJ St. Paul of the Cross Province.
Lacomara, Aelred *c.p.* '57 (MET)[I] South River Passionist Provincial Office.
Lacombe, Robert E. '91 (PRO) Providence, RI St. Bartholomew.
LaCombe, Terrence '87 (GB) Military Chaplains.
LaCorte, Richard '87 (FAR) Grand Forks, ND Holy Family Church of Grand Forks Retired.
Lacovic, Lawrence L. '69 (ALT) Northern Cambria, PA Prince of Peace.
Lacre, Cormac '03 (SAC) On Duty Outside the Diocese.
LaCroix, Charles '05 (FAR)[B] Fargo, ND Shanley High School and Sullivan Middle School; Special Assignment; Fargo, ND Sts. Anne & Joachim Church of Fargo.
Lacroix, Daniel W. '88 (FR) Hyannis, MA St. Francis Xavier's; Auditors.
Lacroix, Maurice R. '53 (MAN)[L] Manchester, NH Monastery of the Precious Blood; DEPARTMENT OF VETERANS AFFAIRS HOSPITALS AND CHAPLAINS Retired.
LaCroix, Robert A. '98 (DET) Dearborn Heights, MI St. Linus.
Lacroix, Stephen A. *c.s.c.* '08 (FTW) South Bend, IN Christ the King.
LaCroix, Wilfred L. *s.j.* '69 (KC)[J] Kansas City, MO Rockhurst Jesuit Community.
LaCruz, Cecilio *sch.p.* '59 (SJN) San Juan, PR Santisimo Salvador; [B] San Juan, PR Colegio Calasanz.
Lacson, Luis Antonio '86 (LA)[J] Burbank, CA Providence Saint Joseph Medical Center.
Lacson, Luis Antonio '86 (SR)[F] Napa, CA Queen of the Valley Medical Center.
LaCuesta, Don A. '06 (DET) Waterford, MI Our Lady of the Lakes; Presbyteral Council.
Lacy, Aidan '93 (PMB) Released from Diocesan Assignment.
Laczko, Rev. Msgr. T. Ansgar '60 (WDC) Washington, DC Assumption; Washington, DC Holy Comforter—St. Cyprian Retired.
Ladamus, Robert G. '70 (HRT) Retired.
Ladd, John O. '79 (GAY) Retired.
Ladda, Paul (BUF) Buffalo, NY Holy Cross.
Ladish, Robert W. '53 (HRT) Retired.
Ladkau, William D. '84 (CHR) Columbia, SC Good Shepherd.
Ladzinski, Rev. Msgr. Casimir H. '62 (TR) Ocean County; Bay Head, NJ Sacred Heart.
Laenen, Henry A. *o.m.i.* '52 (GAL) Alvin, TX St. John the Baptist.
Laenen, Joseph C. *o.praem.* '51 (PH)[Y] Paoli, PA Daylesford Abbey; [S] Darby, PA Mercy Fitzgerald Hospital.
LaFache, Anthony '68 (SY) Utica, NY St. Anthony of Padua.
Laferrera, Rev. Msgr. John J. '73 (NEW) Members; Holy Name Federation; Livingston, NJ St. Philomena.
Laferrera, Robert G. '88 (NEW) Dumont, NJ St. Mary's.
Laferty, Charles P. *o.s.a.* '53 (PH)[C] Villanova University; [Y] Villanova, PA St. Thomas Monastery.
Lafey, Kevin *o.carm* '72 (JOL) Glendale Heights, IL St. Matthew.
Lafferty, Charles L. '55 (BAL) Forest Hill, MD St. Ignatius Retired.
Lafferty, David M. '85 (OKL) Okarche, OK Holy Trinity.
Lafferty, Owen J. '66 (NY) New York, NY Holy Innocents.
Laffey, Matthew T. *o.s.b.* '00 (ALT)[I] University Park, PA Penn State University, University Park; [J] University Park, PA Penn State Catholic Community.
LaFlamme, Julien J. '58 (BUR) Retired.
La Flamme, Steven L. '09 (DUL) Brainerd, MN St. Andrew; Brainerd, MN St. Francis; Brainerd, MN St. Mathias.
LaFleur, Gerard A. '53 (SPR) Chicopee, MA Assumption Retired.
LaFleur, Paul J. '85 (LAF) Breaux Bridge, LA St. Bernard.
Lafond, Donald E. '62 (MAN) Catholic Medical Center Retired.
Lafontaine, James F. *s.j.* '87 (PRT)[I] Portland, ME St. Ignatius Residence (The Jesuits of Maine); Portland, ME St. Patrick's; Portland, ME St. Pius X; Members.
LaFontaine, Paul A. '72 (STP) St. Anthony, MN St. Charles Borromeo.
Laforet, Albert '02 (AUS) Austin, TX St. Mary Cathedral.
LaForge, Paul *s.v.d.* '58 (DUB)[B] Epworth, IA Divine Word College.
LaFramboise, Ronald F. *o.m.i.* '67 (BUF) Buffalo, NY Holy Angels.
Laframboise, Ross '03 (FAR) Napoleon, ND St. Philip's Church of Napoleon; Diocesan College of Consultors; Deanery 8.
LaFrance, Valerian *o.p.* '58 (WDC) Washington, DC St. Dominic Church & Priory.
La Fratta, William '63 (RIC) Retired.
LaFreniere, Thomas '09 (PMB) Palm Springs, FL St. Luke.
Lafrenz, James '54 (ELP) Retired.
Lafrenz, James '54 (LSC) Retired.
Lagacé, Raymond R. *o.f.m.* '59 (PRT) Togus, ME Togus VA Medical Center; DEPARTMENT OF VETERANS AFFAIRS HOSPITALS AND CHAPLAINS.
Lagan, Hugh *s.m.a.* '90 (BO)[U] Dedham, MA African Mission House.
Lager, John *o.f.m.cap.* '79 (DEN)[N] Denver, CO St. Francis of Assisi Friary; Denver, CO; [N] Denver, CO Capuchin Province of Mid–America, Inc.
Lagges, Patrick R. '77 (CHI) College of Consultors; Judges.
Lagges, Patrick R. '77 (TUC) Promoter of Justice – Penal Cases.
Lagges, Patrick (CHI)[U] Chicago, IL University of Chicago Calvert House.
Laghezza, Pasquale V. *ss.cc.* '60 (MO) DEPARTMENT OF VETERANS AFFAIRS HOSPITALS AND CHAPLAINS.
Laghezza, Pasquale V. *ss.cc.* '60 (NY) New York, NY New York City Veterans Administration Hospital; Manhattan, NY U.S.V.A. Medical Center.
Laghezza, Pasquale V. *ss.cc.* '60 (LA)[P] La Verne, CA Congregation of the Sacred Hearts of Jesus and Mary.
Lagiovane, John M. '92 (NY)[E] Poughkeepsie, NY Our Lady of Lourdes High School; [E] Poughkeepsie, NY Our Lady of Lourdes High School; Hyde Park, NY Regina Coeli.
Lago, Danilo *s.x.* '77 (PAT)[N] Wayne Xaverian Missionary Fathers; Wayne, NJ XAVERIAN MISSIONARY FATHERS.
Lagoa, Raul M. '79 (FR) Somerset, MA St. John of God.
Lagodinski, Dale '72 (FAR) Wahpeton, ND St. John's Church of Wahpeton; [I] Wahpeton, ND State College of Science Newman Student Parish; Deanery 1.
La Goe, John P. '61 (GR) Retired.
Lagomarsino, John *s.s.c.* '70 (OM)[K] St. Columbans Missionary Society of St. Columban.
Lagrimas, Miguelito (NY) New York, NY St. Teresa.
Laguna–Vargas, Enrique *o.carm.* '90 (JOL)[L] Darien Carmelite Provincial Office.
Lagunilla, Ariel R. '06 (SAN) Big Spring, TX Holy Trinity Parish.
Lagura, Florencio (PT) Crestview, FL Our Lady of Victory.
Lagututta, Nunzio J. '78 (SJ) On Leave of Absence.
Lah, Peter *s.j.* '95 (STL)[O] St. Louis, MO Leo Brown Jesuit Community.
Lahart, Daniel K. *s.j.* '94 (GAL)[E] Houston, TX Strake Jesuit College Preparatory Inc.; Elected Members.
Lahens, Albert '95 (MIA) Pompano Beach, FL San Isidro.
Lahey, Piers M. '82 (SFR) Pacifica, CA Good Shepherd.
LaHood, Thomas G. (WDC) Leonardtown, MD Our Lady's.
Lahoud, Rev. Msgr. Joseph F. '59 (SAM) Jamaica Plain, MA Our Lady of the Cedars of Lebanon.
Lai, Doan Van '73 (SD) San Diego, CA Holy Spirit; Vietnamese.
Laible, Jeffrey G. '88 (MO) Lincoln, IL Holy Family; Air National Guard Chaplains.
Laicha, Michael '89 (HBG)[F] Danville, PA Holy Family Convent and Infirmary.
Laing, Vincent Thu '87 (SAL) New Almelo, KS St. Joseph Parish; Norton, KS St. Francis of Assisi Parish.
Laini, Valerian '69 (CHI) Libertyville, IL St. Joseph.
Laird, Kenneth W. '75 (BR) Retired.
Laird, Martin L. '08 (ALX) Alexandria, LA Our Lady of Prompt Succor; Hispanic Ministry.
Laird, Martin S. *o.s.a.* '90 (PH)[Y] Villanova, PA St. Thomas Monastery.
Laird, Martin *o.s.a.* '81 (PH)[C] Villanova University.
Laird, Peter A. '97 (STP) Archdiocesan Finance Council (AFC); College of Consultors.
Laird, Peter A. '97 (STP)[A] Saint Paul, MN The Saint Paul Seminary; [C] St. Paul, MN University of St. Thomas; [S] West St. Paul, MN Saint Paul's Outreach, Inc.; Office of Vicar General and Moderator of the Curia; Ex Officio; Archbishop's Commission on Bio–Medical Ethics.
Laird, William F. '75 (ROC) Macedon, NY St. Patrick; Censores Librorum; Priest Consultors; Palmyra, NY St. Anne; Palmyra, NY St. Gregory.
Laiton, Rafael '91 (RCK) Carpentersville, IL St. Monica.
Lajack, Edward F. '68 (CLV) Absent on Sick Leave.
Lajack, Jerome M. '66 (CLV) Cleveland, OH St. Wendelin.
Lajiness, Todd '95 (DET)[A] Detroit, MI Sacred Heart Major Seminary, Inc.
Lajo, Saturnino *o.m.i.* '63 (SAT)[R] San Antonio, TX Oblate Lourdes Grotto Shrine of the Southwest, Tepeyac de San Antonio; [S] San Antonio, TX Oblate Missions.
Lajoie, Marcel *s.m.* '56 (BO)[U] Boston, MA Marist Fathers Lourdes Residence; [Z] Boston, MA Marist Fathers Residence.
Lajoie, Roland *s.m.* '74 (BO)[U] Boston, MA Marist Fathers and Brothers Provincial House.
Lakers, John J. *o.f.m.* '58 (SFD)[B] Quincy, IL Quincy University; [L] Quincy, IL Holy Cross Friary Retired.

Lakkineni, Arogyaswamy '00 (RCK) McHenry, IL St. Patrick.
Lakra, Albert '87 (BAK) Pilot Rock, OR St. Helen.
Lakra, Nonatus '91 (LAN) Owosso, MI St. Paul.
Lakra, Prabhu '02 (LAN) Lansing, MI St. Gerard.
Laksana, Albertus Bagus *s.j.* '03 (BO)[U] Newton, MA The Jesuit Community at Boston College.
Laliberte, George G. '56 (HRT) Retired.
Laliberte, Rev. Msgr. Robert '73 (FAR) Censor Librorum; Fargo, ND St. Anthony of Padua's Church of Fargo.
Lalic, Paul '58 (BGP) Retired.
Lalli, Tony B. *s.x.* '66 (BO)[U] Holliston, MA Xaverian Missionaries.
Lally, Brendan G. *s.j.* '77 (BAL)[S] Towson Maryland Province of the Society of Jesus.
Lally, Rev. Msgr. Dennis M. '65 (GB) New London, WI St. Patrick.
Lally, Joachim *c.s.p.* '65 (GR) Presbyteral Council; Grand Rapids, MI Cathedral of St. Andrew.
Lally, Martin '78 (DEN) Aurora, CO Queen of Peace.
Lally, Owen *c.p.* '59 (BRK)[T] Jamaica, NY Immaculate Conception Monastery.
Lally, Owen *c.p.* '59 (NY)[II] Jamaica, NY The Fellowship of the Beloved Disciple.
Lalonde, Venant *o.f.m.* '54 (SP)[N] St. Petersburg, FL St. Anthony Friary.
Lalor, Thomas '66 (JKS) Priests' Council; Tupelo, MS St. James; Diocesan Consultors.
Lam, Hoang Chi '06 (DET) Clawson, MI Guardian Angels.
Lam, John *s.d.b.* '71 (LA) Los Angeles, CA St. Bridget's Chinese Catholic Church; [P] Los Angeles, CA Dominic Savio Salesian Residence.
Lam, Peter Vu '04 (SD) Oceanside, CA Tri City Hospital; Vista, CA St. Francis of Assisi.
Lam, Theo '08 (GAL) Houston, TX Prince of Peace.
Lama, Michael '84 (SB) Adelanto, CA Christ the Good Shepherd; Appointed Members; High Desert; College of Consultors.
Lamanna, Alfred '49 (ALB) Retired.
Lamanna, Thomas J. *s.j.* '97 (P)[A] Portland, OR Jesuit Novitiate of Sheridan Orgeon.
LaMar, Joseph P. *m.m.* '83 (NY)[EE] Maryknoll Maryknoll Fathers and Brothers Retired.
LaMartina, Liborio J. *s.j.* '67 (BAL)[S] Towson, MD Maryland Province of the Society of Jesus; Towson, MD; [S] Baltimore, MD Colombiere Jesuit Community.
Lamas, Rodolfo '80 (SJN) Caguas, PR Divino Nino Jesus; Subcommission for Sacred Art.
LaMazza, Carmen G. *m.m.* '55 (SJ)[M] Los Altos, CA Maryknoll.
Lamb, Bruce *o.f.m.conv.* '89 (RNO) Reno, NV St. Thomas Aquinas Cathedral.
Lamb, Gary E. '83 (MEM) Lexington, TN St. Andrew the Apostle.
Lamb, Louis J. '61 (OKL) Retired.
Lamb, Matthew L. '62 (MIL) On Duty Outside the Archdiocese.
Lamb, Patrick H. '83 (ALN) Pen Argyl, PA St. Elizabeth of Hungary; [C] Bangor, PA Pius X High School; Forks of the Delaware Serra.
Lamb, Paul T. '96 (FR) Retired.
Lamb, Thomas J. '71 (BO)[T] Cambridge, MA Opus Dei, Prelature of the Holy Cross and Opus Dei; Cambridge.
Lamb, Wes '81 (SAV) Springfield, GA St. Boniface Church.
Lam Ba Trong, Philip M. *c.m.c.* '08 (SPC) Springfield, MO Cathedral of St. Agnes; [B] Springfield, MO Springfield Catholic High School.
Lambeck, Robert W. *s.j.* '49 (MIL)[P] Wauwatosa, WI Jesuit Community at St. Camillus.
Lambelho, Jose Fernando '84 (LA) Cursillo Movement.
Lamberson, Bryan '00 (L) Unassigned.
Lambert, Cornelius F. '83 (CAM) Retired.
Lambert, Curtis '74 (CHI) Prospect Heights, IL St. Alphonsus Liguori.
Lambert, James J. '80 (PT) Retired.
Lambert, James L. *s.j.* '66 (LAF) Council of Priests; Grand Coteau, LA St. Charles Borromeo.
Lambert, John C. '84 (SCR) Conyngham, PA St. John Bosco; Drums, PA Church of the Good Shepherd.
Lambert, Louis *s.j.* '66 (ELP) El Paso, TX Sacred Heart.
Lambert, Paul Francis '09 (PT) Gulf Breeze, FL St. Ann.
Lambert, Richard D. '80 (CR) Commission on Building and Planning.
Lambert, Richard I. '75 (PBR) Youngstown, OH Assumption of the Blessed Virgin; Consultors; Protopresbyters.
Lambert, Rick '80 (CR) Thief River Falls, MN St. Bernards; Priests' Personnel Board; Priests' Council.
Lambert, Timothy J. '92 (MET) Bridgewater, NJ St. Bernard of Clairvaux.
Lambeth, K. Michael '94 (TR) Tuckerton, NJ St. Theresa.
Lambro, Edward (PAT) Secretariat for Catholic Charities; Special Assignment.
Lamela, Juan *c.m.* '62 (PCE) Ponce, PR La Milagrosa.
Lamendola, Salvatore R. '90 (GBG) Avonmore, PA St. Matthew; Slickville, PA St. Sylvester; Avonmore, PA St. Ambrose.
LaMere, Cletus *s.d.s.* (MIL)[P] Milwaukee, WI Salvatorians – Jordan Hall Retired.
Lamica, Alan J. '78 (OG) Malone, NY Barehill Correctional Facility; Ray Brook, NY Federal Correctional Institution; [G] Our Lady of the Adirondacks Community; Advocates; Tupper Lake, NY Sunmount Developmental Center.
Lamitie, James F. '53 (OG) Retired.
Lamitie, Robert O. '57 (OG) Retired.
Lamm, Timothy J. *o.s.b.* '54 (SEA)[L] Lacey, WA St. Martin's Abbey.
Lamm, William *s.j.* '44 (SCR)[C] Scranton, PA The University of Scranton.
Lammeier, Francis G. '55 (CIN) Judges Retired.
Lammers, Rev. Msgr. Donald W. '66 (JC) Russellville, MO St. Michael; Personnel Board.
Lammers, Ralph A. '63 (OM) Retired.
Lammert, Edward H. *o.f.m.* '58 (LEX) Cumberland, KY St. Stephen; Harlan, KY Holy Trinity; Cumberland, KY Church of the Resurrection.
LaMoine, Gary '81 (CR) Barnesville, MN Assumption; Priests Retirement Board of Trustees; Finance Council; Priests' Council.
Lamonde, Rev. Msgr. Joseph R. '74 (PIT) On Duty Outside the Diocese.
LaMontagne, Bernard L. '63 (PRO) On Duty Outside the Diocese.
Lamore, Victor E. '80 (OG) Gabriels, NY Gabriel's Correctional Facility; Ray Brook, NY Adirondack Correctional Facility.
LaMorte, Joseph P. '81 (MO) Poughkeepsie, NY Holy Trinity; Air National Guard Chaplains; Priests Council of the Archdiocese of New York.
LaMorte, Richard '66 (NY)[HH] Poughkeepsie, NY Marist College.
Lamothe, C. Romero '48 (WOR) Retired.
Lamothe, Daniel O. '62 (MAN) Keene, NH St. Bernard; Keene, NH St. Margaret Mary; Keene, NH Immaculate Conception; Cheshire County House of Corrections; Vicars Forane; Keene, NH Mary, Queen of Peace Parish.
Lamothe, Donat R. *a.a.* '62 (WOR)[O] Worcester, MA Assumptionists of Assumption College.
LaMothe, Philip R. '55 (BUR) Retired.
Lamoureux, Matthew *m.i.c.* '05 (JOL) Plano, IL St. Mary; Yorkville, IL St. Patrick.
Lamoureux, Richard *a.a.* '71 (BO)[U] Boston Assumptionist Center.
Lamoureux, Roger E. *o.m.i.* '83 (NOR)[G] Willimantic, CT Missionary Oblates of Mary Immaculate.
Lamoureux, Roger J. *o.m.i.* '59 (NOR) Willimantic, CT St. Mary; Defenders of the Bond.
Lamp, Edward '82 (SP) On Duty Outside the Diocese; DEPARTMENT OF VETERANS AFFAIRS HOSPITALS AND CHAPLAINS.
Lampe, Rev. Msgr. Irvin F. '43 (WCH) Retired.
Lampert, Robert E. '65 (STL) Retired.
Lampert, Robert E. '65 (SAT) Retired.
Lampert, Vincent '91 (IND) Greenwood, IN SS. Francis and Clare of Assisi; Archdiocesan Judges.
Lam Phan, Anthony '62 (OAK) Oakland, CA St. Lawrence O'Toole–St. Cyril of Jerusalem.
Lamping, Thomas E. '84 (CHI) Chicago, IL Queen of Angels; Summit, IL St. Joseph.
Lampitt, Robert '08 (PEO) Champaign, IL St. Matthew.
Lamprea, Gefford C. '00 (SPC) Buffalo, MO St. William; Conway, MO Sacred Heart.
Lampron, Alfred J. '75 (PAT) Wharton, NJ St. Bernard's.
Lampron, Maurice W. '63 (MAN) Retired.
Lamus, Luis Antonio Diaz *c.s.* '98 (NY) Mt. Vernon, NY Our Lady of Victory.
Lamy, Raymond J. '81 (MAN) Absent on Leave.
Lamy, Robert E. *c.m.* '51 (STL)[O] Perryville, MO Congregation of the Mission.
Lan, Augustine Pham Van '63 (CLV) Vietnamese–American Apostolate.
Lanahan, Daniel *o.f.m.* '62 (NEW)[M] East Rutherford, NJ Sacred Heart Friary.
Lancaster, Leo '54 (WOR) Shrewsbury, MA St. Mary's.
Lancaster, Robert '99 (SFE) Albuquerque, NM Sangre de Cristo.
Lancellotti, Vincent A. '68 (NY)[EE] Bronx, NY John Cardinal O'Connor Residence Retired.
Landa, Florencio *c.p.* '63 (SJN) Carolina, PR Nuestra Senora de la Piedad.
Landa, Salvador '94 (ORG) Santa Ana, CA St. Anne's.
Landauer, Joseph P. '78 (POD) Chicago.
Landauer, Joseph P. '78 (CHI) Chicago, IL St. Mary of the Angels; [V] Chicago, IL Midtown Residence.
Landenwitch, Shawn R. '09 (CIN) Cincinnati, OH St. Ann.
Lander, Mark C. '00 (SB) Victorville, CA Holy Innocents; Elected Members.
Landewe, Robert A. '59 (SPC) Retired.
Landeza, Jayson J. '87 (OAK) On Sabbatical.
Landgraff, Thomas A. *o.s.f.s.* '64 (TOL)[C] Toledo, OH St. Francis de Sales High School; [I] Toledo, OH.
Landherr, Clayton '91 (DUB) On Leave of Absence (Not Authorized for Priestly Ministry).
Landi, Lodovico Joseph '90 (SFR) San Francisco, CA St. Cecilia.
Landicho, Rey D. '97 (WH) Williamson, WV Sacred Heart; Nitro, WV Holy Trinity.
Landis, Gabriel *o.s.b.* '04 (KCK) Hiawatha, KS St. Ann's; [I] Atchison, KS St. Benedict's Abbey.
Lando, Camillo *c.s.* '66 (PRO) Providence, RI Holy Ghost.
Landolfi, Paul J. *s.m.* (BRK)[M] Rockaway Park, NY St. John's Residence & School for Boys.
Landrau–Roman, Jose A. (SJN) Instructors.
Landreau, Edward Joseph '57 (LA) Azusa, CA St. Frances of Rome Retired.
Landreville, Norbert B. '58 (MAR) Retired.
Landry, Bartholomew K. *c.s.p.* '07 (SFR) San Francisco, CA Old St. Mary's Cathedral.
Landry, Charles R. '83 (BR) St. Gabriel, LA St. Gabriel the Archangel; Presbyteral Council.
Landry, Francis *c.p.* '76 (SCR) Scranton, PA St. Ann's Basilica Parish; [M] Scranton, PA Saint Ann's Passionist Monastery.
Landry, Gary S. *c.m.* '73 (LA)[P] Montebello, CA DePaul Evangelization Center; [V] Montebello, CA DePaul Evangelization Center.
Landry, Keith '08 (LAF) Broussard, LA Sacred Heart of Jesus.
Landry, Leroy *o.m.i.* '61 (PRT) Howland, ME St. Leo The Great.
Landry, Oneil Anthony '47 (LAF) Retired.
Landry, Philip G. '88 (NO) Deans; Worship Office; Liturgical Commission; New Orleans, LA St. Francis of Assisi.
Landry, Ralph James '62 (LAF) Retired.
Landry, Richard B. *m.s.* '69 (PH) Newtown, PA St. Andrew.
Landry, Richard *m.s.* '69 (MAN)[N] Enfield, NH Shrine of Our Lady of La Salette; [K] Enfield, NH Shrine of Our Lady of La Salette.
Landry, Roger J. '99 (FR) New Bedford, MA St. Anthony of Padua's; Diocesan Newspaper.
Landry, Thomas '83 (WOR) On Medical Leave of Absence.
Landsberger, Nicholas '61 (SCL) Little Falls, MN Holy Family; Little Falls, MN St. Mary; Defensor Vinculi; Directors.
Landsberger, Robert '57 (SCL) Directors; Holdingford, MN St. Columbkille's Retired.
Landwerlen, Paul E. '54 (IND) Shelbyville, IN St. Vincent de Paul; Greensburg, IN Immaculate Conception; Greensburg, IN St. Denis.
Landy, Joseph V. *s.j.* '54 (NY)[EE] New York, NY Murray–Weigel Hall.
Lane, Brian '89 (RC) Eagle Butte, SD All Saints; [E] Eagle Butte, SD CPT, Inc.; Diocesan Consultors; Diocesan Finance Council.
Lane, Edmund C. *s.s.p.* '64 (NY)[B] Staten Island, NY Society of St. Paul; Staten Island, NY.
Lane, Rev. Msgr. Frank P. '67 (COL) Diocesan Judges Retired.
Lane, George A. *s.j.* '67 (CHI)[N] Chicago, IL Woodlawn Jesuit Community; [W] Chicago, IL Loyola Press.
Lane, James M. '07 (VNN) Secretary for the Presbyteral Council & The College of Consultors.
Lane, James '07 (VNN) San Luis Obispo, CA Saint Anne.
Lane, John Thomas *s.s.s.* '92 (CLV) Highland Heights, OH St. Paschal Baylon; [N] Cleveland, OH Congregation of the Blessed Sacrament.
Lane, Mark J. *c.o.* '83 (BRK) Brooklyn, NY St. Boniface; [T] Brooklyn, NY Oratory of Saint Philip Neri, Congregation Pontifical Rite.
Lane, Rev. Msgr. Mark Richard '74 (RIC) Vicar for Clergy; Bishop's Administrative Advisory Council.
Lane, Michael '74 (JOL) Joliet, IL St. Jude; Deans.
Lane, Robert C. '69 (STL) St. Peters, MO All Saints.
Lane, Thomas J. '90 (BAL)[A] Emmitsburg, MD Mount St. Mary's Seminary.
Lane, Thomas V. '64 (YAK) Yakima, WA Holy Family Retired.
Lane, Timothy R. *c.j.* '95 (LA)[B] Santa Maria, CA St. Joseph Seminary (Josephite Fathers' Novitiate).
Lane, William '50 (SEA) Retired.
Lanergan, James F. '61 (BO) Senior Priests. Retired.
Lanese, Pasquale *o.m.i.* '53 (BWN) Brownsville, TX Immaculate Conception Cathedral Retired.
Lang, Arnold *s.v.d.* '53 (WH) Gassaway, WV St. Thomas.
Lang, Arnold *s.v.d.* '53 (CHI)[N] Techny, IL Divine Word Residence.
Lang, Brian G. '98 (SY) Syracuse, NY St. Ann; Syracuse, NY St. Charles Borromeo.
Lang, Rev. Msgr. Charles E. '65 (DUB)[C] Dubuque, IA Loras College Retired.
Lang, Charles F. '75 (CIN) Fairborn, OH Mary Help of Christians.
Lang, Frederick *c.pp.s.* '54 (CIN)[N] Carthagena, OH St. Charles Retired.
Lang, Henry A. '46 (BRK) Bayside, NY St. Robert Bellarmine Retired.

Lang, Hugh J. '56 (PIT) Pittsburgh, PA St. Anne Retired.
Lang, James P. '75 (SY) Syracuse, NY St. James; Special Assignment; Board of Diocesan Consultors; Management Team; Presbyteral Council; Vicar for Parishes; Boy Scouts/Girl Scouts; Building Commission; Priests' Personnel Committee.
Lang, James Paul '75 (Y) Windham, OH St. Michael's.
Lang, Joseph R. *m.m.* '52 (NY)[EE] Retired.
Lang, Joseph '65 (CLV) Life of Prayer and Penance.
Lang, Joseph '05 (DET) Royal Oak, MI National Shrine of the Little Flower.
Lang, Leonard P. '75 (TR) Leave of Absence.
Lang, Michael P. '92 (TR) Millstone Township, NJ St. Joseph.
Langa, Daniel J. '09 (PIT) Pittsburgh, PA St. Louise de Marillac; Priest Council.
Langan, John P. *s.j.* '72 (WDC)[N] Washington, DC The Jesuit Community at Georgetown University; [N] Washington, DC The Jesuit Community at Georgetown University.
Langan, Thomas '59 (HBG) Retired.
Langan, Vincent F. '60 (SCR) Retired.
Langan, William J.P. '77 (SCR) Honesdale, PA St. John the Evangelist; Navy Reserve Chaplains.
Langdon, Robert H. '56 (NEW)[M] Rutherford, NJ St. John Vianney Residence for Priests Retired.
Lange, Donald F. '70 (MAD) Retired.
Lange, George O. '57 (WOR) Retired.
Lange, John J. *m.m.* '58 (FgM) Maryknoll, NY MARYKNOLL.
Lange, John W. *s.j.* '61 (SCR)[C] Scranton, PA The University of Scranton.
Lange, Joshua L. '09 (COV)[B] Alexandria, KY Bishop Brossart High School; Cold Spring, KY St. Joseph.
Lange, Milton R. '52 (LR) Retired.
Lange, Robert A. '86 (ARL) Retired.
Lange, Ronald *s.v.d.* '71 (FgM) Techny, IL.
Lange, Steven J. '02 (RCK) Rochelle, IL St. Patrick.
Lange, Theodore Severin '09 (P) Special Assignment.
Lange, Timothy J. '61 (OM) Retired.
Lange, William S. '92 (PH) Aston, PA St. Joseph.
Langelier, Rev. Msgr. Gerald J. '61 (BRK) Forest Hills, NY Our Lady of Mercy Retired.
Langenbrunner, Norman W. '77 (CIN) Judges.
Langenbrunner, Norman '70 (CIN) Retired.
Langenderfer, Carl J. *o.f.m.* '71 (CIN) Priest Councilors; [C] Cincinnati, OH St. Anthony Shrine, Franciscan Postulancy.
Langenfeld, Thomas G. *c.s.v.* '60 (CHI)[N] Arlington Heights Viatorian Province Center–Clerics of St. Viator.
Langenkamp, August *s.v.d.* '57 (CHI)[N] Techny, IL Divine Word Residence.
Langford, Terry L. '96 (MO) On Duty Outside the Archdiocese; DEPARTMENT OF VETERANS AFFAIRS HOSPITALS AND CHAPLAINS.
Langford, Terry L. (CHI) Hines V.A. Hospital.
Langhans, Victor E. '84 (HEL) Kalispell, MT St. Matthew.
Langheim, Albert *o.f.m.* '55 (GAY) Indian River, MI Cross in the Woods Catholic Shrine.
Langhorst, Randall L. '92 (LIN) Seward, NE St. Vincent de Paul.
Langille, Justin '80 (SD) El Cajon, CA St. Louise de Marillac.
Langley, Barry J. *o.f.m.* '94 (BO)[Z] Boston, MA St. Anthony Shrine.
Langley, Terence *s.c.j.* '79 (JKS) Olive Branch, MS Queen of Peace.
Langlois, Charles '96 (LAF) New Iberia, LA St. Peter; Ecumenism.
Langlois, Frederick M. '91 (HRT) New Milford, CT Our Lady of the Lakes; [U] New Milford, CT Our Lady of the Lakes Corporation.
Langlois, John A. *o.p.* '91 (WDC)[B] Washington, DC Dominican House of Studies.
Langlois, William A. '74 (GR) Grand Haven, MI St. Patrick's.
Langner, Donald '08 (KC)[C] St. Joseph, MO Bishop LeBlond High School.
Langner, Douglas '08 (KC) St. Joseph, MO St. Mary's.
Langone, Robert *s.a.* '89 (NY)[EE] Garrison, NY Franciscan Friars of the Atonement.
Langsch, Gerold M. '72 (MIL)[T] Waukesha, WI Schoenstatt Fathers.
Langsdorf, Karl *s.p.s.* '72 (CHI)[N] Chicago, IL St. Patrick's Missionary Society; Saratoga, CA.
Langston, Micheas *o.s.b.* '65 (IND)[K] St. Meinrad St. Meinrad Archabbey.
Langton, Bernard F. *o.p.* '69 (PRO)[P] Providence St. Thomas Aquinas Priory at Providence College.
Lankeit, John '06 (PHX) Tolleson, AZ Blessed Sacrament Roman Catholic Parish; College of Consultors; Presbyteral Council.
Lankenau, Thomas *s.j.* '04 (P) Portland, OR; [L] Portland, OR Jesuit Provincial Office (Society of Jesus, Oregon Prov.).
Lankenau, Thomas *s.j.* '04 (P)[L] Portland, OR Colombiere Community.
Lankford, Michael G. '92 (MO) On Duty Outside the Diocese; DEPARTMENT OF VETERANS AFFAIRS HOSPITALS AND CHAPLAINS.
Lankford, Michael '92 (TR)[T] West Long Branch, NJ Catholic Center at Monmouth University.
Lanning, Michael J. '78 (CLV) Fairview Park, OH St. Angela Merici.
Lannon, Timothy R. *s.j.* '86 (PH)[Y] Loyola Center and Manresa Hall; [C] Jesuit Fathers.
LaNoue, Bertrand *o.s.b.* '52 (KCK) Atchison, KS St. Joseph's; Atchison, KS St. Patrick's; [I] Atchison, KS St. Benedict's Abbey.
Lanoue, Marc L. '09 (BAL) Glyndon, MD Sacred Heart.
Lansang, Ferdinand *o.carm.* '96 (LA) North Hollywood, CA St. Jane Frances de Chantal.
Lantigua, Ramon Fco. Garcia '01 (PCE)[H] Coto Laurel, PR Diocesan Fathers of Schoenstatt–Santuary of Schoenstatt.
Lantry, Jerome *o.c.d.* '46 (LA) Alhambra, CA St. Therese.
Lantry, Stephen C. *s.j.* '81 (SEA) Tacoma, WA St. Leo the Great.
Lantry, Stephen C. *s.j.* '81 (P)[L] Portland, OR Jesuit Provincial Office (Society of Jesus, Oregon Prov.).
Lantsberger, James *o.m.i.* '57 (SR) Imola, CA Napa State Hospital.
Lantsberger, John '76 (SFS) Watertown, SD Holy Name; Tribunal Judges; Personnel Board.
Lantz, Rev. Msgr. David S. '78 (SFD) Springfield, IL Christ The King; [C] Springfield, IL Springfield College in Illinois; Office for the Diaconate; Office for Ministry Formation.
Lantz, Gary *s.c.j.* '78 (SFS) Retired.
Lanuevo, Edwin C. '94 (NY) Staten Island, NY Our Lady of Pity.
Lanuevo, Victor '75 (MO) On Duty Outside the Diocese; Army Chaplains.
Lanz, Matt '94 (FAR) Retired.
Lanza, Daniel A. *m.m.* '59 (NY)[EE] Retired.
Lanza, Steven M. '81 (CHI) Tinley Park, IL Saint Julie Billiart.
Lanzaderas, Francisco (NY) Staten Island, NY Blessed Sacrament.
Lanzalaco, Joseph M. *c.s.b.* '87 (ROC)[J] Rochester, NY Basilian Residence; [M] Rochester, NY St. John Fisher College.
Lanzrath, Curt *o.f.m.* '54 (CIN)[N] Cincinnati St. Francis Seraph Friary Retired.
Lanzrath, John P. '88 (WCH) Presbyteral Council/ College of Consultors; Ongoing Formation of the Clergy Committee; Stewardship Office.
Lap, Gilbert D. '03 (RVC) West Babylon, NY Our Lady of Grace.
LaPalme, Paul M. '97 (WOR) Millbury, MA St. Brigid; Deans; Presbyteral Council.
La Pan, Kenneth *t.o.r.* '52 (ALT)[G] Newry, PA St. Bernardine Monastery Retired.
LaPastina, Cyprian P. '97 (BGP) Stamford, CT St. Gabriel.
LaPata, Richard C. *o.p.* '59 (CHI)[D] Oak Park, IL Fenwick High School; [N] River Forest, IL St. Thomas Aquinas Priory.
La Patka, Gerald '56 (DUL) Retired.
Lapauw, Joseph A. *c.i.c.m.* '73 (R) Wendell, NC St. Eugene.
La Paz, Rev. Msgr. Gabriel '78 (NY) New York, NY Incarnation; Manhattan (North).
Lape, Lydell T. '90 (OM) Columbus, NE St. Anthony.
Lape, Steven W. '99 (ROC) East Rochester, NY St. Jerome.
Lapensky, John G. '77 (STP) Veseli, MN Most Holy Trinity.
LaPenta, Charles A. *o.s.f.s.* '54 (TOL)[C] Toledo, OH St. Francis de Sales High School Retired.
Lapera, John M. '84 (SCR) Kingston, PA St. Ignatius Loyola, Kingston; Kingston, PA St. Mary's Annunciation; Deans; Diocesan Building Commission.
Laperle, Theodore R. '54 (WOR) Fitchburg, MA St. Bernard Retired.
LaPlante, Bob J. '95 (CR) Detroit Lakes, MN St. Mary of the Lakes; Lake Park, MN St. Francis Xavier's.
La Plante, David W. '78 (MIL) Hartford, WI St. Kilian.
LaPlante, David W. '78 (OM) On Duty Outside the Archdiocese.
LaPlante, Eugene *a.a.* '58 (WOR)[O] Worcester, MA Assumptionists (Augustinians of the Assumption) Retired.
Laplante, Jean-Paul '50 (BUR) Retired.
LaPlante, Joseph A. '54 (WIN) Retired.
Laplante, Laurent R. '57 (PRT) Retired.
LaPlante, Roland M. '62 (HRT) Meriden, CT The Corporation of the Church of the Holy Angels.
LaPointe, Donald '67 (SPR) Holy Childhood Association Retired.
Lapointe, J. Donald R. '67 (SPR) Psychotherapeutic Counselor; Building Commission; Propagation of the Faith; Our Lady of Providence Children's Center, West Springfield.
La Pointe, Jacques *o.f.m.* '97 (NY) New York, NY St. Stephen of Hungary.
LaPointe, John G. '72 (PRO) Johnston, RI St. Robert Bellarmine.
LaPointe, Laurence A.M. '70 (NOR)[L] Willimantic, CT Campus Ministry; [L] New London, CT Connecticut College; College of Consultors; Deans; Campus Ministry; New London; Willimantic; Censor of Books; Presbyteral Council.
Lapomarda, Vincent A. *s.j.* '64 (WOR)[O] Worcester, MA Jesuits of the Holy Cross, Inc.
La Pore, Arthur '76 (JOL) Absent on Leave.
LaPorte, Gerard B. *c.ss.r.* '65 (NO) New Orleans, LA St. Alphonsus.
Laporte, Paul J. '65 (PRO) Retired.
Lappe, Derek '00 (SEA) Bremerton, WA Our Lady, Star of the Sea.
Lapuebla, Enrique C. *m.s.* '80 (SB) Moreno Valley, CA St. Christopher; [I] Moreno Valley, CA Missionaries of Our Lady of La Salette, MS.
LaPuebla, Enrique Canavelar *m.s.* '80 (SB) Morena Valley, CA Riverside County Regional Medical Center.
Laput, T. Noel G. *c.m.* '99 (SFR) Daly City, CA Our Lady of Mercy.
Laquindanum, Phil James '87 (BRK) Long Island City, NY St. Patrick.
Lara, Fernando Alvarez *s.j.* '09 (SEA)[A] Seattle, WA Seattle University; [L] Seattle, WA Arrupe Jesuit Community at Seattle University.
Lara, Rev. Msgr. James C. '57 (SP) Brandon, FL Church of the Nativity Retired.
Lara, Jose Rafael '99 (LA) Los Angeles, CA Presentation of the Mary.
Lara, Josue '94 (RCK) Carpentersville, IL St. Monica.
Lara, Santiago G. '72 (LA)[P] Los Angeles, CA Guadalupe Missioners Procure.
LaRaia, Joseph P. '46 (BO) Senior Priests. Retired.
Laranjinha, Armindo Simao *s.d.b.* (PAT)[O] Haledon, NJ Institute of the Daughters of Mary Help of Christians.
Laranjinha, Armindo *s.d.b.* '02 (NEW)[M] Ramsey, NJ Don Bosco Prep Salesian Residence; [C] Ramsey, NJ Don Bosco Preparatory High School.
Lardner, Gerald V. *s.s.* '67 (BAL)[S] Baltimore Society of St. Sulpice, Province of the United States Retired.
Largaespada, Luis Roger '09 (MIA) Miami, FL Our Lady of Lourdes.
Large, John J. '75 (PH) Philadelphia, PA St. Joan of Arc; Philadelphia, PA Mater Dolorosa.
Largent, Jeffery A. '84 (FTW) Mishawaka, IN St. Monica.
Largente, Laurent '59 (SJ) Retired.
Larger, Raymond E. '77 (CIN) Pastoral Council Secretariat; Cincinnati, OH St. Peter in Chains Cathedral.
Larion, Steven '06 (SD) Presbyteral Council; San Diego, CA St. Brigid.
Lariviere, Robert D. '78 (PRT) Diocesan Priests' Benefit Plan – Trustees; Sanford, ME Saint Therese of Lisieux Parish.
Larkin, Rev. Msgr. Alexander C. '67 (SJ) Retired.
Larkin, Bartholomew *o.carm.* '58 (VEN)[G] Venice, FL Carmel in Venice.
Larkin, Donald L. *s.j.* '66 (BO)[U] Weston, MA Campion Health Center, Inc.
Larkin, Joseph M. '57 (SY) Minetto, NY Our Lady of Perpetual Help.
Larkin, Kevin John '59 (LA) Sherman Oaks, CA St. Francis de Sales Retired.
Larkin, Kirk S. '04 (OKL) Lawton, OK Holy Family.
Larkin, Michael J. '59 (STA) Jacksonville, FL Prince of Peace; Building Commission.
Larkin, Michael T. '68 (SC) Special Assignment.
Larkin, Patrick '57 (WCH) Retired.
Larkin, Rev. Msgr. Robert W. '73 (NY) Bronx, NY Visitation; Canon 1742 Panel of Pastors.
Larko, Ronald P. '82 (PBR) McKees Rocks, PA Holy Ghost; Presbyteral Council.
Larmore, Donald E. '63 (GI) Retired.
LaRocca, Christopher *o.c.d.* '97 (P)[Q] Mt. Angel, OR Carmelite House of Studies; [L] Mount Angel, OR Discalced Carmelite Friars (OCD).
LaRocca, Frank *s.j.* '98 (BUF)[O] Buffalo, NY Canisius Jesuit Community Inc.
LaRocca, John J. *s.j.* '75 (CIN)[N] Cincinnati, OH Jesuit Community at Xavier University.
Laroche, Christopher J. '85 (MO) Air Force Reserve Chaplains.
Laroche, Leonidas B. '61 (BUR) Fairfield, VT St. Patrick.
LaRoche, Victor *o.p.* '02 (SAT)[H] San Antonio, TX Christus Santa Rosa Health Care Corporation; [L] San Antonio, TX Dominican Priory of San Juan Macias; San Antonio, TX St. Ann.
Larochelle, Maurice R. '87 (MAN) Manchester, NH Ste. Marie; Manchester, NH Sacred Heart of Jesus.
LaRocque, Rev. Msgr. Richard P. '63 (NOR) College of Consultors; Members; Part Time; Vicar for Clergy; Bishop's Liaison with Retired Clergy; Stonington, CT St. Mary.
LaRosa, John J. '81 (PH) Huntingdon Valley, PA St. Albert the Great.
LaRosa–Lopez, Manuel '96 (GAL) Richmond, TX St. John Fisher.
La Rosa–Lopez, Manuel '96 (BWN)[K] Brownsville, TX

Asociacion Nacional de Sacerdotes Hispanos.
LaRousse, William J. *m.m.* '80 (FgM) Maryknoll, NY MARYKNOLL.
Larran, Francisco *o.s.a.* '50 (MGZ) San German, PR St. Rose of Lima.
Larrea, Hector '94 (NEW) Union City, NJ Sts. Joseph and Michael.
Larrea, Luis E. *m.f.e.* '77 (TYL) College of Consultors; Hispanic Ministry Advisory Council; Priests' Personnel Board; Presbyteral Council.
Larrea, Luis Eduardo *m.f.e.* '77 (TYL) Tyler, TX St. Peter Claver.
Larrivee, Leo J. *s.s.* '77 (BAL) Catonsville, MD Our Lady of the Angels Catholic Community; [S] Baltimore Society of St. Sulpice, Province of the United States.
Larrivee, Leo J. *s.s.* '77 (SEA) On Duty Outside the Archdiocese.
Larroque, Rev. Msgr. H. Alexandre '55 (LAF)[I] Lafayette, LA Discalced Carmelites; Vicar General; Promoter of the Justice; Judges; Diocesan Consultors.
Larry, Anthony J. *o.s.f.s.* '67 (WIL)[J] Childs, MD Retirement and Assisted Care Facility.
Larsen, Kevin J. '93 (ARL) Springfield, VA St. Bernadette.
Larsen, Matthew '09 (SPK) Spokane Valley, WA St. Mary.
Larson, Bart (JC)[B] Jefferson City, MO St. Mary Health Center.
Larson, Lawrence A. '77 (BGP) Westport, CT Church of the Assumption.
Larson, Paul '79 (DUL) Deer River, MN St. Augustine; Deer River, MN St. Mary.
Larson, Ryan '07 (JOL) Naperville, IL Sts. Peter and Paul.
Larussa, Raymond '74 (COL) Powell, OH St. Joan of Arc.
Las, Stefan '88 (PAT) Vocations Board; Passaic, NJ Holy Rosary.
Las, Wlodzimierz R. *s.d.s.* '86 (BRK) Brooklyn, NY Our Lady of Consolation.
LaSaile, Donald *s.m.m.* (FTW)[B] University of Notre Dame Du Lac.
LaSalle, Donald *s.m.m.* '83 (BRK)[T] Ozone Park Montfort Missionaries Provincialate (Missionaries of the Company of Mary).
LaSana, Andre *l.c.* '01 (CHI)[N] Hillside, IL Legion of Christ.
Lascelle, Roger L. '77 (DEN) Fort Collins, CO St. Joseph.
Lasch, Rev. Msgr. Kenneth E. '62 (PAT) Retired.
Lasecki, Daniel J. '64 (MIL) Retired.
Lasheras, Antonio *o.a.r.* '62 (ELP) El Paso, TX Saint Therese of the Little Flower Parish; St. Paul; Priests' Personnel Advisory Committee; El Paso, TX Augustinian Recollect Fathers; El Paso, TX.
Laska, William M. '88 (E) Brookville, PA Immaculate Conception.
Laske, Kenneth S. '58 (CHI) Retired.
Laskowski, Keith R. '02 (ALN) Easton, PA St. Jane Frances de Chantal.
Laskowski, Norbert F. '79 (NEW) Rochelle Park, NJ Sacred Heart; Archdiocesan Judges.
Lasky, Rev. Msgr. Joseph J. '55 (SCR) Retired.
Lasky, Michael *o.f.m.conv.* '00 (BGP) Danbury, CT Sacred Heart of Jesus; [V] Danbury, CT Newman Center at Western CT State University.
Lasota, Stanislaw *c.r.* (CHI) Chicago, IL St. Hyacinth Basilica.
Lasrado, Francis '80 (RVC) Holbrook, NY Good Shepherd.
Lasrado, Max '92 (RCK) Sublette, IL Our Lady of Perpetual Help; West Brooklyn, IL St. Mary.
Lasseigne, John A. *o.m.i.* '99 (LA) Pacoima, CA Mary Immaculate.
Last, Carl A. '69 (MIL) Milwaukee, WI Cathedral of St. John the Evangelist.
Lastiri, Jean–Michael '85 (FRS) Oakhurst, CA Our Lady of the Sierra; Worship and Evangelization; Priests' Council.
Lasuba, John Lugala '93 (WIN) Rochester, MN St. John the Evangelist.
Laszewski, Richard G. *m.m.* '51 (SJ)[M] Los Altos, CA Maryknoll.
Latcovich, Mark A. '81 (CLV)[A] Wickliffe, OH St. Mary Seminary and Graduate School of Theology.
Lathem, Rev. Msgr. E. Christopher '65 (CHR) Summerville, SC St. John the Beloved; College of Consultors; Personnel Committee; Vicar for Clergy.
Lathrop, Robert '01 (DAV) Keokuk, IA All Saints.
Latkowski, Waldemar *c.ss.r.* '97 (MET) Perth Amboy, NJ St. Stephen; Somerville, NJ Somerset Medical Center; Perth Amboy, NJ St. Mary.
La Torre, Anthony '97 (SFR) San Francisco, CA St. Philip the Apostle.
Latosynski, Roger '84 (PT) Apalachicola, FL St. Patrick.
Latour, Charles L. *o.p.* '02 (NO)[P] Metairie, LA Dominican Friars, Southern Dominican Province of St. Martin de Porres; [P] Metairie, LA Southern Dominican Foundation; [S] Metairie, LA Southern Dominican Foundation; New Orleans, LA St. Anthony of Padua.
Latre, Rev. Msgr. Angel '54 (MGZ) Moca, PR Our Lady of Monserrate.
Latronico, Philip F. '86 (NEW)[R] Rutherford, NJ The Community of God's Love; Archdiocesan Commission of Christain Unity; Archdiocesan Commission for Interreligious Affairs; The Community of God's Love.
Latsko, Andrew '92 (CHL) Retired.
Lattanzio, Sabino *o.f.m.cap.* '72 (LAV) Hospital Apostolate.
Lattas, Joseph '99 (MEM) Retired.
Lattner, Stephen E. *o.s.b.* '07 (MIL)[P] Benet Lake, WI St. Benedict's Abbey; Kenosha, WI Our Lady of Mount Carmel; Kenosha, WI St. Anthony; Kenosha, WI St. Elizabeth.
Latus, Charles J. '68 (ROC) Webster, NY St. Rita.
Latzko, Frank J. '84 (CHI) Chicago, IL St. Teresa of Avila.
Lau, Ignatius '58 (ORG) Santa Ana, CA Immaculate Heart of Mary Retired.
Lau, Michael '61 (P) Retired.
Laubach, Barnabas *o.s.b.* '52 (SCL)[I] Collegeville St. John's Abbey, of the Order of St. Benedict.
Laubacker, Jerome P. *o.de.m.* '74 (CLV) Cleveland, OH Our Lady of Mount Carmel; [N] Cleveland, OH Mercedarians.
Laubenthal, Allan R. '61 (CLV) Associate Judges Retired.
Lauden, Edward J. '05 (NO) New Orleans, LA St. Andrew the Apostle.
Lauder, Robert E. '60 (BRK) Released from Diocesan Assignment.
Laudick, John R. '64 (TOL) Retired.
Lauducci, James V. '57 (SY) Retired.
Laudwein, James R. *s.j.* '62 (P)[L] Portland, OR Colombiere Community.
Lauenstein, Gary *c.ss.r.* '71 (CHI)[N] Glenview, IL The Redemptorists of Glenview, Illinois.
Lauer, Douglas J. '94 (COV) Cynthiana, KY St. Edward.
Lauer, Eric *c.f.p.* (COV)[M] Covington, KY Brothers of the Poor of St. Francis.
Lauer, Eugene F. '61 (PIT) Priest Council Retired.
Lauerman, James P. '70 (FAR) Grafton, ND Sacred Heart Church of Oakwood; Grafton, ND St. Thomas Church of St. Thomas.
Laughery, Kevin '83 (SFD) Auburn, IL Holy Cross; Office for Tribunal Services.
Laughlin, James J. '91 (BO) Wayland, MA St. Ann; Wayland, MA St. Zepherin; Vicariate I; Canonical Affairs Committee.
Laughlin, Joseph R. *s.j.* '57 (BO)[U] Weston, MA Campion Health Center, Inc.
Laughlin, Rev. Msgr. Martin T. '52 (CHR) Finance Council; Building & Renovation Commission; Investment Council; Personnel Committee; Vocations Board; Sites & Boundaries Committee; Office of Ongoing Formation for Recently Ordained Clergy; Vicar General's Office; College of Consultors.
Laughlin, Rev. Msgr. Martin T. '52 (DUB) Retired.
Launderville, Dale *o.s.b.* '79 (SCL)[I] Collegeville, MN St. John's Abbey, of the Order of St. Benedict.
Laurance, John D. *s.j.* '70 (MIL)[P] Milwaukee, WI Jesuit Community at Marquette University.
Laurent, Edward *o.f.m.cap.* '64 (PIT)[M] Pittsburgh, PA St. Augustine Friary.
Laurent, Sterling '02 (MIA) Miami, FL St. James.
Laurenzo, James '69 (DM) Retired.
Lauretti, George F. '56 (HRT) Retired.
Lauri, John F. '73 (NY) Bronx, NY Visitation.
Laurick, Richard *c.s.c.* (FTW)[H] Notre Dame Congregation of Holy Cross, Indiana Province, Provincial House.
Laurinaitis, Saulius P. '48 (COL) Hilliard, OH St. Brendan Retired.
Lauriola, Guglielmo *o.f.m.* '53 (SFR) San Francisco, CA St. Anthony of Padua.
Lause, James A. *o.f.m.* '98 (STL) St. Louis, MO St. Anthony of Padua.
Lause, James *o.f.m.* '98 (STL) Councilors:; [O] St. Louis, MO Franciscan Friary of St. Anthony of Padua.
Lause, Richard L. *c.m.* '77 (STL)[O] St. Louis, MO Lazarist Residence.
Lautermilch, David J. '62 (TOL) Retired.
Lautz, Boniface *o.s.b.* '60 (B)[C] Jerome, ID Monastery of the Ascension.
Lauzon, Kris C. '91 (OG) Au Sable Forks, NY Catholic Community of Holy Name and St. Matthew.
Lavagetto, Xavier M. *o.p.* '96 (SFR) San Francisco, CA St. Dominic; [N] San Francisco, CA St. Dominic Priory.
Lavagetto, Xavier *o.p.* '96 (OAK)[M] Oakland, CA Order of Preachers (Province of the Most Holy Name of Jesus – Western Dominican Province).
LaVallee, Pierre A. '61 (BUR) Deans; Bristol, VT St. Ambrose.
LaValley, Rev. Msgr. Richard G. '64 (BUR) Deans; Vicar for Clergy; [G] Northfield, VT Norwich Newman Apostolate; Winooski, VT St. Francis Xavier.
LaVan, Kenneth G. '58 (STP) Retired.
Lavan, Michael G. '06 (RCK) Special Assignment; Vocations; Rockford, IL St. Rita.
Lavann, Jason '06 (MIL)[H] Waukesha, WI Waukesha Catholic School System, Inc.; Waukesha, WI St. William.
Lavarone, Ken *o.f.m.* '79 (OAK)[M] Oakland, CA Franciscan Friars (Province of St. Barbara).
Lavaroni, Rino '67 (NEW) Jersey City, NJ Holy Rosary.
Lavastida, Jose I. '87 (NO)[A] New Orleans, LA Notre Dame Seminary Graduate School of Theology.
Lavelle, Donald *c.m.f.* '46 (LA)[V] Rancho Dominguez, CA Dominguez Seminary Inc.
Lavelle, Edward R. '63 (HBG) Defender of the Bond; Middletown, PA Seven Sorrows of the Blessed Virgin Mary.
Lavelle, John–Michael '00 (Y) Ravenna, OH Immaculate Conception; Catholic Television Network of Youngstown (CTNY); Council for Catechesis.
Lavelle, Raymond E. '57 (COL) Retired.
Lavely, Charles J. *c.s.c.* '65 (FTW)[H] Notre Dame Congregation of Holy Cross, Indiana Province, Provincial House.
Laver, Eugene F. (PIT) Pittsburgh, PA Prince of Peace.
LaVerde, Calogero N. '68 (CAM) Turnersville, NJ The Church of Saints Peter and Paul, Washington Township, N.J.
Laverde Saldarriaga, Luis Fernando '89 (BRK) Brooklyn, NY St. Rita.
LaVerghetta, Rev. Msgr. Richard D. '86 (TR) Secretary; Marlton, NJ St. Joan of Arc.
Laverone, Kenneth J. *o.f.m.* '79 (MRY) Special Assignment; Judicial Vicar; Judges.
Laverone, Kenneth J. *o.f.m.* '79 (OAK)[A] Berkeley, CA Franciscan School of Theology; Oakland, CA.
Laverone, Kenneth *o.f.m.* (STO) Judges.
Laverty, Seamus '68 (SEA) Tacoma, WA St. Patrick.
Laverty, Tod *o.f.m.* '72 (DET) Detroit, MI St. Patrick; Detroit, MI St. Aloysius.
Laviano, Vincent A. *o.f.m.* '74 (NY) New York, NY St. Francis of Assisi.
Lavich, David *o.c.s.o.* '73 (WOR)[O] Spencer, MA St. Joseph's Abbey.
Lavigne, Maurice D. '68 (MAN) Rye Beach, NH St. Theresa.
Lavilla, Rafael *o.s.j.* '05 (FRS) Madera, CA St. Joachim.
Lavin, Bernard C. '79 (PRO) Lincoln, RI St. Jude.
Lavin, Rev. Msgr. James M. '45 (STP) Saint Paul, MN; [C] St. Paul, MN University of St. Thomas Retired.
Lavin, John J. '64 (PRO) Retired.
Lavin, Thomas *o.f.m.conv.* '87 (BAL)[S] Ellicott City, MD Order of Friars Minor Conventual; [W] Ellicott City, MD Fr. Justin Ministry Fund, Inc.
Lavin, Wayne Patrick '71 (CAM) Retired.
Lavoie, Alfred *o.m.i.* '40 (SAT)[K] San Antonio, TX Oblate Madonna Residence.
LaVoie, Joseph '64 (SFE) Retired.
Lavoie, Merle L. '68 (SPR) Northampton, MA St. John Cantius Retired.
LaVoie, Raymond J. '00 (HBG) Vocations, Office for; [A] Harrisburg, PA Bishop McDevitt High School; Steelton, PA Prince of Peace.
Lavoie, Rene G. '51 (PRT) Retired.
Lavoie, Richard *m.s.* '64 (STL)[O] LaSalette Spirituality Center.
Lavoie, Rev. Msgr. Robert G. '53 (PRT)[G] Waterville, ME Mt. St. Joseph Holistic Care Community Retired.
Lavorgna, John L. '06 (HRT) Torrington, CT St. Francis of Assisi; Torrington, CT Sacred Heart; Torrington, CT St. Mary; Litchfield Deanery; Torrington, CT St. Peter.
Lavoy, Elwood '53 (LAV) Retired.
Lawler, Bruce A. '80 (SC) Schaller, IA St. Joseph's; Storm Lake, IA St. Mary's; [G] Storm Lake, IA St. Mary's Foundation of Storm Lake, Iowa; Liturgy Commission; Priests' Personnel Board; Priests' Pension Plan – Board of Trustees; Catholic School Foundation of the Diocese of Sioux City.
Lawler, David '62 (IND) Indianapolis, IN St. Christopher; Council of Priests.
Lawler, Rev. Msgr. Joseph A. '61 (BEL) McLeansboro, IL St. Clement; McLeansboro, IL St. John the Baptist; Diocesan Deans.
Lawler, Rev. Msgr. Robert L. '56 (OG) Madrid, NY St. John the Baptist; Waddington, NY St. Mary; Diocesan Consultors; Committee on Assignments.
Lawler, Rev. Msgr. Terrance M. '74 (MET) Alpha, NJ St. Mary.
Lawler, Thomas A. *s.j.* '99 (MIL)[P] Milwaukee, WI Arrupe House Jesuit Community; [P] Milwaukee, WI Jesuit Provincial Office, Wisconsin Province.
Lawler, William J. '72 (WIL) Cambridge, MD St. Mary Refuge of Sinners; Liaison for Evangelization.
Lawless, Joseph *m.s.f.* '71 (CC) Corpus Christi, TX St. Joseph.
Lawless, P. Brendan '64 (JC) Retired.
Lawless, Thomas '07 (ALB) Albany, NY Blessed Sacrament.
Lawlor, Brendan '55 (SP) Retired.
Lawlor, David T. *o.praem.* '71 (PH)[Y] Paoli, PA Daylesford Abbey.
Lawlor, Edward J. *s.s.j.* '40 (BAL)[S] Baltimore, MD St.

Joseph's Manor Retired.
Lawlor, Francis X. *o.s.a.* '45 (CHI)[N] Olympia Fields, IL Tolentine Monastery at Tolentine Center.
Lawlor, J. Michael '73 (BO) Needham, MA St. Joseph; College of Consultors; Presbyteral Council.
Lawlor, James F. '63 (ROC) Retired.
Lawlor, John J. *c.m.* '44 (PH)[Y].
Lawlor, Rev. Msgr. Joseph A. '61 (BEL) Dahlgren, IL St. John Nepomucene.
Lawlor, Joseph G. '62 (JC) Retired.
Lawlor, Mark S. '95 (CHL) Charlotte, NC St. Vincent de Paul; Propagation of the Faith.
Lawlor, Rev. Msgr. Timothy F. '43 (SB) Ontario, CA St. George Retired.
Lawrence, Andrew F. '00 (MO) Army Chaplains.
Lawrence, Andrew '00 (DUB) Military Chaplains.
Lawrence, Damian '93 (OKL) Alva, OK Sacred Heart.
Lawrence, David '97 (JOL) Bolingbrook, IL St. Dominic.
Lawrence, David *s.j.* '74 (OAK) Concord, CA St. Bonaventure; Presbyteral Council.
Lawrence, James A. '70 (BUR) Fair Haven, VT Our Lady of Seven Dolors.
Lawrence, John M. '76 (SAC) Redding, CA St. Joseph.
Lawrence, Kenneth F. '60 (HBG) Columbia, PA Holy Trinity; Consultors, College; Deans; Presbyteral Council.
Lawrence, Rev. Msgr. Kevin C. '87 (PH) Philadelphia, PA St. Malachy; Regional Vicars; Priests' Personnel Board.
Lawrence, Martin E. '03 (SFS) Salem, SD St. Mary.
Lawrence, Michael S. '73 (ALN) Retired.
Lawrence, Neal Henry *o.s.b.* '60 (FgM) Collegeville, MN St. John's Abbey.
Lawrence, Peter '99 (SPA) El Cajon, CA St. Michael Chaldean Catholic Church; San Diego, CA Mar Addai Mission.
Lawrence, Richard T. '68 (BAL) Baltimore, MD St. Vincent de Paul; Priest Personnel Board.
Lawrence, Rev. Msgr. Robert E. '66 (HBG) Harrisburg, PA Holy Name of Jesus; Deans.
Lawrence, Rev. Msgr. Robert E. '67 (SB) Special or Other Diocesan Assignment; Defender of the Bond Retired.
Lawrence, William *f.s.s.p.* (LIN)[A] Denton, NE Our Lady of Guadalupe Seminary.
Lawrence, William *f.s.s.p.* '06 (WDC)[B] Washington, DC St. Joseph's Seminary.
Lawrence, *s.m.* '75 (FgM) THE SOCIETY OF MARY.
Lawrenz, Jaroslaw Robert *c.m.* '87 (BRK) Brooklyn, NY St. Stanislaus Kostka.
Lawryniuk, Lawrence *o.s.b.m.* '64 (STF) Bronx, NY St. Mary Protectress.
Lawson, Douglas J. '62 (R) Retired.
Lawson, Harold F. '59 (BO) Senior Priests. Retired.
Lawson, Meinrad J. *o.s.b.* '67 (GBG)[G] Latrobe Saint Vincent Archabbey.
Lawson, Meinrad *o.s.b.* '67 (E) St. Marys, PA St. Mary.
Lawson, Theodore L. *c.ss.r.* (STL)[O] Liguori, MO St. Clement Health Care Center.
Lawton, Robert B. *s.j.* '81 (LA)[C] Los Angeles, CA Loyola Marymount University; [C] Los Angeles, CA Jesuit Community.
Laygo, Kristian *s.d.b.* (OAK)[E] Richmond, CA Salesian High School.
Layton, Richard *o.c.s.o.* '82 (P)[L] Lafayette, OR The Cistercian (Trappist) Abbey of Our Lady of Guadalupe.
Layton, Thomas Michael '09 (P) Junction City, OR St. Rose of Lima; Junction City, OR St. Helen.
Laz, Medard P. '69 (CHI) Other Assignments; [W] La Grange Park, IL Joyful Again.
Lazar, Antony *m.s.c.* '03 (ALN) Nazareth, PA Holy Family.
Lazar, John E. '80 (BRK) On Leave/Unassigned.
Lazar, Rev. Archpriest John '42 (STN) Retired.
Lazarek, Mariusz '04 (SAT) Panna Maria, TX Immaculate Conception of the Blessed Virgin Mary; Karnes City, TX St. Cornelius.
Lazaro Angarita, Jesus Eduardo '06 (TYL) Sulphur Springs, TX St. James.
Lazarski, Marvin I. '62 (MIL) Special Assignment; Spiritual Director.
Lazo, Alonzo *s.m.m.* '07 (BRK)[T] Ozone Park Montfort Missionaries Provincialate (Missionaries of the Company of Mary).
Lazo, Johnny Laura '94 (WIL) Salisbury, MD St. Francis De Sales.
Lazzarato, Mauro *c.s.* '86 (CHI)[N] Chicago, IL Scalabrini House of Theology; Melrose Park, IL Our Lady of Mount Carmel.
Lazzeroni, Gary '07 (SEA) Vancouver, WA St. Joseph.
Le, Anthony Duc *s.v.d.* '06 (FgM) Techny, IL.
Le, Ben '98 (LA) Los Angeles, CA St. Martin of Tours.
Le, Francis *o.p.* '04 (ANC) Anchorage, AK Holy Family Cathedral; Diocesan Consultors.
Le, Hoang V. '99 (BO) Vietnamese; Dorchester, MA St. Ambrose.
Le, Hoang Viet '61 (TLS) Retired.
Le, Hung Viet '01 (TLS) Hartshorne, OK Holy Rosary.
Le, James Vinh '87 (KAL) Mendon, MI St. Edward; Vicksburg, MI St. Martin.
Le, John Hung *s.v.d.* '04 (FgM) Techny, IL.
Le, Joseph Hung *c.ss.r.* '08 (DAL)[J] Dallas, TX St. John Neumann Formation House.
Le, Joseph Thu '03 (GAL) Houston, TX St. Christopher.
Le, Justin '09 (SJ) Los Gatos, CA St. Mary of the Immaculate Conception; [O] San Jose, CA Catholic Professionals.
Le, Khoa T. '06 (RVC) Seaford, NY St. James.
Le, Lam T. '04 (GR) Big Rapids, MI St. Paul's Campus Parish; Big Rapids, MI St. Mary's.
Le, Nhat Hong (CHI) Mt. Prospect, IL St. Raymond de Penafort.
Le, Peter Quang (OKL) Defenders of the Bond.
Le, Peter Tai Thanh '98 (MO) Administrative Leave; Navy Chaplains.
Le, Peter Tan Van '73 (CHL) Vietnamese Apostolate; Charlotte, NC St. Joseph Church.
Le, Peter Tuan '06 (DAL) Allen, TX St. Jude.
Le, Thai '08 (LA) Thousand Oaks, CA St. Paschal Baylon.
Le, Trieu Ngoc '42 (PIT) Retired.
Le, Tuan *s.j.* '99 (CHI)[C] Chicago, IL Jesuit Community at Loyola University Chicago; [J] Maywood, IL Loyola University Medical Center.
Lea, Joseph P. '04 (PH)[D] Fairless Hills, PA Conwell–Egan Catholic High School; Levittown, PA Immaculate Conception B.V.M.
Leach, Gregory '80 (DM) Des Moines, IA St. Mary of Nazareth; Priests' Pension Fund Society.
Leach, Jerome '76 (SFR) Absent on Leave.
Leach, Rev. Msgr. Phillip '85 (R) Retired.
Leach, Thomas F. '73 (BRK) Brooklyn, NY Our Lady of Grace; Presbyteral Council.
Leach, William '58 (STL) St. Louis, MO St. Margaret Mary Alacoque.
Leahey, Patrick R. '77 (ALT) Absent on Leave.
Leahy, Anthony M. '55 (CHI) Chicago, IL St. Barnabas Retired.
Leahy, Edwin D. *o.s.b.* '72 (NEW)[M] Newark, NJ Newark Abbey; [C] Newark, NJ Saint Benedict's Preparatory School; [C] Newark, NJ Saint Benedict's Preparatory School.
Leahy, Juvenal F. *o.f.m.* '58 (FgM) New York, NY Holy Name Province.
Leahy, Liam '72 (TUC) Tucson, AZ Saint Mark Roman Catholic Parish – Tucson.
Leahy, Maurice J. '55 (SB) Retired.
Leahy, William J. '66 (SAV) McRae, GA Holy Redeemer.
Leahy, William P. *s.j.* '78 (BO)[C] Chestnut Hill, MA Boston College; [U] Newton, MA The Jesuit Community at Boston College; [B] Chestnut Hill, MA The Ecclesiastical Faculty at Boston College.
Leahy, William '66 (SAV) Eastman, GA St. Mark.
Leake, Jerome L. '68 (RCK) Aurora, IL St. Joseph.
Leake, Stephen *s.d.b.* '00 (NEW)[M] Orange, NJ The Salesian Community.
Lealofi, Rev. Msgr. Etuale '69 (SPP) Fatuoaiga Multipurpose Cultural and Pastoral Center; Pago Pago, AS Church of the Holy Cross; Adjunct Judicial Vicar; Diocesan Consultors.
Leary, Albert R. '54 (BIS) Retired.
Leary, Daniel P. '97 (WDC) Huntingtown, MD Jesus the Divine Word Parish.
Leary, Donald G. '51 (WIN) Retired.
Leary, James F. '68 (HRT) Hartford Vicariate; West Hartford, CT St. Peter Claver; Suburban Hartford Deanery.
Leary, James *o.f.m.cap.* '70 (LC) Sparta, WI St. Patrick.
Leary, Rev. Msgr. Patrick '76 (LAV) Presbyteral Council for the Diocese of Las Vegas; Executive Director; Board of Trustees; [F] Las Vegas, NV Catholic Charities of Southern Nevada.
Leary, Richard *c.p.* '46 (BRK)[T] Jamaica, NY Immaculate Conception Monastery Retired.
Lease, James E. '06 (HBG) New Cumberland, PA St. Theresa of the Infant Jesus; [A] Camp Hill, PA Trinity High School.
Leatham, Gerald '65 (LUB) Brownfield, TX St. Anthony's; Priests Personnel Board.
Leatherby, Jeremy P. '06 (SAC) Sacramento, CA Presentation of the Blessed Virgin Mary; Presbyteral Council.
Leavey, Rev. Msgr. Thomas G. '51 (RVC) Seaford, NY St. William the Abbot Retired.
Leavins, Brice A. *o.f.m.* '69 (WOR) Auditor; Judges.
Leavins, Brice *o.f.m.* '69 (PRO) Providence, RI Our Lady of Lourdes; Judges; [N] Providence, RI St. Francis Chapel & City Ministry Center.
Leavitt, Robert F. *s.s.* '68 (BAL)[A] Baltimore, MD St. Mary's Seminary and University; [S] Baltimore, MD St. Mary's Seminary & University.
Leavitt, Robert F. *s.s.* '68 (HRT) On Duty Outside the Archdiocese.
Lebanowski, Gerald *m.s.* '59 (MIL)[P] Twin Lakes, WI La Salette Missionaries.
Lebar, Ivan M. *t.o.r.* '58 (WH) Keyser, WV Assumption.
Lebdowicz, Jan Krzystof '80 (NEW) Plainfield, NJ The Parish of St. Bernard and St. Stanislaus.
LeBeau, Philip A. '93 (PAT) Lincoln Park, NJ St. Joseph's.
Lebel, Maurice T. '67 (PRT) Retired.
Lebiedz, Bernard V. *o.s.b.* '59 (LAF)[H] Opelousas, LA Mother of the Redeemer Monastery.
LeBlanc, Alvin J. '82 (HRT) Bristol, CT St. Ann; Judges.
LeBlanc, Charles R. '79 (NOR) North Grosvenordale, CT St. Joseph; Quinebaug, CT St. Stephen; Deans; Part Time; Council of Catholic Women; Diocesan Commission for Ecumenical and Interreligious Affairs.
Le Blanc, Clyde *s.j.* '75 (BR)[J] Convent, LA Manresa House of Retreats.
LeBlanc, Daniel *o.m.i.* '78 (WDC)[N] Washington, DC Oblate Community.
LeBlanc, Etienne '71 (HT) Retired.
LeBlanc, Harold E. '61 (BO) Woburn, MA St. Joseph.
LeBlanc, James L. '96 (CHR) Aiken, SC St. Mary, Help of Christians; Family Life Services.
LeBlanc, Keith P. '96 (BO) Haverhill, MA St. John the Baptist.
LeBlanc, Leo A. '74 (MAN) Plymouth, NH Holy Trinity Parish.
LeBlanc, Leo J. *o.m.i.* '67 (LA) Pacoima, CA Mary Immaculate.
LeBlanc, Leo–Paul J. '79 (WOR) Southbridge, MA Notre Dame; Southbridge, MA Sacred Heart of Jesus.
LeBlanc, Omer *c.j.m.* '61 (SD) El Cajon, CA Our Lady of Grace.
LeBlanc, Paul J. (NY) Bronx, NY St. Joan of Arc.
LeBlanc, Steven C. '77 (LAF) Lafayette, LA St. Pius X.
LeBleu, V. Wayne '95 (LKC) Lake Charles, LA Christ the King.
LeBleu, Wayne '95 (LKC) Propagation of the Faith & Holy Childhood Association; Relief Services Catholic; Pastoral Services, Catholic.
LeBoeuf, Gerard '93 (DET)[D] Madison Heights, MI Bishop Foley Catholic High School; Clawson, MI Guardian Angels.
LeBourgeois, Rev. Msgr. Louis P. '61 (NO) Retired.
Le Bouteiller des Haries, Philippe *o.s.b.* '95 (TLS)[G] Hulbert, OK Our Lady of the Annunciation of Clear Creek Monastery.
Lebrun, Raymond A. *o.m.i.* '68 (WDC)[N] Washington, DC Oblate Community; [R] Washington, DC Basilica of the National Shrine of the Immaculate Conception.
LeCaptain, Douglas E. '93 (GB) Oshkosh, WI St. Raphael the Archangel; Regional Vicars; Omro, WI St. Mary; Winneconne, WI St. Mary.
Lech, Waclaw L. *o.c.d.* '74 (CHI) Chicago, IL St. Camillus.
Lech, Waclaw L. *o.c.d.* '74 (GRY)[H] Munster, IN Discalced Carmelite Fathers Monastery.
Lechiara, Francis J. '59 (PMB) Palm Beach, FL St. Edward; Consultors.
Lechnar, William J. '97 (GBG) Indiana, PA St. Thomas More University Parish; Office for Planning.
Lechner, Rev. Msgr. Roger A. '66 (SD) San Diego, CA Holy Spirit.
Lechtenberg, Rev. Msgr. Edward W. '51 (DUB) Retired.
Leckie, Michael J. '76 (PRO) Hope Valley, RI St. Joseph.
LeClair, Lawrence J. '53 (HRT) Retired.
LeClaire, H. Fred *c.m.f.* '87 (PHX) Chino Valley, AZ St. Catherine Laboure Roman Catholic Mission Chino Valley, A Quasi–Parish; Advocates.
LeClaire, Karl *s.d.s.* '86 (MIL)[P] Milwaukee Salvatorian Provincial Offices.
Leclerc, Rev. Msgr. Leo A. '61 (SPR) Bishop's Cabinet; Chicopee, MA Assumption; Vicars General; Bishop's Commission for Clergy; Diocesan Consultors; Presbyteral Council Retired.
Leclerc, Thomas L. *m.s.* '80 (BO) Cambridge, MA St. John the Evangelist.
LeCompte, Glenn '86 (HT) Continuing Education of the Clergy–Ministry to Priests Program; Worship; Houma, LA Cathedral of St. Francis De Sales.
Lecomte, Gerard *c.j.m.* '78 (SD) Solana Beach, CA St. James.
LeCours, Sylva P. '47 (NOR) Retired.
Lecumberri, Rufino '54 (NY) Bronx, NY Sacred Heart.
Leddy, John *o.m.i.* '51 (BEL)[F] Belleville, IL Shrine of Our Lady of the Snows.
Leddy, Leonard '59 (AUS) Retired.
Leder, Dennis M. *s.j.* '76 (FgM) New York, NY Society of Jesus.
Ledermann, Paul F. '63 (SR) On Duty Outside the Diocese; Veterans Administration Home.
Ledesma, Salvador '99 (STO) Newman Apostolate.
Ledet, Rev. Msgr. Donald '63 (HT) Houma, LA Annunziata Retired.
Ledford, John S. '75 (WH) Stonewood, WV Our Lady of Perpetual Help.
Ledoux, Albert H. '87 (ALT) Gallitzin, PA St. Demetrius.
Ledoux, Damien C. '05 (MAN) Absent on Leave.
LeDoux, Jerome *s.v.d.* (FWT) Fort Worth, TX Our Mother of Mercy.
LeDoux, Louis V. '58 (SAT)[R] San Antonio, TX Our Lady of Czestochowa.
Ledoux, Louis Vernon '52 (LAF) Retired.

Ledoux, Mark '99 (LAF) Krotz Springs, LA St. Anthony of Padua.
Ledoux, Michael Dominic W. *o.f.m.* '86 (ALB)[A] Catskill, NY St. Anthony Friary.
Ledoux, William J. '93 (PRO) Pawtucket, RI St. Mary of the Immaculate Conception; Deans.
LeDuc, Roger D. '60 (FR) Retired.
Ledwidge, Brendan '55 (LAN) Retired.
Ledwith, Harry '74 (TUC) Tucson, AZ Saint Pius X Roman Catholic Parish – Tucson.
Ledwon, Jacob C. '72 (BUF) Council of Priests; [R] Buffalo, NY State University of New York at Buffalo (Main St. South Campus); Buffalo, NY St. Joseph–University; Consultors, College of.
Lee, Andrew H. (NY) Bronx, NY St John Nam.
Lee, Bernard *s.m.* '67 (SAT)[L] San Antonio, TX Ligustrum Marianist Community.
Lee, Borromeo Bongchoon '06 (NEW) Saddle Brook, NJ Korean Martyrs.
Lee, Cha Yong (TR) The Korean Apostolate.
Lee, Rev. Msgr. David M. '68 (BUF)[A] East Aurora, NY Christ the King Seminary; Buffalo, NY St. Ambrose; [G] Buffalo, NY South Buffalo Catholic School; Buffalo, NY St. Agatha.
Lee, Dominic Savio '94 (SFR) San Mateo, CA St. Matthew.
Lee, Eugene '04 (ORG)[H] Anaheim, CA St. Thomas Korean Catholic Center; Liturgical Commission.
Lee, Gabriel '97 (BRK) Flushing, NY St. Paul Chong Ha–Sang Roman Catholic Chapel.
Lee, Gerard *o.f.m.* '71 (ALB)[B] Siena College; [R] Albany, NY St. Francis Chapel.
Lee, Huengwoo '04 (CIN)[U] Cincinnati, OH St. Andrew Kim Korean Catholic Community.
Lee, Jaehee '00 (CHL) Korean Catholic Cultural Center.
Lee, Jaehwa John '07 (PH) Philadelphia, PA Maternity B.V.M.
Lee, James '75 (SEA) Olympia, WA St. Michael.
Lee, Jeffrey E. '92 (TR) Expansion and Restructuring Commission; Trenton, NJ Our Lady of the Angels Parish.
Lee, John Michael *c.p.* '72 (BRK)[V] Jamaica, NY Bishop Molloy Retreat House; [T] Jamaica, NY Immaculate Conception Monastery.
Lee, John R. *c.s.b.* '56 (ROC)[J] Rochester, NY Basilian Residence.
Lee, John T. Matthew '93 (WDC) Absent On Leave.
Lee, Rev. Archimandrite Joseph (Richard) '72 (PHU)[E] Washington, DC Monastery of the Holy Cross.
Lee, Joseph C. '91 (DAL) Duncanville, TX Holy Spirit.
Lee, Joseph P. '57 (LA) Retired.
Lee, Joseph '55 (CHI) Retired.
Lee, Joshua Peter '89 (LA) Pico Rivera, CA St. Hilary.
Lee, Keun–Soo '95 (BR) Morganza, LA St. Ann.
Lee, Rev. Msgr. Lawrence F. (GAL) Retired.
Lee, Lawrence '49 (GAL)[L] Houston, TX Pope John Paul XXIII Priests' Residence Retired.
Lee, Matthew K. '09 (CIN) Botkins, OH St. Lawrence; Wapakoneta, OH St. Joseph; Botkins, OH Immaculate Conception.
Lee, Michael G. '64 (WH) Retired.
Lee, Michael J. *o.praem.* '70 (PH) Philadelphia, PA St. Gabriel; [Y] Paoli, PA Daylesford Abbey; Council of Priests.
Lee, Michael *s.j.* '96 (LA)[C] Los Angeles, CA Jesuit Community.
Lee, Patrick J. '76 (CHI) Chicago, IL Immaculate Conception of the Blessed Virgin Mary; Chicago, IL St. Joseph.
Lee, Patrick J. *s.j.* '78 (P)[L] Portland, OR Jesuit Provincial Office (Society of Jesus, Oregon Prov.); [L] Portland, OR Colombiere Community.
Lee, Patrick J. '68 (SAC) Sacramento, CA Immaculate Conception Retired.
Lee, Patrick J. *s.j.* '78 (FgM) Portland, OR Society of Jesus; Portland, OR.
Lee, Paul D. '83 (WDC) Washington, DC Epiphany; Advocates; Office for Ecumenical and Interreligious Affairs.
Lee, Paul Kyung '06 (NEW) Fort Lee, NJ Madonna.
Lee, R. Anthony '93 (PEO) Peoria, IL St. Jude's.
Lee, Raphael '08 (NEW) Saddle River Borough, NJ St. Gabriel the Archangel.
Lee, Roy '86 (MIL) Personal Leave; Board of Directors:.
Lee, Sang Yil '92 (AUS) Chaplains of the Military.
Lee, Terence J. *m.h.m.* '57 (NY)[EE] Hartsdale, NY Mill Hill Fathers Residence.
Lee, Rev. Msgr. Thaddeus (PAT) Retired.
Lee, Thomas M. '53 (PRT) Retired.
Lee, Thomas '99 (HBG) Korean Ministry.
Lee, William J. *s.s.* '46 (BAL)[S] Baltimore Society of St. Sulpice, Province of the United States Retired.
Lee, William J. *s.s.* '46 (CLV) Retired.
Lee, Won–Tae '92 (DEN) Aurora, CO St. Lawrence Korean Catholic Church.
Lee, Yong Huyk '01 (GAL) Houston, TX St. Andrew Kim.
Lee, Yong–Kyu '96 (SFR) San Francisco, CA St. Michael Korean Catholic Church.
Lee, Young Chan *s.j.* '87 (LA) Los Angeles, CA St. Agnes.
Leeuw, Daniel R. '57 (FTW) Veterans Administration Hospital; [F] Avilla, IN Provena LaVerna Terrace Retired.
Lefebure, Leo D. '78 (WDC) Other Assignments; Washington, DC Our Lady of Victory.
Lefebvre, Rev. Msgr. Gerald M. '56 (BR) Judges Retired.
Lefebvre, James '59 (ALB) Albany, NY St. Mary; Advocates; Priests Retirement Board/Priests Retirement Plan Board.
Lefebvre, Robert R. *m.m.* '57 (NY)[EE] Retired.
Lefebvre, Simon P. *c.s.v.* '56 (CHI)[N] Arlington Heights Viatorian Province Center–Clerics of St. Viator.
LeFevre, Rev. Msgr. Michael C. '82 (DET) Highland Park, MI St. Benedict; Detroit, MI St. Gregory the Great; Detroit, MI Madonna; Detroit, MI Cathedral, Church of the Most Blessed Sacrament; Archdiocesan Vicars; Judges; Pastoral Care for Priests.
LeFevre, Robert J. '66 (ALB) Saratoga Springs, NY St. Peter Retired.
Leffler, Richard J. '78 (MAD) Potosi, WI SS. Andrew and Thomas.
Lefler, John '57 (EVN) Retired.
LeFleur, R. Keith '76 (SAG) Retired.
Lefor, Jason '99 (FAR) Grand Forks, ND St. Thomas Aquinas Newman Church of Grand Forks; [I] Grand Forks, ND St. Thomas Aquinas Newman Church of Grand Forks.
LeFort, David R. '98 (ALB) East Greenbush, NY St. Mary.
LeFrois, Rev. Msgr. Marvin '49 (SAV) Valdosta, GA St. John the Evangelist Retired.
Legal, Wilfred A. *o.s.b.* '94 (GAL) Spring, TX St. Ignatius of Loyola.
Legarra, Francisco J. *o.a.r.* '74 (NEW) Union City, NJ Holy Family; [M] Union City, NJ Augustinian Recollects, St. Nicholas of Tolentine Monastery.
Legarreta, Felipe '93 (JOL) West Chicago, IL St. Mary.
Legarski, Anthony J. '83 (ALT) Hollidaysburg, PA St. Mary's; Altoona, PA Veterans Medical Center.
Legarski, Joseph '83 (MO) DEPARTMENT OF VETERANS AFFAIRS HOSPITALS AND CHAPLAINS.
Legaspi, Alex L. '76 (SFR) Daly City, CA St. Andrew; Navy Reserve Chaplains.
Legaspi, Dennis L. '93 (SB) Desert Hot Springs, CA St. Elizabeth of Hungary; Elected Members.
Legaspi, Fulgencio Paul '89 (MO) Navy Reserve Chaplains.
Legaspi, Fulgencio "Dol" L. '89 (LA) El Monte, CA Nativity.
Legault, Michel *m.s.a.* '71 (NOR)[A] Cromwell, CT Holy Apostles College and Seminary.
Leger, Austin '62 (LAF) Retired.
Leger, G. Robert '71 (SJ) Sunnyvale, CA Church of The Resurrection; Pastoral Resource Committee for Ministry to Gay and Lesbian Catholics; Ongoing Formation of Clergy.
Leger, Jeffrey P. '97 (L) Unassigned.
Leger, Laurie L. *m.s.* '54 (WOR) Fitchburg, MA St. Joseph's.
Leger, Steven L. '86 (BEA) Bridge City, TX St. Henry.
Legerski, John '81 (B) On Duty Outside the Diocese.
Legerski, John '81 (RNO)[A] Reno, NV Bishop Manogue Catholic High School, a Nevada non–profit corporation; On Special Assignment.
Legge, Dominic M. *o.p.* '07 (PRO)[P] Providence St. Thomas Aquinas Priory at Providence College.
Lego, William E. *o.s.a.* '83 (CHI) Chicago, IL St. Rita of Cascia; [N] Olympia Fields, IL The Augustinians–Provincialate; Olympia Fields, IL Province of Our Mother of Good Counsel (Midwestern); Olympia Fields, IL.
Lehane, Brian J. *s.j.* '97 (DET)[E] Detroit, MI University of Detroit Jesuit High School and Academy.
Leheny, Rev. Msgr. Bernard M. '66 (LA) Long Beach, CA St. Bartholomew; Board of Directors.
Leheny, Rev. Msgr. Bernard '66 (LA) Deanery 20.
Lehman, Charles (TUC)[C] Tucson, AZ Carondelet St. Joseph's Hospital.
Lehman, John J. (MAR) Retired.
Lehman, Rev. Msgr. Joseph P. '80 (RIC) Roanoke, VA Our Lady of Nazareth.
Lehman, Joseph *t.o.r.* '96 (BO)[U] Newton, MA The Jesuit Community at Boston College.
Lehman, Paul J. '54 (NEW) Couples for Christ; Secretaries; Newark, NJ St. Antoninus Retired.
Lehmkuhl, Gerhardt B. *s.j.* '74 (STL)[O] St. Louis, MO Jesuit Community Corporation at Saint Louis University – Jesuit Hall.
Lehner, John *o.s.f.s.* '70 (TOL)[C] Toledo, OH St. Francis de Sales High School; [I] Toledo, OH.
Lehnerd, Frank M. '58 (Y) Retired.
Lehnert, Brian '00 (PMB) Wellington, FL St. Therese de Lisieux.
Lehning, Thomas J. '70 (ARL) Clifton, VA St. Clare of Assisi; Defenders of the Bond.
Lehocky, Rev. Msgr. Leigh A. '68 (CHR) Columbia, SC St. Peter.
Lehr, James W. *m.m.* '53 (NY)[EE] Maryknoll Maryknoll Fathers and Brothers Retired.
Lehrberger, James *o.cist.* '76 (DAL)[B] University of Dallas; [J] Irving, TX Cistercian Abbey of Our Lady of Dallas.
Leibenguth, Gerald T. *o.s.b.* '72 (BO)[U] Hingham, MA Glastonbury Abbey.
Leibham, David '87 (AUS) Waco, TX St. Louis; Consultors.
Leibrecht, Robert G. '58 (STL) Retired.
Leidich, Kevin A. *s.j.* '82 (SAC)[D] Sacramento, CA Jesuit High School; [I] Carmichael, CA Sacramento Jesuit Community.
Leies, John A. *s.m.* '56 (SAT)[C] San Antonio, TX St. Mary's University of San Antonio, Texas; [L] San Antonio, TX Marianist Residence; Catholic Physicians Guild.
Leif, Gregory P. '78 (WIN) Caledonia, MN St. Mary; Caledonia, MN St. Patrick's.
Leigh, David J. *s.j.* '68 (SEA)[A] Seattle, WA Seattle University; [L] Seattle, WA Arrupe Jesuit Community at Seattle University.
Leighton, Rev. Msgr. Donald E. '62 (PH) Gladwyne, PA St. John Baptist Vianney.
Leiker, Perry D. '76 (LA) Hawthorne, CA St. Joseph.
Lein, Lambert *s.v.d.* '00 (LAF) Broussard, LA St. Joseph.
Leinen, Ronald *m.s.c.* '57 (ALN)[A] Center Valley, PA Sacred Heart Villa, Missionaries of the Sacred Heart.
Leininger, Charles A. *s.j.* '53 (DAL)[D] Dallas, TX Jesuit College Preparatory School.
Leininger, William '56 (SJ) Retired.
Leiphon, Donald A. '68 (FAR) Liaison with Charismatic Movement Retired.
Leise, Gerald A. '74 (OM) Schuyler, NE Divine Mercy.
Leise, Leo V. *s.j.* '94 (SFE) Albuquerque, NM Immaculate Conception.
Leisen, Leo '54 (SCL) Paynesville, MN St. Agnes Retired.
Leisen, Richard '56 (SCL) Diocesan Priests Pension Plan Trustees Retired.
Leising, Edmund *o.m.i.* '46 (FgM) Washington, DC AMERICAN OBLATE MISSIONS.
Leising, Rev. Msgr. Frederick D. '71 (BUF) Williamsville, NY Nativity of the Blessed Virgin Mary; Finance Council.
Leising, John J. '69 (BUF) Williamsville, NY Nativity of the Blessed Virgin Mary.
Leising, Robert *o.m.i.* '90 (CR) Waubun, MN St. Frances Cabrini; Waubun, MN St. Anne; Waubun, MN St. Ann.
Leisy, Christian *o.s.b.* '88 (SFE)[H] Abiquiu, NM Monastery of Christ in the Desert.
Leitem, Leon *o.f.m.cap.* '57 (HBG) Harrisburg, PA St. Francis of Assisi.
Leiting, Robert L. '67 (SC) Retired.
Leitner, Rev. Msgr. John E. '55 (KC) Presbyteral Council Retired.
Leitner, Thomas Aquinas *o.s.b.* '92 (OM)[K] Schuyler, NE Benedictine Mission House; Religious Orders.
Leiweke, Robert W. *s.j.* '58 (MIL)[P] Milwaukee, WI Jesuit Community at Marquette University.
Le Jacq, Peter M. *m.m.* '87 (NY)[EE] Maryknoll Maryknoll Fathers and Brothers.
LeJeune, Ronald J. '71 (TOL) Bucyrus, OH Holy Trinity.
Lek, Basil L. '04 (NEW) On Duty Outside the Archdiocese.
Leke, Charles '82 (SP) Inverness, FL Our Lady of Fatima.
Leland, Thomas '99 (WCH) Wichita, KS St. Anne.
Leliaert, Richard M. '67 (DET) Redford Township, MI St. Robert Bellarmine.
Lelii, Raymond M. *s.j.* '61 (WDC)[N] Washington, DC The Jesuit Community of St. Aloysius Gonzaga.
Lella, Rev. Msgr. Christopher '79 (PAT) Wayne, NJ Annunciation.
Lelo–Luemba, Albert *c.i.c.m.* '96 (BWN) San Benito, TX St. Ignatius.
Leloczky, Julius *o.cist.* '61 (DAL)[J] Irving, TX Cistercian Abbey of Our Lady of Dallas.
Lelonis, Richard M. '71 (PIT)[N] Pittsburgh, PA Mount Assisi Convent; Judges; Matrimonial Concerns, Officefor; Matrimonial Concerns, Office for.
Lemaine, Calonge '89 (BRK) Brooklyn, NY Our Lady of Miracles.
LeMaire, Francis (BRK) Springfield Gardens, NY Christ the King.
Lemaster, Scott '85 (DAV) Charlotte, IA Assumption and St. Patrick's; Charlotte, IA Ss. Mary and Joseph; Charlotte, IA Immaculate Conception.
Lemay, Donald H. '89 (RIC) Richmond, VA St. Edward The Confessor; Presbyteral Council.
LeMay, Donald *o.s.b.* '57 (SCL)[I] Collegeville, MN St. John's Abbey, of the Order of St. Benedict.
Lemay, Jean M. '75 (MAN) Elliott Hospital; Manchester, NH St. Joseph Cathedral.
Lemay, Larry '99 (BEL) Leave of Absence.
Lembo, Richard '75 (WOR) Gilbertville, MA St. Aloysius.
Le Mieux, Thomas A. '59 (MIL) Retired.
Lemire, Paul W. '89 (WOR) Auburn, MA St. Joseph's.

Lemkuhl, David '79 (CIN) Cincinnati, OH St. Margaret – St. John Parish.
Lemlin, Timothy J. '78 (PRO) Central Falls, RI Holy Spirit Parish.
Lemm, Eugene '57 (SCL) Brandon, MN Church of St. Ann Retired.
Lemme, Christopher *t.o.r.* '98 (ARL) Luray, VA Our Lady of the Valley.
Lemmert, Ronald D. '79 (NY) Bedford Hills, NY Bedford Hills Correctional Facility.
Lemmert, Ronald J. '79 (NY) Ossining, NY Sing Sing Correctional Facility.
Lemming, Patrick W. '81 (MOB) On Leave from the Archdiocese.
Lemoi, Paul R. '75 (PRO) West Warwick, RI Our Lady of Good Counsel; Army National Guard Chaplains.
Lemoine, Russell J. '70 (ALX) Retired.
Lemon, Rev. Msgr. Clement P. '64 (WIL) Wilmington, DE Immaculate Heart of Mary; Vicar for Priests; College of Consultors.
Lemos, Thomas F. *c.s.c.* '74 (COS)[F] Cascade, CO Holy Cross Novitiate.
Lemos, Thomas *c.s.c.* (FTW)[H] Notre Dame Congregation of Holy Cross, Indiana Province, Provincial House.
Lemus, Francisco Arrivillaga *o.s.b.* '95 (SFS)[F] Marvin, SD Blue Cloud Abbey.
Lemus, Raul '02 (SR) Ukiah, CA St. Mary of the Angels; Priests' Council.
Lenaghan, J. Jordan *o.p.* '95 (COL) Columbus, OH St. Patrick.
Lenahan, Claude T. *o.f.m.* '55 (PAT)[N] Butler, NJ St. Anthony Friary.
Lenahan, John B. '49 (L) Retired.
Lenane, Rev. Msgr. William '50 (SJ) Retired.
Lencewicz, Leonard *o.f.m.* '63 (NY)[EE] New York Franciscan Friars, Holy Name Province.
Lenchak, Timothy *s.v.d.* '75 (FgM) Techny, IL.
Lendacky, Francis G. '61 (PH) Philadelphia, PA St. Agnes–St. John Nepomucene; Legion of Mary.
Lendvai, John B. '94 (PIT) West Mifflin, PA Holy Spirit; [P] West Mifflin, PA Community College of Allegheny County – South Campus.
Lenehan, Vincent '54 (SAC) Retired.
Lengerich, Bob J. '07 (FTW) Granger, IN St. Pius X; [C] South Bend, IN Saint Joseph's High School.
Lengerich, Rev. Msgr. Vincent L. '48 (CIN)[N] Carthagena, OH St. Charles; Judges Retired.
Lengwin, Ronald P. '66 (PIT) Pittsburgh, PA St. Mary of Mercy; Clergy Personnel Board; Ecumenical and Interfaith Commission; Mission Office; Pilgrimage Office; Public and Community Affairs, Office for; Society for the Propagation of the Faith.
Lenihan, Daniel F. *o.c.s.o.* '55 (DUB)[K] Peosta, IA New Melleray Abbey, Order of Cistercians of the Strict Observance.
Lenihan, Rev. Msgr. John J. '53 (STA) Retired.
Lenihan, Rev. Msgr. Michael '52 (LA) Redondo Beach, CA St. Lawrence Martyr Retired.
Lenk, Dominic *o.s.b.* '98 (STL)[O] St. Louis, MO The Abbey of St. Mary and St. Louis.
Lenneman, Marc J. '06 (HEL)[A] Helena, MT Carroll College; Presbyteral Council; Borromeo Pre–Seminary Program; [B] Helena, MT Carroll College; Personnel Board.
Lennon, James M. '58 (JOL) Retired.
Lennon, Joseph L. *o.p.* '47 (PRO)[P] Providence St. Thomas Aquinas Priory at Providence College.
Lennon, Rev. Msgr. Peter F. '55 (NEW)[B] School of Diplomacy and Intl. Rels. Retired.
Lennon, Peter F. '55 (NEW) Retired.
Lennon, Raymond T. *s.v.d.* '64 (TR)[N] Bordentown, NJ Society of the Divine Word.
Lennon, Sean M. *o.s.m.* '80 (CHI)[N] Chicago Order of Friar Servants of Mary (Servites) United States of America Province, Inc.
Lenoci, Dominick J. '95 (NEW) Emerson, NJ Church of the Assumption.
Lenox, Peter F. '00 (BGP) Stamford, CT Saint Benedict – Our Lady of Montserrat.
Lenti, Arthur *s.d.b.* '50 (OAK)[A] Berkeley, CA Dominican School of Philosophy and Theology; [M] Berkeley Salesians of Don Bosco.
Lentine, Peter S. '50 (DET) Detroit, MI St. Philomena.
Lentini, James S. '03 (WIL)[A] Magnolia, DE St. Thomas More Preparatory School; Dover, DE Holy Cross.
Lentz, Gerald J. *s.j.* '60 (SJ)[M] Los Gatos, CA Sacred Heart Jesuit Center.
Lentz, Lawrence D. *c.s.v.* '81 (CHI)[N] Arlington Heights Viatorian Province Center–Clerics of St. Viator.
Lentz, Lawrence *c.s.v.* '81 (LAV) Las Vegas, NV Guardian Angel Cathedral.
Lenz, Daniel *o.s.b.* '85 (OM)[C] Elkhorn, NE Mount Michael Benedictine School; [K] Elkhorn, NE Mount Michael Benedictine Abbey.
Lenz, Frank B. '94 (VIC) Meyersville, TX SS. Peter & Paul; Defenders of the Bond.
Lenz, Frank '69 (MAR) Retired.
Lenz, Michael *o.f.m.* '76 (PIT)[M] Pittsburgh, PA Holy Family Friary; Pittsburgh, PA.
Lenz, Rev. Msgr. Paul A. '49 (ALT) Retired.
Lenzini, Donald J. '51 (BEL) Retired.
Lenzner, George '57 (GB) Retired.
Leo, Arthur R. '85 (NY) Absent on Sick Leave.
Leon, Antonio '57 (STA) Jacksonville, FL Immaculate Conception.
Leon, Bartholomew *o.s.b.* '85 (SAM) Greenville, SC St. Rafka Maronite Mission.
Leon, Carlos '98 (ORG) Santa Ana, CA Immaculate Heart of Mary.
Leon, David '05 (SD) UCSD Medical Center; [I] San Diego, CA Nazareth House Retirement Home; San Diego, CA Nazareth House.
Leon, Francisco *o.s.a.* '78 (LAR) Laredo, TX Holy Redeemer; Priests Personnel Board; Ex Officio Members.
Leon, Francisco '93 (SAC) Woodland, CA Holy Rosary.
Leon, Gregorio '88 (LAV) Las Vegas, NV St. Anne.
Leon, Hector (BGP) Danbury, CT Our Lady of Guadalupe.
Leon, Jose M. '81 (OAK) Union City, CA Our Lady of the Rosary; Presbyteral Council.
Leon, Raguiel Rodriguez '08 (FAJ) Humacao, PR Concathedral Dulce Nombre de Jesus.
Leon, Victor *o.s.j.* '00 (SCR) Hazleton, PA Annunciation, Hazelton; Hispanic Ministry Outreach.
Leon–Angulo, Marcos '03 (R) Whiteville, NC Sacred Heart; Deans; Council of Priests.
Leon–Valencia, Rafael A. '04 (R) Burgaw, NC St. Joseph.
Leonard, Albert J. '89 (SCR) Jersey Shore, PA Immaculate Conception of the Blessed Virgin Mary; Williamsport, PA St. Luke.
Leonard, Clyde A. '64 (BO) Senior Priests. Retired.
Leonard, Daniel '94 (DEN) Deaneries; Denver, CO Christ the King; Elected Representatives from Deanery to Presbyteral Council.
Leonard, Derek '96 (FgM) Boston, MA St. James the Apostle, Inc.
Leonard, Edwin M. '84 (CLV) Parma, OH St. Charles Borromeo.
Leonard, Eugene A. '66 (CHR) Retired.
Leonard, Francis B. '50 (BO) Chelmsford, MA St. John the Evangelist; Senior Priests. Retired.
Leonard, John E. '65 (RIC) Retired.
Leonard, John F. '55 (BO) Senior Priests. Retired.
Leonard, John J. *s.j.* '50 (NY)[F] Bronx, NY Fordham Preparatory School; [EE] Jesuit Community, Kohlmann Hall.
Leonard, John J. *o.f.m.* (PAT) Butler, NJ St. Anthony.
Leonard, John (NTN) Retired.
Leonard, Matthew '98 (CHL) Swannanoa, NC St. Margaret Mary.
Leonard, Michael '91 (CHI) Chicago, IL St. Tarcissus.
Leonard, Patrick F. *o.s.a.* '96 (PH)[Y] Villanova, PA St. Augustine Friary.
Leonard, Patrick J. '63 (NEW) Retired.
Leonard, Peter J. *o.s.f.s.* '86 (ALN)[B] Center Valley, PA DeSales University; [K] Center Valley, PA Oblates of St. Francis de Sales.
Leonard, Raymond J. '90 (MET) On Duty Outside the Diocese.
Leonard, Samuel H. *i.v.e.* '04 (WIN) Mankato, MN SS. Peter and Paul's.
Leonard, Sebastian *o.s.b.* '57 (HRT)[E] New Milford, CT Canterbury School.
Leonard, Sebastian *o.s.b.* '57 (IND)[K] St. Meinrad St. Meinrad Archabbey.
Leonard, Rev. Msgr. Thomas P. '56 (NY) New York, NY Holy Trinity; Manhattan (West).
Leonard, William F. '70 (CHR)[H] Charleston, SC Charleston Southern University.
Leonard, William T. '69 (BO) Waltham, MA St. Jude; Pastoral Care.
Leonards, Martin C. '66 (LAF) Duson, LA St. Theresa of the Child Jesus; Duson, LA St. Benedict the Moor.
Leone, Arthur '56 (NY) New York, NY St. Peter Retired.
Leone, James M. '60 (BRK) Retired.
Leone, Rev. Msgr. Kenneth J. '67 (DEN) Denver, CO Church of the Risen Christ; [P] Denver, CO St. Joseph Retreat Center.
Leone, Richard D. *o.s.f.s.* '59 (WIL)[J] Wilmington, DE DeSales House.
Leone, William B. '74 (ROC) Rochester, NY St. Cecilia.
Leonelli, Louis *c.f.r.* '09 (NY)[EE] Yonkers, NY St. Felix Friary.
Leong, Francis J. *m.m.* '87 (NY)[EE] Retired.
Leong, Herman '91 (OAK) Alameda, CA St. Barnabas; Judges.
Leong, Herman '91 (HON) Defender of the Bond and Promoter of Justice.
Leon Guerrero, Felixberto C. *o.f.m.cap.* '86 (AGN) Mangilao, GU Santa Teresita.
Leonhardt, Douglas J. *s.j.* '69 (MIL)[P] Milwaukee, WI Jesuit Community at Marquette University.
Leonhardt, Louis J. '56 (DAV) Hills, IA St. Joseph's; Lone Tree, IA St. Mary's; Nichols, IA St. Mary's; DEPARTMENT OF VETERANS AFFAIRS HOSPITALS AND CHAPLAINS.
Leonhardt, Robert *o.f.m.* '59 (FWT)[H] Crowley, TX St. Maximilian Kolbe Friary.
Leopold, David C. '82 (BGP) Georgetown, CT Sacred Heart.
Leopold, Martin J. '01 (SAT) Ecumenical Affairs; Ecumenical Relations; San Antonio, TX Our Lady of Grace; Administrative Assistant to the Archbishop; Administrative Services Department; Priests Personnel Board; Moderator of the Curia & Director of Administration; Archdiocesan Presbyteral Council; [H] San Antonio, TX San Fernando Health Care Centre of San Antonio; Lay Pension Plan Committee.
Leota, Niko F. '87 (LA) Carson, CA St. Philomena.
LePage, Bradley *t.o.r.* '03 (STU)[A] Steubenville, OH Franciscan University of Steubenville; [H] Steubenville, OH Holy Spirit Friary.
Lepak, Przemyslaw '06 (PRO) Riverside, RI St. Brendan.
Lepak, Roy C. '62 (STP) Special Assignment Retired.
Lepleiter, Robert P. '63 (PH) Retired.
LeQuang, Tuan *c.ss.r.* '00 (WDC)[N] Washington, DC Holy Redeemer College.
Lequin, Thomas '77 (PRT) Farmington, ME St. Joseph's; Jay, ME St. Rose of Lima; [M] Farmington, ME University of Maine at Farmington; Pastoral Associates.
Leroux, Gonzague '09 (OAK) Oakland, CA St. Augustine.
Leroux, Roger *m.s.* '52 (FR)[G] Attleboro, MA La Salette Shrine Retired.
Lery, Bruce *s.m.* '87 (WDC)[N] Washington, DC Marist Center.
Lesak, William P. '75 (NEW) Military Chaplains.
Lescher, Raymond C. '63 (JOL) Joliet, IL Sacred Heart.
Lesczynski, James J. '64 (LC) Retired.
Leser, Rev. Msgr. William J. '63 (LA) Retired.
Leser, Chorbishop William '63 (OLL) Judicial Vicar; Board of Pastors.
Leshney, Michael F. '73 (CIN) Bethel, OH St. Mary; New Richmond, OH St. Peter.
LeSieur, Rev. Msgr. David '76 (LR) Deans; Continuing Education for the Clergy; Minister to Priests; Rogers, AR St. Vincent de Paul; Priests Personnel Board (Diocesan); Vicars for Religious; Presbyteral Council.
Lesigues, Lope '90 (NEW) Upper Saddle River, NJ Church of the Presentation.
Leskovar, Richard J. '68 (ALB) Delmar, NY St. Thomas the Apostle; Ministers to Retired Priests; Priests Retirement Board/Priests Retirement Plan Board Retired.
Leslie, Patrick J. '69 (SR) Santa Rosa, CA Star of the Valley; Sonoma Developmental Center.
Lesniak, David '91 (DET) Dearborn, MI St. Alphonsus.
Lesniak, Marian '50 (LAN) Retired.
Lesniak, Richard D. '66 (MAD) Retired.
Lesnick, John F. '78 (BAL) Hancock, MD St. Peter's; On Duty Outside the Archdiocese.
Lesniewski, Stephen F. '93 (CHI) Chicago, IL Immaculate Conception.
Lesniowski, Stanley '70 (PAT) Passaic, NJ St. Joseph's.
Lesousky, John *c.r.* '56 (L)[L] Louisville, KY Villa Pacis, Resurrectionist Retirement Home; Louisville, KY.
Lessard, Eugene R. '59 (PRO) North Scituate, RI St. Joseph Retired.
Lessard, Gerard *o.p.* '84 (WDC) Washington, DC St. Dominic Church & Priory.
Lessard, Joseph M. '80 (PHX) On Leave.
Lessard, Leo '60 (GB) Retired.
Lessard–Thibodeau, John G. '92 (SPR) Holyoke, MA Our Lady of Guadalupe.
Lesseps, Roland J. *s.j.* '65 (NO)[P] New Orleans, LA Ignatius Residence.
Lester, Rev. Msgr. J. William '45 (FTW) Vicar for Retired Clergy; Consultors; Retired Clergy Committee; [F] Fort Wayne, IN Saint Anne Home & Retirement Community Retired.
Lester, John E. '59 (TOL) Retired.
Lester, John J. '62 (NEW) Scotch Plains, NJ St. Bartholomew Retired.
Lester, Thomas '57 (OAK) San Leandro, CA St. Leander Retired.
Lester, William F. *s.j.* '54 (SJ)[M] Los Gatos, CA Sacred Heart Jesuit Center.
LeStrange, Gregory C. '82 (SY) Camillus, NY St. Joseph; Presbyteral Council.
Leszczynski, Jacek K. *o.f.m.conv.* '98 (R)[F] Elon, NC Conventual Franciscans; Burlington, NC Blessed Sacrament.
Letendre, Theodore *f.i.c.* '97 (PRT)[I] Alfred, ME Notre Dame Institute; [I] Notre Dame Spiritual Center; [L] Alfred, ME Notre Dame Retreat & Spiritual Center.
LeThiez, Alphonse D. '55 (PRO) Retired.
Leto, Nelo A. '54 (DM) Retired.
Letoile, Kenneth R. *o.p.* '74 (PRO) Providence, RI St. Pius V; [P] Providence, RI St. Pius Priory.
Letona, Robert M. '09 (LC)[C] Stevens Point, WI St. Peter Middle School; Stevens Point, WI St. Peter; [C] Stevens Point, WI Pacelli High School.
Letourneau, Daniel J. '06 (OKL) Edmond, OK St. John the Baptist; [B] Oklahoma City, OK Bishop McGuinness Catholic High School.
Letourneau, Larry '00 (SAL) Clyde, KS St. John the Baptist Parish; Board of Trustees; Aurora, KS St.

Peter Parish; Clyde, KS St. Mary Parish.
LeTran, Benjamin T. '05 (BO) Framingham, MA St. George.
Letteer, Michael C. '96 (HBG) York, PA Immaculate Conception of the Blessed Virgin Mary.
Lettic, Edward P. '73 (WOR) Lancaster, MA Immaculate Conception.
Lettre, Raymond '88 (SP) Retired.
LeTure, Theodore J. '49 (RVC) Valley Stream, NY Holy Name of Mary Retired.
Leuluia, Taisali *s.d.b.* '07 (OAK)[M] Berkeley Salesians of Don Bosco.
Leurck, Raymond J. '67 (CIN) Shandon, OH St. Aloysius.
Leute, Charles J. *o.p.* '69 (FAR) Fort Totten, ND St. Jerome's Church of Crow Hill; Fort Totten, ND Seven Dolors; Fort Totten, ND Christ the King Church of Tokio; Fort Totten, ND Christ the King – Tokio; Fort Totten, ND Seven Dolors Indian Mission.
Leva, Stephen F. '88 (PH) Philadelphia, PA St. Timothy.
Levandusky, Edward '65 (PHU) Simpson, PA SS. Peter and Paul.
LeVasseur, Giles '84 (WH) Moorefield, WV Epiphany of the Lord; Petersburg, WV St. Mary's.
LeVasseur, Lawrence A. *c.s.c.* '51 (SAT)[L] San Antonio, TX Holy Cross Community.
LeVecke, John R. *s.j.* '84 (ORG) Rancho Santa Margarita, CA San Francisco Solano Church.
LeVecke, John *s.j.* '84 (LA)[P] Culver City, CA Ignatius House, The Novitiate of the California Province, Society of Jesus.
Leveille, Andre E. *c.s.c.* '78 (FTW)[H] Notre Dame, IN Holy Cross Community, Corby Hall, University of Notre Dame.
Leveille, Rudolph J. '57 (PRT) Retired.
Leven, Marvin F. '59 (OKL) Special Assignment; [L] Okarche, OK New Leaven Ministries Foundation; Charismatic Renewal Retired.
Levenhagen, Robert J. '57 (DUB) Retired.
Levens, Robert J. *s.j.* '81 (BGP)[E] Fairfield, CT Fairfield College Preparatory School; [O] Fairfield, CT The Fairfield Jesuit Community–Fairfield University; Presbyteral Council.
Levesque, Rev. Msgr. Edmond R. '55 (FR) Westport, MA St. George's Retired.
Levesque, Gerald A. '64 (PRT) Retired.
Levesque, Joseph L. *c.m.* '67 (BUF)[O] Niagara University, NY Vincentian Community at Niagara University; [C] Niagara University, NY Niagara University.
Levesque, Robert G. *o.m.i.* '60 (MAN)[K] Colebrook, NH Shrine of Our Lady of Grace.
Levesque, Roger J. '59 (FR) Fall River, MA St. Anne's Retired.
Levesque, Sylvio J. '55 (PRT) Retired.
Levis, Robert J. '48 (E)[B] Erie, PA Gannon University Retired.
Levitt, Donald L. '79 (PEO) Moline, IL Christ the King.
Levko, John J. *s.j.* '78 (SCR)[C] Scranton, PA The University of Scranton.
Levra, Ronald W. '07 (SUP) Weyerhaeuser, WI St. Mary; Weyerhaeuser, WI St. Francis of Assisi; Weyerhaeuser, WI Assumption of the Blessed Virgin Mary; Weyerhaeuser, WI SS. Peter and Paul Retired.
Levreault, Raymond G. '05 (SAV) Douglas, GA St. Paul's; Catholic Cemetery.
Levri, Fid *g.h.m.* '67 (CIN)[N] Cincinnati Headquarters of Glenmary Home Missioners Retired.
Levy, Cyril '53 (GLP) Retired.
Levy, Michael *o.m.i.* '57 (SAT)[K] San Antonio, TX Oblate Madonna Residence.
Lewandowski, Andrew *o.f.m.* '76 (STL)[O] St. Louis, MO Franciscan Friary of St. Anthony of Padua; [Q] St. Louis, MO Franciscan Sisters of Mary Administration.
Lewandowski, Bruce *c.ss.r.* '94 (PH) Philadelphia, PA Visitation B.V.M.
Lewandowski, David J. '55 (HRT) Retired.
Lewandowski, Dennis '85 (JOL) Naperville, IL Holy Spirit Catholic Community.
Lewandowski, Donald R. *o.s.a.* '69 (JOL) New Lenox, IL St. Jude.
Lewandowski, Glen *o.s.c.* '74 (PHX)[F] Crosiers Serving Abroad.
Lewandowski, John '96 (FAR) Retired.
Lewandowski, Leonard A. '77 (PH) Philadelphia, PA St. Josaphat.
Lewandowski, Michael *o.f.m.conv.* '75 (ALT) Davidsville, PA St. Anne.
Lewandowski, Raymond H. '85 (DET) Garden City, MI St. Raphael the Archangel.
Lewandowski, Richard P. '74 (WOR) Retired.
Lewandowski, Ronald C. '95 (CHI) Antioch, IL St. Raphael the Archangel Retired.
Lewandowski, Theodore V. '98 (RCK) Retired.
Lewandowski, Thomas J. '00 (PIT) New Castle, PA St. Camillus; [P] New Castle, PA Westminster College.
Lewanski, Gary J. '82 (CHI) Other Assignments.
Lewett, George *o.f.m.* '88 (FgM) Washington, DC COMMISSARIAT OF THE HOLY LAND.
Lewicki, Roman B. *s.j.* '65 (FgM) Chicago, IL Society of Jesus.
Lewinski, Ronald J. '72 (CHI) Mundelein, IL St. Mary of the Annunciation; Deans; [W] Mundelein, IL Foundation for Adult Catechetical Teaching Aids.
Lewinski, Thomas Cassian *o.p.* '69 (SB)[M] Riverside, CA St. Andrew Newman Center; [I] Riverside, CA St. Vincent Ferrer House; Special or Other Diocesan Assignment; Riverside, CA St. Andrew Newman Center.
Lewis, Alexander '85 (LA) North Hills, CA Our Lady of Peace.
Lewis, Clyde A. '64 (OG) Rouses Point, NY St. Joseph; Rouses Point, NY St. Patrick; Judges; Committee on Assignments.
Lewis, David C. '04 (BO) Peabody, MA St. Adelaide.
Lewis, David J. '66 (GB) New London, WI Most Precious Blood; Hortonville, WI SS. Peter and Paul.
Lewis, David '90 (CI)[C] Tunnuk, Chuuk, FM Vicariate Residence.
Lewis, Dennis J. '75 (MIL) Milwaukee, WI St. Michael; Milwaukee, WI St. Rose.
Lewis, Eric Anthony '69 (LA)[J] West Covina, CA Citrus Valley Medical Center, Queen of the Valley Campus; La Puente, CA St. Louis of France; Hospital Chaplains.
Lewis, Rev. Msgr. Gerald L. '61 (R) New Bern, NC St. Paul Retired.
Lewis, Harry J. '50 (SCR) Retired.
Lewis, James B. (FTW)[B] University of Notre Dame Du Lac.
Lewis, James V. *s.j.* '69 (CLV)[D] Cleveland, OH St. Ignatius High School.
Lewis, James *o.carm.* '83 (JOL)[L] Darien Carmelite Provincial Office.
Lewis, Lawrence J. *m.m.* '75 (NY)[EE] Maryknoll Maryknoll Fathers and Brothers.
Lewis, Leo T. '60 (STL) Retired.
Lewis, Mark *s.j.* '91 (NO)[P] New Orleans, LA Jesuit Provincial Office; New Orleans, LA; New Orleans, LA Immaculate Conception.
Lewis, Ryan P. '99 (OM) Omaha, NE St. Thomas More; Ecumenical Officer; Judges.
Lewis, William M. '09 (OKL) Norman, OK St. Joseph's.
Lewkiewicz, Richard '68 (BRK) Brooklyn, NY Our Lady of Angels.
Lewnau, Richard '04 (DET) Detroit, MI St. Suzanne/ Our Lady Gate of Heaven; Detroit, MI St. Thomas Aquinas.
Lewon, Michal '08 (CHI) Riverside, IL St. Mary.
Lex, Henry V. '51 (BUF) Retired.
Lexa, Robert '70 (GB) Retired.
Ley, Phillip G. *o.f.m.conv.* '84 (SAT)[B] San Antonio, TX San Damiano Friary, Prenovitiate House of Formation; [L] San Antonio, TX San Damiano Friary.
Ley, Richard J. '71 (ARL) Arlington, VA Our Lady of Lourdes.
Ley, Theodore *s.m.* '59 (LA) Los Angeles, CA St. Ann; [F] Marianist Community.
Leyba, John Paul '02 (DEN) Foxfield, CO Our Lady of Loreto.
Leykam, Rev. Msgr. John J. '72 (STL) Archdiocesan Consultors; Ladue, MO Church of the Annunziata.
Leykam, Lambert *o.f.m.* '56 (FWT)[H] Crowley, TX St. Maximilian Kolbe Friary.
Leyland, Thomas J. '65 (TOL) Retired.
Leyrita, Norbert '63 (GR) Retired.
Lhoposo, Jean–Pierre Swamunu *c.i.c.m.* '04 (CHL) Hickory, NC St. Aloysius.
Li, Dong Min (Paul) '07 (HON) Pearl City, HI Our Lady of Good Counsel; Presbyteral Council.
Li, Francis '99 (CHI) Chicago, IL St. Barbara.
Liable, Adrian *o.s.b.* '58 (OM)[K] Elkhorn, NE Mount Michael Benedictine Abbey.
Libaire, Nathan '81 (SFE) Santa Fe, NM St. John the Baptist; Presbyteral Council of the Archdiocese of Santa Fe.
Libanati, Ciro '62 (SB) Elected Members; Victorville, CA St. Joan of Arc.
Libby, Donald L. '05 (GAY) Maple City, MI St. Rita–St. Joseph; Members of the College of Consultors; Cedar, MI Holy Rosary.
Libby, Richard A. '99 (CC)[I] Corpus Christi, TX Search Retreats; Alice, TX St. Joseph.
Libens, John F. *s.j.* '70 (CLV)[D] Cleveland, OH St. Ignatius High School.
Libera, Angelo '57 (SY) Retired.
Libera, Thomas A. '69 (CHI) Evanston, IL St. Athanasius.
Liberatore, David D. '60 (CLV) Parma Heights, OH St. John Bosco.
Liberman–Ormaza, Antonio '85 (DAL) Ennis, TX St. John Nepomucene.
Liberty, Donald *c.ss.r.* '61 (LA) Whittier, CA St. Mary of the Assumption; [P] Whittier, CA Redemptorists of Whittier Retired.
Liberty, Robert S. '03 (DET) Detroit, MI St. Jude.
Libiszewski, Dominik Pawel *o.s.p.p.e.* '07 (NY) New York, NY St. Stanislaus Bishop and Martyr.
Libone, John '80 (DAL) Deans; Dallas, TX St. Thomas Aquinas; Adjutant Judicial Vicars; College of Consultors.
Librandi, Michael A. '78 (RCK) Retired.
Librea, Raphael B. '35 (OM) Springfield, NE St. Joseph Retired.
Licanda, Samuel '94 (MO) Air Force Chaplains.
Licari, John J. '02 (PT) Pensacola, FL St. Anne's.
Licari, Jonathan *o.s.b.* '76 (SCL)[I] Collegeville, MN St. John's Abbey, of the Order of St. Benedict.
Licayan, Ron '97 (ANC) Kodiak, AK St. Mary's.
Licciardi, Fred *c.pp.s.* '82 (CIN)[N] Dayton Provincial Office of the Cincinnati Province of the Society of the Precious Blood.
Licciardi, Fred *c.pp.s.* '82 (CHI) Barrington, IL St. Anne.
Licea–Anguiano, Santos *o.r.c.* '98 (STO) Ceres, CA St. Jude Church (Pastor of).
Lichtefeld, James J. '59 (L) Defenders of the Bond Retired.
Lichtenthal, Rev. Msgr. James J. '63 (BUF) Retired.
Lichter, Mark '92 (SFS) Yankton, SD Sacred Heart; Personnel Board.
Licinsky, Steven *l.c.* '02 (MAN)[A] Center Harbor, NH Immaculate Conception Apostolic School.
Lickman, Peter '68 (PSC) Miami, FL St. Basil; Syncellus; Eparchial College of Consultors; Presbyteral Council.
Lickteig, Anthony '54 (KCK) Overland Park, KS Holy Spirit; Louisburg, KS Retired.
Lickteig, Bernard *o.carm.* '46 (JOL)[L] Darien Carmelite Provincial Office.
Lickteig, Norbert '61 (KCK) Holy Childhood Association; Missions; Pontifical Mission Societies in the United States Retired.
Licznerski, Henry *c.r.* '92 (SB) Blythe, CA St. Joan of Arc; [I] Blythe, CA.
Liddy, Rev. Msgr. Richard M. '63 (NEW)[B] School of Diplomacy and Intl. Rels.
Liderbach, Daniel P. *s.j.* '73 (DET)[K] Clarkston, MI Colombiere Center.
Liebert, William *s.v.d.* '57 (CHI)[N] Techny, IL Divine Word Residence Retired.
Lieberth, Joseph '68 (CLV) Administrative Leave.
Liebhardt, Kevin M. '74 (CLV) Eastlake, OH St. Justin Martyr; [F] Eastlake, OH St. Mary Magdalene–St. Justin Martyr School, Inc.
Liebler, Thomas R. '81 (SFD) Bethalto, IL Our Lady Queen of Peace.
Liebner, David M. '60 (ALN) Girardville, PA St. Vincent de Paul Retired.
Liebner, James *s.v.d.* '85 (FgM) Techny, IL.
Liebscher, Arthur F. *s.j.* '84 (SJ)[B] Santa Clara, CA Jesuit Community.
Liekhus, James C. '05 (STP) Hopkins, MN St. John the Evangelist.
Liem, Joseph Than Van *c.m.c.* '89 (SPC) Kimberling City, MO Our Lady of the Cove.
Lienert, Rev. Msgr. Charles '68 (P) College of Consultors; Area Vicars; Personnel Board.
Lienert, Rev. Msgr. Charles '68 (P) Portland, OR St. Andrew.
Lienert, James *m.s.f.* '54 (BWN) Donna, TX St. Joseph.
Lienhard, Joseph T. *s.j.* '71 (NY)[A] Yonkers, NY St. Joseph's Seminary; [EE] Cardinal Spellman Hall, Jesuit Community.
Lies, C. Jarrod '01 (WCH)[B] Wichita, KS Bishop Carroll Catholic High School; Viola, KS St. John.
Lies, David J. '98 (WCH) Lindsborg, KS St. Bridget of Sweden; McPherson, KS St. Joseph; [K] Mc Pherson, KS Engaged Encounter.
Lies, Eric *o.s.b.* '45 (IND)[K] St. Meinrad, IN St. Meinrad Archabbey.
Lies, James M. *c.s.c.* '97 (FTW)[H] Notre Dame Congregation of Holy Cross, Indiana Province, Provincial House.
Lies, James *c.s.c.* '97 (P)[B] University of Portland; [L] Portland, OR Holy Cross Fathers & Brothers, C.S.C. – University of Portland.
Lies, William M. *c.s.c.* '94 (FTW)[B] University of Notre Dame Du Lac; [H] Notre Dame, IN Holy Cross Community, Corby Hall, University of Notre Dame; Provincial Councilors:; [H] Notre Dame, IN Congregation of Holy Cross, Indiana Province, Provincial House.
Lieser, Gregory '63 (SCL) Defensor Vinculi; Deans; Catholic Women, Council of Retired.
Lieser, Vincent '67 (SCL) Personnel Committee; Melrose, MN St. Mary's; Diocesan Planning Council.
Liewer, David F. '74 (OM) Ponca, NE St. Peter; Ponca, NE St. Joseph; Deans; Deans.
Lifrak, Richard *ss.cc.* '95 (FR)[G] Fairhaven, MA Damien Residence.
Ligato, Anthony F. '95 (ALB) Little Falls, NY Holy Family; Priestly Life and Ministry Council.
Ligato, Anthony '95 (ALB) Wynantskill, NY St. Jude the Apostle; Presbyteral Council; Diocesan Board of Consultors.
Ligeti, Angelus *o.f.m.* '79 (DET) Detroit, MI Holy Cross.
Ligeza, Jan A. '03 (STA) Jacksonville, FL St. Paul's.
Ligeza, Kazimierz '90 (STA) Gainesville, FL Queen of Peace.
Lightner, Michael '05 (MIL)[X] Milwaukee, WI University of Wisconsin – Milwaukee, Newman Center; Special Assignment; Directors.

Ligonde, Jean–Marie Fritz '89 (VEN) Naples, FL St. Finbarr; Haitian Ministry; Lee County; Presbyteral Council.
Ligory, Joseph '83 (NY) Bronx, NY St. Helena.
Ligot, Andres C. '92 (SJ) Judicial Vicar; Judicial Vicar; Diocesan Clergy Personnel Board; Special Assignment.
Ligot, Andres '92 (SJ) Saratoga, CA Church of the Ascension.
Liguori, Christopher '03 (STA) Palm Coast, FL St. Elizabeth Ann Seton.
Liguori, Henry A. '66 (TR) Military Chaplains.
Liistro, Frank J. '74 (WOR) Fitchburg, MA Madonna of the Holy Rosary; Fitchburg, MA Sacred Heart of Jesus.
Lijewski, Thomas F. '70 (MIL) Port Washington, WI St. Peter of Alcantara; Saukville, WI Immaculate Conception; Port Washington, WI St. Mary.
Lijewski, Timothy M. '93 (CHR) North Augusta, SC Our Lady of Peace.
Lill, Kenneth J. '91 (TOL) Fremont, OH Sacred Heart.
Lillpopp, Michael '05 (MO) West Springfield, MA St. Frances Xavier Cabrini Parish; Air Force Reserve Chaplains.
Lilly, Robert A. *m.m.* '62 (NY)[EE] Retired.
Lilly, Robert M. *m.m.* '60 (FgM) Maryknoll, NY MARYKNOLL.
Lilly, Thomas C. '03 (ANC) Anchorage, AK St. Elizabeth Ann Seton; Diocesan Consultors; Air Force Reserve Chaplains; Vocations; Valdez, AK St. Francis Xavier.
Lim, Candido O. *s.j.* '69 (SJ) San Jose, CA St. Victor; [M] Los Gatos Sacred Heart Jesuit Center.
Lim, Carmelo Rey '95 (HON) Waianae, HI Sacred Heart.
Lim, Joseph D. '75 (MO) Air Force Chaplains.
Lim, Marc '07 (OM) Omaha, NE St. Robert Bellarmine.
Lim, Roque G. '06 (BAL) Baltimore, MD St. Joseph.
Lima, J. Bosco '92 (NEW) Newark, NJ Holy Trinity – Epiphany.
Lima, John H. '63 (OAK) Retired.
Lima, Vivian B. '85 (LA) Downey, CA Our Lady of Perpetual Help.
Limbert, William G. '51 (KAL) Retired.
Limmer, George A. '64 (BAL) Retired.
Limpiado, Edwin (MRY) Salinas, CA Madonna Del Sasso; Presbyteral Council.
Lin, Ming Yu "Vincent" '01 (LA) Monterey Park, CA St. Thomas Aquinas.
Lin, Sheng Jiao '08 (BRK)[T] Jamaica, NY Vincentian Residence.
Lin, Vincent '07 (DAL) Plano, TX Sacred Heart of Jesus.
Linago, Deogracias '64 (NY) Staten Island, NY Staten Island University Hospital South.
Linakis, William *s.a.* '77 (NY)[EE] Garrison Franciscan Friars of the Atonement, Minister General Office.
Linan, Jesse S. (GAL) Retired.
Linares, Jose R. '86 (MGZ) Cabo Rojo, PR St. Michael.
Lincoln, Daniel L. '84 (L) Elizabethtown, KY St. John the Baptist; Vine Grove, KY St. Brigid.
Lincoln, Howard A. '91 (SB) Palm Desert, CA Christ of the Desert; Palm Desert, CA Sacred Heart; Elected Members.
Lincon, Joseph B. (TYL) Longview, TX St. Anthony.
Lincon, Joseph '89 (BGP) On Duty Outside the Diocese.
Lind, Rev. Msgr. Joseph G. '65 (BO) Senior Priests.; Wellesley, MA St. Paul Retired.
Lind, Thomas *s.c.j.* '58 (JKS)[E] Nesbit, MS St. Michael Community House.
Lindblad, Karl–Albert '87 (MO) Military Chaplains; Navy Chaplains.
Lindemann, Gene E. '83 (BIS) Bismarck, ND St. Mary; Defensor Vinculi; Presbyteral Council; Office of Worship.
Linden, Emmet *c.p.* '51 (L)[L] Louisville, KY Sacred Heart Retreat.
Linden, John '07 (LAN) Ann Arbor, MI St. Francis of Assisi.
Linden, Michael D. *s.j.* '80 (BO)[U] Watertown, MA The Society of Jesus of New England–Provincial Offices; Presbyteral Council; [U] Weston, MA Campion Jesuit Community.
Linden, Michael J. *s.j.* '80 (FgM) Watertown, MA; Watertown, MA Society of Jesus.
Lindenfelser, Timothy M. '94 (STA) Elkton, FL St. Ambrose.
Lindenfelser, Timothy M. '94 (STA) St. Augustine, FL St. Augustine Diocesan Cemeteries; Judicial Vicar.
Linder, Rev. Msgr. William J. '63 (NEW) Newark, NJ St. Rose of Lima.
Lindle, Lawrence H. '59 (L)[Q] Louisville, KY Perpetual Eucharistic Adoration; [Q] Louisville, KY World Apostolate of Fatima (Blue Army); [Q] Louisville, KY Sacred Heart Apostolate; [Q] Louisville, KY Archdiocesan Marian Committee; Sacred Heart Enthronement Center Retired.
Lindley, Philip '83 (AMA) Unassigned.
Lindner, Jerold W. *s.j.* '76 (SJ)[M] Los Gatos, CA Sacred Heart Jesuit Center.
Lindner, Thomas F. '95 (LC) Stevens Point, WI Newman University Parish; [K] Stevens Point, WI Newman University Parish; Appointed Members.
Lindsay, John *o.s.f.s.* '70 (STO) Modesto, CA St. Stanislaus Church (Pastor of).
Lindsay, Michael P. '87 (MO) Defenders of the Bond; Army National Guard Chaplains.
Lindsay, Michael '87 (LSC) Priests Retirement Fund Committee.
Lindsay, Robert E. *s.j.* '60 (BO)[U] Weston, MA Campion Health Center, Inc.
Lindsay, Stewart M. *o.s.f.s.* '74 (BUF)[K] Lewiston, NY Mount St. Mary's Hospital of Niagara Falls; Niagara Falls, NY Holy Family of Jesus, Mary and Joseph.
Lindsey, Bob *c.ss.r.* '09 (KC)[J] Kansas City, MO Redemptorists Fathers of Kansas City, Missouri.
Lindsey, Robert *c.ss.r.* '09 (KC) Kansas City, MO Our Lady of Perpetual Help.
Lindstrom, Michael *s.v.d.* '82 (FgM) Techny, IL.
Linebach, Martin A. '57 (L) Louisville, KY St. Ignatius; Ecumenical and Interreligious Relations Officer; Louisville, KY Cathedral of the Assumption.
Linehan, Brian *o.f.m.* '67 (PAT)[N] Ringwood, NJ Holy Name Friary, Inc.
Linehan, Cornelius '43 (P) Retired.
Linehan, Maurice F. *m.s.* '52 (HRT)[L] Hartford, CT Missionaries of LaSalette.
Linehan, Michael '71 (CC) Retired.
Linehan, Stephen J. '75 (BO) Military & VA Chaplains.
Lingan, Joseph E. *s.j.* '90 (SY)[A] Syracuse, NY Saint Andrew Hall; Towson, MD.
Lingao, Deogracias (NY) Staten Island, NY Sacred Heart.
Lingle, Brent '07 (SC) Sioux City, IA Cathedral of the Epiphany.
Linhares, William P. *t.o.r.* '84 (WH)[D] Kearneysville, WV Priest Field Pastoral Center; Vicars Forane; Councilors:.
Linhares, William P. *t.o.r.* '84 (ALT)[G] Hollidaysburg, PA Province Econome's Office.
Lininger, Paul *o.f.m.conv.* (WDC)[N] Silver Spring, MD Gemelli House.
Link, David T. '08 (GRY) Indiana State Prison.
Link, David '91 (OAK) Castro Valley, CA Transfiguration; Bishop's Representative for Eastern Rite Catholics.
Link, Fred *o.f.m.* '70 (CIN) Cincinnati, OH St. Clement; [N] Cincinnati, OH St. Clement Friary.
Link, Frederick G. '69 (CAM) Brooklawn, NJ St. Maurice's Church, Brooklawn, N.J.; Westville, NJ St. Anne's Church, Westville, N.J.
Link, Mark J. *s.j.* '60 (CHI)[C] Chicago, IL Jesuit Community at Loyola University Chicago.
Link, Matt *c.pp.s.* (OAK)[M] Berkeley, CA Society of the Precious Blood (Province of Kansas City).
Linkchorst, William J. '73 (ALN) Tamaqua, PA SS. Peter and Paul.
Linn, Matthew L. *s.j.* '73 (STP)[B] St. Paul, MN Jesuit Novitiate.
Linnan, John E. *c.s.v.* '61 (CHI)[N] Arlington Heights Viatorian Province Center–Clerics of St. Viator.
Linnan, Roger J. '62 (SC) Hawarden, IA St. Mary's; Directors; Priests' Pension Plan – Board of Trustees; Presbyteral Council.
Linnane, Brian F. *s.j.* '86 (BO)[U] Boston The Society of Jesus of New England–Provincial Offices.
Linnane, Brian F. *s.j.* '86 (BAL)[B] Timonium, MD Loyola Graduate Center–Timonium Campus; [S] Baltimore, MD Jesuit Community of Loyola University, Inc.; [B] Baltimore, MD Loyola University in Maryland; [B] Jesuit Community of Loyola University, Inc.
Linnebur, Leroy '61 (WCH) Retired.
Linnebur, Michael '08 (WCH) Wichita, KS St. Francis of Assisi.
Linnemann, Eugene C. '80 (BEL) Retired.
Linowski, Eugene R. '57 (PRM) Retired.
Lins, James R. '64 (MAD) Shullsburg, WI St. Peter; [F] Madison, WI Bishop O'Connor Catholic Pastoral Center Retired.
Linse, Henry *c.s.s.* '48 (BO)[X] Waltham, MA Stigmatine Fathers and Brothers Retired.
Linsky, Gary S. '95 (MO) Military Chaplains; Air Force Chaplains.
Linsler, Christopher E. '78 (ROC) Horseheads, NY St. Mary Our Mother.
Linster, Rev. Msgr. Joseph B. '69 (RCK) Saint Charles, IL St. Patrick; Deans.
Linton, Edward *o.s.b.* (CHI) Chicago, IL St. James.
Linton, Edward *o.s.b.* '91 (IND)[K] St. Meinrad St. Meinrad Archabbey.
Lintz, Charles *s.s.c.* '70 (OM)[K] St. Columbans, NE Missionary Society of St. Columban.
Lintz, Charles "Chuck" '70 (OM) Omaha, NE Our Lady of Guadalupe – St. Agnes Parish.
Lintz, Christoph '94 (NEW) On Duty Outside the Archdiocese.
Lintzenich, Stephen P. '74 (EVN) Evansville, IN St. John the Apostle; Evansville, IN St. Joseph; Evansville, IN St. Mary; Clergy Personnel Board; Judges; Diocesan Council of Priests; Special Assignment; Diocesan Consultors.
Linzmaier, Eric G. '00 (LC) Auburndale, WI Nativity of the Blessed Virgin Mary; Hewitt, WI St. Michael.
Lioi, Frank E. '67 (ROC) Auburn, NY St. Mary.
Lion, William J. '58 (CHI) Oak Lawn, IL St. Catherine of Alexandria Retired.
Lionelli, Anthony J. '72 (NEW) Montclair, NJ Our Lady of Mt. Carmel.
Lipareli, Michael A. '80 (PH) Philadelphia, PA Veterans Administration Medical Center.
Lipareli, Michael A. '80 (MO) DEPARTMENT OF VETERANS AFFAIRS HOSPITALS AND CHAPLAINS.
Lipiec, Bartholomew W. '83 (BUF) Depew, NY Our Lady of the Blessed Sacrament.
Lipinski, Edward J. '71 (CAM) Turnersville, NJ The Church of Saints Peter and Paul, Washington Township, N.J.; Judges; Adjutant Judicial Vicars.
Lipinski, Paul M. '73 (RCK) Special Assignment; [B] Rockford, IL Boylan Central Catholic High School.
Lipka, Wieslaw '65 (KAL) Kalamazoo, MI St. Monica.
Lipnicki, Thomas P. '78 (NEW) Oakland, NJ Our Lady of Perpetual Help; Northwest Bergen Region Deanery 1; Cursillo Movement.
Liporace, Francisco *i.v.e.* (CHI) Chicago, IL St. Francis of Assisi.
Lipp, John F. *o.s.a.* '54 (PH)[Y] Villanova, PA St. Thomas Monastery.
Lippert, Donald F. *o.f.m.cap* '85 (WDC)[W] Washington, DC Spanish Catholic Center.
Lippert, Donald *o.f.m.cap.* '85 (FgM) Pittsburgh, PA Province of St. Augustine.
Lippert, Paul R. '61 (MIL) Retired.
Lippincot–Pino, Jamie (ALB) Mount McGregor Correctional Facility.
Lippold, John L. '57 (BAL) Linthicum Heights, MD St. Philip Neri Retired.
Lipps, Rev. Msgr. Frank J. '68 (NO) Slidell, LA Our Lady of Lourdes.
Lipps, Louis J. *s.j.* '52 (CIN)[N] Cincinnati, OH Claver Jesuit Community.
Lippstock, Paul E. '78 (DUB) Preston, IA St. Joseph; Sabula, IA St. Peter; Springbrook, IA SS. Peter and Paul; Maquoketa, IA St. John.
Lippstock, Paul Eldon '78 (MO) Army National Guard Chaplains.
Liprie, James *o.s.b.* '83 (LAF)[H] Opelousas, LA Mother of the Redeemer Monastery.
Lipscomb, John B. (SP)[P] Lutz, FL Bethany Center, Inc.
Lipscomb, N. Alan '94 (RIC) Palmyra, VA Church of the Nativity; Columbia, VA St. Joseph's/Shrine of St. Katharine Drexel; Palmyra, VA Ss. Peter & Paul.
Lipscomb, William W. '97 (GAY) Members of the College of Consultors.
Liptak, Rev. Msgr. David Q. '53 (HRT) Hartford, CT Cathedral of St. Joseph; Special and other Archdiocesan Assignment; [A] Cromwell, CT Holy Apostles College and Seminary; Newspaper; Censor Librorum.
Liptak, Edward *s.d.b.* '59 (SFR) San Francisco, CA Corpus Christi.
Lipton, Mariadas J. '87 (NOR) Durham, CT Notre Dame.
LiPuma, Rev. Msgr. David G. '87 (BUF) Secretary to Diocesan Bishop and Vice Chancellor; [O] Buffalo, NY Bishop's Residence.
Lira, Juan Pineda *m.s.c.* '77 (FRS) Huron, CA St. Frances Cabrini; Avenal, CA St. Joseph.
Lis, Albert *o.f.m.* '86 (MIL)[N] Greenfield, WI Clement Manor Health Center; [Y] Greenfield, WI Clement Manor Retirement Community; Milwaukee, WI St. Anthony of Padua.
Lis, John S. '73 (SPR) Absent on Sick Leave.
Lisante, Rev. Msgr. James P. '81 (RVC) Massapequa Park, NY Our Lady of Lourdes.
Lisbeth, Michael *s.m.* '80 (CIN)[N] Dayton, OH Marianist Community, Novitiate; [C] Dayton, OH Marianist Novitiate.
Lischaa, Rev. Msgr. Sharbel '61 (SAM) Philadelphia, PA St. Maron.
Lischwe, Bruno V. *c.ss.r.* '52 (STL)[O] Liguori, MO St. Clement Health Care Center.
Lisik, Paul A. '81 (GBG) Clymer, PA Church of the Resurrection; Deaneries; College of Consultors; Bishop's Priests Council; College of Deans.
Liska, Richard A. '70 (MIL) Oak Creek, WI St. Stephen.
Lisowski, Brian A. '81 (CHI) Other Assignments.
Lisowski, Edward E. '64 (MO) DEPARTMENT OF VETERANS AFFAIRS HOSPITALS AND CHAPLAINS Retired.
Lisowski, Lawrence M. '84 (CHI) Lemont, IL SS. Cyril and Methodius.
Lisowski, Thomas '86 (SPR) Office of Lay Ministry Formation.
Lisowski, William J. '50 (CHI) Retired.
Liss, Robert C. '62 (STL) Richwoods, MO St. Stephen.
Lisson, Edwin *s.j.* '69 (STL)[C] Saint Louis University; [O] St. Louis, MO Jesuit Community Corporation at Saint Louis University – Jesuit Hall.
List, Brian *s.o.l.t.* '03 (CC)[G] Robstown, TX Society of Our Lady of the Most Holy Trinity.

List, John E. '85 (LEX) Judicial Vicar; Lexington, KY St. Peter.
Liston, Rev. Msgr. Daniel P. '85 (SPR) Springfield, MA St. Michael's Cathedral; Vicar for Canonical Affairs and Chancellor; Judges; Bishop's Commission for Clergy; Bishop's Cabinet; Diocesan Consultors; Presbyteral Council; Mont Marie Health Care Center.
Liston, Paul F. '58 (WDC)[W] Washington, DC Catholic Historical Society of Washington; [M] Washington, DC Cardinal O'Boyle Residence for Priests Retired.
Liszewski, Francis A. '69 (NOR) Retired.
Liszewski, Peter B. '78 (NOR) Westbrook, CT St. Mark; Continuing Education and Formation Commission for the Clergy.
Litak, Czeslaw (STL) Saint Louis, MO St. Agatha Parish, Polish Roman Catholic Church.
Litavec, Edward S. '60 (PIT) Pittsburgh, PA Sacred Heart; McKeesport, PA St. Mary Czestochowa Retired.
Litcheck, Michael P. '71 (SCR) Retired.
Literski, Rev. Msgr. Roy E. '53 (WIN) Tucson, AZ Retired.
Litot, Rev. Msgr. Edward F. '47 (GRY) Judges Retired.
Littelmann, Edward J. '69 (TOL) College of Consultors; Spiritual Directors; Toledo, OH St. Patrick of Heatherdowns.
Little, Rev. Msgr. Anthony B. '82 (ALT) Newry, PA St. Patrick's.
Littlefield, Philaret '87 (NTN) Milwaukee, WI St. George; Associated Melkite Charities; College of Eparchial Consultors; Presbyteral Council.
Litwack, Joshua E. '00 (TLS) Wilburton, OK Sacred Heart.
Litwin, Rev. Msgr. Paul A. '79 (BUF) The Diocese of Buffalo, N.Y.; Chancellor; [O] Buffalo, NY Bishop's Residence; [A] East Aurora, NY Christ the King Seminary; Finance Council.
Litzau, Richard *o.p.* '05 (IND) Bloomington, IN St. Paul Catholic Center.
Litzner, Corey J. '04 (MAR) Stephenson, MI Precious Blood Church; Consultors.
Liu, Daniel '08 (AUS) Austin, TX St. Mary Cathedral.
Liu, Peter T. '60 (RVC) Ronkonkoma, NY St. Joseph's Retired.
Liu, Pius *o.f.m.* '53 (FgM) New York, NY Holy Name Province.
Liuzzi, Kenneth J. '75 (DEN) Denver, CO Blessed Sacrament; [S] Denver, CO Blessed Sacrament Catholic Educational Foundation.
Liuzzi, Peter J. *o.carm.* '65 (LA)[P] Encino, CA Our Lady of Mount Carmel Priory.
Liuzzo, Vincent *o.f.m.cap.* '49 (PAT) Passaic, NJ St. Mary Hospital; Passaic, NJ Our Lady Of Mt. Carmel.
Lively, Gregory '01 (HEL) Eureka, MT Our Lady of Mercy.
Lively, Joseph A. '57 (BUR) Retired.
Livigni, Salvatore '61 (BAL) Baltimore, MD St. Michael Retired.
Livingston, James T. '90 (STP) Minneapolis, MN St. Boniface; North Memorial Hospital.
Livingstone, James L. '03 (SFR) Millbrae, CA St. Dunstan.
Livingstone, James W. '03 (SFR) Serra Club of San Mateo; Burlingame, CA St. Catherine of Siena.
Livinus, William T. '96 (GAY) Harrisville, MI St. Anne; Harrisville, MI St. Raphael.
Livisni, Salvatore '61 (BAL) Office of Pastoral Service for Senior and Retired Clergy.
Livojevich, Ronald '70 (KCK) Retired.
Lizama, Sergio *s.a.c.* '06 (MIL) Milwaukee, WI St. Vincent Pallotti; [P] Milwaukee, WI Pallotti House.
Lizarraga, Candido *rr.t.c.* '41 (SJN)[F] Santurce, PR Casa de Ninos Manuel Fernandez Juncos.
Lizarralde, Jose *c.p.* '69 (MGZ) San Sebastian, PR San Sebastian Martir.
Lizewski, John M. '99 (WOR)[R] Paxton, MA Anna Maria College; West Boylston, MA Our Lady of Good Counsel.
Lizinczyk, Tadeusz '98 (PH)[Y].
Lizio, John R. '57 (BO) Senior Priests. Retired.
Lizor, Rev. Msgr. Joseph S. '58 (BAL) Baltimore, MD St. Luke.
Llamas, Rodolfo D. '93 (SAC) Elk Grove, CA St. Joseph; Priests' Personnel Board, Diocesan.
Llamas, Salvador Diaz *m.n.m.* '04 (ARE) Quebradillas, PR Our Lady of Monserrate.
Llambias, Martin '73 (SJN)[G] Guaynabo, PR Opus Dei; San Juan.
Llanos, Philip S. '78 (LA) Military Chaplains.
Llanos, Phillip S. '78 (MO) Air Force Chaplains.
Lleo, Pedro '76 (MIA) Pompano Beach, FL St. Coleman.
LLona, German *o.ss.t.* '61 (ARE) Isabela, PR Our Lady of Mount Carmel.
Llorente, Amando *s.j.* '48 (MIA)[M] Miami, FL John Paul II Retreat House; Agrupacion Catolica Universitaria (ACU).
Llorente, Ignacio '09 (P) Corvallis, OR St. Mary; [P] Corvallis, OR Newman Center at Oregon State University (Corvallis).
Lloyd, James B. *c.s.p.* '48 (NY)[EE] Jamaica Estates Paulist Fathers Generalate; [EE] New York, NY Paulist Fathers' Motherhouse Retired.
Lloyd, Patrick *s.c.j.* '69 (MIL)[P] Franklin, WI Villa Maria.
Lloyd, Philip P. '78 (GAL) Houston, TX St. Theresa.
Lloyd, Robert J. *m.m.* '62 (NY)[EE] Maryknoll Maryknoll Fathers and Brothers Retired.
Llywelyn, Dorian *s.j.* '90 (LA)[C] Los Angeles, CA Jesuit Community.
Loaiza, Jorge H. '98 (RCK) Aurora, IL Sacred Heart.
Lobacz, James E. '79 (MIL)[B] Hales Corners, WI Sacred Heart School of Theology; Special Assignment.
Lobato, Nicanor '61 (VEN) Retired.
Lobaton, Jose Ruben '73 (TYL) Paris, TX Our Lady of Victory.
Lobert, Richard C. '75 (BAL) On Duty Outside the Archdiocese.
Lobert, Richard C. '75 (LAN)[B] Ann Arbor, MI Father Gabriel Richard High School.
LoBianco, Rev. Msgr. Francis R. '54 (NEW) Retired.
LoBianco, Paschal *s.v.d.* '50 (CHI)[N] Techny, IL Divine Word Residence.
LoBianco, Richard J. '79 (CHI) Norridge, IL Divine Savior.
LoBiondo, Gasper F. *s.j.* '68 (WDC)[N] Washington, DC Woodstock Jesuit Community; [W] Washington, DC Woodstock Theological Center.
Lobo, Benjamin '63 (GF) Retired.
Lobo, Joseph '98 (RVC) East Meadow, NY St. Raphael.
Lobo, Raul Venust '62 (NO) Retired.
Lobo, Stanley M. '65 (NEW) Palisades Park, NJ St. Michael's Retired.
Lobon, Simon *c.ss.p.* '90 (NY) New York, NY St. Mark the Evangelist.
Lobsinger, Daniel *c.r.* '96 (L) Louisville, KY Guardian Angels; Louisville, KY.
Locatelli, Paul L. *s.j.* '74 (SJ)[B] Santa Clara, CA Jesuit Community; Members; Members.
Loch, Richard J. '79 (SCR) Scranton, PA St. Lucy's; Episcopal Vicar for Priests; Catholic Charismatic Renewal; Priests' Purgatorial Society; Priests' Retirement Advisory Board; Locust Grove, VA National Service Committee of the Catholic Charismatic Renewal of the United States, Inc.; Diocesan Consultors.
Lock, Bertram *ss.cc.* '89 (HON) Waialua, HI St. Michael.
Lockard, Rev. Msgr. David A. '75 (ALT) State College, PA Our Lady of Victory.
Locke, James E. '61 (PH) Retired.
Lockey, Paul E. '87 (GAL) Houston, TX St. Elizabeth Ann Seton.
Lockman, James *o.f.m.* (OAK)[R] Board of Directors:.
Lockman, Rev. Msgr. V. James '67 (WDC) Washington, DC Annunciation.
Lockulu, Jean–Paulin '95 (JUN) Diocesan Consultors.
Lockwood, Gregory '88 (STL) Crestwood, MO St. Elizabeth of Hungary; [A] St. Louis, MO Kenrick School of Theology.
Lococo, Donald J. *c.s.b.* '90 (ROC)[J] Rochester, NY Basilian Residence.
Loda, Mauro *s.x.* '99 (FgM)[N] Wayne Xaverian Missionary Fathers; Wayne, NJ XAVERIAN MISSIONARY FATHERS.
Lodge, John G. '73 (CHI)[A] Mundelein, IL University of St. Mary of the Lake/Mundelein Seminary; [A] Mundelein, IL University of St. Mary of the Lake/Mundelein Seminary.
Lodge, Richard J. '69 (CAM) West Collingswood, NJ Church of the Transfiguration, West Collingswood, N.J.
Lodi, George C. '74 (NY) Shrub Oak, NY Saint Elizabeth Ann Seton.
Lody, John '62 (Y) Retired.
Lody, Joseph Delano '03 (BIR) Alexander City, AL St. John the Apostle; Priests'/Presbyteral Council.
Loeb, Karl E. '95 (BUF) Attica, NY SS. Joachim & Anne.
Loebl, Jeffrey R. *s.j.* '82 (MIL)[P] Milwaukee Jesuit Provincial Office, Wisconsin Province.
Loecke, Douglas J. '89 (DUB) Cascade, IA St. Patrick; Investment Committee; Cascade, IA St. Peter; Cascade, IA St. Matthias; Bernard, IA Sacred Heart; Judges; Directors.
Loecker, Craig J. '92 (OM) Omaha, NE St. Philip Neri; Omaha, NE Blessed Sacrament.
Loeffler, Earl A. '51 (TOL) Retired.
Loegering, Leonard '73 (FAR) Milnor, ND St. Arnold's Church of Milnor; Wyndmere, ND St. John the Baptist.
Loehr, Charles D. '47 (MIL) Retired.
Loehr, James P. '67 (MIL) Waukesha, WI St. John Neumann.
Loehrlein, Richard A. *s.m.* '61 (STL)[O] St. Louis Marianists, Province of the United States (Society of Mary).
Loehrlein, Sylvester '56 (EVN) Retired.
Loeper, David J. '83 (ALN) Pottsville, PA St. John the Baptist.
Loeper, Rev. Msgr. Richard J. '50 (ALN) Douglassville, PA Immaculate Conception; Bethlehem, PA Holy Ghost Retired.
Loera, Abel '03 (LA) Los Angeles, CA Mother of Sorrows; Los Angeles, CA St. Malachy; Los Angeles, CA San Antonio de Padua.
Loew, James *o.s.b.* '97 (GBG) Vandergrift, PA St. Gertrude.
Loez–Gambarte, Maximo *sch.p.* (BRK) Brooklyn, NY St. Martin of Tours–Our Lady of Lourdes.
Lofgren, Eric '93 (SAC) Lincoln, CA St. Joseph.
Loftin, Don '94 (AUS) Temple, TX St. Luke.
Lofton, Rev. Msgr. Edward D. '82 (CHR) Summerville, SC St. Theresa the Little Flower; Continuing Education for Priests; Bishop's Missionary Support Committee; Holy Childhood Association; Vocations Board; Propagation of the Faith.
Lofton, James J. '61 (ALN) Retired.
Loftus, David C. '94 (LA) Adult Education; Los Angeles, CA St. Teresa of Avila; English.
Loftus, J. Allan *s.j.* '74 (BO) Newton, MA St. Ignatius Loyola.
Loftus, John Allan *s.j.* '74 (BO)[U] Newton, MA The Jesuit Community at Boston College.
Loftus, Joseph J. '56 (ARL) Arlington, VA Our Lady of Lourdes Retired.
Loftus, Kenneth G. *s.j.* '91 (BO) Newton, MA St. Ignatius Loyola; [U] Newton, MA The Jesuit Community at Boston College.
Loftus, Mel M. *o.s.m.* '62 (CHI)[N] Chicago Order of Friar Servants of Mary (Servites) United States of America Province, Inc.
Loftus, Rev. Msgr. Padraic '62 (LA) Retired.
Loftus, Robert A. '91 (WOR)[R] Worcester, MA Becker College; [R] Worcester, MA Worcester Polytechnic Institute; Campus Ministry; Worcester, MA Holy Family Parish.
Loftus, Steven P. '02 (PEO) Rapids City, IL St. John the Baptist.
Loftus, Thomas *c.ss.r.* '57 (HBG)[G] Ephrata, PA St. Clement's Mission House.
Logan, Aidan (Arthur H.) *o.c.s.o.* '85 (WOR)[O] Spencer, MA St. Joseph's Abbey.
Logan, Aidan Arthur H. *o.c.s.o.* '85 (MO) Navy Chaplains.
Logan, Rev. Msgr. Daniel B. '63 (STA) Ponte Vedra Beach, FL Our Lady Star of the Sea; Associate Judges; Building Commission.
Logan, Gary '93 (SR) Occidental, CA St. Philip.
Logan, J.D. *o.p.* '57 (TYL)[C] Lufkin, TX Monastery of the Infant Jesus.
Logan, James J. '59 (LC) Retired.
Logan, James P. '86 (BAK) Judicial Vicar; Chancellor; Judicial Vicar and Chief Judge; Council of Priests and Diocesan Consultors; Director of Catholic Hospitals; Friends of the Catholic University of America; Sisters, OR St. Edward; Vicar General; Building Committee.
Logan, Rev. Msgr. James T. '54 (FRS) Priests' Council Retired.
Logan, Jerry '79 (PEO) Annawan, IL Sacred Heart; Annawan, IL St. Patrick's.
Logan, John *o.carm.* '64 (NY) Middletown, NY Our Lady of Mt. Carmel.
Logan, William R. '69 (RVC) West Islip, NY Consolation Nursing Home.
LoGatto, Joseph J. '57 (PAT) Retired.
Loggiodice, Omar '09 (ATL) Marietta, GA St. Joseph.
Logrip, Rev. Msgr. Joseph L. '72 (PH) Philadelphia, PA Mother of Divine Grace; Regional Vicars; Priests' Personnel Board; Pastors Review Board; College of Consultors.
Logsdon, L. Peter *c.s.c.* '68 (FgM) New Rochelle, NY Eastern Brothers Province.
Logsdon, Wilfrid *o.f.m.conv.* '59 (SAV) Brunswick, GA St. Francis Xavier.
Logue, Charles D. '48 (BO) Senior Priests. Retired.
Logue, Mark '73 (BAL) West River, MD Our Lady of Sorrows.
Lohan, Louis '71 (BLX) Long Beach, MS St. Thomas the Apostle; College of Consultors; Presbyteral Council.
Lohan, William P. (BO) Dedham, MA St. Mary.
Lohkamp, Nicholas *o.f.m.* '52 (CIN)[N] Cincinnati St. Francis Seraph Friary Retired.
Lohrmeyer, Kenneth P. '70 (SAL) Minneapolis, KS St. Paul Parish; Minneapolis, KS Immaculate Conception of the Blessed Virgin Mary Parish; Judicial Vicar–Officialis; Associate Judges.
Lohrmeyer, Kenneth '70 (SAL) Minneapolis, KS St. Mary Parish.
Lohse, Edward M. '89 (E) Administrative Cabinet; College of Consultors; Promoter of Justice; Chancellor; Members; Board of Members; Vocation Office.
Loi, Nguyen '68 (OM) Omaha, NE Our Lady of Fatima Catholic Community.
Loiacono, James A. *o.m.i.* '79 (LAR) Eagle Pass, TX Our Lady of Refuge; Presbyteral Council.
LoJacono, Joseph *i.v.e.* (SJ) Santa Clara, CA Our Lady of Peace.
Lojek, Robert '03 (CHI) Chicago, IL St. Constance.
Lokanga, Daniel '86 (BUR) St. Albans, VT Holy Angels.
Lolio, Rev. Msgr. John W. '70 (PRO) East Greenwich, RI

Our Lady of Mercy; Deans.
Lomasiewicz, Donald E. '62 (GR) Grand Rapids, MI St. Isidore.
Lomax, Mark '80 (NO) Slidell, LA St. Luke the Evangelist; Deans.
Lombard, Richard J. '53 (SHP) Shreveport, LA St. Joseph; Advocates; Finance Council.
Lombard, Roy A. '47 (WH) Retired.
Lombardi, Albert U. '47 (DET) Retired.
Lombardi, Gary '69 (SR) Petaluma, CA St. Vincent de Paul; Deans; Board of Consultors; Priests' Council; Finance Committee.
Lombardi, John C. *m.s.f.* (STL) St. Louis, MO St. Wenceslaus.
Lombardi, John J. '92 (BAL) St. Vincent de Paul Society.
Lombardi, Joseph L. *s.j.* '75 (PH)[C] Jesuit Fathers; [Y] Loyola Center and Manresa Hall.
Lombardi, Nicholas D. *s.j.* '72 (NY)[EE] Cardinal Spellman Hall, Jesuit Community.
Lombardi, Thomas '75 (FTW) Fort Wayne, IN St. Joseph.
Lombardo, Francis *o.f.m.conv.* '71 (BUF)[D] Athol Springs, NY St. Francis High School; [O] Athol Springs, NY St. Francis of Assisi Friary; Williamsville, NY St. Gregory the Great.
Lombardo, Gerard Michael '86 (NEW) Bayonne, NJ Saint Michael and Saint Joseph.
Lombardo, Joseph A. '85 (TUC) Tucson, AZ Roman Catholic Church of Saint Elizabeth Ann Seton – Tucson.
Lombardo, Michael D. '78 (PAT) Wayne, NJ Our Lady of Consolation.
Lombardo, Robert *c.f.r.* '90 (NY)[EE] New York, NY St. Joseph's Friary.
Lombo, German *o.s.a.* '53 (MGZ) Aguada, PR St. Francis of Assisi.
Lomeli, Pastor Hermosillo *m.s.c.* '79 (FRS) Earlimart, CA St. Jude Thaddeus.
Lomello, Lucian B. *s.d.b.* '48 (LA)[P] Los Angeles, CA Dominic Savio Salesian Residence Retired.
Lomibao, Conrado J. '96 (HON) Honolulu, HI Holy Family.
Lomica, Frank '02 (DEN) Denver, CO Cathedral Basilica of the Immaculate Conception.
LoMonaco, Lawrence M. '02 (CHL) Waynesville, NC St. John the Evangelist.
Lonardo, Alfred C. '63 (PRO) Retired.
Loncar, Stephen *o.f.m.conv.* '88 (GRY) Gary, IN St. Joseph The Worker.
Lonchyna, Taras '77 (PHU) Silver Spring, MD Holy Trinity; Silver Spring, MD Annunciation of the Blessed Virgin Mary; Silver Spring, MD St. John the Baptist; Protopresbyters (Deans); Pro–Life and Family Ministry.
Loncle, John '05 (ROC) Fairport, NY Assumption of the Blessed Virgin Mary.
Londono, Heriberto '84 (SJN) Toa Alta, PR Nuestra Senora de la Medalla Milagrosa.
Londono, Hugo Leon *m.s.c.* '03 (CHI) Chicago, IL St. Joseph.
Londono, Hugo Leon *m.s.c.* '03 (RCK)[G].
Londono, Hugo '62 (ORL) Retired.
Londono Zuluaga, Edwin Alberio '07 (SJN) Vicar for Vocations; Vocations Promoter; Spiritual Directors.
Lone, Henry Saw '94 (SAL) Hill City, KS Immaculate Heart of Mary Parish; Damar, KS St. Joseph Parish.
Lonek, Stephen C. '76 (WIL) Secretary, MD Our Lady of Good Counsel.
Lonergan, David W. '61 (HRT) Wethersfield, CT Corpus Christi; Wethersfield, CT Sacred Heart; Medical Leave.
Lonergan, J. Barry '66 (ALB) Retired.
Lonergan, Lester *m.h.m.* '62 (NY)[EE] Hartsdale, NY Mill Hill Fathers Residence Retired.
Lonergan, Michael J. '93 (PH) Bensalem, PA St. Elizabeth Ann Seton.
Long, Anthony Vu Khac '92 (RCK) DeKalb, IL St. Mary; Special Assignment.
Long, Daniel '94 (CHI) Chicago, IL Epiphany.
Long, David P. '02 (PAT) Absent on Leave.
Long, Galen '91 (SAL) Plainville, KS Sacred Heart Parish; Plainville, KS St. Thomas Parish.
Long, Garrett J. *s.m.* '76 (RVC)[D] Mineola, NY Chaminade High School (Boys); [M] Mineola, NY Provincial Residence and Novitiate; Mineola, NY.
Long, J. William '89 (R) Ahoskie, NC St. Charles Borromeo.
Long, James T. '63 (BEL) Retired.
Long, Jeffrey D. '06 (SFD)[N] Jacksonville, IL Illinois College Newman Catholic Community; [N] Jacksonville, IL MacMurray College Newman Catholic Community; Jacksonville, IL Our Saviour; Jacksonville, IL Jacksonville Correctional Center.
Long, John R. '89 (SUP) Gilman, WI SS. Peter and Paul; Gilman, WI St. Michael; Gilman, WI St. Stanislaus; Gilman, WI St. John the Apostle.
Long, John '61 (JC) Retired.
Long, John '78 (STP) Brooklyn Park, MN St. Vincent de Paul.
Long, Joseph J. *c.s.c.* '59 (ORL)[F] Cocoa Beach, FL Congregation of Holy Cross, Eastern Province Retired.
Long, Joseph J. *c.s.c.* '59 (SCR)[C] Wilkes–Barre, PA King's College Retired.
Long, Mark J. '07 (TUC) Superior, AZ Saint Francis of Assisi Roman Catholic Parish – Superior.
Long, Matthew Tyler '09 (SHP) Monroe, LA Jesus the Good Shepherd.
Long, Melvin '66 (SAL) Retired.
Long, Nathan '08 (LKC) Lake Charles, LA Our Lady Queen of Heaven; Scouting; Vocation Recruiters.
Long, Nguyen Phi *c.ss.r.* '03 (LA)[P] Baldwin Park Vietnamese Redemptorist Mission.
Long, Richard E. (BRK)[E] Brooklyn, NY Campus Ministers and Ministry Centers; Brooklyn, NY St. Cecilia.
Long, Stuart '07 (HEL) Anaconda, MT Anaconda Catholic Community.
Long, Thomas E. *c.s.v.* '69 (CHI)[N] Chicago, IL Viatorian Residence; [N] Arlington Heights Viatorian Province Center–Clerics of St. Viator.
Long, Thomas (GB) Newton, WI St. Thomas the Apostle.
Long, Tom (GB)[O] Green Bay, WI Teens Encounter Christ (TEC), Green Bay Chapter.
Long, Vincent P. '69 (SY) Hinckley, NY St. Ann; Holland Patent, NY St. Leo.
Long, W. Thomas '91 (GB) Serra Clubs; [N] Green Bay, WI Ecumenical Center–UWGB; Vocations and Ongoing Formation of Priests and Parish Directors; Special Assignment.
Longalong, Patrick H. O. '08 (BRK) Floral Park, NY Our Lady of the Snows.
Longanga, Emery (FTW)[A] Notre Dame, IN Moreau Seminary.
Longbucco, John L. '90 (MAR) Baraga, MI The Most Holy Name of Jesus–Blessed Kateri Tekakwitha; Baraga, MI St. Ann; L'Anse, MI Sacred Heart; Baraga, MI The Most Holy Name of Jesus–Blessed Kateri Tekakwitha; [B] L'Anse, MI Sacred Heart School Endowment Fund.
Longe, James '07 (SPR) Westfield, MA St. Mary's.
Longo, Robert *o.f.m.cap.* '85 (CAM) Retired.
Longobucco, Robert '98 (ALB) Schenectady, NY St. Helen; Office of Evangelization, Catechesis and Family Life.
Longtin, Lucien F. *s.j.* '65 (ALN)[A] Wernersville, PA Jesuit Center–Jesuit Community; [N] Wernersville, PA Jesuit Center.
Longua, Rev. Msgr. Paul A. '61 (PAT) Retired.
Long Vu, Michael *s.v.d.* '06 (LAF) Lafayette, LA Immaculate Heart of Mary.
Lonzo, Anthony P. '05 (COL) Dennison, OH Immaculate Conception.
Looby, Christopher J. '01 (OG) Brushton, NY St. Mary's Church; North Bangor, NY St. Augustine.
Looby, John J. '66 (OG) Chateaugay, NY Catholic Community of Burke and Chateaugay; Ellenburg, NY St. Edmund.
Loomis, Rev. Msgr. Richard A. '76 (LA) On Administrative Leave.
Loomis, Richard P. '52 (WIN) Austin, MN St. Edward's Retired.
Loomis, Thomas A. '92 (WIN) Rochester, MN Resurrection; Finance Council; Priest Assignments Committee.
Looney, Daniel A. '71 (SAC) Vacaville, CA St. Joseph; Vicars Forane; Priests' Personnel Board, Diocesan.
Looney, Joseph E. '67 (HRT) Bethlehem, CT Church of the Nativity.
Looney, Mathew D. '58 (NEW) Retired.
Looney, Thomas P. *c.s.c.* '87 (BGP)[O] Bridgeport, CT Provincial Offices of the Priests and Brothers of Holy Cross, Eastern Province.
Loos, Francis *c.i.c.m.* '47 (SAT)[L] San Antonio, TX Missionhurst C.I.C.M. Residence.
Loos, Frederick C. '63 (SAG) Retired.
Lopardo, Vito R. '55 (BEL) Retired.
Lopatesky, Rev. Msgr. Raymond M. '75 (PAT)[Q] Chester, NJ Nazareth Village; Clergy Personnel Office.
Lopera, Rafael I. *c.s.b.* '94 (GAL)[O] Sugar Land Basilian Mission Center.
Loperfido, Ernest '59 (Y) Retired.
Lopes, Richard *o.f.m.cap.* '82 (SFR)[N] Burlingame, CA Capuchin Provincial House.
Lopes, Steven J. *s.t.l.* '01 (SFR) On Duty Outside the Archdiocese.
Lopes, Thomas C. '65 (FR) Diocesan Consultors Retired.
Lopez, Abel '56 (SJ) Retired.
Lopez, Alberto '87 (SJN) Trujillo Alto, PR San Pio X.
Lopez, Alcides Castro '84 (TR) Trenton, NJ St. Mary Cathedral.
Lopez, Alejandro *o.f.m.conv.* '03 (PEO) Peoria, IL Holy Family.
Lopez, Alfred A. *o.p.* '84 (CHI)[N] River Forest, IL St. Thomas Aquinas Priory.
Lopez, Alfred A. *o.p.* '84 (STL)[O] St. Louis, MO Dominican Community of St. Louis.
Lopez, Alvaro M. '86 (STO) Manteca, CA St. Anthony Church of Manteca (Pastor of).
Lopez, Amador *o.m.i.* '58 (SD) Calipatria, CA St. Patrick.
Lopez, Angel *c.ss.r.* '79 (CGS) San Lorenzo, PR Nuestra Senora de la Mercedes.
Lopez, Anthony '08 (NSH) Nashville, TN St. Edward; Hispanic Ministry; Antioch, TN Our Lady of Guadalupe.
Lopez, Antonio Garnica *m.s.c.* '79 (LA) Cudahy, CA Sagrado Corazon y Santa Maria de Guadalupe.
Lopez, Antonio '02 (ORG) Buena Park, CA St. Pius V.
Lopez, Antonio *f.s.c.b.* (BO)[U] Lexington, MA Priestly Fraternity of the Missionaries of St. Charles Borromeo, Inc.; Lexington, MA.
Lopez, Armando *o.f.m.* '90 (SFR) San Francisco, CA St. Boniface.
Lopez, Augustin *sch.p.* (PCE) Ponce, PR Our Lady of Mt. Carmel.
Lopez, Benjamin *s.o.l.t.* '98 (CC)[G] Robstown, TX Society of Our Lady of the Most Holy Trinity.
Lopez, Benjamin (PCE) Aguirre, PR Sacred Heart.
Lopez, Bruce '88 (PEO) Monticello, IL St. Michael; Monticello, IL St. Philomena.
Lopez, Camilo '93 (NEW) Emerson, NJ Church of the Assumption.
Lopez, Carlos A. (BO) Boston, MA Cathedral of the Holy Cross; Roxbury, MA St. Patrick.
Lopez, Carlos A. (ARE) On Duty Outside the Diocese.
Lopez, Carlos Acosta '60 (NY) New York, NY Our Lady of Esperanza.
Lopez, Carlos *o.s.b.* '02 (LA)[P] Valyermo, CA St. Andrew's Abbey.
Lopez, Rev. Msgr. Daniel '63 (FRS) Selma, CA St. Joseph; Federacion Mariana de Guadalupe.
Lopez, Edilberto '97 (ELP) Priests' Retirement and Disability Plan; El Paso, TX St. Luke.
Lopez, Eduardo *c.m.* '70 (GAL) Houston, TX St. Charles Borromeo.
Lopez, Eduardo '03 (TUC) Yuma, AZ Immaculate Conception Roman Catholic Parish & Guadalupe Mission – Yuma.
Lopez, Efrain (SJN)[F] Puerta De Tierra, PR Asylum For The Aged and Infirm.
Lopez, Elpidio (TYL) Mount Pleasant, TX St. Michael.
Lopez, Enrique *c.ss.r.* '64 (LA)[P] Whittier, CA Redemptorists of Whittier; Whittier, CA St. Mary of the Assumption Retired.
Lopez, Enrique '93 (LSC) Presbyteral Council.
Lopez, Enrique '93 (LSC) Deming, NM Holy Family; Deming, NM St. Ann's; Promoter of Justice; Clergy Personnel Board.
Lopez, Ernesto '06 (LUB) Ralls, TX St. Michael; Vocation Team Members; Diocesan Pastoral Liturgy Commission.
Lopez, Ezequiel Padilla *c.r.* '08 (PBL) On Duty Outside the Diocese.
Lopez, Fabian '99 (NY) New York, NY Our Lady of Lourdes.
Lopez, Felipe '59 (NEW) Jersey City, NJ St. Paul's; Hispanic Curia of Hudson County.
Lopez, Francisco Javier *sch.p.* '78 (SJN) San Juan, PR Santisimo Salvador.
Lopez, Frank '93 (ELP) Office of Worship; El Paso, TX St. Frances Xavier Cabrini Parish; Diocesan Building Committee; Our Lady of Guadalupe; Priests' Personnel Advisory Committee.
Lopez, Gabriel Maduro '59 (ARE) Promoter of Justice.
Lopez, Rev. Msgr. Gerard M. '91 (SB) Diocesan Review Committee; Special or Other Diocesan Assignment; Office of the Vicar General/Moderator of the Curia; Ex Officio Member; Diocesan Curia; College of Consultors; Ex Officio.
Lopez, Gustavo '90 (HRT) Torrington, CT St. Francis of Assisi; Torrington, CT St. Mary; Torrington, CT St. Peter; Torrington, CT Sacred Heart.
Lopez, Gustavo '95 (LFT) Lafayette, IN St. Boniface.
Lopez, Gustavo *o.s.j.* (FRS) Madera, CA St. Joachim.
Lopez, Rev. Msgr. Humberto '86 (MGZ) San German, PR San German de Auxerre; Diocesan Consultors.
Lopez, Jairo '94 (AUS) Marble Falls, TX St. John the Evangelist.
Lopez, James F. '04 (DET) Marine City, MI Our Lady on the River.
Lopez, Jesus Francisco '96 (CC) Taft, TX Immaculate Conception.
Lopez, Joel '03 (RCK) Rockford, IL St. Bernadette.
Lopez, Jorge A. Granados '97 (YAK) Cowiche, WA St. Juan Diego.
Lopez, Jose Jesus '08 (PHX) Gilbert, AZ St. Anne Roman Catholic Parish.
Lopez, Jose M. (ARE) On Duty Outside the Diocese.
Lopez, Jose Maria *o.c.d.* '57 (MIL)[P] Milwaukee Provincial Offices – Discalced Carmelites.
Lopez, Jose Miguel '78 (TYL) Tyler, TX Cathedral of the Immaculate Conception.
Lopez, Jose '94 (JKS) Retired.
Lopez, Jose '94 (BRK) Brooklyn, NY St. Rose of Lima.
Lopez, Rev. Msgr. Joseph A. '71 (SAT)[A] San Antonio, TX Assumption Seminary; [C] Oblate School of Theology.
Lopez, Joseph A. '02 (CC) Office of the Bishop; College

of Consultors; Presbyteral Council; Judges; Chancellor; Corpus Christi, TX Corpus Christi Cathedral; Finance Council.
Lopez, Rev. Msgr. Joseph '71 (SAT) Judges.
López, José Refugio *s.s.p.* '83 (LA)[P] Los Angeles, CA The Society of St. Paul.
Lopez, Juan Carlos '03 (AUS) Cameron, TX St. Monica.
Lopez, Juan J. '89 (ARE) On Duty Outside the Diocese.
Lopez, Juan M. '62 (MIA) Miami, FL SS. Peter and Paul.
Lopez, Juan M. '08 (SFR) San Mateo, CA St. Matthew.
Lopez, Kharlosg '77 (FAJ) Humacao, PR Maria Reina de la Paz.
Lopez, Leonardo G. *i.v.e.* '02 (BRK) Brooklyn, NY St. Michael – Saint Malachy.
Lopez, Lionel '96 (BWN) On Assignment Outside the Diocese.
Lopez, Lionel '96 (MIA)[D] Miami, FL Belen Jesuit Preparatory School.
Lopez, Luis E. *c.s.v.* '95 (CHI)[N] Arlington Heights Viatorian Province Center–Clerics of St. Viator.
Lopez, Marco T. '97 (SLC) Milford, UT Saint Bridget LLC 217; Park City, UT Saint Mary of the Assumption LLC 238.
Lopez, Mario *o.carm.* '76 (BO)[Z] Peabody, MA St. Theresa Carmelite Chapel; [U] Peabody, MA Our Lady of the Scapular Priory.
Lopez, Mauricio '92 (SAT) Converse, TX St. Monica.
Lopez, P. Harry '86 (MGZ) Aguadilla, PR St. Charles Borromeo.
Lopez, Pedro J. '81 (LA) Deanery 18; Santa Fe Springs, CA St. Pius X; Members; Liturgical Commision.
Lopez, Primitivo T. '91 (CHK) Saipan, MP San Roque Parish; Finance Officer; Presbyteral Council; El Shaddai Movement; San Roque Parish – Mother of Divine Love Praesidium.
Lopez, Ramon '08 (NY) Bronx, NY St. Raymond.
Lopez, Ramon *o.f.m.cap.* '76 (SJN) San Juan, PR San Francisco de Asis.
Lopez, Renato *s.s.* '86 (BAL)[S] Baltimore, MD St. Mary's Seminary & University; [A] Baltimore, MD St. Mary's Seminary and University.
Lopez, Rev. Msgr. Richard J. '73 (ATL)[C] Atlanta, GA St. Pius X Catholic High School; Special or Other (Arch)Diocesan Assignment.
Lopez, Richard '89 (ELP) Absent on Leave.
Lopez, Romualdo *c.r.s.* '07 (GAL) Houston, TX Christ the King.
Lopez, Sergio '98 (OAK) Graduate Studies.
Lopez, Severino *c.m.f.* '44 (CHI) Chicago, IL Our Lady of Guadalupe; [N] Oak Park Claretian Missionaries USA Eastern Province.
Lopez, Vincent *o.p.* '56 (LA)[Q] Los Angeles, CA Monastery of the Angels (Contemplative).
Lopez, Walter Suarez '96 (SJ) San Jose, CA Sacred Heart of Jesus.
Lopez, Wilfredo Echevarria (SJN) San Juan, PR Ntr. Sra. de la Caridad del Cobre.
Lopez–Bolanos, Eddy E. '09 (PRO) On Special Assignment.
Lopez–Cardinale, Alejandro '91 (NEW)[R] Plainfield, NJ RENEW International; Elizabeth, NJ Blessed Sacrament.
Lopez–Figueroa, Alberto '87 (SJN) for Pastoral Affairs.
Lopez–Restrepo, Eugenio '84 (SAC) Sacramento, CA St. Charles Borromeo.
Lopez Aponte, Nelson '91 (FAJ) Vieques, PR Inmaculada Concepcion.
Lopez Figueroa, Rev. Msgr. Alberto '87 (SJN) Vicar for Pastoral Affairs; Diocesan Consultors.
Lopez Garcia, Mario *s.o.l.t.* '99 (CC)[G] Robstown, TX Society of Our Lady of the Most Holy Trinity.
Lopez Vega, Jose Antonio '92 (PCE) Coto Laurel, PR Our Lady of Mt. Carmel.
LoPinto, Rev. Msgr. Alfred P. '70 (BRK)[M] Brooklyn, NY Catholic Charities; Vicar for Human Services; Howard Beach, NY St. Helen.
Lopoke, Symphorien '94 (ARL) Falls Church, VA St. James.
Lopoke–Ohamamboya, Symphorien (ARL) Advocate & Procurator.
LoPresti, Carl '97 (PEO) Chenoa, IL St. Joseph's; Colfax, IL St. Joseph's.
Lopresti, Julio *i.v.e.* '96 (BGP) Bridgeport, CT St. George; [O] Bridgeport, CT Instituto Verbo Encarnado.
Lopresti, Marcelo R. *i.v.e.* '02 (PH) Philadelphia, PA St. Hugh of Cluny.
Lorance, Douglas '84 (SJP) Lyndora, PA St. Michael; Presbyters.
Lord, David *m.i.c.* '91 (JOL) Darien, IL Our Lady of Peace.
Lord, Robert J. '60 (HRT) Retired.
Lordemann, Francis W. '72 (OM) West Point, NE Assumption B.V.M.
Lorden, Demetrio '70 (SP) Wimauma, FL Our Lady of Guadalupe Mission.
Loredo, Miguel A. *o.f.m.* '64 (SP)[N] St. Petersburg, FL St. Anthony Friary.
Lorei, Brian '09 (ATL) Decatur, GA St. Thomas More.
Loremus, Gabriel (BO) Lynn, MA St. Mary.
Lorenc, Henryk '80 (MO) Army Chaplains.
Lorente, Jose '65 (MET)[M] Stewartsville, NJ Society of Jesus Christ the Priest; New Brunswick, NJ Our Lady of Mt. Carmel.
Lorente, Manuel '68 (MET)[M] Stewartsville, NJ Society of Jesus Christ the Priest; New Brunswick, NJ Our Lady of Mt. Carmel.
Lorenz, Bernard A. '85 (LIN) Imperial, NE St. Patrick's; Apostolate to the Spanish Speaking.
Lorenz, John F. '54 (DM)[G] Des Moines, IA Institute of the Heart of Jesus Retired.
Lorenz, Matthais E. '69 (CHI) On Duty Outside the Archdiocese.
Lorenz, Richard J. *s.a.c.* '60 (MIL)[P] Milwaukee, WI St. Vincent Community.
Lorenzana, Elias (CGS) Cayey, PR Nuestra Senora de la Merced.
Lorenzetti, Rev. Msgr. Dino J. '53 (BUF)[O] Tonawanda, NY O'Hara Residence Retired.
Lorenzo, Avelino *s.d.b.* '60 (LA) Los Angeles, CA St. Mary; [P] Los Angeles, CA Dominic Savio Salesian Residence.
Lorenzo, Eduardo '66 (LAN) Retired.
Lorenzo, Elias R. *o.s.b.* '89 (PAT)[N] Morristown St. Mary's Abbey.
Lorenzo, Joseph F. *o.f.m.* '76 (NY) New York, NY St. Anthony of Padua; Definitors:.
Lorenzo, Juan '93 (VEN) Charismatic Renewal; Clewiston, FL St. Margaret.
Lorenzoni, Larry *s.d.b.* '51 (SFR)[N] San Francisco, CA Salesian Provincial Residence Retired.
Lorfanfant, Ernest P. *s.m.* '68 (RVC)[M] Mineola, NY Provincial Residence and Novitiate.
Lorge, Felix P. '50 (SPK) Retired.
Lorig, Douglas E. '84 (PHX) Scottsdale, AZ St. Maria Goretti Roman Catholic Parish.
Lorig, Jeffrey '04 (OM) O'Neill, NE St. Patrick.
Lorilla, Willy O. (AGN) Piti, GU Assumption of Our Lady.
Lorimer, Daniel S. '04 (WCH) Bushton, KS Holy Name of Jesus; Lyons, KS St. Paul.
Lorio, Rev. Msgr. Joseph O. '54 (NO) Retired.
Lorkowski, A. Robert '77 (CLV) Medina, OH St. Francis Xavier.
Lorrain, Matthew P. '86 (BR) Defenders of the Bond; Board Members; Serra Clubs; Vocations; [K] Baton Rouge, LA Christ the King Parish and Catholic Center; Baton Rouge, LA Christ the King.
Losarcos, Javier '51 (NEW) Newark, NJ St. Benedict's.
Losarcos, Javier '80 (NEW) Retired.
Lo Sasso, John *o.f.m.cap.* '89 (NY) Bronx, NY Immaculate Conception.
LoSasso, John *o.f.m.cap.* '89 (NEW)[M] Union City, NJ Capuchin Friars – Province of the Sacred Stigmata of St. Francis; Definitors:.
LoSasso, John *o.f.m.cap.* '89 (NY)[EE] New York, NY Immaculate Conception Friary.
LosBanes, Hermes '86 (MO) Army Chaplains.
Lo Schiavo, John J. *s.j.* '55 (SFR)[N] San Francisco, CA Loyola House Jesuit Community.
Loseke, Jeffrey S. '00 (OM) Hartington, NE St. Michael; Hartington, NE Holy Trinity; [B] Hartington, NE Cedar Catholic High School; Air Force Reserve Chaplains.
Losh, Joseph F. '64 (COL) Retired.
Losito, Rev. Msgr. Felix A. '58 (ALN) Reading, PA Holy Rosary; National Shut–In Visitation Society; Third Order Secular Carmelites.
Loskot, Donald *s.d.s.* '76 (NSH) Tenn. Tech–Cookeville; Cookeville, TN St. Thomas Aquinas.
Losoya, Jose E. *c.o.* '91 (BWN) Pharr, TX St. Jude Thaddeus; [F] Pharr, TX Pharr Oratory of St. Philip Neri of Pontifical Right; [B] Pharr, TX Oratory Athenaeum for University Preparation; Pharr, TX Oratory School – Athenaeum for University Preparation; [C] Pharr, TX Oratory Academy School of St. Philip Neri; Pharr, TX Oratory Academy School of St. Philip Neri.
Lossing, Larry '84 (ORL) Orlando, FL St. Joseph Retired.
Lostritto, Paul *o.f.m.* '96 (BO)[Z] Boston, MA St. Anthony Shrine.
Loterte, Samuel E. *s.s.s.* '91 (HON) Hilo, HI St. Joseph; Hilo, HI Malia Puka O' Kalani (Mary Gate of Heaven).
Lothamer, James W. *s.s.* '68 (LAN) Fowlerville, MI St. Agnes.
Lothamer, James W. *s.s.* '68 (BAL)[S] Baltimore Society of St. Sulpice, Province of the United States.
Lott, Roger R.S. *o.s.b.* '54 (BIR)[E] Cullman, AL St. Bernard Abbey Retired.
Lotz, Ezekiel *o.s.b.* '00 (P)[A] St. Benedict, OR Mount Angel Seminary; [L] St. Benedict, OR Mt. Angel Abbey.
Lotz, Robert J. '73 (MIL) Sheboygan Falls, WI Blessed Trinity; Kohler, WI St. John Evangelist.
Louapre, Albert C. *s.j.* '60 (ATL)[I] Atlanta, GA Ignatius House.
Loubriel, Harry '05 (MIA)[B] St. Thomas University; Campus Ministry; St. Thomas University; Miami Gardens, FL Visitation.
Loucks, Thomas '77 (B) Kellogg, ID St. Rita's; Wallace, ID St. Alphonsus.
Lougen, Louis *o.m.i.* '79 (FgM) Washington, DC AMERICAN OBLATE MISSIONS.
Lougen, Louis *o.m.i.* '79 (WDC) Washington, DC; [N] Washington, DC Oblate Community; [N] Washington, DC Provincial Offices of the United States Province of the Missionary Oblates of Mary Immaculate.
Lougen, Louis '79 (STP)[S] St. Paul, MN Oblate Media and Communication Corporation.
Loughery, Robert J. *c.s.c.* '89 (P) Portland, OR St. Vincent de Paul.
Loughery, Robert *c.s.c.* (FTW)[H] Notre Dame Congregation of Holy Cross, Indiana Province, Provincial House.
Loughlin, Rev. Msgr. William J. '69 (BGP) Pilgrimages, Office of Diocesan; [O] Stamford, CT The Catherine Dennis Keefe Queen of the Clergy Retired Priests' Residence Retired.
Loughman, Rev. Msgr. Kenneth M. '58 (NY) Retired.
Loughnane, Rev. Msgr. James J. '61 (LA) Diamond Bar, CA St. Denis; Deanery 12; Chair.
Loughnane, John B. '88 (MAN) Pittsfield, NH Our Lady of Lourdes.
Loughran, James *s.a.* '89 (NY)[EE] New York, NY Atonement Friars; [EE] New York, NY Graymoor Ecumenical and Interreligious Institute.
Loughran, John *o.s.f.s.* '80 (LAN) Deerfield, MI St. Alphonsus; Blissfield, MI St. Peter the Apostle.
Loughrey, Vivian '97 (MIA) Plantation, FL St. Gregory.
Louis, Jean Woady '91 (VEN) Bradenton Beach, FL St. Bernard.
Louis, Rev. Msgr. John H. '62 (SCR) Clarks Green, PA St. Gregory; Defenders of the Bond; [G] Clarks Summit, PA St. Gregory Early Childhood Center.
Louis, John *o.m.i.* '43 (BEL)[F] Belleville, IL Shrine of Our Lady of the Snows Retired.
Louis, Kevin C. '89 (LC) Stevens Point, WI St. Peter.
Louis, Olin Pierre '09 (SJN) San Juan, PR San Mateo.
Louis, Pascal '83 (BRK) Brooklyn, NY Holy Cross; Brooklyn, NY Holy Innocents.
Lourdusamy, Joseph '95 (TYL) Chireno, TX Our Lady of Lourdes; Nacogdoches, TX Immaculate Conception – Moral.
Louzon, Bede *o.f.m.cap.* '85 (DET) Hazel Park, MI St. Mary Magdalen.
Lovas, Donald J. '63 (WIN) Rollingstone, MN St. Mary's; Rollingstone, MN Holy Trinity; Rollingstone, MN St. Paul's.
Lovat, Rene *s.x.* '57 (FgM)[N] Wayne Xaverian Missionary Fathers; Wayne, NJ XAVERIAN MISSIONARY FATHERS.
Lovatin, Agostino *c.s.* (CHI) Melrose Park, IL Our Lady of Mount Carmel.
Love, John W. '90 (LA) Fillmore, CA St. Francis of Assisi; [AA] Goleta, CA University of California Santa Barbara; Air National Guard Chaplains.
Love, Lester E. *s.j.* '91 (OAK)[M] Oakland, CA Jesuit Fathers and Brothers.
Love, Lester E. *s.j.* '91 (CHI)[N] Chicago Chicago Province of the Society of Jesus–Provincial Office.
Loveless, William J. '75 (Y) Warren, OH St. Pius X; Priests Council.
Lovell, Allen B. '02 (CAM) Continuing Education & Spiritual Formation of Priests (CESF); Gibbsboro, NJ St. Andrew the Apostle's R.C. Church, Gibbsboro, N.J.
Lovell, John P. '07 (RCK) Vocations; Loves Park, IL St. Bridget; Special Assignment.
Lover, Lawrence E. *c.ss.r.* '51 (BRK)[T] Brooklyn, NY Redemptorist Fathers of New York, Inc.–Baltimore Province; Brooklyn, NY.
Lovett, Gerald F. '59 (SEA) Retired.
Lovrencic, Athanasius *o.f.m.* '48 (CHI)[N] Lemont, IL The Slovene Franciscan Fathers, Order of Friars Minor, Commissariat of the Holy Cross; Councilors:.
Lovric, Ivan (NY) Crestwood, NY Church of the Annunciation.
Lowchy, Gregory '01 (R) Wilson, NC Church of St. Therese.
Lowe, Bryan K. '01 (BIR) Anniston, AL Sacred Heart of Jesus; Diocesan College of Vicars.
Lowe, Francis E. '85 (MO) Air Force Chaplains.
Lowe, Frank E. '85 (SB) On Duty Outside the Diocese.
Lowe, Frank E. '85 (BLX) Keesler Airforce Base.
Lowe, Philip J. '82 (PH) On Special or Other Archdiocesan Assignment; Linwood, PA Holy Saviour.
Lowe, Russell P. '92 (CLV) Cleveland, OH Corpus Christi; Cleveland, OH St. Leo the Great.
Lowe, William C.B. '07 (LA) Military Chaplains.
Lowery, James T. *m.s.* '55 (HRT)[L] Hartford, CT Missionaries of LaSalette.
Lowery, Martin J. *m.m.* '68 (NY)[EE] Maryknoll Maryknoll Fathers and Brothers.
Lowery, Rev. Msgr. Philip A. '76 (TR) Red Bank, NJ St. James.
Lowery, Shaun *o.s.f.s.* (TOL) Toledo, OH Gesu.
Lowery, Stephen *c.o.* '09 (PIT)[P] Pittsburgh, PA Carnegie–Mellon University; [P] Pittsburgh, PA Chatham College; [M] Pittsburgh, PA Congregation

of the Oratory of St. Philip Neri; [P] Pittsburgh, PA University of Pittsburgh.
Lowery, Wil *c.ss.r.* '49 (STP) Brooklyn Center, MN St. Alphonsus.
Lowie, Richard J. '69 (GR) Retired.
Lowisz, Myron *o.f.m.* '60 (GRY)[F] Crown Point, IN Franciscan Communities at St. Anthony Campus; [H] Cedar Lake, IN Our Lady of Lourdes Friary.
Lowney, Jeremiah (HEL) Retired.
Lowrey, Robert *o.m.v.* '78 (BO)[U] Milton, MA Oblate Residence (St. Joseph House); [Z] Boston, MA St. Francis Chapel.
Lowry, Matthew '08 (PHX)[H] Flagstaff, AZ Holy Trinity Catholic Newman Center; Flagstaff, AZ Holy Trinity Newman Center.
Loya, Daniel J. '66 (PBR) Pleasant City, OH St. Michael; Elected Deanery Representatives.
Loya, John F. '74 (CLV)[A] Wickliffe, OH Borromeo Seminary.
Loya, Joseph *o.s.a.* '79 (PH)[C] Villanova University; [Y] Rosemont, PA Saxony Hall.
Loya, Mario *o.carm.* '04 (JOL)[L] Darien Carmelite Provincial Office.
Loya, Thomas '82 (PRM) Homer Glen, IL Annunciation Byzantine Catholic Church; Syncellus for Parishes and Laity; Presbyteral Council; Eparchial Pastoral Council; Office of Youth Ministry; Respect Life Office.
Loyd, Frederick A. '70 (COL) Retired.
Loyson, Michael '92 (DET) St. Clair Shores, MI St. Lucy; Defenders of Bond.
Lozada, Enrique Francisco (CHI) Franklin Park, IL St. Gertrude.
Lozano, Arturo *s.j.* (LKC) Hispanic Ministry; Lake Charles, LA St. Henry; Lake Charles, LA Immaculate Heart of Mary.
Lozano, Rev. Msgr. Jose '65 (PCE) Juana Diaz, PR St. Raymond Nonato; Diocesan Consultors; Parish Priests Consultors.
Lozano, Roland *c.m.f.* '75 (LA) Los Angeles, CA Our Lady Queen of the Angels.
Lozano–Burgos, Jose Y. '01 (LR) Springdale, AR St. Raphael.
Lozier, Donald G. *o.m.i.* '60 (BO)[U] Lowell, MA Andre Garin Retirement Residence; Lowell, MA Holy Family.
Lozier, Timothy R. '88 (STA) Jacksonville, FL Most Holy Redeemer; Presbyteral Council; Cursillos de Cristiandad.
Lozinski, Rev. Msgr. Eugene L. '72 (NU) Sleepy Eye, MN St. Mary; Board of Trustees for Pension Plan for Priests; On Special or Other Diocesan Assignment; Bishop's Delegate for the Permanent Diaconate; Chancellor; Associate Judges; Corporate Board; Priest Personnel Board; Diocesan Council of Catholic Women; College of Consultors; Priests' Council.
Lozinski, Robert W. *c.s.c.* '73 (PSC) Dunmore, PA St. Michael.
Luamanu, Setefano T. '92 (SPP) Auditors; Pago Pago, AS Sacred Heart Parish–Pago Pago.
Luan, Nguyen Truong '98 (LA)[P] Baldwin Park Vietnamese Redemptorist Mission.
Lubeley, Rev. Msgr. Richard J. '49 (STL) Webster Groves, MO Mary, Queen of Peace Retired.
Luberti, Richard *c.ss.r.* '79 (DET) Maybee, MI St. Joseph.
Lubic, Robert T. '96 (GBG) Perryopolis, PA St. John the Baptist; Smock, PA St. Hedwig; [C] Connellsville, PA Geibel Catholic (Middle–High School).
Lubinsky, Michael '78 (SAV) Augusta, GA Church of the Most Holy Trinity.
Lubowa, Francis Muteesasira '02 (SP) Beverly Hills, FL Our Lady of Grace.
Lubrano, Joseph *s.d.s.* '74 (MIL)[P] St. Francis, WI St. Joseph's Salvatorian Community (Novitiate).
Lubrano, Robert '85 (RVC) Medical Leave.
Luca, Edward J. '54 (CLV) Sheffield, OH St. Teresa of Avila; Judges in Second Instance Retired.
Luca, Rev. Msgr. Joseph L. '70 (BAL) Clarksville, MD St. Louis.
Lucas, Christopher D. '85 (PH) Philadelphia, PA St. John the Baptist; [D] Philadelphia, PA John W. Hallahan Catholic Girls High School.
Lucas, Edward M. '61 (PBR) Weirton, WV St. Mary's.
Lucas, Eliseo '01 (SB) Mecca, CA Sanctuary of Our Lady of Guadalupe; Low Desert.
Lucas, Eliseo '59 (SB) Officers.
Lucas, George J. *c.s.c.* '72 (BGP)[O] Bridgeport, CT Provincial Offices of the Priests and Brothers of Holy Cross, Eastern Province.
Lucas, James W. '00 (GB) Combined Locks, WI St. Paul.
Lucas, Jayaselanraj '96 (TYL) Henderson, TX St. Jude; Bradshaw State Facility, Texas Department of Corrections.
Lucas, Jeffery J. '81 (E) West Middlesex, PA Good Shepherd.
Lucas, Rev. Msgr. John J. '65 (E) Warren, PA Holy Redeemer; Deans.
Lucas, John P. '68 (CHI) Oak Park, IL St. Edmund; Provincial Court of Appeals; [W] Chicago, IL Court of Appeals–Province of Chicago.
Lucas, John P. (STN) "New Star" – Eparchial Newspaper.
Lucas, John '66 (STN) Chicago, IL St. Michael's.
Lucas, Lawrence E. '59 (NY) New York, NY Our Lady of Lourdes; East Elmhurst, NY George Vierno Center; Manhattan, NY North General Hospital.
Lucas, Robert F. '02 (PH) Drexel Hill, PA St. Bernadette.
Lucas, Robert *c.m.* '74 (CHI)[N] Chicago, IL Vincentian Community, Congregation of the Mission, Western Province.
Lucas, Theodore '84 (CLV) Willowick, OH St. Mary Magdalene.
Lucas, Thomas M. *s.j.* '85 (SFR)[N] San Francisco, CA Loyola House Jesuit Community.
Lucas, William P. '90 (BIR) Trussville, AL Holy Infant of Prague; Diocesan College of Consultors; Priests'/Presbyteral Council; Diocesan College of Vicars.
Lucasinsky, Raymond *c.m.m.* '62 (DET)[K] Vocation Office.
Lucatero, Heliodoro '86 (SPK) On Duty Outside the Diocese.
Lucatero, Heliodoro '86 (SAT) Office of Worship; San Antonio, TX St. Michael.
Lucavei, Januario *o.s.b.m.* '00 (STF) Long Island City, NY Holy Cross.
Lucavei, Roberto (Tarcisio) *o.s.b.m.* '91 (STF)[B] Glen Cove, NY Basilian Fathers Novitiate of the Order of St. Basil the Great.
Lucavei, Roberto (Tarcisio) *o.s.b.m.* '91 (RVC)[M] Glen Cove, NY St. Josaphat's Monastery, Novitiate and Retreat House.
Lucchetti, Luis R. '97 (LA) San Gabriel, CA St. Anthony.
Lucero, Edward F. '08 (TUC) Yuma, AZ Immaculate Conception Roman Catholic Parish & Guadalupe Mission – Yuma.
Lucero, Jose *s.d.b.* '03 (SFR) San Francisco, CA Corpus Christi.
Lucero, Rev. Msgr. Leo '60 (SFE) Retired.
Lucero, Lorenzo '56 (ELP) Retired.
Lucev, John '65 (SD) Retired.
Lucey, Beatus T. *o.s.b.* '59 (PAT)[N] Morristown, NJ St. Mary's Abbey.
Lucey, Gregory *s.j.* '64 (MOB)[A] Mobile, AL Spring Hill College.
Lucey, Gregory *s.j.* '64 (NO)[P] New Orleans, LA Jesuit Provincial Office.
Lucey, Paul T. *s.j.* '48 (BO)[U] Weston, MA Campion Health Center, Inc.
Lucey, Walter D. '98 (NEW)[B] School of Diplomacy and Intl. Rels.; [A] South Orange, NJ Immaculate Conception Seminary.
Lucey, William F. '51 (BO) Senior Priests.; Pastoral Care Retired.
Lucht, Shannon G. '01 (BIS) Belfield, ND St. Bernard; South Heart, ND St. Mary; Belfield, ND SS. Peter and Paul; Pro–Synodal Judges; Presbyteral Council.
Lucia, Douglas J. '89 (OG) Canton, NY St. Mary; Adjutant Judicial Vicars; Department of Worship; Diocesan Consultors; Committee on Assignments; Episcopal Vicar for Diocesan Service and Director of Seminarians and Vocations; Canton, NY Newman Ministry of St. Mary's Parish: Newman Center; Campus Ministry.
Luciana, Rev. Msgr. Lawrence J. '63 (WH) Huntington, WV St. Joseph's.
Luciano, Edmund A. '09 (MET) Raritan, NJ The Catholic Church of St. Ann.
Luciano, William J. '83 (NY) Priests Council of the Archdiocese of New York; Yonkers, NY Christ the King.
Lucid, Philip *s.j.* '55 (SPK)[J] Spokane, WA Regis Community Retired.
Lucido, John '73 (ELP) Kermit, TX St. Thomas & St. Joseph; Monahans, TX St. John the Apostle and Evangelist; St. Mark and St. Luke; Priests' Personnel Advisory Committee.
Luck, Robert O. '62 (LA) Retired.
Lucree, Rev. Msgr. Lawrence A. '60 (SAV) Americus, GA St. Mary Retired.
Luczak, Andrew E. '70 (CHI) Niles, IL St. Isaac Jogues.
Luczak, Jay R. '92 (TUC) Miami, AZ Our Lady of the Blessed Sacrament Roman Catholic Church – Miami.
Luczak, Thomas *o.f.m.* '70 (BWN) McAllen, TX Sacred Heart; Vicar General; Presbyteral Council.
Luczycki, Rev. Msgr. Matthew C. '45 (SY) Oneida, NY St. Joseph Retired.
Ludden, John J. '97 (VEN) Naples, FL St. John the Evangelist; Presbyteral Council; Vicar for Priests; Propagation of the Faith/Mission Cooperative Program.
Ludeke, Bruce J. '06 (RCK) Crystal Lake, IL St. Elizabeth Ann Seton.
Ludescher, Kenneth F. '61 (STP) Retired.
Ludvik, John J. '71 (SEA) Snoqualmie, WA Our Lady of Sorrows.
Ludwick, Edmond '97 (CI) Chuuk, FM Holy Cross; [C] Tunnuk, Chuuk, FM Vicariate Residence.
Ludwicki, Tomasz *s.ch.* '03 (JOL) Lombard, IL Divine Mercy Polish Mission.
Ludwig, Alexander '58 (SCL) Retired.
Ludwig, Eugene M. *o.f.m.cap.* '71 (SFR) San Francisco, CA Our Lady of Fatima Byzantine Catholic Church; Burlingame, CA Our Lady of Angels.
Ludwig, Eugene *o.f.m.cap.* '71 (OAK)[A] Berkeley, CA Dominican School of Philosophy and Theology.
Ludwig, John P. '74 (DM) Advocates; Norwalk, IA St. John the Apostle Church.
Ludwig, Thomas K. '87 (KC) St. Joseph, MO Our Lady of Guadalupe.
Ludwig, Thomas '87 (MO) Presbyteral Council; Deans; Air National Guard Chaplains.
Ludwikoski, James E. '73 (KCK) Shawnee, KS Good Shepherd.
Luebke, Martial *o.f.m.* '39 (LA)[P] Los Angeles, CA St. Joseph Friary Retired.
Luebking, Rev. Msgr. Thomas A. '71 (TR) Spring Lake, NJ St. Catharine.
Lueckenotte, Daniel I.J. '90 (JC) Iberia, MO St. Anthony; St. Elizabeth, MO St. Lawrence.
Lueras, Charles R. *c.r.i.c.* '81 (LA) Santa Paula, CA Our Lady of Guadalupe; [P] Santa Paula, CA Canons Regular of the Immaculate Conception.
Luerman, John H. '56 (IND) Retired.
Luevano, Rafael '81 (ORG) Orange, CA Cathedral of the Holy Family; Special Assignment.
Luft, Matthew *o.s.b* '05 (SCL)[I] Collegeville, MN St. John's Abbey, of the Order of St. Benedict.
Luft, Raymond P. '68 (PRO) Providence, RI Our Lady of Mt. Carmel.
Luger, Paul P. *s.j.* '42 (SPK)[J] Spokane, WA Regis Community Retired.
Lugger, William R. '89 (LAN) Lansing, MI St. Casimir; Worship Commission.
Lugo, Camillo '70 (RVC) Copiague, NY Our Lady of the Assumption.
Lugo, Joseph W. '62 (PAT) Retired.
Lui, Gabriel '79 (LA) Monterey Park, CA St. Thomas Aquinas.
Lui, Tovia '83 (LA) Torrance, CA St. Catherine Laboure; Altadena, CA Sacred Heart.
Luis, Raymond Rodriquez *s.a.* '09 (NY)[EE] Garrison Franciscan Friars of the Atonement, Minister General Office.
Luisi, Joseph G. '83 (PIT) Monroeville, PA North American Martyrs; Pitcairn, PA St. Michael.
Luiten, Gary '92 (FAR) Fargo, ND Nativity Church of Fargo; Diocesan College of Consultors.
Luiz, Gary M. *c.p.p.s.* '77 (RNO) Defenders of the Bond.
Lukac, Thomas M. '63 (GBG) Retired.
Lukachinsky, Jerome A. '88 (CLV) Euclid, OH SS. Robert & William Retired.
Lukas, Andrew F. '58 (WH) Retired.
Lukas, Joseph S. '46 (BO) Senior Priests. Retired.
Lukas, Martin C. *o.s.f.s.* '80 (TOL)[I] Toledo, OH Provincial Residence; Toledo, OH Gesu.
Lukaschek, Ernest C. *m.m.* '64 (NY)[EE] Maryknoll Maryknoll Fathers and Brothers.
Lukaszewski, Stanley P. '79 (TR) Manasquan, NJ St. Denis.
Lukati, Willy Frank *c.s.c.* (FTW)[H] Notre Dame Congregation of Holy Cross, Indiana Province, Provincial House.
Luke, Eugene *o.s.b.* '61 (LR) Paris, AR St. Joseph.
Lukefahr, Oscar *c.m.* '66 (STL)[O] Perryville, MO Congregation of the Mission; [V] Perryville, MO Catholic Home Study Service.
Lukehart, Frederick '63 (Y) Serra Club of Trumbull County; Catholic Women, Diocesan Council of Retired.
Lukenda, Raymond T. '56 (NEW) Retired.
Lukianiuk, Andrzej '86 (BRK) Brooklyn, NY Guardian Angel; Rockaway Beach, NY St. Rose of Lima.
Lukose, Joseph *c.m.* '84 (MET) Edison, NJ St. Helena.
Lukoskie, Raymond M. '58 (PEO) Retired.
Luksza, Mariusz G. '04 (NEW) Garfield, NJ St. Stanislaus Kostka.
Lukyamuzi, Joseph M. *o.s.b.* '81 (RIC)[K] Richmond, VA Mary Mother of the Church Abbey.
Lule, John '82 (RC) Rapid City, SD Cathedral of Our Lady of Perpetual Help.
Lule, Mugagga '95 (LAV) Vocations; Henderson, NV St. Peter the Apostle.
Lulf, Ken '99 (SFS) Milbank, SD St. Lawrence.
Luljak, Louis P. '61 (MIL) Retired.
Lulko, Leo T. '65 (DET) Highland, MI Church of the Holy Spirit.
Lumbre, Roger '86 (WCH) Wichita, KS Christ the King.
Luminais, Rev. Msgr. J. Anthony '54 (NO) Retired.
Lumpe, Michael J. '04 (COL) Columbus, OH St. Catharine.
Lumpkin, Thomas '64 (DET) Special Assignment.
Lumsden, Patrick L. '96 (DAV) Albia, IA St. Patrick's; Lovilia, IA St. Peter's; Melrose, IA St. Patrick's.
Luna, Ignacio '65 (BWN) San Benito, TX St. Benedict.
Luna, Rev. Msgr. Lambert J. '78 (SFE) Albuquerque, NM Saint Joseph on the Rio Grande; Vicar–General; College of Consultors; Presbyteral Council of the Archdiocese of Santa Fe; Finance Council.
Luna, Luis G. Belmonte *o.c.d.* '07 (SAT)[L] San

Antonio, TX Discalced Carmelite Fathers of San Antonio.
Luna, Luis *m.s.a.* '87 (NOR)[A] Cromwell, CT Holy Apostles College and Seminary.
Luna, Nicolas *e.c.* '64 (STU)[H] Bloomingdale, OH Holy Family Hermitage.
Lund, Donald J. '69 (CHI) Round Lake, IL St. Joseph.
Lundberg, Bjorn C. '06 (ARL) Notaries; Fredericksburg, VA St. Mary of the Immaculate Conception.
Lundberg, Jan *o.c.d.* '93 (LA) Alhambra, CA St. Therese.
Lundberg, John W. '60 (TLS) Retired.
Lundgren, Stephen A. '79 (DUB) Edgewood, IA St. Mark; Medical–Moral Commission; Edgewood, IA St. Patrick.
Lundy, George F. *s.j.* '78 (BR) Baton Rouge, LA Immaculate Conception; [K] Baton Rouge, LA Martin Luther King, Jr. Catholic Student Center.
Lundy, James P. *c.ss.r.* '47 (NY)[EE] New York, NY Redemptorist Priests and Brothers, C.Ss.R.
Lungay, Jose Roel G. '84 (NO) Slidell, LA St. Genevieve.
Luniw, Paul '82 (STF) Diocesan Consultors; Judicial Vicar; Hartford; Presbyteral Council; Terryville, CT St. Michael.
Luniw, Paul (PHU) Adjunct Judicial Vicars.
Lunness, John A. '04 (WIL) New Castle, DE St. Peter the Apostle.
Lunney, William H. '94 (SPR) Orange, MA St. Mary.
Lunnon, William '82 (DET) Special Assignment; Detroit, MI St. Mary's of Redford.
Lunsford, Keith '92 (KCK) Archdiocesan Pastoral Council; Prairie Village, KS St. Ann.
Lunsford, Rev. Msgr. Robert D. '60 (LAN) Retired.
Luo, Matteo *o.f.m.conv.* '59 (BAL)[S] Ellicott City Order of Friars Minor Conventual.
Luong, Tri M. '94 (HBG) Harrisburg, PA Polyclinic Medical Clinic; Harrisburg, PA Our Lady of the Blessed Sacrament.
Luong Minh Tuat, Francis Xavier M. *c.m.c.* '83 (SPC)[F] Carthage, MO Congregation of the Mother Coredemptrix, United States Assumption Province.
Luongo, Anthony V. (BO) Norwood, MA St. Catherine of Siena.
Luongo, John '78 (ORG) Retired.
Luoni, Christopher '05 (Y) Office of Vocations; [O] Kent, OH Kent State University Newman Center; University Parish Newman Center (Kent State); Kent, OH University Parish Newman Center.
Lupico, Samuel '65 (BAL) Baltimore, MD St. Pius X Retired.
Lupo, David *ss.cc.* '91 (FR)[G] Fairhaven, MA Damien Residence.
Lupo, Robert L. '08 (PRT) Saco, ME Good Shepherd Parish.
Lupton, Brendan P. '05 (CHI) Other Assignments.
Lusch, Daniel J. *s.j.* '62 (BO)[U] Boston The Society of Jesus of New England–Provincial Offices.
Lusch, Daniel J. *s.j.* '62 (BUF)[O] Buffalo, NY Canisius Jesuit Community Inc.
Luschen, Timothy D. '88 (OKL) Edmond, OK St. Monica; Council of Priests Archdiocesan.
Lusk, Craig '08 (KAL) Battle Creek, MI St. Joseph.
Lusoski, Thomas J. '57 (CLV) South Euclid, OH St. Margaret Mary Retired.
Lussier, Bonaventure *o.c.d.* '75 (BO)[U] Boston, MA Carmelite Monastery.
Lussier, Louis *m.i.* '90 (MIL)[P] Milwaukee, WI St. Camillus Provincialate; [Y] Wauwatosa, WI St. Camillus Health System, Inc.; [Y] Milwaukee, WI St. Camillus Communities, Inc.; [Y] Wauwatosa, WI St. Camillus Ministries, Inc.; [Y] Wauwatosa, WI San Camillo, Inc.; [Y] Wauwatosa, WI Order of St. Camillus Foundation, Inc.
Lussier, Louis *o.s.cam.* '90 (SAV) Sylvania, GA Our Lady of the Assumption.
Lussier, Robert *o.s.b.* '92 (SFE)[H] Pecos, NM Our Lady of Guadalupe Abbey; [I] Santa Fe, NM Discalced Carmelite Monastery.
Lussier, Robert *s.s.s.* '56 (SAT) San Antonio, TX St. Joseph.
Lusson, David R. '80 (SUP) Cumberland, WI Sacred Heart of Jesus Church; Cumberland, WI St. Anthony Abbot; Cumberland, WI St. Ann; Board of Directors.
Lustan, Ariel G. '94 (TUC) Safford, AZ Saint Rose of Lima Roman Catholic Parish – Safford; [G] Safford, AZ Eastern Arizona Junior College; Council of Priests; Vicars Forane; All Vicars Forane.
Lutgen, Richard '61 (SAL) Retired.
Luther, Benjamin F. '64 (OWN) Central City, KY St. Joseph; Deans/Coordinators; Legion of Mary; Priest Personnel Committee.
Lutjen, George J. '68 (BRK) Retired.
Lutmer, Joseph H. '46 (CIN) Retired.
Lutostanski, Anthony '58 (BUF) Buffalo, NY St. John Kanty Retired.
Luttenberger, Gerard H. *c.m.* '65 (ALB)[M] Albany, NY De Paul Provincial House.
Luttenberger, Gerard H. *c.m.* (RVC)[A] Huntington, NY Diocesan Seminary of the Immaculate Conception; [M] Oyster Bay, NY Vincentian Community.
Lutz, Bernard A. '63 (EVN) Diocesan Council of Priests; Special Assignment; Continuing Education of Clergy; Diocesan Consultors Retired.
Lutz, Donald J. '70 (BUF) Buffalo, NY Our Lady of Perpetual Help.
Lutz, Frederick J. '73 (SPC) Lamar, MO St. Mary.
Lutz, Rev. Msgr. George C. '62 (NEW) Retired.
Lutz, Gerald J. '56 (PIT) Retired.
Lutz, Gerald J. '56 (CHR) Ridgeland, SC St. Anthony.
Lutz, Herman '58 (IND) Archdiocesan Judges; [I] Beech Grove, IN St. Paul Hermitage Retired.
Lutz, Rev. Msgr. James M. '58 (SY) Retired.
Lutz, Joseph L. '87 (RCK) Retired.
Lutz, Kevin F. '78 (COL) Columbus, OH Holy Family.
Lutz, Thomas '93 (NY) Patterson, NY Sacred Heart.
Luu, Khien *s.v.d.* '92 (DUB)[B] Epworth, IA Divine Word College.
Luu, Vinh Dinh '03 (NO) Graduate Studies.
Lux, Joseph W. *s.j.* '71 (NY)[EE] New York, NY St. Ignatius Loyola Residence.
Lux, Thomas J. '85 (LIN) Holdrege, NE All Saints; Diocesan Council of Catholic Women.
Luyet, Gregory T. '95 (LR) Vice Chancellors; Adjutant Judicial Vicars; Judges; Fort Smith, AR Immaculate Conception; Fort Smith, AR St. Leo's; Priests Personnel Board (Diocesan); Presbyteral Council.
Luyet, Gregory '95 (MEM) Judges.
Lwin, Paw Tun '02 (KC) Harrisonville, MO Our Lady of Lourdes.
Lybarger, Curtis F. '77 (STP) Plymouth, MN St. Mary of the Lake.
Lyden, Dennis P. '63 (STU) Retired.
Lydon, John E. *o.p.* '99 (NO) New Orleans, LA St. Anthony of Padua; New Orleans, LA Tulane Catholic Center.
Lydon, Leo B. '50 (WH) Retired.
Lydon, Michael J. '84 (STL) Affton, MO St. Dominic Savio.
Lydon, Michael '74 (SP) New Port Richey, FL St. Thomas Aquinas; [F] New Port Richey, FL St. Thomas Aquinas Early Childhood Center.
Lyle, Dennis J. '91 (CHI)[A] Mundelein, IL University of St. Mary of the Lake/Mundelein Seminary; Mundelein Seminary/University of St. Mary of the Lake; [A] Mundelein, IL University of St. Mary of the Lake/Mundelein Seminary.
Lyle, John W. *o.s.f.s.* '85 (MO) Navy Chaplains.
Lyman, Edward P. '67 (SCR) Unassigned or Leave of Absence.
Lynam, Gerald J. '50 (HEL) Retired.
Lynam, John '00 (PIT) Pittsburgh, PA Madonna del Castello.
Lynam, Robert G. '84 (MET) Kendall Park, NJ St. Augustine of Canterbury; Deans.
Lynch, Antone '81 (BLX) Retired.
Lynch, Brian T. '06 (STP) Woodbury, MN Saint Ambrose of Woodbury.
Lynch, Charles E. *c.s.b.* '58 (GAL) Manvel, TX Sacred Heart of Jesus.
Lynch, Cornelius B. '54 (PRO) Retired.
Lynch, Daniel C. '48 (SC) Retired.
Lynch, Daniel *s.m.a.* '73 (WDC)[N] Takoma Park, MD Lay Missionary Program.
Lynch, Dennis J. '68 (LC)[D] Stevens Point, WI St. Michael's Hospital of Stevens Point, Inc.
Lynch, E. Patrick *c.ss.r.* '69 (STV) Frederiksted, VI Church of St. Patrick; Diocesan Consultors; Catholic Schools Office.
Lynch, E. Patrick *c.ss.r* '69 (FgM) Baltimore Province.
Lynch, Rev. Msgr. Edward J. '57 (BAL) Towson, MD Church of the Immaculate Conception Retired.
Lynch, Francis A. *c.m.* '50 (MOB) Tallassee, AL St. Vincent De Paul.
Lynch, Francis '57 (BRK) Retired.
Lynch, Gerard *o.ss.t.* (BAL)[S] The Trinitarians in New Jersey.
Lynch, Gregory A. *s.j.* '03 (WOR)[O] Worcester, MA Jesuits of the Holy Cross, Inc.
Lynch, James M. *m.m.* '74 (FgM) Maryknoll, NY MARYKNOLL.
Lynch, John A. '60 (ROC) Judges; Rochester, NY St. Anne Retired.
Lynch, John E. *c.s.p.* '51 (WDC)[B] Washington, DC St. Paul's College; [C] Catholic University of America, The Retired.
Lynch, John J. '65 (NY) Woodbourne, NY Immaculate Conception.
Lynch, John J. *s.j.* '66 (MIL)[P] Wauwatosa, WI Jesuit Community at St. Camillus.
Lynch, John S. '63 (E) Retired.
Lynch, John W. (NY) Ellenville, NY St. Mary and St. Andrew.
Lynch, John *m.afr.* '62 (WDC)[N] Washington, DC Missionaries of Africa; Washington, DC MISSIONARIES OF AFRICA; Washington, DC.
Lynch, Joseph P. '53 (CHI) Retired.
Lynch, Joseph *s.m.* '64 (STL)[O] St. Louis Marianists, Province of the United States (Society of Mary).
Lynch, Kevin A. *c.s.p.* '53 (NEW)[M] Mahwah, NJ Paulist Fathers – Paulist Press; [R] Mahwah, NJ Paulist Press.
Lynch, Kevin A. *c.s.p.* '53 (NY)[EE] New York, NY Paulist Fathers' Motherhouse.
Lynch, Kevin A. *m.m.* '61 (FgM) Maryknoll, NY MARYKNOLL.
Lynch, Leo A. '93 (ALT) Williamsburg, PA St. Joseph.
Lynch, Leo X. '56 (BO) Senior Priests. Retired.
Lynch, Michael J. *s.j.* '93 (BAL) Towson, MD Society of Jesus; [S] Towson Maryland Province of the Society of Jesus.
Lynch, Michael '89 (MIA) Catholic Fire Service Ministry; Deerfield Beach, FL St. Ambrose.
Lynch, Michael '88 (BRK) On Leave/Unassigned.
Lynch, Myles M. *o.s.m.* '58 (CHI)[N] Chicago Order of Friar Servants of Mary (Servites) United States of America Province, Inc.
Lynch, Patrick J. '46 (ALB) Retired.
Lynch, Patrick J. *s.j.* '72 (BUF)[O] Buffalo, NY Canisius Jesuit Community Inc.
Lynch, Peter J. '99 (BGP) Presbyteral Council.
Lynch, Robert B. '60 (NOR) Norwich, CT St. Mary; Legion of Mary Retired.
Lynch, Robert *o.f.m.* '43 (PAT)[N] Ringwood, NJ Holy Name Friary, Inc.
Lynch, Shane M. '01 (OG) Speculator, NY St. James Major; Speculator, NY St. Ann's.
Lynch, Stephen P. '77 (BRK) Brooklyn, NY St. Lucy–St. Patrick; [E] Brooklyn, NY Campus Ministers and Ministry Centers.
Lynch, T. Patrick *s.j.* '61 (NEW)[B] Jersey City, NJ Jesuit Center; [M] Jersey City, NJ Jesuits of Saint Peter's College, Inc.
Lynch, Thomas A. '92 (NY) Bronx, NY Our Lady of Angels; [EE] Yonkers, NY Cathedral Preparatory Seminary High School Formation Program.
Lynch, Thomas F. '71 (BGP) Stratford, CT St. James.
Lynch, Thomas P. *o.p.* '86 (DEN)[N] Denver, CO Dominican Friars; Religious Order Representative.
Lynch, William J. *s.j.* '48 (CHL) Mooresville, NC St. Therese; [J] Mooresville, NC Jesuit Community.
Lynes, James F. '79 (GAL) Clute, TX St. Jerome.
Lynes, John G. '87 (MOB) Mobile, AL Little Flower.
Lyness, Stephen J. '98 (ATL) Special or Other (Arch)Diocesan Assignment; Norcross, GA Mary Our Queen Catholic Church; [J] Atlanta, GA Catholic Center Georgia State University.
Lyng, Rev. Msgr. Edward F. '58 (SD) San Diego, CA St. Joseph Cathedral Retired.
Lynn, William D. *s.j.* '54 (ALN)[A] Wernersville, PA Jesuit Center–Jesuit Community.
Lynn, Rev. Msgr. William J. '76 (PH) Downingtown, PA St. Joseph.
Lyon, Rev. Msgr. Gerald F. '49 (SC) Retired.
Lyon, Joseph A. '50 (L) Retired.
Lyons, Denis '58 (ORG) Retired.
Lyons, Edward D. '62 (CAM) Retired.
Lyons, Rev. Msgr. Frederick J. '52 (ALX) Retired.
Lyons, James A. '94 (PH) Philadelphia, PA St. John the Baptist.
Lyons, James D. '60 (BO) Dracut, MA Ste. Marguerite d'Youville; Senior Priests. Retired.
Lyons, James M. '88 (HBG) Consultors, College; Steelton, PA Prince of Peace.
Lyons, James *o.m.i.* '61 (FgM) Washington, DC AMERICAN OBLATE MISSIONS.
Lyons, John F. '46 (Y) Retired.
Lyons, John J. '80 (SAV) Savannah, GA Sacred Heart of Jesus.
Lyons, John P. '88 (TUC) Tucson, AZ Saints Peter and Paul Roman Catholic Parish – Tucson; Special Assignment; Judicial Vicar; Council of Priests.
Lyons, John R. *m.s.a.* '05 (HRT) Waterbury, CT Basilica of the Immaculate Conception.
Lyons, John R. *m.s.a.* '05 (NOR)[G] Cromwell Society of the Missionaries of the Holy Apostles.
Lyons, John T. '74 (PH) Ambler, PA St. Anthony of Padua.
Lyons, John *d.m.v.* '84 (SAC) Sacramento, CA St. Stephen the First Martyr Parish.
Lyons, Lawrence '54 (MIA) Retired.
Lyons, Leo J. (CHI) Retired.
Lyons, Michael J. '70 (DUL) Silver Bay, MN St. Mary; Two Harbors, MN Holy Spirit.
Lyons, Michael P. '96 (BGP) Easton, CT Notre Dame (of Easton).
Lyons, Michael '96 (VIC) Ganado, TX Assumption of the B.V.M.; Defenders of the Bond.
Lyons, Patrick J. '45 (LIN)[E] Lincoln, NE Bonacum House Retired.
Lyons, Patrick M. '70 (CHI) Calumet City, IL Our Lady of Knock.
Lyons, Peter A. *t.o.r.* '66 (BAL) Baltimore, MD St. Ann; Baltimore, MD St. Wenceslaus; Presbyteral Council; Councilors:.
Lyons, Richard J. '74 (MET) North Plainfield, NJ St. Joseph; Judicial Vicar.
Lyons, Timothy V. *c.m.* '86 (PH) Philadelphia, PA St. Francis of Assisi.
Lyons, Timothy '82 (BAL)[S] Ellicott City, MD Friary of St. Joseph Cupertino.
Lyons, William J. '56 (CHI) Retired.

Lyons, Rev. Msgr. William J. '56 (STL) Special Assignment.
Lytle, Gerald A. '60 (HBG) Retired.
Lyttle, Eugene '93 (DUL) Retired.

M

Ma, Peter '55 (NY) New York, NY St. Mary Retired.
Maag, Ronald E. '78 (BAK) Western; Director of Campaign for Human Development; Priests' Continuing Education Committee; Hood River, OR Immaculate Conception; Health and Retirement Board.
Maassen, Jeffrey A. '97 (STL) Arnold, MO St. David.
Mabango, Ashiono Anthony '95 (PAT) Absent on Leave.
Mabon, Rev. Msgr. Thomas K. '57 (ALT) Retired.
Macabalo, Ponciano *o.f.m.* '77 (MIL) Waterford, WI General Secretariat of the Franciscan Missions, Inc.; [Y] Waterford, WI General Secretariat of the Franciscan Missions, Inc.
Macabio, Arnel *m.s.* '03 (SB) Moreno Valley, CA St. Christopher; [I] Moreno Valley, CA Missionaries of Our Lady of La Salette, MS.
Macalintal, Dionisio '63 (SD) National City, CA St. Mary; Filipino.
MacAulay, Gerard '59 (OKL) Defenders of the Bond Retired.
Macaulay, Neil *o.m.i.* '63 (SJN) San Juan, PR Nuestra Sra. de Guadalupe.
Macaya, Miguel '65 (LSC) Dona Ana, NM Our Lady of the Purification.
MacCandless, William J. *o.s.b.* '58 (NO)[P] St. Benedict, LA St. Joseph Abbey.
MacCarthy, John P. *o.praem.* '69 (GB)[J] De Pere St. Norbert Abbey.
MacCarthy, Joseph T. '97 (BO) Medway, MA St. Joseph.
MacCarthy, Justin H. '64 (ORG) La Habra, CA Our Lady of Guadalupe.
MacCarthy, Liam '68 (SAC) Roseville, CA St. Clare; Priests' Personnel Board, Diocesan.
MacCarthy, Timothy '60 (ORG) Laguna Woods, CA St. Nicholas Retired.
MacDonald, Adam *s.v.d.* '00 (CHI)[N] Techny, IL Divine Word Residence.
MacDonald, Rev. Msgr. Arthur F. '52 (GLP) Glenwood, NM Santo Nino Retired.
MacDonald, Rev. Msgr. Colin A. '45 (MAN) Manchester, NH St. Joseph Cathedral Retired.
Macdonald, Colin '81 (SAC) Retired.
MacDonald, Fabian '77 (SEA) Seattle, WA Immaculate Conception.
MacDonald, Hugh J. '64 (HRT) North Haven, CT St. Barnabas.
MacDonald, James H. '67 (SFR) Redwood City, CA St. Pius; Deans.
MacDonald, Kevin M. *c.ss.r.* '91 (FgM) Baltimore Province.
MacDonald, Kevin (STV) Frederiksted, VI Church of St. Patrick.
MacDonald, Paul V. '59 (BO) Senior Priests. Retired.
MacDonald, Richard *s.c.j.* '65 (BWN) Raymondville, TX Our Lady of Guadalupe.
MacDonald, Sebastian *c.p.* '58 (CHI)[N] Chicago, IL Passionist Community–CTU.
MacDonald, Timothy E. '00 (LAN) Burton, MI Holy Redeemer.
MacDonald, Timothy I. *s.a.* '67 (NY)[EE] Garrison, NY Franciscan Friars of the Atonement, Minister General Office; [EE] New York, NY Atonement Friars; General Council.
MacDonald, Vincent *s.c.j.* '58 (MIL)[P] Franklin Villa Maria.
MacDonough, Richard B. *s.s.* '60 (BAL)[S] Baltimore Society of St. Sulpice, Province of the United States Retired.
MacDonough, Richard *s.s.* '60 (PRT) Retired.
MacDougall, James L. *o.s.a.* '59 (MIA)[B] St. Thomas University; [K] Miami Gardens, FL Casa San Lorenzo.
Mace, John D. *s.j.* '68 (MIL)[P] Milwaukee Jesuit Provincial Office, Wisconsin Province; Milwaukee, WI Society of Jesus.
Maceda, Thomas *c.ss.r.* '63 (BRK) Brooklyn, NY Our Lady of Perpetual Help Basilica.
MacEntee, Francis J. *s.j.* '54 (SCR)[C] Scranton, PA The University of Scranton.
MacEwen, Michael W. (BO) Marlborough, MA Immaculate Conception.
Macey, James R. '07 (BIR) Jacksonville, AL St. Charles; [H] Jacksonville, AL Jacksonville State University.
Macey, Richard '75 (DET) Woodhaven, MI Our Lady of the Woods.
Macfarlane, Rev. Msgr. John F. '66 (WDC) Rockville, MD St. Elizabeth.
MacGabhann, Kevin '63 (PMB) Retired.
MacGee, James B. *o.m.i.* '57 (PT) Crawfordville, FL St. Elizabeth Ann Seton; Woodville, FL St. Stephen the Protomartyr.
MacGillivray, John J. *c.m.* '76 (FgM) Philadelphia, PA Eastern Province.
Machado, Clement *s.o.l.t.* '93 (CC)[G] Robstown, TX Society of Our Lady of the Most Holy Trinity.
Machado, Domingos A. *o.a.r.* '95 (LA) Montebello, CA St. Benedict; West Orange, NJ.
Machado, Johnson J. '05 (CC) Benavides, TX Santa Rosa de Lima.
Machado, Jose '93 (WCH) Wichita, KS Our Lady of Perpetual Help.
Machain, David B. '52 (PH) Philadelphia, PA St. Bernard Retired.
Machalski, Thomas C. '85 (BRK) Diocesan Judges.
Machalski, Thomas C. '85 (BRK) Vice Officiale–Associate Judicial Vicar; Bayside, NY St. Josaphat.
Machamire, Cuthbert (CC)[D] Corpus Christi, TX CHRISTUS Spohn Hospital Corpus Christi – Memorial.
Machar, Jerome J. *o.c.s.o.* '75 (ROC)[J] Piffard, NY Abbey of the Genesee; Piffard, NY.
Machira, Paul (SY) Solvay, NY St. Cecilia.
Machlik, Jerome J. '71 (DET) Shelby Twp., MI St. John Vianney Church.
Machnik, Theodore F. '91 (COL) Portsmouth, OH St. Mary; Deanery 13: Scioto County; Presbyteral Council; Parochial Examiners.
Macho, George S. '53 (NEW) Retired.
Machozi, Vincent *a.a.* '94 (BO)[U] Boston, MA Assumptionist Center.
Maciag, Waldemar '97 (ORL) Orlando, FL Holy Family.
Macias, Alonso E. (BO) Vocations; Cambridge, MA St. Mary of the Annunciation.
Macias, Frank '94 (SAT) San Antonio, TX St. Leo.
Macias, Fray Jorge *o.f.m.cap.* (SJN).
Macias, Salvador '82 (OAK) Fremont, CA Corpus Christi.
Maciej, David '80 (SCL) Lastrup, MN Holy Cross; Lastrup, MN St. John Nepomuk; Koinonia Program of Central Minnesota.
Maciejewski, Norbert F. '69 (DET) Retired.
Maciejewski, Tadeusz *c.m.* '88 (BRK) Brooklyn, NY SS. Cyril and Methodius.
MacInnes, Colin '70 (FgM) Boston, MA St. James the Apostle, Inc.
MacInnis, John E. (BO) Designated; Peabody, MA St. John the Baptist.
MacInnis, Michael *o.f.m.* '00 (HRT) New Milford, CT St. Francis Xavier.
MacIntyre, Frederick H. '92 (WDC) Retired.
MacIsaac, Charles (PAT)[Q] Paterson, NJ Cor Jesu Mission Fund Inc.
MacIssac, Charles *o.s.* '83 (PCE) On Duty Outside the Diocese.
Mack, John P. '85 (MO) Air Force Reserve Chaplains; [A] East Aurora, NY Christ the King Seminary.
Mack, John '06 (PRM) Sugar Creek, MO St. Luke, Byzantine Catholic Parish.
Mack, Joseph W. '89 (CHL) Reidsville, NC Holy Infant.
Mack, Rev. Msgr. Robert A. '57 (BUF) Retired.
Mack, Rev. Msgr. Thomas E. '78 (PEO) Cullom, IL St. John's; Pontiac, IL St. Mary's; Vicariates and Vicars.
MacKay, Arthur T. (BO) Woburn, MA St. Charles Borromeo.
Macke, Paul B. *s.j.* '73 (WDC)[N] Washington, DC Leonard Neale House.
Macke, Paul B. *s.j.* '73 (CHI)[N] Chicago Chicago Province of the Society of Jesus–Provincial Office.
Macke, Richard J. '54 (SC) Retired.
MacKenzie, John B. '00 (MAN) Lincoln, NH St. Joseph; Presbyteral Council.
MacKenzie, William M. '66 (BO) Senior Priests. Retired.
Mackert, Albert J. '61 (CLV) Cleveland, OH Immaculate Conception Retired.
Mackey, Alan C. '00 (BIR) Scottsboro, AL St. Jude.
Mackey, James '61 (ALB) Troy, NY St. Michael the Archangel Retired.
Mackiewicz, Richard E. '69 (GBG)[F] Greensburg, PA Neumann House Retired.
Mackin, Eamon *c.h.s.* '70 (ORG) Huntington Beach, CA St. Mary's by the Sea.
Mackin, Kevin *o.f.m.* (NY)[C] Newburgh, NY Mt. St. Mary College.
MacKinnon, Donald *c.ss.r.* '59 (OAK)[M] Berkeley, CA Redemptorist Fathers (Denver Province); Kmhmu/Laotian Pastoral Center.
Mackle, Daniel E. '80 (PH)[A] Wynnewood, PA Theological Seminary of St. Charles Borromeo, Overbrook; Philadelphia, PA St. Patrick.
Mackle, Liam M. *o.s.m.* '58 (CHI)[N] Chicago Order of Friar Servants of Mary (Servites) United States of America Province, Inc.
Macklin, Eckley *s.o.l.t.* '95 (CHY) Lovell, WY St. Joseph's.
Macklin, Eckley *s.o.l.t.* '95 (CC)[G] Robstown, TX Society of Our Lady of the Most Holy Trinity.
Mackowski, Richard M. *s.j.* '61 (DET)[K] Detroit, MI Jesuit Community at the University of Detroit Mercy.
MacLean, Thomas S. '02 (LIN) Advocates; Lincoln, NE St. Mary; Health Care Facilities; Lincoln, NE Nebraska Penal Complex; Building Commission.
MacLellan, Iain G. *o.s.b.* '87 (MAN)[K] Manchester, NH St. Anselm Abbey.
MacLennan, Donald B. '67 (DET) Retired.
MacLeod, Malcolm *m.ss.cc.* '87 (CAM) Linwood, NJ The Church of Our Lady of Sorrows, Linwood, N.J.; [M] Linwood, NJ Villa Pieta. Missionaries of the Sacred Hearts of Jesus & Mary; Linwood, NJ.
MacLoughlin, James '63 (ORL) Casselberry, FL St. Augustine Retired.
MacMahon, Craig *o.m.v.* '90 (BO)[Z] Boston, MA St. Francis Chapel.
MacMahon, Rev. Msgr. Eamon '47 (MRY) Retired.
Mac Mahon, Michael '66 (BIR) Huntsville, AL Holy Spirit; Diocesan College of Consultors; Priests'/Presbyteral Council; Diocesan College of Vicars.
MacMahon, Patrick '69 (SPK) Davenport, WA Immaculate Conception; Harrington, WA St. Francis of Assisi; Davenport, WA St. Michael.
MacMaster, Thomas A. *o.c.s.o.* '57 (DUB)[K] Peosta, IA New Melleray Abbey, Order of Cistercians of the Strict Observance.
MacMillan, Donald A. *s.j.* '72 (BO)[U] Newton, MA The Jesuit Community at Boston College.
MacMillan, Len '91 (B) Meridian, ID Holy Apostles.
MacNamara, Robert C. '51 (ROC) Elmira, NY St. Mary Retired.
MacNew, James '69 (PH)[C] Philadelphia, PA Holy Family University.
Maco, Stephen L. '76 (ALN) Allentown, PA St. Paul.
Macora, Athanasius *o.f.m.* '92 (FgM) Washington, DC COMMISSARIAT OF THE HOLY LAND.
Macoskie, Melvin H. '55 (MIL) Retired.
Macoy, Jose '60 (HON) Hana, HI St. Mary.
MacPhaidin, Bartley *c.s.c.* '63 (FR)[A] North Easton, MA Holy Cross Fathers Religious.
MacPherson, Damian *s.a.* '78 (NY)[EE] Garrison Franciscan Friars of the Atonement, Minister General Office.
MacPherson, Stephen E.C. '86 (SR) On Leave.
MacPherson, Walter E. '55 (BEL) Retired.
Macpherson, Walter '86 (CIN) Retired.
MacQuarrie, John D. '78 (CIN) West Milton, OH Transfiguration.
MacRory, Camillus *o.f.m.cap.* '51 (SFR) Definitors:; [N] Burlingame, CA Capuchin Provincial House Retired.
Macsherry, Hugh *o.f.m.* '09 (BO)[Z] Boston, MA St. Anthony Shrine.
Mactutis, Peter '06 (SEA) Lakewood, WA St. Frances Cabrini.
MacVeigh, Donal T. *s.j.* '72 (NEW)[B] Jersey City, NJ Jesuit Center; [M] Jersey City, NJ Jesuits of Saint Peter's College, Inc.
MacVeigh, Michael C. '56 (PIT)[M] Pittsburgh, PA St. John Vianney Manor Retired.
MacWade, Joseph A. *s.j.* '61 (FgM) Watertown, MA Society of Jesus.
Madanu, Anthaiah *s.v.d.* '92 (LA) Los Angeles, CA St. John, The Evangelist.
Madanu, Santosh *h.g.n.* (LEX) Jenkins, KY St. George.
Madathiparambil, Vinod '98 (SYM) Eparchial Consultors; Procurator; Elmhurst, IL Syro–Malabar Catholic Mission Pittsburgh, PA.
Madathiparampil, George '67 (SYM) Vicar General (Protosyncellus); Eparchial Consultors; Louisville, KY Syro–Malabar Catholic Mission Louisville, Kentucky.
Madden, Benjamin *o.f.m.cap.* '58 (FgM) Pittsburgh, PA Province of St. Augustine.
Madden, Rev. Msgr. Brendan P. '51 (PAT)[Q] Chester, NJ Nazareth Village Retired.
Madden, Rev. Msgr. Edward T. '52 (DEN) Retired.
Madden, Henry *o.f.m.* (PAT)[N] Ringwood, NJ Holy Name Friary, Inc.
Madden, J. Thomas '53 (SFR) Retired.
Madden, James J. *m.m.* '60 (FgM) Maryknoll, NY MARYKNOLL.
Madden, James P. *c.s.c.* '57 (ALB)[L] Valatie, NY St. Joseph Center.
Madden, John F. '84 (WOR) Worcester, MA St. John's.
Madden, John J. *s.j.* '69 (SAV) Special Assignment.
Madden, John P. '86 (Y) McDonald, OH Our Lady of Perpetual Help.
Madden, John R. '70 (SAV) Pine Mountain, GA Christ the King Church.
Madden, Rev. Msgr. John R. '59 (SY) Hamilton, NY St. Mary; Morrisville, NY St. Joan of Arc.
Madden, Joseph *o.f.m.conv.* '62 (R) Siler City, NC St. Julia; [F] Pittsboro, NC Our Lady of Guadalupe Friary; Apex, NC St. Andrew the Apostle.
Madden, Lawrence J. *s.j.* '64 (WDC)[N] Washington, DC The Jesuit Community at Georgetown University.
Madden, Michael J. '95 (BGP) Leave of Absence.
Madden, Michael '75 (EVN) Bloomfield, IN Holy Name; Advocates; Diocesan Council of Priests; Linton, IN St. Peter; Diocesan Consultors.
Madden, Patrick J. '83 (MOB) Grove Hill, AL Sacred Heart.
Madden, Patrick J. '74 (SHP) Greco Institute.
Madden, Patrick '83 (MOB) Butler, AL St. John The Evangelist.
Madden, Stephen J. '88 (BO) Foxborough, MA St. Mary.
Madden, Thomas F. '76 (NY) Haverstraw, NY St. Peter; Canon 1742 Panel of Pastors.
Madden, Rev. Msgr. Thomas G. '55 (NEW) North Arlington, NJ Queen of Peace; [M] Rutherford, NJ

St. John Vianney Residence for Priests Retired.
Madden, Thomas J. *s.j.* '57 (LAF)[J] Grand Coteau, LA Jesuit Spirituality Center (St. Charles College).
Madden, William T. *m.m.* '58 (NY)[EE] Maryknoll Maryknoll Fathers and Brothers; [EE] Maryknoll, NY Maryknoll Fathers and Brothers Charitable Trust; [II] Maryknoll, NY Friends of St. Maria Goretti, U.S.A., Inc. Retired.
Maddineni, Ananda Prasad *m.s.f.s.* '96 (STA) Jacksonville, FL Holy Spirit.
Maddock, Andrew *s.j.* '85 (HEL) St. Ignatius, MT St. Ignatius Mission; Diocesan Consultors.
Maddock, George *o.f.m.cap.* '64 (AGN)[F] Agana Heights, GU St. Fidelis Friary; White Plains, NY Province of St. Mary.
Maddock, Jay T. '75 (FR) East Taunton, MA Holy Family; [K] East Taunton, MA Diocesan Catholic Youth Organization; Judges; Taunton Deanery; Catholic Youth Organization.
Maddock, Laurence F. '56 (CHI)[A] Chicago, IL St. Joseph College Seminary Retired.
Madej, Paul D. '90 (SY) Military Chaplains; Army Chaplains.
Madel, Samuel Tanios *m.l.m.* (OLL)[A] Houston, TX The Congregation of Maronite Lebanese Missionaries.
Madel, Samuel '91 (OLL) West Covina, CA St. Jude Maronite Catholic Church.
Mader, George L. '59 (NEW)[M] Caldwell, NJ The Rev. Msgr. James F. Kelley Residence for Retired Priests Retired.
Mader, Joseph '67 (IND) On Disability Leave.
Mader, Stan P. '92 (STP) Hampton, MN St. Mathias; Vermillion, MN St. John the Baptist; Hampton, MN St. Mary.
Madera, Juan '08 (FRS) Reedley, CA St. Anthony of Padua.
Madera, Luis M. *o.s.a.* '00 (MIA)[K] Miami Gardens, FL Casa San Lorenzo.
Madero, Martin *sch.p.* '02 (LA) Los Angeles, CA Our Lady Help of Christians (Maria Auxiliadora).
Madey, Louis '68 (MO) Navy Reserve Chaplains; On Duty Outside the Diocese.
Madeya, Gregory *b.h.s.* '08 (SJP) McKeesport, PA St. John the Baptist; Presbyters.
Madhichetti, Anthony '00 (GI) Mitchell, NE St. Theresa's.
Madi–Okin, Charles '07 (BO) Somerville, MA St. Joseph.
Madigan, Arthur R. *s.j.* '77 (BO)[U] Newton, MA The Jesuit Community at Boston College.
Madigan, Daniel A. *s.j.* '83 (WDC)[W] Washington, DC Woodstock Theological Center; [N] Washington, DC The Jesuit Community at Georgetown University; [N] Washington, DC Woodstock Jesuit Community.
Madigan, Daniel '64 (SAC) Clarksburg, CA St. Joseph.
Madigan, Daniel (HEL) Helena, MT Cathedral of St. Helena.
Madigan, Henry *o.f.m.conv.* '56 (ALB)[L] Rensselaer, NY Provincialate, Immaculate Conception Friary – Order of Friars Minor Conventual.
Madigan, John A. *o.p.* (RVC)[B] Rockville Centre, NY Molloy College.
Madigan, John C. '74 (SEA) Seattle, WA Holy Rosary; Seattle, WA Our Lady of Mount Virgin; Deans.
Madigan, Rev. Msgr. John J. '54 (WDC) Silver Spring, MD Our Lady of Grace Retired.
Madigan, John R. *o.m.i.* '77 (BEL)[J] Belleville, IL Missionary Association of Mary Immaculate–Missionary Oblates of Mary Immaculate; [F] Belleville, IL Shrine of Our Lady of the Snows.
Madigan, John *o.p.* (RVC) Uniondale, NY St. Martha.
Madigan, Kevin '70 (NY) New York, NY St. Peter.
Madigan, Patrick S. *s.j.* '83 (NO)[P] New Orleans Jesuit Provincial Office.
Madike, Sebastian '00 (BUR) Rutland, VT Christ the King.
Madley, Jeffrey J. '76 (RVC) Southampton, NY Sacred Hearts of Jesus and Mary.
Madori, Peter J. '69 (NY) Wurtsboro, NY St. Joseph.
Madrid, Saul '85 (PHX) On Leave.
Madrigal, Hector '87 (AMA) Advocates; Ex Officio; Vicars Forane; Amarillo, TX St. Joseph's.
Madrigal, Ildefonso M. '57 (LA) Retired.
Madsen, Rev. Msgr. John W. '66 (BUF) Depew, NY St. Barnabas.
Madu, Anthony '93 (RVC) Rockville Centre, NY Mercy Medical Center; Baldwin, NY St. Christopher.
Madu, Ferdinand E. '86 (MO) Army Chaplains.
Maduakor, Casmir '84 (ATL) Marietta, GA Holy Family.
Madumelu, Jerome '94 (RVC) West Islip, NY Good Samaritan Hospital Medical Center.
Maduri, John '87 (BRK) Brooklyn, NY Most Precious Blood; Nocturnal Adoration Society.
Maduro, Gabriel '59 (ARE) Arecibo, PR Cathedral of San Felipe Apostol; Defenders of the Bond.
Maduro, P. Gabriel '59 (ARE) Arecibo Hospital; Susoni Hospital.
Madus, Rev. Msgr. Peter P. '68 (SCR) Diocesan Consultors; Peckville, PA Sacred Heart of Jesus.
Maduzia, Norbert J. '82 (CHI)[T] Chicago, IL National Organization for Continuing Education of Roman Catholic Clergy, Inc.; Spring, TX St. Ignatius of Loyola; Building and Planning Commission; Chicago, IL National Organization for Continuing Education of Roman Catholic Clergy, Inc. (NOCERCC).
Maechler, Edmund Francis '49 (LA) Retired.
Maekawa, Steven *o.p.* '98 (OAK)[M] Oakland, CA Order of Preachers (Province of the Most Holy Name of Jesus – Western Dominican Province); [M] Oakland, CA Order of Preachers (Province of the Most Holy Name of Jesus – Western Dominican Province).
Maes, Allen *o.m.i.* '68 (BEL)[F] Belleville, IL Shrine of Our Lady of the Snows.
Maes, Allen *o.m.i.* '68 (WDC)[N] Washington, DC Provincial Offices of the United States Province of the Missionary Oblates of Mary Immaculate; Councilors:.
Maes, Anthony G. *o.praem.* '82 (SFE)[B] Albuquerque, NM St. Pius X High School; [H] Albuquerque, NM Santa Maria de la Vid Priory.
Maes, Clarence '87 (SFE) Albuquerque, NM Sacred Heart; Presbyteral Council of the Archdiocese of Santa Fe; Presbyteral Council of the Archdiocese of Santa Fe.
Maes, Clark B. '95 (STL) Bloomsdale, MO St. Agnes; Bloomsdale, MO St. Lawrence.
Maes, John J. '67 (DOD) Diocesan Finance Council; College of Consultors Retired.
Maestri, William F. '77 (NO) New Orleans, LA St. Louis Cathedral; On Special Assignment.
Maffei, Vincent R. '64 (BO) Randolph, MA St. Mary; Senior Priests. Retired.
Maffeo, Michael T. '91 (RVC) Ronkonkoma, NY St. Joseph's.
Magabe, Benedict *c.pp.s.* '06 (CIN) Saint Henry, OH St. Bernard; St. Henry, OH St. Aloysius; St. Henry, OH St. Francis; St. Henry, OH St. Henry; Saint Henry, OH St. Wendelin; [N] Dayton, OH Provincial Office of the Cincinnati Province of the Society of the Precious Blood.
Magallanes, Manuel *o.s.b.* '76 (OKL)[I] Shawnee, OK St. Gregory's Abbey.
Magallenes, Alejandro '69 (LA)[B] Santa Ynez, CA San Lorenzo Seminary – Retreat Center.
Magallon, Ernesto '98 (BWN) Edcouch, TX St. Theresa of the Infant Jesus.
Magaña, Alberto O. '01 (YAK) Special Assignment.
Magana, Edgar *o.f.m.* '02 (SJ) San Jose, CA Our Lady of Guadalupe.
Magana, Jose L. '98 (LA) Long Beach, CA St. Anthony.
Magana, Salvador '06 (WIL) Milford, DE St. John the Apostle.
Magapayo, Teodoro P. '89 (SFR) San Mateo, CA St. Bartholomew.
Magary, Thomas A. '66 (STU) Martins Ferry, OH St. Mary.
Magat, Elmer '88 (SFR) San Francisco, CA Star of the Sea.
Magat, Geronimo A. '02 (ARL) Stafford, VA St. William of York.
Magbanua, Celso '01 (CHK) Kristo Rai Parish; Presbyteral Council.
Magbanua, Rev. Msgr. Mario '65 (DAL) Dallas, TX St. James.
Magdaleno, Ricardo '89 (FRS) Children's Hospital Central California; Kaiser Permanente Medical Center; Fresno, CA St. Anthony of Padua.
Magdaong, Joseph '98 (LA) West Covina, CA St. Christopher.
Magdaraog, Vicente '96 (TR) Eatontown, NJ St. Dorothea.
Magee, George P. *o.s.a.* '68 (PH)[Y] Villanova, PA St. Thomas Monastery.
Magee, Rev. Msgr. Michael K. '91 (PH)[A] Wynnewood, PA Theological Seminary of St. Charles Borromeo, Overbrook; Council of Priests.
Magee, Patrick F. '70 (TR) Retired.
Magee, Patrick '81 (FR) On Duty Outside the Diocese.
Magee, Patrick *f.l.h.f.* '81 (PAT) Paterson, NJ St. Therese.
Magee, Raphael M. *f.i.* '98 (FR)[G] New Bedford, MA Marian Friary of Our Lady, Queen of the Seraphic Order.
Magel, John E. '60 (L) Retired.
Mager, Martin J. *o.s.b.* '63 (SFR)[N] Portola Valley, CA Woodside Priory; Portola Valley, CA.
Maghari, E. Pablito (NY) Staten Island, NY St. Peter.
Maghinay, Joseph '74 (STO) Filipino Pastoral Ministry; Stockton, CA St. Luke Church of Stockton (Pastor of).
Maghsoudi, Aron M. '06 (ALT) Altoona, PA Cathedral of the Blessed Sacrament; Cresson, PA State Correctional Institution.
Magiera, Michael W. *f.s.s.p.* '05 (IND) Indianapolis, IN SS. Peter and Paul Cathedral; Indianapolis, IN Holy Rosary.
Maginnis, Andrew F. *s.j.* '52 (SFR)[E] San Francisco, CA St. Ignatius College Preparatory (Coed); [N] San Francisco, CA Jesuit Community at St. Ignatius College Preparatory.
Maginnis, Edward L. *s.j.* '53 (STL)[O] St. Louis, MO Jesuit Community Corporation at Saint Louis University – Jesuit Hall.
Maginot, Michael L. '83 (GRY) Merrillville, IN St. Stephen, Martyr.
Maginot, Richard J. '50 (CHI) Retired.
Magnan, Oscar G. '63 (NEW)[B] Jersey City, NJ Jesuit Center; [M] Jersey City, NJ Jesuits of Saint Peter's College, Inc.
Magnano, Paul A. '67 (SEA) Special Assignment; Vicar for Clergy, Office of; Presbyteral Council; College of Consultors.
Magnano, Paul '67 (SEA) Seattle, WA Christ Our Hope Personal Parish.
Magnaye, Carlo Benjamin *m.f.* '96 (AUS) Mexia, TX St. Mary; Mexia, TX State School.
Magner, Kevin P. '03 (STP) Hamel, MN St. Anne.
Magner, Richard P. *s.j.* (SEA)[L] Seattle, WA Jesuit House, Seattle.
Magni, Daniel D. (BO) Lowell, MA St. Rita; Vicariate II.
Magnuson, Sean R. '06 (STP) Military Chaplains; Army Chaplains.
Mago, Israel E. '07 (MIA) Key Biscayne, FL St. Agnes.
Magoon, R. Dale '60 (GAY) Mancelona, MI St. Anthony of Padua.
Magraw, Rev. Msgr. Daniel E. '75 (E) Erie, PA Blessed Sacrament; Presbyteral Council; College of Consultors.
Maguire, Connell J. '45 (PH) Retired.
Maguire, Daniel J. '69 (SFR) San Francisco, CA St. Thomas the Apostle.
Maguire, Enda J. '59 (STO) Diamond Springs, CA Retired.
Maguire, Francis X. *c.m.* '78 (PH)[Y].
Maguire, Robert *o.cist.* '76 (DAL)[B] University of Dallas; [J] Irving, TX Cistercian Abbey of Our Lady of Dallas.
Maguire, Seamus J. '53 (WH) Retired.
Maguire, Thomas H. '76 (BO) Norwell, MA St. Helen Mother of the Emperor Constantine.
Maguire, Thomas J. '69 (SAC) Alcoholism Advisory Board; Folsom, CA St. John the Baptist Retired.
Maguire, William *c.p.* '02 (PIT)[M] Pittsburgh, PA St. Paul of the Cross Monastery.
Mahalic, Philip A. '75 (MO) Army Reserve Chaplains.
Mahan, Daniel '88 (IND) Board of Consultors.
Mahan, Terrance L. *s.j.* '54 (LA)[C] Los Angeles, CA Jesuit Community.
Mahaney, Hilary F. '69 (CHI) Chicago, IL St. Mary of the Angels; [V] Chicago, IL Midtown Residence; Chicago.
Mahar, Christopher M. '04 (PRO) Graduate Studies.
Mahar, James (BRK)[E] Brooklyn, NY Campus Ministers and Ministry Centers.
Mahar, Raymond J. '58 (BUF)[O] Buffalo, NY Sheehan Residence for Priests Retired.
Maher, Arthur '54 (JOL) Retired.
Maher, Byron G. '50 (CHI) Retired.
Maher, Charles E. '60 (PRO) Retired.
Maher, Daniel J. '62 (ALB) Retired.
Maher, Edmund J. '88 (PH) Blind, Guild for all the; [CC] Philadelphia, PA Catholic League For Persons With Disabilities Retired.
Maher, Edward J. '81 (CAM) Barrington, NJ Church of St. Francis de Sales, Barrington, N.J.
Maher, Francis '54 (JOL) Retired.
Maher, Francis '54 (COS) Colorado Springs, CO St. Joseph's Retired.
Maher, J. David '71 (JC) Jefferson City, MO St. Peter; III. Jefferson City; Personnel Board.
Maher, James J. *c.m.* '90 (BRK)[D] St. John's University; [D] Brooklyn, NY Bread & Life Soup Kitchen; [T] Jamaica, NY St. Vincent's House.
Maher, James J. '92 (LA) Westlake Village, CA St. Maximilian Kolbe; Scouting, Camp Fire Ministry.
Maher, Jerry '94 (MRY) Scotts Valley, CA San Agustin; Clergy Life and Ministry Board.
Maher, John L. *s.j.* '74 (FgM) St. Louis, MO Society of Jesus.
Maher, John T. *c.m.* '81 (BUF)[C] Niagara University, NY Niagara University; [O] Niagara University, NY Vincentian Community at Niagara University; [R] Niagara University, NY Niagara University.
Maher, Michael L. '48 (SAG) Retired.
Maher, Michael N. *ss.cc.* '63 (SB) Cathedral City, CA St. Louis.
Maher, Michael N. *ss.cc* '63 (LA)[P] La Verne, CA Congregation of the Sacred Hearts of Jesus and Mary.
Maher, Michael W. *s.j.* '86 (SPK)[B] Spokane, WA Gonzaga University.
Maher, Patrick '71 (LUB) Littlefield, TX Sacred Heart.
Maher, Patrick '53 (MOB) Coden, AL St. Rose of Lima.
Maher, Paul P. *o.m.i.* '58 (P) Lebanon, OR St. Edward.
Maher, Raymond '44 (SJ) Retired.
Maher, Raymond *o.carm.* '97 (NY) New York, NY St. John the Martyr.
Maher, Rev. Msgr. Robert E. '71 (BWN) Edinburg, TX St. Joseph; Presbyteral Council; Vicar General; College of Consultors; Diocesan Finance Council; [D] Executive Board:.

Maher, Robert G. '57 (WIN) Retired.
Maher, Robert *o.f.m.cap.* '74 (HON) Waimanalo, HI St. George.
Maher, Ryan J. *s.j.* '97 (WDC)[N] Washington, DC The Jesuit Community at Georgetown University.
Maher, Ryan L. '05 (COV) Covington, KY St. Benedict; Diocesan Consultors; Deanery Pastoral Council; Initiation; Office of Worship.
Maher, Sean M. '09 (BO) Duxbury, MA Holy Family.
Maher, T. Patrick '02 (GAY) West Branch, MI Holy Family; West Branch, MI St. Joseph; Members of the College of Consultors; Prescott, MI St. Stephen of Hungary.
Maher, Thomas F. '47 (CHI) Chicago, IL St. Mary of the Woods Retired.
Maher, Thomas *o.m.i.* '57 (FgM) Washington, DC AMERICAN OBLATE MISSIONS.
Maher, William *o.m.i.* '66 (FgM) Washington, DC AMERICAN OBLATE MISSIONS.
Mahimbo, Casimir '97 (ROC) Horseheads, NY St. Mary Our Mother.
Mahler, Clyde '99 (HT) Houma, LA Maria Immacolata; Knights of Columbus.
Mahler, Rev. Msgr. Frank E. '56 (ARL) Alexandria, VA Blessed Sacrament Retired.
Mahlmann, Raymond '85 (GLP) Ecumenical Affairs in New Mexico.
Mahlmann, Raymond '85 (GLP) Milan, NM St. Vivian; Milan, NM San Mateo; Milan, NM San Rafael; Grants, NM St. Teresa of Avila; Seboyeta, NM Our Lady of Sorrows.
Mahon, Ambrose J. '58 (STP) Retired.
Mahon, Rev. Msgr. Dennis (NEW)[B] School of Diplomacy and Intl. Rels.
Mahon, Rev. Msgr. Gerald A. '71 (WIN) Rochester, MN St. John the Evangelist.
Mahon, Joseph F. *c.s.p.* '56 (NY)[EE] New York, NY Paulist Fathers' Motherhouse Retired.
Mahon, Leo T. '51 (CHI) Chicago, IL St. Mary of the Woods Retired.
Mahon, M. Shawn '88 (BAL) Baltimore, MD St. Thomas Aquinas; Presbyteral Council.
Mahon, William A. '92 (NEW) New Providence, NJ Our Lady of Peace.
Mahone, Casey B. '89 (WH) Clarksburg, WV Immaculate Conception.
Mahone, Michael '80 (RNO) Reno, NV Our Lady of the Snows; Seminary Board; Priest Personnel Board.
Mahoney, Bernard '53 (AUS) Retired.
Mahoney, Brian E. '95 (BO) Sherborn, MA St. Theresa of Lisieux.
Mahoney, Daniel C. '70 (GBG) Latrobe, PA Holy Family; Deaneries; Bishop's Priests Council; College of Deans.
Mahoney, Daniel J. '56 (BO) Charlestown, MA St. Francis de Sales.
Mahoney, Gerard J. *o.s.f.s.* '71 (PH)[D] Philadelphia, PA Father Judge High School for Boys; [Y] Philadelphia, PA Father Louis Brisson Residence.
Mahoney, Gordon '56 (JOL)[K] Naperville, IL St. John Vianney Villa Retired.
Mahoney, James M. '92 (BO) Abington, MA St. Bridget.
Mahoney, Rev. Msgr. James T. (PAT) Chatham, NJ Corpus Christi; Vicar General and Moderator of the Curia; Presbyteral Council; Finance Council; College of Consultors; [Q] Clifton, NJ Consortium of Catholic Schools of the Roman Catholic Diocese of Paterson, Inc.; [Q] Sparta, NJ The Catholic Academy of Sussex County, Inc.
Mahoney, Rev. Msgr. John E. '72 (BRK) Jackson Heights, NY Our Lady of Fatima.
Mahoney, John J. '90 (MAN) Diocesan Judges; On Duty Outside the Diocese; Manchester, NH Parish of the Transfiguration.
Mahoney, John '90 (BUR) Judges.
Mahoney, John *o.m.i.* '54 (SAT)[K] San Antonio, TX Oblate Madonna Residence.
Mahoney, Joseph P. '57 (WOR) Worcester, MA St. Stephen's.
Mahoney, Kevin J. '81 (STL) High Ridge, MO St. Anthony of Padua.
Mahoney, Mark A. '86 (BO) Topsfield, MA St. Rose of Lima.
Mahoney, Maurice J. *o.s.a.* '60 (FgM) Villanova, PA Province of St. Thomas of Villanova (Eastern).
Mahoney, Michael *o.f.m.cap.* '74 (SFR) Burlingame, CA Our Lady of Angels.
Mahoney, Rev. Msgr. Neil J. '70 (NEW) Newark, NJ St. John's; Newark, NJ St. Patrick's Pro–Cathedral.
Mahoney, Peter '61 (BRK)[M] Brooklyn, NY Catholic Charities; Brooklyn, NY Assumption of the Blessed Virgin Mary.
Mahoney, Richard J. '58 (STP) Rosemount, MN St. Agatha Retired.
Mahoney, Robert J. '55 (KC) Retired.
Mahoney, Shaun L. '91 (PH) On Special or Other Archdiocesan Assignment; [BB] Philadelphia, PA Temple University; Philadelphia, PA St. Martin De Porres.
Mahoney, Thomas A. '98 (BO) Boston, MA St. Cecilia.
Mahoney, Thomas D. '65 (CLV) Retired.
Mahoney, Thomas E. '68 (WOR) Mendon, MA St. Michael; Advocates.
Mahonge, Augustine Madafa R. '09 (CHI) Blue Island, IL St. Benedict.
Mahony, John '58 (SP) Retired.
Mahowald, Paul A. *s.j.* '68 (OM) Omaha, NE St. John; [K] Omaha, NE Jesuit Community at Creighton University.
Mahowald, Rev. Msgr. Richard J. '55 (SFS) Retired.
Mai, Dan T. *s.j.* '03 (P)[L] Portland Jesuit Provincial Office (Society of Jesus, Oregon Prov.).
Mai, Joseph Khoa Xuan (VIC) Vietnamese American Apostolic Center.
Mai, Khoa L. '05 (LA) Santa Fe Springs, CA St. Pius X.
Mai, Peter Vong (OAK)[M] Saint Conrad Friary.
Mai, Trung Thanh *s.v.d.* '05 (DUB)[B] Epworth, IA Divine Word College.
Mai–Chi–Than, Joseph M. '57 (PEO) Retired.
Maibusch, Henry *o.s.a.* '54 (MIL) Racine, WI St. Rita.
Maichen, Richard F. '54 (DUB) Retired.
Maida, Thaddeus S. '58 (PIT) Retired.
Maier, John '90 (DM) Leavenworth, KS Retired.
Maier, Joseph *c.ss.r.* '65 (FgM) Denver, CO Denver Province.
Maier, Paul '70 (RIC) Abingdon, VA Christ the King; Marion, VA St. John the Evangelist Church.
Maiers, Brennan *o.s.b.* '63 (SCL)[I] Collegeville, MN St. John's Abbey, of the Order of St. Benedict.
Maikowski, Thomas R. '76 (MO) Defenders of the Bond; Air Force Reserve Chaplains.
Maikowski, Thomas '76 (GLP) Page, AZ Immaculate Heart of Mary.
Mailadiyil, Augustine '75 (SP) Sun City Center, FL Prince of Peace.
Mailldoux, Thomas Bernard *c.s.b.* '50 (GAL)[O] Houston, TX Dillon House Retired.
Maillet, Paul A. *s.s.* '01 (BAL) On Duty Outside the Archdiocese; [S] Baltimore Society of St. Sulpice, Province of the United States; Graduate Studies.
Mailloux, Normand F. *m.s.* '55 (HRT)[L] Hartford, CT Missionaries of LaSalette.
Mainardi, Donald G. '64 (ORL) Viera, FL St. John the Evangelist Retired.
Mainza, Peter C. *a.j.* '89 (ALN)[P] Shenandoah, PA Apostles of Jesus.
Mainzer, James S. '87 (WCH) Newton, KS St. Mary; Legion of Mary.
Maione, Francis T. '65 (NEW)[K] Kearny, NJ New Jersey Boystown Retired.
Mair, Henry *s.a.* '62 (BO)[N] Brockton, MA Chapel of Our Savior–Catholic Pastoral and Information Center; [U] Brockton, MA Chapel of Our Savior; [Z] Brockton, MA Chapel of Our Saviour.
Mair, Henry *s.a.* '62 (NY)[EE] Garrison Graymoor Ecumenical and Interreligious Institute.
Mair, Robert G. '65 (CHI) Retired.
Maisano, Richard J. '69 (PH) Avondale, PA St. Gabriel of the Sorrowful Mother.
Maiser, Raymond *c.ss.r.* '64 (SEA)[L] Seattle, WA The Redemptionist Society of Washington; Seattle, WA Sacred Heart of Jesus.
Maisog, Alberic *o.c.s.o.* '00 (SPC)[F] Ava, MO Assumption Abbey (Trappist).
Maison, Gabriel '78 (VIC) Promoter of Justice; Moulton, TX St. Joseph's; Permanent Diaconate Program.
Maisonet–Ortiz, Rev. Msgr. Tomas '45 (SJN) Retired.
Maisonneuve, John *o.carm.* '86 (JOL)[K] Darien, IL Carmelite Carefree Retirement Village.
Maisonneuve, Joseph *o.carm.* (JOL)[L] Darien Carmelite Provincial Office Retired.
Maivelett, Bruce A. *s.j.* '88 (PH)[Y] Philadelphia, PA Jesuit Community, Arrupe House.
Maivelett, Rev. Msgr. Bruce M. *s.j.* '88 (PH)[F] Philadelphia, PA St. Joseph's Preparatory School.
Mai Vinh Loc, Timothy M. *c.m.c.* '77 (SPC)[F] Carthage, MO Congregation of the Mother Coredemptrix, United States Assumption Province.
Maiza, Jesus Maria *s.s.s.* '67 (CGS) Caguas, PR Santisimo Sacramento.
Maj, George C. *s.a.c.* '58 (BUF)[O] North Tonawanda, NY Society of the Catholic Apostolate.
Maj, Jerzy *o.s.p.p.e.* '89 (CHI) Harwood Heights–Norridge, IL St. Rosalie.
Maj, Jerzy *o.s.p.p.e.* '89 (PH)[Y].
Majalla, Roc *s.a.c.* '92 (GR) Fremont, MI St. Michael.
Majarucon, Jon F. '84 (LA) Oxnard, CA Santa Clara; Deanery 3; Santa Barbara Region; Members.
Majcher, Tadeusz *s.d.s.* '87 (GRY)[H] Merrillville, IN Salvatorian Fathers (Society of the Divine Savior).
Majchrowski, Anthony P. '44 (LAN) Flint, MI All Saints.
Majerus, Daniel '57 (SCL) Retired.
Majewski, Edmund W. *s.j.* '83 (NEW)[B] Jersey City, NJ Jesuit Center; [M] Jersey City, NJ Jesuits of Saint Peter's College, Inc.
Majewski, Francis *o.f.m.cap.* '64 (PAT) Passaic, NJ Our Lady Of Mt. Carmel.
Majewski, Joseph B. '66 (RIC) Newport News, VA St. Jerome.
Majewski, Mariusz '08 (B) Boise, ID Cathedral of St. John the Evangelist.
Majic, Timothy *o.f.m.* '39 (CHI)[N] Chicago, IL St. Anthony's Friary.
Majikas, David J. '97 (CLV) Barberton, OH St. Augustine.
Majka, Frank A. *s.j.* '74 (MIL)[P] Milwaukee, WI Jesuit Community at Marquette University; Milwaukee, WI; [P] Milwaukee, WI Jesuit Provincial Office, Wisconsin Province.
Majka, George '72 (MAN) Claremont, NH St. Joseph.
Majka, Philip S. '65 (ARL) Falls Church, VA St. James.
Major, Charles M. '59 (SY) Liverpool, NY St. Joseph the Worker.
Major, Peter *m.h.m.* '68 (NY)[EE] Hartsdale, NY Mill Hill Fathers Residence.
Major, Steven P. '87 (LIN) Beatrice, NE St. Joseph's.
Major, Thomas J. '91 (SCR) Shohola, PA St. Ann's; Lords Valley, PA St. John Neumann.
Majoros, Rev. Msgr. George A. '79 (PH) Secane, PA Our Lady of Fatima; Regional Vicars; Priests' Personnel Board.
Majoros, Stephen R. '57 (TOL) Fraternity of Communion and Liberation Retired.
Majstorovic, Ivica *o.f.m.* '00 (CHI) Chicago, IL Blessed Alojzije Stepinac Croatian Mission; [N] Chicago, IL Croatian Franciscan Fathers.
Maka, Tomek '01 (DET) Ira Township, MI Immaculate Conception.
Makacinas, Stanley *o.carm.* '70 (JOL)[L] Darien Carmelite Provincial Office.
Makarewicz, Rev. Msgr. Marion J. '87 (JC) Argyle, MO St. Aloysius; Vienna, MO Holy Guardian Angels; Vienna, MO Visitation of the Blessed Virgin Mary; Ministry to Priests.
Maki, George S. '88 (MAR) Watersmeet, MI Immaculate Conception.
Makos, Jason M. '05 (BO) Foxborough, MA St. Mary.
Makothakat, John M. '62 (SAT) San Antonio, TX; [C] Oblate School of Theology; Promoter Justitiae; Judges Retired.
Makowski, Douglas T. '66 (CLV) Independence, OH St. Michael Retired.
Makowski, Lee J. *o.s.a.* '80 (PH)[C] Villanova University; [Y] Villanova, PA St. Thomas Monastery.
Makowski, Tomasz '93 (PMB) West Palm Beach, FL Mary Immaculate.
Makranyi, Steven F. '69 (LAN) Retired.
Maksvytis, Jerome J. '74 (MAD) Berlin, WI All Saints.
Maksym, Kevin '01 (SAG) Alma, MI St. Mary; St. Louis, MI St. Joseph.
Maksymowicz, Rev. Msgr. John H. '70 (BRK) Released from Diocesan Assignment.
Makwali, Silvester *c.s.c.* '98 (FTW)[H] Notre Dame Congregation of Holy Cross, Indiana Province, Provincial House.
Malabad, Antonio R. '53 (RIC) Retired.
Malacari, Carmen '93 (CHL) Denver, NC Holy Spirit.
Malachowski, Christopher *o.s.* '58 (PCE) On Duty Outside the Diocese.
Malacrida, Mario *m.c.c.j.* '87 (CHI)[N] Chicago, IL Comboni Missionaries Theologate (M.C.C.J.), Verona Fathers; [W] Chicago, IL The Peace Corner, Incorporated.
Malagesi, Robert *m.ss.cc.* '07 (HBG)[J] Fairfield, PA Missionaries of the Sacred Hearts of Jesus & Mary House of Studies; Fairfield, PA Immaculate Conception of the Blessed Virgin Mary; Fairfield, PA St. Rita.
Malagon, Eduardo '00 (GRY) Cursillos in Christianity; Bishop's Council of Priests; Lake Station, IN St. Francis Xavier.
Malagreca, Rev. Msgr. Joseph P. '76 (BRK) Brooklyn, NY Holy Cross; Renouveau Charismatique of the Diocese of Brooklyn; Renovacion Carismatica of the Diocese of Brooklyn.
Malai, Dominic '90 (SR) Napa, CA St. Apollinaris.
Malain, Dan '66 (BEA)[G] Beaumont, TX Rev. Herman Vincent Scholarship Fund; Nederland, TX St. Charles Borromeo.
Malangon, Julio Cesar Sanchez '09 (AGN) Merizo, GU San Dionisio.
Malanowski, Rev. Msgr. Thaddeus F. '47 (NOR) Stamford, CT Retired.
Malanowski, Rev. Msgr. Thaddeus F. '47 (BGP)[O] Stamford, CT The Catherine Dennis Keefe Queen of the Clergy Retired Priests' Residence.
Malarz, Andrew '92 (VEN) Marco Island, FL San Marco.
Malasi, Wilhelm '87 (CLV) Akron, OH St. Bernard.
Malatesta, Christopher A. '93 (SPR) Dalton, MA St. Agnes; [M] Goshen, MA Holy Cross Camp Grounds; Bishop's Commission for Clergy; Diocesan Consultors; Deans; Presbyteral Council; Diocesan Pastoral Council.
Malave, Jason A. '97 (CHI) Chicago, IL St. Bartholomew.
Malave, Will–Roger '86 (HRT) Waterbury, CT St. Margaret Retired.
Malaver, Daniel '03 (WDC) Silver Spring, MD St. Michael.
Malavolti, Nathan *t.o.r.* '05 (ALT)[A] Loretto, PA St. Francis University.

Malcolm, Lawrence J. '70 (CHI) Oak Lawn, IL St. Gerald.
Malczuk, Dariusz '03 (SAC) Yreka, CA St. Joseph.
Malczyk, Joseph *c.r.* '69 (CHI)[D] Chicago, IL Gordon Tech High School.
Maldari, Donald C. *s.j.* '85 (SY)[Q] Syracuse, NY Jesuits at LeMoyne, Inc.
Maldonado, Angel M. *o.s.m.* '79 (ELP) El Paso, TX St. Ignatius of Loyola.
Maldonado, Edward *o.f.m.cap.* (ARE) Utuado, PR San Miquel.
Maldonado, Fernando '99 (SPK) Pasco, WA St. Patrick.
Maldonado, Francisco '90 (TUC) Rio Rico, AZ Most Holy Nativity of Our Lord Jesus Christ Roman Catholic Parish – Rio Rico; Green Valley, AZ Our Lady of the Valley Roman Catholic Parish – Green Valley; All Vicars Forane.
Maldonado, Fredy Cesar *s.j.* '92 (BGP)[O] Fairfield, CT The Fairfield Jesuit Community–Fairfield University; [B] Fairfield, CT Fairfield University.
Maldonado, Leonardo '64 (RCK) Elgin, IL St. Joseph.
Maldonado, Roberto *l.d.* '05 (PCE) Ponce, PR Church Santisimo Sacramento; [H] Orocovis, PR Santuario Nuestra Senora del Encuentro con Dios – Hilasterio Masculino; [H] Ponce, PR Santuario Nuestra Senora del Encuentro con Dios Hilasterio Femenino.
Malecki, John J. '48 (ALB) Office Retired.
Malene, Rev. Msgr. Robert M. '72 (E) West Middlesex, PA Good Shepherd; College of Consultors.
Malesic, Edward C. '87 (HBG) York Haven, PA Holy Infant; Judicial Vicar; Judicial Vicar.
Maleszyk, Mieczyslaw "Mitch" '00 (SAC) Sacramento, CA Our Lady of Lourdes.
Maletta, Sammie L. '80 (GRY) St. John, IN St. John the Evangelist.
Maletz, Leo J. '73 (ALN) Minersville, PA St. Matthew the Evangelist.
Malewski, Christian '09 (KC) Kansas City, MO St. Elizabeth's.
Mali, Joseph '88 (NY)[X] Poughkeepsie, NY St. Francis Hospital; Poughkeepsie, NY St. Francis Hospital.
Malia, Thomas R. '84 (BAL)[M] Baltimore, MD Mercy Health Services Inc.; Special Assignment; Lansdowne, MD St. Clement.
Maliakkal, Varghese '85 (IND) Indianapolis, IN St. Michael the Archangel.
Malick, Kevin M. '07 (NY) Tuckahoe, NY Immaculate Conception.
Malicki, Jan '73 (MIA) Absent on Leave.
Maliekal, Cyriac '71 (HRT) Milford, CT Christ the Redeemer.
Maliekal, George '01 (SP)[J] Tampa, FL St. Joseph's Hospital, Inc.
Maliekal, Jose *m.s.f.s.* '74 (ATL)[G] Snellville, GA The Missionaries of St. Francis De Sales.
Malik, Rev. Msgr. John E. '53 (LC) Retired.
Malin, Delbert J. '58 (LC) Special Assignment; Ex Officio Retired.
Malin, Don '03 (PBL) Catholic Charismatic Renewal Center; Rocky Ford, CO St. Peter.
Malin, Donald P. '03 (PBL) Presbyteral Council–College of Consultors; Deans; Presbyteral Council.
Malin, Gary J. '86 (CLV) Gates Mills, OH St. Francis of Assisi.
Malinowski, Rev. Msgr. John C. '63 (AUS)[E] Bryan, TX St. Joseph Regional Health Center Retired.
Malinowski, Stanley J. '54 (PEO) Rantoul, IL St. Malachy; Thomasboro, IL St. Elizabeth of Hungary Retired.
Malitz, George M. '97 (PSC) Leave of Absence.
Maliwa, Festus '02 (TLS) Bartlesville, OK St. John's.
Malkiewicz, Edward S. '71 (NEW) Jersey City, NJ St. Aloysius Retired.
Malkiewicz, Stephen E. *o.f.m.* '69 (MIL)[A] St. Francis, WI Saint Francis de Sales Seminary; [B] Hales Corners, WI Sacred Heart School of Theology; Milwaukee, WI St. Anthony of Padua.
Malkov, Leonid *c.ss.r.* '90 (PHU) Newark, NJ St. John the Baptist.
Mallaghan, Thomas P. *c.m.* '60 (PH)[Y].
Mallahan, James '52 (SEA) Retired.
Mallak, Mark S. '88 (NU) Defender of the Bond; [C] Sleepy Eye, MN Divine Providence Community Home & Lake Villa Maria Senior Apts.; Sleepy Eye, MN St. Mary.
Mallari, Arturo O. '07 (RCK) Elgin, IL St. Thomas More.
Mallavarapu, Kasparaj '84 (FBK) Fairbanks, AK St. Mark University Catholic Parish Fairbanks; [C] Fairbanks, AK Kobuk Center.
Mallen, Santiago *c.ss.r.* '47 (CGS) San Lorenzo, PR Nuestra Senora de la Mercedes.
Mallet, Rev. Msgr. Charles J. '55 (LAF) Retired.
Mallet, James '66 (KNX)[H] Chattanooga, TN Newman Foundation of Chattanooga, Inc.
Mallet, W. Curtis '92 (LAF) Lafayette, LA St. Genevieve; Defenders of the Bond.
Mallett, James K. '66 (NSH) General Counsel; Judges; Censor Librorum Retired.
Mallett, James '66 (KNX) University of Tennessee–Chattanooga.
Mallett, Raymond *o.f.m.conv.* '76 (LA) Hermosa Beach, CA Our Lady of Guadalupe.
Mallette, Daniel J. '57 (CHI) Chicago, IL St. Margaret of Scotland Retired.
Malley, Francis '01 (SFE) Ranchos De Taos, NM San Francisco de Asis; Vicars Forane (Deans); Presbyteral Council of the Archdiocese of Santa Fe.
Malley, James B. *s.j.* '64 (BO)[U] Weston, MA Campion Health Center, Inc.
Malley, John *o.carm.* '56 (JOL)[O] Darien, IL Carmelite Mission Office; Councilors:.
Malley, John *o.carm.* '56 (TUC)[A] Tucson, AZ Salpointe Catholic High School; [D] Tucson, AZ Carmelite Priory; Darien, IL Mission Office, Carmelite Missions.
Malley, Kenneth '97 (SP) Clearwater, FL St. Catherine of Siena; Elected Pastors; Personnel Board.
Malley, Raymond *s.m.* '68 (SJ)[M] Cupertino, CA The Marianist Center.
Malley, Vernon *o.carm.* '59 (TUC)[A] Tucson, AZ Salpointe Catholic High School; [D] Tucson, AZ Carmelite Priory Retired.
Malley, William J. *s.j.* '64 (FgM) New York, NY Society of Jesus.
Mallia, Joseph '92 (DET) Allen Park, MI St. Frances Cabrini; Archdiocesan Vicars; Presbyteral Council.
Mallick, Andrew '83 (ORL) Ocala, FL Our Lady of the Springs.
Mallick, Marcus '05 (DEN) Boulder, CO Sacred Heart of Mary.
Mallin, Peter *o.f.m.conv.* '90 (LA) Hospital Chaplains; Hermosa Beach, CA Our Lady of Guadalupe; [J] Torrance, CA Providence Little Company of Mary Hospital.
Mallinson, Arthur D. '81 (DAL) On Leave of Absence.
Mallo, Walter *i.v.e.* '90 (SJ) Santa Clara, CA Our Lady of Peace; [A] Santa Clara, CA Shrine of Our Lady of Peace.
Mallon, Elias D. *s.a.* '71 (NY)[EE] New York, NY Atonement Friars; [II] New York, NY Franciscans International, Inc.; [EE] Garrison, NY Franciscan Friars of the Atonement, Minister General Office; General Council.
Mallonee, Robert *s.v.d.* '67 (BO)[U] Duxbury, MA Society of the Divine Word.
Malloy, Rev. Msgr. David J. '83 (MIL) On Duty Outside the Archdiocese; General Secretary; Staff; Members; Members; Consultants.
Malloy, Edward A. *c.s.c.* '70 (FTW)[H] Notre Dame, IN Holy Cross Community, Corby Hall, University of Notre Dame; [B] University of Notre Dame Du Lac.
Malloy, Francis X. '85 (MO) Air Force Reserve Chaplains; Awaiting Assignment.
Malloy, John *s.d.b.* (OAK)[E] Richmond, CA Salesian High School.
Malloy, Joseph J. '70 (BGP) Stamford, CT St. Clement of Rome.
Malloy, Michael B. '76 (OM) Emerson, NE Sacred Heart; Pender, NE St. John.
Malloy, Peter *s.d.b.* '74 (NY)[GG] Stony Point, NY Marian Shrine; [GG] Stony Point, NY Don Bosco Retreat Center and Marian Shrine.
Malloy, Richard G. *s.j.* '88 (PH)[Y] Loyola Center and Manresa Hall.
Malloy, Stephen J. '96 (BO) Health Leave.
Malloy, Thomas *o.s.f.s.* '67 (R) Fayetteville, NC St. Ann.
Malloy, William E. '73 (CHI) Chicago, IL St. Barnabas.
Mally, Edward J. *s.j.* '61 (NY)[EE] New York Jesuit Provincial's Office.
Mallya, Sabas '91 (PMB) Jupiter, FL St. Peter.
Mallya, Stephen V. *a.j.* (ALN) Fountain Hill, PA St. Ursula.
Malm, Raymond B. '76 (PRO) Newport, RI St. Joseph.
Malnar, Rev. Msgr. Matthew '66 (AMA) Retired.
Malnar, Stan '72 (HEL) Special Assignments.
Malo, Richard C. '87 (PRT) Greenville, ME Holy Family; Jackman, ME St. Anthony.
Malone, Rev. Msgr. Alan '59 (PHX) Retired.
Malone, Rev. Msgr. Bernard G. '50 (LR) Hot Springs Village, AR Sacred Heart of Jesus.
Malone, Edward T. (BO) Reading, MA St. Agnes.
Malone, Rev. Msgr. Francis I. '77 (LR) Little Rock, AR Christ the King; Vicars for Religious; Diocesan Consultors; Deans; Hospitals; Propagation of the Faith; Chancellor for Ecclesial Affairs; Priests Personnel Board (Diocesan); Presbyteral Council.
Malone, Rev. Msgr. Francis I. (OKL) Adjutant Judicial Vicars.
Malone, H. Patrick '69 (WCH) Veterans Administration Hospital; DEPARTMENT OF VETERANS AFFAIRS HOSPITALS AND CHAPLAINS Retired.
Malone, John M. '67 (STP) St. Paul, MN Assumption; [C] St. Paul, MN University of St. Thomas.
Malone, John S. *c.s.sp.* '65 (MO) DEPARTMENT OF VETERANS AFFAIRS HOSPITALS AND CHAPLAINS.
Malone, John (RVC) Northport, NY Veteran's Administration Hospital.
Malone, Michael T. *c.s.sp.* '65 (PRO)[B] Newport, RI Salve Regina University.
Malone, Patrick J. *s.j.* '01 (OM)[K] Omaha, NE Jesuit Community at Creighton University.
Malone, Rev. Msgr. Richard '62 (PH) Upper Darby, PA St. Laurence.
Malone, Robert *c.s.c.* '61 (FR)[A] North Easton, MA Holy Cross Fathers Religious; [F] North Attleboro, MA Madonna Manor Inc.
Maloney, Bernard M. *o.f.m.cap.* '69 (NY) New Paltz, NY St. Joseph; [EE] New Paltz, NY St. Joseph Friary.
Maloney, Daniel *o.s.b.* '68 (BIS)[A] Richardton, ND Assumption Abbey; [B] Bismarck, ND University of Mary; [H] Bismarck, ND Annunciation Monastery.
Maloney, Edward J. '55 (CHI) Retired.
Maloney, Francis G. '60 (R) Retired.
Maloney, Rev. Msgr. J. Christopher '66 (NY) Yonkers, NY St. John the Baptist.
Maloney, James F. *c.m.f.* '60 (CHI)[N] Oak Park Claretian Missionaries USA Eastern Province.
Maloney, James G. '71 (CLV) Norton, OH St. Andrew the Apostle.
Maloney, John P. '66 (BRK) Retired.
Maloney, Rev. Msgr. John W. '75 (BRK) Brooklyn, NY St. Anselm; Assignment Board.
Maloney, Joseph L. '91 (PH) On Special or Other Archdiocesan Assignment.
Maloney, Joseph *o.f.m.cap.* '58 (DET)[K] Detroit St. Bonaventure Friary.
Maloney, Kevin '05 (SY) Syracuse, NY Blessed Sacrament.
Maloney, Malcolm *o.f.m.cap.* '55 (DET)[K] Detroit St. Bonaventure Friary.
Maloney, Patrick H. *c.s.c.* '54 (FTW)[B] University of Notre Dame Du Lac; [H] Notre Dame Congregation of Holy Cross, Indiana Province, Provincial House; [H] Notre Dame, IN Holy Cross Community, Corby Hall, University of Notre Dame.
Maloney, Richard *s.d.s.* '69 (WDC)[B] Silver Spring, MD Salvatorian Community.
Maloney, Richard *s.d.s.* '69 (MIL)[P] Milwaukee Salvatorian Provincial Offices.
Maloney, Robert P. *c.m.* '66 (PH)[Y].
Maloney, Robert S. *s.x.* '57 (BO)[U] Holliston, MA Xaverian Missionaries.
Maloney, Rufino *o.f.m.conv.* '59 (ALB)[L] Rensselaer, NY Provincialate, Immaculate Conception Friary – Order of Friars Minor Conventual.
Maloney, Rev. Msgr. Thomas F. '68 (BUF) Finance Council; Tonawanda, NY St. Amelia.
Maloney, Thomas J. '65 (SCR) Hughestown, PA Blessed Sacrament; Pittston, PA St. Mary, Help of Christians.
Maloney, Thomas P. '70 (RVC) Retired.
Maloney, Wilfred F. '55 (PH) Retired.
Maloney, William J. '48 (E) Retired.
Malovetz, Rev. Msgr. Gregory E. S. '83 (MET) Skillman, NJ St. Charles Borromeo.
Maloy, Dale '54 (PEO) Retired.
Maltese, James L. (NOR) On Duty Outside the Diocese.
Maltese, James L. '65 (RVC) Stony Brook, NY Stony Brook University Hospital; St. James, NY SS. Philip and James.
Malthaner, John P. '93 (E)[C] Oil City, PA Venango Catholic High School; Priest Personnel Board.
Malvey, Killian *o.s.b.* '73 (SEA)[L] Lacey, WA St. Martin's Abbey; [A] Lacey, WA Saint Martin's University.
Malvey, Seamus *o.c.s.o.* '86 (L)[L] Trappist, KY Abbey of Our Lady of Gethsemani, of the Order of Cistercians of the Strict Observance.
Malyarchuk, Roman '95 (STF) Rochester, NY St. Josaphat.
Malzacher, Craig S. '08 (MIA) Miami, FL St. John Neumann.
Mamani, Raul '00 (ARE) Sabana Hoyos, PR Nuestra Senora de Fatima.
Mamich, Joseph R. '06 (CLV) Presbyteral Council; Presbyteral Conveners; Stow, OH Holy Family.
Maminirina, Jacques Cyprien Ranaivotratra *s.j.* '05 (OAK)[M] Berkeley, CA Jesuit Fathers and Brothers.
Mammarella, Dominick '53 (HBG) Retired.
Mamo, Nathan '78 (HON) On Duty Outside the Diocese.
Mampilly, Joy '84 (NY) New York, NY Immaculate Conception.
Mampuzhakkal, Jose Mathai *o.s.h.* '92 (GAL) Missouri City, TX Holy Family.
Manahan, Christopher J. *s.j.* '03 (DET)[B] Berkley, MI Loyola House.
Manahan, John *s.m.* '68 (CIN) Cincinnati, OH St. Francis de Sales; [N] Cincinnati, OH De Sales Crossings Marianist Community.
Manahan, Reynaldo '95 (SD) Pala, CA Mission San Antonio de Pala.
Manahan, Thomas C. *s.j.* '95 (MIL)[P] Milwaukee, WI Jesuit Community at Marquette University; [E] Milwaukee, WI Marquette University High School.
Manalel, Mathew '72 (KAL) Buchanan, MI St. Anthony.
Manalili, Feliciano *o.c.s.o.* '62 (CHR)[E] Moncks Corner, SC Mepkin Abbey.
Manalo, Pantaleon O. '63 (RIC)[E] Portsmouth, VA Bon Secours Maryview Medical Center.
Manalo, Rosendo R. '94 (OAK) Hayward, CA St. Bede.
Manalo, Vincent P. *c.s.p.* '00 (SFR) San Francisco, CA

Old St. Mary's Cathedral.
Manano, Grace '96 (CAM) Richard Stockton College of New Jersey; Egg Harbor City, NJ St. Nicholas' Church, Egg Harbor City; [R] Pomona, NJ Richard Stockton College of New Jersey.
Manappuram, Joseph '69 (GAL) Spring, TX St. James the Apostle.
Manarchuck, Joseph J. '78 (SCR) Wyalusing, PA St. Mary's Assumption; Diocesan Consultors; Wyalusing, PA St. Joachim.
Manase, Michael '77 (HT) Thibodaux, LA St. Charles Borromeo.
Manatt, Timothy *s.j.* '07 (RC) St. Francis, SD St. Francis Mission/Rosebud Educational Society; Rosebud, SD St. Bridget; [C] Howes, SD Kino Jesuit Community; St. Francis, SD St. Charles Borromeo.
Mancha, George '87 (SJ) Santa Clara, CA St. Clare.
Manchapilly, George *c.m.i.* '81 (BLX) Biloxi, MS Cathedral of the Nativity of the Blessed Virgin Mary.
Manchas, Lawrence L. '78 (GBG) Belle Vernon, PA St. Sebastian; College of Consultors.
Manchester, Roman R. '05 (PRO)[K] North Providence, RI St. Joseph Health Services of Rhode Island – Our Lady of Fatima Hospital; Pawtucket, RI St. John the Baptist.
Mancini, Rev. Msgr. Anthony '78 (PRO) Providence, RI Cathedral of SS. Peter and Paul.
Mancini, Domenic '76 (PIT) Imperial, PA St. Columbkille.
Mancini, Rev. Msgr. James E. '66 (LR) Bella Vista, AR St. Bernard of Clairvaux; Charismatic Movement.
Mancini, John *o.s.f.s.* '80 (SAG) Saginaw, MI SS. Simon and Jude; Saginaw, MI St. Christopher.
Mancini, Joseph A. '01 (NEW) Youth and Young Adult Ministries; Boy Scouts of America/Catholic Committee on Scouting; [O] Kearny, NJ Archdiocesan Youth Retreat Center; Kearny, NJ St. Stephen.
Mancini, Marc '92 (PAT) Vocations Board; Green Pond, NJ St. Simon the Apostle; Deans; College of Consultors; Vice Chancellors.
Mancini, Mark A. (PAT) Judge.
Mancini, Nicholas J. '75 (Y) Youngstown, OH St. Stephen of Hungary; Youngstown, OH SS. Cyril and Methodius.
Mancini, Robert *o.s.f.s.* '77 (ARL) Reston, VA St. John Neumann.
Mancuso, Anthony J. '83 (SJ) Special Assignment.
Mancuso, Dennis J. '96 (BUF) Belmont, NY St. Patrick; Council of Priests; Fillmore, NY St. Patrick.
Mancuso, Henry '75 (LKC) Lake Charles, LA Sacred Heart of Jesus; On Leave.
Mancuso, Rev. Msgr. Joseph A. '64 (KC) Gladstone, MO St. Andrew the Apostle; [N] Kansas City, MO Diocesan Council of Catholic Women.
Mancuso, Luke *o.s.b.* '83 (SCL)[I] Collegeville, MN St. John's Abbey, of the Order of St. Benedict.
Mandac, Elmer '96 (SD) Valley Center, CA St. Stephen.
Mandagiri, Jojaiah *m.s.f.s.* '95 (KCK) Kansas City, KS St. Patrick's.
Mandagiri, Jojaiah *m.s.f.s.* '95 (TYL)[B] Whitehouse, TX The Missionaries of St. Francis de Sales.
Mandala, Michael J. *s.j.* '77 (LA) Los Angeles, CA Blessed Sacrament; Deanery 14.
Mandala, Michael *s.j.* (OAK)[R] Oakland, CA PICO National Network.
Mandapati, Lourdumar Reddy '97 (SUP) Bayfield, WI Holy Family; Washburn, WI St. Ann; Bayfield, WI St. Joseph; Bayfield, WI St. Francis; Washburn, WI St. Louis.
Mandato, Kieran '87 (NY) Military Chaplains; Navy Chaplains.
Mandato, Pio *f.m.h.j.* '85 (SCR)[M] Laceyville, PA Franciscan Missionary Hermits of St. Joseph.
Mandel, Brian L. '94 (NU) Kandiyohi, MN St. Patrick; Kandiyohi, MN St. Thomas More.
Manderfield, Paul G. '60 (MAR) Panama Mission Fund.
Manderfield, R.P. Geraldo (MAR) Retired.
Mandile, John J. *s.j.* '57 (BO)[U] Weston, MA Campion Health Center, Inc.
Manding, Benito O. '64 (SJ) Retired.
Manding, Benito (SY) Endicott, NY St. Ambrose.
Mandock, Patrick H. '72 (GBG) Retired.
Mandoli, Richard *o.c.d.* '92 (SJ)[M] San Jose, CA Carmelite Monastery, Novitiate.
Mandry, Stephen (GAL) Retired.
Manenti, Rene *c.s.* '02 (NY)[EE] Staten Island, NY Scalabrinian Missionaries; [II] New York, NY Trust for the Center for Migration Studies in New York.
Manerowski, Joseph '95 (ALB) Priestly Life and Ministry Council; Glens Falls, NY St. Mary.
Maney, Robert L. '51 (MIL) Retired.
Manfred, Donald J. '67 (OG) Massena, NY St. Lawrence; Massena, NY Sacred Heart; Diocesan Consultors.
Manfredonia, Ignatius Mary *f.i.* '05 (NOR)[G] Griswold, CT Marian Friary of Our Lady of Guadalupe.
Mangalath, Augustine '79 (HRT) West Haven, CT St. Paul's; [H] New Haven, CT Hospital of St. Raphael.
Mangalath, Jaison *s.v.d.* '99 (LAF) Opelousas, LA Holy Ghost.
Mangampo, Gil '91 (GLP) Farmington, NM Sacred Heart; Farmington, NM Farmington Area Hospitals.
Manganello, Rev. Msgr. Salvatore '82 (BUF) Due Process; Judicial Vicar; Judges; Buffalo, NY St. Louis; Council of Priests.
Mangano, Charles N. '90 (RVC) Merrick, NY Curé of Ars.
Mangat, B. Thomas *c.m.i.* '89 (SAL) Hoxie, KS St. Frances Cabrini Parish; Hoxie, KS St. Martin Parish.
Manger, Daniel *o.s.b.cam.* '85 (MRY)[F] Big Sur, CA New Camaldoli Hermitage.
Manger, Rev. Msgr. William '62 (BEA) Southeast Texas ACTS Mission Chapter; Central Vicariate; Charismatic Prayer Renewal; Beaumont, TX St. Anne.
Mangesho, Paulinus M. *a.l.c.p.* '91 (SFR) Redwood City, CA Our Lady of Mount Carmel.
Mangiafico, Paul J. '70 (HRT) Medical Leave.
Mangiafico, Paul '70 (SP) St. Petersburg, FL Holy Family.
Mangiaracina, Cayet N. *o.p.* '64 (BR) Hammond, LA Holy Ghost; Tickfaw, LA Our Lady of Pompeii.
Mangiaracina, George *o.c.d.* '93 (BO)[U] Boston, MA Carmelite Monastery.
Mangieri, Thomas '01 (PAT) Mountain Lakes, NJ St. Catherine of Siena.
Mangini, Richard A. '67 (OAK) Concord, CA St. Bonaventure; Deanery #8.
Manglaviti, Leo M. *s.j.* '99 (BO)[A] Weston, MA Blessed John XXIII National Seminary; [U] Boston The Society of Jesus of New England–Provincial Offices; [U] Weston, MA Campion Jesuit Community.
Mangum, Peter B. '90 (SHP) Shreveport, LA St. John Berchmans Cathedral; Judicial Vicar; Judges; Presbyteral Council; Diocesan Liturgy Commission; [A] Shreveport, LA Loyola College Prep; College of Consultors.
Mani, David Lazar (RVC) Northport, NY Veteran's Administration Hospital.
Mani, David '64 (SEA) Veterans Administration Medical Center.
Mani, L. David '64 (MO) DEPARTMENT OF VETERANS AFFAIRS HOSPITALS AND CHAPLAINS.
Maniamkerry, Mathew *o.ss.t.* '84 (BAL)[S] The Trinitarians in India (Bangalore & Trichur).
Maniangat, Joseph '64 (STA) Retired.
Maniangattu, George '89 (ORL) Ocala, FL Our Lady of the Springs.
Manickam, Peter M. '81 (LC) Marshfield, WI Corpus Christi; Marshfield, WI Sacred Heart of Jesus; Appointed Members.
Manickathan, Paulose '98 (WH) St. Marys, WV St. John.
Manickathan, Paulous '96 (WH) Harrisville, WV Christ Our Hope.
Manikuttiyil, Kurian '90 (PT) Florida State Hospital; Blountstown, FL St. Francis of Assisi; Chattahoochee, FL Holy Cross Parish.
Manimala, Thomas '95 (SAN) Fort Stockton, TX St. Agnes; Sanderson, TX St. James; Presbyteral Council; Fort Stockton, TX St. Joseph's.
Maniola, Francis N. '38 (CHI) Chicago, IL St. Symphorosa and Seven Sons Retired.
Manion, Francis *s.s.c.* '52 (OM)[K] St. Columbans Missionary Society of St. Columban.
Manion, Kevin '89 (AUS) On Duty Outside the Diocese.
Manion, Thomas F. '57 (PIT)[Q] Pittsburgh, PA Cardinal Dearden Center Retired.
Maniscalco, Rev. Msgr. Francis J. '71 (RVC) West Hempstead, NY St. Thomas, the Apostle; Respect Life.
Maniscalco, Paul *s.d.b.* '44 (SFR) San Francisco, CA SS. Peter and Paul Retired.
Manista, Clemens D. '74 (WIL) College of Consultors; National Conference for Community and Justice.
Maniyangat, Jose '75 (STA) Macclenny, FL St. Mary's; Civil Institutions; Legion of Mary.
Manjadi, George '67 (WH) Camden, WV St. Boniface.
Manjakunnel, Jose '98 (CAM) Berlin, NJ Saint Simon Stock Parish, Berlin, N.J.
Manjaly, Jose '79 (BIR) Birmingham, AL Blessed Sacrament.
Manjaly, Jose *m.s.* '05 (ATL) Smyrna, GA St. Thomas the Apostle.
Mank, Rev. Msgr. Virgil W. '65 (SFD) Retired.
Mankalonius, Joseph *t.o.r.* '66 (PIT)[M] Pittsburgh, PA Franciscan Friars, T.O.R.
Mankamthanath, Thomas '04 (NY) New York, NY St. Monica.
Mankel, Rev. Msgr. Francis Xavier '61 (KNX)[K] Knoxville, TN Diocesan Council of Catholic Women; [K] Knoxville, TN Ladies of Charity; Presbyteral Council; Diocesan Consultors; Diocesan Finance Council; Diocesan Council of Catholic Women; Knoxville, TN Holy Ghost; Vicar General.
Manko, Andriy *c.ss.r.* '95 (PHU) Newark, NJ St. John the Baptist.
Mankowski, Maciej '01 (Y) Newton Falls, OH St. Mary and St. Joseph Parish.
Mankowski, Marcin *o.p.* '83 (LC) Custer, WI Sacred Heart; Rosholt, WI St. Adalbert.
Mankowski, Marcin *o.p.* '83 (NY)[II] New York, NY Polish Dominicans, Inc.
Mankowski, Paul V. *s.j.* '87 (CHI)[N] Chicago, IL Woodlawn Jesuit Community.
Manley, Bernard A. '87 (CHL) Retired.
Manly, Rev. Msgr. Alexander F. '57 (RVC) Kings Park, NY St. Joseph's Retired.
Mann, Frank '79 (BRK) College Point, NY St. Fidelis.
Mann, Gordon '92 (EVN) Washington, IN Our Lady of Hope.
Mann, Lawrence *s.m.* '45 (SJ)[M] Cupertino, CA The Marianist Center.
Mann, Quentin A. '06 (GB)[N] Oshkosh, WI University of Wisconsin Oshkosh, Newman Center; Special Assignment; [O] Appleton, WI Catholic Youth Expeditions, Inc.; Vocations and Ongoing Formation of Priests and Parish Directors.
Mann, Raymond *o.f.m.* '59 (BO)[Z] Boston, MA St. Anthony Shrine.
Mann, Robert G. '59 (PEO) Retired.
Manna, David '06 (HRT) Leave of Absence.
Manna, Louis '73 (IND) Salem, IN St. Patrick; Scottsburg, IN American Martyrs.
Mannaparambil, Augustine *m.s.f.s.* '04 (TYL)[B] Whitehouse, TX The Missionaries of St. Francis de Sales.
Mannara, Frederick R. '63 (SY) Syracuse, NY Most Holy Rosary.
Mannebach, Thomas M. '99 (CIN) New Bremen, OH Holy Redeemer.
Mannhardt, Daniel C. '57 (DAV) Retired.
Manning, Brian F. '74 (BO) Franklin, MA St. Mary; Members.
Manning, C. Robert '97 (COS) Colorado Springs, CO St. Gabriel the Archangel.
Manning, Charles T. '75 (ROC) Absent on Leave.
Manning, Francis J. '51 (SPR) Bishop's Commission for Clergy; Retired Priests' Service Retired.
Manning, Francis '51 (SPR) Priests' Retirement Program.
Manning, J. Patrick '78 (Y)[B] North Canton, OH Walsh University.
Manning, James J. '75 (CIN) Franklin, OH St. Mary.
Manning, James *s.m.m.* '58 (RVC)[M] Bay Shore, NY Montfort Missionaries.
Manning, John E. '72 (CLV) Cleveland, OH St. Vincent de Paul; College of Consultors; Associate Judges.
Manning, Joseph H. '61 (BO) Senior Priests. Retired.
Manning, Martin B. '43 (DAV) Retired.
Manning, Michael *s.v.d.* '69 (SB)[N] San Bernardino, CA Wordnet, Inc.
Manning, Michael '97 (TR) Rumson, NJ Holy Cross.
Manning, Paul R. '59 (NEW) Retired.
Manning, Paul S. '85 (PAT) Clifton, NJ St. Philip the Apostle; School Division; Education.
Manning, Robert A. '83 (E) Stoneboro, PA St. Columbkille.
Manning, Robert C. '97 (STL) On Duty Outside the Archdiocese.
Mannion, J. Patrick '55 (WCH) Retired.
Mannion, James P. '81 (RVC) Setauket, NY St. James; Procurator & Advocates.
Mannion, John H. '68 (IND)[G] Beech Grove, IN St. Francis Hospital and Health Centers; On Duty Outside the Diocese.
Mannion, Rev. Msgr. M. Francis '73 (SLC) Salt Lake City, UT Saint Vincent de Paul LLC 250.
Mannion, Mark S. '95 (POD)[G] South Bend, IN Prelature of the Holy Cross and Opus Dei; South Bend.
Mannion, Rev. Msgr. Martin J. '62 (CAM) Collingswood, NJ St. John's Catholic Church, Collingswood, N.J.
Mannion, Martin K. '66 (STL) Retired.
Mannion, Rev. Msgr. Michael T. '71 (CAM) Office of Community Relations; Pennsauken, NJ Mary, Queen of All Saints, Pennsauken, N.J.
Mannion, P. John '66 (SAT) On Duty Outside the Archdiocese Retired.
Mannion, Patrick J. '66 (SAT) Retired.
Mannion, Thomas Ignatius '65 (HBG) Catawissa, PA Our Lady of Mercy.
Mannion, William D. '63 (CHI) Rosemont, IL Our Lady of Hope Retired.
Manno, John D. '01 (SY) Syracuse, NY St. James.
Manno, John K. '68 (SCR) Montoursville, PA Our Lady of Lourdes.
Manolev, Kiril '01 (STF) Colchester, CT St. Mary Dormition; Glastonbury, CT St. John The Baptist.
Manondo, Ely '00 (DAL) Kaufman, TX St. Ann.
Manos, James M. '96 (NEW) Bayonne, NJ St. Vincent de Paul; Members.
Manrique, Ramon S. (NY) Bronx, NY St. Rita of Cascia Shrine Church.
Manrique, Wilfredo S. '88 (SJ) Roman Catholic Seminary Corporation; Vicar for Clergy; College of Consultors; Council of Priests; Judges; Office of the Vicar for Clergy; Diocesan Clergy Personnel Board; Ongoing Formation of Clergy; Priests' Retirement Board; Special Assignment; Santa Clara, CA St. Lawrence, the Martyr.
Manriquez, Raymundo '00 (LUB) Plainview, TX Our Lady of Guadalupe.
Mans, Leo J. '53 (ROC) Retired.
Mansell, Kirk '84 (SAV) Kathleen, GA St. Patrick.

Mansfield, John L. '53 (BO) Senior Priests. Retired.
Mansfield, Scott '00 (SFE) Rio Rancho, NM St. Thomas Aquinas; Lovelace Hospital.
Manship, D. Joseph '76 (PRT) St. Mary's Regional Medical Center; [G] Lewiston, ME St. Marguerite d'Youville Pavilion.
Manship, James C. '98 (HRT) New Haven, CT St. Rose of Lima.
Manship, Joseph '76 (PRT)[H] Lewiston, ME St. Mary's Regional Medical Center.
Mansini, Guy *o.s.b.* '77 (IND) Bristow, IN St. Isidore the Farmer; [A] St. Meinrad, IN Saint Meinrad School of Theology; [K] St. Meinrad, IN St. Meinrad Archabbey.
Manso, Robert F. '00 (SPC) Cape Girardeau, MO St. Vincent de Paul.
Manso–Hamilton, John '90 (BRK) Springfield Gardens, NY St. Mary Magdalene.
Manson, Brendan David '06 (ORG) La Habra, CA Our Lady of Guadalupe; Council of Priests.
Manson, Sean '99 (NEW) Ridgewood, NJ Our Lady of Mount Carmel.
Mansoor, Awraha '00 (SPA) Santa Ana, CA St. George Chaldean Catholic Church; [C] Perris, CA St. George Monastery/Retreat Center; Perris, CA St. Hormizdah Mission.
Mansour Abba, Yousif '78 (OLD) Saint Joseph's; Syriac Mission.
Manternach, Rev. Msgr. Albert V. '52 (DUB) Retired.
Manternach, Carl J. '55 (DUB) Retired.
Manternach, Neil J. '85 (DUB) Personnel Advisory Board; Hiawatha, IA St. Elizabeth Ann Seton Parish; Building Commission; Church Design/Renovation Commission; Seminary Admissions and Advisory Board.
Mantia, Armand '85 (NEW) Union, NJ Holy Spirit.
Mantovani, Firmo *c.s.* '73 (SJ) San Jose, CA Holy Cross.
Manuel, Gardenio M. *s.j.* '79 (SJ)[B] Santa Clara, CA Jesuit Community.
Manuel, Herman *s.v.d.* '04 (SB)[I] Riverside, CA Divine Word Seminary.
Manuel, Jose '00 (NEW) Ridgefield, NJ St. Matthew's.
Manuel, Victor '06 (B) Weiser, ID St. Agnes.
Manuel, Vincent '81 (MO) Army Chaplains.
Manuele, Christopher '06 (NTN) Scranton, PA St. Joseph; Presbyteral Council.
Manuppella, Rev. Msgr. Anthony J. '76 (CAM) Merchantville, NJ St. Peter's Catholic Church, Merchantville, N.J.; Appointed Members; Camden West Deanery; Consultants.
Manvelpillai, David '89 (NY) Bronx, NY St. Margaret of Cortona.
Manyama, Augustine *a.j.* '02 (P)[J] Portland, OR Providence Portland Medical Center.
Manz, Michael J. '79 (GAL) Houston; [N] Houston, TX Opus Dei.
Manzo, Fernando L. '83 (TUC) Administrative Leave of Absence.
Manzo, Louis *c.s.c.* '65 (ORL) Viera, FL St. John the Evangelist.
Manzon–Balagat, Arturo J. '75 (SB) On Leave of Absence; Elected Members.
Mapara, Ildefonce *o.s.b.* '00 (BAK) Klamath Falls, OR St. Pius X.
Maples, Frederic A. *s.j.* '72 (BO)[U] Boston The Society of Jesus of New England–Provincial Offices; [U] Boston, MA Loyola House.
Maples, Michael R. '05 (KNX) Cleveland, TN St. Therese of Lisieux.
Marabe, Jose G. (NY) New York, NY Cathedral of St. Patrick.
Marabe, Jose '70 (NY) Defenders of the Bond.
Marable, Gerard C. '88 (CAM) Camden, NJ St. Bartholomew's R.C. Church, Camden, N.J.; Camden, NJ The Church of St. Joan of Arc, West Collingswood, N.J.; Camden, NJ The Church of St. Joan of Arc, West Collingswood, N.J.; Continuing Education & Spiritual Formation of Priests (CESF).
Maraczewski, Edward S. '45 (CHI) Retired.
Maramattam, Jose J. '80 (MAR) Gladstone, MI Holy Family.
Maramot, Faustino '74 (MEM) Federal Correctional Institute at Memphis.
Marandu, Nicolaus '82 (P) Portland, OR Immaculate Heart of Mary.
Marangone, Mark *s.x.* '84 (PAT)[N] Wayne Xaverian Missionary Fathers; Wayne, NJ XAVERIAN MISSIONARY FATHERS.
Marani, Philip *o.carm.* '65 (NY) Tarrytown, NY Transfiguration.
Marankulam, Mathew M. '78 (SAC) Vicars Forane.
Marankulam, Mathew M. '78 (SAC) Anderson, CA Sacred Heart; Presbyteral Council.
Marano, Fred '91 (BRK)[B] Douglaston, NY Cathedral Seminary Residence of the Immaculate Conception; [B] Elmhurst, NY Cathedral Preparatory Seminary of the Immaculate Conception.
Maranowski, Michael J. '87 (PIT) Coraopolis, PA St. Malachy.
Maranto, Charles L. *c.s.v.* '50 (CHI)[N] Arlington Heights, IL Viatorian Province Center–Clerics of St. Viator.
Maranto, Samuel C. *c.ss.r.* '72 (BR) Baton Rouge, LA St. Gerard Majella; [H] Baton Rouge, LA St. Gerard Residence; [L] Baton Rouge, LA Redemptorist Fathers of Baton Rouge, Inc.
Marat, Wojciech A. '88 (CHI) Chicago, IL St. John Fisher; Judges.
Maravi, Raul *o.carm.* '97 (JOL)[L] Darien Carmelite Provincial Office.
Maraya, Felipe '62 (ELP) Absent on Leave.
Marbach, Lawrence J. '52 (SFS) Federal Prison Camp Retired.
Marbury, Cabell B. '64 (ALB) Albany, NY St. James Retired.
Marcaccio, Rev. Msgr. Anthony J. '91 (CHL) Greensboro, NC St. Pius the Tenth; Vice Chancellor; Diocesan Consultors.
Marcaida, Epifanio '83 (NY) Bronx, NY St. Frances de Chantal.
Marcantonio, Clement '59 (PBL) Retired.
Marceau, Emmett L. '67 (SAG) Saginaw, MI St. Helen.
Marceau, Timothy R. *o.s.b.* '52 (JOL)[L] Lisle, IL St. Procopius Abbey.
Marcell, Robert G. '56 (BR) Retired.
Marcello, Albert P. '09 (PRO) Cranston, RI St. Paul.
Marcello, Joseph A. '03 (BGP) Secretary to the Bishop; Assistant Vocation Directors; Pastors' Vocation Advisory Board; Presbyteral Council.
Marcellus, Gordon E. *o.s.a.* '59 (PH)[Y] Rosemont, PA Saxony Hall.
Marcelo, Florante E. '96 (CHY) Jackson, WY Our Lady of the Mountains.
Marcelo, Jeronimo '92 (SAC) South Lake Tahoe, CA St. Theresa.
Marcelo, Jose M. '79 (MET) Bound Brook, NJ St. Joseph.
March, Nathan D. '07 (PRT) Catholic Scouting; Lewiston, ME Prince of Peace Parish.
March, Nicholas B. '04 (DUB) Ex–Officio; Cedar Rapids, IA All Saints.
March, Ralph *o.cist.* '45 (DAL)[B] University of Dallas; [J] Irving, TX Cistercian Abbey of Our Lady of Dallas.
Marcham, David S. '05 (FR) Taunton, MA St. Mary's.
Marchand, Gerald A. '54 (NEW) Retired.
Marchand, Robert A. '52 (MAN) Retired.
Marchesani, Gino *f.d.p.* '56 (BO)[S] East Boston, MA Don Orione Nursing Home.
Marchese, Henry *s.a.* '64 (NY)[EE] New York, NY Atonement Friars Retired.
Marchese, Joseph P. '69 (SPR) On Duty Outside the Diocese.
Marchese, Rev. Msgr. Richard E. '70 (BRK) Released from Diocesan Assignment.
Marchessault, Edward T. *c.s.sp.* '64 (FgM) Bethel Park, PA CONGREGATION OF THE HOLY SPIRIT.
Marchetti, Carlo M. *o.s.m.* '59 (CHI)[N] Chicago Order of Friar Servants of Mary (Servites) United States of America Province, Inc.
Marchetti, Michael H. '82 (SCR) Unassigned or Leave of Absence.
Marchetto, Ezio '82 (NY)[EE] Staten Island, NY Scalabrinian Missionaries.
Marchewka, Jacek '00 (NEW) Upper Saddle River, NJ Church of the Presentation.
Marchionda, James *o.p.* '73 (CHI)[N] Oak Park, IL Dominican Community of St. Martin de Porres.
Marchitelli, Rev. Msgr. Anthony D. '76 (NY)[E] White Plains, NY Archbishop Stepinac High School.
Marchlewski, Michael A. *s.j.* '67 (STL)[F] St. Louis, MO St. Louis University High School, George H. Backer Memorial; [O] Saint Louis, MO St. Louis University High School Jesuit Community.
Marchulones, Kenneth L. '65 (PEO) East Peoria, IL St. Monica Church.
Marchwiany, Robert '03 (CHI) Burbank, IL St. Albert the Great.
Marciano, Robert L. '83 (MO) Air National Guard Chaplains; On Duty Outside the Diocese.
Marcil, Michael *s.j.* '74 (NEW)[B] Jersey City, NJ Jesuit Center.
Marcil, Michel *s.j.* '74 (NEW)[M] Jersey City, NJ Jesuits of Saint Peter's College, Inc.; [R] South Orange, NJ U.S. Catholic China Bureau.
Marciniak, Bartlomiej *o.s.p.p.e.* '93 (PH)[Y].
Marciniak, Rev. Canon Felix R. '79 (NEW) Wallington, NJ Most Sacred Heart of Jesus.
Marciniak, John '56 (NOR) Retired.
Marciniak, Stanislaw P. '86 (SAT) Karnes City, TX St. Cornelius.
Marciniak, Thomas R. *s.j.* '76 (NY)[EE] Loyola Hall, Jesuit Community.
Marco, Michael J. *s.j.* '96 (CLV)[D] Cuyahoga Falls, OH Walsh Jesuit High School.
Marcoe, Timothy D. '07 (HBG) Hanover, PA St. Joseph; [A] York, PA York Catholic High School; Pastoral Council, Diocesan.
Marconato, Tiziano *c.r.s.* '57 (GAL) Houston, TX Assumption.
Marcone, Eugene F. '64 (NEW) Retired.
Marcone, Eugene '64 (NEW) Roselle Park, NJ The Assumption.
Marconi, John E. '87 (LR) Pocahontas, AR St. Paul the Apostle; [K] Pocahontas, AR St. Paul the Apostle Catholic Church – Capital Improvement Trust Fund; Deans; Pocahontas, AR St. John the Baptist; Corning, AR St. Joseph the Worker Church; Vicars for Religious.
Marconi, Joseph Patrick '01 (LR) Tontitown, AR St. Joseph; Fayetteville, AR St. Thomas Aquinas University Parish; [I] Fayetteville, AR University of Arkansas, St. Thomas Aquinas University Parish; Huntsville, AR St. John the Evangelist.
Marconi, Paul M. *c.r.s.p.* '58 (ALN)[K] Bethlehem, PA The Barnabite Fathers Barnabite Spiritual Center.
Marconi, Theodore B. '84 (E) Erie, PA Our Lady of Peace.
Marcotte, David P. *s.j.* '92 (NY)[EE] Cardinal Spellman Hall, Jesuit Community.
Marcotte, Joseph A. '69 (WOR) Webster, MA St. Louis.
Marcotte, Wayne E. '66 (MAR) Retired.
Marcotte, William '60 (SB) Retired.
Marcouiller, Douglas W. *s.j.* '86 (FgM)[O] St. Louis, MO The Jesuits of the Missouri Province; St. Louis, MO Society of Jesus.
Marcouiller, Douglas W. *s.j.* '86 (STL) Saint Louis, MO; [O] St. Louis, MO Sacred Heart Jesuit Community.
Marcoux, A. Stephen '93 (MAN) Windham, NH St. Matthew.
Marcoux, Joseph W. '01 (ROC) Censores Librorum; Clyde, NY St. John the Evangelist; Lyons, NY St. Michael.
Marcucci, John A. '68 (PIT) Glenshaw, PA St. Mary of the Assumption.
Marczewski, Robert '95 (PH) On Duty Outside the Archdiocese.
Marczewski, Robert (DET)[A] Orchard Lake, MI SS. Cyril and Methodius Seminary.
Marczewski, Rev. Msgr. Ronald J. '74 (NEW) Bayonne, NJ Mt. Carmel.
Marczuk, Rev. Msgr. Scott L. '81 (LR) Bentonville, AR St. Stephen; Vice Chancellors; Diocesan Consultors; Priests Personnel Board (Diocesan); Presbyteral Council.
Marczuk, Rev. Msgr. Scott L. (SPP) Judges.
Mardian, Pius '44 (SFS) Retired.
Marecki, Ronald '83 (SP) Homosassa, FL St. Thomas the Apostle.
Marek, Dean V. '65 (WIN) On Special or Other Diocesan Assignment; [D] Rochester, MN Saint Mary Hospital.
Marek, Dean V. '65 (MIL) On Duty Outside the Archdiocese.
Marek, Libor '05 (DET) Sterling Heights, MI SS. Cyril and Methodius.
Marek, Ray John *o.m.i.* '89 (SAT)[C] Oblate School of Theology; [L] San Antonio, TX De Mazenod House.
Marek, Walter '46 (GAY) Retired.
Mares, Philip W. *m.m.* '86 (FgM) Maryknoll, NY MARYKNOLL.
Maresca, Rev. Msgr. Ralph J. '78 (BRK) Astoria, NY St. Francis of Assisi.
Maresh, Mark '94 (GI) Grand Island, NE Blessed Sacrament.
Marflak, Albert *o.s.b.* '75 (CLV)[N] Cleveland, OH; Cleveland, OH.
Marfori, Antonio '78 (SCL) Foley, MN St. Elizabeth of Hungary; Gilman, MN SS. Peter and Paul; Foley, MN St. Joseph's.
Margallo, Roy '00 (MRY) Watsonville, CA St. Patrick.
Margarito, Luis A. Bonilla '00 (ALN) Unassigned.
Margason, Rev. Msgr. James E. '71 (BEL) Lebanon, IL St. Joseph; Judges; Shiloh, IL Corpus Christi.
Margevicius, Thomas '99 (STP)[A] Saint Paul, MN The Saint Paul Seminary.
Margevieus, Thomas '99 (STP)[C] St. Paul, MN University of St. Thomas.
Marggraf, Brian *ss.cc.* '55 (FR)[G] Fairhaven, MA Damien Residence Retired.
Margherio, Ronald L. *o.s.b.* '78 (PEO)[A] Peru, IL St. Bede Abbey; [C] Peru, IL St. Bede Academy.
Marginean, Ovidiu Ioan '06 (ROM) Canton, OH St. Theodore; Chancellor; Finance Council; Canton, OH St. George Cathedral.
Marhafer, Maury *o.f.m.conv.* '54 (FgM) Rensselaer, NY Province of the Immaculate Conception.
Mariani, Guilbert '97 (CC)[G] Robstown, TX Society of Our Lady of the Most Holy Trinity.
Mariani, Paul P. *s.j.* '02 (SJ)[B] Santa Clara, CA Jesuit Community.
Mariano, John M. '58 (BRK) Retired.
Mariano, Miguel (TUC) Office of Worship.
Mariano, Remigio "Miguel" '94 (TUC) Tucson, AZ Saint Joseph Roman Catholic Parish – Tucson; Diocesan Liturgical Coordinators.
Mariasavary, Chinnapparaj '88 (SAN) Odessa, TX St. Elizabeth Ann Seton.
Mariasoosai, Gnanapragasam '81 (CHL) Marion, NC Our Lady of the Angels.
Mariasoosai, Lawrence *o.m.i.* '97 (BEL) Walsh, IL St. Pius V.

Mariasossai, Lawrence *o.m.i.* '97 (BEL) Sparta, IL Our Lady of Lourdes.
Marick, Thomas D. '97 (STN) Retired.
Marickovic, Thomas C. '81 (HBG) Spring Grove, PA Sacred Heart.
Marien, Roy C. '85 (PT) Niceville, FL Christ Our Redeemer; Seminarian Candidate Review Board; Members Appointed.
Marier, Edward '88 (SPK) Colton, WA St. Gall; Colton, WA St. Boniface.
Marigliano, Michael *o.f.m.cap.* '84 (NY) New York, NY Our Lady of Sorrows.
Marin, John L. '85 (MET) On Duty Outside the Diocese.
Marin, Jose G. '93 (TYL) Teague, TX Boyd Unit, Texas Department of Correction.
Marin, Jose '95 (TYL) Teague, TX St. Mary.
Marin, Miguel '78 (ELP) Absent on Leave.
Marin, Moises '95 (CHI) Other Assignments.
Marin, Rev. Msgr. Tomas M. '89 (MIA) Doral, FL Our Lady of Guadalupe; Judges; Deans and Deaneries; Archdiocese of Miami Health Plan Trust; Catholic Physicians' and Dentists' Guild; Catholic Fire Service Ministry; [Q] Miami Shores, FL Bahamas Mission of Florida, Inc.; Pension.
Marin, Rev. Msgr. Tomas '89 (MIA) Members.
Marin–Leon, Rafael '78 (LA) Santa Barbara, CA Our Lady of Guadalupe; Deanery 2.
Marinacci, Rev. Msgr. Nicolas '38 (NY) Retired.
Marinak, Andrew P. '56 (HBG) Retired.
Marincioni, Raniero A. '90 (MET) On Duty Outside the Diocese.
Marine, Rev. Msgr. John C. '76 (PH) Holland, PA St. Bede the Venerable.
Maring, William J. *s.j.* '45 (SJ)[M] Los Gatos, CA Sacred Heart Jesuit Center.
Marini, Francis J. '95 (SAM) Scranton, PA St. Ann; Judicial Vicar; Presbyteral Council; College of Consultors; Board of Pastors.
Marini, Francis J. '95 (SCR) Promoter of Justice.
Marini, Francis J. '95 (ROM) Judicial Vicar.
Marini, Joseph J. '52 (SFR) Retired.
Marini, Michael '72 (MRY) Advocates; Presbyteral Council Retired.
Marino, Christopher '93 (MIA) Miami, FL St. Michael the Archangel; Italian; Catholic Educators' Guild.
Marino, Edward J. *c.s.* '57 (PRO)[M] North Kingstown, RI Scalabrini Villa.
Marino, John J. *o.f.m.* '88 (SP)[N] St. Petersburg, FL St. Anthony Friary.
Marino, Jose Humberto Lopez '98 (SJN) Guaynabo, PR Nuestra Senora de la Paz.
Marino, Rev. Msgr. Joseph T. '75 (PH) Regional Vicars; Priests' Personnel Board; Strafford, PA Our Lady of the Assumption.
Marino, Robert '08 (BUF) Cheektowaga, NY St. Philip the Apostle.
Marino, Rev. Msgr. Ronald T. '73 (BRK) Brooklyn, NY St. Rosalia–Regina Pacis; Catholic Migration Services, Inc.; Vicar for Migrant and Ethnic Apostolates; Assignment Board.
Marinucci, Steven J. '74 (PH) Philadelphia, PA St. Agatha–St. James.
Maristany, Edward G. '80 (CHI)[V] Chicago, IL Prelature of the Holy Cross and Opus Dei; Chicago.
Maristela, Victor '87 (SD) Borrego Springs, CA St. Richard.
Mark, John K. '01 (STV) Charlotte Amalie, VI Our Lady of Perpetual Help; Permanent Diaconate.
Mark, Urey P. *s.v.d.* '07 (STL) St. Louis, MO St. Nicholas.
Markalalonis, Joseph *t.o.r.* (PIT) Allegheny County, PA Mercy Health System of Pittsburgh–Pittsburgh Mercy Hospital.
Markell, John W. '84 (PIT) Retired.
Markellos, Christopher M. '06 (CAM) Williamstown, NJ Our Lady of Peace Parish, Monroe Township, N.J.
Markelz, Carl J. *o.carm.* '91 (CHI)[D] Chicago, IL; [N] Chicago Carmelite Priory of St. Cyril.
Markert, Leo '62 (ALB) Retired.
Markewych, Rev. Archpriest Uriy '65 (PHU) Retired.
Markey, Earle L. *s.j.* '63 (WOR)[O] Worcester, MA Jesuits of the Holy Cross, Inc.
Markey, Greg J. '99 (BGP) Norwalk, CT St. Mary.
Markey, John J. *o.p.* '93 (SAT)[L] San Antonio, TX Dominican Priory of San Juan Macias.
Markey, John *o.p.* '93 (SAT) San Antonio, TX St. Ann.
Markham, Rev. Msgr. James J. '51 (MAN) Manchester, NH Parish of the Transfiguration Retired.
Markham, John C. '03 (SAV) Special Assignment; Savannah, GA St. Frances Xavier Cabrini.
Markiewicz, Stanley T. *o.s.b.* '61 (GBG)[G] Latrobe, PA Saint Vincent Archabbey.
Markley, Edward P. *o.s.b.* '66 (BIR) Florence, AL St. Michael.
Marko, Andrew '98 (SJP) Presbyters Retired.
Markowitch, Robert '01 (STF) Brooklyn, NY St. Nicholas.
Marks, Kevin E. '04 (PBR) Aliquippa, PA St. George the Great Martyr; Ambridge, PA St. Mary's; Vocations; Presbyteral Council.
Marks, Thomas C. '79 (LR) Cherokee Village, AR St. Michael; Horseshoe Bend, AR St. Mary of the Mount.
Marks, William G. '92 (IND) Indianapolis, IN St. Simon the Apostle.
Markunas, Robert '76 (ORL) Palm Bay, FL Our Lady of Grace.
Markus, Anthony L. '80 (CHI) Chicago, IL Nativity of the Blessed Virgin Mary.
Markwell, Benjamin *o.f.m.cap.* '66 (DET) Detroit, MI Province of St. Joseph; [K] Detroit St. Bonaventure Friary.
Markwell, George *m.afr.* '65 (WDC)[L] Silver Spring, MD Holy Cross Hospital of Silver Spring, Inc.; [N] Washington, DC Missionaries of Africa; Washington, DC; Washington, DC MISSIONARIES OF AFRICA.
Marley, John *s.s.c.* '50 (PRO)[P] Bristol, RI St. Columban's Retirement House Retired.
Marley, John *s.s.c.* '50 (OM)[K] St. Columbans Missionary Society of St. Columban.
Marley, William F. *m.m.* '52 (NY)[EE] Retired.
Marneni, Ignatius '69 (PH) Parkesburg, PA Our Lady of Consolation.
Marneni, Julian '67 (WH) Huntington, WV St. Joseph's; Wayne, WV Nativity of Our Lord.
Marney, Matthew D. '07 (WCH) Wichita, KS St. Elizabeth Ann Seton; Ongoing Formation of the Clergy Committee.
Maroney, Frank '92 (DEN) Longmont, CO St. Francis of Assisi; College of Consultors; Ex Officio Members.
Maroney, Maurice J. '67 (HRT) Milford, CT St. Gabriel.
Maroon, Donald M. '67 (COL) Wellston, OH SS. Peter and Paul.
Maroor, Joseph '63 (MIA) Lighthouse Point, FL St. Paul the Apostle.
Marot, Roger L. '50 (PRO) Woonsocket, RI Precious Blood Retired.
Marotta, Michael *c.r.m.* '87 (NEW) Lodi, NJ St. Joseph's.
Marotta, Robert G. '63 (NEW) Retired.
Maroun, George F. '74 (OG) Carthage, NY St. James Minor; Copenhagen, NY St. Mary.
Maroun, Rev. Msgr. Sharbel '89 (OLL) Minneapolis, MN St. Maron Maronite Catholic Church; College of Consultors; Office of Priestly Vocations; Presbyteral Council; Protopresbyters; Personnel Board.
Marquard, Elmer E. '66 (CLV) North Ridgeville, OH St. Julie Billiart.
Marquardt, Donald '51 (GB) Retired.
Marquart, Ernest J. '70 (SPC) Mountain View, MO St. John Vianney; Region V.
Marques, Anthony E. '06 (RIC) Tappahannock, VA St. Timothy.
Marques, Eduardo (BO) Brazilian.
Marques, Jesus *sch.p.* '64 (SJN) San Juan, PR Santisimo Salvador.
Marques, Jose E. (BO) Allston, MA St. Anthony of Padua.
Marquez, Celso *m.sp.s.* '97 (P)[A] Mount Angel, OR Felix Rougier House of Studies; [L] Mount Angel, OR Missionaries of the Holy Spirit, M.Sp.S.
Marquez, Esteban '95 (LA) Lomita, CA St. Margaret Mary Alacoque.
Marquez, Fabian '04 (ELP) Pecos, TX St. Catherine; Pecos, TX Santa Rosa de Lima.
Marquez, Fausto '97 (ATL) Atlanta, GA St. Jude; Atlanta, GA Centro Catolico del Espiritu Santo.
Marquez, Gregory '03 (ORG)[G] Fullerton, CA St. Jude Medical Center; Anaheim, CA St. Boniface.
Marquez, Humberto '05 (DEN) Brighton, CO St. Augustine.
Marquez, Jose E. '99 (NEW) Union City, NJ St. Anthony of Padua.
Marquez–Munoz, Salvador '03 (LR) Siloam Springs, AR St. Mary.
Marquis, Joseph '06 (PRM) Priest's Pension Board; Livonia, MI Sacred Heart.
Marquis, Paul R. '86 (PRT) Portland, ME Maine Medical Center; Portland, ME St. Louis.
Marquis, William P. *o.p.* '83 (PRO)[P] Providence St. Thomas Aquinas Priory at Providence College; Finance Council.
Marr, Thomas P. '70 (MAD) Watertown, WI St. Bernard; Deaneries.
Marra, James *s.d.b.* '83 (NEW)[C] Ramsey, NJ Don Bosco Preparatory High School; [M] Ramsey, NJ Don Bosco Prep Salesian Residence.
Marreddy, Allam '79 (CHR) Abbeville, SC Sacred Heart.
Marreddy, Yeruva Lourdu (GLP) St. Johns, AZ San Rafael; St. Johns, AZ St. John the Baptist.
Marrell, Dennis P. '78 (LA) Los Angeles, CA St. Basil's.
Marren, Rev. Msgr. Hugh M. '76 (ATL) Roswell, GA St. Andrew.
Marren, Martin T. '84 (CHI) Country Club Hills, IL St. Emeric.
Marrero, Adan *s.d.b.* '97 (SJN)[C] Catano, PR Prenoviciado Salesiano.
Marrin, Joseph *c.ss.r.* (BRK) Legion of Mary.
Marrion, Malachy *o.c.s.o.* '54 (ARL)[H] Berryville, VA Cistercian Abbey of Our Lady of the Holy Cross.
Marro, Nicholas A. *c.s.* '63 (CHI) Chicago, IL Santa Lucia–Santa Maria Incoronata.
Marro, Simeon D. *o.carm.* '55 (GBG)[G] Bolivar, PA Mount Carmel Hermitage; Bolivar, PA.
Marrodan, Francisco J. *c.m.* '54 (ARE) Manati, PR Sagrada Familia.
Marron, Leonard J. *m.m.* '57 (FgM) Maryknoll, NY MARYKNOLL.
Marron, Rev. Msgr. Patrick L. '67 (SAT) Retired.
Marrone, Michael V. '07 (PH) Havertown, PA St. Denis.
Marrone, Robert J. '73 (CLV) Cleveland, OH St. Peter.
Marroquin, Luis '86 (WDC) Silver Spring, MD St. Catherine Laboure.
Marrow, Stanley B. *s.j.* '61 (BO)[U] Weston, MA Campion Health Center, Inc.
Marrufo, Ramon '76 (SD) Fallbrook, CA St. Peter.
Marsalek, Peter *s.o.l.t.* '05 (CC)[G] Robstown, TX Society of Our Lady of the Most Holy Trinity.
Marse, John J. '81 (NO) New Orleans, LA Mater Dolorosa; Metairie, LA East Jefferson General Hospital.
Marsh, Ivan *o.carm.* (TUC) Tucson, AZ Saint Cyril of Alexandria Roman Catholic Parish – Tucson.
Marshall, Eugene C. *o.s.b.* '50 (OKL)[I] Shawnee, OK St. Gregory's Abbey.
Marshall, James C. '59 (STL) Retired.
Marshall, James '04 (SFE) Abiquiu, NM St. Thomas Apostle.
Marshall, James *s.j.* '03 (SAT) San Antonio, TX Our Lady of Guadalupe.
Marshall, Joseph Mary *s.m.* '93 (SAT)[L] San Antonio, TX Casa San Juan Marianist Community; San Antonio, TX St. Mary Magdalen.
Marshall, Joseph Mary '93 (SAT)[S] San Antonio, TX Brothers of the Beloved Disciple.
Marshall, Patrick M. '79 (CHI)[U] Chicago, IL University of Illinois at Chicago – John Paul II Newman Center.
Marshall, Paul M. *s.m.* '76 (CIN)[D] Dayton, OH The University of Dayton; [D] Dayton, OH The University of Dayton; [N] Dayton, OH Marianist Community.
Marshall, Peter A. '09 (IND) Indianapolis, IN St. Barnabas.
Marshall, Robert A. '61 (STL) Retired.
Marshall, Robert W. '00 (MEM) Memphis, TN Church of the Ascension; Clergy Personnel Board; Presbyteral Council; College of Consultors.
Marshall, Thomas R. *c.s.p.* '59 (NY)[EE] Jamaica Estates Paulist Fathers Generalate.
Marshall, William '63 (OAK) Retired.
Marsicek, Robert *s.d.s.* '68 (MIL)[P] Milwaukee Salvatorian Provincial Offices; Wauwatosa, WI St. Pius X; Milwaukee, WI Mother of Good Counsel; Consultors:.
Marsick, James J. '72 (CLV) Cuyahoga Falls, OH St. Joseph.
Marstall, David '04 (WCH)[I] Pittsburg, KS St. Pius X Newman Center (Pittsburg State University); Pittsburg, KS Our Lady of Lourdes.
Marszal, Theodore '68 (CLV) Cleveland, OH Cathedral of St. John the Evangelist; [X] Cleveland, OH St. John Cathedral Endowment Trust; Assistant Chancellors; Administrative Assistant to the Bishop.
Marszalek, Paul B. '52 (CHI) Retired.
Marta, Rev. Msgr. Raul '72 (FRS) Tulare, CA St. Aloysius.
Martel, C. James '70 (PRT) Retired.
Martel, Christopher M. '09 (MAN) Newmarket, NH St. Mary; Exeter, NH St. Michael.
Martel, Leo E. '63 (BO) Senior Priests. Retired.
Martel, Luc *a.a.* '73 (BO)[U] Boston Assumptionist Center.
Martel, Marcel I. '79 (MAN) Littleton, NH St. Rose of Lima.
Martell, James J. '88 (MEM) Memphis, TN Holy Rosary; College of Consultors; Presbyteral Council.
Martelli, Jose M. *c.s.c.* '73 (FTW)[H] Notre Dame Congregation of Holy Cross, Indiana Province, Provincial House.
Martello, Ernest *o.s.c.* '70 (SCL)[I] Onamia, MN Crosier Priory.
Martello, Lawrence N. '74 (CLV) Amherst, OH St. Joseph; Associate Judges; South Amherst, OH Nativity of Blessed Virgin Mary.
Martens, L. Gene *s.j.* '63 (STL) Saint Louis, MO; [O] St. Louis, MO The Jesuits of the Missouri Province; [V] St. Louis, MO The Jesuits of the Missouri Province; [O] St. Louis, MO Jesuit Community Corporation at Saint Louis University – Jesuit Hall.
Martensen, Carsten P. *s.j.* '77 (SY)[Q] Syracuse, NY Jesuits at LeMoyne, Inc.
Martensen, Carsten *s.j.* '77 (ROC)[M] Ithaca, NY The Catholic Community of Ithaca College.
Marterior, Raul A. '94 (GAL) Anderson, TX St. Stanislaus; Navasota, TX Christ Our Light.
Marth, Rev. Msgr. Loydell J. '56 (FRS) Retired.
Marthaler, Andrew '90 (SCL) Retired.
Marthaler, Berard L. *o.f.m.conv.* '52 (WDC) Washington, DC St. Anthony; [B] Forestville, MD St. Bonaventure Friary; [C] Catholic University of America, The Retired.
Marti, Antonio *o.f.m.cap.* '96 (LA)[F] La Canada

Flintridge, CA St. Francis High School of La Canada–Flintridge.
Marti, Ramon *sch.p.* '55 (LA) Monrovia, CA Annunciation; Duarte, CA City of Hope Medical Center.
Martignetti, Richard *o.f.m.* '97 (NY)[EE] New York Franciscan Province of the Immaculate Conception.
Martignetti, Richard *o.f.m.* '97 (STU)[A] Steubenville, OH Franciscan University of Steubenville; [H] Steubenville, OH Holy Spirit Friary.
Martignon, John E. '84 (MAR) Houghton, MI St. Ignatius Loyola; Houghton, MI Holy Family; Vicars Forane.
Martin, Rev. Msgr. Andrew E. '67 (CAM)[A] Cherry Hill, NJ Camden Catholic High School, Cherry Hill, N.J.; Members.
Martin, Anselm *o.f.m.cap.* '45 (PH) Philadelphia, PA St. John the Evangelist.
Martin, Benjamin '75 (DOD) Leoti, KS St. Anthony of Padua Catholic Church of Leoti, Kansas; Marienthal, KS St. Mary Catholic Church of Marienthal, Kansas; Tribune, KS St. Joseph the Worker Catholic Church of Tribune, Kansas.
Martin, Benjamin *s.o.l.t.* '06 (CC)[G] Robstown, TX Society of Our Lady of the Most Holy Trinity.
Martin, C. Lou '76 (BAL) Baltimore, MD St. Clare; [J] Baltimore, MD Mother Mary Lange Catholic School.
Martin, Charles A. *c.s.p.* '65 (PMB)[H] Vero Beach, FL Paulist Fathers Residence.
Martin, Christopher M. '06 (STL) St. Charles, MO St. Joseph; [V] St. Louis, MO Archdiocesan Stewardship Education Committee.
Martin, Clarence A. *s.j.* '46 (PH)[Y] Loyola Center and Manresa Hall.
Martin, Clifford A. '76 (SFR) San Francisco, CA Star of the Sea.
Martin, Cristobal *m.id.* '96 (NY) Bronx, NY Santa Maria; [EE] Bronx, NY Idente Missionaries – Santa Maria Residence.
Martin, D. (BAL) Westminster, MD St. John.
Martin, David A. '76 (EVN) Newburgh, IN St. John the Baptist; Diocesan Council of Priests.
Martin, David L. '73 (ARL) Fredericksburg, VA St. Jude.
Martin, Dennis A. '75 (E) Erie, PA St. Vincent's Health Center; [G] Erie, PA Saint Vincent Health Center.
Martin, Dennis C. '67 (DAV) West Branch, IA St. Bernadette; West Liberty, IA St. Joseph's.
Martin, Diosdado '66 (LA) Los Angeles, CA Assumption Retired.
Martin, Donald *s.j.* '82 (NO)[A] New Orleans, LA Notre Dame Seminary Graduate School of Theology.
Martin, Edward '77 (MO) Military Chaplains; Army Chaplains.
Martin, Elijah *o.c.d.* '01 (MIL) Milwaukee, WI St. Florian.
Martin, Rev. Msgr. Emilio '52 (MIA) Hialeah, FL St. John the Apostle.
Martin, Faustino *c.m.* '72 (LA) Artesia, CA Holy Family.
Martin, Francis R. '56 (WDC) Special Ministries Retired.
Martin, Francis '39 (LAN) Retired.
Martin, Gerald R. '89 (BR) Board Members.
Martin, Gerard R. '73 (BR) Baton Rouge, LA St. Patrick; Defenders of the Bond.
Martin, Gilmer '74 (NO) Lacombe, LA St. John of the Cross.
Martin, Harry '66 (SAT) Retired.
Martin, Hilary *o.p.* '55 (OAK)[M] Oakland, CA Order of Preachers (Province of the Most Holy Name of Jesus – Western Dominican Province); [M] Oakland Order of Preachers (Province of the Most Holy Name of Jesus – Western Dominican Province); [A] Berkeley, CA Dominican School of Philosophy and Theology.
Martin, James J. *s.j.* '99 (BO)[U] Boston The Society of Jesus of New England–Provincial Offices.
Martin, James J. *s.j.* '99 (NY)[EE] New York, NY "America;" Residence and publication office of the America Press.
Martin, James J. '63 (PH) Retired.
Martin, James *c.s.c.* '93 (AUS) Austin, TX St. Paul.
Martin, Jeffrey D. '05 (LFT) Logansport, IN All Saints.
Martin, Joel W. *o.s.b.* '91 (BIR)[B] Cullman, AL St. Bernard Preparatory School; [E] Cullman, AL St. Bernard Abbey.
Martin, John F. *s.j.* '74 (WDC)[N] Washington, DC The Jesuit Community at Georgetown University.
Martin, Rev. Msgr. John J. '72 (ALN) Bethlehem, PA Assumption B.V.M.
Martin, John J. '65 (SR) Retired.
Martin, John M. *s.j.* '84 (PHX)[F] Phoenix, AZ Society of Jesus.
Martin, Rev. Msgr. John P. '61 (RVC) Priests' Retirement Board Retired.
Martin, John P. *m.m.* '66 (FgM) Maryknoll, NY MARYKNOLL.
Martin, John '65 (NEW) Elizabeth, NJ St. Mary of the Assumption.
Martin, John '84 (PHX) Phoenix, AZ St. Francis Xavier Roman Catholic Parish.
Martin, Jon C. '65 (BO) Senior Priests. Retired.
Martin, Rev. Msgr. Joseph A. '67 (NY) Fishkill, NY Church of St. Mary, Mother of the Church.
Martin, Joseph I. '56 (BO) Senior Priests. Retired.
Martin, Joseph I. '56 (FgM) Boston, MA St. James the Apostle, Inc.
Martin, Kevin '03 (PRT) Portland, ME St. Peter's; Portland, ME Cathedral of the Immaculate Conception; Portland, ME St. Christopher's; Portland, ME St. Louis; Portland, ME Sacred Heart/St. Dominic.
Martin, Larok '80 (OKL)[K] Tonkawa, OK Northern Oklahoma College.
Martin, Leon J. *s.a.c.* '75 (MIL)[Y] Milwaukee, WI Pallottine Fathers and Brothers, Inc., Disability Trust; [Y] Milwaukee, WI Pallottine Fathers and Brothers, Inc., Educational and Apostolic Ministry Trust; Milwaukee, WI; [P] Milwaukee, WI Pallotti House.
Martin, Leonard A. *s.j.* '73 (WDC)[E] North Bethesda, MD Georgetown Preparatory School.
Martin, Leonard *s.j.* '73 (PSC) Harrisburg, PA St. Ann.
Martin, Malcolm *s.a.* '62 (BO)[N] Brockton, MA Chapel of Our Savior–Catholic Pastoral and Information Center; [U] Brockton, MA Chapel of Our Savior; [Z] Brockton, MA Chapel of Our Saviour Retired.
Martin, Malcolm *s.a.* '62 (NY)[EE] Garrison Graymoor Ecumenical and Interreligious Institute.
Martin, Michael J. *c.s.f.* '77 (PMB)[H] Vero Beach, FL Paulist Fathers Residence.
Martin, Michael *o.f.m.conv.* '89 (BAL)[C] Baltimore, MD Archbishop Curley High School; [S] Baltimore, MD Immaculate Heart of Mary Friary; [V] Baltimore, MD Archbishop Curley High School Endowment Trust.
Martin, Oscar '01 (BO) East Boston, MA Our Lady of the Assumption.
Martin, Patrick A. '78 (NOR) On Duty Outside the Diocese.
Martin, Rev. Msgr. Ralph L. '65 (WIL) Retired.
Martin, Raymond D. '94 (BAL) Special Assignment.
Martin, Reginald *o.p.* '74 (OAK)[M] Oakland, CA Order of Preachers (Province of the Most Holy Name of Jesus – Western Dominican Province).
Martin, Reginald *o.p.* '74 (P) Portland, OR Holy Rosary Parish & Dominican Priory; [L] Portland, OR Holy Rosary Priory.
Martin, Ricardo '03 (MIL)[V] Racine, WI Community of St. Paul, Inc.
Martin, Richard B. '66 (ARL) Burke, VA Church of the Nativity.
Martin, Richard J. '63 (CHI) Retired.
Martin, Robert A. '83 (BUF) Kenmore, NY St. Andrew.
Martin, Robert *c.ss.r.* '50 (FgM) Denver, CO Denver Province.
Martin, Roosevelt '88 (GAL) Retired.
Martin, Samuel A. '99 (LC) Special Assignment; [A] La Crosse, WI Holy Cross Seminary House of Formation; [H] La Crosse, WI Holy Cross (Seminary) Diocesan Center; Office of Ecumenism.
Martin, Sean '81 (DAL) On Duty Outside the Diocese.
Martin, Seán '79 (STL)[B] St. Louis, MO Aquinas Institute of Theology.
Martin, Stephen E. '98 (MOB) Mobile, AL St. Ignatius; Group III; Pastoral Services.
Martin, Rev. Msgr. Thomas A. '79 (KAL) Chancellor; Judicial Vicar; Diocesan Consultors; Delegate for Ecumenical and Interreligious Concerns; Presbyteral Council Members; Presbyteral Council Members; Diocesan Finance Council.
Martin, Thomas P. *s.j.* '66 (BAL)[S] Baltimore, MD Colombiere Jesuit Community.
Martin, Thomas '70 (OAK) Oakland, CA St. Jarlath.
Martin, Rev. Msgr. Thomas '79 (KAL) Kalamazoo, MI St. Augustine Cathedral.
Martin, Thomas *o.c.d.* '61 (MIL)[P] Milwaukee Provincial Offices – Discalced Carmelites.
Martin, Vicente Moreno '75 (VEN) Palmetto, FL Holy Cross Church.
Martin, Victor T. '80 (BGP) Fairfield, CT St. Thomas Aquinas.
Martin, William F. '63 (NY) On Duty Outside the Archdiocese.
Martin, William F. '78 (STP) Oakdale, MN Guardian Angels.
Martin, William J. '71 (L) Louisville, KY Our Mother of Sorrows.
Martin, William *o.m.i.* '61 (BO)[U] Lowell, MA St. Eugene House (Residence).
Martin–Calama, Florian '95 (DEN)[A] Denver, CO Redemptoris Mater House of Formation; The Redemptoris Mater House of Formation; Ex Officio Members.
Martina, Joseph A. '89 (SHP) Many, LA St. John the Baptist; Priests' Retirement Board.
Martine, Michael T. '97 (NY) Staten Island, NY St. Joseph; [A] Yonkers, NY St. Joseph's Seminary; Judicial Vicar.
Martine, Michael T. '97 (ALB) Interdiocesan Tribunal for the Province of NY Archdiocese.
Martineau, Albert P. *o.m.i.* '59 (BO)[Z] Lowell, MA St. Joseph the Worker Residence; [X] Tewksbury, MA Immaculate Heart of Mary Residence.
Martineau, Laurier J. '59 (BO) Senior Priests. Retired.
Martinek, John '73 (FBK) Delta Junction, AK Our Lady of Sorrows Catholic Church Delta Junction.
Martinez, Abelardo Huanca *o.f.m.conv.* '99 (ATL) Jonesboro, GA St. Philip Benizi.
Martinez, Adam '85 (AUS) Killeen, TX St. Joseph.
Martinez, Adolfo '03 (TUC) Tucson, AZ Saint Monica Roman Catholic Parish – Tucson.
Martinez, Alex (WDC) Cheverly, MD St. Ambrose.
Martinez, Alfredo (CGS) Retired.
Martinez, Andres (MAD)[F] Edgerton, WI Koshkonong Pastoral Center.
Martinez, Andrew *o.f.m.conv.* '09 (FTW) Angola, IN St. Anthony.
Martinez, Antonio *o.a.r.* '48 (LSC)[B] Mesilla, NM Augustinian Recollect Fathers.
Martinez, Charlie *o.f.m.* '80 (SAT)[B] San Antonio, TX San Antonio de Padua Friary.
Martinez, Danilo '03 (SJN) Resident Chaplains; San Juan, PR Santa Cecilia.
Martinez, Efrain '04 (FRS) Firebaugh, CA St. Joseph; Priests' Council.
Martinez, Ernest R. *s.j.* '62 (FgM) Los Gatos, CA Society of Jesus.
Martinez, Eusebio '03 (BWN) St. Peter; Edinburg, TX Holy Family.
Martinez, Felipe Antonio '96 (TUC) Administrative Leave of Absence.
Martinez, Felipe J. *c.m.* '55 (STL)[O] Perryville, MO Congregation of the Mission.
Martinez, Francisco Xavier *s.t.l.* '89 (CC)[B] Corpus Christi, TX Holy Family Catholic School; Corpus Christi, TX Holy Family.
Martinez, Gilbert S. *c.s.p.* '95 (NY) New York, NY St. Paul the Apostle; [EE] New York, NY Paulist Fathers' Motherhouse.
Martinez, Guillermo *m.s.p.* '02 (LA) Los Angeles, CA Santa Isabel.
Martinez, Ignacio '93 (MRY) Soledad, CA Our Lady of Solitude; Vicars Forane; Clergy Personnel Board.
Martinez, Ignatius '93 (MRY) Catholic Charities Board.
Martinez, James E. *o.s.a.* '57 (PH) Bryn Mawr, PA Our Mother of Good Counsel; [Y] Bryn Mawr, PA Augustinians Friars (O.S.A.).
Martinez, Jery Rivera '00 (PCE) Ensenada, PR Sacred Heart.
Martinez, Jesus E. '02 (WOR) Holy Spirit; On Administrative Leave of Absence; Gardner, MA Sacred Heart of Jesus.
Martinez, Joaquin *s.j.* (TOL)[C] Toledo, OH St. John's Jesuit High School.
Martinez, John J. *s.j.* '62 (ALN)[A] Wernersville, PA Jesuit Center–Jesuit Community.
Martinez, Jose de Jesus '08 (PBL) Center, CO St. Francis Jerome; Monte Vista, CO Holy Name of Mary; Monte Vista, CO St. Joseph.
Martinez, Jose Luis *o.a.r.* '64 (NY)[GG] Bronx, NY St. Joseph's Center; [II] Bronx, NY St. Joseph's Center.
Martinez, Jose Luis *o.a.r.* '64 (ORG) Santa Ana, CA Our Lady of the Pillar.
Martinez, Jose Rogelio '05 (LSC) Judges; Jal, NM St. Cecilia; Judicial Vicars.
Martinez, Jose Vicente *c.m.f.* '68 (CGS) Caguas, PR Inmaculado Corazon de Maria; Priests Senate.
Martinez, Jose Vicente *c.m.f.* (SJN) Spiritual Directors.
Martinez, Jose '69 (NY) Bronx, NY St. Roch.
Martinez, Jose *o.a.r.* (NY) Bronx, NY St. Anselm.
Martinez, Joyle '91 (SAC) Red Bluff, CA Sacred Heart.
Martinez, Juan *s.d.b.* '73 (SJN) Catano, PR San Francisco de Sales.
Martinez, Rev. Msgr. Leo '63 (SAT)[K] San Antonio, TX Casa De Padres Retired.
Martinez, Leonel *o.s.a.* '74 (LAR) Laredo, TX St. Vincent de Paul.
Martinez, Luis '96 (SR) On Leave.
Martinez, Luis (BRK) Brooklyn, NY St. Catharine of Alexandria.
Martinez, Manuel '66 (SAT) On Duty Outside the Archdiocese.
Martinez, Marcos '59 (CC) Corpus Christi, TX Our Lady of Pillar.
Martinez, Margarito Severino '00 (LA) Los Angeles, CA Our Lady of the Rosary of Talpa.
Martinez, Mario Castro *o.f.m.conv.* (SAT) San Antonio, TX St. Alphonsus.
Martinez, Mark '95 (LA) Los Angeles, CA Norris Cancer and USC University Hospital; Inglewood, CA St. John Chrysostom.
Martinez, Martin S. '93 (TUC) Nogales, AZ Sacred Heart of Jesus Roman Catholic Parish – Nogales.
Martinez, Matthias *o.s.b.* '08 (GBG)[A] Latrobe, PA St. Vincent Seminary; [G] Latrobe, PA Saint Vincent Archabbey.
Martinez, Michael '89 (TUC) Tucson, AZ Christ the King Chapel; Air National Guard Chaplains.
Martinez, Miguel Angel '01 (CHI)[W] Des Plaines, IL Maryville–Our Lady of Guadalupe Chapel.
Martinez, Omar *o.p.* '00 (SB) Cathedral City, CA St. Louis.
Martinez, Oscar '06 (SLC) Team; Cedar City, UT Christ the King LLC 203.
Martinez, Pablo A. '09 (NEW) Plainfield, NJ St. Mary.
Martinez, Pastor *o.s.a.* '78 (LAR) Laredo, TX St.

Vincent de Paul.
Martinez, Peter '04 (CC) On Special Assignment; [A] Corpus Christi, TX John Paul II High School; Corpus Christi, TX SS. Cyril and Methodius.
Martinez, Rafael Suazo '64 (SJN) San Juan, PR San Juan Evangelista.
Martinez, Roberto *o.f.m.cap.* '92 (SJN)[C] San Juan, PR Fraternidad San Antonio; San Juan, PR San Antonio.
Martinez, Roberto *o.f.m.cap.* '96 (WDC)[B] Washington, DC St. Francis Friary–Capuchin College.
Martínez, Roy F. *o.f.m.cap.* '85 (SJN) San Juan, PR San Antonio; [E] Rio Piedras, PR Hospital San Francisco; [C] San Juan, PR Fraternidad San Antonio.
Martinez, Roy *o.f.m.cap.* (SJN) Franciscan Third Order (Secular Franciscan Order).
Martinez, Timothy A. '90 (SFE) Chancellor; College of Consultors; Presbyteral Council of the Archdiocese of Santa Fe; Finance Council; Albuquerque, NM Our Lady of Fatima.
Martinez, Vidal M. *o.s.m.* '75 (CHI)[N] Chicago, IL Order of Friar Servants of Mary (Servites) United States of America Province, Inc.; Chicago, IL Our Lady of Sorrows, Basilica of; [N] Chicago, IL Servite Secular Order; Chicago, IL.
Martinez, Virgilio '65 (SJN) Bayamon, PR Santa Rosa de Lima.
Martinez, Zacharis '04 (ARL) Woodstock, VA St. John Bosco.
Martinez–Irigoyen, Jesus M. '67 (GAL) South Houston, TX Our Lady of Grace.
Martinez–Solis, Eduardo '07 (CHI) Indian Creek, IL St. Mary of Vernon.
Martinez Adorno, Ivan '08 (ARE) Arecibo, PR Our Lady of Hope.
Martinez de Espronceda, Jesus *o.a.r.* '62 (LSC) Las Cruces, NM Our Lady of Health; [B] Mesilla, NM Augustinian Recollect Fathers.
Martínez Galvez, Mariano *o.m.i.* '86 (SJN) San Juan, PR Maria Reina del Mundo.
Martinez Medina, Omar J. *o.p.* '00 (PCE) Ponce, PR Christ the King.
Martinez Tobon, Jose Dario '87 (SJN) Toa Baja, PR Ntra. Sra. de la Candelaria.
Martínez Veliz, Alfredo (FAJ) Canovanas, PR Resurreccion del Señor.
Martinez y Alire, Rev. Msgr. Jerome '76 (SFE) Santa Fe, NM The Cathedral Basilica of St. Francis of Assisi; Santa Fe, NM Cristo Rey; Vicars Forane (Deans); Promoter of Justice; Presbyteral Council of the Archdiocese of Santa Fe; Cerrillos, NM St. Joseph.
Martini, Richard '80 (LA) Chairman; Our Lady of the Angels Region; Los Angeles, CA Transfiguration.
Martinito, Felix S. '90 (CHY) Guernsey, WY St. Anthony's.
Martinka, Stanley V. '61 (NU) Retired.
Martinkovic, Joseph '54 (ALN) Retired.
Martino, José D. Rodriguez (PCE)[B] The Pontifical Catholic University of Puerto Rico.
Martinosky, Joseph A. '57 (STU) Retired.
Martin Pinillos, Ricardo '03 (MIL) Study Leave.
Martins, Carlos '09 (GAL)[S] Houston, TX Catholic Charismatic Center.
Martins, Celso *c.ss.r.* (NEW) Newark, NJ St. James.
Martins, Orlando (CHI) Oak Lawn, IL St. Linus.
Martinson, George G. *s.j.* '73 (FgM) Los Gatos, CA Society of Jesus.
Martinson, Kieth Barry *s.j.* '75 (FgM) Los Gatos, CA Society of Jesus.
Martiny, Leon Martin A. *o.p.* '98 (FgM) New York, NY Province of St. Joseph (Eastern).
Martis, Douglas A. '89 (CHI)[A] Mundelein, IL The Liturgical Institute; [A] Mundelein, IL University of St. Mary of the Lake/Mundelein Seminary.
Martis, Douglas '89 (JOL) On Duty Outside the Diocese.
Martis, Samuel '83 (BGP)[M] Norwalk, CT Notre Dame Convalescent Home.
Martlock, Loville N. '63 (BUF) Retired.
Martocchio, Rev. Msgr. Peter T. '57 (BO) Weymouth, MA St. Jerome; Senior Priests. Retired.
Marton, Bernard *o.cist.* '67 (DAL)[J] Irving, TX Cistercian Abbey of Our Lady of Dallas; Irving, TX.
Martorano, Nicholas *o.s.a.* '77 (PH) Philadelphia, PA St. Nicholas of Tolentine; [Y] Philadelphia, PA Augustinian Community (O.S.A.).
Martos, Rafael E. '96 (SP) Cursillo, Spanish; Plant City, FL St. Clement.
Martyniuk, Pawlo '92 (STF) Hartford, CT St. Michael; League of Ukrainian Catholics; Priest Personnel Board.
Maruca, Dominic W. *s.j.* '58 (BAL)[S] Baltimore, MD Jesuit Community of Loyola University, Inc.
Marucci, Rev. Msgr. Louis A. '87 (CAM) Haddonfield, NJ The Church of St. Vincent Pallotti, Haddon Township, N.J.
Marullo, Lawrence E. '75 (OG) Constableville, NY St. Mary; West Leyden, NY St. Mary's Nativity.
Marus, Andrew G. '71 (BGP) Stratford, CT Holy Name of Jesus.
Marusceac, Vladimir '88 (STF) Cohoes, NY SS. Peter and Paul; Albany.
Marut, Paul *o.f.m.conv.* '72 (HBG) Shamokin, PA Mother Cabrini.
Marut, Thomas '74 (STU) Carrollton, OH Our Lady of Mercy; Waynesburg, OH St. Mary.
Maruthukunnel, James *c.m.i.* '77 (SAL) Park, KS St. Agnes Parish; Park, KS Sacred Heart Parish; Grinnell, KS Immaculate Conception of the Blessed Virigin Mary Parish.
Marva, Robert *o.f.m.cap.* '97 (CLV) Cleveland, OH St. Agnes – Our Lady of Fatima; [N] Cleveland, OH St. Paul Friary; Cleveland, OH Conversion of St. Paul; [N] Cleveland, OH St. Agnes–Our Lady of Fatima.
Marx, Louis N. '66 (SB) Guasti, CA San Secondo d'Asti.
Marx, Paul *o.s.b.* '47 (SCL)[I] Collegeville, MN St. John's Abbey, of the Order of St. Benedict.
Marx, Paul *o.m.i.* '65 (FgM) Washington, DC AMERICAN OBLATE MISSIONS.
Marx, Robert '88 (SJ) On Leave of Absence.
Maryanski, Fabian J. '71 (BUF) Vicars; Sloan, NY St. Andrew; Finance Council.
Maryland, Joseph A. '40 (E) Retired.
Marzan, Eddie Rivera '91 (SJN) San Juan, PR San Luis Gonzaga; [E] San Juan, PR Centro Medico de P.R.
Marzetti, Raul Lopez '85 (PHX) Phoenix, AZ SS. Simon and Jude Roman Catholic Cathedral.
Marzocchi, Mario *s.s.s.* '84 (SAT) San Antonio, TX St. Joseph.
Marzolf, John G. *s.j.* '66 (NY)[EE] New York, NY Murray–Weigel Hall.
Marzolf, John G. *s.j.* '66 (BUF) Buffalo, NY St. Michael.
Marzynski, Janusz (DET) Detroit, MI St. John Hospital.
Masabakhwa, Raphael '95 (DM) Neola, IA St. Patrick; Neola, IA St. Columbanus.
Masad, Frederick F. '60 (CHR) Columbia, SC St. John Neumann.
Masakowski, Edward M. '57 (SCR) Retired.
Mascardo, Editho '83 (STO) Hughson, CA St. Anthony Church of Hughson (Pastor of).
Mascarella, Patrick J. '66 (BR) Retired.
Mascarenhas, Oswald A. *s.j.* '66 (DET)[K] Detroit, MI Jesuit Community at the University of Detroit Mercy.
Mascari, Michael A. *o.p.* '87 (CHI)[N] Chicago Dominicans (Provincial Office); [N] St. Pius V Priory; [W] Chicago, IL St. Thomas Aquinas Foundation; Chicago, IL Province of St. Albert the Great (Central); Chicago, IL.
Masciocchi, Robert *c.s.s.* '54 (BO)[U] Waltham, MA Stigmatine Fathers & Brothers Provincial House; [W] Waltham, MA Espousal Retreat House and Conference Center.
Mascioli, Joseph M. '57 (WH) Retired.
Mascolino, Charles E. '54 (STU) Presbyteral Council; College of Consultors Retired.
Mascorro, Miguel *sch.p.* '96 (LA) Los Angeles, CA St. Lucy; Los Angeles, CA Santa Teresita.
Masello, David W. '78 (PRO) Warren, RI St. Alexander; Defenders of the Bond.
Mash, Wesley M. '90 (PBR) Tarentum, PA Sts. Peter and Paul.
Masiar, Paul E. '69 (ALN)[J] Bethlehem, PA Holy Family Villa.
Masich, Michael *o.f.m.cap.* '98 (BAL) Cumberland, MD SS. Peter and Paul; [S] Cumberland, MD SS. Peter and Paul Friary.
Masiello, John *s.d.b.* '58 (SP)[P] Tampa, FL Salesian Society of Florida, Inc.
Masiello, Rev. Msgr. Joseph P. '69 (NEW) Westfield, NJ Holy Trinity; Members.
Masinde, Steven '00 (NY) Bronx, NY SS. Philip and James.
Maslach, Paul *o.f.m.* '62 (MIL) Milwaukee, WI Sacred Heart; Councilors:.
Maslak, Gregory '72 (PHU) Bristol, PA St. Mary's.
Maslanka, Piotr J. '04 (NEW) Elizabeth, NJ St. Hedwig's.
Maslar, George *o.f.m.conv.* (BGP) Bridgeport, CT Bridgeport Health Care.
Maslejak, Andrzej *s.ch.* '79 (CHI) Chicago, IL Holy Trinity Mission.
Maslowski, Krzysztof '88 (NEW) Roselle, NJ Church of St. Joseph the Carpenter.
Maslowsky, Michael '86 (P)[K] Portland, OR St. Anthony Village (activity of St. Anthony Village Enterprise); [K] Portland, OR Assumption Village (activity of St. Anthony Village Enterprise).
Masluk, Alexander '79 (PH) Philadelphia, PA Saint Martha.
Masnicki, Marek '92 (NOR) Middletown, CT St. Mary of Czestochowa.
Maso, Dario *s.x.* '82 (PAT)[N] Wayne Xaverian Missionary Fathers; Wayne, NJ XAVERIAN MISSIONARY FATHERS.
Mason, Brian G. '93 (MIL) Milwaukee, WI Old St. Mary; Milwaukee, WI Three Holy Women Catholic Parish.
Mason, Carl '64 (NY) Manhattan, NY Hospital for Special Surgery.
Mason, Charlon O. '79 (GR) Pewamo, MI St. Joseph's.
Mason, Dennis *o.f.m.conv.* '78 (BGP) Danbury, CT Sacred Heart of Jesus.
Mason, James E. '01 (SFS) Sioux Falls, SD St. Lambert; Vice Chancellors; Diocesan Consultors; Presbyteral Council.
Mason, Louis *o.p.* '64 (NY) Manhattan, NY Memorial Sloan Kettering Cancer Center; New York, NY St. Catherine of Siena; Manhattan, NY New York Presbyterian Hospital.
Mason, Mark E. '75 (OKL) Weatherford, OK St. Eugene's; [K] Weatherford, OK Southwestern Oklahoma State University.
Mason, Matthew J. (MAN) Laconia, NH St. Joseph; Lakeport, NH Our Lady of the Lakes; Laconia, NH Sacred Heart.
Mason, Robert E. '56 (RVC) Massapequa Park, NY Our Lady of Lourdes Retired.
Mason, William *o.m.i.* '71 (MIA) Miami, FL Christ the King.
Mass, Ronald J. '70 (CHI) Palos Heights, IL Incarnation.
Massa, James '86 (BRK) Released from Diocesan Assignment.
Massa, Mark S. *s.j.* '80 (NY)[EE] Cardinal Spellman Hall, Jesuit Community.
Massar, Richard A. '69 (BUF)[O] Lackawanna, NY Bishop Head Residence Retired.
Massarella, Francis A. '46 (CIN) Priests Commended to a Life of Prayer and Penance Retired.
Massari, John Charles *c.s.* (NY) New York, NY Our Lady of Pompeii.
Massaro, Gabriel *o.f.m.cap.* '66 (NY)[B] Beacon, NY St. Lawrence of Brindisi Friary; [EE] White Plains, NY St. Conrad Friary.
Massaro, Michael *c.s.c.* '81 (PMB) Vero Beach, FL Holy Cross.
Massaro, Thomas J. *s.j.* '93 (NY)[EE] New York, NY "America;" Residence and publication office of the America Press.
Massaro, Thomas *s.j.* '93 (BO)[U] Cambridge, MA Rahner House.
Massart, James P. '66 (GB) Special Assignment; Ecumenical Liaison.
Massawe, Andrew *c.s.c.* '03 (FTW)[H] Notre Dame Congregation of Holy Cross, Indiana Province, Provincial House.
Massawe, Aristides *c.s.c.* '02 (FTW)[H] Notre Dame Congregation of Holy Cross, Indiana Province, Provincial House.
Massett, Rev. Msgr. Robert D. '66 (NO) Metairie, LA St. Mary Magdalen; Council of Catholic School Cooperative Clubs; Serra Club of East Jefferson.
Massetti, Philip *o.s.j.* '76 (SAC)[A] Loomis, CA Mount St. Joseph Novitiate and Seminary.
Massey, Robert E. '66 (MIL) West Allis, WI Holy Assumption.
Massi, Anthony '84 (MIA) Retired.
Massicotte, Bernard *o.s.b.cam.* '57 (MRY)[F] Big Sur, CA New Camaldoli Hermitage.
Massie, Rev. Msgr. Guy A. '83 (BRK) Brooklyn, NY St. Andrew the Apostle; Ecumenical and Interreligious Affairs, Diocesan Commission for; Committee for Catholic–Jewish Relations; Catholic Muslim Dialogue.
Massillon, Nazaire '00 (ORL) Kissimmee, FL St. Catherine of Siena.
Massimino, Jerome *o.f.m.* '77 (NY) New York, NY St. Francis of Assisi; [EE] New York, NY Saint Francis Monastery, Inc.; [II] New York, NY St. Francis Monastery Breadline for the Poor, Inc.
Massingale, Bryan N. '83 (MIL) Special Assignment.
Masson, Paul R. *m.m.* '72 (NY) Maryknoll, NY; Maryknoll, NY; [EE] Maryknoll Maryknoll Fathers and Brothers.
Massoth, Rt. Rev. Charles *o.s.b.* '51 (OKL)[I] Shawnee, OK St. Gregory's Abbey; Shawnee, OK Retired.
Massucci, Joseph D. '70 (CIN)[D] Dayton, OH The University of Dayton; On Duty Outside the Diocese.
Mastalir, Peter '92 (GB) Absent on Leave, Sick or Disabled.
Masters, Burke '02 (JOL) Vocations; [O] Joliet, IL Fiat House of Discernment.
Masters, Gerard G. '66 (HRT) Madison, CT St. Margaret.
Masterson, Thomas D. *s.j.* '64 (PH)[Y] Loyola Center and Manresa Hall.
Mastey, Gregory '95 (SCL) Vocations.
Mastin, Mark *s.c.j.* '07 (MIL)[P] Milwaukee, WI SCJ Community; [P] Hales Corners, WI Priests of the Sacred Heart.
Mastrangelo, David F. *s.j.* '87 (DET)[E] Detroit, MI Loyola High School; [E] Detroit, MI Loyola Work Experience Program, Inc.
Mastrangelo, Mario *o.f.m.cap.* '58 (PCE) Ponce, PR Santa Teresita; [B] The Pontifical Catholic University of Puerto Rico; [E] Ponce, PR Fraternidad Santa Teresita, Frailes Capuchinos; Episcopal Vicar for Religious; Pittsburgh, PA Province of St. Augustine.
Mastrangelo, Nicholas '64 (PIT) Munhall, PA St. Rita; Munhall, PA St. Therese of Lisieux; West Mifflin, PA Resurrection.

Mastria, Angelo *o.carm.* '58 (TUC)[A] Tucson, AZ Salpointe Catholic High School; [B] Tucson, AZ Chaplaincy–Pastoral Ministry to Non–Denominational Nursing Homes; [D] Tucson, AZ Carmelite Priory.
Mastrian, Mark J. '87 (E) Grampian, PA St. Bonaventure; Curwensville, PA St. Timothy.
Mastrobuono, Peter *s.c.j.* '66 (GAL) Houston, TX Our Lady of Guadalupe.
Mastroeni, Anthony J. '72 (PAT)[Q] Paterson, NJ Cor Jesu Mission Fund Inc; Theological Commission; Unassigned.
Mastrolia, Arthur '87 (NY) Congers, NY St. Paul.
Masutti, Federico *f.s.s.p.* '07 (SD) San Diego, CA St. Anne.
Mata, Luke J. '06 (POD) Los Angeles.
Mata, Luke '06 (LA)[W] Los Angeles, CA Prelature of the Holy Cross and Opus Dei.
Mata, Octavio '05 (LA) Los Angeles, CA Immaculate Conception.
Matanic, George M. *o.p.* '70 (SB) Riverside, CA St. Andrew Newman Center; Elected Members; [I] Riverside, CA St. Vincent Ferrer House; [M] Riverside, CA St. Andrew Newman Center.
Matanzonga, Bienvenu *s.j.* '06 (BAL)[S] Baltimore, MD Jesuit Community of Loyola University, Inc.
Matarazzo, Rev. Msgr. Francis '67 (PAT) Clifton, NJ St. Brendan Retired.
Matas, Rev. Msgr. Juan '65 (LA) Montebello, CA Our Lady of the Miraculous Medal; Cursillo Movement.
Matash, Rev. Msgr. Edward M. '56 (NEW) Bayonne, NJ Saint Michael and Saint Joseph; [M] Rutherford, NJ St. John Vianney Residence for Priests Retired.
Matejek, John M. '03 (ATL) Kennesaw, GA St. Catherine of Siena.
Mateljan, Roy A. '67 (MIL) Retired.
Mateo, Marlon *o.carm.* '09 (TUC)[D] Tucson, AZ Carmelite Priory.
Mateo, Mateo *ss.cc.* '47 (SJN) Guaynabo, PR Sagrados Corazones.
Mateo, Miguel *s.f.* '81 (WDC)[B] Silver Spring, MD Holy Family Seminary.
Mateo, Victor Santiago *s.t.* '82 (FgM) Silver Spring, MD MISSIONARY SERVANTS OF THE MOST HOLY TRINITY.
Mateos, Tomas *s.f.o.* '45 (BWN) Retired.
Mateos, Tomas (BWN)[K] Mission, TX Fraternity of Our Lady of Guadalupe Secular Franciscan Order.
Matera, Frank J. '68 (WDC) On Duty Outside the Archdiocese; [C] Catholic University of America, The.
Matera, Philip T. '51 (TR) Retired.
Maternoski, Robert '62 (JOL) Retired.
Materu, Paul *a.l.c.p.* '98 (B) Meridian, ID Holy Apostles.
Mateus, Norberto '81 (ATL) On Leave of Absence.
Mateus–Ariza, Hector '09 (BAL) Westminster, MD St. John.
Mathai, Mani '80 (TYL) Jefferson, TX Immaculate Conception.
Mathaner, John P. '93 (E) Oil City, PA Our Lady Help of Christians.
Matheny, William K. '96 (WH) Morgantown, WV St. John University Parish, Newman Hall.
Mathers, Rev. Msgr. Douglas J. '85 (NY) Vice–Chancellors; Conciliation and Arbitration, Office of; New York, NY St. John the Evangelist.
Mathesius, William P. '76 (WIL) Retired.
Matheu, Santiago '75 (MIA) Cursillos de Cristiandad (Spanish).
Mathew, Abraham P. '97 (BRK) Jamaica, NY St. Nicholas of Tolentine; On Leave/Unassigned.
Mathew, Biju *c.m.i.* '01 (BRK) East Glendale, NY Sacred Heart.
Mathew, Biju *c.f.i.c.* '98 (STP) St. Paul, MN St. Mary; [K] St. Paul, MN Congregation of the Sons of the Immaculate Conception.
Mathew, Charles *o.f.m.* '74 (NSH) Clarksville, TN Immaculate Conception.
Mathew, James '97 (SYM) Cortlandt Manor, NY Knanaya Catholic Mission of Westchester and Bronx, NY; Cortlandt Manor, NY Knanaya Catholic Mission of Rockland, NY.
Mathew, Joel *o.i.c.* '93 (MIA) Miami Beach, FL St. Patrick.
Mathew, Joshy *c.m.i.* '05 (SAC) Roseville, CA St. Rose of Lima.
Mathew, Pius T. '90 (AUS) Waco, TX St. Louis.
Mathew, Sunny *o.carm.* '97 (NY) New York, NY St. John the Martyr.
Mathew, T. Shane '05 (E)[C] Erie, PA Cathedral Preparatory School.
Mathew, Thomas (TYL) On Duty Outside the Diocese.
Mathews, James D. '62 (SY) Syracuse, NY St. Lucy.
Mathews, Michael C. *c.s.c.* '99 (FTW) South Bend, IN Holy Cross; Provincial Councilors:; [H] Notre Dame Congregation of Holy Cross, Indiana Province, Provincial House; Members; [H] Notre Dame, IN Congregation of Holy Cross, Indiana Province, Provincial House.
Mathews, Ronald J. '75 (ALX) On Duty Outside the Diocese.
Mathewson, Dean '73 (COL) Columbus, OH St. Thomas the Apostle.
Mathewson, Robert B. *s.j.* '62 (SJ)[D] San Jose, CA Bellarmine College Preparatory.
Mathias, Edwin J. '67 (TR) Browns Mills, NJ St. Ann.
Mathias, Gregory A. '91 (FR) North Dartmouth, MA St. Julie Billiart; Family Ministry.
Mathias, Jayme *o.f.m.conv.* '01 (AUS) Austin, TX Cristo Rey.
Mathie, D. Edward *s.j.* '68 (MIL)[X] Milwaukee, WI Marquette University/Campus Ministry; [P] Milwaukee, WI Jesuit Community at Marquette University.
Mathie, John *s.j.* (MIL)[C] Marquette University.
Mathieu, Rev. Msgr. Rene T. '77 (PRT) Diocesan Consultors; Personnel Board; Saco, ME Good Shepherd Parish.
Mathieu, Robert E. '76 (GLP) Aztec, NM St. Joseph; Bloomfield, NM St. Rose of Lima; Bloomfield, NM St. Mary; Aztec, NM Holy Trinity; Cursillos.
Mathis, Christian '00 (KNX) Lenoir City, TN St. Thomas the Apostle.
Mathis, George *g.h.m.* '55 (CIN)[N] Cincinnati Headquarters of Glenmary Home Missioners Retired.
Mathis, R. Paul '72 (SY) Cleveland, NY St. Mary of the Assumption.
Mathur, Keith A. '09 (ALN) Allentown, PA St. Thomas More.
Mathy, H. Francis *s.j.* '58 (FgM) Milwaukee, WI Society of Jesus.
Matocha, Rev. Msgr. John L. '47 (SAT) Retired.
Matondo, Thomas *c.i.c.m.* '82 (BWN) Progreso, TX Holy Spirit.
Matonti, Charles J. '60 (BRK) Retired.
Matos, Angel R. '97 (WOR) Worcester, MA St. Paul Cathedral; Diocesan Hispanic Apostolate; St. Paul.
Matro, Justin M. *o.s.b.* '89 (GBG)[A] Latrobe, PA St. Vincent Seminary; [G] Latrobe, PA Saint Vincent Archabbey.
Matt, Erwin H. '56 (MIL) Retired.
Matt, J. Wilson '45 (LAF) Retired.
Matt, Joseph H. '74 (KC) Independence, MO St. Joseph the Worker; Judicial Vicar and Tribunal Director; Special Assignment.
Matta, Pablo '90 (ELP) El Paso, TX San Judas Tadeo; Canutillo, TX St. Patrick; Presbyteral Council; [J] El Paso, TX Cursillos de Cristianidad.
Mattaliano, James R. *s.j.* '90 (BO)[W] Weston, MA Campion Renewal Center; [W] Weston, MA Campion Renewal Center; [U] Weston, MA Campion Jesuit Community.
Mattar, Ghassan *m.l.m.* '96 (OLL) San Antonio, TX St. George Maronite Catholic Church; [A] Houston, TX The Congregation of Maronite Lebanese Missionaries.
Mattas, Louis '60 (SAL) Retired.
Mattathilanickal, Cyriac *m.s.* '99 (FR)[G] Attleboro, MA La Salette Shrine; [I] Attleboro, MA La Salette Retreat Center.
Mattathilanickal, George (NOR)[E] Windham, CT St. Joseph Living Center; Higganum, CT St. Peter; Killingworth, CT St. Lawrence.
Matteo, Rev. Msgr. James P. '72 (PH) Retired.
Mattern, Joseph A. '59 (GB) Redgranite, WI Sacred Heart of Jesus; Redgranite, WI St. Mark Retired.
Matteucig, Giuseppe *s.x.* '84 (BO)[U] Holliston, MA Xaverian Missionaries.
Mattey, Joseph J. '65 (SCR) Freeland, PA Our Lady of the Immaculate Conception.
Matthew, Abraham '97 (BRK) Catholic Hindu/Buddhist Dialogue.
Matthew, Antony *t.o.r.* '96 (FWT) Fort Worth, TX St. Thomas.
Matthews, Andre '84 (ROM) College of Consultors; Cleveland, OH St. Helena; Vicar for Clergy.
Matthews, Armand *o.m.i.* '49 (BWN) Brownsville, TX Immaculate Conception Cathedral.
Matthews, James '74 (OAK) Oakland, CA St. Benedict; Deanery #12.
Matthews, Jay '74 (OAK) Priest Representatives.
Matthews, Michael C. *c.s.c.* '99 (FTW) South Bend, IN St. Stanislaus.
Matthys, Donald R. *s.j.* '68 (MIL)[P] Milwaukee, WI Jesuit Community at Marquette University.
Matti, Wisam '97 (EST) Southfield, MI Our Lady of Chaldeans Cathedral, Mother of God Chaldean Parish; Eparchial College of Consultors.
Mattice, George F. '64 (SY) Retired.
Mattimoe, Edward J. *s.j.* '65 (DET)[K] Detroit Jesuit Provincial Office–Detroit Province of the Society of Jesus.
Mattimoe, Ned *s.j.* '65 (RVC) Huntington, NY St. Patrick's.
Mattimore, John J. *s.j.* '88 (BUF) Buffalo, NY St. Michael; U.S. Department of Immigration & Naturalization Federal Detention Center.
Mattina, Louis A. '95 (MET)[I] Somerset, NJ Maria Regina Residence; Air Force Reserve Chaplains.
Mattingly, Basil *o.s.b.* '46 (SD)[J] Oceanside, CA Prince of Peace Abbey.
Mattingly, John F. *s.s.* '48 (BAL)[O] Baltimore, MD St. Charles Villa; [S] Baltimore Society of St. Sulpice, Province of the United States Retired.
Mattingly, John S. '72 (WDC) Leonardtown, MD St. Francis Xavier.
Mattingly, Lawrence *o.f.m.conv.* '64 (SAT)[B] San Antonio, TX San Damiano Friary, Prenovitiate House of Formation; [L] San Antonio, TX San Damiano Friary; San Antonio, TX Christ the King.
Mattingly, Robert B. '68 (VEN) Retired.
Mattingly, Thomas E. '97 (RIC) Harrisonburg, VA Blessed Sacrament.
Mattison, Thomas V. '73 (BUR) Judges; Manchester Center, VT Christ Our Savior Parish; Elected Members.
Mattler, Albert A. '56 (STL) St. Louis, MO St. Simon the Apostle.
Mattox, Randall '01 (ATL) Ellijay, GA Good Samaritan Catholic Church; Deans.
Mattscheck, John J. '53 (CIN) Consultors; Ex Officio Members Retired.
Mattson, Steven M. '05 (LAN) Priests' Assignment Commission; Department of Education and Catechesis; Superintendent of Schools; Swartz Creek, MI St. Mary.
Mattulke, Arthur E. '97 (BUF) Vicars; Oakfield, NY St. Padre Pio.
Matty, Richard A. '83 (ELP) El Paso, TX St. Patrick Cathedral; Diocesan Review Board; St. Peter; Priests' Personnel Advisory Committee.
Matula, Lawrence '62 (VIC) El Campo, TX St. Robert Bellarmine.
Matula, Stanley '59 (SY) Syracuse, NY Sacred Heart Basilica.
Matulewicz, Ronald '59 (ALB) Retired.
Matunog, Reynaldo B. '91 (LA) Defenders of the Bond; Los Angeles, CA Sacred Heart; Adjutant Judicial Vicar; Judges.
Maturi, Gregory A. (RIC) Charlottesville, VA St. Thomas Aquinas.
Maturi, Gregory *o.p.* '94 (Y) Youngstown, OH St. Dominic.
Matus, Thomas *o.s.b.cam.* '70 (OAK)[M] Berkeley, CA Incarnation Monastery, Camaldolese Benedictines.
Matus, Thomas *o.s.b.conv.* '70 (MRY)[F] Big Sur New Camaldoli Hermitage.
Matus, Walter J. '70 (AUS) Burlington, TX St. Joseph; Burlington, TX SS. Cyril and Methodius Catholic Church – Marak, Texas.
Matusak, Rev. Msgr. Michael W. '75 (GBG) Uniontown, PA St. Therese, the Little Flower of Jesus; Deaneries; College of Consultors; Bishop's Priests Council; College of Deans.
Matuscak, Jerzy *c.r.* (CHI) Bridgeview, IL St. Fabian.
Matusiak, Waldemar *s.ch.* '95 (STP) Minneapolis, MN Holy Cross.
Matusz, Michael A. '89 (CLV) Garfield Heights, OH SS. Peter and Paul.
Matuszak, Edward S. (E) Retired.
Matuszak, Edward S. '55 (LFT) Retired.
Matuszak, Walter L. '58 (BUF) Darien Center, NY Immaculate Heart of Mary Retired.
Matveenko, Michael J. '82 (CAM) Egg Harbor City, NJ St. Nicholas' Church, Egg Harbor City; Galloway, NJ The Church of the Assumption.
Maty, Robert J. '57 (BGP) Retired.
Matya, Robert A. '95 (LIN) Lincoln, NE St. Thomas Aquinas; [I] Lincoln, NE University of Nebraska, Newman Club; Diocesan Consultors; Presbyteral Council; Bishop's Lay Committee for Vocations; Newman Center University of Nebraska; Serra Club; Vocations.
Matysik, Robert B. '84 (CAM) Atlantic City, NJ Church of St. Nicholas, Atlantic City, N.J.
Matz, David S. *c.p.p.s.* '95 (SFR) San Rafael, CA St. Raphael.
Matz, David *c.pp.s.* '95 (OAK)[M] Berkeley, CA Society of the Precious Blood (Province of Kansas City).
Matz, Joseph A. '64 (SCR) Retired.
Matz, Leo '61 (MRY) Retired.
Matz, Rev. Msgr. Michael J. '84 (PH) Flourtown, PA St. Genevieve.
Matzek, William J. '63 (LC) River Falls, WI Nativity of the Blessed Virgin Mary.
Matzinger, Robert J. *c.s.b.* '57 (GAL) Houston, TX St. Clare of Assisi.
Matzko, David G. *s.j.* '79 (RC) Rapid City, SD St. Isaac Jogues; [C] Howes, SD Kino Jesuit Community; Deaneries.
Mau, Nguyen Duc *c.ss.r.* '70 (LA)[P] Baldwin Park Vietnamese Redemptorist Mission.
Mauck, George A. '77 (BEL) Carlyle, IL St. Mary; Carlyle, IL St. Teresa of Avila; Centralia, IL Centralia Correctional Center.
Mauel, James E. *s.j.* '57 (MIL)[P] Milwaukee, WI Jesuit Community at Marquette University.
Mauer, Elmar *o.m.i* '62 (BEL)[F] Belleville, IL Missionary Oblates of Mary Immaculate – St. Henry's Oblate Residence.
Maughan, Richard N. '72 (NO) New Orleans, LA St. James Major.
Mauk, Dismas *s.v.d.* (LAF) On Special Assignment.
Maullon, Alberto A. '82 (GAL) Houston, TX St. Paul.
Maung, Chrysostom Ah '74 (WCH) Columbus, KS St. Joseph; Columbus, KS St. Rose; Columbus, KS St.

Patrick; Columbus, KS St. Bridget's.
Maung, John S. '63 (IND) Unassigned.
Mauntel, Robert J. '49 (CIN) Retired.
Maura, Peter James (CHY) Sundance, WY St. Paul.
Maurer, Carl R. '01 (SAT) San Antonio, TX El Carmen Catholic Church.
Maurer, Daniel J. '97 (PIT) Pittsburgh, PA SS. Simon and Jude.
Maurer, Jacob M. '09 (SEA) Tacoma, WA Holy Rosary; Tacoma, WA Sacred Heart; Tacoma, WA St. Ann; Tacoma, WA St. Joseph; Tacoma, WA Visitation; Tacoma, WA St. John of the Woods.
Maurer, Jeffrey E. '05 (NY) Monroe, NY Sacred Heart Church; Washingtonville, NY St. Mary.
Maurer, Russell J. '60 (PIT) Retired.
Mauric, William *s.p.s.* '92 (NEW)[M] Cliffside Park, NJ St. Patrick's Missionary Society.
Mauricci, Bruno '90 (LAV) Henderson, NV St. Peter the Apostle.
Maurice, Francis *o.f.m.cap.* '88 (NY) New Rochelle, NY Holy Name of Jesus.
Maurice, Francis '98 (NY) Staten Island, NY Our Lady Help of Christians.
Mauriello, Rev. Canon Matthew '88 (BGP) Greenwich, CT St. Roch.
Mauritzen, Joseph H. '96 (FR) Woods Hole, MA St. Joseph's; Falmouth Hospital.
Maurizio, Joseph D. '87 (ALT) Central City, PA Our Lady Queen of Angels.
Maurus, Irsan *s.j.* '03 (BAL)[S] Baltimore, MD Ferdinand Wheeler Jesuit Community.
Maus, Christopher P. '93 (DET) Clarkston, MI St. Daniel.
Maus, Le Roy '66 (SCL) Retired.
Maus, Mark T. '91 (STP) Special Assignment.
Mauthe, Richard '58 (GB) Retired.
Mavin, Fabio *c.ss.r.* (BAL) Annapolis, MD St. Mary.
Mawhinney, John J. *s.j.* '65 (PH)[Y] Loyola Center and Manresa Hall.
Mawn, Francis X. '85 (BO) Lawrence, MA Corpus Christi.
Maxa, Edward J. '59 (CHI) Chicago, IL Immaculate Conception Retired.
Maxfield, Leo *m.s.* '55 (MAN)[K] Enfield, NH Shrine of Our Lady of La Salette; [N] Enfield, NH Shrine of Our Lady of La Salette Retired.
Maxim, Craig '91 (KCK) Shawnee, KS Sacred Heart.
Maximino, Diego *m.i.c.* '94 (JOL) Plano, IL St. Mary.
Maxwell, Daniel J. '09 (BAK) Bend, OR St. Francis of Assisi.
Maxwell, Finbar *s.s.c.* '88 (OM)[K] St. Columbans Missionary Society of St. Columban.
Maxwell, John '59 (OAK) El Cerrito, CA St. John the Baptist.
Maxwell, Palmer '88 (SAT) On Sabbatical.
May, Anthony C. '75 (SD) San Diego, CA St. Mary Magdalene Retired.
May, Darrin M. '99 (WCH) Fort Scott, KS Mary Queen of Angels.
May, Douglas E. *m.m.* '86 (FgM) Maryknoll, NY MARYKNOLL.
May, Gregory *c.ss.r.* '88 (GAL) Houston, TX Holy Ghost.
May, Herbert J. '75 (LAF) Judges.
May, Rev. Archimandrite Herbert J. '75 (LKC) Welsh, LA Our Lady of Seven Dolors; Deans; Diocesan Consultors; Promoter of Justice.
May, Rev. Archimandrite Herbert '75 (LKC) Presbyteral Council.
May, Herbert (NTN) Judges.
May, James '98 (STA) Bunnell, FL St. Stephen; Palm Coast, FL St. Elizabeth Ann Seton.
May, Michael K. *s.j.* '93 (STL)[C] Saint Louis University; [O] St. Louis, MO Jesuit Community Corporation at Saint Louis University – Jesuit Hall.
May, Raymond '93 (KCK) Emporia, KS St. Catherine; [L] Emporia, KS.
May, Ronald P. '86 (HRT) Commission for Priests' Retreats; Appointed; Southington, CT St. Dominic.
May, Thomas P. '83 (CHI) Niles, IL St. John Brebeuf.
Maya–Chavez, Manuel *o.s.m.* '58 (CHI)[N] Chicago Order of Friar Servants of Mary (Servites) United States of America Province, Inc.
Mayall, Daniel G. '77 (CHI) Chicago, IL Holy Name Cathedral; Deans.
Maybrier, Michael J. '86 (WCH) Mulvane, KS St. Michael the Archangel.
Maydya, Gregory (SJP) Alternates.
Mayefske, Thomas J. '62 (GB) Retired.
Mayefske, Thomas '62 (SFE) Presbyteral Council of the Archdiocese of Santa Fe Retired.
Mayemba, Bienvenu *s.j.* '04 (BO)[U] Newton, MA The Jesuit Community at Boston College.
Mayer, Cory A. '09 (VEN) Venice, FL Epiphany Cathedral.
Mayer, David *s.v.d.* '66 (FgM) Techny, IL.
Mayer, Douglas J. '86 (GRY) Valparaiso, IN St. Elizabeth Seton.
Mayer, Gary A. '09 (DUB) Dubuque, IA Holy Ghost; Dubuque, IA Holy Trinity; Dubuque, IA Sacred Heart.
Mayer, James W. *o.de.m.* '93 (PH) Philadelphia, PA Our Lady of Lourdes.
Mayer, John L. '64 (STL) Sunset Hills, MO St. Justin Martyr.
Mayer, Jules Anthony '64 (LA) Retired.
Mayer, Michael A. '98 (ROC) Rochester, NY Light of Christ Roman Catholic Parish.
Mayer, Rev. Msgr. Richard G. '61 (E) Erie, PA Blessed Sacrament.
Mayer, Robert *o.m.i.* '67 (FgM) Washington, DC AMERICAN OBLATE MISSIONS.
Mayer, Walter W. '59 (OAK) Livermore, CA St. Michael Retired.
Mayer, William C. *c.s.v.* '56 (CHI)[N] Arlington Heights, IL Viatorian Province Center–Clerics of St. Viator.
Mayers, Gregory *c.ss.r.* '70 (TUC)[F] Tucson, AZ Redemptorist Society of Arizona Redemptorist Renewal Center.
Mayfield, Olin '96 (LA) Santa Clarita, CA St. Clare.
Mayfield, Phillip *p.i.m.e.* '78 (LAN)[N] Ypsilanti, MI Holy Trinity Student Parish; Ypsilanti, MI Holy Trinity Student Parish.
Mayhew, John A. *c.j.* '65 (LA) Santa Maria, CA St. Louis de Montfort; [B] Santa Maria, CA St. Joseph Seminary (Josephite Fathers' Novitiate).
Maynard, Jack G. '78 (COL) Dresden, OH St. Ann's.
Maynard, Leo E. '47 (HRT) Retired.
Maynard, Lewis H. '69 (BRK) Brooklyn, NY St. Agatha's Retired.
Maynard, Richard C. '56 (PRO) Retired.
Mayne, Kenneth '94 (LAF) Abbeville, LA St. Theresa of the Child Jesus.
Maynigo–Arenas, Joseph Victor '70 (NY) Staten Island, NY St. Patrick.
Mayo, James '76 (P) Portland, OR Church of St. Michael the Archangel; Area Vicars; Judges; Liturgical Commission.
Mayo, John W. '09 (STL) Washington, MO St. Francis Borgia.
Mayo, Rev. Msgr. Joseph M. '73 (SLC) College of Consultors; Salt Lake City, UT Cathedral of the Madeleine LLC 202; Ecumenical Commission; Defenders of the Bond; Board of Directors.
Mayo, Rev. Msgr. Reid C. '63 (BUR) Canon 1742 Panel of Pastors; Elected Members; Diocesan Administrative Board Retired.
Mayona, Rev. Msgr. Inaki *c.p.* (SJN) Spiritual Director.
Mayor, Paul (LA) Hospital Chaplains.
Mayorga, Fulgencio Vincent '98 (AUS) Wimberley, TX St. Mary.
Mayorga, Guadalupe '02 (AMA) Dimmitt, TX Immaculate Conception.
Mayorga, Lupe '02 (AMA) Presbyteral Council.
Mayorga, Victor '95 (AUS) Martindale, TX Immaculate Heart of Mary; Uhland, TX St. Michael.
Mayorga–Fonseca, Joaquin '89 (SJN) Rio Piedras; San Juan, PR Sagrada Familia.
Mayotte, Allan J. '60 (MAR) Retired.
Mayovsky, David L. '97 (SEA) Poulsbo, WA St. Olaf; Presbyteral Council; Deans.
Mayovsky, Frederick P. *s.j.* '75 (SEA)[C] Tacoma, WA Bellarmine Preparatory School; [C] Tacoma, WA Bellarmine Preparatory School.
Mayovsky, Gerald L. '59 (SEA) Seattle, WA Our Lady of Lourdes; Tukwila, WA St. Thomas.
Mayta, Robert A. '95 (LIN) Priests' Continuing Education Committee.
Mayworm, James A. '66 (DET) Retired.
Mayzik, James J. *s.j.* '85 (BGP)[B] Fairfield, CT Fairfield University; [O] Fairfield, CT The Fairfield Jesuit Community–Fairfield University.
Mazanec, James F. '81 (CLV) Amherst, OH St. Joseph.
Mazanowksi, Zygmunt *t.o.r.* (ALT)[I] Loretto, PA St. Francis University (Loretto).
Mazarati, Jean Baptiste *s.j.* '01 (WDC)[N] Washington, DC The Jesuit Community at Georgetown University.
Mazariegos, Edgar '80 (PMB) Palm Beach Gardens, FL Cathedral of St. Ignatius Loyola.
Mazich, Edward M. *o.s.b.* '01 (GBG)[G] Latrobe, PA Saint Vincent Archabbey.
Mazon, Diego *o.f.m.* '60 (SFE)[H] Albuquerque, NM The Province of Our Lady of Guadalupe.
Mazouch, Charles '73 (DOD) Claflin, KS Immaculate Conception Catholic Church of Claflin, Kansas; Ellinwood, KS St. Joseph Catholic Church of Ellinwood, Kansas; Presbyteral Council; Deans; [F] Dodge City, KS The Diocese of Dodge City Priest Retirement Fund, Inc.; [C] Ellinwood, KS St. Joseph School Education Endowment Fund; St. John, KS St. John the Apostle Catholic Church of St. John, Kansas.
Mazur, Francis X. '76 (BUF) Ecumenism; Defenders of the Bond; Erie County Medical Center.
Mazur, Jacek P. '04 (BUF) Niagara Falls, NY Divine Mercy.
Mazur, Jacek '01 (VEN) Port Charlotte, FL San Antonio.
Mazur, Kenneth *p.i.m.e.* '82 (DET)[K] Detroit, MI P.I.M.E. Missionaries; Detroit, MI Pontifical Institute for Foreign Missions, P.I.M.E., Inc.
Mazur, Rev. Msgr. Robert C. '76 (ALT) Liturgy; Altoona, PA Cathedral of the Blessed Sacrament; Parish Life Office; Diocesan Contact for Parish Pastoral Councils; Stewardship.
Mazur, Timothy P. '95 (DET) St. Clair Shores, MI St. Isaac Jogues.
Mazurek, James K. '73 (PIT) On Duty Outside the Diocese.
Mazurkiewicz, Rev. Msgr. Ben '55 (AUS) Retired.
Mazurkiewicz, Rev. Msgr. Harry '51 (AUS) Retired.
Mazurowski, Rafal '05 (STA) Orange Park, FL St. Catherine's.
Mazuryk, Ivan '94 (STF) Auburn, NY SS. Peter and Paul; Presbyteral Council; Youth Apostolate; Youth–For–Christ Association.
Mazza, Rev. Msgr. Louis J. '53 (NY) Sleepy Hollow, NY Immaculate Conception.
Mazza, Mark G. '80 (GRY) On Duty Outside the Diocese.
Mazza, Mark G. '80 (SFR) Pacifica, CA St. Peter.
Mazza, Victor J. '70 (PAT) Clifton, NJ St. Paul.
Mazzarella, Cadmus D. '85 (CAM) Williamstown, NJ Our Lady of Peace Parish, Monroe Township, N.J.
Mazzarella, Frederick *o.f.m.* '61 (NY)[EE] New York Franciscan Province of the Immaculate Conception.
Mazzei, John C. '92 (PRT) Skowhegan, ME Christ the King Parish.
Mazzola, Robert E. '63 (IND) Indianapolis, IN St. Matthew; On Special or Other Archdiocesan Assignment; Auditor.
Mazzone, James S. '99 (WOR) Diocesan Scouts; Vocation Office.
Mazzone, Joseph M. (BO) Weymouth, MA Sacred Heart.
Mazzotta, Rev. Msgr. George J. '66 (PH) Philadelphia, PA Stella Maris.
Mazzuchelli, Matthew C. *o.s.b.* '58 (PEO)[A] Peru, IL St. Bede Abbey.
Mbaegbu, Anthony '92 (BAK) Lakeview, OR St. Patrick.
Mbaegbu, Innocent '92 (RVC) Seaford, NY Maria Regina.
Mbagwu, Brendan O. '95 (LFT) Carmel, IN St. Elizabeth Ann Seton.
Mbala, Felicien '84 (DEN) Loveland, CO St. John the Evangelist.
Mbalo, Firmin Mola *c.m.* '93 (CHI)[N] Chicago DePaul Vincentian Residence.
Mbanefo, Anthony *m.s.p.* '92 (AUS) Gatesville, TX Our Lady of Lourdes Catholic Church – Gatesville, Texas; Hamilton, TX St. Thomas Catholic Church – Hamilton, Texas.
Mbanisi, Victor '93 (NY) Bronx, NY Calvary Hospital; Astoria, NY St. Francis of Assisi.
Mbanu, Celestine '78 (SB) Redlands, CA The Holy Name of Jesus Catholic Community, Inc.
Mbatia, Paul *a.j.* '89 (BAK) Hermiston, OR Our Lady of Angels.
Mbazuigwe, Patrick '93 (LA) Panorama City, CA St. Genevieve.
Mben, Joseph Loic *s.j.* '09 (OAK)[M] Berkeley, CA Jesuit Fathers and Brothers.
Mbidoaka, Eusebius '94 (IND) Indianapolis, IN St. Rita.
Mbinda, Rev. Msgr. John '68 (HON) Kapolei, HI St. Jude.
Mbiti, Jacob Mugo *o.c.d.* '08 (MIL)[P] Milwaukee Provincial Offices – Discalced Carmelites.
Mbonu, Michael '95 (BEL) Fairfield, IL St. Edward; Mount Carmel, IL St. Sebastian.
McAfee, Franklyn M. '71 (ARL) McLean, VA St. John the Beloved.
McAlear, Richard *o.m.i.* '70 (BO)[X] Tewksbury, MA Immaculate Heart of Mary Residence.
McAleenan, Aiden (OAK) Oakland, CA St. Columba.
McAleer, Robert T. '71 (DAV) Bettendorf, IA St. John Vianney; Judges.
McAlister, Richard A. *o.p.* '61 (PRO)[P] Providence St. Thomas Aquinas Priory at Providence College.
McAllister, Alex '86 (SR) On Leave.
McAllister, Donald '71 (PRT) Retired.
McAllister, Donald '71 (MAN)[J] Dover, NH St. Ann Rehabilitation and Nursing Center Retired.
McAloon, Francis X. *s.j.* '92 (OAK)[M] Berkeley, CA Jesuit Fathers and Brothers; [A] Berkeley, CA Jesuit School of Theology at Santa Clara University.
McAlpin, Andrew M. *o.p.* '09 (CHI) River Forest, IL St. Vincent Ferrer.
McAlpin, James C. '64 (SC) Retired.
McAlpin, Leonard J. '69 (GBG)[F] Greensburg, PA St. Anne Home.
McAlpine, Harry D. '87 (SC) Priests' Pension Plan – Board of Trustees Retired.
McAndrew, John P. '86 (ORG) Inactive Leave Retired.
McAndrew, Joseph P. '85 (NY)[X] Warwick, NY St. Anthony Community Hospital, Inc.; [AA] Warwick, NY Villa Frances at the Knolls Retired.
McAndrew, Michael *c.ss.r.* '73 (LA)[P] In Res; Whittier, CA St. Mary of the Assumption.
McAndrew, Michael *c.ss.r.* (FRS) Multicultural and Campesino Ministry (Spanish).
McAndrew, Thomas F. '61 (DUB) Retired.

McAndrews, Rev. Msgr. Donald A. '54 (SCR)[N] Dunmore, PA Villa St. Joseph Retired.
McAndrews, James F. *s.j.* '62 (PH) Philadelphia, PA Old St. Joseph's Retired.
McAndrews, Richard J. '67 (PH) Lansdale, PA Corpus Christi.
McAnerney, Brendan *o.p.* '88 (OAK)[M] Oakland, CA Order of Preachers (Province of the Most Holy Name of Jesus – Western Dominican Province); [A] Berkeley, CA Dominican School of Philosophy and Theology.
McAniff, Bernard F. *s.j.* '03 (CHI)[N] Chicago Chicago Province of the Society of Jesus–Provincial Office.
McArdle, John F. '51 (MAR) Retired.
McArdle, Kevin *o.c.d.* '43 (TUC) Tucson, AZ Saint Margaret Mary Alacoque Roman Catholic Parish – Tucson; [D] Tucson, AZ Discalced Carmelite Friars of St. Margaret Mary's.
McAree, Rev. Msgr. Francis J. '75 (NY) Harrison, NY St. Gregory the Great; Censors Librorum; Canon 1742 Panel of Pastors.
McArthur, Rev. Msgr. John B. '74 (MEM) Memphis, TN St. Louis; [I] Memphis, TN Serra Club of Memphis; College of Consultors; Clergy Personnel Board; Presbyteral Council.
McArtney, Robert J. '60 (BUF) Retired.
McAskill, Kenneth F. '50 (BO) Senior Priests. Retired.
McAtee, John F. *o.s.a.* '66 (FgM) Villanova, PA Province of St. Thomas of Villanova (Eastern).
McAteer, James *i.c.* '64 (SP) Spring Hill, FL St. Theresa.
McAteer, Rev. Msgr. Kenneth P. '73 (PH) Bensalem, PA Saint Ephrem; Approved Advocates.
McAteer, Patrick J. *s.j.* '73 (CHI) Chicago, IL St. Ignatius; [C] Chicago, IL Jesuit Community at Loyola University Chicago.
McAughan, Andrew *o.c.s.o.* '92 (L)[L] Trappist, KY Abbey of Our Lady of Gethsemani, of the Order of Cistercians of the Strict Observance.
McAuley, Edward J. '06 (BGP) Bethel, CT St. Mary.
McAuley, James D. *m.m.* '80 (FgM) Maryknoll, NY MARYKNOLL.
McAuley, John J. *m.m.* '81 (FgM) Maryknoll, NY MARYKNOLL.
McAuliff, R. Richard *s.j.* '92 (FgM) New York, NY Society of Jesus.
McAuliff, Richard *s.j.* (CI)[B] Chuuk, FM Xavier High School.
McAuliffe, Dennis '73 (RIC) Charlottesville, VA Church of the Holy Comforter; Scottsville, VA St. George.
McAuliffe, Rev. Msgr. Kevin W. '90 (LAV) Presbyteral Council for the Diocese of Las Vegas; Board of Trustees; Las Vegas, NV St. Elizabeth Ann Seton; Chancellor and Moderator of the Curia; Diocesan Judges; Building Committee; Director of Clergy Education; Home and Foreign Missions; Information, Communications and Media; Native American and Colored People Commission; Priests' Pension Board; Vicar General; Promoters of Justice; Diocesan Liturgy Committee.
McAuliffe, Kevin '90 (VNN) Defender of the Bond; Judge; Notaries.
McAuliffe, Robert J. '57 (BO) Senior Priests. Retired.
McAvoy, Rev. Msgr. C. John '63 (OG) Retired.
McBeth, Jeffrey R. '06 (TOL) Toledo, OH Good Shepherd; Toledo, OH St. Thomas Aquinas; Youth, Young Adult and Campus Ministry.
McBrearity, Gerald D. *s.s.* '73 (ATL) On Duty Outside the Archdiocese.
McBrearity, Gerald D. *s.s.* '73 (BAL)[S] Baltimore, MD Society of St. Sulpice, Province of the United States; Baltimore, MD.
McBrearity, Gerald D. *s.s.* '73 (WDC)[A] Washington, DC Theological College of the Catholic University of America.
McBrearty, John J. *s.s.j.* '68 (BR) New Roads, LA St. Augustine.
McBriar, David J. *o.f.m.* '64 (R) Ecumenical Commission; Raleigh, NC St. Francis of Assisi.
McBride, Alfred A. *o.praem.* '53 (GB)[J] De Pere, WI St. Joseph Priory.
McBride, Brendan '75 (SFR) San Francisco, CA St. Philip the Apostle; Irish Ministry.
McBride, Daniel '51 (CLV) Administrative Leave.
McBride, Daniel '95 (PHX) Phoenix, AZ Holy Family Roman Catholic Parish; Phoenix, AZ St. Edward Confessor Roman Catholic Parish; Chandler, AZ St. Mary Roman Catholic Parish; Deans.
McBride, Eugene J. *o.s.f.s.* '89 (WIL)[J] Childs, MD Retirement and Assisted Care Facility Retired.
McBride, Henry J. '61 (CAM) Retired.
McBride, Rev. Msgr. James P. '56 (PH) Tresckow, PA Retired.
McBride, John F. '62 (PH) Glenside, PA St. Luke the Evangelist.
McBride, John *s.j.* '61 (P)[L] Portland, OR Colombiere Community.
McBride, Larry '87 (OWN) Sturgis, KY St. Ambrose; Sturgis, KY St. William; Sturgis, KY St. Francis Borgia; Pastoral Office for Worship; Diocesan Liturgical Committee.
McBride, Rev. Msgr. Peter A. '60 (PAT)[Q] Chester, NJ Nazareth Village Retired.
McBride, Robert G. '72 (NEW) Union County Southeast Deanery 24; Archdiocesan Judges; Promoter of Justice; Linden, NJ St. John the Apostle.
McBrien, Kevin F. '86 (BRK) Rosedale, NY St. Clare.
McBrien, Kevin *o.carm.* (CHI) Chicago, IL St. Thomas Apostle.
McBrien, Kevin *o.carm.* '70 (JOL) Glendale Heights, IL St. Matthew.
McBrien, Richard P. '62 (FTW)[B] University of Notre Dame Du Lac.
McBrien, Richard P. '62 (HRT) On Duty Outside the Archdiocese.
McBurney, James D. *o.s.a.* '84 (PH) Philadelphia, PA St. Augustine.
McCabe, Edward D. '68 (MO) Military & VA Chaplains.; Army Reserve Chaplains.
McCabe, James F. *c.s.p.* '57 (NY)[EE] Jamaica Estates Paulist Fathers Generalate.
McCabe, James T. '71 (PH) Philadelphia, PA St. Cecilia.
McCabe, James *c.pp.s.* '58 (CIN)[N] Carthagena, OH St. Charles Retired.
McCabe, John H. '55 (RVC)[M] Amityville, NY St. Pius X Residence Retired.
McCabe, Joseph V. *m.m.* '77 (NY)[EE] Maryknoll Maryknoll Fathers and Brothers.
McCabe, Joseph '77 (RVC) Mission Office.
McCabe, Kenneth *ss.cc.* '65 (LA)[P] La Verne, CA Congregation of the Sacred Hearts of Jesus and Mary.
McCabe, Kevin P. '03 (PH) Malvern, PA St. Patrick; [D] Downingtown, PA Bishop Shanahan High School.
McCabe, Louis J. *s.j.* '71 (STL)[O] St. Louis, MO Sacred Heart Jesuit Community; [O] St. Louis, MO The Jesuits of the Missouri Province.
McCabe, Michael G. '89 (LIN) Nebraska City, NE St. Mary's; [C] Nebraska City, NE Lourdes Central Catholic Schools; [L] Nebraska City, NE Lourdes Central High School Endowment Fund; Members.
McCabe, Patrick A. '61 (CAM) Retired.
McCabe, Peter '70 (AUS) Retired.
McCabe, Ramon J. *m.m.* '56 (FgM) Maryknoll, NY MARYKNOLL.
McCabe, Rev. Msgr. Robert J. '64 (NY) Haverstraw, NY St. Mary of the Assumption.
McCabe, Robert J. '95 (DET) Southgate, MI St. Pius X.
McCabe, Rev. Msgr. Vincent '46 (LA) Retired.
McCafferty, David L. '64 (CLV) Wickliffe, OH Our Lady of Mount Carmel; Akron, OH St. Vincent Retired.
McCafferty, James B. *s.m.* '70 (WH) Paden City, WV Mater Dolorosa; Sistersville, WV Holy Rosary.
McCafferty, Michael F. '67 (CHR) Gaffney, SC Sacred Heart; Union, SC St. Augustine; Spartanburg, SC St. Paul the Apostle.
McCafferty, Richard B. *s.j.* '62 (BO)[U] Boston The Society of Jesus of New England–Provincial Offices.
McCafferty, Richard *s.j.* '62 (OAK) Livermore, CA St. Charles Borromeo Retired.
McCaffrey, Daniel '58 (OKL) Special Assignment; Catholic Physicians Guild.
McCaffrey, Edmund M. '59 (CHR) Retired.
McCaffrey, Gerald *o.f.m.* (PAT)[N] Butler, NJ St. Anthony Friary.
McCaffrey, Rev. Msgr. John A. '76 (AUS) Bryan, TX St. Joseph; [M] Bryan, TX St. Joseph Memorial Endowment Fund; St. Joseph's School Memorial Endowment Fund.
McCaffrey, Joseph C. '99 (PH) Philadelphia, PA St. Bartholomew; [D] Philadelphia, PA Little Flower Catholic High School for Girls.
McCaffrey, Joseph P. '77 (ROC) Wolcott, NY Catholic Community of the Blessed Trinity of Wolcott, NY.
McCaffrey, Joseph R. '87 (PIT) Sewickley, PA Saints John and Paul.
McCaffrey, Kevin '02 (Y) Andover, OH Our Lady of Victory; Andover, OH St. Patrick.
McCaffrey, Kilian '07 (PHX) Phoenix, AZ St. Vincent de Paul Roman Catholic Parish.
McCaffrey, Lawrence X. *s.j.* '51 (NY)[EE] New York, NY Murray–Weigel Hall.
McCaffrey, Patrick J. '59 (WDC) Retired.
McCaffrey, Rev. Msgr. William J. '72 (PRO) Rumford, RI St. Margaret; College of Consultors.
McCahill, Rev. Msgr. Patrick P. '68 (NY) New York, NY St. Elizabeth of Hungary; [P] New York, NY New York Catholic Deaf Center; Deaf, Catholic Center for; [N] Deaf Apostolate.
McCahill, Robert T. *m.m.* '64 (FgM) Maryknoll, NY MARYKNOLL.
McCahon, Rev. Msgr. Joseph F. '75 (SP) Retired.
McCain, Thomas *c.p.* (BAL) Baltimore, MD St. Joseph Passionist Monastery Parish.
McCain, William H. '86 (SFR) Novato, CA Our Lady of Loretto.
McCall, Edward (BGP) On Duty Outside the Diocese.
McCall, Stephen P. '79 (SD) San Diego, CA St. Mary Magdalene.
McCallister, Richard '91 (SEA) Puyallup, WA All Saints.
McCallum, David C. *s.j.* '00 (SY)[Q] Syracuse, NY Jesuits at LeMoyne, Inc.
McCallum, Dougald '97 (HEL) Choteau, MT St. Joseph; Fairfield, MT St. John the Evangelist; Presbyteral Council.
McCallum, Gregory P. '97 (GAY) Alpena, MI St. Anne; Alpena, MI St. Bernard; Alpena, MI St. John the Baptist; Alpena, MI St. Mary; Herron, MI St. Rose of Lima.
McCallum, Paul F. '62 (AUS) Retired.
McCambridge, Paul J. *f.s.s.p.* (PAT) Pequannock, NJ Our Lady of Fatima Chapel (Tridentine).
McCandless, Michael P. '08 (CLV) Painesville, OH St. Mary.
McCandless, William T. *o.s.f.s.* '94 (WIL)[B] Wilmington, DE Salesianum School.
McCandless, William T. *o.s.f.s.* '94 (MO) Navy Reserve Chaplains.
McCann, Arthur L. '62 (DM) Retired.
McCann, Charles '69 (WDC) Clinton, MD Church of St. John the Evangelist.
McCann, James M. *s.j.* '79 (CHI)[N] Chicago Chicago Province of the Society of Jesus–Provincial Office.
McCann, James M. *s.j.* '79 (WDC)[N] Washington, DC Leonard Neale House.
McCann, Rev. Msgr. John B. '85 (ALN) Douglassville, PA Immaculate Conception.
McCann, John H. *s.m.m.* '55 (HRT) Bantam, CT Our Lady of Grace.
McCann, Rev. Msgr. John J. '65 (RVC) Manhasset, NY St. Mary's; North Hempstead Deanery.
McCann, Luke W. '79 (NY) Kingston, NY St. Colman Retired.
McCann, Robert J. '81 (OAK) Judges; Censor; Dublin, CA St. Raymond; Adjutant Judicial Vicars; Pastoral Leadership Placement Board (PLPB).
McCann, Thomas M. '98 (NO) Pearl River, LA SS. Peter and Paul.
McCann, Thomas W. '68 (CLV) Cuyahoga Falls, OH Immaculate Heart of Mary; Associate Judges.
McCann, Thomas *c.p.* '64 (BAL)[S] Baltimore, MD St. Joseph's Passionist Community.
McCann, William '94 (LSC) Roswell, NM Assumption of the Blessed Virgin Mary; Presbyteral Council; Clergy Personnel Board; Priests Retirement Fund Committee; Finance Council.
McCarren, Rev. Msgr. Gerard H. '91 (NEW)[A] South Orange, NJ Immaculate Conception Seminary; [A] South Orange, NJ Immaculate Conception Seminary; [B] School of Diplomacy and Intl. Rels.; Archdiocesan Liturgical Commission; Censores Librorum.
McCarren, Paul J. *s.j.* '74 (WDC)[C] Washington, DC Georgetown University; [N] Washington, DC The Jesuit Community at Georgetown University.
McCarren, Rev. Msgr. Stephen A. '55 (GBG) Retired.
McCarron, Gerard J. '70 (TR)[N] Trenton, NJ Villa Vianney Retired.
McCarron, Rev. Msgr. Michael D. '77 (RIC) Chesapeake, VA St. Stephen, Martyr.
McCarthy, Anthony T. '71 (MIL) North Lake, WI Blessed Teresa of Calcutta.
McCarthy, Brian P. '75 (NY) Bronx, NY St. Margaret of Cortona; Inter–Parish Financing, Commission for.
McCarthy, C. Ryan '01 (IND) Guilford, IN St. John the Baptist; West Harrison, IN St. Joseph.
McCarthy, Carl '95 (OWN) Owensboro, KY SS. Joseph and Paul; Diocesan Liturgical Committee.
McCarthy, Charles A. *c.s.sp.* '51 (PEO) Streator, IL Annunciation of Blessed Virgin Mary; Tonica, IL SS. Peter and Paul's.
McCarthy, Charles *o.f.m.conv.* '79 (ELP) El Paso, TX Our Lady of Mt. Carmel.
McCarthy, Daniel P. '67 (CHI) Chicago, IL St. Tarcissus.
McCarthy, Daniel *o.s.b.* '91 (KCK)[I] Atchison, KS St. Benedict's Abbey.
McCarthy, David J. '60 (CLV) Doylestown, OH SS. Peter and Paul; Cuyahoga Falls, OH St. Joseph Retired.
McCarthy, Donal *ss.cc.* '65 (LA)[P] La Verne, CA Congregation of the Sacred Hearts of Jesus and Mary.
McCarthy, Donald G. '54 (CIN) Imprimatur Censors; Cincinnati, OH St. Ignatius of Loyola Retired.
McCarthy, Donald (SAL) Retired.
McCarthy, Edward J. '71 (ORL) Orlando, FL Basilica of the National Shrine of Mary Queen of the Universe.
McCarthy, Edward *c.pp.s.* '40 (CIN)[N] Carthagena, OH St. Charles Retired.
McCarthy, Emmanuel Charles '81 (NTN) Priests Serving Outside the Eparchy.
McCarthy, Eugene '60 (VEN) Retired.
McCarthy, George B. '56 (PRO) Newport, RI St. Mary.
McCarthy, Gerald A. '57 (FAR) Apostolate for Native Americans; Bisbee, ND Holy Rosary Retired.
McCarthy, J. Joseph '66 (FgM) Boston, MA St. James the Apostle, Inc.
McCarthy, James H. '55 (CHI) Special Religious Education (SPRED) Retired.
McCarthy, James J. '63 (BO) Braintree, MA St. Thomas More.

McCarthy, Jeremiah J. '66 (BO) Society of St. James the Apostle.
McCarthy, Jeremiah J. '72 (TUC) On Duty Outside the Diocese.
McCarthy, Jeremiah J. '78 (SAV) Savannah, GA Most Blessed Sacrament; Officialis; Tribunal Judges; College of Consultors; Presbyteral Council.
McCarthy, Rev. Msgr. Jeremiah J. '72 (SFR)[A] Menlo Park, CA St. Patrick Seminary and University.
McCarthy, Jeremiah *m.s.c.* '50 (SAT)[L] San Antonio, TX Missionaries of the Sacred Heart.
McCarthy, John D. '08 (RVC) Rockville Centre, NY St. Agnes Cathedral.
McCarthy, Rev. Msgr. John F. '55 (HEL) On Duty Outside the Diocese.
McCarthy, Rev. Msgr. John F. '55 (LC)[M] Eastman, WI Marian Academy of the Oblates of Holy Tradition.
McCarthy, Rev. Msgr. John F. '55 (STL)[U] Saint Louis, MO Oblates of Wisdom Study Center.
McCarthy, Rev. Msgr. John J. '84 (HRT) Hartford, CT Cathedral of St. Joseph; Chancellor; Promoter of Justice; College of Consultors; Special and other Archdiocesan Assignment; Ex Officio Members.
McCarthy, John J. *m.s.* '69 (HRT)[L] Hartford, CT Missionaries of LaSalette.
McCarthy, John L. *s.j.* '62 (STL)[O] St. Louis, MO Jesuit Community Corporation at Saint Louis University – Jesuit Hall.
McCarthy, Rev. Msgr. John M. '54 (NY) Staten Island, NY St. Patrick.
McCarthy, John M. (BO) Dorchester, MA St. Brendan.
McCarthy, John *c.ss.r.* '62 (FgM) Denver, CO Denver Province.
McCarthy, John (NY) Staten Island, NY St. Clare.
McCarthy, Joseph F. '48 (SFD) Burlington, VT Retired.
McCarthy, Joseph S. '96 (BO) Pembroke, MA St. Thecla Retired.
McCarthy, Joseph '48 (BUR) Retired.
McCarthy, Joseph *o.f.m.cap.* '60 (MAN) Manchester, NH St. Anne–St. Augustin.
McCarthy, Joseph *o.carm.* '60 (JOL)[L] Darien Carmelite Provincial Office.
McCarthy, Joseph *c.ss.r.* '60 (VEN)[I] Venice, FL Our Lady of Perpetual Help Retreat and Spirituality Center.
McCarthy, Kevin P. '89 (GRY)[L] Valparaiso, IN Newman Apostolate–Valparaiso University; Priests' Personnel Board; Campus Ministry.
McCarthy, Rev. Msgr. Leo F. '59 (BUF) Tonawanda, NY Blessed Sacrament Retired.
McCarthy, Martin F. *s.j.* '54 (BO)[U] Weston, MA Campion Health Center, Inc.
McCarthy, Michael C. *s.j.* '96 (SJ)[B] Santa Clara, CA Jesuit Community.
McCarthy, Patrick R. *m.s.* '78 (HRT)[L] Hartford, CT Missionaries of LaSalette.
McCarthy, Patrick '08 (NY) Bronx, NY St. Barnabas.
McCarthy, Paul J. *s.j.* '57 (SLC) Sandy, UT Saint Thomas More Catholic Church LLC 248.
McCarthy, Paul '84 (FTW) South Bend Office; New Carlisle, IN St. Stanislaus Kostka.
McCarthy, Raymond P. *c.ss.r.* '47 (NY)[EE] New York, NY Redemptorist Priests and Brothers, C.Ss.R.
McCarthy, Richard C. '69 (PRT) Retired.
McCarthy, Rev. Msgr. Robert J. '46 (OG) Retired.
McCarthy, Rev. Msgr. Robert '58 (STL) Retired.
McCarthy, Scott '74 (MRY) Special Assignment.
McCarthy, Sean M. '91 (BO) Health Leave.
McCarthy, Terrence A. '74 (CHI) Retired.
McCarthy, Thomas A. '59 (NEW) Retired.
McCarthy, Thomas H. '07 (CIN) Liberty Township, OH St. Maximilian Kolbe.
McCarthy, Thomas J. '61 (Y) Judges.
McCarthy, Thomas J. '80 (BUF) Retired.
McCarthy, Thomas R. *o.s.a.* '94 (CHI)[D] Chicago, IL St. Rita of Cascia High School; [N] Chicago, IL St. Rita Monastery; Olympia Fields, IL; [N] Olympia Fields, IL The Augustinians–Provincialate.
McCarthy, Thomas *s.j.* '62 (P) Sherwood, OR St. Francis; [L] Portland, OR Colombiere Community.
McCarthy, Thomas '53 (RVC) Retired.
McCarthy, Thomas '61 (Y) Office of Priests' Personnel Advisor; Bishop's Delegate for Retired Priests; Salem, OH St. Paul; Leetonia, OH St. Patrick.
McCarthy, Vincent *s.s.c.* '64 (OM)[K] St. Columbans Missionary Society of St. Columban.
McCarthy, Warren J. '52 (CHI) Retired.
McCarthy, William A. '03 (SC) Marcus, IA St. Catherine's; Remsen, IA St. Mary's.
McCarthy, William E. *m.m.* '58 (NY)[EE] Retired.
McCarthy, William E. *m.m.* '58 (RVC) Retired.
McCarthy, William *m.s.a.* '59 (NOR)[G] Cromwell, CT Society of the Missionaries of the Holy Apostles.
McCarthy, Rev. Msgr. William '63 (PAT) Retired.
McCartney, James J. *o.s.a.* '70 (PH)[Y] Rosemont, PA Saxony Hall.
McCartney, James '84 (LUB) Plainview, TX St. Alice; Vicars Forane; Priests' Retirement Board.
McCartney, John J. '99 (RVC) Dix Hills, NY St. Matthew.
McCarty, Bruce '89 (OWN) Owensboro, KY Precious Blood; Consultors; Serra Club.
McCarty, Joshua A. '09 (OWN) Owensboro, KY St. Stephen Cathedral.
McCarty, Paul T. *s.j.* '67 (BO)[U] Weston, MA Campion Health Center, Inc.
McCarty, Robert E. *s.j.* '67 (NEW)[B] Jersey City, NJ Jesuit Center; [M] Jersey City, NJ Jesuits of Saint Peter's College, Inc.
McCasland, Howard '44 (OG) Churubusco, NY Immaculate Heart of Mary Retired.
McCaslin, Dick *s.j.* '65 (RC) Pine Ridge, SD Holy Rosary.
McCaslin, John O. '55 (OM) Retired.
McCaslin, John Patrick '02 (IND) Indianapolis, IN St. Anthony; Indianapolis, IN Holy Trinity.
McCaslin, John T. *s.j.* '66 (ALN)[A] Wernersville, PA Jesuit Center–Jesuit Community.
McCaslin, R. Patrick '61 (OM) Omaha, NE St. John Vianney.
McCaslin, Richard *s.j.* '65 (RC)[C] Pine Ridge, SD Jesuit Community of Holy Rosary Mission.
McCaughley, Sean '87 (NY) New York, NY.
McCauley, Daniel Thomas *o.c.d.* '55 (MIL)[P] Hubertus, WI Retreat Center Retired.
McCauley, George C. *s.j.* '61 (NY)[EE] Loyola Hall, Jesuit Community.
McCauley, James A. '56 (WIN) Retired.
McCauley, James P. *s.j.* '56 (SJ)[M] Los Gatos, CA Sacred Heart Jesuit Center.
McCaulley, Barbara (DUB)[H] Mason City, IA Mercy Medical Center–North Iowa.
McCaulley, Cornelius W. '66 (PIT) Pittsburgh, PA St. Stephen Retired.
McCawley, Scott M. '93 (JOL) Absent on Leave.
McCawley, William J. '60 (SCR) Retired.
McChesney, Robert W. *s.j.* '81 (OAK)[M] Berkeley, CA Jesuit Fathers and Brothers; [A] Berkeley, CA Jesuit School of Theology at Santa Clara University.
McClain, J. Thomas *s.j.* '77 (LAN) Ann Arbor, MI St. Mary Student Parish; [N] Ann Arbor, MI St. Mary Student Parish; [J] Ann Arbor, MI Detroit Province of the Society of Jesus – Jesuit Residence.
McClain, Joseph P. *c.m.* '49 (PH)[Y].
McClain, Matthew R. '02 (PIT)[A] Pittsburgh, PA Saint Paul Seminary; Priestly Vocations, Office for; Priest Council.
McClanahan, Robert P. '84 (PT) Military Chaplains; Navy Chaplains.
McClane, Michael T. '06 (TR) Defenders of the Bond; Vice Chancellors; New Egypt, NJ The Church of the Assumption.
McClane, Michael T. (ARL) McLean, VA St. John the Beloved.
McClean, Rev. Msgr. John R. '57 (DUB) Pontifical Missions/Mission Awareness; Directors Retired.
McClellan, Keith J. '79 (GRY) Michigan City, IN Notre Dame; Bishop's Council of Priests.
McClellan, Robert J. '81 (RCK) South Beloit, IL St. Peter.
McClintock, James '86 (BEA) Dayton, TX St. Joseph the Worker; Dayton, TX St. Anne Mission.
McClory, Bernard J. '53 (COL) Retired.
McClory, Rev. Msgr. Robert J. '99 (DET)[Q] Detroit, MI Catholic Community Services of the Archdiocese of Detroit, Inc.; Moderator of the Curia; Judges; Archdiocesan Theological Commission.
McCloskey, C. John '81 (POD) Chicago.
McCloskey, Daniel J. '83 (WIL) Georgetown, DE St. Michael the Archangel.
McCloskey, Francis G. '63 (ALB) Retired.
McCloskey, Gary N. *o.s.a.* '73 (PH)[C] Villanova, PA Villanova University; [Y] Villanova, PA St. Thomas Monastery; Counselors:.
McCloskey, J. Terrence *c.ss.r.* '66 (KC)[J] Kansas City, MO Redemptorists Fathers of Kansas City, Missouri.
McCloskey, Rev. Msgr. James A. '46 (SY) Fayetteville, NY Immaculate Conception; Promoters of Justice Retired.
McCloskey, James P. *c.s.sp.* '80 (FgM) Bethel Park, PA CONGREGATION OF THE HOLY SPIRIT.
McCloskey, James P. *c.s.sp.* (PIT)[B] Pittsburgh, PA Duquesne University of the Holy Spirit.
McCloskey, Joseph M. *s.j.* '63 (WDC)[N] Washington, DC The Jesuit Community of St. Aloysius Gonzaga.
McCloskey, Joseph W. '61 (PH) Retired.
McCloskey, Lester '64 (SEA) Retired.
McCloskey, Patrick *o.f.m.* '75 (CIN)[N] Cincinnati, OH St. Clare Friary.
McCloskey, Terry *c.ss.r.* '66 (KC) Kansas City, MO Our Lady of Perpetual Help.
McClosky, Rev. Msgr. Adam S. '67 (GAL) Houston, TX All Saints.
McClure, Jack H. *c.pp.s.* '76 (DUB) Van Horne, IA St. Paul; Van Horne, IA St. Michael; Van Horne, IA Immaculate Conception; Van Horne, IA St. Patrick; Van Horne, IA St. John.
McClure, Jason Wayne '03 (OWN) Murray, KY St. Leo; Priest Personnel Committee.
McClure, Jason '03 (OWN)[I] Murray, KY Murray State University Newman House; Deans/Coordinators.
McClure, John A. '62 (TOL) Retired.
McCluskey, James F. '68 (OM) Laurel, NE St. Mary; [N] Laurel, NE St. Ann Church of Dixon Cemetery Endowment Trust Fund.
McCluskey, Tom *c.ss.r.* '08 (NY) Bronx, NY Immaculate Conception.
McCoart, Charles C. '90 (ARL) Alexandria, VA Good Shepherd.
McCole, John F. '58 (PH) Retired.
McColligan, Raymond '43 (PIT) Retired.
McCollum, Paul '98 (RNO) Gardnerville, NV St. Gall; Diocesan Board of Consultors; Seminary Board; Vocations; Presbyteral Council.
McComiskey, Joseph C. '70 (RVC) Retired.
McConaghy, Robert J. '75 (ALN) Boyertown, PA St. Columbkill.
McConnell, James J. *s.m.a.* '72 (NEW) Newark, NJ Queen of Angels; [M] Tenafly, NJ Society of African Missions, Provincialate, S.M.A. Fathers.
McConnell, James J. '54 (TR)[N] Trenton, NJ Villa Vianney; Diocesan Consultors Retired.
McConnell, John M. *s.j.* '55 (NY)[EE] New York, NY Murray–Weigel Hall.
McConnell, William J. '53 (BO) Senior Priests. Retired.
McConvey, Michael '79 (GLP) On Leave of Absence.
McConville, William E. *o.f.m.* '73 (R) Raleigh, NC St. Francis of Assisi.
McConway, Sean J. *o.p.* '87 (NY) New York, NY St. Catherine of Siena; Manhattan, NY Hospital for Special Surgery; Manhattan, NY Memorial Sloan Kettering Cancer Center; Manhattan, NY New York Presbyterian Hospital.
McCoog, Thomas M. *s.j.* '79 (NY)[EE] Cardinal Spellman Hall, Jesuit Community.
McCool, Naos *c.s.sp.* (PIT)[B] Pittsburgh, PA Duquesne University of the Holy Spirit.
McCool, Patrick *o.s.b.* '63 (OKL)[I] Shawnee, OK St. Gregory's Abbey.
McCord, Kent G. '81 (MO) On Duty Outside the Diocese; DEPARTMENT OF VETERANS AFFAIRS HOSPITALS AND CHAPLAINS.
McCorkell, Patrick M. *s.j.* '74 (STP)[N] Lake Elmo, MN Jesuit Retreat House.
McCorkle, Rev. Msgr. Louis W. '53 (JC) Retired.
McCormac, Rev. Msgr. Michael P. '80 (PH) Fairless Hills, PA St. Frances Cabrini.
McCormack, Douglas '69 (LFT) Retired.
McCormack, John '61 (KC)[I] Kansas City, MO Jeanne Jugan Center Retired.
McCormack, Keith J. '76 (TOL) Mansfield, OH St. Mary of the Snows.
McCormack, Michael J. *o.p.* '87 (WDC)[B] Washington, DC Dominican House of Studies.
McCormack, Rev. Msgr. Robert '47 (NY) Retired.
McCormick, Andrew '82 (PH) Swedesburg, PA Sacred Heart.
McCormick, Brian '66 (TR)[U] Trenton, NJ Martin House; Martin House.
McCormick, Daniel J. '57 (ATL) Dunwoody, GA All Saints; Defenders of the Bond; Promoter of Justice; Dunwoody, GA Atlanta Veterans Administration Hospital.
McCormick, Frank '68 (HEL)[E] Missoula, MT St. Patrick Hospital and Health Sciences Center, Sisters of Providence of Montana Corporation.
McCormick, Gregory *s.p.* '49 (SFE) Jemez Springs, NM Our Lady of the Assumption; [H] Jemez Springs, NM Our Lady of Lourdes; [L] Jemez Springs, NM Fitzgerald Charitable Trust; [L] Jemez Springs, NM EDSA Charitable Trust.
McCormick, Howard W. '57 (SPR)[G] Springfield, MA St. Michael's Residence; Presbyteral Council; Diocesan Consultors Retired.
McCormick, James D. '62 (SC)[F] Auburn, IA Opus Spiritus Sancti; Auburn, IA Opus Spiritus Sancti Retired.
McCormick, James '82 (E)[C] Erie, PA Cathedral Preparatory School; Erie, PA St. James.
McCormick, Jeffrey '96 (MIA) Pembroke Pines, FL St. Maximilian Kolbe.
McCormick, Jerry '73 (MRY) Catholic Charities Board Retired.
McCormick, John J. '56 (BO) Billerica, MA St. Theresa of Lisieux; Senior Priests. Retired.
McCormick, John M. '75 (ORL) Orlando, FL St. James Cathedral; Ethnic Ministries; Propagation of the Faith; Central South.
McCormick, John '99 (SR) Unassigned.
McCormick, Joseph *o.s.a.* (KAL) Edwardsburg, MI Our Lady of the Lake; Presbyteral Council Members; Presbyteral Council Members.
McCormick, Justin J. *c.s.p.* '61 (NY)[EE] Jamaica Estates Paulist Fathers Generalate.
McCormick, Kieran J. '64 (SFR) Retired.
McCormick, Louis M. *o.f.m.* '65 (BUF)[Q] West Clarksville, NY Mount Irenaeus, Franciscan Mountain Retreat & Holy Peace Friary; [C] West Clarksville, NY Holy Peace Friary.
McCormick, Mark '91 (RC) Piedmont, SD Our Lady of the Black Hills; Diocesan Consultors.
McCormick, Rev. Msgr. Maurice M. '58 (SFR) San Francisco, CA St. Cecilia Retired.

McCormick, Myron *o.f.m.* '52 (BO)[Z] Boston, MA St. Anthony Shrine.
McCormick, Patrick G. '96 (PH) Philadelphia, PA St. Timothy.
McCormick, Patrick J. '68 (ATL) Military Chaplains; Navy Chaplains.
McCormick, Patrick J. '68 (HON) Military Chaplains.
McCormick, Rev. Msgr. Patrick Joseph '75 (FRS) Merced, CA Our Lady of Mercy/St. Patrick's; Defenders of the Bond; Master of Ceremonies; Planada, CA Sacred Heart.
McCormick, Rev. Msgr. Patrick '75 (FRS) Personnel Board.
McCormick, Paul *o.cist.* '97 (DAL)[J] Irving, TX Cistercian Abbey of Our Lady of Dallas.
McCormick, Peter M. *c.s.c.* '07 (FTW)[B] University of Notre Dame Du Lac; [A] Notre Dame, IN; [H] Notre Dame Congregation of Holy Cross, Indiana Province, Provincial House; [H] Notre Dame, IN Holy Cross Community, Corby Hall, University of Notre Dame.
McCormick, Robert F. (BGP)[S] Darien, CT Convent of St. Birgitta.
McCormick, Thomas F. *s.j.* '67 (SJ)[M] Los Gatos, CA Sacred Heart Jesuit Center.
McCormick, Thomas '59 (DEN) Retired.
McCormley, Hugh J. '62 (PIT) Pittsburgh, PA; [M] Pittsburgh, PA St. John Vianney Manor Retired.
McCorry, Rev. Msgr. Edward J. '56 (NY) Retired.
McCotter, Daniel E. *c.s.p.* '81 (SFR) San Francisco, CA Holy Family Chinese Mission; San Francisco, CA Old St. Mary's Cathedral.
McCouch, Richard S. *s.j.* '93 (WDC)[E] North Bethesda, MD Georgetown Preparatory School.
McCourt, Rev. Msgr. B. (BRK) Peter Turner Insurance Co.; Diocesan Insurance Committee.
McCourt, Gerald P. *s.j.* '72 (SJ)[M] Los Gatos, CA Sacred Heart Jesuit Center.
McCourt, Rev. Msgr. Robert R. '61 (BRK) St. Albans, NY Our Lady of Light Roman Catholic Church Retired.
McCown, Robert M. *sj* '63 (NO)[P] New Orleans, LA Ignatius Residence Retired.
McCoy, Alfred E. '54 (SC) Retired.
McCoy, Bernard *o.cist.* '95 (LC)[H] Sparta, WI Our Lady of Spring Bank, Cistercian Abbey; Sparta, WI.
McCoy, Charles F. *c.s.c.* '09 (FTW)[H] Notre Dame Congregation of Holy Cross, Indiana Province, Provincial House.
McCoy, Charles *c.s.c.* '09 (P)[B] University of Portland; [L] Portland, OR Holy Cross Fathers & Brothers, C.S.C. – University of Portland.
McCoy, Daniel P. '03 (BO) Saugus, MA Blessed Sacrament; Saugus, MA St. Margaret.
McCoy, Floyd '83 (SJN) On Duty Outside the Archdiocese.
McCoy, James B. '63 (PH)[BB] Chalfont, PA Delaware Valley College of Science and Agriculture.
McCoy, Rev. Msgr. James P. '63 (PH) Chalfont, PA St. Jude; Parish Sites and Boundaries, Commission for.
McCoy, John J. '93 (STU) Amsterdam, OH St. Joseph; Richmond, OH St. John Fisher; Presbyteral Council.
McCoy, John '93 (STU) College of Consultors.
McCoy, Rev. Msgr. Kevin C. '81 (SC)[B] Fort Dodge, IA Fort Dodge Catholic Schools, Inc.; [G] Fort Dodge, IA Saint Edmond Catholic Schools Foundation; [G] Fort Dodge, IA Holy Trinity Parish Cemetery Improvement Society; Fort Dodge, IA Holy Trinity Parish of Webster County; [G] Fort Dodge, IA Holy Trinity Parish Foundation of Webster County; Presbyteral Council.
McCoy, Perry M. *o.s.m.* '93 (CHI)[N] Chicago Order of Friar Servants of Mary (Servites) United States of America Province, Inc.
McCoy, Perry *o.s.m.* '93 (ORG)[I] Anaheim, CA Servite Fathers and Brothers.
McCracken, John E. '79 (GAY) Manistee, MI Guardian Angels; Manistee, MI St. Joseph; Manistee, MI St. Mary of Mt. Carmel Shrine; Members of the College of Consultors; Continuing Spiritual Formation of Clergy, Pastoral Administrators and Women Religious; Elected Members.
McCracken, Rev. Msgr. John T. '44 (OAK) Danville, CA St. Isidore Retired.
McCracken, Kevin *c.m.* '82 (LA)[A] Camarillo, CA St. John's Seminary; Liturgical Commision.
McCrane, Gerard T. *m.m.* '59 (NY)[EE] Maryknoll Maryknoll Fathers and Brothers Retired.
McCrann, Peter J. *s.m.m.* '58 (RVC) Bay Shore, NY Southside Hospital; [M] Bay Shore, NY Montfort Missionaries.
McCrate, D. Stephen *s.t.l.* '89 (BEA) Port Arthur, TX St. Joseph.
McCrate, Stephen '89 (BEA) Diocesan College of Consultors.
McCray, Trinette '81 (MIL)[C] Milwaukee, WI Cardinal Stritch University.
McCreanor, James '78 (MIA) Homestead, FL Sacred Heart.
McCreary, Glenn E. '95 (SCR) Muncy, PA Resurrection; Muncy, PA Muncy Prison.
McCreary, Robert E. *o.f.m.cap.* '64 (PIT)[M] Beaver, PA St. Fidelis Friary.
McCreary, Robert L. *o.f.m.cap.* '64 (CLV)[A] Wickliffe, OH Borromeo Seminary.
McCreedy, Harry E. '72 (PH) Norristown, PA St. Paul.
McCreedy, Justin D. *o.s.b.* '70 (SEA)[L] Lacey, WA St. Martin's Abbey; Puyallup, WA All Saints; [G] Tacoma, WA Catholic Pastoral Care–Hospital Tacoma Ministry.
McCreesh, Thomas P. *o.p.* '72 (PRO)[P] Providence St. Thomas Aquinas Priory at Providence College.
McCreight, James H. '68 (CLV) Cleveland, OH St. Michael the Archangel; [V] Cleveland, OH St. Michael.
McCrone, John M. '82 (NEW) Mountainside, NJ Church of Our Lady of Lourdes; Union Northwest Deanery 22.
McCue, Michael J. *o.s.f.s.* '90 (CAM) Rutgers University; [R] Camden, NJ Rutgers University; Camden, NJ The Church of the Immaculate Conception, Camden, N.J.
McCue, Richard T. '58 (CHL) Retired.
McCue, Scott E. '01 (R) Special Assignment.
McCulken, Rev. Msgr. Michael T. '76 (PH)[CC] Philadelphia, PA Catholic Clinical Consultants; Philadelphia, PA Cathedral Basilica of SS. Peter and Paul.
McCulloch, Lawrence F. *m.m.* '70 (NY)[EE] Maryknoll Maryknoll Fathers and Brothers Retired.
McCullough, Hugh J. '79 (FR) Fall River, MA St. Joseph's.
McCullough, Rev. Msgr. J. Edward '67 (GBG) Dunbar, PA St. Aloysius; Catholic Relief Services Representative; Missions; Apostleship of Prayer; Catholic Daughters of America; Holy Childhood Association; Pilgrimages; Priests' Eucharistic League; Board of Trustees.
McCullough, Michael P. '73 (LA) Los Angeles, CA Transfiguration; L.A. Police Dept.
McCumber, Rev. Msgr. William W. '83 (STL) St. Louis, MO St. Luke the Evangelist; Archdiocesan Office of Worship.
McCune, James L. '58 (BO) Senior Priests; Senior Priests. Retired.
McCurdy, William J. *s.j.* '61 (BUF)[O] Buffalo, NY Canisius Jesuit Community Inc.; [D] Buffalo, NY Canisius High School.
McCurry, James *o.f.m.conv.* '77 (BAL) Ellicott City, MD Province of Saint Anthony of Padua; [S] Ellicott City Order of Friars Minor Conventual.
McDade, Robert *m.ss.cc.* '76 (CAM)[M] Linwood, NJ Villa Pieta. Missionaries of the Sacred Hearts of Jesus & Mary.
McDade, Rev. Msgr. Thomas J. '74 (PAT)[B] Morristown, NJ College of Saint Elizabeth; Mountainside, NJ Church of Our Lady of Lourdes.
McDaid, Henry '63 (BIR) Birmingham (Hoover), AL Prince of Peace Retired.
McDaid, Rev. Msgr. J. Anthony '75 (DEN) On Duty Outside the Archdiocese.
McDaid, Patrick *s.m.* '08 (SAT)[F] San Antonio, TX Central Catholic High School; [L] San Antonio, TX Woodlawn Marianist Community.
McDaniel, George W. '70 (DAV) Davenport, IA Holy Family; [A] St. Ambrose University; Chancellor; Judges; Diocesan Corporate Board; Finance Council; Priests' Aid Society; Propagation of the Faith; Notaries; Archivist.
McDaniel, Isaac '82 (L)[A] Bellarmine University.
McDaniel, John W. *s.j.* '71 (PH)[Y] Loyola Center and Manresa Hall.
McDaniel, Raymond '07 (FWT) Lindsay, TX St. Peter.
McDarby, J. Patrick *o.s.b.* '53 (SCL)[I] Collegeville, MN St. John's Abbey, of the Order of St. Benedict.
McDermott, Brian O. *s.j.* '68 (BAL)[B] Jesuit Community of Loyola University, Inc.; [S] Baltimore, MD Jesuit Community of Loyola University, Inc.
McDermott, Charles B. '73 (NEW) Union, NJ St. Michael's.
McDermott, Charles B. '63 (PRO)[P] Narragansett, RI Christian Brothers' Center Retired.
McDermott, Christopher H. *c.s.sp.* '81 (PH)[Y] Bensalem, PA Congregation of the Holy Spirit; Councilors:; [F] Bensalem, PA Holy Ghost Preparatory School.
McDermott, H. Thomas *c.s.c.* '79 (FgM)[H] Notre Dame, IN Congregation of Holy Cross, Indiana Province, Provincial House; New Rochelle, NY Eastern Brothers Province.
McDermott, John J. '86 (DUB) On Leave of Absence (Not Authorized for Priestly Ministry).
McDermott, Rev. Msgr. John J. '89 (BUR) Members Ex Officio; Vicars General; Chancery Office; Office of Diocesan Pastoral Planning; Promoter of Justice; Diocesan Administrative Board; Diocesan Archives; The Review Board; [G] Burlington, VT University of Vermont–The Catholic Center at UVM; Defenders of the Bond; Diocesan Consultors; Institute for Catholic Enrichment and Lay Apostolate Formation.
McDermott, Joseph M. '95 (PH) Primos, PA St. Eugene.
McDermott, Joseph P. '62 (BO) Stoughton, MA Immaculate Conception.
McDermott, Joseph *s.v.d.* '52 (DUB)[B] Epworth, IA Divine Word College.
McDermott, Martin F. *s.j.* '64 (FgM) Watertown, MA Society of Jesus.
McDermott, Michael A. '66 (PIT) Retired.
McDermott, Michael F. '79 (GI) Grand Island, NE Resurrection; Vicar–Judicial; Judges; Diocesan Consultors; Priests' Advisory Board (Presbyteral Council).
McDermott, Michael J. '75 (WIL) Milford, DE St. John the Apostle.
McDermott, Michael J. '65 (SEA) Tacoma, WA St. Charles Borromeo; College of Consultors; Deans; Presbyteral Council.
McDermott, Neal W. *o.p.* '61 (NO) Archdiocesan Consultors; Members of the Board; Executive Director; Campus Ministry; Rosary Congress Committee; New Orleans, LA St. Anthony of Padua.
McDermott, Robert B. '90 (PH)[A] Wynnewood, PA Theological Seminary of St. Charles Borromeo, Overbrook.
McDermott, Robert J. '81 (STA) Gainesville, FL St. Patrick Church.
McDermott, Rev. Msgr. Robert T. '69 (CAM) Camden, NJ St. Joseph Catholic Church, East Camden, N.J. (Pro–Cathedral); Vicars General; College of Consultors; Camden City Deanery; Ex Officio Members; Ex Officio Members; Ex Officio Members.
McDermott, Robert T. '81 (MIL) On Duty Outside the Archdiocese.
McDermott, Robert T. '81 (STL) St. Louis, MO St. Roch.
McDermott, Robert '83 (STA) Special Assignment.
McDermott, Stephen C. '03 (MO) Military Chaplains; Army Reserve Chaplains.
McDermott, Thomas J. '97 (DUB) Seminary Admissions and Advisory Board; Cedar Rapids, IA St. Ludmila; Directors.
McDermott, Thomas *o.p.* '83 (STL)[A] St. Louis, MO Kenrick School of Theology; [O] St. Louis, MO St. Dominic Priory.
McDermott, William '98 (FAR) Langdon, ND St. Alphonsus Church of Langdon; Langdon, ND St. Michael's; Langdon, ND St. Edward.
McDevitt, Rev. Msgr. Anthony '49 (MOB) Judicial Consultant Retired.
McDevitt, Edward P. *c.o.* '71 (CHR) Fort Mill, SC St. Philip Neri; [E] Rock Hill, SC Oratory of St. Philip Neri, Congregation of the Oratory of Pontifical Rite.
McDevitt, James A. '90 (BGP) On Duty Outside the Diocese.
McDevitt, James '90 (BRK) Brooklyn, NY St. John the Evangelist; Brooklyn, NY Metropolitan Detention Center.
McDevitt, Michael V. '71 (SPC) Springfield, MO Cathedral of St. Agnes; Aurora, MO Holy Trinity; Aurora, MO Sacred Heart; Priests' Eucharistic League Confraternity of The Most Blessed Sacrament; Region IV; Advocates for the Respondent.
McDevitt, Robert *s.j.* '60 (SJ)[M] Los Gatos, CA Sacred Heart Jesuit Center.
McDevitt, Thomas '58 (LAN) Retired.
McDonagh, Donat Michael '74 (SP) On Duty Outside the Diocese; [T] St. Petersburg, FL Marian Servants of the Holy Spirit, Inc.
McDonagh, Edward C. '62 (BO) West Bridgewater, MA St. Ann.
McDonagh, John P. '82 (SPR) On Duty Outside the Diocese.
McDonagh, John P. '81 (NY) Mt. Vernon, NY SS. Peter and Paul.
McDonagh, John P. (R)[I] Durham, NC Newman Catholic Student Center Duke University.
McDonald, A. John '56 (BR) Retired.
McDonald, Alexander F. *s.j.* '47 (SPK)[J] Spokane, WA Regis Community Retired.
McDonald, Allan J. '80 (SAV) Macon, GA St. Joseph.
McDonald, Bernard J. '59 (NY) Retired.
McDonald, C. Alexander '91 (CHR) Clemson, SC St. Andrew; [H] Clemson, SC Clemson University, Southern Wesleyan University & TriCounty Technical College; Administrator for Ecumenical & Interreligious Affairs.
McDonald, Charles J. '65 (LEX) Priests' Retirement Board Retired.
McDonald, Charles P. *c.ss.r.* '71 (NY) New York, NY Most Holy Redeemer.
McDonald, Charles *c.ss.r.* (BAL) Baltimore, MD St. Michael; Baltimore, MD St. Patrick.
McDonald, Daniel C. *s.j.* '81 (MIL)[P] Milwaukee Jesuit Provincial Office, Wisconsin Province.
McDonald, Edward J. *c.s.p.* '41 (NY)[EE] Jamaica Estates Paulist Fathers Generalate.
McDonald, Elmer J. '49 (ROC) Retired.
McDonald, Finian *o.s.b.* '62 (SCL)[I] Collegeville, MN St. John's Abbey, of the Order of St. Benedict.
McDonald, Francis B. '60 (JOL) Roselle, IL St. Walter Retired.
McDonald, G. Malcolm '85 (PIT) Allegheny County, PA Allegheny County Jail.
McDonald, James E. *c.s.c.* '84 (FTW)[B] University of Notre Dame Du Lac; [B] University of Notre Dame Du Lac; Provincial Councilors:; [H] Notre Dame Congregation of Holy Cross, Indiana Province, Provincial House; [H] Notre Dame, IN Holy Cross Community, Corby Hall, University of Notre Dame;

Members; [H] Notre Dame, IN Congregation of Holy Cross, Indiana Province, Provincial House.
McDonald, Rev. Msgr. James M. '67 (RVC) Williston Park, NY St. Aidan's Church; [A] Huntington, NY Diocesan Seminary of the Immaculate Conception; Procurator & Advocates; Apostleship of Prayer; Nocturnal Adoration Society; Legion of Mary.
McDonald, James *c.ss.r.* '90 (TOL) Lima, OH St. Gerard.
McDonald, John G. '07 (BIR)[A] Birmingham, AL John Carroll Catholic High School; Birmingham, AL St. Peter the Apostle; Birmingham, AL St. Francis Xavier; Diocesan College of Vicars.
McDonald, John J. *s.j.* '57 (NY)[EE] Loyola Hall, Jesuit Community.
McDonald, Joseph F. '87 (B) Idaho Falls, ID Holy Rosary; Idaho Falls, ID Christ the King; Promoters of Justice.
McDonald, Kenneth '57 (LAN) Retired.
McDonald, Malcolm '85 (PIT)[M] Pittsburgh, PA St. John Vianney Manor.
McDonald, Mark *m.s.c.* '68 (RCK)[G].
McDonald, Mark *m.s.c.* '68 (FgM) Aurora, IL MISSIONARIES OF THE SACRED HEART.
McDonald, Martin '62 (MRY) Retired.
McDonald, Matthew D. '40 (CHI) Retired.
McDonald, Michael D. '85 (GI) Kearney, NE Prince of Peace; Personnel Board; Propagation of the Faith.
McDonald, Paul F. '51 (DUB) Retired.
McDonald, Perry *o.f.m. cap.* '67 (MAD)[I] Madison, WI San Damiano Friary Retired.
McDonald, Peter '59 (SFR) Ross, CA St. Anselm Retired.
McDonald, Richard '99 (KCK) Further Studies.
McDonald, Thomas F. '52 (NY)[EE] Bronx, NY John Cardinal O'Connor Residence; Yonkers Fire Department Retired.
McDonald, Thomas '52 (NY) Allen Pavilion.
McDonald, Vincent *o.carm.* '47 (NY)[EE] Middletown, NY St. Albert's Priory.
McDonald, William '89 (STO) Absent on Leave.
McDonell, Clint W. '08 (DET) Presbyteral Council; Dearborn, MI Divine Child.
McDonnell, Anthony '70 (LA) On Sick Leave.
McDonnell, David '72 (PAT) Priestly Life Committee; Sparta, NJ Our Lady of the Lake.
McDonnell, Donald C. '47 (SFR) Retired.
McDonnell, Francis E. '51 (RCK) Pro Synodal Judges; Censores Librorum Retired.
McDonnell, Francis P. '58 (HRT) Windsor Locks, CT St. Mary Retired.
McDonnell, John H. '56 (WH) Religious Unity, Diocesan Commission for Retired.
McDonnell, John J. '73 (CHI) Chicago, IL St. Mary, Star of the Sea.
McDonnell, John J. *c.m.* '43 (PH)[Y].
McDonnell, Joseph F. '55 (CHI) Retired.
McDonnell, Rev. Msgr. Joseph '67 (DM) Urbandale, IA St. Pius X.
McDonnell, Joseph '04 (STA) Chiefland, FL St. John the Evangelist.
McDonnell, Kilian *o.s.b.* '51 (SCL)[I] Collegeville, MN St. John's Abbey, of the Order of St. Benedict.
McDonnell, Lawrence V. *c.s.p.* '53 (NY)[EE] Jamaica Estates Paulist Fathers Generalate; [EE] New York, NY Paulist Fathers' Motherhouse Retired.
McDonnell, Rev. Msgr. Martin '68 (PAT) Hawthorne, NJ St. Anthony's.
McDonnell, Michael *o.f.m.* '65 (NY) Mt. Vernon, NY St. Mary; New York, NY Holy Name of Jesus.
McDonnell, Rev. Msgr. P. William '64 (RCK) Freeport, IL St. Thomas Aquinas; Deans.
McDonnell, Patrick J. '73 (TR) Hightstown, NJ St. Anthony of Padua.
McDonnell, Paul A. *o.s.j.* '91 (SCR)[M] Pittston, PA Our Lady of Sorrows Province of the Oblates of St. Joseph; Blue Army of Our Lady of Fatima; Pittston, PA; [B] Pittston, PA St. Joseph's Oblate Seminary.
McDonnell, Sean '88 (PAT) Whippany, NJ Our Lady of Mercy.
McDonnell, Thomas P. *m.m.* '65 (NY)[EE] Maryknoll Maryknoll Fathers and Brothers; [EE] Maryknoll, NY Maryknoll Fathers and Brothers Charitable Trust Retired.
McDonnell, Thomas P. *s.j.* '68 (CHL) Charlotte, NC St. Peter; [J] Mooresville, NC Jesuit Community.
McDonnell, Rev. Msgr. William '64 (RCK) Diocesan Consultors.
McDonough, Edward J. *c.ss.r.* (BO) Healing and Restoration Ministry.
McDonough, James A. *o.p.* '62 (AUS)[G] Austin, TX Dominican Friars of Austin.
McDonough, James A. *s.j.* '61 (NY)[EE] New York, NY Murray–Weigel Hall.
McDonough, James P. '84 (PIT) Judges.
McDonough, Rev. Msgr. James T. '57 (PH) Strafford, PA Our Lady of the Assumption; Pontifical Society of St. Peter Apostle; Pontifical Missionary Union; Pontifical Society for the Propagation of the Faith Retired.
McDonough, Rev. Msgr. John P. '52 (BO) Senior Priests. Retired.
McDonough, John T. '50 (CLV) Akron, OH St. Sebastian; Hinckley, OH Our Lady of Grace; Presbyteral Council Retired.
McDonough, John T. '00 (PHX) Fountain Hills, AZ Ascension Roman Catholic Parish.
McDonough, John '95 (WH) Charleston, WV St. Agnes.
McDonough, Kevin M. '80 (STP) Hispanic Ministry; Office for Safe Environment.
McDonough, Kevin M. '80 (STP) St. Paul, MN St. Peter Claver; Commission for Black Catholics.
McDonough, Patrick M. '68 (WH) St. Albans, WV St. Francis of Assisi.
McDonough, Roger F. '76 (BGP) Fairfield, CT St. Thomas Aquinas.
McDonough, Vincent *s.j.* '62 (ROC)[B] Elmira, NY Notre Dame High School.
McDougal, H. Jon '79 (LR) Fort Smith, AR St. Boniface.
McDougall, James G. '75 (LAN) Ann Arbor, MI St. Francis of Assisi.
McDougall, Jeffrey N. *s.j.* '03 (P)[F] Portland, OR St. Andrew Nativity School; [L] Portland, OR Colombiere Community.
McDougall, Russell K. *c.s.c.* '91 (FTW)[H] Notre Dame Congregation of Holy Cross, Indiana Province, Provincial House; New Rochelle, NY Eastern Brothers Province.
McDowell, John *o.f.m.* '77 (CHL)[M] Stoneville, NC St. Francis Springs Prayer Center; [J] Stoneville, NC Franciscan Friary.
McDowell, Leo G. '94 (MO) Air Force Reserve Chaplains.
McDowell, Leo G. '94 (GF) Fort Benton, MT Immaculate Conception; Boy Scouts; Finance Council; Director of Vocations.
McDowell, Patrick D. '68 (SCR) Weston, PA Sacred Heart.
McDuffie, Paul A. '95 (BR) Defenders of the Bond; Baton Rouge, LA Sacred Heart of Jesus.
McEachern, Bernard *c.p.* '64 (MET)[I] South River Passionist Provincial Office.
McEachern, Xavier (JOL)[K] Darien, IL Carmelite Carefree Retirement Village.
McEachin, Donald J. *c.s.sp.* '81 (FgM) Bethel Park, PA CONGREGATION OF THE HOLY SPIRIT.
McElduff, Edward W. '53 (ALN)[J] Bethlehem, PA Holy Family Villa Retired.
McEleney, Robert J. '58 (RIC) Retired.
McElheron, J. Daniel '01 (HRT) Enfield, CT St. Martha.
McElligott, Thomas J. '69 (OAK)[P] Moraga, CA St. Mary's College Mission and Ministry Center; On Duty Outside the Archdiocese.
McElligott, Thomas (OAK)[B] St. Mary's College.
McElroy, Charles J. '64 (PH) Schwenksville, PA St. Mary.
McElroy, Damian '88 (TR) Moorestown, NJ Our Lady of Good Counsel.
McElroy, David R. *o.praem.* '02 (GB)[B] St. Norbert College; [J] De Pere, WI St. Norbert Abbey.
McElroy, John J. '45 (PRO) Pawtucket, RI St. Teresa of the Child Jesus Retired.
McElroy, John W. '56 (BO) Senior Priests. Retired.
McElroy, Rev. Msgr. Robert W. '80 (SFR) San Mateo, CA St. Gregory; College of Consultors.
McElroy, Thomas *ss.cc.* '67 (FR) Fairhaven, MA St. Joseph's; [G] Fairhaven, MA Sacred Hearts Provincial House; Fairhaven, MA.
McElwee, Robert W. '83 (WCH) Temporary Leave of Absence.
McEnery, James G. '53 (MAD) Retired.
McEnhill, Gerald A. '72 (DET) Orchard Lake, MI Our Lady of Refuge; College of Consultors.
McEnhill, John *s.m.* '56 (SJ)[M] Cupertino, CA The Bordeaux House.
McEnnis, Thomas '45 (SEA) Retired.
McEntee, John B. '61 (STL) Lonedell, MO St. Francis of Assisi.
McEvilly, John W. '64 (BEL) Belleville, IL Blessed Sacrament; Belleville, IL Our Lady Queen of Peace; Belleville, IL Chapel of St. John Children's Home; [C] Belleville, IL Chancery Office; [J] Belleville, IL The Catholic Diocese of Belleville Deposit and Loan Fund; [J] Belleville, IL The Catholic Diocese of Belleville Custodial Fund; [J] Belleville, IL The Catholic Diocese of Belleville Group Health Insurance Fund; [J] Belleville, IL The Catholic Diocese of Belleville Property Insurance Fund; [J] Belleville, IL The Catholic Diocese of Belleville Ministry Formation Fund; Vicar General; Moderator of the Curia; Diocesan Consultors; Diocesan Finance Council.
McEvoy, David *o.carm.* '88 (KCK) Leavenworth, KS Immaculate Conception–St. Joseph.
McEvoy, James '81 (WDC)[N] Washington, DC Holy Redeemer College.
McEvoy, John '76 (SP) Ruskin, FL St. Anne; Diocesan Council of Catholic Women.
McEvoy, William '87 (KCK) Kansas City, KS Blessed Sacrament; Kansas City, KS Our Lady and St. Rose; Kansas City, KS Christ the King.
McEwan, Kevin D. '02 (OG) Morristown, NY The Roman Catholic Community of Morristown, Hammond and Rossie.
McFadden, Frank '83 (BAL) Priests Sick or Absent.
McFadden, J. Michael '74 (HBG) New Cumberland, PA St. Theresa of the Infant Jesus.
McFadden, John R. '62 (PH) Cheltenham, PA Presentation of Blessed Virgin Mary.
McFadden, Rev. Msgr. Leo E. '53 (RNO) Retired.
McFadden, Michael J. *o.s.a.* '67 (LA) Ojai, CA St. Thomas Aquinas.
McFadden, Michael '61 (SAC) Winters, CA St. Anthony; Vacaville, CA St. Mary.
McFadden, Richard K. '05 (PH)[D] Philadelphia, PA Archbishop Ryan High School; Bensalem, PA St. Charles Borromeo.
McFadden, William C. *s.j.* '59 (WDC)[N] Washington, DC The Jesuit Community at Georgetown University.
McFadin, Marcus '92 (ELP) Office of Worship; El Paso, TX St. Stephen, Deacon and Martyr; Diocesan Master of Ceremonies; Diocesan Building Committee.
McFalls, Dean '95 (STO) Deans; Stockton, CA St. Mary of the Assumption Church (Pastor of).
McFarland, Rev. Msgr. Edward J. '55 (COL) Retired.
McFarland, James W. '47 (NEW)[M] Rutherford, NJ St. John Vianney Residence for Priests; Maria Immaculata Curia of Hudson County Retired.
McFarland, Michael C. *s.j.* '84 (WOR)[A] Worcester, MA College of the Holy Cross, Inc.; [O] Worcester, MA Jesuits of the Holy Cross, Inc.
McFarland, Timothy D. *c.pp.s.* '83 (LFT)[A] Rensselaer, IN Saint Joseph's College.
McFarlane, William M. '05 (CHI) Oak Lawn, IL St. Catherine of Alexandria.
McGaffin, Joseph P. '96 (PHX) Tempe, AZ Church of the Resurrection Roman Catholic Parish.
McGahagan, James E. '68 (SCR) Wilkes–Barre, PA St. Boniface; Wilkes–Barre, PA St. Patrick's.
McGahee, Thomas *s.d.b.* '77 (NO)[D] Marrero, LA Archbishop Shaw High School.
McGahren, Joseph J. *m.m.* '51 (NY)[EE] Maryknoll Maryknoll Fathers and Brothers Retired.
McGann, Diarmuid F. '64 (RVC) Blue Point, NY Our Lady of the Snow Retired.
McGann, Rev. Msgr. Francis J. '49 (BO) Needham, MA St. Joseph; Senior Priests.; Presbyteral Council Retired.
McGann, L. Philip '71 (WIL) Retired.
McGann, Thomas A. *c.m.f.* '76 (SPC)[J] Springfield, MO Catholic Campus Ministry O'Reilly Catholic Student Center, Southwest MO State University, Drury College, Ozarks Technical Com; Campus Ministries; [F] Springfield, MO Claretians Missionaries' Residence–Villa Claret; Presbyteral Council.
McGarrigle, Michael R. '49 (PRT) Retired.
McGarril, Colman J. *t.o.r.* '54 (ALT)[G] Loretto, PA St. Francis Friary at Mount Assisi.
McGarrity, Patrick *c.ss.r.* '61 (HBG) Ephrata, PA Mother of Perpetual Help; [G] Ephrata, PA St. Clement's Mission House.
McGarrity, Richard A. *s.j.* '70 (MIL)[P] Milwaukee, WI Jesuit Provincial Office, Wisconsin Province; [P] Milwaukee, WI Jesuit Community at Marquette University.
McGarry, Rev. Msgr. James J. '70 (SCR) Clarks Summit, PA Our Lady of the Snows; Keystone College.
McGarry, John P. *s.j.* '93 (FgM) Los Gatos, CA; Los Gatos, CA Society of Jesus.
McGarry, John P. *s.j.* '93 (SJ)[M] Los Gatos, CA California Province of the Society of Jesus, Jesuit Provincial Office; [M] Santa Clara, CA Casa San Inigo, Jesuit Residence; [B] Santa Clara, CA Jesuit Community.
McGarry, Michael B. *c.s.p.* '75 (NY)[EE] Jamaica Estates Paulist Fathers Generalate.
McGarry, Michael B. (FTW)[B] University of Notre Dame Du Lac.
McGarry, Peter *o.carm.* '69 (CHI)[D] Chicago, IL; [N] Chicago Carmelite Priory of St. Cyril.
McGarry, Rev. Msgr. Thomas '53 (NY) Bronx, NY St. Martin of Tours; Bronx, NY St. Barnabas Hospital Retired.
McGarry, William C. '59 (BUF) Retired.
McGarry, William J. *s.j.* '58 (FgM) New York, NY Society of Jesus.
McGarty, Rev. Msgr. Bernard O. '49 (LC) Retired.
McGaugh, Philip E. '78 (BO) Needham, MA St. Bartholomew.
Mc Gavock, Sabrina '03 (SP)[J] Tampa, FL St. Joseph's Hospital, Inc.
McGeady, Ignatius J. *o.f.m.* '58 (FgM) New York, NY Holy Name Province.
McGee, Rev. Msgr. H. Desmond '71 (E) Clearfield, PA St. Francis; Priest Personnel Board; College of Consultors.
McGee, James J. '85 (OAK) Walnut Creek, CA St. John Vianney.
McGee, John E. *o.s.f.s.* '82 (R) Council of Priests.
McGee, John *o.s.f.s.* '82 (R) Wilmington, NC Immaculate Conception.

McGee, Leo J. '57 (PH) Retired.
McGee, Michael J. '77 (BRK) Brooklyn, NY Good Shepherd.
McGee, Richard *c.r.* '74 (SB)[I] Fontana, CA Congregation of the Resurrection, CR Retired.
McGee, Thomas J. *o.s.f.s.* '71 (ARL) Vienna, VA Our Lady of Good Counsel.
McGee, Rev. Msgr. Timothy H. '87 (CR) Deans; Diocesan Consultors; Detroit Lakes, MN Holy Rosary; Members; Priests' Council; Catechumenal Commission; Finance Council; Members.
McGeean, John T. '86 (JOL) Manhattan, IL St. Joseph.
McGeory, Peter '76 (NY) Military Chaplains.
McGeough, Jude P. '58 (PRO) Retired.
McGeough, Martin *c.m.* (RVC) Procurator & Advocates; Hispanic Apostolate of the South Fork.
McGeown, Rev. Msgr. Joseph P. '65 (PH) Philadelphia, PA Immaculate Heart of Mary.
McGeown, William F. '70 (PH) Feasterville, PA Assumption B.V.M.; Priests' Personnel Board.
McGerity, Francis X. '84 (CC) On Duty Outside the Diocese.
McGettigan, Neil J. *o.s.a.* '53 (PH)[C] Villanova University; [Y] Villanova, PA St. Thomas Monastery.
McGettrick, Rev. Msgr. Tom '56 (CC) Bishop's Office; Deans; College of Consultors; Personnel Board – Priests; Presbyteral Council; Vicar for Priests; Corpus Christi, TX Saint Andrew By the Sea Parish.
McGhee, Jim '95 (AMA) Retired.
McGhee, Rev. Msgr. William P. '82 (BEL) Belleville, IL St. Mary; Co Directors; Diocesan Consultors.
McGill, Joseph P. *s.j.* '60 (NO)[P] New Orleans, LA Ignatius Residence.
McGill, Malachy *c.p.* '46 (BRK)[T] Jamaica, NY Immaculate Conception Monastery Retired.
McGillicuddy, Patrick *c.ss.r.* '79 (FgM) Baltimore Province.
McGillicuddy, Sean *c.ss.r.* (BO) Boston, MA Our Lady of Perpetual Help.
McGilvray, A. Robert *o.s.f.s.* '62 (WIL)[J] Childs, MD Retirement and Assisted Care Facility Retired.
McGing, Thomas '71 (JKS) Clinton, MS Holy Savior; [H] Clinton, MS Mississippi College Newman Center; Defenders of the Bond; Trustees.
McGing, Thomas '71 (BLX) Trustees.
McGinley, Bernard P. '61 (HBG) Harrisburg, PA Holy Family.
McGinley, Jeremiah V. *o.f.m.* '55 (PAT)[N] Butler, NJ St. Anthony Friary.
McGinley, John F. *o.s.f.s.* '68 (WIL) Wilmington, DE St. Anthony of Padua.
McGinn, Anthony F. *s.j.* '79 (NO)[E] New Orleans, LA Jesuit High School; [H] New Orleans, LA Jesuit High School; [S] Metairie, LA 124 Airline Drive, Inc.
McGinn, Daniel *s.s.c.* '53 (PRO)[P] Bristol, RI St. Columban's Retirement House Retired.
McGinn, Daniel *s.s.c.* '53 (OM)[K] St. Columbans Missionary Society of St. Columban.
McGinn, Finian *o.f.m.* '60 (OAK)[M] Oakland Franciscan Friars (Province of St. Barbara).
McGinness, Matthew C. '89 (WCH) Wichita, KS St. Thomas Aquinas; [K] Wichita, KS Priests' Retirement and Education Fund of Wichita; Vicar for Clergy; Apostleship of Prayer; Presbyteral Council/ College of Consultors.
McGinnis, Albin C. '77 (PIT) Pittsburgh, PA St. John Neumann.
McGinnis, Charles E. '06 (WH) Wheeling, WV St. Alphonsus.
McGinnis, J. Donald *m.m.* '53 (FgM) Maryknoll, NY MARYKNOLL.
McGinnis, Jack P. '63 (GAL) On Duty Outside the Archdiocese.
McGinnis, James J. '78 (PH) Retired.
McGinnis, Jay W. '76 (BUF) Kenmore, NY St. Paul.
McGinnis, John Arthur '04 (FAR) Jamestown, ND St. James Basilica of Jamestown.
McGinnis, John P. (GAL) Retired.
McGinnity, John C. '75 (WH) Retired.
McGinnity, John '75 (RIC) Hot Springs, VA The Shrine of the Sacred Heart Retired.
McGinnity, P. J. '91 (KNX) Madisonville, TN St. Joseph the Worker.
McGinnity, Robert F. '55 (CHI) Palos Hills, IL Sacred Heart Retired.
McGivern, Gregory '85 (SFR)[E] San Francisco, CA Mercy High School (Girls).
McGivern, John W. '91 (CHI) Oak Park, IL St. Edmund.
McGivney, Thomas '90 (JOL) Lockport, IL St. Joseph.
McGlinchey, James J. '56 (TLS) Tulsa, OK St. Bernard of Clairvaux Retired.
McGlinn, Rev. Msgr. Charles '67 (KCK) Leawood, KS Curé of Ars; Archdiocesan Consultors.
McGlinn, Robert J. '55 (CHI) Milwaukee, WI Retired.
McGloin, James P. *s.j.* '74 (FgM) Portland, OR Society of Jesus.
McGlone, Gerald J. *s.j.* '87 (PH)[Y] Loyola Center and Manresa Hall.
McGlone, Gerard M. '84 (SCR) Nicholson, PA St. Patrick.
McGlone, Joseph F. '52 (BO) Senior Priests. Retired.
McGlothlin, Eugene J. *o.s.b.* '60 (SCL) Collegeville, MN St. John the Baptist; [I] Collegeville, MN St. John's Abbey, of the Order of St. Benedict.
McGlynn, Daniel J. '82 (WIL) Dover, DE Holy Cross.
McGlynn, Philip M. *o.s.m.* '65 (CHI)[N] Chicago Order of Friar Servants of Mary (Servites) United States of America Province, Inc.
McGlynn, Thomas E. '84 (FR) Fall River, MA Cathedral of St. Mary of the Assumption; Defenders of the Bond; Auditors.
McGoldrick, James F. *s.m* '67 (WH) Wheeling, WV St. Vincent de Paul.
McGoldrick, Rev. Msgr. John T. '38 (B) Retired.
McGoldrick, Kevin B. '03 (PH) Philadelphia, PA Our Lady of Mt. Carmel.
McGoldrick, William J. '43 (DET) Retired.
McGonagle, Douglas '00 (SPR)[N] Amherst, MA The Newman Catholic Center; [N] Amherst, MA University of Massachusetts; Newman Apostolate and Campus Ministry.
McGonegal, James R. '71 (CLV) Cleveland, OH St. Ignatius of Antioch.
McGonigle, Thomas D. *o.p.* '68 (PRO)[P] Providence St. Thomas Aquinas Priory at Providence College.
McGough, Rev. Msgr. James P. '57 (BLX) Pro–Synodal Judge Retired.
McGough, Rev. Msgr. Stephen D. '68 (SCR) Williamsport, PA St. Lawrence; Williamsport, PA St. Boniface.
McGough, Timothy *o.c.d.* '49 (MIL) Milwaukee, WI St. Florian.
McGough, William J. '57 (NO) Retired.
McGourn, Francis T. *m.m.* '64 (FgM)[EE] Maryknoll Maryknoll Fathers and Brothers; Maryknoll, NY MARYKNOLL Retired.
McGovern, Donan *o.f.m.* '55 (BO)[Z] Boston, MA St. Anthony Shrine.
McGovern, Edward J. '51 (PRO)[P] Providence, RI St. John Vianney Residence; Assessor and Auditor Retired.
McGovern, Edward J. *m.m.* '04 (FgM) Maryknoll, NY; Maryknoll, NY; [EE] Maryknoll Maryknoll Fathers and Brothers.
McGovern, Eugene F. '29 (BRK) Retired.
McGovern, Eugene '56 (BRK)[T] Douglaston, NY Bishop Mugavero Residence Retired.
McGovern, Gerald *o.m.i.* '57 (BWN) San Juan, TX St. John the Baptist Retired.
McGovern, Rev. Msgr. James J. '58 (TR) Retired.
McGovern, Rev. Msgr. James O. '67 (BAL) Consultors; Senior Priests' Retirement Board; Consultors Retired.
McGovern, John J. *m.m.* '54 (FgM) Maryknoll, NY MARYKNOLL.
McGovern, John P. '65 (NEW) Cranford, NJ St. Michael's.
McGovern, Joseph J. *s.j.* '48 (PH) Philadelphia, PA Old St. Joseph's Retired.
McGovern, Rev. Msgr. Lawrence '67 (STO) Stockton, CA Presentation Church (Pastor of); College of Consultors/Presbyteral Council; Personnel Board.
McGovern, Mark J. '67 (DUB) On Special or Other Archdiocesan Assignment; Archives.
McGovern, Michael G. '94 (CHI) Lake Forest, IL St. Mary; Deans.
McGovern, Thomas A. '58 (CLV) Akron, OH St. Matthew Retired.
McGovern, Rev. Msgr. Thomas '46 (LA) Retired.
McGovern, Walter J. '64 (BAL) Randallstown, MD Holy Family Retired.
McGovern, William W. '55 (WOR) Retired.
McGowan, Rev. Msgr. Anthony '41 (ORG) San Clemente, CA Our Lady of Fatima Retired.
McGowan, Denis *c.p.* '55 (FgM).
McGowan, Dennis M. *o.s.a.* '83 (PH) Bryn Mawr, PA Our Mother of Good Counsel; [Y] Bryn Mawr, PA Augustinians Friars (O.S.A.).
McGowan, Frederick R. '49 (BO) Senior Priests. Retired.
McGowan, James J. '62 (BO) Quincy, MA Sacred Heart.
McGowan, James '02 (SFE) Portales, NM St. Helen; [K] Portales, NM University Catholic Center – St. Thomas More Chapel; Vicars Forane (Deans); PORTALES: St. Thomas Moore Newman Center; Presbyteral Council of the Archdiocese of Santa Fe.
McGowan, Jeffrey A. '89 (STA) Gainesville, FL Queen of Peace.
McGowan, John *c.ss.r.* '62 (TR)[R] Long Branch, NJ San Alfonso Retreat House.
McGowan, Joseph O. *s.j.* '74 (SEA)[C] Tacoma, WA Bellarmine Preparatory School.
McGowan, Joseph *o.carm.* '62 (NEW) Cresskill, NJ St. Therese of Lisieux.
McGowan, Richard A. *s.j.* '83 (BO)[U] Newton, MA The Jesuit Community at Boston College.
McGowan, Richard W. *s.j.* '60 (SFE) Albuquerque, NM Immaculate Conception.
McGowan, Rev. Msgr. Seamus '57 (CC) Presbyteral Council Retired.
McGowan, Timothy '79 (LA) On Administrative Leave.
McGrade, Kevin M. '85 (BO) Permanent Disability.; Air Force Reserve Chaplains.
McGrail, Charles A. '80 (NOR) Retired.
McGrann, John '67 (P) Retired.
McGrath, Andre *o.f.m.* '67 (SHP) Shreveport, LA Our Lady of the Blessed Sacrament.
McGrath, Brian F. '92 (SPR) Westfield, MA St. Mary's; Bishop's Commission for Clergy; Diocesan Consultors; Deans.
McGrath, Rev. Msgr. Conor '74 (SAT) San Antonio, TX St. Elizabeth Ann Seton.
McGrath, E. Joseph '85 (LKC) Fenton, LA St. Charles Borromeo.
McGrath, Edward F. '80 (WIN) Owatonna, MN St. Joseph's.
McGrath, Felix P. *o.f.m.* '61 (NY) New York, NY St. Francis of Assisi.
McGrath, Rev. Msgr. Frank C. '70 (BGP) Darien, CT St. John.
McGrath, Gerald '58 (MIA) Retired.
McGrath, J. Joseph *s.j.* '51 (BO)[U] Weston, MA Campion Health Center, Inc.
McGrath, James *c.s.c.* (FTW)[H] Holy Cross House.
McGrath, Rev. Msgr. Jeremiah J. '80 (BEA) Ecumenical Interreligious Affairs Officer; Diaconate, Permanent Diaconate; Beaumont, TX St. Anthony Cathedral Basilica.
McGrath, John A. '66 (CIN)[D] Dayton, OH The University of Dayton; [N] Dayton, OH Marianist Community.
McGrath, John F. '44 (CHI) Chicago, IL St. Thomas More Retired.
McGrath, John R. '82 (BLX) Biloxi, MS Cathedral of the Nativity of the Blessed Virgin Mary; Tribunal Judge; Special Delegate for Matrimonial Dispensations; Judicial Vicar; Deans; College of Consultors; Catholic Housing Board; Presbyteral Council.
McGrath, John '59 (MIA) Retired.
McGrath, John *o.m.i.* '53 (SAT)[K] San Antonio, TX Oblate Madonna Residence.
McGrath, Jordan A. *o.p.* '59 (CHI)[N] River Forest, IL St. Thomas Aquinas Priory.
McGrath, Kevin Anthony *o.p.* '96 (WDC)[B] Washington, DC Dominican House of Studies.
McGrath, Kevin D. *o.s.b.* '74 (BIR)[E] Cullman, AL St. Bernard Abbey; Cullman, AL.
McGrath, Lancelot '85 (MET) Hillsborough, NJ Mary, Mother of God.
McGrath, Rev. Msgr. Laurence W. '57 (BO) Senior Priests. Retired.
McGrath, Noel '80 (PMB) Stuart, FL St. Joseph.
McGrath, Patrick E. *s.j.* '06 (CHI)[D] Wilmette, IL Loyola Academy; [W] Wilmette, IL Loyola Recreational Facility Corp.; [E] Chicago, IL Chicago Jesuit Academy.
McGrath, Peter (TYL) Hallsville, TX Our Lady of Grace.
McGrath, Richard J. *o.s.a.* '73 (JOL)[C] New Lenox, IL Providence Catholic High School; [L] New Lenox, IL Augustinian Friary.
McGrath, Robert '67 (DET) Farmington Hills, MI St. Alexander.
McGrath, Rev. Msgr. Roger E. '71 (CAM)[G] Camden, NJ The Frank J. and Rosina W. Suttill Catholic Foundation; [G] Camden, NJ Francis, Elizabeth and Edward Roger Welsh Scholarship Trust; Vicars General; College of Consultors; Ex Officio Members; Ex Officio Members; Office of Vocations; Ex Officio Members; Vocation Advisory Board; Officers; [G] Camden, NJ The Sharkey Family Charitable Trust; Haddonfield, NJ Church of Christ the King, Haddonfield, N.J.
McGrath, Sean J. '91 (DEN) Littleton, CO St. Frances Cabrini.
McGrath, Thomas B. *s.j.* '64 (FgM) Agana, GU Dulce Nombre de Maria Cathedral – Basilica; New York, NY Society of Jesus; [F] Tamuning, GU Society of Jesus Micronesia.
McGrath, Thomas E. '77 (JC) Retired.
McGrath, Thomas J. '59 (SY) Skaneateles, NY St. Mary of the Lake.
McGrath, Thomas (PAT) Special Assignment; Adoption and Counseling Services.
McGrath, William J. *s.j.* '59 (SCR)[C] Scranton, PA The University of Scranton; [E] Scranton, PA Scranton Preparatory School.
McGrath, William '00 (ROC) Caledonia, NY St. Columba; [N] Rochester, NY Catholic Committee on Scouting.
McGratty, John J. '71 (RVC) Patchogue, NY St. Francis de Sales.
McGraw, Howard *o.s.a.* '62 (PH)[Y] Philadelphia, PA Augustinian Community (O.S.A.).
McGraw, Rev. Msgr. John T. '56 (SY) Retired.
McGraw, Rev. Msgr. Michael D. *m.ss.a.* '75 (PMB) Boca Raton, FL St. Joan of Arc.
McGraw, Rene *o.s.b.* '62 (SCL)[I] Collegeville, MN St. John's Abbey, of the Order of St. Benedict.
McGraw, Robert H. '76 (LAN) Jackson, MI Queen of the Miraculous Medal; College of Consultors; Priests' Assignment Commission.
McGraw, Sean D. *c.s.c.* '01 (FTW)[H] Notre Dame

Congregation of Holy Cross, Indiana Province, Provincial House; [B] University of Notre Dame Du Lac; [H] Notre Dame, IN Holy Cross Community, Corby Hall, University of Notre Dame.
McGraw, Stephen F. '01 (ARL) Dale City, VA Holy Family.
McGraw, W. Howard *o.s.a.* '62 (PH) Philadelphia, PA St. Nicholas of Tolentine.
McGray, James '67 (SD) Retired.
McGread, Rev. Msgr. Thomas '53 (WCH) Retired.
McGready, Rev. Msgr. Oliver '62 (WDC) Charlotte Hall, MD St. Mary.
McGreevy, John G. *o.p.* '64 (DEN) Denver, CO St. Dominic; [N] Denver, CO Dominican Friars.
McGreevy, Thomas More J. *o.p.* '64 (P)[L] Portland, OR Holy Rosary Priory; Portland, OR Holy Rosary Parish & Dominican Priory Retired.
McGregor, Mark *s.j.* '96 (SPK)[B] Spokane, WA Gonzaga University.
McGroarty, Rev. Msgr. Charles E. '62 (PH) Philadelphia, PA St. Matthew.
McGroarty, Hugh H. '45 (SCR) Pittston, PA St. John the Evangelist.
McGroarty, William K. *s.j.* '55 (BAL)[S] Baltimore, MD Jesuit Community of Loyola University, Inc.
McGrogan, James P. '64 (GRY) Chesterton, IN St. Patrick Retired.
McGuffey, James W. '95 (MET) Carteret, NJ St. Joseph; Carteret, NJ St. Elizabeth of Hungary.
McGuigan, David *s.m.* '01 (BAL) Eldersburg, MD St. Joseph; [V] Sykesville, MD St. Joseph Catholic Community Endowment Trust.
McGuigan, Hugh J. *o.s.f.s.* '97 (VEN) Fort Myers, FL Our Lady of Light.
McGuigan, Hugh *o.s.f.s.* '97 (VEN) Presbyteral Council.
McGuigan, John J. '68 (PAT) Hopatcong, NJ St. Jude's.
McGuigan, Patrick *o.carm.* '79 (NY) Middletown, NY Our Lady of Mt. Carmel; [EE] Middletown, NY Carmelite Friars (North American Province of St. Elias).
McGuigan, Steven F. '90 (SPR) Springfield, MA St. Michael's Cathedral; Auditors.
McGuill, Martin F. '64 (MO) Air Force Reserve Chaplains.
McGuill, Martin '64 (ARL) McLean, VA St. Luke.
McGuine, Peter M. '90 (MO) Air Force Reserve Chaplains.
McGuine, Peter '90 (SD) Spring Valley, CA Santa Sophia; Clergy Personnel Board.
McGuiness, David '73 (MOB) On Leave from the Archdiocese.
McGuiness, Edward J. '61 (SB) Retired.
McGuinn, Finian *o.f.m.* '60 (SFR) San Francisco, CA St. Boniface.
McGuinn, James T. '88 (PH) Philadelphia, PA St. Mary of the Assumption.
McGuinness, David '77 (ATL) Athens, GA St. Joseph; Deans.
McGuinness, Fergal '86 (SR) Adjutant Judicial Vicar; Diocesan Judges; Santa Rosa, CA Cathedral of St. Eugene.
McGuinness, Gerard J. '60 (SB) Retired.
McGuinness, J. Roger '65 (OG) West Chazy, NY St. Joseph.
McGuire, Anthony E. '65 (SFR) San Mateo, CA St. Matthew; Deans.
McGuire, Rev. Msgr. Anthony W. '57 (PH) Retired.
McGuire, Anthony *o.f.m.* '52 (PAT)[N] Butler, NJ St. Anthony Friary.
McGuire, Bonaventure M. *f.i.* '99 (NOR)[G] Griswold, CT Marian Friary of Our Lady of Guadalupe.
McGuire, Brendan '00 (SJ) San Jose, CA Holy Spirit; Notre Dame Club of San Jose/Silicon Valley; College of Consultors; Council of Priests; Vicar General, Office for Special Projects; Special Assignment; Diocesan Leadership Team.
McGuire, David V. '88 (MO) Military Chaplains; Air Force Chaplains.
McGuire, Frederick J. '81 (CIN) On Duty Outside the Archdiocese.
McGuire, J. Frederick '81 (SP) St. Petersburg, FL Blessed Trinity.
McGuire, James D. *o.a.r.* '54 (LA) Montebello, CA St. Benedict.
McGuire, Rev. Msgr. John A. '50 (RVC) Sound Beach, NY St. Louis de Montfort Retired.
McGuire, John C. '79 (NY) Kingston, NY St. Colman Retired.
McGuire, John F. '76 (P) Coquille, OR Holy Name.
McGuire, John Patrick *o.p.* '73 (NY) New York, NY St. Joseph.
McGuire, John *o.p.* '79 (NY)[HH] New York, NY New York University; [HH] New York, NY Pace University.
McGuire, Joseph E. '65 (DUB) Retired.
McGuire, Ken *c.s.p.* '68 (ALB)[L] Lake George, NY St. Mary of the Lake.
McGuire, Kenneth H. *c.s.p.* '68 (NY)[EE] Jamaica Estates Paulist Fathers Generalate.
McGuire, Paul J. *s.c.j.* '68 (MIL)[P] Franklin, WI St. Francis Residence; [Y] Hales Corners, WI Congregation of the Priests of the Sacred Heart Support and Maintenance Trust; [P] Franklin, WI Dehon Study Center.
McGuire, Richard G. *o.c.s.o.* '57 (CHR)[E] Moncks Corner, SC Mepkin Abbey.
McGuire, Rev. Msgr. Richard J. '60 (E) CIVIL AIR PATROL Retired.
McGuire, Richard '67 (SCL) Greenwald, MN St. Michael's Retired.
McGuire, Richard *o.s.c.* '73 (PHX)[F] Phoenix, AZ; Chandler, AZ St. Andrew the Apostle Roman Catholic Parish.
McGuire, Robert *s.j.* '58 (ALB)[N] Fultonville, NY Shrine of Our Lady of Martyrs; Apostleship of Prayer.
McGuire, Thaddeus '99 (PHX) Scottsdale, AZ St. Daniel the Prophet Roman Catholic Parish.
McGuire, Thomas D. '81 (LIN) Indianola, NE St. Catherine's; Presbyteral Council; Diocesan Area CCD Directors; Diocesan Council of Catholic Women; Advocates.
McGuire, Timothy P. '84 (STU) Cadiz, OH St. Teresa; Cadiz, OH Sacred Heart; Cadiz, OH St. Matthias Mission; Woman's Club; College of Consultors.
McGuire, William A. *o.s.a.* '65 (FgM)[Y] Villanova, PA Provincial Offices of the Order of St. Augustine, Province of St. Thomas of Villanova; [Y] Villanova, PA St. Thomas Monastery; Villanova, PA Province of St. Thomas of Villanova (Eastern); Counselors:; [Y] Rosemont, PA Saxony Hall.
McGuire, William *c.p.* (PIT)[O] Pittsburgh, PA St. Paul of the Cross Retreat Center.
McGuirk, Alan B. *m.s.* '56 (HRT)[L] Hartford, CT Missionaries of LaSalette.
McGuirk, John J. '70 (SC) Early, IA Sacred Heart; Sac City, IA St. Mary's; Wall Lake, IA St. Joseph's; Presbyteral Council.
McGuirk, William C. '82 (GBG) United, PA St. Florian.
McGuirl, Rev. Msgr. John A. '72 (BRK) Forest Hills, NY Our Lady of Mercy.
McGurk, Patrick C. '58 (HEL) Associate Judges Retired.
McGurk, Simon '72 (WDC)[N] Washington, DC St. Anselm's Abbey.
McGurn, Richard H. *s.j.* '75 (CHI)[D] Wilmette, IL Loyola Academy; [E] Chicago, IL Chicago Jesuit Academy.
McHale, John F. '04 (SCR) White Haven, PA St. Patrick's.
McHenry, John P. *s.v.d.* '55 (SB)[I] Riverside, CA Divine Word Seminary.
McHenry, Raymond '00 (DM) Indianola, IA St. Thomas Aquinas; Continuing Education for Clergy.
McHenry, Rev. Msgr. Stephen P. '73 (PH) Ambler, PA St. Anthony of Padua; Council of Priests; Pastors Review Board.
McHenry, V. F. *o.p.* '49 (WDC) Washington, DC St. Dominic Church & Priory.
McHenry, Vincent Ferrer *o.p.* '49 (NY)[EE] New York, NY St. Catherine of Siena Priory.
McHugh, Adrian '92 (RVC) Huntington, NY St. Patrick's.
McHugh, Alphonsus *ss.cc.* '69 (BWN) Harlingen, TX Queen of Peace.
McHugh, Brian J. '88 (BO) Somerville, MA St. Ann; Somerville, MA St. Catherine of Genoa.
McHugh, Conall *o.f.m.conv.* '56 (CHL) Winston–Salem, NC Our Lady of Mercy.
McHugh, Connell A. '72 (SCR) Conyngham, PA St. John Bosco; Drums, PA Church of the Good Shepherd.
McHugh, Dennis (PAT) Retired.
McHugh, Donald '57 (P) Retired.
McHugh, Francis *o.f.m.* '76 (BO)[Z] Boston, MA St. Anthony Shrine.
McHugh, Francis '97 (SAT) San Antonio, TX St. Pius X.
McHugh, James L. '60 (COV) Retired.
McHugh, Jerome *o.f.m.cap.* '60 (NY)[EE] White Plains, NY St. Conrad Friary; [EE] White Plains, NY Capuchin Friars International, Inc.; [EE] White Plains, NY St. Francis of Assisi Foundation; [EE] White Plains, NY Capuchin Friars of North America.
Mc Hugh, John F. *o.m.i.* '73 (BO)[X] Tewksbury, MA Immaculate Heart of Mary Residence.
McHugh, John P. '91 (HRT) Collinsville, CT St. Patrick.
McHugh, John T. '93 (LC) Leave of Absence.
McHugh, John W. '76 (HRT) Avon, CT St. Ann's.
McHugh, John *s.o.l.t.* '52 (CC)[G] Robstown, TX Society of Our Lady of the Most Holy Trinity.
McHugh, John *s.o.l.t.* '52 (SFE) Mora, NM St. Gertrude.
McHugh, John *o.f.m.cap.* '69 (NY)[EE] White Plains, NY St. Conrad Friary.
McHugh, Joseph B. *s.j.* '58 (BO)[U] Weston, MA Campion Jesuit Community; [U] Weston, MA Campion Health Center, Inc.
McHugh, Joseph *s.j.* '83 (BO)[W] Gloucester, MA Eastern Point Retreat House.
McHugh, Rev. Msgr. Kieran A. '70 (PAT)[Q] Sparta, NJ Pope John XXIII High School Special Project Foundation, Inc; [C] Sparta, NJ Pope John XXIII High School; [Q] Sparta, NJ The Catholic Academy of Sussex County, Inc.
McHugh, Michael J. '80 (BRK) Brooklyn, NY St. Jude Shrine Church; Woodside, NY St. Sebastian; On Leave/Unassigned.
McHugh, Patrick Joseph '50 (LA) Torrance, CA Nativity Retired.
McHugh, Paul F. '53 (MAN) Retired.
McHugh, Rev. Msgr. Peter J. '65 (PAT)[Q] Chester, NJ Nazareth Village.
McHugh, Thomas J. '49 (CHI) Retired.
McHugh, William *o.m.i.* '52 (P) Shady Cove, OR Our Lady of Fatima.
McIlhenny, Bernard R. *s.j.* '56 (SCR)[C] Scranton, PA The University of Scranton.
McIlhone, James P. '74 (CHI)[A] Mundelein, IL University of St. Mary of the Lake/Mundelein Seminary.
McIlmail, Edward *l.c.* '01 (PRO)[G] Warwick, RI Overbrook Academy at Our Lady of Providence Center.
McIlvane, Donald W. '52 (PIT) Retired.
McIlwain, Michael A. *o.s.b.* '94 (GBG)[G] Latrobe Saint Vincent Archabbey.
McIndoo, Ed (P)[J] Eugene, OR Sacred Heart Medical Center.
McInerney, Blaise *o.carm.* '54 (JOL)[L] Darien Carmelite Provincial Office.
McInerney, Henry '77 (BLX) Ocean Springs, MS St. Alphonsus.
McInerney, Kieran *o.s.b.* '52 (FgM) Atchison, KS St. Benedict's Abbey.
McInerny, Kieran *o.s.b.* '52 (KCK)[I] Atchison, KS St. Benedict's Abbey.
McInerny, Rev. Msgr. Lawrence B. '79 (CHR) Sullivan's Island, SC Stella Maris.
McInerny, Rev. Msgr. Paul B. '72 (BO) On Duty Outside the Archdiocese.
McInnes, Val A. *o.p.* '61 (NO) New Orleans, LA St. Dominic; [S] New Orleans, LA The Patrons of the Vatican Museums in the South, Inc.; [S] Metairie, LA International Dominican Foundation.
McInnis, Francis L. '56 (GF) Retired.
McInnis, Francis '57 (GF)[B] Great Falls, MT Great Falls Central Catholic High School.
McInnis, Gary '98 (LAN) Egeler Correctional Facility.
McInnis, George L. *c.p.m.* '07 (OWN)[F] Auburn, KY Fathers of Mercy.
McInnis, Thomas J. '57 (LC) Retired.
McIntire, William J. *m.m.* '67 (FgM) Maryknoll, NY MARYKNOLL.
McIntosh, Martin *s.j.* (TUC)[H] Nogales, AZ Kino Border Initiative.
McIntosh, Robert K. *s.j.* '72 (FgM) Milwaukee, WI Society of Jesus.
McIntosh, Thomas *c.ss.r.* '66 (FgM) Denver, CO Denver Province.
McIntyre, Gerald J. *s.j.* '74 (PAT)[J] Morristown, NJ Loyola House of Retreats.
McIntyre, James *o.f.m.cap.* '53 (NY)[EE] Yonkers, NY St. Clare Friary.
McIntyre, Rev. Msgr. John J. '92 (PH) On Special or Other Archdiocesan Assignment; Office of the Cardinal.
McIntyre, John P. *s.j.* '63 (BO)[U] Newton, MA The Jesuit Community at Boston College.
McIntyre, Justin '81 (SR) Retired.
McIntyre, Patrick '60 (FgM) Boston, MA St. James the Apostle, Inc.
McIntyre, Rev. Msgr. Thomas J. '66 (CAM) College of Consultors; Cape May, NJ The Church of Our Lady Star of the Sea, Cape May.
McIntyre, Thomas J. *c.m.* '50 (LA)[P] Montebello, CA DePaul Evangelization Center; [V] Montebello, CA DePaul Evangelization Center Retired.
McIntyre, William *o.f.m.* '95 (R) Durham, NC Immaculate Conception.
McKamy, Eldon J. '63 (OM) Retired.
McKane, Wm. Paul *o.s.b.* '88 (GF) Great Falls, MT St. Joseph; Great Falls, MT St. Luke the Evangelist.
McKarns, James E. '62 (Y) North Canton, OH St. Paul; Priests Council Retired.
McKay, Alistair *c.ss.r.* '75 (RIC) Newport News, VA St. Vincent de Paul; [M] Hampton, VA Holy Family Retreat.
McKay, Douglas M. '82 (PH)[W] Philadelphia, PA Holy Family Home; On Special or Other Archdiocesan Assignment.
McKay, Rev. Msgr. James P. '56 (SFR) Retired.
McKay, James R. *s.m.* '44 (CIN)[N] Dayton, OH Mercy Siena Gardens.
McKay, John F. '73 (WDC) Riverdale Park, MD St. Bernard; Hospital & Nursing Home Ministries; Bethesda, MD St. Jane Frances de Chantal.
McKay, Michael *o.s.b.* '86 (WH)[F] Wheeling, WV Wheeling Hospital.
McKay, Michael *o.s.b.* '86 (GBG)[G] Latrobe Saint Vincent Archabbey.
McKay, Robert '70 (SJ)[H] San Jose, CA O'Connor Hospital.
McKay, Rev. Msgr. William E. '49 (PHX) Retired.
McKean, Dan '87 (LAN) On Leave of Absence.
McKeaney, James J. '69 (PH) Bryn Mawr, PA St. John Neumann.
McKearney, James L. *s.s.* '97 (HRT) On Duty Outside

the Archdiocese.
McKearney, James L. *s.s.* '97 (BAL)[S] Baltimore Society of St. Sulpice, Province of the United States.
McKearney, James L. *s.s.* '97 (SFR)[A] Menlo Park, CA St. Patrick Seminary and University; [A] Menlo Park, CA St. Patrick Seminary and University.
McKee, Francis X. '66 (PH) Philadelphia, PA Holy Family.
McKee, Henry J. '72 (PH) Havertown, PA Sacred Heart.
McKee, Jay R. '02 (WIL) Perryville, MD Church of the Good Shepherd.
McKee, Shane *s.o.l.t.* '07 (CC)[G] Robstown, TX Society of Our Lady of the Most Holy Trinity.
Mckee, Shane *s.o.l.t.* '07 (FAR) Belcourt, ND St. Ann; Belcourt, ND St. Ann.
McKee, William '83 (SEA) Federal Way, WA St. Vincent De Paul.
McKeefry, Brendan '67 (SAC) Carmichael, CA Our Lady of the Assumption.
McKeever, Henry *c.ss.r.* '48 (STL)[O] Liguori, MO St. Clement Health Care Center Retired.
McKelvey, James P. '93 (PH)[T] Immaculata, PA Camilla Hall Nursing Home; On Special or Other Archdiocesan Assignment.
McKelvey, Thomas P. '62 (PH) Retired.
McKenna, Brian *o.f.m.cap.* '66 (SFR) Burlingame, CA Our Lady of Angels.
McKenna, Colin J. '99 (BGP) Georgetown, CT Sacred Heart.
McKenna, Edward J. '65 (CHI) Other Assignments.
McKenna, Rev. Msgr. Enda '64 (SAT) Fredericksburg, TX St. Mary's.
McKenna, Eugene J. '63 (PRO) Retired.
McKenna, F. Charles '60 (ALN)[J] Bethlehem, PA Holy Family Villa Retired.
McKenna, George P. '44 (CHI) Retired.
McKenna, James George '61 (DAL) On Duty Outside the Diocese; Dallas, TX Holy Cross.
McKenna, James *s.d.b.* '80 (NO)[D] Marrero, LA Archbishop Shaw High School; [G] Marrero, LA Archbishop Shaw Junior High School.
McKenna, Jerome *c.p.* '58 (ATL) Atlanta, GA St. Paul of the Cross.
McKenna, John H. *c.m.* '64 (BRK)[T] Jamaica, NY St. Vincent's House.
McKenna, John J. '47 (NY) Sloatsburg, NY St. Joan of Arc Retired.
McKenna, John L. '88 (PIT) Monaca, PA St. John the Baptist.
McKenna, John *c.ss.r.* '77 (WIL) Seaford, DE Our Lady of Lourdes; Deans.
McKenna, Joseph J. *o.s.f.s.* '57 (WIL) Wilmington, DE St. Francis Hospital; [I] Wilmington, DE St. Francis Hospital, Inc.; [J] Wilmington, DE DeSales House.
McKenna, Joseph R. '57 (PRT) Portland, ME St. Joseph's Manor Retired.
McKenna, Kenneth N. *o.s.f.s.* '85 (LAN)[M] Brooklyn, MI Lake Vineyard Camps, Inc., (De Sales Center); Toledo, OH; [J] Brooklyn, MI Thorrez Vocational Trust, Ltd.
McKenna, Kenneth N. *o.s.f.s.* '85 (TOL)[I] Toledo Oblates of St. Francis de Sales.
McKenna, Kevin E. '77 (ROC) Rochester, NY Sacred Heart Cathedral; Priest Consultors; Judges.
McKenna, Peter '57 (SAT) Retired.
McKenna, Philip A. '62 (MOB) Montgomery, AL Church of the Holy Spirit; Sacramental Ministers.
McKenna, Thomas F. *c.m.* '70 (BUF)[O] Niagara University, NY Vincentian Community at Niagara University; [C] Niagara University, NY Niagara University.
McKenna, Timothy J. '79 (MO) Air National Guard Chaplains.
McKenna, Timothy '79 (SEA) Auburn, WA Holy Family.
McKenna, William A. *s.j.* '68 (NEW)[B] Jersey City, NJ Jesuit Center; [M] Jersey City, NJ Jesuits of Saint Peter's College, Inc.
McKenzie, John J. *o.s.a.* '65 (PH)[C] Villanova University; Conshohocken, PA SS. Cosmas and Damian; [Y] Rosemont, PA Saxony Hall.
McKenzie, Mark D. *s.j.* '69 (STL) St. Louis, MO St. Matthew, Apostle; [O] St. Louis, MO St. Matthew Jesuit Community.
McKenzie, William L. '82 (KNX) Oak Ridge, TN St. Mary; Presbyteral Council.
McKeon, Gerard R. *s.j.* '86 (BO)[AA] Salem, MA Salem State College, Catholic Campus Ministry; Salem State College; [D] Dorchester, MA Boston College High School.
McKeon, Gerard R. *s.j.* '86 (NOR)[L] Storrs, CT University of Connecticut.
McKeon, John Aedan *o.p.* '56 (NY)[EE] New York St. Vincent Ferrer Priory.
McKeon, Michael C. '65 (SAC) Roseville, CA St. Rose of Lima Retired.
McKeon, Raymond T. '63 (NEW) Jersey City, NJ St. Paul's Retired.
McKeon, Robert F. '90 (NY) Brewster, NY St. Lawrence O'Toole; Canon 1742 Panel of Pastors.
McKeon, Robert '59 (LAN) Gaines, MI St. Joseph Retired.
McKeough, Brendan J. *o.praem.* '53 (GB)[J] De Pere, WI St. Joseph Priory.
McKeough, James A. *s.j.* '54 (FgM) New York, NY Society of Jesus.
McKeown, Timothy P. '97 (SAV) Statesboro, GA St. Matthew; Statesboro Deanery; Director of Vocations.
McKercher, Mark J. '97 (OM) Omaha, NE St. Cecilia Cathedral.
McKernan, Leo J. '83 (SCR)[M] Laceyville, PA Franciscan Missionary Hermits of St. Joseph.
McKernan, Louis F. *c.s.p.* '54 (NY)[EE] Jamaica Estates Paulist Fathers Generalate.
McKevitt, Gerald L. *s.j.* '75 (SJ)[B] Santa Clara, CA Jesuit Community.
McKiernan, Rev. Msgr. J. Michael '91 (ORG) Council of Priests; Consultors; Liturgical Commission; Building and Renovation Committee of the Liturgical Commission; Santa Ana, CA Christ Our Savior Cathedral.
McKiernan, Vincent W. *c.s.p.* '57 (COL)[J] Columbus, OH Campus Ministry.
McKillin, David *o.s.b.* '76 (LR)[H] Fort Smith, AR St. Scholastica Monastery–Motherhouse.
McKinley, Joseph *s.s.j.* '85 (NO)[P] New Orleans, LA The Josephite Faculty House of St. Augustine High School.
McKinley, Michael J. '85 (LFT) Union City, IN St. Mary; Union City, IN St. Joseph.
McKinley, Stephen *o.f.m.conv.* '94 (CHI)[N] Libertyville, IL Marytown, Our Lady of Fatima Friary.
McKinney, Floyd E. '80 (DOD) Pratt, KS Sacred Heart Catholic Church of Pratt, Kansas; On Duty Outside the Diocese.
McKinney, Michael '93 (LFT) Logansport, IN All Saints; Members.
McKinney, Ronald H. *s.j.* '83 (SCR)[C] Scranton, PA The University of Scranton.
McKinney, Thomas A. '61 (GR) Retired.
McKinnon, Eymard '54 (NY)[EE] Yonkers, NY St. Clare Friary.
McKitrick, James V. '58 (RCK) Retired.
McKnight, Albert *c.s.sp.* '52 (SB)[I] Hemet, CA Congregation of the Holy Spirit Retired.
McKnight, James '59 (SAC) Retired.
McKnight, Kevin F. '94 (PIT) Pittsburgh, PA Saint Elizabeth of Hungary.
McKnight, W. Shawn '94 (WCH) Wichita, KS Blessed Sacrament.
McKone, John '08 (FWT) Vernon, TX St. Joseph; Vernon, TX St. Mary; Vernon, TX Holy Family; Mission Council.
McKusky, Kristoffer '05 (DUL) Brainerd, MN All Saints.
McLachlan, Frederick E. *s.s.e.* '64 (BUR) Putney, VT Our Lady of Mercy.
McLafferty, Joseph M. '00 (NY) Staten Island, NY St. Christopher.
McLain, John J. *s.j.* '98 (P)[L] Portland Jesuit Provincial Office (Society of Jesus, Oregon Prov.).
McLain, Michael D. '08 (SUP) Mellen, WI St. George; Mellen, WI Most Precious Blood; Mellen, WI St. Anthony; Mellen, WI Holy Rosary; Mellen, WI St. Anne.
McLaughlin, Anthony J. '59 (PAT) Unassigned.
McLaughlin, Anthony '97 (TYL) Judges.
McLaughlin, Daniel F. *m.m.* '61 (FgM) Maryknoll, NY MARYKNOLL.
McLaughlin, Daniel J. *o.s.a.* '76 (PH)[Y] Villanova, PA St. Augustine Friary.
McLaughlin, David S. '96 (NEW) Hackensack, NJ Bergen County Correctional Facility; Hackensack, NJ Holy Trinity; Newark, NJ St. John's.
McLaughlin, Don E. '81 (JOL) Wheaton, IL St. Michael.
McLaughlin, Donald E. '67 (NEW) Retired.
McLaughlin, Edward J. '52 (BO) Bridgewater, MA St. Thomas Aquinas; Senior Priests. Retired.
McLaughlin, Edward J. '59 (CHI) Palos Heights, IL Incarnation Retired.
McLaughlin, Farrell E. '71 (PRO) Cranston, RI St. Ann.
McLaughlin, Gerald L. *s.j.* '59 (FgM) Watertown, MA Society of Jesus.
McLaughlin, Gregory '85 (AUS) Salado, TX St. Stephen.
McLaughlin, James J. '70 (PH) Absent on Sick Leave.
McLaughlin, James W. '96 (MET) Retired.
McLaughlin, James '73 (SB) College of Consultors; La Quinta, CA St. Francis of Assisi.
McLaughlin, John R. '95 (BO) On Duty Outside the Archdiocese.
McLaughlin, John R. '95 (MO) Presbyteral Council; Director of Vocations.
McLaughlin, John '61 (SEA) Retired.
McLaughlin, John '66 (MIA) Retired Priests' Committee Retired.
McLaughlin, Joseph J. '66 (PH) Richboro, PA St. Vincent de Paul.
McLaughlin, Joseph J. *s.m.* '72 (FgM) THE SOCIETY OF MARY.
McLaughlin, Joseph M. *s.s.e.* '70 (BUR)[E] Colchester, VT Society of St. Edmund; [A] Colchester, VT St. Michael's College.
McLaughlin, Joseph P. *o.praem.* '70 (PH)[Y] Paoli, PA Daylesford Abbey.
McLaughlin, Joseph P. *o.praem.* '70 (WIL)[B] Claymont, DE Archmere Academy.
McLaughlin, Michael (DM) Greenfield, IA St. John; Massena, IA St. Patrick.
McLaughlin, Neil P. *s.j.* '59 (BAL)[S] Baltimore, MD Colombiere Jesuit Community.
McLaughlin, Patrick A. '05 (OM) Dodge, NE St. Wenceslaus; Deans; Officers; Deans.
McLaughlin, Patrick J. '61 (BO) Medford, MA St. Joseph; Presbyteral Council.
McLaughlin, Patrick J. '74 (SCR) Scranton, PA Immaculate Conception.
McLaughlin, Paul F. '71 (VEN) Bradenton, FL St. Joseph.
McLaughlin, Peter A. '78 (PT) On Duty Outside the Diocese; Pensacola, FL St. Michael.
McLaughlin, Peter '78 (PT) Apostleship of the Sea, Office of the.
McLaughlin, Richard C. '74 (PRT) Members; Auburn, ME Immaculate Heart of Mary Parish; Norway, ME Blessed Teresa of Calcutta Parish.
McLaughlin, Richard P. '68 (BO) Senior Priests. Retired.
McLaughlin, Robert A. '73 (PH) Kimberton, PA St. Basil the Great.
McLaughlin, Rev. Msgr. Thomas C. '56 (VIC) On Special or Other Diocesan Assignment; Vicars General; Chancellor; Diocesan Consultors; Presbyteral Council; Judicial Vicar; Priests' Personnel Board; Diocesan Finance Board; Propagation of the Faith, Holy Childhood Association; Mission Cooperative Plan.
McLaughlin, Thomas D. '76 (SCR) Stroudsburg, PA St. Luke; Diocesan Finance Council; Deans.
McLaughlin, Thomas R. '81 (NEW) Elizabeth, NJ Blessed Sacrament.
McLaughlin, William A. '92 (BRK) Douglaston, NY St. Anastasia.
McLaughlin, William H. '68 (BO) Beverly, MA St. John the Evangelist.
McLaughlin, William J. '70 (TR) Asbury Park, NJ Holy Spirit; Asbury Park, NJ St. Peter Claver; The Haitian Apostolate.
McLaughlin, Rev. Msgr. William '58 (ORG) Retired.
McLaverty, Albert J. '00 (CAM) On Leave of Absence.
McLean, Barry L. '90 (SAN) Diocesan Consultors; Board of Directors; Presbyteral Council; Continuing Education of the Clergy; Vocations.
McLean, Edward J. '52 (HRT) Special and other Archdiocesan Assignment; Catholic Library and Information Center – Catholic Book Store; Glastonbury, CT St. Paul Retired.
McLean, George F. *o.m.i.* '55 (WDC)[N] Washington, DC Oblate Community; [W] Washington, DC Council for Research in Values and Philosophy; Washington, DC The National Center for Urban Ethnic Affairs (1971).
McLean, William '70 (LA) Chatsworth, CA St. John Eudes.
McLearen, Daniel J. '92 (HRT) New Haven, CT St. Francis; New Haven Vicariate.
McLellan, Daniel *o.f.m.* '76 (R) Durham, NC Immaculate Conception.
McLellan, James R. '70 (FR) Retired.
McLellan, Michael F. '76 (BO) Canton, MA St. John the Evangelist.
McLelland, James R. '00 (SHP) Vivian, LA St. Clement; [B] Shreveport, LA Christus Health Northern Louisiana; Priests' Retirement Board.
McLeod, David (PAT) Retired.
McLeod, Frederick G. *s.j.* '62 (BO)[U] Boston The Society of Jesus of New England–Provincial Offices.
McLeod, Frederick G. *s.j.* '62 (STL)[O] St. Louis, MO Jesuit Community Corporation at Saint Louis University – Jesuit Hall.
McLernon, Thomas M. '57 (MIL)[B] Hales Corners, WI Sacred Heart School of Theology.
McLinden, James E. *s.s.j.* '71 (BAL) Baltimore, MD St. Francis Xavier.
McLinden, James E. *s.s.j.* '62 (WDC)[B] Washington, DC Josephite Pastoral Center.
McLoone, Rev. Msgr. Joseph C. '88 (PH) Chester, PA Saint Katharine Drexel; [BB] Chester, PA Widener University.
McLoud, Steven J. '94 (SC) Churdan, IA St. Columbkille; Churdan, IA St. Paul's.
McLoughlan, Daniel *s.j.* '63 (WDC)[N] Adelphi, MD Father Judge Missionary Cenacle.
McLoughlin, Brendan '70 (PAT) On Duty Outside the Diocese.
McLoughlin, Rev. Msgr. James W. '65 (RCK) Deans; Richmond, IL St. Joseph.
McLoughlin, John T. '73 (NY) Mt. Vernon, NY St. Ursula.
McLoughlin, John *c.ss.r.* '92 (HBG) Ephrata, PA Mother of Perpetual Help; [G] Ephrata, PA St. Clement's Mission House.
McLoughlin, Luke '66 (STA) Jacksonville, FL St. Matthew's; Catholic Women, Council of.
McLoughlin, Michael P. '81 (NY) Warwick, NY St. Stephen.

McLoughlin, Nicholas '66 (VEN) Presbyteral Council; Avon Park, FL Our Lady of Grace.
McLoughlin, Paul J. '71 (SPC) Ozark, MO St. Joseph the Worker; Co Directors; Office of Worship; Liturgical Commission; Presbyteral Council; Priests' Mutual Benefit Society; Diocesan Consultors.
McMackin, Thomas P. '63 (ORL) Retired.
McMahan, Timothy M. *s.j.* (STL)[O] St. Louis, MO Bellarmine House of Studies.
McMahon, Albert *o.f.m.* '60 (ALB)[A] Catskill, NY St. Anthony Friary.
McMahon, Aloysius J. '53 (OM) Retired.
McMahon, Bartholomew *o.f.m.* '62 (FgM) New York, NY Holy Name Province.
McMahon, Bernard '48 (NY) Retired.
McMahon, Brian F. '80 (BO) Dorchester, MA St. Brendan.
McMahon, Charles E. *s.s.j.* '58 (BLX) Pascagoula, MS St. Peter the Apostle; College of Consultors.
McMahon, Craig *o.m.v.* '90 (BO)[U] Milton, MA Oblate Residence (St. Joseph House).
McMahon, Edward J. *s.j.* '60 (NY)[EE] New York, NY Xavier Jesuit Community.
McMahon, Francis X. *s.s.e.* '54 (BUR) Putney, VT Our Lady of Mercy Retired.
McMahon, Gerald J. '59 (ROC) Retired.
McMahon, Gerard J. '59 (ROC) Webster, NY Holy Spirit Retired.
McMahon, John A. *o.p.* '68 (WDC) Washington, DC St. Dominic Church & Priory; [N] Washington, DC Center for Assisted Living; New York, NY.
McMahon, Rev. Msgr. John J. '48 (PHX)[G] Phoenix, AZ Mount Claret Roman Catholic Retreat Center Retired.
McMahon, Rev. Msgr. John '66 (PMB) Retired.
McMahon, Joseph R. '71 (WIL) Wilmington, DE St. Mary Magdalen; Apostleship of Prayer.
McMahon, Joseph S. '68 (P) Lake Oswego, OR Our Lady of the Lake; Liturgical Commission; College of Consultors.
McMahon, Joseph V. '84 (NSH) Madison, TN St. Joseph.
McMahon, Joseph (NSH) Deans; Presbyteral Council.
McMahon, Rev. Msgr. Kevin T. '75 (WIL) On Duty Outside the Diocese.
McMahon, Kieran M. '65 (SAC) Sacramento, CA St. Robert.
McMahon, Michael F. '88 (CHI) Antioch, IL St. Peter.
McMahon, Michael J. '04 (PRO) Warwick, RI St. Timothy.
McMahon, Patrick *o.carm.* '76 (WDC)[B] Washington, DC Whitefriars Hall; [B] The Carmelitana Library.
McMahon, Walter M. '73 (SJ) San Jose, CA Church of the Transfiguration.
McManamon, James *o.f.m.* '49 (CLV)[N] Brooklyn, OH St. Anthony of Padua Friary.
McManamon, John M. *s.j.* '80 (CHI)[C] Chicago, IL Jesuit Community at Loyola University Chicago.
McManus, Denis *c.s.sp.* '58 (SFR) San Rafael, CA St. Raphael Retired.
McManus, Dennis Douglas '05 (MOB) On Leave from the Archdiocese.
McManus, Eamon '54 (WDC) Retired.
McManus, Francis J. *s.j.* '73 (BO)[U] Weston, MA Campion Jesuit Community.
McManus, Rev. Msgr. Gerald D. '79 (PH) Military Chaplains; Air Force Chaplains.
McManus, Rev. Msgr. Gerald D. '79 (MO) Presbyteral Council.
McManus, Rev. Msgr. Hugh F. '61 (NY) Scarsdale, NY Our Lady of Fatima.
Mc Manus, Joseph *s.o.l.t.* '96 (CC)[G] Robstown, TX Society of Our Lady of the Most Holy Trinity.
McManus, Michael K. '85 (FR) Raynham Center, MA St. Ann; Chancellor; Diocesan Consultors; Members.
McManus, Michael '48 (SAT)[K] San Antonio, TX Casa De Padres Retired.
McManus, Paul C. '65 (DUB) Retired.
McManus, Paul G. '87 (BO) Lawrence, MA St. Patrick.
McManus, Rev. Msgr. Paul J. '42 (BO) Senior Priests. Retired.
McManus, Richard *o.f.m.* '82 (LA)[P] Santa Barbara, CA Franciscan Friary, Order of Friars Minor (Old Mission).
McManus, Rev. Msgr. Robert T. '52 (PH) Retired.
McManus, Thomas F. *s.j.* '63 (NEW)[C] Jersey City, NJ Jesuit Community; [M] Jersey City, NJ Jesuit Community of St. Peter's Prep, Inc.
McMaster, Brian '01 (AUS) Vocations; Diocesan Institute for Ecclesial Ministry.
McMenamy, Alvin *s.m.* '53 (STL)[O] St. Louis, MO Maryland Avenue Marianist Community.
McMenemie, Rev. Msgr. James P. '53 (NEW) Lyndhurst, NJ St. Michael's; Archdiocesan Judges Retired.
McMichael, Steven J. '03 (STP)[C] St. Paul, MN University of St. Thomas.
McMichael, Steven *o.f.m.conv.* '02 (STP)[N] Prior Lake, MN Franciscan Retreats.
McMichael, Thomas '09 (SEA) Burlington, WA St. Charles; La Conner, WA Sacred Heart; Sedro Woolley, WA Immaculate Heart of Mary; La Conner, WA St. Paul; Mount Vernon, WA Immaculate Conception.
McMillan, Cliff J. '90 (DEN) Glenwood Springs, CO St. Stephen.
McMillan, John F. *c.p.* '56 (PIT)[M] Pittsburgh, PA St. Paul of the Cross Monastery.
McMillan, Robert G. *s.j.* '62 (BO)[U] Boston, MA Loyola House.
McMillan, Robert *s.j.* (BO) Members.
McMillen, Michael *s.c.j.* '67 (JOL) Elmhurst, IL Elmhurst Memorial Hospital.
McMillen, Michael *s.c.j.* '67 (MIL)[P] Hales Corners Priests of the Sacred Heart.
McMillin, Charles '02 (LKC) Jennings, LA Our Lady Help of Christians.
McMorrow, Matthew '05 (RCK) Special Assignment; Scouts; [B] Rockford, IL Boylan Central Catholic High School.
McMullan, John '61 (SEA) Retired.
McMullen, Francis R. '51 (RVC) Retired.
McMullen, John *o.s.b.* '66 (SFS) Wilmot, SD St. Mary; [F] Marvin, SD Blue Cloud Abbey; [I] Marvin, SD Blue Cloud Abbey Retirement Trust.
McMullen, Patrick M. '06 (CIN) Dayton, OH St. Peter.
McMullen, Roger '67 (SHP) Retired.
McMullin, Daniel T. '81 (ROC)[M] Ithaca, NY The Cornell Catholic Community, Inc. (Ithaca); Ithaca, NY Cornell University.
McMurry, John E. *s.s.* '56 (BAL)[S] Baltimore Society of St. Sulpice, Province of the United States; [O] Baltimore, MD St. Charles Villa Retired.
McMurry, John E. *s.s.* '56 (NSH) Retired.
McMurry, Vincent deP. *s.s.* '49 (BAL)[O] Baltimore, MD St. Charles Villa; [S] Baltimore Society of St. Sulpice, Province of the United States Retired.
McMurry, Vincent deP. *s.s.* '49 (NSH) Retired.
McNair, Andrew *l.c.* '97 (PRO) Central Falls, RI Holy Spirit Parish; Black Catholic Ministry.
McNalis, John P. '76 (CHI) Other Assignments.
McNally, Dennis E. *s.j.* '74 (PH)[C] Jesuit Fathers; [Y] Loyola Center and Manresa Hall.
McNally, Edward F. '95 (SY) Absent on Leave.
McNally, Joseph J. '58 (IND) Retired.
McNally, Lawrence R. '77 (CHI) Oak Park, IL Ascension.
McNally, Michael J. '73 (PMB) Fort Pierce, FL St. Mark the Evangelist.
McNally, Michael R. '59 (MO) DEPARTMENT OF VETERANS AFFAIRS HOSPITALS AND CHAPLAINS Retired.
McNally, Nathan *o.f.m.* '57 (STL)[J] St. Louis, MO St. Anthony's Medical Center; [O] St. Louis, MO Franciscan Friary of St. Anthony of Padua Retired.
McNally, Richard *ss.cc.* '75 (FR)[G] Fairhaven National Center of the Enthronement.
McNally, Stephen '86 (RIC) Fincastle, VA Church of the Transfiguration; New Castle, VA Saint John the Evangelist Mission.
McNally, Theodore A. *o.f.m.* '55 (PAT)[N] Ringwood, NJ Holy Name Friary, Inc.
McNally, Thomas *c.s.c.* '59 (FTW)[H] Notre Dame Congregation of Holy Cross, Indiana Province, Provincial House.
McNally, Vincent M. *s.j.* '48 (BUF)[O] Buffalo, NY Canisius Jesuit Community Inc. Retired.
McNamara, Anthony *o.carm.* '69 (JOL)[L] Darien Carmelite Provincial Office.
McNamara, Rev. Msgr. Brian J. '84 (RVC) Priests' Retirement Board; Secretary for Ministerial Personnel; Clergy Personnel; Priests' Personnel Assignment Board; Priests' Personnel Policy Board; Garden City, NY St. Joseph's.
McNamara, Brian J. '84 (MO) Air Force Reserve Chaplains.
McNamara, Daniel J. *s.j.* '80 (FgM) New York, NY Society of Jesus.
McNamara, Dennis L. *s.j.* '76 (WDC)[N] Washington, DC The Jesuit Community at Georgetown University.
McNamara, Donald P. '61 (PH) Retired.
McNamara, Rev. Msgr. Eugene P. '53 (BO) Senior Priests. Retired.
McNamara, Rev. Msgr. James M. '71 (RVC) Smithaven Deanery.
McNamara, James '71 (RVC) Nesconset, NY Church of the Holy Cross.
McNamara, John P. '56 (CHI) Retired.
McNamara, Michael J. '80 (BO) Unassigned.
McNamara, Rev. Msgr. Patrick V. '60 (NY) New Rochelle, NY St. Gabriel.
McNamara, Philip D. '56 (WOR) Retired.
McNamara, Philip *s.a.c.* '58 (FWT) Stephenville, TX St. Brendan; Stephenville, TX Our Lady of Guadalupe; Stephenville, TX Sacred Heart.
McNamara, Robert J. '69 (LA) Woodland Hills, CA St. Bernardine of Siena.
McNamara, Stephen E. '67 (VEN) Fort Myers, FL Church Of The Resurrection Of Our Lord; Treasurer; College of Consultors; Deans; Priest Personnel Board; Priest Personnel Board; Presbyteral Council.
McNamara, Thomas J. '82 (SAG) Saginaw, MI Cathedral of Mary the Assumption; Mount Pleasant, MI St. Joseph the Worker; Vicar General.
McNamara, Thomas *o.f.m.cap.* '07 (NY) New York, NY Our Lady of Sorrows.
McNamara, William '65 (SAT) Elmendorf, TX St. Anthony; Archdiocesan Council of Catholic Women.
McNamee, Rev. Msgr. Charles W. '50 (RCK) Censores Librorum Retired.
McNamee, Francis G. '95 (ATL) Vicars for Clergy; Priest Personnel; College of Consultors; Atlanta, GA Cathedral of Christ the King.
McNamee, James P. '73 (LC) Adams, WI St. Joseph; Oxford, WI St. Ann.
McNamee, John P. '59 (PH) Retired.
McNamee, Patrick '70 (P) Beaverton, OR St. Cecilia; Building Commission.
McNea, Mark C. '89 (WIN) Wells, MN Our Lady of Mount Carmel; Wells, MN St. John the Baptist; Wells, MN St. Casimir's; Elected Deanery Representatives.
McNeeley, William J. '07 (KNX) Townsend, TN St. Francis of Assisi.
McNeely, Matthew *f.s.s.p.* '07 (SAC) "Ecclesia Dei" Community (Latin Mass); Sacramento, CA St. Stephen the First Martyr Parish.
McNeese, Robert J. '98 (SPK) Priests' Personnel Board.
McNeese, Robert J. '98 (SPK) Spokane, WA St. Augustine; Members.
McNeff, Thomas C. '77 (CHI) Chicago, IL St. Jane de Chantal.
McNeil, Aubrey *o.f.m.* '85 (CHR) Anderson, SC St. Mary of the Angels.
McNeil, Joel '87 (DM) On Special Assignment; Des Moines, IA St. Catherine of Siena Catholic Student Center; [I] Des Moines, IA St. Catherine of Siena Catholic Student Center; On Duty Outside the Diocese.
McNeil, Joel (DM) Campus Ministry.
McNeil, John R. '61 (BO) On Duty Outside the Archdiocese. Retired.
McNeil, Lawrence J. '73 (HBG) Hanover, PA Basilica of the Sacred Heart of Jesus; Consultors, College; Presbyteral Council.
McNeil, Lawrence J. '73 (BAL)[A] Emmitsburg, MD Mount St. Mary's Seminary.
McNeill, Donald *c.s.c.* '65 (FTW)[H] Notre Dame Congregation of Holy Cross, Indiana Province, Provincial House; [B] University of Notre Dame Du Lac; [H] Notre Dame, IN Holy Cross Community, Corby Hall, University of Notre Dame.
McNeill, Neil '01 (LAF) Breaux Bridge, LA St. Bernard.
McNeilly, Dennis P. *s.j.* '85 (OM)[K] Omaha, NE Jesuit Community at Creighton University.
McNelis, Paul D. *s.j.* '77 (NY)[EE] Cardinal Spellman Hall, Jesuit Community.
McNellis, Paul *s.j.* '87 (BO)[U] Newton, MA The Jesuit Community at Boston College.
McNerney, Eamonn '86 (B)[B] Cottonwood, ID St. Mary's Hospital; Cottonwood, ID Monastery of St. Gertrude; [D] Cottonwood, ID Monastery of St. Gertrude, Motherhouse and Novitiate; Cottonwood, ID.
McNew, Dwayne A. '95 (COL) Portsmouth, OH Holy Redeemer.
McNichol, Daniel '87 (HON) Retired.
McNicholas, Stephen '53 (ORL) Retired.
McNicholas, Walter F. *o.s.a.* '52 (CHI)[N] Chicago, IL St. Rita Monastery.
McNulty, Edward P. '93 (SD) San Diego, CA St. Agnes; Judicial Vicar; Clergy Personnel Board.
McNulty, Francis J. '52 (NEW)[M] Caldwell, NJ The Rev. Msgr. James F. Kelley Residence for Retired Priests Retired.
McNulty, Gerard J. '67 (LA) VA Chaplains; DEPARTMENT OF VETERANS AFFAIRS HOSPITALS AND CHAPLAINS; Hospital Chaplains.
McNulty, James '03 (DET) Livonia, MI St. Priscilla.
McNulty, John P. '73 (CLV) Euclid, OH Holy Cross; Euclid, OH St. Christine.
McNulty, John T. '74 (PRO) Newport, RI St. Augustin.
McNulty, Joseph D. '69 (CLV) Cleveland, OH St. Augustine; Office of Ministry for Persons with Disabilities.
McNulty, Martin J. '03 (BO) Permanent Disability.
McNulty, Michael T. *s.j.* '73 (WDC)[N] Washington, DC The Jesuit Community of St. Aloysius Gonzaga.
McNulty, Patrick J. '60 (FTW) Retired.
McNulty, Rev. Msgr. Patrick '53 (LA) Los Angeles, CA St. Bernard Retired.
McNulty, Robert E. '56 (NOR) Retired.
McNulty, William J. '61 (CHI) Retired.
McNulty, William J. '64 (NOR) District Moderators Retired.
McPadden, Charles J. *m.m.* '69 (NY)[EE] Maryknoll Maryknoll Fathers and Brothers Retired.
McPartlan, Rev. Msgr. Paul '84 (WDC)[C] Catholic University of America, The.
McPartland, Guy *o.carm.* '55 (NEW) Paramus, NJ Carmelite Chapel of St. Therese.
McPartland, Patrick '08 (TR) Toms River, NJ St. Joseph.
McPartland, Paul G. '57 (BO) Senior Priests. Retired.

McPhail, J. Stuart *o.p.* '69 (PRO)[P] Providence St. Thomas Aquinas Priory at Providence College.
McPhee, Rev. Msgr. Marvin '65 (SFS) Retired.
McPhillips, James G. '83 (CLV) Newbury, OH St. Helen.
McQuade, Brian '94 (RVC) Commack, NY Christ the King.
McQuade, Donald P. *m.m.* '65 (SJ)[M] Los Altos, CA Maryknoll.
McQuade, James F. *c.s.p.* '56 (NY)[EE] New York, NY Paulist Fathers' Motherhouse; Roosevelt Site.
McQuade, Richard E. '57 (BO) Senior Priests. Retired.
McQuaid, Thomas W. '79 (CHI) Berwyn, IL St. Leonard.
McQuesten, Mark A. '87 (MAR) Bark River, MI St. Elizabeth Ann Seton.
McQuillan, Cornelius T. *c.s.sp.* '75 (SJN)[F] Dorado, PR Santuario del Espiritu Santo.
McQuillen, Paul *s.s.e.* '77 (MOB) Montgomery, AL St. Jude Parish; [J] Montgomery, AL City of St. Jude, Inc., The; [G] Selma, AL Edmundite Fathers.
McQuillen, Thomas J. '96 (TOL) On Duty Outside the Diocese; Mission of Accompaniment.
McQuinn, Peter B. '91 (CHI) Mt. Prospect, IL St. Thomas a Becket.
McRae, Rev. Msgr. Cornelius M. '61 (BO) Trustees; Norwood, MA St. Catherine of Siena.
McReavy, Thomas J. *c.s.b.* '59 (GAL)[O] Houston, TX Dillon House Retired.
McReynolds, Eugene *o.s.b.* '70 (OM) Boys Town, NE Immaculate Conception B.V.M.; [I] Boys Town, NE Father Flanagan's Boys' Home; [K] Elkhorn, NE Mount Michael Benedictine Abbey.
McShane, John A. '57 (BRK)[T] Douglaston, NY Bishop Mugavero Residence Retired.
McShane, John '74 (LAV) Caliente, NV Holy Child; Amargosa Valley, NV Christ of the Desert Catholic Church.
McShane, Joseph M. *s.j.* '77 (NY)[C] Bronx, NY Fordham University; [EE] Cardinal Spellman Hall, Jesuit Community.
McShane, Patrick E. '79 (CLV) Retired.
McShane, Thomas S. *s.j.* '60 (OM)[K] Omaha, NE Jesuit Community at Creighton University.
McSherry, John G. *s.j.* '72 (NY)[EE] New York, NY Jesuit Community of the Immaculate Conception.
McSherry, John *s.v.d.* '61 (CHI)[N] Techny, IL Divine Word Residence.
McSherry, Patrick *o.f.m.cap.* '78 (DET)[K] Detroit, MI Provincialate; [K] Detroit St. Bonaventure Friary.
McSherry, Thomas '71 (OKL) Oklahoma City, OK St. Patrick.
McSorley, Aidan *o.s.b.* '69 (KC)[A] Conception, MO Conception Seminary College; [J] Parnell, MO St. Joseph Parish; Parnell, MO St. Joseph's.
McSorley, Gerald '64 (LA) Los Angeles, CA St. Bernard.
McSorley, Matthew T. *o.s.b.* '49 (CHL)[J] Belmont, NC Belmont Abbey.
McSpiritt, John *s.t.* '59 (WDC)[N] Adelphi, MD Father Judge Missionary Cenacle.
McStravog, Patrick B. *o.s.a.* '89 (PH) Philadelphia, PA St. Augustine.
McSweeney, Brian T. '88 (NY) Cold Spring, NY Our Lady of Loretto.
McSweeney, Edward F. '52 (PIT)[Q] Pittsburgh, PA Cardinal Dearden Center Retired.
McSweeney, James '74 (SR) Middletown, CA St. Joseph.
McSweeney, Jeremiah F. '72 (WH) Wheeling, WV St. Michael.
McSweeney, Rev. Msgr. John J. '74 (CHL) Charlotte, NC St. Matthew.
McSweeney, John R. *o.c.d.* '52 (SR)[L] Oakville, CA Carmelite House of Prayer.
McSweeney, Rev. Msgr. John R. '61 (BUR) Judges; Diocesan Consultors Retired.
McSweeney, John '48 (MRY) Retired.
McSweeney, Joseph *s.s.c.* '58 (PRO)[P] Bristol, RI St. Columban's Retirement House.
McSweeney, Joseph *s.s.c.* '58 (OM)[K] St. Columbans Missionary Society of St. Columban.
McSweeney, Liam P. '63 (SAC) Fair Oaks, CA St. Mel.
McSweeney, Rev. Msgr. Thomas J. '71 (E) Erie, PA Holy Trinity.
McSweeney, William *o.m.i.* '52 (BO)[X] Tewksbury, MA Immaculate Heart of Mary Residence.
McSweeny, Joseph *s.s.c.* '90 (FgM)[K] St. Columbans Missionary Society of St. Columban; St Columbans, NE House of Post–Graduate Studies.
McTaggart, Rev. Msgr. Edward P. '55 (SFR) San Mateo, CA St. Gregory; Serra Club of San Francisco (Golden Gate); [S] San Francisco, CA Archdiocesan Council of Catholic Women Retired.
McTavey, Lawrence '55 (ALB) Retired.
McTeigue, Robert J. *s.j.* '97 (BAL)[S] Towson Maryland Province of the Society of Jesus.
McTiernan, Jimmy *m.afr.* '71 (WDC) Washington, DC; Washington, DC MISSIONARIES OF AFRICA; [N] Washington, DC Missionaries of Africa.
McTighe, Edward P. *s.j.* '61 (P)[D].
McTigue, Norman P. '70 (BUF) Retired.
McVean, John J. *o.f.m.* '67 (NY) New York, NY St. Francis of Assisi.
McVeigh, James E. '73 (PH) Collingdale, PA St. Joseph.
McVeigh, John J. '58 (LAV) Retired.
McWeeney, Brian E. '73 (NY) Pleasant Valley, NY St. Stanislaus Kostka.
McWhorter, Michael L. '92 (ATL) Fayetteville, GA St. Gabriel; Special or Other (Arch)Diocesan Assignment.
Mead, James Herbert *s.j.* '62 (NO)[P] New Orleans, LA Ignatius Residence Retired.
Mead, Leland C. '68 (NU) Retired.
Meade, Denis *o.s.b.* '55 (FgM)[I] Atchison, KS St. Benedict's Abbey; [A] Atchison, KS Benedictine College; Atchison, KS St. Benedict's Abbey; Judges.
Meade, James W. '81 (CIN) Cincinnati, OH Corpus Christi.
Meade, James W. '86 (GRY) Chesterton, IN St. Patrick.
Meade, Maurice P. '48 (BO) Senior Priests. Retired.
Meaden, Paul *o.s.b.* '84 (SFE)[H] Pecos, NM Our Lady of Guadalupe Abbey.
Meadw, Pachomius *o.s.b.* '09 (KC)[A] Conception, MO Conception Seminary College.
Meagher, Rt. Rev. Cletus *o.s.b.* '71 (BIR)[I] Cullman, AL St. Bernard Preparatory School Educational Foundation; [I] Cullman, AL St. Bernard Abbey Foundation.
Meagher, Rev. Msgr. Frank J. '60 (COL) College of Consultors; Presbyteral Council Retired.
Meagher, Joseph A. '92 (NEW) Respect Life Office; Jersey City, NJ St. John the Baptist.
Meagher, Rev. Msgr. Michael T. '65 (SY) Binghamton, NY Saints John & Andrew; Priests' Personnel Committee.
Meagher, Thomas L. '64 (DET) White Lake, MI St. Patrick.
Mealey, Mark S. *o.s.f.s.* '79 (ARL) Vienna, VA Our Lady of Good Counsel; [L] Arlington, VA Rooted in Faith–Forward in Hope, Inc.; Vicar General for Administration and Moderator of the Curia; Diocesan Judges; Diocesan Consultors; Provincial Councilors:; Judicial Vicar.
Meaney, Brendan J. '65 (CAM) Retired.
Meaney, Patrick '87 (CC)[G] Hebbronville, TX Catholic Solitudes.
Means, David A. '81 (STL) On Duty Outside the Archdiocese.
Means, David A. '81 (JC) Chamois, MO Most Pure Heart of Mary; Chamois, MO Assumption.
Meany, John J. *o.p.* '87 (CHI)[N] Chicago Dominicans (Provincial Office); Chicago, IL; [W] Chicago, IL The Bolivian Trust of the Dominicans; [N] St. Pius V Priory.
Meany, Michael G. '80 (CHI) Oak Forest, IL St. Damian.
Meany, Neill R. *s.j.* '54 (YAK) Diocesan Consultors; Yakima, WA St. Joseph Parish; Diocesan Catholic Committee on Scouting; Naches, WA St. John.
Meares, Clyde Timberlake '02 (R) Rocky Mount, NC Our Lady of Perpetual Help.
Measer, Donald L. '63 (BUF) Tonawanda, NY St. Amelia Retired.
Meaux, Glenn *s.o.l.t.* '80 (CC)[G] Robstown, TX Society of Our Lady of the Most Holy Trinity.
Mecca, Gregg D. '96 (BGP) Danbury, CT St. Peter.
Meccia, Francis S. *m.m.* '66 (NY)[EE].
Mech, John J. '95 (DET) Troy, MI St. Anastasia.
Mecir, Joseph S. '80 (CLV) Cleveland, OH Sacred Heart of Jesus; Cleveland Clinic Foundation.
Meconi, David V. *s.j.* '03 (CHI)[N] Chicago Chicago Province of the Society of Jesus–Provincial Office.
Meconi, David V. *s.j.* '03 (STL)[C] Saint Louis University; [O] St. Louis, MO Jesuit Community Corporation at Saint Louis University – Jesuit Hall.
Mecwel, Pawel J. '90 (MAR) St. Ignace, MI Immaculate Conception; St. Ignace, MI St. Ignatius Loyola.
Medairos, Anthony J. '73 (BO) Carver, MA Our Lady of Lourdes.
Medas, Michael B. '88 (BO)[CC] Braintree, MA KOLBE Association, Inc.; [A] Brighton, MA St. John Seminary; Air Force Reserve Chaplains.
Medeiros, Antonio S. '54 (BO) Senior Priests. Retired.
Medeiros, Antonio (BO)[B] Chestnut Hill, MA Redemptoris Mater Archdiocesan Missionary House of Formation.
Medeiros, Arnold R. '75 (FR) North Falmouth, MA St. Elizabeth Seton.
Medeiros, Benjamin *t.o.r.* '77 (ALT)[G] Loretto, PA St. Francis Friary at Mount Assisi.
Medeiros, Leonel S. '04 (BGP) Pastors' Vocation Advisory Board; Assistant Vocation Directors; Bridgeport, CT St. Augustine Cathedral.
Medeiros, Paul *o.m.i.* '64 (FgM) Washington, DC AMERICAN OBLATE MISSIONS.
Meder, Stephen A. *s.j.* '43 (DET)[K] Clarkston, MI Colombiere Center.
Medina, David '02 (TLS) Tulsa, OK St. Francis Xavier Church and Diocesan Marian Shrine & Expiatory Temple of Our Lady of Guadalupe; Hispanic Ministry; Vocations; Seminary Board.
Medina, Eduardo '04 (PMB) Port St. Lucie, FL Holy Family; Jupiter, FL St. Peter.
Medina, Efrain '01 (MRY) Gonzales, CA St. Theodore; Clergy Life and Ministry Board.
Medina, Fabio E. '83 (SFR) Menlo Park, CA St. Anthony.
Medina, Rev. Msgr. Francisco '89 (SJN) Istepa.
Medina, George A. '97 (TR) Trenton, NJ St. Joseph.
Medina, George '87 (PCE) On Duty Outside the Diocese.
Medina, Gilbert '07 (ORL) Altamonte Springs, FL St. Mary Magdalen; [A] Orlando, FL Bishop Moore Catholic High School Inc.
Medina, Hector '84 (FWT) Arlington, TX St. Matthew; Presbyteral Council and Consultors.
Medina, Ignazio C. '78 (JC) Bonnots Mill, MO Our Lady Help of Christians; Linn, MO St. George; VIII. Westphalia.
Medina, Jose Antonio '82 (SJ) Sunnyvale, CA St. Martin.
Medina, Jose de Jesus '06 (CHI) Chicago, IL St. Bede the Venerable.
Medina, Jose *f.s.c.b.* (BO)[D] Cambridge, MA North Cambridge Catholic High School, Inc.; Lexington, MA.
Medina, Juan B. '69 (FAJ) Rio Grande, PR San Francisco de Asis.
Medina, Julian '73 (SAC) Marysville, CA St. Joseph; Colusa, CA Our Lady of Lourdes.
Medina, Leonardo '07 (TLS) Tulsa, OK St. Francis Xavier Church and Diocesan Marian Shrine & Expiatory Temple of Our Lady of Guadalupe; Hispanic Ministry.
Medina, Mauricio '64 (B) Cursillo Movement Retired.
Medina, Rolando '71 (MIA) Retired.
Medina, Tito *m.s.c.* '92 (RCK)[G].
Medina–Algaba, Felix P. '04 (DEN) Denver, CO St. James.
Medina–Cruz, Jamie '99 (ALX) Nachitoches, LA St. Anthony of Padua.
Medio, Joseph Paul *f.p.o.* '99 (BO)[U] Lawrence, MA Franciscans of Primitive Observance.
Medley, Robert W. '90 (MET) Plainsboro, NJ Queenship of Mary; Department of Worship and Liturgical Formation; Liturgical Advisor.
Medley, Samuel '08 (CC)[I] Corpus Christi, TX.
Medlin, Douglas S. '02 (ATL) Retired.
Medlock, Scott '96 (ANC) Anchorage, AK St. Patrick; Board Members.
Medow, David '01 (JOL) Plainfield, IL St. Mary Immaculate.
Medrano, Marcus '86 (DEN) Retired.
Medrek, Tomasz '04 (ARL) Alexandria, VA St. Lawrence.
Medve, Kenneth A. '97 (ALN) Elected Members; Lansford, PA St. Katharine Drexel Parish.
Medwid, John M. '90 (ALB) Amsterdam, NY St. Mary.
Mee, Michael (Brian) *o.s.b.* (SPK) Spokane, WA St. Peter.
Mee, Michael *o.s.b.* '78 (P)[L] St. Benedict, OR Mt. Angel Abbey.
Meehan, Barry C. *s.j.* '86 (BUR) West Rutland, VT St. Bridget.
Meehan, Barry M. '78 (PRO) Warwick, RI St. Timothy.
Meehan, Rev. Msgr. Francis X. '61 (PH)[A] Wynnewood, PA Theological Seminary of St. Charles Borromeo, Overbrook Retired.
Meehan, Gabriel '59 (CHL) Retired.
Meehan, Gery G. *o.praem.* '60 (GB)[J] De Pere, WI St. Joseph Priory.
Meehan, James N. *s.j.* '59 (SPK)[B] Spokane, WA Gonzaga University.
Meehan, James T. *s.j.* '63 (FgM) New York, NY Society of Jesus.
Meehan, Rev. Msgr. John T. '64 (NY) Mt. Vernon, NY St. Mary.
Meehan, Joseph J. '61 (PH) Springfield, PA St. Francis of Assisi Retired.
Meehan, Joseph '66 (STA) Retired.
Meehan, Kenneth E. *s.j.* '71 (WDC)[N] Washington, DC The Jesuit Community of St. Aloysius Gonzaga; [E] Washington, DC Gonzaga College High School.
Meehan, Kevin *l.c.* '91 (HRT)[B] Cheshire, CT Novitiate of the Legion of Christ.
Meehan, Peter '68 (NY) New York, NY Our Lady of the Rosary.
Meehan, T. J. '72 (ATL) Atlanta, GA Sacred Heart of Jesus.
Meehan, Terence A. '67 (CIN) Monroe, OH Our Lady of Sorrows Retired.
Meehan, Thomas J. '72 (ATL) Catholic Charities of the Archdiocese of Atlanta, Inc.
Meehan, Thomas J. *o.s.a.* '80 (PH)[F] Malvern, PA Malvern Preparatory School for Boys; [Y] Malvern, PA Augustinian Friars (O.S.A.).
Meehan, Timothy A. '59 (HRT) North Haven, CT St. Therese.
Meehling, Donald J. '58 (SFD) Commission for the Care of Infirm and Retired Priests Retired.
Meeks, Delphyn J. '83 (BEA) Buna, TX St. Francis of Assisi Mission; Mauriceville, TX St. Maurice.
Meenihan, Regis '92 (E)[K] Hermitage, PA John XXIII Home.

Meeuwsen, Jeffrey '07 (P) Forest Grove, OR St. Anthony; [P] Forest Grove, OR Pacific University (Forest Grove).
Megge, Paul '98 (GAY) Cheboygan, MI St. Mary–St. Charles; Pellston, MI St. Clement; Pellston, MI Sacred Heart.
Mehan, Joseph A. '96 (DAL) Garland, TX St. Michael the Archangel; Procurator–Advocates.
Mehm, Richard J. '77 (BO) Malden, MA Immaculate Conception.
Mehrkens, Rev. Msgr. William '50 (CR) Bemidji, MN St. Philip's; Diocesan Board of Conciliation and Arbitration Retired.
Meidl, Gerald S. '74 (NU) Hutchinson, MN Church of St. Anastasia; Stewart, MN Church of St. Boniface.
Meier, Rev. Msgr. Allen J. '51 (COV) Archives Retired.
Meier, Denis E. '63 (MO) DEPARTMENT OF VETERANS AFFAIRS HOSPITALS AND CHAPLAINS.
Meier, Denis '63 (SFS) Retired.
Meier, Emeric *o.f.m.* '68 (BO)[Z] Boston, MA St. Anthony Shrine.
Meier, Gary '98 (STL) Saint Louis, MO Sts. Teresa and Bridget.
Meier, Gerald A. '66 (STL) Webster Groves, MO Mary, Queen of Peace.
Meier, John P. (FTW)[B] University of Notre Dame Du Lac.
Meier, Rev. Msgr. John P. '67 (NY) On Duty Outside the Archdiocese.
Meier, Laverne G. '58 (MAD)[F] Madison, WI Bishop O'Connor Catholic Pastoral Center Retired.
Meier, Timothy J. *s.j.* '91 (DET)[K] Detroit Jesuit Provincial Office–Detroit Province of the Society of Jesus.
Meier, Timothy *s.j.* '91 (MO) Army National Guard Chaplains.
Meik, Thomas J. *c.m.* '48 (STL)[O] Perryville, MO Congregation of the Mission.
Meiklejohn, Norman *a.a.* '54 (WOR)[O] Worcester, MA Assumptionists (Augustinians of the Assumption).
Meiman, Louis J. '87 (L) Louisville, KY St. Francis of Assisi; Ex Officio.
Meinen, Dennis W. '87 (SC) Special Assignment; [D] Sioux City, IA Holy Spirit Retirement Home; [C] Sioux City, IA Mercy Medical Center – Sioux City Retired.
Meiners, Andrew *c.ss.r.* '70 (STL)[O] Liguori, MO Liguori Mission House/Redemptorists.
Meinholz, John M. '77 (MAD) Madison, WI Immaculate Heart of Mary; Elected; Diocesan Consultors.
Meirose, Harold R. *s.j.* '62 (DET)[K] Clarkston, MI Colombiere Center.
Meis, Anthony '72 (JOL) Retired.
Meis, Peter *o.f.m.cap.* '67 (FgM) Denver, CO Province of Mid–America.
Meisel, Rev. Msgr. Charles F. '50 (BAL) Hydes, MD St. John the Evangelist Retired.
Meisel, Gerald A. '61 (LA) Long Beach, CA St. Matthew Retired.
Meismer, Paul J. '69 (PEO) Arlington, IL St. Patrick's; Cherry, IL Holy Trinity.
Meissner, Robert J. '69 (SAG) Bay City, MI St. Vincent de Paul; Diocese of Saginaw Priests' Retirement Association.
Meissner, William W. *s.j.* '61 (BO)[U] Newton, MA The Jesuit Community at Boston College.
Meister, Rev. Msgr. Andrew H. '44 (OM) Retired.
Meitl, Roger K. '59 (SAL) St. Francis, KS St. Joseph Parish; St. Francis, KS St. Francis of Assisi Parish.
Mejia, Gustavo '68 (LA) Los Angeles, CA Resurrection.
Mejia, Hector *m.s.c.* '06 (RCK)[G].
Mejia, Jose '91 (LA) Hospital Chaplains.
Mejia, Manuel J. *m.m.* '63 (SFR) Holy Childhood Association Coordinator.
Mejia, Manuel J. *m.m.* '63 (NY)[EE] Retired.
Mejia, Marvin S. (NEW) Bayonne, NJ St. Vincent de Paul.
Mejia, Miguel '00 (SPK) Rosalia, WA St. Catherine of Alexandria; Rosalia, WA Holy Rosary; St. John, WA Our Lady of Perpetual Help; Rosalia, WA Sacred Heart; Spokane, WA Cathedral of Our Lady of Lourdes.
Mekkat, Benny *c.f.i.c.* (STP) St. Paul, MN St. Mary.
Meladath, Mathew '99 (SYM) Farmington, MI Knanaya Catholic Mission of Detroit.
Melancon, Bill John '93 (LAF) Carencro, LA St. Peter.
Melancon, J. Aaron '97 (LAF) Seminarians; Vocations; Lafayette, LA St. Pius X.
Melancon, Rev. Msgr. Louis J. '63 (LAF) Opelousas, LA Our Lady Queen of Angels.
Melancon, Rev. Msgr. Louis '63 (LKC) Retired.
Melancon, Thomas J. *s.j.* '74 (STL)[O] St. Louis, MO Jesuit Community Corporation at Saint Louis University – Jesuit Hall.
Melaneon, Mark F. '04 (LAF) Washington, LA St. Peter.
Melaniuk, J. Maciej '86 (MET) South Plainfield, NJ Our Lady of Czestochowa.
Melcher, Luke A. '05 (ALX) Pineville, LA Sacred Heart.
Melcher, Michael '92 (LUB) Anson, TX St. Michael; Vicars Forane; Priests' Retirement Board; Presbyteral Council.
Melchior, Carl J. '09 (SP) Clearwater, FL St. Catherine of Siena; Elected Parochial Vicars.
Melchior, Frank '59 (GB) Retired.
Melchior, Gerald P. '90 (OM) Omaha, NE St. Bernard.
Melchior, Thomas '65 (KCK) Retired.
Mele, Carmen *o.p.* '80 (FWT) Pope John Paul II Institute for Lay Ministry.
Mele, Joseph M. '73 (PIT)[A] Pittsburgh, PA Saint Paul Seminary; Post–Ordination Formation, Department for; St. Paul Seminary; Priest Council; Clergy Personnel Board; Vicars General; College of Consultors.
Meledom, Joseph '68 (FWT) Burkburnett, TX St. Jude Thaddeus.
Melendez, Anthony *i.v.e.* '07 (BRK) Brooklyn, NY St. Mary Mother of the Church.
Melendez, Daniel J. '02 (CAM) On Leave of Absence.
Melendez, Elberto '04 (RNO) Battle Mountain, NV St. John Bosco.
Melendez, Hector '80 (PAT) Clifton, NJ SS. Cyril and Methodius.
Melepuram, John P. '78 (PH) Abington, PA Our Lady Help of Christians.
Melepuram, John '78 (SYM) Philadelphia, PA St. Thomas Syro–Malabar Catholic Church; Eparchial Consultors.
Melevage, Rev. Msgr. F. J. '42 (GRY) Retired.
Melfi, F. Patrick '06 (BUF) Limestone, NY St. Patrick; Salamanca, NY Our Lady of Peace.
Melillo, William J. '66 (NEW)[C] West Orange, NJ Seton Hall Preparatory School Retired.
Melito, Ignatius M. *c.m.* '51 (STL) St. Louis, MO St. Catherine Laboure; [O] St. Louis, MO Lazarist Residence.
Melka, John *o.c.d.* '64 (P)[Q] Mt. Angel, OR Carmelite House of Studies.
Melle, James J. '72 (PH) West Chester, PA St. Agnes.
Mellein, John Thomas *o.p.* '07 (WDC)[B] Washington, DC Dominican House of Studies.
Melley, James J. '77 (MIA) Encino, CA St. Cyril Retired.
Mellitt, John *o.f.m.cap.* '75 (RVC) East Patchogue, NY St. Joseph the Worker.
Mello, Jay '07 (FR)[B] North Dartmouth, MA Bishop Stang High School; North Dartmouth, MA St. Julie Billiart.
Mello, Matthew '87 (ORL) Lakeland, FL Church of the Resurrection.
Melloh, John A. *s.m.* '61 (STL)[O] St. Louis Marianists, Province of the United States (Society of Mary).
Mellone, Rev. Msgr. Michael J. '76 (WDC) Washington, DC St. Thomas Apostle; Deans; Silver Spring, MD St. Andrew Apostle.
Mellone, Vincent P. '65 (BO) Woburn, MA St. Barbara; Presbyteral Council.
Melmer, John H. '91 (ARL) Warrenton, VA St. John the Evangelist.
Melnic, Rev. Msgr. James T. '78 (PHU) McAdoo, PA St. Michael's; McAdoo, PA St. Mary's; [D] Philadelphia, PA Ascension Manor, Inc.; Board Members.
Melnick, James P. '09 (LR) Springdale, AR St. Raphael.
Melnick, John E. '86 (SCR) On Duty Outside the Diocese.
Melnick, John P. '00 (HRT) Enfield, CT St. Bernard.
Melnick, John (KCK) Kansas City, KS Holy Family; Kansas City, KS St. Mary–St. Anthony.
Melnick, William D. '75 (WIL) Wilmington, DE St. John the Beloved.
Melo, Fidel C. '96 (CHL) Greensboro, NC Our Lady of Grace.
Melo, Nicholas P. '83 (HRT) Southington, CT St. Thomas.
Melocoton, Carlos L. '09 (WH) Charleston, WV Basilica of the Co–Cathedral of the Sacred Heart.
Melody, William P. *c.s.c.* '59 (FTW)[H] Holy Cross House.
Melone, Rt. Rev. Mark E. '78 (NTN) Sacramento, CA St. George.
Melton, Thomas K. '59 (TLS) Retired.
Meluskey, Andre J. '59 (HBG) Carlisle, PA Saint Patrick Retired.
Melvin, Thomas P. '01 (WIN)[A] Winona, MN Immaculate Heart of Mary Seminary; Vocations; Chaplain; Girl Scouts; Diocese of Winona Incardination Board; [I] Winona, MN St. Thomas Aquinas Newman Center; Elected Deanery Representatives; Priest Assignments Committee.
Memenas, Vytas '57 (JOL) Joliet, IL St. Anthony Retired.
Mena, Abel '02 (SR) Healdsburg, CA St. John the Baptist; Diocesan Judges.
Mena, Antonio '81 (ELP) Fabens, TX Our Lady of Guadalupe.
Mena, J. Roberto *s.t.* '01 (SAV) Bainbridge, GA St. Joseph's.
Mena, Jesus Maria *o.a.r.* '86 (ELP) El Paso, TX Guardian Angel.
Mena, Jose '92 (NY) Poughkeepsie, NY St. Mary.
Mena–Beltran, Rene '05 (CHI) Chicago, IL St. Agnes of Bohemia.
Menapace, James L. '63 (MAR) Retired.
Menard, Bernard D. '07 (OG) Malone, NY Notre Dame.
Menard, Clarence *o.m.i.* '59 (SAT)[K] San Antonio, TX Oblate Madonna Residence.
Menard, Gerard E. *s.j.* '99 (DEN)[D] Denver, CO Arrupe Jesuit High School; [N] Denver, CO Regis Jesuit Community (The Jesuits at Regis University).
Menard, Gilbert B. '55 (OG) Judges Retired.
Menard, J. Godden *c.m.* '55 (GLP) Tuba City, AZ St. Jude.
Menard, Robert *o.f.m.* '72 (ARL) Triangle, VA St. Francis of Assisi.
Menasco, Edward T. '90 (OKL) Norman, OK St. Joseph's; Special Assignment; Priests' Retirement Board; Region I–B.
Menchaca, Luis Gerardo '95 (SJ) On Duty Outside the Diocese.
Mencias, Jaime '90 (ANC) Anchorage, AK St. Elizabeth Ann Seton.
Mencsik, John *c.pp.s.* '74 (CIN) Dayton, OH St. Joseph.
Mende, Dennis W. '83 (BUF) Jamestown, NY Holy Apostles; [G] Jamestown, NY Catholic Academy of the Holy Family.
Mendem, Marianand '93 (KCK) Burlington, KS St. Francis Xavier; Burlington, KS St. Patrick's; Burlington, KS St. Joseph's; Burlington, KS St. Teresa's.
Mendes, Joseph *m.s.f.s.* '63 (ATL) Lawrenceville, GA St. Marguerite D'Youville; [G] Snellville, GA The Missionaries of St. Francis De Sales.
Mendes, Joseph *m.s.f.s.* '63 (TYL)[B] Whitehouse, TX The Missionaries of St. Francis de Sales.
Mendes, Peter *s.a.c.* (DET) Novi, MI Holy Family.
Mendes, Rony '05 (BRK) Brooklyn, NY Holy Innocents.
Mendez, Angel Mendez '90 (MGZ) Sabana Grande, PR Church of San Isidro.
Mendez, Angel (SJN) Clergy Social Security (Prevision Social del Clero).
Mendez, Jose del Carmen '02 (CHI) Maywood, IL St. Eulalia.
Mendez, José Ramón Fernández '59 (SJN) Rio Piedras, PR Asuncion de La Virgen.
Mendez, Juan '73 (SFE) Presbyteral Council of the Archdiocese of Santa Fe; Albuquerque, NM Nativity of the Blessed Virgin Mary.
Mendez, Luis *s.e.m.v.* '95 (STP) St. Paul, MN St. Francis De Sales; St. Paul, MN St. James.
Mendez, Oscar A. *o.f.m.* '89 (OAK) Oakland, CA St. Elizabeth; [M] Oakland, CA Franciscan Friars (Province of Santa Barbara).
Mendez, Oscar *s.j.* '64 (MIA)[K] Miami, FL Villa Javier Retired.
Mendez, Rafael '93 (MGZ) Lajas, PR Our Lady of the Purification.
Mendez, Winston R. '03 (PCE) Ponce, PR Good Shepherd Parish.
Mendez–Cobos, Manuel (MAD) Madison, WI Saint Joseph.
Mendez Laracuente, Carlos F. '09 (MGZ) Moca, PR Our Lady of Monserrate.
Mendicoa, John M. (BO) Roslindale, MA Sacred Heart.
Mendis, Linus (BO) Lynnfield, MA Our Lady of the Assumption.
Mendl, Michael *s.d.b.* '78 (NY)[EE] New Rochelle, NY Salesian Provincial House.
Mendonca, John '79 (BRK) Rego Park, NY Our Lady of the Angelus.
Mendonca, Johnny '91 (RVC) Franklin Square, NY St. Catherine of Sienna.
Mendonca, Robert '00 (OAK) Livermore, CA St. Michael; Deanery #1.
Mendonca, Walter *s.v.d.* '76 (FgM) Techny, IL.
Mendoza, Andres '95 (LUB) Presbyteral Council.
Mendoza, Andres '95 (LUB) Lubbock, TX Our Lady of Guadalupe.
Mendoza, Anthony Maria *o.s.b.* '95 (SAT) San Antonio, TX Santo Nino de Cebu.
Mendoza, Eddy '97 (ELP) El Paso, TX San Judas Tadeo.
Mendoza, Eduardo W. *p.e.s.* '99 (SAC) Dixon, CA St. Peter.
Mendoza, Francis '04 (LA) Los Angeles, CA Cathedral of Our Lady of the Angels; Members.
Mendoza, Gerald *o.p.* (AUS)[G] Austin, TX Dominican Friars of Austin.
Mendoza, Gerardo '88 (SB) Fontana, CA St. George.
Mendoza, Jose Eduardo '84 (SFR) South San Francisco, CA All Souls.
Mendoza, Jose '99 (OM) Omaha, NE Our Lady of Guadalupe – St. Agnes Parish.
Mendoza, R. Anthony '99 (LAR) La Pryor, TX St. Joseph; College of Consultors; Office of Respect Life; Priests Personnel Board; Ex Officio Members.
Mendyuk, Jaroslav '93 (STN).
Mendyuk, Yaroslav '97 (STN) Munster, IN St. Josaphat; Presbyteral Council.
Menegatto, Gaetano *c.s.j.* '42 (CLV)[N] Avon, OH Congregation of St. Joseph.
Menegay, David C. '88 (Y) Louisville, OH St. Louis; On Duty Outside the Diocese.
Menegay, Greg '98 (PHX) Higley, AZ St. Mary Magdalene Roman Catholic Parish; Presbyteral Council.
Menei, Francis T. '67 (PH) On Duty Outside the Archdiocese.

Menei, Francis '67 (HBG) Manheim, PA St. Richard.
Menendez, Adolph *s.x.* '68 (MIL)[B] Franklin, WI Xaverian Missionary Fathers College Seminary.
Menendez, Adolph *s.x.* '69 (PEO)[M] Champaign, IL St. John's Catholic Newman Center at the University of Illinois, Urbana–Champaign; Champaign, IL St. John's Catholic Chapel.
Menendez, Jose L. '77 (MIA) Miami, FL Corpus Christi.
Meneses, Miguel '61 (ELP) Retired.
Meney, Rev. Canon Olivier '00 (MIL) Milwaukee, WI St. Stanislaus.
Menezes, Mark '59 (JOL) Monee, IL St. Boniface.
Menezes, Wade *c.p.m.* '00 (OWN)[F] Auburn, KY Fathers of Mercy.
Meng, David P. '89 (ARL) Lake Ridge, VA St. Elizabeth Ann Seton; Diocesan Consultors.
Meng, Robert A. '45 (ROC) Retired.
Menge, James P. '62 (SPR) Retired.
Mengel, Mark M. *s.s.c.* '71 (SPR) Springfield, MA Holy Name.
Mengel, Mark *s.s.c.* '71 (OM)[K] St. Columbans Missionary Society of St. Columban.
Mengelle, Ervens '91 (COL)[A] Columbus, OH Pontifical College Josephinum; [A] Columbus, OH Pontifical College Josephinum.
Menghini, Peter D. '80 (SCR)[L] Moscow, PA St. Mary's Villa Nursing Home; [L] Moscow, PA St. Mary's Villa Residence; Elmhurst, PA St. Eulalia.
Mengon, Albert *s.d.b.* '66 (MRY)[C] Watsonville, CA St. Francis Youth Center; [F] Watsonville, CA Saint Francis Salesian Community; Watsonville, CA Our Lady Help of Christians.
Menig, Walter J. *c.m.* '47 (PH)[Y].
Menig, Walter T. *c.m.* '47 (BAL) Emmitsburg, MD St. Joseph.
Menihane, Daniel J. '57 (PH)[Y] Villanova, PA St. Thomas Monastery.
Meninger, William *o.c.s.o.* '58 (DEN)[N] Snowmass, CO St. Benedict's Monastery.
Menjiar, Evelis '04 (WDC) Washington, DC St. Matthew Cathedral.
Menjivar–Ayala, Evelio '04 (WDC) Bethesda, MD St. Bartholomew.
Menke, Andrew V. '99 (LIN) Lincoln, NE Cathedral of the Risen Christ; Advocates; Commission for Sacred Liturgy and Sacred Music; [C] Lincoln, NE Pius X Catholic High School.
Menke, George R. *s.j.* '75 (IND)[D] Indianapolis, IN Brebeuf Jesuit Preparatory School, Inc.
Menke, Paul F. '66 (LA) Alhambra, CA St. Thomas More Retired.
Menker, Joseph *o.m.i.* '53 (STP)[K] St. Paul, MN Oblate Residence.
Menkhus, James *o.f.m.cap.* '73 (WDC)[B] Washington, DC St. Francis Friary–Capuchin College.
Menna, F. Dominic '58 (BO) Quincy, MA St. Mary; Senior Priests. Retired.
Menna, Rev. Msgr. Francis A. '64 (PH) Darby, PA Retired.
Menna, Michael J. '99 (PRO) Providence, RI St. Ann.
Menner, Michael L. '93 (PEO) Warsaw, IL Sacred Heart; [O] Moline, IL The Order of the Legion of Little Souls of the Merciful Heart of Jesus.
Menner, Michael '93 (PEO) Penfield, IL St. Lawrence's.
Menner, Robert J. '68 (STL) Manchester, MO St. Joseph.
Mennis, Rev. Msgr. James F. '62 (SAC) Retired.
Menniti, Daniel J. '53 (HBG) Carlisle, PA Saint Patrick Retired.
Mens, Theodore J. '67 (GRY) Griffith, IN St. Ann; Griffith, IN St. Mary; Pro–Life Activities.
Mensah, Gabriel '83 (VIC) On Duty Outside the Diocese; Navy Chaplains.
Mensah, Isaac Ebo (BO) Bedford, MA St. Michael.
Mensah, John M. '86 (NY) Staten Island, NY Holy Family.
Mensah, Paul A. '90 (SJ) Morgan Hill, CA St. Catherine of Alexandria.
Mensah, Philip (CHI) Chicago, IL St. Columbanus.
Mensah, Thomas Oppong (HRT) Enfield, CT Holy Family.
Mensinger, Gary J. '98 (PSC) Old Forge, PA St. Nicholas; Retirement Plan Board; Notary; Presbyteral Council.
Menty, Ronald A. '69 (ALB) Colonie, NY St. Clare.
Menty, Ronald '69 (ALB) Administrative Advocate for Priests; Priestly Life and Ministry Council; Members; Priests Placement Committee; Priests Retirement Board/Priests Retirement Plan Board; Special Assignment.
Menuba, Elias '74 (HRT)[H] Hartford, CT Saint Francis Hospital and Medical Center.
Meny, Hilary G. '40 (IND) Retired.
Menz, Anthony E. *o.c.s.o.* '68 (MO) DEPARTMENT OF VETERANS AFFAIRS HOSPITALS AND CHAPLAINS.
Menzel, William G. '67 (LC) Wisconsin Rapids, WI St. Vincent de Paul.
Meogrossi, Romuald *o.f.m.conv.* (BAL) Baltimore, MD St. Casimir.
Meogrossi, Romuald *o.f.m.conv.* '68 (WDC) Definitors:; [C] Catholic University of America, The.
Meoska, John '82 (PBL)[H] Crestone, CO Spiritual Life Institute of America, Inc.
Mera–Vallejos, Jose E. '09 (HBG) Harrisburg, PA St. Catherine Laboure.
Mercado, Edwin A. '86 (ARE) Arecibo, PR Santa Ana; Diocesan Consultors; Priest's Senate (Consejo Presbiteral).
Mercado, Floyd '03 (FAJ) Humacao, PR Concathedral Dulce Nombre de Jesus.
Mercado, Heriberto '06 (LUB) Morton, TX St. Ann.
Mercado, Jose A. '06 (HRT) Office for Hispanic Evangelization; Hartford, CT St. Augustine; [S] Bloomfield, CT Office for Hispanic Evangelization.
Mercado, Marco A. '98 (CHI) Chicago, IL Good Shepherd.
Mercado, Miguel '83 (ARE) Arecibo, PR Nuestra Senora del Carmen.
Mercado, Rev. Msgr. Thaddeus F. '67 (HON) Wahiawa, HI Our Lady of Sorrows.
Mercado Rivera, Miguel '83 (ARE) Priest's Senate (Consejo Presbiteral).
Mercado Vidvo, Floyd '03 (FAJ) Vocations.
Merced, Miguel A. '00 (CGS) Diocesan Tribunal of Caguas; Fajardo, PR Santisimo Redentor.
Merced, Roberto *o.p.* '06 (DAL) Dallas, TX St. Edward; [J] Irving, TX Dominican Priory of St. Albert the Great and Novitiate.
Merced Reyes, Miguel A. '00 (FAJ) Sec. Chancellor.
Mercer, David '87 (SJ) Ongoing Formation of Clergy; Sunnyvale, CA St. Martin.
Mercer, James G. '97 (ARL) Alexandria, VA St. Lawrence; Defenders of the Bond.
Mercer, Robert *s.a.* '82 (NY)[EE] Garrison Franciscan Friars of the Atonement, Minister General Office.
Mercieca, Anthony '62 (MIA) Retired.
Mercieca, Cyprian J. *t.o.r.* '61 (FWT) Arlington, TX St. Joseph's.
Mercier, Rev. Msgr. Joseph '55 (BLX) Retired.
Mercier, Ronald A. *s.j.* '87 (BO)[U] Boston The Society of Jesus of New England–Provincial Offices.
Mercier, Ronald A. (STL)[O] St. Louis, MO Sacred Heart Jesuit Community.
Mercieri, Dennis J. '05 (NOR) Middletown, CT Middlesex Memorial Hospital; East Hampton, CT St. Patrick.
Mercure, Jerome '79 (BUR) Canon 1742 Panel of Pastors; Waterbury, VT St. Andrew; State Hospital; Deans.
Mercurio, Gregory (BO) Lynn, MA Holy Family.
Merdian, Rev. Msgr. Mark J. '93 (PEO) Champaign, IL St. Matthew.
Merdinger, Philip E. '64 (BO)[A] Brighton, MA St. John Seminary.
Meredith, John R. '80 (OWN)[J] Owensboro, KY Gideon Productions, Inc.; Television and Radio Broadcast Communications.
Meredith, John '80 (OWN) Owensboro, KY Blessed Mother.
Meredith, Richard '78 (OWN) Owensboro, KY St. Pius Tenth; Judges; Ongoing Formation of Priests.
Mergenhagen, John J. '54 (BUF) Retired.
Mericantante, John J. '75 (PMB) Pahokee, FL St. Mary.
Merino, Rev. Msgr. Baudilio '48 (SJN) Rio Piedras, PR Nuestra Senora de la Providencia; Police Chaplains.
Merino, Santiago James '46 (LA) Retired.
Merino Merino, Rev. Msgr. Baudilio '48 (SJN) Catholic Charismatic Renewal.
Meriwether, Stephen A. '83 (SFR) Defenders of the Bond; San Francisco, CA Most Holy Redeemer.
Merkatoris, Ralph '58 (GB) Retired.
Merkel, Thomas *s.j.* (OM)[C] Omaha, NE Creighton Preparatory School.
Merkelis, John D. *o.s.a.* '85 (JOL)[C] New Lenox, IL Providence Catholic High School; [L] New Lenox, IL Augustinian Friary.
Merkle, Charles W. '88 (ARL) Annandale, VA St. Ambrose.
Merkovsky, Paul W. '90 (PIT) Bridgeville, PA Holy Child.
Merkt, Joseph T. '66 (L) Louisville, KY St. Francis of Assisi.
Merkt, Michael F. '81 (MIL) West Allis, WI Mary, Queen of Heaven.
Merlino, Darrin *c.m.f.* '00 (LA)[V] Rancho Dominguez, CA Dominguez Seminary Inc.
Merman, Rev. Msgr. Raymond F. '60 (ALN)[J] Bethlehem, PA Holy Family Villa Retired.
Merold, James E. '71 (CHI) Chicago, IL St. Gabriel.
Merrick, Andrew J. '08 (BR) Baton Rouge, LA Christ the King; [K] Baton Rouge, LA Christ the King Parish and Catholic Center.
Merrifield, Donald P. *s.j.* '65 (SJ)[M] Los Gatos, CA Sacred Heart Jesuit Center.
Merrill, Thomas *o.f.m.conv.* '79 (STP) Bloomington, MN St. Bonaventure; Richfield, MN The Church of the Assumption.
Merris, Christopher '82 (MO) Military Chaplains; Navy Chaplains.
Merry, Paul F. '71 (BGP) Danbury, CT St. Peter.
Mersinger, Norbert A. '55 (STL) Retired.
Mertens, Michael G. '45 (LC)[H] La Crosse, WI Holy Cross (Seminary) Diocesan Center Retired.
Mertensotto, Leon J. *c.s.c.* '56 (FTW)[B] University of Notre Dame Du Lac; [H] Notre Dame, IN Holy Cross Community, Corby Hall, University of Notre Dame.
Mertes, Mark '87 (KCK) Overland Park, KS Holy Cross; Council for Catholic Charismatic Renewal; Archdiocesan Pastoral Council.
Mertes, Robert *s.v.d.* '78 (DUB)[B] Epworth, IA Divine Word College; Religious Priests Representative.
Mertz, Frederick A. '49 (STP) Retired.
Merwald, Melvin J. '71 (OM) Omaha, NE St. Wenceslaus.
Merz, Albert *o.f.m.* '66 (NSH)[H] Nashville, TN Franciscan Friars.
Merz, Daniel J. '98 (KC)[A] Conception, MO Conception Seminary College; Liturgical Commission; On Duty Outside the Diocese.
Merz, Eugene F. *s.j.* '61 (MIL)[P] Milwaukee, WI Arrupe House Jesuit Community.
Merzweiler, David W. '77 (Y) Lake Milton, OH St. Catherine; North Jackson, OH St. James Parish.
Mesa, Jose L. *s.j.* '77 (STA) Gainesville, FL St. Augustine.
Mesa, Luis (STL) On Duty Outside the Archdiocese.
Mesa, Mario *o.f.m.cap.* '64 (SJN) San Juan, PR San Juan de La Cruz; San Juan Bautista Regional Seminary.
Mesa, Ruel Z. '08 (SAC) Citrus Heights, CA Holy Family.
Mescall, Rev. Msgr. John '52 (NY) Rye, NY Resurrection; New Rochelle, NY Holy Family Retired.
Mescall, Thomas J. '04 (CHI) Chicago, IL St. Adrian.
Mescher, Michael J. '83 (DUB) Tama, IA St. Patrick; Tama, IA St. Joseph; Tama, IA St. Boniface; Belle Plaine, IA St. Michael; Deans; Directors.
Mesi, Vincent *o.f.m.* '72 (PHX) Phoenix, AZ St. Mary's Roman Catholic Basilica; Phoenix, AZ Banner Good Samaritan Medical Center.
Meskell, David B. '55 (BO) Senior Priests. Retired.
Meskill, Patrick A. '53 (LA) Retired.
Meskill, Thomas A. '60 (LA) Retired.
Mesley, Jerome T. '73 (GLP) Retired.
Mesmer, William A. '68 (SY) Sherrill, NY St. Helena; Vernon, NY Holy Family.
Messaro, Michael A. *m.ss.cc.* '68 (HBG) Fairfield, PA St. Rita; Fairfield, PA Immaculate Conception of the Blessed Virgin Mary.
Messenger, William P. '77 (LA) On Administrative Leave.
Messer, Joseph V. '61 (BAL) Retired.
Messer, Paul A. *s.j.* '67 (BO)[U] Newton, MA The Jesuit Community at Boston College.
Messer, Terrence *c.f.r.* '94 (NY)[EE] Yonkers, NY St. Felix Friary.
Messick, Severin *o.s.b.* '82 (IND) Greenfield, IN St. Michael; [K] St. Meinrad St. Meinrad Archabbey; Archdiocesan Judges.
Messier, Gerard *a.a.* '58 (BO)[U] Brighton, MA Assumption Guild.
Messier, Gerard *a.a.* (NY) New York, NY St. Vincent de Paul.
Messina, Angelo '68 (ALX) Retired.
Messina, D. Andrew '09 (PRO) North Kingstown, RI St. Francis De Sales.
Messina, John '96 (BAL) Priests Sick or Absent.
Messina, Joseph '72 (CAM) Retired.
Messina, Richard C. '65 (BO) Winchester, MA St. Mary.
Messina, Samuel '65 (JKS) Batesville, MS St. Mary; Priests' Council.
Messina, Victor G. '74 (BR) Retired.
Messing, Francis '59 (MOB) Retired.
Messner, Michael E. '98 (HBG) Lancaster, PA Sacred Heart of Jesus.
Messner, Michael '98 (HBG)[I] Lancaster, PA Franklin and Marshall College, Lancaster.
Messner, Thomas *o.f.m.* '67 (LA)[P] Santa Barbara, CA Franciscan Friary, Order of Friars Minor (Old Mission).
Mestas, Leonard J. '81 (MO) On Assignment Outside the Diocese; DEPARTMENT OF VETERANS AFFAIRS HOSPITALS AND CHAPLAINS.
Mestriparampil, Thomas '89 (NY) East Elmhurst, NY George M. Motchan Detention Center; East Elmhurst, NY Otis Bantum Correctional Center; New York, NY St. Charles Borromeo.
Mesure, Rev. Msgr. Gerard C. '84 (PH) On Special or Other Archdiocesan Assignment; Defenders of the Bond; Promoters of Justice.
Mesure, Rev. Msgr. Gerard C. '84 (PH) Conshohocken, PA St. Mary; West Conshohocken, PA St. Gertrude; The Chancery.
Meszaros, James J. '69 (BRK) Bayside, NY St. Josaphat Retired.
Metcalf, Andrew '86 (SR) Santa Rosa, CA St. Rose of Lima.
Method, Fredrick '66 (DUL) Buhl, MN Our Lady of the Sacred Heart; Chisholm, MN St. Joseph; College of Consultors.
Metrejean, Rev. Msgr. Paul '63 (LAF) Retired.
Metro, LeRoy '63 (SAL) Retired.

Metsy, Rev. Msgr. Norman G. '47 (PRO) Retired.
Metts, Ralph E. *s.j.* '73 (WDC)[N] Washington, DC The Jesuit Community at Georgetown University; [W] Washington, DC Jesuit Secondary Education Association.
Metz, Bradley *c.s.c.* '02 (FTW) South Bend, IN Holy Cross; South Bend, IN St. Stanislaus; [H] Notre Dame Congregation of Holy Cross, Indiana Province, Provincial House.
Metz, David '97 (SAL) Hanover, KS Sacred Heart Parish; Hanover, KS St. John the Baptist Parish; Washington, KS Saints Peter and Paul Parish; Washington, KS St. Augustine Parish.
Metz, Ken (ORL) Sanford, FL All Souls.
Metz, Kenneth J. '65 (MIL) Retired.
Metzbower, Francis X. *s.j.* '63 (BAL)[S] Baltimore, MD Colombiere Jesuit Community.
Metzdorf, William C. '73 (WDC) Retired.
Metzger, Andrew *o.s.b.* '56 (SP)[N] St. Leo, FL St. Leo Abbey.
Metzger, Christopher (NEW)[M] Newark, NJ Franciscan Friars of the Renewal.
Metzger, Clement *s.j.* '65 (CLV) Parma, OH St. Anthony of Padua; [D] Cleveland, OH St. Ignatius High School.
Metzger, Dennis M. '74 (TOL) Sylvania, OH St. Joseph; St. Luke Deanery; Members.
Metzger, Edward *o.f.m.* '59 (SLC) Helper, UT Saint Anthony of Padua Catholic Church LLC 216.
Metzger, Edwin '55 (ROC) Rochester, NY Our Mother of Sorrows Retired.
Metzger, John L. '67 (COL) Retired.
Metzger, Joseph H. '91 (RIC) Norfolk, VA Blessed Sacrament.
Metzger, Rev. Msgr. Paul E. '43 (STU) Retired.
Metzger, Richard '67 (COL) Groveport, OH St. Mary.
Metzger, Rev. Msgr. Robert E. '60 (COL) Retired.
Metzger, Rev. Msgr. Sam S. '59 (TYL) Retired.
Metzger, Stephen A. '70 (COL) Utica, OH Church of the Nativity.
Metzger, Thomas H. '82 (LFT) Noblesville, IN Our Lady of Grace.
Metzger, Thomas '56 (BAL) Priests Sick or Absent.
Metzger, William A. '78 (COL) Columbus, OH St. John the Baptist; Columbus, OH Sacred Heart; Diocesan Judges.
Metzger, William J. *o.s.f.s.* '71 (ARL) Vienna, VA Our Lady of Good Counsel.
Metzger, William J. '62 (COL) Groveport, OH St. Mary Retired.
Metzinger, John R. '82 (OKL) Edmond, OK St. John the Baptist; Council of Priests Archdiocesan.
Metzler, Warren W. '64 (PIT) Pittsburgh, PA St. James.
Metzler, William R. '72 (HRT) Simsbury, CT St. Mary.
Meulemans, Carl P. *m.m.* '60 (NY)[EE] Maryknoll Maryknoll Fathers and Brothers.
Meulemans, Dennis T. '61 (SUP) Board of Directors Retired.
Meulemans, Edward G. '60 (SUP) Retired.
Meulemans, Thomas O. *o.praem.* '59 (PH)[Y] Paoli, PA Daylesford Abbey.
Meuret, Donald L. '84 (LC) Deans; Marshfield, WI Our Lady of Peace.
Mevissen, Richard *c.ss.r.* '66 (DEN)[N] Denver, CO The Redemptorists/Denver Province; Denver, CO.
Meyer, Albert *o.s.b.* '56 (MRY)[F] San Luis Obispo, CA Men's Residence.
Meyer, Arthur D. '61 (PEO) Lacon, IL Immaculate Conception Retired.
Meyer, Benedict *o.s.b.* '54 (IND)[K] St. Meinrad, IN St. Meinrad Archabbey.
Meyer, Bernard A. '59 (SFD) Retired.
Meyer, Blase G. '68 (PHX) Retired.
Meyer, Charles R. '45 (CHI)[A] Mundelein, IL University of St. Mary of the Lake/Mundelein Seminary Retired.
Meyer, Clayton '66 (SEA) Retired.
Meyer, Daniel J. '82 (CIN) Dayton, OH Holy Angels; [U] Dayton, OH Catholic Alumni Club (Dayton Chapter).
Meyer, Dennis J. *m.s.* '70 (STL)[O] St. Louis, MO Missionaries of LaSalette, Province of Mary, Mother of the Americas; [O] St. Louis, MO La Salette Novitiate.
Meyer, Earl *o.f.m.cap.* '60 (KCK)[I] Lawrence, KS St. Conrad's Friary; Lawrence, KS St. John the Evangelist.
Meyer, Emmett F. '64 (OM) Retired.
Meyer, Eric *c.p.* '66 (CHI) Chicago, IL Immaculate Conception; [N] Chicago, IL Passionist Community–Immaculate Conception Monastery.
Meyer, Frederick A. '65 (STL) St. Charles, MO St. Peter.
Meyer, Gerald J. '96 (PEO) Retired.
Meyer, Rev. Msgr. Gilbert '42 (FRS) Retired.
Meyer, Harold K. *o.c.s.o.* '62 (SAC)[A] Vina, CA Abbey of New Clairvaux, Trappist Seminary; [I] Vina, CA Abbey of New Clairvaux, Trappist.
Meyer, Harry J. '64 (CIN) Retired.
Meyer, James A. '94 (FAR) Diocesan College of Consultors.
Meyer, James '94 (FAR) West Fargo, ND Holy Cross Church of West Fargo; Deanery 2.
Meyer, James '60 (DET) Retired.
Meyer, John A. '82 (IND) Madison, IN Prince of Peace; Madison, IN Most Sorrowful Mother of God; Deaneries and Deans; [O] Madison, IN Hanover College; [C] Madison, IN Shawe Memorial Junior–Senior High School.
Meyer, John D. '08 (STP) St. Anthony, MN St. Charles Borromeo.
Meyer, John R. '89 (SFR)[R] San Francisco, CA Prelature of the Holy Cross and Opus Dei; San Francisco.
Meyer, Jonathan P. '03 (IND) North Vernon, IN St. Mary/Nativity of the Blessed Virgin Mary; North Vernon, IN St. Anne; North Vernon, IN St. Joseph.
Meyer, Leo A. '65 (NO) Liaisons Retired.
Meyer, Rev. Msgr. Louis F. '44 (STL) Retired.
Meyer, Luke D. '06 (FAR) Special Assignment; [J] Fargo, ND Catholic Chaplains Association; Chancellor and Secretary to the Bishop; Archivist; Notaries; Corporate Board; Diocesan Finance Council; Office of Worship and Sacraments; Holy Childhood Association; Propagation of the Faith.
Meyer, Michael W. '93 (LA) Temple City, CA St. Luke the Evangelist.
Meyer, Nick '52 (SFD)[L] Springfield, IL Our Lady of Angels Friary.
Meyer, Robert G. '74 (WIN) Diocesan Consultors Retired.
Meyer, Robert J. '64 (PIT) Bridgeville, PA Holy Child; [M] Pittsburgh, PA St. John Vianney Manor.
Meyer, Robert S. '88 (NEW)[B] School of Diplomacy and Intl. Rels.; Defenders of the Bond.
Meyer, Ronald *o.m.i.* '71 (NOR)[G] Willimantic, CT Missionary Oblates of Mary Immaculate.
Meyer, Stephen L. '79 (DUB)[G] Bellevue, IA Bellevue Area Elementary School; Dubuque, IA St. Catherine; Bellevue, IA St. Donatus; Bellevue, IA St. Joseph; [G] Bellevue, IA Marquette High School.
Meyer, Steven J. '90 (FAR) Wimbledon, ND St. Mary's Church of Dazey; Wimbledon, ND St. John's Church of Kensal; Wimbledon, ND St. Boniface Church of Wimbledon.
Meyer, Thomas C. '98 (SFD) Edwardsville, IL St. Mary.
Meyer, Thomas C. '98 (SFD) Comite Diocesano de Ministerio Hispano – Diocesan Committee for Hispanic Ministry.
Meyer, Thomas E. '70 (CIN) Dayton, OH St. Albert the Great.
Meyer, Thomas *o.m.i.* '70 (BEL)[F] Belleville, IL Missionary Oblates of Mary Immaculate – St. Henry's Oblate Residence.
Meyer, William J. *s.m.* '79 (SAT)[C] Oblate School of Theology.
Meyer, William O. '49 (DAV) Davenport, IA Our Lady of Victory Retired.
Meyer, William *s.m.* '79 (STL)[O] St. Louis Marianists, Province of the United States (Society of Mary).
Meyers, James P. '70 (WDC) Rockville, MD St. Raphael.
Meyers, John F. '83 (PH) Bensalem, PA Our Lady of Fatima.
Meyers, Rev. Msgr. John F. '56 (DAL) Dallas, TX St. Monica Retired.
Meyers, John R. '89 (POD) Vicar for California.
Meyers, Rev. Msgr. Michael W. '77 (LA) Clergy, Vicar for; Ex Officio; Altadena, CA St. Elizabeth of Hungary; Vicar for Clergy.
Meyers, Robert V. '87 (MET) Highland Park, NJ St. Paul the Apostle; Canonical Staff.
Meyr, Herbert J. '60 (CHI) Retired.
Meysenburg, James J. '89 (LIN)[C] Lincoln, NE Pius X Catholic High School; [L] Lincoln, NE Pius X Foundation and Pius X Endowment Fund; Lincoln, NE St. Patrick's.
Meystrik, Gregory C. '90 (JC) Jefferson City, MO St. Margaret of Antioch; Jefferson City, MO St. Stanislaus; Chair Couple; Ministry to Priests; Board of Trustees; Scouting.
Meza, Rev. Msgr. Arturo '88 (AMA) Amarillo, TX Blessed Sacrament.
Meza, Fernando '95 (SAC) Lincoln, CA St. Joseph.
Meza, Gonzalo E. '09 (SAT) San Antonio, TX St. Pius X.
Meza, Mario Flores *o.f.m.* (LAR) Laredo, TX Sagrado Corazon de Jesus Mission; Laredo, TX Nuestra Senora del Rosario Independent Mission.
Meza, Misael *s.j.* '02 (BO)[U] Newton, MA The Jesuit Community at Boston College.
Meznar, Joseph A. '58 (DEN) Denver, CO Holy Rosary Retired.
Meznar, Robert P. '60 (DEN) Retired.
Mezquida, Ramon '58 (PCE) On Duty Outside the Diocese.
Mezydlo, James A. '77 (CHI) Chicago, IL St. Florian.
Mfodwo, Francis (NY) Poughkeepsie, NY Our Lady of Mt. Carmel.
Mgaya, Bruno (B) Boise, ID St. Mark's.
Mgbeajuo, Donatus C. *m.s.p.* '97 (SAV) Columbus, GA St. Benedict the Moor.
Mgimba, Thadeo '08 (CHI) Chicago, IL Holy Name of Mary.
Mhagama, Laurent '08 (CHI) Midlothian, IL St. Christopher.
Mhanna, Andre '01 (OLL) Special Assignment.
Miah, Gabriel '77 (RVC) Mineola, NY Corpus Christi; Elmont, NY St. Boniface.
Miani, Titian A. '55 (STO) Diamond Springs, CA Retired.
Miara, James L. '01 (NY) Bronx, NY Our Lady of Mt. Carmel.
Miarecki, Marek '01 (PAT) Passaic, NJ Holy Rosary.
Micallef, Rene Mario *s.j.* '08 (BO)[U] Cambridge, MA Claver House.
Micarelli, Edmond C. '59 (PRO) Retired.
Micca, Louis F. *s.a.c.* '66 (BAL) Baltimore, MD St. Jude Shrine.
Micciulla, Angelo J. '05 (NY) Suffern, NY Sacred Heart.
Micek, Sylvester '51 (SFD)[L] Springfield, IL Our Lady of Angels Friary.
Miceli, John P. '94 (CLV) Cleveland, OH St. Mark.
Miceli, Michael A. '97 (BR) Vacherie, LA Our Lady of Peace.
Miceli, Paul E. '72 (BO)[A] Weston, MA Blessed John XXIII National Seminary.
Miceli, Vincent F. '91 (BRK) Brooklyn, NY St. Fortunata.
Mich, Kenneth A. '70 (MIL) Menomonee Falls, WI Good Shepherd.
Mich, Mario *s.d.b.* '48 (SFR)[K] San Francisco, CA Home for the Aged of the Little Sisters of the Poor.
Michael, Babu '89 (RVC) Holbrook, NY Good Shepherd.
Michael, Rev. Msgr. Chester P. '42 (RIC) Retired.
Michael, David C. '86 (BO) West Roxbury, MA St. John Chrysostom; Jewish Relations; On Duty Outside the Diocese.
Michael, David '96 (CHR) Barnwell, SC St. Andrew; Scouting Programs.
Michael, David '95 (CAM) Marmora, NJ Church of the Resurrection, Marmora, N.J.
Michael, George *v.c.* (SCL) St. Cloud, MN St. Michael; Waite Park, MN St. Joseph's.
Michael, Gnanadhas George '78 (NY) Wappingers Falls, NY St. Mary.
Michael, Rev. Msgr. Kenneth '65 (OLL) Retired.
Michael, Lawrence P. '75 (SAM) Torrington, CT St. Maron.
Michael, Peter *s.v.d.* '40 (FgM) Techny, IL.
Michaels, Dana P. '82 (OAK) Alameda, CA St. Barnabas.
Michaels, James *s.s.c.* '51 (OM)[K] St. Columbans Missionary Society of St. Columban.
Michaels, Patrick T. '82 (SFR) Mill Valley, CA Our Lady of Mt. Carmel.
Michaelson, Sean D. *s.j.* '06 (SFR)[N] San Francisco, CA Loyola House Jesuit Community.
Michalak, Jan *o.s.p.p.e.* '81 (PH)[Y].
Michalak, Jaromir '91 (CAM) Clayton, NJ St. Catherine's Roman Catholic Church, Clayton, N.J.; Franklinville, NJ R.C. Church of the Nativity, Franklinville, N.J.
Michalak, Rev. Msgr. John S. '51 (OM) Retired.
Michalchuk, Jack H. '01 (ALX) Bunkie, LA St. Anthony of Padua.
Michalcka, John J. '59 (OKL) Ponca City, OK Church of St. Mary.
Michalczak, John T. '70 (NEW) Teaneck, NJ Holy Name Hospital; [G] School of Nursing.
Michalek, Rev. Msgr. George C. '78 (LAN) Lansing, MI St. Mary Cathedral; Bishop's Office; Presbyteral Council; Diocesan Archivist; Tribunal Judges.
Michalek, Stanislaw *s.ch.* '88 (SEA) Seattle, WA St. Margaret of Scotland; Polish Speaking, Ministry to.
Michalenko, Alexei '68 (VNN) On Special Assignment.
Michalenko, Seraphim *m.i.c.* '56 (SPR)[H] John Paul II Institute of Divine Mercy; [H] Stockbridge, MA Congregation of Marian Fathers of The Immaculate Conception of the Most Blessed Virgin Mary; [H] Stockbridge, MA Association of Marian Helpers, Marian Helpers Center.
Michaletz, James E. *c.s.v.* '60 (JOL) Bourbonnais, IL Maternity of the Blessed Virgin Mary.
Michaletz, James E. *c.s.v.* '60 (CHI)[N] Arlington Heights Viatorian Province Center–Clerics of St. Viator.
Michalicka, John J. '59 (OKL)[H] Ponca City, OK St. Mary's Housing Foundation.
Michalicka, John '59 (OKL) Region VIII.
Michalik, Gary '80 (DET) Westland, MI St. Theodore of Canterbury.
Michalisin, Gregory J. '92 (PBR) Windber, PA St. Mary (Dormition) Church; Notaries; Elected Deanery Representatives; Windber, PA SS. Peter and Paul.
Michalowski, John W. *s.j.* '81 (BO)[U] Boston The Society of Jesus of New England–Provincial Offices.
Michalowski, John W. *s.j.* '81 (MAN) Salem, NH Mary, Queen of Peace; Salem, NH St. Joseph; Presbyteral Council.
Michalski, Edward (WOR) Leominster, MA St. Cecilia.
Michalski, James L. *s.j.* '72 (OM)[E] Omaha, NE The Jesuit Middle School of Omaha; [K] Omaha, NE Jesuit Community at Creighton University.

Michalski, Jan *s.ch.* '86 (BAL) Baltimore, MD Holy Rosary.
Michalski, Jan *s.ch.* '86 (DET) Hamtramck, MI St. Florian.
Michalski, Melvin E. '70 (MIL) Special Assignment; [B] Hales Corners, WI Sacred Heart School of Theology.
Michalski, Michael F. '76 (MIL)[H] Milwaukee, WI All Saints Catholic East School System, Inc.; Milwaukee, WI SS. Peter and Paul.
Michalski, Simon Felix *o.p.* '08 (JC)[D] Columbia, MO St. Thomas More Newman Center; Columbia, MO St. Thomas More Newman Center, University of Missouri.
Michalski, Simon Felix *o.p.* '08 (JC) Columbia Catholic Hospital Ministry.
Michatek, William C. '66 (ROC) Webster, NY Holy Trinity.
Michaud, Gregory A. '09 (LC)[C] Wausau, WI Newman Catholic High School; Wausau, WI Church of the Resurrection; Wausau, WI St. Michael.
Michaud, James L. '77 (PRT) Special or Other Diocesan Assignment.
Michel, Delix *s.s.l.* '88 (SFD) Alton, IL Ss. Peter and Paul; Black Catholic Advisory Board; Vandalia, IL Vandalia Correctional Center.
Michel, Engelbert G. '66 (PH)[CC] Philadelphia, PA Catholic Kolping Society; Philadelphia, PA St. Christopher.
Michel, Eugene *o.f.m.* '64 (STP) St. Paul, MN Sacred Heart.
Michel, Gabriel (BO) Mattapan, MA St. Angela Merici; Haitian.
Michel, Richard B. *o.s.b.* '86 (GBG)[G] Latrobe Saint Vincent Archabbey.
Michele, Robert P. *c.s.p.* '55 (AUS) Austin, TX St. Austin.
Michele, Robert P. *c.s.p.* '55 (NY)[EE] Jamaica Estates Paulist Fathers Generalate.
Michelini, Edward L. '05 (SCR) Canadensis, PA St. Bernadette.
Michelini, Michael S. '71 (CHI) Chicago, IL St. Adalbert.
Michell, George J. '64 (RVC) Southold, NY St. Patrick's.
Michell, Timothy *o.c.s.o.* '65 (P)[L] Lafayette, OR The Cistercian (Trappist) Abbey of Our Lady of Guadalupe.
Michels, Andrew J. '85 (NU) Boy Scouts; Priests' Council.
Michelson, Chris '80 (KNX) Presbyteral Council; Diocesan Finance Council; Knoxville, TN St. Albert the Great Church.
Michiels, Kenneth J. '91 (ALX) Appointed Members; Leesville, LA St. Michael; College of Consultors; Vocations and Seminarians.
Michiels, Philip F. '69 (SHP) Shreveport, LA St. Elizabeth Ann Seton; Shreveport, LA Overton Brooks Veteran's Administration Medical Center; Defenders of the Bond; Presbyteral Council; Diocesan Liturgy Commission; College of Consultors; DEPARTMENT OF VETERANS AFFAIRS HOSPITALS AND CHAPLAINS.
Michini, F. Joseph *s.j.* '80 (BAL)[D] Baltimore, MD Loyola Blakefield.
Michka, Aaron J. (FgM) New Rochelle, NY Eastern Brothers Province.
Michka, Aaron J. *c.s.c.* '09 (FTW)[H] Notre Dame Congregation of Holy Cross, Indiana Province, Provincial House.
Michler, James R. '75 (STL) On Duty Outside the Archdiocese.
Michlik, Valerian '00 (SJP) Pittsburgh, PA St. George; Liturgical Commission; League of Ukrainian Catholics; Personnel Board; Vice Chancellor; Alternates; Presbyteral Council; Presbyters.
Michniewicz, Martin E. '86 (CHI) Calumet City, IL St. Andrew the Apostle.
Mick, Lawrence E. '72 (CIN) On Special and Archdiocesan Assignment.
Mick, Lawrence J. '49 (CIN) Cincinnati, OH St. Antoninus Retired.
Micka, A. *m.i.c.* '49 (JOL) Retired.
Micketti, Gerald F. '83 (GAY) Acme, MI Christ the King; Archivist.
Mickey, Richard L. '88 (MEM)[F] Cordova, TN Villa Vianney Senior Priests Residence; Archives; Villa Vianney Priests Retirement Residence.
Mickiewicz, David '84 (ALB) Amsterdam, NY St. Stanislaus; Ecumenical and Interreligious Affairs of the Roman Catholic Diocese of Albany, Commission for; Priestly Life and Ministry Council.
Mickiewicz, J. William '62 (MET) Califon, NJ St. John Neumann; Deans.
Mickler, Jeffrey *s.s.p.* '74 (Y)[A] Canfield, OH Society of St. Paul.
Mickus, James J. '72 (OKL) Chandler, OK Our Lady of Sorrows.
Miclot, Brian *ph.d.* '74 (DAV)[A] St. Ambrose University.
Middendorf, Cyril G. *s.m.* '53 (CIN)[N] Dayton, OH Mercy Siena Woods, Nursing Care.
Middlecamp, Eric *s.d.s.* '52 (MIL)[P] Milwaukee, WI Salvatorians – Jordan Hall Retired.
Middleton, Charles '51 (WCH) Retired.
Midor, Adam '91 (TR) Roebling, NJ The Church of Saints Francis and Clare, Florence Township, N.J.
Midura, Rev. Msgr. Francis S. '70 (RVC) Hauppauge, NY St. Thomas More; Judges for Interdiocesan Tribunal.
Midzak, Rt. Rev. Mitred Archpriest Ihor '90 (STF) Priest Personnel Board; Stamford, CT St. Vladimir Cathedral; Vicar General; Diocesan Consultors; Presbyteral Council; Administrative Council; Directors.
Miechielsen, Albert *ss.cc.* '46 (HON)[D] Honolulu, HI St. Patrick's Monastery.
Mieczkowski, Rev. Msgr. Chester J. '45 (BAL) Retired.
Miekina, Stanley *c.m.* '59 (HRT) New Haven, CT St. Stanislaus.
Miele, Joseph J. '56 (TR) Manasquan, NJ St. Denis Retired.
Mielechowicz, Leszek '89 (LA) San Gabriel, CA St. Anthony.
Mien, Francis '65 (SEA) Chaplains.
Mierenfeld, Lawrence E. '73 (CIN) Centerville, OH Incarnation.
Mierzwa, Ronald B. '76 (BUF) Ellicottville, NY Holy Name of Mary.
Mieszala, Raphael *b.g.s.* '05 (MIA)[F] Brothers of the Good Shepherd, Inc.
Mifsud, Carmelo '59 (OAK) Retired.
Mifsud, James J. *s.m.* '65 (SJ) San Jose, CA Queen of Apostles.
Migliore, Angelus *t.o.r.* '64 (SP) Cursillo, English; Cursillo, Spiritual Advisors; Tampa, FL St. Patrick.
Migone, Pablo '09 (SAV) Warner Robins, GA Sacred Heart.
Miguel, Eutiquiano *o.f.m.cap.* '51 (NO) New Orleans, LA St. Theresa of Avila; New Orleans, LA University Hospital.
Miguélez, Rev. Msgr. Valeriano '66 (SJN) San Juan, PR Espiritu Santo; [E] San Juan, PR Hospital Pavia; Police Chaplains; [E] San Juan, PR Centro Medico de P.R.; [B] San Juan, PR Colegio Espiritu Santo.
Miguez, Raul (NY) Bronx, NY Holy Spirit.
Mihalak, James J. '76 (ALN) Retired.
Mihalco, John J. '83 (PBR) Sykesville, PA Holy Trinity; Protopresbyters; Defender of the Bond; Elected Deanery Representatives; Du Bois, PA Nativity of the Mother of God.
Mihalic, Peter M. '76 (CLV) Fairport Harbor, OH St. Anthony of Padua.
Mihalik, Rev. Msgr. Alexis E. '64 (PBR) Retired.
Mihan, Rev. Msgr. John A. '59 (LA) Retired.
Mihayli, Gilbert *o.praem.* '43 (GB)[J] De Pere, WI St. Norbert Abbey.
Mijas, Paul J. '85 (RVC) Kings Park, NY St. Joseph's.
Mikalajunas, John E. '69 (SY) Binghamton, NY Binghamton General Hospital.
Mikalofsky, Hilarion A. '75 (MIL) On Duty Outside the Archdiocese.
Mikalonis, Estanislao '05 (SJ) Mountain View, CA St. Athanasius.
Mikes, Pavel '90 (FAR) On Duty Outside the Diocese.
Mikesch, Rev. Msgr. Gregory R. '75 (STL) Wildwood, MO St. Alban Roe; [V] St. Louis, MO Archdiocesan Stewardship Education Committee.
Mikhael, Elie Hares '95 (SAM) Miami, FL Our Lady of Lebanon; Young Adult Ministry.
Mikkelson, Scott '82 (AUS) Retired.
Mikobi, Alidor *c.j.* '02 (LA) Santa Maria, CA St. Louis de Montfort.
Mikolaitis, Vito E. '43 (CHI) Retired.
Mikolajczyk, Bruno '88 (CC) Retired.
Mikolajczyk, Edward M. '73 (CHI) Evergreen Park, IL Queen of Martyrs; College of Consultors; Presbyteral Council.
Mikonis, Gerald S. '74 (PIT) Port Vue, PA St. Mark.
Miksch, Joseph A. '66 (OM) Columbus, NE St. Isidore.
Mikstay, Michael '81 (Y) Military Chaplains; Navy Chaplains.
Mikula, John Joseph *o.f.m.conv.* '56 (DET)[K] Dearborn Heights, MI All Saints Friary.
Mikulanis, Rev. Msgr. Dennis '77 (SD) Vicars Forane; San Diego, CA San Rafael; Cemetery Committee; Ecumenical and Interreligious Affairs.
Mikulcik, Kenneth '98 (OWN) Mayfield, KY St. Joseph; Scouting Activities; Deans/Coordinators.
Mikulik, Kenneth E. '52 (GAL) Retired.
Mikus, Elemir '57 (DET) Retired.
Milanese, John M. '74 (BUR)[G] Randolph, VT Vermont Technical College; Randolph, VT Our Lady of the Angels.
Milani, Rev. Msgr. Joseph J. '50 (SJ) Cupertino, CA St. Joseph of Cupertino; Diocesan Clergy Personnel Board; [O] Cupertino, CA St. Joseph Cupertino Retirement Residence; Priests' Retirement Board Retired.
Milano, Cleo J. '83 (BR) Plaquemine, LA St. John the Evangelist; Board Members.
Milanowski, Paul '65 (GR) East Grand Rapids, MI St. Stephen Catholic Church.
Milbauer, Robert L. '66 (LA) Granada Hills, CA St. John Baptist de la Salle; Deanery 5.
Milby, Lawrence M. '65 (BUF) Retired.
Milek, Richard '83 (CHI) Burbank, IL St. Albert the Great.
Miles, C. Thomas '99 (CHR) Defenders of the Bond.
Miles, Cassian A. *o.f.m.* '61 (PAT)[N] Ringwood, NJ Holy Name Friary, Inc.
Miles, James '78 (BAL) Baltimore, MD Little Flower, Shrine of.
Miles, James '78 (LKC) On Leave.
Miles, John *c.r.* '51 (L)[L] Louisville, KY Villa Pacis, Resurrectionist Retirement Home; Louisville, KY St. Margaret Mary; Louisville, KY.
Miles, Richard M. '84 (NO) Kenner, LA Our Lady of Perpetual Help.
Miles, Thomas '99 (CHR) Graduate Studies.
Milewski, Casimir '69 (TR) Retired.
Milewski, Douglas J. '89 (NEW)[B][A] South Orange, NJ Immaculate Conception Seminary; [A] South Orange, NJ Immaculate Conception Seminary.
Milewski, John A. '93 (MO) DEPARTMENT OF VETERANS AFFAIRS HOSPITALS AND CHAPLAINS.
Milewski, John '93 (WDC) Washington, DC St. Anthony.
Milewski, John '93 (CLV) Cleveland, OH Veterans Administration Hospitals, Brecksville V.A.; Cleveland, OH Cleveland V.A.
Milewski, Richard R. '83 (TR) Freehold, NJ St. Rose of Lima; [N] Trenton, NJ Villa Vianney.
Milewski, Rev. Msgr. Stanley E. '55 (DET) Priests Conference for Polish Affairs of the Archdiocese of Detroit Retired.
Miley, Eamon '73 (MOB) Troy, AL St. Martin of Tours; [I] Troy, AL University Newman Center.
Milia, Rev. Msgr. Anthony A. '50 (OG) Judges Retired.
Milich, Nicohlas '01 (YAK) On Duty Outside the Diocese.
Milienewicz, Rt. Rev. Frank J. '76 (NTN) Birmingham, AL St. George; Protopresbyters; College of Eparchial Consultors; Presbyteral Council.
Militante, Henry A. '84 (TR) Capital Health System: Mercer Campus & Fluid Campus; Trenton, NJ Blessed Sacrament–Our Lady of the Divine Shepherd Parish.
Militello, Benedict P. '57 (NEW) Northvale, NJ St. Anthony's Retired.
Militello, Cosmo F. '60 (CHI) Retired.
Millan, Jose Luis '00 (SPK) Pullman, WA Sacred Heart; Defensor Vinculi; Members; Priests' Personnel Board.
Millane, Rev. Msgr. Thomas J. '63 (TUC) Directors; Vicar for Retired Priests; Tucson, AZ Roman Catholic Church of Saint Elizabeth Ann Seton – Tucson Retired.
Millard, Glen Michael '06 (BIS) Stanley, ND Queen of the Most Holy Rosary.
Millard, Mike '06 (BIS) Stanley, ND St. Ann.
Millbourn, Richard L. *s.j.* '01 (CHI)[N] Chicago, IL Chicago Province of the Society of Jesus–Provincial Office; [E] Chicago, IL Chicago Jesuit Academy; [W] Chicago, IL Jesuit International Missions, Inc.; [N] Chicago, IL Clark Street Jesuit Residence.
Millea, Thomas V. (CHI) Retired.
Millea, Rev. Msgr. William V. '80 (BGP) On Duty Outside the Diocese.
Miller, Abraham '79 (STN) Seattle, WA Our Lady of Zavarnytsya.
Miller, Arnie (B) Boise, ID St. Mary's.
Miller, B. Henry *s.j.* '54 (NO)[P] New Orleans, LA Ignatius Residence.
Miller, Bert '91 (FAR) West Fargo, ND Blessed Sacrament Church of West Fargo.
Miller, Bertin *o.f.m.* '64 (STL)[S] Dittmer, MO Il Ritiro–The Little Retreat.
Miller, Brendan *o.s.b.* '83 (LR)[A] Subiaco, AR Subiaco Abbey.
Miller, Brian J. *t.o.r.* '53 (SP) St. Petersburg, FL St. Mary Our Lady of Grace.
Miller, Bruce '77 (ALX) Moderator of the Curia; Judges; Pineville, LA Sacred Heart; College of Consultors.
Miller, Byron J. *c.ss.r.* '90 (NO) New Orleans, LA St. Alphonsus; New Orleans, LA National Shrine of Blessed Francis Xavier Seelos.
Miller, C. Anthony '80 (HBG) Lykens, PA Our Lady Help of Christians; Williamstown, PA Sacred Heart of Jesus.
Miller, Casper J. *s.j.* '64 (FgM) Detroit, MI Detroit Province.
Miller, Charles E. '91 (SB) Idyllwild, CA Queen of Angels.
Miller, Charles J. *o.f.m.* '72 (NEW) Bloomfield, NJ Church of St. Thomas the Apostle.
Miller, Charles J. *o.f.m.* '66 (ARL) Triangle, VA St. Francis of Assisi.
Miller, Charles '72 (NEW) Members.
Miller, Christopher J. '08 (LIN) Lincoln, NE St. Joseph; Advocates.
Miller, Christopher T. '93 (LFT) Frankfort, IN St. Mary; Vicar for Hispanic Ministry in White County; Special Assignment.
Miller, Cletus *o.s.b.* '44 (SFS)[F] Marvin, SD Blue Cloud Abbey; Marvin, SD Blue Cloud Abbey.
Miller, David L. '81 (SPC) Cassville, MO St. Edward;

Shell Knob, MO Holy Family; Region II; Apostolate to the Deaf.
Miller, Dennis W. '02 (DUB) Associate Directors; [N] Ames, IA St. Thomas Aquinas Church and Catholic Student Center (Iowa State University); Gilbert, IA SS. Peter and Paul; Ames, IA St. Thomas Aquinas Church (and Catholic Student Center); Deanery Representatives.
Miller, Donald A. *o.f.m.* '72 (CIN)[N] Cincinnati, OH St. Francis Seraph Friary.
Miller, Rev. Msgr. Edward M. '71 (BAL) Baltimore, MD St. Bernardine; Advocates; Presbyteral Council; Priest Personnel Board.
Miller, Francis J. '50 (CIN) Retired.
Miller, Francis *o.c.d.* '49 (WDC)[B] Washington, DC Discalced Carmelite Friars Retired.
Miller, Rev. Msgr. Frank '54 (AUS) Retired.
Miller, Franklin '89 (FAR) Harvey, ND St. Cecilia's Church of Harvey; Selz, ND St. Anthony.
Miller, Frederick L. '72 (NEW) On Duty Outside the Archdiocese.
Miller, Frederick L. '72 (BAL)[A] Emmitsburg, MD Mount St. Mary's Seminary.
Miller, Gary M. '72 (CHI) Evergreen Park, IL St. Bernadette.
Miller, George P. '78 (TOL) Judges.
Miller, Rev. Msgr. George P. '78 (DET) Detroit, MI St. Jude; Judges.
Miller, Gregory *o.s.b.* '73 (SCL)[I] Collegeville, MN St. John's Abbey, of the Order of St. Benedict.
Miller, Jake '01 (FAR) Rolla, ND Immaculate Heart of Mary Church of Rock Lake; Rolla, ND St. Joachim's Church of Rolla.
Miller, James H. '68 (LC) Cashton, WI St. Augustine of Hippo Retired.
Miller, James L. '76 (DUB) Permanent Diaconate Formation Board; Marshalltown, IA St. Mary; [F] Marshalltown, IA Marshalltown Area Catholic Schools.
Miller, James Norman '59 (NSH) Nashville, TN St. Mary of the Seven Sorrows; DEPARTMENT OF VETERANS AFFAIRS HOSPITALS AND CHAPLAINS.
Miller, James *c.pp.s.* '54 (CIN)[N] Carthagena, OH St. Charles Retired.
Miller, James '68 (FWT)[G] Crowley, TX St. Francis Village, Inc. Retired.
Miller, James *o.m.i.* '57 (SAT)[K] San Antonio, TX Oblate Madonna Residence.
Miller, John A. '08 (TOL) Perrysburg, OH St. Rose.
Miller, John C. '95 (BRK) On Leave/Unassigned.
Miller, Rev. Msgr. John J. '64 (PH) Philadelphia, PA Saint Martha.
Miller, John L. '09 (E) Erie, PA St. Peter Cathedral; [C] Erie, PA Cathedral Preparatory School.
Miller, John P. '78 (HEL) Columbia Falls, MT St. Richard.
Miller, John P. '82 (WCH) Cunningham, KS Sacred Heart; Nashville, KS St. Leo the Great; Zenda, KS St. Peter's; Zenda, KS St. John.
Miller, Joseph A. '89 (BRK) On Leave/Unassigned.
Miller, Joseph C. '49 (OWN) Retired.
Miller, Joseph K. '57 (SAG) Pinconning, MI St. Mary; Pinconning, MI St. Michael.
Miller, Joseph *c.pp.s.* '77 (KC) Presbyteral Council; [J] Liberty, MO Precious Blood Society Provincial Office.
Miller, Joseph *s.v.d.* '68 (SD) Missions; Propagation of the Faith.
Miller, Rev. Msgr. Kenneth E. '77 (Y) Youngstown, OH Sacred Heart of Jesus; Boardman, OH St. Luke.
Miller, Rev. Msgr. Lawrence J. '69 (NEW) Bayonne, NJ St. Mary Star of the Sea; Serra Club of Hudson County.
Miller, Leo M. *o.m.i.* '52 (LA) Veterans Affairs Medical Center.
Miller, Leo *o.m.i.* '52 (BEL)[F] Belleville, IL Shrine of Our Lady of the Snows Retired.
Miller, Loran *o.f.m.cap.* '64 (MAD)[I] Madison, WI San Damiano Friary Retired.
Miller, Mardean E. '94 (PH) Philadelphia, PA St. William.
Miller, Mark O. '05 (PEO) Champaign, IL St. Matthew.
Miller, Mark *c.pp.s.* '71 (SAN) Odessa, TX St. Joseph; Odessa, TX St. Anthony; Presbyteral Council; Diocesan Consultors.
Miller, Martin J. '94 (POD) Oak Park.
Miller, Martin J. '94 (TR)[S] Princeton, NJ Opus Dei; Princeton.
Miller, Martin John '02 (CHI)[V] Oak Park, IL Oak Park Study Center.
Miller, Maurice R. '49 (LFT) Lafayette, IN St. Ann Retired.
Miller, Meinrad *o.s.b.* '94 (KCK)[A] Atchison, KS Benedictine College; [I] Atchison, KS St. Benedict's Abbey; Atchison, KS.
Miller, Michael I. *m.s.c.* '85 (RCK) Aurora, IL St. Therese of Jesus; [G] Aurora, IL Missionaries of the Sacred Heart Community.
Miller, Michael J. '72 (MRY) Salinas, CA Sacred Heart.
Miller, Michael J. '96 (STP) Stillwater, MN St. Mary; Stillwater, MN St. Michael; [G] Stillwater, MN St. Croix Catholic School.
Miller, Michael (MRY) Presbyteral Council.
Miller, Michael *o.f.m.conv.* '01 (HRT) Kensington, CT St. Paul.
Miller, Paul A. *c.ss.r.* '62 (ROC)[L] Canandaigua, NY Notre Dame Retreat House.
Miller, Paul D. '44 (FTW) Retired.
Miller, Philip '77 (Y) Ashtabula, OH St. Joseph.
Miller, Randall J. '89 (LAN) Jackson, MI St. John the Evangelist; Jackson, MI St. Joseph.
Miller, Robert J. '80 (PIT) Pittsburgh, PA Our Lady of Loreto; Pittsburgh, PA St. Pius X; [C] Mt. Lebanon, PA Seton–LaSalle Catholic High School, Inc.
Miller, Robert J. '76 (CHI) Chicago, IL St. Dorothy.
Miller, Robert L. '70 (SB) Office of Continuing Formation of Priests; Special or Other Diocesan Assignment; San Bernardino; Appointed Members.
Miller, Robert M. '92 (PIT) Evans City, PA St. Matthias; Zelienople, PA St. Gregory; Clergy Personnel Board.
Miller, Robert M. '02 (Y) Massillon, OH Saint Mary.
Miller, Theodore J. '75 (TOL) Gibsonburg, OH St. Michael Church; Helena, OH St. Mary.
Miller, Thomas C. '93 (STL) St. Louis, MO Epiphany of Our Lord.
Miller, Rev. Msgr. Thomas G. '71 (RIC) Roanoke, VA St. Andrew.
Miller, Thomas M. *c.s.b.* '45 (ROC)[J] Rochester, NY Basilian Residence.
Miller, Thomas R. '77 (PIT) Pittsburgh, PA St. Joseph.
Miller, Tyler '07 (SFD) Absent on Leave.
Miller, Vincent '98 (CR) Bemidji, MN St. Philip's; [D] Bemidji, MN Holy Spirit Newman Center; Vocations.
Miller, Walter *s.v.d.* '69 (SD) San Diego, CA Our Lady of the Sacred Heart.
Miller, Whitney '80 (LKC)[C] Moss Bluff, LA St. Charles Center; Clergy Formation; Counseling; St. Charles Retreat Center.
Miller, William C. '83 (E) Lucinda, PA St. Joseph.
Miller, William T. *s.j.* '55 (DEN)[N] Denver, CO Xavier Jesuit Center.
Miller, William T. *i.c.* '84 (PEO) Abingdon, IL Sacred Heart; Galesburg, IL Corpus Christi; Galesburg, IL St. Patrick's; [A] Peoria, IL Rosminian Novitiate; Diocesan College of Consultors; Peoria, IL.
Miller, William T. *s.j.* '72 (BAL)[S] Baltimore, MD Jesuit Community of Loyola University, Inc.
Miller, William '61 (L) Retired.
Miller, William '91 (LKC) Lake Charles, LA St. Margaret.
Miller, William *c.pp.s.* '63 (JC) Sedalia, MO St. Patrick; Sedalia, MO Sacred Heart.
Miller, William *s.j.* '55 (BAL)[A] Baltimore, MD St. Mary's Seminary and University.
Millican, Ronald C. '81 (P) Portland, OR Our Lady of Sorrows.
Milligan, Richard A. '60 (PHX) Phoenix, AZ St. Luke Roman Catholic Parish.
Milligan, Ronald '72 (DET) Sterling Heights, MI St. Ephrem.
Milliken, Damian J. *o.s.b.* '58 (PAT)[N] Newton St. Paul's Abbey.
Milliken, Damian *o.s.b.* '58 (FgM) Newton, NJ St. Paul's Abbey.
Milliken, David W. '77 (NEW) New Milford, NJ Ascension; Central Bergen Region Deanery 3.
Milling, Robert T. '04 (BO) Plymouth, MA St. Peter.
Millis, Karl '99 (CHY) St. Joseph's Society for Priests (Clergy Mutual Benefit Society); Saratoga, WY St. Ann's; Rawlins, WY Wyoming State Penitentiary.
Millisor, Daniel J. '86 (COL) Reynoldsburg, OH St. Pius X; Diocesan Judges.
Millott, Thirburse F. '75 (WOR) Worcester, MA Christ the King.
Mills, Alexander M. '90 (TUC) Tubac, AZ Saint Ann's Roman Catholic Parish and Missions – Tubac; Vicars Forane; Council of Priests.
Mills, Elias Mary *f.i.* (IND)[K] Bloomington, IN Marian Friary of Our Lady Coredemptrix, Franciscan of the Immaculate.
Mills, Joseph M. '53 (OWN) Defenders of the Bond Retired.
Milon, Augustin *o.f.m.* '70 (CHI)[I] Chicago, IL Port Ministries.
Milosz, Bogdan '80 (DET) Hamtramck, MI Our Lady Queen of Apostles.
Milota, Thomas '92 (JOL) Diocesan Life Office; Naperville, IL Sts. Peter and Paul.
Milsted, Gordon '63 (MOB) Atmore, AL St. Robert Bellarmine.
Milton, Hilary *o.carm.* '63 (NEW) Englewood, NJ St. Cecilia's.
Milton, John W. *c.s.v.* '57 (CHI)[N] Arlington Heights, IL Viatorian Province Center–Clerics of St. Viator.
Milton, Kevin *c.ss.r.* '67 (BAL) Baltimore, MD Our Lady of Fatima; Presbyteral Council.
Milunski, Brad A. *o.f.m.conv.* '93 (WDC)[B] Forestville, MD St. Bonaventure Friary; Rensselaer, NY.
Mimnaugh, Stephen D. *o.f.m.* '09 (NY) New York, NY St. Francis of Assisi.
Mina, John L. '89 (PBR) Clairton, PA Ascension of Our Lord; Archives.
Minch, Richard '69 (SAV) Retired.
Minchak, Paul L. *o.f.m.cap.* '69 (HON) Waipahu, HI Resurrection of the Lord.
Minder, Kevin '89 (YAK) Special Assignment.
Mindling, J. Daniel *o.f.m.cap.* '80 (BAL)[A] Emmitsburg, MD Mount St. Mary's Seminary; Consultants.
Mindling, J. Daniel *o.f.m.cap.* '80 (WDC)[B] Washington, DC St. Francis Friary–Capuchin College; Consultants.
Mindling, Joseph *o.f.m.cap.* '66 (WDC)[B] Washington, DC St. Francis Friary–Capuchin College.
Minelli, Peter A. '63 (MAR) Retired.
Mingollo, Rodrigo '02 (RIC) Onley, VA St. Peter the Apostle.
Minh, Vu Duc '80 (TLS) On Duty Outside the Diocese.
Minh Nguyen, Andrew Tu '69 (BUF) Buffalo, NY Coronation of the Blessed Virgin Mary.
Minhoto, Rev. Msgr. Walter F. '64 (FRS) Retired.
Minh Vu, Joseph P. '80 (COS) Colorado Springs, CO The Vietnamese Holy Martyrs Parish.
Minichello, Arthur G. '73 (BRK) College Point, NY St. Fidelis.
Minifie, Michael J. *c.c.* '05 (GAL) Houston, TX Queen of Peace.
Minigan, William J. '86 (BO) Malden, MA St. Joseph.
Miniscalco, Donald *c.ss.r.* '68 (PH) Philadelphia, PA St. Peter the Apostle.
Minja, Alfons *c.pp.s.* (TOL) Ottawa, OH SS. Peter and Paul.
Minja, Alfons *c.pp.s.* '98 (CIN)[N] Dayton, OH Provincial Office of the Cincinnati Province of the Society of the Precious Blood.
Mink, John J. '85 (WIL) New Castle, DE Our Lady of Fatima; Priests' Personnel Committee; New Castle, DE; Air National Guard Chaplains; Priest Personnel Committee; Coordinator of Institutional Chaplains.
Minkel, William *o.f.m.* '05 (P) Portland, OR Ascension.
Minkler, Jeffrey R. '05 (SPR) Absent on Leave.
Minner, Ronald J. '01 (ALN) St. Joseph the Worker Council #10921, Orefield; McAdoo, PA All Saints Parish.
Minnich, John F. '51 (GRY) Retired.
Minnihan, Paul D. '93 (OAK) Episcopal Liturgies; Provost.
Minniti, Anthony L. '70 (CAM) Collingswood, NJ St. John's Catholic Church, Collingswood, N.J.
Minniti, David V. '72 (CAM) Merchantville, NJ St. Peter's Catholic Church, Merchantville, N.J. Retired.
Minogue, John P. *c.m.* '72 (CHI)[N] Chicago DePaul Vincentian Residence.
Minogue, Michael J. '81 (PHX) Retired.
Minson, Bartholomew *o.f.m.cap.* '61 (ROC) Ovid, NY St. Francis Solanus; Ovid, NY Holy Cross; [J] Interlaken, NY St. Fidelis Friary.
Minsterman, Joseph '61 (GBG) Retired.
Mintjal, Frank '59 (Y) Retired.
Minturn, Joseph '57 (RVC) Retired.
Miodowski, Leonard A. '51 (NEW) Retired.
Mioduszewski, Marcin A. '07 (PRO) Woonsocket, RI St. Stanislaus; Woonsocket, RI St. Joseph.
Miola, Luigi C. '77 (CLV) Maple Heights, OH St. Martin of Tours.
Miotke, Carmel F. *o.f.m.* '60 (BO)[X] Boston, MA Saint Anthony Residence Retired.
Miqueli, Peter A. '91 (NY) Roosevelt Island, NY St. Frances Cabrini.
Miquilena, Iden Jose Bello '05 (LAR) Vocation Office; Vice Chancellor; College of Consultors.
Mirabelli, Daniel J. *c.s.v.* '60 (PEO)[B] Rock Island, IL Alleman High School.
Mirabelli, Daniel J. *c.s.v.* '60 (CHI)[N] Arlington Heights Viatorian Province Center–Clerics of St. Viator.
Miracky, James J. *s.j.* '88 (WOR)[O] Worcester, MA Jesuits of the Holy Cross, Inc.
Miralbes–Drago, Julio E. '72 (MIL) Retired.
Miramontes, Francisco '91 (SJ) San Jose, CA Cathedral Basilica of St. Joseph.
Miranda, Lorenzo '91 (LA) Clergy, Vicar for; Associate Vicar for Clergy; Ex Officio.
Miranda, Luis *o.carm.* '84 (SJN) Carmelite Third Order.
Miranda, Luke '55 (FWT) Retired.
Miranda, R. Dario '92 (LA) Graduate Studies.
Miranne, Paul *o.s.b.* '47 (NO)[P] St. Benedict, LA St. Joseph Abbey.
Mirchuk, Rev. Archpriest Mitrat Roman '76 (PHU) Whippany, NJ St. John the Baptist; Whippany, NJ St. Paul.
Miriani, Gerald C. '62 (BEL) Retired.
Miriani, Gerry '62 (TUC) Tucson, AZ Saint Pius X Roman Catholic Parish – Tucson Retired.
Miriyala, Balachandra '02 (KCK) Sabetha, KS St. Augustine's; Sabetha, KS Sacred Heart; Sabetha, KS St. James.
Mirro, Joseph A. '76 (RVC) Westhampton Beach, NY Immaculate Conception; Procurator & Advocates.
Mirro, Joseph '76 (RVC) Peconic Deanery.
Mirsberger, Richard E. '66 (MIL) Retired.
Mirto, Gregorio L. '65 (DEN) Fort Lupton, CO St. William.
Misakabo, Faustin *o.praem.* '80 (JKS) Port Gibson, MS St. Joseph.

Misal, Pratap *c.m.* '95 (WDC) Washington, DC Providence Hospital.
Misbrener, David M. '95 (Y) Rootstown, OH St. Peter of the Fields.
Miscamble, Wilson D. *c.s.c.* '88 (FTW)[A] Notre Dame, IN Moreau Seminary; [B] University of Notre Dame Du Lac.
Mischke, Bernard *o.s.c.* '51 (SCL)[I] Onamia, MN Crosier Priory.
Mischke, Gerald '64 (SCL) Diocesan Priests Pension Plan Trustees; St. Cloud, MN St. Mary's Cathedral of St. Cloud Retired.
Mischkowiuski, Henry B. '65 (LR) Barling, AR Sacred Heart of Mary; Fort Smith, AR SS. Sabina & Mary Church.
Mischler, Thomas E. '81 (GRY) Gary, IN Holy Rosary; Gary, IN St. Mary of the Lake.
Misenko, John A. '78 (CLV) Avon, OH Holy Trinity.
Misey, Leonard S. '63 (JC) Brunswick, MO St. Boniface; Brunswick, MO St. Raphael.
Mish, Roy L. '60 (LC) Retired.
Misiewicz, Chester J. '73 (WOR) Worcester, MA St. Charles Borromeo.
Misiolek, Frederick '65 (DET) Newport, MI St. Charles Borromeo.
Miskella, Richard '65 (LA) Retired.
Miskiewicz, Paul *o.f.m.conv.* '76 (BRK) Elmhurst, NY St. Adalbert.
Misko, James '07 (AUS) Pflugerville, TX St. Elizabeth.
Misko, Lukasz *o.p.* '07 (NY)[II] New York, NY Polish Dominicans, Inc.; New York, NY Notre Dame.
Miskolczy, Kalman *sch.p.* '45 (PH)[Y] Devon Piarist Fathers (Order of the Pious Schools).
Missimi, Rev. Msgr. Anthony N. '62 (COL) Retired.
Missinne, William *c.i.c.m.* '54 (FgM) Arlington, VA MISSIONHURST.
Missler, John C. '78 (TOL) Port Clinton, OH Immaculate Conception; Our Lady of the Lake Deanery.
Mistor, Todd C. '04 (DET) Absent on Leave.
Misurda, Matthew '77 (ALT) Windber, PA SS. Cyril and Methodius.
Mitas, Rev. Msgr. Matthew M. '79 (STL) Union, MO Immaculate Conception; Deaneries/Deans.
Mitchell, Charles I. '84 (ORL) Altamonte Springs, FL St. Mary Magdalen.
Mitchell, Darell J. '98 (YAK) Special Assignment.
Mitchell, Douglas J. '01 (SFE) Presbyteral Council of the Archdiocese of Santa Fe; Los Lunas, NM San Clemente; Vicars Forane (Deans).
Mitchell, Edward J. '54 (DET) Retired.
Mitchell, Eugene *b.s.o.* '92 (NTN) Miami, FL St. Jude; Methuen, MA Basilian Salvatorian Order; Methuen, MA.
Mitchell, Rev. Msgr. John J. '63 (RCK) Diocesan Consultors Retired.
Mitchell, John J. '96 (STP) White Bear Lake, MN St. Pius X.
Mitchell, John T. *s.j.* '72 (OAK)[M] Berkeley, CA Jesuit Fathers and Brothers.
Mitchell, Joseph P. '79 (SEA) Vancouver, WA Holy Redeemer.
Mitchell, Joseph *c.p.* '81 (L)[L] Louisville, KY Sacred Heart Retreat.
Mitchell, Joseph *c.p.* '00 (L) Louisville, KY St. Agnes.
Mitchell, Mark E. '76 (GR) Retired.
Mitchell, Rev. Msgr. Michael J. '65 (SJ) Retired.
Mitchell, Michael J. '05 (NO) Metairie, LA St. Ann Church and Shrine.
Mitchell, Peter G. '51 (HRT) Retired.
Mitchell, Peter M. '99 (LIN) Ecumenical Affairs, Commission for; [A] Seward, NE St. Gregory the Great Seminary.
Mitchell, Peter '78 (ORL) Bartow, FL St. Thomas Aquinas.
Mitchell, Robert J. '85 (PAT) Budd Lake, NJ St. Jude; Deans; College of Deans.
Mitchell, Robert W. '73 (ORL) Haines City, FL St. Ann.
Mitchell, Royce J. '74 (NO)[N] New Orleans, LA Chateau de Notre Dame; Chateau de Notre Dame Guild Retired.
Mitchell, Rev. Msgr. Salvatore P. '42 (E) Retired.
Mitchell, Thomas R. '79 (HRT) Consultors – Canon 1742; Hartford Deanery; Medical Leave; Farmington, CT St. Patrick.
Mitchell, Walter A. '61 (BRK) Retired.
Mitchell, Walter '91 (MIA) Retired.
Mitchell, William J. '49 (PHX) Retired.
Mitchko, James '77 (PSC) Leave of Absence.
Mitek, Jozef '84 (LA) Granada Hills, CA St. John Baptist de la Salle.
Mitera, Andrzej (STA) Jacksonville, FL Blessed Trinity.
Miti, Peter '07 (HON) Kapaa, HI St. Catherine.
Mitka, John J. '66 (BUF) Elma, NY St. Gabriel.
Mitko, Joseph K. *o.ss.t.* '80 (BAL)[S] The Trinitarian Community in Adelphi, Maryland.
Mitolo, Frank '68 (PIT) Pittsburgh, PA Resurrection.
Mitrano, Joseph Charles *c.s.b.* '69 (GAL)[O] Houston, TX Dillon House Retired.
Mittelstadt, John *o.f.m.* '62 (GLP) Tohatchi, NM St. Mary Church.
Mittempergher, Giancarlo *c.s.s.* '66 (SAC) Special Assignment; Sacramento, CA St. Elizabeth; West Sacramento, CA Holy Cross.
Mitty, Rev. Msgr. Edward J. '50 (NY) New York, NY Our Lady of Victory; [EE] Bronx, NY John Cardinal O'Connor Residence Retired.
Mitulski, James M. '72 (STL) Florissant, MO St. Norbert.
Mitzel, Daniel C. '81 (HBG) Lancaster, PA St. Anthony of Padua; Consultors, College; Appointed.
Mitzi, John (ORL) Retired.
Miyares, Carlos '81 (MIA) Miami Lakes, FL Our Lady of the Lakes.
Miyares, Gustavo '73 (MIA) Retired.
Mizener, Paul '64 (R) New Bern, NC St. Paul; On Duty Outside the Diocese.
Mizener, Paul '64 (R) Oriental, NC Saint Peter the Fisherman.
Mizeur, Thomas R. '73 (PEO) Henry, IL St. Joseph's; Henry, IL St. Mary's; Lacon, IL Immaculate Conception; Air National Guard Chaplains.
Mizicko, Carroll *o.f.m.* '68 (BEL)[F] East St. Louis, IL St. Benedict the Black Friary; East Saint Louis, IL St. Augustine of Hippo.
Mizzi–Gili, Anthony '09 (NY) Bronx, NY Our Lady of the Assumption.
Mlay, Mark *a.l.c.p.* '84 (PMB) Fort Pierce, FL St. Anastasia.
Mlinganisa, Henry '81 (BUR) Troy, VT St. Vincent de Paul; Troy, VT Sacred Heart of Jesus.
Mlsna, Todd A. '98 (LC) La Crosse, WI St. Joseph the Workman Cathedral; [D] La Crosse, WI Franciscan Skemp Healthcare, Mayo Health System, La Crosse Campus Medical Center; [N] La Crosse, WI Franciscan Skemp Medical Center, Inc.
Mmegbuadimma, Maurice '01 (BRK) Ozone Park, NY St. Elizabeth.
Moan, Francis X. *s.j.* '57 (BAL)[S] Baltimore, MD Colombiere Jesuit Community.
Mocarski, Janusz '09 (RVC) East Islip, NY St. Mary's.
Moccia, Bonaventure *c.p.* '52 (MET)[I] South River Passionist Provincial Office Retired.
Mocco, Charles W. '57 (GB) Clergy Credit Union; Diocesan Council of Catholic Women Retired.
Mocio, Stephen J. '76 (DAL) Denison, TX St. Patrick.
Mock, Robert M. '84 (BUF) West Seneca, NY Fourteen Holy Helpers; [C] Buffalo, NY Trocaire College.
Mock, Timothy *c.m.m.* '52 (DET)[K] Vocation Office.
Mockaitis, Timothy '78 (P) Salem, OR Queen of Peace; Justice and Peace/Respect for Life.
Mockel, George E. '75 (OAK) Ex Officio; Moderator of the Curia and Vicar General; Consultors; Diocesan Finance Council; Ex Officio; Diocesan Planning Board; Ex Officio.
Mockevicius, Dominic F. '48 (ROC) Rochester, NY St. George Retired.
Mockler, Patrick J. '79 (MO) Air Force Reserve Chaplains; Presbyteral Council.
Mockler, Patrick J. '79 (BLX) Trustees; Biloxi, MS Our Lady of Fatima; Advocates.
Mockler, Patrick '79 (JKS) Trustees.
Mockler, Peter F. '73 (BLX) Gulfport, MS St. Ann; Deans; College of Consultors; Finance Council; Presbyteral Council.
Moczulski, David *o.f.m.* '93 (PIT)[M] Pittsburgh, PA Holy Family Friary; Pittsburgh, PA.
Moczydlowski, Rev. Msgr. Chester M. '73 (CHR) Mt. Pleasant, SC St. Benedict; Building & Renovation Commission.
Moczydlowski, Stanley M. '02 (ALN) Whitehall, PA St. Elizabeth.
Modde, Brad '97 (STL) St. Louis, MO Immaculate Heart of Mary.
Mode, Daniel L. '92 (ARL) On Duty Outside the Diocese; Military Chaplains; Navy Chaplains.
Mode, Daniel (NOR) New London, CT U.S. Coast Guard Memorial Chapel.
Modebei, Sylvester '03 (PHX) Lake Havasu City, AZ Our Lady of the Lake Roman Catholic Parish.
Modike, Sebastian '00 (BUR) Wallingford, VT St. Patrick.
Modino, Roman '89 (TR) Freehold, NJ St. Rose of Lima.
Modlin, William F. '96 (PRT) Augusta, ME St. Michael Parish.
Modrys, Walter J. *s.j.* '78 (NY)[EE] New York, NY Society of Jesus, New York Province; [EE] New York, NY "America;" Residence and publication office of the America Press.
Modugno, Rev. Msgr. Thomas A. '66 (NY) New York, NY St. Monica; Manhattan (East).
Moeder, August L. '53 (SAL) Retired.
Moeder, John '57 (SAL) Retired.
Moeggenberg, Raymond '56 (SAG) Coleman, MI St. Philip Neri Retired.
Moeglein, James *o.s.c.* '70 (SCL)[I] Onamia, MN Crosier Priory.
Moellenberndt, Rev. Msgr. Duane R. '76 (MAD) Sun Prairie, WI Sacred Hearts of Jesus and Mary; Building Commission; Council of Catholic Women.
Moeller, Rev. Msgr. George B. '62 (BAL) Retired.
Moen, Brian '03 (FAR) St. Michael, ND St. Michael's Church of St. Michael; St. Michael, ND St. Michael's Church of St. Michael.
Moenkedick, Leo '86 (SCL) Little Falls, MN Sacred Heart; Randall, MN St. James; Little Falls, MN St. Stanislaus; Air National Guard Chaplains.
Moerman, Stephen A. '94 (PH) Maple Glen, PA St. Alphonsus.
Moeslein, Rev. Msgr. Francis R. '58 (R) Morehead City, NC St. Egbert; Apostleship of the Sea Retired.
Mofan, Feliciano '79 (SFR) San Rafael, CA St. Isabella.
Moga, Michael D. *s.j.* '64 (FgM) New York, NY Society of Jesus.
Mohammed, Nigel R. '03 (NEW) Ramsey, NJ St. Paul.
Mohan, Bernard N. '61 (NEW) Archdiocesan Judges Retired.
Mohan, Brian Quinn '05 (COS) Elizabeth, CO Our Lady of the Visitation.
Mohan, Oliver *o.m.i.* '48 (PHX) Mesa, AZ St. Timothy Roman Catholic Parish Retired.
Mohl, Andrew S. '84 (BAL) Randallstown, MD Holy Family.
Mohnickey, Ronald J. *t.o.r.* '71 (STU)[A] Steubenville, OH Franciscan University of Steubenville; [H] Steubenville, OH Holy Spirit Friary.
Mohr, J. Patrick *s.j.* '75 (SCR)[C] Scranton, PA The University of Scranton.
Mohr, Richard G. '67 (MO) DEPARTMENT OF VETERANS AFFAIRS HOSPITALS AND CHAPLAINS.
Mohr, Thomas H. '58 (DAV) Retired.
Mohrbacher, Austin '57 (PSC) Retired.
Mohrman, J. Gregory *o.s.b.* '86 (STL)[F] Creve Coeur, MO St. Louis Priory School; [O] St. Louis, MO The Abbey of St. Mary and St. Louis.
Moineau, John A. '87 (GBG) Irwin, PA Immaculate Conception; College of Consultors; Bishop's Priests Council.
Moisant, William C. '01 (P) Tualatin, OR Resurrection Catholic Church; Area Vicars.
Moisin, Michael '88 (ROM) Brookline, MA Romanian Catholic Mission of Boston; Finance Council; College of Consultors; Office to Aid the Church in Romania.
Mojica, Ariel Cortes '96 (TYL) Pittsburg, TX Holy Cross.
Mokarzel, Galeb *o.m.i.* '57 (SAT)[K] San Antonio, TX Oblate Madonna Residence.
Mokluk, John M. *o.s.f.s.* '70 (WIL)[B] Wilmington, DE Salesianum School.
Mokrzycki, M. Joseph '65 (TR) Avon By The Sea, NJ St. Elizabeth; Long Branch, NJ The Church of Christ the King, Long Branch, N.J.
Mol, Joseph C. '77 (CHI) Hickory Hills, IL St. Patricia; Delegate of the Archbishop for Privilege Cases; Advocates.
Molan, Rev. Msgr. John E. '53 (MAN) Auburn, NH St. Peter; Presbyteral Council; College of Consultors; Manchester, NH St. Pius X; New Hampshire State Prison for Women Retired.
Molano, Ernesto '56 (MIA) Judges Retired.
Moleski, Martin X. *s.j.* '81 (BUF)[O] Buffalo, NY Canisius Jesuit Community Inc.
Molewski, Andrew '82 (WIL) Wilmington, DE St. Hedwig.
Moley, Kevin J. *c.ss.r.* '70 (PH) Philadelphia, PA St. Peter the Apostle; College of Consultors.
Molgano, James '03 (PMB) Jensen Beach, FL St. Martin de Porres.
Molina, Alfredo Valdez '02 (PHX) Phoenix, AZ St. Catherine of Siena Roman Catholic Parish.
Molina, Angel '94 (CGS) Caguas, PR Nuestra Senora del Perpetuo Socorro; Sec. Chancellor; Priests Senate.
Molina, Arturo '83 (LEX) Special Assignment.
Molina, Benjamin '82 (DAL) Dallas, TX St. Elizabeth.
Molina, Joe '95 (ELP) El Paso, TX Our Lady of Assumption.
Molina, Jonathan B. '04 (SAC) Redding, CA Our Lady of Mercy.
Molina, Juan Francisco '90 (TOL) Toledo, OH Immaculate Conception; Toledo, OH SS. Peter and Paul; Toledo, OH St. Stephen; Office of Hispanic Ministries.
Molina, Juan *o.ss.t.* '99 (BAL)[S] The Trinitarian Community in Adelphi, Maryland.
Molina, Milhton Scarpetta '01 (SEA) Burlington, WA St. Charles; La Conner, WA Sacred Heart; Mount Vernon, WA Immaculate Conception; Sedro Woolley, WA Immaculate Heart of Mary.
Molina, Rolando *c.m.* '07 (FgM) Philadelphia, PA Eastern Province.
Molina, Seraphim *s.t.* '97 (TUC) Tucson, AZ Blessed Kateri Tekakwitha Roman Catholic Missions Parish – Tucson; [H] South Tucson, AZ Blessed Kateri Tekakwitha Parish Center.
Molina–Juarez, Jaime *m.n.m.* '88 (ATL) Smyrna, GA St. Thomas the Apostle.
Molina–Restrepo, Fernando '99 (ATL) Douglasville, GA St. Theresa.
Molina–Torres, Robeth '08 (CHI) Glenview, IL Our Lady of Perpetual Help.
Molinari, Todd '95 (P) Salem, OR St. Joseph; [P] Salem, OR Willamette University (Salem); College of Consultors.

Molinaro, Kenneth M. *c.s.c.* '76 (FTW)[H] Notre Dame, IN Congregation of Holy Cross, Indiana Province, Provincial House; Notre Dame, IN; Austin, TX.
Molinelli, Louis J. *s.d.b.* '90 (NEW)[M] Ramsey, NJ Don Bosco Prep Salesian Residence; [C] Ramsey, NJ Don Bosco Preparatory High School.
Molini, Thomas M. '85 (STL) Kirkwood, MO St. Gerard Majella; Deaneries/Deans.
Molitor, Donald F. '63 (STL) House Springs, MO Our Lady, Queen of Peace Retired.
Molka, Victor J. '78 (PIT) New Castle, PA Mary, Mother of Hope.
Moll, Daniel '07 (MAR) Iron Mountain, MI St. Mary and St. Joseph.
Moll, Walter J. '85 (ALT) Priests' Retirement Plan; Portage, PA St. Joseph's.
Mollenhauer, Arthur *l.c.* '97 (BGP) Stamford, CT St. Mary.
Molling, Mark '80 (MIL) Genesee Depot, WI St. Paul.
Mollner, Jeffrey J. '08 (OM) Omaha, NE St. Margaret Mary.
Molloy, John *c.p.m.* '46 (OWN)[F] Auburn, KY Fathers of Mercy.
Molloy, Joseph '83 (SFD) Decatur, IL Holy Family; Priests' Personnel Board.
Molloy, Kevin '72 (SP) Tarpon Springs, FL St. Ignatius of Antioch.
Molloy, Rev. Msgr. Thomas E. '70 (RVC) Brentwood, NY St. Luke; Judges for Interdiocesan Tribunal.
Molnar, Jeffrey T. '03 (PIT) Pittsburgh, PA St. Maurice.
Molnar, Jude *t.o.r.* '65 (WH)[O] Fairmont, WV Fairmont State University Newman Center.
Molnar, Michael '76 (DET) Grosse Ile, MI Sacred Heart.
Molodowitz, Augustine '59 (PHU) Retired.
Molokie, Jerome M. *o.praem.* '95 (ORG)[D] Silverado, CA St. Michael's Preparatory School; [I] Silverado, CA Norbertine Fathers of Orange Inc.
Moloney, Rev. Msgr. Alphonsus '63 (SD) Retired.
Moloney, Rev. Msgr. James A. '56 (DET) Dearborn Heights, MI St. Anselm; College of Consultors; Propagation of the Faith (Missions).
Moloney, John C. '91 (PH) Springfield, PA St. Kevin.
Moloney, John Jesus *c.s.j.* '95 (LAR)[D] Laredo, TX St. John Priory, F.J.; Presbyteral Council; [F] Laredo, TX Holy Spirit Retreat and Conference Center.
Moloney, John '72 (LA) Norwalk, CA St. John of God.
Moloney, Patrick W. '77 (NTN) Yonkers, NY Christ the Savior Church.
Moloney, Rev. Msgr. Stephan J. '82 (COL) Columbus, OH Immaculate Conception; Vicar General; College of Consultors; Parochial Examiners; Presbyteral Council; Promoter of Justice; Diocesan Board of Review for the Protection of Children; Diocesan Finance Council; Victim Assistance Coordinator; Bishop's Council.
Molter, Richard J. '64 (MIL) Retired.
Molumby, Donald '56 (SFS) Retired.
Molumby, Edward J. *s.t.* '61 (SB) Rancho Cucamonga, CA Sacred Heart.
Molyn, John '81 (ALB) Valatie, NY St. John the Baptist; Deans.
Molyneux, John *c.m.f.* '97 (CHI)[N] Chicago, IL Claretian Missionaries, St. Jude League, Inc.
Molyneux, John *c.m.f.* '98 (ATL) Stone Mountain, GA Corpus Christi.
Monaco, David *c.p.* '90 (MET)[I] South River Passionist Provincial Office.
Monaco, Harry *o.f.m.* '09 (BUF)[O] St. Bonaventure, NY St. Bonaventure Friary; [C] St. Bonaventure, NY Friar Community.
Monaco, James M. '85 (BUF) Buffalo, NY St. Katharine Drexel.
Monaghan, Rev. Msgr. Charles J. '41 (PH) Retired.
Monaghan, George P. '80 (DAL) Commerce, TX St. Joseph.
Monaghan, J. Fergus '72 (SPC) Springfield, MO Holy Trinity; Region IV; The Mirror Advisory Board.
Monaghan, John T. '63 (NY)[E] Bronx, NY Cardinal Spellman High School.
Monaghan, Joseph F. *s.j.* '52 (PH)[Y] Loyola Center and Manresa Hall.
Monaghan, Justin D. '66 (SPC) Joplin, MO St. Mary; Region I.
Monaghan, Robert '62 (STP) Minneapolis, MN Church of the Incarnation.
Monaghan, Thomas J. '70 (MAD) Reedsburg, WI Sacred Heart.
Monagle, Robert J. '91 (MO) Air Force Chaplains; Military & VA Chaplains.
Monahan, David F. '53 (OKL) Retired.
Monahan, John C. *s.j.* '99 (BO)[U] Boston The Society of Jesus of New England–Provincial Offices.
Monahan, John C. *s.j.* '99 (MO) Navy Chaplains.
Monahan, Joseph E. '77 (DEN) Golden, CO St. Joseph.
Monahan, Joseph R. '62 (STL) Retired.
Monahan, Joseph *t.o.r.* '90 (WIL)[I] Wilmington, DE St. Francis Hospital, Inc.
Monahan, Kieran *o.f.m.* '65 (BO)[U] Boston, MA St. Christopher Friary.
Monahan, Paul '60 (DM) Diocesan Consultors Retired.
Monahan, Richard J. '59 (BGP) Retired.
Monahan, Shawn *o.m.v.* '02 (SFD) Alton, IL St. Mary's.
Monahan, Rev. Msgr. Thomas J. '58 (RCK) Experts; Priests' Eucharistic League Retired.
Monahan, William J. '07 (PH) Southampton, PA Our Lady of Good Counsel.
Monan, J. Donald *s.j.* '55 (BO)[U] Newton, MA The Jesuit Community at Boston College.
Monastere, Bony '07 (BRK) Cambria Heights, NY Sacred Heart.
Moncada, Fabio '81 (FAJ) Canovanas, PR Nuestra Senora del Pilar.
Moncher, Raymond F. '58 (MAR) Wakefield, MI Immaculate Conception of the Blessed Virgin Mary Retired.
Monclova, Michael '97 (PEO) Atkinson, IL St. Anthony's.
Mondello, Rev. Msgr. Donald J. '60 (GBG)[F] Greensburg, PA Neumann House; Diocesan Council of Catholic Women.
Mondiek, Stephen J. '03 (CIN) Hamilton, OH St. Ann; Hamilton, OH St. Joseph.
Mondik, Michael '73 (PSC) Rahway, NJ St. Thomas the Apostle; Syncellus; Eparchial College of Consultors; Building and Properties Commission; Eparchial Liturgy and Art Commission; Presbyteral Council.
Mondji, Jean–Marie '08 (PBL) Pueblo, CO Our Lady of the Meadows; Pueblo, CO Holy Rosary.
Mondor, Christian *o.f.m.* '51 (ORG) Huntington Beach, CA SS. Simon and Jude; Ecumenical and Interreligious Affairs.
Mondragon, Antonio '63 (SFE) Retired.
Mondragon, Ezequiel '62 (DET) Imlay City, MI Sacred Heart.
Mondzelewski, Dominic *o.s.b.* '69 (CLV) Cleveland, OH St. Lawrence; [N] Cleveland, OH.
Moneck, George J. '89 (PIT) California, PA St. Thomas Aquinas; Roscoe, PA St. Joseph; [P] California, PA California University (California).
Moneme, Nnamdi *o.m.v.* '09 (SFD) Alton, IL St. Mary's.
Mones, Benjamin '58 (ELP) El Paso, TX St. Joseph's.
Monestero, John '75 (ORG) Anaheim, CA St. Justin Martyr; Absent on Sick Leave; Ecumenical and Interreligious Affairs.
Monestime, Perard C. *s.j.* '85 (FgM) Watertown, MA Society of Jesus.
Monet, Zachary *o.carm.* '60 (JOL)[L] Darien Carmelite Provincial Office.
Monette, Michael R. '99 (MAN) Plaistow, NH St. Luke the Evangelist Parish.
Moneypenny, John W. '98 (ORG) Santa Ana, CA St. Joseph; Council of Priests.
Monforton, Rev. Msgr. Jeffrey M. '94 (DET)[A] Detroit, MI Sacred Heart Major Seminary, Inc.
Mongelluzzo, Rev. Msgr. James A. '74 (WOR) On Duty Outside the Diocese.
Mongeon, Peter M. '83 (NO) On Medical Leave of Absence.
Mongeon, Peter M. '83 (PRO) Retired.
Mongiello, Anthony P. '80 (ALN) Bethlehem, PA St. Anne; Serra Club of Bethlehem; Trinity Council #313, Bethlehem.
Mongiello, Robert '87 (VEN) Bradenton Beach, FL St. Bernard.
Mongrain, Dennis '77 (LA) Diamond Bar, CA St. Denis.
Moniuk, Evhan '92 (PHU) Palmerton, PA St. Vladimir's.
Moniz, Joseph V. '64 (LA) Pasadena, CA St. Philip the Apostle.
Monnerat, Brian W. '88 (HRT) Forestville, CT St. Matthew; Special and other Archdiocesan Assignment; Holy Childhood Association; Mission Cooperative Planning Office; Mission Office, The.
Monnig, Matthew S. *s.j.* '07 (BO)[U] Boston The Society of Jesus of New England–Provincial Offices.
Monnin, Robert J. '55 (CIN) Retired.
Monogue, Michael G. '85 (STP) United Hospitals, Inc.; United Children's Hospital.
Monohan, Duncan W. '77 (SD) Winterhaven, CA St. Thomas (Indian Mission).
Monostori, Benedict *o.cist.* '44 (DAL)[J] Irving, TX Cistercian Abbey of Our Lady of Dallas.
Monreal, Jesus *o.carm.* '69 (ARE) Morovis, PR Nuestra Senora del Carmen.
Monreal, Melchisedech '95 (SD) Poway, CA St. Michael.
Monroe, Charles F. '75 (WOR) Worcester, MA Our Lady of the Angels.
Monroe, Edward F. *c.ss.r.* '61 (MIL)[S] Oconomowoc, WI The Redemptorist Retreat Center.
Monsalve, Carlos *o.c.d.* '88 (CHI)[A] Mundelein, IL Instituto De Liderazgo Pastoral (Hispanic Programs for Lay Ministry and Permanent Diaconate).
Monsalve, German Barona *m.s.c.* '86 (FgM) Aurora, IL MISSIONARIES OF THE SACRED HEART.
Monson, Eamonn *s.c.a.* '80 (DET)[K] Wyandotte, MI Pallottine Missionary Center (Irish Province).
Montag, John F. *s.j.* '93 (STL)[O] St. Louis, MO Jesuit Community Corporation at Saint Louis University – Jesuit Hall.
Montague, George T. *s.m.* '58 (SAT)[C] San Antonio, TX St. Mary's University of San Antonio, Texas; [L] San Antonio, TX Casa San Juan Marianist Community; [S] San Antonio, TX Brothers of the Beloved Disciple; San Antonio, TX St. Mary Magdalen.
Montague, Hugh *s.o.cist.* '82 (ALN)[K] New Ringgold, PA Cistercian Monastery.
Montalbano, Francis *o.m.i.* '47 (SAT)[K] San Antonio, TX Oblate Madonna Residence.
Montalbano, Joseph E. '55 (ALX) Retired.
Montanaro, Guido G. '69 (BGP) Fairfield, CT Holy Family.
Montanaro, James *o.m.v.* '83 (BO)[U] Milton, MA Oblate Residence (St. Joseph House).
Montanez, Edwin '98 (RIC) Charlottesville, VA Church of the Incarnation.
Montanez, Gustavo *o.p.* '08 (NO)[P] New Orleans Dominican Friars, Southern Dominican Province of St. Martin de Porres; New Orleans, LA St. Anthony of Padua.
Montanez, Melvin '06 (CGS) Caguas, PR Cathedral Dulce Nombre de Jesus.
Montanez, Melvin (CGS) Liturgical Consultor; Master of Ceremonies.
Montanez Lopez, Jose R. *c.p.* '95 (SJN) Carolina, PR Santa Gema Galgani.
Montano, Angel '92 (CC) Defenders of the Bond; Freer, TX St. Mary.
Montavon, Thomas G. '61 (CLV) Brunswick, OH St. Colette; Garfield Heights, OH St. Monica Retired.
Montecalvo, Rev. Msgr. Carlo F. '73 (PRO) Johnston, RI Our Lady of Grace; Deans.
Monteiro, Alfredo '73 (NY) Brewster, NY St. Lawrence O'Toole.
Monteiro, Ralph J. *o.s.a.* '66 (PH)[Y] Villanova, PA St. Thomas Monastery.
Montejano, John G. '94 (LA) Baldwin Park, CA St. John the Baptist; Notaries and Other Officials.
Montelaro, Thomas '75 (LAF) Retired.
Monteleone, Jacob '75 (SP) Clearwater, FL Light of Christ.
Montella, Alban V. *o.f.m.* '55 (NY)[EE] New York Franciscan Province of the Immaculate Conception.
Montemayor, Eduardo *s.o.l.t.* '02 (CC) Bishop's Office; Director for Evangelization Department; Alliance for Human Life; Hispanic Ministry; The Catholic Charismatic Renewal Movement; [G] Robstown, TX Society of Our Lady of the Most Holy Trinity; [I] Corpus Christi, TX Small Catholic Community Ministry.
Montemayor, Ted *s.d.b.* '83 (LA) Bellflower, CA St. Dominic Savio; [V] Rosemead, CA St. Joseph's Salesian Youth Renewal Center.
Montenegro, Blas *o.a.r.* '49 (NEW) Union City, NJ St. Augustine's.
Montenegro, Manuel '01 (AUS) Austin, TX Sacred Heart.
Montero, Alvaro *d.c.j.m.* '04 (DEN) Littleton, CO St. Mary.
Montero, Eduardo G. '83 (PH) Assistant Judicial Vicars; Wynnewood, PA Presentation B.V.M.
Montero, Hugo L. '92 (STP)[C] St. Paul, MN University of St. Thomas.
Montero, Romulo (NY) New York, NY Our Lady of Pompeii.
Montes, Francisco X. '03 (MRY) Arroyo Grande, CA St. Patrick.
Montes, Jesse *s.d.b.* '79 (MRY)[F] Watsonville, CA Saint Francis Salesian Community; Watsonville, CA Our Lady Help of Christians.
Montes, Jose Felipe *c.s.v.* '01 (CHI)[N] Arlington Heights Viatorian Province Center–Clerics of St. Viator.
Montes–Colon, Flavio '05 (MIA) Miami, FL St. Brendan.
Montesanti, Steven G. '99 (MAN) Concord, NH St. John the Evangelist; Recruiters; Lay Ministry Formation Commission.
Montesi, Eugene *s.x.* '62 (FgM)[N] Wayne Xaverian Missionary Fathers; Wayne, NJ XAVERIAN MISSIONARY FATHERS.
Montesino, Efraín '85 (ARE) Arecibo, PR San Juan Bosco.
Montez, Paul *o.s.b.* '97 (DEN) Centennial, CO St. Thomas More.
Montgomery, Joseph T. '58 (HRT) Retired.
Montgomery, Matthias *o.c.d.* '62 (MIL)[P] Hubertus, WI Retreat Center.
Montgomery, William L. '79 (WDC) Special Ministries; [D] Washington, DC Archbishop Carroll High School.
Monti, Dominic *o.f.m.* '71 (NY)[EE] New York, NY Franciscan Friars, Holy Name Province; New York, NY St. Francis of Assisi.
Monti, Robert M. '61 (LC) Retired.
Monti, Robert '61 (MIA)[J] Fort Lauderdale, FL Holy Cross Hospital.
Monticello, Rev. Msgr. Robert V. '51 (DET) Retired.
Montiel, Jose '57 (FRS) Retired.
Montini–Coleman, James '99 (MOB) Associate Judges.
Montminy, Marc R. '77 (MAN) Newmarket, NH St. Mary; Exeter, NH St. Michael.
Montminy, Paul D. '78 (MAN) Co Spiritual Dir.; Manchester, NH St. Catherine.
Montondon, Rev. Msgr. Walter '57 (BEA) Retired.
Montoya, Francisco '00 (SAL) Manhattan, KS Seven

Dolors of the Blessed Virgin Mary Parish; Manhattan, KS St. Patrick Parish.
Montoya, Hector '09 (SAC) Chico, CA St. John the Baptist.
Montoya, Jesus E. '63 (SAC) Sacramento, CA St. Rose.
Montoya, Jose '86 (BGP) Danbury, CT Our Lady of Guadalupe.
Montoya, Juan '89 (MIA) Absent on Sick Leave.
Montoya, Michael *m.j.* '94 (LA) Washington, DC United States Catholic Mission Association; [P] Los Angeles, CA Missionaries of Jesus, Inc.
Montoya, Rev. Msgr. Paul M. '73 (LA) Santa Clarita, CA Our Lady of Perpetual Help; Moderator.
Montoya, Pedro N. '93 (ARE) Camuy, PR St. Joseph.
Monturo, Christopher W. '03 (NY) West Harrison, NY St. Anthony of Padua.
Montz, Jeffrey A. '08 (NO) New Orleans, LA St. Francis of Assisi.
Monzillo, Oneil '53 (NO) Retired.
Moodie, Michael *s.j.* '79 (SJ)[D] San Jose, CA Bellarmine College Preparatory.
Moody, Kenneth J. *m.m.* '70 (FgM) Maryknoll, NY MARYKNOLL.
Moody, Quentin E. '85 (NO) New Orleans, LA St. Augustine.
Moody, Thomas A. '67 (OG) Retired.
Moody, William J. '70 (BAL) Retired.
Mooka, John Mary *a.j.* '99 (PIT) Pittsburgh, PA St. Bede.
Moon, Michael E. '02 (MAD) Albany, WI St. Patrick; Brodhead, WI St. Rose of Lima.
Moon, Michael Ki–Sung '02 (TOL) Bowling Green, OH St. Thomas More University Parish.
Moon, Michael (NY) Staten Island, NY Blessed Sacrament.
Mooney, Dennis M. '77 (PH) Bristol, PA St. Mark.
Mooney, Rev. Msgr. Michael P. '63 (PT) Pensacola, FL Nativity of Our Lord; Priests' Pension Plan, Board for.
Mooney, Richard T. '79 (RIC) Lynchburg, VA St. Thomas More.
Mooney, William C. '68 (STA) St. Augustine, FL Corpus Christi.
Mooney, William J. '68 (PAT) Florham Park, NJ Holy Family.
Mooney, William '55 (SD) Retired.
Moonnanappallil, Joseph '92 (HRT) Glastonbury, CT St. Paul; South Glastonbury, CT St. Augustine.
Moons, Joseph *c.p.* '77 (GAL)[O] Houston, TX Congregation of the Passion, Holy Name Passionist Community and Retreat Center; [Q] Houston, TX Holy Name Retreat Center; Consultors:.
Moons, Joseph *c.p.* '77 (CHI)[N] Chicago, IL Passionist Provincial Office.
Mooradd, Paul '84 (SAM) Worcester, MA Our Lady of Mercy.
Moorby, William A. '82 (ROC) Owego, NY St. Patrick; Owego, NY Blessed Trinity.
Moore, Andrew '97 (BEA) Director of Seminarians; Kountze, TX Holy Spirit Mission; Lumberton, TX Infant Jesus; Presbyteral Council.
Moore, Anthony F. *o.f.m.* '51 (NY) Yulan, NY St. Anthony of Padua.
Moore, Augustine J. '60 (SFE) Espanola, NM Sacred Heart.
Moore, Rev. Msgr. Brian R. '83 (DOD)[F] Dodge City, KS The Diocese of Dodge City Priest Retirement Fund, Inc.
Moore, Rev. Msgr. Brian R. '83 (DOD) Dodge City, KS Cathedral of Our Lady of Guadalupe Catholic Church of Dodge City, Kansas; College of Consultors; Pastoral Ministry Formation; Director of Seminarians; Priest Continuing Formation; Presbyteral Council.
Moore, Christian *o.f.m.conv.* '65 (L) Louisville, KY Incarnation; [L] Louisville, KY St. Francis of Assisi Friary.
Moore, Christopher P. '77 (BAL) Hagerstown, MD St. Joseph; Priest Personnel Board.
Moore, Daniel F. *s.s.* '84 (BAL)[S] Baltimore Society of St. Sulpice, Province of the United States.
Moore, Daniel F. *s.s.* '84 (WDC)[A] Washington, DC Theological College of the Catholic University of America.
Moore, Donald J. *s.j.* '60 (NY)[EE] Loyola Hall, Jesuit Community.
Moore, Rev. Msgr. Edmund J. '59 (SHP) Monroe, LA Jesus the Good Shepherd Retired.
Moore, Edward F. *m.m.* '58 (NY)[EE] Maryknoll Maryknoll Fathers and Brothers.
Moore, F. Thomas (MOB)[E] Mobile, AL Little Sisters of the Poor, Home For the Aged, Inc. Retired.
Moore, Frederick Thomas '75 (STA) Retired.
Moore, George B. '66 (PH) Philadelphia, PA St. Benedict.
Moore, Gregory J. *o.p.* '55 (CHI)[N] St. Pius V Priory.
Moore, James J. *o.p.* '08 (TUC) Tucson, AZ Saint Thomas More Roman Catholic Newman Parish – Tucson; [G] Tucson, AZ University of Arizona.
Moore, Rev. Msgr. James R. '67 (NY) Croton Falls, NY St. Joseph; Archdiocesan Consultors.
Moore, James T. '84 (GAL) Retired.
Moore, James W. *s.j.* '59 (PH)[Y] Loyola Center and Manresa Hall.
Moore, James '88 (SFE) Retired.
Moore, John C. '78 (BAL) Middletown, MD Holy Family Catholic Community Retired.
Moore, Rev. Msgr. John F. '60 (FR) Retired.
Moore, Jon H. '81 (WIN) Austin, MN Queens of Angels Hermitage; [A] Winona, MN Immaculate Heart of Mary Seminary; [H] Austin, MN Annunciation Hermitage, Carmelites of St. Joseph.
Moore, Lawrence *s.j.* '77 (NO)[C] New Orleans, LA Loyola University New Orleans.
Moore, Mark J. '03 (STU)[F] Steubenville, OH Trinity Medical Center, West; Assistant Directors; Hospitals; Steubenville, OH Triumph of the Cross.
Moore, Mark '03 (STU) Steubenville, OH Holy Name Cathedral.
Moore, Michael '97 (FRS) Hanford, CA St. Brigid; Cliffside Park, NJ St. Patrick's Missionary Society.
Moore, Michael *s.p.s.* '84 (SJ) Saratoga, CA; [M] Saratoga, CA St. Patrick's Missionary Society.
Moore, Michael *o.s.f.s.* '68 (FgM) Wilmington, DE OBLATES OF ST. FRANCIS DE SALES MISSIONS.
Moore, Neil '60 (P) Retired.
Moore, Raymond H. '81 (WDC) Washington, DC St. Thomas More; Deans; Priest Council.
Moore, Robert O. *o.c.s.o.* '49 (ROC)[J] Piffard, NY Abbey of the Genesee.
Moore, Stephen P. '04 (ALB) Loudonville, NY St. Pius X.
Moore, Steven C. '76 (ANC) Anchorage, AK St. Benedict; Vicars General; Diocesan Consultors; Unalaska, AK Corp. of St. Christopher By the Sea Church.
Moore, Steven P. '04 (ALB) Priestly Life and Ministry Council; Members.
Moore, Rev. Msgr. Terence M. '67 (SLC) Board of Directors; College of Consultors; Draper, UT Saint John the Baptist LLC 252; Presbyteral Council.
Moore, Thomas *o.s.f.s.* '66 (FgM) Wilmington, DE OBLATES OF ST. FRANCIS DE SALES MISSIONS.
Moore, Ward P. '72 (NEW) Fairfield, NJ St. Thomas More; Serra Club of North Essex.
Moore, Wilbur E. '57 (OKL) Region II–B Retired.
Moore, Rev. Msgr. William C. '68 (STO) Stockton, CA St. Bernadette Church (Pastor of); Deans; Air Force Reserve Chaplains.
Moore, William C. *ss.cc.* '75 (LA)[P] La Verne, CA Congregation of the Sacred Hearts of Jesus and Mary.
Moore, William F. '69 (CAM) Pennsauken, NJ Mary, Queen of All Saints, Pennsauken, N.J.; Continuing Education & Spiritual Formation of Priests (CESF); Vocation Advisory Board.
Moore, Rev. Msgr. William '68 (STO) Diocesan Building Committee.
Moorman, Dennis *m.m.* '98 (NY)[EE] Maryknoll Maryknoll Fathers and Brothers.
Moorman, Raymond J. '46 (STP) Retired.
Moorman, William J. *o.ss.t.* '79 (BAL)[P] Baltimore, MD Trinitarian Counseling Services, Inc.; [S] Baltimore, MD; [M] Towson, MD St. Joseph Medical Center, Inc.
Moors, Clifton *s.m.* '56 (BO)[U] Boston, MA Marist Fathers of Our Lady of Victories (Boston Prov.) Retired.
Moorse, Dunstan *o.s.b.* '78 (SCL)[I] Collegeville, MN St. John's Abbey, of the Order of St. Benedict.
Moortgat, Luke *c.i.c.m.* '65 (FgM) Arlington, VA MISSIONHURST.
Moothasseril, Mathew '83 (SP) Tarpon Springs, FL St. Ignatius of Antioch.
Mooya, Cletus '07 (HON) Mililani Town, HI St. John Apostle and Evangelist.
Mora, Guillermo '96 (NEW) Hillside, NJ St. Catherine of Siena.
Mora, Ismael '02 (SR) Eureka, CA Sacred Heart.
Mora, Pedro M. *c.s.b.* '04 (GAL)[O] Sugar Land Basilian Mission Center.
Mora, Sergio '94 (OAK) Oakland, CA Mary Help of Christians Church; Oakland, CA St. Anthony.
Mora, Tito Abdenago Medina *m.s.c.* '92 (FgM) Aurora, IL MISSIONARIES OF THE SACRED HEART.
Morabito, Vincent R. '87 (PH) Philadelphia, PA St. Agatha–St. James; [BB] Philadelphia, PA Drexel University; On Special or Other Archdiocesan Assignment.
Moraes, Claudio *o.s.b.* '84 (GBG)[G] Latrobe Saint Vincent Archabbey.
Moraga, Cecilio '84 (SD) Julian, CA St. Elizabeth of Hungary.
Moral, Alejandro *o.c.d.* '60 (CGS)[A] Caguas, PR Colegio San Jose Superior; Caguas, PR San Jose.
Morales, Angel L. '83 (SJN).
Morales, Anibal '93 (MIA) Sunrise, FL All Saints.
Morales, Dan '90 (VIC) Port Lavaca, TX Our Lady of the Gulf; Defenders of the Bond; Campaign For Human Development and Catholic Relief Services; Vocations Director; Director of Seminarians.
Morales, Eduardo D. '96 (SAT) San Antonio, TX St. Peter Prince of the Apostles; In Metropolitan Area; Archdiocesan Presbyteral Council; Priests Personnel Board.
Morales, Rev. Msgr. Elias S. '91 (PCE)[A] Ponce, PR Diocesan Seminary; Judicial Vicar; Diocesan Consultors; Vocations.
Morales, Francisco '89 (PCE) On Duty Outside the Diocese.
Morales, Francisco '94 (AUS) Kyle, TX St. Anthony Marie De Claret.
Morales, Geovany *c.m.* '01 (FgM) Philadelphia, PA Eastern Province.
Morales, Gonzalo '85 (FWT) Granbury, TX St. Frances Cabrini.
Morales, Harry Flores *s.m.m.* '09 (BRK)[T] Ozone Park Montfort Missionaries Provincialate (Missionaries of the Company of Mary).
Morales, Hugo '06 (CHI) Cicero, IL Mary, Queen of Heaven.
Morales, Ignacio '09 (ATL) Flowery Branch, GA Prince of Peace.
Morales, Rev. Msgr. John F. '60 (GRY) Retired.
Morales, Jorge Y. (ARE) Corozal, PR Holy Family.
Morales, Juan Bautista '83 (MGZ) Moca, PR Our Lady of Monserrate.
Morales, Raul '75 (PHX) Retired.
Morales, Raul '88 (FAJ) Loiza, PR San Patricio.
Morales, Raymond D. '81 (LA) Long Beach, CA Our Lady of Refuge.
Morales, Ricardo Hernandez '98 (SJN) Spiritual Directors; Guaynabo, PR San Jose.
Morales, Robert P. '66 (BRK) Richmond Hill, NY Our Lady of the Cenacle.
Morales, Romain G. *c.m.* '73 (STL)[O] St. Louis, MO Vincentian Residence.
Morales, Ruben '04 (OAK) Presbyteral Council; Livermore, CA St. Michael.
Morales, Salomon J. '63 (ARE) Angeles, PR Our Lady of Angels.
Morales–Martinez, Armando '05 (CHI) Chicago, IL St. Gall.
Morales Cruz, Oscar *o.p.* (SJN) Bayamon, PR Catalina de Siena.
Morales Figueroa, Angel L. '83 (SJN) San Juan, PR Nuestra Senora de Lourdes.
Moralez Feliu, Francisco '89 (SJN) Carolina, PR Epifania Del Senor.
Moran, Allen Bernard *o.p.* '07 (PRO)[P] Providence St. Thomas Aquinas Priory at Providence College.
Moran, Charles '67 (STU) Chesapeake, OH St. Ann.
Moran, Edward M. '76 (HRT) West Hartford, CT St. Thomas the Apostle.
Moran, Edward '89 (RIC) Retired.
Moran, Edwin *c.p.* '61 (PIT)[M] Pittsburgh, PA St. Paul of the Cross Monastery.
Moran, Gerard K. '71 (OAK) Danville, CA St. Isidore.
Moran, Rev. Msgr. J. Thomas '57 (BUF) Finance Council; Youngstown, NY St. Bernard's.
Moran, James F. '71 (BO) Permanent Disability.
Moran, James M. '74 (HRT) Wethersfield, CT Incarnation.
Moran, James M. '03 (NEW) Elmwood Park, NJ St. Leo's; Engaged Encounter.
Moran, Rev. Msgr. James P. '72 (MET) Edison, NJ Guardian Angels.
Moran, James W. *c.s.p.* '64 (NY)[EE] Jamaica Estates, NY Paulist Fathers Generalate.
Moran, James W. *c.s.p.* (BRK)[T] Jamaica Estates, NY Paulist Fathers – Generalate.
Moran, James *c.o.* '89 (CHR)[E] Rock Hill, SC Oratory of St. Philip Neri, Congregation of the Oratory of Pontifical Rite.
Moran, James (WDC) Washington, DC Washington Hospital Center.
Moran, John J. *m.m.* '66 (NY)[EE] Maryknoll Maryknoll Fathers and Brothers.
Moran, John P. *s.s.c.* '50 (FgM) St Columbans, NE House of Post–Graduate Studies.
Moran, John *s.s.c.* '50 (PRO)[P] Bristol, RI St. Columban's Retirement House Retired.
Moran, John *s.s.c.* '82 (OM)[K] St. Columbans Missionary Society of St. Columban.
Moran, Joseph P. '71 (HEL) Health Leave.
Moran, Kevin '65 (SEA) Federal Way, WA St. Theresa.
Moran, Rev. Msgr. Lawrence J. '52 (IND) Retired.
Moran, Martin O. '88 (CIN) Cincinnati, OH Holy Cross–Immaculata.
Moran, Martin O. '88 (CIN) Cincinnati, OH Old St. Mary.
Moran, Michael F. '82 (MIL) West Bend, WI Immaculate Conception.
Moran, Michael J. '58 (NEW) Retired.
Moran, Michael P. *s.m.a.* '81 (FgM)[M] Tenafly, NJ Society of African Missions, Provincialate, S.M.A. Fathers; Tenafly, NJ SOCIETY OF AFRICAN MISSIONS; Tenafly, NJ; Tenafly, NJ Society of African Missions.
Moran, Rev. Archpriest Michael (VNN) Retired.
Moran, Owen B. '91 (PAT) East Hanover, NJ St. Rose of Lima; Chatham, NJ St. Patrick's.
Moran, Patrick '58 (DUL) Retired.
Moran, Pedro Lopez *c.m.f.* '52 (SJN) Bayamon, PR

Santa Maria.
Moran, Rev. Msgr. Peter C. '65 (LA) Northridge, CA Our Lady of Lourdes.
Moran, Richard S. '61 (BO) Senior Priests. Retired.
Moran, Robert B. '64 (SJ) Mountain View, CA St. Joseph.
Moran, Robert E. '69 (LFT) Portland, IN Immaculate Conception; Deans; Members.
Moran, Robert '64 (SJ) Diocesan Clergy Personnel Board.
Moran, Stephen P. '92 (CLV) Wooster, OH St. Mary of the Immaculate Conception; Rittman, OH St. Anne; [V] Wooster, OH St. Mary of the Immaculate Conception.
Moran, Terence J. '90 (BO) Chelsea, MA St. Rose of Lima.
Moran, Thomas A. '71 (CHI) Northbrook, IL Our Lady of the Brook.
Moran, Thomas D. '88 (SFR) Portola Valley, CA Our Lady of the Wayside; Our Lady of the Wayside Retired.
Moran, Thomas *c.m.f.* '55 (CHI) Chicago, IL Our Lady of Guadalupe; [N] Oak Park Claretian Missionaries USA Eastern Province.
Moran, Rev. Msgr. Timothy J. '76 (BO) Medway, MA St. Joseph; Vicariate IV.
Moran, Timothy '06 (ATL)[G] Alpharetta, GA Norcross Pastoral Center, Inc.
Moran–Rosero, Norman H. '05 (CHI) Chicago, IL St. Jerome.
Morand, Robert '57 (DET) Detroit, MI Our Lady of the Rosary.
Moras, Leo '89 (MO) Army Chaplains.
Moratelli, Ronald J. '69 (HBG) Quarryville, PA St. Catherine of Siena.
Moravitz, Ryan John '08 (DUL) Hibbing, MN Blessed Sacrament.
Morawski, Stefan *o.f.m.conv.* '68 (BGP) Bridgeport, CT St. Michael The Archangel.
Morbeck, George H. '52 (SPK) Republic, WA St. Patrick; Republic, WA Immaculate Conception Retired.
Morbito, Angelo L. '56 (SY)[Q] Syracuse, NY Tommy Coyne Residence Dillon Hall Retired.
Morciniec, Peter J. '70 (SPC) Pierce City, MO St. Mary; Pierce City, MO St. Agnes.
Morcone, Nicholas J. *o.s.b.* '69 (BO)[U] Hingham, MA Glastonbury Abbey.
Moreau, Jean–Marie '92 (OAK) Oakland, CA St. Margaret Mary.
Moreau, Jean–Marie '92 (SJ) Santa Clara, CA Oratory of Our Mother of Perpetual Help.
Moreau, Maurice *o.f.m.cap.* '98 (NY) Yonkers, NY Sacred Heart.
Moreau, Paul *l.c.* '02 (ATL)[L] Norcross, GA Home and Family, Inc.; [D] Atlanta, GA Holy Spirit Preparatory School; [G] Alpharetta, GA Norcross Pastoral Center, Inc.
Moreau, Randall '87 (LAF) Abbeville, LA St. Anne.
Moreau, Raymond J. '85 (OG) Tupper Lake, NY Holy Name of Jesus; Tupper Lake, NY St. Alphonsus; Defenders of the Bond; Committee on Assignments.
Moreeuw, Leroy *c.pp.s.* '68 (CLV) Cleveland, OH Our Lady of Good Counsel.
Moreira, Adelson S. *o.ss.t.* (BAL)[S] The Trinitarians in Texas (Victoria & vicinity).
Moreira, Adelson Silvestre *o.ss.t.* (VIC) Victoria, TX Our Lady of Sorrows.
Moreira, Nelson A. *s.s.j.* '72 (BAL)[S] Baltimore, MD St. Joseph Society of the Sacred Heart House of Central Administration.
Morel, John J. '55 (NEW)[M] Rutherford, NJ St. John Vianney Residence for Priests Retired.
Morel, John *c.i.c.m.* '39 (ARL)[H] Arlington, VA Missionhurst, C.I.C.M.–Central House and Provincialate.
Moreland, J. Gordon *s.j.* '64 (ORG) Special Assignment; [L] Orange, CA House of Prayer for Priests.
Morell, Fernando '87 (ARE) Hatillo, PR Our Lady of Mt. Carmel.
Morell, J. William *o.m.i.* '70 (WDC) Councilors:; [N] Washington, DC Oblate Community; [N] Washington, DC Provincial Offices of the United States Province of the Missionary Oblates of Mary Immaculate.
Morell, William *o.m.i.* '70 (CHI)[W] Chicago, IL Oblates for International Pastoral.
Morell Dominguez, Fernando '87 (ARE) Pastoral Vocational Program; Diocesan Consultors.
Morelle, Edmund J. '53 (SY) Verona, NY Our Lady of Good Counsel.
Morelli, Attilio '98 (NEW) On Duty Outside the Archdiocese.
Morelli, Attilio '98 (PEO) Creve Coeur, IL Sacre Coeur.
Morelli, Gary '81 (DET) Wyandotte, MI Henry Ford Wyandotte Hospital; Inkster, MI Holy Family Parish.
Morello, Carl '83 (CHI) Oak Park, IL St. Giles.
Morello, Peter '78 (GLP) Dulce, NM St. Francis of Assisi Retired.
Morello, Sam Anthony *o.c.d.* '62 (NO)[B] New Orleans, LA St. John of the Cross, Discalced Carmelite House of Studies.
Morelock, George L. '65 (SFD) Retired.
Morency, Raymond P. '87 (PRT) Caribou, ME Parish of the Precious Blood.
Moreno, Antonio O. *o.f.m.conv.* '80 (MO) Air Force Chaplains.
Moreno, Dario *m.s.c.* '04 (RCK)[G].
Moreno, David *s.d.b.* '79 (NEW)[M] Orange, NJ The Salesian Community.
Moreno, Gonzalo *o.f.m.* '08 (SFE) Councilors:; [H] Albuquerque, NM The Province of Our Lady of Guadalupe; Albuquerque, NM Holy Family.
Moreno, Hector C. '05 (LC) Necedah, WI St. Francis of Assisi.
Moreno, James S. '76 (DEN) Denver, CO Holy Family; Judicial Vicar; Metropolitan Judges.
Moreno, Jorge '63 (SD) Brawley, CA Our Lady of Perpetual Help.
Moreno, Jose Alfredo (SD) El Centro, CA Our Lady of Guadalupe.
Moreno, Jose Luis *s.j.* '89 (MIL) Milwaukee, WI Our Lady of Guadalupe Parish; Milwaukee, WI St. Patrick.
Moreno, Jose *s.j.* '89 (MIL)[P] Milwaukee, WI Jesuit Community at Marquette University.
Moreno, Joseph F. '86 (BUF) Buffalo, NY St. Lawrence; Cattaraugus, NY St. Mary.
Moreno, Juan '60 (LSC) Las Cruces, NM St. Genevieve.
Moreno, Luis Carlos '09 (PAT) Succasunna, NJ St. Therese.
Moreno, Martin '03 (DAL) Dallas, TX Doctors Hospital; Dallas, TX St. Bernard of Clairvaux.
Moreno, Robert '93 (STF) Lancaster, NY St. Basil; Alden, NY Erie County Home; Alden, NY Erie County Correctional Facility.
Moreshead, Harold D. '55 (PRT) Portland, ME St. Patrick's Retired.
Moreton, Rev. Msgr. John '64 (FRS) Fresno, CA Our Lady of Victory.
Moretta, Rev. Msgr. John T. '68 (LA) Los Angeles, CA Resurrection; Deanery 9; San Gabriel Region.
Morette, Thomas '05 (ALB) Presbyteral Council.
Moretti, Edward D. '60 (VEN) Bradenton, FL SS. Peter and Paul the Apostles; Vicar General; College of Consultors; Presbyteral Council; Planning and Development Committee.
Moretti, Mark E. '95 (ARL) Reston, VA St. Thomas a Becket.
Morey, Robert E. '96 (BAL) On Duty Outside the Archdiocese.
Morey, Robert E. '96 (CHR) Hilton Head Island, SC Holy Family.
Morfeld, Rev. Msgr. Frank G. '51 (DEN) Denver, CO St. Francis de Sales.
Morfin, John N. '67 (GAL) Retired.
Morgan, Brendan P. '64 (NO) Retired.
Morgan, Charles J. '79 (ALX) Region 5 Chaplain; Dupont, LA Immaculate Conception; Plaucheville, LA Mater Dolorosa.
Morgan, D. Terrence '76 (STA) St. Augustine, FL St. Anastasia.
Morgan, Dare J. *s.j.* '53 (SJ)[M] Los Gatos, CA Sacred Heart Jesuit Center.
Morgan, Drew P. *c.o.* '85 (PIT)[M] Pittsburgh, PA Congregation of the Oratory of St. Philip Neri; Pittsburgh, PA; [Q] Pittsburgh, PA National Institute for Newman Studies.
Morgan, Edward *c.ss.r.* '64 (KC) Kansas City, MO Our Lady of Perpetual Help; [J] Kansas City, MO Redemptorists Fathers of Kansas City, Missouri; Kansas City, MO Our Lady of Sorrows.
Morgan, Guy *o.f.m.* '54 (SP)[N] St. Petersburg St. Anthony Friary Retired.
Morgan, James F. *s.j.* '54 (BO)[U] Weston, MA Campion Health Center, Inc.
Morgan, James P. '01 (SFS) Sioux Falls, SD Holy Spirit; [I] Sioux Falls, SD Holy Spirit School Permanent Trust.
Morgan, James Patrick '91 (ORL) DeLand, FL St. Peter's Church.
Morgan, Jerome L. '62 (SAL) Diocesan Finance Officer; Diocesan Finance Council; College of Consultors; Council of Priests; Art and Architecture Commission; Ex Officio; Consultors; [H] Salina, KS St. Joseph Annex, Inc.; Personnel Board.
Morgan, John A. '40 (ROC) Retired.
Morgan, Rev. Msgr. John W. '58 (B) Retired.
Morgan, John '40 (LA) Camarillo, CA St. Mary Magdalen.
Morgan, John (B) Judges.
Morgan, Joseph A. '81 (OG) Keene, NY St. Brendan; Lake Placid, NY St. Agnes; Defenders of the Bond; Diocesan Consultors.
Morgan, Julian *c.p.* '53 (HRT)[L] West Hartford Holy Family Monastery/Retreat.
Morgan, Martin '70 (TLS) Sand Springs, OK St. Patrick's.
Morgan, Michael P. '01 (STA) Chancellor; Diocesan Consultors; Presbyteral Council; Building Commission; Multicultural Ministry; Ecumenism and Interfaith; Associate Judges; Jacksonville, FL Sacred Heart.
Morgan, Thomas B. '55 (BO) Salisbury, MA Star of the Sea; Ancient Order of Hibernians – Ladies Auxiliary.
Morgan, Rev. Msgr. Thomas J. '65 (CAM) Cherry Hill, NJ The Church of St. Thomas More, Cherry Hill, New Jersey; Representatives by Deaneries; Vocation Advisory Board; College of Consultors.
Morgan, Thomas '84 (SP)[L] Tampa, FL St. Lawrence Housing, Inc.; Vicars Forane; College of Consultors; Tampa, FL St. Lawrence; [L] Tampa, FL St. Lawrence Housing II, Inc.
Morgan, W. Donald '07 (SJ) San Jose, CA Five Wounds Portuguese National Church.
Morgan, William P. '57 (BUR) Retired.
Morgera, Michael A. '85 (MEM) Bartlett, TN Church of The Nativity; [I] Cordova, TN Society of St. Vincent DePaul.
Morgewicz, Robert A. '09 (HRT) West Hartford, CT St. Brigid; West Hartford, CT St. Helena.
Morgia, Robustiano D. '76 (NO) Filipino Catholic Ministry; New Orleans, LA St. Maria Goretti.
Morhous, Robert *o.c.s.o.* '59 (WOR)[O] Spencer, MA St. Joseph's Abbey.
Moriarity, Daniel J. '64 (PH) Philadelphia, PA Nativity of the Blessed Virgin Mary Retired.
Moriarity, Robert T. '92 (SLC)[C] Kearns, UT St. Francis Xavier Regional School; Priests' Personnel Board.
Moriarity, William J. '66 (CHI) Chicago, IL Holy Name Cathedral.
Moriarty, Edward *c.ss.r.* '42 (FgM) Baltimore Province.
Moriarty, James F. '51 (CHI) Retired.
Moriarty, John J. *s.j.* '78 (BO)[A] Weston, MA Blessed John XXIII National Seminary; [U] Boston The Society of Jesus of New England–Provincial Offices; [U] Weston, MA Campion Jesuit Community.
Moriarty, John J. '62 (JOL) Retired.
Moriarty, John '91 (LEX) Lexington, KY St. Elizabeth Ann Seton; College of Consultors; Fayette.
Moriarty, Joseph B. '93 (IND) French Lick, IN Our Lady of the Springs; French Lick, IN Our Lord Jesus Christ the King; [A] St. Meinrad, IN Saint Meinrad School of Theology.
Moriarty, Mark D. '99 (STP) Rogers, MN The Catholic Church of Mary Queen of Peace.
Moriarty, Robert T. '92 (SLC) Kearns, UT Saint Francis Xavier LLC 222.
Moriarty, Thomas '92 (RVC) Hewlett, NY St. Joseph's.
Moriarty, Timothy J. '03 (HEL) Personnel Board; Anaconda, MT Anaconda Catholic Community.
Moriarty, W. Barry *c.m.* '67 (FgM) Earth City, MO Western Province.
Morin, Benjamin R. *s.j.* '56 (DET)[K] Clarkston, MI Colombiere Center.
Morin, Eddy '99 (PRT) Special or Other Diocesan Assignment.
Morin, Francis P. '73 (PRT) Augusta, ME St. Michael Parish.
Morin, George E. '70 (BO) Saugus, MA Blessed Sacrament; Saugus, MA St. Margaret.
Morin, John *o.m.i.* '51 (BO)[Z] Lowell, MA St. Joseph the Worker Residence.
Morin, John *o.m.i.* '51 (NOR)[G] Willimantic, CT Missionary Oblates of Mary Immaculate; [I] Willimantic, CT Immaculata Retreat House; Local Haitian Apostolate/Apostola Ayisyun.
Morin, Joseph J. *c.ss.r.* '64 (CHI)[N] Chicago, IL The Redemptorist Fathers of Chicago; Chicago, IL St. Michael in Old Town.
Morin, Maurice N. '64 (PRT) Lewiston, ME Prince of Peace Parish Retired.
Morin, Michael J. '88 (LIN) Geneva, NE St. Joseph's; Apostleship of Prayer; Diocesan Area CCD Directors; Lincoln, NE Nebraska Penal Complex; Advocates.
Morin, Robert *o.m.i.* '69 (STP)[K] St. Paul, MN Oblate Residence.
Morin, Timothy '77 (STP) Wayzata, MN Holy Name of Jesus.
Morisette, Alfred *s.j.* '61 (SPK)[B] Spokane, WA Gonzaga University.
Morisette, Richard P. '61 (SY) Hannibal, NY Our Lady of the Rosary; Oswego, NY St. Mary.
Morkunas, Andrew M. '09 (WDC) Silver Spring, MD St. Andrew Apostle.
Morlan, Lawrence A. '95 (PEO) On Leave of Absence; Pekin, IL St. Joseph's.
Morley, Craig '01 (SP) Brooksville, FL St. Anthony the Abbot.
Morley, Ed *o.c.s.o.* '83 (ATL)[G] Conyers, GA The Monastery of the Holy Spirit.
Morley, John F. '62 (NEW)[B] School of Diplomacy and Intl. Rels.; [B] School of Diplomacy and Intl. Rels. Retired.
Morley, John J. '04 (MET) Perth Amboy, NJ Holy Spirit; John F. Kennedy Medical Center.
Morley, John M. '61 (NEW) Retired.
Morlino, Rt. Rev. Paschal A. *o.s.b.* '66 (BAL) Baltimore, MD St. Benedict.
Morman, David G. '89 (BIS) Bowman, ND St. Charles; [I] Sentinel Butte, ND Home On The Range Foundation; Bowman, ND St. Mary; Bowman, ND St. Mel; Priests' Benefit Association.
Morman, James *t.o.r.* '92 (STU)[H] Steubenville, OH

Holy Spirit Friary.
Morman, Ken '73 (CIN)[B] Cincinnati, OH Mt. St. Mary's Seminary of the West; [B] Cincinnati, OH Mt. St. Mary's Seminary of the West.
Morman, Kenneth G. '73 (TOL) On Duty Outside the Diocese.
Mormando, Nicholas A. *o.f.m.cap.* '01 (CHL) Hendersonville, NC Immaculate Conception; Union City, NJ.
Mormando, Nicholas A. *o.f.m.cap.* '01 (NEW)[M] Union City, NJ Capuchin Friars – Province of the Sacred Stigmata of St. Francis.
Mormen, James *t.o.r* '92 (STU)[A] Steubenville, OH Franciscan University of Steubenville.
Morocho, Gonzalo *s.d.b.* (NY) Buchanan, NY St. Christopher.
Moroney, Rev. Msgr. James P. '80 (BO) Worcester, MA St. Paul Cathedral; [A] Brighton, MA St. John Seminary.
Moroney, Rev. Msgr. James P. (WOR) Deans; Presbyteral Council.
Moroney, Martin J. '67 (SAC) Rancho Cordova, CA St. John Vianney.
Moroney, Michael J. '71 (BR) Judges; Ecumenical Affairs; Presbyteral Council; Greenwell Springs, LA St. Alphonsus Liguori.
Moroney, William *m.afr.* '61 (FgM) Washington, DC MISSIONARIES OF AFRICA.
Moronta, Andris Alexis *i.v.e.* '02 (PH) Philadelphia, PA St. Hugh of Cluny.
Morosini, Louis *s.m.* '56 (FgM) THE SOCIETY OF MARY.
Morozowich, Mark '91 (SJP) On Assignment Outside the Diocese; Administrative Council; Liturgical Commission; Vocations; [C] Catholic University of America, The; Presbyters.
Morr, Robert F. (SP) Department of Christian Formation.
Morras, Ignacio '49 (MIA) Hialeah, FL St. John the Apostle Retired.
Morras, Rev. Msgr. Xavier '50 (MIA) Retired Priests' Committee Retired.
Morreale, Matthew *o.f.m.* '85 (NY) Bronx, NY Our Lady of Pity.
Morrette, Thomas '05 (ALB) Northville, NY St. Francis of Assisi; Broadalbin, NY St. Joseph; Diocesan Board of Consultors.
Morrier, David *t.o.r.* '97 (STU)[A] Steubenville, OH Franciscan University of Steubenville; [H] Steubenville, OH Holy Spirit Friary; Councilors:.
Morrill, Bruce T. *s.j.* '92 (BO)[U] Boston, MA Loyola House.
Morris, Alan E. '92 (PIT) Bethel Park, PA St. Valentine.
Morris, Alexis P. *o.f.m.* '56 (SP)[N] St. Petersburg St. Anthony Friary Retired.
Morris, Anthony *c.ss.r.* '94 (RIC)[M] Hampton, VA Holy Family Retreat.
Morris, Rev. Msgr. C. Eugene '96 (STL) Brentwood, MO St. Mary Magdalen.
Morris, Charles M. '83 (DET) Wyandotte, MI St. Elizabeth; Wyandotte, MI St. Patrick.
Morris, George O. *s.j.* '68 (SPK)[B] Spokane, WA Gonzaga University.
Morris, Gerald R. '70 (MIA) Marathon, FL San Pablo; Deans and Deaneries.
Morris, James A. '94 (KAL) New Buffalo, MI St. Mary of the Lake.
Morris, James H. '66 (SFR) Menlo Park, CA St. Raymond.
Morris, James '93 (STF) Salem, MA St. John the Baptist; Educational Institutions.
Morris, John J. '60 (NEW) Retired.
Morris, John J. *s.j.* '62 (P)[L] Portland, OR Colombiere Community.
Morris, John S. '62 (BO) Senior Priests. Retired.
Morris, John *o.p.* '66 (OAK)[B] St. Mary's College; [M] Oakland, CA Order of Preachers (Province of the Most Holy Name of Jesus – Western Dominican Province).
Morris, Joseph E. '96 (ATL)[J] Kennesaw, GA Kennesaw State University; Special or Other (Arch)Diocesan Assignment.
Morris, Joseph *s.j.* '59 (LA) Hospital Chaplains; Santa Barbara, CA Our Lady of Sorrows.
Morris, Kenan *o.f.m.* '50 (BO)[X] Boston, MA Saint Anthony Residence Retired.
Morris, Kenan *o.f.m.* '50 (PAT)[N] Ringwood, NJ Holy Name Friary, Inc.
Morris, Kenneth R. *c.s.v.* '54 (CHI)[N] Chicago, IL Viatorian Residence; [N] Arlington Heights Viatorian Province Center–Clerics of St. Viator.
Morris, Kevin '97 (IND) Plainfield, IN St. Susanna.
Morris, Michael E. *s.p.s.* '76 (NEW)[M] Cliffside Park, NJ St. Patrick's Missionary Society; Saratoga, CA; Cliffside Park, NJ St. Patrick's Missionary Society.
Morris, Michael J. '05 (SP) Air Force Reserve Chaplains; On Duty Outside the Diocese.
Morris, Michael T. *o.p.* '77 (OAK)[A] Berkeley, CA Dominican School of Philosophy and Theology.
Morris, Michael '89 (NY)[A] Yonkers, NY St. Joseph's Seminary.
Morris, Michael *o.p.* '77 (OAK)[M] Oakland, CA Order of Preachers (Province of Holy Name of Jesus – Western Dominican Province).
Morris, Rev. Msgr. Philip D. '63 (NEW) Hillsdale, NJ St. John the Baptist Retired.
Morris, Robert A. *o.p.* '50 (PRO)[P] Providence St. Thomas Aquinas Priory at Providence College.
Morris, Robert F. '66 (PT) Destin, FL Corpus Christi; Catholic Daughters of the Americas; Members Elected by Deanery.
Morris, Robert F. '91 (SP) Moderator of the Curia; Executive Committee; Vicar General; College of Consultors; Personnel Board; Ex Officio; Saint Petersburg, FL Cathedral of St. Jude the Apostle; Secretary of Christian Formation.
Morris, Robert J. '04 (NY) White Plains, NY St. Bernard.
Morris, Robert '91 (SP)[H] Spring Hill, FL Father William F. Balfe Memorial Library.
Morris, Sean *o.m.v.* '09 (LA) Hawaiian Gardens, CA St. Peter Chanel.
Morris, Stephen '79 (RVC) Serving Outside the Diocese.
Morris, Thomas A. *o.ss.t.* '81 (PH) Bristol, PA St. Ann.
Morris, Thomas A. *o.ss.t.* '81 (BAL)[S] The Trinitarians in Bristol, Pennsylvania.
Morris, Wayne E. '01 (STU) Caldwell, OH Corpus Christi; Caldwell, OH St. Stephen.
Morris, Wayne '01 (STU) Priests Personnel Board.
Morris, William T. '69 (MET)[B] Watchung, NJ Mount St. Mary Academy.
Morris, William T. '69 (NEW)[N] Englewood Cliffs, NJ St. Michael Villa.
Morrisey, Paul F. *o.s.a.* '67 (PH) Philadelphia, PA St. Augustine.
Morrison, Carl T. '69 (MIA) Miami Shores, FL St. Martha; Promoters of Justice; Defenders of the Bond.
Morrison, Craig *o.carm.* '87 (JOL)[L] Darien Carmelite Provincial Office.
Morrison, Craig *o.carm.* '87 (WDC)[B] Washington, DC Whitefriars Hall.
Morrison, Rev. Msgr. David J. '54 (ALN) Bethlehem, PA Our Lady of Perpetual Help; Judges Retired.
Morrison, Douglas A. '56 (HRT) Retired.
Morrison, Jack '92 (SAM) Ministries (Permanent Deacons and Subdeacons); [E] New Bedford, MA Cedar Holdings, Inc.
Morrison, James J. '74 (PRT) Auburn, ME Immaculate Heart of Mary Parish Retired.
Morrison, James '87 (HT) Administrative Leave.
Morrison, John A. '92 (SAM) New Bedford, MA Our Lady of Purgatory.
Morrison, Larry '79 (RNO) Reno, NV St. Rose of Lima.
Morrison, Michael G. *s.j.* '68 (OM)[K] Omaha, NE Jesuit Community at Creighton University.
Morrison, Thomas A. *o.p.* '55 (CHI)[N] St. Pius V Priory.
Morrison, Thomas F. '76 (CHR) Absent On Leave.
Morrissette, Dominic '45 (JOL) Retired.
Morrissey, Daniel W. *o.p.* '62 (CHI)[N] Chicago Dominicans (Provincial Office).
Morrissey, J. Michael '78 (P) Veneta, OR St. Catherine of Siena.
Morrissey, John '63 (PMB) Fellsmere, FL Our Lady of Guadalupe Mission; Sebastian, FL St. Sebastian.
Morrissey, Michael E. '86 (RCK) Dixon, IL St. Anne.
Morrissey, Rev. Msgr. Michael J. '65 (DAV) Adjutant Judicial Vicar; Judges; Finance Council; Diocesan Consultors; [J] Davenport, IA St. Vincent Center Retired.
Morrissey, Paul F. *s.m.* '75 (STP) St. Paul, MN St. Louis King of France.
Morrissey, Rev. Msgr. Robert O. '83 (RVC) Secretary to the Bishop; Vice Chancellors; Censors of Books; Judges for Interdiocesan Tribunal; Senate of Priests (Presbyteral Council/College of Consultors); Secretary to the Bishop.
Morrissey, Robert '76 (BGP) Leave of Absence.
Morrissy, Dennis M. '06 (RCK) Geneva, IL St. Peter.
Morrone, Louis S. *o.p.* '92 (DEN) Denver, CO St. Dominic; [N] Denver, CO Dominican Friars.
Morroquin, Esvin *c.s.* '07 (LA) Los Angeles, CA St. Peter.
Morrow, Brian '80 (DEN) Longmont, CO St. John the Baptist.
Morrow, Dennis W. '75 (GR) Grand Rapids, MI SS. Peter and Paul; On Special Assignment; Archivist; Grand Rapids, MI St. James.
Morrow, Michael D. (NY) Yonkers, NY St. Eugene.
Morrow, Michael J. '86 (MO) Air Force Reserve Chaplains.
Morrow, Richard B. '55 (ATL) Atlanta, GA Cathedral of Christ the King; Judges; Vicars for Clergy Retired.
Morrow, Thomas G. '82 (WDC) Silver Spring, MD St. Catherine Laboure.
Morse, Frederick '95 (PRT) Bath, ME All Saints Parish.
Morse, James H. '67 (FR) Attleboro, MA St. Stephen's.
Morse, John J. *s.j.* '61 (SPK)[J] Spokane, WA Regis Community.
Morse, Jonathan K. '88 (MO) Army Reserve Chaplains.
Morse, Michael '84 (STA) Absent or Sick Leave.
Morse, Richard E. *o.s.f.s.* '69 (TOL)[I] Toledo, OH; Toledo, OH St. Pius X.
Mort, Ernest C. *c.s.p.* '59 (NY)[EE] Jamaica Estates Paulist Fathers Generalate.
Mortell, Anthony *s.s.c.* '60 (LA)[P] Los Angeles, CA Columban Fathers, Procure House.
Mortell, Anthony *s.s.c.* '85 (OM)[K] St. Columbans, NE Missionary Society of St. Columban.
Mortimer, Rev. Msgr. James E. '52 (PH) Retired.
Morton, Jake *s.j.* '75 (SPK) Inchelium, WA St. Michael's Mission; Nespelem, WA Sacred Heart Mission; Keller, WA St. Rose of Lima; Omak, WA St. Joseph.
Morton, Vincent '86 (SP) Retired.
Morton, William *s.s.c.* '60 (OM)[K] St. Columbans Missionary Society of St. Columban; St Columbans, NE; St Columbans, NE House of Post–Graduate Studies.
Morugudi, Bhaskar '99 (SAN) Rowena, TX St. Boniface.
Mosbrucker, Jacob A. '66 (P) Retired.
Moscaritolo, Mario '64 (KC) Retired.
Mosele, Victor *s.x.* '60 (MIL)[B] Franklin, WI Xaverian Missionary Fathers College Seminary.
Moser, Albert *c.s.p.* '60 (OAK) Berkeley, CA Holy Spirit Parish/Newman Hall.
Moser, Claudio *o.f.m.* '63 (NY)[EE] St. Peter Friary.
Moser, John A. '86 (DUB) Osage, IA Sacred Heart; Osage, IA Church of the Visitation.
Moser, Thomas W. '94 (KNX) Lenoir City, TN St. Thomas the Apostle.
Moses, Patrick '03 (ORG) Cypress, CA St. Irenaeus.
Mosey, Douglas L. *c.s.b.* '74 (NOR)[A] Cromwell, CT Holy Apostles College and Seminary; [M] Cromwell, CT Basilian Fathers of Connecticut, Inc.
Mosha, Benedict Ndeyekiyo *a.l.c.p.* '89 (PMB) Tequesta, FL St. Jude.
Mosher, Robert *s.s.c.* '82 (FgM)[K] St. Columbans Missionary Society of St. Columban; St Columbans, NE House of Post–Graduate Studies.
Mosher, Thomas L. '81 (BUR) Woodstock, VT Our Lady of the Snows; Deans; Elected Members.
Mosimann, John P. '97 (ARL) Leesburg, VA St. John the Apostle; Diocesan Consultors; Defenders of the Bond.
Moskal, Joseph E. '65 (SY) Camden, NY St. Mary.
Mosko, Rt. Rev. Mitred Msgr. Leon '56 (STF) Retired.
Moskus, John T. '63 (HRT) Retired.
Mosley, Charles A. '85 (GRY) Hammond, IN Our Lady of Perpetual Help.
Mosley, Daniel E. '77 (STL) Warson Woods, MO Ste. Genevieve Du Bois.
Mosley, Rev. Msgr. Godfrey T. '79 (WDC) Washington, DC St. Ann; Adjutant Judicial Vicars.
Moslosky, Robert W. *c.s.b.* '74 (DET)[E] Novi, MI Catholic Central High School.
Moss, Brendan *o.s.b.* '01 (IND)[K] St. Meinrad, IN St. Meinrad Archabbey; [A] St. Meinrad, IN Saint Meinrad School of Theology.
Moss, Darius G. C. '97 (HBG) Millersburg, PA Queen of Peace.
Moss, Donald G. '86 (MO) Navy Chaplains; Chaplains of the Military.
Moss, James (PAT) Paterson, NJ Preakness Hospital; Wayne, NJ Our Lady of the Valley.
Moss, James '82 (STA) Jacksonville, FL San Jose.
Moss, Raymond B. '86 (CHY) Cheyenne, WY St. Joseph's.
Moss, Robert D. '69 (BUF) Absent on Leave.
Moss, Robert H. *c.s.c.* '74 (FTW)[B] University of Notre Dame Du Lac; [H] Notre Dame, IN Holy Cross Community, Corby Hall, University of Notre Dame.
Mossa, Mark S. *s.j.* '08 (NY)[EE] Cardinal Spellman Hall, Jesuit Community.
Mossett, Robert C. *o.s.f.s.* '65 (DET) Monroe, MI St. Anne.
Mossholder, Francis D. '88 (LAN) Charlotte, MI St. Mary; Bellevue, MI St. Ann.
Mossi, John P. *s.j.* '73 (SJ)[O] Los Gatos, CA Jesuit Seminary Association; [M] Santa Clara, CA Casa San Inigo, Jesuit Residence; [B] Santa Clara, CA Jesuit Community.
Mostardi, Joseph S. *o.s.a.* '75 (PH)[C] Villanova University; [Y] Villanova, PA Provincial Offices of the Order of St. Augustine, Province of St. Thomas of Villanova; [Y] Villanova, PA Fray de Leon Community; Counselors:.
Mostardi, Joseph S. *o.s.a.* '75 (CAM)[M] Ocean City, NJ Augustinian Friars.
Moster, Humbert *o.f.m.* '57 (CIN)[C] Cincinnati, OH St. Anthony Shrine, Franciscan Postulancy.
Moster, Humbert *o.f.m.* '57 (IND) Brookville, IN St. Peter.
Moster, James *o.f.m.cap.* '76 (KCK)[I] Lawrence, KS St. Conrad's Friary; Denver, CO.
Moster, James *o.f.m.cap.* '76 (MO) DEPARTMENT OF VETERANS AFFAIRS HOSPITALS AND CHAPLAINS.
Moszur, Edward J. '71 (GRY) Highland, IN Our Lady of Grace; Priests' Personnel Board.
Motl, James R. *o.p.* '62 (STL)[O] St. Louis, MO St. Dominic Priory.
Motl, James R. *o.p.* '62 (STP)[C] St. Paul, MN University of St. Thomas Retired.
Motsay, Joseph R. '78 (SCR) Retired.
Motsay, Russell E. '72 (SCR) Carbondale, PA Our Lady

of Mt. Carmel.
Motsett, Rev. Msgr. C. Bourke '34 (PEO) Retired.
Mott, Allen P. '03 (MAR) Chassell, MI St. Anne; Houghton, MI St. Albert the Great University Parish; [G] Houghton, MI St. Albert the Great, University Parish.
Mott, David John Paul *o.p.* '04 (WDC)[B] Washington, DC Dominican House of Studies.
Mott, James A. *o.s.a.* '65 (LA) Los Angeles, CA Our Mother of Good Counsel.
Motta, Anthony '63 (ALB) Haines Falls, NY Sacred Heart–Immaculate Conception Church.
Motta, Jairo '83 (CC) Corpus Christi, TX Sacred Heart.
Motta, Rev. Msgr. Michael J. '72 (HRT) West Hartford, CT St. Mark the Evangelist; Special and other Archdiocesan Assignment; Office of Religious Education; Evangelization.
Mottau, Robert S. '58 (BO) Senior Priests. Retired.
Mottet, Rev. Msgr. Marvin A. '56 (DAV)[J] Davenport, IA St. Vincent Center; [H] Davenport, IA Thomas Merton House, Inc. Retired.
Mouannes, Nabil '84 (OLL) El Cajon, CA St. Ephrem Maronite Catholic Church; Presbyteral Council.
Mouannes, Tanios '05 (SAM) On Duty Outside the Diocese.
Mouch, Rev. Msgr. Frank M. '58 (VEN) Retired.
Moudry, Paul '87 (STP) Golden Valley, MN St. Margaret Mary.
Moudry, Richard P. '50 (STP) Retired.
Mould, Christopher J. '88 (ARL) Alexandria, VA St. Lawrence.
Moulder, John P. '90 (CHI) Chicago, IL St. Gregory, the Great.
Mount, Maurus *o.s.b.* '06 (GBG)[G] Latrobe Saint Vincent Archabbey.
Mount, Maurus *o.s.b.* '06 (PEO)[M] Champaign, IL St. John's Catholic Newman Center at the University of Illinois, Urbana–Champaign; Champaign, IL St. John's Catholic Chapel.
Mountain, Edward C. '47 (WIN) Retired.
Mountain, Rev. Msgr. Joseph W. '52 (WIN) Retired.
Mounteer, Louis A. *s.j.* '56 (NY)[EE] New York, NY Murray–Weigel Hall.
Moussier, Howard R. *o.s.b.* '65 (MOB) Elberta, AL St. Bartholomew.
Moussier, Howard R. *o.s.b.* '65 (BIR)[E] Cullman, AL St. Bernard Abbey.
Moutenot, Charles *s.j.* '84 (PAT)[J] Morristown, NJ Loyola House of Retreats.
Mouthevil, Ambrose (PIT) Allegheny County, PA Kane Regional Center – Ross.
Mouton, Rev. Msgr. Richard von Phul '55 (LAF) Diocesan Consultors; Holy Childhood; Pontifical Mission Societies; Lafayette, LA Cathedral of St. John the Evangelist; Instructors Retired.
Mouton, Thomas Jason '92 (LAF) Youngsville, LA St. Anne.
Mower, Scott M. '97 (PRT) Ellsworth, ME St. Joseph; Ellsworth, ME Stella Maris Parish.
Mowrer, Patrick '97 (PHX) Flagstaff, AZ San Francisco de Asis Roman Catholic Parish; Deans.
Moy, Francis J. *s.j.* '69 (BO)[U] Boston The Society of Jesus of New England–Provincial Offices; [U] Boston, MA Loyola House.
Moy, Francis J. *s.j.* '69 (FR) South Dartmouth, MA St. Mary's.
Moyer, Rev. Msgr. Richard W. '64 (PHX) Priests' Assurance Association Retired.
Moyher, Francis *t.o.r.* '63 (ALT)[G] Loretto, PA St. Francis Friary at Mount Assisi.
Moylan, Thomas '69 (NY)[V] Thornwood, NY Catholic World Mission, Inc.
Moylan, Thomas *l.c.* '69 (PHX) Queen Creek, AZ Our Lady of Guadalupe Roman Catholic Parish.
Moyna, John L. '73 (ALB) Coxsackie, NY St. Mary; Regional Medical Unit; Advocates; Deans.
Moynahan, Michael E. *s.j.* '73 (SAC) Sacramento, CA St. Ignatius of Loyola; [I] Carmichael, CA Sacramento Jesuit Community.
Moynihan, Eugene J. *s.s.j.* '57 (BAL)[S] Baltimore, MD St. Joseph's Manor Retired.
Moynihan, Jeremiah P. '74 (ROC) Elmira, NY Christ the Redeemer.
Moynihan, John C. *m.m.* '67 (FgM) Maryknoll, NY MARYKNOLL.
Moynihan, Michael '79 (BGP) Leave of Absence.
Moynihan, Noel *c.s.sp.* '77 (BRK) Woodside, NY Blessed Virgin Mary, Help of Christians.
Moynihan, T. Joseph '57 (BO) Senior Priests. Retired.
Moys, Rev. Msgr. Gregory '64 (P) St. Paul, OR St. Paul; College of Consultors; Defenders of the Bond.
Mozdyniewicz, Peter '94 (DEN) Denver, CO Notre Dame.
Mozer, Joseph F. '97 (BO) Tribunal Court; Canonical Affairs Committee; Dedham, MA St. Mary.
Mpagi, Anthony '06 (WOR) African Ministry; Worcester, MA St. Joan of Arc; Worcester, MA St. Peter.
Mpanda, Apo T. '88 (DAV) Farmington, IA St. Boniface; West Point, IA Assumption of the Blessed Virgin Mary.
Mpeka, Rogatus '82 (TR) Yardville, NJ St. Vincent de Paul.
Mpuya, Claudius '93 (SP) Largo, FL St. Patrick.
Mraz, Rev. Msgr. John S. '75 (ALN) Emmaus, PA St. Ann; Office of Ecumenical and Interreligious Dialogue.
Mraz, Louis R. *o.s.c.* '59 (PHX)[F] Phoenix, AZ Crosier Community of Phoenix (Canons Regular of the Order of the Holy Cross) Retired.
Mraz, Robert J. '74 (NU) Tracy, MN St. Mary; Walnut Grove, MN St. Paul; Priests' Council.
Mrnarevic, Daniel '84 (FAR) Grand Forks, ND St. Mary.
Mroczkowski, Joseph A. '45 (LIN) Retired.
Mroczkowski, Rev. Msgr. Joseph J. '42 (CHI) Retired.
Mroczynski, Edward *s.ch.* '57 (SJ) San Jose, CA St. Brother Albert Chmielowski Polish Catholic Pastoral Mission.
Mrowka, Chester R. *c.m.* '59 (HRT)[L] Manchester, CT DePaul Provincial Residence.
Mroz, Richard J. '92 (NEW) Irvington, NJ St. Leo's.
Mroziewski, Witold '91 (BRK) Brooklyn, NY Our Lady of Czestochowa–St. Casimir; [S] Polish Apostolate; Attorney and Counselor at Canon Law; Diocesan Judges.
Msaki, Beda *a.l.c.p.* '98 (SLC) Vernal, UT Saint James the Greater LLC 227.
Msongore, Josaphat *c.s.sp.* '63 (FgM) Bethel Park, PA CONGREGATION OF THE HOLY SPIRIT.
Mthembu, Mafanisa *o.s.m.* '90 (CHI)[N] Chicago Order of Friar Servants of Mary (Servites) United States of America Province, Inc.
Mubelo, Jean Willy Moka *s.j.* '07 (OAK)[M] Berkeley, CA Jesuit Fathers and Brothers.
Muc, John *o.cist.* '90 (CHI)[N] Willow Springs, IL Cistercian Fathers, Our Lady Mother of the Church Polish Mission; Argo, IL Our Lady, Mother of the Church Polish Mission.
Mucci, Flavian *o.f.m.* '63 (FgM) New York, NY Franciscan Province of the Immaculate Conception.
Mucci, Robert V. '09 (BRK) Graduate Studies.
Muccilli, Sebastian '57 (MET) Retired.
Muccino, Keith F. *s.j.* '96 (CHI)[C] Chicago, IL Jesuit Community at Loyola University Chicago.
Mucha, Jan '54 (DEN) Denver, CO St. Joseph Polish.
Mucha, Jan '83 (CHI) Chicago, IL St. Ladislaus.
Mucha, John '81 (STU) Bridgeport, OH St. Joseph; Presbyteral Council; Priests Personnel Board.
Mucha, John '81 (STU) Bridgeport, OH St. Anthony of Padua.
Mucha, Jozef '01 (SY) Pulaski, NY Christ Our Light.
Muckenhaupt, Gregory F. *s.j.* '88 (CI) Pohnpei, FM Sacred Heart; [C] Kolonia, Pohnpei, FM Jesuit House.
Muckenhaupt, Gregory F. *s.j.* '88 (FgM) New York, NY Society of Jesus.
Mucowski, Richard J. *o.f.m.* (ROM) Formation Council.
Mucowski, Richard *o.f.m.* (PAT) Consulting Psychologist.
Mucowski, Richard *o.f.m.* '71 (MET) Psychological Consultants.
Muda, Adam '09 (PAT) Hewitt, NJ Our Lady Queen of Peace.
Mudakodiyil, Jose Thomas '02 (BAK) La Pine, OR Holy Redeemer.
Mudavankunnel, Jose *m.s.f.s.* '81 (TYL)[B] Whitehouse, TX The Missionaries of St. Francis de Sales.
Mudavankunnell, Joseph *m.s.f.s.* (MOB) Lillian, AL St. Joseph.
Mudd, David A. '80 (WDC) Military Chaplains; Navy Chaplains.
Mudd, Earl '60 (BEA) Retired.
Mudd, Gerald R. *o.f.m.* '66 (ALB)[B] Siena College; [R] Albany, NY St. Francis Chapel.
Mudd, James T. '64 (L) Louisville, KY St. Gabriel the Archangel Retired.
Mudd, Joachim Mary *f.i.* (IND)[K] Bloomington, IN Marian Friary of Our Lady Coredemptrix, Franciscan of the Immaculate.
Mudd, Joachim *f.i.* '97 (FAR) On Duty Outside the Diocese.
Mudd, John '69 (WDC) Special Ministries; [D] Washington, DC Archbishop Carroll High School.
Mudduse, Lawrence Yawe (CHI) Northbrook, IL Our Lady of the Brook.
Mudrak, Lloyd '62 (DUL) Coleraine, MN Mary Immaculate; Marble, MN St. Mary; Coleraine, MN St. Joseph; Boy Scouts.
Mudry, Lubomyr '51 (STF) Retired.
Mueggenborg, Rev. Msgr. Daniel H. '89 (TLS) Diocesan Consultors; Staff; On Duty Outside the Diocese.
Mueller, Donald R. '61 (TOL) Retired.
Mueller, Eric '09 (TOL) Norwalk, OH St. Paul.
Mueller, Eugene J. '56 (CIN) Retired.
Mueller, Glenn R. *s.j.* '73 (KC) Kansas City, MO Guardian Angels; [J] Kansas City, MO Rockhurst Jesuit Community.
Mueller, James J. '66 (BRK) Brooklyn, NY St. Finbar.
Mueller, James *o.carm.* '69 (JOL)[L] Darien Carmelite Provincial Office.
Mueller, James *s.m.* '53 (LA)[F] Marianist Community.
Mueller, James *o.carm.* '69 (GAL)[A] Houston, TX St. Mary's Seminary.
Mueller, Jerome D. *o.f.m.* '73 (SFE) Albuquerque, NM St. Charles Borromeo.
Mueller, John J. '59 (CLV) Wooster, OH St. Mary of the Immaculate Conception Retired.
Mueller, John J. *s.j.* '75 (STL)[C] Saint Louis University; [O] St. Louis, MO Jesuit Community Corporation at Saint Louis University – Jesuit Hall.
Mueller, Joseph G. *s.j.* '93 (MIL)[P] Milwaukee, WI Jesuit Community at Marquette University.
Mueller, Kevin A. '92 (BAL) Crofton, MD Church of the Holy Apostles.
Mueller, Matthias R. *o.p.* '49 (CHI) Chicago, IL St. Pius V; [N] Chicago, IL Dominican Community.
Mueller, Michael '85 (MO) On Duty Outside the Diocese; Navy Chaplains.
Mueller, Noel *o.s.b.* '68 (IND)[K] St. Meinrad, IN St. Meinrad Archabbey.
Mueller, Paul R. *s.j.* '93 (CHI)[C] Chicago, IL Jesuit Community at Loyola University Chicago.
Mueller, Richard J. '63 (CHI) Northbrook, IL St. Norbert Retired.
Mueller, Richard J. '44 (IND) Retired.
Mueller, Richard J. '66 (PIT) Retired.
Mueller, Richard '44 (IND) Archdiocesan Judges Retired.
Mueller, Robert F. '46 (MIL) Retired.
Mueller, Roman *s.d.s.* '74 (SAC) Orangevale, CA Divine Savior.
Muench, Joseph N. '81 (LEX) Special Assignment.
Muench, Rev. Msgr. R. Francis '81 (RIC) Regional Vicars; Judicial Vicar.
Muench, William G. '59 (OG) Ticonderoga, NY Sacred Heart Church; Ticonderoga, NY St. Mary.
Muenchrath, David '04 (DM)[J] Panora, IA St. Thomas More Center; Vocations; On Special Assignment.
Muenks, Nicholas J. '06 (STL) St. Louis, MO St. Clement.
Mugabe, Pascal *c.s.c.* '05 (FTW)[H] Notre Dame Congregation of Holy Cross, Indiana Province, Provincial House.
Mugabowakigeri, Bernardin '96 (SAC) Alturas, CA Sacred Heart.
Mugan, William L. *s.j.* '55 (MIL)[P] Wauwatosa, WI Jesuit Community at St. Camillus.
Muganyizi, George *c.s.c.* '98 (FTW)[H] Notre Dame Congregation of Holy Cross, Indiana Province, Provincial House.
Mugasha, Chrisanth S. *a.j.* '99 (NY) Bellevue Hospital.
Mugavero, Anthony P. '81 (ROC) Rochester, NY Holy Apostles.
Muggli, Boniface *o.s.b.* '90 (BIS) Richardton, ND St. Mary; [A] Richardton, ND Assumption Abbey; Richardton, ND St. Thomas; Richardton, ND St. Stephen.
Muggli, Florian *o.s.b.* '51 (SCL)[I] Collegeville, MN St. John's Abbey, of the Order of St. Benedict.
Muggli, Odo *o.s.b.* '66 (BIS)[A] Richardton, ND Assumption Abbey; [I] Richardton, ND Sacred Heart Mission.
Muguerza, Octavio '92 (SAT) San Antonio, TX St. John Neumann.
Muha, Joseph '60 (B) Priest Retirement Committee Retired.
Muha, Peter J. '88 (GRY) Merrillville, IN Our Lady of Consolation.
Muhich, Peter '89 (DUL) Duluth, MN Cathedral of Our Lady of the Rosary; Duluth, MN Calvary Cemetery; Diocesan Finance Council; Finance Officer; Mission Outreach and Propagation of the Faith; Moderator of the Curia.
Muhlbaier, Howard E. '65 (CAM) Gibbsboro, NJ St. Andrew the Apostle's R.C. Church, Gibbsboro, N.J.
Muhlen, Micah *o.f.m.* '91 (PHX) Advocates; Phoenix, AZ St. Mary's Roman Catholic Basilica.
Muhm, William M. '95 (NY) Military Chaplains; Navy Chaplains.
Muhr, Michael '83 (PMB)[A] Boynton Beach, FL St. Vincent de Paul Regional Seminary.
Muhr, Michael '83 (SP) On Duty Outside the Diocese.
Muir, Edmund D. '49 (DET) Retired.
Muir, Gavin W. '65 (PH) Riegelsville, PA St. Lawrence.
Muir, John '07 (PHX) Phoenix, AZ St. Joan of Arc Roman Catholic Parish; Worship and Liturgy, Office of; [A] Phoenix, AZ Xavier College Preparatory Roman Catholic High School.
Mujule, Christopher Michael '78 (BEL) Metropolis, IL St. Rose of Lima.
Mujuni, John Bosco (CHI) Chicago, IL St. Benedict the African (West).
Mukalel, Joseph V. '58 (NEW) Retired.
Mukamba, Benoit K. *c.s.sp.* '92 (GAL) Houston, TX St. Benedict the Abbot.
Mukasa, Edoth *s.j.* (FTW)[K] South Bend, IN Jesuit Community.
Mukkoot, Saji George '92 (CHI) Evanston, IL Divine Liturgy–Ascension Church.
Mukkoot, Saji '92 (CHI)[J] Chicago, IL Resurrection Medical Center.
Mukundi, Samson Ngatia '03 (CHI) Grayslake, IL St. Gilbert.

Mulah, Nixon Ambe (BAL) Baltimore, MD St. Francis Xavier.
Mulangattil, Joseph *m.c.b.s.* '74 (MIL)[P] Kenosha, WI Missionary Congregation of the Blessed Sacrament, Inc., Zion Province.
Mulanjanany, Augustine '69 (LKC) Bell City, LA St. John Vianney.
Mularczyk, Mariusz (PIT) Aliquippa, PA St. Frances Cabrini.
Mulavanal, Thomas '89 (SYM) South Gate, CA St. Pius X Knanaya Catholic Mission of Los Angeles.
Mulcahey, Andrew *l.c.* '96 (PRO)[E] Wakefield, RI Immaculate Conception Academy, Inc.
Mulcahy, Daniel R. '79 (WOR) Portuguese Ministry; Milford, MA St. Mary of the Assumption.
Mulcahy, Rev. Msgr. Donal '51 (LA) Ventura, CA Our Lady of the Assumption Retired.
Mulcahy, Gerald F. '62 (CHI) Retired.
Mulcahy, John M. *c.s.c.* '65 (FTW)[H] Notre Dame Congregation of Holy Cross, Indiana Province, Provincial House.
Mulcahy, John P. '05 (WH) Fairmont, WV St. Anthony; Monongah, WV Holy Spirit.
Mulcahy, Louis *o.s.b.* '89 (IND)[K] St. Meinrad, IN St. Meinrad Archabbey.
Mulcahy, Matthew Bernard *o.p.* '03 (WDC)[B] Washington, DC Dominican House of Studies.
Mulcahy, Patrick J. '95 (SD) Bonita, CA Corpus Christi.
Mulcahy, Patrick '06 (JOL) Glen Ellyn, IL St. Petronille.
Mulcahy, Sean '62 (MIA) Retired.
Mulcair, William W. *m.s.* '65 (HRT)[L] Hartford, CT Missionaries of LaSalette.
Mulcrone, Joseph A. '71 (CHI) Chicago, IL St. Francis Borgia; [W] Chicago, IL Catholic Office of the Deaf; Catholic Office of the Deaf.
Mulcrone, Thomas A. '77 (CHI)[L] Chicago, IL St. Mary of Providence; Fire Department Chaplain.
Mulderry, Anthony '67 (MIA) Pompano Beach, FL St. Gabriel; Chaplain—Broward County - Serra Club.
Muldoon, Rev. Msgr. Brendan '64 (SP) Indian Rocks Beach, FL St. Jerome; [F] Largo, FL St. Jerome Early Childhood Center; College of Consultors.
Muldoon, P. Christopher '71 (PAT) Lake Hopatcong, NJ Our Lady Star of the Sea.
Muldowney, Thomas M. '03 (SCR) Scouts of America; Olyphant, PA St. Patrick's; Olyphant, PA St. Michael the Archangel.
Mulemi, Patrick *s.j.* '03 (MIL)[P] Milwaukee, WI Jesuit Community at Marquette University.
Mulewski, Patrick M. '79 (NEW) Old Tappan, NJ St. Pius X.
Mulgrew, John E. '56 (PH) Media, PA St. Mary Magdalen Retired.
Mulhall, Michael *o.carm.* (CHI) Chicago, IL St. Thomas Apostle.
Mulhauser, Daniel J. *s.j.* '60 (SY) Presbyteral Council; [Q] Syracuse, NY Jesuits at LeMoyne, Inc.
Mulhearn, Michael *c.m.* '68 (KC)[J] Independence, MO Vincentian Parish Mission Center.
Mulhern, Kevin P. '76 (SCR) Dalton, PA Our Lady of the Abingtons.
Mulholland, David '02 (SEA) Centralia, WA St. Mary; Chehalis, WA St. Joseph; Pe Ell, WA St. Joseph; Toledo, WA St. Francis Xavier; Winlock, WA Sacred Heart; Presbyteral Council; Deans.
Muli, Killian '01 (CHY) Pine Bluffs, WY St. Paul's.
Mulica, James '67 (CLV) Retired.
Mulinda, Lawrence '95 (STA) Switzerland, FL San Juan Del Rio.
Mulka, Arthur C. '51 (GAY) Retired.
Mulka, Raymond C. '49 (GAY) Retired.
Mulkerin, Terrence J. '61 (BRK) Mission Office; Brooklyn, NY Holy Name; [X] Brooklyn, NY Society of the Immaculate Conception of Brooklyn Retired.
Mulkern, Daniel J. *t.o.r.* '66 (ALT)[G] Loretto, PA St. Francis Friary at Mount Assisi.
Mulkern, Stephen M. '49 (PRT) Retired.
Mull, Thomas P. '76 (ROC) Canadaigua, NY St. Mary; [N] Rochester, NY Apostleship of Prayer; East Bloomfield, NY St. Bridget.
Mullady, Brian T. *o.p.* '72 (P) Portland, OR Holy Rosary Parish & Dominican Priory.
Mullady, Brian T.B. *o.p.* '72 (P)[L] Portland, OR Holy Rosary Priory.
Mullakkara, Joseph *m.s.f.s.* '75 (ATL)[F] Atlanta, GA Our Lady of Perpetual Help Home; Johns Creek, GA St. Benedict.
Mullakkara, Joseph *m.s.f.s.* '75 (ATL)[G] Snellville, GA The Missionaries of St. Francis De Sales; Special or Other (Arch)Diocesan Assignment.
Mullakkara, Joseph *m.s.f.s.* '75 (TYL)[B] Whitehouse, TX The Missionaries of St. Francis de Sales.
Mullally, Gerald F. '76 (SCR) Milford, PA St. Patrick.
Mullally, Thomas A. *s.v.d.* '70 (JKS) Greenville, MS Sacred Heart; Indianola, MS Immaculate Conception; Indianola, MS St. Benedict the Moor; Shaw, MS St. Francis of Assisi.
Mullamangalam, Mathew (LAF) Berwick, LA St. Stephen.
Mullan, Glen F. '94 (CC) Corpus Christi, TX Christ the King.
Mullan, Patrick '67 (PAT)[Q] Chester, NJ Nazareth Village Retired.
Mullan, Raymund A. '62 (FWT) Graham, TX St. Mary; Graham, TX St. Theresa of the Infant Jesus; Deans.
Mullan, William F. *m.m.* '62 (FgM) Maryknoll, NY MARYKNOLL.
Mullane, Bernard J. '56 (RCK) Retired.
Mullane, Thomas '68 (MIA) Big Pine Key, FL St. Peter.
Mullaney, Aidan '52 (ALT)[G] Loretto, PA St. Francis Friary at Mount Assisi.
Mullaney, Cornelius J. '71 (BO) Lynn, MA St. Pius Fifth.
Mullaney, Gregory C. '90 (NOR) Chaplains; Storrs, CT St. Thomas Aquinas.
Mullaney, Lawrence J. '88 (RIC) Tabb, VA Blessed Kateri Tekakwitha.
Mullaney, Leonard M. '62 (FR) Retired.
Mullaney, Mark '03 (ARL) Clifton, VA St. Andrew the Apostle; Notaries.
Mullarkey, John T. '64 (GB) Bear Creek, WI St. Mary; Bear Creek, WI St. Rose Retired.
Mullarkey, Rev. Msgr. Patrick J. '64 (SD) San Diego, CA St. Catherine Laboure.
Mullelly, Thomas J. '80 (TR)[T] Princeton, NJ Campus Ministry for the Diocese of Trenton; Diocesan Consultors; Office of Continuing Education for Priests; Secretary.
Mullen, Rev. Msgr. Austin '65 (SP) Beverly Hills, FL Our Lady of Grace.
Mullen, Bernard *c.pp.s.* '48 (CIN)[N] Carthagena, OH St. Charles Retired.
Mullen, Charles F. *c.pp.s.* '64 (CIN) Fort Recovery, OH Mary Help of Christians; Fort Recovery, OH St. Paul.
Mullen, David J. '82 (BO) Bellingham, MA St. Brendan.
Mullen, Dennis M. '70 (SUP) Frederic, WI St. Dominic; Frederic, WI Immaculate Conception; Board of Directors.
Mullen, Godfrey *o.s.b.* '94 (IND)[A] St. Meinrad, IN Saint Meinrad School of Theology; [K] St. Meinrad, IN St. Meinrad Archabbey.
Mullen, Kevin *o.f.m.* '80 (ALB)[B] Loudonville, NY Siena College; [B] Siena College.
Mullen, Kevin *o.f.m.* '80 (NY)[II] New York, NY The Fratecelli Corporation.
Mullen, Rev. Msgr. Michael '62 (KCK) Kansas City, KS St. Patrick's; Co Directors Seminarians; Archdiocesan Consultors.
Mullen, Michael '75 (VEN) Fort Myers, FL St. Francis Xavier; [K] Fort Myers, FL St. Francis Xavier School Foundation.
Mullen, Owen J. '64 (WIL) On Duty Outside the Diocese.
Mullen, Owen '64 (SD)[B] University of San Diego.
Mullen, Patrick '85 (LA)[A] Camarillo, CA St. John's Seminary.
Mullen, Paul M. '73 (SCR) Milford, PA St. Vincent de Paul.
Mullen, Richard *o.s.a.* '81 (MIA)[K] Miami Gardens, FL Casa San Lorenzo; Hollywood, FL Little Flower.
Mullen, Richard '55 (PEO) Retired.
Mullen, Thomas J. *ss.cc.* '75 (LA)[P] La Verne, CA Congregation of the Sacred Hearts of Jesus and Mary.
Mullen, Rev. Msgr. William J. '51 (HRT) Judges; [A] In Res. at the Archbishop Daniel A. Cronin Retirement Residence at St. Thomas Seminary Retired.
Muller, Anthony '68 (CIN) Cincinnati, OH St. Ann.
Muller, George *o.p.* '59 (WDC) Washington, DC St. Dominic Church & Priory.
Muller, James B. *o.p.* '59 (L) Louisville, KY St. Louis Bertrand; [L] Louisville, KY St. Louis Bertrand Priory.
Muller, Joseph T. *m.s.c.* '58 (ALN)[A] Center Valley, PA Sacred Heart Villa, Missionaries of the Sacred Heart.
Muller, Kennard '66 (BAL) Forest Hill, MD St. Ignatius Retired.
Muller, Rev. Msgr. Martin M. '57 (BIR) Birmingham, AL Our Lady of Sorrows; Diocesan College of Consultors; Priests'/Presbyteral Council; Diocesan College of Vicars.
Muller, Myles '48 (BAL) Retired.
Muller, Peter D. *o.praem.* '93 (ORG)[I] Silverado, CA Norbertine Fathers of Orange Inc.
Muller, Stephen *o.c.s.o.* '06 (ROC)[J] Piffard, NY Abbey of the Genesee.
Muller, William H. *s.j.* '73 (LA)[D] Los Angeles, CA Verbum Dei High School; [F] In Res.
Mullet, John '56 (SAG) Outside the Diocese.
Mullet, John '91 (SP)[J] St. Petersburg, FL St. Anthony's Hospital, Inc.
Mullett, Rev. Msgr. Gene W. '76 (STU) Bellaire, OH St. John; Neffs, OH Sacred Heart; Judges.
Mulligan, Bede J.K. *o.carm.* '58 (GBG)[G] Bolivar, PA Mount Carmel Hermitage; Bolivar, PA.
Mulligan, Bertram *o.f.m.cap.* '49 (SFR)[N] Burlingame, CA Capuchin Provincial House Retired.
Mulligan, Rev. Msgr. Edward '56 (SP) Clearwater, FL St. Brendan Retired.
Mulligan, Gorge B. *c.s.c.* '82 (ORL)[F] Cocoa Beach, FL Congregation of Holy Cross, Eastern Province.
Mulligan, Rev. Msgr. James J. '61 (ALN) Censor of Books; Priestly Life and Ministry Office; Diocesan Medical Ethicist; Northampton, PA Queenship of Mary Parish.
Mulligan, James J. *s.t.l.* '66 (PH) Doylestown, PA Our Lady of Mount Carmel.
Mulligan, James *s.o.l.t.* '06 (CC)[G] Robstown, TX Society of Our Lady of the Most Holy Trinity.
Mulligan, James *s.o.l.t.* (PAT)[J] Branchville, NJ Sanctuary of Mary–Our Lady of the Holy Spirit.
Mulligan, John M. '64 (ROC) Rochester, NY; Vicars General; Judges; Priest Consultors; Rochester, NY Sacred Heart Cathedral Retired.
Mulligan, Rev. Msgr. John T. '64 (NY) Piermont, NY St. John the Baptist.
Mulligan, Joseph E. *s.j.* '73 (FgM)[K] Detroit Jesuit Provincial Office–Detroit Province of the Society of Jesus; Detroit, MI Detroit Province.
Mulligan, Joseph '75 (CHL) Boone, NC St. Elizabeth.
Mulligan, Paul F. '57 (BO) Senior Priests. Retired.
Mulligan, Robert G. *o.s.f.s.* '85 (PH)[Y] Philadelphia, PA Father Louis Brisson Residence.
Mulligan, Robert H. '90 (PH) Philadelphia, PA Holy Cross; Philadelphia, PA St. Madeleine Sophie.
Mulligan, William L. *s.j.* '65 (BO)[CC] Cambridge, MA The Youville House, Inc.; [U] Cambridge, MA Faber House.
Mullin, Douglas *o.s.b.* '07 (SCL)[B] Saint John's University; [I] Collegeville, MN St. John's Abbey, of the Order of St. Benedict.
Mullin, Edward J. *c.m.* '54 (STL)[O] Perryville, MO Congregation of the Mission.
Mullin, Henry *c.s.sp.* '59 (MIA) Fort Lauderdale, FL St. Clement.
Mullin, Hugh J. '46 (KC) Retired.
Mullin, John A. *s.j.* '75 (NEW)[C] Jersey City, NJ Jesuit Community; [M] Jersey City, NJ Jesuit Community of St. Peter's Prep, Inc.; [C] Jersey City, NJ St. Peter's Preparatory School.
Mullin, Patrick J. *c.m.* '75 (LA)[P] Santa Barbara, CA St. Mary's Evangelization Center; [V] Santa Barbara, CA St. Mary's Seminary Center.
Mullin, Thomas J. '65 (MO) DEPARTMENT OF VETERANS AFFAIRS HOSPITALS AND CHAPLAINS.
Mullin, Rev. Msgr. Thomas M. '75 (PH) Uwchlan, PA Saint Elizabeth; Pastors Review Board.
Mullin, Thomas '65 (BRK) Veterans Administration Medical Center.
Mullins, Kevin C. *o.s.a.* '90 (OAK) Castro Valley, CA Our Lady of Grace.
Mullins, Kevin *s.s.c.* '78 (OM)[K] St. Columbans Missionary Society of St. Columban; Council:.
Mullins, Michael E. '05 (ALN) Orefield, PA St. Joseph The Worker.
Mullins, Rev. Msgr. Raymond '52 (PT) Pensacola, FL Nativity of Our Lord Retired.
Mullins, Richard A. '95 (ARL) Alexandria, VA St. Louis; Defenders of the Bond.
Mullonkal, George '71 (SJP) Rossford, OH St. Michael; Presbyters.
Mulloth, Albi G. '98 (ALX) Judges.
Mullowney, Edward J. *s.s.j.* '55 (BAL)[S] Baltimore, MD St. Joseph's Manor.
Mullowney, Thomas E. '55 (GI) Retired.
Mulloy, James *s.d.b.* '85 (NY)[F] New Rochelle, NY Salesian High School.
Mulloy, John F. '70 (BO) Malden, MA St. Joseph.
Mulloy, Matthew '53 (NY)[EE] Bronx, NY Retired.
Mulloy, Michel '79 (RC) Rapid City, SD Cathedral of Our Lady of Perpetual Help; Diocesan Consultors.
Mulqueen, John D. '62 (Y) Retired.
Mulqueen, Rev. Msgr. Joseph C. '57 (BRK) Diocesan Judges Retired.
Mulqueen, Martin B. '74 (PMB) Palm City, FL Holy Redeemer.
Mulranen, Francis J. '82 (PH) Coatesville, PA St. Cecilia.
Mulrenan, Alexius J. *o.f.m.* '60 (SP)[N] St. Petersburg St. Anthony Friary Retired.
Mulroney, Joseph G. '93 (R) Promoter of Justice; Raleigh, NC St. Luke the Evangelist; Adjutant Vicar Judicial.
Mulrooney, Conan P. *o.praem.* '67 (GB)[J] De Pere, WI St. Norbert Abbey.
Mulroy, Timothy *s.s.c.* '95 (CHI)[N] Chicago, IL Columban Fathers Theologate.
Mulroy, Timothy *s.s.c.* '95 (OM)[K] St. Columbans Missionary Society of St. Columban.
Mulvanerty, Rev. Msgr. Thomas F. '79 (RVC)[M] Amityville, NY St. Pius X Residence; Ministry to Senior Priests; Priests' Retirement Board; [M] Amityville, NY St. Pius X Residence; Priests' Personnel Policy Board.
Mulvaney, Andrew R. '68 (OG) Black River, NY St. Paul; Black River, NY St. Rita.
Mulvaney, Francis '08 (BRK) Brooklyn, NY Our Lady of Perpetual Help Basilica.
Mulvaney, James J. '53 (BIR) Retired.
Mulvanity, Francis C. '51 (CLV) Retired.

Mulvany, Michael '88 (KCK) Lawrence, KS Corpus Christi.
Mulvehill, John R. '57 (BO) Cohasset, MA St. Anthony of Padua.
Mulvehill, Louis J. '53 (ALT) Retired.
Mulvey, Gerard *o.f.m.cap.* '91 (NOR) Middletown, CT St. Pius X.
Mulvey, John J. '62 (NEW) Retired.
Mulvihill, David J. '72 (CHI) Retired.
Mulvihill, John E. '64 (CHI) Highwood, IL St. James.
Mulvihill, Martin J. '83 (STL) Pacific, MO St. Bridget Church.
Mulvihill, Michael *c.s.sp.* '66 (BRK) Long Island City, NY Queen of Angels.
Muma, Sama F. '08 (DET) Presbyteral Council; Grosse Pointe Farms, MI St. Paul Catholic Church.
Mumar, Orencio '95 (TLS) Dewey, OK Our Lady of Guadalupe.
Mumba, David *s.o.l.t.* '09 (CC)[G] Robstown, TX Society of Our Lady of the Most Holy Trinity.
Mumper, Edward '63 (JOL) Retired.
Mundackal, Sebastian *o.s.b.* (STL) Fenton, MO St. Paul.
Mundadan, Joe '84 (FAR) Special Assignment.
Mundadan, Jose '84 (FAR) Fargo, ND Holy Spirit Church of Fargo.
Mundakal, Joseph *c.m.i.* '83 (NSH) Lawrenceburg, TN Sacred Heart.
Mundanmani, Paulson '91 (OAK) Walnut Creek, CA St. Mary; Presbyteral Council; Consultors.
Mundanmany, Jaison *c.m.i.* '00 (NY) Mt. Vernon, NY SS. Peter and Paul.
Mundwiller, Edmund *o.f.m.* '81 (STL)[O] St. Louis, MO Franciscan Friary of St. Anthony of Padua.
Mungovan, Reed *s.d.s.* '09 (NSH) Cookeville, TN St. Thomas Aquinas.
Mungujakisa, Alfred '94 (CAM) Brigantine, NJ St. Thomas' Catholic Church, Brigantine, N.J.
Muniz, Alberto '77 (PCE) Salinas, PR Our Lady of Monserrat.
Muniz, Kevin M. (SFD) Absent on Leave.
Muniz, Orlando Rosas '97 (MGZ) Maricao, PR St. John the Baptist.
Muniz, William '94 (MIA)[J] Fort Lauderdale, FL Holy Cross Hospital.
Munjanath, Mathews Kurian '92 (SYM) Phoenix, AZ Holy Family Syro–Malabar Catholic Church.
Munkday–Kukana, Raphael '07 (BRK) Astoria, NY St. Francis of Assisi.
Munkelt, Richard A. '01 (SCR) On Duty Outside the Diocese.
Munley, J. Thomas '93 (LAN) On Leave of Absence.
Munoz, Arcadio '76 (NEW) New Milford, NJ Ascension.
Munoz, Elbano *c.o.* '05 (CHR) York, SC Divine Saviour; [E] Rock Hill, SC Oratory of St. Philip Neri, Congregation of the Oratory of Pontifical Rite.
Munoz, F. Javier '96 (ATL) Atlanta, GA Holy Cross.
Munoz, Jesus M. '01 (ARE) On Duty Outside the Diocese.
Munoz, Jose *o.m.* '82 (CGS) Cayey, PR Nuestra Senora de la Asuncion.
Munoz, Jose '96 (ORL) Orlando, FL St. Isaac Jogues.
Munoz, Juan Francisco *s.d.b.* '73 (LAR) Laredo, TX San Luis Rey.
Munoz, Manuel '98 (ELP) Absent on Leave.
Munoz, Matthew '02 (ORG) Cypress, CA St. Irenaeus.
Munoz, Mauro '91 (ELP)[B] El Paso, TX St. Anthony's School of Theology.
Munoz, Octavio '04 (CHI) Casa Jesus; Chicago, IL Seminary Formation House–Casa Jesus.
Munoz, Oscar '97 (NY) Bronx, NY Our Lady of Mt. Carmel.
Munoz, Rafael '60 (PCE) On Duty Outside the Diocese.
Munoz, Ruben '05 (GAY) Traverse City, MI Immaculate Conception.
Munoz, Theodore G. *s.j.* '83 (CHI)[N] Chicago, IL Chicago Province of the Society of Jesus–Provincial Office.
Munoz, Tomas G. '85 (TUC) Wellton, AZ Saint Joseph the Worker Roman Catholic Parish - Wellton.
Munoz–Capetillo, Octavio '04 (CHI) Other Assignments.
Munoz–Lasalle, Jesus M. '01 (MO) Army Reserve Chaplains.
Munoz–Sanchez, Ariel *o.r.c.* '97 (STO) Ceres, CA St. Jude Church (Pastor of).
Munro, Donald '87 (PMB) Wellington, FL St. Rita.
Munroe, Rev. Msgr. Henry T. '53 (FR) Retired.
Munsch, Christopher Louis '01 (BLX) Lakeshore, MS St. Ann.
Munsch, Nathan J. *o.s.b.* '91 (GBG)[G] Latrobe, PA Saint Vincent Archabbey.
Munsch, Nathan *o.s.b.* (ALT) West Salisbury, PA St. Michael's.
Munsell, Richard F. '79 (GF) Leave of Absence.
Munshower, William G. '58 (IND)[D] Indianapolis, IN Cathedral High School (Cathedral Trustees, Inc.) Retired.
Muntone, Rev. Msgr. Anthony D. *s.t.l.* '64 (ALN) Whitehall, PA St. Elizabeth.
Munz, Theodore G. *s.j.* '83 (CHI) Chicago, IL; Detroit, MI; [N] Evanston, IL Canisius House.
Munz, Theodore G. *s.j.* '83 (DET)[K] Chicago, IL Jesuit Provincial Office–Detroit Province of the Society of Jesus.
Munzing, Joel *o.f.m.* '47 (PAT)[N] Ringwood, NJ Holy Name Friary, Inc.
Muodiaju, Samuel *c.s.sp.* '85 (MIA) Miami Gardens, FL St. Monica.
Muoneke, Romanus O. '74 (GAL) Houston, TX St. Peter Claver.
Muorah, Charles '91 (TR) Medford, NJ St. Mary of the Lakes.
Muppala, Anthony '85 (CC) Corpus Christi, TX Holy Cross.
Mupparathara, Abraham J. *m.c.b.s.* '94 (MAR) Calumet, MI Our Lady of Peace; Calumet, MI Sacred Heart; Calumet, MI St. Paul the Apostle.
Mur, Rev. Msgr. Rogelio *o.carm.* '56 (MGZ) For Pastoral; Diocesan Consultors; Diocesan Board of Administration; Parish Priests Consultors; Development and Planification.
Murasso, Jeremiah N. '79 (HRT) South Windsor, CT St. Francis of Assisi.
Murawka, Slawomir *s.ch.* '94 (DET) Sterling Heights, MI Our Lady of Czestochowa.
Murcko, Rev. Msgr. Charles S. '52 (E) Mercer, PA State Correctional Facility; Mercer, PA Immaculate Heart Retired.
Murd, Francis A. '76 (TOL)[J] Tiffin, OH St. Francis Convent.
Murdock, Paul J. '75 (NOR) Windham, CT Sagrado Corazon de Jesus; Iglesia del Sagrado Corazon de Jesus; Liturgical Commission; Members.
Murhammer, Francis J. '88 (PIT) Pittsburgh, PA St. Margaret.
Murhula, Kafarhire *s.j.* '06 (CHI)[C] Chicago, IL Jesuit Community at Loyola University Chicago.
Murin, Frantisek '04 (VNN) Sacramento, CA St. Philip the Apostle.
Murnan, Sean *o.f.m.* '73 (GLP) Zuni, NM St. Anthony, Our Lady of Guadalupe; Councilors:.
Murnane, Patrick J. '60 (MIA) Hollywood, FL Nativity.
Murnane, Theodore *s.v.d.* '59 (FgM) Techny, IL.
Murnane, Thomas M. *o.s.a.* '65 (PH)[Y] Villanova, PA St. Thomas Monastery.
Murnane, Thomas *o.s.a.* '61 (PH)[C] Villanova University.
Muro, Jose Luis '01 (SD) Brawley, CA St. Margaret Mary.
Muro, Rev. Msgr. Victor S. '66 (CAM)[O] Vineland, NJ Pope John Paul II Retreat Center; Vicar for Hispanics; Ex Officio Members; Vineland, NJ Divine Mercy, Vineland, N.J.
Muroko, Peter (CC)[D] Corpus Christi, TX CHRISTUS Spohn Hospital Corpus Christi – Shoreline.
Murphy, Rev. Msgr. A. Robert '74 (KC) Administrative Committee; Special Assignment; Vicar General; Consultors; Permanent Diaconate.
Murphy, Alfred E. *o.s.a.* '56 (PH)[Y] Villanova, PA St. Augustine Friary.
Murphy, Arthur J. '55 (HRT) West Hartford, CT St. Thomas the Apostle.
Murphy, Austin *o.s.b.* '04 (JOL)[L] Lisle, IL St. Procopius Abbey.
Murphy, Austin *o.s.b.* (FTW)[A] Notre Dame, IN Moreau Seminary.
Murphy, Bartholomew J. *s.j.* '72 (FgM)[L] Portland Jesuit Provincial Office (Society of Jesus, Oregon Prov.); Portland, OR Society of Jesus.
Murphy, Bernard Marie *c.f.r.* '98 (NY)[BB] Bronx, NY St. Elizabeth House; Bronx, NY; [II] Bronx, NY Franciscan Mission Outreach, Inc.; [EE] Bronx, NY Franciscan Friars of the Renewal; [II] Bronx, NY Franciscan Renewal Ministries, Inc.; [EE] Bronx, NY Saint Lawrence Friary.
Murphy, Brendan *o.p.* '00 (PRO)[B] Providence, RI Providence College.
Murphy, Charles J. '60 (BO) Weymouth, MA St. Francis Xavier.
Murphy, Rev. Msgr. Charles M. '61 (PRT) Diaconate Retired.
Murphy, Charles R. '91 (OKL) Oklahoma City, OK St. Francis of Assisi; Council of Priests Archdiocesan.
Murphy, Charles R. '91 (OKL) Personnel Committee.
Murphy, Christopher D. '96 (ARL) Doral, FL San Francisco de Asis, Banica; Doral, FL San Jose, Pedro Santana; On Duty Outside the Diocese.
Murphy, Clarence '47 (FR) Retired.
Murphy, Rev. Msgr. D. Declan '49 (MRY) Retired.
Murphy, Daniel G. '56 (SY)[Q] Binghamton, NY McDevitt Residence for Retired Priests; Pastoral Examiners Retired.
Murphy, Daniel J. '56 (DET) Retired.
Murphy, Daniel S. '70 (BRK) Brooklyn, NY St. Saviour.
Murphy, Daniel T. '62 (MIL) Retired.
Murphy, Daniel W. '73 (PAT) Randolph, NJ St. Matthew the Apostle.
Murphy, David Brendan *o.p.* '00 (PRO)[P] Providence St. Thomas Aquinas Priory at Providence College.
Murphy, David C. '63 (BO) Senior Priests. Retired.
Murphy, David F. '87 (WIL) New Castle, DE; Army National Guard Chaplains; Wilmington, DE St. Joseph on the Brandywine.
Murphy, David M. '53 (ROC) Retired.
Murphy, Declan (SAC)[B] Sacramento, CA University of Sacramento.
Murphy, Dennis '75 (ALB) Members; Schenectady, NY St. Paul the Apostle.
Murphy, Dennis '74 (RIC) Retired.
Murphy, Dominic Sario M. *f.i.* '03 (FR)[G] New Bedford, MA Marian Friary of Our Lady, Queen of the Seraphic Order.
Murphy, Edward A. '98 (FR) Morton Hospital; Diocesan Liaison with Charismatic Groups; Taunton, MA St. Jude the Apostle.
Murphy, Edward F. *c.m.* '79 (STL)[L] St. Louis, MO Guardian Angel Settlement Association; [O] St. Louis, MO Vincentian Residence.
Murphy, Edward J. *s.j.* '68 (NY)[EE] New York, NY Murray–Weigel Hall.
Murphy, Edward W. '92 (STA) Scouts; Jacksonville, FL Immaculate Conception.
Murphy, Emmet *o.f.m.* '86 (PAT)[N] Butler, NJ St. Anthony Friary.
Murphy, Eoin '64 (LAN) St. Johns, MI St. Joseph.
Murphy, Rev. Msgr. Eugene F. '52 (RVC) Mineola, NY Corpus Christi Retired.
Murphy, Rev. Msgr. Francis A. '57 (ANC) Retired.
Murphy, Rev. Msgr. Francis C. '46 (MOB) Mobile, AL St. Dominic Retired.
Murphy, Francis J. *c.s.c.* '86 (FTW)[H] Notre Dame Congregation of Holy Cross, Indiana Province, Provincial House; Provincial Councilors:, [H] Notre Dame, IN Congregation of Holy Cross, Indiana Province, Provincial House.
Murphy, Francis J. '66 (GAY) Cadillac, MI St. Ann; Cadillac, MI St. Edward; Lake City, MI St. Stephen; Lake City, MI St. Theresa; Vicar General; Finance Council, Diocesan.
Murphy, Francis J. '51 (LIN) Retired.
Murphy, Francis J. *s.j.* '56 (STL)[O] St. Louis, MO Jesuit Community Corporation at Saint Louis University – Jesuit Hall.
Murphy, Rev. Msgr. Francis '46 (MOB) Retired.
Murphy, Francis *c.s.c.* '86 (P)[B] University of Portland; [L] Portland, OR Holy Cross Fathers & Brothers, C.S.C. – University of Portland.
Murphy, Rev. Msgr. Frederick J. '57 (BO) Senior Priests.; Danvers, MA St. Mary of the Annunciation Retired.
Murphy, G. Ronald *s.j.* '69 (WDC)[N] Washington, DC The Jesuit Community at Georgetown University.
Murphy, George E. '66 (BLX) Gulfport, MS St. Joseph Catholic Church.
Murphy, George R. *s.j.* '71 (OAK)[A] Berkeley, CA Jesuit School of Theology at Santa Clara University; [M] Berkeley, CA Jesuit Fathers and Brothers; [A] Berkeley, CA Jesuit School of Theology at Santa Clara University.
Murphy, Rt. Rev. Archimandrite Gerasimos '67 (NTN) Judicial Vicar.
Murphy, H. Joseph '61 (BO) Senior Priests. Retired.
Murphy, Harold B. '68 (CHI) Chicago, IL St. Margaret Mary Retired.
Murphy, Harry J. '40 (GBG) Retired.
Murphy, Hugh P. '71 (PAT) Mount Arlington, NJ Our Lady of the Lake.
Murphy, J. Patrick *c.m.* '76 (CHI)[N] Chicago, IL Vincentian Community, Congregation of the Mission, Western Province.
Murphy, J. Wayne '65 (L) Defenders of the Bond Retired.
Murphy, James E. '55 (GI) Retired.
Murphy, James E. '52 (STL) Retired.
Murphy, James F. '70 (PIT) Butler, PA St. Fidelis of Sigmaringen.
Murphy, James G. *s.j.* '64 (CHI)[C] Chicago, IL Jesuit Community at Loyola University Chicago.
Murphy, James H. '81 (MAD) Briggsville, WI St. Mary Help of Christians; Portage, WI St. Mary of the Immaculate Conception; Elected.
Murphy, James J. '45 (PH) Retired.
Murphy, James J. '54 (WH) Retired.
Murphy, James P. '65 (CHI) Retired.
Murphy, Rev. Msgr. James T. '68 (SAC) Presbyteral Council.
Murphy, James W. '48 (MEM) Retired.
Murphy, James Wayne '65 (L) Retired.
Murphy, James '78 (JOL) Elmhurst, IL Immaculate Conception.
Murphy, James '70 (MIA) Miami Lakes, FL Our Lady of the Lakes; Incardination Committee.
Murphy, Rev. Msgr. James '68 (SAC) Moderator of the Curia; Vicar General; Ex Officio; Sacramento, CA Cathedral of the Blessed Sacrament.
Murphy, James *c.s.c.* '58 (ORL)[F] Cocoa Beach, FL Congregation of Holy Cross, Eastern Province.
Murphy, James *c.m.* '85 (CHI)[N] Chicago, IL Vincentian Community, Congregation of the Mission, Western Province.
Murphy, Rev. Msgr. Jeremiah '63 (LA) West Hollywood, CA St. Victor.

Murphy, John C. '65 (SP) Dade City, FL Sacred Heart.
Murphy, John D. *s.j.* '77 (LA)[C] Los Angeles, CA Jesuit Community.
Murphy, John F. '59 (CLV)[A] Wickliffe, OH Borromeo Seminary Retired.
Murphy, John J. '68 (DEN) On Duty Outside the Archdiocese.
Murphy, John J. '68 (E) Eldred, PA St. Raphael; Shinglehouse, PA St. Theresa.
Murphy, Rev. Msgr. John P. '64 (ALN) Allentown, PA St. Thomas More; Pontifical Mission Societies in the United States; Elected Members; College of Consultors; Operation Rice Bowl.
Murphy, John P. *s.j.* '69 (CIN) Cincinnati, OH St. Francis Xavier.
Murphy, Rev. Msgr. John R. '73 (OG) Episcopal Vicar for Pastoral Services and Moderator of the Curia; Advocates; Committee on Assignments; Ogdensburg, NY Notre Dame.
Murphy, John Thaddeus *o.p.* '54 (NY) New York, NY St. Catherine of Siena; [EE] New York, NY St. Catherine of Siena Priory.
Murphy, John V. *s.j.* '52 (P)[L] Portland, OR Colombiere Community.
Murphy, John '94 (ATL) McDonough, GA St. James the Apostle.
Murphy, John *f.m.s.i.* '72 (BO)[B] Framingham, MA Sylva Maria; Framingham, MA.
Murphy, John '57 (ALB) Retired.
Murphy, Joseph A. *s.j.* '73 (COL)[A] Columbus, OH Pontifical College Josephinum.
Murphy, Joseph E. '61 (PAT)[Q] Chester, NJ Nazareth Village; Totowa, NJ St. James of the Marches Retired.
Murphy, Joseph G. '44 (HRT) Retired.
Murphy, Joseph H. '61 (NEW) Retired.
Murphy, Rev. Msgr. Joseph P. '54 (NY)[II] Staten Island, NY Emmaus Ministries, Ltd.
Murphy, Joseph T. '47 (PH) Retired.
Murphy, Joseph V. '67 (GRY) Crown Point, IN Holy Spirit.
Murphy, Jude *o.f.m.* '61 (PAT) Butler, NJ St. Anthony.
Murphy, Kenneth R. '86 (MET) Sayreville, NJ St. Stanislaus Kostka.
Murphy, Kevin F. '81 (NEW) Scotch Plains, NJ St. Bartholomew; [P] Teaneck, NJ Fairleigh Dickinson Univ.–Teaneck Campus.
Murphy, Kevin J. *o.s.b.* '62 (MIL)[P] Benet Lake, WI St. Benedict's Abbey.
Murphy, Kevin P. '68 (ROC) Pittsford, NY St. Louis.
Murphy, Laurence T. *m.m.* '54 (NY)[EE] Retired.
Murphy, Laurence *m.m.* '54 (MET)[I] Somerset, NJ Maria Regina Residence Retired.
Murphy, Lawrence J. *c.ss.r.* '49 (NY)[EE] New York, NY Redemptorist Priests and Brothers, C.Ss.R.
Murphy, Louis Eugene *s.t.* '60 (WDC)[N] Riverdale, MD Holy Spirit Missionary Cenacle.
Murphy, Michael A. '92 (BAL) Special Assignment.
Murphy, Rev. Msgr. Michael D. '66 (LAN) Bishop's Office; College of Consultors; Moderator of the Curia; Victim Assistance Coordinator.
Murphy, Michael D. '77 (PH) Drexel Hill, PA St. Dorothy.
Murphy, Michael F. '83 (SD) Coronado, CA Sacred Heart.
Murphy, Michael G. '87 (STL) Webster Groves, MO Holy Redeemer.
Murphy, Michael P. '89 (JC) Macon, MO Immaculate Conception; Diocesan Consultors; IV. Kirksville; Senators.
Murphy, Michael '83 (SD) Priests; Presbyteral Council.
Murphy, Myles P. *s.t.l.* '90 (NY) New York, NY St. Michael.
Murphy, Owen *s.a.* '52 (NY)[EE] Garrison, NY Franciscan Friars of the Atonement Retired.
Murphy, Owen *s.a.* '52 (PAT)[N] Ringwood, NJ Holy Name Friary, Inc.
Murphy, Patrick E. '85 (MAR) On Duty Outside the Diocese; DEPARTMENT OF VETERANS AFFAIRS HOSPITALS AND CHAPLAINS.
Murphy, Patrick F. '67 (LIN) Manley, NE St. Patrick's.
Murphy, Patrick J. '97 (SD) Clergy Personnel Board; San Diego, CA Our Lady of Mt. Carmel.
Murphy, Patrick L. *s.j.* '67 (MIL)[P] Milwaukee Jesuit Provincial Office, Wisconsin Province.
Murphy, Patrick *c.s.* '80 (KCK) Hispanic Ministry.
Murphy, Patrick *c.s.* (KC) Kansas City, MO Holy Rosary.
Murphy, Patrick '04 (JOL) Hinsdale, IL St. Isaac Jogues.
Murphy, Paul M. *c.m.* (BAL) Emmitsburg, MD St. Joseph; [S] Emmitsburg, MD Vincentian House.
Murphy, Paul P. '78 (MRY) Pacific Grove, CA St. Angela Merici Church; Vicar for Clergy; Diocesan Consultors; Clergy Life & Ministry; Clergy Life and Ministry Board; Clergy Personnel Board; Presbyteral Council; Diocesan Consultors.
Murphy, Paul '96 (BGP) Sherman, CT Holy Trinity.
Murphy, Paul '94 (BGP) Presbyteral Council.
Murphy, Peter P. '68 (PIT) Wexford, PA St. Alphonsus.
Murphy, Ralph *s.d.b.* '56 (SFR)[N] San Francisco, CA Salesian Provincial Residence.
Murphy, Richard D. '96 (BGP) Stratford, CT Our Lady of Peace.
Murphy, Rev. Msgr. Richard J. '73 (BAL) Frederick, MD St. John the Evangelist.
Murphy, Richard M. '65 (ROC)[M] Auburn, NY New York Chiropractic College Retired.
Murphy, Richard '65 (PMB) Vero Beach, FL Holy Cross; [K] Diocesan Property & Liability Insurance Committee; Consultors; Building, Construction, Real Estate Office; Real Estate.
Murphy, Richard '65 (ROC) Auburn, NY St. Francis of Assisi; Auburn, NY St. Hyacinth.
Murphy, Richard '80 (Y) Mineral Ridge, OH St. Mary.
Murphy, Richard '57 (PMB) Retired.
Murphy, Robert A. '93 (NOR) Building Commission.
Murphy, Robert J. *s.j.* '54 (DET)[K] Clarkston, MI Colombiere Center.
Murphy, Rev. Msgr. Robert '74 (KC) Pleasant Hill, MO St. Bridget.
Murphy, Robert *m.s.a.* '93 (NOR) Chester, CT St. Joseph; [G] Cromwell, CT Society of the Missionaries of the Holy Apostles.
Murphy, Robert '93 (VEN) Naples, FL St. William.
Murphy, Rory E. '88 (SFR)[J] Daly City, CA Seton Medical Center; Seton Hospital.
Murphy, T. Austin '03 (BAL) Towson, MD Church of the Immaculate Conception; Special Assignment.
Murphy, T. Austin '03 (BAL)[U] Baltimore, MD Archdiocesan Office–Newman Center; [U] Baltimore, MD Towson University.
Murphy, Theodore *s.m.m.* '58 (RVC)[M] Bay Shore, NY Montfort Missionaries Retired.
Murphy, Thomas E. *o.s.f.s.* '76 (ARL) Reston, VA St. John Neumann.
Murphy, Thomas J. '85 (IND) Retired.
Murphy, Thomas J. '87 (SAV) Hinesville, GA St. Stephen, First Martyr; Presbyteral Council.
Murphy, Thomas K. *o.f.m.* '58 (SP)[N] St. Petersburg St. Anthony Friary.
Murphy, Thomas M. '79 (PRT) Diocesan Priests' Benefit Plan – Trustees; Wells, ME Holy Spirit Parish.
Murphy, Thomas P. *c.s.p.* '62 (NY)[EE] Jamaica Estates Paulist Fathers Generalate; [EE] Jamaica Estates Paulist Fathers Generalate.
Murphy, Thomas R. '36 (PIT) Retired.
Murphy, Thomas R. E. *s.j.* '99 (BO)[U] Boston The Society of Jesus of New England–Provincial Offices.
Murphy, Thomas R.E. *s.j.* '99 (SEA)[A] Seattle, WA Seattle University; [L] Seattle, WA Arrupe Jesuit Community at Seattle University.
Murphy, Thomas *o.f.m.cap.* '71 (NY) Yonkers, NY Sacred Heart; Yonkers, NY St. Joseph's Medical Center; [X] Yonkers, NY St. Joseph's Medical Center.
Murphy, Thomas *s.j.* '57 (NY)[EE] Loyola Hall, Jesuit Community.
Murphy, Rev. Msgr. Thomas '66 (SAT) Defenders of the Bond; San Antonio, TX; [K] San Antonio, TX Casa De Padres; College of Consultors Retired.
Murphy, Timothy J. '63 (BO) Salem, MA Immaculate Conception.
Murphy, Timothy J. '74 (SPR) Hampden, MA St. Mary's; Permanent Diaconate; Diocesan Diaconate Formation Board.
Murphy, Timothy '67 (P)[C] Portland, OR Central Catholic High School.
Murphy, Timothy '60 (VEN) Retired.
Murphy, Timothy '93 (JKS) Pontotoc, MS St. Christopher.
Murphy, Timothy '67 (P) Portland, OR St. Patrick.
Murphy, Tommy *s.s.c.* (FgM).
Murphy, Ultan P. '53 (DOD) Olmitz, KS St. Ann Catholic Church of Olmitz, Kansas.
Murphy, Venard *o.f.m.* '61 (SP)[N] St. Petersburg, FL St. Anthony Friary.
Murphy, Rev. Msgr. Walter C. '58 (BRK)[T] Douglaston, NY Bishop Mugavero Residence; Courage Ministry; Accountants Retired.
Murphy, Warren L. *t.o.r.* '60 (FWT) Fort Worth, TX St. Andrew.
Murphy, William F. '88 (BO) Cambridge, MA St. Paul; [AA] Cambridge, MA Harvard Catholic Student Center.
Murphy, William F. '56 (PRO)[P] Providence St. John Vianney Residence Retired.
Murphy, William F. (COL)[A] Columbus, OH Pontifical College Josephinum.
Murphy, William J. '96 (SUP) Hammond, WI St. John the Baptist; Hammond, WI Immaculate Conception; Hammond, WI St. Bridget; Board of Directors.
Murphy, William J. '57 (DET) Retired.
Murphy, William P. '86 (SPR) Great Barrington, MA St. Peter's; Housatonic, MA Blessed Teresa of Calcutta Parish.
Murphy, William S. '90 (PH) Norristown, PA St. Patrick.
Murphy, William T. '50 (RVC) Retired.
Murphy, William *c.p.* '73 (BAL) Baltimore, MD St. Joseph Passionist Monastery Parish; [S] Baltimore, MD St. Joseph's Passionist Community.
Murphy, William *s.j.* '08 (CLV)[D] Cleveland, OH St. Ignatius High School.
Murphy–O'Connor, James (FTW)[B] University of Notre Dame Du Lac.
Murray, Brendan J. '68 (PAT) Dover, NJ Sacred Heart; Dover, NJ Our Lady Queen of the Most Holy Rosary.
Murray, Charles A. *m.m.* '51 (SJ)[M] Los Altos, CA Maryknoll.
Murray, Cornelius J. '63 (CLV) North Olmsted, OH St. Brendan Retired.
Murray, Cyprian *o.f.m.cap.* '64 (NY) Yonkers, NY Sacred Heart.
Murray, Rev. Msgr. Daniel A. '64 (PH) North Wales, PA St. Rose of Lima.
Murray, Rev. Msgr. Daniel J. '73 (ORG) Administrative Leave.
Murray, Daniel L. '86 (WIN) Absent on Leave.
Murray, Donald J. '61 (MAD) Retired.
Murray, Donnon P. *o.f.m.* '56 (FgM) New York, NY Holy Name Province.
Murray, Edward K. '62 (SFR) St. Mary's Medical Center; [J] San Francisco, CA St. Mary's Medical Center; San Francisco, CA St. Stephen.
Murray, Eugene M. *m.m.* '58 (FgM) Maryknoll, NY MARYKNOLL.
Murray, Francis J. '51 (LAN) Retired.
Murray, Francis K. '53 (SFR)[S] San Francisco, CA Italian Catholic Federation Retired.
Murray, Frank J. '81 (PRT) Ex Officio Members; Seminarians; Bath, ME All Saints Parish.
Murray, Frank K. '53 (SFR) Burlingame, CA St. Catherine of Siena Retired.
Murray, Frank '81 (PRT) Pastoral Associates.
Murray, George B. *s.j.* '65 (BO)[U] Weston, MA Campion Jesuit Community.
Murray, Gerald E. '84 (NY) New York, NY St. Vincent de Paul; Legion of Mary.
Murray, Rev. Msgr. Ignatius L. '57 (PH) Norristown, PA Visitation B.V.M. Retired.
Murray, J–Glenn *s.j.* '79 (WDC)[N] Washington, DC The Jesuit Community of St. Aloysius Gonzaga; Washington, DC St. Aloysius.
Murray, James B. '57 (NSH) Retired.
Murray, Rev. Msgr. James H. '56 (PAT) Retired.
Murray, James M. *o.s.b.* '93 (PEO)[A] Peru, IL St. Bede Abbey.
Murray, James Stephen *o.p.* '50 (L) Springfield, KY St. Rose; [M] St. Catharine, KY Sansbury Care Center, Inc.
Murray, John A. '62 (BO) Senior Priests. Retired.
Murray, John A. '54 (Y) Retired.
Murray, John C. *c.s.b.* '57 (ROC)[J] Rochester, NY Basilian Residence.
Murray, John D. '62 (LA) Burbank, CA St. Francis Xavier Retired.
Murray, John E. '63 (HEL) Retired.
Murray, John F. *c.ss.r.* '73 (TR)[R] Long Branch, NJ San Alfonso Retreat House.
Murray, John F. *c.ss.r.* '94 (ORL) New Smyrna Beach, FL Sacred Heart.
Murray, John Francis *s.m.a.* '57 (NEW)[M] Tenafly, NJ Society of African Missions, Provincialate, S.M.A. Fathers.
Murray, John M. '98 (FR) Attleboro, MA St. Joseph's; Attleboro, MA Holy Ghost; Attleboro.
Murray, John M. '98 (FR) South Yarmouth, MA St. Pius Tenth.
Murray, John P. *s.j.* '87 (BO)[U] Newton, MA The Jesuit Community at Boston College.
Murray, John P. '54 (RVC) Retired.
Murray, John S. '69 (ORL) New Smyrna Beach, FL Our Lady Star of the Sea.
Murray, John W. '68 (CHI) Retired.
Murray, John *c.ss.r.* '94 (NY)[GG] Esopus, NY Mount St. Alphonsus Redemptorist Retreat Center.
Murray, John *c.s.b.* '67 (ROC)[N] Rochester, NY Marriage Encounter Apostolate.
Murray, John '60 (CHY) Retired.
Murray, Rev. Msgr. Joseph W. '61 (PH) King of Prussia, PA Mother of Divine Providence Retired.
Murray, Kevin P. '77 (PH) Rydal, PA St. Hilary of Poitiers.
Murray, Kevin R. *c.ss.r.* '86 (PH) Philadelphia, PA Visitation B.V.M.
Murray, Leo A. *s.j.* '62 (WDC) Washington, DC Holy Trinity.
Murray, Maurice M. *s.j.* '66 (FgM) St. Louis, MO Society of Jesus.
Murray, Rev. Msgr. Michael J. '76 (WDC) Special Ministries.
Murray, Michael S. *o.s.f.s.* '86 (WIL)[J] Wilmington, DE DeSales House; [M] Wilmington, DE De Sales Spirituality Center.
Murray, Paul G. '09 (PRT) Waterville, ME Corpus Christi Parish; Waterville, ME Corpus Christi Parish.
Murray, Peter J. *s.j.* '72 (ALB)[N] Fultonville, NY Shrine of Our Lady of Martyrs; Special Assignment.
Murray, Rev. Msgr. Richard Hayes '43 (LA) Woodland Hills, CA St. Bernardine of Siena Retired.

Murray, Robert J. *o.s.a.* '83 (PH)[C] Villanova University; [Y] Villanova, PA St. Thomas Monastery.
Murray, Robert W. '88 (BO) Haverhill, MA St. James.
Murray, Russel T. *o.f.m.* '98 (WDC)[N] Silver Spring, MD Gemelli House.
Murray, Rev. Msgr. Sean '52 (SD) San Diego, CA St. Brigid Retired.
Murray, Stan '69 (ORL) Deans; Ex Officio Members.
Murray, Steven J. '00 (PBL) Gunnison, CO Queen of All Saints; Gunnison, CO St. Peter.
Murray, Steven M. '88 (OG) Watertown, NY Holy Family.
Murray, Rev. Msgr. Thomas A. '68 (PH) Norristown, PA Visitation B.V.M.
Murray, Thomas F. '57 (BO) Senior Priests. Retired.
Murray, Thomas P. '81 (RVC) Greenport, NY St. Agnes.
Murray, Thomas (RVC) Shelter Island Heights, NY Our Lady of the Isle.
Murray, Trevor '01 (BEL) Royalton, IL St. Aloysius/Sacred Heart.
Murray, Rev. Msgr. William C. '55 (CC) Robstown, TX St. Anthony.
Murray, Rev. Msgr. William F. '45 (PRO) Retired.
Murray, William F. '54 (MIL) Retired.
Murrillo, Juan Pedro *o.f.m.* '95 (ELP)[B] El Paso, TX Roger Bacon College.
Murrin, Donald L. *s.v.d.* '60 (LR) Pine Bluff, AR St. Peter.
Murrin, Raymond J. '57 (BIR) Retired.
Murrin, Robert '99 (MRY) Boulder Creek, CA St. Michael.
Murrman, Jonathan J. *o.s.b.* '65 (GBG)[G] Latrobe, PA Saint Vincent Archabbey.
Murrman, Warren D. *o.s.b.* '65 (GBG)[G] Latrobe, PA Saint Vincent Archabbey.
Murry, Trevor K. '01 (BEL) Diocesan Consultors; West Frankfort, IL St. John the Baptist; Co Directors.
Murtagh, Henry Paul *ss.cc.* '67 (LA)[P] La Verne, CA Congregation of the Sacred Hearts of Jesus and Mary.
Murtagh, James '66 (PMB) West Palm Beach, FL St. Ann; Consultors.
Murtagh, John J. '69 (YAK) Moxee, WA Holy Rosary.
Murtagh, Paul *ss.cc.* '67 (LSC) Artesia, NM Our Lady of Grace; Vicars; Presbyteral Council; Artesia, NM St. Anthony.
Murtaugh, Lewis C. *s.j.* '69 (CHI)[N] Chicago Chicago Province of the Society of Jesus–Provincial Office.
Murtaugh, William A. '72 (STP) Deanery 8; [G] Eagan, MN Faithful Shepherd Catholic School; Eagan, MN St. Thomas Becket.
Murtha, Chester '93 (SFS) Miller, SD St. Ann.
Murtha, John *o.s.b.* '57 (GBG)[G] Latrobe, PA Saint Vincent Archabbey.
Muruli, Martin R. '98 (SFR) San Francisco, CA Star of the Sea.
Musa, Sebastian (BO) Brookline, MA St. Mary of the Assumption.
Musans, Pascal Rumb *s.j.* '09 (BO)[U] Cambridge, MA Rahner House.
Muscalino, Daniel C. '78 (SY) Syracuse, NY St. John the Baptist; Truxton, NY St. Patrick; Special Assignment.
Musco, Joseph '06 (SP) Tampa, FL St. Paul; Elected Parochial Vicars.
Muscolino, Frank J. '68 (BIR) Retired.
Mushalla, Walter '98 (SAT) Somerset, TX Retired.
Mushi, Peter *a.j.* '87 (NY) New York, NY St. Cecilia; Bronx, NY St. Angela Merici.
Mushinsky, John E. (PAT) Retired.
Musial, George '67 (CHI)[N] Chicago, IL St. Peter's Friary.
Musico, Edwin '85 (STO) Stockton, CA St. George Church (Pastor of).
Musinguzi, John Bosco '00 (LA) North Hills, CA Our Lady of Peace; [J] Mission Hills, CA Providence Holy Cross Medical Center.
Musiol, Josef *s.d.s.* '72 (SAT)[L] Falls City, TX Salvatorian Fathers Community of Texas.
Musiol, Jozef *s.d.s.* '72 (AUS) Smithville, TX St. Paul the Apostle; Adjutant Judicial Vicar; Defenders of the Bond.
Musonda, Francis M. *s.s.* '96 (BAL)[S] Baltimore Society of St. Sulpice, Province of the United States.
Musselman, Randall '09 (MIA) Davie, FL St. David.
Mussett, Peter '06 (DEN) Boulder, CO St. Thomas Aquinas.
Musso, David D. *s.m.* '98 (ATL)[D] Atlanta, GA Marist School.
Mustaciuolo, Rev. Msgr. Gregory '90 (NY) New York, NY; Chancellor and Moderator of the Curia; Archdiocesan Consultors.
Musuande, Salvatore *a.a.* '00 (WOR)[O] Worcester, MA Assumptionists of Assumption College.
Musula, Charles E. '07 (CHI) Park Ridge, IL St. Paul of the Cross.
Musumbu, Gilbert Malu '88 (TUC) Douglas, AZ Immaculate Conception Roman Catholic Parish – Douglas; Douglas, AZ Saint Luke Roman Catholic Church – Douglas; Pirtleville, AZ Saint Bernard Roman Catholic Church – Pirtleville; [G] Douglas, AZ Cochise Community College.
Musumeci, James S. '76 (BRK) Released from Diocesan Assignment.
Musuubire, Gerald F. '06 (RIC) Palmyra, VA Ss. Peter & Paul.
Muszkiewicz, Joseph '08 (GAY) Manistee, MI St. Joseph; Manistee, MI Guardian Angels; Manistee, MI St. Mary of Mt. Carmel Shrine.
Muteru, Gabriel '87 (RVC) Roosevelt, NY Queen of the Most Holy Rosary.
Muth, Joseph L. '74 (BAL) Baltimore, MD St. Matthew; [V] Baltimore, MD St. Matthew's Parish Endowment Trust.
Muth, Stephen '82 (PRM) Sugar Creek, MO St. Luke, Byzantine Catholic Parish.
Muthaya, Aloysius *s.a.c.* '76 (FWT) Pilot Point, TX St. Thomas Aquinas.
Mutholath, Abraham '80 (SYM) Eparchial Consultors.
Mutholathu, Abraham '83 (SYM) Maywood, IL Sacred Heart Knanaya Catholic Parish.
Muthu, Anthony Savari '90 (CAM) Cape May Court House, NJ The Church of Our Lady of the Angels, Cape May Court House, N.J.
Muthu, Anthony *h.g.n.* (LEX) Louisa, KY St. Jude.
Muthu, Stanislau '80 (DAL) Dallas, TX All Saints.
Muthukatti, Thomas '66 (BRK) South Richmond Hill, NY St. Benedict Joseph Labre Retired.
Muthuplackal, Joseph *o.ss.t.* '04 (BAL)[S] The Trinitarians in India (Bangalore & Trichur).
Mutibula, Richard Tambwe *s.j.* '09 (OAK)[M] Berkeley, CA Jesuit Fathers and Brothers.
Mutsko, Frank J. '00 (ORL) Lady Lake, FL Retired.
Muwanga, Godfrey '84 (RC) Bonesteel, SD Immaculate Conception; Fairfax, SD St. Anthony's; Gregory, SD St. Joseph; Burke, SD Sacred Heart.
Muweesi, John Vianney *s.d.s.* '86 (MIL)[P] Franklin, WI Salvatorian Formation House.
Muwonge, Charles '93 (LAN)[D] Plymouth, MI Spiritus Sanctus Academy.
Muwonge, Expedito '89 (L) Norton Audubon Hospital.
Mux, Juan Francisco Peren *o.s.b.* '07 (RCK)[G] Aurora, IL Marmion Abbey.
Muyimbwa, Paul (BO) Watertown, MA St. Patrick.
Muzas, Brian Keenan '03 (NEW)[B] School of Diplomacy and Intl. Rels.
Muzdakis, John J. *o.s.f.s.* '65 (WIL)[J] Childs, MD Retirement and Assisted Care Facility Retired.
Muzic, Anthony J. '63 (CLV) Cleveland, OH St. Mark Retired.
Muzzey, Charles H. '65 (WDC) Retired.
Muzzin, Victor *f.d.p.* '72 (NY) New York, NY St. Francis de Sales.
Mvondo, Laurent '81 (SAN) Crane, TX Good Shepherd; McCamey, TX Sacred Heart.
Mwageni, Honoratus Canute (CHI) Chicago, IL SS. Peter and Paul.
Mwakera, Revocatus L. '96 (NU) Appleton, MN St. John; Madison, MN St. Michael.
Mwampela, Ayub '00 (BGP) Greenwich, CT Greenwich Hospital; Stamford, CT St. Maurice.
Mwanamwambwa, Victor '05 (BAL)[S] Baltimore, MD St. Mary's Seminary & University.
Mwangi, Simon *c.s.c.* '05 (FTW)[H] Notre Dame Congregation of Holy Cross, Indiana Province, Provincial House.
Mwinzi, Joseph M. (PEO) Peoria, IL St. Mark's.
Myers, Christopher P. *s.o.l.t.* '90 (MO) Air National Guard Chaplains; DEPARTMENT OF VETERANS AFFAIRS HOSPITALS AND CHAPLAINS.
Myers, Christopher *s.o.l.t.* '90 (CC)[G] Robstown, TX Society of Our Lady of the Most Holy Trinity.
Myers, Edward T. *o.p.* '65 (PRO)[P] Providence St. Thomas Aquinas Priory at Providence College.
Myers, Gabriel *o.s.b.* '99 (WDC)[N] Washington, DC St. Anselm's Abbey.
Myers, Gerald '94 (FAR) Retired.
Myers, J. Edward '55 (NEW) Retired.
Myers, James E. '80 (PEO) On Duty Outside the Diocese.
Myers, James E. *s.s.* '80 (SFR)[A] Menlo Park, CA Vatican II Institute for Clergy Formation.
Myers, James E. *s.s.* '80 (BAL)[S] Baltimore Society of St. Sulpice, Province of the United States.
Myers, Jeremy '84 (DAL) Sherman, TX St. Francis of Assisi (Quasi Parish); Sherman, TX St. Mary.
Myers, Kenneth E. '80 (PIT) Lawrence County, PA Almira Home; Lawrence County, PA Belvedere Residence, Inc.; Lawrence County, PA Golden Hill Nursing, Inc.; Lawrence County, PA Haven Convalescent Home; Lawrence County, PA Highland Hall Care Center; Lawrence County, PA Hillview Manor; Lawrence County, PA Indian Creek Nursing Home; Lawrence County, PA Jack Rees Nursing and Rehabilitation Center; Lawrence County, PA Overlook Nursing Home; Lawrence County, PA Castle Manor; Lawrence County, PA Cedar Manor; Lawrence County, PA Majors Manor; Lawrence County, PA Shenango United Presbyterian Home; Lawrence County, PA Silver Oak Nursing.
Myers, Rawley J. '49 (COS) Retired.
Myers, Regis F. '54 (ALT) Retired.
Myers, Robert *s.v.d.* '49 (CHI)[N] Techny, IL Divine Word Residence.
Myers, Rev. Msgr. William R. '69 (STU) Gallipolis, OH St. Louis; [L] Gallipolis, OH Rio Grande University.
Myers, William '88 (SFR) Menlo Park, CA St. Raymond.
Myers, William '88 (STO) On Duty Outside the Diocese.
Myett, Robert D. *o.p.* '60 (PRO)[P] Providence St. Thomas Aquinas Priory at Providence College.
Myhalyk, Richard *s.s.e.* '71 (MOB)[G] Selma, AL Edmundite Fathers; [J] Selma, AL Edmundite Guild.
Mykyta, Myron '97 (LA) Los Angeles, CA Nativity of Blessed Virgin Mary.
Mykyta, Myron '97 (STN) Hollywood, CA Nativity of B.V.M.; Presbyteral Council.
Myladil, Thomas *o.c.d.* '76 (MET) Bridgewater, NJ Holy Trinity.
Myladiyil, Sebastian *s.v.d.* '99 (BLX) Bay St. Louis, MS St. Rose De Lima.
Myler, John T. '82 (BEL) Belleville, IL Cathedral of St. Peter; [J] Belleville, IL World Apostolate of Fatima, The Blue Army, U.S.A.; Formation of Priests; Advocate; Diocesan Consultors; Diocesan Deans; Holy Childhood Association; Propagation of the Faith.
Myles, John J. '64 (SAC) Williams, CA Sacred Heart Retired.
Mylet, James J. *m.m.* '75 (FgM) Maryknoll, NY MARYKNOLL.
Myronyuk, Myron (PHU) Philadelphia, PA Immaculate Conception of Blessed Virgin Mary, Cathedral.
Myshchuk, Mikhail '94 (STF) Troy, NY Protection of B.V.M.; Watervliet, NY St. Nicholas; Priests' Benevolent Association.
Myslinski, John F. '80 (WDC) Absent On Leave.
Mysliwiec, Haldane '70 (CHI)[J] Des Plaines, IL Holy Family Medical Center.
Mysliwiec, Jan J. *s.d.s.* '62 (NEW)[M] Verona, NJ The Salvatorian Fathers.
Myszel, George G. '53 (MIL) Retired.
Myszka, Rev. Msgr. Daniel J. '58 (BUF) Retired.

N

N'go, Anthony Chinh '94 (L) Louisville, KY St. John Vianney.
N'Guessan, Sess Julien *s.j.* '97 (OAK)[M] Berkeley, CA Jesuit Fathers and Brothers.
N'Zilamba, Norbert *o.praem.* '87 (JKS)[E] Raymond, MS Priory of St. Moses the Black.
Naa, Anayo *c.ss.r.* '03 (PH) Philadelphia, PA St. Athanasius.
Naas, Stephen '78 (KAL) Marshall, MI St. Mary.
Nabbefeld, Grant '95 (SJ) On Leave of Absence.
Nabozny, Peter '54 (ALB) Troy, NY St. Mary Retired.
Nabwana, Charles (ORL) Daytona Beach, FL Basilica of Saint Paul.
Nacarino, Raymond L. '85 (MET) New Brunswick, NJ Our Lady of Mt. Carmel; [M] Stewartsville, NJ Society of Jesus Christ the Priest.
Naccarato, Frank '79 (NY) Staten Island, NY Arthur Kill Correctional Facility.
Nacciarone, Ugo R. *s.j.* '64 (NY)[EE] New York, NY St. Ignatius Loyola Residence; New York, NY St. Ignatius Loyola.
Nace, Rev. Msgr. Arthur J. '57 (PH) Retired.
Nachajski, Richard E. '71 (ALN) Unassigned.
Nacius, Michael A. '89 (CHI) Flossmoor, IL Infant Jesus of Prague; Deans.
Nacke, Xavier *o.s.b.* '63 (KC)[A] Conception, MO Conception Seminary College; [J] Parnell, MO St. Joseph Parish.
Nacorda, Cirilo A. '92 (CLV) North Olmsted, OH St. Brendan.
Nadackal, Zacharias *c.m.i.* '64 (NY) Rye, NY Resurrection.
Nadal, Tomas Ciscar *o.carm.* (ARE) Ciales, PR Holy Rosary.
Naddeo, Henry M. '56 (NEW) Retired.
Nadeau, James L. '88 (PRT) Fort Kent, ME St. John Vianney Parish.
Nadeau, Lance P. *m.m.* '90 (FgM) Maryknoll, NY MARYKNOLL.
Nadeau, Real J. '62 (PRT) Retired.
Nadeau, Richard A. '80 (PRT) Retired.
Nadeau, Roland P. '00 (PRT) Bangor, ME St. Joseph's Hospital; [H] Bangor, ME Pastoral Care Dept.; Bangor, ME Saint Paul the Apostle Parish.
Nadeau, Roland *m.s.* '69 (ORL) Orlando, FL Blessed Trinity.
Nadeau, Thomas D. '05 (BUR) Swanton, VT Nativity of the Blessed Virgin Mary–St. Louis.
Nadeau, Timothy J. '91 (PRT) Bangor, ME Saint Paul the Apostle Parish; Diocesan Priests' Benefit Plan – Trustees.
Nadeau, William '68 (RNO) Incline Village, NV St. Francis of Assisi; Life, Peace & Justice Commission.
Nadicksbernd, Elmer *s.v.d.* (COV)[N] Melbourne, KY St. Anne Convent Retired.
Nadine, Jerome E. '58 (BRK) Retired.
Nadolny, Edmund S. '59 (HRT) East Berlin, CT Sacred Heart.
Nadolny, Paul *s.v.d.* '89 (FgM) Techny, IL.

Nadolny, Stanley J. '68 (TUC) Apache Junction, AZ Saint George Roman Catholic Parish – Apache Junction.
Nadolski, Kevin M. *o.s.f.s.* '97 (WIL)[J] Wilmington, DE Wilmington–Philadelphia Province of the Oblates of St. Francis de Sales.
Nadres, Sergio D. '91 (NEW) Hillside, NJ Christ the King.
Naduvathaniyil, Jerome *o.s.b.* (LC) Loyal, WI St. Anthony of Padua.
Naduvilekoot, Augustine '71 (NOR) Voluntown, CT St. Thomas the Apostle.
Naedele, Rev. Msgr. William B. '49 (NEW) Maplewood, NJ St. Joseph's; Mausoleum Office.
Naegele, Gary P. '79 (WH) Follansbee, WV St. Anthony.
Naegele, Zacchaeus Maria *o.s.b.cam.* '98 (MRY)[F] Big Sur, CA New Camaldoli Hermitage.
Naessens, Philip *o.f.m.cap.* '86 (DET)[K] Detroit St. Bonaventure Friary.
Naffate, Lenin '00 (SAT) Priests Personnel Board; In Metropolitan Area; Archdiocesan Presbyteral Council; San Antonio, TX St. Joseph.
Nagai, Rev. Msgr. Alan A. '58 (HON) Retired.
Nagel, Kurt '97 (SEA) Kirkland, WA Holy Family; College of Consultors.
Nagel, Rick '07 (IND) Young Adult and College Campus Ministry.
Nagengast, Maynard G. *o.s.b.* '62 (NEW)[M] Newark, NJ Newark Abbey.
Nagle, Austin *ss.cc.* '54 (FR)[G] Fairhaven, MA Damien Residence.
Nagle, Edmund W. *s.j.* '63 (PAT)[J] Morristown, NJ Loyola House of Retreats.
Nagle, Gerald J. *m.m.* '57 (NY)[EE] Maryknoll Maryknoll Fathers and Brothers Retired.
Nagle, Rev. Msgr. Joseph P. '71 (BRK) Brooklyn, NY St. Patrick; Peter Turner Insurance Co.; Diocesan Insurance Committee.
Nagle, Michael R. '72 (FR) Vineyard Haven, MA Good Shepherd.
Nagle, Walter M. '99 (NOR) East Hampton, CT St. Patrick; Diocesan Pastoral Council.
Nagle, Rev. Msgr. William A. '49 (BGP)[O] Stamford, CT The Catherine Dennis Keefe Queen of the Clergy Retired Priests' Residence Retired.
Naglich, Robert *s.c.j.* '91 (MIL) Franklin, WI St. Martin of Tours; [P] Milwaukee, WI SCJ Community.
Naguit, Glenn A. '05 (OAK) Concord, CA St. Francis of Assisi.
Nagy, Balint *s.j.* '09 (BO)[U] Cambridge, MA Faber House.
Nahal, John '93 (OLL) Millbrae, CA Our Lady of Lebanon Maronite Catholic Church.
Nahman, Richard *o.s.a.* '65 (NY) Bronx, NY St. Nicholas of Tolentine.
Nahoe, Francisco *o.f.m.conv.* (OAK)[M] Castro Valley, CA Conventual Franciscans (Province of St. Joseph of Cupertino).
Naickamparambil, Varghese '72 (SYM) Southfield, MI St. Thomas Syro–Malabar Catholic Church, Detroit.
Naill, Joseph P. '97 (RCK) McHenry, IL St. Patrick; Divine Worship, Office for; Liturgical Commission, Diocesan; Special Assignment.
Nairki, Modi Abil *m.c.c.j.* '71 (LA) Los Angeles, CA Holy Cross.
Nairki Modi, Abil *m.c.c.j.* '71 (CHI)[N] La Grange Park, IL Comboni Missionaries.
Nairn, Thomas *o.f.m.* '75 (STL)[O] St. Louis, MO Franciscan Friary of St. Anthony of Padua.
Najera, Arthur '09 (SAC) Auburn, CA St. Joseph; Auburn, CA St. Teresa of Avila Parish.
Najim, Michael J. '01 (PRO)[A] Providence, RI Seminary of Our Lady of Providence; Vocations.
Najjar, Samuel A. '84 (SAM) Fayetteville, NC St. Michael the Archangel; Protopresbyters (Deans); Presbyteral Council; Office of Ecumenism and Interreligious Dialogue.
Najmowski, James T. *m.m.* '76 (FgM) Maryknoll, NY MARYKNOLL.
Nakagawa, Francis *s.m.* '57 (HON)[D] Honolulu, HI; Honolulu, HI Latin Mass Community.
Nakagawa, Francis *s.m.* '57 (STL)[O] St. Louis Marianists, Province of the United States (Society of Mary).
Nakowicz, Stanley T. '67 (PRO) East Providence, RI Our Lady of Loreto.
Nakwah, Joseph C. '90 (LC) Hillsboro, WI St. Aloysius; Hillsboro, WI St. Jerome.
Nale, Joseph C. '03 (ALT) McConnellsburg, PA St. Stephen's; Orbisonia, PA St. Mary's.
Nalepa, Rev. Msgr. Damien G. '70 (BAL) Baltimore, MD St. Gregory the Great; Baltimore, MD Baltimore City Detention Center – Men; Vicar for African–American Affairs; Presbyteral Council.
Nalepa, Richard A. *c.p.* '70 (BRK)[T] Jamaica, NY Immaculate Conception Monastery.
Nalepka, Robert *s.ch.* '88 (CHI) Chicago, IL Holy Trinity Mission.
Nall, James M. '87 (BEL) New Athens, IL St. Agatha; Judicial Vicar; Judges.
Nallen, James F. '66 (CHI) Chicago, IL St. Columba.
Nalley, Robert W. '75 (GAY) Traverse City, MI St. Patrick; Elected Members; Tribunal Diocesan.
Nally, Joseph M. '72 (WOR) Worcester, MA St. Stephen's; Diocesan College of Consultors.
Nalty, Rev. Msgr. Christopher '99 (NO) New Orleans, LA Good Shepherd.
Nalugon, Nilo '94 (SAN) Odessa, TX Holy Redeemer.
Nalysnyk, Bohdan '95 (STN) Chicago, IL St. Nicholas Ukrainian Catholic Cathedral.
Nalysnyk, Jaroslaw '90 (STF) Jamaica Plain, MA Christ the King; Boston.
Nam, Heebong '95 (BRK) Brooklyn, NY Holy Spirit; [S] Korean Apostolate.
Nam, Joseph P. *c.m.c.* (BO) Chelsea, MA St. Rose of Lima.
Nam, Peter Tran Van '84 (NO) New Orleans, LA St. Joseph.
Nam, Simon '76 (NY) Bronx, NY St John Nam.
Nam, Tien *s.j.* '05 (SJ) San Jose, CA Most Holy Trinity.
Nambatac, Alner '96 (SFR) San Rafael, CA St. Isabella.
Nambusseril, Thankachan (John) '93 (HT) Raceland, LA Community of St. Anthony; Raceland, LA St. Hilary of Poitiers.
Namie, James B. '54 (STP) Retired.
Namiotka, Edward F. '87 (CAM) Representatives by Deaneries; Landisville, NJ Queen of Angels Parish, Buena Borough, N.J.; Malaga, NJ St. Mary's Roman Catholic Church of Malaga, N.J.; [B] Vineland, NJ Sacred Heart High School.
Namo, Warlito F. '91 (SFR) Ross, CA St. Anselm.
Namocatcat, Felix S. '62 (SFR) Retired.
Nangachiveettil, George Joseph '83 (IND) Oldenburg, IN St. John the Evangelist; Oldenburg, IN St. Anne; Greensburg, IN St. Maurice.
Nangle, Joseph J. *o.f.m.* '58 (NY)[EE] New York Franciscan Friars, Holy Name Province.
Nangle, Thomas R. '70 (CHI) Other Assignments; Police Department Chaplain.
Nangwele, Linus '00 (MIA) Fort Lauderdale, FL St. Anthony.
Nano, Efren '87 (TYL) Mineola, TX St. Peter the Apostle; Presbyteral Council.
Nanz, John D. '71 (PIT) Absent on Sick Leave.
Napier, Robert L. '90 (STA) Interlachen, FL St. John.
Napieralski, Maciej '83 (MO) Army Chaplains.
Naples, Timothy '09 (BUR)[B] Rutland, VT Mount St. Joseph Academy – Rutland Catholic Schools; Rutland, VT Christ the King; Wallingford, VT St. Patrick.
Napoli, Carlo *t.o.r.* '58 (WDC)[L] Washington, DC Providence Hospital.
Napoli, Carol *t.o.r.* (PIT)[M] Pittsburgh, PA Franciscan Friars, T.O.R.
Napoli, Peter *o.f.m.cap.* '73 (NY) Bronx, NY Immaculate Conception; [EE] New York, NY Immaculate Conception Friary.
Napolitano, Joseph V. '76 (HRT) Ansonia, CT Holy Rosary; Ansonia, CT St. Anthony.
Napora, Jacek J. '06 (NEW) Caldwell, NJ St. Aloysius.
Nappo, Michael *o.f.m.* '91 (NY)[GG] Wappingers Falls, NY Mt. Alvernia Retreat House.
Naquin, Roch R. '32 (HT) Cursillo.
Naquin, Roch '62 (HT) Retired.
Naranjo, Francisco '95 (STO) Lathrop, CA Our Lady of Guadalupe Church (Pastor of).
Narciso, Richard A. '07 (PRO) East Providence, RI St. Francis Xavier; Council Members.
Nardoianni, Antonio *o.f.m./i.c.* '74 (BO) Boston, MA St. Leonard of Port Maurice.
Nardoianni, Antonio *o.f.m.* (BO) Italian.
Nardone, Amedeo *o.f.m.* '68 (NY)[EE] New York Franciscan Province of the Immaculate Conception.
Nardone, Richard M. '54 (NEW)[B] School of Diplomacy and Intl. Rels. Retired.
Narez, Juan '93 (ELP) Absent on Leave.
Narichetti, Jesuprathap '92 (CHR) Folly Beach, SC Our Lady of Good Counsel.
Narisetti, Rayanna '98 (SCR) Dunmore, PA Our Lady of Mount Carmel Parish.
Narithookil, James *c.m.i.* '72 (SAC) Sacramento, CA St. Mary.
Narivelil, Victor Z. *c.m.i.* '64 (STA) Jacksonville, FL Sacred Heart.
Narkun, Rev. Msgr. Peter P. '45 (NY)[E] Bronx, NY Cardinal Hayes High School Retired.
Narla, Lourduswamy Dhanraj '67 (LR) Huntsville, AR St. John the Evangelist; Tontitown, AR St. Joseph; Fayetteville, AR St. Thomas Aquinas University Parish.
Narog, Joseph L. *o.s.a.* (BO) Andover, MA St. Augustine.
Nartker, Michael F. *s.m.* '96 (STL)[O] St. Louis Marianists, Province of the United States (Society of Mary).
Nasar, Ayub '85 (GR)[G] Grand Rapids, MI Saint Mary's Health Care.
Nascimento, Daniel '98 (SFR) San Francisco, CA St. Brendan.
Naseman, Alfred *c.pp.s.* '67 (CIN)[N] Carthagena, OH St. Charles.
Nash, Edward H. *s.j.* '50 (PH)[Y] Loyola Center and Manresa Hall.
Nash, Francis J. *s.j.* '69 (BAL)[S] Baltimore, MD Jesuit Community of Loyola University, Inc.; [B] Jesuit Community of Loyola University, Inc.
Nash, James R. '89 (SCR) Nanticoke, PA Holy Trinity; Nanticoke, PA St. Joseph's; Nanticoke, PA St. Mary of Czestochowa; Nanticoke, PA St. Stanislaus; Priests' Retirement Advisory Board.
Nash, James '94 (WIL) Newark, DE Holy Family.
Nash, Robert C. '48 (WH) Retired.
Nash, Robert (RIC) Retired.
Nasini, Gino *s.x.* '65 (FgM)[N] Wayne Xaverian Missionary Fathers; Wayne, NJ XAVERIAN MISSIONARY FATHERS.
Naskar, Lawrence *s.d.b.* '98 (NY) Port Chester, NY Our Lady of Mercy.
Nason, Dennis T. '66 (BO) Haverhill, MA All Saints.
Nasr, Toufic M. '97 (OLL) Fairlawn, OH Our Lady of the Cedars of Mt. Lebanon Maronite Catholic Church.
Nasri, Rev. Msgr. Youssef Bochra '85 (BRK) Brooklyn, NY St. Michael; Brooklyn, NY Resurrection Catholic Coptic Chapel; [S] Arabic Speaking Apostolate.
Nasry, Wafik *s.j.* '01 (LA)[C] Los Angeles, CA Jesuit Community.
Nassal, Joseph *c.pp.s.* '82 (KC)[A] Liberty, MO Society of the Precious Blood Provincial Offices.
Nassal, Joseph *c.p.p.s.* (OAK)[M] Berkeley, CA Society of the Precious Blood (Province of Kansas City).
Nassaney, Daniel *o.m.i.* '74 (BO) Tewksbury, MA St. William.
Nasser, Joseph M. *s.j.* '75 (TYL) Hemphill, TX St. Pius I.
Nassetta, Peter W. *y.a.* '89 (ARL)[K] Fairfax, VA George Mason University, Catholic Campus Ministry; [K] Fairfax, VA St. Robert Bellarmine Chapel; Campus Ministry; [L] McLean, VA Youth Apostles Institute, An Association of Christian Faithful.
Nassr, Martin B. '67 (TOL) Sandusky, OH SS. Peter and Paul.
Nasta, Thomas A. '82 (PH) Stowe, PA St. Gabriel of the Sorrowful Mother; [D] Pottstown, PA St. Pius X High School.
Natad, Diosmar '04 (ATL) Johns Creek, GA St. Brigid; Special or Other (Arch)Diocesan Assignment.
Natale, Sam (RVC)[N] Amityville, NY Queen of the Rosary, Motherhouse.
Natale, Samuel '79 (RIC) Retired.
Natalizia, Louis T. '80 (PRO) North Providence, RI Presentation of the Blessed Virgin Mary.
Nathan, Matthew '09 (JOL) Downers Grove, IL St. Joseph.
Nathan, Sahayanathan (LC) Abbotsford, WI St. Bernard; Abbotsford, WI St. Louis; Owen, WI Holy Rosary.
Nathe, Thomas '04 (SEA) Clallam Bay Correction Center; Clearwater / Olympic Correction Center; Forks, WA St. Anne Parish; Port Angeles, WA Queen of Angels.
Nations, David G. *c.m.* '97 (STL)[O] St. Louis, MO Vincentian Residence.
Natsuhara, Bruce K. '78 (OKL) Oklahoma City, OK St. Joseph; Consultors Archdiocesan; Council of Priests Archdiocesan.
Nattunilam, Dominic *c.m.i.* '86 (MET)[J] Flemington, NJ The Carmel of Mary Immaculate and St. Mary Magdalen.
Nau, Dale '78 (DUL) Duluth, MN St. Raphael; Defender of the Bond; Department of Continuing Formation of Clergy; Safe Environment; Promoter of Justice.
Nau, Thomas R. '78 (STU) Steubenville, OH Holy Name Cathedral; Priests Personnel Board; Steubenville, OH Triumph of the Cross.
Naucke, Alfred E. *s.j.* '65 (SJ)[B] Santa Clara, CA Jesuit Community; [M] Los Gatos, CA California Province of the Society of Jesus, Jesuit Provincial Office; Los Gatos, CA.
Naughton, James J. *s.d.b.* '67 (BIR) Leeds, AL St. Theresa's.
Naughton, Rev. Msgr. John Thomas '49 (LA) Retired.
Naughton, Michael *o.s.b.* '66 (SCL) Albany, MN Seven Dolors; Albany, MN St. Anthony's; [I] Collegeville, MN St. John's Abbey, of the Order of St. Benedict.
Naughton, Patrick J. '91 (MIA) On Duty Outside the Diocese; Coral Springs, FL St. Elizabeth Ann Seton.
Naughton, Thomas J. '61 (BO) Senior Priests.; Milton, MA St. Mary of the Hills Retired.
Naughton, Rev. Msgr. William M. '72 (PAT) Unassigned; Passaic, NJ Adult Medical Day Care Center.
Naugle, John F. '09 (PIT) Pittsburgh, PA St. Sebastian.
Naumann, Paul S. *s.j.* '63 (SY)[Q] Syracuse, NY Jesuits at LeMoyne, Inc.
Naumes, Matthew '63 (SEA) Retired.
Naus, John E. *s.j.* '55 (MIL)[P] Wauwatosa, WI Jesuit Community at St. Camillus.
Nava, Rufino Carlos *o.m.i.* '99 (BWN) San Juan, TX St. John the Baptist.
Naval, Thomas Paul K. '89 (ORG) Anaheim, CA St. Justin Martyr.
Navalo, Hector *c.m.f.* '03 (CHI)[N] Oak Park Claretian Missionaries USA Eastern Province.
Navaratne, Louis–Marie *o.s.b.* '76 (PAT)[N] Clifton, NJ Holy Face of Jesus Monastery.

Navarra, Peter '81 (SD) Chula Vista, CA Our Lady of Guadalupe.
Navarrete, Jesus '87 (MO) Air Force Chaplains.
Navarro, Allen '09 (SJ) San Jose, CA St. Julie Billiart.
Navarro, Edison *c.r.l.* '04 (ARE) Corozal, PR Christ the King.
Navarro, Juan B. (ORG) Fullerton, CA St. Mary's.
Navarro, Luis G. '08 (STO) Turlock, CA Sacred Heart Church of Turlock (Pastor of).
Navarro, Marcelo Javier *i.v.e.* '94 (SJ) San Jose, CA St. Leo the Great.
Navarro, Nicolas *s.d.b.* '69 (SJN) San Juan, PR Maria Auxiliadora; [B] San Juan, PR Colegio San Juan Bosco.
Navarro, Rev. Msgr. Pablo A. '78 (MIA) Miami, FL St. John Neumann; Incardination Committee; Priests' Personnel Board; Consultors.
Navarro, Rev. Msgr. Pablo '78 (MIA) Pax Catholic Communications; Spirit Online Radio – English Language Internet Radio; Radio Paz – WACC, 830 AM. Spanish Language Radio Ministry; Radio Ke Poze – WLQY, 1320 AM. Haitian Radio Ministry; PaxNet/Radio Paz Satelital.
Navarro, Pedro '63 (NEW) Retired.
Navarro, Servando '97 (DEN) Longmont, CO St. John the Baptist.
Navarro Saenz, George Alexander '09 (MAD) Sauk City, WI St. Aloysius.
Nave, Arthur '08 (PHX) Phoenix, AZ St. Thomas the Apostle Roman Catholic Parish.
Nave, Rev. Msgr. Francis A. '92 (ALN) Bath, PA Sacred Heart of Jesus.
Navin, Rev. Msgr. Cyril '45 (LA) Encino, CA St. Cyril Retired.
Navin, Timothy M. '79 (VEN) Marco Island, FL San Marco.
Navins, Robert J. '50 (NY) Staten Island, NY Sacred Heart Retired.
Navit, Zachary W. '94 (PH)[BB] Philadelphia, PA University of the Sciences in Philadelphia; Office for Special Projects/Closures.
Navone, John J. *s.j.* '62 (P)[L] Portland Jesuit Provincial Office (Society of Jesus, Oregon Prov.).
Navoy, Ronald W. '71 (CHI) Mt. Prospect, IL St. Emily.
Nawalaniec, Mariusz '93 (CHI) Burbank, IL St. Albert the Great.
Nawarskas, Rev. Msgr. Frederick '67 (SAN) Abilene, TX Holy Family; Priests' Personnel Board; Diocesan Consultors; Presbyteral Council; Deans; Pastor Review Board; Board of Directors.
Nawrocki, Norman D. '82 (DET) Bloomfield Hills, MI St. Regis; Defenders of Bond.
Nawrocki, Robert W. '61 (MIL) Retired.
Nayak, Alexis *ss.cc.* '00 (FR)[G] Fairhaven National Center of the Enthronement.
Nayak, Christudas '68 (ALX)[B] Alexandria, LA Christus Health Central Louisiana; Alexandria, LA Our Lady of Prompt Succor; Alexandria, LA Christus St. Frances Cabrini Hospital.
Nayak, Prodeep Chandra (NOR) New London, CT St. Joseph.
Nayak, Subal *ss.cc.* (FR)[G] Fairhaven National Center of the Enthronement.
Nayak, Sudhir Cristo Das *ss.cc.* '06 (FR)[G] Fairhaven National Center of the Enthronement.
Nayak, Sudhir *ss.cc.* '03 (FR)[G] Fairhaven National Center of the Enthronement.
Naylor, David W. '00 (L) Shepherdsville, KY St. Benedict; Shepherdsville, KY St. Aloysius.
Naylor, Ronald J. '60 (RIC) Retired.
Nazareth, Andrew L. '87 (FTW) Garrett, IN St. Joseph.
Nazhianpara, Jose *c.m.* '91 (CHI)[N] Chicago DePaul Vincentian Residence.
Nazimek, David '93 (GBG) Monessen, PA The Epiphany of Our Lord.
Nazzani, Ermete *c.s.* '61 (LA)[O] Sun Valley, CA Villa Scalabrini.
Nazzaro, Alfonse *l.c.* '03 (DAL)[J] Irving, TX Legionaries of Christ; [D] Irving, TX The Highlands School; [E] Irving, TX The Highlands School.
Nazzaro, John *s.d.b.* '83 (BO)[M] Boston, MA Orient Heights Unit; Salesian Boys and Girls Club.
Ndagizimana, Isidore '85 (AUS) Austin, TX St. Albert The Great.
Ndeanaefo, Aloysius Okey '05 (SFD) Highland, IL St. Paul; Commission for the Care of Infirm and Retired Priests.
Ndebilie, Valentine '05 (TLS) Poteau, OK Immaculate Conception.
Ndereba, Protasio '96 (CHI) Chicago, IL St. Andrew.
Ndour, Jean–Marie *m.s.c.* '07 (RCK)[G].
Ndugbu, Polycarp '73 (SAC) Represa, CA.
Nduh, Ikeokwu *m.s.p.* '88 (BEA) Liberty, TX Our Mother of Mercy.
Nduka, Pascal E. '96 (IND) Morris, IN St. Anthony of Padua.
Nduke, Emmanuel Lugard '99 (TLS) Stillwater, OK St. John the Evangelist Parish and Newman Center.
Ndulaka, Matthias (NY) Wurtsboro, NY St. Joseph.
Ndylaka, Matthias '78 (NY) Woodbourne, NY Woodbourne Correctional Facility.
Neal, Mark '06 (DM)[C] Council Bluffs, IA Saint Albert Catholic Schools; [A] Council Bluffs, IA St. Albert High School.
Nealon, Rev. Msgr. Joseph A. '61 (STU) Retired.
Neary, Mark '83 (SJ) Absent on Sick Leave.
Neary, Patrick M. *c.s.c.* '91 (FTW)[A] Notre Dame, IN Moreau Seminary; [A] Notre Dame, IN Moreau Seminary; [H] Notre Dame, IN Congregation of Holy Cross, Indiana Province, Provincial House; Provincial Councilors:; Members.
Neault, Armand R. '52 (PRT) Retired.
Nedder, Edward T. '87 (SAM) Lincoln, RI St. George.
Nedeff, George *s.o.l.t.* '07 (CC) Robstown, TX St. Anthony; [G] Robstown, TX Society of Our Lady of the Most Holy Trinity.
Nediakala, Kuriakose *m.c.b.s.* '78 (DUL) Duluth, MN St. Mary Star of the Sea; Duluth, MN St. Peter; Duluth, MN Our Lady of Mercy.
Nedimyer, Raymond *t.o.r.* '97 (PIT)[M] Pittsburgh, PA Franciscan Friars, T.O.R. Retired.
Nediyakala, Jose *c.m.i.* '69 (ALX) St. Joseph, LA St. Joseph.
Nedumankuzhiyil, Joseph '99 (RVC) Elmont, NY St. Vincent de Paul.
Nedumaruthumchalil, George K. '78 (NY) New Rochelle, NY Holy Family.
Nedumcheril, John '90 (DET) Richmond, MI St. Augustine.
Nedungadan, Johnson *c.m.* '91 (BRK) Bellerose, NY St. Gregory the Great.
Neduvelichalumkal, Kurian '91 (SYM) Fremont, CA St. Thomas Syro–Malabar Catholic Church of San Francisco.
Nee, Eugene O. '64 (SAT) Military Chaplains.
Nee, Robert E. '71 (BO) Cambridge, MA St. John the Evangelist; Permanent Disability.
Nee, Robert *o.f.m.* '62 (PAT)[N] Ringwood, NJ Holy Name Friary, Inc.
Nee, Thomas M. '39 (PIT) Retired.
Needles, Brian X. '06 (NEW) Livingston, NJ St. Philomena.
Neeley, Peter *s.j.* (TUC)[H] Nogales, AZ Kino Border Initiative.
Neely, Bradley '03 (B) Grangeville, ID SS. Peter and Paul; College of Consultors; Deans; Priest Personnel Commission.
Neely, Harry M. *o.s.a.* '53 (SD)[J] San Diego, CA Augustinian Community.
Neenan, Benedict *o.s.b.* '88 (KC)[A] Conception, MO Conception Seminary College; [J] Parnell, MO St. Joseph Parish.
Neenan, William B. *s.j.* '61 (BO)[U] Newton, MA The Jesuit Community at Boston College.
Neff, Eugene J. '71 (BEL) Lebanon, IL St. Joseph; Hospitals; Sick and Aged (Ministry); New Baden, IL St. George.
Neff, John '86 (E) Youngsville, PA St. Luke.
Neff, Rev. Msgr. John '52 (SP) Retired.
Neff, Steven V. '05 (PIT) Butler, PA St. Paul; Butler, PA St. Wendelin.
Negley, Phil "Skip" M. *m.s.* '73 (GAL) Friendswood, TX Mary, Queen.
Negley, Phil M. *m.s.* '73 (HRT)[L] Hartford, CT Missionaries of LaSalette Province of Mary, Mother of the Americas.
Negparanon, Nixon '05 (RIC) South Boston, VA St. Paschal Baylon; South Hill, VA Good Shepherd.
Negrete, Wayne *s.j.* '91 (LA) Los Angeles, CA Blessed Sacrament.
Negrillos, Ferdinand *sch.p.* '41 (PH)[F] Devon, PA Devon Preparatory School; [Y] Devon Piarist Fathers (Order of the Pious Schools).
Negro, Fernando *sch.p.* '81 (NY) New York, NY Annunciation; [EE] New York, NY Calasanzian Fathers (Piarists).
Negron, Juan Luis '89 (SJN)[C] Rio Piedras, PR Seminario Mayor Regional San Juan Bautista; San Juan Bautista Regional Seminary.
Negron, Ramon H. *o.f.m.cap.* '97 (SJN) San Juan, PR San Francisco de Asis.
Negron, Ramon Hiram *o.f.m.cap.* (SJN) Vicar for Youth; Youth Ministries.
Nehrig, Robert V. *m.m.* '54 (FgM) Maryknoll, NY MARYKNOLL.
Neidhart, William *c.s.c.* (FTW)[H] Notre Dame Congregation of Holy Cross, Indiana Province, Provincial House.
Neiheisel, Stanley H. '60 (CIN) Cincinnati, OH St. Stephen Retired.
Neilson, James P. *o.praem.* '93 (GB)[B] St. Norbert College; [J] De Pere, WI St. Norbert Abbey.
Neilson, Kieran A. *o.s.b.* '60 (CHL)[J] Belmont, NC Belmont Abbey.
Neilson, Richard J. '83 (NY) Retired.
Neiman, John '86 (LA) Camarillo, CA St. Mary Magdalen.
Neis, William P. '67 (LC) Leave of Absence.
Neissen, John A. *s.v.d.* '45 (SB)[I] Riverside, CA Divine Word Seminary.
Neitzke, Ron P. '89 (MO) Joliet, IL St. Mary Magdalene; Navy Reserve Chaplains.
Nekic, Simon J. '43 (CLV) Lorain, OH St. Vitus.
Nekoliczak, Ted A. '59 (GI) Retired.
Nelan, Francis *m.s.c.* '53 (SAT)[K] San Antonio, TX Padua Place.
Nelan, Rev. Msgr. Kevin J. '77 (NY) New York, NY Our Lady of Guadalupe at St. Bernard's; Manhattan (South); Apostleship of the Sea.
Nelapatti–Thomas, Irudayaraj '97 (AUS) Waco, TX St. Mary of the Assumption.
Nellikunnell, James *c.m.i.* '79 (ALX) Simmesport, LA Christ the King.
Nelliparambil, John '97 (FRS) Fresno, CA St. Helen.
Nelliparambil, Theophane *o.d.d.* (LA) Hospital Chaplains.
Nellis, Thomas F. '66 (ROC) Rochester, NY Holy Ghost.
Nelson, Andrew L. '57 (MIL) Retired.
Nelson, Brian D. '03 (WCH) South Hutchinson, KS Our Lady of Guadalupe; [B] Hutchinson, KS Trinity Catholic High School.
Nelson, Caye A. '88 (BR) Baton Rouge, LA St. Jude the Apostle.
Nelson, Charles T. '87 (SFD) Retired.
Nelson, Daniel C. *o.f.m.* '77 (ALB)[B] Siena College.
Nelson, Dennis (Dan) (STA) Lake City, FL Epiphany.
Nelson, Rev. Msgr. Francis J. '66 (SAV) Savannah, GA St. Frances Xavier Cabrini; Tribunal Judges; Promoter of Justice; College of Consultors.
Nelson, Francis M. '88 (RVC) Brentwood, NY St. Anne's.
Nelson, Francis *c.ss.r.* '64 (ORL) New Smyrna Beach, FL Sacred Heart.
Nelson, Rev. Msgr. Glenn L. '93 (RCK) DeKalb, IL Christ the Teacher, University Parish of Northern Illinois University; Special Assignment; [L] DeKalb, IL Newman Foundation for Catholic Students of Northern Illinois University; Vicars General; Chancellor; Deans; Catholic Office of the Deaf; Newman–Campus Ministry.
Nelson, Greg '97 (PEO) Danville, IL St. Paul's; Clergymen's Aid, Inc.
Nelson, Joseph *o.f.m.* '64 (LSC) Roswell, NM St. Peter.
Nelson, Kevin '00 (PMB) Assessors; Advocates; Lantana, FL Holy Spirit.
Nelson, Linden (LC)[D] Spiritual Services Dept.
Nelson, Martin Lester '97 (BEA) Diocesan Judges; Sour Lake, TX Our Lady of Victory.
Nelson, Patrick *s.d.s.* (BIR) Huntsville, AL St. Joseph's.
Nelson, Paul E. '61 (WIN) Rochester, MN St. Pius X; Priests' Pension Board.
Nelson, Robert W. '77 (LC) Pittsville, WI St. Joachim; Pittsville, WI Holy Rosary; Vesper, WI St. James.
Nelson, Ronald '07 (P) Gervais, OR Sacred Heart–St. Louis.
Nelson, Thomas J. *c.m.* '75 (DEN)[N] Denver, CO Congregation of the Mission Western Province: De Paul House.
Nelson, Thomas W. *o.praem.* '81 (ORG)[A] Silverado, CA St. Michael's Norbertine Postulancy, Novitiate and Juniorate; [I] Silverado, CA Norbertine Fathers of Orange Inc.
Nelson, Thomas *o.praem.* '81 (CHI)[T] Libertyville, IL Institute on Religious Life.
Nelson, Timothy '00 (LAN) Flint, MI Our Lady of Guadalupe; Priests' Assignment Commission.
Nelson, William R. '82 (PBL) Paonia, CO Sacred Heart.
Nemchausky, Matthew '09 (CHI) Evergreen Park, IL Most Holy Redeemer.
Nemec, Rev. Msgr. Joseph J. '84 (LIN) Lincoln, NE St. Teresa's; [G] Lincoln, NE Adoration Convent and Church of Christ the King; Commission for Sacred Liturgy and Sacred Music; Diocesan Director of Liturgy; Evangelization Committee.
Nemecek, Cyril '60 (CHI) Retired.
Nemeck, Francis Kelly *o.m.i.* '61 (SAT)[C] Oblate School of Theology.
Nemeck, Francis Kelly *o.m.i.* '61 (CC)[F] Sarita, TX Lebh Shomea House of Prayer.
Nemer, Lawrence *s.v.d.* '60 (FgM) Techny, IL.
Nemergut, Robert S. '77 (EVN) Special Assignment.
Nemeth, Edward G. '08 (STL) Imperial, MO St. Joseph.
Nemeth, Edward M. *s.j.* '65 (DET)[K] Clarkston, MI Colombiere Center.
Nemeth, Maurus B. *o.s.b.* '72 (SFR)[N] Portola Valley, CA Woodside Priory.
Nemmers, Francis J. '57 (SC) Retired.
Nemmers, Mark R. '66 (DUB) Judges Retired.
Neneman, John '00 (ORG) Special Assignment; Vocations Office.
Nenneau, Thomas D. '81 (LAN) Mount Morris, MI St. Mary; College of Consultors.
Nentwick, John '65 (Y) Retired.
Nereparaampil, Paul *c.m.i.* '85 (SFS) Highmore, SD St. Mary.
Neri, Gregori '92 (FRS)[B] Fresno, CA Saint Agnes Medical Center.
Nerino, Joseph C. *m.m.* '46 (SJ)[M] Los Altos, CA Maryknoll.
Nero, James *o.f.m.* '71 (MIA)[J] Fort Lauderdale, FL Holy Cross Hospital.
Neroda, Edward J. '57 (Y) Youngstown, OH St. Stanislaus Kostka.

Nesbit, Walter G. *s.j.* '59 (STL)[O] St. Louis, MO Jesuit Community Corporation at Saint Louis University – Jesuit Hall.
Nesbitt, John B. '62 (SD) Retired.
Neske, Mark I. '83 (MOB) Mobile, AL Holy Family.
Nespolo, Umberto *o.m.i.* '59 (OAK)[M] Oakland, CA Missionary Oblates of Mary Immaculate United States Province.
Nesrsta, Steven '95 (AUS) Fayetteville, TX St. John the Baptist; Fayetteville, TX St. Mary.
Ness, Bernardine *o.s.b.* '64 (SFS)[F] Marvin, SD Blue Cloud Abbey; Marvin, SD Blue Cloud Abbey.
Nessel, William J. *o.s.f.s.* '56 (HBG) Promoter of Justice Retired.
Nessel, William *o.s.f.s.* '56 (PH)[Y] Philadelphia, PA Father Louis Brisson Residence Retired.
Nesti, Donald S. *c.s.sp.* '63 (GAL)[C] Houston, TX University of St. Thomas; [S] Houston, TX The Society of the Holy Spirit; Houston, TX St. Theresa.
Nestler, David *o.f.m.cap.* '89 (WH)[D] Wheeling, WV Paul VI Pastoral Center; [L] Wheeling, WV Capuchin Hermitage of St. Joseph.
Nestor, Rev. Msgr. Michael '65 (SJP) Presbyters Retired.
Nestor, Robert P. '70 (NEW)[B] School of Diplomacy and Intl. Rels. Retired.
Nestor, Thomas F. '81 (BO) Vicariate III; Vicariate III; Winchester, MA St. Eulalia.
Nesvadba, Rev. Msgr. Reginald R. '66 (GAL) Pearland, TX St. Helen.
Neto, Germano Cord *s.j.* '08 (BO)[U] Cambridge, MA La Farge House.
Netta, John G. '57 (NEW) Retired.
Nettekoven, Joseph M. '75 (ORG) Anaheim, CA San Antonio de Padua Del Cañon Church; Judges; Apostleship of Prayer.
Neu, Rev. Msgr. Hubert '51 (FWT) Building Commission Retired.
Neu, Rev. Msgr. Leon M. '52 (BUF)[O] Lackawanna, NY Bishop Head Residence Retired.
Neubert, Germar *o.s.b.* '65 (OM)[N] Schuyler, NE Benedictine Mission House Endowment Trust; [K] Schuyler, NE Benedictine Mission House; [N] Schuyler, NE St. Benedict Center Endowment Fund; Schuyler, NE.
Neuhaus, Rev. Msgr. William B. '83 (COV) Covington, KY Cathedral, Basilica of the Assumption; Diocesan Consultors; Deans; Ministry Development Program for Lay & Deacons; Permanent Diaconate Formation; Defenders of the Bond.
Neuizil, Lowell Greg '67 (MO) DEPARTMENT OF VETERANS AFFAIRS HOSPITALS AND CHAPLAINS.
Neuman, Eugene C. '70 (MIL) Retired.
Neuman, James L. '71 (SFD) Hillsboro, IL St. Agnes; Litchfield, IL Holy Family; Diocesan Finance Council.
Neuman, James '71 (SFD) Priests' Personnel Board.
Neuman, Matthias *o.s.b.* '67 (IND)[K] St. Meinrad St. Meinrad Archabbey; [L] Beech Grove, IN.
Neuman, Peter *i.c.m.* '80 (BR)[H] Baton Rouge, LA Incarnatio Consecratio Missio.
Neumann, Aloysius J. '60 (RCK) Retired.
Neumann, Don A. '72 (GAL)[S] Houston, TX The Catholic Chaplain Corps; Houston, TX St. Thomas More.
Neumann, Richard J. '65 (HRT) Windsor, CT St. Gabriel.
Neumann, William J. '75 (ORL) Casselberry, FL St. Augustine.
Neumeier, Larry '95 (LA) Woodland Hills, CA St. Mel.
Neurohr, Gilbert N. '54 (MAR) Retired.
Neusch, Tony '04 (AMA) Wellington, TX Our Mother of Mercy; Vocation Development Team.
Neuser, John '62 (GB) Retired.
Neuville, Joseph '46 (P) Retired.
Neuzil, Gregory '67 (KNX) Retired.
Neuzil, Lowell G. '67 (CLV) Cleveland, OH Veterans Administration Hospitals, Brecksville V.A.
Nevares, Eduardo '81 (COL)[A] Columbus, OH Pontifical College Josephinum; [A] Columbus, OH Pontifical College Josephinum.
Nevares, Eduardo '01 (TYL) On Duty Outside the Diocese.
Nevels, Thomas A. '99 (CIN) Miamisburg, OH Our Lady of Good Hope.
Neville, Harold '52 (RCK) Retired.
Neville, Joseph B. *s.j.* '60 (SY)[Q] Syracuse, NY Jesuits at LeMoyne, Inc.
Nevin, Rev. Msgr. Emmet R. '77 (NY) Blauvelt, NY St. Catharine.
Nevins, Donald J. '75 (CHI) Chicago, IL St. Agnes of Bohemia; Deans.
Nevins, Eugene J. *s.j.* '80 (CHI) Chicago, IL John H. Stroger, Jr. Hospital of Cook County; [D] Chicago, IL St. Ignatius Jesuit Community.
Nevins, John J. '57 (PH) Retired.
Nevins, Troy '96 (GR) Grand Rapids, MI Immaculate Heart of Mary.
Nevlud, Gregory J. '82 (SAT) In Rural Area; Priests Personnel Board; Archdiocesan Presbyteral Council; Schertz, TX Church of the Good Shepherd.
New, Gary *s.d.s.* '91 (BIR) Huntsville, AL St. Joseph's; [H] Huntsville, AL Campus Ministry – University of Alabama in Huntsville.
Newbold, Ronan *c.p.* '69 (CHI) Chicago, IL Immaculate Conception; [N] Chicago, IL Passionist Community–Immaculate Conception Monastery.
Newburn, Charles *sch.p.* '79 (MIA)[C] Fort Lauderdale, FL Cardinal Gibbons High School.
Newbury, Robert G. '07 (COS) Parker, CO Ave Maria.
Newbury, Robert (COS) College of Consultors.
Newcomb, Matthew C. '05 (NY) Croton Falls, NY St. Joseph.
Newell, John J. '58 (BRK) Retired.
Newell, Joseph A. *s.j.* '66 (ALN)[A] Wernersville, PA Jesuit Center–Jesuit Community.
Newland, Rev. Msgr. Ronald A. '67 (NEW) Military Chaplains Retired.
Newland, Rev. Msgr. Ronald '67 (BRK) Rockaway Point, NY Blessed Trinity Roman Catholic Church.
Newman, Brian *o.f.m.cap.* '61 (FgM) Pittsburgh, PA Province of St. Augustine.
Newman, Jay Scott '93 (CHR) Greenville, SC St. Mary; [H] Greenville, SC Furman University Campus Ministry.
Newman, Louis I. '58 (RVC) Retired.
Newman, Mark L. *c.j.* '60 (LA) Santa Maria, CA St. Louis de Montfort; [B] Santa Maria, CA St. Joseph Seminary (Josephite Fathers' Novitiate).
Newman, Michael T. (MIL) Kenosha, WI St. Mary; Judges for Second Instance.
Newman, Michael '67 (MIL)[P] Milwaukee Salvatorian Provincial Offices Retired.
Newman, Rev. Msgr. Nelson A. '54 (OM) Central City, NE St. Michael.
Newns, John J. '74 (PH) Phoenixville, PA St. Ann.
Newton, David J. '88 (LFT) Dunkirk, IN St. Mary; Hartford City, IN St. John the Evangelist; Montpelier, IN St. Margaret of Scotland; Associate Judges.
Newton, Joseph L. '08 (IND) Indianapolis, IN St. Luke.
Newton, Stephen P. *c.s.c.* '89 (FTW)[H] Notre Dame Congregation of Holy Cross, Indiana Province, Provincial House.
Newton, Stephen *c.s.c.* '89 (CHI) Mt. Prospect, IL St. Emily.
Newton, Thomas A. '98 (CAM) Appointed Members; Elected Members; Members; Cherry Hill, NJ The Catholic Community of Christ Our Light, Cherry Hill, N.J.; Consultants.
Neylon, Bruce M. '75 (FR) Fall River, MA St. Stanislaus; Procurator–Advocates; Diocesan Guild for the Blind.
Neyra, Hugo R. '84 (LA) Winnetka, CA St. Joseph the Worker.
Neyrey, Jerome H. *s.j.* '70 (LAF)[J] Grand Coteau, LA Our Lady of the Oaks Retreat House.
Ng, Andrew Ping Yee *s.d.b.* '97 (SFR) San Francisco, CA SS. Peter and Paul.
Ng, Francis '09 (ORG) Anaheim, CA St. Justin Martyr.
Ng, Thomas '61 (OAK) Oakland, CA St. Leo the Great Retired.
Ngageno, Robert '97 (CAM) Vineland, NJ The Catholic Church of the Sacred Heart, Vineland, N.J.
Ngalamulume, Maurice Mamba '98 (SEA) Lynnwood, WA St. Thomas More.
Ngan, Joseph M. Vu Kim *c.m.c.* (DEN) Wheat Ridge, CO Queen of Vietnamese Martyrs.
Nganzi, Bernardine '88 (BEL) Lawrenceville, IL Immaculate Conception; Lawrenceville, IL St. Lawrence; Lawrenceville, IL St. Francis Xavier.
Nghiem, Peter '72 (GR) Wyoming, MI Our Lady of LaVang; On Special Assignment; Vietnamese Ministry.
Ngirwa, Apolinari J. '95 (NY) Mount Sinai Medical Center; New York, NY St. Monica.
Ngo, Anthony '94 (RIC) Retired.
Ngo, Chi V. *s.j.* '00 (SJ)[M] Los Gatos, CA California Province of the Society of Jesus, Jesuit Provincial Office; [M] Santa Clara, CA Casa San Inigo, Jesuit Residence; [B] Santa Clara, CA Jesuit Community.
Ngo, Francis Huan Ton '89 (GAL) Houston, TX St. Gregory the Great.
Ngo, Joseph Thong *c.ss.r.* '07 (SEA) Seattle, WA Sacred Heart of Jesus; [L] Seattle, WA The Redemptorist Society of Washington.
Ngo, Lan *s.j.* '04 (WDC)[N] Washington, DC The Jesuit Community at Georgetown University.
Ngo, Peter Thang '93 (LA) Huntington Park, CA St. Matthias; Cursillo Movement.
Ngo, Thich *o.p.* '05 (ARL) Arlington, VA Holy Martyrs of Vietnam.
Ngoc Lien, Joseph To '62 (SPC)[F] Carthage, MO Congregation of the Mother Coredemptrix, United States Assumption Province.
Ngo Duc Vuong, John D.M. *c.m.c.* '91 (SPC)[F] Carthage, MO Congregation of the Mother Coredemptrix, United States Assumption Province.
Ngowke, Emeka (FTW)[A] Notre Dame, IN Moreau Seminary.
Nguyen, Andrew M. '08 (BIR) Birmingham, AL Vietnamese Catholic Community Our Lady of LaVang Parish at St. John Bosco Church.
Nguyen, Andrew V. '05 (SJ) San Jose, CA Holy Spirit.
Nguyen, Andrew *o.s.b.* '07 (SFE)[H] Abiquiu, NM Monastery of Christ in the Desert.
Nguyen, Anh Tuan '98 (ORG) Administrative Leave.
Nguyen, Anh–Tuan Dominic '07 (LA) Pomona, CA St. Joseph.
Nguyen, Anthony G. '66 (BO) Presbyteral Council.
Nguyen, Anthony Lap '96 (HT) Morgan City, LA Thanh Gia.
Nguyen, Anthony Phuc *c.ss.r.* '92 (LA)[P] In Res; Whittier, CA St. Mary of the Assumption.
Nguyen, Anthony Phuc (ORG) Santa Ana, CA Our Lady of La Vang.
Nguyen, Anthony Quyen *c.m.f.* '07 (LA) San Gabriel, CA San Gabriel Mission.
Nguyen, Anthony Tin *s.d.d.* '06 (PT) Panama City, FL SS. Peter & Paul Mission; Panama City, FL St. Dominic.
Nguyen, Anthony Tuong '00 (SJ) San Jose, CA St. Patrick.
Nguyen, Anthony *c.ss.r.* '92 (STL)[B] St. Louis, MO St. John Neumann House.
Nguyen, Benjamin N. '05 (WCH) Coffeyville, KS Holy Name; Ongoing Formation of the Clergy Committee.
Nguyen, Bich '03 (OAK) Graduate Studies.
Nguyen, Bieu Van '00 (MOB) Bayou LaBatre, AL St. Margaret; Coden, AL St. Michael the Archangel.
Nguyen, Binh T. '01 (ORG) Anaheim, CA St. Anthony Claret.
Nguyen, Binh Thanh *s.v.d.* '02 (STL) St. Louis, MO Resurrection of Our Lord.
Nguyen, Binh Van *c.m.* '82 (LA)[P] Montebello, CA DePaul Evangelization Center; [V] Montebello, CA DePaul Evangelization Center.
Nguyen, Brandon *c.s.sp.* '00 (CHI) Chicago, IL St. Mary Magdalene.
Nguyen, Chanh C. *s.j.* '05 (SJ) San Jose, CA Most Holy Trinity.
Nguyen, Charles '89 (SAC) Absent on Leave.
Nguyen, Chau J. '89 (ORL) Vietnamese Ministry; Orlando, FL St. Philip Phan Van Minh Catholic Church; Appointed Members.
Nguyen, Chien '97 (ORL) Orlando, FL St. Philip Phan Van Minh Catholic Church.
Nguyen, Chinh '94 (SR)[J] Penngrove, CA Newman Hall, Sonoma State University, Intercollegiate Catholic Ministries; Vietnamese Martyrs Community.
Nguyen, Christopher T. *s.j.* '01 (LA)[P] Culver City, CA Ignatius House, The Novitiate of the California Province, Society of Jesus.
Nguyen, Cuong H. *m.m.* '98 (FgM) Maryknoll, NY MARYKNOLL.
Nguyen, Dam D. '93 (PIT) Pittsburgh, PA St. Gabriel of the Sorrowful Virgin; Chaplain to Vietnamese Catholic Community.
Nguyen, Daokim '93 (GAL) New Waverly, TX St. Joseph.
Nguyen, Doanh "John" *s.j.* '01 (SJ) San Jose, CA Most Holy Trinity.
Nguyen, Dominic Huyen Duc '64 (NO) New Orleans, LA Our Lady of La Vang.
Nguyen, Dominic Long *c.ss.r.* '03 (DAL)[J] Dallas, TX St. John Neumann Formation House.
Nguyen, Dominic Trung *c.ss.r.* '03 (TUC) Tucson, AZ Our Lady of LaVang Roman Catholic Parish – Tucson.
Nguyen, Dominic '95 (ORG) Administrative Leave.
Nguyen, Dominic *s.j.* '92 (SEA)[C] Tacoma, WA Bellarmine Preparatory School.
Nguyen, Dominic *o.s.b.* '04 (SFE)[H] Abiquiu, NM Monastery of Christ in the Desert.
Nguyen, Dominic *c.ss.r.* '03 (PH) Vietnamese Apostolate.
Nguyen, Dominic '96 (CIN)[U] Cincinnati, OH Vietnamese Catholic Community of Our Lady of Lavang.
Nguyen, Dominic *s.v.d.* (STL) St. Louis, MO Resurrection of Our Lord.
Nguyen, Dovan '93 (TLS) Tulsa, OK St. Joseph Church.
Nguyen, Duc Cong '06 (SEA) Renton, WA St. Anthony.
Nguyen, Duc '09 (KC) Kansas City, MO St. Therese Parish.
Nguyen, Dung '02 (ATL) Milledgeville, GA Sacred Heart of Jesus.
Nguyen, Duong *s.v.d.* '05 (SD) San Diego, CA Our Lady of the Sacred Heart.
Nguyen, Francis Khoi '90 (DOD) Garden City, KS St. Mary Catholic Church of Garden City, Kansas.
Nguyen, Francis Minh Hai *i.c.m.* '92 (BR) Vietnamese Apostolate.
Nguyen, Francis Nhi (BAL) Baltimore, MD Our Lady of La Vang.
Nguyen, Gan *c.ss.r.* '98 (CHI) Chicago, IL St. Michael in Old Town; [N] Chicago, IL The Redemptorist Fathers of Chicago.
Nguyen, Greg Viet *i.c.m.* '98 (GAL) Houston, TX St. Justin Martyr.
Nguyen, Hien Minh '85 (SJ) Special Assignment; [O] San Jose, CA Vietnamese Catholic Center; San Jose, CA St. Patrick.
Nguyen, Hien Paul '00 (WCH) Marion, KS Holy Family.

Nguyen, Hieu Trong *s.v.d.* '06 (OAK) Hayward, CA St. Joachim.
Nguyen, Hieu '69 (SC) Sioux City, IA Cathedral of the Epiphany.
Nguyen, Hoa Van '76 (HBG) Vietnamese Ministry.
Nguyen, Hoa '98 (FWT) Wichita Falls, TX Sacred Heart; Presbyteral Council and Consultors.
Nguyen, Hoai Thanh '06 (NO) Kenner, LA Divine Mercy.
Nguyen, Hoang D. '05 (STP) St. Paul, MN St. Columba.
Nguyen, Hoang H. '04 (CHI) Military Chaplains.
Nguyen, Hoang Peter '04 (MO) Air Force Chaplains.
Nguyen, Hoang (B) Mountain Home A F B, ID St. Mary's.
Nguyen, Huan Tien '66 (CIN) Retired.
Nguyen, Hung Joseph '94 (STO) Lodi, CA St. Anne Church (Pastor of).
Nguyen, Hung Van *s.o.l.t.* '02 (MO) Air Force Reserve Chaplains.
Nguyen, Hung Viet *i.c.m.* '69 (BR)[H] Baton Rouge, LA Incarnatio Consecratio Missio; [L] Baton Rouge, LA St. Michael's Home.
Nguyen, Hung '94 (SEA) Gig Harbor, WA St. Nicholas.
Nguyen, Hung *o.f.m.cap.* '99 (LA)[F] La Canada Flintridge, CA St. Francis High School of La Canada–Flintridge.
Nguyen, Huy H. '09 (BO) Dorchester, MA St. Ambrose; Dorchester, MA Holy Family; Dorchester, MA St. Peter; Dorchester, MA Blessed Mother Teresa of Calcutta.
Nguyen, Huy '95 (LA) Norwalk, CA St. Linus.
Nguyen, Hy K. *s.s.* '97 (BAL)[S] Baltimore Society of St. Sulpice, Province of the United States; [A] Baltimore, MD St. Mary's Seminary and University.
Nguyen, Hy *s.s.* '97 (OAK) On Duty Outside the Diocese.
Nguyen, Ignatius Kinh Hai Duong *c.m.c.* '89 (SB)[I] Corona, CA Congregation of the Mother Co–Redemptrix, C.M.C.; Corona, CA St. Mary Magdalene.
Nguyen, J. Christopher C. '08 (GAL) Houston, TX St. Michael.
Nguyen, J. Duc Minh (ORG) Santa Ana, CA Our Lady of La Vang.
Nguyen, James Bam '01 (LAF) Melville, LA St. John the Evangelist.
Nguyen, Rev. Msgr. Joe Van Anh '68 (AUS) Austin, TX Holy Vietnamese Martyrs Catholic Church – Austin, Texas.
Nguyen, John C. '99 (PH)[D] Warminster, PA Archbishop Wood Catholic High School; Horsham, PA St. Catherine of Siena.
Nguyen, John Hoa '72 (LA) Arcadia, CA Holy Angels.
Nguyen, John Luat *o.f.m.* '94 (SFR) San Francisco, CA St. Boniface.
Nguyen, John Tran E. (SAC) Vacaville, CA St. Mary.
Nguyen, John Tung '07 (WDC) Olney, MD St. Peter.
Nguyen, John Baptist Vuong Duc *o.p.* '00 (ARL) Arlington, VA Holy Martyrs of Vietnam.
Nguyen, Joseph An '92 (CAM) Woodlynne, NJ The Immaculate Heart of Mary, Woodlynne, N.J.; Consultants.
Nguyen, Joseph C. '78 (ORG) Stanton, CA St. Polycarp.
Nguyen, Joseph Chau *s.v.d.* '08 (DUB)[B] Epworth, IA Divine Word College.
Nguyen, Joseph Chinh (BO) Dorchester, MA St. Ambrose.
Nguyen, Joseph D. '08 (ORG) Newport Beach, CA Our Lady Queen of Angels.
Nguyen, Joseph Dau Van '84 (NO) Unassigned.
Nguyen, Joseph Hau Duc '69 (P) Retired.
Nguyen, Joseph Huyen '95 (SAC) Judges.
Nguyen, Joseph Long Kim '02 (ORG) Garden Grove, CA St. Callistus.
Nguyen, Joseph Luan '90 (ORG) Huntington Beach, CA St. Mary's by the Sea.
Nguyen, Joseph Luu '66 (HT) Retired.
Nguyen, Joseph Minh Tri '61 (NEW) Vietnamese Apostolate; Jersey City, NJ Parish of the Resurrection.
Nguyen, Joseph Minh Vu *s.v.d.* '96 (FgM) Techny, IL.
Nguyen, Joseph Phien '92 (RIC) Norfolk, VA Our Lady of Vietnam Chapel; Norfolk, VA Our Lady of Lavang.
Nguyen, Joseph Phiet The '73 (GAL) Hempstead, TX St. Katherine Drexel.
Nguyen, Joseph Quan '05 (LA) Moorpark, CA Holy Cross; Board of Directors.
Nguyen, Joseph Son '89 (ORG) Orange, CA UCI Medical Center.
Nguyen, Joseph Tan Doan *o.f.m.* '86 (FgM) U.S. Religious Serving Elsewhere.
Nguyen, Joseph Thai '95 (CHI) Other Assignments.
Nguyen, Joseph Thai '95 (ORG) Garden Grove, CA St. Columban.
Nguyen, Joseph Thieu '04 (OAK) Berkeley, CA St. Joseph The Worker.
Nguyen, Joseph Trong '69 (LAV) Las Vegas, NV Shrine of Our Lady of La Vang.
Nguyen, Joseph Trong *s.v.d.* '91 (FgM) Techny, IL.
Nguyen, Joseph Tuoc *s.j.* '89 (DEN) Denver, CO St. Ignatius Loyola; [N] Denver, CO Society of Jesus – St. Ignatius Loyola Jesuit Community.
Nguyen, Joseph Xuan Huong '85 (SAC) Vicars Forane.
Nguyen, Joseph '73 (FRS) Fresno, CA St. Francis.
Nguyen, Joseph *o.s.b.* '03 (P)[L] St. Benedict, OR Mt. Angel Abbey; Saint Benedict, OR.
Nguyen, Joseph '05 (OAK) Fremont, CA St. Joseph (Old Mission San Jose).
Nguyen, Joseph *o.p.* '93 (PHX) Phoenix, AZ Vietnamese Martyrs Parish Roman Catholic Parish.
Nguyen, Joseph *s.j.* (SEA)[L] Seattle, WA Jesuit House, Seattle.
Nguyen, Justin M. '09 (AUS) Temple, TX St. Luke.
Nguyen, Khanh Hai (STP)[S] Minneapolis, MN Queen Anne Communities.
Nguyen, Khanh Pham '97 (HON) Honolulu, HI Blessed Sacrament; Honolulu, HI St. Stephen.
Nguyen, Khanh '06 (SEA) Ferndale, WA St. Joseph.
Nguyen, Khiet '96 (TLS) Judges; Skiatook, OK Sacred Heart.
Nguyen, Khoa M. '01 (PH) Absent on Sick Leave.
Nguyen, Khoa *o.f.m.* '94 (FgM) New York, NY Holy Name Province.
Nguyen, Kim Son '87 (SAV) Savannah, GA Sts. Peter and Paul.
Nguyen, Lam *o.f.m.* '97 (WDC)[B] Silver Spring, MD Holy Name College.
Nguyen, Lam (STA) Jacksonville, FL Assumption.
Nguyen, Lich Van '84 (NO) Harvey, LA St. Martha.
Nguyen, Liem *o.s.b.* '94 (P)[A] St. Benedict, OR Mount Angel Seminary.
Nguyen, Linh N. '06 (CIN) On Duty Outside the Archdiocese.
Nguyen, Linh N. (GAL) Kingwood, TX St. Martha.
Nguyen, Linh T. (BO) Randolph, MA St. Bernadette.
Nguyen, Linh Tien '04 (SFR) South San Francisco, CA St. Veronica.
Nguyen, Linh '97 (LEX) Georgetown, KY SS. Francis & John Catholic Church.
Nguyen, Long Phi *s.v.d.* '07 (FgM) Techny, IL.
Nguyen, Long '08 (LA) Lynwood, CA St. Emydius.
Nguyen, Luan D. '08 (P) Lake Oswego, OR Our Lady of the Lake.
Nguyen, Luke Hungdung '02 (NO) New Orleans, LA Mary, Queen of Vietnam.
Nguyen, Mark Huynh Thanh *c.m.c.* '77 (FWT) Fort Worth, TX Our Lady of Fatima.
Nguyen, Martin Lam *c.s.c.* '89 (FTW)[B] University of Notre Dame Du Lac.
Nguyen, Martin Thanh *i.c.m.* '97 (BR)[H] Baton Rouge, LA Incarnatio Consecratio Missio.
Nguyen, Martin '05 (ORG) Brea, CA St. Angela Merici.
Nguyen, Martino Ba Thong '04 (SAV) Presbyteral Council.
Nguyen, Martino '04 (SAV) Grovetown, GA St. Teresa of Avila.
Nguyen, Matthias Huy Chuong *c.m.c.* '81 (SB) Special or Other Diocesan Assignment.
Nguyen, Michael Manh *c.m.* '95 (CHL) Greensboro, NC St. Mary; Consultors:.
Nguyen, Michael Nam Hoang '93 (NO) Terrytown, LA Christ the King.
Nguyen, Michael Quang *s.v.d.* '02 (FgM) Techny, IL.
Nguyen, Michael Tung '03 (ORG) Irvine, CA St. John Neumann.
Nguyen, Minh Hai *i.c.m.* '92 (BR) Baton Rouge, LA Sts. Anthony of Padua and Le Van Phung; [H] Baton Rouge, LA Incarnatio Consecratio Missio.
Nguyen, Minh '08 (SB) Perris, CA St. James.
Nguyen, Nghiem Van '89 (NO) River Ridge, LA St. Matthew the Apostle.
Nguyen, Nguyen Van '02 (NO) New Orleans, LA Chapel of the Vietnamese Martyrs; New Orleans, LA Mary, Queen of Vietnam.
Nguyen, Nhuan D. *m.m.* '93 (FgM) Maryknoll, NY MARYKNOLL.
Nguyen, Odon *o.s.b.* '65 (SFE)[H] Abiquiu, NM Monastery of Christ in the Desert.
Nguyen, Paul Chung '00 (PMB) Palm Springs, FL St. Luke.
Nguyen, Paul Chuong *s.d.b.* '88 (SP)[P] Tampa, FL Salesian Society of Florida, Inc.
Nguyen, Paul Cuong Hung *s.v.d.* (CHI) Wheeling, IL St. Joseph the Worker.
Nguyen, Paul Dean '07 (WDC) Bethesda, MD St. Jane Frances de Chantal.
Nguyen, Paul Hai *c.ss.r.* '97 (DAL) Diocesan Judges.
Nguyen, Paul Van Tung '79 (NO) Covington, LA St. Peter.
Nguyen, Paul '06 (DAL) Dallas, TX St. Patrick.
Nguyen, Paul *c.ss.r.* '97 (DAL) Garland, TX Mother of Perpetual Help.
Nguyen, Peter Duc Hung '97 (SC) Ruthven, IA Sacred Heart.
Nguyen, Peter H. (BRK)[S] Vietnamese Apostolate.
Nguyen, Peter Hung *s.o.l.t.* '02 (CC)[G] Robstown, TX Society of Our Lady of the Most Holy Trinity.
Nguyen, Peter Hung *s.o.l.t.* '00 (SFE) La Joya, NM Our Lady of Sorrows.
Nguyen, Peter Mau *c.ss.r.* '70 (TUC) Tucson, AZ Our Lady of LaVang Roman Catholic Parish – Tucson.
Nguyen, Peter P. *s.j.* '08 (CHI)[N] Chicago Chicago Province of the Society of Jesus–Provincial Office.
Nguyen, Rev. Msgr. Peter Quang '90 (DEN) Denver, CO Our Lady of Lourdes.
Nguyen, Peter Sam Cao *s.v.d.* '86 (FgM) Techny, IL.
Nguyen, Phi '06 (CHI) Oak Forest, IL St. Damian.
Nguyen, Phien T. '92 (CHI) Other Assignments.
Nguyen, Phillip D. '87 (GR) Personal Leave.
Nguyen, Phong Cao *s.v.d.* '06 (FgM) Techny, IL.
Nguyen, Polycarp *c.m.c.* '91 (FWT) Arlington, TX Church of the Vietnamese Martyrs.
Nguyen, Qui–Thac '04 (SEA)[O] Bellingham, WA Western Washington University (Bellingham); Bellingham, WA Sacred Heart.
Nguyen, Quoc *o.f.m.cap.* '02 (SFR)[B] San Francisco, CA Capuchin Franciscan Order San Buenaventura Friary.
Nguyen, Raphael Xuan '02 (ORG) Fountain Valley, CA Holy Spirit.
Nguyen, Scott C. '97 (WCH) On Duty Outside the Diocese.
Nguyen, Scott '97 (SB) Upland, CA St. Joseph.
Nguyen, Son Anh '03 (WOR) Worcester, MA Our Lady of Vilna; [K] Worcester, MA Saint Vincent Hospital, Inc.
Nguyen, Son *s.v.d.* '03 (MO) Air Force Chaplains.
Nguyen, Stephen Kha *s.v.d.* '06 (DUB)[B] Epworth, IA Divine Word College.
Nguyen, Stephen Tan *o.f.m.* '59 (SFR) San Francisco, CA St. Boniface.
Nguyen, Steve '99 (HON) Kailua, HI St. Anthony of Padua.
Nguyen, Steven '99 (HON) Judge.
Nguyen, Sy '91 (ORG)[H] Santa Ana, CA Vietnamese Catholic Center; Cursillo Movement; Adjutant Judicial Vicars; Council of Priests; Consultors.
Nguyen, Tam N. '82 (TLS) Tulsa, OK Christ the King; Diocesan Consultors; Priests' Personnel Committee.
Nguyen, Tam (OKL) Adjutant Judicial Vicars.
Nguyen, Tan Viet *s.v.d.* '03 (CHI)[N] Techny, IL Divine Word Residence.
Nguyen, Tan Viet *s.v.d.* (GAL) Houston, TX St. Mary of the Purification.
Nguyen, Tan '09 (SJ) Campbell, CA St. Lucy.
Nguyen, Tan *s.v.d.* (PIT) Allegheny County, PA UPMC Shadyside Hospital.
Nguyen, Te Van '86 (SFR) San Francisco, CA St. Brendan; Vietnamese Catholic Ministry; Laguna Honda Home.
Nguyen, Thai Hung '09 (SAG)[D] Saginaw, MI St. Mary's of Michigan Medical Center.
Nguyen, Thanh N. '94 (R) Hope Mills, NC Good Shepherd.
Nguyen, Thanh T. '91 (STA) Jacksonville, FL Christ the King; Diocesan Consultors; Presbyteral Council.
Nguyen, Thanh Van '00 (OKL) Oklahoma City, OK Cathedral of Our Lady of Perpetual Help; [B] Oklahoma City, OK Bishop McGuinness Catholic High School.
Nguyen, Thanh Vincent *c.ss.r.* '97 (AUS) Bryan, TX St. Joseph.
Nguyen, Thanh '67 (PRT) Retired.
Nguyen, Thao N. *s.j.* '08 (OAK)[M] Berkeley, CA Jesuit Fathers and Brothers.
Nguyen, That Son Ngoc '90 (WH) Gary, WV Our Lady of Victory; Powhatan, WV Sacred Heart; War, WV Christ the King; Welch, WV St. Peter.
Nguyen, Thien Van '89 (WIN) Plainview, MN St. Joachim's; Plainview, MN Immaculate Conception.
Nguyen, Thien '01 (WOR) Fitchburg, MA Immaculate Conception.
Nguyen, Thien '01 (MAN) Vietnamese Apostolate.
Nguyen, Thinh *s.d.b.* '99 (LA) Bellflower, CA St. Dominic Savio.
Nguyen, Thomas Thanh '69 (LAF) Franklin, LA St. Helena.
Nguyen, Thu Ngoc '93 (GAL) Houston, TX Co–Cathedral of the Sacred Heart; Archdiocesan Judges; Priests Personnel Committee.
Nguyen, Thu Van '92 (VIC) On Duty Outside the Diocese.
Nguyen, Thu '92 (FWT) Fort Worth, TX St. George.
Nguyen, Thuong '91 (OAK) San Leandro, CA Our Lady of Good Counsel; Deanery #19.
Nguyen, Thuy Quang '98 (GAL) Sealy, TX St. Mary; Wallis, TX Guardian Angel.
Nguyen, Tien Duc (ORG) Retired.
Nguyen, Tien–Tri '96 (SFE) Santa Fe, NM Our Lady of Guadalupe.
Nguyen, Timothy '02 (ORG) Laguna Niguel, CA St. Timothy.
Nguyen, Tinh Van '98 (BO) Billerica, MA St. Theresa of Lisieux.
Nguyen, Toan X. '96 (SFR) Novato, CA St. Anthony of Padua.
Nguyen, Tong Ba '09 (SB) La Quinta, CA St. Francis of Assisi.
Nguyen, Trong Joseph *s.v.d.* '91 (SB) Beaumont, CA Blessed Kateri Takakwitha Catholic Community, Inc.
Nguyen, Truc Q. '00 (LA) Los Angeles, CA Cathedral Chapel.
Nguyen, Truc '00 (LA) Defenders of the Bond; Canonical Staff.

Nguyen, Trung V. '94 (GAL)[A] Houston, TX St. Mary's Seminary; Archdiocesan Judges.
Nguyen, Truyen '03 (SJ) San Jose, CA St. Patrick.
Nguyen, Tu T. '07 (SAT) San Antonio, TX St. Joseph.
Nguyen, Tuan John '95 (ORG) Santa Ana, CA St. Barbara Catholic Church.
Nguyen, Tuan Van '86 (JOL) Villa Park, IL St. Alexander.
Nguyen, Tuan '92 (SEA) Tacoma, WA St. Ann; Tacoma, WA St. John of the Woods; Tacoma, WA St. Joseph; Tacoma, WA Holy Rosary; Tacoma, WA Sacred Heart; Tacoma, WA Visitation; College of Consultors; Presbyteral Council.
Nguyen, Tuan *s.d.b.* '88 (STO) Stockton, CA St. Luke Church of Stockton (Pastor of).
Nguyen, Tuan *c.ss.r.* '09 (LA)[P] In Res.
Nguyen, Tuyen '87 (ORG) Garden Grove, CA St. Callistus.
Nguyen, Ty Van '85 (HT) Bourg, LA St. Ann.
Nguyen, Van Hiep *s.v.d.* '99 (FgM) Techny, IL.
Nguyen, Van T. '79 (MO) Navy Reserve Chaplains.
Nguyen, Vandennis '90 (YAK) Richland, WA Christ the King.
Nguyen, vanThanh *s.v.d.* '97 (CHI)[N] Chicago, IL Divine Word Theologate; [B] Chicago, IL The Catholic Theological Union at Chicago.
Nguyen, Vien The '89 (NO) New Orleans, LA Mary, Queen of Vietnam; Vietnamese Catholics Office; Judges; New Orleans, LA Chapel of the Vietnamese Martyrs; [A] New Orleans, LA Notre Dame Seminary Graduate School of Theology.
Nguyen, Vien *s.c.j.* '04 (CHI)[N] Chicago, IL Priests of the Sacred Heart.
Nguyen, Vincent Kien '89 (HON) Vietnamese Catholic Community.
Nguyen, Vincent Liem *o.s.b.* '94 (P)[L] St. Benedict, OR Mt. Angel Abbey.
Nguyen, Vincent Vuong–Quoc '99 (GAL) The Woodlands, TX Sts. Simon and Jude.
Nguyen, Vinh Daniel *s.v.d.* '07 (FgM) Techny, IL.
Nguyen, Vinh Quang '86 (NEW) Fort Lee, NJ Holy Trinity.
Nguyen, Vitus H. *c.s.j.b.* '03 (BRK) Long Island City, NY Our Lady of Mount Carmel.
Nguyen–Thanh–Long, Peter '65 (WDC) Silver Spring, MD Our Lady of Vietnam.
Nguyen Chau Dien, Raymond M. *c.m.c.* '88 (SPC)[F] Carthage, MO Congregation of the Mother Coredemptrix, United States Assumption Province.
Nguyen Chautly, Lawrence M. *c.m.c.* (SPC)[F] Carthage, MO Congregation of the Mother Coredemptrix, United States Assumption Province.
Nguyen Hoan Luong, Dominic M. *c.m.c.* '08 (SPC)[F] Carthage, MO Congregation of the Mother Coredemptrix, United States Assumption Province.
Nguyen Hong An, Andrew M. *c.m.c.* '87 (SPC)[F] Carthage, MO Congregation of the Mother Coredemptrix, United States Assumption Province.
Nguyen Ngoc Ban, Tadeus M. *c.m.c.* '73 (SPC)[F] Carthage, MO Congregation of the Mother Coredemptrix, United States Assumption Province.
Nguyen Trung Chanh, Dominic M. *c.m.c.* '09 (SPC)[F] Carthage, MO Congregation of the Mother Coredemptrix, United States Assumption Province.
Nguyen Tuan Binh, Thomas M. *c.m.c.* '04 (SPC)[J] Joplin, MO Newman Club, Missouri Southern State University; [F] Carthage, MO Congregation of the Mother Coredemptrix, United States Assumption Province; Campus Ministries.
Nguyen Van Quy, Peter *o.f.m.* '71 (NY)[EE] New York Franciscan Province of the Immaculate Conception.
Ngyen, Joseph Liep Van '63 (CC) Retired.
Ngyen, Peter *c.s.j.b.* (BRK)[H] Astoria, NY St. John Preparatory School.
Nhien, Louis M. Vu Minh *c.m.c.* (SPC)[F] Carthage, MO Congregation of the Mother Coredemptrix, United States Assumption Province.
Nho, Do Duy '66 (LR) North Little Rock, AR St. Patrick.
Niblick, Charles W. '74 (GRY) Dyer, IN St. Maria Goretti.
Nicastro, Thomas D. '90 (NEW) Bayonne, NJ Our Lady of the Assumption.
Nicastro, Thomas *o.f.m.* '42 (ALB)[A] Catskill, NY St. Anthony Friary.
Niccolls, Edward D. '74 (WOR) Worcester, MA St. Christopher; Clergy Benefit Plan.
Nicgorski, David *o.m.v.* '91 (BO)[U] Milton, MA Oblate Residence (St. Joseph House).
Nicholas, Gerald A. *o.s.a.* '66 (MIL)[P] Racine, WI Augustinian Novitiate; Racine, WI St. Rita.
Nicholas, William C. '01 (SFR) Novato, CA Our Lady of Loretto.
Nicholl, Rev. Msgr. Rex '67 (AMA) Cursillo Movement; Amarillo, TX St. Martin De Porres Mission.
Nicholl, Rev. Msgr. Rex '67 (AMA) Diocesan Council of Catholic Women; College of Consultors.
Nicholls, Trevor '90 (NY)[E] Bronx, NY Cardinal Spellman High School.
Nichols, Aquinas *o.s.b.* '80 (DM) Des Moines, IA Basilica of Saint John.
Nichols, Harry E. '73 (PIT) Pittsburgh, PA St. Patrick–St. Stanislaus Kostka.
Nichols, Henry P. '70 (MO) Military & VA Chaplains.; DEPARTMENT OF VETERANS AFFAIRS HOSPITALS AND CHAPLAINS; Pastoral Care.
Nichols, Irby C. '01 (SFE) Albuquerque, NM St. Anne.
Nichols, John J. '62 (BO) Senior Priests. Retired.
Nichols, Joseph E. '62 (NOR) Norwich, CT St. Patrick Cathedral Retired.
Nichols, Louis J. '60 (SR) Mendocino, CA St. Anthony; On Duty Outside the Diocese.
Nichols, Roderick '89 (LSC) Silver City, NM St. Vincent de Paul.
Nichols, Rev. Msgr. Timothy E. '73 (LA) Hacienda Heights, CA St. John Vianney; Members.
Nicholson, Francis J. *s.j.* '53 (BO)[U] Weston, MA Campion Health Center, Inc.
Nicholson, Patrick '69 (MOB) On Leave from the Archdiocese.
Nickel, Leander '47 (GB) Retired.
Nickels, Larry *o.f.m.* '86 (BEL) Carlyle, IL St. Felicitas.
Nickels, Lawrence M. *o.f.m.* '86 (BEL) Carlyle, IL St. Teresa of Avila.
Nickels, Lawrence M. *o.f.m.* (STL)[V] St. Louis, MO The Franciscan Connection.
Nickels, Peter *o.f.m.conv.* '60 (LSC)[D] Mesilla Park, NM Holy Cross Retreat and Friary.
Nickerson, Oliver E. *s.j.* '54 (FgM) Watertown, MA Society of Jesus.
Nickle, Fred *o.f.m.cap.* '65 (NY)[EE] Beacon, NY St. Joachim Friary; [Q] Garrison, NY Capuchin Youth and Family Ministries.
Nicknair, Harold W. '61 (PRT) Retired.
Nicknair, Rev. Msgr. Leopold G. '58 (PRT) Madawaska, ME Notre Dame du Mont Carmel Parish Retired.
Nickol, G. Eugene '73 (BAL) Millersville, MD Our Lady of the Fields; Advocates.
Nicks, Matthew '08 (SPK) Pasco, WA St. Patrick.
Nicola, John J. '55 (CHI) Retired.
Nicolas, Jean Vanes '85 (ARL) Falls Church, VA St. Anthony's.
Nicolas, Jeffrey S. '93 (L) Louisville, KY Epiphany; Ex Officio.
Nicolau, Rev. Msgr. Juan '60 (BWN) McAllen, TX Our Lady of Perpetual Help.
Nicoletti, Maurizio *o.cist.* '65 (TR) Mount Laurel, NJ St. John Neumann; [N] Mount Laurel, NJ Cistercian Monastery of Our Lady of Fatima; Mount Laurel, NJ.
Nicolicchia, J. Andrew *o.p.* '65 (WDC) Washington, DC St. Dominic Church & Priory.
Nicoll, Leo A. *s.j.* '61 (NO)[C] New Orleans, LA Loyola University New Orleans.
Nicolo, Rev. Msgr. Joseph J. '74 (PH) Blue Bell, PA St. Helena; Approved Advocates.
Nicolosi, Joseph P. '97 (RCK) Hampshire, IL St. Charles Borromeo.
Nicolosi, Mark Ronald *o.s.b.* '67 (BUR)[E] Weston, VT Priory of Benedictine Monks.
Nicosia, Peter *o.f.m.cap.* '59 (SP) Tampa, FL Most Holy Redeemer.
Nicosia, Vincent *s.o.l.t.* '92 (CC)[G] Robstown, TX Society of Our Lady of the Most Holy Trinity.
Nieberding, Rick *c.pp.s.* '80 (CIN) Minster, OH St. Joseph; Minster, OH St. Augustine.
Nieberding, Robert '56 (LEX) Lexington, KY Mary, Queen of the Holy Rosary Retired.
Nieblas, James *s.d.b.* '86 (LA)[P] Los Angeles, CA Dominic Savio Salesian Residence.
Niebrzydowski, Rev. Msgr. Walter J. '59 (NY) New York, NY Epiphany; New York, NY Our Lady of the Scapular and St. Stephen Retired.
Nieckarz, James P. *m.m.* '66 (NY)[EE] Staten Island, NY St. Adalbert.
Niedergeses, Bernard '50 (NSH) Retired.
Niedermier, Jerome G. '52 (TOL) Retired.
Niehaus, Charles W. *s.j.* '74 (LEX) Lexington, KY St. Paul.
Niehaus, Francis H. '55 (CIN) Retired.
Niehaus, Jonathan J. '94 (MIL)[T] Waukesha, WI Schoenstatt Fathers.
Niehaus, Mark J. '03 (MIL)[T] Waukesha, WI Schoenstatt Fathers.
Niehaus, Thomas M. '08 (WIN) Winona, MN Cathedral of the Sacred Heart.
Niehoff, Edmund A. (Larry) '64 (SHP) Mansfield, LA St. Joseph; Priests' Retirement Board.
Niehoff, Kevin W. *o.p.* '93 (SFE) Presbyteral Council of the Archdiocese of Santa Fe.
Niehoff, Kevin W. *o.p.* '93 (SFE) Albuquerque, NM St. Thomas Aquinas University Parish; Adjutant Judicial Vicar; [K] Albuquerque, NM St. Thomas Aquinas (Newman Center) University Parish.
Niehoff, Robert J. *s.j.* '82 (CLV)[B] University Heights, OH John Carroll University; [B] University Heights, OH John Carroll Jesuit Community.
Niekamp, Philip E. '05 (JC) Freeburg, MO Holy Family; Rich Fountain, MO Sacred Heart; Appointed Members; Diocesan Consultors.
Nieli, Bruce *c.s.p.* '73 (MEM) Memphis, TN St. Patrick's.
Nielsen, Eric H. '95 (MAD) Madison, WI St. Paul University Parish; [I] Madison, WI St. Paul University Catholic Foundation, Inc.
Nielsen, Kenneth M. '80 (BUF) On Duty Outside the Diocese.
Nielson, Kenneth (Karl) '99 (AUS) Chaplains of the Military.
Nielson, Kenneth W. '99 (MO) Army Chaplains.
Nielson, Thomas A. '59 (NY)[II] New York, NY St. Ansgar Scandinavian Catholic League Retired.
Niemann, Paul J. '80 (STL) St. Ann, MO Holy Trinity.
Niemann, Paul '80 (PRM) St. Louis, MO St. Louis Mission.
Niemczyk, Stefan J. '87 (SPR) Three Rivers, MA SS. Peter and Paul; Deans; Three Rivers, MA St. Anne's.
Niemeier, Dennis A. '73 (CIN) Retired.
Niemeier, Dennis '73 (ATL) Military Chaplains.
Niemeyer, Roger *o.f.m.* '40 (SFD)[L] Springfield, IL Our Lady of Angels Friary.
Niemiec, Antoninus *o.p.* '01 (NY)[EE] New York, NY St. Vincent Ferrer Priory.
Niemier, Roch *o.f.m.* '65 (MIL)[P] Provincial Offices of the Franciscan Friars, Assumption BVM Province, Inc.; Provincial Councilors:.
Niemira, Thomas '65 (JKS) Retired.
Nienaber, Paul J. *s.j.* '99 (CHI)[N] Chicago Chicago Province of the Society of Jesus–Provincial Office.
Nienaber, Paul J. *s.j.* '99 (WIN) Additional Diocesan Assignments.
Nienaber, Rev. Msgr. Robert H. '63 (OM) Retired.
Nienhaus, Gerald T. '62 (STL) Chesterfield, MO Incarnate Word.
Nienhaus, Ivan R. '89 (DUB) On Special or Other Archdiocesan Assignment.
Niese, Larry '95 (ATL) Woodstock, GA St. Michael the Archangel.
Nieset, Frank E. '56 (TOL) Retired.
Niespolo, Aelred *o.s.b.* '05 (LA)[P] Valyermo, CA St. Andrew's Abbey.
Nietes, Romeo C. '63 (HON) Honolulu, HI SS Peter and Paul.
Nietfeld, Fred J. '46 (TOL) Retired.
Nieto, Gustavo (NY) New York, NY St. Paul; Bronx, NY St. Jerome's; [EE] New York, NY Institute of the Incarnate Word, Inc.
Nieto, Jose *c.m.f.* '66 (SJN) Bayamon, PR San Antonio Maria Claret.
Nieto–Ruiz, Jesus '94 (OAK) Oakland, CA St. Anthony; Deanery #11; Presbyteral Council.
Nieva, Constantino S. '63 (RVC) Retired.
Nieva, Javier *d.c.j.m.* '00 (DEN) Littleton, CO St. Mary.
Nieves, Angel Valle '08 (MGZ) Rosario, PR Our Lady of Rosary.
Nieves, Carlos '86 (PCE) On Duty Outside the Diocese.
Nieves, Encarnación '83 (CGS) Comerio, PR Santo Cristo de la Salud.
Nieves, Pablo *s.x.* '99 (PAT)[N] Wayne Xaverian Missionary Fathers; Wayne, NJ XAVERIAN MISSIONARY FATHERS.
Niewczas, Taddeus '52 (RVC) Retired.
Niewiadomski, Arthur J. '94 (TOL) Bascom, OH St. Patrick; Bascom, OH St. Andrew.
Niez, Lester *a.m.* (TUC) Tucson, AZ Saint Joseph Roman Catholic Parish – Tucson.
Niggel, Clement '03 (SFE) Chama, NM St. Patrick; San Jose; Tierra Amarilla, NM Santo Nino.
Nigli, Francis A. '97 (OM) O'Neill, NE St. Patrick.
Nijem, Rev. Msgr. Fred J. '68 (SAV) Warner Robins, GA Sacred Heart; Presbyteral Council.
Niklas, Gerald R. '59 (CIN)[K] Cincinnati, OH Good Samaritan Hospital.
Nikodem, Ronald J. *s.m.* '94 (WH) Buckhannon, WV Holy Rosary; [O] Buckhannon, WV West Virginia Wesleyan College Newman Center.
Nikolic, Dennis '02 (NY) Middletown, NY St. Joseph.
Nilema, Nicholas *a.l.c.p./o.s.s.* '88 (P) Seaside, OR Our Lady of Victory.
Nilema, Nicholas *a.l.c.p.* (P) Area Vicars.
Nilles, Rev. Msgr. Allan F. '49 (FAR) Retired.
Nilles, Roger G. '59 (MAD) Madison, WI St. Peter.
Nilsson, Richard A. '71 (RVC) Roslyn, NY St. Mary's.
Nimerichter, Dean '92 (DM) Cumberland, IA St. Timothy; Griswold, IA Our Lady Of Grace; Diocesan Consultors.
Nimocks, Michael '96 (COL) Marion, OH St. Mary.
Nimu, Lusius *ss.cc.* '03 (HON) Honolulu, HI St. Augustine by the Sea.
Nin, Felino Reyes '89 (NY) New York, NY Incarnation.
Ninemire, Kerry '75 (SAL) Salina, KS St. Mary Queen of the Universe Parish; College of Consultors; Vicariate Representatives; Priests' Continuing Formation Committee; Council of Priests.
Ninh van Pham, James '67 (P) College of Consultors.
Niniel, Jovito '93 (HON) Honolulu, HI St. Pius X; Honolulu, HI Sacred Heart.
Nirappel, James '90 (SYM) Hagerstown, MD Syro–Malabar Catholic Mission of Baltimore.
Nirappel, James (BAL) Hagerstown, MD St. Mary.
Nirappel, Joshy T. *c.m.f.* '95 (MET) Perth Amboy, NJ Our Lady of Fatima.
Nirschl, Nicholas E. *o.praem.* '56 (SFE)[H] Albuquerque, NM Santa Maria de la Vid Priory.
Nisari, Joseph '68 (AUS) Granger, TX SS. Cyril and

Methodius; Sts. Cyril & Methodius School Endowment.
Nisbet, James '69 (MRY) Spreckels, CA St. Joseph.
Nischan, James R. '83 (PCE) On Duty Outside the Diocese.
Nishimura, Bryce T. *m.m.* '56 (FgM) Maryknoll, NY MARYKNOLL.
Nishimuta, James K. *m.m.* '54 (NY)[EE] Retired.
Niskanen, Stephen *c.m.f.* '90 (LA) San Gabriel, CA San Gabriel Mission.
Nitoski, Gerald A. '51 (DET) Retired.
Nitz, Eliot *s.d.s.* '68 (WDC)[B] Silver Spring, MD Salvatorian Community.
Niven, Timothy L. '98 (ROC) Victor, NY St. Patrick.
Nix, Albert P. '73 (PAT) Retired.
Nix, Julian *o.s.b.* '87 (BIS)[A] Richardton, ND Assumption Abbey.
Nixon, Joseph J. '85 (RVC) Copiague, NY Our Lady of the Assumption.
Niyitegeka, Cyprien '00 (SPK) Okanogan, WA Our Lady of the Valley.
Niziolek, Terry *m.s.* '48 (ORL) Orlando, FL Good Shepherd.
Njau, Francis *a.j.* '98 (P)[J] Portland, OR Providence St. Vincent Medical Center.
Njoku, Francis '97 (SAN) Garden City, TX St. Lawrence.
Njoku, Hippolytu (SAC) Sacramento, CA St. Paul.
Njoku, Hippolytus *s.m.m.m.* '95 (SAC) Sacramento, CA University of California, Davis Medical Center.
Njoku, Hyacinth '86 (NY) East Elmhurst, NY North Infirmary Command.
Njoku, Titus C. '04 (NEW) Jersey City, NJ St. Anne's.
Njus, Jeffrey '03 (LAN) Lansing, MI St. Mary Cathedral.
Njuu, Augustine R. *a.j.* '83 (SPC) St. John's Regional Health Center; [D] Springfield, MO St. John's Regional Health Center.
Nkachukwu, Michael C. '80 (DET) Presbyteral Council; Detroit, MI Good Shepherd; Archdiocesan Vicars.
Nkuanga, Anselme Malonda *c.i.c.m.* '92 (FgM) Arlington, VA MISSIONHURST; Arlington, VA.
Nkuanga, Anselme Malonda *c.i.c.m.* '92 (ARL)[H] Arlington, VA Missionhurst, C.I.C.M.–Central House and Provincialate.
Nkumbi, Paul '96 (SFE) Roy, NM Holy Family–St. Joseph; Wagon Mound, NM Santa Clara.
Nkwasibwe, L. Frederick *a.j.* '99 (HBG) York, PA Immaculate Conception of the Blessed Virgin Mary; York, PA York Hospital.
Nkyi, Anthony '94 (OM) Omaha, NE St. Pius X.
Nnabaugo, Theodore '00 (BAK) Klamath Falls, OR Sacred Heart.
Nnabuife, Charles Chika '05 (BAK) Council of Priests and Diocesan Consultors; The Dalles, OR St. Peter.
Nnadozie, Edmund C. *m.s.p.* '97 (GAL) Houston, TX St. Francis of Assisi.
Nnajiofor, Polycarp '91 (RVC) Mineola, NY Corpus Christi; Mineola, NY Winthrop Hospital.
Nnamezie, Tema Godwin (PBL)[C] Canon City, CO Centura Health–St. Thomas More Hospital.
Nnaso, Sylvester '02 (RCK) Byron, IL St. Mary.
Nnaukwu, Alex C. '93 (NEW) Hackensack, NJ Hackensack University Medical Center.
Nnorom, Columba A. '74 (RIC) Ebony, VA St. Richard; Ebony, VA St. Peter The Apostle.
Noah, Daniel '50 (CR) Retired.
Noah, Timothy T. '47 (CR) Hallock, MN St. Patrick's.
Nobbe, Scott E. '06 (IND) Seymour, IN Our Lady of Providence; Seymour, IN St. Ambrose.
Nobile, Angelo '53 (MEM) Retired.
Nobiletti, Raymond J. *m.m.* '69 (NY) New York, NY Transfiguration.
Noble, Bruce H. '87 (GAL)[S] Houston, TX The Catholic Chaplain Corps.
Noble, David H. '87 (GAL)[S] Houston, TX The Catholic Chaplain Corps.
Noble, Jeffery J. '86 (E) Hermitage, PA Church of Notre Dame; Deans.
Noble, Paul A. '81 (COL) Gahanna, OH St. Matthew; Diocesan Judges; Diocesan Board of Review for the Protection of Children.
Nobrega, Kenneth '08 (OAK) Pinole, CA St. Joseph.
Nocchi, Martin S. '04 (BAL) Special Assignment; [R] Sparks, MD Msgr. Clare J. O'Dwyer Retreat House.
Nocero, Pascal Francis '48 (LA) Retired.
Noche, Joselito M. '07 (TR) Spring Lake, NJ St. Catharine.
Nochelski, Paul W. *s.j.* '71 (BUF)[O] Buffalo, NY Canisius Jesuit Community Inc.
Nock, James J. '64 (HRT) East Hartford, CT Blessed Sacrament; East Hartford, CT Our Lady of Peace.
Nockunas, Anthony *m.i.c.* (SPR)[H] Stockbridge, MA Congregation of Marian Fathers of The Immaculate Conception of the Most Blessed Virgin Mary.
Noda, Jorge '84 (MIA) Hialeah, FL St. John the Apostle.
Noe, John P. '74 (LEX) Ashland, KY Holy Family; Ashland, KY; [D] Ashland, KY Our Lady of Bellefonte Hospital, Inc.
Noel, Guyma '97 (ATL) Lithonia, GA Christ Our Hope.
Noel, Marc A. '98 (ALX) Moreauville, LA Our Lady of Sorrows; Moreauville, LA Sacred Heart.
Noesen, Rev. Msgr. Gerald '50 (CR) Retired.
Noesen, Rev. Msgr. Jerry '55 (CR) Diocesan Consultors; Priests' Council.
Noesen, Robert '93 (JOL) Coal City, IL Assumption of the Blessed Virgin Mary.
Nofi, Michael *m.s.a.* '74 (NOR)[G] Cromwell Society of the Missionaries of the Holy Apostles.
Noga, Edward P. '76 (Y) Youngstown, OH St. Patrick; Priests Council.
Noga, Gregory J. '79 (PSC) Trenton, NJ St. Mary; Central New Jersey Protopresbyterate; Office for Eastern Christian Formation (formerly: Office of Religious Education).
Noga, Henry *s.v.d.* '96 (ORG)[H] Yorba Linda, CA Pope John Paul II Polish Center.
Noga, John T. '99 (CHI) Chicago, IL St. Daniel the Prophet.
Nogaro, Paul M. '71 (BUF) Grand Island, NY St. Stephen.
Nogosek, Robert J. *c.s.c.* '56 (FTW)[H] Holy Cross House.
Noguera, Dagoberto '83 (BRK) Brooklyn, NY St. Anthony of Padua–St. Alphonsus.
Noguera, Ronald '81 (MIA) Hialeah, FL Immaculate Conception Retired.
Nohs, Joseph E. '93 (RVC) New Hyde Park, NY Holy Spirit.
Noiseux, Donald A. '84 (SPR) On Sabbatical.
Nolan, Brian J. '91 (MET) Watchung, NJ St. Mary–Stony Hill; Deans.
Nolan, Brian P. '01 (BAL)[B] Emmitsburg, MD Mount Saint Mary's University; Special Assignment.
Nolan, Colman J. *s.t.* '56 (B) Post Falls, ID St. George's.
Nolan, Daniel T. *c.s.v.* '83 (CHI)[N] Arlington Heights Viatorian Province Center–Clerics of St. Viator.
Nolan, David E. '95 (NY) Beacon, NY St. John the Evangelist.
Nolan, Emmett J. *c.m.* (BRK)[T] Brooklyn, NY St. John the Baptist Rectory; Brooklyn, NY St. John the Baptist.
Nolan, Eugene A. *s.j.* '71 (WDC)[N] Washington, DC The Jesuit Community at Georgetown University.
Nolan, James L. *o.s.a.* '46 (PH)[Y] Villanova, PA St. Thomas Monastery.
Nolan, Jerome M. '74 (TR) Bradley Beach, NJ Ascension.
Nolan, John '77 (SFD) Chatham, IL St. Joseph the Worker.
Nolan, Joseph A. '60 (ORL) Melbourne Beach, FL Immaculate Conception.
Nolan, Joseph J. *m.s.* '48 (HRT)[L] Hartford, CT Missionaries of LaSalette.
Nolan, Joseph M. '47 (BRK) Cambria Heights, NY Sacred Heart Retired.
Nolan, Joseph T. '53 (WCH) Retired.
Nolan, Justin *o.s.b.* '55 (GBG)[G] Latrobe, PA Saint Vincent Archabbey.
Nolan, Justin *f.s.s.p.* '03 (SCR)[E] Moscow, PA St. Gregory's Academy; [M] Elmhurst, PA Priestly Fraternity of St. Peter (F.S.S.P.), North American District Headquarters.
Nolan, Kevin L. '90 (LA) Culver City, CA St. Augustine; Deanery 13; Members; Army Reserve Chaplains.
Nolan, Kieran *o.s.b.* '59 (FgM)[I] Collegeville St. John's Abbey, of the Order of St. Benedict; Collegeville, MN St. John's Abbey.
Nolan, Michael E. '84 (WCH) Goddard, KS Holy Spirit; Adjutant Judicial Vicar; Judges; Ongoing Formation of the Clergy Committee; Building Commission; Worship Office.
Nolan, Michael F. '87 (KNX) Diocesan Consultors; Kingsport, TN St. Dominic.
Nolan, Michael L. (BO) Waltham, MA St. Mary.
Nolan, Michael '00 (BO)[AA] Bridgewater, MA Bridgewater State College Catholic Center.
Nolan, Paul J. '57 (NEW) Retired.
Nolan, Paul '57 (NEW) South Kearny, NJ Hudson County Correctional Center; Newark, NJ Delaney Hall Assessment Center.
Nolan, Peter P. *c.s.sp.* '59 (BO) Hyde Park, MA Most Precious Blood; Milton, MA St. Pius Tenth.
Nolan, Robert *s.a.c.* '70 (CAM)[C] Pennsauken, NJ Bishop Eustace Prep School.
Nolan, Shawn *o.f.m.conv.* '55 (NY)[EE] Staten Island, NY St. Francis Friary Retired.
Nolan, Rev. Msgr. Terence '66 (SAT)[K] San Antonio, TX Casa De Padres; Chancellor; College of Consultors; Archdiocesan Presbyteral Council; Judicial Vicar; Judges; Catholic Lawyers Guild.
Nolan, Timothy F. '67 (STP) Retired.
Nolan, Timothy M. '02 (WIL) Associate Directors; New Castle, DE Holy Spirit.
Nolan, Timothy '92 (PEO) Pekin, IL St. Joseph's; Vicariates and Vicars.
Nolan, Rev. Msgr. Walter E. '69 (TR) Princeton, NJ St. Paul; Tribunal Judges; Diocesan Consultors.
Nolan, William A. '85 (MAD) Retired.
Nolan, William J. '69 (TR)[N] Trenton, NJ Villa Vianney Retired.
Nolette, Mark P. '87 (PRT) Dexter, ME Our Lady of the Snows Parish; Dexter, ME St. Agnes.
Nolker, Thomas C. '72 (CIN) Cincinnati, OH St. James the Greater; Judges.
Noll, Daniel J. '76 (LEX) Versailles, KY St. Leo; College of Consultors; Priests' Personnel.
Nollette, Louis A. '75 (GI) Ainsworth, NE St. Pius X; Ongoing Formation for Clergy and Liturgy; Priests' Advisory Board (Presbyteral Council); Diocesan Consultors.
Nollette, Neal P. '80 (GI) Chappell, NE St. Joseph's; Priests' Advisory Board (Presbyteral Council); Rural Life Conference.
Nolte, Walter L. '03 (OM) Creighton, NE St. Ludger.
Nombre, Ronnie (NEW) Elizabeth, NJ St. Genevieve's.
Nomellini, Paul J. '77 (MAR) Retired.
Nondorf, Aloysius J. '57 (GRY) Military Chaplains.
Nondorf, Timothy '99 (SAC) Vice Chancellor and Secretary to the Bishop; Priests' Personnel Board, Diocesan.
Nonis, Pattinikuttige Kingsley '93 (BEL) Newman Catholic Student Center; Carterville, IL Church of the Holy Spirit.
Nontol, Lucio *t.o.r.* (NEW) Newark, NJ Immaculate Heart of Mary.
Noon, Rev. Msgr. Robert L. '51 (COL) Retired.
Noonan, Bradford '99 (COS) Castle Rock, CO St. Francis of Assisi.
Noonan, Guy '76 (STA) St. Augustine, FL Our Lady of Good Counsel.
Noonan, Joseph T. '95 (CHI) Archdiocesan Vocations; Chicago, IL Holy Name Cathedral.
Noonan, Mark J. '07 (BUF) Tonawanda, NY St. Amelia.
Noonan, Mark L. '59 (BO) Senior Priests. Retired.
Noonan, Patrick '63 (JKS) Retired.
Noonan, Robert C. '64 (HEL) Defenders of the Bond Retired.
Noonan, Robert (GF)[J] Great Falls, MT Retrouvaille of Montana.
Noonan, Rev. Msgr. Thomas F. '45 (BRK) Brooklyn, NY St. Edmund; Teachers Retired.
Noone, Charles J. '67 (PH) Oreland, PA Holy Martyrs Retired.
Noone, David E. '66 (ALB) Loudonville, NY Christ Our Light Roman Catholic Church.
Noone, John T. '67 (BLX) Kiln, MS Annunciation.
Noone, Rev. Msgr. Kevin B. '70 (BRK) Brooklyn, NY Our Lady of Angels; Assignment Board.
Nooney, Patrick J. '52 (SC) Retired.
Noradounghian, Antoine '96 (OLN) Brooklyn, NY St. Ann's Armenian Catholic Cathedral.
Norbeck, Ernest '84 (JOL) Downers Grove, IL St. Mary of Gostyn.
Norcavage, Albert R. '50 (ALT) Absent on Leave.
Nord, Aaron P. '07 (STL) Special Assignment.
Nord, Paul *o.s.b.* '07 (IND)[K] St. Meinrad, IN St. Meinrad Archabbey; [A] St. Meinrad, IN Saint Meinrad School of Theology.
Nordeman, John J. '01 (PH)[BB] West Chester, PA West Chester University; On Special or Other Archdiocesan Assignment; West Chester, PA St. Maximilian Kolbe.
Norden, Emmett M. '62 (MAR)[C] Escanaba, MI O.S.F. St. Francis Hospital Retired.
Nordenbrock, William *c.pp.s.* '83 (CHI)[W] Chicago, IL Precious Blood Ministry of Reconciliation.
Nordenbrock, William *c.pp.s.* '83 (CIN)[N] Dayton Provincial Office of the Cincinnati Province of the Society of the Precious Blood.
Norder, John '66 (MAD) Cassville, WI St. Charles Borromeo; Cassville, WI St. Mary Help of Christians.
Nordhaus, Jeffrey J. '72 (TOL) Custar, OH St. Louis; Deshler, OH Immaculate Conception; Members.
Nordick, Jack (John) A. '90 (NU) Cottonwood, MN St. Mary; Marshall, MN Holy Redeemer.
Nordick, Jerome '83 (SCL) Rockville, MN Holy Cross; Rockville, MN Mary of the Immaculate Conception.
Nordmeyer, Emeric *o.f.m.* '56 (SFE) Albuquerque, NM Queen of Angels Native American Center and Archdiocesan Shrine to Kateri Tekakwitha; [H] Albuquerque, NM The Province of Our Lady of Guadalupe.
Nordquist, Theodore A. '80 (GRY) Lowell, IN St. Edward; Girl Scout Liaison.
Noreika, Michael *s.s.s.* '70 (CLV)[N] Cleveland, OH Congregation of the Blessed Sacrament.
Norena, Nicholas '94 (MET) Perth Amboy, NJ La Asuncion.
Norfolk, Jeffrey Thomas '09 (SFS) Aberdeen, SD St. Mary.
Norick, Daniel J. '97 (DEN) Denver, CO St. Anthony of Padua; Deaneries; Elected Representatives from Deanery to Presbyteral Council.
Noriega, Arnoldo '75 (TUC) Leave of Absence.
Noriega, Arnoldo '83 (TUC) Retired.
Noriega Puga, Segundo Manuel (SJN) Rio Piedras, PR Santismo Sacramento.
Norkett, Michael '68 (OAK) Oakland, CA St. Paschal Baylon.
Norman, Charles *o.s.f.s.* '65 (ALN)[O] Easton, PA Lafayette College (Easton).
Norman, Clifford A. '60 (PBL) On Duty Outside the Diocese.

Norman, Gary '94 (YAK) Ephrata, WA St. Rose of Lima.
Norman, John (SLC) Magna, UT Our Lady of Lourdes LLC 209.
Norman, Reginald D. '09 (BGP) Bridgeport, CT Blessed Sacrament; Bridgeport, CT Our Lady of Good Counsel.
Norman, Reginald (BGP) African Americans, Apostolate of.
Norman, Richard W. *s.j.* '58 (ALN)[A] Wernersville, PA Jesuit Center–Jesuit Community.
Noronha, Konrad *s.j.* '06 (BAL)[S] Baltimore, MD Jesuit Community of Loyola University, Inc.
Norris, David J. '74 (FRS) School of Ministry; On Special Assignment; [A] Fresno, CA San Joaquin Memorial High School; Fresno, CA St. Paul Newman Center.
Norris, Patrick F. *o.p.* '89 (MAD) Madison, WI Blessed Sacrament; Diocesan Consultors.
Norris, Thomas P. *o.s.f.s.* '73 (R) Goldsboro, NC St. Mary.
Norris, Timothy L. '94 (STP) Shakopee, MN St. Mark.
Norris, Walter A. '73 (CAM) Auditors.
Norris, Walter '73 (CAM) National Park, NJ St. Matthew's Catholic Church, National Park, N.J.
Norsworthy, Richard '85 (SHP) Bastrop, LA St. Joseph.
Northrop, James '97 (SEA) Presbyteral Council; Deans; Bothell, WA St. Brendan.
Northrop, John B. *m.m.* '74 (NY)[EE] Maryknoll Maryknoll Fathers and Brothers.
Northrup, Gerald *s.f.o.* '01 (FRS) Scouting Retired.
Norton, Edward *s.v.d.* '45 (CHI)[N] Techny, IL Divine Word Residence.
Norton, Robert A. '72 (PIT) Pittsburgh, PA St. Athanasius.
Norton, Robert J. *o.f.m.* (PAT) Lincoln Park, NJ St. Joseph's; Wayne, NJ St. Joseph's Wayne Hospital; Pompton Plains, NJ Chilton Memorial Hospital.
Norton, Stephen P. '01 (NY) Hopewell Junction, NY St. Denis.
Norton, Thomas '63 (NEW) Retired.
Nortz, Alfred E. '55 (SY)[Q] Syracuse, NY Tommy Coyne Residence Dillon Hall Retired.
Nortz, Robert '07 (SAM)[B] Petersham, MA Maronite Monks of Adoration Most Holy Trinity Monastery.
Norvel, William L. *s.s.j.* '65 (WDC) Washington, DC Our Lady of Perpetual Help.
Nosbush, Peter C. '70 (NU) North Mankato, MN Holy Rosary.
Nosser, Rev. Msgr. Charles J. '53 (RVC) Floral Park, NY Our Lady of Victory Retired.
Nosser, Rev. Msgr. John C. '64 (RVC) Ocean Beach, NY Our Lady of the Magnificat; Judges for Interdiocesan Tribunal Retired.
Notabartolo, Charles E. '77 (PMB)[K] Diocesan Pension Plan Trust; Vicar General; Moderator of Curia; Consultors; [K] Diocese of Palm Beach Health Plan Trust; Ex Officio; Tequesta, FL St. Jude.
Notaro, Carlo *m.i.* '88 (MIL)[P] Milwaukee, WI St. Camillus Provincialate.
Notarpole, Joseph '49 (STA) Retired.
Notebaart, James C. '71 (STP) Special Assignment; Minneapolis, MN Church of Gichiwaa Kateri.
Nott, David L. '93 (RIC) Tribunal Staff; Petersburg, VA St. John.
Notter, Richard E. '63 (TOL) Retired.
Nourie, Paul *o.m.i.* '64 (SD) Chula Vista, CA Most Precious Blood.
Nouza, Frank M. *o.p.* '58 (CHI)[N] Chicago Dominicans (Provincial Office).
Nouza, Frank (SD)[O] Valley Center, CA North County Magnificat.
Novack, Kevin '81 (PBL) Pueblo, CO Holy Rosary; Pueblo, CO Our Lady of the Meadows; Deans.
Novak, David A. '79 (CLV) Lakewood, OH St. Clement.
Novak, David A. '77 (STL) Retired.
Novak, Francis A. *c.ss.r.* '49 (STL)[O] Liguori, MO St. Clement Health Care Center; Liguori, MO National Catholic Conference for Total Stewardship (NCCTS) Retired.
Novak, Henry *c.ss.r.* '50 (CHI)[N] Glenview, IL The Redemptorists of Glenview, Illinois.
Novak, Joseph A. *s.j.* '57 (NY)[EE] Cardinal Spellman Hall, Jesuit Community.
Novak, Kevin '81 (PBL) Continuing Education and Formation.
Novak, Norbert *o.s.b.* '64 (B)[C] Jerome, ID Monastery of the Ascension.
Novak, Paul M. *o.s.m.* '90 (CHI)[D] Chicago, IL Institute Campus for Young Men; [D] Chicago, IL Lourdes Hall Campus for Young Women; [N] Chicago Order of Friar Servants of Mary (Servites) United States of America Province, Inc.
Novak, Robert J. '42 (CHI) Retired.
Novak, Thomas *s.d.s.* '59 (MIL)[P] Milwaukee, WI Salvatorians – Jordan Hall.
Novak, Vincent M. *s.j.* '55 (NY)[EE] Loyola Hall, Jesuit Community.
Novak, William L. '97 (OKL) Yukon, OK St. John Nepomuk; Region II–A; Vocations and Seminarians.
Novakowski, James E. '95 (GI) Personnel Board; Priests' Advisory Board (Presbyteral Council); Diocesan Consultors; North Platte, NE Holy Spirit.
Novell, Ramon *sch.p.* '66 (LA) Los Angeles, CA St. Lucy; Los Angeles, CA Santa Teresita.
Novelly, Duane R. '79 (DET) Detroit, MI St. Matthew.
Novick, Michael '01 (CHI) Matteson, IL St. Lawrence O'Toole.
Novielli, John Joseph *o.praem.* '74 (PH)[B] Paoli, PA Daylesford Abbey; [Y] Paoli, PA Daylesford Abbey; Paoli, PA.
Noviello, Harold J. '09 (RVC) Bay Shore, NY St. Patrick's.
Novoa, Jose Marino *c.m.f.* '79 (CHI)[N] Oak Park Claretian Missionaries USA Eastern Province.
Novokowsky, Robert '00 (LR)[K] North Little Rock, AR Priestly Fraternity of St. Peter.
Novotny, Allen P. *s.j.* '82 (WDC)[E] Washington, DC Gonzaga College High School; [N] Washington, DC The Jesuit Community of St. Aloysius Gonzaga.
Novotny, James F. '64 (OM) Lindsay, NE Holy Family; St. Edward, NE St. Edward.
Novotny, Jerome *o.m.i.* '68 (FgM) Washington, DC AMERICAN OBLATE MISSIONS.
Novotny, Richard '81 (MO) On Duty Outside the Diocese; Air Force Chaplains.
Novotny, Robert J. '50 (MIL) Retired.
Nowacki, Jerome A. '93 (MAR) Retired.
Nowak, Bernard U. '74 (BUF) Orchard Park, NY Nativity of Our Lord.
Nowak, Christopher *o.s.a.* '97 (RVC) Procurator & Advocates; Long Beach, NY St. Mary of the Isle.
Nowak, Edward C. *c.s.p.* '89 (AUS) Austin, TX St. Austin; [L] Austin, TX University Catholic Center.
Nowak, Eugene J. '70 (CHI) Grayslake, IL St. Gilbert.
Nowak, Jacek *s.ch.* '94 (GAL) Houston, TX Our Lady of Czestochowa.
Nowak, James '67 (JOL)[K] Naperville, IL St. John Vianney Villa Retired.
Nowak, John H. *c.r.* '71 (CHI)[M] Chicago, IL Franciscan Communities; Chicago, IL St. Wenceslaus.
Nowak, Krzysztof '05 (DET) Royal Oak, MI National Shrine of the Little Flower.
Nowak, Lurasz *o.c.d.* '08 (GRY)[H] Munster, IN Discalced Carmelite Fathers Monastery.
Nowak, Mark A. '75 (E) Mc Kean, PA St. Francis Xavier.
Nowak, Michael E. (MIL) Kenosha, WI St. Therese.
Nowak, Randolph *o.f.m.cap.* '52 (FgM)[F] Agana Heights, GU St. Fidelis Friary; White Plains, NY Province of St. Mary.
Nowakowski, Edward S. '48 (GB) Retired.
Nowakowski, Jerome F. '63 (TOL) Toledo, OH Good Shepherd; Ministry To Catholic Charismatic Renewal (MCCR) Retired.
Nowakowski, Rudolph *o.m.i.* '60 (SFD)[A] Godfrey, IL Immaculate Heart of Mary Novitiate.
Nowel, Mark D. *o.p.* '86 (PRO)[P] Providence St. Thomas Aquinas Priory at Providence College.
Nowel, Mark S. *o.p.* '86 (PRO)[B] Providence, RI Providence College.
Nowicki, Andrzej '09 (CHI) Niles, IL St. John Brebeuf.
Nowicki, Gary D. '96 (MIL) Kansasville, WI St. John the Baptist; Kansasville, WI St. Francis Xavier.
Nowinski, Claudius S. *m.s.* '65 (HRT)[L] Hartford, CT Missionaries of LaSalette.
Nowinski, Claudius *m.s.* (BO) Pastoral Care.
Nowinski, Dennis J. '73 (DET) Roseville, MI St. Angela; Absent on Sick Leave.
Nowlan, John T. '66 (DET) Oak Park, MI Our Lady of Fatima Retired.
Noyola, Miguel A. *s.o.l.t.* '07 (CC) Robstown, TX St. Anthony; [G] Robstown, TX Society of Our Lady of the Most Holy Trinity.
Nsongolo, Gaston *c.p.* (FgM) South River, NJ St. Paul of the Cross Province.
Nsongolo, Gaston *c.p.* '91 (MET)[I] South River Passionist Provincial Office.
Ntahondi, Remigius Bukuru '89 (BUR) Rutland, VT Immaculate Heart of Mary.
Ntaiyia, Symon Peter '80 (ROC) Ontario, NY St. Maximilian Kolbe.
Ntsele, Thulani *o.s.m.* '99 (CHI)[N] Chicago Order of Friar Servants of Mary (Servites) United States of America Province, Inc.
Ntsiful–Amissah, Dominic Kofi '79 (MO) DEPARTMENT OF VETERANS AFFAIRS HOSPITALS AND CHAPLAINS.
Ntsiful–Amissah, Kofi '79 (ALB) Black Apostolate.
Ntumba, Ambroise M. '99 (SEA) Buckley, WA St. Aloysius.
Nuanez, Anthony '79 (LA) On Sick Leave.
Nuelle, John R. *m.s.* '64 (HRT)[L] Hartford, CT North American La Salette Mission Center; [U] Hartford, CT North American La Salette Mission Center, Inc.
Nuelle, John *m.s.* '64 (STL)[O] LaSalette Spirituality Center; [O] Saint Louis, MO North American La Salette Mission Center.
Nugent, Anthony A. '72 (JOL) Bradley, IL St. Joseph.
Nugent, Rev. Msgr. Arthur W. '47 (PH) Retired.
Nugent, C. Robert *s.d.s.* '65 (HBG) New Freedom, PA St. John the Baptist.
Nugent, Rev. Msgr. Irvine '54 (PMB) Vero Beach, FL St. Helen Retired.
Nugent, J. Michael '96 (ORL) Port Orange, FL Epiphany.
Nugent, Rev. Msgr. James B. '56 (STU) Retired.
Nugent, James J. *c.ss.r.* '50 (STL)[O] Liguori, MO St. Clement Health Care Center Retired.
Nugent, John G. *c.m.* '49 (PH)[Y].
Nugent, Rev. Msgr. Joseph A. '71 (BRK) Presbyteral Council; Brooklyn, NY St. Vincent Ferrer.
Nugent, Kevin *s.t.* '51 (WDC)[N] Adelphi, MD Father Judge Missionary Cenacle.
Nugent, Rev. Msgr. Peter '62 (LA) Chatsworth, CA St. John Eudes.
Nugent, Robert *s.d.s.* '65 (WDC)[B] Silver Spring, MD Salvatorian Community.
Nunan, Jeremiah '63 (ALB) Cairo, NY Sacred Heart.
Nundwe, Saviour '08 (SPC) Cape Girardeau, MO St. Vincent de Paul; [B] Cape Girardeau, MO Notre Dame Regional High School.
Nunes, Brian '08 (LA) San Pedro, CA Mary, Star of the Sea.
Nunes, James *m.s.* (BRK) Jamaica Hospital – Trump Pavilion.
Nunes, Rui *s.j.* '06 (LA)[C] Los Angeles, CA Jesuit Community.
Nunez, Albert G. '64 (LAF) Washington, LA Immaculate Conception; Catholic Charismatic.
Nunez, Albert Gayle '54 (LAF) Washington, LA Holy Trinity.
Nunez, Baltazar '88 (CGS)[F] Casa del Apostol San Andres.
Nunez, Edward '76 (PBL) Pueblo, CO St. Paul the Apostle.
Nunez, Felix '99 (CGS)[F] Caguas, PR Diocesan Tribunal of Caguas; Diocesan Tribunal of Caguas; Priests Senate; Aguas Buenas, PR Espiritu Santo.
Nunez, Pedro '77 (NO) Mensaje, Inc.
Nunez, Philip '88 (ARE) On Duty Outside the Diocese.
Nunez, Philip (SJN)[E] San Juan, PR Centro Medico de P.R.
Nunez, Rev. Msgr. Reynaldo '69 (MET) Piscataway, NJ St. Frances Cabrini.
Nunez–Carrion, Felipe '88 (SJN) Rio Piedras, PR Inmaculado Corazon de Maria.
Nunning, David H. '69 (EVN) Evansville, IN Sacred Heart; Evansville, IN St. Agnes; Deans.
Nuno, Rafael '69 (ARE) Utuado, PR San Pedro y San Pablo.
Nurnberger, Lothar *s.j.* '44 (DET)[K] Clarkston, MI Colombiere Center.
Nurre, Henry V. *o.s.b.* '56 (MIL)[P] Benet Lake, WI St. Benedict's Abbey; Benet Lake, WI.
Nusbaum, Daniel C. '61 (ALB) Retired.
Nuss, David W. '93 (TOL) Sandusky, OH St. Mary.
Nuss, Francis B. '61 (RVC)[M] Amityville, NY St. Pius X Residence Retired.
Nuthulapati, Jayababu *c.pp.s.* '06 (CIN)[N] Dayton, OH Provincial Office of the Cincinnati Province of the Society of the Precious Blood.
Nutt, Maurice J. *c.ss.r.* '89 (MEM) Memphis, TN Holy Names of Jesus and Mary; [F] Memphis, TN Redemptorists of Tennessee.
Nuttall, J. *o.p.* '69 (FgM) New York, NY Province of St. Joseph (Eastern).
Nutter, Charles W. '06 (BLX) Auditors; Gautier, MS St. Mary.
Nutter, N. John '89 (BR) Propagation of the Faith and Association of Holy Childhood; Presbyteral Council.
Nutter, Nicholas John '89 (BR) Baton Rouge, LA St. Louis, King of France.
Nuttman, Joseph *c.ss.r.* '52 (STL)[O] Liguori, MO St. Clement Health Care Center Retired.
Nuzzi, Ronald J. (FTW)[B] University of Notre Dame Du Lac.
Nuzzi, Ronald '84 (Y) On Duty Outside the Diocese.
Nwabichie, Remigius '89 (BGP) Bridgeport, CT Bridgeport Hospital.
Nwabugwu, Edwin Okey (BRK) Brooklyn, NY Resurrection.
Nwachukwu, Anthony '87 (NY) Manhattan, NY New York University Medical Center; New York, NY Our Lady of the Scapular and St. Stephen.
Nwachukwu, Jude *s.m.m.m.* '06 (BAK) Jordan Valley, OR St. Bernard; Ontario, OR Blessed Sacrament.
Nwachukwu, Oliver '82 (BEL) Tamaroa, IL Immaculate Conception; Dubois, IL St. Charles Borromeo.
Nwachukwu, Peter C. '86 (TUC) Ajo, AZ Immaculate Conception Roman Catholic Church – Ajo.
Nwachukwu, Raymond '87 (BWN) McAllen, TX Our Lady of Perpetual Help.
Nwachukwu, Thomas Kizito '82 (CC) On Special Assignment; [D] Corpus Christi, TX CHRISTUS Spohn Hospital Corpus Christi – Memorial.
Nwachukwu–Udaku, Benedict C. '95 (SB) Rancho Cucamonga, CA Sacred Heart.
Nwagbara, Anselm '96 (BO) Boston, MA St. Katharine Drexel; [O] Brighton, MA Caritas St. Elizabeth's Medical Center of Boston, Inc.; Nigerian.
Nwagbaraocha, John *d.s.* '80 (BUR) Burlington, VT Fletcher Allen Health Care.
Nwagwu, Nicholas '98 (NY) Yonkers, NY Christ the King; Yonkers, NY St. John's Riverside Hospital.

Nwaiwu, Francis '80 (DEN) Fort Collins, CO Blessed John XXIII.
Nwambu, Paul I. '99 (NY) Scarsdale, NY Immaculate Heart of Mary.
Nwankwo, Fidelis *c.s.sp.* '94 (MIA) Miami, FL Holy Redeemer.
Nwankwor, Ruben C. '93 (GAL) Houston, TX St. Bernadette Soubirous.
Nwanonenyi, Benjamin '97 (PH) Lansdale, PA Corpus Christi.
Nwaogu, Sylvester N. '64 (TUC) Tombstone, AZ Sacred Heart of Jesus Roman Catholic Parish – Tombstone.
Nwaogwugwu, Cletus '92 (RVC) West Islip, NY Good Samaritan Hospital Medical Center.
Nwaokeafor, Louis Chijioke '95 (DAL) Richardson, TX St. Joseph.
Nwaorgu, Rev. Msgr. Anselm I. '92 (NEW) Newark, NJ Blessed Sacrament–St. Charles Borromeo; Nigerian IBO Catholic Community.
Nwaru, Romanus N. '95 (MIL) Milwaukee, WI St. Paul; [H] Milwaukee, WI St. Thomas Aquinas Academy Association.
Nwauzor, Reginald '80 (B) Blackfoot, ID St. Bernard's.
Nweke, Ugo *s.j.* '05 (SJ)[B] Santa Clara, CA Jesuit Community.
Nwobi, Paul '88 (RVC) West Islip, NY Good Samaritan Hospital Medical Center.
Nwoga, Laserian '95 (MO) On Duty Outside the Diocese; Air Force Chaplains.
Nwohu, Rev. Msgr. Ambrose O. '66 (TUC) San Manuel, AZ Saint Bartholomew Roman Catholic Parish – San Manuel; Oracle, AZ St. Helen.
Nwokorie, Fabian '90 (BAK) Dufur, OR St. Alphonsus; The Dalles, OR St. Peter.
Nwokoye, Patrick I. '02 (SPC)[J] Cape Girardeau, MO Catholic Campus Ministry Southeast Missouri State University, Newman Center; Campus Ministries; Catholic Scouting; Vocations–Seminarians.
Nwokoye, Peter '99 (SAG) Ruth, MI St. Mary; Palms, MI St. Patrick; Ruth, MI SS. Peter and Paul.
Nwosu, Abuchi '08 (PAT) Highland Lakes, NJ Our Lady of Fatima.
Nwosu, Benjamin '01 (JC) Jefferson City, MO St. Joseph Cathedral; To The Bishop.
Nwosu, Malachy '93 (ROC) Rochester, NY St. Helen.
Nwosuh, Cosmas Okey *m.s.p.* '89 (DOD) Kiowa, KS St. John the Apostle Catholic Church of Kiowa, Kansas; Medicine Lodge, KS Holy Rosary Catholic Church of Medicine Lodge, Kansas; Sharon, KS St. Boniface Catholic Church of Sharon, Kansas.
Nwudah, Anthony '90 (AUS) Diocesan Tribunal Judges; Austin, TX Sacred Heart.
Nyabenda, Sixmund '01 (BUR) Barton, VT Most Holy Trinity.
Nyaki, Casimir Lawrence (PIT)[B] Pittsburgh, PA Duquesne University of the Holy Spirit.
Nyamai Munini, Dominic '97 (ROC) Canadaigua, NY St. Mary; East Bloomfield, NY St. Bridget.
Nyambe, Shoba '03 (BAL)[S] Baltimore, MD St. Mary's Seminary & University.
Nyambo, Callist N. '69 (SP) Clearwater, FL All Saints.
Nyanguf, Frederick O. *a.j.* '98 (NY) Bellevue Hospital, Chapel of Our Lady Helper of the Sick; Bellevue Hospital.
Nyardy, Jeffrey S. *o.s.b.* '90 (SAV)[B] Savannah, GA Benedictine Military School; [E] Savannah, GA The Benedictine Priory.
Nycz, Matt Mieczyslaw '94 (BUF) Angola, NY Most Precious Blood.
Nydegger, Rev. Msgr. Thomas P. '92 (NEW)[A] South Orange, NJ Immaculate Conception Seminary[B]; Members; Chaircouple; Serra Club of the Oranges.
Nyembo, Jean Ngoy *s.j.* (FTW)[K] South Bend, IN Jesuit Community.
Nygaard, Robert C. '64 (STP)[Q] Roseville, MN Catholic Youth Camps, Inc. Retired.
Nyimi, Roger Malonda (R) Garner, NC St. Mary, Mother of the Church.
Nyl, Steven J. *c.ss.r.* '01 (LA) Whittier, CA St. Mary of the Assumption; [P] Whittier, CA Redemptorists of Whittier.
Nyman, Vincent '99 (STL) Fenton, MO St. Paul.
Nyoike, John '82 (WDC)[B] Washington, DC St. Joseph's Seminary.
Nyquist, Raymond J. '54 (GF) Retired.
Nys, Loren *s.d.s.* '67 (GB) Kiel, WI SS. Peter and Paul.
Nzegwu, Anthony '99 (BRK)[S] Nigerian Apostolate; Jamaica, NY St. Nicholas of Tolentine.
Nzehi, Godwin *c.m.f.* (LAF) Port Barre, LA St. Mary.
Nzekwe, Anselm '89 (BGP)[J] Bridgeport, CT St. Vincent's Medical Center.
Nzomo, Boniface '86 (SR) Petaluma, CA St. James.

O

O'Bell, John C. '91 (SCR) Clarks Summit, PA Our Lady of the Snows; [K] Tunkhannock, PA St. Michael's School.
O'Blaney, James *c.ss.r.* '58 (HBG) Lititz, PA St. James; [G] Ephrata, PA St. Clement's Mission House.
O'Brien, Anthony '68 (MIA) Pembroke Pines, FL St. Maximilian Kolbe.
O'Brien, Rev. Msgr. Bartholomew J. '65 (PH) Retired.
O'Brien, Brian D. '07 (TLS)[A] Tulsa, OK Bishop Kelley High School; [J] Tulsa, OK Bishop Kelley High School Endowment Trust.
O'Brien, Brian '07 (TLS) Diocesan Senators; Diocesan Consultors.
O'Brien, Charles *o.p.* '54 (WDC) Washington, DC St. Dominic Church & Priory.
O'Brien, Christian T. *o.praem.* '62 (GB)[J] De Pere, WI St. Norbert Abbey Retired.
O'Brien, Cornelius '55 (ARL) Retired.
O'Brien, Daniel J. *s.j.* '59 (NY)[EE] Cardinal Spellman Hall, Jesuit Community.
O'Brien, Daniel P. '85 (HBG) New Oxford, PA Immaculate Conception of the Blessed Virgin Mary.
O'Brien, David W. *c.s.p.* '56 (COL)[J] Columbus, OH Campus Ministry Retired.
O'Brien, David *o.m.i.* '59 (FgM) Washington, DC AMERICAN OBLATE MISSIONS.
O'Brien, Dennis J. '81 (PT) Milton, FL St. Rose of Lima; Vicars Forane; College of Consultors; Administrative Council; Hispanic Ministry, Office of; Orders & Ministries, Commission for; Seminarian Candidate Review Board.
O'Brien, Dennis J. '77 (WOR) Harvard, MA Holy Trinity.
O'Brien, Donald J. '61 (GI) Cozad, NE Christ the King.
O'Brien, Donald V. *s.j.* '55 (NY)[EE] Loyola Hall, Jesuit Community.
O'Brien, Edmund M. '57 (HRT) Enfield, CT St. Adalbert's.
O'Brien, Edward C. *s.j.* '61 (STL)[O] St. Louis, MO; [S] St. Louis, MO Retreat House.
O'Brien, Elias *o.carm.* '86 (WDC)[B] Washington, DC Whitefriars Hall.
O'Brien, Francis P. '85 (BO) Marlborough, MA St. Matthias.
O'Brien, Frederick W. '50 (BO) Senior Priests.; Institute of the Heart of Jesus Retired.
O'Brien, George L. '58 (WOR) Diocesan College of Consultors Retired.
O'Brien, George '58 (LA) Beverly Hills, CA Good Shepherd.
O'Brien, Gerard C. *s.j.* '59 (BO)[U] Newton, MA The Jesuit Community at Boston College.
O'Brien, Gerard '95 (LA) Pasadena, CA Assumption of the Blessed Virgin Mary.
O'Brien, Howard E. *m.m.* '55 (NY)[EE] Retired.
O'Brien, James A. *s.j.* '60 (WH) Towson, MD; [A] Wheeling, WV Wheeling Jesuit University.
O'Brien, James C. *s.j.* '61 (BO)[U] Boston The Society of Jesus of New England–Provincial Offices.
O'Brien, James C. *s.j.* '61 (PRT) Portland, ME St. Pius X; Portland, ME St. Patrick's.
O'Brien, James E. '60 (Y) Boardman, OH St. Luke Retired.
O'Brien, James J. '60 (CHI) Chicago, IL St. Monica Retired.
O'Brien, James R. '66 (HBG) Chambersburg, PA Corpus Christi; Deans.
O'Brien, James T. '70 (SY) Liverpool, NY St. John.
O'Brien, John E. '87 (BAL) Priests Sick or Absent.
O'Brien, John E. '50 (CHI) Retired.
O'Brien, Rev. Msgr. John F. '61 (PH) Glenside, PA St. Luke the Evangelist Retired.
O'Brien, Rev. Msgr. John H. '62 (BRK) South Richmond Hill, NY St. Benedict Joseph Labre.
O'Brien, John J. *m.m.* '52 (NY)[EE] Retired.
O'Brien, John J. '07 (STL) St. Louis, MO St. Clement.
O'Brien, John M. *o.c.s.o.* '81 (ATL)[G] Conyers, GA The Monastery of the Holy Spirit.
O'Brien, John P. '49 (SPK) Retired.
O'Brien, John W. '67 (BO) Quincy, MA Sacred Heart.
O'Brien, John W. '82 (PRO) Middletown, RI St. Lucy; [U] Middletown, RI Charismatic Renewal.
O'Brien, John '55 (GB) Retired.
O'Brien, John '96 (ALX) Deville, LA St. John the Baptist.
O'Brien, Jon J. *s.j.* '63 (WDC)[C] Catholic University of America, The; [N] Washington, DC The Jesuit Community at Georgetown University Retired.
O'Brien, Joseph E. '51 (PH) Philadelphia, PA St. Leo Retired.
O'Brien, Joseph J. '60 (CHI) Retired.
O'Brien, Joseph L. '55 (TOL)[H] Oregon, OH Sacred Heart Home Retired.
O'Brien, Joseph '91 (ALB) East Greenbush, NY Holy Spirit; Advocates; Presbyteral Council; Diocesan Board of Consultors.
O'Brien, Joseph *o.p.* '78 (LAV)[F] Henderson, NV Saint Therese Center; [C] Las Vegas, NV Dominican Rectory, Fra Angelico House.
O'Brien, Joseph *o.carm.* '63 (NEW) Cresskill, NJ St. Therese of Lisieux.
O'Brien, Rev. Msgr. Joseph '57 (DUB) Retired.
O'Brien, Kevin F. *s.j.* '06 (WDC)[N] Washington, DC The Jesuit Community at Georgetown University.
O'Brien, Kevin J. '81 (OG) Brownville, NY Roman Catholic Community of Brownville and Dexter; Sackets Harbor, NY St. Andrew; Diocesan Consultors.
O'Brien, Kevin J. '79 (RIC) Judges; Richmond, VA St. Edward The Confessor.
O'Brien, Rev. Msgr. Kevin P. '73 (NY) Bronx, NY St. Philip Neri; Canon 1742 Panel of Pastors.
O'Brien, Kevin P. '54 (DET) Retired.
O'Brien, Leo P. '56 (ALB) Albany, NY St. James Retired.
O'Brien, Rev. Msgr. Martin F. '52 (NEW) Haworth, NJ Sacred Heart Retired.
O'Brien, Maurice '68 (SAC) Willows, CA St. Monica.
O'Brien, Michael J. '00 (DEN) Aspen, CO St. Mary.
O'Brien, Michael T. '79 (SP) Seminole, FL St. Justin Martyr.
O'Brien, Michael '72 (JKS) Notaries; Personnel Board; Jackson, MS St. Richard of Chichester; Institute for the Blind, Institute for the Deaf and Speech Impaired; Jackson, MS Holy Family; Priests' Council; Diocesan Consultors.
O'Brien, Michael *m.s.c.* '69 (SAT)[L] San Antonio, TX Missionaries of the Sacred Heart.
O'Brien, Michael '05 (LAN) East Lansing, MI St. Thomas Aquinas.
O'Brien, Nicholas J. '83 (ORL) Lakeland, FL St. Anthony Catholic Church.
O'Brien, Patrick '74 (HT) Houma, LA St. Bernadette; Diocesan Finance Council.
O'Brien, Patrick '69 (SAV) Retired.
O'Brien, Patrick '46 (SEA) Retired.
O'Brien, Patrick *c.ss.r.* '64 (OAK)[O] Oakland, CA Holy Redeemer Center; [M] Oakland, CA Redemptorist Fathers (Denver Province).
O'Brien, Patrick *c.ss.r.* '64 (SEA)[L] Seattle, WA The Redemptionist Society of Washington; Seattle, WA Sacred Heart of Jesus.
O'Brien, Paul A. *m.m.* '59 (NY)[EE] Maryknoll Maryknoll Fathers and Brothers Retired.
O'Brien, Paul B. '91 (BO) Lawrence, MA St. Patrick; Trustees.
O'Brien, Peter *s.j.* '71 (NEW)[M] Jersey City, NJ Jesuits of Saint Peter's College, Inc.; [B] Jersey City, NJ Jesuit Center.
O'Brien, Peter '05 (P) Coos Bay, OR St. Monica.
O'Brien, Raymond C. '75 (WDC) Special Ministries; [C] Catholic University of America, The.
O'Brien, Richard (BO)[O] Methuen, MA Caritas Holy Family Hospital, Inc.
O'Brien, Richard *c.m.* '61 (STL)[O] Perryville, MO Congregation of the Mission.
O'Brien, Robert E. *s.j.* '54 (NY)[EE] New York, NY St. Ignatius Loyola Residence.
O'Brien, Roger '61 (SEA) Retired.
O'Brien, Scott *o.p.* '92 (MIA) Miami, FL St. Dominic; [B] Miami, FL Barry University; [K] Miami, FL Dominican Fathers of Miami, Inc.; Barry University.
O'Brien, Scott *o.p.* '92 (NO)[P] Metairie, LA Southern Dominican Foundation; [S] Metairie, LA Southern Dominican Foundation.
O'Brien, Seamus (MRY) Special Assignment.
O'Brien, Sean P. '93 (SY) Boonville, NY St. Joseph; Forestport, NY St. Patrick.
O'Brien, Sean Patrick '93 (MO) Navy Reserve Chaplains.
O'Brien, Sean *o.f.m.* '98 (SP) Tampa, FL Sacred Heart.
O'Brien, Steven G. '86 (DUB) On Leave of Absence (Not Authorized for Priestly Ministry).
O'Brien, Thomas F. '56 (WOR) Retired.
O'Brien, Thomas F. '83 (STP) Minneapolis, MN Visitation.
O'Brien, Thomas J. *m.m.* '74 (FgM) Maryknoll, NY MARYKNOLL.
O'Brien, Thomas *o.m.i.* '55 (FgM) Washington, DC AMERICAN OBLATE MISSIONS.
O'Brien, Thomas *s.j.* '02 (ROC) Elmira, NY Blessed Sacrament Roman Catholic Church of Elmira, NY; Rochester, NY St. Lawrence.
O'Brien, Timothy A. '94 (HRT) New Hartford, CT Immaculate Conception; Special and other Archdiocesan Assignment.
O'Brien, Timothy J. '69 (MIL) Special Assignment.
O'Brien, Vincent M. *s.j.* '59 (PH)[Y] Loyola Center and Manresa Hall.
O'Brien, William D. '50 (DUB) Retired.
O'Brien, William G. '51 (WOR) Retired.
O'Brien, William J. '78 (BAL) Havre de Grace, MD St. Patrick's.
O'Brien, William J. '80 (E) Girard, PA St. John the Evangelist.
O'Brien, William J. *c.m.* '67 (PH)[Y] Philadelphia Congregation of the Mission[Y].
O'Brien, William P. *s.j.* '02 (CHI)[N] Chicago Chicago Province of the Society of Jesus–Provincial Office.
O'Brien, William P. *s.j.* '02 (STL)[O] St. Louis, MO Sacred Heart Jesuit Community; [O] St. Louis, MO Jesuit Community Corporation at Saint Louis University – Jesuit Hall; [C] Saint Louis University.
O'Brien, William S. '69 (RIC) Retired.
O'Brien, William '90 (GB) Two Rivers, WI St. Peter the Fisherman.
O'Brien, William '61 (NEW) Retired.
O'Brien, Rev. Msgr. William '51 (NY) Retired.
O'Brien, William '88 (VNN) Spokane Valley, WA SS. Cyril & Methodius.

O'Bryan, Michael '06 (NSH) Lebanon, TN St. Frances Cabrini.
O'Byrne, John '61 (LA) Torrance, CA St. Catherine Laboure.
O'Byrne, Patrick J. '60 (LIN) Retired.
O'Callaghan, Rev. Msgr. Eugene '55 (SAT) Retired.
O'Callaghan, John J. *s.j.* '62 (CHI)[C] Chicago, IL Jesuit Community at Loyola University Chicago.
O'Callaghan, Patrick '55 (SAT) Retired.
O'Callaghan, Thomas '54 (SEA) Retired.
O'Callaghan, Tiernan *o.carm.* '56 (PHX)[F] Phoenix, AZ Carmelite Community Retired.
O'Carroll, Eugene '62 (PHX) Retired.
O'Carroll, Patrick J. '54 (ORL) Barefoot Bay, FL St. Luke.
O'Cinnsealaigh, Benedict '93 (CIN)[B] Cincinnati, OH Mt. St. Mary's Seminary of the West; [B] Cincinnati, OH Mt. St. Mary's Seminary of the West; [A] Special Studies Division:.
O'Connell, Anthony M. *o.s.m.* '67 (CHI)[N] Chicago Order of Friar Servants of Mary (Servites) United States of America Province, Inc.
O'Connell, Brendan M. *m.m.* '63 (FgM) Maryknoll, NY MARYKNOLL.
O'Connell, Cuthbert R. '86 (BLX) Waveland, MS St. Clare; College of Consultors; Priests' Continuing Education and Retreat Programs.
O'Connell, Damian *s.j.* '75 (NY)[HH] New York, NY Fordham Lincoln Center.
O'Connell, Daniel C. '83 (BO) Boston, MA St. Joseph.
O'Connell, Daniel C. *s.j.* '58 (STL)[O] St. Louis, MO Ignatius House.
O'Connell, Daniel P. '71 (SAV) Valdosta, GA St. John the Evangelist; Presbyteral Council.
O'Connell, Daniel (BO) Spiritual Life.
O'Connell, David M. *c.m.* '82 (WDC)[C] Washington, DC Catholic University of America, The.
O'Connell, David M. *c.m.* '82 (PH)[Y].
O'Connell, Rev. Msgr. David '79 (LA) Los Angeles, CA St. Michael.
O'Connell, Edward P. *s.j.* '56 (WDC) Port Tobacco, MD St. Ignatius.
O'Connell, James R. *o.f.m.* '83 (NY) New York, NY St. Francis of Assisi.
O'Connell, James *o.f.m.* '82 (NY) Manhattan, NY St. Vincent Hospital & Medical Center.
O'Connell, John R. '73 (NEW) Westwood, NJ St. Andrew's; Members.
O'Connell, Joseph A. '51 (SFR) Retired.
O'Connell, Joseph *s.o.l.t.* '91 (CC)[G] Robstown, TX Society of Our Lady of the Most Holy Trinity.
O'Connell, Kevin G. *s.j.* '69 (FgM) Watertown, MA Society of Jesus.
O'Connell, Mark A. '79 (NEW) Belleville, NJ St. Peter's.
O'Connell, Mark '90 (BO) Judicial Vicar of the Archdiocese; Canonical Affairs Committee; Braintree, MA St. Francis of Assisi; Tribunal Court.
O'Connell, Marvin R. '56 (STP) On Duty Outside the Archdiocese Retired.
O'Connell, Rev. Msgr. Maurice V. '72 (WDC) Washington, DC Blessed Sacrament, Shrine of the Most; Ridge, MD St. Michael.
O'Connell, Michael W. '83 (CHI) Orland Park, IL Our Lady of the Woods.
O'Connell, Michael '67 (STP) Minneapolis, MN Ascension.
O'Connell, Neil J. *o.f.m.* '64 (NY)[HH] Bronx, NY Herbert H. Lehman College; [HH] New York, NY Borough of Manhattan; New York, NY St. Joseph of the Holy Family.
O'Connell, Paul A. '03 (SAV) Waycross, GA St. Joseph's.
O'Connell, Paul T. '60 (WOR) Associate Judicial Vicar; Judges; Shrewsbury, MA St. Anne.
O'Connell, Richard C. '51 (ROC) Retired.
O'Connell, Sean T. '09 (MIL) Brookfield, WI St. Dominic.
O'Connell, Terry J. '92 (MO) Navy Reserve Chaplains.
O'Connell, Terry '92 (P) Grand Ronde, OR St. Michael; McMinnville, OR St. James; McMinnville, OR Good Shepherd.
O'Connell, Thomas P. '63 (KNX) Retired.
O'Connell, Thomas P. '63 (PBR) Knoxville, TN Holy Resurrection Mission.
O'Connell, Rev. Msgr. Timothy P. '63 (LA) Respect Life Office; Chairman and Coordinator of Activities; Hospital Chaplains Retired.
O'Connell, Walter T. *o.p.* '58 (CHI)[N] St. Pius V Priory.
O'Connell, William A. '55 (SFR) Retired.
O'Connell, Rev. Msgr. William '57 (RC) Retired.
O'Connell, William '66 (VEN) Retired.
O'Connell, William *s.m.* '56 (SJ)[M] Cupertino, CA The Marianist Center.
O'Conner, Rev. Msgr. Gerard P. '00 (FR) Acushnet, MA St. Francis Xavier's.
O'Conner, Joseph '05 (SY) Syracuse, NY Blessed Sacrament.
O'Connor, Albert '67 (SAC) Sacramento, CA Holy Spirit.
O'Connor, Andrew M. '87 (NY) Bronx, NY Holy Family.
O'Connor, Andrew '87 (STL) Special Assignment.
O'Connor, Bernard F. *o.s.f.s.* '73 (ALN)[B] Center Valley, PA DeSales University; [K] Center Valley, PA Oblates of St. Francis de Sales.
O'Connor, Bernard *c.m.f.* '50 (LA)[V] Rancho Dominguez, CA Dominguez Seminary Inc.
O'Connor, Charles J. *o.f.m.* '73 (PRO)[N] Providence, RI St. Francis Chapel & City Ministry Center; [P] Providence, RI St. Francis Friary; Providence, RI St. Mary.
O'Connor, Charles T. '83 (MET) Bound Brook, NJ St. Joseph.
O'Connor, Christopher K. '98 (BO)[A] Brighton, MA St. John Seminary.
O'Connor, Christopher M. (BRK) Presbyteral Council.
O'Connor, Christopher '99 (BRK) Jamaica, NY Presentation of the Blessed Virgin Mary; Diocesan Consultors.
O'Connor, Christopher *l.c.* (HRT)[B] Cheshire, CT Novitiate of the Legion of Christ.
O'Connor, Daniel P. '90 (ALX) College of Consultors; Elected Members; Deans; Alexandria, LA Our Lady of Prompt Succor.
O'Connor, Rev. Msgr. Daniel '60 (ATL) Retired.
O'Connor, Daniel '90 (ALX) Diaconate Program.
O'Connor, David H. '86 (DUB) Cedar Rapids, IA All Saints; Priestly Life and Ministry Committee; Permanent Diaconate Formation Board.
O'Connor, David '64 (JKS) Co Chairmen; Natchez, MS Assumption of the B.V.M.; Natchez, MS St. Mary Basilica; Priests' Council.
O'Connor, Dennis '98 (SD) Santa Ysabel, CA Santa Ysabel Indian Mission.
O'Connor, Rev. Msgr. Desmond '80 (NY) LaGrangeville, NY Blessed Kateri Tekakwitha.
O'Connor, Desmond *s.p.s.* '50 (PAT) Mount Arlington, NJ Our Lady of the Lake.
O'Connor, Dominic E. (SCR) On Duty Outside the Diocese.
O'Connor, Donald *s.v.d.* '64 (SB)[I] Riverside, CA Divine Word Seminary.
O'Connor, Donald '64 (JOL) Retired.
O'Connor, Edward D. *c.s.c.* '48 (FTW)[B] University of Notre Dame Du Lac; [H] Notre Dame, IN Holy Cross Community, Corby Hall, University of Notre Dame.
O'Connor, Rev. Msgr. Edward J. '81 (ALN) Pottsville, PA St. Patrick; Vicars Forane; Schuylkill Council #431, Pottsville; Pottsville – Court Santa Maria #26.
O'Connor, Rev. Msgr. Eugene '54 (BIR) Birmingham, AL St. Barnabas.
O'Connor, Francis J. '53 (MAN) Retired.
O'Connor, Frank '62 (ALB) Stuyvesant, NY Church of St. Joseph.
O'Connor, Rev. Msgr. Fred P. '52 (GAL) Retired.
O'Connor, Gerald P. *m.m.* '69 (FgM) Maryknoll, NY MARYKNOLL.
O'Connor, Gerald V. *s.j.* '76 (WDC)[N] Washington, DC The Jesuit Community of St. Aloysius Gonzaga; [E] Washington, DC Gonzaga College High School.
O'Connor, Glenn L. '80 (IND) Indianapolis, IN St. Ann; Indianapolis, IN St. Joseph; Indianapolis International Airport.
O'Connor, James C. '71 (BUF) Getzville, NY St. Pius X.
O'Connor, James E. *o.c.s.o.* '57 (DUB)[K] Peosta, IA New Melleray Abbey, Order of Cistercians of the Strict Observance.
O'Connor, James E. '84 (WH) Grafton, WV St. Augustine.
O'Connor, James J. '54 (CIN) Retired.
O'Connor, James M. '52 (LIN) Retired.
O'Connor, James T. '54 (CHI) Retired.
O'Connor, Rev. Msgr. James T. '66 (NY) Millbrook, NY St. Joseph.
O'Connor, Rev. Msgr. James '70 (LUB) Lubbock, TX St. Elizabeth University Parish; Priests' Retirement Board; Priests Personnel Board.
O'Connor, James '82 (WH) Philippi, WV St. Elizabeth Parish.
O'Connor, Javier *d.c.j.m.* '91 (DEN) Littleton, CO St. Mary.
O'Connor, Rev. Msgr. Jay F. '74 (BAL) Baltimore, MD St. Michael; Special Assignment; Clergy Personnel, Division of; Office of Diaconate; Permanent Deacon Formation Program.
O'Connor, Rev. Msgr. John F. '73 (R) Cary, NC St. Michael the Archangel; Council of Priests.
O'Connor, John F. *o.f.m.* '73 (NY) New York, NY St. Francis of Assisi; [II] New York, NY Foundation of the Order of Friars Minor of the Province of the Most Holy Name; New Milford, CT.
O'Connor, John F. *o.f.m.* '73 (NY)[EE] New York, NY Franciscan Friars, Holy Name Province; [II] New York, NY Shrine of St. Jude, Inc.
O'Connor, John H. (PAT) Retired.
O'Connor, John J. '93 (BRK) Queens Village, NY Incarnation.
O'Connor, John J. '58 (DUB)[F] New Vienna, IA Archbishop Hennessy Catholic School; New Vienna, IA St. Boniface; Dyersville, IA SS. Peter and Paul.
O'Connor, John L. '63 (ROC) Retired.
O'Connor, Rev. Msgr. John Philip '61 (NEW) Scotch Plains, NJ St. Bartholomew Retired.
O'Connor, Rev. Msgr. John '60 (SFR) Absent on Leave.
O'Connor, Joseph X. *o.s.a.* '53 (NY) Staten Island, NY Our Lady of Good Counsel.
O'Connor, Joseph '05 (SY) Vocation Promotion.
O'Connor, Kent '03 (KCK) Kansas City, KS Our Lady of Unity.
O'Connor, Mark *s.a.* '84 (NY)[EE] Garrison, NY Franciscan Friars of the Atonement.
O'Connor, Matthew J. '56 (SPR) Retired.
O'Connor, Matthew '71 (MOB) Daphne, AL Christ the King.
O'Connor, Maurice J. '53 (BO) Senior Priests. Retired.
O'Connor, Michael G. '56 (KC) Kansas City, MO St. Thomas More.
O'Connor, Michael J. '72 (TR) Lakewood, NJ St. Mary of the Lake.
O'Connor, Michael J. '85 (AUS) College Station, TX St. Thomas Aquinas.
O'Connor, Michael J. *o.s.a.* '71 (CHI)[N] Olympia Fields, IL Tolentine Monastery at Tolentine Center.
O'Connor, Michael P. '05 (BLX) Pass Christian, MS Sacred Heart; Cursillo and Retreats; Presbyteral Council; College of Consultors.
O'Connor, Michael S. (MO) CIVIL AIR PATROL.
O'Connor, Neil D. '69 (CLV) Parma, OH St. Columbkille.
O'Connor, Patrick C. '78 (SAG) Essexville, MI St. John the Evangelist; Bay City, MI St. Joseph.
O'Connor, Patrick J. '64 (GBG) Retired.
O'Connor, Patrick T. *o.s.f.s.* '97 (VEN) Fort Myers, FL Jesus the Worker Mission (Jesus Obrero); Fort Myers, FL San Jose Mission.
O'Connor, Patrick *m.s.c.* '52 (SAT)[L] San Antonio, TX Missionaries of the Sacred Heart.
O'Connor, Paul F. *c.s.b.* '70 (MO) DEPARTMENT OF VETERANS AFFAIRS HOSPITALS AND CHAPLAINS.
O'Connor, Paul F. *o.s.b.* (NY) Bronx, NY Veterans Administration Hospital; U.S.V.A. Medical Center.
O'Connor, Rev. Msgr. Paul '45 (CAM) Retired.
O'Connor, Pio *o.f.m.* '94 (SFE) St. Vincent's Hospital; [H] Albuquerque, NM The Province of Our Lady of Guadalupe.
O'Connor, Raymond E. *c.m.f.* '64 (CHI) Chicago, IL Our Lady of Guadalupe; [N] Oak Park, IL Claretian Missionaries USA Eastern Province.
O'Connor, Rev. Msgr. Robert B. '56 (NY) New York, NY Blessed Sacrament.
O'Connor, Robert D. '55 (PEO) Retired.
O'Connor, Robert F. *s.j.* '79 (OM)[K] Omaha, NE Jesuit Community at Creighton University.
O'Connor, Rev. Msgr. Robert W. '48 (PEO) Lewistown, IL St. Mary's.
O'Connor, Shaun '82 (SPR) Hadley, MA Most Holy Redeemer.
O'Connor, Terrence P. '01 (PIT) Ambridge, PA Good Samaritan; Baden, PA St. John the Baptist; Clergy Personnel Board.
O'Connor, Thomas J. '93 (BO)[U] Hingham, MA Glastonbury Abbey.
O'Connor, Thomas *s.j.* '63 (NEW)[M] Jersey City, NJ Jesuit Community of St. Peter's Prep, Inc.; [C] Jersey City, NJ St. Peter's Preparatory School.
O'Connor, Timothy J. '75 (CLV) Avon Lake, OH St. Joseph.
O'Connor, Timothy *c.s.c.* '91 (FTW)[H] Holy Cross House; Notre Dame, IN Sacred Heart.
O'Connor, Vincent M. '48 (SPR) Haydenville, MA Our Lady of the Hills Retired.
O'Connor, William B. '47 (BO) Senior Priests. Retired.
O'Connor, William J. '58 (BO) Senior Priests. Retired.
O'Connor, William J. '66 (LA) Long Beach, CA St. Joseph.
O'Connor, William *c.s.c.* '49 (FTW)[H] Holy Cross House.
O'Conor, Kevin *o.m.i.* '58 (P) Scio, OR Our Lady of Lourdes; Scio, OR St. Bernard.
O'Day, Michael '38 (SB) Retired.
O'Dea, Loren F. '93 (DET) Retired.
O'Dea, Thomas '58 (PHX) Retired.
O'Dell, Kevin '00 (SFS) Sioux Falls, SD St. Michael.
O'Dell, William Paul '93 (SFR) San Bruno, CA St. Robert.
O'Dempsey, Gerard *o.f.m.cap.* '95 (PIT)[M] Allison Park, PA St. Conrad Friary.
O'Doherty, Gerard *s.v.d.* '74 (LA) Los Angeles, CA Our Lady of Lourdes.
O'Doherty, Rev. Msgr. Jude '65 (MIA) Miami, FL Epiphany; Members; Pension.
O'Doherty, Liam T. *o.s.a.* (BO) Lawrence, MA St. Mary of the Assumption.
O'Doherty, Patrick J. '70 (ORL) Ocala, FL Queen of Peace.
O'Donnell, Brian J. '09 (BUR) Middlebury, VT Assumption of the Blessed Virgin Mary.
O'Donnell, Brian P. *s.j.* '86 (WH) Catholic Conference of West Virginia; [A] Wheeling, WV Wheeling Jesuit University; Executive Secretary.
O'Donnell, David P. '95 (BO) Brockton, MA Christ the King.
O'Donnell, Dennis J.W. '74 (PH) On Special or Other

Archdiocesan Assignment; Philadelphia, PA St. Christopher; [Z] Huntingdon Valley, PA Sisters of the Holy Redeemer Provincialate.
O'Donnell, Dennis '83 (GR) Free Soil, MI St. John Cantius; Irons, MI St. Bernard's.
O'Donnell, Edmond G. '64 (SB) Retired.
O'Donnell, Edmond "Ned" G. '64 (SB) Patton, CA Patton State Hospital; Elected Members.
O'Donnell, Rev. Msgr. Edward C. '41 (OM) Retired.
O'Donnell, Rev. Msgr. Edward D. '54 (NY) Rye, NY Resurrection Retired.
O'Donnell, Edward T. *s.j.* '74 (CAM) Runnemede, NJ Church of St. Teresa of the Infant Jesus, Runnemede, N.J.
O'Donnell, Eugene P. '73 (SJ) San Jose, CA St. Francis of Assisi.
O'Donnell, Frank T. *m.m.* '55 (NY)[EE] Retired.
O'Donnell, Gabriel *o.p.* '70 (WDC)[B] Washington, DC Dominican House of Studies.
O'Donnell, Harold F. *s.j.* '64 (NY)[EE] New York, NY Xavier Jesuit Community.
O'Donnell, Harold F.X. *s.j.* '64 (NY) Manhattan, NY Bird S. Coler Memorial Hospital and Home.
O'Donnell, Rev. Msgr. Hugh A. '54 (NEW) Retired.
O'Donnell, Hugh '58 (SFR)[K] San Rafael, CA Nazareth House of San Rafael, Inc. Retired.
O'Donnell, James A. *s.j.* '61 (FgM) New York, NY Society of Jesus.
O'Donnell, James P. '56 (CLV) Cuyahoga County Detention Home; Northeast Pre Release Center; [R] Cleveland, OH Community of Little Brothers and Sisters of the Eucharist, Inc.; Central City Ministry with Poor.
O'Donnell, James *o.s.b.* '42 (PAT)[N] Morristown, NJ St. Mary's Abbey.
O'Donnell, John F. '63 (BO) Senior Priests. Retired.
O'Donnell, Rev. Msgr. John F. '54 (LR)[G] Little Rock, AR St. John Manor; Assistant Directors Retired.
O'Donnell, John *o.s.b.* '98 (BIR) Cullman, AL Sacred Heart; On Special or Other Diocesan Assignment.
O'Donnell, John '72 (DUL) Virginia, MN Sacred Heart; Virginia, MN Holy Spirit; Virginia, MN Sacred Heart; College of Consultors.
O'Donnell, Joseph F. *c.s.c.* '60 (PHX)[F] Phoenix, AZ Holy Cross Congregation/Casa Santa Cruz Retired.
O'Donnell, Joseph P. '76 (CLV) Cleveland, OH St. Leo the Great.
O'Donnell, Joseph *c.s.c.* (FTW)[H] Notre Dame Congregation of Holy Cross, Indiana Province, Provincial House.
O'Donnell, Mark D. '85 (NOR) College of Consultors; Members; Continuing Education and Formation Commission for the Clergy; Diocesan Commission for Ecumenical and Interreligious Affairs; Niantic, CT St. Agnes; Advisory Board.
O'Donnell, Matthew '95 (STO) Stockton, CA St. Luke Church of Stockton (Pastor of).
O'Donnell, Paul J. '02 (PH)[D] Springfield, PA Cardinal O'Hara High School; Havertown, PA Sacred Heart.
O'Donnell, Rev. Msgr. Peter C. '58 (NY)[EE] Bronx, NY John Cardinal O'Connor Residence Retired.
O'Donnell, Philip '58 (LAV) Retired.
O'Donnell, Ralph B. '97 (OM) Omaha, NE St. Bridget; Omaha, NE St. Rose.
O'Donnell, Raymond G. '72 (SD) La Jolla, CA All Hallows; Presbyteral Council.
O'Donnell, Richard A. '55 (PRT) Retired.
O'Donnell, Richard C. '05 (BUR) Brattleboro, VT St. Michael.
O'Donnell, Richard J. '35 (CHI) Retired.
O'Donnell, Richard *m.i.* '64 (MIL)[Y] Wauwatosa, WI St. Camillus Health System, Inc.; [Y] Milwaukee, WI St. Camillus Communities, Inc.; [Y] Wauwatosa, WI St. Camillus Ministries, Inc.; [P] Milwaukee, WI St. Camillus Provincialate; [N] Wauwatosa, WI St. Camillus Health Center, Inc.; [Y] Wauwatosa, WI San Camillo, Inc.; Milwaukee, WI; [Y] Wauwatosa, WI Order of St. Camillus Foundation, Inc.
O'Donnell, Richard *s.s.s.* (CHI) Chicago, IL Blessed Sacrament.
O'Donnell, Robert A. *c.s.p.* '51 (NY)[EE] Jamaica Estates Paulist Fathers Generalate; [EE] New York, NY Paulist Fathers' Motherhouse Retired.
O'Donnell, Robert J. '74 (STP) Minneapolis, MN St. Lawrence–Newman Center; [K] Minneapolis, MN Paulist Fathers; [R] Minneapolis, MN Newman Center at St. Lawrence.
O'Donnell, Simon *o.s.b.* '68 (LA)[P] Valyermo, CA St. Andrew's Abbey.
O'Donnell, Terrence *s.d.b.* '70 (NY)[EE] New Rochelle, NY Salesian Provincial House.
O'Donnell, Thomas D. *s.m.* '44 (WDC)[N] Washington, DC Marist Center Retired.
O'Donnell, Thomas M. '61 (HEL) East Helena, MT SS. Cyril and Methodius; Personnel Board; Vocations Office.
O'Donnell, Thomas M. '60 (PIT) Pittsburgh, PA St. Mary of Mercy; Judges; Pittsburgh, PA Retired.
O'Donnell, Thomas V. '67 (CLV) Cleveland, OH Holy Name; College of Consultors.
O'Donnell, Walter *s.t.* '55 (PT)[E] Tallahassee, FL Missionary Servants of the Most Holy Trinity.
O'Donnell, William J. '52 (ALN)[J] Bethlehem, PA Holy Family Villa Retired.
O'Donnell, William J. '66 (NO) Retired.
O'Donnell, Rev. Msgr. William J. J. '52 (PH) Priests' Personnel Board; Council of Priests Retired.
O'Donnell, William *c.pp.s.* '77 (CIN) Dayton, OH Precious Blood; Dayton, OH St. Rita.
O'Donnell, William *o.m.i.* '70 (WDC)[N] Washington, DC Provincial Offices of the United States Province of the Missionary Oblates of Mary Immaculate; [N] Washington, DC Oblate Community.
O'Donoghue, Brendan W. '50 (WOR) Retired.
O'Donoghue, Rev. Msgr. James P. '43 (SD) Retired.
O'Donoghue, John '64 (SAT) San Antonio, TX Blessed Sacrament.
O'Donoghue, Kevin J. '58 (BRK)[T] Douglaston, NY Bishop Mugavero Residence Retired.
O'Donoghue, Neil Xavier '00 (NEW)[A] Kearny, NJ Redemptoris Mater Archdiocesan Missionary Seminary; Members.
O'Donoghue, Patrick '61 (BIR) Retired.
O'Donohue, James A. (BO) Canonical Affairs Committee.
O'Donohue, John M. '00 (ARL) Kilmarnock, VA St. Francis de Sales.
O'Donohue, Neville *s.m.* '02 (STL)[O] St. Louis Marianists, Province of the United States (Society of Mary).
O'Donovan, Rev. Msgr. Dennis '69 (P)[Q] Portland, OR Oregon Catholic Conference; Vicar General and Moderator of the Curia; Pastoral Services; College of Consultors; Ex Officio; Building Commission; Finance Council; Oregon Catholic Conference; Pastoral Services; Secretary–Treasurer; Cemeteries.
O'Donovan, Donal '50 (WH) Retired.
O'Donovan, Leo J. *s.j.* '66 (NY)[EE] New York, NY "America;" Residence and publication office of the America Press.
O'Donovan, Martin E. '78 (CHI) Winnetka, IL SS. Faith, Hope and Charity; Members.
O'Donovan, Patrick G. '72 (PAT) New Vernon, NJ Christ the King.
O'Donovan, Thomas P. '70 (CC) Retired.
O'Donovan, Rev. Msgr. Timothy John '49 (B) Retired.
O'Dowd, Bernard J. *o.s.a.* '58 (PH)[Y] Villanova, PA St. Thomas Monastery.
O'Dowd, Francis '01 (TYL) Tyler Catholic Committee on Scouting; Gun Barrel City, TX St. Jude.
O'Driscoll, James (BO) Rockland, MA Holy Family.
O'Dwyer, Dominick '66 (MIA) Tamarac, FL St. Malachy.
O'Dwyer, James '65 (STO) Diamond Springs, CA Retired.
O'Dwyer, Michael *s.a.c.* '61 (LUB) Retired.
O'Dwyer, Thomas '70 (MIA) Hollywood, FL Little Flower; Deans and Deaneries; Archdiocesan Vocations Review Board.
O'Farrell, Donal *s.s.c.* '53 (OM)[K] St. Columbans, NE Missionary Society of St. Columban.
O'Farrell, John V. '02 (RVC) Priests' Personnel Assignment Board; Floral Park, NY Our Lady of Victory.
O'Flaherty, Edward F. *s.j.* (BO) Ecumenical and Interreligious Affairs.
O'Flaherty, Edward M. *s.j.* '65 (BO)[U] Newton, MA The Jesuit Community at Boston College.
O'Flaherty, Michael '75 (PMB) Boca Raton, FL St. John the Evangelist.
O'Flanagan, Thomas P. '95 (PMB) Released from Diocesan Assignment; Navy Chaplains.
O'Flynn, John '61 (PBL) Retired.
O'Flynn, Seamus '59 (STA) Retired.
O'Friel, Rev. Msgr. John '45 (FRS) Retired.
O'Gara, James R. *c.s.p.* '61 (NY)[EE] Jamaica Estates Paulist Fathers Generalate.
O'Gara, Stephen R. '71 (STP) St. Paul, MN Assumption.
O'Gorman, Rev. Msgr. Charles Francis '49 (LA) Oxnard, CA Santa Clara Retired.
O'Gorman, Eamon T. '67 (ORG) Laguna Beach, CA St. Catherine of Siena.
O'Gorman, Rev. Msgr. Michael B. '64 (SAT) San Antonio, TX St. Gregory's.
O'Gorman, Thomas H. *s.j.* '63 (FgM) New York, NY Society of Jesus.
O'Grady, Columkille *c.p.* '71 (HRT)[L] West Hartford Holy Family Monastery/Retreat.
O'Grady, Columkille *c.p.* '71 (MET)[I] South River Passionist Provincial Office.
O'Grady, Dennis R. '61 (CLV) Cleveland, OH St. Michael the Archangel Retired.
O'Grady, Frank (PAT) Military Chaplains.
O'Grady, J. Frank '69 (MO) Army Chaplains.
O'Grady, James F. '58 (LA) Los Angeles, CA Visitation Retired.
O'Grady, James Francis '54 (LA) Retired.
O'Grady, John F. '66 (ALB) Retired.
O'Grady, Rev. Msgr. Michael '58 (PHX) Retired.
O'Grady, Peter '63 (NO) Retired.
O'Grady, Robert A. '72 (HRT) Windsor Locks, CT St. Mary; Windsor Locks, CT St. Robert Bellarmine; Hartford, CT Hartford Correctional Institution; Special and other Archdiocesan Assignment; Hartford Vicariate.
O'Grady, Robert M. '78 (BO) Boston Catholic Directory; Arlington, MA St. Camillus.
O'Guinn, Jon '93 (BEL) Leave of Absence.
O'Hagan, James P. '47 (DET) Waterford, MI Retired.
O'Hagan, Patrick J. *ss.cc.* '48 (SB) Chino Hills, CA St. Paul the Apostle; [I] Chino Hills, CA Congregation of the Sacred Hearts of Jesus & Mary, SS.CC.; Appointed Members; West End; Council for Consecrated Life; College of Consultors.
O'Hagan, Patrick J. *ss.cc* '65 (LA) Veterans Administration Medical Center; [P] La Verne, CA Congregation of the Sacred Hearts of Jesus and Mary.
O'Hala, Stephen '88 (MIA) On Duty Outside the Archdiocese.
O'Hala, Steven '88 (PMB)[A] Boynton Beach, FL St. Vincent de Paul Regional Seminary.
O'Hallaran, John *s.s.j.* '85 (JKS) Fayette, MS St. Anne; Natchez, MS Holy Family.
O'Halloran, Edward P. '78 (NY) Yonkers, NY; Yonkers, NY St. Denis.
O'Halloran, Richard F. '51 (FRS)[C] Los Banos, CA New Bethany Residential Care and Skilled Nursing Community.
O'Halloran, Richard '51 (MRY) Retired.
O'Hanlon, Michael A. '57 (GF) Retired.
O'Hara, Charles R. '70 (PH) Spring City, PA St. Joseph.
O'Hara, Daniel J. '87 (MO) Air Force Reserve Chaplains; Liverpool, NY Immaculate Heart of Mary.
O'Hara, Edward '60 (SAC) Retired.
O'Hara, Eugene *o.f.m.cap.* '61 (ROC)[J] Interlaken, NY St. Fidelis Friary.
O'Hara, Francis A. '56 (BO) Senior Priests. Retired.
O'Hara, Francis W. '59 (PRO) Retired.
O'Hara, James T. '66 (E) Legion of Mary; Erie, PA Our Mother of Sorrows.
O'Hara, John J. '84 (NY) Staten Island, NY St. Teresa.
O'Hara, John T. '80 (ARL) Arlington, VA St. Charles Borromeo.
O'Hara, John '79 (PRT) Bar Harbor, ME Holy Redeemer; Bar Harbor, ME St. Ignatius.
O'Hara, Joseph M. '01 (LC) Leave of Absence.
O'Hara, Martin '53 (SFD) Retired.
O'Hara, Michael D. '60 (BUF) Retired.
O'Hara, Michael *o.m.i.* '76 (NY) New York, NY Metropolitan Correctional Center.
O'Hara, Thomas J. *c.s.c.* '78 (SCR)[C] King's College; [C] Holy Cross Community; Prov. Councilors:.
O'Hare, Daniel G. *s.j.* '79 (NY)[EE] New York, NY St. Ignatius Loyola Residence.
O'Hare, Daniel M. '65 (NY) Maybrook, NY Church of the Assumption.
O'Hare, Daniel '65 (NY) Montgomery, NY Holy Name of Mary.
O'Hare, Donal J. '54 (WCH) Retired.
O'Hare, John B. '53 (PMB) Vero Beach, FL Holy Cross Retired.
O'Hare, Joseph A. *s.j.* '61 (NY)[EE] New York, NY "America;" Residence and publication office of the America Press.
O'Hare, Keith M. '02 (ARL) On Duty Outside the Diocese.
O'Hare, Keith M. '97 (ARL) Doral, FL San Francisco de Asis, Banica; Doral, FL San Jose, Pedro Santana.
O'Hare, Robert V. *s.j.* '95 (NY)[F] New York, NY Xavier High School.
O'Hare, Robert V. *s.j.* '95 (NEW)[C] Jersey City, NJ Jesuit Community; [M] Jersey City, NJ Jesuit Community of St. Peter's Prep, Inc.
O'Hearn, Michael J. '95 (FR)[G] Fall River, MA Priests' Hostel.
O'Hern, Mark '02 (E) Meadville, PA St. Brigid.
O'Hogan, Patrick '09 (SEA) Olympia, WA St. Michael.
O'Hotto, Kenneth L. '80 (STP) West St. Paul, MN St. Michael.
O'Kane, James D. '65 (GI) Retired.
O'Kane, John J. '08 (MET) Sayreville, NJ Our Lady of Victories.
O'Kane, John '04 (ALB) Chestertown, NY Parish of St. Isaac Jogues; North Creek, NY St. James.
O'Kane, Patrick J. '77 (SC) Salix, IA St. Joseph's; Onawa, IA St. John.
O'Keefe, Daniel Paul *o.s.b.* '93 (GBG) Latrobe, PA St. Vincent Basilica; [G] Latrobe, PA Saint Vincent Archabbey.
O'Keefe, J. Kevin '95 (ARL) Burke, VA Church of the Nativity.
O'Keefe, Rev. Msgr. John J. '72 (NY) Pearl River, NY St. Margaret of Antioch.
O'Keefe, John J. '68 (DET) Pontiac, MI St. Damien of Molokai Parish.
O'Keefe, Joseph L. '75 (BUR) Veterans Administration Hospital.
O'Keefe, Joseph M. *s.j.* '86 (BO)[U] Newton, MA The Jesuit Community at Boston College; [C] Lynch School of Education; [C] Lynch Graduate School of Education.
O'Keefe, Joseph '75 (ALB) Retired.
O'Keefe, Lawrence J. '70 (GLP) Gallup, NM Cathedral of the Sacred Heart; Crownpoint, NM St. Paul;

Adjutant Judicial Vicar; Judges; Presbyteral Council; Diocesan Consultors.
O'Keefe, Mark *o.s.b.* '83 (IND)[K] St. Meinrad St. Meinrad Archabbey; [A] St. Meinrad, IN Saint Meinrad School of Theology.
O'Keefe, Mark *o.s.b.* '83 (EVN) Huntingburg, IN Visitation of the Blessed Virgin Mary.
O'Keefe, Martin D. *s.j.* '66 (STL)[O] St. Louis, MO Jesuit Community Corporation at Saint Louis University – Jesuit Hall.
O'Keefe, Michael *o.carm.* '75 (JOL) Darien, IL Our Lady of Mount Carmel.
O'Keefe, Patrick T. '96 (BUF) Awaiting Assignment.
O'Keefe, William F. '60 (HRT) Thomaston, CT St. Thomas.
O'Keefe, Rev. Msgr. William Joseph '59 (LA) Retired.
O'Keeffe, Dennis J. '84 (LFT) Zionsville, IN St. Alphonsus.
O'Keeffe, Jeremiah E. '66 (LA) Northridge, CA Our Lady of Lourdes.
O'Keeffe, Joseph '75 (MO) DEPARTMENT OF VETERANS AFFAIRS HOSPITALS AND CHAPLAINS.
O'Keeffe, Michael '68 (ORL) Ocala, FL Blessed Trinity.
O'Keeffe, Michael '68 (SAV) Retired.
O'Keeffe, Rev. Msgr. Richard W. '59 (TUC) Yuma, AZ Immaculate Conception Roman Catholic Parish & Guadalupe Mission – Yuma; Special Assignment; Council of Priests; Episcopal Vicar; Episcopal Vicar.
O'Keeffe, Rev. Msgr. William J. '59 (LA) Long Beach, CA Our Lady of Refuge.
O'Kelly, P. Colm '64 (SAC) El Dorado Hills, CA Holy Trinity Retired.
O'Kennedy, Philip N. '71 (BIR) Madison, AL St. John the Baptist; [I] Madison, AL St. John's Educational Foundation.
O'Kielty, James P. '54 (PAT) Retired.
O'Konsky, Stanley J. *s.j.* '72 (NY)[F] Bronx, NY Fordham Preparatory School; [EE] Jesuit Community, Kohlmann Hall.
O'Kruta, Francis A. '94 (WH) Wheeling, WV St. Alphonsus.
O'Laughlin, Rev. Msgr. Patrick J. '67 (STL) Wentzville, MO St. Patrick.
O'Leary, Arthur P. '75 (BO) Senior Priests. Retired.
O'Leary, Barry P. '07 (PIT) McKees Rocks, PA Holy Trinity; SCI Pittsburgh.
O'Leary, Cornelius F. '56 (WOR) Retired.
O'Leary, Rev. Msgr. Cornelius P. '48 (CAM) Retired.
O'Leary, Daniel F. *o.m.i.* '50 (BUF) Buffalo, NY Holy Angels.
O'Leary, David M. '85 (BO) Belmont, MA St. Joseph.
O'Leary, Rev. Msgr. Finbarr '60 (FgM) Boston, MA St. James the Apostle, Inc.
O'Leary, Harold V. *c.s.b.* '49 (GAL)[O] Houston, TX Residence of the Basilian Fathers of the University of St. Thomas.
O'Leary, Hilary *o.s.b.* '68 (PAT)[N] Morristown, NJ St. Mary's Abbey.
O'Leary, James E. '68 (BO) Arlington, MA St. Camillus.
O'Leary, James J. *s.j.* '65 (MIL)[P] Milwaukee, WI Jesuit Community at Marquette University.
O'Leary, James J. '56 (DET) Retired.
O'Leary, James M. *s.j.* '91 (CHI)[N] Chicago Chicago Province of the Society of Jesus–Provincial Office.
O'Leary, James M. *s.j.* '91 (FgM) Chicago, IL Society of Jesus.
O'Leary, James M. *s.j.* (STL)[O] St. Louis, MO Jesuit Community Corporation at Saint Louis University – Jesuit Hall.
O'Leary, James S. '61 (KAL) Parchment, MI St. Ambrose.
O'Leary, John A. '78 (CAM) Cape May Court House, NJ The Church of Our Lady of the Angels, Cape May Court House, N.J.
O'Leary, John P. '54 (BIS)[G] Bismarck, ND Emmaus Place Retired.
O'Leary, John '67 (MIA) On Duty Outside the Archdiocese; Boston, MA St. James the Apostle, Inc.
O'Leary, John *s.j.* '60 (SEA)[L] Seattle, WA Jesuit House, Seattle.
O'Leary, John '67 (BRK) The Brooklyn Hospital.
O'Leary, Kevin J. '95 (BO) Boston, MA Cathedral of the Holy Cross; Boston, MA St. James the Greater; Vicariate III.
O'Leary, Lawrence J. '56 (RVC) West Brentwood, NY Pilgrim Psychiatric Center Retired.
O'Leary, Rev. Msgr. Lawrence '53 (LA) Los Angeles, CA St. Martin of Tours Retired.
O'Leary, Malcolm *s.v.d.* '61 (JKS) Vicksburg, MS St. Mary.
O'Leary, Mark *o.p.* '85 (OAK)[M] Oakland, CA Order of Preachers (Province of the Most Holy Name of Jesus – Western Dominican Province).
O'Leary, Matthew L. '03 (SEA) Battle Ground, WA Sacred Heart; Presbyteral Council; Deans.
O'Leary, Michael *f.s.s.p.* '93 (SCR) Scranton, PA St. Michael's; [M] Elmhurst, PA Priestly Fraternity of St. Peter (F.S.S.P.), North American District Headquarters.
O'Leary, Niall Finbarr '60 (LA) South Pasadena, CA Holy Family Retired.
O'Leary, Patrick B. *s.j.* '61 (SEA)[A] Seattle, WA Seattle University; [L] Seattle, WA Arrupe Jesuit Community at Seattle University.
O'Leary, Patrick D. '51 (Y) Retired.
O'Leary, Peter P. '01 (BUR) Hardwick, VT Mary Queen of All Saints Parish.
O'Leary, Raymond J. '62 (ORL) Retired.
O'Leary, Richard *o.s.a.* '73 (PH) Rosemont, PA St. Thomas of Villanova Parish.
O'Leary, Robert A. '53 (NEW) Retired.
O'Leary, Sean '61 (SAC) Retired.
O'Leary, Rev. Msgr. Thomas M. '57 (NEW) Hillsdale, NJ St. John the Baptist Retired.
O'Leary, Rev. Msgr. Timothy F. (BO) Boston, MA St. Stephen; Society of Saint James the Apostle.
O'Leary, Rev. Msgr. Todd '58 (TUC) Tucson, AZ Saint Thomas the Apostle Roman Catholic Parish – Tucson; Diocesan Building Committee.
O'Leary, William F. *s.j.* '62 (OM)[C] Omaha, NE Creighton Preparatory School.
O'Loghlen, Martin P. *ss.cc.* '61 (LA) San Dimas, CA Holy Name of Mary; [P] La Verne, CA Congregation of the Sacred Hearts of Jesus and Mary.
O'Loughlin, Francis A. '80 (PRO) Newport, RI Jesus Saviour; Newport Hospital.
O'Loughlin, Frank '65 (PMB) Retired.
O'Loughlin, Michael '05 (VNN) Denver, CO Holy Protection of the Mother of God; Vocations Office.
O'Loughlin, Padhraic *s.s.c.* '57 (FgM) St Columbans, NE House of Post–Graduate Studies.
O'Loughlin, Patrick J. '99 (MIL) Oak Creek, WI St. Matthew.
O'Mahony, Jerome *m.s.c.* '50 (LA) Sherman Oaks, CA St. Francis de Sales Retired.
O'Mahony, Maurice K. '67 (LA) Santa Barbara, CA Our Lady of Mount Carmel Retired.
O'Malley, James E. '46 (SFR) Retired.
O'Malley, James F. '56 (CHI) Highwood, IL St. James Retired.
O'Malley, John A. '55 (BWN) Retired.
O'Malley, John J. *o.p.* '59 (CHI) River Forest, IL St. Vincent Ferrer.
O'Malley, John J. '65 (PIT) Retired.
O'Malley, John L. *s.j.* '63 (FgM) Chicago, IL Society of Jesus.
O'Malley, John W. *s.j.* '57 (WDC)[N] Washington, DC The Jesuit Community at Georgetown University.
O'Malley, Joseph M. '50 (DEN) Retired.
O'Malley, Kenneth *c.p.* '64 (CHI)[N] Chicago, IL Passionist Community–CTU.
O'Malley, Leonard F. '74 (BO) Appointed; Cambridge, MA St. Peter.
O'Malley, Mark (NEW)[B] School of Diplomacy and Intl. Rels.; [A] South Orange, NJ Immaculate Conception Seminary.
O'Malley, Patrick J. '57 (CHI)[A] Mundelein, IL University of St. Mary of the Lake/Mundelein Seminary Retired.
O'Malley, Paul *s.s.c.* '57 (OM)[K] St. Columbans Missionary Society of St. Columban Retired.
O'Malley, Terence *s.c.j.* '60 (OAK) Dublin, CA St. Raymond.
O'Malley, Thomas J. '66 (SCR) Ashley, PA St. Leo's.
O'Malley, Timothy J. '97 (CHI) Round Lake, IL St. Joseph.
O'Malley, Vincent J. *c.m.* '73 (BAL) Emmitsburg, MD St. Joseph; [S] Emmitsburg, MD Vincentian House.
O'Malley, William J. *s.j.* '63 (NY)[F] Bronx, NY Fordham Preparatory School.
O'Malley, William J. *s.j.* '51 (NY)[EE] Jesuit Community, Kohlmann Hall.
O'Malley, William M. '62 (SPK)[J] Spokane, WA Regis Community Retired.
O'Malley, William *o.carm.* '65 (NEW) Teaneck, NJ St. Anastasia's.
O'Mannion, Sean '08 (SPR) Northampton, MA Sacred Heart.
O'Mara, Dennis *s.s.c.* '61 (OM)[K] St. Columbans Missionary Society of St. Columban.
O'Mara, Dennis '04 (WOR) Westborough, MA St. Luke the Evangelist.
O'Mara, Michael E. '88 (IND) Indianapolis, IN St. Mary/Immaculate Conception.
O'Mara, William T. '58 (CHI) Retired.
O'Meara, Gerard J. '56 (BO) Senior Priests. Retired.
O'Meara, Gerard '56 (FgM) Boston, MA St. James the Apostle, Inc.
O'Meara, Gregory J. *s.j.* '02 (MIL)[P] Milwaukee, WI Jesuit Community at Marquette University.
O'Meara, Joseph P. '53 (NY) New York, NY Retired.
O'Meara, Joseph '67 (BAL) Baltimore, MD St. Rose of Lima Retired.
O'Meara, Joseph '52 (NY) New York, NY Our Lady of Guadalupe at St. Bernard's.
O'Meara, Noel P. *c.s.sp.* '65 (BRK)[T] Long Island City, NY Holy Ghost Fathers of Ireland; [X] Long Island City, NY World Compassion Link; Councilors:.
O'Meara, Thomas F. *o.p.* '62 (CHI)[N] River Forest, IL St. Thomas Aquinas Priory.
O'Melia, Edward A. '77 (DAV) Davenport, IA St. Mary's.
O'Neal, James E. '80 (MO) On Duty Outside the Diocese; Army Chaplains.
O'Neal, Norman B. *s.j.* '59 (NO)[E] New Orleans, LA Jesuit High School.
O'Neal, Shawn '00 (CHL) Bryson City, NC St. Joseph.
O'Neil, Edward '63 (NY) Mamaroneck, NY St. Vito.
O'Neil, Flann *o.f.m.* '52 (GLP) Ganado, AZ All Saints; St. Michaels, AZ St. Michael.
O'Neil, James W. *s.j.* '57 (BO)[D] Dorchester, MA Boston College High School.
O'Neil, James '85 (GF)[J] Malta, MT St. Mary's Catholic Education Trust.
O'Neil, Jim '85 (GF) Malta, MT St. Mary.
O'Neil, Joseph M. *m.s.* '93 (HRT)[L] Hartford, CT Missionaries of LaSalette.
O'Neil, Kevin *c.ss.r.* '81 (WDC)[N] Washington, DC Holy Redeemer College.
O'Neil, Michael '59 (SEA) Retired.
O'Neil, Patrick *o.p.* '95 (SAC) Benicia, CA St. Dominic.
O'Neil, Rev. Msgr. Philip E. '54 (RCK) Rockford, IL St. Bernadette Retired.
O'Neil, Robert J. *m.h.m.* '65 (NY) New York, NY St. Mary.
O'Neil, Thomas D. '69 (PIT) Washington, PA St. Hilary.
O'Neill, Blane *o.f.m.* '51 (SHP) Ruston, LA St. Thomas Aquinas.
O'Neill, Brian E. '68 (CAM) Ministry with the Deaf and Persons with Disabilities.
O'Neill, Charles E. *s.j.* '57 (NO)[P] New Orleans, LA Ignatius Residence Retired.
O'Neill, Daniel J. '76 (ALT) Somerset, PA St. Peter's.
O'Neill, Daniel *o.carm.* '69 (NEW) Teaneck, NJ St. Anastasia's.
O'Neill, Dennis B. '73 (CHI) Morton Grove, IL St. Martha.
O'Neill, Rev. Msgr. Edward M. '71 (MET) Colonia, NJ St. John Vianney; Diocesan Council of Catholic Women.
O'Neill, Rev. Msgr. Felix M. '55 (CAM) Retired.
O'Neill, Francis J. *s.j.* '50 (BO)[U] Weston, MA Campion Health Center, Inc.
O'Neill, George F. '97 (BGP) Brookfield, CT St. Joseph.
O'Neill, Hugh '77 (GLP) Retired.
O'Neill, James M. *c.s.b.* '86 (DET)[E] Novi, MI Catholic Central High School.
O'Neill, James W. *m.m.* '55 (NY)[EE] Retired.
O'Neill, James '57 (ALB) Troy, NY St. Mary Retired.
O'Neill, Rev. Msgr. James '54 (CHY) Casper, WY Saint Patrick's Retired.
O'Neill, James '07 (TR) Moorestown, NJ Our Lady of Good Counsel.
O'Neill, James '85 (GF) Diocesan Consultors; Priests' Council.
O'Neill, Jeremiah '59 (LA) Alhambra, CA St. Thomas More Retired.
O'Neill, Jeremy *o.s.b.* '00 (LAF)[H] Opelousas, LA Mother of the Redeemer Monastery.
O'Neill, John B. Charles '99 (KNX) Fairfield Glade, TN St. Francis of Assisi.
O'Neill, John D. *s.j.* '60 (DET)[K] Detroit, MI Jesuit Community at the University of Detroit Mercy.
O'Neill, John J. *m.s.* '62 (NOR) Danielson, CT St. James.
O'Neill, John J. (MO) Navy Reserve Chaplains.
O'Neill, John M. *o.s.f.s.* '73 (WIL)[J] Childs, MD Retirement and Assisted Care Facility.
O'Neill, John '67 (SFR) Olema, CA Sacred Heart.
O'Neill, John *i.v.dei.* '00 (BRK) Woodside, NY Corpus Christi.
O'Neill, Joseph J. *m.m.* '49 (NY)[EE] Retired.
O'Neill, Keith *o.f.m.conv.* '66 (SAV) Jesup, GA St. Joseph.
O'Neill, Rev. Msgr. Kevin P. '77 (SCR) Unassigned or Leave of Absence.
O'Neill, Rev. Msgr. Kevin S. '77 (HEL) Diocesan Pastoral Council; Helena, MT Cathedral of St. Helena; Presbyteral Council; Vicar General; Diocesan Consultors; Diocesan Finance Council; Deaneries; Personnel Board.
O'Neill, Rev. Msgr. Kevin T. '61 (BUF)[G] Cheektowaga, NY Mary Queen of Angels Catholic School; [O] Lackawanna, NY Bishop Head Residence Retired.
O'Neill, Michael *i.c.* '70 (SP) Seffner, FL St. Francis of Assisi.
O'Neill, Patrick G. '53 (SEA) Retired.
O'Neill, Patrick H. '67 (MIA) Special Assignment; Catholic Office for Inter–Faith Activities and Catholic–Jewish Relations Commission; Christian Unity Commission.
O'Neill, Patrick J. '90 (CHI) Palos Heights, IL St. Alexander.
O'Neill, Rev. Msgr. Patrick J. '47 (SAC) Retired.
O'Neill, Rev. Msgr. Patrick J. '45 (SD) La Mesa, CA St. Martin of Tours Retired.
O'Neill, Patrick '67 (MIA) Coordinator of Special Projects.
O'Neill, Raymond F. '66 (SP) Spring Hill, FL Saint Joan of Arc.
O'Neill, Richard V. '54 (SY) Marcy, NY Central New York Psychiatric Center; Pastoral Examiners Retired.
O'Neill, Robert '95 (STO) On Duty Outside the Diocese.

O'Neill, Seamus '74 (NY)[II] New York, NY St. Patrick's International Inc.
O'Neill, Sean F. '03 (PH) Oxford, PA Sacred Heart.
O'Neill, Thomas D. '68 (PRO) West Warwick, RI St. Mary.
O'Neill, Thomas H. *s.j.* '90 (SFR)[E] San Francisco, CA St. Ignatius College Preparatory (Coed); [N] San Francisco, CA Jesuit Community at St. Ignatius College Preparatory.
O'Neill, Thomas '62 (FRS) Frazier Park, CA Our Lady of the Snows Mission.
O'Neill, Timothy H. '67 (Y) Hubbard, OH St. Patrick.
O'Neill, William J. '65 (PRO) Jamestown, RI St. Mark.
O'Neill, Rev. Msgr. William O. '67 (SAV) Savannah, GA Cathedral of St. John the Baptist.
O'Neill, William P. '61 (CLV) Hinckley, OH Our Lady of Grace; Judges in Second Instance.
O'Neill, William R. *s.j.* '81 (OAK)[A] Berkeley, CA Jesuit School of Theology at Santa Clara University; [M] Berkeley, CA Jesuit Fathers and Brothers.
O'Nyamwaro, Richard *a.j.* (CHI) Chicago, IL St. Mary of the Lake; [J] Chicago, IL Saint Joseph Hospital.
O'Rafferty, Patrick '51 (SAC) Retired.
O'Regan, Hugh H. '57 (BO) Senior Priests. Retired.
O'Reilly, Aidan '60 (SAC) Retired.
O'Reilly, Rev. Msgr. Alvin J. '51 (NO) Retired.
O'Reilly, Andrew *c.pp.s.* '73 (CIN)[N] Dayton, OH Provincial Office of the Cincinnati Province of the Society of the Precious Blood.
O'Reilly, Bernard M. '69 (PRO) Harrisville, RI St. Patrick.
O'Reilly, Daniel '03 (NY)[D] Yonkers, NY University Apostolate –Campus Ministry; [HH] Yonkers, NY University Apostolate; [HH] Bronx, NY New York Maritime College; [A] Yonkers, NY St. John Neumann Seminary College At St. Joseph's Seminary Dunwoodie; [A] Yonkers, NY St. Joseph's Seminary.
O'Reilly, Desmond T. '90 (SAC) Sacramento, CA St. Charles Borromeo.
O'Reilly, Edward M. '68 (NY) Military Chaplains Retired.
O'Reilly, Gabriel '67 (MIA) Davie, FL St. David; Members.
O'Reilly, Gerald K. '85 (CHI) Chicago, IL St. Daniel the Prophet.
O'Reilly, James E. *s.j.* '57 (DET) Detroit, MI St. Peter Claver; [E] Detroit, MI Loyola High School.
O'Reilly, Joseph F. '56 (WH) Retired.
O'Reilly, Joseph '49 (SFD) Retired.
O'Reilly, Kevin P. '84 (WDC) Suitland, MD St. Bernardine; Barnesville, MD St. Mary Church and Shrine of Our Lady of Fatima.
O'Reilly, Kevin '96 (NY)[A] Yonkers, NY St. Joseph's Seminary.
O'Reilly, Michael '96 (SAC) Roseville, CA St. Rose of Lima.
O'Reilly, Patrick J. '65 (OG) Retired.
O'Reilly, Rev. Msgr. Peter A. '61 (LA) Claremont, CA Our Lady of the Assumption Retired.
O'Reilly, Vincent P. '62 (SAC) Vacaville, CA St. Joseph.
O'Riley, Dennis H. '59 (PEO) Retired.
O'Riordan, James '64 (JKS) Retired.
O'Riordan, Jeremiah '67 (PAT)[Q] Chester, NJ Nazareth Village Retired.
O'Riordan, William '85 (NO) Belle Chasse, LA Our Lady of Perpetual Help.
O'Rorke, Rev. Msgr. James H. '61 (PAT) Presbyteral Council; College of Consultors Retired.
O'Rourke, Charles *s.s.c.* '57 (OM)[K] St. Columbans, NE Missionary Society of St. Columban.
O'Rourke, Daniel '88 (GF) Lewistown, MT St. Leo; [J] Lewistown, MT St. Leo's Catholic Education Trust; Personnel Board.
O'Rourke, David K. *o.p.* '62 (OAK)[M] Oakland, CA Order of Preachers (Province of Holy Name of Jesus – Western Dominican Province); Defenders of the Bond; Point Richmond, CA Our Lady of Mercy.
O'Rourke, Dennis '80 (PHX)[H] Phoenix, AZ Catholic Committee on Scouting; The Catholic Scouting Program; Cave Creek, AZ St. Gabriel Roman Catholic Parish; Deans.
O'Rourke, Edmund F. *o.s.f.s.* '56 (WIL)[J] Childs, MD Retirement and Assisted Care Facility Retired.
O'Rourke, Francis J. *c.ss.r.* '62 (NY)[EE] New York, NY Redemptorist Priests and Brothers, C.Ss.R.
O'Rourke, Francis J. '75 (CHL) Charlotte, NC St. Gabriel Retired.
O'Rourke, James J. '58 (BO) Senior Priests.; Brighton, MA St. Columbkille Retired.
O'Rourke, John F. *o.s.a.* '61 (VEN) Cape Coral, FL Saint Katharine Drexel.
O'Rourke, Kevin *o.p.* '54 (CHI) River Forest, IL St. Vincent Ferrer.
O'Rourke, Matthew J. *s.s.j.* '47 (BAL)[S] Baltimore, MD St. Joseph's Manor.
O'Rourke, Michael K. '69 (GB) Appleton, WI St. Mary.
O'Rourke, Michael *o.p.* '96 (NO) New Orleans, LA St. Dominic.
O'Rourke, P. Gerard '50 (SFR) San Francisco, CA St. Gabriel Retired.
O'Rourke, Peter J. '99 (SCR) Scranton, PA St. Patrick's.
O'Rourke, Peter *c.p.* '64 (MET)[I] South River Passionist Provincial Office.
O'Rourke, Peter '64 (RVC) Stony Brook, NY L.I. State Veterans' Home.
O'Rourke, Richard *m.s.c.* '65 (AUS) Harker Heights, TX St. Paul Chong Hasang.
O'Rourke, Robert *s.s.c.* '58 (PRO)[P] Bristol, RI St. Columban's Retirement House Retired.
O'Rourke, Robert *s.s.c.* '58 (OM)[K] St. Columbans Missionary Society of St. Columban Retired.
O'Rourke, Thomas J. '64 (HRT) Hamden, CT Ascension.
O'Rourke, William D. '58 (RVC) Franklin Square, NY St. Catherine of Sienna.
O'Ryan, Colm '55 (LA) Beverly Hills, CA Good Shepherd Retired.
O'Shaughnessy, Denis (STA) Jacksonville, FL Mary Queen of Heaven.
O'Shaughnessy, Donald J. *s.j.* '55 (DET)[K] Clarkston, MI Colombiere Center.
O'Shaughnessy, Gerard *s.s.c.* '60 (SB) Fontana, CA St. Mary.
O'Shaughnessy, Gerard *s.s.c.* '60 (OM)[K] St. Columbans Missionary Society of St. Columban.
O'Shaughnessy, James J. '68 (NY)[E] Bronx, NY Cardinal Spellman High School.
O'Shaughnessy, Rev. Msgr. Michael A. '50 (VIC) Retired.
O'Shaughnessy, Patrick '68 (BLX) Retired.
O'Shaughnessy, Richard *s.m.* '47 (SAT)[K] San Antonio, TX Marianist Residence: Skilled Nursing.
O'Shea, Daniel *s.a.* '64 (NY)[EE] Garrison Graymoor Ecumenical and Interreligious Institute.
O'Shea, David T. '61 (PT) Retired.
O'Shea, Gerard '66 (NY) Retired.
O'Shea, Howard *o.f.m.* '58 (NY)[EE] New York Franciscan Friars, Holy Name Province.
O'Shea, James B. '65 (WOR) Worcester, MA Our Lady of Lourdes; Deans; Presbyteral Council.
O'Shea, James D. '64 (SFD) Retired.
O'Shea, James *c.p.* '89 (FgM)[I] South River Passionist Provincial Office; South River, NJ St. Paul of the Cross Province; South River, NJ; [I] South River Passionist Provincial Office.
O'Shea, James *c.p.* (BRK) Brooklyn, NY All Saints.
O'Shea, Jeremiah T. '64 (PIT) Bethel Park, PA St. Valentine; Priest Council.
O'Shea, John G. '60 (YAK) Kennewick, WA Holy Spirit.
O'Shea, John J. '50 (WCH) Retired.
O'Shea, John L. '81 (PIT) Meadow Lands, PA Our Lady of the Miraculous Medal.
O'Shea, Joseph '61 (SEA) Vancouver, WA St. John the Evangelist Retired.
O'Shea, Rev. Msgr. Lawrence '56 (DUL) Retired.
O'Shea, Michael James *o.f.m.* '54 (SFR) Burlingame, CA Our Lady of Angels.
O'Shea, Michael '52 (LA) Retired.
O'Shea, Morty *s.o.l.t.* '97 (CC)[G] Robstown, TX Society of Our Lady of the Most Holy Trinity.
O'Shea, Patrick '61 (LA) On Duty Outside the Archdiocese.
O'Shea, Patrick '61 (MIA) Hollywood, FL Little Flower.
O'Shea, Patrick *m.s.c.* '73 (SAT)[L] San Antonio, TX Missionaries of the Sacred Heart.
O'Shea, Philip *o.f.m.* '75 (BO)[Z] Boston, MA St. Anthony Shrine.
O'Shea, William D. '62 (PMB) North Palm Beach, FL St. Clare.
O'Shea, William J. '63 (JOL) Naperville, IL St. Margaret Mary Retired.
O'Sullivan, Brendan *s.s.c.* '54 (SB) Fontana, CA St. Mary.
O'Sullivan, Brendan *s.s.c.* '70 (FgM) St Columbans, NE House of Post–Graduate Studies.
O'Sullivan, Brendan *s.s.c.* '70 (LA)[P] Los Angeles, CA Columban Fathers, Procure House.
O'Sullivan, Brendan *s.s.c.* '70 (OM)[K] St. Columbans Missionary Society of St. Columban.
O'Sullivan, Carrol '51 (LA) Santa Barbara, CA Our Lady of Mount Carmel Retired.
O'Sullivan, Cyril '80 (SFR) Lagunitas, CA St. Cecilia.
O'Sullivan, Daniel A. '63 (LA) Ventura, CA Sacred Heart Retired.
O'Sullivan, Daniel '60 (DET) Retired.
O'Sullivan, Daniel '70 (FgM) Boston, MA St. James the Apostle, Inc.
O'Sullivan, Denis A. '72 (SR) Santa Rosa, CA St. Rose of Lima.
O'Sullivan, Rev. Msgr. Francis G. '47 (BO) Peabody, MA St. John the Baptist; Senior Priests. Retired.
O'Sullivan, Rev. Msgr. Jeremiah '58 (SD) Coronado, CA Sacred Heart Retired.
O'Sullivan, John V. '68 (PT) Tallahassee, FL Blessed Sacrament.
O'Sullivan, John '50 (B) Retired.
O'Sullivan, Rev. Msgr. John '68 (PT) Orders & Ministries, Commission for; Priests' Pension Plan, Board for; Priest Personnel Board.
O'Sullivan, Michael J. '55 (WDC)[M] Washington, DC Cardinal O'Boyle Residence for Priests Retired.
O'Sullivan, Peter '83 (KCK) Topeka, KS Christ the King.
O'Sullivan, Rev. Msgr. Peter '34 (LA) Retired.
O'Sullivan, Raymond S. '68 (BO) Society of St. James the Apostle.; Boston, MA St. James the Apostle, Inc.
O'Sullivan, Sarsfield '51 (HEL) Retired.
O'Sullivan, Sean A. *s.j.* '99 (CHI)[N] Chicago, IL Miguel Pro Jesuit Community.
O'Sullivan, Sean '64 (MIA) Coral Gables, FL Little Flower Retired.
O'Sullivan, Rev. Msgr. T. Brendan '56 (SAC) Members; Sacramento, CA St. Anthony Retired.
O'Sullivan, Thomas Carrol '51 (LA) Retired.
O'Sullivan, Thomas P. '71 (SR) Point Arena, CA St. Aloysius.
O'Sullivan, Timothy F. '94 (PH) Levittown, PA Immaculate Conception B.V.M.
O'Sullivan, Tracy *o.carm.* '62 (LA) Los Angeles, CA St. Raphael.
O'Toole, Brian P. '86 (WOR) Diocesan College of Consultors; Gardner, MA Sacred Heart of Jesus.
O'Toole, Coleman P. '61 (PRT) Old Orchard Beach, ME St. Margaret's.
O'Toole, James '64 (FWT) Retired.
O'Toole, John M. '67 (PIT) Retired.
O'Toole, John *c.ss.r.* '53 (ALB)[L] Saratoga Springs, NY St. John Neumann Residence.
O'Toole, Lawrence J. *s.j.* '58 (BO)[U] Weston, MA Campion Health Center, Inc.
O'Toole, Matthew L. '95 (STL)[F] St. Louis, MO Christian Brothers College High School (C.B.C.).
O'Toole, Matthew '95 (STL) Chesterfield, MO Ascension.
O'Toole, Rev. Msgr. Patrick F. '60 (BRK) Retired.
O'Toole, Robert F. *s.j.* '67 (NY)[EE] New York, NY "America;" Residence and publication office of the America Press; [II] New York, NY Gregorian University Foundation, The.
O'Toole, Thomas F. *c.ss.r.* '51 (ALB)[L] Saratoga Springs, NY St. John Neumann Residence.
O'Toole, Thomas '69 (OKL) Ardmore, OK St. Mary; Region III.
O'Toole, Timothy '89 (PMB) Released from Diocesan Assignment.
O'Toole, William F. '96 (GRY) Hammond, IN St. Casimir; Bishop's Council of Priests; East Chicago, IN St. Patrick.
O'Toole, Rev. Msgr. William P. '61 (LA) Alhambra, CA All Souls Retired.
Oajaca–Lopez, Gonzalo '08 (RVC) Brentwood, NY St. Anne's; Senate of Priests (Presbyteral Council/College of Consultors).
Oakes, Eathan '03 (BEA) Beaumont, TX Our Lady of the Assumption.
Oakes, Edward T. *s.j.* '79 (CHI)[A] Mundelein, IL University of St. Mary of the Lake/Mundelein Seminary.
Oakham, Ronald A. *o.carm.* '77 (TUC) Tucson, AZ Saint Cyril of Alexandria Roman Catholic Parish – Tucson.
Oakshott, Ward B. '77 (SEA) Lynnwood, WA St. Thomas More.
Oates, Eugene M. *c.ss.r.* '44 (STL)[O] Liguori, MO St. Clement Health Care Center Retired.
Oates, Thomas F. '63 (BO) Society of St. James the Apostle.
Oates, Thomas '63 (FgM) Boston, MA St. James the Apostle, Inc.
Obando, Gustavo '87 (CC) Corpus Christi, TX Corpus Christi Cathedral.
Obasi, Augustine I. (SB) Ontario, CA St. Elizabeth Ann Seton.
Obasi, John (PIT) Allegheny County, PA UPMC University of Pittsburgh Medical Center.
Obatama, Raphael '87 (BIR) Bessemer, AL St. Francis of Assisi.
Obayashi, Hal N. '02 (BO) Health Leave.
Obaza, Theodore L. '61 (SCR) Wilkes Barre Township, PA St. Joseph Retired.
Obba, Thaddeus '86 (NY) Yonkers, NY St. Ann.
Obee, Gregory *o.s.b.* '56 (RCK)[G] Aurora, IL Marmion Abbey Retired.
Obele, Oliver O. *m.s.p.* '95 (GAL) Houston, TX St. Anne de Beaupre.
Obelosi, Dominick (BRK) Brooklyn, NY Our Lady of Mount Carmel Shrine Church.
Obeng, Simon '89 (STV) On Duty Outside the Diocese.
Obeng, Simon (OG) U.S. Army Headquarters.
Obeng–Kyeremeh, Simon '89 (MO) Army Chaplains.
Ober, Lawrence M. *s.j.* '77 (CLV)[D] Cleveland, OH St. Ignatius High School.
Oberch, Rev. Msgr. Rick J. '85 (PEO) Defender of the Bond; [L] East Peoria, IL Mt. Alverno Novitiate; Promoter of Justice.
Oberg, Paul *s.s.j.* '85 (BIR) Birmingham, AL Our Lady of Fatima; [I] Birmingham, AL The Fatima Educational Foundation.
Oberle, Gerard *c.ss.r.* '55 (NEW) Newark, NJ St. James.
Oberle, James P. *s.s.* '87 (WDC) On Duty Outside the Archdiocese.
Oberle, James P. *s.s.* '87 (BAL)[S] Baltimore Society of St. Sulpice, Province of the United States.

Oberle, James P. *s.s.* '87 (DAL)[A] Irving, TX Holy Trinity Seminary.
Obermeyer, Robert A. '61 (CIN) Cincinnati, OH Our Lord, Christ the King; Judges; Cincinnati, OH St. Stephen.
Obermiller, Edwin H. *c.s.c.* '96 (FTW) Notre Dame, IN; [B] University of Notre Dame Du Lac; [H] Notre Dame, IN Holy Cross Community, Corby Hall, University of Notre Dame; [H] Notre Dame, IN Congregation of Holy Cross, Indiana Province, Provincial House.
Obero, Eduardo '93 (SJ) San Jose, CA St. John Vianney.
Obersinner, Joseph L. *s.j.* '57 (SPK)[J] Spokane, WA Regis Community.
Oberstar, Richard G. *m.s.f.* (DUL) Brainerd, MN St. Mathias Retired.
Obersteiner, Ernest '77 (GLP) On Leave of Absence.
Oberto, Rev. Msgr. Peter '78 (MAR) Negaunee, MI St. Paul; [B] Negaunee, MI Negaunee St. Paul Endowment Fund; Judicial Vicar; Diocesan Judge.
Oberts, David P. '69 (SUP) Rice Lake, WI St. John Evangelist; Rice Lake, WI Our Lady of Lourdes; Rice Lake, WI Holy Trinity; Board of Directors.
Obiatuegwu, Thomas '95 (LFT) Kokomo, IN St. Patrick; [F] Kokomo, IN Maria Regina Mater Monastery; Kokomo, IN St. Joan of Arc.
Obidiegwu, Celestine '04 (TLS) Langley, OK St. Frances of Rome; Pryor, OK St. Mark's.
Obiechina, Jude M. *c.m.f.* '83 (LAF) Opelousas, LA St. Joseph.
Obiekezie, Matthew U. (BRK) Brooklyn, NY SS. Simon and Jude.
Obijokwu, Francis *s.m.m.m.* '06 (BAK) La Grande, OR Our Lady of the Valley.
Obikwelu, Evaristus Uche '09 (AUS) Austin, TX St. Vincent de Paul.
Obin, Arthur *o.m.i.* '64 (PMB) Riviera Beach, FL St. Francis of Assisi.
Obin, Gilbert *c.i.c.m.* '67 (SAT) San Antonio, TX St. Martin de Porres.
Obinwa, Charles '95 (TOL) Lima, OH St. Rita Hospital and Medical Center; [G] Lima, OH St. Rita's Medical Center; Delphos, OH St. John the Evangelist.
Obisike, Bonaventure '01 (SPK) Special Ministry.
Obiudu, Alfred '05 (WH) Ravenswood, WV St. Matthew.
Oblinger, Joseph B. '46 (HEL) West Yellowstone, MT Our Lady of the Pines Retired.
Obloj, Stanislaw '93 (DET) Plymouth, MI Our Lady of Good Counsel; Absent on Sick Leave.
Obniski, Jeffrey *i.v.e.* '07 (SJ) Santa Clara, CA Our Lady of Peace.
Oboi, Robert Nyeko (CLV) Bedford, OH Our Lady of Hope.
Oborny, Paul J. '63 (WCH) Harvest House; [K] Wichita, KS Marriage Encounter Retired.
Oborny, Rudolf F. '71 (LIN) Hebron, NE Sacred Heart; Diocesan Area CCD Directors; Deaneries and Deans.
Obrikwe, Kenneth (ALX) Cloutierville, LA St. John the Baptist.
Obrimski, Paul '70 (PH) Philadelphia, PA Immaculate Heart of Mary.
Obu–Mends, Francis JoJo '92 (BRK) Rockaway Point, NY Blessed Trinity Roman Catholic Church.
Obwona, Martin Larok *f.c.* '80 (OKL) Blackwell, OK St. Joseph's; Tonkawa, OK St. Joseph's.
Ocampo, Arturo M. *o.f.m.* '85 (IND) Indianapolis, IN St. Patrick.
Ocampo, P. Ramón Conde *o.de.m.* '59 (PCE) Ponce, PR La Merced.
Ocariz, Rev. Msgr. Fernando '71 (POD) Vicar General.
Ocasro, Edgardo Acosta '83 (MGZ) Sabana Grande, PR Church of San Isidro; Cursillos de Cristiandad.
Occeno, Adolfo (NY) Fishkill, NY Church of St. Mary, Mother of the Church.
Occhiuto, Joseph L. '79 (MRY) Santa Cruz, CA Holy Cross; Administrative Committee Priests' Pension Plan.
Ochalek, Arkadiusz '99 (MO) Army Reserve Chaplains.
Ochalek, Arkdiusz '61 (BAL) Military Chaplains.
Ochasi, Aloysius '01 (PH) Roslyn, PA St. John of the Cross.
Ochej, Tomasz '00 (VEN) Absent on Leave.
Ochetti, Jerome '02 (SB) Upland, CA St. Joseph; Special or Other Diocesan Assignment; Office of Vocations.
Ochiabuto, Isidore '01 (SAN) Big Lake, TX St. Margaret of Cortona.
Ochieze, Oliver '88 (LR) Fairfield Bay, AR St. Francis Assisi; Clinton, AR St. Jude Church.
Ochiltree, Richard *c.ss.r.* '53 (OAK)[M] Berkeley, CA Redemptorist Fathers (Denver Province).
Ochoa, David '72 (LA) Los Angeles, CA Immaculate Heart of Mary.
Ochoa, Einer '85 (SAT) Cursillos of Christianity of the Archdiocese of San Antonio; San Antonio, TX St. Agnes.
Ochoa, Rafael '78 (LA) Los Angeles, CA Immaculate Conception.
Ochoa–Lugo, Adrian *o.de.m.* '97 (SB) Riverside, CA St. Anthony of Padua.
Ochs, Daniel L. '76 (COL) Columbus, OH St. Agatha.
Ochs, Robert J. *s.j.* '61 (CHI)[N] Chicago Chicago Province of the Society of Jesus–Provincial Office.
Ochs, Robert J. *s.j.* '61 (OAK)[M] Berkeley, CA Jesuit Fathers and Brothers.
Ochu, Austin Charles *s.m.a.* '92 (WDC)[N] Takoma Park, MD House of Studies.
Ochu, Austin Charles *s.m.a.* '92 (MO) DEPARTMENT OF VETERANS AFFAIRS HOSPITALS AND CHAPLAINS.
Ocilka, John A. '94 (CLV) Absent on Sick Leave.
Ock Jin Cho, Peter '77 (P) Portland, OR Korean Martyrs Catholic Church.
Ocun, Godfred *a.j.* '96 (P)[J] Portland, OR Providence St. Vincent Medical Center; [M] Beaverton, OR Sisters of St. Mary of Oregon.
Oddo, Peter A. '61 (NEW) On Duty Outside the Archdiocese.
Odemokpa, Paschal '79 (MO) DEPARTMENT OF VETERANS AFFAIRS HOSPITALS AND CHAPLAINS.
Odenbrett, Stephen *o.s.b.* '46 (MRY)[F] San Luis Obispo, CA Men's Residence.
Odermann, John *o.s.b.* '55 (BIS)[A] Richardton, ND Assumption Abbey Retired.
Odermann, Valerian *o.s.b.* '73 (BIS)[A] Richardton, ND Assumption Abbey; [B] Bismarck, ND University of Mary.
Odhiambo Okola, Peter *a.j.* '98 (ARL) Springfield, VA St. Raymond of Penafort.
Odien, Terry M. '73 (CAM) Ex Officio Members; Vicar for Clergy; Ex Officio Members; Advanced Studies for Priests; Ex Officio Members; Consultants; Cherry Hill, NJ The Catholic Community of Christ Our Light, Cherry Hill, N.J.
Odikanoro, Vincent I. '83 (NY) Middletown, NY Holy Cross.
Odina, Christopher C. (BRK) Rosedale, NY St. Pius X.
Odiong, Anthony '93 (AUS) West, TX St. Mary, Church of the Assumption; [L] Waco, TX St. Peter Catholic Student Center at Baylor University.
Odor, Luke U. '83 (MO) DEPARTMENT OF VETERANS AFFAIRS HOSPITALS AND CHAPLAINS.
Odorizzi, Thomas A. *c.o.* '92 (MET) New Brunswick, NJ St. Peter the Apostle; [I] New Brunswick, NJ The New Brunswick Congregation of the Oratory of St. Philip Neri; New Brunswick, NJ.
Odozor, Paulinus I. *c.ss.p.* (FTW)[B] University of Notre Dame Du Lac.
Odunze, Damian *c.s.sp.* (GAL) Houston, TX St. Peter Claver.
Oduori, Constantine *a.j.* '03 (ALN) Easton, PA Our Lady of Mercy Parish.
Oduro, Charles Akoto '89 (BRK) Brooklyn, NY St. Catherine of Genoa; [S] Ghanaian Apostolate; Brooklyn, NY St. Vincent Ferrer.
Oedy, Thomas E. '71 (TOL) Columbus Grove, OH St. Anthony of Padua.
Oehmler, Gary W. '83 (PIT) Pittsburgh, PA St. Teresa of Avila.
Oehrlein, Rev. Msgr. Felix G. '65 (MAD) Wisconsin Dells, WI St. Cecilia.
Oelrich, Anthony '92 (SCL) St. Cloud, MN St. Mary's Cathedral of St. Cloud; St. Cloud, MN St. Augustine; [L] St. Cloud, MN Newman Center, Inc.; Campus Ministry; Continuing Formation of Priests; St. Cloud, MN Christ Church.
Oen, Edward J. *c.pp.s.* '64 (KCK) Baileyville, KS Sacred Heart; St. Benedict, KS St. Mary's.
Oenbrink, Michael J. '99 (CHR) Hilton Head Island, SC St. Francis By the Sea; Deans; Vocations Board; College of Consultors; Personnel Committee.
Oesterle, John G. '67 (PIT) Allegheny County, PA Mercy Health System of Pittsburgh–Pittsburgh Mercy Hospital.
Oestreich, Brian W. '93 (NU) Silver Lake, MN Church of the Holy Family; Committee on Parishes; Priests' Council.
Offeh, Joseph Mary '91 (SY) Binghamton, NY St. Mary of the Assumption; Binghamton, NY St. Paul.
Offerman, Paul '57 (SFS) Bridgewater, SD St. Stephen.
Offor, Celsius '95 (LKC) Jennings, LA Our Lady of Perpetual Help; Welsh, LA St. Joseph.
Offor, Oliver (NY) Pelham Manor, NY Our Lady of Perpetual Help.
Offutt, Rev. Msgr. Bradley S. '86 (KC) Chancellor; Consultors; Building Commission; Special Assignment; Kansas City, MO Cathedral of Immaculate Conception.
Offutt, J. James '62 (JC) Centralia, MO Holy Spirit; Judges.
Ofodum, Anselm '95 (GF) Special Assignment; Wolf Point, MT Immaculate Conception.
Oforchukwu, Joachim *c.s.sp.* '90 (CAM) Blue Anchor, NJ Parish of Blessed John the Twenty–Third, Blue Anchor, N.J.; New Jersey State Psychiatric Hospital.
Ofori–Domah, John '81 (LC) Camp Douglas, WI St. James; Camp Douglas, WI St. Michael.
Ogbemure, Raymond '74 (OAK) El Cerrito, CA St. John the Baptist.
Ogbonna, Christian Iheanyichukwu '79 (ALX) Winnfield, LA Our Lady of Lourdes.
Ogbonna, Joseph (SAN) Eden, TX St. Charles.
Ogbonna, Leonard '93 (BEA)[B] Beaumont, TX CHRISTUS Health Southeast Texas – CHRISTUS Hospital – St. Elizabeth.
Ogbonna, Stanislaus *c.s.sp.* '73 (NY) Monticello, NY St. Peter; Fallsburg, NY Sullivan Correctional Facility.
Ogbuji, Udochukwu Vincent '97 (LR) Little Rock, AR Christ the King.
Ogden, Louis P. '85 (HBG) Middletown, PA Seven Sorrows of the Blessed Virgin Mary; Consultors, College; Presbyteral Council.
Oge, Raymond J. '67 (STL) Retired.
Ogg, Thomas '68 (CHY) Sheridan, WY Holy Name; Ex Officios, Non–Voting; St. Joseph's Society for Priests (Clergy Mutual Benefit Society); Diocesan Schools Advisory Group.
Oggero, Roy J. *c.s.b.* '61 (GAL)[B] Sugar Land, TX Basilian Fathers of Sugarland Retired.
Oggioni, Paul *sd.c* '70 (PH)[L] Springfield, PA Divine Providence Village; [B] Springfield, PA Servants of Charity.
Ogle, Rev. Msgr. Sean G. '77 (BRK) Long Island City, NY Our Lady of Mount Carmel; Presbyteral Council.
Ogonwa, Stephen '01 (ORL) Port Orange, FL Our Lady of Hope.
Ogorevc, Metod *o.f.m.* '92 (CHI) Lemont, IL Slovenian Catholic Mission; [N] Lemont, IL The Slovene Franciscan Fathers, Order of Friars Minor, Commissariat of the Holy Cross.
Ogorzaly, Adam '85 (ROC) Rochester, NY St. Stanislaus.
Ogrodowski, Rev. Msgr. William M. '75 (PIT) Priest Council; Clergy Personnel Board; Vicariate 3; College of Consultors.
Oguagua, Thomas E. *s.j.* '05 (CHI)[C] Chicago, IL Jesuit Community at Loyola University Chicago.
Oguamana, Mark E. '83 (WIL) Veterans Admin.
Oguamanam, Mark '83 (MO) DEPARTMENT OF VETERANS AFFAIRS HOSPITALS AND CHAPLAINS.
Ogumere, Augustine *c.s.sp.* '82 (PHX) Sun City, AZ St. Clement of Rome Roman Catholic Parish.
Ogumoro, Isidro T. '89 (CHK) Tinian, MP San Jose; Presbyteral Council.
Ogun, David O. *s.j.* '00 (NY)[EE] Loyola Hall, Jesuit Community.
Ogurchock, John J. *m.m.* '54 (FgM) Maryknoll, NY MARYKNOLL.
Oh, Paul Saewan '83 (OM) Omaha, NE St. Andrew Kim Taegon Catholic Community.
Oh, Taegon–Seil *s.j.* '04 (BO)[U] Newton, MA The Jesuit Community at Boston College.
Ohajunwa, Martin E. '00 (BEL) Flora, IL St. Stephen.
Ohanete, Michael '96 (LA) Lancaster, CA Sacred Heart.
Ohankwere, Desmond C. *m.s.p.* '92 (GAL) Houston, TX St. Nicholas.
Ohlig, John '95 (AMA) Amarillo, TX St. Joseph's.
Ohlinger, Vincent *s.v.d.* '68 (MIL)[P] East Troy, WI Divine Word Missionaries.
Ohm, Edward U. '92 (MO) On Duty Outside the Diocese; Army Chaplains.
Ohmann, Daniel F. *m.m.* '55 (FgM) Maryknoll, NY MARYKNOLL.
Ohner, John M. *o.s.a.* '74 (JOL) Homer Glen, IL Our Mother of Good Counsel.
Ohno, Ignatius F. *s.j.* '92 (SEA)[A] Seattle, WA Seattle University; [L] Seattle, WA Arrupe Jesuit Community at Seattle University.
Ohuche, Evaristus '02 (NY) New York, NY St. Elizabeth.
Oiland, Kevin '09 (SPK) Walla Walla, WA Assumption of the Blessed Virgin Mary; Walla Walla, WA St. Francis of Assisi; Walla Walla, WA St. Patrick.
Ojeda, Uriel '07 (SAC) Redding, CA Our Lady of Mercy.
Oji, Joseph Kalu *c.s.sp.* (R) Cary, NC St. Michael the Archangel.
Ojibway, Paul *s.a.* '77 (OAK) Orinda, CA Santa Maria.
Ojibway, V. Paul *s.a.* '78 (NY)[EE] Garrison, NY Franciscan Friars of the Atonement, Minister General Office; [EE] Garrison Graymoor Ecumenical and Interreligious Institute; General Council.
Okafor, Bernard E. '85 (CLV) Akron, OH St. Bernard.
Okafor, Gabriel (DEN)[H] Denver, CO Saint Joseph Hospital.
Okafor, Gregory '88 (TUC) Tucson, AZ Saint Mark Roman Catholic Parish – Tucson.
Okafor, Jerome '83 (FAR) Fessenden, ND St. Augustine's Church of Fessenden; Fessenden, ND St. Patrick's Church of Hurdsfield; Fessenden, ND Holy Family.
Okafor, Jude '96 (FAR) Fargo, ND Sts. Anne & Joachim Church of Fargo.
Okafor, Patrick Chudi '92 (RVC) Stony Brook, NY Stony Brook University Hospital.
Okafor, Patrick '96 (RVC) Stony Brook, NY Stony Brook University Hospital.
Okagbue, Bartholomew '88 (GR)[G] Muskegon, MI Mercy Health Partners.
Okeahialam, George *m.s.p.* '02 (BEA) Raywood, TX Sacred Heart.
Okeahialam, Uju Patrick *c.s.s.p.* '94 (PBL) Pueblo, CO St. Francis Xavier.
Okechukwu, Emmanuel '86 (HRT) Waterbury, CT

Basilica of the Immaculate Conception.
Okeiyi, Athanasius N. '91 (LR) Brinkley, AR St. John the Baptist; Forrest City, AR St. Francis of Assisi; Brinkley, AR St. Mary of the Lake Church.
Okeiyi, Emmanuel '03 (RVC) Roslyn, NY St. Francis Hospital.
Okeke, Anselm '98 (RVC) Smithtown, NY St. Catherine of Siena Hospital; Smithtown, NY St. Patrick.
Okeke, Felix '96 (SAN) Ozona, TX Our Lady of Perpetual Help.
Okeke, Gerald '01 (IND) Richmond, IN Holy Family; Richmond, IN St. Andrew; Richmond, IN St. Mary.
Okeke, Kizito '95 (ATL) Gainesville, GA St. Michael.
Okeke, Stephen '96 (NY) Manhattan, NY New York University Medical Center; New York, NY Our Lady of the Scapular and St. Stephen.
Okello, Maxwell '96 (OWN) Hardinsburg, KY St. Mary–of–the–Woods; Judges; Hardinsburg, KY St. Anthony.
Okenedo, Marcelinus *s.m.m.m.* '04 (FRS) Kerman, CA St. Patrick; Tranquillity, CA St. Paul.
Okere, Michael C. '91 (CHR) Orangeburg, SC Holy Trinity.
Okere, Remigius C. *c.s.sp.* '94 (DM) Granger, IA Assumption of the Blessed Virgin Mary.
Okhuoya, Kizito Raphael '94 (OM) Omaha, NE St. Thomas More.
Okiria, Richard P. '86 (HRT) West Hartford, CT St. Thomas the Apostle.
Okochi, Augustine '93 (RVC) Valley Stream, NY Franklin Medical Center Hospital.
Okochi, Chux '88 (RVC) Malverne, NY Our Lady of Lourdes.
Okochi, Chux '88 (NY) Bronx, NY Calvary Hospital; [Y] Bronx, NY Calvary Hospital.
Okodua, Michael (MOB) Mobile, AL Cathedral of the Immaculate Conception.
Okogba, Joseph '80 (FAR) Drayton, ND St. Edward's Church of Drayton; Pembina, ND Assumption Church of Pembina.
Okoli, Christopher '92 (RVC) Bay Shore, NY Southside Hospital; Islip Terrace, NY St. Peter the Apostle.
Okoli, Eugene '93 (GR) Lowell, MI St. Mary's.
Okoli, Francis '00 (NY) Manhattan, NY Beth Israel Medical Center.
Okoli, Jovita '96 (DET) Judges; Grosse Pointe, MI Our Lady Star of the Sea.
Okolie, Maxwell '88 (LKC) Elton, LA St. Joseph's.
Okon, Alan J. '98 (PH)[D] Norristown, PA Kennedy–Kenrick Catholic High School; [D] Pottstown, PA St. Pius X High School; Norristown, PA Holy Saviour.
Okonkwo, Ben '84 (IND)[G] Indianapolis, IN St. Vincent Hospital and Health Care Center, Inc.
Okonkwo, Ignatius '98 (BEL) Eldorado, IL St. Mary; Elizabethtown, IL St. Joseph; Harrisburg, IL St. Mary.
Okonkwo, Jovita '97 (TLS) Sapulpa, OK Sacred Heart.
Okonkwo, Patrick E. '04 (NU) Hutchinson, MN Church of St. Anastasia.
Okonmah, Emmanuel '97 (FAR) Absent on Leave.
Okonski, Joseph F. '90 (PH) Philadelphia, PA St. Athanasius.
Okonski, Maciej *o.p.* '07 (NY)[II] New York, NY Polish Dominicans, Inc.
Okore, Innocent '93 (LR) Hot Springs National Park, AR St. John the Baptist; Hot Springs National Park, AR St. Mary of the Springs.
Okorie, Christopher '94 (BRK) Forest Hills, NY Our Lady of Mercy.
Okorie, Ferdinand *c.m.f.* '09 (CHI)[N] Oak Park Claretian Missionaries USA Eastern Province.
Okorie, Onyema '99 (MO) Air Force Chaplains; On Duty Outside the Diocese.
Okorn, Dusan A. '47 (HEL) Retired.
Okoro, Alexander A. '86 (MO) Veterans Hospital; DEPARTMENT OF VETERANS AFFAIRS HOSPITALS AND CHAPLAINS.
Okoro, Bonaventure '02 (RCK) Lee, IL St. James.
Okoro, George (STO) Stockton, CA Presentation Church (Pastor of).
Okoro, John '95 (OWN) Calhoun, KY St. Sebastian; Calhoun, KY St. Charles.
Okoro, Martin *c.m.f.* '97 (NEW) Hoboken, NJ Our Lady of Grace and Saint Joseph Parish.
Okoroafor, Augustine (HRT) Meriden, CT St. Mary; Meriden, CT St. Joseph.
Okorobia, Gregory (MOB) Enterprise, AL St. John.
Okoroh, Patrick (GRY)[D] Crown Point, IN Saint Anthony Medical Center.
Okoroji, Ignatius *s.d.v.* '04 (PAT)[N] Florham Park, NJ Father Justin Vocationary; Florham Park, NJ.
Okorougo, Charles '87 (LKC)[B] Lake Charles, LA CHRISTUS Health Southwestern Louisiana.
Okoth, Crispin '90 (SEA) Seattle, WA St. John the Evangelist.
Okoth, George '89 (MO) Army Chaplains.
Okoye, Charles '92 (NEW) Hackensack, NJ Hackensack University Medical Center.
Okoye, James C. *c.s.sp.* '70 (CHI) Chicago, IL St. Mary Magdalene; [B] Chicago, IL The Catholic Theological Union at Chicago.
Okpalauwaekwe, Emmanuel '91 (NY) Manhattan, NY Harlem Hospital.
Okpara, Benson Claret '91 (Y) Canton, OH St. Benedict; Canton, OH St. Mary of the Immaculate Conception.
Okpara, Theophilus '96 (LR) Lake Village, AR Holy Spirit Church; Lake Village, AR Our Lady of the Lake.
Okpechi, Chukwubikem *o.p.* '76 (HBG) Hershey, PA St. Joan of Arc; Hershey, PA Milton J. Hershey Medical Center.
Okpogba, Desmond '89 (TLS) Sallisaw, OK St. Francis Xavier.
Okumu, Richard U. '81 (DAV) Camanche, IA Church of the Visitation.
Okumu, Stephen '86 (SEA) Seattle, WA St. Therese.
Okwara, Marcel Emeka *c.ss.r* '07 (MEM)[F] Memphis, TN Redemptorists of Tennessee; Memphis, TN Holy Names of Jesus and Mary.
Okwir, Martin '90 (BO) Charlestown, MA St. Francis de Sales; [S] Cambridge, MA Youville Hospital & Rehabilitation Center, Inc.
Okwumuo, Patrick '00 (BEL) Belleville, IL St. Augustine of Canterbury.
Okwuzu, Augustine *s.m.m.m.* '04 (BAK) Wasco, OR St. Mary.
Olazo, Marco Hurtado '02 (NEW) Roselle, NJ Church of St. Joseph the Carpenter.
Olbrys, Mariusz '07 (BGP) Ridgefield, CT St. Mary.
Olczak, Joseph M. *o.s.p.p.e.* '65 (NOR)[A] Cromwell, CT Holy Apostles College and Seminary.
Olczak, Joseph M. *o.s.p.p.e.* '65 (PH)[Y].
Oldani, Louis J. *s.j.* '64 (KC)[J] Kansas City, MO Rockhurst Jesuit Community.
Oldenski, Kenneth E. '66 (PIT) Gibsonia, PA Saint Richard.
Oldershaw, Robert H. '62 (CHI) Retired.
Oldfield, Albert E. '59 (SCR) Retired.
Oldfield, John *o.a.r.* '63 (NY) Bronx, NY St. John's.
Oldham, David A. '03 (LIN) Rulo, NE Immaculate Conception; [C] Falls City, NE Sacred Heart School; Advocates.
Olds, Daryl *c.m.f.* '92 (PHX) Prescott, AZ Sacred Heart Roman Catholic Parish; San Gabriel, CA.
Olds, Daryl *c.m.f.* '92 (LA)[V] San Gabriel, CA Claretian Missionaries – Western Province, Inc.
Olds, Steven '88 (PMB) On Duty Outside the Diocese; [A] Boynton Beach, FL St. Vincent de Paul Regional Seminary; Censor of Books.
Olek, Ralph F. *s.m.* '74 (ATL)[D] Atlanta, GA Marist School.
Oleksiak, Donald P. '89 (CLV) Lakewood, OH St. Hedwig; Clergy Personnel Board; Garfield Heights, OH SS. Peter and Paul; Presbyteral Council.
Oleksy, Kazimierz *s.d.s.* '92 (SAT) Jourdanton, TX St. Matthew's; [L] Falls City, TX Salvatorian Fathers Community of Texas.
Oleksy, Stanislaw *s.d.s.* '82 (SAT) Bandera, TX St. Stanislaus; [L] Falls City, TX Salvatorian Fathers Community of Texas.
Olendzki, Rev. Msgr. Joaquim J. '58 (NY) Red Hook, NY St. Christopher; Tivoli, NY St. Sylvia.
Olenick, John *c.ss.r.* '03 (PH) Philadelphia, PA Visitation B.V.M.
Olenowski, Mark '85 (PAT) Priestly Life Committee; Vocations Board; Long Valley, NJ Our Lady of the Mountain.
Olesik, William J. '72 (NOR) Members; Pontifical Association of the Holy Childhood; Pontifical Society for the Propagation of the Faith.
Olesik, William '72 (NOR) Jewett City, CT St. Mary.
Olges, H. Anthony '70 (L) Louisville, KY St. Elizabeth of Hungary; Louisville, KY Holy Family; Louisville, KY St. Therese.
Olguin, Jacinto '74 (LAR) Presbyteral Council; Laredo, TX St. Patrick.
Olguin, Luis '92 (SY) Utica, NY St. John; Utica, NY St. Mary of Mt. Carmel/Blessed Sacrament; Rome, NY Walsh Facility; Special Assignment.
Oliagba, Dominic (BRK) Brooklyn, NY St. Sylvester.
Oligschlaeger, P. Gregory '93 (JC) Martinsburg, MO St. Joseph; Martinsburg, MO Church of the Resurrection; V. Mexico; Appointed Members; Judges; Diocesan Consultors.
Olinoyo, Julius (NO) Reserve, LA Our Lady of Grace.
Olisaemeka, Justin '01 (BEL) Centralia, IL St. Mary; Sandoval, IL St. Lawrence.
Oliva, G. Max *s.j.* '72 (SJ)[D] San Jose, CA Bellarmine College Preparatory.
Olivares, Jesus *c.s.* '97 (KCK) Hispanic Ministry.
Olivares, Jesus *c.s.* (KC) Kansas City, MO Holy Rosary.
Olivares, Romeo D. *c.i.c.m.* '74 (SAT) Lytle, TX St. Andrew.
Olivars, Jesus *c.s.* (CHI) Melrose Park, IL Our Lady of Mount Carmel.
Olivas, J. Alfredo '81 (ELP) Absent on Leave.
Olive, Alphonsus *c.ss.r.* '86 (BAL) Annapolis, MD St. Mary.
Olive, Rodney J. *c.ss.r.* '86 (FgM) Brooklyn, NY AMERICAN REDEMPTORIST FATHERS.
Oliveira, Edivaldo daSilva '09 (AGN) Barrigada, GU San Vicente Ferrer.
Oliveira, Gastao A. '72 (FR) Fall River, MA Santo Christo.
Oliveira, Joel D. '54 (PRO) Retired.
Oliveira, John J. '77 (FR) New Bedford, MA Our Lady of Mt. Carmel; New Bedford, MA St. John the Baptist; Diocesan Consultors; New Bedford Deanery; Director of Portuguese Ministry; Mentoring Program for Priests.
Oliveira, Rev. Msgr. John J. *p.a.* '67 (FR) New Bedford, MA St. Mary's.
Oliveira, Rev. Msgr. John J. '66 (FR) Holy Childhood Association, The; Missionary Cooperative Plan; Permanent Diaconate Program; Propagation of the Faith.
Oliveira, Manoel J. '04 (NEW) Newark, NJ St. Augustine's; Newark, NJ St. Benedict's.
Oliveira, Robert A. '77 (FR) New Bedford, MA Holy Name of the Sacred Heart of Jesus.
Oliveira, Vitor '73 (SPR) Ludlow, MA Our Lady of Fatima.
Olivencia, Ramon '97 (ARE) Vega–Baja, PR Our Lady of Lourdes.
Oliver, James M. '88 (PH) On Special or Other Archdiocesan Assignment; Philadelphia, PA St. Philip Neri; The Chancery; Defenders of the Bond; Promoters of Justice.
Oliver, Rev. Msgr. John A. '52 (TUC) Retired.
Oliver, John '82 (STA) Absent or Sick Leave.
Oliver, Marc K. '89 (NY)[HH] Kingston, NY Culinary Institute of America; [HH] Kingston, NY Dutchess Community College; Kingston, NY St. Peter.
Oliver, Marc (NY) Hyde Park, NY Hyde Park, P.J. Kenedy Memorial Chapel of Our Lady of the Way.
Oliver, Robert W. '00 (BO)[A] Brighton, MA St. John Seminary.
Oliver, Robert (BO) Associates.
Oliver, William A. '77 (GAL) Houston, TX St. Thomas More.
Olivera, Carlos Alberto '84 (SJ) Chinese Catholic Community; Santa Clara, CA Chinese Catholic Community; Santa Clara, CA St. Clare.
Oliveras, Evaristo *c.m.* '88 (SJN) San Juan, PR San Vicente de Paul; Santurce, PR Hospital Pavia–Santurce; [E] San Juan, PR Centro Medico de P.R.; [B] San Juan, PR Colegio San Vicente de Paul.
Oliveras, Jose '95 (ARE) Morovis, PR Nuestra Senora del Carmen.
Olivere, Michael S. '94 (PH) Philadelphia, PA Divine Mercy Parish.
Oliveri, Armand *s.d.b.* '50 (SFR) San Francisco, CA SS. Peter and Paul.
Oliveri, Richard H. '66 (PAT) Pompton Plains, NJ Our Lady of Good Counsel Retired.
Oliverio, Rev. Msgr. Francis E. '56 (NY) Retired.
Olivero, Michael A. '74 (CHI) Mt. Prospect, IL St. Cecilia.
Olivier, David S. '62 (SPK)[J] Spokane, WA Regis Community Retired.
Olivier, Harry T. *s.j.* '57 (PHX)[F] Phoenix, AZ Society of Jesus.
Olivier, John H. *s.s.* '47 (BAL)[O] Baltimore, MD St. Charles Villa; [S] Baltimore Society of St. Sulpice, Province of the United States Retired.
Olivier, John H. *s.s.* '47 (MAR) Retired.
Oliviera, Humbert '77 (MAN) Retired.
Oliviera, Joel D. '54 (BO) Senior Priests. Retired.
Olivo, Stephen G. *s.j.* '69 (SJ)[M] Los Gatos, CA Sacred Heart Jesuit Center.
Ollendick, William *o.f.m.* '01 (DET) Southfield, MI Church of the Transfiguration.
Ollison, Vernetta (P)[J] Portland, OR Providence Portland Medical Center.
Olmer, Vernon *o.f.m.* '62 (SFD) Montrose, IL St. Rose of Lima; Teutopolis, IL St. Francis of Assisi; [L] Teutopolis, IL St. Francis Assisi Friary.
Olmo, Luis S. *o.f.m.* '85 (SJN) Carolina, PR Santa Clara de Asis.
Olmstead, Daryl '75 (SAL) Vicariate Representatives; Hays, KS St. Nicholas of Myra Parish; Munjor, KS St. Francis of Assisi Parish; Council of Priests.
Olnhausen, James Robert '70 (AUS) Giddings, TX St. Margaret; Giddings, TX St. Mary; State School.
Olobo, Leonard *c.s.c.* '04 (FTW)[H] Notre Dame Congregation of Holy Cross, Indiana Province, Provincial House.
Olona, Rev. Msgr. Richard '70 (SFE) Albuquerque, NM Risen Savior Catholic Community; Ecumenical Commission and Interreligious Affairs; College of Consultors.
Olowin, Rev. Msgr. Jan C. '68 (E) Emlenton, PA St. Michael; [P] Emlenton, PA Clarion University of Pennsylvania.
Ols, James R. '75 (CLV) Elyria Township, OH St. Vincent de Paul.
Olsavsky, John R. '62 (CLV) Judges in Second Instance; College of Consultors; Presbyteral Council; Chagrin Falls, OH St. Joan of Arc Retired.
Olsavsky, John R. (Y) Judges.
Olsem, Andrew D. '67 (WIN) Retired.
Olsen, Arthur J. '99 (CHI) Chicago, IL St. Hilary.

Olsen, Brian A. '04 (RCK) Polo, IL St. Mary's.
Olsen, Charles R. *s.j.* '68 (SAC)[D] Sacramento, CA Jesuit High School; [I] Carmichael, CA Sacramento Jesuit Community.
Olsen, Eric F. '09 (STL) Florissant, MO St. Norbert.
Olsen, Eric S. '02 (OM) Wynot, NE Holy Family Church of Cedar County.
Olsen, Ken '73 (P)[J] Eugene, OR Sacred Heart Medical Center.
Olsen, Thomas F. '53 (NEW) Retired.
Olson, David P. '98 (LC) La Crosse, WI Blessed Sacrament.
Olson, Eric E. '84 (MAR) Escanaba, MI St. Joseph & St. Patrick.
Olson, Hans M. '83 (SEA) Everett, WA St. Mary Magdalen.
Olson, Hans M. '83 (SEA) Presbyteral Council; College of Consultors.
Olson, James P. '88 (PH) East Lansdowne, PA St. Cyril of Alexandria; [A] Wynnewood, PA Theological Seminary of St. Charles Borromeo, Overbrook; [D] Drexel Hill, PA Monsignor Bonner and Archbishop Prendergast Catholic High School.
Olson, John E. '07 (WIL) Easton, MD SS. Peter and Paul.
Olson, Michael F. '94 (FWT) On Duty Outside the Diocese.
Olson, Michael F. '94 (DAL)[A] Irving, TX Holy Trinity Seminary.
Olson, Michael P. '94 (GR) Muskegon, MI Our Lady of Grace; Muskegon, MI St. Thomas the Apostle.
Olson, Randy G. '90 (LC) Leave of Absence.
Olson, Ronald *o.f.m.conv.* '58 (SUP) Superior, WI Holy Assumption of the B.V.M.; Pastoral Consultors.
Olson, Theodore '72 (ORG) Buena Park, CA St. Pius V; Council of Priests; Judges; Consultors.
Olson, Thomas '73 (SCL) Kimball, MN Church of Saint Anne; Kimball, MN St. Nicholas; Defensor Vinculi; Diocesan Priests Pension Plan Trustees.
Olsovsky, George J. '56 (GAL) Retired.
Olszamowski, Leon M. *s.m.* '76 (DET)[D] Pontiac, MI Notre Dame Preparatory School and Marist Academy.
Olszewski, Clarence A. '57 (HBG) Retired.
Olszewski, Daniel D. '51 (SCR) Retired.
Olszewski, Edward T. '60 (MIA) Retired.
Olszewski, Gregory J. '06 (CLV) Brunswick, OH St. Ambrose.
Olszewski, John S. '47 (NEW) Retired.
Olszewski, Laurence *c.s.c.* '64 (ORL)[F] Cocoa Beach, FL Congregation of Holy Cross, Eastern Province.
Olszewski, Michael '03 (SAC) Vallejo, CA St. Catherine of Siena.
Olszewski, Paul A. '93 (CAM) Millville, NJ The Church of Saint Mary Magdalen, Millville.
Olszewski, Ronald W. E. *o.s.f.s.* '74 (TOL) Toledo, OH Christ the King; [C] Toledo, OH St. Francis de Sales High School; [I] Toledo, OH; [I] St. Francis de Sale High School Endowment Fund, Inc.; Toledo, OH.
Olszyk, Thomas P. '71 (MIL) On Duty Outside the Archdiocese.
Olszyk, Rev. Msgr. Thomas P. '71 (MO) Judicial Vicar.
Olugbami, Godwin '00 (WDC)[B] Washington, DC St. Joseph's Seminary.
Olvida, Victor A. '82 (SEA) Sequim, WA St. Joseph.
Olzacki, Tadeuz (ORL) Summerfield, FL St. Mark the Evangelist.
Omalanga, Jules Omba '93 (STP) Minneapolis, MN St. Philip.
Omana, Max B. '79 (MO) Air Force Chaplains.
Ombao, Manny '70 (AGN) Agana, GU San Juan Bautista.
Omboga, John Orenge '96 (ROC) Penn Yan, NY St. Michael; Penn Yan, NY Our Lady of the Lakes Catholic Community; Stanley, NY St. Theresa.
Ombok, Gregory '95 (SCL) Freeport, MN St. Francis of Assisi; Bowlus, MN St. Stanislaus Kostka; Bowlus, MN St. Edward's; Bowlus, MN St. Mary.
Omeaku, Fidelis C. '08 (LA) Palmdale, CA St. Mary.
OMearain, Rev. Msgr. Ciaran P. '60 (CAM) Gibbsboro, NJ St. Andrew the Apostle's R.C. Church, Gibbsboro, N.J.
Omenihu, Anthony (NY) Washingtonville, NY St. Mary; Judges.
Omernick, Kenneth E. '74 (MIL) Hartland, WI St. Charles.
Omollo, Peter Otieno *s.j.* '05 (CHI)[C] Chicago, IL Jesuit Community at Loyola University Chicago.
Omorogbe, Edwin '03 (COV) Defenders of the Bond.
Omotu, Charles '94 (RVC) Bellmore, NY St. Barnabas the Apostle.
Omwando, George O. '07 (CHI) Chicago Ridge, IL Our Lady of the Ridge.
Ondeck, Douglas A. '07 (WH) Parkersburg, WV St. Margaret Mary.
Onderko, John M. '62 (PEO) Retired.
Ondo, Michael A. '54 (LFT) Retired.
Ondreyka, Richard J. *m.s.* '54 (CLV) Lakewood, OH SS. Cyril and Methodius Retired.
Onegiu, Benedict '93 (PHX) Cave Creek, AZ St. Gabriel Roman Catholic Parish.
Oneko, Chrispin Q. B. '90 (OWN) Hawesville, KY Immaculate Conception; Lewisport, KY St. Columba.
Oneyeabor, Ukachukwu '86 (TUC)[C] Tucson, AZ Carondelet St. Mary's Hospital.
Ong, Antonio '92 (P)[J] Portland, OR Providence St. Vincent Medical Center.
Ongaro, Mario *m.c.c.j.* '51 (CIN)[N] Cincinnati, OH Comboni Missionaries (Verona Fathers)–Comboni Mission Center Retired.
Oni, Andrew (NY) Elmsford, NY Our Lady of Mt. Carmel.
Oniskiewicz, Mieczyslaw T. '92 (MAR) On Duty Outside the Diocese.
Oniskiewicz, Mieczyslaw '92 (SAG) Kinde, MI St. Mary–St. Edward.
Onogbosele, Jude (ARL) Manassas, VA Sacred Heart.
Onsongo, Raymond Achuka *o.c.d.* '09 (MIL)[P] Milwaukee Provincial Offices – Discalced Carmelites.
Ontiveros, Omar '06 (SLC) Salt Lake City, UT Cathedral of the Madeleine LLC 202.
Ontiveros, Roy *o.carm.* '78 (TUC)[A] Tucson, AZ Salpointe Catholic High School.
Onubugo, Charles '88 (SFR) Igbo Nigerian Ministry; San Francisco, CA St. Anthony of Padua.
Onuchukwu, Jude O. '92 (PRO) Providence, RI Holy Name of Jesus; Judges.
Onuegbe, Paul '95 (LAF) Loreauville, LA Our Lady of Victory; Loreauville, LA St. Joseph.
Onumaegbu, Ted '02 (NY) Irvington–on–the–Hudson, NY Immaculate Conception.
Onunkwo, Vincent '92 (BUR) Wilmington, VT Our Lady of Fatima.
Onunwa, Paschal U. '74 (PH) Doylestown, PA Our Lady of Mount Carmel.
Onuoha, Christopher N. '06 (OM) Omaha, NE Mary Our Queen.
Onuoha, Gerald '93 (SB) Apple Valley, CA St. Mary Medical Center.
Onuoha, Silas '91 (CC)[D] Corpus Christi, TX CHRISTUS Spohn Hospital Corpus Christi – Memorial; On Special Assignment.
Onuora, Felix A. *c.s.sp.* '79 (DM) Lacona, IA Holy Trinity Church of Southeast Warren County.
Onushco, William J. '76 (ALN) Unassigned.
Onuwmere, Leonard *j.p.* '90 (MO) DEPARTMENT OF VETERANS AFFAIRS HOSPITALS AND CHAPLAINS.
Onwere, Callistus '82 (STA) Jacksonville, FL Church of the Crucifixion; Jacksonville, FL St. Pius the Fifth; Jacksonville, FL Holy Rosary.
Onwubiko, Augustas (NY) Bronx, NY St. Mary Star of the Sea.
Onwuegbule, Stanley I. '93 (SB) Loma Linda, CA Loma Linda Community Hospital; Loma Linda, CA Loma Linda U.M.C. East Campus.
Onwughalu, Jerome *c.s.sp.* (CHI)[J] Chicago, IL Resurrection Medical Center.
Onwumelu, Benjamin '94 (GLP) Shiprock, NM Christ the King.
Onyeayana, Daniel *c.m.f.* '00 (ATL) Stone Mountain, GA Corpus Christi.
Onyegbule, Cletus S. '02 (ALN) Sinking Spring, PA St. Ignatius Loyola.
Onyeihe, Cyprian (NY) Bronx, NY St. Barnabas.
Onyejegbu, Cyriacus N. '03 (GAL) Houston, TX St. Paul.
Onyekuru, Michael U. '00 (ATL) Archdiocesan Judges; Adjutant Judicial Vicars.
Onyekwelu, Anthony '93 (NEW) Summit, NJ Overlook Hospital.
Onyekwere, Godfrey C. '03 (GR) Grand Rapids, MI St. Mary Magdalen; Presbyteral Council; College of Consultors; Inclusion/Diversity Initiatives; Black Catholic Ministry; On Special Assignment.
Onyemaobi, Nnaemeka A. '09 (NEW) Bloomfield, NJ Church of St. Thomas the Apostle.
Onyenagubo, Innocent (SY) Syracuse, NY University Hospital.
Onyenobi, Christopher '83 (LA)[J] Torrance, CA Providence Little Company of Mary Hospital; Hospital Chaplains.
Onyeocha, Chinemere R.U. '08 (ALT) Altoona, PA Cathedral of the Blessed Sacrament.
Onyia, Joseph Bernardine '95 (NY) Bronx, NY St. Augustine; Bronx, NY Bronx–Lebanon Hospital Center.
Onze, Robert E. '64 (BGP) Retired.
Oonnooney, George '91 (NY) Yonkers, NY Most Holy Trinity.
Oonnoonny, George '91 (NY) Bronx, NY Christ the King; Judges.
Opalalic, Agustin '77 (SD) Vista, CA St. Francis of Assisi.
Opalda, Jose (BAL) Millersville, MD Our Lady of the Fields.
Opara, Christopher '92 (MO) Army Chaplains.
Opara, Isaac '88 (MO) Army Chaplains.
Opara, Peter Ben '88 (DET)[H] Livonia, MI St. Mary Mercy Hospital.
Opara, Vitalis N. '88 (BRK) Brooklyn, NY Holy Family.
Oparaekwe, Godfrey '83 (TUC) Bisbee, AZ Saint Patrick Roman Catholic Parish – Bisbee.
Opat, Kenneth *o.s.c.* '69 (SCL)[I] Onamia, MN Crosier Priory.
Opeil, Cyril *s.j.* '94 (BO)[U] Newton, MA The Jesuit Community at Boston College.
Opem, Anthony '68 (SFS) Dakota Dunes, SD Blessed Teresa of Calcutta Catholic Church; Ecumenical Commission.
Opendi, Richard *o.c.d.* '08 (MIL)[P] Milwaukee Provincial Offices – Discalced Carmelites.
Ophals, Donald J. '61 (ALB) Watervliet, NY Immaculate Heart of Mary Retired.
Opira, Simon Peter '93 (STV) Kingshill, VI Church St. Ann.
Opoka, Lloyd E. '68 (KC) Kansas City, MO St. Matthew The Apostle.
Opondo–Owora, Charles '93 (SY) Endicott, NY St. Joseph.
Oppenheim, Frank M. *s.j.* '55 (DET)[K] Clarkston, MI Colombiere Center.
Oppenheim, Frank M. *s.j.* '55 (CHI)[N] Chicago Chicago Province of the Society of Jesus–Provincial Office.
Oppido, Harold J. *s.j.* '55 (NEW)[C] Jersey City, NJ St. Peter's Preparatory School.
Oppitz, Joseph *c.ss.r.* '53 (ALB)[L] Saratoga Springs, NY St. John Neumann Residence.
Oppong, Charles '96 (RVC) Port Jefferson, NY St. Charles Hospital, Port Jefferson, New York.
Opris, Gheorghe '71 (ROM) Dearborn, MI St. Mary.
Orama, Raymond '08 (PAT) English Cursillos; Kinnelon, NJ Our Lady of the Magnificat.
Orandi, Nazareno '61 (NEW) Lyndhurst, NJ Our Lady of Mount Carmel.
Oranefo, Francis '94 (RVC) Rockville Centre, NY St. Agnes Cathedral; Rockville Centre, NY Mercy Medical Center.
Orapankal, Abraham '83 (NEW)[R] Plainfield, NJ RENEW International.
Oravanamthadathil, Jacob *h.g.n.* '99 (LEX) Mount Sterling, KY St. Patrick; Winchester, KY St. Joseph; Bluegrass East.
Oravec, Christian R. *t.o.r.* '64 (ALT)[G] Loretto, PA St. Francis Friary at Mount Assisi; Loretto, PA THIRD ORDER REGULAR MISSIONS.
Oravetz, Robert F. '97 (PBR) Hawk Run, PA St. John the Baptist; Archives; Evangelization, Mission Activity and Ecumenism; State College, PA State College PA Byzantine Catholic Community.
Orbanek, Rev. Msgr. Gerald L. '66 (E) Pleasant Ridge Manor East; The Bishop's Theological Advisory Committee.
Orchik, Michael J. '73 (BAL) Baltimore, MD Little Flower, Shrine of.
Orci, Ernesto '09 (SJ) Santa Clara, CA St. Lawrence, the Martyr.
Ordax, Rev. Msgr. Emiliano '48 (MIA) Retired.
Ordiales Reniva, Cary '09 (P) Medford, OR Sacred Heart of Jesus.
Ordonez, Jose Naul '99 (CC) Corpus Christi, TX Holy Family.
Ordonez, Ricky V. '08 (TUC) Tucson, AZ Saints Peter and Paul Roman Catholic Parish – Tucson.
Orel, Paul '84 (PHX) On Leave.
Orellana, Jose A. *i.v.e.* '03 (BRK) Brooklyn, NY St. Mary Mother of the Church.
Orellana, Roberto '01 (ATL) Covington, GA St. Augustine of Hippo.
Orellara, Jose '93 (LR) De Queen, AR St. Barbara.
Orengo, Rev. Msgr. Juan Rodriguez '79 (PCE) Ponce, PR Christ the King; Episcopal Vicar for Pastoral Coordination; Parish Priests Consultors; Children of Mary; Ecumenism; Legion of Mary; [B] The Pontifical Catholic University of Puerto Rico.
Oreshoski, Gary '88 (RC) Presho, SD St. Martin; Presho, SD Christ the King; [E] Philip, SD Priest Retirement and Aid Association/Pension Plan Board.
Orf, Rev. Msgr. Raymond V. '55 (SPC) Springfield, MO Immaculate Conception; Priests' Mutual Benefit Society Retired.
Organ, Patrick C. '71 (VEN) North Port, FL San Pedro.
Ori, Kevin (MIL)[K] Milwaukee, WI Wheaton Franciscan Healthcare – St. Francis, Inc.
Oria, Enrique *o.carm.* '58 (ARE) Morovis, PR Nuestra Senora del Carmen.
Orians, Thomas *s.a.* '92 (NY)[EE] Garrison, NY Franciscan Friars of the Atonement.
Orimaco, Domingo '72 (SFR) Half Moon Bay, CA Our Lady of the Pillar.
Oriole, Philip M. '70 (E) Albion, PA St. Lawrence; Erie County Prison.
Orique, David *o.p.* '01 (P) Eugene, OR St. Thomas More Church.
Orjianioke, Martin M. '95 (MEM) Cordova, TN St. Francis of Assisi.
Orlandi, Joseph J. '73 (PAT) Wayne, NJ Holy Cross.
Orlando, Gerard A. *c.p.* '46 (BRK)[T] Jamaica, NY Immaculate Conception Monastery Retired.
Orlando, Vincent A. *s.j.* '74 (NO)[P] New Orleans, LA Ignatius Residence.
Orlik, Dale A. '67 (SAG) Bay City, MI St. Boniface; Bay

City, MI St. Joseph.
Orlikiewicz, Stanley '53 (JOL) Retired.
Orlinski, Richard A. '73 (GRY) Hammond, IN St. John Bosco; Hammond, IN St. Joseph; Bishop's Council of Priests.
Orloski, Raymond J. '62 (HBG) Retired.
Orlosky, Anselm '53 (PBR) Wall, PA Holy Trinity; [C] Butler, PA Holy Trinity Monastery; Butler, PA.
Orlowski, Joseph *f.s.s.p.* '04 (Y) Vienna, OH Queen of the Holy Rosary.
Orlowski, Robert J. '97 (BUF) Corfu, NY St. Maximilian Kolbe Parish.
Orlowski, Rev. Msgr. Walter C. '79 (BGP) Norwalk, CT St. Matthew; Diocesan Consultors; Parochial Examiners; Presbyteral Council.
Orlowsky, Michael T. '93 (ARL) Madison, VA Our Lady of the Blue Ridge.
Ormechea, John B. *c.p.* '65 (FgM).
Ormechea, John B. *c.p.* '65 (CHI)[N] Chicago Passionist Provincial Office.
Ormond, Henry *o.carm.* '77 (JOL)[L] Darien Carmelite Provincial Office.
Ormond, Henry *o.carm.* '77 (OAK)[A] Berkeley, CA Dominican School of Philosophy and Theology.
Orndorff, Christopher M. '97 (TUC) Yuma, AZ Saint Francis of Assisi Roman Catholic Parish – Yuma.
Orndorff, Jared P. '08 (CLV) Mentor, OH St. John Vianney.
Ornowski, Gerald *m.i.c.* '62 (FBK) Presbyteral Council; Consultors.
Oroffa, Francis *m.s.p.* '91 (NY) Yonkers, NY St. Bartholomew.
Oropel, James '07 (SB) Victorville, CA Holy Innocents; Elected Members.
Orosa, Augustin *m.i.* '94 (MIL)[P] Milwaukee, WI St. Camillus Provincialate; [N] Wauwatosa, WI St. Camillus Health Center, Inc.
Orosco, James '81 (DAL) Terrell, TX St. John.
Orozco, Argemiro '92 (YAK) East Wenatchee, WA Holy Apostles; Diocesan Consultors; Presbyteral Council Executive Committee; [F] East Wenatchee, WA Holy Apostles Parish.
Orozco, Avelino '04 (ORG) Orange, CA La Purisima.
Orozco, Edicson '99 (BGP)[U] St. Charles Outreach Program.
Orozco, Edicson '99 (BGP) Bridgeport, CT St. Charles Borromeo.
Orozco, Isaac '07 (FWT) Keller, TX St. Elizabeth Ann Seton.
Orozco, Ramon '95 (LA) Santa Maria, CA St. John Neumann.
Orozco–Lopez, Francisco J. '90 (DAL) Dallas, TX Blessed Sacrament.
Orpilla, Julito R. '06 (SAC) Fairfield, CA Holy Spirit.
Orr, James R. '79 (PIT) Pittsburgh, PA St. Albert the Great.
Orr, John Arthur '01 (KNX) Knoxville, TN Holy Ghost.
Orr, Joseph T. '82 (ALT) Scouting; Tyrone, PA St. Matthew's.
Orr, Sherman A. '91 (WCH) Wichita, KS Church of the Resurrection.
Orr, Rev. Msgr. Stephen L. '74 (DM) Ankeny, IA Our Lady's Immaculate Heart; Judges.
Orr, Rev. Msgr. Stephen '74 (DM) Diocesan Consultors.
Orrigo, Mario J. '96 (BO) Stoneham, MA St. Patrick.
Orru, Bruno *s.x.* '63 (PAT)[N] Wayne Xaverian Missionary Fathers; Wayne, NJ XAVERIAN MISSIONARY FATHERS.
Orsborn, Bruce J. '81 (SD)[N] San Diego, CA Newman Center – SDSU; Presbyteral Council; Vicars Forane; San Diego, CA Blessed Sacrament.
Orsborn, Bruce '81 (SD) College of Consultors.
Orsi, Michael P. '76 (CAM) On Duty Outside the Diocese.
Orsini, James '74 (HON)[B] Wailuku, HI St. Anthony Junior–Senior High School.
Orsini, Joseph E. '64 (CAM) Retired.
Orsino, Jerry *o.m.i.* (CR) Waubun, MN St. Ann.
Orso, Clair *c.s.* '91 (DAL) Irving, TX St. Luke.
Orsolits, Norbert F. '65 (BUF) Retired.
Orsulak, Rev. Msgr. Thomas J. '90 (ALN) Reading, PA St. Peter the Apostle.
Orsy, Ladislas *s.j.* '51 (WDC)[N] Washington, DC The Jesuit Community at Georgetown University.
Orszulak, Henry A. '67 (BUF) Judges.
Orta, Abel Guerrero '00 (ATL) Clarkesville, GA St. Mark.
Ortega, Carlos '99 (SR) Sonoma, CA St. Leo; Sonoma, CA St. Francis Solano; Renovacion Carismatica Catolica.
Ortega, Eduardo '95 (BWN) San Juan, TX Basilica of Our Lady of San Juan del Valle–National Shrine; [I] San Juan, TX The Basilica of Our Lady of San Juan del Valle–National Shrine; Catholic Relief Services.
Ortega, Efren '72 (DAL) Retired.
Ortega, Fernando '08 (STP) Faribault, MN Divine Mercy Catholic Church; Kenyon, MN St. Michael; Shieldsville, MN St. Patrick.
Ortega, Jose F. *l.c.* '01 (PRO)[U] Wakefield, RI Overbrook, Incorporated; [U] Wakefield, RI Ocean Pastoral Center, Inc.; [U] Greenville, RI Vocation Action Circle, Inc.; [U] Greenville, RI LC Pastoral Services, Inc.
Ortega, Jose F. *l.c.* (ATL)[L] Alpharetta, GA LCNA Atlanta, Incorporated; [L] Alpharetta, GA College Compass, Inc.; [L] Alpharetta, GA Youth for the Third Millennium, Inc.
Ortega, Jose F. *l.c.* '01 (CHI)[E] Lemont, IL Everest Academy of Lemont, Inc.
Ortega, Jose Felix *l.c.* '01 (HRT)[U] Hamden, CT Helping Hand Investments, Inc.; [U] Hamden, CT Racebrook, Inc.; [U] Hamden, CT Rossotto, Inc.; [U] Hamden, CT Horizons Institute, Inc.; [U] Hamden, CT The Legion of Christ, Incorporated; [U] Hamden, CT Logos, Inc.; [U] Hamden, CT LUX ET VITA, INC.; [C] Cheshire, CT Legion of Christ College, Inc.
Ortega, Jose Felix *l.c.* '01 (NY)[C] Mt. Kisco, NY Legion of Christ College, Inc.; [CC] Thornwood, NY Challenge NA, Inc.; [II] Thornwood, NY Familia USA, Inc.; [II] Thornwood, NY Catholic Net, Inc.; [II] Thornwood, NY Mission Network Programs USA, Inc.; [II] Thornwood, NY Youth and Family Encounter, Inc.; [II] Mt. Kisco, NY Regina Apostolorum, Inc.; [II] Thornwood, NY Consolidated Catholic Administrative Services, Inc.; [II] Rye, NY Pastoral Support Services, Inc.; [II] Rye, NY Legion of Christ North America, Inc.; [II] Thornwood, NY Nueva Primavera Inc.; [II] Thornwood, NY Legion of Christ and Consecrated Regnum Christi Members Assistance Foundation; [II] Thornwood, NY Arke, Inc.
Ortega, Jose Felix *l.c.* (STL)[V] Chesterfield, MO Gateway Academy Incorporated; [V] Wildwood, MO Gateway Educational Foundation, Inc.
Ortega, Jose Felix *l.c.* '01 (WDC)[W] Bethesda, MD Woodmont Educational Foundation, Inc.; [W] Bethesda, MD Mission Network Young Mens Program USA, Inc.
Ortega, Jose Felix *l.c.* '01 (MAD)[I] Edgerton, WI Oaklawn Incorporated; [F] Edgerton, WI Koshkonong Pastoral Center.
Ortega, Jose Felix *l.c.* '01 (DET)[T] Bloomfield Hills, MI Opdyke, Inc.
Ortega, Jose Felix *l.c.* '01 (MAN)[K] Center Harbor, NH L.C. Center Harbor, Inc.
Ortega, Jose Luis *m.sp.s.* '88 (DAL) Waxahachie, TX St. Joseph.
Ortega, Leo '08 (LA) Los Angeles, CA St. Thomas the Apostle.
Ortega, Marco Antonio '95 (NY) New York, NY Our Lady Queen of Martyrs.
Ortega, Miguel Angel '09 (BWN) Hidalgo, TX St. Frances Xavier Cabrini.
Ortega, Ovidio '83 (SJN) Resident Chaplains; [F] Puerta De Tierra, PR Asylum For The Aged and Infirm.
Ortega, Russel *o.s.a.* '86 (VEN) Naples, FL St. Elizabeth Seton.
Ortega, Santos L. '96 (SB) Hesperia, CA Holy Family.
Ortega–Ruiz, Agustin '93 (JOL) Bensenville, IL St. Alexis.
Ortega Lemus, Ovidio '83 (SJN) San Juan, PR Sagrado Corazon de Jesus.
Ortega y Ortiz, Adam L. '92 (SFE) College of Consultors.
Ortega y Ortiz, Adam Lee '92 (SFE) Santa Fe, NM Santa Maria de la Paz Catholic Community; Defenders of the Bond.
Ortez, Sofonias '96 (VEN) Secretariado Hispano de Cursillos; Arcadia, FL St. Paul.
Orth, Anthony F. '75 (PH) Essington, PA St. Margaret Mary Alacoque.
Orthel, Joseph A. '89 (SPC) Special Assignment.
Orthmann, James *o.c.s.o.* '94 (ARL)[H] Berryville, VA Cistercian Abbey of Our Lady of the Holy Cross.
Ortigas, Jose Ignacio A. '09 (BGP) Newtown, CT St. Rose of Lima.
Ortiz, Alex *c.ss.r.* '76 (BRK)[C] Bronx, NY St. Alphonsus Formation Residence.
Ortiz, Angel '87 (MGZ) Cabo Rojo, PR St. Michael.
Ortiz, Arnold *o.s.j.* '72 (SAC)[A] Loomis, CA Mount St. Joseph Novitiate and Seminary; Loomis, CA St. Joseph Marello.
Ortiz, Benedicto '57 (BWN) Retired.
Ortiz, Edsil *o.f.m.* '98 (SJ) Santa Clara, CA St. Justin.
Ortiz, Emerito Gomez '82 (FAJ) Palmer, PR Cristo Rey.
Ortiz, Emerito '96 (WOR) St. Francis; Fitchburg, MA St. Francis of Assisi.
Ortiz, J.C. '91 (PHX) West Sedona, AZ St. John Vianney Roman Catholic Parish.
Ortiz, Jorge '04 (BRK) Brooklyn, NY St. Joseph.
Ortiz, Jose A. '66 (LA) South El Monte, CA Epiphany.
Ortiz, Jose Juan *c.o.* '05 (BWN) Pharr, TX St. Jude Thaddeus; Pharr, TX Oratory Academy School of St. Philip Neri; [B] Pharr, TX Oratory Athenaeum for University Preparation; [C] Pharr, TX Oratory Academy School of St. Philip Neri; [F] Pharr, TX Pharr Oratory of St. Philip Neri of Pontifical Right; Pharr, TX Oratory School – Athenaeum for University Preparation.
Ortiz, Jose '00 (CC) Gregory, TX Immaculate Conception.
Ortiz, Jose '06 (SJN) Bayamon, PR San Agustin.
Ortiz, Leo W. '00 (SFE) Santa Fe, NM St. Anne's.
Ortiz, Marco A. *o.m.i.* '08 (GAL) Houston, TX Immaculate Conception.
Ortiz, Marco Antonio '00 (LA) Graduate Studies.
Ortiz, Mario (SAN) Wall, TX St. Ambrose.
Ortiz, Maximo J. *o.s.a.* '74 (WDC) Washington, DC St. Elizabeth's Hospital (Government Operated).
Ortiz, Michael '56 (SD) Retired.
Ortiz, Miguel Angel *o.f.m.cap.* '86 (SFR)[N] Burlingame, CA Capuchin Provincial House; Definitors:.
Ortiz, Pedro '82 (CGS) Caguas, PR Nuestra Senora de la Providencia.
Ortiz, Roberto '09 (NEW) Special Assignment in the Archdiocese.
Ortiz, Rodrigo *o.f.m.* '73 (OAK)[M] Oakland Franciscan Friars (Province of St. Barbara).
Ortiz, Victor G. '86 (CGS) Caguas, PR El Salvador.
Ortiz, Victor (SJN)[A] Bayamon Central University.
Ortiz–Mangual, Julio '02 (SJN) Carolina, PR San Juan de Dios.
Ortiz–Montelongo, Ruben '07 (WCH)[C] Wichita, KS St. Francis Campus.
Ortiz–Padilla, Jose A. '66 (LA) Los Angeles, CA Our Lady of Guadalupe.
Ortman, John '82 (DET) Romeo, MI St. Clement of Rome.
Ortman, William '57 (SD) San Diego, CA St. Joseph Cathedral Retired.
Ortmeier, Paul R. '72 (OM) Lyons, NE Holy Cross; Lyons, NE St. Joseph.
Ortmeier, Richard J. '56 (SFS) Retired.
Oruko, William Dickson *a.j.* '99 (KNX) Athens, TN St. Mary.
Orum, Vincent '92 (CAM) Pennsauken, NJ St. Stephen's R.C. Church, Pennsauken Township, N.J.
Orzech, Eric '93 (CLV) Presbyteral Council; Westlake, OH St. Bernadette; Presbyteral Conveners.
Orzech, Eric '93 (SAT)[S] San Antonio, TX Polish American Priest Association (P.A.P.A.).
Orzechowski, Jacek *o.f.m.* '02 (WDC) Silver Spring, MD St. Camillus.
Orzechowski, Walter B. '49 (MIL) Retired.
Orzel, David J. '79 (SY) Utica, NY St. Peter.
Osbahr, Theodore W. '67 (NEW) Roseland, NJ Our Lady of the Blessed Sacrament.
Osborn, Douglas '68 (LAN) Retired.
Osborn, Rev. Msgr. Michael A. '92 (KAL) St. Joseph, MI St. Joseph.
Osborn, William '66 (SFS) Redfield, SD St. Bernard.
Osborne, Kenan B. *o.f.m.* '55 (OAK)[A] Berkeley, CA Franciscan School of Theology.
Osborne, Paul J. *o.f.m.* '64 (FgM) New York, NY Holy Name Province.
Osborne, R. Benjamin *s.j.* '09 (BO)[U] Cambridge, MA Hopkins House.
Osborne, Robert E. '54 (L) Defenders of the Bond Retired.
Osborne, Robert *s.m.* '66 (STL)[O] St. Louis, MO Maryland Avenue Marianist Community.
Osborne, Stanley J. '59 (L) Retired.
Osborne, Thomas L. *o.s.a.* '66 (CHI)[N] Olympia Fields, IL Tolentine Monastery at Tolentine Center.
Osburg, Frank C. '60 (LEX) College of Consultors; Priests' Retirement Board Retired.
Osburg, Gregory E. '77 (COV) Newport, KY Holy Spirit; Defenders of the Bond.
Oschwald, Daniel D. '98 (R) Raleigh, NC Cathedral of the Sacred Heart; Council of Priests.
Osebold, Richard A. '60 (DET) Redford, MI St. John Bosco.
Oseguera, Melvin '94 (NEW) Jersey City, NJ St. Paul of the Cross.
Osei–Fosu, Paul (NY) Pearl River, NY St. Margaret of Antioch.
Osendorf, James *c.m.* '80 (LA)[P] Montebello, CA DePaul Evangelization Center; [V] Montebello, CA DePaul Evangelization Center.
Oser, Donald J. '53 (Y) North Canton, OH St. Paul Retired.
Oser, Lance '01 (SFS) Hoven, SD St. Anthony of Padua.
Oser, Ronald E. '92 (ORL) Ormond Beach, FL Prince of Peace.
Osiander, Alfons M. '73 (BUF)[A] East Aurora, NY Christ the King Seminary; Sardinia, NY St. Jude.
Osias, Jean Max '94 (NEW) East Orange, NJ Holy Spirit–Our Lady Help of Christians.
Osinski, Ronald V. '72 (ALT) Air Force Reserve Chaplains; Allegheny Deanery; Portage, PA Our Lady of the Sacred Heart.
Osom, John *m.s.p.* '85 (BR) Napoleonville, LA St. Benedict the Moor.
Osondu, Chidi E. '05 (SAV) On Duty Outside the Diocese.
Osorio, Abel *c.m.* '08 (PH) Philadelphia, PA St. Vincent de Paul.
Osorio, Celimo '87 (ELP) San Elizario, TX San Felipe de Jesus.
Osorio, Flover A. '85 (CC) Instructor.
Osorio, Francisco Javier '86 (PMB) Judges.
Osorio, Francisco '86 (PMB) Wellington, FL St. Rita; Elected Members.

Osorio, Jose Fernando *o.p.* '04 (SJN) Bayamon, PR Invencion de la Santa Cruz.
Osorio, Louis '58 (CHL) On Duty Outside the Diocese.
Osorio, Luis '00 (ORL) Rockledge, FL St. Mary's.
Osorio, Rudolfo B. '55 (NEW) Retired.
Osorio Mourino, Jose Benito *o.de.m.* '62 (SJN) San Juan, PR Nuestra Senora de la Merced.
Osowski, Chester J. '49 (LC) Retired.
Ospina, Diego '05 (RCK) Belvidere, IL St. James.
Ospina, Walter '02 (R) Red Springs, NC St. Andrew.
Ossa, Pedro N. '63 (BRK) Brooklyn, NY St. Martin of Tours–Our Lady of Lourdes Retired.
Ossamora, Diego A. '89 (SP) Land O'Lakes, FL Our Lady of the Rosary.
Ossino, Angelo '57 (DEN) Retired.
Ossola, Rev. Msgr. John R. '64 (SFD) Springfield, IL Little Flower; Commission for the Care of Infirm and Retired Priests.
Ostaszewski, Andrew '84 (NEW) Newark, NJ St. Casimir's.
Ostaszewski, Andrzej '84 (NEW) Polish Apostolate.
Ostdick, Rupert *o.s.b.* '48 (IND)[K] St. Meinrad, IN St. Meinrad Archabbey.
Ostdiek, Gilbert *o.f.m.* '60 (CHI)[B] Chicago, IL The Catholic Theological Union at Chicago; [N] Chicago, IL Holy Spirit Friary, Order of Friars Minor.
Ostdiek, John Leonard *o.f.m.* '49 (SFD)[L] Quincy, IL Holy Cross Friary Retired.
Ostendorf, Mark '81 (SCL) Special Assignment.
Osterhage, Louis *c.pp.s.* '58 (CIN)[N] Carthagena, OH St. Charles Retired.
Osterhaus, Mark '85 (DUB) Cedar Rapids, IA St. Matthew.
Osterhout, Conrad *c.f.r.* '83 (NY)[EE] Yonkers, NY St. Leopold's Friary.
Osterle, Paul *s.j.* '59 (NO) New Orleans, LA Immaculate Conception.
Osterman, Gerald J. '67 (BO) Everett, MA Immaculate Conception; Boston, MA St. Katharine Drexel.
Osterman, Richard '69 (GF) Retired.
Ostini, Anthony H. *s.j.* '72 (LAF)[J] Grand Coteau, LA Jesuit Spirituality Center (St. Charles College).
Ostler, David M. '87 (PHX) Sun City West, AZ Our Lady of Lourdes Roman Catholic Parish.
Ostrander, Gary L. '71 (OM) Ralston, NE St. Gerald; Age Groups.
Ostrowski, David T. '89 (STP) Minnetonka, MN Immaculate Heart of Mary.
Ostrowski, Eugene S. '77 (WH) Wheeling, WV Corpus Christi; Vicars Forane.
Ostrowski, John T. '98 (CLV) Rocky River, OH St. Christopher.
Ostrowski, Joseph C. '52 (SCR)[N] Dunmore, PA Villa St. Joseph Retired.
Ostrowski, Theodore L. '81 (CHI) Chicago, IL St. Denis.
Ostrowski, Walter *s.v.d.* '65 (PIT)[M] Pittsburgh, PA Society of The Divine Word.
Osuagwu, Denis A. '89 (LAF) Lawtell, LA Holy Family; Lawtell, LA St. Ann.
Osuch, Michal *c.r.* '80 (CHI) Chicago, IL St. Hyacinth Basilica; Deans.
Osudibia, Kizito '93 (COS) Bailey, CO St. Mary of the Rockies.
Osuegbu, Cyprian '03 (RVC) East Meadow, NY Nassau University Medical Center; Levittown, NY St. Bernard.
Osugi, Cletus (P)[J] Roseburg, OR Mercy Medical Center, Inc.
Osuji, Ngozi '81 (BRK) Brooklyn, NY Holy Family–Saint Thomas Aquinas.
Osuji, Peter I. (PIT)[B] Pittsburgh, PA Duquesne University of the Holy Spirit.
Osuji, Urban *c.m.* '86 (BEL) Valmeyer, IL Seven Dolors of the B.V.M.
Osuna, E. Donald '63 (OAK) Retired.
Oswald, John '61 (LR)[G] Little Rock, AR St. John Manor Retired.
Oswald, Leo P. '78 (PH) Absent on Sick Leave.
Oswald, Norman R. '72 (MIL) Wood, WI Veterans Administration Medical Center; Special Assignment; DEPARTMENT OF VETERANS AFFAIRS HOSPITALS AND CHAPLAINS.
Oswald, Randall J. '97 (CHY) Kemmerer, WY St. Patrick's; Advocates.
Oswald, Rev. Msgr. Richard '65 (LR)[G] Little Rock, AR St. John Manor.
Oswald, Robert '02 (GF) Circle, MT St. Francis Xavier; Miles City, MT Sacred Heart; Diocesan Consultors; Vicars Forane; D.C.C.W.; Priests' Council.
Oswalt, M. Price '96 (OKL) Prague, OK St. Wenceslaus, National Shrine of the Infant Jesus of Prague.
Otanga, Thomas Ochieng *o.c.d.* '03 (WDC)[B] Washington, DC Discalced Carmelite Friars.
Otellini, Rev. Msgr. Steven D. '78 (SFR) Menlo Park, CA The Church of the Nativity; Knights of Malta.
Otero, Rev. Msgr. Henry '62 (WDC) Retired.
Otero, Jose Colon '01 (ARE) Advocate.
Otero, Lino O. *l.c.* '01 (SAC) Sacramento, CA Our Lady of Guadalupe Shrine; Vicars Forane; Presbyteral Council.
Otillio, Peter *o.p.* '57 (FgM)[N] Chicago Dominicans (Provincial Office); Chicago, IL Province of St. Albert the Great (Central).
Otor, Patrick A. '92 (SAV) Waynesboro, GA Sacred Heart.
Otsiwah, Charles E. '85 (VIC) Victoria, TX Our Lady of Victory Cathedral.
Ott, Rev. Msgr. Alfred R. '60 (ALN) Allentown, PA Cathedral of St. Catharine of Siena; [J] Bethlehem, PA Holy Family Villa Retired.
Ott, Jeffery M. *o.p.* '02 (NO) New Orleans, LA St. Anthony of Padua.
Ott, Richard W. *s.j.* '72 (OM)[K] Omaha, NE Jesuit Community at Creighton University.
Ottagan, Anthoni *h.g.n.* '03 (OWN) Hopkinsville, KY SS. Peter and Paul.
Otten, Lammert B. *s.j.* '65 (FgM) St. Louis, MO Society of Jesus.
Otterbacher, John *g.h.m.* '56 (CIN)[N] Cincinnati Headquarters of Glenmary Home Missioners Retired.
Otting, Loras C. '62 (DUB) Archives Retired.
Otting, Paul J. '66 (DUB) Retired.
Ottman, Timothy *o.s.b.* '78 (HON)[D] Waialua, HI Benedictine Monastery of Hawaii/Retreat Center.
Otto, David C. '77 (KAL) Niles, MI St. Mary of the Imm. Conception Church.
Otto, James C. '97 (PH) Philadelphia, PA St. Ignatius of Loyola; Philadelphia, PA Our Mother of Sorrows.
Otto, Leo '56 (SCL) Retired.
Otto, Thomas '73 (PMB) Retired.
Ottonello, Pedro *o.a.d.* '47 (SJ) Santa Clara, CA Oratory of Our Mother of Perpetual Help.
Otusafo, Joshua Elvis *c.s.sp.* '04 (CIN) Dayton, OH St. Benedict the Moor; Dayton, OH St. Mary.
Otusafo, Joshua *c.ss.p.* (CIN) Germantown, OH St. Augustine.
Otuwurenne, Michael (NEW) Paramus, NJ Bergen Regional Medical Center.
Otuwurunne, Onyedika Michael '96 (NEW) Dumont, NJ St. Mary's.
Oubre, Carroll L. '91 (ARL) Arlington, VA St. Agnes.
Oubre, Louis T. '86 (BR) St. James, LA St. James; Vacherie, LA St. Philip.
Oubre, Sinclair '86 (BEA) Diocesan Judges; Apostleship of the Sea; Port Arthur, TX St. John; [H] Port Arthur, TX Apostleship of the Sea of the United States of America (AOSUSA); Port Arthur, TX Apostleship of the Sea of the United States of America (AOSUSA).
Ouderkirk, Lloyd Paul '59 (DUB) Retired.
Ouedraogo, Evariste '94 (NY) New York, NY Holy Name of Jesus.
Ouellet, Maurice F. *s.s.e.* '52 (MOB)[G] Selma, AL Edmundite Fathers.
Ouellette, Anthony '06 (KCK) Osage City, KS St. Francis of Assisi; Osage City, KS St. Patrick; Osage City, KS St. Patrick's.
Ouellette, Francis *o.m.i.* '52 (BO)[X] Tewksbury, MA Immaculate Heart of Mary Residence.
Ouellette, John C. '95 (CC) Premont, TX St. Theresa of the Infant Jesus.
Ouellette, Kent R. '05 (PRT) Bangor, ME Saint Paul the Apostle Parish.
Ouellette, Louis M. *m.s.* '61 (HRT)[L] Hartford, CT Missionaries of LaSalette.
Ouellette, Paul *o.m.i.* (BO) Lowell, MA St. Patrick.
Ouellette, Richard R. '75 (PRT) Retired.
Ouellette, Richard T. *m.m.* '63 (NY)[EE] Retired.
Ouellette, Richard *m.m.* '63 (LA)[P] Los Angeles, CA Retired.
Ouillette, Arthur A. '55 (WOR) Retired.
Oulds, John V. '68 (PH) Coatesville, PA St. Joseph; Coatesville, PA St. Stanislaus Kostka.
Ouletta, James F. '60 (CHI) Retired.
Oulvey, William T. *s.j.* '85 (FgM) St. Louis, MO Society of Jesus.
Ouper, John J. '84 (JOL) Glen Ellyn, IL St. James the Apostle.
Ours, Donald J. *c.m.* '94 (NO) New Orleans, LA St. Joseph; [P] New Orleans, LA Congregation of the Mission Western Province (Vincentians); New Orleans, LA Good Shepherd.
Ours, Donald *c.m.* '94 (CHI)[N] Chicago DePaul Vincentian Residence.
Ours, Robert A. '80 (SY) Special Assignment; [C] Binghamton, NY Seton Catholic Central High School of Broome County; Binghamton, NY St. Christopher; Endicott, NY St. Joseph.
Ouseph, Kuriakose '87 (CC) Corpus Christi, TX Corpus Christi Cathedral.
Ovalle, Thomas *o.m.i.* '77 (SAT)[L] San Antonio, TX Oblate Benson Residence (Southwest Area); [S] San Antonio, TX Oblate Missions; [L] San Antonio, TX Missionary Oblates of Mary Immaculate.
Ovalle, Thomas *o.m.i.* '77 (WDC)[N] Washington, DC Provincial Offices of the United States Province of the Missionary Oblates of Mary Immaculate.
Ovando, Sergio '93 (SJ) On Duty Outside the Diocese.
Overbaugh, Rev. Msgr. Hugh A. '61 (HBG) Consultors, College; Appointed Retired.
Overbeck, Kenneth C. '97 (BO) Manomet, MA St. Bonaventure.
Overbeck, T. Jerome *s.j.* '74 (CHI)[C] Chicago, IL Jesuit Community at Loyola University Chicago.
Overman, Rev. Msgr. Robert F. '45 (STL) Retired.
Overmann, William J. '62 (SFD) Robinson, IL Our Lady of Lourdes; Robinson, IL St. Elizabeth.
Overmyer, John '97 (FTW) Advisory Board.
Overton, Troy '89 (L) Bardstown, KY Basilica of St. Joseph Proto–Cathedral.
Oviedo, Francisco *o.a.r.* '69 (LSC)[B] Mesilla, NM Augustinian Recollect Fathers; Las Cruces, NM Santa Rosa de Lima.
Ovienloba, Andrew '98 (NY) Bronx, NY Montefiore Medical Center.
Ovienloba, Andrew '95 (NY) Bronx, NY St. Ann.
Ovsak, William '99 (FAR)[G] Wahpeton, ND Carmel of Mary Retired.
Owen, Michael '09 (CHI) Hickory Hills, IL St. Patricia.
Owens, Bernard C. *c.s.b.* '67 (GAL)[O] Sugar Land Basilian Mission Center.
Owens, Bernard J. *s.j.* '72 (DET)[P] Bloomfield Hills, MI Manresa Jesuit Retreat House.
Owens, Edward *o.ss.t.* '80 (LA)[A] Camarillo, CA St. John's Seminary.
Owens, J. Edward *o.ss.t.* '80 (BAL) Councilors:; [S] Individuals in Other Locations:.
Owens, J. Edward *o.ss.t.* '80 (SAT)[C] Oblate School of Theology; [L] San Antonio, TX Trinitarian Residence.
Owens, John J. '49 (BIS) Retired.
Owens, Joseph V. *s.j.* '71 (BO)[U] Weston, MA Campion Jesuit Community.
Owens, Leroy E. '64 (BO) Medfield, MA St. Edward the Confessor.
Owens, Michael J. '84 (HON) Honolulu, HI Blessed Sacrament.
Owens, Michael (STN) Honolulu, HI St. Sophia Byzantine Missions.
Owens, S. Brian '95 (WH) Charles Town, WV St. James.
Owens, Rev. Msgr. Thomas J. '74 (PH) Maple Glen, PA St. Alphonsus.
Owino, Felix *a.j.* (WH) Weirton, WV St. Paul's.
Owuamanam, Remigius *s.m.m.m.* '95 (ALX) Alexandria, LA St. James Memorial; Alexandria, LA St. Juliana.
Owusa–Mensah, Sebastian '01 (RVC) East Meadow, NY Nassau University Medical Center; Hicksville, NY Holy Family.
Owusu–Achiaw, John '92 (DET) Detroit, MI St. Mary.
Owusu–Ansah, Edward '94 (BRK) Brooklyn, NY St. Vincent Ferrer.
Owusu–Boateng, Johnson '85 (VIC) Vanderbilt, TX St. John Bosco; Procurator Advocate.
Owusu–Sekyere, Augustine (ARL) Falls Church, VA St. Anthony's.
Oxley, Walter R. '03 (COL)[A] Columbus, OH Pontifical College Josephinum; [A] Columbus, OH Pontifical College Josephinum.
Oyafemi, Clement '94 (CHI) Chicago, IL St. Francis de Sales.
Oye, Paul *o.p.* '94 (LAV) Ely, NV Sacred Heart.
Oyo, Charles *c.s.c.* (FTW)[A] Notre Dame, IN Moreau Seminary.
Ozbun, John W. '84 (WIN) Retired.
Ozele, Anthony M. (BRK) Brooklyn, NY Good Shepherd.
Ozella, John '07 (PBL) Pueblo, CO St. Anne; Office of Worship and Spiritual Life.
Ozimek, Adam Z. '94 (ATL) Marietta, GA Holy Family.
Ozimek, Anthony J. *o.s.b.* '68 (CLV)[N] Billings, MT.
Ozminkowski, Clyde *o.carm.* '54 (KCK) Garnett, KS St. Therese; Garnett, KS St. Boniface Retired.
Ozuagu, Cosmas U. (BRK) Brooklyn, NY St. Francis of Paola.
Ozug, John C. '77 (FR) New Bedford, MA Our Lady of Fatima.

P

Paala, Jonathan '75 (SFR) Foster City, CA St. Luke.
Pabellan, Rolan '91 (SAC) Oroville, CA St. Thomas the Apostle.
Pabin, Chester J. '92 (STU) Cambridge, OH Christ Our Light Parish.
Pabis, Dariusz Grzegorz *c.ss.r.* (CHI) Cicero, IL St. Mary of Czestochowa.
Pable, Martin *o.f.m.cap.* '58 (MIL)[P] Milwaukee, WI St. Conrad Friary.
Pablo, Calixto A. '83 (SFR) San Francisco, CA St. Patrick.
Pablo, Maximo Asencios *m.s.a.* '68 (NOR)[G] Cromwell Society of the Missionaries of the Holy Apostles.
Pabst, Peter *s.j.* '86 (SJ)[E] San Jose, CA Sacred Heart Nativity School; [M] Santa Clara, CA Casa San Inigo, Jesuit Residence; [B] Santa Clara, CA Jesuit Community.
Pace, Paul J. '66 (HRT) Waterbury, CT St. Francis Xavier; Waterbury Vicariate.
Pace, Woodrow H. '95 (LC) Neillsville, WI St. Mary; Deans; Personnel Council.
Pacecho–Sanchez, Luis (MIL) Milwaukee, WI St. Rafael the Archangel.
Pachana, Robert A. '98 (NEW) Bayonne, NJ Mt. Carmel.

Pacheco, Rev. Msgr. Agostinho S. '60 (BWN) Edinburg, TX Doctor's Hospital at Renaissance Retired.
Pacheco, Alexandre '68 (STO) Linden, CA Holy Cross Church (Pastor of).
Pacheco, John '09 (FWT) Arlington, TX St. Matthew.
Pacheco, Luis '00 (VEN) Bonita Springs, FL St. Leo; Presbyteral Council.
Pacheco, Mario '76 (LA) Hawthorne, CA St. Joseph.
Pacheco, Norbert A. *m.m.* '79 (FgM) Maryknoll, NY MARYKNOLL.
Pacheco, Philip *o.f.m.* '07 (HRT) New Milford, CT St. Francis Xavier.
Pacheco, Victor *c.m.* '84 (LA) Artesia, CA Holy Family.
Pacheco–Sanchez, Luis (MIL) Milwaukee, WI St. Adalbert.
Pachence, Ron '74 (SD)[B] University of San Diego Retired.
Pachence, Ronald A. '74 (SAV) On Duty Outside the Diocese.
Pachla, Stanley L. '83 (DET) Eastpointe, MI St. Veronica.
Pacholczyk, Tadeusz '99 (PH) Ardmore, PA St. Colman.
Pacholczyk, Tadeusz '99 (FR) On Duty Outside the Diocese.
Pacholec, Daniel S. '96 (SPR) Westfield, MA Our Lady of the Blessed Sacrament.
Pacini, Peter *c.s.c.* '00 (SB)[I] Coachella, CA Congregation of Holy Cross.
Pacini, Peter *c.s.c.* (FTW)[H] Notre Dame Congregation of Holy Cross, Indiana Province, Provincial House.
Pacitti, Gary '89 (PH) Philadelphia, PA Annunciation B.V.M.
Packard, Walter E. '71 (E) Warren, PA St. Joseph.
Packuvettithara, George '94 (MIA) Miami Beach, FL St. Joseph.
Pacocha, Edwin D. '62 (CHI) Retired.
Pacquing, Joseph '83 (LSC) Hobbs, NM St. Helena.
Paculan, Wilson A. '07 (NEW) Union, NJ St. Michael's.
Pacwa, Mitchell C. *s.j.* '76 (CHI)[N] Chicago Chicago Province of the Society of Jesus–Provincial Office.
Paczesny, John R. '61 (MIL) Whitefish Bay, WI St. Monica Retired.
Paczkowski, Vincent *s.d.b.* '86 (NY) Port Chester, NY Corpus Christi.
Padamattummal, Bosco '92 (LAN) Fenton, MI St. John; Catholic Deaf Ministry.
Padavick, William B. '63 (CLV) Retired.
Padavick, William '63 (CLV) Oberlin, OH Sacred Heart Retired.
Padazinski, C. Michael '88 (SFR) South San Francisco, CA Mater Dolorosa; Deans; Judicial Vicar and Director; Archbishop's Cabinet; On Special Assignment; College of Consultors; Chancellor.
Padazinski, Michael C. '88 (MO) Air Force Reserve Chaplains.
Padberg, John W. *s.j.* '57 (STL)[O] St. Louis, MO Jesuit Community Corporation at Saint Louis University – Jesuit Hall; [V] St. Louis, MO Institute of Jesuit Sources.
Paddack, Rev. Msgr. John N. '84 (NY)[E] Staten Island, NY Monsignor Farrell High School.
Paddock, Richard W. '59 (RCK) Retired.
Padelli, Emilio P. '62 (HRT) Broad Brook, CT St. Catherine; East Windsor, CT St. Philip's.
Paderon, Gerardo '94 (MET) Alpha, NJ St. Mary.
Padget, Leo L. '01 (SFE) Albuquerque, NM Santuario San Martin de Porres.
Padgett, Gary T. '99 (L) Louisville, KY Ascension of Our Lord; Archdiocesan Examiners.
Padilla, Aquino '60 (SFR) Daly City, CA Our Lady of Perpetual Help Retired.
Padilla, Glibert '55 (TUC) Retired.
Padilla, Jose D. *o.p.* '04 (NO)[P] New Orleans Dominican Friars, Southern Dominican Province of St. Martin de Porres; Metairie, LA St. Martin de Porres Province (Southern Dominican Province).
Padilla, Jose Manuel '03 (TUC) Tucson, AZ Our Lady of Fatima Roman Catholic Parish – Tucson.
Padilla, Lionel Pacheco *c.p.* '96 (SJN) Toa Baja, PR Espiritu Santo.
Padilla, Luis Alfonso '04 (SJN) Guaynabo, PR Sagrados Corazones.
Padilla, Manuel G. '99 (CHI) Chicago, IL Maternity of the Blessed Virgin Mary.
Padilla, Norberto '90 (SJN) Bayamon, PR Santa Maria.
Padilla, Rafael '89 (VEN) Promoter of Justice; Judges; Hispanic, Migrant and Spanish Speaking Apostolates; Port Charlotte, FL St. Maximilian Kolbe.
Padilla, Rafael '03 (AUS) Bryan, TX Santa Teresa; Associate Directors.
Padinjarepeedika, Joseph L.F. *c.m.i.* '72 (LAF) St. Martinville, LA St. Elizabeth.
Padit, Jose Pelagio A. '96 (SFR) Colma, CA Holy Angels.
Pado, Thomas '75 (ORG) Irvine, CA St. Elizabeth Ann Seton.
Padovani, Martin *s.v.d.* '60 (TR)[N] Bordentown, NJ Society of the Divine Word.
Padrez, Mark *o.p.* '95 (OAK)[M] Oakland, CA Order of Preachers (Province of Holy Name of Jesus – Western Dominican Province); [M] Oakland, CA Order of Preachers (Province of the Most Holy Name of Jesus – Western Dominican Province).
Padrez, Mark *o.p.* '95 (SAC) Benicia, CA St. Dominic; Oakland, CA.
Padrnos, David *s.s.c.* '71 (FgM) St Columbans, NE House of Post–Graduate Studies.
Padula, Armand *o.f.m.* '56 (NY)[GG] Wappingers Falls, NY Mt. Alvernia Retreat House.
Paez, Abelavido Mojica (SJN) Bayamon, PR Nuestra Sra. del Rosario.
Paffel, Gregory '01 (SCL) Battle Lake, MN Our Lady of the Lake; Fergus Falls, MN Our Lady of Victory; Underwood, MN Church of Saint James at Maine; Presbyteral Council.
Pagan, Angel M. '83 (ARE) On Duty Outside the Diocese.
Pagan, Antonio (ORL) Retired.
Pagan, Jose R. Linares (PCE)[B] The Pontifical Catholic University of Puerto Rico.
Pagan, Miguel '04 (WOR) Chaplains; Clinton, MA St. John the Evangelist; St. John.
Pagano, Nicholas A. '06 (LEX) Lexington, KY Mary, Queen of the Holy Rosary.
Pagano, Peter E. '52 (SPR) Retired.
Page, Anthony J. '69 (LA) La Mirada, CA Beatitudes of Our Lord.
Page, Bryan '06 (NEW) Verona, NJ Our Lady of the Lake.
Page, David '58 (ORL) Indialantic, FL Holy Name of Jesus.
Page, Hugh R. '80 (FTW)[B] University of Notre Dame Du Lac.
Page, Joselito '05 (SJ) San Jose, CA St. Martin of Tours.
Page, Leon J. '56 (DET) Retired.
Page, Stephen C. '87 (DAV) Fairfield, IA St. Mary's.
Page, Thomas P. '79 (GR) Grand Rapids, MI St. Jude; On Special Assignment; Associate Vicar for Priests; Associate Vicar for Clergy.
Pagel, John M. '80 (CHL) On Sabbatical.
Pagliara, Alfonso D. *o.f.m.cap.* '81 (SP) Tampa, FL Most Holy Redeemer.
Pagliari, Robert M. '75 (BRK)[T] Brooklyn, NY Redemptorist Fathers of New York, Inc.–Baltimore Province.
Pagliari, Robert *c.ss.r.* '75 (NY)[EE] New York, NY Redemptorist Priests and Brothers, C.Ss.R.
Pagnotta, James V. '69 (NEW) Jersey City, NJ St. Joseph.
Pagones, Peter '68 (ALB) Schenectady, NY St. Paul the Apostle; Presbyteral Council; Deans; Diocesan Board of Consultors.
Paguaga, Juan Carlos '00 (MIA) Miami, FL St. John Bosco; Archdiocesan Vocations Review Board.
Pahamtang, Leonardo '77 (LUB) Muleshoe, TX Immaculate Conception; Priests' Retirement Board.
Pahler, Robert E. '57 (CLV) Cuyahoga Falls, OH Immaculate Heart of Mary; Uniontown, OH Queen of Heaven Retired.
Paider, Paul J. '92 (GB) Francis Creek, WI St. Anne; Francis Creek, WI St. Augustine; Mishicot, WI Holy Cross; College of Consultors.
Paillacho, Jose J. '87 (MOB) Montgomery, AL St. Bede the Venerable Catholic Church; Sacramental Ministers.
Painter, George F. *m.m.* '44 (NY)[EE] Retired.
Painunkal, Sajeev *s.j.* '04 (CHI)[C] Chicago, IL Jesuit Community at Loyola University Chicago.
Pais, Rohwin *o.f.m.* '89 (NY)[EE] New York Franciscan Province of the Immaculate Conception.
Paisley, James J. '85 (SCR) Shavertown, PA St. Therese.
Paisley, John C. '62 (DUB) Retired.
Paiva, Antonio M. '49 (PRO) Providence, RI Our Lady of the Rosary Retired.
Paiz, William *c.m.f.* '79 (FRS) Fowler, CA St. Lucy.
Pajarillo, Cesar C. '03 (RCK) Aurora, IL St. Rita of Cascia.
Pajerski, Daniel *l.c.* '04 (DET)[T] Bloomfield Hills, MI Logos, Inc. (Michigan); [T] Clarkston, MI Clarkston Pastoral Center, Inc.
Pajik, Thomas J. '87 (CLV) Chagrin Falls, OH St. Joan of Arc.
Pajor, Robert M. '07 (CHI) Chicago, IL St. Ferdinand.
Pak, Ki–Jun Lawrence '88 (LA) Los Angeles, CA St. Basil's.
Pakianather, Aloysius '78 (RVC) Massapequa, NY St. Rose of Lima.
Pakosta, Francis J. '52 (SUP) Retired.
Pakula, Michael G. '73 (PEO) Geneseo, IL St. Malachy's.
Pala, Manuel Soler *m.ss.cc.* '70 (SJN)[A] Bayamon Central University.
Palacino, Joseph '82 (BGP) Norwalk, CT St. Jerome Retired.
Palacio, Guillermo *o.ss.t.* '90 (PCE) Ponce, PR La Santisima Trinidad.
Palacio, Jorge M. *o.s.m.* '79 (ELP) El Paso, TX St. Ignatius of Loyola.
Palacios, Antonio *o.a.r.* '71 (NY) Bronx, NY St. Anselm.
Palacios, Benjamin *d.v.m.* (NY) Bronx, NY St. Anthony of Padua.
Palacios, Joseph M. '87 (LA) On Duty Outside the Archdiocese.
Palackal, Joseph *c.m.i.* '79 (BRK) Maspeth, NY St. Stanislaus Kostka.
Palacpac, Luello N. '86 (SFR) San Francisco, CA Mission Dolores Basilica.
Paladino, John J. '91 (NEW) Scotch Plains, NJ St. Bartholomew; Union County Southwest Deanery 26; Members.
Palafax, Lorenzo J. *s.j.* '67 (SJ)[M] Los Gatos, CA Sacred Heart Jesuit Center.
Palakudy, James *s.a.c.* '78 (MIL)[P] Milwaukee, WI Pallotti House.
Palakudy, James *s.a.c.* '78 (SFD) Decatur, IL Our Lady of Lourdes; Decatur, IL St. Thomas the Apostle.
Palanca, Mario S. '83 (AGN) Tamuning, GU St. Anthony and St. Victor.
Palang, Mansueto P. '77 (BR) Retired.
Palang, Mansueto P. '77 (ATL) Alpharetta, GA St. Thomas Aquinas.
Palaparambil, John '97 (NY) Highland Mills, NY St. Patrick.
Palardy, William B. '85 (BO)[A] Weston, MA Blessed John XXIII National Seminary; Elected.
Palasits, John A. '58 (NEW) Retired.
Palathara, Jose *c.m.i.* '70 (ALX) Mansura, LA Our Lady of Prompt Succor.
Palathingal, Joseph '90 (SFR) Daly City, CA Our Lady of Mercy; Seton Hospital; [J] Daly City, CA Seton Medical Center.
Palatucci, John F. '04 (NY) Staten Island, NY St. Joseph, St. Thomas; DEPARTMENT OF VETERANS AFFAIRS HOSPITALS AND CHAPLAINS.
Palazzo, Michael L. '87 (NY) Hyde Park, NY Regina Coeli.
Palazzolo, Anthony P. '93 (STA) Special Assignment.
Palcheck, Gerald F. '67 (SD) Descanso, CA Our Lady of Light.
Palcisko, Raymond '58 (CR) Retired.
Palermo, Angelo *s.a.c.* '60 (NY) Bronx, NY St. Benedict.
Palermo, Frank C. '55 (SPC) Springfield, MO Holy Trinity; St. Francis de Sales Association Retired.
Palermo, Jason P. '07 (BR) French Settlement, LA St. Joseph; Maurepas, LA St. Stephen the Martyr.
Palermo, Joseph S. '94 (NO)[A] New Orleans, LA Notre Dame Seminary Graduate School of Theology; St. Thomas More Catholic Lawyers Association; Archdiocesan Consultors.
Palica, Jacek *o.c.d.* '96 (GRY)[H] Munster, IN Discalced Carmelite Fathers Monastery; Munster, IN.
Palick, George '58 (PIT) Butler, PA St. Fidelis of Sigmaringen.
Paligutan, Alvin *o.s.a.* '07 (SD)[C] San Diego, CA St. Augustine High School; [J] San Diego, CA Augustinian Community.
Palis, Theo '45 (OAK) Retired.
Palisada, Arthur *s.s.p.* '68 (NY)[B] Staten Island, NY Society of St. Paul.
Palisada, Arthur *s.s.p.* (DET)[K] Dearborn, MI Society of St. Paul.
Paliwoda, Rev. Canon Steven '94 (SJP) Lorain, OH St. John the Baptist; Chancellor; Consultors; Eparchial Corporation; Western Protopresbytery; Presbyteral Council; Personnel Board; St. Josaphat Sacerdotal Society; Presbyters.
Palka, Bernard *s.a.* '72 (NY)[BB] Garrison, NY St. Christopher's Inn; [EE] Garrison, NY St. Christopher's Inn.
Palka, Bogdan *s.d.s.* '92 (BAL)[M] Towson, MD St. Joseph Medical Center, Inc.; Baltimore, MD St. Pius X.
Palka, Bogdan *s.d.s.* '92 (WDC)[B] Silver Spring, MD Salvatorian Community.
Palka, Edwin '96 (SP) San Antonio, FL St. Anthony of Padua.
Palko, John A. '54 (PIT) Retired.
Palko, Raymond (STF) Buffalo, NY St. Nicholas; Niagara Falls, NY Protection of B.V.M.
Palkowski, Jan '76 (PH) Clifton Heights, PA Sacred Heart.
Palkowski, Matthew *o.f.m.cap.* '05 (PH) Philadelphia, PA St. John the Evangelist.
Palladino, Rev. Msgr. Alfonso G. '43 (BO) Melrose, MA St. Mary of the Annunciation; Senior Priests. Retired.
Palladino, Robert J. '58 (P) Retired.
Palladino, William C. '06 (BO) South Boston, MA St. Brigid; South Boston, MA Gate of Heaven.
Pallardy, James G. '87 (PEO) Kewanee, IL St. Francis of Assisi; Kewanee, IL St. Mary's Catholic Church; Vicariates and Vicars; Finance Council (Canon 492).
Palliparambil, Jose Simon '62 (RVC) Plainview, NY North Shore Hospital at Plainview.
Pallipparambil, Binochan *o.s.b.silv.* '02 (ALX) Glenmora, LA St. Louis.
Pallipurath, Jose *o.s.b.silv.* '01 (ALX) Marksville, LA St. Genevieve; Marksville, LA St. Joseph's.
Pallo, Joseph L. '61 (LR) Blytheville, AR Immaculate Conception; Osceola, AR St. Matthew; [K] Blytheville, AR Immaculate Conception Trust Fund.
Palluck, M. Charles '66 (SEA) Retired.

Palma, Raul *sch.p.* '58 (LA)[P] Los Angeles, CA Piarist Fathers.
Palmatier, David *o.s.b.* '59 (RCK)[G] Aurora, IL Marmion Abbey.
Palmer, Frank S. '62 (DM) Retired.
Palmer, Herbert *o.s.b.* '39 (SD)[J] Oceanside, CA Prince of Peace Abbey.
Palmer, John M. *c.s.v.* '71 (CHI)[N] Arlington Heights Viatorian Province Center–Clerics of St. Viator.
Palmer, John *c.s.v.* '71 (JOL)[A] Lisle, IL Benedictine University.
Palmer, Michael C. '63 (BGP) Wilton, CT Our Lady of Fatima.
Palmer, Richard *o.s.a.* '87 (FgM) Olympia Fields, IL Province of Our Mother of Good Counsel (Midwestern).
Palmer, Rev. Msgr. Thomas '48 (SAT) Retired.
Palmer, William '03 (TYL) Malakoff, TX Mary, Queen of Heaven Church.
Palmese, Anthony '76 (ORL) Retired.
Palmieri, Armando M. *s.d.v.* '98 (NEW) Palisades Park, NJ St. Nicholas.
Palmieri, Frank *c.r.m.* '62 (CHR) Spartanburg, SC Jesus Our Risen Savior.
Palmieri, Louis R. '93 (BO) Avon, MA St. Michael.
Palmieri, Luigi '67 (ALN)[J] Bethlehem, PA Holy Family Villa Retired.
Palmigiano, James '88 (WOR)[O] Spencer, MA St. Joseph's Abbey.
Palmiotto, Paul C. '82 (BRK) Ozone Park, NY Nativity of the Blessed Virgin Mary; Ozone Park, NY St. Stanislaus Bishop and Martyr.
Palmisano, Joseph R. *s.j.* '08 (BO)[U] Boston The Society of Jesus of New England–Provincial Offices.
Palmisano, Peter J. '93 (NEW) Garfield, NJ Our Lady of Mt. Virgin; Our Lady of Fatima First Saturday Family.
Palmitessa, Paul '56 (SD) Retired.
Palo, Anthony *o.carm.* '64 (NEW) Englewood, NJ St. Cecilia's.
Paloma, Victor E. '70 (NEW) Jersey City, NJ Our Lady of Victories.
Palomanes–Vega, Jesus *s.t.* '92 (FAJ) Loiza, PR Santiago Apostol, El Mayor.
Palomera, Ramon '99 (LA) Los Angeles, CA St. Aloysius Gonzaga.
Palomino, Esviardo '49 (NY) New York, NY St. Lucy Retired.
Palomino, Humberto *p.e.s.* (STP) St. Paul, MN St. Mark.
Palomino, Ignacio '85 (HBG) Chambersburg, PA Corpus Christi.
Palomo, Benigno *o.s.a.* '66 (SJN) Bayamon, PR Santa Rita de Casia.
Palos, Anthony *o.a.r.* '60 (ORG) Santa Ana, CA Our Lady of the Pillar; [I] Santa Ana, CA Our Lady of the Pillar.
Paloso, Nicasio G. '75 (SFR) San Francisco, CA Holy Name of Jesus.
Palsa, Steven M. '79 (PIT) New Castle, PA St. Vincent de Paul.
Paluch, Krzysztof '05 (CHI) Wauconda, IL Transfiguration.
Paluck, Casimir S. '61 (BIS) Priests' Benefit Association Retired.
Palumbo, Eugene *s.d.b.* '51 (NEW)[M] Ramsey, NJ Don Bosco Prep Salesian Residence; [C] Ramsey, NJ Don Bosco Preparatory High School.
Palumbos, Edward L. '72 (ROC) Fairport, NY Assumption of the Blessed Virgin Mary; Board of Directors.
Palys, Daniel J. '69 (BUF) Evangelization Commission; Elma, NY St. Gabriel.
Pambello, Louis M. '81 (NEW) Montclair, NJ Immaculate Conception; West Orange, NJ Kessler Institute for Rehabilitation.
Pamintuan, Edison *m.s.* '02 (HON) Kalaheo, HI Holy Cross.
Pamment, Duaine H. '64 (LAN) Laingsburg, MI St. Isidore.
Pampackal, Joseph *s.d.b.* '83 (OAK)[M] Berkeley Salesians of Don Bosco.
Pamplaniyil, Mathew V. '76 (FAR) West Fargo, ND Holy Cross Church of West Fargo.
Pamula, Robert '87 (MO) Army Reserve Chaplains.
Panackachira, Mathew Joseph *m.c.b.s.* '95 (MEM) Memphis, TN Church of the Holy Spirit.
Panackal, Philip '89 (CC) Deans; College of Consultors; Personnel Board – Priests; Presbyteral Council; Refugio, TX Our Lady of Refuge.
Panagia, Sal J. '73 (PAT) Paterson, NJ Our Lady of Pompei.
Panagoplos, Christopher *t.o.r.* '76 (ALT)[G] Newry, PA St. Bernardine Monastery; [E] Altoona, PA Altoona Regional Health System – Bon Secours Hospital Campus.
Panakal, Alex *o.c.d.* '75 (ORL) Ocala, FL Queen of Peace.
Panakal, Thomson '60 (JOL) Lockport, IL St. Dennis.
Panaligan, Vicente '77 (LAV) Las Vegas, NV Our Lady of Las Vegas; Hospital Apostolate.
Panares, Auxentius '62 (WDC) Retired.
Panaretos, Paul D. *s.j.* '84 (CLV) University Heights, OH Gesu; [B] University Heights, OH John Carroll Jesuit Community.
Panchot, Daniel A. *c.s.c.* '65 (FgM) New Rochelle, NY Eastern Brothers Province.
Pancorbo, Rev. Msgr. Marcos A. '58 (PCE) Ponce, PR Cathedral of Our Lady of Guadalupe; [H] Penuelas, PR Congregacion San Juan Evangelista; Diocesan Consultors; Diocesan Board of Administration; Parish Priests Consultors.
Panczuk, Bernard J. *o.s.b.m.* '63 (STF) New York, NY St. George; Missionaries, Diocesan; Presbyteral Council.
Pane, Andrew '87 (NY) Retired.
Panek, Andrezej K. '83 (LC) Cazenovia, WI St. Anthony de Padua; Richland Center, WI Nativity of the Blessed Virgin Mary; Cazenovia, WI Sacred Heart.
Panek, Edward B. '91 (CHI) Mt. Prospect, IL St. Thomas a Becket.
Panek, Robert M. '70 (NY) Gardiner, NY St. Charles Borromeo.
Panepinto, Vincent P. '67 (ROC) Rochester, NY Our Lady of the Americas of Rochester, NY.
Panes, Romeo *o.s.j.* '86 (NEW) Newark, NJ St. Francis Xavier.
Pangratz, Clement *o.s.b.* '47 (SEA)[L] Lacey, WA St. Martin's Abbey; Lacey, WA.
Paniagua, Edwin *o.f.m.* '00 (NY)[EE] New York Franciscan Province of the Immaculate Conception; [EE] New York Franciscan Province of the Immaculate Conception.
Paniagua, Jose L. '62 (MIA) Hialeah, FL St. Benedict.
Paniagua, Pablo '59 (SAT)[K] San Antonio, TX Padua Place Retired.
Paniagua–Monroy, Carlos *s.v.d.* '00 (MEM) Hispanic Catholic Ministry; [F] Memphis, TN Society of the Divine Word (Chicago Province).
Paninski, John *m.s.* '61 (PEO) Georgetown, IL St. Isaac Jogues; [K] Georgetown, IL La Salette Missionaries.
Pankanin, Krzysztof '02 (CHI) Chicago, IL St. James.
Panke, Rev. Msgr. Robert J. '96 (WDC) Washington, DC St. Patrick; Washington, DC St. Stephen Martyr; Pastoral Center Special Ministries; Vocations for Men; Secretariat for Ministerial Leadership and Vicar for Clergy.
Pankiraj, Theesmas '90 (NEW) Saddle Brook, NJ St. Philip the Apostle.
Pankratz, Richard L. *s.s.c.* '74 (FgM) St Columbans, NE House of Post–Graduate Studies.
Panlasigui, Renato *r.c.j.* '88 (FRS) Sanger, CA St. Mary; Sanger, CA St. Katherine.
Panlilio, Christopher '91 (NEW) Jersey City, NJ Our Lady of Victories.
Panos, Rev. Msgr. Patrick G. '68 (PAT) Ringwood, NJ St. Catherine of Bologna.
Panossian, Antoine '66 (OLN) Los Angeles, CA Our Lady Queen of Martyrs.
Panossian, Antoine *p.i.a.* '66 (LA) Los Angeles, CA Our Lady Queen of Martyrs.
Panqueva, Alvaro '98 (DEN) Aurora, CO St. Therese.
Panthalanickal, Abraham M. '88 (NSH) Joelton, TN St. Lawrence; [I] Nashville, TN Mercy Convent.
Pantle, G. Donald *s.j.* '60 (SCR)[C] Scranton, PA The University of Scranton.
Pantoja, Franklin (NY) Ossining, NY St. Ann.
Pantoja, Lucas '05 (MRY) Clergy Life and Ministry Board; Los Osos, CA St. Elizabeth Ann Seton; Vocations Board.
Pantuso, John *s.d.s.* '67 (NSH) Sparta, TN St. Andrew.
Pantyra, Anthony '78 (RCK) Rockford, IL St. Edward.
Panula, Arne A. '73 (POD) Washington.
Panula, Arne A. '73 (WDC)[U] Washington, DC Prelature of the Holy Cross and Opus Dei; [S] Washington, DC Catholic Information Center.
Panuska, Joseph A. *s.j.* '60 (BAL)[S] Baltimore, MD Colombiere Jesuit Community.
Panza, Rev. Msgr. Paul D. '54 (ALT) Retired.
Panza, Paulo Sergio *o.s.b.* '03 (GBG)[G] Latrobe Saint Vincent Archabbey.
Panzer, Joel '94 (LIN) Army Chaplains; On Duty Outside the Diocese.
Paolicelli, Lawrence '84 (NY) Highland, NY St. Augustine.
Paolino, Stephen H. '07 (PH) Warrington, PA St. Robert Bellarmine.
Paolo, Francis de Sales *o.f.m.* '58 (FR) Buzzards Bay, MA St. Margaret.
Paolozzi, Joseph L. '61 (MEM) Martin, TN St. Jude's; [H] Martin, TN Interfaith Student Center; College of Consultors; Presbyteral Council.
Paonessa, Ralph *o.f.m.* '63 (NY)[EE] New York Franciscan Province of the Immaculate Conception; Definitors:.
Papa, Charles E. '67 (RVC) Sound Beach, NY St. Louis de Montfort.
Papa, Christopher J. '89 (PH) Glenolden, PA St. George.
Papa, Dominic '60 (BRK)[T] Jamaica, NY Immaculate Conception Monastery.
Papa, Frank *s.o.l.t.* '89 (CC)[G] Robstown, TX Society of Our Lady of the Most Holy Trinity.
Papaiah, Joseph '93 (AMA) Stratford, TX St. Joseph's; Sunray, TX Christ the King.
Papaj, Joseph J. *s.j.* '70 (NEW)[B] Jersey City, NJ Jesuit Center; [M] Jersey City, NJ Jesuits of Saint Peter's College, Inc.
Papalia, Pasquale A. '74 (TR) Whiting, NJ St. Elizabeth Ann Seton.
Pape, William H. '70 (ALB) Albany, NY Cathedral of the Immaculate Conception; [R] Albany, NY The Cathedral Restoration Corp.
Papen, Gerald T. *c.s.c.* '63 (FTW)[H] Notre Dame Congregation of Holy Cross, Indiana Province, Provincial House; New Rochelle, NY Eastern Brothers Province.
Papera, Rev. Msgr. Lewis V. '67 (NEW) Hasbrouck Heights, NJ Corpus Christi; Members.
Papera, Rev. Msgr. Lewis V. '67 (NEW) South Bergen Region Deanery 7.
Papes, Joseph M. '01 (PMB) Elected Members; Lake Worth, FL Sacred Heart.
Papes, Rudy *c.ss.r.* '65 (GR) Grand Rapids, MI St. Alphonsus; [L] Grand Rapids, MI The Society of the Redemptorists of the City of Grand Rapids.
Papesh, Michael (PBL) Office of Lifelong Catechesis; O.C.I.A. (R.C.I.A.); Catechetical Ministry.
Papineau, Andre *s.d.s.* '65 (MIL)[P] Greendale, WI; [B] Hales Corners, WI Sacred Heart School of Theology.
Papineau, Daniel R. '98 (SPR) Lee, MA St. Mary's.
Papp, Edward E. '60 (OG) Fort Covington, NY St. Joseph Retired.
Pappalliyil, Xavier *o.c.d.* '80 (SR)[L] Oakville, CA Carmelite House of Prayer.
Pappu, Rev. Msgr. Xavier '81 (TYL) Vicar General; College of Consultors; Diocesan Finance Council; Ex Officio; Priests' Pension Board; Priests' Personnel Board; Presbyteral Council; Longview, TX St. Matthew Catholic Church.
Paquet, Fernand *m.m.* '56 (NY)[EE] Maryknoll Maryknoll Fathers and Brothers Retired.
Paquet, Hubert J. '55 (PRT) Retired.
Paquet, Joseph A. *s.j.* '59 (BO)[U] Weston, MA Campion Health Center, Inc.
Paquette, Francis '57 (DUL) Silver Bay, MN St. Mary Retired.
Paquette, Joseph '78 (PRO) Pawtucket, RI St. Teresa of the Child Jesus.
Paquette, Neil *o.c.s.o.* '94 (DUB)[K] Peosta, IA New Melleray Abbey, Order of Cistercians of the Strict Observance; Peosta, IA.
Parackal, George '67 (OKL) Oklahoma City, OK St. Joseph; Special Assignment; [E] Oklahoma City, OK St. Anthony Hospital.
Paraday, Mark *o.p.* '88 (CHI)[N] St. Pius V Priory.
Paradis, Donald *m.s.* '58 (FR)[G] Attleboro, MA La Salette Shrine Retired.
Paradis, James D. *o.s.a.* '91 (PH) Philadelphia, PA St. Augustine; [Y] Villanova, PA Provincial Offices of the Order of St. Augustine, Province of St. Thomas of Villanova; [C] Villanova, PA Villanova University.
Paradis, Rev. Msgr. Wilfrid H. '49 (MAN) Retired.
Paragas, Rudsend *s.s.s.* (CHI) Chicago, IL Blessed Sacrament.
Paraguya, Felipe '68 (SAC) Sacramento, CA Sacred Heart of Jesus.
Parakkal, Baiju *o.ss.t.* '05 (BAL)[S] The Trinitarians in India (Bangalore & Trichur).
Paramo, Raymond *c.s.b.* '66 (DET)[E] Novi, MI Catholic Central High School.
Parampakattil, Jacob Christy '90 (SYM) Missouri City, TX St. Joseph Syro–Malabar Catholic Church.
Parampath, Joseph K. '53 (BGP) Judges; [O] Stamford, CT The Catherine Dennis Keefe Queen of the Clergy Retired Priests' Residence Retired.
Paraniuk, Michael A. '81 (CIN) Hillsboro, OH St. Mary; Greenfield, OH St. Benignus.
Parappally, Rev. Msgr. James '59 (MIA) Deerfield Beach, FL Our Lady of Mercy.
Parathanal, Jose '90 (LA) South Pasadena, CA Holy Family.
Paratore, Matthew R. '09 (MET) Metuchen, NJ Cathedral of St. Francis of Assisi; Auditors.
Parayno, Martin *o.s.b.* '94 (SAT) San Antonio, TX Santo Nino de Cebu.
Parchem, Peter *o.f.m.conv.* '51 (MRY) Pismo Beach, CA St. Paul the Apostle.
Parcher, Adrian *o.s.b.* (SPK) Members.
Pardee, Charles D. '84 (JC) Saint James, MO St. Anthony; St. James, MO Immaculate Conception; Jefferson City, MO Jefferson City Correctional Center; St. James, MO Missouri Veterans' Home.
Pardo, Miguel Angel Cervantes '09 (AGN) Tamuning, GU St. Anthony and St. Victor.
Pardue, John '88 (ALX) Woodworth, LA Congregation of Mary, Mother of Jesus Roman Catholic Church, Woodworth, Louisiana.
Pare, Arthur H. *s.j.* '60 (BO)[U] Boston The Society of Jesus of New England–Provincial Offices.
Pare, Arthur *s.j.* '60 (MAN) Salem, NH St. Joseph Retired.
Pare, Paul M. '53 (PRT) Lewiston, ME Prince of Peace Parish Retired.

Pare, Paul *o.f.m.* '00 (SUP) Ashland, WI St. Mary; Ashland, WI Our Lady of the Lake Catholic Community.
Pare, Robert '79 (SAG) Caseville, MI St. Roch; Kinde, MI St. Felix; Territorial Vicars.
Paredes, Edmundo B. '85 (DAL) Deans; Dallas, TX St. Cecilia; Personnel Board.
Paredes, Gabriel '91 (SFE) Albuquerque, NM San Jose; Albuquerque, NM St. Francis Xavier; Vicars Forane (Deans); Presbyteral Council of the Archdiocese of Santa Fe.
Paredes, Jorge '95 (ARE) Vega–Baja, PR Holy Rosary.
Paredes Monjaras, Antonio Francisco *s.s.p.* (LA)[P] Los Angeles, CA The Society of St. Paul.
Parekatt, Chako '73 (MEM)[F] Memphis, TN Society of the Divine Word (Chicago Province).
Parekkat, Winson '68 (BRK) Brooklyn, NY St. Bernard of Clairvaux; Brooklyn, NY Holy Family.
Parekkatt, Joseph *s.d.b.* '74 (OAK) Deanery #3; Walnut Creek, CA St. Anne.
Parel, Joseph '67 (HRT) Northford, CT St. Monica.
Parella, Francis J. *s.s.p.* '47 (NY)[B] Staten Island, NY Society of St. Paul Retired.
Parent, Basil R. '86 (NTN) Priests Serving Outside the Eparchy.
Parent, Rev. Msgr. J. Wilfrid '91 (WDC) Waldorf, MD St. Peter; Deans.
Parent, Lawrence *o.f.m.* '98 (NY)[EE] St. Francis Center for Religious.
Parent, Norman E. *o.m.i.* (BO)[Z] Lowell, MA St. Joseph the Worker Residence; Lowell, MA Holy Family.
Parent, Philip *s.m.* '81 (BRK) Brooklyn, NY St. Francis of Assisi–St. Blaise.
Parent, Rene L. *m.s.* '76 (SPR) Westfield, MA Holy Trinity.
Parent, Robert '86 (PRT) Latin Mass.
Parent, Royal J. '56 (PRT) Retired.
Parente, Lino S. *o.cist.* '65 (TR) Mount Laurel, NJ St. John Neumann; [N] Mount Laurel, NJ Cistercian Monastery of Our Lady of Fatima; Mount Laurel, NJ.
Parenti, Thomas M. '74 (MO) Sausalito, CA St. Mary Star of the Sea; Navy Reserve Chaplains.
Paretsky, Albert *o.p.* '81 (OAK) Berkeley, CA St. Mary Magdalen; [A] Berkeley, CA Dominican School of Philosophy and Theology.
Paretsky, J. Albert *o.p.* '81 (NY)[EE] New York St. Vincent Ferrer Priory.
Parfienczyk, Rev. Msgr. Stanislaw (BO) Salem, MA St. John the Baptist.
Parham, William J. '76 (MEM) Collierville, TN Church of the Incarnation.
Paril, Rico '98 (MET) Martinsville, NJ Blessed Sacrament.
Parillo, Emery *o.f.m.* '51 (NY)[EE] New York Franciscan Province of the Immaculate Conception.
Parinello, Frank *f.s.s.p.* (HBG) Harrisburg, PA Cathedral Parish of St. Patrick.
Pariogua–Monray, Carlos *s.v.d.* '00 (MEM) Memphis, TN St. Joseph's.
Paris, Basil '98 (STN)[A] Eagle Harbor, MI Holy Transfiguration Skete.
Paris, Benedetto J. '95 (MAR) Marquette, MI St. Louis the King (Harvey); Executive Board; Apostleship of the Sea; Chancellor; Administrator and Notary; Vicars Forane; Knights of Columbus; Promoter of Justice.
Paris, John U. '50 (BO)[D] Needham, MA St. Sebastian's School, Inc.; Malden, MA Immaculate Conception.
Paris, John *s.j.* '69 (BO)[U] Newton, MA The Jesuit Community at Boston College.
Parise, Michael '79 (BO) Billerica, MA St. Andrew.
Parisi, Frank J. '85 (RVC) Malverne, NY Our Lady of Lourdes.
Parisi, Joseph L. '74 (STL) Overland, MO St. Jude.
Parisi, Michael R. '28 (BRK) Retired.
Parisi, Michael '55 (BRK) Flushing, NY St. Kevin Retired.
Parisi, Michael '82 (MO) Military Chaplains; Navy Chaplains.
Parizek, Rev. Msgr. James F. '72 (DAV) Davenport, IA Our Lady of Victory; [M] Davenport, IA Quad Cities Catholic Deaf Ministry; Promoters of Justice.
Park, Adam Y. '05 (WDC) Secretary to the Archbishop; Pastoral Center Special Ministries.
Park, Andrew J. '09 (NEW) Bloomfield, NJ Sacred Heart.
Park, Rev. Msgr. Augustin C. '61 (NEW) Maplewood, NJ St. Andrew Kim; [R] Orange, NJ Mee Joo Catholic Inc.
Park, Rev. Msgr. Augustin '61 (NEW) Our Lady Mother of God Curia (Korean); Our Lady, Gate of Heaven Curia (Korean) Retired.
Park, Austin N. *s.j.* '55 (NO)[P] New Orleans, LA Ignatius Residence Retired.
Park, Hongshik Don Bosco '01 (NEW) Saddle Brook, NJ Korean Martyrs.
Park, Hyo–Geun '95 (BWN) McAllen, TX Our Lady of Sorrows.
Park, John Sung Woo '93 (PH) Philadelphia, PA Holy Angels; Korean Apostolate.
Park, Jun–Hyuk '00 (NO) Metairie, LA Hanmaum Korean Catholic Chapel; Hanmaum Korean Catholic Chapel.
Park, Robert G. '57 (WH) Wheeling, WV St. Joseph's Cathedral; Behavioral Counseling and Ministry.
Park, Shin–Hwa (LA) Hospital Chaplains.
Park, Thomas R. '65 (SEA) Port Orchard, WA St. Gabriel.
Park, Yoon Jo (CHL) Korean Catholic Cultural Center.
Parke, Frederick R. '75 (STA) Jacksonville, FL Assumption; Presbyteral Council.
Parke, James E. '65 (RIC) Virginia Beach, VA Church of the Ascension; Virginia Beach, VA Church of the Holy Apostles.
Parker, Adam '00 (BAL) Special Assignment.
Parker, Adam '94 (BAL) Baltimore, MD Basilica of the National Shrine of the Assumption of the Blessed Virgin Mary.
Parker, Carroll *o.m.i.* '61 (FgM) Washington, DC AMERICAN OBLATE MISSIONS.
Parker, Charles '71 (PHX) Retired.
Parker, Frank J. *s.j.* '73 (BO)[U] Newton, MA The Jesuit Community at Boston College.
Parker, Glenn D. *c.ss.r.* '85 (ORL)[F] New Smyrna Beach, FL Redemptorist Fathers of the Vice Province of Richmond; New Smyrna Beach, FL Sacred Heart; Consultors:.
Parker, James W. '03 (RCK) East Dubuque, IL St. Mary; East Dubuque, IL Nativity of the Blessed Virgin Mary.
Parker, James '82 (MO) CIVIL AIR PATROL Retired.
Parker, John W. '70 (CHI) Chicago, IL All Saints–St. Anthony.
Parker, Kenneth '65 (R) Retired.
Parker, Larry '84 (WCH) Oswego, KS Mother of God.
Parker, Michael J. '83 (BUF) Kenmore, NY St. John the Baptist.
Parker, Nicholas '08 (SAL)[A] Salina, KS Sacred Heart Junior–Senior High School; Salina, KS St. Mary Queen of the Universe Parish.
Parker, Rick '77 (OKL) Absent on Sick Leave.
Parker, Theodore K. '72 (DET) Detroit, MI St. Cecilia; Detroit, MI St. Leo; College of Consultors.
Parker, William C. '64 (TOL) Judges Retired.
Parker, William J. *c.ss.r.* '73 (TUC)[F] Cortaro, AZ Redemptorist Society of Arizona Desert House of Prayer.
Parkerson, Paul M. '98 (R) Dunn, NC Sacred Heart.
Parkes, Gregory '99 (ORL) Vicar General and Chancellor for Canonical Affairs; Defenders of the Bond; Celebration, FL Corpus Christi; Ex Officio Members.
Parkes, Joseph P. *s.j.* '76 (NY)[F] New York, NY Cristo Rey New York High School, Inc.; [EE] New York, NY "America;" Residence and publication office of the America Press; [F] New York, NY Cristo Rey New York High School, Inc.
Parkes, Stephen D. '98 (ORL)[G] Orlando, FL Catholic Campus Ministry at the University of Central Florida; Deans; Oviedo, FL Most Precious Blood Catholic Church; Ex Officio Members; Catholic Campus Ministry at University of Central Florida.
Parkos, John F. '64 (STP) Retired.
Parks, Jonathan *s.d.b.* '78 (NO) Harvey, LA St. Rosalie.
Parks, Rev. Msgr. Richard E. '59 (BAL) Baltimore, MD Sacred Heart of Mary Retired.
Parks, Richard L. *c.p.* '70 (SAC)[I] Citrus Heights, CA Christ the King Retreat.
Parlante, Rev. Msgr. Gregory J. '82 (PH) Chadds Ford, PA St. Cornelius; Permanent Diaconate Department.
Parle, Richard '56 (SEA) Retired.
Parlet, Stephen J. '97 (COS) Buena Vista, CO St. Rose of Lima; Presbyteral Council.
Parlette, Thomas L. '89 (DAV) Davenport, IA St. Alphonsus; Buffalo, IA St. Peter's.
Parnassas, Rev. Msgr. George John '53 (LA) West Hollywood, CA St. Victor Retired.
Parnell, Dennis R. *s.j.* '93 (SJ)[M] Los Gatos, CA California Province of the Society of Jesus, Jesuit Provincial Office; [B] Santa Clara, CA Jesuit Community.
Parqualetto, Vicente *s.t.* '70 (FAJ) Vicar General.
Parr, Charles J. '73 (PAT) Theological Commission; Wayne, NJ Holy Cross; Ecumenical Officer.
Parr, John L. '78 (LC) Cashton, WI Sacred Heart of Jesus.
Parra, Andres '05 (SJ) San Jose, CA Sacred Heart of Jesus.
Parra, Jose '09 (SAG) Saginaw, MI St. Thomas Aquinas.
Parra, Pedro *c.s.c.* '99 (FTW)[H] Notre Dame Congregation of Holy Cross, Indiana Province, Provincial House.
Parrinello, Frank P. '00 (OM) On Duty Outside the Archdiocese.
Parrinello, Frank *f.s.s.p.* '99 (HBG) Mater Dei Community.
Parrish, Bryan K. '88 (BO) Trustees.
Parrish, Bryan K. '88 (BO) Duxbury, MA Holy Family.
Parrish, L. Jerome '04 (CHI) Other Assignments.
Parrott, Gregory '09 (WIN) Owatonna, MN Sacred Heart.
Parrotta, Michael '01 (FAR) Retired.
Parrotta, Michael '01 (PMB) Delray Beach, FL St. Vincent Ferrer.
Parry, Rev. Msgr. Charles J. '81 (WDC) Bowie, MD Sacred Heart; Deans.
Parry, Denis '94 (FgM) Boston, MA St. James the Apostle, Inc.
Parsch, David L. '80 (SAG) Saginaw, MI Holy Spirit.
Parson, Donald J. '90 (BAL) Oakland, MD St. Peter the Apostle; Presbyteral Council; Advocates.
Parsons, Harry E. '56 (PIT)[M] Pittsburgh, PA St. John Vianney Manor Retired.
Parsons, LaSalle *o.f.m.cap.* '57 (FgM) White Plains, NY Province of St. Mary.
Parsons, Samuel *o.p.* '57 (OAK)[M] Oakland, CA Order of Preachers (Province of the Most Holy Name of Jesus – Western Dominican Province); [M] Oakland, CA Order of Preachers (Province of Holy Name of Jesus – Western Dominican Province).
Parsons, Vincent L. '01 (GI) Scottsbluff, NE St. Agnes; Priests' Advisory Board (Presbyteral Council).
Partain, Chad A. '03 (ALX) Elected Members; Mansura, LA St. Paul the Apostle.
Partee, Chrysostom *o.f.m.* '50 (SFE)[H] Albuquerque, NM The Province of Our Lady of Guadalupe.
Partensky, Leonard J. '42 (DET) Retired.
Parthie, Ralph *o.f.m.* '75 (GRY)[H] Cedar Lake, IN San Damiano Friary.
Partida, Rafael A. '86 (SB) On Duty Outside the Diocese; Special or Other Diocesan Assignment.
Partika, Richard '51 (DUL) Retired.
Partridge, Bede *o.s.b.* '58 (P)[L] St. Benedict, OR Mt. Angel Abbey.
Partridge, Francis C. '60 (GAY) Retired.
Partusch, Frank A. '72 (OM) Omaha, NE St. Anthony; Omaha, NE SS. Peter and Paul.
Parzymies, Joseph K. '78 (HRT) Retired.
Pasadilla, Nicolas O. '72 (GAL) Magnolia, TX St. Matthias the Apostle.
Pasala, Balaswamy (CC) Beeville, TX St. James.
Pasala, Lourdu '80 (GRY) Hobart, IN Assumption of the Blessed Virgin Mary; Defender of the Bond; Judges.
Pasalic, Nikola *o.f.m.* (NY) New York, NY SS. Cyril and Methodius – St. Raphael.
Pascazi, Louis F. '80 (PIT) Ellwood City, PA Holy Redeemer Parish.
Pasche, Fred *o.f.m.conv.* '64 (FTW) Angola, IN St. Anthony.
Pasciak, Marcel J. '74 (CHI) Hickory Hills, IL St. Patricia.
Pasciuto, Joseph C. '91 (BRK) On Leave/Unassigned.
Pascoe, Louis B. *s.j.* '64 (NY)[EE] Loyola Hall, Jesuit Community.
Pascual, Antonio S. '60 (RVC) Defenders of the Bond; Wantagh, NY St. Frances de Chantal Retired.
Pascual, Celestino V. (BO) Filipino; Boston, MA St. Joseph.
Pascual, Lope D. '82 (MET)[M] Stewartsville, NJ Society of Jesus Christ the Priest.
Pascual, Manuel '46 (FRS) Retired.
Pascucci, Philip *s.d.b.* (NY) Port Chester, NY Our Lady of the Rosary Retired.
Pashak, Lawrence M. '63 (SAG) Freeland, MI St. Agnes.
Pashby, John J. '60 (FgM) Boston, MA St. James the Apostle, Inc.; Senior Priests. Retired.
Pashley, Rev. Msgr. Wilfred J. '63 (PH) Philadelphia, PA St. Barbara; Philadelphia, PA St. Rose of Lima.
Pasieczny, Roman '80 (DET) Warren, MI St. Martin de Porres; Presbyteral Council.
Pasik, Mark A. '76 (SY) Utica, NY St. Mark.
Paskey, Robert V. *s.j.* '66 (BO)[U] Weston, MA Campion Jesuit Community.
Paskey, Robert V. *s.j.* '66 (MAN) Concord Hospital.
Paskowicz, Marian '54 (ALN) Retired.
Pasley, Robert C. '82 (CAM)[P] Berlin, NJ Mater Ecclesiae Mission; Berlin, NJ Mater Ecclesiae Church.
Pasqualetto, Vicente *s.t.* '70 (FAJ) Luquillo, PR San Jose.
Pasqualetto, Vicente *s.t.* '70 (SJN) Apostolado Del Cenaculo Misionero.
Pasquinelli, Rev. Msgr. Frederick A. '52 (STU) Retired.
Pasquini, John J. '98 (PMB) Vero Beach, FL St. John of the Cross.
Passalacqua, Robert '83 (SJ) Retired.
Passamonti, Paul G. '95 (WDC) Military Chaplains; Army Chaplains.
Passant, Paul A. '98 (NEW) On Duty Outside the Archdiocese.
Passant, Paul '98 (PHX) Scottsdale, AZ St. Daniel the Prophet Roman Catholic Parish.
Passauer, Gregory P. '86 (E) Crown, PA St. Mary.
Passenant, Francis J. (BRK) Forest Hills, NY Our Lady, Queen of Martyrs.
Passeri, Richard *o.f.m.* '47 (BO)[U] Boston, MA St. Christopher Friary Retired.
Passero, Ernest F. *s.j.* '70 (BO)[U] Weston, MA Campion Health Center, Inc.
Passos, Preston P. '08 (LA) North Hollywood, CA St. Charles Borromeo.
Pastick, Joseph A. (CHI) Retired.

Pastick, Joseph A. '49 (SP) New Port Richey, FL Our Lady Queen of Peace Retired.
Pastirik, Joachim *o.s.b.* '69 (CLV)[N] Cleveland, OH.
Pastizzo, Michael H. *s.j.* '70 (BUF)[O] Buffalo, NY Canisius Jesuit Community Inc.
Pastorius, Thomas M. '03 (STL) St. Louis, MO St. Mark.
Pastors, Jerome P. '98 (GB) Kaukauna, WI St. Katharine Drexel.
Pastro, Vincent '78 (SEA) Kent, WA Holy Spirit Parish.
Pasupalety, Sebastian '81 (CC) Corpus Christi, TX Our Lady of Mount Carmel.
Pasupil, Philip T. '74 (LUB) Shallowater, TX St. Philip Benizi.
Patalano, Anthony M. *o.p.* '86 (P) Portland, OR Holy Rosary Parish & Dominican Priory; [L] Portland, OR Holy Rosary Priory.
Patalinghug, Leo E. '99 (BAL) Special Assignment.
Patalinghug, Leo '99 (BAL)[A] Emmitsburg, MD Mount St. Mary's Seminary.
Patau, Siaosi E. '04 (DET) Armada, MI St. Mary Mystical Rose.
Patella, Michael *o.s.b.* '90 (SCL)[A] Collegeville, MN St. John's School of Theology and Seminary; [I] Collegeville, MN St. John's Abbey, of the Order of St. Benedict.
Patenaude, Gilbert A. '46 (PRT) Retired.
Pateno, Pelagio Calambia *s.v.d.* (TR) Lakewood, NJ St. Anthony Claret.
Pater, Aurel '90 (ROM) Aurora, IL St. Michael; Finance Council; College of Consultors; Aurora Deanery.
Pater, Daniel R. '79 (CIN) Priests On Administrative Leave.
Pater, Giles H. '58 (CIN) Imprimatur Censors Retired.
Paternoster, Alejandro '94 (LFT) Wheatfield, IN Sorrowful Mother.
Patete, Michael A. '62 (NEW) Berkeley Heights, NJ Church of the Little Flower Retired.
Pathe, Eugene '56 (PT) Charismatic Renewal, Diocesan Commission for.
Pathenveedu, Louis Charuvila '99 (RVC) Hempstead, NY St. John Chrysostom Malankara Mission.
Pathiyamoola, Paul '70 (SFS) Canton, SD St. Dominic.
Pathiyamoola Ouseph, Jolly '02 (GF) Special Assignment; Wibaux, MT St. Peter.
Pathiyil, Jaimon Kurian *o.s.h.* '03 (GAL)[O] Missouri City, TX The Society of the Oblates of Sacred Heart; Houston, TX St. Cecilia.
Pathiyil, Joseph *m.f.* '88 (OAK) San Leandro, CA St. Felicitas.
Pathmarajah, T. Pius '72 (ROC) Judges; Rochester, NY St. John the Evangelist.
Patillo, Rev. Msgr. Bennie J. '67 (BEA) Diocesan College of Consultors; Clergy Personnel Board; Diocesan Judges; Port Neches, TX St. Elizabeth; Presbyteral Council.
Patin, Lawrence *c.ss.r.* '63 (FgM) Denver, CO Denver Province.
Patino, Eliecer '07 (AUS) Austin, TX St. Julia.
Patino, Jose R. *s.d.b.* (ARE) Orocovis, PR San Juan Bautista.
Patino, Ruben M. *c.s.p.* '79 (AUS) Horseshoe Bay, TX St. Paul the Apostle.
Patino Villa, Carlos Alberto '00 (FR) Cape Cod; Nantucket.
Patnode, Rev. Msgr. Michael '72 (CR) Diaconate Office; Georgetown, MN St. John; Moorhead, MN St. Francis de Sales.
Patnode, Ronald J. '61 (YAK) Retired.
Patout, Rivers '67 (GAL) Houston, TX St. Alphonsus; Apostleship of the Sea (Port Ministry); Area Representatives.
Patricius, J. M. '57 (NEW) Bayonne, NJ Saint Michael and Saint Joseph Retired.
Patrick, Michael '83 (P) Oregon City, OR St. Philip Benizi; Area Vicars; Judges.
Patrick, Richard Martin *o.p.* '65 (GAL)[O] Houston, TX Dominican Friars, St. Mark Priory, Inc.
Patrick, William J. '58 (CLV) Released from Diocesan Assignment.
Patrick, William '58 (ORG) Retired.
Patriquin, Garry D. '84 (PIT) Absent on Sick Leave.
Patrizio, Anthony '66 (CAM) Mays Landing, NJ Church of St. Vincent de Paul, Mays Landing, N.J.
Patron, Charles A. '62 (SB) Barstow, CA St. Joseph; Barstow, CA St. Philip Neri; Barstow, CA St. Madeleine Sophie Barat; Elected Members.
Patrylak, Frank '62 (PHU) Retired.
Patte, Steven W. '69 (CHI) Other Assignments.
Pattee, Daniel *t.o.r* '87 (STU)[A] Steubenville, OH Franciscan University of Steubenville; [H] Steubenville, OH Holy Spirit Friary.
Patten, Patrick A. *c.s.sp.* '78 (FgM) Bethel Park, PA CONGREGATION OF THE HOLY SPIRIT.
Patterson, Alfred *o.s.b.* '90 (ALT) Summerhill, PA St. John.
Patterson, Bruce '86 (ORG) Huntington Beach, CA St. Bonaventure; Council of Priests.
Patterson, Bryan D. '99 (BRK) Cambria Heights, NY Sacred Heart; Censors of Books.
Patterson, Rev. Msgr. Charles '51 (JC) Retired.
Patterson, David L. '68 (ATL) On Duty Outside the Archdiocese.
Patterson, Frank '67 (SAV) Columbus, GA Holy Family.
Patterson, James *c.ss.r.* '50 (STL)[O] Liguori, MO St. Clement Health Care Center Retired.
Patterson, John H. *s.o.l.t.* '02 (CC)[G] Robstown, TX Society of Our Lady of the Most Holy Trinity.
Patterson, Patrick *c.pp.s.* '65 (COL) Columbus, OH St. James–the–Less.
Patterson, Ralph '03 (OWN) On Duty Outside the Diocese.
Patterson, Randall P. '70 (ALB) Troy, NY Our Lady of Victory; Deans; Architecture and Building Commission.
Patterson, Terrence R. '66 (OG) Retired.
Patti, Angelo J. '82 (ALT) Presbyteral Council; Johnstown, PA St. Andrew.
Patti, Steve *o.f.m.* '01 (R) Durham, NC Immaculate Conception.
Pattison, Rev. Msgr. W. Francis '58 (SD) San Diego, CA St. Rita.
Patton, James J. '65 (CLV) Perry, OH St. Cyprian Retired.
Patton, Mel *o.s.b.* '56 (IND)[K] St. Meinrad St. Meinrad Archabbey.
Patton, Mel *o.s.b.* '56 (SFS)[G] Yankton, SD Sacred Heart Monastery.
Patton, Patrick G. '78 (HEL) Whitefish, MT St. Charles Borromeo.
Patullo, Michael '02 (DUL) Crosslake, MN Immaculate Heart; Emily, MN St. Emily; College of Consultors.
Paul, Benedict '84 (NY) Bronx, NY St. Michael.
Paul, David *s.m.* '70 (STL)[O] St. Louis Marianists, Province of the United States (Society of Mary).
Paul, Dennis '93 (JOL) Bloomingdale, IL St. Isidore.
Paul, Gregory *c.p.* '58 (HRT)[L] West Hartford Holy Family Monastery/Retreat; [P] West Hartford, CT Holy Family Passionist Retreat Center.
Paul, John F. *s.j.* '92 (NO)[P] New Orleans, LA Ignatius Residence.
Paul, John J. *m.s.c.* '58 (ALN) Diocesan Tribunal; [A] Center Valley, PA Sacred Heart Villa, Missionaries of the Sacred Heart.
Paul, John M. *s.j.* '80 (MIL)[P] Milwaukee, WI Jesuit Provincial Office, Wisconsin Province; Milwaukee, WI; [P] Milwaukee, WI Arrupe House Jesuit Community.
Paul, John P. '72 (PH) Philadelphia, PA Our Lady of Calvary.
Paul, Kasiano '02 (CI) Our Lady of Mercy.
Paul, Raphael '87 (SFD) Brighton, IL St. Alphonsus; Brighton, IL St. John the Evangelist.
Paul, Raphael (STL)[J] Bridgeton, MO SSM De Paul Health Center Foundation.
Paul, Raymond L. '62 (Y) Massillon, OH St. Joseph; Defenders of the Bond.
Paul, Thomas Elmus '07 (ALX) Alexandria, LA St. Frances Xavier Cabrini.
Paul, Thomas '77 (JOL) Naperville, IL St. Elizabeth Seton; [D] Naperville, IL All Saints Catholic Academy.
Paulin, Jeremy *o.m.v.* '06 (DEN) Denver, CO Holy Ghost.
Paulino, Felino '77 (SEA) Seattle, WA St. Edward; Seattle, WA St. George; Seattle, WA St. Paul; Seattle, WA St. Mary.
Paulino, P. Samuel Fernandez *o.c.d.* (CGS)[A] Caguas, PR Colegio San Jose Elemental.
Paulish, W. Jeffrey '88 (SCR) Bear Creek, PA St. Elizabeth; DEPARTMENT OF VETERANS AFFAIRS HOSPITALS AND CHAPLAINS; Veteran's Administration Hospital.
Paulissen, Richard E. *m.m.* '63 (GAL)[O] Houston Maryknoll Fathers and Brothers.
Paulissen, Richard E. *m.m.* '63 (NY)[EE] Retired.
Paulits, Walter J. '72 (BAL) Pasadena, MD Our Lady of the Chesapeake Retired.
Paulli, Kenneth *o.f.m.* '90 (ALB)[B] Loudonville, NY Siena College; [B] Siena College.
Paulos, George Maliekal '01 (SYM) Tampa, FL St. Joseph Syro–Malabar Catholic Church.
Paulose, Antony *c.m.i.* '97 (GAL) Houston, TX St. Vincent de Paul.
Paulose, Wilson Kidangan '80 (CAM) Lindenwold, NJ Our Lady of Guadalupe Parish, Lindenwold, N.J.
Paulsen, Timothy W. *o.m.i.* '97 (BWN) Brownsville, TX St. Eugene De Mazenod.
Paulson, Brian G. *s.j.* '92 (CHI)[D] Chicago, IL St. Ignatius College Prep; [D] Chicago, IL St. Ignatius Jesuit Community.
Paulson, Harold P. '78 (TYL) Tennessee Colony, TX Coffield Unit, Texas Department of Corrections; Tennessee Colony, TX Gurney Unit; Tennessee Colony, TX Michael Unit Retired.
Paulson, Jerome E. '76 (NU) Arlington, MN St. Mary; Gaylord, MN St. Michael; Green Isle, MN St. Brendan; College of Consultors; Priests' Council.
Paur, Roman *o.s.b.* '66 (SCL)[I] Collegeville St. John's Abbey, of the Order of St. Benedict.
Paurazas, Peter P. '55 (CHI) Retired.
Pausche, Frederick F. '78 (CLV) Concord Twp., OH St. Gabriel.
Pauselli, Francis L. '75 (SCR) Scranton, PA Divine Mercy; Scranton, PA Immaculate Conception.
Pautler, Mark '74 (SPK) Spokane, WA Sacred Heart; Chancellor; Judicial Vicar; Members.
Pavamkott, George *o.praem.* '92 (SFE) University Hospital; [H] Albuquerque, NM Santa Maria de la Vid Priory.
Pavela, Wayne (OM) Humphrey, NE St. Francis.
Pavelis, Harold '51 (SCL) Retired.
Pavia, Nicholas S. '00 (BGP) Vicariate IV (East Bridgeport, Stratford, Trumbull, Monroe, Shelton); Shelton, CT St. Joseph; Presbyteral Council.
Pavich, Philip *o.f.m.* '57 (CHI)[N] Chicago, IL St. Anthony's Friary.
Pavignano, Steven *o.f.m.* '78 (NY) New York, NY All Saints; [EE] New York, NY All Saints Friary.
Pavis, Rev. Msgr. Victor S. '43 (NY)[EE] Bronx, NY Retired.
Pavkovic, Miljenko '08 (DEN) Boulder, CO Sacred Heart of Jesus.
Pavlak, Andrew J. '00 (SFE) Socorro, NM San Miguel.
Pavlakovich, Michael '87 (DEN) Littleton, CO Light of the World Parish.
Pavlicek, Edward '83 (SAT) Somerset, TX St. Mary's.
Pavlicek, Rev. Msgr. Louis '71 (AUS) Georgetown, TX St. Helen.
Pavlick, Raymond A. '71 (NY) Castle Point, NY V.A. Hudson Valley Healthcare.
Pavlick, Raymond A. '71 (MO) On Duty Outside the Diocese; DEPARTMENT OF VETERANS AFFAIRS HOSPITALS AND CHAPLAINS.
Pavlik, Albert *o.carm.* '61 (ALB) Troy, NY St. Joseph.
Pavlik, David P. '78 (CHI) Chicago, IL Saint Ita.
Pavlik, John *o.f.m.cap.* '78 (FgM)[M] Pittsburgh, PA St. Augustine Friary; Pittsburgh, PA Province of St. Augustine; Pittsburgh, PA.
Pavlik, John *o.f.m.cap.* '78 (NY)[EE] White Plains, NY Capuchin Friars of North America.
Pavlik, Mark L. '03 (STP) Minneapolis, MN St. Olaf.
Pavlik, Paul R. *t.o.r.* '59 (FgM) Loretto, PA THIRD ORDER REGULAR MISSIONS.
Pavlock, Martin L. '66 (BUF) Retired.
Pavlosky, John J. '71 (ALN) Retired.
Pavlovsky, Wencil C. '91 (GAL) Houston, TX St. Augustine; William P. Hobby Airport; Central Vicariate; Appointees; College of Consultors.
Pavone, Frank '88 (AMA) On Duty Outside the Diocese.
Pavur, Claude N. *s.j.* '84 (STL)[C] Saint Louis University; [O] St. Louis, MO Jesuit Community Corporation at Saint Louis University – Jesuit Hall.
Pawelec, Henryk '04 (MIA) Miami Shores, FL St. Rose of Lima.
Pawelk, Steve *g.h.m.* '89 (CIN)[N] Fairfield, OH; Cincinnati, OH.
Pawell, Robert '66 (CHI)[N] Chicago, IL Holy Evangelists Friary.
Pawlaczyk, Miroslaw '92 (NY) Mahopac, NY St. John the Evangelist.
Pawlicki, James *s.v.d.* '73 (BLX)[D] Bay St. Louis, MS Media Production Center; [D] Bay St. Louis, MS St. Augustine's Residence; [D] Bay St. Louis, MS Southern Province of St. Augustine – Provincial Offices; [D] Bay St. Louis, MS Media Production Center "In A Word"; Bay Saint Louis, MS Southern Province; Bay Saint Louis, MS.
Pawlik, Walter M. *s.d.s.* '58 (GRY)[H] Merrillville, IN Salvatorian Fathers (Society of the Divine Savior).
Pawlikowski, John M. *o.s.m.* '67 (CHI) Chicago, IL Assumption of the Blessed Virgin Mary; [B] Chicago, IL The Catholic Theological Union at Chicago; [N] Chicago, IL Assumption Priory.
Pawlikowski, Matthew '97 (NEW) Military Chaplains; Army Chaplains.
Pawlikowski, Matthew '97 (NY) West Point, NY Catholic Chapel of the Most Holy Trinity.
Pawloski, Gregory P. '74 (LIN) Auburn, NE St. Joseph's.
Pawlowski, Dariusz '87 (SHP) Scouting; Shreveport, LA St. Mary of the Pines.
Pawlowski, Joseph M. '73 (GRY) Valparaiso, IN St. Paul; Finance Council.
Pawson, Rev. Msgr. Robert J. '66 (BRK) Queens Village, NY Our Lady of Lourdes.
Pax, Ulric *o.f.m.* '59 (SFE)[H] Albuquerque, NM The Province of Our Lady of Guadalupe.
Paxton, Philip *c.p.* '95 (BIR) Fairfield, AL St. Mary's.
Paxton, Philip *c.p.* '95 (CHI)[N] Chicago, IL Passionist Provincial Office; Consultors:.
Payea, Gerald *o.carm.* '70 (FgM) Darien, IL Provincial Headquarters, Carmelite Provincial Office.
Payea, Gerald *o.carm.* '70 (JOL)[L] Darien Carmelite Provincial Office.
Payer, Emil S. '71 (GBG) Yukon, PA Seven Dolors.
Payikat, Zacharias *c.m.i.* '70 (NSH) Presbyteral Council; Clergy Personnel Board; Nashville, TN Cathedral of the Incarnation.
Payikat, Zachary *c.m.i.* '70 (NSH)[K] Liberty, TN Carmel Center of Spirituality.
Payne, Charles E. *o.f.m.* (CHI)[N] Chicago, IL Holy

Spirit Friary, Order of Friars Minor.
Payne, Gary '85 (OWN) Absent on Leave.
Payne, Jeremiah L. '07 (ORL) On Duty Outside the Diocese.
Payne, John J. '01 (NO) Metairie, LA St. Edward the Confessor; Defenders of the Bond.
Payne, John Michael *o.c.d.* '70 (LR)[A] Little Rock, AR Marylake – Carmelite Novitiate.
Payne, Mark M. *o.s.b.* '81 (NEW)[M] Newark, NJ Newark Abbey; Newark, NJ.
Payne, Mark '94 (MIL) Milwaukee, WI St. Veronica.
Payne, Stephen J. '71 (GAL) Huntsville, TX St. Thomas the Apostle.
Payne, Steven *o.c.d.* '82 (MIL)[P] Milwaukee Provincial Offices – Discalced Carmelites.
Payne, Thomas H. '50 (SAV) Retired.
Payo, Reuben '84 (DEN) Wheat Ridge, CO SS. Peter and Paul.
Paysse, Wayne C. '87 (NO) On Duty Outside the Archdiocese; Board of Directors:; Board of Directors:; Board of Directors; Consultants.
Pazdan, Benedykt M. '06 (CHI) Streamwood, IL St. John the Evangelist.
Pazdzioch, Pawel '96 (ORL) Haines City, FL St. Ann.
Paz en la Casa, Vincente '66 (PBL) Florence, CO St. Benedict.
Pazhayakari, Philip *c.m.i.* '62 (SHP) Rayville, LA Sacred Heart.
Pazhayapurackal, Emmanuel J. *c.m.i.* '75 (STA) Gainesville, FL Holy Faith.
Pazhayaveetil, Binu Joseph *o.praem* '04 (SFE)[H] Albuquerque, NM Santa Maria de la Vid Priory; Lovelace Hospital.
Pazheparambil, Thomas J. '00 (BLX) Diberville, MS Sacred Heart.
Pazheveettil, Jose *m.s.t.* '97 (DAL) McKinney, TX St. Gabriel the Archangel.
Pazhoor, Mathew (NY) Mamaroneck, NY Most Holy Trinity.
Pazhukkathara, Shaji Joseph '02 (SUP) Winter, WI St. Peter; Winter, WI Sacred Heart.
Pazmany, Geza *sch.p.* '61 (PH)[F] Devon, PA Devon Preparatory School; [Y] Devon Piarist Fathers (Order of the Pious Schools).
Peach, D. Patrick '06 (BAL) On Duty Outside the Archdiocese.
Peach, Patrick Peter *o.carm.* '06 (STP) Lake Elmo, MN; [K] Lake Elmo, MN Carmelite Hermitage of the Blessed Virgin Mary.
Peacha, Thomas James '59 (LA) Los Angeles, CA Holy Trinity Retired.
Peacock, Francis A. '53 (PHX) Phoenix, AZ Our Lady of Fatima.
Peacock, Mark E. '07 (GR) Ada, MI St. Patrick's.
Peacock, Thomas E. *s.j.* '63 (BAL)[S] Baltimore, MD Colombiere Jesuit Community.
Peak, James '07 (SPK) Absent on Leave.
Peake, Rev. Msgr. Daniel A. '49 (NY) Bronx, NY St. Margaret of Cortona; [EE] Bronx, NY John Cardinal O'Connor Residence Retired.
Pearce, Donald *s.j.* '59 (NO)[P] New Orleans, LA Ignatius Residence Retired.
Pearce, John S. *c.m.* '57 (PH)[Y].
Pearce, Joseph Francis *c.o.* '99 (CHR)[E] Rock Hill, SC Oratory of St. Philip Neri, Congregation of the Oratory of Pontifical Rite.
Pearsall, William T. '53 (BO) Senior Priests. Retired.
Pearson, Everett '91 (WDC) Washington, DC Holy Name.
Pearson, John A. '66 (NU) Committee for Continuing Education of Clergy; Litchfield, MN St. Gertrude.
Pearson, John H. *c.s.c.* '73 (FTW)[A] Notre Dame, IN Moreau Seminary.
Pearson, Rev. Msgr. Robert A. '65 (SPK) Spokane, WA; Vicar for Priests; Priests' Personnel Board Retired.
Pearson, Robert A. '78 (TR) Retired.
Pease, Raymond A. *s.j.* '68 (FgM) St. Louis, MO Society of Jesus.
Peatee, Gregory L. '92 (TOL) Toledo, OH St. Charles Borromeo; Toledo, OH St. Hyacinth; College of Consultors.
Pecaric, Alfred F. '82 (BGP) Defenders of the Bond; Fairfield, CT Holy Cross.
Pecchie, Paul '95 (SP) Largo, FL St. Patrick; Elected Pastors.
Pecci, Ronald J. *o.f.m.* '83 (WIL) Wilmington, DE St. Paul's.
Pecevich, Conrad S. '77 (WOR) Blackstone, MA St. Paul's.
Pecharroman, Ovidio '61 (WDC)[B] Washington, DC Diocesan Laborer Priests, House of Studies.
Pechillo, Arthur C. '01 (PRT) Retired.
Pecht, Gerard J. *c.ss.r.* '50 (STL)[O] Liguori, MO St. Clement Health Care Center Retired.
Peck, David A. '94 (RCK)[B] Elgin, IL St. Edward Central Catholic High School; Special Assignment.
Peck, John J. *o.s.b.* '89 (HBG) Annville, PA St. Paul the Apostle; [I] Annville, PA Lebanon Valley College.
Pecklers, Keith F. *s.j.* '91 (NY)[EE] New York Jesuit Provincial's Office.
Pecklers, Keith (FTW)[B] University of Notre Dame Du Lac.
Peckman, R. William '97 (JC) Bowling Green, MO St. Clement; Priestly and Religious Vocations Committee.
Pecoraro, John C. '02 (MEM) Absent on Leave.
Pecotte, Robert '04 (FAR) Cavalier, ND St. Brigid of Ireland Church of Cavalier; Cavalier, ND St. Patrick's Church of Crystal.
Peddicord, Richard A. *o.p.* '86 (STL)[B] St. Louis, MO Aquinas Institute of Theology; [O] St. Louis, MO Dominican Community of St. Louis.
Pedersen, Bryan J. B. '03 (STP) Robbinsdale, MN Sacred Heart.
Pedi, Mario *o.s.b.* '57 (RCK)[G] Aurora, IL Marmion Abbey; [C] Aurora, IL Marmion Academy.
Pedigo, Jon '91 (SJ) San Jose, CA St. Julie Billiart; Ongoing Formation of Clergy.
Pednekar, Joseph C. *m.s.f.s.* '62 (CLV) Cleveland, OH St. Patrick.
Pednekar, Joseph Charles *m.s.f.s.* '62 (TYL)[B] Whitehouse, TX The Missionaries of St. Francis de Sales.
Pedone, Rev. Msgr. F. Stephen '78 (WOR) Worcester, MA Blessed Sacrament; Judicial Vicar and Vicar for Canonical Affairs; Judges; Diocesan College of Consultors; Presbyteral Council.
Pedrano, Stephanos *o.s.b.* '91 (SD)[J] Oceanside, CA Prince of Peace Abbey.
Pedretti, Raymond J. '56 (LC) Retired.
Pedretti, Robert F. '64 (LC) Retired.
Pedrizetti, Raymond *o.s.b.* '58 (SCL)[I] Collegeville, MN St. John's Abbey, of the Order of St. Benedict.
Pedroso, Rafael '64 (MIA) Retired.
Pedrotti, Frank L. *s.j.* '70 (STL)[O] St. Louis, MO Jesuit Community Corporation at Saint Louis University – Jesuit Hall.
Pedroza, Salvador '81 (LAR) Asherton, TX Immaculate Conception.
Pedzich, Henry J. '72 (SY) Syracuse, NY St. Michael & St. Peter.
Pedzik, Vitalis B. '61 (RVC) Retired.
Peek, Joseph '02 (ATL) Norcross, GA Saint Patrick.
Peek, Kevin T. '98 (MO) Military Chaplains; Army Chaplains.
Peelo, Adrian *o.f.m.* '83 (SD) Oceanside, CA Mission San Luis Rey.
Peeters, John N. *c.s.v.* '83 (CHI)[N] Arlington Heights Viatorian Province Center–Clerics of St. Viator.
Peeters, John N. *c.s.v.* '83 (JOL) Kankakee, IL St. Patrick.
Peffley, Francis J. '90 (ARL) Gainesville, VA Holy Trinity.
Pegnam, William '67 (SJ) San Jose, CA Santa Teresa Retired.
Pehl, Jeffrey '95 (SAT)[A] San Antonio, TX Assumption Seminary.
Pehler, Gerald *o.f.m.cap.* (LC) Wausau, WI Holy Name of Jesus.
Pehrsson, Alfred R. *c.m.* '58 (PH)[Y].
Peiffer, James E. '67 (TOL) Ecumenical and Interreligious Affairs Commission Retired.
Peil, William L. '49 (GRY) Retired.
Peil, William '49 (FTW) Retired.
Peinemann, Michael '05 (SAT) Kerrville, TX Notre Dame.
Peiris, Richard '62 (OAK) Retired.
Peixotto, Joseph *c.s.c.* '61 (FgM) New Rochelle, NY Eastern Brothers Province.
Pejza, John P. *o.s.a.* '61 (SD)[J] San Diego, CA Augustinian Community.
Pekar, Athanasius B. *o.s.b.m.* '46 (RVC)[M] Glen Cove, NY St. Josaphat's Monastery, Novitiate and Retreat House.
Pekar, Athanasius B. *o.s.b.m.* '46 (STF)[B] Glen Cove, NY Basilian Fathers Novitiate of the Order of St. Basil the Great.
Pekar, Rev. Msgr. Joseph W. '57 (BGP) Bridgeport, CT SS. Cyril and Methodius.
Pekarske, Daniel *s.d.s.* '90 (MIL)[P] Milwaukee Salvatorian Provincial Offices; [B] Hales Corners, WI Sacred Heart School of Theology.
Peklo, Edward *s.v.d.* '69 (MIL)[P] East Troy, WI Divine Word Missionaries.
Pekola, David J. '86 (MET) Hackettstown, NJ Assumption of the Blessed Virgin Mary.
Pelaez, Andres Fernandez–Lopez '04 (NY) New Rochelle, NY Sound Shore Medical Center.
Pelaez, Oskar '94 (STO) Absent on Leave.
Pelak, Anthony M. '03 (GR) North Muskegon, MI Prince of Peace.
Pelc, Timothy R. '74 (DET) Grosse Pointe Park, MI St. Ambrose; Presbyteral Council.
Pelczar, Edward A. '62 (PH) On Special or Other Archdiocesan Assignment; Philadelphia, PA St. Helena.
Pelczarski, Wojciech *s.d.s.* (NOR) Fishers Island, NY Our Lady of Grace.
Peles, David S. '84 (ALT) Johnstown, PA St. Benedict's.
Pelkington, Robert Leo '68 (WDC) Washington, DC St. Dominic Church & Priory.
Pellegrini, Frederick J. *s.j.* '84 (NY) New York, NY St. Aloysius; Manhattan (Central Harlem).
Pellegrino, Rev. Msgr. Francis B. '51 (SLC) Retired.
Pellegrino, Joseph A. '77 (SP) Tarpon Springs, FL St. Ignatius of Antioch; [F] Tarpon Springs, FL St. Ignatius Early Childhood Center; Diocesan Finance Council; Executive Committee; Elected Pastors; Personnel Board.
Pellerin, Keith '98 (LKC) Lake Charles, LA St. Martin dePorres.
Pelletier, Adrien O. *s.m.* '56 (BO)[W] Framingham, MA The Marist House Retired.
Pelletier, Emile '94 (PHX) Phoenix, AZ St. Gregory Roman Catholic Parish.
Pelletier, Norman B. *s.s.s.* '69 (CLV)[N] Highland Heights, OH Congregation of the Blessed Sacrament Provincial House; [N] Cleveland, OH Congregation of the Blessed Sacrament; Cleveland, OH.
Pelletier, Walter R. *s.j.* '60 (BGP)[O] Fairfield, CT The Fairfield Jesuit Community–Fairfield University Retired.
Pellini, Robert R. *m.m.* '59 (FgM) Maryknoll, NY MARYKNOLL.
Pellissier, Francois *g.h.m.* '81 (CIN)[N] Fairfield, OH.
Peloso, John P. '96 (MIA) Tavernier, FL San Pedro; Spiritual Moderators.
Pelotte, Dana *s.s.s.* '99 (GAL) Houston, TX Corpus Christi.
Pelous, Donald '77 (LAF) Retired.
Pelrine, Edward '01 (CHI) Elk Grove Village, IL Queen of the Rosary.
Pelton, Robert S. *c.s.c.* '49 (FTW)[B] University of Notre Dame Du Lac; [H] Notre Dame, IN Holy Cross Community, Corby Hall, University of Notre Dame.
Pelton, Thomas '66 (CHI) Chicago, IL Maternity of the Blessed Virgin Mary.
Peltz, Carl F. '77 (KAL) Albion, MI St. John the Evangelist.
Peltzer, Michael '80 (WCH) Harper, KS St. Joan of Arc.
Peluse, Dominic *s.c.j.* '74 (GB) Sturgeon Bay, WI SS. Peter and Paul; Sturgeon Bay, WI St. Joseph.
Peluso, Frank *o.a.r.* '61 (NY) St. Joseph's Cursillo Center.
Pelzel, Bradley C. '02 (SC) Diocesan Consultors; Vocations; Sioux City, IA St. Joseph; Presbyteral Council; [A] Sioux City, IA Briar Cliff University.
Pemberton, James '05 (FWT) Gainesville, TX St. Mary; Vocations and Seminarians.
Pemberton, Joseph '77 (FWT) Fort Worth, TX Holy Family; Deans; Continuing Pastoral Formation.
Pena, Cesar E. '08 (MIA) Southwest Ranches, FL St. Mark.
Pena, Luis '97 (MGZ) Cabo Rojo, PR St. Michael.
Pena, Richard '92 (SAT) San Antonio, TX St. Gabriel.
Pena, Roberto *o.m.i.* '55 (LAR) Eagle Pass, TX Sacred Heart.
Pena–Jimenez, Rodrigo (CHI) Chicago, IL Providence of God.
Pena–Moredo, Rev. Msgr. Wilfredo '74 (SJN) San Juan, PR Santa Bernardita Soubirous; Vicar of Family Affairs.
Penafiel, Fausto '83 (PHX) Phoenix, AZ St. Mark Roman Catholic Parish; Phoenix, AZ St. Philip the Deacon Roman Catholic Mission, A Quasi–Parish; Special Assignment.
Penalba, Vicente *c.m.f.* '69 (SJN) Bayamon, PR Santa Maria.
Penalba, Vincent '69 (CGS) Caguas, PR Inmaculado Corazon de Maria.
Penaloza, Jorge A. '60 (LA) Pico Rivera, CA St. Francis Xavier Retired.
Penaloza, Luis M. '99 (SR) Clearlake, CA Our Lady, Queen of Peace.
Penas, Perfecto Fondevila '62 (SJN) San Juan, PR Cristo Rey.
Penchi, Edward J. '56 (LC) Retired.
Pendergast, Richard J. *s.j.* '63 (NY)[EE] New York, NY Murray–Weigel Hall.
Penderghest, William T. *ss.cc.* '67 (BWN) Harlingen, TX Queen of Peace.
Pendergraft, Gregory *f.s.s.p.* '05 (SCR)[M] Elmhurst, PA Priestly Fraternity of St. Peter (F.S.S.P.), North American District Headquarters; Elmhurst, PA.
Pendergraft, Michael '81 (STA) Lake City, FL Epiphany; Presbyteral Council; Rural Life Director; Diocesan Consultors.
Pendleton, Arthur J. *o.s.b.* '64 (CHL)[J] Belmont, NC Belmont Abbey.
Pendolphi, Richard J. '76 (COL) Worthington, OH St. Michael.
Pendrick, Thomas E. '03 (NEW)[C] Oradell, NJ Bergen Catholic; Ridgewood, NJ Our Lady of Mount Carmel.
Pendzick, John S. '97 (ALN) Allentown, PA Our Lady Help of Christians.
Penez, Francisco '00 (AMA) Vicars Forane.
Peng, John B. (CHI) Retired.
Penhallurick, Robert '96 (COL) Newark, OH St. Francis de Sales; [C] Newark, OH Newark Catholic High School.
Penisten, Edmund J. '02 (JUN) Ketchikan, AK Holy Name; Diocesan Consultors; Port Chaplains; Vocations.

Penkala, Rev. Msgr. Edmund S. '45 (SCR)[N] Dunmore, PA Villa St. Joseph Retired.
Penko, Francis '60 (SD) Retired.
Penn, Churchill '96 (BGP) Bridgeport, CT St. Ambrose.
Penn, Michael W. '03 (JC) Glasgow, MO St. Mary; Slater, MO St. Joseph; To The Bishop; Senators.
Penna, Rev. Msgr. Joseph P. '67 (NY) Pearl River, NY St. Aedan.
Penna, Michael Della *o.f.m.* '99 (FgM)[EE] St. Francis Center for Religious; New York, NY Franciscan Province of the Immaculate Conception.
Penna, Tony (BO) Boston College.
Pennett, Frederick J. '71 (MAN) Hampstead, NH St. Anne; Vicars Forane.
Pennings, Gary '01 (KCK) Vicars General; Department of Parish Ministries; Ex Officio; Archdiocesan Consultors; Archdiocesan Council on Finances; Archdiocesan Administrative Team; Savior Pastoral Center; Overland Park, KS St. Michael the Archangel.
Pennington, John F. *s.j.* '70 (CHI)[N] Chicago Chicago Province of the Society of Jesus–Provincial Office.
Pennington, John F. *s.j.* '70 (DET)[K] Clarkston, MI Colombiere Center.
Pennington, Rev. Msgr. John R. '79 (WDC) Silver Spring, MD St. John the Evangelist.
Pennington, Matthew '88 (MRY) Capitola, CA St. Joseph; Vicars Forane; Presbyteral Council; Diocesan Consultors; Diocesan Consultors.
Pennock, Michael '95 (JOL) Gilman, IL Immaculate Conception; Piper City, IL St. Peter.
Penonzek, Edward M. *o.s.m.* '58 (CHI)[N] Chicago Order of Friar Servants of Mary (Servites) United States of America Province, Inc.
Penonzek, Edward M. *o.s.m.* '58 (ORG)[I] Anaheim, CA Servite Fathers and Brothers.
Penta, Leo J. '78 (BRK) Released from Diocesan Assignment.
Pentareddy, John Paul *p.v.* '94 (CHR) Cheraw, SC St. Peter.
Pentecost, Denver B. '69 (NO) Marrero, LA West Jefferson General Hospital; Marrero, LA Wynhoven Health Care Center.
Pentello, Richard J. '79 (Y) Kent, OH St. Patrick's.
Pentis, William F. *c.o.* '66 (CHR)[E] Rock Hill, SC Oratory of St. Philip Neri, Congregation of the Oratory of Pontifical Rite; Catholic Women, Council of; York, SC Divine Saviour.
Pentony, Liam '55 (JKS) Retired.
Pepe, Robert F. '50 (WCH) Retired.
Pepel, Clement '82 (MET) On Duty Outside the Diocese.
Pepin, Darryl J. '78 (MAR) Ironwood, MI Our Lady of Peace; [B] Ironwood, MI Our Lady of Peace School Educational Fund.
Pepin, Normand A. *s.j.* '63 (BO)[U] Boston The Society of Jesus of New England–Provincial Offices.
Pepin, Normand A. *s.j.* '63 (FBK)[A] Fairbanks, AK Monroe Catholic Junior–Senior High School; [E] Fairbanks, AK House of Prayer; Hispanic Ministry; [E] St. Marys, AK Brother Joe Prince Jesuit Community; [B] Fairbanks, AK Immaculate Conception Grade School.
Pepka, Edward '77 (SAC) Sacramento, CA St. Charles Borromeo.
Peplansky, Joseph *c.m.f.* '60 (CHI)[N] Oak Park, IL Claretian Missionaries USA Eastern Province.
Peplowski, Sigmund A. '75 (PAT) Rockaway, NJ Sacred Heart; Rockaway, NJ St. Cecilia's.
Pepowski, Bert '61 (GRY)[H] Cedar Lake, IN Our Lady of Lourdes Friary.
Peppard, Patrick F. *s.j.* '73 (DET)[E] Detroit, MI University of Detroit Jesuit High School and Academy.
Pepper, J. David '58 (DUB) Retired.
Peprah, Rev. Msgr. Raphael (BRK) Brooklyn, NY Holy Name.
Pera, Sylvano *o.f.m.* '52 (SFD)[L] Teutopolis, IL St. Francis Assisi Friary; Teutopolis, IL St. Francis of Assisi; Effingham, IL St. Mary Help of Christians; Comite Diocesano de Ministerio Hispano – Diocesan Committee for Hispanic Ministry.
Perales, Jorge '78 (MIA) Miami, FL St. Kevin.
Perata, Stephen F. '58 (SJ) San Jose, CA St. Victor.
Percell, Lawrence J. '03 (SJ) Deans.
Percell, Lawrence P. '03 (SJ) Los Altos, CA St. Nicholas.
Perdomo–Peidomo, Eli *ss.c.c.* '94 (SJN) Guaynabo, PR Sagrados Corazones; San Juan, PR San Juan M. Vianney.
Perdue, John *m.ss.cc.* '90 (CAM)[I] Pleasantville, NJ Our Lady's Residence, Pleasantville, N.J.; Linwood, NJ; [M] Linwood, NJ Villa Pieta. Missionaries of the Sacred Hearts of Jesus & Mary.
Perea, Donald '98 (SEA) Seattle, WA St. Bernadette; Special Assignment.
Perea, Michael U. *o.praem.* '90 (LA) Wilmington, CA SS. Peter and Paul.
Pereda, Rev. Msgr. James F. '81 (RVC) Judicial Vicar.
Pereda, Rev. Msgr. James *c.r.c.* '81 (BRK)[U] Queens Village, NY St. Ann's Novitiate, Little Sisters of the Poor.
Peredes, Hernan *s.j.* '95 (NY) Staten Island, NY Our Lady of Mt. Carmel–St. Benedicta.
Perehubka, Jozef '84 (HEL) Libby, MT St. Joseph.
Pereida, Alex '08 (SAT) San Antonio, TX Holy Trinity.
Pereira, Anand *s.j.* '00 (OM)[K] Omaha, NE Jesuit Community at Creighton University.
Pereira, Anthony '82 (SJ) On Leave of Absence.
Pereira, Brian *s.j.* '02 (BAL)[S] Baltimore, MD Ferdinand Wheeler Jesuit Community.
Pereira, Cyril F. '54 (ALB) Troy, NY St. Patrick Retired.
Pereira, Herivelto Jeder *c.ss.r.* '02 (WOR) Brazilian Ministry.
Pereira, Joseph '74 (HT) Galliano, LA St. Joseph.
Pereira, Luciano J. '54 (FR) Retired.
Pereira, Robert J. '62 (STO) Diamond Springs, CA Retired.
Pereira, Roy *s.j.* '97 (BO)[U] Newton, MA The Jesuit Community at Boston College.
Perelli, Robert J. *c.j.m.* '76 (BUF)[O] Buffalo, NY The Eudists – Congregation of Jesus and Mary.
Pereppadan, Jose *c.m.i.* '79 (COV) Fort Mitchell, KY Blessed Sacrament.
Perera, Denzil M. '58 (NO) Retired.
Perera, J. Bosco '69 (FTW) Geneva, IN St. Mary of the Presentation.
Perera, Jude *t.o.r.* (STP) Minneapolis, MN St. Bridget.
Peres, Mark *c.pp.s.* '85 (CIN)[N] Dayton Provincial Office of the Cincinnati Province of the Society of the Precious Blood.
Peretti, Peter L. '73 (GBG) New Salem, PA St. Thomas; New Salem, PA St. Procopius.
Perez, Angel A. '02 (P) Woodburn, OR St. Luke.
Perez, Angel Antonio *c.p.* '87 (MGZ) San Sebastian, PR San Sebastian Martir.
Perez, Angel '05 (DEN) Graduate Studies.
Perez, Armando S. '02 (SEA) Vancouver, WA St. John the Evangelist.
Perez, Armando '62 (MIA) Fort Lauderdale, FL Our Lady Queen of Martyrs.
Perez, Aurelio H. '86 (MIL) Wind Lake, WI St. Clare.
Perez, Boris Espinoza '78 (CGS) Las Piedras, PR Inmaculada Concepcion.
Perez, Carlos '92 (B) Bonners Ferry, ID St. Ann's.
Perez, David Guzman *m.x.y.* '88 (NY) Bronx, NY Our Saviour.
Perez, David '87 (MGZ) Moca, PR Our Lady of Monserrate.
Perez, Eduardo '95 (STO) Riverbank, CA St. Frances of Rome Church (Pastor of).
Perez, Edwin E. '01 (ARL)[D] Alexandria, VA Bishop Ireton High School; Alexandria, VA St. Rita.
Perez, Francisco '00 (AMA) Advocates; Ex Officio; Chancellor; Vocation Development Team; Pampa, TX St. Vincent de Paul; Priests' Pension Plan Retirement Committee; College of Consultors.
Perez, Gabino *o.a.r.* '51 (ORG) Santa Ana, CA Our Lady of the Pillar.
Perez, Hector A. '07 (MIA) Pembroke Pines, FL St. Maximilian Kolbe.
Perez, Hector R.G. '81 (PT) Pensacola, FL St. Stephen; Legion of Mary.
Perez, Horacio *s.x.* '03 (PAT)[N] Wayne Xaverian Missionary Fathers; Wayne, NJ XAVERIAN MISSIONARY FATHERS.
Perez, Isidro '81 (MIA) Miami, FL St. Brendan.
Perez, Javier H. '93 (TUC) Somerton, AZ Immaculate Heart of Mary Roman Catholic Parish – Somerton; Vicars Forane; All Vicars Forane; Council of Priests.
Perez, Jesse L. '74 (PBL) Retired.
Perez, John C. '96 (MO) Army Chaplains.
Perez, John Jairo '03 (BGP) Stamford, CT St. Mary.
Perez, John Mary *s.o.l.t.* '00 (CC)[G] Robstown, TX Society of Our Lady of the Most Holy Trinity.
Perez, Jose Manuel '05 (KNX) Knoxville, TN Cathedral of the Sacred Heart of Jesus.
Perez, Jose '99 (BRK) On Leave/Unassigned.
Perez, Jose '64 (COL) Columbus, OH Santa Cruz Parish.
Perez, Joseph '69 (GAL) On Duty Outside the Archdiocese.
Perez, Juan '98 (SAC) Roseville, CA St. Rose of Lima.
Perez, Juan (L) Cursillo Movement.
Perez, Lazaro '89 (MET)[G] New Brunswick, NJ Saint Peter's University Hospital; Spotswood, NJ Immaculate Conception.
Perez, Leo *o.m.i.* '83 (SAT)[L] San Antonio, TX Oblate Benson Residence (Southwest Area).
Perez, Leon '60 (ARE) Retired.
Perez, Leopoldo G. *o.m.i.* '84 (SAT)[C] Oblate School of Theology; [R] San Antonio, TX Oblate Lourdes Grotto Shrine of the Southwest, Tepeyac de San Antonio.
Perez, Luis A. '95 (MIA) Cutler Bay, FL Our Lady of the Holy Rosary.
Perez, Rev. Msgr. Manuel Garcia '75 (SJN) San Juan, PR San Luis Rey.
Perez, Marcos Rene '03 (LUB) Lubbock, TX St. Theresa's.
Perez, Modesto L. '84 (LA) Alhambra, CA All Souls.
Perez, Modesto Lewis '84 (LA) Cursillo Movement.
Perez, Rev. Msgr. Nelson J. '89 (PH) West Chester, PA St. Agnes.
Perez, Nicolas '03 (PCE) Patillas, PR Inmaculado Corazon de Maria.
Perez, Oscar A. '03 (OM) South Sioux City, NE St. Michael.
Perez, Ovidio '00 (ARE)[A] Arecibo, PR Seminario de Jesus Maestro; Director of Youth; Seminario Jesus Maestro College Seminary; Seminary Board and Vocation Program; Retreat House, Centro Diocesano Mons. Mendez; Vocations; Pastoral Vocational Program.
Perez, Rev. Msgr. Pedro Luis '52 (MIA) Retired.
Pérez, Perfecto (MGZ) Aguadilla, PR La Milagrosa.
Perez, Rafael *o.s.b.* '79 (FAJ)[B] Humacao, PR San Antonio Abad Abbey of the Order of St. Benedict.
Perez, Raymond L. *o.praem.* '88 (LA) Wilmington, CA SS. Peter and Paul.
Perez, Rene '03 (LUB) Vocation Team Members.
Perez, Restituto *o.p.* '60 (MIA) Miami, FL St. Dominic; [K] Miami, FL Dominican Fathers of Miami, Inc.
Perez, Robert R. '86 (CHI) Chicago, IL St. Michael the Archangel.
Perez, Ronald '08 (NY) LaGrangeville, NY Blessed Kateri Tekakwitha.
Perez, Salvador '61 (FWT) Retired.
Perez, Samuel '03 (TLS) Tulsa, OK St. Thomas More; Diocesan Consultors; Defender of the Bond; Promoter of Justice; Diocesan Senators; Hispanic Ministry.
Perez, Viktor *o.f.m.conv.* '89 (FRS) Coalinga, CA St. Paul The Apostle.
Perez, William A. *o.s.a.* '62 (TLS)[B] Tulsa, OK Cascia Hall Preparatory School.
Perez–Barrera, Jesus Alejandro '02 (TUC) San Luis, AZ Saint Jude Thaddeus Roman Catholic Parish – San Luis.
Perez–Cobo, Raul '06 (CR) Moorhead, MN St. Joseph's.
Perez–Diaz, German '97 (KAL) Bridgman, MI Our Lady Queen of Peace.
Perez–Lerena, Francisco *s.j.* '58 (MIA)[D] Miami, FL Belen Jesuit Preparatory School; [K] Miami, FL Villa Javier.
Perez–Martinez, Jose Ramon '80 (SAT) San Antonio, TX Cathedral of San Fernando.
Perez–Ojeda, Juan Antonio *o.ss.t.* (BAL)[S] Novitiate House (Victoria, Texas); [S] Baltimore, MD.
Perez–Pupo, Joaquin '76 (MIA) Hialeah, FL Immaculate Conception.
Perez–Rodriguez, Arturo '72 (CHI) Jail Ministry/Kolbe House; [W] Chicago, IL Kolbe House; Kolbe House.
Perez Gonzalez, Osvaldo *c.s.sp.* (SJN)[C] Bayamon, PR Seminario Misionero del Espiritu Santo.
Perez Vazquez, Juan De La Cruz '96 (SJN) Military Services.
Perfetto, Richard A. '66 (DET) Canton, MI Resurrection.
Pergjini, Nikolin '99 (NY) Bronx, NY St. Lucy.
Perham, Arnold E. *c.s.v.* '56 (CHI)[D] Arlington Heights, IL St. Viator High School; [N] Arlington Heights, IL Viatorian Province Center–Clerics of St. Viator.
Peri, Asuramonil F. '79 (NY) Sleepy Hollow, NY St. Teresa of Avila.
Peri, Paul '71 (P) Finance Council; [A] St. Benedict, OR Mount Angel Seminary.
Periannan, Selvaraj *m.s.f.x.* '88 (BIS) Kenmare, ND St. Anthony; Kenmare, ND St. Joseph (Bowbells); Kenmare, ND St. Agnes.
Pericone, Nicholas P. '96 (NO) Defenders of the Bond; Metairie, LA St. Catherine of Siena.
Peries, Angelito '74 (SR) Windsor, CA Our Lady of Guadalupe; Deans; Board of Consultors; Priests' Council.
Perikala, Alfhones '02 (SCR) Susquehanna, PA St. John the Evangelist; Great Bend, PA St. Lawrence; Jackson, PA St. Martin of Tours.
Perin, Glen W. '53 (CIN) Retired.
Perini, Rev. Msgr. Armando J. '56 (MET) Retired.
Perino, John M. '79 (NO) Luling, LA Holy Family.
Perissinotto, Rodrigo *o.s.b.* '04 (KCK)[I] Atchison, KS St. Benedict's Abbey.
Perkin, David R. '78 (NSH) Nashville, TN St. Patrick; On Special Assignment; Vicar General; Moderator of the Curia and Vicar General; Adjutant Judicial Vicar; Judges; Presbyteral Council; Diocesan Finance Board; Clergy Personnel Board.
Perkins, Charles J. '78 (HT) Raceland, LA St. Mary's Nativity; Priests Council; College of Consultors; South Lafourche Deanery.
Perkins, Dennis M. '95 (NOR) Pawcatuck, CT St. Michael; Members; Continuing Education and Formation Commission for the Clergy; Priests' Retirement Plan Board; Diocesan Panel of Pastors, Canon 1742; Advisory Ministry Evaluation Committee.
Perkins, Joseph F. '68 (WDC) Garrett Park, MD Holy Cross.
Perkins, Rev. Msgr. Robert M. '71 (RIC) Hampton, VA Immaculate Conception.
Perkinton, Rev. Msgr. John J '85 (LIN)[F] Waverly, NE Our Lady of Good Counsel Retreat House; [H] Lincoln, NE Villa Marie School and Home for the Educable Mentally Handicapped; Diocesan Consultors; Presbyteral Council; Building Commission; Priests' Continuing Education Committee; Schools;

Diocesan Housing Ministries, Inc.; [L] Lincoln, NE Blessed John XXIII Diocesan Center.
Perkl, James M. '84 (STP) Hastings, MN St. Elizabeth Ann Seton; College of Consultors.
Perko, Richard '04 (STA) Live Oak, FL St. Francis Xavier.
Perkovic, Anton '46 (NO) Retired.
Perkovich, Frank '54 (DUL) Retired.
Perl, Richard D. *s.j.* '78 (FgM) St. Louis, MO Society of Jesus.
Perlinski, Daniel A. '57 (TLS) Retired.
Perlite, John J. *s.j.* '49 (SJ)[M] Los Gatos, CA Sacred Heart Jesuit Center.
Perluzzi, James *o.f.m.* '65 (CHI)[N] Chicago, IL St. Peter's Friary.
Permuy, Francisco *s.j.* '06 (MIA)[D] Miami, FL Belen Jesuit Preparatory School.
Permuy, Jose F. *s.j.* '06 (MIA)[K] Miami, FL Villa Javier.
Pernia, Rev. Msgr. John R. '58 (SFR) San Francisco, CA Star of the Sea Retired.
Perozich, Richard L. '92 (SD) Escondido, CA St. Mary.
Perreault, Joseph A. '75 (CAM) Sea Isle City, NJ St. Joseph's Catholic Church, Sea Isle City, N.J.; Cape May Deanery.
Perreault, Leonard J. '54 (SPR)[G] Holyoke, MA Mont Marie Health Care Center, Inc. Retired.
Perretta, Andrew T. '75 (PAT) Clifton, NJ Sacred Heart.
Perri, Dean Patrick '02 (PRO) Graduate Studies.
Perri, Rogerio Silva '01 (BGP) Bridgeport, CT St. Charles Borromeo.
Perricone, Charles A. '74 (PAT) Sussex, NJ St. Monica.
Perricone, John A. '76 (NEW) On Duty Outside the Archdiocese.
Perriello, Robert A. '76 (WH) Fairmont, WV St. Peter the Fisherman Catholic Church.
Perrier, Monroe *c.ss.r.* '58 (SAT) San Antonio, TX St. Gerard Majella; [L] San Antonio, TX Redemptorists of Texas–San Antonio #1.
Perrin, Thomas *s.d.s.* '97 (MIL)[P] St. Francis, WI St. Joseph's Salvatorian Community (Novitiate).
Perron, Gary *a.a.* '66 (BO)[U] Boston Assumptionist Center.
Perron, Richard J. '46 (BO) Senior Priests. Retired.
Perron, Robert P. '81 (PRO) Pawtucket, RI Holy Family Parish, Pawtucket; Finance Council.
Perrone, Eduard '78 (DET) Detroit, MI Assumption Grotto.
Perrone, James *s.m.a.* '59 (NEW)[M] Tenafly, NJ Society of African Missions, Provincialate, S.M.A. Fathers Retired.
Perry, Carmen J. '77 (SCR) Stroudsburg, PA St. Luke.
Perry, David A. '01 (E) Frenchville, PA St. Mary of the Assumption.
Perry, Francis J. '50 (DUB) Retired.
Perry, Francis '98 (R) Retired.
Perry, Rev. Msgr. John A. '63 (FR) Falmouth, MA St. Patrick's; Diocesan Consultors; Members; Diocesan Pastoral Council; Vicar General.
Perry, John J. '83 (FR) Auditors; Diocesan Director of Cemeteries; Taunton, MA St. Jude the Apostle.
Perry, Lee '75 (VNN) Olympia, WA St. George Byzantine Catholic Church; Pro–Life Coordinator.
Perry, Michael A. '71 (BRK) Brooklyn, NY Our Lady of Refuge.
Perry, Michael E. *o.de.m.* '85 (SP)[N] St. Petersburg, FL St. Peter Nolasco Residence.
Perry, Michael *o.f.m.* '84 (STL)[O] St. Louis Franciscan Friary of St. Anthony of Padua.
Perry, Paul E. '67 (SFR) Kentfield, CA St. Sebastian.
Perry, Richard *s.j.* '70 (HEL) Missoula, MT St. Francis Xavier; Presbyteral Council.
Perry, Robert U. *o.p.* '59 (NO)[P] Metairie, LA Dominican Friars, Southern Dominican Province of St. Martin de Porres.
Perry, Ronald V. *s.j.* '76 (BO)[D] Dorchester, MA Boston College High School.
Persha, Gerald J. *m.m.* '70 (FgM) Maryknoll, NY MARYKNOLL.
Pershe, Joseph N. *s.j.* '66 (MIL)[P] Wauwatosa, WI Jesuit Community at St. Camillus.
Persia, William *c.s.c.* '62 (SP) Dade City, FL St. Rita.
Persich, Roy A. *c.m.* '60 (LA)[P] Santa Barbara, CA St. Mary's Evangelization Center; [V] Santa Barbara, CA St. Mary's Seminary Center Retired.
Persico, Rev. Msgr. Lawrence T. '77 (GBG) New Alexandria, PA St. James; College of Consultors; Vicar General/Chancellor; Defender of Bond; Bishop's Priests Council; Finance Council; Members of the Corporation; Board of Members of the Corporation; Greensburg Catholic Accent and Communications, Inc.; Bishop's Delegate; Vice President; St. Luke Society for Health Care Professionals.
Persico, Philip T. '99 (NY) Valhalla, NY Holy Name of Jesus.
Persing, Charles L. '88 (HBG) Dallastown, PA St. Joseph; Presbyteral Council.
Persinger, Patrick '87 (FRS) Wofford Heights, CA St. Jude.
Perumpally, Mathew '73 (NSH) Dickson, TN St. Christopher.
Perunilam, Thomas V. '64 (MET) Retired.
Perupayikkad, Thomas Babu '99 (RNO) Reno, NV St. Michael's.
Perzan, Stephen B. '73 (PH) Philadelphia, PA St. Helena.
Pesanka, Nicholas A. '75 (PIT)[M] Pittsburgh, PA St. John Vianney Manor; Absent on Sick Leave.
Pesarchick, Robert A. '91 (PH)[A] Wynnewood, PA Theological Seminary of St. Charles Borromeo, Overbrook; Censores Librorum.
Pesaresi, Thomas E. *m.m.* '85 (NY)[EE] Maryknoll Maryknoll Fathers and Brothers.
Pesaresi, Thomas *m.m.* '85 (MO) DEPARTMENT OF VETERANS AFFAIRS HOSPITALS AND CHAPLAINS.
Pescatello, Joseph A. '89 (PRO) Mapleville, RI Our Lady of Good Help; [S] Smithfield, RI Bryant University.
Pesce, John Baptist *c.p.* '51 (HRT)[L] West Hartford Holy Family Monastery/Retreat.
Pesch, Elroy *o.f.m.cap.* '63 (MIL)[P] Mount Calvary, WI St. Lawrence Friary Retired.
Peschel, Roland A. '60 (OM) Retired.
Peschiera, Rev. Msgr. Bruno '54 (SFR) Italian Ministry.
Pesci, Thomas A. *s.j.* '79 (BAL)[D] Baltimore, MD Loyola Blakefield.
Pesek, Anthony '65 (SAT) New Braunfels, TX SS. Peter and Paul.
Pesek, Fred C. '89 (CHI) Lansing, IL St. Ann.
Peshu, Kombo L. '01 (CHI) Bellwood, IL St. Simeon.
Pesola, Joseph G. '97 (IND) Fortville, IN St. Thomas the Apostle.
Pesola, Joseph '97 (LFT) Pendleton, IN Indiana State Reformatory, St. Christopher Chapel; Pendleton, IN Correctional Industrial Complex Ecumenical Chapel.
Pesongco, Rudy '82 (RVC) Garden City, NY St. Anne.
Pestano, Leonardo '94 (SEA) Federal Way, WA St. Vincent De Paul.
Pestun, Aloysius J. *s.d.b.* '59 (SFR) San Francisco, CA Corpus Christi.
Petcavage, Paschal *o.s.b.* '81 (CLV) Broadview Heights, OH Assumption; [N] Cleveland, OH.
Pete, Joseph P. '76 (WIN) Rushford, MN St. Peter's; Rushford, MN St. Joseph's; Deposit and Loan Board; Rushford, MN St. Mary's.
Petekiewicz, Robert P. '91 (LAV) Unassigned.
Peter, Abednecco Wambua *o.c.d.* '09 (MIL)[P] Milwaukee Provincial Offices – Discalced Carmelites.
Peter, Arul Rajan '84 (NOR) Canterbury, CT St. Augustine; Plainfield, CT St. John the Apostle.
Peter, David J. '66 (BUF) Retired.
Peter, Martin A. '67 (IND) Retired.
Peter, Patrick N. '75 (BEL) Breese, IL St. Dominic.
Peter, Valentine J. '59 (OM) Boys Town, NE Immaculate Conception B.V.M.; [I] Boys Town USA.
Petering, Michael '99 (VIC) Edna, TX St. Agnes; Presbyteral Council.
Peterka, Dale C. '68 (CIN) Cincinnati, OH St. John the Evangelist; On Special and Archdiocesan Assignment.
Peterka, Sylvester *c.m.* '76 (BAL) Baltimore, MD St. Cecilia; Baltimore, MD Immaculate Conception; Presbyteral Council.
Peterlini, Luciano *s.x.* '63 (PAT)[N] Wayne Xaverian Missionary Fathers; Wayne, NJ XAVERIAN MISSIONARY FATHERS.
Peterman, Thomas J. '57 (WIL) Retired.
Petermeier, Virgil *o.s.c.* '77 (FgM) Phoenix, AZ CROSIER FATHERS MISSIONS.
Petermeier, Virgil *o.s.c.* '77 (PHX)[F] Crosiers Serving Abroad.
Peters, Aaron *o.s.b.* '77 (KCK)[I] Atchison, KS St. Benedict's Abbey.
Peters, Claudio *f.d.p.* '97 (BO)[S] East Boston, MA Don Orione Nursing Home.
Peters, David L. '58 (SFD) Commission for the Care of Infirm and Retired Priests; Vicar for Clergy Retired.
Peters, Eric '80 (SP) Citrus Springs, FL St. Elizabeth Ann Seton.
Peters, John B. *c.i.c.m.* '53 (ARL)[H] Arlington, VA Missionhurst, C.I.C.M.–Central House and Provincialate.
Peters, John C. '74 (VIC) Hallettsville, TX Sacred Heart; Hallettsville, TX St. Mary; Hallettsville, TX St. John the Baptist; Diocesan Consultors; Hallettsville Deanery; Presbyteral Council; Priests' Personnel Board.
Peters, Rev. Msgr. John '60 (ELP) El Paso, TX St. Luke; Priests' Retirement and Disability Plan.
Peters, Jude *o.c.d.* '89 (MIL)[P] Hubertus, WI Discalced Carmelite Monastery – Holy Hill Basilica of the National Shrine of Mary, Help of Christians, Holy Hill.
Peters, Julian *o.s.b.* '88 (IND)[K] St. Meinrad, IN St. Meinrad Archabbey; [A] St. Meinrad, IN Saint Meinrad School of Theology.
Peters, Kenan *c.p.* '60 (BRK)[T] Jamaica, NY Immaculate Conception Monastery.
Peters, Kevin '90 (Y) Youngstown, OH St. Christine.
Peters, Lyle '96 (DM) Leave of Absence.
Peters, Michael G. '88 (DM) Guthrie Center, IA St. Patrick; Guthrie Center, IA St. Mary; Guthrie Center, IA St. Cecilia.
Peters, Paul R. '62 (DUB) Strawberry Point, IA St. Mary; Volga, IA Sacred Heart; Elkader, IA St. Joseph.
Peters, Stephen '67 (ELP) El Paso, TX Blessed Sacrament; Adjutant Vicars; Judges; [A] El Paso, TX St. Charles Seminary.
Peters, Timothy J. '03 (ORG) Education Leave.
Petersen, Rev. Msgr. E. James '59 (FRS) Diocesan Consultors; Personnel Board Retired.
Petersen, Michael C. '92 (MIL) Fond du Lac, WI Sons of Zebedee: Saints James and John.
Petersen, Todd J. '99 (NU) Lucan, MN Our Lady of Victory; Wabasso, MN St. Mary; Wabasso, MN St. Anne; Wabasso, MN St. Mathias; Priest Personnel Board; Vocations Team; On Special or Other Diocesan Assignment.
Petersen, Vincent *o.f.m.conv.* '85 (LSC) Mesilla Park, NM Shrine and Parish of Our Lady of Guadalupe; [D] Mesilla Park, NM Holy Cross Retreat and Friary.
Peterson, Bradley L. *o.carm.* '92 (PHX) Phoenix, AZ St. Agnes Roman Catholic Parish.
Peterson, Bruce '57 (STP) Bellechester, MN St. Mary; Goodhue, MN St. Columbkill.
Peterson, C. Vincent '74 (SEA) Special Assignment Retired.
Peterson, Casimir M. '47 (BAL)[W] Baltimore, MD Reparation Society of the Immaculate Heart of Mary, Inc. Retired.
Peterson, Charles J. *s.j.* '69 (FBK) Bethel, AK Immaculate Conception Catholic Church Bethel; Presbyteral Council; [E] St. Marys, AK Brother Joe Prince Jesuit Community; Consultors.
Peterson, Dennis M. '06 (MRY) Jolon, CA San Antonio Mission.
Peterson, Eric '89 (MEM) Memphis, TN St. Mary Church.
Peterson, Francis '60 (HON) Retired.
Peterson, Frederick *o.s.b.* '95 (RCK)[G] Aurora, IL Marmion Abbey.
Peterson, Frederick *o.s.b.* '95 (ROM) Aurora, IL St. George.
Peterson, Gerald *g.h.m.* '56 (CIN)[N] Cincinnati Headquarters of Glenmary Home Missioners Retired.
Peterson, Harry *s.d.b.* '61 (FgM) New Rochelle, NY SALESIANS OF DON BOSCO.
Peterson, Rev. Msgr. James W. '47 (E)[L] Erie, PA Maria House Project Retired.
Peterson, Jay H. '78 (GF) Finance Council; Moderator of the Curia; Newspaper; Pastoral Outreach; Vicar General; Priests' Council.
Peterson, Jay H. '78 (GF) Great Falls, MT St. Joseph; Great Falls, MT St. Luke the Evangelist; Black Eagle, MT Most Blessed Sacrament; [J] Great Falls, MT St. Joseph's Education Trust.
Peterson, John P. *y.a.* '89 (ARL)[K] Arlington, VA Marymount University; [L] McLean, VA Youth Apostles Institute, An Association of Christian Faithful.
Peterson, John S. *o.p.* '62 (PRO)[P] Providence St. Thomas Aquinas Priory at Providence College.
Peterson, John W. *o.f.m.* '63 (LSC) Tularosa, NM St. Francis de Paula.
Peterson, Joseph L. '75 (WH) Parkersburg, WV St. Margaret Mary; Diocesan Consultors; Vicars Forane; Presbyteral Council.
Peterson, Leonard N. '67 (PH) Hatfield, PA St. Maria Goretti.
Peterson, Louis P. '74 (BEL) Retired.
Peterson, Maurice F. '87 (YAK) Retired.
Peterson, Michael *o.s.b.* '06 (SFS)[F] Marvin, SD Blue Cloud Abbey.
Peterson, Paul *s.j.* '61 (IND)[D] Indianapolis, IN Brebeuf Jesuit Preparatory School, Inc.
Peterson, Steve *o.s.j.* '04 (FRS) Bakersfield, CA Our Lady of Guadalupe.
Peterson, Steven J. '73 (RVC) Port Washington, NY Our Lady of Fatima.
Peterson, Steven J. '94 (WIN) Spring Valley, MN St. Finbarr's; Spring Valley, MN St. Patrick's; Spring Valley, MN St. Ignatius; Priests' Pension Board.
Peterson, William F. '59 (RCK) Retired.
Peterson, William *g.h.m.* '59 (SAV) Retired.
Peterson, William *c.ss.r.* '67 (SEA)[L] Seattle, WA The Redemptionist Society of Washington; Seattle, WA Sacred Heart of Jesus.
Petilla, Antonio G. '61 (SFR) Daly City, CA Our Lady of Perpetual Help.
Petilla, Rev. Msgr. Cesar '77 (SP) Palm Harbor, FL St. Luke the Evangelist.
Petinge, Roland *o.f.m.* '61 (BO)[U] Andover St. Francis Friary; [W] Andover, MA Franciscan Center – Retreat House.
Petit, Leo *m.s.c.* '50 (ALN)[A] Center Valley, PA Sacred Heart Villa, Missionaries of the Sacred Heart.
Petkash, Donald J. *s.j.* '71 (CLV)[D] Cuyahoga Falls, OH Walsh Jesuit High School.
Petosa, Joseph '55 (SEA) Retired.
Petracca, Anthony '85 (ALT) Absent on Leave.
Petraitis, David *o.s.a.* '79 (CHI)[J] Chicago, IL St.

Anthony Hospital; [N] Chicago, IL St. John Stone Friary.
Petraitis, Donald S. *m.i.c.* '64 (CHI)[N] Chicago, IL Congregation of Marian Fathers of the Immaculate Conception.
Petraitis, Joseph *m.i.c.* (SPR)[H] On Duty Outside of the USA:.
Petrarulo, John D. '53 (PIT) New Castle, PA St. Vitus.
Petras, David M. '67 (PBR)[A] Pittsburgh, PA Byzantine Catholic Seminary of SS. Cyril and Methodius.
Petras, Rev. Archpriest David M. '67 (PRM) On Duty Outside the Diocese.
Petras, Rev. Archpriest David '67 (PRM) Eparchial Consultors; Eparchial Censor; Sacred Liturgy; Building Commission; Cantors' Institute Faculty; Seminary Education Formation Board; Office of Ecumenical Activity.
Petrasic, Martin J. '43 (OM) Retired.
Petrauskas, John *m.i.c.* '43 (NOR)[C] Thompson, CT Congregation of Marians of the Immaculate Conception; [G] Thompson, CT Marian Fathers.
Petri, Gregg *o.f.m.* (PEO) Bloomington, IL St. Mary's.
Petri, Jacob *o.p.* '09 (PRO)[P] Providence St. Thomas Aquinas Priory at Providence College.
Petri, John C. '45 (TR)[N] Trenton, NJ St. Lawrence Rehabilitation Center Retired.
Petrich, John C. '83 (DUL) Duluth, MN St. Margaret Mary; St. Luke's Hospital; Northeast Regional Correctional Institution.
Petrie, Michael J. '87 (MIL) Horicon, WI Sacred Heart.
Petrie, Roderic *o.f.m.* '59 (SP)[N] St. Petersburg St. Anthony Friary.
Petrie, William F. *ss.cc.* '69 (FR)[G] Fairhaven, MA Sacred Hearts Provincial House.
Petrikovic, John J. *o.f.m.cap.* '81 (PIT)[M] Pittsburgh, PA St. Augustine Friary.
Petrillo, Rev. Msgr. Joseph A. '77 (NEW) West Orange, NJ Our Lady of Lourdes; Priest Personnel Policy Board; Office of Clergy Personnel; Archdiocesan Priest Personnel.
Petrillo, Thomas F. '83 (NY) Larchmont, NY SS. John and Paul.
Petrillo, Thomas J. '59 (NEW) Retired.
Petrillo, Thomas '59 (TR) Jackson, NJ Church of St. Monica.
Petrimoulx, Leo *o.f.m.cap.* '66 (MAD)[D] Madison, WI St. Mary's Hospital; [I] Madison, WI San Damiano Friary Retired.
Petringa, Gerard (BO) Belmont, MA St. Luke; Presbyteral Council.
Petrino, Juan Daniel '84 (ORL) Orlando, FL Blessed Trinity.
Petriv, Vasyl '92 (SJP) Parma, OH St. Josaphat Cathedral; Presbyters.
Petriv, Volodymyr '89 (STN) Dearborn Heights, MI Our Lady of Perpetual Help; Detroit; Presbyteral Council.
Petro, Rev. Archpriest John G. '68 (PBR) Beaver, PA Saint Nicholas Chapel; [A] Pittsburgh, PA Byzantine Catholic Seminary of SS. Cyril and Methodius; Presbyteral Council; Diaconate Program.
Petro, Thomas J. '00 (SCR) On Duty Outside the Diocese.
Petro, William '70 (WH) Absent on Sick Leave.
Petrocelli, John N. '71 (PRO) Absent on Leave.
Petron, David Jeffrey '06 (SCL) Carlos, MN St. Nicholas; Osakis, MN Immaculate Conception.
Petron, William G. '57 (DET) Retired.
Petronek, Rev. Msgr. Thomas C. '65 (STU) Retired.
Petronio, Rolando C. '77 (STO) College of Consultors/ Presbyteral Council; Angels Camp, CA St. Patrick Church of Angels Camp (Pastor of).
Petroske, Peter '84 (DET) Dearborn, MI Sacred Heart.
Petroski, Michael A. '00 (LAN) Leslie, MI SS. Cornelius and Cyprian.
Petrosky, Arnold *t.o.r.* '57 (ALT)[G] Loretto, PA St. Francis Friary at Mount Assisi.
Petrovsky, Felix *o.f.m. cap.* '55 (COS)[I] Colorado Springs, CO Catholic Center at the Citadel; [F] Colorado Springs, CO Solanus Casey Friary.
Petrovsky, James F. '68 (GBG) Smock, PA St. Hedwig.
Petroy, Dominic J. *o.s.b.* '87 (GBG)[G] Latrobe, PA Saint Vincent Archabbey.
Petru, Augustine *o.m.i.* '53 (FgM) Washington, DC AMERICAN OBLATE MISSIONS.
Petru, Rev. Msgr. Stanley J. '48 (VIC) La Grange, TX Holy Rosary; La Grange, TX SS. Peter and Paul.
Petrucci, Peter J. *m.m.* '49 (NY)[EE] Retired.
Petrucci, Raymond K. '73 (BGP) Danbury, CT St. Joseph; Danbury, CT Danbury Hospital.
Petruha, Louis *o.f.m.cap.* '65 (HBG) York, PA St. Joseph; Appointed.
Petrunak, William '59 (Y) Struthers, OH Holy Trinity; [F] Warren, OH Notre Dame School, Inc., John F. Kennedy Jr. and Sr. High School.
Petruska, Christopher '59 (PSC) Retired.
Petruska, Gregory '53 (PBR) Retired.
Petruska, William M. '73 (SCR) Military Chaplains.
Petruska, William M. '73 (SD) Presbyteral Council.
Petry, Thomas G. '78 (COL) Columbus, OH Saint Anthony.
Petryshak, Roman '02 (PHU) Plymouth, PA SS. Peter and Paul; Nanticoke, PA Transfiguration of Our Lord.
Petsch, Rev. Msgr. Joseph '50 (SAT)[K] San Antonio, TX Casa De Padres Retired.
Petsche, Daniel *o.s.b.* '67 (KC)[A] Conception, MO Conception Seminary College; Conception, MO.
Petta, Gerard *m.s.a.* '84 (NOR)[G] Cromwell Society of the Missionaries of the Holy Apostles.
Pettei, Thomas G. '86 (BRK) Jamaica, NY St. Nicholas of Tolentine.
Petter, Rev. Msgr. Henry V. '76 (DAL) Deans; Consultors of Pastors; Plano, TX St. Elizabeth Ann Seton; Personnel Board; College of Consultors.
Pettingill, David M. '62 (SFR) San Francisco, CA St. Emydius Retired.
Pettit, Edward G. '51 (PBL) Retired.
Pettit, Joseph H. '56 (HRT) Retired.
Pettit, Joseph '55 (GR) Retired.
Pettke, Lawrence A. '81 (DET) Clinton Twp., MI St. Louis.
Peyton, Mark J. '77 (CLV) Parma, OH St. Francis de Sales.
Peyton, Thomas A. *m.m.* '58 (FgM) Maryknoll, NY MARYKNOLL.
Peyton, Thomas J. '74 (SAV) Tybee Island, GA St. Michael.
Pezzullo, Angelo B. '62 (BRK) Ozone Park, NY Nativity of the Blessed Virgin Mary Retired.
Pezzulo, Neil *g.h.m.* '99 (LR) Waldron, AR Saint Andrew Church; Waldron, AR St. Jude Thaddeus Church.
Pfab, Cletus H. *s.j.* '69 (MIL)[P] Milwaukee, WI Arrupe House Jesuit Community.
Pfaff, Aaron '96 (IND) Leopold, IN St. Augustine; St. Croix, IN Holy Cross; St. Meinrad, IN St. Martin of Tours.
Pfaff, Joseph A. '75 (BRK) East Glendale, NY Sacred Heart.
Pfalzer, Miles *o.f.m.* '47 (ALN)[K] Easton, PA St. Francis Friary.
Pfander, Timothy '04 (BIR) Winfield, AL Holy Spirit.
Pfannenstiel, Donald F. '75 (SAL) WaKeeney, KS Christ the King Parish; Board of Trustees.
Pfannenstiel, John *o.f.m.cap.* '82 (PIT)[Q] Pittsburgh, PA The Capuchin Franciscan Volunteer Corps, Inc.; Pittsburgh, PA.
Pfannenstiel, Jonn *o.f.m.cap.* '82 (PIT)[M] Pittsburgh, PA St. Augustine Friary.
Pfannenstiel, Richard '93 (NEW) South Orange, NJ Our Lady of Sorrows.
Pfau, Bernard '65 (FAR) New Rockford, ND Sts. Peter & Paul Church of McHenry; New Rockford, ND St. John's Church of New Rockford.
Pfeffer, Rev. Msgr. Edward B. '56 (DM) Judges Retired.
Pfeifer, Francis *o.m.i.* '59 (FgM) Washington, DC AMERICAN OBLATE MISSIONS.
Pfeifer, Francis *o.m.i.* '59 (SAT)[K] San Antonio, TX Oblate Madonna Residence.
Pfeifer, Frederick A. '93 (NEW) East Orange, NJ Saint Joseph Parish; Newark, NJ Sacred Heart.
Pfeifer, James *o.m.i.* '51 (BWN) Mission, TX Our Lady of Guadalupe.
Pfeifer, John M. '65 (BIS) Watford City, ND Epiphany; Watford City, ND Our Lady of Consolation.
Pfeifer, John M. '07 (CLV) Concord Twp., OH St. Gabriel.
Pfeiffer, David L. *m.m.* '66 (FgM) Maryknoll, NY MARYKNOLL.
Pfeiffer, Rev. Msgr. Joseph C. '58 (BRK) Howard Beach, NY St. Helen Retired.
Pfeiffer, Mark S. '82 (LIN) Grant, NE Mother of Sorrows; Wallace, NE St. Mary's.
Pfeiffer, Matthew E. '09 (CLV) Akron, OH St. Sebastian.
Pfeiffer, Robert F. '61 (CLV) Medina, OH Holy Martyrs; Judges in Second Instance Retired.
Pfeiffer, Robert F. (Y) Judges.
Pfister, John F. '66 (FTW) Huntington, IN St. Mary; Budget Committee.
Pfister, John '66 (FTW) Presbyteral Council.
Pfister, Neal A. '90 (DEN) Denver, CO Church of the Good Shepherd.
Pfisterer, Robert *o.f.m.* '51 (LA)[P] Los Angeles, CA St. Joseph Friary Retired.
Pfleger, Michael L. '75 (CHI) Chicago, IL St. Sabina.
Pfleger, Phillip C. '79 (TR) Marlton, NJ St. Isaac Jogues.
Pflomm, Rev. Msgr. Peter J. '70 (RVC) Seaford, NY Maria Regina; Senate of Priests (Presbyteral Council/ College of Consultors); Seaford Deanery; Priests' Personnel Assignment Board.
Pflumm, Robert '60 (KCK) Retired.
Pfnausch, Edward G. '68 (HRT) North Haven, CT St. Frances Cabrini.
Pfundstein, George A. '63 (BRK) Flushing, NY St. Ann Retired.
Phalan, James H. *c.s.c.* '92 (FR)[A] North Easton, MA Holy Cross Fathers Religious; [M] North Easton, MA Holy Cross Family Ministries.
Phalen, John L. '59 (DET) Retired.
Phalen, John P. *c.s.c.* '74 (ALB)[R] North Easton, MA Crusade for Family Prayer, Inc.
Phalen, John P. *c.s.c.* '74 (FR)[M] North Easton, MA Holy Cross Family Ministries; Prov. Councilors:; Taunton, MA St. Mary's.
Pham, Anh Tuan *c.ss.r.* '99 (GAL) Houston, TX Holy Ghost.
Pham, Ansgar *s.d.d.* '05 (DAL) Grand Prairie, TX St. Joseph Vietnamese Parish.
Pham, Anthony Tam H. (GAL) Houston, TX St. Vincent de Paul.
Pham, Bartholomew Dat H. *s.d.d.* '03 (P) Portland, OR Our Lady of Lavang.
Pham, Bryan Viet-Hung *s.j.* '04 (P)[L] Portland Jesuit Provincial Office (Society of Jesus, Oregon Prov.).
Pham, Charles *c.m.c.* '05 (SAC) Sacramento, CA Vietnamese Martyrs Church.
Pham, Chau *s.v.d.* '95 (FTW) Fort Wayne, IN St. Patrick.
Pham, Christopher Tuan '07 (ORG) Los Alamitos, CA St. Hedwig.
Pham, Cuong M. '01 (BRK) Graduate Studies; Queens Village, NY Our Lady of Lourdes.
Pham, Doan The '98 (LA) El Monte, CA Nativity.
Pham, Dominic Chinh *i.c.m.* '95 (DAL) Dallas, TX St. Peter Vietnamese.
Pham, Dominic Thao '98 (ALN)[P] Bath, PA Blue Army of Our Lady of Fatima; Emmaus, PA St. Ann; Blue Army of Our Lady of Fatima.
Pham, Dominic *l.c.* '02 (ATL)[L] Norcross, GA Home and Family, Inc.; [G] Alpharetta, GA Norcross Pastoral Center, Inc.
Pham, Dominic *c.ss.r.* '05 (LA)[P] Baldwin Park Vietnamese Redemptorist Mission.
Pham, Francis Han *c.ss.r.* '93 (SAT) San Antonio, TX St. Gerard Majella; San Antonio, TX Vietnamese Martyrs Catholic Center; [L] San Antonio, TX Redemptorists of Texas–San Antonio #1.
Pham, Hanh Duc *s.j.* '08 (OAK)[M] Berkeley, CA Jesuit Fathers and Brothers.
Pham, Hung Q. '89 (WCH) Wichita, KS St. Anthony.
Pham, Huy (John) Quoc '02 (PEO) Lincoln, IL Holy Family.
Pham, James Chau *c.ss.r.* '96 (BLX) Biloxi, MS Church of the Vietnamese Martyrs.
Pham, Rev. Msgr. James Ninh Van '67 (P) Retired.
Pham, Joseph Hung '70 (SFR) San Mateo, CA St. Gregory.
Pham, Joseph Luong '01 (CAM) On Leave of Absence.
Pham, Joseph Luong T. '98 (CAM) Atlantic City, NJ St. Michael's Church, Atlantic City, N.J.; Atlantic City, NJ Our Lady, Star of the Sea, Atlantic City, N.J.; Atlantic South Deanery; Vocation Advisory Board; Ethnic Ministries.
Pham, Rev. Msgr. Joseph Thang '85 (RIC) Richmond, VA Church of the Vietnamese Martyrs.
Pham, Joseph The *c.ss.r.* '98 (STL)[O] St. Louis, MO Redemptorist Fathers.
Pham, Joseph '70 (BRK) Long Island City, NY Our Lady of Mount Carmel.
Pham, Khoi '94 (STO) Modesto, CA Our Lady of Fatima Church (Pastor of).
Pham, Le–Minh '93 (AUS) Cedar Park, TX St. Margaret Mary; Associate Directors.
Pham, Linh *s.v.d.* '09 (DUB)[B] Epworth, IA Divine Word College.
Pham, M. Anthony Hanh Si *o.cist.* '04 (SB)[I] Lucerne Valley, CA The Cistercian Congregation of the Holy Family, St. Joseph Monastery.
Pham, Marty '04 (GAL) Lake Jackson, TX St. Michael.
Pham, Michael '99 (SD) San Diego, CA Holy Family; Clergy Personnel Board.
Pham, Minn J. *c.m.* '90 (LA) Los Angeles, CA St. Vincent De Paul.
Pham, Peter Nghi Duc *s.o.l.t.* '99 (CC) Rockport, TX St. Peter's Parish.
Pham, Peter T. '98 (CHL) Charlotte, NC St. John Neumann.
Pham, Peter *s.o.l.t.* '99 (CC)[G] Robstown, TX Society of Our Lady of the Most Holy Trinity.
Pham, Quyet A. '04 (ALN) Reading, PA St. Paul.
Pham, Robert Tan *s.j.* '04 (ORG) Newport Beach, CA Our Lady of Mount Carmel.
Pham, Thang John '07 (BLX) Vancleave, MS Holy Spirit Catholic Church.
Pham, Thanh Q. '07 (CAM) Haddon Heights, NJ Church of St. Rose, Haddon Heights, N.J.
Pham, Thi *s.v.d.* '02 (FgM) Techny, IL.
Pham, Thi *s.c.j.* '07 (MIL)[P] Milwaukee, WI SCJ Community; [P] Hales Corners, WI Priests of the Sacred Heart.
Pham, Thinh Duc '02 (LA) Graduate Studies.
Pham, Thomas *c.ss.r.* '09 (STP) Brooklyn Center, MN St. Alphonsus.
Pham, Thuy (RIC) Retired.
Pham, Tin Cosmas Kim '95 (GAL) Brazoria, TX St. Joseph on the Brazos.
Pham, Tri '04 (PMB) Vero Beach, FL St. Helen.
Pham, Tuan Anh '99 (NO) Reserve, LA St. Peter.
Pham, Rev. Msgr. Tuan Joseph '94 (ORG) Director of Clergy Personnel; Secretary to the Bishop; Adjutant Judicial Vicars; Clergy Personnel Board; Staff; Staff;

Staff; Council of Priests; Special Assignment; Building and Renovation Committee of the Liturgical Commission.
Pham, Tuan Ngoc '88 (ORG) Westminster, CA Blessed Sacrament.
Pham, Tuan '94 (ORG) Liturgical Commission.
Pham, Vincent Hung '97 (ORG) Orange, CA La Purisima.
Pham, Vincent '97 (ORG) Clergy Personnel Board.
Pham Kim Ban, Albert M. *c.m.c.* '03 (SPC)[F] Carthage, MO Congregation of the Mother Coredemptrix, United States Assumption Province.
Pham Minh Van, Bartholomew *c.m.c.* '77 (SPC)[F] Carthage, MO Congregation of the Mother Coredemptrix, United States Assumption Province.
Pham Van Lan, Augustine '63 (CLV) Cleveland, OH St. Boniface; Translators.
Pham Van Tue, Joseph '73 (NO) Marrero, LA St. Agnes Le Thi Thanh.
Phan, An Duy '06 (OM) Omaha, NE St. Leo.
Phan, Anthony Lam '62 (OAK) Retired.
Phan, Cho Dink Peter '72 (DAL) On Duty Outside the Diocese.
Phan, Dominic T.H. '09 (LIN) Hastings, NE St. Michael's; Advocates.
Phan, Dominic '70 (BLX) Retired.
Phan, John '05 (JOL) Downers Grove, IL St. Mary of Gostyn.
Phan, Joseph Duong '93 (OAK) Apostleship of the Sea; San Leandro, CA Assumption of the Blessed Virgin Mary.
Phan, Joseph Son Thanh '03 (GAL) Damon, TX Sts. Cyril and Methodius; Needville, TX St. Michael.
Phan, Joseph '93 (OAK) Presbyteral Council.
Phan, Khoi '09 (ORG) Buena Park, CA St. Pius V.
Phan, Loc D. '02 (GAL) Houston, TX Vietnamese Martyrs.
Phan, Long N. '09 (OKL) Edmond, OK St. John the Baptist.
Phan, Minh Cong '97 (NO) Graduate Studies.
Phan, Ngoan '07 (SFR) San Rafael, CA St. Raphael.
Phan, Nguyen Van *c.ss.r.* '93 (LA)[P] Baldwin Park, CA Vietnamese Redemptorist Mission.
Phan, Paul Cuong '99 (SJ) San Jose, CA St. Victor.
Phan, Philip S. '85 (NY) New York, NY Guardian Angel.
Phan, Phu T. '92 (AMA) Judicial Vicar; Canyon, TX St. Ann's.
Phan, Phu '92 (AMA) Ex Officio; Vicar General; Ex Officio; College of Consultors; Vocation Development Team.
Phan, Vincent Huo '95 (MOB) Mobile, AL St. Ignatius.
Phan Bao Luyen, Francis Xavier (SAC)[I] Walnut Grove, CA Monastery of Chau Son Sacramento.
Phat, Rev. Msgr. Peter Tran Van '67 (NY) Otisville, NY Holy Name.
Phelan, Cornelius Noel '59 (LA) Los Angeles, CA St. Basil's Retired.
Phelan, Edward '63 (SFR) Novato, CA St. Anthony of Padua Retired.
Phelan, Nicholas '52 (SAC) Grass Valley, CA St. Patrick Retired.
Phelan, Thomas E. '76 (BEA) Diocesan College of Consultors; Orange, TX St. Francis of Assisi; Presbyteral Council.
Phelan, Thomas '53 (SEA) Retired.
Phelan, Walter M. '49 (MO) DEPARTMENT OF VETERANS AFFAIRS HOSPITALS AND CHAPLAINS Retired.
Phelps, Anthony '08 (LUB) Lubbock, TX Cathedral Christ the King.
Phelps, John *c.ss.r.* '68 (STL)[O] Liguori, MO Liguori Mission House/Redemptorists.
Phelps, Lawrence J. *o.s.b.* '63 (NO)[P] St. Benedict, LA St. Joseph Abbey.
Phelps, Robert *o.f.m.cap.* '66 (RVC) East Patchogue, NY St. Joseph the Worker.
Philbin, Patrick B. *s.m.* '72 (ORG)[L] Orange, CA House of Prayer for Priests; [M] Irvine, CA U.C.I. Interfaith Center.
Philbin, Patrick '72 (ORG) Special Assignment.
Philbin, Patrick *s.m.* '52 (STL)[O] St. Louis Marianists, Province of the United States (Society of Mary).
Philen, Michael *c.m.f.* '99 (LA)[V] Rancho Dominguez, CA Dominguez Seminary Inc.; Veterans Affairs Medical Center.
Philibert, Paul J. *o.p* '63 (R)[F] Raleigh, NC Dominican Priory.
Philion, Richard *o.m.i.* '61 (BWN) Roma, TX Our Lady of Refuge.
Philip, Thomas M. '98 (LA)[J] Lynwood, CA St. Francis Medical Center.
Philiposki, Richard *s.ch.* (TOL) Toledo, OH St. Adalbert; Toledo, OH St. Hedwig.
Philippe, Jean Claude Jean *c.m.* (PCE) Ponce, PR San Vicente–Cantera.
Philippe, Jean–Rony '99 (BGP) Haitian American Catholic Center of Greater Stamford; [W] Stamford, CT Haitian American Catholic Center.
Philips, Ligory Johnson '91 (SYM) West Hempstead, NY St. Mary Syro–Malabar Catholic Church.
Philipsen, Todd K. '89 (GI) Grand Island, NE Blessed Sacrament.
Philius, Vilaire '09 (ORL)[A] Orlando, FL Bishop Moore Catholic High School Inc.; Winter Park, FL St. Margaret Mary.
Phillip, Alan *c.p.* '67 (LA)[P] Sierra Madre, CA Passionist Residence.
Phillippino, Michael L. '79 (NOR) Middletown, CT St. John; Members; Seminarian Advisory Board; Deans.
Phillips, Ambrose *t.o.r.* '71 (WDC)[N] Washington, DC St. Louis Friary.
Phillips, Benet C. *o.s.b.* '92 (MAN)[K] Manchester, NH St. Anselm Abbey.
Phillips, C. Frank *c.r.* '77 (CHI) Chicago, IL St. John Cantius; [P] Chicago, IL Canons Regular of Saint John Cantius.
Phillips, Christopher G. '83 (SAT) San Antonio, TX Our Lady of the Atonement Catholic Church.
Phillips, Clyde *m.m.* '78 (FgM)[EE] New York, NY Maryknoll House; Maryknoll, NY MARYKNOLL.
Phillips, Edward J. *m.m.* '74 (NY)[EE] Maryknoll Maryknoll Fathers and Brothers.
Phillips, Gene D. *s.j.* '65 (CHI)[N] Evanston, IL Canisius House.
Phillips, Rev. Msgr. George M. '40 (OG) Ogdensburg, NY Notre Dame; Ogdensburg, NY Retired.
Phillips, Glenn '66 (CHI)[N] Chicago, IL St. Peter's Friary.
Phillips, Gregory *o.s.b.* '01 (WOR)[O] Petersham, MA St. Mary's Monastery.
Phillips, John M. '87 (STA) Gainesville, FL Holy Faith; Priests' Spirituality Committee.
Phillips, John '55 (ROC) Retired.
Phillips, Joseph H. '68 (SY) Special Assignment; [L] Syracuse, NY Family Life Education; Management Team; Family Life Education; Propagation of the Faith.
Phillips, Kenneth G. '91 (BIS) Mandan, ND Christ the King; Priests' Benefit Association; Priests' Personnel Board.
Phillips, Louis J. '81 (PRT) Portland, ME Cathedral of the Immaculate Conception; Portland, ME St. Louis; Portland, ME St. Peter's; Portland, ME St. Christopher's; Portland, ME Sacred Heart/St. Dominic.
Phillips, Louis J. '81 (PRT) Members.
Phillips, Rev. Msgr. Michael J. '60 (BRK) Retired.
Phillips, Michael T. '69 (DAV) Iowa City, IA St. Wenceslaus; Priests Eucharistic League.
Phillips, Randall '83 (DET) Sterling Heights, MI St. Blase.
Phillips, Randy '97 (SFS) Ipswich, SD Holy Cross; Ipswich, SD Our Lady of Perpetual Help.
Phillips, Rene F. *o.f.m.* '56 (NY)[EE] New York Franciscan Friars, Holy Name Province.
Phillips, Robert *s.j.* '72 (BAL)[M] Towson, MD St. Joseph Medical Center, Inc.
Phillips, Rev. Msgr. Thomas L. '71 (BAL) Baltimore, MD St. Gabriel; Presbyteral Council.
Phillips, Walter W. '55 (GI) Retired.
Phillipson, David '03 (SFE) On Duty Outside the Archdiocese.
Philominsamy, Michaelraj '91 (SR) Fort Bragg, CA Our Lady of Good Counsel; Clergy Personnel Committee; Parish Priest Consultors; Clergy Formation.
Phinn, Paul A. '57 (BO) Senior Priests. Retired.
Phipps, Charles T. *s.j.* '59 (SJ)[B] Santa Clara, CA Jesuit Community.
Phipps, Ricardo M. '02 (JKS) Jackson, MS St. Mary; Jackson, MS Christ the King; Co Chairmen; [H] Jackson, MS Jackson State University Newman Center; Defenders of the Bond.
Pho, Luan *o.p.* '08 (ARL) Arlington, VA Holy Martyrs of Vietnam.
Phongo, Jean–Marie Mvumbi *c.i.c.m.* '03 (SAT) San Antonio, TX Divine Providence.
Phuc, Tran Dinh *c.ss.r.* '56 (LA)[P] Baldwin Park Vietnamese Redemptorist Mission.
Phung, Chi Peter '90 (TLS) Henryetta, OK St. Michael; Henryetta, OK St. Stephen's.
Phung, Joseph P. V. '00 (DAV) Mount Pleasant, IA St. Alphonsus.
Phung, Le Quang *c.ss.r.* '69 (LA)[P] Baldwin Park Vietnamese Redemptorist Mission.
Phung, Vincent '96 (DEN) Englewood, CO Holy Name.
Phuoc Hoa, Dang *c.ss.r.* '03 (LA)[P] Baldwin Park Vietnamese Redemptorist Mission.
Phuong, Rev. Msgr. Francis '66 (ATL) Vicars for Clergy.
Piacentini, David A. '71 (PRO) North Providence, RI St. Lawrence.
Piano, Timothy '77 (MIA) Absent on Leave.
Piansay, Victor '64 (FRS) Riverdale, CA St. Ann.
Piasecki, Adam *c.r.* (CHI) Chicago, IL St. Hyacinth Basilica.
Piasecki, Timothy '73 (RCK) Aurora, IL St. Mary.
Piasta, Chris *o.f.m.* '95 (BRK) Douglaston, NY St. Anastasia.
Piatt, Charles E. *s.t.* '03 (SB) Riverside, CA Our Lady of Perpetual Help.
Piazza, Rev. Msgr. Benjamin A. '49 (NEW) Caldwell, NJ St. Aloysius Retired.
Picado, Rodrigo '71 (NO) On Duty Outside the Archdiocese.
Picard, Daniel '79 (LAF) Lawtell, LA St. Bridget.
Picard, Rev. Msgr. Michael C. '66 (PH) Newtown, PA St. Andrew; Council of Priests.
Picard, Raymond '65 (PRT) Yarmouth, ME Sacred Heart.
Picardi, Aubert Marie *o.f.m.* '62 (BO)[U] Boston, MA St. Christopher Friary.
Picardi, John M. '83 (BO) Unassigned.
Picarella, Dale '84 (BAL) Linthicum Heights, MD St. Philip Neri.
Picariello, Anthony R. *s.j.* '80 (BO)[U] Weston, MA Campion Health Center, Inc.
Picciano, Rev. Msgr. Daniel A. '71 (RVC) Lake Ronkonkoma, NY St. Elizabeth Ann Seton.
Piccinini, Claudio *c.p.* '72 (MET)[I] South River Passionist Provincial Office.
Piccinino, Corey V. '86 (BGP) Bethel, CT St. Mary.
Piccola, Michael J. '78 (SCR) Pittston, PA Church of the Holy Redeemer; West Pittston, PA Immaculate Conception.
Piccoli, Gino L. *o.f.m.* '65 (TUC) San Carlos, AZ San Carlos Apache Roman Catholic Community – San Carlos.
Piccolomini, Rev. Msgr. Rocco M. '85 (WOR) Diocesan College of Consultors; Worcester State Hospital; Worcester, MA Our Lady of Mt. Carmel and St. Ann.
Pichard, Rev. Msgr. Lawrence '73 (DAL) Consultors of Pastors; Frisco, TX St. Francis of Assisi.
Pichardo, Nelson '95 (NY) New York, NY St. Gregory.
Piche, Donald J. '77 (STP) Maple Grove, MN St. Joseph the Worker.
Piche, Marc A. '68 (BO) Newburyport, MA Immaculate Conception; Presbyteral Council.
Pichette, Rev. Msgr. Fernand L. '58 (MAN) Retired.
Pichiamuthu, Victor Paulraj *m.s.f.x.* '99 (BIS) Foxholm, ND St. Mary; Glenburn, ND St. Philomena; Minot, ND St. Leo.
Picinic, John P. *s.a.c.* '05 (CAM) Woodstown, NJ St. Joseph's Catholic Church, Woodstown, N.J.
Pick, Anthony '67 (SC) Coon Rapids, IA Annunciation; Dedham, IA St. Joseph's.
Pick, Edward '60 (VEN) Retired.
Pickard, William B. '76 (SCR) Scranton, PA Saint John Neumann, Scranton; [J] Scranton, PA St. Joseph's Center.
Pickard, Rev. Msgr. William M. '54 (GAL) Defenders of the Bond Retired.
Pickarts, Bernard J. '55 (MAD) Retired.
Pickens, David '09 (PAT) Little Falls, NJ Our Lady of the Holy Angels.
Pickett, James B. '61 (OAK) Retired.
Pickett, Robert T. '55 (TLS) Retired.
Pico, Fernando *s.j.* '71 (SJN)[H] Hato Rey, PR Jesuit Community – Casa Claver.
Picone, Alfonso '00 (NEW) On Duty Outside the Archdiocese.
Picone, Alfonso '00 (BGP) Bridgeport, CT St. Raphael.
Picos, Martin '06 (SLC) Ogden, UT Saint Joseph LLC 230.
Picton, James D. '75 (SEA) Bellevue, WA St. Madeleine Sophie; Presbyteral Council.
Picton, Thomas D. *c.ss.r.* '71 (DEN)[N] Denver, CO The Redemptorists/Denver Province.
Picton, Thomas *c.ss.r.* '71 (FgM) Silver Spring, MD; Denver, CO Denver Province; Consultants.
Piderit, John J. *s.j.* '71 (CHI)[W] Chicago, IL The Catholic Education Institute.
Piderit, John J. *s.j.* '71 (NY) Bronx, NY St. Anthony.
Pidgeon, John '87 (PH) Philadelphia, PA Epiphany of Our Lord.
Pieber, Carl L. *c.m.* '80 (PH)[CC] Philadelphia, PA The Central Association of the Miraculous Medal; Philadelphia, PA Immaculate Conception; [B] Philadelphia, PA St. Vincent's Seminary.
Piechocki, Rev. Msgr. Bruce '84 (FTW) Fort Wayne, IN Our Lady of Good Hope; On Special Assignment; Presbyteral Council; Judicial Vicar; Pro–Synodal Judges; Consultors.
Piechocki, Raymond S. '47 (ALB) Retired.
Piechota, Lech '89 (SFR) On Duty Outside the Archdiocese.
Pieczara, Stanislaw '76 (MO) Air Force Chaplains.
Pieczara, Stanislaw *s.d.s.* '76 (GRY)[H] Merrillville, IN Salvatorian Fathers (Society of the Divine Savior).
Pied, Wilfrid L. '51 (BO) Senior Priests. Retired.
Piedra, Ruskin *c.ss.r.* '60 (BRK) Brooklyn, NY Our Lady of Perpetual Help Basilica.
Piedrahita, Jose Gabriel *m.x.y.* '87 (NY) New York, NY St. Benedict the Moor; New York, NY Sacred Heart of Jesus.
Piekarczyk, Marian A. *s.d.s.* '80 (MO) DEPARTMENT OF VETERANS AFFAIRS HOSPITALS AND CHAPLAINS; Army Reserve Chaplains.
Piekarczyk, Marian *s.d.s.* '80 (SAT) San Antonio, TX Our Lady of Sorrows; San Antonio, TX Methodist Hospital.
Piekarski, Joseph J. '86 (WIL) Elkton, MD Immaculate Conception; Associate Directors.
Pieniazek, Tadeusz *s.d.s.* '92 (NEW) Westfield, NJ St. Helen.
Pienkos, Zbigniew *c.ss.r.* (CHI) Cicero, IL St. Mary of Czestochowa.

Pienkowski, Marek *o.p.* '80 (NY)[II] New York, NY Polish Dominicans, Inc.; New York, NY Notre Dame; [HH] New York, NY Columbia University.
Pienta, Robert J. '99 (LAN) Jackson, MI St. Joseph.
Pientek, Placid *o.s.b.* '44 (CLV)[N] Cleveland, OH.
Pieper, Herbert *s.m.* '38 (SAT)[K] San Antonio, TX Marianist Residence: Skilled Nursing.
Pieper, Rev. Msgr. James E. '57 (STL) St. Louis, MO St. Clement.
Pieper, Theodore X. '62 (STL) Cadet, MO St. Joachim; Cadet, MO St. Joseph.
Piepmeyer, Ronald J. '97 (CIN) Morrow, OH St. Philip the Apostle.
Pierce, Bradley *m.s.a.* '83 (NOR)[A] Cromwell, CT Holy Apostles College and Seminary; [G] Cromwell, CT Society of the Missionaries of the Holy Apostles.
Pierce, Brian J. *o.p.* '83 (FgM) Metairie, LA St. Martin de Porres Province (Southern Dominican Province).
Pierce, Edward J. '72 (SFS) Aberdeen, SD Sacred Heart.
Pierce, James L. *s.j.* '77 (NY)[EE] New York, NY Xavier Jesuit Community.
Pierce, John J. *o.f.m.* '63 (PAT)[N] Butler, NJ St. Anthony Friary.
Pierce, Joseph B. '92 (WDC) Cheverly, MD St. Ambrose.
Pierce, Larry E. '58 (SAL) Retired.
Pierce, Mark R. '81 (LC) La Crosse, WI Roncalli Newman Parish; [K] La Crosse, WI Roncalli Newman Parish; Newman Campus Ministry; Appointed Members.
Pierce, William C. '71 (CAM) Millville, NJ The Church of St. John Bosco, Millville, N.J.
Pierceall, Patrick L. '69 (JC) Retired.
Pierini, Raymond G. *m.m.* '87 (NY)[EE].
Pierino, Vicente '64 (SJN) On Duty Outside the Archdiocese.
Pierjok, Peter Augustine H. *o.s.b.* '88 (GBG) Whitney, PA St. Cecilia; Whitney, PA Sacred Heart; [G] Latrobe, PA Saint Vincent Archabbey.
Piermarini, Rev. Msgr. Louis R. '69 (WOR) Oxford, MA St. Roch.
Pierog, Stanislaw '76 (VEN) Arcadia, FL St. Paul.
Pieroni, Edward L. '85 (PRO) Providence, RI St. Raymond; Providence, RI Miriam Hospital.
Pierre, Adrien *o.m.i.* '98 (BRK) Brooklyn, NY Our Lady of Refuge.
Pierre, Andre *o.f.m.cap.* (WDC) Washington, DC Shrine of the Sacred Heart.
Pierre, Brunache Michel (BRK) Brooklyn, NY St. Gregory the Great.
Pierre, Darren *o.p.* '04 (CIN) Cincinnati, OH St. Gertrude; [N] Cincinnati, OH St. Gertrude Priory.
Pierre, Jaccius Jean '01 (NY) White Plains, NY St. John the Evangelist.
Pierre, Jean Y. (BRK) Far Rockaway, NY St. Mary Star of the Sea and St. Gertrude.
Pierre, Rev. Msgr. Jean '88 (MIA) Miami, FL St. James; Consultors; Priests' Personnel Board; Ministry to Cultural Groups (Non–Hispanic Ethnicities); Haitians; Native Americans; Archdiocesan Vocations Review Board; Pontifical Mission Societies.
Pierre, Kenneth J. '63 (STP) Retired.
Pierre, Lucien E. '07 (MIA) Cutler Bay, FL Our Lady of the Holy Rosary.
Pierre, Roger P. '63 (STP) White Bear Lake, MN St. Mary of the Lake.
Pierre–Jules, Oswald Pierre *s.s.j.* '06 (WDC) Washington, DC Our Lady of Perpetual Help.
Pierre–Louis, Andre Dumarsais '01 (PMB)[B] West Palm Beach, FL Cardinal Newman High School, Inc.; West Palm Beach, FL St. Ann.
Pierro, Sebastian C. '82 (BUF) Lewiston, NY St. Peter.
Pierse, Rev. Msgr. James J. '44 (ORG) Seal Beach, CA Holy Family Retired.
Pierson, Robert *o.s.b.* '84 (SCL)[I] Collegeville, MN St. John's Abbey, of the Order of St. Benedict.
Pierzchala, Ireneusz '08 (NEW) Saddle Brook, NJ St. Philip the Apostle.
Pietramale, John L. '92 (OM) Omaha, NE St. Pius X; Age Groups.
Pietras, Robert E. '62 (JOL)[K] Naperville, IL St. John Vianney Villa Retired.
Pietraszko, Andrzej '03 (MIA) Sunny Isles Beach, FL St. Mary Magdalen; Miami, FL St. Brendan.
Pietropaoli, David '84 (BAL) Priests Sick or Absent.
Pietropinto, Joseph P. '70 (NEW) Secaucus, NJ Immaculate Conception.
Pietrowski, Stephen J. '92 (RVC) Leave of Absence.
Pietrucha, Edward S. *c.s.p.* '57 (TUC) Tucson, AZ Saint Cyril of Alexandria Roman Catholic Parish – Tucson Retired.
Pietrzak, Bernard J. '81 (CHI) Barrington, IL St. Anne; Deans.
Pietrzyk, Joseph Pius *o.p.* '08 (COL) Zanesville, OH St. Thomas Aquinas.
Pietrzyk, Paul J. *o.de.m.* '02 (CLV) Cleveland, OH St. Rocco.
Pietrzyk, Paul *o.de.m.* '02 (CLV) Lutheran Medical Center.
Pifher, Cletus *o.f.m.conv.* '64 (SAV) Brunswick, GA St. Francis Xavier.
Pifher, William A. '94 (TOL) Monroeville, OH St. Joseph; Monroeville, OH St. Alphonsus Liguori.
Piga, Stephen M. '02 (TR) Freehold, NJ St. Rose of Lima.
Piggford, George *c.s.c.* '05 (FR)[A] North Easton, MA Holy Cross Fathers Religious; [A] North Easton, MA Stonehill College.
Pighini, Richard J. *c.s.v.* '85 (CHI) Arlington Heights, IL; [N] Arlington Heights Viatorian Province Center–Clerics of St. Viator.
Pighini, Richard *c.s.v.* '85 (JOL) Bourbonnais, IL Maternity of the Blessed Virgin Mary.
Pignato, David A. '01 (FR) Graduate Studies.
Pignato, Salvatore A. '68 (PSC) Orlando, FL St. Nicholas of Myra; Vocations; Retirement Plan Board; Presbyteral Council.
Pigott, Edward L. *s.j.* '68 (CIN)[F] Cincinnati, OH St. Xavier High School; [N] Cincinnati, OH Jesuit Community at St. Xavier High School.
Pijnenburg, Carlos *o.p.* '54 (SJN)[E] Bayamon, PR Hospital Hermanos Melendez.
Pijoan, L. Adrian M. Figuerola '71 (NO) Retired.
Pikula, Zygmunt '55 (NEW) Retired.
Pikulinski, Jerzy *o.f.m.* '01 (NEW) Wyckoff, NJ St. Elizabeth.
Pilaczynski, John E. *o.m.i.* '58 (STP)[K] St. Paul, MN Oblate Residence.
Pilande, Benildo M. '02 (SFR) San Francisco, CA St. John the Evangelist.
Pilarski, Bernard '56 (DET) Wayne, MI Oakwood Annapolis Hospital; Garden City, MI Garden City Hospital.
Pilarski, Chester J. '50 (SAG) Retired.
Pilarski, Peter R. '59 (PIT) Plum, PA St. Januarius.
Pilarz, Scott R. *s.j.* '92 (SCR)[C] Scranton, PA The University of Scranton.
Pilat, Edmund S. '56 (SY) Retired.
Pilato, Sabato A. '92 (LA) Superintendent Secondary Schools; Advisory Members to the Commission.
Pilato, Sal A. '92 (LA) Members; Inglewood, CA St. John Chrysostom.
Pilatowski, Augustine *o.f.m.conv.* '59 (HRT)[J] New Britain, CT St. Lucian's Residence, Inc.; [L] New Britain, CT Conventual Franciscans.
Pilatowski, Eugene L. '60 (NOR) District Moderators; Norwich, CT St. Joseph Retired.
Pilcher, Gregory *o.s.b.* '78 (LR) El Dorado, AR Holy Redeemer.
Pilcher, John '99 (KCK) Wamego, KS Holy Family; Wamego, KS St. Joseph; Paxico, KS Sacred Heart; Wamego, KS St. Bernard's.
Pileggi, Anthony M. '07 (WIL) Berlin, MD St. John Neumann Roman Catholic Church.
Pileggi, Anthony '81 (KC) On Duty Outside the Diocese.
Pileggi, Francis J. *o.s.f.s.* '61 (WIL)[B] Wilmington, DE Salesianum School.
Piletic, William R. *c.m.* '77 (LA)[P] Los Angeles, CA Amat Residence 1.
Pilger, G. Richard *i.c.* '79 (SP) Seminole, FL Blessed Sacrament.
Pilgram, Paul C. *s.j.* '70 (STL)[O] St. Louis, MO Ignatius House.
Pilipie, John P. '82 (PAT) Ogdensburg, NJ St. Thomas of Aquin; Deans.
Pilla, P. Carl '54 (SY)[Q] Syracuse, NY Tommy Coyne Residence Dillon Hall Retired.
Pilla, Raju '91 (PH) Penndel, PA Our Lady of Grace.
Pillai, Joseph Anthony Rex *c.ss.r.* (CHI) Barrington, IL St. Anne.
Pillari, Moses de Jesus '07 (SAT) Special Assignment.
Pilli, Anthony '96 (SFD) Petersburg, IL Holy Family; Petersburg, IL St. Peter.
Pilola, Joseph '87 (HT) Thibodaux, LA St. Thomas Aquinas; Vocations; Campus Ministry; Serra Club of Thibodaux.
Pilon, Rev. Msgr. Daniel J. '76 (FAR) Enderlin, ND St. Patrick's Church of Enderlin; Enderlin, ND Holy Trinity Church of Fingal; Enderlin, ND Our Lady of the Scapular Church of Sheldon; Defensor Vinculi.
Pilon, James F. '67 (HRT) Retired.
Pilon, Jean–Pierre G. '02 (SCR) On Duty Outside the Diocese.
Pilon, Mark A. '75 (ARL) Springfield, VA St. Raymond of Penafort.
Pilon, Peter A. '00 (PEO) Campus, IL Sacred Heart; Odell, IL St. Paul's.
Pilones, Loji C. '86 (LA) Palmdale, CA St. Mary.
Pilsner, Joseph E. *c.s.b.* '91 (GAL)[O] Houston, TX Residence of the Basilian Fathers of the University of St. Thomas; [C] Houston, TX University of St. Thomas.
Pilsner, Peter R. '89 (NY)[E] Bronx, NY Cardinal Spellman High School.
Pilus, Jaroslaw '98 (DET) Shelby Twp., MI St. Therese of Lisieux.
Pimentel, Joseph W. *o.p.* '90 (MO) Navy Reserve Chaplains.
Pina, Martin '93 (LUB) Lubbock, TX St. Joseph's; Director of Hispanic Affairs; Director of Vocations; Presbyteral Council.
Pinapati, Lucas Raj '98 (OKL) McLoud, OK St. Vincent de Paul.
Pincelli, Thomas L. '70 (BWN) Harlingen, TX St. Anthony; Parish Priests Consultors and Priests' Personnel Board.
Pinchock, Joseph '72 (ORL) Port Orange, FL Our Lady of Hope.
Pinciaro, Albert G. '84 (BGP) Stamford, CT St. Maurice.
Pincince, Gerald P. '65 (PRO) Retired.
Pinczewski, Philip '87 (E) Priest Personnel Board.
Pinczewski, Phillip A. '87 (E) Kane, PA St. Callistus; Deans; Eastern Vicariate.
Pineda, Juan G. '90 (BGP) Norwalk, CT St. Mary.
Pineda, Vincent '05 (SJ) Sunnyvale, CA Church of The Resurrection.
Pineiro, Juan Colon '95 (CGS) Barranquitas, PR Church of St. Anthony of Padua.
Pinero, Geraldo J. '91 (PH) Philadelphia, PA Incarnation of Our Lord.
Pinette, Stuart H. '95 (HRT) Rocky Hill, CT St. Elizabeth Seton.
Pinillos, Ricardo Martin '03 (ARL) Alexandria, VA Good Shepherd.
Pinizzotto, Anthony J. *o.s.f.s.* '78 (ARL) Chantilly, VA St. Timothy.
Pinkerton, Samuel J. '95 (WCH) Garden Plain, KS Immaculate Conception; Garden Plain, KS St. Anthony.
Pinne, Chris *s.j.* '87 (DEN)[N] Centennial, CO Regis High Jesuit Community.
Pinne, Christopher P. *s.j.* '87 (DEN)[D] Aurora, CO Regis Jesuit High School Corporation.
Pino, Justin P. '07 (E) Punxsutawney, PA SS. Cosmas and Damian; Punxsutawney, PA St. Anthony of Padua.
Pinon, Gilberto *o.m.i.* '71 (FgM) Washington, DC AMERICAN OBLATE MISSIONS.
Pins, Herbert J. '71 (HEL) Dillon, MT St. Rose of Lima; Warm Springs State Hospital; [G] Dillon, MT University of Montana – Western.
Pins, Rev. Msgr. Joseph D. '70 (STL) St. Louis, MO Cathedral Basilica of Saint Louis; Archdiocesan Newspaper "The St. Louis Review".
Pins, Joseph (DM) Creston, IA Holy Spirit; Creston, IA St. Edward.
Pintacura, Michael '93 (STO) On Duty Outside the Diocese.
Pinti, Domenico C. '85 (TUC) Diocesan Consultors; Apache Junction, AZ Saint George Roman Catholic Parish – Apache Junction; Council of Priests; Vicars Forane; Directors; All Vicars Forane.
Pinto, Agnelo '71 (BRK) Brooklyn, NY St. Augustine.
Pinto, Alex (NEW) Serra Club of Union County West.
Pinto, Danny '63 (FTW) Churubusco, IN St. John Bosco; Churubusco, IN Immaculate Conception.
Pinto, Edgaro '80 (SJN) Bayamon, PR Nuestra Senora de la Milagrosa.
Pinto, Franco *s.d.b.* (NEW)[M] South Orange, NJ Salesian Office of Youth Ministry & Vocations; [M] South Orange, NJ Don Bosco Vocation Office.
Pinto, P. Francis *s.d.b.* (NEW)[R] Offices of Vocation and Youth Ministry.
Pinto, Santan '77 (CC)[G] Robstown, TX Society of Our Lady of the Most Holy Trinity.
Pintye, Louis M. *o.f.m.* '90 (BGP) Fairfield, CT St. Emery.
Pinyan, Charles '92 (NEW) Allendale, NJ Guardian Angel; Members.
Pinzon, Alvaro '91 (MIA) Miami, FL St. Mary's Cathedral; Judges.
Pinzon, Eduardo *s.j.* '60 (CHI) Chicago, IL St. Bartholomew Retired.
Pinzon, Steven V. '05 (CAM) Swedesboro, NJ St. Joseph's Church, Swedesborough.
Pinzon Umana, Eduardo *s.j.* '60 (CHI)[C] Chicago, IL Jesuit Community at Loyola University Chicago.
Piontkowski, Richard L. '82 (MO) Army Reserve Chaplains.
Piontkowski, Richard L. '82 (GI) Adjutant Vicars–Judicial; Judges; Diocesan Consultors; Grand Island, NE Cathedral of the Nativity of the Blessed Virgin Mary.
Piorkowski, Darlusz *s.j.* '07 (BO)[U] Newton, MA The Jesuit Community at Boston College.
Piorkowski, Robert '76 (STN) Madison, IL St. Mary's.
Piorkowski, Rev. Msgr. Stanley W. '51 (SCR)[N] Dunmore, PA Villa St. Joseph Retired.
Piotrowski, Adrian *o.s.c.* '64 (SCL)[I] Onamia, MN Crosier Priory.
Piotrowski, Leonard '93 (SP) Tampa, FL St. Paul; [F] Tampa, FL St. Paul Child Enrichment; Secretary for Priest Personnel; College of Consultors; Personnel Board; Ex Officio.
Piovan, Benjamin '64 (NO) Retired.
Piovan, Benjamin '64 (BLX) Latin American Apostolate.
Piovan, Benjamin (JKS)[I].
Pipp, Thomas J. *s.j.* '92 (TOL)[C] Toledo, OH St. John's Jesuit High School; [M] Toledo, OH Saint John's Jesuit High School Foundation.

Pipta, Robert M. '94 (VNN) Vocations Office; Liturgy & Music Commission; San Diego, CA Holy Angels; College of Consultors; Personnel Board.
Piquado, Thomas G. *s.j.* '72 (SAC) Sacramento, CA St. Ignatius of Loyola; [I] Carmichael, CA Sacramento Jesuit Community.
Pira, Reginald Paul S. '98 (HON) Lanai City, HI Sacred Hearts of Jesus and Mary Parish.
Piraro, Don '67 (LKC)[C] Moss Bluff, LA St. Charles Center; St. Charles Retreat Center; Presbyteral Council; Diocesan Consultors.
Pires, Francisco '84 (SLC) Riverton, UT Saint Andrew Catholic Church LLC 233; College of Consultors.
Pires, Francisco (SLC) Finance Council; Board of Directors; Team.
Piro, Francis '54 (PH) Philadelphia, PA St. Philip Neri Retired.
Piro, Frank R. '62 (SFR) Retired.
Piro, Gerald J. '79 (BRK) On Leave/Unassigned.
Pirrera, Aaron *o.s.b.* '85 (LR) Subiaco, AR St. Benedict.
Pirrone, Roberto '88 (LA) La Puente, CA St. Joseph.
Pirros, Rafael *s.t.* (PAT) Migrant Ministry.
Pirrung, George '54 (PHX) Retired.
Pisaneschi, Joseph J. '01 (SCR) Hunlock Creek, PA Our Lady of Mount Carmel.
Pisano, Joseph Daniel '07 (WH) Wheeling, WV St. Michael.
Pisano, Mario *o.m.* '68 (LA)[P] Los Angeles, CA Minim Fathers; Los Angeles, CA All Saints; Los Angeles, CA.
Pisano, Stephen *s.j.* '75 (FgM) Los Gatos, CA Society of Jesus.
Pisarcik, John G. (PAT) Retired.
Pisciotta, Justin M. *o.s.m.* '64 (CHI)[N] Chicago Order of Friar Servants of Mary (Servites) United States of America Province, Inc.
Pisciotta, Justin M. *o.s.m.* '64 (ORG) Fullerton, CA St. Philip Benizi.
Piscitello, Primo *o.f.m.* '60 (NY)[EE] New York Franciscan Province of the Immaculate Conception.
Pisegna, Cedric *c.p.* '91 (GAL)[O] Houston, TX Congregation of the Passion, Holy Name Passionist Community and Retreat Center.
Piselli, Costanzo J. '69 (PRT) Retired.
Pish, Robert H. '05 (STP)[A] Saint Paul, MN The Saint Paul Seminary.
Pish, Robert '05 (STP)[C] St. Paul, MN University of St. Thomas; Graduate Studies.
Piskura, Joseph '54 (CLV) Retired.
Pisors, John A. *c.s.v.* '66 (CHI)[N] Arlington Heights Viatorian Province Center–Clerics of St. Viator.
Pistacchio, Gene *o.f.m.* '89 (BO)[Z] Boston, MA St. Anthony Shrine.
Pistacchio, Gene *o.f.m.* '89 (WDC)[V][V] West Bethesda, MD Missionaries of the Kingship of Christ.
Pistone, Benardo '73 (HBG) Gettysburg, PA St. Francis Xavier's; Appointed.
Pistone, Dominic J. '78 (GAL) Houston, TX St. Clare of Assisi.
Pistone, Dominic (GAL) Southern Vicariate.
Pistorius, Francis X. *s.j.* '72 (NO) New Orleans, LA Immaculate Conception.
Pisut, Christopher '02 (DM) Chariton, IA Sacred Heart; Leon, IA St. Brendan; Judicial Vicar; Judges; Chariton, IA St. Francis.
Piszker, James '91 (E)[B] Erie, PA Mercyhurst College; [P] Erie, PA Mercyhurst College.
Pitcavage, William *s.c.j.* '76 (SFS) Chamberlain, SD St. James; Presbyteral Council.
Pitre, Eric J. '81 (GAL) Sealy, TX Immaculate Conception; Archdiocesan Judges; Western Vicariate.
Pitroipa, Anatole France *s.j.* '07 (WDC)[N] Washington, DC The Jesuit Community at Georgetown University.
Pitstick, Martin John '08 (COV) California, KY Sts. Peter and Paul.
Pitstick, Rory '94 (P)[A] St. Benedict, OR Mount Angel Seminary.
Pitt, Rev. Msgr. William L. '61 (RIC) Retired.
Pittapilly, Thomas '61 (GF) Special Assignment.
Pittard, Wayne M. '83 (GF) Big Timber, MT St. Joseph; Livingston, MT St. Mary.
Pittman, Robert S. *s.s.s.* '58 (WDC)[W] Washington, DC Black Leadership and Christ's Kingdom Society.
Pitts, Joseph *o.m.i.* '59 (BEL)[F] Belleville, IL Shrine of Our Lady of the Snows.
Pitts, William L. '70 (R) Pinehurst, NC Sacred Heart.
Pitula, Roman '98 (PHU) Presbyteral Council; Hillsborough, NJ St. Michael's; New Brunswick, NJ Nativity of B.V.M.
Pitzer, John M. *o.p.* '99 (MEM) Memphis, TN St. Peter Church; [F] Memphis, TN The Dominican Friars of Memphis, Inc.
Pivarnik, R. Gabriel *o.p.* '97 (PRO)[P] Providence St. Thomas Aquinas Priory at Providence College.
Pivonka, David *t.o.r.* '96 (WDC)[N] Washington, DC St. Louis Friary.
Pivonka, Rev. Msgr. Leonard '77 (CC) Bishop's Office; Deans; College of Consultors; Personnel Board – Priests; Presbyteral Council; Judges; Alice, TX St. Elizabeth of Hungary.
Piwowar, Stanley J. '51 (MAN) Retired.
Pizmoht, Louis A. '66 (CLV) Willoughby, OH Immaculate Conception.
Pizzamiglio, Rev. Msgr. Ernest E. '66 (PEO) Galesburg, IL Immaculate Heart of Mary; Vicariates and Vicars.
Pizzarelli, Francis *s.m.m.* '79 (RVC) Port Jefferson, NY Most Precious Blood; [M] Bay Shore, NY Montfort Missionaries; Senate of Priests (Presbyteral Council/ College of Consultors).
Pizzo, Anthony B. *o.s.a.* '84 (CHI) Chicago, IL St. Rita of Cascia; Deans.
Pizzo, Philip J. '77 (BRK) Long Island City, NY St. Rita.
Pizzonia, Domenico '05 (GF) Black Eagle, MT Most Blessed Sacrament.
Pizzuto, Alfred '55 (NY)[EE] Bronx, NY John Cardinal O'Connor Residence Retired.
Placa, Rev. Msgr. Alan J. '70 (RVC) Great Neck, NY St. Aloysius; Unassigned.
Place, Michael D. '70 (CHI) Members.
Placette, David D. '04 (BEA) Nederland, TX St. Charles Borromeo.
Plagens, Rev. Msgr. James A. '65 (SAN) Promoter Justitiae; Midland, TX St. Ann's.
Plaisted, Eugene D. *o.s.c.* '61 (SCL)[I] Onamia, MN Crosier Priory.
Plakut, Peter *o.c.s.o.* '58 (P)[L] Lafayette, OR The Cistercian (Trappist) Abbey of Our Lady of Guadalupe.
Plammoottil, Sunny Joseph *o.s.h.* '93 (GAL)[O] Missouri City, TX The Society of the Oblates of Sacred Heart; Missouri City, TX Holy Family.
Plamondon, Donald J. '72 (DUB) Independence, IA St. Patrick; Independence, IA St. John the Evangelist; Defenders of the Bond.
Planas, Salvador '54 (MIA) Retired.
Plancher, Christian *s.m.m.* '96 (MIA) Pembroke Pines, FL St. Edward.
Planea, John '82 (NO) On Duty Outside the Archdiocese.
Plank, Stephen J. *o.s.b.* '94 (OM)[C] Elkhorn, NE Mount Michael Benedictine School; [K] Elkhorn, NE Mount Michael Benedictine Abbey.
Planning, Stephen W. *s.j.* '99 (DEN)[D] Denver, CO Arrupe Jesuit High School; [N] Denver, CO Regis Jesuit Community (The Jesuits at Regis University).
Plans, John F. *s.f.* '67 (WDC) Silver Spring, MD Christ the King.
Plant, Christopher M. '08 (GAL) Conroe, TX Sacred Heart.
Plante, Georges J. '53 (PRT)[G] Waterville, ME Mt. St. Joseph Holistic Care Community Retired.
Plante, Rev. Msgr. Jacques L. '82 (PRO) Deans; West Warwick, RI SS. John and James Parish.
Plante, Paul A. '71 (PRT) Oquossoc, ME Our Lady of the Lakes; Vicar for Priests; Ex Officio Members; Diocesan Consultors; Ministry to Priests.
Plante, Pierre J. '78 (PRO) Pawtucket, RI St. Cecilia.
Plante, Roger J. *m.s.* '61 (MAN)[K] Enfield, NH Shrine of Our Lady of La Salette; [N] Enfield, NH Shrine of Our Lady of La Salette.
Planty, Donald J. '93 (ARL) Dale City, VA Holy Family; Defenders of the Bond.
Plasker, Alexander *o.s.b.* '62 (P)[L] St. Benedict, OR Mt. Angel Abbey.
Plasse, Eugene J. '72 (SPR) Palmer, MA St. Bartholomew's; Palmer, MA St. Thomas the Apostle.
Plaster, George F. '80 (IND) Indianapolis, IN St. Mark the Evangelist; Priests' Personnel Board.
Plaster, George '80 (IND) Council of Priests.
Plastino, James L. '94 (MRY) Retired.
Plata, Gregory *o.f.m.* '85 (JKS) Greenwood, MS Immaculate Heart of Mary; Greenwood, MS St. Francis of Assisi; Lexington, MS St. Thomas; Winona, MS Sacred Heart; [H] Lexington, MS Holmes Community College Newman Center; Co Chairmen; Priests' Council.
Plate, Brian G. '96 (NEW) Summit, NJ St. Teresa's.
Plathanam, Ignatius J. *c.m.i.* '72 (STA) Palatka, FL St. Monica.
Plathe, Anthony H. '63 (NU) Retired.
Plathottam, Mathew '67 (PHX) Phoenix, AZ St. Theresa Roman Catholic Parish.
Plathottam, Thomas *c.s.t.* '74 (NOR) Ellington, CT St. Luke.
Plathottam, Thomas *c.s.t.* '74 (HRT) Enfield, CT Carl Robinson Correctional Institution; Enfield, CT Enfield Correctional Institute.
Platt, Philip Wallace *c.s.b.* '50 (GAL)[O] Sugar Land Basilian Mission Center.
Platt, Stewart '51 (Y) Retired.
Plaushin, Mark *o.s.f.s.* '89 (MO) Army Reserve Chaplains.
Plaushin, Mark *o.s.f.s.* '89 (ALN)[B] Center Valley, PA DeSales University; [K] Center Valley, PA Oblates of St. Francis de Sales.
Plavcan, Jon J. '94 (GRY) Gary, IN Cathedral of Holy Angels; Deans; Administrative Assistant to the Bishop; Bishop's Council of Priests; Consultors; Priests' Personnel Board.
Plavec, Timothy J. '86 (CLV) Mentor, OH St. Bede the Venerable.
Plawecki, Joseph A. '83 (DET) Richmond, MI St. Augustine.
Plazewski, Leonard '91 (SP) Saint Petersburg, FL Cathedral of St. Jude the Apostle; Vocations Office; Elected Parochial Vicars; Huntington, NY National Conference of Diocesan Vocation Directors (1962); Personnel Board.
Pleban, Alexander L. '57 (GBG) Uniontown, PA St. Joseph; Bishop's Priests Council.
Pleban, Leo '60 (Y) Retired.
Pleho, Anthony J. '79 (NY)[AA] New York, NY Kateri Residence.
Pleier, David J. '75 (GB) Green Bay, WI St. Bernard; Green Bay, WI St. Philip the Apostle; Cursillo.
Pleiman, Kenneth F. *c.pp.s.* '70 (CLV) Cleveland, OH St. Adalbert.
Pleiman, Kenneth F. *c.pp.s.* '70 (CIN)[T] Dayton, OH Community Support Charitable Trust.
Pleiness, Gregg A. '81 (LAN) Howell, MI St. Augustine.
Plesa, Andrew J. '56 (RCK) Elgin, IL St. Thomas More Retired.
Pleskac, Rev. Msgr. Myron J. '60 (LIN)[G] Lincoln, NE School Sisters of Christ the King, Villa Regina Motherhouse & Novitiate; Lincoln, NE St. Luke's Czech Catholic Shrine; Presbyteral Council; Deaneries and Deans; Priests' Continuing Education Committee; Lincoln, NE Nebraska Penal Complex; Evangelization Committee.
Pleus, Adrian C.H. '99 (ATL) Dallas, GA St. Vincent de Paul.
Pleva, Gerald *s.m.* '77 (HON) Wailuku, HI St. Anthony of Padua; [D] Wailuku, HI Wailuku Marianist Community.
Plewka, Rev. Msgr. Mark A. '76 (PBL) Chancellor; Judicial Vicar; Judge; Presbyteral Council–College of Consultors; Presbyteral Council; Tribunal.
Pliauplis, Christopher '87 (NY) New York, NY Cathedral of St. Patrick.
Plishka, Andrew '06 (STN) St. Louis, MO Assumption B.V.M.
Plishka, Richard '08 (PRM) Notaries; Priest Secretary to the Bishop; Young Adults.
Plo, Rev. Msgr. John '61 (NY) Retired.
Ploch, Jacek '08 (PRO) Warwick, RI St. Kevin.
Ploch, Timothy *s.d.b.* '76 (FgM) St. Francis Central Coast Catholic High School, Inc.; San Francisco, CA; San Francisco, CA Salesian Provincial House.
Ploch, Timothy *s.d.b.* '76 (SFR)[N] San Francisco, CA Salesian Provincial Residence.
Plocharczyk, Rev. Msgr. Daniel J. '74 (HRT) Hartford Vicariate; New Britain, CT Sacred Heart of Jesus.
Plocke, Donald J. *s.j.* '84 (BO)[U] Newton, MA The Jesuit Community at Boston College.
Plomillo, Ronald S. '95 (CHI) Skokie, IL St. Lambert.
Plominski, Walter J. '68 (ROC) Rochester, NY Unity Health System; Rochester, NY St. Theodore.
Ploof, Gerald '75 (LAN) Clio, MI SS. Charles and Helena; Otisville, MI St. Francis Xavier.
Ploplis, Theodore '77 (CHI)[J] Chicago, IL Saint Joseph Hospital.
Plotkowski, Jerome '65 (SFE) Judicial Vicar; Judicial Vicar; Delegate for Matrimonial Dispensations; Albuquerque, NM Risen Savior Catholic Community.
Plotkowski, John S. '74 (CHI) Des Plaines, IL St. Zachary.
Ploude, Thomas E. '64 (CAM) Retired.
Plough, James H. '58 (PBL) Retired.
Plourde, Carroll W. *s.s.e.* '87 (MOB) Orrville, AL Immaculate Conception; Selma, AL Our Lady Queen of Peace; [G] Selma, AL Edmundite Fathers; [I] Selma, AL Marion Institute Newman Center; Councilors:.
Plourde, James S. '82 (PRT) Calais, ME Blessed Kateri Tekakwitha Parish; Machias, ME Saint Peter the Fisherman Parish.
Plow, Gregory *t.o.r.* '08 (STU)[A] Steubenville, OH Franciscan University of Steubenville; [H] Steubenville, OH Holy Spirit Friary.
Pluciennik, Marcin P. '09 (HRT) Manchester, CT St. Bartholomew; Manchester, CT St. Bridget.
Plummer, James '58 (CAM) Retired.
Plunkett, Craig '06 (FRS) Clovis, CA Our Lady of Perpetual Help.
Plunkett, Rev. Msgr. Joseph P. '60 (NEW) Newark, NJ Our Lady of Good Counsel Retired.
Pluth, Paul R. '96 (SEA) Judges; Adjunct Judicial Vicar.
Plutz, Stanley *s.v.d.* '53 (BLX)[D] Bay St. Louis, MS St. Augustine's Residence.
Po, Thanh Ha '63 (ORG) Retired.
Poandl, Robert '68 (SAV) Claxton, GA St. Christopher.
Poblocki, Richard M. I. '83 (BUF) Apostleship of Prayer; Cheektowaga, NY St. Josaphat.
Pocernich, Eugene '74 (MIL)[K] Milwaukee, WI Columbia St. Mary's Hospital Milwaukee, Inc.; Special Assignment.
Pocetto, Alexander T. *o.s.f.s.* '55 (ALN)[B] Center Valley, PA DeSales University; [K] Center Valley, PA Oblates of St. Francis de Sales.
Poche, Daniel M. '78 (HT) Morgan City, LA Holy Cross; Defender of the Bond; College of Consultors; Upper Lafourche Deanery; Priests Council.

Poche, Louis *s.j.* '55 (NO)[P] New Orleans, LA Ignatius Residence Retired.
Poczworowski, Luke *o.f.m.conv.* '67 (PEO) Wenona, IL St. John the Baptist's; Minonk, IL St. Patrick's; Wenona, IL St. Mary's.
Podeszwik, Wladyslaw (CHI) Chicago, IL St. Constance Retired.
Podhajsky, Christopher R. '01 (DUB) Cedar Rapids, IA Immaculate Conception; Cedar Rapids, IA St. Wenceslaus.
Podhajsky, Michael J. '03 (DUB) On Special or Other Archdiocesan Assignment.
Podimattam, Thomas *c.m.i.* '77 (SFS) Herreid, SD St. Michael.
Podlesny, James F. *o.s.b.* '80 (HBG) Palmyra, PA Church of the Holy Spirit.
Podraza, Timothy '97 (OM) Butte, NE Sacred Heart Parish of Boyd County.
Podsiadlo, Jack *s.j.* '72 (BRK)[K] Brooklyn, NY Brooklyn Jesuit Prep.
Podsiedlik, Slawomir S. *o.c.d.* '02 (STA) Bunnell, FL St. Mary; [H] Bunnell, FL Discalced Carmelite Fathers of Florida.
Podvin, Albert J. '62 (SFE) Retired.
Podwysocki, Grzegorz '08 (JOL) Romeoville, IL St. Andrew the Apostle.
Podymniak, Miroslaw *o.f.m.conv.* '92 (BRK) Elmhurst, NY St. Adalbert.
Poecking, David G. '96 (PIT) Carnegie, PA St. Elizabeth Ann Seton; Continuing Education of Clergy, Office for.
Poecking, Kevin G. '04 (PIT)[Q] Pittsburgh, PA Christ Child Society of Pittsburgh; Slippery Rock, PA St. Peter; [P] Slippery Rock, PA Slippery Rock University, Newman Center (Slippery Rock).
Poehlmann, Edward J. '67 (DEN) Denver, CO Presentation of Our Lady.
Poerio, John '59 (LKC) Advocates Retired.
Poettgen, Edward '80 (ORG) Santa Ana, CA Immaculate Heart of Mary; Consultors; Council of Priests; Land Advisory Board.
Poetzel, Richard K. *c.ss.r.* '63 (BAL) Baltimore, MD Our Lady of Fatima.
Poff, Edward '58 (JOL) Retired.
Poff, Pius *o.f.m.conv.* '61 (IND) Floyds Knobs, IN St. Mary.
Poggemeyer, Joseph T. '97 (TOL) Toledo, OH St. Joseph; [B] Toledo, OH Central Catholic High School.
Pogorelc, Anthony J. *s.s.* '88 (SAT) On Duty Outside the Archdiocese.
Pogorelc, Anthony J. *s.s.* '88 (WDC)[C] Catholic University of America, The.
Pogorelc, Anthony J. *s.s.* '88 (BAL)[S] Baltimore Society of St. Sulpice, Province of the United States.
Pogorelce, Anthony J. *s.s.* '88 (WDC)[A] Washington, DC Theological College of the Catholic University of America.
Pogorzelski, Andrzej '77 (HRT) New Britain, CT Sacred Heart of Jesus.
Pohl, Rev. Msgr. Daniel J. '53 (LIN)[E] Lincoln, NE Bonacum House Retired.
Pohl, Jerome H. '67 (PH) Retired.
Pohl, Leon H. '56 (KAL) Retired.
Pohl, Stephen A. '85 (L) Louisville, KY St. Margaret Mary.
Pohlman, Stephen J. '84 (SFD) Godfrey, IL St. Michael; Godfrey, IL St. Ambrose.
Pohlmeier, Erik '98 (LR) Hot Springs National Park, AR St. John the Baptist; Hot Springs National Park, AR St. Mary of the Springs; Assistant Directors.
Pohlmeier, Loren G. '82 (GI) Mullen, NE St. Mary's.
Pohorlak, Joseph '61 (PRM) Retired.
Pohto, P. Thomas *o.s.a.* '67 (CHL) Maggie Valley, NC St. Margaret of Scotland.
Pointek, Rev. Msgr. Francis J. '40 (FRS) Retired.
Poirier, David *s.a.* '77 (NY)[EE] Garrison Franciscan Friars of the Atonement, Minister General Office.
Poirier, Robert L. *s.j.* '77 (STL)[O] St. Louis, MO Leo Brown Jesuit Community; [C] Saint Louis University.
Poirier, Vincent J. '85 (BO) Senior Priests. Retired.
Poirot, Jeff '01 (FWT) Mineral Wells, TX Our Lady of Lourdes.
Poissant, Rev. Msgr. Leeward J. '63 (OG) Keeseville, NY St. John the Baptist (The Roman Catholic Community of Keeseville); Deans.
Poisson, Thomas L. '78 (MAR) Retired.
Poitras, Robert A. '05 (BO) Milton, MA St. Agatha.
Pojol, Peter *s.j.* '02 (BO)[U] Cambridge, MA Hopkins House.
Pokorsky, Jerry '90 (ARL) Annandale, VA St. Michael.
Pokrzewinski, Justus M. *o.p.* '60 (CHI)[N] Chicago Dominicans (Provincial Office).
Pokrzewinski, Justus *o.p.* '60 (FgM) Chicago, IL Province of St. Albert the Great (Central).
Poku, John '98 (RVC) East Rockaway, NY St. Raymond's.
Pokusa, Rev. Msgr. Joseph W. '70 (CAM) On Duty Outside the Diocese.
Polak, Michael J. '58 (PIT)[M] Pittsburgh, PA St. John Vianney Manor Retired.
Polando, Rev. Msgr. Peter M. '80 (Y) Finance Council; Youngstown, OH St. Matthias; Adjutant Judicial Vicar; Youngstown, OH Holy Name of Jesus.
Polansky, Lawrence E. '09 (CAM) Vineland, NJ The Church of Saint Isidore the Farmer, Vineland, N.J.
Polasek, Jeffrey S. '91 (TLS) Tahlequah, OK St. Brigid; [I] Tahlequah, OK Northeastern State University Catholic Student Organization.
Polczyk, Stanislaus '82 (TR) Leave of Absence; [N] Trenton, NJ St. Lawrence Rehabilitation Center.
Polczynski, Alan N. '07 (GBG)[C] Greensburg, PA Greensburg Central Catholic High School; Greensburg, PA St. Bruno; Greensburg, PA St. Benedict.
Polednak, John V. '76 (SCR) Wyoming, PA Our Lady of Sorrows; Wyoming, PA St. Joseph's; Episcopal Vicars.
Polek, David *c.ss.r.* '62 (STL) St. Louis, MO St. Alphonsus Liguori; [O] St. Louis, MO Redemptorist Fathers.
Polek, Ryszard (WOR) Worcester, MA Our Lady of Czestochowa.
Polenz, Gordon '82 (ALB) Sidney, NY Sacred Heart.
Polgar, Capistran L. *o.f.m.* '67 (MET) New Brunswick, NJ St. Ladislaus.
Poliadlo, Gregorz (NEW) Bayonne, NJ Mt. Carmel.
Poliafico, David A. '95 (COL) Marysville, OH Our Lady of Lourdes.
Policetti, Julian '81 (FRS) Hanford, CA St. Brigid.
Polich, David J. '76 (DM) Perry, IA St. Patrick; Defenders of the Bond.
Polich, James C. '71 (DM) Des Moines, IA St. Augustin's.
Polichnowski, Nicholas *t.o.r.* '77 (STU)[A] Steubenville, OH Franciscan University of Steubenville; [H] Steubenville, OH Holy Spirit Friary.
Policicchio, Luke *o.s.b.* '88 (RIC) Virginia Beach, VA St. Gregory the Great.
Polidano, Carmel F. '81 (CAM) Hammonton, NJ St. Anthony of Padua Roman Catholic Church, Hammonton, N.J.
Polifka, Charles *o.f.m.cap.* '71 (DEN) Denver, CO; [N] Denver, CO St. Francis of Assisi Friary; [N] Denver, CO Capuchin Province of Mid–America, Inc.
Polifka, Charles *o.f.m.cap.* '71 (FgM) Denver, CO Province of Mid–America.
Polifka, Charles *o.f.m.cap.* '71 (NY)[EE] White Plains, NY Capuchin Friars of North America.
Polito, Martin F. '76 (CLV) Cleveland, OH Holy Redeemer; Presbyteral Council; Presbyteral Conveners.
Polito, Victor V.J. '54 (MAN) Retired.
Polizzi, Rev. Msgr. Salvatore E. '56 (STL) St. Louis, MO St. Roch; Archdiocesan Office of Urban and Community Affairs; Washington, DC The National Center for Urban Ethnic Affairs (1971).
Poljicak, Vlatko '65 (LA) Los Angeles, CA St. Anthony.
Polk, Page E. *o.f.m.* '86 (GAL)[S] Houston, TX The Catholic Chaplain Corps; Catholic Chaplain Corps (Hospital Chaplains).
Polk, Page *o.f.m.* '86 (CIN)[N] Cincinnati, OH St. Francis Seraph Friary.
Polk, Thomas T. '67 (BAL) Retired.
Poll, Jeff A. '05 (LAN) Jackson, MI Queen of the Miraculous Medal.
Pollack, Anthony '55 (ALT) Retired.
Pollard, Christopher J. '98 (ARL) On Duty Outside the Diocese.
Pollard, John E. '74 (CHI) Wilmette, IL St. Joseph.
Pollard, John L. '83 (STA) Absent or Sick Leave.
Pollard, Marcus A. '90 (ARL) Springfield, VA St. Bernadette.
Pollard, Patrick J. '72 (CHI) Chicago, IL Notre Dame de Chicago; Hillside, IL Central Office; College of Consultors; Catholic Cemeteries.
Pollard, Rev. Msgr. Raymond J. '50 (NEW) Retired.
Pollard, Roy F. '66 (WIL) Governor Bacon Health Center; Delaware City, DE St. Paul.
Pollard, Thomas W. '66 (WDC) Clinton, MD Church of St. John the Evangelist.
Pollie, A. Frank '67 (DET) Rochester Hills, MI St. Irenaeus.
Pollis, Robert G. '57 (BO) Senior Priests. Retired.
Pollock, Jonah F. *o.p.* '09 (WDC)[B] Washington, DC Dominican House of Studies.
Pollock, Paul E. *s.j.* '73 (FgM) Los Gatos, CA Society of Jesus.
Pollock, Rev. Msgr. Robert C. '48 (SLC) Retired.
Polmounter, Richard J. '78 (SCR) Tunkhannock, PA St. Mary of the Lake; Tunkhannock, PA Nativity of Blessed Virgin Mary; Diocesan Finance Council.
Polo, Antonio *s.d.b.* '56 (SJN) San Juan, PR Maria Auxiliadora.
Poloche, Pedro '98 (ATL) Vicars for Clergy; Advocates.
Polosky, Michael '91 (SJP) Ambridge, PA Ss. Peter and Paul; Consultors; Youth Ministries; Presbyteral Council; Personnel Board; Presbyters.
Poloway, Rev. Msgr. Mitred Michael '54 (SJP) Presbyters Retired.
Polselli, Leo *c.s.c.* '70 (FR)[A] North Easton, MA Holy Cross Fathers Religious.
Polson, Mikel Anthony '02 (LAF) Iota, LA St. Joseph.
Poltorak, Stanley '82 (SAC) Rocklin, CA SS. Peter and Paul.
Poltorek, George *s.a.c.* (BRK) Ridgewood, NY St. Aloysius.
Poluikis, John A. *c.s.b.* '51 (ROC)[J] Rochester, NY Basilian Residence.
Polyak, Anthony V. *m.m.* '62 (FgM) Maryknoll, NY MARYKNOLL.
Polyak, John V. '69 (MET) North Brunswick, NJ Our Lady of Peace.
Polycarpe, Pierre G. '99 (RCK) Special Assignment; Rockford, IL St. Bernadette.
Pomerleau, Claude *c.s.c.* '65 (P)[B] University of Portland; [L] Portland, OR Holy Cross Fathers & Brothers, C.S.C. – University of Portland; New Rochelle, NY Eastern Brothers Province.
Pomerleau, Claude *c.s.c.* (FTW)[H] Notre Dame Congregation of Holy Cross, Indiana Province, Provincial House.
Pomerleau, William A. '79 (SPR) Springfield, MA Our Lady of the Sacred Heart; Diocesan Commission for Ecumenism.
Pomeroy, Thomas '93 (GB) Kaukauna, WI Holy Cross.
Pomilio, Matthew J. '62 (BRK) Retired.
Pommier, Richard *o.m.i.* '66 (FgM) Washington, DC AMERICAN OBLATE MISSIONS.
Pompei, Francis *o.f.m.* '74 (BUF)[T] Buffalo, NY Franciscan Mystery Players, Inc.; [O] Buffalo, NY St. Patrick Friary.
Pompei, Frederick A. '66 (SY) Syracuse, NY Our Lady of Pompei/St. Peter; Special Assignment.
Pomposello, Peter A. '04 (NY) Bronx, NY Holy Cross.
Ponce, Demetrio '88 (ELP) Absent on Leave.
Ponce, Francisco '67 (NEW) Jersey City, NJ St. Joseph.
Ponce, James '01 (COS) On Duty Outside Diocese.
Ponce, Jesus *o.f.m.* '06 (SJN) Sabana Seca, PR San Jose Obrero.
Ponce, Juan Manuel '00 (SAC) Corning, CA Immaculate Conception.
Poncelet, Frank '87 (SCL) Retired.
Poncini, John '05 (SJ) Diocesan Clergy Personnel Board; Vocation Office; Special Assignment; Ongoing Formation of Clergy; Council of Priests; San Jose, CA Cathedral Basilica of St. Joseph.
Poncini, Laurence *o.c.d.* '07 (SEA) Stanwood, WA St. Cecilia.
Pondo, Stanley '98 (IND) Beech Grove, IN Holy Name; Defenders of the Bond.
Ponessa, Joseph '74 (GF) Glendive, MT Sacred Heart; Personnel Board.
Ponnet, Chris '83 (LA) Director & Cardinal Liaison.
Ponnet, Christopher D. '83 (LA) Los Angeles, CA St. Camillus De Lellis; Los Angeles, CA Norris Cancer and USC University Hospital; AIDS/AIDS Council; AIDS/HIV Ministry; Hospital Chaplains.
Pons, Miguel '53 (SJN) Trujillo Alto, PR San Judas Tadeo.
Pons, Ramon '88 (SR) Santa Rosa, CA St. Rose of Lima.
Pontarelli, Michael M. *o.s.m.* '82 (CHI)[N] Chicago Order of Friar Servants of Mary (Servites) United States of America Province, Inc.; Chicago, IL; [N] San Juan Capistrano, CA Servite Vocation Team Coordinator; [N] Chicago, IL Order of Friar Servants of Mary (Servites) United States of America Province, Inc.
Pontarelli, Michael M. *o.s.m.* '82 (ORG)[I] Anaheim, CA Servite Fathers and Brothers; San Juan Capistrano, CA Mission Basilica – San Juan Capistrano.
Pontes, Scott J. '04 (PRO) Bristol, RI St. Elizabeth.
Ponthokkan, Bosco *s.d.b.* '88 (OAK) Berkeley, CA St. Ambrose.
Ponticello, Robert D. '81 (MEM) Union City, TN Immaculate Conception.
Pontzer, Stephen '07 (SAV) On Duty Outside the Diocese.
Ponzini, Thomas V. '96 (GAL) Texas City, TX St. Mary.
Pookkattu, George *c.m.i.* '72 (ALX) Vidalia, LA Our Lady of Lourdes.
Pool, Jefferson *s.v.d.* '92 (TR)[N] Bordentown, NJ Society of the Divine Word.
Poole, Michael P. '98 (HEL) Bonner, MT St. Ann.
Poole, Richard '94 (MO) Absent on Leave; Air Force Chaplains.
Poole, Stafford *c.m.* '56 (LA)[P] Los Angeles, CA Amat Residence II Retired.
Poole, Steven F. '96 (BEL) Christopher, IL St. Andrew; Sesser, IL St. Mary.
Poole, William G. '63 (LEX) Retired.
Pooler, Alfred *c.p.* '60 (LA)[P] Sierra Madre, CA Passionist Residence; [V] Sierra Madre, CA Mater Dolorosa Passionist Retreat Center, Inc.
Poon, Stanislaus '62 (OAK) Retired.
Poonoly, Joy *c.ss.r.* (TOL) Lima, OH St. Gerard.
Poore, Charles '89 (Y) Lowellville, OH Our Lady of the Holy Rosary.
Poorman, Mark L. *c.s.c.* '82 (FTW)[B] University of Notre Dame Du Lac; [B] University of Notre Dame Du Lac; [H] Notre Dame, IN Holy Cross Community, Corby Hall, University of Notre Dame.
Poorten, William P. *s.j.* '63 (PAT)[J] Morristown, NJ Loyola House of Retreats.

Poovakulam, Antony P. '63 (TR) Retired.
Poovakulam, Antony P. '63 (LAV) Tonopah, NV St. Patrick.
Poovathinal, Emmanuel *c.m.i.* '03 (NY) Dobbs Ferry, NY Sacred Heart.
Poovathumkudy, Kuriakose (NY) Garnerville, NY St. Gregory Barbarigo.
Pop, Carlos Antonio *o.s.b.* '99 (SFS)[F] Marvin, SD Blue Cloud Abbey.
Popadick, Rev. Msgr. Peter J. '70 (BUF) Cheektowaga, NY St. Aloysius Gonzaga.
Pope, Rev. Msgr. Charles E. '89 (WDC)[W] Silver Spring, MD Archdiocese of Washington Division, The Blue Army; Archdiocesan College of Consultors; Priest Council.
Pope, George F. *c.s.c.* '58 (FgM) New Rochelle, NY Eastern Brothers Province.
Pope, L. Michael *s.j.* '81 (YAK) Yakima, WA St. Joseph Parish; Presbyteral Council Executive Committee.
Pope, Nicholas F. *s.j.* '72 (MIL)[P] Milwaukee, WI Jesuit Community at Marquette University.
Popelka, Joseph '92 (SAL) Manhattan, KS Seven Dolors of the Blessed Virgin Mary Parish; Manhattan, KS St. Patrick Parish.
Popesh, Rev. Msgr. Bernard '49 (DUL) Retired.
Popivchak, Rev. Msgr. Ronald P. '67 (PHU) Bridgeport, PA SS. Peter and Paul; Protopresbyters (Deans); Censor.
Popochock, James L. '68 (GBG) Farmington, PA St. Joan of Arc.
Popov, Pavlo '09 (STN) Chicago, IL St. Nicholas Ukrainian Catholic Cathedral.
Popovich, Peter '85 (NY) Hartsdale, NY Church of Our Lady of Shkodra.
Popovich, Stephen '81 (Y) Youngstown, OH Immaculate Heart of Mary; Office of Continuing Education and Formation of Priests.
Popovici, Olvian '98 (STF) Lindenhurst, NY Holy Family.
Popowski, Stanley (HEL) Leave of Absence.
Popp, Kenneth '83 (SCL) Breckenridge, MN St. Mary of the Presentation; Kent, MN St. Thomas; [G] Breckenridge, MN St. Francis Medical Center; [H] Breckenridge, MN St. Francis Home.
Poppa, Chester *o.f.m.cap.* '53 (GF) Broadus, MT St. David.
Popravak, Christopher *o.f.m.cap.* (DEN)[N] Denver, CO Capuchin Province of Mid–America, Inc.
Popson, Michael G. '87 (PSC) Danbury, CT St. Nicholas; Presbyteral Council.
Popyk, Volodymyr '97 (PHU) Presbyteral Council; Trenton, NJ St. Josaphat's; Department of Religious Education.
Porada, Casey '89 (LIN) Lincoln, NE Blessed Sacrament; Health Care Facilities.
Porpiglia, Joseph D. '86 (MO) Navy Reserve Chaplains; Council of Priests; Eggertsville, NY St. Benedict.
Porpora, Robert '90 (NY) Middletown, NY Holy Cross.
Porras, Adrian '01 (CHL) Arden, NC St. Barnabas.
Port, Dennis R. '74 (STL) St. Louis, MO St. Matthias.
Portalatin, Antonio '91 (ARE) Hatillo, PR Perpetual Help.
Portalatin Rodriguez, Antonio (PCE)[B] The Pontifical Catholic University of Puerto Rico.
Portasik, Richard *o.f.m.* '52 (PIT)[M] Pittsburgh, PA Holy Family Friary Retired.
Portela, Carlos '95 (KAL) Bronson, MI St. Mary's.
Porter, Charles Daniel *c.s.b.* '75 (GAL)[O] Sugar Land Basilian Mission Center.
Porter, Jack W. '75 (IND) On Special or Other Archdiocesan Assignment; Archdiocesan Historian Retired.
Porter, John E. '56 (CIN) Retired.
Porter, Rev. Msgr. John F. '57 (GR) Retired.
Porter, John F. '57 (GAY) Frankfort, MI St. Ann Retired.
Porter, Lawrence B. '74 (NEW)[A] South Orange, NJ Immaculate Conception Seminary; [A] South Orange, NJ Immaculate Conception Seminary; [B] School of Diplomacy and Intl. Rels.; Censores Librorum.
Porter, Robert G. '81 (HEL) Deer Lodge, MT Immaculate Conception; Montana State Prison.
Porter, Robert N. '64 (SFD) Retired.
Porter, Rocco '97 (DEN) Greeley, CO St. Peter.
Porter, Stephen C. '81 (SB) Rialto, CA St. Catherine of Siena.
Porter, William J. '75 (WIL) Pocomoke City, MD Holy Name of Jesus.
Porter, William '80 (KCK) Overland Park, KS St. Michael the Archangel; Archdiocesan Consultors.
Porterfield, David J. *c.s.c.* '79 (FTW)[H] Holy Cross House Retired.
Porterfield, Mark A. '94 (JC) St. Thomas, MO St. Cecilia; St. Thomas, MO St. Thomas the Apostle; Promoter of Justice; Judges; Senators.
Portes, Oscar Jimenez *o.s.a.* (SJN) San Juan, PR Ntra. Sra. de la Monserrate.
Portland, Paul *s.d.s.* '76 (MIL)[P] Milwaukee Salvatorian Provincial Offices.
Portman, Rev. Msgr. John R. '56 (SD) Retired.
Portzer, Joseph *f.s.s.p.* '99 (LIN)[A] Denton, NE Our Lady of Guadalupe Seminary.
Posadas, J. Antonio *o.f.m.* '95 (SAT) San Antonio, TX San Jose y San Miguel.
Posch, Christopher J. *o.f.m.* '95 (WIL) Wilmington, DE St. Paul's; Wilmington Office.
Poschen, Rev. Msgr. Ed '53 (FRS) Retired.
Poser, Gregory *o.s.c.* '75 (SCL)[I] Onamia, MN Crosier Priory; Hillman, MN St. Rita's; Onamia, MN The Church of the Holy Cross of Onamia; Onamia, MN St. Therese, Little Flower Indian Mission; Wahkon, MN Sacred Heart; Pastoral Council.
Posey, Patrick L. '91 (ARL) Falls Church, VA St. James; Propagation of the Faith.
Posey, Thaddeus J. *o.f.m.cap.* '71 (SAL)[D] Victoria, KS St. Fidelis Friary.
Posey, Thaddeus *o.f.m.cap.* '71 (WDC)[B] Washington, DC St. Francis Friary–Capuchin College.
Posiewala, John *s.a.c.* '76 (BUF)[O] North Tonawanda, NY Society of the Catholic Apostolate; North Tonawanda, NY.
Posluszny, Francis '62 (BGP) On Duty Outside the Diocese.
Post, Joseph S. '07 (STL) Florissant, MO St. Ferdinand.
Post, Robert J. '82 (BGP) Darien, CT St. Thomas More.
Postell, Philip S. *s.j.* '70 (DAL)[D] Dallas, TX Jesuit College Preparatory School.
Poster, James M. '03 (MAD) Palmyra, WI St. Mary; Fort Atkinson, WI St. Joseph; Elected.
Poston, J. Collin '03 (BAL) Hagerstown, MD St. Mary.
Poszwa, Stanislaw *s.ch.* '83 (DAL) Dallas, TX St. Peter.
Potaczek, John A. '99 (LC) Deans; Stevens Point, WI St. Bartholomew; Stevens Point, WI St. Stephen; Consultors; Ex Officio.
Poth, Thomas D. *s.m.m.* '83 (BRK)[T] Ozone Park Montfort Missionaries Provincialate (Missionaries of the Company of Mary).
Pothier, Glen J. '95 (PMB) West Palm Beach, FL Mary Immaculate; Adjutant Judicial Vicar; Judges.
Pothireddy, Marreddy '94 (WIN) Appointed Members.
Pothireddy, Marreddy '94 (WIN) Lewiston, MN St. Anthony's; Lewiston, MN St. Rose of Lima; Lewiston, MN Immaculate Conception.
Pothireddy, Swaminatha R. '93 (WIN) New Richland, MN St. Aidan; New Richland, MN St. Mary; New Richland, MN All Saints.
Pottamplackal, Efrem *m.c.b.s.* '74 (NY) Bronx, NY St. Margaret of Cortona.
Pottamplackal, Ephrem *m.c.b.s.* '74 (NY) Bronx, NY Montefiore Medical Center.
Pottemmel, Joseph *m.s.f.s.* (TUC) Tucson, AZ Saints Peter and Paul Roman Catholic Parish – Tucson.
Pottemmel, Joseph *m.s.f.s.* '76 (TYL)[B] Whitehouse, TX The Missionaries of St. Francis de Sales.
Pottenparambil, Joseph '90 (MIL)[P] Kenosha, WI Missionary Congregation of the Blessed Sacrament, Inc., Zion Province.
Potter, Gerald '54 (FAR) Retired.
Potter, Harold G. '09 (KAL) Kalamazoo, MI St. Augustine Cathedral.
Potter, Rev. Msgr. Joseph D. '54 (BGP) On Duty Outside the Diocese Retired.
Potthast, Richard L. *c.s.c.* '67 (FgM) New Rochelle, NY Eastern Brothers Province; [H] Notre Dame Congregation of Holy Cross, Indiana Province, Provincial House.
Potthoff, Donald William '49 (LA) Diamond Bar, CA St. Denis Retired.
Potthoff, Rev. Msgr. Fred E. '44 (LFT) Associate Judges Retired.
Pottokaran, Jose *c.m.i.* '67 (GRY)[D] Michigan City, IN Saint Anthony Memorial Health Centers.
Pottorff, Lisle J. '49 (DOD) Retired.
Potts, Donald G. '60 (KAL) Cassopolis, MI St. Ann; Presbyteral Council Members; Presbyteral Council Members.
Potts, Robert J. '64 (ALN) Fountain Hill, PA St. Ursula.
Potts, Ronald A. '89 (WDC) La Plata, MD Sacred Heart; Priest Council; Archdiocesan Chaplain – Catholic Committee on Girl Scouts.
Potts, Thomas *s.v.d.* '61 (BLX)[D] Bay St. Louis, MS St. Augustine's Residence; [D] Bay St. Louis, MS Province Development Office.
Potts, Thomas *s.v.d.* '61 (JKS)[F] Chatawa, MS St. Mary of the Pines; [G] Chatawa, MS St. Mary of the Pines.
Potvin, Leo F. '64 (ALB) Retired.
Potvin, Raymond H. '58 (SPR) On Duty Outside the Diocese Retired.
Potvin, Raymond J. '80 (MAN) Penacook, NH Immaculate Conception; Presbyteral Council; Public Policy Commission.
Poulang Mot, Rigobert '01 (BWN) Edinburg, TX Doctor's Hospital at Renaissance.
Poulin, Arthur *o.s.b.cam.* '81 (MRY)[F] Big Sur New Camaldoli Hermitage.
Poulin, Arthur *o.s.b.cam.* '81 (OAK)[M] Berkeley, CA Incarnation Monastery, Camaldolese Benedictines.
Poulin, Calvin H. *s.j.* '62 (FgM) New York, NY Society of Jesus.
Poulin, Edward C. *s.m.* '54 (NOR) Retired.
Poulin, Edward C. '54 (NOR) Willimantic, CT St. Mary Retired.
Pouliot, Francis A. '58 (STP) Deanery 18; St. Paul, MN Maternity of the Blessed Virgin.
Poulose, Skariya *m.s.t.* '86 (CHI)[J] Chicago, IL Saints Mary and Elizabeth Medical Center.
Poulsen, James '68 (SD) La Mesa, CA St. Martin of Tours; Clergy Personnel Board.
Poulsen, Thomas R. *o.p.* '67 (LFT)[I] West Lafayette, IN Dominicans, Community of St. Thomas Aquinas, Inc.
Poulsen, Tom *o.p.* '67 (LFT)[H] West Lafayette, IN St. Thomas Aquinas Parish and Foundation for Catholic Students Attending Purdue University; West Lafayette, IN St. Thomas Aquinas.
Poulson, David L. '79 (E) Fryburg, PA St. Michael; World Apostolate of Fatima (Blue Army).
Poumade, James M. '01 (ARL) Advocates; McLean, VA St. John the Beloved.
Poupore, J. Gareth *c.s.b.* '53 (ROC)[J] Rochester Basilian Residence.
Poupore, Norman E. '50 (OG) Retired.
Poussard, Bertrand R. '67 (PRT) Retired.
Pousson, Donald '66 (LAF) Crowley, LA St. John the Baptist; Mermentau, LA St. John the Evangelist; Morse, LA Immaculate Conception.
Poveromo, Robert J. '72 (NY) New York, NY St. Vincent de Paul; [E] New York, NY Cathedral High School; Staten Island, NY Our Lady Star of the Sea.
Povish, Robert W. '90 (PH) Collegeville, PA St. Eleanor; Graterford, PA Graterford State Correctional Institution.
Powell, Bernard F. '58 (PMB) Retired.
Powell, Daniel F.X. '92 (HBG) Harrisburg, PA St. Margaret Mary Alacoque.
Powell, Edward F. '54 (SUP) Retired.
Powell, Rev. Msgr. Eric S. '90 (PEO) Normal, IL Epiphany.
Powell, John J. *s.j.* '56 (DET)[K] Clarkston, MI Colombiere Center.
Powell, Leon A. '71 (LC) Special Assignment; [H] La Crosse, WI Holy Cross (Seminary) Diocesan Center; Vice–Chancellor; Ecclesiastical Notaries.
Powell, Marc L. '03 (SEA) Vashon, WA St. John Vianney.
Powell, Matthew D. *o.p.* '75 (PRO)[P] Providence St. Thomas Aquinas Priory at Providence College.
Powell, Michael '89 (JOL)[I] Kankakee, IL Provena St. Mary's Hospital.
Powell, Paul '48 (OWN) Roman Catholic Diocese of Owensboro Charitable Trust Fund, Inc. Retired.
Powell, Philip Neri *o.p.* (NO)[P] New Orleans Dominican Friars, Southern Dominican Province of St. Martin de Porres.
Powell, Philip *o.p.* '05 (FgM) Metairie, LA St. Martin de Porres Province (Southern Dominican Province).
Powell, Robert J. '76 (FR) Orleans, MA St. Joan of Arc.
Powell, Rev. Msgr. Robert J. '74 (PH) Jamison, PA St. Cyril of Jerusalem; Defenders of the Bond.
Power, David N. *o.m.i., s.t.d.* '56 (WDC)[N] Washington, DC Oblate Community.
Power, Eugene J. *s.j.* '51 (PH)[Y] Loyola Center and Manresa Hall.
Power, Frank *s.v.d.* '73 (FgM) Techny, IL.
Power, Gerard *o.carm.* '99 (JOL)[L] Darien Carmelite Provincial Office.
Power, J. Timothy '66 (STP) Retired.
Power, James F. '62 (BO) Senior Priests. Retired.
Power, Patrick *c.ss.r.* '66 (KC) Kansas City, MO Our Lady of Perpetual Help; [J] Kansas City, MO Redemptorists Fathers of Kansas City, Missouri.
Powers, Aloysius '48 (OWN) Retired.
Powers, Rev. Msgr. Bernard '52 (OWN) Daughters of Isabella Retired.
Powers, Bruce J. '73 (RVC) Manorville, NY Sts. Peter & Paul; Chaplains of the Suffolk County Police Department.
Powers, Charles '97 (MIA) Absent on Leave.
Powers, Daniel *s.j.* '68 (HEL) Heart Butte, MT St. Anne (Blackfeet Reservation).
Powers, Glenn E. '87 (MIL) Sheboygan, WI SS. Cyril and Methodius; Sheboygan, WI Immaculate Conception.
Powers, Isaias *c.p.* '61 (BRK)[T] Jamaica, NY Immaculate Conception Monastery Retired.
Powers, James P. '90 (SUP) Rice Lake, WI St. Joseph; Adjutant Judicial Vicar; Board of Directors.
Powers, John J. '51 (CHI) South Holland, IL St. Jude the Apostle Retired.
Powers, John *c.p.* '77 (NY)[GG] Bronx, NY The Passionist Spiritual Center/Cardinal Spellman Retreat House; [EE] Riverdale, NY Passionist Spiritual Center.
Powers, Joseph '79 (KC) St. Joseph, MO Co–Catherdral of St. Joseph.
Powers, Richard E. '56 (E) Retired.
Powers, Rev. Msgr. Richard T. '63 (PH) Philadelphia, PA Epiphany of Our Lord.
Powers, Richard '59 (OWN) Curdsville, KY St. Elizabeth; Owensboro, KY St. Alphonsus Retired.
Powers, Robert M. '92 (BRK) Brooklyn, NY Saint Paul and Saint Agnes Roman Catholic Church.

Powers, Thomas F. '66 (BO) Wellesley, MA St. John the Evangelist.
Powers, Thomas J. (BO) Lynnfield, MA St. Maria Goretti.
Powers, Thomas J. *s.j.* '95 (SJ)[B] Santa Clara, CA Jesuit Community.
Powers, Thomas M. '62 (ALB) Retired.
Powers, Thomas M. '49 (CHI) Wilmette, IL St. Joseph Retired.
Powers, Thomas '97 (BGP) On Duty Outside the Diocese.
Powers, Troy David '87 (SAC) Sacramento, CA Presentation of the Blessed Virgin Mary; Absent on Leave.
Powers, William V. '58 (PBL) Retired.
Powhida, Robert '78 (ALB) Schenectady, NY St. Madeleine Sophie; Schenectady, NY St. Gabriel the Archangel.
Powis, Rev. Msgr. John J. '59 (BRK) Retired.
Poyatt, Rev. Msgr. William F. '49 (CAM) Retired.
Pozdol, Henry '50 (CHI) Summit, IL St. Joseph Retired.
Pozen, Matthew '01 (JOL) Absent on Leave.
Pozza, Aldo *m.c.c.j.* '66 (CHI) Franklin Park, IL St. Gertrude.
Prabell, Paul '72 (LEX) Defenders of the Bond; Promoter of Justice; [L] Morehead, KY Catholic Student Center–Morehead State University; Morehead, KY Church of Jesus Our Savior.
Prachar, Andrew M. '90 (NEW) Berkeley Heights, NJ Church of the Little Flower.
Pracz, Thaddeus '66 (PEO) Danville, IL Holy Family; Diocesan College of Consultors; Vicariates and Vicars.
Prada, John J. '09 (NEW) Secaucus, NJ Immaculate Conception.
Prada, Mario '07 (CR) Mahnomen, MN St. Michael's Parish; Hispanic Ministry; Commission on Hispanic Affairs.
Prado, A. Benito '04 (NEW) Hoboken, NJ SS. Peter and Paul's; Part–time Staff.
Prado, Amilcar B. '04 (NEW)[P] Hoboken, NJ Catholic Campus Ministry at Stevens Institute of Technology.
Prado, Giopre '09 (OAK) Oakley, CA St. Anthony.
Prado, Manuel *c.m.* '62 (PCE) Ponce, PR La Milagrosa.
Prado, Rodolfo '04 (LA) On Administrative Leave.
Prado, Teodoro Tim Y. '77 (GAL)[S] Houston, TX The Catholic Chaplain Corps.
Praem, Jude Lucier O. '74 (ORG) Garden Grove, CA St. Callistus.
Pragasam, Albert Susai *o.s.m.* (STL) Affton, MO Seven Holy Founders.
Pragasam, John Peter '05 (STO) Modesto, CA St. Joseph Church of Modesto (Pastor of).
Prager, John P. *c.m.* '82 (FgM) Philadelphia, PA Eastern Province.
Prakash, Gnana '80 (NY) Bronx, NY Our Lady of the Assumption.
Prakash, Madineni '92 (OKL) Elgin, OK St. Ann.
Prakuzhy, Zacharias *c.m.i.* '68 (SHP) Lake Providence, LA St. Patrick; Oak Grove, LA Sacred Heart.
Prall, Arthur J. *m.m.* '52 (FgM) Maryknoll, NY MARYKNOLL.
Prall, Arthur J. *m.m.* '52 (NY)[EE] Retired.
Pranaitis, Mark S. *c.m.* '93 (STL)[O] Earth City, MO Congregation of the Mission Western Province (Vincentians).
Pranzo, Joseph F. *c.s.* '71 (MIA) Margate, FL St. Vincent.
Prasad, Ananda *m.s.f.s.* '96 (TYL)[B] Whitehouse, TX The Missionaries of St. Francis de Sales.
Praski, Jacek *c.r.* '91 (CHI) Chicago, IL St. Wenceslaus.
Prass, Charles *o.m.i.* '45 (BEL)[F] Belleville, IL Shrine of Our Lady of the Snows Retired.
Prasser, Jeffery A. '89 (MIL) West Allis, WI St. Rita; West Allis, WI St. Aloysius Gonzaga.
Prati, Jason M. '02 (STU) On Leave.
Prati, Jason '02 (STU) College of Consultors.
Pratico, Rev. Msgr. Patrick J. '79 (SCR) Dickson City, PA Visitation of the Blessed Virgin Mary; Judges; Procurator/Advocates.
Pratscher, Matthew '08 (JOL) Elmhurst, IL Visitation.
Pratt, Dean '97 (DAL) Retired.
Pratt, Edward '08 (CIN) Dayton, OH St. Rita; Dayton, OH Precious Blood.
Pratt, James F.X. *s.j.* '86 (BO)[U] Boston The Society of Jesus of New England–Provincial Offices.
Pratt, James *s.m.* '46 (SFR)[K] San Francisco, CA Home for the Aged of the Little Sisters of the Poor Retired.
Pratt, Lawrence E. '62 (BO) Presbyteral Council; Senior Priests. Retired.
Pratt, Oscar J. '96 (BO) West Roxbury, MA Holy Name.
Pravetz, Matthew A. *o.f.m.* '79 (NY) New York, NY Holy Name of Jesus.
Pray, Joseph N. '50 (BUR) Retired.
Prechtl, Ronald G. '80 (WH) Morgantown, WV St. Luke the Evangelist.
Preciado, Guillermo '02 (FRS) Fresno, CA St. John Cathedral.
Preciado, Rudolph J. '69 (ORG) Anaheim, CA St. Anthony Claret.
Precourt, Peter *a.a.* '76 (WOR) Fiskdale, MA St. Anne's and St. Patrick's.
Predelus, Dessier (NY) Spring Valley, NY St. Joseph.
Predmore, John A. *s.j.* '05 (PRT)[C] Portland, ME Cheverus High School.
Pregana, Craig A. '89 (FR) Special Assignment.
Prehn, James S. *s.j.* '99 (DET) Chicago, IL; [K] Chicago, IL Jesuit Provincial Office–Detroit Province of the Society of Jesus; Detroit, MI.
Prehn, James S. *s.j.* '99 (CHI)[N] Chicago, IL Chicago Province of the Society of Jesus–Provincial Office; [N] Evanston, IL Canisius House.
Preisinger, Robert F. '63 (OM) Fort Calhoun, NE St. John the Baptist.
Premarini, Peter *m.c.c.j.* (CHI) Chicago, IL St. Martin De Porres.
Prenatt, David E. '95 (E) North East, PA St. Gregory Thaumaturgus.
Prendergast, Edmond '73 (MIA) Davie, FL St. Bonaventure.
Prendergast, Fergus J. '94 (MOB) On Leave from the Archdiocese.
Prendergast, Rev. Msgr. John J. '76 (PEO) Ransom, IL St. Patrick's; Streator, IL Immaculate Conception; Streator, IL St. Anthony of Padua; Streator, IL St. Casimir; Streator, IL St. Stephen's; Diocesan College of Consultors.
Prendergast, Joseph *c.s.sp.* '54 (SJ) Santa Clara, CA St. Justin Retired.
Prendergast, Noel '58 (JKS) Retired.
Prendergast, Richard J. '79 (CHI) Chicago, IL St. Josaphat.
Prendergast, Robert E. '50 (PEO) Retired.
Prendergast, Rev. Msgr. Thomas '56 (SD) San Diego, CA Immaculate Conception Retired.
Prendeville, Thomas (MRY) St. Francis Central Coast Catholic High School, Inc.
Prendiville, Edmond P. '63 (PRO) On Duty Outside the Diocese.
Prendiville, Eugene *o.m.i.* '58 (SFD) Madison, IL St. Mary and St. Mark.
Prendiville, Kerry '84 (RC) Lead, SD St. Ambrose; Lead, SD St. Patrick's; Continuing Education of Clergy; Director of Ongoing Formation.
Prendiville, Thomas *s.d.b.* '56 (SFR)[N] San Francisco, CA Salesian Provincial Residence.
Preneta, Henry S. '67 (GBG)[F] Greensburg, PA Neumann House Retired.
Prengaman, Leo P. *s.j.* (SLC) West Haven, UT Saint Mary LLC 237.
Prensa, Pedro Velez '04 (PHX) Scottsdale, AZ St. Daniel the Prophet Roman Catholic Parish.
Prentice, Theodore R. '04 (P) Tigard, OR St. Anthony.
Presenti, Richard *s.d.b.* '68 (SFR)[N] San Francisco, CA Salesian Provincial Residence.
Preske, Venantius '52 (LR) Retired.
Preskenis, James T. *c.s.c.* '75 (BUR) The Review Board; Bennington, VT Sacred Heart St. Francis de Sales; Deans; Canon 1742 Panel of Pastors.
Presley, Joseph *i.c.* '01 (PEO) Galesburg, IL Corpus Christi; Abingdon, IL Sacred Heart; Galesburg, IL St. Patrick's.
Presmanes, Jorge L. *o.p.* '91 (MIA)[K] Miami, FL Dominican Fathers of Miami, Inc.; Miami, FL St. Dominic; [B] Miami, FL Barry University.
Presta, James '86 (CHI)[A] Chicago, IL St. Joseph College Seminary; [A] Chicago, IL St. Joseph College Seminary; St. Joseph College Seminary at Loyola University; The Tuite Program at St. Joseph College Seminary.
Preston, Laurence *m.s.a.* '94 (NOR)[G] Cromwell Society of the Missionaries of the Holy Apostles.
Presutti, Robert *l.c.* '98 (SAC) Sacramento, CA Our Lady of Guadalupe Shrine; [B] Sacramento, CA University of Sacramento.
Pretto, Franklin D. '72 (SFE) Santa Fe, NM San Isidro.
Preuss, David *o.f.m.cap.* '79 (MIL)[P] Milwaukee, WI St. Conrad Friary; Milwaukee, WI St. Martin de Porres.
Preuss, Richard *c.m.* '73 (FgM) Earth City, MO Western Province.
Previtali, Joseph F. '09 (SFR) Graduate Studies.
Previte, Joseph '07 (CLV) Parma, OH St. Columbkille.
Prevost, Robert F. *o.s.a.* '82 (CHI)[N] Olympia Fields, IL Tolentine Monastery at Tolentine Center.
Prevosto, Paul '96 (NEW) Hackensack, NJ Holy Trinity.
Prez, Daniel J. '74 (E) Cambridge Springs Correction Institution; Pleasant Ridge Manor West; Erie, PA St. Patrick.
Pribek, James M. *s.j.* '99 (BUF)[O] Buffalo, NY Canisius Jesuit Community Inc.
Pribonic, Phillip '67 (PIT) South Park, PA St. Joan of Arc.
Pribula, Duane '70 (CR) Nevis, MN Our Lady of the Pines; Nevis, MN St. Theodore of Tarsus – Laporte.
Pribyl, Ross *s.j.* '99 (CHI)[D] Chicago, IL St. Ignatius College Prep; [D] Chicago, IL St. Ignatius Jesuit Community.
Pricco, Rev. Msgr. Richard A. '62 (PEO) Macomb, IL St. Paul's; Rushville, IL St. Rose; Vicariates and Vicars.
Price, Bede *o.s.b.* '96 (STL)[O] St. Louis, MO The Abbey of St. Mary and St. Louis; [F] Creve Coeur, MO St. Louis Priory School; Creve Coeur, MO Saint Gregory the Great and Saint Augustine of Canterbury Oratory.
Price, James A. *c.p.* '94 (FgM) South River, NJ St. Paul of the Cross Province; South River, NJ.
Price, James *c.p.* '94 (MET)[I] South River Passionist Provincial Office.
Price, John R. '66 (CHI) Other Assignments.
Price, Rothell '88 (SHP) Shreveport, LA St. Mary of the Pines; Adjutant Judicial Vicar; Judges; Black Catholic Commission; Church Vocations Board & Vocations Office.
Pridons, Dominique (BAL) Clarksville, MD St. Louis.
Priebe, Rev. Msgr. Norman F. '67 (LA) Los Angeles, CA St. Jerome.
Priest, Rev. Msgr. Gerald A. '68 (TYL) Texarkana, TX Sacred Heart; Texarkana, TX Federal Corrections Institution; College of Consultors; Deans; Priests' Pension Board; Priests' Personnel Board.
Priestly, Joseph *s.m.* '55 (HON)[D] Honolulu, HI Marianist Hall Community.
Prieto, Carlos '00 (RVC) Brentwood, NY St. Luke.
Prieto, Frank '64 (SFE) Retired.
Prietto, Mario J. *s.j.* '73 (SFR)[N] San Francisco, CA Loyola House Jesuit Community.
Prill, Mark P. '08 (DET) Troy, MI St. Anastasia.
Primavera, Mauro '09 (NEW) Nutley, NJ Holy Family.
Primich, John '95 (MET) Flemington, NJ St. Magdalen de Pazzi.
Primor, Salvino '99 (LAF) Lafayette, LA St. Genevieve.
Prince, Joseph A. '71 (BGP) Ridgefield, CT St. Elizabeth Seton.
Prince, Leo R. '86 (NY) Staten Island, NY St. Roch.
Prince, Michael J. '98 (DET) Absent on Leave.
Principe, Francis J. '53 (NY)[E] Bronx, NY Cardinal Spellman High School.
Prindiville, Gerald T. '96 (NEW) On Duty Outside the Archdiocese.
Prinelli, John '78 (RIC) Christiansburg, VA Holy Spirit Catholic Church; Pearisburg, VA Holy Family.
Pringle, John R. '72 (MET) Bridgewater, NJ Holy Trinity.
Printy, Michael G. '57 (OM) Retired.
Prior, Felix *o.carm.* '58 (BO)[Z] Peabody, MA St. Theresa Carmelite Chapel; [U] Peabody, MA Our Lady of the Scapular Priory.
Prior, James G. *c.m.* '53 (ALN) Roseto, PA Our Lady of Mt. Carmel.
Prior, Rev. Msgr. Joseph G. '90 (PH)[A] Wynnewood, PA Theological Seminary of St. Charles Borromeo, Overbrook; St. Charles Borromeo Seminary; Censores Librorum.
Prior, Richard '01 (SY) Syracuse, NY Holy Family.
Prior, Robert *c.m.* '92 (PH)[Y].
Prior, Thomas W. *c.m.* '59 (ALN) Roseto, PA Our Lady of Mt. Carmel.
Priscaro, Jerry S. '93 (E) Erie, PA Our Mother of Sorrows.
Prist, Wayne F. '67 (CHI) Chicago, IL Queen of All Saints Basilica.
Pritt, Phillip P. '62 (CLV) Rittman, OH St. Anne; Parma, OH St. Matthias Retired.
Pritzl, Kurt *o.p.* '91 (WDC)[B] Washington, DC Dominican House of Studies; [C] Washington, DC Catholic University of America, The; [C] Catholic University of America, The.
Prive, Francis R. '69 (BUR) Morrisville, VT The Parish of the Holy Name of Jesus.
Privett, John *s.j.* '72 (SJ)[M] Los Gatos, CA Sacred Heart Jesuit Center.
Privett, Stephen A. *s.j.* '72 (SFR)[C] San Francisco, CA University of San Francisco; [N] San Francisco, CA Loyola House Jesuit Community.
Proback, Adrian *o.c.s.o.* '54 (WOR)[O] Spencer, MA St. Joseph's Abbey.
Probst, R. Dean '81 (SFD) Rochester, IL St. Jude; Office for Tribunal Services.
Procaccini, David C. '93 (PRO) Providence, RI Holy Cross.
Procella, Rev. Msgr. Paul '87 (GAL) Retired.
Prochaska, John '93 (OAK) Fremont, CA Our Lady of Guadalupe; Deanery #14; Priest Representative; Pastoral Leadership Placement Board (PLPB).
Prochnow, Josef *o.f.m.* (OAK)[O] Danville, CA San Damiano Retreat.
Procopio, Clement *o.f.m.* '44 (NY)[EE] New York Franciscan Province of the Immaculate Conception.
Proctor, John '72 (SD) Presbyteral Council.
Procyk, Marijan '80 (STF) Buffalo, NY St. Nicholas; Buffalo; Presbyteral Council; Apostleship of Prayer; League of Ukrainian Catholics.
Prodanets, Mykhaylo '01 (PSC) Kingston, PA St. Mary's.
Prodehl, Richard B. '66 (JOL) Retired.
Proehl, Douglas '74 (CLV) Absent on Leave.
Proenza, Rafael *o.p.* '96 (FgM)[P] New Orleans Dominican Friars, Southern Dominican Province of St. Martin de Porres; Metairie, LA St. Martin de Porres Province (Southern Dominican Province).
Profeta, Salvatore '50 (PMB) Retired.

Proffitt, James (BAL) Severna Park, MD St. John the Evangelist.
Profota, James H. '75 (DET) Retired.
Prokes, Francis A. *s.j.* '57 (OM)[K] Omaha, NE Jesuit Community at Creighton University.
Prokopiw, Taras *o.s.b.m.* '58 (RVC)[M] Glen Cove, NY St. Josaphat's Monastery, Novitiate and Retreat House.
Prokopiw, Taras *o.s.b.m.* '58 (STF)[B] Glen Cove, NY Basilian Fathers Novitiate of the Order of St. Basil the Great.
Promesso, William J. '87 (DET) Riverview, MI St. Cyprian.
Promis, Christopher *c.s.sp.* '72 (BAL)[S] Baltimore, MD Congregation of the Holy Spirit.
Pronesti, Salvatore J. '67 (PH) Bridgeport, PA Our Lady of Mt. Carmel.
Proppe, John *o.f.m.cap.* '47 (NY)[EE] Yonkers, NY St. Clare Friary.
Propst, Sergius *o.p.* '73 (OAK)[M] Oakland, CA Order of Preachers (Province of the Most Holy Name of Jesus – Western Dominican Province); [A] Berkeley, CA Dominican School of Philosophy and Theology.
Prospero, William *s.j.* '98 (SAG) Mount Pleasant, MI St. Mary University Parish.
Prost, Charles E. *c.m.* '78 (STL)[O] Perryville, MO Congregation of the Mission.
Protack, Thomas J. *s.t.l.* '96 (WIL) Berlin, MD St. John Neumann Roman Catholic Church.
Protano, Joseph '63 (PRO) Block Island, RI St. Andrew.
Proterra, Michael *s.j.* '71 (R) Raleigh, NC St. Raphael the Archangel; [F] Raleigh Jesuit Community.
Protopapas, George *o.m.i.* '43 (SAT)[K] San Antonio, TX Oblate Madonna Residence.
Proulx, Arthur J. '80 (SP) Brandon, FL Church of the Nativity.
Proulx, Arthur '70 (SP) Vicars Forane; College of Consultors.
Proulx, Raymond G. '60 (HRT) Retired.
Prout, Thomas S. *s.j.* '92 (NY)[EE] New York, NY Murray–Weigel Hall.
Provanzano, Thomas *s.d.b.* (NY)[F] New Rochelle, NY Salesian High School.
Provenza, Rev. Msgr. Earl V. '64 (SHP) Shreveport, LA Holy Trinity; Vicars Forane; Deans; Priests' Retirement Board; College of Consultors; Ex Officio Members.
Provenza, John F. '90 (LA) San Pedro, CA Mary, Star of the Sea.
Provinsal, Thomas G. *s.j.* '75 (FBK)[E] St. Marys, AK Brother Joe Prince Jesuit Community.
Provinzano, Rocco '66 (NEW) Retired.
Provost, John T. '73 (ALB) Nassau, NY St. Mary.
Provost, John T. '73 (ALB) Priests Retirement Board/ Priests Retirement Plan Board; Averill Park, NY St. Henry.
Proxell, Leo J. '77 (HEL) Bozeman, MT Holy Rosary; Diocesan Consultors; Deaneries.
Prucha, Francis Paul *s.j.* '57 (MIL)[P] Milwaukee, WI Jesuit Community at Marquette University.
Pruett, Bill '79 (OKL) Guymon, OK St. Peter's; [K] Goodwell, OK Oklahoma Panhandle State University; Region VI.
Prunty, Brian J. *o.praem.* '65 (GB)[J] De Pere, WI St. Joseph Priory; [B] St. Norbert College.
Prus, Edward J. '61 (DET) Retired.
Prus, Rev. Msgr. Eugene '64 (MET) Martinsville, NJ Blessed Sacrament.
Prusaitis, John P. '78 (BO) Maynard, MA St. Bridget.
Prusakowski, Gerald A. *o.f.m.* '65 (GB)[J] Wausaukee, WI Villa Alverna; Sobieski, WI St. Maximilian Kolbe.
Pruss, Rodney Lee A. '69 (GI) Retired.
Prusynski, Chester *c.s.c.* '62 (P)[B][L] Portland, OR Holy Cross Fathers & Brothers, C.S.C. – University of Portland Retired.
Prusynski, Chester *c.s.c.* (FTW)[H] Notre Dame Congregation of Holy Cross, Indiana Province, Provincial House.
Pruys, George L. '75 (STN) Wilton, ND SS. Peter and Paul.
Prybis, Raymond A. *o.m.i.* '67 (STP)[N] Buffalo, MN Christ the King Retreat Center.
Pryor, G. Robert '55 (CR) Retired.
Przepiora, Mieczyslaw "Mitchell" '90 (AMA) Defenders of the Bond; Propagation of the Faith; Panhandle, TX St. Theresa; White Deer, TX Sacred Heart.
Przybilla, Troy D. '05 (STP) Lonsdale, MN Immaculate Conception; Deanery 7.
Przybocki, Rev. Msgr. Bernard A. '58 (ALT) Retired.
Przybyla, Kenneth '77 (COS) Littleton, CO Pax Christi Catholic Church; Presbyteral Council; College of Consultors.
Przybyla, Philip J. '70 (PIT) Verona, PA St. Joseph.
Przybylski, Donald L. '74 (LC) Mosinee, WI St. Paul.
Przybysz, Joseph J. '75 (TOL) Fort Jennings, OH St. Joseph.
Przybysz, Mark C. '90 (GR) Grand Rapids, MI St. Anthony of Padua; On Special Assignment; Continuing Education for Clergy.
Przygocki, Edward *m.s.a.* '81 (NOR)[G] Cromwell Society of the Missionaries of the Holy Apostles.
Przystasz, Wojciech '98 (LAR) Laredo, TX Blessed Sacrament; Presbyteral Council.
Ptacek, John P. '55 (DUB) Retired.
Ptak, Slawomir '03 (BEL) Dahlgren, IL St. John Nepomucene; McLeansboro, IL St. Clement; McLeansboro, IL St. John the Baptist.
Ptak, Walter J. '87 (DET) Wyandotte, MI St. Stanislaus Kostka; Wyandotte, MI Our Lady of Mt. Carmel.
Ptaszynski, Thomas E. '73 (HRT) West Hartford, CT St. Mark the Evangelist; Glastonbury, CT St. Dunstan.
Pu, Matthew '53 (B) Retired.
Pua'auli, Kelemete '01 (SPP) Pago Pago, AS Co–Cathedral of St. Joseph the Worker; Faculty Members; Auditors; Diocesan Consultors.
Pucar, August '63 (BEA) Retired.
Pucci, Alfred '54 (NY) Staten Island, NY Holy Family Retired.
Pucciarelli, George W. '74 (BO) On Duty Outside the Archdiocese.
Puccinelli, Alfred *s.m.* '66 (FgM) THE SOCIETY OF MARY.
Puchalski, Andrzej '75 (PAT) Passaic, NJ St. Joseph's.
Puchenski, Anthony C. '71 (CHI) Des Plaines, IL St. Zachary.
Puchner, Augustine R. *o.praem.* '97 (ORG)[I] Silverado, CA Norbertine Fathers of Orange Inc.; Costa Mesa, CA St. John the Baptist.
Pucke, Michael U. '73 (CIN) Hamilton, OH St. Julie Billiart; Priest Councilors; Consultors.
Pucke, Michael '73 (CIN) Imprimatur Censors.
Pudhota, Arul '92 (OKL) Oklahoma City, OK St. Charles Borromeo.
Pudhota, Paul L. '92 (SCR) Wilkes–Barre, PA Holy Trinity.
Pudichery, Joseph P. '62 (PIT) Chicora, PA Mater Dolorosa; Chicora, PA St. Joseph.
Pudota, Joseph Sundar Raju '82 (OKL) Altus, OK Prince of Peace.
Pudota, Rayanna '01 (OKL)[C] Oklahoma City, OK Mount St. Mary High School; Oklahoma City, OK Sacred Heart.
Pudota, Shouraiah '79 (SFR) San Francisco, CA Church of the Epiphany.
Pudota, Thomas (GLP) Aztec, NM St. Joseph; Aztec, NM Holy Trinity.
Pudussery, Devasia '80 (BAL)[S] Emmitsburg, MD Vincentian House.
Puente, Benjamin '07 (STO) Stockton, CA Cathedral of the Annunciation (Pastor of).
Puente, Francisco '00 (SAT) San Antonio, TX St. Joan of Arc.
Puentes, Jesus '86 (CHI) Chicago, IL St. Philomena.
Puentes–Mejia, Abraham '94 (AUS) Austin, TX St. Louis.
Puerta, Jorge '89 (MIA) Absent on Sick Leave.
Puetz, Richard W. '45 (LFT) Retired.
Puga, Gerardo '94 (DEN) Denver, CO Church of the Ascension.
Pugat, Gaudencio G. *s.v.d.* '85 (RIC) Tazewell, VA Holy Family Parish.
Pugh, James L. '67 (MEM) Memphis, TN St. Paul The Apostle.
Pugliese, Francis A. '68 (NY) Military Chaplains.
Pugliese, Rev. Msgr. Frank A. '68 (MO) Vicar General & Moderator of the Curia; Presbyteral Council.
Pugliese, Steven J. *s.j.* '93 (NY)[EE] New York, NY St. Ignatius Loyola Residence.
Puglisi, James F. *s.a.* '73 (NY)[EE] Garrison, NY Franciscan Friars of the Atonement, Minister General Office; [EE] Garrison Franciscan Friars of the Atonement, Minister General Office; General Council.
Puguscik, Jerzy *o.f.m.conv.* (HRT)[M] Provincial House.
Puhak, Rev. Msgr. Nicholas I. '57 (PSC) Freeland, PA St. Mary's.
Puhlman, Robert W. '84 (LAV) Overton, NV St. John the Evangelist; Priests' Pension Board; Mesquite, NV La Virgen de Guadalupe.
Puigbo, Juan A. '01 (WDC)[B] Washington, DC Diocesan Laborer Priests, House of Studies; Washington, DC Diocesan Laborer Priests.
Puisis, John C. *c.s.v.* '45 (CHI)[N] Arlington Heights Viatorian Province Center–Clerics of St. Viator.
Puisis, Leonard '52 (MIA) Retired.
Puiyanampattayil, Tomy Joseph *m.s.f.s.* '94 (SYM) Loretto, TN Blessed Mother Theresa Syro–Malabar Mission Nashville, TN.
Pujante, P. Jesus Monreal *o.carm.* '69 (ARE) Diocesan Consultors.
Pujdak, Steve *s.c.j.* '69 (SP)[N] Pinellas Park, FL Priests of the Sacred Heart.
Pujos, Nathanael '04 (DEN)[R] Denver, CO The Catholic Community of the Beatitudes; Denver, CO St. Catherine of Siena.
Pulaski, Joseph S. *m.m.* '47 (NY)[EE] Retired.
Puleo, Augustus C. '05 (PH) Philadelphia, PA Our Lady of Mt. Carmel.
Puleo, Edward C. '88 (MET) Far Hills, NJ St. Elizabeth; College of Consultors; Department of Clergy and Religious Personnel; Office for Priest Personnel.
Pulgarin, Rene Mauricio '04 (TR) Princeton, NJ St. Paul.
Pulice, John J. '66 (MIL) Milwaukee, WI St. Roman Retired.
Pulickal, Sony G. '83 (OG) Deans; Indian Lake, NY St. Mary's.
Pulickaparambil, Alex '05 (GF) Miles City, MT Sacred Heart; Special Assignment.
Pulido, Felipe '02 (YAK) Moses Lake, WA Our Lady of Fatima; Diocesan Consultors; Vocations; Presbyteral Council Executive Committee; Moses Lake, WA Queen of All Saints.
Puling, Tarsisius *s.v.d.* '04 (JKS) Shaw, MS St. Francis of Assisi; Greenville, MS Sacred Heart; Indianola, MS St. Benedict the Moor; Indianola, MS Immaculate Conception.
Pulivelil, Peter *c.m.i.* '72 (SHP) Grambling, LA St. Benedict the Black; [F] Grambling, LA Student Center.
Puliynampattayil, Tomy *m.s.f.s.* '94 (TYL)[B] Whitehouse, TX The Missionaries of St. Francis de Sales.
Puljic, Marko *o.f.m.* '81 (CHI)[N] Chicago, IL Croatian Franciscan Custody of the Holy Family; Chicago, IL.
Pullambryayil, Baby George '93 (FWT) Hillsboro, TX Our Lady of Mercy; Abbott, TX Immaculate Heart of Mary; Penelope, TX Nativity of the Blessed Virgin Mary.
Pullikattil, Joseph '00 (HRT)[H] Waterbury, CT Saint Mary's Hospital.
Pullukattu, Anthony *o.ss.t.* '04 (BAL)[S] The Trinitarians in India (Bangalore & Trichur).
Pulparayil, George '67 (NY) Monroe, NY Sacred Heart Church.
Pulskamp, Rev. Msgr. James E. '67 (SR) Vicar General; Chancellor; Director of Clergy Personnel; Notaries; Board of Consultors; Priests' Council; Finance Committee; Diocesan Building Committee; Review Board; Archivist; Clergy Personnel Committee; Custodian of Records; Santa Rosa, CA Cathedral of St. Eugene.
Puma, Rev. Msgr. Vincent E. (PAT) Retired.
Punakkattu, Sojan '00 (SP) Lutz, FL St. Timothy.
Punch, Nicholas W. *o.p.* '66 (SUP)[H] Webster, WI Thomas More Center for Preaching and Prayer, Inc.
Punchayil, Mathew '72 (SYM) Darnestown, MD Syro–Malabar Catholic Mission of Greater Washington; Darnestown, MD Our Lady of the Visitation.
Punderson, Rev. Msgr. Joseph R. '76 (TR) On Duty Outside the Diocese.
Pung, Karl L. '97 (LAN) Brighton, MI St. Patrick; College of Consultors; Priestly Life and Ministry.
Pung, Karl '97 (LAN) Priests' Assignment Commission.
Punnackal, Antony *c.m.i.* '92 (AMA) Vega, TX Immaculate Conception.
Punnakunnel, John '79 (BGP) Bridgeport, CT Holy Rosary Retired.
Punnolil, George '80 (CAM) Haddonfield, NJ Church of Christ the King, Haddonfield, N.J.
Punnoose, Siby '98 (SC) Fonda, IA Our Lady of Good Counsel; Fonda, IA St. Columbkille's.
Puntal, Pedro (Peter) '82 (ORL) Filipino Ministry; Winter Haven, FL St. Joseph's.
Puntal, Peter '82 (ORL) Deans; Ex Officio Members.
Punti, George '55 (RVC) Elmont, NY St. Boniface Retired.
Puntino, John *s.d.b.* '78 (NY)[GG] Stony Point, NY Don Bosco Retreat Center and Marian Shrine; [GG] Stony Point, NY Marian Shrine.
Puntrello, Philip *r.c.j.* '63 (FRS) Sanger, CA St. Katherine; Sanger, CA St. Mary; Sanger, CA.
Punzalan, Manolo '92 (NEW) Maplewood, NJ St. Joseph's.
Puodziunas, John *o.f.m.* '87 (MIL)[P] Provincial Offices of the Franciscan Friars, Assumption BVM Province, Inc.
Puopolo, Rocco *s.x.* '77 (WDC)[W] Washington, DC Africa Faith & Justice Network.
Pupius, George '63 (OKL) Oklahoma City, OK Immaculate Conception.
Pupsys, Adam '52 (NOR) Retired.
Puraidam, George *m.s.f.s.* '75 (TYL)[B] Whitehouse, TX The Missionaries of St. Francis de Sales.
Puravakkatt, Titus Augustine *c.m.i.* '99 (SFE) Arroyo Seco, NM La Santisima Trinidad.
Purawan, Lucito T. '96 (NY) Staten Island, NY St. John Neumann.
Purayidathil, Thomas '80 (HON) Aiea, HI St. Elizabeth; College of Consultors; Diocesan Theological Commission; Office of Clergy Priest Retirement Committee.
Purcaro, Arthur P. *o.s.a.* '75 (FgM) Villanova, PA Province of St. Thomas of Villanova (Eastern).
Purcell, Rev. Msgr. Lawrence M. '65 (SD) Rancho Santa Fe, CA Church of the Nativity; Vicars Forane.
Purcell, Mark *o.s.b.* '05 (RIC)[K] Richmond, VA Mary Mother of the Church Abbey.
Purcell, Rev. Msgr. Paul J. '54 (SCR)[N] Dunmore, PA Villa St. Joseph Retired.
Purcell, Richard P. *o.f.m.* '68 (SFR) San Francisco, CA St. Boniface.
Purcell, Robert '74 (ALB) Retired.

Purdy, David *s.d.b.* '70 (OAK)[M] Berkeley Salesians of Don Bosco.
Purfield, James R. '54 (DEN) Denver, CO All Saints.
Purpura, Peter J. '07 (BRK) Graduate Studies.
Purta, Jerome J. *o.s.b.* '61 (GBG)[G] Latrobe, PA Saint Vincent Archabbey.
Purtell, Jack *s.o.l.t.* '95 (CC)[G] Robstown, TX Society of Our Lady of the Most Holy Trinity.
Purtell, John J. '68 (DUB) Retired.
Purtell, Thomas J. '61 (CHI) Chicago, IL St. John Fisher; Chicago, IL St. Christina Retired.
Purtell, Thomas W. '53 (DUB) Retired.
Purvey, John J. '84 (BAL) Retired.
Puryear, Stan '95 (OWN) Bowling Green, KY St. Joseph's.
Pusak, Ronald '61 (MIA) Defenders of the Bond Retired.
Pusateri, Christian *o.s.b.* '55 (RCK)[G] Aurora, IL Marmion Abbey.
Pusateri, Joseph M. *s.m.* '66 (WDC)[N] Washington, DC Marist Center Retired.
Pusateri, Samuel D. *o.s.b.* '79 (PEO)[A] Peru, IL St. Bede Abbey.
Pusch, Richard '71 (SHP) Forcht Wade Correctional Center; Jail–Prison Ministry.
Pushpanathan, Zacarias '81 (HRT) Hartford, CT St. Anne–Immaculate Conception.
Putano, John P. '70 (SY) Vestal, NY Our Lady of Sorrows; Southern Area Vicar; Presbyteral Council; Board of Diocesan Consultors.
Putenparambil, James '80 (CC) Mathis, TX Sacred Heart.
Putera, Vasyl '96 (PHU) Jersey City, NJ SS. Peter and Paul.
Putharayil, Benny D. '94 (BIS) Tioga, ND St. Thomas; Tioga, ND St. Michael; Tioga, ND St. James.
Puthenangady, Paul (CC) Kingsville, TX Our Lady of Good Counsel.
Puthenkulathil, Joseph '76 (SFS) Tabor, SD St. Wenceslaus.
Puthenpeedika, George '79 (LAN) Flint, MI Holy Rosary.
Puthenpurackal, Binoj Mathew *o.ss.t.* '08 (BAL)[S] The Trinitarians in India (Bangalore & Trichur).
Puthenpurakal, Bitaju *o.ss.t.* '01 (BAL)[S] The Trinitarians in India (Bangalore & Trichur).
Puthenveettil, Pradeep *o.ss.t.* '05 (BAL)[S] The Trinitarians in India (Bangalore & Trichur).
Puthenveettil, Pradeep *o.ss.t.* '05 (TR) Trenton, NJ The Church of the Incarnation–St. James.
Puthiaparampil, Abraham *m.s.f.s.* '98 (ATL)[G] Snellville, GA The Missionaries of St. Francis De Sales.
Puthiyadom, Thomas '66 (SYM) Hartford, CT St. Thomas Syro–Malabar Mission of Hartford.
Puthiyadom, Thomas '66 (HRT)[H] Hartford, CT Saint Francis Hospital and Medical Center; West Hartford, CT St. Helena.
Puthiyaparampil, Johnny *m.s.f.s.* '98 (TYL)[B] Whitehouse, TX The Missionaries of St. Francis de Sales.
Puthoff, Chad *s.d.s.* '71 (NSH) Cookeville, TN St. Thomas Aquinas.
Puthota, Charles '89 (SFR) South San Francisco, CA St. Veronica.
Puthumayil, Chacko '71 (GAL) La Marque, TX Queen of Peace.
Puthuparambil, Jacob P. *o.s.b.* (LUB) Petersburg, TX Sacred Heart.
Puthuppally, Joseph '66 (SHP) Monroe, LA St. Matthew; Vicars Forane; Deans; College of Consultors; Ex Officio Members.
Puthusseril, George '79 (MIA) Coral Springs, FL St. Andrew; Deans and Deaneries; Priests' Personnel Board.
Puthusseril, Thomas Joseph *o.s.h.* '78 (GAL) Houston, TX St. Luke the Evangelist; [O] Missouri City, TX The Society of the Oblates of Sacred Heart.
Puthussery, Jojo *m.f.* '02 (OAK) Alameda, CA St. Philip Neri; Alameda, CA St. Albert.
Putich, Michael J. *o.f.m.* '68 (BUF) Boy Scouts; Buffalo, NY St. Clare; Veterans Hospital.
Putich, Michael J. *o.f.m.* '68 (MO) DEPARTMENT OF VETERANS AFFAIRS HOSPITALS AND CHAPLAINS.
Putka, John S. *s.m.* '69 (CIN)[D] Dayton, OH The University of Dayton.
Putnam, John T. '92 (CHL) Salisbury, NC Sacred Heart; Judicial Vicar; Diocesan Consultors.
Putnam, Richard *s.d.b.* '89 (BO)[M] Salesian Staff:.
Putrimas, Rev. Msgr. Edmond '85 (LIT).
Putten, Angelo Van der *f.s.s.p.* '96 (TLS) Tulsa, OK Parish of Saint Peter.
Putthoff, Jeffrey P. *s.j.* '98 (PH)[Y] Philadelphia, PA Jesuit Community, Arrupe House.
Putthoff, Jeffrey *s.j.* (CAM)[V] Camden, NJ Hopeworks N Camden, Inc.
Putti, Anthony '01 (KCK) Beattie, KS St. Malachy's; Marysville, KS St. Gregory's.
Putz, Kenneth '73 (PH) West Grove, PA Assumption B.V.M.
Puza, Paul G. '87 (ALN) Retired.
Puzio, Thomas '70 (DET) Centerline, MI St. Clement; Warren, MI St. Teresa of Avila.
Puznakoski, Gilbert Z. '75 (PIT) Allegheny County, PA West Penn Allegheny Health System–Allegheny General; Pittsburgh, PA St. Raphael.
Pyda, Janusz *o.p.* (HRT) New Haven, CT St. Mary's Priory.
Pyka, Frank *c.m.f.* '46 (LA)[V] Rancho Dominguez, CA Dominguez Seminary Inc. Retired.
Pyo, Michael Yang–Gwon '98 (ORL) Korean Ministry; Orlando, FL St. Ignatius Kim Korean Mission.
Pyso, Volodymyr '73 (STF) Kerhonkson, NY Holy Trinity.

Q

Quade, Alvin '54 (SCL) Retired.
Quadrini, Angelo '65 (EVN)[D] Jasper, IN Providence Home, Nursing Home for the Needy.
Quaine, Michael W. '85 (DET) Sterling Heights, MI St. Michael.
Quainoo, Clement '82 (VIC) El Campo, TX St. Andrew.
Qualizza, Franco *s.x.* '71 (FgM)[N] Wayne Xaverian Missionary Fathers; Wayne, NJ XAVERIAN MISSIONARY FATHERS.
Quang, John '70 (SAV) Military Chaplains.
Quang Chau, Peter Do '73 (NSH) Ashland City, TN St. Martha.
Quang Le, Peter '79 (LR) Barling, AR Sacred Heart of Mary.
Quant, Roberto '91 (OKL) Judicial Vicar; Hennessey, OK St. Joseph's.
Quante, Paul E. *o.s.a.* '84 (OAK) Castro Valley, CA Our Lady of Grace.
Quanz, Paul E. *c.s.b.* '84 (GRY)[B] Merrillville, IN Andrean High School; [H] Merrillville, IN Basilian Fathers Residence.
Quarato, Robert A. '91 (NY) Bronx, NY Holy Rosary.
Quarshie, Felix '92 (BRK) Brooklyn, NY Holy Name.
Quartana, Donald F. '53 (MIL) Retired.
Quartier, Rev. Msgr. Neal E. '76 (SY) Syracuse, NY St. John the Evangelist; Special Assignment.
Quartier, Rev. Msgr. Neal '76 (SY) Syracuse, NY The Cathedral of the Immaculate Conception; Personal Resource Center.
Quattropane, Joseph *o.f.m.cap.* '72 (SB) Colton, CA Immaculate Conception; Colton, CA San Salvador.
Que, Dinh Ngoc *c.ss.r.* '56 (LA)[P] Baldwin Park Vietnamese Redemptorist Mission.
Queally, Kevin *t.o.r.* '77 (ALT)[G] Loretto, PA St. Francis Friary at Mount Assisi.
Quealy, Philip J. '83 (NY) White Plains, NY Our Lady of Sorrows; [E] White Plains, NY Archbishop Stepinac High School.
Quebedeaux, Carl J. *c.m.f.* '82 (CHI) Chicago, IL Our Lady of Guadalupe; [N] Oak Park, IL Claretian Missionaries Community Support Trust; Deans; Oak Park, IL; [N] Oak Park Claretian Missionaries USA Eastern Province.
Quejadas, Mario S. '00 (JOL) Roselle, IL St. Walter.
Quelin, Aldo M. *o.s.m.* '93 (ELP) El Paso, TX Our Lady of Sorrows.
Quenum, Henri Elphege *s.j.* '09 (BO)[U] Cambridge, MA Zipoli House.
Querijero, Andres F. *o.c.d.* '97 (NEW) Linden, NJ St. Elizabeth of Hungary.
Querin, Michele *c.m.v.* (ARE) Sabana Hoyos, PR Nuestra Senora de Fatima.
Quetchenbach, Raymond *s.v.d.* '57 (CHI)[N] Techny, IL Divine Word Residence.
Quevedo, Alfredo S. *s.j.* '56 (NY)[EE] New York, NY Murray–Weigel Hall.
Quezada, Francisco J. '88 (COS) Colorado Springs, CO St. Mary Cathedral; Hispanic Ministry; Vicar for Hispanic Ministry; Presbyteral Council; College of Consultors.
Quezada, Joel *m.sp.s.* '05 (P)[A] Mount Angel, OR Felix Rougier House of Studies; [A] St. Benedict, OR Mount Angel Seminary; [L] Mount Angel, OR Missionaries of the Holy Spirit, M.Sp.S.
Quezada, Ramon E. *s.d.b.* '09 (MGZ) San Antonio, PR San Jose Obrero.
Quezada, Sixto '81 (NY) New York, NY Ascension.
Qui, Vincent '68 (NO) Retired.
Quic, Cristobal Coche *o.s.b.* '92 (RCK)[G] Aurora, IL Marmion Abbey.
Quiceno, Francisco Jose '72 (SJN) Carolina, PR San Valentin.
Quigley, Eugene J. *s.j.* '55 (NY)[EE] New York, NY Murray–Weigel Hall.
Quigley, James Ferrer *o.p.* '65 (PRO)[P] Providence St. Thomas Aquinas Priory at Providence College.
Quigley, John *o.f.m.* '72 (CIN)[U] Cincinnati, OH Franciscans Network; [N] Cincinnati, OH Pleasant Street Friary.
Quigley, Joseph P. '60 (BRK) Brooklyn, NY St. Mark; Coney Island Hospital.
Quigley, William G. *c.i.c.m.* (R)[I] Greenville, NC Newman Catholic Student Center of East Carolina University.
Quijano, Antonio '92 (RNO) Lovelock, NV St. John the Baptist; Lovelock Prison.
Quijano, Carlos *s.j.* '98 (BRK) Brooklyn, NY St. Ignatius.
Quijano, Carlos–Bartolome *o.p.* '96 (NY) New York, NY St. Catherine of Siena; Manhattan, NY New York Presbyterian Hospital.
Quijano, Jose Juan '73 (PMB)[A] Boynton Beach, FL St. Vincent de Paul Regional Seminary.
Quijano, Jose Juan '73 (MIA) On Duty Outside the Archdiocese.
Quilcate, Jose '99 (RVC) Hicksville, NY St. Ignatius Loyola.
Quill, J. Michael '82 (WDC) Beltsville, MD St. Joseph.
Quill, James E. '53 (COV) Fort Wright, KY St. Agnes; [I] Edgewood, KY St. Elizabeth Medical Center, Inc.; Censor Librorum Retired.
Quill, John A. '74 (NEW) Roselle, NJ Church of St. Joseph the Carpenter.
Quill, John '74 (NEW) Elizabeth, NJ Trinitas Regional Medical Center.
Quillen, Andrew M. '91 (BO)[U] Hingham, MA Glastonbury Abbey.
Quilligan, Michael '71 (MIA) West Hollywood, FL Annunciation.
Quindlen, Joseph J. '73 (PH) Plymouth Meeting, PA Epiphany of Our Lord.
Quinlan, Edward J. '78 (HBG) Dauphin, PA St. Matthew, Apostle and Evangelist; [J] Harrisburg, PA The Neumann Scholarship Foundation; Secretary for Education.
Quinlan, Jack '97 (DET) Monroe, MI St. John The Baptist.
Quinlan, James V. '76 (CHI) Other Assignments.
Quinlan, John J. '70 (PAT) Swartswood, NJ Our Lady of Mt. Carmel.
Quinlan, Joseph M. '52 (NEW) Serra Club of Bergen County; Lincroft, NJ St. Leo the Great Retired.
Quinlan, Thomas J. '58 (RIC) Virginia Beach, VA Retired.
Quinlan, William M. '99 (BGP) Judges; Stamford, CT St. Leo.
Quinlivan, Anthony F. *c.ss.r.* '71 (ORL) Cocoa, FL Blessed Sacrament.
Quinlivan, Frank J. *c.s.c.* '70 (FgM) New Rochelle, NY Eastern Brothers Province.
Quinlivan, Thomas J. '72 (BUF) Vicars; West Seneca, NY Queen of Heaven; Clergy Personnel Board.
Quinlivan, William J. '95 (BUF) Tonawanda, NY Blessed Sacrament.
Quinn, Alban *o.carm.* '49 (JOL)[L] Darien Carmelite Provincial Office.
Quinn, Bernard J. *c.m.* '72 (STO) College of Consultors/ Presbyteral Council; Deans; Patterson, CA Sacred Heart Church of Patterson (Pastor of).
Quinn, Brendan '74 (NEW) Elizabeth, NJ Immaculate Conception; Elizabeth, NJ Trinitas Regional Medical Center.
Quinn, Bruce *o.f.m.cap.* '57 (NOR) Middletown, CT St. Pius X Retired.
Quinn, Charles J. '61 (WIN) Elected Senior Member Retired.
Quinn, Charles P. '66 (PRO) Retired.
Quinn, Desmond *s.s.c.* '54 (FgM) St Columbans, NE House of Post–Graduate Studies.
Quinn, Donald A. '83 (IND) Greenwood, IN Our Lady of the Greenwood.
Quinn, Edward J. *m.m.* '47 (SJ)[M] Los Altos, CA Maryknoll.
Quinn, Edward *s.s.c.* '55 (FgM)[K] St. Columbans, NE Missionary Society of St. Columban; St Columbans, NE House of Post–Graduate Studies.
Quinn, J. Patrick '84 (ORL)[E] Winter Park, FL San Pedro Spiritual Development Center; [F] Winter Park, FL Franciscan Friars, T.O.R., San Pedro Friary.
Quinn, James A. '67 (MIA) Hallandale Beach, FL St. Matthew; Catholic Fire Service Ministry.
Quinn, James E. '54 (MIA) Retired.
Quinn, James F. '58 (SY) Cicero, NY Sacred Heart.
Quinn, Jarlath '96 (NY) Staten Island, NY Our Lady Help of Christians.
Quinn, John F. '71 (NY) Armonk, NY St. Patrick.
Quinn, John L. '62 (NY) On Duty Outside the Archdiocese.
Quinn, John M. '57 (SY) New Hartford, NY St. Thomas.
Quinn, Rev. Msgr. John P. '68 (MAN) Priest Personnel Board; Bedford, NH St. Elizabeth Seton; Presbyteral Council; College of Consultors; Vicars Forane.
Quinn, John T. '67 (SD) Retired.
Quinn, John *s.j.* '92 (LA)[F] Los Angeles, CA Loyola High School of Los Angeles.
Quinn, Rev. Msgr. Joseph G. '85 (SCR) Defenders of the Bond.
Quinn, Rev. Msgr. Joseph G. '85 (SAM) Defender of the Bond.
Quinn, Rev. Msgr. Joseph '45 (NY)[C] Bronx, NY Fordham University.
Quinn, Kenneth B. (BO) Hingham, MA Resurrection of Our Lord and Savior Jesus Christ.
Quinn, Kevin P. *s.j.* '85 (SJ)[B] Santa Clara, CA Jesuit Community.
Quinn, Kieran *o.f.m.cap.* '44 (WH) Charleston, WV St.

Anthony; [L] Charleston, WV Capuchins–St. Anthony Friary Retired.
Quinn, Lawrence J. '71 (NY) Mount Vernon, NY Our Lady of Mount Carmel.
Quinn, Liam '83 (MIA) Fort Lauderdale, FL St. Sebastian.
Quinn, Michael F. '70 (JC) Hannibal, MO Holy Family; Judges; Coordinators.
Quinn, Michael F. '09 (SFR) San Francisco, CA St. Brendan; [S] San Francisco, CA Italian Catholic Federation.
Quinn, Michael P. *c.ss.r.* '72 (STL)[O] Liguori, MO St. Clement Health Care Center.
Quinn, Patrick T. *s.j.* '88 (STL)[O] St. Louis, MO Jesuit Community Corporation at Saint Louis University – Jesuit Hall; [C] Saint Louis University.
Quinn, Patrick *t.o.r.* '84 (ORL) Cemetery, San Pedro; San Pedro Spiritual Development Center; Representative for Religious Priests; Foundations for Lay Ministry Program Retired.
Quinn, Peter F. '72 (BO) Westford, MA St. Catherine of Alexandria; Presbyteral Council.
Quinn, Peter N. '75 (PH) Upper Darby, PA St. Alice; Vietnamese Apostolate.
Quinn, Peter '50 (ORL) Retired.
Quinn, Richard J. *m.m.* '54 (FgM) Maryknoll, NY MARYKNOLL.
Quinn, Richard *c.ss.r* '62 (KC)[J] Kansas City, MO Redemptorists Fathers of Kansas City, Missouri; Kansas City, MO Our Lady of Perpetual Help.
Quinn, Robert C. '61 (ALN) Mohnton, PA St. Benedict's Retired.
Quinn, Robert F. *c.s.p.* '53 (NY)[EE] Jamaica Estates Paulist Fathers Generalate.
Quinn, Terence *o.p.* '55 (NY) Pleasantville, NY Holy Innocents.
Quinn, Thomas J. *s.j.* '68 (NY) Staten Island, NY St. Mary of the Assumption Retired.
Quinn, Thomas J. *s.j.* '68 (PBL) Retired.
Quinn, Thomas Patrick '05 (NEW) Ridgewood, NJ Our Lady of Mount Carmel.
Quinn, Thomas '62 (SEA) Retired.
Quinn, Rev. Msgr. W. Louis '45 (WDC) Bethesda, MD Our Lady of Lourdes Retired.
Quinn, Walter J. *o.s.a.* '61 (PH)[Y] Villanova, PA St. Thomas Monastery.
Quinn, William P. '55 (SFR) Retired.
Quinn, Rev. Msgr. William '62 (CAM) College of Consultors.
Quinnan, Edward J. *s.j.* '87 (NY) New York, NY; [GG] Staten Island, NY Mount Manresa Jesuit Retreat House; Staten Island, NY Our Lady of Mt. Carmel–St. Benedicta.
Quinnan, Michael F. '86 (SCR) Brodheadsville, PA Our Lady Queen of Peace; Diocesan Consultors.
Quinones, Francisco Javier '82 (SJN) Guaynabo, PR Maria Madre de Mi Senor; [B] San Juan, PR Academia Sagrado Corazon.
Quinones, Leoncio '46 (PCE) On Duty Outside the Diocese.
Quinones–Rivera, Leoncio '46 (SJN) Retired.
Quinones Murillo, Luis H. '97 (FAJ) Canovanas, PR Resurreccion del Señor.
Quint, Dennis J. '96 (DUB) Reinbeck, IA Holy Family Church, Reinbeck, Iowa; Personnel Advisory Board; Worship Commission; Priestly Life and Ministry Committee; Witness Advisory Committee.
Quintal, Gerald '65 (P) Retired.
Quintana, Jose '96 (GR) Grand Rapids, MI Shrine of St. Francis Xavier and Our Lady of Guadalupe; On Special Assignment.
Quintana–Puente, Rev. Msgr. Carlos '02 (SJN) Santurce, PR Ntra. Sra. del Perpetuo Socorro; Staff; Staff.
Quinter, Paul S. '82 (PH) Philadelphia, PA Maternity B.V.M.
Quintero, Gilberto '88 (SP) Clearwater, FL St. Cecelia.
Quintero, Gustavo V. '80 (STO) Stockton, CA St. Linus Church (Pastor of).
Quintero, John Fredy '02 (HON) Kailua–Kona, HI St. Michael The Archangel.
Quintero, Manuel '81 (LAV) Las Vegas, NV St. Francis de Sales; Priests' Pension Board.
Quintero–Angueira, Jose Francisco '89 (SJN) Vicar for Priests.
Quinto, Armand *s.d.b.* '75 (NEW) Orange, NJ Our Lady of the Valley.
Quinto, Jupeter *r.c.j.* '99 (FRS) Sanger, CA St. Mary; Sanger, CA St. Katherine.
Quiogue, Roy Milton *c.i.c.m.* '82 (SAT)[L] San Antonio, TX Missionhurst C.I.C.M. Residence.
Quioque, Roy *c.i.c.m.* '82 (SAT) San Antonio, TX Santa Rosa Hospital System; [H] San Antonio, TX Christus Santa Rosa Health Care Corporation.
Quiray, Danilo '90 (CAM) Turnersville, NJ The Church of Saints Peter and Paul, Washington Township, N.J.
Quirk, Rev. Msgr. Kevin M. '93 (WH) Wheeling, WV St. Joseph's Cathedral; Assistant to the Bishop; Judicial Vicar; Apostleship of Prayer; Censor Librorum.
Quirk, Richard J. '78 (STL) St. Louis, MO Basilica of St. Louis, King of France.
Quiroz, Heriberto Palacios '95 (LA) Fillmore, CA St. Francis of Assisi.
Quiroz, Jesus Salvador '96 (OAK) Pittsburg, CA St. Peter, Martyr of Verona.
Quiroz, Robinson Sierra *s.a.* '95 (BRK) Jackson Heights, NY Blessed Sacrament.
Quispe, Cirilo (DAL) Plano, TX St. Mark the Evangelist.
Quitugua, Rev. Msgr. David C. '84 (AGN) Agana, GU Dulce Nombre de Maria Cathedral – Basilica; Moderator of the Curia and Vicar General; Archdiocesan College of Consultors; Archdiocesan Presbyteral Council; Judicial Vicar; Pontifical Holy Childhood Association & Pontifical Society for the Propagation of the Faith; Legion of Mary; Judicial Vicar.
Quitugua, Rev. Msgr. David I.A. '64 (AGN) Agana, GU San Juan Bautista; Archdiocesan Presbyteral Council.
Quyet, Anthony '83 (JKS) On Leave for Studies.

R

Raab, John *c.m.f.* '76 (LA)[V] Los Angeles, CA Tepeyac House (Novitiate).
Raab, Ronald P. *c.s.c.* '83 (P) Portland, OR St. Vincent de Paul.
Raab, Ronald *c.s.c.* (FTW)[H] Notre Dame Congregation of Holy Cross, Indiana Province, Provincial House.
Raaser, Eric P. '85 (NY) Tuckahoe, NY Immaculate Conception; Tuckahoe, NY Assumption.
Raaz, Paul A. '70 (SAT) Gonzales, TX St. James; Gonzales, TX Sacred Heart.
Rabalais, Rusty P. '97 (ALX) Marksville, LA St. Joseph's.
Rabbat, Rt. Rev. Archimandrite Robert '94 (NTN) West Roxbury, MA Annunciation Cathedral; College of Eparchial Consultors; Presbyteral Council; Diocese of Newton for the Melkites in the USA, Inc., a Massachusetts Corporation; Vocations Office; "Sophia" (A Journal).
Rabe, David L. '83 (NO) Westwego, LA Our Lady of Prompt Succor.
Rabenarivo, Rolland *s.j.* '03 (BAL)[S] Baltimore, MD Jesuit Community of Loyola University, Inc.
Rabenecker, David *o.s.b.* '91 (IND)[K] St. Meinrad St. Meinrad Archabbey.
Rabiy, Andriy '01 (PHU) College of Archeparchial Consultors; Presbyteral Council; Archeparchial Seminary Advisory and Admissions Board; Victim Assistance Coordinator; Reading, PA Nativity of Blessed Virgin Mary; Archdiocesan Bulletin; Auditor; Vice Chancellor.
Rable, Cyril J. '56 (HBG)[F] Danville, PA Maria Hall, Inc. Retired.
Rable, Cyril J. '56 (SCR)[N] Dunmore, PA Villa St. Joseph.
Racco, Philip G. '77 (CLV) Cleveland, OH Holy Rosary.
Rached, José J. *c.ss.r.* '70 (PCE) Guayama, PR St. Anthony of Padua.
Rachford, Nicholas '71 (PRM) Boy Scout Chaplain; Lorain, OH St. Nicholas; Presbyteral Council; Eparchial Consultors; Vicar Judicialis; Cantors' Institute Faculty.
Rachunek, Henry C. '62 (GAL) Hungerford, TX St. Wenceslaus Mission.
Rachunek, Henry C. '62 (VIC) Hungerford, TX St. John the Baptist.
Racine, Michael S. '95 (FR) Assonet, MA St. Bernard's.
Racivitch, Herve P. *s.j.* '62 (NO)[P] New Orleans, LA Ignatius Residence Retired.
Racki, Rev. Msgr. Leonard E. '62 (PBL) Pueblo, CO Sacred Heart Cathedral; Clergy Assemblies Retired.
Racos, Irinel (RVC)[C] Hicksville, NY Holy Trinity Diocesan High School.
Raczka, Rt. Rev. Philip '80 (NTN) Hammond, IN St. Michael the Archangel; South Bend, IN St. John of Damascus; West Roxbury, MA Seminary of St. Gregory the Theologian; Protopresbyters; Presbyteral Council; Vocations Office.
Raczynski, Paul L. '72 (MIL) Sturtevant, WI St. Sebastian.
Raczynski, Theodore T. '56 (HRT) Suffield, CT Sacred Heart Retired.
Radaich, Thomas '70 (DUL) Duluth, MN St. Michael.
Radano, Rev. Msgr. John A. '65 (NEW)[B] School of Diplomacy and Intl. Rels.
Radano, Rev. Msgr. John A. '65 (NY)[A] Yonkers, NY St. Joseph's Seminary.
Radasky, Robert '56 (ALT) Johnstown, PA St. Clement's.
Radde, James M. *s.j.* '72 (MIL)[P] Milwaukee Jesuit Provincial Office, Wisconsin Province.
Radecki, Dane J. *o.praem.* '77 (GB)[O] Green Bay, WI Notre Dame de la Baie Foundation, Inc.; [J] De Pere, WI St. Norbert Abbey; [D] Green Bay, WI Notre Dame de la Baie Academy.
Radek, James '89 (JOL) Absent on Leave.
Rademacher, Germain P. '58 (NU) Retired.
Rademacher, John R. '70 (GI) Retired.
Rademacher, Robert *g.h.m.* '55 (CIN)[N] Cincinnati Headquarters of Glenmary Home Missioners Retired.
Rademacher, Robert (RIC) Retired.
Rader, John '91 (SFS) Parkston, SD Sacred Heart.
Radermacher, Michael '06 (SEA) Vancouver, WA Our Lady of Lourdes.
Radetski, John J. '77 (MIL) Sheboygan, WI St. Dominic.
Radetski, Paul J. '82 (GB) Menasha, WI St. John; Menasha, WI St. Mary; Menasha, WI St. Patrick.
Radice, Lawrence D. *m.m.* '85 (FgM) Maryknoll, NY MARYKNOLL.
Radke, Barnabas '09 (AMA) Amarillo, TX St. Francis.
Radloff, James A. '93 (BAK) Council of Priests and Diocesan Consultors; Director of Youth Ministry; Vocation Promoter; Sisters, OR St. Edward; Director of Religious Education.
Radloff, Thomas H. *s.j.* '61 (TOL)[C] Toledo, OH St. John's Jesuit High School; Associate Vicar for Priests.
Radocha, Rev. Msgr. Stephen J. '77 (ALN) Easton, PA St. Jane Frances de Chantal; Vicars Forane; College of Consultors.
Radomski, Joseph A. '62 (TR)[N] Trenton, NJ Villa Vianney Retired.
Radosevich, Eugene A. '90 (PEO) Eureka, IL St. Luke.
Radosevich, George '68 (SFD) Livingston, IL Sacred Heart; Staunton, IL St. Michael the Archangel.
Radowicz, Michael R. '05 (MAD) Hollandale, WI Immaculate Conception; Hollandale, WI St. Patrick; Hollandale, WI Holy Redeemer; Advocate/Procurator (cc.1481–1490).
Radtke, Fred *o.f.m.* '67 (JOL) Joliet, IL St. John the Baptist; [L] Joliet, IL St. John the Baptist Friary.
Radvansky, Joseph R. '65 (TOL) Retired.
Radwan, John Z. '05 (NEW) Closter, NJ St. Mary.
Raef, Scott '94 (AMA) Ex Officio; Vicars Forane; Vocation Development Team; Dalhart, TX St. Anthony of Padua.
Raeke, Joseph K. '80 (BO) Bridgewater, MA St. Thomas Aquinas; [CC] Braintree, MA Caritas Christi Retirement Plan and Trust; Health Benefit Trust, Insurance and Pension Trusts, Caritas Christi Retirement Plan.
Raether, Philip '04 (SEA) Oak Harbor, WA St. Augustine.
Rafacz, Joseph J. '56 (LC) Schofield, WI St. Agnes; Appointed Members.
Rafaj, Elias L. '99 (PBR) Houston, TX St. John Chrysostom; Irving, TX St. Basil the Great; Protopresbyters; Office of Religious Education.
Raffaeta, George J. '56 (HRT) Retired.
Raffel, Godfrey '53 (FRS) Retired.
Rafferty, Brian M. '62 (BAL) Pasadena, MD Our Lady of the Chesapeake.
Rafferty, Brian '94 (RIC) Norfolk, VA Christ the King.
Rafferty, Gerard F. *s.s.l.* '79 (NY) West Nyack, NY St. Francis of Assisi; [A] Yonkers, NY St. Joseph's Seminary.
Rafferty, James A. '94 (SCR) On Duty Outside the Diocese.
Rafferty, James F. '63 (BO) Hingham, MA St. Paul.
Rafferty, James R. '01 (DET) Rockwood, MI St. Mary.
Rafferty, James '72 (SD) La Jolla, CA Mary, Star of the Sea.
Rafferty, Lawrence B. '67 (RVC) Woodbury, NY Holy Name of Jesus.
Rafferty, Michael J. '57 (SCR)[N] Dunmore, PA Villa St. Joseph Retired.
Rafferty, Michael *o.a.r.* '03 (LA) Montebello, CA St. Benedict.
Rafferty, Raymond J. '54 (PRO)[P] Providence St. John Vianney Residence Retired.
Rafferty, Raymond M. '66 (NY) New York, NY Corpus Christi.
Rafferty, Thomas F. '83 (GAL) The Woodlands, TX St. Anthony of Padua.
Rafferty, Thomas S. '05 (BO) Swampscott, MA St. John the Evangelist.
Raffo, Cesar '85 (LA) Los Angeles, CA St. Frances Xavier Cabrini.
Raffo, Frank M. '98 (R) Tarboro, NC St. Catherine of Siena.
Raftery, Paul C. *o.p.* '55 (OAK) Berkeley, CA St. Mary Magdalen.
Raftery, Paul *o.p.* '84 (LA)[C] Santa Paula, CA Thomas Aquinas College.
Raftery, William J. *s.j.* '57 (BO)[U] Weston, MA Campion Health Center, Inc.
Raftis, Sean *s.j.* (HEL) Missoula, MT St. Francis Xavier.
Ragan, Gerald '79 (SAV) Augusta, GA St. Mary on the Hill; Augusta Deanery; College of Consultors.
Ragan, James A. '98 (PBR) Charleroi, PA Holy Ghost.
Rager, Patrick F. '85 (PIT) Absent on Sick Leave.
Ragis, Gerald '63 (BUR) Retired.
Ragni, Richard R. '66 (PIT)[Q] Pittsburgh, PA Cardinal Dearden Center Retired.
Ragnoni, James V. '60 (CLV) Akron, OH St. Anthony of Padua.
Ragsdale, Rev. Msgr. Patrick '72 (SAT) In Metropolitan Area; San Antonio, TX Shrine of St. Padre Pio of

Pietrelcina; Archdiocesan Presbyteral Council; Priests Personnel Board.
Ragusa, Salvatore *s.d.s.* '88 (OAK)[P] Moraga, CA St. Mary's College Mission and Ministry Center; [B] St. Mary's College.
Raharjo, Johanes Teguh *c.i.c.m.* '06 (R) Wendell, NC St. Eugene.
Rahilly, Paul '81 (RVC) Cedarhurst, NY St. Joachim; Senate of Priests (Presbyteral Council/College of Consultors).
Rahoy, Nicholas P. '77 (CI) Chuuk, FM Immaculate Heart of Mary Cathedral; [C] Tunnuk, Chuuk, FM Vicariate Residence; Diocesan Consultors; Chuuk; Defenders of the Bond.
Rai, Kevin '74 (AUS) Austin, TX San Jose.
Raia, Jonathan D. '09 (AUS) Round Rock, TX St. William.
Raible, Daniel *c.pp.s.* '43 (CIN)[N] Carthagena, OH St. Charles Retired.
Raible, Roland *o.f.m.cap.* '35 (PIT)[M] Allison Park, PA St. Conrad Friary.
Raica, Rev. Msgr. Steven J. '78 (LAN) Durand, MI St. Mary; Bishop's Office; Victim Assistance Coordinator; Lansing, MI St. Mary Cathedral; Tribunal Judges; College of Consultors.
Raiche, Brian '95 (ALB) Leave of Absence.
Raila, Donald *o.s.b.* '83 (GBG)[G] Latrobe, PA Saint Vincent Archabbey.
Raimer, Chester J. '74 (GBG) Blairsville, PA SS. Simon and Jude; Torrance, PA Torrance State Hospital.
Raimondi, Michele A. '50 (SFR) Retired.
Rainaldo, John H. *s.j.* '64 (MIL)[P] Wauwatosa, WI Jesuit Community at St. Camillus.
Rainforth, Thomas G. '73 (PAT)[K] Paterson, NJ St. Joseph's Hospital and Medical Center; Paterson, NJ St. Joseph Hospital.
Rainone, John J. '70 (PRO)[K] Providence, RI St. Joseph Health Services of Rhode Island – St. Joseph Hospital for Specialty Care; [K] North Providence, RI St. Joseph Health Services of Rhode Island – Our Lady of Fatima Hospital; [P] Providence St. John Vianney Residence.
Rainville, Marcel R. *s.s.e.* '71 (BUR) Leap; [E] South Burlington, VT Edmundnite House of Formation.
Rainville, Paul *m.s.* '65 (TYL) Lufkin, TX St. Patrick.
Rainwater, Randall '96 (STO) Diocesan Finance Council; Stockton, CA DeWitt Nelson Training Center; College of Consultors/Presbyteral Council.
Raj, Arul Xavier *o.f.m.cap.* (NY) Staten Island, NY St. Teresa.
Raj, Joseph '74 (NY) Staten Island, NY Staten Island University Hospital South.
Raja, Joseph Anthony *ss.cc.* '06 (FR)[G] Fairhaven National Center of the Enthronement.
Raja, Joseph (LC) Boyd, WI Sacred Heart of Jesus–St. Joseph; Stanley, WI Holy Family.
Raja, Tiburtis Antony '96 (HBG) Lancaster, PA St. Leo the Great.
Rajamanickam, Masilamani '95 (AUS) Austin, TX St. Catherine of Siena.
Rajanayagam, Thomas M. '66 (STO) Riverbank, CA St. Frances of Rome Church (Pastor of).
Rajappa, Dominic Savio '92 (FRS) Fresno, CA St. Alphonsus; Community Regional Medical Center & University Medical Center; Fresno, CA Veterans Administration Medical Center.
Rajareegam, Paul (CC) Sinton, TX Sacred Heart.
Rajayan, Antony William '96 (WIL) Newark, DE Holy Family.
Rajayan, Antony William '96 (WIL) Wilmington, DE Wilmington Hospital.
Raj Kocherla, Sundar '76 (JOL) Clarendon Hills, IL Notre Dame.
Raj Samala, Arokia '02 (AMA) Clarendon, TX St. Mary's; Groom, TX Immaculate Heart of Mary.
Rakoczy, Richard S. '59 (DET) Retired.
Rakoczy, Walter J. '78 (GRY) Michigan City, IN St. Mary of the Immaculate Conception; Michigan City, IN Sacred Heart Mission.
Rakotondraibe, Romuald '96 (WDC)[N] Washington, DC La Salette Formation Community.
Rakotovoavy, R. Francois *m.s.f.* (STL) St. Louis, MO St. Wenceslaus.
Rakowicz, William J. *s.j.* '80 (CI) Judical Vicar.
Rakowicz, William J. *s.j.* '80 (PAT)[J] Morristown, NJ Loyola House of Retreats.
Rakowski, Helmut *o.f.m.cap.* (FgM) AMERICAN CAPUCHIN MISSIONS.
Ralko, Martin J. '84 (COL) Zanesville, OH St. Nicholas; [C] Zanesville, OH Bishop Rosecrans High School; [L] Zanesville, OH St. Nicholas Foundation.
Ralph, John '55 (WH) Retired.
Ralph, Sean P. '09 (CLV) Olmsted Falls, OH St. Mary of the Falls.
Ralph, Rev. Msgr. Thomas J. '56 (DUB) Retired.
Ram, Anthony Raj '00 (OKL) Oklahoma City, OK Church of the Epiphany of the Lord.
Ramacciotti, Gabriel M. *o.s.m.* '51 (CHI)[N] Chicago Order of Friar Servants of Mary (Servites) United States of America Province, Inc.
Ramacciotti, Gabriel M. *o.s.m.* '51 (DEN) Denver, CO Our Lady of Mount Carmel.
Ramacciotti, Rev. Msgr. James J. '85 (STL) Lemay, MO St. Martin of Tours; [A] St. Louis, MO Kenrick School of Theology.
Ramaeker, Victor '61 (SC) Whittemore, IA St. Joseph's; Whittemore, IA St. Michael's.
Ramaekers, Timothy '82 (ORG) Placentia, CA St. Joseph.
Ramat, Martin '07 (SAC) Yuba City, CA St. Isidore.
Ramatowski, Edward F. '03 (STL) St. Louis, MO Immaculate Heart of Mary; Air National Guard Chaplains.
Ramelow, Anselm *o.p.* '03 (OAK)[A] Berkeley, CA Dominican School of Philosophy and Theology.
Ramelow, Anselm *o.p.* '03 (SFR)[N] San Francisco, CA St. Dominic Priory; San Francisco, CA St. Dominic.
Ramen, Paul F. '60 (NOR) Retired.
Ramenaden, Bernard *o.s.b.* '75 (FTW) Rome City, IN St. Gaspar del Bufalo.
Ramer, Rev. Msgr. James K. '86 (PEO) Pesotum, IL St. Mary; Pesotum, IL St. Joseph; Philo, IL St. Thomas.
Ramirez, Allen *o.f.m.conv.* (OAK)[M] Castro Valley, CA Conventual Franciscans (Province of St. Joseph of Cupertino).
Ramirez, Carlos Reyes *c.s.* '05 (WDC) Riverdale, MD Our Lady of Fatima Parish.
Ramirez, Cesar Rebolledo '97 (CAM) International Priests Representatives.
Ramirez, Charles J. '87 (LA) Claremont, CA Our Lady of the Assumption.
Ramirez, Cornelio C. *s.a.c.* '67 (LUB) Retired.
Ramirez, David (NSH) Presbyteral Council.
Ramirez, Enrique Espinosa *m.sp.s.* '79 (LA) Huntington Park, CA St. Martha.
Ramirez, Fernando '78 (SD) Escondido, CA Church of St. Timothy.
Ramirez, Fernando '04 (ORL) Orlando, FL St. Charles Borromeo.
Ramirez, Francisco Javier *c.m.* (PCE) Ponce, PR San Vicente–Cantera.
Ramirez, Francisco X. '79 (LA) Los Angeles, CA St. Patrick.
Ramirez, Francisco *o.f.m.cap.* '04 (DEN) Denver, CO Annunciation; [N] Denver, CO San Antonio Friary.
Ramirez, Gerardo '91 (PCE) Mercedita, PR Church of the Resurrection; Cursillos de Cristiandad.
Ramirez, Hernando J. *s.j.* '75 (LAF)[J] Grand Coteau, LA Jesuit Spirituality Center (St. Charles College).
Ramirez, J. Jesus '86 (YAK) Royal City, WA St. Michael the Archangel.
Ramirez, Jairo H. '88 (STO) Lodi, CA St. Anne Church (Pastor of).
Ramirez, Jorge '06 (B) On Duty Outside the Diocese.
Ramirez, Jorge '06 (KC) St. Joseph, MO St. Patrick.
Ramirez, Jose Alfredo *o.f.m.* '99 (ELP)[B] El Paso, TX St. Anthony's School of Theology.
Ramirez, Jose de Jesus '86 (YAK) Spanish.
Ramirez, Jose Nieves '79 (ELP) Absent on Leave.
Ramirez, Jose *s.m.* '69 (STL)[O] Eureka, MO Marycliff Marianist Community; [O] St. Louis, MO Marianist Community; [S] Eureka, MO Marianist Retreat & Conference Center.
Ramirez, Juan Carlos '07 (LSC) Presbyteral Council; Hobbs, NM St. Helena.
Ramirez, Luis Ariel *c.m.* '94 (LA) Los Angeles, CA St. Vincent De Paul.
Ramirez, Mario *s.t.b.* '05 (DEN) Denver, CO St. Joseph.
Ramirez, Mario '82 (NY) Staten Island, NY Our Lady, Queen of Peace.
Ramirez, Oran de Jesus '67 (PCE) Jayuya, PR Our Lady of Monserrate.
Ramirez, Oscar Martinez (LAR) Laredo, TX San Agustin Cathedral.
Ramirez, Rev. Msgr. Pedro '74 (SPK) Priests' Personnel Board.
Ramirez, Rafael '94 (SAT)[A] San Antonio, TX Assumption Seminary.
Ramirez, Renelmo '85 (TYL) Palestine, TX Sacred Heart.
Ramirez, Roland B. '08 (SAC) Carmichael, CA St. John the Evangelist.
Ramirez, Salvador '04 (BWN) Brownsville, TX Holy Family.
Ramirez, Thielo '09 (PHX) Avondale, AZ St. Thomas Aquinas Roman Catholic Parish.
Ramirez, Ybain F. '96 (ORL) Orlando, FL St. James Cathedral; Hispanic Ministry.
Ramirez–Alejos, Rev. Msgr. Pedro '74 (SPK) Spokane, WA St. Thomas More.
Ramirez–Portugal, Daniel '91 (LAR) Laredo, TX St. John Neumann; Persons with Disabilities.
Ramiriz, Cesar A. Rebolledo *o.f.m.* '97 (CAM) Millville, NJ The Church of Saint Mary Magdalen, Millville.
Ramler, Michael J. '74 (LEX) Priests' Retirement Board; Somerset, KY St. Mildred; Mountain West; Whitley City, KY Good Shepherd Chapel.
Ramon, Rev. Msgr. Gustavo J. '92 (LA) Los Angeles, CA Assumption; Los Angeles, CA San Antonio de Padua; Board of Directors.
Ramon, Valentin '64 (PHX) Prescott, AZ Sacred Heart Roman Catholic Parish.
Ramon–Jimenez, Edilberto '04 (CHI) Other Assignments.
Ramon–Landry, Kenneth G. '87 (BLX) Hattiesburg, MS Sacred Heart.
Ramos, A.W. '94 (SFS) South Dakota State Penitentiary & Minnehaha County Correctional Centers.
Ramos, Alex (BRK) Ridgewood, NY St. Aloysius.
Ramos, Andres '88 (SD) Ramona, CA Immaculate Heart of Mary.
Ramos, Angel Roman '90 (MGZ) Rincon, PR St. Rose of Lima.
Ramos, Antonio (ARE) Barceloneta, PR Our Lady of Victory.
Ramos, Cipriano '52 (SAC) Retired.
Ramos, Danilo '79 (DAL) Corsicana, TX Immaculate Conception.
Ramos, Rev. Msgr. Hector Rivera '82 (MGZ) Parish Priests Consultors.
Ramos, Juancho D. *s.s.s.* (CHI) Chicago, IL Blessed Sacrament.
Ramos, Julio *m.g.* '01 (LA) Los Angeles, CA St. Paul.
Ramos, Justin S. *o.praem.* '95 (ORG)[D] Silverado, CA St. Michael's Preparatory School; [I] Silverado, CA Norbertine Fathers of Orange Inc.
Ramos, Marcos *o.p.* '01 (FgM) Metairie, LA St. Martin de Porres Province (Southern Dominican Province).
Ramos, Marcos *o.p.* '01 (NO)[P] New Orleans Dominican Friars, Southern Dominican Province of St. Martin de Porres.
Ramos, Orlando *o.c.d.* '93 (PCE) Ponce, PR San Jose.
Ramos, Ponciano *s.v.d.* '45 (SB)[I] Riverside, CA Divine Word Seminary.
Ramos, Sergio '99 (ORG) San Clemente, CA Our Lady of Fatima; Santa Ana, CA Our Lady of La Vang.
Ramos, Victor Raul '84 (LA) Los Angeles, CA Mother of Sorrows; Los Angeles, CA St. Malachy.
Ramos, Victoriano '54 (SJN) Union Eucaristica Reparadora (UNER) Retired.
Ramos Cintron, Israel '08 (CGS) Aibonito, PR Church of St. Joseph.
Ramoso, Rene R. '89 (SFR) South San Francisco, CA St. Augustine; Deans.
Ramotso, Gerard (ARL) Purcellville, VA St. Francis de Sales.
Ramsey, James Boniface '73 (NY) New York, NY St. Joseph; [II] New York, NY Patrons of the Arts in Vatican Museums.
Ramsey, James '84 (GAL) Houston, TX Our Lady of Walsingham.
Ramson, Ronald *c.m.* '59 (DAL)[A] Irving, TX Holy Trinity Seminary.
Ranada, Arnel '98 (NY) Staten Island, NY St. Joseph, St. Thomas.
Ranalletti, Richard A. *c.s.b.* '73 (DET)[E] Novi, MI Catholic Central High School.
Ranallo, Albert D. '07 (PRO) Providence, RI St. Augustine.
Rances, Ronan B. '01 (SAC) Vallejo, CA St. Vincent Ferrer.
Randall, Rev. Msgr. Edward '64 (GAL) Retired.
Randall, John F. '53 (PRO) Retired.
Randall, Jude D. *o.s.b.* '60 (JOL)[C] Lisle, IL Benet Academy; [L] Lisle, IL St. Procopius Abbey.
Randall, Rev. Msgr. Kevin S. '92 (NOR) On Duty Outside the Diocese; Air Force Reserve Chaplains.
Randall, Robert J. '51 (PRO) Retired.
Randazzo, Anthony J. '86 (NEW) North Caldwell, NJ Notre Dame; West Essex Deanery 15.
Randl, Ewald '98 (NEW) On Duty Outside the Archdiocese.
Randone, Michael C. '95 (BO) Unassigned.
Randrianary, Jacques *s.j.* '09 (OAK)[M] Berkeley, CA Jesuit Fathers and Brothers.
Ranek, Jerome '91 (SFS) Kimball, SD St. Margaret; Propagation of the Faith.
Raneri, Carmine B. '55 (HRT) Bristol, CT St. Gregory the Great Retired.
Raney, Richard E. '38 (PEO) Retired.
Rangel, Carlos '98 (TYL) Carthage, TX St. William of Vercelli; Henderson, TX St. Jude.
Rangel, Maximino J. *o.f.m.* '95 (ELP)[B] El Paso, TX St. Anthony's School of Theology.
Rangel, Romauldo *o.f.m.* '87 (ELP)[B] El Paso, TX Roger Bacon College.
Ranges, Charles H. *s.s.e.* '72 (BUR) Elected Members; Essex Junction, VT Holy Family–St. Lawrence.
Ranieri, John J. '82 (NEW)[B] School of Diplomacy and Intl. Rels.
Ranieri, Rev. Msgr. Joseph A. '57 (WDC) Pastoral Center Special Ministries; Pastoral Care of Priests; Archdiocesan Building Commission.
Ranieri, Rev. Msgr. Joseph '57 (WDC) Secretariat for Ministerial Leadership and Vicar for Clergy.
Ranin, Geraldo J. '06 (SAC) Jackson, CA St. Patrick's; Sutter Creek, CA Immaculate Conception; Ione, CA Sacred Heart of Jesus.
Ranjo, Carlito '96 (HON) Pahoa, HI Sacred Heart.
Rank, Ronald G. '58 (MAD) Retired.
Rankin, Joseph M. '79 (L) Louisville, KY St. Luke; Louisville, KY St. Rita; College of Consultors; Ex Officio.

Rankin, Robert '80 (VNN) Tucson, AZ St. Melany; Youth.
Ranly, Ernest W. *c.pp.s.* '56 (CIN)[N] Carthagena, OH St. Charles Retired.
Rannazzisi, Gregory '09 (RVC) Academic Leave.
Ranoa, Bernardo '84 (SD) San Diego, CA Blessed Sacrament.
Ranola, Hildritho '04 (SPP) Pago Pago, AS Cathedral of the Holy Family; Auditors.
Ransom, Donald B. '64 (NEW) Retired.
Ranzino, Thomas C. '78 (BR) Baton Rouge, LA St. Jean Vianney; Chancellor; Diocesan Corporation (The Roman Catholic Church of the Diocese of Baton Rouge); Worship, Office of; [A] St. Benedict, LA St. Joseph Seminary College.
Ranzino, Tom (NO)[A] St. Benedict, LA St. Joseph Seminary College.
Rapaglia, Eric '00 (NY) Bronx, NY Our Lady of Mt. Carmel.
Raphael, John J. *s.s.j.* '95 (NO)[H] New Orleans, LA St. Augustine High School; [P] New Orleans, LA The Josephite Faculty House of St. Augustine High School; [E] New Orleans, LA St. Augustine High School.
Raphael, John *s.s.j.* '95 (WDC)[T] Washington, DC Howard Univ. Newman Center.
Raphael, Mark S. '98 (NO)[A] New Orleans, LA Notre Dame Seminary Graduate School of Theology.
Rapisarda, John '08 (BAL) Baltimore, MD Our Lady of Mount Carmel.
Rapose, Mario D. '00 (OM) Blair, NE St. Francis Borgia.
Raposo, John A. '77 (FR)[F] Fall River, MA Catholic Memorial Home Inc.; Fall River, MA Holy Name.
Rapp, Bernard A. '77 (SD) Vista, CA St. Francis of Assisi Retired.
Rappold, Norbert F. '99 (LR) Mena, AR St. Agnes; Mount Ida, AR All Saints Church.
Rapposelli, Stephen J. '98 (CAM) Cape May Court House, NJ The Church of Our Lady of the Angels, Cape May Court House, N.J.
Raptosh, Joseph R. '87 (PBR) Elected Deanery Representatives.
Raptosh, Richard Joseph '87 (PBR) Monroeville, PA Church of the Resurrection.
Raquepo, Mario '79 (HON) Honolulu, HI St. John the Baptist; [C] Honolulu, HI St. Francis Healthcare System of Hawaii.
Rara, Clarito Z. '75 (MO) DEPARTMENT OF VETERANS AFFAIRS HOSPITALS AND CHAPLAINS.
Rareshide, Rev. Msgr. Lanaux J. '61 (NO) Slidell, LA St. Margaret Mary; Liaisons.
Rasby, Rev. Msgr. James W. '52 (DEN) Retired.
Rasch, Richard S. *o.de.m.* '84 (CLV) Cleveland, OH Our Lady of Mount Carmel; Presbyteral Council; [N] Cleveland, OH Mercedarians.
Rascher, Joseph C. '81 (BEL) Caseyville, IL St. Stephen.
Raschke, Bernard L. '58 (LC) Retired.
Raschko, Michael '75 (SEA) Special Assignment; Censor Librorum; Theological Resources.
Rashford, John *s.j.* '71 (SEA)[L] Seattle, WA Jesuit House, Seattle.
Rashford, Nicholas J. *s.j.* '71 (PH)[C] Jesuit Fathers; [Y] Loyola Center and Manresa Hall.
Rasing, Linus E. '53 (DUB) Retired.
Rask, Phillip J. '72 (STP) Shoreview, MN St. Odilia.
Rasky, Joseph G. *s.m.* '65 (SAT)[L] San Antonio, TX Central Catholic Marianist Community; Movimiento de Apostolado Familiar & Marriage Encounter (Rural).
Rasmussen, Harry W. *s.d.b.* '62 (MRY) Watsonville, CA Our Lady Help of Christians; [F] Watsonville, CA Saint Francis Salesian Community.
Rasner, David L. '82 (LFT) Attica, IN St. Francis Xavier; Covington, IN St. Joseph; Officialis; Presiding Judges; Censor Librorum.
Raso, Anthony F. '75 (BRK) Brooklyn, NY St. Sylvester.
Raspudic, Bruno *o.f.m.* '43 (CHI)[N] Chicago, IL St. Anthony's Friary.
Rasquinha, G. Ignatius '65 (SB) Joshua Tree, CA St. Christopher of the Desert.
Rassley, George *c.ss.r.* '53 (DEN)[N] Denver The Redemptorists/Denver Province.
Rassmussen, Terry '79 (STP) New Hope, MN St. Joseph.
Rastrelli, Thomas P. '02 (DUB) On Leave of Absence (Not Authorized for Priestly Ministry).
Rasura, James I. *s.j.* '56 (SD) San Diego, CA Our Lady of Guadalupe.
Raszeja, Norbert W. *c.r.* '72 (CHI)[N] Chicago Provincial Office of the Congregation of the Resurrection.
Rata, Jovito '07 (SAC) On Duty Outside the Diocese.
Ratajczak, Justin A. *o.f.m.conv.* '77 (ALT) Davidsville, PA St. Anne; Boswell, PA All Saints.
Ratajczak, Michael '75 (SD) Oceanside, CA St. Thomas More; Presbyteral Council.
Ratajczak, Richard C. '58 (SAG) Retired.
Ratazak, Bernard A. '76 (RCK) Retired.
Ratchford, Robert J. *s.j.* '61 (NO) Gretna, LA Jefferson Parish Correctional Center; [P] New Orleans, LA Ignatius Residence Retired.
Raterman, Herbert J. *s.j.* '55 (CIN)[U] Cincinnati, OH Living Monuments of Reparation.
Raterman, Herbert J. *s.j.* '55 (DET)[K] Clarkston, MI Colombiere Center.
Ratermann, Rev. Msgr. David A. '51 (STL) Retired.
Ratermann, George H. *m.m.* '47 (NY)[EE] Maryknoll Maryknoll Fathers and Brothers Retired.
Ratermann, Jerome B. '57 (BEL) Retired.
Rath, Martin *o.s.b.* '83 (SCL)[I] Collegeville, MN St. John's Abbey, of the Order of St. Benedict.
Rath, Richard J. '88 (STL) St. Louis, MO St. John the Baptist.
Rath, Thomas V. '49 (CLV) Lorain, OH St. John the Baptist Retired.
Rathfon, John R. '54 (CLV) Cuyahoga Falls, OH Immaculate Heart of Mary Retired.
Rathgeb, Rev. Msgr. William R. '67 (GBG) Judicial Vicar; Greensburg, PA St. Paul.
Rathinam, Bala '74 (RVC) Seaford, NY St. William the Abbot.
Rathschmidt, John *o.f.m.cap.* '69 (BO)[U] Jamaica Plain, MA St. Francis of Assisi Friary.
Ratigan, Patrick A. '83 (OG) Brasher Falls, NY St. Patrick; Brasher Falls, NY St. Lawrence; [I] Brasher Falls, NY St. Patrick's Cemetery Association of Brasher Falls, N.Y.
Ratigan, Shawn '04 (KC) Kansas City, MO St. Patrick.
Ratnasamy, Charles *s.d.b.* '90 (DET) Clinton Twp., MI St. Thecla.
Ratsimbazafy, Fulgence *s.j.* '02 (OAK)[M] Berkeley, CA Jesuit Fathers and Brothers.
Ratterman, Kevin J. '94 (OKL) Enid, OK St. Francis Xavier; Region VII.
Ratzenberger, Raymond '85 (TUC) Tucson, AZ Our Lady of Fatima Roman Catholic Parish – Tucson.
Ratzmann, George '87 (VEN) Naples, FL St. William; Presbyteral Council.
Rau, Rev. Msgr. Donald E. '56 (STL) Retired.
Rau, Peter J. '85 (ATL) Roswell, GA St. Peter Chanel; Deans.
Rauch, David E. '70 (STL) St. Louis, MO Our Lady of Providence.
Rauch, Edward L. *o.s.f.s.* '64 (PH) Philadelphia, PA Our Lady of Ransom; [Y] Philadelphia, PA Father Louis Brisson Residence Retired.
Rauch, Laszlo F. '49 (TR)[N] Trenton, NJ St. Lawrence Rehabilitation Center Retired.
Raudabaugh, Joseph R. '62 (CIN) Retired.
Raudes, Santiago '02 (SAC) Adjutant Judicial Vicar; Sacramento, CA Immaculate Conception.
Raulli, Enrico *s.j.* '65 (NEW)[C] Jersey City, NJ St. Peter's Preparatory School.
Raulli, Enrico *s.j.* '65 (NY)[EE] New York, NY Jesuit Community of the Immaculate Conception.
Raun, Rev. Msgr. Douglas A. '82 (SFE) Rio Rancho, NM St. Thomas Aquinas; Vicars Forane (Deans); Presbyteral Council of the Archdiocese of Santa Fe.
Rausch, Clyde *o.m.i.* '68 (FgM) Washington, DC AMERICAN OBLATE MISSIONS.
Rausch, Dale J. '68 (DUB) West Union, IA Holy Name; Clermont, IA St. Peter.
Rausch, Dennis '80 (MIA) Retired.
Rausch, John W. '47 (MIL) Retired.
Rausch, John *o.f.m.* '76 (STL)[O] St. Louis, MO Franciscan Friary of St. Anthony of Padua.
Rausch, John *g.h.m.* '72 (LEX)[M] Martin, KY The Catholic Committee of Appalachia.
Rausch, Leon S. *s.j.* '59 (MIL)[P] Wauwatosa, WI Jesuit Community at St. Camillus.
Rausch, Thomas P. *s.j.* '72 (LA)[C] Los Angeles, CA Jesuit Community; Co Chairmen.
Rauscher, Rev. Msgr. Joseph G. '67 (SCR) Wilkes–Barre, PA St. Nicholas.
Rauscher, Rev. Msgr. Martin F. '60 (PAT) Retired.
Rauscher, Russell G. '75 (CLV) Strongsville, OH St. John Neumann.
Rausseo Gomez, Jose Gregorio '07 (SLC) Orem, UT St. Francis of Assisi LLC 221.
Rautenberg, Joseph F. '73 (IND) Cambridge City, IN St. Elizabeth of Hungary; Knightstown, IN St. Rose; New Castle, IN St. Anne; Vicariate for Advocacy to Priests; Council of Priests.
Rauth, Philip J. '59 (LIN) Retired.
Raux, Redmond P. '82 (MO) Military & VA Chaplains.; Air Force Chaplains.
Rauzi, Mario *c.s.* '45 (CIN) Cincinnati, OH Sacred Heart.
Ravenkamp, Michael W. *s.j.* '96 (LA) Santa Barbara, CA Our Lady of Sorrows.
Ravey, Donald J. '61 (BUR) Richmond, VT Our Lady of the Holy Rosary; Williston, VT Immaculate Heart of Mary.
Ravi, Joseph (AMA) Pampa, TX St. Vincent de Paul.
Ravizza, Mark A. *s.j.* '99 (SJ)[B] Santa Clara, CA Jesuit Community.
Rawa, Jerome D. *s.m.* '55 (WH) Richwood, WV Holy Family.
Rawden, Rev. Msgr. John A. '55 (LA) Retired.
Ray, Daniel *l.c.* '06 (SAC) Sacramento, CA St. Maria Goretti.
Rayappan, Philip S. '98 (SCR) West Hazleton, PA Transfiguration; West Hazleton, PA St. Francis of Assisi.
Rayar, Thomas '93 (STP) Northfield, MN Annunciation of the B.V.M.
Rayder, Peter J. '02 (BRK) Brooklyn, NY Our Lady Help of Christians; Presbyteral Council.
Rayen, Germanus *o.f.m.cap.* '72 (AUS) Austin, TX St. Mary Cathedral.
Rayer, Daniel J. '99 (LIN) Chancellor; Judge; Diocesan Consultors; Catholic Relief Services; Liturgical Ministries; Permanent Deacon Continuing Education Committee; Diocesan Housing Ministries, Inc.; Presbyteral Council; Priests' Continuing Education Committee; [J] Lincoln, NE Mass Stipends.
Rayes, Emanuel '54 (EST) Retired.
Raymond, David R. '89 (SPR) Cheshire, MA St. Mary of the Assumption.
Raymond, David R. '03 (PRT) Houlton, ME St. Mary of the Visitation; Houlton, ME St. Agnes.
Raymond, Wilfred *c.s.c.* '71 (FR)[M] North Easton, MA Holy Cross Family Ministries.
Raymond, Willie *c.s.c.* '71 (LA) Santa Monica, CA St. Monica.
Raymundo, Gregorio G. '46 (LA) Retired.
Rayson, Robert '99 (PEO) Dalzell, IL St. Thomas More; Presbyteral Council.
Rayson, Robert '99 (PEO) La Salle, IL Shrine of Queen of the Holy Rosary; La Salle, IL St. Hyacinth's; La Salle, IL Resurrection; La Salle, IL St. Patrick's.
Razov, Elvis '94 (WDC) Washington, DC St. Blaise.
Re, Angelo '60 (SJ) Retired.
Read, Ignacio *o.c.d.* '56 (MIL)[P] Milwaukee Provincial Offices – Discalced Carmelites.
Reade, John M. '09 (COL)[C] Lancaster, OH William V. Fisher Catholic High School.
Reading, Edward '72 (PAT) On Duty Outside the Diocese.
Ready, Frank J. '59 (ARL) Vicar for Religious; Diocesan Consultors; Diaconal Formation Program; Vicar General for Pastoral Services; Arlington, VA St. Agnes.
Reagan, Robert '04 (ORL) Retired.
Real, Fernando *m.id.* '81 (NY) Bronx, NY Santa Maria; [EE] Bronx, NY Idente Missionaries – Santa Maria Residence.
Reale, Frank *s.j.* '81 (STL)[C] Saint Louis University; [C] Saint Louis University; [O] St. Louis, MO Bellarmine House of Studies; [C] Madrid Spain Campus.
Realmuto, George *m.s.a.* '87 (NOR)[G] Cromwell, CT Society of the Missionaries of the Holy Apostles.
Reamer, Mark G. *o.f.m.* '91 (MO) Navy Reserve Chaplains.
Reamer, Mark G. *o.f.m.* '91 (R) Council of Priests; Raleigh, NC St. Francis of Assisi.
Reamer, William G. '87 (OG) Plattsburgh, NY Champlain Valley Physicians Hospital Medical Center; Advocates.
Reardon, Daniel '97 (KC) On Duty Outside the Diocese.
Reardon, Dennis A. '72 (PRO) Wickford, RI St. Bernard.
Reardon, Francis '78 (PMB) Boca Raton, FL Our Lady of Lourdes.
Reardon, James A. '01 (MO) Tidioute, PA St. John; DEPARTMENT OF VETERANS AFFAIRS HOSPITALS AND CHAPLAINS.
Reardon, John D. '73 (PH) Roslyn, PA St. John of the Cross; Defenders of the Bond.
Reardon, John F. '76 (BO) Canton, MA St. John the Evangelist.
Reardon, John F. '50 (NY) Staten Island, NY St. Rita; [EE] Bronx, NY John Cardinal O'Connor Residence Retired.
Reardon, Jonathan '08 (SPR) West Springfield, MA St. Thomas the Apostle.
Reardon, Joseph D. '97 (MO) Navy Chaplains.
Reardon, Michael '74 (LA) Whittier, CA St. Bruno.
Reardon, Michael *s.d.v.* '99 (BUR) Derby Line, VT St. Edward; Newport, VT St. Mary Star of the Sea.
Reardon, Robert J. '59 (PIT)[M] Pittsburgh, PA St. John Vianney Manor; Pittsburgh, PA Retired.
Reasbeck, Rev. Msgr. David E. '56 (STU) Retired.
Reasoner, Mark J. '98 (DUB) Directors; Cedar Rapids, IA St. Jude; Deanery Representatives.
Reaume, Michael R. *s.m.* '69 (STL)[O] St. Louis Marianists, Province of the United States (Society of Mary).
Reaves, Phillip A. '94 (LR) Monticello, AR St. Mark; Warren, AR St. Luke Church; Monticello, AR Holy Child Church.
Rebacz, Jerzy (LC) Hatley, WI St. Florian.
Rebamontan, Marito F. '70 (ORG) Laguna Beach, CA St. Catherine of Siena.
Rebanal, Rev. Msgr. Jeremias R. '55 (NEW) Elizabeth, NJ St. Mary of the Assumption Retired.
Rebaque, Jose *s.a.c.* '70 (BGP) Bridgeport, CT St. Peter.
Rebatzki, George M. '64 (MIL) Retired.
Rebeck, Rev. Msgr. Eugene M. '65 (TR) Holmdel, NJ St. Catharine; Monmouth County; Tribunal Judges.
Rebel, John W. '65 (PIT) New Bedford, PA St. James; Lawrence County, PA Youth Development Center.
Rebel, Patrick M. '85 (SP) Largo, FL St. Matthew.
Rebello, Valentine D. '89 (RVC) Bellmore, NY St.

Barnabas the Apostle.
Rebeyro, Lloyd '70 (ALB) Albany, NY St. Mary.
Rebman, Rev. Msgr. Joseph F. '60 (WIL) Wilmington, DE St. Joseph on the Brandywine; Vicar General for Pastoral Services; Secretary, Pastoral Services Department; Catholic Cemeteries; Ecumenical Liaison; Marian Devotions; College of Consultors; Catholic Cemeteries, Inc.; Catholic Diocese of Wilmington, Inc.
Rebman, Rev. Msgr. Joseph F. '61 (WIL) Priests' Council; Black & Native American Missions.
Rebol, Anthony '56 (CLV) Administrative Leave; Cleveland, OH St. Lawrence.
Reboli, John P. *s.j.* '70 (WOR)[O] Worcester, MA Jesuits of the Holy Cross, Inc.
Rebong, Nestor D. '86 (LA) West Covina, CA St. Christopher; Cursillo Movement.
Rebong, Nestor '86 (LA) Deanery 11; Members.
Rebosura, Sabino B. '87 (HT) Raceland, LA Community of St. Anthony; Raceland, LA St. Hilary of Poitiers.
Rebovich, John '67 (PRM) Absent on Leave.
Rebuldela, Alfred '72 (HON) Captain Cook, HI St. Benedict.
Reburiano, Vincent "Mark" '05 (SFR) San Mateo, CA St. Gregory.
Recaido, Florentino E. '02 (CHK) Director of Youth Ministry; Presbyteral Council; Adult Leaders; Children of God the Father, Inc.
Recaido, Florentino E. '02 (CHK) Saipan, MP Cathedral of Our Lady of Mt. Carmel.
Recchuti, William A. *o.s.a* '61 (PH) Philadelphia, PA St. Rita of Cascia.
Receconi, Edward R. *o.s.b.* '79 (SEA)[L] Lacey, WA St. Martin's Abbey.
Recera, Manuel '85 (RCK) Freeport, IL St. Thomas Aquinas.
Rechenburg, Basil *o.s.b.* '68 (WOR)[O] Still River, MA Benedictine Monks, St. Benedict Abbey.
Recio, Dennis C. *s.j.* '04 (SFR)[N] San Francisco, CA Loyola House Jesuit Community.
Reck, Donald W. *s.j.* '65 (DEN)[N] Denver, CO Xavier Jesuit Center.
Recker, Anthony L. '09 (TOL) Toledo, OH St. Joan of Arc.
Recker, Odo *o.s.b.* '78 (P)[L] St. Benedict, OR Mt. Angel Abbey.
Recker, Philip F. '59 (DUB) Retired.
Recker, Ralph *o.s.b.* '09 (P)[A] St. Benedict, OR Mount Angel Seminary; [L] St. Benedict, OR Mt. Angel Abbey.
Reckinger, Robert A. '51 (DET) Retired.
Reckker, Stephen C. '63 (DET) Romeo, MI St. Clement of Rome.
Reczek, Felix *o.f.m.* (MIL)[P] Burlington, WI Queen of Peace Friary.
Reczek, Paul *o.f.m.* '72 (MIL)[P] Provincial Offices of the Franciscan Friars, Assumption BVM Province, Inc.
Red, Armando '74 (SEA) Seattle, WA Holy Family.
Redcay, Christopher '89 (PH) Philadelphia, PA Our Lady of Ransom.
Redden, Chris (NO)[A] St. Benedict, LA St. Joseph Seminary College.
Redden, Michael J. '72 (ATL) Retired.
Reddick, E. Peter '72 (SY) Syracuse, NY Blessed Sacrament.
Reddy, Louis Maram '89 (NY) White Plains, NY St. Bernard; White Plains, NY White Plains Hospital.
Reddy, Reginald J. *o.f.m.* '61 (ALB)[B] Siena College; [R] Albany, NY St. Francis Chapel.
Redfern, Damian Joseph '06 (LC) Altoona, WI St. Mary.
Reding, Michael A. '97 (STP) Wayzata, MN St. Bartholomew.
Redington, James D. *s.j.* '78 (PH)[C] Jesuit Fathers; [Y] Philadelphia, PA St. Alphonsus House.
Redlon, Reginald *o.f.m.* '49 (BO)[X] Boston, MA Saint Anthony Residence Retired.
Redmond, Arthur S. '55 (LC) Stratford, WI St. Andrew Retired.
Redmond, Daniel P. '96 (CLV) Parma, OH Holy Family.
Redmond, Donald *o.s.b* '57 (KCK)[I] Atchison, KS St. Benedict's Abbey Retired.
Redmond, Paul V. '54 (ALB) Retired.
Redmond, Paul V. '54 (BAL)[B] Emmitsburg, MD Mount Saint Mary's University Retired.
Redolad, Esteban '96 (MIL) Racine, WI Cristo Rey; Racine, WI St. Patrick.
Redstone, James '90 (NEW) Retired.
Redulla, Arsenio C. '74 (LUB) Plainview, TX Sacred Heart; Presbyteral Council; Priests Personnel Board.
Redulla, Flordito *s.v.d.* '83 (FRS) Fresno, CA Shrine of St. Therese.
Redwanski, Dale H. *o.s.c.* '71 (DET) Absent on Sick Leave.
Reece, Richard T. *o.s.f.s.* '65 (PH)[Y] Wyndmoor, PA Villa de Sales Oblate Residence.
Reece, Robert G. *o.s.f.s.* '65 (PH)[Y] Wyndmoor, PA Villa de Sales Oblate Residence.
Reed, Albert *c.pp.s.* '54 (CIN)[N] Carthagena, OH St. Charles Retired.
Reed, Daniel J. '84 (CLV) Parma, OH St. Charles Borromeo.
Reed, David '05 (FRS) Kerman, CA St. Patrick; Tranquillity, CA St. Paul.
Reed, Douglas '71 (R) Edenton, NC St. Anne.
Reed, Jeffrey Allen '09 (GAL) Houston, TX St. Ambrose.
Reed, Rev. Msgr. Michael V. '84 (PT) College of Consultors.
Reed, Rev. Msgr. Michael V. '84 (PT) Pensacola, FL Cathedral of the Sacred Heart; Pensacola, FL St. Anthony of Padua; Chancellor; Vicar for Religious; Promoter of Justice; Administrative Council; Building & Renovation, Diocesan Commission for; Finance, Diocesan Commission for; Holy Name Society; Orders & Ministries, Commission for; Moderator of the Curia; Priests' Pension Plan, Board for; Members Ex Officio.
Reed, Robert J. '61 (ALN)[J] Bethlehem, PA Holy Family Villa Retired.
Reed, Robert P. '85 (BO) Radio; Boston, MA St. Joseph; Catholic Television.
Reed, William C. '71 (NEW) Newark, NJ Sacred Heart.
Reedy, Gerard *s.j.* '70 (NY)[EE] Cardinal Spellman Hall, Jesuit Community.
Reen, Jeremiah *s.d.b.* '71 (PMB) Belle Glade, FL St. Philip Benizi.
Reese, Benjamin '91 (PEO) Northlake, IL St. John Vianney, Cure of Ars; On Duty Outside the Diocese.
Reese, Charles T. '49 (CHL) Retired.
Reese, David '08 (RCK) Huntley, IL St. Mary.
Reese, Edward *s.j.* '73 (PHX)[B] Phoenix, AZ Brophy College Preparatory; [F] Phoenix, AZ Society of Jesus.
Reese, Francis X. *s.j.* '60 (CHL)[J] Mooresville, NC Jesuit Community.
Reese, Matthew A. '02 (ALT) Johnstown, PA St. Patrick's.
Reese, Robert P. '89 (ALT) South Fork, PA Most Holy Trinity.
Reese, Thomas J. *s.j.* '74 (WDC)[N] Washington, DC Woodstock Jesuit Community; [W] Washington, DC Woodstock Theological Center.
Reesman, Nathan D. '06 (MIL) West Bend, WI St. Frances Cabrini; West Bend, WI Holy Angels.
Reeson, David G. '80 (OM) Military Chaplains.
Reeson, David G. '80 (MO) Air Force Reserve Chaplains.
Reeves, Harold Smith '06 (WDC) Absent On Leave.
Reeves, Joseph '76 (BAK) Retired.
Reeves, Marc *s.j.* '05 (LA)[C] Los Angeles, CA Jesuit Community.
Reeves, Mark Thomas '02 (MIA) Judges.
Reeyes–Garcia, Jose *o.de.m.* (SJN) San Juan, PR Ntra. Sra. de Fatima.
Refermat, Thomas '94 (CHI) Northlake, IL St. John Vianney, Cure of Ars.
Refosco, Fabio *c.o.* '04 (CHR)[E] Rock Hill, SC Oratory of St. Philip Neri, Congregation of the Oratory of Pontifical Rite.
Regado, Justo Beltran '69 (BRK) Maspeth, NY St. Stanislaus Kostka.
Regalado, Luis *o.s.b.* '84 (SFE)[H] Abiquiu, NM Monastery of Christ in the Desert.
Regales, Oriol '01 (MIL)[V] Racine, WI Community of St. Paul, Inc.; On Duty Outside the Archdiocese.
Regan, Rev. Msgr. Charles W. '58 (WCH) Presbyteral Council/College of Consultors Retired.
Regan, Columkille '49 (NY)[EE] Bronx, NY Passionist Residence.
Regan, Rev. Msgr. Dennis M. '64 (RVC) Senate of Priests (Presbyteral Council/College of Consultors); Hampton Bays, NY St. Rosalie's.
Regan, Desmond '46 (BIR) Birmingham, AL St. Paul's Cathedral Retired.
Regan, Francis A. '53 (BO) Senior Priests. Retired.
Regan, Gerald T. *s.j.* '64 (MIL)[P] Wauwatosa, WI Jesuit Community at St. Camillus.
Regan, James J. *s.j.* '67 (FgM) Detroit, MI Detroit Province.
Regan, Rev. Msgr. John D. '53 (HRT)[A] In Res. at the Archbishop Daniel A. Cronin Retirement Residence at St. Thomas Seminary; Appointed Members Retired.
Regan, Rev. Msgr. John J. '53 (FR) Retired.
Regan, John '89 (JOL) Absent on Leave.
Regan, Kevin '08 (WDC) Washington, DC St. Matthew Cathedral.
Regan, Michael J. '62 (BO) Senior Priests. Retired.
Regan, Richard J. *s.j.* '63 (NY)[EE] Loyola Hall, Jesuit Community.
Regan, Richard J. '85 (SAN) Retired.
Regan, Robert F. *s.j.* '59 (BO)[U] Boston The Society of Jesus of New England–Provincial Offices.
Regan, Robert F. *s.j.* '59 (PRT) Portland, ME St. Patrick's; Portland, ME St. Pius X.
Regan, Terrence P. '68 (GF) Stanford, MT St. Rose of Lima.
Regan, Terry '68 (GF) Clerical Benefit Association.
Regan, Thomas J. *s.j.* '87 (BO)[U] Boston The Society of Jesus of New England–Provincial Offices.
Regan, Thomas *s.j.* '87 (LA)[C] Los Angeles, CA Jesuit Community.
Regan, Timothy J. '91 (DAV) Special Assignment.
Regan, William P. '56 (SY)[Q] Syracuse, NY Tommy Coyne Residence Dillon Hall Retired.
Reger, George L. '69 (BUF) Buffalo, NY Blessed Trinity.
Reginald, Francis Xavier '91 (NY) Bronx, NY St. Helena.
Reginato, Julian '64 (GR) Muskegon, MI St. Francis de Sales Retired.
Regoli, Rev. Msgr. John A. '61 (GBG)[F] Greensburg, PA Neumann House Retired.
Regotti, Benjamin *o.f.m.cap.* '79 (PH) Philadelphia, PA St. John the Evangelist.
Regula, Gary R. '00 (PHX) Advocates; Phoenix, AZ St. Benedict Roman Catholic Parish; Presbyteral Council.
Regula, Ronald R. '57 (NEW) Retired.
Regynski, Larry '95 (SFS) Mitchell, SD Holy Family.
Rehkemper, Rev. Msgr. Robert C. '49 (DAL) Retired.
Rehling, Paul L. '56 (CIN) Cincinnati, OH St. William Retired.
Rehrauer, Matthew J. '92 (SPC) Houston, MO St. Mark; South Central Correctional Center.
Rehrauer, Stephen *c.ss.r.* '80 (CHI)[N] Chicago Redemptorist Theology Residence.
Reich, John C. '84 (WH) Mullens, WV St. John the Evangelist.
Reich, Paul A. *s.m.* '57 (BAL) Eldersburg, MD St. Joseph.
Reichel, Bill *o.f.m.* '61 (CIN)[N] Cincinnati, OH St. John the Baptist Friary.
Reichenbacher, Charles *o.s.b.* '67 (RCK)[G] Aurora, IL Marmion Abbey.
Reicher, A. Paul '62 (CHI) Chicago, IL St. John Berchmans Retired.
Reichert, Eldon (CIN)[N] Dayton, OH Mercy Siena Woods, Nursing Care.
Reichert, J. Lawrence '71 (COL) Johnstown, OH Church of the Ascension.
Reichert, Rev. Msgr. James J. '71 (ALN) Martins Creek, PA St. Rocco; College of Consultors.
Reichert, James *o.s.b.* '59 (SCL)[I] Collegeville, MN St. John's Abbey, of the Order of St. Benedict.
Reichert, Kenneth *o.s.b.* '59 (KC)[J] Conception, MO Conception Abbey.
Reichert, Ralph J. '49 (TOL) Retired.
Reichlen, Gregory A. '08 (SCR) On Duty Outside the Diocese.
Reichling, David *o.f.m.cap.* '67 (GF) Billings, MT St. Bernard; Diocesan Consultors; Priests' Council.
Reichling, Paul *o.f.m.cap.* '65 (GF) Billings, MT Little Flower; Billings, MT Our Lady of Guadalupe.
Reichmann, James B. *s.j.* '53 (SEA)[A] Seattle, WA Seattle University; [L] Seattle, WA Arrupe Jesuit Community at Seattle University.
Reicks, Allan A. '76 (SC) Sioux Rapids, IA Sacred Heart; Sioux Rapids, IA St. Joseph.
Reid, Adam R. '05 (WOR) Shrewsbury, MA St. Mary's.
Reid, David P. *ss.cc.* '66 (FR)[G] Fairhaven National Center of the Enthronement.
Reid, George B. '53 (WDC) Retired.
Reid, Gerard E. '77 (BO) Woburn, MA St. Barbara.
Reid, Henry W. '06 (RVC) Hicksville, NY Holy Family.
Reid, Malcolm '57 (CHY) Retired.
Reid, Mark Robert '07 (ALT) Ebensburg, PA Holy Name.
Reid, Rev. Msgr. Michael J. '78 (BRK)[X] Brooklyn, NY Compostela Fund of the Roman Catholic Diocese of Brooklyn; Diocesan Budget Committee; Catholic Cemetery Guild; Diocesan Finance Council; Secretariat for Financial Administration/Econome; Diocesan Consultors.
Reid, Michael P. '00 (HBG) Lebanon, PA Assumption of the Blessed Virgin Mary; Consultors, College; Presbyteral Council.
Reid, R. Michael '69 (RVC) Uniondale, NY Holly Patterson Geriatric Center.
Reid, R. Michael '67 (RVC) Hicksville, NY Holy Family.
Reid, Timothy S. '04 (CHL) Charlotte, NC St. Ann.
Reidman, John '62 (SAT) Kerrville, TX Notre Dame.
Reidman, Joseph G. '56 (IND) Retired.
Reidy, James E. '56 (STP)[C] St. Paul, MN University of St. Thomas Retired.
Reidy, Richard F. '94 (WOR) Graduate Studies.
Reidy, Robert J. '75 (CLV) Cleveland, OH Sagrada Familia; [V] Cleveland, OH Hispanic Parishes: Iglesia La Sagrada Familia.
Reidy, Rev. Msgr. Robert '62 (Y) Retired.
Reidy, Rev. Msgr. Thomas E. '67 (SPC) Springfield, MO St. Elizabeth Ann Seton; Vicar General; Chancellor; Catholic Foundation Of The Diocese Of Springfield–Cape Girardeau; Judicial Vicar; Vicar For The Religious; Catholic Relief Services; Cemeteries; National Shrine Of The Immaculate Conception; Priests' Mutual Benefit Society; Diocesan Consultors; Appointed Member; Judges.
Reif, Bryan T. '01 (CIN) Batavia, OH Holy Trinity; Batavia, OH St. Ann.
Reif, John '65 (ROC) Rochester, NY Holy Cross Retired.

Reifel, Mark *t.o.r.* '55 (ALT) Windber, PA St. Anthony of Padua.
Reifenberg, Philip D. '79 (MIL) Cudahy, WI Nativity of the Lord Parish; Judges for Second Instance; Promoter of Justice.
Reiff, Dale E. '67 (SC) Halbur, IA St. Augustine's; Halbur, IA Holy Angels; Halbur, IA Sacred Heart.
Reiff, Dennis E. '81 (NEW) Nutley, NJ Our Lady of Mount Carmel; Archdiocesan Council of Catholic Women (N.C.C.W.); District Moderators and Officers.
Reigle, Gordon P. '05 (LAN)[B] Lansing, MI Lansing Catholic Central High School; Priests' Assignment Commission.
Reiker, John H. '78 (STL) St. Charles, MO St. Charles Borromeo.
Reiker, Robert J. '73 (STL) Dardenne Prairie, MO Immaculate Conception.
Reiley, Robert J. *m.m.* '59 (NY)[EE] Maryknoll Maryknoll Fathers and Brothers Retired.
Reilly, A. Leo *c.s.b.* '62 (DET) Detroit, MI Ste. Anne de Detroit.
Reilly, Bernard '73 (LAN) Lansing, MI St. Mary Cathedral.
Reilly, Cristobal *s.t.* '55 (PCE) Coamo, PR St. Blase.
Reilly, David F. '75 (CIN) Priests On Administrative Leave.
Reilly, Denis *o.p.* '70 (SLC) Midvale, UT Saint Therese of the Child Jesus LLC 246.
Reilly, Donald F. *o.s.a.* '74 (PH)[C] Villanova, PA Villanova University; [Y] Villanova, PA Provincial Offices of the Order of St. Augustine, Province of St. Thomas of Villanova; [Y] Villanova, PA St. Thomas of Villanova Friary; Villanova, PA Province of St. Thomas of Villanova (Eastern).
Reilly, Rev. Msgr. Edward W. '54 (STL) St. Charles, MO St. Elizabeth Ann Seton Retired.
Reilly, F. Joseph '58 (STL) Ste. Genevieve, MO St. Catherine of Alexandria; Ste. Genevieve, MO SS. Philip and James.
Reilly, Francis E. '80 (SPR) Longmeadow, MA St. Mary's.
Reilly, George M. '60 (NEW) New Milford, NJ St. Joseph's.
Reilly, James F. '68 (NEW) Palisades Park, NJ St. Michael's.
Reilly, James J. '68 (NEW) Kearny, NJ Our Lady of Sorrows.
Reilly, John E. *s.j.* '59 (DET)[K] Clarkston, MI Colombiere Center.
Reilly, Rev. Msgr. Joseph R. '91 (NEW)[A] South Orange, NJ Seton Hall University College Seminary; Censores Librorum.
Reilly, Joseph '91 (NEW)[B] School of Diplomacy and Intl. Rels.
Reilly, Kevin M. '03 (NOR) Office of the Bishop; Oakdale, CT Our Lady of the Lakes; Seminarian Advisory Board.
Reilly, Lawrence T. '64 (YAK) Vicar for Priests; Clergy Personnel Board; Cle Elum, WA St. John the Baptist; Cle Elum, WA Immaculate Conception; Diocesan Consultors.
Reilly, Liam '00 (FgM) Boston, MA St. James the Apostle, Inc.
Reilly, Mark R. '97 (OG) Evans Mills, NY St. Mary; Antwerp, NY St. Michael; [A] Watertown, NY Immaculate Heart Central High School; Navy Reserve Chaplains.
Reilly, Michael J. '01 (PH) Exton, PA SS. Philip and James.
Reilly, Michael P. '92 (NY)[F] Staten Island, NY St. Joseph by the Sea, High School; [T] Staten Island, NY Mission of the Immaculate Virgin.
Reilly, Rev. Msgr. Patrick '58 (LA) Burbank, CA St. Robert Bellarmine Retired.
Reilly, Rev. Msgr. Philip J. '60 (BRK) Special Assignment; [U] Brooklyn, NY Monastery of the Sisters Adorers of the Precious Blood Retired.
Reilly, Rembert F. *o.s.b.* '59 (PAT)[N] Morristown, NJ St. Mary's Abbey.
Reilly, Robert E. '58 (L) Retired.
Reilly, Rev. Msgr. Robert J. '45 (E) Retired.
Reilly, Scott *l.c.* '97 (ATL)[G] Norcross, GA Legionaries of Christ, Incorporated.
Reilly, Scott *l.c.* '97 (DET)[F] Clarkston, MI Everest Academy.
Reilly, Steven *l.c.* '94 (WDC)[N] Potomac, MD Legionaries of Christ.
Reilly, Terence *o.p.* '59 (OAK)[M] Oakland, CA Order of Preachers (Province of Holy Name of Jesus – Western Dominican Province).
Reilly, Thomas A. *m.s.* '72 (ATL) Marietta, GA St. Ann.
Reilly, Thomas J. '00 (BO) North Reading, MA St. Theresa of Lisieux.
Reilly, Thomas J. '67 (BO) Senior Priests. Retired.
Reilly, Thomas J. *s.j.* '95 (SJ)[M] Los Gatos, CA Sacred Heart Jesuit Center.
Reilly, Thomas *m.afr.* '78 (FgM) Washington, DC; Washington, DC MISSIONARIES OF AFRICA.
Reilly, Timothy D. '03 (PRO) Advocate; Vice Chancellor; [A] Providence, RI Seminary of Our Lady of Providence; Seminary of Our Lady of Providence.
Reilly, Rev. Msgr. William J. '65 (NEW) Garfield, NJ Holy Name; Southwest Bergen Region Deanery 4; Multicultural Affairs.
Reilman, Thomas J. '61 (DAV) Retired.
Reily, Dennis *o.p.* (SLC) West Valley City, UT Saints Peter and Paul LLC 243.
Reim, Dan *s.j.* (LAN) Ann Arbor, MI St. Mary Student Parish.
Reim, Daniel T. *s.j.* '95 (LAN)[J] Ann Arbor, MI Detroit Province of the Society of Jesus – Jesuit Residence.
Reimer, Edward J. '67 (SY) Chittenango, NY St. Patrick; Jamesville, NY Jamesville Penitentiary.
Reina, Nicholas J. *s.d.b.* '78 (OAK)[E] Richmond, CA Salesian High School.
Reina, Richard A. '70 (BUF)[A] East Aurora, NY Christ the King Seminary.
Reinbold, Charles '56 (NEW) Retired.
Reinders, David H. '97 (TUC) Tucson, AZ U.S. Veterans Hospital; DEPARTMENT OF VETERANS AFFAIRS HOSPITALS AND CHAPLAINS.
Reinersman, Gerald L. '79 (COV) Cold Spring, KY St. Joseph; Continuing Education of Priests; Diocesan Consultors.
Reinert, Duane F. *o.f.m.cap.* '76 (KCK) Haskell Institute; [I] Lawrence, KS St. Conrad's Friary; [L] Lawrence, KS Haskell Catholic Campus Center.
Reinert, Duane F. *o.f.m.cap.* '76 (KC)[A] Conception, MO Conception Seminary College.
Reinert, Rev. Msgr. James M. '83 (LIN) On Duty Outside the Diocese.
Reinhard, William *o.m.i.* '61 (FgM) Washington, DC AMERICAN OBLATE MISSIONS.
Reinhardt, Leo J. '78 (ROC) Ithaca, NY Immaculate Conception.
Reinhardt, Leo S. '55 (BEL) Retired.
Reinhardt, Mark S. '96 (PRT) Camden, ME Saint Brendan the Navigator Parish.
Reinhart, Blaise R. *o.f.m.* '55 (ALB)[B] Siena College.
Reinhart, David A. '98 (TOL)[D] Oregon, OH The Kateri Catholic School System; Members; Martin, OH Our Lady of Mt. Carmel.
Reinhart, Kenneth *o.f.m.cap.* '68 (DET)[P] Washington, MI Capuchin Retreat.
Reinhart, Robert J. '61 (TOL) Toledo, OH Our Lady of Perpetual Help.
Reinhart, Robert *c.pp.s.* '53 (CIN)[N] Carthagena, OH St. Charles Retired.
Reinheimer, George E. '50 (NY) Retired.
Reinig, Joseph '98 (BAK) Central; Board of Education; Bend, OR St. Francis of Assisi.
Reinke, Francis P. '57 (GB) Retired.
Reinke, Robert J. '57 (COV) Covington, KY St. Augustine; Ludlow, KY Sts. Boniface and James Retired.
Reinke, Robert J. '49 (COV) Retired.
Reinkemeyer, John C. '51 (WCH) Garden Plain, KS Immaculate Conception.
Reinkemeyer, John '57 (WCH) Retired.
Reis, Daniel O. '75 (FR) New Bedford, MA Our Lady of the Immaculate Conception.
Reis, Justin J. '69 (COL) Columbus, OH St. Peter.
Reis, Lancelot '67 (PAT) Haskell, NJ St. Francis of Assisi.
Reis, Michael J. '67 (COL) Heath, OH St. Leonard.
Reis, Ronival '90 (WOR) Brazilian Ministry.
Reis, Timothy P. '86 (FR) Taunton, MA Saint Andrew the Apostle Parish.
Reisch, Rev. Msgr. Milton L. '60 (NO) Liaisons Retired.
Reischl, Fred P. '55 (DM) Retired.
Reischman, Virgil '69 (STU) Marietta, OH St. John the Baptist.
Reiser, Richard J. '80 (OM) Omaha, NE St. James.
Reiser, Robert E. *s.j.* '97 (NEW)[C] Jersey City, NJ St. Peter's Preparatory School; [M] Jersey City, NJ Jesuit Community of St. Peter's Prep, Inc.
Reiser, William E. *s.j.* '72 (WOR)[O] Worcester, MA Jesuits of the Holy Cross, Inc.; Our Lady of Providence.
Reisert, Gregory *o.f.m.cap.* '64 (SP)[N] Seminole, FL Capuchin Franciscan Residence.
Reising, Christopher (DM) Des Moines, IA Our Lady of the Americas.
Reisinger, Walter J. *c.m.* '55 (JC) Dixon, MO St. Cornelius; Dixon, MO St. Theresa.
Reiss, John E. '69 (Y) Retired.
Reissmann, Richard A. '63 (WIL) Retired.
Reist, Thomas *o.f.m.conv.* '79 (BAL)[S] Ellicott City Order of Friars Minor Conventual.
Reisteter, William *o.f.m.* '71 (ALN)[K] Easton, PA St. Francis Friary.
Reisz, Leonard '50 (OWN) Retired.
Reiter, James '90 (MO) CIVIL AIR PATROL.
Reites, James W. *s.j.* '71 (SJ)[B] Santa Clara, CA Jesuit Community.
Reith, David H. '76 (MIL) Brookfield, WI St. Dominic.
Reitmeyer, Larry (LSC) Retired.
Reitz, Andrew J. *o.f.m.* '71 (SP) Tampa, FL Sacred Heart; Appointed Members.
Reitz, Glenn (STL)[J] Bridgeton, MO SSM De Paul Health Center Foundation.
Reitz, Joseph A. '53 (GAY) Retired.
Reitz, Louis M. *s.s.* '55 (BAL)[S] Baltimore Society of St. Sulpice, Province of the United States Retired.
Reitz, William J. '47 (GR) Retired.
Rejsek, Rev. Msgr. J. Brian '86 (PEO) Judges; Marseilles, IL St. Joseph's; Diocesan Hispanic Ministry Office.
Rekasi, Joseph S. *o.praem.* '46 (GB)[J] De Pere, WI St. Joseph Priory; [O] De Pere, WI Canons Regular of Magnovarad, Ltd.
Reker, Timothy T. '82 (WIN) Rochester, MN St. Francis of Assisi; Deans; Censors of Books and Periodicals; Commission on Sacred Liturgy.
Rekofke, Robert F. *s.j.* '59 (SPK)[J] Spokane, WA Regis Community.
Relihan, Thomas '47 (SAC) Ione, CA Sacred Heart of Jesus Retired.
Reller, Gary W. '71 (HEL) Missoula, MT St. Anthony; Presbyteral Council; Diocesan Consultors; Episcopal Vicar for Clergy; Defenders of the Bond; Personnel Board.
Remick, Todd M. '06 (BUF) Chautauqua Catholic Community, Chautauqua Institution; Bemus Point, NY St. Mary of Lourdes.
Remillard, Andre N. '70 (WOR) Jefferson, MA St. Mary.
Remke, Raymond J. '88 (BIR) Decatur, AL Annunciation of the Lord; Propagation of the Faith and Holy Childhood; Priests'/Presbyteral Council; Diocesan College of Consultors; Diocesan College of Vicars.
Remm, George F. '60 (PEO) Retired.
Remmel, William *s.d.s.* '67 (TUC) Tucson, AZ Most Holy Trinity Roman Catholic Parish – Tucson.
Remmerswaal, James H. *o.s.c.* '65 (SCL) Foreston, MN St. Louis Bertrand; Milaca, MN St. Mary's; [I] Onamia, MN Crosier Priory.
Remmes, Richard R. '62 (SC) Retired.
Rempe, Melvin '65 (LIN) York, NE St. Joseph's.
Remski, Howard L. *f.s.s.p.* '00 (OKL) Bethany, OK Latin Mass Community; Bethany, OK Latin Mass Community.
Remuzgo, Jorge *o.carm.* '83 (JOL)[L] Darien Carmelite Provincial Office.
Remy, David P. '67 (DUB) Military Chaplains.
Renard, Eugene C. *s.j.* '60 (STL)[S] St. Louis, MO Retreat House; [O] St. Louis, MO.
Renard, Peter J. *o. praem.* '68 (GB) Pastoral Care; Knights of Columbus; [J] De Pere, WI St. Joseph Priory.
Render, Patrick W. *c.s.v.* '68 (LAV) Henderson, NV St. Thomas More; Presbyteral Council for the Diocese of Las Vegas.
Render, Patrick W. *c.s.v.* '68 (CHI)[N] Arlington Heights Viatorian Province Center–Clerics of St. Viator.
Rendon, Anthony *o.m.i.* '67 (FgM) Washington, DC AMERICAN OBLATE MISSIONS.
Rendon, Luis A. '73 (PAT) Paterson, NJ St. Agnes; Passaic County Jail.
Rendon, Mathias *o.f.m.* (OG) U.S. Army Headquarters.
Rendon, Matthias *o.f.m.* '92 (FgM) Washington, DC COMMISSARIAT OF THE HOLY LAND.
Rendon, Rev. Msgr. Nicolas '76 (LUB) Slaton, TX St. Joseph's; Chancellor; Moderator of the Curia; Presbyteral Council; Priests Personnel Board; Director of Scouting; Priests' Retirement Board; Propagation of the Faith; Diocesan Building Commission.
Rendon, Samuel '92 (LA) Wilmington, CA Holy Family.
Renehan, Rev. Msgr. Edmond M. '58 (LA) Santa Clarita, CA St. Clare Retired.
Renfroe, Frank *s.j.* '73 (ELP) El Paso, TX Sacred Heart.
Rengers, Christopher *o.f.m.cap.* '42 (WDC)[B] Washington, DC St. Francis Friary–Capuchin College.
Rengers, Christopher *o.f.m.cap.* '42 (RCK)[M] St. Charles, IL Queen of Americas Guild.
Rengers, Christopher *o.f.m.cap.* '42 (PIT)[M] Allison Park, PA St. Conrad Friary Retired.
Renggli, John J. '68 (SEA) Tacoma, WA Holy Cross.
Rengifo, Jesus Orlando '85 (NEW) West New York, NJ St. Joseph of the Palisades.
Renic, Stipe *o.f.m.* (NY) New York, NY SS. Cyril and Methodius – St. Raphael.
Renken, Rev. Msgr. John '79 (SFD) On Duty Outside the Diocese.
Renna, Anton J. *s.j.* '65 (SJ)[M] Los Gatos, CA Sacred Heart Jesuit Center.
Renner, Christopher A. '91 (DEN) Evergreen, CO Christ the King.
Renner, Frank G. '81 (EVN) Sullivan, IN St. Mary; Sullivan, IN St. Joan of Arc.
Renner, Louis *s.j.* '57 (SPK)[B] Spokane, WA Gonzaga University.
Renner, Ralph C. *s.j.* '70 (STL)[O] St. Louis, MO Jesuit Community Corporation at Saint Louis University – Jesuit Hall.
Renninger, Michael A. '93 (RIC) Vicar for Vocations.
Rensing, William F. '55 (BEL) Retired.
Renteria, Javier *sch.p.* '83 (NY) New York, NY Annunciation; [EE] New York, NY Calasanzian Fathers (Piarists).
Renteria–Torres, Jaime *m.n.m.* '89 (SAT) Del Rio, TX Our Lady of Guadalupe.
Rentner, Randall C. *c.s.c.* '90 (FTW)[H] Notre Dame Congregation of Holy Cross, Indiana Province, Provincial House; [B] University of Notre Dame Du Lac; [H] Notre Dame, IN Holy Cross Community, Corby

Hall, University of Notre Dame.
Rento, Richard G. '58 (PAT) Retired.
Renz, Christopher J. *o.p.* '97 (OAK)[A] Berkeley, CA Dominican School of Philosophy and Theology; [M] Oakland, CA Order of Preachers (Province of the Most Holy Name of Jesus – Western Dominican Province).
Repenning, Robert B. '01 (NY) Fishkill, NY Church of St. Mary, Mother of the Church.
Repenshek, Jerome V. '63 (MIL) Retired.
Repko, Cyril *o.f.m.cap.* '62 (FgM) Pittsburgh, PA Province of St. Augustine.
Repko, Joseph '95 (PRM) Bedford, OH St. Eugene; Solon, OH St. John the Baptist; Eparchial Pastoral Council.
Repole, Charles *o.f.m.cap.* '43 (NY)[EE] Yonkers, NY St. Clare Friary.
Repole, Charles *o.f.m.cap.* (BRK) Legion of Mary; [Q] Queens Village, NY Queen of Peace Residence.
Reppen, Robert B. *o.praem.* '46 (GB)[J] De Pere, WI St. Norbert Abbey.
Reque, Francis M. *o.s.b.* '00 (BIR)[E] Cullman, AL St. Bernard Abbey.
Reschick, Joseph W. '77 (PIT) Pittsburgh, PA St. Rosalia.
Resconich, Emil *t.o.r.* '54 (ALT)[G] Loretto, PA St. Francis Friary at Mount Assisi.
Resen, William Patrick '07 (KNX) Copperhill, TN St. Catherine Laboure; Madisonville, TN St. Joseph the Worker.
Resicki, Timothy P. *s.j.* '94 (CHI)[N] Chicago, IL Chicago Province of the Society of Jesus–Provincial Office.
Reskey, George A. '73 (MOB) On Leave from the Archdiocese.
Resko, Blane L. *o.s.b.* '57 (GBG)[G] Latrobe, PA Saint Vincent Archabbey.
Resma, Luis V. '62 (SAC) Vallejo, CA St. Vincent Ferrer.
Resop, Michael A. '79 (MAD) Plain, WI St. Luke; Spring Green, WI St. John the Evangelist.
Ressler, Clint C. '93 (GAL) Houston, TX St. Rose of Lima; Priests Personnel Committee.
Ressler, Mark A. '76 (DUB) Dubuque, IA St. Joseph the Worker.
Ressler, Rev. Msgr. Wayne A. '64 (DUB)[G] Dubuque, IA Holy Family Catholic Schools; Dubuque, IA St. Raphael Cathedral.
Restrepo, Francisco '88 (DET) Sterling Heights, MI St. Matthias.
Restrepo, George A. *s.j.* '65 (BUF)[O] Buffalo, NY Canisius Jesuit Community Inc.
Restrepo, Jairo '92 (B) Defenders of the Bond; Idaho Falls, ID Christ the King; Idaho Falls, ID Holy Rosary; Judges.
Restrepo, John *o.p.* '04 (SAT) San Antonio, TX St. Ann.
Restrepo, Martin '86 (R) Kenansville, NC Maria, Reina De Las Americas.
Restrepo, Nelson *o.d.c.* '01 (SP) Ruskin, FL St. Anne.
Restrepo, Ruben D. *c.m.* '97 (LA) Los Angeles, CA St. Vincent De Paul.
Restrick, Jacob *o.p.* '89 (BUF)[P] Buffalo, NY Monastery of Our Lady of the Rosary.
Restrick, Jacob *o.p.* '89 (NY)[EE] New York St. Vincent Ferrer Priory.
Restropo, John J. *o.p.* '93 (SAT)[L] San Antonio, TX Dominican Priory of San Juan Macias.
Reszel, Marc W. '88 (CHI) Buffalo Grove, IL St. Mary.
Retar, John C. '03 (CLV) Mentor, OH St. John Vianney.
Reteneller, Charles E. '60 (L) Retired.
Rethinger, Omer '53 (TOL) Retired.
Retnazihamoni, Joy Antony '98 (ALX) Deville, LA St. John the Baptist.
Retortillo, Benito *o.p.* '62 (CC) San Diego, TX St. Francis de Paula; [G] San Diego, TX Vicariate of Holy Rosary; San Diego, TX.
Rettger, Thaddeus E. *o.s.b.* '74 (ALT) Hastings, PA St. Bernard.
Rettig, Donald R. '71 (CIN) Cincinnati, OH St. Vincent de Paul; [E] Cincinnati, OH Elder High School.
Rettig, Kevin E. '84 (LA) Winnetka, CA St. Joseph the Worker.
Retzel, Joseph R. *s.j.* '60 (GF) Hays, MT St. Paul's Indian Mission.
Retzner, James P. *o.s.a.* '95 (LA) Los Angeles, CA Our Mother of Good Counsel.
Reuse, Patrick *s.j.* '73 (SLC) Brigham City, UT Saint Henry LLC 225.
Reusing, James M. '94 (BAL) Special Assignment; [M] Baltimore, MD Good Samaritan Hospital; [N] Baltimore, MD Good Samaritan Nursing Center; [N] Baltimore, MD Belvedere Green at Good Samaritan.
Reuter, Arnold F. '52 (LC)[H] La Crosse, WI Holy Cross (Seminary) Diocesan Center Retired.
Reuter, Christian *o.f.m.* '66 (BEL)[F] East St. Louis, IL St. Benedict the Black Friary; Vienna, IL Shawnee Correctional Center; Vienna Correctional Center.
Reuter, James B. *s.j.* '46 (FgM) New York, NY Society of Jesus.
Reuter, John F. '67 (GB) On Duty Outside the Diocese.
Reuter, Lawrence *s.j.* '71 (CHI)[C] Chicago, IL Jesuit Community at Loyola University Chicago; [J] Maywood, IL Loyola University Medical Center.
Reuter, Leon *o.f.m.* '62 (STL)[O] St. Louis Franciscan Friary of St. Anthony of Padua.
Reuter, Lloyd E. '57 (DUB) Retired.
Reuther, John N. *i.m.c.* '73 (BUF)[O] Williamsville, NY Consolata Fathers.
Reutter, James G. '04 (CIN) Cincinnati, OH Our Lady of Victory.
Revent, Michael (KAL) Benton Harbor, MI Ss. John & Bernard.
Revilla, Francisco '54 (STA) Retired.
Revilla, Isaias *o.s.a.* '60 (MGZ) Aguada, PR St. Francis of Assisi; Censor Librorum.
Revuelto, Manuel '59 (NEW) Retired.
Rewak, William *s.j.* '64 (LA)[C] Los Angeles, CA Jesuit Community; [C] Los Angeles, CA Jesuit Community.
Rewtiuk, Rev. Msgr. Mitred Michael '69 (SJP) On Leave; Presbyters Retired.
Rey, Francisco J. Arizcuren '93 (SJN)[F] Santurce, PR Casa de Ninos Manuel Fernandez Juncos.
Reyaan, Amandus *m.s.c.* '82 (MI) Majuro, MH Sacred Heart of Jesus; Prefecture Consultors.
Reyburn, Calvin (GB)[G] Appleton, WI St. Elizabeth Hospital, Inc.
Reycraft, Robert J. '75 (DEN) Englewood, CO St. Louis.
Reyes, Andres J. '70 (NEW) Jersey City, NJ St. Paul of the Cross; Jersey City North Region Deanery 10.
Reyes, Armando I. '76 (MO) Army Chaplains.
Reyes, Eider '05 (PAT) Presbyteral Council; College of Consultors.
Reyes, Eider '05 (PAT) Paterson, NJ St. Anthony's.
Reyes, Emilio *s.v.d.* '85 (SB)[I] Riverside, CA Divine Word Seminary.
Reyes, Gaylord '02 (LA) Bellflower, CA St. Bernard.
Reyes, Jaime *o.s.b.* '64 (FAJ)[B] Humacao, PR San Antonio Abad Abbey of the Order of St. Benedict.
Reyes, Javier *o.f.m.* '98 (SJ) San Jose, CA Our Lady of Guadalupe.
Reyes, Jesse T. '07 (CHK) Saipan, MP San Jose Parish; Presbyteral Council; Legion of Mary at San Jose Parish/Rainan i Gef Santos Na Lisayo; Prison Chaplaincy; Police and Fire Departments Chaplaincy; Director of Vocations; Confraternity of Christian Mothers.
Reyes, Jesus *c.s.* '93 (CHI)[N] Chicago, IL Scalabrini House of Theology.
Reyes, Jorge A. *o.s.a.* '96 (BO) Counselors:; Lawrence, MA St. Mary of the Assumption; Secular Augustinians.
Reyes, Jorge *o.s.a.* (MAN) Salem Hispanic Apostolate.
Reyes, Jose Angel Rodriguez (SJN) Toa Alta, PR San Fernando Rey.
Reyes, Juan Alberto Torres '96 (PCE) Santa Isabel, PR St. James.
Reyes, Rev. Msgr. Lonnie C. '69 (AUS) Retired.
Reyes, Marco D. '85 (LA) Lynwood, CA St. Emydius.
Reyes, Noel B. '05 (CHI) Chicago, IL Our Lady of Mercy.
Reyes, Pedro L. '90 (SJN) Spiritual Directors.
Reyes, Raul *o.c.d.* '69 (OKL) Oklahoma City, OK Our Lady of Mount Carmel and St. Therese Little Flower.
Reyes, Raymund M. '88 (SFR) San Francisco, CA St. John of God.
Reyes, Raymund '88 (SFR) San Francisco, CA St. Anne; Deans.
Reyes, Saul '08 (B) Nampa, ID St. Paul's.
Reyes, Victor J. '94 (ATL) Canton, GA Our Lady of LaSalette; Advocates.
Reyes, Xamie M. '00 (CHI) Hanover Park, IL St. Ansgar.
Reyes–Cedillo, Jose *o.r.c.* '78 (STO) Ceres, CA St. Jude Church (Pastor of).
Reyes Lebrón, Pedro L. '90 (SJN) Judicial Vicar; [C] Rio Piedras, PR Seminario Mayor Regional San Juan Bautista; Diocesan Consultors.
Reyesmedina, Carlos '87 (DET) Retired.
Reyes Pichardo, Elky '09 (NEW) Newark, NJ St. Aloysius.
Reyling, Mark D. '98 (BEL) Freeburg, IL St. Joseph.
Reymann, James J. '58 (CLV) Wellington, OH St. Patrick.
Reyna, Alan '83 (WIL) Wilmington, DE St. Catherine of Siena.
Reyna, Cecilio C. '94 (LAN) Jackson, MI St. Mary Star of the Sea.
Reyna, Jose Jaime Maldonado '02 (SPK) Walla Walla, WA St. Francis of Assisi; Walla Walla, WA St. Patrick.
Reyna, Marcos '86 (LSC) Silver City, NM St. Francis Newman Center Parish; Diocesan Consultors; Presbyteral Council; Clergy Personnel Board; Office of Vocations; Campus Ministry; Members; Priestly Life and Ministry Committee.
Reynalte, Fabian '87 (SB) Ontario, CA St. George.
Reynebeau, Thomas J. '87 (GB) College of Consultors; Oshkosh, WI St. Jude the Apostle.
Reynierse, Peter '95 (WDC) Retired.
Reynolds, Brad R. *s.j.* '77 (P)[L] Portland, OR Colombiere Community.
Reynolds, Daniel '53 (P) Retired.
Reynolds, Fred G. *s.j.* '78 (NO)[P] New Orleans, LA Ignatius Residence.
Reynolds, George J.D. *o.p.* '59 (SFE)[K] Albuquerque, NM St. Thomas Aquinas (Newman Center) University Parish.
Reynolds, George '97 (LA) Long Beach, CA St. Barnabas.
Reynolds, J. Patrick '80 (OWN) Paducah, KY St. Thomas More.
Reynolds, Rev. Msgr. James B. '50 (MIA) Retired.
Reynolds, James J. '84 (BRK)[T] Douglaston, NY Bishop Mugavero Residence; On Leave/Unassigned.
Reynolds, Jeffrie S. '90 (BIR) On Duty Outside the Diocese Retired.
Reynolds, John C. '90 (KCK) Atchison, KS Corpus Christi; Nortonville, KS St. Joseph's; Nortonville, KS St. Mary's Immaculate Conception.
Reynolds, John '83 (STA) Jacksonville, FL Holy Family.
Reynolds, Rev. Msgr. Joseph F. '59 (NY) Harriman, NY St. Anastasia; [FF] Monroe, NY Queen of Apostles Convent.
Reynolds, Kirk R. *s.j.* '79 (PAT)[J] Morristown, NJ Loyola House of Retreats.
Reynolds, Paul F. '65 (PRO) East Providence, RI St. Martha Retired.
Reynolds, Rev. Msgr. Paul H. '63 (ATL) Johns Creek, GA St. Brigid; Judges.
Reynolds, Rev. Msgr. Roger A. '43 (NEW)[M] Rutherford, NJ St. John Vianney Residence for Priests Retired.
Reynolds, Rubin R. '79 (BR) Gonzales, LA St. Mark.
Reynolds, Stephen B. '89 (GAL) Sugar Land, TX St. Theresa; Western Vicariate.
Reynolds, Thomas P. *s.s.c.* '61 (FgM) St Columbans, NE U.S. Foundation & Administration.
Reynolds, Thomas *s.s.c.* '61 (OM)[K] St. Columbans Missionary Society of St. Columban.
Reynolds, William E. '81 (DAV) Newton, IA Sacred Heart; Defenders of the Bond; Deans; Colfax, IA Immaculate Conception.
Reynolds., George J.D. *o.p.* '59 (SFE) Albuquerque, NM St. Thomas Aquinas University Parish.
Reynoso, Oscar '05 (SB) Upland, CA St. Joseph.
Rezac, Keith D. '87 (OM) Pierce, NE St. Joseph; Plainview, NE St. Paul; Diaconate Program.
Rezac, Robert *i.m.c.* '77 (BUF)[O] Williamsville, NY Consolata Fathers.
Rezula, Leon J. '69 (CHI) Elk Grove Village, IL St. Julian Eymard.
Rezumov, Victor (PAT)[K] Denville, NJ Saint Clare's Hospital, Inc.
Rhinehart, R. William *c.m.* (STL) Perryville, MO Christ the Savior; Perryville, MO Our Lady of Victory.
Rhoades, Terance *o.f.m.* '43 (GLP) Tohatchi, NM St. Mary Church.
Rhodes, Rev. Msgr. David W. '65 (Y) Youngstown, OH St. Christine; Judges; College of Consultors; Priests Council.
Rhodes, Joseph '41 (OWN) Retired.
Rhomberg, Thomas W. '53 (DUB) Retired.
Rhyner, Robert E. '59 (GB) Retired.
Riani, Rev. Msgr. Peter R. '55 (OG) Elizabethtown, NY St. Elizabeth; Elizabethtown, NY St. Philip Neri; Promoter of Justice; Deans.
Riano, Camilo *c.m.f.* '47 (SJN) Bayamon, PR San Jose.
Ribaudo, Rev. Msgr. Charles A. '67 (RVC) Retired.
Ribbens, William H. *o.praem.* '62 (GB)[J] De Pere, WI St. Norbert Abbey.
Ribble, Rev. Msgr. James M. '57 (SPK) Retired.
Ribeiro, Alvaro *s.j.* '87 (WDC)[N] Washington, DC The Jesuit Community at Georgetown University.
Ribeiro, Georger *s.a.* '67 (NY)[EE] Garrison, NY Franciscan Friars of the Atonement.
Ribera–Ribo, Francisco J. '54 (SJN) Retired.
Ribits, Thomas A. *o.s.f.s.* '82 (TOL)[I] Toledo Oblates of St. Francis de Sales.
Ribits, Thomas *o.s.f.s.* '82 (BUF)[T] Buffalo, NY Salesian Studios; [R] Buffalo, NY D'Youville College; [C] Buffalo, NY D'Youville College.
Ricafort, Jovencio D. '82 (SD) Chula Vista, CA Mater Dei.
Ricard, David F. '69 (PRO) Warwick, RI St. Gregory the Great; Kent County Memorial Hospital.
Ricard, Richard J. '98 (NOR) Rockville, CT St. Bernard; Members; Part Time; Diocesan Panel of Pastors, Canon 1742.
Ricard, Richard '98 (NOR) Seminarian Advisory Board.
Ricard, Rodney Anthony '95 (NO) New Orleans, LA Our Lady Star of The Sea.
Ricbe, Todd '80 (IND)[C] Richmond, IN Seton Catholic High School.
Ricca, Francis '05 (MAR) Newberry, MI St. Gregory.
Riccardi, Salvatore *c.p.* '62 (BRK) Jamaica, NY Immaculate Conception; [T] Jamaica, NY Immaculate Conception Monastery.
Riccardo, John '96 (DET) Plymouth, MI Our Lady of Good Counsel; Office of Evangelization and Catechesis.
Riccardo, Rev. Msgr. Joseph J. '75 (E) Punxsutawney, PA St. Joseph, Huband of Mary; Punxsutawney, PA SS. Cosmas and Damian; Punxsutawney, PA St. Anthony of Padua; Deans.
Ricchini, Joseph *o.f.m.* '64 (CIN)[C] Cincinnati, OH St.

Anthony Shrine, Franciscan Postulancy.
Ricci, Alfred V. '80 (PRO) Warwick, RI St. Gregory the Great.
Ricci, Andrew P. '97 (SUP) Superior, WI Cathedral of Christ the King.
Ricci, Daniel A. *c.m.* '74 (STL)[O] St. Louis, MO Vincentian Residence.
Ricci, Lorenzo '06 (DEN) Westminster, CO Holy Trinity.
Ricci, Rev. Msgr. Philip C. '65 (PH) North Wales, PA Mary, Mother of the Redeemer.
Ricciardelli, Albert '84 (TR)[M] Lawrenceville, NJ Morris Hall–Saint Lawrence, Inc.; [K] Lawrenceville, NJ Morris Hall/Saint Lawrence, Inc.
Ricciardi, August A. '83 (SCR) Matamoras, PA St. Joseph; Deans.
Ricciardi, Robert P. '79 (HRT) Cheshire, CT St. Bridget.
Riccio, Antonio *o.f.m.* '70 (NY)[EE] New York Franciscan Province of the Immaculate Conception.
Riccio, Fred A. '77 (OAK) Alameda, CA St. Joseph Basilica.
Riccio, Fred '77 (OAK) Pastoral Leadership Placement Board (PLPB); Deanery #9.
Riccio, Salvatore M. '66 (PH) Springfield, PA St. Francis of Assisi.
Riccitelli, Dennis '85 (PHX) Retired.
Riccomini, Rev. Msgr. Dino '57 (FRS) Retired.
Rice, Anthony *s.j.c.* '08 (CHI) Volo, IL St. Peter; [P] Chicago, IL Canons Regular of Saint John Cantius.
Rice, Charles '01 (BAL) Priests Sick or Absent.
Rice, Rev. Msgr. Edward M. '87 (STL) Office of Consecrated Life; Office of Vocations; Webster Groves, MO Holy Redeemer.
Rice, G. Nicholas '67 (L) Louisville, KY Our Lady of Lourdes; [Q] Louisville, KY Mass of the Air.
Rice, Gregory P. *m.h.m.* '72 (NY)[EE] Hartsdale, NY Mill Hill Fathers Residence.
Rice, Gregory P. *m.h.m.* '72 (PHX) Special Assignment.
Rice, John '03 (WH) Montgomery, WV Immaculate Conception.
Rice, Joseph P. '77 (NEW)[M] Rutherford, NJ St. John Vianney Residence for Priests Retired.
Rice, Lawrence *c.s.p.* '89 (COL)[J] Columbus, OH Campus Ministry.
Rice, Michael D. '64 (KC) Retired.
Rice, Morgan *c.s.b.* '09 (ROC) Rochester, NY St. Salome; Rochester, NY Christ the King; Rochester, NY St. Thomas the Apostle.
Rice, Patrick '74 (PAT) Sparta, NJ Blessed Kateri Tekakwitha; Justice and Peace Commission; Presbyteral Council; College of Consultors.
Rice, Richard P. '60 (PRT) Charismatic Renewal.
Rice, Richard P. '60 (PRT) Retired.
Rice, Robert A. *s.j.* '53 (FgM) New York, NY Society of Jesus.
Rice, Rev. Msgr. Thomas G. '77 (DET) Warren, MI St. Louise; Office of Digital Media.
Rice, William A. '63 (E) Retired.
Rich, John A. *m.m.* '58 (NY)[EE] Retired.
Rich, Joseph '74 (SJ) On Duty Outside the Diocese.
Richard, Edward J. *m.s.* '91 (STL)[A] St. Louis, MO Kenrick School of Theology; [D] St. Louis, MO Paul VI Institute of Catechetical and Pastoral Studies.
Richard, Edward *m.s.* '91 (STL)[O] LaSalette Spirituality Center.
Richard, Edward '41 (TLS) Retired.
Richard, Joseph E. '58 (SFR) Retired.
Richard, Louis J. '81 (LAF) Broussard, LA Sacred Heart of Jesus.
Richard, Normand P. '72 (PRT) Resource Center; Portland, ME St. Patrick's.
Richard, Raymond *o.f.m.cap.* '72 (FgM) White Plains, NY Province of St. Mary.
Richard, Rusty P. '97 (LAF) On Special Assignment.
Richard, Timothy '92 (LAF) Lafayette, LA St. Edmond.
Richards, Damian '92 (SAL) Tipton, KS St. Boniface Parish; Salina Diocesan Council of Catholic Women (S.D.CC.W.); Tipton, KS Saints Peter and Paul Parish; Cursillo.
Richards, Edward W. '59 (BRK)[T] Douglaston, NY Bishop Mugavero Residence Retired.
Richards, George J. '95 (NOR) Judges; Norwich, CT SS. Peter and Paul.
Richards, Lawrence R. '89 (E) Erie, PA St. Joseph; Bread of Life Community.
Richards, Mark R. '93 (SAC)[N] Sacramento, CA Catholic Committee on Scouting; Judicial Vicar; Presbyteral Council; Due Process; Members; Scouting, Diocesan Catholic Committee on; Theological Commission; College of Consultors; Sacramento, CA Cathedral of the Blessed Sacrament.
Richards, Paul *o.s.b.* (SCL)[I] Collegeville, MN St. John's Abbey, of the Order of St. Benedict.
Richards, Peter M. '98 (STP) St. Michael, MN St. Michael.
Richards, Ronald '04 (DET) Garden City, MI St. Dunstan.
Richardson, David P. '03 (PEO) Peoria, IL St. Philomena; Assistant Directors.
Richardson, Donald '57 (GLP) Retired.
Richardson, Francis X. '93 (ATL) Cumming, GA Good Shepherd.
Richardson, James *s.c.* '92 (HRT) New Haven, CT Sacred Heart.
Richardson, James '06 (KAL)[E] Kalamazoo, MI St. Philip Neri House; Diocesan Finance Council; [A] Kalamazoo, MI Msgr. Hackett Catholic Central High School.
Richardson, John L. '54 (R) Retired.
Richardson, John M. *o.f.m.* '56 (PAT)[N] Butler, NJ St. Anthony Friary.
Richardson, John T. *c.m.* '49 (FgM)[C] Chicago, IL De Paul University; Earth City, MO Western Province.
Richardson, M. Paul '91 (ARL) Springfield, VA St. Bernadette.
Richardson, Paul *s.s.c.* '54 (FgM)[K] St. Columbans Missionary Society of St. Columban; St Columbans, NE House of Post–Graduate Studies.
Richardson, Paul *s.s.c.* '54 (PRO)[P] Bristol, RI St. Columban's Retirement House Retired.
Richardson, Robert C. '71 (WDC) Retired.
Richardson, Stephen S. '03 (BAL) Priests Sick or Absent.
Richardson, William J. *s.j.* '53 (BO)[U] Newton, MA The Jesuit Community at Boston College.
Richardson, Rev. Msgr. William M. '72 (HBG) Lewisburg, PA Sacred Heart of Jesus.
Richardson, William *s.f.o.* (WDC)[W] Washington, DC Catholic Historical Society of Washington.
Richardt, J. Lawrence '63 (IND) Retired.
Richardt, Lawrence J. '62 (IND) Archdiocesan Judges.
Richart, Paul F. '61 (IND) Sellersburg, IN St. Paul.
Richel, Michael C. '87 (MAD) Personnel Board; Deaneries; Montello, WI St. John the Baptist; Montello, WI Good Shepherd.
Richetta, John J. '55 (MIL) Retired.
Richey, Rev. Msgr. Terrence '64 (LA) Los Angeles, CA St. Basil's; Alcohol and Substance Abuse; Alcohol and Substance Abuse Ministry Retired.
Richling, Theodore L. '71 (OM) Retired.
Richmeier, Garry *c.pp.s.* '83 (KC)[A] Kansas City, MO Gaspar Mission House; Kansas City, MO St. James; Liberty, MO; [A] Liberty, MO Society of the Precious Blood Provincial Offices.
Richmond, Troy A. '03 (DAV) Fort Madison, IA Holy Family; Montrose, IA St. Joseph's.
Richstatter, Thomas *o.f.m.* '66 (IND)[A] St. Meinrad, IN Saint Meinrad School of Theology.
Richter, Anthony Charles '03 (DET) Lincoln Park, MI Christ the Good Shepherd.
Richter, David A. '00 (BIS) Beach, ND St. John the Baptist.
Richter, David T. '86 (SHP) Vicar General and Moderator of the Curia; Judges; Corporate Council; Finance Council; Campaign for Human Development; Catholic Relief Services; Church Vocations; Church Vocations Board & Vocations Office; Mission Director; Propagation of the Faith; College of Consultors; Ex Officio Members.
Richter, David '00 (BIS)[F] Sentinel Butte, ND Home On The Range; Beach, ND St. Mary (Medora); Pro–Synodal Judges; Beach, ND St. Mary's Golva.
Richter, Helmut W. '94 (OAK) Pittsburg, CA Good Shepherd.
Richter, Rev. Msgr. John A. '64 (NU) New Ulm, MN Cathedral of The Holy Trinity; New Ulm, MN St. John the Baptist; Priest Personnel Board.
Richter, Kevin M. '88 (SC) Le Mars, IA St. Joseph's; [B] Le Mars, IA Gehlen Catholic School.
Richter, Robert J. '67 (MIL) Personal Leave.
Richter, Robert J. '67 (ARL) Arlington, VA Our Lady, Queen of Peace.
Richter, Thomas J. '96 (BIS) Bismarck, ND St. Anne; Office of Vocations; Vicar for Deacons; Priests' Personnel Board.
Richtsteig, Erik J. '94 (MO) Air Force Reserve Chaplains; Ogden, UT Saint James the Just LLC 226.
Ricker, John Michael '55 (TOL) Retired.
Rickert, William '45 (GB) Retired.
Rickey, James E. '69 (PEO) Dwight, IL St. Patrick's; Dwight, IL Dwight Correctional Center.
Rickle, William C. *s.j.* '79 (BAL)[S] Towson, MD Maryland Province of the Society of Jesus; [S] Baltimore, MD Colombiere Jesuit Community.
Rickles, Gary A. '96 (GAL) La Porte, TX St. Mary.
Ricks, Paul '78 (SAC) Sacramento, CA University of California, Davis Medical Center; Sacramento, CA Presentation of the Blessed Virgin Mary.
Rico, Dairo '03 (ATL) Norcross, GA Saint Patrick.
Rico, Jose Luis '01 (FRS) Parlier, CA Our Lady of Sorrows.
Rico–Rostro, Lino '98 (ARL) Sterling, VA Christ the Redeemer.
Ridella, Joseph '52 (VNN) Retired.
Ridgeway, Kenneth *s.m.* '69 (BUR) White River Junction, VT St. Anthony.
Ridgley, Lawrence P. '02 (BUR) Alburgh, VT St. Amadeus; South Hero, VT St. Rose of Lima.
Ridgway, John *s.j.* '82 (P)[L] Portland, OR Colombiere Community; Portland, OR St. Ignatius.
Ridick, George J. '73 (WOR) Advocates; Worcester, MA Sacred Heart of Jesus–St. Catherine of Sweden.
Riding, Raymond *s.t.* '75 (FgM) Silver Spring, MD MISSIONARY SERVANTS OF THE MOST HOLY TRINITY.
Ridore, Danis '67 (PMB) Legion of Mary, Palm Beach Curia; Delray Beach, FL St. Vincent Ferrer.
Riebe, Bruce '85 (PRM) Brecksville, OH St. Joseph; Presbyteral Council; Office of Youth Ministry.
Riebe, Todd M. '80 (IND) Richmond, IN Holy Family; Richmond, IN St. Andrew; Richmond, IN St. Mary; Richmond State Hospital; [O] Richmond, IN Earlham College.
Riebe–Estrella, Gary L. *s.v.d.* '71 (CHI)[B] Chicago, IL The Catholic Theological Union at Chicago; [B] Chicago, IL The Catholic Theological Union at Chicago; [N] Chicago, IL Edward McGuinn, S.V.D. Residence.
Riedel, Richard R. *c.pp.s.* '52 (CIN) Celina, OH Immaculate Conception of the Blessed Virgin Mary.
Riedemann, Kenneth '64 (SCL) Retired.
Rieder, Donald '55 (SCL) Retired.
Rieder, Michael J. '94 (RVC) Montauk, NY St. Therese of Lisieux.
Rieder, Ronald *o.f.m.cap.* '63 (FTW) Huntington, IN SS. Peter and Paul.
Riedman, Boniface *s.a.* '45 (PAT)[N] Ringwood, NJ Holy Name Friary, Inc.
Riedman, John '62 (SFS) Retired.
Riedmann, Boniface *s.a.* '45 (NY)[EE] Garrison Graymoor Ecumenical and Interreligious Institute Retired.
Rieger, Alan J. *o.c.d.* '61 (MIL)[P] Milwaukee Provincial Offices – Discalced Carmelites.
Riegger, Patrick M. '01 (RVC) Smithtown, NY St. Patrick.
Riegler, Frederick J. '67 (PH) Quakertown, PA St. Isidore.
Riehl, Christopher '09 (KNX) Knoxville, TN Cathedral of the Sacred Heart of Jesus.
Riel, Robert H. '80 (SPR) Chicopee, MA St. George's.
Rieman, Richard W. '58 (POD)[T] Newton, MA Prelature of the Holy Cross and Opus Dei; Chestnut Hill.
Riemeh, Lawrence H. '95 (DAL) On Duty Outside the Diocese.
Riemer, Robert *s.v.d.* '60 (FgM) Techny, IL.
Rien, Robert '74 (OAK) Antioch, CA St. Ignatius of Antioch.
Riendeau, Alfred A. '98 (BGP) Westport, CT St. Luke.
Riendeau, Richard A. '57 (SPR) Holyoke, MA Blessed Sacrament Retired.
Riener, Vincent (SFR) South San Francisco, CA; Archdiocesan Board of Education.
Ries, Carl A. '70 (DUB) Nashua, IA St. Michael; Charles City, IA Immaculate Conception.
Ries, Donald C. '59 (SC) Grand Junction, IA St. Brigid's; Jefferson, IA St. Joseph's.
Ries, James C. '93 (ORG) Fullerton, CA St. Mary's.
Ries, Richard S. '63 (SC) Manson, IA St. Thomas; Manson, IA St. Mary's; Rockwell City, IA St. Francis of Assisi; Calhoun County State Reformatory, Minimum Security for Men.
Riesberg, Leo L. '57 (SC) Retired.
Riesenberg, John J. '60 (COV) Edgewood, KY St. Pius X Retired.
Rietti, John '57 (JKS) Retired.
Riffle, David '67 (B) Retired.
Riffle, Donald J. '62 (B) Retired.
Riffle, Douglas H. '57 (B) Retired.
Riffle, Henry J. '70 (SP) Hudson, FL St. Michael the Archangel.
Riffle, Patrick J. '08 (WDC) Olney, MD St. Peter.
Riffle, Rev. Msgr. Raymond E. '79 (GBG) Greensburg, PA Our Lady of Grace; Catholic Charities of the Diocese of Greensburg, PA, Inc.; Catholic Charities; Victim Assistance Coordinators; Diocese of Greensburg – Managing Directors.
Rigali, Joseph *o.f.m.* '58 (NO) New Orleans, LA St. Mary of the Angels.
Rigali, Norbert *s.j.* '59 (SD)[B] University of San Diego.
Rigali, Norbert '64 (LA)[C] Los Angeles, CA Jesuit Community Retired.
Rigatuso, Leo '94 (OM) Howells, NE Holy Trinity; Howells, NE SS. Peter and Paul; Howells, NE St. John Nepomucene; [D] Howells, NE Howells Community Catholic School.
Rigdon, Vincent J. '77 (WDC) Poolesville, MD Our Lady of the Presentation; Judges.
Rigert, James *c.s.c.* (FTW)[H] Notre Dame Congregation of Holy Cross, Indiana Province, Provincial House.
Rigert, James *c.s.c.* '66 (P)[L] Portland, OR Holy Cross Fathers & Brothers, C.S.C. – University of Portland Retired.
Rightor, Harold W. '02 (IND) Seelyville, IN Holy Rosary; Brazil, IN Annunciation of the Blessed Virgin Mary.
Rigney, Rev. Msgr. Dennis A. '66 (ALN) Retired.
Rigoberto Rodriguez, J. '89 (LA) Los Angeles, CA Our Lady of Guadalupe.
Rigoli, Anthony *o.m.i.* '72 (NO) International Shrine of St. Jude; New Orleans, LA Our Lady of Guadalupe /International Shrine of St. Jude; New Orleans, LA Shrine of St. Jude Thaddeus.

Rigonan, Antonio R. '88 (MO) Air Force Chaplains.
Riha, Francis A. *m.m.* '68 (FgM) Maryknoll, NY MARYKNOLL.
Rihn, Rev. Msgr. Roy '42 (SAT)[K] San Antonio, TX Casa De Padres Retired.
Riley, Andrew (CHR) North Charleston, SC St. Thomas The Apostle.
Riley, Daniel J. '84 (BO) Weymouth, MA Sacred Heart.
Riley, Daniel P. *o.f.m.* '71 (BUF)[Q] West Clarksville, NY Mount Irenaeus, Franciscan Mountain Retreat & Holy Peace Friary; [R] St. Bonaventure, NY St. Bonaventure University; [C] West Clarksville, NY Holy Peace Friary.
Riley, David J. '64 (BGP) Stamford, CT St. Cecilia.
Riley, Dennis S. '79 (CHI) Retired.
Riley, Edward H. *o.p.* '60 (FgM)[N] Chicago Dominicans (Provincial Office); Chicago, IL Province of St. Albert the Great (Central).
Riley, Edward M. (BO) Holbrook, MA St. Joseph.
Riley, Eric D. '98 (OWN) Beaver Dam, KY Holy Redeemer; Fordsville, KY St. John the Baptist; Morgantown, KY Holy Trinity; Teens Encounter Christ.
Riley, Finian A. *o.f.m.* '54 (PAT)[N] Ringwood, NJ Holy Name Friary, Inc.
Riley, George F. *o.s.a.* '62 (PH)[C] Villanova University; [Y] Villanova, PA St. Thomas Monastery.
Riley, James F. *s.j.* '74 (DET)[E] Detroit, MI University of Detroit Jesuit High School and Academy; [K] Detroit Jesuit Provincial Office–Detroit Province of the Society of Jesus.
Riley, James H. '58 (BO) Senior Priests. Retired.
Riley, John A. '03 (KCK) Chancellor; Archdiocesan Council on Finances; Archdiocesan Consultors.
Riley, John F. '56 (ALB) Retired.
Riley, John F. '55 (STP)[C] St. Paul, MN University of St. Thomas Retired.
Riley, John J. '91 (ARL) Spotsylvania, VA St. Matthew.
Riley, John P. *c.s.c.* '94 (FTW) South Bend, IN St. Joseph.
Riley, John '03 (KCK) Archdiocesan Administrative Team; Ex Officio.
Riley, John '06 (KCK) Shawnee, KS St. Joseph.
Riley, Kenneth A. '92 (KC) Kansas City, MO St. Charles Borromeo.
Riley, Leo P. '82 (VEN) Punta Gorda, FL Sacred Heart.
Riley, Mark J. (BO) Wellesley, MA St. Paul.
Riley, Mark R. '95 (CLV) Casa Parroquial San Pedro Teotepeque.
Riley, Miles O'Brien '63 (SFR) Retired.
Riley, Patric '81 (KCK) Eudora, KS Holy Family; Regional Pastoral Leaders.
Riley, Patrick '48 (SCL) Retired.
Riley, Walter J. '06 (WOR) Worcester, MA Christ the King.
Rimelspach, Jeffrey J. '85 (COL) Columbus, OH St. Margaret of Cortona.
Rimes, Robert B. *s.j.* '55 (MOB)[A] Mobile, AL Spring Hill College; Vicars for Religious.
Rimmele, Leo R. *o.s.b.* '55 (MO) DEPARTMENT OF VETERANS AFFAIRS HOSPITALS AND CHAPLAINS.
Rimmele, Leo R. *o.s.b.* '55 (SEA) Veterans Admin. Medical Center.
Rimmele, Leo *o.s.b.* '55 (P)[L] St. Benedict, OR Mt. Angel Abbey.
Rimselis, Victor *m.i.c.* '43 (CHI)[N] Chicago, IL Congregation of Marian Fathers of the Immaculate Conception Retired.
Rimshaw, Joseph J. *s.s.j.* '48 (BAL)[S] Baltimore, MD St. Joseph Society of the Sacred Heart House of Central Administration Retired.
Rimshaw, Joseph J. *s.s.j.* '48 (ORL) Melbourne, FL Our Lady of Lourdes Retired.
Rinaldi, Francis *o.s.f.s.* '69 (WIL) Wilmington, DE St. Anthony of Padua.
Rinaldo, Joseph *s.c.* '67 (LAN)[E] Chelsea, MI St. Louis Center for Exceptional Children & Adults; [P] Grass Lake, MI The Pious Union of St. Joseph.
Rindos, Paul T. '59 (HBG) Harrisburg, PA Retired.
Riney, C. Phillip '48 (OWN) Board Members; Roman Catholic Diocese of Owensboro Charitable Trust Fund, Inc.
Riney, Jerry '75 (OWN) Priest Personnel Committee; Consultors.
Riney, Maury D. '77 (OWN)[E] Owensboro, KY Carmel Home; Non–Parochial Assignments.
Riney, Philip C. '48 (OWN) Retired.
Riney, W. Jerry '75 (OWN) Bowling Green, KY Holy Spirit.
Ring, Bob '82 (ROC) Penn Yan, NY St. Michael; Stanley, NY St. Theresa.
Ring, Daniel J. '68 (TOL) Judges; Marblehead, OH St. Joseph.
Ring, John K. '61 (SFR) San Francisco, CA St. Vincent de Paul.
Ring, Joseph G. '88 (SFD) Riverton, IL St. James; Corporate Board Directors; Commission for the Care of Infirm and Retired Priests; Vicar for Clergy; Priests' Personnel Board; Illiopolis, IL Resurrection Parish.
Ring, Paul L. '95 (BO) Pepperell, MA Our Lady of Grace.
Ring, Robert P. '82 (ROC) Penn Yan, NY Our Lady of the Lakes Catholic Community; [M] Penn Yan, NY Keuka College c/o St. Michael's Church.
Ring, Vincent D. '64 (SFR) San Bruno, CA St. Robert Retired.
Ringenback, Gerard A. '72 (RVC) Levittown, NY St. Bernard; Hicksville Deanery; Catholic Youth Organization of Nassau and Suffolk.
Ringenberger, Harry '69 (MIA) Fort Lauderdale, FL St. Pius X.
Ringholz, Benedict E. '45 (TOL) Retired.
Ringley, F. John '01 (BGP) Shelton, CT St. Lawrence; [C] Bridgeport, CT Kolbe–Cathedral High School.
Ringwood, Joseph D. *s.j.* '59 (SPK)[J] Spokane, WA Regis Community Retired.
Rini, John '67 (ELP)[A] Conception, MO Conception Seminary College Retired.
Rink, George '57 (SEA) Retired.
Rink, Louis W. *c.s.c.* '58 (FTW)[H] Holy Cross House Retired.
Rinn, Richard A. *c.s.v.* '81 (LAV) Las Vegas, NV St. Viator.
Rinn, Richard A. *c.s.v.* '81 (CHI)[N] Arlington Heights Viatorian Province Center–Clerics of St. Viator.
Rinzel, Jerome A. '64 (MIL) Retired.
Riordan, Rev. Msgr. Brendan P. '70 (RVC) Great Neck, NY St. Aloysius; Senate of Priests (Presbyteral Council/College of Consultors).
Riordan, Eugene *s.m.a.* '53 (NEW)[M] Tenafly, NJ Society of African Missions, Provincialate, S.M.A. Fathers Retired.
Riordan, John B. *o.f.m.cap.* '71 (NY)[HH] New York, NY Fashion Institute of Technology (SUNY); New York, NY St. John the Baptist.
Riordan, Patrick M. '90 (PEO) Princeville, IL St. Mary of the Woods; Clergymen's Aid, Inc.
Rios, Francisco Alanis '01 (SFE)[H] Abiquiu, NM Monastery of Christ in the Desert.
Rios, Francisco '91 (SJ) San Jose, CA St. John Vianney; Special Assignment; Deans.
Rios, Guadalupe '09 (FRS) Los Banos, CA St. Joseph.
Rios, Juan Carlos '93 (MIA)[A] Miami, FL St. John Vianney College Seminary.
Rios, Luis Alfredo '97 (RCK) Aurora, IL St. Nicholas.
Rios, Manuel D. '86 (NEW) Union City, NJ Saint Rocco/Saint Brigid; Boy Scouts of America/Catholic Committee on Scouting.
Rios, Matthew *o.s.b.* '05 (LA)[P] Valyermo, CA St. Andrew's Abbey.
Rios, Ruben *i.v.e.* '06 (CHI) Chicago, IL St. Francis of Assisi.
Rios, Secundino *c.m.* '01 (FgM) Philadelphia, PA Eastern Province.
Rios, Teodoro A. *c.m.* '76 (FgM) Philadelphia, PA Eastern Province.
Rios Matos, P. Angel Luis '85 (MGZ) Mayaguez, PR Sacred Heart; Hormigueros, PR El Salvador.
Rios Ruiz, Moises (SJN) Carolina, PR Nuestra Senora de la Piedad.
Rioux, J. Robert *c.s.c.* '56 (FR)[G] North Dartmouth, MA St. Joseph's Hall; [G] North Dartmouth, MA Holy Cross Residence Retired.
Rioux, Ray '94 (SR) Guerneville, CA St. Elizabeth.
Ripko, DePaul *o.f.m.cap.* '53 (PIT)[M] Butler, PA St. Mary's Friary.
Riplog, Duane T. '84 (CHR) Retired.
Ripp, Anthony *m.s.c.* '68 (PH) Ottsville, PA St. John the Baptist.
Ripperger, Chad *f.s.s.p.* '97 (B) St. Joan of Arc.
Ripperger, Mark *o.cist.* '93 (DAL)[J] Irving, TX Cistercian Abbey of Our Lady of Dallas.
Ripperger, William '55 (IND) Retired.
Rippinger, Joel *o.s.b.* '74 (RCK)[G] Aurora, IL Marmion Abbey.
Rippy, Robert J. '84 (ARL) Arlington, VA Cathedral of St. Thomas More; Deans; Diocesan Consultors.
Riquelme, Alvaro A. *c.ss.r.* '97 (CHL) Kannapolis, NC St. Joseph Church.
Risacher, James E. '52 (TOL) Retired.
Risacher, James (BAL) Baltimore, MD Immaculate Heart of Mary.
Rischmann, Edward '48 (NEW) Retired.
Risley, John C. *o.p.* '65 (MAD)[G] Sinsinawa, WI Dominican Motherhouse.
Ristuccia, Leon C. *o.f.m.* '45 (PAT)[N] Butler, NJ St. Anthony Friary.
Rita, Thomas L. '70 (FR) Seekonk, MA St. Mary's; Judges.
Ritari, Raymond J. '83 (PHX) Phoenix, AZ St. Matthew Roman Catholic Parish.
Ritchey, Timothy M. '85 (B) St. Maries, ID St. Mary Immaculate; College of Consultors; Priest Personnel Commission; Priest Retirement Committee.
Ritchie, David L. '01 (TOL) Genoa, OH Our Lady of Lourdes; Oak Harbor, OH St. Boniface.
Ritchie, Gerald T. '68 (E) Harborcreek, PA Our Lady of Mercy.
Ritchie, Robert T. '71 (NY)[R] New York, NY Society of St. Vincent De Paul, Archdiocesan Central Council of New York.
Ritchie, Rev. Msgr. Robert '71 (NY) New York, NY Cathedral of St. Patrick.
Riter, Dennis G. '71 (BUF) Vicars; Dunkirk, NY St. Elizabeth Ann Seton.
Ritt, Paul E. '81 (BO) Chelmsford, MA St. John the Evangelist; Vicariate I; Presbyteral Council.
Ritter, Edward '57 (DET) Retired.
Ritter, Eric '03 (SAT) San Antonio, TX St. Dominic.
Ritter, Nicholas J. '65 (LAN) Retired.
Ritter, Patrick '74 (SEA) Bellevue, WA Sacred Heart.
Ritter, Patrick *s.d.s.* '76 (MIL)[P] Milwaukee, WI Salvatorians – Jordan Hall Retired.
Ritz, Eugene P. '09 (ALN) Reading, PA St. Catharine of Siena.
Ritz, Robert G. *c.s.b.* '51 (GAL)[O] Houston, TX Dillon House Retired.
Ritzert, William J. '64 (PIT) DEPARTMENT OF VETERANS AFFAIRS HOSPITALS AND CHAPLAINS Retired.
Ritzman, Joseph M. *s.j.* (BAL)[S] Baltimore, MD Colombiere Jesuit Community.
Riva, Gerald '68 (JOL) Woodridge, IL St. Scholastica; Deans.
Riva, Hugo *m.c.c.j.* '50 (CHI) Blue Island, IL St. Donatus.
Riva, Paul *c.r.s.* '96 (MAN)[H] Allenstown, NH Pine Haven Boys Center.
Rivard, Robert *f.m.s.i.* '77 (BO) Norfolk, MA St. Jude; [B] Framingham, MA Sylva Maria.
Rivard, Rev. Msgr. Roland J. '56 (BUR) Retired.
Rivas, David '85 (ARE) Lares, PR St. Judas Tadeos.
Rivas, Jose Antonio *l.c.* '03 (DET)[T] Clarkston, MI Clarkston Pastoral Center, Inc.
Rivas, Juan *l.c.* '82 (LA)[P] Arcadia, CA Legionaries of Christ; [BB] El Monte, CA Hombre Nuevo.
Rivas, Manuel de Jesus '92 (ATL) Kennesaw, GA St. Catherine of Siena; Marietta, GA Holy Family.
Rivas, Rigoberto Caloca *o.f.m.* (OAK)[R] Board of Directors:.
Rivas, Romeo '59 (MIA) Retired.
Rivera, Adalin '77 (PCE)[B] The Pontifical Catholic University of Puerto Rico; Censores Librorum.
Rivera, Adrian Alicea (FAJ) Ceiba, PR San Antonio de Padua.
Rivera, Anastacio *s.j.* '74 (LA)[C] Los Angeles, CA Jesuit Community.
Rivera, Andres *s.d.b.* '74 (SJN) San Juan, PR Maria Auxiliadora.
Rivera, Felix '91 (FAJ) Humacao, PR Maria Reina de la Paz.
Rivera, Guadalupe '49 (SFE) Retired.
Rivera, Rev. Msgr. Hector E. '82 (MGZ) For Diocesan Administration; Chancellor; Legion of Mary.
Rivera, Isreal '04 (HRT) Bristol, CT St. Joseph.
Rivera, Jaime '07 (ATL) Woodstock, GA St. Michael the Archangel.
Rivera, Librado Godinez *i.v.e.* '77 (PHX) Phoenix, AZ St. Anthony Roman Catholic Parish.
Rivera, Luis J. '06 (ARE) Hatillo, PR Our Lady of Mt. Carmel.
Rivera, Luis M. Miranda *o.carm.* '83 (SJN) San Juan, PR Santa Teresita Del Nino Jesus.
Rivera, Luis R. '84 (MIA) Miami, FL Our Lady of Divine Providence; Knights of Columbus (English and Spanish).
Rivera, Miguel '83 (ARE) Corozal, PR Our Lady of the Seven Sorrows.
Rivera, Miguel *s.d.b.* '86 (SJN) San Juan, PR San Juan Bosco.
Rivera, Oscar '79 (CGS) Cayey, PR San Esteban Protomartir; Diocesan Consultors; Priests Senate.
Rivera, P. Eliud Aponte '86 (PCE) Orocovis, PR Our Lady Mother of Divine Providence.
Rivera, Pedro '06 (SD) San Diego, CA St. Jude.
Rivera, Raymond L. '86 (PCE) Guayanilla, PR Immaculate Conception.
Rivera, Rolando '94 (LAV) Las Vegas, NV St. Francis de Sales; Diocesan Advocates.
Rivera, Walter Espinoza '99 (MRY) Watsonville, CA Our Lady of the Assumption.
Rivera–Marzan, Eddie '90 (SJN)[E] San Juan, PR VA Medical Center.
Rivera–Soto, Orlando '90 (PCE) Juana Diaz, PR Santa Teresita del Nino Jesus.
Rivera–Vigo, Milton Agustin '05 (SJN) Vicar of Social Communication; Television Station; Diocesan Consultors.
Rivera Maldonado, Jose A. '84 (FAJ) Canovanas, PR Santa Maria Madre de Dios.
Rivera Perez, Marco Antonio '06 (SJN) San Juan, PR San Francisco Javier; Diocesan Consultors.
Rivera Ramos, Rev. Msgr. Hector E. '82 (MGZ) Mayaguez, PR Cathedral of Our Lady of Purification.
Rivero, Andres *o.f.m.* '75 (SD) Hispanic; [J] Oceanside, CA Mission San Luis Rey.
Rivero, Eduardo *o.carm.* '02 (JOL)[L] Darien Carmelite Provincial Office.
Rivero, Jordi '82 (MIA)[O] West Park, FL Respect Life Ministry; Respect Life Ministry.

Rivero, Jordi '82 (MIA) Miami, FL St. Timothy.
Rivero, Juan '72 (FWT) Glen Rose, TX St. Rose of Lima; Granbury, TX St. Frances Cabrini; Priests' Pension Plan Trustees; Vicar for Priests.
Rivero, Julio *t.o.r.* (SP) St. Petersburg, FL St. Mary Our Lady of Grace.
Rivero, Leonides '78 (ELP) Priests' Retirement and Disability Plan; El Paso, TX St. Mark; Presbyteral Council.
Riveroll, Jesus R. *s.j.* '88 (FgM) St. Louis, MO Society of Jesus.
Riveros, Wilfredo '97 (CGS) Cayey, PR Nuestra Senora de la Merced.
Rivers, Robert S. *c.s.p.* '68 (BO)[U] Boston, MA Paulist Fathers Residence.
Rivituso, Rev. Msgr. Mark S. '88 (STL) Judicial Vicar; St. Louis, MO Cure' of Ars.
Rizk, Antoine *b.s.o.* '96 (NTN) Brooklyn, NY Church of the Virgin Mary; Methuen, MA; Presbyteral Council.
Rizo, Sergio '89 (FWT) Cleburne, TX St. Joseph.
Rizzo, David R. '99 (ALT) Tribunal; Altoona, PA Our Lady of Lourdes.
Rizzo, Giovanni '00 (AGN)[A] Yona, GU Redemptoris Mater Archdiocesan Missionary Seminary.
Rizzo, Mark '68 (ELP) Retired.
Rizzo, Matteo (BRK) Brooklyn, NY St. Francis of Paola.
Rizzo, Robert C. '74 (CHI) Hoffman Estates, IL St. Hubert.
Rizzuto, Mariano J. *s.m.* '59 (NO)[P] New Orleans, LA Marist Fathers.
Ro, Matheus B. *s.v.d.* '07 (WH) Gassaway, WV St. Thomas; Maysel, WV Risen Lord; Webster Springs, WV St. Anne's.
Roa, Daniel E. '08 (SAG) Bay City, MI St. Stanislaus Kostka.
Roach, Daniel *o.p.* '56 (FgM) Chicago, IL Province of St. Albert the Great (Central).
Roach, Francis J. '56 (STP) Retired.
Roach, Francis J. '73 (WOR) Worcester, MA Our Lady of Lourdes; University of Mass Medical Center.
Roach, John A. '58 (SPR) Presbyteral Council.
Roach, Joseph W. *s.a.g.* '48 (SAG) Retired.
Roach, Michael J. '71 (BAL) Manchester, MD St. Bartholomew; [A] Emmitsburg, MD Mount St. Mary's Seminary.
Roach, Michael '81 (KC) Kansas City, MO St. Therese Parish.
Roach, Thomas *s.j.* '69 (SCR)[C] Scranton, PA The University of Scranton.
Roache, James P. '59 (CHI) Retired.
Roarden, Patrick *o.p.* '60 (DEN)[N] Denver, CO Dominican Friars.
Roark, John D. '56 (SY) Retired.
Roark, Michael B. '70 (WIL) Marydel, MD Immaculate Conception.
Robak, Anthony G. '74 (NEW) North Bergen, NJ Sacred Heart.
Robb, Dennis E. '74 (SEA) Aberdeen, WA St. Mary; Aberdeen, WA SS. Peter and Paul; Aberdeen, WA Our Lady of Good Help; Aberdeen, WA St. Jerome.
Robb, Kevin D. *o.p.* '77 (PRO)[P] Providence St. Thomas Aquinas Priory at Providence College.
Robb, Paul V. *s.j.* '60 (CHI)[N] Chicago, IL Chicago Province of the Society of Jesus–Provincial Office; Chicago, IL; [N] Chicago, IL Woodlawn Jesuit Community.
Robbins, Hugh W. *c.s.v.* '52 (CHI)[N] Arlington Heights Viatorian Province Center–Clerics of St. Viator.
Robbins, John F. *c.s.b.* '72 (GAL) Houston, TX St. Anne.
Robbins, Robert J. '74 (NY) New York, NY Holy Family; Office of Ecumenical and Interreligious Affairs.
Robbins, Rev. Msgr. Roger P. '63 (SAT) Schertz, TX Church of the Good Shepherd.
Robbins, Thomas P. '74 (COV)[B] Covington, KY Holy Cross High School; Air Force Reserve Chaplains; Edgewood, KY St. Pius X.
Roberge, Francis A. '78 (WOR) Baldwinville, MA St. Vincent De Paul; Winchendon, MA Immaculate Heart of Mary.
Roberge, Richard A. '85 (MAN) Vicars Forane; Berlin, NH Good Shepherd; Gorham, NH Holy Family; Northern New Hampshire Correctional Facility; Priest Personnel Board.
Roberson, Henry '71 (OKL) Retired.
Roberson, Michael '74 (NO) Metairie, LA Our Lady of Divine Providence.
Roberson, Ronald G. *c.s.p.* '77 (WDC)[B] Washington, DC St. Paul's College; Staff.
Roberson, Shawn *t.o.r.* '02 (ALT)[I] Loretto, PA St. Francis University (Loretto); [G] Loretto, PA St. Francis Friary at Mount Assisi; [G] Loretto, PA St. Bonaventure Friary; [A] Loretto, PA St. Francis University.
Robert, Darin T. '71 (LAN) DEPARTMENT OF VETERANS AFFAIRS HOSPITALS AND CHAPLAINS Retired.
Robert, Rene '89 (STA) Fleming Island, FL Sacred Heart.
Roberts, Allan '80 (LA) Los Angeles, CA St. Bernadette.
Roberts, Anthony P. *s.j.* '56 (PH)[Y] Loyola Center and Manresa Hall.
Roberts, Arthur *c.s.b.* '55 (LSC)[B] Las Cruces, NM Basilian Fathers; Las Cruces, NM Cathedral of the Immaculate Heart of Mary.
Roberts, Benjamin A. '09 (CHL) Greensboro, NC St. Paul the Apostle.
Roberts, Christopher George '07 (LFT) Carmel, IN Our Lady of Mount Carmel.
Roberts, Don J. '78 (SFD) Hardin, IL St. Francis of Assisi; Brussels, IL Blessed Trinity.
Roberts, Edward *s.s.s.* '60 (CLV)[N] Cleveland Congregation of the Blessed Sacrament Provincial House.
Roberts, Edward *s.s.c.* '60 (OM)[K] St. Columbans Missionary Society of St. Columban.
Roberts, Eugene J. '75 (TR) Marlboro, NJ St. Gabriel.
Roberts, G. Richard '91 (LC) Fountain City, WI St. Lawrence; Fountain City, WI Immaculate Conception.
Roberts, Guy R. '98 (IND) Indianapolis, IN St. Joan of Arc.
Roberts, Joseph L. '02 (ORL) Deltona, FL Our Lady of the Lakes.
Roberts, Marshall M. '96 (SCR) Unassigned or Leave of Absence.
Roberts, Nathanael *o.s.b.* '03 (RCK)[G] Aurora, IL Marmion Abbey.
Roberts, Ralph O. '98 (GAL) Sweeny, TX Our Lady of Perpetual Help.
Roberts, Ralph *s.s.s.* '75 (CLV)[N] Cleveland Congregation of the Blessed Sacrament Provincial House.
Roberts, Stephen '07 (LEX) Vocations.
Roberts, Thomas C. '84 (NEW) Newark, NJ Northern State Prison; Bayonne, NJ Our Lady of the Assumption.
Robertson, Douglas C. '96 (LC) La Crosse, WI Mary, Mother of the Church.
Robertson, Eugene G. '78 (STL) Marthasville, MO St. Vincent de Paul.
Robertson, James E. '77 (AUS) Copperas Cove, TX Holy Family.
Robertson, John W. '71 (HEL) Special Assignments; Diocesan Pastoral Council; Episcopal Vicar for Canonical Services; Chancellor; Diocesan Tribunal; Judicial Vicar; Office of Due Process; Program of Formation for the Permanent Diaconate; Diocesan Finance Council.
Robertson, John W. '71 (GF) Promoter of Justice.
Robertson, John W. '71 (HEL) Permanent Deacons.
Robertson, John (HEL) Helmville, MT St. Thomas.
Robertson, Luke *t.o.r.* '99 (FWT) Fort Worth, TX St. Andrew.
Robertson, Thomas M. '65 (STL) St. Louis, MO St. George.
Robeson, Robert J. '03 (IND) Bishop Simon Brute College Seminary.
Robeson, Steven P. '84 (STL) Imperial, MO St. John.
Robichaud, Armand *s.m.* '50 (BO)[U] Boston, MA Marist Fathers of Our Lady of Victories (Boston Prov.).
Robichaud, Paul G. *c.s.p.* '75 (MO) Navy Reserve Chaplains.
Robichaud, Paul G. *c.s.p.* '75 (WDC) Washington, DC American Catholic Historical Association (1919); [B] Washington, DC St. Paul's College.
Robichaux, Rev. Msgr. Robie E. '76 (LAF) Lafayette, LA St. Leo the Great; Judicial Vicar; Clergy Personnel Advisory Board.
Robicheaux, David J. '98 (NO) New Orleans, LA Our Lady of The Rosary; Deans.
Robideau, Jeffrey '97 (LAN) Michigan Center, MI Our Lady of Fatima.
Robillard, Joseph '84 (ORG) Anaheim, CA St. Justin Martyr; Council of Priests.
Robin, Richard A. *s.j.* '67 (LA)[C] Los Angeles, CA Loyola Marymount University; [C] Los Angeles, CA Jesuit Community.
Robine, Paul M. '59 (ALT) Retired.
Robins, Dean L. '87 (NO) Covington, LA Most Holy Trinity.
Robinson, Charles *o.f.m.cap.* '70 (GF) Crow Agency, MT St. Dennis.
Robinson, Christopher S. *c.m.* '89 (CHI) Chicago, IL St. Vincent de Paul; [N] Chicago, IL Vincentian Community, Congregation of the Mission, Western Province.
Robinson, David C. *s.j.* '92 (ORG)[H] Yorba Linda, CA Pope John Paul II Polish Center; [H] Orange, CA Loyola Institute for Spirituality; [I] Anaheim, CA Manresa Jesuit Residence.
Robinson, David J. '90 (PHX)[F] Phoenix, AZ Society of Jesus.
Robinson, Denis *o.s.b.* '93 (IND)[K] St. Meinrad, IN St. Meinrad Archabbey; [A] St. Meinrad, IN Saint Meinrad School of Theology.
Robinson, Donald A. '80 (OG) Watertown, NY St. Anthony.
Robinson, Edmund J. *s.j.* '55 (SPK)[J] Spokane, WA Regis Community Retired.
Robinson, Edward M. *o.p.* '41 (DAL)[J] Irving, TX Dominican Priory of St. Albert the Great and Novitiate.
Robinson, Edwin F.D. *o.f.m.* '68 (NY) Dobbs Ferry, NY St. Cabrini Nursing Home.
Robinson, Edwin F.D. *o.f.m.* '68 (PAT)[N] Butler, NJ St. Anthony Friary.
Robinson, Edwin *o.f.m.* '68 (NY)[AA] Dobbs Ferry, NY Cabrini of Westchester.
Robinson, Gerald H. *s.j.* '77 (SAC)[K] Applegate, CA Our Lady of the Oaks Villa; Vicars Forane; [I] Carmichael, CA Sacramento Jesuit Community.
Robinson, Jack Clark *o.f.m.* '86 (LA)[P] Santa Barbara, CA Franciscan Friary, Order of Friars Minor (Old Mission).
Robinson, Jack Clark *o.f.m.* '80 (SAT)[B] San Antonio, TX San Antonio de Padua Friary.
Robinson, Rev. Msgr. James P. *s.s.e.* '57 (DET) Detroit, MI Cathedral, Church of the Most Blessed Sacrament.
Robinson, Jerome '75 (BEA) On Leave from the Archdiocese; [B] Port Arthur, TX CHRISTUS Health Southeast Texas – CHRISTUS Hospital – St. Mary; [B] Beaumont, TX CHRISTUS Health Southeast Texas – CHRISTUS Hospital – St. Elizabeth.
Robinson, John A. '71 (CHI) Other Assignments.
Robinson, John C. '54 (MOB) Retired.
Robinson, John '54 (BIR) Birmingham, AL St. Peter the Apostle.
Robinson, John *s.o.l.t.* '09 (CC)[G] Robstown, TX Society of Our Lady of the Most Holy Trinity.
Robinson, Joseph A. '64 (CIN) Cincinnati, OH St. Boniface; Vicarri Foranei (Deans).
Robinson, Joseph P. '68 (BO) Burlington, MA St. Margaret.
Robinson, Ken '92 (FWT) Muenster, TX Sacred Heart.
Robinson, Lawrence F. *s.j.* '65 (P)[D].
Robinson, Michael '96 (SD) San Diego, CA Good Shepherd.
Robinson, Monte E. '75 (MAD) Belmont, WI St. Philomena; Belmont, WI St. Michael; Belmont, WI Immaculate Conception.
Robinson, Patrick '91 (PHX) Scottsdale, AZ Blessed Sacrament Roman Catholic Parish.
Robinson, Paul F. *o.carm.* '67 (FR) Judicial Vicar; Judges.
Robinson, Paul *o.carm.* '67 (JOL)[L] Darien Carmelite Provincial Office.
Robinson, Perry L. *s.j.* '72 (OM) Ralston, NE St. Gerald; [K] Omaha, NE Jesuit Community at Creighton University.
Robinson, Ralph C. '03 (CHR) Absent On Leave.
Robinson, Richard J. '63 (MIL) Big Bend, WI St. Joseph.
Robinson, Robert M. '69 (BRK) Queens Village, NY SS. Joachim and Anne.
Robinson, Tyrone '79 (DET) Detroit, MI St. Luke; Detroit, MI St. Mary's of Redford.
Robinson, William *o.f.m.conv.* '74 (CHL) Winston–Salem, NC Our Lady of Mercy; Rensselaer, NY.
Robisch, David C. '62 (CIN) Retired.
Robitaille, Jean–Claude *m.afr.* '73 (WDC) Washington, DC; Washington, DC MISSIONARIES OF AFRICA; [N] Washington, DC Missionaries of Africa.
Robitaille, Raymond '47 (LAF) Retired.
Robledo, Jaime '90 (SAT)[A] San Antonio, TX Assumption Seminary.
Robles, Antonio *s.d.b.* '61 (ARE) Orocovis, PR San Juan Bautista.
Robles, Ariel (TR) Red Bank, NJ St. James.
Robles, Daniel '01 (SPC) Springfield, MO Sacred Heart.
Robles, Juan Pablo '07 (BWN) Brownsville, TX St. Luke.
Robles, Vidal '98 (ELP) Promoter of Justice; Defenders of the Bond; La Tuna Federal.
Robles–Sanchez, Jose A. '95 (ALX) Liturgy Commission; Alexandria, LA St. Frances Xavier Cabrini.
Robotnik, Lawrence R. '57 (COV)[N] Erlanger, KY Monastery of the Sacred Passion Retired.
Robu, Emil '98 (MRY) Carmel Valley, CA Our Lady of Mt. Carmel; Defenders of the Bond; Promoter of Justice.
Roby, Brian '96 (OWN) Paducah, KY St. Francis de Sales; Paducah, KY Rosary Chapel; Deans/Coordinators; Paducah, KY Mt. Carmel Interparochial Cemetery.
Roby, Bruce '09 (BGP) Stratford, CT St. James.
Roca, Albert L. '77 (MET) Retired.
Roca, Casimiro *s.f.* '43 (SFE) Chimayo, NM Holy Family.
Rocca, Peter D. *c.s.c.* '74 (FTW)[A] Notre Dame, IN Moreau Seminary; [A] Notre Dame, IN Moreau Seminary; [B] University of Notre Dame Du Lac; Liturgical Commission.
Rocchi, Frank J. '82 (NEW) Irvington, NJ Good Shepherd.
Rocco, Daniel M. '90 (CAM) Blackwood, NJ The R.C. Church of St. Jude, Gloucester Township, N.J.
Rocha, Antonio Nuno '06 (NEW) Newark, NJ Our Lady of Fatima.
Rocha, Constantino '95 (FTW) Goshen, IN St. John the Evangelist; Goshen.
Rocha, Rev. Msgr. Ivo D. '66 (STO) Tracy, CA St. Bernard Church (Pastor of).
Rocha, Jose F. '04 (PRO) Pawtucket, RI St. Anthony.
Rocha, Leonardo *c.s.* '06 (DAL) Irving, TX St. Luke.

Rocha, Michael '88 (LA) Venice, CA St. Mark.
Rocha, Richard '02 (KC) Vocations; Special Assignment; Kansas City, MO St. Peter's.
Rocha, Victor J. '53 (PIT) Pittsburgh, PA Resurrection Retired.
Roche, Amalraj *m.s.f.x.* '98 (BIS) New Salem, ND St. Pius V; Center, ND St. Martin; New Salem, ND St. Mary, Queen of Peace.
Roche, David '58 (PEO) Retired.
Roche, Edward *s.o.l.t.* '97 (CC)[G] Robstown, TX Society of Our Lady of the Most Holy Trinity.
Roche, John F. *s.s.c.* '56 (PRO)[P] Bristol, RI St. Columban's Retirement House Retired.
Roche, John J. *s.d.b.* '86 (OAK)[A] Berkeley, CA Dominican School of Philosophy and Theology.
Roche, John *ss.cc.* '82 (LA) San Dimas, CA Holy Name of Mary; [P] La Verne, CA Congregation of the Sacred Hearts of Jesus and Mary.
Roche, John *c.ss.r.* '63 (FgM) Baltimore Province.
Roche, John *s.d.b.* (OAK)[M] Berkeley Salesians of Don Bosco.
Roche, John *s.s.c.* '56 (OM)[K] St. Columbans Missionary Society of St. Columban.
Roche, Joseph L. *s.j.* '58 (FgM) New York, NY Society of Jesus.
Roche, Matthew F. *s.j.* '81 (NY)[GG] Staten Island, NY Mount Manresa Jesuit Retreat House; Staten Island, NY Our Lady of Mt. Carmel–St. Benedicta.
Roche, Randall *s.j.* '68 (LA)[C] Los Angeles, CA Jesuit Community.
Roche, Robert *o.s.b.* '62 (ALT) Patton, PA Queen of Peace.
Roche, Ron '61 (PBL) Retired.
Roche, Stanley *o.s.b.* '47 (SCL)[I] Collegeville, MN St. John's Abbey, of the Order of St. Benedict.
Roche, Rev. Msgr. William H. '50 (BO) Senior Priests.; [CC] Boston, MA Sancta Maria House, Inc. Retired.
Rochford, John J. '47 (CHI) Retired.
Rochford, Thomas M. *s.j.* '76 (STL)[O] St. Louis, MO Leo Brown Jesuit Community.
Rochon, Robert A. '74 (PRO) Johnston, RI St. Brigid.
Rochuparathanathu, Augustine *v.c.* (FTW) Huntington, IN SS. Peter and Paul.
Rock, John J. *s.j.* '87 (BAL)[S] Towson Maryland Province of the Society of Jesus.
Rock, Larry G. '00 (BAL)[D] Hagerstown, MD St. Maria Goretti High School; Special Assignment.
Rock, Martin I. *s.j.* '59 (SLC) West Haven, UT Saint Mary LLC 237.
Rock, Michael R. *o.de.m.* '86 (BUF)[O] LeRoy, NY Order of the BVM of Mercy/Mercedarian Friars; LeRoy, NY Our Lady of Mercy; [O] LeRoy, NY St. Raymond Nonnatus Novitiate; Bergen, NY St. Brigid.
Rock, Richard J. *c.m.* '73 (PH) Philadelphia, PA St. Vincent de Paul.
Rock, Rev. Msgr. Russell L. '62 (CAM) Runnemede, NJ Church of St. Maria Goretti, Runnemede, N.J.; College of Consultors.
Rock, Stephen B. '74 (BO) Reading, MA St. Agnes.
Rock, William J. *o.p.* '58 (Y) Youngstown, OH St. Dominic.
Rocker, Stephen '79 (OG) Gouverneur, NY Sacred Heart; Gouverneur, NY St. James.
Rockers, Alfred '62 (KCK) Basehor, KS Holy Angels.
Rocks, Jason T. '02 (CAM) Magnolia, NJ St. Gregory's Church, Magnolia, N.J.
Rocus, John George '01 (LAN) Brighton, MI Holy Spirit; W. J. Maxey Boys Training School.
Rodak, Joseph *c.pp.s.* (CLV) Cleveland, OH Our Lady of Good Counsel.
Rodak, Joseph *c.pp.s.* '62 (CIN)[N] Dayton Provincial Office of the Cincinnati Province of the Society of the Precious Blood.
Rodak, Michael '07 (PAT) Presbyteral Council; College of Consultors; Sparta, NJ Our Lady of the Lake.
Rodakowski, Louis '42 (P) Retired.
Rodas, Mauro G. '65 (IND) Greenwood, IN Our Lady of the Greenwood Retired.
Rodell, Jeremiah J. '47 (CHI) Retired.
Roden, Raymond '81 (BRK) Special Assistant to Vicar for Clergy; Long Island City, NY Our Lady of Mount Carmel.
Roden–Lucero, Edward Paul '82 (ELP) El Paso, TX San Juan Diego Parish.
Roden–Lucero, Edward '82 (SAT) Defenders of the Bond.
Rodenfels, Jerome P. '74 (COL) New Albany, OH Church of the Resurrection.
Roder, Terry A. '88 (SC) Anthon, IA St. Joseph's; Danbury, IA St. Mary's; Board of Education.
Rodes, Kenneth J. '81 (MO) Navy Chaplains.
Rodgers, Rev. Msgr. Arthur E. '65 (PH) Bala Cynwyd, PA St. Matthias; Regional Vicars; Priests' Personnel Board.
Rodgers, Hilary R. '04 (WIL) Ridgely, MD St. Benedict.
Rodgers, Philip F. '81 (ALN) Mohnton, PA St. Benedict's.
Rodgers, Rev. Msgr. William J. '49 (BRK)[Q] Queens Village, NY Queen of Peace Residence Retired.
Rodgriguez, Astor *c.m.* '93 (BRK) Brooklyn, NY St. John the Baptist.
Rodia, James C. *o.praem.* '72 (PH)[Y] Paoli, PA Daylesford Abbey.
Rodighiero, Dominic *c.s.* '61 (WDC)[M] Mitchellville, MD Villa Rosa Nursing Home, Inc.
Rodighiero, Dominic *c.s.* (BO) Everett, MA St. Anthony of Padua.
Rodillas, Raynato '97 (SLC) St. George, UT St. George LLC 223.
Rodis, James '60 (STL) Retired.
Rodlach, Alexander *s.v.d.* '90 (CHI)[N] Techny, IL Divine Word Residence.
Rodney, John *s.v.d.* '60 (WDC)[N] Washington, DC Divine Word House.
Rodney, Joseph C. *s.s.j.* '68 (NO) Reserve, LA Our Lady of Grace.
Rodoni, Rick '91 (SJ) Los Gatos, CA St. Mary of the Immaculate Conception; College of Consultors.
Rodrigalvarez, Jose Antonio *o.a.r.* (NY) Bronx, NY St. Anselm.
Rodrigo, Niranjan *s.s.s.* '99 (NY) Goshen, NY St. John the Evangelist.
Rodrigo, Salvador *o.carm.* '62 (SJN) San Juan, PR Santa Teresita Del Nino Jesus.
Rodrigo, Stephen *s.j.* '75 (KAL) Byron Center, MI St. Mary's Visitation.
Rodrigue, Josh (NO)[A] St. Benedict, LA St. Joseph Seminary College.
Rodrigue, Joshua John '02 (HT) Houma, LA St. Anthony of Padua; Priests Council.
Rodrigue, Raymond E. '97 (NEW) Midland Park, NJ Nativity.
Rodrigues, Allen *s.t.* '07 (PT)[E] Tallahassee, FL Missionary Servants of the Most Holy Trinity.
Rodrigues, Amancio J. '66 (P) Lincoln City, OR St. Augustine.
Rodrigues, Carlos R. '95 (BGP) Stamford, CT Sacred Heart; [K] Stamford, CT St. Camillus Health Center.
Rodrigues, Charles *s.j.* '08 (CHI)[N] Chicago Chicago Province of the Society of Jesus–Provincial Office.
Rodrigues, Ignatius '66 (SB) Loma Linda, CA St. Joseph the Worker.
Rodrigues, Jeremy J. '08 (PRO) Greenville, RI St. Philip.
Rodrigues, Joseph *s.d.s.* '93 (TUC)[H] Tucson, AZ Jordan Ministry Team, Inc.
Rodrigues, Sabbas '61 (RVC) Hampton Bays, NY St. Rosalie's.
Rodrigues, Tommy '69 (TOL) New Washington, OH St. Bernard.
Rodrigues, Wenceslaus '91 (NY) Hartsdale, NY Sacred Heart.
Rodrigues, William '00 (FR) New Bedford, MA Our Lady of Mt. Carmel.
Rodriguez, Agustin *m.sp.s.* '06 (LA) Oxnard, CA Our Lady of Guadalupe Parish.
Rodriguez, Alberto E. *o.ss.t.* '87 (DAL) Dallas, TX Santa Clara.
Rodriguez, Alberto *o.p.* '71 (MIA) Miami, FL St. Dominic; [K] Miami, FL Dominican Fathers of Miami, Inc.
Rodriguez, Alejandro J. '08 (MIA) Miami, FL Our Lady of Lourdes.
Rodriguez, Ambiorix '97 (NY) Bronx, NY Our Lady of Mercy.
Rodriguez, Antonio L. '49 (BUF) Retired.
Rodriguez, Antonio Salvador '68 (DAL) Dallas, TX St. Cecilia.
Rodriguez, Antonio '63 (LA) Long Beach, CA St. Lucy.
Rodriguez, Antonio '93 (PAT) Passaic, NJ Holy Trinity; Deans; Presbyteral Council; College of Consultors.
Rodriguez, Armando J. '55 (GAL)[L] Houston, TX Pope John Paul XXIII Priests' Residence Retired.
Rodriguez, Arturo Perez '72 (CHI) Chicago, IL Assumption.
Rodriguez, Astor *c.m.* '93 (BRK)[T] Brooklyn, NY St. John the Baptist Rectory.
Rodriguez, Rev. Msgr. Benigno Antonio '66 (LA) Retired.
Rodriguez, Bernardo C. '80 (BGP) Bridgeport, CT St. Patrick Church; Bridgeport, CT Bridgeport Community Correctional Facility.
Rodriguez, Carlos L. *c.p.* '99 (ARE) Lares, PR St. Joseph.
Rodriguez, Carlos *o.c.s.o.* '70 (L)[L] Trappist, KY Abbey of Our Lady of Gethsemani, of the Order of Cistercians of the Strict Observance.
Rodriguez, Carlos '87 (NY) Bronx, NY St. John Chrysostom; Archdiocesan Consultors.
Rodriguez, David *o.f.m.* '89 (CHI)[D] Chicago, IL Hales Franciscan High School, Inc.; [N] Chicago, IL Holy Spirit Friary, Order of Friars Minor.
Rodriguez, Delfin '86 (ARE) Corozal, PR Holy Family.
Rodriguez, Domingo *s.t.* '67 (WDC)[N] Adelphi, MD Our Lady Missionary Cenacle.
Rodriguez, Edgar A. Carlo '97 (MGZ) Aguadilla, PR St. Charles Borromeo.
Rodriguez, Edgar '03 (CHI) La Grange, IL St. Cletus.
Rodriguez, Edmundo '66 (FWT)[J] Lake Dallas, TX Montserrat Jesuit Retreat House.
Rodriguez, Eduardo *o.c.s.o.* '69 (ATL)[G] Conyers, GA The Monastery of the Holy Spirit.
Rodriguez, Rev. Msgr. Elias S. Morales (PCE)[B] The Pontifical Catholic University of Puerto Rico.
Rodriguez, Epifanio *o.p.* '54 (CC) San Diego, TX St. Francis de Paula; San Diego, TX; [G] San Diego, TX Vicariate of Holy Rosary.
Rodriguez, Fabian *s.j.* '66 (FAJ) Canovanas, PR Sagrado Corazon de Jesus.
Rodriguez, Feliciano '85 (CGS) Priests Senate; Pastoral Vicar.
Rodriguez, Felix M. '97 (YAK) On Duty Outside the Diocese.
Rodriguez, Fernando E. '07 (SAT) San Antonio, TX St. Luke.
Rodriguez, Fidel (ORL) Winter Park, FL Saints Peter and Paul.
Rodriguez, Florencio *t.o.r.* '80 (SAT) San Antonio, TX St. Lawrence.
Rodriguez, Francis *o.c.s.o.* '55 (WOR)[O] Spencer, MA St. Joseph's Abbey.
Rodriguez, Franklin '64 (CGS) San Lorenzo, PR Sagrado Corazon de Jesus y 12 Apostoles.
Rodriguez, Gilbert '74 (SAN) Midland, TX St. Stephen's.
Rodriguez, Guillermo '69 (LA) Long Beach, CA St. Matthew.
Rodriguez, Guillermo '56 (SFR) Retired.
Rodriguez, Gustavo Ortega *o.f.m.* (LAR) Hebbronville, TX Our Lady of Guadalupe.
Rodriguez, Henry '86 (SD) Unassigned.
Rodriguez, Hernan Queuedo '97 (ATL) Hapeville, GA St. John the Evangelist.
Rodriguez, Isnardo Serrano '97 (SAC) Vallejo, CA St. Vincent Ferrer.
Rodriguez, Israel J. '09 (BO) Marlborough, MA Immaculate Conception.
Rodriguez, James '08 (BRK)[H] Astoria, NY St. John Preparatory School; Long Island City, NY Most Precious Blood.
Rodriguez, Jesus A. '93 (ARE) Vega–Baja, PR Our Lady of Carmen–Playa.
Rodriguez, Jesus *s.j.* '95 (MOB)[A] Mobile, AL Spring Hill College.
Rodriguez, Joaquin '72 (MIA) Miami, FL St. Thomas the Apostle.
Rodriguez, Rev. Msgr. John F. '59 (SFR) San Francisco, CA St. John the Evangelist Retired.
Rodriguez, Jorge I. '86 (PAT) Paterson, NJ St. Mary's.
Rodriguez, Jorge Luis *c.o.r.c.* '08 (SB)[I] Corona, CA Confraternity of Operarios Del Reino De Cristo, C.O.R.C.; Corona, CA St. Edward.
Rodriguez, Jorge '87 (DEN)[A] Denver, CO Saint John Vianney Theological Seminary.
Rodriguez, Rev. Msgr. Jose A. '64 (SFR) San Francisco, CA St. John the Evangelist; College of Consultors; Hispanic & Haitian Ministry; Archbishop's Cabinet; On Special Assignment.
Rodriguez, Jose A. '95 (WOR) Worcester, MA St. Joan of Arc; Director of Priest Personnel; Priests' Personnel Board; Director of Priest Personnel; St. Joan of Arc.
Rodriguez, Jose A. '80 (ARE) On Duty Outside the Diocese.
Rodriguez, Jose Alberto '05 (AGN) San Vicente Ferrer Parish; Barrigada, GU San Vicente Ferrer.
Rodriguez, Jose Diego '81 (PCE) Coamo, PR St. Blase; Parish Priests Consultors.
Rodriguez, Rev. Msgr. Jose '64 (SFR) Episcopal Vicar for the Spanish Speaking.
Rodriguez, Jose Alberto '05 (AGN) Archdiocesan College of Consultors; Archdiocesan Presbyteral Council.
Rodriguez, L. Antonio '49 (BUF)[O] Lackawanna, NY Bishop Head Residence Retired.
Rodriguez, Lawrence '52 (LA) Retired.
Rodriguez, Lilson '97 (CHR) Goose Creek, SC Immaculate Conception.
Rodriguez, Luis F. '01 (NO) Metairie, LA St. Clement of Rome; Serra Club of New Orleans; Vocation Office.
Rodriguez, Luis R. '93 (HBG) Mount Joy, PA Mary, Mother of the Church.
Rodriguez, Luis *s.j.* '65 (FgM) Milwaukee, WI Society of Jesus; Milwaukee, WI.
Rodriguez, Luis *s.j.* '65 (MIL)[Y] Milwaukee, WI The Jesuit Partnership; [P] Milwaukee, WI Jesuit Provincial Office, Wisconsin Province; [P] Milwaukee, WI Jesuit Community at Marquette University.
Rodriguez, Manuel (BRK) Brooklyn, NY St. Michael.
Rodriguez, Mario *m.sp.s.* '00 (LA) Huntington Park, CA St. Martha.
Rodriguez, Marlon *o.c.d.* '96 (DEN) Centennial, CO St. Thomas More.
Rodriguez, Martin S. *c.o.r.c.* '92 (SB)[I] Corona, CA Confraternity of Operarios Del Reino De Cristo, C.O.R.C.; Riverside, CA Sacred Heart.
Rodriguez, Matias '66 (TYL) Kilgore, TX Christ the King.
Rodriguez, Michael '96 (ELP) El Paso, TX San Juan Bautista.
Rodriguez, Michael '90 (SAN) Sweetwater, TX Holy Family; Sweetwater, TX Immaculate Heart of Mary.
Rodriguez, Nestor '93 (PMB) Indiantown, FL Holy Cross; Elected Members; Damas Catolicas en Acion.
Rodriguez, Rev. Msgr. Pablo M. '61 (RVC) Hempstead, NY Our Lady of Loretto.

Rodriguez, Pablo Ponce '02 (AGN)[A] Yona, GU Redemptoris Mater Archdiocesan Missionary Seminary.
Rodriguez, Pedro Poloche '98 (ATL) Atlanta, GA Sacred Heart of Jesus.
Rodriguez, Pedro *o.carm.* '09 (MGZ) Anasco, PR St. Anthony Abbot.
Rodríguez, Rafael *s.j.* '84 (SJN)[A] Sacred Heart University; [D] San Juan, PR Centro Universitario Catolico; [H] San Juan, PR; UPR Catholic Student Center.
Rodriguez, Rafael '04 (MIL) Whitewater, WI St. Patrick.
Rodriguez, Ray '94 (CHY) Vocation Office.
Rodriguez, Reyes G. '67 (SLC) Retired.
Rodriguez, Robert A. '08 (TUC) Tucson, AZ Saint Joseph Roman Catholic Parish – Tucson.
Rodriguez, Robert '53 (MIL) Retired.
Rodriguez, Roberto *m.m.* '95 (FgM) Maryknoll, NY MARYKNOLL.
Rodriguez, Santos '70 (SFR) San Bruno, CA St. Bruno.
Rodriguez, Tobias '02 (NEW)[A] Kearny, NJ Redemptoris Mater Archdiocesan Missionary Seminary.
Rodriguez, William H. '02 (R) Roxboro, NC Sts. Mary and Edward.
Rodriguez, William '79 (LA) Los Angeles, CA St. Thomas the Apostle.
Rodríguez, Wilson Montes '06 (MGZ) Mayaguez, PR Sacred Heart.
Rodriguez–Delgado, Emerson *o.f.m.* '07 (NY)[EE] New York Franciscan Friars, Holy Name Province.
Rodriguez–Fuentes, Rafael '07 (LIN) Advocates; Seward, NE St. Vincent de Paul.
Rodriguez–Hernandez, Edwin '95 (ALX) Hessmer, LA St. Martin of Tours; Hessmer, LA St. Alphonsus.
Rodriguez–Jimenes, Rev. Msgr. Leonardo J. '90 (SJN) Bayamon, PR Sagrada Familia; Moderator; Subcommission for Ministries; for Administration of Temporalities; Commission for Sacred Liturgy and Popular Piety; Vicars General.
Rodriguez–Leon, Mario '91 (SJN)[A] Bayamon Central University.
Rodriguez–Otero, Rev. Msgr. Efrain '74 (SJN) Carolina, PR San Fernando; Vicar of Cultural Affairs.
Rodriguez–Toloza, Marco Lino '90 (SAT) Rocksprings, TX Sacred Heart of Mary.
Rodriguez De La Vuda, Jorge '01 (MIA) Miami, FL Good Shepherd.
Rodriguez de Yurre, Prudencio *c.m.* '65 (DEN)[N] Denver, CO Congregation of the Mission Western Province: De Paul House.
Rodriguez Jimenes, Rev. Msgr. Leonardo J. '90 (SJN) Diocesan Consultors; Subcommission for Sacred Art.
Rodriguez Ochoa, Leonardo '91 (FAJ) Naguabo, PR Nuestra Senora del Rosario.
Rodriguez Orengo, Rev. Msgr. Juan '79 (PCE) Diocesan Consultors.
Rodriques, Carlos '95 (BGP) Greenwich, CT St. Roch.
Rodriquez, Alberto *o.ss.t.* (BAL)[S] (Dallas, Texas).
Rodriquez, Feliciano '85 (CGS) Pastoral Social; Juncos, PR Inmaculada Concepcion.
Rodriquez, Felix (TUC) Casa Grande, AZ Saint Anthony of Padua Roman Catholic Parish – Casa Grande.
Rodriquez, Rev. Msgr. Pablo M. '61 (RVC) Hispanic Ministry.
Roebert, Michael '66 (LA) Long Beach, CA St. Lucy.
Roebuck, John H. '76 (PH) Glen Mills, PA St. Thomas the Apostle.
Roedig, Robert L. '53 (STL) Retired.
Roehrich, Andrew '50 (FAR) Retired.
Roehrich, David '84 (SFS) Elk Point, SD St. Joseph; Jefferson, SD St. Peter.
Roehrio, Matthew *s.s.p.* '84 (NY)[B] Staten Island, NY Society of St. Paul.
Roemer, Richard *c.f.r.* '98 (NY)[EE] Bronx, NY Franciscan Friars of the Renewal; Counselors:; [II] Bronx, NY St. Anthony Shelter for Renewal.
Roensch, Frederick J. '55 (MIL) Retired.
Roensch, Rev. Msgr. Roger '57 (WDC) On Duty Outside the Archdiocese.
Roesch, David H. '67 (ALT) Cemetery Commission; Bellwood, PA St. Joseph's; Altoona, PA Veterans Medical Center; DEPARTMENT OF VETERANS AFFAIRS HOSPITALS AND CHAPLAINS.
Roesch, Joseph *m.i.c.* (SPR)[H] On Duty Outside of the USA:.
Roesch, Karl J. *o.s.b.* '60 (CHR) Hartsville, SC St. Mary the Virgin Mother; [H] Hartsville, SC Coker College; Deans; College of Consultors.
Roesch, Karl J. *o.s.b.* '60 (PAT)[N] Morristown St. Mary's Abbey.
Roesch, Karl *o.s.b.* '60 (CHR) Personnel Committee.
Roeten, Rev. Msgr. Winus '48 (NO) Retired.
Roetzel, Robert E. *c.s.c.* '87 (FTW)[H] Notre Dame Congregation of Holy Cross, Indiana Province, Provincial House.
Roetzel, Robert E. *c.s.c.* '87 (MO) Army Chaplains.
Roetzer, James M. '98 (MAR) Norway, MI St. Mary; Vulcan, MI St. Barbara; Advocates.
Roetzer, Russell G. '64 (MIL) Retired.
Rog, Francis *c.r.* '55 (CHI) Chicago, IL St. Hyacinth Basilica; College of Consultors.
Rog, Stanislaw (HEL) Conrad, MT St. Michael; Dutton, MT St. William.
Rog, Theodore C. '64 (BUF)[O] Lackawanna, NY Bishop Head Residence Retired.
Rogaczewski, Dan '00 (ATL)[C] Atlanta, GA St. Pius X Catholic High School.
Rogala, Gerald E. '66 (CHI) Des Plaines, IL St. Stephen Protomartyr.
Rogalla, William G. '93 (LAF) Morgan City, LA St. Bernadette.
Rogan, Brian '03 (SB) Retired.
Rogawski, Ralph *o.p.* '59 (AUS)[G] Austin, TX Dominican Friars of Austin.
Roger, Francis *s.s.c.* '57 (OM)[K] St. Columbans Missionary Society of St. Columban.
Roger, Richard G. '64 (WOR) Worcester, MA Holy Family Parish.
Rogers, Christopher B. '00 (PH) On Special or Other Archdiocesan Assignment; Havertown, PA Annunciation B.V.M.; Vocation Office for Diocesan Priesthood.
Rogers, Daniel J. '53 (DUB) Retired.
Rogers, Gary P. '72 (BRK) Brooklyn, NY Holy Name.
Rogers, James '39 (EVN) Retired.
Rogers, James '39 (IND)[I] Beech Grove, IN St. Paul Hermitage.
Rogers, Jerry '76 (CR) Red Lake, MN St. Mary's Mission Church; Diocesan Consultors; Priests' Council.
Rogers, Joel C. *c.p.m.* '00 (L) Glasgow, KY St. Helen.
Rogers, Joseph Everett '06 (WDC) Rockville, MD St. Patrick.
Rogers, Joseph '54 (DAV)[I] Davenport, IA Kahl Home for the Aged and Infirm Retired.
Rogers, Nicholas P. '55 (MAN) Suncook, NH St. John the Baptist Retired.
Rogers, Patrick D. *s.j.* '02 (WDC)[C] Washington, DC Georgetown University; [N] Washington, DC The Jesuit Community at Georgetown University.
Rogers, Patrick W. '82 (MO) Columbus, OH St. Philip The Apostle; Air National Guard Chaplains.
Rogers, Paul E. '77 (RVC) Leave of Absence.
Rogers, Peter J. *o.p.* '02 (SLC)[H] Salt Lake City, UT University of Utah, Newman Center.
Rogers, Peter S. *s.j.* '74 (NO)[C] New Orleans, LA Loyola University New Orleans.
Rogers, Peter *o.p.* '02 (SLC) Salt Lake City, UT Saint Catherine of Siena LLC 218.
Rogers, Philip E. '80 (Y) Boardman, OH St. Charles Borromeo.
Rogers, Robert C. '92 (HT) Lockport, LA Holy Savior; Priests Council.
Rogers, Roy (GB)[G] Appleton, WI St. Elizabeth Hospital, Inc.
Rogers, Sean '04 (SR) Petaluma, CA St. Vincent de Paul; Priests' Council.
Rogers, Steven C. '06 (KC) Raytown, MO Our Lady of Lourdes.
Rogers, Vince '93 (KC) Trenton, MO St. Joseph's.
Rogerson, David '77 (SEA) Redmond, WA St. Jude; Duvall, WA Holy Innocents.
Roggenbuck, Robert '03 (LAN) Ypsilanti, MI St. John.
Rogina, Walter '85 (SR) Healdsburg, CA St. John the Baptist.
Rogliano, Joseph S. '85 (BUF) West Seneca, NY Fourteen Holy Helpers; Council of Priests.
Rogmans, Gerard *c.i.c.m.* '55 (FgM) Arlington, VA MISSIONHURST.
Roh, Raymond V. *o.s.b.* '59 (MRY)[F] San Luis Obispo, CA Men's Residence.
Roh, Rev. Msgr. Robert A. '65 (LIN) Falls City, NE SS. Peter and Paul; [C] Falls City, NE Sacred Heart School; [L] Falls City, NE Sacred Heart High School Endowment Fund; Deaneries and Deans.
Rohan, John P. '72 (HRT) East Hartford, CT St. Isaac Jogues; East Hartford, CT St. Mary; East Hartford, CT St. Rose.
Rohleder, Earl '63 (EVN) Santa Fe, NM Santa Maria de la Paz Catholic Community Retired.
Rohlfing, Cory J. '01 (STP) Kilkenny, MN St. Canice; Montgomery, MN Most Holy Redeemer; Appointees.
Rohlfs, Rev. Msgr. Steven P. '76 (PEO) On Duty Outside the Diocese.
Rohlfs, Rev. Msgr. Steven P. '76 (BAL)[B] Emmitsburg, MD Mount Saint Mary's University; [A] Emmitsburg, MD Mount St. Mary's Seminary.
Rohling, Rev. Msgr. George W. '39 (NSH) Nashville, TN St. Mary Villa Parish Community; [L] Nashville, TN Ladies of Charity Welfare Agency, Inc.
Rohling, Rev. Msgr. Paul L. '75 (BIR) Birmingham, AL Our Lady of the Valley; [I] Birmingham, AL Catholic Housing of Birmingham, Inc.; Diocesan College of Vicars; Priests'/Presbyteral Council; Diocesan College of Consultors.
Rohling, Rev. Msgr. Paul '75 (BIR) Judges.
Rohr, Jerome M. '94 (DEN) Denver, CO St. Rose of Lima.
Rohr, John J. *s.j.* '60 (NY)[EE] New York, NY Murray–Weigel Hall.
Rohr, Richard *o.f.m.* '70 (SFE) Albuquerque, NM Holy Family; [L] Albuquerque, NM Center for Action and Contemplation; [H] Albuquerque, NM The Province of Our Lady of Guadalupe.
Rohrer, Richard '94 (PSC) Cary, NC SS. Cyril & Methodius Byzantine Catholic.
Rohrich, Robert R. *c.m.* '61 (CHI)[N] Chicago DePaul Vincentian Residence.
Rohrkemper, Charles '43 (CIN)[N] Carthagena, OH St. Charles Retired.
Roia, Martino *s.x.* '82 (FgM)[N] Wayne Xaverian Missionary Fathers; Wayne, NJ XAVERIAN MISSIONARY FATHERS.
Roide, Russell J. *s.j.* '70 (HON) Honolulu, HI Newman Center–Holy Spirit Parish; [D] Honolulu, HI Jesuit Fathers House.
Roig, Vicente Perez '58 (PCE) Coamo, PR St. Blase.
Roig Lorenzo, Ricardo Augusto '97 (SJN) Graduate Studies.
Rojas, Alberto '97 (CHI)[A] Mundelein, IL University of St. Mary of the Lake/Mundelein Seminary.
Rojas, Benito *m.s.p.* '03 (LA) Los Angeles, CA Our Lady of Solitude.
Rojas, Carlos '06 (SP) Plant City, FL St. Clement; Appointed Members.
Rojas, Francisco '85 (MIL)[T] Waukesha, WI Schoenstatt Fathers.
Rojas, Hugo Marcelo '97 (SJ) Gilroy, CA St. Mary.
Rojas, Jaime '86 (PCE) Jayuya, PR Our Lady of Monserrate.
Rojas, Joaquín J. *m.n.m.* '02 (ARE) Quebradillas, PR Our Lady of Monserrate.
Rojas, Juan Carlos *c.s.b.* '06 (GAL)[O] Sugar Land Basilian Mission Center.
Rojas, Loreto '00 (SAC) Davis, CA St. James; Evangelization and Catechetical Commission; Theological Commission.
Rojas, Loretto B. '00 (SAC) Vicars Forane.
Rojas, Melquiades '91 (ARE) Arecibo, PR Church of Sagrado Corazon de Jesus.
Rojas, Oscar Borda '99 (CHR) Greer, SC Blessed Trinity; Spartanburg, SC Jesus Our Risen Savior.
Rojas, Roberto Adrian '96 (SJ) Council of Priests.
Rojas, Roberto P. *c.s.b.* '98 (GAL)[O] Sugar Land Basilian Mission Center.
Rojas, Roberto '96 (SJ) Morgan Hill, CA St. Catherine of Alexandria.
Rojas, Tito Nels '68 (ORL) Sanford, FL All Souls; Judges.
Rojas, Victor '85 (ARE) Barceloneta, PR Church of Our Lady of Mt. Carmel; Diocesan Consultors; Priest's Senate (Consejo Presbiteral); Pastoral Vocational Program.
Rojas Paniagua, Oscar E. *c.ss.r* '87 (CHL) Concord, NC St. James.
Rokicki, Klaudiusz *m.i.c.* '00 (BEA) Beaumont, TX St. Anthony Cathedral Basilica.
Rokos, Richard V. '56 (PRT) Retired.
Rokosz, Charles W. '70 (SCR) Duryea, PA Holy Rosary; Duryea, PA Sacred Heart of Jesus.
Rokusek, Robert J. '66 (WDC)[E] Washington, DC Gonzaga College High School.
Roland, Glynn (Bud) '99 (AUS) Austin, TX St. John Neumann; Consultors.
Roldan, Basilio *c.m.* '59 (SJN) San Juan, PR Jesus Maestro.
Roldan, Jovito B. '98 (STO) Judicial Vicar; Stockton, CA St. Gertrude Church (Pastor of); Defenders of the Bond.
Roldan, Juan '56 (SJN) On Duty Outside the Archdiocese.
Roleke, H. James *s.j.* '62 (BUF) Buffalo, NY St. Michael.
Rolewicz, Richard S. *m.m.* '65 (FgM) Maryknoll, NY MARYKNOLL.
Rolf, Rev. Msgr. John J. '57 (LEX) Retired.
Rolfes, Robert '77 (SCL) St. Cloud, MN St. Mary Help of Christians; Chancellor; Notaries; Diocesan Corporate Board; Clerical Aid Association; Diocesan Priests Pension Plan Trustees; Director of Retired Priests; Legion of Decency; Defensor Vinculi.
Rolfes, Robert '77 (CR) Defenders of the Bond.
Rolfs, Richard W. *s.j.* '61 (LA)[C] Los Angeles, CA Jesuit Community.
Rolheiser, Ronald *o.m.i.* '72 (SAT)[C] San Antonio, TX Oblate School of Theology; [C] San Antonio, TX The United Colleges of San Antonio; [L] San Antonio, TX.
Roll, Bertin *o.f.m.cap.* '42 (PIT)[M] Pittsburgh, PA St. Augustine Friary Retired.
Roll, David H. '70 (SD) Retired.
Roll, Robert J. '77 (CHI) Chicago, IL St. Bride.
Rolland, Daniel *o.p.* '93 (OAK)[M] Oakland, CA Order of Preachers (Province of the Most Holy Name of Jesus – Western Dominican Province).
Rolland, Daniel *o.p.* '93 (P) Eugene, OR St. Thomas More Church; [P] Eugene, OR University of Oregon (Eugene).
Rolland, Michael *o.p.* '88 (OAK)[M] Oakland Order of Preachers (Province of the Most Holy Name of Jesus – Western Dominican Province).
Rolland, Miguel *o.p.* '88 (PHX)[F] Tempe, AZ Dominicans (Dominican Community–Jordan House).
Rolland, Miguel *o.p.* '88 (FgM) Oakland, CA Province of the Holy Name (Western Dominican Province).

Roller, John W. '60 (CHI) Mt. Prospect, IL St. Emily Retired.
Rolling, Brendan *o.s.b.* '00 (KCK)[A] Atchison, KS Benedictine College; [I] Atchison, KS St. Benedict's Abbey.
Rolon, Alfredo '02 (MIA) Coral Gables, FL Little Flower.
Rolon Torres, Julio A. '93 (PCE)[A] Ponce, PR Diocesan Seminary; [B] The Pontifical Catholic University of Puerto Rico.
Rolph, Edward *s.p.* '70 (SFE)[H] Jemez Springs, NM Our Lady of Lourdes; Jemez Springs, NM Our Lady of the Assumption.
Rolwing, Rev. Msgr. Richard C. '53 (SPC) Retired.
Rom, Gregory A. '75 (CHI) Chicago, IL St. Felicitas.
Roman, Carlos R. (STL) St. Louis, MO St. Cecilia.
Roman, Carlos '89 (PCE) On Duty Outside the Diocese.
Roman, Charles '70 (HEL) Retired.
Roman, Jorge A. '81 (STO) Tracy, CA St. Bernard Church (Pastor of).
Roman, Jose Antonio Landrau '90 (SJN) San Juan, PR San Francisco de Monte Alvernia.
Roman, Julio I. '00 (NEW) On Duty Outside the Archdiocese.
Roman, Julio '73 (LA)[J] Los Angeles, CA St. Vincent Medical Center; Hospital Chaplains Retired.
Roman, Manuel R. '56 (BAL) Retired.
Roman, Paul '71 (ALB) Retired.
Roman, Pedro *o.p.* '84 (VEN) Naples, FL St. Peter the Apostle.
Roman, Stephen '57 (SEA) Aberdeen, WA St. Jerome Retired.
Roman, Victor '84 (DET) Ecorse, MI St. Francis Xavier.
Romanek, Janusz '07 (MAR) Baraga, MI The Most Holy Name of Jesus–Blessed Kateri Tekakwitha; Baraga, MI The Most Holy Name of Jesus–Blessed Kateri Tekakwitha; Baraga, MI St. Ann; L'Anse, MI Sacred Heart.
Romanello, Carmelo '06 (MIA) Coral Gables, FL St. Augustine.
Romanet, Antoine De '95 (WDC) Washington, DC Church of St. Louis.
Romano, Blase *t.o.r.* '89 (ORL) Mount Dora, FL St. Patrick's.
Romano, Charles '79 (RVC) Port Jefferson, NY Infant Jesus.
Romano, Eugene C. '57 (PAT)[J] Chester, NJ Hermits of Bethlehem in the Heart of Jesus.
Romano, Harry A. '57 (PH) Retired.
Romano, Joseph L. '63 (DET) Retired.
Romano, Joseph '63 (BUR) Pittsford, VT St. Alphonsus Liguori.
Romano, Michael M. '07 (CAM)[A] Haddonfield, NJ Paul VI High School, Haddon Township, N.J.; Mantua, NJ R.C. Church of the Incarnation, Township of Mantua, New Jersey.
Romano, Robert J. '77 (BRK) Police Department.
Romano, Rev. Msgr. Robert '78 (BRK) Brooklyn, NY Our Lady of Guadalupe.
Romanoski, Joseph V. '86 (MET) South Amboy, NJ Sacred Heart.
Romanowski, Aloysius *o.f.m.conv.* '57 (CHI)[N] Chicago Conventual Franciscans of St. Bonaventure Province.
Romanowski, Brian J. '03 (NOR) Mystic, CT St. Patrick; [B] Uncasville, CT Saint Bernard School.
Romanowski, Jerome C. '64 (CAM) Retired.
Romanowski, Slawomir *c.ss.r.* '99 (MET) Manville, NJ Christ the King.
Romans, Jeffrey V. '03 (HRT) Secretary to the Archbishop; Assistant Chancellor; Special and other Archdiocesan Assignment.
Romanski, Aloysius *o.f.m.conv.* '57 (CHI)[L] Lake Zurich, IL Mt. St. Joseph Home.
Romanski, Edward '75 (CHI) Harvey, IL St. John the Baptist.
Romanski, Gregory A. '77 (AUS) Retired.
Romanyuk, Ruslan '09 (PHU) Cherry Hill, NJ St. Michael's.
Romea, Jonas '82 (SFE) Cerrillos, NM St. Joseph.
Romeo, Peter A. '72 (LAV) Las Vegas, NV Our Lady of Las Vegas.
Romeo, Peter '72 (VNN) Promoter of Justice.
Romeo, Peter '72 (RNO) Judges.
Romeo, Robert A. '87 (RVC) Sea Cliff, NY St. Boniface Martyr.
Romeo, Robert '87 (RVC) Procurator & Advocates.
Romerde, Manuel R. '08 (NEW) Jersey City, NJ Our Lady of Mercy.
Romero, Alejandro *c.s.b.* '00 (GAL)[O] Sugar Land Basilian Mission Center.
Romero, Anthony E. '05 (SFE) Retired.
Romero, David H. *s.j.* '91 (NO)[P] New Orleans Jesuit Provincial Office.
Romero, Domingo *o.f.m.cap.* '00 (FWT) Fort Worth, TX Our Lady of Guadalupe.
Romero, Donald '91 (DEN) Air Force Chaplains; On Duty Outside the Archdiocese.
Romero, Elmer '03 (CHI) Chicago, IL St. Mark.
Romero, Fortunato '60 (NY) Bronx, NY St. Jerome's; Bronx, NY St. Pius V.
Romero, Gilbert Claude '61 (LA) Retired.
Romero, Giovani '99 (BRK) Brooklyn, NY Our Lady of Solace.
Romero, Rev. Msgr. J. Robert '75 (LAF) Opelousas, LA St. Landry.
Romero, Jose *o.s.a.* (GAL) Pasadena, TX St. Juan Diego.
Romero, Joseph J. '69 (BEA) Retired.
Romero, Juan R. '64 (LA) Retired.
Romero, M. Ross *s.j.* '05 (BO)[U] Newton, MA The Jesuit Community at Boston College.
Romero, Marion P. '90 (LAF) Ville Platte, LA Our Lady Queen of All Saints.
Romero, P. Jesus *sch.p.* '03 (PCE)[C] Coto Laurel, PR Colegio Ponceno.
Romero, Ruben '91 (LSC) Hobbs, NM Our Lady of Guadalupe.
Romero–Rios, Adolfo '88 (NY) Bronx, NY St. Pius V.
Romfh, Paul *o.s.b.* '63 (SP)[N] St. Leo, FL St. Leo Abbey.
Romito, Rev. Msgr. Donald '74 (ORG) Irvine, CA St. John Neumann; Clergy Personnel Board.
Romo, Jose Valdez *m.s.c.* '95 (LA) Los Angeles, CA San Miguel.
Romo, Sergio '93 (CHI) Chicago, IL St. Andrew.
Romo–romo, Juan Antonio *s.v.d.* '05 (WDC)[N] Washington, DC Divine Word House.
Romza, Rev. Msgr. Victor G. '54 (PBR) Campbell, OH St. Michael.
Ronaghan, John J. '80 (BO) Quincy, MA St. Ann; Presbyteral Council.
Ronaipe, Jose '94 (BO)[U] Boston, MA Marist Fathers of Our Lady of Victories (Boston Prov.).
Ronald, Rev. Msgr. Roy K. '60 (BUF) Retired.
Ronan, Eugene *m.s.f.* '93 (SAT) New Braunfels, TX Our Lady of Perpetual Help.
Ronan, Gerald C. '74 (PH) Hatboro, PA St. John Bosco.
Ronan, Rev. Msgr. Hugh F. '61 (TR) Diocesan Consultors; [N] Trenton, NJ Villa Vianney Retired.
Ronan, James J. '82 (BO) Boston, MA St. Mary – St. Catherine of Siena.
Roncancio, Luis Alphonse '95 (TYL) Centerville, TX St. Leo the Great; Hilltop Lakes, TX St. Thomas More.
Roncase, Robert A. '82 (PH) Pennsburg, PA St. Philip Neri.
Ronchi, Vincenzo *c.s.* '91 (PMB) Delray Beach, FL Our Lady Queen of Peace.
Rondeau, Lawrence J. '58 (BO) Salem, MA St. James; Senior Priests. Retired.
Roney, George '78 (LUB) Stamford, TX St. Ann; Priests' Retirement Board.
Ronik, Rev. Msgr. Michael '57 (Y) Retired.
Rono, Rev. Msgr. Voltaire '80 (ALN) Douglassville, PA Immaculate Conception.
Ronquest, Rev. Msgr. John T. '45 (STL) Retired.
Roock, John D. '59 (SY)[Q] Syracuse, NY Tommy Coyne Residence Dillon Hall Retired.
Roodbeen, Henry W. '75 (DET) Livonia, MI St. Colette.
Roof, Frank '72 (OWN) Non–Parochial Assignments.
Rookey, Peter M. *o.s.m.* '41 (CHI)[N] Chicago Order of Friar Servants of Mary (Servites) United States of America Province, Inc.
Rooks, Charles W. '52 (COV) Retired.
Rooney, Donald J. '94 (ARL) Fredericksburg, VA St. Mary of the Immaculate Conception; Ecumenical and Interreligious Affairs Commission; Carbondale, IL Catholic Association of Diocesan Ecumenical and Interreligious Officers (CADEIO).
Rooney, Edward K. '62 (STA) Middleburg, FL St. Luke; Diocesan Schools and Social Action Appeal.
Rooney, Eugene M. *s.j.* '57 (BAL)[S] Towson Maryland Province of the Society of Jesus; Towson, MD Society of Jesus.
Rooney, Francis V. *s.j.* '60 (NY)[EE] New York, NY Murray–Weigel Hall.
Rooney, James T. '64 (BRK) Flushing, NY Mary's Nativity.
Rooney, John C. '89 (LIN) Shelby, NE Sacred Heart; Building Commission; Deaneries and Deans; Commission on Alcohol and Drug Abuse.
Rooney, John J. '62 (ALB) Retired.
Rooney, John '01 (GAL) Ecumenism and Interreligious Affairs Commission; Missouri City, TX St. Angela Merici.
Rooney, Jordon *o.carm.* '54 (JOL)[L] Darien Carmelite Provincial Office.
Rooney, Joseph S. *s.j.* '66 (SLC) Payson, UT Saint Patrick LLC 257; Payson, UT San Andres LLC 212.
Rooney, Kevin E. '62 (BUR) Northfield, VT St. John the Evangelist.
Rooney, Martin *m.s.a.* '93 (NOR)[G] Cromwell Society of the Missionaries of the Holy Apostles.
Rooney, Martin '93 (PAT) Paterson, NJ St. Joseph Hospital; [K] Paterson, NJ St. Joseph's Hospital and Medical Center.
Rooney, Robert B. '63 (GI) Retired.
Rooney, Sean *s.d.b.* '66 (NY)[EE] New Rochelle, NY Salesian Provincial House.
Rooney, Stephen '85 (DET) Temperance, MI Our Lady of Mt. Carmel.
Rooney, Rev. Msgr. Thaddeus '47 (RVC) Deer Park, NY SS. Cyril and Methodius; [M] Amityville, NY St. Pius X Residence Retired.
Rooney, Thomas J. '91 (PH) Philadelphia, PA St. Timothy.
Rooney, William *o.f.m.* '81 (CLV) Cleveland, OH St. Rose of Lima; [N] Brooklyn, OH St. Anthony of Padua Friary.
Roos, Rev. Msgr. H. Jules '56 (PIT) On Duty Outside the Diocese.
Roos, John R. '55 (ALB) Censor Librorum.
Roos, John '55 (ALB) Cherry Valley, NY St. Thomas the Apostle Retired.
Roos, Rev. Msgr. Jules '56 (FgM) Boston, MA St. James the Apostle, Inc.
Roos, Lee R. '90 (ARL) Arlington, VA St. Agnes; Adjutant Judicial Vicar; Diocesan Judges.
Roos, Richard H. *s.j.* '74 (BO)[U] Boston, MA Loyola House.
Roost, Joseph F. '89 (DAV) Marengo, IA St. Patrick's; North English, IA St. Joseph's; Williamsburg, IA St. Mary's; Personnel Board.
Root, James A. '84 (SAM) Brooklyn, NY Cathedral of Our Lady of Lebanon; Presbyteral Council; Vocations; Protopresbyters (Deans).
Root, Richard '90 (SPK) Absent on Leave.
Ropel, Mark *s.o.l.t.* '02 (CC)[G] Robstown, TX Society of Our Lady of the Most Holy Trinity.
Ropel, Mark *s.o.l.t.* '02 (FAR) Belcourt, ND St. Ann; Belcourt, ND St. Anthony; Belcourt, ND St. Ann.
Roppolo, Rev. Msgr. Ignatius M. '54 (NO) Retired.
Roque, Alejandro *o.m.i.* '88 (MIA) Miramar, FL St. Stephen.
Roque, Eduardo *m.j.* '95 (GAL) Houston, TX St. Stephen.
Roque, Reynoldo (SD) Brawley, CA Sacred Heart.
Roque, Sigifredo Martin '02 (LA) Los Angeles, CA Presentation of the Mary.
Roque, Ubaldo Huerta '08 (WIN) Winona, MN Cathedral of the Sacred Heart.
Ros, Manuel '60 (BRK) Corona, NY Our Lady of Sorrows Retired.
Rosa, Rev. Msgr. Joseph '76 (BRK) Legion of Mary.
Rosa, Rolando De la '95 (SFR) Menlo Park, CA The Church of the Nativity.
Rosa, Salvatore J. '41 (HRT) Derby, CT St. Jude.
Rosack, Rev. Msgr. Edward V. '54 (PBR) Retired.
Rosaforte, Rev. Msgr. Anthony S. '70 (NOR) Norwich, CT St. Patrick Cathedral; College of Consultors; Members; Diocesan Panel of Pastors, Canon 1742.
Rosal, Rey '88 (CHK) Saipan, MP San Vicente Parish; Presbyteral Council.
Rosales, Deo G. '82 (POD) New York.
Rosales, Deogracias '82 (NY)[JJ] New York, NY Prelature of the Holy Cross and Opus Dei.
Rosales, Freddi A. '92 (BRK) Brooklyn, NY Guardian Angel.
Rosales, Fruto '70 (RVC) Hempstead, NY Our Lady of Loretto.
Rosales, Raul "Rudy" H. '93 (TUC) Globe, AZ Holy Angels Roman Catholic Church – Globe.
Rosales, Samuel *s.j.* '73 (ELP) El Paso, TX Sacred Heart.
Rosalinas, Rogel *s.o.l.t.* '94 (CC)[G] Robstown, TX Society of Our Lady of the Most Holy Trinity.
Rosario, Angel Cuevas '90 (SJN) Carolina, PR Ntra. Sra. Reina de la Paz.
Rosario, Jacinto *o.c.d.* '91 (PCE) Ponce, PR San Jose.
Rosario, Mario S. '90 (MO) Army Reserve Chaplains.
Rosas, Orlando '97 (MGZ) Vocations.
Rosato, Philip J. *s.j.* '71 (WDC)[E] North Bethesda, MD Georgetown Preparatory School.
Rosca, Paschal *o.de.m.* '63 (CLV) Cleveland, OH St. Rocco.
Roscioli, Dominic J. '74 (MIL) Retired.
Rose, Alphonse G. '56 (BAL) Retired.
Rose, Rev. Msgr. Donald '53 (GB) Retired.
Rose, Frank '90 (NEW) Plainfield, NJ The Parish of St. Bernard and St. Stanislaus; Archdiocesan Judges.
Rose, Geoff *o.s.f.s.* '02 (LAN)[B] Jackson, MI Lumen Christi Catholic High School; Toledo, OH.
Rose, James '57 (FTW) U.S. Veteran's Hospital Retired.
Rose, John F. '72 (SY) Pastoral Examiners.
Rose, John *s.j.* '99 (SJ)[B] Santa Clara, CA Jesuit Community.
Rose, Joseph '76 (BRK) Brooklyn, NY Most Precious Blood.
Rose, Justin '95 (NTN) San Bernardino, CA St. Philip; MAYA (Melkite Assoc. of Young Adults).
Rose, Michael F. '81 (WOR) Shrewsbury, MA St. Mary's; Deans; Presbyteral Council.
Rose, William J. '96 (TOL) Toledo, OH Christ the King.
Rosebrough, Robert T. '69 (STL) Ferguson, MO Blessed Teresa of Calcutta.
Roselada, Eoli *o.f.m.* '93 (CHI)[J] Evanston, IL Saint Francis Hospital.
Roselada, Eulogio '93 (CHI)[N] Chicago, IL Holy Evangelists Friary.
Roselli, Marc J. *s.j.* '85 (RVC)[O] Manhasset, NY St. Ignatius Retreat House, Inisfada.
Rosemeyer, John C. '58 (CHI) Westchester, IL Divine Providence Retired.

Rosemeyer, Paul F. '52 (CHI) Palatine, IL St. Theresa Retired.
Rosen, Cyprian *o.f.m.cap.* '62 (WIL)[J] Wilmington, DE Capuchin Franciscan Friars, St. Francis Renewal Center; [M] Wilmington, DE St. Francis Renewal Center; Defenders of the Bond.
Rosenau, Alan '88 (LR)[D] Hot Springs National Park, AR St. Joseph's Mercy Health Center; Hot Springs National Park, AR St. John the Baptist; Hot Springs National Park, AR St. Mary of the Springs.
Rosenbaum, Mark '07 (JOL) Plainfield, IL St. Mary Immaculate.
Rosenbaum, William E. '76 (ALT) Johnstown, PA St. Clement's.
Rosensweig, Rev. Msgr. Walter F. '53 (TUC) Retired.
Rosette, Fabian Maria *o.carm.* '80 (SAN)[A] Christoval, TX Hermits of the Blessed Virgin Mary of Mount Carmel.
Rosevear, Anthony R. *o.p.* '78 (SFR) San Francisco, CA St. Dominic; [N] San Francisco, CA St. Dominic Priory.
Rosevear, Anthony *o.p.* '78 (OAK)[M] Oakland, CA Order of Preachers (Province of the Most Holy Name of Jesus – Western Dominican Province).
Rosie, Rev. Msgr. Joseph N. '90 (TR) Lawrenceville, NJ St. Ann; Chancellor; Diocesan Pastoral Council; Diocesan Finance Council; Censores Librorum.
Rosimo, Cosmenio '91 (HON) Ewa Beach, HI Our Lady of Perpetual Help.
Rosin, Richard *s.d.b.* '95 (NEW)[C] Ramsey, NJ Don Bosco Preparatory High School; [M] Ramsey, NJ Don Bosco Prep Salesian Residence.
Rosing, Paul J. '73 (CLV) Stow, OH Holy Family; College of Consultors; Presbyteral Council; Associate Judges.
Rosing, Robert C. '53 (COV)[N] Park Hills, KY Provincial House of the Sisters of Notre Dame; [I] Edgewood, KY St. Elizabeth Medical Center, Inc. Retired.
Rosinski, Bernard J. *s.c.j.* '59 (RC) Lower Brule, SD St. Mary's; [C] Lower Brule, SD SCJ Community House.
Rosinski, Bernard *s.c.j.* '59 (SFS) Fort Thompson, SD St. Joseph; Lower Brule, SD Immaculate Conception.
Rosinski, Edward B. '63 (CAM) Retired.
Rosinski, Richard A. '91 (RCK) St. Charles, IL St. John Neumann.
Rosko, Ladislaus '52 (CLV) Retired.
Rosloniec, Rev. Msgr. Leo S. '54 (GR) Conklin, MI St. Joseph's.
Roslovich, Peter J. *s.j.* '63 (NY)[EE] New York, NY Murray–Weigel Hall.
Rosolen, Emil '86 (AMA) On Duty Outside the Diocese.
Rosolowski, Romulus *o.f.m.conv.* '74 (BUF) Lackawanna, NY Our Lady of Victory National Shrine.
Rosonke, Steven J. '82 (DUB) Dubuque, IA St. Mary; Dubuque, IA St. Patrick.
Rosonke, Vince G. '75 (DM) Waukee, IA St. Boniface.
Ross, Bob *s.j.* (GLP) Tohatchi, NM St. Mary Church.
Ross, Brendan '87 (NY) Absent on Sick Leave.
Ross, Christopher M. *o.s.m.* '54 (CHI)[N] Chicago Order of Friar Servants of Mary (Servites) United States of America Province, Inc.
Ross, Daniel J. *s.j.* '66 (FgM) Los Gatos, CA Society of Jesus.
Ross, David M. '75 (TOL) Promoter of Justice; Judges; Lima, OH St. John the Evangelist; Lima, OH St. Rose of Lima; College of Consultors; Priests' Council.
Ross, Gregory S. *o.c.d.* '95 (NO)[B] New Orleans, LA St. John of the Cross, Discalced Carmelite House of Studies.
Ross, Joseph R. '69 (OKL) Personnel Committee; Ministry to Priests Program; Lawton, OK Blessed Sacrament; Special Assignment.
Ross, Joseph *m.s.* '55 (MAN)[K] Enfield, NH Shrine of Our Lady of La Salette; [N] Enfield, NH Shrine of Our Lady of La Salette Retired.
Ross, Justin *o.f.m.conv.* '08 (BUF)[D] Athol Springs, NY St. Francis High School; [O] Athol Springs, NY St. Francis of Assisi Friary.
Ross, Mark J. '88 (SAV) Savannah, GA St. James.
Ross, Raymond J. *c.m.* '48 (STL)[O] Perryville, MO Congregation of the Mission.
Ross, Richard '67 (JOL) Joliet, IL St. Bernard; Joliet, IL Dept. of Corrections.
Ross, Robert J. *s.j.* '72 (CIN)[N] Cincinnati, OH.
Ross, Theodore *s.j.* '67 (CIN)[B] Cincinnati, OH Mt. St. Mary's Seminary of the West.
Ross, William B. '54 (OKL) Health Panel, Archdiocesan; Oklahoma City, OK St. Eugene's Retired.
Rossa, Peter '03 (PHX) Scottsdale, AZ St. Bernadette Roman Catholic Parish.
Rosse, John '54 (ROC) Rochester, NY St. Margaret Mary Retired.
Rossell, Richard *o.f.m.conv.* '61 (TR) Seaside Heights, NJ Our Lady of Perpetual Help.
Rossello, Nicholas A. '60 (BUF) Retired.
Rossetti, Rev. Msgr. Stephen '84 (SY) On Duty Outside the Diocese.
Rossey, Stephen J. *o.praem.* '59 (GB)[J] De Pere, WI St. Norbert Abbey.
Rossi, Anthony T. '09 (PH) Willow Grove, PA St. David.
Rossi, Desmond '92 (ALB) Leave of Absence.
Rossi, Domenic A. *o.praem.* '74 (PH) Paoli, PA St. Norbert; [Y] Paoli, PA Daylesford Abbey.
Rossi, Rev. Msgr. Frank H. '83 (GAL) Houston, TX St. Michael; Ex Officio Members; College of Consultors; Priests Personnel Committee; Vicars General.
Rossi, John A. '09 (CAM) On Duty Outside the Diocese.
Rossi, Joseph M. '84 (BO) Lynn, MA St. Pius Fifth.
Rossi, Joseph S. *s.j.* '80 (BAL)[B] Timonium, MD Loyola Graduate Center–Timonium Campus; [S] Baltimore, MD Jesuit Community of Loyola University, Inc.; [B] Jesuit Community of Loyola University, Inc.
Rossi, Pat F. '82 (NY) Bronx, NY St. Michael.
Rossi, Paul J. '74 (SFR) San Rafael, CA St. Raphael; Serra Club of Marin; Deans.
Rossi, Philip J. *s.j.* '71 (MIL)[P] Milwaukee, WI Arrupe House Jesuit Community.
Rossi, Raymond R. '58 (LR) Retired.
Rossi, Robert J. *o.s.c.* '70 (PHX)[F] Phoenix, AZ Crosier Community of Phoenix (Canons Regular of the Order of the Holy Cross).
Rossi, Ronald J. *o.praem.* '70 (PH)[B] Paoli, PA Daylesford Abbey; [Y] Paoli, PA Daylesford Abbey; Paoli, PA.
Rossi, Thomas J. *o.praem.* '73 (PH)[Y] Paoli, PA Daylesford Abbey; Philadelphia, PA St. Edmond.
Rossi, Thomas P. (BO) Lowell, MA St. Michael.
Rossi, Rev. Msgr. Walter R. '87 (SCR) On Duty Outside the Diocese; [R] Washington, DC Basilica of the National Shrine of the Immaculate Conception.
Rossi, Rev. Msgr. Walter R. '87 (WDC)[C] Catholic University of America, The.
Rossier, Francois *s.m.* (CIN)[D] Dayton, OH The University of Dayton; [N] Dayton, OH Marianist Community.
Rossiter, John F. '58 (KCK) Topeka, KS Mater Dei Retired.
Rossman, Christopher '07 (KCK) Topeka, KS Mother Teresa of Calcutta.
Rossman, Richard '71 (P) Eugene, OR St. Mark; Eugene, OR St. Peter; Area Vicars.
Rosso, Mario A. *s.d.b.* '49 (SFR) San Francisco, CA SS. Peter and Paul.
Rosso, Norbert T. *c.s.sp.* '54 (PIT)[O] Bethel Park, PA The Spiritan Center.
Rosson, John P. '75 (ALB) Cooperstown, NY St. Mary.
Rosswog, Ken *o.f.m.* '50 (SFD) Montrose, IL St. Rose of Lima.
Rosswog, Kenneth *o.f.m.* '57 (SFD) Teutopolis, IL St. Francis of Assisi; [L] Teutopolis, IL St. Francis Assisi Friary; Comite Diocesano de Ministerio Hispano – Diocesan Committee for Hispanic Ministry.
Rost, Rev. Msgr. George W. '51 (HBG) Retired.
Rost, Louis B. *m.m.* '55 (FgM) Maryknoll, NY MARYKNOLL.
Rost, Robert '74 (KC) Hamilton, MO Sacred Heart.
Roszko, Edward J. *o.s.f.s.* '70 (WIL)[B] Wilmington, DE Salesianum School.
Roszkowski, Donald F. '97 (PEO) Metamora, IL St. Mary's.
Roten, Johann B.G. *s.m.* '69 (CIN)[D] Dayton, OH The University of Dayton; [D] The Marian Library/International Marian Research Institute (IMRI); [N] Dayton, OH Marianist Community.
Rotert, Matthew '94 (KC) Independence, MO St. Mary's.
Rotert, Norman '57 (KC) Retired.
Roth, Donald *c.ss.r.* '75 (FgM) Baltimore Province.
Roth, James J. '46 (WCH) Retired.
Roth, James *m.m.* '54 (SJ)[M] Los Altos, CA Maryknoll.
Roth, Rev. Msgr. Joseph R. '79 (CHR) Myrtle Beach, SC St. Andrew; Judges; College of Consultors; Finance Council; Investment Council; Diaconate, Office of; Personnel Committee; Vocations Board.
Roth, Timothy *m.i.c.* '74 (NOR)[C] Thompson, CT Marianapolis Preparatory School; [G] Thompson, CT Marian Fathers; Provincial Councilors:.
Roth, Timothy *m.i.c.* '74 (SPR)[H] Provincial Office.
Rothan, Michael W. '04 (HBG) Lebanon, PA St. Benedict the Abbot; [A] Lebanon, PA Lebanon Catholic School.
Rothe, James A. '56 (LA) Retired.
Rother, Michael J. '07 (VIC) Hallettsville, TX Sacred Heart; Hallettsville, TX St. John the Baptist; Procurator Advocate.
Rothermel, Paul L. '94 (ALN) Sinking Spring, PA St. Ignatius Loyola.
Rothfuchs, Gregory '95 (JOL) Joliet, IL St. Paul the Apostle.
Rothrauff, Leo P. *o.s.b.* '56 (GBG)[G] Latrobe, PA Saint Vincent Archabbey.
Rothrauff, Noel H. *o.s.b.* '54 (GBG)[G] Latrobe, PA Saint Vincent Archabbey; Latrobe, PA St. Vincent Archabbey.
Rothrock, Theodore D. '83 (LFT) Carmel, IN St. Elizabeth Ann Seton; Deans; Diocesan Consultors; Building Commission; Members.
Rothschild, Paul J. '84 (STL)[A] St. Louis, MO Kenrick School of Theology.
Rothwell, Joseph T. '52 (BO) Senior Priests. Retired.
Rotola, Albert C. *s.j.* '68 (STL)[O] St. Louis, MO Jesuit Community Corporation at Saint Louis University – Jesuit Hall; [C] Saint Louis University.
Rotondi, Paul *o.f.m.* '56 (HRT)[Q] New Britain, CT Central Connecticut State University Newman House; New Britain, CT St. Francis of Assisi.
Rott, Bernard E. '79 (MAD) Dickeyville, WI Holy Ghost; Kieler, WI Immaculate Conception.
Rott, Jeffrey M. '09 (PH) West Chester, PA SS. Simon and Jude.
Rottgers, Robert A. '09 (COV) Fort Thomas, KY St. Catherine of Siena.
Rottman, Gary '03 (TYL) Crockett, TX St. Francis of the Tejas.
Rotunno, Anthony R. '61 (PRT) Retired.
Rotunno, Floyd '70 (NEW) Mahwah, NJ Immaculate Heart of Mary.
Rotunno, Philip J. '66 (NEW) West New York, NJ Our Lady of Libera; Charismatic Renewal.
Rouch, Nicholas J. '89 (E)[A] Erie, PA St. Mark's Seminary; [M] Erie, PA Holy Family Monastery; Administrative Cabinet; Vicar for Catholic Education; St. Mark Seminary.
Rouech, Chris W. '96 (GR) Grandville, MI St. Pius X; Worship; On Special Assignment.
Rougeau, Marc *s.d.b.* '77 (LA)[V] Rosemead, CA St. Joseph's Salesian Youth Renewal Center.
Rougeau, Marc *s.d.b.* '77 (MRY)[F] Watsonville, CA Saint Francis Salesian Community; Watsonville, CA Our Lady Help of Christians.
Rouleau, Francis C. '00 (NOR) Diocesan Commission for Ecumenical and Interreligious Affairs.
Rourke, John '63 (VEN) Retired.
Rouse, C. Paul '67 (BO) Senior Priests. Retired.
Rouse, Charles Owen '76 (BAL) Priests Sick or Absent.
Rouse, Silvan *c.p.* '49 (ALT)[K] Bedford, PA St. Mary's House of Greater Solitude.
Rouse, Warren *o.f.m.* '57 (LA)[V] Malibu, CA Serra Retreat.
Rousseau, Jean–Jacques (BGP) Bridgeport, CT St. Charles Borromeo.
Rousseau, Julian *s.s.s.* '50 (CLV)[N] Cleveland, OH Congregation of the Blessed Sacrament.
Rousseau, Peter A. '49 (BUR) Retired.
Rousseau, Richard W. *s.j.* '54 (BO)[U] Weston, MA Campion Health Center, Inc.
Rousseau, Robert J. '67 (HRT) North Branford, CT St. Augustine.
Rousseau, Sean K. '95 (ARL) Chantilly, VA Corpus Christi Mission.
Rousseau, Rev. Msgr. Stanlislaus B. '56 (BGP) Fairfield, CT St. Pius X Retired.
Rousseau, William C. '95 (SPR) Chicopee, MA St. Anne's.
Routhier, Rev. Msgr. Peter A. '77 (BUR) Members Ex Officio; Vicars General; Advocate; Ex Officio Members; Liturgical Commission; Diocesan Administrative Board; Diocesan Consultors; Ecumenical Commission; Ex Officio/Consultant; Victim's Advocacy Committee; Burlington, VT St. Joseph's Co–Cathedral.
Roux, Christopher A. '01 (CHL) Charlotte, NC St. Patrick Cathedral.
Roux, Christopher Alan '01 (CHL) Special Assignment.
Roux, G. Albert '66 (PRT) Retired.
Roux, Philippe D. '73 (SPR) South Deerfield, MA Holy Family Parish.
Roux, Randy P. '79 (NO) On Administrative Leave.
Roverse, Michael E. '84 (SAV) Grovetown, GA St. Teresa of Avila.
Rowan, Rev. Msgr. John J. '61 (RVC) Wantagh, NY St. Frances de Chantal Retired.
Rowan, John M. '89 (BO) Framingham, MA St. George.
Rowan, Mark P. '91 (RVC) Serving Outside the Diocese; Air Force Chaplains.
Rowan, Stephen C. (P)[B] College of Arts and Sciences.
Rowe, Charles '99 (KC) Weston, MO Holy Trinity; Deans; Weston, MO Twelve Apostles Parish.
Rowe, Donald F. *s.j.* '72 (CHI)[C] Chicago, IL Jesuit Community at Loyola University Chicago.
Rowe, William J. '64 (BEL) Mount Carmel, IL St. Mary.
Rowgh, Matthew T. '75 (MO) DEPARTMENT OF VETERANS AFFAIRS HOSPITALS AND CHAPLAINS.
Rowgh, T. Matthew '75 (WH) Shepherdstown, WV St. Agnes.
Rowland, Rev. Msgr. Charles H. '70 (CHR) Johns Island, SC Church of the Holy Spirit; Office of Tribunal; College of Consultors.
Rowland, Edward P. '53 (JOL)[K] Naperville, IL St. John Vianney Villa Retired.
Rowland, James '09 (TYL) Paris, TX Our Lady of Victory.
Rowland, Thomas '49 (ELP) On Duty Outside of Diocese.
Rowland, William F. *c.j.m.* '70 (SD) Carlsbad, CA St. Patrick.
Rowland, William *s.m.* '79 (BO)[U] Boston, MA Marist Fathers of Our Lady of Victories (Boston Prov.).
Rowntree, Stephen C. *s.j.* '75 (NO)[C] New Orleans, LA Loyola University New Orleans; [P] New Orleans, LA Jesuit Provincial Office; New Orleans, LA.
Rowsome, Rev. Msgr. Morgan J. '70 (CC) Deans; College of Consultors; Presbyteral Council; Corpus

Christi, TX St. Peter Prince of Apostles; Personnel Board – Priests; Finance Council.
Roxas, Rodolfo P. (SAV) Retired.
Roy, Rev. Msgr. Allen J. '54 (NO) New Orleans, LA Holy Spirit.
Roy, Dick (P) Salem, OR Santiam Correctional Institution; Salem, OR Mill Creek Correctional Facility.
Roy, Donald J. '70 (BUR) Bradford, VT Our Lady of Perpetual Help.
Roy, Duane *o.s.b.* '67 (FgM)[I] Atchison, KS St. Benedict's Abbey; Atchison, KS St. Benedict's Abbey.
Roy, Rev. Msgr. F. Gilles '57 (WOR) On Duty Outside the Diocese.
Roy, George *o.m.i.* '73 (CHI) Chicago, IL St. Malachy.
Roy, James R. *m.m.* '61 (NY)[EE] Retired.
Roy, James '61 (ALX) Retired.
Roy, Jean–Paul *m.s.a.* '54 (NOR)[A] Cromwell, CT Holy Apostles College and Seminary.
Roy, Maurice J. '73 (BUR) Deans; St. Albans, VT Holy Angels; Canon 1742 Panel of Pastors.
Roy, Michael J. '75 (WOR) Webster, MA Sacred Heart of Jesus.
Roy, Neil (FTW)[A] Notre Dame, IN Moreau Seminary.
Roy, Paul A. *m.s.* '58 (HRT)[L] Hartford Our Lady of Sorrows Rectory.
Roy, Richard M. '75 (FR) Attleboro, MA St. John the Evangelist.
Roy, Richard *m.afr.* '71 (FgM) Washington, DC; Washington, DC MISSIONARIES OF AFRICA.
Roy, Richard *m.afr.* '71 (WDC)[N] Washington, DC Missionaries of Africa.
Roy, Robert E. '69 (L) Fairdale, KY Blessed Teresa of Calcutta.
Roy, Robert P. '94 (HRT) East Hartford, CT St. Mary; East Hartford, CT St. Rose; East Hartford, CT St. Isaac Jogues; Appointed.
Royal, Rev. Msgr. Kevin T. '85 (BGP) Episcopal Vicar for Clergy; Office for Clergy Personnel; Office for the Continuing Education of Clergy; Members of the Clergy Personnel Committee; Presbyteral Council; Pastors' Vocation Advisory Board.
Royals, Andrew Francis '06 (WDC) Bowie, MD Sacred Heart.
Royce, Thomas *s.j.* '56 (P) Portland, OR St. Ignatius; [L] Portland, OR Colombiere Community.
Royer, Rev. Msgr. Ronald Edmund '58 (LA) Retired.
Royer, Rev. Msgr. Ronald '58 (FRS) Porterville, CA St. Anne Retired.
Royer, Thomas J. '60 (PEO) Champaign, IL St. Mary's.
Royer, Yvon J. '90 (BUR) Daughters of Isabella; Vergennes, VT St. Peter; Canon 1742 Panel of Pastors.
Royik, Ihor '92 (PHU) Melrose Park, PA Annunciation of the B.V.M.; The Way – Online Newspaper.
Roza, Andrew J. '07 (OM)[B] Columbus, NE Scotus Central Catholic High School; Columbus, NE St. Bonaventure.
Rozansky, Joseph G. *o.f.m.* (NY)[EE] New York Franciscan Friars, Holy Name Province.
Rozario, Christal '00 (PH) Philadelphia, PA St. Francis de Sales; [S] Darby, PA Mercy Fitzgerald Hospital.
Rozario, William '90 (OAK) Pleasanton, CA The Catholic Community of Pleasanton.
Rozek, Piotr '88 (RVC) Copiague, NY Our Lady of the Assumption.
Rozembajgier, John M. '04 (MET) Spotswood, NJ Immaculate Conception.
Rozic, Peter *s.j.* '07 (WDC)[N] Washington, DC The Jesuit Community at Georgetown University.
Rozman, Thomas J. '86 (HBG) Harrisburg, PA Cathedral Parish of St. Patrick.
Rozmarynowycz, Mychail '95 (PRM) Sterling Heights, MI St. Basil.
Rozniak, Rev. Msgr. Ronald J. '71 (NEW) Ridgewood, NJ Our Lady of Mount Carmel; Members; Administration; [R] Catholic Health and Human Services Corporation; Newark, NJ Cathedral Healthcare Systems; Members; Members; [R] Newark, NJ Trinity Management & Technology Corp.; Cathedral Foundation, Inc.; Cathedral/Columbus Group, Inc.; [F] Newark, NJ Cathedral Healthcare System, Inc.; [R] Newark, NJ University Heights Property Company, Inc.
Rozum, George A. *c.s.c.* '68 (FTW)[B] University of Notre Dame Du Lac; [H] Notre Dame, IN Holy Cross Community, Corby Hall, University of Notre Dame.
Rozycki, George '70 (SP) Zephyrhills, FL St. Joseph Catholic Church.
Rozycki, Rev. Msgr. Isidore '68 (AUS) West, TX St. Martin; West, TX St. Joseph.
Ruan, Joseph (NY) New York, NY St. Joseph.
Ruane, Dennis *s.s.s.* '59 (CLV)[N] Cleveland Congregation of the Blessed Sacrament Provincial House.
Ruane, Dennis '59 (SLC) Copperton, UT Immaculate Conception LLC 206.
Ruane, Edward *o.p.* '69 (CHI)[N] Chicago Dominicans (Provincial Office).
Ruane, George '73 (NEW) Edgewater, NJ Holy Rosary.
Ruane, Gerald P. '60 (NEW) Retired.
Ruane, John P. *s.j.* '49 (NEW)[B] Jersey City, NJ Jesuit Center; [M] Jersey City, NJ Jesuits of Saint Peter's College, Inc.
Ruane, Martin '63 (JKS) Grenada, MS St. Peter.
Ruane, Michael J. '69 (BAL) Mount Airy, MD St. Michael.
Ruba, Rev. Msgr. Nicholas J. '51 (SC) Retired.
Rubadue, Paul E. *o.s.b.* '86 (GBG)[G] Latrobe, PA Saint Vincent Archabbey.
Rubaj, Leon B. '60 (SAT)[K] San Antonio, TX Casa De Padres Retired.
Rubaj, Leon '60 (SAT) San Antonio, TX Retired.
Rubbelke, Ronald J. '64 (STL) O'Fallon, MO Assumption.
Rubey, Charles T. '66 (CHI)[G] Chicago, IL Catholic Charities of the Archdiocese of Chicago–Archdiocesan Offices; [G] Chicago, IL Catholic Charities of the Archdiocese of Chicago–Archdiocesan Offices; Office for Persons with Disabilities; Office for Persons with Disabilities; Associate Administrators Retired.
Rubiano, Cesar A. '96 (TR) Secretary to the Bishop.
Rubiano, Luis Eduardo *o.f.m.cap.* '81 (NY)[EE] White Plains, NY Capuchin Friars International, Inc.
Rubino, Vincent *o.f.m.conv.* '00 (PMB) Port St. Lucie, FL St. Lucie.
Rubio, Jose Antonio '80 (SJ) Special Assignment; Ecumenical and Interreligious Affairs.
Rubio, Jose Antonio '80 (SFR)[A] Menlo Park, CA St. Patrick Seminary and University.
Rubio, Juan *o.f.m.* '03 (AMA) Amarillo, TX St. Laurence Cathedral.
Rubio, Santiago '80 (NY) Bronx, NY Sacred Heart.
Rubio–Boitel, Fernando '75 (SFE) Albuquerque, NM Queen of Heaven Retired.
Ruby, David C. '91 (GB) Egg Harbor, WI Stella Maris.
Rucando, Anthony M. '70 (BRK) Howard Beach, NY Our Lady of Grace.
Ruchgy, Rev. Canon Wayne J. '66 (STN) Dearborn, MI St. Michael's.
Ruchgy, Rev. Canon Wayne '66 (STN) Protosyncellus; Diocesan Consultors; Personnel Board; Presbyteral Council.
Ruchinski, David '07 (STA) Vocations; Gainesville, FL St. Augustine.
Rucinski, Willard *o.s.f.s.* '65 (R) Fayetteville, NC St. Elizabeth Ann Seton.
Rucker, Lawrence *s.c.j.* '66 (MIL)[P] Franklin, WI Villa Maria.
Rucker, Martha H *b.c.c.* (LEX)[D] Ashland, KY Our Lady of Bellefonte Hospital, Inc.
Rudcki, Stanley R. '53 (CHI) Retired.
Rudd, Thad B. '91 (ATL) Gainesville, GA St. Michael Retired.
Rudden, Matthew T. '59 (RCK) Retired.
Ruddy, Paul *o.s.f.s.* '64 (LAN) Clinton, MI St. Dominic Oratory.
Rudecki, Marek *s.a.c.* '83 (BRK) Ridgewood, NY St. Aloysius.
Rudemiller, Edward L. '58 (CIN) Retired.
Rudjak, Joseph '00 (Y) Youngstown, OH SS. Peter and Paul; Youngstown, OH Our Lady of Hungary.
Rudnick, Kenneth *s.j.* '91 (LA)[C] Los Angeles, CA Jesuit Community; [AA] Los Angeles, CA Loyola Law School.
Rudnicki, Wladyslaw '56 (RVC) Retired.
Rudnicki, Zbigniew A. '90 (PMB) Royal Palm Beach, FL Our Lady Queen of Peace Catholic Cemetery, Inc.; Royal Palm Beach, FL Our Lady Queen of the Apostles; Cemetery: Our Lady Queen of Peace.
Rudnik, John J. '61 (CHI) Chicago, IL Transfiguration of Our Lord Retired.
Rudnik, Tadeusz '55 (SY) Syracuse, NY Transfiguration.
Rudolf, Rosendo '07 (CI) Chancellor; Finance Committee; [C] Tunnuk, Chuuk, FM Vicariate Residence.
Rudolph, Michael L. '05 (STP) Hamel, MN St. Thomas the Apostle; Deanery 11.
Rudolph, Patrick '88 (ORG) Orange, CA St. Norbert.
Rudolph, Thomas J. '61 (LC) Stratford, WI St. Andrew; Stratford, WI St. Joseph.
Rudolphi, Stephen A. '79 (BEL) Carmi, IL St. Polycarp (German); Carmi, IL St. Patrick.
Rudolphi, Timothy C. '89 (STP) Monticello, MN St. Henry.
Rudy, Noel '53 (SAG) Harrison, MI St. Athanasius Retired.
Rudy, Richard E. '76 (PH) Bensalem, PA Saint Ephrem.
Rudzewicz, Jan '83 (OAK) On Sabbatical.
Ruede, Ernest J. '66 (R) Jacksonville, NC Shrine of the Infant of Prague, Church of the Holy Spirit; Diocesan Consultors; Deans; Council of Priests.
Ruedisueli, Robert A. '69 (DET) Warren, MI St. Mark.
Ruef, Rev. Msgr. James L.T. '78 (COL) Retired.
Ruef, Rev. Msgr. James L.T. '78 (COL) Judicial Vicar; Presiding Judge in Second Instance.
Rueger, William J. '75 (BRK) Brooklyn, NY St. Francis Xavier.
Ruekert, Thomas E. *s.d.b.* '73 (NY) Port Chester, NY Corpus Christi.
Ruelle, Gerald *o.s.b.* '50 (BIS)[A] Richardton, ND Assumption Abbey Retired.
Ruessmann, John J. *m.m.* '79 (NY)[EE].
Rueter, Joseph J. '46 (COV) Retired.
Ruetz, Edward J. '62 (FTW) Retired.
Ruff, Anthony *o.s.b.* '93 (SCL)[I] Collegeville, MN St. John's Abbey, of the Order of St. Benedict.
Ruff, Charles R. '46 (STL) Retired.
Ruff, Daniel M. *s.j.* '86 (PH) Philadelphia, PA Old St. Joseph's.
Ruff, Frank *g.h.m.* '63 (OWN) Elkton, KY St. Susan; Guthrie, KY Sts. Mary & James; Deans/Coordinators.
Ruff, Frank *g.h.m.* '63 (CIN)[N] Cincinnati Headquarters of Glenmary Home Missioners Retired.
Ruffalo, Michael R. '08 (PIT) McMurray, PA St. Benedict the Abbot.
Ruffing, Joseph R. '55 (LFT) Retired.
Ruffing, Norman '63 (OAK) Retired.
Ruffo, John *o.f.m.conv.* '74 (SY) Syracuse, NY Assumption B.V.M.; Presbyteral Council.
Ruffolo, George *c.m.f.* '59 (CHI) Chicago, IL Holy Cross/Immaculate Heart of Mary; [N] Oak Park Claretian Missionaries USA Eastern Province.
Rufo, Henry '01 (P) Rainier, OR Nativity B.V.M.
Rufo, Nicholas (CIN)[N] Dayton, OH Mercy Siena Support Community.
Rugaragu, Innocent Balthazary *s.j.* '09 (OAK)[M] Berkeley, CA Jesuit Fathers and Brothers.
Ruge, Fernando '94 (AMA) Tulia, TX Church of the Holy Spirit.
Ruge, Paul '97 (FAR) Retired.
Rugen, Patrick J. '76 (CHI) Waukegan, IL St. Dismas.
Ruggere, Peter L. *m.m.* '68 (NY)[EE] Maryknoll Maryknoll Fathers and Brothers.
Ruggeri, Joseph A. '65 (BO) Senior Priests. Retired.
Ruggeri, Salvatore M. '99 (CLV) Cleveland, OH St. John of the Cross.
Ruggieri, James T. '95 (PRO) Providence, RI St. Casimir; Providence, RI St. Patrick; Officers.
Ruggieri, Joseph '95 (Y) Ashtabula, OH Our Lady of Mt. Carmel; Ashtabula, OH Mother of Sorrows.
Ruggieri, Pasquale *f.d.p.* '52 (NY) New York, NY St. Ann.
Ruggiero, James S. '70 (PIT) Retired.
Ruggiero, Philip '81 (TR) Matawan, NJ St. Clement.
Ruggles, Christopher V. '79 (TYL) Judges; On Duty Outside the Diocese.
Ruggles, Christopher V. '79 (CAM) Procurator–Advocate; Cherry Hill, NJ St. Mary's R.C. Church, Delaware Township, N.J.
Ruhl, Matthew D. *s.j.* '92 (KC) Kansas City, MO St. Francis Xavier; [J] Kansas City, MO Rockhurst Jesuit Community.
Ruhl, William J. *o.s.f.s.* '62 (ARL) Vienna, VA Our Lady of Good Counsel; Diocesan Judges.
Ruhlin, James '02 (SP) Hudson, FL St. Michael the Archangel.
Ruhnke, Robert A. *c.ss.r.* '66 (SAT)[L] San Antonio, TX Redemptorists of Texas–San Antonio #1.
Ruisanchez, Jose P. '86 (BO)[T] Newton, MA Prelature of the Holy Cross and Opus Dei; Chestnut Hill.
Ruiz, Albert Capello '73 (AUS) Austin, TX Nuestra Senora De Dolores.
Ruiz, Alberto M. *c.m.f.* '84 (SAT) San Antonio, TX Immaculate Heart of Mary.
Ruiz, Antonio A. '71 (TUC) Retired.
Ruiz, Carlos A. (NY) Bronx, NY St. Joan of Arc.
Ruiz, Dominic *o.s.b.* '83 (SCL)[I] Collegeville, MN St. John's Abbey, of the Order of St. Benedict.
Ruiz, Eddie '99 (SD) Holtville, CA St. Joseph; Vicars Forane; Presbyteral Council.
Ruiz, Edgar '01 (PAT) Passaic, NJ Assumption of the Blessed Virgin Mary.
Ruiz, Enrique '56 (SAT) On Leave.
Ruiz, Faustino C. '91 (MET) On Duty Outside the Diocese.
Ruiz, Faustino *s.j.s.* '91 (MAD) Merrimac, WI St. Mary, Health of the Sick; Sauk City, WI St. Aloysius; Sauk City, WI St. Norbert.
Ruiz, Gabriel *c.m.f.* '89 (FRS) Fresno, CA St. Anthony Claret; Priests' Council.
Ruiz, Giovanni (CGS) San Lorenzo, PR Sagrado Corazon de Jesus y 12 Apostoles.
Ruiz, Jean–Pierre '82 (BRK) Released from Diocesan Assignment; Queens Village, NY SS. Joachim and Anne.
Ruiz, John '55 (HT) Retired.
Ruiz, Jose Domingo '89 (STO) Stockton, CA St. Linus Church (Pastor of); Spanish.
Ruiz, Joseph B. '66 (CHI) Evergreen Park, IL Most Holy Redeemer Retired.
Ruiz, Juan Antonio *c.m.* '65 (DAL) Dallas, TX Holy Trinity; [J] Dallas, TX Congregation of the Mission, Western Province.
Ruiz, Lorenzo '63 (SJN) San Juan, PR San Juan Bosco.
Ruiz, Luis M. '85 (FAJ) Culebra, PR Nuestra Senora del Carmen.
Ruiz, Luis '68 (SAT) San Antonio, TX St. Stephen.
Ruiz, Manuel '98 (BIR) Guntersville, AL St. William.
Ruiz, Miguel *s.v.d.* '95 (SB) Riverside, CA Queen of Angels.
Ruiz, Orlando *o.f.m.* '06 (NY)[EE] New York Franciscan Province of the Immaculate Conception.
Ruiz, Oscar Ramirez '94 (NEW) Rahway, NJ St. Mary's.

Ruiz, Raul Gomez *s.d.s.* '87 (MIL)[P] Franklin, WI Salvatorian Formation House; [B] Hales Corners, WI Sacred Heart School of Theology.
Ruiz, Rick '92 (ELP) Absent on Leave.
Ruiz, Ruben Romero '91 (LSC) Presbyteral Council.
Ruiz, Rudy '79 (MRY) Vicars Forane; Hollister, CA Sacred Heart/St. Benedict Catholic Community.
Ruiz, Ryan Thomas '08 (CIN) Centerville, OH Incarnation.
Ruiz–Mayorga, John Martin *o.p.* '08 (PRO) Providence, RI St. Pius V; [P] Providence, RI St. Pius Priory.
Ruiz–Santos, Carlos '03 (SAL) Salina, KS Sacred Heart Cathedral Parish; Council of Priests; Office of Hispanic Ministry.
Rukavina, Steven '87 (B) Boise, ID St. Mark's.
Rukstalis, Simeon *o.f.m.conv.* '64 (SY) Binghamton, NY SS. Cyril and Method; Binghamton, NY Holy Trinity.
Rukuratwa, Avitus L. '06 (CHI) Winnetka, IL Sacred Heart.
Rule, Philip C. *s.j.* '62 (WOR)[O] Worcester, MA Jesuits of the Holy Cross, Inc.
Rule, Steven R. '75 (RIC) Richmond, VA Church of the Epiphany.
Rumble, Clarence F. '86 (SY) Endwell, NY Church of the Holy Family.
Rumin–Dominguez, Juan R. *o.f.m.* '95 (MIA) Miami, FL St. John Neumann.
Runde, David H. '57 (MAD)[F] Madison, WI Bishop O'Connor Catholic Pastoral Center Retired.
Runde, Luis *o.f.m.* '65 (FWT)[H] Crowley, TX St. Maximilian Kolbe Friary.
Runde, Raymond E. '56 (MAD) Retired.
Rundzio, Mark A. '81 (MAN) Retired.
Runnion, David A. '06 (CHR) Chester, SC St. Joseph; Lancaster, SC St. Catherine; Vice–Chancellor.
Runtu, Lukas '00 (PH) Brookhaven, PA Our Lady of Charity.
Runyon, Jacob '09 (FTW) South Bend, IN St. Matthew Cathedral.
Ruoff, Lou '84 (RIC) Colonial Heights, VA St. Ann.
Rupert, Rev. Msgr. Dalegord '77 (SCR) On Duty Outside the Diocese.
Rupp, Daniel J. '98 (BUR) Burlington, VT Christ the King–St. Anthony; Elected Members; Canon 1742 Panel of Pastors.
Rupp, Daniel N. '66 (MAR) Retired.
Rupp, Edward F. '60 (CLV) Life of Prayer and Penance.
Ruppenkamp, Raymond '50 (DAV) Retired.
Ruppert, Alan E. '78 (BEL) Leave of Absence.
Ruppert, David '05 (FTW) Fort Wayne, IN St. Therese; [C] Fort Wayne, IN Bishop Luers High School; Presbyteral Council.
Ruppert, Donald R. '78 (VIC) East Bernard, TX Holy Cross; Diocesan Finance Board.
Rurangirwa, Romain (BO) Carlisle, MA St. Irene.
Rusatsi, Andrew *s.j.* '81 (WDC)[N] Washington, DC The Jesuit Community at Georgetown University.
Rusay, Leonard E. '85 (MET) Whitehouse Station, NJ Our Lady of Lourdes.
Rusch, Donald '61 (LAN) Retired.
Ruschman, Albert E. '53 (COV) Fort Thomas, KY St. Thomas Retired.
Rusconi, Rev. Msgr. Richard A. '72 (PAT) Clifton, NJ St. Andrew the Apostle.
Ruse, Fred R. '76 (ORL) On Duty Outside the Diocese.
Rush, Ernest G. '02 (NEW) Bayonne, NJ Mt. Carmel.
Rush, Rev. Msgr. J. Kenneth '71 (RIC) Lynchburg, VA Holy Cross; Regional Vicars; Judges.
Rush, James C. '68 (HRT) Retired.
Rush, James P. '72 (CAM) Margate, NJ Church of the Blessed Sacrament, Margate City, New Jersey.
Rush, Joseph E. '64 (CAM) Retired.
Rush, Michael P. '73 (CAM) Ocean City, NJ St. Augustine's Catholic Church, Ocean City, N.J.
Rush, Patrick J. '69 (KC) Kansas City, MO Visitation of the Blessed Virgin Mary.
Rush, Thomas *o.m.i.* '73 (FgM) Washington, DC AMERICAN OBLATE MISSIONS.
Rush, Rev. Msgr. Vincent '72 (RVC) West Babylon, NY Our Lady of Grace.
Rushford, William A. '55 (BIS)[G] Bismarck, ND Emmaus Place Retired.
Rushofsky, John R. '79 (PIT) Pittsburgh, PA St. Sebastian.
Rusin, Joseph C. '46 (SCR) Dickson City, PA Visitation of the Blessed Virgin Mary Retired.
Rusin, Krzysztof '07 (MEM) Germantown, TN Our Lady Of Perpetual Help.
Rusk, Richard M. '90 (MET) Episcopal Vicars.
Rusk, Richard M. '90 (MET) Belvidere, NJ St. Patrick; Oxford, NJ St. Rose of Lima; [M] Oxford, NJ The Anawim Community.
Rusk, Richard M. '90 (ROC)[N] Corning, NY Anawim Community Center.
Rusk, Ron '68 (SB) Blythe, CA Ironwood State Prison.
Ruskamp, Robert L. '85 (ARL) Alexandria, VA St. Mary's.
Ruskoski, William Paul '74 (LAF) Rayne, LA St. Joseph.
Ruskowski, Clifford F. '62 (DET) Retired.
Rusnak, Anton *o.c.s.o.* '03 (L)[L] Trappist, KY Abbey of Our Lady of Gethsemani, of the Order of Cistercians of the Strict Observance.
Rusnak, Melvin E. '70 (Y) Geneva, OH Assumption B.V.M.
Rusnak, Tadeusz *s.ch.* '85 (P) Portland, OR St. Stanislaus.
Russeau, Kevin M. *c.s.c.* '01 (FTW)[A] Notre Dame, IN Old College; [B] University of Notre Dame Du Lac; [H] Notre Dame, IN Holy Cross Community, Corby Hall, University of Notre Dame; [A] Notre Dame, IN Moreau Seminary.
Russell, Alfred J. '66 (KAL) Hastings, MI St. Rose of Lima.
Russell, Anselm *o.s.b.* '97 (CHI) Evanston, IL St. Mary.
Russell, Anselm *o.s.b.* '97 (IND)[K] St. Meinrad St. Meinrad Archabbey.
Russell, David P. '81 (WDC) North Beach, MD St. Anthony.
Russell, David '64 (MIA) Retired.
Russell, Dean E. '00 (RCK) Rockford, IL St. James.
Russell, Edward '83 (NY) New York, NY Our Lady of Esperanza; New York, NY St. Rose of Lima.
Russell, James A. *s.m.* '64 (CIN)[N] Huntsville, OH St. George Chapel of Marianist Community.
Russell, James D. '60 (WIN) Retired.
Russell, John F. *o.carm.* '60 (NEW)[A] South Orange, NJ Immaculate Conception Seminary; [A] South Orange, NJ Immaculate Conception Seminary; [B] School of Diplomacy and Intl. Rels.
Russell, John *o.carm.* '60 (JOL)[L] Darien Carmelite Provincial Office.
Russell, Kenneth '58 (OAK) Retired.
Russell, Nock W. '08 (AUS) College Station, TX St. Thomas Aquinas.
Russell, Rev. Msgr. Paul F. '87 (BO) On Duty Outside the Archdiocese.
Russell, Raymond R. '56 (BUF)[O] Buffalo, NY Sheehan Residence for Priests Retired.
Russell, Richard R. '61 (HRT)[A] In Res. at the Archbishop Daniel A. Cronin Retirement Residence at St. Thomas Seminary Retired.
Russell, Robert L. *s.s.* '55 (BAL)[S] Baltimore Society of St. Sulpice, Province of the United States Retired.
Russell, Robert *s.s.* (DET) Retired.
Russell, Samuel *o.s.b.* '94 (KC)[A] Conception, MO Conception Seminary College; [J] Stanberry, MO St. Peter Parish.
Russell, Stanley J. '61 (WIL) Wilmington, DE St. Helena; Deans.
Russell, William C. *s.j.* '65 (BO)[U] Newton, MA The Jesuit Community at Boston College.
Russi, Fred '67 (LKC) Diocesan Consultors; Presbyteral Council Retired.
Russi, John *s.m.* '67 (SJ)[C] San Jose, CA Archbishop Mitty High School; [M] Cupertino, CA The Bordeaux House.
Russick, Matthew '09 (ALT)[G] Loretto, PA St. Francis Friary at Mount Assisi.
Russo, Anthony J. '00 (BR) Retired.
Russo, Anthony P. *s.c.j.* '66 (MIL)[P] Franklin, WI St. Francis Residence.
Russo, Anthony S. '00 (GR) Rockford, MI Our Lady of Consolation.
Russo, Anthony T. *c.ss.r.* '65 (PH) Deaf Apostolate; Philadelphia, PA Visitation B.V.M.
Russo, Caesar '74 (STA) Defenders of the Bond; Diocesan Tribunal.
Russo, Rev. Msgr. Charles J. (PAT) Retired.
Russo, Francis X. *o.f.m.cap.* '59 (WDC)[B] Washington, DC St. Francis Friary–Capuchin College.
Russo, Frank '81 (LA) On Sick Leave.
Russo, Michael A. '71 (NEW) On Duty Outside the Archdiocese; [B] St. Mary's College.
Russo, Michael '89 (LAF) Lafayette, LA Our Lady of Fatima.
Russo, Peter '76 (ALB) Scotia, NY St. Joseph.
Russo, Reginald *o.f.m.cap.* '67 (PIT) Pittsburgh, PA Our Lady of the Angels; [N] Pittsburgh, PA Sisters of Charity of Nazareth.
Russo, Ricardo *o.f.m.* '74 (MO) Army National Guard Chaplains.
Russo, Ricardo *o.f.m.* '74 (SFE)[I] Santa Fe, NM Discalced Carmelite Monastery.
Russo, Richard M. '82 (RCK) Marengo, IL Sacred Heart.
Russo, Robert T. '61 (HRT)[A] In Res. at the Archbishop Daniel A. Cronin Retirement Residence at St. Thomas Seminary Retired.
Russo, Rt. Rev. Roman V. (BRK)[S] Russian Apostolate.
Russo, Rt. Rev. Roman V. '77 (NY) New York, NY St. Michael Chapel.
Russo, Rt. Rev. Romanos V. '77 (NTN) Priests Serving Outside the Eparchy.
Rust, Adam M. '09 (MEM) Bartlett, TN Church of The Nativity; Graduate Studies.
Ruston, Robert L. '76 (ALT) Johnstown, PA SS. Gregory & Barnabas.
Ruszel, Henry *c.r.* '54 (SB)[I] Fontana, CA Congregation of the Resurrection, CR; Fontana, CA Blessed John XXIII Catholic Community, Inc. Retired.
Ruszel, Humphrey *c.r.* '46 (SB) Fontana, CA Blessed John XXIII Catholic Community, Inc.; [I] Fontana, CA Congregation of the Resurrection, CR Retired.
Ruteaga, Rogelio Martinez *o.f.m.* '03 (JOL) Joliet, IL St. John the Baptist; [L] Joliet, IL St. John the Baptist Friary.
Ruth, John C. '85 (SCR) Scranton, PA St. Mary of the Assumption; Hispanic Ministry Outreach.
Ruth, Robert F. '60 (RIC) Retired.
Ruther, William E. '90 (LA) Carson, CA St. Philomena.
Rutherford, Donald I. '81 (ALB) Military Chaplains.
Rutherford, Rev. Msgr. Donald L. '81 (MO) Presbyteral Council; Army Chaplains.
Rutherford, H. *c.s.c.* (FTW)[H] Notre Dame Congregation of Holy Cross, Indiana Province, Provincial House.
Rutherford, Mark J. '09 (LAN) Brighton, MI St. Patrick.
Rutherford, Richard *c.s.c.* '64 (P)[B] University of Portland; [L] Portland, OR Holy Cross Fathers & Brothers, C.S.C. – University of Portland; Liturgical Commission.
Rutkowski, George A. '60 (DET) Retired.
Rutkowski, James '77 (SAT)[A] San Antonio, TX Diaconate Program; Permanent Diaconate Program; [O] San Antonio, TX Catholic Counseling and Consultation Center; San Antonio, TX Purisima Concepcion; San Antonio, TX Purisima Concepcion.
Rutkowski, Ronald J. '69 (GBG) Retired.
Rutkowski, Theodore A. '63 (PIT) Retired.
Rutkowski, William '87 (SAG) Bay City, MI St. Stanislaus Kostka; Bay Area Catholic Schools; Territorial Vicars.
Rutledge, William G. '53 (PIT) Retired.
Rutledge, William M. *o.s.f.s.* '89 (ARL) Reston, VA St. John Neumann.
Rutler, George W. '81 (NY) New York, NY Our Saviour; [II] New York, NY Guild of Catholic Lawyers, The.
Rutten, Erich '05 (STP)[C] St. Paul, MN University of St. Thomas; Ecumenical and Interreligious Affairs.
Rutten, Paul A. '02 (SFS) Vocations.
Rutten, Paul J. '58 (LIN)[E] Lincoln, NE Bonacum House Retired.
Ruttenberg, Gari *o.m.i.* '95 (STP)[N] Buffalo, MN Christ the King Retreat Center.
Ruttle, Paul *c.p.* '80 (MET)[I] South River Passionist Provincial Office.
Ruttle, Paul *c.p.* (FgM) South River, NJ St. Paul of the Cross Province.
Rutz, Rev. Msgr. Gilbert J. '66 (COV) Vicars General; Diocesan Consultors.
Ruvo, Rev. Msgr. John A. '54 (NY) New Rochelle, NY St. Joseph.
Ruwaainenyi, Deogratias M. '06 (CLV) Cleveland Heights, OH Communion of Saints Parish.
Ruwe, Paul A. '05 (CIN) On Special and Archdiocesan Assignment.
Ruyechan, Matthew J. '80 (E) Oil City, PA St. Stephen; Oil City, PA St. Venantius.
Ruygt, Hans P. '85 (PHX) Surprise, AZ St. Clare of Assisi Roman Catholic Parish; Presbyteral Council.
Ruzicka, Gary '76 (CHY) Cheyenne, WY St. Mary's Cathedral; Ex Officios, Voting; Diocese of Cheyenne, Board of Directors; Liturgical Commission; Diocesan Schools Advisory Group; [G] Cheyenne, WY St. Mary's School Foundation; Building Committee; Cheyenne, WY Olivet Cemetery.
Rwechungura, Siffredus B. '99 (NEW) On Duty Outside the Archdiocese.
Rwegasira, Deogratias *a.j.* '96 (ALN) Easton, PA Our Lady of Mercy Parish.
Rweyongeza, Rev. Msgr. Deogratias (PEO) La Salle, IL Shrine of Queen of the Holy Rosary; La Salle, IL St. Patrick's.
Rwezaura, Deogratias Mutayoba *s.j.* '05 (OAK)[M] Berkeley, CA Jesuit Fathers and Brothers.
Ryan, Adam *o.s.b.* '90 (KC)[J] Stanberry, MO St. Peter Parish; [A] Conception, MO Conception Seminary College.
Ryan, Alan J. *m.m.* '60 (SJ)[M] Los Altos, CA Maryknoll.
Ryan, Albert J. '58 (FR) Retired.
Ryan, C. Duane '54 (JC) Versailles, MO St. Philip Benizi.
Ryan, C. Duane '54 (KC) Retired.
Ryan, Cornelius *c.s.c.* '66 (FTW) South Bend, IN St. Therese, Little Flower; [H] Notre Dame Congregation of Holy Cross, Indiana Province, Provincial House.
Ryan, Daniel J. '89 (TR) Willingboro, NJ Corpus Christi.
Ryan, David '79 (CHI) Lake Zurich, IL St. Francis de Sales.
Ryan, Denis J. *c.ss.r.* '06 (GR)[L] Grand Rapids, MI The Society of the Redemptorists of the City of Grand Rapids; Grand Rapids, MI St. Alphonsus.
Ryan, Dennis K. '66 (DEN) Frisco, CO St. Mary Retired.
Ryan, Dennis M. '74 (GB) Appleton, WI St. Bernard; Xavier Guild.
Ryan, Donald P. '63 (L)[L] Louisville, KY Bishop David Apartments Retired.

Ryan, Edmund K. *o.p.* '65 (OAK)[M] Oakland, CA Order of Preachers (Province of the Most Holy Name of Jesus – Western Dominican Province).
Ryan, Rev. Msgr. Edward A. '71 (BRK) Ridgewood, NY Our Lady of the Miraculous Medal.
Ryan, Edward J. '53 (ALB) Retired.
Ryan, Edward M. '74 (WOR) Worcester, MA Our Lady of Providence Parish.
Ryan, Eugene '69 (VEN) Retired.
Ryan, F. Lee '68 (JOL) Watseka, IL St. Edmund.
Ryan, Francis J. *s.j.* '56 (FgM) Watertown, MA Society of Jesus.
Ryan, Francis X. *s.j.* '84 (CLV)[B] University Heights, OH John Carroll Jesuit Community.
Ryan, Francis '58 (PEO) Retired.
Ryan, Frank A. *o.m.i.* '54 (BEL)[F] Belleville, IL Shrine of Our Lady of the Snows Retired.
Ryan, G. Philip '88 (ATL) Greensboro, GA Christ Our King and Savior.
Ryan, Rev. Msgr. George J. '62 (BRK) Douglaston, NY St. Anastasia.
Ryan, Rev. Msgr. Gerald E. '55 (DM) Retired.
Ryan, Rev. Msgr. Gerald J. '45 (NY) Bronx, NY St. Luke.
Ryan, Herbert J. *s.j.* '62 (LA)[C] Los Angeles, CA Jesuit Community.
Ryan, J. Patrick '76 (PAT) Paterson, NJ Blessed Sacrament.
Ryan, Jack '76 (HON) Honolulu, HI St. John the Baptist; Diocesan Ecumenical Commission; Presbyteral Council.
Ryan, James G. *o.s.a.* '49 (LAN) Flint, MI St. Matthew.
Ryan, James M. '75 (COV) Adjutant Judicial Vicars.
Ryan, James M. '75 (COV) Elsmere, KY St. Henry.
Ryan, Rev. Msgr. James W. '48 (BRK) Brooklyn, NY St. Fortunata Retired.
Ryan, John A. '70 (SFR) Burlingame, CA St. Catherine of Siena.
Ryan, John Chrysostom *c.p.* '48 (BRK)[T] Jamaica, NY Immaculate Conception Monastery Retired.
Ryan, John J. '71 (ORL) Ormond Beach, FL St. Brendan.
Ryan, John J. *c.s.c.* '90 (SCR)[C] King's College; [C] Holy Cross Community; Prov. Councilors:.
Ryan, John J. *s.j.* '67 (BUF)[O] Buffalo, NY Canisius Jesuit Community Inc.; [D] Buffalo, NY Canisius High School.
Ryan, John M. '64 (CHI) Retired.
Ryan, Rev. Msgr. John M. '55 (BUF) Buffalo, NY Assumption Retired.
Ryan, John P. '63 (NEW) Retired.
Ryan, John '74 (NO) Lafitte, LA St. Anthony.
Ryan, Rev. Msgr. John '50 (SB) Retired.
Ryan, John '54 (ALX) Retired.
Ryan, Joseph A. *o.m.i.* '42 (BO)[X] Tewksbury, MA Immaculate Heart of Mary Residence.
Ryan, Joseph G. *o.s.a.* '87 (PH)[Y] Villanova, PA St. Thomas Monastery.
Ryan, Joseph J. '51 (STL) Retired.
Ryan, Joseph *o.s.a.* '83 (PH)[C] Villanova University.
Ryan, Kenan *s.t.* '59 (JKS) Philadelphia, MS Holy Cross.
Ryan, Rev. Msgr. Kevin E. '70 (SAT) San Antonio, TX St. Mark the Evangelist; Defenders of the Bond.
Ryan, Laurence D. *s.j.* '77 (BGP)[E] Fairfield, CT Fairfield College Preparatory School; [O] Fairfield, CT The Fairfield Jesuit Community–Fairfield University.
Ryan, Lawrence A. '42 (SAC) Retired.
Ryan, Rev. Msgr. Leo P. '54 (PAT)[Q] Chester, NJ Nazareth Village Retired.
Ryan, Rev. Msgr. Martin P. '76 (BGP) New Fairfield, CT St. Edward the Confessor; Presbyteral Council; Vicariate V (Bethel, Brookfield, Danbury, Georgetown, Newtown, New Fairfield, Redding, Ridgefield, Sherman).
Ryan, Michael G. '66 (SEA) Seattle, WA St. James Cathedral; [P] Seattle, WA Fulcrum Foundation; Seattle, WA St. Peter.
Ryan, Michael J. '72 (PH) Oreland, PA Holy Martyrs.
Ryan, Michael J. '68 (SEA) Retired.
Ryan, Milton F. *c.m.* '91 (STL) Perryville, MO St. Vincent De Paul.
Ryan, Patrick J. *s.j.* '59 (BO)[U] Weston, MA Campion Health Center, Inc.
Ryan, Patrick J. *s.j.* '68 (NY)[EE] Cardinal Spellman Hall, Jesuit Community.
Ryan, Patrick '70 (STL) St. Charles, MO St. Robert Bellarmine.
Ryan, Rev. Msgr. Paul T. '58 (BO) Senior Priests.; Norwood, MA St. Catherine of Siena Retired.
Ryan, Paul *s.m.* '45 (SAT)[K] San Antonio, TX Marianist Residence: Skilled Nursing.
Ryan, Peter F. *s.j.* '87 (BAL)[A] Emmitsburg, MD Mount St. Mary's Seminary; [S] Baltimore, MD Jesuit Community of Loyola University, Inc.
Ryan, Philip V. '57 (DAV) Brooklyn, IA St. Patrick Retired.
Ryan, Philip '57 (SR) Retired.
Ryan, Raymond R. *o.s.a.* '57 (JOL)[L] New Lenox, IL Augustinian Friary; [C] New Lenox, IL Providence Catholic High School.
Ryan, Regis J. '66 (PIT) McKees Rocks, PA St. John of God.
Ryan, Rev. Msgr. Richard J. '73 (STO) Stockton, CA St. Michael Church of Stockton (Pastor of); Vicar General; Vice–Officialis; College of Consultors/Presbyteral Council; Diocesan Building Committee; Diocesan Finance Council; Personnel Board.
Ryan, Richard R. *c.m.* '69 (DEN)[N] Denver, CO Congregation of the Mission Western Province: De Paul House.
Ryan, Robin *c.p.* '84 (MET)[I] South River Passionist Provincial Office.
Ryan, Robin *c.p.* '84 (CHI)[N] Chicago, IL Passionist Community–CTU; [B] Chicago, IL The Catholic Theological Union at Chicago.
Ryan, Stephen Desmond *o.p.* '93 (WDC)[B] Washington, DC Dominican House of Studies.
Ryan, Stephen M. *o.s.m.* '55 (CHI)[N] Chicago Order of Friar Servants of Mary (Servites) United States of America Province, Inc.
Ryan, Stephen M. '95 (NY) Absent on Sick Leave.
Ryan, Stephen R. *o.s.m.* '55 (P) Cottage Grove, OR Our Lady of Perpetual Help.
Ryan, Steve *s.d.b.* '92 (NEW)[M] South Orange, NJ Salesian Office of Youth Ministry & Vocations; [R] Offices of Vocation and Youth Ministry; [M] South Orange, NJ Don Bosco Vocation Office.
Ryan, Rev. Msgr. T. Peter '62 (RVC) Centerport, NY Our Lady Queen of Martyrs; Huntington Deanery.
Ryan, Terrance '77 (SFR) San Francisco, CA Old St. Mary's Cathedral.
Ryan, Thomas A. '64 (GI) Defender of the Bond; Schools; Ord, NE Our Lady of Perpetual Help.
Ryan, Thomas F. '93 (MET) Sayreville, NJ Our Lady of Victories.
Ryan, Thomas J. '79 (SY) Priests' Personnel Committee; Fayetteville, NY Immaculate Conception.
Ryan, Thomas '73 (BAL) Special Assignment; [U] Baltimore, MD Johns Hopkins University.
Ryan, Thomas *c.s.p.* '75 (WDC)[B] Washington, DC St. Paul's College.
Ryan, Rev. Msgr. Timothy A. '57 (CAM) Cape May, NJ The Church of Our Lady Star of the Sea, Cape May Retired.
Ryan, Timothy K. '62 (SAV) Special Assignment.
Ryan, William A. *o.s.a.* '66 (P) Myrtle Creek, OR All Souls; [L] Myrtle Creek, OR Augustinian Community.
Ryan, William A. '59 (PEO) Retired.
Ryan, William F. '62 (CAM) Cape May Court House, NJ Retired.
Ryan, William F. *s.j.* '62 (SPK)[B] Spokane, WA Gonzaga University.
Ryan, Rev. Msgr. William H. '48 (ELP) El Paso, TX Immaculate Conception Retired.
Ryan, William P. *s.j.* '94 (BAL)[S] Towson, MD Maryland Province of the Society of Jesus; Towson, MD; [S] Baltimore, MD Colombiere Jesuit Community.
Ryan, William '55 (JOL) Retired.
Ryan, William '68 (STO) Absent on Leave.
Ryba, Charles J. '69 (CLV) Columbia Station, OH St. Elizabeth Ann Seton; Grafton Correctional Institution; Lorain, OH Lorain Correctional Institution.
Rybansky, Eugene '00 (CHI) Tinley Park, IL St. George.
Rybarczyk, Melvin *c.r.* '69 (VNN) Sherman Oaks, CA Cathedral of St. Mary.
Rybchuk, Bogdan (STN) Warren, MI St. Vladimir's.
Ryberg, James C. '57 (OM) Retired.
Rybicki, Daryl '79 (FTW) South Bend, IN Corpus Christi.
Rybicki, David G. '09 (LC) Durand, WI St. Mary's Assumption; Durand, WI Holy Rosary; Durand, WI Sacred Heart of Jesus.
Rybicky, Walter *o.s.b.m.* '83 (STN) Warren, MI St. Josaphat.
Rybolt, John E. *c.m.* '67 (CHI)[N] Chicago, IL DePaul Vincentian Residence.
Rydelek, Rev. Msgr. Theodore F. '89 (TYL) Buffalo, TX Blessed Kateri Tekakwitha Church.
Ryder, Joseph F. '46 (DET) Retired.
Rydzon, Walter G. '73 (PIT) Pittsburgh, PA St. Justin; Allegheny County, PA Depaul Institution; Disabilities, Dept. for Persons with.
Rye, Gary *o.s.a.* '65 (CHI)[N] Chicago, IL St. Augustine Friary.
Rykowski, Jerome A. '55 (PBL) Grand Junction, CO Retired.
Rykwalder, David L. '85 (GI) Bridgeport, NE All Souls.
Ryland, Raymond '83 (SD) Retired.
Rymdeika, Joseph F. '82 (PH) Horsham, PA St. Catherine of Siena.
Rynda, Reynold *o.f.m.cap.* '54 (PIT)[M] Allison Park, PA St. Conrad Friary.
Rynes, Theodore J. *s.j.* '62 (SJ)[B] Santa Clara, CA Jesuit Community.
Rynne, Thomas J. '56 (PMB) Jensen Beach, FL St. Martin de Porres Retired.
Ryscavage, Richard J. *s.j.* '77 (BGP)[B] Fairfield, CT Fairfield University; [O] Fairfield, CT The Fairfield Jesuit Community–Fairfield University.
Ryu, Hyong–Nyol *s.j.* (ATL) Doraville, GA Korean Martyrs Catholic Church.
Rywalt, Lawrence *c.p.* '92 (MET)[I] South River Passionist Provincial Office; South River, NJ St. Paul of the Cross Province.
Rywalt, Lawrence *c.p.* '92 (BRK)[T] Jamaica, NY Immaculate Conception Monastery.
Rzadca, Janusz '95 (PAT)[C] Paterson, NJ Paterson Catholic Regional High School; Paterson, NJ Our Lady of Victories.
Rzasowski, Jerzy '85 (MO) Army Chaplains.
Rzeczkowski, Eugene M. *o.p.* '69 (WDC)[B] Washington, DC Dominican House of Studies.
Rzepiela, Thomas R. '72 (CHI) Palatine, IL St. Thomas of Villanova.
Rzeszutek, Martin *m.i.c.* '51 (SPR)[H] Stockbridge, MA Congregation of Marian Fathers of The Immaculate Conception of the Most Blessed Virgin Mary.
Rzonca, Michael W. '73 (PH) Phoenixville, PA Holy Trinity; Phoenixville, PA Sacred Heart.

S

Sa, Dominic Phan '88 (PT) Pensacola, FL St. Mary.
Saad, Hector Vazquez '08 (ORL) Kissimmee, FL Holy Redeemer.
Saad, Chorbishop Richard D. '72 (OLL) Spiritual Director for the National Apostolate of Maronites.
Saad, Chorbishop Richard D. '72 (OLL) Birmingham, AL St. Elias Maronite Catholic Church; Birmingham, AL Maronite Catholic Community of Louisiana; St. Louis, MO St. Sharbel Maronite Catholic Mission; College of Consultors; Office of Communications; Presbyteral Council; Protopresbyters; Personnel Board; Board of Pastors; Advisor for Priests.
Saade, Bassam '92 (SAM) Orlando, FL St. Jude; Presbyteral Council.
Saade, Elie '06 (PH)[B] Springfield, PA Servants of Charity.
Saah–Buckman, Michael *s.s.j.* (NO) New Orleans, LA All Saints.
Saale, Richard T. '50 (KC) Retired.
Saato, Fred '67 (NTN) Leave of Absence.
Saavedra, Joven S. *d.s.* '99 (GAL) Houston, TX St. Matthew the Evangelist.
Saavedra, Joven Vincent Romuald *d.s.* '99 (GAL)[O] Houston, TX St. Matthew the Evangelist.
Saavedra, Ramon '96 (MO) DEPARTMENT OF VETERANS AFFAIRS HOSPITALS AND CHAPLAINS.
Saawuan, Stephen '03 (WDC)[B] Washington, DC St. Joseph's Seminary.
Saba, Joseph J. '70 (BGP) Retired.
Saba, Joseph '74 (JUN) On Duty Outside the Diocese.
Saba, Joseph '74 (TUC) Tucson, AZ St. Mary's Hospital; [C] Tucson, AZ Carondelet St. Mary's Hospital.
Saban, Michael J. '89 (PH) Norristown, PA Visitation B.V.M.
Sabando, Manuel '92 (DAL) Mesquite, TX Divine Mercy of Our Lord.
Sabariar, Thobias *m.c.* '92 (LEX) Lancaster, KY St. William; Lancaster, KY St. Sylvester.
Sabatini, Francis J. '63 (PH) Philadelphia, PA St. Lucy.
Sabatino, Rev. Msgr. Robert '56 (Y) Retired.
Sabatos, Daniel C. '62 (BRK) Retired.
Sabatté, Frank *c.s.p.* '80 (NY)[EE] New York, NY Paulist Fathers' Motherhouse.
Sabbagh, Stephen F. *o.f.m.* '59 (WDC)[N] Washington, DC Franciscan Monastery USA Inc.; Washington, DC Retired.
Sabel, David '09 (PEO) Pontiac, IL St. Mary's.
Sabella, Charles A. '94 (MET) Somerville, NJ Immaculate Conception.
Sabia, Rev. Msgr. John B. '64 (BGP) Monroe, CT St. Jude.
Sabio, Generoso *m.s.c.* (SB) Riverside, CA St. Catherine of Alexandria.
Sabio, Lennard '97 (RVC) Farmingdale, NY St. Kilian.
Sabio, Rev. Msgr. Raymundo T. *m.s.c.* (MI) Majuro, MH.
Sabio, Rev. Msgr. Raymundo T. *m.s.c.* '71 (MI) Cathedral of the Assumption; Majuro, MH Outer Island Parish; Vocations.
Sable, Rev. Msgr. Robert M. '74 (DET) On Duty Outside the Archdiocese.
Sable, Thomas F. *s.j.* '75 (SCR)[C] Scranton, PA The University of Scranton.
Sabo, Edward J. *t.o.r.* '68 (ALT) Altoona, PA Our Lady of Mt. Carmel; [E] Altoona, PA Altoona Regional Health System – Bon Secours Hospital Campus; Altoona, PA Altoona Hospital Campus; Catholic Chaplaincy Ministry.
Sabo, Gerald J. *s.j.* '80 (CLV)[B] University Heights, OH John Carroll Jesuit Community.
Sabo, Paul P. '69 (BUF) Council of Catholic Men; Holy Name Society; Adjunct Judicial Vicar; Judges; Eggertsville, NY St. Benedict.
Sabo, Steven M. '03 (RCK) Wonder Lake, IL Christ the King.
Sabog, Henry '60 (HON) Retired.
Sabourin, Rev. Msgr. Gerard O. '60 (PRO) Exeter, RI Blessed Kateri Tekakwitha Catholic Community;

Handicapped Persons Apostolate; Eleanor Slater Hospital.
Sabourin, Leo F. '58 (DET) Taylor, MI St. Constance.
Saburo, Rusk R. '93 (CI) Palau, PW Sacred Heart; [C] Manresa Jesuit House.
Saburo, Rusk '88 (CI) Diocesan Consultors; Palau; Defenders of the Bond.
Sacca, Raymond '79 (OAK) Clergy Services; Deacon Council; Alameda, CA St. Joseph Basilica; Ex Officio.
Saccacio, Rev. Msgr. Robert J. '61 (RVC) Retired.
Sacco, Carmine J. *s.j.* '57 (SEA) Tacoma, WA St. Rita of Cascia.
Saccoccia, Todd C. '02 (RVC) Mastic Beach, NY St. Jude.
Sachs, John R. *s.j.* '76 (BO)[U] Cambridge, MA La Farge House.
Sackevich, Paul '84 (BUR) Barre, VT St. Monica.
Sacks, Rev. Msgr. Edward R. '64 (ALN) Bethlehem, PA Our Lady of Perpetual Help; Elected Members.
Sacks, Francis W. *c.m.* '67 (MET)[I] Princeton, NJ Vincentian Residence.
Sacksteder, Rev. Msgr. Thomas B. '73 (COV) Florence, KY St. Paul.
Sacus, Rev. Msgr. Samuel S. '66 (WH) Beckley, WV St. Francis De Sales; Diocesan Consultors; Vicars Forane.
Sada, Luis *ss.cc.* '60 (SJN) Guaynabo, PR Sagrados Corazones.
Sadek, Rev. Msgr. Ignace '57 (SAM)[A] Washington, DC Our Lady of Lebanon Maronite Seminary Retired.
Sadie, Rev. Msgr. P. Edward '57 (WH) Charleston, WV Basilica of the Co–Cathedral of the Sacred Heart; Diocesan Consultors; Vicars Forane; Catholic Conference of West Virginia; Director.
Sadlack, Robert J. '70 (BRK) East Elmhurst, NY St. Gabriel.
Sadlowski, Ronald F. '72 (SPR) Russell, MA Holy Family Parish; Huntington, MA St. Thomas; Russell, MA Our Lady of the Rosary.
Sadowski, Izydor *s.d.b.* (NOR)[H] Putnam, CT Matulaitis Nursing Home Inc.
Sadowski, Marek *c.m.* '94 (HRT) New Haven, CT St. Stanislaus.
Sadowsky, James A. *s.j.* '57 (NY)[EE] Loyola Hall, Jesuit Community.
Sadusky, Rev. Msgr. Joseph F. '70 (WDC) Washington, DC St. Peter; Pastoral Center Special Ministries; Judicial Vicar.
Saeed, Rev. Msgr. Chorbishop Saeed D. '98 (SPA) Chancellor; Director of Finance; Judicial Officer; Glendale, AZ Holy Family Mission.
Saelzler, Richard J. '76 (TOL)[J] Toledo, OH Ursuline Convent of the Sacred Heart.
Saena, Poao '93 (SEA) Tacoma, WA St. Ann; Tacoma, WA St. John of the Woods; Tacoma, WA Sacred Heart; Samoan, Ministry to; Tacoma, WA Holy Rosary; Tacoma, WA St. Joseph; Tacoma, WA Visitation.
Saengthien, Peter P. *s.j.* '06 (STL)[O] St. Louis, MO St. Matthew Jesuit Community.
Saenz, Alonso '97 (PHX) Phoenix, AZ St. Catherine of Siena Roman Catholic Parish.
Saenz, Christopher *s.s.c.* '00 (FgM) St Columbans, NE House of Post–Graduate Studies.
Saenz, David (CC)[D] Corpus Christi, TX CHRISTUS Spohn Hospital Corpus Christi – Shoreline; [D] Corpus Christi, TX CHRISTUS Spohn Hospital Corpus Christi – Memorial.
Saenz, Jorge L. '03 (MIA) On Duty Outside the Archdiocese.
Saenz, José '04 (DEN) Carbondale, CO St. Vincent de Paul.
Saenz, Nester (CHI) Chicago, IL Our Lady of Fatima.
Saenz, Roberto B. *s.j.* '57 (SPK)[J] Spokane, WA Regis Community Retired.
Saenz, Urbano *o.s.a.* '70 (MGZ) San German, PR St. Rose of Lima.
Saenz Ramos, Jorge (SJN) Dorado, PR San Antonio de Padua.
Saez, Solh '67 (DAL) Dallas, TX St. Augustine Catholic Church.
Saez Munoz, Raul '82 (SJN) Toa Alta, PR San Esteban, Protomartir.
Saffirio, John *i.m.c.* '65 (MET)[I] Somerset, NJ Consolata Society for Foreign Missions.
Safiejko, Edward M. '48 (MIL) Retired.
Safko, Gerard F. '90 (SCR) Montrose, PA Holy Name of Mary.
Safko, Steven '73 (PSC) Phillipsburg, NJ SS. Peter and Paul; Retirement Plan Board.
Safranek, William J. '96 (OM) Beemer, NE Holy Cross; Wisner, NE St. Joseph; [N] Ewing, NE St. Theresa Church of Clearwater Cemetery Endowment Trust Fund.
Safraniec, Joseph N. '76 (MO) On Duty Outside the Diocese; Air Force Reserve Chaplains.
Sagardia, Reinaldo '79 (SJN) San Juan, PR Nuestra Senora de Belen.
Sagardoy, Angel '60 (LA) Retired.
Sagayam, Andrew '02 (RIC) Richmond, VA St. Elizabeth.
Saglio, Charles A. '74 (RIC) Franklin, VA St. Jude.
Sagorski, Peter A. '95 (ORL) Wildwood, FL St. Vincent de Paul.
Sagra, Rev. Msgr. Andrés '65 (DAL) Dallas, TX Mary Immaculate.
Saguto, Gerard *f.s.s.p.* (SEA) Seattle, WA North American Martyrs Personal Quasi–Parish.
Saharic, Michael C. '88 (MET) Hampton, NJ St. Ann.
Sahd, Christopher S. '01 (SCR) Eynon, PA St. Mary of Czestochowa; Archbald, PA St. Thomas Aquinas.
Sahuc, Allan Fredrick *c.m.f.* '07 (CHI)[N] Oak Park Claretian Missionaries USA Eastern Province.
Saint Jean, Kidney M. '92 (MIA) North Lauderdale, FL Our Lady Queen of Heaven.
Saint Martin, Jeremy P. (BO) Newton, MA Sacred Heart.
Saint Pierre, Ronald L. '83 (BO) Tyngsborough, MA St. Mary Magdalen.
Sajda, Michael *o.f.m.conv.* '79 (BUF)[O] Athol Springs, NY St. Francis of Assisi Friary; [D] Athol Springs, NY St. Francis High School.
Sajdak, John *s.m.* '71 (DET)[K] Livonia, MI Marist Fathers & Brothers Community.
Sajdak, Ronald P. '96 (BUF) Peace and Justice (Diocesan Commission); Buffalo, NY St. Martin de Porres; Clergy Personnel Board.
Sajgo, Szabolcs *s.j.* '74 (ATH) Hungarian Priests' Association in Canada.
Sakano, Rev. Msgr. Donald '71 (NY) New York, NY St. Patrick's Old Cathedral; [II] New York, NY The Housing Fund of the Archdiocese of New York.
Sakowicz, Gregory '79 (CHI) Chicago, IL St. Mary of the Woods.
Sakowski, Derek '03 (LC) On Duty Outside the Diocese.
Sakowski, John J. '05 (SFR) San Carlos, CA St. Charles.
Sala, Manuel I. (PCE) Guayama, PR SS. Peter and Paul.
Sala, Michael J. *s.j.* '77 (NY) Metropolitan Hospital; [EE] New York, NY St. Ignatius Loyola Residence.
Salach, Conrad *o.f.m.conv.* '71 (BO) Amesbury, MA Holy Family.
Salada, Urbano '59 (SD) Retired.
Saladna, George E. '58 (PIT) Springdale, PA St. Alphonsus.
Salah, Michael A. '91 (WDC) Forestville, MD Mt. Calvary; Silver Spring, MD St. Catherine Laboure; Priest Council; Archdiocesan College of Consultors.
Salamon, John *c.ss.r.* '45 (ALB)[L] Saratoga Springs, NY St. John Neumann Residence.
Salamone, Charles E. '75 (BO)[O] Brighton, MA Caritas St. Elizabeth's Medical Center of Boston, Inc.
Salamoni, Vincent *m.s.a.* '84 (MO) Navy Chaplains.
Salamoni, Vincent *m.s.a.* '84 (NOR)[G] Cromwell Society of the Missionaries of the Holy Apostles.
Salanga, Victor *s.j.* '74 (NY)[EE] Loyola Hall, Jesuit Community.
Salanitro, Alfred J. '89 (OM) Bellevue, NE St. Bernadette; Deans; Deans.
Salanitro, Carl A. '70 (OM) Omaha, NE Holy Cross.
Salapata, Andrzej *s.ch.* '97 (SJ) San Jose, CA St. Brother Albert Chmielowski Polish Catholic Pastoral Mission.
Salas, Raul *o.m.i.* '80 (SAT)[B] San Antonio, TX George Sexton House of Studies.
Salas, Rev. Msgr. Sipio '50 (SFE) Retired.
Salatino, John C. '94 (SPR) Pittsfield, MA St. Mark's; [N] Pittsfield, MA Berkshire Community College.
Salazar, Rev. Msgr. Alejandro '91 (LAR) Laredo, TX San Martin de Porres; Laredo, TX Santa Teresita Mission.
Salazar, Cesar '93 (ORG) Administrative Leave.
Salazar, Donald *o.f.m.* '67 (FgM) New York, NY Franciscan Province of the Immaculate Conception.
Salazar, Edward '74 (ATL)[I] Atlanta, GA Ignatius House.
Salazar, Enrique '08 (DEN) Aurora, CO Queen of Peace.
Salazar, Eusebio C. Fernandez '71 (SJN) San Juan, PR Santa Catalina Laboure.
Salazar, Franklin '75 (ORL) Lakeland, FL St. Joseph's; Lakeland, FL St. Anthony Catholic Church.
Salazar, George '67 (SFE) LAS VEGAS: Newman Center; State Hospital; Las Vegas, NM Immaculate Conception.
Salazar, Jose A. (NY) Manhattan, NY U.S.V.A. Medical Center; New York, NY New York City Veterans Administration Hospital.
Salazar, Jose *m.s.a.* '77 (NOR)[G] Cromwell Society of the Missionaries of the Holy Apostles.
Salazar, Jose '85 (CC)[A] Houston, TX St. Mary's Seminary; On Duty Outside the Diocese.
Salazar, Jose Luis S. *s.j.* '01 (NEW)[M] Jersey City, NJ Jesuits of Saint Peter's College, Inc.; [B] Jersey City, NJ Jesuit Center.
Salazar, Marco Antonio '06 (AMA) Dumas, TX SS. Peter and Paul.
Salazar, Mario A. '61 (YAK) Quincy, WA St. Pius X; Vicar for Priests; Clergy Personnel Board.
Salazar, Mario P. '90 (YAK) Granger, WA Our Lady of Guadalupe.
Salazar, Rev. Msgr. Ralph C. '69 (GAL) Houston, TX St. Christopher.
Salazar, Thomas *l.c.* '01 (SAT)[G] San Antonio, TX Rolling Hills Academy, Inc.; [S] San Antonio, TX San Antonio Rolling Hills, Inc.
Salazar Castano, Jairo (SJN) Toa Baja, PR San Pedro Apostol.
Salberg, James G. '69 (PIT) Butler, PA St. Andrew.
Salca, Louis '65 (SD) Retired.
Salcedo, Luis G. '89 (WDC) Retired.
Salcedo, Osiris *s.d.b.* (NY) New York, NY St. Elizabeth.
Salcedo, Reginaldo '89 (SAG) Saginaw, MI SS. Casimir & St. George; Bay City, MI Our Lady of Guadalupe.
Saldana, Jesus '82 (MIA) Miami, FL St. Kevin.
Saldana, Luis F. '99 (NY)[A] Yonkers, NY Cathedral Prep Program; [A] Yonkers, NY St. John Neumann Seminary College At St. Joseph's Seminary Dunwoodie; [A] Yonkers, NY St. Joseph's Seminary.
Saldana, Wilson (BAL) Baltimore, MD St. Gabriel.
Saldana–Taneco, Ermeregildo *s.t.* '94 (TUC)[H] South Tucson, AZ Blessed Kateri Tekakwitha Parish Center; Tucson, AZ Blessed Kateri Tekakwitha Roman Catholic Missions Parish – Tucson.
Saldanha, Reginald '97 (KCK) Osawatomie, KS Our Lady of Lourdes; Osawatomie, KS Sacred Heart Shrine to St. Philippine Duchesne; Osawatomie, KS St. Philip Neri.
Saldarriaga, Reinaldo A. (BRK) Flushing, NY St. Michael; Diocesan Judges; Richmond Hill, NY Holy Child Jesus.
Salditos, Henry '89 (LAV) Las Vegas, NV St. James the Apostle.
Salditos, Rey '83 (LAV) Las Vegas, NV Our Lady of Las Vegas; Hospital Apostolate.
Salditos, Ricardito P. '80 (MO) Air Force Chaplains.
Saldivar, Roberto *m.sp.s.* '00 (LA) Oxnard, CA Our Lady of Guadalupe Parish.
Saldua, Max Ernesto M. '78 (MO) DEPARTMENT OF VETERANS AFFAIRS HOSPITALS AND CHAPLAINS.
Saldua, Max '78 (LA) West Los Angeles, CA Chaplain Service.
Salemi, Rev. Msgr. Cajetan P. '61 (NEW) Woodcliff Lake, NJ Our Lady Mother of the Church Retired.
Salemi, Paul S. '00 (BUF) Williamsville, NY St. Gregory the Great.
Salen, Enrique V. *d.s.* '90 (GAL)[S] Houston, TX The Catholic Chaplain Corps; [O] Houston, TX Disciples of Hope (Texas).
Salera, Alfredo J. '77 (CHI) Glenview, IL St. Catherine Laboure.
Salerno, Emilio J. '59 (BRK) Retired.
Salerno, Joseph A. '65 (CAM) Millville, NJ The Church of Saint Mary Magdalen, Millville; Judges; Adjutant Judicial Vicars.
Salerno, Joseph A. '80 (SY) Utica, NY Our Lady of Lourdes; Eastern Area Vicars; Pastoral Examiners; Presbyteral Council; Priests' Personnel Committee; Board of Diocesan Consultors.
Sales, Kenneth '04 (OAK) Hayward, CA St. Clement.
Saletrik, E. George '96 (GBG) Scottdale, PA St. John the Baptist; Diocesan Catholic Scoutmaster.
Salgado, Gerardo Francisco '99 (ELP) El Paso, TX Our Lady of Guadalupe.
Salgado, Manuel E. *o.ss.t.* (ARE) Isabela, PR St. Anthony.
Saliba, John A. *s.j.* '65 (DET)[K] Detroit, MI Jesuit Community at the University of Detroit Mercy.
Salicone, Aniello *s.x.* '66 (CHI) Chicago, IL St. Therese Catholic Chinese Church.
Saliga, Christopher M. *o.p.* '05 (Y) Youngstown, OH St. Dominic; Walsh University; [B] North Canton, OH Walsh University.
Saligumba, Carlos *s.o.l.t.* '91 (KC) Kansas City, MO St. Louis.
Salim, Anthony J. (SAM) Brockton, MA St. Theresa.
Salim, Anthony '74 (OLL) Special Assignment.
Salinas, Andres '93 (RCK) Aurora, IL St. Nicholas.
Salinas, Octavio *o.f.m.* (BRK) Brooklyn, NY Our Lady of Peace.
Salinas, Romeo (CC) Kingsville, TX St. Joseph.
Salisbury, Keith R. '06 (NU) Henderson, MN St. John–Assumption; Henderson, MN St. Joseph; Henderson, MN St. Thomas (Oratory); Priests' Council.
Salisbury, Paschal D. *o.p.* '67 (SFR)[N] San Francisco, CA St. Dominic Priory; San Francisco, CA St. Dominic.
Salko, John H. '60 (PBR) Scottdale, PA St. John the Baptist; Protopresbyters.
Salkovski, Basil *o.s.b.m.* '88 (STN) Presbyteral Council.
Salkovski, Varcilio Basil *o.s.b.m.* '88 (STN) Palos Park, IL Nativity of B.V.M.; Diocesan Consultors; Chicago.
Saller, Neil *t.o.r.* '56 (PH)[Y] Fairless Hills, PA St. Anthony Friary.
Sallese, Albert J. '66 (BO) Senior Priests.; Bellingham, MA St. Blaise Retired.
Sallis, Steven '80 (SEA) Seattle, WA St. Benedict; Presbyteral Council; Seattle, WA St. Anne; College of Consultors.
Sallot, Steven '80 (ORG) Dana Point, CA San Felipe de Jesus; Dana Point, CA St. Edward the Confessor;

Membership; Consultors; Council of Priests.
Salmani, Frank S. '82 (PRO) Warwick, RI St. William; [U] Warwick, RI.
Salmi, Richard P. *s.j.* '82 (MOB)[A] Mobile, AL Spring Hill College.
Salmon, Edward F. *s.j.* '85 (NY)[EE] New York, NY "America;" Residence and publication office of the America Press; [F] New York, NY Regis High School.
Salmon, Edward P. '59 (CHI) Oak Park, IL St. Giles Retired.
Salmon, James F. *s.j.* '64 (BAL)[B] Timonium, MD Loyola Graduate Center–Timonium Campus; [S] Baltimore, MD Jesuit Community of Loyola University, Inc.; [B] Jesuit Community of Loyola University, Inc.
Salmon, William F. '65 (BO) Weymouth, MA Immaculate Conception.
Salmonowicz, Philip P. '03 (GR) Greenville, MI St. Charles Borromeo.
Salnicky, Michael '93 (PSC) Pocono Summit, PA St. Nicholas; [C] Cresco, PA Carpathian Village; Saint Nicholas Shrine – Carpathian Village.
Salocks, Stephen E. '80 (BO)[A] Brighton, MA St. John Seminary.
Salois, Philip G. *m.s.* '84 (MO) DEPARTMENT OF VETERANS AFFAIRS HOSPITALS AND CHAPLAINS.
Salois, Philip *m.s.* (BO) Pastoral Care.
Salomon, Elias M. '79 (SFR) San Francisco, CA St. Elizabeth.
Salomon, Victor '98 (WDC)[B] Washington, DC Diocesan Laborer Priests, House of Studies.
Salomone, Gregory R. *o.p.* '72 (WDC) Washington, DC St. Dominic Church & Priory.
Salomone, Ramon A. *s.j.* '65 (NY) New York, NY Society of Jesus; [EE] New York, NY Society of Jesus, New York Province; [EE] New York, NY St. Ignatius Loyola Residence.
Saloy, Lee John '72 (NO) Metairie, LA St. Philip Neri; Defenders of the Bond.
Saloy, Thomas '88 (RVC) Unassigned.
Saltar, William '08 (MGZ) Mayaguez, PR Our Lady of Mt. Carmel.
Saltarin, Jose '67 (NEW) Jersey City, NJ St. Anne's.
Salter, Bartholomew *c.s.c.* '71 (MAN) Catholic Medical Center; Manchester, NH St. Joseph Cathedral.
Salus, Jude S. *o.s.b.* '75 (PAT) Cedar Knolls, NJ Notre Dame of Mt. Carmel; [N] Morristown St. Mary's Abbey; Deans; Presbyteral Council.
Salvador, Cruz Buitrago (CHI) Northlake, IL St. John Vianney, Cure of Ars.
Salvador, Stephen B. '74 (FR) Fall River, MA SS. Peter and Paul; Irving, TX National Catholic Committee on Scouting Executive Committee (1934).
Salvagna, Michael J. *c.p.* '69 (NY)[EE] Pelham Manor, NY St. Vincent's Residence.
Salvagna, Michael *c.p.* '69 (SCR) Scranton, PA St. Ann's Basilica Parish; [R] Scranton, PA Saint Ann's Media, Inc.
Salvagna, Michael *c.p.* '69 (SCR)[M] Scranton, PA Saint Ann's Passionist Monastery.
Salvas, John *o.f.m.cap.* '88 (CHL) Hendersonville, NC Immaculate Conception.
Salvatori, Chris *s.a.c.* '99 (NY) Yonkers, NY Our Lady of Mt. Carmel.
Salvi, Americo *c.r.m.* '55 (NEW) Lodi, NJ St. Joseph's.
Salwowski, Andrezej '86 (BRK) Ozone Park, NY St. Stanislaus Bishop and Martyr; Ozone Park, NY Nativity of the Blessed Virgin Mary.
Saly, Rev. Msgr. Robert J. '85 (ALT) Dmitri Manor – Priests' Residence – St. Mary's Lane; [F] Hollidaysburg, PA Dmitri Manor Priests' Residence; Duncansville, PA St. Catherine of Siena.
Salz, Marvin C. '64 (DUB) St. Lucas, IA St. Luke; Waucoma, IA St. Mary; Lawler, IA Our Lady of Mt. Carmel; Deans; Protivin, IA St. John Nepomucene; Protivin, IA Assumption of the B.V.M.; Protivin, IA Holy Trinity.
Salzillo, Raphael Mary *o.p.* '09 (SEA) Seattle, WA Blessed Sacrament.
Salzmann, George S. *o.s.f.s.* '77 (BO) Cambridge, MA St. Paul; [AA] Cambridge, MA Harvard Catholic Student Center.
Samaha, Jeffrey F. '78 (WDC) Hospital & Nursing Home Ministries; Forestville, MD Church of the Holy Spirit.
Samaha, Rt. Rev. Victor *b.c.o.* (NTN) Retired.
Samala, Savio J. '89 (GB)[O] Green Bay, WI Society for Faith and Children's Education, Inc.
Samaniego, Eduardo *s.j.* '69 (SJ) San Jose, CA Most Holy Trinity.
Samaniego, Tarsicio *l.c.* (HRT)[B] Cheshire, CT Novitiate of the Legion of Christ.
Samay, Sebastian A. *o.s.b.* '59 (GBG)[G] Latrobe, PA Saint Vincent Archabbey; [G] Latrobe, PA Saint Vincent Archabbey.
Samayoa, Emmanuel G. '89 (ROM) Detroit, MI St. John the Baptist; Formation Council.
Sambor, David R. '78 (SY) Special Assignment.
Sambu, Jean Olivier M. '02 (BWN) Roma, TX Sacred Heart.
Samele, Christopher J. '03 (BGP)[C] Trumbull, CT St. Joseph High School.
Samiano, Marvin '92 (HON) Judicial Vicar and Director of Canonical Affairs; Missionary Coopertive Program.
Sammarco, Bruno S. '08 (NEW) On Duty Outside the Archdiocese.
Sammons, Charles *o.f.m.cap.* '07 (NY) Yonkers, NY Sacred Heart.
Sammut, George '99 (PT) Pensacola, FL Cathedral of the Sacred Heart.
Sammut, Tito '52 (GB) Retired.
Samonie, Jacob '56 (DET) Retired.
Samoylo, Francis J. '01 (NY) Cortlandt Manor, NY St. Columbanus.
Samperi, Charles J. '96 (GAL) Spring, TX St. James the Apostle.
Sampson, Elric '85 (CHI)[N] Chicago, IL St. Peter's Friary.
Sampson, James *s.p.* '65 (SFE)[H] Jemez Springs, NM Our Lady of Lourdes; Albuquerque, NM Annunciation.
Sampson, Kenneth '08 (P) Astoria, OR St. Mary, Star of the Sea.
Samra, Basil '86 (NTN) Akron, OH St. Joseph.
Sams, Ronald W. *s.j.* '59 (BUF) Consultors, College of; Buffalo, NY St. Michael; Council of Priests.
Samsa, Bertin L. *o.f.m.cap.* '56 (GB) Manawa, WI Sacred Heart; Weyauwega, WI SS. Peter and Paul.
Samsa, John Francis *o.f.m.cap.* '61 (GB)[J] Appleton, WI St. Fidelis Friary Retired.
Samson, Arokiaswamy '89 (HBG) Lancaster General Hospital and Lancaster Community Hospital; Lancaster, PA Sacred Heart of Jesus.
Samson, Robert J. '79 (STL) St. Louis, MO St. Gabriel the Archangel.
Samson, Rodrigo S. '75 (NEW) Nutley, NJ Our Lady of Mount Carmel.
Samter, James W. '87 (GB) Retired.
Samuel, Francis A. *o.c.i.* '72 (RVC) Babylon, NY St. Joseph.
Samuels, Reginald Wayne '09 (GAL) Sugar Land, TX St. Laurence.
Samway, Patrick H. *s.j.* '69 (PH)[C] Jesuit Fathers; [Y] Philadelphia, PA St. Alphonsus House; [CC] Philadelphia, PA Apostleship of Prayer.
Samy, Ed '67 (SJ) Sunnyvale, CA St. Martin Retired.
Sana, Yoshia '84 (SPA) Campbell, CA St. Mary Assyrian–Chaldean Parish.
Sanabria, Rafael *c.s.v.* '96 (CHI)[N] Arlington Heights Viatorian Province Center–Clerics of St. Viator.
Sanaghan, John J. '72 (CHI) Chicago, IL St. Matthias.
Sanahuja, Manuel *sch.p.* '67 (LA) Los Angeles, CA Our Lady Help of Christians (Maria Auxiliadora); Hispanic Liturgy and Ministry Coordinator; Ex Officio.
San Andres, Vito '79 (AGN) Dededo, GU Santa Barbara.
Sanches, Joseph A. '70 (ATL) Retired.
Sanchez, Adrian *o.praem.* (ORG) Santa Ana, CA All Adult and Juvenile Jail Facilities; [I] Silverado, CA Norbertine Fathers of Orange Inc.
Sanchez, Albert N. '73 (MO) Air Force Chaplains.
Sanchez, Alejandro '93 (STV) On Duty Outside the Diocese.
Sanchez, Angel '90 (PCE) Villalba, PR Our Lady of Mt. Carmel.
Sanchez, Antero *m.s.c.* '65 (FRS) McFarland, CA St. Elizabeth.
Sanchez, Antonio '90 (MRY) Salinas, CA Christ the King.
Sanchez, Castor G. '61 (TR) Retired.
Sanchez, David '02 (L) Louisville, KY Holy Name; Louisville, KY St. Joseph.
Sanchez, Edgar *m.sp.s.* '97 (SEA) Mill Creek, WA St. Elizabeth Ann Seton.
Sanchez, Esequiel '95 (CHI) Cicero, IL Mary, Queen of Heaven.
Sanchez, Felix '65 (SP) Tampa, FL St. Joseph.
Sánchez, Rev. Msgr. Fernando Benicio Felices '82 (SJN) Trujillo Alto, PR Gruta de Lourdes.
Sanchez, German '90 (LA) Los Angeles, CA St. Sebastian.
Sanchez, Humberto '97 (GAL) Katy, TX St. Bartholomew the Apostle.
Sanchez, James *s.o.l.t.* '01 (CC)[G] Robstown, TX Society of Our Lady of the Most Holy Trinity.
Sanchez, James *s.o.l.t.* '01 (SFE) Mora, NM St. Gertrude.
Sanchez, Jose L. *c.m.f.* '95 (LA)[V] San Gabriel, CA Claretian Missionaries – Western Province, Inc.
Sanchez, Jose M. '58 (GAL)[L] Houston, TX Pope John Paul XXIII Priests' Residence Retired.
Sanchez, Jose '61 (BRK) Corona, NY St. Paul the Apostle.
Sanchez, Juan Luis '84 (MIA) Miami, FL SS. Peter and Paul.
Sanchez, Marcos '09 (B) Rupert, ID St. Nicholas; Burley, ID St. Theresa.
Sanchez, Margarito *s.o.l.t.* '03 (CC)[G] Robstown, TX Society of Our Lady of the Most Holy Trinity.
Sanchez, Miguel Angel '98 (ELP) Vocations & Seminarians.
Sanchez, Nicolas '91 (LA) Santa Clarita, CA Our Lady of Perpetual Help.
Sanchez, Oscar '90 (FAJ) Pastoral Vicar.
Sanchez, Pablo *m.sp.s.* '05 (P) Hillsboro, OR St. Matthew.
Sanchez, Rev. Msgr. Paul R. '71 (BRK) Rego Park, NY Resurrection–Ascension; Queens; Assignment Board.
Sanchez, Rev. Msgr. Paul '71 (BRK) Presbyteral Council.
Sanchez, Prudencio *c.m.* '59 (MGZ) Mayaguez, PR San Vicente.
Sanchez, Raul N. '74 (GLP) On Leave of Absence.
Sanchez, Rev. Msgr. Raul '93 (FRS) Fresno, CA St. John Cathedral; Diocesan Consultors; Personnel Board; Priests' Council; Vicar Urbanis.
Sanchez, Raul '02 (OKL) Guymon, OK St. Peter's.
Sanchez, Ricardo '99 (CHL) Biscoe, NC Our Lady of the Americas.
Sanchez, Rodolfo '01 (DAL) On Duty Outside the Diocese.
Sanchez, Rudolfo '01 (GAL) Houston, TX Blessed Sacrament.
Sanchez, Stephen A. '82 (SFE) Albuquerque, NM Our Lady of Fatima; Lovelace Hospital.
Sanchez, Stephen *o.c.d.* '92 (DAL)[H] Dallas, TX Mount Carmel Center; [J] Dallas, TX Mt. Carmel Center.
Sanchez, Steve '07 (SFE) Vaughn, NM St. Mary; Fort Sumner, NM St. Anthony of Padua.
Sanchez, Steven A. '07 (SFE) Anton Chico, NM San Jose.
Sanchez, Victor '91 (ARE) Manati, PR Our Savior.
Sanchez, William E. '83 (SFE) Albuquerque, NM St. Edwin.
Sanchez–Espinoza, Juan '93 (CHI) Other Assignments.
Sanchez–Lopez, Oscar Alberto '90 (FAJ) Canovanas, PR San Jose.
Sanchez–Maya, Rigoberto '01 (SB) Hesperia, CA Holy Family.
Sanchez–Munoz, Alejandro '66 (MO) Army National Guard Chaplains.
Sanchez Chan, Ramiro V. *c.s.* '03 (LA)[B] Sun Valley, CA Scalabrini House of Discernment (Seminary).
Sanchez Mendoza, Marco Antonio *s.t.* '92 (MOB) Fort Mitchell, AL St. Joseph; Sacramental Ministers.
Sancho, Jesus *o.c.d.* '64 (DAL) Dallas, TX St. Mary of Carmel.
Sancho Piquer, Enrique '50 (PCE) On Duty Outside the Diocese.
Sand, John '55 (SPK) Retired.
Sandberg, Kevin *c.s.c.* '05 (FTW)[H] Notre Dame Congregation of Holy Cross, Indiana Province, Provincial House.
Sandberg, Kevin *c.s.c.* '03 (NY) Bronx, NY Holy Family.
Sandberg, Stuart '68 (NY)[II] White Plains, NY Company of St. Paul; White Plains, NY Company of St. Paul (Lay People and Priests).
Sande, Michael Oduor '07 (CHI) Harvey, IL Ascension–St. Susanna.
Sander, Reginald *o.s.b.* '63 (KC) Tarkio, MO St. Paul the Apostle.
Sander, Timothy *o.s.b.* '41 (P)[L] St. Benedict, OR Mt. Angel Abbey.
Sander, Timothy *o.s.b.* '41 (FBK) Beginning Experience.
Sanderfoot, Brian P. '04 (WDC) Pastoral Center Special Ministries; Adjutant Judicial Vicars.
Sanderfoot, Brian '96 (WDC) Washington, DC St. Patrick.
Sanders, Daniel J. '78 (MIL) Fontana, WI St. Benedict.
Sanders, Dennis *c.r.* '67 (CHI)[N][N] Chicago, IL Provincial Office of the Congregation of the Resurrection.
Sanders, Edwin J. *s.j.* '59 (ALN)[A] Wernersville, PA Jesuit Center–Jesuit Community.
Sanders, Gary *o.s.a.* '75 (SD)[J] Office of the Provincial; [J] San Diego, CA Augustinian Provincialate; [J] San Diego, CA Monica House – Augustinian Community.
Sanders, Rev. Msgr. John C. '73 (BGP)[O] Stamford, CT The Catherine Dennis Keefe Queen of the Clergy Retired Priests' Residence Retired.
Sanders, Joseph P. '61 (ALN)[A] Wernersville, PA Jesuit Center–Jesuit Community.
Sanders, Larry *c.ss.r.* '93 (STL)[B] St. Louis, MO St. John Neumann House.
Sanders, Lawrence *c.ss.r.* '88 (MIL)[S] Oconomowoc, WI The Redemptorist Retreat Center.
Sanders, Patrick B. '90 (NO) On Administrative Leave.
Sanders, Peter C. '84 (MRY)[F] Monterey, CA Oratorian Community–Congregation of the Oratory of Pontifical Right; Monterey, CA.
Sanders, Philip A. '05 (NEW) Bloomfield, NJ Church of St. Thomas the Apostle.
Sanders, William F. '75 (WOR) Worcester, MA Our Lady of the Rosary; Advocates; Deans; Presbyteral Council.
Sandersfeld, Rev. Msgr. John '66 (SJ) Los Altos, CA St. William Retired.
Sanderson, William E. '83 (OM) Omaha, NE St. Francis Assisi; Omaha, NE St. Mary.

Sandhage, Martin J. '86 (LFT) Winamac, IN St. Peter.
Sandi, Rev. Msgr. Thomas P. '73 (NY) Shrub Oak, NY Saint Elizabeth Ann Seton.
Sandman, Greg '80 (MRY)[A] Salinas, CA Christian Brothers Institute of California, Inc.
Sandman, Gregory '80 (MRY) Administrative Committee Priests' Pension Plan; Clergy Personnel Board; Watsonville, CA Our Lady of the Assumption.
Sandmann, Augustus C. *o.s.a.* '47 (PH)[Y] Villanova, PA St. Thomas Monastery.
Sandor, Albert *o.f.m.cap.* '82 (DET)[K] Detroit St. Bonaventure Friary.
Sandor, George *o.f.m.conv.* '72 (SY) Binghamton, NY SS. Cyril and Method; Binghamton, NY Holy Trinity.
Sandoval, Adan '06 (CHI) Orland Park, IL St. Michael.
Sandoval, Clarence J. '87 (SLC) Hyde Park, UT Saint Thomas Aquinas LLC 247.
Sandoval, Francisco *o.a.r.* '04 (NY) Bronx, NY St. John's.
Sandoval, Jairo *o.p.* '08 (NO) New Orleans, LA St. Anthony of Padua.
Sandoval, Lazaro *o.f.m.conv.* '07 (LA) Hermosa Beach, CA Our Lady of Guadalupe.
Sandoval, Luis '74 (SAT) On Leave.
Sandoval, Norberto '05 (MIL) Milwaukee, WI St. Alexander; [H] Milwaukee, WI Holy Wisdom Academy; Milwaukee, WI St. John Kanty; Milwaukee, WI St. Helen.
Sandoval–Manzo, Ismael '03 (CHI) Blue Island, IL St. Benedict.
Sandoz, Robert J. *o.f.m.* (NEW)[C] Newark, NJ Christ the King Preparatory School of Newark, N.J., Corp.; [C] Newark, NJ Christ the King Work Study Program; Jersey City, NJ St. John the Baptist.
Sandrick, Philip *o.s.b.m.* (STF)[E] Locust Valley, NY Provincialate of Basilian Fathers; Religious Communities, Vicar.
Sands, Joseph C. *s.j.* '92 (BAL)[S] Towson Maryland Province of the Society of Jesus.
Sands, Maurice Henry '05 (DET) Taylor, MI St. Alfred; Consultants.
Sandstrom, Philip '62 (NY) On Duty Outside the Archdiocese.
Sandweg, Michael J. '79 (STL) On Medical Leave.
Sanella, Nicholas A. (BO) Presbyteral Council.
San Eufrasio, Angel *o.a.r.* (NEW) Centro Guadalupe.
Sanfelippo, Frank J. '58 (MIL) Retired.
Sanfilippo, David '94 (PHX) Vicar General; College of Consultors; Priest Personnel; Advisory Board for the Continuing Formation of Priests; Priestly Life and Ministry Board; Priests' Placement Board; Office of Ethnic Ministries; Presbyteral Council; Phoenix, AZ St. Martin de Porres Roman Catholic Parish; Phoenix, AZ St. Gregory Roman Catholic Parish.
Sanford, James R. *o.s.f.s.* '86 (TOL) Toledo, OH Immaculate Conception; Toledo, OH SS. Peter and Paul.
Sanford, L. Harold *s.j.* '75 (DET)[K] Clarkston, MI Colombiere Center.
Sanford, Stephen J. *s.j.* '94 (BO)[U] Boston The Society of Jesus of New England–Provincial Offices.
Sanford, Stephen J. *s.j.* '94 (RC) Pine Ridge, SD Sacred Heart; Pine Ridge, SD Holy Rosary; [C] Pine Ridge, SD Jesuit Community of Holy Rosary Mission.
Sang, Francis D. '73 (RVC) Deer Park, NY SS. Cyril and Methodius.
Sang–Ki, Jeong (BIR) Birmingham, AL Korean Catholic Community, St. Luke Hwang.
Sangermano, Rev. Msgr. Charles L. '78 (PH) Norristown, PA Holy Saviour; College of Consultors; [A] Wynnewood, PA Theological Seminary of St. Charles Borromeo, Overbrook.
Sangiovanni, William F. '77 (BGP)[C] Fairfield, CT Notre Dame Catholic High School.
Sankar, Paul (BGP) Norwalk, CT St. Joseph.
Sankoorikal, George S. '71 (BGP) Brookfield, CT St. Marguerite Bourgeoys.
Sankoorikal, Paul L. '59 (LC) Retired.
Sankovitz, Rev. Msgr. John P. '47 (STP) Retired.
Sanks, T. Howland *s.j.* '65 (OAK)[A] Berkeley, CA Jesuit School of Theology at Santa Clara University; [M] Berkeley, CA Jesuit Fathers and Brothers.
San Martin, Francisco J. *s.j.* (MOB) Sacramental Ministers.
San Martin, Javier *s.j.* '71 (MOB)[A] Mobile, AL Spring Hill College.
Sannella, Nicholas A. (BO) Lowell, MA Immaculate Conception.
Sanner, Rev. Msgr. James E. '59 (E) Retired.
San Nicasio, Julian *s.d.b.* (CGS)[C] Aibonito, PR Casa Salesiana de Retiros.
San Nicolas, Jeffrey C. '97 (AGN) Yigo, GU Our Lady of Lourdes; Formation Program for the Permanent Diaconate; Our Lady of Lourdes Parish.
San Nicolas, Jeffrey '97 (AGN) Archdiocesan Presbyteral Council.
Sans, Pablo '53 (BRK) Richmond Hill, NY Our Lady of the Cenacle Retired.
Sans, Theodore R. '59 (L) Louisville, KY St. Margaret Mary Retired.
Sanson, Robert J. '67 (CLV) Strongsville, OH St. Joseph; College of Consultors; Judges in Second Instance.
Sansone, Anthony J. '80 (BRK) Brooklyn, NY Sacred Hearts of Jesus and Mary and St. Stephen.
Sant, Ivan '08 (NEW) Plainfield, NJ St. Mary.
Santa, Michael *o.s.b.* '56 (KCK)[I] Atchison, KS St. Benedict's Abbey Retired.
Santa, Thomas *c.ss.r.* '78 (TUC)[F] Tucson, AZ Redemptorist Society of Arizona Redemptorist Renewal Center.
Santa–Bibiana, Joseph *s.d.b.* '66 (PMB) Belle Glade, FL St. Philip Benizi; Religious; Episcopal Delegates.
Santaballa, Francisco Javier '02 (WDC) Priest Council; Archdiocesan College of Consultors.
Santaballa, Francisco Javier (WDC)[A] Hyattsville, MD Redemptoris Mater Archdiocesan Missionary Seminary.
Santaballa, Javier '02 (WDC) Bethesda, MD Our Lady of Lourdes.
Santa Barbara, Robert L. '90 (MET) New Brunswick, NJ St. Mary of Mount Virgin.
Santa Cruz, Ramon *s.o.l.t.* '99 (SEA) Kirkland, WA St. John Mary Vianney.
Santa Cruz, Ramon *s.o.l.t.* '99 (CC)[G] Robstown, TX Society of Our Lady of the Most Holy Trinity.
Santaella, Esteban '58 (PCE) Mercedita, PR Church of the Resurrection.
Santaliz, Edgardo Sanabria '96 (SJN) San Juan, PR Maria Madre de La Iglesia.
Santamaria, Max '56 (MRY) Retired.
Santamaria, Roberto '98 (NEW)[A] Kearny, NJ Redemptoris Mater Archdiocesan Missionary Seminary.
Santana, Edward '86 (MO) Air National Guard Chaplains; On Duty Outside the Diocese.
Santana, Edward '86 (MIA) Judges.
Santana, Franklin '72 (MGZ) San Antonio, PR San Jose Obrero.
Santana, Ramon '89 (FAJ) Punta Santiago, PR Nuestra Senora del Carmen.
Santana, Sady Nelson '93 (SAT) Poteet, TX St. Philip Benizi.
Santangelo, Christopher *ss.cc.* '99 (FR) New Bedford, MA Our Lady of the Assumption.
Santangelo, Michael A. '95 (TR) Scouting.
Santarosa, Scott *s.j.* '00 (LA) Los Angeles, CA Dolores Mission.
Santeliz, William '07 (PAT) Parsippany, NJ St. Peter the Apostle.
Santen, Thomas J. '70 (STL) Manchester, MO St. Joseph.
Santerre, Richard R. '82 (BO) Senior Priests. Retired.
Santhiyagu, Arockiyasamy *m.s.f.s.* '96 (LAN) Flint, MI St. Michael.
Santiago, Alberto '85 (HT) Larose, LA Our Lady of the Rosary.
Santiago, Florentino F. '78 (HT) Theriot, LA St. Eloi.
Santiago, Jorge *s.d.b.* (CGS)[C] Aibonito, PR Casa Salesiana de Retiros.
Santiago, Jose M. *o.p.* '93 (STP) Minneapolis, MN Holy Rosary.
Santiago, Jose *o.p.* '93 (STL)[B] St. Louis, MO Aquinas Institute of Theology; [O] St. Louis, MO St. Dominic Priory.
Santiago, José A. *o.ss.t.* '93 (SJN) Bayamon, PR Espiritu Santo.
Santiago, Juan José *s.j.* '64 (SJN)[D] San Juan, PR Centro Universitario Catolico; [H] San Juan, PR.
Santiago, Leoncio S. '73 (MO) DEPARTMENT OF VETERANS AFFAIRS HOSPITALS AND CHAPLAINS.
Santiago, Manuel '85 (PCE) Ponce, PR San Jose Obrero; Associate Judicial Vicars.
Santiago, Marc A. '88 (ARE) Vega–Baja, PR Holy Rosary.
Santiago, Samuel '76 (PCE) Ponce, PR Santa Maria Reina; Cursillos de Cristiandad.
Santiago, Xavier S. '94 (NY) Red Hook, NY St. Christopher.
Santich, Jan '90 (CHY) Wheatland, WY St. Patrick's.
Santillanes, Jose Flavio '65 (SFE) Santa Fe, NM N.S. de Guadalupe del Valle de Pojoaque.
Santilli, Francis C. '80 (PRO) Cranston, RI St. Paul.
Santitoro, Francis E. '66 (TR) Toms River, NJ St. Maximilian Kolbe.
Santo, Sergio *o.f.m.* '85 (OAK)[M] Oakland Franciscan Friars (Province of St. Barbara).
Santoalla, Rev. Msgr. Jesús Portomene '57 (SJN) Retired.
Santone, John M. '00 (HRT) Judges; Simsbury, CT St. Mary.
Santor, John E. '65 (E) Erie, PA St. Patrick.
Santora, Alexander M. '82 (NEW) Hoboken, NJ Our Lady of Grace and Saint Joseph Parish.
Santoro, David J. *o.p* '77 (DET)[L] Farmington Hills, MI Monastery of the Blessed Sacrament.
Santoro, Michael C. '80 (NEW) Jersey City, NJ St. John the Baptist; Jersey City, NJ Our Lady of Mt. Carmel.
Santorsola, Albert J. '86 (PH) Broomall, PA St. Pius X.
Santos, Angel M. '77 (ARE) Almirante Sur Station, PR The Blessed Trinity.
Santos, Cesar E. '93 (ARE) Florida, PR Our Lady of Mercy.
Santos, Ferdinand '98 (MIA)[A] Miami, FL St. John Vianney College Seminary.
Santos, Francisco M. '97 (CHK) Saipan, MP San Antonio Parish; Household Leaders; Knights of Columbus; Legion of Mary at San Antonio Parish/ Mother of Perpetual Help Praesidium; Presbyteral Council.
Santos, Rev. Msgr. Francisco Medina '89 (SJN) Guaynabo, PR Buen Pastor; [A] Guaynabo, PR ISTEPA (Instituto Superior de Teologia y Pastoral).
Santos, Gregory *o.c.s.o.* '59 (SLC)[F] Huntsville Abbey of Our Lady of the Holy Trinity of the Order of Cistercians.
Santos, John Richard F. '98 (WIL)[J] Dover, DE Oblate Apostles of the Two Hearts.
Santos, Joseph D. '89 (PRO) Providence, RI Holy Name of Jesus.
Santos, Maximiano *c.m.* '66 (SJN) San Juan, PR Nuestra Senora del Pilar.
Santos, Nicky *s.j.* '00 (SJ)[B] Santa Clara, CA Jesuit Community.
Santos, Raúl '63 (CGS) Barranquitas, PR San Andres Apostol.
Santos, Sergio *o.f.m.* '85 (FgM) Oakland, CA St. Barbara Province.
Santos, Tomas '95 (ARE) Morovis, PR St. Paul Apostle.
Santos–Lecturer, Francisco Medina (PCE)[B] The Pontifical Catholic University of Puerto Rico.
Santos Rodriguez, Tomas '95 (ARE) Priest's Senate (Consejo Presbiteral); Pastoral Vocational Program.
Santre, William *t.o.r.* '61 (ALT) Altoona, PA Our Lady of Mt. Carmel Retired.
Santry, Robert '86 (HON) On Duty Outside the Diocese.
Santucci, Louis '74 (Y) Retired.
Sanvicente, Noel '85 (SJ) San Jose, CA Queen of Apostles.
Sanz, Florentino '65 (SJN) Retired.
Sanz, Jose A. *d.l.p.* '73 (SB)[A] Grand Terrace, CA Blessed Junipero Serra House of Formation; [I] Grand Terrace, CA Diocesan Laborer Priests, DLP; Office of Seminarians; Blessed Junipero Serra House of Formation; Special or Other Diocesan Assignment.
Sanz, Jose *d.l.p.* '73 (WDC) On Duty Outside the Archdiocese.
Sanz, Julian '77 (TUC) Administrative Leave of Absence.
Sapeta, Joseph S. '47 (NEW) Retired.
Saporito, Rev. Msgr. Cosmo G. '54 (BRK) Brooklyn, NY St. Bernadette Retired.
Saporito, Louis R. *s.s.j.* '60 (BAL)[S] Baltimore, MD St. Joseph Society of the Sacred Heart House of Central Administration Retired.
Saporito, Michael A. '92 (NEW) Maplewood, NJ St. Joseph's; South Essex Deanery 18; Elected Members.
Saporito, Peter M. '78 (CAM) Vineland, NJ St. Padre Pio Parish, Vineland, N.J.; Representatives by Deaneries.
Sappenfield, John P. '98 (NSH) Unassigned.
Sappenfield, Mark '08 (NSH) MTSU–Murfreesboro; Murfreesboro, TN St. Rose of Lima.
Saprano, Samuel '71 (STU) Shadyside, OH St. John Vianney; Shadyside, OH St. Mary's.
Sara, Solomon I. *s.j.* '63 (WDC)[N] Washington, DC The Jesuit Community at Georgetown University.
Sara, Solomon I. *s.j.* '63 (BO)[U] Boston The Society of Jesus of New England–Provincial Offices.
Sarauskas, Rev. Msgr. R. George '73 (CHI) Riverside, IL St. Mary; Members.
Sardina, John J. '60 (BUF)[O] Clarence, NY Regional Motherhouse of Brothers of Mercy; [M] Clarence, NY Brothers of Mercy Nursing & Rehabilitation Center; [M] Clarence, NY Brothers of Mercy Sacred Heart Home, Inc.; Cheektowaga, NY Queen of Martyrs.
Sardinas, Juan Carlos (TYL) Daingerfield, TX Our Lady of Fatima.
Sare, Burt '96 (RIC) Staunton, VA St. Francis of Assisi.
Sarge, John S. '73 (SAG) Birch Run, MI Sacred Heart; Bridgeport, MI Assumption of the Blessed Virgin Mary.
Sargent, Anthony G. *o.s.b.* '02 (PAT)[N] Morristown St. Mary's Abbey.
Sargent, Anthony *o.s.b.* '02 (NEW) Linden, NJ St. Elizabeth of Hungary.
Sariego, Francis *o.f.m.cap.* '69 (WIL)[J] Wilmington, DE Capuchin Franciscan Friars, St. Francis Renewal Center; [M] Wilmington, DE St. Francis Renewal Center.
Sariego, Francis *o.f.m.cap.* (PH)[T] Aston, PA Assisi House.
Sarihadduk, Silvaster '98 (BRK) Ridgewood, NY St. Matthias.
Sarjeant, Francis X. *s.j.* '61 (BO)[U] Weston, MA Campion Health Center, Inc.
Sarmiento, Nicanor *o.m.i.* '99 (OAK) Oakland, CA Sacred Heart.
Sarmiento–Diaz, Carlos *o.f.m.* '99 (FgM) New York, NY Holy Name Province.
Sarnecki, Thomas G. '02 (SCR) On Duty Outside the

Diocese; DEPARTMENT OF VETERANS AFFAIRS HOSPITALS AND CHAPLAINS.
Sarnicki, Peter *o.f.m.conv.* '94 (RCK) Rockford, IL St. Stanislaus Kostka.
Sarno, Rev. Msgr. Robert J. '73 (BRK) Released from Diocesan Assignment.
Saroki, Anthony '05 (SD) Finance Council; San Diego, CA Ascension; Priestly Vocations; [A] San Diego, CA St. Francis De Sales Center; Presbyteral Council; Assistant to the Bishop.
Saroyan, Antoine '85 (OLN) Glendale, CA St. Gregory Armenian Catholic Church.
Sarrazin, Edward *o.f.m.* '07 (TUC) Tucson, AZ San Xavier Mission Roman Catholic Parish – Tucson.
Sarrazine, Kenneth J. '62 (FTW) Roanoke, IN St. Catharine; Roanoke, IN St. Joseph.
Sarsfield, Emmett (YAK) Retired.
Sarto, Stephen Joseph *ss.cc.* '06 (FR)[G] Fairhaven National Center of the Enthronement.
Sartorelli, Otto '50 (MAR) Retired.
Sartori, Hector *c.s.* '54 (PMB) Delray Beach, FL Our Lady Queen of Peace.
Sarzynski, Rev. Msgr. Edward W. '79 (ALN)[L] Reading, PA Sacred Heart Convent; [L] Reading, PA St. Joseph Villa.
Sas, Thomas J. '76 (HRT) West Hartford, CT St. Peter Claver; Special and other Archdiocesan Assignment; Office of Ministry Enrichment for Priests; Commission for Priests' Retreats.
Sasin, Jan '77 (NEW) Newark, NJ St. Francis Xavier; North Newark Essex Deanery 19.
Sasmita, Ignatius Hadimulia *s.j.* (BRK)[S] Indonesian Apostolate.
Sasmita, Ignatius *s.j.* '07 (OAK)[M] Berkeley, CA Jesuit Fathers and Brothers.
Saso, Michael '61 (SJ) On Duty Outside the Diocese.
Sass, Pawel '09 (WDC) Gaithersburg, MD St. Martin of Tours.
Sassani, John E. '80 (BO) Newton, MA Our Lady Help of Christians; Spiritual Life; Cursillo.
Sassano, Rock '63 (P) Retired.
Sasse, John '02 (EVN) Fort Branch, IN St. Bernard; Fort Branch, IN Holy Cross; Haubstadt, IN SS. Peter and Paul.
Sasso, Frank M. '73 (CHI) Chicago, IL St. Thaddeus.
Sasso, Joseph M. '58 (ROC) Retired.
Sasway, Rev. Msgr. John R. '62 (ALT) Lilly, PA Our Lady of the Alleghenies.
Satoun, Arbogaste '99 (SCR) West Pittston, PA Immaculate Conception; Pittston, PA Church of the Holy Redeemer.
Sattler, Frederick F. '70 (ALN)[J] Bethlehem, PA Holy Family Villa Retired.
Sattler, Henry *c.ss.r.* '76 (RVC) Bethpage, NY St. Martin of Tours.
Saucci, Ronald R. *m.m.* '65 (FgM) Maryknoll, NY MARYKNOLL.
Sauchelli, James J. '63 (TR) Retired.
Saucier, Thomas *o.p.* '96 (JC) Columbia, MO St. Thomas More Newman Center, University of Missouri; [D] Columbia, MO St. Thomas More Newman Center; Columbia Catholic Hospital Ministry.
Saucier, William Patrick '01 (MOB) Chickasaw, AL St. Thomas the Apostle.
Saudis, Richard B. '55 (CHI) Berwyn, IL St. Odilo; Associate Vicars.
Sauer, Anthony P. *s.j.* '71 (SFR)[E] San Francisco, CA St. Ignatius College Preparatory (Coed); [N] San Francisco, CA Jesuit Community at St. Ignatius College Preparatory.
Sauer, Bonaventure *o.c.d.* '92 (NO)[B] New Orleans, LA St. John of the Cross, Discalced Carmelite House of Studies.
Sauer, Gerard J. '01 (BRK) Woodside, NY St. Sebastian; Pilgrimage Office.
Sauer, James '77 (EVN) Jasper, IN St. Joseph.
Sauer, John M. '85 (WIN) Owatonna, MN Holy Trinity; Owatonna, MN Sacred Heart; Censors of Books and Periodicals; Diocese of Winona Incardination Board; Elected Deanery Representatives.
Sauer, Stephen J. *s.j.* '98 (NO) New Orleans, LA Immaculate Conception.
Sauer, Timothy '76 (SEA) Seattle, WA St. Bridget; Presbyteral Council; College of Consultors.
Sauerbier, Paul *c.m.* (DAL)[J] Dallas, TX Congregation of the Mission, Western Province.
Saulaitis, Antanas *s.j.* '69 (CHI) Lemont, IL Blessed Jurgis Matulaitis Mission; [N] Lemont, IL Baltic Jesuits Advancement Office.
Saumell, Amaro '92 (SB) Needles, CA St. Ann.
Saunders, Allan L. '86 (SPC) Kennett, MO St. Cecilia; Portageville, MO St. Eustachius; Region VIII.
Saunders, Donald E. *s.j.* '84 (NO)[E] New Orleans, LA Jesuit High School.
Saunders, Rev. Msgr. Douglas Wm. '65 (LA) Long Beach, CA St. Maria Goretti.
Saunders, Thomas C. *m.m.* '65 (NY)[EE] Maryknoll Maryknoll Fathers and Brothers Retired.
Saunders, William P. '84 (ARL) Potomac Falls, VA Our Lady of Hope; Deans; Diocesan Consultors.
Sauppe, Timothy J. '92 (PEO) Westville, IL St. Mary's.
Sauriamakkel, Joseph '75 (SYM) Mesquite, TX Knanaya Catholic Mission Dallas/Fortworth.
Sauriol, Mark A. '99 (PRO) Council Members; Woonsocket, RI All Saints Parish.
Sauter, David A. *s.j.* '72 (BAL)[W] Towson, MD Jesuit Educational Association of Maryland, Inc.; [S] Towson, MD Maryland Province of the Society of Jesus.
Sauter, John '85 (GLP) Overgaard, AZ Our Lady of Assumption; Vicars Forane; Presbyteral Council; Alpine, AZ St. Helena.
Sautner, Scott '00 (FAR) Fairmount, ND St. Anthony's Church of Fairmount; Hankinson, ND St. Philip's Church of Hankinson.
Savage, James W. '70 (BO) Cambridge, MA St. Paul.
Savage, Paul J. '57 (PIT) Retired.
Savage, Robert *s.d.b.* '46 (NY)[EE] New Rochelle, NY Salesian Provincial House.
Savage, Roger A. '77 (MIL) Bristol, WI Holy Cross.
Savage, Thomas J. '47 (MAN) Retired.
Savage, Warren J. '79 (SPR) Agawam, MA St. John the Evangelist.
Savaia, Giuseppe '95 (PMB) North Palm Beach, FL St. Clare.
Savandra, Edwin '72 (STP) Madison Lake, MN Immaculate Conception of Marysburg.
Savard, John D. *s.j.* '91 (WOR)[O] Worcester, MA Jesuits of the Holy Cross, Inc.
Savari, Thumma '93 (SCR) Wilkes–Barre, PA St. Aloysius; Wilkes–Barre, PA St. Casimir's.
Savarimathu, Simonraj (BAL)[M] Baltimore, MD St. Agnes HealthCare, Inc.
Savarimuthu, Eugene K. '97 (TR) Hamilton, NJ Our Lady of Sorrows–St. Anthony Parish.
Savarimuthu, Jesuraj '80 (LIN) Alma, NE St. Joseph's.
Savarimuthu, Pancras '80 (TYL) Athens, TX St. Edward Church.
Savary, James '60 (LR) Retired.
Savastano, Rev. Msgr. Anthony J. '56 (RVC)[M] Amityville, NY St. Pius X Residence Retired.
Savchyn, Vasyl '79 (STN) The Colony, TX St. Sophia Ukrainian Catholic Church.
Savela, Erwin M. *c.s.v.* '71 (CHI)[N] Arlington Heights Viatorian Province Center–Clerics of St. Viator.
Savelesky, Michael J. '73 (SPK) Spokane, WA Assumption of the Blessed Virgin Mary; Director of Deacon Formation; Censor Liborum; Members.
Savial, Clarence J. '89 (LAV) Las Vegas, NV St. Joseph, Husband of Mary.
Saviano, Frederick L. '68 (BGP) Pontifical Association of the Holy Childhood; Propagation of the Faith; Weston, CT St. Francis of Assisi.
Savickas, Michael G. '74 (DET) Walled Lake, MI St. William.
Savidge, Peter M. '89 (KC) Holden, MO St. Patrick's.
Savilla, Edmund '77 (SFE) Albuquerque, NM Ascension.
Savilla, Edmund '77 (SFE) Pilgrimage for Vocations.
Savino, Michael A. '82 (CIN) North Bend, OH St. Joseph.
Savino–Gyimah, Joseph '92 (HRT) East Hartford, CT St. Mary.
Savinski, Rev. Msgr. John M. '71 (PH) Morton, PA Our Lady of Perpetual Help.
Savio, John '67 (CHY) Douglas, WY St. James.
Savio, Michael G. '92 (MIL) Mukwonago, WI St. James.
Saviour, Joseph *o.f.m.cap.* '98 (WDC)[B] Washington, DC St. Francis Friary–Capuchin College.
Savitt, Alan F. '73 (PAT) On Duty Outside the Diocese.
Savoie, Johnny '95 (MOB) Monroeville, AL St. Joseph; Monroeville, AL Annunciation; [I] Monroeville, AL Alabama Southern Community College Newman Center.
Savoree, John M. '63 (SFD) Retired.
Savyo, Dominic '99 (TOL) Toledo, OH Christ the King.
Saw, Benjamin '90 (SAL) Logan, KS St. John Parish; Phillipsburg, KS Saints Philip and James Parish; Priests' Continuing Formation Committee.
Sawicki, Gregory *s.d.s.* '86 (SAT) Falls City, TX Holy Trinity; Hobson, TX St. Boniface; In Rural Area; Archdiocesan Presbyteral Council; Priests Personnel Board.
Sawicki, Gregory *s.d.s.* '86 (SAT)[L] Falls City, TX Salvatorian Fathers Community of Texas.
Sawicki, John A. *c.s.sp.* '86 (PIT)[B] Pittsburgh, PA Duquesne University of the Holy Spirit; Councilors:.
Sawicki, Jonathan P. '09 (HBG) Gettysburg, PA St. Francis Xavier's.
Sawicki, Mitchell *o.f.m.conv.* '05 (NOR) Cromwell, CT St. John.
Sawyer, Benjamin S. '09 (WCH) Wichita, KS St. Thomas Aquinas.
Sawyer, Rev. Msgr. Donald J. '74 (OLL) Austin, TX Our Lady's Maronite Parish; Office for Missions.
Sawyer, Lucien A. *o.m.i.* '49 (BO)[U] Lowell, MA St. Eugene House (Residence).
Sawyer, Michael *o.s.b.* '74 (HON)[D] Waialua, HI Benedictine Monastery of Hawaii/Retreat Center; [G] Waialua, HI Benedictine Monastery of Hawaii/ Retreat Center.
Saxon, JaVan '83 (R) Laurinburg, NC St. Mary.
Say, Celestino '58 (VIC) Victoria, TX Our Lady of Lourdes; Judges.
Say, James K. '60 (TOL) Retired.
Sayegh, Rt. Rev. Fouad '79 (NTN) Northlake, IL St. John the Baptist.
Sayer, Robert J. '99 (CHR) Batesburg–Leesville, SC St. John of the Cross; Lexington, SC Corpus Christi.
Sayers, Glen W. *s.d.s.* '97 (BIR) Huntsville, AL St. Mary of the Visitation.
Sayers, James M. '58 (CHI) Retired.
Sayers, Monty '86 (E) Clarion, PA Immaculate Conception.
Sayers, Raymond J. '64 (DET) Retired.
Sayes, Ronald E. '57 (DET) Retired.
Saylor, Brian R. '99 (ALT) Vocation; Altoona, PA St. Rose of Lima; Coupon, PA St. Joseph's; [K] Loretto, PA Office of Vocations.
Saylor, Rev. Msgr. Philip '55 (ALT) Retired.
Sayre, Dismas '08 (OAK) Antioch, CA Most Holy Rosary.
Sayuk, Rev. Msgr. Mitred Thomas A. '74 (SJP) On Leave; Presbyters.
Sazama, Warren J. *s.j.* '77 (MIL)[P] Milwaukee, WI Arrupe House Jesuit Community; [E] Milwaukee, WI Marquette University High School.
Sbordone, Gaetano J. '83 (BRK) Brooklyn, NY St. Frances Cabrini.
Scafidi, William A. *m.ss.a.* '83 (NY) Newburgh, NY St. Mary; Newburgh, NY Sacred Heart.
Scaglione, Paul A. '73 (L) Office of Pastoral Care.
Scagnelli, Peter J. '76 (PRO) Absent on Leave.
Scahill, James J. '74 (SPR) East Longmeadow, MA St. Michael's.
Scala, Thomas A. '73 (HBG) Milton, PA St. Joseph; Consultors, College; Presbyteral Council.
Scales, Donald F. *o.s.b.* '55 (RIC)[K] Richmond, VA Mary Mother of the Church Abbey; Richmond, VA.
Scales, George '88 (FR) Chatham, MA Holy Redeemer.
Scalese, Mark P. *s.j.* '97 (BGP)[B] Fairfield, CT Fairfield University; [O] Fairfield, CT The Fairfield Jesuit Community–Fairfield University.
Scaletty, Thomas F. '63 (WCH) Retired.
Scalf, Kevin *c.pp.s.* '09 (LFT)[A] Rensselaer, IN Saint Joseph's College.
Scalia, Paul D. '96 (ARL) McLean, VA St. John the Beloved.
Scanlan, Rev. Msgr. Edward J. '53 (BUF) Retired.
Scanlan, Francis G. '61 (CHI) Oak Forest, IL St. Damian Retired.
Scanlan, Michael R. (NEW)[C] Newark, NJ Saint Benedict's Preparatory School.
Scanlan, Michael *t.o.r.* '64 (STU)[A] Steubenville, OH Franciscan University of Steubenville; [H] Steubenville, OH Holy Spirit Friary.
Scanlan, Thomas R. '57 (BAK) Retired.
Scanlan, William A. '72 (BO) Permanent Disability.
Scanlin, Joseph T. '89 (HBG) Lebanon, PA St. Cecilia.
Scanlon, Charles *s.v.d.* '54 (CHI)[N] Techny, IL Divine Word Residence.
Scanlon, Edward *o.p.* '59 (SFR) San Francisco, CA St. Dominic.
Scanlon, Francis P. '83 (NY) Bronx, NY St. Ann.
Scanlon, James M. *m.m.* '52 (NY)[EE] Retired.
Scanlon, Michael J. *o.s.a.* '64 (PH)[C] Villanova University; [Y] Villanova, PA St. John Stone Friary.
Scanlon, Paul *o.p.* '59 (SFR)[N] San Francisco, CA St. Dominic Priory.
Scanlon, Peter J. '57 (WOR)[R] Worcester, MA Campus Ministry.
Scanlon, Regis *o.f.m.cap.* '72 (DEN)[N] Denver, CO Capuchin Province of Mid–America, Inc.
Scanlon, Rev. Msgr. Thomas F. '49 (NY) Mt. Vernon, NY SS. Peter and Paul Retired.
Scanlon, Rev. Msgr. Thomas J. '59 (PH) Retired.
Scanlon, William J. *s.j.* '70 (NY)[EE] New York, NY Murray–Weigel Hall.
Scannel, Anthony *o.f.m.cap.* '55 (LA)[F] La Canada Flintridge, CA St. Francis High School of La Canada–Flintridge.
Scannell, Timothy J. '69 (NY) Dobbs Ferry, NY Sacred Heart; Dobbs Ferry, NY Our Lady of Pompeii; [A] Yonkers, NY St. Joseph's Seminary.
Scantlebury, Neil '95 (STV) St. Thomas, VI Holy Family Parish; Chancellor; Diocesan Consultors.
Scantlin, Rev. Msgr. Joseph S. '59 (FWT) Arlington, TX Most Blessed Sacrament; Deans.
Scaramuzzo, Peter C. '66 (NY) West Harrison, NY St. Anthony of Padua.
Scarangella, Joseph A. '92 (NEW) Montclair, NJ Immaculate Conception.
Scarangello, John R. *o.f.m.* '81 (BRK) Brooklyn, NY Our Lady of Peace.
Scaravelli, Volmar *c.s.* '82 (MIA) Brazilian and Portuguese Apostolate; Margate, FL St. Vincent.
Scarborough, Henry *o.c.s.o.* '63 (WOR)[O] Spencer, MA St. Joseph's Abbey.
Scarcella, Philip J. '77 (CHL) Charlotte, NC Our Lady of the Assumption.
Scarcello, Michael S. '56 (B) Retired.
Scarcia, John J. '74 (PH) Retired.
Scardella, Joseph E. '81 (SY) Building Commission;

Formation for Ministry and Liturgy; Management Team.
Scarfia, Gabriel *o.f.m.* '64 (BUF)[A] East Aurora, NY Christ the King Seminary.
Scaria, Anthony *c.f.i.c.* (STP) St. Paul, MN St. Mary.
Scaria, Job Edathinatt *c.m.i.* '94 (SHP) Monroe, LA Our Lady of Fatima; [F] Monroe, LA Catholic Campus Ministry at the University of Louisiana at Monroe.
Scarlata, Ronald E. '66 (CHI) Retired.
Scarry, Benignus *o.f.m.cap.* (DEN)[N] Denver, CO San Antonio Friary.
Scepaniak, Russell G. '93 (WIN) Chatfield, MN St. Mary's; Chatfield, MN St. Patrick; Chatfield, MN St. Columban.
Scerbo, Joseph *s.a.* '70 (NY)[EE] Garrison Franciscan Friars of the Atonement, Minister General Office.
Sceski, Alfred P. '91 (HBG) Elysburg, PA Queen of the Most Holy Rosary.
Scesney, Everard *o.f.m.* '68 (GB) Birnamwood, WI St. Boniface; Birnamwood, WI St. Philomena; [J] Wausaukee, WI Villa Alverna.
Schaab, Dennis *c.pp.s.* '68 (DAV) Centerville, IA St. Mary's.
Schaab, Denny M. '76 (STL) Valley Park, MO Sacred Heart.
Schaab, R. Michael '71 (PEO) Rock Island, IL St. Pius X.
Schaab, Thomas J. '74 (STL) Clayton, MO St. Joseph.
Schabel, Joseph A. '56 (SAG) Retired.
Schabowski, Henry F. '60 (TR) Retired.
Schack, Stephen '99 (PHX) El Mirage, AZ Santa Teresita Roman Catholic Parish.
Schad, Joseph J. *s.j.* '91 (BO)[U] Boston The Society of Jesus of New England–Provincial Offices.
Schad, Joseph *s.j.* '91 (PRT) Portland, ME Mercy Hospital; [H] Portland, ME Mercy Hospital.
Schad, Marco Federico '08 (WDC) Bethesda, MD Our Lady of Lourdes.
Schaedel, Rev. Msgr. Joseph F. '82 (IND) Indianapolis, IN SS. Peter and Paul Cathedral; Indianapolis, IN Holy Rosary; Vicar General and Moderator of the Curia; Board of Consultors; Council of Priests; Finance Council; Roman Catholic Archdiocese of Indianapolis Properties; Mission Office.
Schaedel, Rev. Msgr. Joseph '82 (IND)[P] Indianapolis, IN Hearts and Hands Corporation of Indiana.
Schaefer, Bernard *o.s.b.* '56 (RCK)[G] Aurora, IL Marmion Abbey.
Schaefer, Rev. Msgr. Dennis R. '75 (BEL) Red Bud, IL St. John the Baptist; Red Bud, IL St. Patrick.
Schaefer, Edgar J. '54 (WIN) Retired.
Schaefer, Edward F. '75 (BEL) Carlyle, IL St. Felicitas; St. Rose, IL St. Rose.
Schaefer, James F. '61 (LC) Retired.
Schaefer, James W. '56 (STL) St. Mary, MO Sacred Heart.
Schaefer, Rev. Msgr. Kenneth J. '74 (BEL) Herrin, IL Our Lady of Mount Carmel.
Schaefer, Rev. Msgr. Kenneth '73 (BEL) Johnston City, IL St. Paul.
Schaefer, Les F. *c.s.b.* '61 (GAL)[E] Houston, TX St. Thomas High School.
Schaefer, Martin T. '92 (WIN) Waseca, MN Sacred Heart; Pathways TEC (Teens Encounter Christ); [A] Winona, MN Immaculate Heart of Mary Seminary; Appointed Members.
Schaefer, Philip *c.p.* '58 (L)[L] Louisville, KY Sacred Heart Retreat.
Schaefer, Richard L. '68 (DUB)[H] Dubuque, IA Mercy Medical Center–Dubuque.
Schaefer, Roman J. '42 (NU) Retired.
Schaefer, Thomas '82 (PBR) Pittsburgh, PA St. John the Baptist.
Schaeffer, Bradley M. *s.j.* '77 (BO)[U] Cambridge, MA Faber House.
Schaeffer, Bradley M. *s.j.* '77 (CHI)[N] Chicago Chicago Province of the Society of Jesus–Provincial Office.
Schaeffer, Martin T. '92 (WIN) Advocates.
Schaeffer, Richard C. '83 (MAR) Leave of Absence.
Schaeper, Lawrence A. '09 (COV) Fort Thomas, KY St. Thomas.
Schafer, Dennis R. '89 (BIS) Williston, ND St. Joseph; Williston, ND St. John the Baptist; Presbyteral Council.
Schafer, Dennis *o.f.m.* '80 (JOL) Joliet, IL St. John the Baptist; [L] Joliet, IL St. John the Baptist Friary; [O] Joliet, IL The Upper Room Crisis Hotline (TURCH).
Schafer, Peter '05 (GR) Newaygo, MI St. Bartholomew's.
Schafer, Raymond E. '89 (IND) Unassigned.
Schafer, William *s.d.b.* '61 (LA)[P] Los Angeles, CA Dominic Savio Salesian Residence.
Schaff, Tyrone J. '73 (SPK) Spokane, WA Our Lady of Fatima; Members.
Schaffer, Gregory J. '94 (STP) On Duty Outside the Archdiocese.
Schaffer, Rev. Msgr. Gregory T. '60 (NU) On Duty Outside the Diocese; San Lucas Mission Office.
Schaffer, J. Darrell '90 (DEN) Lakewood, CO St. Jude.
Schaffer, Patrick *o.f.m.* '08 (GLP) Gallup, NM St. Francis of Assisi.
Schaffner, Mark *o.carm.* '89 (VEN) Englewood, FL St. Raphael.
Schaftlein, Steven '78 (IND) Charlestown, IN St. Michael; Charlestown, IN St. Francis Xavier.
Schaicoski, Daniel *o.s.b.m.* '89 (STN) Hamtramck, MI Immaculate Conception of B.V.M.
Schak, John R. *s.j.* '61 (MIL)[P] Milwaukee Jesuit Provincial Office, Wisconsin Province; Milwaukee, WI Society of Jesus.
Schalk, David A. '08 (COL) Delaware, OH St. Mary.
Schalk, Sebastian *o.praem.* '60 (JKS)[E] Raymond, MS Priory of St. Moses the Black.
Schall, James V. *s.j.* '63 (WDC)[N] Washington, DC The Jesuit Community at Georgetown University.
Schallberger, Meinrad *o.s.b.* '64 (B)[C] Jerome, ID Monastery of the Ascension.
Schaller, Robert A. '87 (LC) Holmen, WI St. Elizabeth Ann Seton.
Schamber, Richard Lee '07 (PT) Tallahassee, FL Blessed Sacrament.
Schanberger, J. Lawrence *m.m.* '49 (FgM) Maryknoll, NY MARYKNOLL.
Schapfel, Michael '83 (WDC) McLean, VA Nativity of the Blessed Virgin (German Mission); [W] McLean, VA German Speaking Catholic Mission, Washington DC.
Schappler, Norbert *o.s.b.* '52 (KC)[J] Stanberry, MO St. Peter Parish.
Schardt, William B. '75 (ARL) Middleburg, VA St. Stephen the Martyr.
Scharf, David E. '85 (PIT)[M] Pittsburgh, PA St. John Vianney Manor.
Scharf, David E.F. '85 (PIT)[N] Baden, PA Sisters of St. Joseph.
Scharfenberger, Rev. Msgr. Edward B. '73 (BRK) Ridgewood, NY St. Matthias; Mediation and Arbitration, Board of; Lawyers.
Schariah, Abraham P. (SYM) Loganville, GA St. Alphonsa Syro–Malabar Catholic Church, Atlanta.
Scharitz, Peter *c.ss.r.* '76 (STL)[O] Liguori, MO Liguori Mission House/Redemptorists.
Schartz, Kenneth E. '84 (CIN) Cincinnati, OH St. Mary.
Schatteman, Rene J. '60 (POD)[L] Pittsburgh, PA Prelature of the Holy Cross and Opus Dei; Pittsburgh.
Schatz, David A. '00 (DUB)[A] Dubuque, IA Seminary of St. Pius X; Vocation Awareness; On Special or Other Archdiocesan Assignment.
Schatzel, John E. '61 (BO) Senior Priests. Retired.
Schatzle, Michael J. '74 (BR) Baton Rouge, LA St. George; College of Consultors; Presbyteral Council.
Schauerman, Rev. Msgr. Henry J. '51 (E) Retired.
Schaukowitch, James V. *s.j.* '79 (SFR)[E] San Francisco, CA St. Ignatius College Preparatory (Coed); [N] San Francisco, CA Jesuit Community at St. Ignatius College Preparatory.
Schaut, Gregory F. '85 (CLV) Fairview Park, OH St. Angela Merici.
Schawe, Wesley W. '04 (DOD) Garden City, KS St. Dominic Catholic Church of Garden City, Kansas; Ingalls, KS St. Stanislaus Catholic Church of Ingalls, Kansas; Advocates.
Scheaffer, Rev. Msgr. Walter T. '66 (ALN) Kutztown, PA St. Mary.
Schebera, Richard *s.m.m.* '64 (BRK)[T] Ozone Park, NY Montfort Missionaries Provincialate (Missionaries of the Company of Mary).
Scheble, Carl J. '83 (STL) Florissant, MO St. Rose Philippine Duchesne.
Scheckel, Roger J. '84 (LC) La Crosse, WI St. James the Less; [L] La Crosse, WI Father Joseph Walijewski Orphanage Endowment Trust; Holy Childhood Association; Propagation of the Faith.
Scheckenback, Robert C. '89 (RVC) West Islip, NY Our Lady of Lourdes.
Schecker, Robert J.W. '71 (TR) Fair Haven, NJ Church of the Nativity.
Scheel, Rev. Msgr. Daniel L. '69 (GAL) Houston, TX St. Jerome; Western Vicariate; Appointees; College of Consultors; Council of Catholic Women.
Scheeler, Jeffrey *o.f.m.* '80 (CIN)[N] Cincinnati, OH St. Francis Seraph Friary; Cincinnati, OH.
Scheer, Allen '95 (SAL) Salina, KS Sacred Heart Cathedral Parish; College of Consultors; Council of Priests; Rural Life Conference.
Scheer, John R. *s.a.c.* '70 (MIL)[P] Milwaukee, WI Pallotti House; [P] Milwaukee, WI St. Vincent Community.
Scheerger, Michael Therese *c.s.j.* (LAR) Campus Ministry.
Scheets, Francis K. *o.s.c.* '51 (PHX)[F] Phoenix, AZ Retired.
Scheetz, Daniel L. '65 (SAL) Promoter of Justice and Guardian.
Scheetz, Daniel '65 (SAL) Retired.
Scheetz, Joseph '54 (SAL) Retired.
Schefers, Eberhard '64 (SCL) Retired.
Scheff, Philip J. '01 (VEN) Port Charlotte, FL St. Charles Borromeo.
Scheffler, Mark *c.ss.r.* (STL)[O] Liguori, MO St. Clement Health Care Center.
Schehr, Timothy P. '73 (CIN)[B] Cincinnati, OH Mt. St. Mary's Seminary of the West; Imprimatur Censors.
Scheib, Joseph C. '76 (PIT) Pittsburgh, PA St. Basil; Judges.
Scheible, Ronald E. *o.s.a.* '57 (CHI)[N] Chicago, IL St. Monica Monastery.
Scheich, Eugene '66 (L) Retired.
Scheick, James C. '63 (DET) Retired.
Scheiding, Philip '81 (MIA) On Duty Outside the Archdiocese.
Scheidler, David *c.s.c.* '94 (FTW) South Bend, IN St. Adalbert; South Bend, IN St. Casimir; [H] Notre Dame Congregation of Holy Cross, Indiana Province, Provincial House.
Scheidt, Daniel D. '01 (FTW) Mishawaka, IN Queen of Peace; Consultors; Environment and Art.
Scheier, Steven '73 (WCH) Caldwell, KS St. Martin of Tours.
Scheierl, LeRoy '91 (SCL) Brandon, MN Church of St. Ann; Brandon, MN Seven Dolors; Parkers Prairie, MN Church of St. William; Parkers Prairie, MN Sacred Heart; Boy Scouts.
Scheiner, Richard *c.p.* '60 (MET)[I] South River Passionist Provincial Office.
Scheiner, Richard *c.p.* '60 (BRK)[T] Jamaica, NY Immaculate Conception Monastery.
Scheinost, Douglas P. '92 (OM) Verdigre, NE St. Wenceslaus; Verdigre, NE St. William; [O] Lynch, NE Niobrara Valley House of Renewal.
Scheip, Michael A. '94 (VEN) Cursillo Movement.
Scheip, Michael '93 (VEN) Sarasota, FL Incarnation.
Schelble, Michael T. (LC)[H] La Crosse, WI Holy Cross (Seminary) Diocesan Center.
Schelble, T. Michael '61 (LC) Retired.
Schelich, Theodosius A. *o.f.m.* '59 (SFD)[I] Litchfield, IL St. Francis Hospital.
Schelich, Theodosius A. *o.f.m.* '59 (STL)[O] St. Louis Franciscan Friary of St. Anthony of Padua.
Schellberg, Eugene '60 (MET) Retired.
Schellberg, Eugene (CHL) Charlotte, NC St. Matthew.
Schellenberg, James E. '77 (SAT) San Antonio, TX Brooke Army Medical Center.
Schemel, Francis *s.j.* '58 (WDC)[N] Washington, DC The Jesuit Community at Georgetown University.
Schemm, Michael '93 (WCH) Augusta, KS St. James.
Schempp, Albert *m.i.* '04 (MIL)[Y] Wauwatosa, WI San Camillo, Inc.; [Y] Milwaukee, WI St. Camillus Communities, Inc.; [P] Milwaukee, WI St. Camillus Provincialate; [Y] Wauwatosa, WI St. Camillus Health System, Inc.; [Y] Wauwatosa, WI St. Camillus Ministries, Inc.; [Y] Wauwatosa, WI Order of St. Camillus Foundation, Inc.
Schempp, Albert *m.i.* '04 (PIT) Allegheny County, PA Mercy Health System of Pittsburgh–Pittsburgh Mercy Hospital; Pittsburgh, PA St. Patrick–St. Stanislaus Kostka.
Schenck, Stephen *s.d.b.* '81 (NY) Port Chester, NY Our Lady of the Rosary.
Schenden, Gregory A. *s.j.* '08 (WDC) Washington, DC Holy Trinity.
Schendt, Richard L. '63 (CHI)[V] Oak Park, IL Oak Park Study Center; Oak Park.
Schenick, Joseph D. '51 (PRO)[P] Providence St. John Vianney Residence Retired.
Schenk, Francis *g.h.m.* '55 (CIN)[N] Cincinnati Headquarters of Glenmary Home Missioners Retired.
Schenk, Raymond C. '70 (BAL) Priests Sick or Absent.
Schenk, Richard *o.p.* '78 (OAK)[A] Berkeley, CA Dominican School of Philosophy and Theology; [M] Oakland, CA Order of Preachers (Province of the Most Holy Name of Jesus – Western Dominican Province); [M] Oakland, CA Order of Preachers (Province of the Most Holy Name of Jesus – Western Dominican Province).
Schenkel, Dennis '08 (MEM) Memphis, TN St. Louis.
Schenning, Rev. Msgr. Kevin T. '81 (BAL) Baltimore, MD St. Joseph; Priest Personnel Board; Presbyteral Council.
Schepers, M. B. *o.p.* '56 (FgM) New York, NY Province of St. Joseph (Eastern).
Scherba, Raymond M. '82 (BGP) Danbury, CT St. Gregory the Great.
Scherer, Albert *o.f.m.conv.* (SY) Bridgeport, NY St. Francis of Assisi.
Scherer, Donald R. '67 (NEW) Retired.
Scherer, Donald R. '67 (NO) Retired.
Scherer, Gary *c.pp.s.* '67 (GRY) Whiting, IN St. John the Baptist.
Scherer, Gerald N. '54 (RC) Retired.
Scherer, James F. '64 (ATL) Retired.
Scherer, Philip M. *o.s.m.* '55 (CHI)[N] Chicago Order of Friar Servants of Mary (Servites) United States of America Province, Inc.
Scherger, Herman F. '58 (TOL) Retired.
Scherrer, Rev. Msgr. Carl E. '73 (BEL) Columbia, IL Immaculate Conception of the B.V.M.
Scherrer, Steven S. *m.m.* '72 (NY)[EE] Retired.
Scherrey, Michael G. '05 (GAL)[S] Houston, TX Catholic Charismatic Center.
Scherschel, Michael G. '07 (CHI) Chicago, IL St. William.

Schetelick, Rev. Msgr. Paul D. '76 (NEW) Bayonne Deanery 13; Bayonne, NJ St. Andrew's.
Scheuer, James '59 (DUL) Retired.
Scheuerell, Charles A. '57 (MIL) Retired.
Scheuerman, Edward L. '50 (DET) Retired.
Schevers, Joel *o.carm.* '42 (VEN) Venice, FL Epiphany Cathedral; Defenders of the Bond.
Schexnayder, Francis F. *m.m.* '64 (FgM) Maryknoll, NY MARYKNOLL.
Schexnayder, Gary '69 (LAF) Crowley, LA St. Michael Archangel; Diocesan Consultors; Scouting.
Schexnayder, James '64 (OAK) Retired.
Scheyd, Rev. Msgr. William J. '65 (BGP) New Canaan, CT St. Aloysius; Vicars General; Diocesan Consultors; Presbyteral Council; Finance Council; Pastors' Vocation Advisory Board.
Schiavi, Giulio *p.i.m.e.* '63 (DET) Clinton Twp., MI San Francesco Community.
Schiavo, John Lo *s.j.* '55 (SFR)[C] San Francisco, CA University of San Francisco.
Schiavo, Sylvan *c.s.j.* '63 (LA) San Pedro, CA St. Peter.
Schiavone, Jeldo J. '52 (LFT) Retired.
Schiavone, Robert W. '69 (GB) On Duty Outside the Diocese.
Schiavone, Robert W. '69 (MIL)[B] Hales Corners, WI Sacred Heart School of Theology.
Schiavonne, John S. '73 (LA) Whittier, CA St. Gregory the Great.
Schiblin, Richard *c.ss.r.* '61 (OAK)[M] Berkeley, CA Redemptorist Fathers (Denver Province).
Schiblin, Richard *c.ss.r.* '61 (STL)[B] St. Louis, MO St. John Neumann House Retired.
Schiblin, Richard *c.ss.r.* '61 (BRK)[C] Bronx, NY St. Alphonsus Formation Residence.
Schichtel, Kenneth H. '62 (GR) Retired.
Schieber, Brian '99 (KCK) Topeka, KS Most Pure Heart of Mary; Vicars General; Archdiocesan Consultors; Archdiocesan Administrative Team.
Schieber, Joachim *o.s.b.* '44 (KC)[J] Stanberry, MO St. Peter Parish.
Schiel, Nicholas E. *s.j.* '55 (FgM)[P] Milwaukee Jesuit Provincial Office, Wisconsin Province; Milwaukee, WI Society of Jesus.
Schiele, John D. '93 (PH) Hilltown, PA Our Lady of the Sacred Heart; [D] Lansdale, PA Lansdale Catholic High School.
Schifalacqua, Ildebrando E. '43 (PH) Retired.
Schifano, Albert I. '01 (TUC) Special Assignment; Diocesan Consultors; Council of Priests; Tucson, AZ Saints Peter and Paul Roman Catholic Parish – Tucson; [H] Tucson, AZ Catholic Foundation for the Diocese of Tucson; Vicars General; Moderator of the Curia; Ex Officio; Diocesan Building Committee; Moderator of the Curia.
Schifano, James *s.c.j* '75 (MIL)[P] Hales Corners, WI Priests of the Sacred Heart.
Schifano, Vincent '00 (RVC) Seaford, NY St. James.
Schiferl, David E. '01 (P) Cornelius, OR St. Alexander.
Schiffelbein, Matthew '09 (KCK) Overland Park, KS Church of the Ascension.
Schiffer, James *c.p.* '71 (ALB) Greenville, NY St. John the Baptist; Windham, NY St. Theresa of Child Jesus.
Schiffer, James '71 (ALB) Members.
Schifferli, Jerome F. '45 (ROC) Retired.
Schik, Jerome *o.s.c.* '75 (SCL) Onamia, MN St. Therese, Little Flower Indian Mission; Hillman, MN St. Rita's; Onamia, MN The Church of the Holy Cross of Onamia; Wahkon, MN Sacred Heart.
Schik, Jerry *o.s.c.* '75 (SCL)[I] Onamia, MN Crosier Priory.
Schik, LeRoy '03 (SCL) Battle Lake, MN Our Lady of the Lake; Fergus Falls, MN Our Lady of Victory; Underwood, MN Church of Saint James at Maine.
Schild, Eric P. '07 (TOL) Fostoria, OH St. Wendelin.
Schilder, David M. '68 (COL) Retired.
Schilken, Karl '80 (FWT) Fort Worth, TX St. John the Apostle.
Schill, Damien '87 (FAR) Veterans Administration Medical Center; On Duty Outside the Diocese.
Schill, Frederick J. '57 (TOL) Retired.
Schill, Gerald F. (Damien) '87 (MO) DEPARTMENT OF VETERANS AFFAIRS HOSPITALS AND CHAPLAINS.
Schill, Paul A. '80 (E) Greenville, PA St. Michael Retired.
Schiller, Francis E. '65 (NEW) Jersey City, NJ St. Patrick and Assumption/All Saints Church; [R] Jersey City, NJ Trinity Child Care Center; [R] Jersey City, NJ St. Patrick and Assumption All Saints Foundation.
Schiller, Thomas A. '55 (GR) Retired.
Schilli, Richard J. '77 (STL) Eureka, MO Sacred Heart.
Schillinger, James A. '84 (ATL) Atlanta, GA Immaculate Heart of Mary; Judges; Deans.
Schiltz, Roger J. '68 (WIN) Retired.
Schimelpfening, James *s.m.* '80 (CIN)[N] Dayton, OH Marianist Community; [D] Dayton, OH The University of Dayton; [R] Dayton, OH University of Dayton Campus Ministry.
Schiml, Ronald J. *c.pp.s.* '55 (LFT) Star City, IN St. Joseph.
Schimmel, Eric *c.s.c.* (FTW)[H] Notre Dame Congregation of Holy Cross, Indiana Province, Provincial House.
Schimmel, Eric *c.s.c.* '02 (PHX)[J] Phoenix, AZ Andre House of Arizona.
Schimmelmann, Wayne *c.m.f.* '86 (CHI)[N] Chicago, IL Claret House.
Schimmer, Robert J. '68 (SC) Sheldon, IA St. Patrick's.
Schimscheiner, Francis M. *o.s.f.s.* '65 (BUF) Lockport, NY All Saints.
Schindler, Carl *c.ss.r.* '63 (SAT)[L] San Antonio, TX Redemptorists of Texas–San Antonio #1; Bexar County Detention Ministries.
Schindler, Paul E. '67 (CLV) Casa Parroquial Inmaculada Concepcion.
Schindler–McGraw, Kevin *o.f.m.conv.* '84 (LA) Hermosa Beach, CA Our Lady of Guadalupe; Redondo Beach, CA St. Lawrence Martyr.
Schineller, J. Peter *s.j.* '70 (NY)[II] New York, NY Catholic Medical Mission Board, Inc.; [EE] New York, NY Society of Jesus, New York Province.
Schinelli, Giles A. *t.o.r.* '70 (STP) Brooklyn Park, MN St. Gerard Majella; [K] Brooklyn Park, MN St. Gerard Friary.
Schinn, Bernard *o.s.b.* '99 (PAT)[N] Clifton, NJ Holy Face of Jesus Monastery.
Schinski, Rev. Msgr. Stanley E. '51 (PAT)[Q] Chester, NJ Nazareth Village Retired.
Schipp, John H. '64 (EVN) Vincennes, IN Basilica of St. Francis Xavier; [H] Vincennes, IN Old Cathedral Library & Museum, Inc.; Advocates; Vincennes, IN St. Thomas The Apostle.
Schipp, Ralph '65 (EVN) Retired.
Schipper, Carl A. '68 (SFR) Retired.
Schipper, William *o.s.b.* '94 (SCL)[I] Collegeville, MN St. John's Abbey, of the Order of St. Benedict.
Schiro, Nicholas T. *s.j.* '57 (NO)[E] New Orleans, LA Jesuit High School.
Schiska, Paul A. '57 (MAR) Retired.
Schissel, Gregory A. *s.j.* '79 (MIL)[P] Milwaukee Jesuit Provincial Office, Wisconsin Province.
Schitmeyer, James '81 (AMA) Childress, TX Holy Angels.
Schlachter, Eric A. '81 (JC) Absent on Leave.
Schladen, Robert '59 (PEO) Retired.
Schlaf, John E. '64 (GI) Concordia, KS Retired.
Schlaf, John '64 (SAL)[E] Concordia, KS Nazareth Convent & Academy Corporation Sisters of St. Joseph of Concordia.
Schlafer, Joseph M. '75 (RVC) Garden City, NY St. Joseph's.
Schlageter, Robert *o.f.m.conv.* '84 (WDC)[C] Washington, DC Catholic University of America, The.
Schlagheck, Regis *o.f.m.conv.* '66 (IND) Clarksville, IN St. Anthony of Padua.
Schlangen, Louis '57 (SFD) Retired.
Schlarb, Greg '97 (PHX) Gilbert, AZ St. Anne Roman Catholic Parish; Presbyteral Council.
Schlarb, Gregory '77 (PHX) Stewardship Office.
Schlatter, Fredric *s.j.* '56 (SPK)[B] Spokane, WA Gonzaga University.
Schlautman, Wayne W. '65 (OM) Retired.
Schlaver, David E. *c.s.c.* '71 (FTW)[H] Notre Dame Congregation of Holy Cross, Indiana Province, Provincial House.
Schlaver, David *c.s.c.* (PRT) Old Orchard Beach, ME St. Margaret's.
Schlax, Charles H. '66 (CHI) Des Plaines, IL St. Mary.
Schlegel, Daniel F. '88 (CLV) Chagrin Falls, OH Holy Angels.
Schlegel, Rev. Msgr. George J. '66 (COL) New Philadelphia, OH Sacred Heart; College of Consultors.
Schlegel, John P. *s.j.* '73 (OM)[A] Omaha, NE Creighton University; [K] Omaha, NE Jesuit Community at Creighton University.
Schlegel, Lawrence *o.s.b.* '54 (MAN)[K] Manchester, NH St. Anselm Abbey Retired.
Schleicher, Edward '83 (PIT) Glenshaw, PA St. Mary of the Assumption.
Schleicher, James R. '54 (CLV) Akron, OH St. Francis de Sales Retired.
Schleisman, Jeffrey '00 (SC) Larchwood, IA St. Mary; Rock Rapids, IA Holy Name; Presbyteral Council.
Schlenker, Richard J. '56 (MIL) Retired.
Schlert, Rev. Msgr. Alfred A. '87 (ALN) Hellertown, PA St. Theresa of the Child Jesus; Vicar General; Defenders of the Bond; College of Consultors; Ex Officio Members; Finance Council.
Schlesselmann, Rev. Msgr. Gregory J. '93 (FAR) Special Assignment; [A] Fargo, ND Cardinal Muench Seminary; [B] Fargo, ND Fargo Catholic Schools Network; Notaries.
Schleter, Edward J. '67 (TOL) Wauseon, OH St. Caspar.
Schlett, Francis J. '70 (PH) Retired.
Schleupner, Rev. Msgr. G. Michael '72 (BAL) Consultors; Consultors; Bel Air, MD St. Margaret.
Schlichte, Carl *o.p.* '98 (SJ) Stanford, CA Catholic Community at Stanford.
Schlick, Regis *o.f.m.cap.* '65 (WH)[L] Charleston, WV Capuchins–St. Anthony Friary.
Schlick, Regis *o.f.m.cap.* '65 (PIT)[M] Pittsburgh St. Augustine Friary.
Schliessmann, Thomas L. '89 (IND) Edinburgh, IN Holy Trinity; Franklin, IN St. Rose of Lima; [O] Franklin, IN Franklin College.
Schlight, Harry J. *o.s.f.s.* '44 (FgM) Wilmington, DE OBLATES OF ST. FRANCIS DE SALES MISSIONS.
Schlim, Robert J. *s.j.* '62 (SPK)[J] Spokane, WA Regis Community.
Schlimm, Chrysostom V. *o.s.b.* '61 (GBG)[G] Latrobe, PA Saint Vincent Archabbey.
Schlitt, Dale *o.m.i.* '69 (WDC)[N] Washington, DC Provincial Offices of the United States Province of the Missionary Oblates of Mary Immaculate; Washington, DC AMERICAN OBLATE MISSIONS.
Schlitt, Rev. Msgr. Harry G. '64 (SFR)[S] San Francisco, CA Catholics for Truth & Justice; College of Consultors; Archbishop's Cabinet; Moderator of the Curia and Vicar for Administration; On Special Assignment.
Schloeder, Paul '87 (SAC) Retired.
Schloemer, Bernard J. '60 (STL) St. Louis, MO St. Gabriel the Archangel Retired.
Schloemer, Leo *g.h.m.* '56 (CIN)[N] Cincinnati Headquarters of Glenmary Home Missioners Retired.
Schloemer, Paul *o.f.m.conv.* '04 (L)[L] Louisville, KY St. Francis of Assisi Friary.
Schloemer, Paul *o.f.m.conv.* '01 (IND)[K] Pleasure Ridge Park, KY St. Paul Friary.
Schloemer, Thomas N. *s.j.* '68 (MIL)[P] Milwaukee, WI Jesuit Community at Marquette University.
Schloesser, Stephen *s.j.* '92 (BO)[U] Newton, MA The Jesuit Community at Boston College.
Schlosser, Richard '74 (GF) Great Falls, MT Holy Spirit; Clerical Benefit Association; Vicars Forane.
Schloth, Brian D. *m.s.* '89 (HRT)[L] Hartford, CT Missionaries of LaSalette Province of Mary, Mother of the Americas; [L] Hartford, CT Our Lady of Sorrows Rectory; Hartford, CT Our Lady of Sorrows.
Schludecker, Andre *o.f.m.* '64 (SFD)[M] Springfield, IL St. Francis Convent; [L] Springfield, IL Our Lady of Angels Friary.
Schluter, Rev. Msgr. O. Charles '78 (MAD) Platteville, WI St. Mary; Platteville, WI St. Augustine University Parish; Office for the Continuing Education of Priests; [I] Platteville, WI St. Augustine Newman Center.
Schmalhofer, John D. '74 (HBG) New Holland, PA Our Lady of Lourdes.
Schmaltz, Bernard '73 (NO) Retired.
Schmalzried, Bernard R. '69 (Y) Warren, OH St. Mary.
Schmeid, Thomas *o.f.m.cap.* '69 (DET)[K] Detroit St. Bonaventure Friary.
Schmeidler, John *o.f.m.cap.* '97 (KCK) Lawrence, KS St. John the Evangelist; [I] Lawrence, KS St. Conrad's Friary; Denver, CO.
Schmelz, Damian *o.s.b.* '58 (EVN) Ferdinand, IN St. Henry.
Schmelz, Damian *o.s.b.* '58 (IND)[K] St. Meinrad St. Meinrad Archabbey.
Schmelzer, Rev. Msgr. Delbert L. '56 (MAD) Appointed; Holy Childhood, Pontifical Association; Propagation of the Faith; [F] Madison, WI Bishop O'Connor Catholic Pastoral Center Retired.
Schmelzer, Ronald '02 (SCL) Staples, MN St. Michael's; Staples, MN Sacred Heart.
Schmenk, Cleo S. '53 (TOL) Retired.
Schmid, Wayne L. '68 (WCH) Derby, KS St. Mary; Ongoing Formation of the Clergy Committee.
Schmid, Will '09 (PHX) Chandler, AZ St. Mary Roman Catholic Parish; [A] Chandler, AZ Seton Roman Catholic High School.
Schmidberger, Richard '57 (DET) Retired.
Schmidt, Anthony '50 (SFD) Retired.
Schmidt, Carl '50 (SFD) Retired.
Schmidt, Charles J. *m.m.* '48 (NY)[EE] Retired.
Schmidt, David R. '81 (GB) Florence, WI Immaculate Conception; Wabeno, WI St. Ambrose; Priests' Personnel Board; Armstrong Creek, WI St. Stanislaus Kostka; Goodman, WI St. Joan of Arc; Lakewood, WI St. Mary of the Lake.
Schmidt, David '77 (SFD) Absent on Leave.
Schmidt, Dennis C. '80 (STL) Ste. Genevieve, MO Ste. Genevieve.
Schmidt, Donald '73 (MIL) Retired.
Schmidt, Edward P. *s.j.* '71 (FgM) Chicago, IL Society of Jesus.
Schmidt, Edward W. *s.j.* '73 (CHI)[N] Chicago, IL Clark Street Jesuit Residence.
Schmidt, Edwin A. '63 (JC) Jefferson City, MO St. Martin.
Schmidt, Florian J. '61 (DUB) Retired.
Schmidt, Francis J. '58 (MAD) Retired.
Schmidt, Rev. Msgr. Francis X. '57 (PH) Retired.
Schmidt, George E. '70 (KNX) Chattanooga, TN SS. Peter and Paul; Chattanooga, TN Mount Olivet Cemetery; Deans of the Diocese; Diocesan Finance Council; Cemeteries; Ministries of the Chattanooga Deanery; Presbyteral Council.
Schmidt, Rev. Msgr. Gregory L. '61 (STL) Old Monroe,

MO Immaculate Conception; Deaneries/Deans.
Schmidt, Henry '57 (SFD) Carrollton, IL St. John the Evangelist; Greenfield, IL St. Michael; Carrollton, IL All Saints.
Schmidt, Jan Kevin '90 (CIN) Loveland, OH St. Margaret of York.
Schmidt, Jerome J. '49 (BRK)[T] Douglaston, NY Bishop Mugavero Residence Retired.
Schmidt, John K. *c.ss.r.* '89 (CHI)[N] Chicago, IL Redemptorist Theology Residence.
Schmidt, Joseph F. '66 (B) Moscow, ID St. Mary's.
Schmidt, Kenneth W. '81 (KAL) Kalamazoo, MI St. Thomas More Student Parish; [H] Kalamazoo, MI Western Michigan University, Kalamazoo College, Kalamazoo Valley Community College; Priestly Life and Ministry Office; Judges.
Schmidt, Leo C. '56 (COV) Covington, KY St. Augustine.
Schmidt, Leslie *g.h.m.* '61 (RIC) Jonesville, VA Church of the Holy Spirit; Big Stone Gap, VA Sacred Heart.
Schmidt, Pale Teofilo '06 (SPP) Pago Pago, AS Sts. Peter & Paul.
Schmidt, Paul J. '64 (OAK) Pinole, CA St. Joseph; Presbyteral Council.
Schmidt, Paul Lester *s.v.d.* '81 (SB)[I] Riverside, CA Divine Word Seminary.
Schmidt, Paul (OAK) Consultors.
Schmidt, Peter *o.c.s.o.* '75 (WOR)[O] Spencer, MA St. Joseph's Abbey.
Schmidt, Raymond F. '60 (BRK) Retired.
Schmidt, Raymond F. '84 (WDC) Hollywood, MD St. John Francis Regis.
Schmidt, Richard C. *s.j.* '61 (WDC)[Q] Faulkner, MD Loyola Retreat House.
Schmidt, Robert H. *s.j.* '69 (FgM) Detroit, MI Detroit Province.
Schmidt, Rev. Msgr. Robert '57 (DAV) Retired.
Schmidt, Sebastian *o.s.b.* '60 (BIS)[A] Richardton, ND Assumption Abbey; Richardton, ND.
Schmidt, Teofilo '06 (SPP) Pago Pago, AS Christ the King.
Schmidt, Thomas W. '99 (CIN) Centerville, OH St. Francis of Assisi; Priest Councilors.
Schmidt, Rev. Msgr. W. Robert '57 (DAV) Holy Childhood, Pontifical Association.
Schmidt, William F. *s.a.* '59 (ARL) Sterling, VA Christ the Redeemer.
Schmidt, William T. '76 (BO) Stoneham, MA St. Patrick.
Schmied, Rev. Msgr. Michael S. '71 (RIC) Richmond, VA St. Augustine.
Schmieder, Mark C. '66 (CIN) On Special and Archdiocesan Assignment; Cincinnati, OH American Catholic Correctional Chaplains Association.
Schmiesing, Julian *o.s.b.* '58 (SCL)[I] Collegeville, MN St. John's Abbey, of the Order of St. Benedict.
Schmit, Arthur G. *o.s.b.* '57 (PEO)[A] Peru, IL St. Bede Abbey.
Schmit, Fred J. *s.d.s.* '46 (NSH) Retired.
Schmit, George V. '68 (NU) Bird Island, MN St. Mary; Building Committee; Committee on Parishes; Priest Personnel Board.
Schmit, Rev. Msgr. Jerome Lucien '57 (LA) Altadena, CA Sacred Heart Retired.
Schmit, Jerome '57 (LA) San Gabriel, CA St. Anthony.
Schmit, Kenneth A. '79 (ORG) Los Alamitos, CA St. Hedwig; Diocesan Construction Board; Council of Priests.
Schmit, Louis *c.pp.s.* '63 (CIN)[N] Carthagena, OH St. Charles Retired.
Schmit, Rev. Msgr. Ralph R. '46 (MIL) Retired.
Schmit, Roger *o.s.b.* '62 (KCK) Kansas City, KS Christ the King.
Schmit, Ronald G. '85 (OAK) Byron, CA St. Anne.
Schmit, Ronald '85 (OAK) Presbyteral Council.
Schmit, Stanley T. '94 (OM) Albion, NE St. Michael; Petersburg, NE St. John the Baptist.
Schmitmeyer, Daniel J. '06 (CIN) Sidney, OH Holy Angels.
Schmitmeyer, James M. '81 (CIN) On Duty Outside the Archdiocese.
Schmitt, Adam '57 (FTW) Fort Wayne, IN St. Joseph Retired.
Schmitt, Bill Bernardo '68 (OM) Omaha, NE Our Lady of Guadalupe – St. Agnes Parish.
Schmitt, Bowan M. '97 (PEO) Hoopeston, IL St. Anthony Church; [B] Danville, IL Schlarman High School.
Schmitt, Carl E. '05 (GB) Sturgeon Bay, WI Corpus Christi; Vicariate.
Schmitt, Rev. Msgr. Carl L. '61 (DUB)[E] New Hampton, IA St. John School of Religion; New Hampton, IA Holy Family; New Hampton, IA Immaculate Conception; Nashua, IA St. Boniface; College of Consultors; Deans; Building Commission; Directors.
Schmitt, Charles R. '59 (E) Retired.
Schmitt, Christopher '60 (POD) Miami.
Schmitt, Christopher '61 (MIA)[P] Miami, FL Prelature of the Holy Cross and Opus Dei.
Schmitt, Conrad *s.t.* (PAT)[N] Stirling, NJ Holy Spirit Missionary Cenacle.
Schmitt, David J. '67 (WH) Point Pleasant, WV Sacred Heart.
Schmitt, Eugene '00 (EVN) Chrisney, IN St. Martin; Rockport, IN St. Bernard; Diocesan Council of Priests; Clergy Personnel Board.
Schmitt, Frank J. *s.j.* '83 (OKL) Union City, OK St. Joseph's; El Reno, OK Sacred Heart.
Schmitt, Gregory *c.ss.r.* '69 (NO) New Orleans, LA St. Mary's Assumption; New Orleans, LA St. Mary's Chapel; New Orleans, LA St. Alphonsus.
Schmitt, Harold F. '59 (PEO)[I] Lacon, IL St. Joseph Nursing Home; Lacon, IL Immaculate Conception.
Schmitt, James C. '66 (GI) Retired.
Schmitt, James '51 (LAN) Retired.
Schmitt, Rev. Msgr. Joseph J. '55 (AUS) Lago Vista, TX Our Lady of the Lake Catholic Church – Lago Vista, Texas.
Schmitt, Kent A. '73 (MAD) Madison, WI St. Dennis; Elected.
Schmitt, Michael T. '71 (ALB) Retired.
Schmitt, Philip E. '56 (DUB) Mount Vernon, IA St. John the Baptist.
Schmitt, Phillip E. '56 (DUB) Engaged Encounter; Family Life & Marriage Advisory Committee Retired.
Schmitt, Silverius '58 (SCL) Retired.
Schmitt, Theodore J. '02 (CHI) Chicago, IL St. Monica.
Schmitt, Thomas F. '91 (BO)[A] Weston, MA Blessed John XXIII National Seminary.
Schmitt, Thomas F. '91 (SPR) On Duty Outside the Diocese.
Schmitt, William *s.s.c.* '68 (OM)[K] St. Columbans, NE Missionary Society of St. Columban.
Schmitter, Philip '71 (LAN) Flint, MI Christ the King.
Schmittgens, Kevin V. '83 (STL) Union, MO St. Joseph.
Schmitz, Aloysius F. *s.j.* '59 (MIL)[P] Wauwatosa, WI Jesuit Community at St. Camillus.
Schmitz, Bartley *s.v.d.* '44 (FgM) Techny, IL.
Schmitz, Rev. Msgr. Bernard A. '74 (DEN) Vicar for Clergy; Ex Officio Members; Denver, CO Mother of God; College of Consultors; Vicar for Clergy.
Schmitz, Charles *s.j.* '72 (SPK)[J] Spokane, WA Regis Community.
Schmitz, Donald J. '80 (WIN) Rochester, MN Holy Spirit; Elected Deanery Representatives.
Schmitz, Rev. Msgr. Donald P. '64 (WIN) Harmony, MN The Assumption; Harmony, MN The Nativity of the Blessed Virgin; Harmony, MN St. Olaf; [A] Winona, MN Immaculate Heart of Mary Seminary; Diocesan Consultors; Vicar for Senior Priests.
Schmitz, George R. '69 (CIN) Cincinnati, OH Our Lady of Victory; Cincinnati, OH St. Teresa of Avila.
Schmitz, Rev. Msgr. Gerard G. '68 (HRT) Special and other Archdiocesan Assignment; [A] Bloomfield, CT St. Thomas Seminary; Office of Vicar For Priests; Ex Officio; Office of Coordinator for Retired Priests.
Schmitz, James P. '86 (CLV) Lorain, OH St. Joseph; West Salem, OH St. Stephen.
Schmitz, John A. '52 (MIL) Retired.
Schmitz, John J. '91 (JC) Mexico, MO St. Brendan; Senators; Priestly and Religious Vocations Committee.
Schmitz, Michael D. '96 (OM) Crofton, NE St. Andrew; Crofton, NE St. Rose of Lima.
Schmitz, Michael '03 (DUL) Campus Ministry; Department of Youth and Young Adult Ministry; [F] Duluth, MN Newman Catholic Campus Ministry.
Schmitz, Rev. Msgr. R. Michael '82 (CHI)[N] Chicago, IL Institute of Christ the King Sovereign Priest.
Schmitz, Robert A. '55 (OM) Retired.
Schmitz, Robert E. '75 (CIN) Cincinnati, OH Good Shepherd.
Schmoll, John *o.s.b. oblate* '85 (FRS) Lamont, CA St. Augustine.
Schmoll, John '85 (FRS) Priests' Council.
Schmolt, Johnathan P. '08 (E) Erie, PA St. Jude the Apostle.
Schmuhl, Lawrence R. *s.m.* '47 (ATL)[D] Atlanta, GA Marist School Retired.
Schnacky, Paul '53 (ROC) Hornell, NY Our Lady of the Valley Retired.
Schnakenberg, John Gregory *o.p.* '09 (WDC)[B] Washington, DC Dominican House of Studies.
Schnaubelt, Joseph C. *o.s.a.* '57 (PH)[Y] Villanova, PA St. Thomas Monastery.
Schneck, Richard J. *s.j.* '72 (FgM) Los Gatos, CA Society of Jesus.
Schneebeck, Paul Otto *c.m.* '69 (STL) St. Louis, MO St. Vincent de Paul.
Schneibel, Jeffrey A. *c.s.c.* '85 (COS) Monument, CO St. Peter.
Schneible, Peter *o.f.m.* '89 (BUF)[O] St. Bonaventure, NY St. Bonaventure Friary; [C] St. Bonaventure, NY Friar Community.
Schneider, Aquinas *o.f.m.* '54 (PEO) Peoria, IL Sacred Heart Retired.
Schneider, Bernard '67 (FAR) Manvel, ND St. Timothy's Church of Manvel; Altru Hospital; [J] Manvel, ND Beginning Experience Apostolate.
Schneider, Charles *s.v.d.* '46 (CHI)[N] Techny, IL Divine Word Residence.
Schneider, Daniel Mary *m. carm.* '98 (CHY)[D] Powell, WY Monks of the Most Blessed Virgin Mary of Mt. Carmel.
Schneider, Edward (ORL) Retired.
Schneider, Rev. Msgr. Ernest '77 (GR) Grand Rapids, MI St. Paul the Apostle; Deans; College of Consultors.
Schneider, Rev. Msgr. Francis J. '83 (RVC) Melville, NY St. Elizabeth; Censors of Books; Priests' Personnel Policy Board; Senate of Priests (Presbyteral Council/College of Consultors).
Schneider, Fred *o.f.m.* '49 (SFD)[L] Springfield, IL Our Lady of Angels Friary.
Schneider, Gilbert *o.f.m.* '64 (GLP) Navajo, NM St. Berard; Fort Defiance, AZ Our Lady of Blessed Sacrament; St. Michaels, AZ St. Michael; [E] Gallup, NM Southwest Indian Foundation; Vicars Forane; Presbyteral Council; Diocesan Consultors.
Schneider, Harold E. '62 (COL) Retired.
Schneider, Harold F. '74 (KCK) Kansas City, KS Cathedral of St. Peter the Apostle.
Schneider, Henry W. '53 (BIS) Retired.
Schneider, Herbert *s.j.* '70 (FgM) New York, NY Society of Jesus.
Schneider, J. Daniel *m.m.* '45 (NY)[EE] Maryknoll Maryknoll Fathers and Brothers Retired.
Schneider, Jerzy *s.d.b.* '53 (NEW)[M] Ramsey, NJ Don Bosco Prep Salesian Residence; [C] Ramsey, NJ Don Bosco Preparatory High School Retired.
Schneider, John H. '68 (STL) Bonne Terre, MO St. Joseph's; DEPARTMENT OF VETERANS AFFAIRS HOSPITALS AND CHAPLAINS.
Schneider, John '83 (CHL) Absent On Leave.
Schneider, Joseph M. '74 (DUB) Waukon, IA St. Patrick; Waukon, IA St. Mary; Waukon, IA St. Mary.
Schneider, Karl J. '59 (MIL) West Allis, WI Immaculate Heart of Mary.
Schneider, Kevin C. *s.j.* '94 (OM)[C] Omaha, NE Creighton Preparatory School.
Schneider, Lance J. '03 (MAD) Madison, WI St. Dennis.
Schneider, Leo J. '83 (STP) Minneapolis, MN Holy Name; Maplewood, MN St. John's Hospital.
Schneider, Michael '94 (GF) Columbus, MT St. Mary; Defender of the Bond.
Schneider, Michael '81 (SFS) Howard, SD St. Agatha; Howard, SD St. William of Vercelli.
Schneider, Rev. Msgr. Nicholas A. '56 (STL) Retired.
Schneider, Nick L. '09 (BIS) Graduate Studies.
Schneider, Philip *o.f.m.conv.* '61 (FTW) Angola, IN St. Anthony; Angola, IN St. Paul Chapel.
Schneider, Ric *o.f.m.* '59 (PEO) Bloomington, IL St. Mary's.
Schneider, Rev. Msgr. Robert E. '57 (COL) Retired.
Schneider, Robert J. '81 (SP) Safety Harbor, FL Espiritu Santo.
Schneider, Robert J. '78 (WIN) Madison Lake, MN All Saints; Madison Lake, MN Immaculate Conception.
Schneider, Ronald F. '67 (GR) Baldwin, MI St. Ann's; Deans; Presbyteral Council.
Schneider, Ronald '75 (GB) Absent on Leave, Sick or Disabled.
Schneider, Terrance L. '79 (CIN) Beavercreek, OH St. Luke.
Schneider, Todd '85 (SCL) Sauk Centre, MN St. Paul's.
Schneider, William T. '63 (TR) Retired.
Schneller, Michael J. '72 (NO) Metairie, LA St. Ann Church and Shrine; Metairie, LA St. Ann National Shrine.
Schnipke, Eugene H. *c.pp.s.* '80 (CIN) Maria Stein, OH Nativity of the Blessed Virgin Mary; Maria Stein, OH Most Precious Blood; Maria Stein, OH St. John the Baptist; Maria Stein, OH St. Rose; Maria Stein, OH St. Sebastian; [N] Dayton Provincial Office of the Cincinnati Province of the Society of the Precious Blood.
Schnipke, Kenneth *c.pp.s.* '90 (CIN)[N] Dayton, OH Provincial Office of the Cincinnati Province of the Society of the Precious Blood; [N] Dayton Provincial Office of the Cincinnati Province of the Society of the Precious Blood; Provincial Council:.
Schnippel, Kyle E. '04 (CIN) Cincinnati, OH Our Lady of Lourdes; Vocations Office.
Schnobrich, Jon–Daniel '07 (BUR) House of Discernment; [G] Burlington, VT University of Vermont–The Catholic Center at UVM.
Schnur, Edward '91 (EVN) Evansville, IN St. Wendel; Poseyville, IN St. Francis Xavier.
Schock, Ronald A. '96 (TOL) Swanton, OH Holy Trinity; Priests' Personnel Board; Members.
Schoeberle, Bradford C. *c.s.p.* '00 (GR) Allendale, MI St. Luke University Parish; [K] Allendale, MI St. Luke University Parish and Catholic Campus Ministry.
Schoellmann, Edward R. *m.m.* '65 (GAL)[O] Houston, TX Maryknoll Fathers and Brothers.
Schoemann, Robert L. '66 (DM) Priests' Pension Fund Society.
Schoemann, Robert (DM) Retired.
Schoen, Thomas A. *s.m.* '87 (CIN)[N] Dayton, OH Mercy Siena Gardens.
Schoen, Timothy *o.s.b.* '64 (KC)[A] Conception, MO Conception Seminary College; [J] Stanberry, MO St.

Peter Parish.
Schoenauer, Francis P. '73 (ALN) Walnutport, PA St. Nicholas.
Schoenbaechler, Charles *c.r.* '42 (L)[L] Louisville, KY Villa Pacis, Resurrectionist Retirement Home; Louisville, KY.
Schoenberg, Oscar *o.s.c.* '48 (SCL)[I] Onamia, MN Crosier Priory.
Schoenberger, James T. '57 (STP) Retired.
Schoenfeldt, Arthur *c.s.c.* (FTW)[H] Notre Dame Congregation of Holy Cross, Indiana Province, Provincial House.
Schoenfield, Andrew '02 (ATL) On Leave of Absence.
Schoenhofen, Darr F. '82 (SY) Priests' Personnel Committee.
Schoenig, Stephen A. *s.j.* '85 (STL)[C] Saint Louis University.
Schoenig, Steven A. *s.j.* '01 (NY)[EE] New York, NY Xavier Jesuit Community.
Schoenig, Steven A. (STL)[O] St. Louis, MO Sacred Heart Jesuit Community.
Schoening, Sylvester H. '58 (PBL) Retired.
Schoenstene, Robert L. '75 (CHI)[A] Mundelein, IL University of St. Mary of the Lake/Mundelein Seminary; On Duty Outside the Diocese.
Schoepppe, F. Warren *s.j.* '58 (SJ)[M] Los Gatos, CA Sacred Heart Jesuit Center.
Schoettelkotte, Lawrence L. *s.m.* '70 (CIN)[N] Cincinnati, OH Marianist Community.
Schoffelmeer, Arnold L. '56 (SPK) Retired.
Scholander, Anthony E. *s.j.* '84 (OAK)[M] Berkeley, CA Jesuit Fathers and Brothers.
Scholl, Jerel A. '01 (LIN) Mead, NE St. James; Advocates.
Scholla, Robert W. *s.j.* '86 (LA)[C] Los Angeles, CA Jesuit Community; [C] Los Angeles, CA Jesuit Community.
Scholz, Mark A. '02 (KNX) Dunlap, TN Shepherd of the Valley; South Pittsburg, TN Our Lady of Lourdes.
Schommer, George *o.p.* '94 (CIN) Cincinnati, OH St. Gertrude; [N] Cincinnati, OH St. Gertrude Priory.
Schommer, Rev. Msgr. Mark J. '63 (GB) Leo Benevolent Association Retired.
Schommer, Michael '93 (FAR) Valley City, ND St. Catherine's Church of Valley City.
Schon, Randy L. '88 (SC) Wesley, IA Sacred Heart; Wesley, IA St. Benedict's; Wesley, IA St. Joseph's; Catholic Youth Organization; Presbyteral Council.
Schonberger, Micah *o.c.s.o.* '05 (DEN)[N] Snowmass, CO St. Benedict's Monastery.
Schons, Rev. Msgr. Gerard '47 (SAC) Retired.
Schooler, Rev. Msgr. William C. '74 (FTW) Granger, IN St. Pius X; Liturgical Commission.
Schopfer, John C. '69 (SY) Syracuse, NY The Cathedral of the Immaculate Conception; Syracuse, NY Public Safety Building; Special Assignment; [U] Syracuse, NY Brady Faith Center, Inc.
Schopp, George L. '74 (CHI) Chicago, IL Our Lady of Grace.
Schoppe, Charles K. '49 (GAL)[L] Houston, TX Pope John Paul XXIII Priests' Residence Retired.
Schork, John *c.p.* '76 (CHI)[N] Chicago, IL Passionist Provincial Office.
Schork, John *c.p.* '76 (L)[L] Louisville, KY Sacred Heart Retreat.
Schorp, W. Franz *s.m.* '64 (SAT)[C] San Antonio, TX St. Mary's University of San Antonio, Texas; [L] San Antonio, TX Marianist Residence.
Schorr, James D. '68 (CLV) Retired.
Schorr, James '68 (SD) Scripps Mercy Hospital; [H] San Diego, CA Scripps Mercy Hospital.
Schorr, W. David '73 (PIT) Munhall, PA St. Rita; West Mifflin, PA Resurrection.
Schott, James E. '61 (NO) Retired.
Schott, Kevin J. '90 (NEW) Maywood, NJ Our Lady Queen of Peace.
Schott, Paul *s.j.* '60 (NO) New Orleans, LA Holy Name of Jesus.
Schott, Timothy R. '70 (SC) Carroll, IA St. Lawrence; Lidderdale, IA Holy Family.
Schott, Timothy '70 (SC) Deans; Building Commission; Presbyteral Council.
Schotzko, Philip M. '77 (NU) St. Peter, MN Church of St. Peter; Propagation of the Faith/Holy Childhood Association; On Special or Other Diocesan Assignment; Ex Officio.
Schouten, Francis L. '55 (CHI) Retired.
Schrad, Merlin J. '77 (SC) Sioux City, IA Blessed Sacrament; Presbyteral Council; Diocesan Consultors; Deans.
Schrader, James C. '76 (LIN) Campbell, NE St. Anne; Deaneries and Deans.
Schrader, James *c.pp.s* '56 (KC)[J] Liberty, MO Precious Blood Center.
Schrader, Robert J. '78 (ROC) Rochester, NY Peace of Christ Roman Catholic Parish of Rochester, NY; Priests' Council; Priest Consultors; Board of Directors.
Schrader, Thomas *o.carm.* '01 (LA)[F] Encino, CA Crespi Carmelite High School; [P] Encino, CA Our Lady of Mount Carmel Priory.
Schramel, Michael J. '80 (ROC) Rochester, NY St. Jude the Apostle.
Schramm, Charles H. '71 (MIL) Hales Corners, WI St. Mary.
Schramm, Rev. Msgr. Donald C. '67 (STL) St. Charles, MO St. Charles Borromeo.
Schramm, Mark *s.v.d.* '75 (CHI)[N] Chicago, IL Edward McGuinn, S.V.D. Residence.
Schramm, Robert *o.s.f.s.* '69 (LAN) Adrian, MI St. Mary of Good Counsel.
Schratz, Martin A. *o.f.m.cap.* (CHL) Charlotte, NC Our Lady of Consolation.
Schray, Karl '65 (P) North Bend, OR Holy Redeemer; Area Vicars; North Bend, OR Shutter Creek Correctional Institution.
Schreck, Rev. Msgr. Christopher J. '77 (SAV) On Duty Outside the Diocese.
Schreck, Rev. Msgr. Christopher '77 (COL)[A] Columbus, OH Pontifical College Josephinum; [A] Columbus, OH Pontifical College Josephinum.
Schreck, J. Gerard '83 (SAV) Columbus, GA St. Anne; [A] Columbus, GA Pacelli Catholic High School; Defender of the Bond; Columbus Deanery.
Schreck, Kim J. '07 (PIT) Pittsburgh, PA St. Paul Cathedral.
Schreck, Paul C. '45 (BUF)[O] Buffalo, NY Sheehan Residence for Priests Retired.
Schreiber, Francis Anton '02 (GF) Poplar, MT Our Lady of Lourdes; Wolf Point, MT Immaculate Conception.
Schreiber, Francis '02 (GF) Membership; Vicars Forane.
Schreiber, Gerard '54 (HBG)[G] Ephrata, PA St. Clement's Mission House.
Schreiber, Martin J. *s.j.* '09 (CHI)[C] Chicago, IL Jesuit Community at Loyola University Chicago.
Schreiber, Stephen J. '99 (E) Religious Education; Vocation Office; [A] Erie, PA St. Mark's Seminary; St. Mark Seminary.
Schreiber, William A. '79 (SC) Spencer, IA Sacred Heart.
Schreiber, William A. '79 (SC) Deans.
Schreiner, Robert '89 (CR) Chancellor; Crookston, MN Cathedral of the Immaculate Conception; Finance Council; Priests' Council.
Schreiter, John P. '69 (MIL) Beaver Dam, WI St. Katharine Drexel.
Schreiter, Robert *c.pp.s.* '75 (CHI)[B] Chicago, IL The Catholic Theological Union at Chicago.
Schreitmueller, Henry '56 (NEW) Nutley, NJ St. Mary's Retired.
Schremmer, Robert A. '76 (DOD) Wright, KS St. Andrew Catholic Church of Wright, Kansas; Vicar General and Moderator of the Curia; Presbyteral Council; College of Consultors; Advocates; Pratt, KS St. Joseph Catholic Church of Greensburg, Kansas.
Schrenger, Arthur C. '75 (MOB) On Administrative Leave.
Schriber, Robert T. '96 (R) Garner, NC St. Mary, Mother of the Church.
Schriver, Ragan '95 (KNX) Seymour, TN Holy Family; Catholic Charities of East Tennessee, Inc.; Catholic Campaign for Human Development.
Schrodel, Lawrence '07 (NY)[DD] Yonkers, NY Casa Juan Diego, Inc.
Schroder, John F. *s.j.* '53 (NO) Retired.
Schroedal, Lawrence '07 (NY)[EE] Yonkers, NY St. Felix Friary.
Schroeder, Dennis A. '61 (TOL) Judges; Clyde, OH St. Mary; St. Philomena Deanery.
Schroeder, Edward H. '58 (BUF) Depew, NY Retired.
Schroeder, Eugene A. '79 (EVN) Evansville, IN St. Joseph; Cemeteries.
Schroeder, George J. '42 (PEO) Rock Island, IL St. Mary Retired.
Schroeder, Rev. Msgr. George '62 (DEN) Retired.
Schroeder, Rev. Msgr. George '62 (PHX) Scottsdale, AZ St. Patrick Roman Catholic Parish.
Schroeder, James *s.c.j.* '70 (MIL)[P] Hales Corners Priests of the Sacred Heart.
Schroeder, Jerome *o.f.m.cap.* '70 (MIL)[S] South Milwaukee, WI The Dwelling Place; Milwaukee, WI St. Benedict the Moor; Milwaukee, WI St. Francis Institute Milwaukee.
Schroeder, Kenneth J. *c.pp.s.* '65 (CIN)[N] Dayton Provincial Office of the Cincinnati Province of the Society of the Precious Blood; [N] Carthagena, OH St. Charles.
Schroeder, Kevin M. '08 (STL) St. Louis, MO Cathedral Basilica of Saint Louis; Archdiocesan Master of Ceremonies.
Schroeder, Matthew '02 (SJP) Miami, FL Assumption of B.V.M.; Presbyters.
Schroeder, Richard F. '45 (CHI) Retired.
Schroeder, Roger P. *s.v.d.* '79 (CHI)[B] Chicago, IL The Catholic Theological Union at Chicago; [N] Chicago, IL Divine Word Theologate.
Schroeder, Stephen L. '01 (TOL) Edgerton, OH St. Mary; Hicksville, OH St. Michael.
Schroeder, Tait C. '02 (MAD) Advocate/Procurator (cc.1481–1490); Vicar for Permanent Deacons; Graduate Studies; [F] Madison, WI Bishop O'Connor Catholic Pastoral Center.
Schroeder, Thomas H. '64 (MAD)[F] Madison, WI Bishop O'Connor Catholic Pastoral Center Retired.
Schroeder, Timothy '88 (FAR) Grafton, ND St. John the Evangelist's Church of Grafton; Hispanic Ministry.
Schroer, Joseph *o.c.s.o.* '52 (SLC)[F] Huntsville, UT Abbey of Our Lady of the Holy Trinity of the Order of Cistercians.
Schroer, Thomas A. *s.m.* '72 (CIN) Dayton, OH Queen of Apostles; [N] Dayton, OH Mercy Siena Support Community.
Schroth, Raymond A. *s.j.* '67 (NEW)[B] Jersey City, NJ Jesuit Center; [M] Jersey City, NJ Jesuits of Saint Peter's College, Inc.
Schu, Walter *l.c.* '94 (HRT)[B] Cheshire, CT Novitiate of the Legion of Christ.
Schubeck, Thomas L. *s.j.* '68 (CLV)[B] University Heights, OH John Carroll Jesuit Community.
Schubert, Gerard J. *o.s.f.s.* '59 (ALN)[B] Center Valley, PA DeSales University; [K] Center Valley, PA Oblates of St. Francis de Sales.
Schubert, Gerold *o.f.m.* '54 (JOL)[L] Joliet, IL St. John the Baptist Friary Retired.
Schubert, Herbert '56 (MIL) Retired.
Schubert, Roy R. '63 (PBR) Sheffield, PA St. Michael.
Schuckenbrock, Harry *o.m.i.* '59 (BWN) Port Isabel, TX Our Lady Star of the Sea.
Schuckman, Kenneth J. '92 (WCH) Colwich, KS Sacred Heart; [K] Wichita, KS Serra Club of Wichita – Downtown.
Schudde, Derk (ORL) Winter Park, FL Saints Peter and Paul.
Schuele, Francis '68 (KC) Sugar Creek, MO St. Cyril.
Schuele, John '76 (KC) Odessa, MO St. George.
Schuelkens, Dennis R. '06 (WH) Vocations Promoters; Wheeling, WV Our Lady of Peace; Diocesan Committee on Scouting.
Schueller, Anthony *s.s.s.* '77 (NY) New York, NY St. Jean Baptiste.
Schueller, La Verne L. '66 (DUB) Retired.
Schueller, Michael G. '97 (DUB)[G] Mason City, IA Newman High School; [G] Mason City, IA Newman Elementary School; Mason City, IA Holy Family.
Schuerger, Anthony J. '77 (CLV) Cleveland, OH St. Malachi; Diaconate Office.
Schuerman, James T. '86 (MIL) Delavan, WI St. Andrew.
Schuessler, Peter *s.d.s.* '80 (MIL)[B] Hales Corners, WI Sacred Heart School of Theology.
Schuessler, William R. '67 (RCK) Active Outside the Diocese.
Schuetze, John W. '97 (MO) Air Force Reserve Chaplains; Manitowoc, WI St. Francis of Assisi; Military Chaplains.
Schuetze, John (BIS) Minot, ND Minot Air Force Base Chapel.
Schuh, Rev. Msgr. John H. '65 (GB) Priests' Personnel Board Retired.
Schuh, Karl Christopher '09 (NOR) Rockville, CT St. Bernard.
Schuler, Rev. Msgr. A. John '74 (STL) Florissant, MO St. Ferdinand; Deaneries/Deans.
Schuler, Emett J. *o.f.m.cap.* '69 (MO) DEPARTMENT OF VETERANS AFFAIRS HOSPITALS AND CHAPLAINS.
Schuler, Robert J. '89 (JOL) Clarendon Hills, IL Notre Dame.
Schuler, Steven *s.v.d.* '79 (TR)[N] Bordentown, NJ Society of the Divine Word.
Schulmeister, Lawrence *o.f.m.* (BAL) University of Maryland– R. Adams Crowley Shock Trauma.
Schulte, Carl G. *c.m.* '48 (KC)[J] Independence, MO Vincentian Parish Mission Center.
Schulte, Francisco *o.s.b.* '79 (SCL)[I] Collegeville St. John's Abbey, of the Order of St. Benedict.
Schulte, Gary '72 (DET) Warren, MI St. Sylvester.
Schulte, Rev. Msgr. John R. '77 (COV) Walton, KY All Saints; Deans; Judges.
Schulte, Lyle L. '60 (LC) Retired.
Schulte, Mark A. '97 (SFD) Springfield, IL St. Aloysius.
Schulte, Rev. Msgr. Robert C. '75 (FTW) Fort Wayne, IN Cathedral of the Immaculate Conception; Board of Directors; Finance Council; Vicar General–Chancellor; Episcopal Vicar for Education; Consultors; Advisory Board; Budget Committee; Continuing Education of the Clergy; Presbyteral Council; Ecumenical Affairs; Retired Clergy Committee.
Schulte, William P. '52 (NEW) Retired.
Schultenover, David G. *s.j.* '69 (MIL)[Y] Milwaukee, WI Theological Studies, Inc.; [P] Milwaukee, WI Jesuit Community at Marquette University.
Schultheis, Raymond *c.pp.s.* '56 (CIN)[N] Carthagena, OH St. Charles Retired.
Schultz, Blaine *o.s.b.* '60 (KCK)[A] Atchison, KS Benedictine College; [I] Atchison, KS St. Benedict's Abbey.
Schultz, Brian '82 (DUL) Retired.
Schultz, Bruce B. *o.p.* '88 (R)[I] Durham, NC North Carolina Central University Catholic Campus Ministry; [F] Raleigh, NC Dominican Priory.
Schultz, Charles F. '80 (SB) Retired.
Schultz, Dustin P. '08 (PEO) Peoria, IL St. Vincent De Paul.

Schultz, George E. *s.j.* '81 (SJ)[L] Los Altos, CA Jesuit Retreat Center of Los Altos.
Schultz, Joel P. '00 (MEM) Absent on Leave.
Schultz, John A. '65 (LC) Eau Claire, WI St. James the Greater.
Schultz, John C. '57 (LFT) Retired.
Schultz, John M. '82 (E) Erie, PA St. Boniface.
Schultz, Mark A. '03 (SFE) Albuquerque, NM Holy Ghost.
Schultz, Raymond C. '91 (BEL) Fairview Heights, IL Holy Trinity Catholic Church; Diocesan Deans.
Schultz, Robert '01 (CHI) Schiller Park, IL St. Beatrice.
Schultz, Stephen J. '09 (ARL) Chantilly, VA St. Timothy.
Schultz, Stephen '99 (SFE) Belen, NM Our Lady of Belen; Defenders of the Bond.
Schultz, Rev. Msgr. William F. '64 (BGP) Stratford, CT Our Lady of Grace.
Schultze, George E. *s.j.* '94 (SFR)[A] Menlo Park, CA St. Patrick Seminary and University.
Schulyer, David H. *s.m.* '60 (SLC) Judges.
Schulz, Rev. Msgr. Donald C. '53 (COL) Retired.
Schulz, James W. *s.j.* '77 (CHI)[N] Chicago, IL Woodlawn Jesuit Community.
Schulz, James W. *s.j.* '77 (GRY) Hammond, IN St. Margaret Mary.
Schulz, Ronald '68 (PMB) Lantana, FL Holy Spirit Retired.
Schulz, Wilfred G. *o.s.b.* '53 (PAT)[N] Morristown, NJ St. Mary's Abbey.
Schulze, Robert R. '69 (TR) Prison Ministry.
Schumacher, Rev. Msgr. Andrew '59 (B) Defenders of the Bond; College of Consultors; Censor Librorum Retired.
Schumacher, Anthony J. '60 (MAD)[A] Madison, WI Edgewood College Retired.
Schumacher, Jacob J. '52 (BIS)[G] Bismarck, ND Emmaus Place Retired.
Schumacher, James '95 (CHY) Laramie, WY St. Laurence O'Toole; Diocesan Schools Advisory Group; [G] Laramie, WY St. Laurence School Foundation.
Schumacher, John N. *s.j.* '57 (FgM) New York, NY Society of Jesus.
Schumacher, Rev. Msgr. Joseph A. '57 (FWT) Retired.
Schumacher, Patrick A. '93 (BIS) Mandan, ND St. Joseph; Presbyteral Council.
Schumacher, Paul A. '62 (NU) Ivanhoe, MN SS. Peter & Paul; Ivanhoe, MN St. John Cantius; AIDS Ministry; Catholic Charities Advisors.
Schumacher, Paul A. '62 (NU) Tyler, MN St. Genevieve; Tyler, MN St. Dionysius.
Schumacher, Paul '48 (GB) Retired.
Schumm, Nicholas Frank '06 (PT) Members Elected by Deanery; Milton, FL St. Rose of Lima.
Schuster, Anthony J. '70 (GF) Retired.
Schuster, Charles G. *c.m.* '55 (FgM) Philadelphia, PA Eastern Province.
Schuster, Daniel J. '08 (GB) Manitowoc, WI St. Francis of Assisi.
Schuster, Frank J. '00 (BIS) Underwood, ND St. Bonaventure.
Schuster, Frank '00 (BIS) Underwood, ND St. Edwin's Church; Underwood, ND St. Catherine.
Schuster, Frank '99 (SEA) Woodinville, WA Blessed Teresa of Calcutta.
Schuster, Rev. Msgr. George M. '57 (BRK) Ridgewood, NY Our Lady of the Miraculous Medal; St. John's Priests Relief Society Retired.
Schuster, Paul R. '93 (FAR) Bottineau, ND St. Mark's Church of Bottineau; Westhope, ND St. Andrew's Church of Westhope; Prison Apostolate.
Schuster, Peter L. '95 (WIN) Jackson, MN Good Shepherd; Jackson, MN St. Luke's; Jackson, MN St. Joseph.
Schuster, Raymond '93 (SAT) San Antonio, TX St. Bonaventure.
Schuster, Robert '95 (DET) Roseville, MI Holy Innocents–St. Barnabas.
Schuster, Roy *o.f.m.cap* '59 (WH)[L] Charleston, WV Capuchins–St. Anthony Friary; Charleston, WV St. Anthony Retired.
Schuster, Rev. Msgr. Wilfred J. '46 (MAD)[F] Madison, WI Bishop O'Connor Catholic Pastoral Center Retired.
Schute, Arthur B. '67 (NEW) On Duty Outside the Archdiocese Retired.
Schute, Bruce J. *s.a.c.* '60 (MIL)[P] Milwaukee, WI Pallotti House.
Schutte, James R. '79 (CIN) Cincinnati, OH St. Leo the Great.
Schutten, Rev. Msgr. Marion F. '45 (NO) Retired.
Schutter, Thomas '68 (JOL) Carol Stream, IL St. Luke.
Schutty, John J. '83 (JC) Retired.
Schuwey, Emil *c.pp.s.* '49 (CIN)[N] Carthagena, OH St. Charles Retired.
Schuyler, David H. *s.m.* '60 (LAV) Diocesan Judges.
Schuyler, David *s.m.* '60 (SJ)[M] Cupertino, CA The Alcalde House.
Schuyler, David *s.m.* '60 (MRY) Judges.
Schuyler, David *s.m.* '60 (RNO) Advocates.
Schwab, Elwin '60 (P) Portland, OR St. Charles; Board Members.
Schwab, James '81 (JOL) Roselle, IL St. Walter.
Schwab, Joseph C. *o.m.i.* '53 (PT) Madison, FL St. Vincent de Paul.
Schwab, Joseph *o.f.m.* '08 (PHX)[G] Scottsdale, AZ Franciscan Renewal Center, Inc. (Casa de Paz Y Bien).
Schwab, Rev. Msgr. Robert C. '41 (BUF) Retired.
Schwab, Steven C. '90 (IND) Indianapolis, IN St. Thomas Aquinas; Indianapolis Metropolitan Police Department.
Schwab, Thomas E. '56 (CHI) Rosemont, IL Our Lady of Hope Retired.
Schwaegel, Rev. Msgr. Joseph R. '65 (BEL) Retired.
Schwall, J. J. '06 (SLC) Salt Lake City, UT Our Lady of Lourdes LLC 211.
Schwalm, Donald '52 (KCK) Retired.
Schwalm, Donald (STP) Minneapolis, MN St. Hedwig Retired.
Schwan, Paul Mark *o.c.s.o.* '88 (SAC)[A] Vina, CA Abbey of New Clairvaux, Trappist Seminary; [I] Vina, CA Abbey of New Clairvaux, Trappist.
Schwan, Paul (MIL)[K] Mequon, WI St. Mary's Hospital Ozaukee, Inc.
Schwanger, Rev. Msgr. Kenneth K. '90 (MIA) Miami, FL Our Lady of Lourdes; [C] Miami, FL Archbishop Coleman Carroll High School; Adjutant Judicial Vicar; Archdiocesan Vocations Review Board; Permanent Diaconate; Promoters of Justice.
Schwantes, John *s.j.* '69 (GB)[M] Oshkosh, WI Jesuit Retreat House.
Schware, Richard A. '75 (ALN) Ringtown, PA St. Mary; Sheppton, PA St. Joseph.
Schwarting, J. Donald '66 (GAL) Retired.
Schwartz, Edwin V. '60 (ALN) Allentown, PA Immaculate Conception Retired.
Schwartz, Hugh F. '56 (OM) Retired.
Schwartz, James A. '68 (ROC) Penfield, NY St. Joseph; Office of Seminarians.
Schwartz, John T. '81 (SFR) St. Anne's Home; [K] San Francisco, CA Home for the Aged of the Little Sisters of the Poor.
Schwartz, Norman R. '69 (MIL) On Duty Outside the Archdiocese.
Schwartz, Norman (WDC)[L] Washington, DC Georgetown University Hospital.
Schwartz, Robert M. '67 (STP) Edina, MN Our Lady of Grace.
Schwartz, Rodney A. '92 (SFD) Pittsfield, IL St. Mary; Winchester, IL St. Mark.
Schwartz, Rev. Msgr. William H. *p.a.* '68 (RCK) Special Assignment; Permanent Diaconate Program Diocesan; Pro Synodal Judges.
Schwartz, William J. '68 (PIT) Beaver County, PA Heritage Valley Beaver; Beaver, PA SS. Peter and Paul; Beaver County, PA Friendship Ridge Skilled Nursing.
Schwartzlose, John A. '00 (L) Cox's Creek, KY St. Gregory; Defenders of the Bond.
Schwarz, Elmer C. '53 (OKL)[K] Chickasha, OK University of Science & Arts of Oklahoma; Defenders of the Bond Retired.
Schwarz, Frank L. '01 (BRK) Oakland Gardens, NY American Martyrs.
Schwarz, Joseph Patrick '08 (OKL) Ponca City, OK Church of St. Mary.
Schwarz, Robert '65 (MRY) Retired.
Schwarz, Thomas *s.j.* '01 (SJ)[B] Santa Clara, CA Jesuit Community; San Jose, CA Most Holy Trinity.
Schwarzhaupt, Robert W. '86 (HON) Kamuela, HI Church of the Annunciation.
Schwebs, Daniel L. *o.s.j.* '86 (SCR) Pittston, PA Our Lady of Mt. Carmel; Pittston, PA St. Rocco.
Schweda, Phillip '79 (LAN) Tribunal Judges; Okemos, MI St. Martha.
Schweder, Rev. Msgr. John F. '60 (DET) Retired.
Schweers, Gregory *o.cist.* '81 (DAL)[J] Irving, TX Cistercian Abbey of Our Lady of Dallas.
Schweigardt, Erwin H. '67 (ALB) Priests Retirement Board/Priests Retirement Plan Board.
Schweigardt, Erwin '67 (ALB) Retired.
Schweiger, Troy J. '95 (LIN) Hastings, NE St. Cecilia's; [C] Hastings, NE St. Cecilia's Middle School/High School; [L] Hastings, NE St. Cecilia High School Endowment Fund.
Schweikert, John *m.s.c.* '96 (RCK)[G] Aurora, IL Missionaries of the Sacred Heart Community.
Schweitzer, Rev. Msgr. Francis X. '45 (COL) Retired.
Schweitzer, Gerald H. '71 (GRY) Wanatah, IN St. Mary; Wanatah, IN Sacred Heart; Deans; Bishop's Council of Priests; Consultors; Priests' Personnel Board; Marriage Dispensations.
Schweitzer, Joachim B. *o.s.b.* '58 (PAT)[N] Morristown, NJ St. Mary's Abbey.
Schweitzer, Paul A. *s.j.* '70 (FgM) Watertown, MA Society of Jesus.
Schweitzer, Robert J. '67 (PIT) New Castle, PA St. Joseph the Worker.
Schweitzer, Thomas '82 (LA) Glendale, CA Church of the Incarnation; Vernon, CA Holy Angels Parish of the Deaf.
Schweizer, Paul *o.carm.* '62 (NEW) Bogota, NJ St. Joseph's.
Schwendeman, Daniel P. '01 (LEX) Harrodsburg, KY St. Andrew.
Schwenzer, Ronald G. *c.s.b.* '68 (GAL)[E] Houston, TX St. Thomas High School.
Schwer, Albert *c.p.* '55 (L) Louisville, KY St. Agnes; [L] Louisville, KY Sacred Heart Retreat.
Schwermer, Paul '82 (LAN) McLaren Regional Medical Center; Hurley Regional Medical Center.
Schwertley, James F. '61 (OM) Omaha, NE St. Mary Magdalene Retired.
Schwertner, Rev. Msgr. Timothy '65 (LUB) Rotan, TX St. Joseph.
Schwet, Edward N. '82 (CLV) Fairview General Hospital; Cleveland, OH St. Patrick.
Schwieters, Severin '50 (SCL) Retired.
Schwinger, Rev. Msgr. William A. '58 (BUF) Retired.
Schwinghamer, David J. *m.m.* '73 (NY)[EE].
Scianna, Bernard C. *o.s.a.* '93 (TLS)[B] Tulsa, OK Cascia Hall Preparatory School; Diocesan Consultors.
Scianna, Bernard C. *o.s.a.* (PH)[C] Villanova, PA Villanova University.
Sciarrotta, Lee L. *s.m.* '67 (CIN) Dayton, OH Emmanuel; [N] Dayton, OH Marianist Community.
Sciarrotta, Paul J. '62 (CLV)[O] Chardon, OH Provincial House of the Sisters of Notre Dame, Juniorate, Novitiate Retired.
Sciberras, Ivan '99 (NEW) Belleville, NJ St. Peter's.
Sciberras, Michael J. '67 (GBG) East Vandergrift, PA Our Lady, Queen of Peace.
Sciera, Rev. Msgr. Ronald P. '61 (BUF) Retired.
Scillieri, Charles P. '73 (MET) Jamesburg, NJ St. James the Less.
Scioli, Richard A. *c.s.s.* '79 (WOR) Milford, MA Sacred Heart of Jesus.
Scirghi, Thomas J. *s.j.* '86 (NY)[EE] Cardinal Spellman Hall, Jesuit Community.
Sciumbato, Michael R. '94 (SLC) Salt Lake City, UT Our Lady of Guadalupe LLC 208.
Sciurba, Salvatore *o.c.d.* '71 (BO)[U] Boston, MA Carmelite Monastery.
Scocco, Victor *o.ss.t.* (BAL)[S] Leadership; [S] Baltimore, MD.
Scolamiero, Dominic A. '69 (PAT) Unassigned.
Scollen, Rev. Msgr. Francis J. '71 (WOR) Worcester, MA St. Peter; [R] Worcester, MA Clark University; Diocesan College of Consultors; Black Catholics: African American.
Scopa, Joseph *c.s.* '48 (PRO) Retired.
Scornaienchi, Frank *t.o.r.* '79 (ALT) Altoona, PA Our Lady of Mt. Carmel.
Scorzello, Joseph F. '69 (BO)[A] Brighton, MA St. John Seminary.
Scotchie, David '93 (ORL) Orlando, FL St. Maximilian Kolbe.
Scott, Alfonso A. '59 (LA) Long Beach, CA St. Cyprian Retired.
Scott, Brendan T. *s.j.* '78 (NY)[EE] New York, NY Murray–Weigel Hall.
Scott, Craig '96 (ALX) Vicar for Clergy; Appointed Members.
Scott, Daniel J. *m.s.* '73 (HRT) New Haven, CT St. John the Baptist; [L] Hartford, CT Missionaries of LaSalette.
Scott, Daniel J. *m.s.* (NOR) Brooklyn, CT Our Lady of La Salette.
Scott, Daniel J. *m.s.* '73 (MO) DEPARTMENT OF VETERANS AFFAIRS HOSPITALS AND CHAPLAINS.
Scott, Daniel V. *m.s.* '73 (HRT) West Haven, CT V.A. CT Health Care System.
Scott, Delroy Thomas '86 (MGZ) Rincon, PR St. Rose of Lima; Christian Family Movement; Vocations.
Scott, Derrek D. '01 (PBL) Alamosa, CO Sacred Heart; Deans; Continuing Education and Formation.
Scott, Edward R. '56 (SCR)[N] Dunmore, PA Villa St. Joseph Retired.
Scott, James C. '74 (PAT) Absent on Leave.
Scott, Joe *c.s.p.* '73 (LA) Los Angeles, CA St. Paul the Apostle.
Scott, John V. '69 (GRY) Knox, IN St. Thomas Aquinas; Priests' Personnel Board.
Scott, John *o.s.b.* '72 (SEA)[L] Lacey, WA St. Martin's Abbey.
Scott, Joseph P. *s.v.d.* '75 (SB)[I] Riverside, CA Divine Word Seminary.
Scott, Joseph '75 (SB)[N] San Bernardino, CA Ministerio Biblico Verbo Divino (MBVD).
Scott, Kenny *o.f.m.* '58 (OAK)[M] Oakland, CA Franciscan Friars (Province of Santa Barbara).
Scott, Rev. Msgr. Leonard G. '64 (CAM) Oaklyn, NJ St. Aloysius Catholic Church, Oaklyn, N.J.
Scott, Mark *o.c.s.o.* '87 (SAC)[A] Vina, CA Abbey of New Clairvaux, Trappist Seminary.
Scott, Michael Craig *v.c.* '96 (ALX) Alexandria, LA St. Rita; [A] Alexandria, LA Holy Savior Menard Central.

Scott, Michael P. '87 (MET) Office of Prison Ministry; Matawan, NJ Most Holy Redeemer.
Scott, Rev. Msgr. Patrick J. '60 (PAT) Pompton Plains, NJ Our Lady of Good Counsel.
Scott, Philip P. '79 (PSC) Roswell, GA Epiphany Byzantine Church.
Scott, Philip '89 (SP) On Duty Outside the Diocese.
Scott, Raymond '48 (DAL) Retired.
Scott, Robert T. *c.s.p.* '49 (AUS) Austin, TX St. Austin.
Scott, Robert T. *c.s.p.* '49 (NY)[EE] Jamaica Estates Paulist Fathers Generalate.
Scott, Samuel V. '95 (BGP) Pastors' Vocation Advisory Board; Office for Ecumenical and Interreligious Affairs; [A] Stamford, CT St. John Fisher Seminary Residence.
Scott, Timothy *o.c.s.o.* '05 (WOR)[O] Spencer, MA St. Joseph's Abbey.
Scott, Vincent J. '75 (OAK) San Leandro, CA Assumption of the Blessed Virgin Mary.
Scotti, P. Paschal *o.s.b.* '89 (PRO)[P] Portsmouth, RI Abbey of St. Gregory the Great.
Scotto, Dominic *t.o.r.* '67 (STU)[A] Steubenville, OH Franciscan University of Steubenville; [H] Steubenville, OH Holy Spirit Friary.
Scrima, Claude *o.f.m./i.c.* '61 (BO) Boston, MA St. Leonard of Port Maurice.
Scroggin, Christopher *l.c.* '04 (DAL)[E] Irving, TX The Highlands School; [D] Irving, TX The Highlands School; [J] Irving, TX Legionaries of Christ.
Scuderi, Carmen *o.f.m.* '83 (PSC) Hazleton, PA St. John the Baptist Church; [A] Sybertsville, PA Holy Dormition Friary; Presbyteral Council.
Scuderi, Michael *o.s.a.* '09 (PH) Philadelphia, PA St. Rita of Cascia.
Scull, Rev. Msgr. Edward J. '51 (BGP) Retired.
Scullin, Robert J. *s.j.* '76 (DET) Detroit, MI Gesu; [K] Detroit, MI Jesuit Community at the University of Detroit Mercy; Presbyteral Council.
Scullion, James *o.f.m.* (TR) Brant Beach, NJ St. Francis of Assisi.
Scully, John J. '72 (TR) Matawan, NJ St. Clement; Tribunal Judges.
Scully, John T. *s.s.e.* '55 (BUR)[E] Colchester, VT Society of St. Edmund.
Scully, Rev. Msgr. John '48 (SP) Valrico, FL St. Stephen Retired.
Scully, Michael G. *s.j.* '86 (HON) Laupahoehoe, HI St. Anthony; Papaikou, HI Immaculate Heart of Mary; Vicars Forane; Presbyteral Council.
Scully, Michael *o.f.m.cap.* '65 (SAL) Victoria, KS St. Fidelis Parish; Victoria, KS St. Boniface Parish; [D] Victoria, KS St. Fidelis Friary; [F] Victoria, KS Capuchin Center for Spiritual Life; Victoria, KS St. Ann Parish.
Scully, Patrick A. '56 (SHP) Retired.
Scully, Robert E. *s.j.* '96 (SY)[Q] Syracuse, NY Jesuits at LeMoyne, Inc.
Scully, Timothy R. *c.s.c.* '81 (FTW)[B] University of Notre Dame Du Lac; [H] Notre Dame, IN Holy Cross Community, Corby Hall, University of Notre Dame.
Scully, William *o.f.m.* (NY) Narrowsburg, NY St. Francis Xavier.
Scurti, Louis J. '73 (PAT) North Jersey Developmental Center; [P] Haledon, NJ William Paterson University of New Jersey; Directors; Office of Campus Ministry.
Seabo, Frank J. '00 (CHL) Candler, NC St. Joan of Arc.
Seabold, John P. '88 (CLV) Grafton, OH Our Lady Queen of Peace Parish.
Seabridge, Thomas L. '88 (SAC) Jackson, CA St. Patrick's; Sutter Creek, CA Immaculate Conception; Ione, CA Sacred Heart of Jesus.
Seagraves, Richard '90 (NY) New York, NY Cathedral of St. Patrick Retired.
Seagriff, Edward M. '81 (RVC) Massapequa Park, NY Our Lady of Lourdes.
Seaman, Cyril *o.f.m.* '56 (BO)[X] Boston, MA Saint Anthony Residence Retired.
Seaman, Paul G. '85 (CHI) Chicago, IL St. Pascal; Deans.
Seamus, *o.s.a.prim.* '75 (ORL)[F] Deland, FL Augustinian Monks of the Primitive Observance.
Seans, George '05 (NY) New York, NY St. Rose of Lima.
Searby, James R. '05 (ARL) Lake Ridge, VA St. Elizabeth Ann Seton.
Searles, Lawrence P. *s.j.* '87 (SJN)[D] San Juan, PR Centro De Espiritualidad Ignaciana Pedro Arrupe (CEIPA).
Searles, Thaddeus '56 (SAV) Retired.
Searles, Rev. Msgr. Wendell H. '55 (BUR) Winooski, VT St. Stephen Retired.
Sears, Rev. Msgr. Eugene A. '58 (KAL) Presbyteral Council Members; Presbyteral Council Members Retired.
Sears, G. David '63 (SY) New Hartford, NY St. Thomas.
Sears, Gerald *o.c.s.o.* '73 (WOR)[O] Spencer, MA St. Joseph's Abbey.
Sears, Michael '94 (LA) Los Nietos, CA Our Lady of Perpetual Help.
Sears, Robert T. *s.j.* '66 (CHI)[N] Chicago, IL Woodlawn Jesuit Community.
Sears, William F. '84 (PRO) Cumberland, RI St. Aidan Retired.
Seasoltz, Kevin *o.s.b.* '56 (SCL)[I] Collegeville, MN St. John's Abbey, of the Order of St. Benedict.
Seaver, Paul E. *o.p.* '59 (PRO)[P] Providence St. Thomas Aquinas Priory at Providence College.
Seavey, Michael J. '86 (PRT) Norway, ME Blessed Teresa of Calcutta Parish; Portland, ME Cathedral of the Immaculate Conception; Portland, ME St. Christopher's; Portland, ME St. Louis; Portland, ME St. Peter's; Portland, ME Sacred Heart/St. Dominic.
Seay, Robert '76 (LAF) Lafayette, LA St. Paul The Apostle.
Sebaali, Rev. Msgr. George M. '83 (SAM) Glen Allen, VA St. Anthony; Presbyteral Council; Communications; (Diocesan Newspaper) "The Maronite Voice"; College of Consultors; Board of Pastors.
Sebaali, Rev. Msgr. George (OLL) Eparchial Newsletter.
Sebahar, John '58 (JOL)[K] Naperville, IL St. John Vianney Villa Retired.
Sebastian, Angelos '01 (ORG) Huntington Beach, CA St. Bonaventure.
Sebastian, Jolly *m.c.b.s.* '00 (MEM) Germantown, TN Our Lady Of Perpetual Help.
Sebastian, Sony *s.v.d.* '92 (SB)[I] Riverside, CA Divine Word Seminary; [N] San Bernardino, CA Wordnet, Inc.
Sebasty, Joseph '85 (P) Rockaway, OR St. Mary by the Sea; Tillamook, OR Sacred Heart.
Sebaugh, Rev. Msgr. Thomas '59 (LR) Information Systems; On Special or Other Diocesan Assignment.
Sebescak, Gary '94 (BEL) Leave of Absence.
Sebesta, James A. *s.j.* '70 (STL)[C] Saint Louis University; [O] St. Louis, MO Jesuit Community Corporation at Saint Louis University – Jesuit Hall.
Sebo, Martin *s.j.* '05 (BO)[U] Cambridge, MA Zipoli House.
Sebra, Anthony G. '72 (STA) Jacksonville, FL Assumption.
Secor, Gary L. '77 (HON) Vicars Forane; Honolulu, HI Holy Trinity; Office of Clergy Priest Retirement Committee; [F] Board of Directors:; Members; Presbyteral Council; Office of Clergy: Diocesan Screening Committee.
Secora, James L. '75 (DUB) Ames, IA St. Cecilia.
Secrist, Jeremy A. '04 (JC) To The Bishop; Ministry to Priests; Secretary to the Bishop; Vice–Chancellors; Cemeteries; Historical Archives; Owensville, MO Immaculate Conception; Belle, MO St. Alexander.
Seculoff, James F. '62 (FTW) New Haven, IN St. John the Baptist; Retired Clergy Committee; Presbyteral Council.
Seda, Jon M. '88 (DUB) Gilbert, IA SS. Peter and Paul; [N] Ames, IA St. Thomas Aquinas Church and Catholic Student Center (Iowa State University); Ames, IA St. Thomas Aquinas Church (and Catholic Student Center).
Sedar, Adam C. '98 (ALN) Appointed Members; Minersville, PA St. Michael the Archangel Parish.
Sederevicius, Arturas *s.j.* '96 (CHI)[C] Chicago, IL Jesuit Community at Loyola University Chicago.
Sedita, Rev. Msgr. Vincent '72 (LKC) Judges Retired.
Sedjeu, Janvier '03 (STV) Charlotte Amalie, VI Cathedral of Sts. Peter and Paul.
Sedlacek, Richard D. '79 (YAK) Benton City, WA St. Frances Xavier Cabrini; Kennewick, WA St. Joseph's; Presbyteral Council Executive Committee.
Sedlak, John A. '82 (GBG) Everson, PA St. Joseph; [J] Everson, PA Ladies of Charity; St. Vincent de Paul Society.
Sedlak, Kenneth *c.ss.r.* '72 (CHI) Chicago, IL St. Michael in Old Town; [N] Chicago, IL The Redemptorist Fathers of Chicago.
Sedley, Joseph *c.p.* '69 (PIT)[M] Pittsburgh, PA St. Paul of the Cross Monastery.
Sedlmayer, Lauro Colen '85 (MET) Perth Amboy, NJ Our Lady of the Rosary of Fatima; Portuguese Apostolate.
Sedlock, David W. '91 (MAR) Retired.
Sedlock, Stephen J. *c.s.c.* '66 (FTW)[H] Notre Dame Congregation of Holy Cross, Indiana Province, Provincial House.
Sedlock, Stephen J. '66 (PHX)[F] Phoenix, AZ Holy Cross Congregation/Casa Santa Cruz.
Seeberger, Claude *o.s.b.* '49 (BIS)[A] Richardton, ND Assumption Abbey.
Seeberger, Claude *o.s.b.* '49 (FAR)[G] Valley City, ND Sisters of Mary of the Presentation; Special Assignment.
Seed, Michael *s.a.* '86 (NY)[EE] Garrison Franciscan Friars of the Atonement, Minister General Office.
Seegar, Kenneth M. '87 (SCR) Wilkes–Barre, PA Holy Saviour.
Seekamp, Walter J. '79 (BGP) Stratford, CT Our Lady of Grace.
Seelman, Patrick *t.o.r.* '63 (ORL)[E] Winter Park, FL San Pedro Spiritual Development Center; [F] Winter Park, FL Franciscan Friars, T.O.R., San Pedro Friary Retired.
Seeman, Robert L. '79 (PIT) Jefferson Hills, PA St. Thomas A'Becket.
Seethaler, Scott *o.f.m.cap.* '69 (PIT)[M] Pittsburgh, PA St. Augustine Friary.
Seeton, Philip M. '91 (OKL) Oklahoma City, OK St. Charles Borromeo; [K] Lawton, OK Cameron University.
Seewald, Carl H. *s.v.d.* '68 (OAK) Hayward, CA All Saints.
Sefcik, Dennis L. '65 (SC) Retired.
Segaric, Rev. Msgr. John '48 (LA) Retired.
Segatta, Bruno '74 (B) On Duty Outside the Diocese.
Seger, Michael A. '88 (CIN)[B] Cincinnati, OH Mt. St. Mary's Seminary of the West; Imprimatur Censors.
Seger, Oscar H. '70 (CIN) Wapakoneta, OH St. John; St. Marys, OH St. Patrick.
Segerblom, Kevin Lee '07 (RIC) Salem, VA Our Lady of Perpetual Help.
Segotta, Vincent *c.p.* '77 (PIT)[M] Pittsburgh, PA St. Paul of the Cross Monastery.
Segovia, Norman '67 (SJ) Milpitas, CA St. John the Baptist.
Segovia, Normandy '06 (SJ) Cupertino, CA St. Joseph of Cupertino.
Segreve, Richard J. *c.s.c.* '61 (FR)[A] North Easton, MA Holy Cross Fathers Religious.
Seguin, Robert J. *c.s.b.* '69 (GAL)[O] Sugar Land Basilian Mission Center.
Segura, Anastacio (ALB) Schenectady, NY Our Lady of Mt. Carmel.
Segura, Luis Alfonso *m.s.c.* '99 (RCK) Aurora, IL MISSIONARIES OF THE SACRED HEART[G].
Seher, Philip O. '65 (CIN) Retired.
Sehler, Michael E. *s.j.* '73 (NY)[F] New York, NY Loyola School; [EE] New York, NY "America;" Residence and publication office of the America Press.
Seibert, Gary G. *s.j.* '73 (STL)[O] St. Louis, MO Leo Brown Jesuit Community; [C] Saint Louis University.
Seibert, James C. *c.pp.s.* '77 (CIN)[N] Carthagena, OH St. Charles; Vicarri Foranei (Deans); [U] Carthagena, OH The Society of the Precious Blood Senior Housing Corporation.
Seid, David *o.p.* '08 (FgM) Metairie, LA St. Martin de Porres Province (Southern Dominican Province).
Seidel, George J. *o.s.b.* '58 (SEA)[L] Lacey, WA St. Martin's Abbey; [A] Lacey, WA Saint Martin's University.
Seidel, Thomas E. *c.s.c.* '57 (FTW)[H] Holy Cross House; South Bend, IN Holy Cross; South Bend, IN St. Stanislaus.
Seidel, Victor *s.t.* '61 (SAV) Blakely, GA Holy Family Retired.
Seidl, Larry J. '75 (GB) Green Bay, WI St. Matthew; Green Bay, WI SS. Peter and Paul; Regional Vicars.
Seifert, Michael D. '84 (Y) Alliance, OH Regina Coeli.
Seifert, William N. '81 (ALN) Allentown, PA St. Stephen of Hungary.
Seifert, William *s.v.d.* '67 (CHI)[N] Techny, IL Divine Word Residence; [N] Techny, IL Divine Word Novitiate.
Seifferly, Richard R. '63 (GAY) Retired.
Seifner, Thomas J. '92 (JC) Bonnots Mill, MO St. Louis; Loose Creek, MO Immaculate Conception.
Seifried, Rev. Msgr. Kenneth A. '63 (SC) Deans; Priests' Personnel Board; Holstein, IA Our Lady of Good Counsel.
Seigel, Timothy J. '91 (RCK) Genoa, IL St. Catherine of Genoa.
Seiker, Rev. Msgr. Daniel J. '87 (LIN) Valparaiso, NE Sts. Mary and Joseph's; Catholic Lawyers Guild; Vicars For Religious; Deaneries and Deans; Priests' Continuing Education Committee; Victim Assistance Coordinator; Promoters Justitiae.
Seiker, Leo V. '91 (LIN) Cortland, NE St. James; Building Commission; Permanent Deacon Continuing Education Committee; Pro Life.
Seiker, Mark E. '84 (LIN) North Platte, NE St. Elizabeth Ann Seton; Deaneries and Deans; Cursillo.
Seil, Paul D. '89 (BUF) Orchard Park, NY St. Bernadette.
Seiler, Andrew J. '88 (WCH) Conway Springs, KS St. Joseph.
Seiler, Gerald L. '90 (NO) Chancellor; Adjutant Judicial Vicar; Members of the Board; Censores Librorum; Canonical Permissions and Dispensations; Metairie, LA St. Edward the Confessor.
Seiler, John A. '59 (COV)[N] Fort Thomas, KY Sisters of the Good Shepherd; [I] Edgewood, KY St. Elizabeth Medical Center, Inc. Retired.
Seimas, Peter '02 (SJ) Cupertino, CA St. Joseph of Cupertino.
Seipp, William J. '63 (MAD) Lancaster, WI St. Clement; Personnel Board.
Seis, Michael '93 (GB) On Duty Outside the Diocese.
Seisser, Edward J. '98 (RCK) Elgin, IL St. Mary.
Seiter, George C. '83 (CAM) Office of Propagation of the Faith and Diocesan Missions; Cherry Hill, NJ Holy Eucharist Parish, Cherry Hill, N.J.
Seiter, Joseph A. *c.s.sp.* '62 (GAL)[O] Houston, TX Congregation of the Holy Spirit, Province of the United States.

Seitz, Gilbert J. '82 (BAL) Special Assignment; Judicial Vicar; Presbyteral Council.
Seitz, Rev. Msgr. J. Mark '80 (DAL) Dallas, TX St. Rita.
Seitz, James J. '94 (WIN) Adams, MN Sacred Heart; Adams, MN St. John's; Adams, MN Queen of Peace; Adams, MN St. Peter's; Appointed Members.
Seitz, Joseph W. '58 (CHI) Retired.
Seitz, Patrick K. '92 (BWN) Weslaco, TX St. Pius X; St. Matthew; Presbyteral Council; College of Consultors.
Seitz, Paul F.X. '58 (CHR) Retired.
Seitz, Wolfgang *o.r.c.* '02 (DET)[K] Grosse Pointe, MI Order of Canons Regular of the Holy Cross.
Seiwert, Charles F. '99 (WCH) Arkansas City, KS Sacred Heart; Presbyteral Council/College of Consultors; Defenders of the Bond.
Seiwert, James K. '09 (SAT) Selma, TX Our Lady of Perpetual Help.
Sejba, Anthony F. '99 (CLV) Medina, OH St. Francis Xavier.
Sekellick, Rev. Msgr. John T. '69 (PSC) Jessup, PA Holy Ghost; Northern Pennsylvania/Northern New York Protopresbyterate; Judicial Vicar; Family Life; Presbyteral Council.
Sekere, Joseph (TOL) Lima, OH St. Charles Borromeo.
Seland, John *s.v.d.* '68 (FgM) Techny, IL.
Seleccion, Romeo N. *m.s.* '82 (SB)[I] Moreno Valley, CA Missionaries of Our Lady of La Salette, MS; Elected Members.
Seleccion, Romeo N. *m.s.* '70 (SB) College of Consultors; Ex Officio Member; San Bernardino Pastoral Region; San Bernardino, CA Our Lady of Hope Catholic Community, Inc.; Special or Other Diocesan Assignment; Grand Terrace, CA Christ the Redeemer; Rancho Cucamonga, CA Our Lady of Mount Carmel; Rancho Cucamonga, CA Sacred Heart; Redlands, CA The Holy Name of Jesus Catholic Community, Inc.; Upland, CA St. Anthony; Yucaipa, CA St. Frances Xavier Cabrini; Diocesan Curia.
Selemobri, Efiri Matthias *m.s.p.* '91 (DOD) Garden City, KS St. Mary Catholic Church of Garden City, Kansas.
Seli, Rev. Msgr. John J. '46 (PIT) Retired.
Seli, William *s.m.* '58 (WH) Wheeling, WV St. Vincent de Paul.
Selker, Raymond *o.f.m.* (CHR) Greenville, SC St. Anthony of Padua.
Sell, Rev. Msgr. Robert L. '78 (LFT) De Motte, IN St. Cecilia; Special Assignment; [I] Board Members:; Vicar General; Chancellor and Moderator of the Curia; Diocesan Consultors; Administrative Causes; Building Commission; Corporation; Finance Council; Members; Propagation of the Faith.
Sella, Donald J. '83 (PAT) Retired.
Selladurai, Selvaraj (GRY) Michigan City, IN Queen of All Saints.
Sellars, Charles *o.m.i.* '54 (NO) Medjugorje Star.
Sellars, Charles *o.m.i.* '54 (SAT)[K] San Antonio, TX Oblate Madonna Residence.
Sellas, Joseph '89 (CHI) Northbrook, IL Our Lady of the Brook.
Selleck, John P. '57 (CAM) Retired.
Selleck, John '57 (PT) Panama City, FL St. Dominic; Gulf Coast Institution; Washington Correctional Institution.
Selvam, Panneer '81 (P) Roseburg, OR St. Joseph; Roseburg, OR St. Francis Xavier.
Selvanayakam, Darnis *m.s.f.x.* '03 (BIS) Killdeer, ND St. Paul; Killdeer, ND St. Joseph.
Selvaraj, Balapa '86 (ATL) Graduate Studies.
Selvaraj, Bose Raja '73 (BGP) Greenwich, CT Sacred Heart.
Selvaraj, Peter '82 (NY) On Leave of Absence.
Selvaraj, Rakshaganathan '94 (AUS) Waco, TX St. Jerome.
Selvaraj Pilla, Raju B. '81 (PH) Indian Apostolate, Latin Rite.
Selvester, Guy W. '97 (MET)[I] Raritan, NJ Clairvaux House; [L] Raritan, NJ Shrine Chapel of the Blessed Sacrament; Diocesan Eucharistic League.
Selzer, Eugene P. '61 (PRM) St. Louis, MO St. Louis Mission.
Selzer, Eugene P. '61 (STL) Retired.
Semancik, Rev. Msgr. Joseph F. '53 (GRY) East Chicago, IN Sacred Heart; Bishop's Council of Priests.
Sember, Benjamin '07 (GB) Defenders of the Bond; Green Bay, WI Nativity of Our Lord.
Sember, Joel A. '07 (GB) Oshkosh, WI St. Jude the Apostle; De Pere, WI St. Francis Xavier; De Pere, WI St. Mary.
Semeniuk, Gregory J. *c.m* '89 (RVC)[M] Oyster Bay, NY Vincentian Community.
Semik, Leszek '94 (LA) Glendora, CA St. Dorothy.
Seminara, Ronald S. *s.j.* '74 (CHY)[G] St. Stephens, WY St. Stephens Indian Mission Foundation; Saint Stephens, WY St. Stephen's; [D] Saint Stephens, WY St. Stephens Mission – Jesuit Community.
Seminatore, Joseph '69 (CLV) Administrative Leave.
Semko, Edward '69 (PSC) Carteret, NJ St. Elias.
Semler, Albert J. '67 (PIT) Butler, PA Holy Sepulcher.
Semmer, Dean F. '79 (CHI) Antioch, IL St. Peter.
Semonin, James R. '71 (CLV) Parma Community Hospital; Parma, OH St. Bridget.
Sempa, Rev. Msgr. John J. '80 (SCR) Wilkes–Barre, PA Sacred Heart–St. John; Wilkes–Barre, PA St. Stanislaus Kostka.
Sempko, Walter A. '50 (HBG) Retired.
Semple, James '61 (SLC) Salt Lake City, UT Retired.
Sena, Charles A. '92 (PBL) Continuing Education and Formation.
Sena, Charlie '92 (PBL) Holly, CO St. Frances of Rome; Lamar, CO St. Francis De Sales–Our Lady of Guadalupe; Springfield, CO Annunciation.
Sena, Sotero A. '81 (SFE) Clovis, NM Our Lady of Guadalupe.
Senchur, Becket G. *o.s.b.* '73 (GBG)[G] Latrobe Saint Vincent Archabbey.
Sendlein, Thomas *c.m.* '72 (FgM) Philadelphia, PA Eastern Province.
Senecal, Gerard *o.s.b.* '54 (KCK) Atchison, KS St. Benedict's; Atchison, KS Sacred Heart; Regional Pastoral Leaders; [I] Atchison, KS St. Benedict's Abbey.
Senetsky, Rev. Msgr. Robert '60 (PSC) Peekskill, NY SS. Peter and Paul.
Senger, Rev. Msgr. Joseph '54 (FAR) Retired.
Senger, William L. *m.m.* '73 (NY)[EE] Maryknoll Maryknoll Fathers and Brothers.
Senghas, Richard E. '98 (PRT) Ecumenical & Interreligious Services Retired.
Senior, Donald *c.p.* '67 (CHI)[B] Chicago, IL The Catholic Theological Union at Chicago; [B] Chicago, IL The Catholic Theological Union at Chicago; [N] Chicago, IL Passionist Community–CTU; [W] Mundelein, IL Foundation for Adult Catechetical Teaching Aids.
Seniw, John '82 (PHU) Berwick, PA SS. Cyril and Methodius; Protopresbyters (Deans); Board Members.
Senk, Christopher '76 (VEN) Sanibel, FL St. Isabel.
Sensat, Clinton M. '09 (LAF) Ville Platte, LA Sacred Heart of Jesus; Ville Platte, LA St. Joseph.
Sensenig, Andrew *o.m.i.* '97 (ANC) Pastoral Team:; Pastoral Team:; Pastoral Team:.
Senvello, Robert '94 (YAK) Retired.
Senz, Augustine *o.s.b.* '07 (WOR)[O] Still River, MA Benedictine Monks, St. Benedict Abbey.
Seo, Jeongseob (NSH) Korean Catholic Community of St. Joseph.
Sepe, Kevin M. '86 (BO) Braintree, MA St. Francis of Assisi; Elected.
Seper, John M. '83 (STL) St. Louis, MO Assumption; Archdiocesan Consultors.
Sepich, Lawrence '74 (MIL) Retired.
Sepulveda, Edgar '89 (R) Kenansville, NC Maria, Reina De Las Americas.
Sepulveda, Miguel A. '02 (MIA) Miami, FL St. Timothy.
Sepulveda, Thomas W. *c.s.b.* '74 (DET) Detroit, MI Ste. Anne de Detroit; [T] Detroit, MI Gabriel Richard Historical Society.
Sequeira, Jose '00 (CHI) Chicago, IL St. Nicholas of Tolentine.
Sequeira, Michael '66 (NOR) Clinton, CT St. Mary of the Visitation; St. Mary of the Visitation Church – Spanish Apostolate.
Sequiera, Eustace *s.j.* '75 (DEN) Denver, CO St. Ignatius Loyola.
Sequiera–Ruiz, Marcos '91 (NEW) Jersey City, NJ Parish of the Resurrection.
Sera, Enrique J. '78 (ORG) Costa Mesa, CA St. Joachim; Clergy Personnel Board; Navy Reserve Chaplains; Sexual Misconduct and Oversight Review Board (SMORB).
Serafin, Thomas J. '93 (MET) Three Bridges, NJ St. Elizabeth Ann Seton.
Serafini, Augustine '62 (GB)[J] Oshkosh, WI Community of Our Lady.
Seran, Augustinus *s.v.d.* '99 (LAF) St. Martinville, LA Notre Dame de Perpetuel Secours.
Serano, Joseph A. *o.praem.* '69 (PH)[B] Paoli, PA Daylesford Abbey; [Y] Paoli, PA Daylesford Abbey; Paoli, PA.
Serban, Ron '93 (SR) Lakeport, CA St. Mary; Deans; Board of Consultors; Priests' Council.
Serena, Edward T. '81 (BO) Senior Priests. Retired.
Sereno, David '86 (SD) Imperial, CA St. Anthony of Padua.
Sergi, Michael '79 (ROC)[L] Canandaigua, NY Notre Dame Retreat House.
Sergott, Joseph *o.p.* '96 (SD)[N] San Diego, CA University of California at San Diego (Campus Ministry).
Sergott, Lawrence J. '01 (GAY) Copemish, MI St. Raphael; Onekama, MI St. Joseph; Cursillo.
Serio, Anthony '67 (NO) Retired.
Serio, John *s.d.b.* '82 (WDC) Washington, DC Nativity; [D] Washington, DC Don Bosco Cristo Rey High School of the Archdiocese of Washington.
Sermak, Ronald *o.f.m.conv.* '60 (BUF)[O] Athol Springs, NY St. Maximilian Kolbe Friary.
Serna, Alfonso *o.ss.t.* '09 (BAL)[S] The Trinitarians in Egypt (Cairo).
Serna, J. Patrick '01 (CC) Banquete, TX Saint Michael the Archangel.
Serna, Juan '00 (STO) Personnel Board; College of Consultors/Presbyteral Council; Modesto, CA Holy Family Church (Pastor of).
Serna, Mark F. *o.s.b.* '86 (BO)[U] Hingham, MA Glastonbury Abbey.
Sernett, Rev. Msgr. Michael D. '70 (SC) Graettinger, IA Immaculate Conception; Defenders of the Bond.
Serour, George J. '59 (SAG) Bay City, MI St. Maria Goretti Retired.
Serowik, James P. '87 (SY) Priests' Personnel Committee; Endicott, NY St. Anthony of Padua.
Serpa, Vincent *o.p.* '68 (OAK)[M] Oakland, CA Order of Preachers (Province of the Most Holy Name of Jesus – Western Dominican Province).
Serra, Dominic F. '72 (WDC)[C] Catholic University of America, The.
Serra, Dominic '72 (NY) On Duty Outside the Archdiocese.
Serraglio, Rev. Msgr. Mario '58 (COL) Retired.
Serraino, Fred *c.s.c.* '68 (FR)[G] North Dartmouth, MA Holy Cross Residence.
Serrano, Dionisio '97 (PCE) On Duty Outside the Diocese.
Serrano, Edgar '87 (SD) San Diego, CA Metropolitan Correction Center; [N] San Diego, CA Newman Center – SDSU.
Serrano, Heriberto '67 (SAC) Woodland, CA Holy Rosary.
Serrano, Jose I. '95 (NY) Bronx, NY St. John Vianney, Cure of Ars.
Serrano, Rodrigo '01 (FWT) Fort Worth, TX Holy Name of Jesus.
Serrano, Sergio *o.p.* '07 (NO) New Orleans, LA St. Dominic.
Serrano Prada, Cesar A. '01 (ARL) Purcellville, VA St. Francis de Sales.
Serrano Rivera, Ivan '87 (SJN) San Juan, PR Santa Teresa Jornet.
Serrao, Ronald *c.s.c.* '92 (SUP) Tomahawk, WI St. John the Baptist; Tomahawk, WI St. Augustine.
Serraon, Mel '82 (OAK) San Leandro, CA St. Leander.
Serrick, James K. *s.j.* '62 (DET)[K] Detroit, MI Jesuit Community at the University of Detroit Mercy.
Serva, Donald M. *s.j.* '78 (WH)[A] Wheeling, WV Wheeling Jesuit University.
Servatius, Rev. Msgr. Robert R. '64 (SLC) Sandy, UT Blessed Sacrament LLC 201; College of Consultors; Board of Directors; Defenders of the Bond.
Servatius, Thomas R. '03 (SY) Waterville, NY St. Bernard; Vocation Formation.
Servera, Rafael Sastre '51 (MGZ) Mayaguez, PR Cathedral of Our Lady of Purification.
Servinsky, Rev. Msgr. Michael E. '70 (ALT) Vicar General; Priests' Personnel Board; Treasurer; Altoona, PA Holy Rosary.
Serwa, Gregory P. *s.a.c.* '70 (MIL)[P] Milwaukee, WI Pallotti House.
Sesana, Giuseppe *i.m.c.* '74 (MET)[I] Somerset, NJ Consolata Society for Foreign Missions; Somerset, NJ Mission International, Inc.
Sescon, Albert C. '86 (DET) Detroit, MI Our Lady Queen of Angels.
Sescon, Esteban '77 (ELP) El Paso, TX St. Francis Xavier.
Sessions, Phillip D. '80 (LAN) On Duty Outside the Diocese.
Sestito, Joseph N. '59 (OG) On Duty Outside the Diocese.
Sesto, Gennaro J. *s.d.b.* '50 (NEW) Elizabeth, NJ St. Anthony's.
Setelik, James '84 (RNO) Carson City, NV Corpus Christi.
Setonga, Mansuetus '86 (DAV)[J] Iowa City, IA O'Keefe Hall.
Setter, H. Jay '88 (WCH) Wichita, KS All Saints.
Settimo, Scott R. '06 (JUN) Sitka, AK St. Gregory of Nazianzen; Diocesan Consultors.
Settle, Matthew W. '04 (GB) Goodman, WI St. Joan of Arc; Lakewood, WI St. Mary of the Lake; Wabeno, WI St. Ambrose; Wausaukee, WI St. Augustine; Niagara, WI St. Anthony; Pembine, WI St. Margaret; Niagara, WI Sacred Heart; Florence, WI Immaculate Conception.
Settles, Dennis F. '65 (JOL) Kankakee, IL St. Martin of Tours.
Seubert, Xavier *o.f.m.* '71 (BUF)[C] St. Bonaventure, NY Friar Community; [O] St. Bonaventure, NY St. Bonaventure Friary.
Seuferling, George '56 (KCK) Retired.
Seung–Chul Im, Thomas Aquinas '88 (SEA) Koreans, Ministry to.
Seuntjens, LeRoy L. '60 (SC) Retired.
Severt, William H. '74 (CLV) University Hospitals.
Severt, William '74 (CLV) North Olmsted, OH St. Brendan.
Sevilla, Dennis '69 (SEA)[G] Tacoma, WA St. Joseph Medical Center; Special Assignment.
Sevola, Frank *o.f.m.* '91 (PRO) Providence, RI St. Mary; [N] Providence, RI St. Francis Chapel & City Ministry Center; [P] Providence, RI St. Francis Friary; Council Members.

Sewell, Jack '78 (ORG) San Clemente, CA Our Lady of Fatima; Judges; Air Force Reserve Chaplains.
Sewvello, Robert '94 (GF) Glasgow, MT St. Raphael; Diocesan Consultors; Priests' Council.
Sexstone, James H. '69 (ATL) Retired.
Sexton, Rev. Msgr. Michael F. '61 (BIR) Priests'/ Presbyteral Council; Diocesan College of Consultors; Diocesan College of Vicars.
Sexton, Rev. Msgr. Michael R. '61 (BIR) Pell City, AL Our Lady of the Lake.
Seyer, James A. '50 (SPC) Retired.
Seyer, Lawrence '97 (LA) Los Angeles, CA Our Saviour Catholic Center; Los Angeles, CA Transfiguration; [AA] Los Angeles, CA University of Southern California.
Seymour, Rev. Msgr. Francis R. '63 (NEW) Archdiocesan/ University Archives; [B] School of Diplomacy and Intl. Rels.
Seymour, James W. '87 (OG) Heuvelton, NY St. Raphael's; Lisbon, NY SS. Philip and James; Ogdensburg, NY Riverview Correctional Facility; Ogdensburg, NY Ogdensburg Correctional Facility; Episcopal Vicar for Clergy and Director Priest Personnel and Deacons.
Seymour, Jay W. '87 (OG) Committee on Assignments.
Seymour, John *s.t.* '70 (LA) Compton, CA Our Lady of Victory.
Seymour, Scott R. '99 (OG) Morrisonville, NY The Roman Catholic Community of St. Alexander and St. Joseph.
Sezzi, Michael J. '96 (LA) Hacienda Heights, CA St. John Vianney.
Sgarioto, Michael *o.carm.* '85 (JOL)[L] Darien Carmelite Provincial Office.
Sgarioto, Michael *o.carm.* '85 (FgM) Darien, IL Provincial Headquarters, Carmelite Provincial Office.
Shackelford, Christopher '91 (GAL) Channelview, TX St. Andrew.
Shadwell, Damian '90 (WDC) Hillcrest Heights, MD Holy Family; St. Mary's City, MD St. Cecilia.
Shadwell, Steven (PAT) West Milford, NJ St. Joseph.
Shaefer, Konrad *o.s.b.* '80 (FgM) Saint Benedict, OR Mount Angel Abbey.
Shafer, Rev. Msgr. Drake R. '73 (DAV) Long Grove, IA St. Ann's.
Shafer, James A. '75 (FTW) Fort Wayne, IN St. Elizabeth Ann Seton.
Shafer, Robert J. '99 (DET) Trenton, MI St. Timothy; Gibraltar, MI St. Victor.
Shaffer, G. Scott '89 (TR) Jackson, NJ St. Aloysius; Jackson, NJ Church of St. Monica.
Shaffer, Gregory W. '06 (WDC) Washington, DC St. Stephen Martyr; Special Ministries.
Shafran, Steve *s.d.b.* '85 (WDC) Washington, DC Nativity; Priest Council; [D] Washington, DC Don Bosco Cristo Rey High School of the Archdiocese of Washington; [W] Washington, DC Don Bosco Cristo Rey Work–Study of the Archdiocese of Washington.
Shah, Bruno M. *o.p.* '09 (WDC)[B] Washington, DC Dominican House of Studies.
Shaheen, Joseph '59 (SAM) Retired.
Shaiju, Thomas *h.g.n.* '99 (OWN) Eddyville, KY St. Mark Church; Princeton, KY St. Paul; [J] Princeton, KY Heralds of Good News of St. Paul, Inc.
Shaji, Jose '92 (SFR) Menlo Park, CA St. Denis.
Shaldone, Robert *s.o.l.t.* '97 (CC)[G] Robstown, TX Society of Our Lady of the Most Holy Trinity.
Shaleta, Emanuel Isho '84 (EST) Eparchial College of Consultors; Shelby Twp., MI St. George Caldean Catholic Church.
Shallbetter, Martin '69 (STP) Cologne, MN St. Bernard; Norwood, MN Ascension.
Shallow, Edmund J. '81 (MET) Carteret, NJ Holy Family; Carteret, NJ Sacred Heart.
Shallow, Zachory Of the Mother of God *s.o.l.t.* '04 (CC)[G] Robstown, TX Society of Our Lady of the Most Holy Trinity.
Shamleffer, Rev. Msgr. John B. '83 (STL) Judicial Vicar; Archdiocesan Consultors; Clayton, MO St. Joseph.
Shanahan, Daniel *o.p.* '62 (NO) New Orleans, LA St. Dominic.
Shanahan, John *t.o.r.* '08 (WDC)[N] Washington, DC St. Louis Friary.
Shanahan, Michael J. '92 (CHI) Chicago, IL Our Lady of Lourdes.
Shanahan, Michael *ss.cc.* '62 (FR)[G] Fairhaven, MA Damien Residence.
Shanahan, Thomas J. *s.j.* '67 (OM)[K] Omaha, NE Jesuit Community at Creighton University.
Shananhan, Kevin *m.s.c.* '86 (SAT) San Antonio, TX St. Anthony of Padua.
Shane, Donald W. '69 (OM) Omaha, NE St. Robert Bellarmine.
Shaner, Simon *o.s.p.p.e.* (ORL) Summerfield, FL St. Mark the Evangelist.
Shanfelt, Thomas '78 (ALN)[J] Orwigsburg, PA St. Francis Villa for Priests.
Shangraw, Philip '79 (GR) Hart, MI St. Joseph's; On Special Assignment.
Shanley, Brian J. *o.p.* '87 (PRO)[B] Providence, RI Providence College; [P] Providence St. Thomas Aquinas Priory at Providence College.
Shanley, Charles M. *c.m.* '55 (PH)[Y].
Shanley, Gerry *ss.cc.* '61 (FR)[G] Fairhaven National Center of the Enthronement.
Shanley, James A. '80 (HRT) East Haven, CT Our Lady of Pompeii.
Shanley, Matthias *ss.cc.* (FR)[G] Fairhaven, MA Damien Residence.
Shanley, Owen F. '53 (ALB) Retired.
Shannon, Brendan '62 (MIA) Retired.
Shannon, Francis T. '87 (BRK) Brooklyn, NY Blessed Sacrament.
Shannon, Michael *l.c.* '93 (LA)[P] Arcadia, CA Legionaries of Christ.
Shannon, Richard J. '59 (CHI) Retired.
Shannon, Timothy J. '75 (STU) Pastoral Staff; Vocations.
Shannon, Rev. Msgr. William H. '43 (ROC)[K] Rochester, NY Sisters St. Joseph of Rochester; Censores Librorum Retired.
Shannon, William '71 (HON) Office of Clergy: Diocesan Screening Committee; Vicars Forane; Diocesan Planning and Building Commission; Lihue, HI Immaculate Conception; College of Consultors; Presbyteral Council.
Shantillo, Gerald W. '09 (SCR) On Duty Outside the Diocese.
Shao, Evod E. *c.s.sp.* (BAL) Baltimore, MD St. Edward.
Shapiro, Matthew *o.s.b.* '86 (TLS)[G] Hulbert, OK Our Lady of the Annunciation of Clear Creek Monastery.
Shappelle, James '48 (CIN) Cincinnati, OH St. Bernard; Cincinnati, OH Mother of Christ; Priest Councilors; Consultors.
Sharbel, Joseph M. '85 (KC) Kansas City, MO St. Gabriel Archangel.
Sharkey, Gregory C. *s.j.* '88 (FgM) Watertown, MA Society of Jesus.
Sharkey, Rev. Msgr. John A. '56 (PH) Retired.
Sharkey, Owen *c.p.* '45 (HRT)[L] West Hartford Holy Family Monastery/Retreat.
Sharkey, Peter *s.j.* '74 (CIN)[N] Cincinnati, OH Faber Jesuit Community.
Sharkey, Philip J. '98 (HRT) Hamden, CT St. Rita.
Sharkey, Rev. Msgr. Thomas F. '48 (CAM) Defenders of the Bond Retired.
Sharkey, Thomas P. *c.s.sp.* '50 (PIT)[O] Bethel Park, PA The Spiritan Center.
Sharland, David M. *y.a.* '99 (ARL)[A] Arlington, VA Marymount University; [K] Arlington, VA Marymount University; [L] McLean, VA Youth Apostles Institute, An Association of Christian Faithful.
Sharland, David '99 (FR) On Duty Outside the Diocese.
Sharman, Robert F. '84 (HBG) New Bloomfield, PA St. Bernard; Consultors, College; Missions, Office of (Home and Foreign); Appointed.
Sharon, Charles *s.a.* '72 (NY)[EE] New York, NY Atonement Friars; [EE] Garrison, NY Franciscan Friars of the Atonement, Minister General Office.
Sharon, Norbert *s.t.* '48 (WDC)[N] Adelphi, MD Father Judge Missionary Cenacle.
Sharp, Donald B. *s.j.* '71 (SFR) San Francisco, CA St. Agnes.
Sharp, George F. '89 (NEW) Nutley, NJ St. Mary's; Elizabeth, NJ Elizabeth Federal Detention Center.
Sharp, James '84 (DAL) Retired.
Sharpe, Peter '09 (FAR) Devils Lake, ND St. Joseph's Church of Devils Lake.
Sharrett, Victor F. '65 (PH) Kennett Square, PA St. Patrick.
Sharum, Peter *o.s.b.* '52 (LR) Charleston, AR Sacred Heart.
Shashy, Daniel '91 (STA) Retired.
Shatzel, Richard J. '69 (ROC) Aurora, NY Good Shepherd Catholic Community; [M] Aurora, NY Wells College, c/o Good Shepherd Catholic Community.
Shaughnessey, James *s.j.* (BO) Pastoral Care.
Shaughnessey, Rusty *o.f.m.* '73 (OAK)[O] Danville, CA San Damiano Retreat.
Shaughnessy, Angelus *o.f.m.cap.* '55 (PIT) Clairton, PA St. Clare of Assisi.
Shaughnessy, James M. *s.j.* '79 (BO)[U] Boston, MA Loyola House; Watertown, MA; [U] Watertown, MA The Society of Jesus of New England–Provincial Offices.
Shaughnessy, James '73 (KCK) Frankfort, KS St. Monica – St. Elizabeth; Frankfort, KS Annunciation; Frankfort, KS St. Joseph's; Regional Pastoral Leaders.
Shaughnessy, Martin G. *s.j.* '63 (BGP)[E] Fairfield, CT Fairfield College Preparatory School; [O] Fairfield, CT The Fairfield Jesuit Community–Fairfield University.
Shaughnessy, Paul J. *s.j.* '87 (MO) Navy Chaplains.
Shaughnessy, Paul J. *s.j.* '87 (BAL)[S] Towson Maryland Province of the Society of Jesus.
Shaughnessy, Thomas *o.f.m.* '60 (SFD) Quincy, IL St. Francis Solanus; [L] Quincy, IL St. Francis Solanus Friary; Comite Diocesano de Ministerio Hispano – Diocesan Committee for Hispanic Ministry.
Shaughnessy, Thomas *s.s.c.* '66 (OM)[K] St. Columbans, NE Missionary Society of St. Columban.
Shaughnessy, William G. '92 (POD) Washington.
Shaughnessy, William G. '92 (WDC)[U] Washington, DC Prelature of the Holy Cross and Opus Dei.
Shaum, David W. '46 (BAL)[B] Emmitsburg, MD Mount Saint Mary's University Retired.
Shaute, Joseph '01 (ATL) Calhoun, GA St. Clement.
Shaver, James R. '89 (LAN) Jackson, MI St. John the Evangelist; Cotton Facility; Regional Vicars.
Shaver, James '89 (LAN) Jackson, MI St. Joseph.
Shaw, Brian A. '66 (HRT) Milford, CT St. Ann.
Shaw, Charles E. '51 (HRT) Retired.
Shaw, David '68 (SR) Santa Rosa, CA Resurrection; [N] Santa Rosa, CA Catholic Community Foundation; Defender of the Bond; Priests' Council; Finance Committee; Catholic Community Foundation; Clergy Personnel Committee.
Shaw, David '06 (P) Gresham, OR St. Anne.
Shaw, Dennis '74 (ROC) Auburn, NY Holy Family.
Shaw, John M. '57 (YAK) Toppenish, WA St. Aloysius; Cursillo, English; Native American; Presbyteral Council Executive Committee; Native American Ministries Retired.
Shaw, Richard D. '68 (ALB) Coxsackie Correctional Facility; Greene Correctional Facility; Special Assignment; Athens, NY St. Patrick; Catskill, NY St. Patrick.
Shaw, Thomas W. '01 (PEO) Lincoln, IL Logan Correctional Center; Elkhart, IL St. Patrick.
Shaw, William E. '57 (YAK) White Swan, WA St. Mary's; Clergy Personnel Board.
Shay, Michael *s.d.s.* '73 (TUC) O.F.C. Members; Sahuarita, AZ Roman Catholic Parish of San Martin De Porres – Sahuarita.
Shayo, Barnabas *a.j.* (P)[J] Portland, OR Providence Portland Medical Center.
Shayo, Jude *a.j.* '90 (OKL) Mangum, OK Sacred Heart.
Shea, Baldwin *o.c.s.o.* '53 (SLC)[F] Huntsville, UT Abbey of Our Lady of the Holy Trinity of the Order of Cistercians.
Shea, Daniel B. '69 (HEL) Helena, MT Our Lady of the Valley; [B] Helena, MT Carroll College; Personnel Board.
Shea, Rev. Msgr. Donald '62 (HEL) Bigfork, MT Pope John Paul II; Presbyteral Council; Diocesan Consultors.
Shea, Ed *o.f.m.* '87 (CHI)[N] Chicago, IL St. Joseph Interprovincial Post–Novitiate Formation House.
Shea, James E. *c.ss.r.* '65 (SAT) San Antonio, TX St. Gerard Majella; [L] San Antonio, TX Redemptorists of Texas–San Antonio #1.
Shea, James J. *sch.p.* '92 (PH)[F] Devon, PA Devon Preparatory School; [Y] Devon Piarist Fathers (Order of the Pious Schools).
Shea, James M. *s.j.* '75 (FgM) Towson, MD Society of Jesus; Towson, MD.
Shea, James M. *s.j.* '75 (FgM) Washington, DC National Headquarters.
Shea, James M. '65 (BUR) Venice, FL Epiphany Cathedral Retired.
Shea, James M. *s.j.* '75 (BAL)[S] Baltimore, MD Jesuit Community of Loyola University, Inc.; [S] Towson, MD Maryland Province of the Society of Jesus.
Shea, James P. '02 (BIS)[B] Bismarck, ND University of Mary.
Shea, John J. '61 (BO) Senior Priests. Retired.
Shea, John J. *s.j.* '75 (FgM) New York, NY Society of Jesus.
Shea, Joseph P. '78 (LA) Simi Valley, CA St. Rose of Lima; Board of Directors; Treasurer.
Shea, Leo B. *m.m.* '66 (FgM) Maryknoll, NY MARYKNOLL.
Shea, Lewis M. *o.p.* '66 (CHI)[N] Chicago Dominicans (Provincial Office).
Shea, Lewis M. *o.p.* '52 (FgM) New York, NY Province of St. Joseph (Eastern); Chicago, IL Province of St. Albert the Great (Central).
Shea, Michael J. *c.m.* '70 (GR)[J] Spring Lake, MI St. Lazare Retreat House.
Shea, Michael J. '76 (SFE) Albuquerque, NM Prince of Peace Catholic Community.
Shea, Michael M. *c.m.* '70 (PH)[Y].
Shea, Michael *c.ss.r.* '64 (FgM) Denver, CO Denver Province.
Shea, Mike '76 (SFE) College of Consultors.
Shea, Peter G. *c.s.p.* '62 (SFR) San Francisco, CA Old St. Mary's Cathedral.
Shea, Rev. Msgr. Richard J. '61 (BGP) Trumbull, CT St. Catherine of Siena.
Shea, Robert F. '55 (R) Retired.
Shea, Roy *c.i.c.m.* '86 (FgM) Arlington, VA MISSIONHURST.
Shea, Thomas M. '66 (SPR) South Hadley, MA St. Patrick's; Bishop's Commission for Clergy; Presbyteral Council.
Shea, Thomas '73 (PEO) Bloomington, IL St. Patrick Church of Merna.
Shea, Thomas '49 (SJ) Retired.
Shea, Thomas *c.s.c.* '67 (SP) Brandon, FL Church of the Nativity.

Shea, Timothy J. '61 (BO) Woburn, MA St. Charles Borromeo.
Shea, William *s.v.d.* '64 (DUB)[B] Epworth, IA Divine Word College.
Sheaffer, John K. '93 (SPR) Springfield, MA St. Catherine of Siena; Presbyteral Council.
Sheahan, Rev. Msgr. Donal C. '60 (SD) San Diego, CA Our Mother of Confidence.
Sheahan, John A. '60 (ORG) Retired.
Sheahan, Rev. Msgr. Richard D. '69 (PRO) Cranston, RI Holy Apostles; Finance Council.
Sheahan, William T. *s.j.* '08 (KC)[D] Kansas City, MO Rockhurst High School; [J] Kansas City, MO Rockhurst Jesuit Community.
Shearer, Thomas M. '78 (CIN) Dayton, OH St. Henry.
Sheary, Pat *s.j.* '80 (LA) Long Beach, CA St. Cornelius.
Shebuski, Charles J. '65 (GB) Absent on Leave, Sick or Disabled.
Shecterle, Rev. Msgr. Ross A. '86 (MIL) On Duty Outside the Archdiocese; Consultant.
Sheeds, Gerald E. '68 (KCK) Retired.
Sheedy, Edward J. '72 (BUF) Olean, NY St. John.
Sheedy, Patrick J. '65 (ORL) Ocala, FL Blessed Trinity; [A] Ocala, FL Trinity Catholic High School, Inc.
Sheedy, Timothy J. '76 (DAV) Bettendorf, IA Our Lady of Lourdes.
Sheedy, Val '55 (ORL) Retired.
Sheehan, Augustine J. '55 (RVC) Retired.
Sheehan, Daniel J. '53 (BO) South Boston, MA St. Brigid; Senior Priests. Retired.
Sheehan, Rev. Msgr. Dennis F. '63 (BO) Designated; Presbyteral Council; Newton, MA Our Lady Help of Christians.
Sheehan, Donald P. '68 (NEW) Ridgefield, NJ St. Matthew's.
Sheehan, Edward *s.m.* '61 (BO)[U] Boston, MA Marist Fathers of Our Lady of Victories (Boston Prov.).
Sheehan, Rev. Msgr. George F. '61 (SY)[Q] East Syracuse, NY Vianney House; Board of Diocesan Consultors; Management Team; Special Assignment.
Sheehan, Gerard J. *s.o.l.t.* '85 (CC)[G] Robstown, TX Society of Our Lady of the Most Holy Trinity.
Sheehan, J. Peter '56 (BIR) Retired.
Sheehan, James C. '79 (NY) New York, NY St. Columba.
Sheehan, Rev. Msgr. James M. '98 (NEW) Newark, NJ Cathedral Basilica of the Sacred Heart; Judicial Vicar; Metropolitan Tribunal; Members.
Sheehan, James '79 (NY)[HH] Bronx, NY Bronx Community College; [HH] Bronx, NY Hostos Community College.
Sheehan, John P. '89 (NY) Bronx, NY St. Frances of Rome.
Sheehan, John R. *s.j.* '92 (NY)[II] New York, NY Xavier Society for the Blind; [EE] New York, NY St. Ignatius Loyola Residence.
Sheehan, Joseph A. '59 (ALN)[J] Bethlehem, PA Holy Family Villa Retired.
Sheehan, Joseph G. '48 (NEW) Holy Name Federation Retired.
Sheehan, Joseph *o.carm.* '63 (SFS)[A] Aberdeen, SD Presentation College.
Sheehan, Justin R. *o.c.s.o.* '91 (ROC)[J] Piffard, NY Abbey of the Genesee.
Sheehan, Mark S. '63 (BO) Bedford, MA St. Michael.
Sheehan, Maurice *o.f.m.cap.* '55 (NOR)[A] Cromwell, CT Holy Apostles College and Seminary.
Sheehan, Maurice *o.f.m.cap.* '55 (PIT)[M] Pittsburgh, PA St. Augustine Friary.
Sheehan, Michael J. '78 (NEW) River Edge, NJ St. Peter the Apostle; Office of Divine Worship.
Sheehan, Michael J. '64 (PH) Philadelphia, PA Sacred Heart of Jesus.
Sheehan, Myles N. *s.j.* '94 (BO)[U] Watertown, MA The Society of Jesus of New England–Provincial Offices; [U] Boston The Society of Jesus of New England–Provincial Offices; [U] Newton, MA The Jesuit Community at Boston College; Watertown, MA; Watertown, MA Society of Jesus.
Sheehan, Myles *s.j.* '94 (FgM) Washington, DC National Headquarters.
Sheehan, Peter J. '04 (PRO) Coventry, RI SS. John and Paul.
Sheehan, Richard *o.m.i.* '61 (SAT)[K] San Antonio, TX Oblate Madonna Residence.
Sheehan, Thomas F. *o.f.m.* '60 (NY)[EE] New York Franciscan Friars, Holy Name Province.
Sheehan, Thomas J. *s.j.* '99 (WOR)[O] Worcester, MA Jesuits of the Holy Cross, Inc.
Sheehan, Thomas W. '70 (CLV) Retired.
Sheehan, William J. *c.s.b.* '66 (ROC)[J] Rochester Basilian Residence.
Sheehan, William *o.m.i.* '65 (BO)[U] Lowell, MA Missionary Oblates of Mary Immaculate; [U] Lowell, MA St. Eugene House (Residence).
Sheehy, Charles I. '44 (BO) Senior Priests. Retired.
Sheehy, Michael *c.m.m.* '64 (DET)[K] Vocation Office.
Sheehy, Vincent J. '61 (VEN) Venice, FL Our Lady of Lourdes Retired.
Sheehy, Wilfred '60 (SR) Retired.
Sheehy, Yvon *s.c.j.* '78 (MIL)[P] Hales Corners, WI Priests of the Sacred Heart; [P] Milwaukee, WI SCJ Community; Franklin, WI St. Martin of Tours.
Sheekey, Philip P. '64 (WIL) Wilmington, DE St. Mary Magdalen.
Sheeran, Fintan '56 (WDC) Seat Pleasant, MD St. Margaret.
Sheeran, Michael J. *s.j.* '70 (DEN)[B] Denver, CO Regis University; [N] Denver, CO Regis Jesuit Community (The Jesuits at Regis University).
Sheeran, Rev. Msgr. Robert T. '70 (NEW)[A] South Orange, NJ Immaculate Conception Seminary; [A] South Orange, NJ Seton Hall University College Seminary; [B] South Orange, NJ Seton Hall University; [B] School of Diplomacy and Intl. Rels.
Sheerger, Michael T. '07 (LAR)[D] Laredo, TX St. John Priory, F.J.; [F] Laredo, TX Holy Spirit Retreat and Conference Center.
Sheerin, Rev. Msgr. James O. '56 (NEW)[M] Rutherford, NJ St. John Vianney Residence for Priests Retired.
Sheerin, Philip F. *m.m.* '44 (SJ)[M] Los Altos, CA Maryknoll.
Sheets, James P. '75 (SAC) Sacramento, CA Sutter General Hospital; Sacramento, CA Sutter Memorial Hospital.
Sheets, Joseph B. '57 (IND) Retired.
Sheganoski, Fabian *t.o.r.* '65 (ALT)[G] Newry, PA St. Bernardine Monastery Retired.
Sheil, James '66 (CLV) Military Chaplains; Army Chaplains.
Shelander, Donald E. '70 (CIN) Retired.
Shelby, Charles F. *c.m.* '68 (CHI)[N] Chicago DePaul Vincentian Residence.
Sheldon, Alexander J. '01 (BR) Baton Rouge, LA St. Pius X.
Sheldon, William W. *c.m.* '52 (PH)[Y].
Sheldon, William W. *c.m.* '52 (ALB) Special Assignment; [M] Albany, NY De Paul Provincial House.
Shellem, John J. '52 (PH) Retired.
Shelley, John J. '61 (PH) Willow Grove, PA St. David Retired.
Shelley, Jonathan P. '95 (STP) Hugo, MN St. John the Baptist.
Shelley, Rev. Msgr. Thomas J. '62 (NY) New York, NY St. Thomas More; On Duty Outside the Archdiocese.
Shelley, William M. '50 (NY) New York, NY Cathedral of St. Patrick Retired.
Shellito, Edward D. *m.m.* '90 (FgM) Maryknoll, NY MARYKNOLL.
Shellman, Richard L. '86 (HRT)[A] In Res. at the Archbishop Daniel A. Cronin Retirement Residence at St. Thomas Seminary Retired.
Shelly, Eamonn *l.c.* '02 (ATL)[L] Norcross, GA Home and Family, Inc.; [D] Cumming, GA Pinecrest Academy, Inc.; [G] Alpharetta, GA Norcross Pastoral Center, Inc.
Shelly, Roy '78 (MRY) Vocations Director; Diocesan Consultors; Vocations Board.
Shelly, Roy '78 (MRY)[I] Monterey, CA Department of Campus Ministry; Office of Faith Formation; Campus Ministry Department; Permanent Diaconate; Presbyteral Council; Clergy Personnel Board; Pastoral Support; Permanent Diaconate Advisory Board; Moderator of the Curia; Carmel, CA San Carlos Borromeo Basilica; Diocesan Consultors; Special Assignment.
Shelton, Charles M. *s.j.* '82 (DEN)[N] Denver, CO Regis Jesuit Community (The Jesuits at Regis University).
Shelton, Charles *o.f.m.conv.* '81 (MRY)[F] Arroyo Grande, CA St. Joseph Cupertino Friary.
Shelton, Henry '69 (JKS) Retired.
Shelton, James Brent Allen '01 (KNX) Alcoa, TN Our Lady of Fatima.
Shelton, Lawrence '66 (LA) Los Angeles, CA St. Anselm.
Sheltz, Rev. Msgr. George A. '71 (GAL) Secretariat For Clergy Formation and Chaplaincy Services; College of Consultors; Priests Personnel Committee; Building and Planning Commission; Secretariat for Clergy Formation and Chaplaincy Services; Ex Officio Members.
Shema, George T. '67 (PAT)[Q] Chester, NJ Nazareth Village Retired.
Shemuga, Kevin C. '83 (CLV) Strongsville, OH St. Joseph.
Shen, Raphael *s.j.* '70 (DET)[K] Detroit, MI Jesuit Community at the University of Detroit Mercy.
Shenk, Bertrand J. '37 (TOL) Retired.
Shenosky, Joseph T. '00 (PH)[D] Philadelphia, PA Archbishop Ryan High School; Censores Librorum; Philadelphia, PA Christ the King.
Shenoy, Leslie '76 (FRS) Retired.
Shenrock, Rev. Msgr. Joseph C. '53 (TR) Whiting, NJ St. Elizabeth Ann Seton; Tribunal Judges Retired.
Shepanzyk, Thomas '09 (BRK) Brooklyn, NY Our Lady of Czestochowa–St. Casimir.
Shepard, Eugene '76 (AUS) Retired.
Shepard, Thomas B. '77 (HRT) New Haven, CT St. Brendan; New Haven, CT St. Aedan; New Haven Deanery.
Shepard, Timothy J. '82 (CLV)[D] Cuyahoga Falls, OH Walsh Jesuit High School.
Sheperd, Raymond C. '57 (TOL) Retired.
Shepherd, Baby *c.m.i.* (SYM) Falmouth, KY Blessed Chavara Syro–Malabar Catholic Church Cincinnati, OH.
Shepley, Brian J. '92 (DAV) Brooklyn, IA St. Patrick; Victor, IA St. Bridget; DEPARTMENT OF VETERANS AFFAIRS HOSPITALS AND CHAPLAINS.
Sherba, Rev. Msgr. Girard M. '79 (R) Vicar Judicial; Ex Officio; Bishops' Delegates for Religious; Vicar Judicial & Chancellor; Diocesan Consultors.
Sherbno, John C. '49 (TOL) Retired.
Sherbo, Albert '87 (DM) Adel, IA St. John.
Sherburne, Richard F. *s.j.* '56 (MIL)[P] Wauwatosa, WI Jesuit Community at St. Camillus.
Sherdel, Lawrence W. '81 (HBG) McSherrystown, PA Annunciation of the Blessed Virgin Mary.
Sherer, Richard B. '58 (HRT) Retired.
Sheridan, Brian R. *m.s.* '83 (ORL) Orlando, FL Good Shepherd.
Sheridan, Daniel '79 (RVC) Unassigned.
Sheridan, Denis J. '81 (RVC)[M] Amityville, NY St. Pius X Residence Retired.
Sheridan, Edward J. '63 (CHL) Asheville, NC St. Eugene Retired.
Sheridan, Edward M. '07 (RVC) Franklin Square, NY St. Catherine of Sienna.
Sheridan, Eugene F. *c.m.* '68 (PH) Philadelphia, PA St. Francis of Assisi.
Sheridan, James J. *o.s.a.* '61 (DET) Grosse Pointe Park, MI St. Clare of Montefalco.
Sheridan, John E. '90 (BO) Salem, MA St. James.
Sheridan, John J. *o.s.a.* '85 (PH)[Y] Villanova, PA Provincial Offices of the Order of St. Augustine, Province of St. Thomas of Villanova; [Y] Villanova, PA St. Thomas Monastery; Counselors:.
Sheridan, Rev. Msgr. John Virgilius '43 (LA) Malibu, CA Our Lady of Malibu Retired.
Sheridan, Mark *o.s.b.* '65 (WDC)[N] Washington, DC St. Anselm's Abbey.
Sheridan, Matthew W. '54 (BRK)[T] Douglaston, NY Bishop Mugavero Residence Retired.
Sheridan, Patrick L. '98 (CIN) Bellefontaine, OH St. Patrick.
Sheridan, Paul G. *s.j.* '75 (SJ)[D] San Jose, CA Bellarmine College Preparatory.
Sheridan, Rev. Msgr. Paul W. '56 (SFD) Retired.
Sheridan, Peter *o.f.m.* (PAT)[N] Ringwood, NJ Holy Name Friary, Inc.
Sheridan, Philip A. '51 (HRT) Retired.
Sheridan, Sean O. *t.o.r.* '06 (WDC)[N] Washington, DC St. Louis Friary; [C] Catholic University of America, The.
Sheridan, Thomas L. *s.j.* '57 (NEW)[B] Jersey City, NJ Jesuit Center; [M] Jersey City, NJ Jesuits of Saint Peter's College, Inc.; Elizabeth, NJ Elizabeth Federal Detention Center.
Sheridan, Thomas '64 (CHY) Green River, WY Immaculate Conception.
Sheridan, William H. '54 (CHI) Chicago, IL St. Philip Neri Retired.
Sheridan, William J. '72 (CHI) Wilmette, IL St. Francis Xavier.
Sheridan, William P. '89 (NEW) Mahwah, NJ Immaculate Conception; [P] Mahwah, NJ Ramapo College.
Sherliza, Michael S. '99 (ATL) Marietta, GA St. Joseph.
Sherlock, James C. '64 (PH) Ardmore, PA St. Colman.
Sherlock, John P. '69 (WCH) Wichita, KS Cathedral of the Immaculate Conception; Sedgwick County Adult Local Detention Facility; Presbyteral Council/College of Consultors.
Sherlock, R. Marc '79 (CIN) Tipp City, OH St. John the Baptist; Judges.
Sherman, Rev. Msgr. Anthony F. '70 (BRK) Released from Diocesan Assignment; Staff; Staff.
Sherman, Daniel J. *m.m.* '47 (NY)[EE] Retired.
Sherman, Edward '56 (FAR) Native American Ministries Retired.
Sherman, Gary D. '85 (TLS)[E] Tulsa, OK St. John Medical Center, Inc.; [F] Tulsa, OK St. John Villas, Inc.; Special Assignment.
Sherman, Rt. Rev. Kenneth '80 (NTN) Rochester, NY St. Nicholas; Presbyteral Council.
Sherman, Richard T. '00 (SLC) Central Utah Correctional Facility; Central Valley, UT Saint Elizabeth LLC 220; [H] Ephraim, UT St. Jude Catholic Center; Correctional Institution Ministry.
Sherman, William C. '55 (FAR) Retired.
Sherrer, Charles D. *c.s.c.* '61 (P)[B] University of Portland; [L] Portland, OR Holy Cross Fathers & Brothers, C.S.C. – University of Portland Retired.
Sherrer, Charles *c.s.c.* (FTW)[H] Notre Dame Congregation of Holy Cross, Indiana Province, Provincial House.
Sherry, Brendan '52 (AMA) Retired.
Sherry, Bryan W. '62 (TUC) Retired.
Sherry, Edward F. '68 (BO) Merrimac, MA Holy Redeemer.
Sherry, Frank *c.p.m.* '89 (OWN)[F] Auburn, KY Fathers of Mercy.
Sherry, Robert N. '66 (RCK) McHenry, IL Church of

Holy Apostles; Cursillo Movement.
Shershanovich, Rev. Msgr. Michael '74 (SPR) Pittsfield, MA St. Joseph's; Vicars for the Clergy; Presbyteral Council.
Sherwin, Michael S. *o.p.* '91 (OAK)[M] Oakland Order of Preachers (Province of the Most Holy Name of Jesus – Western Dominican Province).
Sherwood, Lan S. '75 (PHX) On Leave.
Sherwood, Stephen K. *c.m.f.* '71 (SAT) San Antonio, TX Immaculate Heart of Mary; [C] Oblate School of Theology.
Sherwood, Timothy H. '93 (SP) St. Petersburg, FL St. Joseph; [F] Saint Petersburg, FL Immaculate Conception Early Childhood Center.
Sheslo, Charles '61 (SD) Retired.
Shetler, John '92 (PHX) On Leave; Mesa, AZ Holy Cross Roman Catholic Parish.
Shetler, Joseph L. '06 (JC) Columbia, MO Our Lady of Lourdes; Columbia Catholic Hospital Ministry.
Shetter, John '57 (ORG) Retired.
Shevlin, John *s.v.d.* '60 (LA)[D] Lakewood, CA Saint Joseph High School.
Shidler, Anthony *o.s.b.* '64 (KC)[J] Conception, MO Conception Abbey.
Shields, David M. *s.j.* '73 (MIL)[Y] Milwaukee, WI Casa Romero Renewal Center, Inc.; [P] Milwaukee, WI Jesuit Community at Marquette University.
Shields, Rev. Msgr. Hugh Joseph '72 (PH) On Special or Other Archdiocesan Assignment; Philadelphia, PA Our Lady of Ransom; Vicar for Hispanic Catholics.
Shields, Rev. Msgr. James J. '63 (PH) North Wales, PA Mary, Mother of the Redeemer.
Shields, Rev. Msgr. Joseph A. '49 (PH) Gladwyne, PA St. John Baptist Vianney Retired.
Shields, Rev. Msgr. Maurice L. '57 (MOB)[E] Daphne, AL Mercy Medical Retired.
Shields, Michael '79 (ANC) On Duty Outside Archdiocese; Magadan Mission.
Shields, Patrick J. '64 (CLV) Stow, OH Holy Family.
Shields, Robert J. '64 (YAK) Retired.
Shields, Stephen L. '74 (CLV) Sheffield Lake, OH St. Thomas the Apostle.
Shields, W. Bry '84 (MOB)[B] Mobile, AL McGill–Toolen Catholic High School; Mobile, AL St. Pius X.
Shiffer, James *s.s.c.* '65 (LA)[P] Los Angeles, CA Columban Fathers, Procure House; Defenders of the Bond.
Shiffer, James *s.s.c.* '65 (SPP) Judges.
Shiffer, James *s.s.c.* '65 (OM)[K] St. Columbans Missionary Society of St. Columban.
Shigo, Francis L. *s.v.d.* '60 (LA)[J] San Pedro, CA Providence Little Company of Mary San Pedro Hospital; [J] San Pedro, CA Providence Little Company of Mary San Pedro Peninsula Hospital Pavilion.
Shikany, Paul M. '79 (IND) Indianapolis, IN St. Matthew; Adjunct Vicars Judicial; Priests' Personnel Board.
Shikaputo, Victor S. *s.s.* '94 (BAL)[S] Baltimore Society of St. Sulpice, Province of the United States.
Shillcox, Timothy D. *o.praem.* '87 (GB) De Pere, WI Our Lady of Lourdes; [J] De Pere, WI St. Joseph Priory.
Shimek, Joseph J. '07 (MIL) Kenosha, WI St. Mary.
Shimkus, John Martin *o.s.b.* '03 (DET)[B] Oxford, MI St. Benedict Monastery.
Shimotsu, John M. '94 (ORG) Military Chaplains; Navy Chaplains; On Duty Outside the Diocese.
Shimsky, James B. '01 (SCR) Scott Twp., PA St. John Vianney; Clifford, PA St. Pius X.
Shin, Ki Ryong (TR) Trenton, NJ The Church of the Korean Martyrs.
Shin, Peter Dong Ho *c.p.* '94 (AUS) Harker Heights, TX St. Paul Chong Hasang.
Shin, Stephen *o.f.m.cap.* (HBG) York, PA St. Joseph.
Shindelar, Vincent J. '56 (RCK) Retired.
Shine, Edward J. '57 (CIN) Harrison, OH St. John the Baptist Retired.
Shine, John V. '63 (LA)[P] Santa Barbara, CA St. Mary's Evangelization Center Retired.
Shine, John *c.m.* '63 (LA)[V] Santa Barbara, CA St. Mary's Seminary Center.
Shine, Robert W. '55 (SAG) Retired.
Shinkut, Stanley (BRK) Brooklyn, NY St. Finbar.
Shinney, Robert J. *s.j.* '68 (SJ)[D] San Jose, CA Bellarmine College Preparatory.
Shinnick, Edward P. '56 (GF) Retired.
Shinnick, Lawrence E. '05 (BIR) Demopolis, AL St. Leo; Livingston, AL St. Francis of Assisi.
Shipley, Rev. Msgr. William '54 (SD) Retired.
Shipp, Edmund N. '61 (SFR) Retired.
Shipps, Bede *o.p.* '85 (WDC) Washington, DC St. Dominic Church & Priory.
Shirey, Joseph *s.j.* '56 (SPK)[J] Spokane, WA Regis Community.
Shirley, John T. *o.s.a.* '65 (CHI)[N] Olympia Fields, IL Tolentine Monastery at Tolentine Center.
Shirley, Rev. Msgr. Richard '67 (CC) Office of the Bishop; College of Consultors; Finance Council; Personnel Board – Priests; Presbyteral Council; Defenders of the Bond; Vicar General; [I] Corpus Christi, TX Journey to Damascus, Inc.; Corpus Christi, TX St. Pius X; [I] Corpus Christi, TX Hope, Faith & Love, Inc.; Consultors.
Shirley, Ronald '73 (MRY) Aptos, CA Resurrection.
Shiroda, Donald L. '59 (MAR) Retired.
Shiverski, John J. '68 (MAR) Defensore Vinculi Retired.
Shiyo, Evarist (B) Boise, ID Sacred Heart.
Shlesinger, Bernard (Ned) '96 (R)[J] Raleigh, NC Vocations Office.
Shlesinger, Bernard E. '96 (R) Special Assignment; Office for Vocations and Seminarian Formation.
Shmaruk, Richard J. '65 (BO) Woburn, MA St. Anthony of Padua.
Shnob, Alan D. '78 (OG) Peru, NY St. Augustine; Defenders of the Bond.
Shoback, Thomas P. '77 (SCR) Jermyn, PA Sacred Hearts of Jesus & Mary, Jermyn.
Shockey, Benjamin D. '04 (WCH)[B] Wichita, KS Kapaun Mt. Carmel Catholic High School; Wichita, KS St. Thomas Aquinas.
Shocklee, Christopher R. '09 (LFT) Lafayette, IN St. Lawrence; Lafayette, IN St. Mary Cathedral.
Shoda, D. Brian '87 (WH) Inwood, WV St. Leo.
Shoemaker, David A. '05 (BO) Absent on Leave.
Shoemaker, David M. '00 (MOB) Eufaula, AL Holy Redeemer; Ventress Correctional Institution; Bullock County Correctional Facility; Vocations.
Shoemaker, Rev. Msgr. Samuel E. '66 (PH) Yardley, PA St. Ignatius of Antioch; Archdiocesan Judges.
Shoemaker, Thomas '90 (FTW) Fort Wayne, IN St. Jude; Consultors; Presbyteral Council.
Shoemaker, Victor *c.s.j.* '03 (NEW) Orange, NJ Mt. Carmel.
Shofany, Saba '95 (NTN) San Diego, CA St. Jacob Mission; Vocations Office.
Shofany, Saba (SD)[B] University of San Diego.
Shofner, Christopher '05 (STP) Le Center, MN St. Mary; Le Center, MN Church of St. Henry.
Shonebarger, Thomas '69 (COL) Retired.
Shonis, Anthony J. '71 (OWN) Deans/Coordinators; Henderson, KY Holy Name of Jesus.
Shooner, Jeffrey P. '04 (L) Louisville, KY St. Lawrence; College of Consultors; Ex Officio; Vocations.
Shore, Zachary J. '81 (SFR) Retired.
Shori, Nicholas R. '74 (Y) New Middletown, OH St. Paul the Apostle.
Short, Anthony J. *s.j.* '71 (STL)[O] St. Louis, MO Jesuit Community Corporation at Saint Louis University – Jesuit Hall.
Short, Gregory *o.m.v.* '79 (BO)[B] Boston, MA Oblate Provincialate.
Short, James M. *s.j.* '61 (STL)[O] St. Louis, MO Bellarmine House of Studies; [V] St. Louis, MO The Jesuits of the Missouri Province.
Short, John '99 (SFS) Mobridge, SD St. Joseph.
Short, Redemptus *o.c.d.* '47 (MIL)[P] Hubertus, WI Discalced Carmelite Monastery – Holy Hill Basilica of the National Shrine of Mary, Help of Christians, Holy Hill Retired.
Shortall, Robert '74 (DAV) Retired.
Shorter, Melvin *c.p.* '86 (NY)[EE] Pelham Manor, NY St. Vincent's Residence.
Shortt, David J. '89 (PBR) Youngstown, OH St. Nicholas; CIVIL AIR PATROL.
Shortt, Patrick J. '66 (JC) Eldon, MO Sacred Heart; Eugene, MO Our Lady of the Snows; Senators.
Shott, Stephen *o.s.f.s.* '95 (VEN) Naples, FL St. Ann.
Shoup, Steven L. '84 (CIN) Fort Loramie, OH St. Michael; Fort Loramie, OH SS. Peter and Paul; Priest Councilors; Vicarri Foranei (Deans); Consultors.
Shovelton, Gerald T. '56 (FR) Retired.
Shovelton, Gerald '56 (ORL) Lady Lake, FL St. Timothy Retired.
Shovelton, William J. '46 (FR) Retired.
Showalter, Joseph L. '57 (SPK)[J] Spokane, WA Regis Community Retired.
Showalter, Rev. Msgr. Paul E. '66 (PEO) Peoria, IL St. Mary's Cathedral; Peoria, IL St. Bernard's; Peoria, IL St. Peter's; Vicar General; Diocesan College of Consultors; Finance Council (Canon 492); Catholic Relief Services; Clergymen's Aid, Inc.; Conciliation and Arbitration Process; Diocesan Pastoral Council; Diocesan Personnel Board; Holy Childhood Association; Propagation of the Faith; Priests' Purgatorial Society; Peoria, IL Catholic Cemetery Association of Peoria, IL.
Showalter, Thomas *s.o.l.t.* '97 (CC)[G] Robstown, TX Society of Our Lady of the Most Holy Trinity; Robstown, TX St. John Nepomucene.
Showfety, Rev. Msgr. Joseph '55 (CHL) Greensboro, NC Retired.
Showraiah, Marneni *o.f.m.* '90 (NSH) Franklin, TN St. Philip.
Shramko, John '02 (ATL) On Leave of Absence.
Shreenan, Timothy J. *o.f.m.* '84 (NY) New York, NY St. Francis of Assisi.
Shreve, Rev. Msgr. Thomas F. '61 (RIC) Vicar General; Holy Childhood Association; Propagation of the Faith; Bishop's Administrative Advisory Council; Building and Renovation Committee; Propagation of the Faith.
Shreve, Rev. Msgr. Thomas (BAL) Judicial Vicar.
Shroeder, Danielmose *o.f.m.* '91 (FgM) Washington, DC COMMISSARIAT OF THE HOLY LAND.
Shrum, Jack D. '08 (SEA) Sumner, WA St. Andrew.
Shuda, Paul R. '60 (HBG) Legion of Mary; Harrisburg, PA Retired.
Shudrak, Jaroslav '08 (SJP) On Assignment Outside the Diocese; Presbyters.
Shuey, Mark '07 (SJP) Raleigh, NC St. Basil The Great Mission; Raleigh, NC St. Nicholas Mission; Mid–Atlantic Protopresbytery; Presbyters.
Shugrue, Rev. Msgr. Michael P. '66 (R) Fayetteville, NC St. Patrick; Diocesan Consultors; Council of Priests.
Shugrue, Rev. Msgr. Timothy J. '73 (NEW) Cranford, NJ St. Michael's.
Shuley, Keith J. '92 (MO) Navy Chaplains.
Shuley, Keith *c.c.* '92 (CC) Military Chaplains.
Shulik, Bernard P. '74 (PIT)[N] Coraopolis, PA Our Lady of the Sacred Heart Convent.
Shultz, Rev. Msgr. William E. '70 (ALT) Roaring Spring, PA St. Thomas More.
Shumway, Lynn M. '03 (BUF) Grand Island, NY St. Stephen.
Shuping, Kenneth J. '03 (RIC) Christiansburg, VA St. Jude.
Shuppert, William T.J. '71 (TUC) Tucson, AZ Saint Francis de Sales Roman Catholic Parish – Tucson.
Shurtleff, F. James '66 (OG) Ogdensburg, NY Notre Dame.
Shuter, Alex (PSC) Williamsburg, VA Ascension of Our Lord.
Shutt, Paul–Alexander *o.s.b.* '98 (GBG)[G] Latrobe, PA Saint Vincent Archabbey.
Shuttleworth, Edward J. '90 (LC) Prescott, WI St. Joseph.
Sia, Joseph M. '08 (DAV) Muscatine, IA SS. Mary and Mathias of Muscatine; Columbus Junction, IA St. Joseph.
Siamoo, Peter '99 (P)[J] Portland, OR Providence St. Vincent Medical Center.
Siani, Angelo *o.m.i.* '65 (FgM) Washington, DC AMERICAN OBLATE MISSIONS.
Sibel, John J. '72 (PH) Linwood, PA Holy Saviour.
Sibenik, Simeon B. '81 (PBR) Consultors.
Sibenik, Simeon B. '81 (PBR) Ernest, PA St. Jude Thaddeus; Punxsutawney, PA SS. Peter and Paul.
Siberski, John R. *s.j.* '07 (WDC)[N] Washington, DC The Jesuit Community at Georgetown University.
Siberski, John R. *s.j.* '07 (BO)[U] Boston The Society of Jesus of New England–Provincial Offices.
Sibilano, Joseph D. *o.s.j.* '65 (SCR) Pittston, PA St. Anthony of Padua; [M] Pittston, PA Our Lady of Sorrows Province of the Oblates of St. Joseph; Councilors:; [B] Pittston, PA St. Joseph's Oblate Seminary.
Sibirnij, Volodymyr '04 (STF) Troy, NY Protection of B.V.M.; Watervliet, NY St. Nicholas.
Sibley, Bryce '00 (LAF) Mamou, LA St. Ann; Diocesan Consultors.
Sica, Joseph F. '82 (SCR) Scranton, PA Immaculate Conception.
Sicard, Kenneth *o.p.* '90 (PRO)[P] Providence St. Thomas Aquinas Priory at Providence College; New York, NY; [B] Providence, RI Providence College.
Sicari, Rev. Msgr. Joseph J. '82 (BUF) Catholic Charities; Catholic Charities Appeal; Propagation of the Faith; Consultors, College of; Council of Priests; [H] Appeal Administration and Publicity Offices; Snyder, NY Christ the King; [T] Buffalo, NY Delta Development of Western New York, Inc.
Siceloff, John C. '04 (MET) Dunellen, NJ St. John the Evangelist.
Sichko, James W. '98 (LEX) Richmond, KY St. Mark; Special Assignment; [L] Richmond, KY St. Stephen Newman Center–St. Mark Church.
Siciliano, Donald L. '93 (CIN) Cincinnati, OH St. Bernard.
Siciliano, Jude *o.p.* '69 (R)[F] Raleigh, NC Dominican Priory.
Sickler, Robert *m.s.a.* '87 (NOR)[G] Cromwell, CT Society of the Missionaries of the Holy Apostles.
Sickler, Thomas *m.s.* '73 (NOR) Danielson, CT St. James.
Siconolfi, Rev. Msgr. Constantine V. '59 (SCR) Retired.
Siconolfi, Michael T. *s.j.* '72 (NY)[EE] Jesuit Community, Kohlmann Hall.
Siconolfi, Thomas J. *c.ss.r.* '70 (TR)[R] Long Branch, NJ San Alfonso Retreat House.
Sidney, Walter T. *s.j.* '78 (STL)[F] St. Louis, MO De Smet Jesuit High School; [O] St. Louis, MO De Smet Jesuit High School Community.
Sidor, Sidney '04 (PRM) Indianapolis, IN St. Athanasius Church; Priest's Pension Board.
Siebenaler, John M. '61 (STP) Retired.
Siebenaler, Leonard (STP) Retired.
Siebenaler, Martin '59 (STP) Retired.
Siebenand, Ambrose F. '41 (NU) Retired.
Siebenand, Paul Alcuin '60 (LA) Avalon, CA St. Catherine of Alexandria.

Sieber, Patrick *o.f.m.* '71 (CAM) Camden, NJ The Church of St. Joan of Arc, West Collingswood, N.J.
Sieber, Patrick *o.f.m.* '71 (PH)[Y] Philadelphia, PA Order of Friars Minor of the Province of the Most Holy Name.
Siebert, Edward J. *s.j.* '97 (LA)[BB] Culver City, CA Loyola Productions, Inc.; [P] Culver City, CA Ignatius House, The Novitiate of the California Province, Society of Jesus.
Siebert, Paul S. '86 (E) Emporium, PA St. Mark.
Siebert, Stephen A. '94 (DEN) Greeley, CO Our Lady of Peace.
Siebert, William P. '81 (DET) Retired.
Siebor, John '58 (RVC) Hempstead, NY St. Ladislaus Retired.
Sieczynski, Jerzey '00 (SAT) On Leave.
Siefer, Rev. Msgr. Richard R. '75 (E) Du Bois, PA St. Catherine; Clergy Continuing Education and Formation.
Siefert, John S. (STL) Affton, MO St. Dominic Savio.
Siefert, John '89 (STL)[V] St. Louis, MO Archdiocesan Stewardship Education Committee.
Siefert, Ralph A. *s.m.* '73 (STL)[F] Creve Coeur, MO Chaminade College Preparatory School Inc.; [G] Creve Coeur, MO Chaminade College Preparatory; [O] Saint Louis, MO Marybrook Marianist Community.
Sieg, Leslie M. '76 (P) Tigard, OR St. Anthony; Building Commission.
Sieg, Robert *o.f.m.* '75 (CLV) Cleveland, OH St. Rose of Lima.
Sieg, Thomas H. '71 (STP) Prior Lake, MN St. Michael; College of Consultors.
Siegel, Kenan *o.f.m.cap.* '56 (MIL)[P] Mount Calvary, WI St. Lawrence Friary Retired.
Siekierski, Rev. Msgr. John J. '67 (GRY) East Chicago, IN Holy Trinity; East Chicago, IN St. Stanislaus; Vicar General; Deans; Bishop's Council of Priests; Consultors; Priests' Personnel Board.
Sielski, Joseph *m.i.c.* '41 (WDC)[N] Brookeville, MD Marian Monastery–Brookeville.
Siemianowski, John S. '89 (CHI) Chicago Heights, IL St. Agnes; Chicago Heights, IL St. Paul.
Siendo, Ralph C. (NEW) Jersey City, NJ Our Lady of Mercy.
Sienkiewicz, Matthew '59 (FTW) Retired.
Siepka, Rev. Msgr. Richard W. '82 (BUF)[A] East Aurora, NY Christ the King Seminary; Co–Directors; Kenmore, NY St. Andrew.
Siepker, Daniel '93 (DM) Atlantic, IA SS. Peter and Paul; Anita, IA St. Mary.
Sierminski, Vernon '56 (SAG) Retired.
Sierotowicz, Felicjan '90 (ROC) Auburn, NY; Moravia, NY Cayuga Correctional; Red Creek, NY Butler Correctional Facility; [H] Auburn, NY Mercy Health & Rehabilitation Center Nursing Home Co., Inc.; Auburn, NY Sacred Heart; Auburn, NY St. Hyacinth.
Sierra, Angel '80 (SFD) New Berlin, IL Visitation B.V.M.; New Berlin, IL Sacred Heart of Jesus; New Berlin, IL Sacred Heart of Mary; New Berlin, IL St. Sebastian.
Sierra, John A. *s.f.* '40 (WDC)[B] Silver Spring, MD Holy Family Seminary.
Sierra, Rolando A. *c.ss.r.* '99 (LA) Bell Gardens, CA St. Gertrude.
Sierra–Posada, Pedro J. '76 (ALX) Lecompte, LA St. Martin.
Sievel, Thomas A. '78 (HRT) East Haven, CT St. Vincent de Paul.
Siewiera, Bogdan '98 (COS) Salida, CO St. Joseph.
Siffert, Etienne *s.m.* '58 (SFR) San Francisco, CA Notre Dame des Victoires.
Siffrin, Rev. Msgr. Robert J. '79 (Y) Finance Council; Vicar General & Moderator of the Curia; College of Consultors; Youngstown, OH St. Edward.
Siffrin, Rev. Msgr. Robert '79 (Y) Priests Council.
Sigaran, Mamerto '60 (SFR) Retired.
Sigler, Gary L. '79 (FTW) Fort Wayne, IN Queen of Angels.
Sigler, John W. '94 (LA) Hospital Chaplains.
Sigman, Louis A. '67 (PHX) Retired.
Sigmund, Andrew J. '64 (STL) Washington, MO St. Francis Borgia.
Signorelli, Francis *s.x.* '59 (BO)[U] Holliston, MA Xaverian Missionaries; [Z] Holliston, MA Our Lady of Fatima Shrine.
Siguere, Roberto *o.f.m.* '65 (FgM) New York, NY Franciscan Province of the Immaculate Conception.
Siguere, Roberto *o.f.m.* (NY)[EE] New York Franciscan Province of the Immaculate Conception.
Sihuay, Francis X. *o.f.m.* '51 (WDC)[N] Washington, DC Franciscan Monastery USA Inc. Retired.
Sikandar Chanan, Anthony '90 (BRK) Jackson Heights, NY St. Joan of Arc.
Siket, Bruce '07 (PRT)[M] Castine, ME Maine Maritime Academy; Ellsworth, ME St. Joseph; Ellsworth, ME Stella Maris Parish.
Siklodi, Sandor '71 (CLV) Cleveland, OH St. Emeric.
Sikon, Michael P. '96 (GBG) Delmont, PA St. John Baptist de La Salle; Export, PA St. Mary; Office for Worship.
Sikora, James R. '67 (GF)[A] Great Falls, MT University of Great Falls; [A] University of Great Falls; Clerical Benefit Association.
Sikora, James '67 (GF) Special Assignment.
Sikora, Stanley J. '57 (HRT)[A] In Res. at the Archbishop Daniel A. Cronin Retirement Residence at St. Thomas Seminary Retired.
Sikora, Thomas More *o.s.b.* '97 (GBG)[G] Latrobe, PA Saint Vincent Archabbey.
Sikorski, Allan '08 (RVC) Manhasset, NY St. Mary's.
Sikorski, Harold R. '56 (SAG) Retired.
Sikorski, Jeffery P. '73 (TOL) Huron, OH St. Peter.
Sikorski, Leszek '97 (MO) Navy Chaplains.
Sikorski, Leszek '97 (VEN) Military Chaplains.
Sikorski, Louis S. '64 (GAL) Retired.
Sikorsky, Charles *l.c.* '02 (WDC)[N] Potomac, MD Legionaries of Christ.
Sikorsky, Charles *l.c.* (ARL)[B] Arlington, VA The Institute for the Psychological Sciences, Inc.
Silagan, Gorgonio '01 (SEA) Special Assignment.
Silayo, Constantine L. '82 (IND)[G] Beech Grove, IN St. Francis Hospital and Health Centers.
Silcox, John D. '95 (PH) Drexel Hill, PA St. Dorothy.
Sileo, Joseph (WDC) Great Mills, MD Holy Face.
Siler, Paschal *o.f.m.cap.* '60 (GF) Ashland, MT St. Labre; Lame Deer, MT Blessed Sacrament.
Siler, Robert M. '01 (YAK) Notaries; Presbyteral Council Executive Committee; Diocesan Finance Council; Moderator of the Curia; Chancellor; Campaign for Human Development; Press (Central Washington Catholic); Clergy Personnel Board; Diocesan Consultors.
Silio, Antonio R. '88 (MIA) Pembroke Pines, FL St. Boniface.
Sill, Theodore K. '89 (COL) London, OH St. Patrick.
Silos, Gerardo (LAR) Zapata, TX Our Lady of Lourdes.
Silva, Alvaro '74 (POD) Chestnut Hill.
Silva, Alvaro '87 (ARE) Manati, PR Nuestra Senora del Mar.
Silva, Bryan *o.m.i.* '85 (WDC)[N] Washington, DC Oblate Community; [N] Washington, DC Provincial Offices of the United States Province of the Missionary Oblates of Mary Immaculate.
Silva, Caesar '74 (HT) Montegut, LA Sacred Heart; Air National Guard Chaplains.
Silva, David E. '54 (CLV) Retired.
Silva, Edwin Lugo '89 (MGZ) Mayaguez, PR Nuestra Senora De Fatima.
Silva, Eleazar '01 (SLC) Kearns, UT Saint Francis Xavier LLC 222.
Silva, Ethiege *o.m.i.* (NEW) Palisades Park, NJ St. Michael's.
Silva, Eusbio F. '66 (MAN) Plymouth, NH Holy Trinity Parish.
Silva, Frank J. '76 (BO) Appointed; Newton, MA Corpus Christi – St. Bernard.
Silva, Hilary '89 (FRS) Hilmar, CA Holy Rosary.
Silva, Ismael '79 (ORG) Garden Grove, CA St. Callistus.
Silva, John '04 (EVN) Evansville, IN St. John the Evangelist.
Silva, Jorge de *s.m.* '72 (STL)[O] St. Louis Marianists, Province of the United States (Society of Mary).
Silva, Juan '92 (LA) Pomona, CA Sacred Heart.
Silva, Langes J. '95 (SLC) Priests' Personnel Board; Salt Lake City, UT Cathedral of the Madeleine LLC 202; Vice Chancellor; Ecumenical Commission; Judicial Vicar; Judges.
Silva, Langes J. '95 (LAV) Diocesan Judges.
Silva, Luis '98 (CR) On Duty Outside the Diocese.
Silva, Miguel '84 (SAC) Gridley, CA Sacred Heart.
Silva, Raul '06 (NEW) New Milford, NJ St. Joseph's.
Silva, Raul '79 (FRS) Avenal, CA St. Joseph.
Silva, Rev. Msgr. Robert J. '65 (STO) Continuing Education of Clergy; Diaconate Formation; Office for Pastoral Leadership Development; Ongoing Education for Clergy; Office for Deacon Formation.
Silva, Rolando '06 (GAY) Alpena, MI St. Anne; Alpena, MI St. Bernard; Alpena, MI St. John the Baptist; Alpena, MI St. Mary.
Silva, Rosendo *l.c.* (ORG) Lake Forest, CA Santiago de Compostela.
Silva, Susith '87 (HRT) Waterbury, CT Basilica of the Immaculate Conception.
Silva, Vajira *t.o.r.* (STP) Minneapolis, MN St. Bridget.
Silva, Victor T. '07 (PRO) Cranston, RI St. Matthew.
Silva Arredondo, Raul '79 (FRS) Huron, CA St. Frances Cabrini.
Silveira, Eduino T. '87 (SAC) Priests' Personnel Board, Diocesan; Sacramento, CA St. Philomene.
Silver, Bertram *o.m.i.* '54 (FgM) Washington, DC AMERICAN OBLATE MISSIONS.
Silver, Jeffrey P. '84 (CIN) Oxford, OH St. Mary Church and Catholic Campus Ministry; [R] Oxford, OH Miami University Catholic Campus Ministry.
Silver, John E. '93 (OG) Conway, SC St. James Retired.
Silveri, Donato P. '64 (PH) Spring City, PA St. Joseph; Spring City, PA Southeastern Pennsylvania Veterans Center.
Silverio, Gilbert J. *o.f.m.* '59 (FR)[G] Onset, MA St. Joseph Friary–Franciscan Friars.
Silvester, Peter *s.v.d.* '78 (CHI)[N] Techny, IL Divine Word Residence.
Silvestrini, Dino F. '85 (MAR) Leave of Absence.
Silvia, Kenneth J. *c.s.c.* '64 (ORL)[F] Cocoa Beach, FL Congregation of Holy Cross, Eastern Province.
Silwinski, Philip A. '97 (GR) Ravenna, MI St. Catherine; Conklin, MI St. Francis Xavier.
Sima, John R. *s.j.* '71 (FgM)[N] Chicago Chicago Province of the Society of Jesus–Provincial Office; Chicago, IL Society of Jesus.
Simango, Lucas K. '87 (CHY) Pinedale, WY Our Lady of Peace.
Simas, Rev. Msgr. Manuel C. '61 (OAK) Fremont, CA St. Joseph (Old Mission San Jose).
Simboli, Ronald L. '75 (GBG) Belle Vernon, PA St. Anne.
Simburger, Joseph '79 (SFD) Altamont, IL St. Clare; Altamont, IL St. Anne; Altamont, IL St. Mary.
Simeone, Francis '61 (FRS) Retired.
Simeone, Gary F. '75 (HRT) Wallingford, CT Holy Trinity.
Simeone, Rev. Msgr. Ronald P. '82 (PRO) Woonsocket, RI St. Anthony; Vicar for Judicial Matters; Judicial Vicar; Secretary; Council Members.
Simien, Gregory M. '99 (LAF) Maurice, LA Our Lady of Perpetual Help.
Simington, Rev. Msgr. Ralph P. '62 (DUB) Directors; Retired Priests' Representatives Retired.
Simko, James G. '91 (VEN) Fort Myers, FL St. Francis Xavier.
Simko, James '91 (DEN) On Duty Outside the Archdiocese.
Simlik, Frank P. '54 (PHX) Retired.
Simmons, Franklin '79 (GAL) Houston, TX St. Ambrose Retired.
Simmons, Jerome S. '68 (E) Erie, PA Sacred Heart; [M] Erie, PA Sisters of Saint Joseph of Northwestern Pennsylvania; [O] Erie, PA Ecclesia Ministry.
Simmons, Joseph C. '61 (BAL) Joppa, MD Church of the Holy Spirit.
Simmons, Mark '07 (BRK) Brooklyn, NY St. Patrick.
Simmons, Matthew P. '03 (JKS) Approved Advocate and Auditors; Personnel Board; Brookhaven, MS St. Francis; [H] Brookhaven, MS Lincoln Junior College Newman Center.
Simmons, Rev. Msgr. Walter E. '55 (RVC) Port Washington, NY St. Peter of Alcantara Retired.
Simmons, William B. *c.s.c.* '52 (FTW)[B] University of Notre Dame Du Lac; [H] Notre Dame, IN Holy Cross Community, Corby Hall, University of Notre Dame.
Simms, Robert A. *s.j.* '46 (STL)[O] St. Louis, MO Jesuit Community Corporation at Saint Louis University – Jesuit Hall.
Simo, Philip *o.s.b.* '97 (WDC)[N] Washington, DC St. Anselm's Abbey.
Simon, Akan S. '98 (RCK) Crystal Lake, IL St. Thomas the Apostle.
Simon, Ambrose *o.f.m.cap.* '50 (GB)[J] Appleton, WI St. Fidelis Friary Retired.
Simon, Brian '96 (SFS) Clear Lake, SD St. Mary; Presbyteral Council.
Simon, Carl A. '71 (LAN) Brooklyn, MI St. Joseph Shrine; Gus Harrison Regional Facility.
Simon, George Howard '57 (LAF) Retired.
Simon, John L. '73 (MIL) North Fond du Lac, WI Presentation of the Blessed Virgin Mary; Eldorado, WI Our Risen Savior.
Simon, Rev. Msgr. Joseph M. '71 (STL) Oakville, MO Queen of All Saints; [V] St. Louis, MO Archdiocesan Stewardship Education Committee.
Simon, Richard T. '75 (CHI) Skokie, IL St. Lambert.
Simon, Robert G. *c.s.c.* '61 (FTW)[H] Notre Dame Congregation of Holy Cross, Indiana Province, Provincial House; New Rochelle, NY Eastern Brothers Province.
Simon, Robert J. '90 (SCR) Moscow, PA St. Catherine of Siena.
Simon, Thomas *m.s.a.* '79 (NOR)[G] Cromwell, CT Society of the Missionaries of the Holy Apostles.
Simonar, Mathew J. '97 (GB) Brillion, WI Holy Family; Vicariate.
Simonds, Donald D. *m.s.* '63 (HRT)[L] Hartford, CT Missionaries of LaSalette.
Simonds, Thomas A. *s.j.* '99 (OM)[K] Omaha, NE Jesuit Community at Creighton University.
Simone, Earl Francis '77 (CIN) Dayton, OH St. Peter.
Simone, Michael A. *m.m.* '56 (NY)[EE] Maryknoll Maryknoll Fathers and Brothers Retired.
Simone, Michael M. '03 (WCH) Wichita, KS Christ the King; [K] Wichita, KS Serra Club of Wichita – Metro; Vocations.
Simone, Michael *s.j.* '07 (BAL)[S] Baltimore, MD Ferdinand Wheeler Jesuit Community.
Simoneau, Norman J. '67 (MAN) Retired.
Simoneau, Roland L. '78 (PRO) Warwick, RI St. Benedict.
Simoneaux, Jody '82 (LAF) Jeanerette, LA St. John the Evangelist.
Simonelli, Gerald '90 (JOL) Bloomingdale, IL St. Isidore.

Simonetti, David J. '05 (CHI) Sauk Village, IL St. James.
Simonin, Rev. Msgr. John A. '47 (CHR) Retired.
Simonnet, Philippe *s.s.e.* '52 (BUR)[E] Colchester, VT Society of St. Edmund; Colchester, VT SOCIETY OF ST. EDMUND.
Simons, Derek *s.v.d.* '70 (CHI)[N] Chicago, IL Angels Studio.
Simons, James L. '00 (CIN) Bradford, OH Immaculate Conception; Covington, OH St. Teresa of the Infant Jesus.
Simons, Thomas G. '77 (GR) Alpine, MI Holy Trinity.
Simonson, Earl C. '69 (STP) Minneapolis, MN St. Clement.
Simpson, Brian L. '72 (CHI) Military Chaplains; Navy Chaplains.
Simpson, David L. *o.carm.* '70 (JOL) Commissary Provincials:; [L] Darien, IL St. Simon Stock Priory; [L] Darien, IL Carmelite Provincial Office; [N] Darien, IL Carmelite Spiritual Center.
Simpson, Kenneth C. '78 (CHI) Chicago, IL St. Clement.
Simpson, Mauro *o.s.b.* '52 (FAJ)[B] Humacao, PR San Antonio Abad Abbey of the Order of St. Benedict.
Simpson, Robert '65 (RNO) Retired.
Simpson, Roger '52 (SFD) Retired.
Sims, John D. *o.p.* '04 (BR) Ponchatoula, LA St. Joseph.
Sims, Robert W. '71 (IND) Indianapolis, IN Immaculate Heart of Mary.
Simutowe, Patrick *s.s.* '96 (BAL)[S] Baltimore Society of St. Sulpice, Province of the United States.
Sinasac, Alvin A. *c.s.b.* '79 (GAL) Houston, TX St. Anne.
Sinatra, Leonard '67 (PHU) Retired.
Sinatra, Robert L. '04 (CAM) On Duty Outside the Diocese.
Sinatra, William D. '64 (DET) Presbyteral Council Retired.
Sinclair, Alexander B. '57 (KC) Grandview, MO Coronation of Our Lady; Consultors Retired.
Sindik, Rev. Msgr. George '59 (PT) Pensacola, FL Cathedral of the Sacred Heart Retired.
Sindik, Matthew A. '62 (MOB) Montgomery, AL St. Jude Parish Retired.
Singarayar, Philip *o.m.i.* '64 (OAK) Oakland, CA Sacred Heart.
Singarayer, Arulraj S. '99 (MET) Parlin, NJ St. Bernadette.
Singelyn, Robert K. '60 (DET) Monroe, MI St. Mary Retired.
Singer, Christopher J. '03 (E) On Duty Outside Diocese.
Singer, Jerome C. '63 (DET) Detroit, MI Nativity of Our Lord.
Singer, Thomas J. *o.m.i.* '57 (BEL)[F] Belleville, IL Missionary Oblates of Mary Immaculate – St. Henry's Oblate Residence.
Singler, Charles E. '84 (TOL) Toledo, OH Queen of the Most Holy Rosary Cathedral; Office of Worship and Liturgical Music; Members.
Singler, James E. '82 (CLV) Cleveland Heights, OH Communion of Saints Parish.
Singler, John P. '82 (CLV) Twinsburg, OH SS. Cosmas and Damian; Presbyteral Conveners; Presbyteral Council.
Singleton, Jeremiah '65 (MIA) Fort Lauderdale, FL St. Anthony; Deans and Deaneries.
Singleton, Rev. Msgr. William V. '50 (RVC) East Rockaway, NY St. Raymond's Retired.
Sinibaldi, Daniel J. '96 (MAN) Farmington, NH St. Peter; Rochester, NH St. Mary.
Sinisi, Daniel *t.o.r.* '66 (ALT) Ecumenical Minister; [A] Loretto, PA St. Francis University.
Sinkler, Michael '81 (LR) Paragould, AR St. Mary; Walnut Ridge, AR Immaculate Heart of Mary.
Sinnappan, Selvaraj '97 (TYL) Canton, TX St. Therese.
Sinnema, Paul *o.f.m.* '63 (NEW) Wood Ridge, NJ Our Lady of the Assumption.
Sinnerud, James A. *s.j.* '72 (OM)[C] Omaha, NE Creighton Preparatory School.
Sinnott, Andrew R. '99 (SCR) Hanover Township, PA Exaltation of the Holy Cross; Wilkes–Barre, PA St. Aloysius; Priests' Retirement Advisory Board; Wilkes–Barre, PA St. Casimir's.
Sinnott, James P. *m.m.* '60 (FgM) Maryknoll, NY MARYKNOLL.
Sinnott, Thomas G. '00 (SCR) Unassigned or Leave of Absence.
Sinor, Michael '88 (SD) San Diego, CA St. Didacus.
Sinski, Norbert J. *c.s.c.* '77 (FTW)[H] Notre Dame Congregation of Holy Cross, Indiana Province, Provincial House.
Sinz, Eugene R. '60 (STL) Webster Groves, MO Holy Redeemer Retired.
Siok, Slawomir *s.a.c.* '90 (BUF) Niagara Falls, NY St. John de La Salle.
Sioleti, Andrew *o.f.m.* (NY) Manhattan, NY U.S.V.A. Medical Center.
Sioleti, Andrew *i.v.dei.* '84 (MO) DEPARTMENT OF VETERANS AFFAIRS HOSPITALS AND CHAPLAINS.
Sioleti, Andrew *o.f.m. conv.* (BRK) Veterans Affairs Extended Care Center, St. Albans, NY.
Sioli, Joseph E. *c.o.* '97 (PIT) Washington, PA Immaculate Conception; [P] Washington, PA Washington and Jefferson College (Washington).
Siordia, Oscar O. '06 (BWN) Santa Rosa, TX St. Mary.
Sipaco, Cecilio E. '67 (MET)[G] New Brunswick, NJ Saint Peter's University Hospital.
Sipe, Robert J. '59 (STP) Retired.
Sipitkowski, James A. '74 (SPR) Easthampton, MA Sacred Heart.
Siple, Donald M. *o.s.m.* '92 (CHI)[N] Chicago Order of Friar Servants of Mary (Servites) United States of America Province, Inc.
Siple, Donald *o.s.m.* '92 (STL) Affton, MO Seven Holy Founders.
Siple, William P. '92 (PIT) Natrona Heights, PA Our Lady of the Most Blessed Sacrament.
Sippel, Bernard S. '65 (MIL) Franklin, WI St. James; Judges for First Instance; Judges for Second Instance Retired.
Sippel, Edward F. '47 (MIL) Retired.
Sipperly, Edward '54 (ALB) Retired.
Sipulski, Vianney *o.f.m.* '60 (MIL)[P] Burlington, WI Queen of Peace Friary.
Siracus, Aloysius *o.f.m.* '47 (PAT)[N] Ringwood, NJ Holy Name Friary, Inc.
Siracuse, Guy F. '67 (BUF) Retired.
Sirangelo, J. Peter *s.m.p.* '05 (SPC)[F] Marionville, MO The Society of Our Mother of Peace, Sons of Our Mother of Peace.
Sirba, Joseph A. '87 (DUL) Longville, MN St. Edward; Longville, MN St. Paul.
Sirianni, Anthony M. '89 (MET) Edison, NJ St. Helena.
Sirianni, Klaus J. '78 (WDC) Washington, DC St. Stephen Martyr.
Sirianni, Louis A. '74 (ROC) Rochester, NY St. Mark; Judicial Vicar; Judicial Vicar; Judges.
Sirianni, Louis A. (CHY) Defenders of the Bond.
Sirianni, Richard D. '78 (P) Portland, OR St. Thomas More; Ecumenical and Interreligious Affairs; Air National Guard Chaplains; Finance Council.
Sirianni, Sam A. '89 (TR) Office of Worship.
Sirico, Robert '89 (KAL) Kalamazoo, MI St. Mary; [E] Kalamazoo, MI St. Philip Neri House.
Siriwa, Avitus *a.j.* '02 (ALN) Easton, PA Our Lady of Mercy Parish.
Sirois, Rev. Msgr. Joseph V. '51 (WOR) Retired.
Siroki, David '93 (PSC) On Duty Outside Diocese.
Sirolli, Francis A. *o.s.a.* '65 (PH)[Y] Bryn Mawr, PA Augustinians Friars (O.S.A.); Bryn Mawr, PA Our Mother of Good Counsel.
Siroskey, Paul Larry '80 (DET) Absent on Sick Leave.
Sirvent, Francisco '88 (PCE) On Duty Outside the Diocese.
Siry, Philip L. '62 (WIL) Retired.
Sis, Rev. Msgr. Michael J. '86 (AUS) Austin, TX St. Thomas More; Consultors.
Sisco, Michael A. '97 (PRO) Bristol, RI Our Lady of Mount Carmel; [S] Bristol, RI Roger Williams University.
Sisk, Robert *t.o.r.* '61 (BAL) Baltimore, MD St. Elizabeth of Hungary.
Sison, Alden J. '87 (LA) Panorama City, CA St. Genevieve.
Sison, Dave Thomas N. '04 (NEW) Newark, NJ St. Anthony's.
Sison, Ronnie '03 (VEN) Fort Myers, FL Blessed Pope John XXIII.
Sistare, Juniper Mary *c.f.r.* '03 (NY)[EE] Yonkers, NY St. Leopold's Friary.
Sisul, Paul *c.m.* '72 (CHI)[N] Chicago DePaul Vincentian Residence.
Sitar, Richard T. '79 (GAY) Retired.
Sitko, Joseph S. '68 (SCR) Simpson, PA St. Michael.
Sitzmann, Eugene E. '62 (SC) Retired.
Sitzmann, Richard A. '62 (SC) Sioux City, IA St. Boniface; Mercy Medical Center; [C] Sioux City, IA Mercy Medical Center – Sioux City.
Siu, Peter Kin Chung *s.j.* '93 (SJ)[M] Santa Clara, CA Casa San Inigo, Jesuit Residence; Santa Clara, CA Chinese Catholic Community.
Siu, Peter *s.j.* '93 (SJ)[B] Santa Clara, CA Jesuit Community.
Siu, Robert K.C. '54 (CHY) Lander, WY Holy Rosary Retired.
Siurys, Petraj *l.i.c.* '91 (LIT) Pontifical Lithuanian College of St. Casimir.
Siva, Renier C. '05 (SAC) Portola, CA Holy Family.
Sivalon, John C. *m.m.* '65 (NY)[EE] Maryknoll Maryknoll Fathers and Brothers.
Sivillo, Rev. Msgr. Nicholas W. '64 (BRK) Middle Village, NY St. Margaret Retired.
Sivinskyi, Vasyl '92 (PHU) Baltimore, MD St. Michael's.
Siviramatu, Antony (NY) Bronx, NY St. Gabriel.
Siwek, Daniel S. '73 (CHI)[A] Mundelein, IL University of St. Mary of the Lake/Mundelein Seminary.
Sizemore, David W. '96 (COL) Sunbury, OH St. John Neumann.
Sizing, Theodore C. '55 (SY) Syracuse, NY St. Vincent de Paul Retired.
Skagen, Robert '70 (PHX) Retired.
Skaj, John P. *c.s.sp.* '63 (PIT) Pittsburgh, PA Sacred Heart.
Skalski, Francis S. '56 (DET) Retired.
Skalsky, Ted A. '72 (DOD) Dodge City, KS Cathedral of Our Lady of Guadalupe Catholic Church of Dodge City, Kansas; College of Consultors; Deans; Advocates; Deacon Personnel.
Skarbek, Richard *m.s.a.* '86 (NOR)[G] Cromwell, CT Society of the Missionaries of the Holy Apostles.
Skarda, David *c.ss.r.* (ORL)[F] New Smyrna Beach, FL St. Alphonsus Villa–Redemptorist Fathers and Brothers.
Skaria, Antony *c.f.i.c.* '96 (STP) Ramsey County Correctional Facilities; [K] St. Paul, MN Congregation of the Sons of the Immaculate Conception; Regions Medical Center.
Skaria, Sunnychan Vadakkedath *o.c.d.* (ALN) Reading Hospital and Medical Center.
Skarich, William '99 (DUL) Babbitt, MN St. Pius X; Ely, MN St. Anthony; Cursillo Movement.
Skeabeck, Andrew *c.ss.r.* '47 (ALB)[L] Saratoga Springs, NY St. John Neumann Residence.
Skechus, Francis E. *s.j.* '75 (PH)[F] Philadelphia, PA St. Joseph's Preparatory School; [Y] Loyola Center and Manresa Hall.
Skeehan, William K. '60 (TLS) Retired.
Skehan, James W. *s.j.* '54 (BO)[U] Weston, MA Campion Health Center, Inc.
Skehan, John A. '52 (PMB) Delray Beach, FL St. Vincent Ferrer Retired.
Skehan, John R. '86 (PRT) Kittery, ME St. Raphael's; York, ME St. Christopher–by–the–Sea; Berwick, ME Our Lady of the Angels; Personnel Board.
Skehan, Rev. Msgr. Martin O. '44 (YAK) Moses Lake, WA Our Lady of Fatima Retired.
Skeldon, John Robert '00 (FWT) Wichita Falls, TX Our Lady of Guadalupe.
Skelly, Francis G. *c.ss.r.* '72 (NY) Bronx, NY Immaculate Conception.
Skelly, Rev. Msgr. John J. '53 (RVC) Manhasset, NY St. Mary's; [M] Amityville, NY St. Pius X Residence Retired.
Skelly, Rev. Msgr. Richard J. '54 (PH) Aston, PA St. Joseph Retired.
Skelskey, David A. *s.j.* '80 (FgM) Watertown, MA Society of Jesus.
Skelton, Paul H. '64 (SFD) Villa Grove, IL St. Michael; Villa Grove, IL Sacred Heart.
Skenderovic, Ivan '76 (BUF) Niagara Falls, NY St. Raphael.
Skeris, Robert A. '61 (MIL) Retired.
Skerl, Alphonse '55 (GRY) East Chicago, IN Holy Trinity.
Skerry, Donald *s.v.d.* '62 (BO)[U] Brighton, MA Divine Word Missionaries.
Skertich, Mark J. '77 (PIT) Pittsburgh, PA Sacred Heart.
Skiba, Walter F. '56 (SCR) Priests' Retirement Advisory Board Retired.
Skidmore, Harold G. *c.m.* '50 (PH)[Y].
Skillin, Rev. Msgr. Harmon '60 (STO) College of Consultors/Presbyteral Council; Personnel Board; Vicar for Priests; Judges; Diamond Springs, CA Retired.
Skillingstad, M. Delmar '60 (SPK)[B] Spokane, WA Gonzaga University.
Skillman, David P. '09 (STL) St. Charles, MO St. Elizabeth Ann Seton.
Skindeleski, Thomas J. '71 (PMB) Delray Beach, FL St. Vincent Ferrer; Vicars Forane; Ex Officio; Knights of Columbus.
Skinner, Charles D. '53 (E) Retired.
Skirtich, John W. '90 (PIT) Pittsburgh, PA St. Maurice; College of Consultors; Clergy Personnel Board; Priest Council.
Skitzki, Francis P. '70 (SCR) Retired.
Sklar, Louis E. '01 (ALX) Ferriday, LA St. Patrick; Appointed Members.
Skluzacek, Michael C. '80 (STP) New Brighton, MN St. John the Baptist.
Skluzacek, Richard F. '57 (STP) Retired.
Skok, Charles '52 (SPK) Spokane Valley, WA St. John Vianney Retired.
Skoneki, Rev. Msgr. William J. '87 (MOB) Auburn, AL St. Michael; [I] Auburn, AL Auburn University Newman Center; Archdiocesan Consultors.
Skonezny, Raymond '61 (ORG) Retired.
Skonseng, Rev. Msgr. Dennis A. '82 (FAR) Special Assignment; Diocesan College of Consultors; [A] Fargo, ND Cardinal Muench Seminary.
Skornia, Bernard L. '57 (SAG) Retired.
Skorup, Ildephonse *o.f.m.* '59 (JOL)[L] Joliet, IL St. John the Baptist Friary.
Skowron, Greg '89 (JOL) Frankfort, IL St. Anthony.
Skriba, Raymond F. '57 (CHI) Retired.
Skrincosky, Rev. Msgr. Peter (STF) Retired.
Skrobutt, Andrew '06 (RCK) St. Charles, IL St. John Neumann.
Skrocki, Michael K. '00 (NTN) Sophia Press; Danbury, CT St. Ann; Judges; Presbyteral Council.
Skrocki, Michael K. '00 (PBR) Pro–Synodal Judges.

Skrogky, Michael '00 (BGP) Judges.
Skrzypek, Jaroslaw Z. '04 (SPC) Monett, MO St. Lawrence; Monett, MO SS. Peter and Paul; Presbyteral Council.
Skrzypiec, Andrzej '82 (SLC) Salt Lake City, UT Saint Ambrose LLC 214; Team.
Skublics, Mate '09 (NEW) Newark, NJ St. Benedict's.
Skudlarek, William *o.s.b.* '64 (SCL)[I] Collegeville St. John's Abbey, of the Order of St. Benedict.
Skufca, Ronald J. '79 (MAR) Army National Guard Chaplains; Menominee, MI Holy Spirit.
Skupien, Rev. Msgr. Francis M. '51 (BUF)[O] Lackawanna, NY Bishop Head Residence Retired.
Skura, Mark David *o.f.m.conv.* '82 (BUF)[P] Hamburg, NY Immaculate Conception Convent; [D] Athol Springs, NY St. Francis High School; Athol Springs, NY St. Francis of Assisi.
Skurla, Anthony *o.f.m.* '54 (PSC)[A] Sybertsville, PA Holy Dormition Friary.
Skurla, Robert J. '56 (PSC) Retired.
Slaby, Joseph A. *m.m.* '66 (FgM) Maryknoll, NY MARYKNOLL.
Slaby, Stanislaw *c.ss.r.* '99 (MET) Manville, NJ Sacred Heart of Jesus; Manville, NJ Christ the King.
Sladicka, Phillip J. '76 (SCR) Avoca, PA St. Mary's; Avoca, PA SS. Peter and Paul; Cursillo Movement.
Slampak, John A. '66 (RCK) North Aurora, IL Blessed Sacrament Catholic Church; Parish Services and Directors.
Slane, Anthony P. *c.ss.r.* '42 (STL)[O] Liguori, MO St. Clement Health Care Center Retired.
Slate, William '55 (SEA) Retired.
Slater, Dennis '62 (SY) Retired.
Slater, William T. '77 (RVC) New Hyde Park, NY Notre Dame.
Slatterie, Leo '51 (LAV) Retired.
Slattery, Edmund J. *s.s.s.* '50 (CLV)[N] Cleveland Congregation of the Blessed Sacrament Provincial House; [N] Richfield, OH Regina Health Center.
Slattery, Rev. Msgr. John F. '57 (COS)[G] Colorado Springs, CO Sisters of St. Francis of Perpetual Adoration Retired.
Slattery, Joseph A. '66 (RIC) Virginia Beach, VA Holy Family.
Slattery, Kevin '86 (JKS) Gluckstadt, MS St. Joseph; Diocesan Judges; Personnel Board; Canton, MS Sacred Heart; Canton, MS Holy Child Jesus; Diocesan Consultors; Adjutant Judicial Vicar.
Slattery, Kirk '08 (COS) Cheyenne Wells, CO Sacred Heart; Colorado Springs, CO Holy Apostles.
Slattery, Michael J. *o.s.a.* '77 (JOL)[C] New Lenox, IL Providence Catholic High School; [L] New Lenox, IL Augustinian Friary.
Slattery, Rev. Msgr. Michael J. '62 (LA) Santa Clarita, CA Blessed Kateri Tekakwitha.
Slattery, Michael J. *o.s.a.* '77 (CHI)[N] Olympia Fields, IL The Augustinians–Provincialate; Olympia Fields, IL.
Slaughter, Martin '85 (LA) Los Angeles, CA St. Gerard Majella.
Slaven, Rev. Msgr. Frederick '59 (Y) Retired.
Sledesky, Stephen M. '93 (HRT) Manchester, CT St. Bridget; Manchester, CT St. Bartholomew.
Sledziona, John S. *c.m.* '70 (MAN) Concord, NH Sacred Heart; Office of Clergy Formation.
Sleiman, Elias *m.l.m.* '98 (OLL) Los Angeles, CA Our Lady of Mt. Lebanon–St. Peter Maronite Catholic Cathedral; [A] Houston, TX The Congregation of Maronite Lebanese Missionaries; Procurator/ Advocate; Office of Young Adult Ministry.
Slepicka, Rev. Msgr. Joseph J. '55 (DUB) Retired.
Slevin, Henry '62 (WDC) Washington, DC St. Francis de Sales; On Duty Outside the Archdiocese.
Slevin, Patrick C. '57 (MIA) Fort Lauderdale, FL St. Pius X.
Sleyman, Kenneth C. *m.m.* '90 (FgM) Maryknoll, NY MARYKNOLL.
Slezak, Raymond P. '74 (ALN) Allentown, PA SS. Peter and Paul.
Slight, William J. *m.s.* '65 (TYL) Lufkin, TX St. Patrick.
Sliney, Michael *l.c.* '98 (WDC)[N] Potomac, MD Legionaries of Christ.
Slinger, Rev. Msgr. Joseph T. '70 (NEW) Paramus, NJ Our Lady of the Visitation; Newark, NJ Cathedral Healthcare Systems; [R] Newark, NJ University Heights Property Company, Inc.; Cathedral Health Services, Inc.; Cathedral Affiliated Group at Orange, Inc.; Cathedral Affiliated Group at Montclair, Inc.; Montclair Community Hospital; University Heights Property Co., Inc.
Slipe, Rev. Msgr. Robert H. '73 (NEW) Cedar Grove, NJ St. Catherine of Siena.
Slisz, Charles E. '71 (BUF) Tonawanda, NY St. Christopher.
Sliwiak, Rev. Msgr. Stanley A. '66 (LAR) Vicar General; College of Consultors; Finance Council; Laredo, TX Blessed Sacrament.
Sliwiak, Rev. Msgr. Stanley A. '66 (LAR) Ex Officio Members.
Sliwinski, Philip '97 (GR) On Special Assignment.
Sliwinski, Richard *s.d.b.* (NOR) Pomfret, CT Most Holy Trinity.
Sloan, Daniel '82 (MET) Monmouth Junction, NJ St. Cecilia; College of Consultors.
Sloan, James D. *c.pp.s.* '62 (OAK)[M] Berkeley, CA Society of the Precious Blood (Province of Kansas City).
Slobig, John '90 (PHX) Sun City, AZ St. Clement of Rome Roman Catholic Parish.
Sloboda, Michael J. *m.m.* '85 (FgM) Maryknoll, NY MARYKNOLL.
Slobogin, Roland D. '73 (PH) Drexel Hill, PA St. Charles Borromeo; Council of Priests; Pastors Review Board.
Slocum, Samuel B. '80 (E) Bradford, PA St. Francis of Assisi; Lewis Run, PA Our Mother of Perpetual Help.
Slodowski, Bruno '68 (MIL) Not Assigned.
Slomba, Eugene S. '64 (BUF) Albion Correctional Facility; Batavia, NY Ascension; Orleans Correction Facility.
Slominski, Fabian B. '48 (DET) Retired.
Slominski, Leon '58 (SCL) Retired.
Slomski, Joseph P. '53 (WCH) Retired.
Slon, Thomas R. *s.j.* '90 (FgM)[EE] New York, NY "America;" Residence and publication office of the America Press; [EE] New York, NY Society of Jesus, New York Province; New York, NY; New York, NY Society of Jesus.
Sloneker, Patrick L. '97 (CIN) Botkins, OH Immaculate Conception; Botkins, OH St. Lawrence; Wapakoneta, OH St. Joseph.
Slota, Frederick V. '53 (PRO) Retired.
Slovacek, Emil C. '54 (DAL) Retired.
Slovikovski, John J. '96 (ALT) On Duty Outside the Diocese.
Slovikovski, John J. '96 (BAL)[S] Baltimore, MD St. Mary's Seminary & University.
Slovikovski, John (WDC)[A] Washington, DC Theological College of the Catholic University of America.
Slowiak, Allan L. '73 (LC) Rothschild, WI St. Mark.
Slowik, Joseph S. '72 (RIC) Retired.
Slowinski, Jerome '90 (DET) Sterling Heights, MI St. Jane Frances de Chantal; Adjutant Judicial Vicars.
Slowinski, Thomas F. '81 (MO) Navy Reserve Chaplains; Rochester, MI St. Andrew.
Sloyan, Gerard S. '44 (TR) Retired.
Slubecky, Rev. Msgr. David S. '73 (BUF) Finance Council; Consultors, College of; Council of Priests; Vicars General; Moderator of the Curia; The Diocese of Buffalo, N.Y.; Buffalo, NY St. Joseph's Cathedral; [T] Buffalo, NY St. Joseph Investment Fund, Inc.
Slusser, Michael S. '66 (STP) Retired.
Slusz, Michael J. '03 (HRT) Naugatuck, CT St. Francis of Assisi; Cheshire–Naugatuck Deanery.
Smail, Brian E. *o.f.m.* '99 (NY)[EE] New York, NY The Franciscan Vocation Ministry of Holy Name Province; New York, NY St. Francis of Assisi; New York, NY.
Smaistrla, Benjamin '72 (GAL) Houston, TX St. Ambrose.
Smalarz, James '04 (DET) Detroit, MI St. Christopher.
Small, Andrew *o.m.i.* '99 (WDC)[N] Washington, DC Oblate Community.
Small, Bryan '02 (ATL)[J] Atlanta, GA Emory University, Agnes Scott College; Special or Other (Arch)Diocesan Assignment.
Small, Edward J. *s.j.* '70 (BGP)[O] Fairfield, CT The Fairfield Jesuit Community–Fairfield University; Fairfield, CT Holy Family.
Small, Edward J. *s.j.* '70 (BO)[U] Boston The Society of Jesus of New England–Provincial Offices.
Small, James *c.ss.r.* '54 (HBG)[G] Ephrata, PA St. Clement's Mission House.
Small, Jeffrey '93 (PEO) On Leave of Absence.
Small, William T. '77 (PH) Absent on Sick Leave.
Smar, Michael J. '69 (Y) Retired.
Smarsh, Charles F. '64 (NY) On Duty Outside the Archdiocese.
Smart, Raymond W. '70 (PH) Pennsburg, PA St. Philip Neri Retired.
Smedile, Anselm *o.s.b.* '03 (MAN)[A] Manchester, NH St. Anselm Abbey Seminary; [K] Manchester, NH St. Anselm Abbey; Presbyteral Council.
Smegal, John T. '77 (SPR) Amherst, MA St. Brigid's; Continuing Education for Priests.
Smegelsky, John J. '66 (SY) Central Square, NY St. Michael.
Smeltzer, Stuart M. '96 (WCH) Wichita, KS St. Joseph; Defenders of the Bond.
Smereka, John '83 (SJP) Carnegie, PA Holy Trinity; Presbyters.
Smet, Joachim *o.carm.* '42 (JOL)[L] Darien Carmelite Provincial Office.
Smet, Joachim *o.carm.* '42 (WDC)[B] Washington, DC Whitefriars Hall.
Smet, Leroy R. '59 (GB) Retired.
Smetanka, Gary T. '82 (DET) Grosse Pointe, MI Our Lady Star of the Sea.
Smialek, Jeffrey *o.carm.* '07 (TUC)[A] Tucson, AZ Salpointe Catholic High School; [D] Tucson, AZ Carmelite Priory.
Smialowski, Raymond S. '82 (HRT) Bristol, CT St. Stanislaus.
Smiech, Charles *o.f.m.* '81 (CIN)[N] Cincinnati St. Francis Seraph Friary.
Smiga, George '75 (CLV) Willoughby Hills, OH St. Noel.
Smigiel, Walter J. '50 (PBL) Retired.
Smilanic, Daniel A. '73 (CHI) Park Ridge, IL St. Paul of the Cross; Canonical Services; Adjutant Judicial Vicar; Judges.
Smiley, Douglas J. '00 (R) Morehead City, NC St. Egbert.
Smilga, Zenon '50 (NOR) Putnam, CT Retired.
Smit, Gerard C. '50 (LKC) Retired.
Smith, Alberic *o.f.m.* (SPK) Spokane, WA St. Francis of Assisi.
Smith, Albert J. *o.s.f.s.* '65 (PH)[Y] Wyndmoor, PA Villa de Sales Oblate Residence.
Smith, Rt. Rev. Alexei R. '87 (LA) El Segundo, CA St. Andrew; Ecumenical and Interreligious Affairs; Commission for Ecumenical and Interreligious Affairs; Members.
Smith, Rt. Rev. Alexei '87 (NTN) El Segundo, CA St. Paul; Protopresbyters; College of Eparchial Consultors; Presbyteral Council; Continuing Education of Clergy Office.
Smith, Rev. Msgr. Alfred D. '53 (TR)[N] Trenton, NJ St. Lawrence Rehabilitation Center Retired.
Smith, Rev. Msgr. Alfred E. '56 (BAL) Williamsport, MD St. Augustine Retired.
Smith, Alvin '89 (ORG)[G] Fullerton, CA St. Jude Medical Center.
Smith, Andrew Charles '09 (CHI) Chicago, IL St. Ailbe.
Smith, Andrew T. *o.s.b.* '64 (PAT)[N] Morristown, NJ St. Mary's Abbey.
Smith, Aquinas '59 (SD) Retired.
Smith, Arthur J. '71 (BUF) Buffalo, NY St. Thomas Aquinas; Buffalo Fire Department and Erie County Emergency Services; Buffalo, NY St. Martin.
Smith, Bernard *o.f.m.cap.* '64 (NY)[EE] Beacon, NY St. Joachim Friary.
Smith, Bernard '90 (SP)[J] Tampa, FL St. Joseph's Hospital, Inc.
Smith, Bob (OM)[H] Omaha, NE New Cassel Retirement Center.
Smith, Brian P. '03 (BO) Brockton, MA St. Edith Stein.
Smith, Brian '98 (SJ) On Leave of Absence.
Smith, Charles C. '06 (ARL) Notaries.
Smith, Charles D. '65 (PH) Huntingdon Valley, PA St. Albert the Great.
Smith, Charles F. *s.v.d.* '88 (MO) DEPARTMENT OF VETERANS AFFAIRS HOSPITALS AND CHAPLAINS.
Smith, Christopher L. '03 (FTW) Goshen, IN St. John the Evangelist.
Smith, Christopher '78 (ORG) Vicar for Priests; Priests' Relief; Ministry to Priests; Special Assignment.
Smith, Christopher '05 (CHR) Hilton Head Island, SC St. Francis By the Sea.
Smith, Clifford G. '96 (DAL) Plano, TX St. Mark the Evangelist.
Smith, Craig '05 (PT) Advocate; Auditors; Fort Walton Beach, FL St. Mary Church.
Smith, D. Stephen '73 (MAD) McFarland, WI Christ the King.
Smith, Daniel *o.carm.* '46 (NEW) Paramus, NJ Carmelite Chapel of St. Therese.
Smith, Daniel '99 (VEN) Naples, FL St. John the Evangelist.
Smith, David A. *m.m.* '85 (FgM) Maryknoll, NY MARYKNOLL.
Smith, David L. *s.j.* '85 (DM)[J] Griswold, IA Creighton University Retreat Center.
Smith, David L. *s.j.* '85 (OM)[K] Omaha, NE Jesuit Community at Creighton University.
Smith, David W. '64 (STP)[C] St. Paul, MN University of St. Thomas; Censores Librorum.
Smith, David '82 (MIA) Miami, FL St. Raymond.
Smith, Dean M. '99 (RCK) Stockton, IL Holy Cross.
Smith, Dennis '75 (FWT) Keller, TX St. Elizabeth Ann Seton.
Smith, Donald R. '57 (SC) Retired.
Smith, Douglas *c.s.c.* (FTW)[A] Notre Dame, IN Moreau Seminary.
Smith, Edmund *o.s.b.* '65 (P)[L] St. Benedict, OR Mt. Angel Abbey; [N] St. Benedict, OR Mount Angel Abbey Retreat House.
Smith, Edward E. '82 (MOB) On Leave from the Archdiocese.
Smith, Edward J. '65 (BRK) Jackson Heights, NY Blessed Sacrament; Jackson Heights, NY Blessed Sacrament.
Smith, Edward J. '01 (CLV) Sheffield, OH St. Teresa of Avila.
Smith, Edward P. '82 (CIN)[A] Cincinnati, OH The Athenaeum of Ohio; [B] Cincinnati, OH Mt. St. Mary's Seminary of the West; [B] Cincinnati, OH Mt. St. Mary's Seminary of the West.
Smith, Elmer W. '50 (CIN) Cincinnati, OH St. Cecilia; [U] Cincinnati, OH Legion of Mary Retired.
Smith, Eugene M. *o.s.m.* '84 (CHI)[N] Chicago Order of Friar Servants of Mary (Servites) United States of

America Province, Inc.
Smith, Eugene M. *o.s.m.* '88 (ORG)[I] Anaheim, CA Servite Fathers and Brothers.
Smith, Eugene P. '50 (LC) Boyd, WI Sacred Heart of Jesus–St. Joseph Retired.
Smith, F. Harold '50 (L) Retired.
Smith, Rev. Msgr. Francis J. '67 (ELP) El Paso, TX St. Raphael; Vicars General; Ex Officio Members; Advocates; Finance Council; Priests' Personnel Advisory Committee; Priests' Retirement and Disability Plan; [J] El Paso, TX Knights of Columbus; [J] El Paso, TX Knights of the Holy Sepulchre; [J] El Paso, TX Ladies of the Holy Sepulchre.
Smith, Francis J. *s.j.* '52 (DET)[K] Clarkston, MI Colombiere Center.
Smith, Francis R. *s.j.* '70 (SJ)[B] Santa Clara, CA Jesuit Community.
Smith, Francis X.J. (ORL) Winter Park, FL St. Margaret Mary Retired.
Smith, Gabriel J. '82 (CHR) Charleston, SC St. Joseph.
Smith, Gary N. *s.j.* '71 (P)[L] Portland Jesuit Provincial Office (Society of Jesus, Oregon Prov.).
Smith, Gary N. *s.j.* '71 (FgM) Portland, OR Society of Jesus.
Smith, Gene F. '84 (CHI) Chicago, IL St. Barnabas.
Smith, Geoffrey C. '74 (HRT) Hamden, CT St. Rita; New Haven, CT Yale–New Haven Hospital; Special and other Archdiocesan Assignment.
Smith, Gerald S. '64 (PH) North Wales, PA St. Rose of Lima.
Smith, Gerald '65 (AUS) Retired.
Smith, Herbert F. *s.j.* '62 (PH)[Y] Loyola Center and Manresa Hall.
Smith, Howard C. *s.m.* '72 (WDC)[N] Washington, DC Marist Center.
Smith, Ignatius E. *o.f.m.* '56 (NY) Callicoon, NY Holy Cross.
Smith, Ignatius *o.s.b.* '54 (KCK)[I] Atchison, KS St. Benedict's Abbey.
Smith, Jacob–Matthew *o.f.m.* (WDC)[N] Washington, DC Franciscan Monastery USA Inc.; Washington, DC.
Smith, James A.D. '56 (PAT)[Q] Chester, NJ Nazareth Village.
Smith, James B. '85 (WIL) Hockessin, DE St. Mary of the Assumption.
Smith, James D. '87 (STP) Special Assignment.
Smith, James E. *c.m.* '61 (PH)[Y].
Smith, James F. *s.j.* '62 (SY)[Q] Syracuse, NY Jesuits at LeMoyne, Inc.
Smith, James G. *o.praem.* '77 (ORG)[D] Silverado, CA St. Michael's Preparatory School; [I] Silverado, CA Norbertine Fathers of Orange Inc.
Smith, James H. '63 (HRT) Retired.
Smith, James R. '67 (SC) Spirit Lake, IA St. Mary's.
Smith, James T. '65 (COL) Columbus, OH St. Matthias.
Smith, James (PAT) Retired.
Smith, Rev. Msgr. James '60 (ALN) Retired.
Smith, Johannes Michael Mary *f.i.* '04 (SY)[U] Maine, NY Mount St. Francis Hermitage, Inc.
Smith, Rev. Msgr. John F.X. '61 (NY) Tuxedo, NY Our Lady of Mt. Carmel.
Smith, Rev. Msgr. John J. '59 (FR) Retired.
Smith, John K. '04 (LUB) Hale Center, TX St. Theresa's.
Smith, John *s.s.c.* (CHI)[N] Chicago, IL Korean Catholic Center.
Smith, John *s.s.c.* '62 (OM)[K] St. Columbans Missionary Society of St. Columban.
Smith, Joseph A. '96 (SAV) Richmond Hill, GA St. Anne.
Smith, Joseph J. *s.j.* '57 (FgM) New York, NY Society of Jesus.
Smith, Rev. Msgr. Joseph P.T. '60 (ALN) Orefield, PA St. Joseph The Worker.
Smith, Rev. Msgr. K. Bartholomew '98 (WDC) Silver Spring, MD St. Bernadette.
Smith, Kenneth G. '84 (HBG) Orrtanna, PA St. Ignatius Loyola.
Smith, Rev. Msgr. Kenneth J. '64 (NY) New York, NY St. Catherine of Genoa; Judges.
Smith, Kevin M. '88 (RVC) Oyster Bay, NY St. Dominic's; Nassau County, Fire Chiefs, Council of; Chaplain of the Nassau County Firemen's Association.
Smith, Lawrence C. *s.j.* '82 (BO)[U] Boston The Society of Jesus of New England–Provincial Offices.
Smith, Lawrence R. '76 (PIT) Pittsburgh, PA Most Holy Name of Jesus; Pittsburgh, PA St. Aloysius.
Smith, Leland J. '53 (WIN) Retired.
Smith, Leo Joseph '06 (VEN) Port Charlotte, FL St. Charles Borromeo.
Smith, Leonard A. '91 (WH) Berkeley Springs, WV St. Vincent de Paul.
Smith, LeRoy J. '78 (BRK) Retired.
Smith, Leroy '78 (SPR) Pittsfield, MA Berkshire Medical Center.
Smith, Lester E. '75 (SY) Sherburne, NY St. Malachy; New Berlin, NY St. Theresa of the Infant Jesus.
Smith, M. Christopher '83 (JC) Palmyra, MO St. Joseph.
Smith, Mark Leo '05 (WDC) Kensington, MD Holy Redeemer; Pomfret, MD St. Joseph.
Smith, Mark S. '96 (JC) Westphalia, MO St. Anthony of Padua; Westphalia, MO St. Joseph; Judges; Priestly and Religious Vocations Committee.
Smith, Martin L. *o.s.a.* '77 (PH)[Y] Villanova, PA St. Thomas Monastery.
Smith, Michael B. '74 (CLV) Akron, OH Immaculate Conception.
Smith, Michael H. '66 (SAV) Retired.
Smith, Michael M. '77 (HEL) Retired.
Smith, Michael N. *s.j.* '67 (PBL) Fruita, CO Sacred Heart.
Smith, Michael R. '00 (SP) Lecanto, FL St. Scholastica Church.
Smith, Michael S. '92 (NOR) Hebron, CT The Church of the Holy Family; Members; Continuing Education and Formation Commission for the Clergy; Advisory Board.
Smith, Nicholas P. '65 (PRO) Wakefield, RI St. Francis of Assisi; South County Hospital.
Smith, Nicholas W. '94 (STL) St. Louis, MO St. Joan of Arc.
Smith, Norman '50 (GLP) Retired.
Smith, Patrick A. '90 (WDC) Priest Council.
Smith, Patrick '67 (PHX) Scottsdale, AZ Scottsdale Healthcare Osborn; Scottsdale, AZ Our Lady of Perpetual Help Roman Catholic Parish.
Smith, Patrick '03 (JKS) Woodville, MS St. Joseph.
Smith, Paul F. '73 (CLV) Thompson, OH St. Patrick.
Smith, Paul O. '64 (COL) Retired.
Smith, Paul '59 (ALB) Altamont, NY St. Lucy; Albany, NY St. James Retired.
Smith, Paul '59 (HON) Honolulu, HI Diocesan Hospital Ministry.
Smith, Peter '00 (P) Portland, OR St. Rose of Lima; Judges.
Smith, Peter '00 (P)[Q] Portland, OR Brotherhood of the People of Praise.
Smith, Philip T. *o.praem.* '84 (ORG) Costa Mesa, CA St. John the Baptist.
Smith, R. Douglas *o.s.f.s.* '62 (PH) Philadelphia, PA Our Mother of Consolation.
Smith, R. Leroy '54 (COV) Retired.
Smith, Ramon *o.f.m.* '53 (SFE)[I] Rio Rancho, NM Felician Sisters; [H] Albuquerque, NM The Province of Our Lady of Guadalupe.
Smith, Richard A. '56 (MAN) Retired.
Smith, Richard G. (NY) Bronx, NY St. Benedict.
Smith, Richard P. *m.m.* '76 (FgM) Maryknoll, NY MARYKNOLL.
Smith, Richard '98 (FRS) Laton, CA Shrine of Our Lady of Fatima.
Smith, Richard '84 (JKS) Booneville, MS St. Francis of Assisi; Corinth, MS St. James.
Smith, Richard '76 (JOL) Morris, IL Immaculate Conception of the Blessed Virgin Mary.
Smith, Richard '00 (WIL) Ocean City, MD St. Luke and St. Andrew.
Smith, Richard '09 (PH) Morton, PA Our Lady of Perpetual Help.
Smith, Rev. Msgr. Robert J. '70 (E)[J] Erie, PA Bishop Michael J. Murphy Residence for Retired Priests; Vicar General; Northern Vicariate; Administrative Cabinet; College of Consultors; Ex Officios; Priest Personnel Board; Members; Matrimonial Judges; Board of Members; Clergy Personnel.
Smith, Robert J. '55 (OM) Retired.
Smith, Robert J. '83 (RVC) Setauket, NY St. James; Censors of Books; Senate of Priests (Presbyteral Council/College of Consultors); Priests' Personnel Assignment Board.
Smith, Robert S. '58 (RVC) Retired.
Smith, Robert V. '61 (CAM) Liaison with Retired Priests Retired.
Smith, Robert '53 (ROC)[M] Ithaca, NY The Cornell Catholic Community, Inc. (Ithaca) Retired.
Smith, Robert '97 (FAR) Lidgerwood, ND Sts. Peter & Paul Church of Cayuga; Geneseo, ND St. Martin's Church of Geneseo; Lidgerwood, ND St. Boniface Church of Lidgerwood.
Smith, Roger J. '73 (SEA) Morton, WA Sacred Heart.
Smith, Rev. Msgr. Roger R. '76 (CC) Presbyteral Council; Judges; Corpus Christi, TX St. Patrick; Members.
Smith, Ronald T. '73 (HRT) New Britain, CT St. Andrew; New Britain, CT St. John the Evangelist; New Britain, CT The Hospital of Central Connecticut (New Britain General Hospital); Special and other Archdiocesan Assignment; New Britain Deanery.
Smith, Russell E. '80 (RIC) Unassigned.
Smith, S. Douglas *c.s.c.* '76 (FTW)[H] Notre Dame Congregation of Holy Cross, Indiana Province, Provincial House; [B] University of Notre Dame Du Lac.
Smith, Rev. Msgr. Sherrill '55 (SAT)[K] San Antonio, TX Padua Place Retired.
Smith, Simon E. *s.j.* '61 (BO)[G] Roxbury, MA Nativity Preparatory School.
Smith, Simon E. *s.j.* '61 (WOR)[O] Worcester, MA Jesuits of the Holy Cross, Inc.
Smith, Stanley C. *o.s.a.* '60 (PH)[Y] Villanova, PA St. Thomas Monastery.
Smith, Stephen *o.p.* '58 (R) Ex Officio; Defender of the Bond; [F] Raleigh, NC Dominican Priory; Vicar for Priests.
Smith, Terrance W. '73 (CIN) Judges; Cincinnati, OH Good Shepherd.
Smith, Terrence *t.o.r.* '73 (STP) Brooklyn Park, MN St. Gerard Majella; [K] Brooklyn Park, MN St. Gerard Friary.
Smith, Thomas A. '83 (L) Louisville, KY Holy Spirit; College of Consultors; Priests' Council.
Smith, Thomas A. *o.f.m.conv.* '79 (L) Louisville, KY St. Rita.
Smith, Thomas E. *s.j.* '74 (NY) Wallkill, NY Wallkill Correctional Facility; [EE] Loyola Hall, Jesuit Community; Napanoch, NY Eastern Correctional Facility; Wallkill, NY Shawangunk Correctional Facility; Napanoch, NY Ulster Correctional Facility.
Smith, Thomas E. '51 (PIT) Retired.
Smith, Thomas F. *o.c.s.o.* '58 (ATL)[G] Conyers, GA The Monastery of the Holy Spirit.
Smith, Rev. Msgr. Thomas H. '57 (HBG) Lancaster, PA St. Joseph; Cursillo Movement.
Smith, Thomas J. '60 (LC)[H] La Crosse, WI Holy Cross (Seminary) Diocesan Center Retired.
Smith, Thomas J. '82 (NOR) On Duty Outside the Diocese.
Smith, Thomas R. '81 (CLV) Lorain, OH St. John the Baptist; Associate Judges; Lorain, OH St. Vitus.
Smith, Thomas W. *c.s.c.* '72 (FTW)[H] Notre Dame Congregation of Holy Cross, Indiana Province, Provincial House; South Bend, IN St. Adalbert; Notre Dame, IN HOLY CROSS MISSION CENTER.
Smith, Thomas '51 (ORL) Altamonte Springs, FL St. Mary Magdalen Retired.
Smith, Tom *o.f.m.conv.* '79 (IND) Clarksville, IN St. Anthony of Padua.
Smith, Trevor '67 (MIA) Retired.
Smith, Vernon '89 (FAR) On Duty Outside the Diocese.
Smith, Vernon (DM) Shenandoah, IA St. Mary; Hamburg, IA St. Mary.
Smith, Vincent E. *o.s.f.s.* '85 (PH)[Y] Philadelphia, PA Father Louis Brisson Residence.
Smith, Rev. Msgr. Vincent J. '55 (HBG) Mechanicsburg, PA Saint Katharine Drexel; Mechanicsburg, PA Saint Katharine Drexel Retired.
Smith, Vincent Leo '66 (DEN) Retired.
Smith, W. Andrew '80 (LR) Jacksonville, AR St. Jude the Apostle.
Smith, Walter J. *s.j.* '72 (BO)[U] Boston The Society of Jesus of New England–Provincial Offices.
Smith, Walter J. *s.j.* '72 (NY)[EE] New York Jesuit Provincial's Office.
Smith, Wilfred T. '56 (CLV) Madison, OH Immaculate Conception; Mentor, OH St. Mary of the Assumption Retired.
Smith, William A. '74 (BRK) South Ozone Park, NY St. Anthony of Padua.
Smith, William A. '03 (CLV) Parma Heights, OH St. John Bosco.
Smith, William G. '79 (BRK) St. Albans, NY Our Lady of Light Roman Catholic Church.
Smith, William J. '47 (PH) Retired.
Smith, William J. '81 (MET) Port Reading, NJ St. Anthony of Padua; Woodbridge, NJ Our Lady of Mount Carmel.
Smith, William P. *o.m.i.* '45 (BO) Lexington, MA St. Brigid; [X] Tewksbury, MA Immaculate Heart of Mary Residence.
Smith, William *c.s.sp.* '74 (PIT)[O] Bethel Park, PA The Spiritan Center.
Smith, William '74 (DEN) Glenwood Springs, CO St. Stephen.
Smith, Wilton S. '58 (SFR)[K] San Rafael, CA Nazareth House of San Rafael, Inc. Retired.
Smith–Soucier, Martin D. '79 (MO) On Duty Outside the Diocese; DEPARTMENT OF VETERANS AFFAIRS HOSPITALS AND CHAPLAINS.
Smith–Sourcier, Martin D. (ROC) Canandaigua, NY Veteran's Hospital.
Smithson, Thomas *s.s.s.* '02 (CHI) Chicago, IL Blessed Sacrament.
Smits, Ken *o.f.m.cap.* '64 (MIL)[P] Mount Calvary, WI St. Lawrence Friary.
Smits, Lee '71 (CHI)[J] Maywood, IL Loyola University Medical Center.
Smochko, Rev. Msgr. Basil '46 (PRM) Retired.
Smolarski, Dennis C. *s.j.* '79 (SJ)[B] Santa Clara, CA Jesuit Community.
Smolenski, Stanley '68 (HRT) On Duty Outside the Archdiocese.
Smolenski, Stanley *s.p.m.a.* '68 (CHR) Marian Programs; [J] Kingstree, SC Shrine of Our Lady of South Carolina–Our Lady of Joyful Hope.
Smoley, Rudolph F. '69 (PIT) Elizabeth, PA St. Michael.
Smolich, Thomas H. *s.j.* '86 (FgM) Washington, DC National Headquarters; Washington, DC; Washington, DC Jesuit Conference, Inc.
Smolich, Thomas H. *s.j.* '86 (WDC)[W] Washington, DC Jesuit Conference, Inc.; [N] Washington, DC Leonard Neale House.

Smolik, Peter K. '02 (BGP) Shelton, CT St. Lawrence.
Smolinski, Clarence D. '53 (GAY) Posen, MI St. Casimir Retired.
Smolinski, Joseph J. '48 (NY) Retired.
Smolko, John F. '57 (BGP) On Duty Outside the Diocese Retired.
Smolley, Robert '82 (STF) Manchester, NH Protection of B.V.M.
Smuda, Alfred J. *o.s.f.s.* '66 (FgM) Wilmington, DE OBLATES OF ST. FRANCIS DE SALES MISSIONS.
Smullen, Martin J. '82 (NO) Metairie, LA St. Mary Magdalen.
Smutelovic, Peter '95 (NEW) On Duty Outside the Archdiocese.
Smyka, James *o.f.m.conv.* (ALT) Johnstown, PA Memorial Medical Center Lee Campus; Johnstown, PA Good Samaritan Medical Center.
Smyth, James '56 (NY) Hastings–on–Hudson, NY St. Matthew.
Smyth, James '57 (NY) Retired.
Smyth, John P. '62 (CHI)[D] Niles, IL Notre Dame College Prep.
Smyth, John *c.ss.r.* '64 (RIC)[M] Hampton, VA Holy Family Retreat.
Smyth, Joseph P. '59 (BO) Senior Priests. Retired.
Sneck, William J. *s.j.* '71 (ALN)[A] Wernersville, PA Jesuit Center–Jesuit Community; [N] Wernersville, PA Jesuit Center.
Snedeker, Arthur '74 (CLV) Metro Health Medical Center & Rehabilitation Center; Cleveland, OH Our Lady of Mercy.
Snell, Francis '91 (HRT) New Haven, CT Sacred Heart.
Snell, Roger K. '72 (FAR) Retired.
Sneyd, Derrick '70 (FTW) Auburn, IN Immaculate Conception; Consultors; Advisory Board.
Snider, Harold *o.f.m.cap.* '89 (LA) Solvang, CA Old Mission Santa Ines.
Snider, Mike (TYL) Tyler, TX Cathedral of the Immaculate Conception.
Snieg, Peter '93 (CHI)[A] Chicago, IL St. Joseph College Seminary.
Sniezyk, Rev. Msgr. Richard S. '62 (SPR) Retired.
Sniosek, Jaroslaw '98 (VEN) Auditors; Judges; Venice, FL Epiphany Cathedral.
Snipes, Roy Lee *o.m.i.* '80 (BWN) Mission, TX Our Lady of Guadalupe.
Snitily, Steven P. '09 (LIN) Lincoln, NE North American Martyrs.
Snitily, Steven '09 (LIN) Advocates.
Snock, Bernard C. '62 (GAL) Retired.
Snodgrass, Thomas A. '76 (CIN) Cincinnati, OH St. Peter in Chains Cathedral; Assistant Chancellor; Judges.
Snoich, Stephen *o.s.b.* '72 (LFT) Lake Village, IN St. Augusta.
Snoich, Stephen *o.s.b.* '72 (IND)[K] St. Meinrad St. Meinrad Archabbey.
Snoke, F. Richard '65 (COL) Danville, OH St. Luke; Deanery 9: Knox Licking; Presbyteral Council; Parochial Examiners.
Snopek, Charles J. '86 (CHR) Retired.
Snouffer, Philip T. '62 (BAL) Retired.
Snow, Glenn *o.carm.* '89 (TUC) Tucson, AZ Saint Cyril of Alexandria Roman Catholic Parish – Tucson.
Snow, Rev. Msgr. Harry K. '77 (OG) Norwood, NY St. Andrew; Judicial Vicar and Vicar for Canonical Affairs; Deans.
Snow, Lorn J. *s.j.* '99 (CLV) University Heights, OH Gesu; [B] University Heights, OH John Carroll Jesuit Community; Presbyteral Council; Presbyteral Conveners.
Snyder, Alexander '59 (OAK) Retired.
Snyder, Brian '79 (SEA) Renton, WA St. Stephen the Martyr.
Snyder, Chester P. '77 (HBG) Mechanicsburg, PA St. Joseph; Consultors, College; Appointed.
Snyder, Donald E. '73 (CLV) Westlake, OH St. Ladislas; Associate Judges.
Snyder, Frederick J. '52 (TOL) Swanton, OH Holy Trinity Retired.
Snyder, Frederick '52 (GI) Retired.
Snyder, Gary B. '74 (SC) Sioux City, IA St. Michael; Priests' Pension Plan – Board of Trustees.
Snyder, George '07 (SAC) Fair Oaks, CA St. Mel.
Snyder, Guy Christopher *p.i.m.e.* '98 (DET)[K] Detroit, MI P.I.M.E. Missionaries; Detroit, MI All Saints.
Snyder, John F. *s.j.* '55 (STL)[O] St. Louis, MO Jesuit Community Corporation at Saint Louis University – Jesuit Hall.
Snyder, Rev. Msgr. John R. '54 (E) Retired.
Snyder, Larry J. '88 (STP) Special Assignment.
Snyder, Michael E. '97 (BLX) Picayune, MS St. Charles Borromeo.
Snyder, Michael J. *m.m.* '79 (FgM) Maryknoll, NY MARYKNOLL.
Snyders, William J. *s.j.* '66 (FgM) St. Louis, MO Society of Jesus.
Snyderwine, Rev. Msgr. L. Thomas '68 (E) Erie, PA St. Luke; Apostleship of the Sea and Chaplain to the Port of Erie.
Snyers, Peter '53 (SCL) Retired.
Soares, John P. '92 (PRO) Providence, RI St. Thomas.
Soares, Rev. Msgr. Nicholas J. '64 (NY) Staten Island, NY St. Clement; Staten Island, NY St. Michael.
Sobarzo, Jose '05 (RNO) Gardnerville, NV St. Gall.
Sobczak, Marek W. *c.m.* '81 (BRK) Brooklyn, NY St. Stanislaus Kostka.
Soberal, Jose D. '60 (ARE) Arecibo, PR Church of Santa Teresita; Vicar General; Diocesan Consultors; Priest's Senate (Consejo Presbiteral); Pastoral Vocational Program.
Sobiech, Slawomir '01 (BRK) On Leave/Unassigned.
Sobiech, Stanley *o.f.m.conv.* '62 (SPR) Holyoke, MA Mater Dolorosa.
Sobiecki, Peter S. '66 (HRT) Retired.
Sobierajski, Rev. Msgr. Edward J. '61 (BUF)[O] Tonawanda, NY O'Hara Residence Retired.
Sobierajski, Joseph A. *s.j.* '74 (CHL)[J] Mooresville, NC Jesuit Community.
Sobiesiak, Rev. Msgr. Joseph R. '76 (ALN) Allentown, PA St. Paul.
Sobieszczyk, David '64 (DEN) Retired.
Sobolewski, Edward F. '69 (CAM) Rosenhayn, NJ St. Mary's Church, Rosenhayn, N.J.
Sobolewski, Wlodzimierz *c.r.* (BO) Court Advocate/ Petitioner.
Sobolik, Joseph T. '09 (DUL) Duluth, MN Cathedral of Our Lady of the Rosary.
Sobon, Walter A. '67 (PIT) McDonald, PA St. Alphonsus; Oakdale, PA St. Patrick.
Sobotka, DePaul *o.f.m.* '63 (MIL)[P] Burlington, WI Queen of Peace Friary.
Sobus, James M. '86 (WH) Huntington, WV Our Lady of Fatima; Ona, WV St. Stephen.
Socha, Bogdan Mikolaj *o.s.p.p.e.* '93 (NY) New York, NY St. Stanislaus Bishop and Martyr.
Socha, Bronislaw F. *o.c.d.* '89 (GRY)[H] Munster, IN Discalced Carmelite Fathers Monastery.
Socha, Michael I. *o.f.m. conv.* '98 (PAT) Clifton, NJ St. John Kanty.
Sochulak, Pavol *s.v.d.* '92 (SB) San Bernardino, CA Our Lady of the Rosary Cathedral.
Socias, James '78 (POD) Oak Park.
Socias, James '78 (CHI)[V] Chicago, IL Midtown Residence.
Sockol, Timothy '77 (PMB) Delray Beach, FL Emmanuel.
Sodano, Thomas M. '91 (PH)[D] Philadelphia, PA St. Hubert's Catholic High School for Girls; Philadelphia, PA St. Bernard.
Sodini, Pierre G. '68 (PIT) Avella, PA St. Michael.
Sodja, Richard H. '65 (HEL)[B] Helena, MT Carroll College Retired.
Sodoro, Carl F. '77 (OM)[G] Omaha, NE Archbishop Bergan Mercy Medical Center; Omaha, NE St. Adalbert.
Soeherman, Miguel Marie *m.f.v.a.* '04 (BIR)[E] Birmingham, AL Franciscan Missionaries of the Eternal Word, A Public Association of the Christian Faithful.
Soehner, Mark *o.f.m.* '87 (CHI)[N] Chicago, IL St. Joseph Interprovincial Post–Novitiate Formation House.
Soerries, Denis *o.s.b.* '56 (LR) New Blaine, AR St. Scholastica; [J] New Blaine, AR Hesychia House of Prayer.
Sofie, J. Francis '94 (MOB) Mobile, AL Little Flower; [B] Mobile, AL McGill–Toolen Catholic High School.
Sogliuzzo, Louis P. *s.j.* '87 (SY)[T] Syracuse, NY LeMoyne College Campus Ministry; [Q] Syracuse, NY Jesuits at LeMoyne, Inc.
Soh, Christopher *s.j.* '05 (LA) Santa Barbara, CA Our Lady of Sorrows.
Soha, Roderick N. *t.o.r.* '95 (ALT) Windber, PA St. Anthony of Padua.
Sohm, Andrew L. '05 (OM) Omaha, NE St. Stephen the Martyr.
Sohm, John E. '58 (SFD) Sullivan, IL St. Columcille.
Soileau, Charles '57 (LKC) Retired.
Sojka, Jeremiusz H. '95 (RIC) Blacksburg, VA St. Mary; Salem, VA Salem VA Medical Center.
Sojka, Louis L. *o.s.b.* '90 (OM)[C] Elkhorn, NE Mount Michael Benedictine School; [K] Elkhorn, NE Mount Michael Benedictine Abbey; Elkhorn, NE.
Sokalski, Marcel *o.f.m.conv.* '59 (BUF)[O] Athol Springs, NY St. Maximilian Kolbe Friary.
Sokol, Nathaniel '04 (LAN) On Duty Outside the Diocese.
Sokol, Stanislaw '85 (SPR) Springfield, MA Our Lady of the Rosary.
Sokolowski, Rev. Msgr. Robert S. '65 (WDC) On Duty Outside the Archdiocese; [C] Catholic University of America, The.
Sokolowski, Thomas J. '79 (SCR)[N] Dunmore, PA Villa St. Joseph; Unassigned or Leave of Absence.
Sokolowski, William R. '65 (HRT) Wolcott, CT St. Maria Goretti.
Sokolski, John *o.m.i.* '55 (SAT)[K] San Antonio, TX Oblate Madonna Residence.
Solan, Lawrence T. '80 (COS) Colorado Springs, CO St. Patrick.
Solana, Fermin '70 (MIA) Miami, FL Our Lady of Divine Providence.
Solano, Julio R. '93 (MIA) Miami, FL Mother of Christ.
Solari, James K. '55 (CHL) Retired.
Solarski, John E. (POD) Irving.
Solarski, John E. '76 (DAL)[I] Irving, TX Opus Dei.
Solazzo, Michael J. '76 (CHI) Evanston, IL St. Mary.
Solcia, Louis M. *c.r.s.p.* '57 (SD) San Diego, CA Our Lady of the Rosary; [O] San Diego, CA Magnificat (Central) San Diego Chapter.
Soler, Jean–Paul '07 (NY) New York, NY Our Lady Queen of Martyrs.
Soler, Lawrence *t.o.r.* '51 (AUS) Waco, TX Sacred Heart Catholic Church – Waco, Texas.
Soler, Manuel A. '98 (MIA) Police Chaplains; Miami, FL Corpus Christi.
Soler, Roberto '62 (MGZ) Aguada, PR Santuario Protomartires de la Concepcion.
Solera, Eugenio '86 (RVC) West Babylon, NY Our Lady of Grace.
Soley, Roger A. '78 (WDC) Upper Marlboro, MD Church of the Most Holy Rosary.
Solis, Francisco J. '06 (BWN) San Juan, TX Basilica of Our Lady of San Juan del Valle–National Shrine; [I] San Juan, TX The Basilica of Our Lady of San Juan del Valle–National Shrine.
Solis, Marco '97 (LA) Guadalupe, CA Our Lady of Guadalupe.
Solis, Olman '97 (OAK) Oakley, CA St. Anthony; Deanery #6.
Solis, Ralph '93 (ELP) Horizon City, TX Holy Spirit.
Solis, Sergio '00 (CHI) Cicero, IL St. Anthony of Padua.
Solivan, Roberto (CGS) Priests Senate.
Soliván, Roberto '81 (CGS) Cidra, PR Nuestra Senora de Fatima.
Solla, Santiago '53 (PCE) Juana Diaz, PR St. Raymond Nonato.
Solma, Martin A. *s.m.* '78 (STL)[O] St. Louis Marianists, Province of the United States (Society of Mary); [O] St. Louis, MO Maryland Avenue Marianist Community.
Soloman, Louis E. *s.j.* '64 (NY)[EE] New York, NY Murray–Weigel Hall.
Solomon, Marc J. '06 (E) Sykesville, PA Assumption of Blessed Virgin Mary; Priest Personnel Board; Reynoldsville, PA St. Mary.
Solors, Stephen '91 (DUL) Deer River, MN St. Joseph; Deer River, MN Sacred Heart.
Solorzano, Marcelo *o.p.* '95 (FgM) Metairie, LA St. Martin de Porres Province (Southern Dominican Province).
Solorzano, Marcelo *o.p.* '96 (MIA)[K] Miami, FL Dominican Fathers of Miami, Inc.
Solorzano, Mario '06 (JKS) New Albany, MS St. Francis of Assisi.
Solorzano, Miguel A. '93 (GAL) Houston, TX St. Charles Borromeo.
Soltero, Gilberto Monico '02 (LA) Lynwood, CA St. Philip Neri.
Soltis, John F. *m.m.* '62 (NY)[EE] Maryknoll Maryknoll Fathers and Brothers Retired.
Soltys, Daniel F. '68 (OM) Omaha, NE St. Joan of Arc.
Soltys, Raymond A. '79 (SPR) Ludlow, MA Christ the King.
Somarriba, Marcos A. '93 (MIA) Miami, FL St. Kieran.
Sombilon, Edmundo '93 (NEW) Fort Lee, NJ Holy Trinity.
Somera, Romelo '99 (HON) Kapaa, HI St. Catherine.
Somers, Eldon K. '51 (E) Retired.
Somers, Michael '82 (GB) Absent on Leave, Sick or Disabled.
Somers, Richard '66 (JKS) Greenville, MS St. Joseph.
Somerville, Alvin *o.f.m.conv.* '58 (ALB) Albany, NY Holy Family Parish.
Somerville, Conrad *o.f.m.conv.* '54 (SY) Syracuse, NY Assumption B.V.M.
Sommer, Allan J. '66 (MIL) CIVIL AIR PATROL; Milwaukee, WI St. Bernadette.
Sommer, Gerald J. *m.s.c.* '47 (Y)[I] Canton, OH House of Loreto Retired.
Sommer, Harold *s.j.* '65 (CIN)[N] Cincinnati, OH Faber Jesuit Community.
Sommer, Rev. Msgr. Jerome '40 (JC) Retired.
Sommer, Rev. Msgr. Ralph '83 (RVC) Westbury, NY St. Brigid.
Sommermeyer, Gary H. '91 (BRK) Retired.
Sommers, Edward P. '73 (CAM) Retired.
Somoza, Jose I. *o.f.m.* '65 (MIA) Miami, FL St. Timothy.
Son, Doan Trong *c.ss.r.* '99 (LA)[P] Baldwin Park, CA Vietnamese Redemptorist Mission.
Son, Eun Seok (BRK) Flushing, NY St. Paul Chong Ha–Sang Roman Catholic Chapel.
Son, Kyungsu *m.m.* '79 (FgM) Maryknoll, NY MARYKNOLL.
Sonefeld, Raymond G. '48 (KAL) Retired.
Song, James '00 (SAT) Boerne, TX Korean Martyrs Catholic Church.
Songy, Rev. Msgr. James B. '54 (HT) Retired.
Sonnberger, Albert W. '56 (LC) Bloomer, WI St. John the Baptist Retired.
Sonnier, Cedric '97 (LAF) Eunice, LA St. Thomas More; Diocesan Co Chaplains.
Sonnier, Charles '64 (VIC) Sweet Home, TX St. John

the Baptist; Sweet Home, TX Queen of Peace; Presbyteral Council.
Soo–Gil Chae, Cyril '04 (ATL) Norcross, GA Saint Patrick.
Soosaimanickam, Benjamin V. '90 (NOR) Willimantic, CT St. Joseph.
Soosairaj, Michael '88 (NY) Rhinebeck, NY The Good Shepherd.
Soper, Paul R. '90 (BO) Weymouth, MA St. Albert the Great.
Sopiak, Donald A. '78 (DET) Detroit, MI Our Lady Queen of Heaven.
Sopoliga, Michael '79 (PSC) Fort Pierce, FL SS. Cyril and Methodius.
Sopp, Michael '75 (SJP) On Leave; Presbyters.
Soprano, Ernest R. '79 (CAM) North Cape May, NJ The Church of St. John of God, North Cape May, N.J.
Soprych, Marion '75 (CHI) Chicago, IL St. John Fisher.
Soranno, Joseph M. '74 (SPR) Wilbraham, MA St. Cecilia's.
Sorce, John J. '52 (CHR) Absent On Leave.
Sorci, Rev. Msgr. Francis P. '42 (BUF) Retired.
Sordillo, Ronald '74 (PAT) Retired.
Soreng, Birendra '96 (BGP) Stratford, CT St. Mark.
Sorensen, Bartley A. '76 (PIT) Pittsburgh, PA Immaculate Conception–St. Joseph; Allegheny County, PA West Penn Allegheny Health System–West Penn Hospital.
Sorensen, Bryan '88 (RC) Martin, SD Our Lady of the Sacred Heart; Deaneries.
Sorensen, Jonathan D. '09 (GI) Grand Island, NE Cathedral of the Nativity of the Blessed Virgin Mary.
Sorenson, Kris '08 (FRS) California City, CA Our Lady of Lourdes.
Sorgie, Anthony D. '82 (NY) Carmel, NY St. James the Apostle.
Soria, Manuel B. '81 (SAC) Rio Vista, CA St. Joseph.
Soriano, Danilo '78 (JOL) Braidwood, IL Immaculate Conception.
Soriano, Jesus T. '70 (SAC) Vallejo, CA St. Catherine of Siena.
Sork, Rev. Msgr. David A. '70 (LA) Rancho Palos Verdes, CA St. John Fisher; Members.
Sorohan, Rev. Msgr. David V. '59 (COL) Retired.
Sorra, James L. '06 (BAL) Baltimore, MD St. Michael; Clarksville, MD St. Louis.
Sortino, Anthony *l.c.* '06 (WDC)[N] Potomac, MD Legionaries of Christ.
Sorys, Luke *c.m.* '09 (MAN) Concord, NH St. Peter; Concord, NH Sacred Heart.
Sosa, Anulfo del Rosario *c.m.* '92 (SJN) San Juan, PR San Vicente de Paul.
Sosa, Emilio '06 (SAN) Midland, TX St. Ann's.
Sosa, Jose *sch.p.* '04 (LA) Los Angeles, CA Our Lady Help of Christians (Maria Auxiliadora).
Sosa, Juan J. '72 (MIA) Miami, FL St. Catherine of Siena; Committee on Popular Piety; Archdiocesan Vocations Review Board; Washington, DC Instituto Nacional Hispano de Liturgia, Inc.; Consultants.
Soseman, Rev. Msgr. Richard '92 (PEO) On Duty Outside the Diocese.
Sosing, Rev. Msgr. Romualdo '77 (RVC) New Hyde Park, NY Notre Dame; Oyster Bay, NY St. Dominic's.
Sosnowski, Ted *c.r.* '97 (PT) Panama City Beach, FL St. Bernadette.
Sostrich, John L. '62 (SD) Retired.
Sotak, John J. *o.s.a.* '92 (JOL)[C] New Lenox, IL Providence Catholic High School; [L] New Lenox, IL Augustinian Friary.
Sotelo, A. Richard *s.j.* '87 (BAL)[S] Towson Maryland Province of the Society of Jesus.
Sotelo, Angel '91 (FRS) Chowchilla, CA St. Columba.
Sotelo, Antonio '58 (PHX) Special Assignment Retired.
Sotelo–Pena, Fabio A. '99 (ATL) Gainesville, GA St. Michael.
Sotiroff, Stephen T. '81 (SFD) Maryville, IL Mother of Perpetual Help.
Soto, Angel Leonides (MGZ)[B] San German, PR Hospital of the Immaculate Conception.
Soto, Antonio *o.carm.* (ARE) Ciales, PR Holy Rosary.
Soto, Calixto '85 (SJN) Toa Alta, PR San Jose.
Soto, Charles *o.f.m.* '70 (NY)[EE] New York Franciscan Province of the Immaculate Conception Retired.
Soto, Charles *o.f.m.* '70 (MO) DEPARTMENT OF VETERANS AFFAIRS HOSPITALS AND CHAPLAINS Retired.
Soto, Edward P. '58 (LA) Maywood, CA St. Rose of Lima Retired.
Soto, Jose (NY) Spring Valley, NY St. Joseph.
Soto, Randy '91 (STL)[A] St. Louis, MO Kenrick School of Theology.
Soto Tanon, Carmelo '89 (SJN) Instructors.
Sottocornola, Frank *s.x.* '69 (FgM) Wayne, NJ XAVERIAN MISSIONARY FATHERS.
Sottocornula, Frank *s.x.* '59 (PAT)[N] Wayne Xaverian Missionary Fathers.
Souber, Michael A. '69 (STP) Minneapolis, MN St. Olaf.
Soucey, Louis A. '74 (MAN) Retired.
Souckar, Rev. Msgr. Michael A. '88 (MIA)[Q] Miami Shores, FL Archdiocese of Miami Millennium Appeal, Inc.; [Q] Miami Shores, FL Archdiocese of Miami, Inc.; Chancellor; Secretary to the Archbishop; Judges; Incardination Committee; Priests' Personnel Board; Chancellor's Office; Consultors; Special Assignment; Members.
Souckar, Rev. Msgr. Michael (NTN) Judges.
Soucy, A. Francis *o.f.m.* '67 (PAT)[N] Ringwood, NJ Holy Name Friary, Inc.
Soucy, Neil *s.m.* '62 (FgM) THE SOCIETY OF MARY.
Soucy, Robert P. '62 (BO) Senior Priests. Retired.
Souffrant, Claude *s.j.* '67 (CHI) Chicago, IL St. Margaret of Scotland.
Soukup, Paul A. *s.j.* '79 (SJ) Catholic Scouting; [B] Santa Clara, CA Jesuit Community.
Soule, Becket *o.p.* '93 (MAN) Hanover, NH St. Denis.
Soulliere, Richard '76 (MIA) Legion of Mary; Marian Movements & Devotions Retired.
Sousa, Edward A. '03 (PRO) Warwick, RI St. Catherine; [K] North Providence, RI St. Joseph Health Services of Rhode Island – Our Lady of Fatima Hospital.
Sousa, Manuel F. '80 (STO) Turlock, CA Our Lady of the Assumption of the Portuguese Church (Pastor of).
Sousa, Peter E. *c.ss.r.* '78 (MO) Army Reserve Chaplains.
Sousa, Peter *c.ss.r.* '78 (ORL)[F] New Smyrna Beach, FL Redemptorist Fathers of the Vice Province of Richmond.
Sousa, Peter *c.ss.r.* '78 (RIC) Fort Monroe, VA St. Mary Star of the Sea; Hampton, VA St. Joseph.
Souse, Stephen J. *o.s.b.* '43 (PEO)[A] Peru, IL St. Bede Abbey.
Southcombe, Michael (STL)[J] Bridgeton, MO SSM De Paul Health Center Foundation.
Soutis, Anibal (SJP) Presbyters.
Soutos, Hannibal '06 (SJP) On Assignment Outside the Diocese.
Soutus, Hugo '94 (STN) Phoenix, AZ Assumption of B.V.M.; Presbyteral Council.
Soutuyo, Raul S. '93 (MIA) Miami, FL St. Agatha.
Souza, Jason '98 (LA) Long Beach, CA St. Cyprian.
Sowa, Artur '06 (CHI) Tinley Park, IL Saint Julie Billiart.
Sowada, Arlie '73 (SCL) Elbow Lake, MN St. Olaf; Tintah, MN St. Gall.
Soy, Esteban '52 (VEN) Retired.
Soyer, Christoph *s.j.* '07 (CHI)[C] Chicago, IL Jesuit Community at Loyola University Chicago.
Soyka, Giles *o.f.m.cap.* '50 (GB)[J] Appleton, WI St. Fidelis Friary Retired.
Spacek, Frank W. '97 (BRK) Brooklyn, NY St. Brendan.
Spacek, William F. '95 (BAL) Baltimore, MD St. Alphonsus, Shrine of; Special Assignment.
Spacht, Andres *c.ss.r.* '61 (CGS) San Lorenzo, PR Nuestra Senora de la Mercedes.
Spacht, Harold *c.ss.r.* '61 (CGS)[B] Aguas Buenas, PR Casa Cristo Redentor.
Spadaro, Rev. Msgr. Thomas L. '64 (RVC) Holbrook, NY Good Shepherd; Senate of Priests (Presbyteral Council/ College of Consultors).
Spagnolo, Nicholas *c.s.s.* '52 (BO)[U] Waltham, MA Bertoni Hall – Formation House.
Spahn, James A. *o.p.* '81 (STP) Minneapolis, MN St. Albert the Great.
Spahn, James '00 (DEN) Windsor, CO Our Lady of the Valley; Elected Representatives from Deanery to Presbyteral Council.
Spahn, Stephen F. *s.j.* '04 (WDC) Washington, DC Holy Trinity.
Spahr, Matthew D. '92 (SD)[A] San Diego, CA St. Francis De Sales Center; Priestly Formation — St. Francis Center; College of Consultors; Presbyteral Council; San Diego, CA The Immaculata Church USD Campus.
Spain, John H. *m.m.* '70 (FgM) Maryknoll, NY MARYKNOLL.
Spalatin, Christopher A. *s.j.* '71 (FgM) Milwaukee, WI Society of Jesus.
Spalding, J. Mark '91 (L) LaGrange, KY Immaculate Conception; Judicial Vicar and Director; College of Consultors; Ex Officio.
Spalding, Leon C. '59 (L) Louisville, KY Retired.
Spanel, Hubert J. '59 (GI) Retired.
Spangenberg, George J. *c.s.sp.* (WDC)[W] Wheaton, MD U.S. Foundation for the Congregation of the Holy Ghost and the Immaculate Heart of Mary, Inc.
Spangenberg, George *c.s.sp.* '76 (LR) Conway, AR St. Joseph.
Spanier, Marian *s.t.l.* '81 (NEW) Harrison, NJ Our Lady of Czestochowa.
Spanjers, John J. '59 (SUP) Retired.
Spanley, Anthony L. '68 (GRY) Hamlet, IN Holy Cross.
Spannagel, Luke A. '03 (PEO)[M] Champaign, IL St. John's Catholic Newman Center at the University of Illinois, Urbana–Champaign; Champaign, IL St. John's Catholic Chapel.
Spano, Philip F. '82 (BR) Donaldsonville, LA Ascension of Our Lord Jesus Christ; Donaldsonville, LA St. Francis of Assisi.
Sparacino, Thomas A. '98 (PIT) Pittsburgh, PA St. Benedict the Moor; [P] Pittsburgh, PA Robert Morris College, Downtown Pittsburgh Campus; [P] Pittsburgh, PA Art Institute of Pittsburgh; Pittsburgh, PA Epiphany; Priest Council; [P] Pittsburgh, PA Point Park College; Pittsburgh, PA St. Mary of Mercy.
Sparklin, Paul C. '91 (BAL)[W] Baltimore, MD Johns Hopkins Hospital; Baltimore, MD Our Lady, Queen of Peace; Johns Hopkins Hospital; Special Assignment.
Sparks, Kenneth A. '95 (PIT) Pittsburgh, PA St. Gabriel of the Sorrowful Virgin.
Sparks, Richard *c.s.p.* '78 (CHI) Chicago, IL Old St. Mary.
Sparough, J. Michael *s.j.* '78 (CHI)[C] Chicago, IL Jesuit Community at Loyola University Chicago.
Spatt, John *c.pp.s.* '43 (CIN)[N] Carthagena, OH St. Charles Retired.
Spaulding, Donald E. '57 (EVN) Retired.
Spaulding, John D. '71 (PHX)[J] Mesa, AZ Paz de Cristo Community Center; Mesa, AZ St. Timothy Roman Catholic Parish.
Spaulding, Robert '09 (CHY) Sheridan, WY Holy Name.
Specht, Joseph E. *s.j.* '69 (HON)[D] Honolulu, HI Jesuit Fathers House; [C] Honolulu, HI St. Francis Healthcare System of Hawaii.
Specht, Terry W. '96 (ARL) Child Protection and Safety; Diocesan Consultors; Annandale, VA Holy Spirit.
Speck, Gregory *s.c.j.* '76 (SP)[N] Pinellas Park, FL Priests of the Sacred Heart.
Speck, James A. '50 (WIN) Retired.
Speckman, Harry *o.f.m.* '61 (GAY) Indian River, MI Cross in the Woods Catholic Shrine.
Speerstra, William F. '59 (SUP) Retired.
Speice, Rev. Msgr. Lawrence T. '61 (E) Cambridge Springs, PA St. Anthony; Deans.
Speicher, Charles W. '75 (PIT) Judges; Sewickley, PA St. James.
Speicher, David J. '86 (LAN) Howell, MI St. Joseph.
Speier, Francis J. '75 (TOL) Milan, OH St. Anthony; Norwalk, OH St. Mary, Mother of the Redeemer; St. John Neumann Deanery.
Speier, Thomas *o.f.m.* '58 (CIN) Cincinnati, OH St. Monica–St. George Parish Newman Center; [R] Cincinnati, OH University of Cincinnati Newman Center; [N] Cincinnati, OH St. Francis Seraph Friary.
Speiser, Thomas M. '77 (DAL) On Leave of Absence.
Speitel, Edmond J. '55 (PH) Retired.
Speitel, Mark M. '08 (HBG) Harrisburg, PA Holy Name of Jesus.
Spekschate, John '42 (LAF) Retired.
Spellerberg, Joseph R. *s.j.* '53 (BUF) Buffalo, NY St. Michael.
Spellman, John P. *o.s.f.s.* '66 (WIL)[B] Wilmington, DE Salesianum School.
Spellman, Paul J. '01 (LA) Los Angeles, CA Holy Name of Jesus.
Spellman, Robert M. '74 (WOR) Berlin, MA St. Joseph the Good Provider.
Spenard, James *o.s.a.* '72 (ALB) Troy, NY St. Augustine.
Spencer, F. Richard '88 (MO) Military Chaplains; Army Chaplains.
Spencer, Gregory D. '89 (R) Havelock, NC Annunciation.
Spencer, Jeremiah L. '65 (KCK) Kansas City, KS Holy Name; Kansas City, KS K.U. Medical Center and Chapel; Hospitals; Nurses Association.
Spencer, John P. *s.j.* '79 (BO)[U] Boston, MA Loyola House.
Spencer, Matthew *o.s.j.* '09 (FRS) Bakersfield, CA Our Lady of Guadalupe.
Spencer, Robert A. '98 (CHR) Military Chaplains; Navy Chaplains.
Spencer, Robert K. '85 (WCH) Frontenac, KS Sacred Heart.
Spencer, Robert M. '82 (RIC) Richmond, VA Our Lady of Lourdes.
Spencer, William *o.f.m.* '74 (FgM) Saint Louis, MO Sacred Heart Province; Saint Louis, MO.
Spencer, William '07 (SAG) Harbor Beach, MI Our Lady of Lake Huron; Harbor Beach, MI St. Anthony.
Spencer, William *o.f.m.* '74 (STL)[O] St. Louis, MO Franciscan Friary of St. Anthony of Padua.
Spengler, Rev. Msgr. James F. '68 (BRK) Rockaway Beach, NY St. Rose of Lima.
Spenner, Jerome I. '64 (OM) Retired.
Speno, Eugene '60 (SB) Retired.
Spera, James F. '77 (NEW)[A] South Orange, NJ Seton Hall University College Seminary; [B] Seton Hall University; [B] School of Diplomacy and Intl. Rels.
Sperger, Herbert J. '79 (PH) Philadelphia, PA St. Thomas Aquinas.
Sperl, August J. '54 (SFD) Retired.
Sperlak, Charles S. '64 (ALN) Reading, PA SS. Cyril and Methodius.
Spexarth, Aaron '08 (WCH) Wichita, KS Church of the Magdalen.
Spexarth, Daniel J. '84 (WCH) Wichita, KS St. Catherine of Siena.
Spexarth, James '55 (WCH) Retired.
Spexarth, Jerome J. '01 (WCH) Presbyteral Council/ College of Consultors; Ongoing Formation of the Clergy Committee; Wichita, KS St. Patrick.

Spexarth, Joachim *o.s.b.* '65 (OKL)[I] Shawnee, OK St. Gregory's Abbey; Consultors Archdiocesan; Council of Priests Archdiocesan; Shawnee, OK.
Speyrer, Jules '45 (LAF) Retired.
Spezia, Leo J. '76 (STL) St. Louis, MO St. John the Baptist.
Spezia, Robert '97 (DET)[A] The College of Liberal Arts.
Speziale, Michael G. '09 (PH) Newtown Square, PA St. Anastasia.
Spicer, Kevin P. *c.s.c.* '92 (FR)[A] North Easton, MA Stonehill College.
Spicer, Leo M. *o.s.m.* '76 (CHI)[N] Chicago Order of Friar Servants of Mary (Servites) United States of America Province, Inc.
Spicer, Richard J. '86 (SEA) Langley, WA St. Hubert.
Spiegel, John D. '76 (DAV) Ottumwa, IA St. Patrick's.
Spiegel, Rev. Msgr. Robert H. '66 (DAV) Military Chaplains.
Spiegel, Thomas J. '67 (DAV) Oskaloosa, IA St. Mary's.
Spiekermeier, Michael J. '69 (DAV) Davenport, IA St. Paul the Apostle; Deans; [M] Davenport, IA Davenport Deanery; [M] Davenport, IA St. Paul the Apostle Foundation.
Spieler, Joseph G. *s.j.* '75 (LA) Los Angeles, CA Dolores Mission.
Spielman, Paul J. '61 (STL) St. Louis, MO St. John Nepomuk Chapel; St. Louis, MO St. Mary of Victories.
Spielmann, Henry V. *o.s.a.* '39 (TLS)[B] Tulsa, OK Cascia Hall Preparatory School.
Spier, Mathias *o.s.b.* '58 (SCL)[I] Collegeville, MN St. John's Abbey, of the Order of St. Benedict.
Spies, Dennis '02 (JOL) Gibson City, IL Our Lady of Lourdes.
Spiess, Kevin J. '86 (JOL) Other Assignments; Joliet, IL St. Francis Xavier.
Spilka, Anthony Francis *o.f.m.conv.* '69 (ALT) Bishop's Vicar for Religious; Johnstown, PA St. Michael's; Johnstown, PA St. Francis of Assisi.
Spillane, Emmanuel *o.c.s.o.* '44 (SLC)[F] Huntsville, UT Abbey of Our Lady of the Holy Trinity of the Order of Cistercians.
Spillane, William *c.ss.r.* '57 (RIC) Hampton, VA St. Joseph; Fort Monroe, VA St. Mary Star of the Sea.
Spillett, Thomas '64 (SP) St. Petersburg, FL St. Raphael; Elected Parochial Vicars.
Spilly, Alphonse *c.pp.s.* '67 (CIN)[N] Dayton Provincial Office of the Cincinnati Province of the Society of the Precious Blood.
Spilly, Alphonse *c.pp.s.* (GRY)[A] Whiting, IN Calumet College of St. Joseph.
Spilly, William V. '74 (ROC) Hamlin, NY St. Elizabeth Ann Seton.
Spilman, Robert D. '96 (PEO) Spring Valley, IL Immaculate Conception; Spring Valley, IL St. Anthony; Vicariates and Vicars; Clergymen's Aid, Inc.; Finance Council (Canon 492).
Spilman, Robert '96 (PEO) Spring Valley, IL SS. Peter and Paul's.
Spina, Douglas J. '76 (PRO) East Providence, RI St. Martha.
Spine, William J. '73 (CHI)[N] Chicago Chicago Province of the Society of Jesus–Provincial Office.
Spinelli, Joseph A. *o.s.a.* '55 (PH)[Y] Villanova, PA St. Thomas Monastery.
Spinler, Ruben C. '94 (WIN) Retired.
Spino, John J. '90 (NEW) Retired.
Spinosa, Rev. Msgr. Anthony '83 (OLL) Office for Missions; Office of Inter–faith/Ecumenical Affairs; [C] North Jackson, OH National Shrine of Our Lady of Lebanon; [E] North Jackson, OH Father Tobia Retirement Home.
Spirko, Nicholas A. '72 (PIT) Washington, PA Immaculate Conception.
Spisak, Stephen M. '82 (CLV) Cleveland, OH St. Mary; Absent on Sick Leave.
Spishak, Carl A. '59 (ALT) Altoona, PA St. Rose of Lima Retired.
Spiteri, George (NY) Yonkers, NY St. Denis.
Spiteri, Rev. Msgr. Laurence J. '78 (LA) On Duty Outside the Archdiocese.
Spittler, Ernest G. *s.j.* '62 (CLV)[B] University Heights, OH John Carroll Jesuit Community.
Spitz, Gregory M. '67 (MIL) Milwaukee, WI Our Lady Queen of Peace.
Spitzer, Michael H. '98 (PH)[A] Wynnewood, PA Theological Seminary of St. Charles Borromeo, Overbrook.
Spitzer, Robert J. *s.j.* '83 (SPK)[B] Spokane, WA Gonzaga University.
Spitzley, Denis R. '75 (LAN) Concord, MI St. Catherine Laboure.
Splain, Tom *s.j.* '71 (SFR)[C] Belmont, CA Notre Dame de Namur University.
Splawski, Bernard *o.f.m.* '63 (CAM)[M] Margate, NJ Franciscan Friary.
Spleet, Julius A. '62 (SAG) Retired.
Spodnik, A. Leo '48 (HRT) Retired.
Spohrer, Dennis E. '03 (PEO) Alexis, IL St. Theresa's.
Spolny, Joseph R. '78 (CLV) Cleveland, OH SS. Philip and James.
Sponder, John '93 (JOL) Wayne, IL Resurrection Catholic Community.
Spong, William '79 (FWT) On Duty Outside the Diocese.
Spontak, James A. '75 (PBR) Portage, PA SS. Peter and Paul; Consultors; Presbyteral Council.
Spors, Roman '58 (DUL) Retired.
Sportino, Salvatore '90 (NY) Bronx, NY St. Joseph.
Spranger, William J. '56 (GRY) San Pierre, IN All Saints.
Sprauer, Michael '72 (P) Absent on Leave.
Sprecace, Rev. Msgr. Francis A. '55 (CAM) Retired.
Sprietsma, Leo *o.f.m.* '53 (LA)[P] Santa Barbara, CA Franciscan Friary, Order of Friars Minor (Old Mission).
Spriggs, Robert '65 (SFD) Effingham, IL Sacred Heart; Comite Diocesano de Ministerio Hispano – Diocesan Committee for Hispanic Ministry; Priests' Personnel Board.
Sprigler, William A. '75 (NU) Benson, MN St. Francis; Benson, MN St. Malachy; Benson, MN Church of the Visitation (Oratory); Benson, MN St. Bridget.
Spring, Mark P. '80 (DAV) Fort Madison, IA Holy Family.
Spring, Mark P. '80 (DAV) Montrose, IA St. Joseph's.
Springer, Francis *s.m.* '55 (SFR)[N] San Francisco, CA Marist Center of the West Retired.
Springer, Lawrence F. '59 (CHI) Des Plaines, IL St. Zachary Retired.
Springer, William A. '72 (SD) San Diego, CA Mission Basilica San Diego De Alcala.
Springman, Donald W. '67 (L) Louisville, KY St. Martha.
Sprott, Robert *o.f.m.* (GLP) Houck, AZ St. John the Evangelist; Fort Defiance, AZ Our Lady of Blessed Sacrament; St. Michaels, AZ St. Michael.
Spruill, Mark T. '07 (BIR) Fort Payne, AL Our Lady of the Valley; [A] Huntsville, AL Pope John Paul II Catholic High School; Madison, AL St. John the Baptist.
Sprute, Mel '69 (B) Retired.
Spurr, Michael R. '08 (R) Cary, NC St. Michael the Archangel.
Spychala, Daniel S. '84 (ARL) Ashburn, VA St. Theresa.
Spyrka, Edward C. *o.c.d.* '62 (GRY)[H] Munster, IN Discalced Carmelite Fathers Monastery.
Squeo, Eugene P. '71 (NEW) Jersey City, NJ St. Patrick and Assumption/All Saints Church; [R] Jersey City, NJ St. Patrick's Housing Corp.
Squiller, Rt. Rev. Mitred Msgr. John '56 (STF) Retired.
Srampical, Roy *c.p.* '96 (BRK)[T] Jamaica, NY Immaculate Conception Monastery.
Sreboth, Michael J. (MOB) Prison Ministry.
Sreboth, Michael R. '86 (MOB) Montgomery, AL Our Lady Queen of Mercy; [I] Montgomery, AL Huntington College Newman Center.
Sredzinski, Joseph L. '70 (GBG)[H] Greensburg, PA Benedictine Nuns.
Srenn, Thomas E. '77 (CHI) Chicago, IL Our Lady of Mount Carmel.
Srion, Charles N. '78 (RVC) Centereach, NY Assumption of the Blessed Virgin Mary.
Srnec, Rev. Msgr. Stanley J. '42 (STP) Saint Paul, MN Retired.
Srode, John S. *c.pp.s.* '72 (MO) Air Force Chaplains.
Srode, John S. *c.pp.s.* '72 (CIN)[N] Dayton Provincial Office of the Cincinnati Province of the Society of the Precious Blood.
Sroka, Gerald A. '60 (GRY) Retired.
Ssebadduka, George '78 (KC) Richmond, MO Immaculate Conception.
Ssegawa, John R. *a.j.* '94 (PHX) Glendale, AZ St. James Roman Catholic Parish.
Ssekiranda, Remigious '98 (VEN) Cape Coral, FL St. Andrew.
Ssekyole, Patrick '09 (WOR) Worcester, MA St. Joan of Arc.
Ssemakula, Luke '97 (OAK) Hayward, CA All Saints.
Ssemakula, Yozefu B. '93 (PT) Lanark Village, FL Sacred Heart of Jesus.
Sseriiso, Henry M. *i.m.c.* '06 (SB) Rancho Cucamonga, CA Sacred Heart.
Ssozi, John Mary (MIL) Shorewood, WI St. Robert.
St–Godard, Edward G. '64 (PRO) Woonsocket, RI Holy Family.
St. Amand, Kenneth J. '69 (NEW) Retired.
St. Andre, Jonathan *t.o.r.* '06 (PIT)[M] Pittsburgh, PA Franciscan Friars, T.O.R.
St. Clair, Robert L. *s.j.* '58 (SJ)[B] Santa Clara, CA Jesuit Community.
St. Croix, Ben '01 (GAL) Houston, TX Our Lady of Mt. Carmel.
St. Cyr, John *o.m.i.* '61 (FgM) Washington, DC AMERICAN OBLATE MISSIONS.
St. Fleur, Maxis '01 (ATL) On Leave of Absence.
St. Forte, Elifete '08 (PMB) Royal Palm Beach, FL Our Lady Queen of the Apostles; Elected Members.
St. George, John P. *s.j.* '66 (NY)[EE] New York, NY Murray–Weigel Hall.
St. George, Peter T. '95 (CIN) Cincinnati, OH St. Ignatius of Loyola.
St. Germain, Rt. Rev. Andre '96 (NTN) Manchester, NH Our Lady of the Cedars Retired.
St. Germain, Brian '88 (PRM) Absent on Leave.
St. Hilare, Kenneth T. '07 (SPK)[A] Spokane, WA Bishop White Seminary; Spokane, WA St. Francis Xavier; Spokane, WA St. Patrick.
St. Jean, Marcel '96 (BGP) Shelton, CT St. Joseph.
St. John, George G. '52 (ALB) Albany, NY Blessed Sacrament; Ministers to Retired Priests Retired.
St. Jules, Stephen '79 (RCK) Cary, IL SS. Peter & Paul; Diocesan Consultors.
St. Laurent, Daniel A. '71 (MAN) Nashua, NH St. Aloysius.
St. Louis, Richard E. '00 (MAN) Newport, NH St. Patrick; Priest Personnel Board; Co Spiritual Dir.
St. Marie, Denis L. '59 (CLV) Amherst, OH St. Joseph; South Amherst, OH Nativity of Blessed Virgin Mary Retired.
St. Marie, Michael '93 (B) Buhl, ID Immaculate Conception; Twin Falls, ID St. Edward The Confessor; Shoshone, ID St. Peter's; [F] Twin Falls, ID College of Southern Idaho; Deans; College of Consultors; Gooding, ID St. Elizabeth's.
St. Martin, Jean–Claude '08 (PAT) Rockaway, NJ St. Cecilia's; Rockaway, NJ Sacred Heart.
St. Martin, Jeremy P. '02 (BO) Director.
St. Martin, Robert J. '56 (HRT) Unionville, CT St. Mary Retired.
St. Martin, Robert *o.f.m.conv.* '77 (STP) Bloomington, MN St. Bonaventure.
St. Paul, Michael '05 (ORG) Anaheim, CA St. Anthony Claret; Clergy Personnel Board.
St. Peter, Dallas T. '07 (BUR) Burlington, VT St. Joseph's Co–Cathedral.
St. Pierre, Roland *o.m.i.* '52 (BO)[U] Lowell, MA Missionary Oblates of Mary Immaculate Retired.
St. Vil, Romane *m.m.* '03 (NY)[EE] Maryknoll Maryknoll Fathers and Brothers.
Staab, Gregory *o.m.v.* '84 (BO)[B] Boston, MA Our Lady of Grace Seminary; [Z] Boston, MA St. Francis Chapel.
Staak, John *o.m.i.* '95 (SAT)[B] San Antonio, TX George Sexton House of Studies.
Staal, David E. '90 (OAK) Livermore, CA St. Michael; Office of the Bishop; Officers; Officers.
Staar, Robert J. '77 (NY) Port Chester, NY Our Lady of Mercy.
Stab, Herbert J. '59 (MET)[I] Somerset, NJ Maria Regina Residence; Piscataway, NJ Our Lady of Fatima Retired.
Stabene, Edmondo '45 (STU) Retired.
Stabeno, John M. '00 (CAM) Sicklerville, NJ The Church of St. Charles Borromeo, Washington Township, N.J.
Stabile, Thomas *t.o.r.* '87 (FWT) Fort Worth, TX St. Andrew.
Stacer, John R. *s.j.* '63 (NO)[P] New Orleans Jesuit Provincial Office.
Stachacz, James T. '98 (RVC) Lindenhurst, NY Our Lady of Perpetual Help.
Stacherczak, Idzi '75 (CHI) Chicago, IL St. Priscilla.
Stachnik, Kenneth R. '86 (GAY) Traverse City, MI St. Francis of Assisi.
Stachowiak, Conrad P. '74 (BUF) Deaf; Cheektowaga, NY Resurrection.
Stachura, Thaddeus X. '64 (WOR) Worcester, MA Our Lady of Czestochowa; Apostleship of Prayer and Eucharistic Crusade; Diocesan Building Commission Members.
Stachurski, David *o.f.m.conv.* (TR) Delran, NJ The Church of the Resurrection, Delran Township, N.J.
Stachurski, Miroslav '03 (BGP) Redding Ridge, CT St. Patrick.
Stachyra, Kenneth '01 (RCK) Rockford, IL St. Bernadette.
Stack, Daniel '82 (ATL) Cartersville, GA St. Francis of Assisi.
Stack, Gabriel D. *o.praem.* '82 (ORG)[D] Silverado, CA St. Michael's Preparatory School; [I] Silverado, CA Norbertine Fathers of Orange Inc.
Stack, James M. '86 (WDC) Hyattsville, MD St. Jerome.
Stack, Jerome P. *c.pp.s.* '72 (CIN)[N] Dayton Provincial Office of the Cincinnati Province of the Society of the Precious Blood.
Stack, Jerome *c.pp.s.* (GRY)[A] Whiting, IN Calumet College of St. Joseph.
Stack, John J. '88 (DAV)[G] Clinton, IA Mercy Medical Center – Clinton.
Stack, John J. '53 (HRT) Retired.
Stack, John P. *o.s.a.* '74 (PH)[C] Villanova University; [Y] Villanova, PA St. Thomas Monastery.
Stack, John P. '55 (WDC) Retired.
Stack, Rev. Msgr. Richard J. '56 (E) Matrimonial Judges; Erie, PA Blessed Sacrament Retired.
Stack, Thomas Mannix '73 (MIA) Southwest Ranches, FL St. Mark.
Stadmeyer, Raymond *o.f.m.cap.* '92 (DET) Detroit, MI St. Charles Borromeo.

Stadtmueller, Roman *s.d.s.* '54 (WDC)[B] Silver Spring, MD Salvatorian Community Retired.
Stadtmueller, Roman *s.d.s.* (MIL)[P] Milwaukee Salvatorian Provincial Offices.
Staebell, Francis J. *s.j.* '50 (BUF) Buffalo, NY St. Michael.
Staehler, Adrian *o.f.m.cap.* '67 (GB)[M] Appleton, WI Monte Alverno Retreat & Spirituality Center.
Staes, Robert F. *o.p.* '71 (DEN) Denver, CO St. Dominic; [N] Denver, CO Dominican Friars.
Staff, Stephen M. '90 (MOB) On Leave from the Archdiocese.
Stafford, Dennis '91 (CHI) Deerfield, IL Holy Cross; [A] Mundelein, IL Diaconate Formation Program.
Stafford, Edward G. *t.o.r.* '99 (PIT) Allegheny County, PA Mercy Health System of Pittsburgh–Pittsburgh Mercy Hospital.
Stafford, Edward G. *t.o.r.* '99 (WH) Moundsville, WV St. Francis Xavier's.
Stafford, James D.M. '61 (OKL) Lawton, OK Blessed Sacrament.
Stafford, Rev. Msgr. Joseph L. '57 (BRK) Flushing, NY Holy Family Retired.
Stafford, Michael *o.s.b.* '58 (PRO)[P] Portsmouth, RI Abbey of St. Gregory the Great.
Stagaman, David J. *s.j.* '66 (CHI)[C] Chicago, IL St. Joseph's Seminary; [C] Chicago, IL Jesuit Community at Loyola University Chicago; [A] Chicago, IL St. Joseph College Seminary.
Stagg, Robert B. '75 (NEW) Upper Saddle River, NJ Church of the Presentation.
Stagnaro, John J. '76 (BO) Watertown, MA Sacred Heart; Laboure College.
Stahl, Allen M. '75 (COS) On Duty Outside the Diocese Retired.
Stahl, David A. '91 (DEN) Brush, CO St. Mary.
Stahmer, Andrew J. '05 (HBG) Kulpmont, PA Holy Angels.
Stahura, Joseph L. '81 (HBG) Greencastle, PA St. Mark the Evangelist.
Staib, Donald F. '61 (R) Apex, NC St. Mary Magdalene.
Staigers, Del '87 (CIN) Dayton, OH Corpus Christi; Dayton, OH Our Lady of Mercy; Dayton, OH Queen of Martyrs.
Stainwall, Bernal '80 (NY) Staten Island, NY Holy Rosary.
Stajkowski, James *m.s.* '73 (MIL)[P] Twin Lakes, WI La Salette Missionaries.
Stajkowski, Leo S. '66 (ALN) Reading, PA St. Mary.
Stake, Ronald P. '85 (MO) Military Chaplains; Navy Chaplains.
Stakem, Gary *o.f.m.cap.* '51 (PIT)[M] Butler, PA St. Mary's Friary.
Stakem, Ward G. *o.f.m.cap.* '78 (MO) Air Force Reserve Chaplains.
Stakem, Ward *o.f.m.cap.* '78 (PIT) Cabot, PA St. Joseph; Butler, PA St. Mary of the Assumption; [M] Butler, PA St. Mary's Friary.
Staley, Robert P. '95 (R) Fuquay–Varina, NC St. Bernadette.
Stalla, Michael J. '03 (CLV) Casa Parroquial San Pedro Teotepeque.
Stalter, Rev. Msgr. Cal '94 (AMA) Retired.
Stalzer, Joseph '59 (JOL) Retired.
Stammitti, Anthony O. '91 (LIN) Advocates; Apostolate to the Elderly; Lincoln, NE Cristo Rey; Health Care Facilities.
Stampiglia, Fausto *s.a.c.* '60 (VEN) Sarasota, FL St. Martha; [F] Sarasota, FL St. Martha's Housing, Inc.; [F] Sarasota, FL St. Martha's Housing II, Inc.; College of Consultors; Deans; Presbyteral Council; Theologian to the Bishop; Diaconate.
Stamschror, Robert P. '61 (WIN) Retired.
Stanbery, Stephen L. '80 (TOL) Holgate, OH St. Mary; New Bavaria, OH Sacred Heart of Jesus.
Stanchik, Dennis P. '59 (LC) Retired.
Stander, Charles *s.m.* '81 (SAT)[C] San Antonio, TX St. Mary's University of San Antonio, Texas; [L] San Antonio, TX Woodlawn Marianist Community.
Stander, Edwin L. '63 (LIN)[D] Lincoln, NE St. Elizabeth Regional Medical Center; Health Care Facilities.
Stanfield, Francis E. '80 (GLP) Retired.
Stanfield, George *c.p.* '68 (SAC)[I] Citrus Heights, CA Christ the King Retreat.
Stanfield, William L. '76 (MIL)[A] St. Francis, WI Saint Francis de Sales Seminary; Special Assignment.
Stang, Charles L. *s.j.* '67 (MIL)[P] Milwaukee, WI Pere Marquette Jesuit Community; [E] Milwaukee, WI Marquette University High School.
Stang, Mark '90 (SCL) Holdingford, MN St. Hedwig's; Holdingford, MN St. Mary's; Holdingford, MN Our Lady of Mt. Carmel; Holdingford, MN Immaculate Conception; Holdingford, MN St. Columbkille's; Presbyteral Council; Diocesan Consultors.
Stang, William J. *c.pp.s.* '77 (MO) Army National Guard Chaplains.
Stang, William J. *c.pp.s.* '77 (LFT)[A] Rensselaer, IN Saint Joseph's College.
Stanganelli, Anthony M. '79 (RVC) St. James, NY SS. Philip and James; Priests' Personnel Policy Board.
Stange, James R. '95 (P) Scappoose, OR St. Wenceslaus.
Stangel, Mark J. '65 (MIL) Retired.
Stanger, Edward J. '91 (STL) Florissant, MO Sacred Heart.
Stanger, Harold B. '77 (CHI) Deerfield, IL Holy Cross.
Stangl, Alfred '63 (SCL) Presbyteral Council Retired.
Stanibula, Krzysztof '95 (FR) Fall River, MA St. Anne's.
Stanichar, Rt. Rev. Joseph '68 (VNN) Seattle, WA St. John Chrysostom.
Stanichar, Rt. Rev. Joseph '68 (VNN) Director of Evangelization.
Stanievich, J. Walter '46 (DET) Retired.
Stanis, Casimir M. '01 (SCR) Friendsville, PA St. Francis Xavier; Friendsville, PA St. Joseph.
Staniskis, Daniel '84 (PAT) Whippany, NJ Our Lady of Mercy.
Stanislaus, Samineni '87 (OKL) Anadarko, OK St. Patrick's.
Staniszewski, Ignatius *s.s.p.* '64 (Y)[A] Canfield, OH Society of St. Paul.
Staniszewski, Stanley *c.m.* '63 (HRT)[L] Manchester, CT DePaul Provincial Residence.
Staniukiewicz, Edward *o.f.m.conv.* '87 (RCK) Algonquin, IL St. Margaret Mary.
Stankard, Albert H. '59 (BO) Framingham, MA St. Stephen.
Stanko, Andrew C. '70 (ALT) Johnstown, PA St. John Vianney's.
Stankus, Gregory A. '78 (BRK) Brooklyn, NY SS. Simon and Jude.
Stanley, Brian L. '96 (KAL) Florence Crane Correctional Facility for Women; Camp Branch; Lakeland Correctional Facility for Men.
Stanley, Charles R. '71 (BO) Peabody, MA St. Ann.
Stanley, Colm *s.s.c.* '69 (OM)[K] St. Columbans, NE Missionary Society of St. Columban.
Stanley, Matthew D. '91 (SJ) San Jose, CA Holy Family; Priests' Retirement Board.
Stanley, Michael *o.s.a.* '81 (ALB) Waterford, NY St. Mary of the Assumption.
Stanley, Peter '09 (CC) Corpus Christi, TX St. Joseph; Bishop's Office; St. Paul School of Catechesis; Religious Education; Presbyteral Council; [I] Corpus Christi, TX Lifelong Faith Formation Board; On Special Assignment.
Stanley, Richard J. *s.j.* '74 (BO)[U] Boston, MA Loyola House; [W] Gloucester, MA Eastern Point Retreat House.
Stanley, Ron '67 (NEW) Midland Park, NJ Nativity.
Stanley, Ronald *o.p.* (NY)[HH] Orangeburg, NY Dominican College; [C] Dominican College.
Stanley, Thomas *s.m.* '50 (CIN)[N] Dayton, OH Mercy Siena Gardens.
Stano, Luke M. *o.s.m.* '61 (CHI)[N] Chicago, IL Order of Friar Servants of Mary (Servites) United States of America Province, Inc.
Stanonik, Anthony '82 (SD) On Duty Outside the Diocese.
Stanosz, Paul A. '84 (MIL)[Y] Milwaukee, WI The Korean Catholic Community of Milwaukee; Milwaukee, WI St. Mary Magdalen.
Stanowski, Bartlomiej *o.c.d.* '06 (GRY)[H] Munster, IN Discalced Carmelite Fathers Monastery.
Stansberry, Richard D. '92 (OKL) Oklahoma City, OK Christ the King; Judicial Vicar; Consultors Archdiocesan; Archdiocesan Finance Council.
Stansley, Rev. Msgr. Ralph W. '73 (TR) West Trenton, NJ Our Lady of Good Counsel; Tribunal Judges; Office of Permanent Deacons.
Stanton, Finbarr P. '67 (SAV) Albany, GA St. Teresa.
Stanton, Francis M. '51 (COL) Retired.
Stanton, Joseph E. '51 (COL) Retired.
Stanton, Thomas F. (BO) Massachusetts Correctional Institution – Cedar Junction; Bay State Correctional Facility.
Stanton, Thomas J. '91 (BO) Needham, MA St. Bartholomew.
Stanton, Rev. Msgr. William J. '56 (SPC) St. Francis de Sales Association; Diocesan School Board Retired.
Stapenhorst, Verne P. '61 (SC) Retired.
Staples, Terrence R. '95 (ARL) Orange, VA St. Isidore the Farmer.
Stapleton, Gerard P. '85 (NO) Port Sulphur, LA St. Patrick.
Starasinich, James E. '99 (NEW) Lyndhurst, NJ Sacred Heart.
Starbuck, James '48 (OAK) Retired.
Starbuck, James '90 (DUB) Advisory Committee in Partnership with Persons with Disabilities.
Starczewski, John F. '04 (CHL) Hamlet, NC St. James.
Stark, Paul V. *s.j.* '55 (STL)[O] St. Louis, MO Jesuit Community Corporation at Saint Louis University – Jesuit Hall; [C] Saint Louis University.
Stark, Philip M. '71 (PRO) Retired.
Stark, Ronald P. *o.f.m.* '66 (NY)[II] New York, NY Franciscan Missionary Charities, Inc.
Stark, Ronald *o.f.m.* '66 (WDC)[B] Silver Spring, MD Holy Name College.
Starkey, Brian Denis *m.afr.* '77 (FgM) Washington, DC MISSIONARIES OF AFRICA; Washington, DC; [N] Washington, DC Missionaries of Africa.
Starkey, Donald '52 (SFE) Retired.
Starman, Bernard '06 (OM) Omaha, NE St. Elizabeth Ann; [B] Omaha, NE Roncalli Catholic High School of Omaha.
Starmann, Joseph W. '63 (JC) Retired.
Staron, Stanley R. '74 (HRT)[H] Waterbury, CT Saint Mary's Hospital; Special and other Archdiocesan Assignment.
Starzynski, Stefan P. '96 (ARL) Fairfax, VA St. Mary of Sorrows.
Stash, Robert '82 (PRM) Akron, OH St. Michael the Archangel.
Stashek, Brian E. '02 (LC) Leave of Absence.
Stasiak, Grzegorz '99 (BRK) Maspeth, NY Holy Cross.
Stasiak, Kurt *o.s.b.* '80 (IND)[A] St. Meinrad, IN Saint Meinrad School of Theology.
Stasik, Thaddeus '60 (NEW)[M] Rutherford, NJ St. John Vianney Residence for Priests Retired.
Stasiowski, John '65 (FWT) Lewisville, TX St. Philip the Apostle.
Stasker, R. Louis '65 (GR) Grand Rapids, MI Basilica of St. Adalbert; Catholic Secondary Schools Pastor and President; On Special Assignment.
Staskevicius, Vytautas (LIT) Lithuanian R. Catholic Priests' League of Canada.
Staszewski, Robert M. (PIT) Bulger, PA St. Ann.
Statkus, Rev. Msgr. Francis J. '46 (PH) Retired.
Statnick, Rev. Msgr. Roger A. '73 (GBG) Greensburg, PA Blessed Sacrament Cathedral; Office for the Permanent Diaconate.
Statt, Thomas R. '58 (ROC) Rochester, NY St. Charles Borromeo Retired.
Stattmiller, John E. '66 (COL) Columbus, OH Corpus Christi; Columbus, OH St. Ladislas; College of Consultors; Parochial Examiners.
Statz, James '84 (SCL) Sauk Centre, MN Our Lady of the Angels; Sauk Centre, MN St. Alexius.
Statz, Jeffrey P. '05 (MAN) Berlin, NH Good Shepherd; Woodsville, NH St. Catherine of Siena; Woodsville, NH St. Joseph; Gorham, NH Holy Family; Grafton County House of Corrections; Priest Personnel Board.
Staublin, Daniel J. '82 (IND) Board of Consultors.
Staudenmaier, John M. *s.j.* '70 (DET)[K] Detroit, MI Jesuit Community at the University of Detroit Mercy; [C] Detroit, MI Dental School.
Stauder, Paul W. '48 (BEL) Retired.
Staudinger, Gregory '81 (GF) Sidney, MT St. Matthew; Personnel Board; [J] Great Falls, MT Big Sky Cum Christo/Cursillo.
Staudt, Joseph W. '78 (RVC) Cutchogue, NY Sacred Heart.
Staunton, Rev. Msgr. Patrick Joseph '60 (LA) La Puente, CA St. Joseph Retired.
Stauter, Andrew '57 (MOB)[E] Mobile, AL Little Sisters of the Poor, Home For the Aged, Inc. Retired.
Stavoy, Stephen J. '79 (MO) Wilkes–Barre, PA St. Nicholas; Veteran's Administration Hospital; Military Chaplains; DEPARTMENT OF VETERANS AFFAIRS HOSPITALS AND CHAPLAINS; Navy Reserve Chaplains.
Stawarczyk, Pawel '96 (PHX) Cottonwood, AZ Immaculate Conception Roman Catholic Parish.
Stawasz, David *s.c.* '04 (LAN)[E] Chelsea, MI St. Louis Center for Exceptional Children & Adults.
Stawasz, James '53 (HON) Retired.
Stawasz, John B. '53 (HON) Kailua–Kona, HI St. Michael The Archangel Retired.
Stawiarski, Waldemar '03 (CHI) Chicago, IL St. Helen.
Staysniak, Dale W. '75 (CLV) Parma, OH St. Anthony of Padua.
Stead, Julian *o.s.b.* '52 (PRO)[P] Portsmouth, RI Abbey of St. Gregory the Great.
Stearns, Joseph E. '72 (VEN) Sarasota, FL St. Michael the Archangel.
Steber, Michael J. '86 (MAR) Vicars General; Consultors; Charismatic Prayer Groups; Marquette, MI St. Peter Cathedral.
Stec, John '74 (MET) Carteret, NJ Holy Family; Carteret, NJ Sacred Heart.
Stec, Joseph C. '57 (PH) Retired.
Stec, Mark D. '88 (BEL) Equality, IL St. Joseph; Shawneetown, IL St. Patrick; Ridgway, IL St. Joseph; Shawneetown, IL St. Mary.
Stec, Michael S. '94 (LIN) Syracuse, NE St. Paulinus; Diocesan Area CCD Directors; Deaf Ministry.
Stec, Robert G. '88 (CLV) Brunswick, OH St. Ambrose.
Stecher, John E. '72 (DAV) On Duty Outside the Diocese.
Stecher, Kenneth C. '68 (DUB)[G] Gilbertville, IA Gilbertville–Raymond Consolidation; Jesup, IA St. Athanasius; Dunkerton, IA St. Francis; Waterloo; Deanery Representatives.
Stechmann, Michael *o.a.r.* '08 (LA)[P] Oxnard, CA St. Augustine Priory O.A.R.; Los Angeles, CA Cristo Rey.
Stechschulte, Barry J. '09 (CIN) Coldwater, OH St. Anthony; Coldwater, OH Holy Trinity; Coldwater, OH St. Mary.
Steck, Christopher W. *s.j.* '94 (WDC)[N] Washington, DC The Jesuit Community at Georgetown University.

Steckel, Gregory A. '81 (DUB) Lost Nation, IA Sacred Heart; Lost Nation, IA St. James; Lost Nation, IA Sacred Heart.
Stecklein, Warren L. '90 (DOD) Scott City, KS St. Joseph Catholic Church of Scott City, Kansas; Dighton, KS St. Theresa Catholic Church of Dighton, Kansas; [F] Dodge City, KS The Diocese of Dodge City Priest Retirement Fund, Inc.
Steckler, Gerard *s.j.* '57 (P) Waldport, OR St. Anthony; [L] Portland, OR Colombiere Community.
Steckler, Kenneth '96 (EVN) Mount Vernon, IN St. Matthew; New Harmony, IN Holy Angels.
Stecz, Jeffrey M. '99 (PH) Sellersville, PA St. Agnes.
Steele, J. *c.s.c.* '97 (P) Portland, OR Holy Redeemer.
Steele, Joseph S. '97 (LIN) Bellwood, NE Presentation; [C] David City, NE Aquinas/St. Mary's Schools.
Steele, Michael L. '77 (BO) Marblehead, MA Our Lady, Star of the Sea; Presbyteral Council.
Steele, Philip G. *s.j.* '80 (DEN)[D] Aurora, CO Regis Jesuit High School Corporation; [N] Centennial, CO Regis High Jesuit Community.
Steele, Thomas J. *s.j.* '64 (SFE) Albuquerque, NM Immaculate Conception.
Steen, Raymond *o.m.i.* '60 (BO)[X] Tewksbury, MA Immaculate Heart of Mary Residence.
Steenson, Jeffery N. '09 (SFE) On Duty Outside the Archdiocese.
Stefanelli, Joseph *s.m.* '51 (SJ)[M] Cupertino, CA The Marianist Center.
Stefaniak, James S. *m.m.* '50 (SJ)[M] Los Altos, CA Maryknoll.
Stefanko, Rev. Msgr. Paul F. '76 (PRT) Officialis; Office Coordinator; Diocesan Consultors; Department of Canonical Services; Cape Elizabeth, ME St. Bartholomew; Scarborough, ME St. Maximilian Kolbe; South Portland, ME Church of the Holy Cross; South Portland, ME St. John the Evangelist.
Stefanowich, Paul *i.m.c.* '72 (MET)[I] Somerset, NJ Consolata Society for Foreign Missions.
Stefanski, Gery W. '79 (CHI) Other Assignments.
Steffan, Carl J. '58 (HBG) Retired.
Steffen, Arnold *s.v.d.* '57 (FgM) Techny, IL.
Steffen, Francis J. '57 (MAD) Hazel Green, WI Retired.
Steffen, Rev. Msgr. Kenneth C. '84 (SFD) Marine, IL St. Elizabeth; Marine, IL St. James.
Steffen, Mark (JC)[B] Jefferson City, MO St. Mary Health Center.
Steffens, Terrence J. '82 (GRY) Dyer, IN St. Joseph.
Steffensmeier, Ralph J. '59 (OM) Cedar Rapids, NE St. Anthony.
Steffes, James P. '93 (WIN) Vicar General; Vicar General; Continuing Formation and Education for Clergy; Ex Officio; Moderator of the Curia; Diocesan Board of Administration; Priest Assignments Committee; Diocesan Consultors; Finance Council; Deposit and Loan Board; Priests' Pension Board; Diocese of Winona Incardination Board; Misconduct Issues; Winona, MN Cathedral of the Sacred Heart.
Steffes, LuVerne W. '95 (OM) Atkinson, NE St. Joseph; Stuart, NE St. Boniface.
Steffes, Marvin J. *c.pp.s.* '58 (CIN)[N] Carthagena, OH St. Charles Retired.
Steffes, Raymond *o.s.c.* '58 (SCL)[I] Onamia, MN Crosier Priory; Legion of Mary.
Steffl, Mark S. '05 (NU) Committee for Continuing Education of Clergy; New Ulm, MN Cathedral of The Holy Trinity.
Steffy, David *l.c.* '94 (MAN)[A] Center Harbor, NH Immaculate Conception Apostolic School; Presbyteral Council.
Stefula, Salvator *t.o.r.* '74 (VEN) Bradenton, FL Sacred Heart; Judges.
Stefun, Bonaventure *o.f.m.cap.* '56 (PIT) Clairton, PA St. Clare of Assisi.
Steger, Francis R. *o.c.s.o.* '56 (ROC)[J] Piffard, NY Abbey of the Genesee.
Steggert, Bruce A. *s.j.* '93 (WDC)[N] Washington, DC The Jesuit Community of St. Aloysius Gonzaga; [E] Washington, DC Gonzaga College High School.
Stegman, Leonard F. '43 (ELP) Retired.
Stegman, Thomas D. *s.j.* '95 (BO)[U] Cambridge, MA Hopkins House.
Stegman, Vincent G. *c.s.sp.* '62 (FgM) Bethel Park, PA CONGREGATION OF THE HOLY SPIRIT.
Stegmann, Robert '95 (GB) Wautoma, WI St. Joseph; Redgranite, WI Sacred Heart of Jesus; Plainfield, WI St. Paul; Redgranite, WI St. Mark.
Stehlik, Thomas *c.m.* '96 (LR) North Little Rock, AR St. Anne.
Stehling, Larry '88 (AUS) San Marcos, TX St. John the Evangelist.
Stehly, Rev. Msgr. Dennis R. '77 (STL) Chesterfield, MO Ascension.
Stehly, James '83 (LA) Camarillo, CA St. Mary Magdalen.
Stehly, Mark '66 (SEA) Special Assignment Retired.
Stehly, Thomas J. '61 (LA) Retired.
Steier, Charles '73 (SAL) Russell, KS St. Mary Queen of Angels Parish; College of Consultors; Personnel Board; Council of Priests.
Steiger, Rev. Msgr. Richard A. '67 (PAT) Andover, NJ Good Shepherd; Presbyteral Council; College of Consultors.
Steigmeyer, Robert C. *c.s.c.* '47 (FTW)[H] Holy Cross House Retired.
Steik, Dennis *s.m.* '69 (SFR) San Francisco, CA Notre Dame des Victoires.
Steimel, Craig E. '89 (DUB) Mason City, IA St. Joseph.
Steimel, Rev. Msgr. Paul T. '52 (DUB) Retired.
Stein, E. J. *o.f.m.* (GAL) Galveston, TX Holy Family.
Stein, Mark J. '02 (TUC) Willcox, AZ Sacred Heart of Jesus Roman Catholic Church – Willcox.
Stein, Paul '01 (CHI) Chicago, IL St. Sylvester.
Stein, Robert E. '81 (CLV) Doylestown, OH SS. Peter and Paul.
Stein, Robert *s.d.b.* '78 (LA) Los Angeles, CA St. Mary; [P] Los Angeles, CA Dominic Savio Salesian Residence.
Stein, Rev. Msgr. Timothy P. '84 (ALT) "The Catholic Register"; Altoona, PA Immaculate Conception.
Steinacker, Anthony '06 (FTW) Fort Wayne; Fort Wayne, IN St. Charles Borromeo.
Steinbacher, Wil *g.h.m.* '62 (CIN)[N] Cincinnati Headquarters of Glenmary Home Missioners Retired.
Steinbauer, Joseph R. '79 (TOL) Toledo, OH Little Flower of Jesus; Members.
Steinbeisser, Joseph A. '86 (NU) Litchfield, MN St. Philip.
Steinbock, Leo E. '54 (LA) Retired.
Steinbrunner, Jerry *c.pp.s.* '74 (CIN) Cincinnati, OH St. Andrew; Cincinnati, OH St. Mark the Evangelist.
Steinbugler, Thomas B. *s.j.* '61 (FgM) New York, NY Society of Jesus.
Steiner, Daniel R. '79 (CHI)[J] Chicago, IL Saints Mary and Elizabeth Medical Center.
Steiner, Edward F. '82 (NSH) Nashville, TN Cathedral of the Incarnation; Presbyteral Council; Priest Benefit Foundation.
Steiner, Edward '82 (NSH) Continuing Education of Clergy.
Steiner, Rev. Msgr. John M. '69 (SPK) Vicars General; Defensor Vinculi.
Steiner, John W. '74 (LC) Black River Falls, WI St. Joseph; Melrose, WI St. Kevin; Ex Officio; Consultors.
Steiner, Rev. Msgr. John '69 (SPK) Spokane Valley, WA St. Mary; Continuing Education of Priests.
Steiner, Luke *o.s.b.* '56 (SCL)[I] Collegeville, MN St. John's Abbey, of the Order of St. Benedict.
Steiner, William H. (Carlos) *c.ss.r.* '54 (FgM) Denver, CO Denver Province.
Steingraeber, John *c.ss.r.* '74 (DEN)[N] Denver The Redemptorists/Denver Province.
Steingreaber, Paul *o.s.b.* '65 (KCK)[I] Atchison, KS St. Benedict's Abbey.
Steinhauser, Kenneth B. '70 (JC) On Duty Outside the Diocese.
Steinhauser, Michael G. '67 (BRK) On Leave/Unassigned.
Steinhiber, Richard *s.s.c.* '51 (OM)[K] St. Columbans, NE Missionary Society of St. Columban.
Steinhoff, Henry '67 (B) Retired.
Steinkerchner, Scott *o.p.* '98 (STL)[O] St. Louis, MO St. Dominic Priory.
Steinle, Christopher C. *o.s.a.* '98 (FgM) Olympia Fields, IL Province of Our Mother of Good Counsel (Midwestern).
Steinle, Christopher C. *o.s.a.* '98 (CHI)[N] Olympia Fields, IL Tolentine Monastery at Tolentine Center.
Steinle, David G. '79 (DAV) West Burlington, IA St. Mary's; West Burlington, IA SS. Mary and Patrick; Diocesan Consultors; Deans.
Steinle, James '53 (TOL) Retired.
Steinman, Robert E. *o.s.a.* '50 (PH)[Y] Villanova, PA St. Thomas Monastery.
Steinmetz, Gerald *o.f.m.* '71 (SFE) Albuquerque, NM Holy Family; [H] Albuquerque, NM The Province of Our Lady of Guadalupe.
Steinmetz, Paul B. *s.j.* '59 (MIL)[P] Wauwatosa, WI Jesuit Community at St. Camillus.
Steinmetz, Ricardo *s.j.* '55 (FgM) St. Louis, MO Society of Jesus.
Steinmetz, Thomas P. '02 (NTN) Manchester, NH Our Lady of the Cedars; National Association of Melkite Youth; DEPARTMENT OF VETERANS AFFAIRS HOSPITALS AND CHAPLAINS.
Steinmiller, Alex *c.p.* '70 (BIR)[B] Birmingham, AL Holy Family Cristo Rey Catholic High School; Birmingham, AL Holy Family; [I] Birmingham, AL Congregation of the Passion: Holy Family Community, Inc.
Steinwachs, David *o.s.b.* '58 (SP)[N] St. Leo, FL St. Leo Abbey.
Steller, Paul W. '65 (BUF)[A] East Aurora, NY Christ the King Seminary; Lancaster, NY St. Mary of the Assumption.
Stellini, Robert J. '07 (MEM) Cordova, TN St. Francis of Assisi.
Stelmach, Jerome J. '80 (BUF) Awaiting Assignment.
Stelmach, Rev. Canon Michael '70 (STN) Minneapolis, MN St. Constantine; Diocesan Consultors; Minneapolis.
Stelmaszczyk, Miroslaw '77 (PIT) Creighton, PA Holy Family.
Stelten, Anthony Mary *m.f.v.a.* '00 (BIR)[E] Birmingham, AL Franciscan Missionaries of the Eternal Word, A Public Association of the Christian Faithful.
Stelten, Leo F. '50 (FAR) Retired.
Steltenkamp, Michael F. *s.j.* '76 (WH)[A] Wheeling, WV Wheeling Jesuit University.
Stelter, Richard T. '80 (RVC) Amityville, NY St. Martin of Tours.
Stelzer, Mark S. '83 (SPR) Springfield, MA Sacred Heart; Censor of Books.
Stembler, James G. '89 (CC) Seminary Formation & Vocations; Corpus Christi, TX St. Paul the Apostle; Bishop's Office; Diocesan Council of Catholic Women.
Stemmann, Joseph '63 (LAF)[G] New Iberia, LA Consolata Home Retired.
Stemn, Paul G. '09 (CHI) Winnetka, IL SS. Faith, Hope and Charity.
Stempeck, Rev. Msgr. Martin '55 (BAL) Bel Air, MD St. Margaret.
Stempora, Daniel F. '60 (JOL)[K] Naperville, IL St. John Vianney Villa; Roselle, IL St. Walter Retired.
Stempsey, William E. *s.j.* '92 (WOR)[O] Worcester, MA Jesuits of the Holy Cross, Inc.
Stenberg, Jim '01 (ROC)[J] Rochester Basilian Residence.
Stenberg, Jim *c.b.* '01 (SY) Syracuse, NY Assumption B.V.M.
Stencil, Rallen '63 (GB) Retired.
Stencil, Steven G. '81 (TUC) Administrative Leave of Absence.
Stengel, Rev. Msgr. Charles G. '56 (NEW) Jersey City, NJ St. Aloysius Retired.
Stengel, Mark *o.s.b.* '72 (LR)[A] Subiaco, AR Subiaco Abbey.
Stengel, Michael Joseph *c.p.* '57 (L)[L] Louisville, KY Sacred Heart Retreat.
Stengel, Rev. Msgr. Paul F. '59 (BUF)[O] Lackawanna, NY Bishop Head Residence Retired.
Stengel, William J. '57 (GB) Porterfield, WI SS. Joseph & Edward Retired.
Stenger, James R. '81 (CLV) Brook Park, OH Assumption of Mary; Brook Park, OH St. Peter the Apostle.
Stenger, Joseph *c.ss.r.* '57 (STP) Brooklyn Center, MN St. Alphonsus.
Stenger, William J. '94 (WH) Retired.
Stenson, Patrick J. *m.s.c.* '63 (CHR) Pawleys Island, SC Precious Blood of Christ.
Stenson, Paul J. '98 (PH) Absent on Sick Leave.
Stenzel, Duane *o.f.m.* '54 (CIN)[N] Cincinnati St. Francis Seraph Friary.
Stenzel, Eugene F. '67 (WIN) Retired.
Stenzel, William J. '75 (CHI) Chicago, IL St. Bede the Venerable.
Stepanich, Martin *o.f.m.* '41 (CHI)[N] Lemont, IL The Slovene Franciscan Fathers, Order of Friars Minor, Commissariat of the Holy Cross.
Stepanski, Thomas K. '62 (IND) Retired.
Stepek, Robert A. '81 (CHI) Burbank, IL St. Albert the Great.
Stephan, M. Jeffrey '01 (KC) Plattsburg, MO St. Ann's; Easton, MO St. Joseph's.
Stephan, Matthew J. '83 (CC) Falfurrias, TX Sacred Heart.
Stephen, John *c.r.* '38 (CHI)[M] Des Plaines, IL Nazarethville.
Stephens, Anthony M. *c.p.m.* '05 (OWN)[F] Auburn, KY Fathers of Mercy; Auburn, KY.
Stephens, Timothy J. *s.j.* '99 (WDC)[N] Washington, DC The Jesuit Community of St. Aloysius Gonzaga; [E] Washington, DC Gonzaga College High School.
Stephenson, Alfonse J. '75 (MO) Air National Guard Chaplains.
Stephenson, Alphonse J. '75 (PAT) On Duty Outside the Diocese.
Stephenson, Patrick '68 (SR) American Canyon, CA Holy Family.
Stephenson, Robert B. '78 (SY) Fulton, NY Holy Family–St. Michael's.
Stepien, Allen F. '65 (PAT) Retired.
Steriti, Edward *o.c.s.o.* '57 (WOR)[O] Spencer, MA St. Joseph's Abbey.
Sterling, Donald A. '74 (BAL) Baltimore, MD The New All Saints.
Sterling, John J. '96 (COV) Erlanger, KY St. Barbara.
Stern, Benjamin '07 (BEL) Breese, IL St. Dominic; Carlyle, IL St. Felicitas.
Stern, Rev. Msgr. Robert L. '58 (NY) On Duty Outside the Archdiocese; [II] New York, NY Catholic Near East Welfare Association (CNEWA).
Stern, Rev. Archimandrite Robert L. (WDC)[W] Silver Spring, MD Catholics Committed to Support the Pope.
Sternberg, Eric G. '05 (MAD) Advocate/Procurator (cc.1481–1490); Madison, WI St. Paul University Parish; Appointed.
Sternemann, Reinhard J. *o.s.a.* '66 (CHI)[N] Chicago, IL St. John Stone Friary.
Sterner, James M. '70 (HBG) Littlestown, PA St. Aloysius.

Sterowski, Scott P. '91 (SCR) Scranton, PA St. Francis; Scranton, PA Saint Paul of the Cross, Scranton; Priests' Retirement Advisory Board.
Stessman, Rev. Msgr. Gerald '59 (DM) West Des Moines, IA Retired.
Stetson, Rev. Msgr. William H. '62 (GAL)[N] Houston, TX Opus Dei.
Stetson, Rev. Msgr. William H. '62 (POD) Houston.
Stetz, Allan *o.s.b.* '66 (KC) Conception Junction, MO St. Columba; [J] Stanberry, MO St. Peter Parish.
Stetz, Mark '90 (MRY) Cambria, CA Santa Rosa.
Steuben, Rev. Msgr. Lawrence '55 (SAT)[K] San Antonio, TX Casa De Padres Retired.
Steuernol, Slider '96 (P) Portland, OR St. Agatha; Continuing Education for Clergy.
Steuterman, James M. '75 (WOR) Sterling, MA St. Richard of Chichester.
Stevens, Clifford J. '56 (OM) Boys Town, NE Immaculate Conception B.V.M. Retired.
Stevens, David E. '98 (MO) Air National Guard Chaplains.
Stevens, David '98 (SFS) Parker, SD St. Christina; Tea, SD St. Nicholas.
Stevens, Gladstone H. *s.s.* '00 (BAL)[S] Baltimore, MD St. Mary's Seminary & University.
Stevens, Gladstone H. *s.s.* '00 (SFR)[A] Menlo Park, CA St. Patrick Seminary and University; [A] Menlo Park, CA St. Patrick Seminary and University.
Stevens, Gladstone H. *s.s.* '00 (L) On Duty Outside the Archdiocese.
Stevens, Joshua R. '09 (WH) Beckley, WV St. Francis De Sales.
Stevens, Shane '07 (SFS) De Smet, SD St. Thomas Aquinas; Presbyteral Council.
Stevensky, Rev. Msgr. Mitred John '63 (SJP) St. Petersburg, FL Epiphany of Our Lord; Southern Protopresbytery; Presbyteral Council; Arbitration Board; Presbyters.
Stevenson, Dennis E. '88 (COL) Presiding Judges of First Instance; Columbus, OH St. Aloysius.
Stevenson, Francis '92 (SAC) Elk Grove, CA Good Shepherd Catholic Church.
Stevenson, Roy Anthony '81 (OWN) Calvert City, KY St. Pius Tenth; Grand Rivers, KY St. Anthony of Padua.
Stevenson, William J. '82 (LAN) Saline, MI St. Andrew.
Stevenson, William '86 (SD) San Diego, CA St. Therese.
Stevko, Victor *s.v.d.* '57 (FgM) Techny, IL.
Stewart, August '94 (COS) Leadville, CO Holy Family Parish; Western Deanery; Vicars Forane.
Stewart, Claudio (NY) New York, NY St. Paul.
Stewart, Columba *o.s.b.* '90 (SCL)[B] Saint John's University; [I] Collegeville, MN St. John's Abbey, of the Order of St. Benedict.
Stewart, Edward R. '89 (BRK) On Leave/Unassigned.
Stewart, George R. '94 (NY) Bronx, NY St. Brendan.
Stewart, J. Patrick *s.j.* '61 (P)[L] Portland, OR Colombiere Community.
Stewart, Keith '93 (MEM) College of Consultors; Seminarians; Vocations; Memphis, TN St. Anne's; Presbyteral Council.
Stewart, Michael L. '75 (MEM) Judges Retired.
Stewart, Patrick F. '78 (LEX) London, KY St. William.
Stewart, Paul '73 (PT) Military Chaplains; Air Force Reserve Chaplains.
Stewart, Robert H. '82 (KC) Lee's Summit, MO St. Margaret of Scotland Catholic Church.
Stewart, Rev. Msgr. Terrence L. '70 (GR) Sparta, MI Holy Family.
Sthokal, Edward S. *s.j.* '54 (STP)[N] Lake Elmo, MN Jesuit Retreat House.
Sticco, Peter T. *s.a.c.* '69 (NEW) Fairview, NJ Our Lady of Grace; [M] South Orange, NJ Pallottine Fathers & Brothers; South Orange, NJ; [R] South Orange, NJ Pallottine Intra–Community Operating Corporation.
Sticco, Peter T. *s.a.c.* '69 (BAL)[S] Baltimore, MD Pallottine Center for Apostolic Causes.
Stice, Randy '07 (KNX) Worship and Liturgy.
Sticha, Cory D. '08 (GF) Circle, MT St. Francis Xavier.
Stickle, William '50 (RIC) Retired.
Stieferman, Lowell '63 (OKL) Del City, OK St. Paul, Apostle; Defenders of the Bond.
Stiefvater, Robert X. '77 (MIL) Fond du Lac, WI Holy Family.
Stiegeler, A. Francis *s.j.* '78 (SFR)[E] San Francisco, CA St. Ignatius College Preparatory (Coed); [N] San Francisco, CA Jesuit Community at St. Ignatius College Preparatory.
Stieger, Rev. Msgr. Joseph '50 (MRY) Retired.
Stiene, Paul *i.c.* '90 (PEO) Elmwood, IL St. Patrick's; [A] Peoria, IL Rosminian Novitiate.
Stikel, Roman '88 (MIL) Kenosha, WI St. Anthony; Kenosha, WI St. Elizabeth.
Stikhin, Innokentij '91 (PRM) Bay City, MI Saint George; Omer, MI St. John.
Stiles, J. Roy '63 (L) Vicar for Retired Clergy; Louisville, KY St. Bartholomew Retired.
Stiles, Wallis '61 (SAT) D'Hanis, TX Holy Cross; In Rural Area; Archdiocesan Presbyteral Council; Priests Personnel Board.
Stillmock, Martin *c.ss.r.* '58 (STP) Brooklyn Center, MN St. Alphonsus.
Stillmunks, Steven J. '77 (OM) Omaha, NE Christ the King.
Stilwell, Dennis R. '71 (GAY) Petoskey, MI St. Francis Xavier.
Stimpson, Adam '09 (PEO) La Salle, IL Resurrection; La Salle, IL St. Hyacinth's; La Salle, IL St. Patrick's.
Stine, Robert F. '73 (BR) New Roads, LA St. Mary of False River; Clergy Personnel.
Stine, Robert (NO)[A] St. Benedict, LA St. Joseph Seminary College.
Stingel, Louis F. '60 (MET)[I] Somerset, NJ Maria Regina Residence Retired.
Stingle, Lawrence A. '41 (GB) Retired.
Stinson, Michael *f.s.s.p.* '09 (SAC) Sacramento, CA St. Stephen the First Martyr Parish.
Stirniman, Jeffrey D. '95 (PEO) Clergymen's Aid, Inc.; Princeton, IL St. Louis.
Stirpe, Carlo C. '65 (SY) Camden, NY St. John the Evangelist.
Stislow, Louis *o.f.m.* (MIL)[P] Burlington, WI Queen of Peace Friary.
Stiteler, Francis Michael *o.c.s.o.* '83 (ATL)[G] Conyers, GA The Monastery of the Holy Spirit; Conyers, GA.
Stites, John F. '76 (TOL) Cloverdale, OH St. Barbara; Ottoville, OH Immaculate Conception.
Stitt, Bryan D. '03 (OG) Colton, NY St. Patrick; Catholic Scouting; Associate Vocations Director.
Stluka, Jerome D. '69 (COL) Columbus, OH Holy Cross.
Stobba, Joseph G. *o.s.a.* '59 (MIL) Racine, WI St. Rita; Archdiocesan Consultors.
Stober, Rev. Msgr. William P. '73 (PAT) Branchville, NJ Our Lady Queen of Peace; Vicar for Pastoral Administration; Pastoral Administration.
Stobie, Stephen A. '96 (P) Wilsonville, OR St. Cyril.
Stobie, Stephen '81 (P) Board Members.
Stochl, John J. *s.j.* '54 (FgM) St. Louis, MO Society of Jesus.
Stochmal, Marek '95 (DET) Absent on Leave.
Stock, Thomas E. '98 (CLV) North Royalton, OH St. Albert the Great.
Stockbridge, Kevin J. '09 (MEM) Collierville, TN Church of the Incarnation.
Stockelman, William R. '78 (CIN) Amelia, OH St. Bernadette's.
Stocker, Bede *o.s.b.* '42 (RCK)[G] Aurora, IL Marmion Abbey Retired.
Stockert, Harold R. '63 (PSC) New York, NY SS. Peter and Paul.
Stockhausen, Gerard L. *s.j.* '79 (DET)[K] Detroit, MI Jesuit Community at the University of Detroit Mercy; [C] Detroit, MI Dental School.
Stockman, Gerald W. '64 (JC) Retired.
Stockton, Marc '02 (E) Falls Creek, PA St. Bernard; [C] Du Bois, PA DuBois Area Catholic School; [C] Du Bois, PA Du Bois Area Catholic School.
Stockus, Edward S. '91 (CHI) Retired.
Stodola, Francis '80 (MO) Army National Guard Chaplains.
Stodola, Francisco '89 (LAR) Cotulla, TX Sacred Heart.
Stoeckig, Robert E. '89 (LAV) Boulder City, NV St. Andrew's.
Stoecklein, Ted D. '01 (DOD) College of Consultors; Spearville, KS St. John the Baptist Catholic Church of Spearville, Kansas; Dodge City, KS Cathedral of Our Lady of Guadalupe Catholic Church of Dodge City, Kansas; Youth/Family Ministry and Religious Formation; [F] Dodge City, KS The Diocese of Dodge City Priest Retirement Fund, Inc.
Stoegbauer, Carlton C. '82 (CAM) Retired.
Stoeger, James A. *s.j.* '75 (CHI)[N] Chicago Chicago Province of the Society of Jesus–Provincial Office.
Stoeger, James A. *s.j.* '74 (WDC)[W] Washington, DC Jesuit Secondary Education Association; [N] Washington, DC Leonard Neale House.
Stoeger, John D. '72 (LA) Cardinal Manning House of Prayer for Priests.
Stoeger, William R. *s.j.* '72 (TUC)[D] Tucson, AZ Jesuit Community of the Vatican Observatory.
Stoerlein, Rev. Msgr. Joseph G. '49 (CAM) Retired.
Stoetzel, Charles D. '80 (LC) Marshfield, WI St. John the Baptist; Marshfield, WI Christ the King.
Stoffel, Richard J. '79 (MIL) Slinger, WI St. Peter; Allenton, WI Resurrection.
Stohrer, Walter J. *s.j.* '60 (MIL)[P] Milwaukee, WI Jesuit Community at Marquette University.
Stoia, Aurelio '09 (AGN) Hagatna, GU Nuestra Senora de la Paz y Buen Viaje.
Stojic, Damir *s.d.b.* '02 (WDC) Washington, DC St. Blaise.
Stokes, David F. '63 (BAL)[S] Towson Maryland Province of the Society of Jesus.
Stokes, David L. '02 (PRO) Providence, RI St. Sebastian; Censors of Books.
Stokes, Thomas A. *s.m.* '63 (SP) Tampa, FL Our Lady of Perpetual Help.
Stokowski, Lucjan '77 (CLV) Cleveland, OH St. Barbara; Cleveland, OH St. John Cantius.
Stolcis, Ronald '68 (CHY) Sheridan, WY Holy Name.
Stoley, Lawrence '91 (LIN)[F] Waverly, NE Our Lady of Good Counsel Retreat House; Commission for Sacred Liturgy and Sacred Music; Retreat Program; Schools.
Stolinski, Dennis R. '69 (OM) Bellevue, NE St. Matthew The Evangelist Church of Bellevue.
Stoll, Mark J. '92 (SC) Moville, IA Immaculate Conception; Vice Chancellor; Moville, IA St. Michael's.
Stollenwerk, Charles J. '73 (CLV) North Olmsted, OH St. Richard; Associate Judges.
Stoltz, John J. '90 (L) Louisville, KY St. Gabriel the Archangel; Defenders of the Bond; Ex Officio.
Stoltz, Richard L. '74 (STL) New Melle, MO Immaculate Heart of Mary.
Stolz, William K. *s.j.* '62 (SAC)[D] Sacramento, CA Jesuit High School; [I] Carmichael, CA Sacramento Jesuit Community.
Stommel, Russel J. '67 (MIL) Retired.
Stone, Bob '01 (CR) Argyle, MN St. Rose of Lima; Strandquist, MN Assumption – Church of Florian; Stephen, MN St. Stephen's.
Stone, Jeffrey E. '05 (SFD) Liberty, IL St. Brigid; Liberty, IL St. Edward; Liberty, IL St. Joseph.
Stone, John Colm *o.c.d.* '63 (SJ)[M] San Jose, CA Carmelite Monastery, Novitiate.
Stone, Michael J. '68 (ALN) Schuylkill Haven, PA St. Ambrose; Elected Members.
Stone, Robert J. (PH)[Y].
Stone, Robert '90 (KC) Independence, MO Nativity of Mary Parish.
Stone, Ronald G. '01 (SFE) Mountainair, NM St. Alice.
Stone, Theodore '52 (CHI) Park Ridge, IL Mary, Seat of Wisdom Retired.
Stoneberg, Jeffery '90 (JOL) Channahon, IL St. Ann Parish; Presbyteral Council.
Stoner, John Bosco *o.s.b.* '76 (LA)[P] Valyermo, CA St. Andrew's Abbey.
Stoner, Timothy L. '96 (GI) Chadron, NE St. Patrick's.
Stookey, Gerald L. *o.p.* '78 (DEN)[N] Denver, CO Dominican Friars; Denver, CO St. Dominic.
Stopyra, David M. *o.f.m.conv.* '60 (FR) Taunton, MA Our Lady of the Holy Rosary; Diocesan Consultors.
Storan, William '61 (SAC) Retired.
Storck, Edward J. '52 (WIL) Retired.
Storey, Kevin J. '92 (GAL)[E] Houston, TX St. Thomas High School.
Storey, Richard '04 (KCK) Overland Park, KS Holy Spirit.
Stormes, James R. *s.j.* '79 (SFR)[N] San Francisco, CA Loyola House Jesuit Community.
Stortz, Donald L. '64 (OM) Retired.
Stortz, Rev. Msgr. Mario '49 (AMA) Happy, TX Holy Name of Jesus Retired.
Stout, O. Hugh '61 (CAM) Retired.
Stout, Richard E. *c.s.c.* '71 (FgM)[H] Notre Dame Congregation of Holy Cross, Indiana Province, Provincial House; New Rochelle, NY Eastern Brothers Province.
Stout, William *o.f.m.* '00 (JKS) Greenwood, MS St. Francis of Assisi; Greenwood, MS Immaculate Heart of Mary.
Stoviak, Leonard W. '73 (GBG) North Huntingdon, PA St. Elizabeth Ann Seton.
Stowe, Gregory P. '06 (PRO) Wakefield, RI St. Francis of Assisi; [C] Wakefield, RI The Prout School.
Stowe, John *o.f.m.conv.* '95 (ELP) El Paso, TX Our Lady of Mt. Carmel; Finance Council; Vicars General; Moderator of the Curia; Chancellor; Diocesan Pastoral Staff; Ex Officio Members; Priests' Retirement and Disability Plan; Missions Office/Propagation of the Faith/Catholic Relief Services; Priests' Personnel Advisory Committee; [J] El Paso, TX Franciscans, Secular Order of Franciscans.
Stoyle, James '91 (FTW) Kendallville, IN Immaculate Conception; Fort Wayne, IN Cathedral of the Immaculate Conception.
Strabala, Matthew T.D. *o.p.* '00 (SFE) Albuquerque, NM St. Thomas Aquinas University Parish; [K] Albuquerque, NM St. Thomas Aquinas (Newman Center) University Parish; [L] Albuquerque, NM Dominican Ecclesial Institute (D.E.I.).
Strachota, Michael D. '79 (MIL) Nashotah, WI St. Joan of Arc.
Strader, Mark A. '91 (LA) Santa Barbara, CA St. Raphael.
Stradinger, Stephen J. '74 (MIL) Racine, WI St. Mary by the Lake.
Stradomski, Ryszard '83 (SP) Crystal River, FL St. Benedict.
Stragapede, Michele *m.c.c.j.* '83 (CHI) Chicago, IL St. Martin De Porres.
Strahan, Rev. Msgr. Francis V. '59 (BO) Framingham, MA St. Bridget; Trustees.
Strain, Eugene R. '53 (DET) Retired.
Straka, Francis P. '90 (ALN) Northampton, PA Assumption of the Blessed Virgin Mary; Saint Vincent De Paul Society.
Straley, Michael '83 (PHX) Phoenix, AZ St. Paul Roman Catholic Parish; Presbyteral Council.
Strand, Luke N. '09 (MIL) Fond du Lac, WI Holy Family.
Strand, Ralph S. '64 (CHI) Retired.
Strange, J. Michael *s.s.* '65 (SFR) San Francisco, CA St.

Vincent de Paul.
Strange, J. Michael *s.s.* '65 (BAL)[S] Baltimore Society of St. Sulpice, Province of the United States.
Strange, Todd O. '09 (SEA) Centralia, WA St. Mary; Pe Ell, WA St. Joseph; Toledo, WA St. Francis Xavier; Winlock, WA Sacred Heart; Chehalis, WA St. Joseph.
Strano, Rev. Msgr. Edward '56 (TR) Belmar, NJ; [N] Trenton, NJ Villa Vianney Retired.
Stransky, Thomas F. *c.s.p.* '57 (NY)[EE] Jamaica Estates Paulist Fathers Generalate.
Strasser, John R. '76 (DOD) Kinsley, KS St. Nicholas Catholic Church of Kinsley, Kansas; College of Consultors; Kinsley, KS St. Joseph Catholic Church of Offerle, Kansas; Diocesan Finance Council; Diocesan Review Board; [F] Dodge City, KS The Diocese of Dodge City Priest Retirement Fund, Inc.
Strasz, James *s.m.* '80 (DET)[D] Pontiac, MI Notre Dame Preparatory School and Marist Academy.
Straten, William R. '09 (AUS) Georgetown, TX St. Helen.
Stratman, Joseph '77 (BEA) Retired.
Stratman, Raymond '55 (LEX) Retired.
Stratman, Thomas F. '50 (DAV)[J] Davenport, IA St. Vincent Center Retired.
Straub, David R. '94 (CHI) Des Plaines, IL St. Zachary; Lake Villa, IL Prince of Peace.
Straub, Rev. Msgr. Edward F. '65 (NY) Liberty, NY St. Peter; Sullivan.
Strausser, George '77 (PH) Philadelphia, PA St. Agatha–St. James.
Stravinskas, Peter M.J. '77 (B) On Duty Outside the Diocese.
Strawn, Nicholas *s.v.d.* '62 (FgM) Techny, IL.
Strazicich, Mel '07 (SEA) Kelso, WA Immaculate Heart of Mary; Castle Rock, WA St. Mary.
Strebel, Roger W. '66 (GB) Elcho, WI Holy Family; Pickerel, WI St. Mary.
Strebig, John J. '52 (GRY) Retired.
Strebler, Charles F. '94 (CLV) Cleveland, OH Cathedral of St. John the Evangelist; Adjunct Judicial Vicars.
Strecok, Lubomir J. '98 (ALT)[K] Hollidaysburg, PA Conference of Slovak Clergy; Clarence, PA Queen of Archangels.
Streichardt, Wolfgang '82 (SAG) Bannister, MI St. Cyril.
Streicher, Bernard J. *s.j.* '60 (CLV)[D] Cleveland, OH St. Ignatius High School.
Streifel, Keith N. '99 (BIS) Dickinson, ND St. Joseph; Pro–Synodal Judges.
Streit, David *s.v.d.* '69 (FgM) Techny, IL.
Streit, Thomas G. *c.s.c.* '86 (FTW)[B] University of Notre Dame Du Lac; [H] Notre Dame, IN Holy Cross Community, Corby Hall, University of Notre Dame.
Streitenberger, Adam A. '07 (COL) Gahanna, OH St. Matthew.
Strelecki, Rev. Msgr. Richard T. '69 (NEW)[M] Rutherford, NJ St. John Vianney Residence for Priests Retired.
Strelick, Charles J. '56 (MAR) Retired.
Strelinski, Ernest '65 (PIT) Allison Park, PA St. Ursula.
Strempeck, Rev. Msgr. Martin R. '55 (BAL) Retired.
Stretton, Noel '59 (DUL) Duluth Federal Prison Retired.
Streveler, Robert A. '69 (LC) Edgar, WI St. John the Baptist.
Streza, Charles V. '43 (ROM) Retired.
Stricker, Robert A. '48 (CIN) Cincinnati, OH St. Therese, The Little Flower; Imprimatur Censors Retired.
Strickland, Rev. Msgr. Joseph E. '85 (TYL) Tyler, TX Cathedral of the Immaculate Conception; College of Consultors; Deans; Judicial Vicar; Judges; Priests' Pension Board; Priests' Personnel Board; Presbyteral Council; Diocesan Finance Council; Diocesan Implementation Committee On Ethics and Integrity Policy for Church Personnel.
Strieder, Leon '76 (AUS) On Duty Outside the Diocese.
Strieder, Leon '76 (GAL) Houston, TX St. Michael.
Striedl, Max J. '96 (RCK) Lena, IL St. Joseph.
Striedl, Max J. '96 (RCK) Warren, IL St. Joseph; Warren, IL St. Ann.
Striegel, Robert M. '73 (DAV)[J] Iowa City, IA O'Keefe Hall; Veteran's Administration Hospital; DEPARTMENT OF VETERANS AFFAIRS HOSPITALS AND CHAPLAINS; Richland, IA Ss. Joseph and Cabrini.
Stringini, John L. '79 (RCK) Special Assignment; [F] Rockford, IL Provena Cor Mariae Center Retired.
Stripe, Keith A. '96 (TOL) Maumee, OH St. Joseph; Members.
Strittmatter, Andre *t.o.r.* '61 (ALT)[G] Loretto, PA St. Francis Friary at Mount Assisi.
Strittmatter, Paul J. *s.j.* '77 (DM) Dunlap, IA St. Patrick; Dunlap, IA Sacred Heart; Dunlap, IA Holy Family.
Strittmatter, Paul J. *s.j.* '77 (OM)[K] Omaha, NE Jesuit Community at Creighton University.
Strittmatter, Robert '66 (FWT) Fort Worth, TX San Mateo; Fort Worth, TX St. Mary of the Assumption.
Strmecki, Ivan M. *o.f.m.* '05 (CHI) Chicago, IL St. Jerome.
Strobl, Andrew '09 (KCK)[B] Overland Park, KS Saint Thomas Aquinas High School, Inc.; Olathe, KS Prince of Peace.
Strock, Richard M. '65 (LR)[G] Little Rock, AR St. John Manor Retired.
Strohmeyer, George E. '64 (E)[B] Erie, PA Gannon University; Priest Personnel Board; [P] Erie, PA Gannon University.
Stroik, Placid *o.f.m.* '63 (NEW)[N] Lodi, NJ Immaculate Conception Convent.
Strollo, Charles P. *c.m.* '73 (PH)[B] Philadelphia, PA St. Vincent's Seminary; [B] Philadelphia, PA DePaul Novitiate; [Y] Philadelphia Congregation of the Mission; Philadelphia, PA Eastern Province; Philadelphia, PA.
Strom, Charles W. '72 (HEL) Retired.
Stromberg, James S. '57 (STP)[C] St. Paul, MN University of St. Thomas Retired.
Strommer, James *c.p.* '70 (FgM)[N] Chicago, IL Passionist Provincial Office; Chicago, IL Holy Cross Province (Western); Consultors:; [N] Chicago, IL Passionist Community–Immaculate Conception Monastery.
Stromski, Adam F.X. '46 (STU) Retired.
Strong, Barry R. *o.s.f.s.* '84 (WIL)[J] Wilmington, DE Wilmington–Philadelphia Province of the Oblates of St. Francis de Sales.
Stronkowski, John '85 (BGP) Bridgeport, CT St. Ambrose.
Stroot, Thomas J. '70 (WCH) Pittsburg, KS Our Lady of Lourdes; [B] Pittsburg, KS St. Mary–Colgan High School.
Strother, Michael A. '05 (BEA) Woodville, TX Our Lady of the Pines.
Struik, Felix A.P. *o.p.* '58 (SJN)[A] Bayamon Central University.
Strumski, Matthew J. '48 (PRO) Retired.
Strupp, James A. '67 (MIL) Retired.
Strupp, Joachim *o.f.m.cap.* '63 (MIL)[P] Mount Calvary, WI St. Lawrence Friary Retired.
Strus, Walter A. '94 (CHI) Other Assignments.
Struzik, Edward J. '85 (MET)[I] Somerset, NJ Maria Regina Residence Retired.
Struzynski, Robert *o.f.m.* '63 (BUF)[C] West Clarksville, NY Holy Peace Friary; [Q] West Clarksville, NY Mount Irenaeus, Franciscan Mountain Retreat & Holy Peace Friary; [R] St. Bonaventure, NY St. Bonaventure University.
Struzzieri, Andrew L. '75 (BRK) Brooklyn, NY St. Matthew.
Struzzo, John A. *c.s.c.* '65 (FTW)[H] Notre Dame Congregation of Holy Cross, Indiana Province, Provincial House.
Strycharz, Stanislaw '91 (VEN) Bonita Springs, FL St. Leo.
Stryker, Peter R. *c.p.m.* '98 (OWN) Russellville, KY Sacred Heart; [F] Auburn, KY Fathers of Mercy.
Strynkowski, Rev. Msgr. John '63 (BRK) Brooklyn, NY The Cathedral–Basilica of St. James; Committee for Catholic–Protestant Relations; Vicar for Higher Education; [E] Brooklyn, NY Campus Ministers and Ministry Centers.
Strzadala, Wieslaw P. *s.d.s.* '90 (NEW) Hackensack, NJ St. Joseph's; [M] Verona, NJ The Salvatorian Fathers.
Strzalkowski, Dariusz '00 (DET) Taylor, MI Our Lady of the Angels.
Strzok, James J. *s.j.* '70 (MIL)[P] Milwaukee Jesuit Provincial Office, Wisconsin Province.
Strzok, James J. *s.j.* '70 (FgM) Milwaukee, WI Society of Jesus.
Strzyz, Stanislaus '68 (BAK) Health and Retirement Board; Redmond, OR St. Thomas; Council of Priests and Diocesan Consultors Retired.
Stua, Ronald *c.m.f.* '81 (CHI)[N] Oak Park, IL Claretian Missionaries USA Eastern Province; Oak Park, IL; [N] Oak Park, IL Claretian Missionaries Community Support Trust; [N] Chicago, IL Claret House.
Stuart, Francis *o.s.b.* '61 (JC) Retired.
Stuart, George E. '89 (WDC) Bethesda, MD Little Flower; Pastoral Center Special Ministries; Archivist; Judges; Defenders of the Bond; Vice Chancellor.
Stubbs, Michael C. '78 (KCK) Lansing, KS St. Francis de Sales.
Stubeda, Anthony J. '85 (NU) St. Pius X; Committee on Parishes.
Stubna, Kris D. '85 (PIT) Pittsburgh, PA SS. Simon and Jude; [Q] Pittsburgh, PA Scholastic Opportunity Scholarship Program; Secretary for Catholic Education; Diocesan Development Board.
Stuchlik, Richard '68 (WCH) Wichita, KS St. Margaret Mary.
Stuczko, Richard J. '54 (SY) Oriskany, NY Oneida County Jail Retired.
Studeny, Colman *o.f.m.cap.* '61 (FgM) Pittsburgh, PA Province of St. Augustine.
Studer, Louis *o.m.i.* '70 (STP)[N] Buffalo, MN Christ the King Retreat Center.
Studerus, Rev. Msgr. Gregory J. '80 (NEW) West New York, NJ St. Joseph of the Palisades.
Studniewski, Gary R. '95 (WDC) Military Chaplains; Army Chaplains.
Studwell, Joachim *o.f.m.* '87 (GRY)[H] Cedar Lake, IN San Damiano Friary.
Studzinski, Raymond *o.s.b.* '69 (IND)[K] St. Meinrad St. Meinrad Archabbey.
Studzinski, Raymond *o.s.b.* '69 (WDC)[C] Catholic University of America, The.
Stuebben, Rev. Msgr. Lawrence J. '55 (SAT)[Q] San Antonio, TX Archdiocese of San Antonio Endowment Fund for Parishes, School and Ministries; [Q] San Antonio, TX Mary Jane Ihle Clark Endowment Fund for Ministry to Persons with Disabilities; College of Consultors Retired.
Stueber, Edwin *o.s.b.* '46 (SCL)[I] Collegeville, MN St. John's Abbey, of the Order of St. Benedict.
Stuecker, Henry C. '38 (L) Retired.
Stuempel, Robert L. '75 (L) Louisville, KY St. Bernard.
Stuglik, Robert '03 (CHI) Summit, IL St. Joseph.
Stuhrenberg, James '06 (CHL) Greensboro, NC Our Lady of Grace.
Stulb, Joseph A. '61 (NEW)[M] Rutherford, NJ St. John Vianney Residence for Priests Retired.
Stump, David X. *s.j.* '71 (NEW)[B] Jersey City, NJ Jesuit Center; [M] Jersey City, NJ Jesuits of Saint Peter's College, Inc.
Stump, James M. *o.f.m.cap.* '88 (MO) DEPARTMENT OF VETERANS AFFAIRS HOSPITALS AND CHAPLAINS.
Stump, James *o.f.m.cap.* '88 (SFR)[N] Burlingame, CA Capuchin Provincial House.
Stumpf, Michael J. '01 (PIT) Pittsburgh, PA St. Mary of the Mount.
Stumpf, Walter P. '06 (GB) Crivitz, WI St. Mary.
Stumpf, William F. '85 (IND) Bloomington, IN St. Charles Borromeo; Board of Consultors; Council of Priests; Brookville, IN St. Peter; Deaneries and Deans.
Stunek, Howard *o.f.m.* (MIL)[P] Burlington, WI Queen of Peace Friary.
Stunek, Leonard *o.f.m.* '60 (CLV) Cleveland, OH St. Stanislaus; [N] Cleveland, OH St. Stanislaus Friary.
Stupca, Edward L. '61 (HEL) Retired.
Sturm, Donald E. '58 (KC) St. Joseph, MO Seven Dolors; Legion of Mary.
Sturm, John G. *s.j.* '50 (BUF) Buffalo, NY St. Michael.
Sturm, Michael O. '69 (MIL) Waupun, WI St. Mary; Waupun, WI St. Joseph; Waupun, WI St. Brendan.
Sturm, Samuel L. '99 (KNX) Dayton, TN St. Bridget.
Sturn, Michael L. '77 (SB) Ontario, CA St. George.
Sturtz, Richard S. '56 (OG) Schroon Lake, NY St. Joseph; Schroon Lake, NY Our Lady of Lourdes.
Stybor, Marek *o.f.m.conv.* '99 (SPR) Chicopee, MA St. Stanislaus Basilica.
Styles, Kenneth A. *s.j.* '72 (CLV)[D] Cleveland, OH St. Ignatius High School.
Suan, Charito E. '85 (SFR) San Francisco, CA St. Elizabeth; Deans.
Suarez, Carlos *o.s.b.* '86 (FgM) Richardton, ND Assumption Abbey.
Suarez, Carlos *o.s.b.* '86 (BIS)[A] Richardton, ND Assumption Abbey.
Suarez, Edgar *c.s.v.* '04 (CHI)[N] Arlington Heights Viatorian Province Center–Clerics of St. Viator.
Suarez, Gildardo '92 (PRO) Providence, RI Assumption of the Blessed Virgin Mary; Council Members.
Suarez, Jesus E. '86 (GAL) Houston, TX St. Philip of Jesus.
Suarez, John–Jairo (PAT) Paterson, NJ Our Lady of Lourdes.
Suarez, Leo '88 (STO) Absent on Leave.
Suarez, Octavio '64 (TYL) Mount Pleasant, TX St. Michael.
Suarez, Pedro A. *s.j.* '72 (MIA)[B] Miami, FL Barry University; [D] Miami, FL Belen Jesuit Preparatory School; [K] Miami, FL Villa Javier; Comunidad de Vida Cristiana, Regina Mundi, South Florida Region.
Suaybaguio, Evangelio R. '75 (NY) Staten Island, NY St. Joseph, St. Thomas.
Suazo Martínez, Rafael (SJN).
Suberlak, Donald *c.r.* '67 (KAL) Three Oaks, MI St. Mary of the Assumption.
Subiza, Innocent '01 (SAC)[L] Davis, CA Newman Catholic Student Community Davis; Davis, CA St. James.
Subler, Carl A. '04 (COL) Military Services; Army Chaplains.
Subocz, Adam C. '86 (HRT)[M] Hartford, CT SS. Cyril & Methodius Convent; Hartford, CT SS. Cyril and Methodius.
Subosa, Cristobal *f.i.m.* '01 (SB) San Jacinto, CA St. Anthony; Rancho Cucamonga, CA Sacred Heart.
Suchan, Rev. Msgr. Aleksander '88 (DUL) Floodwood, MN Immaculate Conception; Floodwood, MN St. Louis; Floodwood, MN St. Mary.
Suchan, Robert J. *s.j.* '56 (FgM) New York, NY Society of Jesus.
Sucharski, Michael M. *s.v.d.* '83 (LAF) Lafayette, LA St. Anthony.
Sucher, Frederick *c.p.* '44 (L)[L] Louisville, KY Sacred Heart Retreat.
Suchnicki, Michael *o.f.m.cap.* '88 (DEN)[N] Denver, CO St. Francis of Assisi Friary.
Suchocki, James A. '62 (GAY) Miami, FL St. Mary's

Cathedral Retired.
Suchocki, Marek '86 (NY) Staten Island, NY St. Stanislaus Kostka; Judges.
Sucholet, James '91 (NOR) Tolland, CT St. Matthew.
Suchy, Theodore D. *o.s.b.* '67 (JOL)[A] Lisle, IL Benedictine University; [L] Lisle, IL St. Procopius Abbey.
Sudano, Glenn *c.f.r.* '84 (BRK)[V] Brooklyn, NY Grassroots Renewal Project, Inc.
Sudano, Glenn *c.f.r.* '84 (NEW)[M] Newark, NJ Franciscan Friars of the Renewal.
Sudario, Rev. Msgr. Antonio '69 (SB) San Bernardino, CA St. Bernardine Medical Center.
Sudekum, Rev. Msgr. Edward J. '61 (STL) University City, MO Our Lady of Lourdes.
Sudlik, Leonard '76 (GR) Diocesan Finance Council Membership.
Sudlik, Richard M. *o.m.i.* '72 (BO)[U] Tewksbury, MA Oblate World/Missionary Association of Mary Immaculate; [U] Lowell, MA Missionary Oblates of Mary Immaculate; [U] Lowell, MA St. Eugene House (Residence).
Sudlik, Richard *o.m.i.* '72 (WDC)[N] Washington, DC Provincial Offices of the United States Province of the Missionary Oblates of Mary Immaculate; Councilors:; Lowell, MA.
Sudol, Ignatius *o.h.* (LA)[BB] Ojai, CA St. Joseph's H. & RC Foundation.
Suehr, Philip *o.s.c.* '66 (PHX)[F] Phoenix, AZ Crosier Community of Phoenix (Canons Regular of the Order of the Holy Cross).
Suellentrop, Anthony J. '73 (DOD) Retired.
Suelzer, Rev. Msgr. John N. '65 (FTW) Fort Wayne, IN St. Charles Borromeo; Budget Committee; Retired Clergy Committee.
Suenram, John Magdalene *o.c.d.* '87 (LR)[A] Little Rock, AR Marylake – Carmelite Novitiate.
Sueper, Alban *s.s.c.* '53 (OM)[K] St. Columbans Missionary Society of St. Columban Retired.
Sueper, Alban *s.s.c.* '53 (PRO)[P] Bristol, RI St. Columban's Retirement House Retired.
Suess, Milton M. '63 (GB) Luxemburg, WI Immaculate Conception; Casco, WI Holy Trinity; Censores Librorum.
Suffrin, Paul '80 (MIA) Miami, FL St. Joachim.
Sughrue, Paul S. '70 (BO) Braintree, MA St. Clare.
Sugrue, John F. '62 (CAM) Retired.
Sugrue, Patrick *o.c.d.* '64 (SJ)[M] San Jose, CA Carmelite Monastery, Novitiate.
Suh, Daniel '95 (BRK) Woodside, NY St. Sebastian; Graduate Studies.
Suhaka, Peter '86 (MET) Pittstown, NJ St. Catherine of Siena; [K] Milford, NJ Bethany Ridge.
Suhoza, John E. '68 (PIT) Pittsburgh, PA St. Gabriel of the Sorrowful Virgin; Allegheny County, PA St. Joseph House of Hospitality; [N] Pittsburgh, PA Sisters of St. Francis of the Providence of God.
Sui, Peter Kin Chung *s.j.* '93 (SJ) Chinese Catholic Community.
Suibielski, Kenneth J. '77 (PRO) Misquamicut, RI St. Clare.
Suing, Benedict *o.s.b.* '54 (P)[L] St. Benedict, OR Mt. Angel Abbey.
Suing, Benedict *o.s.b.* '54 (STU)[J] Hopedale, OH The Order of the Sacred and Immaculate Hearts of Jesus and Mary.
Suit, Robert J. '74 (STL) Valley Park, MO Sacred Heart.
Sujono, Yohanes *m.s.c.* '95 (MI) Marshall Islands, MH Queen of Peace; Prefecture Consultors.
Sukovaty, G. L. *o.p.* '51 (FgM) New York, NY Province of St. Joseph (Eastern).
Sulaiman, Selwan A. (OLD) Jacksonville, FL Saint Ephrem.
Sularz, Tom '71 (JOL) Wheaton, IL St. Daniel the Prophet Church.
Suleimanovs, Gabriel *o.s.p.p.e.* (NOR) Rockville, CT St. Joseph.
Sulistya, Francis *o.carm* '07 (WDC)[B] Washington, DC Whitefriars Hall.
Sulkowski, Anthony P. '86 (DET) Eastpointe, MI St. Basil.
Sullins, Paul '02 (WDC) Hyattsville, MD St. Mark; [C] Catholic University of America, The.
Sullivan, Andrew A. '94 (BIR) Florence, AL St. Joseph's; [H] Florence, AL University of North Alabama.
Sullivan, Brendan V. '60 (CAM) Retired.
Sullivan, Brian '03 (PAT) Hawthorne, NJ St. Anthony's; Presbyteral Council; College of Consultors.
Sullivan, Charles D. *s.j.* '72 (NY)[F] Bronx, NY Fordham Preparatory School; [EE] Jesuit Community, Kohlmann Hall.
Sullivan, Charles J. '66 (PH) Priests' Personnel Board; Levittown, PA St. Michael the Archangel.
Sullivan, Charles K. '64 (VEN) Retired.
Sullivan, D. Edward '42 (CHL) Retired.
Sullivan, Daniel F. '57 (CHI) Lake Villa, IL Prince of Peace Retired.
Sullivan, Daniel J. '53 (CHI) Retired.
Sullivan, Daniel J. *s.j.* '61 (NY)[EE] Loyola Hall, Jesuit Community.
Sullivan, Rev. Msgr. Daniel J. '77 (PH) On Special or Other Archdiocesan Assignment; Office of the Vicar for Clergy; Priests' Personnel Board; Diocesan Priests' Compensation and Benefits Committee; College of Consultors; Council of Priests.
Sullivan, Daniel J. *s.j.* '72 (PHX) Phoenix, AZ St. Francis Xavier Roman Catholic Parish; [F] Phoenix, AZ Society of Jesus.
Sullivan, Daniel James '63 (HRT) Hamden, CT Our Lady of Mt. Carmel.
Sullivan, Daniel Jeremiah '63 (HRT) South Windsor, CT St. Margaret Mary.
Sullivan, Daniel *c.p.* '68 (PIT)[M] Pittsburgh, PA St. Paul of the Cross Monastery.
Sullivan, David C. '58 (STL) Retired.
Sullivan, Donal P. '90 (STA) Vicar for Priests.
Sullivan, Donal '64 (STA) Fleming Island, FL Sacred Heart.
Sullivan, E. Paul '63 (BO) Senior Priests. Retired.
Sullivan, Edward Hartrick *c.m.* '46 (STL)[O] Perryville, MO Congregation of the Mission.
Sullivan, Edward *o.f.m.* (NY)[GG] Warwick, NY Franciscan Sisters of the Poor Convent.
Sullivan, Emmanuel *s.a.* '55 (NY)[EE] Garrison, NY Franciscan Friars of the Atonement.
Sullivan, Eugene P. '68 (BO) Weymouth, MA St. Francis Xavier.
Sullivan, Rev. Msgr. Eugene '59 (CHY) Retirees' Representative; St. Joseph's Society for Priests (Clergy Mutual Benefit Society) Retired.
Sullivan, F. Norman '62 (BUF) Retired.
Sullivan, Francis A. *s.j.* '51 (BO)[U] Newton, MA The Jesuit Community at Boston College.
Sullivan, Francis E. *c.ss.r.* '59 (ALB) Saratoga Springs, NY St. Clement.
Sullivan, Francis E. '88 (BO) Billerica, MA St. Mary.
Sullivan, Francis X. '48 (SPR) Retired.
Sullivan, Frederick J. '53 (NY)[EE] Bronx, NY Retired.
Sullivan, Gael E. *s.d.b.* '76 (OAK)[M] Berkeley Salesians of Don Bosco.
Sullivan, Gael *s.d.b.* '76 (LA) Cursillo Movement.
Sullivan, George *s.j.* '75 (OM)[C] Omaha, NE Creighton Preparatory School; Religious Orders.
Sullivan, George '76 (LA) La Mirada, CA St. Paul of the Cross.
Sullivan, J. David *m.m.* '60 (NY)[EE] Retired.
Sullivan, J. Richard '77 (L) Louisville, KY St. Michael.
Sullivan, James B. '58 (NEW) Roseland, NJ Our Lady of the Blessed Sacrament Retired.
Sullivan, James F. '87 (PH) Drexel Hill, PA St. Andrew.
Sullivan, James L. '43 (BO) Senior Priests. Retired.
Sullivan, James M. '60 (HEL) Retired.
Sullivan, James M. '66 (STL) Chesterfield, MO Incarnate Word.
Sullivan, James M. *o.p.* '95 (L) Ex Officio; [L] Louisville, KY St. Louis Bertrand Priory; Louisville, KY St. Louis Bertrand.
Sullivan, Rev. Msgr. James P. '70 (NY) Poughkeepsie, NY St. Martin de Porres.
Sullivan, James '06 (OAK) Fremont, CA Our Lady of Guadalupe.
Sullivan, Jan C. P. '91 (COL) Washington Court House, OH St. Colman; Deanery 12: Chillicothe; Presbyteral Council; Parochial Examiners.
Sullivan, Jeremiah D. *c.s.p.* '59 (NY)[EE] New York, NY Paulist Fathers' Motherhouse Retired.
Sullivan, Jeremiah '62 (HEL) Retired.
Sullivan, John D. '54 (JOL) Glen Ellyn, IL St. Petronille Retired.
Sullivan, John J. '77 (CHI) Glenwood, IL St. John.
Sullivan, John J. '67 (CLV) Wickliffe, OH Our Lady of Mount Carmel.
Sullivan, John J. *o.s.f.s.* '81 (PH)[Y] Philadelphia, PA Father Louis Brisson Residence.
Sullivan, John J. '66 (DET) Retired.
Sullivan, John J. *s.m.* '65 (ATL) Atlanta, GA Our Lady of the Assumption.
Sullivan, John L. '74 (BO) Canton, MA St. Gerard Majella.
Sullivan, John L. *o.p.* '49 (PRO) Providence, RI St. Pius V; [P] Providence, RI St. Pius Priory.
Sullivan, John L. '71 (SPR)[G] Springfield, MA St. Michael's Residence; Sisters of Providence Care Centers, Inc.; Judges Retired.
Sullivan, John M. '91 (BO) Melrose, MA St. Mary of the Annunciation; Courage.
Sullivan, John M. '90 (FR) Wareham, MA St. Patrick's.
Sullivan, John P. '65 (HRT) New Haven, CT St. Joseph's.
Sullivan, John P. '72 (SAC) Presbyteral Council Retired.
Sullivan, John P. *m.s.* '70 (FR)[G] Attleboro, MA La Salette Shrine.
Sullivan, John R. '94 (LIN) Lincoln, NE Blessed Sacrament; Diocesan Finance Council; Priests' Continuing Education Committee.
Sullivan, John *o.f.m.* '59 (SFD)[L] Springfield, IL Our Lady of Angels Friary.
Sullivan, John *m.m.* '60 (WDC)[B] Washington, DC Maryknoll Fathers and Brothers.
Sullivan, John *o.c.d.* '68 (MIL)[P] Milwaukee, WI Provincial Offices – Discalced Carmelites.
Sullivan, Joseph D. '56 (NY) Montgomery, NY Holy Name of Mary Retired.
Sullivan, Rev. Msgr. Joseph P. '53 (SFR)[K] San Rafael, CA Nazareth House of San Rafael, Inc. Retired.
Sullivan, Joseph '03 (SPK) Newport, WA Our Lady of Sorrows; Ione, WA St. Bernard; Metaline Falls, WA St. Joseph; Newport, WA St. Anthony; Newport, WA St. Jude.
Sullivan, Kenneth J. *m.m.* '57 (FgM) Maryknoll, NY MARYKNOLL.
Sullivan, Kevin B. '63 (SFD) Retired.
Sullivan, Rev. Msgr. Kevin L. '76 (NY) New York, NY Corpus Christi; [I] New York, NY The Catholic Charities of the Archdiocese of New York; [I] New York, NY Roman Catholic Fund for Children and Other Purposes; [I] New York, NY Catholic Charities Alliance; [II] New York, NY Carmel Housing Development Fund Co., Inc.; [II] New York, NY The Housing Fund of the Archdiocese of New York; [II] New York, NY Cor Mariae Development Fund Corporation; [II] New York, NY Cor Mariae Housing Development Fund, Inc.; Catholic Charities; [J] New York, NY Catholic Charities Department of Housing, Housing Development Institute, Inc.
Sullivan, Lawrence F. *o.c.d.* '60 (BO)[U] Boston, MA Carmelite Monastery.
Sullivan, Lawrence F. '56 (BO) Senior Priests. Retired.
Sullivan, Lawrence J. '92 (CHI) Chicago, IL St. Christina; College of Consultors; Presbyteral Council.
Sullivan, Mervyn '69 (SJ) On Leave of Absence.
Sullivan, Michael Bruce *c.s.c.* '75 (FTW)[B] University of Notre Dame Du Lac; [H] Notre Dame, IN Holy Cross Community, Corby Hall, University of Notre Dame.
Sullivan, Michael D. '91 (TR) Point Pleasant, NJ St. Martha.
Sullivan, Michael P. '66 (MIA) Retired.
Sullivan, Michael P. *o.s.a.* '67 (PH)[Y] Villanova, PA St. Thomas Monastery.
Sullivan, Michael *o.f.m.cap.* '84 (CHI) Chicago, IL St. Clare of Montefalco.
Sullivan, Michael '81 (STP) Maple Grove, MN St. Joseph the Worker.
Sullivan, Michael '04 (NY) Staten Island, NY Our Lady Star of the Sea.
Sullivan, Neil S. '97 (HBG) Harrisburg, PA St. Catherine Laboure.
Sullivan, Neil '97 (HBG) Worship, Office of.
Sullivan, Patrick A. '82 (CR) Dilworth, MN St. Elizabeth; Hawley, MN St. Andrew; Priests Retirement Board of Trustees.
Sullivan, Patrick J. *s.j.* '50 (NY)[EE] New York, NY Murray–Weigel Hall.
Sullivan, Patrick J. *s.j.* (RVC) Oceanside, NY St. Anthony.
Sullivan, Patrick J. *c.s.c.* '56 (FR)[A] North Easton, MA Holy Cross Fathers Religious.
Sullivan, Patrick M. *o.s.b.* '87 (MAN)[K] Manchester, NH St. Anselm Abbey.
Sullivan, Patrick T. *s.j.* '64 (NY)[EE] New York, NY Murray–Weigel Hall.
Sullivan, Patrick *o.f.m.cap.* '71 (FgM) White Plains, NY Province of St. Mary.
Sullivan, Patrick '09 (KCK) Lenexa, KS Holy Trinity.
Sullivan, Patrick *c.s.c.* (BO) Labor Guild; Labor Guild.
Sullivan, Paul G. '07 (PHX) Vocations; [G] Phoenix, AZ Mount Claret Roman Catholic Retreat Center.
Sullivan, Paul M. *s.j.* '83 (BO)[W] Gloucester, MA Eastern Point Retreat House.
Sullivan, Paul V. (BO) Needham, MA St. Joseph.
Sullivan, Peter J. '70 (ALB) Special Assignment; Adjutant Vicar Judicial; Judges; Bishop's Delegate for Marriage Dispensations.
Sullivan, Philip *o.c.d.* '07 (TUC)[D] Tucson, AZ Discalced Carmelite Friars of St. Margaret Mary's; Tucson, AZ Saint Margaret Mary Alacoque Roman Catholic Parish – Tucson.
Sullivan, R. William *o.s.a.* '67 (JOL) New Lenox, IL St. Jude.
Sullivan, Raymond F. *m.m.* '54 (NY)[EE] Maryknoll Maryknoll Fathers and Brothers Retired.
Sullivan, Rev. Msgr. Richard J. '58 (E) Erie, PA St. Andrew.
Sullivan, Robert E. '80 (BO) On Duty Outside the Archdiocese.
Sullivan, Robert E. (FTW)[B] University of Notre Dame Du Lac.
Sullivan, Robert J. '78 (BO) Unassigned.
Sullivan, Robert J. '63 (SY) Special Assignment; Vestal, NY St. Vincent de Paul; Binghamton, NY Saints John & Andrew Retired.
Sullivan, Robert J. '93 (BIR) Birmingham, AL St. Francis Xavier; Navy Reserve Chaplains.
Sullivan, Robert L. *s.j.* (DEN)[D] Aurora, CO Regis Jesuit High School Corporation.
Sullivan, Sean *t.o.r.* '57 (ALT)[G] Loretto, PA St. Francis Friary at Mount Assisi.
Sullivan, Rev. Msgr. Terrence J. '64 (SJ) Retired.
Sullivan, Rev. Msgr. Thomas J. '77 (WOR) Chancery

Office; Diocesan Director of Fiscal Affairs; Director of Catholic Relief Services; Diocesan Expansion Fund; Diocesan College of Consultors; Archivist; The Annual Partners in Charity Appeal; Diocesan Building Commission Members; Stewardship and Development Office; Finance Office; Presbyteral Council; Worcester, MA St. Paul Cathedral; Diocesan College of Consultors.
Sullivan, Thomas K. '52 (STA) Retired.
Sullivan, Thomas *c.p.m.* '04 (OWN) Auburn, KY; [F] Auburn, KY Fathers of Mercy.
Sullivan, Timothy F. *c.s.p.* '85 (MEM) Memphis, TN St. Patrick's; [I] Memphis, TN St. Patrick's Center; Episcopal Vicar for Social Ministry.
Sullivan, Timothy '90 (BUR) Burlington, VT Fletcher Allen Health Care; South Burlington, VT St. John Vianney.
Sullivan, Vincent B. *s.j.* '76 (NY)[B] Bronx, NY Ciszek Hall.
Sullivan, Vincent '99 (ATL) Cleveland, GA St. Paul the Apostle.
Sullivan, Rev. Msgr. W. Jerome '61 (BUF) Promoter of Justice; Consultors, College of; Council of Priests; Cheektowaga, NY Infant of Prague.
Sullivan, William F. *s.s.c.* '56 (PRO)[P] Bristol, RI St. Columban's Retirement House.
Sullivan, William J. '59 (HBG) Retired.
Sullivan, William J. *o.s.b.* '71 (MAN)[K] Manchester, NH St. Anselm Abbey.
Sullivan, William J. *o.s.s.t.* '81 (MIA)[C] Fort Lauderdale, FL St. Thomas Aquinas High School; Fort Lauderdale, FL St. John the Baptist.
Sullivan, William J. *s.j.* '61 (MIL)[P] Wauwatosa, WI Jesuit Community at St. Camillus.
Sullivan, William M. '81 (BO) Absent on Leave.
Sullivan, William *o.ss.t.* '81 (BAL)[S] Individuals in Other Locations:.
Sullivan, William '72 (FTW) Elkhart, IN St. Thomas the Apostle; Advisory Board; Presbyteral Council.
Sullivan, William *s.j.* '66 (NY)[EE] New York, NY Murray–Weigel Hall.
Sullivan, William *s.s.c.* '56 (OM)[K] St. Columbans Missionary Society of St. Columban.
Sulmosy, Daniel *o.f.m.* '85 (CHI)[N] Chicago, IL St. Joseph Interprovincial Post–Novitiate Formation House.
Sum, Robert *o.s.b.* '05 (JOL)[L] Lisle, IL St. Procopius Abbey; [A] Lisle, IL Benedictine University.
Sumampong, Jed *c.p.* '84 (BRK)[T] Jamaica, NY Immaculate Conception Monastery; Jamaica, NY Immaculate Conception.
Sumanga, Oscar B. '95 (TR) Tribunal Judges; Associate Judicial Vicars; Hamilton, NJ Our Lady of Sorrows–St. Anthony Parish.
Sumler, Kevin '82 (BEA) Retired.
Sumler, Paul '80 (BEA) Vidor, TX Our Lady of Lourdes.
Summers, Bryan F. *c.o.* '72 (GBG) Cadogan, PA St. Lawrence.
Summers, John '54 (Y) Retired.
Summers, Randall R. '07 (IND) Indianapolis, IN St. Barnabas.
Summitt, James A. '81 (BIR) Absent on Leave.
Sumpter, Gary '79 (SR) Fortuna, CA St. Joseph; Garberville, CA Our Lady of the Redwoods; Scotia, CA St. Patrick.
Sun, Kieran Jianjun *s.v.d.* '98 (MEM)[F] Memphis, TN Society of the Divine Word (Chicago Province).
Sunberg, David A. '92 (CIN) Cincinnati, OH Our Lady of Lourdes.
Sundaram, Joseph '94 (PH) Indian Apostolate, Syro Malankara Rite; Philadelphia, PA Maternity B.V.M.
Sundaram, Manuel '90 (CR) Roseau, MN Sacred Heart.
Sundararaj, Joseph Rajpaul '95 (STL) Florissant, MO St. Rose Philippine Duchesne.
Sundborg, Stephen V. *s.j.* '74 (SEA)[A] Seattle, WA Seattle University; [L] Seattle, WA Arrupe Jesuit Community at Seattle University.
Sundholm, Conrad '55 (ROC) Retired.
Sunds, Rev. Msgr. Elvin '73 (JKS) Office of Vicar General; Chancellor; Co Chairmen; Defenders of the Bond; Priests' Council; Diocesan Consultors; Personnel Board; Parish Pastoral Councils; Jackson, MS St. Richard of Chichester.
Suneet, Joseph *i.m.s.* '94 (AUS) Burlington, TX St. Ann; Burlington, TX St. Michael.
Sungcad, Nemesio '76 (SD) El Cajon, CA Holy Trinity.
Sunghera, Gilbert *s.j.* '02 (DET)[K] Detroit, MI Jesuit Community at the University of Detroit Mercy.
Sunkara, Hrudayaraju '95 (NY) Pearl River, NY St. Aedan.
Sun Kim, Simon Chung '98 (ORG) Education Leave.
Sunnenberg, Scott M. '02 (SPC) Marshfield, MO Holy Trinity; [B] Springfield, MO Springfield Catholic High School.
Suntum, James *s.f.* '84 (SFE) Chimayo, NM Holy Family.
Sunwoo, Richard '09 (LA) Redondo Beach, CA St. Lawrence Martyr.
Su O, Chang '91 (CLV) Korean Catholic Apostolate; Cleveland, OH St. Andrew Kim Pastoral Center.
Supancheck, Norman A. '68 (LA) Sylmar, CA St. Didacus.
Suparno, Ignatius *c.m.* '99 (PH) Indonesian Apostolate; Philadelphia, PA St. Vincent de Paul.
Super, David J. '80 (CR) Diocesan Board of Review for the Protection of Children and Young People; Deans; Fosston, MN St. Mary's; Bagley, MN St. Joseph.
Supnet, Romeo *o.s.a.* '84 (SD) R.J. Donovan Correctional Facility.
Suppa, F. Thomas '78 (E) Union City, PA St. Teresa of Avila.
Supple, Richard *o.carm.* '02 (NEW) Bogota, NJ St. Joseph's.
Suquilvide, Abel '55 (LA) Retired.
Surafka, Michael *o.f.m.* '91 (CLV) Cleveland, OH St. Stanislaus.
Suran, Joaquin '50 (BRK) Corona, NY St. Leo Retired.
Surban, Denis S. '90 (NEW) Clark, NJ St. Agnes.
Suren, Richard H. '53 (STL) St. Louis, MO St. Raphael The Archangel Retired.
Suresh, Rajaian *s.a.c.* '00 (DET) Dryden, MI St. Cornelius; Allenton, MI St. John the Evangelist; Capac, MI St. Nicholas.
Surette, John E. *s.j.* '67 (BO)[U] Boston The Society of Jesus of New England–Provincial Offices.
Surette, John E. *s.j.* '67 (CHI)[C] Chicago, IL Jesuit Community at Loyola University Chicago.
Surges, Robert F. '64 (MIL) St. Francis, WI Sacred Heart of Jesus.
Suriani, Raymond N. '85 (PRO) Westerly, RI St. Pius X; College of Consultors; Council Members.
Suriano, Thomas '64 (MIL) Milwaukee, WI St. Catherine Retired.
Surman, Darrell '62 (YAK) Retired.
Surman, Stanley '56 (SAG) Retired.
Surmeier, William J. '65 (SAL) Gorham, KS St. Mary Help of Christians Parish; Catholic Charities Outreach Office – Hays; Consultors.
Surowiec, Jude *o.f.m.conv.* '75 (NOR) Stafford Springs, CT St. Edward; [A] Cromwell, CT Holy Apostles College and Seminary; Definitors:.
Surprenant, Paul W. '73 (WIN) Byron, MN Christ the King; Byron, MN Holy Family; Priest Assignments Committee.
Surufka, Michael *o.f.m.* '91 (CLV)[N] Cleveland, OH St. Stanislaus Friary; [Y] Cleveland, OH Pulaski Franciscan Community Development Corp.
Survil, Bernard '67 (GBG)[E] Greensburg, PA Clelian Heights School for Exceptional Children; [H] Greensburg, PA Apostles of the Sacred Heart of Jesus.
Surwilo, Rev. Msgr. Edward R. '63 (BGP) Stamford, CT Our Lady Star of the Sea.
Susa, Robert P. '61 (E) Retired.
Susai, Barnabas Maria *i.m.s.* '90 (LR) Scranton, AR SS. Peter and Paul; Scranton, AR St. Ignatius; Scranton, AR St. Meinrad Church.
Susaimanickam, Leon J. '79 (NOR) Dayville, CT St. Joseph.
Susann, Robert F. *m.s.* '73 (ORL) Orlando, FL Blessed Trinity; Airport Ministry, Orlando International Airport.
Susi, Rev. Msgr. Joseph M. '50 (ALX) Archivist and Chancellor; College of Consultors; Appointed Members Retired.
Susin, Angelo J. *c.s.* '38 (PRO) Retired.
Suskey, Robert G. '90 (PH) Chalfont, PA St. Jude.
Susko, Rev. Msgr. Martin S. '61 (Y) Judges Retired.
Suslenko, Mark S. '86 (HRT) Prospect, CT St. Anthony's.
Suslowicz, Michael S. '80 (PIT) Pittsburgh, PA St. Thomas More.
Susnik, Bernardin *o.f.m.* '59 (CHI)[N] Lemont, IL The Slovene Franciscan Fathers, Order of Friars Minor, Commissariat of the Holy Cross.
Suso, Anthony J. '09 (CLV) Akron, OH St. Francis de Sales.
Suss, Thomas J. '73 (SEA) Retired.
Sustarsic, John '52 (DUL) Retired.
Sustayta, Paul A. '91 (LA) Pasadena, CA St. Andrew.
Suszko, Robert K. '02 (NEW) Cedar Grove, NJ St. Catherine of Siena.
Suszynski, Edward F. '08 (CLV) Parma, OH St. Charles Borromeo.
Suszynski, Michael '86 (SP) Tampa, FL Incarnation; College of Consultors.
Sutherland, Raphael (JOL)[K] Darien, IL Carmelite Carefree Retirement Village.
Sutherland, Thomas J. '60 (DET) Retired.
Sutherland, Rev. Msgr. William E. '83 (E) Co Directors.
Sutherland, William E. '83 (E)[P] Edinboro, PA Edinboro University of PA; Edinboro, PA Our Lady of the Lake.
Sutil, Florencio '44 (SJN) On Duty Outside the Archdiocese.
Sutter, Conrad *o.f.m.conv.* '93 (IND)[J] Mount St. Francis, IN Mount Saint Francis Friary and Retreat Center.
Sutter, Conrad *o.f.m.conv.* '93 (L) Norton Hospitals.
Sutter, Raymond A. '73 (CLV) Parma, OH St. Matthias.
Sutton, Alphonsus M. *f.i.* '57 (FR)[G] New Bedford, MA Marian Friary of Our Lady, Queen of the Seraphic Order.
Sutton, Brian F. '06 (WIN) Mapleton, MN St. Teresa's; Mapleton, MN St. Joseph; Mapleton, MN St. Matthew.
Sutton, Douglas B. '02 (WH) Mannington, WV St. Peter's; Mannington, WV St. Patrick's.
Sutton, ST '96 (OLD) Special Assignment; Chancellor; Officialis.
Sutton, Stephen '84 (BAL) Forest Hill, MD St. Ignatius.
Sutton, Thomas E. '73 (SAG) Auburn, MI St. Anthony/St. Joseph.
Suvakkin, Masilamani *h.g.n.* '01 (OWN) Bardwell, KY St. Charles; Bardwell, KY St. Denis.
Suwalsky, David J. *s.j.* '95 (STL) Saint Louis, MO; [O] St. Louis, MO The Jesuits of the Missouri Province; [C] Saint Louis University; [O] St. Louis, MO Bellarmine House of Studies.
Svarczkopf, Rev. Msgr. Mark '74 (IND) Greenwood, IN Our Lady of the Greenwood.
Svetelj, Tone *s.j.* '01 (BO)[U] Newton, MA The Jesuit Community at Boston College.
Svida, Wayne A. '02 (CHI) Chicago Ridge, IL Our Lady of the Ridge; Blue Island, IL St. Benedict.
Svirchuk, Taras *c.ss.r.* '06 (PHU) Newark, NJ St. John the Baptist.
Svirskas, Joseph J. '51 (BO) Senior Priests. Retired.
Svitan, Martin '79 (NY) New York, NY St. John Nepomucene.
Svobodny, Aloysius *o.m.i.* '49 (STP)[N] Buffalo, MN Christ the King Retreat Center.
Swacha, Stanley J. '79 (E) Sharon, PA St. Stanislaus Kostka–Holy Trinity.
Swain, Kenneth J. '72 (ALB) Johnstown, NY Holy Trinity Parish.
Swain, Robert *c.m.* '59 (PH)[Y].
Swalina, Rev. Msgr. Michael F. '70 (SPC) Lebanon, MO St. Francis De Sales; Region III; Defender of the Bond; Holy Childhood Association; Missionary Apostolate; Mission of the Laity; Diocesan Consultors; Presbyteral Council.
Swaner, Rev. Msgr. James J. '61 (PEO) Utica, IL St. Mary.
Swanson, Charles F. '66 (OM) Springfield, NE St. Joseph.
Swanson, Gerald '86 (SD)[H] San Diego, CA Scripps Mercy Hospital.
Swantek, David S. '08 (TR) Middletown, NJ St. Mary.
Swanton, Michael '05 (OM) Omaha, NE St. Wenceslaus.
Swarick, Joachim *o.f.m.* '52 (GB)[J] Green Bay, WI St. Mary of the Angels Friary; [J] Green Bay, WI St. Mary of the Angels Friary; [J] Pulaski, WI Friary.
Swartvagher, Marc E. '96 (BRK)[B] Douglaston, NY Cathedral Seminary Residence of the Immaculate Conception; Howard Beach, NY Our Lady of Grace; Graduate Studies.
Swartz, Michael R. '87 (BUF) Absent on Leave.
Sweany, Thomas M. '80 (CLV) Chesterland, OH St. Anselm.
Swearingen, Eric '87 (FRS) Fresno, CA Holy Spirit.
Sweeney, Callistus *o.f.m.* '53 (FgM) New York, NY Holy Name Province.
Sweeney, D. Gilbert *s.j.* '54 (ALN)[A] Wernersville, PA Jesuit Center–Jesuit Community.
Sweeney, Daniel *s.j.* '94 (MO) Air Force Reserve Chaplains.
Sweeney, Denis '58 (GBG) Retired.
Sweeney, E. Daniel '82 (PIT) Munhall, PA St. Therese of Lisieux; Homestead, PA St. Maximilian Kolbe.
Sweeney, Edward '88 (AMA) Retired.
Sweeney, Ernest S. *s.j.* '63 (LA)[C] Los Angeles, CA Jesuit Community.
Sweeney, Eugene *s.m.* '78 (STL)[O] St. Louis, MO Marianist Community; [O] Eureka, MO Marycliff Marianist Community; [S] Eureka, MO Marianist Retreat & Conference Center Retired.
Sweeney, Francis M. *c.s.p.* '61 (NY)[EE] New York, NY Paulist Fathers' Motherhouse Retired.
Sweeney, Frank M. *c.s.p.* '61 (NY)[EE] Jamaica Estates Paulist Fathers Generalate.
Sweeney, Frederick E. '52 (BO) Senior Priests. Retired.
Sweeney, James H. '81 (BRK) Brooklyn, NY Our Lady of the Presentation–Our Lady of Loreto; Brooklyn, NY Holy Name; Ozone Park, NY Nativity of the Blessed Virgin Mary.
Sweeney, John Maria *f.p.o.* '98 (BO)[U] Lawrence, MA Franciscans of Primitive Observance.
Sweeney, John P. '73 (PIT) Charismatic Prayer Groups; Glenshaw, PA St. Bonaventure.
Sweeney, John T. '70 (GBG) West Newton, PA Holy Family.
Sweeney, Joseph J. '61 (PH) Retired.
Sweeney, Kevin J. '97 (BRK) Brooklyn, NY St. Michael; Vocations, Office of.
Sweeney, Kevin '94 (MO) Military Chaplains; Navy Chaplains; On Duty Outside the Diocese.
Sweeney, Rev. Msgr. Lawrence P. '54 (SLC) Retired.
Sweeney, Luke M. '01 (NY)[A] Yonkers, NY Cathedral Prep Program; [A] Yonkers, NY St. John Neumann

Seminary College At St. Joseph's Seminary Dunwoodie; [A] Yonkers, NY St. Joseph's Seminary.
Sweeney, Michael '79 (KNX) Harriman, TN Blessed Sacrament; Lancing, TN St. Ann; Deans of the Diocese; Presbyteral Council; Ministries of the Cumberland Mtn. Deanery.
Sweeney, Michael *o.p.* '79 (OAK)[A] Berkeley, CA Dominican School of Philosophy and Theology; Berkeley, CA St. Mary Magdalen.
Sweeney, Rev. Msgr. Patrick E. '72 (PH) Collegeville, PA St. Eleanor; [BB] Collegeville, PA Ursinus College.
Sweeney, Peter T. '61 (WDC) Damascus, MD St. Paul; Silver Spring, MD Our Lady of Grace.
Sweeney, Richard R. '86 (TR) Retired.
Sweeney, Robert J. '82 (NY) Greenwood Lake, NY Holy Rosary.
Sweeney, Rev. Msgr. Robert J. '69 (RCK) Pecatonica, IL St. Mary; Secretary for Administrative Processes; Propagation of the Faith; Special Assignment.
Sweeney, Timothy *o.s.b.* '61 (IND)[K] St. Meinrad, IN St. Meinrad Archabbey; [A] St. Meinrad, IN Saint Meinrad School of Theology.
Sweeney, William F. '81 (BRK)[H] Fresh Meadows, NY St. Francis Preparatory School.
Sweeney, William F. *s.s.c.* (BO) Readville, MA St. Anne.
Sweeney, William F. *s.s.c.* '75 (PRO)[P] Bristol, RI St. Columban's Retirement House.
Sweeney, William *s.s.c.* '75 (OM)[K] St. Columbans Missionary Society of St. Columban.
Sweeney, William '81 (BRK) Oakland Gardens, NY American Martyrs.
Sweeny, Daniel *s.j.* '94 (SCR)[C] Scranton, PA The University of Scranton.
Sweeny, Rev. Msgr. Edward A. '57 (RVC) Long Beach, NY St. Ignatius Martyr.
Sweet, Daniel J. '01 (PRO) Providence, RI St. Anthony; [C] Pawtucket, RI St. Raphael Academy.
Sweetser, Thomas P. *s.j.* '70 (MIL)[P] Milwaukee, WI Arrupe House Jesuit Community; Milwaukee, WI The Parish Evaluation Project.
Sweitzer, Raymond M. *s.j.* '75 (NY)[F] Bronx, NY Fordham Preparatory School; [EE] Jesuit Community, Kohlmann Hall.
Swencki, John T. '79 (BO) Whitman, MA Holy Ghost.
Swengros, William J. '91 (SP) Valrico, FL St. Stephen; Judges.
Swenson, Rev. Msgr. Roger A. '70 (NO) Metairie, LA St. Catherine of Siena; Priests for Life.
Swetland, Rev. Msgr. Stuart W. '91 (PEO) On Duty Outside the Diocese.
Swetland, Rev. Msgr. Stuart W. '91 (BAL)[A] Emmitsburg, MD Mount St. Mary's Seminary.
Swetnam, James H. *s.j.* '58 (FgM) St. Louis, MO Society of Jesus.
Swett, Charles J. '57 (TLS) Retired.
Swett, Rev. Msgr. Ronald J. '67 (FRS) Bakersfield, CA St. Philip the Apostle.
Swiader, Rev. Msgr. James P. '75 (RVC)[A] Huntington, NY Diocesan Seminary of the Immaculate Conception; Priestly Life and Ministry; Priests' Personnel Policy Board.
Swiat, James R. '67 (LAN) Retired.
Swiatocha, Bruno '56 (RVC) Retired.
Swichtenberg, William D. '83 (GB) Algoma, WI St. Mary; Kewaunee, WI Holy Rosary.
Swickard, John L. '74 (COL) Grove City, OH Our Lady of Perpetual Help.
Swiderski, Jan '94 (NOR) Killingworth, CT St. Lawrence; Higganum, CT St. Peter.
Swiderski, Stan '63 (LR) Mountain Home, AR St. Peter the Fisherman; Mountain View, AR St. Mary Church.
Swiercz, Pawel A. '94 (FR) Awaiting Assignment; [G] Fall River, MA Priests' Hostel.
Swierczynski, Joseph E. '64 (PIT) Pittsburgh, PA Immaculate Heart of Mary.
Swierz, Michael '85 (Y) Campbell, OH St. Elizabeth; Campbell, OH St. Joseph the Provider.
Swierzbiolek, Waclaw *s.d.b.* '62 (NY)[GG] Stony Point, NY Marian Shrine; [GG] Stony Point, NY Don Bosco Retreat Center and Marian Shrine.
Swierzowski, Stanislaus J. '56 (ALB) Retired.
Swietochowski, Andrew '78 (SFS) Mitchell, SD Holy Spirit; Personnel Board.
Swift, Bruce *o.s.b.* '60 (KCK)[I] Atchison, KS St. Benedict's Abbey.
Swift, Daniel F. '89 (TR) Holmdel, NJ St. Benedict.
Swift, James E. *c.m.* '78 (STL)[O] St. Louis, MO Lazarist Residence.
Swift, William J. '44 (TLS) Tulsa, OK Church of St. Mary.
Swift, William V. '44 (TLS) Retired.
Swing, R. John '70 (LC) Nekoosa, WI Sacred Heart of Jesus; Port Edwards, WI St. Alexander; [L] Port Edwards, WI St. Alexander's Church, Port Edwards Endowment Trust; Deans.
Swink, Lawrence '06 (WDC)[W] Bowie, MD Sodality Union; Bowie, MD St. Pius X.
Swirczynski, Gary *o.f.m.* '87 (OAK)[M] Oakland Franciscan Friars (Province of St. Barbara).
Swirski, Thaddeus M. '54 (CLV) Retired.
Swisshelm, Germain *o.s.b.* '60 (IND)[K] St. Meinrad, IN St. Meinrad Archabbey.
Swistovich, John '98 (FWT) Wichita Falls, TX Our Lady Queen of Peace; Deans.
Switanowski, Robert Joseph *o.f.m.conv.* '90 (MIL) Definitors:; [A] St. Francis, WI Saint Francis de Sales Seminary.
Swoger, Rev. Msgr. John W. '63 (E) Oil City, PA St. Joseph; Western Vicariate; College of Consultors; Finance Council; Administrative Cabinet; Oil City, PA Assumption of the Blessed Virgin Mary.
Swope, John W. *s.j.* '86 (BAL)[D] Baltimore, MD Cristo Rey Jesuit High School.
Swope, Mark G. '90 (PH)[Z] Huntingdon Valley, PA Sisters of the Holy Redeemer Provincialate; On Special or Other Archdiocesan Assignment.
Swope, Rev. Msgr. Timothy J. '66 (ALT) Prince Gallitzin Deanery; Ongoing Formation of the Clergy; Loretto, PA Basilica of St. Michael the Archangel; [K] Loretto, PA Office of Ongoing Formation of Clergy.
Sybertz, Donald F. *m.m.* '55 (FgM) Maryknoll, NY MARYKNOLL.
Sybirnyy, Volodymyr '04 (STF) Liturgical Commission.
Sydorovych, Roman '05 (STF) Rochester, NY Epiphany of Our Lord.
Sykora, Paul M. *m.m.* '76 (FgM) Maryknoll, NY MARYKNOLL.
Sylva, Eugene R. (PAT) Office of the Permanent Diaconate.
Sylva, Geno (PAT) Secretariat for Evangelization; Evangelization; [H] Madison, NJ St. Paul Inside The Walls: The Catholic Center for Evangelization at Bayley–Ellard; Morristown, NJ Assumption of the Blessed Virgin Mary.
Sylvain, Daniel *s.a.* '01 (NY)[EE] Garrison, NY St. Christopher's Friary; [EE] Garrison, NY Franciscan Friars of the Atonement.
Sylvester, Emmanuel '88 (CR) Warren, MN SS. Peter and Paul.
Sylvester, Sean '99 (DET) Absent on Leave.
Sylvia, Albert A. '66 (BO) EnCourage.
Sylvia, William M. '08 (FR) Mansfield, MA St. Mary's.
Symolon, Lawrence S. '75 (HRT) Consultors – Canon 1742; Guilford, CT St. George.
Synek, Roger A. '98 (BIS) Parshall, ND St. Bridget; Parshall, ND St. Elizabeth; Parshall, ND Sacred Heart.
Sypek, Rev. Msgr. Stanislaus T. '43 (BO) Hyde Park, MA St. Adalbert.
Syracuse, Ross *o.f.m.conv.* '78 (BAL) Baltimore, MD St. Casimir.
Sys, Joseph *m.afr.* '41 (SP)[N] St. Petersburg, FL Missionaries of Africa.
Syslo, Alan M. *c.s.v.* '66 (CHI)[N] Arlington Heights Viatorian Province Center–Clerics of St. Viator.
Syverson, David '99 (FAR) Carrington, ND Sacred Heart Church of Carrington; Sykeston, ND St. Elizabeth's Church of Skyeston.
Syverstad, Daniel *o.p.* '82 (SEA) Seattle, WA Blessed Sacrament.
Szabelski, Joseph R. '70 (CHI) Other Assignments Retired.
Szabo, Ferenc *s.j.* '62 (ATH) "Tavlatok".
Szabo, Marcel '71 (PSC) Passaic, NJ St. Michael Cathedral; Northern New Jersey Protopresbyterate.
Szada, John A. '78 (HBG) Hanover, PA St. Vincent; World Apostolate of Fatima.
Szakaly, Anthony V. *c.s.c.* '92 (FTW)[H] Notre Dame, IN Congregation of Holy Cross, Indiana Province, Provincial House; Notre Dame, IN; Austin, TX.
Szal, George L. *s.m.* '75 (BO) Revere, MA Immaculate Conception.
Szal, George *s.m.* '75 (BO) Trustees.
Szal, Ignatius J. '44 (PH) Retired.
Szamocki, Piotr '91 (CAM) Waterford, NJ St. Anthony's Church, Waterford, N.J.
Szanto, Hubert S. *o.praem.* '48 (ORG)[D] Silverado, CA St. Michael's Preparatory School; [I] Silverado, CA Norbertine Fathers of Orange Inc.
Szantyr, Eugene R. '78 (BGP) Bridgeport, CT St. Andrew.
Szanyi, Mark *o.f.m.conv.* '78 (PMB) Port St. Lucie, FL St. Lucie.
Szarek, Eugene *c.r.* '67 (CHI) Chicago, IL St. Hedwig.
Szarek, Mitchell '57 (DET) Detroit, MI SS. Peter and Paul.
Szarek, Mitchell '54 (DET) Retired.
Szarnicki, Henry A. '55 (PIT)[M] Pittsburgh, PA St. John Vianney Manor Retired.
Szaroleta, Rev. Msgr. Andrew L. '77 (MET) Edison, NJ Our Lady of Peace.
Szarwark, Stanley *c.i.c.m.* '64 (FgM) Arlington, VA MISSIONHURST.
Szatkowski, David *s.c.j.* '02 (MIL)[P] Hales Corners Priests of the Sacred Heart.
Szcurek, Victor S. *o.praem.* '00 (ORG)[I] Silverado, CA Norbertine Fathers of Orange Inc.
Szczapa, Stanley J. '71 (NOR) Bolton, CT St. Maurice; Vernon, CT Sacred Heart.
Szczechowski, Glen '05 (CHY) June Priests' Retreat; Powell, WY St. Barbara; [F] Powell, WY NorthWest College; College of Consultors.
Szczepanik, John '88 (MET) South River, NJ St. Stephen Protomartyr.
Szczepankiewicz, Gary J. '75 (BUF) Buffalo, NY St. Casimir; Buffalo, NY St. Bernard.
Szczesnawicz, Andrzej (COS) Colorado Springs, CO Saint Paul.
Szczesniak, Harry F. '72 (BUF) Buffalo, NY Our Lady of Czestochowa.
Szczesny, John S. '75 (GBG) Youngwood, PA Holy Cross.
Szczesny, Walter J. '90 (BUF) Vocations; [A] East Aurora, NY Christ the King Seminary.
Szczotka, Krzysztof *s.d.s.* '88 (NEW) Elizabeth, NJ Saint Adalbert and Saints Peter & Paul.
Szczykutowicz, Rev. Msgr. Francis S. '58 (PT) Sunny Hills, FL St. Theresa; Propagation of the Faith, Office of; Members Elected by Deanery; Priest Personnel Board.
Szczypula, Marcin '08 (CHI) Lemont, IL SS. Cyril and Methodius.
Szebenyi, Andrew L. *s.j.* '61 (SY)[Q] Syracuse, NY Jesuits at LeMoyne, Inc.
Szekula, Augustin *o.mech.* '44 (OLN) Tujunga, CA Mekhitarist School.
Szeman, Stephen J. '53 (SEA) Retired.
Szemborski, Chester *s.d.b.* '50 (NY)[GG] Stony Point, NY Don Bosco Retreat Center and Marian Shrine; [GG] Stony Point, NY Marian Shrine.
Szendrey, J. Edward *m.m.* '62 (NY)[EE] Maryknoll, NY Maryknoll Fathers and Brothers Charitable Trust; [EE] Maryknoll Maryknoll Fathers and Brothers.
Szewczyk, Grzegorz *s.d.s.* '91 (SAT) Poth, TX Blessed Sacrament; [L] Falls City, TX Salvatorian Fathers Community of Texas.
Szews, George R. '78 (LC) Eau Claire, WI Newman Community; [K] Eau Claire, WI Newman Parish.
Szinos, Charles '99 (NY)[A] Yonkers, NY St. Joseph's Seminary.
Szippl, Richard *s.v.d.* '81 (FgM) Techny, IL.
Szklarski, Joseph '62 (NEW) Lyndhurst, NJ St. Michael's.
Szkredka, Slawomir '02 (LA) Graduate Studies.
Szlezak, Emeric *o.f.m.* '44 (SP)[N] St. Petersburg St. Anthony Friary Retired.
Szlezak, Emeric (BGP) Retired.
Szmyd, John S. '96 (CHI)[A] Mundelein, IL University of St. Mary of the Lake/Mundelein Seminary.
Szobonya, James *c.ss.r* '06 (RVC) Bethpage, NY St. Martin of Tours.
Szolack, Joseph T. '88 (CAM) Representatives by Deaneries; Elected Members.
Szolack, Joseph T. '88 (CAM) Vocation Advisory Board.
Szopa, Daniel F. '76 (MAN) Absent on Sick Leave; Concord Hospital.
Szorc, Andrzej *c.ss.r.* '86 (STV) Christiansted, VI Church of the Holy Cross.
Szparagowski, George J. '02 (PH) Blue Bell, PA St. Helena.
Szpiech, Edward P. '67 (NEW) Garfield, NJ St. Stanislaus Kostka.
Szpieg, Edmund L. '94 (PMB) Port St. Lucie, FL St. Elizabeth Ann Seton.
Szpilski, Joseph *c.m.* '56 (BRK) Brooklyn, NY St. Stanislaus Kostka.
Sztandera, Tomasz '99 (CHI) Chicago, IL St. Ferdinand.
Sztorc, Richard E. '69 (CHI) Evanston, IL St. Athanasius.
Sztuber, Tomasz '86 (NOR) Norwich, CT St. Joseph.
Szudarek, Ronald J. '81 (CLV) Retired.
Szudera, Ted F. '77 (GF) Belt, MT St. Mark the Evangelist; Diocesan Consultors; Priests' Council.
Szufel, Adam '64 (SAV) Retired.
Szufel, Adam *o.f.m.* '64 (GB)[J] Wausaukee, WI Villa Alverna.
Szukalski, John *s.v.d.* '97 (WDC)[N] Washington, DC Divine Word House.
Szulwach, Joseph '87 (MET) South River, NJ St. Mary of Ostrabrama Retired.
Szumilo, Julian *c.m.* '50 (HRT)[L] Manchester DePaul Provincial Residence.
Szupa, Joseph '92 (PHU) Elizabeth, NJ St. Vladimir's; Procurator/Advocate; Protopresbyters (Deans); Presbyteral Council; College of Archeparchial Consultors.
Szupper, Rev. Msgr. Michael F. '57 (WIL) Retired.
Szura, John *o.s.a.* '66 (CHI)[N] Chicago, IL St. John Stone Friary.
Szura, Thomas *c.m.m.* '78 (DET)[K] Vocation Office.
Szurek, Pawel F. '05 (PAT) Clifton, NJ St. Philip the Apostle; Priestly Life Committee.
Szuster, Jacek '01 (SAV) Thomasville, GA St. Augustine; Albany Deanery.
Szwach, Joseph F. '55 (WOR) Dudley, MA St. Andrew Bobola; Diocesan College of Consultors.
Szybka, Joseph P. '83 (TOL) Tiffin, OH St. Joseph; Precious Blood of Jesus Deanery.
Szybka, Stanley '80 (TOL) Plymouth, OH St. Joseph; Willard, OH St. Francis Xavier.
Szyda, Arkadiusz '99 (SAT) San Antonio, TX Holy Name.

Szydlik, Thomas '03 (PEO) Nauvoo, IL SS. Peter and Paul; Nauvoo, IL Immaculate Conception.
Szydlowski, Joel F. *o.f.m.* '67 (TR) St. Francis Medical Center; [J] Schools for Nurses.
Szydlowski, Joel *o.f.m.* '67 (GB)[G] Manitowoc, WI Holy Family Memorial, Inc.
Szydlowski, Robert L. '62 (STL) Hazelwood, MO St. Martin de Porres.
Szylar, Jan *c.m.* '94 (BRK) Brooklyn, NY St. Stanislaus Kostka.
Szymakowski, Andrew *f.s.s.p.* '04 (BAK) Nyssa, OR St. Bridget of Kildare.
Szymanski, Edward S. '99 (BAL) Special Assignment; Ellicott City, MD Resurrection.
Szymanski, Rev. Msgr. John B. '57 (MET)[I] Somerset, NJ Maria Regina Residence; Vicars General Retired.
Szymaszek, Leszek P. '97 (BGP) Stamford, CT St. Leo.

T

Ta, Binh T. *c.ss.r.* (GAL)[R] Houston, TX Rice University/ Texas Medical Center Schools; Catholic Student Center.
Tabak, Thaddeus *s.d.s.* '77 (SAT) San Antonio, TX Our Lady of Sorrows; [L] Falls City, TX Salvatorian Fathers Community of Texas.
Tabalanza, Celso *c.i.c.m.* '96 (BWN) Mercedes, TX Sacred Heart Church.
Tabbert, Robert D. '79 (VEN) Fort Myers, FL Blessed Pope John XXIII; Presbyteral Council.
Taberski, Richard M. '64 (HRT) Goshen, CT St. Thomas of Villanova.
Tabigue, Joseph *c.r.s.p.* '05 (SD) San Diego, CA Our Lady of the Rosary.
Tabios, Walter '82 (SAC) Placerville, CA St. Patrick's.
Tabo, Virgilio "Jojo" '05 (TUC) Tucson, AZ Our Mother of Sorrows Roman Catholic Parish – Tucson.
Tabon, Raymond *o.s.j.* '60 (SCR) Pittston, PA St. Anthony of Padua.
Tabone, Marcel M. '85 (CAM) On Leave of Absence.
Tabor, Stanley '84 (JOL) Naperville, IL Edward Hospital.
Tabujara, Oscar '75 (SJ) Mountain View, CA St. Athanasius.
Tacastacas, Rene C. *s.j.* '99 (STL)[O] St. Louis, MO Jesuit Community Corporation at Saint Louis University – Jesuit Hall.
Tacay, Archie *c.i.c.m.* (SAT) San Antonio, TX St. James the Apostle.
Tacelli, Ronald K. *s.j.* '82 (BO)[U] Newton, MA The Jesuit Community at Boston College.
Tachias, Alfred A. '59 (GLP)[D] Gallup, NM Villa Guadalupe Home for the Aged Retired.
Tack, Theodore E. *o.s.a.* '53 (TLS)[B] Tulsa, OK Cascia Hall Preparatory School.
Tackney, John P. '74 (BO) Cambridge, MA Sacred Heart; Elected.
Taddy, Jerome J. '60 (GB) Retired.
Tadena, Arnold '89 (SD) San Diego, CA St. Charles.
Tadeo, Abran R. '00 (TUC) Marana, AZ Saint Christopher Roman Catholic Parish – Marana.
Tadeo, Victor C. '71 (MO) Army Chaplains.
Tadla, Casmir T. *c.r.* '48 (SB)[I] Fontana, CA Congregation of the Resurrection, CR; Fontana, CA Blessed John XXIII Catholic Community, Inc. Retired.
Tadyszak, Leonard *s.c.j.* '51 (SP)[N] Pinellas Park, FL Priests of the Sacred Heart Retired.
Tae, Jinu Andrew (TUC) Korean Catholic Community.
Taft, Robert F. *s.j.* '63 (BO)[U] Boston The Society of Jesus of New England–Provincial Offices.
Taft, Robert F. (FTW)[B] University of Notre Dame Du Lac.
Tagg, Joseph L. '88 (MEM) Defenders of the Bond; Promoter of Justice.
Taggart, Bruce *o.carm.* '97 (JOL)[L] Darien Carmelite Provincial Office.
Taggart, Frederick H. *o.s.a.* '65 (LAN) Flint, MI St. Matthew; College of Consultors.
Taggart, James E. *o.m.i.* '85 (BO) Lowell, MA St. Patrick.
Taglianetti, Bernard J. '05 (PH) Yardley, PA St. Ignatius of Antioch.
Tah, Philip P. '96 (NY) Hartsdale, NY Sacred Heart.
Taheny, Mark V. '95 (SFR) Kentfield, CA St. Sebastian.
Taheny, Robert R. *s.j.* '59 (SJ)[M] Los Gatos, CA Sacred Heart Jesuit Center.
Taheny, Theodore T. *s.j.* '56 (SJ)[M] Los Gatos, CA Sacred Heart Jesuit Center.
Tai, John Busco Pham V. *c.m.c.* '94 (STP) Minneapolis, MN Church of St. Anne – St. Joseph Hien.
Taillon, Marcel L. '94 (PRO) Narragansett, RI St. Thomas More; Ongoing Formation of Priests.
Tajak, Ralph *o.s.b.* '94 (PIT) Pittsburgh, PA St. Peter; [P] Pittsburgh, PA Community College of Allegheny County – Northside Campus.
Tajonera, R. Joyalito F. *m.m.* '02 (FgM) Maryknoll, NY MARYKNOLL.
Takoudjou, Rodrigue *s.j.* '06 (WDC)[N] Washington, DC The Jesuit Community at Georgetown University.
Takuski, Walter J. '95 (CHI) Bartlett, IL St. Peter Damian.
Talafous, Don *o.s.b.* '52 (SCL)[I] Collegeville, MN St. John's Abbey, of the Order of St. Benedict.
Talaisis, Bernardas *o.f.m.* '52 (SP)[N] St. Pete Beach, FL Franciscan Friary; St. Pete Beach, FL St. Casimir Lithuanian Mission.
Talamo, John '98 (NO) Mandeville, LA Our Lady of the Lake Roman Catholic Church.
Talar, Charles J. '79 (GAL) Houston, TX St. John Vianney.
Talar, Charles J.T. '79 (BGP) On Duty Outside the Diocese.
Talarico, Anthony M. '70 (CHI) South Holland, IL Holy Ghost.
Talarico, Matthew L. '07 (CHI) Chicago, IL; [N] Chicago, IL Institute of Christ the King Sovereign Priest.
Talaska, Richard J. '68 (MIL) Retired.
Talavera, Carlos '96 (HT) Houma, LA St. Louis.
Talbot, Christopher '04 (DET) Ray Township, MI St. Francis of Assisi–St. Maximilian Kolbe.
Talbot, James F. *s.j.* '68 (BO)[U] Weston, MA Campion Jesuit Community.
Talbot, Ralph W. '04 (STP) Mahtomedi, MN St. Jude of the Lake.
Talbot, Ralph '04 (STP) Rush City, MN Sacred Heart; Deanery 1; College of Consultors.
Talbott, Ronald *o.f.m.cap.* '81 (LA)[B] Santa Ynez, CA San Lorenzo Seminary – Retreat Center.
Talcott, Peter '75 (SR) Unassigned.
Talentino, William *o.f.m.cap.* '67 (FgM) Pittsburgh, PA Province of St. Augustine.
Talesfore, John J. '89 (SFR) San Francisco, CA Cathedral of St. Mary (Assumption); Deans.
Taliercio, Pasquale *m.s.a.* '92 (NOR)[G] Cromwell, CT Society of the Missionaries of the Holy Apostles.
Talkin, Ralph *s.j.* '57 (DEN)[J] Denver, CO Little Sisters of the Poor.
Tallarida, Thomas C. *c.s.c.* '51 (FTW)[B] University of Notre Dame Du Lac; [H] Notre Dame, IN Holy Cross Community, Corby Hall, University of Notre Dame.
Talley, Charles *o.f.m.* '99 (SD) Oceanside, CA Mission San Luis Rey.
Talley, Rev. Msgr. David P. '71 (ATL) Lilburn, GA St. John Neumann.
Tallman, Gilmary *o.f.m.cap.* '60 (SAL) Hays, KS St. Joseph Parish; [D] Hays, KS St. Joseph's Friary.
Tallman, John '88 (ALB) Albany, NY Parish of Mater Christi; St. Peter's Hospital; Special Assignment; [H] Albany, NY St. Peter's Hospital of the City of Albany.
Tallman, Stephen '59 (HEL) Retired.
Talocci, Peter '86 (PH) Malvern, PA St. Patrick.
Tam, Francis P. '87 (TR) Howell, NJ St. William the Abbot; Keyport, NJ St. Joseph.
Tam, Thomas '50 (STP) St. Paul, MN St. Adalbert.
Tamara, Eder '90 (NY) Harriman, NY St. Anastasia.
Tamayo, Alberto W. '07 (TR) Bayville, NJ St. Barnabas.
Tamayo, Alfredo L. '77 (SAC) Elk Grove, CA Good Shepherd Catholic Church.
Tamayo, Dante '93 (OAK) El Cerrito, CA St. Jerome.
Tamayo, Rev. Msgr. Elias '72 (PAT) Sabbatical.
Tambornino, James M. *s.o.l.t.* '91 (MIL)[R] Slinger, WI Carmelite Hermit of the Trinity – CHT.
Tambornino, James *s.o.l.t.* '91 (CC)[G] Robstown, TX Society of Our Lady of the Most Holy Trinity.
Tamburello, Dennis *o.f.m.* '80 (ALB)[B] Siena College.
Tamburrini, Joseph '64 (Y) Retired.
Tamburro, Francis J. '74 (HBG) Berwick, PA Immaculate Conception of the Blessed Virgin Mary; Deans.
Tamburro, Joseph '99 (SJP) Northern Cambria, PA Immaculate Conception; Examiners of Clergy; Priests' Continuing Education; Presbyteral Council; Presbyters.
Tamez, Benito '02 (DAL) Dallas, TX Baylor University Medical Center.
Tamiian, Calin '02 (ROM) Sherman Oaks, CA St. Mary Romanian Catholic Mission.
Tamminga, Robert G. '71 (TUC) Tucson, AZ Saint Francis de Sales Roman Catholic Parish – Tucson.
Tamoro, Briccio *s.v.d.* '72 (SB)[I] Riverside, CA Divine Word Seminary.
Tampe, Luis A. *s.j.* '02 (BO)[U] Boston The Society of Jesus of New England–Provincial Offices.
Tampe, Luis A. *s.j.* '02 (BAL)[B] Jesuit Community of Loyola University, Inc.; [S] Baltimore, MD Jesuit Community of Loyola University, Inc.
Tamulis, John J. '40 (GAY) Retired.
Tanck, Norman C. *c.s.b.* '74 (ROC) Rochester, NY Christ the King; Rochester, NY St. Salome; Rochester, NY St. Thomas the Apostle.
Tancredi, Carl T. '67 (HBG) York, PA St. Rose of Lima; [I] York, PA Penn State University, York Campus; [I] York, PA York College.
Tancrell, William Luke *o.p.* '59 (COL) Somerset, OH Holy Trinity; Somerset, OH St. Joseph's.
Tandoh, Francis *c.s.sp.* '93 (CIN) Dayton, OH St. Benedict the Moor; Germantown, OH St. Augustine; Dayton, OH St. Mary; Dayton, OH Holy Family; Dayton, OH St. Mary's.
Taneo, Teodulo G. *s.v.d.* '89 (YAK) Richland, WA Christ the King.
Tang, George Donkor '87 (CAM) Cherry Hill, NJ The Church of St. Thomas More, Cherry Hill, New Jersey.
Tang, Michael '90 (LA) Hawthorne, CA St. Joseph.
Tangorra, Philip–Michael '09 (PAT) Graduate Studies.
Tanguay, Andre *o.m.i.* '53 (BO)[U] Lowell, MA Missionary Oblates of Mary Immaculate Retired.
Tanguay, William H. '69 (PRO) Retired.
Tanilong, Rev. Msgr. Gerardo J. '62 (ORG) Retired.
Tank, Rev. Msgr. Thomas '67 (KCK) Overland Park, KS Church of the Ascension; Archdiocesan Consultors.
Tanon, Carmelo Soto '89 (SJN) Guaynabo, PR Maria Madre de la Misericordia.
Tanto, Henry '07 (NY)[FF] Warwick, NY Mt. Alverno Center, Bon Secours Charity Health System Retired.
Tanto, Henry (PAT)[K] Denville, NJ Saint Clare's Hospital, Inc.; Dover, NJ Dover General Hospital.
Tanu, Emanuel *s.v.d.* (LKC) Lake Charles, LA St. Margaret; Iowa, LA St. Raphael.
Tanzini, Paolo '08 (NEW) Linden, NJ St. John the Apostle.
Taormina, Rev. Msgr. Andrew C. '62 (NO) Metairie, LA St. Francis Xavier; Judges; Deans; Serra Club of Downtown New Orleans; Strategic Planning Coordinating Committee.
Taosan, Yohanes K. '96 (GAL)[S] Houston, TX The Catholic Chaplain Corps.
Tape, Bernard '00 (SAC) Fort Jones, CA Sacred Heart; Rancho Cordova, CA St. John Vianney.
Tapel, Rene '84 (RVC) Ronkonkoma, NY St. Joseph's.
Tapella, Joseph '78 (JOL) Joliet, IL The Cathedral of St. Raymond; Vicar General; Moderator of the Curia; Judicial Vicar; Judges.
Taphorn, Joseph C. '97 (OM) Chancellor; Judges; Finance Council; Censor Librorum; Archbishop's Appointees; Omaha, NE St. Margaret Mary.
Tapia, Gilberto Mora '88 (SEA) Tacoma, WA St. Ann; Tacoma, WA St. John of the Woods; Tacoma, WA Holy Rosary; Tacoma, WA St. Joseph; Tacoma, WA Sacred Heart; Tacoma, WA Visitation.
Tapia, Ignacio '04 (BWN)[A] Mission, TX The Saint Joseph and Saint Peter Seminary.
Tapia, Ignacio '04 (BWN) Parish Priests Consultors and Priests' Personnel Board.
Taponi, Selwan Sulaiman '94 (STA) Jacksonville, FL St. Ephrem Syriac Antiochian Catholic Church.
Tapp, John '84 (SP) St. Petersburg, FL Holy Family; College of Consultors; Worship, Office of; Executive Committee; Elected Pastors.
Tappe, Walter J. '85 (WDC) Greenbelt, MD Saint Hugh of Grenoble.
Tapper, John W. '61 (CHI) Retired.
Tarabay, Paul *o.m.m.* '06 (OLL)[A] Ann Arbor, MI Maronite Order of the Blessed Virgin Mary; Ann Arbor, MI.
Taran, Peter '60 (NY)[EE] Garrison, NY Franciscan Friars of the Atonement.
Tarantino, James T. '81 (SFR) Tiburon, CA St. Hilary; [S] Tiburon, CA Charismatic Movement; College of Consultors.
Tarantino, John F. '78 (PAT) Pequannock, NJ Holy Spirit.
Taranto, James '81 (KC) Independence, MO St. Mark; Deans.
Tarasi, Carlo D. '72 (CHL) Unassigned.
Taras Miles, Michael '70 (STN) Belfield, ND St. John the Baptist; Belfield, ND St. Demetrius.
Tarazona, Ramiro '08 (AUS) Temple, TX St. Matthew; Temple, TX Our Lady of Guadalupe Catholic Church – Temple, Texas.
Tardiff, Edward *c.ss.r.* '42 (ALB)[L] Saratoga Springs, NY St. John Neumann Residence.
Targonski, Conrad A. *o.f.m.* '75 (MO) Navy Chaplains.
Targonski, George '02 (MET) Edison, NJ St. Matthew the Apostle.
Tarlizzo, David *o.m.i.* '68 (SAT)[L] San Antonio, TX Oblate Benson Residence (Southwest Area).
Tarlton, Allen *o.s.b.* '55 (SCL)[I] Collegeville, MN St. John's Abbey, of the Order of St. Benedict.
Tarnawski, Wiktor '81 (ARE) Ciales, PR N.S. Madre del Redentor.
Tarrant, Rev. Msgr. Edward L. '50 (RVC) Hicksville, NY St. Ignatius Loyola; Mineola, NY Corpus Christi Retired.
Tarrant, Patrick J. '53 (GF) Retired.
Tarrillion, Joseph A. *s.m.* '66 (SAT)[K] San Antonio, TX Marianist Residence: Skilled Nursing.
Tarro, Michael *c.s.* '58 (PRO) Johnston, RI St. Rocco Retired.
Tarsio, Anastarsio '99 (NY) New York, NY St. Agnes.
Tartaglia, Paul '58 (ALB) Retired.
Tartaglia, Richard V. '72 (PAT) Denville, NJ St. Mary's.
Tasca, Marco *o.f.m.conv.* '83 (IND)[K] Curia Generalizia.
Tasch, Hugh *o.s.b.* '48 (KC)[J] Conception, MO Conception Abbey; [K] Savannah, MO Sisters of St. Francis Provincial House.
Taschetta, Anthony '71 (JOL) Elmhurst, IL Mary, Queen of Heaven.
Tash, Rev. Msgr. Joseph T. '62 (AMA) Advocates; Presbyteral Council; Priests' Pension Plan Retirement Committee; Amarillo, TX St. Thomas the Apostle; College of Consultors.
Tasler, Mark A. '90 (LIN) York, NE St. Joseph's;

Lincoln, NE Nebraska Penal Complex.
Tassone, Salvatore A. *s.j.* '63 (SJ)[B] Santa Clara, CA Jesuit Community.
Tassone, Thomas W. '08 (RVC) Williston Park, NY St. Aidan's Church.
Taste, Frank A. *c.s.c.* '60 (ORL)[F] Cocoa Beach, FL Congregation of Holy Cross, Eastern Province.
Tasto, Harold J. '68 (STP) Minneapolis, MN St. Thomas the Apostle.
Tasto, John P. *o.s.a.* '67 (FgM)[N] Olympia Fields, IL Tolentine Monastery at Tolentine Center; Olympia Fields, IL Province of Our Mother of Good Counsel (Midwestern).
Tatarczuk, Rev. Msgr. Vincent A. '49 (PRT) Diocesan Consultors Retired.
Tate, Joseph *c.s.c.* '81 (FR)[G] North Dartmouth, MA Holy Cross Residence Retired.
Tatel, Orlando G. '65 (STP) Jordan, MN St. Patrick of Cedar Lake Township.
Tatino, Tagaloa Timoteo '91 (SPP) Pago Pago, AS Sacred Heart of Jesus Parish, Vailoa.
Tatman, Robert '04 (VEN) Ave Maria, FL Quasi–Parish of Ave Maria Oratory.
Taton, Thomas P. '61 (BUF) Buffalo, NY Assumption.
Taton, Thomas P. '60 (BUF) Millard Fillmore Hospital.
Tatro, Joseph C. '00 (WCH)[A] Wichita, KS Newman University.
Tatro, Kenneth J. '76 (SPR) West Springfield, MA St. Thomas the Apostle.
Tatro, Timothy M. '99 (JC) Absent on Leave.
Tatum, Gregory T. *o.p.* '89 (OAK)[M] Oakland Order of Preachers (Province of the Most Holy Name of Jesus – Western Dominican Province).
Taube, Sylvester '64 (DET) Retired.
Tauber, Jerome A. '02 (ALN) Hellertown, PA St. Theresa of the Child Jesus; Appointed Members.
Taubitz, Leo A. '56 (KAL) Dowagiac, MI Holy Maternity of Mary.
Taufen, Rev. Msgr. Daniel J. '56 (SCL) Retired.
Taugher, Timothy J. '78 (SY) Binghamton, NY St. Catherine of Siena; Binghamton, NY St. Christopher.
Tauke, Michael L. '74 (DUB) Waverly, IA St. Mary.
Taurasi, David '88 (CC) On Duty Outside the Diocese.
Tauscher, Donald *o.s.b.* '65 (SCL)[I] Collegeville, MN St. John's Abbey, of the Order of St. Benedict.
Tavarro, Elly S. '81 (ORG)[G] Orange, CA St. Joseph Hospital of Orange.
Tavella, Thomas *c.s.p.* '81 (GR) Grand Rapids, MI Cathedral of St. Andrew; Evangelization.
Taveras, Teodoro Mata '98 (VEN) Wauchula, FL St. Michael.
Taveras Reymoso, Julio Cesar *m.ss.cc.* (SJN) Bayamon, PR Santiago Apostol.
Tavis, Gordon *o.s.b.* '58 (SCL)[I] Collegeville, MN St. John's Abbey, of the Order of St. Benedict.
Tawiah, Rev. Msgr. Francis Yaw '81 (BRK) St. Albans, NY Our Lady of Light Roman Catholic Church.
Tawiah, Gabriel Oduro '97 (VIC) Nada, TX St. John Nepomucene.
Tawiah, Raphael Amoako '07 (NY) Hyde Park, NY Regina Coeli.
Tax, Samuel Perez '01 (NU) Benson, MN St. Francis; Murdock, MN Church of the Sacred Heart.
Tay, Rev. Msgr. Peter P. '54 (PBR) Retired.
Tayag, Edison '08 (ROC) Rochester, NY Sacred Heart Cathedral.
Tayar, Hanna *o.m.m.* '96 (OLL) Flint, MI Our Lady of Lebanon Maronite Catholic Church; Ann Arbor, MI; [A] Ann Arbor, MI Maronite Order of the Blessed Virgin Mary.
Taylor, Augustus R. '66 (PIT) On Duty Outside the Diocese.
Taylor, Benedict M. *o.f.m.* '60 (NY)[EE] New York Franciscan Friars, Holy Name Province.
Taylor, Brian P. '06 (NY) Bronxville, NY St. Joseph.
Taylor, Brian '06 (LAF) Basile, LA St. Augustine.
Taylor, Rev. Msgr. Charles F. '53 (CHY) Promoter of Justice; Defenders of the Bond; Retirees' Representative; St. Joseph's Society for Priests (Clergy Mutual Benefit Society) Retired.
Taylor, Daniel '75 (TUC) Administrative Leave of Absence.
Taylor, David H. '74 (PIT) Pittsburgh, PA St. Charles Lwanga Parish.
Taylor, Douglas D. '97 (TOL) New London, OH Our Lady of Lourdes; Wakeman, OH St. Mary.
Taylor, Gordon A. '85 (B) Salmon, ID St. Charles Retired.
Taylor, James E. *o.m.i.* '56 (BEL)[F] Belleville, IL Missionary Oblates of Mary Immaculate – St. Henry's Oblate Residence.
Taylor, Jon '64 (GF)[A] University of Great Falls.
Taylor, Jon '64 (LAN) Retired.
Taylor, Joseph C. '53 (CHI) Chicago, IL St. Edward Retired.
Taylor, Kenneth '78 (IND) Deaneries and Deans; Priests' Personnel Board; Commission for Multicultural Ministry; Indianapolis, IN Holy Angels; Board of Directors:.
Taylor, Mel *o.s.b.* '67 (SCL)[I] Collegeville St. John's Abbey, of the Order of St. Benedict.
Taylor, Michael G. '93 (ARL) Fredericksburg, VA St. Patrick.
Taylor, Michael J. *s.j.* '54 (SPK)[J] Spokane, WA Regis Community Retired.
Taylor, Michael S. '97 (MAN) Somersworth, NH St. Mary; Somersworth, NH Saint Ignatius of Loyola; Diocesan Judges.
Taylor, Paul R. *o.s.b.* '92 (GBG)[G] Latrobe, PA Saint Vincent Archabbey.
Taylor, Peter '74 (GB) Retired.
Taylor, Philip *s.p.* '04 (STL) Cedar Hill, MO; [S] Dittmer, MO Vianney Renewal Center.
Taylor, Reynaldo S. '07 (CIN) Cincinnati, OH St. Joseph.
Taylor, Robert H. '56 (WIN) Absent on Leave.
Taylor, Roger H. '64 (MAD) Retired.
Taylor, Senan *o.f.m.cap.* '70 (NY)[EE] Yonkers, NY St. Clare Friary.
Taylor, Thomas '83 (PEO) Peoria Heights, IL St. Thomas.
Taylor, William R. '67 (SAG) Retired.
Taylor, William '64 (B) Retired.
Taylor, William '67 (SAG) Saginaw, MI St. Stephen; Clergy Personnel Board Retired.
Tcheou, Pang S. '06 (HBG)[I] Millersville, PA Millersville University.
Tchinqui, Antonio Jorge '97 (HRT) Hartford, CT Our Lady of Fatima.
Teague, Bruce N. '80 (BO) On Duty Outside the Diocese; Brookline, MA St. Mary of the Assumption.
Teague, Bruce (BO) Pastoral Care.
Teall, Richard *c.s.c.* '50 (FTW)[H] Holy Cross House Retired.
Teater, Kristian C. '00 (STL) Special Assignment; [A] St. Louis, MO Kenrick School of Theology.
Tebalt, Timothy D. '04 (CHR) Beaufort, SC St. Peter; [H] Beaufort, SC University of South Carolina, Beaufort Extension; [H] Greenwood, SC Lander University.
Tebbe, Francis S. *o.f.m.* '75 (CIN)[N] Cincinnati St. Francis Seraph Friary.
Tebbe, Francis S. *o.f.m.* '75 (CHI)[C] Saint Xavier University.
Tedesco, Joseph A. '79 (TR) On Duty Outside the Diocese.
Tedesco, Joseph P. *s.m.* '83 (CIN)[N] Dayton, OH Marianist Community; [D] Dayton, OH The University of Dayton.
Tedone, Michael G. '91 (BRK) Queens Village, NY Our Lady of Lourdes; [E] Brooklyn, NY Campus Ministers and Ministry Centers.
Teeling, John P. *s.j.* '55 (STL)[O] St. Louis, MO Jesuit Community Corporation at Saint Louis University – Jesuit Hall.
Tegeder, Michael '78 (STP) Bloomington, MN St. Edward.
Tegeler, Herbert L. '53 (DUB) Earlville, IA St. Joseph.
Teichert, Isaiah *o.s.b.cam.* '90 (MRY)[F] Big Sur, CA New Camaldoli Hermitage.
Tejada, Francisco R. '95 (ARE) Arecibo, PR Church of San Martin de Porres.
Tejada, Jose '92 (SP) Land O'Lakes, FL Our Lady of the Rosary.
Tekkoliekal, Antony *o.s.b.silv.* '03 (STL) Florissant, MO St. Angela Merici.
Teles, Dennis J. '65 (GRY) Retired.
Telesz, Rev. Msgr. Leo '39 (CLV) Retired.
Telken, Paul E. '73 (STL) Sullivan, MO St. Anthony.
Telles, John '75 (ELP)[A] El Paso, TX St. Charles Seminary; Vocations & Seminarians.
Tellez, Eric '86 (PHX) Scottsdale, AZ St. Patrick Roman Catholic Parish.
Tellez, Jairo A. '62 (SAT) Military Chaplains.
Tellez, Jairo '62 (MIA)[J] Miami, FL Mercy Hospital.
Tellez, Tomas Vasquez '04 (YAK) Religious Education and Hispanic Catechesis.
Tellis, Cyprian *s.j.* '02 (BO)[U] Cambridge, MA La Farge House.
Tello, Carlos Ochoa '09 (WIL) Dover, DE Holy Cross.
Telnack, Methodius *o.c.s.o.* '57 (ATL)[G] Conyers, GA The Monastery of the Holy Spirit.
Telthorst, Rev. Msgr. James T. '68 (STL) St. Louis, MO Mary, Mother of the Church.
Temba, Camillus *a.l.c.p.* '91 (PMB) West Palm Beach, FL St. Juliana.
Temba, Leopold *c.s.c.* '09 (FTW)[H] Notre Dame Congregation of Holy Cross, Indiana Province, Provincial House.
Tempel, Theodore '64 (EVN)[D] Evansville, IN St. John's Home for the Aged Retired.
Templado, Josefino P. '69 (GAL) Galena Park, TX Our Lady of Fatima.
Temple, Matthew *o.carm.* '82 (ROC)[J] Rochester, NY Whitefriars Priory.
Templeton, Rev. Msgr. Robert E. '88 (NEW) Newark, NJ St. Michael Medical Center.
Templin, Kenneth A. *s.m.* '79 (HON)[A] Honolulu, HI Chaminade University of Honolulu; [D] Honolulu, HI Center Marianist Community Retired.
Tenbarge, Timothy '73 (EVN) St. Anthony, IN St. Anthony; Schnellville, IN Sacred Heart.
Teneza, Vicente '01 (SAC) Sacramento, CA St. Paul.
Tenhundfeld, Carl Anthony (GAL) Retired.
Tenhundfeld, Paul F. '54 (COV) Fort Mitchell, KY Blessed Sacrament; [I] Edgewood, KY St. Elizabeth Medical Center, Inc. Retired.
Tenorio, Michael C. *o.f.m.cap.* '99 (MO) Air Force Chaplains.
Tenorio, Michael *o.f.m.cap.* '99 (AGN)[F] Agana Heights, GU St. Fidelis Friary.
Tensi, Lawrence R. '79 (CIN) Loveland, OH St. Columban.
Tentativa, Jose '92 (NY) New York, NY St. Thomas More.
Teo, Eduardo C. '90 (LUB) O'Donnell, TX St. Pius X; Presbyteral Council; Wilson, TX Blessed Sacrament.
Terdine, Richard G. '65 (PIT)[Q] Pittsburgh, PA Cardinal Dearden Center Retired.
Terembula, Tadeusz *s.v.d.* '96 (SJ) Gilroy, CA St. Mary.
Terga, Richard *c.i.c.m.* '73 (NY) New York, NY Our Lady of Good Counsel.
Terico, Nicholas R. *o.praem.* '89 (PH)[Y] Paoli, PA Daylesford Abbey.
Terlecky, Rt. Rev. Mitred Msgr. John '76 (STF) Ansonia, CT SS. Peter and Paul; Econome; Diocesan Consultors; Presbyteral Council; Administrative Council; Directors; Ukrainian Museum and Library of Stamford, Inc.
Termine, Vincent J. '44 (BRK) Retired.
Termyna, James J. '70 (PAT) Dover, NJ St. Clement, Pope and Martyr.
Ternes, Gary '79 (SFS) South Dakota State Penitentiary & Minnehaha County Correctional Centers; Tribunal Judges.
Ternullo, Joseph P. '73 (SAC) Special Assignment; Absent on Leave.
Tero, Richard D. '74 (MO) Diocesan Consultors; Air Force Reserve Chaplains.
Tero, Richard '74 (ANC) Seward, AK Sacred Heart; Anchorage, AK St. Patrick.
Terra, J. *f.s.s.p.* '89 (PHX) Phoenix, AZ Mater Misericordiae Roman Catholic Mission.
Terra, Rev. Msgr. Russell G. '62 (SAC) Retired.
Terranova, Robert *o.s.a.* '73 (NY) Bronx, NY St. Nicholas of Tolentine.
Terrebonne, Burnick J. '77 (NO) Metairie, LA St. Louis King of France.
Terrera, C. Bernardo '89 (SCR) On Duty Outside the Diocese.
Terrien, Douglas J. '79 (DET) Lapeer, MI Immaculate Conception of the Blessed Virgin Mary.
Terrien, Lawrence B. *s.s.* '72 (BAL)[S] Baltimore Society of St. Sulpice, Province of the United States; [A] Baltimore, MD St. Mary's Seminary and University.
Terrien, Lawrence B. *s.s.* '72 (ARL) On Duty Outside the Diocese.
Terriquez, Enrique '63 (B) College of Consultors; Deans; Pocatello, ID Holy Spirit Catholic Community.
Terry, Brian *s.a.* '97 (NY)[EE] Garrison Franciscan Friars of the Atonement, Minister General Office.
Terry, John S. '75 (SCR) Wilkes–Barre, PA Maternity of the Blessed Virgin Mary; [Q] Wilkes–Barre, PA Catholic Youth Center.
Teruela, Alvaro Huerga (PCE)[B] The Pontifical Catholic University of Puerto Rico.
Terza, William R. '69 (PIT) Pittsburgh, PA St. Sebastian.
Terzano, John D. '74 (CLV) Peninsula, OH Mother of Sorrows.
Tesek, Albert J. '51 (CLV) North Royalton, OH St. Albert the Great; Associate Judges Retired.
Tesha, Prosper *c.s.c.* '09 (FTW)[H] Notre Dame Congregation of Holy Cross, Indiana Province, Provincial House.
Teske, Roland J. *s.j.* '65 (MIL)[P] Milwaukee, WI Jesuit Community at Marquette University.
Teslovic, Eugene '77 (RIC) Retired.
Testa, Genaro J. '47 (HRT) Retired.
Testa, Jess '88 (JOL)[K] Naperville, IL St. John Vianney Villa Retired.
Testa, Richard '67 (ALB) Retired.
Testa, Rev. Msgr. Steve J. '64 (ALX) College of Consultors; Appointed Members; Deans; Holy Childhood Association; Propagation of the Faith and Foreign Mission Education; Bordelonville, LA St. Peter; Bordelonville, LA St. Michael.
Teteh, Lawrence *c.s.sp.* '71 (FTW) South Bend, IN Our Lady of Hungary.
Teter, Patrick A. '92 (SPC) Mount Vernon, MO St. Susanne.
Tetherow, Gabriel Francis '02 (SCR) Unassigned or Leave of Absence.
Teti, James V. '97 (NEW) Paramus, NJ Church of the Annunciation; Office of the Permanent Diaconate.
Tetlow, John H. '84 (STA) Switzerland, FL San Juan Del Rio.
Tetlow, Joseph *s.j.* '60 (FWT)[J] Lake Dallas, TX Montserrat Jesuit Retreat House.
Tetrault, Raymond L. '60 (PRO) Retired.
Tetreault, Maynard *o.f.m.* '60 (CIN)[U] Cincinnati, OH

Franciscan Central Purchasing; Councillors:.
Tetreault, Maynard *o.f.m.* '60 (LEX) Cumberland, KY St. Stephen.
Tetreault, Raymond A. '71 (PRO) Slatersville, RI St. John the Evangelist.
Tetteh, Edward *s.v.d.* (TR) Trenton, NJ Blessed Sacrament–Our Lady of the Divine Shepherd Parish.
Tetu, Richard B. '69 (MAN) Manchester, NH Ste. Marie.
Teuth, Michael V. *s.j.* '71 (NY)[EE] New York, NY "America;" Residence and publication office of the America Press.
Teverzczuk, William J. '73 (PH) North Wales, PA Mary, Mother of the Redeemer.
Tewes, John Edwin Thayer '96 (ARL) Annandale, VA St. Ambrose.
Tewes, Rev. Msgr. Thomas J. '63 (BAL) Retired.
Texada, David Ker '80 (NO) Retired.
Tezie, John M. '59 (CLV) South Amherst, OH Nativity of Blessed Virgin Mary Retired.
Thaar, Gerald *o.s.c.* '65 (PHX)[F] Phoenix, AZ Retired.
Thach, Nguyen Van *c.ss.r.* '01 (LA)[P] Baldwin Park Vietnamese Redemptorist Mission.
Thachet, Joseph '53 (KAL) Retired.
Thachil, Joy *s.a.c.* (STL) St. Louis, MO Our Lady of Sorrows.
Thaclathil, Chacko *o.s.b.* '94 (LUB) Slaton, TX Our Lady of Guadalupe.
Thadathilkunnel, Benny Joseph *m.s.* '99 (GAL) Friendswood, TX Mary, Queen.
Thaden, Roy W. *s.j.* '73 (FgM) Portland, OR Society of Jesus.
Thaden, William A. '88 (CLV) Lorain, OH Sacred Heart Chapel; [V] Lorain, OH Sacred Heart Chapel.
Thai, Bao Q. '03 (ORG) Orange, CA Cathedral of the Holy Family.
Thai, Thomas V. '54 (LEX) Defenders of the Bond Retired.
Thai Hoc, Mark Kieu (SAC)[I] Walnut Grove, CA Monastery of Chau Son Sacramento.
Thaikoottathil, James '84 (NOR) Middletown, CT St. Sebastian.
Thainase, Irudaya Nathan *o.f.m. cap.* (LC) Ettrick, WI St. Ansgar; Ettrick, WI St. Bridget.
Thaiparambil, Joy Vincent (DM) Clarinda, IA Sacred Heart; Clarinda, IA St. Joseph; Clarinda, IA St. Clare.
Thai Tran, Joseph '94 (SP) Largo, FL Holy Martyrs of Vietnam.
Thalakulam, Cherian *c.m.i.* '76 (CHR) North Augusta, SC St. Edward.
Thalanany, Joseph *v.c.* '67 (SFS) Dimock, SD SS. Peter and Paul.
Thaler, Joseph L. *m.m.* '77 (FgM) Maryknoll, NY MARYKNOLL.
Thaliyan, Jesudas *c.m.i.* '70 (SFS) Platte, SD St. Peter the Apostle.
Thamert, Mark *o.s.b.* '79 (SCL)[I] Collegeville, MN St. John's Abbey, of the Order of St. Benedict.
Thames, Robert '64 (FWT) On Duty Outside the Diocese.
Than, M. Timothy Qui Van *o.cist.* '75 (SB)[I] Lucerne Valley, CA The Cistercian Congregation of the Holy Family, St. Joseph Monastery.
Thanavelil, Joseph *o.s.b.* '81 (LUB) Denver City, TX St. William; Presbyteral Council.
Thanh, Nguyen Duc *c.ss.r.* '97 (LA)[P] Baldwin Park Vietnamese Redemptorist Mission.
Thanh Ngoc Nguyen, Michael M. '95 (NO) La Place, LA St. Joan of Arc.
Thanh Va, Joseph '85 (GAL) Ethnic Vicars.
Thanugundla, Joji '94 (CHI) Arlington Heights, IL St. James.
Thapwa, Stephen M. '76 (WCH) Fredonia, KS Sacred Heart; Neodesha, KS St. Ignatius.
Tharackal, Joseph '93 (SYM) Cortlandt Manor, NY Knanaya Catholic Mission of Newark New Jersey; Ambler, PA St. Antony Knanaya Catholic Mission of Greater Philadelphia; Cortlandt Manor, NY Knanaya Catholic Mission of Brooklyn, NY.
Tharappel, Augustine *m.s.f.s.* '70 (TYL) Tyler, TX Cathedral of the Immaculate Conception; [B] Whitehouse, TX Fransalian Center for Spirituality; [B] Whitehouse, TX The Missionaries of St. Francis de Sales.
Tharayil, Jose J. (GAL) Sugar Land, TX St. Theresa.
Tharcius, Arul *s.s.s.* (GAL) Houston, TX Corpus Christi.
Tharp, Larry R. '77 (CIN) Fairfield, OH Sacred Heart of Jesus; Judges.
Tharp, Shane I. '00 (OKL) Nicoma Park, OK Our Lady of Fatima; [K] Alva, OK Northwestern Oklahoma State College.
Thavelil, Joseph '81 (LUB) Priests Personnel Board.
Thawale, John '88 (NY) Bronx, NY St. Benedict.
Thayer, David D. *s.s.* '75 (HRT) On Duty Outside the Archdiocese.
Thayer, David D. *s.s.* '75 (WDC)[A] Washington, DC Theological College of the Catholic University of America; [C] Catholic University of America, The.
Thayer, David D. *s.s.* '75 (BAL)[S] Baltimore Society of St. Sulpice, Province of the United States.
Thayil, Mathew *m.s.f.s.* '67 (TYL)[B] Whitehouse, TX The Missionaries of St. Francis de Sales.
Thayil, Matthew *m.s.f.s.* '67 (ALX) Colfax, LA St. Joseph.
Thayilkuzhithottu, George Kutty *m.s.f.s.* '97 (LC) Stevens Point, WI St. Stanislaus.
Thayilkuzhithottu, George *m.s.f.s.* '97 (TYL)[B] Whitehouse, TX The Missionaries of St. Francis de Sales.
Theby, James D. '08 (STL) O'Fallon, MO Assumption.
Theempalangattu, Philip Chacko '80 (SHP)[B] Monroe, LA St. Francis Medical Center.
Thein, Edward '79 (ATL) Hapeville, GA St. John the Evangelist.
Theis, Gerald *s.v.d.* '80 (FgM) Techny, IL.
Theisen, Eugene A. *m.m.* '53 (FgM) Maryknoll, NY MARYKNOLL.
Theisen, Eugene J. '99 (MO) Air Force Chaplains.
Theisen, John J. '59 (MIL) Retired.
Theisen, Kenneth *o.s.b.* '84 (RCK) Aurora, IL; [G] Aurora, IL Marmion Abbey.
Theisen, Wilfred *o.s.b.* '56 (SCL)[I] Collegeville, MN St. John's Abbey, of the Order of St. Benedict.
Theisz, Paul '09 (HBG) Lancaster, PA St. John Neumann.
Thekkan, Pauly *c.m.i.* '89 (MET) John F. Kennedy Medical Center; Edison, NJ Our Lady of Peace.
Thekkekara, Antony '97 (GI) Stapleton, NE St. John the Evangelist.
Thekkel, Hugh *o.s.b.* '76 (LUB) Seminole, TX St. James.
Thekkemury, James Dominic '87 (SHP)[B] Monroe, LA St. Francis Medical Center.
Thekkinen, Jolly Pappachan *o.ss.t.* '08 (BAL)[S] The Trinitarians in India (Bangalore & Trichur).
Thekkudan, Johnson L. *c.m.i.* '02 (COV) Alexandria, KY St. Mary of the Assumption.
Thekkummatthil, George '90 (PT) Cantonment, FL St. Jude Thaddeus.
Thekumthala, Ouseph '75 (TYL) Wills Point, TX St. Luke.
Thelakkatt, Xavier '80 (STP) Albertville, MN St. Albert; Dayton, MN St. John the Baptist.
Thelapilly, Walter *c.m.i.* '86 (BRK) Brooklyn, NY Holy Family.
Thelapilly, Walter *c.m.i.* '84 (BRK)[T] Brooklyn, NY Carmelites of Mary Immaculate, Inc.
Thelappilly, Babu *s.d.v.* '08 (NEW) Palisades Park, NJ St. Nicholas.
Thelen, Albert R. *s.j.* '68 (OM) Omaha, NE St. Benedict the Moor; [K] Omaha, NE Jesuit Community at Creighton University.
Thelen, Bert *s.j.* '68 (OM) Omaha, NE St. John.
Thelen, Frederick L. '80 (LAN) Lansing, MI Cristo Rey.
Thelen, Rev. Msgr. Robert J. '70 (BRK)[B] Douglaston, NY Cathedral Seminary Residence of the Immaculate Conception; Sanitation Department.
Thelen, Rev. Msgr. Robert '70 (BRK) Presiding Judge of the Appellate Court.
Thell, Richard *o.s.b.* '74 (OM)[C] Elkhorn, NE Mount Michael Benedictine School; [K] Elkhorn, NE Mount Michael Benedictine Abbey; Elkhorn, NE.
Thelly, Matthew '71 (TR) Deal, NJ St. Mary of the Assumption.
Then, Antonio *o.s.a.* '03 (MGZ) Aguada, PR St. Francis of Assisi.
Thenan, Peter (CC) Corpus Christi, TX Mary, Mother of the Church Mission.
Theneth, Thomas *c.m.i.* '84 (JOL) Winfield, IL St. John the Baptist.
Thennattil, George *t.o.r.* '76 (FWT) Fort Worth, TX St. Mary of the Assumption; Hospital Chaplaincy.
Theobald, Charles '58 (NEW) Retired.
Theoret, Glenn J. '99 (MAR) Manistique, MI St. Francis de Sales.
Thepe, Theodore C. *s.j.* '55 (CIN)[N] Cincinnati, OH Jesuit Community at Xavier University.
The Pham, Vincent Tung '85 (PH) Philadelphia, PA Holy Innocents.
The Phan, Peter Luc '90 (SJ) San Jose, CA Holy Family.
Theriault, Francis *s.v.d.* '55 (CHI)[N] Techny, IL Divine Word Residence.
Theriault, H. '60 (NY) Tivoli, NY St. Sylvia.
Theriot, Donald C. '57 (LAF) Retired.
Theroux, Bertrand L. '67 (PRO) North Kingstown, RI St. Francis De Sales.
Theroux, David *s.s.e.* '74 (BUR)[E] Colchester, VT Society of St. Edmund.
Theroux, Denis B. '88 (DET) Northville, MI Our Lady of Victory.
Theroux, Rev. Msgr. Paul D. '77 (PRO) Vicars General; Secretary for Diocesan Administration; Vicars General; Moderator of the Curia; Judges; Finance Council; College of Consultors; Council Members; Secretariat for Diocesan Administration; Rumford, RI St. Margaret.
Theroux, Raymond C. '65 (PRO) Cumberland, RI St. John Baptist Mary Vianney.
Therrien, Shawn M. '87 (MAN) Claremont, NH St. Mary; Sullivan County House of Corrections.
Thesing, Gilbert J. *o.p.* '75 (CHI)[N] Chicago Dominicans (Provincial Office).
Thesing, Gilbert *o.p.* '75 (FgM) Chicago, IL Province of St. Albert the Great (Central).
Thesing, Kenneth F. *m.m.* '69 (FgM) Maryknoll, NY MARYKNOLL.
Thesing, Mark B. *c.s.c.* '86 (FTW)[B] University of Notre Dame Du Lac; [H] Notre Dame, IN Holy Cross Community, Corby Hall, University of Notre Dame.
Thesing, Robert J. *s.j.* '76 (CHI)[C] Chicago, IL Jesuit Community at Loyola University Chicago.
Thess, William C. '00 (STL) Warrenton, MO Holy Rosary.
Thessing, Charles '88 (LR) Morrilton, AR Sacred Heart.
Thet–Kyaw, Marcian '95 (CHR) Dillon, SC St. Louis.
Thevarkunnel, Anselm '57 (DUL) Cass Lake, MN St. Charles.
Thevenin, Donelson '05 (BRK) Brooklyn, NY Holy Cross; [S] Haitian Apostolate.
Thi, Andrew '85 (NY) New York, NY St. Patrick's Old Cathedral.
Thibault, Donald P. *o.p.* '68 (NY) Pleasantville, NY Holy Innocents.
Thibault, Rodney E. '01 (FR) East Sandwich, MA Corpus Christi; Judges; St. Luke's Hospital.
Thibeau, Richard *s.v.d.* '57 (FgM) Techny, IL.
Thibodeau, Andre M. '71 (MAN) Advocates Retired.
Thibodeau, Clement D. '58 (PRT) Retired.
Thibodeau, Kenneth *s.m.* '68 (BUR) White River Junction, VT St. Anthony.
Thibodeau, Raynold *o.f.m.cap.* '85 (BUR) Rutland, VT St. Peter.
Thibodeau, Richard *c.ss.r.* '76 (CHI) Chicago, IL St. Michael in Old Town; [N] Chicago, IL The Redemptorist Fathers of Chicago.
Thibodeau, Scott A. '98 (DET) Beverly Hills, MI Our Lady Queen of Martyrs.
Thibodeaux, Charles B. *s.j.* '59 (NO)[P] New Orleans Jesuit Provincial Office.
Thibodeaux, Mark E. *s.j.* '01 (LAF)[A] Grand Coteau, LA St. Charles College.
Thibodeaux, Paul '48 (LAF) Retired.
Thiede, John S. *s.j.* '03 (CHI)[N] Chicago Chicago Province of the Society of Jesus–Provincial Office.
Thiede, John S. *s.j.* '03 (FTW)[K] South Bend, IN Jesuit Community.
Thiel, Chris *o.f.m.cap.* '90 (LA)[F] La Canada Flintridge, CA St. Francis High School of La Canada–Flintridge.
Thiel, Lloyd *o.f.m.cap.* '56 (DET)[K] Detroit St. Bonaventure Friary.
Thiele, Richard *c.ss.r.* '54 (FgM) Denver, CO Denver Province.
Thiele, Robert A. '55 (SC) Retired.
Thielen, Jeffrey M. '74 (MIL) Awaiting Assignment.
Thielman, Kenneth '55 (SCL) Retired.
Thieman, Donald J. *c.pp.s.* '53 (CIN)[N] Dayton Provincial Office of the Cincinnati Province of the Society of the Precious Blood.
Thierry, Jude W. '09 (LAF) Mamou, LA St. Ann.
Thiers, Georges G. *c.o.* '70 (PH) Philadelphia, PA St. Francis Xavier; [Y] Philadelphia, PA The Philadelphia Congregation of The Oratory of St. Philip Neri.
Thieryoung, John '96 (PEO) Aledo, IL St. Catherine's Church; Aledo, IL St. Anthony's Church.
Thiesen, Eugene '99 (STP) Military Chaplains.
Thiess, Daniel R. '90 (STL)[O] St. Louis, MO Lazarist Residence.
Thiessen, Dennis *s.d.s.* '78 (SAC)[D] Sacramento, CA Jesuit High School; Consultors:; Orangevale, CA Divine Savior.
Thill, Richard '81 (PBL) Absent on Leave.
Thimm, Donald H. '76 (MIL) Pleasant Prairie, WI St. Anne.
Thimmesh, Hilary *o.s.b.* '54 (SCL)[I] Collegeville, MN St. John's Abbey, of the Order of St. Benedict.
Thinnes, John M. '64 (CHI) Retired.
Thiruchiluvai, Roche Iruthayaraj *ss.cc.* '06 (FR)[G] Fairhaven National Center of the Enthronement.
Thirumangalam, George *c.m.i.* '76 (SAN) Abilene, TX St. Francis of Assisi.
Thirunelliparamabil, Lukose '92 (CC) Beeville, TX Our Lady of Victory; Deans; College of Consultors; Personnel Board – Priests; Presbyteral Council.
Thissen, Donald R. '70 (WCH) Retired.
Thoa, Ngo Dinh *c.ss.r.* '62 (LA)[P] Baldwin Park, CA Vietnamese Redemptorist Mission.
Thoai Ngoc Tran, Aloysius *c.m.c.* '92 (SB)[I] Corona, CA Congregation of the Mother Co–Redemptrix, C.M.C.
Thoennes, James '64 (SCL) Retired.
Thoennes, Roger '90 (SCL) Lowry, MN Our Lady of the Runestone; Lowry, MN St. John Nepomuk.
Thoguru, Cyprian '82 (RCK) Amboy, IL St. Patrick; Amboy, IL St. Flannen; Amboy, IL St. Mary; Amboy, IL St. Patrick.
Thole, Simeon J. *o.s.b.* '62 (SCL)[I] Collegeville, MN St. John's Abbey, of the Order of St. Benedict.
Thole, Thomas *o.s.b.* '58 (SCL)[I] Collegeville, MN St. John's Abbey, of the Order of St. Benedict.
Tholen, John '62 (YAK) Retired.
Thoma, Steven *c.r.* '91 (LA)[A] Camarillo, CA St. John's Seminary.
Thoman, Dwayne J. '76 (DUB) Dubuque, IA Church of

the Nativity; Deans; Deanery Representatives; Priests' Council.
Thoman, James *c.p.* '75 (DET)[K] Detroit, MI St. Paul of the Cross Community, Congregation of the Passion; [P] Detroit, MI St. Paul of the Cross Passionist Retreat and Conference Center, Inc.
Thomas, Alan E. '92 (ALT) Johnstown, PA Resurrection Roman Catholic Church.
Thomas, Alan J. (NY) New York, NY St. Francis of Assisi.
Thomas, Andrew '05 (P) Board Members; Bandon, OR Holy Trinity.
Thomas, Anil *s.v.d.* '06 (BEA) Jasper, TX St. Michael; Jasper, TX Our Lady of La Salette Mission; Liberty, TX Immaculate Conception.
Thomas, Antoine *c.s.j.* '92 (PEO)[K] Princeville, IL Congregation of St. John.
Thomas, C. Theodore '73 (COL) Columbus, OH St. Mary Church.
Thomas, Charles T. '73 (COL) Diocesan Judges.
Thomas, Clyde '02 (LKC) Lake Arthur, LA Our Lady of the Lake.
Thomas, Curtis '87 (NO) Avondale, LA St. Bonaventure; Waggaman, LA Our Lady of the Angels.
Thomas, David T. '52 (STL) Retired.
Thomas, Dominic *m.c.b.s.* '87 (MIL)[P] Kenosha, WI Missionary Congregation of the Blessed Sacrament, Inc., Zion Province; Kenosha, WI St. James.
Thomas, Donald K. *m.s.* '57 (HRT)[L] Hartford, CT Missionaries of LaSalette.
Thomas, Gary '83 (SJ) Saratoga, CA Sacred Heart.
Thomas, George L. '48 (SFR) Retired.
Thomas, George '97 (CC) Mathis, TX Saint Patrick Mission; Mathis, TX St. Pius X Mission – Sandia.
Thomas, Jacob '76 (ALX) Natchez, LA St. Augustine's.
Thomas, James J. '76 (ALN) On Duty Outside the Diocese.
Thomas, James P. '76 (BEL) Salem, IL St. Elizabeth Ann Seton; Salem, IL St. Theresa of Avila.
Thomas, Jerald '56 (SR) Retired.
Thomas, Jerald '56 (SFR)[K] San Rafael, CA Nazareth House of San Rafael, Inc.
Thomas, Jeremy '92 (CHI) Chicago, IL St. Jerome.
Thomas, Jesudoss '02 (TYL) Young Adult/Campus Ministries.
Thomas, Jesudoss '93 (TYL) Nacogdoches, TX Nacogdoches, St. Mary's Chapel, Stephen F. Austin State University; [D] Nacogdoches, TX Stephen F. Austin University Catholic Student Center; Co Directors.
Thomas, Joby Cheradi *m.s.* '98 (TYL) Overton, TX Billy Max Moore Private Prison; Overton, TX Our Lady Queen of Angels.
Thomas, John D. '54 (WOR) Retired.
Thomas, John M. '66 (SC) Presbyteral Council; Diocesan Consultors.
Thomas, John M. '93 (OWN) Hopkinsville, KY SS. Peter and Paul; Priest Personnel Committee.
Thomas, John '94 (SYM) Columbus, OH St. Raphel Syro–Malabar Mission Cleveland, OH; Columbus, OH St. Mary Syro–Malabar Catholic Mission Columbus, OH.
Thomas, Joseph M. *m.c.b.s.* '74 (DUL) Cook, MN St. Mary; Orr, MN Holy Cross; Tower, MN St. Martin.
Thomas, Joseph S. '52 (CHI) Retired.
Thomas, Joseph *b.s.o.* '71 (NTN) Methuen, MA Seminary of St. Basil the Great; Methuen, MA Basilian Salvatorian Order.
Thomas, Juniper J. '70 (RVC) Ronkonkoma, NY St. Joseph's.
Thomas, Kevin '88 (DET) Livonia, MI St. Aidan.
Thomas, LaVerne (Pike) '86 (SHP) Bossier City, LA St. Jude; Presbyteral Council; Diocesan Liturgy Commission; Clergy Continuing Formation Director; Master of Ceremonies, Diocese of Shreveport; College of Consultors.
Thomas, Mark A. '96 (PIT) Pittsburgh, PA St. Norbert.
Thomas, Mark L. '93 (PIT) Ellwood City, PA Holy Redeemer Parish.
Thomas, Merwyn J. *c.s.c.* '67 (FTW)[B] University of Notre Dame Du Lac; [H] Notre Dame, IN Holy Cross Community, Corby Hall, University of Notre Dame.
Thomas, Chorbishop Michael G. '83 (SAM) Protosyncellus (Vicar General); Chancellor; Finance Council; Judges; Presbyteral Council.
Thomas, Milton '64 (LIN) Retired.
Thomas, Norman P. '55 (DET) Detroit, MI Sacred Heart of Jesus; Detroit, MI St. Elizabeth.
Thomas, Paschal *o.s.b.* '57 (KC)[J] Conception, MO Conception Abbey.
Thomas, Paul K. '63 (BAL) Retired.
Thomas, Paul *o.s.b.* '82 (P)[L] St. Benedict, OR Mt. Angel Abbey.
Thomas, Phillip *o.c.d.* '79 (MIL)[P] Milwaukee Provincial Offices – Discalced Carmelites.
Thomas, Ralph W. '65 (CLV) Akron, OH St. Paul.
Thomas, Raymond J. '72 (Y) Conneaut, OH Saint Mary/Saint Frances Cabrini.
Thomas, Richard L. '66 (GB) Green Bay, WI St. Francis Xavier Cathedral Retired.
Thomas, Robert W. '61 (BO) Senior Priests. Retired.
Thomas, Robert '61 (FgM) Boston, MA St. James the Apostle, Inc.
Thomas, Rev. Msgr. Royce R. '69 (MO) Judicial Vicar; Clergy Welfare Board; Army National Guard Chaplains; Vice Chancellors; Little Rock, AR Our Lady of the Holy Souls; Priests Personnel Board (Diocesan).
Thomas, Sebastian Vettath '93 (CC) Skidmore, TX Immaculate Conception.
Thomas, Shaji R. '88 (TOL) Findlay, OH St. Michael the Archangel.
Thomas, Tom *m.s.f.s.* '98 (TYL)[B] Whitehouse, TX The Missionaries of St. Francis de Sales.
Thomas, Tom (CHI)[J] Hoffman Estates, IL St. Alexius Medical Center.
Thomas, Tomi *i.m.s.* '94 (BGP) Norwalk, CT St. Matthew.
Thomas, Wilbur N. *v.f.* '73 (CHL) Asheville, NC Basilica of St. Lawrence.
Thomas, William F. '93 (LR) Russellville, AR St. John.
Thomas, William V. '62 (CIN) Retired.
Thome, Edwin A. '54 (GAY) Traverse City, MI St. Joseph Retired.
Thome, Edwin J. '51 (LC) La Crosse, WI; [H] La Crosse, WI Holy Cross (Seminary) Diocesan Center Retired.
Thome, John J. '46 (SAG) Retired.
Thompson, Andrew J. *c.ss.r.* '81 (GR)[L] Grand Rapids, MI The Society of the Redemptorists of the City of Grand Rapids; Grand Rapids, MI St. Alphonsus.
Thompson, August L. '57 (ALX) Retired.
Thompson, Augustine '85 (RIC) Charlottesville, VA St. Thomas Aquinas.
Thompson, Augustine *o.p.* '85 (OAK)[M] Oakland, CA Order of Preachers (Province of the Most Holy Name of Jesus – Western Dominican Province); [A] Berkeley, CA Dominican School of Philosophy and Theology.
Thompson, Charles C. '87 (L) Louisville, KY Holy Trinity; Vicar General; Promoter of Justice; College of Consultors; Ex Officio; L.A.M.P.; [A] St. Meinrad, IN Saint Meinrad School of Theology; [Q] Louisville, KY Catholic Bicentennial Initiative Fund, Inc.
Thompson, D. Timothy '82 (FWT) Presbyteral Council and Consultors; Tribunal; Priests' Pension Plan Trustees; Denton, TX St. Mark.
Thompson, Dennis '89 (STP) Farmington, MN St. Michael.
Thompson, Edward C. '59 (NEW) Retired.
Thompson, Edward J. '51 (ORL) Altamonte Springs, FL St. Mary Magdalen.
Thompson, George M. '52 (PEO) Retired.
Thompson, Rev. Msgr. George P. '65 (NY) Bedford, NY St. Patrick; Northern Westchester and Putnam.
Thompson, Gregory S. '06 (ARL) Manassas, VA All Saints; Defenders of the Bond.
Thompson, J. Noel '54 (SD) Retired.
Thompson, J. Timothy *s.j.* '70 (FgM) St. Louis, MO Society of Jesus.
Thompson, James A. '44 (TR) Retired.
Thompson, James D. *o.p.* '03 (PHX)[F] Tempe, AZ Dominicans (Dominican Community–Jordan House); [H] Tempe, AZ Arizona State University; Tempe, AZ All Saints Roman Catholic Newman Center.
Thompson, James *o.s.a.* '71 (CHI)[N] Chicago, IL St. John Stone Friary; [J] Evergreen Park, IL Little Company of Mary Hospital and Health Care Centers.
Thompson, Jefferson M. *c.s.b.* '91 (DET)[E] Novi, MI Catholic Central High School.
Thompson, Jerald Wayne '94 (LA) In Transition.
Thompson, Jerome H. '60 (LA) Retired.
Thompson, John F. *s.m.* '99 (SFR)[N] San Francisco, CA Marianist Community.
Thompson, John *s.d.b.* '79 (FgM) New Rochelle, NY SALESIANS OF DON BOSCO.
Thompson, Kevin J. *o.f.m.cap.* '97 (HBG) Harrisburg, PA St. Francis of Assisi.
Thompson, Kevin *o.f.m.cap.* '97 (WDC) Washington, DC Shrine of the Sacred Heart.
Thompson, Kizito *o.c.s.o.* '70 (WOR)[O] Spencer, MA St. Joseph's Abbey.
Thompson, Matthew E. '79 (WDC) Retired.
Thompson, Melvin F. '67 (DEN) Centennial, CO St. Thomas More.
Thompson, Michael L. *s.s.j.* '04 (BR) Baton Rouge, LA St. Francis Xavier.
Thompson, Michael '96 (STA) Absent or Sick Leave.
Thompson, Nils *o.f.m.* (GAL) Galveston, TX Holy Family.
Thompson, Rev. Msgr. Patrick '60 (LA) Lomita, CA St. Margaret Mary Alacoque.
Thompson, Patrick *o.m.i.* '60 (SD) Chula Vista, CA Most Precious Blood.
Thompson, Philip E. '78 (DUB) Ex–Officio; [D] Cedar Rapids, IA Xavier High School Foundation; Cedar Rapids, IA St. Patrick; Priests' Council; Deanery Representatives; [D] Cedar Rapids, IA Xavier High School; Hiawatha, IA St. Elizabeth Ann Seton Parish; Church Design/Renovation Commission.
Thompson, Philip E. '78 (DUB)[F] Cedar Rapids, IA LaSalle Middle School; [F] Cedar Rapids, IA Holy Family Consolidated School.
Thompson, Richard B. '69 (MAN) College of Consultors; Presbyteral Council; Priest Personnel Board; Institutional Ministries Office; Vicar for Clergy; Manchester, NH St. Pius X.
Thompson, Richard J. '96 (PIT) Waynesburg, PA St. Ann; [P] Waynesburg, PA Waynesburg College (Waynesburg).
Thompson, Richard R. '59 (SY) Retired.
Thompson, Richard '95 (P) Portland, OR All Saints; Board Members.
Thompson, Thomas A. *s.m.* '68 (CIN)[D] Dayton, OH The University of Dayton; [D] The Marian Library/International Marian Research Institute (IMRI); [N] Dayton, OH Marianist Community; Dayton, OH Mariological Society of America (1949).
Thompson, Thomas E. '92 (SUP) Osceola, WI Assumption of the Blessed Virgin Mary; Osceola, WI St. Joseph; Personnel Placement Board; Vocations, Officeof; Presbyteral Council & Diocesan Consultors; Board of Directors.
Thompson, Thomas W. '64 (LAN) Retired.
Thompson, Thomas '82 (SD) Scripps Hospital; Thornton Hospital.
Thompson, William J. '71 (WDC) Indian Head, MD St. Mary Star of the Sea; [M] Washington, DC Cardinal O'Boyle Residence for Priests.
Thompson, Rev. Msgr. William P.A. '54 (CC) Retired.
Thompson, William '08 (WIN) Rochester, MN St. Francis of Assisi; [C] Rochester, MN Lourdes High School of Rochester, Inc.
Thoms, Jeffrey (HBG) Lewistown, PA Sacred Heart of Jesus; Mifflintown, PA St. Jude.
Thomsen, Steven '86 (LAN) On Leave of Absence.
Thomson, J. Garret (BO) Plainville, MA St. Martha.
Thomson, Sean P. '04 (FBK)[C] Fairbanks, AK Kobuk Center.
Thon, Andrew J. *s.j.* '74 (MIL)[P] Milwaukee, WI Jesuit Community at Marquette University.
Thoni, Rev. Msgr. Philip F. '49 (KNX) Fairfield Glade, TN St. Francis of Assisi Retired.
Thoonkuzhy, Joseph '58 (BEL) Tulsa, OK Retired.
Thoppil, Scaria T. *c.m.i.* '80 (JOL) Lisle, IL St. Joan of Arc.
Thorburn, Rev. Msgr. Timothy J. '83 (LIN) Lincoln, NE Bishop Bonacum Chancery; [J] Lincoln, NE The Catholic Foundation of the Diocese of Lincoln; Moderator of the Curia; Vicar General; Promoters Justitiae; Defensores Vinculi; Diocesan Consultors; Presbyteral Council; Building Commission; Censores Librorum; Clergy Relief Society—The Saint John Vianney Association; Diocesan Finance Council; Diocesan Health Ministries, Inc.; Diocesan Housing Ministries, Inc.; Evangelization Committee; Insurance; Priests' Continuing Education Committee; [J] Lincoln, NE Crossing the Threshold Campaign; [J] Lincoln, NE Charity and Stewardship Appeal (DDP).
Thorn, Robert C. '99 (LC) Wausau, WI St. Matthew; Special Assignment; [C] Wausau, WI Newman Catholic Middle School at St. Matthew Parish.
Thorne, Carrol W. *c.p* '60 (MET)[I] South River Passionist Provincial Office.
Thorne, Stephen D. '98 (PH) Philadelphia, PA Saint Cyprian; On Special or Other Archdiocesan Assignment; Office for Black Catholics; College of Consultors.
Thorne, Thomas P. '76 (BGP) Westport, CT Church of the Assumption; Diocesan Consultors; Vicariate II (Norwalk, New Canaan, Wilton, Weston, Westport); Navy Reserve Chaplains; Presbyteral Council.
Thornsberry, Michael J. '91 (BAL) Priests Sick or Absent.
Thornton, James W. *c.s.c.* '64 (PHX)[F] Phoenix, AZ Holy Cross Congregation/Casa Santa Cruz Retired.
Thornton, James *c.s.c.* (FTW)[H] Notre Dame Congregation of Holy Cross, Indiana Province, Provincial House.
Thornton, Rev. Msgr. Michael J. '69 (BLX) Waynesboro, MS St. Bernadette; Laurel, MS Immaculate Conception; College of Consultors; Promoter of Justice; South Mississippi Correctional Facility; Personnel Board; South Mississippi Correctional Institution; Defenders of the Bond; Association of Priests (Diocese of Biloxi and Jackson).
Thornton, Rev. Msgr. Michael '69 (JKS) Association of Priests.
Thornton, William H. '09 (SFR) Novato, CA St. Anthony of Padua.
Thorsen, Henry '53 (BIR) Retired.
Thorsen, Robert J. '56 (CIN) Retired.
Thottamkara, Joseph *c.m.* '91 (NO) New Orleans, LA St. Joseph.
Thottamkara, Joseph *c.m.* '87 (NO)[P] New Orleans, LA Congregation of the Mission Western Province (Vincentians); New Orleans, LA Good Shepherd.
Thottankara, Raju '95 (MO) Gregory, TX Immaculate Conception; Navy Reserve Chaplains.
Thottapally, James J. '71 (OAK) El Sobrante, CA St. Callistus; Deanery #23.
Thottathil, Jose K. '83 (TLS)[F] Tulsa, OK St. John Villas, Inc.
Thottiyil, Mathew *m.s.f.s.* '78 (TYL)[B] Whitehouse, TX The Missionaries of St. Francis de Sales.

Thottiyil, Matthew *m.s.f.s.* '78 (GAL) Houston, TX St. Bernadette Soubirous.
Thottukulappananiyil, John *o.f.m.cap.* (NEW) Elizabeth, NJ Saint Adalbert and Saints Peter & Paul.
Thottungal, Thomas '70 (NEW) Harrison, NJ Holy Cross; Asian–Indian Apostolate.
Thottuvelil, Zacharias '83 (SYM) Coral Springs, FL Our Lady of Health Catholic Church, Florida.
Thottuvelil, Zacharias '83 (MIA) Indians.
Thoyalil, James '91 (PT) Pensacola, FL Cathedral of the Sacred Heart.
Thrasher, Robert W. '62 (SPR) Defenders of the Bond; [G] Springfield, MA St. Michael's Residence; Vice–Chancellor Retired.
Thuer, William J. '46 (HRT)[A] In Res. at the Archbishop Daniel A. Cronin Retirement Residence at St. Thomas Seminary Retired.
Thuerauf, Jason M. '99 (DEN) Fort Morgan, CO St. Helena; Elected Representatives from Deanery to Presbyteral Council.
Thuerauf, Jeffrey P. '89 (TUC) Leave of Absence.
Thuma, Clifton M. '96 (BO) Health Leave.
Thumbi, Francis '87 (SEA) Everett, WA St. Mary Magdalen.
Thumma, Jacob '93 (NY) Bronx, NY St. Theresa of the Infant Jesus; Staten Island, NY St. Sylvester.
Thumma, Lucas '76 (SD) El Cajon, CA Our Lady of Grace.
Thumma, Rayappa '86 (NY) Cortlandt Manor, NY St. Columbanus.
Thundathil, Antony C. '91 (SYM) Bellwood, IL Mar Thoma Sleeha Cathedral; Eparchial Consultors.
Thundathil, Mathew '78 (MIA) Coral Springs, FL St. Andrew.
Thuong, Rev. Msgr. Philippe Le–Xuan '70 (GAL) Houston, TX Christ, The Incarnate Word; Archdiocesan Judges.
Thurber, David G. '08 (PRO) Cranston, RI St. Mary.
Thurston, Anthony '82 (OAK) On Duty Outside the Diocese.
Thury, Gerald '67 (SFS) Tyndall, SD St. Leo.
Thychery, George '60 (LAF) Retired.
Thylstrup, Edward J. *s.j.* '67 (FgM) Los Gatos, CA Society of Jesus.
Tiano, Christopher M. '89 (HRT) Torrington, CT St. Francis of Assisi; Torrington, CT St. Mary; Torrington, CT St. Peter; Waterbury Vicariate; Torrington, CT Sacred Heart.
Tibainuguka, Thomas (PEO) Rushville, IL St. Rose.
Tibay, Ernesto C. '76 (NEW) Bergenfield, NJ St. John the Evangelist; Filipino Apostolate.
Tibbetts, Richard '98 (ATL) Atlanta, GA Holy Cross.
Tibbs, Thomas T. '74 (GRY) Kouts, IN St. Mary.
Tibesar, Leo J. '68 (STP) Minneapolis, MN St. Frances Cabrini.
Tiboni, Rev. Msgr. Vito '69 (NEW) On Duty Outside the Archdiocese.
Tice, Cecil '81 (CHL) Absent On Leave.
Tichacek, Charles P. '94 (STL) Silex, MO St. Alphonsus.
Tickerhoof, Bernard *t.o.r.* '78 (ALT)[G] Loretto, PA St. Bonaventure Friary; [G] Loretto, PA St. Francis Friary at Mount Assisi.
Tickerhoof, David *t.o.r.* '67 (SFS) Marty, SD St. Paul's Church.
Ticllasuca, Rolando *m.r.s.m.* '94 (RVC) Glen Cove, NY St. Patrick's.
Ticona, Fidel *c.s.c.* '00 (SCR)[C] Wilkes–Barre, PA King's College.
Tiegs, James R. '74 (OM) Omaha, NE St. Stephen the Martyr.
Tiell, Florian *o.f.m.conv.* (TOL) Carey, OH Our Lady of Consolation, Basilica–National Shrine.
Tiell, Maurice J. '50 (OWN) Bowling Green, KY St. Joseph's Retired.
Tien, Dominic Hoang Minh '06 (PH) Philadelphia, PA Saint Cyprian.
Tiendrebeogo, Anatole A. '87 (OAK) Oakland, CA St. Leo the Great.
Tiercelin, Harry '47 (NY) Retired.
Tierney, Charles *o.m.i.* '73 (FgM) Washington, DC AMERICAN OBLATE MISSIONS.
Tierney, Gary M. '67 (DET) Judges Retired.
Tierney, Rev. Msgr. James E. '50 (BO) Senior Priests. Retired.
Tierney, Joseph P. (NY)[E] Bronx, NY Cardinal Hayes High School.
Tierney, Michael E. '69 (KC) Kansas City, MO Christ the King; Presbyteral Council; Deans.
Tierney, Michael J. '67 (RCK) Algonquin, IL St. Margaret Mary.
Tierney, Patrick J. '69 (BIR) Albertville, AL Retired.
Tietjen, Kenneth F. *o.c.s.o.* '56 (DUB)[K] Peosta, IA New Melleray Abbey, Order of Cistercians of the Strict Observance.
Tietjen, Michael Eugene '06 (WDC) Silver Spring, MD St. John the Baptist.
Tiffany, Eugene W. '72 (STP) Priestly Life and Ministry.
Tifft, Thomas W. '69 (CLV)[A] Wickliffe, OH St. Mary Seminary and Graduate School of Theology; Presbyteral Council.
Tigges, James J. '71 (SC) Humboldt, IA St. John's; Humboldt, IA St. Mary's; Council of Catholic Women.
Tighe, Dermot F. '54 (DOD)[F] Dodge City, KS The Diocese of Dodge City Priest Retirement Fund, Inc. Retired.
Tighe, James '70 (BRK) Flushing, NY Queen of Peace.
Tighe, Leonard J. '73 (BO) Emergency Response Group.; Unassigned.
Tighe, Philip M. '00 (R) Wake Forest, NC St. Catherine of Siena; Council of Priests.
Tighe, Timothy P. *c.s.p.* '69 (BRK) Brooklyn, NY St. Saviour.
Tighe, Timothy P. *c.s.p.* '69 (NY)[EE] New York, NY Paulist Fathers' Motherhouse.
Tigreros, Ernesto *s.s.p.* '66 (NY)[B] Staten Island, NY Society of St. Paul; Staten Island, NY.
Tigyer, Jeffrey E. '00 (COL) Powell, OH St. Joan of Arc.
Tigyer, Paul '54 (PSC) Retired.
Tijerina, Richard '85 (AUS) Austin, TX Seton/ Brackenridge Hospital.
Tikalsky, Russell F. '56 (MIL) Retired.
Tilford, John E. '66 (CHI) Chicago, IL St. Michael the Archangel.
Tillekeratne, Sujith *s.s.s.* '00 (NY) New York, NY St. Jean Baptiste.
Tillerkerante, Ralph *s.s.s.* '00 (NY) Manhattan, NY Lenox Hill Hospital.
Tilley, Charles J. *s.j.* '85 (SJ) Los Gatos, CA; [M] Santa Clara, CA Casa San Inigo, Jesuit Residence.
Tillia, Marc '59 (KCK) On Duty Outside the Archdiocese.
Tillman, Rev. Msgr. Richard H. '65 (BAL) Commission for Ecumenical and Interreligious Affairs; Priest Personnel Board.
Tillman, Robert J. *s.j.* '77 (OM)[C] Omaha, NE Creighton Preparatory School; [K] Omaha, NE Jesuit Community at Creighton University.
Tillotson, Frederick J. *o.carm.* '69 (WDC)[B] Washington, DC Washington Theological Union; [B] Washington, DC Whitefriars Hall.
Tillrock, Raymond J. '69 (CHI) Other Assignments.
Tilly, Charles *s.j.* '85 (SJ)[B] Santa Clara, CA Jesuit Community.
Tillyer, Rev. Msgr. Herbert K. '68 (PAT) Theological Commission; Parsippany, NJ St. Peter the Apostle; [Q] Bloomfield, NJ Riese Corporation; [Q] Paterson, NJ Martin de Porres Village Corporation; Pro–Synodal Judges; Diocesan Cemeteries Office.
Tilman, Richard H. '65 (BAL) Columbia, MD St. John the Evangelist.
Tilp, John R. '69 (DUB) Clear Lake, IA St. Patrick.
Timar, Frank John *m.s.c.* '58 (RCK) Sycamore, IL St. Mary; [K] Sycamore, IL St. Mary's Educational Foundation, Ltd.; [G] Aurora, IL Missionaries of the Sacred Heart Community.
Timbre, Roland '61 (HT) Kenner, LA Retired.
Timby, Bryan P. '83 (MEM) Memphis, TN Our Lady of Sorrows.
Timchak, Robert M. '92 (SCR) Unassigned or Leave of Absence.
Timko, Philip S. *o.s.b.* '69 (JOL)[A] Lisle, IL Benedictine University; [L] Lisle, IL St. Procopius Abbey.
Timko, Philip *o.s.b.* '69 (CHI)[A] Mundelein, IL University of St. Mary of the Lake/Mundelein Seminary.
Timlin, John P. *c.m.* (CHL) Greensboro, NC St. Mary.
Timm, Richard W. *c.s.c.* '49 (FgM) New Rochelle, NY Eastern Brothers Province.
Timmel, Gerald L. '56 (L) Louisville, KY St. Ignatius; [P] Louisville, KY Society of St. Vincent de Paul, Council of Louisville Retired.
Timmerman, Bart D. '01 (MAD) Bloomington, WI St. Mary; Bloomington, WI St. John; Appointed.
Timmerman, Craig A. '05 (NU) Canby, MN St. Peter; St. Leo, MN St. Leo; Committee for Continuing Education of Clergy; Vocations Team; On Special or Other Diocesan Assignment.
Timmerman, David W. '87 (MAD) Cambridge, WI St. Pius X; Edgerton, WI St. Joseph; Elected.
Timmerman, Paul D. '07 (NU) Committee on Parishes; Ecumenism and Interreligious Affairs; Sleepy Eye, MN St. Mary; On Special or Other Diocesan Assignment; Committee for Evangelization & Catechesis.
Timmerman, Randy J. '93 (MAD) Janesville, WI St. John Vianney; Janesville; Elected.
Timmerman, Sean M. '03 (LIN) Dwight, NE Assumption; Diocesan Area CCD Directors; Advocates.
Timmermans, Rev. Msgr. John '52 (ALX) Retired.
Timmers, Jozef *o.f.m.cap.* '00 (FgM) Detroit, MI Province of St. Joseph.
Timmings, Thomas '70 (FRS) Atwater, CA St. Anthony; Ecclesiastical Notaries.
Timock, Ronald K. '83 (MAR) Gwinn, MI St. Anthony.
Timone, Richard F. *s.j.* '64 (NY)[EE] New York, NY Murray–Weigel Hall.
Timoney, Conan H. *c.p.* '68 (MO) DEPARTMENT OF VETERANS AFFAIRS HOSPITALS AND CHAPLAINS.
Timoney, Conan H. '68 (PSC) Baltimore, MD Patronage of the Mother of God; Syncellus; Presbyteral Council.
Timoney, Francis '69 (LAV) Retired.
Timony, Brian '56 (OAK) Pleasant Hill, CA Christ the King Retired.
Timp, Frederick *s.v.d.* '71 (FgM) Techny, IL.
Tindall, Harold '78 (SD) Poway, CA St. Gabriel Retired.
Tindall, William '89 (DET) Livonia, MI St. Michael; College of Consultors.
Tinder, Rev. Msgr. F. Dennis '68 (BAL) Towson, MD Church of the Immaculate Conception; [V] Towson, MD The Immaculate Conception Elementary School Endowment Trust; Presbyteral Council; [V] Towson, MD Towson Catholic High School Endowment Trust.
Tinder, Rev. Msgr. Frederick D. '68 (BAL) Retired.
Tinh, Joseph Nguyen '57 (SJ) Retired.
Tinkatumire, Leo '92 (CHI) Chicago, IL St. Kilian.
Tinney, Richard W. '65 (BUR) Essex Junction, VT St. Pius X.
Tino, John '01 (BRK) Brooklyn, NY St. Dominic.
Tino, Robert F. '71 (MIL) On Duty Outside the Archdiocese.
Tino, Robert '71 (SEA) Western State Hospital.
Tinsley, Rev. Msgr. Edmond T. '51 (WOR)[J] Leicester, MA McAuley Nazareth Home for Boys; [S] Worcester, MA Monsignor Thomas Griffin Foundation; Diocesan College of Consultors; Worcester, MA St. John's Retired.
Tintle, Raymond *o.f.m.* '69 (MRY)[F] San Miguel, CA Franciscan Friars, O.F.M.; Presbyteral Council; San Miguel, CA San Miguel.
Tiongson, Joselito S. '92 (MO) Navy Chaplains.
Tiplaca, Arnulfo '94 (NY) Staten Island, NY St. Patrick.
Tippmann, Laurence '69 (FTW) Retired.
Tipton, Prentice '08 (SAG) Merrill, MI Sacred Heart; Merrill, MI St. Patrick.
Tiqual, Robert (WIL)[J] Dover, DE Oblate Apostles of the Two Hearts.
Tirabassi, Camillo '59 (FTW)[C] South Bend, IN Saint Joseph's High School; South Bend, IN Holy Family Retired.
Tirado, Orlando *c.m.* '99 (SJN) Military Services.
Tirado, Ramon Orlando *c.m.* '86 (MO) Air National Guard Chaplains.
Tirado, Ramon Orlando '86 (SJN) San Juan, PR San Lucas.
Tirkey, Dominic '98 (GR) Rockford, MI Our Lady of Consolation.
Tirpak, Adrian *t.o.r.* '60 (ALT) Windber, PA St. Anthony of Padua.
Tiscornia, Thomas A. *m.m.* '73 (FgM) Maryknoll, NY MARYKNOLL.
Tissera, Edward J. '89 (HRT) Waterbury, CT St. Joseph; Waterbury, CT St. Patrick.
Titko, Stephen '79 (PRM) Office of Evangelization and Missionary Activity.
Titland, Peter R. *s.j.* '70 (FgM) Portland, OR Society of Jesus.
Tito, Joseph P. '96 (CHI) Chicago, IL Our Lady of Mercy.
Tito, Joseph '88 (NOR) Baltic, CT St. Mary of the Immaculate Conception.
Tito, Rocco A. '55 (E) Meadville, PA St. Brigid; Meadville, PA Crawford County Care Center.
Titonea, Radu N. '09 (ROM) Long Island City, NY.
Titotto, Mario *c.s.* '72 (PRO) Johnston, RI St. Rocco.
Titta, Santino '60 (ALB) Retired.
Tittler, Leo R. '63 (BAL) Retired.
Titus, Austin E. '92 (NY) Staten Island, NY Holy Family.
Titus, Fernando '05 (CI) Chuuk, FM St. Francis Assisi; [C] Tunnuk, Chuuk, FM Vicariate Residence; Chuuk, FM Assumption of the Blessed Virgin Mary.
Titus, John M. '89 (SFD) Charleston, IL St. Charles Borromeo; [N] Charleston, IL Eastern Illinois University Newman Catholic Center.
Titus, Rodney '95 (PMB) Vero Beach, FL St. Helen.
Titus, Steven Matthew '08 (CHY) Cheyenne, WY St. Mary's Cathedral.
Tiu, Jimmy Lim '00 (FAR) On Duty Outside the Diocese.
Tivadar, Vasile '95 (STF) Priest Personnel Board; Ozone Park, NY St. Mary Protectress; Brooklyn.
Tivenan, John J. '72 (BRK) On Leave/Unassigned.
Tivy, Gerald '64 (JOL) Retired.
Tivy, Thomas A. '62 (CHI) Chicago, IL Resurrection Retired.
Tix, Michael '92 (STP) Savage, MN St. John the Baptist.
Tizio, John *c.ss.r.* '85 (RVC) Bethpage, NY St. Martin of Tours.
Tizio, Joseph *c.ss.r.* '75 (BRK) Brooklyn, NY Our Lady of Perpetual Help Basilica.
Tizziani, Mario J. '06 (COV) Legion of Mary; Independence, KY St. Cecilia.
Tjaya, Thomas *s.j.* '03 (BO)[U] Newton, MA The Jesuit Community at Boston College.
Tjaya, Thomas (MAN) Indonesian Apostolate.
Tkachuk, William '81 (CHI) Evanston, IL St. Nicholas.
Tkel, Wayne *s.j.* '02 (CI) Palau, PW St. Thomas Apostle; [C] Manresa Jesuit House.
Tkocz, Peter '01 (ALB) Cohoes, NY St. Michael.
Tlapa, Richard J. (CHI) Retired.
Tlucek, Edward G. *o.f.m.* '78 (GRY) Cedar Lake, IN Holy Name; Provincial Councilors:; [H] Cedar Lake, IN Our Lady of Lourdes Friary.

To'alepai, Etuale *m.f.* '98 (SPP) Pago Pago, AS Our Lady of Fatima; Director of Propagation of the Faith.
Toal, Bernard E. *s.s.c.* '43 (SB) Fontana, CA St. Mary Retired.
Toal, Bernard *s.s.c.* '43 (OM)[K] St. Columbans Missionary Society of St. Columban.
Toal, James Aloysius '58 (LA) North Hollywood, CA St. Charles Borromeo Retired.
Toal, James F. *o.f.m.* '75 (SP)[N] St. Petersburg, FL St. Anthony Friary.
Toale, Rev. Msgr. Thomas E. '81 (DUB)[L] Dubuque, IA St. Joseph's Convent, Mount Carmel; Monona, IA St. Mary; Monona, IA St. Patrick; Monona, IA St. Bridget; Vicar General and Episcopal Vicar for Dubuque Region; College of Consultors; Archdiocesan Pastoral Center; The Archdiocese of Dubuque Corporate Board; Catholic Charities Board of Directors; Finance Council; Pastoral Council; Ex Officio Members; Board of Directors/Priest Pension Plan Board of Trustees; Archbishop's Cabinet; On Special or Other Archdiocesan Assignment; Archdiocese of Dubuque Deposit & Loan Fund Board; Archdiocese of Dubuque Education Fund Board; Archdiocese of Dubuque Perpetual Care Fund Board; Archdiocese of Dubuque Seminarian Education Fund Board; Due Process Board; School Tuition Organization Board of Directors; St. Mary's Home Board of Directors.
Toan, Hoang (GAL)[L] Houston, TX Pope John Paul XXIII Priests' Residence Retired.
Tobias, Joseph F. *m.s.c.* '66 (ALN) Nazareth, PA Holy Family; Elected Members.
Tobin, Charles P. '68 (KC) Belton, MO St. Sabina's; Deans.
Tobin, David *c.ss.r.* '63 (OAK)[M] Berkeley, CA Redemptorist Fathers (Denver Province).
Tobin, Eamon '72 (ORL) Melbourne, FL Ascension.
Tobin, George W. '50 (OG) Retired.
Tobin, James M. *s.m.* '69 (STL)[O] St. Louis, MO Marianist Community, Our Lady of the Pillar Parish; St. Louis, MO Our Lady of the Pillar.
Tobin, Jeremy *o.praem.* '69 (JKS) Carthage, MS St. Anne; [E] Raymond, MS Priory of St. Moses the Black; [H] Raymond, MS Hinds Community College Catholic Student Organization.
Tobin, Joseph W. *c.ss.r.* '78 (DEN)[N] Denver The Redemptorists/Denver Province.
Tobin, Patrick '56 (KC) Kansas City, MO St. Therese Parish Retired.
Tobin, Paul R. '64 (Y) Campbell, OH St. Joseph the Provider Retired.
Tobin, Robert V. *m.m.* '57 (FgM) Maryknoll, NY MARYKNOLL Retired.
Tobin, T. Michael '93 (L) Hodgenville, KY Our Lady of Mercy.
Tobin, Terence *o.f.m.conv.* '55 (FgM) Mount Saint Francis, IN Province of Our Lady of Consolation.
Tobin, Thomas F. *s.j.* '65 (FgM) Detroit, MI Detroit Province.
Tobin, Thomas H. *s.j.* '73 (CHI)[C] Chicago, IL Jesuit Community at Loyola University Chicago.
Tobin, Thomas '59 (GF) Finance Council; Baker, MT St. John the Evangelist.
Tobin, Tom '05 (SP) Pinellas Park, FL Sacred Heart.
Tobin, Vincent *o.s.b.* '59 (IND)[K] St. Meinrad, IN St. Meinrad Archabbey.
Tobolski, James F. '84 (SUP) Superior, WI St. Francis Xavier; Judicial Vicar; Vicar for Canonical Affairs; Northwest Deanery; Presbyteral Council & Diocesan Consultors; Personnel Placement Board; Ecumenical Commission.
Tobolski, Robert *m.s.c.* '55 (ALN) Reading, PA St. Mary.
Toborowsky, Jonathan S. '98 (MET) Laurence Harbor, NJ St. Lawrence; Deans.
Tocco, Rev. Msgr. Anthony M. '65 (DET) Bloomfield Hills, MI St. Hugo of the Hills; College of Consultors.
Tochtrop, Randolph G. '96 (SPC) Advance, MO St. Joseph; Charleston, MO Southeast Correctional Center; Oran, MO Guardian Angel.
Toczek, Melchior *o.f.m.* '49 (SFD)[L] Springfield, IL Our Lady of Angels Friary.
Todd, Richard *c.m.f.* '55 (MET) Perth Amboy, NJ Our Lady of Fatima.
Todd, Wilmer '63 (HT) Retired.
Toepfer, John *o.f.m.cap.* '86 (COS) Colorado Springs, CO St. Mary Cathedral; Hispanic Ministry; [F] Colorado Springs, CO Our Lady of the Angels Friary.
Tofani, Rev. Msgr. Richard L. '79 (TR) Hainesport, NJ Our Lady Queen of Peace; New York, NY A. The Pontifical Society for the Propagation of the Faith; Burlington County.
Togni, Peter J. *s.j.* '85 (SJ)[L] Los Altos, CA Jesuit Retreat Center of Los Altos.
Toilolo, Damien *o.s.b.* '05 (LA) Valyermo, CA; [P] Valyermo, CA St. Andrew's Abbey.
Tokarczyk, Joseph M. '79 (NY) Florida, NY St. Joseph; Pine Island, NY St. Stanislaus.
Tokarski, Gregory '99 (DET) Farmington Hills, MI St. Clare of Assisi.
Tokarski, Stan '93 (DET) Detroit, MI SS. Peter and Paul.
Tokarski, Stephen L. '69 (GF) Billings, MT St. Pius X; Personnel Board.
Tokarz, David J. '91 (MOB) Mobile, AL Our Savior; [J] Mobile, AL Cursillo; Ecumenical Commission.
Tokarz, Thomas M. '77 (WOR) Gardner, MA Holy Spirit; Gardner, MA St. Joseph's.
Tokaz, John *o.f.m.cap.* '78 (ROC) Trumansburg, NY St. James the Apostle; [J] Interlaken, NY St. Fidelis Friary.
Toland, Charles M. *o.s.m.* '56 (CHI)[N] Chicago Order of Friar Servants of Mary (Servites) United States of America Province, Inc.
Toland, Eugene W. *m.m.* '64 (FgM) Maryknoll, NY MARYKNOLL.
Toland, Terrence *s.j.* '52 (PH) Philadelphia, PA Old St. Joseph's Retired.
Tolang, Jaime '58 (SEA) Seattle, WA Immaculate Conception Retired.
Toledo, Joseph '09 (DEN) Fort Collins, CO St. Elizabeth Ann Seton.
Tolentino, Cesar (TR) Red Bank, NJ St. James.
Tolentino, Rev. Msgr. Eddie E. '84 (WDC) Deans; Silver Spring, MD St. Michael; Priest Council; Archdiocesan College of Consultors.
Tolentino, Eric N. '06 (ALN) Easton, PA St. Jane Frances de Chantal.
Tolentino, Rommel P. '05 (LKC) Hackberry, LA St. Peter Apostle; Presbyteral Council; Diocesan Consultors.
Tolentino, Virgilio T. '82 (MET) Middlesex, NJ Our Lady of Mount Virgin.
Tolentino de la Rosa, Lorenzo Maria *o.cart.* '92 (BUR)[E] Arlington, VT Carthusian Foundation in America, Inc., Charterhouse of the Transfiguration.
Tolg, Killian '04 (NO)[A] St. Benedict, LA St. Joseph Seminary College; [P] St. Benedict, LA St. Joseph Abbey.
Tollefson, Rolf R. '01 (STP)[A] St. Paul, MN St. John Vianney Seminary; [C] St. Paul, MN University of St. Thomas.
Tolleson, William Barton '07 (HEL) Helena, MT St. Mary.
Tollini, Frederick P. *s.j.* '65 (SJ)[B] Santa Clara, CA Jesuit Community.
Tolve, Paul *o.f.m.cap.* '84 (NY) Valhalla, NY Westchester County Jail.
Toma, Rev. Msgr. Zouhair '68 (EST) Troy, MI St. Joseph Chaldean Parish.
Toma, Zuhair G. (ORG) Santa Ana, CA St. George (Chaldean Catholic).
Toma, Zuhair G. '00 (SPA) Las Vegas, NV St. Barbara Assyrian–Chaldean Catholic Church.
Tomas, Efren A. *m.s.* '81 (HON) Vicars Forane; Kahului, HI Christ the King; College of Consultors; Presbyteral Council.
Tomas, Peter '95 (SJP) Austintown, OH St. Anne; St. Josaphat Sacerdotal Society; Presbyters.
Tomasek, Richard A. *s.j.* '73 (MIL)[P] Milwaukee, WI Jesuit Community at Marquette University.
Tomaselli, Rev. Msgr. Samuel J. '59 (ALT) Retired.
Tomasi, Lydio F. *c.s.* '63 (WDC) Washington, DC Holy Rosary.
Tomasiewicz, Edward J. *c.m.* '74 (CHI)[N] Chicago DePaul Vincentian Residence.
Tomasiewicz, Frank '65 (SCL) Retired.
Tomasiewicz, Mark A. '91 (OM) Tekamah, NE St. Patrick; Air Force Reserve Chaplains.
Tomasko, Andrew J. '91 (DET) Shelby Twp., MI St. Therese of Lisieux.
Tomaskovic, Emil *s.a.* '71 (NY)[EE] Garrison, NY Franciscan Friars of the Atonement.
Tomasone, Richard C. '80 (E)[C] Du Bois, PA DuBois Area Catholic School; [K] Du Bois, PA Christ the King Manor, Inc.
Tomasovich, Rev. Msgr. John A. '48 (NO) Retired.
Tomasso, Paul J. '81 (ROC) Geneva, NY Our Lady of Peace Roman Catholic Church of Geneva, NY; [M] Geneva, NY Hobart and William Smith College; [N] Rochester, NY Family Rosary For Peace, Inc.
Tomaszewski, Rev. Msgr. Michael J. '58 (GRY) Retired.
Tomczak, Peter A. '05 (NO) Metairie, LA St. Angela Merici.
Tomich, Daniel W. '76 (CHI) Oak Lawn, IL St. Louis De Montfort.
Tomichek, Rev. Msgr. George *d.c.* '74 (PH) Philadelphia, PA St. Peter the Apostle.
Tomicky, Ronald '75 (CLV) Retired.
Tomiczek, Damian *s.d.s.* '82 (NEW)[M] Verona, NJ The Salvatorian Fathers.
Tomiczek, Damian *s.d.s.* (NOR) Moosup, CT All–Hallows; Wauregan, CT Sacred Heart.
Tomikeh, Tomy '88 (SPA) North Hollywood, CA St. Paul Assyrian–Chaldean Catholic Parish; North Hollywood, CA St. Paul Assyrian–Chaldean.
Tomkins, Robert J. '88 (SB) Retired.
Tomkosky, Richard B. '00 (ALT)[I] Lock Haven, PA Lock Haven University (Lock Haven); Lock Haven, PA Immaculate Conception.
Tomlinson, Brian *o.f.m.cap.* '65 (NEW) Hackensack, NJ Church of St. Francis of Assisi; [M] Union City, NJ Capuchin Friars – Province of the Sacred Stigmata of St. Francis.
Tomlinson, Richard '09 (CHR) Sullivan's Island, SC Stella Maris.
Tommaseo, Ellis '98 (BRK) Long Island City, NY Most Precious Blood; [S] Croatian Apostolate.
Tompkins, John Mary *o.s.b.* '93 (GBG) Latrobe, PA Excela Health – Latrobe Area Hospital; [G] Latrobe, PA Saint Vincent Archabbey.
Tompkins, Terrence P. '82 (P)[A] St. Benedict, OR Mount Angel Seminary.
Tompkins, Terry '82 (OAK) On Duty Outside the Diocese.
Tomson, Lucas Ethan '07 (SPK) Spokane, WA Assumption of the Blessed Virgin Mary.
Tomzik, Fred W. '84 (CHI) La Grange Park, IL St. Louise de Marillac.
Ton, Anthony '66 (SEA) Retired.
Tonary, David *m.s.f.* '81 (SAT) Seguin, TX Our Lady of Guadalupe.
Tonelli, Robert F. '72 (CHI) Streamwood, IL St. John the Evangelist; Deans.
Tonelotto, Walter *c.s.* '74 (NY) New York, NY St. James; New York, NY St. Joseph.
Tonelotto, Walter *c.s.* '74 (BRK)[X] Ridgewood, NY Friends of RADIO MARIA, Inc.
Toner, Edward R. '52 (COV) Retired.
Toner, Oliver '71 (VEN) Fort Myers, FL Church Of The Resurrection Of Our Lord.
Toner, Patrick A. '75 (COL) Plain City, OH St. Joseph; Deanery 5: West; Presbyteral Council; Ohio Reformatory for Women; Parochial Examiners.
Tong, Peter *o.c.s.o.* '68 (L)[L] Trappist, KY Abbey of Our Lady of Gethsemani, of the Order of Cistercians of the Strict Observance.
Tonkin, John W. '05 (CIN) Anna, OH Sacred Heart of Jesus.
Tonos, Joseph '94 (JKS) Approved Advocate and Auditors; Oxford, MS St. John the Evangelist; [H] Oxford, MS Ole Miss Campus Ministries.
Tonto, Henry *s.m.m.m.* '87 (NY) Warwick, NY St. Anthony Community Hospital.
Toof, Daniel R. '94 (ATL) Monroe, GA St. Anna.
Toohey, Richard '01 (E)[P] Meadville, PA Allegheny College; Meadville, PA St. Mary of Grace.
Toohey, Timothy J. '65 (STL) Washington, MO St. John's Mercy Hospital; [J] Washington, MO St. John's Mercy Hospital.
Toohy, Rev. Msgr. William J. '61 (NY) New York, NY Blessed Sacrament; [I] New York, NY The Ladies of Charity of the Catholic Charities of the Archdiocese of New York.
Toole, Arthur A. '58 (ALB) Troy, NY St. Michael the Archangel Retired.
Toole, Lawrence E. '67 (PRO) Cumberland, RI St. Patrick.
Toole, Patrick D. '07 (CHL) Charlotte, NC St. Matthew.
Toolis, Martin '70 (GR) Retired.
Tooman, Robert E. '77 (NEW) Bayonne, NJ St. Vincent de Paul.
Toomey, Daniel A. '03 (SCR) Dallas, PA Gate of Heaven; Harveys Lake, PA Our Lady of Victory.
Toomey, John M. '61 (BO) Senior Priests. Retired.
Toomey, Kevin G. '78 (BO) Medford, MA St. Raphael.
Topel, L. John *s.j.* '65 (SEA) Port Townsend, WA St. Mary Star of the Sea; [L] Seattle, WA Arrupe Jesuit Community at Seattle University.
Topf, Thomas J. '63 (SC) Retired.
Topper, Charles J. '68 (HBG) On Duty Outside the Diocese.
Topper, John M. *o.s.m.* '87 (CHI)[N] Chicago, IL Order of Friar Servants of Mary (Servites) United States of America Province, Inc.; [N] Chicago Order of Friar Servants of Mary (Servites) United States of America Province, Inc.; Chicago, IL.
Topper, John M. *o.s.m.* '87 (P)[L] Portland, OR The Grotto, The National Sanctuary of Our Sorrowful Mother.
Topper, Rev. Msgr. Vincent J. '36 (HBG) Harrisburg, PA St. Catherine Laboure Retired.
Toppo, Deepak *s.j.* '07 (CHI)[C] Chicago, IL Jesuit Community at Loyola University Chicago.
Torak, George (NY)[FF] Sparkill, NY Dominican Convent of Our Lady of the Rosary.
Torba, Zdzislaw J. '91 (CHI) Chicago, IL St. Ferdinand.
Torborg, Elmer '55 (SCL) Retired.
Torchia, Joseph *o.p.* '01 (PRO)[P] Providence St. Thomas Aquinas Priory at Providence College.
Torgerson, Rev. Msgr. Lloyd A. '65 (LA) Santa Monica, CA St. Monica.
Torm, Agustin '93 (CHR) Aiken, SC St. Mary, Help of Christians.
Torma, Andrew *m.s.c.* '76 (RCK)[G].
Tormey, Daniel '55 (ROC) Newly Ordained Priests Retired.
Tormey, James D. '78 (SY) Johnson City, NY Blessed Sacrament; Vestal, NY St. Vincent de Paul; Truxton, NY St. Patrick.
Tornes, Dale F. '70 (STU) Colerain, OH St. Frances Cabrini.
Tornes, Dale '70 (STU) Deans; Members.
Torney, Rev. Msgr. John R. '39 (MET) Bernardsville, NJ Our Lady of Perpetual Help; [I] Somerset, NJ Maria

Regina Residence Retired.
Toro, Carlos Perez '88 (SJN) San Juan, PR Santa Rosa de Lima.
Toro–Rivas, Gabriel '02 (BRK) Brooklyn, NY St. Athanasius.
Torok, Rev. Msgr. Dezso '48 (Y) East Palestine, OH Our Lady of Lourdes Retired.
Torok, George J. *c.o.* '58 (NY)[II] Sparkill, NY Hallel Institute; Tappan, NY Our Lady of the Sacred Heart; [II] Sparkill, NY New York Oratory of St. Philip Neri, Inc.
Torpey, Charles L. '69 (GI) Priests' Advisory Board (Presbyteral Council); Grand Island, NE St. Leo; Vicar General; Adjutant Vicars–Judicial; Promoter Justitiae; Judges; Diocesan Consultors.
Torpey, James M. '83 (ALN) Hamburg, PA St. Mary.
Torpey, Matt G. *o.c.s.o.* '56 (ATL)[G] Conyers, GA The Monastery of the Holy Spirit.
Torpey, Michael J. '68 (RVC) Patchogue, NY Our Lady of Mt. Carmel.
Torquato, James R. '89 (PIT) Pittsburgh, PA St. Basil.
Torre, Emilio Diaz *l.c.* '93 (NY)[II] Thornwood, NY Helping Hands Medical Missions, Inc.
Torre, Gonzalo De Jesus *o.f.m.* '08 (NY) New York, NY Holy Name of Jesus.
Torre, Jesse *o.f.m.cap.* '60 (FWT) Fort Worth, TX Immaculate Heart of Mary.
Torrens, Jim *s.j.* '61 (FRS) Fresno, CA St. Alphonsus.
Torrente, Lorenzo '75 (RNO) On Special Assignment.
Torres, A. Ernesto *c.j.m.* (SD) Solana Beach, CA St. James.
Torres, Adrian '75 (PMB) Palm Springs, FL St. Luke.
Torres, Agustino Miguel *c.f.r.* '08 (NY)[EE] Bronx, NY Franciscan Friars of the Renewal.
Torres, Angel Pagan '80 (SJN) Dorado, PR Ntra. Sra. de La Salud; Bayamon.
Torres, Daniel A. '96 (LKC) Vicar General and Moderator of the Curia; Diocesan Consultors; Director of Seminarians; Parish Boundaries Commission; Personnel Board; Seminary Advisory Board; Vocation Director; Lake Charles, LA St. Henry; Presbyteral Council.
Torres, Ernesto '72 (DAL) Mesquite, TX Divine Mercy of Our Lord.
Torres, Fernando *sch.p.* '93 (PCE)[C] Coto Laurel, PR Colegio Ponceno; Coto Laurel, PR.
Torres, Fernando '85 (R) Clinton, NC Immaculate Conception; Council of Priests.
Torres, Francisco Santiago '05 (PCE) Yauco, PR Santo Domingo de Guzman.
Torres, Frank D. '94 (GRY) Hammond, IN St. Casimir.
Torres, Fredi Gomez '02 (PEO) Mendota, IL Holy Cross; Mendota, IL SS. Peter and Paul.
Torres, Gabriel M. (SJN)[B] San Juan, PR Nuestra Senora de la Altagracia.
Torres, Heriberto *c.r.* '04 (PBL) Pueblo, CO Holy Family.
Torres, Hipólito '85 (CGS)[F] Caguas, PR Movimiento Juan XXIII; Diocesan Consultors; Priests Senate; Caguas, PR Sagrado Corazon de Jesus.
Torres, Ivan J. '88 (MO) DEPARTMENT OF VETERANS AFFAIRS HOSPITALS AND CHAPLAINS; DEPARTMENT OF VETERANS AFFAIRS HOSPITALS AND CHAPLAINS.
Torres, Jorge '05 (ORL) Secretary; Appointed Members; Oviedo, FL Most Precious Blood Catholic Church; [G] Orlando, FL Catholic Campus Ministry at the University of Central Florida.
Torres, Jose Angel *o.f.m.cap.* '01 (PCE)[E] Ponce, PR Fraternidad Santa Teresita, Frailes Capuchinos.
Torres, Jose *o.m.i.* '74 (CC) Kingsville, TX St. Martin.
Torres, Juan M. *o.p.* (GAL) Houston, TX Holy Rosary.
Torres, Juan R. '04 (MIA) Coconut Grove, FL St. Hugh.
Torres, Lonilo R. (AGN) Inarajan, GU St. Joseph.
Torres, Mario Alberto *s.j.* '01 (SJN)[B] San Juan, PR Colegio San Ignacio de Loyola; [H] San Juan, PR Comunidad Jesuita.
Torres, Mario '96 (LA) Huntington Park, CA St. Matthias.
Torres, Mark '98 (LA) Los Angeles, CA Dolores Mission.
Torres, Miguel A. *c.ss.r.* '99 (CGS) Aguas Buenas, PR Church of Tres Santos Reyes.
Torres, Nestor (CHI) Waukegan, IL Most Blessed Trinity.
Torres, Nohe '04 (CHL) Salisbury, NC Sacred Heart.
Torres, Rafael *c.ss.r.* '64 (CGS) San Lorenzo, PR Nuestra Senora de la Mercedes.
Torres, Rolando '07 (BGP) Greenwich, CT St. Mary.
Torres, Victor *o.m.i.* '95 (SJN) Toa Alta, PR San Judas Tadeo.
Torres–Pagan, William '91 (SJN) Bayamon, PR N. Sra. de la Providencia; Vicar of Ecumenism.
Torres–Rico, Rafael '07 (COS) Colorado Springs, CO St. Gabriel the Archangel.
Torres–Rivera, Gabriel M. '95 (SJN) Trujillo Alto, PR San Francisco de Asis.
Torres Graciani, Ivan '88 (SJN) On Duty Outside the Archdiocese.
Torreto, Benjamin '85 (ANC) Vocations; Eagle River, AK St. Andrew.
Torretto, Joseph '75 (RIC) Martinsville, VA St. Joseph.
Torrez, Basil '56 (SAL) Retired.
Torrez, John '98 (KCK) Olathe, KS St. Paul.
Torsiello, Ralph C. '58 (WDC) Retired.
Torson, Daniel L. *c.pp.s.* '90 (JOL)[A] Romeoville, IL Lewis University.
Tortora, James '72 (NEW) Jersey City, NJ Our Lady of Victories.
Tortorelli, Kevin *o.f.m.* '73 (NY) New York, NY St. Francis of Assisi.
Torwel, Vitalis '92 (DAV)[J] Iowa City, IA O'Keefe Hall.
Tos, Aldo J. '53 (NY) Retired.
Toscano, Javier '07 (AUS) Cedar Park, TX St. Margaret Mary.
Toscano, Pasquale A. '44 (HRT) Retired.
Toschi, Larry *o.s.j.* '76 (FRS) Bakersfield, CA Our Lady of Guadalupe; Councilors:.
Tosco, Lawrence *c.s.j.* '70 (CLV)[N] Avon, OH Congregation of St. Joseph.
Tosco, Lorenzo *s.s.d.* '70 (CLV)[A] Wickliffe, OH St. Mary Seminary and Graduate School of Theology.
Tosello, Matthew '62 (PIT) Prospect, PA St. Christopher at the Lake.
Tosi, Rev. Msgr. John C. '73 (BRK) Whitestone, NY St. Luke.
Tosti, Rev. Msgr. Ronald A. '62 (FR) Retired.
Tosto, Louis F. '97 (RCK) Rock Falls, IL St. Andrew.
Totah, Sami '71 (NY) Yonkers, NY Immaculate Conception; Good Shepherd Arabic Community of St. Mary.
Totaro, Dominic J. *s.j.* '67 (BAL)[S] Towson Maryland Province of the Society of Jesus; Towson, MD Society of Jesus.
Toth, Stephen J. '02 (NEW) Lodi, NJ St. Francis de Sales; Ridgewood, NJ Valley Hospital.
Totten, Raymond F. '48 (COL) Retired.
Tottle, Gregg '91 (SP) Clearwater, FL St. Michael The Archangel.
Totton, Joseph '04 (KC) St. Joseph, MO St. James.
Tou, Ivan *c.s.p.* '02 (LA) Los Angeles, CA St. Paul the Apostle.
Tou, John B. '57 (NY) Retired.
Tou, Louis A. '56 (WDC)[M] Washington, DC Cardinal O'Boyle Residence for Priests Retired.
Touchette, Marc L. '57 (ALB) Retired.
Tougas, Paul J. '64 (WOR) Boylston, MA St. Mary of the Hills.
Toups, David '97 (SP) On Duty Outside the Diocese.
Toups, Earl J. *c.ss.r.* '48 (STL)[O] Liguori, MO St. Clement Health Care Center.
Toups, Mark '01 (HT) Houma, LA St. Lucy; Thibodaux, LA St. Luke; Seminarians.
Tourangeau, John M. *o.praem.* '86 (GB)[A] De Pere, WI St. Norbert Abbey; [J] De Pere, WI St. Norbert Abbey.
Tourigny, William A. '80 (SPR) Chicopee, MA St. Rose de Lima; Bishop's Commission for Clergy.
Tourville, David E. '09 (BUF) Kenmore, NY St. John the Baptist.
Tovar, Emilio *c.m.* '50 (ARE) Manati, PR La Candelaria.
Tovar, Ireneo Lopez '50 (CAM) Retired.
Tovar–Encinas, Jesus (ORL) DeLand, FL St. Peter's Church.
Towey, Damian *c.p.* '56 (PMB)[H] North Palm Beach, FL Our Lady of Florida Spiritual Center; Promoter of Justice.
Towle, Joseph C. *s.j.* '66 (NY)[EE] New York, NY Jesuit Community of the Immaculate Conception.
Towle, Joseph W. *m.m.* '65 (NY)[EE] Maryknoll Maryknoll Fathers and Brothers Retired.
Townsend, Charles L. '91 (LIN) Wahoo, NE St. Wenceslaus; [C] Wahoo, NE Bishop Neumann Jr.–Sr. High School; [L] Wahoo, NE Bishop Neumann High School Endowment Fund.
Townsend, Joe C. '88 (TLS) Broken Arrow, OK St. Benedict; Coweta, OK St. Vincent de Paul.
Townsend, Ralph V. *o.p.* '50 (L) Louisville, KY St. Louis Bertrand; [L] Louisville, KY St. Louis Bertrand Priory.
Towsley, Peter J. '91 (BGP) Bridgeport, CT St. Ann.
Toyinbo, Andrew *m.s.p.* '86 (MOB) Mount Vernon, AL St. Peter the Apostle.
Tozzi, Anthony G. '09 (CIN) Mason, OH St. Susanna.
Tozzi, Ross '01 (FBK) Presbyteral Council; Consultors; Vocation Director; Kotzebue, AK St. Francis Xavier Catholic Church Kotzebue; Nome, AK St. Joseph Catholic Church Nome.
Trabold, Rev. Msgr. George R. '73 (NEW) Short Hills, NJ St. Rose of Lima.
Tracey, Bernard M. *c.m.* '74 (PH)[B] Philadelphia, PA St. Vincent's Seminary; [Y] Philadelphia Congregation of the Mission[Y].
Tracey, Michael '72 (BLX) Bay St. Louis, MS Our Lady of the Gulf.
Tracey, Thomas S. '63 (CAM) Retired.
Tracey, William *c.ss.r.* '55 (FgM) Baltimore Province.
Tracy, David W. '63 (BGP) On Duty Outside the Diocese.
Tracy, Eugene '91 (SPK) Spokane, WA St. Charles.
Tracy, Rev. Msgr. James R. '60 (CAM) Sicklerville, NJ The Church of St. Charles Borromeo, Washington Township, N.J.; Camden–Gloucester Deanery; College of Consultors.
Tracy, John P. '48 (HRT) Retired.
Tracy, Rev. Msgr. Joseph A. '92 (PH) Lansdale, PA St. Stanislaus.
Tracy, Laurence C. '66 (ROC) Rochester, NY St. Michael; Rochester, NY Our Lady of Perpetual Help; Rochester, NY Our Lady of Perpetual Help.
Tracy, Philip A. '88 (PRT) Deans; Skowhegan, ME Christ the King Parish; Waterville, ME Corpus Christi Parish.
Tracy, Philip Michael '60 (PRT) Retired.
Tracy, Robert D. *o.carm.* '63 (NY) FDR DVA Hospital.
Tracy, T. Shawn *o.s.a.* '66 (PH)[Y] Villanova, PA St. Augustine Friary.
Traczyk, Edward W. *s.ch.* '78 (NY) Poughkeepsie, NY St. Joseph.
Trader, William A. '74 (PH) Berwyn, PA St. Monica.
Trahan, Charles N. '81 (LAF) Port Barre, LA Sacred Heart of Jesus.
Trahan, Clint James '08 (LAF) Rayne, LA St. Joseph.
Trahan, Harold '69 (LAF) Lafayette, LA St. Mary, Mother of the Church.
Trainor, Daniel M. '61 (PRO) Council Members; College of Consultors Retired.
Trainor, Henry J. '73 (SFR) Retired.
Trainor, Michael S.P. '07 (NEW) Short Hills, NJ St. Rose of Lima.
Trainor, Michael *o.p.* '75 (NY) New York, NY St. Catherine of Siena; Manhattan, NY Hospital for Special Surgery; Manhattan, NY Memorial Sloan Kettering Cancer Center; Manhattan, NY New York Presbyterian Hospital.
Trainor, Richard F. '77 (WOR) North Oxford, MA St. Ann; Minister to Priests.
Trainor, Rev. Msgr. Robert M. '57 (NY) Bronx, NY Sacred Heart.
Trammell, Ian W. '05 (TR) Hamilton Square, NJ St. Gregory the Great; Office of Life and Justice Ministries.
Tran, Albert Sang V. '92 (LA) Oxnard, CA St. Anthony.
Tran, Andrew *o.praem.* '06 (ORG) Costa Mesa, CA St. John the Baptist.
Tran, Anh Q. '90 (SAT) Defenders of the Bond.
Tran, Anh '90 (FWT) Deans; Scouting; Grapevine, TX St. Francis of Assisi.
Tran, Anh *s.j.* (WDC)[N] Washington, DC The Jesuit Community at Georgetown University.
Tran, Anthony Doan '88 (BLX) Laurel, MS Immaculate Conception; Waynesboro, MS St. Bernadette.
Tran, Anthony Hung N. *o.p.* '92 (GAL)[O] Houston, TX Dominican Friars, St. Mark Priory, Inc.
Tran, Anthony Lan '70 (SEA) Chaplains.
Tran, Augustine Hoa T. '98 (ATL) Roswell, GA St. Peter Chanel.
Tran, Augustine Minh Hai '04 (ARL) Notaries; Leesburg, VA St. John the Apostle.
Tran, Augustine '98 (ATL)[C] Roswell, GA Blessed Trinity Catholic High School.
Tran, Benjamin Philip '06 (ORG) Garden Grove, CA St. Callistus.
Tran, Bennet '08 (STP) Anoka, MN St. Stephen.
Tran, Binh K. '92 (PEO) Chatsworth, IL SS. Peter and Paul.
Tran, Christopher H. '08 (OKL) Duncan, OK Assumption.
Tran, Cong Bang *s.v.d.* '00 (FgM) Techny, IL.
Tran, Dac T. *o.f.m.* '89 (CHR) Greenville, SC Our Lady of the Rosary; Administrator for Vietnamese Ministry.
Tran, Dominic Dat '99 (PT) Niceville, FL Holy Name of Jesus.
Tran, Dominic Dieu '01 (HT) Morgan City, LA Thanh Gia.
Tran, Dominic Hung (SAC)[I] Walnut Grove, CA Monastery of Chau Son Sacramento.
Tran, Dominic '90 (PH) Vietnamese Apostolate.
Tran, Dominic *s.d.b.* '03 (NEW)[M] Orange, NJ The Salesian Community.
Tran, Dominic '09 (ATL) Marietta, GA Church of the Transfiguration.
Tran, Dung Anton '02 (GR) Muskegon, MI St. Francis de Sales.
Tran, Francis Vu *s.c.j.* '05 (MIL)[P] Milwaukee, WI SCJ Community; [P] Hales Corners, WI Priests of the Sacred Heart; Franklin, WI St. Martin of Tours.
Tran, Francis *c.m.c.* '99 (KC)[A] Conception, MO Conception Seminary College.
Tran, Hieu Chi '08 (LA) Lancaster, CA Sacred Heart.
Tran, Hoi '01 (SFE) Peralta, NM Our Lady of Guadalupe.
Tran, Hung Ba '98 (LA) Monrovia, CA Immaculate Conception.
Tran, Hung M. (CIN)[U] Dayton, OH Catholic Vietnamese Community of Dayton.
Tran, James Taiviet *s.j.* '04 (SEA)[L] Seattle, WA Arrupe Jesuit Community at Seattle University.
Tran, John Kha '89 (GAL) Katy, TX St. Bartholomew the Apostle.
Tran, John Lan *s.j.* '08 (STL)[F] St. Louis, MO St. Louis University High School, George H. Backer Memorial; [O] Saint Louis, MO St. Louis University High School Jesuit Community.

Tran, John Nghi '71 (LA) Claremont, CA Our Lady of the Assumption.
Tran, John Quy V. '05 (LA) Long Beach, CA St. Lucy.
Tran, John R. '00 (L) On Duty Outside the Archdiocese.
Tran, John Tinh *c.m.c.* '96 (BEA) Port Arthur, TX Queen of Vietnam.
Tran, John Tuyen Kim (KAL) Battle Creek, MI St. Jerome.
Tran, John '95 (NY) Monticello, NY St. Peter.
Tran, John *s.v.d.* '96 (SB)[I] Riverside, CA Divine Word Seminary.
Tran, John '00 (SAV) Albany, GA St. Teresa.
Tran, John–Nhan '92 (NO) La Place, LA St. Joan of Arc; Deans.
Tran, Joseph Chuc *m.m.* '03 (SB) San Bernardino, CA Our Lady of Hope Catholic Community, Inc.
Tran, Joseph Huynh *s.v.d.* '03 (FgM) Techny, IL.
Tran, Joseph M. '95 (NO) Pointe A La Hache, LA St. Thomas.
Tran, Joseph M. Duykim N. '90 (NEW) On Duty Outside the Archdiocese.
Tran, Joseph T. Sai *s.v.d.* '05 (LAF) Eunice, LA St. Lawrence.
Tran, Joseph Thang Dinh '96 (NO) Slidell, LA St. Luke the Evangelist.
Tran, Joseph Thuong '05 (ORG) Orange, CA Cathedral of the Holy Family.
Tran, Joseph Tu '99 (HT) Terrebonne General Medical Center.
Tran, Joseph '74 (LAN) Lansing, MI St. Andrew Dung–Lac.
Tran, Joseph '95 (NY) Bronx, NY St. Nicholas of Tolentine.
Tran, Joseph '04 (CC) Corpus Christi, TX St. Patrick.
Tran, Joseph '04 (DEN) Julesburg, CO St. Anthony.
Tran, Joseph '02 (OAK) Fremont, CA Holy Spirit; Military Chaplains.
Tran, Joseph '05 (HRT) Hartford, CT St. Lawrence O'Toole.
Tran, Joseph Thai Minh *s.s.s.* '94 (CLV)[N] Cleveland Congregation of the Blessed Sacrament Provincial House.
Tran, Kiem Van '91 (ORG) Garden Grove, CA St. Columban.
Tran, Loc '08 (ORG) Dana Point, CA St. Edward the Confessor.
Tran, Luan Quach '94 (MO) St. Helens, OR St. Frederic; Air Force Reserve Chaplains.
Tran, Luan '94 (P) Vernonia, OR St. Mary of Immaculate Conception; Area Vicars.
Tran, Luc Nghi '96 (SB) Fontana, CA St. Joseph.
Tran, Luke '01 (NEW) Linden, NJ St. John the Apostle.
Tran, Luong Quang '89 (BEA) Diocesan College of Consultors; Judicial Vicar; Diocesan Judges; [H] Beaumont, TX St. Thomas More Society of Southeast Texas; China, TX Our Lady of Sorrows; Presbyteral Council.
Tran, Manh *s.j.* '04 (LA)[C] Los Angeles, CA Jesuit Community.
Tran, Martin Duc '90 (ORG) Fountain Valley, CA Holy Spirit.
Tran, Martin Vanban *c.m.c.* '94 (BEA) Port Arthur, TX Queen of Vietnam.
Tran, Michael X '93 (SD) Lakeside, CA Blessed Kateri Tekakwitha.
Tran, Mike '02 (HT) Grand Isle, LA Our Lady of the Isle.
Tran, Nhi Dinh '71 (ARL) On Leave of Absence.
Tran, Paul Tam X. '00 (WDC) Silver Spring, MD Our Lady of Vietnam.
Tran, Peter Tam *s.v.d.* '98 (FgM) Techny, IL.
Tran, Peter '73 (RIC) Newport News, VA Our Lady of Mount Carmel.
Tran, Peter '99 (MET) Woodbridge, NJ St. James.
Tran, Philip B. *c.m.c.* '03 (SAC) Sacramento, CA Vietnamese Martyrs Church.
Tran, Phuong D. '65 (SEA) Centralia, WA St. Mary; Chehalis, WA St. Joseph; Pe Ell, WA St. Joseph; Toledo, WA St. Francis Xavier; Winlock, WA Sacred Heart.
Tran, Quan H. '96 (PH) Elkins Park, PA St. James; [D] Wyncote, PA Bishop McDevitt High School.
Tran, Quang Mihn '70 (MO) DEPARTMENT OF VETERANS AFFAIRS HOSPITALS AND CHAPLAINS.
Tran, Quang Minh (LAN) Veterans' Hospital.
Tran, Quynh Dinh '93 (SPR) Southeast Asian Apostolate; Springfield, MA St. Paul the Apostle.
Tran, Tam X. '00 (WDC) Forestville, MD Church of the Holy Spirit.
Tran, Tan Van '92 (DM) Corning, IA St. Patrick's; Lenox, IA St. Patrick; [D] Corning, IA Alegent Health Mercy Hospital.
Tran, Thang '96 (NO) Slidell, LA St. Luke the Evangelist.
Tran, Thienan '05 (SY) Asian Apostolate; Syracuse, NY Our Lady of Pompei/St. Peter; Syracuse, NY St. John the Evangelist.
Tran, Thoai "Aloysius" Ngoc *c.m.c.* '92 (SB) Riverside, CA Our Lady of Perpetual Help.
Tran, Tien '09 (NSH) Unassigned.
Tran, Trong Binh '04 (DOD) Ulysses, KS St. Bernadette Catholic Church of Johnson, Kansas; On Special Diocesan Assignment; Ulysses, KS Mary, Queen of Peace Catholic Church of Ulysses, Kansas.
Tran, Trong '04 (DOD) Vietnamese Ministry.
Tran, Tuan Quoc '97 (ATL) Holy Vietnamese Martyr's Mission.
Tran, Tung '03 (CC) Corpus Christi, TX Christ the King.
Tran, Vang Cong *c.ss.r.* (CHL) Concord, NC St. James.
Tran, Victor Dinh '99 (SJ) Milpitas, CA St. Elizabeth.
Tran, Vincent '07 (GAL) Houston, TX St. Jerome.
Tran, Vu Phong '04 (SEA) Anacortes, WA St. Mary.
Tran–Khac–Hy, Hilarius '57 (WDC) Retired.
Tran Cao Tuong, Andrew '75 (NO) Avondale, LA Assumption of Mary.
Trance, F. Raymond '94 (PIT) Glenshaw, PA St. Bonaventure.
Tranchida, Blaise *o.f.m.* '50 (NY)[EE] New York Franciscan Province of the Immaculate Conception.
Tranchina, Joseph '68 (NO) Retired.
Trancone, Gerard A. '69 (WDC) Special Ministries; [T] Washington, DC Gallaudet University Catholic Community; [W] Landover Hills, MD The Center for Deaf Ministries of the Archdiocese of Washington; Ministry for the Deaf.
Tranel, Daniel D. '56 (RCK) Retired.
Tranel, Don *g.h.m.* '88 (LR) Booneville, AR Church of Our Lady of the Assumption; Ratcliff, AR St. Anthony.
Tran Mai, Michael M. *c.m.c.* '93 (SPC)[A] Carthage, MO Congregation of the Mother Co–Redemptrix; [F] Carthage, MO Congregation of the Mother Coredemptrix, United States Assumption Province; Carthage, MO.
Tran Minh Man, Matthias M. *c.m.c.* '63 (SPC)[F] Carthage, MO Congregation of the Mother Coredemptrix, United States Assumption Province.
Tran Quoc Toan, John M. *c.m.c.* '05 (SPC)[F] Carthage, MO Congregation of the Mother Coredemptrix, United States Assumption Province.
Trapani, Anthony M. '73 (RVC) Lindenhurst, NY Our Lady of Perpetual Help.
Trapasso, Rev. Msgr. Thomas J. '49 (PAT) Pro–Synodal Judges; Catholic Deaf Society; [Q] Chester, NJ Nazareth Village Retired.
Trapp, Andrew '07 (CHR) Garden City, SC St. Michael.
Trapp, Arthur L. *c.m.* '56 (STL)[O] Perryville, MO Congregation of the Mission.
Trapp, Daniel J. '84 (DET)[A] The School of Theology; Detroit, MI St. Augustine and St. Monica.
Trapp, Joseph J. '96 (COL) Zaleski, OH St. Sylvester; Jackson, OH Holy Trinity; Corrections Reception Center.
Trapp, Joseph L. '59 (BEL) Benton, IL St. Joseph.
Trask, David R. '86 (CLV) Macedonia, OH Our Lady of Guadalupe; Auditors/Assessors.
Traub, George W. *s.j.* '67 (CIN)[Q] Milford, OH Jesuit Spiritual Center at Milford.
Traub, Robert '39 (FTW)[F] Fort Wayne, IN Saint Anne Home & Retirement Community Retired.
Traufler, John F. '57 (WIN) Retired.
Traupman, Robert '69 (ORL) Retired.
Travaglione, Michael *o.f.m.* '66 (MO) Army Chaplains.
Travaglione, Michael *o.f.m.* '66 (NY)[EE] New York Franciscan Province of the Immaculate Conception; [EE] New York Franciscan Province of the Immaculate Conception.
Travassos, Horace J. '73 (FR) Westport, MA Our Lady of Grace.
Travers, Alan '83 (NY) Staten Island, NY Holy Child.
Travers, David O. *s.j.* '68 (BO)[U] Boston The Society of Jesus of New England–Provincial Offices.
Travers, David O. *s.j.* '68 (HON) Honolulu, HI SS Peter and Paul.
Travers, Gerard P. '65 (NY) Highland Mills, NY St. Patrick.
Travers, Luke L. *o.s.b.* '86 (PAT)[N] Morristown, NJ St. Mary's Abbey; Morristown, NJ.
Travers, Patrick J. '93 (JUN) Juneau, AK St. Paul The Apostle; Chancellor; Diocesan Consultors; Judicial Vicar; Finance Council; Air Force Reserve Chaplains; Episcopal Delegate of the Apostolic Administrator.
Travers, Patrick *ss.cc.* '62 (LA)[D] La Verne, CA Damien High School; [P] La Verne, CA Congregation of the Sacred Hearts of Jesus and Mary.
Travers, Patrick '93 (FBK) Judicial Vicar.
Travers, Thomas *c.ss.r.* (NY)[EE] Esopus, NY Redemptorist Priests and Brothers C.Ss.R. (Province of Baltimore).
Traverso, Leonard '72 (SJ) Retired.
Travieso, Ernesto Fernandez *s.j.* '73 (MIA)[D] Miami, FL Belen Jesuit Preparatory School; [K] Miami, FL Villa Javier.
Travis, Adam Frederick '07 (ALX) Continuing Education of the Clergy; Alexandria, LA St. Rita.
Travis, Francis J. '81 (CHR) Camden, SC Our Lady of Perpetual Help.
Travis, James M. *m.m.* '67 (NY)[EE] Maryknoll Maryknoll Fathers and Brothers Retired.
Travis, Leo *c.ss.r.* '54 (FgM) Denver, CO Denver Province.
Travis, Robert '07 (MRY) Santa Margarita, CA Santa Margarita de Cortona.
Travnikar, Rock *o.f.m.* '76 (CIN)[N] Cincinnati St. Francis Seraph Friary.
Trawick, Gregory G. '85 (OWN) Cloverport, KY St. Rose; Irvington, KY Holy Guardian Angels.
Traxl, William L. '60 (HRT) Retired.
Traylor, William '76 (EVN) On Leave.
Traynor, Anthony '58 (SAC) Sacramento, CA Our Lady of Lourdes Retired.
Traynor, John J. '45 (RVC) Retired.
Traynor, Scott '00 (SFS) Tribunal Judges.
Traynor, Scott '00 (SFS)[H] Vermillion, SD University of South Dakota; Presbyteral Council.
Treacy, Jerome F. *s.j.* '61 (DET)[K] Clarkston, MI Colombiere Center.
Treacy, John P. *s.j.* '90 (SJ)[B] Santa Clara, CA Jesuit Community.
Treacy, Paul C. '06 (STP) Minneapolis, MN Our Lady of Peace; Deanery 14.
Treacy, William '44 (SEA) Retired.
Treanor, Boniface J. *o.s.b.* '56 (NEW)[M] Newark, NJ Newark Abbey.
Trebels, Xavier *o.praem.* '06 (ORG)[I] Silverado, CA Norbertine Fathers of Orange Inc.
Trebtoske, Everett '59 (AUS) Wimberley, TX St. Mary Retired.
Treglio, Vincent (PAT) Absent on Leave.
Trejo, Alejandro E. '03 (YAK) White Salmon, WA St. Joseph.
Trela, Norman J. '66 (CHI) Chicago, IL St. Symphorosa and Seven Sons.
Trela, Tadeusz '82 (NEW) Irvington, NJ Sacred Heart of Jesus.
Treloar, John L. *s.j.* '70 (MIL)[Y] Milwaukee, WI Theological Studies, Inc.; Milwaukee, WI; [P] Milwaukee, WI Arrupe House Jesuit Community; [P] Milwaukee, WI Jesuit Provincial Office, Wisconsin Province.
Tremari, Albert *s.j.c.* '03 (CHI) Chicago, IL St. John Cantius; [P] Chicago, IL Canons Regular of Saint John Cantius.
Tremblay, Albert J. '97 (MAN) Belmont, NH St. Joseph; Priest Personnel Board; Belknap County House of Corrections.
Tremblay, J. Normand '53 (WOR) Charlton City, MA St. Joseph's.
Tremblay, Marc P. '80 (FR) Norton, MA St. Mary's.
Tremblay, Nellis '54 (ALB) Retired.
Tremie, Eugene R. '71 (LAF) Ville Platte, LA Sacred Heart of Jesus; Ville Platte, LA St. Joseph.
Treml, Richard L. '99 (DET) North Branch, MI St. Mary's Burnside; North Branch, MI SS. Peter and Paul; Presbyteral Council; Archdiocesan Vicars.
Tremmel, Benjamin *o.s.b.* '66 (KCK) Effingham, KS St. Ann; Effingham, KS St. Louis; [I] Atchison, KS St. Benedict's Abbey.
Trempe, James F. '96 (LC) Plover, WI St. Bronislava.
Trench, Rev. Msgr. Edmond J. '57 (RVC) Southampton, NY Sacred Hearts of Jesus and Mary; Procurator & Advocates Retired.
Trenchera, Manuel '80 (AGN) Mongmong, GU Nuestra Senora de las Aguas.
Trenchs, Juan *sch.p.* '40 (LA)[P] Los Angeles, CA Piarist Fathers.
Trent, James F. '62 (DET) Retired.
Trenta, Christopher J. '09 (CLV) Wooster, OH St. Mary of the Immaculate Conception; [V] Wooster, OH St. Mary of the Immaculate Conception.
Trepanier, James R. *c.s.c.* '55 (FTW)[H] Holy Cross House Retired.
Treppa, Terence '67 (DET) Westland, MI St. Richard.
Tressic, David L. '96 (ALB) Leave of Absence.
Tressler, Rev. Msgr. David L. '85 (SCR) Carbondale, PA St. Rose of Lima; Deans.
Treston, Rev. Msgr. James A. '60 (ALN) Sinking Spring, PA St. Ignatius Loyola.
Treston, Kevin *o.f.m.* '81 (WDC) Washington, DC; [N] Washington, DC Franciscan Monastery USA Inc.
Trevino, Alberto T. *m.s.f.* '84 (BWN) Donna, TX St. Joseph.
Trevino, Raciel '03 (PMB) Fellsmere, FL Our Lady of Guadalupe Mission.
Trevizo, Raul P. '88 (TUC) Vicars General; Tucson, AZ Saint John the Evangelist Roman Catholic Parish – Tucson; Special Assignment; Diocesan Consultors; Council of Priests.
Trexler, Donald P. '98 (GBG)[F] Greensburg, PA Neumann House.
Treyes, Reynaldo B. '78 (JOL) Steger, IL St. Liborius.
Trezza, Richard *o.f.m.* (NEW)[M] East Rutherford, NJ Sacred Heart Friary.
Tria, Noel '98 (CHR) Edgefield, SC St. Mary of the Immaculate Conception; Ward, SC St. William.
Tribuiani, Raymond F. '73 (PH) On Special or Other Archdiocesan Assignment; Oreland, PA Holy Martyrs.
Trick, James F. '60 (CIN)[N] Carthagena, OH St. Charles Retired.
Triggs, Thomas J. '75 (TR) Colts Neck, NJ St. Mary's.

Trigilio, John P. '88 (HBG) Marysville, PA Our Lady of Good Counsel.
Trigueros, Raul '69 (ELP) El Paso, TX Cristo Rey Church; St. Matthew; Priests' Personnel Advisory Committee; Catholic Communications Ministry.
Trinchard, Paul '66 (NO) Retired.
Trindade, Leonard J. '95 (FRS) Gustine, CA Shrine of Our Lady of Miracles.
Tringhese, James D. '74 (GBG) Trafford, PA St. Regis; Bishop's Priests Council.
Trinh, Danh Ngoc '05 (ORG) Westminster, CA Blessed Sacrament.
Trinh, Dominic Huy The *o.p.* '75 (GAL) Houston, TX Our Lady of Lavang Church.
Trinh, Hoang T. *o.f.m.* '01 (SFR) San Francisco, CA St. Boniface.
Trinh, Joseph Hoa Duc '93 (DAL) Grand Prairie, TX St. Michael the Archangel.
Trinh, Rev. Msgr. Joseph T. '91 (PH) Philadelphia, PA St. Helena; Vietnamese Apostolate.
Trinh, Joseph Truong Q. '99 (BLX) Presbyteral Council.
Trinh, Loc '92 (GR) Reed City, MI St. Philip Neri.
Trinh, Paul H. '90 (CAM) On Sick Leave.
Trinh, Quan M. '02 (PH) Philadelphia, PA Our Lady of Calvary.
Trinh, Thai Paul Minh '05 (ORG) Laguna Woods, CA St. Nicholas.
Trinh, Thai Z. '90 (RIC) Unassigned.
Trinh, Truong Quang '99 (BLX) Lumberton, MS Our Lady of Perpetual Help.
Trinh, Vinh The *s.v.d.* '07 (FgM) Techny, IL.
Trinidad, Justin *o.c.s.o.* '97 (SPC)[F] Ava, MO Assumption Abbey (Trappist).
Trinidad, Mel *s.d.b.* '85 (LA)[V] Rosemead, CA St. Joseph's Salesian Youth Renewal Center; Councilors:; [D] Rosemead, CA Don Bosco Technical Institute.
Trinidad, Miguel '00 (SJN) Subcommission for Sacred Music.
Trinidad, Nelson '88 (LA) Pico Rivera, CA St. Hilary.
Trinidad–Fonseca, Miguel Angel '00 (SJN) Bayamon, PR Nuestra Senora del Rosario.
Trinity, Rev. Msgr. Bernard J. '54 (PH) Havertown, PA St. Denis Retired.
Trinka, Joseph C. '59 (SUP) Retired.
Trinkle, Clarence M. '92 (ARL) Retired.
Tripi, Ronald *c.s.c.* '62 (FTW) South Bend, IN Christ the King; [H] Notre Dame Congregation of Holy Cross, Indiana Province, Provincial House.
Triplett, Michael '07 (BAL) Ellicott City, MD Resurrection.
Tripole, Martin R. *s.j.* '67 (PH)[Y] Loyola Center and Manresa Hall.
Trippel, Edward G. '55 (CIN) Cincinnati, OH Retired.
Trisco, Rev. Msgr. Robert F. '54 (CHI) On Duty Outside the Archdiocese; [C] Catholic University of America, The Retired.
Trisolini, John *s.d.b.* '67 (FgM) New Rochelle, NY SALESIANS OF DON BOSCO.
Triulzi, Daniel *s.m.* '81 (SJ)[M] Cupertino, CA The Marianist Center.
Trivison, Louis J. '48 (CLV) Solon, OH Resurrection of Our Lord Retired.
Trocha, Lukasz Pawel '00 (BRK) Brooklyn, NY St. Rose of Lima; Brooklyn, NY St. Catharine of Alexandria.
Troche, Sigfrido *m.ss.cc.* '98 (CAM) Landisville, NJ Queen of Angels Parish, Buena Borough, N.J.
Trocinski, LaVern F. '60 (WIN) Retired.
Troha, Michael J. '80 (CLV) Translators; Willoughby, OH Immaculate Conception.
Troiano, Rev. Msgr. Leonard F. '79 (TR) Lavallette, NJ The Church of St. Pio of Pietreclina, Lavallette, N.J.
Troiano, Louis *o.f.m.* '57 (NY)[EE] New York, NY Padua Friary.
Trojcak, Ronald '62 (SFD) Special or Other Diocesan Assignment.
Troncale, Rev. Msgr. F. Charles '65 (MOB) Montgomery, AL Church of the Holy Spirit; Group I; Vicars Forane.
Trong, John T.B. '71 (ARL) Annandale, VA St. Michael.
Trongo, Nicholas M. '67 (GBG) Retired.
Trosch, David '82 (MOB) On Leave from the Archdiocese.
Trosley, Anthony J. '78 (PEO) Nauvoo, IL Immaculate Conception; Nauvoo, IL SS. Peter and Paul.
Trotta, Louis P. *c.m* '52 (PH)[Y].
Trouille, Alan P. '97 (LKC) Lake Charles, LA Our Lady of Good Counsel; [F] Lake Charles, LA Catholic Student Center.
Trout, John *s.p.s.* '89 (CHI) Buffalo Grove, IL St. Mary; Chicago, IL Queen of All Saints Basilica.
Trout, Richard W. '85 (ORL) Sanford, FL All Souls; Priestly Life and Ministry.
Troutman, Richard E. '68 (TUC) Tucson, AZ Saint Odilia Roman Catholic Community – Tucson; Council of Priests; Vicars Forane; All Vicars Forane.
Trovato, Joseph A. *c.s.b.* '56 (ROC) Rochester, NY Christ the King; Rochester, NY St. Thomas the Apostle; Rochester, NY St. Salome.
Troxell, Christopher '92 (LA) Claremont, CA Our Lady of the Assumption.
Troy, Gabriel (BO) Cambridge, MA St. Mary of the Annunciation.
Troyan, Rev. Archpriest Daniel '82 (PHU) Evangelization Center; Presbyteral Council; Archeparchial Museum; Special Assignment; Director of Evangelization.
Trucksis, Fred E. '64 (Y) Warren, OH St. Joseph.
Trudeau, Rev. Msgr. Marc V. '81 (LA) Los Angeles, CA Cathedral of Our Lady of the Angels; Priest Secretary/ Master of Ceremonies.
Trudel, Guy Albert *o.p.* '94 (PRO)[P] Providence, RI St. Pius Priory; Providence, RI St. Pius V.
True, Isaac *o.s.b.* '66 (KC) Bethany, MO Blessed Sacrament; [A] Conception, MO Conception Seminary College; [J] Conception, MO Conception Abbey.
Truhan, Luke *o.c.s.o.* '82 (WOR)[O] Spencer, MA St. Joseph's Abbey.
Trujillo, Carlos B. '76 (PBL) Absent on Leave.
Trujillo, Francisco '05 (PEO) Moline, IL St. Mary's.
Trujillo, Ivan R. '85 (BUF) Attica Correctional Facility; Batavia, NY Resurrection; Council of Priests.
Trujillo, Robert '07 (STA) Presbyteral Council; Orange Park, FL St. Catherine's.
Trujillo, Teofilo '89 (CHR) Simpsonville, SC St. Mary Magdalene; Vocations Board.
Trujillo, Vincent *o.s.b.* '82 (P)[L] St. Benedict, OR Mt. Angel Abbey; College of Consultors; [N] St. Benedict, OR Mount Angel Abbey Retreat House.
Trujillo–Gonzalez, Francisco de Asis '05 (NEW) On Duty Outside the Archdiocese.
Trull, Jason '02 (STA) Jacksonville, FL Resurrection.
Trullols, Charles '06 (POD)[L] Pittsburgh, PA Prelature of the Holy Cross and Opus Dei; Pittsburgh.
Trung, Nguyen Dinh *c.ss.r.* '03 (LA)[P] Baldwin Park Vietnamese Redemptorist Mission.
Trung Dinh Hoang, Louis '95 (DOD) On Duty Outside the Diocese.
Truong, James Thuc Van *o.s.b.* '62 (SPC)[F] Carthage, MO Congregation of the Mother Coredemptrix, United States Assumption Province.
Truong, Peter '99 (PMB) Boynton Beach, FL St. Thomas More.
Truong, Tri Vinh '08 (CHL) Clemmons, NC Holy Family.
Trupkovich, Joseph V. '97 (GBG) Leechburg, PA Christ The King.
Trupkovich, Thomas S. '97 (GBG) Ford City, PA Christ, Prince of Peace Parish; Murrysville, PA Mother of Sorrows.
Trussel, Christopher '92 (SCL) Special Assignment; [C] St. Cloud, MN Cathedral High and John XXIII Middle School.
Trutter, Carl *o.p.* '54 (DAL)[J] Irving, TX Dominican Priory of St. Albert the Great and Novitiate.
Trzeciakowski, Edward J. '55 (PIT)[M] Pittsburgh, PA St. John Vianney Manor Retired.
Trzecieski, Stephen P. *c.m.* '60 (BAL) Emmitsburg, MD St. Joseph; [S] Emmitsburg, MD Vincentian House.
Trzil, Louis J. '50 (DUB) Lansing, IA Immaculate Conception; Lansing, IA St. Pius; Lansing, IA St. Ann–St. Joseph.
Tsang, Augustine H. *s.j.* '94 (FgM) Los Gatos, CA Society of Jesus.
Tsang, Peter '59 (LA) Retired.
Tschakert, Gregory '82 (SFS) Dell Rapids, SD St. Mary's; Judicial Vicar; Defenders of the Matrimonial Bond; Diocesan Consultors; Presbyteral Council.
Tscherne, David D. '77 (TOL) Grand Rapids, OH St. Patrick.
Tseu, Rev. Msgr. Andrew Stanislaus '56 (LA) Pomona, CA St. Madeleine Retired.
Tshibambe, Henri '81 (DEN) Aurora, CO St. Michael the Archangel.
Tshingimba, Zacharie B. '75 (LC) Wisconsin Rapids, WI Our Lady, Queen of Heaven.
Tsiquaye, Paschal B. '66 (NEW) Hohokus, NJ St. Luke's.
Tuan, Bui Quang *c.ss.r.* '97 (LA)[P] Baldwin Park Vietnamese Redemptorist Mission.
Tuan, Camillus M. Nguyen Duc *c.m.c.* '84 (SPC)[F] Carthage, MO Congregation of the Mother Coredemptrix, United States Assumption Province.
Tubbs, Leo *o.p.* '66 (OAK)[M] Oakland, CA Order of Preachers (Province of Holy Name of Jesus – Western Dominican Province).
Tubridy, James J. '53 (NY)[EE] Bronx, NY John Cardinal O'Connor Residence Retired.
Tuchscherer, Vincent '55 (FAR) Retired.
Tucker, James A. '01 (ARL) On Leave of Absence.
Tucker, James G. '06 (NEW) Cliffside Park, NJ Epiphany.
Tucker, James S. *s.s.* '69 (SAT)[A] San Antonio, TX Assumption Seminary; [C] Oblate School of Theology.
Tucker, James S. *s.s.* '69 (BAL)[S] Baltimore Society of St. Sulpice, Province of the United States.
Tucker, James '69 (LA) On Active Leave.
Tucker, Lawrence E. *s.o.l.t.* '97 (CC)[G] Robstown, TX Society of Our Lady of the Most Holy Trinity.
Tucker, Mark E. '89 (WDC) Silver Spring, MD St. John the Evangelist; Judges.
Tucker, Patrick M. '74 (CHI) Palos Hills, IL Sacred Heart.
Tucker, Richard '58 (SY) Retired.
Tucker, Robert F. '70 (HRT) Litchfield, CT St. Anthony of Padua.
Tucker, Rev. Msgr. Robert G. '89 (LIN) Lincoln, NE Cathedral of the Risen Christ.
Tucker, Robert *s.c.j.* '82 (JKS) Southaven, MS Christ the King; Hernando, MS Holy Spirit; Senatobia, MS St. Gregory the Great; Robinsonville, MS Good Shepherd Catholic Church; [E] Nesbit, MS St. Michael Community House.
Tucker, Thomas J. *o.s.f.s.* '66 (WIL)[J] Childs, MD Retirement and Assisted Care Facility Retired.
Tufail, Augustine '80 (ALB) Troy, NY Sacred Heart; Special Assignment.
Tufaro, Douglas '83 (BGP)[K] Danbury, CT The Pope John Paul II Center for Health Care, Inc.
Tufo, Berard *o.f.m.* '51 (BO)[U] Boston, MA St. Christopher Friary Retired.
Tufts, Donn '80 (GR) Montague, MI St. James; Twin Lake, MI St. Mary of the Woods.
Tugwell, Rev. Msgr. Michael W. '75 (PT) Tallahassee, FL Co–Cathedral of St. Thomas More; College of Consultors; Vocations, Office of; Members Appointed; [D] Tallahassee, FL Casa Calderon, Inc.; Seminarian Candidate Review Board.
Tuite, Howard A. '54 (CHI) Retired.
Tuite, Thomas P. '86 (RVC) Hicksville, NY Our Lady of Mercy; Huntington, NY St. Patrick's.
Tuka, Cleophas Oseso '95 (SY)[U] Canastota, NY Catholic Diocese of Nakuru Mission Office, Inc.; Syracuse, NY St. Margaret.
Tulko, Richard *o.f.m.* '64 (GB)[A] Green Bay, WI St. Mary of the Angels Friary.
Tulko, Richard *o.f.m.* (MIL)[P] Burlington, WI Queen of Peace Friary.
Tull, Terry *c.ss.r.* '85 (PCE) Guayama, PR St. Anthony of Padua.
Tuller, John '84 (CHL) Retired.
Tully, Eugene D. '68 (BO) Billerica, MA St. Theresa of Lisieux.
Tully, Eugene M. '73 (PH) Ambler, PA St. Joseph.
Tully, Gerard P. *c.s.p.* '94 (P) Portland, OR St. Philip Neri; [Q] Portland, OR Paulist Fathers Catholic Center for Evangelization.
Tully, Henry F. '77 (IND) New Albany, IN St. Mary.
Tully, John P. '69 (Y) Hanoverton, OH St. Philip Neri; Hanoverton, OH St. Patrick; Hanoverton, OH St. John.
Tully, Thomas S. (R) Hillsborough, NC Holy Family.
Tumaca, Delfin '03 (CHK) Rota, MP San Francisco de Borja Parish.
Tumicki, Ted F. '97 (NOR) Norwich, CT St. Joseph; Judges; Bishop's Delegate for Safe Environments; Safe Environments, Office of; Members; Theological Advisor; Newspaper.
Tumino, Frank C. '98 (BRK) Woodhaven, NY St. Thomas Apostle; Diocesan Liturgy Office; Art and Architecture Commission; Liturgical Commission; Music Commission.
Tumminelli, Lawrence *b.s.o.* '96 (NTN) Methuen, MA Basilian Salvatorian Order; Methuen, MA.
Tumosa, John Joseph '69 (CAM) Newfield, NJ St. Rose's Catholic Church.
Tumulty, Matthias *o.f.m.* '59 (P) Portland, OR Ascension.
Tumulty, Michael J. *c.m.* '51 (PH)[Y].
Tunarosa, Rafael '98 (RCK) Crystal Lake, IL St. Thomas the Apostle.
Tungol, Eugene D. '75 (SFR) San Francisco, CA Church of the Epiphany; College of Consultors.
Tunink, Shawn '08 (KCK) Topeka, KS Most Pure Heart of Mary.
Tunney, Kenneth '63 (ALB) Schenectady, NY St. Gabriel the Archangel Retired.
Tunney, Michael F. *s.j.* '88 (BUF)[O] Buffalo, NY Canisius Jesuit Community Inc.
Tunney, Thomas P. *c.s.sp.* '60 (ARL) Arlington, VA Our Lady, Queen of Peace.
Tunnicliff, Jeffrey '07 (ROC) Elmira, NY St. Mary.
Tunny, Kenneth J. '63 (ALB) Retired.
Tuoc, Ignatius '71 (SP) Tampa, FL Epiphany of Our Lord.
Tuohey, John F. '81 (SPR) On Duty Outside the Diocese.
Tuong, Hoang Minh '01 (NO) Madisonville, LA St. Anselm.
Tuozzolo, Leonard J. *c.s.sp.* '59 (PIT)[O] Bethel Park, PA The Spiritan Center.
Tupa, Allan '97 (SP) St. Pete Beach, FL St. John Vianney.
Tupa, Jerome *o.s.b.* '82 (SCL)[B] Saint John's University; [I] Collegeville, MN St. John's Abbey, of the Order of St. Benedict.
Tupa, Michael J. '91 (SUP) Webster, WI Sacred Hearts of Jesus and Mary; Webster, WI Our Lady of Perpetual Help; Webster, WI St. John the Baptist; Presbyteral Council & Diocesan Consultors; Pastoral Consultors.
Tupasi, Cecilio '92 (SAC) Nevada City, CA St. Canice;

Downieville, CA Immaculate Conception; Grass Valley, CA St. Patrick.
Tupper, Dale E. '67 (WIN) Austin, MN Queen of Angels; Austin, MN Our Lady of Loretto; Deans.
Tuptynski, Marek S. '97 (FR) Somerset, MA St. Patrick's; Diocesan Department of Pastoral Care for the Sick.
Tupuola, Iosefo Vaitele (SPP) Pago Pago, AS Christ the King.
Turano, Steven Jordan *o.p.* '04 (COL) Zanesville, OH St. Thomas Aquinas.
Turati, Fortunato *s.c.* '67 (LAN) Camp Cassidy Lake; [E] Chelsea, MI St. Louis Center for Exceptional Children & Adults; [P] Grass Lake, MI The Pious Union of St. Joseph.
Turcich, Ronald R. *o.s.a.* '58 (CHI)[N] Olympia Fields, IL Tolentine Monastery at Tolentine Center.
Turco, Alfredo *s.x.* '88 (MIL)[B] Franklin, WI Xaverian Missionary Fathers College Seminary.
Turczany, Christopher J. '83 (BRK) Flushing, NY St. Mel; Peter Turner Insurance Co.; Diocesan Insurance Committee.
Turek, Rev. Msgr. Michael E. '76 (STL) Deaneries/Deans; St. Louis, MO St. Joan of Arc.
Turek, Ronald J. '74 (CLV) Orrville, OH St. Agnes.
Tureman, Thomas *s.d.s.* '88 (MIL)[P] Greendale, WI; Lexington, KY U.S.A. Procurator.
Turgeon, Armand A. '43 (MAN) Retired.
Turi, John J. '55 (SCR) Retired.
Turillo, B. Samuel '46 (PRO) Retired.
Turley, Sean F. '71 (WIL) On Duty Outside the Diocese.
Turnbull, Paul E. '73 (ALT) Johnstown Deanery; Johnstown, PA Our Mother of Sorrows.
Turnbull, William '67 (ALB) Retired.
Turner, Andrew B. '06 (CLV) Wickliffe, OH Our Lady of Mount Carmel.
Turner, Christopher M. '05 (WH) Vocations Promoters; Clarksburg, WV Immaculate Conception.
Turner, David *o.s.b.* '63 (JOL)[A] Lisle, IL Benedictine University; [L] Lisle, IL St. Procopius Abbey.
Turner, James M. *o.s.f.s.* '81 (CHL) Thomasville, NC Our Lady of the Highways.
Turner, James '84 (PHX) Glendale, AZ St. Thomas More Roman Catholic Parish.
Turner, Jerome R. '64 (MAD) Retired.
Turner, Paul '79 (KC) Cameron, MO St. Munchin.
Turner, Richard M. '80 (SPR) Chicopee, MA St. Anne's; Chicopee, MA St. Patrick's.
Turner, Richard W. '91 (R) Retired.
Turner, Robert D. '82 (SPK) Dayton, WA St. Joseph; Pomeroy, WA Holy Rosary; Dayton, WA St. Mark.
Turner, Robert D. '88 (MIL) Milwaukee, WI Blessed Sacrament.
Turner, Robert G. '59 (PIT) Homestead, PA St. Maximilian Kolbe Retired.
Turner, Thomas W. '82 (KC)[L] Kansas City, MO Bishop Sullivan Center.
Turner, William J. '75 (IND) Rushville, IN Immaculate Conception/St. Mary.
Turner, William J. '79 (LAN) Chelsea, MI St. Mary; Camp Cassidy Lake.
Turon, Louis Luke *o.p.* '55 (COL) Zanesville, OH St. Thomas Aquinas.
Turro, Rev. Msgr. James C. '48 (NEW) Park Ridge, NJ Our Lady of Mercy; [B] School of Diplomacy and Intl. Rels. Retired.
Turro, Rev. Msgr. James '48 (NOR)[A] Cromwell, CT Holy Apostles College and Seminary.
Turyatoranwa, Julius (PEO) Normal, IL Epiphany.
Turyk, Ivan '03 (PHU) Millville, NJ St. Nicholas; Toms River, NJ St. Stephen's.
Tuscan, Joseph A. *o.f.m.cap.* '97 (HBG) York, PA St. Joseph.
Tushar, David '76 (DUL) Carlton, MN St. Francis; Carlton, MN SS. Mary & Joseph.
Tusky, Richard J. '73 (PIT) Bellevue, PA Assumption of the Blessed Virgin Mary on the Beautiful River.
Tustin, Joseph E. *o.s.f.s.* '67 (PH) Philadelphia, PA Resurrection of Our Lord.
Tutas, Stephen *s.m.* '53 (SJ)[M] Cupertino, CA The Marianist Center; Councilors:.
Tutone, John J. '71 (RVC) Island Park, NY Sacred Heart; Judges for Interdiocesan Tribunal; Five Towns Deanery.
Tutor, Edwin '97 (SD) Chula Vista, CA St. Pius X.
Tuttle, Arthur *c.ss.r.* '65 (ALB) Saratoga Springs, NY St. Clement.
Tuttle, Charles W. '74 (BEL) Beckemeyer, IL St. Anthony; Breese, IL St. Augustine; [A] Breese, IL Mater Dei High School.
Tuttle, Patrick *o.f.m.* '94 (CHR) Greenville, SC St. Anthony of Padua.
Tuttle, Richard J. '76 (STU) College of Consultors; Medical Leave.
Tuxbury, James *o.f.m.* '63 (ALB)[A] Catskill, NY St. Anthony Friary.
Tuyn, William R. '62 (BUF) North Evans, NY St. Vincent; Council of Priests.
Tuzeneu, Rev. Msgr. Kenard J. '79 (TR) Barnegat, NJ St. Mary; Diocesan Consultors; Secretary.
Tuzik, Robert L. '73 (CHI) Chicago, IL St. Gall; Diocesan Priests' Placement Board; Chicago, IL Notre Dame de Chicago; Divine Worship, Office for.
Tvrdik, Roy *s.m.m.* '93 (RVC)[M] Eastport, NY Shrine of Our Lady of the Island.
Tvrdy, Julius '73 (LIN) Crete, NE Sacred Heart; Apostolate to the Spanish Speaking.
Twaddell, Gerald E. '67 (COV) Camp Springs, KY St. Joseph; Defenders of the Bond.
Twardzik, Francis M. *s.d.b.* '70 (PSC) Scranton, PA St. Mary's; Syncellus; Eparchial College of Consultors; Presbyteral Council; Olean, NY St. Mary's.
Twardzik, Michael W.T. '70 (SPR) On Duty Outside the Diocese.
Twardzik, Michael '70 (ROC) Wayland, NY Holy Family Catholic Community.
Twarog, Jerome '82 (CHI) Chicago, IL St. Eugene.
Twele, Robert *o.f.m.conv.* '81 (BAL)[S] Ellicott City, MD Order of Friars Minor Conventual; [W] Baltimore, MD Catholic Relief Services Foundation, Inc.
Twene, Eric (NY) Brewster, NY St. Lawrence O'Toole.
Twiggs, Matthew J. '73 (PAT) Stockholm, NJ St. John Vianney.
Twohig, Michael J. '83 (SPR) Absent on Leave.
Twohig, Richard H. *s.j.* '65 (DET)[T] Jesuit International Missions; [K] Clarkston, MI Colombiere Center; [K] Chicago, IL Jesuit Provincial Office–Detroit Province of the Society of Jesus.
Twohy, Patrick J. *s.j.* '70 (P)[L] Portland, OR Jesuit Provincial Office (Society of Jesus, Oregon Prov.); Portland, OR.
Twohy, Patrick *s.j.* '70 (SEA) Seattle, WA Our Lady of Mount Virgin; [L] Seattle, WA Arrupe Jesuit Community at Seattle University.
Twomey, Daniel F. '75 (BO) Unassigned.
Twomey, Gerald S. '81 (RVC)[M] Amityville, NY St. Pius X Residence; Unassigned.
Twomey, John E. '52 (MIL) Retired.
Ty, Jesus G. '98 (PHX) Chandler, AZ St. Mary Roman Catholic Parish.
Ty, Roch Keresz '60 (DAL)[B] University of Dallas.
Tybor, Karol '09 (CHI) Chicago, IL St. Christina.
Tyburski, Zbigniew '73 (PAT) Boonton, NJ SS. Cyril and Methodius.
Tydlacka, Rev. Msgr. George '44 (AUS) Retired.
Tyhovych, Ivan '69 (MO) Army Reserve Chaplains.
Tykhovytch, Ivan '94 (STF) Brooklyn, NY Holy Ghost.
Tylenda, Joseph N. *s.j.* '60 (SCR)[O] Scranton, PA Pascucci Family Our Lady of Peace Residence; [C] Scranton, PA The University of Scranton.
Tyler, Bernard L. '61 (GAY) Higgins Lake, MI St. Hubert; Higgins Lake, MI St. James Retired.
Tyler, Jason '05 (LR) Little Rock, AR St. Edward.
Tyler, Thomas L. '79 (E) Force, PA St. Joseph; Deans.
Tylka, Louis J. '96 (CHI) North Riverside, IL Mater Christi; Presbyteral Council.
Tyma, John A. *o.s.a.* '59 (FgM) Olympia Fields, IL Province of Our Mother of Good Counsel (Midwestern).
Tyman, Gary L. '86 (ROC) Rochester, NY St. Anne; Rochester, NY Our Lady of Lourdes.
Tymko, Piotr *o.f.m.conv.* '94 (SPR) Chicopee, MA St. Stanislaus Basilica.
Tymoszuk, Leszek '97 (TR) Trenton, NJ Divine Mercy Parish.
Tynan, Desmond A. '67 (FgM) Society of St. James the Apostle.; Boston, MA St. James the Apostle, Inc.
Tynan, John C. *m.m.* '62 (NY)[EE] Retired.
Tynski, Robert M. '89 (TR) Leave of Absence.
Tyrasinski, Lucius *o.s.p.p.e.* '56 (PH)[Y].
Tyrell, Wilfred *s.a.* '94 (NY)[EE] Garrison, NY Franciscan Friars of the Atonement.
Tyrrell, Bernard J. *s.j.* '65 (SPK)[B] Spokane, WA Gonzaga University.
Tyrrell, Joseph J. '89 (NY) New York, NY Cathedral of St. Patrick.
Tyrrell, Michael A. *s.j.* '76 (P)[L] Portland, OR Jesuit Provincial Office (Society of Jesus, Oregon Prov.); [L] Portland, OR Colombiere Community.
Tyrrell, Patrick *s.j.* '67 (CHI) Glenview, IL Our Lady of Perpetual Help.
Tyrrell, Wilfred *s.a.* '94 (NY)[EE] New York, NY Atonement Friars; [EE] New York, NY Atonement Friars.
Tyrrell, William *s.a.* (NY)[HH] Purchase, NY Manhattanville College.
Tyrtania, Joachim B. '83 (RCK) Maple Park, IL St. Mary.
Tyson, David T. *c.s.c.* '75 (FTW)[H] Notre Dame, IN Congregation of Holy Cross, Indiana Province, Provincial House; Notre Dame, IN; Austin, TX.
Tyson, Joseph V. *s.s.j.* '55 (BAL)[S] Baltimore, MD St. Joseph's Manor.
Tyson, Michael *o.f.m.* '59 (WIL) Wilmington, DE St. Paul's.
Tywoniak, Robert F. '83 (MIA) Oakland Park, FL Blessed Sacrament.
Tzanakas, George M. '62 (AUS) Retired.

U

Uba, Alban *s.m.m.m.* '99 (SAC) Carmichael, CA St. John the Evangelist.
Uba, Livinus '94 (WH) Huntington, WV Sacred Heart; Huntington, WV St. Peter Claver.
Ubaka, Victor O. (BRK) Brooklyn, NY St. Matthew.
Ubalde, Ulysses L. '93 (MO) Navy Chaplains.
Ubalde, Ulysses '93 (NEW) Military Chaplains.
Ubanii, Angelo B. *s.m.m.m.* '97 (MO) DEPARTMENT OF VETERANS AFFAIRS HOSPITALS AND CHAPLAINS.
Ubben, Michael Luke '05 (CHI)[N] Chicago, IL St. Peter's Friary.
Ubel, John L. '89 (STP) St. Paul, MN St. Agnes; St. Paul, MN.
Uche, Jude *c.s.sp.* '85 (PHX) Flagstaff, AZ San Francisco de Asis Roman Catholic Parish.
Udahemuka, Fidelis *s.j.* '05 (SJ)[B] Santa Clara, CA Jesuit Community.
Udayar, Santiago D. '89 (SAN) Odessa, TX St. Mary's; Presbyteral Council.
Udeani, Christopher *c.m.f.* '90 (SAT)[M] San Antonio, TX Cordi–Marian Missionary Sisters.
Udechukuu, Bedemoore (NO) New Orleans, LA St. Raymond–St. Leo the Great.
Udegbunam, Michael '81 (SAN) Colorado City, TX St. Ann's.
Udeze, Joseph '91 (NEW) Jersey City, NJ St. Paul's.
Udeze, Kieran O. '95 (PH) African Outreach; Philadelphia, PA Cathedral Basilica of SS. Peter and Paul.
Udick, William S. *s.j.* '55 (STL)[O] St. Louis, MO Jesuit Community Corporation at Saint Louis University – Jesuit Hall.
Udogu, Anthony '95 (NEW) Hackensack, NJ Hackensack University Medical Center.
Udoh, Emmanuel (NY) New York, NY St. Elizabeth.
Udoh, Michael '93 (BRK) Bayside, NY Our Lady of the Blessed Sacrament.
Udokang, Charles (NY) Bronx, NY Our Lady of Grace.
Udomah, Justin '93 (AUS) Austin, TX St. Theresa.
Udovic, Edward R. *c.m.* '84 (CHI)[C] Chicago, IL De Paul University; [N] Chicago, IL Vincentian Community, Congregation of the Mission, Western Province; [C] De Paul University.
Udulutsch, Robert *o.f.m.cap.* '56 (GB)[J] Appleton, WI St. Fidelis Friary Retired.
Uebler, Michael G. '82 (BUF) Tonawanda, NY St. Francis of Assisi.
Uecker, Joseph H. *c.pp.s.* '68 (SAN) Odessa, TX St. Anthony; Odessa, TX St. Joseph.
Uehlein, Christopher *o.s.b.* '60 (SFS)[F] Marvin, SD Blue Cloud Abbey.
Uftring, Richard A. '76 (BO) Gloucester, MA Our Lady of Good Voyage; [Z] Boston, MA Our Lady of the Airways Chapel; Seaport Chaplaincy; Airport Chaplaincy.
Ugalde, Jose *m.sp.s.* '09 (SEA) Mill Creek, WA St. Elizabeth Ann Seton.
Ugbor, Leonard (BRK) Flushing, NY St. Michael.
Ugliano, Bruno A. *o.s.b.* '67 (PAT) Morristown, NJ; [N] Morristown, NJ St. Mary's Abbey.
Ugliano, Bruno A. *o.s.b.* '67 (TR)[T] Trenton, NJ Emmaus House, Rider University; [T] Hamilton Township, NJ Mercer County Community College.
Uglietto, Peter J. '77 (BO)[A] Weston, MA Blessed John XXIII National Seminary; Presbyteral Council; College of Consultors.
Ugo, Charles Chidindu '06 (ALT) State College, PA Our Lady of Victory.
Ugochukwu, Sebastian A. '79 (MO) DEPARTMENT OF VETERANS AFFAIRS HOSPITALS AND CHAPLAINS.
Ugochukwu, Sebastian A. (BO) Pastoral Care.
Uguoji, Matthew (NY) New York, NY Bayview Correctional Facility; New York, NY Edgecombe Correctional Facility; Bronx, NY Fulton Correctional Facility; New York, NY Lincoln Correctional Facility.
Ugwoji, Matthew (BRK) Brooklyn, NY St. Cecilia.
Ugwu, Ejiofor *m.s.p.* '00 (PT) Tallahassee, FL St. Eugene, Florida A&M University; Tallahassee–Florida Agricultural & Mechanical University, St. Eugene Chapel.
Ugwu, Stephen '02 (LAF) Parks, LA St. Joseph.
Ugwuanya, Valentine C. '94 (MO) Military Chaplains; Army Chaplains.
Ugwuegbu, Ambrose '87 (SAC) Vicars Forane; Colfax, CA St. Dominic.
Ugwuegbulem, Longinus N. '93 (NEW) Newark, NJ Blessed Sacrament–St. Charles Borromeo.
Uhde, Peter M. '81 (MO) Army Chaplains.
Uhde, Peter '81 (NEW) Military Chaplains.
Uhen, Cletus V. '42 (MIL) Retired.
Uhen, Timothy J. '96 (MIL)[O] Brookfield, WI Prelature of the Holy Cross and Opus Dei Layton Study Center; Brookfield.
Uhl, Anthony C. '68 (COS) Salida, CO St. Joseph Retired.
Uhlenkott, Benjamin '06 (B) College of Consultors; Deans; Priest Personnel Commission; Boise, ID Risen Christ Catholic Community.
Uhlenkott, Gary D. *s.j.* '80 (SPK)[B] Spokane, WA Gonzaga University.
Uhler, Carl A. '56 (CLV) West Salem, OH St. Stephen.
Uhlman, Laurence *t.o.r.* '90 (STU)[H] Steubenville, OH

Holy Spirit Friary; [A] Steubenville, OH Franciscan University of Steubenville.
Uhrig, A. Gregory '73 (MET) North Plainfield, NJ St. Luke.
Uira Alvarez, Victor Hugo *ss.cc.* (SJN) San Juan, PR San Juan M. Vianney.
Uju, Ikechukwu Eliseus '03 (SB) Corona, CA St. Edward.
Ukaegbu, John Lloyd '62 (LA) Baldwin Park, CA St. John the Baptist.
Ukaegbu–Onuoha, Emmanuel '95 (SB) Norco, CA St. Mel.
Ukanide, Akama *m.s.p.* (MOB) Mobile, AL St. Francis Xavier; Prichard, AL Our Mother of Mercy.
Uko, Joseph M. '88 (BLX) Presbyteral Council.
Uko, Joseph '88 (BLX) Gulfport, MS St. John the Evangelist.
Ukomadu, Linus '90 (LR) Arkadelphia, AR St. Mary; Malvern, AR St. John the Baptist.
Ukwanda, Sebastine '09 (BGP) New Fairfield, CT St. Edward the Confessor.
Ukwe, Stan '94 (WDC)[M] Hyattsville, MD Sacred Heart Home Inc.
Ulak, Robert T. '70 (NEW) Park Ridge, NJ Our Lady of Mercy.
Ulam, Richard *o.s.b.* '82 (WH) Fairmont, WV Immaculate Conception.
Ulaszeski, Rev. Msgr. Edward J. '52 (BUF) Retired.
Ulincy, Andrew A. '66 (ALN) Reading, PA St. Paul.
Uline, Cyprian *o.f.m.conv.* '70 (LSC) Carlsbad, NM St. Edward; Presbyteral Council.
Ullery, Kirk J. '65 (SFR) Retired.
Ullmer, James Louis '09 (TLS)[G] Hulbert, OK Our Lady of the Annunciation of Clear Creek Monastery.
Ulloa, Daniel *o.p.* '70 (NY) Yonkers, NY St. John the Baptist.
Ullrich, David *o.m.i.* '71 (FgM) Washington, DC AMERICAN OBLATE MISSIONS.
Ullrich, John R. *o.f.m.* '76 (TR) Brant Beach, NJ St. Francis of Assisi.
Ullrich, Rev. Msgr. Mark C. '78 (STL) Deaneries/Deans; Catholic Charities; St. Louis, MO Cathedral Basilica of Saint Louis.
Ullrich, Peter *o.s.b.* '87 (KC) Savannah, MO St. Rose of Lima; [J] Conception, MO Conception Abbey.
Ulm, John F. '58 (GAL) Houston, TX St. Maximilian Kolbe.
Ulman, Stanley A. '73 (DET) Presbyteral Council; Rochester Hills, MI St. Mary of the Hills; Archdiocesan Vicars; College of Consultors.
Ulrich, Eugene P. '74 (BUF) Elma, NY Annunciation of the Blessed Virgin Mary.
Ulrich, John *s.m* '86 (MRY) Campus Ministry Department; [F] San Luis Obispo, CA Society of Mary (Marists)–S.M.; [I] San Luis Obispo, CA California State Polytechnic Institute/Cuesta College.
Ulrich, Steve '90 (OWN) Absent on Leave.
Ulrick, Stephen D. '82 (STP) Bloomington, MN Nativity of the Blessed Virgin Mary.
Ulshafer, Thomas R. *s.s.* (BAL)[S] Baltimore, MD Society of St. Sulpice, Province of the United States; Baltimore, MD.
Ulshafer, Thomas *s.s.* '70 (WDC) On Duty Outside the Archdiocese.
Ulto, Victor A. '80 (PMB) Port St. Lucie, FL St. Bernadette.
Umaña, German '96 (SLC) Wendover, UT San Felipe LLC 251.
Umana, Pedro *o.f.m.* '89 (FRS) Shafter, CA St. Therese.
Umberg, Andrew J. '91 (CIN) Cincinnati, OH St. William.
Umberger, Patrick A. '80 (LC) Onalaska, WI St. Patrick.
Umbras, Thomas *s.v.d.* '81 (BO)[U] Duxbury, MA Society of the Divine Word.
Ume, Michael '93 (LA) Bellflower, CA St. Bernard.
Umekwe, Peter Obinna '01 (BAK) Condon, OR St. Francis; Condon, OR St. John.
Umeobi, Jude '97 (LA) Pastoral Team:; Montebello, CA Our Lady of the Miraculous Medal.
Umeokeke, Damian '98 (NY) Manhattan, NY Beth Israel Medical Center; New York, NY Our Lady of the Scapular and St. Stephen.
Umhoefer, Stephen J. '66 (MAD) Elected.
Umhoefer, Stephen '66 (MAD) Janesville, WI Nativity of St. Mary.
Umoenoh, Clement '96 (NY) Bronx, NY St. Joseph.
Umukoro, Fidelis O. *o.p.* '01 (SEA) Seattle, WA Our Lady of Fatima; Aberdeen, WA Our Lady of Good Help.
Umunnakwe, Eze Venantius *c.s.sp.* '87 (CHI) Blue Island, IL St. Isidore.
Underdahl, Mark J. '96 (STP) Lino Lakes, MN St. Joseph.
Underwood, Eric Christopher '06 (LFT) Lafayette, IN St. Mary Cathedral; Lafayette, IN St. Lawrence.
Underwood, Gary E. '80 (TUC) Administrative Leave of Absence.
Underwood, Joseph '63 (BIR) Retired.
Underwood, Scott J. *o.s.b.* '76 (NO)[P] St. Benedict, LA St. Joseph Abbey; [A] St. Benedict, LA St. Joseph Seminary College.
Undralla, Deva '97 (SCR) Gouldsboro, PA St. Rita.
Ungashick, Thomas '76 (Y) Maximo, OH St. Joseph.
Unger, Rev. Msgr. John M. '65 (STL) Warson Woods, MO Ste. Genevieve Du Bois.
Unger, Robert P. '99 (FAR) Park River, ND St. Mary; Grafton, ND St. Luke's Church of Veseleyville.
Unger, Steve (RVC) Stony Brook, NY Stony Brook University Hospital.
Unger, Todd '82 (BAK) Board of Education; Health and Retirement Board; [D] Bend, OR The Health and Retirement Association of the Diocese of Baker, Oregon; Redmond, OR St. Thomas.
Universal, Patrick J. '75 (BO) Boston, MA St. Stephen Retired.
Universal, Patrick '75 (BO) Boston, MA St. James the Apostle, Inc.; [U] Boston, MA The Society of St. James the Apostle, Inc.
Unni, John J. '92 (BO) Boston, MA St. Cecilia.
Unsworth, John E. '76 (PRO) Riverside, RI St. Brendan; Deans.
Untereiner, Harry P. '72 (PSC) New Brunswick, NJ St. Joseph; Retirement Plan Board.
Unterreiner, James J. '70 (SPC) Ironton, MO Ste. Marie Du Lac; Region VI; Region VI; Diocesan Consultors; Presbyteral Council; Diocesan Council of Catholic Women (DCCW).
Unverdorben, Ernest *o.c.d.* '66 (MIL)[P] Hubertus, WI Discalced Carmelite Monastery – Holy Hill Basilica of the National Shrine of Mary, Help of Christians, Holy Hill.
Unverferth, Steven R. '89 (BEL) Leave of Absence.
Unz, Thomas E. '83 (CHI) Westchester, IL Divine Providence.
Uong, Luong *c.ss.r.* '95 (GAL) Houston, TX Holy Ghost.
Upah, William J. '98 (R) Henderson, NC St. James.
Uppani, Jose '67 (LR) North Little Rock, AR St. Mary.
Uppena, Rev. Msgr. James J. '68 (MAD) Milton, WI St. Mary; Elected.
Upson, Michael '76 (ROC) Avon, NY St. Agnes.
Upton, Edward F. '69 (CHI) Orland Park, IL St. Francis of Assisi; Deans.
Upton, John '83 (GAL) Spring, TX Christ the Good Shepherd.
Uralikunnel, George V. '67 (MO) DEPARTMENT OF VETERANS AFFAIRS HOSPITALS AND CHAPLAINS.
Uram, Rev. Msgr. Kenneth J. '59 (STU) Retired.
Urarte, Carmelo '59 (ARE) Quebradillas, PR Sacred Heart; Diocesan Consultors; Priest's Senate (Consejo Presbiteral).
Urassa, Nicodemus *a.j.* '96 (CLV) Cleveland, OH Lakewood Hospital.
Urassa, Rogatian '83 (BAK) Klamath Falls, OR Sacred Heart.
Urban, Anthony M. '73 (SCR) Retired.
Urban, Carl A. '66 (ALB) Schenectady, NY Church of St. Adalbert.
Urban, Charles T. *o.praem.* '54 (PH)[Y] Paoli, PA Daylesford Abbey.
Urban, John L. '59 (MAD) Retired.
Urban, Joseph (NEW) Jersey City, NJ St. Anthony of Padua.
Urban, Rev. Msgr. Lonnie A. '67 (AUS) Taylor, TX St. Mary of the Assumption; Consultors.
Urban, Peter '58 (DEN) Retired.
Urban, Reginald A. '77 (DOD) Great Bend, KS Prince of Peace Catholic Church of Great Bend, Kansas; Presbyteral Council.
Urban, Robert M. '60 (SUP) Retired.
Urban, Thomas E. '02 (DET) Graduate Studies.
Urbanek, Raymond J. '68 (LAN) Ovid, MI Holy Family.
Urbaniak, Andrzej *o.f.m.conv.* '98 (BO) South Boston, MA Our Lady of Czestochowa; Polish.
Urbaniak, Rev. Msgr. Bernard J. '68 (E) Deans; Erie, PA St. Stanislaus.
Urbaniak, Jan *c.m.* '71 (BRK) Brooklyn, NY St. Stanislaus Kostka.
Urbaniak, Lawrence M. '61 (RCK) Retired.
Urbaniak, Lucian '85 (SY) Rome, NY Transfiguration.
Urbanic, James A. *c.pp.s.* '71 (KC) Warrensburg, MO Sacred Heart; [A] Liberty, MO Society of the Precious Blood Provincial Offices; [J] Liberty, MO Precious Blood Society Provincial Office; Liberty, MO; [J] Liberty, MO Precious Blood Center; [N] Liberty, MO St. Gaspar Society.
Urbanowski, Konrad *s.ch.* '43 (DET) Sterling Heights, MI Our Lady of Czestochowa.
Urbanski, Louis '64 (P) Aloha, OR St. Elizabeth Ann Seton.
Urbina, Carlos *o.s.a.* '04 (CHI) Chicago, IL St. Rita of Cascia.
Urbonas, Rev. Msgr. Ignatius L. '35 (GRY) Lemont, IL Blessed Jurgis Matulaitis Mission Retired.
Urcia, Daniel C. '89 (SJ) Milpitas, CA St. Elizabeth; Ongoing Formation of Clergy.
Ureel, Wayne G. '90 (DET) Dryden, MI St. Cornelius; Allenton, MI St. John the Evangelist; Capac, MI St. Nicholas.
Urell, Rev. Msgr. John '78 (ORG) Laguna Niguel, CA St. Timothy.
Urian, Thomas R. '90 (PH) Secane, PA Our Lady of Fatima; [D] Drexel Hill, PA Monsignor Bonner and Archbishop Prendergast Catholic High School.
Urias, Jose Garibaldi Ballesteros '97 (PHX) Phoenix, AZ St. Augustine Roman Catholic Parish.
Uribe, Arturo *c.ss.r.* '95 (CHI) Chicago, IL St. Michael in Old Town; [N] Chicago, IL The Redemptorist Fathers of Chicago.
Uribe, Jose Maria Solano '96 (SJN) Carolina, PR Santisima Trinidad.
Uribe, Saul de Jesus '80 (ELP) El Paso, TX Sts. Peter and Paul.
Uribe–Guzman, Francisco J. '58 (SAT) Del Rio, TX Retired.
Urizalqui, Rev. Msgr. Richard '77 (FRS) Tulare, CA St. Aloysius; Advocates; Priests' Council.
Urlage, Robert J. '58 (COV) Retired.
Urmston, Benjamin J. *s.j.* '59 (CIN)[N] Cincinnati, OH Jesuit Community at Xavier University.
Urnick, Charles B. '74 (LAV) Laughlin, NV St. John the Baptist Catholic Mission.
Uroda, Stanley *s.v.d.* '74 (CHI)[N] Chicago, IL Divine Word Theologate.
Urrea, Miguel A. '87 (SB) Colton, CA Arrowhead Regional Medical Center.
Urrego, Luis Ido '01 (SAC) Sacramento, CA St. Anne.
Urriza, Luis *o.s.a.* '44 (BEA) Beaumont, TX Cristo Rey; Beaumont, TX.
Uschold, Raymond F. '64 (BUF)[O] Lackawanna, NY Bishop Head Residence Retired.
Useche, Teofilo '84 (VEN) Palmetto, FL Holy Cross Church; Presbyteral Council.
Usenza, Robert J. '61 (BGP) Retired.
Ustaski, William B. *c.r.i.c.* '77 (LA) Santa Clarita, CA St. Clare; [P] Santa Paula, CA Canons Regular of the Immaculate Conception.
Uter, Frank M. '69 (BR) Denham Springs, LA Immaculate Conception; Judges; Cemeteries.
Uthuppu, Augustine '88 (HON) Koloa, HI St. Raphael.
Utrup, Eugene E. '59 (STL) Retired.
Utz, Raymond M. '63 (PIT)[Q] Pittsburgh, PA Cardinal Dearden Center Retired.
Utzig, Albert *s.s.c.* '83 (OM)[K] St. Columbans Missionary Society of St. Columban.
Uvietta, Joseph *s.m.* '61 (STL)[O] St. Louis, MO Cure of Ars Marianist Community.
Uwasomba, Benet '78 (RVC) Freeport, NY Our Holy Redeemer.
Uwusomba, Benet '78 (RVC) Manhasset, NY North Shore Univ. Hospital.
Uzbuegbuman, Benjamin (NY) Mt. Vernon, NY Sacred Heart.
Uzoh, Louis N. '73 (BRK) Rosedale, NY St. Pius X.
Uzondu, Gabriel *s.o.l.t.* '01 (CC)[G] Robstown, TX Society of Our Lady of the Most Holy Trinity.
Uzondu, Gabriel *s.o.l.t.* '01 (AUS) Llano, TX Holy Trinity Catholic Church – Llano, Texas; Llano, TX St. Joseph.
Uzukwu, Eugene *c.s.sp.* (PIT)[B] Pittsburgh, PA Duquesne University of the Holy Spirit.
Uzzilio, Robert A. '65 (BGP) Stratford, CT St. James.

V

Vacca, Daniel L. '95 (WCH) Cherryvale, KS St. Francis Xavier's; Independence, KS St. Andrew.
Vaccari, Rev. Msgr. Andrew J. '86 (BRK) Defenders of the Marriage Bond; Brooklyn, NY St. Mary Mother of Jesus.
Vaccari, Rev. Msgr. Peter I. '77 (BRK) Censors of Books; Released from Diocesan Assignment.
Vaccari, Peter I. '77 (RVC)[A] Huntington, NY Diocesan Seminary of the Immaculate Conception; Censors of Books.
Vaccaro, Christopher T. '08 (ARL) Annandale, VA Holy Spirit; Notaries.
Vaccaro, Joseph V. *o.carm.* '58 (STP)[K] Lake Elmo, MN Carmelite Hermitage of the Blessed Virgin Mary; Lake Elmo, MN.
Vacco, James *o.f.m.* '82 (BUF) Council of Priests; [O] St. Bonaventure, NY St. Bonaventure Friary; [C] St. Bonaventure, NY Friar Community.
Vacek, Carl E. *t.o.r.* '79 (WH) Charles Town, WV St. James.
Vacek, Edward V. *s.j.* '73 (BO)[U] Cambridge, MA Hopkins House.
Vadakathalakal, Augustine Varghese *o.ss.t.* '08 (BAL)[S] The Trinitarians in India (Bangalore & Trichur).
Vadakemuriyil, Thomas John *c.m.i.* '92 (SHP)[B] Shreveport, LA Christus Health Northern Louisiana; [B] Shreveport, LA Christus Schumpert Highland.
Vadakevattukula, Tomy *m.s.t.* '01 (CHI)[J] Evanston, IL Saint Francis Hospital; Chicago, IL St. Edward; [J] Chicago, IL Our Lady of the Resurrection Medical Center.
Vadakin, Rev. Msgr. Royale M. '64 (LA) Moderator of the Curia and Vicar General; President; Members; Ex Officio Members; Ex Officio; Los Angeles, CA St. Anastasia.
Vadakkan, Johnny *m.s.* '00 (MAN) Enfield, NH St. Helena.

Vadakkan, Lawrence *s.d.b.* '90 (SFR) Tiburon, CA St. Hilary.
Vadakkekara, Abey '98 (SYM) Valrico, FL Sacred Heart Knanaya Catholic Mission.
Vadakkekara, J. Philip '69 (MET) Retired.
Vadakumcherry, Joseph (CHI) Chicago, IL St. Priscilla.
Vadakumkara, Shijo *h.g.n.* '04 (OWN) Clinton, KY St. Jude; Fulton, KY St. Edward; Hickman, KY Sacred Heart.
Vadana, Kuriakose '81 (SYM) Framingham, MA St. Thomas Syro–Malabar Catholic Church.
Vader, Anthony J. '52 (CHI) Retired.
Vaeth, Paul *c.p.* '68 (PIT)[M] Pittsburgh, PA St. Paul of the Cross Monastery; [O] Pittsburgh, PA St. Paul of the Cross Retreat Center.
Vaghetto, Benedetto P. '78 (PIT) Pittsburgh, PA St. Raphael; Judges; College of Consultors; Priest Council.
Vaghi, Rev. Msgr. Peter J. '85 (WDC)[W] Glen Echo, MD John Carroll Society; [W] Glen Echo, MD The John Carroll Society; Advocates; Deans; Bethesda, MD Little Flower; Archdiocesan College of Consultors; Priest Council.
Vaglienty, Felipe '00 (CHI) Chicago, IL St. Ann.
Vahi, Salvador S. '85 (BO)[T] Newton, MA Prelature of the Holy Cross and Opus Dei.
Vahi, Salvador S. (POD) Chestnut Hill.
Vail, Nathan *f.s.s.p.* (NY)[E] White Plains, NY Archbishop Stepinac High School.
Vail, Thomas '51 (ALB) Retired.
Vaillancourt, Joseph *o.m.i.* '46 (FgM) Washington, DC AMERICAN OBLATE MISSIONS.
Vaillancourt, Mark G. '94 (NY)[E] Somers, NY John F. Kennedy Catholic High School.
Vaillancourt, Raymond *m.s.* '89 (NOR) Retired.
Vaillancourt, Robert C. '82 (PRT) Vocations; Special or Other Diocesan Assignment.
Vainavicz, Anthony C. '61 (GR) Diocesan Council of Catholic Women; On Special Assignment Retired.
Vairo, Carmen *s.d.b.* (LA)[P] Los Angeles, CA Dominic Savio Salesian Residence.
Vakayil, Joseph Varghese '78 (CC) Pettus, TX Sacred Heart Mission.
Vakko, Justin *o.c.d.* '98 (ORL) Longwood, FL Church of the Nativity.
Vakulskas, John A. '69 (SC) Ashton, IA St. Mary's Catholic Church; Sibley, IA St. Andrew's.
Vala, Thomas M. '09 (TR) Long Branch, NJ The Church of Christ the King, Long Branch, N.J.
Valachanath, Cyriac John '93 (SYM) Pharr, TX Divine Mercy Malabar Catholic Church.
Valachanath, Kuriachan Cyriac '93 (CC) Ben Bolt, TX St. Peter Mission.
Valades, Reuben '70 (RC) Retired.
Valadez, Arturo '88 (LA) Pico Rivera, CA St. Francis Xavier.
Valainis, Vitolds '66 (DAV)[J] Iowa City, IA O'Keefe Hall; State University of Iowa Hospital.
Valastro, Rev. Msgr. George J. '56 (NY) Orange; Middletown, NY St. Joseph Retired.
Valavanickal, Thomas *c.m.i.* '96 (NY) Scarsdale, NY Immaculate Heart of Mary.
Valayath, Jacob John '99 (CC) Agua Dulce, TX St. Frances of Rome.
Valayil, Bijoy Francis *o.praem.* '05 (SFE)[H] Albuquerque, NM Santa Maria de la Vid Priory; Belen, NM Our Lady of Belen.
Valbuena, Jairo A. *m.x.y.* '94 (NY) Bronx, NY Our Saviour; [EE] Bronx, NY Yarumal Mission Society, Inc.
Valcin, Fritzner '99 (COL)[L] Columbus, OH Haitian Catholic Coalition of Ohio; Haitian Catholic Coalition of Ohio; Columbus, OH St. Francis of Assisi.
Valdazo, Stephen '58 (BRK) Jackson Heights, NY St. Joan of Arc.
Valderrama, Viliulfo '96 (TUC) Nogales, AZ San Felipe de Jesus Roman Catholic Parish – Nogales; Council of Priests; Vocations.
Valdes, Bert W. '65 (WH) Retired.
Valdez, Carlos Reynoso *o.r.c.* '96 (PCE) Adjuntas, PR St. Joachim.
Valdez, John '91 (AMA) Hereford, TX St. Anthony's; Vicars Forane; Ex Officio; College of Consultors; Vocation Development Team.
Valdez, Jose Pedro '69 (LSC) San Miguel, NM San Miguel.
Valdez, Paul R. *k.c.h.s.* '82 (MRY) Marina, CA St. Jude Parish Community; Defenders of the Bond; Administrative Committee Priests' Pension Plan; Finance Council; Insurance Committee; Vicar for Retired Priests.
Valdez, Pedro G. '98 (LA) Los Angeles, CA Our Lady of Victory; Pacoima, CA Guardian Angel; Hospital Chaplains.
Valdez, Raul Adrain '04 (ORL) Clermont, FL Blessed Sacrament.
Valdivia, Rev. Msgr. Adolfo '81 (SAT) San Antonio, TX Resurrection of the Lord.
Valdivia, Rev. Msgr. Antonio '63 (OAK) Pastoral Leadership Placement Board (PLPB) Retired.
Valdovinos, Francisco *s.t.* '94 (LA) Compton, CA Our Lady of Victory; Members.
Vale, Avelino '89 (LAF) Crowley, LA St. Michael Archangel.
Valencheck, John A. '98 (CLV) Akron, OH St. Sebastian.
Valencia, Ariel '03 (RCK) Carpentersville, IL St. Monica.
Valencia, Braulio '87 (PHX) Chandler, AZ St. Mary Roman Catholic Parish.
Valencia, Carlos D. '85 (BRK) Brooklyn, NY Visitation of the Blessed Virgin Mary.
Valencia, Victor '93 (STP) Annandale, MN St. Ignatius.
Valenciano, Luis '77 (SD) Centinela State Prison.
Valenta, John G. '62 (STL)[O] St. Louis, MO Jesuit Community Corporation at Saint Louis University – Jesuit Hall.
Valenta, Stephen *o.f.m.conv.* '51 (NY)[EE] Staten Island, NY St. Francis Friary Retired.
Valente, Michael '58 (JOL) Retired.
Valente, Palmo *s.f.* '52 (WDC)[B] Silver Spring, MD Holy Family Seminary.
Valenti, Thomas J. '76 (ROC) On Duty Outside the Diocese.
Valenti, Thomas '76 (NY) Yonkers, NY St. John the Baptist.
Valentine, Charles R. '54 (TR) Freehold, NJ St. Robert Bellarmine Retired.
Valentine, Daniel A. '74 (PIT) Sewickley, PA St. James.
Valentine, Joseph *f.s.s.p.* '93 (JOL) Naperville, IL Sts. Peter and Paul.
Valentine, Keveny M. '73 (WDC) Hospital & Nursing Home Ministries.
Valentine, Lambert F. *o.f.m.* '43 (PAT)[N] Ringwood, NJ Holy Name Friary, Inc.
Valentine, Richard A. '74 (PRO) Georgiaville, RI St. Michael.
Valentine, Timothy S. *s.j.* '85 (MO) Army Chaplains.
Valentine, Timothy *s.j.* '85 (NY) West Point, NY Catholic Chapel of the Most Holy Trinity.
Valentino, Francis P. *s.j.* '68 (NY)[EE] New York, NY Murray–Weigel Hall.
Valentino, Rev. Msgr. Frederick A. '50 (TR) Manasquan, NJ St. Denis Retired.
Valenton, Randy '06 (SJ) Los Altos, CA St. Simon.
Valenzano, Rev. Msgr. Arthur F. '75 (BAL) Westminster, MD St. John; Consultors; Consultors.
Valenzuela, Rev. Msgr. Bayani '76 (NY) Monroe, NY Sacred Heart Church.
Valenzuela, James Paul '05 (PT) Priest Personnel Board; Pensacola, FL Nativity of Our Lord; Campus Ministry.
Valenzuela, Luciano '87 (SAC) Absent on Leave.
Valenzuela, Pablo '53 (SJN) San Juan, PR Corpus Christi.
Valenzuela, Ruben '06 (SD) El Centro, CA Our Lady of Guadalupe.
Valera, Edmundo '02 (PBL) Grand Junction, CO St. Joseph; Presbyteral Council; Presbyteral Council–College of Consultors.
Valera, Ramon G. '75 (LA) Northridge, CA Our Lady of Lourdes.
Valerio, Francis D. '06 (OM) Omaha, NE Mary Our Queen.
Valerio, Raymond A. '59 (MAR) Retired.
Valiquette, Hilaire *o.f.m.* '64 (SFE) Isleta, NM St. Augustine; [H] Albuquerque, NM The Province of Our Lady of Guadalupe.
Valit, Robert L. '61 (STP) Stillwater, MN St. Mary; Stillwater, MN St. Michael Retired.
Valiyannoor, Paulson *c.m.f.* '98 (LA)[V] Los Angeles, CA Tepeyac House (Novitiate).
Valka, Christopher *c.s.b.* '09 (DET)[E] Novi, MI Catholic Central High School.
Valker, Richard J. '57 (CHI) Northbrook, IL St. Norbert Retired.
Valko, Rev. Msgr. George J. '77 (ALT) Retired.
Valla, Dominic J. '63 (HRT) Oxford, CT St. Thomas the Apostle.
Valladares, Alejandro E. '00 (MOB)[I] Mobile, AL Sacred Heart of Jesus Catholic Student Center at University of South Alabama; Vocations.
Vallamattam, Thomas *s.j.* '64 (BO)[U] Weston, MA Campion Jesuit Community.
Vallayil, Abraham *c.m.i.* '76 (NY) Blauvelt, NY St. Catharine.
Valle, Miguel (TR) Hightstown, NJ St. Anthony of Padua.
Valle–Reyes, Tomas Del '79 (NY) New York, NY St. Malachy's; [II] New York, NY Descubriendo El Siglo XXI, Inc. (Discovering XXI Century Inc.).
Vallecorsa, Daniele '93 (PIT) Pittsburgh, PA St. Paul Cathedral; Pittsburgh, PA St. Regis; Chaplain to Latino Catholic Community.
Vallee, Robert '87 (MIA)[A] Miami, FL St. John Vianney College Seminary.
Vallejo, Adam '08 (AMA) Amarillo, TX St. Laurence Cathedral.
Vallejo, Rev. Msgr. Arquimedes '89 (RCK) Promoter of Justice.
Vallejo, Rev. Msgr. Arquimedes '89 (RCK) Aurora, IL Sacred Heart; Special Assignment; Hispanic Ministry Offices; Adjunct Judical Vicar; Loves Park, IL St. Bridget; Defenders of the Bond.
Vallejo, Gilberto '02 (SAT) Archdiocesan Presbyteral Council; In Rural Area; Priests Personnel Board; Pleasanton, TX St. Andrew.
Vallejo, William '97 (RCK) Rochelle, IL St. Patrick.
Vallelonga, J. Stephen '90 (WH) Weston, WV St. Patrick's; Glenville, WV Good Shepherd.
Valleroy, Paul J. '74 (KNX) Kingsport, TN St. Dominic.
Valleroy, Rickey J. '93 (STL) Farmington, MO St. Joseph.
Valley, John '60 (CLV) Retired.
Valley, Paul *s.p.* '64 (SFE)[H] Jemez Springs, NM Our Lady of Lourdes.
Vallier, John F. '87 (GR) Grand Rapids, MI Holy Spirit.
Valliere, Timothy C. '91 (NOR) Absent on Leave.
Vallina, Rev. Msgr. Emilio '52 (MIA) Retired.
Valliparambil, Jose '83 (GF) Chinook, MT St. Gabriel; Special Assignment.
Valliyamthadathil, Joseph *m.c.b.s.* '78 (DUL) Gilbert, MN St. Joseph.
Vallone, Louis F. '73 (PIT) Crescent, PA St. Catherine of Siena; McKees Rocks, PA St. John of God.
Valls, Richard '57 (KAL) Retired.
Valmonte, Arturo '93 (RNO) On Special Assignment; [B] Reno, NV Saint Mary's Regional Medical Center.
Valmorida, Mario '83 (SAC) Quincy, CA St. John; Westwood, CA Our Lady of the Snows.
Valone, Fred W. '94 (GAL) Tomball, TX St. Anne; Northern Vicariate.
Valoret, Joseph '83 (MIA) Retired.
Valtierra, David D. *c.o.* '76 (CHR) Rock Hill, SC St. Mary; [E] Rock Hill, SC Oratory of St. Philip Neri, Congregation of the Oratory of Pontifical Rite; [H] Rock Hill, SC Winthrop University, York Co. Tech Center.
Vamos, Joseph E. '66 (GRY) Bishop's Council of Priests Retired.
Vamos, Joseph L. '61 (TOL) Toledo, OH; Defenders of the Bond; Toledo, OH St. Stephen Retired.
Van, Bartholomew M. Pham Minh *c.m.c.* '77 (SPC)[I] Carthage, MO Shrine of Immaculate Heart of Mary.
Van Abel, John W. '72 (MIL) Retired.
Van Alstine, Mark N. '05 (SAV) Presbyteral Council; Augusta, GA St. Mary on the Hill.
Van Alstyne, Donald J. *m.i.c.* '81 (MO) Army Chaplains.
Van Alstyne, Donald *m.i.c.* (SPR)[H] On Duty Outside of House:.
Vanasse, Bernard '78 (FR)[F] Taunton, MA Marian Manor Inc.; [G] Fall River, MA Priests' Hostel.
Vanasse, Roman R. *o.praem.* '60 (GB)[J] De Pere, WI St. Norbert Abbey.
VanBeek, Alois '73 (MIL) Neosho, WI St. Mary; Rubicon, WI St. John.
Van Beek, Dennis E. '69 (MIL) Plymouth, WI St. John the Baptist; Elkhart Lake, WI St. Thomas Aquinas.
Van Bergen, Francis G. '56 (CLV) Retired.
Van Cauwenbergh, Roger *c.i.c.m.* '51 (ARL)[H] Arlington, VA Missionhurst, C.I.C.M.–Central House and Provincialate.
Vance, Rev. Msgr. Charles P. '70 (PH) Lafayette Hill, PA St. Philip Neri.
Vance, Greg *s.j.* '98 (SPK)[D] Spokane, WA Gonzaga Preparatory School.
Vance, James L. '63 (SFE) Corrales, NM San Ysidro.
Vance, Rev. Msgr. Leslie A. '76 (SAT) San Antonio, TX St. Brigid; Adjutant Judicial Vicar.
Van Cleve, Michael S. '01 (GAL) Houston, TX St. Jerome; [S] Houston, TX The Catholic Chaplain Corps.
Vandal, Roland G. *m.s.* '49 (HRT)[L] Hartford, CT Missionaries of LaSalette.
Van Damme, Larry P. '93 (MAR) Marquette, MI St. Michael; [G] Marquette, MI Catholic Campus Ministry–Northern Michigan University; Consultors; St. Joseph Association.
Vandannoor, Joseph Augustine *m.s.t.* '81 (MAR) Menominee, MI Holy Redeemer.
Vandeberg, Joseph '89 (SCL) Brown's Valley, MN St. Anthony's; Wheaton, MN Ave Maria.
Vandebroek, Felix J. *ss.cc.* '54 (HON) Kalaupapa, HI St. Francis.
van de Crommert, Paul H. '88 (NU) Olivia, MN St. Aloysius; College of Consultors; Priests' Council.
Vandegrift, J. Raymond *o.p.* '60 (WDC)[B] Washington, DC Dominican House of Studies.
Vandegrift, William S. '80 (CAM) Villas, NJ St. Raymond's Catholic Church, Wildwood Villas, N.J.
Vandehey, Kelly '96 (P) Adjutant Judicial Vicar; Judges; Vocations.
Vandehey, Scott A. '66 (P) Forest Grove, OR Visitation B.V.M.
Van De Kreeke, William L. '63 (GB) Judges Retired.
Van Del, Curtis E. *s.j.* '65 (DEN)[N] Denver, CO Xavier Jesuit Center.
Van De Loo, Willard J. '55 (GB) Retired.
Van De Moortell, Raymond (BO) Peabody, MA St. Adelaide; [A] Brighton, MA St. John Seminary.
Vandenberg, James '77 (PBL) Absent on Leave.
Vandenberg, Robert H. '58 (GB) Retired.
Vandenberg, Thomas L. '62 (SEA) College of Consultors Retired.

Vanden Boogard, Richard J. *o.praem.* '88 (MO) Navy Chaplains.
Vanden Boogard, Steven J. *o.praem.* '88 (GB)[J] De Pere, WI St. Norbert Abbey.
VandenBossche, John V. *c.s.c.* '51 (FTW)[H] Notre Dame Congregation of Holy Cross, Indiana Province, Provincial House.
Van Den Bussche, Hugo *o.m.i.* '53 (SAT)[L] San Antonio, TX.
Van den Eynde, Stephen *ss.cc.* '48 (HON)[D] Honolulu, HI St. Patrick's Monastery.
Vanden Hogen, Rev. Msgr. James '64 (GB) Retired.
Vanden Hogen, Paul '54 (GB) Retired.
Vandenkker, John P. *c.c.* '85 (GAL) Houston, TX Queen of Peace.
Van De Paer, John *c.i.c.m.* '47 (PH) Parkesburg, PA Our Lady of Consolation.
Vander Heyden, William F. '70 (MO) Veterans Affairs Medical Center; On Duty Outside the Diocese; National Conference of Veterans Affairs Catholic Chaplains, Inc.; DEPARTMENT OF VETERANS AFFAIRS HOSPITALS AND CHAPLAINS.
Vanderholt, Rev. Msgr. James '57 (BEA) Silsbee, TX St. Mark the Evangelist Retired.
Vanderholt, Joseph *s.j.* '68 (SFE) Albuquerque, NM Immaculate Conception.
Vanderkolk, Peter J. '83 (LFT) Delphi, IN St. Joseph; Associate Judges.
Vanderley, Louis *o.s.b.* '66 (OKL) Edmond, OK St. John the Baptist; [I] Shawnee, OK St. Gregory's Abbey; [K] Edmond, OK University of Central Oklahoma; Shawnee, OK.
Vanderlin, Philip *o.s.b.* '70 (BIS)[A] Richardton, ND Assumption Abbey.
Vanderlin, Philip *o.s.b.* '80 (FgM) Richardton, ND Assumption Abbey.
VanderLoop, Anthony G. '03 (STP) Deanery 15.
VanderLoop, Tony '03 (STP) Richfield, MN St. Peter.
van der Peet, Michael *s.c.j.* '53 (MIL)[P] Franklin, WI Villa Maria; [B] Hales Corners, WI Sacred Heart School of Theology.
Vander Ploeg, Jon '01 (STP) Ham Lake, MN Church of Saint Paul; [P] St. Paul, MN The Companions of Christ.
Vander Steeg, Mark P. '99 (GB) Appleton, WI St. Edward; Greenville, WI St. Mary.
Vanderweel, Richard L. *s.s.e.* '62 (BUR) Censor Librorum; [E] Colchester, VT Society of St. Edmund.
Van der Werff, Rev. Msgr. Martin '50 (NO) Retired.
VanderWeyst, Peter '07 (SCL) Presbyteral Council; Chokio, MN St. Mary's; Chokio, MN St. Charles; Morris, MN Assumption of the Blessed Virgin Mary.
Vander Woude, Thomas P. '92 (ARL) Alexandria, VA Queen of Apostles.
Van Deuren, John H. '59 (GB) Luxemburg, WI St. Louis Retired.
Van De Ven, Kenneth A. '71 (PHX) Retired.
Vandewalle, Matthew J. '00 (LIN) Colon, NE St. Joseph's; Advocates.
Van De Water, Richard '82 (LA) Pomona, CA St. Joseph.
VanDoan, Vincent '86 (MO) DEPARTMENT OF VETERANS AFFAIRS HOSPITALS AND CHAPLAINS; Milan, MI Immaculate Conception.
Van Dorn, James *o.f.m.conv.* '67 (STP)[N] Prior Lake, MN Franciscan Retreats.
Van Durme, Patrick '00 (ROC) Military Chaplains; Army Chaplains; On Duty Outside the Diocese.
Van Dyke, James R. *s.j.* '93 (NY)[F] New York, NY Xavier High School; [EE] New York, NY St. Ignatius Loyola Residence.
Vanecko, William E. '65 (CHI) Chicago, IL St. Kilian.
Vanegas, Albeyro *c.s.v.* '90 (CHI)[N] Arlington Heights Viatorian Province Center–Clerics of St. Viator.
Vanejas, Javier *sch.p.* (NY)[EE] New York, NY Calasanzian Fathers (Piarists).
Van Fossen, Brian F. '05 (SCR) Dunmore, PA Our Lady of Mount Carmel Parish.
Vang, Chue '93 (STP) Brooklyn Park, MN St. Vincent de Paul.
Van Guilder, Alphonse *o.f.m.conv.* '64 (MRY) Pismo Beach, CA St. Paul the Apostle.
VanHaight, Christopher *o.f.m.* '08 (PAT) Paterson, NJ St. Bonaventure.
Van Haverbeke, Kenneth S. '91 (WCH) Wichita, KS St. Elizabeth Ann Seton; Ongoing Formation of the Clergy Committee; Presbyteral Council/College of Consultors.
Van Hook, John E. *o.f.m.* '55 (ALB)[B] Siena College.
Van House, Joseph *o.cist.* '09 (DAL)[J] Irving, TX Cistercian Abbey of Our Lady of Dallas.
Vanin, Dino *p.i.m.e.* '72 (DET)[K] Detroit, MI P.I.M.E. Missionaries.
Vanissery, Matthew '64 (OAK) Hospital Ministry; Berkeley, CA St. Joseph The Worker.
Vanitvelt, Milton H. '49 (MAR) Retired.
Vaniyepurackal, George '85 (MAR) DeTour, MI Sacred Heart; Goetzville, MI St. Stanislaus Kostka.
Vankeirsbilck, Paul *e.c.* '90 (STU)[H] Bloomingdale, OH Holy Family Hermitage.
Van Kempen, Robert '93 (FTW) Bristol, IN St. Mary of the Annunciation.
Van Kuren, Corey S. '86 (SY)[T] Vestal, NY Binghamton University Newman Center.
Van Lai, Joseph Khuyen '74 (SD) Lakeside, CA Our Lady of Perpetual Help.
Van Leeuwen, Joseph *c.p.* '64 (FgM)[N] Chicago Passionist Provincial Office.
Van Liefde, Rev. Msgr. Christian M. '73 (LA) On Administrative Leave.
Van Loon, Rev. Msgr. Neil J. '79 (SCR) Williamsport, PA St. Luke.
Van Loon, Rev. Msgr. Neil J. '79 (SCR) Episcopal Vicars; Williamsport, PA St. Boniface; Jersey Shore, PA Immaculate Conception of the Blessed Virgin Mary; Diocesan Consultors.
Van Massenhove, David L. '83 (SLC) Sandy, UT Saint Thomas More Catholic Church LLC 248.
Van Nguyen, James '08 (TLS) Tulsa, OK Holy Family Cathedral.
Van Nguyen, Joseph Son '82 (DAL) Appointed Members; Carrollton, TX Sacred Heart of Jesus Christ.
Van Nguyen, Peter '60 (PMB) Boca Raton, FL Ascension; Lake Worth, FL Sacred Heart.
Van Nguyen, Thanh (HRT) Unassigned.
Vannicola, Michael '06 (VEN) Naples, FL St. Ann.
Van Nquyen, Joseph Huyen '95 (SAC) Knights Landing, CA St. Paul.
Van Nuyen, Paul *c.h.c.* '06 (VEN) The Vietnam Catholic Community of Our Lady of Lavang; Sarasota, FL St. Martha.
Van Ommeren, Rev. Msgr. William '52 (SPK) Spokane, WA St. Joseph; [M] Spokane, WA Immaculate Heart Retreat Center Retired.
Vanoncini, Robert R. '63 (FRS) Dos Palos, CA Sacred Heart.
Vanorny, Ed '98 (RC) Rapid City, SD Cathedral of Our Lady of Perpetual Help.
Van Pham, Hanh '92 (CC) Corpus Christi, TX St. Philip The Apostle.
Van Pham, Phien '77 (SD) San Diego, CA Good Shepherd.
Van Phuong, Rev. Msgr. Francis Pham '66 (ATL) Riverdale, GA Our Lady of Vietnam.
Vanrell, Bartolome '53 (SJN)[E] San Juan, PR Centro Medico de P.R.
Van Sickler, Robert '93 (MO) CIVIL AIR PATROL Retired.
Van Sloun, Michael '95 (STP) Anoka, MN St. Stephen; Deanery 12.
Van Son, Rev. Msgr. Henry Adrian '49 (LA) Retired.
VanTassell, Malachi *t.o.r.* '04 (ALT)[A] Loretto, PA St. Francis University; [G] Loretto, PA St. Francis Friary at Mount Assisi.
Van Thanh, Louis '94 (NY) Newburgh, NY St. Patrick.
Van Thanh, Louis '94 (ALB) Vietnamese Apostolate; Special Assignment.
Vanthu, Joseph N. '71 (SJ) Sunnyvale, CA Church of The Resurrection Retired.
Van Tran, Nahn *s.v.d.* '00 (DUB)[B] Epworth, IA Divine Word College.
Van Tran, Tri '02 (JOL) Park Forest, IL St. Mary.
Van Vlaenderen, Leonard S. '88 (MIL) Retired.
Van Vliet, Charles *f.s.s.p.* '96 (LIN)[A] Denton, NE Our Lady of Guadalupe Seminary; Denton, NE.
VanVurst, James *o.f.m.* '61 (CIN)[N] Cincinnati, OH St. John the Baptist Friary.
Van Wiel, John E. *c.s.v.* '66 (CHI)[D] Arlington Heights, IL St. Viator High School; [N] Arlington Heights, IL Viatorian Province Center–Clerics of St. Viator.
Van Winkle, Charles *c.s.c.* '78 (AUS)[G] Austin, TX Brother Andre Residence.
Van Wormer, Giles *o.f.m.conv.* '57 (ALB)[L] Rensselaer, NY Provincialate, Immaculate Conception Friary – Order of Friars Minor Conventual.
Vanyo, Stephen *c.ss.r.* '62 (FgM) Baltimore Province.
Vanzillotta, Gino *o.m.* '54 (LA) Los Angeles, CA All Saints; [P] Los Angeles, CA Minim Fathers.
Vap, Rev. Msgr. Ivan F. '54 (LIN) Building Commission Retired.
Varano, Andrew R. '58 (BRK) Retired.
Varela, Enrique *o.carm.* '08 (JOL)[L] Darien Carmelite Provincial Office.
Varela, Jose *c.o.r.c.* '90 (SB) Corona, CA St. Edward; [I] Corona, CA Confraternity of Operarios Del Reino De Cristo, C.O.R.C.
Varela, Mariano O. '97 (WIN) Mankato, MN SS. Peter and Paul's; [J] Mankato, MN IVE Formation Program.
Varela–Nungaray, Enrique *o.carm.* (JOL) Joliet, IL Mount Carmel.
Varettoni, Rev. Msgr. Julian B. '55 (PAT) Clifton, NJ Sacred Heart Retired.
Varga, Rev. Msgr. Andrew G. '78 (BGP) Westport, CT St. Luke; Diocesan Consultors.
Varga, Paul *o.f.m.conv.* (TR) Point Pleasant Beach, NJ St. Peter's.
Varga, Wayne F. '74 (PAT) Montague, NJ St. James the Greater; Sandyston, NJ St. Thomas the Apostle.
Vargas, Alex J. '02 (PMB) Boynton Beach, FL St. Thomas More.
Vargas, Eric *s.v.d.* '75 (CHI)[N] Techny, IL Divine Word Residence.
Vargas, Gabriel F. '89 (B) Soda Springs, ID Good Shepherd Catholic Community.
Vargas, George R. '96 (OAK) El Cerrito, CA St. Jerome.
Vargas, German *c.s.* '05 (MIA) Brazilian and Portuguese Apostolate; Margate, FL St. Vincent.
Vargas, John C. *c.ss.r.* '78 (STL)[O] Liguori, MO Alphonsian Foundation.
Vargas, Jose Carlos '92 (PCE) Guanica, PR St. Anthony Abbot.
Vargas, Lenin '06 (JKS) Priests' Council; Meridian, MS St. Joseph; Meridian, MS St. Patrick; Co Chairmen; Office of Vocations.
Vargas, Leonardo J. '85 (PHX) Bagdad, AZ St. Francis of Assisi Roman Catholic Parish.
Vargas, Leonel M. '91 (ORG) Santa Ana, CA St. Joseph.
Vargas, Luis A. *t.o.r.* (NEW) Newark, NJ Immaculate Heart of Mary.
Vargas, Luis '98 (SJ) Alviso, CA Our Lady, Star of the Sea; Deans; College of Consultors; Council of Priests.
Vargas, Luis (WIN) Madelia, MN St. Mary; St. James, MN St. James.
Vargas, Victor '65 (LA) Huntington Park, CA St. Matthias.
Vargas Cruz, Gerardo A. *o.f.m.* '06 (SJN) Sabana Seca, PR San Jose Obrero.
Varghese, Benny Mekkatt *c.f.i.c.* '04 (STP)[K] St. Paul, MN Congregation of the Sons of the Immaculate Conception; Minneapolis, MN Hennepin County Medical Center.
Varghese, Bernard *o.f.m.cap.* '99 (IND) Batesville, IN St. Louis.
Varghese, Jacob *v.c.* (COV) Union, KY St. Timothy.
Varghese, Josekutty '92 (HT) Priests Council; College of Consultors; Schriever, LA St. Lawrence.
Varghese, Joseph P. *v.c.* '70 (CAM) Blackwood, NJ The R.C. Church of St. Jude, Gloucester Township, N.J.
Varghese, Peter *c.m.i.* '91 (BLX) Pass Christian, MS Holy Family Parish.
Varghese, Rejimon *s.v.d.* '02 (WDC)[N] Washington, DC Divine Word House.
Varghese, Shaji '94 (CC) Sinton, TX Our Lady of Guadalupe.
Varghese, T.J. '95 (PRO) Chepachet, RI St. Eugene.
Varghese, Thunkuchan Steve *s.a.c.* (MIL)[P] Milwaukee, WI Pallotti House.
Vargo, Robert B. '89 (HRT) Poquonock, CT St. Joseph's; Special and other Archdiocesan Assignment; Judicial Vicar (Officialis).
Variath, Davis (P)[L] Portland Holy Cross Fathers & Brothers, C.S.C. – University of Portland.
Varickamackal, Joseph '77 (AUS) La Grange, TX Sacred Heart of Jesus.
Varkey, George *m.s.f.s.* '75 (LAN) Davison, MI St. John the Evangelist.
Varkey, George *m.s.t.* '90 (SP) New Port Richey, FL St. Thomas Aquinas.
Varkey, Joy '95 (RVC) Hampton Bays, NY St. Rosalie's.
Varkey, Matthew '96 (CHI)[J] Elk Grove Village, IL Alexian Brothers Medical Center.
Varney, Lawrence F. '60 (TOL) Retired.
Varno, John J. '66 (ALB) Retired.
Varno, John N. '66 (ALB) Ballston Lake, NY Our Lady of Grace.
Varo, Jose Luis '56 (FRS) Retired.
Varone, Normand G. '75 (SPC) Priests' Mutual Benefit Society Retired.
Varsanyi, Rev. Msgr. William I. '52 (NY)[II] New York, NY Hungarian Catholic League of America, Inc.
Varsanyi, Rev. Msgr. William I. '46 (ATH) Providence, RI Our Lady of Charity; [M] Pawtucket, RI Jeanne Jugan Residence; Hungarian Catholic League of America, Inc.; Delegate for Canonical Affairs; Promoter of Justice; Propagation of the Faith; Catholic Relief Services; Holy Childhood Association.
Vartzelis, George D. '53 (BO) Senior Priests. Retired.
Varuvel, Paul L. '72 (BUF)[A] East Aurora, NY Christ the King Seminary.
Vas, Joseph S. '79 (OKL) Newkirk, OK St. Francis of Assisi Retired.
Vas, Laszlo (PAT) Passaic, NJ St. Stephen's.
Vasek, Stephen *o.m.i.* '71 (BUF) Buffalo, NY Holy Angels.
Vashon, Randall J. '00 (MET) Clinton, NJ Immaculate Conception; Office of Vocations; Board for Seminary Education.
Vasile, Louis A. '72 (ROC) Auburn, NY St. Alphonsus.
Vaske, Philip '06 (CHY)[F] Casper, WY St. Francis Newman Center; Casper, WY St. Anthony of Padua.
Vasko, Christopher P. '83 (TOL) Assessors; Toledo, OH Historic Church of Saint Patrick; Toledo, OH St. Martin de Porres; Judicial Vicar; Members.
Vasko, Peter *o.f.m.* '87 (FgM) Washington, DC COMMISSARIAT OF THE HOLY LAND.
Vaskov, Nicholas '09 (PIT) Graduate Studies.
Vasquez, Adrian '08 (B) Pocatello, ID Holy Spirit Catholic Community.
Vasquez, James '06 (CC) Catholic Engaged Encounter; Family Life Office; Catholic Singles in Christ; On Special Assignment; Marriage Encounter; Corpus

Christi, TX Our Lady Star of the Sea.
Vasquez, Jose '08 (BLX) Laurel, MS Immaculate Conception.
Vasquez, Julio '95 (NY) Yonkers, NY St. Peter; Bronx, NY Our Lady of Victory.
Vasquez, Oscar *s.m.* '05 (STL)[O] Saint Louis, MO Chaminade Community; Councilors:.
Vasquez, Paul L. '98 (OM) Omaha, NE St. John Vianney; Special Assignment.
Vasquez, Pedro *o.f.m.* '71 (LA)[P] Santa Barbara, CA Franciscan Friary, Order of Friars Minor (Old Mission).
Vasquez, Perfecto L. '98 (RCK) Virgil, IL SS. Peter and Paul.
Vasquez, Rev. Msgr. Perfecto '59 (BRK)[V] Brooklyn, NY Ss. Peter and Paul Spirituality Center Brooklyn Campus; Woodside, NY St. Teresa.
Vasquez, Roberto Vera '01 (MRY) Castroville, CA Our Lady of Refuge.
Vasquez, Rodolfo D. '03 (CC) Corpus Christi, TX Our Lady of Guadalupe.
Vasquez–Martinez, Jose Alberto '02 (MRY) Clergy Life and Ministry Board; Salinas, CA St. Mary of the Nativity.
Vasquez–Rubio, Juan *o.ss.t.* (BAL)[S] Baltimore, MD.
Vass, Robert *s.d.v.* (PAT) Paterson, NJ St. Gerard Majella; Paterson, NJ St. Michael the Archangel.
Vassalotti, Thomas F. '07 (BRK) Brooklyn, NY St. Agatha's.
Vassar, Paul R. '71 (OAK) San Leandro, CA St. Leander.
Vater, Robert L. '45 (COV) Retired.
Vath, William R. '72 (LFT) Defender of the Bond; Lafayette, IN St. Boniface; Special Assignment; Defenders of the Bond.
Vathalloor, Joseph *c.m.i.* '74 (SAN) Eldorado, TX Our Lady of Guadalupe.
Vathappallil, Thomas *m.c.b.s.* '01 (MIL)[P] Kenosha, WI Missionary Congregation of the Blessed Sacrament, Inc., Zion Province; West Allis, WI St. Aloysius Gonzaga; West Allis, WI St. Rita.
Vathyiakaril–Eapen, Philip '87 (HT) Thibodaux, LA St. Joseph Co–Cathedral; Thibodaux Regional Medical Center.
Vattakudiyil, Francis P. '63 (RVC) Kings Park, NY St. Joseph's.
Vattakunnel, James C. '88 (BGP) Wilton, CT Our Lady of Fatima.
Vattakunnel, Jose '90 (LKC) Oakdale, LA Sacred Heart; [D] Oakdale, LA Herald of Good News, Inc.
Vattapara Devasia, George *m.s.f.s.* '95 (GAL) The Woodlands, TX St. Anthony of Padua.
Vattappara, George *m.s.f.s.* '95 (TYL)[B] Whitehouse, TX The Missionaries of St. Francis de Sales.
Vatter, Joseph E. '78 (BUF) Lockport, NY All Saints.
Vatterot, William (STL)[V] St. Louis, MO Archdiocesan Stewardship Education Committee.
Vatterott, William F. '03 (STL) St. Louis, MO St. Cecilia.
Vaudreuil, Paul *a.a.* '64 (WOR)[O] Worcester, MA Assumptionists (Augustinians of the Assumption).
Vaughan, Rev. Msgr. Gregory D. '72 (TR)[N] Trenton, NJ Villa Vianney; Vicar General and Moderator of the Curia; Diocesan Consultors; Diocesan Finance Council; Office of Vocations.
Vaughan, James '50 (ALB) Troy, NY Sacred Heart Retired.
Vaughan, Rev. Msgr. John J. '67 (MIA) Miami Beach, FL St. Patrick.
Vaughan, John R. '74 (OWN) Owensboro, KY St. Stephen Cathedral; Judges; Deans/Coordinators.
Vaughan, Thomas *s.s.c.* '56 (OM)[K] St. Columbans Missionary Society of St. Columban Retired.
Vaughey, Rev. Msgr. James K. '65 (NY) Briarcliff Manor, NY St. Theresa; Trustees of St. Patrick's Cathedral in the City of New York, Inc.
Vaughn, John *o.f.m.* '55 (LA)[BB] Santa Barbara, CA The Cause of Blessed Junipero Serra; [P] Santa Barbara, CA Franciscan Friary, Order of Friars Minor (Old Mission).
Vaughn, Mason '50 (SAG) Retired.
Vaughn, Richard P. *s.j.* '50 (SJ)[M] Los Gatos, CA Sacred Heart Jesuit Center.
Vaughn, Robert William *o.p.* '71 (NY)[EE] New York St. Vincent Ferrer Priory.
Vaughn, Roland G. '71 (LKC) Fenton, LA St. Charles Borromeo.
Vaught, Michael '73 (OKL) Pauls Valley, OK St. Catherine of Siena; Purcell, OK Our Lady of Victory.
Vavasseur, Henry C. '58 (BR) Retired.
Vaverek, Gavin N. '90 (TYL) Longview, TX St. Mary; College of Consultors; Defender of the Bond; Diocesan Building Board; Priests' Pension Board; Presbyteral Council; Diocesan Council of Catholic Women; Respect Life Program; Diocesan Implementation Committee On Ethics and Integrity Policy for Church Personnel; Diocesan Liturgical Commission; Victim Assistance Coordinator; Diocesan Christian Initiation Team.
Vaverek, Hayden J. '94 (MO) Anderson, SC St. Joseph; Cursillo Movement; Air Force Reserve Chaplains.
Vaverek, Timothy V. '85 (AUS) Waco, TX St. Joseph.
Vavonese, Charles S. '73 (SY) Special Assignment; Catholic Schools; Public Policy; DeWitt, NY Holy Cross.
Vavrick, Eugene B. '93 (TR) Wayside, NJ St. Anselm.
Vavrina, Kenneth P. '62 (OM) Omaha, NE St. Therese of the Child Jesus; Omaha, NE St. Benedict the Moor.
Vaz, Gregorio Dafonte (CGS) Cayey, PR Nuestra Senora de la Merced.
Vaz, Richard *s.v.d.* '78 (CHI)[N] Techny, IL Divine Word Residence; [T] Techny, IL Divine Word Missionaries, Inc.
Vazhappilly, Antony *s.d.b.* (OAK) Fremont, CA St. James The Apostle.
Vazhappilly, Mathew *c.m.i.* '74 (SFS) Scotland, SD St. George.
Vazneparambil, Thomas '69 (LUB) Retired.
Vazquez, Albert *c.m.f.* '55 (FRS) Fresno, CA St. Anthony Claret.
Vazquez, Armando (TR) Trenton, NJ Divine Mercy Parish.
Vazquez, Carlos R. '89 (WIL) Absent on Sick Leave.
Vazquez, Jose Luis '87 (MAD) Madison, WI Cathedral Parish of St. Raphael.
Vazquez, Luis A. '91 (ARE) Vega–Baja, PR Perpetuo Socorro; Police Chaplain.
Vazquez, Manuel *m.sp.s.* '76 (LA) Huntington Park, CA St. Martha.
Vazquez, Rev. Msgr. Perfecto '56 (BRK) Retired.
Vazquez, Raymundo Chavez '00 (AUS) Bryan, TX Santa Teresa.
Vazquez, Tomas (YAK) Ellensburg, WA St. Andrew's.
Vazquez–Rubio, Juan *o.ss.t.* (BAL) Hanover, MD St. Lawrence Martyr.
Vazquez Colon, Antonio Jose '90 (SJN)[E] San Juan, PR Centro Medico de P.R.
Vazquez Colon, Rev. Msgr. Antonio Jose '90 (SJN) Condado, San Juan, PR Stella Maris.
Vead, Victor P. '92 (BEA) Beaumont – Federal Correctional Complex; On Duty Outside the Diocese.
Veasey, Edward '62 (FgM) Boston, MA St. James the Apostle, Inc.
Vebelun, Edward *o.s.b.* '04 (SCL)[I] Collegeville St. John's Abbey, of the Order of St. Benedict.
Vecchiato, Rinaldo *c.s.* '67 (BO) Framingham, MA St. Tarcisius; Staten Island, NY.
Vecchio, Michael J. '50 (PIT) Retired.
Veeneman, Dismas J. *o.f.m.conv.* '69 (L) Louisville, KY St. Paul.
Vega, Aglayde Rafael '06 (BWN) Lyford, TX Prince of Peace.
Vega, Carlos '89 (MIA) Leisure City, FL St. Martin de Porres Catholic Church.
Vega, Cesar M. (YAK) Yakima, WA Holy Family.
Vega, Donald M. *s.j.* '65 (SJN) San Juan, PR San Ignacio de Loyola; [H] San Juan, PR Comunidad Jesuita.
Vega, Edwin Vazquez (PCE)[B] The Pontifical Catholic University of Puerto Rico.
Vega, Erasmo Rodriguez '72 (ELP) El Paso, TX Our Lady of Guadalupe.
Vega, Fernando *c.m.f.* '40 (LA) San Gabriel, CA San Gabriel Mission.
Vega, Hector R. *i.sch.* '74 (CC)[I] Corpus Christi, TX Secular Institute of the Schoenstatt Fathers.
Vega, Hector R. *c.c.* '74 (MIL)[T] Waukesha, WI Secular Institute of Schoenstatt Fathers.
Vega, Jose Antonio *s.j.* '00 (FgM) St. Louis, MO Society of Jesus.
Vega, Jose L. *o.m.* '69 (LA) Los Angeles, CA All Saints; [P] Los Angeles, CA Minim Fathers.
Vega, Jose Luis '54 (FRS) Retired.
Vega, Raymond *s.c.j.* '73 (SP)[N] Pinellas Park, FL Priests of the Sacred Heart Retired.
Vega, Richard '83 (LA) Chicago, IL The National Federation of Priests' Councils (1968); On Duty Outside the Archdiocese.
Vega, Roberto '87 (ARE) Arecibo, PR Cathedral of San Felipe Apostol; Priest's Senate (Consejo Presbiteral); Pastoral Vocational Program; Cathedral of San Felipe Apostol; Arecibo, PR Church of Santa Cecilia.
Vega–Alvarenga, Salvador '01 (LR) Rogers, AR St. Vincent de Paul.
Vega–Garcia, Emilio *ss.cc.* '68 (BWN) Edinburg, TX Sacred Heart.
Vega–Medina, Leonel *m.s.p.* '06 (SB) Riverside, CA St. John the Evangelist.
Veik, Alan D. *o.f.m.cap.* '67 (MIL)[Y] Milwaukee, WI House of Peace; Kenosha, WI Our Lady of the Holy Rosary.
Veit, David J. '98 (JC) Jefferson City, MO Immaculate Conception; Priestly and Religious Vocations Committee.
Veith, William E. '70 (CHI)[J] Elk Grove Village, IL Alexian Brothers Medical Center.
Vela, Edison '91 (DAL) Dallas, TX St. Edward.
Vela, Fabian '56 (MRY) Hollister, CA Sacred Heart/St. Benedict Catholic Community Retired.
Vela, Jesus *o.f.m.cap.* '98 (LA) Los Angeles, CA St. Lawrence of Brindisi; Definitors:.
Vela, Rudy *s.m.* '84 (SAT)[L] San Antonio, TX Ligustrum Marianist Community; [C] San Antonio, TX St. Mary's University of San Antonio, Texas.
Velas, Vincent P. '64 (PIT) McKeesport, PA St. Patrick.
Velasco, Arturo '86 (LA) Los Angeles, CA St. Ignatius of Loyola.
Velasco, Fernando Rogelio '00 (SFR) Menlo Park, CA St. Anthony.
Velasquez, Bernardo (PAT) Passaic, NJ Our Lady of Fatima; Passaic, NJ Holy Trinity.
Velasquez, Francisco '90 (SAC) College of Consultors.
Velasquez, Marcos '89 (TUC) Maricopa, AZ Our Lady of Grace Roman Catholic Parish – Maricopa.
Velazquez, Carlos B. '90 (SAT) San Antonio, TX Holy Spirit.
Velazquez, David M. '80 (LA) Maywood, CA St. Rose of Lima.
Velazquez, Francisco '90 (SAC) Sacramento, CA St. Joseph's.
Velazquez, Luis A. '75 (ARE) On Duty Outside the Diocese.
Velazquez, Osvaldo F. *o.m.i.* '07 (GAL) Houston, TX St. Patrick.
Velazquez, Paul Jesus '06 (LA) Pico Rivera, CA St. Mariana de Paredes.
Velazquez, Rafael '06 (NEW) Plainfield, NJ St. Mary.
Velazquez, Yamil A. '05 (CGS) Naranjito, PR San Miguel Arcangel; Priests Senate.
Velazquez–Morales, Luis R. (SJN) Carolina, PR San Andres.
Velez, Antonio *t.c.* '89 (BAL) Columbia, MD St. John the Evangelist.
Velez, Juan R. '98 (POD) Los Angeles.
Velez, Juan '98 (LA)[W] Los Angeles, CA Prelature of the Holy Cross and Opus Dei.
Velez, Victor Sanchez '91 (ARE) Priest's Senate (Consejo Presbiteral).
Velez–Cardona, Miguel '08 (KNX) Chattanooga, TN St. Jude.
Velichore, Jesudasan '72 (STO) Turlock, CA Sacred Heart Church of Turlock (Pastor of).
Vella, Rev. Msgr. Desmond J. '59 (NY) New York, NY Immaculate Conception; Judges.
Vella, Edward P. *c.ss.r.* '85 (GR) Grand Rapids, MI St. Alphonsus; [L] Grand Rapids, MI The Society of the Redemptorists of the City of Grand Rapids.
Vella, Joseph '68 (BRK) Brooklyn, NY St. Mark.
Vellankal, Mathew *s.d.b.* '87 (OAK) Fremont, CA Holy Spirit.
Vellapallil, Thomas (LKC) Presbyteral Council.
Vellaplackil, George (HRT) Windsor Locks, CT St. Robert Bellarmine; Windsor Locks, CT St. Mary.
Vellappallil, Thomas *m.s.* '94 (LKC) Sulphur, LA St. Theresa.
Vellaramparampil, Aaron T. '71 (RVC) Glen Cove, NY St. Rocco.
Vellardita, Guy *o.f.m.* '58 (FgM) New York, NY Franciscan Province of the Immaculate Conception.
Vellenga, R. Stephen '81 (CLV) Painesville, OH St. Mary; [V] Painesville, OH St. Mary's – Painesville; Mission Office, Society for the Propagation of the Faith; Cleveland, OH Cathedral Square Plaza.
Vellian, Rev. Msgr. Jacob (SYM) San Jose, CA St. Mary Knanaya Catholic Mission of San Jose.
Vellicig, Cyril L. *m.m.* '51 (SJ)[M] Los Altos, CA Maryknoll.
Velliydathupathlil, Tomykkutty '91 (STA) Jacksonville Beach, FL St. Paul's.
Velloorattil, George '78 (CHI) Forest Park, IL St. Bernardine.
Velo, Rev. Msgr. Kenneth (CHI) Rosemont, IL Our Lady of Hope.
Velten, Robert *o.s.b.* '54 (SP)[N] St. Leo, FL St. Leo Abbey.
Veltri, Dennis J. '93 (E) Guys Mills, PA St. Hippolyte.
Veltrie, James V. *s.j.* '65 (STL)[C] Saint Louis University; [O] St. Louis, MO Jesuit Community Corporation at Saint Louis University – Jesuit Hall.
Veluz, Edward T. (NEW) Jersey City, NJ St. Anne's.
Vences, Marco Antonio *s.s.p.* '06 (LA) Los Angeles, CA; [P] Los Angeles, CA The Society of St. Paul.
Vendetti, Michael A. '64 (BRK) Retired.
Venditti, J. Michael '87 (MET) On Duty Outside the Diocese.
Venditti, J. Michael '87 (PSC) Allentown, PA St. Michael.
Vendramin, Aldo *c.s.* '75 (CHI)[N] Oak Park, IL Scalabrini Development Office.
Venegas, Rafael '07 (LA) Glendale, CA Holy Family.
Veneklase, Michael G. *o.c.d.* '93 (GRY)[H] Munster, IN Discalced Carmelite Fathers Monastery.
Veneklase, Michael G. *o.c.d.* '93 (CHI) Chicago, IL St. Camillus.
Veneroso, Joseph R. *m.m.* '78 (BRK).
Veneroso, Joseph R. *m.m.* '78 (NY)[EE] Maryknoll Maryknoll Fathers and Brothers.
Venezia, Arthur '71 (PMB) North Palm Beach, FL St. Paul of the Cross; Consultors.
Vengayil, Thomas '59 (PMB) Tequesta, FL St. Jude.
Venker, Josef V. *s.j.* '87 (SEA)[A] Seattle, WA Seattle

University; [L] Seattle, WA Arrupe Jesuit Community at Seattle University.
Venne, Douglas F. *m.m.* '59 (FgM) Maryknoll, NY MARYKNOLL.
Venne, R. Thomas '62 (MIL) Milwaukee, WI Cathedral of St. John the Evangelist Retired.
Venne, Samuel J. '78 (BUF) Awaiting Assignment.
Venneri, Michael D. '82 (SPK) Special Ministry; [F] Spokane, WA Sacred Heart Medical Center & Children's Hospital.
Vennetti, Robert C. *m.i.c.* '06 (MO) DEPARTMENT OF VETERANS AFFAIRS HOSPITALS AND CHAPLAINS.
Vennitti, Thomas A. '73 (STU) Toronto, OH St. Francis of Assisi; Toronto, OH St. Joseph's.
Vennix, James J. '56 (GB) Retired.
Venters, Darrell '89 (OWN) Fancy Farm, KY St. Jerome; Clergy Personnel Director; Vicar of Clergy; Priest Personnel Committee; Consultors.
Ventiquattro, Jude '88 (ALT)[G] Loretto, PA St. Francis Friary at Mount Assisi.
Ventline, Lawrence M. '76 (DET) Special Assignment.
Ventura, Anthony C. '78 (HRT) Retired.
Ventura, Gennaro J. '43 (ROC) Retired.
Ventura, Octavio *l.c.* '96 (SAC) Sacramento, CA Our Lady of Guadalupe Shrine.
Ventura, William N. '06 (BO) Chelmsford, MA St. John the Evangelist.
Venturini, Fabio '02 (CHI) On Duty Outside the Archdiocese; Franklin Park, IL St. Gertrude.
Venvertloh, Kenneth J. '67 (SFD) Jacksonville, IL Our Saviour; Jacksonville Deanery; Lay Employees' Pension Plan Administrative Committee.
Venza, Felix F. '72 (TR) Bordentown, NJ St. Mary.
Venzor, Jesse C. '80 (FRS) Woodlake, CA St. Frances Cabrini.
Ver, Alex '67 (NEW) Jersey City, NJ St. Nicholas.
Ver'Schneider, Neil L. *s.j.* '66 (PH)[H] Philadelphia, PA The Gesu School; [Y] Philadelphia, PA Jesuit Community, Arrupe House; [Y] Philadelphia, PA Gesu School Jesuit Community and Outreach Center (S.J.).
Vera, Francis (POD) Delray Beach.
Vera, Francisco '07 (MIA)[P] Miami, FL Prelature of the Holy Cross and Opus Dei.
Vera, Jude '89 (SP) Tampa, FL St. Mary.
Vera, Luis A. *o.s.a.* '96 (PH)[C] Villanova, PA Villanova University.
Vera, Luis A. *o.s.a.* '97 (CHI)[N] Chicago, IL St. Augustine Friary.
Vera, Roberto '01 (MRY)[K] Salinas, CA Magnificat the Monterey Bay Chapter; Vocations Board; Presbyteral Council; Diocesan Consultors; Diocesan Consultors.
Vera, Romulo E. *c.s.c.* '89 (FTW)[H] Notre Dame Congregation of Holy Cross, Indiana Province, Provincial House.
Vera, Vicente Antonio '85 (TOL) Sylvania, OH St. Joseph.
Vera–Perez, Jose *o.f.m.* '78 (ELP)[B] El Paso, TX Roger Bacon College.
Veras, Richard '96 (NY) Staten Island, NY St. Rita.
Verber, Thomas G. *o.s.a.* '99 (SD) San Diego, CA St. Patrick; [J] San Diego, CA Augustinian Community.
Verberg, Richard R. '71 (MIL) Retired.
Verbest, Stephen *o.c.s.o.* '98 (DUB)[K] Peosta, IA New Melleray Abbey, Order of Cistercians of the Strict Observance; Peosta, IA.
Verboomen, Willy *c.i.c.m.* '63 (SAT)[K] San Antonio, TX Padua Place Retired.
Verbryke, William L. *s.j.* '83 (CHI)[N] Chicago Chicago Province of the Society of Jesus–Provincial Office.
Verbryke, William L. *s.j.* '83 (DET)[B] Berkley, MI Loyola House.
Vercellone, Anthony '80 (LAV) On Duty Outside the Diocese.
Vercellone, Anthony '80 (RNO) Reno, NV Our Lady of the Snows; Diocesan Board of Consultors; Lists of Deans; Presbyteral Council.
Verdegan, Albert L. '60 (SUP) Retired.
Verdelotti, Anthony W. '86 (PRO) Cranston, RI St. Mark; Cemeteries.
Verdelotti, James J. '78 (PRO) Cranston, RI St. Mary; Deans.
Verdi, Ralph *c.pp.s.* (CLV) Cleveland, OH Our Lady of Good Counsel.
Verdia Nay, Carlos '85 (SJN) San Juan, PR Ntra. Sra. de la Medalla Milagrosa.
Verdick, Jerome F. '58 (WIN) Retired.
Verdun, Gerald J. '72 (PEO) Delavan, IL St. Mary's.
Verduzco–Peregrino, Marlon M. '00 (SFR) San Francisco, CA St. Peter.
Vereb, Jerome *c.p.* '72 (PIT)[M] Pittsburgh, PA St. Paul of the Cross Monastery.
VerEecke, Robert F. *s.j.* '78 (BO) Newton, MA St. Ignatius Loyola; [U] Newton, MA The Jesuit Community at Boston College; Roxbury, MA St. Mary of the Angels.
Verespy, Joseph D. '79 (SCR) Dupont, PA Sacred Heart of Jesus.
Vergara, Arlon M. '90 (RIC) Williamsburg, VA St. Bede.
Vergara, Armando '73 (STO) Hughson, CA St. Anthony Church of Hughson (Pastor of); Personnel Board.
Vergara, Heriberto (STA) Jacksonville, FL San Jose.
Vergara, Jaime *c.m.* '56 (SJN) San Juan, PR Sagrado Corazon de Jesus; [B] San Juan, PR Colegio Sagrado Corazon de Jesus.
Verghase, Steve *s.a.c.* (MIL) South Milwaukee, WI Divine Mercy.
Verhaeghe, Ronald '92 (KC) Lees Summit, MO Holy Spirit; Finance Council.
Verhagen, Norbert M. *m.m.* '39 (NY)[EE] Retired.
Verhalen, Charles J. '47 (MIL)[W] Wauwatosa, WI Legion of Mary Retired.
Verhalen, David H. *c.s.c.* '54 (FTW)[H] Notre Dame Congregation of Holy Cross, Indiana Province, Provincial House.
Verhalen, Peter *o.cist.* '81 (DAL)[D] Irving, TX Cistercian Preparatory School; [J] Irving, TX Cistercian Abbey of Our Lady of Dallas; Irving, TX.
Verhasselt, David A. '89 (MIL) Oconomowoc, WI St. Catherine.
Verheggen, Peter A. *o.f.m.* '49 (LSC) Tularosa, NM St. Francis de Paula.
Verhelst, Steven J. '90 (NU) Willmar, MN St. Mary; College of Consultors; Board of Trustees for Pension Plan for Priests; Priests' Council.
Verhoff, Melvin T. '91 (TOL) Delphos, OH St. John the Evangelist.
Verhoye, Gerard A. '49 (PEO) Retired.
Verley, Jude *o.s.c.* '79 (SCL) Hillman, MN St. Rita's; Onamia, MN The Church of the Holy Cross of Onamia; Wahkon, MN Sacred Heart; Onamia, MN St. Therese, Little Flower Indian Mission; [I] Onamia, MN Crosier Priory.
Vernon, Donald '55 (LFT)[E] Lafayette, IN Emmaus House Retired.
Vernon, William F. '97 (MAD) Verona, WI St. William; Verona, WI St. Andrew.
Veronesi, Giulio *c.r.s.* '75 (GAL) Houston, TX Christ the King.
Verrengio, Rocco F. '70 (BRK) Retired.
Verrier, John M. '95 (PEO) Brimfield, IL St. Joseph's.
Verrigni, Robert J. '77 (NY) Rye, NY Resurrection.
Verrill, O. Wendell '63 (BO) Senior Priests. Retired.
Verrilli, William F. '79 (BGP) Bridgeport, CT St. Andrew; Judges.
Verruni, Samuel A. '86 (PH) Norwood, PA St. Gabriel.
Verschaeve, C. Michael '77 (DET) Lake Orion, MI St. Joseph.
Verstreken, Alfred *c.j.* '73 (LA) Santa Barbara, CA Holy Cross.
Verzosa, Rev. Msgr. Antonio (STV) St. John, VI Our Lady of Mt. Carmel Parish.
Vesbit, Thomas '64 (GR) Retired.
Vesely, James J. '54 (CLV) Cleveland, OH St. Leo the Great; Brooklyn, OH St. Thomas More Retired.
Vesey, John E. '68 (FgM) Maryknoll, NY MARYKNOLL; Released from Diocesan Assignment.
Vesga, Mario '62 (SD) Chula Vista, CA St. Rose of Lima Retired.
Vessels, John L. *s.j.* '57 (ELP)[J] El Paso, TX Our Lady's Youth Center; El Paso, TX Sacred Heart.
Veszelovszky, Albin V. *o.praem.* '44 (GB)[J] De Pere, WI St. Norbert Abbey; [O] De Pere, WI Canons Regular of Magnovarad, Ltd.
Vetrano, Michael A. '79 (RVC) West Islip, NY Our Lady of Lourdes; Procurator & Advocates; Senate of Priests (Presbyteral Council/College of Consultors).
Vetter, Austin '93 (BIS) Minot, ND St. Leo; Continuing Education for Clergy.
Vetter, Joseph G. '73 (R)[I] Durham, NC Newman Catholic Student Center Duke University; Diocesan Consultors; Council of Priests; Campus Ministry.
Vetter, Rev. Msgr. Wendelyn '60 (FAR) Judges Retired.
Vettickal, Sebastian *c.m.i.* '91 (LA) Diamond Bar, CA St. Denis.
Vettiyolil, Abraham (NY) Pelham Manor, NY Our Lady of Perpetual Help.
Vettuvelil, Stephen J. '96 (SYM) Pembroke Pines, FL Syro–Malabar Knanaya Catholic Mission of South Florida.
Vevik, Paul '77 (SPK) Spokane, WA Mary Queen.
Vezhaparambil, Paul '64 (RVC) Massapequa, NY St. Rose of Lima.
Via, Anthony P. *s.j.* '62 (SPK)[B] Spokane, WA Gonzaga University.
Viall, James A. '54 (CLV) Administrative Leave.
Viall, John L. '59 (CLV) North Royalton, OH St. Albert the Great Retired.
Vialpando, Kenneth L. '91 (SLC) Priests' Personnel Board; Ogden, UT Saint Joseph LLC 230; [C] Ogden, UT St. Joseph Catholic Elementary School; Deans; Team.
Vicari, Marc A. '97 (NEW)[P] Newark, NJ The Newman Catholic Center at University Heights (Rutgers/Newark/NJIT); Family Life Ministries; Members.
Vicedo, Hermenegildo '63 (SJN) San Juan, PR Nuestra Senora de la Providencia.
Vicens, Hipolito *c.ss.r.* '94 (CGS)[B] Aguas Buenas, PR Casa Cristo Redentor.
Vicente, Francisco V. *o.p.* '55 (OAK) Promoter of Justice; Antioch, CA Most Holy Rosary.
Vicente, Isidore V. *o.p.* '64 (GAL) Houston, TX Holy Rosary.
Vicente, Julio '08 (B) Mountain Home, ID Our Lady of Good Counsel.
Vicentini, Joseph *c.s.* '55 (KC) Kansas City, MO Holy Rosary.
Vichich, Michael T. '74 (MAR) Spalding, MI St. John Neumann; Nadeau, MI St. Bruno.
Vicini, Andrea *s.j.* '96 (BO)[U] Newton, MA The Jesuit Community at Boston College.
Vick, James L. '99 (KNX) Chattanooga, TN Our Lady of Perpetual Help.
Vickery, Richard F. '48 (MAN) Retired.
Victor, Jose Helbert (NEW) Irvington, NJ St. Leo's.
Victor, P. R. '88 (CC) Corpus Christi, TX SS. Cyril and Methodius.
Victor, Ronald J. '78 (DET) Roseville, MI St. Athanasius.
Victoria, John J. '08 (SCR)[D] Wilkes–Barre, PA Holy Redeemer High School; Wilkes–Barre, PA St. Nicholas.
Victoria, Robert '91 (LA) El Segundo, CA St. Anthony.
Victoria–Tovar, Jose Helber '07 (NEW) Wyckoff, NJ St. Elizabeth.
Victorino, Florentino *m.s.c.* '01 (LA) Cudahy, CA Sagrado Corazon y Santa Maria de Guadalupe.
Vida, Rev. Msgr. George N. '57 (VNN) Anaheim, CA Annunciation; Building and Sacred Arts; Pension Committee.
Vidad, Gerald '97 (SB) Twentynine Palms, CA Blessed Sacrament.
Vidal, David *i.v.e.* '01 (WDC) Chillum, MD St. John Baptist de la Salle.
Vidal, Gregoire '92 (DEN) Denver, CO St. Catherine of Siena.
Vidal, Gustavo '97 (SLC) St. George, UT St. George LLC 223.
Vidal, Jesus Hernandez '94 (OAK) Oakland, CA St. Louis Bertrand.
Vidal, Robert S. '66 (ORG) Seal Beach, CA St. Anne's.
Vidal, Tomas '09 (YAK) Moses Lake, WA Queen of All Saints; Moses Lake, WA Our Lady of Fatima.
Vidarte, Jose Luis '08 (TYL) Center, TX St. Therese; Diocesan Liturgical Commission.
Vidmar, John C. *o.p.* '80 (PRO)[P] Providence St. Thomas Aquinas Priory at Providence College.
Vidra, Rev. Msgr. Thomas '59 (SD) Retired.
Vidrine, Jason '06 (LAF) Gueydan, LA St. Peter the Apostle; [L] Lafayette, LA Our Lady of Wisdom Catholic Student Center.
Vidrine, Richard '95 (LAF) Absent on Sick Leave.
Viego, Carlos M. '98 (NEW) Newark, NJ St. Lucy's.
Viego, Carlos '98 (NEW) Hispanic Curia of Essex and Union Counties.
Vieira, John S. '97 (SB) Ontario, CA St. Elizabeth Ann Seton.
Vieira, Rev. Msgr. Victor M. '67 (PRO) East Providence, RI St. Francis Xavier.
Vieites, Jesus *ss.cc.* '62 (SJN) Guaynabo, PR Corazon de Jesus.
Viejo, Carlos (NEW) Elizabeth, NJ Union County Jail.
Vien, John Rogers '93 (STL) St. Louis, MO St. Pius V.
Vientos, Luis A. Rodriguez (PCE)[B] The Pontifical Catholic University of Puerto Rico.
Viera, Edwin Mercado '86 (ARE) Diocesan Tribunal of Arecibo.
Viera, Manuel *o.f.m.* '82 (CIN) Judicial Vicar; [N] Cincinnati, OH St. Francis Seraph Friary.
Vieras, Richard (NY)[E] White Plains, NY Archbishop Stepinac High School.
Vierra, Theodore A. '60 (LA) Los Angeles, CA St. Paul the Apostle Retired.
Vieson, Paul F. *s.m.* '84 (CIN)[D] Dayton, OH The University of Dayton; [N] Dayton, OH Marianist Community.
Viet, Nguyen Ngoc *c.ss.r.* (LA)[P] Baldwin Park Vietnamese Redemptorist Mission.
Viet Tran, Bac–Hai '84 (NO) Jefferson, LA St. Agnes.
Vieyra, Eladio '08 (B) Caldwell, ID Our Lady of the Valley.
Vigeant, Wilfrid J. *s.j.* '46 (BO)[U] Weston, MA Campion Health Center, Inc.
Vigil, Edwin '07 (SAT) San Antonio, TX Holy Spirit.
Vigil, Joe '80 (SFE) Albuquerque, NM Our Lady of Guadalupe.
Vigil, Joseph A. '06 (PBL) Monte Vista, CO St. Joseph; Center, CO St. Francis Jerome; Monte Vista, CO Holy Name of Mary.
Vigil, Michael A. '85 (GLP) Farmington, NM St. Mary's; Presbyteral Council; Judicial Vicar; Judges.
Vigil, Paul E. '91 (LA) Los Angeles, CA St. Timothy.
Vigilanti, John A. '72 (NY)[F] Bronx, NY Academy of Mount St. Ursula; Judge; Army Reserve Chaplains.
Vigliotta, Thomas F. *o.f.m.* '85 (ATL)[J] Athens, GA University of Georgia – Catholic Student Center; Athens, GA Catholic Student Center at The University of Georgia; Special or Other (Arch)Diocesan Assignment.
Vignato, Joe *s.x.* '93 (FgM)[N] Wayne Xaverian Missionary Fathers; Wayne, NJ XAVERIAN MISSIONARY FATHERS.

Vignoe, Joseph M. '58 (BUR) Retired.
Vignola, Robert R. *c.m.* '50 (PH)[Y].
Vignone, John J. '75 (CAM) Egg Harbor Township, NJ The Church of Saint Katharine Drexel, McKee City, New Jersey; Appointed Members; Consultants.
Vigoa, Richard J. '08 (MIA) Miami, FL St. Michael the Archangel.
Vigues, Gabriel '93 (MIA) Miami Beach, FL St. Francis de Sales.
Vijayan, Joseph '80 (NY) Bronx, NY Holy Spirit.
Vila, Carlos S. '83 (AGN) Associate Judges; Tamuning, GU St. Anthony and St. Victor.
Vila, Richard C. '02 (TR) Medford, NJ St. Mary of the Lakes; Holmdel, NJ St. Benedict.
Viladesau, Richard R. '69 (RVC) Elmont, NY St. Vincent de Paul; Saltaire, NY Our Lady Star of the Sea, Mission Chapel; Serving Outside the Diocese; Seaford, NY St. William the Abbot.
Vilana, Tony '96 (SAT)[Q] San Antonio, TX Historical Centre Foundation.
Vilano, Tony '96 (SAT) Archdiocesan Presbyteral Council; San Antonio, TX Cathedral of San Fernando; Vicar for Clergy; Department of Clergy and Consecrated Life.
Vilaplana, Jose *s.j.* '63 (NY)[EE] Loyola Hall, Jesuit Community.
Vilar, Juan Diaz '69 (NEW)[B] Jersey City, NJ Jesuit Center.
Vileo, Stephen L. '87 (DET) Monroe, MI St. Michael.
Vilkauskas, Edward J. *c.ss.p.* '73 (DET) Detroit, MI Holy Family; Detroit, MI St. Mary.
Villa, Carlos Patino (FR) West Harwich, MA Holy Trinity.
Villa, Eduardo '80 (BWN) Presbyteral Council; Parish Priests Consultors and Priests' Personnel Board; Garciasville, TX St. Paul the Apostle Parish; [A] Mission, TX The Saint Joseph and Saint Peter Seminary.
Villa, James *o.f.m.* '69 (NY)[EE] Mount Vernon, NY St. Bernardine of Siena Friary.
Villa, Joseph L. '97 (IND) Clinton, IN Sacred Heart; Rockville, IN St. Joseph; Universal, IN St. Joseph.
Villa, Leonard F. '86 (NY) Yonkers, NY St. Eugene.
Villa, Richard *s.m.* (FWT)[B] Fort Worth, TX Nolan Catholic High School.
Villa, Robert '02 (HRT) Waterbury, CT St. Margaret.
Villabon, German *o.s.a.* '54 (RVC) Rockville Centre, NY St. Agnes Cathedral.
Villaescusa, Gregory T. '03 (SCR) Canton, PA St. Michael; Towanda, PA SS. Peter and Paul.
Villafan, Alberto *o.f.m.* '05 (LA) Los Angeles, CA St. Francis of Assisi.
Villafan, Alberto *o.f.m.* (OAK)[M] Oakland, CA Franciscan Friars (Province of St. Barbara).
Villafan, Ignacio '99 (FRS) Tulare, CA St. Rita.
Villafranca, Eugenio *c.m.* '53 (SJN)[E] Hato Rey, PR Hospital Auxilio Mutuo; [E] San Juan, PR Centro Medico de P.R.
Villagomez, Jose *o.f.m.cap.* '74 (AGN)[F] Agana Heights, GU St. Fidelis Friary; Promoter of Justice; Knights of Columbus; Agana Heights, GU San Francisco d'Assisi.
Villagran, Gonzalo *s.j.* '08 (BO)[U] Cambridge, MA Hopkins House.
Villalobos, Alberto '85 (LA) El Monte, CA Nativity.
Villalobos, David '96 (SR) On Leave.
Villalobos, Manuel *c.m.f.* '04 (CHI) Chicago, IL Holy Cross/Immaculate Heart of Mary; [N] Oak Park Claretian Missionaries USA Eastern Province.
Villalon, Jose M. '89 (BWN) Weslaco, TX San Martin de Porres; Vicar for Priests.
Villaluz, Anastacio *c.r.m.* '01 (NEW) Lodi, NJ St. Joseph's.
Villamayor, Elmer '01 (HT) Houma, LA Cathedral of St. Francis De Sales.
Villamide, Rev. Msgr. Aniceto '67 (BGP) Bridgeport, CT St. Peter; [W] Bridgeport, CT Hispanic Social Ministries of Fairfield County, Inc.; Episcopal Vicar for Hispanics; Diocesan Consultors; Presbyteral Council; Pastors' Vocation Advisory Board; Cursillos of Fairfield County, Inc.
Villamor, Manuel '99 (FAJ) Rio Grande, PR Nuestra Senora del Carmen.
Villamor, Ronilo '83 (HT) Golden Meadow, LA Our Lady of Prompt Succor.
Villamthanam, George *c.s.t.* (NOR) Ellington, CT St. Luke.
Villani, Rev. Msgr. Rocco D. '61 (BRK) Brooklyn, NY St. Mary Mother of Jesus; Brooklyn, NY St. Brendan Retired.
Villano, Mark *c.s.p.* '88 (LA) Manhattan Beach, CA American Martyrs.
Villano, Mark (LA)[AA] Palos Verdes Peninsula, CA Marymount College (Rancho Palos Verdes).
Villano, Richard R. '58 (STP) Minneapolis, MN St. Helena.
Villanova, Richard A. '67 (NEW) Garwood, NJ Church of St. Anne.
Villanueva, Edgar '93 (MO) Army Chaplains.
Villanueva, Edgar '08 (RNO) Carson City, NV St. Teresa of Avila.
Villanueva, Efrain '04 (AUS) Taylor, TX Our Lady of Guadalupe.
Villanueva, Felix Oliveras '82 (CGS) Naranjito, PR San Miguel Arcangel; Board of Diocesan Government; Economic Administrator.
Villanueva, Gary T. '04 (WDC) Rockville, MD St. Mary.
Villanueva, Jose A. '63 (SAT) Dilley, TX St. Joseph's.
Villaran, Jose A. *o.f.m.cap.* '05 (ARE) Utuado, PR San Miquel.
Villaroya, Ernesto '93 (DAL) Retired.
Villarreal, Louis J. *o.m.i.* '65 (BO)[U] Lowell, MA Missionary Oblates of Mary Immaculate.
Villarreal, Manuel "Meme" *o.m.i.* '78 (LA) San Fernando, CA St. Ferdinand.
Villarreal, Manuel '08 (SD) Fallbrook, CA St. Peter.
Villarreal, Ricardo A. '98 (YAK) Presbyteral Council Executive Committee; Clergy Personnel Board.
Villarreal, Ricardo '98 (YAK) Chelan, WA St. Anne's; Chelan, WA St. Francis de Sales.
Villarroya, Pedro *c.m.* '59 (LA)[P] Los Angeles, CA Amat Residence II.
Villarrubia, Roger '99 (HT) Vicar for Priests; Houma, LA Our Lady of the Most Holy Rosary Retired.
Villarson, Gardy *o.m.i.* '86 (PH) Philadelphia, PA Incarnation of Our Lord; Haitian Apostolate.
Villaruel, Alvin M. '94 (SR) Santa Rosa, CA Cathedral of St. Eugene; [B] Santa Rosa, CA Cardinal Newman High School.
Villas, Manuelito '98 (LA) El Segundo, CA St. Anthony.
Villaverde, Tirso S. '96 (CHI) Chicago, IL St. Bartholomew.
Villaviza, Catalino S. '95 (NY) New York, NY St. Agnes.
Villegas, Diego '74 (BRK) Corona, NY St. Leo.
Villegas, Efraim *o.s.b.* '88 (FgM)[A] Richardton, ND Assumption Abbey; Richardton, ND Assumption Abbey.
Villegas, Francisco Munoz '94 (AUS) Austin, TX Our Lady of Guadalupe.
Villegas, Gonzalo J. '92 (TUC) All Vicars Forane; Diocesan Consultors; Tucson, AZ Our Lady Queen of All Saints Roman Catholic Parish – Tucson; Vicars Forane; Council of Priests.
Villegas, Hector '02 (STO) Newman, CA St. Joachim Church of Newman (Pastor of).
Villegas, Hernando '57 (MIA) Retired.
Villegas, Jorge C. '66 (E) Erie, PA St. Stephen; Hispanic Apostolate.
Villegas, Jorge *o.carm.* '97 (JOL)[L] Darien Carmelite Provincial Office.
Villegas, Juan C. *s.j.* '75 (FgM) New York, NY Society of Jesus.
Villegas, Robert *c.s.c.* '63 (LSC) Chamberino, NM San Luis Rey.
Villemaire, Arthur '51 (SP) Retired.
Villero, Melchor *m.j.* '76 (LA)[P] Los Angeles, CA Missionaries of Jesus, Inc.; Los Angeles, CA Precious Blood; Los Angeles, CA St. Kevin.
Villerot, Henry E. '41 (DET) Retired.
Villerot, Rev. Msgr. Thomas H. '43 (DET) Retired.
Villifan, Alberto *o.f.m.* '05 (SJ) San Jose, CA Our Lady of Guadalupe.
Villote, Augusto E. '03 (SFR) Larkspur, CA St. Patrick.
Viloria, Filadelfo Secundo Angulo '06 (AUS) Buda, TX Santa Cruz.
Vima, Benjamin A. '71 (TLS) Okmulgee, OK St. Anthony's.
Vincent, David P. '64 (CIN) Versailles, OH Holy Family; Versailles, OH St. Denis.
Vincent, Michael A. *s.j.* '82 (CLV)[D] Cleveland, OH St. Ignatius High School.
Vincent, Rev. Msgr. Robert G. '57 (NO) Retired.
Vincenzo, Dennis J. '91 (HRT) Newington, CT St. Mary.
Vinci, Rev. Msgr. Guy '59 (NY) Bronxville, NY St. Joseph.
Vinci, Terzo *s.a.c.* '58 (NY) Yonkers, NY Our Lady of Mt. Carmel.
Vincke, Gerald L. '99 (LAN) Department of Formation and Lay Ministry; Director of Seminarians; Joseph H. Albers Trust Fund for Diocesan Vocations; Emmaus House.
Vinh, Paul Bao *c.ss.r.* '81 (WDC)[N] Washington, DC Holy Redeemer College.
Vinh Ngoc Nguyen, Michael Joseph '90 (NO) New Orleans, LA The Resurrection Of Our Lord.
Vinh Van Vu, Francis Xavir M. *c.m.c.* '00 (AMA) Amarillo, TX Our Lady of Vietnam.
Vinsko, John J. *m.m.* '62 (SJ)[M] Los Altos, CA Maryknoll.
Vinslauski, Robert B. '71 (SFS) Madison, SD St. Thomas Aquinas.
Vinson, Anthony *o.s.b.* '05 (IND)[K] St. Meinrad St. Meinrad Archabbey; St. Meinrad, IN St. Boniface; St. Meinrad, IN St. Meinrad.
Viola, Jose '00 (WIL)[J] Dover, DE Oblate Apostles of the Two Hearts.
Viola, William L. '84 (BAL) Odenton, MD St. Joseph.
Virella, Jorge L. '97 (ARE) Arecibo, PR Santisimo Sacramento.
Virella, Miguel *s.v.d.* '96 (TR) Neptune, NJ Our Lady of Providence.
Virella Vazquez, Jorge L. '97 (ARE) Priest's Senate (Consejo Presbiteral); Chancellor; Adjutant Judges; Movimiento Familiar Cristiano (CFM); Diocesan Consultors; Pastoral Vocational Program.
Virgen, Javier G. '93 (SLC) Priests' Personnel Board; College of Consultors; Hispanic Affairs; Board For Formation of Priests; Vocation Office.
Virginia, Stephen G. '79 (COL) Columbus, OH St. Peter; Medical Experts.
Virnig, Laurn '63 (SCL) Royalton, MN Holy Cross; Royalton, MN Holy Trinity; Directors.
Virrey, Armando '03 (ORG) San Juan Capistrano, CA Mission Basilica – San Juan Capistrano; Council of Priests.
Virus, Keith M. '92 (GRY) Highland, IN St. James the Less.
Visbisky, Richard W. '62 (BO)[O] Brockton, MA Caritas Good Samaritan Medical Center, Inc.; Pastoral Care.
Viscardi, Christopher J. *s.j.* '76 (MOB) Sacramental Ministers.
Viscardi, Christopher J. *s.j.* '76 (MOB)[A] Mobile, AL Spring Hill College.
Visich, Eduard C. '53 (BRK) Retired.
Visnovsky, Marek '04 (PRM) Brunswick, OH St. Emilian.
Visperas, Joseph '86 (LA) La Mirada, CA St. Paul of the Cross.
Vistal, Felix '87 (MO) DEPARTMENT OF VETERANS AFFAIRS HOSPITALS AND CHAPLAINS.
Vit, William J. '05 (MO) Sioux City, IA Cathedral of the Epiphany; Liturgy Commission; St. Joseph Education Society; Air National Guard Chaplains.
Vita, Mariano L. '42 (CHI) Retired.
Vitacolonna, Xavier *c.p.* '74 (NEW)[M] "Compassion" Magazine.
Vitaglione, Robert P. '76 (BRK) Brooklyn, NY Mary of Nazareth.
Vitale, Louis *o.f.m.* '63 (OAK)[A] Berkeley, CA Franciscan School of Theology; [M] Oakland, CA Franciscan Friars (Province of Santa Barbara).
Vitali, James V. *o.s.a.* '81 (PH)[Y] Villanova, PA St. Augustine Friary.
Vitali, John *c.r.s.* '71 (MAN)[H] Allenstown, NH Pine Haven Boys Center.
Vitali, Theodore *c.p.* '69 (MET)[I] South River Passionist Provincial Office.
Vitaliano, Dominic J. '91 (PEO) On Duty Outside the Diocese; Air Force Chaplains.
Vitela, Francisco '68 (LA) El Monte, CA Our Lady of Guadalupe.
Vithanage, Denzil J. '99 (TYL) Diocesan Catholic School Advisory Council.
Vithanage, Denzil '93 (TYL) Marshall, TX St. Joseph.
Vitillo, Robert J. '72 (PAT) On Duty Outside the Diocese.
Vito, Alfred J. '84 (SCR) East Stroudsburg, PA St. John.
Vitro, Thomas J. '66 (CHI) Other Assignments.
Vitte, Jules '49 (NO) Retired.
Vittengl, Donald J. *m.m.* '56 (NY)[EE] Retired.
Vitturino, Saverio T. '67 (WDC) Benedict, MD St. Francis de Sales.
Vitus, Frank '75 (JOL) Winfield, IL St. John the Baptist.
Viuya, Melanio *m.j.* '95 (LA)[P] Los Angeles, CA Missionaries of Jesus, Inc.; Los Angeles, CA St. Kevin; Los Angeles, CA Precious Blood.
Viveiros, Joseph F. '74 (FR) Swansea, MA St. Dominic's.
Vivero, David P. '90 (ORL) Belleview, FL St. Theresa.
Viveros, Ricardo Henry '08 (LA) Hacienda Heights, CA St. John Vianney; Panorama City, CA St. Genevieve.
Viveros, Roberto *o.f.m.cap.* '09 (DAL)[J] Dallas, TX Capuchin Franciscan Friars, Vice Province of Texas; [M] Dallas, TX Dallas Cursillo Center; Dallas, TX Our Lady of Lourdes.
Viviano, Benedict T. *o.p.* '66 (CHI)[N] Chicago Dominicans (Provincial Office).
Viviano, Charles '89 (ORL) Winter Haven, FL St. Matthew; Western.
Viviano, Nino '64 (ALX) Retired.
Vivona, Anthony '53 (BRK) Retired.
Vivona, Rt. Rev. Archimandrite Francis M. '69 (LAV) Las Vegas, NV St. Elizabeth Ann Seton; Diocesan Tribunal Office–Judicial Vicar; Presbyteral Council for the Diocese of Las Vegas.
Vivona, Rt. Rev. Francis M. '69 (VNN) Judicial Vicar; Censor; Commission for the Implementation of the Particular Law.
Vivona, Rt. Rev. Francis '69 (VNN) Las Vegas, NV Our Lady of Wisdom Italo–Greek; College of Consultors.
Vizcaino, Mario B. *sch.p.* '60 (MIA)[O] Miami, FL Southeast Pastoral Institute; [O] Miami, FL Southeast Regional Office for Hispanic Ministry, Inc.; Washington, DC.
Vladyka, Vasyl (PHU) Carteret, NJ St. Mary's.
Vlasz, Melvyn J. '63 (RCK) Retired.
Vlaun, Rev. Msgr. James C. '88 (RVC)[P] Uniondale, NY TELECARE of the Diocese of Rockville Centre; Television (Telecare/TV 29); Williston Park, NY St. Aidan's Church.
Vo, Andrew Bao '07 (SC) Dow City, IA St. Boniface; Dow City, IA St. Marys.
Vo, John K. '86 (LA) El Monte, CA Nativity.

Vo, John '86 (LA) Torrance, CA St. Catherine Laboure.
Vo, Khoa Phi '07 (BLX) Gulfport, MS St. James.
Vo, Peter Son '06 (OAK) Oakland, CA St. Anthony.
Vo, Peter '88 (NEW) Rahway, NJ St. Mary's.
Vodoklys, Edward J. *s.j.* '91 (WOR)[O] Worcester, MA Jesuits of the Holy Cross, Inc.
Voelker, David A. '74 (BEL) Military Chaplains; Air Force Chaplains.
Voelker, Harold H. '54 (STL) Retired.
Voelker, James A. '69 (BEL) Waterloo, IL St. Michael.
Voelker, Karl D. *s.j.* '72 (MIL) Milwaukee, WI Gesu Parish; [P] Milwaukee, WI Jesuit Community at Marquette University.
Voelker, Lawrence '66 (IND) Indianapolis, IN Holy Cross; Indiana Women's Prison.
Voelker, Nicholas A. '02 (WCH) Hutchinson, KS St. Teresa; Lyons, KS Holy Trinity; [K] Wichita, KS Serra Club of Reno County; Kansas State Industrial Reformatory.
Voelker, Peter H. *c.ss.r.* '61 (GAL) Houston, TX Holy Ghost.
Voellmecke, Francis W. '59 (CIN) Cincinnati, OH St. Veronica; [B] Cincinnati, OH Mt. St. Mary's Seminary of the West; Judges; Imprimatur Censors.
Vogan, Howard L. '69 (DET) Livonia, MI St. Genevieve; Livonia, MI St. Maurice.
Vogan, Robert C. '70 (PH) Aston, PA St. Joseph; Building Committee.
Vogel, Arthur '57 (SCL) Retired.
Vogel, Caleb '04 (B) Moscow, ID St. Augustine's; [F] Moscow, ID St. Augustine Catholic Center; Priest Personnel Commission.
Vogel, David '06 (RCK) Rockford, IL Holy Family.
Vogel, Gerhard *s.v.d.* '65 (TR)[N] Bordentown, NJ Society of the Divine Word.
Vogel, John J. '86 (LA) Glendora, CA St. Dorothy.
Vogel, Joseph '87 (SFS) Sioux Falls, SD St. Katharine Drexel Catholic Church; Personnel Board.
Vogel, Marcel '89 (GF) Special Assignment.
Vogel, Walter J. '58 (MIL) Retired.
Vogel, William *s.j.* '75 (YAK) Social Justice and Human Life Commission.
Vogelpohl, Daniel J. '75 (COV) Fort Mitchell, KY Blessed Sacrament; Deans.
Vogelsang, Clifford R. '63 (IND) Board of Consultors; Archdiocesan Judges; Council of Priests Retired.
Vogelsang, Clifford '63 (IND) Indianapolis, IN St. Andrew the Apostle.
Vogl, John C. '00 (YAK) Special Assignment.
Vogl, Rev. Msgr. Robert R. '47 (DUB)[I] Dubuque, IA Marian Hall Infirmary Retired.
Vogler, J. Edward '65 (STL) St. Louis, MO Visitation–St. Ann's Shrine.
Vogler, J. Edward (STL) Criminal Justice Ministry.
Vogler, Jean '70 (EVN) Evansville, IN Holy Trinity; Permanent Diaconate Program.
Vogt, Dick *s.j.* '63 (STL) Saint Louis, MO Our Lady of Guadalupe.
Vogt, Emmerich W. *o.p.* '78 (OAK)[M] Oakland, CA Order of Preachers (Province of the Most Holy Name of Jesus – Western Dominican Province); [R] Oakland, CA Dominican Community Support Charitable Trust; [M] Oakland, CA Order of Preachers (Province of the Most Holy Name of Jesus – Western Dominican Province); Oakland, CA Province of the Holy Name (Western Dominican Province); Oakland, CA.
Vogt, Eric *o.s.b.* '79 (E) St. Marys, PA Sacred Heart of Jesus.
Vogt, Otto J. '50 (ROC) Retired.
Vogt, Richard J. *s.j.* '63 (STL)[O] St. Louis, MO Jesuit Community Corporation at Saint Louis University – Jesuit Hall.
Vogt, Robert W. '62 (BUF) Advocates Retired.
Voida, Paul '05 (ROM) McKeesport, PA St. Mary; Evangelization.
Voiss, James K. *s.j.* '88 (STL)[C] Saint Louis University; [O] St. Louis, MO Leo Brown Jesuit Community.
Voity, Rev. Msgr. Maurice '79 (SAN) San Angelo, TX Cathedral of the Sacred Heart; Board of Directors; Judges.
Vojtek, John C. '76 (PIT) Russellton, PA Transfiguration.
Vojtik, James P. '62 (MIL) Retired.
Vola Vola, Simione *m.s.c.* '01 (ALN) Nazareth, PA Holy Family.
Volertas, Vytautas (BRK) Maspeth, NY Transfiguration; [S] Lithuanian.
Volk, Rev. Msgr. Marvin C. '74 (BEL) Millstadt, IL St. James; Diaconate, Office of Permanent.
Volk, Michael '92 (MRY) Seaside, CA St. Francis Xavier.
Volk, Norman *o.m.i.* '68 (SFS) Sisseton, SD St. Catherine; Sisseton, SD St. Peter.
Volkert, Daniel P. '01 (MIL) Greenfield, WI St. John the Evangelist.
Volkert, James T. '90 (MIL) Waukesha, WI St. Mary.
Volkmer, Michael *c.pp.s.* '68 (DAV) Albia, IA St. Mary's.
Voll, Walter Urban *o.p.* '49 (PRO)[P] Providence St. Thomas Aquinas Priory at Providence College.
Vollkommer, Andrew J. '86 (CHR) Chapin, SC Our Lady of the Lake.
Vollmer, Daniel '02 (PHX) Prescott Valley, AZ St. Germaine Roman Catholic Parish; College of Consultors; Presbyteral Council.
Vollmer, Gary L. '77 (STL) Flint Hill, MO St. Theodore.
Vollmer, William C. '58 (COS) Retired.
Vollmer, William J. '97 (CHI) Northbrook, IL St. Norbert.
Vollmer–Konig, Josef '01 (DAL) Dallas, TX St. Patrick.
Vollor, John '79 (JKS) Mound Bayou, MS St. Gabriel; Clarksdale, MS St. Elizabeth; Clarksdale, MS Immaculate Conception.
Vollor, William J. '63 (BLX) Hattiesburg, MS Holy Rosary.
Volmi, Dennis G. '75 (WIL) Retired.
Volpert, Robert C. '61 (L) Retired.
Voltaggio, Fred '71 (CAM) Retired.
Volz, Anthony R. '85 (IND) Indianapolis, IN Christ The King.
Volz, Edward *o.s.p.p.e.* '88 (GBG) Freeport, PA St. Mary; [G] Kittanning, PA Pauline Fathers Monastery.
Volz, Gerald '92 (KCK) Regional Pastoral Leaders.
Volz, Jerry '92 (KCK) Topeka, KS St. Matthew.
Vomund, Jeffrey G. '97 (STL) St. Louis, MO St. Elizabeth, Mother of John the Baptist; Archdiocesan Council of Priests.
Vona, Michael S. '68 (TR) Farmingdale, NJ St. Catherine of Siena.
von Arx, Jeffrey P. *s.j.* '81 (BGP)[B] Fairfield, CT Fairfield University; [O] Fairfield, CT The Fairfield Jesuit Community–Fairfield University.
von Behren, Thomas R. *c.s.v.* '83 (CHI)[N] Arlington Heights, IL Viatorian Province Center–Clerics of St. Viator.
Vonderhaar, Eugene F. '59 (CIN) Retired.
Vonderhaar, Ralph E. *s.j.* '57 (STL)[O] St. Louis, MO Jesuit Community Corporation at Saint Louis University – Jesuit Hall.
Vondras, John J. '85 (NY) Newburgh, NY St. Francis of Assisi.
von Duerbeck, Julian *o.s.b.* '76 (JOL)[A] Lisle, IL Benedictine University; [L] Lisle, IL St. Procopius Abbey.
Von Essen, Pacificus *s.a.* '53 (NY)[EE] Garrison Franciscan Friars of the Atonement, Minister General Office.
Von Euw, Vincent P. '66 (BO) Senior Priests. Retired.
Von Fauer, Stephen C. '53 (BUR) Retired.
Von Handorf, Joseph '75 (LEX) Hispanic Ministry.
Von Kaenel, George E. *s.j.* '58 (CHY) Glenrock, WY St. Louis.
Von Kerssenbrock, Joachim *s.j.* '59 (NY)[II] Bronx, NY American St. Boniface Society, Incorporated; [EE] Loyola Hall, Jesuit Community.
Von Kobs, Allan G. *o.f.m.* '82 (NY) New York, NY St. Stephen of Hungary.
Von Lehmen, Jeffrey D. '85 (COV) Covington, KY St. Patrick.
von Maluski, Kris M. '01 (PRO)[B] Newport, RI Salve Regina University.
von Menshengen, Richard '00 (TUC) St. Gianna Oratory.
von Nell, Boniface *o.s.b.* '91 (WDC)[N] Washington, DC St. Anselm's Abbey.
Von Tobel, James E. *s.j.* '67 (DET)[T] Detroit, MI Jesuit Seminary Association.
Von Tobel, James *s.j.* (WIN) Windom, MN St. Francis Xavier's; Windom, MN Sacred Heart; Windom, MN Sacred Heart; Waseca, MN Sacred Heart.
Voor, Joseph H. '50 (L) Louisville, KY St. Brigid; Louisville, KY St. James; Clergy Personnel Commission Retired.
Voores Rivera, Gabriel (SJN) San Juan, PR Nuestra Senora de la Altagracia.
Voorhes, Rev. Msgr. Fred R. '71 (BUF) Awaiting Assignment; Buffalo, NY St. John the Evangelist.
Voorhies, Bennett J. '83 (SFE) Albuquerque, NM Annunciation; Presbyteral Council of the Archdiocese of Santa Fe; Vicars Forane (Deans); Presbyteral Council of the Archdiocese of Santa Fe.
Voorhies, Thomas P. '90 (LAF) Scott, LA Sts. Peter and Paul.
Voorhies, Thomas '90 (LAF) Diocesan Consultors.
Voors, David W. '81 (FTW) Consultors; Decatur, IN St. Mary of the Assumption.
Vorderlandwehr, Adrian *o.s.b.* '67 (OKL) Konawa, OK Sacred Heart.
Voris, Francis *o.f.m.cap.* '73 (SAG) Saginaw, MI St. Anthony of Padua.
Vorisek, Rudolph T. *c.s.p.* '56 (NY)[EE] Jamaica Estates Paulist Fathers Generalate; [EE] New York, NY Paulist Fathers' Motherhouse Retired.
Vorwald, Aloysius J. '64 (DUB) Retired.
Vorwek, James *s.v.d.* '69 (FgM) Techny, IL.
Vorwoldt, James F. *s.j.* '71 (CHI)[D] Chicago, IL St. Ignatius Jesuit Community.
Vorwoldt, James S. *s.j.* '70 (CHI)[D] Chicago, IL St. Ignatius College Prep.
Vos, Jude '96 (FAR) Absent on Leave.
Vos, Thomas *o.f.m.* '61 (GAY) Indian River, MI Cross in the Woods Catholic Shrine.
Vos, William '64 (SCL) Catholic Relief Services; Holy Childhood Association; Diocesan Consultors Retired.
Vosen, Gerald P. '61 (MAD) Leave of Absence.
Vosko, Richard '69 (ALB) Special Assignment.
Voss, Dennis F. '64 (BEL) Oakdale, IL St. Anthony; St. Libory, IL St. Liborius; Clergymen's Aid Society; Diocesan Council of Catholic Women; Diocesan Finance Council.
Voss, Donald J. '93 (PBR) McKeesport, PA St. Nicholas.
Voss, Marcus J. *o.s.b.* '71 (BIR)[B] Cullman, AL St. Bernard Preparatory School; [E] Cullman, AL St. Bernard Abbey.
Voss, Robert D. *s.j.* '72 (FgM) St. Louis, MO Society of Jesus.
Voss, Robert J. '70 (PHX) Retired.
Voss, Steven '07 (DEN) Newly Ordained Representative; Arvada, CO Spirit of Christ Catholic Community.
Vossler, Brian E. '91 (E) Ridgway, PA St. Leo the Great.
Votraw, Wilbur J. '55 (SY) Syracuse, NY St. Vincent de Paul; Syracuse, NY St. Vincent de Paul.
Votruba, George L. '54 (SUP) Retired.
Votto, Silvano P. *s.j.* '73 (SJ)[M] Los Gatos, CA Sacred Heart Jesuit Center.
Vowells, John J. *s.j.* '90 (KC)[J] Kansas City, MO Rockhurst Jesuit Community; Presbyteral Council; Consultors.
Vowels, G. Timothy '77 (STL) Chesterfield, MO Incarnate Word.
Voyt, Stephen A. '85 (PT) Military Chaplains; Air Force Chaplains.
Voyt, Steve '85 (HON) Military Chaplains.
Voytek, John *o.f.m.conv.* '82 (BAL)[S] Ellicott City Order of Friars Minor Conventual.
Voytek, Leonard E. '74 (ALT) Cambria Deanery; Windber, PA St. Elizabeth Ann Seton.
Voytovich, Steven '92 (HRT)[H] New Haven, CT Hospital of St. Raphael.
Vrabel, George A. '87 (CLV) Berea, OH St. Mary.
Vrana, John G. '67 (CLV) Westlake, OH St. Ladislas; College of Consultors; Presbyteral Council.
Vrana, John P. '56 (OKL) Retired.
Vrana, Joseph L. '65 (VIC) Nada, TX Nativity of the Blessed Virgin Mary.
Vrazel, Edward J. *o.m.i.* '58 (LAR) Laredo, TX Our Lady of Guadalupe.
Vrba, James J. '77 (DAV) Wilton, IA St. Mary's; Presbyteral Council.
Vreteau, Robert *o.m.i.* '46 (SAT)[K] San Antonio, TX Oblate Madonna Residence.
Vu, An N. '95 (WDC) Priest Council.
Vu, Andy Dinh *s.v.d.* '07 (FgM) Techny, IL.
Vu, Anthony Hien T. '09 (ORG) Irvine, CA St. John Neumann.
Vu, Augustine Bich '06 (ORG) Anaheim, CA St. Boniface.
Vu, Dat '04 (B) Lewiston, ID St. James; Lewiston, ID Our Lady of Lourdes; Lewiston, ID St. Stanislaus.
Vu, Diem Joseph Quang '06 (ARL) Notaries.
Vu, Duc *s.j.* '02 (SJ)[M] Los Gatos, CA Sacred Heart Jesuit Center.
Vu, Dustin L. '04 (DUB) Cedar Rapids, IA John XXIII; Fairfax, IA St. Patrick; Seminary Admissions and Advisory Board.
Vu, Ignatius '94 (NY) Jeffersonville, NY St. George–St. Francis.
Vu, J.B Han '65 (NO) Retired.
Vu, Jack '02 (LR) Jonesboro, AR Blessed John Newman University Parish; [I] Jonesboro, AR Arkansas State University, Blessed John Newman University Parish; Weiner, AR St. Anthony; Marked Tree, AR St. Norbert.
Vu, Joachim '63 (ORG) Retired.
Vu, John Francis *s.j.* '97 (ORG)[H] Yorba Linda, CA Pope John Paul II Polish Center; [I] Anaheim, CA Manresa Jesuit Residence; [M] Irvine, CA U.C.I. Interfaith Center.
Vu, John Francis *s.j.* '98 (ORG) Newman Apostolate; Council of Priests.
Vu, Joseph Dang–Hai *s.d.d.* '02 (MO) Air Force Reserve Chaplains.
Vu, Joseph Dao *s.v.d.* '88 (MEM)[F] Memphis, TN Society of the Divine Word (Chicago Province).
Vu, Joseph Dao *s.v.d.* (MEM) Vietnamese Catholic Ministry.
Vu, Joseph Duc '70 (MO) DEPARTMENT OF VETERANS AFFAIRS HOSPITALS AND CHAPLAINS.
Vu, Joseph Duc '70 (DET) Detroit, MI John D. Dingell Veterans Administration Medical Center.
Vu, Joseph Phiet Trong *c.ss.r.* '95 (P) Portland, OR Our Lady of Lavang.
Vu, Joseph Q. '06 (ARL) Falls Church, VA St. Philip.
Vu, Joseph Thanh '68 (GAL) Houston, TX Vietnamese Martyrs.
Vu, Joseph Tri Van *s.v.d.* '85 (FgM) Techny, IL.
Vu, Joseph Van '09 (LA) San Pedro, CA Holy Trinity.
Vu, Joseph '90 (BRK) College Point, NY St. Fidelis.
Vu, Khue '04 (CHI) Berwyn, IL St. Leonard; Chicago, IL Saint Ita.
Vu, Leo Dinh Huyen *c.m.c.* '94 (DEN) Wheat Ridge, CO Queen of Vietnamese Martyrs.

Vu, Lieu '91 (SJ) San Jose, CA St. Frances Cabrini.
Vu, Louis Lam '85 (LAF) Patterson, LA St. Joseph; Vietnamese Catholic Ministry.
Vu, Luke Van *o.f.m.conv.* '06 (OAK) San Pablo, CA St. Paul.
Vu, Minh '94 (STP) St. Paul, MN St. Adalbert.
Vu, Peter Duc '96 (ATL) Riverdale, GA Our Lady of Vietnam.
Vu, Peter G. '97 (GR) Belmont, MI Assumption of the Blessed Virgin Mary.
Vu, Quyen Kim *s.j.* '04 (BO)[U] Newton, MA The Jesuit Community at Boston College.
Vu, Than N. '84 (BR) Baton Rouge, LA Christ the King; [K] Baton Rouge, LA Christ the King Parish and Catholic Center; Vicar General/Moderator of the Curia; Defenders of the Bond; College of Consultors; Diocesan Corporation (The Roman Catholic Church of the Diocese of Baton Rouge); Campus Ministry; Presbyteral Council.
Vu, Thomas Hein '01 (LAF) Franklin, LA St. Jules.
Vu, Toan Quoc *s.v.d.* '06 (FgM) Techny, IL.
Vu, Tung Duc *c.ss.r.* '07 (LA)[P] Baldwin Park Vietnamese Redemptorist Mission.
Vu Dinh Huyen, Leo M. *c.m.c.* '94 (SPC)[F] Carthage, MO Congregation of the Mother Coredemptrix, United States Assumption Province.
Vuelvas–Arias, David '75 (ORG) Santa Ana, CA Our Lady of Guadalupe; Cursillo Movement.
Vujs, Joseph E. '57 (HRT) Retired.
Vujs, Robert W. *m.m.* '61 (NY)[EE] Maryknoll Maryknoll Fathers and Brothers Retired.
Vuky, Michael '05 (P) Special Assignment.
Vular, Robert J. '01 (PIT) Pittsburgh, PA St. Teresa of Avila; [P] Pittsburgh, PA Community College of Allegheny County – North Hills Campus.
Vung Le, Paul *s.v.d.* '85 (LA) Norwalk, CA St. Linus.
Vuong, John M. Ngo Duc *c.m.c.* '91 (SPC)[F] Carthage, MO Congregation of the Mother Coredemptrix, United States Assumption Province.
Vuong, Joseph–Quoc T. '07 (STP) Wayzata, MN Holy Name of Jesus.
Vuong, Rt. Rev. M. John Lam Dinh *o.cist.* '57 (SB)[I] Lucerne Valley, CA The Cistercian Congregation of the Holy Family, St. Joseph Monastery Retired.
Vuoso, Pasquale *c.r.i.c.* '87 (LA) Santa Paula, CA St. Sebastian; [P] Santa Paula, CA Canons Regular of the Immaculate Conception.
Vu Quang Huy, John E. M. *c.m.c.* '85 (SPC)[F] Carthage, MO Congregation of the Mother Coredemptrix, United States Assumption Province.
Vuturo, Paul V. '73 (MIA) Miramar, FL St. Bartholomew; Sacred Art & Architecture.
Vuturo, Paul '73 (MIA) Members.
Vwankor, Roben C. '93 (GAL) Houston, TX St. Mary of the Purification.
Vyverman, Mark J. '93 (KAL) Three Rivers, MI Immaculate Conception; Diocesan Consultors; Presbyteral Council Members; Presbyteral Council Members.

W

Wach, Anthony J. *s.j.* '72 (MIL)[P] Milwaukee Jesuit Provincial Office, Wisconsin Province; Milwaukee, WI Society of Jesus.
Wachdorf, Paul H. '75 (CHI) Chicago, IL St. Gregory, the Great.
Wachowiak, Duane A. '98 (GAY) Boyne City, MI St. Matthew; Boyne City, MI St. Augustine; Worship and Liturgical Formation, Secretariat for; Boyne City, MI St. John Nepomucene.
Wachter, Robert B. '76 (WCH) Iola, KS St. Joseph; Iola, KS St. John.
Wack, Neil F. *c.s.c.* '04 (FTW) South Bend, IN Christ the King; [H] Notre Dame Congregation of Holy Cross, Indiana Province, Provincial House; [C] South Bend, IN Saint Joseph's High School; [H] Notre Dame, IN Congregation of Holy Cross, Indiana Province, Provincial House.
Wack, Neil *c.s.c.* '04 (FTW) Presbyteral Council.
Wack, William A. *c.s.c.* '94 (AUS) Austin, TX St. Ignatius Martyr.
Wack, William *c.s.c.* (FTW)[H] Notre Dame Congregation of Holy Cross, Indiana Province, Provincial House.
Wackerman, John F. '98 (PH) Newtown, PA St. Andrew.
Waclawik, Leszek J. '84 (LAR) Laredo, TX St. Joseph; Presbyteral Council.
Wadas, Rev. Msgr. Ignatius C. '53 (ALT) Retired.
Wadas, Joseph S. '91 (MOB) On Leave from the Archdiocese.
Wadas, Raymond J. '72 (WDC) Takoma Park, MD Our Lady of Sorrows; Priest Council.
Waddell, Paul M. '84 (NY) Katonah, NY St. Mary of the Assumption.
Waddill, Dale T. '64 (P) Retired.
Wade, Ed *c.c.* '72 (GAL) Houston, TX Queen of Peace; [S] Houston, TX Catholic Charismatic Center.
Wade, Edward C. '72 (CAM) Retired.
Wade, Gerald T. *s.j.* '68 (SJ)[D] San Jose, CA Bellarmine College Preparatory.
Wade, Hubert '77 (SAN) Ballinger, TX St. Mary Star of the Sea; Board of Directors; Diocesan Consultors; Presbyteral Council; Director of Seminarians.
Wade, Jarrell D. *s.j.* '65 (FgM) St. Louis, MO Society of Jesus.
Wade, John J. '56 (TLS) Diocesan Consultors Retired.
Wadelton, Christopher '09 (IND) Indianapolis, IN Holy Spirit.
Wadeson, John '69 (SFR) San Francisco, CA St. Charles Borromeo.
Wadowski, Stanislaw '97 (RVC) Lindenhurst, NY Our Lady of Perpetual Help; Farmingdale, NY St. Kilian.
Wafzig, James E. '55 (L) Retired.
Wagener, John M. '61 (NU) Military Chaplains Retired.
Wagenhoffer, Josef A. '65 (CAM) Somers Point, NJ St. Joseph's Church, Somers Point, N.J.; Atlantic North Deanery.
Wager, Terrence J. *o.s.b.* '64 (SEA) Yelm, WA St. Columban; [L] Lacey, WA St. Martin's Abbey; Presbyteral Council.
Waggoner, David (P)[J] Eugene, OR Sacred Heart Medical Center.
Wagner, Alan *s.d.s.* '76 (SR)[F] Napa, CA Queen of the Valley Medical Center.
Wagner, Donald '87 (SCL) Bluffton, MN St. John the Baptist; Wadena, MN St. Ann's; Deans; Personnel Committee.
Wagner, Edward *o.ss.t.* '80 (BAL)[S] Individuals in Other Locations:.
Wagner, Edward *o.ss.t.* (LAV)[A] Las Vegas, NV Bishop Gorman High School.
Wagner, Rev. Msgr. Harold '55 (BUF) Retired.
Wagner, Jay '87 (RIC) Petersburg, VA Church of the Sacred Heart.
Wagner, Rev. Msgr. John A. '49 (SAT) Retired.
Wagner, John F. '64 (SB) Temecula, CA St. Catherine of Alexandria; Elected Members.
Wagner, John J. '87 (RIC) Petersburg, VA St. John.
Wagner, John P. '62 (SY) Retired.
Wagner, Rev. Msgr. John '49 (SAT)[K] San Antonio, TX Casa De Padres; Vicar for Retired Priests; Archdiocesan Presbyteral Council; Vicar for Retired Priests Retired.
Wagner, Rev. Msgr. Joseph '65 (SFS) Brandon, SD Risen Savior.
Wagner, Joseph *s.j.* '98 (CIN)[N] Cincinnati, OH Jesuit Community at Xavier University.
Wagner, Joshua J. '04 (COL) Columbus, OH Community of Holy Rosary and St. John; Columbus, OH Christ the King.
Wagner, Leon R. '49 (CHI) Retired.
Wagner, Mark '88 (STO) Turlock, CA Sacred Heart Church of Turlock (Pastor of); College of Consultors/Presbyteral Council.
Wagner, Philip C. '98 (CHY) Newcastle, WY Corpus Christi.
Wagner, Richard F. *s.s.j.* '59 (LAF) Rayne, LA Our Mother of Mercy.
Wagner, Robert J. '57 (LC)[H] La Crosse, WI Holy Cross (Seminary) Diocesan Center Retired.
Wagner, Robert J. '09 (ARL) On Duty Outside the Diocese.
Wagner, Robert *s.d.s.* '46 (BIR) Huntsville, AL St. Joseph's Retired.
Wagner, Robert *s.d.s.* '46 (MIL)[P] Milwaukee, WI Salvatorians – Jordan Hall Retired.
Wagner, Ronald F. '79 (SAG) Saginaw, MI Holy Family; Saginaw, MI St. Andrew; Vicar for Priests; Ministry to Priests.
Wagner, Thomas A. '83 (PIT) Natrona Heights, PA Our Lady of the Most Blessed Sacrament; Natrona Heights, PA St. Joseph.
Wagner, Rev. Msgr. Van A. '61 (TUC) Tucson, AZ Saints Peter and Paul Roman Catholic Parish – Tucson; Holy Childhood Association Retired.
Wagner, Vernon *o.f.m.cap.* '53 (MIL)[P] Mount Calvary, WI St. Lawrence Friary Retired.
Wagner, Walter C. *o.p.* '93 (CIN) Cincinnati, OH St. Gertrude; [C] Cincinnati, OH Dominican Novitiate; [N] Cincinnati, OH St. Gertrude Priory.
Wagner, William C. '73 (CIN) Cincinnati, OH St. Thomas More; Vicarri Foranei (Deans); Consultors; Priest Councilors.
Wagner, William F. '63 (L) Retired.
Waguespack, Clarence J. '62 (BR) Pierre Part, LA St. Joseph the Worker.
Wah, Joseph C. '05 (LA) Temple City, CA St. Luke the Evangelist.
Wahal, Stephen J. '00 (PBR) Monessen, PA Assumption of the Blessed Virgin; Donora, PA St. Michael.
Wahl, Joseph A. *c.o.* '56 (CHR)[E] Rock Hill, SC Oratory of St. Philip Neri, Congregation of the Oratory of Pontifical Rite; Rock Hill, SC; Rock Hill, SC St. Anne.
Wahl, Rev. Msgr. Raymond J. '52 (RCK) Pro Synodal Judges; Diocesan Consultors Retired.
Wahl, Richard A. *c.s.b.* '73 (GAL)[E] Houston, TX St. Thomas High School; Adjutant Judicial Vicar.
Wahl, Thomas *o.s.b.* '58 (SCL)[I] Collegeville St. John's Abbey, of the Order of St. Benedict; Collegeville, MN St. John's Abbey.
Wai, Thomas Than '92 (WCH) Haysville, KS St. Cecilia.
Waibel, Philip *o.s.b.* '83 (P) Mt. Angel, OR St. Mary; [L] St. Benedict, OR Mt. Angel Abbey.
Waick, Edward F. *m.m.* '56 (NY)[EE] Maryknoll Maryknoll Fathers and Brothers Retired.
Waickman, Thomas L. '84 (JC) Richmond Heights, MO Retired.
Wainwright, Patrick '97 (DET)[K] Plymouth, MI Miles Christi.
Wainwright, Walter L. '65 (ROC)[M] Elmira, NY Elmira College Retired.
Waiss, John R. '87 (NY)[JJ] Overlook Study Center; New Rochelle.
Wait, Dennis '72 (KCK) Special Assignment.
Waite, James A. '04 (BUF) Lockport, NY St. John the Baptist.
Waite, Patrick J. '54 (SC) Retired.
Waitekus, Christopher J. '91 (SPR) West Stockbridge, MA St. Patrick's; Lenox, MA St. Ann's; Lenox Dale, MA St. Vincent de Paul's.
Waites, Michael J. '83 (TR) Riverton, NJ Sacred Heart.
Waithaka, Paul Maina '02 (CHI) Posen, IL St. Stanislaus Bishop and Martyr.
Waithaka, Paul Maina '02 (CHI) Glenview, IL St. Catherine Laboure.
Waiwood, Richard '89 (ELP) Kermit, TX St. Thomas & St. Joseph; Monahans, TX St. John the Apostle and Evangelist Retired.
Wajda, Mark R. '08 (ORL) Longwood, FL Annunciation.
Wake, John F. '74 (TR) Maple Shade, NJ Our Lady of Perpetual Help.
Wakefield, Alan J. '75 (LAN) Mason, MI St. James.
Wakefield, Christopher L. '96 (ALN) Pottsville, PA St. Patrick; [C] Pottsville, PA Nativity B.V.M. High School.
Wakefield, Michael '81 (LA) Sherman Oaks, CA St. Francis de Sales.
Wakim, Rodolph '96 (SAM) Carnegie, PA Our Lady of Victory.
Wal, Edward '79 (SP) Spring Hill, FL St. Frances Xavier Cabrini; Spring Hill, FL St. Theresa.
Walczak, Melvin '68 (ROC) Absent on Leave.
Walczyk, Rafal *o.s.p.p.e.* '05 (CHI) Harwood Heights–Norridge, IL St. Rosalie.
Walczyk, Rafal *o.s.p.p.e.* '05 (PH)[Y].
Wald, Rev. Msgr. Jeffrey '92 (FAR) Fargo, ND Holy Spirit Church of Fargo; Vice Chancellor.
Wald, Kenneth J. '57 (BIS) Retired.
Waldbilling, Brian T. '01 (LC) Leave of Absence.
Walden, Rev. Msgr. Ellsworth R. '71 (RVC) Smithtown, NY St. Patrick.
Walder, Keith A. '03 (PEO) East Moline, IL St. Anne; Silvis, IL Our Lady of Guadalupe; East Moline, IL St. Mary's.
Waldie, Paul *o.m.i.* '65 (WDC)[N] Washington, DC Oblate Community.
Walding, Eugene F. '66 (SC) Retired.
Waldman, Noah A. '08 (STL) St. Charles, MO Sts. Joachim and Ann.
Waldow, Rev. Msgr. Harold L. '70 (AMA) Ex Officio; Rite of Christian Initiation of Adults Commission; A.C.T.S. Movement; Continuing Education of Clergy; Moderator of the Curia; Vicar of Clergy; Ex Officio; College of Consultors; Diocesan Pastoral Council; [I] Amarillo, TX Monsignor B.A. Erpen Trust Fund; Amarillo, TX St. Mary's.
Waldrep, Jeffrey '90 (JKS) Jackson, MS St. Peter Cathedral; [H] Jackson, MS University of Mississippi Medical Center – Newman Center; Vice Chancellor; Propagation of the Faith; Judicial Vicar; Engaged Encounter; Diocesan Judges; Priests' Council; [H] Jackson, MS Belhaven College Newman Center; [H] Jackson, MS Millsaps College Newman Center.
Waldrep, John W. *m.m.* '90 (FgM) Maryknoll, NY MARYKNOLL.
Waldron, Rev. Msgr. John E. '66 (BRK)[B] Douglaston, NY Cathedral Seminary Residence of the Immaculate Conception Retired.
Waldron, John R. '56 (NEW) Retired.
Waldron, John '66 (P) Canby, OR St. Patrick.
Waldron, Richard P. '61 (HBG) Mechanicsburg, PA St. Elizabeth Ann Seton.
Waldron, Robert J. '68 (BO) Senior Priests. Retired.
Waldron, Walter J. '64 (BO) Roxbury, MA St. Patrick; Trustees.
Waldron, William '50 (PHX) Retired.
Waldrop, Gregory S. *s.j.* '99 (NY)[EE] Cardinal Spellman Hall, Jesuit Community.
Waldschmidt, Valens J. *o.f.m.* '47 (CIN)[U] Cincinnati, OH St. Dymphna Ministry; [N] Cincinnati St. Francis Seraph Friary Retired.
Walega, Stanley J. '64 (MET) Retired.
Walk, Donald J. '67 (VEN) Retired.
Walk, Edward J. '78 (E)[C] Du Bois, PA DuBois Area Catholic School.
Walka, Marcin '09 (PAT) Parsippany, NJ St. Christopher.
Walker, Anselm '56 (GAL) Retired.
Walker, Brian *o.p.* '86 (STP) Minneapolis, MN St. Albert the Great.
Walker, Charles D. '81 (L) Elizabethtown, KY St. Ambrose; Elizabethtown, KY St. James; White Mills, KY St. Ignatius; Deans.

Walker, Rev. Msgr. David M. '64 (HRT) Branford, CT St. Therese; Special and other Archdiocesan Assignment; North Haven, CT Catholic Cemeteries Association of the Archdiocese of Hartford, Inc.; New Haven Vicariate; East Shore Deanery; Catholic Cemeteries Association.
Walker, Donald L. '58 (DET) Redford, MI St. Hilary; Dearborn Heights, MI Our Lady of Grace Retired.
Walker, Douglas '99 (FRS) Lone Pine, CA Santa Rosa.
Walker, Earl Gordon '48 (LA) Los Angeles, CA Cathedral Chapel Retired.
Walker, Edmund *o.f.m.cap.* '63 (NEW) Hoboken, NJ St. Ann's.
Walker, Francisco J. '87 (BRK) Brooklyn, NY St. Agatha's.
Walker, Gerald Bernard '55 (LA) Retired.
Walker, Gerard T. '80 (BRK) Jamaica, NY Our Lady of the Skies Chapel.
Walker, Gilbert R. *c.m.* '87 (FgM) Earth City, MO Western Province.
Walker, Henry *o.m.i.* '85 (SAT)[F] San Antonio, TX St. Anthony Catholic High School; [L] San Antonio, TX De Mazenod House.
Walker, J. Kenneth '81 (EVN) Special Assignment; Judicial Vicar; Diocesan Consultors; Diocesan Council of Priests; Censors of Books.
Walker, J. Patrick '88 (STO) Manteca, CA St. Anthony Church of Manteca (Pastor of); Deans.
Walker, James E. '99 (GLP) Gallup, NM St. John Vianney; Vicar General; Presbyteral Council; Diocesan Consultors.
Walker, James P. '77 (Y) Warren, OH SS. Cyril and Methodius; Warren, OH Christ Our King.
Walker, John Paul *o.p.* '02 (WDC)[B] Washington, DC Dominican House of Studies.
Walker, Kent A. '89 (ORL) St. Cloud, FL St. Thomas Aquinas.
Walker, Michael '62 (KC) Retired.
Walker, Mike '99 (P) Central Point, OR Shepherd of the Valley.
Walker, Paul '72 (STU) McConnelsville, OH St. James.
Walker, Robert L. *o.p.* '56 (WDC) Washington, DC St. Dominic Church & Priory.
Walker, Ronald *o.m.i.* '61 (FgM) Washington, DC AMERICAN OBLATE MISSIONS.
Walker, Thomas J. '90 (STP) Executive Director; Woodbury, MN Saint Ambrose of Woodbury; College of Consultors.
Walker, Thomas J. '89 (MIL) Special Assignment; Services for Senior Priests Coordinator.
Walkowiak, David J. '79 (CLV) Chagrin Falls, OH St. Joan of Arc; Judges in Second Instance.
Wall, Antoninus *o.p.* '50 (OAK)[M] Oakland, CA Order of Preachers (Province of the Most Holy Name of Jesus – Western Dominican Province).
Wall, Augustine *s.v.d.* '91 (BLX)[D] Bay St. Louis, MS St. Augustine's Residence; [D] Bay St. Louis, MS St. Augustine's Retreat Center.
Wall, Barry W. '62 (FR) Diocesan Archives; Legion of Mary Retired.
Wall, Rev. Msgr. G. Warren '76 (MOB) Grand Bay, AL St. John Baptist.
Wall, Rev. Msgr. James E. '63 (BUF) Co–Directors; Priests, Vicar for; Consultors, College of; Council of Priests.
Wall, Rev. Msgr. John A. '60 (R)[I] Chapel Hill, NC Newman Catholic Student Center; Chapel Hill, NC Newman Catholic Student Center, University of North Carolina Retired.
Wall, John E. '57 (CIN) Consultors; Cincinnati, OH St. Ignatius of Loyola; Ex Officio Members Retired.
Wall, John J. '68 (CHI) Chicago, IL Old St. Patrick; Chicago, IL Catholic Church Extension Society of the United States of America, The; [T] Chicago, IL Catholic Church Extension Society.
Wall, Sherman B. *o.m.i.* '57 (SPC) Willow Springs, MO Sacred Heart.
Wall, Terence Damian *c.ss.r.* '65 (SJN)[I] San Juan, PR Casa San Clemente.
Wall, Terence Damian *c.ss.r.* '65 (CGS)[B] Aguas Buenas, PR Casa Cristo Redentor.
Wallace, Basil J. *o.s.b.* '78 (PAT)[N] Morristown, NJ St. Mary's Abbey.
Wallace, Cavana '92 (SD) Oceanside, CA St. Margaret.
Wallace, Donald L. '62 (JC) Retired.
Wallace, Rev. Msgr. Francis T. '63 (LA) Promoter of Justice; Burbank, CA St. Robert Bellarmine.
Wallace, Francis X. '47 (FR) Retired.
Wallace, Harry C. '56 (SY) On Duty Outside the Diocese.
Wallace, James *c.ss.r.* '70 (WDC)[N] Washington, DC Holy Redeemer College.
Wallace, John *f.m.s.i.* '60 (BO)[B] Framingham, MA Sylva Maria.
Wallace, Joseph D. '85 (CAM) Ecumenical and Inter–Religious Affairs; Members.
Wallace, Kenneth F. '00 (CLV)[I] Garfield Heights, OH Marymount Hospital, Inc.; Pastoral Care Services; [M] Garfield Heights, OH Village at Marymount.
Wallace, Rev. Msgr. Murrough C. '60 (SAC) South Lake Tahoe, CA St. Theresa; Please direct all inquiries to Retired.
Wallace, Philip '65 (SEA) Retired.
Wallace, Regis P. *o.s.b.* '60 (PAT)[N] Morristown, NJ St. Mary's Abbey; Pro–Synodal Judges.
Wallace, Richard '86 (MO) Navy Reserve Chaplains.
Wallace, Rev. Msgr. Thomas M. '80 (SB) College of Consultors; Elected Members; Hemet, CA Holy Spirit; Moreno Valley, CA St. Patrick; Yucca Valley, CA St. Mary of the Valley; Special or Other Diocesan Assignment; Ex Officio Member; Riverside Pastoral Region; Indio, CA Our Lady of Perpetual Help; Diocesan Curia.
Wallace, William J. *o.s.a.* '74 (NY) Bronx, NY St. Nicholas of Tolentine.
Wallack, Michael '04 (TR) Marlton, NJ St. Joan of Arc.
Walleman, Kenneth T. *s.j.* '59 (MIL)[P] Wauwatosa, WI Jesuit Community at St. Camillus.
Wallen, Charles L. *c.s.c.* '54 (FR)[G] North Dartmouth, MA Holy Cross Residence Retired.
Wallenfelsz, Scott *s.d.s.* '69 (SUP)[H] Ladysmith, WI Servants of Mary Continuing Care Trust.
Wallenfelsz, Scott *s.d.s.* '69 (MIL)[P] Milwaukee Salvatorian Provincial Offices; [Y] Milwaukee, WI Salvatorian Institute of Philosophy and Theology, Inc.; [Y] Milwaukee, WI Lay Salvatorians, Inc.; Milwaukee, WI.
Waller, Charles J. '73 (PAT) Graduate Studies; Paterson, NJ St. Gerard Majella.
Waller, Robert C. '75 (CIN) Milford, OH St. Andrew.
Wallin, John T. '06 (STP) Dayton, MN St. John the Baptist.
Wallin, Rev. Msgr. Kevin W. '84 (BGP) Bridgeport, CT St. Augustine Cathedral; [R] Bridgeport, CT Inner–City Foundation For Charity & Education; Presbyteral Council; Inner–City Foundation for Charity and Education.
Walling, Gerald C. *s.j.* '61 (DET)[K] Clarkston, MI Colombiere Center.
Walling, Lawrence M. *o.s.m.* '79 (CHI)[N] Chicago Order of Friar Servants of Mary (Servites) United States of America Province, Inc.
Walling, Richard W. '78 (CIN) Coldwater, OH Holy Trinity; Coldwater, OH St. Mary; Coldwater, OH St. Anthony; Imprimatur Censors.
Wallis, Jonathan '07 (FWT) Arlington, TX St. Matthew.
Wallis, William H. '82 (SPR) Westfield, MA St. Peter and St. Casimir.
Wallner, Gerhard '89 (FBK) Leave of Absence.
Walls, John *s.m.* '72 (ATL)[D] Atlanta, GA Marist School.
Walmesley, John '74 (SEA) Seattle, WA Our Lady of Guadalupe.
Walpole, Donald *o.s.b.* '43 (IND)[K] St. Meinrad, IN St. Meinrad Archabbey.
Walsh, Aidan J. '70 (BO) Defenders of the Bond; Milton, MA St. Elizabeth.
Walsh, Andrew J. '66 (NY) Bronx, NY St. Margaret of Cortona.
Walsh, Arthur '85 (CC) Retired.
Walsh, Brendan J. '93 (LAN) Dexter, MI St. Joseph; Regional Vicars; College of Consultors.
Walsh, Brendan *s.c.a.* '98 (DET)[K] Wyandotte, MI Pallottine Peer Ministry; [S] Dearborn, MI Archdiocesan Catholic Campus Ministry Association, Gabriel Richard Campus Ministry; [S] Dearborn, MI Univ. of Michigan, Dearborn, Henry Ford Community College Newman Center.
Walsh, Rev. Msgr. Christopher J. '87 (BGP) Shelton, CT St. Joseph; Diocesan Censors.
Walsh, Christopher M. '99 (PH) Philadelphia, PA St. Raymond of Penafort; Philadelphia, PA St. Therese of the Child Jesus.
Walsh, Clyde J. '51 (PRO)[M] Pawtucket, RI Jeanne Jugan Residence Retired.
Walsh, Daniel L. *c.s.sp.* '91 (GAL)[O] Houston, TX Congregation of the Holy Spirit, Province of the United States; [R] Houston, TX Satellite Office; [R] Houston, TX Catholic Newman Association at the University of Houston Central Campus.
Walsh, Daniel P. '68 (BUF) Gowanda, NY St. Joseph; Cattaraugus, NY St. Mary.
Walsh, Daniel *c.s.sp.* (GAL)[R] Houston, TX Texas Southern University Catholic Newman Hall.
Walsh, Denis '66 (TYL)[B] Palestine, TX Hermitage.
Walsh, Dennis G. '92 (TOL) Toledo, OH St. Patrick of Heatherdowns; College of Consultors.
Walsh, Dennis *s.o.l.t.* '04 (CC) Robstown, TX St. Anthony; [G] Robstown, TX Society of Our Lady of the Most Holy Trinity.
Walsh, E. Corbett *s.j.* '71 (BO)[U] Weston, MA Campion Jesuit Community.
Walsh, Flannan J. '65 (STA) Retired.
Walsh, Flavian A. *o.f.m.* '56 (BO)[Z] Boston, MA St. Anthony Shrine.
Walsh, Rev. Msgr. Francis E. '66 (SPR) Retired.
Walsh, Francis M. *c.s.c.* '56 (FR)[A] North Easton, MA Stonehill College; [A] North Easton, MA Holy Cross Fathers Religious.
Walsh, Francis M. '67 (WDC) On Duty Outside the Archdiocese; Washington, DC Holy Name.
Walsh, Francis P. '57 (CLV) Lakewood, OH St. Luke.
Walsh, Gerald G. '95 (CHI)[A] Chicago, IL St. Joseph College Seminary.
Walsh, Rev. Msgr. Gerald J. '55 (BIS) Retired.
Walsh, Harry A. '60 (STP) Special Assignment.
Walsh, J. Patrick *s.j.* '63 (STL)[O] St. Louis, MO Jesuit Community Corporation at Saint Louis University – Jesuit Hall.
Walsh, J. Thomas '89 (HRT) New Britain, CT St. Ann; New Britain, CT St. Mary's.
Walsh, James B. '65 (SAC) Portola, CA Holy Family Retired.
Walsh, James F. *s.j.* '72 (BO)[U] Boston The Society of Jesus of New England–Provincial Offices; [U] Boston, MA Loyola House.
Walsh, James J. '93 (ALB) Loudonville, NY St. Pius X; Priests Placement Committee.
Walsh, James J. '73 (SCR) Defenders of the Bond; Scranton, PA St. Patrick's.
Walsh, James J. '68 (CIN) Vicarri Foranei (Deans); Ex Officio Members; Consultors.
Walsh, James P. '73 (MAN) Greenville, NH Sacred Heart of Jesus; Greenville, NH Sacred Heart.
Walsh, James P. *s.j.* '66 (STL)[O] St. Louis, MO Jesuit Community Corporation at Saint Louis University – Jesuit Hall.
Walsh, James P.M. *s.j.* '70 (WDC)[N] Washington, DC The Jesuit Community at Georgetown University.
Walsh, James '93 (ALB) Formation for Priesthood/ Vocation Awareness; Vocations and Vocation Awareness Program; Board of Advisors.
Walsh, Rev. Msgr. James '69 (SJ) San Jose, CA St. Christopher.
Walsh, Jay Francis *c.s.b.* '65 (GAL) Houston, TX St. Anne.
Walsh, Jeffrey J. '94 (SCR) Throop, PA Blessed Sacrament, Throop; Throop, PA St. Bridget's; Scranton, PA St. Paul's.
Walsh, Jerome M. *o.p.* '58 (CHI)[N] Chicago Dominicans (Provincial Office).
Walsh, Jerome Matthias *o.p.* (MAD) Madison, WI.
Walsh, Jerome '69 (DET) On Duty Outside the Archdiocese.
Walsh, Jim J. '68 (CIN) Cincinnati, OH St. Dominic.
Walsh, John A. '80 (E) Conneautville, PA St. Peter; Linesville, PA St. Philip.
Walsh, John A. '61 (SCR) On Duty Outside the Diocese.
Walsh, John D. *m.m.* '56 (FgM) Maryknoll, NY MARYKNOLL.
Walsh, John E. '55 (SAL) Retired.
Walsh, John J. *m.m.* '61 (NY)[EE] Maryknoll Maryknoll Fathers and Brothers.
Walsh, John J. '57 (DUB) Retired.
Walsh, John J. *s.j.* '71 (BO) Gloucester, MA Holy Family; [U] Weston, MA Campion Jesuit Community.
Walsh, John J. *s.j.* (NOR)[L] Storrs, CT University of Connecticut.
Walsh, John M. '47 (PH) Retired.
Walsh, John P. '77 (ATL) Marietta, GA St. Joseph.
Walsh, John T. '44 (ROC) Rochester, NY Our Lady Queen of Peace Retired.
Walsh, John '76 (PIT) Pittsburgh, PA Epiphany; Arden Courts North Hills.
Walsh, John '77 (ATL) College of Consultors; Deans.
Walsh, John '61 (ORL) Orlando, FL Holy Cross.
Walsh, Joseph M. '86 (LIN) Hastings, NE St. Cecilia's.
Walsh, Joseph R. '64 (SFR) San Francisco, CA St. Stephen.
Walsh, Kenneth *c.p.* '50 (SCR)[M] Scranton, PA Saint Ann's Passionist Monastery.
Walsh, Kevin B. '92 (ARL) Falls Church, VA St. Philip.
Walsh, Kevin V. *o.c.s.o* '78 (CHR)[E] Moncks Corner, SC Mepkin Abbey.
Walsh, Laurence '45 (NO) Retired.
Walsh, Rev. Msgr. Lawrence '54 (SAT) San Antonio, TX Our Lady of Grace.
Walsh, Leo '94 (ANC) On Duty Outside Archdiocese.
Walsh, Martin de Porres *o.p.* '69 (FgM) Oakland, CA Province of the Holy Name (Western Dominican Province); San Francisco, CA St. Dominic.
Walsh, Martin *o.p.* '69 (OAK)[M] Oakland, CA Order of Preachers (Province of the Most Holy Name of Jesus – Western Dominican Province).
Walsh, Martin *o.p.* '69 (SFR)[S] San Francisco, CA Shrine of St. Jude Thaddeus; [N] San Francisco, CA St. Dominic Priory.
Walsh, Matthew S. *s.j.* '09 (MIL)[P] Milwaukee, WI Arrupe House Jesuit Community; Milwaukee, WI Gesu Parish.
Walsh, Michael F. *c.m.* '72 (STO) Patterson, CA Sacred Heart Church of Patterson (Pastor of).
Walsh, Michael J. '56 (CHI) Retired.
Walsh, Rev. Msgr. Michael J. '73 (TR) Middletown, NJ St. Mary; Diocesan Consultors.
Walsh, Michael P. *m.m.* '88 (NY)[EE] Maryknoll Maryknoll Fathers and Brothers.
Walsh, Michael '53 (DEN) Retired.
Walsh, Rev. Msgr. Michael '38 (LA) Retired.
Walsh, Michael '58 (LA)[F] La Canada Flintridge, CA St. Francis High School of La Canada–Flintridge.
Walsh, Michael (BRK) South Ozone Park, NY Our Lady

of Perpetual Help.
Walsh, Miles D. '80 (BR) Baton Rouge, LA Our Lady of Mercy; Presbyteral Council.
Walsh, Milton T. '78 (SFR) Absent on Leave.
Walsh, P. Brian (LEX)[L] Richmond, KY St. Stephen Newman Center–St. Mark Church.
Walsh, Patrick E. *s.j.* '60 (MIL) Milwaukee, WI Gesu Parish.
Walsh, Patrick F. '72 (P) Estacada, OR St. Aloysius; Sandy, OR St. Michael the Archangel.
Walsh, Patrick '69 (SC) Board of Education; [B] Sioux City, IA Bishop Heelan Catholic Schools.
Walsh, Patrick *c.s.c.* '81 (BUR) North Bennington, VT St. John the Baptist.
Walsh, Peter J. *c.s.c.* (HRT)[Q] New Haven, CT Yale University–St. Thomas More Catholic Center and Chapel.
Walsh, Peter '59 (JC) Retired.
Walsh, Richard (Denis) L. '66 (TYL) Retired.
Walsh, Richard A. '62 (PRO)[M] Newport, RI St. Clare Home Retired.
Walsh, Richard '68 (ORL) Winter Park, FL St. Margaret Mary; Priest Personnel; Central North.
Walsh, Robert E. '06 (WDC) Vocations for Men; Pastoral Center Special Ministries.
Walsh, Robert T. *s.j.* '80 (SFR)[E] San Francisco, CA St. Ignatius College Preparatory (Coed); [N] San Francisco, CA Jesuit Community at St. Ignatius College Preparatory.
Walsh, Robert (WDC) Secretariat for Ministerial Leadership and Vicar for Clergy.
Walsh, Ronald J. '54 (NY) Retired.
Walsh, Seamus '66 (DUL) Grand Marais, MN St. John; Grand Marais, MN Holy Rosary.
Walsh, Sebastian *o.praem.* '05 (ORG)[D] Silverado, CA St. Michael's Preparatory School.
Walsh, Terrance G. *s.j.* '82 (BO)[U] Boston The Society of Jesus of New England–Provincial Offices.
Walsh, Terrence P. '04 (BGP) Stamford, CT The Basilica of Saint John the Evangelist.
Walsh, Theodore *c.p.* '59 (BRK)[T] Jamaica, NY Immaculate Conception Monastery.
Walsh, Thomas A. '42 (PHX) Scottsdale, AZ Blessed Sacrament Roman Catholic Parish Retired.
Walsh, Thomas E. *o.f.m.conv.* '80 (BAL) Baltimore, MD Annunciation; Baltimore, MD St. Clement Mary Hofbauer.
Walsh, Thomas F. *s.j.* '55 (PAT)[J] Morristown, NJ Loyola House of Retreats.
Walsh, Thomas J. '67 (BO) Marshfield, MA St. Christine.
Walsh, Thomas J. '94 (MET) East Brunswick, NJ St. Bartholomew; College of Consultors.
Walsh, Thomas M. *s.s.c.* '57 (BUF)[M] Silver Creek, NY St. Columbans on the Lake, Home for the Aged.
Walsh, Thomas P. '86 (CHI) Chicago, IL St. Agatha.
Walsh, Thomas P. '72 (STA) St. Augustine, FL San Sebastian.
Walsh, Rev. Msgr. Thomas R. '59 (CHL) Retired.
Walsh, Thomas R. '94 (LIN) Lincoln, NE Sacred Heart; Society of St. Vincent de Paul – Lincoln Council.
Walsh, Thomas V. '67 (WOR) Clinton, MA St. John the Evangelist.
Walsh, Thomas *s.s.c.* '57 (OM)[K] St. Columbans Missionary Society of St. Columban.
Walsh, Rev. Msgr. Vincent M. '62 (PH) Archdiocesan Judges Retired.
Walsh, William F. *o.s.f.s.* '68 (R) Kitty Hawk, NC Holy Redeemer by the Sea.
Walsh, William K. '49 (SAC) Rio Vista, CA St. Joseph Retired.
Walsh, William P. *s.j.* '67 (RVC)[O] Manhasset, NY St. Ignatius Retreat House, Inisfada.
Walsh, William *s.j.* '67 (BAL)[S] Baltimore, MD Ferdinand Wheeler Jesuit Community.
Walshe, Sebastian A. *o.praem.* '05 (ORG)[A] Silverado, CA St. Michael's Norbertine Postulancy, Novitiate and Juniorate; [I] Silverado, CA Norbertine Fathers of Orange Inc.
Walsman, Paul *o.f.m.* '58 (CIN)[N] Cincinnati St. Francis Seraph Friary.
Walter, Anthony *o.f.m.* '59 (CIN)[N] Cincinnati, OH St. John the Baptist Friary.
Walter, Chris B. '58 (BIS) Mohall, ND St. Johns; Mohall, ND St. James; Mohall, ND St. Jerome Retired.
Walter, Chris B. '58 (FAR) Lansford, ND St. John's Church of Lansford.
Walter, David A. '63 (STL) Retired.
Walter, Francis *o.f.m.* '77 (BO)[U] Boston, MA St. Bonaventure Friary, Franciscan Friars.
Walter, Francis *o.f.m.* '77 (NY)[EE] New York Franciscan Province of the Immaculate Conception.
Walter, James A. '62 (COL) Sugar Grove, OH St. Joseph; Parochial Examiners; Deanery 11: Lancaster.
Walter, James A. '69 (BUF) Clergy Personnel Board; Springbrook, NY St. Vincent.
Walter, Joseph L. *c.s.c.* '61 (FTW)[B] University of Notre Dame Du Lac; [H] Notre Dame, IN Holy Cross Community, Corby Hall, University of Notre Dame.
Walter, Marius *o.s.b.* '98 (P)[L] St. Benedict, OR Mt. Angel Abbey.
Walter, Marius *o.s.b.* '98 (BUF) Westfield, NY St. Dominic.
Walter, Mark J. '88 (CHI) Midlothian, IL St. Christopher.
Walter, Rev. Msgr. Robert J. '45 (DAV)[J] Davenport, IA St. Vincent Center Retired.
Walter, Steven P. '77 (CIN) Cincinnati, OH St. John Fisher.
Walter, William '61 (KC) St. Joseph, MO St. Francis Xavier.
Walters, Erik T.A. '02 (MOB) On Leave from the Archdiocese.
Walters, Frederick '87 (PAT) Hewitt, NJ Our Lady Queen of Peace; Deans.
Walters, Gary R. '79 (TOL) Sycamore, OH St. Pius X; Tiffin, OH St. Mary.
Walters, Hilarion *c.p.* '47 (FgM) South River, NJ St. Paul of the Cross Province.
Walters, James *s.c.j.* '78 (MIL)[Y] Hales Corners, WI Congregation of the Priests of the Sacred Heart Support and Maintenance Trust; [B] Hales Corners, WI Sacred Heart School of Theology; [P] Hales Corners, WI Priests of the Sacred Heart.
Walters, Michael M. '81 (NEW) Archdiocesan Judges; Section III Coordinator; Boy Scouts of America/ Catholic Committee on Scouting.
Walters, Michael M. '81 (PSC) Defender of the Bond.
Walters, Mitch (NEW) Ministerial Development Center.
Walters, Neil G. '89 (CLV) Garfield Heights, OH St. Therese; Cuyahoga County Jail.
Walters, Ron *o.f.m.* '78 (SFE) Albuquerque, NM; Councilors:; [I] Rio Rancho, NM Felician Sisters.
Walters, Theodore W. *s.j.* '56 (FgM)[K] Detroit Jesuit Provincial Office–Detroit Province of the Society of Jesus; Detroit, MI Detroit Province.
Walters, Thomas *o.f.m.* (NY) New York, NY St. Francis of Assisi.
Walters, Vincent '54 (SB) Retired.
Walterscheid, Kyle '02 (FWT) Ranger, TX St. Francis Xavier; Vocations and Seminarians; Ranger, TX Holy Rosary; Ranger, TX St. Rita; Ranger, TX St. John.
Waltersheid, William J. '92 (HBG) Secretary for Clergy and Religious Life; Permanent Diaconate, Office for; Camp Hill, PA Good Shepherd.
Walther, James *o.m.v.* '95 (SFD) Alton, IL St. Mary's.
Walton, James *o.f.m.* '91 (CHI)[N] Countryside, IL St. Gratian Friary, Franciscan Friars.
Walton, James *o.f.m.* '91 (JOL) Hinsdale, IL Hinsdale Hospital.
Walton, Rev. Msgr. Robert P. '74 (SAC) Sacramento, CA Sacred Heart of Jesus; Defenders of the Bond; College of Consultors; Priests' Personnel Board, Diocesan.
Waltz, Joshua K. '07 (BIS)[C] Bismarck, ND St. Mary's Central High School.
Waltz, Justin P. '08 (BIS) Minot, ND St. Leo; [I] Minot, ND Bishop Ryan High School.
Walz, Daniel '03 (SCL) Bertha, MN St. Joseph; Dent, MN Sacred Heart; Henning, MN Church of St. Edward of Henning; Perham, MN St. Lawrence.
Walz, Richard '88 (SCL) Long Prairie, MN St. Mary of Mt. Carmel.
Walz, Richard *o.s.b.* '67 (LR)[A] Subiaco, AR Subiaco Abbey.
Walz, Rev. Msgr. W. Dean '53 (DUB) Council of Catholic Women; Judges Retired.
Wamara, Serapio *c.s.c.* '03 (FTW)[H] Notre Dame Congregation of Holy Cross, Indiana Province, Provincial House.
Wamayose, Bernard *a.j.* '02 (HBG) New Freedom, PA St. John the Baptist.
Wambach, John W. *s.j.* '64 (MIL)[P] Wauwatosa, WI Jesuit Community at St. Camillus.
Wambach, Joseph *s.d.s.* '67 (MIL)[P] Milwaukee Salvatorian Provincial Offices.
Wampach, Frank J. '84 (STP) Watertown, MN Immaculate Conception.
Wanat, Mitchell *c.m.* '71 (HRT) Ansonia, CT St. Joseph.
Wanaurny, John *s.s.c.* '59 (OM)[K] St. Columbans Missionary Society of St. Columban.
Wanaurny, John *s.s.c.* '59 (FgM) St Columbans, NE House of Post–Graduate Studies.
Wanaurny, John *s.s.c.* '59 (LA)[P] Los Angeles, CA Columban Fathers, Procure House.
Wanda, Michael J. '91 (CHI) Westchester, IL Divine Infant.
Wander, Paul '90 (B) Salmon, ID St. Charles; Priest Personnel Commission.
Wandless, John H. '97 (KC) Retired.
Wang, Francis X. *s.j.* '52 (SJ)[M] Los Gatos, CA Sacred Heart Jesuit Center.
Wang, Ignatius C. (SFR) Retired.
Wang, John '54 (HEL) Retired.
Wang, John (STO) Diamond Springs, CA Retired.
Wangai, Patrick M. '07 (CHI) Arlington Heights, IL Our Lady of the Wayside.
Wangler, Rev. Msgr. Donald R. '57 (BUF) Retired.
Wangler, Leonard *o.s.b.* '70 (LR)[A] Subiaco, AR Subiaco Abbey; Presbyteral Council.
Wangler, Rev. Msgr. William O. '63 (BUF) Retired.
Wangwe, Fred *a.j.* '00 (HBG)[I] Lewisburg, PA Bucknell University.
Wanish, David A. '02 (MAD) Argyle, WI St. Michael; Argyle, WI St. Joseph; Argyle, WI St. Joseph; Gratiot, WI St. John.
Wankerl, Gary A. '80 (MAD) De Forest, WI St. Olaf; De Forest, WI St. Joseph.
Wannemuehler, Robert '51 (EVN) Retired.
Wanser, George V. *s.j.* '76 (SAC)[I] Carmichael, CA Sacramento Jesuit Community.
Wanser, George *s.j.* (SAC)[L] Sacramento, CA Newman Catholic Community at Sacramento State University.
Wantland, Thomas A. '67 (MAR) Retired.
Wapen, Francis A. '70 (SY) Taberg, NY St. Patrick.
Wapenski, Robert '05 (FAR) Anamoose, ND St. Francis Xavier Church of Anamoose; Drake, ND St. Margaret Mary.
Waraksa, Alex J. '90 (KNX) Soddy Daisy, TN Holy Spirit Catholic Church.
Warburton, John *o.s.j.* '80 (MRY) Santa Cruz, CA Shrine of St. Joseph Guardian of the Redeemer; [F] Shrine of St. Joseph; Santa Cruz, CA.
Ward, Bruce *s.t.* '60 (FgM) Silver Spring, MD MISSIONARY SERVANTS OF THE MOST HOLY TRINITY.
Ward, Daniel *o.s.b.* '71 (SCL)[I] Collegeville St. John's Abbey, of the Order of St. Benedict; President's Council:; Silver Spring, MD The Resource Center for Religious Institutes.
Ward, Daniel *o.s.b.* (WDC)[W] Silver Spring, MD National Association for Treasurers of Religious Institutes.
Ward, Donald M. *s.j.* '70 (CHL)[J] Mooresville, NC Jesuit Community; Mooresville, NC St. Therese.
Ward, Edward M. *o.m.i.* (GAL) Houston, TX Immaculate Heart of Mary.
Ward, Edward *o.carm.* '73 (JOL) Darien, IL Our Lady of Mount Carmel.
Ward, Rev. Msgr. Gerald T. '79 (PEO) Diocesan College of Consultors; Bloomington, IL St. Patrick Church of Merna; Downs, IL St. Mary's; Vicariates and Vicars.
Ward, James G. *c.m.* '77 (STL)[V] Perryville, MO Association of the Miraculous Medal; [O] Perryville, MO Congregation of the Mission.
Ward, James J. '73 (ALN) Jim Thorpe, PA Immaculate Conception; Lafayette Council #2522, Palmerton; Jim Thorpe – Court Ryan #911.
Ward, Jerome A. *o.m.i.* '67 (CHR) Retired.
Ward, John B. '86 (BAL) Baltimore, MD Our Lady of Hope; Adjutant Judicial Vicar.
Ward, John B. '86 (MO) Judges.
Ward, John J. '55 (SFR) Retired.
Ward, John J. *c.s.b.* '70 (DET)[E] Novi, MI Catholic Central High School.
Ward, John P. '65 (CAM) Vineland, NJ The Catholic Church of the Sacred Heart, Vineland, N.J.
Ward, Mark *c.p.* '76 (WH) Kingwood, WV St. Sebastian's; Kingwood, WV St. Zita's; Vicars Forane.
Ward, Michael G. '97 (NEW) East Newark, NJ St. Anthony's; Kearny, NJ St. Cecilia's; West Hudson Region Deanery 14; Members.
Ward, Neal A. '57 (WDC) Retired.
Ward, Paul T. '04 (DET) Detroit, MI Assumption Grotto.
Ward, Richard E. '68 (PIT) Bridgeville, PA St. Barbara.
Ward, Richard J. '93 (SEA) Retired.
Ward, Samuel W. '03 (LA) South Gate, CA St. Helen.
Ward, Thomas I. '97 (SY) Greene, NY Immaculate Conception; Greene, NY St. Joseph.
Ward, Thomas '62 (KC) Retired.
Ward, Rev. Msgr. William P. '57 (SCR)[N] Dunmore, PA Villa St. Joseph Retired.
Wardanski, Rev. Msgr. Joseph V. '67 (E) Erie, PA St. Patrick; [K] Erie, PA Saint Mary's Home of Erie.
Warden, Daniel L. '66 (GAL) Retired.
Warden, Joel M. *c.o.* '99 (BRK) Brooklyn, NY St. Boniface; [T] Brooklyn, NY Oratory of Saint Philip Neri, Congregation Pontifical Rite.
Warden, T. Patrick *c.s.b.* '65 (GAL)[O] Houston, TX Residence of the Basilian Fathers of the University of St. Thomas.
Wardenski, Robert W. '72 (BUF) East Aurora, NY Immaculate Conception.
Wardhana, Budi '09 (LA) Simi Valley, CA St. Rose of Lima.
Ware, Brandon M. '07 (STO) Lodi, CA St. Anne Church (Pastor of).
Ware, Donald *c.p.* '72 (PIT)[M] Pittsburgh, PA St. Paul of the Cross Monastery.
Wargel, William '65 (EVN) Retired.
Wargo, Rev. Msgr. Robert J. '72 (ALN) Orefield, PA St. Joseph The Worker.
Waris, Gerald R. '67 (KC) Retired.
Warkulwiz, Victor P. *m.s.s.* '91 (PH) Bensalem, PA Our Lady of Fatima; Bensalem, PA.
Warman, William C. '64 (MO) On Duty Outside the Archdiocese; U.S. Veterans Medical Center; DEPARTMENT OF VETERANS AFFAIRS HOSPITALS AND CHAPLAINS.

Warmuz, Gregory W. *o.cist.* '94 (CHI) Chicago, IL St. Priscilla.
Warmuz, Grzegorz (CHI) Tinley Park, IL St. Stephen, Deacon and Martyr.
Warnakula, Anthony B. *c.h.s.p.* '88 (SAC) Susanville, CA California Correctional Center.
Warner, James P. '69 (GI) Retired.
Warner, John B. *s.j.* '74 (FgM) St. Louis, MO Society of Jesus.
Warner, John F. '70 (Y) Canal Fulton, OH SS. Philip and James; Defenders of the Bond.
Warner, Joseph A. '03 (CLV) Fairlawn, OH St. Hilary; Akron, OH Blessed Trinity.
Warner, Richard V. *c.s.c.* '66 (FTW)[H] Notre Dame, IN Holy Cross Community, Corby Hall, University of Notre Dame; [B] University of Notre Dame Du Lac.
Warnimont, Ronald R. '76 (TOL) Defenders of the Bond; College of Consultors; Judges.
Warnisher, Maximilian M. *f.i.* '94 (FR)[G] New Bedford, MA Marian Friary of Our Lady, Queen of the Seraphic Order.
Warnock, Damian J. *o.s.b.* '79 (GBG)[G] Latrobe, PA Saint Vincent Archabbey.
Warnstedt, Mark '96 (LA) Downey, CA Our Lady of Perpetual Help.
Warosh, James B. *s.j.* '67 (MIL)[P] Milwaukee, WI Jesuit Community at Marquette University.
Warren, Anthony *s.s.p.* '85 (Y)[A] Canfield, OH Society of St. Paul.
Warren, Arthur '63 (LAF) Retired.
Warren, Martin L. '78 (STP)[C] St. Paul, MN University of St. Thomas.
Warren, Michael *o.m.v.* '08 (DEN) Denver, CO Holy Ghost.
Warren, Paul '78 (SFR) San Francisco, CA St. Teresa.
Warren, Robert *s.a.* '81 (NY)[EE] Garrison, NY St. Christopher's Inn; [EE] Garrison, NY St. Christopher's Friary.
Warren, Robert '64 (RIC) Retired.
Warsey, Robert M. *o.s.m.* '85 (CHI)[N] Chicago Order of Friar Servants of Mary (Servites) United States of America Province, Inc.; [N] Chicago, IL Servite Marian Center; Chicago, IL; [N] Chicago, IL National Shrine of Our Lady of Sorrows; [N] Chicago, IL Order of Friar Servants of Mary (Servites) United States of America Province, Inc.
Warsnak, Richard '07 (KCK) Emporia, KS Sacred Heart.
Warzocha, Rev. Msgr. Frank S. '53 (BUR) West Rutland, VT St. Stanislaus Kostka.
Wasek, Piotr (RVC) Hempstead, NY St. Ladislaus.
Waseline, Nicholas R. *o.s.f.s.* '80 (PH) Philadelphia, PA Our Mother of Consolation; [D] Philadelphia, PA Northeast Catholic High School for Boys.
Wash, Pat J. '68 (WH) Absent on Leave.
Washabaugh, Robert '78 (NOR) New London, CT St. Mary, Star of the Sea; College of Consultors; Members; Part Time; St. Mary, Star of the Sea Church – Spanish Apostolate; Advisory Board.
Washington, Christopher T. '06 (SCR)[D] Dunmore, PA Holy Cross High School; Ex Officio; Vocations; Scranton, PA St. Peter's Cathedral; Diocesan Office for Parish Life and Evangelization.
Washington, Freddy *c.s.sp.* '92 (CHI) Chicago, IL St. Ambrose; Chicago, IL St. Mary Magdalene.
Washko, Robert M. '77 (GBG) Seward, PA Holy Family.
Washko, Rt. Rev. Stephen G. '78 (VNN) Phoenix, AZ St. Stephen; Protosyncellus; Building Commission; Eparchial Finance Commission; Commission for the Implementation of the Particular Law; [B] Phoenix, AZ St. Stephen Senior Citizen Apartments; College of Consultors; Finance Council.
Washko, Rt. Rev. Stephen '78 (VNN) Ecclesiatical Notaries; Liturgy & Music Commission; Director of Ecumenical Affairs; Building and Sacred Arts; Pension Committee; Personnel Board; Ecumenism.
Wasiecko, Allan *o.f.m.cap.* '68 (FgM) Pittsburgh, PA Province of St. Augustine.
Wasielewski, Henry R. '64 (PHX) Retired.
Wasikowski, Ronald S. '75 (OM) Omaha, NE St. Patrick (Elkhorn).
Wasilewski, Kenneth P. *s.t.l.* '03 (RCK) Rockford, IL St. Peter Cathedral.
Wasinger, Mark Shane '94 (STP) North Branch, MN St. Gregory the Great.
Wasko, Anthony J. *o.s.a.* '58 (SD)[J] San Diego, CA Augustinian Community Retired.
Waskowiak, Harlan D. P. '98 (LIN) Orleans, NE St. Mary's; Diocesan Consultors; Presbyteral Council.
Waslo, Rev. Msgr. Peter D. '86 (PHU) Protosyncellus; Chancellor; College of Archeparchial Consultors; Archeparchial Corporation; Judicial Vicar; Ecumenical Relations; The Way – Online Newspaper; Office of Vocations; Presbyteral Council; Archeparchial Council for Economic Affairs; Archdiocesan Bulletin; Director of Communication; [D] Philadelphia, PA Ascension Manor, Inc.
Waslo, Rev. Msgr. Peter '86 (PBR) Pro–Synodal Judges; Secretary.
Wasnewski, Richard P. '53 (BO) Senior Priests. Retired.
Wasnie, Blane *o.s.b.* '66 (SCL) Avon, MN St. Benedict's; [I] Collegeville, MN St. John's Abbey, of the Order of St. Benedict.
Wasowski, Ronald *c.s.c.* '73 (P)[B] University of Portland; [L] Portland, OR Holy Cross Fathers & Brothers, C.S.C. – University of Portland.
Wasowski, Ronald *c.s.c.* (FTW)[H] Notre Dame Congregation of Holy Cross, Indiana Province, Provincial House.
Wassef, Pafnuzio '79 (MET) South River, NJ St. Mary of Ostrabrama.
Wassel, Rev. Msgr. Anthony F. '60 (ALN) Retired.
Wassell, John E. '97 (NEW) Elizabeth, NJ Our Lady of Most Holy Rosary/St. Michael; Elizabeth Deanery 25; Members.
Wasser, James *m.s.f.* '74 (SAT)[B] San Antonio, TX MSF Formation Community.
Wassie, Stephen M. '79 (Y) Jefferson, OH St. Joseph Calasanctius; Kingsville, OH St. Andrew.
Wassmuth, Rev. Msgr. Dennis '73 (B) Boise, ID Our Lady of the Rosary; Boise, ID Sacred Heart; Vicars General; Notaries; Ex Officio; Priest Personnel Commission; Finance Council; Priest Retirement Committee; Building Commission; Catholic Liturgical Commission.
Wastag, Michael *o.carm.* '97 (NY)[II] New Rochelle, NY The Center for Spirituality and Justice.
Wastog, Michael J. *o.carm.* '97 (NEW)[O] Mahwah, NJ Carmel Retreat.
Waszczenko, Andrew '98 (SAT) Stockdale, TX St. Ann's.
Waszczenko, Andrzej *s.d.s.* '89 (SAT) Falls City, TX Nativity of the Blessed Virgin Mary; [L] Falls City, TX Salvatorian Fathers Community of Texas.
Watanabe, Rev. Msgr. Terrence A.M. '77 (HON) Kihei, HI St. Theresa.
Watanabe, Rev. Msgr. Terrence '77 (HON) Master of Ceremonies for Episcopal Functions and Coordinator of Diocesan Major Events; Diocesan Planning and Building Commission; St. Anthony Jr./Sr. High School Board of Education (Maui).
Waterman, Gerald *o.f.m.conv.* '85 (R) Burlington, NC Blessed Sacrament; [F] Elon, NC Conventual Franciscans; [I] Elon, NC Elon University.
Waters, Bernard F. '69 (LAV) Unassigned.
Waters, Edward '77 (ORL) Lady Lake, FL St. Timothy.
Waters, J. Kevin *s.j.* '64 (SPK)[B] Spokane, WA Gonzaga University.
Waters, John J. *s.j.* '68 (DEN)[N] Denver, CO Xavier Jesuit Center; [H] Denver, CO Saint Joseph Hospital; [N] Denver, CO Xavier Jesuit Center.
Waters, Joseph L. '87 (SP) Judges.
Waters, Joseph '56 (CHL) Retired.
Waters, Joseph '87 (SP) Saint Petersburg, FL Cathedral of St. Jude the Apostle; Vicars Forane.
Waters, Mark S. '90 (STA) Atlantic Beach, FL St. John the Baptist.
Waters, Philip J. *o.s.b.* '72 (NEW) Newark, NJ St. Mary's; [M] Newark, NJ Newark Abbey; Central Newark Deanery 20.
Waters, Robert E. '69 (BUF) Batavia, NY Resurrection.
Waters, Robert J. '60 (CHR) Aiken, SC St. Mary, Help of Christians.
Waters, William F. *o.s.a.* '71 (BO)[AA] North Andover, MA Merrimack College Campus Ministry Center; [C] Our Mother of Good Counsel Monastery.
Wathen, Ambrose G. *o.s.b.* '65 (NO)[P] St. Benedict, LA St. Joseph Abbey.
Wathen, Daniel '06 (GF) Roundup, MT St. Benedict; Diocesan Consultors; Clerical Benefit Association; Priests' Council.
Wathen, David *o.f.m.* '99 (FgM) Washington, DC; Washington, DC COMMISSARIAT OF THE HOLY LAND.
Wathen, David *o.f.m.* '99 (WDC)[N] Washington, DC Franciscan Monastery USA Inc.
Wathier, Douglas O. '84 (DUB)[L] Dubuque, IA Mt. Loretto Convent; [C] Loras College.
Watin, Nestor '82 (RVC) Freeport, NY Our Holy Redeemer.
Watkins, Charles W. '03 (CHI) La Grange, IL St. Cletus.
Watkins, Clarence N. '67 (ARL) Retired.
Watkins, Rev. Msgr. James D. '89 (WDC) Washington, DC Immaculate Conception; Deans; Priest Council.
Watkins, Mark T. '91 (CIN) Cincinnati, OH St. Lawrence.
Watkins, Paul D. *o.p.* '90 (MEM)[F] Memphis, TN The Dominican Friars of Memphis, Inc.; Memphis, TN St. Peter Church.
Watroba, Boleslaus M. '35 (ALB) Retired.
Watson, Cletus M. *t.o.r.* '66 (SP) St. Petersburg, FL St. Mary Our Lady of Grace.
Watson, David E. *s.j.* '92 (DET)[K] Detroit, MI Jesuit Community at the University of Detroit Mercy.
Watson, Eric J. *s.j.* '09 (SEA)[A] Seattle, WA Seattle University; [L] Seattle, WA Arrupe Jesuit Community at Seattle University.
Watson, Joseph G. '92 (PH) Philadelphia, PA St. William; Office for Pastoral Care for Migrants and Refugees.
Watson, Joseph *o.cist.* '09 (LC)[H] Sparta, WI Our Lady of Spring Bank, Cistercian Abbey.
Watson, Mark A. '96 (SHP) Monroe, LA Jesus the Good Shepherd; Advocates; Presbyteral Council; Church Vocations Board & Vocations Office; College of Consultors.
Watson, Michael B. '86 (COL) Columbus, OH St. Andrew; Deanery 2: Northwest; Diocesan Finance Council; Parochial Examiners; Presbyteral Council.
Watson, Timothy *c.ss.r.* '90 (DEN)[N] Denver The Redemptorists/Denver Province.
Watson, Walter *s.j.* '70 (DEN)[N] Denver, CO Xavier Jesuit Center; Wheat Ridge, CO SS. Peter and Paul.
Watson, Rev. Msgr. William A. '62 (PEO) Peoria Heights, IL St. Thomas; [B] Peoria, IL Peoria Notre Dame Scholarship Trust.
Watson, William M. *s.j.* '85 (SEA)[L] Seattle, WA Arrupe Jesuit Community at Seattle University.
Watt, Gerald *c.r.* (CHI)[N].
Watters, Timothy J. '71 (CHR) Absent On Leave.
Watters, William J. *s.j.* '65 (BAL) Baltimore, MD St. Ignatius Church.
Watterson, John E. '62 (PRO) Retired.
Wattigny, Patrick B. '94 (NO) Metairie, LA St. Benilde.
Watts, Albert W. '59 (BGP) Retired.
Watts, Rev. Msgr. Roger J. '59 (BGP) Retired.
Watts, Thomas H. '57 (ROC) Owego, NY Blessed Trinity; Owego, NY St. Patrick Retired.
Watts, Trent L. '93 (R) Southport, NC Sacred Heart.
Watts, Wayne F. '90 (CHI) Chicago, IL St. John Berchmans; [G] Chicago, IL Catholic Charities of the Archdiocese of Chicago–Archdiocesan Offices; Associate Administrators.
Watzke, James N. *c.s.c.* '63 (FTW)[H] Notre Dame Congregation of Holy Cross, Indiana Province, Provincial House.
Waudby, Lawrence '90 (BAL) Priests Sick or Absent.
Waugh, John G. '55 (PEO) Wedron, IL St. Joseph's; Illinois Industrial School for Boys.
Wawerski, Rev. Msgr. Edward '61 (RVC) Floral Park, NY St. Hedwig's; Hempstead, NY St. Ladislaus.
Waweru, Gabriel '07 (DUL) Hibbing, MN Blessed Sacrament; [G] Hibbing, MN Hibbing Catholic Schools Endowment Fund.
Wawiorka, Ray W. '56 (MIL) Retired.
Wawryszuk, Zdzislaw F. '85 (RCK) Prophetstown, IL St. Catherine.
Wawrzycki, Andrew '70 (ORL) Retired.
Wawrzyniakowski, Edward J. '57 (MIL) Retired.
Way, Edmund J. *o.p.* '43 (WDC) Washington, DC St. Dominic Church & Priory.
Wayne, David A. *s.j.* '68 (DEN)[D] Aurora, CO Regis Jesuit High School Corporation; [N] Centennial, CO Regis High Jesuit Community.
Wdowiak, Boleslaw '65 (SAC) Retired.
Wea, Raymundus *s.v.d.* '82 (SD) Sharp Memorial Hospital; San Diego, CA Children's Hospital; San Diego, CA Our Lady of the Sacred Heart.
Weakley, Robert *o.f.m.* '68 (PEO) Peoria, IL St. Joseph.
Wearden, Rev. Msgr. Francis G. '54 (GAL) Oremus Pro Invicem Retired.
Weare, Kenneth M. '01 (SFR) Fairfax, CA St. Rita; Archdiocesan Board of Education; [P] San Francisco, CA Catholic Charities CYO of the Archdiocese of San Francisco.
Wearsch, Ronald '92 (CLV) Willowick, OH St. Mary Magdalene.
Weary, William M. '84 (HBG) Lewistown, PA Sacred Heart of Jesus; Mifflintown, PA St. Jude.
Weaver, Cyprian *o.s.b.* '72 (FgM) Collegeville, MN St. John's Abbey; [I] Collegeville St. John's Abbey, of the Order of St. Benedict.
Weaver, Jeffrey '82 (CLV) Absent on Leave.
Weaver, John G. '70 (HRT) Enfield, CT St. Patrick.
Weaver, Mark *o.f.m.conv.* '77 (FTW) Angola; LaGrange, IN St. Joseph; Angola, IN St. Anthony; LaGrange.
Weaver, Richard '63 (DAL) Retired.
Webb, Raymond J. '67 (CHI)[A] Mundelein, IL University of St. Mary of the Lake/Mundelein Seminary; [A] Mundelein, IL University of St. Mary of the Lake/ Mundelein Seminary; Mundelein Seminary/University of St. Mary of the Lake.
Webber, Rev. Msgr. Donald S. '62 (SB) Special or Other Diocesan Assignment; Judges; Sun City, CA Retired.
Webber, Donald *c.p.* '73 (CHI)[N] Chicago, IL Passionist Provincial Office; [N] Chicago, IL Passionist Community–Immaculate Conception Monastery; Chicago, IL Holy Cross Province (Western).
Webber, Lawrence E. *o.f.m.cap.* '80 (DET)[K] Detroit, MI St. Mary's Friary; [T] Detroit, MI Solanus Casey Center.
Weber, Alan '84 (SP)[S] Temple Terrace, FL Catholic Student Center, University of South Florida; Incardination Committee.
Weber, Allen *o.f.m.* '65 (BUF)[O] St. Bonaventure, NY St. Bonaventure Friary; [C] St. Bonaventure, NY Friar Community.
Weber, Arnold *o.s.b.* '52 (SCL)[I] Collegeville, MN St. John's Abbey, of the Order of St. Benedict.
Weber, Bernard *c.p.* '81 (L)[L] Louisville, KY Sacred Heart Retreat.
Weber, Charles P. '57 (BO) Senior Priests. Retired.
Weber, Christopher H. '02 (CLV) Cleveland, OH Holy Rosary.

Weber, David '77 (CLV) Administrative Leave.
Weber, Dennis M. *sd.c* '97 (PH)[L] Springfield, PA Don Guanella School; [L] Springfield, PA Cardinal Krol Center; [Y] Springfield, PA Servants of Charity (S.C.); [B] Springfield, PA Servants of Charity.
Weber, Donald E. '58 (GR) On Special Assignment; Vicar For Priests; Vicar for Clergy Retired.
Weber, Rev. Msgr. Edward J. '76 (NY) West Nyack, NY St. Francis of Assisi; Rockland.
Weber, Eric Christopher '01 (LAN) On Duty Outside the Diocese.
Weber, Fidelis F. *t.o.r.* '55 (PH)[Y] Fairless Hills, PA St. Anthony Friary.
Weber, Rev. Msgr. Francis J. '59 (LA) Mission Hills, CA San Fernando Rey Mission; Archives.
Weber, Frank N. '72 (GB)[I] Kaukauna, WI St. Paul Home; Special Assignment.
Weber, Frank W. '62 (PAT) Clifton, NJ St. Brendan.
Weber, Gabriel M. *o.s.m.* '49 (CHI)[N] Chicago Order of Friar Servants of Mary (Servites) United States of America Province, Inc.
Weber, Gabriel M. *o.s.m.* '49 (DEN) Denver, CO Our Lady of Mount Carmel.
Weber, George *c.m.* '54 (NO)[P] New Orleans, LA Congregation of the Mission Western Province (Vincentians) Retired.
Weber, Gerald *o.m.i.* '62 (SAT)[K] San Antonio, TX Oblate Madonna Residence.
Weber, Gerard P. '43 (CHI) Retired.
Weber, Herbert F. '74 (TOL) Perrysburg, OH Blessed John XXIII; College of Consultors; Members.
Weber, Jacques *s.j.* '49 (GAL) Houston, TX St. Cecilia Retired.
Weber, Jamie '04 (CIN) Cincinnati, OH St. Cecilia.
Weber, Rev. Msgr. John George '43 (SAL) Retired.
Weber, John R. *c.s.sp.* '61 (PIT)[O] Bethel Park, PA The Spiritan Center.
Weber, John R. '09 (PH) Lansdale, PA St. Stanislaus.
Weber, John S. '73 (LSC) Fairacres, NM San Jose Mission; Diocesan Tribunal; Finance Council; Judicial Vicars; Judges.
Weber, John '73 (LSC) Presbyteral Council.
Weber, John–Benedict *o.carm.* '77 (JOL)[L] Darien Carmelite Provincial Office.
Weber, Joseph A. '76 (PRM) St. Louis, MO St. Louis Mission.
Weber, Joseph A. '76 (MO) Sunset Hills, MO St. Justin Martyr; Air National Guard Chaplains.
Weber, Joseph O. '57 (SCR) Retired.
Weber, Keith '83 (SAL) Manhattan, KS St. Isidore Catholic Student Center Parish; [G] Manhattan, KS St. Isidore's Catholic Student Center.
Weber, Kevin '93 (SAL) Hays, KS Immaculate Heart of Mary Parish; Personnel Board; Art and Architecture Commission; Board of Trustees.
Weber, Leo F. *s.j.* '56 (DEN) Denver, CO St. Ignatius Loyola; [N] Denver, CO Society of Jesus – St. Ignatius Loyola Jesuit Community.
Weber, Mark *s.v.d.* '82 (CHI)[N] Techny, IL S.V.D. Funds, Inc.; Techny, IL Chicago Province; Techny, IL; [N] Techny, IL Divine Word Residence; [N] Techny, IL Society of the Divine Word, Provincial Headquarters–Chicago Prov.
Weber, Mark *b.c.c.* (SD)[H] Chula Vista, CA Scripps Mercy Chula Vista.
Weber, Matthew '90 (CAM) Glassboro, NJ St. Bridget's Catholic Church, Glassboro, N.J.
Weber, Michael J. *o.praem.* '77 (MO) Air Force Chaplains.
Weber, Michael J. *o.praem.* '77 (GB)[J] De Pere, WI St. Norbert Abbey.
Weber, Mike '77 (HON) Military Chaplains.
Weber, Norbert B. *m.s.c.* '57 (RCK)[G] Aurora, IL Missionaries of the Sacred Heart Community.
Weber, Randall '91 (SAL) Vicars General; Procurator and Advocate; College of Consultors; Council of Priests; Personnel Board; Art and Architecture Commission; Ex Officio; Ex Officio; Consultors; Office of Ecumenical and Interreligious Affairs; Salina, KS Sacred Heart Cathedral Parish; Moderator of the Curia.
Weber, Robert C. '81 (SY) Holland Patent, NY St. Leo; Marcy, NY Mid–State Correctional Facility; Special Assignment.
Weber, Robert P. '65 (CAM) Delmont, NJ Southern State Correctional Facility; Bridgeton, NJ Southwoods State Prison Retired.
Weber, Robson Luis '76 (ALN) Bethlehem, PA Holy Infancy.
Weber, Samuel *o.s.b.* '96 (IND)[K] St. Meinrad St. Meinrad Archabbey.
Weber, Terry '85 (SFS) On Duty Outside the Diocese.
Weber, Theodore '55 (P) Retired.
Weber, Thomas L. '74 (CLV) Westlake, OH St. Bernadette; Retirement Board.
Weberg, Paul *o.s.b.* '03 (RCK)[G] Aurora, IL Marmion Abbey.
Weberg, Paul *o.s.b.* '03 (MO) Army National Guard Chaplains.
Webster, Robert E. '86 (ORL) Liturgy; Washington, DC Federation of Diocesan Liturgical Commissions Retired.
Webster, Robert '86 (ORL) Clermont, FL Blessed Sacrament.
Wechter, David *o.c.s.o.* '58 (WIN)[A] Winona, MN Immaculate Heart of Mary Seminary; [G] Houston, MN Hermits of St. Mary of Carmel, (H.S.M.C.); Associate Judges.
Weckerle, Leo F. '58 (BAK) Defenders of the Bond and Promoters of Justice Retired.
Weckert, Paul M. *o.s.b.* '99 (SEA)[L] Lacey, WA St. Martin's Abbey.
Wedeking, Patrick '88 (MO) Air Force Reserve Chaplains.
Wedig, James M. '93 (CIN) Wilmington, OH St. Columbkille; [R] Wilmington, OH Wilmington College Campus Ministry.
Wedig, Mark *o.p.* '86 (MIA) Miami, FL St. Dominic; [B] Miami, FL Barry University; [K] Miami, FL Dominican Fathers of Miami, Inc.
Wedow, Robert L. '01 (DEN) Sterling, CO St. Anthony; Deaneries.
Wedziuk, Leszek *s.ch.* (TOL) Toledo, OH St. Adalbert; Toledo, OH St. Hedwig.
Wee, Damien E. '04 (OM) Papillion, NE St. Columbkille.
Weekly, Christopher S. '98 (P) Portland, OR St. Ignatius; [L] Portland, OR Colombiere Community.
Weeks, James M. *m.s.* '62 (HRT)[L] Hartford, CT Missionaries of LaSalette.
Weeks, Sean '04 (P) Ashland, OR Our Lady of the Mountain; [P] Ashland, OR Southern Oregon University (Ashland); Area Vicars; Personnel Board.
Weerakkody, Oliver '65 (AUS) Austin, TX St. Louis.
Weerasinghe, Felix M. '64 (RVC) Retired.
Weezorak, Dennis R. '86 (MET) South Amboy, NJ St. Mary.
Wegher, William '91 (LAN) Pinckney, MI St. Mary; Ecumenical Officer.
Weglicki, Michael '79 (LEX) Beattyville, KY Queen of All Saints; Defenders of the Bond; Catholic Scouting.
Wegman, Richard H. '90 (MAN) Retired.
Wegner, Gary *o.f.m.cap.* '89 (MIL)[P] Mount Calvary, WI St. Lawrence Friary; [B] Mount Calvary, WI St. Lawrence Seminary.
Wego, Benignus *s.v.d.* '95 (BLX)[D] Bay St. Louis, MS St. Augustine's Residence.
Wehby, Albert *b.a.o.* '63 (NTN) North Hollywood, CA St. Anne.
Wehinger, Thomas E. '61 (TOL) Retired.
Wehman, Jack W. '80 (CIN) Wyoming, OH St. James of the Valley.
Wehmann, Mark H. '03 (STP) Lindstrom, MN St. Bridget of Sweden.
Wehmeyer, Curtis C. '01 (STP) St. Paul, MN Blessed Sacrament; St. Paul, MN St. Thomas The Apostle.
Wehn, Timothy '79 (LAV) Propagation of the Faith; Las Vegas, NV St. Joan of Arc; Presbyteral Council for the Diocese of Las Vegas.
Wehner, Edwin P. '69 (BIS) Bismarck, ND St. Anne.
Wehner, Eugene C. *o.c.d.* '75 (MIL)[P] Milwaukee Provincial Offices – Discalced Carmelites.
Wehner, James A. '95 (PIT) On Duty Outside the Diocese.
Wehner, James A. '95 (COL)[A] Columbus, OH Pontifical College Josephinum; [A] Columbus, OH Pontifical College Josephinum.
Wehnert, Donald R. *c.s.v.* '63 (JOL) Kankakee, IL St. Patrick Retired.
Wehnert, Donald R. *c.s.v.* '63 (CHI)[N] Arlington Heights Viatorian Province Center–Clerics of St. Viator.
Wehr, Arthur J. *s.j.* '90 (SAC) Sacramento, CA St. Ignatius of Loyola; [I] Carmichael, CA Sacramento Jesuit Community.
Wehri, Francis *o.s.b.* '61 (BIS)[A] Richardton, ND Assumption Abbey; Richardton, ND Assumption Abbey.
Wehrle, Jonathan '78 (LAN) Okemos, MI St. Martha; Building Commission; Priest Pension Board.
Wehrle, Peter G. '99 (NEW) North Bergen, NJ Our Lady of Fatima.
Wehrlen, Rev. Msgr. John B. '59 (PAT) Seaside Park, NJ Retired.
Wehrley, Charles *c.ss.r.* '01 (TUC)[F] Tucson, AZ Redemptorist Society of Arizona Redemptorist Renewal Center.
Wehrlin, Leo J. '93 (Y) Hiram College; Garrettsville, OH St. Ambrose.
Wehrmeyer, Richard *c.m.* '91 (FgM) Earth City, MO Western Province.
Wei, Luke '60 (BRK) Retired.
Weibl, Nicholas '64 (TOL) Fostoria, OH St. Wendelin.
Weible, Thomas C. '59 (LA) Retired.
Weidenbenner, Joseph '07 (SPC) West Plains, MO St. Mary; Presbyteral Council.
Weider, Gregory '63 (ALB)[H] Amsterdam, NY St. Mary's Hospital; Special Assignment.
Weider, Henry '89 (OWN) Absent on Leave.
Weidner, Halbert *c.o.* '74 (CHR)[E] Rock Hill, SC Oratory of St. Philip Neri, Congregation of the Oratory of Pontifical Rite.
Weidner, Halbert *c.o.* '74 (NOR) Middletown, CT St. Francis of Assisi; Middletown; [L] Middletown, CT Wesleyan University–The University Ministry.
Weidner, Larry W. '80 (PHX) Sun City, AZ Banner Boswell Medical Center.
Weidner, Mark *o.c.s.o.* '54 (P)[L] Lafayette, OR The Cistercian (Trappist) Abbey of Our Lady of Guadalupe.
Weidner, S. Anthony '05 (OM) Omaha, NE St. Peter.
Weigand, Dom Peter *o.s.b.* '70 (WDC)[E] Washington, DC St. Anselm's Abbey School, Inc.
Weigand, John J. '67 (CLV) Lakewood, OH St. James.
Weigand, Joseph C. '62 (CLV) Elyria, OH St. Mary Retired.
Weigand, Peter *o.s.b.* '70 (WDC)[N] Washington, DC St. Anselm's Abbey.
Weigard, Joseph C. '62 (CLV) Cuyahoga Falls, OH Immaculate Heart of Mary Retired.
Weighner, James C. '07 (LC) Appointed Members; Prairie du Chien, WI St. Gabriel; Prairie du Chien, WI St. John Nepomucene; Wauzeka, WI Sacred Heart.
Weighner, Robert *l.c.* (LC) Genoa, WI St. Charles Borromeo.
Weigman, Joseph A. '91 (TOL)[H] Oregon, OH Sacred Heart Home.
Weik, Terence *s.m.* '80 (BAL) Eldersburg, MD St. Joseph; [V] Sykesville, MD St. Joseph Catholic Community Endowment Trust.
Weikart, G. David '03 (Y) Orwell, OH St. Mary; Rock Creek, OH Sacred Heart.
Weiksnar, William J. *o.f.m.* '94 (CAM) Camden, NJ St. Anthony of Padua Roman Catholic Church, Camden, N.J.
Weiksner, Jerome M. '55 (GBG) Retired.
Weil, Frank *o.carm.* '67 (JOL)[L] Darien Carmelite Provincial Office.
Weiler, Michael F. *s.j.* '88 (LA)[P] Culver City, CA Ignatius House, The Novitiate of the California Province, Society of Jesus.
Weinandy, Thomas *o.f.m.cap.* '72 (WDC)[B] Washington, DC St. Francis Friary–Capuchin College.
Weinberger, Paul L. '89 (DAL) Greenville, TX St. William; Quinlan, TX Our Lady of Fatima.
Weiner, James J. '88 (NEW) Hohokus, NJ St. Luke's.
Weiner, Rev. Archpriest Philip Canon '91 (STF) Priest Personnel Board; Yonkers, NY St. Michael; Chancellor & Archivist; Diocesan Consultors; New York; Presbyteral Council; Administrative Council; Directors; Diaconate, Permanent; Liturgical Commission.
Weinert, Allan *c.ss.r.* '72 (DEN)[N] Denver, CO The Redemptorists/Denver Province.
Weingartz, Francis A. '54 (DET) Retired.
Weinlader, Wayne T. *m.m.* '68 (FgM) Maryknoll, NY MARYKNOLL Retired.
Weinzapfel, Rev. Msgr. Thomas '45 (DAL) Retired.
Weir, Bernard E. '86 (DAV) Ottumwa, IA St. Mary of the Visitation.
Weis, Denis P. '63 (MIL) Retired.
Weis, Eugene R. '62 (ROC) Lady Lake, FL St. Timothy Retired.
Weis, John H. '66 (PAT) On Duty Outside the Diocese.
Weis, John '66 (SAG) Pigeon, MI St. Francis Borgia; Sebewaing, MI Holy Family.
Weisbeck, Paul '70 (SJ) Santa Clara County Sheriffs Dept.; Special Assignment.
Weisbecker, Thomas W. '96 (OM) Columbus, NE St. Bonaventure; Deans; Deans; [M] Elkhorn, NE Apostolic Sodales.
Weisbrod, Daren *l.c.* (GRY)[C] Rolling Prairie, IN Sacred Heart Apostolic School, Inc.
Weiscopf, Daniel J. '90 (BRK) Retired.
Weise, Thomas D. '62 (MOB) Phenix City, AL St. Patrick; Phenix City, AL Mother Mary Parish.
Weise, Thomas L. '02 (JUN) Juneau, AK Cathedral of the Nativity of The Blessed Virgin Mary; Diocesan Consultors; Port Chaplains.
Weisenbeck, Jude *s.d.s.* '60 (MIL)[P] Milwaukee Salvatorian Provincial Offices Retired.
Weisenberger, Gary '77 (SEA) Fife, WA St. Martin of Tours.
Weisenberger, Leon *m.s.c.* '59 (RCK)[G] Aurora, IL MISSIONARIES OF THE SACRED HEART.
Weisenberger, Richard J. '79 (LFT) Gas City, IN Holy Family; Marion, IN St. Paul.
Weisenburger, Rev. Msgr. Edward J. '87 (OKL) Oklahoma City, OK Cathedral of Our Lady of Perpetual Help; Vicar General; Judges; Consultors Archdiocesan; Council of Priests Archdiocesan; Priests' Medical Fund; Vicar General.
Weisensel, Cyril O. '67 (MAD) Hazel Green, WI St. Francis de Sales; Hazel Green, WI St. Joseph.
Weiser, Charles B. '66 (TR) West End, NJ St. Michael.
Weishaar, Leo '84 (MOB)[D] Mobile, AL Providence Hospital.
Weishar, Paul M. '48 (MIL) Retired.
Weisman, Raymond F. '76 (WIL) Salisbury, MD St. Francis De Sales.
Weiss, Earl A. *s.j.* '54 (DET)[K] Clarkston, MI Colombiere Center.

Weiss, Jerome P. '77 (DUL) Grand Rapids, MN St. Joseph; Grand Rapids, MN St. John; Warba, MN St. Paul.
Weiss, Jerome (DUL) College of Consultors.
Weiss, Joseph E. *s.j.* '85 (STP) St. Paul, MN St. Thomas More.
Weiss, Mark E. '04 (HBG) Lancaster, PA St. Philip the Apostle.
Weiss, Peter C. *s.s.j.* '79 (BAL)[S] Baltimore, MD St. Joseph Society of the Sacred Heart House of Central Administration.
Weiss, Peter *s.s.j.* '79 (WDC)[B] Washington, DC St. Joseph's Seminary.
Weiss, Richard '80 (ELP) Retired.
Weiss, Rev. Msgr. Robert E. '73 (BGP) Newtown, CT St. Rose of Lima.
Weiss, Robert F. *s.j.* '59 (STL)[V] St. Louis, MO The Jesuits of the Missouri Province; Saint Louis, MO; [O] St. Louis, MO The Jesuits of the Missouri Province; [O] St. Louis, MO Jesuit Community Corporation at Saint Louis University – Jesuit Hall.
Weiss, Robert *c.p.* '65 (DET)[K] Detroit, MI St. Paul of the Cross Community, Congregation of the Passion.
Weissbeck, Reinhold '72 (DEN) Greeley, CO St. Mary; Deaneries.
Weist, Edward F. '69 (CLV) Litchfield, OH Our Lady Help of Christians Parish; Judges in Second Instance.
Weithman, Raymond *c.ss.r.* '56 (NY)[EE] Esopus, NY Redemptorist Priests and Brothers C.Ss.R. (Province of Baltimore).
Weithman, Robert J. '55 (TOL) Retired.
Weitzel, Eugene J. *c.s.v.* '59 (CHI)[N] Arlington Heights Viatorian Province Center–Clerics of St. Viator.
Weitzel, Stephen D. '90 (HBG) Mechanicsburg, PA Saint Katharine Drexel; Presbyteral Council.
Weitzel, Theodore '68 (JOL) Naperville, IL St. Raphael.
Weixelman, Richard *o.m.i.* '65 (FgM) Washington, DC AMERICAN OBLATE MISSIONS.
Wekerle, Ronald '90 (B) Jerome, ID St. Jerome's; Sun Valley, ID Our Lady of the Snows.
Wekesa, Pius S. '95 (ROC) Spencerport, NY St. John the Evangelist.
Wekesa, Pius S. '95 (R) Roanoke Rapids, NC St. John the Baptist.
Welbers, Rev. Msgr. Thomas '68 (LA) Liturgical Commission.
Welch, Bernard J. '81 (MO) Military Chaplains; Navy Chaplains.
Welch, Christopher J. '94 (ALB) Hancock, NY St. Paul the Apostle; [C] Saratoga Springs, NY Saratoga Central Catholic High School.
Welch, D. Michael '70 (IND) Indianapolis, IN St. Christopher.
Welch, Gregory T. '67 (STP) Edina, MN St. Patrick.
Welch, John A. *m.s.* '93 (FR)[G] Attleboro, MA La Salette Shrine; [I] Attleboro, MA La Salette Retreat Center.
Welch, John E. *m.s.* '60 (NOR) Danielson, CT St. James Retired.
Welch, John F. *o.carm.* '65 (JOL)[L] Darien, IL St. Simon Stock Priory; [L] Darien, IL Carmelite Provincial Office; Darien, IL Provincial Headquarters, Carmelite Provincial Office; [O] Darien, IL Provincial Office of Lay Carmelites and Scapular Center.
Welch, Richard L. *c.ss.r.* '80 (NY) Judges; [EE] New York, NY Redemptorist Priests and Brothers, C.Ss.R.; Associate Judicial Vicar.
Welch, Robert J. *s.j.* '60 (LA)[C] Los Angeles, CA Jesuit Community.
Welch, William J. '55 (GLP) Snowflake, AZ Our Lady of the Snows.
Weldgen, Rev. Msgr. Francis G. '59 (BUF) Retired.
Welding, Brian J. '91 (PIT) Judicial Vicar; Canon and Civil Law Services, Dept. for; Canonical Services, Office for; Assistant Director, Department for Canon and Civil Law Services; Vice Chancellor; Pittsburgh, PA St. Paul Cathedral.
Weldishofer, Bernard J. '92 (CIN) Lebanon, OH St. Francis de Sales.
Weldon, C. Michael *o.f.m.* '81 (MIL)[B] Hales Corners, WI Sacred Heart School of Theology.
Weldon, Eric M. '00 (WCH) Wichita, KS St. Paul Parish; [I] Wichita, KS St. Paul Newman Center (Wichita State University).
Weldon, James '98 (WCH) Kingman, KS St. Patrick.
Weldon, Michael *o.f.m.* '81 (OAK)[M] Oakland Franciscan Friars (Province of St. Barbara).
Weldon, Michael *o.f.m.* '81 (MIL)[P] Provincial Offices of the Franciscan Friars, Assumption BVM Province, Inc.
Weldu, Awte *o.cist.* '80 (TR)[N] Mount Laurel, NJ Cistercian Monastery of Our Lady of Fatima; Tribunal Judges; Mount Laurel, NJ.
Weliams–Figueredo, Esteban '03 (SJN) San Juan, PR Resurreccion del Senor.
Weling, John *s.j.* '81 (ORG)[C] Santa Ana, CA Mater Dei High School; Newport Beach, CA Our Lady of Mount Carmel.
Welk, Thomas *c.pp.s.* '69 (WCH)[F] Wichita, KS Adorers of the Blood of Christ U.S. Region.
Wellar, Thomas '80 (CC) Ingleside, TX Our Lady of the Assumption.
Welle, Anthony R. '07 (ORL) Indialantic, FL Holy Name of Jesus.
Welle, Jacob *m.s.c.* '50 (ALN)[A] Center Valley, PA Sacred Heart Villa, Missionaries of the Sacred Heart.
Wellems, Bruce L. *c.m.f.* '86 (CHI) Oak Park, IL; Chicago, IL Holy Cross/Immaculate Heart of Mary; [N] Oak Park, IL Claretian Missionaries Community Support Trust; [N] Oak Park Claretian Missionaries USA Eastern Province.
Weller, Andre *o.f.m.cap.* '63 (DET) Detroit, MI Province of St. Joseph; [K] Detroit St. Bonaventure Friary.
Weller, Joseph W. '64 (KAL) Retired.
Welles, Timothy J. '06 (LC) Rudolph, WI St. Philip; Wisconsin Rapids, WI St. Lawrence.
Wellman, Rev. Msgr. Dale L. '64 (PEO) Vicariates and Vicars; Moline, IL Sacred Heart; Diocesan College of Consultors; Catholic Women, Council of.
Wellman, Rev. Msgr. Dale '64 (PEO) Clergymen's Aid, Inc.
Wells, James *o.f.m.* '82 (NY)[EE] St. Peter Friary.
Wells, Rev. Msgr. Patrick R. '93 (GAL) Retired.
Wells, Peter B. '91 (TLS) On Duty Outside the Diocese.
Wells, Peter V.B. '84 (PAT) Clifton, NJ St. Clare's.
Wells, Philip J. '83 (SAC) Davis, CA St. James.
Welna, Floyd '50 (SAG) Retired.
Welsch, Gerard R. '66 (STL) Maryland Heights, MO St. John Bosco.
Welschmeyer, Joseph J. '00 (STL) Potosi, MO St. James.
Welsh, Charles A. *s.j.* '72 (FgM) Los Gatos, CA Society of Jesus.
Welsh, Christopher '82 (DET) Royal Oak, MI Beaumont Hospital.
Welsh, Garry A. '01 (OM) On Leave of Absence.
Welsh, Patrick J. '98 (CIN) Cincinnati, OH St. Bartholomew.
Welsh, Patrick J. '00 (PH)[A] Wynnewood, PA Theological Seminary of St. Charles Borromeo, Overbrook.
Welsh, Peter J. '80 (PH) Chester, PA Saint Katharine Drexel.
Welsh, Richard C. '60 (DET) Retired.
Welsh, Robert J. *s.j.* '67 (CLV)[D] Cleveland, OH St. Ignatius High School.
Welsh, Vincent F. '89 (PH) Defenders of the Bond; Norristown, PA St. Francis of Assisi.
Welsh, William P. '60 (CHI) Retired.
Welstead, Flavian *o.f.m.cap.* '67 (SFR) Burlingame, CA Our Lady of Angels.
Welter, Brian T. '05 (CHI) Orland Hills, IL St. Elizabeth Seton.
Weltin, Richard W. '83 (SFD) Decatur, IL Our Lady of Lourdes; Decatur, IL St. Thomas the Apostle; Comite Diocesano de Ministerio Hispano – Diocesan Committee for Hispanic Ministry.
Welton, Arthur T. '69 (NY) Absent on Sick Leave.
Welzbacher, George A. '51 (STP) St. Paul, MN St. John of St. Paul; Censores Librorum.
Wempe, Richard C. '52 (KCK) Retired.
Wenani, Kizito '08 (SPC) Poplar Bluff, MO Sacred Heart.
Wendel, Alfred W. '78 (MO) Army Chaplains.
Wendel, Arthur G. *c.ss.r.* (NY) New York, NY Most Holy Redeemer.
Wendel, Fred W. '78 (ATL) Fort McPherson, GA Office of the Garrison Chaplain; Military Chaplains.
Wendel, Paul G. *c.s.c.* '55 (FTW)[H] Holy Cross House.
Wendelken, Robert M. '61 (CLV) Solon, OH St. Rita; Lyndhurst, OH St. Clare; Judges Retired.
Wendell, Arthur *c.ss.r.* (NY)[II] Clinton Corners, NY Catholic Women's Union of New York, Inc.
Wendell, Richard '06 (MIL) Reeseville, WI Holy Family; Reeseville, WI St. John; Reeseville, WI St. Columbkille.
Wenderoth, Joseph R. '62 (BAL) Retired.
Wendler, Patrick '08 (MAD) Waunakee, WI St. John the Baptist.
Wendling, Francis *o.f.m.* '63 (CIN)[N] Cincinnati St. Francis Seraph Friary.
Wendling, Mark *s.o.l.t.* '03 (CC)[G] Robstown, TX Society of Our Lady of the Most Holy Trinity.
Wendrychowicz, Rev. Msgr. John B. '73 (PH) Archdiocesan Boy Scouts; Sellersville, PA St. Agnes.
Wendt, Patrick '79 (MIL) Port Washington, WI St. Mary; Saukville, WI Immaculate Conception; Port Washington, WI St. Peter of Alcantara.
Wendzikowski, Rev. Msgr. Mecislaus S. '59 (BUF) Retired.
Wenger, Sean A. *c.c.* '95 (GAL) Houston, TX Our Lady of Mt. Carmel.
Wenig, Laurin J. '73 (MIL) Elm Grove, WI St. Mary's Visitation.
Wenke, Leonard C. '79 (CIN) Cincinnati, OH St. Anthony; Priest Councilors; Vicarri Foranei (Deans); Priests' Personnel Director.
Wenninger, Magnus *o.s.b.* '45 (SCL)[I] Collegeville, MN St. John's Abbey, of the Order of St. Benedict.
Wensing, Michael '76 (SFS) Diocesan Consultors; On Duty Outside the Diocese.
Wenthe, Christopher T. '03 (STP) Delano, MN St. Joseph; Delano, MN St. Peter.
Wentink, William R. '70 (RCK)[D] East Peoria, IL Saint Anthony Medical Center; Special Assignment.
Wentz, Aelred W. *o.c.s.o.* '85 (ROC)[J] Piffard, NY Abbey of the Genesee.
Wenz, Robert '82 (CLV) Northfield, OH St. Barnabas.
Wenzel, James *o.s.a.* '56 (BO)[C] North Andover, MA Merrimack College.
Wenzel, Timothy '66 (SCL) Rice, MN Immaculate Conception; Sauk Rapids, MN Annunciation.
Wenzinger, George E. '78 (TOL) Leipsic, OH St. Mary; St. George Deanery; College of Consultors.
Wenzinger, Mark Edward *o.s.b.* '95 (GBG)[G] Latrobe, PA Saint Vincent Archabbey.
Wenzinger, Rev. Msgr. Robert D. '82 (FRS) Fresno, CA St. Anthony of Padua; Personnel Board.
Werbicki, Walter '57 (BUF) Lakeview Shock Incarceration Correctional Facility; Dunkirk, NY St. Elizabeth Ann Seton.
Weria, Theobold *a.l.c.p.* '98 (SP) Zephyrhills, FL St. Joseph Catholic Church.
Werkhoven, Michael E. '02 (MEM) Humboldt, TN St. Matthew Mission; Presbyteral Council; Search; Humboldt, TN Sacred Heart.
Werling, Wolf '99 (JOL)[F] Momence, IL Good Shepherd Manor.
Werner, Benjamin '64 (LAN) Retired.
Werner, Rev. Msgr. Cyril J. '45 (OM) Retired.
Werner, George J. *s.m.m.* '57 (RVC)[M] Bay Shore, NY Montfort Missionaries; Counselors:.
Werner, Gerald *o.c.d.* '74 (SR)[K] Oakville, CA Carmelite House of Prayer; [L] Oakville, CA Carmelite House of Prayer.
Werner, John J. '00 (MET) Old Bridge, NJ St. Ambrose.
Werner, John P. '51 (COV) Retired.
Werner, Jon K. '82 (SY) Syracuse, NY Holy Trinity; Syracuse, NY St. John the Baptist; Priests' Personnel Committee.
Werner, Justin '58 (GB) Retired.
Werner, Leo E. '51 (WH) Retired.
Werner, Steven (SPK)[N] Pullman, WA "St. Thomas More Catholic Student Center" – Washington State University.
Werning, David H. '98 (WDC) Washington, DC Our Lady of Victory.
Wertanen, Steven A. '97 (DET) Royal Oak, MI St. Mary; Ferndale, MI St. James.
Werth, Alvin '59 (SAL) Retired.
Werth, Charles M. '53 (BUF) Retired.
Werth, Frederick H. '07 (CHL) Mars Hill, NC St. Andrew the Apostle.
Werth, Joshua '09 (SAL) Hays, KS Immaculate Heart of Mary Parish.
Werth, Loren J. '56 (SAL) Board of Trustees Retired.
Werth, Robert Thomas '79 (ROC) Rochester, NY Peace of Christ Roman Catholic Parish of Rochester, NY; Monroe County Jail.
Wertin, Matthew '06 (PBL) Pueblo, CO Our Lady of Mt. Carmel.
Wertman, Raymond '72 (OG) On Duty Outside the Diocese.
Wertz, Jerry *s.d.b.* '88 (SFR)[N] San Francisco, CA Salesian Provincial Residence.
Wesdock, Thomas J. '00 (PBR) Uniontown, PA St. John the Baptist.
Wesely, Eugene L. '57 (CR) Detroit Lakes, MN Retired.
Wesely, Mark '93 (SAL) Herington, KS St. Columba Parish; Herington, KS St. John the Evangelist Parish; Herington, KS St. Phillip Parish; Vicariate Representatives; Council of Priests.
Wesley, Andrew '80 (DET) Hamtramck, MI St. Ladislaus; Detroit, MI Transfiguration–Our Lady Help of Christians.
Wesley, Shaun C. '05 (LR) Berryville, AR St. Anne; Office of Worship; Eureka Springs, AR St. Elizabeth of Hungary.
Weslin, Norman V. *o.s.* '86 (PCE) On Duty Outside the Diocese.
Wesloh, Ferdinand J. '64 (STL) Hazelwood, MO St. Martin de Porres.
Wesnofske, Matthias *o.f.m.cap.* '67 (NY) New York, NY St. John the Baptist.
Wesoloski, Richard J. '72 (PIT) Pittsburgh, PA St. Bernard.
Wesolowski, Anthony P. *o.s.b.* '72 (SAV)[B] Savannah, GA Benedictine Military School; [E] Savannah, GA The Benedictine Priory.
Wesolowski, Edmund C. '48 (PH) Retired.
Wesolowski, Tomasz '02 (PHX) On Leave.
Wesolowski, Victor R. '08 (COL) Corning, OH St. Bernard; New Lexington, OH Church of the Atonement; New Lexington, OH St. Patrick; New Lexington, OH St. Rose of Lima.
Wessel, John F. '57 (CLV) Translators Retired.
Wessell, Harold (ALB) Fort Edward, NY St. Joseph.
Wesselsky, Rev. Msgr. Emil J. '56 (SAT) San Antonio, TX St. Henry.
Wessling, Floyd A. '64 (OM) Retired.
Wessling, John E. '58 (CIN)[F] Cincinnati, OH Ursuline Academy of Cincinnati; Imprimatur Censors Retired.
West, Don J. '90 (CIN) West Chester, OH St. John.

West, Gerald F. '59 (BAL)[T] Baltimore, MD St. Clare of Assisi, Inc. Retired.
West, Gregory '91 (CHR) Absent On Leave.
West, James P. '86 (LR) North Little Rock, AR Immaculate Conception.
West, Joseph *o.f.m.conv.* '92 (CLV) Lorain, OH St. Anthony of Padua.
West, Rev. Msgr. Mauricio W. '79 (CHL) Special Assignment; [Q] Charlotte, NC Catholic Diocese of Charlotte Housing Corp.; Vicar General, Chancellor, and Moderator of the Curia; Diocesan Consultors; Permanent Diaconate.
West, Patrick J. '81 (BRK) Brooklyn, NY Our Lady of Solace; Parish Services Corp.; Peter Turner Insurance Co.; Diocesan Insurance Committee.
West, Peter J. '91 (NY) Staten Island, NY Immaculate Conception.
West, Peter '91 (NEW) On Duty Outside the Archdiocese.
West, Stephen C. '79 (GBG) Derry, PA St. Joseph; New Derry, PA St. Martin.
West, Thomas B. *o.f.m.* '86 (SFR)[S] San Francisco, CA St. Anthony Foundation; San Francisco, CA St. Boniface.
West, Thomas *o.f.m.* '86 (OAK)[A] Berkeley, CA Franciscan School of Theology.
West, William '70 (HRT)[H] New Haven, CT Hospital of St. Raphael.
West, Rev. Msgr. Willis W. '63 (NOR) Retired.
Westbrook, J. Severyn '62 (SPK) Retired.
Westcott, Matthew J. '07 (BO) Scituate, MA St. Mary of the Nativity.
Wester, Charles H. '59 (MIL) Eden, WI Shepherd of the Hills (Good Shepherd) Retired.
Wester, Donald R. '78 (STL) St. Peters, MO All Saints.
Westerhoff, Ralph A. '62 (CIN) Retired.
Westfall, Joseph B. '93 (MO) On Duty Outside the Diocese; DEPARTMENT OF VETERANS AFFAIRS HOSPITALS AND CHAPLAINS.
Westfield, Carlton J. '71 (BUF) Fredonia, NY St. Anthony.
Westhoven, Thomas *s.c.j.* '66 (MIL)[P] Franklin, WI Villa Maria.
Weston, Michael D. '02 (WDC) On Duty Outside the Diocese; [R] Washington, DC Basilica of the National Shrine of the Immaculate Conception.
Weston, Thomas C. *s.j.* '78 (OAK)[M] Oakland, CA Jesuit Fathers and Brothers.
Westray, Kenneth M. '81 (SFR) San Rafael, CA St. Isabella; African American Ministry.
Wetmore, John J. '73 (STL) On Medical Leave.
Wetta, Augustine *o.s.b.* '03 (STL)[F] Creve Coeur, MO St. Louis Priory School; [O] St. Louis, MO The Abbey of St. Mary and St. Louis.
Wetter, Rev. Msgr. Richard L. '57 (BUF)[O] Tonawanda, NY O'Hara Residence Retired.
Wetterer, Rev. Msgr. Edward V. '64 (BRK) Flushing, NY St. Michael.
Wetterholm, Lawrence E. '56 (BO) Senior Priests. Retired.
Wetzel, Steven P. *o.s.f.s.* '03 (PH) Philadelphia, PA St. Joachim.
Wetzler, Daniel '63 (SPK) Charismatic Renewal Retired.
Wevita, Bede '91 (LAV) North Las Vegas, NV St. John Neumann; Presbyteral Council for the Diocese of Las Vegas.
Wewers, William *o.s.b.* '67 (LR) Clarksville, AR Holy Redeemer.
Wey, Richard '50 (SCL) Retired.
Weyker, James *s.d.s.* '69 (FgM) Milwaukee, WI SALVATORIAN MISSIONS.
Weymes, Gerald '74 (ARL) Chantilly, VA St. Timothy.
Weyne, Marie Joseph '85 (LAR)[D] Laredo, TX St. John Priory, F.J.
Weyne, Mary Joseph '85 (LAR)[F] Laredo, TX Holy Spirit Retreat and Conference Center.
Weyrens, Ronald '82 (SCL) Sauk Rapids, MN Sacred Heart; Diocesan Finance Council.
Whalen, Daniel W. '00 (PIT) Pittsburgh, PA Holy Spirit; Pittsburgh, PA St. Nicholas; Priest Council; Clergy Personnel Board.
Whalen, David *o.s.f.s.* '71 (TOL)[I] Toledo, OH Provincial Residence; Toledo, OH; [C] Toledo, OH St. Francis de Sales High School; Toledo, OH Gesu.
Whalen, Rev. Msgr. Edmund J. '84 (NY) Staten Island, NY St. Joseph, St. Thomas; [II] Staten Island, NY North American College of Rome, Alumni Assoc. of; Canon 1742 Panel of Pastors.
Whalen, Edward J. *m.m.* '61 (FgM) Maryknoll, NY MARYKNOLL.
Whalen, John J. '69 (DAV) Retired.
Whalen, John '94 (BUR) Retired.
Whalen, Joseph T. '71 (ALN) Barnesville, PA St. Richard.
Whalen, Joseph *m.s.* '89 (NOR) Danielson, CT St. James Retired.
Whalen, Joseph '99 (STP) Fridley, MN St. William; Fairview University Medical Center.
Whalen, Michael D. *c.m.* '83 (BRK)[T] Jamaica, NY St. Vincent's House.
Whalen, Paul A. '82 (GBG) Retired.
Whalen, Robert B. '51 (BUR) Retired.
Whalen, Rev. Msgr. Thomas J. '67 (BGP) Shelton, CT St. Margaret Mary.
Whalen, Timothy F. '78 (PIT) On Duty Outside the Diocese.
Whalen, Timothy '78 (DET)[A] Orchard Lake, MI SS. Cyril and Methodius Seminary; [E] Orchard Lake, MI St. Mary's Preparatory.
Whalen, William '60 (MIL) Retired.
Wharff, Jonah *o.c.s.o.* '08 (DUB)[K] Peosta, IA New Melleray Abbey, Order of Cistercians of the Strict Observance.
Wharton, Paul J. '82 (WH) Bluefield, WV Sacred Heart; Princeton, WV Sacred Heart.
Whatley, Christopher '70 (BAL) Catonsville, MD St. Mark; Presbyteral Council.
Whatley, Francis *o.ss.t.* (LA) Hospital Chaplains.
Whatley, Frank *o.ss.t.* (BAL)[S] The Trinitarians in California.
Whatley, Frank *o.ss.t.* '88 (LA) Los Angeles, CA St. Agatha.
Whealen, Martin J. *s.j.* '62 (DEN)[N] Denver, CO Xavier Jesuit Center.
Wheatley, Carroll '75 (OWN) Retired.
Wheatley, Charles '68 (MIL) Retired.
Wheatley, Dennis *o.f.m.* '84 (BO) Waltham, MA Sacred Heart; Definitors:.
Wheatley, Herbert '67 (P)[J] Portland, OR Providence Portland Medical Center.
Wheatley, R. Carroll (MEM)[C] Jackson, TN Sacred Heart of Jesus High School.
Wheaton, Michael F. '03 (CHI) Flossmoor, IL Infant Jesus of Prague.
Wheaton, William F. '92 (SLC) Moab, UT Saint Pius X LLC 244; Monticello, UT Saint Joseph LLC 229.
Whedbee, Dominic *o.c.s.o.* '77 (WOR)[O] Spencer, MA St. Joseph's Abbey.
Whedbee, George *c.m.f.* '69 (LA)[V] San Gabriel, CA Claretian Missionaries – Western Province, Inc.
Wheelahan, Michael '80 (OKL) Medford, OK St. Mary's; Scouting.
Wheelan, Mark *s.o.l.t.* '04 (CC)[G] Robstown, TX Society of Our Lady of the Most Holy Trinity.
Wheelan, Mark *s.o.l.t.* '04 (FAR) St. John, ND St. Benedict's Church of Belcourt; St. John, ND St. John's Church of St. John; Belcourt, ND St. Benedict.
Wheeland, Thomas H. '66 (ROC) Rochester, NY Holy Cross; Clergy Relief Society; Pension Committee (Lay and Priests).
Wheeler, Ambrose *c.s.c.* (FTW)[H] Notre Dame Congregation of Holy Cross, Indiana Province, Provincial House.
Wheeler, Arthur F. *c.s.c.* '84 (P)[B] University of Portland; [L] Portland, OR Holy Cross Fathers & Brothers, C.S.C. – University of Portland.
Wheeler, Arthur *c.s.c.* (FTW)[H] Notre Dame Congregation of Holy Cross, Indiana Province, Provincial House.
Wheeler, Charles '79 (JOL) Kankakee, IL St. Rose of Lima; Deans.
Wheeler, Clarence *m.s.* '54 (JC) Retired.
Wheeler, Daniel '75 (LAN) Clinton, MI St. Dominic Oratory; Tecumseh, MI St. Elizabeth; Regional Vicars; Finance Council; College of Consultors.
Wheeler, James D. *s.j.* '54 (KC)[J] Kansas City, MO Rockhurst Jesuit Community.
Wheeler, James J. *s.j.* '68 (NY)[EE] New York, NY Murray–Weigel Hall.
Wheeler, James J. *s.j.* '68 (RVC)[O] Patchogue, NY St. Joseph's Prayer Center.
Wheeler, James *o.f.m.* '66 (SFD) Quincy, IL St. Francis Solanus; [L] Quincy, IL St. Francis Solanus Friary.
Wheeler, Thomas F.X. *s.j.* '62 (PH)[Y] Merion Station St. Alphonsus House.
Wheeler, Wayne B. '79 (GR) Ludington, MI St. Simon's; Ludington, MI St. Stanislaus.
Wheelock, Joseph P. '96 (OG) Absent on Sick Leave, Disabled.
Whelan, Charles M. *s.j.* '58 (NY)[EE] New York, NY "America;" Residence and publication office of the America Press.
Whelan, Daniel '04 (L) Albany, KY Emmanuel Catholic.
Whelan, Dennis '65 (RVC) Franklin Square, NY St. Catherine of Sienna.
Whelan, Fintan *o.f.m.cap.* '60 (SFR)[N] Burlingame, CA Capuchin Provincial House.
Whelan, James J. '73 (PH) West Chester, PA SS. Peter and Paul.
Whelan, James P. '93 (NEW) Weehawken, NJ St. Lawrence's; Central Hudson Region Deanery 9.
Whelan, John F. (RVC) Retired.
Whelan, Paul *o.m.i.* (LAR) Eagle Pass, TX Sacred Heart.
Whelan, Robert J. '83 (BRK) Bayside, NY Our Lady of the Blessed Sacrament.
Whelan, Steven *s.d.b.* '69 (OAK)[M] Berkeley Salesians of Don Bosco.
Whelan, Rev. Msgr. William S. '57 (OM)[M] Omaha, NE Cor Unum Family Inc. Retired.
Whelton, Rev. Msgr. Daniel P. '70 (SR) Cotati, CA St. Joseph; Vicar for Priests; Judicial Vicar; Board of Consultors; Diocesan Judges; Priests' Council.
Whetstone, Richard J. '83 (PBR) Promoter of Justice.
Whetstone, Richard (PHU) Adjunct Judicial Vicars.
Whetstone, Richard '83 (Y) Poland, OH Holy Family.
Whewell, Glenn *s.o.l.t.* '01 (CC)[G] Robstown, TX Society of Our Lady of the Most Holy Trinity.
Whipple, Donald W. *c.s.c.* '57 (FR)[G] North Dartmouth, MA Holy Cross Residence Retired.
Whistle, Brad '81 (OWN) Owensboro, KY Our Lady of Lourdes; Committee for Administration.
Whitaker, Cyril W. '09 (CIN) Cincinnati, OH St. Francis Xavier.
White, Anthony J. '55 (NO) Retired.
White, Bernard C. '52 (CHI) Elmwood Park, IL St. Celestine Retired.
White, Bernard L. '77 (ALT) Dudley, PA Immaculate Conception.
White, Charles H. '65 (BRK) Far Rockaway, NY St. Mary Star of the Sea and St. Gertrude Retired.
White, Charles '09 (DET) Plymouth, MI Our Lady of Good Counsel.
White, Cosmas *o.s.b.* '61 (P)[L] St. Benedict, OR Mt. Angel Abbey.
White, Daniel E. '04 (BUR) Diocesan Consultors; Vocations and Seminarians; Chancery Office; Secretary to the Most Rev. Bishop; Deans; Diocesan Coordinator of the Vietnamese Ministry; Office of Communications; Diocesan Master of Ceremonies; Members Ex Officio; Consultants; Office of Permanent Diaconate Ministry; Burlington, VT St. Joseph's Co–Cathedral.
White, Daniel *s.j.* '01 (LAF)[A] Grand Coteau, LA St. Charles College.
White, David F. *s.j.* '67 (BUF)[O] Buffalo, NY Canisius Jesuit Community Inc.
White, David P. '94 (BO) Westford, MA St. Catherine of Alexandria.
White, Denis '67 (JOL) Retired.
White, Edward Goodwin '05 (SEA) Renton, WA St. Stephen the Martyr.
White, Francis P. *c.s.v.* '44 (CHI)[N] Arlington Heights, IL Viatorian Province Center–Clerics of St. Viator.
White, Gale '56 (DAL) Retired.
White, James D. '69 (TLS) Retired.
White, Rev. Msgr. James E. '83 (NY) Bronx, NY Blessed Sacrament.
White, James R. '80 (NEW) Hohokus, NJ St. Luke's.
White, James *s.j.* '71 (KCK) Minister to Priests.
White, James *c.ss.r.* '81 (MIL)[S] Oconomowoc, WI The Redemptorist Retreat Center.
White, John R. '81 (CIN) Greenville, OH St. Mary; Judges.
White, John V. *s.j.* '65 (CLV)[D] Cuyahoga Falls, OH Walsh Jesuit High School.
White, John '83 (RVC) Leave of Absence.
White, Joseph M. '91 (BO) South Boston, MA St. Vincent de Paul.
White, Kenneth R. '68 (PIT) Aspinwall, PA St. Scholastica.
White, Kevin R. *s.j.* '99 (BO)[U] Weston, MA Campion Jesuit Community.
White, Rev. Msgr. Lawrence E. '70 (CC) Deans; College of Consultors; Personnel Board – Priests; Presbyteral Council; Corpus Christi, TX SS. Cyril and Methodius.
White, Rev. Msgr. Leo J. '56 (BRK) Brooklyn, NY Holy Family–Saint Thomas Aquinas Retired.
White, Mark D. '03 (WDC) Washington, DC Holy Comforter—St. Cyprian.
White, Michael J. '84 (BAL) Timonium, MD Church of the Nativity.
White, Michael J. '48 (BIR) Birmingham, AL Our Lady of the Valley Retired.
White, Michael *c.ss.p.* '83 (SD)[B] University of San Diego; [B] University of San Diego.
White, Morgan '02 (TYL) Clarksville, TX St. Joseph; Paris, TX Our Lady of Victory; Diocesan Liturgical Commission.
White, Nathan R. '02 (STO) Diamond Springs, CA Retired.
White, Paul C. '89 (RCK) Harvard, IL St. Joseph.
White, Paul R. *c.pp.s.* '53 (LFT) Rensselaer, IN St. Francis Solano; Rensselaer, IN St. Henry; [A] Rensselaer, IN Saint Joseph's College Retired.
White, Paul T. '83 (PT) Mary Esther, FL St. Peter; Liturgy, Office of; Permanent Deacon Formation Team; Building & Renovation, Diocesan Commission for.
White, Paul *s.s.c.* '58 (LA)[P] Los Angeles, CA Columban Fathers, Procure House.
White, Paul '83 (PT) Permanent Deacon Formation Board.
White, Paul *s.s.c.* '58 (OM)[K] St. Columbans, NE Missionary Society of St. Columban.
White, Peter H. '62 (WOR) Leicester, MA St. Aloysius–St. Jude.
White, Richard *c.m.f.* '79 (CHI)[N] Oak Park Claretian Missionaries USA Eastern Province.
White, Robert A. *s.j.* '62 (FgM) St. Louis, MO Society of Jesus.

White, Robert Kevin '61 (SFR) Tomales, CA Church of the Assumption.
White, Robert L. '74 (STP) Victoria, MN St. Victoria; Deanery 10.
White, Robert S. *c.s.s.* '73 (SPR) Springfield, MA Our Lady of Mt. Carmel; Waltham, MA.
White, Robert '70 (SD) On Duty Outside the Diocese.
White, Rodney '03 (SAN) San Angelo, TX St. Joseph.
White, Roger *o.f.m.cap.* (BAL)[S] Baltimore, MD St. Ambrose Friary; Baltimore, MD Transfiguration Catholic Community; Baltimore, MD St. Ambrose.
White, Seth Thomas Joseph *o.p.* '08 (WDC)[B] Washington, DC Dominican House of Studies.
White, Stephen C. '86 (PH) Retired.
White, Stephen '98 (DUL) Retired.
White, Stephen *m.s.c.* '46 (SAT)[L] San Antonio, TX Missionaries of the Sacred Heart.
White, Thomas J. '59 (JOL) Wheaton, IL St. Daniel the Prophet Church Retired.
White, Thomas '64 (BLX) Ocean Springs, MS St. Alphonsus.
White, Thomas '78 (LA) Palmdale, CA St. Mary; Lancaster, CA California State Prison, L.A. County.
White, William A. '90 (NY) Pine Plains, NY St. Anthony; Bangall, NY Immaculate Conception.
Whited, Rev. Msgr. Walter M. '66 (STL) Richmond Heights, MO Immacolata.
Whitehead, Joseph '84 (STA) Absent or Sick Leave.
Whiteing, Richard J. '80 (OM) Fullerton, NE St. Peter; Fullerton, NE St. Peter.
Whiteside, Daniel '92 (CHI) Oak Park, IL St. Catherine of Siena–St. Lucy.
Whiteside, David '97 (PEO) Bloomington, IL St. Patrick's.
Whitestone, David A. '89 (ARL) Fairfax, VA St. Leo's; Diocesan Judges; Diocesan Consultors.
Whitley, John R. *c.s.b.* '54 (GAL)[O] Houston, TX Residence of the Basilian Fathers of the University of St. Thomas.
Whitley, Rufus J. *o.m.i.* '76 (CHI)[W] Chicago, IL Oblates for International Pastoral; Members.
Whitman, Andrew P. *s.j.* '63 (TUC)[D] Tucson, AZ Jesuit Community of the Vatican Observatory.
Whitman, Dan G. '83 (KNX) Jefferson City, TN Holy Trinity Catholic Church; [K] Knoxville, TN Diocesan Council of Catholic Women.
Whitman, David R. '05 (CHR) Summerton, SC St. Mary; Santee, SC St. Ann.
Whitman, Glenn R. '75 (E) Sharon, PA St. Joseph; Priest Personnel Board.
Whitman, Mark '95 (STL) Arnold, MO Immaculate Conception.
Whitman, Thomas J. '87 (E) Waterford, PA All Saints.
Whitmore, James R. *m.m.* '59 (NY)[EE] Retired.
Whitmore, Rev. Msgr. Paul E. '54 (OG) Watertown, NY Holy Family Retired.
Whitney, John *s.j.* (SEA) Seattle, WA St. Joseph; [L] Seattle, WA Jesuit House, Seattle.
Whitney, Patrick J. '68 (RVC) Port Washington, NY St. Peter of Alcantara; Priests' Personnel Assignment Board.
Whitney, Rev. Msgr. Paul J. '58 (BUF) Retired.
Whitson, Robley E. '58 (NY) Retired.
Whitt, Dwight Reginald *o.p.* '76 (STP)[C] St. Paul, MN University of St. Thomas.
Whittaker, Kenneth '77 (MIA) Retired.
Whittel, Joseph B. '03 (NOR) Quaker Hill, CT Our Lady of Perpetual Help; Justice & Peace, Catholic Action for; Commission for Human Life and Justice; Members; Vicar for Ministry; Advisory Ministry Evaluation Committee.
Whitten, Carlton E. *s.j.* '61 (SJ)[M] Los Gatos, CA Sacred Heart Jesuit Center.
Whittier, William O. '61 (STP) Retired.
Whittingham, Jose '70 (SD) San Ysidro, CA Our Lady of Mt. Carmel.
Whittington, Justin *s.j.* '99 (ALN)[A] Wernersville, PA Jesuit Center–Jesuit Community.
Whittington, Kenneth L. '88 (CHL) Morganton, NC St. Charles Borromeo.
Whittington, Paul De Porres *o.p.* (CHI) Chicago, IL St. Benedict the African (West).
Whittington, Shaun P. '05 (IND) Osgood, IN St. John; Osgood, IN St. Mary Magdalen.
Whorton, David '98 (LA) Pasadena, CA St. Philip the Apostle.
Whorton, Jeffrey T. '08 (MO) Army National Guard Chaplains.
Whyte, Edmond F. '64 (MIA) Southwest Ranches, FL St. Mark.
Whyte, Michael G. '03 (HRT) West Simsbury, CT St. Catherine of Siena.
Wiant, George '61 (ROC) Penn Yan, NY Our Lady of the Lakes Catholic Community Retired.
Wiatrowski, Ralph E. '74 (CLV) Northfield, OH St. Barnabas; Vicars General; Judges in Second Instance.
Wibers, Rev. Msgr. Michael J. '72 (JC) Buildings and Properties.
Wible, Charles M. '96 (BAL) Abingdon, MD St. Francis de Sales.
Wichlan, David L. '57 (STL) St. Louis, MO St. Rita; Spiritual Directors.
Wichman, Edwin J. '80 (PIT) Pittsburgh, PA St. Wendelin.
Wichmanowski, Walter F. '52 (PIT) Retired.
Wickenhauser, Gerald M. *m.m.* '62 (NY)[EE] Retired.
Wicker, Paul F. '63 (COS) Colorado Springs, CO Holy Apostles; Metro–North Deanery (Colorado Springs); Calhan, CO St. Michael's; Vicars Forane.
Wickersham, James A. '08 (OKL) Oklahoma City, OK St. Charles Borromeo; [B] Oklahoma City, OK Bishop McGuinness Catholic High School.
Wickham, William E. *c.s.c.* '81 (P) Portland, OR Department of Veterans' Affairs Medical Center[B]; [L] Portland, OR Holy Cross Fathers & Brothers, C.S.C. – University of Portland.
Wickham, William E. *c.s.c.* '81 (MO) DEPARTMENT OF VETERANS AFFAIRS HOSPITALS AND CHAPLAINS.
Wickham, William *c.s.c.* (FTW)[H] Notre Dame Congregation of Holy Cross, Indiana Province, Provincial House.
Wicklum, Paul R. '61 (LFT) Retired.
Wickowski, Leroy A. '66 (CHI) River Forest, IL St. Luke.
Wickrematunge, Vernon P. '87 (NY) Peekskill, NY Assumption.
Wicks, W. Jared *s.j.* '62 (CLV)[B] University Heights, OH John Carroll Jesuit Community.
Widiatmojo, Stephanus Heruyanto '81 (LA) Monterey Park, CA St. Stephen Martyr.
Widmann, Phillip A. '77 (FTW) Fort Wayne, IN St. Mary; Fort Wayne, IN St. Peter; [K] Fort Wayne, IN Cathedral Museum; Retired Clergy Committee.
Widner, Thomas C. *s.j.* '69 (IND)[D] Indianapolis, IN Brebeuf Jesuit Preparatory School, Inc.
Widomski, Stanislaus *o.f.m.* '62 (FgM) New York, NY Holy Name Province.
Wieber, Donald A. '57 (KAL) Retired.
Wiecek, Ronald *c.pp.s.* '71 (MRY) Special Assignment; Salinas, CA Sacred Heart.
Wieczorek, Edward R. '65 (Y) Mogadore, OH St. Joseph.
Wieczorek, Matthew S. '57 (SY) Endicott, NY St. Casimir.
Wiedel, Thomas L. '90 (LIN) Steinauer, NE St. Anthony.
Wiederholt, Clarence E. '55 (JC) Retired.
Wiederholt, Thomas W. '63 (KC) Retired.
Wiedmann, Paul A. '63 (PH) Retired.
Wiegand, William R. '05 (DAV)[J] Davenport, IA St. Vincent Center Retired.
Wieging, James F. '67 (DET) River Rouge, MI Our Lady of Lourdes.
Wieladek, Waldemar *c.ss.r.* (CHI) Cicero, IL St. Mary of Czestochowa.
Wieland, Dennis J. '91 (CR) On Duty Outside the Diocese.
Wieland, Dennis J. '91 (MIL) Menomonee Falls, WI St. Anthony.
Wielebski, John T. '78 (BAL) Laurel, MD Resurrection of Our Lord.
Wielgus, Rev. Msgr. Bronislaw '62 (NEW) Linden, NJ St. Theresa of the Child Jesus.
Wieliczko, Andrzej '99 (MET) Belvidere, NJ St. Patrick.
Wieliczko, Krysztof *o.s.p.p.e.* (NOR) Rockville, CT St. Joseph.
Wieling, Raymond P. '49 (SC) Retired.
Wielinski, Alan '84 (SCL) St. Cloud, MN St. Paul; St. Cloud, MN St. Peter.
Wiener, Michael K. '99 (STL) St. Louis, MO Oratory of St. Francis de Sales.
Wienhoff, Paul R. '78 (BEL) Dupo, IL Sacred Heart of Jesus; Promoter Justitiae; Defensores Vinculi; Cahokia, IL Holy Family; Diocesan Consultors.
Wiera, Stefan '68 (SAT) Pleasanton, TX St. Luke–Loire.
Wierichs, Paul *c.p.* '78 (PMB)[H] North Palm Beach, FL Our Lady of Florida Spiritual Center; Elected Members.
Wierzba, Alan P. '01 (LC) Wisconsin Rapids, WI Our Lady, Queen of Heaven; Wisconsin Rapids, WI SS. Peter and Paul; Ex Officio.
Wierzbicki, Melvin *o.f.m.* '53 (GB)[J] Pulaski, WI Friary.
Wierzchowski, Marian *s.a.c.* (BRK) Brooklyn, NY St. Frances de Chantal.
Wiese, Rev. Msgr. Melvern A. '57 (OM) Retired.
Wiese, Miro *o.f.m.* '57 (GAY) Indian River, MI Cross in the Woods Catholic Shrine.
Wiese, Stephen *s.c.j.* '63 (MIL)[P] Franklin, WI Villa Maria.
Wieseler, Larry '69 (BWN) Rio Grande City, TX Starr County Memorial Hospital Retired.
Wiesenbaugh, Robert *s.j.* '71 (R) Raleigh, NC St. Raphael the Archangel; [F] Raleigh Jesuit Community.
Wieser, Stanley '68 (SCL) Elizabeth, MN St. Elizabeth; Pelican Rapids, MN St. Leonard's; Diocesan Priests Pension Plan Trustees; Diocesan Consultors.
Wieslaw, Strzadala *s.d.s.* '90 (NEW)[M] Verona, NJ The Salvatorian Fathers.
Wiesmann, Gary '83 (MIA)[J] Fort Lauderdale, FL Holy Cross Hospital.
Wiesner, Mark '95 (OAK) Oakland, CA St. Augustine.
Wieszczek, Rudolph *o.f.m.* (MIL)[P] Burlington, WI Queen of Peace Friary.
Wietensteiner, Joseph M. '66 (SPK) Retired.
Wiethorn, William *o.f.m.cap.* '66 (CLV) Cleveland, OH Conversion of St. Paul; [N] Cleveland, OH St. Paul Friary.
Wigand, William '83 (STL) Ste. Genevieve, MO Our Lady, Help of Christians.
Wigger, Brian K. '97 (COV) Fort Wright, KY St. Agnes; [C] Park Hills, KY Notre Dame Academy, Inc.
Wiggins, Frank '86 (RIC) Hopewell, VA St. James Church.
Wiggins, Timothy S. '02 (NY) White Plains, NY St. John the Evangelist.
Wigginton, Ellsworth T. '76 (FWT) Fort Worth, TX St. Paul the Apostle.
Wight, Jonathan C. '86 (TOL) Bellevue, OH Immaculate Conception.
Wightman, Paul *o.m.i.* '55 (SPC) Ava, MO Immaculate Heart of Mary; Mountain Grove, MO Sacred Heart.
Wightman, William R. *s.m.* '59 (STL) St. Louis, MO Our Lady of the Pillar; [O] St. Louis, MO Marianist Community, Our Lady of the Pillar Parish.
Wikarski, Tomasz '06 (DEN) Frisco, CO St. Mary.
Wiktor, Ronald A. *c.m.* '63 (HRT)[L] Manchester DePaul Provincial Residence.
Wiktorek, Wladyslaw '81 (MET) Perth Amboy, NJ Holy Trinity.
Wilber, Stewart '91 (ATL) Special or Other (Arch)Diocesan Assignment.
Wilbers, Rev. Msgr. Michael J. '72 (JC) Lake Ozark, MO Our Lady of the Lake; Episcopal Vicars; Diocesan Consultors; Personnel Board; Ex Officio Members; Finance Committee; Board of Trustees.
Wilborn, Jeffrey '00 (DEN) Denver, CO St. Mary Magdalene; Lakewood, CO Our Lady of Fatima.
Wilbricht, Stephen S. *c.s.c.* '97 (FTW)[H] Notre Dame Congregation of Holy Cross, Indiana Province, Provincial House.
Wilbricht, Stephen S. *c.s.c.* '97 (FR)[A] North Easton, MA Holy Cross Fathers Religious; [A] North Easton, MA Stonehill College.
Wilcox, C. Thomas *m.m.* '51 (NY)[EE] Retired.
Wilczek, Walter *c.r.* '53 (CHI) Chicago, IL St. Hedwig Retired.
Wild, Alexander '89 (DUB) On Special or Other Archdiocesan Assignment.
Wild, J. Jerome '81 (PH) Feasterville, PA Assumption B.V.M.
Wild, Jon Anthony '82 (DUL) Duluth, MN St. Elizabeth.
Wild, Michael L. '84 (MIL) Fox Lake, WI Annunciation.
Wild, Robert A. *s.j.* '70 (MIL)[P] Milwaukee, WI Jesuit Community at Marquette University; [C] Marquette University.
Wild, Robert A. '70 (BUF) On Duty Outside the Diocese.
Wilde, Adrian *o.carm.* '72 (VEN) Englewood, FL St. Francis of Assisi.
Wilde, Denis G. *o.s.a.* '70 (PH)[Y] Philadelphia, PA Augustinian Community (O.S.A.); Philadelphia, PA St. Nicholas of Tolentine.
Wilder, Alfred W. *o.p.* '65 (FgM) Metairie, LA St. Martin de Porres Province (Southern Dominican Province).
Wilder, Daniel J. '96 (PEO) Walnut, IL Immaculate Conception Church; Walnut, IL St. John the Evangelist.
Wilder, Frank T. *o.a.r.* '91 (NY)[B] Suffern, NY Tagaste Monastery; Suffern, NY Good Samaritan Hospital.
Wilder, Frank T. *o.a.r.* '91 (LA) Oxnard, CA Mary Star of the Sea; [P] Oxnard, CA St. Augustine Priory O.A.R.
Wilderotter, Paul C. '74 (CHL) On Duty Outside the Diocese.
Wildes, Kevin *s.j.* '86 (NO)[C] New Orleans, LA Loyola University New Orleans.
Wiley, Leo A. '56 (OG) Watertown, NY Holy Family Retired.
Wilgenbusch, Rev. Msgr. Lyle L. '66 (DUB) On Special or Other Archdiocesan Assignment; Episcopal Vicar for Waterloo Region; College of Consultors; Continuing Formation of Priests; American Martyrs Retreat House Advisory Board; Pastoral Council; Ex Officio Members; Stewardship Committee; Archbishop's Cabinet; Archdiocesan Pastoral Center; Priestly Life and Ministry Committee.
Wilger, Norbert J. '49 (LC) Retired.
Wilhelm, Chad F. '94 (FAR) Fargo, ND St. Mary's Cathedral of Fargo; Apostleship of Prayer.
Wilhelm, Dean E. '88 (AUS) Round Rock, TX St. William.
Wilhelm, Edward *c.ss.r.* '47 (CHI)[N] Chicago, IL The Redemptorist Fathers of Chicago; Chicago, IL St. Michael in Old Town Retired.
Wilhelm, H. Joseph *s.m.* '59 (WDC)[N] Washington, DC Marist Center Retired.
Wilhelm, Patrick R.C. '71 (NEW) Kearny, NJ Our Lady of Sorrows Retired.
Wilhelm, Paul W. *o.m.i.* '68 (FgM) Washington, DC

AMERICAN OBLATE MISSIONS.
Wilhelm, Robert J. '59 (TOL) Retired.
Wilhite, Philip A. '90 (GAL) Houston, TX St. Albert of Trapani.
Wilimek, Louis '50 (MIL) Retired.
Wilk, Brian J. '03 (MAD) Watertown, WI St. Henry; Advocate/Procurator (cc.1481–1490); Elected.
Wilk, Joseph M. '81 (CHI) Chicago, IL St. Cornelius.
Wilk, Mitchell S. '70 (SPC) Leave of Absence Retired.
Wilke, David M. '95 (BEL) Fairmont City, IL Holy Rosary; Diocesan Consultors; Co Directors.
Wilke, James B. '89 (STL)[N] Kirkwood, MO St. Agnes Home for the Elderly.
Wilkening, David F. '79 (DAV) Solon, IA St. Mary's; Deans.
Wilkening, Henry '47 (JOL) Winfield, IL Central DuPage Hospital; Winfield, IL St. John the Baptist Retired.
Wilker, Ronald H. '71 (CIN) Retired.
Wilkerson, Rev. Msgr. Jerome F. '50 (STL) Retired.
Wilkerson, Wayne W. '99 (GAL) Houston, TX St. Francis de Sales.
Wilkes, Michael '09 (DET) Bloomfield Hills, MI St. Hugo of the Hills.
Wilkie, John J. '92 (SEA) Tacoma, WA Our Lady, Queen of Heaven.
Wilkie, William E. '54 (DUB)[C] Retired.
Wilkins, Bernard J. '61 (STL) Washington, MO St. Gertrude Retired.
Wilkinson, Bruce W. '81 (ATL) Atlanta, GA Most Blessed Sacrament.
Wilkinson, George A. '01 (WDC) College Park, MD Holy Redeemer.
Wilkinson, John H. '59 (BRK) Brooklyn, NY St. Brigid Retired.
Wilkinson, Neal J. *s.j.* '00 (OM)[K] Omaha, NE Jesuit Community at Creighton University.
Wilkinson, Rick *c.s.c.* '79 (AUS)[A] St. Edward's University.
Wilkosz, William '95 (CHI) Palos Heights, IL Incarnation.
Wilks, Bede *o.p.* '62 (TUC) Tucson, AZ Saint Thomas More Roman Catholic Newman Parish – Tucson; [G] Tucson, AZ University of Arizona Retired.
Will, Lowell '68 (EVN) Boonville, IN St. Clement; Newburgh, IN St. Rupert.
Will, Ronald L. *c.pp.s.* '75 (KC) St. Joseph, MO St. Francis Xavier.
Willard, Donald B. *c.ss.r.* '08 (LA) Whittier, CA St. Mary of the Assumption; [P] Whittier, CA Redemptorists of Whittier.
Willard, Stephen A. '93 (PEO) Champaign, IL Holy Cross.
Willenberg, Lukasz J. '08 (PRO) Barrington, RI St. Luke.
Willenborg, Daniel L. '05 (SFD) Comite Diocesano de Ministerio Hispano – Diocesan Committee for Hispanic Ministry.
Willenborg, Daniel L. '05 (SFD) Nokomis, IL St. Louis.
Willenbring, Mark '57 (SCL) Grey Eagle, MN St. Joseph's; Grey Eagle, MN St. John the Baptist.
Willenburg, Rev. Msgr. Francis J. '54 (SY) Utica, NY St. Agnes.
Willett, John *c.ss.r.* '61 (KC) Kansas City, MO Our Lady of Perpetual Help; [J] Kansas City, MO Redemptorists Fathers of Kansas City, Missouri; Kansas City, MO Our Lady of Sorrows.
Willette, Donald C. '84 (DEN) Fort Collins, CO Blessed John XXIII; [S] Fort Collins, CO West African Development Support Organization.
Willette, Donald C. '84 (MO) Air Force Reserve Chaplains.
Willey, Dennis B. '94 (CHR) Charleston, SC Church of Christ the Divine Teacher; Charleston, SC Sacred Heart.
Willger, Gerard I. '86 (SUP) Medford, WI Our Lady of the Holy Rosary; Medford, WI Our Lady of Perpetual Help; Moderator; Presbyteral Council & Diocesan Consultors.
Willhite, Rev. Msgr. Robert J. '63 (RCK) Aurora, IL St. Joseph Retired.
William, Noel *o.f.m.* '42 (CIN)[N] Cincinnati St. Francis Seraph Friary Retired.
Williams, Anthony C. '83 (KCK) Olpe, KS St. Mary's; Olpe, KS St. Joseph's.
Williams, Baykil *s.o.l.t.* '06 (PBL) Capulin, CO St. Joseph.
Williams, Brady *s.o.l.t.* '04 (CC)[G] Robstown, TX Society of Our Lady of the Most Holy Trinity.
Williams, Clarence *c.pp.s.* '78 (CIN)[N] Dayton Provincial Office of the Cincinnati Province of the Society of the Precious Blood; [N] Dayton, OH Provincial Office of the Cincinnati Province of the Society of the Precious Blood.
Williams, Claude *o.praem.* '09 (ORG)[D] Silverado, CA St. Michael's Preparatory School.
Williams, David '98 (AUS) Diocesan Tribunal Judges.
Williams, Donald J. '83 (SCR)[C] Misericordia University; Wyoming, PA St. Frances Cabrini.
Williams, Edward *o.m.i.* '57 (FgM) Washington, DC AMERICAN OBLATE MISSIONS.
Williams, Francis '77 (LAN) Retired.
Williams, George S. *s.j.* '72 (WDC)[E] North Bethesda, MD Georgetown Preparatory School.
Williams, George T. *s.j.* '04 (BO) Watertown, MA; [U] Weston, MA Campion Jesuit Community.
Williams, George W. '96 (DET) Canton, MI Saint John Neumann; Judges.
Williams, George *s.j.* (BO) Northeast Correctional Center; Massachusetts Correctional Institution – Concord.
Williams, Glenn *s.j.* '56 (DET)[K] Clarkston, MI Colombiere Center.
Williams, H. Brendan '65 (TR) Howell, NJ St. Veronica; Charismatic Renewal.
Williams, Ian J. '96 (GRY) La Porte, IN Sacred Heart; Boy Scouts Liaison.
Williams, J. Gerald *o.carm.* '80 (KCK) Garnett, KS St. Therese; Garnett, KS St. Boniface.
Williams, James C. *s.m.* '98 (RVC)[D] Mineola, NY Chaminade High School (Boys).
Williams, James J. '70 (MAR) Retired.
Williams, James M. '97 (COS) Vocations; Colorado Springs, CO Holy Trinity; Vice Chancellor; Vice Chancellor.
Williams, James '65 (SEA) Retired.
Williams, Rev. Msgr. John J. '78 (R) Raleigh, NC St. Joseph.
Williams, John L. '91 (HRT) Cheshire, CT Church of the Epiphany.
Williams, Jonathan *o.f.m.cap.* '71 (FgM) Pittsburgh, PA Province of St. Augustine.
Williams, Joseph A. '02 (STP) Minneapolis, MN St. Stephen.
Williams, Joseph S. *c.m.* '87 (STL) Perryville, MO St. Vincent De Paul; Perryville, MO St. Rose of Lima; [V] Perryville, MO St. Vincent De Paul Educational Foundation.
Williams, Kenneth '63 (SHP) Retired.
Williams, Manuel *c.r.* '87 (MOB) Montgomery, AL Resurrection Catholic Mission; Montgomery, AL Resurrection Catholic Church; [J] Montgomery, AL Resurrection Catholic Missions.
Williams, Matthew M. '03 (BO) New Evangelization of Youth and Young Adults; Holbrook, MA St. Joseph.
Williams, Matthew '94 (TUC) Miami, AZ Our Lady of the Blessed Sacrament Roman Catholic Church – Miami.
Williams, Matthew *o.c.d.* '90 (SB)[I] Redlands, CA Discalced Carmelites, OCD.
Williams, Michael A. *s.j.* '75 (MOB)[A] Mobile, AL Spring Hill College.
Williams, Michael E. '97 (OWN)[I] Bowling Green, KY Western Kentucky University Newman Center.
Williams, Michael J. '95 (LAN) Lansing, MI St. Therese; Diocesan Mission Office.
Williams, Michael S. '64 (STA) Keystone Heights, FL St. William; Presbyteral Council; Diocesan Consultors.
Williams, Michael '97 (OWN) Consultors.
Williams, Michael '09 (LSC) Lordsburg, NM St. Joseph.
Williams, Oliver F. *c.s.c.* '70 (FTW)[B] University of Notre Dame Du Lac; [H] Notre Dame, IN Holy Cross Community, Corby Hall, University of Notre Dame.
Williams, Patrick J. '93 (NO) Executive Director; New Orleans, LA St. Pius X; Members of the Board.
Williams, Patrick J. '93 (NO)[A] New Orleans, LA Notre Dame Seminary Graduate School of Theology; [H] New Orleans, LA Holy Cross School; [E] New Orleans, LA Holy Cross School; [E] New Orleans, LA Mount Carmel Academy.
Williams, Paul D. '96 (ATL) Dalton, GA St. Joseph's; College of Consultors.
Williams, Paul M. *o.f.m.* '86 (CHR) Columbia, SC Saint Martin de Porres; [H] Columbia, SC Allen University, Benedict College; Deans; Administrator for African-American Catholics; Personnel Committee; College of Consultors.
Williams, Paul '95 (ATL) Special or Other (Arch)Diocesan Assignment.
Williams, Peter J. '04 (STP)[C] St. Paul, MN University of St. Thomas; St. Paul, MN Maternity of the Blessed Virgin; Vocations; Appointees; College of Consultors.
Williams, Peter Y. '87 (BUR) Springfield, VT Maternity of the Blessed Virgin Mary.
Williams, Rayner F. *o.f.m.* '56 (PAT)[N] Butler, NJ St. Anthony Friary.
Williams, Richard B. *o.p.* '71 (SAT) Defenders of the Bond.
Williams, Richard C. '65 (PH) Glen Mills, PA St. Thomas the Apostle.
Williams, Robert Hayes '82 (DET) Hazel Park, MI St. Justin; Adjutant Judicial Vicars.
Williams, Robert L. '68 (LFT) Anderson, IN St. Mary; Deans; Diocesan Consultors; Presbyteral Council; Anderson, IN St. Ambrose.
Williams, Robert '91 (DAL) At Large Members; [M] Dallas, TX Commission on Ecumenism; Garland, TX Good Shepherd; College of Consultors.
Williams, Robert *o.f.m.cap.* '09 (NY) Bronx, NY Immaculate Conception; [EE] New York, NY Immaculate Conception Friary.
Williams, Ronald '02 (CIN) Cincinnati, OH Our Lady of the Sacred Heart.
Williams, Steven T. '91 (MOB) Fairhope, AL St. Lawrence; [J] Fairhope, AL Boy Scouts; Group II.
Williams, Thomas G. *s.j.* '60 (SEA)[C] Tacoma, WA Bellarmine Preparatory School.
Williams, Thomas *s.j.* '60 (SPK)[J] Spokane, WA Regis Community.
Williams, W. Ray '97 (CHL) Sylva, NC St. Mary.
Williams, Rev. Msgr. William E. '59 (NY) Saugerties, NY St. John the Evangelist; Ulster.
Williams, William G. '69 (BO) Dedham, MA St. Mary; Presbyteral Council.
Williams, William M. '96 (ATL) Thomson, GA Queen of Angels.
Williams, William M. '05 (IND) Brookville, IN St. Michael; Brookville, IN Holy Guardian Angels.
Williams, William W. *s.j.* '68 (DEN)[N] Denver, CO Xavier Jesuit Center.
Williamson, Christopher '88 (ATL) Washington, GA St. Joseph.
Williamson, John A. '00 (BAL) Baltimore, MD Ascension; Priest Personnel Board.
Williamson, Michael G. '86 (CLV) Akron, OH St. Matthew.
Williamson, Rev. Msgr. Robert J. '62 (BUF) Akron, NY St. Teresa of Avila.
Williamson, Thomas '96 (CHL) Absent On Leave.
Willie, Arthur H. *m.m.* '51 (NY)[EE] Retired.
Willingham, Charles W. *o.praem.* '95 (ORG)[I] Silverado, CA Norbertine Fathers of Orange Inc.
Willingham, Charles *o.praem.* '95 (LA)[C] Santa Paula, CA Thomas Aquinas College.
Willis, Glen *s.d.s.* '69 (WDC)[B] Silver Spring, MD Salvatorian Community; [H] Rockville, MD The Frost Center, Society of the Divine Savior; [W] Silver Spring, MD Camp St. Charles, Inc.
Willis, Kevin '93 (FAR) Forman, ND St. Mary; Oakes, ND St. Charles Church of Oakes.
Willis, Thomas S. '84 (STA) St. Augustine, FL Cathedral – Basilica of St. Augustine; [K] St. Augustine, FL Flagler College Newman Center; Deans; Office of Liturgy; Respect Life Activities.
Willmering, John H. *s.j.* '68 (FgM) St. Louis, MO Society of Jesus.
Willoughby, Malcolm Sylvester *o.p.* '49 (WDC)[B] Washington, DC Dominican House of Studies.
Wills, Nathan D. *c.s.c.* '06 (FTW)[H] Notre Dame Congregation of Holy Cross, Indiana Province, Provincial House.
Willson, David '88 (E) Johnsonburg, PA St. Anne.
Wilmot, John P. '77 (WIN) Mankato, MN Holy Family; Mankato, MN St. Joseph the Worker.
Wilmoth, James R. '65 (IND) Indianapolis, IN St. Roch; Deaneries and Deans; [C] Indianapolis, IN Roncalli High School; Indianapolis Fire Department.
Wilmsen, Gerald *s.s.c.* '59 (OM)[K] St. Columbans Missionary Society of St. Columban Retired.
Wilson, Alan *o.f.m.cap* '69 (SFR)[B] San Francisco, CA Capuchin Franciscan Order San Buenaventura Friary.
Wilson, Albert L. '51 (L)[L] Louisville, KY Bishop David Apartments Retired.
Wilson, Anthony *o.f.m.* '87 (FgM) New York, NY Holy Name Province.
Wilson, C. Patrick *s.a.c.* '05 (VEN) Sarasota, FL St. Martha.
Wilson, Cedric M. *o.s.a.* '78 (ARL) Arlington, VA St. Agnes.
Wilson, Daniel *l.c.* '02 (WDC)[N] Potomac, MD Legionaries of Christ.
Wilson, David J. '88 (E) Johnsonburg, PA Holy Rosary.
Wilson, Dennis M. *o.f.m.* '92 (NY) New York, NY St. Stephen of Hungary; [EE] New York, NY Franciscan Friars, Holy Name Province.
Wilson, Edward J. '01 (PRO) Warwick, RI Sts. Rose & Clement.
Wilson, Eugene C. '02 (PH) Penndel, PA Our Lady of Grace.
Wilson, F. Philip *o.s.b.* '53 (PRO)[P] Portsmouth, RI Abbey of St. Gregory the Great.
Wilson, George B. *s.j.* '59 (CIN)[N] Cincinnati, OH Jesuit Community at Xavier University.
Wilson, Gregory B. '01 (CHR) Charleston, SC Cathedral of St. John the Baptist; Charleston, SC St. Mary of the Annunciation.
Wilson, Guy *s.t.* '78 (MOB) Fort Mitchell, AL St. Joseph.
Wilson, Joel R. '09 (TR) Belmar, NJ St. Rose.
Wilson, John M. *c.s.b.* '47 (GAL)[O] Houston, TX Dillon House Retired.
Wilson, Jonathan F. '03 (COL) Newark, OH Church of the Blessed Sacrament.
Wilson, Joseph F. '86 (BRK) Middle Village, NY St. Margaret.
Wilson, Lawrence Clifton '09 (GAL) Dickinson, TX Shrine of the True Cross.
Wilson, Method *o.f.m.* '52 (SFD)[L] Springfield, IL Our Lady of Angels Friary.
Wilson, Rev. Msgr. Michael '75 (WDC) Laurel, MD St. Mary; Deans.

Wilson, Richard D. '97 (FR)[J] Fall River, MA Spanish Apostolate; Diocesan Apostolate to Hispanics; New Bedford; New Bedford, MA Our Lady of Guadalupe.
Wilson, Steven *c.ss.r.* '01 (BLX) Biloxi, MS Our Mother of Sorrows; Biloxi, MS Blessed Francis Xavier Seelos; Presbyteral Council.
Wilson, Stuart T. '67 (BAL) Retired.
Wilson, Thomas R. '75 (PIT) Pittsburgh, PA St. John Vianney.
Wilson, Thomas '96 (STP) Lakeville, MN All Saints.
Wilson, William P. '69 (NEW) On Duty Outside the Archdiocese Retired.
Wilt, George A. '59 (PIT)[M] Pittsburgh, PA St. John Vianney Manor Retired.
Wilton, David M. *c.p.m.* '93 (OWN)[F] Auburn, KY Fathers of Mercy.
Wilutis, John P. '55 (RVC)[M] Amityville, NY St. Pius X Residence Retired.
Wilwerding, Anthony P. '46 (OM) Retired.
Wilwerding, Glen '04 (DM) Osceola, IA St. Bernard; Osceola, IA St. Patrick; Osceola, IA St. Joseph.
Wilz, John C. '64 (PH) Retired.
Wimett, Leo J. '60 (SY) North Bay, NY St. John.
Wimmer, Joseph F. *o.s.a.* '64 (WDC) Beltsville, MD St. Joseph.
Wimsett, Scott J. '88 (L) Mount Washington, KY St. Francis Xavier.
Winca, Harry S. '45 (CLV) Middlefield, OH St. Lucy; Parkman, OH St. Edward Retired.
Winchel, Scott '09 (SAV) Columbus, GA St. Anne.
Winchester, George P. *s.j.* '65 (BO)[U] Boston, MA Loyola House.
Windhaus, Edward A. '72 (PH) On Special or Other Archdiocesan Assignment; [BB] Newtown Square, PA Tri–College Newman Cluster–Bryn Mawr, Haverford and Swarthmore Colleges; Newtown Square, PA St. Anastasia.
Windholtz, Barry M. '88 (CIN) Cincinnati, OH St. Rose of Lima; Adjutant Judicial Vicars.
Windholtz, Barry M. '88 (COV) Judges.
Windholtz, Barry '88 (LEX) Associate Judges.
Windish, Adolf *s.m.* '61 (SAT)[K] San Antonio, TX Marianist Residence: Skilled Nursing.
Windle, Raymond L. *s.j.* '59 (STL)[O] St. Louis, MO Jesuit Community Corporation at Saint Louis University – Jesuit Hall.
Windolph, Nestor *o.f.m.* '55 (FgM) Saint Louis, MO Sacred Heart Province.
Windsor, David E. *c.m.* '74 (MIL)[A] St. Francis, WI Saint Francis de Sales Seminary.
Windy, Jeff (PEO) On Leave of Absence.
Wing, Kenneth A. '59 (GR) Retired.
Wingate, Arthur K. '57 (FR) Retired.
Wingert, D. William '60 (SC) Retired.
Wingert, Gerald R. '47 (SC) Retired.
Winiarski, James M. *m.s.* '66 (LKC) Sulphur, LA Our Lady of LaSalette.
Winikates, Thomas '70 (CHI) Westchester, IL Divine Infant.
Winkel, Thomas J. '71 (CLV) Absent on Sick Leave.
Winkelbauer, Phillip J. '75 (KCK) Leavenworth, KS Sacred Heart–St. Casimir; Regional Pastoral Leaders; Easton, KS St. Joseph–St. Lawrence.
Winkeljohn, James Christian '08 (PT) Tallahassee, FL Good Shepherd.
Winkelmann, Luke E. '05 (CHI) Skokie, IL St. Peter.
Winkels, Michael A. *o.p.* '76 (CHI)[D] Oak Park, IL Fenwick High School; [N] Oak Park, IL Dominican Community of St. Martin de Porres.
Winkler, Chauncey '03 (PHX) Lake Havasu City, AZ Our Lady of the Lake Roman Catholic Parish.
Winkler, Eugene '50 (MIL) Retired.
Winkler, Jude *o.f.m.conv.* '81 (BAL)[S] Ellicott City, MD Friary of St. Joseph Cupertino.
Winkowski, Eugene R. '71 (CHI) Chicago, IL Our Lady of Victory.
Winkowski, Michael *c.pp.s.* '70 (CIN)[N] Dayton Provincial Office of the Cincinnati Province of the Society of the Precious Blood.
Winn, Frank A. '98 (BGP) Greenwich, CT St. Paul.
Winne, George R. '83 (ALN) McAdoo, PA All Saints Parish; [C] Tamaqua, PA Marian Catholic High School.
Winnicki, Tadeusz *s.ch.* '72 (SFR) San Francisco, CA Nativity; Polish, Croatian, Slovenian Mission.
Winshman, Alfred O. *s.j.* '65 (BO)[U] Weston, MA Campion Jesuit Community.
Winslow, Patrick J. '99 (CHL) Tryon, NC St. John the Baptist.
Winter, Donald J. *c.ss.r.* '55 (ORL)[F] New Smyrna Beach, FL St. Alphonsus Villa–Redemptorist Fathers and Brothers Retired.
Winter, Harry *o.m.i.* '64 (STP) St. Paul, MN St. Casimir.
Winterer, Rev. Msgr. Michael J. '60 (SLC) Cedar City, UT Christ the King LLC 203; Deans.
Winterlin, John R. '68 (GRY) Retired.
Wintermyer, John S. '62 (WDC) Retired.
Winters, Alfred H. '62 (CLV) Lakewood, OH St. Clement Retired.
Winters, Darvin E. '99 (IND) Terre Haute, IN St. Ann; Terre Haute, IN Sacred Heart of Jesus; Air National Guard Chaplains.
Winters, Martin N. '52 (CHI)[O] Oak Forest, IL Missionary Sisters of St. Benedict of Illinois, Inc. Retired.
Winters, Sean G. '87 (MET) Office of Hospital Chaplaincy; Perth Amboy, NJ Holy Spirit; Perth Amboy, NJ Raritan Bay Medical Center.
Winters, Vaughn P. '93 (LA) Palmdale, CA St. Mary.
Winters, William H. *o.f.m.cap.* (RVC) East Patchogue, NY St. Joseph the Worker.
Wintz, Jack R. *o.f.m.* '63 (CIN)[N] Cincinnati, OH Pleasant Street Friary.
Winzenburg, George *s.j.* '74 (RC)[C] Howes, SD Kino Jesuit Community; [E] Howes, SD The Diocese of Rapid City Mahpiya na Maka Okogna; Diocesan Consultors; Permanent Diaconate Program, Sioux Spiritual Center.
Winzerling, James L. '61 (STL) Retired.
Wiorkiewicz, Marek *s.d.s.* '89 (NEW) Garfield, NJ St. Stanislaus Kostka; [M] Verona, NJ The Salvatorian Fathers.
Wippel, Rev. Msgr. John '60 (STU) On Duty Outside the Diocese; [C] Catholic University of America, The.
Wirkes, Stephen P. '80 (SY) Fulton, NY Immaculate Conception; Board of Diocesan Consultors.
Wirkowski, Mariusz '04 (SY) Syracuse, NY The Cathedral of the Immaculate Conception.
Wironen, John *c.s.c.* '79 (P) Portland, OR Holy Cross Catholic Church[B]; [L] Portland, OR Holy Cross Fathers & Brothers, C.S.C. – University of Portland.
Wironen, John *c.s.c.* (FTW)[H] Notre Dame Congregation of Holy Cross, Indiana Province, Provincial House.
Wirth, Geoffrey D. '67 (RCK) Elgin, IL St. Thomas More; Diocesan Consultors.
Wirth, Jerry E. '68 (BEL) Olney, IL St. Joseph.
Wirth, Justus *o.f.m.* '62 (CIN)[N] Cincinnati St. Francis Seraph Friary.
Wisdon, Andrew–Carl *o.p.* '87 (CHI)[N] Chicago Dominicans (Provincial Office); [N] St. Pius V Priory.
Wise, Mark *c.ss.r.* '70 (PH) Philadelphia, PA St. Peter the Apostle.
Wise, Paul C. '74 (CAM) Atlantic City, NJ St. Monica's Catholic Church, Atlantic City, N.J.
Wise, Richard P. '81 (ATL) Blairsville, GA St. Francis of Assisi; Deans.
Wise, Thomas F. *c.s.v.* '56 (CHI)[N] Arlington Heights, IL Viatorian Province Center–Clerics of St. Viator.
Wiseman, Eric '05 (ANC) Eagle River, AK St. Andrew.
Wiseman, James A. *o.s.b.* '70 (WDC)[C] Catholic University of America, The; [N] Washington, DC St. Anselm's Abbey.
Wiseman, Joseph F. '52 (BRK) Flushing, NY Mary's Nativity Retired.
Wiseman, Robert *c.s.c.* '77 (SP) Indian Rocks Beach, FL St. Jerome; Elected Parochial Vicars.
Wiseman, Vincent *o.p.* '71 (FgM) New York, NY Province of St. Joseph (Eastern).
Wisner, John H. '72 (KCK) Roeland Park, KS St. Agnes.
Wisneski, Edward '67 (NOR) Retired.
Wisneski, John A. '57 (LC) Retired.
Wisneski, John J. '64 (GR) Retired.
Wisneski, Jonathan J. '98 (GBG) On Duty Outside the Diocese.
Wisniefski, Robert W. '80 (PAT) Paterson, NJ St. Joseph's.
Wisniewski, Joseph F. '07 (WIL) Newark, DE Holy Family.
Wisniewski, Joseph *c.m.* '65 (BRK) Brooklyn, NY SS. Cyril and Methodius.
Wisniewski, Robert W. '89 (CLV) Parma, OH St. Bridget.
Wisniewski, Thomas S. '80 (NEW) Glen Rock, NJ St. Catharine.
Wisniewski, Thomas '76 (MIA) Parkland, FL Mary Help of Christians Church.
Wissel, Rev. Msgr. Francis C. '77 (BGP) Greenwich, CT St. Mary; [T] Bridgeport, CT St. Peter's Parish, St. Maximillian Kolbe House of Studies.
Wissler, Thomas '83 (STL) Troy, MO Sacred Heart.
Wissman, J. Patrick '64 (SPC) Bolivar, MO Sacred Heart; Region III.
Wister, Rev. Msgr. Robert J. '68 (NEW)[A] South Orange, NJ Immaculate Conception Seminary; [B] School of Diplomacy and Intl. Rels.
Wit, Mieczyslaw *o.f.m.conv.* '95 (SPR) Chicopee, MA St. Stanislaus Basilica.
Witalec, Dennis J. '82 (PH) Absent on Sick Leave; Philadelphia, PA Epiphany of Our Lord.
Witchousky, Peter *o.p.* '69 (SFD)[M] Springfield, IL Dominican Sisters of Springfield, Il.
Witcoskie, Stanley L. '93 (CAM) On Leave of Absence.
Witczak, Michael G. '77 (MIL) On Duty Outside the Archdiocese; [C] Catholic University of America, The.
Witek, John W. *s.j.* '65 (WDC)[N] Washington, DC The Jesuit Community at Georgetown University.
Witek, Stanley '87 (KAL) Dorr, MI St. Stanislaus.
With, William A. '72 (BRK) Middle Village, NY St. Margaret.
Witherup, Ronald D. *s.s.* '76 (BAL)[S] Baltimore, MD Society of St. Sulpice, Province of the United States.
Witherup, Ronald *s.s.* (E) On Duty Outside Diocese.
Withrow, Justin *o.s.b.* '90 (GBG) Greensburg, PA Excela Health – Westmoreland Hospital; Latrobe, PA Excela Health – Latrobe Area Hospital; [G] Latrobe, PA Saint Vincent Archabbey.
Witkowski, Rev. Msgr. Bernard E. '62 (PH) Philadelphia, PA Maternity B.V.M.
Witkowski, Phillip J. '75 (GR) Shelby, MI Our Lady of the Assumption; Shelby, MI Our Lady of Fatima.
Witkowski, Robert J. '61 (DET) Warren, MI St. Edmund.
Witmer, Joseph W. '67 (Y) Aurora, OH Our Lady of Perpetual Help; College of Consultors; Ecumenism; Priests Council.
Witon, Russell F. '63 (MIL) Retired.
Witsken, Gary J. '69 (CIN) Retired.
Witt, Edward G. *s.j.* '91 (RC) White River, SD St. Ignatius; White River, SD Sacred Heart; St. Francis, SD St. Francis Mission/Rosebud Educational Society; Deaneries; [C] Howes, SD Kino Jesuit Community.
Witt, George M. *s.j.* '06 (NY)[EE] New York, NY St. Ignatius Loyola Residence; New York, NY St. Ignatius Loyola.
Witt, Michael J. '90 (STL)[A] St. Louis, MO Kenrick School of Theology.
Witt, Michael J. '75 (STL) Archdiocesan Office of the Permanent Diaconate.
Witt, Rev. Msgr. Paul K. '71 (LIN) Plattsmouth, NE Church of the Holy Spirit; Deaneries and Deans; Ecumenical Affairs, Commission for; Evangelization Committee.
Witt, William '49 (Y) Retired.
Witte, Mark G. '95 (COV) Leave of Absence.
Witte, Steven D. '92 (BEL) Leave of Absence.
Wittenbrink, Boniface *o.m.i.* '41 (BEL)[F] Belleville, IL Shrine of Our Lady of the Snows Retired.
Witthauer, Paul G. '60 (BAL) Retired.
Wittkop, Scott '05 (SCL) Verndale, MN St. Hubert; Verndale, MN The Church of the Assumption of Our Lady of Menahga; Verndale, MN St. Frederick.
Wittliff, Thomas F. '64 (MIL) Retired.
Wittman, Peter C. '75 (STP) Shakopee, MN St. Mary of the Purification; Shakopee, MN Church of St. Mary.
Wittmann, Christopher T. *s.m.* '94 (CIN)[D] Dayton, OH The University of Dayton; [N] Dayton, OH Marianist Community; [R] Dayton, OH University of Dayton Campus Ministry.
Wittouck, Frank A. *s.c.j.* '65 (BWN) Raymondville, TX Our Lady of Guadalupe.
Wittrock, Daniel L. '93 (OM) South Sioux City, NE St. Michael; Age Groups; Consultors; Ex Officio (Consultors).
Wittstock, Joseph *o.c.s.o.* '84 (ARL)[H] Berryville, VA Cistercian Abbey of Our Lady of the Holy Cross.
Witucki, Roy R. '05 (LC) Ellsworth, WI St. Francis of Assisi.
Witz, Dennis M. '76 (MIL) Milwaukee, WI St. Matthias.
Witzemann, B. Gerald '61 (COV) Warsaw, KY St. Joseph Retired.
Witzmann, Hugh *o.s.b.* '55 (SCL)[I] Collegeville, MN St. John's Abbey, of the Order of St. Benedict.
Wixted, Rev. Msgr. Matthew O. '62 (SLC) Apostleship of Prayer Retired.
Wizeman, William L. *s.j.* '98 (NY)[EE] New York, NY Xavier Jesuit Community; New York, NY Corpus Christi.
Wleczyk, Rev. Msgr. Leo '65 (GAL) Lake Jackson, TX St. Michael; Southern Vicariate; Appointees; College of Consultors.
Wocken, Jeffrey *s.d.s.* '99 (MIL)[P] Milwaukee Salvatorian Provincial Offices; Milwaukee, WI.
Wodecki, Jeremi '07 (CHR) Charleston, SC Cathedral of St. John the Baptist.
Wodniak, John L. '43 (CHI) Chicago, IL St. James Retired.
Wodziak, Michael '48 (RVC) Retired.
Woempner, Michael A. '79 (MAR) Kingsford, MI St. Mary Queen of Peace; Vicars Forane; Consultors.
Woerter, Dennis C. *o.p.* '97 (CHI) River Forest, IL St. Vincent Ferrer.
Woerth, Thomas '66 (DEN) Retired.
Woerz, Christian H. *s.d.b.* '76 (LA)[V] Rosemead, CA St. Joseph's Salesian Youth Renewal Center.
Woestman, William H. *o.m.i.* '56 (CHI) Associate Vicars; Promoter of Justice; Defenders of the Bond; Chicago, IL Holy Name Cathedral.
Wohinc, Karl R. '63 (WH) Shinnston, WV St. Ann's.
Wohler, Gil *o.f.m.* '62 (CIN)[N] Cincinnati St. Francis Seraph Friary.
Wohlwend, Paul W. *c.pp.s.* '54 (CIN)[N] Carthagena, OH St. Charles Retired.
Wojcicki, Miroslaus A. '62 (PIT) East Pittsburgh, PA Holy Cross.
Wojcicki, Rev. Msgr. Ted L. '75 (STL)[A] St. Louis, MO Kenrick School of Theology; Kenrick–Glennon Seminary.
Wojcicki, Wojciech '90 (DET) Retired.
Wojciechowski, Edward C. '81 (PRM) Retired.
Wojciechowski, Richard P. '63 (BAL) Retired.
Wojciechowski, Robert J. '83 (DET) Detroit, MI St.

Francis D'Assisi; Detroit, MI St. Hedwig.
Wojciechowski, Thomas *o.f.m.* '75 (GB) Green Bay, WI St. Mary of the Angels; [J] Green Bay, WI St. Mary of the Angels Friary; Appointed Members.
Wojciechowski, Tomasz *c.r.* '08 (CHI) Chicago, IL St. Hedwig[N].
Wojcik, Eugene H. '74 (BEL) Chester, IL St. Mary Help of Christians; Diaconate, Office of Permanent.
Wojcik, Grzegorz '08 (CHI) Palos Hills, IL Sacred Heart.
Wojcik, Joseph J. '69 (CHI) La Grange Park, IL St. Louise de Marillac.
Wojcik, Przemyslaw '08 (CHI) Wilmette, IL St. Francis Xavier.
Wojcik, Richard J. '49 (CHI)[A] Mundelein, IL University of St. Mary of the Lake/Mundelein Seminary Retired.
Wojcinski, Anthony A. '85 (PBL) Pueblo, CO St. Leander.
Wojslaw, Robert *s.ch.* '00 (CHI) Chicago, IL Five Holy Martyrs.
Wojtan, Andrezj '83 (ORL) Mims, FL Holy Spirit.
Wojtek, Robert *c.ss.r.* (BAL) Baltimore, MD St. Michael; Baltimore, MD St. Patrick.
Wojtewicz, Eugene E. '57 (DET) Retired.
Wojtun, Daniel T. '07 (HRT) Southington, CT Immaculate Conception.
Wolak, Edmund '92 (SY) Absent on Leave.
Wolanski, Edward *c.p.* '72 (R) Greenville, NC St. Peter's.
Wolbach, Rev. Msgr. Richard A. '56 (OM) DEPARTMENT OF VETERANS AFFAIRS HOSPITALS AND CHAPLAINS Retired.
Wolbert, Jerome J. *o.f.m.* '08 (PIT)[M] Pittsburgh, PA Holy Family Friary.
Wolbert, Jerome J. *o.f.m.* '08 (PBR) Upper St. Clair, PA St. Gregory Nazianzus; Sybertsville, PA Assumption B.V.M. Province; On Duty Outside the Diocese.
Wolbert, Jerome *o.f.m.* '09 (PSC)[A] Sybertsville, PA Holy Dormition Friary.
Woldai, Gebriel '93 (OAK) Berkeley, CA St. Joseph The Worker; Eritrean Pastoral Center.
Wolensky, Paul '94 (PHU) Scranton, PA St. Vladimir's.
Wolesky, John '67 (SAL) Solomon, KS St. Patrick Parish; Solomon, KS Immaculate Conception of the Blessed Virgin Mary Parish.
Wolf, Anthony J. '96 (LC) Leave of Absence.
Wolf, Dennis G. '72 (BUF) West Seneca, NY Blessed John XXIII.
Wolf, Donald J. '81 (OKL) Shawnee, OK St. Benedict.
Wolf, Eugene J. '63 (LC) Seneca, WI St. Patrick; Deans.
Wolf, Eugene *o.f.m.cap.* '54 (MIL)[P] Mount Calvary, WI St. Lawrence Friary Retired.
Wolf, George C. '63 (RNO) Promoter of Justice; Defenders of the Bond Retired.
Wolf, George '80 (P) Portland, OR Cathedral of the Immaculate Conception; College of Consultors; Personnel Board.
Wolf, George *o.s.b.* '44 (FgM) Collegeville, MN St. John's Abbey; [I] Collegeville, MN St. John's Abbey, of the Order of St. Benedict.
Wolf, Rev. Msgr. James J. '69 (FTW) Warsaw, IN Sacred Heart; Retired Clergy Committee.
Wolf, Rev. Msgr. John V. '45 (COL) Censor of Books Retired.
Wolf, John *c.pp.s.* '69 (KC) Kearney, MO Church of the Annunciation.
Wolf, Joseph A. '68 (MIL) Retired.
Wolf, Joseph B. '54 (STL) Retired.
Wolf, Joseph D. '87 (BUF) Buffalo, NY Holy Spirit.
Wolf, Joseph M. '94 (DAV) Vice–Chancellors; Judicial Vicar; Notaries; Judges; LeClaire, IA Our Lady of the River.
Wolf, Joseph *o.f.m.cap.* '64 (MIL)[P] Mount Calvary, WI St. Lawrence Friary Retired.
Wolf, Lawrence Robert *o.s.b.m.* '75 (PSC)[A] Matawan, NJ Basilian Fathers of Mariapoch.
Wolf, Michael H. '42 (SAG) Retired.
Wolf, Norbert G. '47 (E) Retired.
Wolf, Paul L. '83 (NU) Marshall, MN St. Clotilde; Marshall, MN Holy Redeemer; Associate Judges.
Wolf, Stephen J. '97 (NSH) Nashville, TN St. Henry.
Wolf, Werner *o.f.m.cap.* '58 (MIL)[P] Mount Calvary, WI St. Lawrence Friary; [B] Mount Calvary, WI St. Lawrence Seminary.
Wolfe, Allan F. '92 (HBG) Lancaster, PA Iglesia Catolica San Juan Bautista.
Wolfe, Joseph M. *m.f.v.a.* '93 (BIR)[E] Birmingham, AL Franciscan Missionaries of the Eternal Word, A Public Association of the Christian Faithful.
Wolfe, Michael '09 (ALT) Johnstown, PA St. Benedict's.
Wolfe, Robert A. *o.carm.* '75 (NEW) Englewood, NJ St. Cecilia's.
Wolfe, William P. '70 (LA) West Hollywood, CA St. Ambrose.
Wolfee, Robert '98 (NEW) Union, NJ St. Michael's; Part–time Staff.
Wolfel, Daniel C. *o.s.b.* '54 (E) St. Marys, PA Queen of the World; St. Marys, PA St. Mary.
Wolfer, Robert R. '48 (CIN) Retired.
Wolff, Alec J. '81 (CHI) Highland Park, IL Immaculate Conception; [W] Wilmette, IL Musica Pacis; Judges.
Wolff, Jim '54 (SFE) Santa Fe, NM Santa Maria de la Paz Catholic Community.
Wolff, Rev. Msgr. Robert C. '50 (CLV) Copley, OH Guardian Angels Retired.
Wolfgram, Daniel '97 (SFS) Big Stone City, SD St. Charles.
Wolford, Donald L. '79 (SFD) Moweaqua, IL St. Frances de Sales; Shelbyville, IL Immaculate Conception; Board of Catholic Education; Assumption, IL Assumption B.V.M.
Wolfram, Frank *s.d.b.* '62 (NY)[EE] New Rochelle, NY Salesian Provincial House.
Wolken, Louis J. *m.m.* '46 (NY)[EE] Retired.
Wolkovits, Paul Dennis '93 (LA) On Sick Leave.
Wollering, Carl J. '66 (CIN) Cincinnati, OH St. Jerome.
Wollesen, Charles A. *s.j.* '52 (SPK)[J] Spokane, WA Regis Community.
Wolnik, James G. '79 (STP) St. Paul, MN Holy Childhood.
Wolnowski, Kenneth J. '65 (CLV) Lorain, OH St. Peter; College of Consultors Retired.
Woloszczuk, Rev. Mitred Archpriest Wolodymyr '81 (SJP) Obnova Societies; Presbyters Retired.
Wolski, Adalbert *t.o.r.* '59 (ALT)[G] Hollidaysburg, PA St. Joseph Friary Retired.
Wolski, Mark J. '67 (BUF) Finance Council; Hamburg, NY SS. Peter and Paul.
Wolter, Richard J. '59 (STP) Retired.
Wolter, Thomas '66 (JOL)[K] Naperville, IL St. John Vianney Villa Retired.
Wolverton, R. Ambrose *o.s.b.* '65 (PRO)[P] Portsmouth, RI Abbey of St. Gregory the Great.
Won, Rev. Msgr. John P. H. '58 (LA) Retired.
Won, Raymond (STP) St. Paul, MN St. Andrew Kim.
Wonch, Charles *s.c.j.* '02 (MIL)[P] Hales Corners, WI Priests of the Sacred Heart.
Wong, Joseph *o.s.b.cam.* '74 (MRY)[F] Big Sur New Camaldoli Hermitage.
Wong, Jules *o.f.m.* '73 (Y)[J] Youngstown, OH Mt. Alverna Friary; Youngstown, OH.
Wood, Charles A. '00 (P) Area Vicars; Gresham, OR St. Henry.
Wood, D. Mark '87 (LR) Little Rock, AR St. Theresa.
Wood, Edson J. *o.s.a.* '72 (NY) West Point, NY Catholic Chapel of the Most Holy Trinity.
Wood, Gregg D. *s.j.* '75 (FBK)[E] St. Marys, AK Brother Joe Prince Jesuit Community; Superior Regular; Presbyteral Council; Consultors.
Wood, James L. '72 (RVC) Bohemia, NY St. John Nepomucene.
Wood, Kenneth E. '89 (RIC) Newport News, VA Our Lady of Mount Carmel.
Wood, Mark '87 (LR) Priests Personnel Board (Diocesan); Vicars for Religious; Presbyteral Council.
Wood, Michael '84 (AMA) Retired.
Wood, Norbert J. *o.praem.* '81 (ORG) Costa Mesa, CA St. John the Baptist.
Wood, Paul A. '80 (BRK) Maspeth, NY St. Stanislaus Kostka; Maspeth, NY Transfiguration; [E] Brooklyn, NY Campus Ministers and Ministry Centers.
Wood, Raymond B. '64 (SY) Retired.
Wood, Robert T. '87 (OKL) Oklahoma City, OK St. James The Greater; Council of Catholic Women, Archdiocesan; Master of Ceremonies.
Wood, Robert W. '74 (BUF) Retired.
Wood, Robert *c.m.* '56 (FgM) Earth City, MO Western Province.
Wood, Simon Paul *c.p.* '43 (HRT)[L] West Hartford Holy Family Monastery/Retreat.
Wood, Tyson J. '69 (MO) Military Chaplains; Army Chaplains.
Wood, William Andrew '73 (GAL) Sugar Land, TX St. Laurence.
Wood, William J. *s.j.* '65 (SJ)[M] Los Gatos, CA Sacred Heart Jesuit Center.
Woodarek, Richard *c.s.s.* '57 (BO)[U] Waltham, MA Stigmatine Fathers & Brothers Provincial House.
Woodeshick, Martin E. '69 (PH) Sharon Hill, PA Holy Spirit.
Woodhall, Jonathan A. '99 (R) Retired.
Woodhall, Jonathan (BAL)[A] Baltimore, MD St. Mary's Seminary and University.
Woodland, Stephen '88 (LA) On Active Leave.
Woodman, Gerald '78 (SEA) Woodland, WA St. Philip.
Woodrow, Brian P. '06 (TR) Jackson, NJ St. Aloysius.
Woodruff, Mark '72 (SAN) Odessa, TX St. Elizabeth Ann Seton; Defensores Vinculi.
Woodruff, William F. '82 (NY) Maybrook, NY Church of the Assumption.
Woods, James A. *s.j.* '61 (BO)[C] Summer Session; [C] Woods College of Advancing Studies; [U] Newton, MA The Jesuit Community at Boston College.
Woods, Keith A. '95 (WDC) Morganza, MD St. Joseph; [T] Washington, DC American University Catholic Community.
Woods, Michael '66 (KNX) Knoxville, TN All Saints Catholic Church; [K] Knoxville, TN Diocesan Council of Catholic Women.
Woods, Michael *s.j.* '04 (SPK)[B] Spokane, WA Gonzaga University.
Woods, Patrick F. *c.ss.r.* '75 (BRK)[T] Brooklyn, NY Redemptorist Fathers of New York, Inc.–Baltimore Province; Brooklyn, NY AMERICAN REDEMPTORIST FATHERS; Brooklyn, NY.
Woods, Richard J. *o.p.* '69 (CHI)[N] River Forest, IL St. Thomas Aquinas Priory.
Woods, Scott '02 (WDC) St. Inigoes, MD St. Peter Claver; Archdiocesan Chaplain – Catholic Committee on Boy Scouts.
Woods, Thomas F. '02 (BIR) Sylacauga, AL St. Jude; Talladega, AL St. Francis of Assisi; [H] Talladega, AL Talladega College Catholic Campus Ministry.
Woods, Thomas Matthew '05 (WDC) Absent On Leave.
Woods, Walter J. '69 (BO) Acton, MA St. Elizabeth of Hungary; Canonical Affairs Committee.
Woodward, John *s.j.* '58 (PH)[Y] Loyola Center and Manresa Hall.
Woolever, James '74 (SY) On Duty Outside the Diocese.
Woolley, Michael J. '99 (PRO) Woonsocket, RI St. Joseph; Council Members.
Woolson, Herbert '82 (LFT) Rochester, IN St. Ann; Monterey, IN St. Anne; Rochester, IN St. Joseph.
Woolway, Rev. Msgr. John S. '80 (LA) Compton, CA Sagrado Corazon, Sacred Heart; San Pedro Region.
Woost, David G. '91 (CLV) Kirtland, OH Divine Word; [Y] Kirtland, OH St. Philip Neri/Divine Word Church in the City Partnership Inc.
Woost, Michael G. '84 (CLV)[A] Wickliffe, OH St. Mary Seminary and Graduate School of Theology; [A] Wickliffe, OH Borromeo Seminary.
Woost, Thomas G. '97 (CLV) North Olmsted, OH St. Brendan.
Wooton, Jerry A. '96 (ARL) Gainesville, VA Holy Trinity.
Wopperer, Thomas J. '64 (BUF) Dunkirk, NY Blessed Mary Angela Parish Retired.
Woracek, Rev. Msgr. Thomas J. '46 (STL) Retired.
Worbleski, Sergius *o.f.m.* '46 (GRY)[H] Cedar Lake, IN Our Lady of Lourdes Friary.
Worcester, Thomas W. *s.j.* '91 (WOR)[O] Worcester, MA Jesuits of the Holy Cross, Inc.
Worch, Donald P. '67 (WDC) Potomac, MD Our Lady of Mercy.
Wordekemper, Thomas *o.s.b.* '94 (BIS)[A] Richardton, ND Assumption Abbey.
Workman, Jamie R. '06 (ARL) Arlington, VA Cathedral of St. Thomas More; Advocates.
Workman, Joseph G. '04 (CLV) Barberton, OH St. Augustine; Wadsworth, OH Sacred Heart of Jesus.
Worland, Christopher J. '01 (CIN) Kettering, OH Ascension.
Worley, Jason '99 (BAL) Libertytown, MD St. Peter.
Worm, Paul F. '88 (LR) Batesville, AR St. Cecilia; Batesville, AR St. Mary.
Worman, Jeremiah F. '67 (GB) White Lake, WI SS. James–Stanislaus.
Worman, Jeremiah F. '67 (GB) Deerbrook, WI St. Wenceslaus; Pembine, WI St. Margaret; College of Consultors; Florence, WI Immaculate Conception Retired.
Wormek, Joseph E. '76 (STL) Crystal City, MO Sacred Heart.
Worn, G. Peter '77 (SY) Cazenovia, NY St. James; [T] Cazenovia, NY Cazenovia College Newman Center.
Worner, William H. '45 (SFR) Retired.
Woroniewicz, Michael A. '85 (DET) Dundee, MI St. Irene; Ida, MI St. Joseph.
Worry, Benedict M. *o.s.b.* '87 (PAT)[N] Morristown St. Mary's Abbey.
Worry, Benedict Michael *o.s.b.* '87 (NEW) Linden, NJ St. Elizabeth of Hungary.
Worschak, D. George '78 (PHU)[F] Fox Chase Manor, PA Provincial Motherhouse of the Sisters of St. Basil the Great.
Worsley, Rev. Msgr. Stephen C. '84 (R) Sanford, NC St. Stephen The First Martyr.
Worster, John R. '87 (MO) Army National Guard Chaplains.
Worster, John '87 (B) Blackfoot, ID St. Bernard's; On Sabbatical; Priest Retirement Committee.
Worth, James '01 (NEW) Springfield, NJ St. James the Apostle.
Worthley, Jason W. '04 (BO) Middleborough, MA Sacred Heart.
Worthy, Donald L. '62 (DET) Retired.
Wortmann, Joseph F. '58 (NEW)[B] Retired.
Worzalla, Dennis A. '50 (GB) Retired.
Wosman, Richard *s.m.* '93 (SAT)[L] San Antonio, TX Woodlawn Marianist Community; [C] San Antonio, TX St. Mary's University of San Antonio, Texas.
Woster, Rev. Msgr. Michael '82 (RC) Winner, SD St. Isidore; Winner, SD Immaculate Conception; [E] Philip, SD Priest Retirement and Aid Association/ Pension Plan Board; Vicar for Retired Priests.
Wotelko, Matthew S. *o.s.b.* '67 (NEW)[M] Newark, NJ Newark Abbey; Newark, NJ.
Woy, Rev. Msgr. Richard W. '79 (BAL) Consultors; Consultors; Special Assignment.
Woy, Rev. Msgr. Richard '79 (BAL) Vicars General; Moderator of the Curia.
Woytek, Robert '91 (PSC) Leave of Absence.
Woytyna, Christopher *o.s.b.m.* '61 (STF) Long Island

City, NY Holy Cross.
Wozniak, Anthony A. '59 (GBG)[F] Greensburg, PA Neumann House.
Wozniak, Casimir '68 (E)[B] Erie, PA Gannon University; The Bishop's Theological Advisory Committee; [M] Erie, PA Congregation of the Divine Spirit.
Wozniak, James E. '97 (GRY) Crown Point, IN St. Matthias; Bishop's Council of Priests.
Wozniak, Rev. Msgr. Louis '51 (AUS) Retired.
Wozniak, Richard *c.m.f.* '52 (PHX) Prescott, AZ Sacred Heart Roman Catholic Parish.
Wozniak, Robert A. '72 (WIL) Wilmington, DE Immaculate Heart of Mary.
Wozniak, Robert A. '88 (BUF) Newfane, NY St. Brendan on the Lake.
Wozniak, Ronald E. *s.j.* '77 (BO)[U] Weston, MA Campion Jesuit Community; [U] Weston, MA Campion Health Center, Inc.
Wozniak, Tim '74 (STP) Burnsville, MN Church of the Risen Savior.
Woznica, Miroslaw '90 (FBK) Fairbanks, AK Immaculate Conception Catholic Church Fairbanks; [C] Fairbanks, AK Kobuk Center.
Woznicki, Donald C. '02 (CHI) Lake Forest, IL St. Mary; [W] Lake Forest, IL New Ethos.
Wozniczka, Stephen Z. *o.s.p.p.e.* '60 (PH)[Y].
Wozny, Jacek '88 (NY) Staten Island, NY St. Ann.
Wray, Joseph M. '96 (OM) Battle Creek, NE St. Patrick's; On Medical Leave.
Wrenn, Lawrence G. '53 (HRT) Hartford, CT Cathedral of St. Joseph Retired.
Wrenn, Lawrence '77 (WH) Retired.
Wright, Addison G. *s.s.* '57 (BAL)[S] Baltimore Society of St. Sulpice, Province of the United States Retired.
Wright, Addison G. *s.s.* '60 (BGP) Retired.
Wright, Arthur J. (BO) Milton, MA St. Mary of the Hills.
Wright, Bryan B. '00 (SCR) Tobyhanna, PA St. Ann; [F] Cresco, PA Monsignor McHugh Elementary School; Mount Pocono, PA St. Mary of the Mount.
Wright, D. Ralph *o.s.b.* '70 (STL)[F] Creve Coeur, MO St. Louis Priory School; [O] St. Louis, MO The Abbey of St. Mary and St. Louis.
Wright, David *o.p.* '68 (STL)[O] St. Louis, MO St. Dominic Priory.
Wright, Francis *c.s.sp.* (BRK) Brooklyn, NY Our Lady of Guadalupe.
Wright, Frank *s.m.a.* '93 (WDC)[N] Takoma Park, MD Lay Missionary Program.
Wright, Frank *s.m.a.* (HEL) Butte, MT St. John the Evangelist.
Wright, Frank *s.m.a.* (NEW)[M] Tenafly, NJ Society of African Missions, Provincialate, S.M.A. Fathers.
Wright, Gary R. *s.j.* '80 (DET)[S] McNichols Campus; [K] Detroit, MI Jesuit Community at the University of Detroit Mercy.
Wright, Gerald *o.m.v.* '80 (E) Veterans Administration Hospital; Erie, PA St. Joseph.
Wright, John A. '56 (CHY) Retired.
Wright, John A. '82 (MAN) Retired.
Wright, John J. '78 (CLV) Bedford, OH Our Lady of Hope.
Wright, Rev. Msgr. John M. '62 (IND) Retired.
Wright, Michael H. '95 (SEA) Seattle, WA St. Bernadette.
Wright, Moses (ROM)[A] Pearblossom, CA Holy Resurrection Monastery.
Wright, Rev. Msgr. Richard J. '45 (PH) Retired.
Wright, Robert E. *o.m.i.* '74 (SAT)[C] Oblate School of Theology; [L] San Antonio, TX; [L] San Antonio, TX Joseph Gerard House.
Wright, Rev. Msgr. Rupert A. '56 (BUF) Clergy Personnel Board; [O] Tonawanda, NY O'Hara Residence Retired.
Wright, Russell *s.t.l.* '88 (VEN) Naples, FL St. Peter the Apostle.
Wright, Tennant C. *s.j.* '62 (SJ)[B] Santa Clara, CA Jesuit Community.
Wright, Warren J. *s.j.* '82 (SFR)[E] San Francisco, CA St. Ignatius College Preparatory (Coed); [N] San Francisco, CA Jesuit Community at St. Ignatius College Preparatory.
Wright, William *c.ss.r.* '60 (FgM) Denver, CO Denver Province.
Wrightson, Mark *o.s.f.s.* '86 (VEN)[G] Fort Myers, FL Oblates of St. Francis de Sales.
Wrigley, Franklin '52 (OKL) Retired.
Wrigley, Michael '03 (BIR) Birmingham, AL St. Barnabas.
Wrobleski, Edward D. *c.s.p.* '62 (LA) Los Angeles, CA St. Paul the Apostle Retired.
Wroblewski, Anthony '95 (DUL) Brainerd, MN St. Andrew; Brainerd, MN St. Francis; Brainerd, MN St. Mathias; Brainerd, MN St. Thomas; College of Consultors.
Wroblewski, Brendan *o.f.m.* '55 (GB)[J] Pulaski, WI Friary.
Wroblewski, Edward D. *c.s.p.* '62 (NY)[EE] Jamaica Estates Paulist Fathers Generalate.
Wroblewski, Edward M. *m.m.* '52 (NY)[EE] Maryknoll Maryknoll Fathers and Brothers Retired.
Wroblewski, John J. '92 (NY) Staten Island, NY St. Anthony.
Wroblewski, Lawrence J. *s.j.* '74 (ROC)[B] Rochester, NY McQuaid Jesuit High School.
Wroblewski, Marion *c.r.* '65 (CHI) Chicago, IL St. Hyacinth Basilica.
Wroblicky, Theodore P. '99 (STN) Sacramento, CA Holy Wisdom.
Wronski, John C. *s.j.* '04 (BO)[U] Newton, MA The Jesuit Community at Boston College.
Wrozek, Timothy A. '88 (FTW) Fort Wayne; Fort Wayne, IN St. Joseph.
Wrynn, John F. *s.j.* '70 (NEW)[M] Jersey City, NJ Jesuits of Saint Peter's College, Inc.
Wrynn, John P. '70 (NEW)[B] Jersey City, NJ Jesuit Center.
Wtorek, Krzysztof '94 (CAM) Ventnor, NJ St. James Catholic Church, Ventnor, N.J.
Wtulich, John '72 (BRK) Belle Harbor, NY St. Francis de Sales.
Wtyklo, Jacek S. '98 (MAR) Perkins, MI St. Joseph; Rapid River, MI St. Charles Borromeo; Trenary, MI St. Rita.
Wu, Jay Jay '07 (LA) Arcadia, CA Holy Angels.
Wu, Peter A. *m.m.* '61 (FgM) Maryknoll, NY MARYKNOLL.
Wudarski, Dariusz P. '96 (SPR) Springfield, MA Immaculate Conception.
Wuerth, James E. *m.s.f.* '71 (STL) St. Louis, MO St. Wenceslaus.
Wuest, George *s.j.* '58 (FgM) Chicago, IL Society of Jesus.
Wueste, Andrew *o.m.i.* '54 (SAT)[K] San Antonio, TX Oblate Madonna Residence.
Wulinski, Stanley F. '80 (MO) Air Force Reserve Chaplains; On Leave/Unassigned.
Wulsch, Michael A. '72 (CHI) Skokie, IL St. Peter; Deans.
Wunderlich, Dale P. '74 (STL) St. Louis, MO Shrine of St. Joseph.
Wurm, Robert L. '60 (DET) Retired.
Wurst, Wayne H. '80 (CHI) Oak Forest, IL Oak Forest Hospital.
Wurth, Elmer P. *m.m.* '56 (FgM) Maryknoll, NY MARYKNOLL.
Wurth, Richard W. '99 (COV) Erlanger, KY Mary, Queen of Heaven; Diocesan Consultors.
Wurtz, Camillus *o.s.b.* '53 (KCK)[I] Atchison, KS St. Benedict's Abbey Retired.
Wurtz, Michael *c.s.c.* '04 (FTW)[H] Notre Dame Congregation of Holy Cross, Indiana Province, Provincial House.
Wurz, George E. '60 (SY) Oswego, NY St. Peter.
Wurzel, Richard T. '59 (TOL) Retired.
Wydeven, John L. '79 (OAK) Providence, RI Veterans Administration Hospital; DEPARTMENT OF VETERANS AFFAIRS HOSPITALS AND CHAPLAINS; On Duty Outside the Diocese.
Wydeven, John '79 (PRO) Providence, RI Holy Name of Jesus.
Wydmanski, Mateusz *o.s.p.p.e.* '92 (BUF) Buffalo, NY Corpus Christi.
Wyffels, Rev. Msgr. Robert J. '60 (NU) Morgan, MN St. Joseph (Oratory); Morgan, MN St. Michael.
Wykes, John *o.m.v.* '98 (BO)[Z] Boston, MA St. Francis Chapel.
Wymelenberg, M. John *s.j.* '60 (OM)[K] Omaha, NE Jesuit Community at Creighton University.
Wymer, Seth T. '07 (STU) Marietta, OH St. Mary's.
Wymes, John F. *m.m.* '54 (NY)[EE] Retired.
Wymes, John F. *m.m.* '54 (RVC) Malverne, NY Our Lady of Lourdes Retired.
Wynants, Paul G. *c.i.c.m.* '51 (ARL)[L] Vienna, VA Mount Tabor Society, Inc.
Wyndaele, William *c.i.c.m.* '59 (ARL)[H] Arlington, VA Missionhurst, C.I.C.M.–Central House and Provincialate.
Wyndham, Thomas F. '69 (BO) Senior Priests. Retired.
Wynne, James *o.m.i.* '55 (BEL)[F] Belleville, IL Missionary Oblates of Mary Immaculate – St. Henry's Oblate Residence.
Wynne, Robert F. *m.m.* '74 (FgM) Maryknoll, NY MARYKNOLL.
Wynnycky, John '92 (DET) Grosse Pointe Farms, MI St. Paul Catholic Church.
Wypych, Andrew P. '79 (CHI) Chicago, IL St. Francis Borgia; Deans.
Wyrostek, Andrzej '00 (RC) Rapid City, SD Blessed Sacrament.
Wyrsch, Thomas W. '78 (STL) St. Louis, MO St. Margaret of Scotland.
Wyse, James B. '87 (GR) Howard City, MI St. Francis de Sales; Howard City, MI Christ the King; Remus, MI St. Michael's.
Wysochansky, Demetrius *o.s.b.m.* '59 (STN) Palos Park, IL Nativity of B.V.M.; Eparchial Censor.
Wysochansky, John '57 (PHU) Retired.
Wysochansky, Rev. Canon Walter '64 (SJP) Ambridge, PA Ss. Peter and Paul; Presbyters Retired.
Wysocki, Joseph A. '71 (SCR) Unassigned or Leave of Absence.
Wysocki, Marek B. '85 (NEW) Lyndhurst, NJ Sacred Heart.
Wysocki, Paul '64 (CLV) Retired.
Wysoczanski, Jaroslaw *o.f.m.conv.* (FgM) AMERICAN CONVENTUAL FRANCISCAN MISSIONS.
Wysong, William H. '72 (CIN)[J] Cincinnati, OH St. Rita School for the Deaf; Defenders of the Bond.
Wyszynski, Darius W. '58 (LAN) Retired.
Wytrwal, Alexander J. '50 (DET) Retired.
Wyvill, Christopher *o.s.b.* '65 (WDC)[N] Washington, DC St. Anselm's Abbey.
Wyzykiewicz, Richard S. *sch.p.* '71 (PH)[F] Devon, PA Devon Preparatory School; [Y] Devon Piarist Fathers (Order of the Pious Schools).

X

Xavariapitchai, Udayakumar (BO) Revere, MA St. Anthony of Padua.
Xavier, Antony Pullukattu (MOB) Andalusia, AL Christ the King; Greenville, AL St. Elizabeth.
Xavier, Antony '60 (RVC) Manhasset, NY North Shore Univ. Hospital.
Xavier, Godwin '85 (SAC) Vacaville, CA California Medical Facility.
Xavier, Joseph *m.s.f.s.* '96 (KAL) Paw Paw, MI St. Mary; Gobles, MI St. Jude.
Xavier, Joseph *m.s.f.s.* '96 (TYL)[B] Whitehouse, TX The Missionaries of St. Francis de Sales.
Xotta, Tomas M. *o.s.m.* '64 (ELP) El Paso, TX Our Lady of Sorrows.
Xuereb, Paul D. '45 (DET) Retired.
Xuereb, Publius '68 (FWT) Aledo, TX Holy Redeemer Parish.

Y

Yabes, Arturo '87 (SJ) Sunnyvale, CA St. Cyprian.
Yablonsky, Gabriel '59 (Y) Retired.
Yabut, Ronald (TUC)[C] Tucson, AZ Carondelet St. Joseph's Hospital.
Yackanich, Eugene P. '65 (PBR) Munhall, PA St. Elias; Consultors; Protopresbyters; Finance Council; Presbyteral Council.
Yacobi, Francis *o.f.m.cap.* '90 (PH) Philadelphia, PA St. John the Evangelist.
Yacyshyn, Gregory '98 (RVC) Mastic Beach, NY St. Jude.
Yadron, Michael J. '83 (GRY) Munster, IN St. Thomas More; Bishop's Council of Priests; Priests' Personnel Board; Deans; Consultors.
Yadron, Raymond A. '63 (CHI) Palatine, IL St. Thomas of Villanova Retired.
Yaeger, Joseph J. '89 (R) Farmville, NC St. Elizabeth.
Yagaza, Severine (SY) East Syracuse, NY St. Matthew.
Yagesh, Richard C. '78 (PIT) Bridgeville, PA Holy Child.
Yaghi, Milad T. *m.l.m.* '88 (OLL) Houston, TX Our Lady of the Cedars Maronite Catholic Church; [A] Houston, TX The Congregation of Maronite Lebanese Missionaries.
Yahner, Gordon A. '63 (CLV) Fairlawn, OH St. Hilary; Akron, OH St. Vincent Retired.
Yakaitis, Michael T. '78 (CHI) Other Assignments.
Yaksick, Michael L. '94 (PIT) Midland, PA St. Blaise.
Yakubu, Peter (STP) Mercy Hospital.
Yakubu, Victor '96 (PHX) Phoenix, AZ St. Edward Confessor Roman Catholic Parish.
Yaldo, Basel '02 (EST) Shelby Twp., MI St. George Caldean Catholic Church.
Yali, Jacob '77 (STP) Clearwater, MN St. Luke.
Yalong, Oliver '99 (NEW) Jersey City, NJ St. Aedan's.
Yammine, Jean *m.l.m.* '00 (OLL) Thousand Oaks, CA Saints Peter and Paul Maronite Catholic Mission; [A] Houston, TX The Congregation of Maronite Lebanese Missionaries.
Yanas, John '84 (ALB) Troy, NY Sacred Heart.
Yander, Steven L. '74 (ATL)[E] Atlanta, GA Saint Joseph's Hospital of Atlanta, Inc.
Yanez, Horacio '75 (SEA) Seattle, WA Holy Family.
Yanez, Jaime *o.f.m.* '47 (ELP)[B] El Paso, TX St. Anthony's School of Theology.
Yanez, Jose *c.m.* '56 (SJN) San Juan, PR Sagrado Corazon de Jesus; [B] San Juan, PR Colegio Sagrado Corazon de Jesus.
Yang, Benedict '07 (ORG) Orange, CA St. Norbert.
Yang, Dominic Hyi Jeong '05 (ARL) Fairfax, VA St. Paul Chung.
Yang, Joseph '96 (LA) Temple City, CA St. Luke the Evangelist.
Yanju, Henry M. '96 (MO) Air Force Reserve Chaplains; Military & VA Chaplains.
Yankauskas, David *o.m.v.* '88 (BO)[Z] Boston, MA St. Francis Chapel; [U] Milton, MA Oblate Residence (St. Joseph House).
Yannarell, James J. *s.j.* '71 (NY)[EE] New York, NY Society of Jesus, New York Province; [EE] New York, NY Xavier Jesuit Community; New York, NY.
Yanos, Richard M. '83 (CHI) Lake Villa, IL Prince of Peace.
Yanovsky, Stepan (STF) Ansonia, CT SS. Peter and Paul.

Yanowski, Stephen (STF) Sodalities, B.V.M.
Yanta, Timothy J. '05 (STP) Jordan, MN St. John the Baptist.
Yanus, Gary D. '81 (CLV) Cleveland, OH St. Ignatius of Antioch; Judicial Vicar.
Yanus, Gary D. (Y) Judges.
Yanus, Gary D. (TOL) Defenders of the Bond.
Yarbrough, Rev. Msgr. Michael '80 (SAT) San Antonio, TX St. Matthew's; In Metropolitan Area; Archdiocesan Presbyteral Council; Priests Personnel Board.
Yarce, Eugenio '92 (SLC) Salt Lake City, UT Sacred Heart LLC 210.
Yargeau, Rev. Msgr. Ronald G. '73 (SPR) Greenfield, MA Holy Trinity; Vicars for the Clergy.
Yarno, Kenneth E. *c.s.v.* '59 (CHI)[N] Arlington Heights Viatorian Province Center–Clerics of St. Viator.
Yarno, Kenneth *c.s.v.* '59 (JOL) Bourbonnais, IL Maternity of the Blessed Virgin Mary Retired.
Yaroch, Kenneth E. '67 (SAG) Retired.
Yaroch, Paul *o.f.m.cap.* '64 (MIL)[P] Mount Calvary, WI St. Lawrence Friary Retired.
Yarrish, Rev. Msgr. Bernard E. '76 (SCR) Retired.
Yasso, Jacob O. '60 (EST) Detroit, MI Sacred Heart Chaldean Parish; Eparchial College of Consultors.
Yast, Robert A. '56 (FTW) Retired.
Yastishock, Charles '77 (PSC) Toms River, NJ Our Lady of Perpetual Help; Presbyteral Council.
Yaszcz, Thomas A. '75 (SCR) On Special or Other Diocesan Assignment.
Yates, John L. *c.s.sp.* '54 (LR) Center Ridge, AR St. Joseph.
Yatkauskas, Matthew '89 (NY) New York, NY St. Joseph.
Yavarone, Mark *o.m.v.* (BO)[B] Boston, MA Oblate Provincialate.
Yavorsky, Stephen T. *s.j.* '77 (DEN) Denver, CO St. Ignatius Loyola; [N] Denver, CO Society of Jesus – St. Ignatius Loyola Jesuit Community.
Yawo Azah, Francis Perry '97 (NY) Pleasant Valley, NY St. Stanislaus Kostka.
Yaya, Louis '79 (NY) Kingston, NY Benedictine Hospital.
Ybarra, Manuel *o.f.m.* '86 (WDC) Washington, DC; [N] Washington, DC Franciscan Monastery USA Inc.
Ybiernas, Bernard *o.c.d.* '55 (MIL)[P] Milwaukee Provincial Offices – Discalced Carmelites.
Yeakel, James *o.s.f.s.* '79 (NY) Harrison, NY Saint Vincent's Westchester; New York, NY Holy Trinity.
Yeazel, Rev. Msgr. J. Robert '67 (SY) DeWitt, NY Holy Cross; Vicar General; Presbyteral Council; Clerical Fund Society of the Roman Catholic Diocese of Syracuse; Finance Committee; Board of Diocesan Consultors.
Yeboah–Amanfo, Peter '83 (VIC) Schulenburg, TX St. Rose of Lima.
Yebra, Bernardino S. '88 (CHR) Blythewood, SC Transfiguration; Army Reserve Chaplains.
Yeddanapalli, George William '90 (AMA) Bovina, TX St. Ann's; Friona, TX St. Teresa of Jesus.
Yee–Mon, Ronald '85 (HT) Dulac, LA Holy Family.
Yee Mon, Ronald '85 (FAR) On Duty Outside the Diocese.
Yelenc, Joseph *t.o.r.* '71 (STU)[A] Steubenville, OH Franciscan University of Steubenville; [H] Steubenville, OH Holy Spirit Friary; Presbyteral Council.
Yelinko, Flavian G. *o.s.b.* '33 (GBG)[G] Latrobe, PA Saint Vincent Archabbey.
Yelle, Ronald R. '79 (HRT) Granby, CT St. Therese; Appointed.
Ye Myint, Sixtus '78 (WCH) Caney, KS Sacred Heart; Moline, KS St. Mary's; Moline, KS St. Robert Bellarmine.
Yender, Basil *o.s.b.* '71 (RCK)[A] Aurora, IL Marmion Abbey; [G] Aurora, IL Marmion Abbey; Aurora, IL.
Yenkevich, Daniel J. '90 (SCR) Retired.
Yennock, Rev. Msgr. Eugene M. '50 (SY) Syracuse, NY St. Daniel.
Yenushosky, Rev. Msgr. Daniel J. '77 (ALN) Whitehall, PA Holy Trinity; Vicars Forane; Serra Club of Allentown.
Yeo, Junkoo '91 (SEA) Koreans, Ministry to.
Yeo, Wilfred '58 (NEW) Retired.
Yeom, Dominic Dong Kyr *s.d.b.* '92 (SP) Tampa, FL Mary Help of Christians; [P] Tampa, FL Salesian Society of Florida, Inc.
Yepes, Walter '01 (CHI) Chicago, IL St. Roman.
Yerrnini, Chinnaiah '90 (PRO) Providence, RI Rhode Island Hospital; Cranston, RI St. Matthew.
Yesalonia, Dennis J. *s.j.* '85 (BO)[U] Watertown, MA The Society of Jesus of New England–Provincial Offices; [U] Boston, MA Loyola House.
Yetman, Robert C. '05 (PH) Philadelphia, PA St. Christopher.
Yetsko, Robert '84 (ALT)[G] Loretto, PA St. Francis Friary at Mount Assisi.
Yetter, Robert M. '73 (BUF) Swormville, NY St. Mary.
Yew, Edward Y. '02 (TLS) Wagoner, OK Holy Cross.
Yi, Ju Hyung Paul '08 (BR) Baton Rouge, LA Our Lady of Mercy.
Yi, Odilo *o.s.b.* '85 (PAT)[N] Newton, NJ St. Paul's Abbey.
Yi, Seung Yong *s.d.b.* '02 (OAK)[M] Berkeley Salesians of Don Bosco.
Yiengst, Rev. Msgr. George B. '62 (BUF) Retired.
Yiftheg, Cuthbert '89 (CI) Our Lady of Mercy.
Yikore, Venantius '95 (LA) Santa Monica, CA St. Monica.
Yim, Louis H. '57 (HON) Retired.
Yllana, Rio Antonio C. '84 (LA) Los Angeles, CA Our Lady of Guadalupe.
Ymson, Enrique *m.j.* '75 (LA)[P] Los Angeles, CA Missionaries of Jesus, Inc.; Los Angeles, CA St. Kevin; Los Angeles, CA Precious Blood.
Yncierto, Frank '75 (LAV) Las Vegas, NV St. Bridget Catholic Church.
Yoakam, Lee R. *o.s.b.* '01 (MO) Army Chaplains.
Yoakam, Lee R. *o.s.b.* '01 (GBG)[G] Latrobe Saint Vincent Archabbey.
Yockey, Aelred *o.s.b.* '93 (P)[K] Mount Angel, OR Providence Benedictine Nursing Center; [L] St. Benedict, OR Mt. Angel Abbey.
Yockey, John G. '70 (MIL) Oconomowoc, WI St. Jerome.
Yohe, Robert A. '89 (HBG) Mount Carmel, PA Divine Redeemer.
Yokum, Joseph T. '07 (COL) New Boston, OH St. Monica; Wheelersburg, OH St. Peter.
Yonas, Deebar *s.v.d.* '07 (SB) Riverside, CA Queen of Angels.
Yonkovig, John R. '77 (OG) Plattsburgh, NY St. Peter; Defenders of the Bond.
Yontz, Rev. Msgr. George W. '59 (STU) Steubenville, OH St. Peter's.
Yori, Robert O. '61 (CAM) Retired.
York, Kenneth J. '88 (BEL) East St. Louis, IL Immaculate Conception; Fayetteville, IL St. Pancratius; Belleville, IL St. Henry; Chancellor for Canonical Affairs; Diocesan Consultors; Diocesan Finance Council.
York, Patrick G. '90 (WCH) Wichita, KS Church of the Magdalen.
York, Paul '64 (LIN) Crete, NE Sacred Heart.
York, Richard '73 (VEN) Venice, FL Epiphany Cathedral.
York, Rev. Msgr. Vincent P. '68 (ALN) Pen Argyl, PA St. Elizabeth of Hungary.
Yossa, Kenneth F. '88 (ROM) Unassigned.
Yost, Alan *s.j.* '06 (SEA)[C] Tacoma, WA Bellarmine Preparatory School.
Yost, Alan *s.j.* '06 (YAK) Yakima, WA St. Joseph Parish.
Yost, Charles *s.c.j.* '80 (SP)[N] Pinellas Park, FL Priests of the Sacred Heart Retired.
Yost, Herbert C. *c.s.c.* '75 (FTW)[H] Notre Dame Congregation of Holy Cross, Indiana Province, Provincial House; Notre Dame, IN.
Yost, Richard J. *o.s.f.s.* '76 (DET)[Q] Warren, MI St. John's Deaf Center.
You, Jae Hun '98 (BUF) Tonawanda, NY St. Andrew Kim.
You, Simon (Kwanggun) '94 (ALB) Korean Apostolate of the Roman Catholic Diocese of Albany, New York; Special Assignment.
Youkhanna, Sanharib (EST) Chicago, IL Mart Mariam Parish.
Younan, Andrew '04 (SPA) El Cajon, CA St. Peter Chaldean Cathedral; [A] El Cajon, CA Seminary of Mar Abba the Great.
Younan, Andrew (SD) El Cajon, CA St. Peter Cathedral.
Younes, Jean '98 (SAM) Danbury, CT St. Anthony; Presbyteral Council.
Young, Bernard L. '63 (NO) Retired.
Young, Rev. Msgr. Bill '70 (GAL) Western Vicariate.
Young, Daniel A. '95 (BUF) North Tonawanda, NY Good Shepherd.
Young, David E. '95 (COL) West Portsmouth, OH Our Lady of Lourdes; West Portsmouth, OH Our Lady of Sorrows.
Young, David H. '02 (SEA) Black Diamond, WA St. Barbara.
Young, David J. '04 (COL) Ada, OH Our Lady of Lourdes; Deanery 7: Marion; Parochial Examiners; Presbyteral Council.
Young, Dennis M. '80 (STA) Special Assignment; DEPARTMENT OF VETERANS AFFAIRS HOSPITALS AND CHAPLAINS.
Young, DeSales *o.f.m.cap.* '48 (PIT)[M] Pittsburgh, PA St. Augustine Friary.
Young, Dismas *o.f.m.cap.* '66 (WH)[D] Wheeling, WV Paul VI Pastoral Center; [L] Wheeling, WV Capuchin Hermitage of St. Joseph.
Young, Dominic G. '79 (LFT) Lafayette, IN St. Ann.
Young, Rev. Archpriest Edward P. '83 (STF) Ludlow, MA SS. Peter and Paul; South Deerfield, MA Holy Ghost.
Young, Edward P. (STF) Censor; Ecumenical Commission; Diocesan Consultors.
Young, Frank '70 (SY) Brewerton, NY St. Agnes.
Young, Gary *c.r.* '76 (L)[M] Nazareth, KY Generalate, Motherhouse and Novitiate of the Sisters of Charity of Nazareth.
Young, Gerald A. '72 (LA) On Duty Outside the Archdiocese.
Young, Gerard F. '63 (BR) Retired.
Young, Rev. Msgr. James E. '74 (TYL) Nacogdoches, TX Sacred Heart; College of Consultors; Deans; Diocesan Finance Council; Priests' Pension Board; Priests' Personnel Board; Presbyteral Council; Office of Clergy Development/Continuing Education.
Young, James G. '69 (PIT) Munhall, PA St. Therese of Lisieux.
Young, Jerome *o.s.b.* '86 (P)[L] St. Benedict, OR Mt. Angel Abbey.
Young, John L. *c.s.c.* '71 (HRT)[L] New Haven, CT Priests of the Congregation of Holy Cross.
Young, Rev. Msgr. John Melvin '47 (LA) Retired.
Young, John (KAL) Retired.
Young, Larry E. '81 (OAK) Rodeo, CA St. Patrick; Consultors; Presbyteral Council.
Young, Lawrence A. '03 (WDC) Bryantown, MD St. Mary.
Young, Otis W. '01 (NO) Marrero, LA St. Joseph the Worker.
Young, Park Chi (STL) University City, MO St. Andrew Kim.
Young, Peter G. '47 (PRO) North Providence, RI St. Lawrence Retired.
Young, Richard '95 (SAV) Apostleship of the Sea; Savannah, GA Sacred Heart of Jesus.
Young, Robert '94 (SP) On Duty Outside the Diocese.
Young, Robert *o.f.m.* '82 (OAK)[M] Oakland Franciscan Friars (Province of St. Barbara).
Young, Ronald E. '75 (DAV) On Duty Outside the Diocese.
Young, Ronald W. *o.m.i.* '88 (SAT)[C] Oblate School of Theology; Washington, DC AMERICAN OBLATE MISSIONS.
Young, Ronald *o.m.i.* '88 (WDC)[N] Washington, DC Provincial Offices of the United States Province of the Missionary Oblates of Mary Immaculate.
Young, Samuel V. '90 (BAL) Aberdeen, MD St. Joan of Arc.
Young, Rev. Msgr. Terry W. '72 (ATL) Deans; Jackson, GA Saint Mary, Mother of God Catholic Church.
Young, Valentine *o.f.m.* '56 (CIN)[N] Cincinnati St. Francis Seraph Friary.
Young, Valentine *o.f.m.* (LEX) Regina Pacis Community.
Young, Vincent J. '78 (SCR) Unassigned or Leave of Absence.
Young, Rev. Msgr. William L. '70 (GAL) Boy and Girl Scouts; Houston, TX St. Vincent de Paul.
Young, William T. *s.s.s.* '64 (CLV) Highland Heights, OH St. Paschal Baylon; Cleveland Clinic Foundation; [N] Cleveland, OH Congregation of the Blessed Sacrament.
Young, William W. '76 (SFR) San Francisco, CA Most Holy Redeemer Retired.
Young, William '90 (SFE) College of Consultors; Moriarty, NM Estancia Valley Catholic Parish.
Youngberg, Vincent *c.p.* '67 (RVC)[O] Shelter Island Heights, NY St. Gabriel's Spiritual Center for Youth.
Youngberg, Vincent *c.p.* '67 (PMB)[H] North Palm Beach, FL Our Lady of Florida Spiritual Center.
Youngkamp, Vincent J. *s.s.c.* '59 (FgM) St Columbans, NE House of Post–Graduate Studies.
Youngs, Fred A. '90 (BR) Baton Rouge, LA St. Isidore the Farmer; Separated and Divorced.
Youtz, Rev. Msgr. Richard A. '66 (HBG) Lancaster, PA St. John Neumann; Deans; Diocesan Judges.
Yrlas, Raynaldo '97 (CC) Propagation of the Faith Office; Alice, TX Our Lady of Guadalupe.
Yslas, Martin *o.s.b.* '87 (LA)[P] Valyermo, CA St. Andrew's Abbey.
Yu, Celso A. *m.f.* '92 (AUS) Bremond, TX St. Mary; [G] Bremond, TX Clerical Congregation Missionaries of Faith.
Yu, Reynaldo '83 (SEA) Forks, WA St. Anne Parish; Clallam Bay Correction Center; Clearwater / Olympic Correction Center; Port Angeles, WA Queen of Angels.
Yudin, Raynald *o.f.m.conv.* '62 (SY) Bridgeport, NY St. Francis of Assisi; Bridgeport, NY St. Mary.
Yuenger, Paul D. '00 (WH) Oak Hill, WV SS. Peter and Paul.
Yuhas, Edward L. '97 (PIT) Monroeville, PA St. Bernadette.
Yuhaus, Cassian J. *c.p.* '51 (SCR)[R] Scranton, PA Ministry for Religious Research and Consultancy.
Yuhaus, Cassian *c.p.* '51 (SCR)[M] Scranton, PA Saint Ann's Passionist Monastery.
Yulfo–Hoffman, Nestor '92 (SJN) Carolina, PR Santo Cristo de los Milagros; Carolina.
Yunk, Rev. Msgr. Michael J. '57 (BUF) Retired.
Yurchak, Thomas D. '76 (P) Eugene, OR St. Jude.
Yurco, Roy *ss.cc.* '62 (FR)[G] Fairhaven, MA Damien Residence Retired.
Yurista, Michael J. '67 (PSC) Bayonne, NJ St. John the Baptist; Retirement Plan Board; Presbyteral Council.
Yurkovic, Dale E. '91 (GF) Havre, MT St. Jude Thaddeus; [J] Havre, MT St. Jude's Education Trust; Diocesan Consultors; Priests' Council.
Yurochko, Dennis P. *s.t.l.* '02 (PIT)[A] Pittsburgh, PA Saint Paul Seminary; Pre–Ordination Formation,

Department for; St. Paul Seminary.

Z

Zabala, Antonio *o.a.r.* '95 (NY) Bronx, NY St. John's.
Zabala, Efrain '67 (CGS) Caguas, PR Santisima Trinidad.
Zabala, Efrain (SJN) "El Visitante".
Zabala, Wilmar '03 (YAK) Vocations; [G] Ellensburg, WA Catholic Campus Ministry at Central Washington University; Youth/Young Adult Director.
Zaballa, Pedro Luis '57 (SJN) San Juan, PR Nuestra Senora de la Caridad del Cobre; [E] San Juan, PR Centro Medico de P.R.
Zabarian, Georges '72 (OLN) Vicar General.
Zabelskas, John A. '56 (GAL) Highlands, TX St. Jude Thaddeus; Northern Vicariate.
Zabler, Charles G. '77 (MIL) Milwaukee, WI Our Lady of Good Hope.
Zaborowski, Paul *o.f.m.cap.* '97 (WDC) Washington, DC Shrine of the Sacred Heart.
Zaborowski, Paul *o.f.m.cap.* '97 (BAL) Baltimore, MD St. Ambrose; [S] Baltimore, MD St. Ambrose Friary.
Zabrocki, Patrick '88 (GF) Plentywood, MT St. Joseph; Scobey, MT St. Philip Bonitus; Diocesan Consultors; Clerical Benefit Association; Priests' Council.
Zabrocki, Stephen J. '89 (GF) Finance Council; Vicars Forane; Liturgical Commission.
Zabrocki, Stephen '89 (GF) Billings, MT St. Thomas the Apostle.
Zaccagnigno, Raffaele '68 (BRK) Retired.
Zaccagnini, Kenneth G. '82 (GBG) Harrison City, PA St. Barbara; Deaneries; College of Consultors; Bishop's Priests Council; College of Deans.
Zaccardo, Rev. Msgr. Peter J. '64 (NEW) Retired.
Zaccone, Paul *ss.cc.* '87 (HON)[D] Kaneohe, HI Sacred Hearts Center.
Zach, Charles E. '73 (P) Gresham, OR St. Henry.
Zach, Kenneth M. '81 (RVC) Procurator & Advocates.
Zach, Kenneth '81 (RVC) Massapequa, NY St. Rose of Lima.
Zachariadis, Rt. Rev. Archimandrite Nicholas (ROM)[A] Pearblossom, CA Holy Resurrection Monastery.
Zachariah, Kurian '85 (ALX) Boyce, LA St. Margaret.
Zacharias, Michael J. '02 (TOL) Van Wert, OH St. Mary of the Assumption.
Zachary, John S. (ATL)[L] Covington, GA Society of Our Lady of the Most Holy Trinity.
Zacheis, Dennis B. '75 (STL) On Leave of Absence.
Zachman, Clarence *o.m.i.* '48 (BEL)[F] Belleville, IL Missionary Oblates of Mary Immaculate – St. Henry's Oblate Residence.
Zacker, Mark '96 (COS) Colorado Springs, CO Corpus Christi; Presbyteral Council; College of Consultors.
Zaczynski, Piotr F. '04 (BUF) On Duty Outside the Diocese.
Zaczynski, Piotr '04 (MAR) Sault Sainte Marie, MI St. Joseph.
Zadora, Boleslaw *s.d.s.* '74 (SAT) St. Hedwig, TX Annunciation of the Blessed Virgin Mary.
Zadora, Charles J. '67 (BUF) Fredonia, NY St. Joseph.
Zadorozny, Tadeusz '99 (NOR) Oakdale, CT Our Lady of the Lakes.
Zadroga, Clinton P. '01 (PIT) On Duty Outside the Diocese.
Zafe, Peter V. '64 (TOL) Philippine–American Catholic Council (PACC).
Zagar, Janko *o.p.* '48 (OAK)[M] Oakland, CA Order of Preachers (Province of the Most Holy Name of Jesus – Western Dominican Province).
Zagarella, John C. *o.praem.* '86 (PH) Paoli, PA St. Norbert; [Y] Paoli, PA Daylesford Abbey.
Zagone, Frederick P. *s.j.* '93 (MIL)[P] Milwaukee, WI Jesuit Community at Marquette University.
Zagorc, Francis D. *c.s.c.* '58 (FTW)[H] Notre Dame Congregation of Holy Cross, Indiana Province, Provincial House.
Zagorski, Jan '02 (MOB) Prattville, AL St. Joseph Church.
Zagst, Bernard L. '61 (ALX) Retired.
Zahler, Paul J. *o.s.b.* '62 (OKL)[I] Shawnee, OK St. Gregory's Abbey; [L] Shawnee, OK National Institute on Development Delays, Inc.
Zahn, George E. '68 (RIC) Richmond, VA St. Paul; Cemeteries.
Zahn, John H. '72 (LFT) Noblesville, IN Our Lady of Grace.
Zahn, Robert R. *m.m.* '55 (NY)[EE] Retired.
Zahuta, Marcin '06 (CHR)[H] Columbia, SC St. Thomas More Center.
Zaiats, Volodymyr '73 (STN) Milwaukee, WI St. Michaels.
Zaidan, Abdallah E. *m.l.m.* '86 (OLL) Los Angeles, CA Our Lady of Mt. Lebanon–St. Peter Maronite Catholic Cathedral; [A] Houston, TX The Congregation of Maronite Lebanese Missionaries; College of Consultors; Commission for Lebanon; Procurator/Advocate; Presbyteral Council; Protopresbyters; Personnel Board; Board of Pastors.
Zaidan, Abdallah *m.l.m.* '86 (OLL)[A] Los Angeles, CA The Congregation of Maronite Lebanese Missionaries.
Zajac, Maciej J. '07 (NEW) Summit, NJ St. Teresa's.
Zajchowski, Zbigniew *o.f.m.conv.* '94 (RCK) Rockford, IL SS. Peter and Paul.
Zajdel, Bernard *o.f.m.conv.* '64 (STP) Bloomington, MN St. Bonaventure.
Zajdel, Robert J. '80 (PIT) McKees Rocks, PA St. John of God; Crescent, PA St. Catherine of Siena.
Zak, Daniel '67 (TOL) Swanton, OH St. Richard.
Zak, Stanislaw '75 (OAK) Oakland, CA St. Margaret Mary.
Zak, Timothy *s.d.b.* '91 (CHI) Chicago, IL St. John Bosco.
Zake, Louis J. '60 (CHI) Retired.
Zakowicz, Giles *o.f.m.conv.* '75 (FgM)[S] Ellicott City Order of Friars Minor Conventual; Ellicott City, MD Province of Saint Anthony of Padua.
Zakowicz, Jorge *o.c.d.* '09 (SB)[I] Redlands, CA Discalced Carmelites, OCD.
Zakshesky, Francis '81 (TYL) Absent on Sick Leave Retired.
Zalacca, Joseph A. '03 (BUF) Franklinville, NY St. Philomena; Council of Priests.
Zalecki, Dennis M. '76 (CHI) Rolling Meadows, IL St. Colette.
Zaleski, Daniel '80 (DET) Dearborn Heights, MI St. Albert the Great.
Zaleski, Gary A. '77 (STU) Administrative Leave.
Zalewski, Francis '78 (TR) Retired.
Zalewski, Peter Lawrence '97 (PT) Panama City, FL St. Dominic; Vicars Forane; College of Consultors; Air Force Reserve Chaplains; Members Appointed.
Zalewski, Thomas *o.carm.* '79 (NY)[EE] Middletown, NY The National Shrine of Our Lady of Mount Carmel; [GG] Middletown, NY National Shrine of Our Lady of Mount Carmel; [EE] Middletown, NY St. Albert's Priory.
Zalewski, Tomasz '06 (VEN) Presbyteral Council; Naples, FL St. Agnes.
Zaloga, Daniel S. '67 (MAR) Iron Mountain, MI St. Mary and St. Joseph.
Zalubski, Czeslaw (NEW) Bayonne, NJ Saint Michael and Saint Joseph.
Zamarripa, Jesus *s.v.d.* '01 (SB) Beaumont, CA Blessed Kateri Takakwitha Catholic Community, Inc.
Zamary, Joseph '01 (Y) Waynesburg, OH St. James.
Zamborsky, Bill '74 (ORL) Ormond Beach, FL Prince of Peace.
Zammit, Francis X. '66 (ORL) Retired.
Zammit, Jimmy *o.f.m.* '81 (NY)[EE] New York Franciscan Province of the Immaculate Conception.
Zammit, Rev. Msgr. Joseph J. '56 (NY) New York Police Department.
Zamora, Arnold '86 (SFR) San Francisco, CA Holy Name of Jesus.
Zamora, Clarence '05 (OAK) Walnut Creek, CA St. John Vianney.
Zamora, Emmanuel F. '07 (LEX)[L] Lexington, KY The Newman Center Holy Spirit Parish University of Kentucky; Lexington, KY The Newman Center, Holy Spirit.
Zamorano, Richard '93 (ELP) On Duty Outside of Diocese.
Zamorski, Rev. Msgr. Robert J. '72 (MET) Episcopal Vicars; College of Consultors; Metuchen, NJ Cathedral of St. Francis of Assisi.
Zampelli, Michael A. *s.j.* '93 (SJ)[B] Santa Clara, CA Jesuit Community.
Zampino, Ignatius *o.f.m.cap.* '61 (PAT) Passaic, NJ Our Lady Of Mt. Carmel.
Zanatta, Albert *c.r.s.* '74 (GAL) Central Vicariate; Houston, TX Assumption.
Zanatta, Remo *c.r.s.* '98 (MAN)[H] Allenstown, NH Pine Haven Boys Center.
Zancan, Robert D. '82 (BUF) Retired.
Zandri, William A. '84 (RC) Rapid City, SD St. Therese the Little Flower; Rapid City, SD St. John the Evangelist.
Zandy, Edward J. '70 (SY) Endicott, NY Our Lady of Good Counsel.
Zanetti, Gordon '06 (VEN) Bradenton, FL SS. Peter and Paul the Apostles.
Zang, Richard P. *c.s.c.* '69 (FTW)[H] Notre Dame Congregation of Holy Cross, Indiana Province, Provincial House.
Zaniewski, Jaroslaw '93 (NEW) Jersey City, NJ Holy Rosary; Families for Nazareth.
Zaniolo, Michael G. '88 (CHI) Des Plaines, IL St. Stephen Protomartyr; Chicago, IL Chicago Airports Catholic Chaplaincy; [W] Chicago, IL Chicago Airports Catholic Chaplaincy; Chicago Airports Catholic Chaplaincy; Chicago, IL National Conference of Catholic Airport Chaplains (NCCAC).
Zanni, Frank L. '90 (Y) Vienna, OH St. Vincent de Paul; Masury, OH St. Bernadette.
Zanon, Romano A. '90 (BRK) Retired.
Zanon, Romano '66 (BRK) East Glendale, NY Sacred Heart.
Zanoni, Charles *c.s.* '62 (PRO) Johnston, RI St. Rocco.
Zanoni, John '60 (JOL)[K] Naperville, IL St. John Vianney Villa Retired.
Zanoni, Richard *s.j.* '75 (NY)[B] Bronx, NY Ciszek Hall.
Zanoni, Ron '05 (LAV) North Las Vegas, NV St. Christopher; Italian Catholic Federation; Building Committee; Presbyteral Council for the Diocese of Las Vegas; Priests' Pension Board.
Zanotti, Rev. Msgr. Charles F. '53 (NY) Glasco, NY St. Joseph.
Zanotti, Richard *c.s.* '80 (LA) Sun Valley, CA Our Lady of the Holy Rosary.
Zanotto, Luigi *m.c.c.j.* '68 (NEW) Newark, NJ St. Lucy's; [M] Montclair, NJ Comboni Missionaries of the Heart of Jesus (Verona Fathers).
Zaorski, Edward F. '90 (DET) Detroit, MI SS. Andrew and Benedict; Detroit, MI St. Stephen–Mary Mother of the Church.
Zapalac, David J. *c.s.b.* '93 (GAL) Manvel, TX Sacred Heart of Jesus.
Zapalac, William E. *o.m.i.* '70 (SAT)[N] San Antonio, TX Oblate Renewal Center.
Zapata, Antonio '68 (ORG) Huntington Beach, CA St. Vincent de Paul.
Zapata, Carlos M. '88 (HRT) Hartford, CT Sacred Heart.
Zapata, Emiliano *o.p.* '95 (NO) New Orleans, LA St. Anthony of Padua; [P] Metairie, LA Dominican Friars, Southern Dominican Province of St. Martin de Porres; [P] Metairie, LA Southern Dominican Foundation; [S] Metairie, LA Southern Dominican Foundation; Metairie, LA.
Zapata, Jose German (MIL) Milwaukee, WI Prince of Peace/Principe de Paz; Milwaukee, WI St. Hyacinth; Milwaukee, WI St. Vincent de Paul.
Zapata, Juan Carlos '05 (NEW) Jersey City, NJ St. Aloysius.
Zapata, Pedro '99 (ORL) Bushnell, FL St. Lawrence.
Zapata, Urian Pèrez '97 (MGZ) Lajas, PR De la Merced Parish.
Zapf, Albert L. '80 (PIT) Harwick, PA Our Lady of Victory.
Zapfel, Rev. Msgr. Robert E. '81 (BUF) Vicars; [L] Buffalo, NY St. Francis of Buffalo, Inc.; Amherst, NY St. Leo the Great; Consultors, College of; Council of Priests; Finance Council; Bishop's Representative for Health Care.
Zapien, Jose B. *m.n.m.* '05 (ARE) Camuy, PR Our Lady of the Miraculous Medal.
Zapien Gomez, Jose B. *m.n.m.* '05 (ARE) Priest's Senate (Consejo Presbiteral).
Zapotocki, Henry E. '48 (SCR) Retired.
Zapp, John '72 (Y) Uniontown, OH Holy Spirit.
Zappa, James C. '76 (STP) Burnsville, MN Mary, Mother of the Church.
Zappitelli, Francis '62 (PHX) Retired.
Zarate, Ramon M. *s.d.b.* '90 (SFR) San Francisco, CA Corpus Christi.
Zarate–Suarez, Jose Edmundo '96 (SD) National City, CA St. Anthony of Padua.
Zarazaga, Rodrigo Esteban *s.j.* '03 (BO)[U] Cambridge, MA Jogues House.
Zarazaga, Rodrigo Esteban *s.j.* '03 (OAK)[M] Berkeley, CA Jesuit Fathers and Brothers.
Zareski, Joseph S. '80 (SY) New Hartford, NY St. John the Evangelist; Pastoral Examiners; Priests' Personnel Committee.
Zarichny, Steven '78 (SJP) Youngstown, OH Holy Trinity; Presbyters.
Zarsky, Brion '07 (AUS) Waco, TX St. Jerome.
Zasacla, Hubert *s.ch.* '02 (CHI) Chicago, IL Holy Trinity Mission.
Zaslona, Jerzy R. '02 (NEW) Hasbrouck Heights, NJ Corpus Christi.
Zastoupil, Stephen R. '61 (BIS) Retired.
Zastrow, John A. '56 (LIN)[E] Lincoln, NE Bonacum House Retired.
Zatalava, James D. '70 (ALT) Altoona, PA Our Lady of Fatima.
Zaucha, Finian Andrew *o.f.m.* '68 (GB)[K] Manitowoc, WI Holy Family Convent of Franciscan Sisters of Christian Charity.
Zavacki, Richard A. '57 (SCR) Freeland, PA Our Lady of the Immaculate Conception Retired.
Zavage, Michael A. '09 (PIT) Pittsburgh, PA St. Anne.
Zavala, Genaro *m.s.p.* '97 (SB) Riverside, CA St. John the Evangelist.
Zavaski, William J. '69 (CHI) Arlington Heights, IL St. James.
Zavell, Edward '61 (PRM) Retired.
Zawacki, Robert *s.s.j.* '77 (BEA) Beaumont, TX Blessed Sacrament; Beaumont, TX Our Mother of Mercy.
Zawada, Joseph F. *o.c.d.* '64 (STA)[H] Bunnell, FL Discalced Carmelite Fathers of Florida.
Zawadski, Justin '68 (SJ) Retired.
Zawadzki, Ryszard *s.v.d.* '87 (LR) Little Rock, AR St. Bartholomew; Little Rock, AR Our Lady of Good Counsel.
Zawadzki, Victor C. '50 (SCR) Retired.
Zayas, Antonio '59 (PCE) On Duty Outside the Diocese.
Zayas, Hector '93 (ARE) Jayuya, PR Our Lady of Monserrate Retired.
Zborowski, Pawel '06 (DEN) Littleton, CO St. Frances Cabrini.

Zborowski, Richard M. '78 (CHI) Palatine, IL St. Theresa.
Zdancewicz, Carl *o.f.m.conv.* '77 (ATL) Lithia Springs, GA St. John Vianney; Deans.
Zdilla, Valentine D. '96 (HEL) Bozeman, MT Resurrection; [G] Bozeman, MT Montana State University; Presbyteral Council.
Zebron, Samuel *o.f.m.conv.* '58 (PMB) Boynton Beach, FL St. Mark.
Zebrowski, Arnold '73 (VEN) Venice, FL Our Lady of Lourdes.
Zec, John '70 (TR)[A] Lakewood, NJ Georgian Court University.
Zeck, George '70 (DUL) Nisswa, MN St. Christopher; Pequot Lakes, MN St. Alice; Pine River, MN Our Lady of Lourdes.
Zee, Louis C. '59 (GAL) Alief, TX Ascension Chinese Mission.
Zee, Louis C. '59 (DUB) Retired.
Zegar, David E. '79 (P) Portland, OR St. Peter.
Zegeer, Eric D. '05 (MIA) Spiritual Moderators; Sunrise, FL All Saints.
Zehler, Steven '07 (STA) Jacksonville, FL Christ the King.
Zehnle, Daren J. '05 (SFD) Virden, IL St. Patrick; Virden, IL Sacred Heart.
Zehrem, Dennis '04 (STP) Coon Rapids, MN Church of the Epiphany.
Zeid, Nadim Abou *m.l.m.* (OLL) Las Vegas, NV St. Sharbel Maronite Catholic Mission; [A] Houston, TX The Congregation of Maronite Lebanese Missionaries.
Zeiler, Donald '01 (DAL) At Large Members; McKinney, TX St. Gabriel the Archangel.
Zeimet, Richard E. *m.m.* '64 (NY)[EE] Retired.
Zein, Milad (SAM) Lawrence, MA St. Anthony.
Zeis, Gabriel *t.o.r.* '80 (ALT)[A] Loretto, PA St. Francis University.
Zeisler, Warren *o.f.m.* '50 (CIN)[N] Cincinnati, OH St. John the Baptist Friary.
Zeitler, Rev. Msgr. Edward J. '58 (E) Hermitage, PA Church of Notre Dame; Hermitage, PA Retired.
Zeitler, Rev. Msgr. John W. '64 (BUF) Lake View, NY Our Lady of Perpetual Help.
Zelaya, Christian '02 (TYL) Texarkana, TX Sacred Heart; Texarkana, TX Federal Corrections Institution.
Zelik, Richard J. *o.f.m.cap.* '77 (PIT) Clairton, PA St. Clare of Assisi.
Zelinski, James *o.f.m.cap.* '61 (MIL) Milwaukee, WI St. Benedict the Moor.
Zelker, Thomas '83 (ALB) Granville, NY St. Mary's Roman Catholic Church Roman Catholic Community of Granville; Deans.
Zeller, Leonard H. '73 (BAL) Priests Sick or Absent.
Zelonis, Christopher M. '03 (ALN) Reading, PA Holy Guardian Angels.
Zelonis, Richard *s.c.j.* '79 (MIL)[P] Franklin Villa Maria.
Zemaitis, Kestutis '65 (CLV)[M] Cleveland, OH Jennings Center for Older Adults.
Zemanik, Rev. Msgr. Edward S. '81 (ALN) Easton, PA St. Anthony of Padua; Easton – Court Easton #358.
Zemczak, Pawel '05 (CHI) Chicago, IL St. Pascal.
Zemelko, John J. '87 (GRY) Valparaiso, IN Our Lady of Sorrows; Mission Office; Ministry to Deaf.
Zemlik, Edward J. *s.c.j.* '01 (JKS) Senatobia, MS St. Gregory the Great; Southaven, MS Christ the King; [E] Nesbit, MS St. Michael Community House; Priests' Council; Hernando, MS Holy Spirit.
Zemlik, Edward *s.c.j.* '01 (JKS) Robinsonville, MS Good Shepherd Catholic Church.
Zemula, Antoni *s.a.c.* '78 (BRK) Brooklyn, NY St. Frances de Chantal.
Zender, Gary '86 (SEA) Renton, WA St. Anthony.
Zendzian, Rev. Msgr. Peter W. '79 (BRK) Maspeth, NY Holy Cross; Presbyteral Council.
Zengierski, Patrick J. '91 (BUF) Newman Club Chaplains; [R] Buffalo, NY Buffalo State College.
Zeni, Rev. Msgr. Dino M. '59 (BRK)[T] Douglaston, NY Bishop Mugavero Residence; Little Neck, NY Retired.
Zenk, Donald W. '54 (WIN)[F] Austin, MN Sacred Heart Care Center, Inc. Retired.
Zenk, Rev. Msgr. Richard E. '54 (SC) Akron, IA St. Patrick; Promoter of Justice; Defenders of the Bond; Holy Childhood Association; Propagation of the Faith, Association of the Holy Childhood, Catholic Students' Mission Crusade.
Zenkel, Edward B. '62 (ROC) Retired.
Zenorini, Henry J. *s.j.* '61 (NY)[EE] New York, NY Xavier Jesuit Community.
Zensen, Gerald F. '49 (SC) Mapleton, IA St. Mary's Retired.
Zenthoefer, Alex '05 (EVN)[A] Evansville, IN Reitz Memorial High School; [A] Evansville, IN Mater Dei High School; Evansville, IN Holy Rosary; Associate Directors; Special Assignment.
Zenz, Rev. Msgr. John P. '78 (DET)[T] Detroit, MI Christ Child Society; Birmingham, MI Holy Name; College of Consultors.
Zepczyk, Gabriel C. '62 (SUP) Retired.
Zepecki, Ronald P. '95 (HRT) Wallingford, CT SS. Peter and Paul.
Zepeda, Alejandro '06 (SPK) Oroville, WA Immaculate Conception; Oroville, WA Holy Rosary.
Zeps, Michael J. *s.j.* '71 (MIL)[P] Milwaukee, WI Jesuit Community at Marquette University.
Zercie, David *m.s.a.* '69 (NOR)[A] Cromwell, CT Holy Apostles College and Seminary; [G] Cromwell Society of the Missionaries of the Holy Apostles.
Zerfas, Rev. Msgr. Herman H. '47 (GR) Retired.
Zeringue, Guy '75 (HT) Thibodaux, LA St. John The Evangelist.
Zerkel, Donald F. '57 (MIL) Racine, WI St. John Nepomuk Retired.
Zermeno, Joseph *o.f.m.* '68 (MRY)[F] San Miguel, CA Franciscan Friars, O.F.M.; San Miguel, CA San Miguel.
Zerr, Dennis P. '03 (CC) Corpus Christi, TX St. Patrick.
Zerr, Gary L. '97 (P) Keizer, OR St. Edward; Area Vicars.
Zerr, Maurice J. *m.m.* '51 (NY)[EE] Maryknoll Maryknoll Fathers and Brothers Retired.
Zerwas, Rick '91 (SFE) Rio Rancho, NM Church of the Incarnation.
Zeth, Allen P. '86 (ALT) New Baltimore, PA St. John the Baptist.
Zettel, David H. '66 (L)[B] Louisville, KY Trinity High School.
Zetzl, Ralph *o.f.m.* '65 (SFD)[I] Effingham, IL St. Anthony's Memorial Hospital; [L] Teutopolis, IL St. Francis Assisi Friary.
Zeugner, Raymond L. '67 (MAR) Retired.
Zeuner, Karl A. '71 (PH) Swarthmore, PA Notre Dame de Lourdes.
Zewe, M. Donald *s.j.* '56 (SY)[Q] Syracuse, NY Jesuits at LeMoyne, Inc.
Zeyack, John '65 (PSC) Retired.
Zeyen, Charles *m.s.f.* '53 (SAT)[K] San Antonio, TX Padua Place.
Zeyen, Thomas E. *s.j.* '54 (SPK)[J] Spokane, WA Regis Community.
Zglejszewski, Andrzej '90 (RVC) Procurator & Advocates; Worship; Rockville Centre, NY St. Agnes Cathedral.
Zgunda, Ronald S. '77 (EVN) Princeton, IN St. Joseph; Oakland City, IN Blessed Sacrament; Deans; Clergy Personnel Board.
Zhai, Peter *s.v.d.* '06 (LA) Rowland Heights, CA St. Elizabeth Ann Seton.
Zhang, Dehua *c.s.j.b.* '76 (BRK)[T] Elmhurst, NY Congregation of St. John the Baptist of China; [T] Elmhurst, NY Our Lady of China Chapel.
Zhang, Edward *c.s.j.b.* (BRK) Elmhurst, NY Our Lady of China Chapel; Flushing, NY St. John Vianney.
Ziccardi, Rev. Msgr. C. Anthony '90 (NEW)[B] School of Diplomacy and Intl. Rels.; Censores Librorum.
Zieba, Jerzy W. *c.r.* '92 (PT) Panama City, FL St. John the Evangelist.
Zieba, Jerzy *c.r.* '92 (CHI)[N].
Ziebacz, Wieslaw M. '92 (SCR) Sayre, PA Church of the Epiphany.
Ziebowicz, Dariusz *s.d.s.* '88 (SAT)[L] Falls City, TX Salvatorian Fathers Community of Texas.
Ziebowicz, Dariusz *s.d.s.* '88 (AUS) Bastrop, TX Sacred Heart; Bastrop, TX St. Mary of the Assumption.
Ziegelmaier, David A. '60 (LC) Retired.
Ziegler, Ambrose M. '61 (LFT) Retired.
Ziegler, John A. '96 (ARL) Colonial Beach, VA St. Elizabeth of Hungary.
Ziegler, Michael Tod '01 (KCK) On Sabbatical.
Ziegler, Thomas G. '69 (Y) Columbiana, OH St. Jude.
Ziegmann, Rev. Msgr. Leonard M. '59 (SC) Retired.
Zielezienski, Raymond '81 (OAK) San Ramon, CA St. Joan of Arc; Deanery #2.
Zielinski, Brian A. *o.praem.* '71 (BAL) Baltimore, MD St. Thomas More.
Zielinski, Brian *o.praem.* '71 (WIL)[J] Middletown, DE Immaculate Conception Priory of the Canons Regular of Premontre; [J] Middletown, DE Norbertine Fathers of Delaware, Inc.
Zielinski, Chad W. '96 (GAY) Special Assignment; Air Force Chaplains.
Zielinski, Francis A. '62 (DET) Retired.
Zielinski, Martin '78 (CHI)[A] Mundelein, IL University of St. Mary of the Lake/Mundelein Seminary; [A] Mundelein, IL University of St. Mary of the Lake/ Mundelein Seminary; [A] Mundelein, IL Ongoing Formation.
Zielinski, Ryszard '83 (CC) Three Rivers, TX Sacred Heart.
Zielke, Michael *o.f.m.conv.* '89 (SPR) Chicopee, MA St. Stanislaus Basilica; Presbyteral Council.
Zielonka, Rev. Msgr. Dariusz J. '95 (BGP) Diocesan Consultors.
Ziemba, Howard '79 (Y)[I] Louisville, OH Emmaus House; Louisville, OH Sacred Heart of Mary.
Ziemba, Rev. Msgr. Walter J. '51 (DET) Retired.
Ziemkiewicz, Frank '84 (SAV)[B] Savannah, GA Benedictine Military School; [E] Savannah, GA The Benedictine Priory.
Ziemniak, Jan '80 (LAR) College of Consultors; Priests Personnel Board; Laredo, TX Nuestra Senora del Rosario Independent Mission; Ex Officio Members.
Ziemnicki, Edward '96 (HRT) Meriden, CT St. Stanislaus.
Zientarski, Nicholas A. '03 (RVC) Silver Spring, MD St. Bernadette; Academic Leave.
Zientek, Rev. Msgr. Benedict '58 (SAN) Retired.
Zientek, Rev. Msgr. Benedict '58 (AUS) Retired.
Zientek, Rev. Msgr. Boleslaus '59 (GAL) Sealy, TX Immaculate Conception Retired.
Zientek, Theodore '00 (STN)[A] Redwood Valley, CA Holy Transfiguration Monastery.
Ziezulewicz, George F. '64 (HRT) Retired.
Zigmond, Kenneth *o.s.b.* '57 (JOL) Lisle, IL St. Joan of Arc; [L] Lisle, IL St. Procopius Abbey.
Ziliak, Jerome *s.v.d.* '47 (CHI)[N] Techny, IL Divine Word Residence.
Ziliak, Joseph '62 (EVN) Newburgh, IN St. John the Baptist; Deans; Censors of Books.
Zilimu, Johndamasceni '95 (PEO) Normal, IL Epiphany.
Zilliox, Robert W. '08 (BUF) Swormville, NY St. Mary.
Zilonka, Paul *c.p.* '71 (MET)[I] South River Passionist Provincial Office.
Zilonka, Paul *c.p.* '71 (CHI)[N] Chicago, IL Passionist Community–CTU.
Zilverberg, Kevin '07 (SFS) Aberdeen, SD Sacred Heart.
Ziminski, James C. '91 (MAR) Special Assignment; Garden, MI St. Mary Magdalene; Garden, MI St. John the Baptist; Garden, MI St. Andrew; [F] Garden, MI Marygrove Retreat Center; Ongoing Formation of Priests; Cursillo; Retreats.
Zimmer, Anthony J. '86 (MIL) Milwaukee, WI St. Charles Borromeo.
Zimmer, David L. '88 (BIS) Minot, ND St. John the Apostle; Defensor Vinculi; Priests' Personnel Board; Promoter of Justice.
Zimmer, Ellis *o.f.m.cap.* '55 (GB)[J] Appleton, WI St. Fidelis Friary Retired.
Zimmer, Eric A. *s.j.* '94 (MO) Air Force Reserve Chaplains.
Zimmer, Eric A. *s.j.* '94 (BAL)[S] Towson Maryland Province of the Society of Jesus.
Zimmer, James '76 (SFS) Sioux Falls, SD Christ the King.
Zimmer, Nicholas '57 (SCL) Retired.
Zimmer, Thomas J. '52 (LFT) Associate Judges Retired.
Zimmer, William E. '91 (CHI) Other Assignments.
Zimmerman, David M. '95 (GB) Cato, WI Immaculate Conception; Whitelaw, WI St. Michael; College of Consultors.
Zimmerman, David '97 (SFD) Paris, IL St. Aloysius; Paris, IL St. Mary; Decatur Deanery; Board of Catholic Education.
Zimmerman, Donald D. '73 (SAL) Manhattan, KS St. Thomas More Parish; Art and Architecture Commission; Catholic Charities Board.
Zimmerman, Rev. Msgr. Donald F. '73 (DAL) Dallas, TX Christ the King.
Zimmerman, John M. '03 (CHR) Florence, SC St. Anne; [H] Florence, SC Francis Marion University.
Zimmerman, Joseph *o.f.m.* '62 (SFD)[B] Quincy, IL Quincy University; Task Force For Racial Justice; [L] Quincy, IL Holy Cross Friary Retired.
Zimmerman, Mitchel '04 (KCK) Vocations Office; Co Directors Seminarians.
Zimmerman, Ralph '76 (SCL) Browerville, MN Christ the King; Clarissa, MN St. Joseph; Personnel Committee.
Zimmerman, Rex A. '67 (LC) Hatley, WI St. Ladislaus; Wittenberg, WI St. Joseph.
Zimmerman, Rev. Msgr. Roland George '51 (LA) Monrovia, CA Annunciation Retired.
Zimmermann, Dominic *s.o.l.t.* '01 (CC)[G] Robstown, TX Society of Our Lady of the Most Holy Trinity.
Zimmers, Michael J. *s.j.* '54 (SJ)[M] Los Gatos, CA Sacred Heart Jesuit Center.
Zimmerschied, Daniel '97 (DEN) Denver, CO St. Vincent De Paul.
Zimodro, Slawomir '08 (RCK) Algonquin, IL St. Margaret Mary.
Zimpfer, Eugene A. *s.j.* '65 (BUF)[O] Buffalo, NY Canisius Jesuit Community Inc.; [D] Buffalo, NY Canisius High School.
Zina, George '86 (SAM) On Leave.
Zingales, A. Jonathan '76 (CLV) Associate Judges; Akron, OH Visitation of Mary.
Zingaro, Joseph J. '78 (PH) Philadelphia, PA St. John Cantius.
Zink, David L. '90 (CIN) Osgood, OH St. Louis; Osgood, OH St. Nicholas; Imprimatur Censors.
Zink, William F. '68 (GR) Deans; College of Consultors; Marne, MI St. Mary's; Ravenna, MI St. Catherine; Conklin, MI St. Francis Xavier.
Zinkula, Thomas R. '90 (DUB) Dubuque, IA Holy Ghost; Judicial Vicar; Judicial Vicar; Judges; Personnel Advisory Board; Directors; Dubuque, IA Holy Trinity; Dubuque, IA Sacred Heart.
Zinn, Donald *c.r.* '72 (CHI)[D] Chicago, IL Gordon Tech High School.

Zinno, Henry P. '82 (PRO) Bristol, RI Our Lady of Mount Carmel.
Zins, Charles A. '77 (BIS) Mott, ND St. Vincent de Paul; Regent, ND St. Henry; Mott, ND St. John the Baptist.
Zinser, Robert E. '68 (STL) On Leave of Absence.
Zinthefer, Neil G. '69 (MIL) Campbellsport, WI St. Kilian; Campbellsport, WI St. Martin; Campbellsport, WI St. Matthew.
Zinzer, Walter W. '64 (STL) Retired.
Ziolkowski, Adam *o.f.m.conv.* '72 (HBG) Shamokin, PA Mother Cabrini.
Ziomek, Dennis A. '78 (CHI) Chicago, IL St. Barbara.
Zipay, Michael J. '68 (SCR) Luzerne, PA Holy Family.
Zirilli, David A. '08 (MIA) Pinecrest, FL St. Louis.
Zirimenya, Paul '07 (SFR) San Francisco, CA St. Benedict Parish at St. Francis Xavier Church[S]; San Francisco, CA St. Gabriel.
Zirnheld, Matthew J. '93 (BUF) Strykersville, NY St. John Neumann; Council of Priests.
Zirra, Benjamin (NY) Maybrook, NY Church of the Assumption.
Zitek, Bradley '89 (LIN) Superior, NE St. Joseph's.
Zivic, Richard A. '94 (ATL) Without Archdiocesan Assignment or Faculties.
Zivkovic, Robert M. *o.s.m.* '66 (CHI)[N] Chicago Order of Friar Servants of Mary (Servites) United States of America Province, Inc.
Zlock, Charles '94 (PH) Bridgeport, PA St. Augustine; On Special or Other Archdiocesan Assignment; Office of the Vicar for Clergy.
Zlotkowski, Frank *c.s.c.* '76 (AUS) Austin, TX Seton/ Brackenridge Hospital.
Zmarlicki, Andrzej '92 (NEW) Elizabeth, NJ St. Hedwig's.
Zmozynski, Francis J. '57 (BUF) Retired.
Zmuda, Christopher J. '01 (NOR) District Moderators.
Zmuda, Christopher '01 (NOR) Norwich, CT SS. Peter and Paul.
Zmudzinski, Charles *c.p.m.* '02 (OWN) Auburn, KY; [F] Auburn, KY Fathers of Mercy; Judges.
Zobler, Alan D. *o.s.f.s.* '07 (TOL)[I] Toledo, OH; [C] Toledo, OH St. Francis de Sales High School; Toledo, OH St. Clement.
Zoeller, Eugene '58 (L) Retired.
Zoellner, Michael *o.s.b.* '80 (KCK)[J] Leavenworth, KS Motherhouse of the Sisters of Charity of Leavenworth; [I] Atchison, KS St. Benedict's Abbey.
Zogby, Edward G. *s.j.* '67 (NY)[EE] New York, NY Jesuit Community of the Immaculate Conception; New York, NY Our Lady of the Rosary.
Zoghby, James F. '71 (MOB) Mobile, AL Corpus Christi; Vicars Forane; Officers; Priests' Personnel Committee.
Zoghby, Paul G. '93 (MOB) Foley, AL St. Margaret Queen of Scotland; Vicars Forane.
Zohlen, Ray '53 (SFR) Retired.
Zollinger, Rev. Msgr. Richard '55 (GRY) Retired.
Zomerfeld, Zbigniew '93 (DET) Port Huron, MI St. Mary.
Zoni, Pierino *s.x.* '61 (FgM)[N] Wayne Xaverian Missionary Fathers; Wayne, NJ XAVERIAN MISSIONARY FATHERS.
Zonneveld, Leo J. *c.i.c.m.* '58 (ARL) Culpeper, VA Precious Blood; Deans.
Zorjan, Peter '07 (PEO) Rock Island, IL St. Pius X.
Zoromski, Herbert P. '51 (LC) Retired.
Zotter, Thomas A. '76 (SFE) Albuquerque, NM Shrine of St. Bernadette.
Zoubek, Ronald '89 (BAL) Retired.
Zoucha, Carl J. '98 (OM) Omaha, NE Our Lady of Guadalupe – St. Agnes Parish; [M] Elkhorn, NE Apostolic Sodales.
Zoufal, Michael L. '87 (CHI) Argo, IL St. Blasé.
Zowada, Stanislaw *o.m.i.* '00 (LA) San Fernando, CA Santa Rosa.
Zsolczai, Raymond (MIL)[P] Burlington, WI Queen of Peace Friary.
Zube, Rev. Msgr. Joseph A. '53 (PEO) Special Residence; Vice Chancellors; Priests' Eucharistic League.
Zuber, Thaddeus F. '50 (NEW)[M] Rutherford, NJ St. John Vianney Residence for Priests Retired.
Zuberbueler, Matthew H. '96 (ARL) Dale City, VA Holy Family; Defenders of the Bond; [D] Dumfries, VA Pope John Paul the Great Catholic High School.
Zubik, Rudolf '64 (NEW) Harrison, NJ Our Lady of Czestochowa.
Zubizarreta Mugica, Jose Ramon *c.p.* '72 (SJN) Toa Baja, PR Espiritu Santo.
Zuccaro, James E. '06 (BUR) Chester, VT St. Joseph.
Zuchowski, Robert J. '72 (GAY) Elk Rapids, MI Sacred Heart.
Zuelke, Michael *o.f.m.cap.* '74 (MIL)[P] Mount Calvary, WI St. Lawrence Friary.
Zuercher, John D. *s.j.* '59 (OM)[K] Omaha, NE Jesuit Community at Creighton University; [P] Omaha, NE Christian Life Community–North Central Region (CLC).
Zuerlein, Damian J. '81 (OM) Papillion, NE St. Columbkille; Officers; Age Groups; [O] Papillion, NE IXIM, Spirit of Solidarity.
Zuerlein, Damian '81 (OM) Finance Council.
Zuffoletto, Michael P. '72 (BUF) On Duty Outside the Diocese.
Zugaj, Piotr W. '04 (VEN) Bradenton, FL St. Joseph.
Zugger, Christopher L. '81 (VNN) Albuquerque, NM Our Lady of Perpetual Help Retired.
Zuk, Richard P. '05 (BRK) Jamaica, NY St. Joseph.
Zukas, Stephan (BO) Lithuanian.
Zukas, Stephen P. '93 (BO) South Boston, MA St. Peter.
Zukowski, Nicholas '82 (DET) New Baltimore, MI St. Mary Queen of Creation.
Zuleger, Donald M. '76 (GB) Appleton, WI St. Bernadette; Regional Vicars; Appointed Members.
Zuleta, Fernando '06 (CHI) Chicago, IL Resurrection.
Zuletta, Nondier (B) On Duty Outside the Diocese.
Zuliani, Vincent *s.d.b.* '56 (NY)[GG] Stony Point, NY Don Bosco Retreat Center and Marian Shrine; [GG] Stony Point, NY Marian Shrine.
Zulkie, Lambert *o.carm.* '88 (JOL)[K] Darien, IL Carmelite Carefree Retirement Village Retired.
Zuluaga, Edwin Londono '07 (SJN) Bayamon, PR Santa Teresa de Jesus.
Zulueta, Johnny *c.m.* '87 (LA) Artesia, CA Holy Family; [BB] Artesia, CA Filipino Pastoral Ministry.
Zumaya, David '77 (SAT) Retired.
Zuniga, Carlos '98 (BWN) McAllen, TX Saint Juan Diego Cuauhtlatoatzin.
Zuniga, Domingo *c.m.f.* '52 (LA) Los Angeles, CA Our Lady Queen of the Angels.
Zuniga, Juan M. *m.m.* '88 (NY)[EE] Maryknoll Maryknoll Fathers and Brothers.
Zuniga, Victor *m.s.p.* (CHI) Chicago, IL Queen of the Universe.
Zunmas, Oby '00 (OKL) Madill, OK Holy Cross Church.
Zunno, Michael O. *m.m.* (BRK) Brooklyn, NY Our Lady of Mount Carmel Shrine Church.
Zunno, Michael O. '53 (NY)[EE] Maryknoll Maryknoll Fathers and Brothers Retired.
Zupez, John *s.j.* (OKL) Oklahoma City, OK Corpus Christi.
Zupka, Anselm *o.s.b.* '67 (CLV)[D] Cleveland, OH Benedictine High School; [N] Cleveland Benedictine Order of Cleveland.
Zurat, Hugh *o.s.b.* '62 (CHI)[O] Chicago, IL Mother of Good Counsel Provincialate.
Zurat, Hugh *o.f.m.* '62 (CHI)[N] Chicago, IL Holy Name Friary.
Zuraw, Rev. Msgr. John A. '87 (Y) Youngstown, OH Immaculate Conception; Defenders of the Bond; Promoter of Justice; Vicar for Administration; Office of Permanent Diaconate.
Zurawski, Lawrence '85 (DET) Westland, MI St. Damian.
Zurcher, Thomas *c.s.c.* '72 (FgM) New Rochelle, NY Eastern Brothers Province.
Zurcher, Thomas *c.s.c.* (FTW)[H] Notre Dame Congregation of Holy Cross, Indiana Province, Provincial House.
Zurek, John '04 (CHI) Orland Park, IL St. Francis of Assisi.
Zurek, Lawrence W. *o.f.m.* '85 (PEO) Peoria, IL Sacred Heart; Peoria, IL St. Joseph.
Zurovetz, Jerome G. '67 (CC) Portland, TX Our Lady of Mount Carmel.
Zuschmidt, Joseph C. *o.s.f.s.* '65 (CHL) High Point, NC Immaculate Heart of Mary.
Zuziak, Joseph R. *s.d.s.* '66 (GRY)[H] Merrillville, IN Salvatorian Fathers (Society of the Divine Savior).
Zuzik, John E. '91 (Y) Canton, OH St. Therese Little Flower.
Zvarych, Petro '00 (PHU) West Easton, PA Holy Ghost; West Easton, PA St. Nicholas.
Zvijak, John *c.pp.s.* '63 (CIN)[N] Carthagena, OH St. Charles.
Zwack, Jeffrey '84 (BIS) Dickinson, ND Queen of Peace Church.
Zwaska, Victor L. '56 (MIL) Retired.
Zwilling, Robert J. '05 (BEL) Radom, IL St. Michael; Scheller, IL St. Barbara.
Zwirn, Ralph H. '85 (CHI) Chicago, IL St. Turibius.
Zwolenkiewicz, Raphael *o.f.m.conv.* '79 (PAT) Clifton, NJ St. John Kanty.
Zygadlo, Mitchell '82 (MO) Military Chaplains; Air Force Chaplains.
Zygas, Arvydas (NOR)[H] Putnam, CT Immaculate Conception Convent, Spiritual Renewal Center and Novitiate.
Zyla, Ludwik *o.cist.* '91 (CHI)[N] Willow Springs, IL Cistercian Fathers, Our Lady Mother of the Church Polish Mission; Argo, IL Our Lady, Mother of the Church Polish Mission.
Zylla, Paul '45 (SCL) Censores Librorum Retired.
Zywan, Paul J. '86 (PIT) Wexford, PA St. Alexis.

Necrology

BISHOPS

✠ D'Antonio, Most Rev. Nicholas, *o.f.m.* (NO) Prelate Emeritus, Ordinary of Olancho, Honduras, C.A. —Died Aug. 1, 2009
✠ Kaffer, Most Rev. Roger L. (JOL) Retired Auxiliary Bishop of Joliet. —Died May 28, 2009
✠ Matthiesen, Most Rev. Leroy T. (AMA) Retired Bishop of Amarillo. —Died March 22, 2010
✠ McDowell, Most Rev. John B. (PIT) Retired Auxiliary Bishop of Pittsburgh. —Died Feb. 25, 2010
✠ Minder, Most Rev. John B., *o.s.f.s.* Bishop Emeritus of Keimoes–Upington, South Africa. —Died Aug. 13, 2009
✠ Moeddel, Most Rev. Carl K. (CIN) Retired Auxiliary Bishop of Cincinnati. —Died Aug. 25, 2009
✠ Pelotte, Most Rev. Donald E., *s.s.s.* (GLP) Retired Bishop of Gallup. —Died Jan. 7, 2010
✠ Puscas, Most Rev. Louis (ROM) Bishop Emeritus for the Romanian Catholic Diocese of Canton. —Died Oct. 3, 2009
✠ Saltarelli, Most Rev. Michael A. (WIL) Bishop Emeritus of Wilmington. —Died Oct. 8, 2009
✠ Ziemann, Most Rev. G. Patrick (SR) Retired Bishop of Santa Rosa. —Died Oct. 22, 2009

ABBOTS

✠ Boultwood, Rt. Rev. Alban, *o.s.b.* (WDC) (Retired). —Died March 25, 2009
✠ Cassell, Rt. Rev. Leonard G., *o.s.b.* (PAT) (Retired). —Died Nov. 13, 2009
✠ Duss, Rt. Rev. Benedict, *o.s.b.* (HRT) Bethlehem, CT Abbey of Regina Laudis. —Died 2009
✠ Jones, Rt. Rev. James, *o.s.b.* (KC) (Retired). —Died May 5, 2009
✠ West, Rt. Rev. Robert, *o.s.b.* (BIS) (Retired). —Died Aug. 30, 2009

PRIESTS

† Aaron, Robert, *o.m.i.* (BEL) Belleville, IL King's House Retreat and Renewal Center. —Died Aug. 17, 2009
† Abeywickrema, Lionel Augustin (SFE). —Died Nov. 12, 2008
† Adamo, Joseph A. (WOR) (Retired). —Died April 20, 2009
† Agar, Tom (MRY) Monterey, CA Cathedral of San Carlos Borromeo. —Died May 1, 2009
† Aherne, Gregory D., *s.j.* (SJ) (Retired). —Died March 2, 2009
† Aherne, Rev. Msgr. John P. (MOB) (Retired). —Died April 27, 2009
† Ahles, Jerome, *o.f.m.* (LA) Santa Barbara, CA Franciscan Friary. —Died Feb. 7, 2009
† Albert, Xavier (STL) (Retired). —Died April 9, 2009
† Aldasoro, Rev. Msgr. Francisco (SD) (Retired). —Died Sept. 9, 2009
† Alliegro, Rev. Msgr. Michael J. (MET) Metuchen, NJ Cathedral of St. Francis of Assisi Rector. —Died Aug. 17, 2009
† Alwell, Juniper, *o.f.m.conv.* (NY) Staten Island, NY St. Francis Friary. —Died Sept. 10, 2009
† Amar, Mubarak Anwar, *f.s.s.p.* (PEO) (On Leave of Absence). —Died Dec. 26, 2008
† Amengual, Miguel (LA) (Retired). —Died June 17, 2009
† Andalikiewicz, Charles (KCK) Louisburg, KS Immaculate Conception. —Died April 2, 2009
† Andres, Joseph P. (CIN) (Retired). —Died Feb. 2, 2009
† Angelo, Girard F. (SCR) Harleigh, PA Church of the Sacred Heart Pastor Emeritus. —Died June 20, 2009
† Anger, Raymond G. (WOR) (Retired). —Died Oct. 8, 2009
† Arango, Heriberto Londono (SJN). —Died June 4, 2009
† Armstrong, Rev. Msgr. Peter G. (SFR) (Retired). —Died Nov. 17, 2009
† Arsenault, Raymond J., *s.m.* (BO) Framingham, MA The Marist House. —Died Sept. 1, 2009
† Aspinall, Campion William, *c.j.* (LA) Santa Maria, CA St. Louis de Montfort.. —Died Sept. 28, 2009
† Asturi, Bruno (PBR) Upper St. Clair, PA St. Gregory Nazianzus. —Died Jan. 26, 2009
† Baggarly, John D., *s.j.* (DET) Clarkston, MI Colombiere Center. —Died Sept. 2, 2009
† Bagge, Carl J., *m.s.* (PT) (Retired). —Died Aug. 20, 2009
† Bailey, Justin J., *o.f.m.* (SP) St. Petersburg, FL St. Anthony Friary. —Died July 4, 2009
† Baillargeon, Anatole, *o.m.i.* (BO) Lowell, MA Missionary Oblates of Mary Immaculate. —Died Dec. 18, 2008
† Bain, Thomas J., *s.j.* (DET) Clarkston, MI Colombiere Center. —Died Oct. 7, 2009
† Baker, Donald H. (WOR) Gardner, MA Sacred Heart of Jesus. —Died April 9, 2009
† Balbi, Mario, *s.d.b.* (NEW) Orange, NJ Our Lady of the Valley. —Died Feb. 23, 2009
† Balker, Rev. Msgr. Joseph W. (FRS) (Retired). —Died April 1, 2009
† Ballman, Thomas J. (CIN) (Retired). —Died March 1, 2009
† Ballor, Milton, *c.pp.s.* (CIN) (Retired). —Died July 21, 2009
† Bamberg, Callistus M., *o.f.m.* (BO) (Retired). —Died March 12, 2009
† Banks, Evan F., *o.f.m.* (PAT) (Retired). —Died March 21, 2009
† Barnes, Joseph A. (ALN) Douglassville, PA Immaculate Conception Pastor Emeritus. —Died Feb. 2, 2009
† Barry, Thomas M. (WOR) (Retired). —Died Dec. 14, 2009
† Basile, Nicholas F. (NY) Mount Vernon, NY St. Francis of Assisi Pastor Emeritus. —Died April 6, 2009
† Battocletti, Richard L. (STU) (Retired). —Died March 23, 2009
† Bayne, David C., *s.j.* (DET) Detroit, MI Jesuit Provincial Office. —Died April 8, 2009
† Bayne, Robert C., *m.m.* (FgM) Maryknoll Foreign Mission. —Died Aug. 14, 2009
† Beach, Raymond P., *o.f.m.* (PAT) (Retired). —Died Sept. 14, 2009
† Beattie, Thomas W. (SEA) (Retired). —Died June 23, 2009
† Becker, Ronald R. (TR). —Died Jan. 21, 2009
† Bedessem, Henry W. (GB) (Retired). —Died Feb. 11, 2009
† Behler, Donald A. (CIN) (Retired). —Died June 17, 2009
† Beischel, Richard, *c.pp.s.* (CIN) Dayton, OH Society of the Precious Blood. —Died April 27, 2009
† Beitzinger, George J. (MIL) (Retired). —Died March 17, 2009
† Belair, Eugene (SCL) (Retired). —Died June 18, 2009
† Beller, Frederic, *o.s.b.* (JOL) Lisle, IL St. Procopius Abbey. —Died Nov. 13, 2008
† Bench, John F. (CHR) (Retired). —Died June 6, 2009
† Berg, Paul C. (DET) (Retired). —Died Jan. 26, 2009
† Berg, Rev. Msgr. S. Theodore (BUF) (Retired). —Died April 16, 2009
† Berry, Thomas, *c.p.* (MET) South River, NJ South River Passionist Provincial Office. —Died June 1, 2009
† Bertke, Erwin J. (CIN) (Retired). —Died Dec. 1, 2009
† Bezuszka, Stanley J., *s.j.* (BO) Weston, MA Campion Health Center. —Died Dec. 27, 2008
† Bielskas, Edward J. (GR) (Retired). —Died Dec. 31, 2008
† Bionda, Bonaventure, *o.f.m.* (ALB) Palenville, NY Sacred Heart. —Died Sept. 17, 2009
† Bir, Stanley, *o.f.m.* (CIN) Cincinnati, OH St. Clement. —Died March 23, 2009
† Birdsall, John M. (RC) (Retired). —Died Sept. 4, 2009
† Birkmeyer, John R., *c.s.c.* (FTW) Notre Dame, IN Notre Dame Congregation of Holy Cross. —Died July 16, 2009
† Birringer, Raphael, *s.d.s.* (MIL) (Retired). —Died March 8, 2009
† Bischof, Simon Robert, *o.s.b.* (SCL) (Retired). —Died Feb. 23, 2009
† Bleaux, Floyd J. (OG) Bombay, NY St. Joseph; Fort Covington, NY St. Mary; Hogansburg, NY St. Patrick. —Died Sept. 2, 2009
† Blough, William G. (PIT) (Retired). —Died Oct. 24, 2008
† Blumm, John L., *m.s.* (LKC) (Retired). —Died Jan. 16, 2009
† Boddie, John D. (RIC) Topping, VA Church of the Visitation; Mathews, VA Church of Francis de Sales. —Died May 19, 2009
† Boensch, Gregory A. (CC) (Retired). —Died Jan. 31, 2009
† Bofto, Robert C. (GF) (Retired). —Died Dec. 2, 2008
† Bolduc, Paul J. (BO) (Retired). —Died Dec. 29, 2009
† Bolerasky, Rev. Msgr. Peter E. (PEO) (Retired). —Died Oct. 30, 2009
† Bolger, Rev. Msgr. John F. (SP) St. Petersburg, FL Transfiguration Pastor Emeritus. —Died 2009
† Boller, Robert J. (STP) (Retired). —Died Nov. 9, 2009
† Bondi, Paul (ALB) (Retired). —Died Feb. 27, 2009
† Bonjean, Richard (MRY) (Retired). —Died Dec. 9, 2009
† Bonnell, Robert A. (CLV) Oberlin, OH Sacred Heart Pastor Emeritus. —Died March 5, 2009
† Bortolotti, Serafino (SFE) (Retired). —Died July 22, 2009
† Boruta, Alexander, *o.f.m.* (GAY) Prescott, MI St. Stephen. —Died Jan. 12, 2009
† Boucher, Maurice U., *s.s.e.* (BUR) (Retired). —Died Aug. 23, 2009
† Bowes, Vincent, *o.c.d.* (BO) Brighton, MA Carmelite Monastery. —Died April 19, 2009
† Boyd, Rev. Msgr. Joseph J. (NY) Wesley Hills, NY St. Boniface; Larchmont, NY SS. John & Paul Pastor Emeritus. —Died Dec. 20, 2009
† Braden, Rev. Msgr. Leroy H. (GAL) (Retired). —Died July 23, 2009
† Bradley, Harold C., *s.j.* (MIL) Wauwatosa, WI Jesuit Community at St. Camillus. —Died July 10, 2009
† Bradower, Theodore, *t.o.r.* (ALT) Loretto, PA St. Francis Friary at Mt. Assisi. —Died 2009
† Brady, Coman V. (BRK) Brooklyn, NY St. Vincent Ferrer. —Died July 20, 2009
† Brady, James, *s.o.l.t.* (CC) Robstown, TX Society of Our Lady of the Most Holy Trinity. —Died 2009
† Branch, Leslie (WDC) (Retired). —Died June 22, 2009
† Brand, William, *o.f.m.* (LA) Los Angeles, CA St. Anne. —Died 2009
† Brantome, Oscar (MIA) (Retired). —Died Feb. 11, 2009
† Braud, Dominic, *o.s.b.* (NO) St. Benedict, LA St. Joseph Abbey. —Died Jan. 1, 2009
† Braun, David L. (BEL) Wendelin, IL Holy Cross; Stringtown, IL St. Joseph.. —Died Dec. 30, 2009
† Braun, Donald B. (MIL) (Retired). —Died Nov. 3, 2009
† Braun, Robert, *o.m.i.* (BEL) Belleville, IL Missionary Oblates of Mary Immaculate. —Died Jan. 10, 2009
† Breunig, Robert L. (DEN) (Retired). —Died Oct. 15, 2009
† Brinker, Paul J. (COV) (Retired). —Died Dec. 27, 2008
† Bronder, Joseph, *o.s.b.* (GBG) Latrobe, PA St. Vincent College. —Died Nov. 5, 2008
† Brown, Henry P. (IND) Beech Grove, IN St. Paul Hermitage. —Died June 21, 2009
† Browne, Joseph T., *s.j.* (NY) New York, NY Murray–Weigel Hall. —Died May 9, 2009
† Buetow, Harold A. (BRK) (Retired). —Died Oct. 17, 2009
† Burgos, Jose Casco (ARE) (Retired). —Died June 16, 2009
† Burke, Edward T., *s.j.* (SJ) (Retired). —Died Feb. 27, 2009
† Burke, James, *o.p.* (DAL) Irving, TX Dominican Priory of St. Albert the Great. —Died Oct. 6, 2009
† Burke, Sean P., *m.m.* (FgM) Maryknoll Foreign Mission. —Died May 5, 2009
† Burke, Vincent dePaul, *o.s.f.s.* (WIL) (Retired). —Died April 7, 2009
† Burke, Walter E. (DET) (Retired). —Died Nov. 25, 2009

† Burkhart, John J., *o.s.a.* (LAN) Fllint, MI St. Matthew. —Died Dec. 8, 2008
† Burn, William C. (CHR) (Retired). —Died May 29, 2009
† Burns, Dennis J. (BO) (Retired). —Died Aug. 25, 2009
† Burns, Robert I., *s.j.* (SJ) (Retired). —Died Nov. 22, 2008
† Burns, Thomas (CAM) (Retired). —Died June 11, 2009
† Busch, Rev. Msgr. Aloysius J. (PAT) (Retired). —Died Oct. 19, 2009
† Bushell, Ralph, *c.pp.s.* (KC) Liberty, MO Precious Blood Center. —Died March 2, 2009
† Buttinelli, Antonio (NY) (Retired). —Died Feb. 12, 2009
† Caffrey, Joseph (PT) (Retired). —Died July 22, 2009
† Cahalane, Timothy, *m.s.c.* (LA) (Retired). —Died 2009
† Cahill, John (WOR) (Retired). —Died Sept. 24, 2009
† Callaghan, George J., *o.s.a.* (PH) Villanova, PA St. Thomas Monastery. —Died Dec. 24, 2008
† Callanan, Edward E., *s.j.* (SAC) (Retired). —Died June 10, 2009
† Campbell, Rev. Msgr. Bernard (STV) Kingshill, VI St. Ann. —Died Jan. 23, 2009
† Campbell, John J., *s.j.* (STL) St. Louis, MO Jesuit Community at St. Camillus. —Died April 10, 2009
† Canavan, Francis P., *s.j.* (NY) New York, NY Murray–Weigel Hall. —Died Feb. 26, 2009
† Canning, John, *o.carm.* (NY) (Retired). —Died Oct. 6, 2009
† Cano, Emilio (PCE) (Retired). —Died Feb. 8, 2008
† Caponi, Jerome (VIC) (Retired). —Died Feb. 27, 2009
† Carbone, Roland J., *o.s.b.* (KC) (Retired). —Died March 9, 2009
† Carbone, Vito J. (PH) (Absent on Sick Leave). —Died April 17, 2009
† Cardiff, Rev. Msgr. John I. (CHI) Oak Lawn, IL St. Linus Pastor Emeritus. —Died Oct. 3, 2009
† Carolan, Charles B. (VIC) (Retired). —Died Oct. 9, 2009
† Carrieri, Leonard R., *m.ss.cc.* (CAM) (Retired). —Died June 20, 2009
† Carrigan, John Thaddeus, *o.p.* (COL) (Retired). —Died Sept. 7, 2009
† Carrillo, Victor M. (SAT) San Antonio, TX Assumption Seminary. —Died Nov. 18, 2009
† Casey, Francis M. (RVC) (Retired). —Died March 13, 2009
† Cassidy, Thomas, *s.v.d.* (FgM) Society of the Divine Word Foreign Mission. —Died Feb. 4, 2009
† Cassiero, Daniel A. (NY) Chap., U.S. Air Force. —Died Oct. 31, 2009
† Caulfield, John F., *s.j.* (BO) Weston, MA Campion Health Center. —Died Feb. 13, 2009
† Cestaro, Joseph J. (NEW) (Retired). —Died July 19, 2009
† Chambers, John E., *s.j.* (FgM) Society of Jesus Foreign Mission. —Died 2009
† Chanh, John Chan Tran (GAL) (Retired). —Died Oct. 25, 2009
† Charlebois, Rev. Msgr. John J. (GRY). —Died Sept. 22, 2009
† Chavez, Rev. Msgr. Adolphus (SB) (Retired). —Died Dec. 28, 2008
† Chonko, Michael J. (Y) (Retired). —Died April 18, 2009
† Christ, Raymond J., *o.s.f.s.* (PH) Wyndmoor, PA Villa de Sales Oblate Residence. —Died Aug. 5, 2009
† Chueca, Ubaldo, *s.d.b.* (MRY) Watsonville, CA Our Lady Help of Christians. —Died Oct. 21, 2008
† Ciani, Francis P. (ALB) (Retired). —Died March 7, 2009
† Cibulskis, Peter, *m.i.c.* (MIL) Kenosha, WI St. Peter. —Died Sept. 28, 2009
† Ciemiega, Ernest D. (CHI) (Retired). —Died March 27, 2009
† Cilinski, Rev. Msgr. John T. (ARL) (Retired). —Died Aug. 14, 2009
† Claerr, Francis, *c.m.m.* (DET) (Retired). —Died July 30, 2009
† Clancy, Thomas H., *s.j.* (NO) (Retired). —Died April 13, 2009
† Clarke, Arthur A., *s.j.* (NY) New York, NY St. Ignatius Loyola Residence. —Died Aug. 2, 2009
† Clarke, John (DM) (Retired). —Died Oct. 23, 2009
† Cleary, Edward M. (SFR) (Retired). —Died July 7, 2009
† Cleary, Richard E., *o.s.f.s.* (WIL) (Retired). —Died May 24, 2009
† Cleary, Richard T., *s.j.* (BO) Weston, MA Campion Health Center. —Died Oct. 7, 2009
† Clifford, Donald G., *s.j.* (PH) Philadelphia, PA Loyola Center. —Died May 4, 2009
† Clifford, Francis M. (MAN) (Retired). —Died March 7, 2009
† Cody, Michael, *s.s.c.* (FgM) Society of St. Columban Foreign Mission. —Died April 21, 2009
† Coghlan, John A. (STO) (Retired) Pastor Emeritus. —Died Sept. 25, 2009
† Colaiacovo, Arthur J. (PAT) Convent Station, NJ Saint Thomas More. —Died March 16, 2009
† Colton, Bradford (HRT) (Retired). —Died Oct. 5, 2009
† Commings, Leo, *m.s.* (ATL) Smyrna, GA St. Thomas the Apostle. —Died Sept. 14, 2009
† Concagh, Thomas V., *c.m.* (PH) Philadelphia, PA Congregation of the Mission. —Died Feb. 11, 2009
† Concepcion, Rev. Msgr. Francisco (ARE) Vega–Alta, PR Immaculate Conception of Blessed Virgin Mary. —Died Oct. 22, 2009
† Condon, Louis (PEO). —Died Feb. 17, 2009
† Condren, William (PT) (Retired). —Died Nov. 3, 2009
† Conley, Rev. Msgr. Raymond J. (DM) (Retired). —Died Feb. 9, 2009
† Conlin, John A., *s.j.* (PH) Philadelphia, PA Loyola Center. —Died March 10, 2009
† Connellan, Thomas J., *c.s.p.* (PMB) Vero Beach, FL Paulist Fathers Residence. —Died Dec. 26, 2008
† Connolly, Rev. Msgr. Edward J. (SB) San Bernardino, CA Diocesan Pastoral Center. —Died March 4, 2009
† Connolly, Joseph A., *o.s.f.s.* (WIL) (Retired). —Died Feb. 9, 2009
† Conover, Sylvan, *o.f.m.cap.* (NY) Yonkers, NY St. Clare Friary. —Died May 25, 2009
† Conroy, Thomas J. (STP) (Retired). —Died March 12, 2009
† Conway, Thomas D. (BO) (Retired). —Died Oct. 25, 2009
† Cook, John N. (GI) (Retired). —Died July 4, 2009
† Corcoran, Rev. Msgr. Lawrence J. (COL) (Retired). —Died Aug. 31, 2009
† Cornell, Robert John, *o.praem.* (GB) DePere, WI St. Joseph. —Died May 10, 2009
† Cosgrove, Thomas H., *c.ss.r.* (STL) (Retired). —Died 2009
† Cote, Joseph A. (MAN). —Died March 19, 2009
† Coughlin, Conall, *o.s.b.* (PAT) Morristown, NJ St. Mary's Abbey. —Died March 1, 2009
† Countie, Charles, *o.carm.* (BO) Peabody, MA Our Lady of the Scapular Priory. —Died 2009
† Cox, Rev. Msgr. John F. (PRO) (Retired). —Died March 8, 2009
† Coyle, Alcuin F., *o.f.m.* (NY) (Retired). —Died Dec. 4, 2008
† Creagan, Daniel J., *s.j.* (MOB) Mobile, AL Spring Hill College. —Died March 6, 2009
† Creedon, James, *m.s.a.* (PH) (Retired). —Died Dec. 25, 2008
† Cregan, Robert G., *s.j.* (NY) Bronx, NY Fordham Preparatory School. —Died Jan. 4, 2009
† Crehan, Joseph, *s.s.c.* (PRO) (Retired). —Died April 1, 2008
† Cronin, Francis C. (STU) (Retired). —Died Aug. 2, 2009
† Croston, John J., *c.s.c.* (FTW) (Retired). —Died July 26, 2009
† Crotty, Rev. Msgr. Matthew M. (BAK) (Special Assignment) Vicar Gen.. —Died Sept. 24, 2009
† Crouse, William S. (ALT) (Retired). —Died July 11, 2009
† Culkin, Henry M. (BRK) (Retired). —Died Aug. 2, 2009
† Culley, Thomas D., *s.j.* (NO) (Retired). —Died July 14, 2009
† Culver, Rev. Msgr. T. Joseph (GAL) (Retired). —Died April 7, 2009
† Cummings, Leo B., *m.s.* (ATL) Smyrna, GA St. Thomas the Apostle. —Died Sept. 14, 2009
† Cung, Ephrem M. Vu Khiem, *c.m.c.* (BO) (Retired). —Died Oct. 2, 2009
† Cunningham, Rev. Msgr. Richard G. (BO) (Retired). —Died Dec. 28, 2009
† Curran, Joseph F., *s.j.* (STL) St. Louis, MO Jesuit Society. —Died Sept. 3, 2009
† Currier Quinn, Frank, *o.p.* (COL) Columbus, OH. —Died Oct. 31, 2008
† Cushing, Alan (SFE) (Retired). —Died June 22, 2009
† Czechowicz, Walter (ALB) (Retired). —Died May 11, 2009
† D'Amato, James J. (BRK) (Retired). —Died Jan. 30, 2009
† D'Aurizio, Joseph F. (ROC) (Retired). —Died Sept. 5, 2009
† Daily, Leo J. (HRT) (Retired). —Died May 30, 2009
† Daly, Claude R., *s.j.* (NO) (Retired). —Died June 19, 2009
† Dambrauskas, Stephen (SP) (Retired). —Died Dec. 30, 2009
† Darbouze, Rev. Msgr. Gerard (MIA) North Miami, FL Saint James. —Died March 21, 2009
† Darkowski, Rev. Msgr. Leon S. (PIT) (Retired). —Died Aug., 2009
† Daschbach, Edwin, *s.v.d.* (WH) Glenville, WV Good Shepherd. —Died Aug. 15, 2009
† Davis, Charles A. (AUS) (Retired). —Died Dec. 18, 2009
† Decker, Maurice C. (DET) (Retired). —Died June 23, 2009
† DeGante, Adalberto (DEN) (Retired). —Died Oct. 31, 2009
† Dehner, Philip, *o.c.s.o.* (ATL) (Retired). —Died Dec. 4, 2008
† de la Vega, Francis, *o.a.r.* (LA) Oxnard, CA St. Augustine Priory. —Died Jan. 1, 2009
† Delos, Bernard M. (ALB) (Retired). —Died Aug. 20, 2009
† De Louw, Joseph, *o.s.c.* (SCL) Onamia, MN Onamia Crossier Priory. —Died July 5, 2009
† Demasi, Michael A. (BUR) (Retired). —Died May 19, 2009
† DeMott, Lester T., *c.m.* (PH) Philadelphia, PA Congregation of the Mission. —Died June 24, 2009
† Demski, Rev. Msgr. Arthur A. (BRK) (Retired). —Died Dec. 10, 2009
† DePriest, Ellis L., *s.m.* (NO) New Orleans, LA Marist Fathers. —Died Feb. 6, 2009
† Deyo, Paul, *ss.cc.* (FR) (Retired). —Died March 25, 2008
† Dicks, Leon, *o.f.m.conv.* (ALB) Fonda, NY St. Cecilia. —Died Oct. 3, 2009
† Dietzel, Rev. Msgr. Elmer J. (MAD) (Retired). —Died Oct. 27, 2009
† Dillon, William, *s.a.* (NY) Garrison, NY Franciscan Friars of the Atonement. —Died Jan. 15, 2009
† Dionne, Leo, *o.m.i.* (MIA) Miramar, FL St. Stephen. —Died July 29, 2009
† Dittoe, Rev. Msgr. John T. (COL) (Retired). —Died Sept. 14, 2009
† DiVito, John, *c.s.* (CHI) (Retired). —Died June 14, 2009
† Divizia, John, *s.d.b.* (NY) Stony Point, NY Don Bosco Retreat Center and Marian Shrine. —Died 2009
† Dodds, Perry W. (B) (Retired). —Died May 17, 2009
† Doherty, Rev. Msgr. Patrick G. (FRS) (Retired). —Died Sept. 7, 2009
† Dokupil, Rev. Msgr. Edward J. (AUS) Bastrop, TX Ascension. —Died Jan. 18, 2009
† Dolan, James J. (RVC) (Retired). —Died May 23, 2009
† Dollar, Robert J. (BEL) (Retired). —Died Dec. 1, 2009
† Dolsina, Stanley (DUL) (Retired). —Died July 27, 2009
† Dombrowski, Robert J. (FTW) (Retired). —Died April 22, 2009
† Donahue, Joseph P. (HRT) (Retired). —Died Jan. 1, 2009
† Donegan, Augustine, *t.o.r.* (ALT) Loretto, PA St. Francis Friary at Mt. Assisi. —Died July 26, 2009
† Donnelly, James J., *s.j.* (FgM) Society of Jesus Foreign Mission. —Died Aug. 17, 2009
† Donnelly, Sean (SPK) (Retired). —Died Feb. 10, 2009
† Donoghue, Rev. Msgr. John F. (B) (Retired). —Died Jan. 5, 2009
† Donohue, Timothy, *o.carm.* (NY) (Retired). —Died Feb. 6, 2009
† Donovan, Gerald Brian, *o.p.* (GAL) Houston, TX St. Mark Priory. —Died March 21, 2009
† Doogan, Joseph H. (SEA) Adjunct Judicial Vicar. —Died May 12, 2009
† Dooley, Henry J., *c.s.p.* (BO) (Retired). —Died July 19, 2009
† Dougherty, Charles (SJ) (Retired). —Died Jan. 27, 2009
† Douglas, Marian, *o.f.m.* (CIN) (Retired). —Died March 22, 2009
† Dower, Douglas (RVC) West Islip, NY Good Samaritan Hospital Medical Center. —Died Oct. 15, 2009
† Doyle, John A., *c.m.* (PH) Philadelphia, PA Congregation of the Mission. —Died July 7, 2009
† Doyle, Joseph F., *s.j.* (NO) New Orleans, LA Ignatius Residence. —Died Dec. 6, 2008
† Dreier, Rev. Msgr. Bruce A. (SFR) San Bruno, CA St. Robert. —Died Aug. 10, 2009
† Driscoll, Rev. Msgr. Maurice F. (BEL) (Retired). —Died Sept. 9, 2009
† Drummond, Richard (SY) (Retired). —Died May 1, 2009
† Dudink, Edward, *s.v.d.* (BO) Duxbury, MA Society of the Divine Word. —Died June 8, 2009
† Duffy, Edwin J. (HON) (Retired). —Died March 19, 2009
† Duffy, Eugene J. (LA) (Retired). —Died Jan. 2, 2009
† Duffy, Vincent, *s.d.b.* (NY) New Rochelle, NY Salesian Provincial. —Died March 21, 2009
† Dufour, Clement E. (FR) (Retired). —Died Sept. 26, 2009
† Dugal, William (JOL) (Absent on Sick Leave). —Died April 4, 2009
† Duggan, Charles T. (BO) (Retired). —Died May 18, 2009
† Duggan, Thomas J. (JC) (Retired). —Died Sept. 29, 2009
† Duggan, Thomas R., *c.ss.r.* (STL) (Retired). —Died 2009
† Duggan, William E. (SFR) (Retired). —Died March 19, 2009
† Dunn, Richard C. (TOL) (Retired). —Died March 10, 2009

† Duritsa, George M. (Y) (Retired). —Died June 4, 2009
† Duvelsdorf, Peter L. (RVC) (Retired). —Died June 13, 2009
† Dwyer, Dennis E. (COS) (Retired). —Died Jan. 15, 2009
† Eberly, Herbert, *c.p.* (PIT) Pittsburgh, PA St. Paul of the Cross Monastery. —Died Oct. 28, 2008
† Eickholt, Henry C. (SAG) (Retired). —Died July 27, 2009
† Eikmeier, Rev. Msgr. Bernard J. (HON) (Retired). —Died July 8, 2009
† Escala, Rafael (MIA) (Retired). —Died Jan. 27, 2009
† Estrada, Domingo, *o.m.i.* (SAT) (Retired). —Died Sept. 21, 2009
† Euresti, Jesse E. (AUS) Austin, TX Christo Rey. —Died April 5, 2009
† Everling, Robert M. (SCR) Great Bend, PA Saint Lawrence Parish Pastor Emeritus. —Died April 1, 2009
† Ewing, Richard A. (MET) (Retired). —Died April 23, 2009
† Fallon, David F. (CLV) Cleveland, OH Sagrada Familia. —Died May 1, 2009
† Fanning, Leo M. (PAT) (Retired). —Died Dec. 29, 2008
† Farrell, James "Jim", *c.ss.r.* (OAK) Berkeley, CA Redemptorist Fathers. —Died June 10, 2009
† Faschan, Matthew John (BR) (Retired). —Died Jan. 3, 2009
† Fauser, Arthur W. (DET) (Retired). —Died April 1, 2009
† Fay, Michael Jude (BGP) (Leave of Absence). —Died Aug. 22, 2009
† Fenlon, Thomas J. (HEL) (Retired). —Died April 21, 2009
† Ferens, Joseph F. (DET) (Retired). —Died Nov. 30, 2009
† Fernandez, Jose Maria (GAL) (Retired). —Died Oct. 15, 2009
† Finch, G. William (WDC) Rockville, MD St. Raphael. —Died April 9, 2009
† Finnell, Eugene (PEO) (Retired). —Died Dec. 27, 2008
† Finnerty, William (KCK) (Retired). —Died Oct. 7, 2009
† Finucan, Rev. Msgr. James P. (LC) (Retired). —Died June 12, 2009
† Fischer, Louis A. (SLC) (Retired). —Died Feb. 6, 2009
† Fisher, Charles M. (RIC) Richmond, VA Our Lady of Lourdes. —Died Jan. 9, 2009
† Fitch, David, *s.j.* (SJ) (Retired). —Died Jan. 30, 2009
† Fitzgerald, Donald J. (BUF) (Retired). —Died Sept. 1, 2009
† Fitzgerald, J. Vincent, *o.m.i.* (BEL) Belleville, IL Missionary Oblates of Mary Immaculate. —Died Sept. 27, 2009
† Fitzgerald, James E. (BUF) (Retired). —Died Dec. 13, 2009
† Fitzpatrick, Thomas J., *o.s.f.s.* (WIL) (Retired). —Died March 16, 2009
† Flach, LaVern J., *o.s.a.* (CHI) Olympia Fields, IL St. Nicholas of Tolentine. —Died Nov. 17, 2008
† Flaherty, Kenneth, *t.o.r.* (ALT) Loretto, PA St. Francis Friary at Mt. Assisi. —Died Feb. 22, 2009
† Flanery, Joseph–Mary, *o.c.d.* (MIL) (Retired). —Died May 31, 2009
† Fleck, Richard Ambrose, *o.p.* (BO) (Retired). —Died Aug. 7, 2009
† Flegge, William (SLC). —Died April 4, 2009
† Fleming, Rev. Msgr. Edward J. (NEW) (Retired). —Died Dec. 25, 2008
† Flinn, Rev. Msgr. George B. (ALT) Johnstown, PA St. John Gualbert Cathedral. —Died Sept. 6, 2009
† Flood, Rev. Msgr. Patrick (FRS) (Retired). —Died July 12, 2009
† Flores, Virgilio M. (LSC) Deming, NM St. Ann's. —Died Nov. 5, 2009
† Flynn, Robert P, *s.j.* (FgM) Society of Jesus Foreign Mission. —Died 2009
† Flynn, Stephen F.X. (ALN) Bath, PA Sacred Heart of Jesus Pastor Emeritus. —Died Feb. 1, 2009
† Fodor, Nicholas, *sch.p.* (PH) Devon, PA Piarist Fathers. —Died Feb. 3, 2009
† Fogarty, Daniel F. (NY) (Retired). —Died Aug. 21, 2009
† Folliard, Rev. Msgr. John P. (LA) (Retired). —Died June 22, 2009
† Forest, Gerald, *m.s.* (FR) (Retired). —Died 2009
† Forst, William (JC) (Retired). —Died Sept. 13, 2009
† Foster, Patrick (EVN) (Retired). —Died April 10, 2009
† Fox, Joseph F. (SCR) Bastress, PA Immaculate Conception Parish Pastor Emeritus. —Died July 26, 2009
† Fox, Robert J. (SFS) (Retired). —Died Nov. 26, 2009
† Frankhauser, William E., *s.j.* (BUF) (Retired). —Died May 3, 2009
† Fratus, James F. (BO) (Retired). —Died April 8, 2009
† Freeswick, William J. (PAT) Denville, NJ Saint Francis Health Resort Chap.. —Died Sept. 12, 2009
† Freyne, Bernard (SJ) (Retired). —Died Feb. 2, 2009
† Frisbie, Kenneth J. (HRT) (Retired). —Died Jan. 17, 2009
† Fritz, Germain, *o.s.b.* (PAT) Morristown, NJ St. Mary's Abbey. —Died April 3, 2009
† Frizelle, Rev. Msgr. John D. (AUS) (Retired). —Died Feb. 19, 2009
† Fry, Richard C. (SJ) (Retired). —Died Feb. 24, 2009
† Fusco, Blaise, *o.f.m.cap.* (PIT) Pittsburgh, PA Vincention Motherhouse. —Died Nov. 2, 2008
† Fye, Rev. Msgr. Lawrence C. (Y) (Retired). —Died July 25, 2009
† Gadarowski, Rev. Msgr. Bronislaw A. (NOR) (Retired). —Died Nov. 10, 2009
† Gagnon, Adelard J. (BO) (Retired). —Died May 2, 2009
† Gallagher, Thomas J., *s.j.* (BO) Boston, MA Loyola House. —Died Oct. 2, 2009
† Gamba, John J. (COL) (Retired). —Died Nov. 21, 2009
† Gambon, John A. (STL) (Retired). —Died July 7, 2009
† Ganley, Charles (SAG) (Retired). —Died Dec. 11, 2008
† Garofalo, Kenneth, *o.f.m.* (BO) South Boston, MA St. Christopher Friary. —Died Sept. 29, 2009
† Garrett, Mark A., *o.s.a.* (PH) Villanova, PA St. Thomas Monastery. —Died April 23, 2009
† Garrett, Sean (SAT) (On Duty Outside the Archdiocese). —Died Dec. 11, 2008
† Garrett, Thomas, *o.s.a.* (SD) (Retired). —Died Nov. 25, 2008
† Garvey, John M. (SFS) (Retired). —Died Feb. 4, 2009
† Gavigan, Rev. Msgr. Peter J. (NY) Bronx, NY Our Lady of Victory. —Died March 17, 2009
† Gefell, Rev. Msgr. Gerard J. (OG) (Retired). —Died Feb. 6, 2010
† Geiger, William G., *c.ss.r.* (HBG) Ephrata, PA St. Clement's Mission House. —Died 2009
† Gerones, Florencio (LA) Westlake Village, CA St. Jude. —Died 2009
† Gesuale, Valentine, *o.f.m.* (FgM) Franciscan Friars Foreign Mission. —Died 2009
† Geyer, Raymond J., *o.s.b.* (CHL) Belmont, NC Belmont Abbey. —Died July 26, 2009
† Gibbons, James M. (BO) (Retired). —Died Aug. 21, 2009
† Giblin, Rev. Msgr. Lawrence E. (SY) (Retired). —Died Sept. 26, 2009
† Gicewicz, Edward, *c.m.* (HRT) (Retired). —Died March 17, 2009
† Gilmartin, Daniel J. (BO) (Retired). —Died Oct. 8, 2009
† Gilmore, Raymond V. (HEL) (Retired). —Died May 25, 2009
† Glynn, Rev. Msgr. Gerard N. (STL) (Retired). —Died Feb. 4, 2009
† Golik, Stanislaus (OM) (Retired). —Died Sept. 7, 2009
† Gomez, Rene J. (SFR) (Retired). —Died June 7, 2009
† Good, Rev. Msgr. Clarence P. (STL) (Retired). —Died May 21, 2009
† Gorham, Peter P. (PRT). —Died Sept. 14, 2009
† Gothing, Donald B. (WOR) (Retired). —Died Oct. 19, 2009
† Grace, Rev. Msgr. James P. (BRK) Queens, NY St. Andrew Avellino. —Died March 3, 2009
† Graven, John P. (FAR) (Retired). —Died Aug. 29, 2009
† Gray, John Hugh, *s.j.* (SJ). —Died Jan. 11, 2009
† Gray, Paul (DAL) Dallas, TX All Saints. —Died Oct. 1, 2009
† Gray, Theodoro (SJN). —Died Sept. 13, 2009
† Graziani, Joseph A. (HRT) (Retired). —Died May 3, 2009
† Greaney, John (HBG) (Retired). —Died March 31, 2009
† Green, Thomas H., *s.j.* (FgM) Society of Jesus Foreign Mission. —Died 2009
† Greene, Thomas S. (SPR) (Retired). —Died Sept. 9, 2009
† Griffin, George J. (ARL) Orange, VA St. Isidore the Farmer. —Died Dec. 25, 2008
† Grollig, Anthony J., *s.j.* (FgM) Society of Jesus Foreign Mission. —Died Oct. 11, 2009
† Gross, Lawrence C. (HBG) (Retired). —Died March 24, 2009
† Gruchot, Stanley J. (CHI) (Retired). —Died Nov. 12, 2009
† Grzeskowiak, Edward S. (STP) (Retired). —Died March 24, 2009
† Guido, Rev. Msgr. William F. (NY) New York, NY Our Savior Pastor Emeritus. —Died April 30, 2009
† Guillen, Arthur H. (LA) (Retired). —Died May 27, 2009
† Guiltnane, Justin Thomas, *s.c.j.* (MIL) (Retired). —Died Feb. 7, 2009
† Gunti, Frederick W. (LR) (On Duty Outside Diocese). —Died Jan. 29, 2009
† Gurski, John K. (NEW) (Retired). —Died April 10, 2009
† Guyder, Thomas F. (SY) (Retired). —Died April 25, 2009
† Gyhra, Lawrence J. (LIN) (Retired). —Died May 17, 2009
† Hacker, John "Jack", *c.ss.r.* (STL) (Retired). —Died March 7, 2009
† Hahn, James Cornelius, *o.p.* (CHI) Chicago, IL St. Pius V Priory. —Died Nov. 8, 2008
† Hall, Jerome M., *s.j.* (WDC) Washington, DC Gonzaga College High School. —Died March 11, 2009
† Haller, Joseph A., *s.j.* (WDC) Washington, DC The Jesuit Community at Georgetown University. —Died Dec. 14, 2008
† Halliwell, Robert J. (NEW) (Retired). —Died May 11, 2009
† Halloran, John (HON) (Retired). —Died May 5, 2009
† Hand, Rev. Msgr. Kevin (AMA) (Retired). —Died Aug. 9, 2009
† Hanna, Don Michael (RIC) (Retired). —Died Nov. 15, 2009
† Harrington, Rev. Msgr. John (NY) Pearl River, NY St. Margaret of Antioch. —Died Aug. 22, 2009
† Harris, David T. (MAR) (Retired). —Died Feb. 24, 2009
† Harrold, James, *s.m.a.* (NEW) (Retired). —Died Aug. 30, 2009
† Hart, Robert P., *s.j.* (MIL) Wauwatosa, WI Jesuit Community at St. Camillus. —Died Nov. 29, 2008
† Hartnett, Rev. Msgr. James R. (STL) (Retired). —Died March 29, 2009
† Hay, Francis J. (WCH) (Retired). —Died Nov. 12, 2008
† Hayes, Rev. Msgr. Thomas P. (STO) Lodi, CA St. Anne (Pastor of). —Died April 13, 2009
† Healy, Joseph (SFR) San Francisco, CA Most Holy Redeemer. —Died Dec. 4, 2009
† Heaney, Rev. Msgr. John P. (SFR) (Retired). —Died Jan. 29, 2010
† Heavey, Edward J., *s.j.* (NEW) Jersey City, NJ Jesuit Center. —Died March 23, 2009
† Heberle, Frederick L. (SPR) (Retired). —Died Nov. 10, 2009
† Hebert, Joseph L., *s.j.* (STL) St. Louis, MO Jesuit Community at St. Louis Univ.. —Died Aug. 8, 2009
† Heck, Theodore, *o.s.b.* (IND) St. Meinrad, IN St. Meinrad. —Died April 29, 2009
† Heffernan, Thomas A. (BRK) (Retired). —Died Aug. 6, 2009
† Hegener, Wilbert, *o.f.m.* (SFD) (Retired). —Died July 15, 2009
† Heid, Richard J. (SCL) Brandon, MN Church of St. Ann. —Died Feb. 1, 2009
† Heidelberger, Ronald L. (DET) (Retired). —Died Jan. 29, 2009
† Heim, Gerald B., *c.ss.r.* (STL) (Retired). —Died June 17, 2009
† Heim, Howard J., *s.j.* (PH) Philadelphia, PA Loyola Center. —Died Dec. 12, 2008
† Heinecke, Gary Leo, *c.ss.r.* (MIL) Oconomowoc, WI The Redeptionist Retreat Center. —Died Feb. 21, 2009
† Helmich, George F., *c.s.p.* (PMB) Vero Beach, FL Paulist Fathers Residence. —Died April 9, 2009
† Hendel, Rev. Msgr. Thomas W. J. (BRK) (Retired). —Died Jan. 6, 2009
† Hendricks, Joseph, *ss.cc.* (HON) Kalaupapa, HI St. Francis. —Died Nov. 3, 2008
† Hendrickson, Frederick (L) (Retired). —Died April 5, 2009
† Herdegen, Rev. Msgr. Anthony (FRS) (Retired). —Died March 17, 2009
† Herman, Jerome A. (DET) (Retired). —Died Oct. 18, 2009
† Hermanns, Harold T. (NEW) (Retired). —Died Oct. 7, 2009
† Hermley, Robert J., *o.s.f.s.* (WIL) (Retired). —Died Aug. 30, 2009
† Herron, Rev. Msgr. Bernard J. (PH) (Retired). —Died Aug. 29, 2009
† Hess, Richard J. (DUB) (Retired). —Died Sept. 1, 2009
† Hessian, Rev. Msgr. Patrick J. (STP) (Retired). —Died 2009
† Hewitt, Rev. Msgr. Bernard P. (CAM) (Retired). —Died Nov. 6, 2009
† Higgins, James P., *s.j.* (SY) Syracuse, NY Jesuits at LeMoyne. —Died Jan. 20, 2009
† Higgins, John F. (WDC) (Retired). —Died July 29, 2009
† Hill, Timothy (BIR) (Retired). —Died April 18, 2009
† Hinds, Edward J. (PAT) Chatham, NJ St. Patrick's. —Died Oct. 22, 2009
† Hirsch, Robert M. (DUB) (Retired). —Died March 21, 2009
† Hitchcock, Rev. Msgr. James R. (NSH) (Retired). —Died Dec. 9, 2008
† Hoban, Paul, *o.carm.* (JOL) (Retired). —Died Aug. 27, 2009

† Hogan, William D., *s.s.j.* (BAL) (Retired). —Died June 14, 2009
† Homa, Thomas D. (PH) (Retired). —Died Sept. 16, 2009
† Horgan–Kung, Rev. Msgr. John V. (BGP) (Retired). —Died Oct. 16, 2009
† Hotze, Leo, *s.v.d.* (CHI) (Retired). —Died Jan. 18, 2009
† Houdek, Francis J., *s.j.* (OAK) Lafayette, CA St. Perpetua. —Died April 23, 2009
† Hourihane, Francis (RVC) (Retired). —Died Oct. 23, 2009
† Howard, Anthony (L) (Retired). —Died July 2, 2009
† Hrebic, Alban, *o.s.b.* (FgM) Benedictine Monks Foreign Mission. —Died Sept. 10, 2009
† Hren, Joseph Innocent, *o.p.* (CHI) Chicago, IL St. Pius V Priory. —Died April 12, 2009
† Hughes, John J. (ARL) (Retired). —Died Feb. 13, 2009
† Hughes, Patrick Michael (LA) (Retired). —Died April 12, 2009
† Hughes, Royce (GAL) (Retired). —Died May 2, 2009
† Hurley, Joseph T., *c.ss.r.* (WIL) Seaford, DE Our Lady of Lourdes. —Died Oct. 30, 2009
† Hynes, James F., *o.f.m.* (NY) New York, NY Franciscan Friary. —Died Nov. 2, 2008
† Iglesias, Luis Fernando (CC) (Retired). —Died Nov. 8, 2009
† Immel, A. William (DET) (Retired). —Died June 16, 2009
† Ireland, Donald J. (MIA) (Retired). —Died April 15, 2009
† Irizarry, Rafael (ARE) (Retired). —Died March 27, 2009
† Jacimerski, Jan (NY) (Retired). —Died July 22, 2009
† Jackson, Gerald, *o.f.m.* (CIN) (Retired). —Died March 25, 2009
† Jamroz, Waclaw, *s.d.s.* (CHI) Chicago, IL Our Lady of the Snows. —Died 2009
† Janesko, Rev. Msgr. John A. (LR) Stuttgart, AR Holy Rosary. —Died June 19, 2009
† Jansen, Rev. Msgr. James H. (BEL) (Retired). —Died Feb. 11, 2009
† Jenks, Francis C. (CHI) (Retired). —Died July 16, 2009
† Jennings, Earl, *t.o.r.* (ALT) Loretto, PA St. Francis Friary at Mt. Assisi. —Died July 15, 2009
† Jette, Donald, *s.s.s.* (CLV) Cleveland, OH Blessed Sacrament. —Died Aug. 31, 2009
† Jillisky, William F. (ALB) (Retired). —Died Aug. 27, 2009
† Jimenez, Rev. Msgr. Armando (WDC) (Retired). —Died Dec. 9, 2008
† Johnson, Harold J. (BO) (Retired). —Died Dec. 22, 2009
† Johnson, J. Raymond, *s.j.* (NY) New York, NY Loyola Hall. —Died Feb. 24, 2009
† Johnson, William J. (CLV) (Retired). —Died Jan. 6, 2009
† Jones, Rev. Msgr. John L. (ALB) (Retired). —Died July 10, 2009
† Jones, Patrick M. (JKS) (Retired). —Died Nov. 16, 2009
† Juaire, Joseph, *o.m.i.* (SB) (Retired). —Died April 13, 2009
† Jude, Rev. Msgr. Walter F. (GR) (Retired). —Died May 5, 2009
† Jurasko, Joseph Jerome, *o.p.* (COL) (Retired). —Died Jan. 26, 2009
† Jurich, James P., *s.j.* (NY) New York, NY Murray–Weigel Hall. —Died Aug. 9, 2009
† Justi, Marvin, *o.f.m.cap.* (PIT) Butler, PA VA Medical Center. —Died Feb. 11, 2009
† Kadlec, Josef, *s.j.* (PH) Philadelphia, PA Loyola Center. —Died Nov. 2, 2008
† Kaminski, Ladislaus J. (HRT) (Retired). —Died Aug. 21, 2009
† Kane, Eugene J. (PEO) (Retired). —Died July 28, 2009
† Kane, Thomas Cornelius, *o.p.* (WDC) (Retired). —Died March 1, 2009
† Karl, Rev. Msgr. Edward B. (BGP) (Retired). —Died Sept. 20, 2009
† Karl, Ralph, *o.m.i.* (BO) Lowell, MA Missionary Oblates of Mary Immaculate. —Died Aug. 20, 2009
† Kasarda, John (PBR) (Retired). —Died Dec. 8, 2008
† Kattady, Augustine (TUC) Apache Junction, AZ St. George Parish. —Died Jan. 24, 2009
† Kaucky, Francis M. (CHI) (Retired). —Died Aug. 18, 2009
† Kaylor, Gary (OKL) (Retired). —Died Jan. 4, 2009
† Keane, Joseph P. (BRK) (Retired). —Died June 10, 2009
† Keane, Patrick J. (SFR) (Retired). —Died Jan. 20, 2009
† Kearns, Robert M., *s.s.j.* (MOB) Mobile, AL Most Pure Heart of Mary. —Died Dec. 6, 2008
† Keefer, John E., *o.p.* (SAT) San Antonio, TX St. Ann. —Died Dec. 17, 2008
† Kekeisen, William (SFD) (Retired). —Died Aug. 29, 2009
† Kelley, David J. (CIN) (Administrative Leave). —Died June 6, 2009
† Kelley, Paul G. (BO) (Retired). —Died Oct. 11, 2009
† Kelly, Daniel J. (DAV) (Retired). —Died Jan. 23, 2009
† Kelly, John Edward (SAT) San Antonio, TX San Francesco di Paola. —Died Jan. 18, 2009
† Kelly, Michael C. (ARL) Purcellville, VA St. Francis de Sales. —Died Dec. 31, 2008
† Kelly, Philip, *o.f.m.conv.* (SY) (Retired). —Died Sept. 7, 2009
† Kemp, Patrick W. (WDC) (Retired). —Died Nov. 18, 2008
† Kempczynski, Rev. Msgr. John (BUF) (Retired). —Died Jan. 25, 2009
† Kennedy, Rev. Msgr. Christopher J. (LA) Long Beach, CA St. Barnabas Pastor Emeritus. —Died March 2, 2009
† Kennedy, Hugh A., *s.j.* (PH) Merion Station, PA Loyola Center. —Died Sept. 6, 2009
† Kennedy, Joseph J. (PH) (Retired). —Died Dec. 22, 2008
† Kennedy, William J., *s.j.* (BGP) Fairfield, CT Fairfield Univ. Jesuit Community. —Died May 16, 2009
† Kenney, Francis P. (WIL) (Absent on Sick Leave). —Died Feb. 14, 2009
† Kenny, Rev. Msgr. James T. (SLC) (Retired). —Died May 31, 2009
† Kenny, Kevin, *o.f.m.conv.* (ALB) Fonda, NY St. Cecilia. —Died Oct. 16, 2009
† Kerner, Timothy J., *c.ss.r.* (BR) Baton Rouge, LA Our Lady of the Lake Regl. Medical Center. —Died Oct. 10, 2009
† Kerr, Rev. Msgr. William A. (PT) Tallahassee, FL Pres., Casa Calderon, Inc.. —Died May 13, 2009
† Kerwin, Rev. Msgr. Eugene H. (OM) (Retired). —Died June 23, 2009
† Kieffer, Henry (SAL) (Retired). —Died Jan. 10, 2009
† King, Thomas J. (ALN) Bethlehem, PA Holy Family Villa Pastor Emeritus. —Died April 4, 2009
† King, Thomas M., *s.j.* (WDC) Washington, DC Georgetown Univ.. —Died June 23, 2009
† King, William F., *s.j.* (DET) Clarkston, MI Colombiere Center. —Died Aug. 20, 2009
† King, William M., *s.j.* (PH) Merion Station, PA Loyola Center. —Died Sept. 3, 2009
† Kita, August, *s.d.b.* (NY) Stony Point, NY Don Bosco Retreat Center and Marian Shrine. —Died 2009
† Kitko, Joseph F. (BAL) Laurel, MD Resurrection of Our Lord Pastor Emeritus. —Died July 22, 2009
† Klamet, Frank X. (CLV) (Released from Diocesan Assignment). —Died April 19, 2009
† Klaus, Joseph J. (R) (Retired). —Died Dec. 30, 2008
† Knauf, Rev. Msgr. Edwin L. (LC) (Retired). —Died Oct. 27, 2009
† Knipe, William T., *m.m.* (NY) (Retired). —Died Aug. 14, 2009
† Knoke, Kenneth (FAR) (Retired). —Died June 8, 2009
† Kobza, John, *m.i.c.* (WDC) Brookeville, MD Marian Monastery. —Died Oct. 4, 2009
† Koenig, Bernard (HEL) (Retired). —Died Dec. 28, 2009
† Koerber, George M. (TOL) (Retired). —Died 2009
† Kohuch, Robert Andrew (PIT) (Leave of Absence). —Died July 1, 2008
† Kokjohn, Joseph E. (DAV) (Retired). —Died May 21, 2009
† Komechak, Michael, *o.s.b.* (JOL) Lisle, IL St. Procopius. —Died Aug. 30, 2009
† Kostelnick, Albert T. (PH) (Retired). —Died March 30, 2009
† Koth, Arthur R. (MAD) (Retired). —Died Nov. 11, 2009
† Kouba, John, *s.d.s.* (MIL) (Retired). —Died March 20, 2009
† Kowal, William D. (R) (Absent on Leave). —Died Dec. 21, 2008
† Kowalski, Ralph E. (DET) (Retired). —Died Jan. 6, 2009
† Kownacki, Francis J., *s.j.* (NY) New York, NY Murray–Weigel Hall. —Died May 31, 2009
† Kraft, Thomas, *o.p.* (SEA) Seattle, WA Blessed Sacrament. —Died Jan. 22, 2009
† Kraus, Rev. Msgr. Conrad (E) (Retired). —Died May 13, 2009
† Kreft, Henry S. (DET) (Retired). —Died Aug. 15, 2009
† Kretz, Edward J. (GBG) (Retired). —Died Aug. 3, 2009
† Krings, James A. (STL) St. Louis, MO St. Joseph. —Died June 27, 2009
† Krivanek, George E., *s.j.* (SJ) (Retired). —Died Oct. 12, 2008
† Kubat, Alphonse M. (STP) (Retired). —Died 2009
† Kucingis, Rev. Msgr. John A. (LA) Los Angeles, CA St. Casimir. —Died Jan. 6, 2009
† Kucyk, Rev. Msgr. Herman W. (DET) Dearborn, MI Divine Child Pastor Emeritus. —Died May 15, 2009
† Kuenzig, Aloysius A. (PIT) (Retired). —Died June 18, 2009
† Kuhn, Thomas W. (TOL) (Retired). —Died Dec. 3, 2009
† Kumontis, Rev. Msgr. Francis M. (HBG). —Died Jan. 27, 2009
† Kunda, Brendan J. (SUP) (Retired). —Died May 14, 2009
† Kurth, Earl J., *s.j.* (MIL) Wauwatosa, WI Jesuit Community at St. Camillus. —Died Sept. 2, 2009
† Lachapelle, Alphonsus, *o.cist.* (ALN) New Ringgold, PA St. Mary's Monastery. —Died Dec. 25, 2008
† LaCoste, James P., *m.m.* (SJ) Los Altos, CA Maryknoll Fathers and Brothers. —Died Oct. 27, 2009
† Lagan, Hugh (SP) (Retired). —Died June 25, 2009
† LaHart, Rev. Msgr. Richard T. (PH) (Retired). —Died Sept. 17, 2009
† Lahey, John (SAL) (Retired). —Died Nov. 3, 2008
† Lambert, Rollins E. (CHI) (Retired). —Died Jan. 25, 2009
† Lang, Jovian, *o.f.m.* (SFD) Springfield, IL Our Lady of Angels Friary. —Died Nov. 5, 2009
† Lange, Raymond L. (WOR) (Retired). —Died July 10, 2009
† Langell, Michael, *g.h.m.* (R) Windsor, NC The Glenmary Home Missioners. —Died April 29, 2009
† LaPenta, Charles A., *o.s.f.s.* (TOL) (Retired). —Died Aug. 1, 2009
† Larkin, Edward A., *s.j.* (MIL) Wauwatosa, WI Jesuit Community at St. Camillus. —Died Dec. 13, 2008
† Larner, James M. (BO). —Died Aug. 24, 2009
† Latella, Joseph A., *s.j.* (NY) New York, NY St. Ignatius Loyola Residence. —Died 2009
† Latko, Ernest, *o.f.m.* (JOL) (Retired). —Died Dec. 12, 2008
† Laudati, Joseph J. (NEW) (Retired). —Died Jan. 15, 2009
† Lavelle, Thomas E., *m.m.* (NY) (Retired). —Died July 16, 2009
† LaVerdiere, Eugene, *s.s.s.* (NY) (Retired). —Died Nov. 20, 2008
† Lazor, Joseph (STF). —Died Sept. 23, 2009
† Leahy, Rev. Msgr. Patrick Joseph (DOD) (Retired). —Died April 30, 2009
† Leeber, Victor F., *s.j.* (BO) Weston, MA Campion Health Center. —Died Aug. 14, 2009
† Legendre, Rev. Msgr. Francis (HT) (Retired). —Died Jan. 15, 2009
† LeMarre, Theodore E. (SAG) (Retired). —Died June 16, 2009
† Lemoyne, William (ALB) (Retired). —Died Aug. 15, 2009
† Lennon, Rev. Msgr. Robert T. (NEW) (Retired). —Died Dec. 1, 2008
† Leonard, Rev. Msgr. William P. (DUB) (Retired). —Died Dec. 10, 2008
† Letourneau, Rev. Msgr. Paul R. (BUF) (Retired). —Died Oct. 23, 2009
† Lettau, David (Y) (Retired). —Died May 21, 2009
† LeVasseur, Angelo B. (PRT) Rumford, ME Parish of the Holy Savior. —Died May 31, 2009
† Lieb, Marianus, *t.o.r.* (ALT) Loretto, PA St. Francis Friary at Mt. Assisi. —Died July 14, 2009
† Lihvar, Francis P., *s.j.* (CLV) University Heights, OH John Carroll Univ.. —Died Jan. 8, 2009
† Linehan, Eugene J., *s.j.* (PH) Philadelphia, PA Loyola Center. —Died May 23, 2009
† Link, Paul, *c.pp.s.* (CIN) (Retired). —Died May 27, 2009
† Linnenbrink, Harry H. (DAV) (Retired). —Died June 17, 2009
† Llaria, Vincente Ibanez (VEN) Lake Placid, FL St. James. —Died Feb. 6, 2009
† Locke, John K., *s.j.* (FgM) Society of Jesus Foreign Mission. —Died March 18, 2009
† Logan, Joseph P., *s.j.* (PH) Philadelphia, PA Loyola Center. —Died May 4, 2009
† Lomasney, John P., *m.m.* (NY) (Retired). —Died Aug. 13, 2009
† Lommel, George D. (FAR) (Retired). —Died Dec. 30, 2008
† London, Lawrence (RCK) (Retired). —Died Nov. 1, 2009
† Longres, Joaquin S. (BRK) (Retired). —Died Feb. 11, 2009
† Lotito, Floyd, *o.f.m.* (SFR) San Francisco, CA St. Boniface. —Died July 14, 2009
† Lucca, Augustine, *s.d.s.* (MIL) (Retired). —Died Aug. 16, 2009
† Lucking, Aloysius (MIA) (Retired). —Died Sept. 16, 2009
† Luna, Roger, *s.d.b.* (SFR) (Retired). —Died Dec. 13, 2008
† Luzzi, Anthony, *s.d.b.* (NY) Stony Point, NY Don Bosco Retreat Center and Marian Shrine. —Died 2009
† Lynch, Robert G., *s.j.* (CHY) Pinedale, WY Our Lady of Peace. —Died Oct. 20, 2009
† Lyon, George, *o.s.b.* (SFS) Marvin, SD Blue Cloud Abbey. —Died Sept. 3, 2009
† Lyons, Francis (MIA) (Retired). —Died Oct. 17, 2009

† Lyons, Thomas J. (BRK) (Retired). —Died Jan. 22, 2009
† Macchi, William (OAK) (Retired). —Died Oct. 9, 2009
† Macedo, Charles (SJ) (Retired). —Died Oct. 1, 2009
† MacNevin, Stanley F., *c.s.p.* (BO) Boston, MA Paulist Fathers Residence. —Died Dec. 21, 2008
† Madden, Rev. Msgr. James J. (GAL) (Retired). —Died Sept. 6, 2009
† Maguire, Rev. Msgr. Hugh (MOB) Grand Bay, AL St. John the Baptist. —Died Feb. 21, 2009
† Maher, David Martin, *s.c.j.* (FgM) Priests of the Sacred Heart Foreign Mission. —Died Sept. 19, 2008
† Mahler, Michael J. (ROC) Ithaca, NY St. Catherine of Siena. —Died June 29, 2009
† Mahnke, Ronald, *o.s.b.* (CLV) Cleveland, OH Benedictine Order. —Died 2009
† Mahoney, Edward P. (R) (Retired). —Died Jan. 8, 2009
† Mahoney, Robert (AUS) (Retired). —Died Sept. 12, 2009
† Mahony, Thomas J., *o.s.a.* (PH) Villanova, PA St. Thomas Monastery. —Died Sept. 1, 2009
† Malanga, Salvatore T. (NEW) (Retired). —Died Aug. 13, 2009
† Malinowski, Hilary L. (SCR) Simpson, PA Saint Micahel Parish Pastor Emeritus. —Died Oct. 1, 2009
† Malley, Rev. Msgr. James (NY) (Retired). —Died March 28, 2009
† Malone, Edward F., *m.m.* (NY) (Retired). —Died Nov. 4, 2009
† Maloney, Rev. Msgr. Thomas (PEO) (Retired). —Died Aug. 7, 2009
† Mangan, James (SPK). —Died Jan. 11, 2009
† Manieri, Rev. Msgr. Frank P. (STU) (Retired). —Died June 28, 2009
† Marley, Thomas J., *c.s.p.* (PMB) Vero Beach, FL Paulist Fathers Residence. —Died Jan. 29, 2009
† Maroon, Rev. Msgr. William J. (COL) (Retired). —Died Jan. 30, 2009
† Marra, Rev. Msgr. Anthony C. (SCR) Dunmore, PA Saint Anthony of Padua Parish Pastor Emeritus. —Died May 12, 2009
† Marron, James F. (BRK) Rosedale, NY St. Pius X. —Died March 16, 2009
† Martin, Joseph C., *s.s.* (BAL) (Retired). —Died March 9, 2009
† Martin, Thomas F., *o.s.a.* (PH) Villanova, PA Villanova University. —Died Feb. 20, 2009
† Martinez, Belisario, *o.s.a.* (SJN) San Juan, PR Ntra. Sra. de la Monserrate. —Died April 14, 2009
† Maschman, Elvan, *o.f.m.* (STL) St. Louis, MO Franciscan Friary of St. Anthony of Padua. —Died 2009
† Matocha, Rev. Msgr. Edward C. (AUS) (Retired). —Died Nov. 11, 2009
† Matyas, Francis B. (STL) (Retired). —Died Jan. 21, 2009
† Mausolf, James H. (GAY) (Retired). —Died Aug. 6, 2009
† Maxcy, Walter J., *m.m.* (NY) (Retired). —Died July 6, 2009
† Maynard, Robert J. (PRO) (Retired). —Died Feb. 8, 2009
† Mazurchuk, Michael T., *c.m.* (PH) Philadelphia, PA St. Vincent de Paul. —Died June 13, 2009
† McAnulty, John D., *s.j.* (LA) (Retired). —Died April 4, 2009
† McCabe, Michael, *o.f.m.* (SFD) (Retired). —Died Jan. 8, 2009
† McCabe, Rev. Msgr. Richard (AUS) (Retired). —Died Sept. 12, 2009
† McCarren, Rev. Msgr. Edgar (RVC) (Retired). —Died Jan. 13, 2009
† McCarthy, Leo, *o.carm.* (VEN) Venice, FL Carmel in Venice. —Died Nov. 18, 2009
† McCarthy, William D., *m.m.* (NY) (Retired). —Died April 30, 2009
† McCarthy, William R. (BO) (Retired). —Died July 24, 2009
† McCartin, Francis, *o.m.i.* (BO) Tewksbury, MA Immaculate Heart of Mary Residence. —Died June 24, 2009
† McCarty, Kieran, *o.f.m.* (TUC) (Retired). —Died Dec. 27, 2008
† McConville, Philip G. (BO) (Retired). —Died Nov. 13, 2009
† McCoy, Alan, *o.f.m.* (LA) (Retired). —Died Oct. 15, 2009
† McCoy, Charles J. (BO) (Retired). —Died Nov. 30, 2009
† McDermott, Rev. Msgr. Thomas J. (SD) (Retired). —Died Nov. 5, 2008
† McDonnell, Rev. Msgr. Thomas J. (BO) (Retired). —Died June 14, 2009
† McDowell, Rev. Msgr. Patrick (DUL) (Retired). —Died May 19, 2009
† McGill, Joseph P., *s.j.* (LAF) Grand Coteau, LA Our Lady of the Oaks Retreat House. —Died 2009
† McGinn, Sylvester P. (NY) (Retired). —Died May 15, 2009
† McGloin, Peter M. (TUC). —Died June 15, 2009
† McGowan, Rev. Msgr. Myles (BAL) Baltimore, MD St. Ursula Pastor Emeritus. —Died Aug. 29, 2009
† McGrath, Patrick (SAC) (Retired). —Died July 12, 2009
† McHugh, Owen Joseph (COS) (Retired). —Died Feb. 24, 2009
† McInerney, Maurice (DEN) (Retired). —Died Jan. 4, 2009
† McInnes, William C., *s.j.* (BO) Weston, MA Campion Health Center. —Died Dec. 8, 2009
† McKee, William F., *c.ss.r.* (STL) (Retired). —Died Oct. 10, 2009
† McKeirnan, Michael J., *m.m.* (NY) (Retired). —Died Sept. 22, 2009
† Mckenna, William J., *s.s.j.* (BAL) (Retired). —Died 2009
† McKnight, Robert J. (BUR) (Retired). —Died June 29, 2009
† McLellan, Alan J., *c.m.* (PH) Philadelphia, PA Congregation of the Mission. —Died April 13, 2009
† McLernon, Thomas M. (HBG) (On Duty Outside the Diocese). —Died Dec. 25, 2009
† McMahon, Gerald J., *s.j.* (NY) New York, NY Murray–Weigel Hall. —Died Aug. 19, 2009
† McMahon, Joseph M. (P) (Retired). —Died May 5, 2009
† McMahon, Joseph W. (CLV) (Retired). —Died Sept. 6, 2009
† McMahon, Rev. Msgr. Lawrence J. (BGP) (Retired). —Died Dec. 15, 2009
† McMahon, Martin, *o.m.i.* (BUF) Buffalo, NY Our Lady of Hope. —Died Feb. 14, 2009
† McMenamin, John J., *o.s.f.s.* (TOL) (Retired). —Died 2009
† McNamara, Patrick M., *o.s.m.* (CHI) Chicago, IL Chicago Order of Friar Servants of Mary. —Died 2009
† McNamara, Peter J. (CC) (Retired). —Died March 11, 2009
† McNamara, Robert F. (ROC) (Retired). —Died May 22, 2009
† McNicholas, Raymond, *s.s.c.* (BUF) (Retired). —Died Sept. 21, 2009
† McQuaid, Rev. Msgr. Eugene (PAT) (Retired). —Died Dec. 20, 2008
† McVey, Thomas Chrysostom, *o.p.* (NY) (Retired). —Died June 29, 2009
† Meehan, Rev. Msgr. James H. (PH) (Retired). —Died June 26, 2009
† Meehan, Rev. Msgr. Joseph P. (NY) (Retired). —Died Dec. 18, 2009
† Mele, Thomas (SPK) (Absent on Leave). —Died April 19, 2009
† Melzer, Howard, *s.c.j.* (MIL) (Retired). —Died April 11, 2009
† Menard, Francis A. (OG) (Retired). —Died Jan. 17, 2009
† Mendez, Enrique, *s.d.b.* (SJN) San Juan, PR San Juan Bosco. —Died April 18, 2009
† Mercer, John E. (NY) Staten Island, NY Our Lady of Pity. —Died Nov. 30, 2009
† Meskenas, Vincent A. (BEL) (Retired). —Died Feb. 27, 2010
† Meurder, Edward E. (BUF) (Retired). —Died Jan. 13, 2009
† Meyer, Sebastian, *o.carm.* (SAC) Fairfield, CA Our Lady of Mt. Carmel. —Died June 24, 2009
† Meyers, Frederick (BWN) Edinburg, TX Sacred Heart. —Died Aug. 30, 2008
† Miceli, James A. (ATL) (Retired). —Died Dec. 8, 2009
† Michaels, John L. (PIT) (Retired). —Died July 13, 2008
† Mignot, Rev. Msgr. John W. (E) Reynoldsville, PA St. Mary. —Died Feb. 19, 2009
† Miklas, Sebastian, *o.f.m.cap.* (WDC) Washington, DC Catholic University. —Died March 5, 2009
† Mikolajczyk, George M., *m.m.* (NY) (Retired). —Died 2009
† Mikulski, Isidore J. (GAY) (Retired). —Died Oct. 6, 2009
† Miller, Neil R. (ROC) (Retired). —Died Dec. 27, 2009
† Miller, Richard G. (TOL) (Retired). —Died March 30, 2009
† Misho, Lloyd P. (BEL) (Retired). —Died July 31, 2009
† Mistretta, Rev. Msgr. Vito F. (SAC) Citrus Heights, CA Holy Family Pastor Emeritus. —Died Oct. 13, 2009
† Mitchell, Conan, *o.f.m.* (SUP) (Retired). —Died March 13, 2009
† Mitchell, William, *ss.cc.* (FR) (Retired). —Died March 21, 2009
† Moeller, Louis (SAN) (Retired). —Died Dec. 29, 2008
† Moelter, Joel, *o.carm.* (SR) (Retired). —Died Nov. 23, 2009
† Mokris, Michael (PBR) (Retired). —Died April 22, 2009
† Mollan, Ralph R. (CHI) (Retired). —Died April 14, 2009
† Montplaisir, Roland A. (MAN) (Retired). —Died June 21, 2009
† Moore, Clark Thomas, *o.p.* (CHI) Chicago, IL Chicago Dominicans. —Died July 5, 2009
† Moore, Donald C. (OKL) (Retired). —Died Oct. 7, 2009
† Moore, Tom (TUC) (Retired). —Died July 5, 2009
† Moran, Daniel F. (BO) (Retired). —Died April 9, 2009
† Moretti, Rev. Msgr. August (LA) Pasadena, CA Assumption of the Blessed Virgin Mary Pastor Emeritus. —Died March 14, 2009
† Morgan, George R., *o.s.a.* (BO) Andover, MA St. Augustine. —Died Jan. 5, 2009
† Morgan, George, *c.m.f.* (CHI) Chicago, IL Oak Park Claretian Missionaries. —Died 2009
† Morgan, Rev. Msgr. Thomas (MRY) (Retired). —Died April 19, 2009
† Moriarty, Philip M. (JC) Wien, MO St. Mary of the Angels. —Died June 18, 2009
† Moriones, Francisco, *o.a.r.* (NY) Suffern, NY Tagaste Monastery. —Died Nov. 29, 2008
† Morris, Rev. Msgr. John E. (PAT) (Retired). —Died Sept. 17, 2009
† Morris, Lester G. (NOR) (Retired). —Died March 24, 2009
† Morrissey, Dunstan, *o.s.b.* (PEO) (Retired). —Died Feb. 25, 2009
† Morrissey, Lawrence P. (PEO) (Retired). —Died Feb. 5, 2009
† Muckerman, Norman J., *c.ss.r.* (STL) (Retired). —Died May 19, 2009
† Mulhall, Rev. Msgr. Francis X. (BRK) (Retired). —Died Sept. 23, 2009
† Mulhern, Raymond F. (COV) (Retired). —Died July 22, 2009
† Mullin, Francis Raymond, *o.p.* (WDC) (Retired). —Died April 14, 2009
† Mulvanerty, Thomas M. (NY) New York, NY St. Monica; Bronx, NY Christ the King & Our Lady of Solace Pastor Emeritus. —Died April 2, 2009
† Murawski, Edward J., *s.j.* (BO) Weston, MA Campion Health Center. —Died July 3, 2009
† Murphy, Brian, *o.carm.* (ROC). —Died Sept. 21, 2009
† Murphy, Charles C., *s.j.* (MIL) Wauwatosa, WI Jesuit Community at St. Camillus. —Died Aug. 1, 2009
† Murphy, Denis J. (LA) (Retired). —Died Jan. 24, 2009
† Murphy, Edward J., *s.j.* (FgM) Society of Jesus Foreign Mission. —Died April 10, 2005
† Murphy, Rev. Msgr. Patrick J. (ALX) (Retired). —Died 2009
† Murphy, Romeo J. "Pete", *o.m.i.* (BO) Lowell, MA St. Eugene House. —Died May 23, 2009
† Murphy, Rev. Msgr. Terrance J. (STP) (Retired). —Died 2009
† Murphy, William P. (CHI) Evergreen Park, Queen of Martyrs Pastor Emeritus. —Died May 22, 2009
† Murray, Rev. Msgr. Andrew L. (BLX) Gulfport, MS St. John the Evangelist. —Died Oct. 20, 2009
† Murray, Edward (SC) Spencer, IA Sacred Heart. —Died Oct. 6, 2009
† Murray, Paul Edward (WDC) (Retired). —Died Jan. 31, 2009
† Murzyn, John A. (GRY) (Retired). —Died April 20, 2009
† Mylchreest, William F. (MIA) Fort Lauderdale, FL Saint Sebastian. —Died July 29, 2009
† Mysliwiec, Austin, *o.f.m.* (ROC) (Retired). —Died May 31, 2009
† Nacu, Jose R., *m.s.* (SB) (Retired). —Died 2009
† Nally, J. Brendan (WOR) (Retired). —Died Nov. 3, 2009
† Nazimek, Francis A. (PIT). —Died July 30, 2008
† Nealon, Joseph W. (NEW) (Retired). —Died May 25, 2009
† Nebus, Vincent J. (MET) (Retired). —Died June 5, 2009
† Negele, Philip, *o.c.s.o.* (DEN) Denver, CO St. Joseph Hospital. —Died March 26, 2009
† Negri, Francisco, *m.s.* (ATL) Smyrna, GA St. Thomas the Apostle. —Died Sept. 28, 2009
† Neuhaus, Richard J. (NY) New York, NY Immaculate Conception. —Died Jan. 8, 2009
† Neville, Franklin A. (WH) Proctor, WV St. Joseph's; Proctor, WV St. Martin. —Died Nov. 16, 2009
† Newman, William Andrew, *o.p.* (WDC) (Retired). —Died April 28, 2009
† Newton, John G. (CAM) (Retired). —Died Feb. 6, 2009
† Nghiem, Vu Minh, *c.ss.r.* (LA) Baldwin Park, CA Vietnamese Redemptorist Mission. —Died Nov. 15, 2008
† Ngo, Joseph Trong (SB) (Retired). —Died July 11, 2009
† Nguyen, Augustine Hue (PT) (Retired). —Died May 12, 2009
† Nguyen Huy Chuong, Matthias M., *c.m.c.* (SB) Corona, CA The Shrine of the Presentation. —Died Jan. 28, 2009
† Nichols, Edward P. (SPC) (Retired). —Died Aug. 5, 2009

† Nicholson, David, *o.s.b.* (P) (Retired). —Died June 9, 2009
† Niland, John, *o.f.m.cap.* (HON) Pearl City, HI Our Lady of Good Counsel. —Died Aug. 5, 2009
† Ninedorf, Robert W. (CHR) (Retired). —Died July 6, 2009
† Nirrengarten, Andrew G. (RVC) (Retired). —Died Jan. 25, 2009
† Nissel, John J., *s.j.* (FgM) Society of Jesus Foreign Mission. —Died 2009
† Nist, Arthur (Y) (Retired). —Died Sept. 10, 2009
† Nistler, Edward A. (CR) (Retired). —Died March 18, 2009
† Noel, Donald Claude, *o.praem.* (GB) DePere, WI St. Norbert. —Died Nov. 21, 2008
† Nolen, Joseph C., *c.ss.r.* (MIL) Oconomowoc, WI Redemptorist Retreat Center. —Died Sept. 12, 2009
† Noone, Sean (CC) (Retired). —Died Oct. 31, 2009
† Norrell, Rev. Msgr. Albert V. (PH) (Retired). —Died March 25, 2009
† Norton, John B., *o.p.* (NO) New Orleans, LA St. Anthony of Padua. —Died July 23, 2009
† Nowak, Stanley F. (BUF) (Retired). —Died July 15, 2009
† Nugent, Rev. Msgr. Michael A. (Andy) (COL) (Retired). —Died June 30, 2009
† Nugent, Rev. Msgr. Richard T. (BUF) (Retired). —Died Oct. 16, 2009
† Nugent, Robert (ALB) (Retired). —Died April 14, 2009
† Nuwer, Harold M. (BUF) (Retired). —Died May 28, 2009
† Nuytten, Raphael H., *c.i.c.m.* (SAT) San Antonio, TX Padua Place. —Died Nov. 29, 2008
† O'Brien, James, *s.s.c.* (PRO) (Retired). —Died March 20, 2009
† O'Brien, Rev. Msgr. John J. (SCR) Scranton, PA Saint Paul Parish Pastor Emeritus. —Died Dec. 27, 2009
† O'Brien, John P. (NY) Scarsdale, NY St. Pius X. —Died Dec. 9, 2009
† O'Brien, John T. (BLX) (Retired). —Died May 18, 2009
† O'Callaghan, Matthias J. (SAC) Willows, CA St. Monica Pastor Emeritus. —Died April 9, 2009
† O'Connell, Rev. Msgr. James P. (STL) (Retired). —Died Dec. 24, 2008
† O'Connor, David, *s.t.* (WDC) University Park, MD Holy Trinity Missionary Cenacle. —Died Sept. 2, 2009
† O'Connor, Gerald T. (ROC) (Retired). —Died Nov. 20, 2009
† O'Connor, John F.X., *c.ss.r.* (NY) New York, NY Redemptorist Priests and Brothers. —Died Feb. 13, 2009
† O'Connor, John P. (PH) (Retired). —Died July 26, 2009
† O'Connor, Maurice (NY) (Retired). —Died March 29, 2009
† O'Connor, Robert C., *s.j.* (CIN) Cincinnati, OH St. Francis Xavier. —Died May 23, 2009
† O'Donnell, Francis P., *s.j.* (CHI) Chicago, IL Clark Street Jesuit Residence. —Died 2009
† O'Donnell, Joseph M., *c.m.* (PH) Philadelphia, PA Congregation of the Mission. —Died March 17, 2009
† O'Donnell, Joseph, *g.h.m.* (CIN) (Retired). —Died Aug. 25, 2009
† O'Donnell, Thomas D., *s.m.* (WDC) (Retired). —Died Nov. 19, 2008
† O'Donnell, Rev. Msgr. William F. (WDC) (Retired). —Died April 23, 2009
† O'Donohoe, James A. (BO) (Retired). —Died Oct. 27, 2009
† O'Dwyer, Patrick (LA) Westlake Village, CA St. Maximilian Kolbe. —Died July 13, 2009
† O'Leary, David A. (WCH) (Retired). —Died Aug. 24, 2009
† O'Malley, Thomas P., *s.j.* (BO) Newton, MA The Jesuit Community at Boston College. —Died Nov. 4, 2009
† O'Neil, W. Laurence, *s.j.* (BGP) Fairfield, CT Fairfield Univ.. —Died Oct. 19, 2009
† O'Neill, Francis J., *s.j.* (BO) Weston, MA Campion Health Center, Inc.. —Died Oct. 28, 2009
† O'Neill, Thomas M. (LC) Chap., La Cross, WI Viterbo Univ.. —Died Sept. 2, 2009
† O'Rourke, Paul, *s.s.c.* (PRO) (Retired). —Died Oct. 28, 2008
† O'Shea, Robert J. (BEL) (Retired). —Died Oct. 20, 2009
† O'Sullivan, Daniel J. (CHI) Park Forest, IL St. Irenaeus. —Died Dec. 15, 2008
† Oetgen, John A., *o.s.b.* (CHL) Belmont, NC Belmont Abbey. —Died Oct. 10, 2009
† Onofrey, Robert, *c.pp.s.* (CIN) Dayton, OH Society of the Precious Blood. —Died April 28, 2009
† Ontiveros, Roy, *o.carm.* (TUC) Tucson, AZ Salpointe Catholic High School. —Died Jan. 2, 2009
† Oppido, Harold J., *s.j.* (NEW) Jersey City, NJ Jesuit Community of St. Peter's Prep. —Died Oct. 2, 2009
† Orians, David (Retired). —Died Oct. 26, 2009
† Orlett, Ray, *g.h.m.* (CIN) (Retired). —Died May 22, 2009
† Orozco, Raphael R. (CHI) (Retired). —Died Dec. 21, 2008
† Orumpakatt, James, *c.m.i.* (CHR) Folly Beach, SC Our Lady of Good Counsel. —Died Jan. 19, 2009
† Ostdiek, Harold Dana, *o.p.* (STP). —Died May 26, 2009
† Ouellette, Roger J. (PRT) (Retired). —Died Jan. 31, 2009
† Paa, Donald R. (KC) (Retired). —Died July 25, 2009
† Pacho, Jesus (PCE) (Retired). —Died May 10, 2009
† Pakenham, Daniel J. (MIL) Elm Grove, WI St. Mary's Visitation. —Died Jan. 15, 2009
† Palm, John B., *s.j.* (SJ) Los Gatos, CA Sacred Heart Jesuit Center. —Died Sept. 8, 2009
† Palmieri, Rev. Msgr. Alexander J. (PH) Chancellor, Diocese of Philadelphia. —Died Aug. 1, 2009
† Pandolfo, Lawrence L., *o.p.* (NO) Jefferson, LA Elmwood Partners. —Died Aug. 2, 2009
† Park, Rev. Msgr. Morton (P) (Retired). —Died Nov. 15, 2009
† Parmisano, Stanley Fabian, *o.p.* (OAK) Oakland, CA St. Albert Priory. —Died June 18, 2009
† Pax, Bart, *o.f.m.* (NO) New Orleans, LA Saint Mary of Angels. —Died July 23, 2009
† Pena, Vincente M., *o.p.* (SAT) San Antonio, TX St. Ann. —Died Jan. 15, 2009
† Pepe, Mario P. (HRT) (Retired). —Died Sept. 17, 2009
† Perez, Anthony R., *s.s.* (BAL) Baltimore, MD St. Mary's Seminary and Univ.. —Died 2009
† Perez, Antonio (AGN) (On Duty Outside the Archdiocese). —Died Sept. 12, 2009
† Perjak, Edmond J. (BEL) (Retired). —Died Sept. 3, 2009
† Perrier, Thomas E., *o.s.b.* (NO) St. Benedict, LA St. Joseph Abbey. —Died Oct. 26, 2009
† Peterman, Charles O. (MIA) Deerfield Beach, FL Saint Ambrose. —Died Dec. 11, 2009
† Petrie, Harry F. (PIT) (Retired). —Died Sept. 24, 2008
† Piccione, John T., *o.f.m.* (NEW) East Rutherford, NJ Sacred Heart Friary. —Died Feb. 22, 2009
† Pick, Philip E., *s.j.* (MIL) St. Louis, MO Jesuit Provincial Office. —Died Aug. 14, 2009
† Pierce, George R. (GBG) (Retired). —Died Nov. 17, 2009
† Pisors, Thomas J., *c.s.v.* (CHI) (Retired). —Died April 25, 2009
† Pistulka, Celestine C. (NU) (Retired). —Died March 16, 2009
† Plasker, Robert L., *c.s.c.* (FTW) Notre Dame, IL Notre Dame Congregation of Holy Cross. —Died Jan. 7, 2009
† Plevyak, Valentine R. (SCR) Sugar Notch, PA Holy Family Parish Pastor Emeritus. —Died May 30, 2009
† Plokhooy, Christopher H. (WIL) (Retired). —Died March 2, 2009
† Poelker, Rev. Msgr. Gerard L. (JC) (Retired). —Died Aug. 3, 2009
† Polewczak, Michael J. (ALB) (On Duty Outside the Diocese). —Died June 23, 2009
† Pomeroy, Joseph B., *s.j.* (WOR) Worcester, MA Jesuits of Holy Cross, Inc.. —Died July 16, 2009
† Pope, Benedict, *o.f.m.cap.* (PIT) Pittsburgh, PA Pittsburgh VA Hospital. —Died Dec. 9, 2008
† Popovich, George (Y) (Retired). —Died June 18, 2009
† Porazzo, Francis J. (TR) (Retired). —Died Oct. 10, 2009
† Porcari, Ernest (DET) (Retired). —Died June 21, 2009
† Powell, John J., *s.j.* (DET) Clarkston, MI Colombiere Center. —Died Sept. 24, 2009
† Powers, Richard J., *s.j.* (NY) New York, NY Murray-Weigel Hall. —Died Sept. 9, 2009
† Prag, Thomas S., *s.j.* (STL) St. Louis, MO Retreat Dir.. —Died Sept. 17, 2009
† Prebula, David "William", *o.s.b.* (SEA) Lacey, WA St. Martin's Abbey. —Died Oct. 4, 2009
† Prendergast, Edward F. (CLV) Rocky River, OH St. Christopher Pastor Emeritus. —Died Dec. 14, 2008
† Prescott, Herbert W. (KNX) (Retired). —Died Nov. 26, 2009
† Probstfield, Regis, *o.s.b.* (KC) Stanberry, MO St. Peter. —Died 2009
† Prokop, Roger (LAN) (Retired). —Died May 22, 2009
† Prushinski, Carl T. (SCR) (Retired). —Died Dec. 31, 2009
† Ptaszynski, Stephen F. (HRT) (Retired). —Died Jan. 5, 2009
† Purcell, James (PEO) (Retired). —Died Oct. 19, 2009
† Purcell, Robert F., *s.j.* (MIL) Wauwatosa, WI Jesuit Community at St. Camillus. —Died Jan. 16, 2009
† Pusateri, Philip A., *s.j.* (NOR) Norwich, CT SS. Peter & Paul. —Died Feb. 23, 2009
† Quinn, Frank Currier, *o.p.* (STL) St. Louis, MO St. Dominic Priory. —Died Oct. 31, 2008
† Quinn, Rev. Msgr. John J. (NY) (Retired). —Died Sept. 24, 2009
† Quinn, John M., *o.s.a.* (PH) Villanova, PA St. Thomas Monastery. —Died Oct. 3, 2008
† Quinn, Joseph L., *s.j.* (SCR) (Retired). —Died Sept. 7, 2009
† Rainville, Laurence P., *o.f.m.* (PAT) (Retired). —Died April 13, 2009
† Ramellini, Rev. Msgr. P. Lino (GBG) (Retired). —Died Aug. 28, 2009
† Ramenaden, Ronald (FTW) North Manchester, IN St. Robert Bellarmine. —Died Sept. 9, 2009
† Randall, Edward, *o.m.i.* (BO) Tewksbury, MA Immaculate Heart of Mary Residence. —Died Oct. 2, 2009
† Rau, Rev. Msgr. Raymond F. (BRK) (Retired). —Died Sept. 20, 2009
† Reale, Sante, *c.pp.s.* (CIN) (Retired). —Died June 27, 2009
† Reardon, Thomas J. (LC) (Retired). —Died Jan. 10, 2010
† Reichert, Henry J. (JC) Tipton, MO St. Andrew & California, MO Annunciation. —Died June 20, 2009
† Reis, Raymond H., *s.j.* (STL) St. Louis, MO Jesuit Community at St. Louis Univ.. —Died July 19, 2009
† Reising, Raymond (EVN) (Retired). —Died July 14, 2009
† Remaklus, Charles W. (LFT) (Retired). —Died Aug. 23, 2009
† Remy, Adrien T. (SPR) (Retired). —Died Feb. 28, 2009
† Renda, Xavier F. (BGP) (Retired). —Died June 22, 2009
† Repsys, Ricardas Southfield, MI Divine Providence. —Died 2010
† Resta, Vincent Anthony (NY) (Retired). —Died July 19, 2009
† Reyes, Reynaldo (LUB) Levelland, TX St. Michael. —Died Aug. 16, 2009
† Reynolds, John C., *c.s.p.* (NY) (Retired). —Died Oct. 3, 2008
† Reynolds, Robert E. (PEO) (Retired). —Died Oct. 27, 2009
† Rice, John A. (SEA) (Retired). —Died Nov. 24, 2009
† Ridgell, John E. (RIC) (Retired). —Died March 1, 2009
† Riehle, James L., *c.s.c.* (FTW) (Retired). —Died 2009
† Riepe, Charles K. (BAL) (Retired). —Died Feb. 7, 2009
† Ripoli, Roland R., *o.s.b.* (GBG) (Retired). —Died July 10, 2009
† Rivi, Geno G. (GBG) (Retired). —Died March 15, 2009
† Roach, Richard R., *s.j.* (SEA) Vashon, WA St. John Vianney. —Died Nov. 7, 2008
† Robello, Louis J. (SFR) (Retired). —Died Nov. 27, 2009
† Robichaud, George H. (MAN). —Died Aug. 30, 2009
† Robillard, Rev. Msgr. Thomas J. (OG) Norfolk, NY Church of the Visitation. —Died March 19, 2009
† Rocheford, Dennis J (WOR) North Oxford, MA St. Ann. —Died Sept. 10, 2009
† Rodrigues, Anthony (RIC) (Retired). —Died Oct. 11, 2009
† Roedel, Robert H. (PH) (Retired). —Died April 5, 2009
† Rogge, Norman J., *s.j.* (NO) (Retired). —Died Feb. 4, 2009
† Romagosa, Edward J., *s.j.* (BR) Convent, LA Manresa House of Retreats. —Died April 4, 2009
† Rompa, John (SPK) Spokane, WA St. Ann. —Died Nov. 13, 2008
† Ronald, Robert J., *s.j.* (FgM) Society of Jesus Foreign Mission. —Died Jan. 2, 2009
† Ropke, John (SJP) (On Leave). —Died June 7, 2009
† Rosage, Rev. Msgr. David E. (SPK) (Retired). —Died Nov. 14, 2009
† Rosebaugh, Lawrence, *o.m.i.* (FgM) Missionary Oblates of Mary Immaculate Foreign Mission. —Died May 18, 2009
† Rossbach, J. Robert, *c.ss.r.* (STL) (Retired). —Died Jan. 29, 2009
† Rossie, Arthur R., *c.ss.r.* (STL) (Retired). —Died 2009
† Roughan, Richard F. (NOR) (Retired). —Died Oct. 5, 2009
† Roy, Kenneth Jude (ALX) Alexandria, LA Pres., Holy Savior Menard Central High School. —Died June 16, 2009
† Rudolph, Frederick, *s.v.d.* (CHI) Techny, IL Society of the Divine Word. —Died Aug. 26, 2009
† Ruland, Vernon J., *s.j.* (SJ) (Retired). —Died April 2, 2009
† Rupiper, Darrell, *o.m.i.* (SFD) Godfrey, IL Immaculate Heart of Mary Novitiate. —Died Feb. 10, 2009
† Russo, Alfred E. (BGP) (Retired). —Died Dec. 14, 2009
† Ruzzo, Paul F. (MAN) Pelham, NH St. Patrick. —Died Nov. 23, 2009
† Ryan, James Patrick (JUN) (Retired). —Died Feb. 15, 2009

† Ryan, Joseph (SAG) (Retired). —Died April 20, 2009
† Ryan, Joseph, *o.m.i.* (BO) Tewksbury, MA Immaculate Heart of Mary Residence. —Died Oct. 2, 2009
† Ryan, Martin E., *s.j.* (BO) Weston, MA Campion Health Center. —Died Feb. 22, 2009
† Ryan, Noel, *s.s.c.* (OM) St. Columbans, NE Society of St. Columban. —Died Nov. 17, 2008
† Ryan, William A., *s.j.* (PH) Merion Station, PA Loyola Center. —Died July 19, 2009
† Rykowski, Valerian J. (MIL) (Retired). —Died March 1, 2009
† Saez, Jose Vincente (ELP) (Retired). —Died Oct. 24, 2008
† Sakalys, Raphael, *o.f.m.* (PRT) Kennebunkport, ME St. Anthony's Friary. —Died Oct. 18, 2008
† Sanchez, Eliseo (LA) (Retired). —Died Dec. 7, 2008
† Saner, Daniel J. (COV) Brooksville, KY St. James. —Died Oct. 20, 2009
† Sanfilippo, Ronald J., *s.j.* (SJ) (Retired). —Died Jan. 30, 2009
† Sapio, Thaddeus M., *o.f.m.* (CHR) Anderson, SC St. Mary of the Angels. —Died Sept. 17, 2009
† Sardina, Jorge J., *s.j.* (MIA) (Retired). —Died Feb. 9, 2008
† Schaffner, William E., *s.j.* (PH) Merion Station, PA Loyola Center. —Died Sept. 15, 2009
† Schellemans, Francis, *ss.cc.* (HON) Honolulu, HI St. Patrick Monastery. —Died Nov. 5, 2008
† Schettler, Charles H. (OKL) (Retired). —Died Dec. 17, 2009
† Schiavone, Alphonse A., *m.m.* (NY) (Retired). —Died Jan. 28, 2009
† Schlueter, Clemens M. (TUC) (Retired). —Died Sept. 14, 2009
† Schmidlin, Donald L. (IND) Indianapolis, IN St. Andrew the Apostle. —Died Feb. 5, 2009
† Schneider, Rev. Msgr. Alfred (GB) (Retired). —Died April 25, 2009
† Schneider, Barry, *o.f.m.* (STP) (Retired). —Died Aug. 9, 2009
† Schneider, Charles J. (WH) (Retired). —Died June 10, 2009
† Schneider, Edward (EVN) Petersburg, IN Sts. Peter and Paul. —Died Dec. 28, 2008
† Schnurr, Thomas, *o.s.b.* (BIR) (Retired). —Died April 5, 2009
† Schoeberle, John, *o.m.i.* (BEL) Belleville, IL Missionary Oblates of Mary Immaculate. —Died Feb. 7, 2009
† Schoenhofen, Roger, *o.m.i.* (SFD) Alton, IL SS. Peter and Paul. —Died Feb. 25, 2009
† Scholsky, Martin J. (HRT) (Retired). —Died July 5, 2009
† Schott, Victor P. (LFT) (Retired). —Died Dec. 15, 2008
† Schreiner, Bernard P. (NU) (Retired). —Died March 15, 2009
† Schroering, Raymond A. (EVN) (Retired). —Died July 19, 2009
† Schuer, Robert J. (COL) (Retired). —Died Jan. 12, 2009
† Schumacher, Eugene T. (SC) (Retired). —Died May 13, 2009
† Schwarz, John S., *s.j.* (SPK) (Retired). —Died June 26, 2009
† Schweifler, Michael, *o.s.a.* (JOL) New Lenox, IL St. Jude. —Died July 26, 2009
† Schwemin, Ralph H. (SPK) (Retired). —Died Oct. 31, 2009
† Schwinn, Thomas J. (DUB) (Retired). —Died July 19, 2009
† Scully, John J., *s.j.* (NY) New York, NY Loyola Hall. —Died Aug. 18, 2009
† Seginak, Theodore, *o.s.b.* (PBR) Butler, PA Holy Trinity Monastery. —Died Jan. 24, 2009
† Seifert, Raymond, *c.pp.s.* (CIN) (Retired). —Died Sept. 14, 2009
† Selle, Paulinus J., *o.s.b.* (GBG) (Retired). —Died Feb. 8, 2009
† Senske, Joseph A. (PH) (Retired). —Died Jan. 1, 2009
† Sepp, Michael P. (NY) Bronx, NY Sacred Heart. —Died March 13, 2009
† Servodidio, Rev. Msgr. John T. (NY) Staten Island, NY St. Joseph. —Died March 22, 2009
† Sevcik, Lawrence, *o.s.b.* (CLV) Cleveland, OH Benedictine Order. —Died 2009
† Sevigny, Robert J. (HT) (Retired). —Died Dec. 27, 2008
† Shaefer, Thomas S. (WDC) (Retired). —Died July 22, 2009
† Sharkey, Robert Urban, *o.p.* (NY) (Retired). —Died Feb. 21, 2009
† Shea, Patrick (CHY) (Retired). —Died Nov. 15, 2009
† Sheehan, David M., *s.s.c.* (FgM) Society of St. Columban Foreign Mission. —Died 2009
† Sheehan, Thomas J. (WDC) (Retired). —Died Aug. 24, 2009
† Sheeran, Kevin, *o.s.b.* (JOL) Lisle, IL St. Procopius Abbey. —Died March 28, 2009
† Sheetz, Steven (HBG) (Retired). —Died Oct. 17, 2009
† Shelley, Owen, *o.f.m.cap.* (NY) Yonkers, NY St. Clare Friary. —Died June 5, 2009
† Shelton, Matthew (Y) (Absent on Sick Leave). —Died June 11, 2009
† Shmauz, Donald A. (MIL) (On Duty Outside the Archdiocese). —Died Oct. 10, 2009
† Sicilia, Rev. Msgr. Pablo (SAT) (Retired). —Died Aug. 24, 2009
† Siciliano, Ronald, *o.f.m.* (NY) New York, NY Franciscan Province of the Immaculate Conception. —Died 2009
† Siedlecki, Edmund J. (CHI) (Retired). —Died Sept. 27, 2009
† Silko, Herbert, *o.f.m.* (GB) (Retired). —Died March 22, 2009
† Simon, Robert C., *c.ss.r.* (STL) Liquori, MO Community Vicar. —Died 2009
† Sitnyein, Isidore, *s.o.l.t.* (CC) Robstown, TX St. Anthony of Padua. —Died May 14, 2009
† Slattery, Kenneth F., *c.m.* (BRK) Jamaica, NY Vincential Residence. —Died 2009
† Slipski, William P. (Y) (Retired). —Died March 7, 2009
† Slough, Charles R. (HBG) (Retired). —Died Aug. 8, 2009
† Slyva, Joseph W. (BO). —Died Feb. 20, 2009
† Smiraldo, Rev. Msgr. Onofrio R. (BUF) (Retired). —Died May 15, 2009
† Smith, Cyril J., *o.s.a.* (MIA) Miami, FL Casa San Lorenzo. —Died July 23, 2009
† Smith, Paschal, *c.p.* (BRK) (Retired). —Died Dec. 21, 2009
† Smith, Raymond K. (SFR) (Retired). —Died March 30, 2009
† Smith, Rev. Msgr. William B. (NY) Yonkers, NY St. Joseph's Seminary. —Died Jan. 24, 2009
† Snyder, Joachim, *o.carm.* (NY) (Retired). —Died May 16, 2009
† Soares, Manuel Bernardo (MRY) (Retired). —Died May 19, 2009
† Sokolowski, Bernard T. (BUF) (Retired). —Died March 8, 2009
† Solozabal, Vincente Egurola (SJN). —Died July 8, 2009
† Soto, Rev. Msgr. Rafael Fontanez (SJN). —Died Feb. 3, 2009
† Soucy, Bertrand, *s.m.* (FgM) Society of Mary Foreign Mission. —Died 2009
† Soucy, Timothy J. (OG) Lowville, NY St. Peter's. —Died March 14, 2009
† Spendov, Vendelin, *o.f.m.* (CHI) Lemont, IL Slovene Franciscan Fathers. —Died July 1, 2009
† Sperry, Rev. Msgr. James E. (E) (Retired). —Died May 17, 2009
† Spoletini, Pasquale M., *s.j.* (SPK) (Retired). —Died May 21, 2009
† St. Jacques, Clement, *s.a.* (WDC) (Retired). —Died April 26, 2009
† St. John, Norman, *s.v.d.* (TR) Bordentown, NJ Society of the Divine Word. —Died May 10, 2009
† Stange, A. Henry (ALT) (Retired). —Died July 21, 2009
† Stanion, Robert, *c.f.r.* (NY) New York, NY St. Felix Friary. —Died March 23, 2009
† Steidle, Mark A. (COV) (Administrative Leave). —Died Aug. 30, 2009
† Stiller, Ludwig F., *s.j.* (FgM) Society of Jesus Foreign Mission. —Died March 10, 2009
† Stokes, David F., *s.j.* (VEN) Sebring, FL St. Catherine. —Died Sept. 24, 2009
† Stout, Thomas (BEL) Red Bud, IL St. John the Baptist. —Died Sept. 18, 2009
† Strassner, Henry E. (ALN) (Retired). —Died Nov. 20, 2009
† Stull, Neal, *s.o.l.t.* (CC) Robstown, TX Society of Our Lady of the Most Holy Trinity. —Died Sept. 27, 2009
† Su Chao, Rev. Msgr. Tomas (SJN) San Juan, PR Segrada Familia. —Died June 4, 2009
† Suellentrop, Daniel Mark, *o.s.b.* (OKL) (Retired). —Died Oct. 12, 2009
† Sullivan, Alan P., *o.f.m.* (PAT) Ringwood, NJ Holy Name Friary. —Died Nov. 3, 2008
† Sullivan, Edward G. (RVC) (Retired). —Died Oct. 6, 2009
† Sullivan, Rev. Msgr. Edwin V. (NEW) (Retired). —Died Feb. 4, 2009
† Sullivan, Emmanuel, *o.c.d.* (BO) Brighton, MA Carmelite Monastery. —Died April 27, 2009
† Sullivan, John Andrew (LAV) Office of the Tribunal. —Died June 10, 2009
† Surban, Rev. Msgr. Edmundo A. (NEW) (Retired). —Died Dec. 29, 2008
† Surprenant, John L. (NOR) (Inactive). —Died Nov. 14, 2009
† Sweeney, Charles J., *s.j.* (DET) Clarkston, MI Colombiere Center. —Died March 8, 2009
† Sweeney, John, *o.f.m.* (SFD) (Retired). —Died March 13, 2009
† Swiatecki, Emilian (VEN) (Retired). —Died Jan. 12, 2009
† Swietek, Walter (VEN) Lehigh Acres, FL St. Raphael. —Died April 16, 2009
† Szabajkowicz, Dominik (VEN) Cape Coral, FL St. Andrew. —Died Nov. 23, 2009
† Szura, Carl, *t.o.r.* (FWT) Fort Worth, TX St. Andrew. —Died Aug. 16, 2009
† Tampe, Eric, *s.a.* (NY) (Retired). —Died April 11, 2009
† Tang, Emery, *o.f.m.* (ORG) Huntington Beach, CA Ss Simon and Jude. —Died June 9, 2009
† Tasker, Franklin, *o.carm.* (VEN) Nokomis, FL Carmel at Mission Valley. —Died Nov. 8, 2009
† Tavai, Van Camp (SPP) Pago Pago, AS Immaculate Conception. —Died April 30, 2009
† Teahan, Timothy J. (BRK) (Retired). —Died Oct. 3, 2009
† Tellers, Marven H., *o.s.c.* (SCL) Onamia, MN Onamia Crossier Priory. —Died Sept. 1, 2009
† Tengler, Rev. Msgr. Alvin (CC) (Retired). —Died July 1, 2009
† Thanh-Hung, John B. (MIL) (Retired). —Died July 1, 2009
† Theisen, Donald J. (LC) (Retired). —Died Oct. 4, 2009
† Thomas, Aquinas, *s.a.* (NY) (Retired). —Died July 1, 2009
† Thompson, William, *o.s.b.* (KCK) (Retired). —Died May 30, 2009
† Thurmond, Rev. Msgr. Benton (VIC) (Retired). —Died Nov. 7, 2009
† Tierney, Rev. Msgr. Patrick M. (CAM) (Retired). —Died June 13, 2009
† Tingerthal, James, *o.s.b.* (SCL) Collegeville, MN St. John's Abbey. —Died July 4, 2009
† Tobin, Rev. Msgr. Neil W. (DUB) (Retired). —Died Feb. 10, 2009
† Tokus, William J., *m.m.* (NY) (Retired). —Died Aug. 17, 2009
† Tolbert, George T., *s.j.* (DET) Clarkston, MI Colombiere Center. —Died June 11, 2009
† Tomasulo, Anthony, *o.s.a.* (CHL) Charlotte, NC St. John Neumann. —Died June 11, 2009
† Tracy, Rev. Msgr. George E. (PRT) (Retired). —Died Sept. 5, 2009
† Trainor, Rev. Msgr. Patrick (SP) St. Pete Beach, FL St. John Vianney. —Died Feb. 7, 2009
† Tran, John Chinh Chan (GAL). —Died Oct. 25, 2009
† Travers, Joseph A., *o.s.f.s.* (WIL) (Retired). —Died Aug. 22, 2009
† Trejo, Ramiro, *o.f.m.cap* (SAG) Saginaw, MI St. Joseph. —Died Oct. 3, 2009
† Trombetta, Jonah P., *o.s.b.* (BRK) (Retired). —Died Oct. 31, 2009
† Tubridy, James M. (NY) West Point, NY Most Holy Trinity Pastor Emeritus. —Died Oct. 17, 2009
† Turnbull, David, *o.f.m.* (CIN) Cincinnati, OH Mercy Hospital. —Died July 16, 2009
† Twarog, Theodore S. (SD) (Retired). —Died Dec. 31, 2008
† Twiddy, Paul (WDC) (Retired). —Died July 2, 2009
† Tyminski, Joseph, *s.d.b.* (SP) (Retired). —Died Oct. 15, 2009
† Tyrrell, Robert D. (BO) (Retired). —Died Feb. 15, 2009
† Ugolik, Richard A. (DET) (Retired). —Died July 16, 2009
† Urtubia, Jorge, *c.s.c.* (FTW) Notre Dame, IN Notre Dame Congregation of Holy Cross. —Died July 9, 2009
† Uzdrowski, Mel R., *o.s.b.* (JOL) Lisle, IL St. Procopius Abbey. —Died April 21, 2009
† Vakoc, Timothy H. (STP). —Died June 20, 2009
† Valles, Carlos, *c.ss.r.* (SJN) San Juan, PR San Agustin. —Died Nov., 2009
† Vallone, Louis A. (BUF) (Retired). —Died April 5, 2009
† Vande Hey, Robert, *o.praem.* (GB) De Pere, WI St. Joseph. —Died June 10, 2009
† Van Der Horst, John (GB) (Retired). —Died Sept. 11, 2009
† VandeVelde, J. Richard, *s.j.* (CHI) Chicago, IL Jesuit Community at Loyola Univ.. —Died Aug. 11, 2009
† VanTrieste, Martin, *s.t.* (WDC) (Retired). —Died 2009
† Vanyo, Leo V. (PIT) (Retired). —Died March 7, 2009
† Varley, John J. (SPR) (Retired). —Died March 31, 2009
† Vasil, James (GBG) (Retired). —Died Jan. 24, 2009
† Vecsey, Stephen N. (LA) (Retired). —Died March 9, 2009
† Verbrugghe, Albert E. (TUC) (Retired). —Died Aug. 20, 2009
† Verhoff, Werner, *c.pp.s.* (CIN) (Retired). —Died Sept. 10, 2009
† Vieck, Hilary F. (EVN) Linton, IN St. Peter. —Died Nov. 27, 2008
† Vieweg, Robert R. (CLV) (Retired). —Died July 16, 2009
† Vogel, Charles P. (BRK) Brooklyn, NY St. Sylvester. —Died Feb. 10, 2009

† Voss, Rev. Msgr. Bernard L. (BEL) Belleville, IL St. Henry. —Died May 12, 2009
† Wagner, Raymond J. (LC) (Retired). —Died Oct. 14, 2009
† Wahmhoff, Andrew, *o.s.b.* (RCK) Aurora, IL Marmion Academy. —Died April 10, 2009
† Wald, Edward, *s.v.d.* (CHI) Techny, IL Divine Word Residence. —Died 2009
† Wall, Edward, *s.v.d.* (CHI) (Retired). —Died Dec. 9, 2008
† Walsh, James A. (TOL) (Retired). —Died Feb. 8, 2009
† Walsh, James P., *s.j.* (BO) Weston, MA Campion Health Center. —Died April 13, 2009
† Walsh, Joseph E. (PH) (Retired). —Died Dec. 29, 2008
† Walsh, Rev. Msgr. Richard J. (ALT) (Retired). —Died Aug. 15, 2009
† Walter, John F. (MIL) (Retired). —Died June 14, 2009
† Ward, John A., *s.s.* (BAL) (Retired). —Died 2009
† Ward, Rev. Msgr. John C. (NU) (Retired). —Died Jan. 17, 2009
† Watson, Joseph T., *s.j.* (NY) New York, NY Murray-Weigel Hall. —Died Sept. 22, 2009
† Weber, Charles E. (COV) (Retired). —Died May 24, 2009
† Weber, Gordon A. (MIL) (Retired). —Died July 4, 2009
† Weckesser, James R., *m.m.* (FgM) Maryknoll Foreign Mission. —Died March 21, 2009
† Weimer, Rev. Msgr. John C. (BUF) (Retired). —Died Oct. 1, 2009
† Weninger, Ronald J. "Marcos", *c.ss.r.* (STL) (Retired). —Died Aug. 21, 2009
† Wessels, Cletus John, *o.p.* (STP) St. Paul, MN St. Albert the Great. —Died Aug. 12, 2009
† Wheeler, Rev. Msgr. David A. (DUB) (Retired). —Died March 26, 2009
† White, George, *o.m.i.* (BO) Tewksbury, MA Immaculate Heart of Mary Residence. —Died June 18, 2009
† White, Lloyd W. (SC) (Retired). —Died May 22, 2009
† White, William J. (CHI) Oak Lawn, IL St. Gerald Pastor Emeritus. —Died Dec. 31, 2008
† Whitsell, John L. (TYL) (Retired). —Died July 28, 2009
† Wichmann, Edward W. (BWN) (Retired). —Died June 28, 2009
† Wiekierak, Joseph F. (GAY) (Retired). —Died Dec. 3, 2008
† Wiemeyer, Raymond G. (CIN) (Retired). —Died Oct. 14, 2009
† Wilkinson, James S. (WCH) (Retired). —Died Jan. 1, 2009
† Wilus, Rev. Msgr. John M. (TR) (Retired). —Died 2007
† Winance, Eleutherius, *o.s.b.* (LA) Valyermo, CA St. Andrew's Abbey. —Died Aug. 15, 2009
† Wojtycha, Rev. Msgr. Edward F. (NEW) (Retired). —Died June 8, 2009
† Wolber, Ferdinand A. (DET) (Retired). —Died Jan. 4, 2009
† Wollmering, Bruce, *o.s.b.* (SCL) Collegeville, MN St. John's Abbey. —Died Feb. 4, 2009
† Wozniak, Philip, *o.f.m.conv.* (CHI) Libertyville, IL Marytown. —Died April 14, 2009
† Wraszczak, Chester (P) (Retired). —Died April 29, 2009
† Wright, John H., *s.j.* (SPK) Spokane, WA Jesuit Fathers and Brothers. —Died April 9, 2009
† Wright, Joseph R., *c.m.* (PH) Philadelphia, PA Congregation of the Mission. —Died June 13, 2009
† Wright, William A. (PH) Drexel Hill, PA St. Bernadette Pastor Emeritus. —Died Dec. 24, 2008
† Wu, Stan (SFR) (Retired). —Died Nov. 5, 2009
† Wuellner, George E. (PEO) (Retired). —Died Aug. 8, 2009
† Young, Valentine W., *o.f.m.cap.* (STL) St. Louis, MO St. Patrick. —Died 2009
† Zaborowski, Edward, *m.s.f.* (SAT) San Antonio, TX Padua Place. —Died March 11, 2009
† Zach, Placidus, *o.s.b.* (P) (Retired). —Died Dec. 1, 2008
† Zak, Rev. Msgr. Casimir A. (BUF) (Retired). —Died July 22, 2009
† Zakens, Michael W. (ALB) Albany, NY St. Mary Pastor Emeritus. —Died April 29, 2009
† Zedar, Thomas (SY) (Retired). —Died Feb. 8, 2009
† Zeeb, Charles M. (DET) (Retired). —Died Sept. 9, 2009
† Zepp, Anthony W. (CLV) Garfield Hts., OH SS. Peter & Paul Pastor Emeritus. —Died April 27, 2009
† Zylla, Robert V., *o.s.c.* (BAL) Emmitsburg, MD St. Mary Seminary. —Died July 29, 2009

	*Mobile AL	Birmingham AL	ALABAMA TOTAL	*Anchorage AK	Fairbanks AK	Juneau AK	2010 U.S. GRAND TOTAL
Cardinals	–	–	–	–	–	–	**13**
Archbishops	2	–	2	2	–	–	**59**
Bishop	–	2	2	–	1	1	**390**
Abbots	–	2	2	–	–	–	**110**
Diocesan Priests	97	84	181	16	13	10	**27,614**
Religious Priests	36	27	63	11	7	2	**13,174**
Total Priests in Diocese	133	111	244	27	20	12	**40,788**
Newly Ordained Priests	–	–	–	–	1	–	**472**
Total Permanent Deacons	55	56	111	19	30	3	**17,165**
Total Brothers	10	22	32	2	2	–	**4,737**
Total Sisters	112	155	267	25	12	3	**58,724**
Number of Parishes	76	54	130	23	46	9	**18,372**
Missions	10	19	29	6	–	17	**2,680**
Pastoral Centers	3	–	3	–	2	–	**619**
New Parishes	–	–	–	–	–	–	**83**
Catholic Hospitals	1	4	5	1	–	1	**561**
Patients Assisted Annually	170,433	689,500	859,933	82,396	–	45,000	**86,525,713**
Health Care Centers	3	1	4	5	–	–	**380**
Patients Assisted Annually	6,119	42,000	48,119	18,273	–	–	**6,332,721**
Specialized Homes	5	–	5	1	–	–	**1,593**
Total Assisted Anually	1,623	–	1,623	641	–	–	**1,600,986**
Residential Care of Children (Orphanages)	1	–	1	2	–	–	**358**
Total Assisted Anually	65	–	65	19	–	–	**28,663**
Day Care and Extended Day Care Centers	4	–	4	–	–	1	**975**
Total Assisted Anually	365	–	365	–	–	100	**121,593**
Special Centers for Social Services	11	19	30	3	1	1	**2,863**
Total Assisted Anually	58,653	87,323	145,976	33,751	2,000	10,000	**24,865,474**
Diocesan Seminaries	–	–	–	–	–	–	**72**
Students	–	–	–	–	–	–	**3,319**
Religious Seminaries	–	–	–	–	–	–	**108**
Students	–	–	–	–	–	–	**1,812**
Colleges and Universities	1	–	1	–	–	–	**234**
Total Students	1,867	–	1,867	–	–	–	**768,541**
High Schools, Diocesan and Parish	3	5	8	1	1	–	**748**
Total Students	1,526	203	1,729	80	210	–	**335,956**
High Schools, Private	–	1	1	–	–	–	**590**
Total Students	–	160	160	–	–	–	**311,290**
Elementary Schools, Diocesan and Parish	15	18	33	3	1	1	**5,614**
Total Students	4,523	3,809	8,332	306	266	125	**1,457,160**
Elementary Schools, Private	–	1	1	–	–	–	**376**
Total Students	–	247	247	–	–	–	**90,052**
Non–residential Schools for the Disabled	–	1	1	–	–	–	**66**
Total Students	–	120	120	–	–	–	**6,329**
Religious Education High School Students	709	1,775	2,484	743	312	452	**687,174**
Religious Education Elementary Students	3,442	6,902	10,344	1,797	848	82	**3,055,645**
Priests Teaching	2	4	6	1	–	–	**1,346**
Scholastics Teaching	–	–	–	–	–	–	**99**
Brothers Teaching	5	1	6	2	–	–	**882**
Sisters Teaching	5	14	19	2	–	–	**4,956**
Lay Teachers	504	263	767	67	54	10	**162,555**
Infant Baptisms	1,060	2,436	3,496	474	309	60	**857,410**
Adult Baptisms	216	206	422	26	17	8	**43,279**
Received into Full Communion	302	576	878	79	23	7	**75,724**
First Communions	857	1,948	2,805	451	223	86	**806,576**
Confirmations	1,127	1,369	2,496	272	104	74	**628,362**
Marriages	327	411	738	96	54	13	**179,576**
Deaths	566	628	1,194	120	119	28	**429,539**
Total Catholics	69,317	89,489	158,806	37,089	15,071	10,000	**68,503,456**
Total Population	1,717,010	2,944,890	4,661,900	401,610	167,000	75,000	**310,252,317**
Catholic Population Percentage	4	3	3	9	9	13	**22**

Archdioceses = 37; Dioceses = 169; Apostolates = 3

2010 GENERAL SUMMARY

	ALASKA TOTAL	Samoa–Pago Pago AS	Phoenix AZ	Tucson AZ	ARIZONA TOTAL	Little Rock AR	2010 U.S. GRAND TOTAL
Cardinals	–	–	–	–	–	–	**13**
Archbishops	2	–	–	–	–	–	**59**
Bishop	2	1	2	1	3	2	**390**
Abbots	–	–	–	–	–	1	**110**
Diocesan Priests	39	15	147	93	240	67	**27,614**
Religious Priests	20	2	95	81	176	37	**13,174**
Total Priests in Diocese	59	17	242	174	416	104	**40,788**
Newly Ordained Priests	1	1	3	1	4	2	**472**
Total Permanent Deacons	52	31	239	113	352	81	**17,165**
Total Brothers	4	–	17	20	37	27	**4,737**
Total Sisters	40	11	190	200	390	181	**58,724**
Number of Parishes	78	16	92	75	167	88	**18,372**
Missions	23	–	23	46	69	38	**2,680**
Pastoral Centers	2	1	3	–	3	1	**619**
New Parishes	–	–	–	–	–	–	**83**
Catholic Hospitals	2	–	2	3	5	12	**561**
Patients Assisted Annually	127,396	–	590,420	470,500	1,060,920	862,562	**86,525,713**
Health Care Centers	5	–	1	1	2	5	**380**
Patients Assisted Annually	18,273	–	15,460	41,500	56,960	42,029	**6,332,721**
Specialized Homes	1	1	43	–	43	27	**1,593**
Total Assisted Anually	641	20	6,236	–	6,236	1,102	**1,600,986**
Residential Care of Children (Orphanages)	2	–	1	–	1	–	**358**
Total Assisted Anually	19	–	3	–	3	–	**28,663**
Day Care and Extended Day Care Centers	1	1	9	–	9	27	**975**
Total Assisted Anually	100	40	777	–	777	1,329	**121,593**
Special Centers for Social Services	5	1	27	2	29	5	**2,863**
Total Assisted Anually	45,751	84	1,480,618	430,000	1,910,618	46,875	**24,865,474**
Diocesan Seminaries	–	–	–	–	–	–	**72**
Students	–	–	–	–	–	–	**3,319**
Religious Seminaries	–	–	3	–	3	–	**108**
Students	–	–	–	–	–	–	**1,812**
Colleges and Universities	–	–	–	–	–	–	**234**
Total Students	–	–	–	–	–	–	**768,541**
High Schools, Diocesan and Parish	2	1	5	–	5	4	**748**
Total Students	290	225	3,761	–	3,761	1,011	**335,956**
High Schools, Private	–	–	1	6	7	2	**590**
Total Students	–	–	1,270	2,034	3,304	665	**311,290**
Elementary Schools, Diocesan and Parish	5	2	32	18	50	28	**5,614**
Total Students	697	313	9,581	4,519	14,100	5,556	**1,457,160**
Elementary Schools, Private	–	–	–	3	3	–	**376**
Total Students	–	–	–	627	627	–	**90,052**
Non–residential Schools for the Disabled	–	–	–	–	–	–	**66**
Total Students	–	–	–	–	–	–	**6,329**
Religious Education High School Students	1,507	830	3,334	3,131	6,465	2,105	**687,174**
Religious Education Elementary Students	2,727	2,443	24,768	12,746	37,514	9,484	**3,055,645**
Priests Teaching	1	4	7	1	8	3	**1,346**
Scholastics Teaching	–	–	–	–	–	–	**99**
Brothers Teaching	2	–	3	6	9	4	**882**
Sisters Teaching	2	7	33	24	57	9	**4,956**
Lay Teachers	131	62	857	414	1,271	544	**162,555**
Infant Baptisms	843	244	7,640	5,748	13,388	2,733	**857,410**
Adult Baptisms	51	80	354	234	588	228	**43,279**
Received into Full Communion	109	48	1,342	515	1,857	510	**75,724**
First Communions	760	305	8,233	5,511	13,744	2,638	**806,576**
Confirmations	450	322	10,474	3,250	13,724	1,649	**628,362**
Marriages	163	54	1,130	813	1,943	587	**179,576**
Deaths	267	61	2,737	2,118	4,855	863	**429,539**
Total Catholics	62,160	14,600	764,140	204,629	968,769	122,842	**68,503,456**
Total Population	643,610	68,000	4,494,940	1,822,276	6,317,216	2,855,390	**310,252,317**
Catholic Population Percentage	10	21	17	11	15	4	**22**

*Indicates Archdioceses.

†Certain Diocese traverse state lines.

	*Los Angeles CA	*San Francisco CA	Fresno CA	Monterey in California CA	Oakland CA	Orange in California CA	2010 U.S. GRAND TOTAL
Cardinals	1	–	–	–	–	–	13
Archbishops	1	2	–	–	–	–	59
Bishop	8	3	1	2	2	3	390
Abbots	1	–	–	–	–	1	110
Diocesan Priests	531	204	124	81	160	175	27,614
Religious Priests	548	163	40	27	200	84	13,174
Total Priests in Diocese	1,079	367	164	108	360	259	40,788
Newly Ordained Priests	9	5	5	2	1	7	472
Total Permanent Deacons	315	79	45	19	120	101	17,165
Total Brothers	103	38	1	30	92	12	4,737
Total Sisters	1,956	744	110	87	336	323	58,724
Number of Parishes	287	90	88	46	84	57	18,372
Missions	9	11	43	7	1	5	2,680
Pastoral Centers	15	21	–	–	17	5	619
New Parishes	–	–	–	–	–	–	83
Catholic Hospitals	14	3	3	1	–	3	561
Patients Assisted Annually	2,500,227	568,365	703,694	–	–	796,750	86,525,713
Health Care Centers	5	4	–	–	–	5	380
Patients Assisted Annually	9,127	288,408	–	–	–	26,973	6,332,721
Specialized Homes	6	25	2	–	8	6	1,593
Total Assisted Anually	2,723	9,100	220	–	20,517	388	1,600,986
Residential Care of Children (Orphanages)	1	2	–	–	–	–	358
Total Assisted Anually	250	500	–	–	–	–	28,663
Day Care and Extended Day Care Centers	19	2	–	–	1	2	975
Total Assisted Anually	1,053	300	–	–	462	150	121,593
Special Centers for Social Services	29	21	6	4	4	13	2,863
Total Assisted Anually	272,617	16,432	200,000	12,557	664,718	501,899	24,865,474
Diocesan Seminaries	1	1	–	–	–	–	72
Students	91	94	–	–	–	–	3,319
Religious Seminaries	11	1	–	–	4	–	108
Students	12	3	–	–	375	–	1,812
Colleges and Universities	5	3	–	–	2	–	234
Total Students	12,999	12,627	–	–	5,149	–	768,541
High Schools, Diocesan and Parish	26	4	2	2	3	3	748
Total Students	14,908	3,543	1,245	566	1,792	4,381	335,956
High Schools, Private	24	10	–	3	6	4	590
Total Students	13,467	4,551	–	1,034	4,131	2,294	311,290
Elementary Schools, Diocesan and Parish	214	54	20	11	45	32	5,614
Total Students	50,010	15,051	4,708	2,588	11,776	11,752	1,457,160
Elementary Schools, Private	9	9	–	3	2	3	376
Total Students	2,320	2,041	–	664	121	1,328	90,052
Non–residential Schools for the Disabled	–	–	–	–	–	–	66
Total Students	–	–	–	–	–	–	6,329
Religious Education High School Students	37,103	1,764	8,974	753	6,005	11,214	687,174
Religious Education Elementary Students	89,119	10,283	28,457	3,069	19,870	32,061	3,055,645
Priests Teaching	30	8	1	1	48	17	1,346
Scholastics Teaching	2	–	–	–	–	–	99
Brothers Teaching	15	8	–	–	37	6	882
Sisters Teaching	217	49	24	8	50	29	4,956
Lay Teachers	3,612	1,643	368	282	1,933	1,681	162,555
Infant Baptisms	82,432	6,341	21,212	6,917	8,415	14,806	857,410
Adult Baptisms	1,597	289	455	139	297	487	43,279
Received into Full Communion	6,315	551	752	233	398	1,618	75,724
First Communions	47,220	4,940	12,263	4,715	8,443	11,920	806,576
Confirmations	27,799	3,682	5,778	1,408	4,755	6,309	628,362
Marriages	7,776	1,060	1,951	1,004	1,073	2,212	179,576
Deaths	11,834	2,275	3,334	1,182	2,478	2,763	429,539
Total Catholics	4,180,859	444,008	1,074,941	196,274	431,212	1,280,159	68,503,456
Total Population	11,669,322	1,850,035	2,756,266	981,371	2,517,141	3,010,759	310,252,317
Catholic Population Percentage	36	24	39	20	17	43	22

Archdioceses = 37; Dioceses = 169; Apostolates = 3

2010 GENERAL SUMMARY

	Sacramento CA	San Bernardino CA	San Diego CA	San Jose in California CA	Santa Rose in California CA	Stockton CA	2010 U.S. GRAND TOTAL
Cardinals	–	–	–	–	–	–	**13**
Archbishops	–	–	–	–	–	–	**59**
Bishop	3	2	1	2	1	1	**390**
Abbots	3	–	1	–	–	–	**110**
Diocesan Priests	170	112	178	139	72	61	**27,614**
Religious Priests	82	123	87	208	10	11	**13,174**
Total Priests in Diocese	252	235	265	347	82	72	**40,788**
Newly Ordained Priests	3	2	–	7	–	–	**472**
Total Permanent Deacons	148	108	137	20	32	45	**17,165**
Total Brothers	22	19	23	64	26	4	**4,737**
Total Sisters	161	156	271	334	42	62	**58,724**
Number of Parishes	104	93	99	49	42	34	**18,372**
Missions	40	11	15	2	18	12	**2,680**
Pastoral Centers	5	–	–	4	8	–	**619**
New Parishes	1	–	–	–	–	–	**83**
Catholic Hospitals	6	2	2	2	5	2	**561**
Patients Assisted Annually	646,111	203,618	37,000	220,000	712,727	560,832	**86,525,713**
Health Care Centers	–	1	–	1	–	1	**380**
Patients Assisted Annually	–	1,200	–	70	–	10,239	**6,332,721**
Specialized Homes	2	1	9	1	1	2	**1,593**
Total Assisted Anually	299	150	83,289	141	48	1,100	**1,600,986**
Residential Care of Children (Orphanages)	–	–	1	–	1	–	**358**
Total Assisted Anually	–	–	200	–	119	–	**28,663**
Day Care and Extended Day Care Centers	–	–	1	1	–	–	**975**
Total Assisted Anually	–	–	400	100	–	–	**121,593**
Special Centers for Social Services	11	15	2	1	9	1	**2,863**
Total Assisted Anually	269,007	46,601	179,520	50,000	32,000	61,866	**24,865,474**
Diocesan Seminaries	–	1	–	–	–	–	**72**
Students	–	17	–	–	–	–	**3,319**
Religious Seminaries	–	–	–	–	–	–	**108**
Students	–	–	2	–	–	10	**1,812**
Colleges and Universities	1	–	2	1	–	–	**234**
Total Students	118	–	7,826	8,490	–	–	**768,541**
High Schools, Diocesan and Parish	3	2	3	2	2	2	**748**
Total Students	603	854	2,719	1,932	802	1,503	**335,956**
High Schools, Private	3	1	2	4	3	–	**590**
Total Students	2,409	340	1,477	4,712	1,133	–	**311,290**
Elementary Schools, Diocesan and Parish	41	27	44	28	11	11	**5,614**
Total Students	9,429	5,886	12,019	9,343	2,385	2,909	**1,457,160**
Elementary Schools, Private	1	1	3	2	1	–	**376**
Total Students	28	460	934	352	80	–	**90,052**
Non–residential Schools for the Disabled	–	–	1	–	–	–	**66**
Total Students	–	–	274	–	–	–	**6,329**
Religious Education High School Students	2,779	7,890	8,399	5,500	1,430	790	**687,174**
Religious Education Elementary Students	21,452	25,674	25,926	12,862	4,895	19,584	**3,055,645**
Priests Teaching	5	3	3	6	1	3	**1,346**
Scholastics Teaching	2	–	–	–	–	–	**99**
Brothers Teaching	2	–	1	3	1	2	**882**
Sisters Teaching	10	11	30	22	5	2	**4,956**
Lay Teachers	761	310	1,117	1,056	322	279	**162,555**
Infant Baptisms	9,632	10,746	10,301	8,351	3,265	6,428	**857,410**
Adult Baptisms	410	926	356	305	104	139	**43,279**
Received into Full Communion	630	892	253	499	95	158	**75,724**
First Communions	7,098	14,950	8,464	5,582	2,495	4,649	**806,576**
Confirmations	5,013	6,936	5,919	3,203	1,068	2,948	**628,362**
Marriages	1,263	1,708	1,865	971	538	802	**179,576**
Deaths	2,810	2,525	2,712	1,707	873	1,453	**429,539**
Total Catholics	980,650	1,167,208	981,211	575,000	169,567	218,605	**68,503,456**
Total Population	3,533,652	4,168,603	3,118,990	1,748,976	909,361	1,299,404	**310,252,317**
Catholic Population Percentage	28	28	31	33	19	17	**22**

*Indicates Archdioceses.

†Certain Diocese traverse state lines.

	CALIFORNIA TOTAL	The Caroline Islands CI	*Denver CO	Colorado Springs CO	Pueblo CO	COLORADO TOTAL	2010 U.S. GRAND TOTAL
Cardinals	1	–	–	–	–	–	13
Archbishops	3	–	1	–	–	1	59
Bishop	29	1	1	2	2	5	390
Abbots	6	–	1	–	–	1	110
Diocesan Priests	2,007	13	183	36	63	282	27,614
Religious Priests	1,583	15	108	18	19	145	13,174
Total Priests in Diocese	3,590	28	291	54	82	427	40,788
Newly Ordained Priests	41	1	4	–	2	6	472
Total Permanent Deacons	1,169	65	190	38	44	272	17,165
Total Brothers	434	2	15	4	2	21	4,737
Total Sisters	4,582	34	272	112	56	440	58,724
Number of Parishes	1,073	29	119	37	53	209	18,372
Missions	174	2	24	5	46	75	2,680
Pastoral Centers	75	–	–	1	–	1	619
New Parishes	1	–	1	–	1	2	83
Catholic Hospitals	43	–	4	2	5	11	561
Patients Assisted Annually	6,949,324	–	296,114	350,528	925,000	1,571,642	86,525,713
Health Care Centers	17	–	6	3	2	11	380
Patients Assisted Annually	336,017	–	26,125	1,809	5,000	32,934	6,332,721
Specialized Homes	63	–	8	3	1	12	1,593
Total Assisted Anually	117,975	–	2,084	1,809	850	4,743	1,600,986
Residential Care of Children (Orphanages)	5	–	–	–	–	–	358
Total Assisted Anually	1,069	–	–	–	–	–	28,663
Day Care and Extended Day Care Centers	26	–	11	–	–	11	975
Total Assisted Anually	2,465	–	1,346	–	–	1,346	121,593
Special Centers for Social Services	116	–	19	1	1	21	2,863
Total Assisted Anually	2,307,217	–	97,922	75,000	5,700	178,622	24,865,474
Diocesan Seminaries	3	–	2	–	–	2	72
Students	202	–	103	–	–	103	3,319
Religious Seminaries	16	–	–	–	–	–	108
Students	402	–	–	4	–	4	1,812
Colleges and Universities	14	–	2	–	–	2	234
Total Students	47,209	–	15,061	–	–	15,061	768,541
High Schools, Diocesan and Parish	54	3	2	–	–	2	748
Total Students	34,848	620	938	–	–	938	335,956
High Schools, Private	60	1	5	1	–	6	590
Total Students	35,548	175	3,017	346	–	3,363	311,290
Elementary Schools, Diocesan and Parish	538	4	37	5	3	45	5,614
Total Students	137,856	1,221	9,075	1,418	796	11,289	1,457,160
Elementary Schools, Private	34	–	2	–	1	3	376
Total Students	8,328	–	578	–	95	673	90,052
Non–residential Schools for the Disabled	1	–	1	–	–	1	66
Total Students	274	–	85	–	–	85	6,329
Religious Education High School Students	92,601	798	4,267	2,701	2,280	9,248	687,174
Religious Education Elementary Students	293,252	1,309	23,917	6,151	5,575	35,643	3,055,645
Priests Teaching	126	–	5	–	–	5	1,346
Scholastics Teaching	4	2	–	–	–	–	99
Brothers Teaching	75	2	3	–	–	3	882
Sisters Teaching	457	24	29	–	7	36	4,956
Lay Teachers	13,364	134	966	118	99	1,183	162,555
Infant Baptisms	188,846	1,424	10,510	1,348	1,582	13,440	857,410
Adult Baptisms	5,504	113	424	103	205	732	43,279
Received into Full Communion	12,394	–	498	154	–	652	75,724
First Communions	132,739	1,171	7,996	1,512	1,113	10,621	806,576
Confirmations	74,818	886	5,450	1,268	758	7,476	628,362
Marriages	22,223	276	1,314	208	278	1,800	179,576
Deaths	35,946	–	2,618	480	1,857	4,955	429,539
Total Catholics	11,699,694	77,733	533,809	82,540	98,400	714,749	68,503,456
Total Population	37,563,880	140,368	3,248,652	978,124	650,000	4,876,776	310,252,317
Catholic Population Percentage	31	55	16	8	15	22	22

Archdioceses = 37; Dioceses = 169; Apostolates = 3

2010 GENERAL SUMMARY

	*Hartford CT	Bridgeport CT	† Norwich CT	CONNECTICUT TOTAL	† Wilmington DE	*† Washington DC	2010 U.S. GRAND TOTAL
Cardinals	–	–	–	–	–	2	**13**
Archbishops	2	–	–	2	–	1	**59**
Bishop	2	1	1	4	1	4	**390**
Abbots	–	–	–	–	–	2	**110**
Diocesan Priests	311	233	115	659	125	290	**27,614**
Religious Priests	96	46	52	194	87	377	**13,174**
Total Priests in Diocese	407	279	167	853	212	667	**40,788**
Newly Ordained Priests	2	6	1	9	2	8	**472**
Total Permanent Deacons	272	112	72	456	110	199	**17,165**
Total Brothers	28	–	24	52	34	99	**4,737**
Total Sisters	715	344	203	1,262	256	562	**58,724**
Number of Parishes	213	87	76	376	57	140	**18,372**
Missions	1	–	6	7	19	9	**2,680**
Pastoral Centers	–	–	10	10	–	–	**619**
New Parishes	–	–	–	–	–	–	**83**
Catholic Hospitals	3	1	–	4	1	3	**561**
Patients Assisted Annually	889,526	206,000	–	1,095,526	174,158	574,982	**86,525,713**
Health Care Centers	2	2	–	4	1	5	**380**
Patients Assisted Annually	4,901	22,453	–	27,354	150	89,176	**6,332,721**
Specialized Homes	8	33	2	43	9	46	**1,593**
Total Assisted Anually	3,119	1,368	239	4,726	461	16,919	**1,600,986**
Residential Care of Children (Orphanages)	–	–	–	–	1	1	**358**
Total Assisted Anually	–	–	–	–	10	280	**28,663**
Day Care and Extended Day Care Centers	9	6	–	15	3	6	**975**
Total Assisted Anually	350	230	–	580	170	382	**121,593**
Special Centers for Social Services	86	9	1	96	15	27	**2,863**
Total Assisted Anually	52,000	490,000	85	542,085	194,300	181,000	**24,865,474**
Diocesan Seminaries	1	1	–	2	–	2	**72**
Students	–	19	–	19	–	104	**3,319**
Religious Seminaries	1	–	1	2	–	11	**108**
Students	150	–	30	180	–	152	**1,812**
Colleges and Universities	2	3	–	5	–	3	**234**
Total Students	4,349	11,373	–	15,722	–	12,250	**768,541**
High Schools, Diocesan and Parish	4	5	3	12	5	2	**748**
Total Students	2,000	2,402	1,892	6,294	2,784	786	**335,956**
High Schools, Private	5	2	2	9	3	16	**590**
Total Students	2,677	1,218	411	4,306	1,713	9,354	**311,290**
Elementary Schools, Diocesan and Parish	56	33	19	108	22	65	**5,614**
Total Students	11,680	7,769	2,839	22,288	7,530	16,687	**1,457,160**
Elementary Schools, Private	2	1	–	3	5	12	**376**
Total Students	216	480	–	696	1,007	1,741	**90,052**
Non–residential Schools for the Disabled	–	2	–	2	1	1	**66**
Total Students	–	98	–	98	80	61	**6,329**
Religious Education High School Students	13,499	2,245	1,688	17,432	1,063	2,917	**687,174**
Religious Education Elementary Students	45,807	34,946	14,974	95,727	10,012	30,680	**3,055,645**
Priests Teaching	9	15	2	26	13	22	**1,346**
Scholastics Teaching	–	2	–	2	–	–	**99**
Brothers Teaching	12	–	7	19	8	12	**882**
Sisters Teaching	23	30	27	80	28	66	**4,956**
Lay Teachers	1,052	1,322	325	2,699	1,153	2,368	**162,555**
Infant Baptisms	6,236	4,217	1,706	12,159	2,673	4,300	**857,410**
Adult Baptisms	228	126	67	421	143	774	**43,279**
Received into Full Communion	308	564	304	1,176	225	548	**75,724**
First Communions	7,773	5,569	2,327	15,669	2,502	5,470	**806,576**
Confirmations	7,192	5,314	2,107	14,613	2,241	4,602	**628,362**
Marriages	1,427	913	449	2,789	643	1,545	**179,576**
Deaths	7,827	2,992	2,004	12,823	1,689	2,680	**429,539**
Total Catholics	624,230	401,136	238,388	1,263,754	233,000	592,769	**68,503,456**
Total Population	1,911,158	884,050	697,653	3,492,861	1,314,050	2,694,405	**310,252,317**
Catholic Population Percentage	33	45	34	36	18	22	**22**

*Indicates Archdioceses.

†Certain Diocese traverse state lines.

	*Miami FL	Orlando FL	Palm Beach FL	Pensacola–Tallahassee FL	St. Augustine FL	St. Petersburg FL	2010 U.S. GRAND TOTAL
Cardinals	–	–	–	–	–	–	**13**
Archbishops	1	–	–	–	–	–	**59**
Bishop	4	2	2	1	2	2	**390**
Abbots	–	–	–	–	–	1	**110**
Diocesan Priests	261	136	120	70	104	149	**27,614**
Religious Priests	76	37	32	18	15	116	**13,174**
Total Priests in Diocese	337	173	152	88	119	265	**40,788**
Newly Ordained Priests	4	1	2	–	–	2	**472**
Total Permanent Deacons	128	181	91	67	62	118	**17,165**
Total Brothers	48	7	2	5	1	52	**4,737**
Total Sisters	277	87	115	27	100	210	**58,724**
Number of Parishes	101	79	50	49	52	75	**18,372**
Missions	4	12	3	8	8	6	**2,680**
Pastoral Centers	2	2	–	–	–	–	**619**
New Parishes	–	–	–	–	1	–	**83**
Catholic Hospitals	2	–	–	1	1	2	**561**
Patients Assisted Annually	837,923	–	–	44,631	164,059	300,000	**86,525,713**
Health Care Centers	10	1	–	–	–	7	**380**
Patients Assisted Annually	10,938	148	–	–	–	35,000	**6,332,721**
Specialized Homes	7	1	5	2	2	15	**1,593**
Total Assisted Anually	5,406	18	435	893	43,836	969	**1,600,986**
Residential Care of Children (Orphanages)	2	–	–	–	–	–	**358**
Total Assisted Anually	255	–	–	–	–	–	**28,663**
Day Care and Extended Day Care Centers	7	12	5	–	–	16	**975**
Total Assisted Anually	3,211	564	700	–	–	1,350	**121,593**
Special Centers for Social Services	16	7	18	4	9	65	**2,863**
Total Assisted Anually	28,695	58,620	17,500	21,000	82,200	25,000	**24,865,474**
Diocesan Seminaries	1	–	1	–	–	–	**72**
Students	74	–	66	–	–	–	**3,319**
Religious Seminaries	–	–	–	–	–	–	**108**
Students	–	–	–	–	–	–	**1,812**
Colleges and Universities	2	–	–	–	–	1	**234**
Total Students	11,000	–	–	–	–	14,339	**768,541**
High Schools, Diocesan and Parish	9	5	3	2	4	4	**748**
Total Students	9,197	2,653	1,573	680	2,448	1,997	**335,956**
High Schools, Private	4	–	–	–	–	2	**590**
Total Students	3,270	–	–	–	–	1,000	**311,290**
Elementary Schools, Diocesan and Parish	50	31	14	7	27	26	**5,614**
Total Students	20,331	11,438	4,501	1,891	8,111	7,726	**1,457,160**
Elementary Schools, Private	2	–	2	–	–	2	**376**
Total Students	1,120	–	543	–	–	941	**90,052**
Non–residential Schools for the Disabled	2	1	–	–	1	2	**66**
Total Students	1,143	60	–	–	119	102	**6,329**
Religious Education High School Students	3,647	3,861	4,598	1,081	1,013	2,094	**687,174**
Religious Education Elementary Students	36,340	22,359	11,987	3,915	8,465	17,765	**3,055,645**
Priests Teaching	32	1	–	3	1	2	**1,346**
Scholastics Teaching	–	–	–	–	2	–	**99**
Brothers Teaching	25	4	–	–	–	10	**882**
Sisters Teaching	66	10	16	9	14	22	**4,956**
Lay Teachers	4,086	979	545	201	655	829	**162,555**
Infant Baptisms	13,692	6,286	4,043	976	2,191	4,902	**857,410**
Adult Baptisms	640	334	180	107	192	–	**43,279**
Received into Full Communion	785	557	415	225	591	506	**75,724**
First Communions	11,269	6,260	3,966	1,063	2,652	5,206	**806,576**
Confirmations	8,246	4,740	2,656	923	2,055	3,983	**628,362**
Marriages	2,093	1,105	686	276	572	1,137	**179,576**
Deaths	4,129	3,540	2,395	538	1,121	4,002	**429,539**
Total Catholics	703,950	413,643	279,823	62,420	171,000	424,951	**68,503,456**
Total Population	4,221,722	4,074,074	1,970,000	1,381,566	1,966,314	2,875,177	**310,252,317**
Catholic Population Percentage	17	10	14	5	9	15	**22**

Archdioceses = 37; Dioceses = 169; Apostolates = 3

2010 GENERAL SUMMARY

	Venice FL	FLORIDA TOTAL	*Atlanta GA	Savannah GA	GEORGIA TOTAL	*Agana GUAM	2010 U.S. GRAND TOTAL
Cardinals	–	–	–	–	–	–	13
Archbishops	–	1	2	–	2	1	59
Bishop	2	15	1	2	3	–	390
Abbots	–	1	1	–	1	–	110
Diocesan Priests	106	946	185	81	266	46	27,614
Religious Priests	69	363	67	24	91	11	13,174
Total Priests in Diocese	175	1,309	252	105	357	57	40,788
Newly Ordained Priests	3	12	8	4	12	4	472
Total Permanent Deacons	97	744	232	59	291	19	17,165
Total Brothers	19	134	9	3	12	2	4,737
Total Sisters	91	907	81	88	169	90	58,724
Number of Parishes	57	463	87	55	142	24	18,372
Missions	14	55	12	24	36	–	2,680
Pastoral Centers	1	5	–	11	11	–	619
New Parishes	–	1	–	–	–	–	83
Catholic Hospitals	–	6	5	1	6	–	561
Patients Assisted Annually	–	1,346,613	348,724	200,000	548,724	–	86,525,713
Health Care Centers	–	18	–	–	–	–	380
Patients Assisted Annually	–	46,086	–	–	–	–	6,332,721
Specialized Homes	10	42	3	–	3	1	1,593
Total Assisted Anually	651	52,208	99	–	99	60	1,600,986
Residential Care of Children (Orphanages)	–	2	–	1	1	–	358
Total Assisted Anually	–	255	–	13	13	–	28,663
Day Care and Extended Day Care Centers	1	41	–	–	–	4	975
Total Assisted Anually	49	5,874	–	–	–	592	121,593
Special Centers for Social Services	29	148	5	15	20	2	2,863
Total Assisted Anually	39,966	272,981	7,350	27,000	34,350	8,109	24,865,474
Diocesan Seminaries	–	2	–	–	–	1	72
Students	–	140	–	–	–	36	3,319
Religious Seminaries	1	1	8	–	8	–	108
Students	1	1	–	–	–	–	1,812
Colleges and Universities	1	4	1	–	1	–	234
Total Students	825	26,164	240	–	240	–	768,541
High Schools, Diocesan and Parish	3	30	3	2	5	4	748
Total Students	1,440	19,988	2,217	421	2,638	927	335,956
High Schools, Private	–	6	4	3	7	1	590
Total Students	–	4,270	1,857	1,092	2,949	353	311,290
Elementary Schools, Diocesan and Parish	10	165	15	16	31	7	5,614
Total Students	2,863	56,861	6,266	4,344	10,610	3,158	1,457,160
Elementary Schools, Private	–	6	4	–	4	–	376
Total Students	–	2,604	1,473	–	1,473	–	90,052
Non-residential Schools for the Disabled	2	8	–	–	–	–	66
Total Students	110	1,534	–	–	–	–	6,329
Religious Education High School Students	1,398	17,692	11,383	695	12,078	1,837	687,174
Religious Education Elementary Students	11,631	112,462	34,088	5,305	39,393	2,370	3,055,645
Priests Teaching	9	48	14	2	16	5	1,346
Scholastics Teaching	–	2	–	–	–	–	99
Brothers Teaching	3	42	2	1	3	2	882
Sisters Teaching	14	151	7	15	22	35	4,956
Lay Teachers	355	7,650	957	450	1,407	349	162,555
Infant Baptisms	4,185	36,275	11,070	1,755	12,825	1,838	857,410
Adult Baptisms	425	1,878	496	161	657	64	43,279
Received into Full Communion	307	3,386	1,260	349	1,609	476	75,724
First Communions	3,710	34,126	9,599	1,566	11,165	1,246	806,576
Confirmations	3,060	25,663	4,853	1,464	6,317	1,122	628,362
Marriages	572	6,441	1,575	361	1,936	227	179,576
Deaths	2,237	17,962	1,331	608	1,939	585	429,539
Total Catholics	237,368	2,293,155	850,000	77,473	927,473	142,000	68,503,456
Total Population	1,959,795	18,448,648	6,887,670	2,800,000	9,687,670	166,000	310,252,317
Catholic Population Percentage	12	12	12	3	10	86	22

*Indicates Archdioceses.

†Certain Diocese traverse state lines.

	Honolulu HI	Boise ID	*Chicago IL	Belleville IL	Joliet in Illinois IL	Peoria IL	2010 U.S. GRAND TOTAL
Cardinals	–	–	1	–	–	–	13
Archbishops	–	–	–	–	–	–	59
Bishop	1	1	10	2	3	1	390
Abbots	–	–	–	–	2	3	110
Diocesan Priests	58	83	807	122	182	198	27,614
Religious Priests	58	15	787	36	110	30	13,174
Total Priests in Diocese	116	98	1,594	158	292	228	40,788
Newly Ordained Priests	2	2	16	–	3	2	472
Total Permanent Deacons	67	65	643	28	209	158	17,165
Total Brothers	33	5	269	6	63	9	4,737
Total Sisters	165	86	1,966	90	496	215	58,724
Number of Parishes	66	51	357	119	120	159	18,372
Missions	24	29	11	–	10	28	2,680
Pastoral Centers	–	28	8	–	–	5	619
New Parishes	–	–	1	–	–	–	83
Catholic Hospitals	–	5	19	5	3	9	561
Patients Assisted Annually	–	648,274	3,026,299	434,372	759,596	3,861,879	86,525,713
Health Care Centers	2	–	2	–	–	–	380
Patients Assisted Annually	1,687	–	17,157	–	–	–	6,332,721
Specialized Homes	1	–	51	4	17	5	1,593
Total Assisted Anually	29	–	7,139	200	85,905	432	1,600,986
Residential Care of Children (Orphanages)	–	–	2	–	–	–	358
Total Assisted Anually	–	–	2,959	–	–	–	28,663
Day Care and Extended Day Care Centers	1	4	33	3	4	2	975
Total Assisted Anually	440	168	1,802	212	1,630	244	121,593
Special Centers for Social Services	1	19	100	3	5	1	2,863
Total Assisted Anually	242	380,000	716,648	250,000	33,651	36,746	24,865,474
Diocesan Seminaries	2	–	2	–	–	–	72
Students	2	–	217	–	–	–	3,319
Religious Seminaries	–	–	1	–	–	–	108
Students	–	–	106	–	–	–	1,812
Colleges and Universities	1	–	6	–	3	1	234
Total Students	2,688	–	51,175	–	14,619	425	768,541
High Schools, Diocesan and Parish	3	1	7	3	3	7	748
Total Students	893	629	1,380	1,227	1,823	2,734	335,956
High Schools, Private	4	–	33	–	4	–	590
Total Students	2,107	–	24,953	–	3,584	–	311,290
Elementary Schools, Diocesan and Parish	23	13	206	30	54	42	5,614
Total Students	5,705	2,227	60,730	4,488	17,151	10,022	1,457,160
Elementary Schools, Private	4	–	9	–	–	–	376
Total Students	772	–	2,065	–	–	–	90,052
Non–residential Schools for the Disabled	–	–	5	–	–	–	66
Total Students	–	–	450	–	–	–	6,329
Religious Education High School Students	2,365	2,350	8,118	340	4,561	1,037	687,174
Religious Education Elementary Students	5,039	5,778	88,176	5,020	47,873	7,489	3,055,645
Priests Teaching	5	–	27	3	23	13	1,346
Scholastics Teaching	–	–	–	–	–	–	99
Brothers Teaching	12	–	32	–	21	2	882
Sisters Teaching	46	1	113	5	31	10	4,956
Lay Teachers	846	210	5,517	549	2,295	990	162,555
Infant Baptisms	2,542	2,596	35,151	1,073	8,075	1,828	857,410
Adult Baptisms	121	168	1,630	127	205	213	43,279
Received into Full Communion	210	203	1,028	186	598	377	75,724
First Communions	1,774	2,401	27,273	1,256	9,638	2,056	806,576
Confirmations	1,097	1,191	21,379	1,375	8,268	2,434	628,362
Marriages	535	464	6,519	492	1,592	584	179,576
Deaths	1,603	732	13,235	1,150	3,460	1,463	429,539
Total Catholics	237,206	167,620	2,338,000	91,550	655,415	161,242	68,503,456
Total Population	1,285,498	1,523,816	5,989,502	850,200	1,888,772	1,465,840	310,252,317
Catholic Population Percentage	18	11	39	11	35	11	22

Archdioceses = 37; Dioceses = 169; Apostolates = 3

2010 GENERAL SUMMARY

	Rockford IL	Springfield in Illinois IL	ILLINOIS TOTAL	*Indianapolis IN	Evansville IN	Fort Wayne–South Bend IN	2010 U.S. GRAND TOTAL
Cardinals	–	–	1	–	–	–	**13**
Archbishops	–	–	–	1	–	–	**59**
Bishop	3	1	20	–	1	2	**390**
Abbots	3	–	8	4	–	–	**110**
Diocesan Priests	203	110	1,622	151	76	78	**27,614**
Religious Priests	42	54	1,059	87	5	137	**13,174**
Total Priests in Diocese	245	164	2,681	238	81	215	**40,788**
Newly Ordained Priests	2	1	24	8	1	5	**472**
Total Permanent Deacons	136	34	1,208	26	52	11	**17,165**
Total Brothers	11	28	386	29	–	142	**4,737**
Total Sisters	120	540	3,427	621	250	489	**58,724**
Number of Parishes	105	131	991	139	69	80	**18,372**
Missions	–	–	49	12	–	1	**2,680**
Pastoral Centers	–	–	13	–	7	3	**619**
New Parishes	–	–	1	–	–	–	**83**
Catholic Hospitals	3	6	45	2	2	2	**561**
Patients Assisted Annually	562,134	697,343	9,341,623	1,237,087	922,897	216,965	**86,525,713**
Health Care Centers	17	–	19	–	1	4	**380**
Patients Assisted Annually	231,610	–	248,767	–	60	56,731	**6,332,721**
Specialized Homes	7	1	85	5	4	7	**1,593**
Total Assisted Anually	3,261	99	97,036	1,281	187	2,291	**1,600,986**
Residential Care of Children (Orphanages)	–	1	3	–	–	–	**358**
Total Assisted Anually	–	30	2,989	–	–	–	**28,663**
Day Care and Extended Day Care Centers	1	1	44	1	1	1	**975**
Total Assisted Anually	33	142	4,063	93	156	119	**121,593**
Special Centers for Social Services	12	–	121	16	10	11	**2,863**
Total Assisted Anually	24,025	–	1,061,070	140,000	159,075	216,883	**24,865,474**
Diocesan Seminaries	–	–	2	1	–	–	**72**
Students	–	–	217	25	–	–	**3,319**
Religious Seminaries	–	–	1	1	–	1	**108**
Students	–	–	106	111	–	18	**1,812**
Colleges and Universities	–	2	12	2	–	5	**234**
Total Students	–	1,850	68,069	3,820	–	16,557	**768,541**
High Schools, Diocesan and Parish	6	5	31	7	4	4	**748**
Total Students	3,190	1,324	11,678	3,641	1,518	3,180	**335,956**
High Schools, Private	2	1	40	4	1	–	**590**
Total Students	962	793	30,292	2,237	6	–	**311,290**
Elementary Schools, Diocesan and Parish	41	42	415	61	24	39	**5,614**
Total Students	10,580	9,213	112,184	16,937	5,802	9,701	**1,457,160**
Elementary Schools, Private	–	–	9	1	–	–	**376**
Total Students	–	–	2,065	75	–	–	**90,052**
Non–residential Schools for the Disabled	–	–	5	–	–	–	**66**
Total Students	–	–	450	–	–	–	**6,329**
Religious Education High School Students	7,118	1,915	23,089	3,431	2,036	1,309	**687,174**
Religious Education Elementary Students	25,312	8,087	181,957	12,311	4,587	9,054	**3,055,645**
Priests Teaching	32	–	98	5	–	–	**1,346**
Scholastics Teaching	–	–	–	–	–	–	**99**
Brothers Teaching	9	1	65	2	–	–	**882**
Sisters Teaching	14	29	202	18	8	5	**4,956**
Lay Teachers	1,370	648	11,369	1,749	477	745	**162,555**
Infant Baptisms	6,016	1,899	54,042	4,064	1,180	2,596	**857,410**
Adult Baptisms	203	193	2,571	428	92	163	**43,279**
Received into Full Communion	333	310	2,832	506	142	474	**75,724**
First Communions	6,845	2,056	49,124	3,914	1,281	2,964	**806,576**
Confirmations	3,959	2,290	39,705	3,194	1,047	2,770	**628,362**
Marriages	1,041	744	10,972	1,010	436	789	**179,576**
Deaths	2,036	1,555	22,899	2,007	800	1,370	**429,539**
Total Catholics	451,509	146,692	3,844,408	226,216	85,079	171,499	**68,503,456**
Total Population	1,850,609	1,138,450	13,183,373	2,430,606	496,795	1,262,788	**310,252,317**
Catholic Population Percentage	24	13	29	9	17	14	**22**

*Indicates Archdioceses.

†Certain Diocese traverse state lines.

	Gary IN	Lafayette in Indiana IN	INDIANA TOTAL	*Dubuque IA	Davenport IA	De Moines IA	2010 U.S. GRAND TOTAL
Cardinals	–	–	–	–	–	–	**13**
Archbishops	–	–	1	2	–	–	**59**
Bishop	1	1	5	–	2	2	**390**
Abbots	–	–	4	3	–	–	**110**
Diocesan Priests	102	121	528	199	101	86	**27,614**
Religious Priests	46	14	289	30	2	8	**13,174**
Total Priests in Diocese	148	135	817	229	103	94	**40,788**
Newly Ordained Priests	–	1	15	2	–	2	**472**
Total Permanent Deacons	58	18	165	97	39	77	**17,165**
Total Brothers	13	3	187	24	1	–	**4,737**
Total Sisters	75	67	1,502	737	159	65	**58,724**
Number of Parishes	69	63	420	176	80	82	**18,372**
Missions	4	–	17	–	–	–	**2,680**
Pastoral Centers	6	–	16	1	–	–	**619**
New Parishes	–	–	–	–	–	1	**83**
Catholic Hospitals	6	9	21	7	3	3	**561**
Patients Assisted Annually	1,167,973	1,074,224	4,619,146	1,235,282	347,853	1,693,252	**86,525,713**
Health Care Centers	–	–	5	2	–	–	**380**
Patients Assisted Annually	–	–	56,791	181	–	–	**6,332,721**
Specialized Homes	4	1	21	4	4	2	**1,593**
Total Assisted Anually	926	590	5,275	657	347	787	**1,600,986**
Residential Care of Children (Orphanages)	2	–	2	–	–	–	**358**
Total Assisted Anually	200	–	200	–	–	–	**28,663**
Day Care and Extended Day Care Centers	2	–	5	–	–	–	**975**
Total Assisted Anually	500	–	868	–	–	–	**121,593**
Special Centers for Social Services	7	–	44	3	–	5	**2,863**
Total Assisted Anually	10,000	–	525,958	570	–	43,690	**24,865,474**
Diocesan Seminaries	–	–	1	1	–	–	**72**
Students	–	–	25	11	–	–	**3,319**
Religious Seminaries	1	–	3	1	–	–	**108**
Students	6	–	135	90	–	–	**1,812**
Colleges and Universities	1	3	11	3	1	1	**234**
Total Students	1,275	6,121	27,773	4,436	3,729	778	**768,541**
High Schools, Diocesan and Parish	3	2	20	7	5	2	**748**
Total Students	1,225	838	10,402	2,570	1,236	1,497	**335,956**
High Schools, Private	1	–	6	–	–	–	**590**
Total Students	36	–	2,279	–	–	–	**311,290**
Elementary Schools, Diocesan and Parish	21	18	163	44	13	15	**5,614**
Total Students	4,947	4,116	41,503	9,731	3,632	4,817	**1,457,160**
Elementary Schools, Private	–	–	1	–	–	–	**376**
Total Students	–	–	75	–	–	–	**90,052**
Non–residential Schools for the Disabled	–	–	–	–	–	–	**66**
Total Students	–	–	–	–	–	–	**6,329**
Religious Education High School Students	808	3,103	10,687	5,187	1,645	2,067	**687,174**
Religious Education Elementary Students	8,982	9,637	44,571	13,460	6,013	10,610	**3,055,645**
Priests Teaching	–	1	6	–	–	2	**1,346**
Scholastics Teaching	–	–	–	–	–	4	**99**
Brothers Teaching	–	3	5	–	–	–	**882**
Sisters Teaching	4	8	43	14	–	4	**4,956**
Lay Teachers	400	392	3,763	900	419	449	**162,555**
Infant Baptisms	1,650	1,860	11,350	2,621	1,405	1,842	**857,410**
Adult Baptisms	64	191	938	101	151	113	**43,279**
Received into Full Communion	238	359	1,719	225	135	253	**75,724**
First Communions	2,040	2,291	12,490	2,931	1,619	1,927	**806,576**
Confirmations	1,972	1,639	10,622	2,330	1,940	1,994	**628,362**
Marriages	486	442	3,163	1,018	518	486	**179,576**
Deaths	1,603	761	6,541	2,031	1,122	747	**429,539**
Total Catholics	184,750	100,691	768,235	205,252	100,777	100,943	**68,503,456**
Total Population	790,527	1,296,384	6,277,100	980,903	753,144	742,190	**310,252,317**
Catholic Population Percentage	23	8	12	21	13	14	**22**

Archdioceses = 37; Dioceses = 169; Apostolates = 3

2010 GENERAL SUMMARY

	Sioux City IA	IOWA TOTAL	*Kansas City in Kansas KS	Dodge City KS	Salina KS	Wichita KS	2010 U.S. GRAND TOTAL
Cardinals	–	–	–	–	–	–	**13**
Archbishops	–	2	2	–	–	–	**59**
Bishop	2	6	–	2	2	2	**390**
Abbots	–	3	3	–	–	–	**110**
Diocesan Priests	143	529	102	30	60	118	**27,614**
Religious Priests	1	41	56	5	16	1	**13,174**
Total Priests in Diocese	144	570	158	35	76	119	**40,788**
Newly Ordained Priests	–	4	3	–	1	1	**472**
Total Permanent Deacons	39	252	3	8	7	5	**17,165**
Total Brothers	–	25	14	–	1	–	**4,737**
Total Sisters	69	1,030	510	68	151	278	**58,724**
Number of Parishes	113	451	110	48	86	90	**18,372**
Missions	–	–	–	1	–	–	**2,680**
Pastoral Centers	–	1	–	–	–	22	**619**
New Parishes	–	1	–	–	–	–	**83**
Catholic Hospitals	3	16	3	2	–	7	**561**
Patients Assisted Annually	213,160	3,489,547	577,426	178,847	–	493,471	**86,525,713**
Health Care Centers	–	2	4	–	–	2	**380**
Patients Assisted Annually	–	181	21,540	–	–	56,574	**6,332,721**
Specialized Homes	3	13	3	–	5	8	**1,593**
Total Assisted Anually	316	2,107	647	–	412	1,203	**1,600,986**
Residential Care of Children (Orphanages)	–	–	–	–	–	–	**358**
Total Assisted Anually	–	–	–	–	–	–	**28,663**
Day Care and Extended Day Care Centers	–	–	2	–	–	–	**975**
Total Assisted Anually	–	–	164	–	–	–	**121,593**
Special Centers for Social Services	5	13	5	4	–	1	**2,863**
Total Assisted Anually	3,457	47,717	33,292	6,220	–	22,734	**24,865,474**
Diocesan Seminaries	–	1	–	–	–	–	**72**
Students	–	11	–	–	–	–	**3,319**
Religious Seminaries	–	1	–	–	–	–	**108**
Students	–	90	2	–	–	–	**1,812**
Colleges and Universities	1	6	3	–	–	1	**234**
Total Students	1,158	10,101	4,611	–	–	2,557	**768,541**
High Schools, Diocesan and Parish	8	22	6	–	4	4	**748**
Total Students	1,685	6,988	3,355	–	375	2,524	**335,956**
High Schools, Private	–	–	1	–	1	–	**590**
Total Students	–	–	178	–	225	–	**311,290**
Elementary Schools, Diocesan and Parish	17	89	38	7	11	35	**5,614**
Total Students	4,575	22,755	12,017	1,050	1,756	8,283	**1,457,160**
Elementary Schools, Private	–	–	3	–	–	–	**376**
Total Students	–	–	160	–	–	–	**90,052**
Non-residential Schools for the Disabled	–	–	–	–	–	–	**66**
Total Students	–	–	–	–	–	–	**6,329**
Religious Education High School Students	2,766	11,665	2,359	1,387	1,646	1,803	**687,174**
Religious Education Elementary Students	6,442	36,525	14,197	3,547	4,171	5,068	**3,055,645**
Priests Teaching	2	4	–	–	3	7	**1,346**
Scholastics Teaching	–	4	–	–	–	–	**99**
Brothers Teaching	–	–	–	–	–	–	**882**
Sisters Teaching	4	22	15	1	2	11	**4,956**
Lay Teachers	546	2,314	1,106	87	230	668	**162,555**
Infant Baptisms	1,535	7,403	3,730	1,081	875	2,389	**857,410**
Adult Baptisms	46	411	270	48	76	223	**43,279**
Received into Full Communion	166	779	498	67	149	379	**75,724**
First Communions	1,515	7,992	3,742	1,109	759	2,536	**806,576**
Confirmations	1,378	7,642	3,593	1,072	840	2,021	**628,362**
Marriages	570	2,592	1,012	240	368	694	**179,576**
Deaths	1,138	5,038	1,438	358	630	892	**429,539**
Total Catholics	94,821	501,793	202,006	44,182	46,255	115,023	**68,503,456**
Total Population	455,297	2,931,534	1,300,373	215,585	315,983	962,097	**310,252,317**
Catholic Population Percentage	21	17	16	20	15	12	**22**

*Indicates Archdioceses.

†Certain Diocese traverse state lines.

	KANSAS TOTAL	*Louisville KY	Covington KY	Lexington KY	Owensboro KY	KENTUCKY TOTAL	2010 U.S. GRAND TOTAL
Cardinals	–	–	–	–	–	–	**13**
Archbishops	2	2	–	–	–	2	**59**
Bishop	6	–	2	2	2	6	**390**
Abbots	3	3	–	–	–	3	**110**
Diocesan Priests	310	150	86	50	73	359	**27,614**
Religious Priests	78	56	12	24	18	110	**13,174**
Total Priests in Diocese	388	206	98	74	91	469	**40,788**
Newly Ordained Priests	5	–	4	1	2	7	**472**
Total Permanent Deacons	23	120	29	57	3	209	**17,165**
Total Brothers	15	59	5	3	1	68	**4,737**
Total Sisters	1,007	697	313	91	179	1,280	**58,724**
Number of Parishes	334	102	47	50	79	278	**18,372**
Missions	1	9	6	13	–	28	**2,680**
Pastoral Centers	22	–	–	–	–	–	**619**
New Parishes	–	2	–	–	–	2	**83**
Catholic Hospitals	12	2	5	11	1	19	**561**
Patients Assisted Annually	1,249,744	210,500	829,973	777,247	268,590	2,086,310	**86,525,713**
Health Care Centers	6	1	–	4	–	5	**380**
Patients Assisted Annually	78,114	5,689	–	54,000	–	59,689	**6,332,721**
Specialized Homes	16	5	3	1	3	12	**1,593**
Total Assisted Anually	2,262	1,200	833	209	226	2,468	**1,600,986**
Residential Care of Children (Orphanages)	–	2	2	–	–	4	**358**
Total Assisted Anually	–	850	360	–	–	1,210	**28,663**
Day Care and Extended Day Care Centers	2	6	1	–	3	10	**975**
Total Assisted Anually	164	300	86	–	218	604	**121,593**
Special Centers for Social Services	10	8	4	1	2	15	**2,863**
Total Assisted Anually	62,246	40,000	85,859	8,000	9,469	143,328	**24,865,474**
Diocesan Seminaries	–	–	–	–	–	–	**72**
Students	–	–	–	–	–	–	**3,319**
Religious Seminaries	–	–	–	–	1	1	**108**
Students	2	–	–	–	–	–	**1,812**
Colleges and Universities	4	3	1	–	1	5	**234**
Total Students	7,168	5,595	1,860	–	719	8,174	**768,541**
High Schools, Diocesan and Parish	14	4	7	1	3	15	**748**
Total Students	6,254	2,256	2,546	842	732	6,376	**335,956**
High Schools, Private	2	5	2	1	–	8	**590**
Total Students	403	4,181	790	68	–	5,039	**311,290**
Elementary Schools, Diocesan and Parish	91	36	26	14	15	91	**5,614**
Total Students	23,106	13,927	6,487	2,928	3,267	26,609	**1,457,160**
Elementary Schools, Private	3	3	2	1	–	6	**376**
Total Students	160	562	479	142	–	1,183	**90,052**
Non–residential Schools for the Disabled	–	1	–	–	–	1	**66**
Total Students	–	75	–	–	–	75	**6,329**
Religious Education High School Students	7,195	1,009	310	717	1,155	3,191	**687,174**
Religious Education Elementary Students	26,983	6,025	4,165	3,265	3,274	16,729	**3,055,645**
Priests Teaching	10	7	–	2	2	11	**1,346**
Scholastics Teaching	–	–	–	–	–	–	**99**
Brothers Teaching	–	4	1	–	–	5	**882**
Sisters Teaching	29	23	20	9	16	68	**4,956**
Lay Teachers	2,091	1,883	709	345	325	3,262	**162,555**
Infant Baptisms	8,075	2,258	1,119	861	908	5,146	**857,410**
Adult Baptisms	617	195	155	85	110	545	**43,279**
Received into Full Communion	1,093	450	106	188	240	984	**75,724**
First Communions	8,146	2,508	1,568	843	1,023	5,942	**806,576**
Confirmations	7,526	2,657	1,558	848	947	6,010	**628,362**
Marriages	2,314	705	485	210	364	1,764	**179,576**
Deaths	3,318	1,542	784	299	553	3,178	**429,539**
Total Catholics	407,466	192,450	89,491	46,798	51,241	379,980	**68,503,456**
Total Population	2,794,038	1,219,650	464,629	1,567,853	867,967	4,120,099	**310,252,317**
Catholic Population Percentage	15	16	19	3	6	22	**22**

Archdioceses = 37; Dioceses = 169; Apostolates = 3

2010 GENERAL SUMMARY

	*New Orleans LA	Alexandria LA	Baton Rouge LA	Houma–Thibodaux LA	Lafayette LA	Lake Charles LA	2010 U.S. GRAND TOTAL
Cardinals	–	–	–	–	–	–	13
Archbishops	4	–	–	–	–	–	59
Bishop	2	1	1	1	1	2	390
Abbots	1	–	–	–	–	–	110
Diocesan Priests	208	55	72	62	156	47	27,614
Religious Priests	153	14	32	7	40	12	13,174
Total Priests in Diocese	361	69	104	69	196	59	40,788
Newly Ordained Priests	3	–	2	–	3	–	472
Total Permanent Deacons	189	6	59	31	79	25	17,165
Total Brothers	59	4	18	6	16	1	4,737
Total Sisters	449	32	95	29	158	16	58,724
Number of Parishes	108	49	68	39	121	38	18,372
Missions	10	23	–	3	29	8	2,680
Pastoral Centers	2	–	–	–	–	–	619
New Parishes	–	–	–	–	–	–	83
Catholic Hospitals	–	1	3	–	1	1	561
Patients Assisted Annually	–	210,657	637,597	–	107,667	79,988	86,525,713
Health Care Centers	12	1	–	–	–	–	380
Patients Assisted Annually	120,980	350	–	–	–	–	6,332,721
Specialized Homes	29	–	12	2	43	1	1,593
Total Assisted Anually	6,725	–	1,016	120	11,473	118	1,600,986
Residential Care of Children (Orphanages)	1	–	–	–	–	–	358
Total Assisted Anually	16	–	–	–	–	–	28,663
Day Care and Extended Day Care Centers	8	–	–	1	–	2	975
Total Assisted Anually	952	–	–	116	–	74	121,593
Special Centers for Social Services	72	8	8	–	6	3	2,863
Total Assisted Anually	106,500	840	225,335	–	100,445	2,402	24,865,474
Diocesan Seminaries	2	–	–	–	–	–	72
Students	141	–	–	–	–	–	3,319
Religious Seminaries	3	–	–	–	1	–	108
Students	14	–	–	–	15	–	1,812
Colleges and Universities	3	–	1	–	–	–	234
Total Students	9,666	–	2,016	–	–	–	768,541
High Schools, Diocesan and Parish	10	3	6	3	9	1	748
Total Students	5,004	684	2,286	1,919	3,553	656	335,956
High Schools, Private	13	–	2	–	1	–	590
Total Students	9,438	–	1,962	–	120	–	311,290
Elementary Schools, Diocesan and Parish	56	7	24	10	30	7	5,614
Total Students	23,074	1,925	11,481	3,955	10,699	2,066	1,457,160
Elementary Schools, Private	5	–	–	–	2	–	376
Total Students	1,617	–	–	–	781	–	90,052
Non–residential Schools for the Disabled	1	–	–	–	–	–	66
Total Students	191	–	–	–	–	–	6,329
Religious Education High School Students	3,623	1,028	3,496	2,552	6,834	2,124	687,174
Religious Education Elementary Students	9,938	2,144	7,456	4,901	14,525	4,979	3,055,645
Priests Teaching	26	–	1	–	–	–	1,346
Scholastics Teaching	4	–	–	–	–	–	99
Brothers Teaching	16	3	4	4	–	–	882
Sisters Teaching	79	8	12	4	2	1	4,956
Lay Teachers	3,199	185	1,051	373	995	233	162,555
Infant Baptisms	4,470	660	2,257	1,310	4,094	1,055	857,410
Adult Baptisms	163	48	105	50	65	49	43,279
Received into Full Communion	140	152	264	55	307	49	75,724
First Communions	4,281	600	2,455	1,233	3,885	1,105	806,576
Confirmations	3,183	465	2,155	992	3,068	902	628,362
Marriages	1,525	194	700	323	1,072	294	179,576
Deaths	3,491	520	1,648	1,272	3,442	1,080	429,539
Total Catholics	471,783	44,003	211,149	105,836	322,507	75,983	68,503,456
Total Population	1,179,459	387,579	935,440	202,000	568,154	284,611	310,252,317
Catholic Population Percentage	40	11	23	52	57	27	22

*Indicates Archdioceses.

†Certain Diocese traverse state lines.

	Shreveport LA	LOUISIANA TOTAL	Portland (in Maine) ME	Marshall Islands	*Baltimore MD	*Boston MA	2010 U.S. GRAND TOTAL
Cardinals	–	–	–	–	1	1	**13**
Archbishops	–	4	–	–	2	–	**59**
Bishop	2	10	2	–	3	6	**390**
Abbots	–	1	–	–	–	1	**110**
Diocesan Priests	36	636	156	–	254	744	**27,614**
Religious Priests	13	271	32	4	246	491	**13,174**
Total Priests in Diocese	49	907	188	4	500	1,235	**40,788**
Newly Ordained Priests	1	9	1	–	4	6	**472**
Total Permanent Deacons	21	410	32	1	158	258	**17,165**
Total Brothers	5	109	19	–	69	144	**4,737**
Total Sisters	43	822	318	6	934	1,945	**58,724**
Number of Parishes	27	450	66	4	153	291	**18,372**
Missions	14	87	20	7	6	–	**2,680**
Pastoral Centers	1	3	–	–	–	1	**619**
New Parishes	–	–	6	–	–	–	**83**
Catholic Hospitals	2	8	3	–	5	8	**561**
Patients Assisted Annually	1,113	1,037,022	557,936	–	1,665,874	708,219	**86,525,713**
Health Care Centers	3	16	–	–	4	3	**380**
Patients Assisted Annually	429,108	550,438	–	–	2,690	7,511	**6,332,721**
Specialized Homes	1	88	5	–	31	36	**1,593**
Total Assisted Anually	190	19,642	2,057	–	4,346	4,554	**1,600,986**
Residential Care of Children (Orphanages)	–	1	–	–	9	1	**358**
Total Assisted Anually	–	16	–	–	1,050	921	**28,663**
Day Care and Extended Day Care Centers	3	14	2	–	7	11	**975**
Total Assisted Anually	208	1,350	230	–	2,220	1,110	**121,593**
Special Centers for Social Services	23	120	2	–	56	43	**2,863**
Total Assisted Anually	38,356	473,878	475	–	659,558	206,000	**24,865,474**
Diocesan Seminaries	–	2	–	–	2	3	**72**
Students	–	141	–	–	216	139	**3,319**
Religious Seminaries	–	4	–	1	–	1	**108**
Students	–	29	–	–	–	37	**1,812**
Colleges and Universities	–	4	1	–	4	6	**234**
Total Students	–	11,682	2,691	–	11,673	24,900	**768,541**
High Schools, Diocesan and Parish	2	34	1	2	8	3	**748**
Total Students	656	14,758	275	207	3,753	1,150	**335,956**
High Schools, Private	–	16	2	–	13	29	**590**
Total Students	–	11,520	733	–	7,641	15,155	**311,290**
Elementary Schools, Diocesan and Parish	5	139	12	3	53	79	**5,614**
Total Students	1,292	54,492	2,482	623	18,544	24,067	**1,457,160**
Elementary Schools, Private	–	7	1	–	7	9	**376**
Total Students	–	2,398	177	–	1,338	2,264	**90,052**
Non–residential Schools for the Disabled	–	1	–	–	1	2	**66**
Total Students	–	191	–	–	121	139	**6,329**
Religious Education High School Students	466	20,123	1,031	50	3,199	26,624	**687,174**
Religious Education Elementary Students	1,891	45,834	6,421	320	24,955	97,419	**3,055,645**
Priests Teaching	–	27	4	–	34	7	**1,346**
Scholastics Teaching	–	4	–	–	–	–	**99**
Brothers Teaching	–	27	1	–	18	31	**882**
Sisters Teaching	2	108	6	4	79	91	**4,956**
Lay Teachers	157	6,193	282	65	3,487	3,177	**162,555**
Infant Baptisms	410	14,256	1,443	84	6,229	15,718	**857,410**
Adult Baptisms	60	540	117	13	483	347	**43,279**
Received into Full Communion	140	1,107	122	–	910	387	**75,724**
First Communions	534	14,093	2,032	149	6,099	18,643	**806,576**
Confirmations	472	11,237	2,161	48	5,529	14,842	**628,362**
Marriages	127	4,235	598	10	1,512	3,716	**179,576**
Deaths	329	11,782	2,532	17	4,510	15,642	**429,539**
Total Catholics	40,290	1,271,551	187,306	4,875	499,529	1,681,533	**68,503,456**
Total Population	793,222	4,350,465	1,316,456	59,000	3,093,068	3,682,588	**310,252,317**
Catholic Population Percentage	5	29	14	8	16	46	**22**

Archdioceses = 37; Dioceses = 169; Apostolates = 3

2010 GENERAL SUMMARY

	Fall River MA	Springfield in Massachusetts MA	Worcester MA	MASS. TOTAL	*Detroit MI	Gaylord MI	2010 U.S. GRAND TOTAL
Cardinals	–	–	–	1	2	–	**13**
Archbishops	–	–	–	–	1	–	**59**
Bishop	1	3	3	13	3	2	**390**
Abbots	–	–	3	4	–	–	**110**
Diocesan Priests	155	145	189	1,233	396	62	**27,614**
Religious Priests	103	37	106	737	199	6	**13,174**
Total Priests in Diocese	258	182	295	1,970	595	68	**40,788**
Newly Ordained Priests	2	–	2	10	5	1	**472**
Total Permanent Deacons	88	78	106	530	205	22	**17,165**
Total Brothers	17	14	74	249	75	–	**4,737**
Total Sisters	182	427	427	2,981	1,245	32	**58,724**
Number of Parishes	91	86	116	584	271	80	**18,372**
Missions	12	9	4	25	1	–	**2,680**
Pastoral Centers	–	–	–	1	–	–	**619**
New Parishes	–	–	2	2	–	–	**83**
Catholic Hospitals	1	1	1	11	10	3	**561**
Patients Assisted Annually	204,595	172,612	228,139	1,313,565	1,096,535	375,000	**86,525,713**
Health Care Centers	–	1	5	9	4	–	**380**
Patients Assisted Annually	–	7,000	–	14,511	4,987	–	**6,332,721**
Specialized Homes	7	9	6	58	34	1	**1,593**
Total Assisted Anually	1,232	454	300	6,540	21,466	250	**1,600,986**
Residential Care of Children (Orphanages)	1	1	1	4	–	4	**358**
Total Assisted Anually	100	36	24	1,081	–	295	**28,663**
Day Care and Extended Day Care Centers	1	1	14	27	–	11	**975**
Total Assisted Anually	45	18	1,500	2,673	–	342	**121,593**
Special Centers for Social Services	4	8	7	62	45	23	**2,863**
Total Assisted Anually	43,727	40,550	65,000	355,277	35,843	28,972	**24,865,474**
Diocesan Seminaries	–	–	–	3	2	–	**72**
Students	–	–	–	139	101	–	**3,319**
Religious Seminaries	–	–	–	1	2	–	**108**
Students	–	–	–	37	21	–	**1,812**
Colleges and Universities	1	1	3	11	3	–	**234**
Total Students	2,430	1,323	8,917	37,570	13,004	–	**768,541**
High Schools, Diocesan and Parish	5	4	4	16	9	4	**748**
Total Students	2,871	1,170	1,879	7,070	3,597	501	**335,956**
High Schools, Private	–	–	5	34	12	–	**590**
Total Students	–	–	1,524	16,679	6,535	–	**311,290**
Elementary Schools, Diocesan and Parish	22	16	19	136	76	16	**5,614**
Total Students	4,824	4,046	4,601	37,538	22,852	1,882	**1,457,160**
Elementary Schools, Private	–	–	3	12	1	–	**376**
Total Students	–	–	450	2,714	354	–	**90,052**
Non–residential Schools for the Disabled	–	–	1	3	–	–	**66**
Total Students	–	–	30	169	–	–	**6,329**
Religious Education High School Students	4,077	6,398	5,647	42,746	5,751	745	**687,174**
Religious Education Elementary Students	23,961	12,822	17,942	152,144	55,644	2,660	**3,055,645**
Priests Teaching	9	1	15	32	19	–	**1,346**
Scholastics Teaching	–	–	–	–	–	–	**99**
Brothers Teaching	3	–	1	35	5	–	**882**
Sisters Teaching	12	26	31	160	88	1	**4,956**
Lay Teachers	730	357	1,127	5,391	2,586	186	**162,555**
Infant Baptisms	3,109	2,466	2,634	23,927	9,544	577	**857,410**
Adult Baptisms	58	96	75	576	704	64	**43,279**
Received into Full Communion	186	153	150	876	960	124	**75,724**
First Communions	3,702	2,506	3,290	28,141	11,768	815	**806,576**
Confirmations	3,546	2,246	2,757	23,391	10,481	845	**628,362**
Marriages	943	632	536	5,827	2,775	271	**179,576**
Deaths	3,613	3,546	3,167	25,968	9,496	853	**429,539**
Total Catholics	319,853	217,391	305,000	2,523,777	1,434,622	60,837	**68,503,456**
Total Population	826,616	816,953	784,992	6,111,149	4,438,006	507,722	**310,252,317**
Catholic Population Percentage	39	27	39	41	32	12	**22**

*Indicates Archdioceses.

†Certain Diocese traverse state lines.

	Grand Rapids MI	Kalamazoo MI	Lansing MI	Marquette MI	Saginaw MI	MICHIGAN TOTAL	2010 U.S. GRAND TOTAL
Cardinals	–	–	–	–	–	2	**13**
Archbishops	–	–	–	–	–	1	**59**
Bishop	3	3	2	3	1	17	**390**
Abbots	–	–	–	–	–	–	**110**
Diocesan Priests	107	66	149	85	93	958	**27,614**
Religious Priests	17	8	42	7	7	286	**13,174**
Total Priests in Diocese	124	74	191	92	100	1,244	**40,788**
Newly Ordained Priests	2	4	1	2	3	18	**472**
Total Permanent Deacons	41	36	102	47	15	468	**17,165**
Total Brothers	1	2	8	–	–	86	**4,737**
Total Sisters	326	217	429	49	94	2,392	**58,724**
Number of Parishes	91	46	86	72	106	752	**18,372**
Missions	12	13	–	22	–	48	**2,680**
Pastoral Centers	1	1	2	–	–	4	**619**
New Parishes	–	–	–	–	–	–	**83**
Catholic Hospitals	2	3	5	1	1	25	**561**
Patients Assisted Annually	1,737,952	467,065	1,511,775	196,495	318,460	5,703,282	**86,525,713**
Health Care Centers	–	5	6	–	1	16	**380**
Patients Assisted Annually	–	623,455	20,967	–	1,294	650,703	**6,332,721**
Specialized Homes	18	8	6	1	4	72	**1,593**
Total Assisted Anually	4,406	733	505	109	305	27,774	**1,600,986**
Residential Care of Children (Orphanages)	–	–	–	–	3	7	**358**
Total Assisted Anually	–	–	–	–	177	472	**28,663**
Day Care and Extended Day Care Centers	–	16	1	–	11	39	**975**
Total Assisted Anually	–	430	100	–	357	1,229	**121,593**
Special Centers for Social Services	4	7	11	8	5	103	**2,863**
Total Assisted Anually	212,080	40,469	290,083	2,100	7,544	617,091	**24,865,474**
Diocesan Seminaries	–	–	–	–	–	2	**72**
Students	–	–	–	–	–	101	**3,319**
Religious Seminaries	–	–	6	–	–	8	**108**
Students	–	–	–	–	–	21	**1,812**
Colleges and Universities	1	–	1	–	–	5	**234**
Total Students	2,312	–	2,365	–	–	17,681	**768,541**
High Schools, Diocesan and Parish	3	3	4	–	3	26	**748**
Total Students	1,456	651	2,123	–	660	8,988	**335,956**
High Schools, Private	1	–	1	–	–	14	**590**
Total Students	203	–	40	–	–	6,778	**311,290**
Elementary Schools, Diocesan and Parish	27	19	33	9	22	202	**5,614**
Total Students	4,433	2,656	7,165	1,260	2,856	43,104	**1,457,160**
Elementary Schools, Private	1	–	2	–	–	4	**376**
Total Students	286	–	347	–	–	987	**90,052**
Non–residential Schools for the Disabled	–	–	–	–	–	–	**66**
Total Students	–	–	–	–	–	–	**6,329**
Religious Education High School Students	2,168	1,443	3,526	875	1,036	15,544	**687,174**
Religious Education Elementary Students	10,818	6,050	18,249	2,587	6,501	102,509	**3,055,645**
Priests Teaching	–	–	2	–	1	22	**1,346**
Scholastics Teaching	–	–	–	–	–	–	**99**
Brothers Teaching	–	–	1	–	–	6	**882**
Sisters Teaching	3	2	8	1	–	103	**4,956**
Lay Teachers	397	230	555	96	265	4,315	**162,555**
Infant Baptisms	2,829	1,277	2,687	559	1,122	18,595	**857,410**
Adult Baptisms	338	194	266	26	80	1,672	**43,279**
Received into Full Communion	544	195	464	90	309	2,686	**75,724**
First Communions	3,234	1,203	3,482	589	1,237	22,328	**806,576**
Confirmations	2,132	1,116	3,298	189	1,593	19,654	**628,362**
Marriages	1,939	340	787	313	483	6,908	**179,576**
Deaths	1,188	828	1,991	1,325	1,566	17,247	**429,539**
Total Catholics	178,000	105,844	217,672	48,630	110,563	2,156,168	**68,503,456**
Total Population	1,283,717	949,063	1,790,849	300,000	708,764	9,978,121	**310,252,317**
Catholic Population Percentage	14	11	12	16	16	22	**22**

Archdioceses = 37; Dioceses = 169; Apostolates = 3

2010 GENERAL SUMMARY

	*St. Paul and Minneapolis MN	Crookston MN	Duluth MN	New Ulm MN	St. Cloud MN	Winona MN	2010 U.S. GRAND TOTAL
Cardinals	–	–	–	–	–	–	**13**
Archbishops	2	–	–	–	–	–	**59**
Bishop	1	2	1	1	1	2	**390**
Abbots	–	–	–	–	2	1	**110**
Diocesan Priests	340	45	78	66	111	115	**27,614**
Religious Priests	96	3	9	–	103	8	**13,174**
Total Priests in Diocese	436	48	87	66	214	123	**40,788**
Newly Ordained Priests	3	–	2	–	1	1	**472**
Total Permanent Deacons	215	16	42	3	48	28	**17,165**
Total Brothers	34	1	–	–	56	21	**4,737**
Total Sisters	722	84	115	62	464	387	**58,724**
Number of Parishes	219	66	94	76	135	114	**18,372**
Missions	5	–	–	–	–	–	**2,680**
Pastoral Centers	4	–	–	–	–	2	**619**
New Parishes	–	–	–	–	–	–	**83**
Catholic Hospitals	4	3	2	1	4	2	**561**
Patients Assisted Annually	228,000	79,723	456,954	8,718	310,748	86,550	**86,525,713**
Health Care Centers	8	–	–	2	–	1	**380**
Patients Assisted Annually	30,000	–	–	9,054	–	1,236	**6,332,721**
Specialized Homes	11	3	5	6	12	10	**1,593**
Total Assisted Anually	2,850	624	697	292	1,084	817	**1,600,986**
Residential Care of Children (Orphanages)	2	–	–	–	1	–	**358**
Total Assisted Anually	1,000	–	–	–	392	–	**28,663**
Day Care and Extended Day Care Centers	2	1	1	–	–	3	**975**
Total Assisted Anually	150	49	95	–	–	17,935	**121,593**
Special Centers for Social Services	17	–	–	–	60	7	**2,863**
Total Assisted Anually	5,200	–	–	–	46,476	4,563	**24,865,474**
Diocesan Seminaries	2	–	–	–	–	1	**72**
Students	240	–	–	–	–	57	**3,319**
Religious Seminaries	1	–	–	–	1	–	**108**
Students	–	–	–	–	–	–	**1,812**
Colleges and Universities	3	–	1	–	2	1	**234**
Total Students	17,000	–	3,746	–	4,127	1,404	**768,541**
High Schools, Diocesan and Parish	10	1	–	3	1	4	**748**
Total Students	8,000	94	–	389	654	996	**335,956**
High Schools, Private	4	–	–	–	1	–	**590**
Total Students	600	–	–	–	328	–	**311,290**
Elementary Schools, Diocesan and Parish	91	9	12	16	31	21	**5,614**
Total Students	30,000	1,349	1,623	1,918	4,658	4,097	**1,457,160**
Elementary Schools, Private	3	–	–	–	–	–	**376**
Total Students	500	–	–	–	–	–	**90,052**
Non–residential Schools for the Disabled	–	–	–	–	–	–	**66**
Total Students	–	–	–	–	–	–	**6,329**
Religious Education High School Students	16,500	1,457	2,949	2,719	5,199	3,375	**687,174**
Religious Education Elementary Students	40,000	3,083	3,455	5,445	11,290	7,874	**3,055,645**
Priests Teaching	41	–	1	–	9	1	**1,346**
Scholastics Teaching	–	–	–	–	–	–	**99**
Brothers Teaching	9	–	–	–	10	–	**882**
Sisters Teaching	115	8	5	3	15	2	**4,956**
Lay Teachers	500	120	305	157	760	325	**162,555**
Infant Baptisms	8,755	498	679	849	2,101	1,807	**857,410**
Adult Baptisms	293	9	29	15	71	27	**43,279**
Received into Full Communion	1,285	57	123	76	206	125	**75,724**
First Communions	9,425	456	702	914	2,103	1,572	**806,576**
Confirmations	7,849	421	717	932	1,818	1,621	**628,362**
Marriages	2,229	204	254	326	757	545	**179,576**
Deaths	4,502	328	831	690	1,391	1,048	**429,539**
Total Catholics	650,000	35,285	63,423	63,011	142,576	131,280	**68,503,456**
Total Population	3,000,000	252,944	439,543	281,802	558,890	573,635	**310,252,317**
Catholic Population Percentage	22	14	14	22	26	23	**22**

*Indicates Archdioceses.

†Certain Diocese traverse state lines.

	MINNESOTA TOTAL	Biloxi MS	Jackson MS	MISSISSIPPI TOTAL	*St. Louis MO	Jefferson City MO	2010 U.S. GRAND TOTAL
Cardinals	–	–	–	–	–	–	**13**
Archbishops	2	–	–	–	1	–	**59**
Bishop	8	2	2	4	1	1	**390**
Abbots	3	–	–	–	3	–	**110**
Diocesan Priests	755	51	55	106	373	93	**27,614**
Religious Priests	219	24	29	53	358	12	**13,174**
Total Priests in Diocese	974	75	84	159	731	105	**40,788**
Newly Ordained Priests	7	1	–	1	5	–	**472**
Total Permanent Deacons	352	35	7	42	274	47	**17,165**
Total Brothers	112	9	9	18	130	1	**4,737**
Total Sisters	1,834	39	172	211	1,426	62	**58,724**
Number of Parishes	704	42	75	117	190	95	**18,372**
Missions	5	11	26	37	–	15	**2,680**
Pastoral Centers	6	–	–	–	–	–	**619**
New Parishes	–	–	1	1	–	–	**83**
Catholic Hospitals	16	–	1	1	12	1	**561**
Patients Assisted Annually	1,170,693	–	119,754	119,754	1,790,768	258,234	**86,525,713**
Health Care Centers	11	–	2	2	–	16	**380**
Patients Assisted Annually	40,290	–	9,142	9,142	–	130,171	**6,332,721**
Specialized Homes	47	7	8	15	48	–	**1,593**
Total Assisted Anually	6,364	469	6,963	7,432	31,040	–	**1,600,986**
Residential Care of Children (Orphanages)	3	–	3	3	3	–	**358**
Total Assisted Anually	1,392	–	352	352	1,706	–	**28,663**
Day Care and Extended Day Care Centers	7	–	2	2	8	–	**975**
Total Assisted Anually	18,229	–	227	227	26,416	–	**121,593**
Special Centers for Social Services	84	9	17	26	8	2	**2,863**
Total Assisted Anually	56,239	362,661	21,488	384,149	10,500	–	**24,865,474**
Diocesan Seminaries	3	–	–	–	2	–	**72**
Students	297	–	–	–	113	–	**3,319**
Religious Seminaries	2	–	–	–	2	–	**108**
Students	–	–	–	–	47	–	**1,812**
Colleges and Universities	7	–	3	3	2	–	**234**
Total Students	26,277	–	42	42	15,534	–	**768,541**
High Schools, Diocesan and Parish	19	4	4	8	12	2	**748**
Total Students	10,133	1,117	1,198	2,315	4,933	956	**335,956**
High Schools, Private	5	1	–	1	16	–	**590**
Total Students	928	375	–	375	8,564	–	**311,290**
Elementary Schools, Diocesan and Parish	180	11	15	26	108	37	**5,614**
Total Students	43,645	2,717	3,102	5,819	30,162	6,494	**1,457,160**
Elementary Schools, Private	3	–	–	–	9	–	**376**
Total Students	500	–	–	–	1,868	–	**90,052**
Non–residential Schools for the Disabled	–	–	–	–	4	–	**66**
Total Students	–	–	–	–	179	–	**6,329**
Religious Education High School Students	32,199	1,287	1,120	2,407	132	2,350	**687,174**
Religious Education Elementary Students	71,147	3,168	3,753	6,921	22,324	3,575	**3,055,645**
Priests Teaching	52	–	–	–	46	8	**1,346**
Scholastics Teaching	–	–	–	–	–	–	**99**
Brothers Teaching	19	5	3	8	21	1	**882**
Sisters Teaching	148	3	9	12	87	11	**4,956**
Lay Teachers	2,167	339	353	692	3,925	605	**162,555**
Infant Baptisms	14,689	996	924	1,920	5,711	1,168	**857,410**
Adult Baptisms	444	140	66	206	323	134	**43,279**
Received into Full Communion	1,872	181	209	390	497	303	**75,724**
First Communions	15,172	1,014	742	1,756	6,619	1,279	**806,576**
Confirmations	13,358	847	439	1,286	6,723	1,096	**628,362**
Marriages	4,315	286	257	543	2,072	507	**179,576**
Deaths	8,790	657	416	1,073	4,110	826	**429,539**
Total Catholics	1,085,575	62,494	50,114	112,608	531,770	80,708	**68,503,456**
Total Population	5,106,814	775,538	2,111,593	2,887,131	2,232,379	876,490	**310,252,317**
Catholic Population Percentage	21	8	2	4	24	9	**22**

Archdioceses = 37; Dioceses = 169; Apostolates = 3

2010 GENERAL SUMMARY

	Kansas City – St. Joseph MO	Springfield – Cape Girardeau	MISSOURI TOTAL	Great Falls – Billings MT	Helena MT	MONTANA TOTAL	2010 U.S. GRAND TOTAL
Cardinals	–	–	–	–	–	–	**13**
Archbishops	–	–	1	–	1	1	**59**
Bishop	2	2	6	2	1	3	**390**
Abbots	1	2	6	–	–	–	**110**
Diocesan Priests	96	65	627	64	78	142	**27,614**
Religious Priests	87	53	510	14	6	20	**13,174**
Total Priests in Diocese	183	118	1,137	78	84	162	**40,788**
Newly Ordained Priests	3	6	14	1	–	1	**472**
Total Permanent Deacons	58	16	395	5	28	33	**17,165**
Total Brothers	34	55	220	1	3	4	**4,737**
Total Sisters	242	82	1,812	56	31	87	**58,724**
Number of Parishes	86	66	437	55	57	112	**18,372**
Missions	12	18	45	52	39	91	**2,680**
Pastoral Centers	–	4	4	–	14	14	**619**
New Parishes	–	–	–	–	–	–	**83**
Catholic Hospitals	3	7	23	2	2	4	**561**
Patients Assisted Annually	307,377	1,032,337	3,388,716	463,532	284,212	747,744	**86,525,713**
Health Care Centers	–	–	16	–	–	–	**380**
Patients Assisted Annually	–	–	130,171	–	–	–	**6,332,721**
Specialized Homes	11	1	60	1	–	1	**1,593**
Total Assisted Anually	2,338	362	33,740	84	–	84	**1,600,986**
Residential Care of Children (Orphanages)	–	–	3	–	–	–	**358**
Total Assisted Anually	–	–	1,706	–	–	–	**28,663**
Day Care and Extended Day Care Centers	8	1	17	7	3	10	**975**
Total Assisted Anually	1,663	39	28,118	347	129	476	**121,593**
Special Centers for Social Services	7	–	17	–	–	–	**2,863**
Total Assisted Anually	223,949	–	234,449	–	–	–	**24,865,474**
Diocesan Seminaries	1	–	3	–	1	1	**72**
Students	116	–	229	–	–	–	**3,319**
Religious Seminaries	–	2	4	–	–	–	**108**
Students	–	6	53	–	–	–	**1,812**
Colleges and Universities	2	–	4	1	1	2	**234**
Total Students	5,609	–	21,143	858	1,428	2,286	**768,541**
High Schools, Diocesan and Parish	4	3	21	2	2	4	**748**
Total Students	1,209	936	8,034	421	334	755	**335,956**
High Schools, Private	4	–	20	1	–	1	**590**
Total Students	2,367	–	10,931	121	–	121	**311,290**
Elementary Schools, Diocesan and Parish	28	23	196	9	4	13	**5,614**
Total Students	7,766	3,580	48,002	1,463	960	2,423	**1,457,160**
Elementary Schools, Private	1	–	10	4	–	4	**376**
Total Students	320	–	2,188	478	–	478	**90,052**
Non–residential Schools for the Disabled	–	–	4	–	–	–	**66**
Total Students	–	–	179	–	–	–	**6,329**
Religious Education High School Students	1,901	1,288	5,671	922	867	1,789	**687,174**
Religious Education Elementary Students	6,672	3,408	35,979	2,620	2,759	5,379	**3,055,645**
Priests Teaching	5	–	59	2	1	3	**1,346**
Scholastics Teaching	–	–	–	–	–	–	**99**
Brothers Teaching	5	1	28	1	2	3	**882**
Sisters Teaching	18	5	121	4	1	5	**4,956**
Lay Teachers	1,548	317	6,395	294	121	415	**162,555**
Infant Baptisms	2,159	878	9,916	654	573	1,227	**857,410**
Adult Baptisms	242	122	821	58	–	58	**43,279**
Received into Full Communion	412	185	1,397	51	140	191	**75,724**
First Communions	2,510	1,182	11,590	673	719	1,392	**806,576**
Confirmations	1,823	817	10,459	799	742	1,541	**628,362**
Marriages	781	325	3,685	156	194	350	**179,576**
Deaths	1,109	532	6,577	698	817	1,515	**429,539**
Total Catholics	135,966	68,147	816,591	47,773	54,460	102,233	**68,503,456**
Total Population	1,489,890	1,226,079	5,824,838	434,299	551,627	985,926	**310,252,317**
Catholic Population Percentage	9	6	14	11	10	22	**22**

*Indicates Archdioceses.

†Certain Diocese traverse state lines.

	Chalan Kanoa MP	*Omaha NE	Grand Island NE	Lincoln NE	NEBRASKA TOTAL	Las Vegas NV	2010 U.S. GRAND TOTAL
Cardinals	–	–	–	–	–	–	**13**
Archbishops	–	2	–	–	2	–	**59**
Bishop	1	1	1	1	3	1	**390**
Abbots	–	3	–	–	3	–	**110**
Diocesan Priests	16	196	68	152	416	39	**27,614**
Religious Priests	1	80	–	10	90	19	**13,174**
Total Priests in Diocese	17	276	68	162	506	58	**40,788**
Newly Ordained Priests	–	–	3	7	10	1	**472**
Total Permanent Deacons	–	237	3	3	243	16	**17,165**
Total Brothers	–	23	–	–	23	4	**4,737**
Total Sisters	–	288	61	137	486	3	**58,724**
Number of Parishes	12	132	36	133	301	28	**18,372**
Missions	1	16	33	1	50	6	**2,680**
Pastoral Centers	1	–	–	5	5	–	**619**
New Parishes	–	–	–	–	–	–	**83**
Catholic Hospitals	–	4	–	3	7	–	**561**
Patients Assisted Annually	–	239,337	–	218,396	457,733	–	**86,525,713**
Health Care Centers	–	–	2	–	2	–	**380**
Patients Assisted Annually	–	–	178,000	–	178,000	–	**6,332,721**
Specialized Homes	1	5	1	3	9	–	**1,593**
Total Assisted Anually	262	9,411	75	256	9,742	–	**1,600,986**
Residential Care of Children (Orphanages)	–	–	–	–	–	–	**358**
Total Assisted Anually	–	–	–	–	–	–	**28,663**
Day Care and Extended Day Care Centers	–	31	–	1	32	–	**975**
Total Assisted Anually	–	4,166	–	29	4,195	–	**121,593**
Special Centers for Social Services	2	11	–	21	32	24	**2,863**
Total Assisted Anually	2,232	98,231	–	26,748	124,979	6,300,000	**24,865,474**
Diocesan Seminaries	–	–	–	1	1	–	**72**
Students	–	–	–	43	43	–	**3,319**
Religious Seminaries	–	–	–	1	1	–	**108**
Students	–	–	–	75	75	–	**1,812**
Colleges and Universities	–	2	–	–	2	–	**234**
Total Students	–	8,485	–	–	8,485	–	**768,541**
High Schools, Diocesan and Parish	–	13	4	6	23	1	**748**
Total Students	–	3,167	495	1,764	5,426	1,169	**335,956**
High Schools, Private	–	5	–	–	5	–	**590**
Total Students	–	2,576	–	–	2,576	–	**311,290**
Elementary Schools, Diocesan and Parish	3	55	6	25	86	7	**5,614**
Total Students	462	14,201	932	5,302	20,435	2,649	**1,457,160**
Elementary Schools, Private	–	1	–	–	1	–	**376**
Total Students	–	72	–	–	72	–	**90,052**
Non-residential Schools for the Disabled	–	1	–	1	2	–	**66**
Total Students	–	57	–	13	70	–	**6,329**
Religious Education High School Students	618	3,631	2,177	1,941	7,749	2,996	**687,174**
Religious Education Elementary Students	528	15,428	3,961	5,019	24,408	10,442	**3,055,645**
Priests Teaching	1	18	–	30	48	2	**1,346**
Scholastics Teaching	–	2	–	–	2	–	**99**
Brothers Teaching	–	4	–	–	4	–	**882**
Sisters Teaching	4	20	2	38	60	–	**4,956**
Lay Teachers	36	1,539	106	442	2,087	225	**162,555**
Infant Baptisms	606	4,271	916	1,088	6,275	5,965	**857,410**
Adult Baptisms	18	160	61	121	342	341	**43,279**
Received into Full Communion	–	483	161	148	792	876	**75,724**
First Communions	597	4,181	869	1,487	6,537	4,590	**806,576**
Confirmations	618	3,712	670	1,526	5,908	1,835	**628,362**
Marriages	58	1,309	292	445	2,046	653	**179,576**
Deaths	169	1,728	478	677	2,883	804	**429,539**
Total Catholics	43,000	224,920	54,644	95,445	375,009	716,000	**68,503,456**
Total Population	71,850	909,580	301,328	580,275	1,791,183	1,925,000	**310,252,317**
Catholic Population Percentage	60	25	18	16	21	37	**22**

Archdioceses = 37; Dioceses = 169; Apostolates = 3

2010 GENERAL SUMMARY

	Reno NV	NEVADA TOTAL	Manchester NH	*Newark NJ	Camden NJ	Metuchen NJ	2010 U.S. GRAND TOTAL
Cardinals	–	–	–	–	–	–	13
Archbishops	–	–	–	2	–	–	59
Bishop	2	3	4	7	1	2	390
Abbots	–	–	1	1	–	–	110
Diocesan Priests	30	69	188	729	289	188	27,614
Religious Priests	6	25	59	165	36	42	13,174
Total Priests in Diocese	36	94	247	894	325	230	40,788
Newly Ordained Priests	–	1	2	13	1	3	472
Total Permanent Deacons	23	39	55	167	152	164	17,165
Total Brothers	3	7	18	74	12	20	4,737
Total Sisters	34	37	439	1,003	286	309	58,724
Number of Parishes	28	56	98	222	125	103	18,372
Missions	6	12	14	–	7	6	2,680
Pastoral Centers	–	–	–	–	30	3	619
New Parishes	–	–	3	–	–	–	83
Catholic Hospitals	1	1	2	5	1	1	561
Patients Assisted Annually	94,486	94,486	433,644	621,226	309,187	398,274	86,525,713
Health Care Centers	2	2	–	1	2	4	380
Patients Assisted Annually	27,707	27,707	–	8,000	19,304	37,702	6,332,721
Specialized Homes	–	–	9	10	7	11	1,593
Total Assisted Anually	–	–	1,150	1,461	2,515	2,011	1,600,986
Residential Care of Children (Orphanages)	–	–	2	–	–	–	358
Total Assisted Anually	–	–	45	–	–	–	28,663
Day Care and Extended Day Care Centers	3	3	–	4	2	2	975
Total Assisted Anually	268	268	–	575	215	279	121,593
Special Centers for Social Services	9	33	11	23	1	9	2,863
Total Assisted Anually	38,000	6,338,000	69,000	71,803	5,588	20,772	24,865,474
Diocesan Seminaries	–	–	–	3	–	–	72
Students	–	–	–	164	–	–	3,319
Religious Seminaries	–	–	–	–	–	–	108
Students	–	–	–	35	–	–	1,812
Colleges and Universities	–	–	4	4	–	–	234
Total Students	–	–	4,338	17,544	–	–	768,541
High Schools, Diocesan and Parish	1	2	3	11	7	3	748
Total Students	613	1,782	1,454	6,244	6,400	2,114	335,956
High Schools, Private	–	–	2	21	3	2	590
Total Students	–	–	901	8,134	1,385	1,149	311,290
Elementary Schools, Diocesan and Parish	4	11	20	84	39	32	5,614
Total Students	1,133	3,782	3,956	18,406	10,003	9,353	1,457,160
Elementary Schools, Private	–	–	5	5	1	–	376
Total Students	–	–	816	1,170	46	–	90,052
Non–residential Schools for the Disabled	–	–	–	–	2	1	66
Total Students	–	–	–	–	974	45	6,329
Religious Education High School Students	1,148	4,144	4,602	4,042	1,400	1,135	687,174
Religious Education Elementary Students	3,730	14,172	10,816	70,021	28,184	35,956	3,055,645
Priests Teaching	–	2	–	30	8	–	1,346
Scholastics Teaching	–	–	–	–	–	–	99
Brothers Teaching	1	1	–	16	6	10	882
Sisters Teaching	–	–	11	16	40	49	4,956
Lay Teachers	135	360	391	2,482	1,038	935	162,555
Infant Baptisms	1,706	7,671	2,584	13,936	5,640	4,839	857,410
Adult Baptisms	101	442	94	301	–	110	43,279
Received into Full Communion	371	1,247	271	216	393	293	75,724
First Communions	1,460	6,050	3,341	12,224	5,370	6,313	806,576
Confirmations	708	2,543	2,645	9,576	5,260	5,756	628,362
Marriages	245	898	517	2,831	1,412	1,055	179,576
Deaths	352	1,156	2,697	9,883	3,846	3,554	429,539
Total Catholics	127,749	843,749	309,987	1,318,557	500,326	566,087	68,503,456
Total Population	753,132	2,678,132	1,315,809	2,784,183	1,610,641	1,347,827	310,252,317
Catholic Population Percentage	17	32	24	47	31	42	22

*Indicates Archdioceses.

†Certain Diocese traverse state lines.

	Paterson NJ	Trenton NJ	NEW JERSEY TOTAL	*Santa Fe NM	† Gallup NM	Las Cruces NM	2010 U.S. GRAND TOTAL
Cardinals	–	–	–	–	–	–	**13**
Archbishops	–	–	2	2	–	–	**59**
Bishop	2	2	14	–	2	1	**390**
Abbots	7	–	8	1	–	–	**110**
Diocesan Priests	248	241	1,695	132	40	33	**27,614**
Religious Priests	126	58	427	86	17	44	**13,174**
Total Priests in Diocese	374	299	2,122	218	57	77	**40,788**
Newly Ordained Priests	9	3	29	2	–	2	**472**
Total Permanent Deacons	212	357	1,052	216	28	40	**17,165**
Total Brothers	30	70	206	70	8	3	**4,737**
Total Sisters	728	366	2,692	176	100	41	**58,724**
Number of Parishes	111	111	672	92	52	45	**18,372**
Missions	–	6	19	217	22	46	**2,680**
Pastoral Centers	5	–	38	4	–	1	**619**
New Parishes	–	1	1	–	–	–	**83**
Catholic Hospitals	3	2	12	1	–	–	**561**
Patients Assisted Annually	949,712	476,350	2,754,749	162,000	–	–	**86,525,713**
Health Care Centers	–	7	14	1	–	–	**380**
Patients Assisted Annually	–	4,500	69,506	1,500	–	–	**6,332,721**
Specialized Homes	8	5	41	3	2	–	**1,593**
Total Assisted Anually	1,940	630	8,557	2,125	74	–	**1,600,986**
Residential Care of Children (Orphanages)	1	1	2	–	–	–	**358**
Total Assisted Anually	70	24	94	–	–	–	**28,663**
Day Care and Extended Day Care Centers	6	6	20	1	–	1	**975**
Total Assisted Anually	1,600	550	3,219	48	–	50	**121,593**
Special Centers for Social Services	12	29	74	6	12	1	**2,863**
Total Assisted Anually	64,000	27,750	189,913	367,809	75,000	8,000	**24,865,474**
Diocesan Seminaries	–	–	3	–	–	–	**72**
Students	–	–	164	–	–	–	**3,319**
Religious Seminaries	2	–	2	–	–	–	**108**
Students	4	3	42	–	–	–	**1,812**
Colleges and Universities	2	1	7	–	–	–	**234**
Total Students	2,156	3,045	22,745	–	–	–	**768,541**
High Schools, Diocesan and Parish	4	8	33	1	1	–	**748**
Total Students	2,518	5,980	23,256	884	95	–	**335,956**
High Schools, Private	4	3	33	1	1	–	**590**
Total Students	1,342	1,181	13,191	768	42	–	**311,290**
Elementary Schools, Diocesan and Parish	41	36	232	15	10	–	**5,614**
Total Students	10,130	12,290	60,182	3,488	1,060	–	**1,457,160**
Elementary Schools, Private	3	3	12	–	1	5	**376**
Total Students	521	677	2,414	–	120	597	**90,052**
Non–residential Schools for the Disabled	–	1	4	–	–	–	**66**
Total Students	–	17	1,036	–	–	–	**6,329**
Religious Education High School Students	9,572	1,077	17,226	4,651	782	2,487	**687,174**
Religious Education Elementary Students	33,344	62,728	230,233	16,493	2,702	5,540	**3,055,645**
Priests Teaching	16	–	54	3	–	–	**1,346**
Scholastics Teaching	–	–	–	–	–	–	**99**
Brothers Teaching	8	15	55	1	–	–	**882**
Sisters Teaching	60	68	233	12	18	–	**4,956**
Lay Teachers	838	952	6,245	380	138	53	**162,555**
Infant Baptisms	6,977	8,048	39,440	5,203	550	1,892	**857,410**
Adult Baptisms	128	905	1,444	297	89	57	**43,279**
Received into Full Communion	219	295	1,416	465	58	259	**75,724**
First Communions	6,998	9,925	40,830	5,242	743	1,691	**806,576**
Confirmations	4,942	9,563	35,097	3,677	475	1,055	**628,362**
Marriages	1,289	1,718	8,305	1,120	155	329	**179,576**
Deaths	3,216	6,343	26,842	3,065	523	822	**429,539**
Total Catholics	424,722	831,707	3,641,399	314,183	61,990	132,646	**68,503,456**
Total Population	1,129,405	2,021,917	8,893,973	1,227,277	495,000	498,308	**310,252,317**
Catholic Population Percentage	38	41	41	26	13	27	**22**

Archdioceses = 37; Dioceses = 169; Apostolates = 3

2010 GENERAL SUMMARY

	NEW MEXICO TOTAL	*New York NY	Albany NY	Brooklyn NY	Buffalo NY	Ogdensburg NY	2010 U.S. GRAND TOTAL
Cardinals	–	1	–	–	–	–	**13**
Archbishops	2	1	–	–	–	–	**59**
Bishop	3	9	1	8	4	1	**390**
Abbots	1	–	–	–	–	–	**110**
Diocesan Priests	205	637	213	525	334	130	**27,614**
Religious Priests	147	868	79	174	115	5	**13,174**
Total Priests in Diocese	352	1,505	292	699	449	135	**40,788**
Newly Ordained Priests	4	5	1	3	2	–	**472**
Total Permanent Deacons	284	374	111	159	125	70	**17,165**
Total Brothers	81	324	76	138	42	8	**4,737**
Total Sisters	317	2,799	702	868	964	113	**58,724**
Number of Parishes	189	371	136	197	171	105	**18,372**
Missions	285	–	16	–	1	10	**2,680**
Pastoral Centers	5	–	5	–	2	–	**619**
New Parishes	–	–	14	–	6	–	**83**
Catholic Hospitals	1	7	3	–	4	–	**561**
Patients Assisted Annually	162,000	862,000	1,250,000	–	1,451,025	–	**86,525,713**
Health Care Centers	1	2	17	10	1	–	**380**
Patients Assisted Annually	1,500	4,800	72,000	10,284	960	–	**6,332,721**
Specialized Homes	5	43	44	35	12	1	**1,593**
Total Assisted Anually	2,199	137,964	1,526	10,400	8,688	128	**1,600,986**
Residential Care of Children (Orphanages)	–	31	4	1	–	–	**358**
Total Assisted Anually	–	2,617	135	6,800	–	–	**28,663**
Day Care and Extended Day Care Centers	2	375	3	28	3	–	**975**
Total Assisted Anually	98	4,856	269	5,403	206	–	**121,593**
Special Centers for Social Services	19	629	75	90	5	4	**2,863**
Total Assisted Anually	450,809	293,664	110,972	108,000	259,503	30,000	**24,865,474**
Diocesan Seminaries	–	2	–	1	1	–	**72**
Students	–	85	–	24	16	2	**3,319**
Religious Seminaries	–	8	–	1	1	–	**108**
Students	–	125	–	13	2	–	**1,812**
Colleges and Universities	–	10	3	3	7	–	**234**
Total Students	–	43,252	6,670	20,659	17,201	–	**768,541**
High Schools, Diocesan and Parish	2	12	4	4	–	2	**748**
Total Students	979	4,418	1,249	2,037	–	352	**335,956**
High Schools, Private	2	43	3	17	15	–	**590**
Total Students	810	23,202	975	14,362	5,221	–	**311,290**
Elementary Schools, Diocesan and Parish	25	187	23	104	55	13	**5,614**
Total Students	4,548	51,290	5,146	33,494	11,976	2,020	**1,457,160**
Elementary Schools, Private	6	29	2	3	3	–	**376**
Total Students	717	4,820	321	413	689	–	**90,052**
Non–residential Schools for the Disabled	–	8	–	2	1	–	**66**
Total Students	–	153	–	103	399	–	**6,329**
Religious Education High School Students	7,920	7,810	8,393	3,727	9,051	1,552	**687,174**
Religious Education Elementary Students	24,735	96,623	20,749	33,051	26,688	6,016	**3,055,645**
Priests Teaching	3	18	3	–	37	2	**1,346**
Scholastics Teaching	–	–	–	–	–	–	**99**
Brothers Teaching	1	33	–	43	24	–	**882**
Sisters Teaching	30	104	13	117	90	10	**4,956**
Lay Teachers	571	4,310	545	2,864	2,527	186	**162,555**
Infant Baptisms	7,645	23,494	3,315	17,095	4,110	1,075	**857,410**
Adult Baptisms	443	938	74	624	132	32	**43,279**
Received into Full Communion	782	828	156	828	224	32	**75,724**
First Communions	7,676	21,638	3,982	11,045	5,201	1,039	**806,576**
Confirmations	5,207	18,273	3,067	10,612	5,167	990	**628,362**
Marriages	1,604	4,679	1,008	2,696	1,515	360	**179,576**
Deaths	4,410	13,180	3,686	9,103	6,217	1,668	**429,539**
Total Catholics	508,819	2,608,299	331,908	1,440,000	656,760	108,078	**68,503,456**
Total Population	2,220,585	5,796,221	1,312,642	4,798,388	1,529,043	491,438	**310,252,317**
Catholic Population Percentage	23	45	25	30	43	22	**22**

*Indicates Archdioceses.

†Certain Diocese traverse state lines.

	Rochester NY	Rockville Centre NY	Syracuse NY	NEW YORK TOTAL	Charlotte NC	Raleigh NC	2010 U.S. GRAND TOTAL
Cardinals	–	–	–	1	–	–	**13**
Archbishops	–	–	–	1	–	–	**59**
Bishop	1	6	3	33	2	2	**390**
Abbots	4	–	–	4	2	–	**110**
Diocesan Priests	185	366	242	2,632	117	90	**27,614**
Religious Priests	46	30	36	1,353	49	49	**13,174**
Total Priests in Diocese	231	396	278	3,985	166	139	**40,788**
Newly Ordained Priests	2	4	1	18	1	–	**472**
Total Permanent Deacons	127	265	85	1,316	96	40	**17,165**
Total Brothers	29	80	6	703	12	3	**4,737**
Total Sisters	481	1,131	317	7,375	122	52	**58,724**
Number of Parishes	124	133	136	1,373	73	78	**18,372**
Missions	4	1	11	43	19	18	**2,680**
Pastoral Centers	–	–	–	7	1	5	**619**
New Parishes	3	–	–	23	–	–	**83**
Catholic Hospitals	2	5	3	24	–	–	**561**
Patients Assisted Annually	250,000	593,750	677,000	5,083,775	–	–	**86,525,713**
Health Care Centers	2	3	2	37	16	–	**380**
Patients Assisted Annually	1,200	31,040	500,000	620,284	67,000	–	**6,332,721**
Specialized Homes	12	12	57	216	6	–	**1,593**
Total Assisted Anually	2,220	4,245	2,625	167,796	677	–	**1,600,986**
Residential Care of Children (Orphanages)	–	3	–	39	–	–	**358**
Total Assisted Anually	–	340	–	9,892	–	–	**28,663**
Day Care and Extended Day Care Centers	1	–	1	411	13	–	**975**
Total Assisted Anually	180	–	182	11,096	1,000	–	**121,593**
Special Centers for Social Services	76	31	2	912	4	10	**2,863**
Total Assisted Anually	845,000	41,002	1,500	1,689,641	24,079	42,545	**24,865,474**
Diocesan Seminaries	–	1	–	5	–	–	**72**
Students	–	40	–	167	–	–	**3,319**
Religious Seminaries	–	–	1	11	–	–	**108**
Students	–	–	14	154	–	–	**1,812**
Colleges and Universities	–	1	1	25	1	–	**234**
Total Students	–	3,500	3,479	94,761	1,638	–	**768,541**
High Schools, Diocesan and Parish	1	5	5	33	2	1	**748**
Total Students	95	4,827	1,654	14,632	1,956	1,185	**335,956**
High Schools, Private	6	5	1	90	–	1	**590**
Total Students	3,308	7,749	750	55,567	–	114	**311,290**
Elementary Schools, Diocesan and Parish	24	53	22	481	16	31	**5,614**
Total Students	5,159	18,624	3,261	130,970	5,738	7,776	**1,457,160**
Elementary Schools, Private	3	4	–	44	–	–	**376**
Total Students	418	1,418	–	8,079	–	–	**90,052**
Non–residential Schools for the Disabled	–	1	–	12	–	–	**66**
Total Students	–	70	–	725	–	–	**6,329**
Religious Education High School Students	5,260	2,698	6,939	45,430	3,237	4,050	**687,174**
Religious Education Elementary Students	17,578	107,584	21,303	329,592	15,173	15,079	**3,055,645**
Priests Teaching	7	14	4	85	5	2	**1,346**
Scholastics Teaching	–	–	–	–	–	–	**99**
Brothers Teaching	–	50	3	153	3	–	**882**
Sisters Teaching	26	57	21	438	11	5	**4,956**
Lay Teachers	798	1,851	461	13,542	762	559	**162,555**
Infant Baptisms	2,579	17,174	3,291	72,133	3,462	5,579	**857,410**
Adult Baptisms	197	601	128	2,726	235	176	**43,279**
Received into Full Communion	292	429	385	3,174	625	–	**75,724**
First Communions	2,797	18,506	3,519	67,727	5,465	4,947	**806,576**
Confirmations	2,579	18,131	3,369	62,188	3,457	2,369	**628,362**
Marriages	1,049	3,956	1,059	16,322	806	958	**179,576**
Deaths	3,509	12,026	3,806	53,195	1,172	1,003	**429,539**
Total Catholics	309,773	1,521,842	284,000	7,260,660	171,909	217,225	**68,503,456**
Total Population	1,485,097	3,513,536	1,173,146	20,099,511	4,792,483	4,432,901	**310,252,317**
Catholic Population Percentage	21	43	24	36	4	5	**22**

Archdioceses = 37; Dioceses = 169; Apostolates = 3

2010 GENERAL SUMMARY

	NORTH CAROLINA TOTAL	Bismarck ND	Fargo ND	NORTH DAKOTA TOTAL	*Cincinnati OH	Cleveland OH	2010 U.S. GRAND TOTAL
Cardinals	–	–	–	–	–	–	**13**
Archbishops	–	–	–	–	2	–	**59**
Bishop	4	1	1	2	–	5	**390**
Abbots	2	2	–	2	–	2	**110**
Diocesan Priests	207	67	136	203	280	405	**27,614**
Religious Priests	98	29	9	38	213	101	**13,174**
Total Priests in Diocese	305	96	145	241	493	506	**40,788**
Newly Ordained Priests	1	3	1	4	7	7	**472**
Total Permanent Deacons	136	79	45	124	176	210	**17,165**
Total Brothers	15	20	–	20	121	58	**4,737**
Total Sisters	174	95	124	219	925	1,073	**58,724**
Number of Parishes	151	99	132	231	218	201	**18,372**
Missions	37	–	–	–	–	1	**2,680**
Pastoral Centers	6	–	–	–	–	2	**619**
New Parishes	–	–	–	–	–	8	**83**
Catholic Hospitals	–	4	8	12	9	3	**561**
Patients Assisted Annually	–	329,137	160,090	489,227	1,577,130	413,766	**86,525,713**
Health Care Centers	16	–	–	–	–	1	**380**
Patients Assisted Annually	67,000	–	–	–	–	259	**6,332,721**
Specialized Homes	6	4	14	18	13	30	**1,593**
Total Assisted Anually	677	570	126,075	126,645	3,273	6,055	**1,600,986**
Residential Care of Children (Orphanages)	–	–	–	–	1	1	**358**
Total Assisted Anually	–	–	–	–	1,269	355	**28,663**
Day Care and Extended Day Care Centers	13	–	–	–	1	9	**975**
Total Assisted Anually	1,000	–	–	–	267	906	**121,593**
Special Centers for Social Services	14	–	5	5	4	22	**2,863**
Total Assisted Anually	66,624	–	10,348	10,348	36,308	292,821	**24,865,474**
Diocesan Seminaries	–	–	1	1	1	2	**72**
Students	–	–	10	10	36	54	**3,319**
Religious Seminaries	–	–	–	–	–	–	**108**
Students	–	–	–	–	–	13	**1,812**
Colleges and Universities	1	1	1	2	4	3	**234**
Total Students	1,638	2,830	480	3,310	20,450	7,154	**768,541**
High Schools, Diocesan and Parish	3	3	1	4	18	6	**748**
Total Students	3,141	627	337	964	10,359	3,216	**335,956**
High Schools, Private	1	–	–	–	4	16	**590**
Total Students	114	–	–	–	3,317	10,262	**311,290**
Elementary Schools, Diocesan and Parish	47	11	12	23	88	98	**5,614**
Total Students	13,514	1,537	1,685	3,222	29,337	33,493	**1,457,160**
Elementary Schools, Private	–	–	–	–	6	9	**376**
Total Students	–	–	–	–	1,844	2,453	**90,052**
Non–residential Schools for the Disabled	–	–	–	–	1	1	**66**
Total Students	–	–	–	–	97	107	**6,329**
Religious Education High School Students	7,287	1,713	1,949	3,662	5,356	4,926	**687,174**
Religious Education Elementary Students	30,252	5,026	5,957	10,983	27,472	38,991	**3,055,645**
Priests Teaching	7	3	1	4	12	19	**1,346**
Scholastics Teaching	–	–	–	–	–	–	**99**
Brothers Teaching	3	–	–	–	9	20	**882**
Sisters Teaching	16	6	1	7	41	112	**4,956**
Lay Teachers	1,321	186	158	344	2,217	3,261	**162,555**
Infant Baptisms	9,041	894	1,262	2,156	5,955	7,009	**857,410**
Adult Baptisms	411	34	36	70	471	694	**43,279**
Received into Full Communion	625	81	146	227	731	573	**75,724**
First Communions	10,412	912	1,028	1,940	7,135	9,139	**806,576**
Confirmations	5,826	1,050	1,120	2,170	7,336	9,045	**628,362**
Marriages	1,764	338	386	724	2,025	2,592	**179,576**
Deaths	2,175	738	874	1,612	4,719	7,655	**429,539**
Total Catholics	389,134	61,271	85,229	146,500	468,204	744,000	**68,503,456**
Total Population	9,225,384	264,082	377,979	642,061	3,023,332	2,855,767	**310,252,317**
Catholic Population Percentage	4	23	23	23	15	26	**22**

*Indicates Archdioceses.

†Certain Diocese traverse state lines.

	Columbus OH	Steubenville OH	Toledo OH	Youngstown OH	OHIO TOTAL	*Oklahoma City OK	2010 U.S. GRAND TOTAL
Cardinals	–	–	–	–	–	–	**13**
Archbishops	–	–	–	–	2	1	**59**
Bishop	2	3	2	1	13	–	**390**
Abbots	–	–	–	–	2	4	**110**
Diocesan Priests	162	86	189	153	1,275	87	**27,614**
Religious Priests	27	28	39	17	425	27	**13,174**
Total Priests in Diocese	189	114	228	170	1,700	114	**40,788**
Newly Ordained Priests	1	2	8	–	25	2	**472**
Total Permanent Deacons	102	9	199	80	776	100	**17,165**
Total Brothers	1	7	8	13	208	8	**4,737**
Total Sisters	267	57	526	198	3,046	97	**58,724**
Number of Parishes	106	58	128	113	824	67	**18,372**
Missions	3	3	–	2	9	44	**2,680**
Pastoral Centers	–	–	–	–	2	–	**619**
New Parishes	–	1	–	–	9	–	**83**
Catholic Hospitals	6	1	8	4	31	5	**561**
Patients Assisted Annually	803,176	243,845	1,266,598	53,269	4,357,784	289,950	**86,525,713**
Health Care Centers	–	–	4	29	34	1	**380**
Patients Assisted Annually	–	–	30,275	1,307,395	1,337,929	108	**6,532,721**
Specialized Homes	20	–	8	15	86	6	**1,593**
Total Assisted Anually	3,125	–	1,366	2,587	16,406	385	**1,600,986**
Residential Care of Children (Orphanages)	–	–	–	–	2	–	**358**
Total Assisted Anually	–	–	–	–	1,624	–	**28,663**
Day Care and Extended Day Care Centers	–	–	–	1	11	2	**975**
Total Assisted Anually	–	–	–	120	1,293	122	**121,593**
Special Centers for Social Services	6	1	7	14	54	–	**2,863**
Total Assisted Anually	210,428	23,743	11,806	44,244	619,350	–	**24,865,474**
Diocesan Seminaries	1	1	–	–	5	–	**72**
Students	120	2	–	–	212	–	**3,319**
Religious Seminaries	–	–	–	–	–	–	**108**
Students	–	–	–	–	13	–	**1,812**
Colleges and Universities	2	1	2	1	13	1	**234**
Total Students	3,849	2,449	3,161	2,936	39,999	709	**768,541**
High Schools, Diocesan and Parish	11	3	10	6	54	2	**748**
Total Students	4,808	494	3,162	2,321	24,360	1,033	**335,956**
High Schools, Private	–	–	4	–	24	–	**590**
Total Students	–	–	2,553	–	16,132	–	**311,290**
Elementary Schools, Diocesan and Parish	42	13	66	32	339	18	**5,614**
Total Students	10,496	1,559	13,453	6,155	94,493	4,175	**1,457,160**
Elementary Schools, Private	2	–	2	2	21	2	**376**
Total Students	82	–	351	345	5,075	391	**90,052**
Non–residential Schools for the Disabled	–	–	1	–	3	–	**66**
Total Students	–	–	53	–	257	–	**6,329**
Religious Education High School Students	876	362	4,973	2,920	19,413	3,394	**687,174**
Religious Education Elementary Students	14,037	1,206	22,362	12,032	116,100	10,065	**3,055,645**
Priests Teaching	15	1	16	4	67	6	**1,346**
Scholastics Teaching	–	–	–	–	–	–	**99**
Brothers Teaching	–	2	–	–	31	2	**882**
Sisters Teaching	5	6	56	9	229	7	**4,956**
Lay Teachers	1,137	178	1,375	561	8,729	384	**162,555**
Infant Baptisms	3,536	415	2,784	1,877	21,576	2,313	**857,410**
Adult Baptisms	317	68	359	191	2,100	210	**43,279**
Received into Full Communion	437	80	410	301	2,532	501	**75,724**
First Communions	3,627	489	3,717	2,238	26,345	2,593	**806,576**
Confirmations	3,838	520	3,521	2,258	26,518	1,393	**628,362**
Marriages	1,053	207	1,224	765	7,866	625	**179,576**
Deaths	1,646	675	2,840	2,766	20,301	720	**429,539**
Total Catholics	257,374	38,693	321,516	201,857	2,031,644	108,871	**68,503,456**
Total Population	2,511,332	230,391	1,461,436	1,193,021	11,275,279	2,998,568	**310,252,317**
Catholic Population Percentage	10	17	22	17	18	4	**22**

Archdioceses = 37; Dioceses = 169; Apostolates = 3

2010 GENERAL SUMMARY

	Tulsa OK	OKLAHOMA TOTAL	*Portland in Oregon OR	Baker OR	OREGON TOTAL	*Philadelphia PA	2010 U.S. GRAND TOTAL
Cardinals	–	–	–	–	–	2	**13**
Archbishops	–	1	1	–	1	–	**59**
Bishop	1	1	1	2	3	6	**390**
Abbots	–	4	5	–	5	2	**110**
Diocesan Priests	74	161	153	36	189	598	**27,614**
Religious Priests	29	56	152	15	167	369	**13,174**
Total Priests in Diocese	103	217	305	51	356	967	**40,788**
Newly Ordained Priests	–	2	9	1	10	6	**472**
Total Permanent Deacons	57	157	63	12	75	245	**17,165**
Total Brothers	18	26	79	–	79	101	**4,737**
Total Sisters	49	146	400	11	411	2,763	**58,724**
Number of Parishes	76	143	124	36	160	267	**18,372**
Missions	2	46	24	23	47	7	**2,680**
Pastoral Centers	–	–	1	–	1	17	**619**
New Parishes	–	–	–	–	–	–	**83**
Catholic Hospitals	4	9	9	5	14	7	**561**
Patients Assisted Annually	1,200,000	1,489,950	1,488,560	481,068	1,969,628	842,614	**86,525,713**
Health Care Centers	1	2	13	–	13	1	**380**
Patients Assisted Annually	5,703	5,811	324,986	–	324,986	153	**6,332,721**
Specialized Homes	7	13	14	4	18	38	**1,593**
Total Assisted Anually	878	1,263	3,777	220	3,997	7,854	**1,600,986**
Residential Care of Children (Orphanages)	–	–	–	–	–	2	**358**
Total Assisted Anually	–	–	–	–	–	530	**28,663**
Day Care and Extended Day Care Centers	–	2	4	3	7	1	**975**
Total Assisted Anually	–	122	1,993	80	2,073	59	**121,593**
Special Centers for Social Services	7	7	13	7	20	18	**2,863**
Total Assisted Anually	45,756	45,756	1,072,019	72,469	1,144,488	108,279	**24,865,474**
Diocesan Seminaries	–	–	1	–	1	1	**72**
Students	–	–	137	–	137	144	**3,319**
Religious Seminaries	–	–	1	–	1	1	**108**
Students	–	–	29	–	29	14	**1,812**
Colleges and Universities	–	1	2	–	2	11	**234**
Total Students	–	709	5,508	–	5,508	41,151	**768,541**
High Schools, Diocesan and Parish	1	3	3	–	3	20	**748**
Total Students	842	1,875	1,408	–	1,408	17,903	**335,956**
High Schools, Private	1	1	7	–	7	15	**590**
Total Students	556	556	3,993	–	3,993	7,662	**311,290**
Elementary Schools, Diocesan and Parish	9	27	39	5	44	180	**5,614**
Total Students	2,094	6,269	8,407	592	8,999	54,677	**1,457,160**
Elementary Schools, Private	2	4	2	–	2	17	**376**
Total Students	1,096	1,487	453	–	453	4,669	**90,052**
Non–residential Schools for the Disabled	–	–	–	–	–	5	**66**
Total Students	–	–	–	–	–	226	**6,329**
Religious Education High School Students	1,340	4,734	3,460	687	4,147	1,249	**687,174**
Religious Education Elementary Students	5,324	15,389	14,752	1,829	16,581	52,643	**3,055,645**
Priests Teaching	4	10	1	–	1	92	**1,346**
Scholastics Teaching	–	–	–	–	–	–	**99**
Brothers Teaching	4	6	4	–	4	35	**882**
Sisters Teaching	5	12	17	–	17	430	**4,956**
Lay Teachers	346	730	961	50	1,011	8,919	**162,555**
Infant Baptisms	1,557	3,870	5,727	977	6,704	13,918	**857,410**
Adult Baptisms	128	338	363	37	400	431	**43,279**
Received into Full Communion	342	843	580	208	788	457	**75,724**
First Communions	1,342	3,935	5,073	1,166	6,239	12,750	**806,576**
Confirmations	996	2,389	2,629	844	3,473	12,772	**628,362**
Marriages	345	970	960	178	1,138	4,455	**179,576**
Deaths	458	1,178	1,896	237	2,133	11,369	**429,539**
Total Catholics	57,938	166,809	409,864	32,799	442,663	1,464,938	**68,503,456**
Total Population	1,635,000	4,633,568	3,269,195	493,996	3,763,191	3,892,194	**310,252,317**
Catholic Population Percentage	4	4	13	7	12	38	**22**

*Indicates Archdioceses.

†Certain Diocese traverse state lines.

	Allentown PA	Altoona-Johnstown PA	Erie PA	Greensburg PA	Harrisburg PA	Pittsburgh PA	2010 U.S. GRAND TOTAL
Cardinals	–	–	–	–	–	–	13
Archbishops	–	–	–	–	–	–	59
Bishop	2	1	1	2	–	2	390
Abbots	–	–	–	1	–	–	110
Diocesan Priests	208	123	193	114	142	387	27,614
Religious Priests	63	61	6	69	32	98	13,174
Total Priests in Diocese	271	184	199	183	174	485	40,788
Newly Ordained Priests	4	4	2	2	4	6	472
Total Permanent Deacons	108	32	56	2	46	41	17,165
Total Brothers	12	9	–	47	1	29	4,737
Total Sisters	350	71	350	198	359	1,143	58,724
Number of Parishes	104	91	120	85	89	212	18,372
Missions	2	5	18	–	8	–	2,680
Pastoral Centers	26	–	–	–	–	–	619
New Parishes	13	1	2	–	–	–	83
Catholic Hospitals	2	1	1	–	1	1	561
Patients Assisted Annually	488,955	407,279	480,800	–	254,408	227,840	86,525,713
Health Care Centers	2	1	–	–	–	–	380
Patients Assisted Annually	4,356	253	–	–	–	–	6,332,721
Specialized Homes	12	3	7	2	7	14	1,593
Total Assisted Anually	774	390	1,722	264	745	3,830	1,600,986
Residential Care of Children (Orphanages)	–	–	–	–	1	–	358
Total Assisted Anually	–	–	–	–	30	–	28,663
Day Care and Extended Day Care Centers	1	–	1	–	–	8	975
Total Assisted Anually	39	–	110	–	–	1,723	121,593
Special Centers for Social Services	7	2	24	6	18	7	2,863
Total Assisted Anually	24,983	25,712	49,900	15,916	2,844	102,673	24,865,474
Diocesan Seminaries	–	–	1	–	–	1	72
Students	–	–	19	–	–	16	3,319
Religious Seminaries	–	–	–	1	–	–	108
Students	–	–	–	24	–	–	1,812
Colleges and Universities	2	2	2	2	–	3	234
Total Students	6,117	4,322	7,454	3,930	–	13,919	768,541
High Schools, Diocesan and Parish	8	3	6	2	7	8	748
Total Students	3,641	953	1,648	655	3,819	3,487	335,956
High Schools, Private	–	–	1	–	–	4	590
Total Students	–	–	595	–	–	720	311,290
Elementary Schools, Diocesan and Parish	45	20	32	15	38	95	5,614
Total Students	9,485	3,608	5,326	2,915	8,563	18,306	1,457,160
Elementary Schools, Private	–	–	1	3	1	4	376
Total Students	–	–	236	238	24	785	90,052
Non-residential Schools for the Disabled	3	–	–	–	–	2	66
Total Students	116	–	–	–	–	164	6,329
Religious Education High School Students	206	3,094	5,658	1,794	1,624	4,648	687,174
Religious Education Elementary Students	16,252	6,708	8,130	7,330	16,402	39,990	3,055,645
Priests Teaching	10	2	9	10	1	2	1,346
Scholastics Teaching	–	–	–	–	–	–	99
Brothers Teaching	–	1	–	4	–	17	882
Sisters Teaching	54	8	10	11	34	66	4,956
Lay Teachers	916	322	534	299	778	1,793	162,555
Infant Baptisms	3,043	974	1,543	1,329	2,075	5,705	857,410
Adult Baptisms	117	62	119	65	321	258	43,279
Received into Full Communion	–	136	90	302	390	553	75,724
First Communions	3,363	1,251	2,021	1,625	3,549	6,624	806,576
Confirmations	3,824	1,928	1,962	1,737	3,030	7,359	628,362
Marriages	935	491	617	680	756	2,142	179,576
Deaths	3,101	1,523	2,542	2,419	2,245	8,282	429,539
Total Catholics	272,300	94,284	221,958	161,959	232,117	673,801	68,503,456
Total Population	1,161,932	638,969	860,340	673,477	2,156,331	1,908,721	310,252,317
Catholic Population Percentage	23	15	26	24	11	35	22

Archdioceses = 37; Dioceses = 169; Apostolates = 3

2010 GENERAL SUMMARY

	Scranton PA	PENN. TOTAL	*San Juan Puerto Rico	Arecibo Puerto Rico	Caguas Puerto Rico	Fajardo–Humacao Puerto Rico	2010 U.S. GRAND TOTAL
Cardinals	–	2	1	–	–	–	**13**
Archbishops	–	–	1	–	–	–	**59**
Bishop	4	18	3	1	3	1	**390**
Abbots	–	3	–	–	–	–	**110**
Diocesan Priests	292	2,057	89	61	48	19	**27,614**
Religious Priests	60	758	166	45	36	10	**13,174**
Total Priests in Diocese	352	2,815	255	106	84	29	**40,788**
Newly Ordained Priests	3	31	3	1	–	1	**472**
Total Permanent Deacons	65	595	165	3	102	26	**17,165**
Total Brothers	8	207	18	6	–	6	**4,737**
Total Sisters	523	5,757	459	170	96	27	**58,724**
Number of Parishes	130	1,098	143	59	34	21	**18,372**
Missions	54	94	143	241	–	–	**2,680**
Pastoral Centers	–	43	–	–	–	–	**619**
New Parishes	–	16	–	–	–	–	**83**
Catholic Hospitals	5	18	5	–	–	–	**561**
Patients Assisted Annually	606,270	3,308,166	33,641	–	–	–	**86,525,713**
Health Care Centers	2	6	4	–	–	–	**380**
Patients Assisted Annually	118,714	123,476	76,944	–	–	–	**6,332,721**
Specialized Homes	13	96	10	5	2	–	**1,593**
Total Assisted Anually	2,164	17,743	37,643	264	186	–	**1,600,986**
Residential Care of Children (Orphanages)	5	8	8	3	–	–	**358**
Total Assisted Anually	682	1,242	936	45	–	–	**28,663**
Day Care and Extended Day Care Centers	9	20	1	–	–	1	**975**
Total Assisted Anually	418	2,349	20	–	–	35	**121,593**
Special Centers for Social Services	13	95	10	1	–	1	**2,863**
Total Assisted Anually	211,798	542,105	33,062	858	–	31	**24,865,474**
Diocesan Seminaries	–	3	1	1	2	–	**72**
Students	–	179	21	14	11	–	**3,319**
Religious Seminaries	1	3	4	–	–	–	**108**
Students	2	40	14	–	–	–	**1,812**
Colleges and Universities	4	26	2	1	–	–	**234**
Total Students	13,190	90,083	9,284	685	–	–	**768,541**
High Schools, Diocesan and Parish	4	58	20	9	2	6	**748**
Total Students	1,529	33,635	4,095	4,926	–	1,599	**335,956**
High Schools, Private	2	22	28	5	7	–	**590**
Total Students	924	9,901	6,904	7,068	–	–	**311,290**
Elementary Schools, Diocesan and Parish	21	446	28	5	2	5	**5,614**
Total Students	6,019	108,899	8,393	4,926	–	1,171	**1,457,160**
Elementary Schools, Private	–	26	41	5	7	–	**376**
Total Students	–	5,952	13,498	2,142	–	–	**90,052**
Non–residential Schools for the Disabled	1	11	1	–	–	–	**66**
Total Students	17	523	120	–	–	–	**6,329**
Religious Education High School Students	4,885	23,158	10,999	1,372	–	–	**687,174**
Religious Education Elementary Students	23,096	170,551	25,223	19,740	–	–	**3,055,645**
Priests Teaching	4	130	41	10	–	–	**1,346**
Scholastics Teaching	–	–	76	–	–	–	**99**
Brothers Teaching	–	57	18	3	–	–	**882**
Sisters Teaching	30	643	459	25	–	–	**4,956**
Lay Teachers	483	14,044	2,257	445	–	–	**162,555**
Infant Baptisms	3,484	32,071	6,221	3,150	3,421	618	**857,410**
Adult Baptisms	81	1,454	–	363	275	138	**43,279**
Received into Full Communion	111	2,039	6	–	–	–	**75,724**
First Communions	4,014	35,197	4,895	3,489	3,645	606	**806,576**
Confirmations	4,236	36,848	4,166	3,500	2,757	434	**628,362**
Marriages	1,096	11,172	1,139	557	511	132	**179,576**
Deaths	4,881	36,362	–	2,000	1,942	350	**429,539**
Total Catholics	323,047	3,444,404	944,508	370,000	350,000	97,869	**68,503,456**
Total Population	1,091,320	12,383,284	1,259,344	603,469	503,000	293,000	**310,252,317**
Catholic Population Percentage	30	28	75	61	70	33	**22**

*Indicates Archdioceses.

†Certain Diocese traverse state lines.

	Mayaguez Puerto Rico	Ponce Puerto Rico	PUERTO RICO TOTAL	Providence RI	Charleston SC	Rapid City SD	2010 U.S. GRAND TOTAL
Cardinals	–	–	1	–	–	–	13
Archbishops	–	–	1	1	–	–	59
Bishop	1	2	11	6	2	1	390
Abbots	–	–	–	3	–	–	110
Diocesan Priests	47	78	342	278	81	37	27,614
Religious Priests	23	50	330	123	38	14	13,174
Total Priests in Diocese	70	128	672	401	119	51	40,788
Newly Ordained Priests	2	–	7	3	1	1	472
Total Permanent Deacons	22	82	400	104	103	29	17,165
Total Brothers	6	7	43	83	23	3	4,737
Total Sisters	106	181	1,039	477	136	43	58,724
Number of Parishes	29	43	329	147	92	88	18,372
Missions	–	–	384	5	24	29	2,680
Pastoral Centers	–	186	186	22	1	4	619
New Parishes	–	–	–	3	–	–	83
Catholic Hospitals	1	–	6	1	3	–	561
Patients Assisted Annually	39,771	–	73,412	200,000	296,399	–	86,525,713
Health Care Centers	–	7	11	1	–	1	380
Patients Assisted Annually	–	336,690	413,634	240	–	15,733	6,332,721
Specialized Homes	4	12	33	11	1	1	1,593
Total Assisted Anually	527	325,288	363,908	44,756	25	7,709	1,600,986
Residential Care of Children (Orphanages)	–	1	12	–	–	1	358
Total Assisted Anually	–	22	1,003	–	–	6	28,663
Day Care and Extended Day Care Centers	–	2	4	2	–	1	975
Total Assisted Anually	–	10,052	10,107	115	–	35	121,593
Special Centers for Social Services	1	4	17	6	8	6	2,863
Total Assisted Anually	15,000	52,823	101,774	62,300	43,131	21,941	24,865,474
Diocesan Seminaries	–	1	5	1	–	–	72
Students	–	22	68	22	–	–	3,319
Religious Seminaries	–	2	6	–	–	–	108
Students	–	9	23	–	–	–	1,812
Colleges and Universities	1	1	5	2	–	–	234
Total Students	1,888	9,679	21,536	7,689	–	–	768,541
High Schools, Diocesan and Parish	4	12	53	4	2	1	748
Total Students	658	1,558	12,836	2,124	1,182	247	335,956
High Schools, Private	4	5	49	8	2	1	590
Total Students	890	806	15,668	3,673	582	209	311,290
Elementary Schools, Diocesan and Parish	5	17	62	33	28	1	5,614
Total Students	860	5,046	20,396	7,777	5,598	568	1,457,160
Elementary Schools, Private	6	4	63	4	–	1	376
Total Students	1,193	1,762	18,595	1,456	–	345	90,052
Non–residential Schools for the Disabled	–	–	1	–	–	–	66
Total Students	–	–	120	–	–	–	6,329
Religious Education High School Students	426	2,469	15,266	8,075	2,502	955	687,174
Religious Education Elementary Students	12,963	7,606	65,532	23,718	10,393	2,434	3,055,645
Priests Teaching	–	18	69	53	2	1	1,346
Scholastics Teaching	–	–	76	–	–	–	99
Brothers Teaching	5	3	29	29	1	–	882
Sisters Teaching	2	16	502	56	22	1	4,956
Lay Teachers	325	946	3,973	1,555	700	119	162,555
Infant Baptisms	3,345	3,126	19,881	4,030	3,324	549	857,410
Adult Baptisms	178	515	1,469	133	201	26	43,279
Received into Full Communion	62	5,477	5,545	318	404	81	75,724
First Communions	2,611	4,190	19,436	4,501	3,057	463	806,576
Confirmations	2,282	3,997	17,136	4,345	2,304	459	628,362
Marriages	337	707	3,383	1,299	682	165	179,576
Deaths	2,203	–	6,495	5,164	1,186	399	429,539
Total Catholics	402,010	445,053	2,609,440	619,964	184,728	25,229	68,503,456
Total Population	502,515	593,388	3,754,716	1,050,788	4,394,300	227,211	310,252,317
Catholic Population Percentage	80	75	69	59	4	11	22

Archdioceses = 37; Dioceses = 169; Apostolates = 3

2010 GENERAL SUMMARY

	Sioux Falls SD	SOUTH DAKOTA TOTAL	Knoxville TN	Memphis TN	Nashville TN	TENNESSEE TOTAL	2010 U.S. GRAND TOTAL
Cardinals	–	–	–	–	–	–	**13**
Archbishops	–	–	–	–	–	–	**59**
Bishop	1	2	1	1	1	3	**390**
Abbots	3	3	–	–	–	–	**110**
Diocesan Priests	116	153	62	62	42	166	**27,614**
Religious Priests	28	42	11	19	26	56	**13,174**
Total Priests in Diocese	144	195	73	81	68	222	**40,788**
Newly Ordained Priests	2	3	2	6	1	9	**472**
Total Permanent Deacons	36	65	53	64	73	190	**17,165**
Total Brothers	8	11	10	30	2	42	**4,737**
Total Sisters	299	342	27	55	231	313	**58,724**
Number of Parishes	150	238	45	42	53	140	**18,372**
Missions	–	29	2	5	3	10	**2,680**
Pastoral Centers	–	4	2	1	2	5	**619**
New Parishes	–	–	–	–	2	2	**83**
Catholic Hospitals	11	11	2	–	4	6	**561**
Patients Assisted Annually	720,000	720,000	388,772	–	615,143	1,003,915	**86,525,713**
Health Care Centers	–	1	1	–	–	1	**380**
Patients Assisted Annually	–	15,733	310	–	–	310	**6,332,721**
Specialized Homes	–	1	3	5	2	10	**1,593**
Total Assisted Anually	–	7,709	1,669	1,452	338	3,459	**1,600,986**
Residential Care of Children (Orphanages)	–	1	–	–	–	–	**358**
Total Assisted Anually	–	6	–	–	–	–	**28,663**
Day Care and Extended Day Care Centers	–	1	–	5	3	8	**975**
Total Assisted Anually	–	35	–	850	783	1,633	**121,593**
Special Centers for Social Services	20	26	7	1	8	16	**2,863**
Total Assisted Anually	50,400	72,341	50,455	12,000	55,858	118,313	**24,865,474**
Diocesan Seminaries	–	–	–	–	–	–	**72**
Students	–	–	–	–	–	–	**3,319**
Religious Seminaries	–	–	–	–	–	–	**108**
Students	–	–	–	–	–	–	**1,812**
Colleges and Universities	2	2	–	1	1	2	**234**
Total Students	1,800	1,800	–	1,773	1,983	3,756	**768,541**
High Schools, Diocesan and Parish	3	4	2	4	2	8	**748**
Total Students	991	1,238	1,135	1,488	1,508	4,131	**335,956**
High Schools, Private	–	1	–	3	1	4	**590**
Total Students	–	209	–	1,229	265	1,494	**311,290**
Elementary Schools, Diocesan and Parish	21	22	8	22	16	46	**5,614**
Total Students	4,157	4,725	2,170	5,065	3,862	11,097	**1,457,160**
Elementary Schools, Private	–	1	–	1	2	3	**376**
Total Students	–	345	–	676	633	1,309	**90,052**
Non–residential Schools for the Disabled	–	–	–	1	–	1	**66**
Total Students	–	–	–	6	–	6	**6,329**
Religious Education High School Students	6,114	7,069	1,375	795	1,454	3,624	**687,174**
Religious Education Elementary Students	7,188	9,622	3,581	3,421	6,416	13,418	**3,055,645**
Priests Teaching	7	8	2	1	–	3	**1,346**
Scholastics Teaching	–	–	–	–	–	–	**99**
Brothers Teaching	–	–	–	7	–	7	**882**
Sisters Teaching	2	3	6	14	44	64	**4,956**
Lay Teachers	332	451	203	657	640	1,500	**162,555**
Infant Baptisms	1,571	2,120	1,203	1,359	1,669	4,231	**857,410**
Adult Baptisms	50	76	105	91	172	368	**43,279**
Received into Full Communion	242	323	259	252	427	938	**75,724**
First Communions	1,506	1,969	1,074	1,429	1,677	4,180	**806,576**
Confirmations	1,703	2,162	742	1,101	1,321	3,164	**628,362**
Marriages	525	690	259	229	424	912	**179,576**
Deaths	951	1,350	308	437	497	1,242	**429,539**
Total Catholics	124,972	150,201	60,295	74,254	75,593	210,142	**68,503,456**
Total Population	524,153	751,364	2,330,795	1,503,679	2,248,497	6,082,971	**310,252,317**
Catholic Population Percentage	24	20	3	5	3	22	**22**

*Indicates Archdioceses.

†Certain Diocese traverse state lines.

	*Galveston – Houston TX	*San Antonio TX	Amarillo TX	Austin TX	Beaumont TX	Brownsville TX	2010 U.S. GRAND TOTAL
Cardinals	1	–	–	–	–	–	13
Archbishops	1	1	–	–	–	–	59
Bishop	1	4	2	2	1	2	390
Abbots	–	–	–	–	–	–	110
Diocesan Priests	200	150	41	131	49	84	27,614
Religious Priests	199	205	5	50	22	38	13,174
Total Priests in Diocese	399	355	46	181	71	122	40,788
Newly Ordained Priests	4	10	2	5	–	2	472
Total Permanent Deacons	386	352	52	197	40	69	17,165
Total Brothers	15	86	1	46	1	20	4,737
Total Sisters	456	726	97	107	23	13	58,724
Number of Parishes	146	139	38	101	44	69	18,372
Missions	6	34	11	22	7	45	2,680
Pastoral Centers	19	–	–	1	2	2	619
New Parishes	1	–	–	–	–	1	83
Catholic Hospitals	2	6	–	4	2	–	561
Patients Assisted Annually	226,461	400,000	–	1,508,356	406,633	–	86,525,713
Health Care Centers	9	5	–	–	–	3	380
Patients Assisted Annually	133,462	37,800	–	–	–	5,486	6,332,721
Specialized Homes	9	13	4	5	–	2	1,593
Total Assisted Anually	5,857	3,696	432	334,413	–	226	1,600,986
Residential Care of Children (Orphanages)	4	3	–	–	–	–	358
Total Assisted Anually	661	989	–	–	–	–	28,663
Day Care and Extended Day Care Centers	37	9	1	2	–	1	975
Total Assisted Anually	3,675	983	89	300	–	38	121,593
Special Centers for Social Services	11	9	1	7	3	6	2,863
Total Assisted Anually	737,241	12,828	4,500	24,524	32,140	23,287	24,865,474
Diocesan Seminaries	1	1	–	–	–	1	72
Students	89	82	–	–	–	4	3,319
Religious Seminaries	5	4	–	–	–	–	108
Students	10	25	–	–	–	–	1,812
Colleges and Universities	1	5	–	1	–	–	234
Total Students	3,246	13,994	–	5,285	–	–	768,541
High Schools, Diocesan and Parish	–	5	1	4	1	–	748
Total Students	–	1,127	139	615	437	–	335,956
High Schools, Private	9	6	–	2	–	3	590
Total Students	4,201	2,584	–	550	–	949	311,290
Elementary Schools, Diocesan and Parish	44	31	5	16	5	8	5,614
Total Students	11,849	8,026	723	3,626	1,260	2,193	1,457,160
Elementary Schools, Private	7	6	–	1	–	3	376
Total Students	2,060	1,730	–	367	–	932	90,052
Non–residential Schools for the Disabled	–	–	–	–	–	–	66
Total Students	–	–	–	–	–	–	6,329
Religious Education High School Students	20,125	11,361	1,723	8,108	1,439	9,018	687,174
Religious Education Elementary Students	67,747	32,315	4,081	29,416	6,632	29,980	3,055,645
Priests Teaching	–	26	1	6	–	1	1,346
Scholastics Teaching	–	–	–	–	–	–	99
Brothers Teaching	–	24	–	3	–	7	882
Sisters Teaching	21	62	5	13	2	10	4,956
Lay Teachers	1,428	1,573	80	629	139	274	162,555
Infant Baptisms	11,534	9,980	1,211	8,182	1,272	8,681	857,410
Adult Baptisms	1,782	426	53	467	139	170	43,279
Received into Full Communion	775	701	181	1,107	–	804	75,724
First Communions	19,588	9,162	921	7,453	1,407	7,023	806,576
Confirmations	9,857	5,846	498	4,308	670	3,700	628,362
Marriages	3,472	1,964	214	1,600	301	1,190	179,576
Deaths	3,720	4,530	345	1,676	776	2,778	429,539
Total Catholics	1,146,908	702,547	40,310	321,197	73,327	1,021,861	68,503,456
Total Population	5,811,010	2,315,988	422,500	2,699,324	597,684	1,202,189	310,252,317
Catholic Population Percentage	20	30	10	12	12	85	22

Archdioceses = 37; Dioceses = 169; Apostolates = 3

2010 GENERAL SUMMARY

	Corpus Christi TX	Dallas TX	El Paso TX	Fort Worth TX	Laredo TX	Lubbock TX	2010 U.S. GRAND TOTAL
Cardinals	–	–	–	–	–	–	**13**
Archbishops	–	–	–	–	–	–	**59**
Bishop	3	5	1	1	1	1	**390**
Abbots	–	1	–	–	–	–	**110**
Diocesan Priests	111	99	77	70	30	47	**27,614**
Religious Priests	35	77	41	52	19	7	**13,174**
Total Priests in Diocese	146	176	118	122	49	54	**40,788**
Newly Ordained Priests	7	2	–	2	–	1	**472**
Total Permanent Deacons	85	148	25	143	34	49	**17,165**
Total Brothers	7	25	10	9	6	–	**4,737**
Total Sisters	145	133	127	65	6	19	**58,724**
Number of Parishes	68	67	57	89	32	62	**18,372**
Missions	32	6	19	2	17	–	**2,680**
Pastoral Centers	3	3	–	–	–	–	**619**
New Parishes	–	–	–	–	–	–	**83**
Catholic Hospitals	6	–	–	–	–	2	**561**
Patients Assisted Annually	516,150	–	–	–	–	290,800	**86,525,713**
Health Care Centers	6	–	2	–	–	20	**380**
Patients Assisted Annually	75,385	–	62,885	–	–	57,600	**6,332,721**
Specialized Homes	4	1	1	4	1	–	**1,593**
Total Assisted Anually	2,160	49	330	342	762	–	**1,600,986**
Residential Care of Children (Orphanages)	–	–	–	–	1	–	**358**
Total Assisted Anually	–	–	–	–	57	–	**28,663**
Day Care and Extended Day Care Centers	–	1	–	–	–	–	**975**
Total Assisted Anually	–	100	–	–	–	–	**121,593**
Special Centers for Social Services	13	7	3	18	2	1	**2,863**
Total Assisted Anually	206,562	57,109	40,878	82,939	151,685	30,000	**24,865,474**
Diocesan Seminaries	–	2	1	–	–	–	**72**
Students	–	65	13	–	–	–	**3,319**
Religious Seminaries	1	1	1	–	–	–	**108**
Students	6	17	12	–	–	–	**1,812**
Colleges and Universities	1	1	–	1	–	–	**234**
Total Students	20	2,883	–	50	–	–	**768,541**
High Schools, Diocesan and Parish	1	3	–	5	1	1	**748**
Total Students	380	2,349	–	1,479	436	49	**335,956**
High Schools, Private	1	4	3	–	–	–	**590**
Total Students	314	2,341	1,130	–	–	–	**311,290**
Elementary Schools, Diocesan and Parish	14	28	8	16	5	2	**5,614**
Total Students	2,416	9,704	2,444	4,753	1,209	411	**1,457,160**
Elementary Schools, Private	3	2	2	1	1	–	**376**
Total Students	620	524	460	180	580	–	**90,052**
Non–residential Schools for the Disabled	–	1	–	–	–	–	**66**
Total Students	–	144	–	–	–	–	**6,329**
Religious Education High School Students	3,726	6,882	6,974	10,135	2,586	1,885	**687,174**
Religious Education Elementary Students	10,160	41,360	11,762	21,320	6,458	4,552	**3,055,645**
Priests Teaching	10	17	–	–	1	–	**1,346**
Scholastics Teaching	–	3	–	–	–	–	**99**
Brothers Teaching	6	8	6	–	1	–	**882**
Sisters Teaching	37	23	13	15	7	2	**4,956**
Lay Teachers	282	1,259	290	525	147	52	**162,555**
Infant Baptisms	2,517	16,931	4,662	5,658	2,692	1,163	**857,410**
Adult Baptisms	188	1,037	165	257	55	150	**43,279**
Received into Full Communion	294	762	215	753	56	132	**75,724**
First Communions	2,649	11,271	4,721	5,941	3,100	1,134	**806,576**
Confirmations	1,427	7,444	3,697	3,767	1,450	860	**628,362**
Marriages	847	1,485	749	1,150	428	276	**179,576**
Deaths	1,737	1,363	2,108	1,077	1,056	541	**429,539**
Total Catholics	391,182	1,181,980	649,648	573,529	279,046	80,742	**68,503,456**
Total Population	558,831	3,785,477	826,611	3,189,134	328,290	451,995	**310,252,317**
Catholic Population Percentage	70	31	79	18	85	18	**22**

*Indicates Archdioceses.

†Certain Diocese traverse state lines.

	San Angelo TX	Tyler TX	Victoria in Texas TX	TEXAS TOTAL	Salt Lake City UT	Burlington VT	2010 U.S. GRAND TOTAL
Cardinals	–	–	–	1	–	–	**13**
Archbishops	–	–	–	2	–	–	**59**
Bishop	1	1	1	27	1	2	**390**
Abbots	–	–	–	1	3	–	**110**
Diocesan Priests	52	75	55	1,271	53	105	**27,614**
Religious Priests	9	11	6	776	24	37	**13,174**
Total Priests in Diocese	61	86	61	2,047	77	142	**40,788**
Newly Ordained Priests	–	3	1	39	–	4	**472**
Total Permanent Deacons	61	93	29	1,763	80	50	**17,165**
Total Brothers	–	1	2	229	10	22	**4,737**
Total Sisters	17	54	85	2,073	40	121	**58,724**
Number of Parishes	47	44	50	1,053	48	77	**18,372**
Missions	22	28	17	268	19	37	**2,680**
Pastoral Centers	–	1	–	31	–	1	**619**
New Parishes	–	–	–	2	–	2	**83**
Catholic Hospitals	–	3	–	25	–	–	**561**
Patients Assisted Annually	–	1,167,073	–	4,515,473	–	–	**86,525,713**
Health Care Centers	–	–	–	45	–	–	**380**
Patients Assisted Annually	–	–	–	372,618	–	–	**6,332,721**
Specialized Homes	–	–	–	44	1	4	**1,593**
Total Assisted Anually	–	–	–	348,267	1,100	175	**1,600,986**
Residential Care of Children (Orphanages)	–	–	–	8	–	–	**358**
Total Assisted Anually	–	–	–	1,707	–	–	**28,663**
Day Care and Extended Day Care Centers	–	–	–	51	4	–	**975**
Total Assisted Anually	–	–	–	5,185	485	–	**121,593**
Special Centers for Social Services	–	9	–	90	3	1	**2,863**
Total Assisted Anually	–	25,000	–	1,428,693	47,500	10,364	**24,865,474**
Diocesan Seminaries	–	–	–	6	–	–	**72**
Students	–	–	–	253	–	–	**3,319**
Religious Seminaries	–	–	–	12	1	–	**108**
Students	–	–	–	70	–	–	**1,812**
Colleges and Universities	–	–	–	10	–	2	**234**
Total Students	–	–	–	25,478	–	2,924	**768,541**
High Schools, Diocesan and Parish	–	1	2	25	3	2	**748**
Total Students	–	221	190	7,422	1,713	451	**335,956**
High Schools, Private	–	–	1	29	–	–	**590**
Total Students	–	–	407	12,476	–	–	**311,290**
Elementary Schools, Diocesan and Parish	3	5	11	201	13	10	**5,614**
Total Students	764	814	2,141	52,333	3,862	1,393	**1,457,160**
Elementary Schools, Private	–	–	1	27	–	2	**376**
Total Students	–	–	357	7,810	–	477	**90,052**
Non–residential Schools for the Disabled	–	–	–	1	–	–	**66**
Total Students	–	–	–	144	–	–	**6,329**
Religious Education High School Students	4,324	1,191	2,478	91,955	1,745	1,713	**687,174**
Religious Education Elementary Students	8,362	5,703	5,767	285,615	7,825	5,041	**3,055,645**
Priests Teaching	–	2	–	64	1	1	**1,346**
Scholastics Teaching	–	–	–	3	–	–	**99**
Brothers Teaching	–	–	–	55	–	–	**882**
Sisters Teaching	1	–	16	227	2	–	**4,956**
Lay Teachers	51	108	238	7,075	313	398	**162,555**
Infant Baptisms	1,795	2,492	1,547	80,317	4,108	870	**857,410**
Adult Baptisms	176	102	57	5,224	326	64	**43,279**
Received into Full Communion	239	367	96	6,482	724	121	**75,724**
First Communions	1,581	2,056	1,349	79,356	3,161	999	**806,576**
Confirmations	1,303	2,948	1,019	48,794	1,880	897	**628,362**
Marriages	373	355	429	14,833	452	406	**179,576**
Deaths	609	338	894	23,548	551	1,383	**429,539**
Total Catholics	84,520	67,594	152,612	6,767,003	250,000	118,000	**68,503,456**
Total Population	792,891	1,359,507	276,846	24,618,277	2,736,424	623,000	**310,252,317**
Catholic Population Percentage	11	5	55	27	9	19	**22**

Archdioceses = 37; Dioceses = 169; Apostolates = 3

2010 GENERAL SUMMARY

	St. Thomas Virgin Islands	Arlington VA	Richmond VA	VIRGINIA TOTAL	*Seattle WA	Spokane WA	2010 U.S. GRAND TOTAL
Cardinals	–	–	–	–	–	–	13
Archbishops	–	–	–	–	2	–	59
Bishop	2	2	2	4	2	1	390
Abbots	–	3	1	4	2	1	110
Diocesan Priests	13	160	149	309	196	83	27,614
Religious Priests	4	62	27	89	92	79	13,174
Total Priests in Diocese	17	222	176	398	288	162	40,788
Newly Ordained Priests	–	3	1	4	6	–	472
Total Permanent Deacons	29	63	82	145	118	53	17,165
Total Brothers	2	15	–	15	18	7	4,737
Total Sisters	23	140	–	140	420	189	58,724
Number of Parishes	8	68	146	214	144	82	18,372
Missions	1	6	4	10	27	2	2,680
Pastoral Centers	–	–	–	–	9	1	619
New Parishes	–	–	–	–	1	–	83
Catholic Hospitals	–	–	10	10	11	6	561
Patients Assisted Annually	–	–	680,000	680,000	1,192,915	562,984	86,525,713
Health Care Centers	–	–	–	–	2	–	380
Patients Assisted Annually	–	–	–	–	12,517	–	6,332,721
Specialized Homes	–	2	25	27	29	5	1,593
Total Assisted Anually	–	–	13,000	13,000	7,941	2,749	1,600,986
Residential Care of Children (Orphanages)	–	–	–	–	227	1	358
Total Assisted Anually	–	–	–	–	553	31	28,663
Day Care and Extended Day Care Centers	–	–	2	2	3	1	975
Total Assisted Anually	–	–	100	100	276	241	121,593
Special Centers for Social Services	3	10	–	10	111	17	2,863
Total Assisted Anually	700	29,162	–	29,162	48,842	194,049	24,865,474
Diocesan Seminaries	–	–	–	–	–	1	72
Students	–	–	–	–	–	20	3,319
Religious Seminaries	–	–	–	–	–	–	108
Students	–	–	–	–	–	–	1,812
Colleges and Universities	–	4	–	4	2	1	234
Total Students	–	6,122	–	6,122	9,438	7,701	768,541
High Schools, Diocesan and Parish	2	4	5	9	5	1	748
Total Students	197	3,456	1,091	4,547	2,459	113	335,956
High Schools, Private	–	2	3	5	6	2	590
Total Students	–	724	842	1,566	3,727	1,103	311,290
Elementary Schools, Diocesan and Parish	3	38	23	61	57	14	5,614
Total Students	526	13,025	7,336	20,361	15,772	3,305	1,457,160
Elementary Schools, Private	–	1	2	3	5	–	376
Total Students	–	200	750	950	1,059	–	90,052
Non–residential Schools for the Disabled	–	–	–	–	–	–	66
Total Students	–	–	–	–	–	–	6,329
Religious Education High School Students	139	2,794	5,358	8,152	6,580	753	687,174
Religious Education Elementary Students	389	34,659	16,169	50,828	29,850	2,140	3,055,645
Priests Teaching	1	–	1	1	13	–	1,346
Scholastics Teaching	–	–	–	–	–	–	99
Brothers Teaching	1	–	4	4	3	–	882
Sisters Teaching	–	19	16	35	11	–	4,956
Lay Teachers	75	803	943	1,746	1,465	229	162,555
Infant Baptisms	234	6,692	3,388	10,080	6,822	1,259	857,410
Adult Baptisms	10	553	42	595	482	127	43,279
Received into Full Communion	16	1,211	852	2,063	436	136	75,724
First Communions	212	8,291	3,425	11,716	6,015	1,321	806,576
Confirmations	132	6,373	2,266	8,639	4,300	1,620	628,362
Marriages	66	1,444	1,011	2,455	1,365	313	179,576
Deaths	169	1,630	1,695	3,325	2,685	592	429,539
Total Catholics	30,000	431,386	232,456	663,842	579,500	103,000	68,503,456
Total Population	120,917	2,826,999	4,942,090	7,769,089	5,202,500	792,306	310,252,317
Catholic Population Percentage	25	15	5	9	11	13	22

*Indicates Archdioceses.

†Certain Diocese traverse state lines.

	Yakima WA	WASHINGTON TOTAL	Wheeling-Charleston WV	*Milwaukee WI	Green Bay WI	La Crosse WI	2010 U.S. GRAND TOTAL
Cardinals	–	–	–	–	–	–	13
Archbishops	–	2	–	2	–	–	59
Bishop	1	4	2	3	3	–	390
Abbots	–	3	–	3	2	–	110
Diocesan Priests	75	354	112	342	187	166	27,614
Religious Priests	7	178	52	321	97	18	13,174
Total Priests in Diocese	82	532	164	663	284	184	40,788
Newly Ordained Priests	4	10	3	8	2	–	472
Total Permanent Deacons	26	197	45	171	133	42	17,165
Total Brothers	3	28	12	61	36	4	4,737
Total Sisters	33	642	163	1,402	489	393	58,724
Number of Parishes	41	267	111	210	157	165	18,372
Missions	3	32	20	–	2	–	2,680
Pastoral Centers	1	11	4	–	17	–	619
New Parishes	–	1	–	–	–	–	83
Catholic Hospitals	–	17	3	10	8	9	561
Patients Assisted Annually	–	1,755,899	723,835	1,212,268	1,050,383	608,548	86,525,713
Health Care Centers	1	3	–	1	–	–	380
Patients Assisted Annually	73,658	86,175	–	10,250	–	–	6,332,721
Specialized Homes	–	34	1	21	19	16	1,593
Total Assisted Anually	–	10,690	16	5,255	9,082	10,921	1,600,986
Residential Care of Children (Orphanages)	–	228	1	–	–	–	358
Total Assisted Anually	–	584	17	–	–	–	28,663
Day Care and Extended Day Care Centers	1	5	2	4	2	2	975
Total Assisted Anually	174	691	200	580	110	144	121,593
Special Centers for Social Services	5	133	11	12	8	2	2,863
Total Assisted Anually	49,389	292,280	41,723	160,627	214,584	3,085	24,865,474
Diocesan Seminaries	–	1	–	1	–	1	72
Students	–	20	–	21	–	8	3,319
Religious Seminaries	–	–	–	2	1	–	108
Students	–	–	–	149	3	–	1,812
Colleges and Universities	–	3	1	5	2	1	234
Total Students	–	17,139	1,288	25,418	3,677	3,088	768,541
High Schools, Diocesan and Parish	–	6	7	7	5	7	748
Total Students	–	2,572	1,649	3,541	1,329	1,565	335,956
High Schools, Private	1	9	–	6	1	–	590
Total Students	190	5,020	–	2,960	720	–	311,290
Elementary Schools, Diocesan and Parish	6	77	25	104	55	63	5,614
Total Students	1,572	20,649	4,784	27,407	9,132	7,138	1,457,160
Elementary Schools, Private	–	5	–	2	–	–	376
Total Students	–	1,059	–	203	–	–	90,052
Non-residential Schools for the Disabled	–	–	–	1	–	–	66
Total Students	–	–	–	11	–	–	6,329
Religious Education High School Students	1,862	9,195	861	6,501	9,075	3,798	687,174
Religious Education Elementary Students	5,709	37,699	4,205	29,545	20,320	12,471	3,055,645
Priests Teaching	–	13	–	53	3	10	1,346
Scholastics Teaching	–	–	–	–	–	–	99
Brothers Teaching	3	6	2	12	–	–	882
Sisters Teaching	6	17	4	110	14	17	4,956
Lay Teachers	112	1,806	469	4,124	740	832	162,555
Infant Baptisms	3,315	11,396	812	7,298	3,729	2,307	857,410
Adult Baptisms	109	718	173	192	102	150	43,279
Received into Full Communion	205	777	185	442	190	227	75,724
First Communions	2,501	9,837	872	7,776	3,725	2,529	806,576
Confirmations	1,164	7,084	885	5,664	3,143	2,491	628,362
Marriages	442	2,120	387	1,942	1,216	818	179,576
Deaths	521	3,798	967	4,969	2,954	1,983	429,539
Total Catholics	78,317	760,817	82,996	657,519	304,614	196,246	68,503,456
Total Population	649,846	6,644,652	1,814,468	2,315,958	989,997	849,626	310,252,317
Catholic Population Percentage	12	11	5	28	31	23	22

Archdioceses = 37; Dioceses = 169; Apostolates = 3

2010 GENERAL SUMMARY

	Madison WI	Superior WI	WISCONSIN TOTAL	† Cheyenne WY	EASTERN RITE *Philadelphia	EASTERN RITE *Pittsburgh	2010 U.S. GRAND TOTAL
Cardinals	–	–	–	–	–	–	13
Archbishops	–	–	2	–	2	1	59
Bishop	3	2	11	2	1	–	390
Abbots	–	–	5	–	–	1	110
Diocesan Priests	136	65	896	52	47	55	27,614
Religious Priests	18	7	461	9	5	7	13,174
Total Priests in Diocese	154	72	1,357	61	52	62	40,788
Newly Ordained Priests	3	2	15	1	1	1	472
Total Permanent Deacons	20	71	437	22	7	16	17,165
Total Brothers	6	–	107	–	–	3	4,737
Total Sisters	396	77	2,757	16	55	80	58,724
Number of Parishes	132	105	769	36	66	79	18,372
Missions	–	–	2	36	–	2	2,680
Pastoral Centers	–	–	17	–	–	3	619
New Parishes	–	–	–	–	–	–	83
Catholic Hospitals	3	6	36	–	–	–	561
Patients Assisted Annually	444,437	328,992	3,644,628	–	–	–	86,525,713
Health Care Centers	3	2	6	–	–	–	380
Patients Assisted Annually	137,095	195	147,540	–	–	–	6,332,721
Specialized Homes	6	12	74	2	2	2	1,593
Total Assisted Anually	567	363	26,188	104	280	553	1,600,986
Residential Care of Children (Orphanages)	–	–	–	1	–	–	358
Total Assisted Anually	–	–	–	242	–	–	28,663
Day Care and Extended Day Care Centers	23	2	33	–	–	–	975
Total Assisted Anually	909	256	1,999	–	–	–	121,593
Special Centers for Social Services	14	7	43	4	–	–	2,863
Total Assisted Anually	45,588	2,985	426,869	10,804	–	–	24,865,474
Diocesan Seminaries	–	–	2	–	1	1	72
Students	–	–	29	–	14	8	3,319
Religious Seminaries	–	–	3	–	–	–	108
Students	–	–	152	–	–	–	1,812
Colleges and Universities	1	–	9	–	1	–	234
Total Students	2,550	–	34,733	–	969	–	768,541
High Schools, Diocesan and Parish	–	–	19	–	–	–	748
Total Students	–	–	6,435	–	–	–	335,956
High Schools, Private	2	–	9	–	1	–	590
Total Students	739	–	4,419	–	380	–	311,290
Elementary Schools, Diocesan and Parish	44	16	282	7	4	–	5,614
Total Students	7,198	2,482	53,357	975	674	–	1,457,160
Elementary Schools, Private	2	–	4	–	–	–	376
Total Students	313	–	516	–	–	–	90,052
Non–residential Schools for the Disabled	–	–	1	–	–	–	66
Total Students	–	–	11	–	–	–	6,329
Religious Education High School Students	6,212	2,142	27,728	811	120	311	687,174
Religious Education Elementary Students	12,326	4,996	79,658	2,987	509	933	3,055,645
Priests Teaching	–	–	66	–	1	–	1,346
Scholastics Teaching	–	–	–	–	–	–	99
Brothers Teaching	2	–	14	–	–	–	882
Sisters Teaching	10	5	156	2	6	–	4,956
Lay Teachers	587	244	6,527	103	64	–	162,555
Infant Baptisms	2,522	788	16,644	926	222	159	857,410
Adult Baptisms	81	23	548	127	7	16	43,279
Received into Full Communion	171	79	1,109	139	52	44	75,724
First Communions	2,667	855	17,552	982	217	189	806,576
Confirmations	2,146	747	14,191	818	250	193	628,362
Marriages	742	274	4,992	301	69	68	179,576
Deaths	1,667	873	12,446	578	417	458	429,539
Total Catholics	278,578	78,826	1,515,783	51,467	14,980	58,763	68,503,456
Total Population	996,348	454,412	5,606,341	532,000	–	–	310,252,317
Catholic Population Percentage	28	17	27	10			22

*Indicates Archdioceses.

†Certain Diocese traverse state lines.

	EASTERN RITE (con't.) Lady of Deliverance	Lady of Lebanon	Lady of Nareg	Newton	Parma	Passaic	2010 U.S. GRAND TOTAL
Cardinals	–	–	–	–	–	–	13
Archbishops	–	–	–	1	–	–	59
Bishop	1	2	1	2	1	2	390
Abbots	–	–	–	–	–	–	110
Diocesan Priests	11	34	3	46	42	70	27,614
Religious Priests	–	15	8	14	1	13	13,174
Total Priests in Diocese	11	49	11	60	43	83	40,788
Newly Ordained Priests	–	–	–	–	–	–	472
Total Permanent Deacons	3	17	1	51	13	27	17,165
Total Brothers	–	–	–	–	–	1	4,737
Total Sisters	–	5	7	–	8	17	58,724
Number of Parishes	9	28	7	40	30	84	18,372
Missions	4	10	–	4	5	4	2,680
Pastoral Centers	–	–	–	–	1	–	619
New Parishes	–	–	–	–	–	–	83
Catholic Hospitals	–	–	–	–	–	–	561
Patients Assisted Annually	–	–	–	–	–	–	86,525,713
Health Care Centers	–	–	–	–	–	–	380
Patients Assisted Annually	–	–	–	–	–	–	6,332,721
Specialized Homes	–	–	–	–	–	–	1,593
Total Assisted Anually	–	–	–	–	–	–	1,600,986
Residential Care of Children (Orphanages)	–	1	–	–	–	–	358
Total Assisted Anually	–	25	–	–	–	–	28,663
Day Care and Extended Day Care Centers	–	1	–	–	1	–	975
Total Assisted Anually	–	150	–	–	57	–	121,593
Special Centers for Social Services	–	–	–	–	5	–	2,863
Total Assisted Anually	–	–	–	–	16,500	–	24,865,474
Diocesan Seminaries	–	–	–	–	–	–	72
Students	–	–	–	–	–	–	3,319
Religious Seminaries	–	–	–	1	–	–	108
Students	–	–	–	2	–	–	1,812
Colleges and Universities	–	–	–	–	–	–	234
Total Students	–	–	–	–	–	–	768,541
High Schools, Diocesan and Parish	–	–	–	–	–	–	748
Total Students	–	–	–	–	–	–	335,956
High Schools, Private	–	–	1	–	–	–	590
Total Students	–	–	76	–	–	–	311,290
Elementary Schools, Diocesan and Parish	–	–	3	–	1	–	5,614
Total Students	–	–	1,048	–	170	–	1,457,160
Elementary Schools, Private	–	1	–	–	–	–	376
Total Students	–	39	–	–	–	–	90,052
Non–residential Schools for the Disabled	–	–	–	–	–	–	66
Total Students	–	–	–	–	–	–	6,329
Religious Education High School Students	54	555	–	200	118	184	687,174
Religious Education Elementary Students	324	1,456	–	1,199	375	752	3,055,645
Priests Teaching	–	–	–	–	–	–	1,346
Scholastics Teaching	–	–	–	–	–	–	99
Brothers Teaching	–	–	–	–	–	–	882
Sisters Teaching	–	–	–	–	3	–	4,956
Lay Teachers	–	1	–	–	9	–	162,555
Infant Baptisms	54	406	81	210	73	124	857,410
Adult Baptisms	6	32	4	10	6	5	43,279
Received into Full Communion	6	16	–	12	19	6	75,724
First Communions	60	348	39	219	50	131	806,576
Confirmations	60	411	87	230	69	126	628,362
Marriages	38	134	61	69	22	48	179,576
Deaths	22	192	–	–	138	478	429,539
Total Catholics	18,200	45,232	25,000	24,791	8,752	17,360	68,503,456
Total Population	–	–	–	–	–	–	310,252,317
Catholic Population Percentage							22

Archdioceses = 37; Dioceses = 169; Apostolates = 3

2010 GENERAL SUMMARY

	EASTERN RITE (con't.) Romanian	St. Josaphat	St. Maron	St. Nicholas	St. Peter the Apostle	St. Thomas the Apostle	2010 U.S. GRAND TOTAL
Cardinals	–	–	–	–	–	–	13
Archbishops	–	–	1	–	–	–	59
Bishop	1	1	2	2	1	1	390
Abbots	1	–	1	1	–	–	110
Diocesan Priests	20	47	51	34	13	15	27,614
Religious Priests	3	1	12	8	5	–	13,174
Total Priests in Diocese	23	48	63	42	18	15	40,788
Newly Ordained Priests	1	4	–	2	–	–	472
Total Permanent Deacons	3	8	17	8	9	120	17,165
Total Brothers	5	3	7	–	–	–	4,737
Total Sisters	4	3	1	4	12	11	58,724
Number of Parishes	13	38	34	40	9	8	18,372
Missions	5	4	5	6	–	–	2,680
Pastoral Centers	–	–	1	1	–	–	619
New Parishes	–	–	–	–	–	–	83
Catholic Hospitals	–	–	–	–	–	–	561
Patients Assisted Annually	–	–	–	–	–	–	86,525,713
Health Care Centers	–	–	–	–	–	–	380
Patients Assisted Annually	–	–	–	–	–	–	6,332,721
Specialized Homes	–	3	–	–	2	1	1,593
Total Assisted Anually	–	173	–	–	96	60	1,600,986
Residential Care of Children (Orphanages)	–	–	–	–	–	–	358
Total Assisted Anually	–	–	–	–	–	–	28,663
Day Care and Extended Day Care Centers	–	–	–	–	–	–	975
Total Assisted Anually	–	–	–	–	–	–	121,593
Special Centers for Social Services	–	–	–	–	–	1	2,863
Total Assisted Anually	–	–	–	–	–	130	24,865,474
Diocesan Seminaries	–	–	1	–	–	–	72
Students	–	–	8	–	–	–	3,319
Religious Seminaries	–	–	–	–	–	–	108
Students	–	–	–	–	–	–	1,812
Colleges and Universities	–	–	–	–	–	–	234
Total Students	–	–	–	–	–	–	768,541
High Schools, Diocesan and Parish	–	–	–	–	–	–	748
Total Students	–	–	–	–	–	–	335,956
High Schools, Private	–	–	–	–	–	–	590
Total Students	–	–	–	–	–	–	311,290
Elementary Schools, Diocesan and Parish	–	–	–	2	–	–	5,614
Total Students	–	–	–	245	–	–	1,457,160
Elementary Schools, Private	–	–	–	–	–	–	376
Total Students	–	–	–	–	–	–	90,052
Non–residential Schools for the Disabled	–	–	–	–	–	–	66
Total Students	–	–	–	–	–	–	6,329
Religious Education High School Students	47	43	315	40	–	–	687,174
Religious Education Elementary Students	68	20	1,597	105	–	–	3,055,645
Priests Teaching	–	–	–	–	–	–	1,346
Scholastics Teaching	–	–	–	–	–	–	99
Brothers Teaching	–	–	–	–	–	–	882
Sisters Teaching	–	–	–	2	–	–	4,956
Lay Teachers	–	–	–	20	–	–	162,555
Infant Baptisms	39	89	391	150	401	901	857,410
Adult Baptisms	2	5	17	4	2	14	43,279
Received into Full Communion	8	–	18	7	–	–	75,724
First Communions	39	32	320	132	333	609	806,576
Confirmations	38	94	461	161	405	–	628,362
Marriages	15	37	108	48	123	342	179,576
Deaths	23	189	264	183	111	194	429,539
Total Catholics	5,869	10,685	30,200	13,915	49,563	120,000	68,503,456
Total Population	–	–	–	–	–	–	310,252,317
Catholic Population Percentage							22

*Indicates Archdioceses.

†Certain Diocese traverse state lines.

	EASTERN RITE (con't.) St. Thomas Syro-Malabar	Stamford	Van Nuys	EASTERN RITE TOTAL	*Military Archdiocese		2010 U.S. GRAND TOTAL
Cardinals	–	–	–	–	–	–	13
Archbishops	–	–	–	5	2	–	59
Bishop	1	2	1	22	4	–	390
Abbots	–	–	–	4	–	–	110
Diocesan Priests	35	36	25	584	–	–	27,614
Religious Priests	9	17	1	119	–	–	13,174
Total Priests in Diocese	45	53	26	703	–	–	40,788
Newly Ordained Priests	–	–	–	9	–	–	472
Total Permanent Deacons	–	10	11	321	–	–	17,165
Total Brothers	–	1	2	22	–	–	4,737
Total Sisters	15	33	3	258	–	–	58,724
Number of Parishes	18	51	19	573	–	–	18,372
Missions	38	3	1	91	–	–	2,680
Pastoral Centers	–	–	–	5	–	–	619
New Parishes	4	–	–	4	–	–	83
Catholic Hospitals	–	–	–	–	–	–	561
Patients Assisted Annually	–	–	–	–	–	–	86,525,713
Health Care Centers	–	–	–	–	–	–	380
Patients Assisted Annually	–	–	–	–	–	–	6,332,721
Specialized Homes	–	1	–	11	–	–	1,593
Total Assisted Anually	–	21	–	1,183	–	–	1,600,986
Residential Care of Children (Orphanages)	–	–	–	1	–	–	358
Total Assisted Anually	–	–	–	25	–	–	28,663
Day Care and Extended Day Care Centers	–	1	–	3	–	–	975
Total Assisted Anually	–	44	–	251	–	–	121,593
Special Centers for Social Services	–	–	–	6	–	–	2,863
Total Assisted Anually	130	–	–	16,630	–	–	24,865,474
Diocesan Seminaries	–	1	–	4	–	–	72
Students	–	3	–	33	–	–	3,319
Religious Seminaries	–	–	–	1	–	–	108
Students	–	–	–	2	–	–	1,812
Colleges and Universities	–	–	–	1	–	–	234
Total Students	–	–	–	969	–	–	768,541
High Schools, Diocesan and Parish	–	1	–	1	–	–	748
Total Students	–	200	–	200	–	–	335,956
High Schools, Private	–	–	–	2	–	–	590
Total Students	–	–	–	456	–	–	311,290
Elementary Schools, Diocesan and Parish	–	2	–	12	–	–	5,614
Total Students	–	200	–	2,337	–	–	1,457,160
Elementary Schools, Private	–	–	–	1	–	–	376
Total Students	–	–	–	39	–	–	90,052
Non–residential Schools for the Disabled	–	–	–	–	–	–	66
Total Students	–	–	–	–	–	–	6,329
Religious Education High School Students	1,492	330	82	3,891	–	–	687,174
Religious Education Elementary Students	3,139	919	328	11,824	–	–	3,055,645
Priests Teaching	–	–	–	2	–	–	1,346
Scholastics Teaching	–	–	–	–	–	–	99
Brothers Teaching	–	–	–	–	–	–	882
Sisters Teaching	–	5	–	16	–	–	4,956
Lay Teachers	–	20	–	114	–	–	162,555
Infant Baptisms	259	183	73	3,815	4,926	–	857,410
Adult Baptisms	38	4	12	184	825	–	43,279
Received into Full Communion	57	2	–	247	358	–	75,724
First Communions	617	137	95	3,567	2,771	–	806,576
Confirmations	633	186	96	3,500	2,165	–	628,362
Marriages	77	78	24	1,361	701	–	179,576
Deaths	42	347	27	3,085	–	–	429,539
Total Catholics	85,000	16,000	2,561	546,871	–	–	68,503,456
Total Population	–	–	–	–	–	–	310,252,317
Catholic Population Percentage				–	–	–	22

Archdioceses = 37; Dioceses = 169; Apostolates = 3

2010 GENERAL SUMMARY

					2000 GRAND TOTAL	2009 GRAND TOTAL	2010 U.S. GRAND TOTAL
Cardinals	–	–	–	–	9	13	**13**
Archbishops	–	–	–	–	50	58	**59**
Bishop	–	–	–	–	366	391	**390**
Abbots	–	–	–	–	114	111	**110**
Diocesan Priests	–	–	–	–	30,940	28,061	**27,614**
Religious Priests	–	–	–	–	15,465	13,428	**13,174**
Total Priests in Diocese	–	–	–	–	46,603	41,489	**40,788**
Newly Ordained Priests	–	–	–	–	463	482	**472**
Total Permanent Deacons	–	–	–	–	12,862	16,935	**17,165**
Total Brothers	–	–	–	–	5,736	4,905	**4,737**
Total Sisters	–	–	–	–	81,161	60,715	**58,724**
Number of Parishes	–	–	–	–	19,627	18,674	**18,372**
Missions	–	–	–	–	2,965	2,790	**2,680**
Pastoral Centers	–		–	–	1,147	661	**619**
New Parishes	–	–	–	–	49	91	**83**
Catholic Hospitals	–	–	–	–	593	562	**561**
Patients Assisted Annually	–	–	–	–	77,006,804	85,283,351	**86,525,713**
Health Care Centers	–	–	–	–	557	373	**380**
Patients Assisted Annually	–	–	–	–	5,868,006	6,703,167	**6,332,721**
Specialized Homes	–	–	–	–	1,414	1,643	**1,593**
Total Assisted Anually	–	–	–	–	504,558	936,900	**1,600,986**
Residential Care of Children (Orphanages)	–	–	–	–	149	403	**358**
Total Assisted Anually	–	–	–	–	78,858	33,952	**28,663**
Day Care and Extended Day Care Centers	–	–	–	–	1,152	963	**975**
Total Assisted Anually	–	–	–	–	108,240	111,576	**121,593**
Special Centers for Social Services	–	–	–	–	2,271	3,009	**2,863**
Total Assisted Anually	–	–	–	–	20,134,669	27,213,486	**24,865,474**
Diocesan Seminaries	–	–	–	–	74	78	**72**
Students	–	–	–	–	3,088	3,274	**3,319**
Religious Seminaries	–	–	–	–	113	111	**108**
Students	–	–	–	–	1,437	1,699	**1,812**
Colleges and Universities	–	–	–	–	235	234	**234**
Total Students	–	–	–	–	701,240	795,823	**768,541**
High Schools, Diocesan and Parish	–	–	–	–	796	751	**748**
Total Students	–	–	–	–	381,311	361,653	**335,956**
High Schools, Private	–	–	–	–	557	590	**590**
Total Students	–	–	–	–	303,544	312,727	**311,290**
Elementary Schools, Diocesan and Parish	–	–	–	–	6,721	5,772	**5,614**
Total Students	–	–	–	–	1,940,285	1,518,886	**1,457,160**
Elementary Schools, Private	–	–	–	–	360	361	**376**
Total Students	–	–	–	–	92,967	90,501	**90,052**
Non–residential Schools for the Disabled	–	–	–	–	82	66	**66**
Total Students	–	–	–	–	18,342	6,304	**6,329**
Religious Education High School Students	–	–	–	–	821,833	722,599	**687,174**
Religious Education Elementary Students	–	–	–	–	3,607,108	3,080,838	**3,055,645**
Priests Teaching	–	–	–	–	1,794	1,569	**1,346**
Scholastics Teaching	–	–	–	–	49	27	**99**
Brothers Teaching	–	–	–	–	1,135	916	**882**
Sisters Teaching	–	–	–	–	9,255	5,169	**4,956**
Lay Teachers	–	–	–	–	150,561	167,861	**162,555**
Infant Baptisms	–	–	–	–	1,022,014	887,145	**857,410**
Adult Baptisms	–	–	–	–	83,157	42,629	**43,279**
Received into Full Communion	–	–	–	–	87,799	81,775	**75,724**
First Communions	–	–	–	–	884,570	821,917	**806,576**
Confirmations	–	–	–	–	629,762	622,641	**628,362**
Marriages	–	–	–	–	267,517	191,265	**179,576**
Deaths	–	–	–	–	473,724	439,347	**429,539**
Total Catholics	–	–	–	–	62,391,484	68,115,001	**68,503,456**
Total Population	–	–	–	–	273,961,528	307,630,068	**310,252,317**
Catholic Population Percentage	–	–	–	–	23	22	**22**

*Indicates Archdioceses.

†Certain Diocese traverse state lines.

U.S. Census Bureau estimate of Total Population as of Jan. 1, 2010: 309,052,808
U.S. Census Bureau estimate of Total Population as of Jan. 1, 2009: 306,207,846
U.S. Census Bureau estimate of Total Population as of Jan. 1, 2000: 274,023,981

Catholic Dioceses

2300 Wisconsin Ave NW Suite 400
Washington, DC 20007
cara.georgetown.edu

in the United States

This map shows boundaries of the Latin Rite dioceses whose bishops belong to the United States Conference of Catholic Bishops (USCCB). Archdioceses are indicated by capital letters and Ecclesiastical Provinces are grouped by color. USCCB regions are shown within maroon lines and indicated by Roman numerals. Dashed lines show where dioceses cross state lines. This map does not show the Diocese of St. Thomas in the U.S. Virgin Islands, which is part of the Ecclesiastical Province of Washington, or the Archdiocese for the Military Services.

The Official Catholic Directory

Products and Services Guide

Index to Advertisers

AUDIO & VIDEO—General

ighthouse Catholic Media, NFP
03 E. State Street
ycamore, IL 60178
el: 866-767-3155 (toll free)
ax: 815-895-0333
-mail: Tim@LighthouseCatholicMedia.org
Vebsite: www.LigthouseCatholicMedia.org

ype of Business:

Lighthouse Catholic Media, NFP is a not for profit organization dedicated to providing high quality Catholic audio CDs as an affordable and convenient way for parishioners to hear faith-filled presentations from the best Catholic speakers of our day.

These recordings provide an easy and effective way to foster catechesis, and provide parishioners with a powerful way to reach out to their family members, friends, etc.

"These CDs helped make the Mass come alive and left me with a hunger to learn more. What a blessing!"

Our FAITHRAISER Kiosk Program is proven effective, with over 3,000 parish customers, and the program is primarily self-funding.

We have over 150 CD titles available in English and Spanish, and our Starter Kit comes complete with a beautiful display stand, CDs, and pamphlets. We also provide a proven success plan, support, and assistance to make your program a success.

For more information, please call 866-767-3155.

ersonnel:

Mark Middendorf (President, Board of Directors)
Terry Barber (Chairman of the Board)
Dave Durand (Vice President of Sales)
Tim Truckenbrod (Vice President of Marketing and Operations)

Cassettes, Audio & Video

Holy Cross Family Ministries
amily Rosary
amily Theater Productions
ather Peyton Family Institute
amily Rosary International
518 Washington Street
North Easton, MA 02356
Tel: 508-238-4095
Fax: 508-238-3953
Website: www.hcfm.org

Type of Business:

Continuing the mission of our founder, Servant of God Father Patrick Peyton, C.S.C., Holy Cross Family Ministries serves Jesus Christ and His Church throughout the world by promoting and supporting the spiritual well-being of the family through products and programs.

Personnel:

Fr. John Phalen, C.S.C. (President)
Susan Wallace (Director of External Relations)
Beth Mahoney (Mission Director)

BUSINESS & FINANCE—General

United States Conference of Catholic Bishops
Office of National Collections
3211 Fourth Street, N.E.
Washington, DC 20017
Tel: 202-541-3400
Website: www.usccb.org/nationalcollections

Type of Business:

The national collections administered by the United States Conference of Catholic Bishops (USCCB) have been established by either the Holy Father or the bishops of the United States. The national collections support the Church's works of social justice, evangelization, and education, both domestically and around the globe.

Every Catholic participates in a global community of faith by contributing and acting as faithful stewards of the gifts God has given them. The national collections of the USCCB are a powerful way to express your solidarity with this community.

Capital Campaigns

Cosgriff Company
209 South 19th Street
Omaha, NE 68102
Tel: 800-456-9902
Fax: 402-341-8590
E-mail: cosgriff@cosgriffco.com
Website: www.cosgriff.com

Type of Business:

Celebrating 50 years of campaign excellence to Catholic parishes and schools. Our Catholic staff understands our mission and actively carries it out each day with prayer and hard work. We have delivered on our mission of providing successful counsel for Campaign and Feasibility Study work across the United States and abroad on over 800 projects and raised over $4.8 billion for churches and schools.

We are specialists in leadership motivation, donor solicitation strategy and low-key solicitations. We are one of the only firms to continue to provide true, full time, residential service for the duration of your campaign to assure we are attuned to every detail helping to assure your success.

Our services include free pre-study and pre-campaign guidance, advice, services and preparation. Our feasibility studies have been called, "the best in the business" because of our attention to detail and thoroughness and our campaigns have been exceeding goal since our founding in 1960.

We would be honored to talk to you about your plans and goals.
"Our only goal is to ensure you make yours." Bob Cosgriff

Personnel:

Robb Spence (Principle, President & CEO)

Guidance in Giving, Inc.
Full Service Stewardship, Development and Campaign Consultants
225 Snedecor Avenue
Bayport, NY 11705
Tel: 888-757-5444; Cell: 631-553-9064
E-mail: mcusack@guidanceingiving.com
Website: www.guidanceingiving.com

Type of Business:

Guidance In Giving, Inc. is a Catholic organization that truly understands the mission of the Catholic Church. Serving as stewardship, development and campaign counsel to dioceses, parishes and schools, our firm has extensive experience in conducting capital campaigns and implementing stewardship throughout the United States. In all of our development efforts we utilize techniques that are continuously tested and refined. Services include: diocesan capital campaigns; diocesan annual appeals; diocesan development audits and feasibility studies; parish capital campaigns; implementing stewardship; parish feasibility studies, school development audits, school feasibility studies, major gifts solicitations and school capital campaigns. Additionally, the firm has an Hispanic Division and offers bilingual services. To discuss your individual situation or to get a cost free analysis of your potential, please contact Michael R. Cusack, President and CEO at 888-757-5444.

Personnel:

Michael R. Cusack (President and CEO)
Michael V. Goodwin (Executive Vice President)
Joseph W. Zamorano (Executive Vice President)
Stephen A. Babcock (Vice President)
Joseph Neville (Vice President)
Carlos Proaño (Vice President, Hispanic Division)

Walsh & Associates
Church Fundraising and Stewardship Specialists
"Helping Churches and Church Members Reach New Heights"™

Walsh & Associates
Church Fundraising and Stewardship Specialists
1601 East Highway 13, Suite 200
Burnsville, MN 55337
Tel: 800-894-3863
Fax: 952-882-5270
E-mail: info@walshfundraising.com
Website: www.walshfundraising.com

Type of Business:

Walsh & Associates, Church Fundraising & Stewardship Specialists, has been helping Catholic churches and church members reach new heights since 1984. Our services include helping churches to prepare for and conduct successful capital campaigns and stewardship efforts. Our capital campaign services include pre-campaign feasibility and planning studies, campaign implementation and follow-up & fulfillment services and support. Our stewardship services include stewardship program evaluations, stewardship formation & education, and volunteer and financial stewardship efforts. So if you're ready to reach new heights in your fund development and stewardship efforts, give us a call. We'd be happy to help.

Personnel:

Michael A. Walsh (President)

Chaplain Services

Army Chaplain Recruiting
Commander,
U.S. Army Recruiting Command
1307 Third Avenue
Fort Knox, KY 40121
Tel: 1-800-USA-ARMY
E-mail: goarmy@usarec.army.mil
Website: chaplain.goarmy.com

Type of Business:

Chaplains are the spiritual leaders of the U.S. Army. As a Chaplai you will provide the tools that Soldiers and their Families need to st spiritually strong. If you are ordained, we have both part-time and fu time opportunities to serve our Soldiers. If you are still a seminary stude discerning your call to ministry, we can provide a part-time look into th Army Chaplain ministry allowing you to weigh any obligation against ar benefits you would receive. You have answered the Call to serve Go Now the Catholic Soldiers and their families are asking you to serve the spiritual needs. Would you consider this important call to serve God an country? The U.S. Army Chaplaincy may be the exciting opportunity yo have been seeking.
Chaplain.goarmy.com 1-800-872-2769

Personnel:

Chaplain (Captain) Paul Halladay (Roman Catholic Chaplain Recruiter)
E-mail: paul.halladay@usarec.army.mil
Chaplain (Captain) John Brocato (Roman Catholic Chaplain Recruiter)
E-mail: john.brocato@usarec.army.mil

U.S. Navy Chaplain Corps
Tel: 1-800-USA-NAVY, 1-800-USA-USNR
Websites: navy.com/chaplain; facebook.com/NavyChaplain

Type of Business:

Expand your ministry. Serve your country. Reach more individuals seekin understanding and purpose in life. And gain valuable experience to shar with your congregation at home. As a Chaplain and Priest in the Nav Chaplain Corps.
All Navy Chaplains are committed to a common cause: providing for th spiritual well-being of all Sailors and Marines, regardless of faith group.
Imagine counseling young men and women preparing to deploy overseas Offering critical moral and spiritual support to the families they leav behind. Providing a conduit to the things of God. Even helping to se policies and procedures. In short, expanding your holy service to thos who face some of life's greatest challenges.
The Navy's need for men of God is great. Learn more about the impact yo can have in the Navy Chaplain Corps – whether it be full-time or part-time Visit navy.com/chaplain for information.

DRILL SERGEANTS STRENGTHEN THEIR MINDS
CHAPLAINS STRENGTHEN THEIR SOULS
There's strong. Then there's Chaplain strong. Do your part to spiritually strengthen our troops and their Families by joining the U.S. Army Chaplaincy. Serve on the frontline of the Soldiers' lives, developing close-knit relationships rarely found in any other ministry. Will you consider the call? For more information, visit www.goarmy.com/info/chaplain/j497.
U.S.ARMY
ARMY STRONG.
©2010. Paid for by the United States Army. All rights reserved.

Church Registers

D.P. Murphy Co., Inc.
945 Grand Boulevard
Deer Park, NY 11729
Tel: 1-800-424-8724
E-mail: sales@dpmurphy.com
Website: www.dpmurphy.com

Type of Business:

For over 135 years, D. P. Murphy Company has been serving the religious community by creating quality items and providing satisfaction with both our products and service with an unconditional guarantee. With a wide range of products from simple stationery products to sophisticated Stewardship and Tithing Programs; from collections envelope systems to contribution recording and a variety of mailing services. Our commitment—to help your church fulfill their financial and administrative responsibilities by providing an innovative mailing service designed specifically for your parish, a complete line of the finest liturgical products available, quality service and all backed by a 100% Satisfaction Guarantee. For a free catalog, call 1-800-4-Church or visit us on the web at www.dpmurphy.com.

Personnel:

Timothy Murphy Schratwieser (President)

Computers & Software

PowerChurch Software
601 Alliance Court
Asheville, NC 28806
Tel: 800-486-1800
Fax: 828-665-1999
E-mail: info@powerchurch.com
Website: www.powerchurch.com

Type of Business:

PowerChurch Plus is an all-in-one software solution that helps you streamline administrative tasks and manage your Membership, Contributions, Accounting, and Event scheduling. PowerChurch Plus records comprehensive membership information, including photographs, for up to 100,000 families. Tracks contributions and pledges, and prepares contribution statements for mailing or e-mailing. Features a complete fund accounting system specially designed for churches. The Event scheduling module allows you to keep track of upcoming events, and generate Event Calendars for your website or word processing documents. Since 1984, over 31,000 churches have found that PowerChurch Plus is truly "Church Management Made Easy!" Visit www.powerchurch.com to download a free demo or to request a demo CD.

Consultants

Guidance in Giving, Inc.
Full Service Stewardship, Development and Campaign Consultants
225 Snedecor Avenue
Bayport, NY 11705
Tel: 888-757-5444; Cell: 631-553-9064
E-mail: mcusack@guidanceingiving.com
Website: www.guidanceingiving.com

Type of Business:

Guidance In Giving, Inc. is a Catholic organization that truly understands the mission of the Catholic Church. Serving as stewardship, development and campaign counsel to dioceses, parishes and schools, our firm has extensive experience in conducting capital campaigns and implementing stewardship throughout the United States. In all of our development efforts we utilize techniques that are continuously tested and refined. Services include: diocesan capital campaigns; diocesan annual appeals; diocesan development audits and feasibility studies; parish capital campaigns; implementing stewardship; parish feasibility studies, school development audits, school feasibility studies, major gifts solicitations and school capital campaigns. Additionally, the firm has an Hispanic Division and offers bilingual services. To discuss your individual situation or to get a cost free analysis of your potential, please contact Michael R. Cusack, President and CEO at 888-757-5444.

Personnel:

Michael R. Cusack (President and CEO)
Michael V. Goodwin (Executive Vice President)
Joseph W. Zamorano (Executive Vice President)
Stephen A. Babcock (Vice President)
Joseph Neville (Vice President)
Carlos Proaño (Vice President, Hispanic Division)

Rohn & Associates Design, Inc.
1113 Creedmoor Avenue
Pittsburgh, PA 15226
Tel: 412-561-1228; 800-245-1288; Fax: 412-561-1201
E-mail: rolfrohn@rohndesign.com; Website: www.rohndesign.com
Blog: http://catholicliturgicalarts.blogspot.com/
Facebook: Catholic Liturgical Arts Journal

Type of Business:

Liturgical Designers, Artists & Artisans
TRADITION. Over the past 58 years, we have assisted the Catholic Church by designing, budgeting and implementing liturgical spaces.
COLLABORATION. We work side-by-side with our clients and collaborators to design and create appropriate and quality sacred art, interior finishes, lighting systems, acoustical systems, liturgical furnishings and appointments to create a rich devotional experience for your parishioners.
EXPERIENCE. We draw upon decades of experience and from a rich treasury of designers, architectural staff and contributing artists.
SCOPE OF SERVICES: Liturgical Design; Interior Design & Decorating; Sacred Artwork; Mosaics; Art Glass; Statuary; Liturgical Appointments; Liturgical Furniture; Metalwork.
ADDITIONAL LOCATIONS: 17515 Spring Cypress, Ste C PMB #246 Cypress, TX 77429. Tel. & Fax: 281-304-7736; 719 S. Flores St., Suite 200, San Antonio, TX 78204. Tel.: 210-231-0377; Fax: 210-231-0366
Contact us to arrange a complimentary project review.

Personnel:

Rolf R. Rohn (President - Liturgical Designer-Consultant)
Kathleen L. Maglicco (Vice President, Design)
Renate Rohn (Vice President, Art)
Francesca Lofaro (Director, Sales)

Donor Walls & Trees of Life

W&E BAUM
Designers and Manufacturers
Donor Walls • Plaques • Awards • Memorials

W & E Baum
89 Bannard Street
Freehold, NJ 07728
Tel: 800-922-7377; 732-866-1881
Fax: 732-866-8978
E-mail: info@webaum.com
Website: www.webaum.com/Church-Products.html

Type of Business:

W&E BAUM, celebrating 86 years and three generations, specializes in the design and fabrication of symbols of recognition and generosity. Additional income for churches can be generated by using many of our innovative products. Our Donor Walls, Bronze Memorials, Giving Trees, Plaques, Awards, Sculptures and more, promote fund-raising efforts and acknowledge gifts of all kinds. Quality, creativity and personal attention to detail are the elements that capture the attention of potential contributors in today's sophisticated world.

To thank, to honor, to reward, to commemorate, to memorialize, W & E Baum stands ready to help you translate your vision into reality.

Our Bronze Memorial Designs are a new and innovative way for your parishioners to permanently memorialize their loved ones. These memorials provide a steady stream of income for many years.

Contact us for more details.

Personnel:

Richard Baum (President)
Maurice Zagha (CEO)
Heshy Spira (Vice President)

Financial Services

KNIGHTS OF COLUMBUS
IN SERVICE TO ONE. IN SERVICE TO ALL.

Knights of Columbus Church Loan
1 Columbus Plaza
New Haven, CT 06510
Tel: 800-380-9995
E-mail: churchloan@kofc.org
Website: kofc.org/churchloan

Type of Business:

Since 1896, the Knights of Columbus ChurchLoan program has been a leader in project financing in the United States and Canada. To date, ChurchLoan has approved more than $600 million in loans to Catholic dioceses, parishes, schools, hospitals, religious orders and other institutions. ChurchLoan serves as an investment supporting K of C insurance policyholders as well as a practical opportunity for the organization to further the growth of the worldwide Catholic community.

Secured loans may be used to replace a construction loan, purchase property or refinance existing debt. ChurchLoan offers competitive fixed rates and maturities up to 20 years. Each loan requires approval and guarantee by the appropriate diocese or religious order and a loan-to-value ratio of 75 percent or less. Unsecured loans are also available for up to five years in amounts of $500,000 or less.

Investment Advisors

CBIS Christian Brothers Investment Services, Inc.

Christian Brothers Investment Services, Inc.
90 Park Avenue, 29th Floor
New York, NY 10016-1301
Tel: 800-592-8890 or 212-490-0800
Fax: 212-490-6092
Website: www.cbisonline.com

Type of Business:

Christian Brothers Investment Services, Inc. (CBIS) manages nearly $3.6 billion for Catholic organizations seeks to combine faith and finance through the responsible stewardship of Catholic assets. CBIS' combination of premier institutional asset managers, diversified product offerings, and careful risk-control strategies constitutes a unique investment approach for Catholic institutions and their fiduciaries. CBIS strives to integrate faith-based values into the investment process through a disciplined approach to socially responsible investing that includes principled purchasing (stock screens), active ownership strategies (proxy voting, dialogues, and shareholder resolutions), and community investing. The firm contributes a portion of all profits to support the Church's educational and social ministry.

For Catholic organizations seeking to unify faith and finance, CBIS welcomes the opportunity to serve you.

Please contact Fred Devlin at 877-550-2247 ext. 0823 or e-mail: fdevlin@cbisonline.com.

Personnel:

Michael W. O'Hern, FSC (President & CEO)
Fred Devlin (Vice President)

CHURCH ART—General

BOTTI STUDIO OF ARCHITECTURAL ARTS, INC.

Botti Studio of Architectural Arts, Inc.
919 Grove Street
Evanston, IL 60201
Tel: 800-524-7211; 847-869-5933
Fax: 847-869-5996
E-mail: botti@bottistudio.com
Website: www.bottistudio.com

Type of Business:

Since 1864, Botti Studio has specialized in serving the ecclesiastic environment through design, fabrication, delivery, and installation. Experts on staff in new design commissions, repair, restoration, conservation, and repair provide a source for experienced project management – from conception through completion. Services include: stained, faceted, sandblasted, carved and painted glass, wood / metal / stone frames / protective glazing, murals, marble, mosaics, bronze, statuary, gilding, painting and decorating, complete interiors, new and restorations, historic discovery, documentation and consultation to owner / architect.

Our staff of 45 includes internationally recognized ecclesiastic artists / designers working in conjunction with highly skilled craftspeople / artisans / conservators.

Locations: New York, NY / (212) 362-6085, LaPorte, IN / (219) 362-5934, Chicago, IL / (847) 869-5933, San Diego, CA / (760) 753-0705, Sarasota, FL / (941) 951-0978, Nassau, Bahamas / (242) 327-2992, Agropoli, Italy / (800) 524-7211.

Personnel:

Ettore Christopher Botti (Principal)
Ethlyn Panzironi Botti (Principal)

Conrad Schmitt Studios Inc.

Excellence in Artistry Since 1889

onrad Schmitt Studios, Inc.
405 S. 162nd Street
ew Berlin, WI 53151
l: 800-969-3033; 262-786-3030
x: 262-786-9036
mail: studio@conradschmitt.com
ebsite: www.conradschmitt.com

pe of Business:

ince 1889, our Studio has been privileged to have decorated and estored churches of all sizes and styles throughout the country. Due to ur extensive scope of work, we have the ability to be a single source to rovide a variety of services. Our experienced, full-time staff of artists nd craftsmen is skilled in various decorative painting, restoration and onservation techniques, including the investigation and documentation f original decorative schemes, plaster and scagliola conservation, gilding, lazing, marbleizing, stenciling and trompe l'oeil. Our Studio has been esigning and executing new stained glass and conserving historic stained lass for over a century. We also design and conserve murals, statuary, culpture and fitments. The Studio can help generate enthusiasm and inancial support by assisting projects in the early stages with renderings, ecorative samples and fundraising materials. We enjoy working as part f a team, to create the best projects in terms of function, longevity and esthetics.

EVERGREENE
Architectural Arts

verGreene Architectural Arts, Inc.
50 West 31 Street, 7th Floor
el: 212-244-2800
ax: 212-244-6204
-mail: info@evergreene.com
Vebsite: www.evergreene.com

ype of Business:

For more than 30 years, EverGreene has designed and implemented sacred artwork, decorative painting, plasterwork, and associated services for the Catholic Church nationwide. EverGreene works with clients to develop solutions that are beautiful and enduring, and offers consultation for budget estimates and value engineering. With a permanent staff that includes some of the world's finest ecclesiastical artists, along with skilled designers and project managers, EverGreene is a resource for projects that will enhance the experience of any worship space and inspire generations to come.

Notable projects: Basilica of the Assumption, Baltimore, MD; St. Thomas Aquinas College Chapel, Santa Paula, CA; Cathedral of the Blessed Sacrament, Sacramento, CA.

The EverGreene team includes project managers, ecclesiastical designers, fine artists, ornamental plaster sculptors, decorative painters, and craftspeople. Call for a free consultation on design or restoration, including practical approaches and budget recommendations.

ersonnel:

Jeff Greene (President)
Kim Lovejoy (Vice President, Director of Restoration)
Terry Vanderwell (Director of Restoration, Midwest)

GASPARD
HANDCRAFTED VESTMENTS AND PARAMENTS
MADE IN THE USA

Gaspard, Inc.
(formerly The Robert Gaspard Company, Inc.)
200 N. Janacek Road
Brookfield, WI 53045
Tel: 800-784-6868 (toll free)
Fax: 800-784-7567
E-mail: mail@gaspardinc.com
Website: www.gaspardinc.com

Type of Business:

For more than five decades customers have looked to Gaspard for fine quality, handcrafted vestments and paraments made in the USA. Offerings include the exquisite Castle Craft® collection; wardrobe essentials such as albs, surplices, cassocks, robes, and clergy shirts; extensive metalware offerings, fair linens, altar accessories, and communion ware.

Because your vestment and parament selections are made to order in our one and only location in Brookfield, Wisconsin, special sizes and custom designs are not a problem. One of our friendly Customer Service Representatives will be happy to help you find just the right size and style to enhance your spiritual expression. Please visit us online or call for a free catalog.

Personnel:

Jason R. Gaspard (President)
Joann Gaspard (Vice President)

RAMBUSCH
SINCE 1898

Rambusch
160 Cornelison Avenue
Jersey City, NJ 07304
Tel: 201-333-2525
Fax: 201-433-3355
Website: www.rambusch.com

Type of Business:

Creativity and Quality are Rambusch Hallmarks. A small, highly personal business, where everything is custom. Each inquiry is handled by a principal, who guides the client through a myriad of possibilities. The chosen solution is then made tangible by our supremely skilled craftspeople.

Rambusch creates complete interiors, shrines, individual art works, stained glass and mosaics. New work, renovations, and restorations all receive the same attention, resulting in beautiful, fitting solutions for your unique commission. Our design rooms, art metal workshops and stained glass studios are in-house, ensuring seamless crafting of all designs. Rambusch-patented lighting fixtures, the recognized industry standard for church lighting, are individually built on our own worktables. Rambusch custom engineered lighting systems make everything look its best!

Call/or come visit our intriguing design rooms and workshops for an initial courtesy consultation. We look forward to hearing from you. Remember Rambusch – on time, within budget, designed just for you.

Personnel:

Edwin P. Rambusch
Martin V. Rambusch
Viggo B.A. Rambusch, Senior Advisor

UNIVERSAL ART STUDIO

67 Mountain Spring Drive
Sparta, NJ 07871
Tel: 973-726-0835
E-mail: yuri@uasrestoration.com
Website: uasrestoration.com

Type of Business:

HISTORICAL RESTORATION — CONSERVATION OF ART

With very few exceptions we shall repair any object of aesthetic, ecclesiastical, spiritual, historical, sentimental or simply monetary value. We offer following services: Complete restoration projects, including: architectural planning, management and execution. Design and fabrication of church furnishings and fixtures. Restoration of paintings, including: murals, frescoes, Greek or Russian icons. Canvas repairs, relining, cleaning, stretching. Custom framing. Goldleafing. Repairs of statuary made of gypsum, marble, wood, composit materials. Repairs of mosaics, tile, ceramics, plaster, terrazzo. Restoration of antique furniture and woodcarvings.

Our Art Gallery creates a range of fine art from ecclesiastical to contemporary, to church interiors, to decoration of living space.

Honestly, Yuri Mironoff

TOUJOURS

ADRIAN HAMERS®
CHURCH INTERIORS

Adrian Hamers, Inc.
2 Madison Avenue
Larchmont, NY 10538
Tel: 914-834-7780
Fax: 914-834-0712
Website: www.adrianhamers.com

Type of Business:

Custom designers and manufacturers of Sacred Vessels. Since 1887, t Hamers name has been synonymous with expert Silversmithing througho the world in the field of Liturgical Art. Please contact us for those hard find items, as we always have a large selection of Adrian Hamers Esta Collection pieces in stock. We have a large collection of antique chur stained glass windows available (both full sets and individual). We a experts in: Church Interiors from design to execution, Renovatior Altars, Sacred Vessels, Gold and Silver Plating & Repairing, Appraisa Tabernacles, Marble, Statuary, Woodwork & Woodcarving, Stained Glas Pews & Chairs, Gold Leafing, Frescoes, Restoration, Trompe-l'oeuil, W Murals (repair and conservation cleaning), Ornamental Plaster, Herald Designs & Bishop Regalia. Please call us for a free 36-page Sacred Vesse color catalog, or our free 80-page color Woodcarvings catalog.

Conrad Schmitt Studios Inc.
Excellence in Artistry Since 1889

Conrad Schmitt Studios, Inc.
2405 S. 162nd Street
New Berlin, WI 53151
Tel: 800-969-3033; 262-786-3030
Fax: 262-786-9036
E-mail: studio@conradschmitt.com
Website: www.conradschmitt.com

Type of Business:

Since 1889, our Studio has been privileged to have decorated ar restored churches of all sizes and styles throughout the country. Due t our extensive scope of work, we have the ability to be a single source provide a variety of services. Our experienced, full-time staff of artis and craftsmen is skilled in various decorative painting, restoration an conservation techniques, including the investigation and documentatio of original decorative schemes, plaster and scagliola conservation, gildin glazing, marbleizing, stenciling and trompe l'oeil. Our Studio has bee designing and executing new stained glass and conserving historic staine glass for over a century. We also design and conserve murals, statuar sculpture and fitments. The Studio can help generate enthusiasm an financial support by assisting projects in the early stages with rendering decorative samples and fundraising materials. We enjoy working as pa of a team, to create the best projects in terms of function, longevity an aesthetics.

INRI

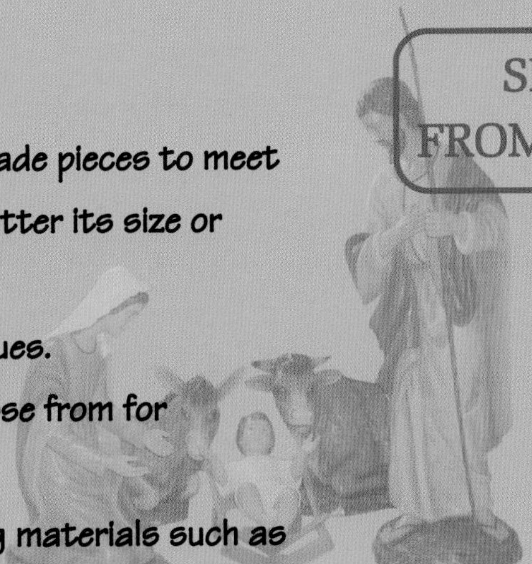

Inspired Artisans, Ltd.
816 W. National Avenue
Milwaukee, WI 53204
Tel: 888-442-9141
Fax: 414-672-9479
E-mail: gianfranco@inspiredart.com
Website: www.inspiredart.com

Type of Business:

Inspired Artisans, Ltd. has been serving the Catholic Church in the design and creation of sacred art since 1997. We take particular pride in personal care for each client and superior attention to detail. Recent commissions: Art and Statuary:
Georgetown University, Washington DC; Our Lady of Peace, North Augusta SC; OFM General Curia, Rome, Italy; College of the Holy Cross, Worcester MA; Monastery of the Infant Jesus, Lufkin TX; St. Dennis, Crow Agency MT; St. Augustine of Canterbury, Toronto, Canada: St. Henry, Nashville TN; Holy Rosary Convent, Ontario OR; Our Lady of Fatima, Saratoga CA; St. Raphael Cathedral, Madison WI; Pius X, Urbandale IA; St. Luke, Houston TX; Holy Angels, Basehor, KS; see our ad under Church Art.
We invite you to visit our website for a full introduction to our studio, a complete list of commissions or to request a portfolio.

Personnel:

Gianfranco Tassara (President)

Rohn & Associates Design, Inc.
1113 Creedmoor Avenue
Pittsburgh, PA 15226
Tel: 412-561-1228; 800-245-1288
Fax: 412-561-1201
E-mail: rolfrohn@rohndesign.com; Website: www.rohndesign.com
Blog: http://catholicliturgicalarts.blogspot.com/
Facebook: Catholic Liturgical Arts Journal

Type of Business:

Liturgical Designers, Artists & Artisans
TRADITION. Over the past 58 years, we have assisted the Catholic Church by designing, budgeting and implementing liturgical spaces.
COLLABORATION. We work side-by-side with our clients and collaborators to design and create appropriate and quality sacred art, interior finishes, lighting systems, acoustical systems, liturgical furnishings and appointments to create a rich devotional experience for your parishioners.
EXPERIENCE. We draw upon decades of experience and from a rich treasury of designers, architectural staff and contributing artists.
SCOPE OF SERVICES: Liturgical Design; Interior Design & Decorating; Sacred Artwork; Mosaics; Art Glass; Statuary; Liturgical Appointments; Liturgical Furniture; Metalwork.
ADDITIONAL LOCATIONS: 17515 Spring Cypress, Ste C PMB #246 Cypress, TX 77429. Tel. & Fax: 281-304-7736; 719 S. Flores St., Suite 200, San Antonio, TX 78204. Tel.: 210-231-0377; Fax: 210-231-0366
Contact us to arrange a complimentary project review.

Personnel:

Rolf R. Rohn (President - Liturgical Designer-Consultant)
Kathleen L. Maglicco (Vice President, Design)
Renate Rohn (Vice President, Art)
Francesca Lofaro (Director, Sales)

Sacred Spaces Liturgical Design Studios, Inc.
312 Montgomery Street, Suite 100
Alexandria, VA 22314
Tel: 703-519-9800; 1-888-519-4599 (toll free)
Fax: 703-519-4599
E-mail: info@sacredspacesinc.com
Website: www.SacredSpacesInc.com

Type of Business:

Sacred Spaces is a liturgical design team of international artists and maste craftsmen with experience spanning four decades in the design of worshi environments: new construction, renovation and restoration. Our Service include Liturgical Design Consulting, Custom Design, Appointments Removals, Consignments and Facsimiles. Specializing in marble, bronz and stone, we custom design altars, ambos, tabernacle thrones an baptismal fonts. We also offer Master Planning Services and Educationa Programs for pastoral teams and parish-wide Town Hall meetings. Sacre Spaces - Excellence in Liturgical Design, Artistry and Craftsmanship.

Personnel:

J. Michael Carrigan (President/CEO)
John Grosvenor (Project Director)
Francisco M. Cano (Art Director)

Santa Teresita Statuary Co.
Art Studio Lima – PERU
Northamerican Office
136290 13th Line
St. Marys, ON N4X 1C7 Canada
Tel: 519-349-2712; 1-877-349-2712 (toll free)
Fax: 519-349-2508

Type of Business:

Since 1927 we are specialized in the art of religious statuary following ou Italian tradition, our statues are made in plaster, fibreglass, resin, woo and bronze, from a large line of standard models to any kind and size o custom made pieces for indoors or outdoors. Our standard line includes, Jesus, Mary, Saints, Crucifixes, Stations of the Cross and Nativity Sets. We offer quality statuary for a reasonable cost.
Shipping for the USA is from Miami, FL

Personnel:

Giovanni Pierinelli
Mariangela Cavassa

Gold Leafing & Painted Murals

ARTECH CHURCH INTERIORS INC.

Artech Church Interiors, Inc.
12 Mill Plain Road
Danbury, CT 06811
Tel: 800-222-7397 (toll free); 203-744-2600
Fax: 203-744-0630
Website: http://www.artechchurchinteriors.com/

Type of Business:

Artech Church Interiors is a third generation family-run business, with over 45 years of personal experience in Church Seating, Church Renovation, and Church Restoration. Artech brings to every job the skill and dedication of master craftsmen. Our specialists will restore your Church's unique interior, or develop an innovative design to completely transform the Church.

Our Services Include: Interior restoration services include: Liturgical design and renderings, Plaster Restoration, Mold making and casting, Interior painting including specialty finishes, Murals, Restoration of Statues and Stations of the Cross, Pew restoration and refinishing, Church Seating, Church Furniture, Pew Cushions and Upholstery, Flooring including carpet, tile, marble, and wood, New and refurbished lighting, Audio and Video, Electric Candle stands.

Exterior restoration services include: Window frame restoration, Buy and Sell Stained Glass windows, Protective Covering and Venting for Windows, Door restoration and new doors, Exterior painting, Bells and Carillon Systems.

Personnel:

Thomas Burns (President) tom@artechchurchinteriors.com
William Burns (Vice President) bill@artechchurchinteriors.com

Conrad Schmitt Studios Inc.
Excellence in Artistry Since 1889

Conrad Schmitt Studios, Inc.
2405 S. 162nd Street
New Berlin, WI 53151
Tel: 800-969-3033; 262-786-3030
Fax: 262-786-9036
E-mail: studio@conradschmitt.com
Website: www.conradschmitt.com

Type of Business:

Since 1889, our Studio has been privileged to have decorated and restored churches of all sizes and styles throughout the country. Due to our extensive scope of work, we have the ability to be a single source to provide a variety of services. Our experienced, full-time staff of artists and craftsmen is skilled in various decorative painting, restoration and conservation techniques, including the investigation and documentation of original decorative schemes, plaster and scagliola conservation, gilding, glazing, marbleizing, stenciling and trompe l'oeil. Our Studio has been designing and executing new stained glass and conserving historic stained glass for over a century. We also design and conserve murals, statuary, sculpture and fitments. The Studio can help generate enthusiasm and financial support by assisting projects in the early stages with renderings, decorative samples and fundraising materials. We enjoy working as part of a team, to create the best projects in terms of function, longevity and aesthetics.

UNIVERSAL ART STUDIO

67 Mountain Spring Drive
Sparta, NJ 07871
Tel: 973-726-0835
E-mail: yuri@uasrestoration.com
Website: uasrestoration.com

Type of Business:

HISTORICAL RESTORATION — CONSERVATION OF ART

With very few exceptions we shall repair any object of aesthetic, ecclesiastical, spiritual, historical, sentimental or simply monetary value. We offer following services: Complete restoration projects, including: architectural planning, management and execution. Design and fabrication of church furnishings and fixtures. Restoration of paintings, including: murals, frescoes, Greek or Russian icons. Canvas repairs, relining, cleaning, stretching. Custom framing. Goldleafing. Repairs of statuary made of gypsum, marble, wood, composit materials. Repairs of mosaics, tile, ceramics, plaster, terrazzo. Restoration of antique furniture and woodcarvings.

Our Art Gallery creates a range of fine art from ecclesiastical to contemporary, to church interiors, to decoration of living space.

Honestly, Yuri Mironoff

Mosaics

Baker Liturgical Art, LLC
Church Restoration / Church Renovation

Baker Liturgical Art, LLC
136 Curtiss Street
Southington, CT 06489
Tel: 860-621-7471
Fax: 860-621-7607
E-mail: bakerart@sbcglobal.net
Website: www.bakerliturgicalart.com

Type of Business:

Baker Liturgical Art, LLC offers a full range of construction and renovation services. These services encompass architectural specifications and liturgical design as well as sound system and lighting design.

Our liturgical design talents result in beautiful altar furnishings of hand-carved wood or of fine imported Italian marble. Stained glass and sacred artwork (painted, wood-carved or chiseled from marble) are the final accents to complete prayerful settings in every worship space from the smallest Chapel to the grandest Cathedral! Baker Liturgical Art, LLC prides itself in offering uncompromising quality in its products and services.

Our Services Include: Liturgical Design, Architectural Services, Liturgical Furnishings, Sculpture & Artwork, Flooring, Millwork, Multi-Media Systems, Stained Glass Fabrication & Restoration.

Additional location: 1300 Gulfshore Blvd., North #510 Naples, FL 34102
P: 860-818-3799.

INSPIRED ARTISANS

Inspired Artisans, Ltd.
816 W. National Avenue
Milwaukee, WI 53204
Tel: 888-442-9141
Fax: 414-672-9479
E-mail: gianfranco@inspiredart.com
Website: www.inspiredart.com

Type of Business:

Inspired Artisans, Ltd. has been serving the Catholic Church in the design and creation of sacred art since 1997. We take particular pride in personal care for each client and superior attention to detail. Recent commissions: Mosaics:
St. Joseph, South Bend IN; Santa Maria Mediatrice, Rome, Italy; OFM Curia, Rome, Italy; Holy Cross Greek Orthodox, Middletown NY; Annunciation Greek Orthodox, Milwaukee WI; Marquette University, Milwaukee WI; St. Adalbert Cemetery, Milwaukee WI; Holy Sepulcher, Coram NY; see our ad under Church Art.
We invite you to visit our website for a full introduction to our studio, a complete list of commissions, or to request a portfolio.

Personnel:

Gianfranco Tassara (President)

RAMBUSCH
SINCE 1898

Rambusch
160 Cornelison Avenue
Jersey City, NJ 07304
Tel: 201-333-2525
Fax: 201-433-3355
Website: www.rambusch.com

Type of Business:

Creativity and Quality are Rambusch Hallmarks. A small, highly personal business, where everything is custom. Each inquiry is handled by a principal, who guides the client through a myriad of possibilities. The chosen solution is then made tangible by our supremely skilled craftspeople.
Rambusch creates complete interiors, shrines, individual art works, stained glass and mosaics. New work, renovations, and restorations all receive the same attention, resulting in beautiful, fitting solutions for your unique commission. Our design rooms, art metal workshops and stained glass studios are in-house, ensuring seamless crafting of all designs. Rambusch-patented lighting fixtures, the recognized industry standard for church lighting, are individually built on our own worktables. Rambusch custom engineered lighting systems make everything look its best!
Call/or come visit our intriguing design rooms and workshops for an initial courtesy consultation. We look forward to hearing from you. Remember Rambusch – on time, within budget, designed just for you.

Personnel:

Edwin P. Rambusch
Martin V. Rambusch
Viggo B.A. Rambusch, Senior Advisor

Sculpture

Conrad Schmitt Studios Inc.
Excellence in Artistry Since 1889

Conrad Schmitt Studios, Inc.
2405 S. 162nd Street
New Berlin, WI 53151
Tel: 800-969-3033; 262-786-3030
Fax: 262-786-9036
E-mail: studio@conradschmitt.com
Website: www.conradschmitt.com

Type of Business:

Since 1889, our Studio has been privileged to have decorated and restored churches of all sizes and styles throughout the country. Due to our extensive scope of work, we have the ability to be a single source to provide a variety of services. Our experienced, full-time staff of artists and craftsmen is skilled in various decorative painting, restoration and conservation techniques, including the investigation and documentation of original decorative schemes, plaster and scagliola conservation, gilding, glazing, marbleizing, stenciling and trompe l'oeil. Our Studio has been designing and executing new stained glass and conserving historic stained glass for over a century. We also design and conserve murals, statuary, sculpture and fitments. The Studio can help generate enthusiasm and financial support by assisting projects in the early stages with renderings, decorative samples and fundraising materials. We enjoy working as part of a team, to create the best projects in terms of function, longevity and aesthetics.

INSPIRED ARTISANS

Inspired Artisans, Ltd.
816 W. National Avenue
Milwaukee, WI 53204
Tel: 888-442-9141
Fax: 414-672-9479
E-mail: gianfranco@inspiredart.com
Website: www.inspiredart.com

Type of Business:

Inspired Artisans, Ltd. has been serving the Catholic Church in the design and creation of sacred art since 1997. We take particular pride in personal care for each client and superior attention to detail. Recent commissions: Sculpture:
St. Anthony Shrine, Ellicot City MO; Poor Clares Monastery, Roswell NM; St. Gertrude Mausoleum, Newark NJ; Nuestra Senora de Guadalupe, Danbury CT; St. Charles Borromeo, Hallandale FL; Brescia University, Owensboro KY; Cuore Immacolato di Maria, San Marino CA; Catholic Cemeteries, Denver CO; St. Andrews, Ellensburg WA; Pax Christi, Rochester MN; Sacred Heart, Waseca MN; St. Gregory, San Mateo CA; Catholic Cemeteries, Syracuse NY; see our ad under Church Art.
We invite you to visit our website for a full introduction to our studio, a complete list of commissions, or to request a portfolio.

Personnel:

Gianfranco Tassara (President)

Stations
Crucifixes
Saints
Angels
Fine bronzes...

Kircher & Associates, Inc.
Sculpture Studio
P.O. Box 53
Jaroso, CO 81138
Tel: 719-672-3063
Website: www.kirchersculpture.com

Type of Business:

Since 1992 we have installed over 200 sculptures in 15 states, 2 foreign countries and the Vatican Collection. Drawing upon classical themes, careful research and the contemporary aspirations of parish leaders, Lynn Kircher crafts his sculptures first in clay and then in bronze using the lost wax process in US foundries and local craftsmen. Professionally trained, gifted and dedicated to his art, Lynn brings powerful expression to each piece. This work is designed to inspire, uplift and create wonder. Your new facilities or the renovation of your existing ones benefit from the freshness of superior custom bronzes. Lynn's existing portfolio of crucifixes, angels and saints contains a selection of sculptures suitable for indoor and outdoor spaces. Commissions for new works are invited. Inquire about our commissioning process. The Kircher studio is located at the Colorado – New Mexico border. We welcome clients and visitors from throughout the country.

Personnel:

Lynn Kircher (Sculptor)
Jane Kircher (Patination & Business)
Jennifer Hunt (Studio Assistant)

RAMBUSCH
SINCE 1898

Rambusch
160 Cornelison Avenue
Jersey City, NJ 07304
Tel: 201-333-2525
Fax: 201-433-3355
Website: www.rambusch.com

Type of Business:

Creativity and Quality are Rambusch Hallmarks. A small, highly personal business, where everything is custom. Each inquiry is handled by a principal, who guides the client through a myriad of possibilities. The chosen solution is then made tangible by our supremely skilled craftspeople.
Rambusch creates complete interiors, shrines, individual art works, stained glass and mosaics. New work, renovations, and restorations all receive the same attention, resulting in beautiful, fitting solutions for your unique commission. Our design rooms, art metal workshops and stained glass studios are in-house, ensuring seamless crafting of all designs. Rambusch-patented lighting fixtures, the recognized industry standard for church lighting, are individually built on our own worktables. Rambusch custom engineered lighting systems make everything look its best!
Call/or come visit our intriguing design rooms and workshops for an initial courtesy consultation. We look forward to hearing from you. Remember Rambusch – on time, within budget, designed just for you.

Personnel:

Edwin P. Rambusch
Martin V. Rambusch
Viggo B.A. Rambusch, Senior Advisor

ROHN
& Associates Design, Inc.

Rohn & Associates Design, Inc.
1113 Creedmoor Avenue
Pittsburgh, PA 15226
Tel: 412-561-1228; 800-245-1288
Fax: 412-561-1201
E-mail: rolfrohn@rohndesign.com
Website: www.rohndesign.com
Blog: http://catholicliturgicalarts.blogspot.com/
Facebook: Catholic Liturgical Arts Journal

Type of Business:

Liturgical Designers, Artists & Artisans
TRADITION. Over the past 58 years, we have assisted the Catholic Church by designing, budgeting and implementing liturgical spaces.
COLLABORATION. We work side-by-side with our clients and collaborators to design and create appropriate and quality sacred art, interior finishes, lighting systems, acoustical systems, liturgical furnishings and appointments to create a rich devotional experience for your parishioners.
EXPERIENCE. We draw upon decades of experience and from a rich treasury of designers, architectural staff and contributing artists.
SCOPE OF SERVICES: Liturgical Design; Interior Design & Decorating; Sacred Artwork; Mosaics; Art Glass; Statuary; Liturgical Appointments; Liturgical Furniture; Metalwork.
ADDITIONAL LOCATIONS: 17515 Spring Cypress, Ste C PMB #246 Cypress, TX 77429. Tel. & Fax: 281-304-7736; 719 S. Flores St., Suite 200, San Antonio, TX 78204. Tel.: 210-231-0377; Fax: 210-231-0366
Contact us to arrange a complimentary project review.

Personnel:

Rolf R. Rohn (President - Liturgical Designer-Consultant)
Kathleen L. Maglicco (Vice President, Design)
Renate Rohn (Vice President, Art)
Francesca Lofaro (Director, Sales)

SANTA TERESITA
statuary company
SINCE 1927

Santa Teresita Statuary Co.
Art Studio Lima – PERU
Northamerican Office
136290 13th Line
St. Marys, ON N4X 1C7 Canada
Tel: 519-349-2712; 1-877-349-2712 (toll free)
Fax: 519-349-2508

Type of Business:

Since 1927 we are specialized in the art of religious statuary following our Italian tradition, our statues are made in plaster, fibreglass, resin, wood and bronze, from a large line of standard models to any kind and size of custom made pieces for indoors or outdoors. Our standard line includes, Jesus, Mary, Saints, Crucifixes, Stations of the Cross and Nativity Sets. We offer quality statuary for a reasonable cost.
Shipping for the USA is from Miami, FL

Personnel:

Giovanni Pierinelli
Mariangela Cavassa

CHURCH FURNISHINGS—General

TOUJOURS

ADRIAN HAMERS®
CHURCH INTERIORS

Adrian Hamers, Inc.
2 Madison Avenue
Larchmont, NY 10538
Tel: 914-834-7780
Fax: 914-834-0712
Website: www.adrianhamers.com

Type of Business:

Custom designers and manufacturers of Sacred Vessels. Since 1887, the Hamers name has been synonymous with expert Silversmithing throughout the world in the field of Liturgical Art. Please contact us for those hard to find items, as we always have a large selection of Adrian Hamers Estate Collection pieces in stock. We have a large collection of antique church stained glass windows available (both full sets and individual). We are experts in: Church Interiors from design to execution, Renovations, Altars, Sacred Vessels, Gold and Silver Plating & Repairing, Appraisals, Tabernacles, Marble, Statuary, Woodwork & Woodcarving, Stained Glass, Pews & Chairs, Gold Leafing, Frescoes, Restoration, Trompe-l'oeuil, Wall Murals (repair and conservation cleaning), Ornamental Plaster, Heraldic Designs & Bishop Regalia. Please call us for a free 36-page Sacred Vessels color catalog, or our free 80-page color Woodcarvings catalog.

ARTECH
CHURCH INTERIORS INC.

Artech Church Interiors, Inc.
12 Mill Plain Road
Danbury, CT 06811
Tel: 800-222-7397 (toll free); 203-744-2600
Fax: 203-744-0630
Website: http://www.artechchurchinteriors.com/

Type of Business:

Artech Church Interiors is a third generation family-run business, with over 45 years of personal experience in Church Seating, Church Renovation, and Church Restoration. Artech brings to every job the skill and dedication of master craftsmen. Our specialists will restore your Church's unique interior, or develop an innovative design to completely transform the Church.

Our Services Include: Interior restoration services include: Liturgical design and renderings, Plaster Restoration, Mold making and casting, Interior painting including specialty finishes, Murals, Restoration of Statues and Stations of the Cross, Pew restoration and refinishing, Church Seating, Church Furniture, Pew Cushions and Upholstery, Flooring including carpet, tile, marble, and wood, New and refurbished lighting, Audio and Video, Electric Candle stands.

Exterior restoration services include: Window frame restoration, Buy and Sell Stained Glass windows, Protective Covering and Venting for Windows, Door restoration and new doors, Exterior painting, Bells and Carillon Systems.

Personnel:

Thomas Burns (President) tom@artechchurchinteriors.com
William Burns (Vice President) bill@artechchurchinteriors.com

Baker Liturgical Art, LLC
Church Restoration / Church Renovation

Baker Liturgical Art, LLC
136 Curtiss Street
Southington, CT 06489
Tel: 860-621-7471
Fax: 860-621-7607
E-mail: bakerart@sbcglobal.net
Website: www.bakerliturgicalart.com

Type of Business:

Baker Liturgical Art, LLC offers a full range of construction and renovation services. These services encompass architectural specifications and liturgical design as well as sound system and lighting design.

Our liturgical design talents result in beautiful altar furnishings of hand carved wood or of fine imported Italian marble. Stained glass and sacred artwork (painted, wood-carved or chiseled from marble) are the final accents to complete prayerful settings in every worship space from the smallest Chapel to the grandest Cathedral! Baker Liturgical Art, LLC prides itself in offering uncompromising quality in its products and services.

Our Services Include: Liturgical Design, Architectural Services, Liturgical Furnishings, Sculpture & Artwork, Flooring, Millwork, Multi-Media Systems, Stained Glass Fabrication & Restoration.

Additional location: 1300 Gulfshore Blvd., North #510 Naples, FL 34102
P: 860-818-3799.

Conrad Schmitt Studios Inc.
Excellence in Artistry Since 1889

Conrad Schmitt Studios, Inc.
2405 S. 162nd Street
New Berlin, WI 53151
Tel: 800-969-3033; 262-786-3030
Fax: 262-786-9036
E-mail: studio@conradschmitt.com
Website: www.conradschmitt.com

Type of Business:

Since 1889, our Studio has been privileged to have decorated and restored churches of all sizes and styles throughout the country. Due to our extensive scope of work, we have the ability to be a single source to provide a variety of services. Our experienced, full-time staff of artists and craftsmen is skilled in various decorative painting, restoration and conservation techniques, including the investigation and documentation of original decorative schemes, plaster and scagliola conservation, gilding, glazing, marbleizing, stenciling and trompe l'oeil. Our Studio has been designing and executing new stained glass and conserving historic stained glass for over a century. We also design and conserve murals, statuary, sculpture and fitments. The Studio can help generate enthusiasm and financial support by assisting projects in the early stages with renderings, decorative samples and fundraising materials. We enjoy working as part of a team, to create the best projects in terms of function, longevity and aesthetics.

EVERGREENE Architectural Arts

verGreene Architectural Arts, Inc.
50 West 31 Street, 7th Floor
el: 212-244-2800
ax: 212-244-6204
-mail: info@evergreene.com
Vebsite: www.evergreene.com

ype of Business:
For more than 30 years, EverGreene has designed and implemented sacred artwork, decorative painting, plasterwork, and associated services for the Catholic Church nationwide. EverGreene works with clients to develop solutions that are beautiful and enduring, and offers consultation for budget estimates and value engineering. With a permanent staff that includes some of the world's finest ecclesiastical artists, along with skilled designers and project managers, EverGreene is a resource for projects that will enhance the experience of any worship space and inspire generations to come.
Notable projects: Basilica of the Assumption, Baltimore, MD; St. Thomas Aquinas College Chapel, Santa Paula, CA; Cathedral of the Blessed Sacrament, Sacramento, CA.
The EverGreene team includes project managers, ecclesiastical designers, fine artists, ornamental plaster sculptors, decorative painters, and craftspeople. Call for a free consultation on design or restoration, including practical approaches and budget recommendations.

Personnel:
Jeff Greene (President)
Kim Lovejoy (Vice President, Director of Restoration)
Terry Vanderwell (Director of Restoration, Midwest)

RAMBUSCH SINCE 1898

Rambusch
160 Cornelison Avenue
Jersey City, NJ 07304
Tel: 201-333-2525
Fax: 201-433-3355
Website: www.rambusch.com

Type of Business:
Creativity and Quality are Rambusch Hallmarks. A small, highly personal business, where everything is custom. Each inquiry is handled by a principal, who guides the client through a myriad of possibilities. The chosen solution is then made tangible by our supremely skilled craftspeople.
Rambusch creates complete interiors, shrines, individual art works, stained glass and mosaics. New work, renovations, and restorations all receive the same attention, resulting in beautiful, fitting solutions for your unique commission. Our design rooms, art metal workshops and stained glass studios are in-house, ensuring seamless crafting of all designs. Rambusch-patented lighting fixtures, the recognized industry standard for church lighting, are individually built on our own worktables. Rambusch custom engineered lighting systems make everything look its best!
Call/or come visit our intriguing design rooms and workshops for an initial courtesy consultation. We look forward to hearing from you. Remember Rambusch – on time, within budget, designed just for you.

Personnel:
Edwin P. Rambusch
Martin V. Rambusch
Viggo B.A. Rambusch, Senior Advisor

ROHN & Associates Design, Inc.

Rohn & Associates Design, Inc.
1113 Creedmoor Avenue
Pittsburgh, PA 15226
Tel: 412-561-1228; 800-245-1288
Fax: 412-561-1201
E-mail: rolfrohn@rohndesign.com
Website: www.rohndesign.com
Blog: http://catholicliturgicalarts.blogspot.com/
Facebook: Catholic Liturgical Arts Journal

Type of Business:
Liturgical Designers, Artists & Artisans
TRADITION. Over the past 58 years, we have assisted the Catholic Church by designing, budgeting and implementing liturgical spaces.
COLLABORATION. We work side-by-side with our clients and collaborators to design and create appropriate and quality sacred art, interior finishes, lighting systems, acoustical systems, liturgical furnishings and appointments to create a rich devotional experience for your parishioners.
EXPERIENCE. We draw upon decades of experience and from a rich treasury of designers, architectural staff and contributing artists.
SCOPE OF SERVICES: Liturgical Design; Interior Design & Decorating; Sacred Artwork; Mosaics; Art Glass; Statuary; Liturgical Appointments; Liturgical Furniture; Metalwork.
ADDITIONAL LOCATIONS: 17515 Spring Cypress, Ste C PMB #246 Cypress, TX 77429. Tel. & Fax: 281-304-7736; 719 S. Flores St., Suite 200, San Antonio, TX 78204. Tel.: 210-231-0377; Fax: 210-231-0366
Contact us to arrange a complimentary project review.

Personnel:
Rolf R. Rohn (President - Liturgical Designer-Consultant)
Kathleen L. Maglicco (Vice President, Design)
Renate Rohn (Vice President, Art)
Francesca Lofaro (Director, Sales)

Altars, Tabernacles, etc.

TOUJOURS
ADRIAN HAMERS® CHURCH INTERIORS

Adrian Hamers, Inc.
2 Madison Avenue
Larchmont, NY 10538
Tel: 914-834-7780
Fax: 914-834-0712
Website: www.adrianhamers.com

Type of Business:
Custom designers and manufacturers of Sacred Vessels. Since 1887, the Hamers name has been synonymous with expert Silversmithing throughout the world in the field of Liturgical Art. Please contact us for those hard to find items, as we always have a large selection of Adrian Hamers Estate Collection pieces in stock. We have a large collection of antique church stained glass windows available (both full sets and individual). We are experts in: Church Interiors from design to execution, Renovations, Altars, Sacred Vessels, Gold and Silver Plating & Repairing, Appraisals, Tabernacles, Marble, Statuary, Woodwork & Woodcarving, Stained Glass, Pews & Chairs, Gold Leafing, Frescoes, Restoration, Trompe-l'oeuil, Wall Murals (repair and conservation cleaning), Ornamental Plaster, Heraldic Designs & Bishop Regalia. Please call us for a free 36-page Sacred Vessels color catalog, or our free 80-page color Woodcarvings catalog.

RAMBUSCH

SINCE 1898

Rambusch
160 Cornelison Avenue
Jersey City, NJ 07304
Tel: 201-333-2525
Fax: 201-433-3355
Website: www.rambusch.com

Type of Business:

Creativity and Quality are Rambusch Hallmarks. A small, highly personal business, where everything is custom. Each inquiry is handled by a principal, who guides the client through a myriad of possibilities. The chosen solution is then made tangible by our supremely skilled craftspeople.
Rambusch creates complete interiors, shrines, individual art works, stained glass and mosaics. New work, renovations, and restorations all receive the same attention, resulting in beautiful, fitting solutions for your unique commission. Our design rooms, art metal workshops and stained glass studios are in-house, ensuring seamless crafting of all designs. Rambusch-patented lighting fixtures, the recognized industry standard for church lighting, are individually built on our own worktables. Rambusch custom engineered lighting systems make everything look its best!
Call/or come visit our intriguing design rooms and workshops for an initial courtesy consultation. We look forward to hearing from you. Remember Rambusch – on time, within budget, designed just for you.

Personnel:

Edwin P. Rambusch
Martin V. Rambusch
Viggo B.A. Rambusch, Senior Advisor

SACRED SPACES INC
LITURGICAL DESIGN STUDIOS

Sacred Spaces Liturgical Design Studios, Inc.
312 Montgomery Street, Suite 100
Alexandria, VA 22314
Tel: 703-519-9800; 1-888-519-4599 (toll free)
Fax: 703-519-4599
E-mail: info@sacredspacesinc.com
Website: www.SacredSpacesInc.com

Type of Business:

Sacred Spaces is a liturgical design team of international artists and master craftsmen with experience spanning four decades in the design of worship environments: new construction, renovation and restoration. Our Services include Liturgical Design Consulting, Custom Design, Appointments, Removals, Consignments and Facsimiles. Specializing in marble, bronze and stone, we custom design altars, ambos, tabernacle thrones and baptismal fonts. We also offer Master Planning Services and Educational Programs for pastoral teams and parish-wide Town Hall meetings. Sacred Spaces - Excellence in Liturgical Design, Artistry and Craftsmanship.

Personnel:

J. Michael Carrigan (President/CEO)
John Grosvenor (Project Director)
Francisco M. Cano (Art Director)

Antiques, Religious

TOUJOURS

ADRIAN HAMERS®
CHURCH INTERIORS

Adrian Hamers, Inc.
2 Madison Avenue
Larchmont, NY 10538
Tel: 914-834-7780
Fax: 914-834-0712
Website: www.adrianhamers.com

Type of Business:

Custom designers and manufacturers of Sacred Vessels. Since 1887, the Hamers name has been synonymous with expert Silversmithing throughout the world in the field of Liturgical Art. Please contact us for those hard to find items, as we always have a large selection of Adrian Hamers Estate Collection pieces in stock. We have a large collection of antique church stained glass windows available (both full sets and individual). We are experts in: Church Interiors from design to execution, Renovations, Altars, Sacred Vessels, Gold and Silver Plating & Repairing, Appraisals, Tabernacles, Marble, Statuary, Woodwork & Woodcarving, Stained Glass, Pews & Chairs, Gold Leafing, Frescoes, Restoration, Trompe-l'oeuil, Wall Murals (repair and conservation cleaning), Ornamental Plaster, Heraldic Designs & Bishop Regalia. Please call us for a free 36-page Sacred Vessels color catalog, or our free 80-page color Woodcarvings catalog.

Baptismal Fonts

RAMBUSCH

SINCE 1898

Rambusch
160 Cornelison Avenue
Jersey City, NJ 07304
Tel: 201-333-2525
Fax: 201-433-3355
Website: www.rambusch.com

Type of Business:

Creativity and Quality are Rambusch Hallmarks. A small, highly personal business, where everything is custom. Each inquiry is handled by a principal, who guides the client through a myriad of possibilities. The chosen solution is then made tangible by our supremely skilled craftspeople.
Rambusch creates complete interiors, shrines, individual art works, stained glass and mosaics. New work, renovations, and restorations all receive the same attention, resulting in beautiful, fitting solutions for your unique commission. Our design rooms, art metal workshops and stained glass studios are in-house, ensuring seamless crafting of all designs. Rambusch-patented lighting fixtures, the recognized industry standard for church lighting, are individually built on our own worktables. Rambusch custom engineered lighting systems make everything look its best!
Call/or come visit our intriguing design rooms and workshops for an initial courtesy consultation. We look forward to hearing from you. Remember Rambusch – on time, within budget, designed just for you.

Personnel:

Edwin P. Rambusch
Martin V. Rambusch
Viggo B.A. Rambusch, Senior Advisor

Bells, Carillons, Etc.

The Verdin Co.
444 Reading Road
Cincinnati, OH 45202
800-543-0488 (toll free)
Tel: 513-241-4010; Fax: 513-241-1855
E-mail: info@verdin.com
Website: www.verdin.com

Type of Business:

America's Bell Ringer
For almost two centuries The Verdin Company has been the world's premier manufacturer and restorer of bells, carillons and clocks. We distinguish ourselves by blending innovative technology with superior customer service. Today, we feature the same high quality bells and clocks as our fathers and grandfathers before us. Our Verdin legacy is the sound of bells ringing from more than 30,000 churches all over the world.
Family owned for five generations, The Verdin Company emphasizes honesty, integrity and trust while bringing the sound of bells to parishioners everywhere.

Personnel:

Robert J. Verdin (CEO)
James R. Verdin (President)
David E. Verdin (Vice President)
Suzanne Sizer (Marketing Manager)

Bishop's Regalia

Adrian Hamers, Inc.
2 Madison Avenue
Larchmont, NY 10538
Tel: 914-834-7780
Fax: 914-834-0712
Website: www.adrianhamers.com

Type of Business:

Custom designers and manufacturers of Sacred Vessels. Since 1887, the Hamers name has been synonymous with expert Silversmithing throughout the world in the field of Liturgical Art. Please contact us for those hard to find items, as we always have a large selection of Adrian Hamers Estate Collection pieces in stock. We have a large collection of antique church stained glass windows available (both full sets and individual). We are experts in: Church Interiors from design to execution, Renovations, Altars, Sacred Vessels, Gold and Silver Plating & Repairing, Appraisals, Tabernacles, Marble, Statuary, Woodwork & Woodcarving, Stained Glass, Pews & Chairs, Gold Leafing, Frescoes, Restoration, Trompe-l'oeuil, Wall Murals (repair and conservation cleaning), Ornamental Plaster, Heraldic Designs & Bishop Regalia. Please call us for a free 36-page Sacred Vessels color catalog, or our free 80-page color Woodcarvings catalog.

C.M. Almy
Three American Lane, P.O. Box 2644
Greenwich, CT 06836-2644
Tel: 800-225-2569
Fax: 800-426-2569
E-mail: almyaccess@almy.com
Website: www.almy.com
Showroom in Old Greenwich, CT

Type of Business:

Almy was founded in 1892. We design and make virtually all of our products in our Maine shop. It is our mission to design furnishings that will grace your worship and to ensure their value by making them with the highest quality materials and craftsmanship. We make a complete line of vestments, haberdashery, choir robes, candles, communion bread, linens, processional and altar appointments, and eucharistic vessels. We also offer custom design and fabrication of all Almy products, and repair and refurbishing of old metal appointments. Quik Ship© delivery of many popular items. All orders backed by The Almy Guarantee. Call, write, or e-mail for a free catalog.

Interior Design/Restoration

Artech Church Interiors, Inc.
12 Mill Plain Road
Danbury, CT 06811
Tel: 800-222-7397 (toll free); 203-744-2600
Fax: 203-744-0630
Website: http://www.artechchurchinteriors.com/

Type of Business:

Artech Church Interiors is a third generation family-run business, with over 45 years of personal experience in Church Seating, Church Renovation, and Church Restoration. Artech brings to every job the skill and dedication of master craftsmen. Our specialists will restore your Church's unique interior, or develop an innovative design to completely transform the Church.
Our Services Include: Interior restoration services include: Liturgical design and renderings, Plaster Restoration, Mold making and casting, Interior painting including specialty finishes, Murals, Restoration of Statues and Stations of the Cross, Pew restoration and refinishing, Church Seating, Church Furniture, Pew Cushions and Upholstery, Flooring including carpet, tile, marble, and wood, New and refurbished lighting, Audio and Video, Electric Candle stands.
Exterior restoration services include: Window frame restoration, Buy and Sell Stained Glass windows, Protective Covering and Venting for Windows, Door restoration and new doors, Exterior painting, Bells and Carillon Systems.

Personnel:

Thomas Burns (President) tom@artechchurchinteriors.com
William Burns (Vice President) bill@artechchurchinteriors.com

Baker Liturgical Art, LLC
Church Restoration / Church Renovation

Baker Liturgical Art, LLC
136 Curtiss Street
Southington, CT 06489
Tel: 860-621-7471
Fax: 860-621-7607
E-mail: bakerart@sbcglobal.net
Website: www.bakerliturgicalart.com

Type of Business:

Baker Liturgical Art, LLC offers a full range of construction and renovation services. These services encompass architectural specifications and liturgical design as well as sound system and lighting design.

Our liturgical design talents result in beautiful altar furnishings of hand-carved wood or of fine imported Italian marble. Stained glass and sacred artwork (painted, wood-carved or chiseled from marble) are the final accents to complete prayerful settings in every worship space from the smallest Chapel to the grandest Cathedral! Baker Liturgical Art, LLC prides itself in offering uncompromising quality in its products and services.

Our Services Include: Liturgical Design, Architectural Services, Liturgical Furnishings, Sculpture & Artwork, Flooring, Millwork, Multi-Media Systems, Stained Glass Fabrication & Restoration.

Additional location: 1300 Gulfshore Blvd., North #510 Naples, FL 34102 P: 860-818-3799.

Conrad Schmitt Studios Inc.
Excellence in Artistry Since 1889

Conrad Schmitt Studios, Inc.
2405 S. 162nd Street
New Berlin, WI 53151
Tel: 800-969-3033; 262-786-3030
Fax: 262-786-9036
E-mail: studio@conradschmitt.com
Website: www.conradschmitt.com

Type of Business:

Since 1889, CSS has been privileged to decorate and restore churches of all sizes and styles throughout the country. Our experienced staff assists projects in the early stages to help assemble the master plan, communicate the vision and generate the enthusiasm and funding needed to make the plan a reality. Some of the tools used to accomplish these goals include renderings, on-site samples, budgetary estimates and fundraising materials.

Our comprehensive scope of services allows us to be a single source for a variety of needs, creating the best projects in terms of function, longevity and aesthetics. Our services include the investigation and documentation of original decorative schemes, gilding, glazing, marbleizing, stenciling, trompe l'oeil and faux finishing.

Recent decorating commissions include the Cathedral of the Immaculate Conception, Springfield, IL; St. Mary Magdalen Catholic Church, Abbeville, LA; St. Joseph Cathedral, Sioux Falls, SD; and St. John Neumann Catholic Church, Knoxville, TN.

Daprato Rigali Studios, Inc.
6030 N. Northwest Highway
Chicago, IL 60631
Tel: 773-763-5511
Fax: 773-763-5522
E-mail: info@dapratorigali.com
Website: www.dapratorigali.com

Type of Business:

Church decoration and restoration of correct plan and execution requires, above all else, the facilities of an artist organization competent to consider and solve in advance, all problems of color and design as well as a thorough understanding of the art of church embellishment and its relationship to existing liturgical needs. Daprato Rigali Studios possesses these necessary qualifications for superior performance in all areas of church restoration for over one hundred and fifty years. Churches seeking decoration, marble, stained glass, wood, bronze, mosaic, therefore, will find it very much worth while to contact Daprato Rigali.

Liturgical Consulting, Design, Decoration Restoration Stained Glass, Statuary, Furnishings in Marble & Wood

Personnel:

John Rigali
Lisa Rigali Galvin
Robert Rigali
Mike Rigali

Kosinski architecture, inc.
Architecture, Planning, Liturgical Design

Kosinski Architecture, Inc.
1401 E. Broward Boulevard, Suite 201
Fort Lauderdale, FL 33301
Tel: 954-627-6988
Fax: 954-627-6955
E-mail: info@kosinskiarchitecture.com
Website: www.kosinskiarchitecture.com

Type of Business:

Kosinski Architecture, Inc., Architects Planners, with offices in Fort Lauderdale, Florida and Branford, Connecticut provides award winning design nationally. The firm's portfolio spans a variety of project types, including religious, educational, housing, and mixed use projects.

The firm is adept at working in both modern and traditional idioms, providing adroit responses to program and technical requirements regardless of stylistic genre.

Kosinski's extensive knowledge of liturgy and of the history of church architecture allows it to provide church clients with exceptional architectural and liturgical design services. Our full range of in-house professional services, including master-planning, the design of all liturgical elements, and interior design gives its clients a single point of contact for complete project delivery. As certified restoration experts, Kosinski's knowledge and appreciation of architectural history is apparent in its extensive restoration portfolio.

Personnel:

Peter R. Kosinski, AIA, NCARB (Contact)

RAMBUSCH

SINCE 1898

ambusch
60 Cornelison Avenue
ersey City, NJ 07304
el: 201-333-2525
ax: 201-433-3355
Vebsite: www.rambusch.com

ype of Business:

Creativity and Quality are Rambusch Hallmarks. A small, highly personal business, where everything is custom. Each inquiry is handled by a principal, who guides the client through a myriad of possibilities. The chosen solution is then made tangible by our supremely skilled craftspeople.

Rambusch creates complete interiors, shrines, individual art works, stained glass and mosaics. New work, renovations, and restorations all receive the same attention, resulting in beautiful, fitting solutions for your unique commission. Our design rooms, art metal workshops and stained glass studios are in-house, ensuring seamless crafting of all designs. Rambusch-patented lighting fixtures, the recognized industry standard for church lighting, are individually built on our own worktables. Rambusch custom engineered lighting systems make everything look its best!

Call/or come visit our intriguing design rooms and workshops for an initial courtesy consultation. We look forward to hearing from you. Remember Rambusch – on time, within budget, designed just for you.

Personnel:

Edwin P. Rambusch
Martin V. Rambusch
Viggo B.A. Rambusch, Senior Advisor

Lighting of Liturgical Space

ARTECH
CHURCH INTERIORS INC.

Making Church Lighting Better for Over 30 Years

Artech Church Interiors, Inc.
12 Mill Plain Road
Danbury, CT 06811
Tel: 800-222-7397 (toll free); 203-744-2600
Fax: 203-744-0630
Website: http://www.artechchurchinteriors.com/

Type of Business:

Artech can supply you with all types of Church lighting solutions, nationwide. Our Services Include Lighting Solutions to increase illumination, efficiency, and maintenance. New Standard Light Fixtures with energy efficient lighting layouts. New Custom Light Fixtures to enhance new designs. Refurbish, update, retrofit and modify existing fixtures. LED, energy-efficient fixtures. Recent Project at St. Benedict's Roman Catholic Church, Bronx, NY, Refurbished 14 Nave Chandeliers including glass diffusers. Tripled the light output at half the wattage utilizing energy efficient lamps. Replaced old wiring and sockets. Restored original finish including gold accents. Provided a new lighting layout including downlighting, general lighting, and uplighting. Notable Projects include Cathedral of the Immaculate Conception, Albany, NY, St. Rita's Parish, Lowell, MA, St. Luke's Parish, Ho-Ho-Kus, NJ, St. Mary Byzantine Catholic Church, Trenton, NJ, Holy Apostles College & Seminary, Cromwell, CT.

Personnel:

Thomas Burns (President) tom@artechchurchinteriors.com
William Burns (Vice President) bill@artechchurchinteriors.com

RAMBUSCH

SINCE 1898

Rambusch
160 Cornelison Avenue
Jersey City, NJ 07304
Tel: 201-333-2525
Fax: 201-433-3355
Website: www.rambusch.com

Type of Business:

Creativity and Quality are Rambusch Hallmarks. A small, highly personal business, where everything is custom. Each inquiry is handled by a principal, who guides the client through a myriad of possibilities. The chosen solution is then made tangible by our supremely skilled craftspeople.

Rambusch creates complete interiors, shrines, individual art works, stained glass and mosaics. New work, renovations, and restorations all receive the same attention, resulting in beautiful, fitting solutions for your unique commission. Our design rooms, art metal workshops and stained glass studios are in-house, ensuring seamless crafting of all designs. Rambusch-patented lighting fixtures, the recognized industry standard for church lighting, are individually built on our own worktables. Rambusch custom engineered lighting systems make everything look its best!

Call/or come visit our intriguing design rooms and workshops for an initial courtesy consultation. We look forward to hearing from you. Remember Rambusch – on time, within budget, designed just for you.

Personnel:

Edwin P. Rambusch
Martin V. Rambusch
Viggo B.A. Rambusch, Senior Advisor

Liturgical Design

ARTECH
CHURCH INTERIORS INC.

Artech Church Interiors, Inc.
12 Mill Plain Road
Danbury, CT 06811
Tel: 800-222-7397 (toll free); 203-744-2600
Fax: 203-744-0630
Website: http://www.artechchurchinteriors.com/

Type of Business:

Artech Church Interiors is a third generation family-run business, with over 45 years of personal experience in Church Seating, Church Renovation, and Church Restoration. Artech brings to every job the skill and dedication of master craftsmen. Our specialists will restore your Church's unique interior, or develop an innovative design to completely transform the Church.

Our Services Include: Interior restoration services include: Liturgical design and renderings, Plaster Restoration, Mold making and casting, Interior painting including specialty finishes, Murals, Restoration of Statues and Stations of the Cross, Pew restoration and refinishing, Church Seating, Church Furniture, Pew Cushions and Upholstery, Flooring including carpet, tile, marble, and wood, New and refurbished lighting, Audio and Video, Electric Candle stands.

Exterior restoration services include: Window frame restoration, Buy and Sell Stained Glass windows, Protective Covering and Venting for Windows, Door restoration and new doors, Exterior painting, Bells and Carillon Systems.

Personnel:

Thomas Burns (President) tom@artechchurchinteriors.com
William Burns (Vice President) bill@artechchurchinteriors.com

Baker Liturgical Art, LLC
Church Restoration Church Renovation

Baker Liturgical Art, LLC
136 Curtiss Street
Southington, CT 06489
Tel: 860-621-7471
Fax: 860-621-7607
E-mail: bakerart@sbcglobal.net
Website: www.bakerliturgicalart.com

Type of Business:

Baker Liturgical Art, LLC offers a full range of construction and renovation services. These services encompass architectural specifications and liturgical design as well as sound system and lighting design.
Our liturgical design talents result in beautiful altar furnishings of hand-carved wood or of fine imported Italian marble. Stained glass and sacred artwork (painted, wood-carved or chiseled from marble) are the final accents to complete prayerful settings in every worship space from the smallest Chapel to the grandest Cathedral! Baker Liturgical Art, LLC prides itself in offering uncompromising quality in its products and services.
Our Services Include: Liturgical Design, Architectural Services, Liturgical Furnishings, Sculpture & Artwork, Flooring, Millwork, Multi-Media Systems, Stained Glass Fabrication & Restoration.
Additional location: 1300 Gulfshore Blvd., North #510 Naples, FL 34102 P: 860-818-3799.

INSPIRED
ARTISANS

Inspired Artisans, Ltd.
816 W. National Avenue
Milwaukee, WI 53204
Tel: 888-442-9141
Fax: 414-672-9479
E-mail: gianfranco@inspiredart.com
Website: www.inspiredart.com

Type of Business:

Inspired Artisans, Ltd. has been serving the Catholic Church in the design and creation of sacred art since 1997. We take particular pride in personal care for each client and superior attention to detail. Recent commissions: Liturgical design: St. Augustine, Thomasville GA; Marquette University HS, Milwaukee WI; St. Anne, Barrington IL; Holy Spirit, Montgomery AL; St. Mary Cathedral, Cheyenne WY; Bellarmine Jesuit Retreat Center, Barrington IL; St. Elizabeth, Rockville MD; Poor Clares Monastery, Palos Park IL; Our Lady of Lourdes, Harrisonville MO; Santa Marianita, Galapagos, Ecuador; St. Joseph, Vancouver WA; All Saints Cemetery, Des Plaines IL; St. Catherine, Portage WI; Basilica of St. Josephat, Milwaukee WI; see our ad under Church Art.
We invite you to visit our website for a full introduction to our studio, a complete list of commissions, or to request a portfolio.

Personnel:

Gianfranco Tassara (President)

Kosinski architecture, inc.
Architecture, Planning, Liturgical Design

Kosinski Architecture, Inc.
1401 E. Broward Boulevard, Suite 201
Fort Lauderdale, FL 33301
Tel: 954-627-6988
Fax: 954-627-6955
E-mail: info@kosinskiarchitecture.com
Website: www.kosinskiarchitecture.com

Type of Business:

Kosinski Architecture, Inc., Architects Planners, with offices in Fort Lauderdale, Florida and Branford, Connecticut provides award winning design nationally. The firm's portfolio spans a variety of project types including religious, educational, housing, and mixed use projects.
The firm is adept at working in both modern and traditional idioms providing adroit responses to program and technical requirements regardless of stylistic genre.
Kosinski's extensive knowledge of liturgy and of the history of church architecture allows it to provide church clients with exceptional architectural and liturgical design services. Our full range of in-house professional services, including master-planning, the design of all liturgical elements, and interior design gives its clients a single point of contact for complete project delivery. As certified restoration experts, Kosinski's knowledge and appreciation of architectural history is apparent in its extensive restoration portfolio.

Personnel:

Peter R. Kosinski, AIA, NCARB (Contact)

RAMBUSCH
SINCE 1898

Rambusch
160 Cornelison Avenue
Jersey City, NJ 07304
Tel: 201-333-2525
Fax: 201-433-3355
Website: www.rambusch.com

Type of Business:

Creativity and Quality are Rambusch Hallmarks. A small, highly personal business, where everything is custom. Each inquiry is handled by a principal, who guides the client through a myriad of possibilities. The chosen solution is then made tangible by our supremely skilled craftspeople.
Rambusch creates complete interiors, shrines, individual art works, stained glass and mosaics. New work, renovations, and restorations all receive the same attention, resulting in beautiful, fitting solutions for your unique commission. Our design rooms, art metal workshops and stained glass studios are in-house, ensuring seamless crafting of all designs. Rambusch-patented lighting fixtures, the recognized industry standard for church lighting, are individually built on our own worktables. Rambusch custom engineered lighting systems make everything look its best!
Call/or come visit our intriguing design rooms and workshops for an initial courtesy consultation. We look forward to hearing from you. Remember Rambusch – on time, within budget, designed just for you.

Personnel:

Edwin P. Rambusch
Martin V. Rambusch
Viggo B.A. Rambusch, Senior Advisor

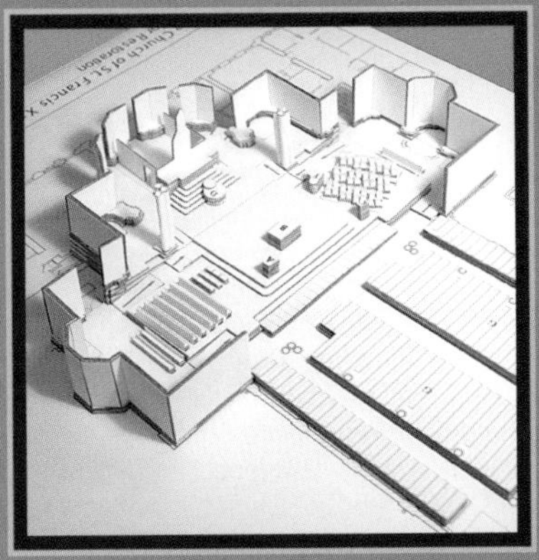

SACRED SPACES INC
LITURGICAL DESIGN STUDIOS

Sacred Spaces Liturgical Design Studios, Inc.
312 Montgomery Street, Suite 100
Alexandria, VA 22314
Tel: 703-519-9800; 1-888-519-4599 (toll free)
Fax: 703-519-4599
E-mail: info@sacredspacesinc.com
Website: www.SacredSpacesInc.com

Type of Business:

Sacred Spaces is a liturgical design team of international artists and master craftsmen with experience spanning four decades in the design of worship environments: new construction, renovation and restoration. Our Services include Liturgical Design Consulting, Custom Design, Appointments, Removals, Consignments and Facsimiles. Specializing in marble, bronze and stone, we custom design altars, ambos, tabernacle thrones and baptismal fonts. We also offer Master Planning Services and Educational Programs for pastoral teams and parish-wide Town Hall meetings. Sacred Spaces - Excellence in Liturgical Design, Artistry and Craftsmanship.

Personnel:

J. Michael Carrigan (President/CEO)
John Grosvenor (Project Director)
Francisco M. Cano (Art Director)

Organs

RODGERS®

Rodgers Instruments Corporation
1300 NE 25th Avenue
Hillsboro, Oregon 97124
Tel: 503-648-4181
Fax: 503-681-0444
E-mail: marketing@rodgers.rain.com
Website: www.rodgersinstruments.com.

Type of Business:

Rodgers is the world's leading builder of stereo imaged digital church organs and pipe-digital combination organs. The sound of Rodgers organs sets them apart from all other products available today, thanks to the development of Parallel Digital Imaging®, which captures true pipe organ sound. Rodgers is part of Roland Corporation, a world leader in digital musical instrument technologies and digital musical instrument sales and manufacturing. The Rodgers/Roland partnership brings together hundreds of engineers specializing in high-resolution stereophonic musical instrument sound generation and the resources of a recognized industry leader with approximately $1 billion per year in revenues. Rodgers introduced many of the most notable advances in organ technology, and it remains the only company to use stereo sampling in church organs. Rodgers organs are played today in major cathedrals, concert halls and universities around the world.

Pews, Chairs, Kneelers

ARTECH
CHURCH INTERIORS INC.

Church seating specialists for over 30 years

Artech Church Interiors, Inc.
12 Mill Plain Road
Danbury, CT 06811
Tel: 800-222-7397 (toll free); 203-744-2600
Fax: 203-744-0630
Website: http://www.artechchurchinteriors.com/

Type of Business:

Church seating specialists for over 30 years, nationwide. Our Service Include: New Pews, straight or curved. Pew refinishing, on or off site New kneelers and pads. Pew cushions and upholstery. Move and reinsta pews for new flooring. Choir chairs, Chapel chairs, Cathedral chairs Notable Projects include Cathedral Basilica of the Sacred Heart, Newark NJ, Holy Apostles College & Seminary, Cromwell, CT, Most Sacred Hear of Jesus Parish, Wallington, NJ, St. Augustine's Roman Catholic Church Ossining, NY, St. Bartholomew the Apostle Church, Scotch Plains, NJ, St Denis Church, Manasquan, NJ, St. Lawrence Roman Catholic Church Weehawkin, NJ, St. Luke's Catholic Church, Irving, TX, St. Patrick' Catholic Church, Chicago, IL.

Personnel:

Thomas Burns (President) tom@artechchurchinteriors.com
William Burns (Vice President) bill@artechchurchinteriors.com

Plaques & Memorials

W&E BAUM
Designers and Manufacturers
Donor Walls • Plaques • Awards • Memorials

W & E Baum
89 Bannard Street
Freehold, NJ 07728
Tel: 800-922-7377; 732-866-1881
Fax: 732-866-8978
E-mail: info@webaum.com
Website: www.webaum.com/Church-Products.html

Type of Business:

W&E BAUM, celebrating 86 years and three generations, specializes in the design and fabrication of symbols of recognition and generosity. Additional income for churches can be generated by using many of our innovative products. Our Donor Walls, Bronze Memorials, Giving Trees, Plaques, Awards, Sculptures and more, promote fund-raising efforts and acknowledge gifts of all kinds. Quality, creativity and personal attention to detail are the elements that capture the attention of potential contributors in today's sophisticated world.

To thank, to honor, to reward, to commemorate, to memorialize, W & E Baum stands ready to help you translate your vision into reality.

Our Bronze Memorial Designs are a new and innovative way for your parishioners to permanently memorialize their loved ones. These memorials provide a steady stream of income for many years.

Contact us for more details.

Personnel:

Richard Baum (President)
Maurice Zagha (CEO)
Heshy Spira (Vice President)

CHURCH GLASS—General

Excellence in Artistry Since 1889

Conrad Schmitt Studios, Inc.
2405 S. 162nd Street
New Berlin, WI 53151
Tel: 800-969-3033; 262-786-3030
Fax: 262-786-9036
E-mail: studio@conradschmitt.com
Website: www.conradschmitt.com

Type of Business:

CSS, in its 121 years of existence, has contributed to the art glass heritage of America through both creation and conservation. The Studio continually works to preserve and advance the techniques that facilitate work in the industry. Clients have commissioned work in a variety of styles. Many recent requests have been for new, traditional-style windows to complement more classically inspired architecture. Contemporary designs are also created in figural, geometric and abstract compositions. Full-time artisans conserve and restore stained glass, including priceless windows by John La Farge, Louis Comfort Tiffany, Mayer of Munich, Thomas O'Shaughnessy, and McCully and Miles.

Recent new stained glass commissions include St. John the Baptist Catholic Church, Costa Mesa, CA; the University of Notre Dame, Notre Dame, IN; and St. Anne Catholic Church, Sherman, TX.

Recent stained glass conservation projects include St. Vincent de Paul Catholic Church, Petaluma, CA and St. Mary Magdalen Catholic Church, Abbeville, LA.

EverGreene Architectural Arts, Inc.
450 West 31 Street, 7th Floor
Tel: 212-244-2800
Fax: 212-244-6204
E-mail: info@evergreene.com
Website: www.evergreene.com

Type of Business:

For more than 30 years, EverGreene has designed and implemented sacred artwork, decorative painting, plasterwork, and associated services for the Catholic Church nationwide. EverGreene works with clients to develop solutions that are beautiful and enduring, and offers consultation for budget estimates and value engineering. With a permanent staff that includes some of the world's finest ecclesiastical artists, along with skilled designers and project managers, EverGreene is a resource for projects that will enhance the experience of any worship space and inspire generations to come.

Notable projects: Basilica of the Assumption, Baltimore, MD; St. Thomas Aquinas College Chapel, Santa Paula, CA; Cathedral of the Blessed Sacrament, Sacramento, CA.

The EverGreene team includes project managers, ecclesiastical designers, fine artists, ornamental plaster sculptors, decorative painters, and craftspeople. Call for a free consultation on design or restoration, including practical approaches and budget recommendations.

Personnel:

Jeff Greene (President)
Kim Lovejoy (Vice President, Director of Restoration)
Terry Vanderwell (Director of Restoration, Midwest)

Glass Heritage, llc
234 W. 3rd Street
Davenport, IA 52801
Tel: 563-324-4300
Fax: 563-324-4321
E-mail: info@glassheritage.com
Website: www.glassheritage.com

Type of Business:

Specializing in restoration, design and fabrication of custom stained glass windows for ecclesiastical environments, Glass Heritage, llc is dedicated to standards of excellence in glass. Our goal is to create a finished work of art that enhances the spiritual mission of your church and creates a space of meditative enrichment. While we specialize in historic restorations and maintenance of leaded glass, Glass Heritage also supplies custom design and fabrication services for stained and leaded glass, faceted glass, etched glass and custom blown glass.

When you choose Glass Heritage, llc, you choose creative, dedicated craftsmen who will meet the needs of your sacred space. All our glasswork is handcrafted, never manufactured. Our reputation for personalized and affordable service is unsurpassed.

Glass Heritage, llc is a Fully Accredited studio member of The Stained Glass Association of America.

SINCE 1898

Rambusch
160 Cornelison Avenue
Jersey City, NJ 07304
Tel: 201-333-2525
Fax: 201-433-3355
Website: www.rambusch.com

Type of Business:

Creativity and Quality are Rambusch Hallmarks. A small, highly personal business, where everything is custom. Each inquiry is handled by a principal, who guides the client through a myriad of possibilities. The chosen solution is then made tangible by our supremely skilled craftspeople.

Rambusch creates complete interiors, shrines, individual art works, stained glass and mosaics. New work, renovations, and restorations all receive the same attention, resulting in beautiful, fitting solutions for your unique commission. Our design rooms, art metal workshops and stained glass studios are in-house, ensuring seamless crafting of all designs. Rambusch-patented lighting fixtures, the recognized industry standard for church lighting, are individually built on our own worktables. Rambusch custom engineered lighting systems make everything look its best!

Call/or come visit our intriguing design rooms and workshops for an initial courtesy consultation. We look forward to hearing from you. Remember Rambusch – on time, within budget, designed just for you.

Personnel:

Edwin P. Rambusch
Martin V. Rambusch
Viggo B.A. Rambusch, Senior Advisor

ROHN
&Associates Design, Inc.

Rohn & Associates Design, Inc.
1113 Creedmoor Avenue
Pittsburgh, PA 15226
Tel: 412-561-1228; 800-245-1288
Fax: 412-561-1201
E-mail: rolfrohn@rohndesign.com
Website: www.rohndesign.com
Blog: http://catholicliturgicalarts.blogspot.com/
Facebook: Catholic Liturgical Arts Journal

Type of Business:

Liturgical Designers, Artists & Artisans
TRADITION. Over the past 58 years, we have assisted the Catholic Church by designing, budgeting and implementing liturgical spaces.
COLLABORATION. We work side-by-side with our clients and collaborators to design and create appropriate and quality sacred art, interior finishes, lighting systems, acoustical systems, liturgical furnishings and appointments to create a rich devotional experience for your parishioners.
EXPERIENCE. We draw upon decades of experience and from a rich treasury of designers, architectural staff and contributing artists.
SCOPE OF SERVICES: Liturgical Design; Interior Design & Decorating; Sacred Artwork; Mosaics; Art Glass; Statuary; Liturgical Appointments; Liturgical Furniture; Metalwork.
ADDITIONAL LOCATIONS: 17515 Spring Cypress, Ste C PMB #246 Cypress, TX 77429. Tel. & Fax: 281-304-7736; 719 S. Flores St., Suite 200, San Antonio, TX 78204. Tel.: 210-231-0377; Fax: 210-231-0366
Contact us to arrange a complimentary project review.

Personnel:

Rolf R. Rohn (President - Liturgical Designer-Consultant)
Kathleen L. Maglicco (Vice President, Design)
Renate Rohn (Vice President, Art)
Francesca Lofaro (Director, Sales)

WILLET HAUSER
Architectural Glass, Inc.

Willet Hauser Architectural Glass, Inc.
811 East Cayuga Street
Philadelphia, PA 19124
Tel: 800-533-3960
Fax: 877-495-9486
Website: www.willethauser.com

Type of Business:

Since 1896 Willet Hauser Architectural Glass has a century-old legacy of glass design and over six decades of renowned restoration. Willet Hauser is the preeminent stained glass studio in the country and operates facilities in Winona, Minnesota, and Philadelphia, Pennsylvania. Willet Hauser has created or restored over 15,000 projects, including some of the most magnificent stained glass windows for religious buildings within the United States and in 14 countries around the world.
The proof of our artistry is in the projects that we have designed and restored. Here are just a few prominent examples of the thousands of churches and institutions that have been our clients during the last century: The National Cathedral, Washington, DC; The Church Center, United Nations, NY; The Cathedral of St. Mary of the Assumption, San Francisco, CA; Cathedral of Mary Our Queen, Baltimore, MD; Princeton University Chapel; The Cadet Chapel, United States Military Academy, West Point; Arlington National Cemetery Chapel; The Cathedral of Christ the King, Atlanta, GA.
When you choose Willet Hauser to create or preserve your legacy in stained glass, you are placing it in the experienced hands of artists, designers and craftspeople whose sole purpose is to ensure that every detail reflects your unique vision in a tribute of glass, color, and light.
...You can trust your legacy to our legacy.

Antiqued Stained Glass

TOUJOURS
ADRIAN HAMERS®
CHURCH INTERIORS

Adrian Hamers, Inc.
2 Madison Avenue
Larchmont, NY 10538
Tel: 914-834-7780
Fax: 914-834-0712
Website: www.adrianhamers.com

Type of Business:

Custom designers and manufacturers of Sacred Vessels. Since 1887, th Hamers name has been synonymous with expert Silversmithing throughou the world in the field of Liturgical Art. Please contact us for those hard t find items, as we always have a large selection of Adrian Hamers Estat Collection pieces in stock. We have a large collection of antique churc stained glass windows available (both full sets and individual). We ar experts in: Church Interiors from design to execution, Renovations Altars, Sacred Vessels, Gold and Silver Plating & Repairing, Appraisals Tabernacles, Marble, Statuary, Woodwork & Woodcarving, Stained Glass Pews & Chairs, Gold Leafing, Frescoes, Restoration, Trompe-l'oeuil, Wa Murals (repair and conservation cleaning), Ornamental Plaster, Heraldi Designs & Bishop Regalia. Please call us for a free 36-page Sacred Vessel color catalog, or our free 80-page color Woodcarvings catalog.

Conrad Schmitt Studios Inc.
Excellence in Artistry Since 1889

Conrad Schmitt Studios, Inc.
2405 S. 162nd Street
New Berlin, WI 53151
Tel: 800-969-3033; 262-786-3030
Fax: 262-786-9036
E-mail: studio@conradschmitt.com
Website: www.conradschmitt.com

Type of Business:

CSS, in its 121 years of existence, has contributed to the art glass heritag of America through both creation and conservation. The Studio continuall works to preserve and advance the techniques that facilitate work in th industry. Clients have commissioned work in a variety of styles. Many recen requests have been for new, traditional-style windows to complemen more classically inspired architecture. Contemporary designs are als created in figural, geometric and abstract compositions. Full-time artisan conserve and restore stained glass, including priceless windows by Joh La Farge, Louis Comfort Tiffany, Mayer of Munich, Thomas O'Shaughnessy and McCully and Miles.
Recent new stained glass commissions include St. John the Baptist Catholi Church, Costa Mesa, CA; the University of Notre Dame, Notre Dame, IN and St. Anne Catholic Church, Sherman, TX.
Recent stained glass conservation projects include St. Vincent de Pau Catholic Church, Petaluma, CA and St. Mary Magdalen Catholic Church Abbeville, LA.

WILLET HAUSER

Architectural Glass, Inc.

Willet Hauser Architectural Glass, Inc.
811 East Cayuga Street
Philadelphia, PA 19124
Tel: 800-533-3960
Fax: 877-495-9486
Website: www.willethauser.com

Type of Business:

Since 1896 Willet Hauser Architectural Glass has a century-old legacy of glass design and over six decades of renowned restoration. Willet Hauser is the preeminent stained glass studio in the country and operates facilities in Winona, Minnesota, and Philadelphia, Pennsylvania. Willet Hauser has created or restored over 15,000 projects, including some of the most magnificent stained glass windows for religious buildings within the United States and in 14 countries around the world.

The proof of our artistry is in the projects that we have designed and restored. Here are just a few prominent examples of the thousands of churches and institutions that have been our clients during the last century: The National Cathedral, Washington, DC; The Church Center, United Nations, NY; The Cathedral of St. Mary of the Assumption, San Francisco, CA; Cathedral of Mary Our Queen, Baltimore, MD; Princeton University Chapel; The Cadet Chapel, United States Military Academy, West Point; Arlington National Cemetery Chapel; The Cathedral of Christ the King, Atlanta, GA.

When you choose Willet Hauser to create or preserve your legacy in stained glass, you are placing it in the experienced hands of artists, designers and craftspeople whose sole purpose is to ensure that every detail reflects your unique vision in a tribute of glass, color, and light.

...You can trust your legacy to our legacy.

Etched Glass

WILLET HAUSER

Architectural Glass, Inc.

Willet Hauser Architectural Glass, Inc.
811 East Cayuga Street
Philadelphia, PA 19124
Tel: 800-533-3960
Fax: 877-495-9486
Website: www.willethauser.com

Type of Business:

Since 1896 Willet Hauser Architectural Glass has a century-old legacy of glass design and over six decades of renowned restoration. Willet Hauser is the preeminent stained glass studio in the country and operates facilities in Winona, Minnesota, and Philadelphia, Pennsylvania. Willet Hauser has created or restored over 15,000 projects, including some of the most magnificent stained glass windows for religious buildings within the United States and in 14 countries around the world.

The proof of our artistry is in the projects that we have designed and restored. Here are just a few prominent examples of the thousands of churches and institutions that have been our clients during the last century: The National Cathedral, Washington, DC; The Church Center, United Nations, NY; The Cathedral of St. Mary of the Assumption, San Francisco, CA; Cathedral of Mary Our Queen, Baltimore, MD; Princeton University Chapel; The Cadet Chapel, United States Military Academy, West Point; Arlington National Cemetery Chapel; The Cathedral of Christ the King, Atlanta, GA.

When you choose Willet Hauser to create or preserve your legacy in stained glass, you are placing it in the experienced hands of artists, designers and craftspeople whose sole purpose is to ensure that every detail reflects your unique vision in a tribute of glass, color, and light.

...You can trust your legacy to our legacy.

Faceted Glass

WILLET HAUSER

Architectural Glass, Inc.

Willet Hauser Architectural Glass, Inc.
811 East Cayuga Street
Philadelphia, PA 19124
Tel: 800-533-3960
Fax: 877-495-9486
Website: www.willethauser.com

Type of Business:

Since 1896 Willet Hauser Architectural Glass has a century-old legacy of glass design and over six decades of renowned restoration. Willet Hauser is the preeminent stained glass studio in the country and operates facilities in Winona, Minnesota, and Philadelphia, Pennsylvania. Willet Hauser has created or restored over 15,000 projects, including some of the most magnificent stained glass windows for religious buildings within the United States and in 14 countries around the world.

The proof of our artistry is in the projects that we have designed and restored. Here are just a few prominent examples of the thousands of churches and institutions that have been our clients during the last century: The National Cathedral, Washington, DC; The Church Center, United Nations, NY; The Cathedral of St. Mary of the Assumption, San Francisco, CA; Cathedral of Mary Our Queen, Baltimore, MD; Princeton University Chapel; The Cadet Chapel, United States Military Academy, West Point; Arlington National Cemetery Chapel; The Cathedral of Christ the King, Atlanta, GA.

When you choose Willet Hauser to create or preserve your legacy in stained glass, you are placing it in the experienced hands of artists, designers and craftspeople whose sole purpose is to ensure that every detail reflects your unique vision in a tribute of glass, color, and light.

...You can trust your legacy to our legacy.

Stained Glass

Toujours

Adrian Hamers®
Church Interiors

Adrian Hamers, Inc.
2 Madison Avenue
Larchmont, NY 10538
Tel: 914-834-7780
Fax: 914-834-0712
Website: www.adrianhamers.com

Type of Business:

Custom designers and manufacturers of Sacred Vessels. Since 1887, the Hamers name has been synonymous with expert Silversmithing throughout the world in the field of Liturgical Art. Please contact us for those hard to find items, as we always have a large selection of Adrian Hamers Estate Collection pieces in stock. We have a large collection of antique church stained glass windows available (both full sets and individual). We are experts in: Church Interiors from design to execution, Renovations, Altars, Sacred Vessels, Gold and Silver Plating & Repairing, Appraisals, Tabernacles, Marble, Statuary, Woodwork & Woodcarving, Stained Glass, Pews & Chairs, Gold Leafing, Frescoes, Restoration, Trompe-l'oeuil, Wall Murals (repair and conservation cleaning), Ornamental Plaster, Heraldic Designs & Bishop Regalia. Please call us for a free 36-page Sacred Vessels color catalog, or our free 80-page color Woodcarvings catalog.

Baker Liturgical Art, LLC
Church Restoration / Church Renovation

Baker Liturgical Art, LLC
136 Curtiss Street
Southington, CT 06489
Tel: 860-621-7471
Fax: 860-621-7607
E-mail: bakerart@sbcglobal.net
Website: www.bakerliturgicalart.com

Type of Business:

Baker Liturgical Art, LLC offers a full range of construction and renovation services. These services encompass architectural specifications and liturgical design as well as sound system and lighting design.

Our liturgical design talents result in beautiful altar furnishings of hand-carved wood or of fine imported Italian marble. Stained glass and sacred artwork (painted, wood-carved or chiseled from marble) are the final accents to complete prayerful settings in every worship space from the smallest Chapel to the grandest Cathedral! Baker Liturgical Art, LLC prides itself in offering uncompromising quality in its products and services.

Our Services Include: Liturgical Design, Architectural Services, Liturgical Furnishings, Sculpture & Artwork, Flooring, Millwork, Multi-Media Systems, Stained Glass Fabrication & Restoration.

Additional location: 1300 Gulfshore Blvd., North #510 Naples, FL 34102 P: 860-818-3799.

BOTTI STUDIO OF ARCHITECTURAL ARTS, INC.

Botti Studio of Architectural Arts, Inc.
919 Grove Street
Evanston, IL 60201
Tel: 800-524-7211; 847-869-5933
Fax: 847-869-5996
E-mail: botti@bottistudio.com
Website: www.bottistudio.com

Type of Business:

Since 1864, Botti Studio has specialized in serving the ecclesiasti environment through design, fabrication, delivery, and installation. Exper on staff in new design commissions, repair, restoration, conservatio and repair provide a source for experienced project management – fror conception through completion. Services include: stained, facete sandblasted, carved and painted glass, wood / metal / stone frames protective glazing, murals, marble, mosaics, bronze, statuary, gildin painting and decorating, complete interiors, new and restorations, histori discovery, documentation and consultation to owner / architect.

Our staff of 45 includes internationally recognized ecclesiastic artists designers working in conjunction with highly skilled craftspeople / artisar / conservators.

Locations: New York, NY / (212) 362-6085, LaPorte, IN / (219) 362-5934 Chicago, IL / (847) 869-5933, San Diego, CA / (760) 753-0705, Sarasota FL / (941) 951-0978, Nassau, Bahamas / (242) 327-2992, Agropoli, Ital / (800) 524-7211.

Personnel:

Ettore Christopher Botti (Principal)
Ethlyn Panzironi Botti (Principal)

Conrad Schmitt Studios Inc.
Excellence in Artistry Since 1889

Conrad Schmitt Studios, Inc.
2405 S. 162nd Street
New Berlin, WI 53151
Tel: 800-969-3033; 262-786-3030
Fax: 262-786-9036
E-mail: studio@conradschmitt.com
Website: www.conradschmitt.com

Type of Business:

CSS, in its 121 years of existence, has contributed to the art glas heritage of America through both creation and conservation. The Studi continually works to preserve and advance the techniques that facilitat work in the industry. Clients have commissioned work in a variety c styles. Many recent requests have been for new, traditional-style window to complement more classically inspired architecture. Contemporar designs are also created in figural, geometric and abstract compositions Full-time artisans conserve and restore stained glass, including priceles windows by John La Farge, Louis Comfort Tiffany, Mayer of Munich Thomas O'Shaughnessy, and McCully and Miles.

Recent new stained glass commissions include St. John the Baptist Catholi Church, Costa Mesa, CA; the University of Notre Dame, Notre Dame, IN and St. Anne Catholic Church, Sherman, TX.

Recent stained glass conservation projects include St. Vincent de Pau Catholic Church, Petaluma, CA and St. Mary Magdalen Catholic Church Abbeville, LA.

Glass Heritage, llc
[illegible]34 W. 3rd Street
Davenport, IA 52801
Tel: 563-324-4300
Fax: 563-324-4321
E-mail: info@glassheritage.com
Website: www.glassheritage.com

Type of Business:

Specializing in restoration, design and fabrication of custom stained glass windows for ecclesiastical environments, Glass Heritage, llc is dedicated to standards of excellence in glass. Our goal is to create a finished work of art that enhances the spiritual mission of your church and creates a space of meditative enrichment. While we specialize in historic restorations and maintenance of leaded glass, Glass Heritage also supplies custom design and fabrication services for stained and leaded glass, faceted glass, etched glass and custom blown glass.

When you choose Glass Heritage, llc, you choose creative, dedicated craftsmen who will meet the needs of your sacred space. All our glasswork is handcrafted, never manufactured. Our reputation for personalized and affordable service is unsurpassed.

Glass Heritage, llc is a Fully Accredited studio member of The Stained Glass Association of America.

HIEMER & COMPANY
Stained Glass Studio

Hiemer & Company Stained Glass Studio
141 Wabash Avenue
Clifton, NJ 07011
Tel: 973-772-5081
Fax: 973-772-0325
E-mail: jevanwie@hiemco.com
Website: www.hiemco.com

Type of Business:

Bold Liturgical statements and traditional Biblical portrayals are executed in magnificent color schemes by the artists and craftsmen at Hiemer & Company. Four generations of the Hiemer family have dedicated their careers to excellence in stained glass and promotion of faith through art. The studio members are highly skilled and experienced with large scale restorations, artistic replications and window renovations. The permanent staff works from concept to installation to the client's complete satisfaction. Over 1,100 Churches served in North America. Fabricators of stained, faceted, and etched glass. Exceptional figure portrayals are a specialty. Information and quotations submitted without obligation.

Personnel:

Gerhard E. Hiemer (C.E.O.)
Judith Hiemer Van Wie (President)
James E. Van Wie (Vice President)

RAMBUSCH
SINCE 1898

Rambusch
160 Cornelison Avenue
Jersey City, NJ 07304
Tel: 201-333-2525
Fax: 201-433-3355
Website: www.rambusch.com

Type of Business:

Creativity and Quality are Rambusch Hallmarks. A small, highly personal business, where everything is custom. Each inquiry is handled by a principal, who guides the client through a myriad of possibilities. The chosen solution is then made tangible by our supremely skilled craftspeople.

Rambusch creates complete interiors, shrines, individual art works, stained glass and mosaics. New work, renovations, and restorations all receive the same attention, resulting in beautiful, fitting solutions for your unique commission. Our design rooms, art metal workshops and stained glass studios are in-house, ensuring seamless crafting of all designs. Rambusch-patented lighting fixtures, the recognized industry standard for church lighting, are individually built on our own worktables. Rambusch custom engineered lighting systems make everything look its best!

Call/or come visit our intriguing design rooms and workshops for an initial courtesy consultation. We look forward to hearing from you. Remember Rambusch – on time, within budget, designed just for you.

Personnel:

Edwin P. Rambusch
Martin V. Rambusch
Viggo B.A. Rambusch, Senior Advisor

EST. 1920 ROHLF STUDIO

Rohlf's Stained & Leaded Glass Studio, Inc.
783 South Third Avenue
Mt. Vernon, NY 10550
Toll Free: 800-969-4106
Tel: 914-699-4848
Fax: 914- 699- 7091
E-mail: rohlf1@aol.com
Website: www.rohlfstudio.com

Type of Business:

For Three Generations our family owned and operated Studio together with our affiliate, George L. Payne Studio have been dedicated to excellence in Stained Glass Art. Our team of International designers and Master Craftspersons have created stained glass windows for over a thousand Churches and Institutions Worldwide. Our reputation and experience in the field of Restoration, Replication and Preservation is well known. We would be pleased to assist you in the early stages of planning and design, working with your Architect and/or committee to achieve your desired goals. From concept to completion, we are dedicated to serve you.

Personnel:

Peter A. Rohlf (Chairman & CEO)
Peter Hans Rohlf (President)
Gregory Rohlf (Vice President)

WILLET HAUSER
Architectural Glass, Inc.

Willet Hauser Architectural Glass, Inc.
811 East Cayuga Street
Philadelphia, PA 19124
Tel: 800-533-3960
Fax: 877-495-9486
Website: www.willethauser.com

Type of Business:

Since 1896 Willet Hauser Architectural Glass has a century-old legacy of glass design and over six decades of renowned restoration. Willet Hauser is the preeminent stained glass studio in the country and operates facilities in Winona, Minnesota, and Philadelphia, Pennsylvania. Willet Hauser has created or restored over 15,000 projects, including some of the most magnificent stained glass windows for religious buildings within the United States and in 14 countries around the world.

The proof of our artistry is in the projects that we have designed and restored. Here are just a few prominent examples of the thousands of churches and institutions that have been our clients during the last century: The National Cathedral, Washington, DC; The Church Center, United Nations, NY; The Cathedral of St. Mary of the Assumption, San Francisco, CA; Cathedral of Mary Our Queen, Baltimore, MD; Princeton University Chapel; The Cadet Chapel, United States Military Academy, West Point; Arlington National Cemetery Chapel; The Cathedral of Christ the King, Atlanta, GA.

When you choose Willet Hauser to create or preserve your legacy in stained glass, you are placing it in the experienced hands of artists, designers and craftspeople whose sole purpose is to ensure that every detail reflects your unique vision in a tribute of glass, color, and light.

...You can trust your legacy to our legacy.

CLERICAL APPAREL—General

CM ALMY
OUTFITTERS TO THE CHURCH & CLERGY
NOW INCLUDING THE KERRY COLLECTION

C.M. Almy
Three American Lane, P.O. Box 2644
Greenwich, CT 06836-2644
Tel: 800-225-2569
Fax: 800-426-2569
E-mail: almyaccess@almy.com
Website: www.almy.com
Showroom in Old Greenwich, CT

Type of Business:

Almy was founded in 1892. We design and make virtually all of our products in our Maine shop. It is our mission to design furnishings that will grace your worship and to ensure their value by making them with the highest quality materials and craftsmanship. We make a complete line of vestments, haberdashery, choir robes, candles, communion bread, linens, processional and altar appointments, and eucharistic vessels. We also offer custom design and fabrication of all Almy products, and repair and refurbishing of old metal appointments. Quik Ship© delivery of many popular items. All orders backed by The Almy Guarantee. Call, write, or e-mail for a free catalog.

GASPARD
HANDCRAFTED VESTMENTS AND PARAMENTS
MADE IN THE USA

Gaspard, Inc.
(formerly The Robert Gaspard Company, Inc.)
[illegible]00 N. Janacek Road
Brookfield, WI 53045
Tel: 800-784-6868 (toll free)
Fax: 800-784-7567
E-mail: mail@gaspardinc.com
Website: www.gaspardinc.com

Type of Business:

For more than five decades customers have looked to Gaspard for fine quality, handcrafted vestments and paraments made in the USA. Offerings include the exquisite Castle Craft® collection; wardrobe essentials such as albs, surplices, cassocks, robes, and clergy shirts; extensive metalware offerings, fair linens, altar accessories, and communion ware.

Because your vestment and parament selections are made to order in our one and only location in Brookfield, Wisconsin, special sizes and custom designs are not a problem. One of our friendly Customer Service Representatives will be happy to help you find just the right size and style to enhance your spiritual expression. Please visit us online or call for a free catalog.

Personnel:

Jason R. Gaspard (President)
Joann Gaspard (Vice President)

Renzetti - Magnarelli Clergy Apparel, Inc.

Renzetti – Magnarelli Clergy Apparel, Inc
2216 S. Broad Street
Philadelphia, PA 19145
Tel: 1-888-439-0164 (toll free); 215-339-0558
Fax: 215-463-0161
Website: www.clergyapparel.com

Type of Business:

Renzetti – Magnarelli Clergy Apparel has been serving the vesturing needs of various religious orders and church organizations since 1945. Renzetti – Magnarelli is known for its high quality garments at extremely reasonable prices. We custom manufacture a complete line of cassocks, clerical vests, rabots and vestments. Our garments are made with Old World craftsmanship passed down from generation to generation and are made according to your individual measurements and specifications at a cost that is less than ready made garments, a value we feel cannot be matched.

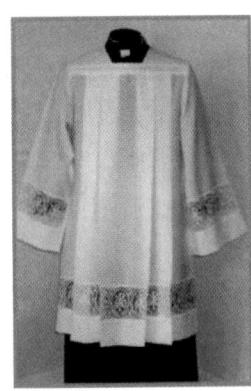

SLABBINCK®

Art Studio Slabbinck
Headquarters:
L. Bauwensstraat 18
8200 Brugge, Belgium
Tel: +32-50-312557
Fax: +32-50-318358
Website: www.slabbinck.com

Type of Business:

Since 1903, Slabbinck is a family owned business that made church vestments in Bruges, Belgium. We make chasubles, stoles, albs, copes, deaconstoles, dalmatics, altar and lectern covers, altar linens and cloths, tapestries and banners. Chalices, ciboria, patens and pyxes are also available. "Slabbinck Speed Service", which allows delivery within 48 hrs, is offered for many items in our catalog. For more information, a free catalog, or a dealer nearest you, visit www.slabbinck.be, e-mail us at info@slabbinck.be , call us at 1-800-423-3224 or fax us at 1-800-284-9000.

CM ALMY
OUTFITTERS TO THE CHURCH & CLERGY

NOW INCLUDING · THE KERRY COLLECTION ·

C.M. Almy
Three American Lane, P.O. Box 2644
Greenwich, CT 06836-2644
Tel: 800-225-2569
Fax: 800-426-2569
E-mail: almyaccess@almy.com
Website: www.almy.com
Showroom in Old Greenwich, CT

Type of Business:

Almy was founded in 1892. We design and make virtually all of our products in our Maine shop. It is our mission to design furnishings that will grace your worship and to ensure their value by making them with the highest quality materials and craftsmanship. We make a complete line of vestments, haberdashery, choir robes, candles, communion bread, linens, processional and altar appointments, and eucharistic vessels. We also offer custom design and fabrication of all Almy products, and repair and refurbishing of old metal appointments. Quik Ship© delivery of many popular items. All orders backed by The Almy Guarantee. Call, write, or e-mail for a free catalog.

THE HOLY ROOD GUILD
for the Sacred Liturgy

The Holy Rood Guild
St. Joseph's Abbey
167 North Spencer Road
Spencer, MA 01562-1233
Tel: 866-383-7292
E-mail: customerservice@holyroodguild.com
Website: www.holyroodguild.com

Type of Business:

Designers and crafters of ecclesiastical vesture for over 60 years. Inspire by our monastic tradition, we seek to unite in our work simplicity i design, quality in materials and excellence in craftsmanship. The resul is vesture that enhances the liturgical celebration with visual grace an order. Our artists—both monks and laypersons—are available for custom design work and consultation.

House of Hansen
4223 West Irving Park Road
Chicago, IL 60641
Tel: 773-736-5858
Fax: 773-736-6715

Type of Business:

Clerical tailoring specialists for over 85 years. We specialize in Prelatial Appointments and Custom Tailored cassocks made by our professional staff. Custom tailored vestments and albs. A full line of ready-made clerical apparel.

Renzetti - Magnarelli Clergy Apparel, Inc.

enzetti – Magnarelli Clergy Apparel, Inc
216 S. Broad Street
hiladelphia, PA 19145
el: 1-888-439-0164 (toll free); 215-339-0558
ax: 215-463-0161
Vebsite: www.clergyapparel.com

ype of Business:

Renzetti – Magnarelli Clergy Apparel has been serving the vesturing needs of various religious orders and church organizations since 1945. Renzetti – Magnarelli is known for its high quality garments at extremely reasonable prices. We custom manufacture a complete line of cassocks, clerical vests, rabots and vestments. Our garments are made with Old World craftsmanship passed down from generation to generation and are made according to your individual measurements and specifications at a cost that is less than ready made garments, a value we feel cannot be matched.

Renzetti - Magnarelli Clergy Apparel, Inc.

Renzetti – Magnarelli Clergy Apparel, Inc
2216 S. Broad Street
Philadelphia, PA 19145
Tel: 1-888-439-0164 (toll free); 215-339-0558
Fax: 215-463-0161
Website: www.clergyapparel.com

Type of Business:

Renzetti – Magnarelli Clergy Apparel has been serving the vesturing needs of various religious orders and church organizations since 1945. Renzetti – Magnarelli is known for its high quality garments at extremely reasonable prices. We custom manufacture a complete line of cassocks, clerical vests, rabots and vestments. Our garments are made with Old World craftsmanship passed down from generation to generation and are made according to your individual measurements and specifications at a cost that is less than ready made garments, a value we feel cannot be matched.

ARTECH CHURCH INTERIORS INC.

Artech Church Interiors, Inc.
12 Mill Plain Road
Danbury, CT 06811
Tel: 800-222-7397 (toll free); 203-744-2600
Fax: 203-744-0630
Website: http://www.artechchurchinteriors.com/

Type of Business:

Artech Church Interiors is a third generation family-run business, with over 45 years of personal experience in Church Seating, Church Renovation, and Church Restoration. Artech brings to every job the skill and dedication of master craftsmen. Our specialists will restore your Church's unique interior, or develop an innovative design to completely transform the Church.

Our Services Include: Interior restoration services include: Liturgical design and renderings, Plaster Restoration, Mold making and casting, Interior painting including specialty finishes, Murals, Restoration of Statues and Stations of the Cross, Pew restoration and refinishing, Church Seating, Church Furniture, Pew Cushions and Upholstery, Flooring including carpet, tile, marble, and wood, New and refurbished lighting, Audio and Video, Electric Candle stands.

Exterior restoration services include: Window frame restoration, Buy and Sell Stained Glass windows, Protective Covering and Venting for Windows, Door restoration and new doors, Exterior painting, Bells and Carillon Systems.

Personnel:

Thomas Burns (President) tom@artechchurchinteriors.com
William Burns (Vice President) bill@artechchurchinteriors.com

Baker Liturgical Art, LLC
Church Restoration / Church Renovation

Baker Liturgical Art, LLC
136 Curtiss Street
Southington, CT 06489
Tel: 860-621-7471
Fax: 860-621-7607
E-mail: bakerart@sbcglobal.net
Website: www.bakerliturgicalart.com

Type of Business:

Baker Liturgical Art, LLC offers a full range of construction and renovation services. These services encompass architectural specifications and liturgical design as well as sound system and lighting design.

Our liturgical design talents result in beautiful altar furnishings of hand-carved wood or of fine imported Italian marble. Stained glass and sacred artwork (painted, wood-carved or chiseled from marble) are the final accents to complete prayerful settings in every worship space from the smallest Chapel to the grandest Cathedral! Baker Liturgical Art, LLC prides itself in offering uncompromising quality in its products and services.

Our Services Include: Liturgical Design, Architectural Services, Liturgical Furnishings, Sculpture & Artwork, Flooring, Millwork, Multi-Media Systems, Stained Glass Fabrication & Restoration.

Additional location: 1300 Gulfshore Blvd., North #510 Naples, FL 34102
P: 860-818-3799.

EVERGREENE Architectural Arts

EverGreene Architectural Arts, Inc.
450 West 31 Street, 7th Floor
Tel: 212-244-2800
Fax: 212-244-6204
E-mail: info@evergreene.com
Website: www.evergreene.com

Type of Business:

For more than 30 years, EverGreene has designed and implemented sacred artwork, decorative painting, plasterwork, and associated services for the Catholic Church nationwide. EverGreene works with clients to develop solutions that are beautiful and enduring, and offers consultation for budget estimates and value engineering. With a permanent staff that includes some of the world's finest ecclesiastical artists, along with skilled designers and project managers, EverGreene is a resource for projects that will enhance the experience of any worship space and inspire generations to come.

Notable projects: Basilica of the Assumption, Baltimore, MD; St. Thomas Aquinas College Chapel, Santa Paula, CA; Cathedral of the Blessed Sacrament, Sacramento, CA.

The EverGreene team includes project managers, ecclesiastical designers, fine artists, ornamental plaster sculptors, decorative painters, and craftspeople. Call for a free consultation on design or restoration, including practical approaches and budget recommendations.

Personnel:

Jeff Greene (President)
Kim Lovejoy (Vice President, Director of Restoration)
Terry Vanderwell (Director of Restoration, Midwest)

GG Guidance In Giving, Inc.

Guidance in Giving, Inc.
Full Service Stewardship, Development and Campaign Consultants
225 Snedecor Avenue
Bayport, NY 11705
Tel: 888-757-5444; Cell: 631-553-9064
E-mail: mcusack@guidanceingiving.com
Website: www.guidanceingiving.com

Type of Business:

Guidance In Giving, Inc. is a Catholic organization that truly understands the mission of the Catholic Church. Serving as stewardship, development and campaign counsel to dioceses, parishes and schools, our firm has extensive experience in conducting capital campaigns and implementing stewardship throughout the United States. In all of our development efforts we utilize techniques that are continuously tested and refined. Services include: diocesan capital campaigns; diocesan annual appeals; diocesan development audits and feasibility studies; parish capital campaigns; implementing stewardship; parish feasibility studies, school development audits, school feasibility studies, major gifts solicitations and school capital campaigns. Additionally, the firm has an Hispanic Division and offers bilingual services. To discuss your individual situation or to get a cost free analysis of your potential, please contact Michael R. Cusack, President and CEO at 888-757-5444.

Personnel:

Michael R. Cusack (President and CEO)
Michael V. Goodwin (Executive Vice President)
Joseph W. Zamorano (Executive Vice President)
Stephen A. Babcock (Vice President)
Joseph Neville (Vice President)
Carlos Proaño (Vice President, Hispanic Division)

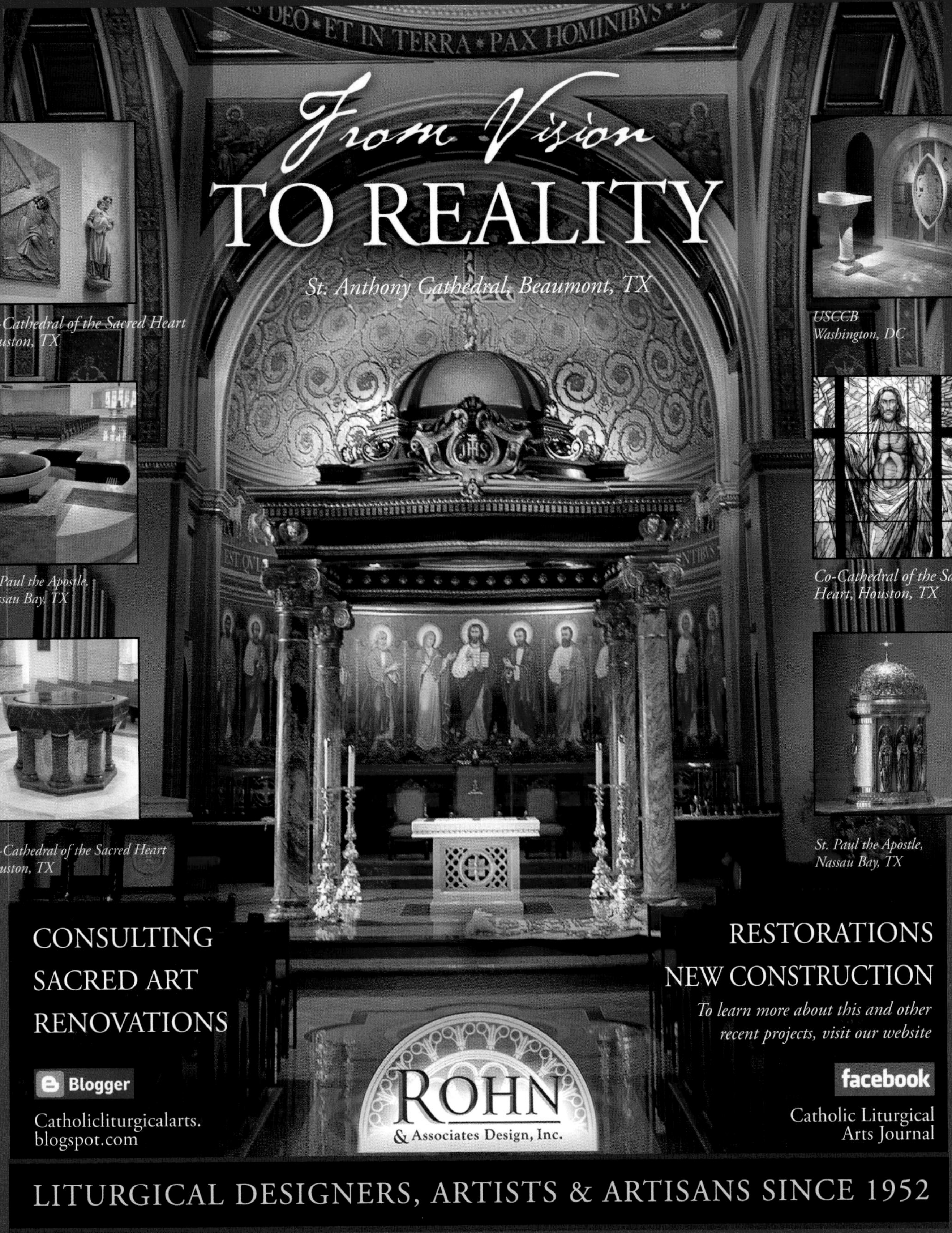
DEO • ET IN TERRA • PAX HOMINIBVS
From Vision
TO REALITY
St. Anthony Cathedral, Beaumont, TX
Co-Cathedral of the Sacred Heart
Houston, TX
USCCB
Washington, DC
St. Paul the Apostle,
Nassau Bay, TX
Co-Cathedral of the Sacred
Heart, Houston, TX
Co-Cathedral of the Sacred Heart
Houston, TX
St. Paul the Apostle,
Nassau Bay, TX
CONSULTING
SACRED ART
RENOVATIONS
RESTORATIONS
NEW CONSTRUCTION
To learn more about this and other recent projects, visit our website
Blogger
Catholicliturgicalarts.
blogspot.com
ROHN
& Associates Design, Inc.
facebook
Catholic Liturgical
Arts Journal
LITURGICAL DESIGNERS, ARTISTS & ARTISANS SINCE 1952

Kosinski architecture, inc.

Architecture, Planning, Liturgical Design

Kosinski Architecture, Inc.
1401 E. Broward Boulevard, Suite 201
Fort Lauderdale, FL 33301
Tel: 954-627-6988
Fax: 954-627-6955
E-mail: info@kosinskiarchitecture.com
Website: www.kosinskiarchitecture.com

Type of Business:

Kosinski Architecture, Inc., Architects Planners, with offices in Fort Lauderdale, Florida and Branford, Connecticut provides award winning design nationally. The firm's portfolio spans a variety of project types, including religious, educational, housing, and mixed use projects.

The firm is adept at working in both modern and traditional idioms, providing adroit responses to program and technical requirements regardless of stylistic genre.

Kosinski's extensive knowledge of liturgy and of the history of church architecture allows it to provide church clients with exceptional architectural and liturgical design services. Our full range of in-house professional services, including master-planning, the design of all liturgical elements, and interior design gives its clients a single point of contact for complete project delivery. As certified restoration experts, Kosinski's knowledge and appreciation of architectural history is apparent in its extensive restoration portfolio.

Personnel:

Peter R. Kosinski, AIA, NCARB (Contact)

ROHN

&Associates Design, Inc.

Rohn & Associates Design, Inc.
1113 Creedmoor Avenue
Pittsburgh, PA 15226
Tel: 412-561-1228; 800-245-1288
Fax: 412-561-1201
E-mail: rolfrohn@rohndesign.com
Website: www.rohndesign.com
Blog: http://catholicliturgicalarts.blogspot.com/
Facebook: Catholic Liturgical Arts Journal

Type of Business:

Liturgical Designers, Artists & Artisans

TRADITION. Over the past 58 years, we have assisted the Catholic Church by designing, budgeting and implementing liturgical spaces.

COLLABORATION. We work side-by-side with our clients and collaborators to design and create appropriate and quality sacred art, interior finishes, lighting systems, acoustical systems, liturgical furnishings and appointments to create a rich devotional experience for your parishioners.

EXPERIENCE. We draw upon decades of experience and from a rich treasury of designers, architectural staff and contributing artists.

SCOPE OF SERVICES: Liturgical Design; Interior Design & Decorating; Sacred Artwork; Mosaics; Art Glass; Statuary; Liturgical Appointments; Liturgical Furniture; Metalwork.

ADDITIONAL LOCATIONS: 17515 Spring Cypress, Ste C PMB #246 Cypress, TX 77429. Tel. & Fax: 281-304-7736; 719 S. Flores St., Suite 200, San Antonio, TX 78204. Tel.: 210-231-0377; Fax: 210-231-0366

Contact us to arrange a complimentary project review.

Personnel:

Rolf R. Rohn (President - Liturgical Designer-Consultant)
Kathleen L. Maglicco (Vice President, Design)
Renate Rohn (Vice President, Art)
Francesca Lofaro (Director, Sales)

SACRED SPACES INC

Liturgical Design Studios

Sacred Spaces Liturgical Design Studios, Inc.
312 Montgomery Street, Suite 100
Alexandria, VA 22314
Tel: 703-519-9800; 1-888-519-4599 (toll free)
Fax: 703-519-4599
E-mail: info@sacredspacesinc.com
Website: www.SacredSpacesInc.com

Type of Business:

Sacred Spaces is a liturgical design team of international artists and master craftsmen with experience spanning four decades in the design of worship environments: new construction, renovation and restoration. Our Services include Liturgical Design Consulting, Custom Design, Appointments, Removals, Consignments and Facsimiles. Specializing in marble, bronze and stone, we custom design altars, ambos, tabernacle thrones and baptismal fonts. We also offer Master Planning Services and Educational Programs for pastoral teams and parish-wide Town Hall meetings. Sacred Spaces - Excellence in Liturgical Design, Artistry and Craftsmanship.

Personnel:

J. Michael Carrigan (President/CEO)
John Grosvenor (Project Director)
Francisco M. Cano (Art Director)

WILLET HAUSER

Architectural Glass, Inc.

Willet Hauser Architectural Glass, Inc.
811 East Cayuga Street
Philadelphia, PA 19124
Tel: 800-533-3960
Fax: 877-495-9486
Website: www.willethauser.com

Type of Business:

Since 1896 Willet Hauser Architectural Glass has a century-old legacy of glass design and over six decades of renowned restoration. Willet Hauser is the preeminent stained glass studio in the country and operates facilities in Winona, Minnesota, and Philadelphia, Pennsylvania. Willet Hauser has created or restored over 15,000 projects, including some of the most magnificent stained glass windows for religious buildings within the United States and in 14 countries around the world.

The proof of our artistry is in the projects that we have designed and restored. Here are just a few prominent examples of the thousands of churches and institutions that have been our clients during the last century: The National Cathedral, Washington, DC; The Church Center, United Nations, NY; The Cathedral of St. Mary of the Assumption, San Francisco, CA; Cathedral of Mary Our Queen, Baltimore, MD; Princeton University Chapel; The Cadet Chapel, United States Military Academy, West Point; Arlington National Cemetery Chapel; The Cathedral of Christ the King, Atlanta, GA.

When you choose Willet Hauser to create or preserve your legacy in stained glass, you are placing it in the experienced hands of artists, designers and craftspeople whose sole purpose is to ensure that every detail reflects your unique vision in a tribute of glass, color, and light.

...You can trust your legacy to our legacy.

FRANCK & LOHSEN
ARCHITECTS
FRANCKLOHSEN.COM ~ (202) 223-9449

ranck & Lohsen Architects Inc
715 N Street, N.W.
Vashington, DC 20036-2801
el: 202-223-9449
ax: 202-223-9484
-mail: art@francklohsen.com
Vebsite: www.francklohsen.com

ype of Business:

Architectural design, Master Planning, new construction, historic renovations and additions of Churches and Religious facilities. Design of liturgical elements and furnishings including mosaics, altars, lighting fixtures, statuary, custom vestments, interiors, etc. Our firm provides services nationally from our offices in Washington, DC.
We are dedicated to producing the highest quality work through a thoughtful and sophisticated combination of classical approaches and modern sensibilities in keeping with the established traditions and norms of the Church. Please feel free to inquire with any questions.

ersonnel:

Arthur Lohsen, AIA, LEED, NCARB, RIBA (President)
Michael Franck, AIA, NCARB, RIBA (Vice President)

Kosinski architecture, inc.
Architecture, Planning, Liturgical Design

Kosinski Architecture, Inc.
1401 E. Broward Boulevard, Suite 201
Fort Lauderdale, FL 33301
Tel: 954-627-6988
Fax: 954-627-6955
E-mail: info@kosinskiarchitecture.com
Website: www.kosinskiarchitecture.com

Type of Business:

Kosinski Architecture, Inc., Architects Planners, with offices in Fort Lauderdale, Florida and Branford, Connecticut provides award winning design nationally. The firm's portfolio spans a variety of project types, including religious, educational, housing, and mixed use projects.
The firm is adept at working in both modern and traditional idioms, providing adroit responses to program and technical requirements regardless of stylistic genre.
Kosinski's extensive knowledge of liturgy and of the history of church architecture allows it to provide church clients with exceptional architectural and liturgical design services. Our full range of in-house professional services, including master-planning, the design of all liturgical elements, and interior design gives its clients a single point of contact for complete project delivery. As certified restoration experts, Kosinski's knowledge and appreciation of architectural history is apparent in its extensive restoration portfolio.

Personnel:

Peter R. Kosinski, AIA, NCARB (Contact)

BOTTI STUDIO OF
ARCHITECTURAL ARTS, INC.

Botti Studio of Architectural Arts, Inc.
919 Grove Street
Evanston, IL 60201
Tel: 800-524-7211; 847-869-5933
Fax: 847-869-5996
E-mail: botti@bottistudio.com
Website: www.bottistudio.com

Type of Business:

Since 1864, Botti Studio has specialized in serving the ecclesiastic environment through design, fabrication, delivery, and installation. Experts on staff in new design commissions, repair, restoration, conservation, and repair provide a source for experienced project management – from conception through completion. Services include: stained, faceted, sandblasted, carved and painted glass, wood / metal / stone frames / protective glazing, murals, marble, mosaics, bronze, statuary, gilding, painting and decorating, complete interiors, new and restorations, historic discovery, documentation and consultation to owner / architect.
Our staff of 45 includes internationally recognized ecclesiastic artists / designers working in conjunction with highly skilled craftspeople / artisans / conservators.
Locations: New York, NY / (212) 362-6085, LaPorte, IN / (219) 362-5934, Chicago, IL / (847) 869-5933, San Diego, CA / (760) 753-0705, Sarasota, FL / (941) 951-0978, Nassau, Bahamas / (242) 327-2992, Agropoli, Italy / (800) 524-7211.

Personnel:

Ettore Christopher Botti (Principal)
Ethlyn Panzironi Botti (Principal)

Conrad Schmitt Studios Inc.
Excellence in Artistry Since 1889

Conrad Schmitt Studios, Inc.
2405 S. 162nd Street
New Berlin, WI 53151
Tel: 800-969-3033; 262-786-3030
Fax: 262-786-9036
E-mail: studio@conradschmitt.com
Website: www.conradschmitt.com

Type of Business:

Since 1889, CSS has been privileged to decorate and restore churches of all sizes and styles throughout the country. Our experienced staff assists projects in the early stages to help assemble the master plan, communicate the vision and generate the enthusiasm and funding needed to make the plan a reality. Some of the tools used to accomplish these goals include renderings, on-site samples, budgetary estimates and fundraising materials.
Our comprehensive scope of services allows us to be a single source for a variety of needs, creating the best projects in terms of function, longevity and aesthetics. Our services include the investigation and documentation of original decorative schemes, gilding, glazing, marbleizing, stenciling, trompe l'oeil and faux finishing.
Recent decorating commissions include the Cathedral of the Immaculate Conception, Springfield, IL; St. Mary Magdalen Catholic Church, Abbeville, LA; St. Joseph Cathedral, Sioux Falls, SD; and St. John Neumann Catholic Church, Knoxville, TN.

Conservation

Conrad Schmitt Studios Inc.

Excellence in Artistry Since 1889

Conrad Schmitt Studios, Inc.
2405 S. 162nd Street
New Berlin, WI 53151
Tel: 800-969-3033; 262-786-3030
Fax: 262-786-9036
E-mail: studio@conradschmitt.com
Website: www.conradschmitt.com

Type of Business:

Since 1889, CSS has been privileged to decorate and restore churches of all sizes and styles throughout the country. Our experienced staff assists projects in the early stages to help assemble the master plan, communicate the vision and generate the enthusiasm and funding needed to make the plan a reality. Some of the tools used to accomplish these goals include renderings, on-site samples, budgetary estimates and fundraising materials.

Our comprehensive scope of services allows us to be a single source for a variety of needs, creating the best projects in terms of function, longevity and aesthetics. Our services include the investigation and documentation of original decorative schemes, gilding, glazing, marbleizing, stenciling, trompe l'oeil and faux finishing.

Recent decorating commissions include the Cathedral of the Immaculate Conception, Springfield, IL; St. Mary Magdalen Catholic Church, Abbeville, LA; St. Joseph Cathedral, Sioux Falls, SD; and St. John Neumann Catholic Church, Knoxville, TN.

Liturgical Consultants

Kosinski architecture, inc.

Architecture, Planning, Liturgical Design

Kosinski Architecture, Inc.
1401 E. Broward Boulevard, Suite 201
Fort Lauderdale, FL 33301
Tel: 954-627-6988
Fax: 954-627-6955
E-mail: info@kosinskiarchitecture.com
Website: www.kosinskiarchitecture.com

Type of Business:

Kosinski Architecture, Inc., Architects Planners, with offices in Fort Lauderdale, Florida and Branford, Connecticut provides award winning design nationally. The firm's portfolio spans a variety of project types, including religious, educational, housing, and mixed use projects.

The firm is adept at working in both modern and traditional idioms, providing adroit responses to program and technical requirements regardless of stylistic genre.

Kosinski's extensive knowledge of liturgy and of the history of church architecture allows it to provide church clients with exceptional architectural and liturgical design services. Our full range of in-house professional services, including master-planning, the design of all liturgical elements, and interior design gives its clients a single point of contact for complete project delivery. As certified restoration experts, Kosinski's knowledge and appreciation of architectural history is apparent in its extensive restoration portfolio.

Personnel:

Peter R. Kosinski, AIA, NCARB (Contact)

Restoration/Refinishing

TOUJOURS

ADRIAN HAMERS® CHURCH INTERIORS

Adrian Hamers, Inc.
2 Madison Avenue
Larchmont, NY 10538
Tel: 914-834-7780
Fax: 914-834-0712
Website: www.adrianhamers.com

Type of Business:

Custom designers and manufacturers of Sacred Vessels. Since 1887, the Hamers name has been synonymous with expert Silversmithing throughout the world in the field of Liturgical Art. Please contact us for those hard to find items, as we always have a large selection of Adrian Hamers Estate Collection pieces in stock. We have a large collection of antique church stained glass windows available (both full sets and individual). We are experts in: Church Interiors from design to execution, Renovations, Altars, Sacred Vessels, Gold and Silver Plating & Repairing, Appraisals, Tabernacles, Marble, Statuary, Woodwork & Woodcarving, Stained Glass, Pews & Chairs, Gold Leafing, Frescoes, Restoration, Trompe-l'oeuil, Wall Murals (repair and conservation cleaning), Ornamental Plaster, Heraldic Designs & Bishop Regalia. Please call us for a free 36-page Sacred Vessels color catalog, or our free 80-page color Woodcarvings catalog.

BOTTI STUDIO OF ARCHITECTURAL ARTS, INC.

Botti Studio of Architectural Arts, Inc.
919 Grove Street
Evanston, IL 60201
Tel: 800-524-7211; 847-869-5933
Fax: 847-869-5996
E-mail: botti@bottistudio.com
Website: www.bottistudio.com

Type of Business:

Since 1864, Botti Studio has specialized in serving the ecclesiastic environment through design, fabrication, delivery, and installation. Experts on staff in new design commissions, repair, restoration, conservation, and repair provide a source for experienced project management – from conception through completion. Services include: stained, faceted, sandblasted, carved and painted glass, wood / metal / stone frames / protective glazing, murals, marble, mosaics, bronze, statuary, gilding, painting and decorating, complete interiors, new and restorations, historic discovery, documentation and consultation to owner / architect.

Our staff of 45 includes internationally recognized ecclesiastic artists / designers working in conjunction with highly skilled craftspeople / artisans / conservators.

Locations: New York, NY / (212) 362-6085, LaPorte, IN / (219) 362-5934, Chicago, IL / (847) 869-5933, San Diego, CA / (760) 753-0705, Sarasota, FL / (941) 951-0978, Nassau, Bahamas / (242) 327-2992, Agropoli, Italy / (800) 524-7211.

Personnel:

Ettore Christopher Botti (Principal)
Ethlyn Panzironi Botti (Principal)

Conrad Schmitt Studios Inc.

Excellence in Artistry Since 1889

Conrad Schmitt Studios, Inc.
2405 S. 162nd Street
New Berlin, WI 53151
Tel: 800-969-3033; 262-786-3030
Fax: 262-786-9036
E-mail: studio@conradschmitt.com
Website: www.conradschmitt.com

Type of Business:

Since 1889, CSS has been privileged to decorate and restore churches of all sizes and styles throughout the country. Our experienced staff assists projects in the early stages to help assemble the master plan, communicate the vision and generate the enthusiasm and funding needed to make the plan a reality. Some of the tools used to accomplish these goals include renderings, on-site samples, budgetary estimates and fundraising materials.

Our comprehensive scope of services allows us to be a single source for a variety of needs, creating the best projects in terms of function, longevity and aesthetics. Our services include the investigation and documentation of original decorative schemes, gilding, glazing, marbleizing, stenciling, trompe l'oeil and faux finishing.

Recent decorating commissions include the Cathedral of the Immaculate Conception, Springfield, IL; St. Mary Magdalen Catholic Church, Abbeville, LA; St. Joseph Cathedral, Sioux Falls, SD; and St. John Neumann Catholic Church, Knoxville, TN.

RAMBUSCH

SINCE 1898

Rambusch
160 Cornelison Avenue
Jersey City, NJ 07304
Tel: 201-333-2525
Fax: 201-433-3355
Website: www.rambusch.com

Type of Business:

Creativity and Quality are Rambusch Hallmarks. A small, highly personal business, where everything is custom. Each inquiry is handled by a principal, who guides the client through a myriad of possibilities. The chosen solution is then made tangible by our supremely skilled craftspeople.

Rambusch creates complete interiors, shrines, individual art works, stained glass and mosaics. New work, renovations, and restorations all receive the same attention, resulting in beautiful, fitting solutions for your unique commission. Our design rooms, art metal workshops and stained glass studios are in-house, ensuring seamless crafting of all designs. Rambusch-patented lighting fixtures, the recognized industry standard for church lighting, are individually built on our own worktables. Rambusch custom engineered lighting systems make everything look its best!

Call/or come visit our intriguing design rooms and workshops for an initial courtesy consultation. We look forward to hearing from you. Remember Rambusch – on time, within budget, designed just for you.

Personnel:

Edwin P. Rambusch
Martin V. Rambusch
Viggo B.A. Rambusch, Senior Advisor

EST. 1920 ROHLF STUDIO

Rohlf's Stained & Leaded Glass Studio, Inc.
783 South Third Avenue
Mt. Vernon, NY 10550
Toll Free: 800-969-4106
Tel: 914-699-4848
Fax: 914- 699- 7091
E-mail: rohlf1@aol.com
Website: www.rohlfstudio.com

Type of Business:

For Three Generations our family owned and operated Studio together with our affiliate, George L. Payne Studio have been dedicated to excellence in Stained Glass Art. Our team of International designers and Master Craftspersons have created stained glass windows for over a thousand Churches and Institutions Worldwide. Our reputation and experience in the field of Restoration, Replication and Preservation is well known. We would be pleased to assist you in the early stages of planning and design, working with your Architect and/or committee to achieve your desired goals. From concept to completion, we are dedicated to serve you.

Personnel:

Peter A. Rohlf (Chairman & CEO)
Peter Hans Rohlf (President)
Gregory Rohlf (Vice President)

UNIVERSAL ART STUDIO

67 Mountain Spring Drive
Sparta, NJ 07871
Tel: 973-726-0835
E-mail: yuri@uasrestoration.com
Website: uasrestoration.com

Type of Business:

HISTORICAL RESTORATION — CONSERVATION OF ART

With very few exceptions we shall repair any object of aesthetic, ecclesiastical, spiritual, historical, sentimental or simply monetary value.

We offer following services: Complete restoration projects, including: architectural planning, management and execution. Design and fabrication of church furnishings and fixtures. Restoration of paintings, including: murals, frescoes, Greek or Russian icons. Canvas repairs, relining, cleaning, stretching. Custom framing. Goldleafing. Repairs of statuary made of gypsum, marble, wood, composit materials. Repairs of mosaics, tile, ceramics, plaster, terrazzo. Restoration of antique furniture and woodcarvings.

Our Art Gallery creates a range of fine art from ecclesiastical to contemporary, to church interiors, to decoration of living space.

Honestly, Yuri Mironoff

WILLET HAUSER
Architectural Glass, Inc.

Willet Hauser Architectural Glass, Inc.
811 East Cayuga Street
Philadelphia, PA 19124
Tel: 800-533-3960
Fax: 877-495-9486
Website: www.willethauser.com

Type of Business:

Since 1896 Willet Hauser Architectural Glass has a century-old legacy of glass design and over six decades of renowned restoration. Willet Hauser is the preeminent stained glass studio in the country and operates facilities in Winona, Minnesota, and Philadelphia, Pennsylvania. Willet Hauser has created or restored over 15,000 projects, including some of the most magnificent stained glass windows for religious buildings within the United States and in 14 countries around the world.

The proof of our artistry is in the projects that we have designed and restored. Here are just a few prominent examples of the thousands of churches and institutions that have been our clients during the last century: The National Cathedral, Washington, DC; The Church Center, United Nations, NY; The Cathedral of St. Mary of the Assumption, San Francisco, CA; Cathedral of Mary Our Queen, Baltimore, MD; Princeton University Chapel; The Cadet Chapel, United States Military Academy, West Point; Arlington National Cemetery Chapel; The Cathedral of Christ the King, Atlanta, GA.

When you choose Willet Hauser to create or preserve your legacy in stained glass, you are placing it in the experienced hands of artists, designers and craftspeople whose sole purpose is to ensure that every detail reflects your unique vision in a tribute of glass, color, and light.

...You can trust your legacy to our legacy.

Educational Opportunities

HGI
GUEST HOUSE INSTITUTE

Guest House Institute
1601 Joslyn Road
Lake Orion, MI 48360
Tel: 800-626-6910; 248-391-4445
Fax: 248-391-0210
E-mail: crichards@guesthouse.org
Website: www.guesthouseinstitute.org

Type of Business:

Just as Guest House's treatment services have grown within the last decade, so too has its service to the Church's leadership in the area of education. In an effort to consolidate, focus and accelerate our education efforts, we created the Guest House Institute.

The mission of Guest House Institute is to promote health and spiritual wellness of Catholics by providing educational services regarding alcoholism and other addictions, and by promoting and providing research in alcoholism and other addictions affecting the Catholic Church.

Personnel:

Daniel A. Kidd (President & Chief Executive Officer)
Michael P. Morton (Executive Director)
Colleen Richards (Project Assistant)

NCCA

National Catholic Council on Alcoholism and Related Drug Problems
1601 Joslyn Road
Lake Orion, MI 48360
Tel: 248-391-4445, ext. 1200
Fax: 248-391-0210
E-mail: ncca@guesthouse.org
Website: www.nccatoday.org

Type of Business:

The NCCA, affiliated with the U.S. Conference of Catholic Bishops, an under the auspices of Guest House, Inc., is dedicated to the promotio of adequate treatment for all clergy, men and women religious, and lait who are suffering from alcoholism and other drug dependencies. NCC also provides educational programs including workshops for dioceses, a annual Conference, also educational and "Spirituality Support" resources including a free booklet: "Prayers for Addicted Persons and Their Love Ones"; also a publication: "When They Won't (or Can't) Quit Alcohol c Drugs". The NCCA seeks to help those struggling to overcome an addictio and those engaged in pastoral ministry, including outreach to the nation' jail and prison ministries.

Personnel:

Richard Thibodeau (Executive Director)

Seton Hall University
Immaculate Conception Seminary School of Theology
400 South Orange Avenue
South Orange, NJ 07079
Tel: 973-761-9575
Fax: 973-761-9577
E-mail: theology@shu.edu
Website: theology.shu.edu

Type of Business:

Immaculate Conception Seminary School of Theology (ICSST) is the schoo of theology of Seton Hall University and the major seminary of the Catholic Archdiocese of Newark. With a 150-year tradition of preparing committe Catholics for service to the Church, ICSST admits both seminarian studying for the Catholic priesthood and lay students. ICSST offers thre graduate degree programs—the Master of Arts in Theology, the Master o Arts in Pastoral Ministry and the Master of Arts in Divinity—in addition t a Bachelor of Arts in Catholic Theology.

Personnel:

Rev. Monsignor Robert F. Coleman, J.C.D. (Rector/Dean)
Rev. Thomas Nydegger, M.Div. (Vice Rector/Business Manager)
Rev. Joseph Chapel, S.T.D. (Associate Dean)
Dianne M. Traflet, J.D., S.T.D. (Associate Dean)

HOLY CROSS FAMILY MINISTRIES

Holy Cross Family Ministries
Family Rosary
Family Theater Productions
Father Peyton Family Institute
Family Rosary International
518 Washington Street
North Easton, MA 02356
Tel: 508-238-4095
Fax: 508-238-3953
Website: www.hcfm.org

Type of Business:

Continuing the mission of our founder, Servant of God Father Patrick Peyton, C.S.C., Holy Cross Family Ministries serves Jesus Christ and His Church throughout the world by promoting and supporting the spiritual well-being of the family through products and programs.

Personnel:

Fr. John Phalen, C.S.C. (President)
Susan Wallace (Director of External Relations)
Beth Mahoney (Mission Director)

LIGHTHOUSE CATHOLIC MEDIA™ A NOT FOR PROFIT CORPORATION

Lighthouse Catholic Media, NFP
303 E. State Street
Sycamore, IL 60178
Tel: 866-767-3155 (toll free)
Fax: 815-895-0333
E-mail: Tim@LighthouseCatholicMedia.org
Website: www.LigthouseCatholicMedia.org

Type of Business:

Lighthouse Catholic Media, NFP is a not for profit organization dedicated to providing high quality Catholic audio CDs as an affordable and convenient way for parishioners to hear faith-filled presentations from the best Catholic speakers of our day.
These recordings provide an easy and effective way to foster catechesis, and provide parishioners with a powerful way to reach out to their family members, friends, etc.
"These CDs helped make the Mass come alive and left me with a hunger to learn more. What a blessing!"
Our FAITHRAISER Kiosk Program is proven effective, with over 3,000 parish customers, and the program is primarily self-funding.
We have over 150 CD titles available in English and Spanish, and our Starter Kit comes complete with a beautiful display stand, CDs, and pamphlets. We also provide a proven success plan, support, and assistance to make your program a success.
For more information, please call 866-767-3155.

Personnel:

Mark Middendorf (President, Board of Directors)
Terry Barber (Chairman of the Board)
Dave Durand (Vice President of Sales)
Tim Truckenbrod (Vice President of Marketing and Operations)

MERCY CENTER CONFERENCES, RETREATS & SPIRITUAL PROGRAMS

Mercy Center
Spirituality & Conference Center
2300 Adeline Drive
Burlingame, CA 94010-5540
Tel: 650-340-7474
Fax: 650-340-1299
E-mail: mc@mercyburl.org
Website: www.mercy-center.org

Type of Business:

Mercy Center Burlingame Conference and Retreat Center
We are known worldwide for pioneering work in spiritual direction, Taizé prayer and East-West meditation. Educational and spiritual conferences, retreats and training programs are offered year round on our beautiful, wooded campus. We offer summer internships in spiritual direction, on-going training in Centering Prayer, directed retreats and a personal sabbatical program. We will be glad to spend time with you finding the right program or retreat that fits your need. Limited scholarships available. Check out the videos on our website www.mercy-center.org to find out what our past program participants say about our transformational contemplative programs. Contact Colleen Shannon Soracco 650-340-7495 in our Program office for assistance.

Personnel:

Suzanne Buckley (Director)
Sue Thourson (Conference Services/Reservations)

SELECT International

Select International Tours
85 Park Avenue
Flemington, NJ 08822
Tel: 800-842-4842
Fax: 908-237-9263
E-mail: sales@select-intl.com
Website: www.selectinternationaltours.com

Type of Business:

Join our 25th anniversary celebration by receiving a valuable thank you gift from Select International Tours, when you book a group with us and mention this listing from OCD.
Through our network of partner offices in Europe, Mexico and the Holy Land we offer you many choices for custom designed or scheduled group departures. New for 2011 are guaranteed departures to the Holy Land, Egypt, Turkey, Greece, Medjugorje and Italy. Plus cruises with 1 free for every 10 booked and World Youth Day in Madrid, Spain. Call us at 800-842-4842 for our brochures, group quotes or check out our web site for the latest news about pilgrimage travel www.selectinternationaltours.com.
We do all the work to make your pilgrimage experience excellent and easy from beginning to end.

FUNDRAISING—General

CHURCHSUPPLIER.COM
Jewelry, Fundraising, Stewardship, Supplies ■ Division of Neibauer Press

ChurchStewardship and Growth Center
20 Industrial Drive
Warminster, PA 18974 USA
Tel: 800-322-6203; 215-322-6200
Fax: 215-322-2495
E-mail: Sales@ChurchSupplier.com; Nathan@ChurchSupplier.com
Website: www.ChurchSupplier.com

Type of Business:

Church Supplier is a unique church and parish resource for inexpensive self-directed stewardship giving programs. These programs require volunteers to run. Our proven programs include Pony Express - a stewardship program, Let Love Guide You - a canvas program, Give in Grace, We are Family and many church giving brochures. We also write, design and print custom giving programs, envelopes and mailings. We design and manufacture many items for donations including coin folders, coin boxes, and lucite collection boxes for institutions. We design and sell church supplies, childrens' camp and school giveaways for churches on a limited budget. We operate a complete printing and mailing company. We manufacture value priced custom jewelry, bracelets, coins and lapel pins for churches and their men's, ladies and children's fellowships. No fancy consultants. No fancy fees. We labor for the Lord in helping to find solutions for parishes since 1967.

Personnel:

Pastor Walt Waddell (Sales Manager)
Nathan Neibauer (President)

COSGRIFF COMPANY
CAPITAL CAMPAIGN COUNSEL

Cosgriff Company
209 South 19th Street
Omaha, NE 68102
Tel: 800-456-9902
Fax: 402-341-8590
E-mail: cosgriff@cosgriffco.com
Website: www.cosgriff.com

Type of Business:

Celebrating 50 years of campaign excellence to Catholic parishes and schools. Our Catholic staff understands our mission and actively carries it out each day with prayer and hard work. We have delivered on our mission of providing successful counsel for Campaign and Feasibility Study work across the United States and abroad on over 800 projects and raised over $4.8 billion for churches and schools.

We are specialists in leadership motivation, donor solicitation strategy and low-key solicitations. We are one of the only firms to continue to provide true, full time, residential service for the duration of your campaign to assure we are attuned to every detail helping to assure your success.

Our services include free pre-study and pre-campaign guidance, advice, services and preparation. Our feasibility studies have been called, "the best in the business" because of our attention to detail and thoroughness and our campaigns have been exceeding goal since our founding in 1960.

We would be honored to talk to you about your plans and goals.

"Our only goal is to ensure you make yours." Bob Cosgriff

Personnel:

Robb Spence (Principle, President & CEO)

Fundraising Counseling

CCS
Fund Raising • Development Services • Strategic Consulting

CCS
461 Fifth Avenue
New York, NY 10017
Tel: 800-223-6733
Fax: 212-967-6451
E-mail: info@ccsfundraising.com
Website: www.ccsfundraising.com

Type of Business:

CCS is proud of our more than 60 years of service to the Church. One of the largest, most widely recommended firms, CCS provides fund-raising counsel and management services to Catholic institutions worldwide. Our methodology has helped to shape some of the most successful and complex fund-raising campaigns in the Catholic world, including the Archdioceses of Philadelphia, St. Louis, and Washington DC, and the Dioceses of Arlington, Austin, Biloxi, Brooklyn, Honolulu, Springfield, Stockton, and Tucson, among many others. CCS successfully plans and manages campaigns and stewardship initiatives for dioceses, parishes, universities, colleges, high schools, hospitals, homes for the aged, social service agencies, seminaries, and religious communities. CCS offices are located in New York, Boston, Baltimore, Washington, Chicago, St. Louis, Seattle, San Francisco, Los Angeles, Toronto, London, and Dublin. To learn more visit www.ccsfundraising.com or contact us at info@ccsfundraising.com or (800) 223-6733.

Graham-Pelton
CONSULTING, INC.

Graham-Pelton Consulting, Inc.
Offices across North America
Tel: 800-608-7955
E-mail: contact@grahampelton.com
Website: www.grahampelton.com; www.catholic-fundraising.com

Type of Business:

At Graham-Pelton, our professional staff sets the standard throughout the industry for creative and effective ways to respond to the evolving challenges Catholic organizations face. Through the years we have built a sterling reputation at the national, regional, and community levels for delivering fundraising solutions that overcome the challenges of today. Graham-Pelton helps dioceses, parishes, religious communities and faith-based charities reach their mission and ministry goals by overcoming funding obstacles to raise needed capital. We offer Campaign Management, Capital Campaign, Endowment Campaign, Increased Giving/Stewardship Campaign, Staff and Volunteer Training, Annual Appeal, Planning Studies, Major Gift Counsel, Planned Giving Management, Development Operation Assessment, Interim Staffing, Database Management Training, Electronic Philanthropy Services and Prospect Screening services. Graham-Pelton is committed to your success.

Personnel:

Craig J. Leach (President & CEO)
Craig C. Hall (Executive Vice President and Managing Director)

Fundraising Services

Walsh & Associates
Church Fundraising and Stewardship Specialists
"Helping Churches and Church Members Reach New Heights"

Valsh & Associates
:hurch Fundraising and Stewardship Specialists
601 East Highway 13, Suite 200
urnsville, MN 55337
el: 800-894-3863
ax: 952-882-5270
-mail: info@walshfundraising.com
Vebsite: www.walshfundraising.com

ype of Business:

Walsh & Associates, Church Fundraising & Stewardship Specialists, has been helping Catholic churches and church members reach new heights since 1984. Our services include helping churches to prepare for and conduct successful capital campaigns and stewardship efforts. Our capital campaign services include pre-campaign feasibility and planning studies, campaign implementation and follow-up & fulfillment services and support. Our stewardship services include stewardship program evaluations, stewardship formation & education, and volunteer and financial stewardship efforts. So if you're ready to reach new heights in your fund development and stewardship efforts, give us a call. We'd be happy to help.

ersonnel:

Michael A. Walsh (President)

CCS
Fund Raising • Development Services • Strategic Consulting

CCS
461 Fifth Avenue
New York, NY 10017
Tel: 800-223-6733
Fax: 212-967-6451
E-mail: info@ccsfundraising.com
Website: www.ccsfundraising.com

Type of Business:

CCS is proud of our more than 60 years of service to the Church. One of the largest, most widely recommended firms, CCS provides fund-raising counsel and management services to Catholic institutions worldwide. Our methodology has helped to shape some of the most successful and complex fund-raising campaigns in the Catholic world, including the Archdioceses of Philadelphia, St. Louis, and Washington DC, and the Dioceses of Arlington, Austin, Biloxi, Brooklyn, Honolulu, Springfield, Stockton, and Tucson, among many others. CCS successfully plans and manages campaigns and stewardship initiatives for dioceses, parishes, universities, colleges, high schools, hospitals, homes for the aged, social service agencies, seminaries, and religious communities. CCS offices are located in New York, Boston, Baltimore, Washington, Chicago, St. Louis, Seattle, San Francisco, Los Angeles, Toronto, London, and Dublin. To learn more visit www.ccsfundraising.com or contact us at info@ccsfundraising.com or (800) 223-6733.

Cosgriff Company
209 South 19th Street
Omaha, NE 68102
Tel: 800-456-9902
Fax: 402-341-8590
E-mail: cosgriff@cosgriffco.com
Website: www.cosgriff.com

Type of Business:

Celebrating 50 years of campaign excellence to Catholic parishes and schools. Our Catholic staff understands our mission and actively carries it out each day with prayer and hard work. We have delivered on our mission of providing successful counsel for Campaign and Feasibility Study work across the United States and abroad on over 800 projects and raised over $4.8 billion for churches and schools.

We are specialists in leadership motivation, donor solicitation strategy and low-key solicitations. We are one of the only firms to continue to provide true, full time, residential service for the duration of your campaign to assure we are attuned to every detail helping to assure your success.

Our services include free pre-study and pre-campaign guidance, advice, services and preparation. Our feasibility studies have been called, "the best in the business" because of our attention to detail and thoroughness and our campaigns have been exceeding goal since our founding in 1960.

We would be honored to talk to you about your plans and goals.

"Our only goal is to ensure you make yours." Bob Cosgriff

Personnel:

Robb Spence (Principle, President & CEO)

Graham-Pelton Consulting, Inc.
Offices across North America
Tel: 800-608-7955
E-mail: contact@grahampelton.com
Website: www.grahampelton.com; www.catholic-fundraising.com

Type of Business:

At Graham-Pelton, our professional staff sets the standard throughout the industry for creative and effective ways to respond to the evolving challenges Catholic organizations face. Through the years we have built a sterling reputation at the national, regional, and community levels for delivering fundraising solutions that overcome the challenges of today. Graham-Pelton helps dioceses, parishes, religious communities and faith-based charities reach their mission and ministry goals by overcoming funding obstacles to raise needed capital. We offer Campaign Management, Capital Campaign, Endowment Campaign, Increased Giving/Stewardship Campaign, Staff and Volunteer Training, Annual Appeal, Planning Studies, Major Gift Counsel, Planned Giving Management, Development Operation Assessment, Interim Staffing, Database Management Training, Electronic Philanthropy Services and Prospect Screening services. Graham-Pelton is committed to your success.

Personnel:

Craig J. Leach (President & CEO)
Craig C. Hall (Executive Vice President and Managing Director)

Guidance in Giving, Inc.
Full Service Stewardship, Development and Campaign Consultants
225 Snedecor Avenue
Bayport, NY 11705
Tel: 888-757-5444; Cell: 631-553-9064
E-mail: mcusack@guidanceingiving.com
Website: www.guidanceingiving.com

Type of Business:

Guidance In Giving, Inc. is a Catholic organization that truly understand the mission of the Catholic Church. Serving as stewardship, developmen and campaign counsel to dioceses, parishes and schools, our firm ha extensive experience in conducting capital campaigns and implementin stewardship throughout the United States. In all of our developmen efforts we utilize techniques that are continuously tested and refined Services include: diocesan capital campaigns; diocesan annual appeals diocesan development audits and feasibility studies; parish capita campaigns; implementing stewardship; parish feasibility studies, schoo development audits, school feasibility studies, major gifts solicitations an school capital campaigns. Additionally, the firm has an Hispanic Divisio and offers bilingual services. To discuss your individual situation or to ge a cost free analysis of your potential, please contact Michael R. Cusack President and CEO at 888-757-5444.

Personnel:

Michael R. Cusack (President and CEO)
Michael V. Goodwin (Executive Vice President)
Joseph W. Zamorano (Executive Vice President)
Stephen A. Babcock (Vice President)
Joseph Neville (Vice President)
Carlos Proaño (Vice President, Hispanic Division)

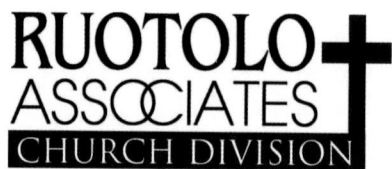

Ruotolo Associates Inc.
Horizon Square
29 Broadway, Suite 210
Cresskill, NJ 07626
Tel: 800-786-8656
Fax: 201-568-8783
E-mail: info@ruotoloassoc.com; info@churchdivision.com
Website: www.ruotoloassoc.com

Type of Business:

Since 1979, Ruotolo Associates has provided fundraising and public relations counsel to Catholic dioceses, parishes, schools, religious orders and social service agencies nationwide. Our services include: Stewardship efforts, feasibility/planning studies, comprehensive development programs, capital campaigns, annual funds, planned giving, strategic planning, marketing, public relations, executive search, student/membership recruitment, staff/volunteer training, seminars/workshops, TESS (Temporary Executive Staffing Services). Please call us to discuss an individualized creative strategy and solution for your advancement requirements.

Personnel:

George C. Ruotolo, Jr., CFRE (Chairman and CEO)
Joseph J. Caporale, CFRE (President and COO)
Theresa A. Shubeck (Executive Vice President)
Douglas R. Held (Senior Associate)

Walsh & Associates
Church Fundraising and Stewardship Specialists
1601 East Highway 13, Suite 200
Burnsville, MN 55337
Tel: 800-894-3863
Fax: 952-882-5270
E-mail: info@walshfundraising.com
Website: www.walshfundraising.com

Type of Business:

Walsh & Associates, Church Fundraising & Stewardship Specialists, has been helping Catholic churches and church members reach new heights since 1984. Our services include helping churches to prepare for and conduct successful capital campaigns and stewardship efforts. Our capital campaign services include pre-campaign feasibility and planning studies, campaign implementation and follow-up & fulfillment services and support. Our stewardship services include stewardship program evaluations, stewardship formation & education, and volunteer and financial stewardship efforts. So if you're ready to reach new heights in your fund development and stewardship efforts, give us a call. We'd be happy to help.

Personnel:

Michael A. Walsh (President)

Fundraising Supplies

D.P. Murphy Co., Inc.
945 Grand Boulevard
Deer Park, NY 11729
Tel: 1-800-424-8724
E-mail: sales@dpmurphy.com
Website: www.dpmurphy.com

Type of Business:

For over 135 years, D. P. Murphy Company has been serving the religious community by creating quality items and providing satisfaction with both our products and service with an unconditional guarantee. With a wide range of products from simple stationery products to sophisticated Stewardship and Tithing Programs; from collections envelope systems to contribution recording and a variety of mailing services. Our commitment—to help your church fulfill their financial and administrative responsibilities by providing an innovative mailing service designed specifically for your parish, a complete line of the finest liturgical products available, quality service and all backed by a 100% Satisfaction Guarantee. For a free catalog, call 1-800-4-Church or visit us on the web at www.dpmurphy.com.

Personnel:

Timothy Murphy Schratwieser (President)

LITURGICAL & CHURCH GOODS—General

Adrian Hamers, Inc.
2 Madison Avenue
Larchmont, NY 10538
Tel: 914-834-7780
Fax: 914-834-0712
Website: www.adrianhamers.com

Type of Business:

Custom designers and manufacturers of Sacred Vessels. Since 1887, the Hamers name has been synonymous with expert Silversmithing throughout the world in the field of Liturgical Art. Please contact us for those hard to find items, as we always have a large selection of Adrian Hamers Estate Collection pieces in stock. We have a large collection of antique church stained glass windows available (both full sets and individual). We are experts in: Church Interiors from design to execution, Renovations, Altars, Sacred Vessels, Gold and Silver Plating & Repairing, Appraisals, Tabernacles, Marble, Statuary, Woodwork & Woodcarving, Stained Glass, Pews & Chairs, Gold Leafing, Frescoes, Restoration, Trompe-l'oeuil, Wall Murals (repair and conservation cleaning), Ornamental Plaster, Heraldic Designs & Bishop Regalia. Please call us for a free 36-page Sacred Vessels color catalog, or our free 80-page color Woodcarvings catalog.

Church Budget Envelope & Mailing Company
271 South Ellsworth Avenue
Salem, OH 44460
Tel: 800-446-9780
Fax: 330-337-5990
E-mail: info@churchbudget.com
Website: www.churchbudget.com

Type of Business:

An Offering Envelope Company In Touch With the Needs of Today's Catholic Parish! Since 1917, we have provided appealing offering envelope products that effectively translate the image and traditions of your Catholic Community.
Offertory Products include: Boxed Sets, Periodic Mail Sets, Mailback Return Booklets, Prestige Series Holy Day Envelopes, Children Collection Envelopes, and Diocesan Mailing Services.
No Phone Trees - Personal Service!

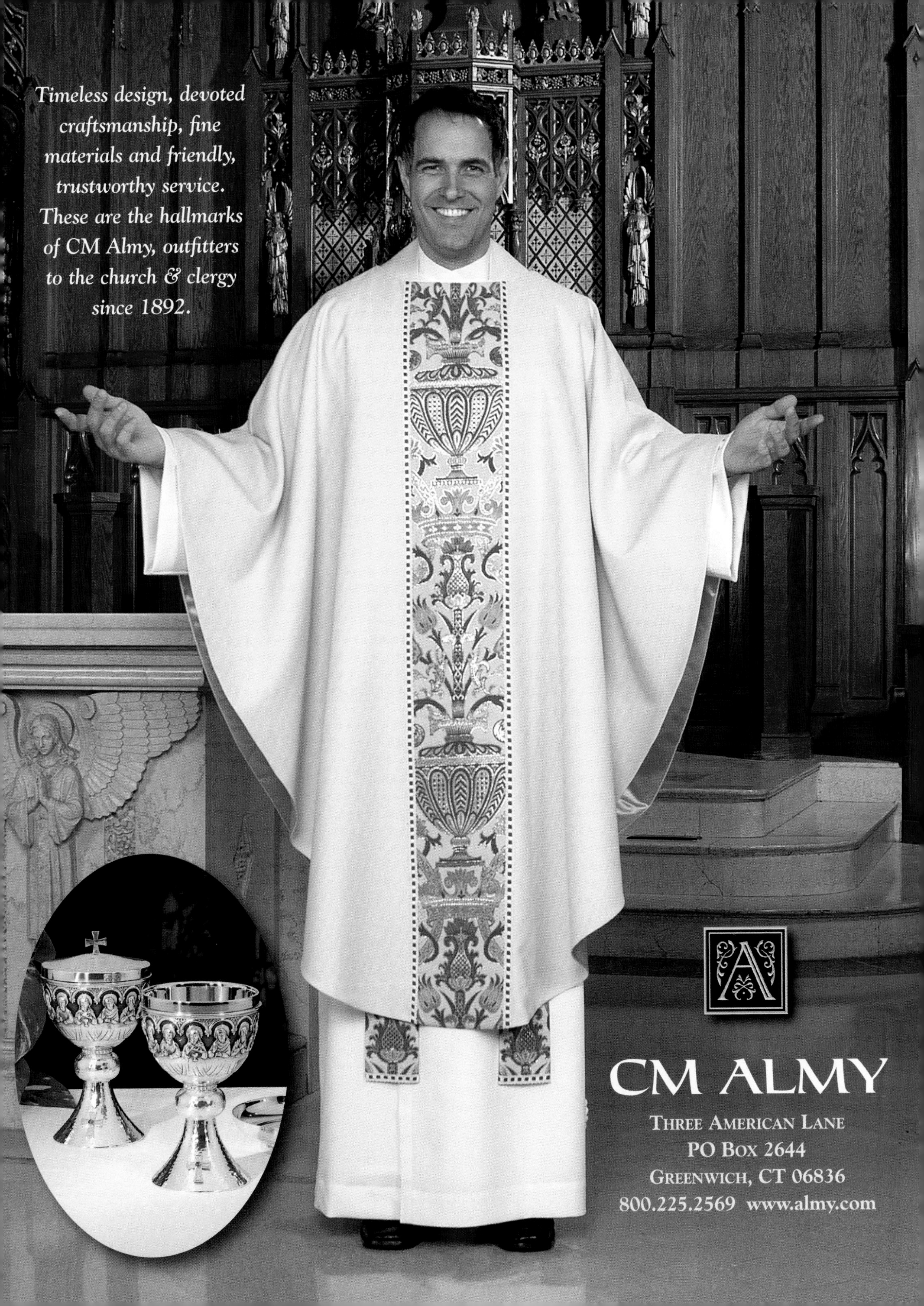
Timeless design, devoted craftsmanship, fine materials and friendly, trustworthy service. These are the hallmarks of CM Almy, outfitters to the church & clergy since 1892.
A
CM ALMY
Three American Lane
PO Box 2644
Greenwich, CT 06836
800.225.2569 www.almy.com

ChurchSupplier.com
Jewelry, Fundraising, Stewardship, Supplies ■ Division of Neibauer Press

ChurchStewardship and Growth Center
20 Industrial Drive
Warminster, PA 18974 USA
Tel: 800-322-6203; 215-322-6200
Fax: 215-322-2495
E-mail: Sales@ChurchSupplier.com; Nathan@ChurchSupplier.com
Website: www.ChurchSupplier.com

Type of Business:

Church Supplier is a unique church and parish resource for inexpensive self-directed stewardship giving programs. These programs require volunteers to run. Our proven programs include Pony Express - a stewardship program, Let Love Guide You - a canvas program, Give in Grace, We are Family and many church giving brochures. We also write, design and print custom giving programs, envelopes and mailings. We design and manufacture many items for donations including coin folders, coin boxes, and lucite collection boxes for institutions. We design and sell church supplies, childrens' camp and school giveaways for churches on a limited budget. We operate a complete printing and mailing company. We manufacture value priced custom jewelry, bracelets, coins and lapel pins for churches and their men's, ladies and children's fellowships. No fancy consultants. No fancy fees. We labor for the Lord in helping to find solutions for parishes since 1967.

Personnel:

Pastor Walt Waddell (Sales Manager)
Nathan Neibauer (President)

GASPARD
HANDCRAFTED VESTMENTS AND PARAMENTS
MADE IN THE USA

Gaspard, Inc.
(formerly The Robert Gaspard Company, Inc.)
200 N. Janacek Road
Brookfield, WI 53045
Tel: 800-784-6868 (toll free)
Fax: 800-784-7567
E-mail: mail@gaspardinc.com
Website: www.gaspardinc.com

Type of Business:

For more than five decades customers have looked to Gaspard for fine quality, handcrafted vestments and paraments made in the USA. Offerings include the exquisite Castle Craft® collection; wardrobe essentials such as albs, surplices, cassocks, robes, and clergy shirts; extensive metalware offerings, fair linens, altar accessories, and communion ware.

Because your vestment and parament selections are made to order in our one and only location in Brookfield, Wisconsin, special sizes and custom designs are not a problem. One of our friendly Customer Service Representatives will be happy to help you find just the right size and style to enhance your spiritual expression. Please visit us online or call for a free catalog.

Personnel:

Jason R. Gaspard (President)
Joann Gaspard (Vice President)

THE HOLY ROOD GUILD
for the Sacred Liturgy

The Holy Rood Guild
St. Joseph's Abbey
167 North Spencer Road
Spencer, MA 01562-1233
Tel: 866-383-7292
E-mail: customerservice@holyroodguild.com
Website: www.holyroodguild.com

Type of Business:

Designers and crafters of ecclesiastical vesture for over 60 years. Inspired by our monastic tradition, we seek to unite in our work simplicity in design, quality in materials and excellence in craftsmanship. The result is vesture that enhances the liturgical celebration with visual grace and order. Our artists—both monks and laypersons—are available for custom design work and consultation.

SACRED SPACES INC
LITURGICAL DESIGN STUDIOS

Sacred Spaces Liturgical Design Studios, Inc.
312 Montgomery Street, Suite 100
Alexandria, VA 22314
Tel: 703-519-9800; 1-888-519-4599 (toll free)
Fax: 703-519-4599
E-mail: info@sacredspacesinc.com
Website: www.SacredSpacesInc.com

Type of Business:

Sacred Spaces is a liturgical design team of international artists and master craftsmen with experience spanning four decades in the design of worship environments: new construction, renovation and restoration. Our Services include Liturgical Design Consulting, Custom Design, Appointments, Removals, Consignments and Facsimiles. Specializing in marble, bronze and stone, we custom design altars, ambos, tabernacle thrones and baptismal fonts. We also offer Master Planning Services and Educational Programs for pastoral teams and parish-wide Town Hall meetings. Sacred Spaces - Excellence in Liturgical Design, Artistry and Craftsmanship.

Personnel:

J. Michael Carrigan (President/CEO)
John Grosvenor (Project Director)
Francisco M. Cano (Art Director)

ROOT®

THE BEST CANDLE IN AMERICA

The A.I. Root Company d/b/a Root Candles
623 W Liberty Street
Medina, OH 44256
Tel: 800-289-7668
Fax: 330-725-5624
E-mail: church@rootcandles.com
Website: www.rootcandles.com

Type of Business:

Since 1869, every Root candle has been made using premium waxes featuring the finest beeswax and natural woven wicks for pure, clean flames that burn nearly one-third longer than ordinary liturgical altar candles. Root's devotion to purity, honesty and uncompromising quality has created "The Best Liturgical Candle in America."
Root's Full Line of Liturgical Candles, Church Goods & Services: Altar, Sacramental, Hand-Decorated Paschals, Advent, Special Occasions, Votives, Devotional, Sanctuary Lights and Jubilee Candles; Altar Bread/ Wine, Palms/Ashes, Inspirational Gifts, Replating/Refinishing Services; Patron Saint & Custom Decal Candles for Grottos, Shrines or Chapels.
Two factory locations: Medina, OH & San Antonio, TX.
Free 200+ page color catalog. 800-BUY-ROOT

Personnel:

Brad Root (President)

SINCE 1897
Cathedral
CANDLE COMPANY

Cathedral Candle Corp/eximious ®
Website: www.cathedralcandles.com

Type of Business:

Classical symbolism and expressive liturgical design in the luxurious hand decorated artistry of SCULPTWAX, created and mastercrafted here in the United States... exclusively at Cathedral Candle Co.
Now in stock at your nearest church goods dealer.

CM ALMY
OUTFITTERS TO THE CHURCH & CLERGY

NOW INCLUDING · THE KERRY COLLECTION

C.M. Almy
Three American Lane, P.O. Box 2644
Greenwich, CT 06836-2644
Tel: 800-225-2569
Fax: 800-426-2569
E-mail: almyaccess@almy.com
Website: www.almy.com
Showroom in Old Greenwich, CT

Type of Business:

Almy was founded in 1892. We design and make virtually all of our products in our Maine shop. It is our mission to design furnishings that will grace your worship and to ensure their value by making them with the highest quality materials and craftsmanship. We make a complete line of vestments, haberdashery, choir robes, candles, communion bread, linens, processional and altar appointments, and eucharistic vessels. We also offer custom design and fabrication of all Almy products, and repair and refurbishing of old metal appointments. Quik Ship© delivery of many popular items. All orders backed by The Almy Guarantee. Call, write, or e-mail for a free catalog.

Chalices, Crosses & Metalware

Adrian Hamers, Inc.
2 Madison Avenue
Larchmont, NY 10538
Tel: 914-834-7780
Fax: 914-834-0712
Website: www.adrianhamers.com

Type of Business:

Custom designers and manufacturers of Sacred Vessels. Since 1887, the Hamers name has been synonymous with expert Silversmithing throughout the world in the field of Liturgical Art. Please contact us for those hard to find items, as we always have a large selection of Adrian Hamers Estate Collection pieces in stock. We have a large collection of antique church stained glass windows available (both full sets and individual). We are experts in: Church Interiors from design to execution, Renovations, Altars, Sacred Vessels, Gold and Silver Plating & Repairing, Appraisals, Tabernacles, Marble, Statuary, Woodwork & Woodcarving, Stained Glass, Pews & Chairs, Gold Leafing, Frescoes, Restoration, Trompe-l'oeuil, Wall Murals (repair and conservation cleaning), Ornamental Plaster, Heraldic Designs & Bishop Regalia. Please call us for a free 36-page Sacred Vessels color catalog, or our free 80-page color Woodcarvings catalog.

C.M. Almy
Three American Lane, P.O. Box 2644
Greenwich, CT 06836-2644
Tel: 800-225-2569
Fax: 800-426-2569
E-mail: almyaccess@almy.com
Website: www.almy.com
Showroom in Old Greenwich, CT

Type of Business:

Almy was founded in 1892. We design and make virtually all of our products in our Maine shop. It is our mission to design furnishings that will grace your worship and to ensure their value by making them with the highest quality materials and craftsmanship. We make a complete line of vestments, haberdashery, choir robes, candles, communion bread, linens, processional and altar appointments, and eucharistic vessels. We also offer custom design and fabrication of all Almy products, and repair and refurbishing of old metal appointments. Quik Ship© delivery of many popular items. All orders backed by The Almy Guarantee. Call, write, or e-mail for a free catalog.

Gold & Silver Plating, Brass Restoration & Repairs

Adrian Hamers, Inc.
2 Madison Avenue
Larchmont, NY 10538
Tel: 914-834-7780
Fax: 914-834-0712
Website: www.adrianhamers.com

Type of Business:

Custom designers and manufacturers of Sacred Vessels. Since 1887, the Hamers name has been synonymous with expert Silversmithing throughout the world in the field of Liturgical Art. Please contact us for those hard to find items, as we always have a large selection of Adrian Hamers Estate Collection pieces in stock. We have a large collection of antique church stained glass windows available (both full sets and individual). We are experts in: Church Interiors from design to execution, Renovations, Altars, Sacred Vessels, Gold and Silver Plating & Repairing, Appraisals, Tabernacles, Marble, Statuary, Woodwork & Woodcarving, Stained Glass, Pews & Chairs, Gold Leafing, Frescoes, Restoration, Trompe-l'oeuil, Wall Murals (repair and conservation cleaning), Ornamental Plaster, Heraldic Designs & Bishop Regalia. Please call us for a free 36-page Sacred Vessels color catalog, or our free 80-page color Woodcarvings catalog.

Offering Envelopes

Church Budget Envelope & Mailing Company
271 South Ellsworth Avenue
Salem, OH 44460
Tel: 800-446-9780
Fax: 330-337-5990
E-mail: info@churchbudget.com
Website: www.churchbudget.com

Type of Business:

An Offering Envelope Company In Touch With the Needs of Today's Catholic Parish! Since 1917, we have provided appealing offering envelope products that effectively translate the image and traditions of your Catholic Community.
Offertory Products include: Boxed Sets, Periodic Mail Sets, Mailback Return Booklets, Prestige Series Holy Day Envelopes, Children Collection Envelopes, and Diocesan Mailing Services.
No Phone Trees - Personal Service!

D.P. MURPHY CO., INC. — Serving the Catholic Community Since 1873

D.P. Murphy Co., Inc.
945 Grand Boulevard
Deer Park, NY 11729
Tel: 1-800-424-8724
E-mail: sales@dpmurphy.com
Website: www.dpmurphy.com

Type of Business:
For over 135 years, D. P. Murphy Company has been serving the religious community by creating quality items and providing satisfaction with both our products and service with an unconditional guarantee. With a wide range of products from simple stationery products to sophisticated Stewardship and Tithing Programs; from collections envelope systems to contribution recording and a variety of mailing services. Our commitment — to help your church fulfill their financial and administrative responsibilities by providing an innovative mailing service designed specifically for your parish, a complete line of the finest liturgical products available, quality service and all backed by a 100% Satisfaction Guarantee. For a free catalog, call 1-800-4-Church or visit us on the web at www.dpmurphy.com.

Personnel:
Timothy Murphy Schratwieser (President)

Sacred Vessels

ADRIAN HAMERS® CHURCH INTERIORS

Adrian Hamers, Inc.
2 Madison Avenue
Larchmont, NY 10538
Tel: 914-834-7780
Fax: 914-834-0712
Website: www.adrianhamers.com

Type of Business:
Custom designers and manufacturers of Sacred Vessels. Since 1887, the Hamers name has been synonymous with expert Silversmithing throughout the world in the field of Liturgical Art. Please contact us for those hard to find items, as we always have a large selection of Adrian Hamers Estate Collection pieces in stock. We have a large collection of antique church stained glass windows available (both full sets and individual). We are experts in: Church Interiors from design to execution, Renovations, Altars, Sacred Vessels, Gold and Silver Plating & Repairing, Appraisals, Tabernacles, Marble, Statuary, Woodwork & Woodcarving, Stained Glass, Pews & Chairs, Gold Leafing, Frescoes, Restoration, Trompe-l'oeuil, Wall Murals (repair and conservation cleaning), Ornamental Plaster, Heraldic Designs & Bishop Regalia. Please call us for a free 36-page Sacred Vessels color catalog, or our free 80-page color Woodcarvings catalog.

CM ALMY
OUTFITTERS TO THE CHURCH & CLERGY

NOW INCLUDING THE KERRY COLLECTION

C.M. Almy
Three American Lane, P.O. Box 2644
Greenwich, CT 06836-2644
Tel: 800-225-2569
Fax: 800-426-2569
E-mail: almyaccess@almy.com
Website: www.almy.com
Showroom in Old Greenwich, CT

Type of Business:

Almy was founded in 1892. We design and make virtually all of our products in our Maine shop. It is our mission to design furnishings that will grace your worship and to ensure their value by making them with the highest quality materials and craftsmanship. We make a complete line of vestments, haberdashery, choir robes, candles, communion bread, linens, processional and altar appointments, and eucharistic vessels. We also offer custom design and fabrication of all Almy products, and repair and refurbishing of old metal appointments. Quik Ship© delivery of many popular items. All orders backed by The Almy Guarantee. Call, write, or e-mail for a free catalog.

PROFESSIONAL ASSOCIATIONS & ORGANIZATIONS —General

CFCA®

Christian Foundation for Children and Aging (CFCA)
1 Elmwood Avenue
Kansas City, KS 66103
Tel: 913-384-6500 or 800-875-6564
Fax: 913-384-2211
E-mail: mail@cfcausa.org
Website: www.hopeforafamily.org

Type of Business:

Christian Foundation for Children and Aging is an international movement serving those living in poverty in 24 developing countries. CFCA's Hope for a Family sponsorship program connects individual sponsors with a child, youth or elderly person in need of encouragement and support. Hope for a Family sponsorship helps provide food, education, health care and livelihood programs, but it does more. It gives families hope that they can create a path out of poverty for their children. Founded by lay Catholics acting on the Gospel call to serve those living in poverty, the CFCA movement includes people of all faiths.

FOOD FOR THE POOR, INC.

Food for the Poor Inc.
6401 Lyons Road
Coconut Creek, FL 33073
Tel: 954-427-2222; Fax: 954-570-7654
Website: www.foodforthepoor.org

Type of Business:

Food For The Poor is the largest international relief and development organization in the United States, aiding the destitute of 17 countries in the Caribbean and Latin America through churches and missionaries. Since its founding in 1982, FFP has distributed more than 52,000 containers of assistance valued over $7.3 billion to the region and maintains an operating expense ratio under 4%. Food For The Poor provides food, housing, healthcare, water projects, education, emergency relief and micro-enterprise assistance to millions of the poor in the region.

Personnel:

Robin G. Mahfood (President/CEO)
Angel A. Aloma (Executive Director)
Vicki Kaufmann (Director, Speakers Bureau)
Joan C. Vidal (Manager, Church Relations)

Priests For Life

Priests for Life
P.O. Box 141172
Staten Island, NY 10314
Tel: 888-735-3448; 718-980-4400; Fax: 718-980-6515
E-mail: mail@priestsforlife.org
Website: www.priestsforlife.org

Type of Business:

Priests for Life is the largest ministry in the Catholic Church working exclusively to end abortion and euthanasia. Priests for Life helps both clergy and laity to present the pro-life message effectively, and to work strategically to advance the protection of life. We provide Resources, Networking with Priests Worldwide, Seminars on Abortion, Regular Newsletter, Pro-Life Strategies, Consultation and assist with Organizing Activities. Subscribe to our biweekly column (free) at: subscribe@priestsforlife.org.

Fraternal Organizations

KNIGHTS OF COLUMBUS
IN SERVICE TO ONE. IN SERVICE TO ALL.

nights of Columbus
Columbus Plaza
ew Haven, CT 06510
el: 203-752-4000; Customer service (insurance): 800-380-9995
Vebsite: kofc.org

ype of Business:

The Knights of Columbus is the worldís largest Catholic family fraternal service organization. Founded by Father Michael J. McGivney in 1882 as a fraternal benefit society, the K of C has maintained its original mission to render financial assistance to members and their families. In addition, social and supportive fellowship is promoted among members through a variety of educational, charitable, religious, community and other service program and initiatives. The K of C has nearly 1.8 million members throughout North and Central America, the Philippines, the Caribbean, Poland, Guam and Saipan.

The organization's history shows the foresight of Father McGivney, whose cause for sainthood is under consideration by the Holy See. Father McGivneyís ideals have helped families obtain financial security through fraternal programs for more than 125 years. Beyond this, the Knights of Columbus contributes time and money worldwide to service to the Church and charitable initiatives. Last year, Knights contributed $150 million and 68 million volunteer service hours to worthy causes across the globe.

Private Associations of Lay Faithful

he Coming Home Network International
.O. Box 8290
anesville, OH 43701
el: 740-450-1175
-mail: info@chnetwork.org
Vebsite: www.chnetwork.org

ype of Business:

CHN exists to offer support/fellowship for non-catholic ministers on their journey to the Catholic Church.

In 1993, out of the seemingly isolated experiences of several Protestant clergy and their spouses converting CHN began. Upon leaving their pastorates to enter the Catholic Church, these clergy discovered the need to assist others in the same situation. CHN now assists thousands of pastors and laymen on their journeys home.

ersonnel:

Marcus Grodi (Founder/President)
Fr. Ray Ryland (Chaplain/Vice-President)
Jim Anderson (Director, Pastoral Care)
Rob Rodgers (Director, Administration)
Ann Moore (Financial Coordinator)
Sharon Coen (Administrative Assistant)

PUBLISHERS—General

OCP
(Oregon Catholic Press)
5536 NE Hassalo
Portland, OR 97213-3638
Tel: 1-800-LITURGY (548-8749)
Fax: 1-800-462-7329
E-mail: liturgy@ocp.org
Website: ocp.org

Type of Business:

Are you looking for innovative solutions to engage, unite and inspire your multicultural and intergenerational congregation? Look no further. Nearly all Catholic churches in the United States turn to OCP for worship resources to meet their changing needs. These include quarterly and annual missals (Today's Missal, Breaking Bread w/ Readings, Misal del Día, Unidos en Cristo/United in Christ); hymnals with traditional and contemporary music for liturgy and prayer (Spirit & Song, Flor y Canto, Segunda Edición, One Faith, Una Voz, Thán Ca Dân Chúa); choral resources, books and music for multicultural communities; online liturgy planning tools (Liturgy.com, LicenSingOnline.org) and Pastoral Press books. OCP, a not-for-profit organization based in Portland, Oregon, has been in operation for over 80 years, is distributed worldwide and known for its excellent customer service. Call us today and find out why! Custom workshops and conferences available.

Personnel:

John J. Limb (Publisher)
Tim Dooley (Customer Service Manager)
Mónica Rada (Marketing Manager)

spiritandsong.com®
a division of ocp

spiritandsong.com
5536 NE Hassalo
Portland, OR 97213-3638
Tel: 1-800-548-8749
Fax: 1-800-462-7329
E-mail: support@spiritandsong.com
Website: spiritandsong.com

Type of Business:

If you are looking to reach youth and young adults with the best contemporary songs for Catholic worship, look no further. A division of OCP, spiritandsong.com is the place for the latest releases from both big-name composers (including Steve Angrisano, Tom Booth, Sarah Hart, Matt Maher, Jesse Manibusan) and emerging talents (including Jackie François and Ike Ndolo). It is also home to the popular streaming video program The Commons, giving visitors live, in-studio performances, artist interviews and a behind-the-scenes look at their favorite songs. OCP, a not-for-profit organization based in Portland, Oregon, has been in operation for over 80 years and is distributed worldwide. Nearly all Catholic churches in the United States turn to OCP for innovative solutions to engage, unite and inspire their multicultural and intergenerational congregation. More information is available at ocp.org and 1-800-548-8749.

Personnel:

Robert Feduccia (General Manager)
Tom Booth (Associate Director, Artist Relations and Product Development)
Mónica Rada (Marketing Manager)

Parish Directories

olan mills

Catholic Partnership

Olan Mills Parish Directories and Portraits
P.O. Box 23456
Chattanooga, TN 37422-3456
Tel: 800-845-1157
Fax: 423-629-8181
E-mail: dchurch@olanmills.com
Website: www.olanmillsdirectories.com

Type of Business:

More parishes choose Olan Mills for their parish family albums and family portraits than anyone else. That's because Olan Mills delivers the highest quality portraits and directories quickly and at NO COST to your parish. Every family photographed receives a FREE Pictorial Directory and a FREE 8 x 10 Signature Portrait. Plus, with the complimentary OM Plus+ Online Directory, family and staff photos as well as your entire Parish roster are easily updatable – at NO CHARGE! Olan Mills makes it easier than ever for your parish with online photography scheduling, expert directory design services and helpful customer service. Contact Olan Mills today for our special offers and fundraising opportunities.

Personnel:

David Butler (President)
Ed Carpenter (Vice President – Marketing)

Photography

olan mills

Catholic Partnership

Olan Mills Portraits and Parish Directories
P.O. Box 23456
Chattanooga, TN 37422-3456
Tel: 800-845-1157
Fax: 423-629-8181
E-mail: dchurch@olanmills.com
Website: www.olanmillsdirectories.com

Type of Business:

Olan Mills signature portraits are your lasting gift to your congregation and a unique opportunity for creating professional images of your church families. More parishes choose Olan Mills for their parish family albums and family portraits than anyone else. That's because Olan Mills provides renowned quality portraits for your families. Every family photographed receives a FREE 8 x 10 Signature Portrait and a FREE Pictorial Directory. Your parishioners will look their best with the poses and styles that have made Olan Mills Portraits famous the world over. Other features include online photography scheduling, helpful customer service, and creative new portrait products as well as portrait fundraising programs. Contact Olan Mills today for details on the easiest program available and special offers.

Personnel:

David Butler (President)
Ed Carpenter (Vice President – Marketing)

SPECIAL CARE FACILITIES—General

Guest House®

Guest House, Inc.
1601 Joslyn Road
Lake Orion, MI 48360
Tel: 800-626-6910; 248-391-4445; Fax: 248-391-0210
E-mail: info@guesthouse.org
Website: www.guesthouse.org

Type of Business:

Guest House, Inc. is a lay-owned, lay-operated nonprofit corporatic established in 1956. With the approbation of the Catholic hierarchy, operates special residential treatment centers for Catholic priests, deacon brothers, sisters and seminarians with addictions from all over the worl The facilities are licensed and accredited.
GUEST HOUSE FOR WOMEN RELIGIOUS Tel.: 800-626-6910; 248-39 3100; Fax: 248-393-0186; E-mail: ghousemi@guesthouse.org
GUEST HOUSE FOR CLERGY AND MEN RELIGIOUS Tel.: 800-634-415 507-288-4693; Fax: 507-288-1240; E-mail: ghousemn@tds.net

Personnel:

Daniel A. Kidd (President and Chief Executive Officer)

Guest House® at Saint John Vianney Center 1946

151 Woodbine Road
Downingtown, PA 19335-3057
Tel: 888-599-9787
E-mail: kspitz@sjvcenter.org
Website: www.guesthouse.org

Type of Business:

Under the Guest House Program at St. John Vianney, men and wome in religious life who suffer from co-occurring addictive and psychiatri disorders will be able to receive treatment at the same time and in th same place. In the past, dual diagnosis issues were dealt with by treatin each difficulty separately. When a person is treated separately for the addiction and their psychiatric issues, they are often given conflictin information that produces poor results. This program addresses thes concerns by treating each issue simultaneously and is designed to treat th whole person – physically, mentally and spiritually.

Personnel:

Kathleen Spitz (Director)

The Saint Louis Consultation Center

The St. Louis Consultation Center
2039 N. Geyer Road
St. Louis, MO 63131
Tel: 314-909-4620
E-mail: information@stlconsult.org
Website: www.stlconsult.org

Type of Business:

The St. Louis Consultation Center is an out-patient facility founded in 1992 for clergy and vowed men and religious women. Dedicated, highly skilled, lay and religious professionals offer a program which provides: an intensive therapeutic experience utilizing professional services of the highest caliber in a faith-filled environment which recognizes the importance of spirituality and its place in the treatment process; and an affordable cost-effective program which serves as a viable alternative to more expensive residential or hospital-based programs. The St. Louis Consultation Center offers comprehensive psychological evaluations, candidate assessments, and an Intensive Treatment Program. We specialize in the treatment of depression, anxiety, addictions, alcoholism, behavioral problems, anger management, sexual misconduct, compulsive behavior and vocation discernment. Please visit our website for further information about The St. Louis Consultation Center: www.stlconsult.org.

Personnel:

Dr. Paul M. Midden (Clinical Director)

Catholic Travel Centre — "The Most Trusted Name in Religious Group Travel" — Worldwide Tours & Pilgrimages

Catholic Travel Centre
4444 Riverside Drive, Ste. 301
Burbank, CA 91505
Tel: 800-553-5233; 818-848-9449
Fax: 818-848-0712
E-mail: Groups@GoCatholicTravel.com
Website: www.GoCatholicTravel.com

Type of Business:

A reputation for extraordinary quality has made Catholic Travel Centre the choice of groups that demand exacting service and exceptional attention to detail. With meticulous detail, we will plan a one-of-a-kind pilgrimage tour catering to your group's specific interests. We can work within the constraints of any budget.

Our client list includes prestigious Catholic institutions nationwide, returning year-after-year to Catholic Travel Centre. To start planning your tour please call 800-553-5233 or visit our web site at GoCatholicTravel.com.

Go with Catholic Travel Centre, "The most trusted name in customized religious group travel."

Personnel:

J. Scott Scherer (President)
Inga Duranovic (Director of Operations)

TRAVEL & TOURISM—General

ALTURA® TOURS — World Vacation Generators™

Altura Tours
1060 Brickell Ave. Ste.1801
Miami, FL 33131
Tel: 800-242-4122; 305-374-7007 (local)
Fax: 305-374-7024
E-mail: info@alturatours.com
Website: www.alturatours.com

Type of Business:

Since 1992, ALTURATOURS has provided meaningful spiritual experiences to Catholic Pilgrims around the world.

Whether your choice is a fully-planned itinerary from Altura's Spiritual Pilgrimage Group Planner, or a customized program, our religious department's team of professionals will assist you in planning all aspects of your trip.

We carefully design our programs with special consideration to devotion, prayer and reflection, including reliable scheduled flights, comfortable first class accommodations, experienced tour directors, comprehensive sightseeing, deluxe land transportation and exceptional meals.

Group travel is an excellent way to raise funds, and a Pilgrimage Tour can serve this purpose. The group organizer can travel free of cost and the participants are rewarded with a memorable spiritual experience and group benefits not possible with independent travel.

Let us take you and your group on your next Pilgrimage of joy and peace to experience your journey of a lifetime!

Personnel:

Diego Linares (President)
Ivonne Gero (Vice President Operations - Groups)

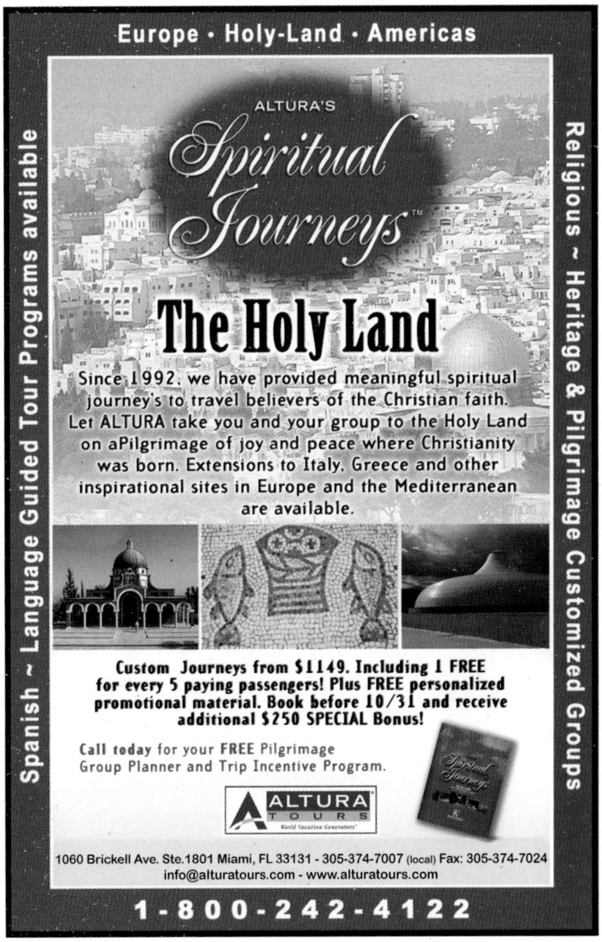

Europe • Holy-Land • Americas
ALTURA'S
Spiritual Journeys™
The Holy Land
Since 1992, we have provided meaningful spiritual journey's to travel believers of the Christian faith. Let ALTURA take you and your group to the Holy Land on aPilgrimage of joy and peace where Christianity was born. Extensions to Italy, Greece and other inspirational sites in Europe and the Mediterranean are available.
Custom Journeys from $1149. Including 1 FREE for every 5 paying passengers! Plus FREE personalized promotional material. Book before 10/31 and receive additional $250 SPECIAL Bonus!
Call today for your FREE Pilgrimage Group Planner and Trip Incentive Program.
ALTURA TOURS
1060 Brickell Ave. Ste.1801 Miami, FL 33131 - 305-374-7007 (local) Fax: 305-374-7024
info@alturatours.com - www.alturatours.com
1-800-242-4122
Spanish ~ Language Guided Tour Programs available
Religious ~ Heritage & Pilgrimage Customized Groups

Visit Israel

You'll never be the same.

Israel Ministry of Tourism
800 Second Avenue, 16th Floor
Yitzhak Rabin Way
New York, NY 10017
Tel: 212-499-5650
Fax: 212-499-5655
E-mail: igtonewyork@imot.org

Type of Business:

Israel is breathtaking, invigorating, enlightening, and transforming. The Ministry of Tourism does not sell services but provides resources and information regarding travel to the Land of the Bible. The Ministry of Tourism of the State of Israel works very closely with priests and Church leaders in order to help them take their congregations to Israel, and would be happy to provide them with a toolkit to help them organize a pilgrimage. We are always eager to assist you. Visit Israel — you will never be the same!

Keane International Impressions   KNOCK

Keane International Impressions
P.O. Box 240242
Charlotte, NC 28224
Tel: 704-287-1763; Fax: 704-553-9065 (office)
E-mail: info@catholictravel.org
Website: www.catholictravel.org

Type of Business:

Bringing you the world via pilgrimages of distinction is the specialty of Keane International Impressions. Utilizing 30+ years of travel expertise, we prepare a very personalized Catholic pilgrimage experience. We operate one pilgrimage at a time–assuring exceptional attention to every detail. Our Catholic travel professionals both here and abroad, possess vast insight, knowledge and expertise second to none.

We hold the distinction of being endorsed as specialist tour operator for Our Lady of KNOCK Shrine in Ireland. Our pilgrimage specialists work closely with you in designing your itinerary, taking into consideration the focus of your group, creating a specialized pilgrimage of distinction. Our same mission is to ensure your experience will be as meaningful to you, as spiritual director, as your pilgrims. We see to each group from beginning to end on their faith-filled and spiritual journey of a lifetime: Offering the highest quality, while providing the best value.

The Leo House
332 West 23rd Street
New York, NY 10011
Tel: 212-929-1010; Fax: 212-366-6801

Type of Business:

Centrally located in Manhattan, The Leo House is a quiet, not-for-profit, Catholic Christian guesthouse with an old world charm. We provide Christian hospitality to travelers of all races and religions, both foreign and domestic. The dedicated staff includes the Sisters of St. Agnes and lay people. We offer single and double rooms with private or shared baths (all rooms have a sink and toilet). Rooms are equipped with color cable TV and we have a new telephone system. A wonderful buffet-style breakfast is served every day except Sunday (7:30 to 10:30 am) at a cost of $9 per person. We also have an a la carte breakfast menu. Baking is performed on premise. Relax in our peaceful garden, meditate or pray in our chapel; we also have a Wi-Fi in several locations in the guesthouse.

The neighborhood (Chelsea) offers a wide variety of entertainment, reasonably priced restaurants, and is in walking distance to Broadway's theater district, Madison Square Garden and the Fashion District. Transportation to many other tourist attractions such as, Greenwich Village, Little Italy and Chinatown, are within a half a block walking distance. You can make future reservations by telephone, fax, or in writing. Single and double rooms are $95 to $130 a night. We accept Visa/Mastercard, Cash or Travelers Checks. BOOK EARLY — WE RECOMMEND RESERVATIONS TWO MONTHS IN ADVANCE.

For reservations phone: (212) 929-1010 ext 219 or Fax your request to (212) 366-6801.

Personnel:

Frank J. Castro (Executive Director)
Lucy Morales (Front Desk Manager)

MAGNIFICAT TRAVEL
HOLYTRAVELS.COM

Magnificat Travel
P.O. Box 4801
Lafayette, LA 70502
Tel: 337-291-1933
Fax: 337-291-1935
E-mail: info@holytravels.org
Website: www.holytravels.org

Type of Business:

Since its founding on the feast day of Our Lady of Lourdes in 2001 Magnificat Travel has specialized in custom domestic and international group pilgrimage and mission experiences for church parishes and schools. These experiences are designed to celebrate and promote the rich traditions and dynamic devotions that are unique to Catholic Christianity. Magnificat Travel's pilgrimage destinations span the globe, from the Holy Land, reaching out to Italy, Ireland, Germany, Poland, Switzerland, France, Canada, Mexico, Portugal, Spain, Australia, and America.

Magnificat Travel is an apostolate that seeks to "Magnify the Lord" by supporting the ongoing conversion of pilgrims and missionaries. The ministry of Magnificat Travel is intended to aid in building the Kingdom of God while reverencing the multi-dimensional call to conversion that Jesus places on the heart of every disciple. Join Magnificat Travel in its 10th anniversary year of Taking Pilgrims to Holy Places™ .

Personnel:

Maria Tregre (Founder and Director of Travels)

Nawas International Travel

The Leader in Catholic Pilgrimages for 61 years

Nawas International Travel
777 Post Road, Suite 305
Darien, CT 06820-4721
Tel: 800-221-4984
Fax: 203-655-1577
E-mail: George@Nawas.com
Website: www.NAWAS.com

Type of Business:

NAWAS INTERNATIONAL proudly celebrates 61 years of operating inspiring and affordable pilgrimages to the Holy Land, Rome, Italy and other important Catholic Shrines. We are also offering several pilgrimages including World Youth Day 2011 in Madrid.

Since 1949 Nawas has been designing and operating pilgrimages to the Holy Land, Italy, Lourdes, Fatima, Santiago de Compostela, the Shrines of Europe, Ireland, Poland, Greece, Turkey with the Steps of St. Paul, and more. We are dedicated to delivering high quality programs and the finest pilgrimages available at the most competitive prices. Plus, we offer excellent tour host benefits—you can travel FREE with as few as 6 or 8 paying passengers! Thousands of Catholic leaders have organized their travel plans through Nawas. Call us toll free and we'll show you how to promote your pilgrimage and travel FREE!

Personnel:

Soli Nawas (President)
George Khoury (Executive Vice President)
Sami Nawas (Vice President)
Neil Dellis (Vice President)

SELECT International

Select International Tours
85 Park Avenue
Flemington, NJ 08822
Tel: 800-842-4842
Fax: 908-237-9263
E-mail: sales@select-intl.com
Website: www.selectinternationaltours.com

Type of Business:

Join our 25th anniversary celebration by receiving a valuable thank you gift from Select International Tours, when you book a group with us and mention this listing from OCD.

Through our network of partner offices in Europe, Mexico and the Holy Land we offer you many choices for custom designed or scheduled group departures. New for 2011 are guaranteed departures to the Holy Land, Egypt, Turkey, Greece, Medjugorje and Italy. Plus cruises with 1 free for every 10 booked and World Youth Day in Madrid, Spain. Call us at 800-842-4842 for our brochures, group quotes or check out our web site for the latest news about pilgrimage travel www.selectinternationaltours.com.

We do all the work to make your pilgrimage experience excellent and easy from beginning to end.

Conference & Retreat Centers

MERCY CENTER
CONFERENCES, RETREATS & SPIRITUAL PROGRAMS

Mercy Center
Spirituality & Conference Center
2300 Adeline Drive
Burlingame, CA 94010-5540
Tel: 650-340-7474
Fax: 650-340-1299
E-mail: mc@mercyburl.org
Website: www.mercy-center.org

Type of Business:

Mercy Center Burlingame Conference and Retreat Center

Experience peace, tranquility and gracious hospitality for all of your meeting and conference needs.

Close to SF airport and downtown, transportation.We accomodate groups from 4-200. 85 guest rooms; 2 dining rooms, chapel, Labyrinth garden, internet, A/V and more.

Discounts for first time groups and weekday events. www.mercy-center.org

Personnel:

Suzanne Buckley (Director)
Sue Thourson (Conference Services/Reservations)

Pilgrimages

ALTURA TOURS®
World Vacation Generators™

Altura Tours
1060 Brickell Ave. Ste.1801
Miami, FL 33131
Tel: 800-242-4122; 305-374-7007 (local)
Fax: 305-374-7024
E-mail: info@alturatours.com
Website: www.alturatours.com

Type of Business:

Since 1992, ALTURA TOURS has provided meaningful spiritual experiences to Catholic Pilgrims around the world.

Whether your choice is a fully-planned itinerary from Altura's Spiritual Pilgrimage Group Planner, or a customized program, our religious department's team of professionals will assist you in planning all aspects of your trip.

We carefully design our programs with special consideration to devotion, prayer and reflection, including reliable scheduled flights, comfortable first class accommodations, experienced tour directors, comprehensive sightseeing, deluxe land transportation and exceptional meals.

Group travel is an excellent way to raise funds, and a Pilgrimage Tour can serve this purpose. The group organizer can travel free of cost and the participants are rewarded with a memorable spiritual experience and group benefits not possible with independent travel.

Let us take you and your group on your next Pilgrimage of joy and peace to experience your journey of a lifetime!

Personnel:

Diego Linares (President)
Ivonne Gero (Vice President Operations - Groups)

Experience the difference.

At Catholic Heritage Tours, each group tour is designed and prepared from the ground up for each particular group's interests and needs. Being a Catholic tour operator, we offer more than just travel arrangements — we offer spiritual enrichment. Each pilgrim is provided with detailed information on the sites, saints, and shrines visited on their journey, so as to enhance their spiritual lives. And if you are the group leader, you can travel for free! Call us today for a price quote for your group.

Custom-Tailored Tours & Pilgrimages for Catholic Groups

- One-of-a-kind, customized program for each group
- True, vast expertise on Catholic saints and shrines
- Faith-focused itineraries, emphasizing religious sites
- Group coordinators can travel for free

UNA ✠ SANCTA ✠ CATHOLICA ✠ APOSTOLICA ✠ ECCLESIA

Catholic Heritage Tours

DISCOVERING CATHOLIC TREASURES AND TRADITIONS

(800) 290-3876 ✠ (785) 437-2191

www.catholicheritagetours.com

"I want to thank you for all you have done for us, you hav[e] been most helpful. I take tour groups most years and this the first time I have used Catholic Heritage Tours, has bee[n] the most helpful and thorough service. Thank you once again and may God continue to bless your pilgrimage ministry!" - *Fr. P.O., Immaculate Conception Cathedral*

Catholic Heritage Tours
P.O. Box 67
411 W. Mission Street
Saint Mary's, KS 66536
Tel: 800-290-3876; 785-437-2191
Fax: 785-437-3093
E-mail: info@catholicheritagetours.com
Website: www.catholicheritagetours.com

Type of Business:

Catholic Heritage Tours is a full-service Catholic tour operator specializing in customized travel for Catholic groups, such as parishes, schools, and organizations. Each tour is designed with a unique itinerary according to the group's particular interests and needs, focusing on Catholic sites of interest. Since we are a Catholic company, and understand the value of spiritual journeys, we not only take care of all travel arrangements, we also do our best to pass on our Catholic heritage by ensuring that pilgrims attain the highest spiritual fulfillment possible. We supply each group with a custom-made booklet containing information on the saints, sites, and shrines visited each day of the trip. In the cities you choose to visit, our professional guides will point out and explain the Catholic treasures and sites. Experience the difference with Catholic Heritage Tours. Group coordinators have the option of traveling for free. For more information, please call us at 800-290-3876.

Personnel:

Luis De la Serna (General Manager)
Cristina Bolton (Customer Service Manager)

"The Most Trusted Name in Religious Group Travel"

Catholic Travel Centre
4444 Riverside Drive, Ste. 301
Burbank, CA 91505
Tel: 800-553-5233; 818-848-9449
Fax: 818-848-0712
E-mail: Groups@GoCatholicTravel.com
Website: www.GoCatholicTravel.com

Type of Business:

A reputation for extraordinary quality has made Catholic Travel Centre the choice of groups that demand exacting service and exceptional attention to detail. With meticulous detail, we will plan a one-of-a-kind pilgrimage tour catering to your group's specific interests. We can work within the constraints of any budget.

Our client list includes prestigious Catholic institutions nationwide, returning year-after-year to Catholic Travel Centre. To start planning your tour please call 800-553-5233 or visit our web site at GoCatholicTravel.com.

Go with Catholic Travel Centre, "The most trusted name in customized religious group travel."

Personnel:

J. Scott Scherer (President)
Inga Duranovic (Director of Operations)

Visit Israel
You'll never be the same.

Israel Ministry of Tourism
800 Second Avenue, 16th Floor
Yitzhak Rabin Way
New York, NY 10017
Tel: 212-499-5650
Fax: 212-499-5655
E-mail: igtonewyork@imot.org

Type of Business:

Israel is breathtaking, invigorating, enlightening, and transforming. The Ministry of Tourism does not sell services but provides resources and information regarding travel to the Land of the Bible. The Ministry of Tourism of the State of Israel works very closely with priests and Church leaders in order to help them take their congregations to Israel, and would be happy to provide them with a toolkit to help them organize a pilgrimage. We are always eager to assist you. Visit Israel — you will never be the same!

Magnificat Travel
P.O. Box 4801
Lafayette, LA 70502
Tel: 337-291-1933
Fax: 337-291-1935
E-mail: info@holytravels.org
Website: www.holytravels.org

Type of Business:

Since its founding on the feast day of Our Lady of Lourdes in 2001, Magnificat Travel has specialized in custom domestic and international group pilgrimage and mission experiences for church parishes and schools. These experiences are designed to celebrate and promote the rich traditions and dynamic devotions that are unique to Catholic Christianity. Magnificat Travel's pilgrimage destinations span the globe, from the Holy Land, reaching out to Italy, Ireland, Germany, Poland, Switzerland, France, Canada, Mexico, Portugal, Spain, Australia, and America.

Magnificat Travel is an apostolate that seeks to "Magnify the Lord" by supporting the ongoing conversion of pilgrims and missionaries. The ministry of Magnificat Travel is intended to aid in building the Kingdom of God while reverencing the multi-dimensional call to conversion that Jesus places on the heart of every disciple. Join Magnificat Travel in its 10th anniversary year of Taking Pilgrims to Holy Places™ .

Personnel:

Maria Tregre (Founder and Director of Travels)

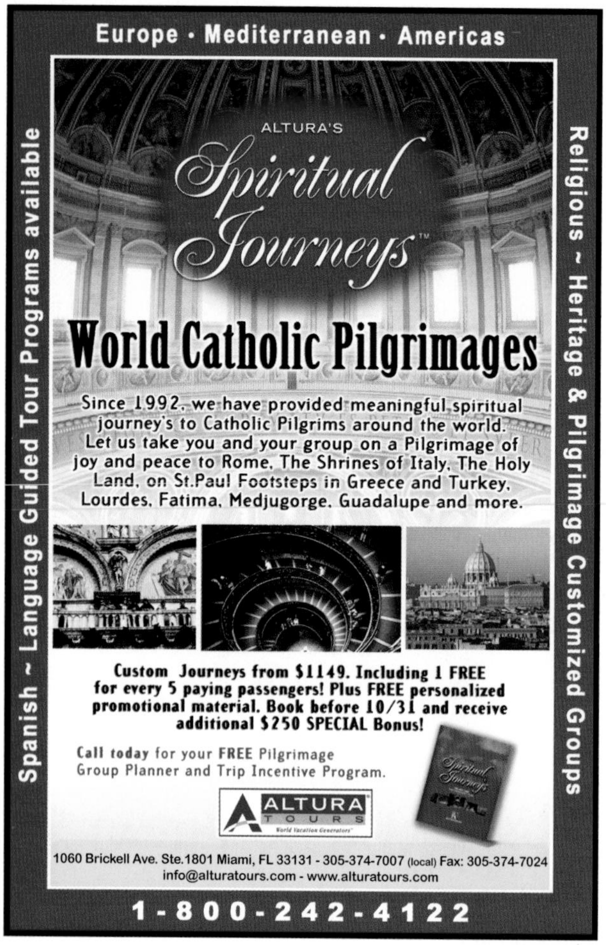

Nawas International Travel
The Leader in Catholic Pilgrimages for 61 years

Nawas International Travel
777 Post Road, Suite 305
Darien, CT 06820-4721
Tel: 800-221-4984
Fax: 203-655-1577
E-mail: George@Nawas.com
Website: www.NAWAS.com

Type of Business:

NAWAS INTERNATIONAL proudly celebrates 61 years of operating inspiring and affordable pilgrimages to the Holy Land, Rome, Italy and other important Catholic Shrines. We are also offering several pilgrimages including World Youth Day 2011 in Madrid.

Since 1949 Nawas has been designing and operating pilgrimages to the Holy Land, Italy, Lourdes, Fatima, Santiago de Compostela, the Shrines of Europe, Ireland, Poland, Greece, Turkey with the Steps of St. Paul, and more. We are dedicated to delivering high quality programs and the finest pilgrimages available at the most competitive prices. Plus, we offer excellent tour host benefits—you can travel FREE with as few as 6 or 8 paying passengers! Thousands of Catholic leaders have organized their travel plans through Nawas. Call us toll free and we'll show you how to promote your pilgrimage and travel FREE!

Personnel:

Soli Nawas (President)
George Khoury (Executive Vice President)
Sami Nawas (Vice President)
Neil Dellis (Vice President)

Passages by Peter's Way
Custom Designed Pilgrimages • Clergy Retreats • Educational/Study Tours

Passages by Peter's Way
500 North Broadway, Suite 221
Jericho, NY 11753
Tel: 516-605-1551; 800-225-7662
Fax: 516-605-1555
E-mail: passages@petersway.com
Website: www.petersway.com/passages.html

Type of Business:

PILGRIMAGES, CLERGY RETREATS, STUDY TOURS
Passages by Peter's Way will customize your group retreat or parish pilgrimage. Leaders, like you, know what sacrifices and preparations are required for a good pilgrimage experience. Whether you travel to the Holy Land, Italy, European Shrines, or to special ecclesial events, let us take care of the details, giving you the freedom to focus on the journey.

Personnel:

Peter Bahou (President)
Karen Rohrecker (Pilgrimage Director)

Peter's Way Tours Inc.
Specializing in Custom Performance Tours and Pilgrimages

Peter's Way Tours Inc.
500 North Broadway, Suite 221
Jericho, NY 11753
Tel: 516-605-1551; 800-443-6018; 800-225-7662
Fax: 516-605-1555
E-mail: annette@peterswaysales.com; peter@petersway.com
Website: www.petersway.com

Type of Business:

CUSTOM PERFORMANCE TOURS AND PILGRIMAGES
As the leader in choir pilgrimages, we invite your music minister to join us for an annual complimentary preview tour to one of our most popular destinations. Experience our level of service, witness liturgy and performance in a variety of venues and settings, and even select your preferred hotels. We'll then work with you to customize a pilgrimage that best fits the needs of your group - and provide you with a trip for two to raffle!

Personnel:

Peter Bahou (President)
Annette Molinari (Director)

Regina Tours

Regina Tours
94 Eighth Avenue, 22nd Floor
New York, NY 10001
Tel: 800-CATHOLIC (800-228-4654)
Fax: 212-594-7073
E-mail: regina@groupist.com
Website: www.1800CATHOLIC.com

Type of Business:

Regina Tours has been the leader in Catholic Pilgrimages since 1984. Our Pilgrimages include Fatima, Lourdes, the shrines of Italy (Assisi, Florence, Rome, San Giovanni Rotondo – Padre Pio - Pompeii, & Sicily), Greece (following St. Paul), Mexico (Our Lady of Guadalupe), Poland, Ireland, Israel and the Holy land. We understand the true meaning of a Pilgrimage and will provide our expertise for you and your Pilgrims. Contact us for our free color brochure. Learn how you can travel for free and/or use travel as a fundraiser. Mention this ad and receive a gift. For more information, visit our website. Midwest office & custom groups 800-HOLYCROSS (800-465-9276)

Personnel:

Nicholas Mancino (President)
Raymond Masillo (Vice President)
Angela Scharf (Custom Groups)
Bill, Maria, Loretta, Lucille, & Zelda (Travel Experts)

SELECT International

Select International Tours
85 Park Avenue
Flemington, NJ 08822
Tel: 800-842-4842
Fax: 908-237-9263
E-mail: sales@select-intl.com
Website: www.selectinternationaltours.com

Type of Business:

Join our 25th anniversary celebration by receiving a valuable thank you gift from Select International Tours, when you book a group with us and mention this listing from OCD.

Through our network of partner offices in Europe, Mexico and the Holy Land we offer you many choices for custom designed or scheduled group departures. New for 2011 are guaranteed departures to the Holy Land, Egypt, Turkey, Greece, Medjugorje and Italy. Plus cruises with 1 free for every 10 booked and World Youth Day in Madrid, Spain. Call us at 800-842-4842 for our brochures, group quotes or check out our web site for the latest news about pilgrimage travel www.selectinternationaltours.com.

We do all the work to make your pilgrimage experience excellent and easy from beginning to end.

Shrines

206 Tours
333 Marcus Blvd.
Hauppauge, NY 11788
Tel: 631-361-4644, ext. 206 or 800-260-TOUR (8687)
Fax: 631-361-3682
E-mail: sales@206tours.com
Websites: www.pilgrimages.com or www.206tours.com

Type of Business:

206 Tours is a highly respected 25 year old Catholic Pilgrimage Operator. Offers include regularly scheduled all-Inclusive pilgrimages to sacred sites & Marian Shrines. Trips include Mass daily, Catholic Priest as Spiritual Director, superior accommodations, meals, flights & more! We plan your air arrangements, hotel accommodations, meals, ground transportation, sightseeing and professional tour guides.

We also personalize services for individuals, special groups and conferences. Each one of our clients is handled with care, attention and respect. 206 Tours will provide you with a free 116-page color brochure, that covers every detail of what we do and explains our policies. Additional pilgrimages are on our website www.206tours.com. 206 Tours is proud to have an A+ rating by BBB.

Learn how you can travel for FREE www.206Tours.com/groups

Why 206 Tours? We are proud to share letters from our clients www.206tours.com/letters.

When you deal with 206 Tours, you can rest assure that we will emphasize the highest quality and care of each person.

Personnel:

Milanka M. Lachman (President)
Eva Manise-Relyea (Vice President)
Sandra Lippold (Director of Operations)

The Black Madonna of Czestochowa Shrine and Grottos
100 Saint Joseph's Hill Road
Pacific, MO 63069
Tel: 636-938-5361
E-mail: Shrine1OLC@AOL.com
Website: www.FranciscanCaring.org

Type of Business:

A Franciscan-Marian Shrine in honor of Poland's Queen of Peace and Mercy, Our Lady of Czestochowa. Built by Franciscan Brother Bronislaus, the Shrine is a shining example of what one man with faith can achieve. The inspirational rock grottos depict the Stations of the Cross, Seven Joys of Mary, St. Francis, St. Joseph, Our Lady of Perpetual Help, The Nativity, Our Lady of Sorrows and the Agony in the Garden. This wonderful work of faith is a welcome tonic for body and soul, sacred to pilgrims and inspiring to tourists. Located 35 miles west of downtown St. Louis, Missouri, in the beautiful foothills of the Ozark's, on the grounds of the Franciscan Missionary Brothers. We welcome group tours, families and individuals.

Personnel:

Michael Scully (Shrine Director)
Sr. Mary Francis (Assistant Director)

Catholic Travel Centre
Worldwide Tours & Pilgrimages

"THE MOST TRUSTED NAME IN RELIGIOUS GROUP TRAVEL"

Catholic Travel Centre
4444 Riverside Drive, Ste. 301
Burbank, CA 91505
Tel: 800-553-5233; 818-848-9449
Fax: 818-848-0712
E-mail: Groups@GoCatholicTravel.com
Website: www.GoCatholicTravel.com

Type of Business:

A reputation for extraordinary quality has made Catholic Travel Centre the choice of groups that demand exacting service and exceptional attention to detail. With meticulous detail, we will plan a one-of-a-kind pilgrimage tour catering to your group's specific interests. We can work within the constraints of any budget.

Our client list includes prestigious Catholic institutions nationwide, returning year-after-year to Catholic Travel Centre. To start planning your tour please call 800-553-5233 or visit our web site at GoCatholicTravel.com.

Go with Catholic Travel Centre, "The most trusted name in customized religious group travel."

Personnel:

J. Scott Scherer (President)
Inga Duranovic (Director of Operations)

Keane International Impressions

KNOCK

Keane International Impressions
P.O. Box 240242
Charlotte, NC 28224
Tel: 704-287-1763; Fax: 704-553-9065 (office)
E-mail: info@catholictravel.org
Website: www.catholictravel.org

Type of Business:

Bringing you the world via pilgrimages of distinction is the specialty of Keane International Impressions. Utilizing 30+ years of travel expertise, we prepare a very personalized Catholic pilgrimage experience. We operate one pilgrimage at a time–assuring exceptional attention to every detail. Our Catholic travel professionals both here and abroad, possess vast insight, knowledge and expertise second to none.

We hold the distinction of being endorsed as specialist tour operator for Our Lady of KNOCK Shrine in Ireland. Our pilgrimage specialists work closely with you in designing your itinerary, taking into consideration the focus of your group, creating a specialized pilgrimage of distinction. Our same mission is to ensure your experience will be as meaningful to you, as spiritual director, as your pilgrims. We see to each group from beginning to end on their faith-filled and spiritual journey of a lifetime: Offering the highest quality, while providing the best value.

MOUNT ST. MARY'S UNIVERSITY
NATIONAL SHRINE GROTTO OF OUR LADY OF LOURDES

National Shrine Grotto of Our Lady of Lourdes at Mount St. Mary's University
16300 Old Emmitsburg Road
Emmitsburg, MD 21727
Tel: 301-447-5318
Fax: 301-447-5917
E-mail: tronolone@msmary.edu

Type of Business:

The National Shrine Grotto of Our Lady of Lourdes at Mount St. Mary's University is the oldest known replica of the revered French shrine, dating to about 1875 (the original Lourdes apparitions were in 1858). The Grotto has been in use since 1805 when Fr. John Dubois founded it as a place of prayer and devotion.

The National Shrine Grotto of Lourdes is located just south of Emmitsburg, MD, off of US Route 15.

Grotto Hours: April through September 7:30 a.m. to 7:30 p.m.; October through March 7:30 a.m. to 5:30 p.m.

Schedule of Services: Saturday Mass at 12 Noon; Sunday Confessions 11–11:45 a.m. & Mass at Noon; April 5–Nov. 2 Mass at 12:30 p.m. Monday through Friday

Personnel:

William V. Tronolone (Director of the Grotto)

Nawas International Travel
The Leader in Catholic Pilgrimages for 61 years

Nawas International Travel
777 Post Road, Suite 305
Darien, CT 06820-4721
Tel: 800-221-4984
Fax: 203-655-1577
E-mail: George@Nawas.com
Website: www.NAWAS.com

Type of Business:

NAWAS INTERNATIONAL proudly celebrates 61 years of operating inspiring and affordable pilgrimages to the Holy Land, Rome, Italy and other important Catholic Shrines. We are also offering several pilgrimages including World Youth Day 2011 in Madrid.

Since 1949 Nawas has been designing and operating pilgrimages to the Holy Land, Italy, Lourdes, Fatima, Santiago de Compostela, the Shrines of Europe, Ireland, Poland, Greece, Turkey with the Steps of St. Paul, and more. We are dedicated to delivering high quality programs and the finest pilgrimages available at the most competitive prices. Plus, we offer excellent tour host benefits—you can travel FREE with as few as 6 or 8 paying passengers! Thousands of Catholic leaders have organized their travel plans through Nawas. Call us toll free and we'll show you how to promote your pilgrimage and travel FREE!

Personnel:

Soli Nawas (President)
George Khoury (Executive Vice President)
Sami Nawas (Vice President)
Neil Dellis (Vice President)

Tours

206 Tours
333 Marcus Blvd.
Hauppauge, NY 11788
Tel: 631-361-4644, ext.206 or 800-260-TOUR (8687)
Fax: 631-361-3682
E-mail: sales@206tours.com
Website: www.pilgrimages.com or www.206tours.com

Type of Business:

206 Tours is a highly respected 25 year old Catholic Pilgrimage Operator. Offers include regularly scheduled all-Inclusive pilgrimages to sacred sites & Marian Shrines. Trips include Mass daily, Catholic Priest as Spiritual Director, superior accommodations, meals, flights & more! We plan your air arrangements, hotel accommodations, meals, ground transportation, sightseeing and professional tour guides.

We also personalize services for individuals, special groups and conferences. Each one of our clients is handled with care, attention and respect. 206 Tours will provide you with a free 116-page color brochure, that covers every detail of what we do and explains our policies. Additional pilgrimages are on our website www.206tours.com. 206 Tours is proud to have an A+ rating by BBB.

Learn how you can travel for FREE www.206Tours.com/groups

Why 206 Tours? We are proud to share letters from our clients www.206tours.com/letters.

When you deal with 206 Tours, you can rest assure that we will emphasize the highest quality and care of each person.

Personnel:

Milanka M. Lachman (President)
Eva Manise-Relyea (Vice President)
Sandra Lippold (Director of Operations)

Catholic Heritage Tours
DISCOVERING CATHOLIC TREASURES AND TRADITIONS

Catholic Heritage Tours
P.O. Box 67
411 W. Mission Street
Saint Mary's, KS 66536
Tel: 800-290-3876; 785-437-2191
Fax: 785-437-3093
E-mail: info@catholicheritagetours.com
Website: www.catholicheritagetours.com

Type of Business:

Catholic Heritage Tours is a full-service Catholic tour operator specializing in customized travel for Catholic groups, such as parishes, schools, and organizations. Each tour is designed with a unique itinerary according to the group's particular interests and needs, focusing on Catholic sites of interest. Since we are a Catholic company, and understand the value of spiritual journeys, we not only take care of all travel arrangements, we also do our best to pass on our Catholic heritage by ensuring that pilgrims attain the highest spiritual fulfillment possible. We supply each group with a custom-made booklet containing information on the saints, sites, and shrines visited each day of the trip. In the cities you choose to visit, our professional guides will point out and explain the Catholic treasures and sites. Experience the difference with Catholic Heritage Tours. Group coordinators have the option of traveling for free. For more information, please call us at 800-290-3876.

Personnel:

Luis De la Serna (General Manager)
Cristina Bolton (Customer Service Manager)

Catholic Travel Centre
"THE MOST TRUSTED NAME IN RELIGIOUS GROUP TRAVEL"
Worldwide Tours & Pilgrimages

Catholic Travel Centre
4444 Riverside Drive, Ste. 301
Burbank, CA 91505
Tel: 800-553-5233; 818-848-9449
Fax: 818-848-0712
E-mail: Groups@GoCatholicTravel.com
Website: www.GoCatholicTravel.com

Type of Business:

A reputation for extraordinary quality has made Catholic Travel Centre the choice of groups that demand exacting service and exceptional attention to detail. With meticulous detail, we will plan a one-of-a-kind pilgrimage tour catering to your group's specific interests. We can work within the constraints of any budget.

Our client list includes prestigious Catholic institutions nationwide, returning year-after-year to Catholic Travel Centre. To start planning your tour please call 800-553-5233 or visit our web site at GoCatholicTravel.com.

Go with Catholic Travel Centre, "The most trusted name in customized religious group travel."

Personnel:

J. Scott Scherer (President)
Inga Duranovic (Director of Operations)

Nawas International Travel
The Leader in Catholic Pilgrimages for 61 years

Nawas International Travel
777 Post Road, Suite 305
Darien, CT 06820-4721
Tel: 800-221-4984
Fax: 203-655-1577
E-mail: George@Nawas.com
Website: www.NAWAS.com

Type of Business:

NAWAS INTERNATIONAL proudly celebrates 61 years of operating inspiring and affordable pilgrimages to the Holy Land, Rome, Italy and other important Catholic Shrines. We are also offering several pilgrimages including World Youth Day 2011 in Madrid.

Since 1949 Nawas has been designing and operating pilgrimages to the Holy Land, Italy, Lourdes, Fatima, Santiago de Compostela, the Shrines of Europe, Ireland, Poland, Greece, Turkey with the Steps of St. Paul, and more. We are dedicated to delivering high quality programs and the finest pilgrimages available at the most competitive prices. Plus, we offer excellent tour host benefits—you can travel FREE with as few as 6 or 8 paying passengers! Thousands of Catholic leaders have organized their travel plans through Nawas. Call us toll free and we'll show you how to promote your pilgrimage and travel FREE!

Personnel:

Soli Nawas (President)
George Khoury (Executive Vice President)
Sami Nawas (Vice President)
Neil Dellis (Vice President)